Cassell's Dictionary of Slang

2ND EDITION

Cassell's Dictionary of Slang

2ND EDITION

Jonathon Green

WEIDENFELD & NICOLSON

For Susan Ford

Weidenfeld & Nicolson
Wellington House, 125 Strand, London WC2R 0BB

First edition published in 1998
This second edition published in 2005

1 3 5 7 9 10 8 6 4 2

British Library Cataloguing in Publication Data
A catalogue entry for this book is available from the British Library

ISBN 0 304 366366

Typeset in Great Britain by Gem Graphics, Trenance, Cornwall
Printed and bound in Finland by WS Bookwell

The Orion Publishing Group Ltd
Orion House, 5 Upper Saint Martin's Lane, London WC2H 9EA
www.orionbooks.co.uk

Contents

Introduction to the Second Edition

Cassell's Dictionary of Slang was published in late 1998; it offered some 74,500 entries, covering worldwide anglophone slang from the early 16th century to the late 20th. The last seven years have moved the world into a new century, and this second edition, adding 13,000 headwords, as well as a number of new definitions for those terms already included, reflects slang's onward expansion. The great themes: sex and the bodily parts with which we pursue it, money, drink, drugs, criminality, insults and the like, are unchanged, but slang's underlying need for originality, even for secrecy – however shortlived such secrecy may be in this media-savvy, trend-conscious world – remains. The terms mutate, develop, re-emerge in a newborn form, the older ones are subsumed in the fresh creations. Thus has it been for a half a millennium of slang's collection, thus it will undoubtedly continue.

This second edition is not, however, a simple expansion of its predecessor. It is hugely and significantly informed by my work in progress, a multi-volume work 'on historical principles', in other words, a dictionary that offers 'citations' or usage examples. Research for that work has covered thousands of books, plays, journals, newspapers, magazines, TV and movie scripts, comics, rock, blues and rap lyrics and much more. In addition to which the ever-expanding archives, typically of old newspapers, that are coming online have made all forms of lexicographical research a matter not so much of painstakingly ferreting out the material, but of finding time to look into the wealth of potential sources that is now available. That is an on-going task. (To this end, I have decided to omit the ever-expanding bibliography from this edition, since the sources which it would list are more useful in the context of citations.)

The main knock-on effect for this single-volume work has been in what I hope is substantially improved dating. Dating without citations is always hard; without as best possible a certified 'earliest use' one tends to fall back on one's predecessors: for instance, is it in dictionary A? then it dates to approximately year X, if it is not in dictionary B, appearing 50 years later, then it has become obsolete in the interim between publications. If it is, then one looks on to dictionary C, yet more decades down the line. Citations change that radically and offer much improvement. In many cases what we have read has pushed back our knowledge of when a given slang word or phrase entered the language, but in others we have found that supposedly 'dead' words are in fact thriving. The constraints of a non-cited dictionary mean that entries must still be given relatively 'broadbrush' dates, e.g. [mid-17C–early 19C] or [20C+], but those who compare the two editions will see that many of these have been changed. That our researches are on-going means that even the improvements are not invariably 'the last word' – a hitherto unknown citation can mean a new predating – but I hope they represent a substantial step in the right chronological direction. Similarly the geographical labels, e.g. (*Aus.*) or (*US*), have been changed when, as is often the case, it transpires that a term has been less limited in use than had hitherto appeared. Finally, the reading for citations has shown that many existing terms have been used in ways that I had missed or which had yet to be coined when I put together the original 1998 edition. I have included these extra definitions, some of which may be quite old, others very new, at the relevant headword. While I doubt that many of the dictionary's users will have the desire to check 1998 against 2005, I can assure them that this edition, while no more finite than any dictionary can ever be, is as up-to-date and accurate a collection of terms as is possible.

Jonathon Green AUGUST 2005

Introduction

Slang is the counter-language. A jackanapes lexicon of the dispossessed. The language of the rebel, the outlaw, the despised, the marginal, the young. Above all it is the language of the city – urgent, pointed, witty, cruel, capable both of excluding and including, of mocking and confirming. Its origins lie in the Scandinavian *sleng*, which also renders standard English's *sling*, and means a slinging, a device, a strategy. Thus slang is both literally and figuratively a 'slung' or 'thrown' language, tossed cunningly, as it were, into the hearer's face and ears. At its worst it can be no more than vulgar for vulgarity's sake, stupid, depressingly obvious, the stuff of insult and obscenity. At its best it can be apropos, apposite, delightfully and even subtly humorous, a vibrant subset of the English language of which, like its 'neighbours' jargon, dialect and colloquialism, it provides one more part.

Reviled and proscribed by pedants and purists, it is endlessly resilient, inventive and untameable. Its age is that of speech itself. If there has always been a standard, inevitably there has been an alternative: slang, to tease, to provoke and expand our ways of communication. It is hugely enriching, the spice in the greater linguistic dish, enhancing quotidian ingredients with its brash new flavours.

This dictionary

This dictionary represents the first brand-new attempt to codify the slang vocabulary to appear in the UK since the first edition of Partridge's *Dictionary of Slang and Unconventional English* appeared in 1937. It is not, of course, the first slang dictionary to be published since then; Partridge's own work went into eight editions (the last posthumous); there have been a variety of others of greater or lesser extent, and my own *Dictionary of Contemporary Slang* is in its third edition. All that said, this dictionary is the first in 60 years to go back to the early 16th century and make its way on from

there. It also covers an unprecedentedly wide range of territory, looking at the slangs of a variety of English-speaking countries. Its 70,000 words and phrases range across the globe.

What is slang?

Among the many descriptions of slang, both positive and negative, one thing stands out: it is a good way from mainstream English. It can and does share the same vocabulary at times, but slang definitions underpin its rogue status. Whether, as one observer suggests, it is the working man of language, doing the lexicon's 'dirty work' or, as another suggests, it stands up for the disenfranchised, offering 'the poor man's poetry' or, as its many critics still proclaim, it has nothing but the most deleterious effects on 'proper speech', slang remains a law unto itself. Nor is it easy to define of itself. The official (*Oxford English Dictionary*) definition runs, 'The special vocabulary used by any set of persons of a low or disreputable character; language of a low or vulgar type,' and adds, 'Language of a highly colloquial type, considered as below the level of standard educated speech, and consisting either of new words or of current words employed in some special sense.' All that is true, but others have essayed their opinion and I offer mine above. Between them they provide, try as they might, as much a theoretical, 'atmospheric' take on their subject as a hard, lexicographical one. Perhaps the best definition, of many, is that of John Camden Hotten, written in 1859 but equally pertinent today:

> Slang represents that evanescent, vulgar language, ever changing with fashion and taste, [...] spoken by persons in every grade of life, rich and poor, honest and dishonest [...]. Slang is indulged in from a desire to appear familiar with life, gaiety, town-humour and with the transient nick names

and street jokes of the day [...] slang is the language of street humour, of fast, high and low life [...]. Slang is as old as speech and the congregating together of people in cities. It is the result of crowding, and excitement, and artificial life.

Yet stand alone as it does, the isolation of slang from its linguistic 'neighbours', and especially from colloquialism, is never cut and dried. Jargon, by which I mean 'occupational or professional slang' (rather than the obscurantisms, deliberate or otherwise, which are also described, often in relation to governmental or corporate pronouncements, as jargon) offers a relatively minor problem. Although one more *OED* definition of slang, excluded above, equates it with this occupational jargon, I would draw a hard line and, with certain exceptions, I have not listed such terminology here. I have, for instance, chosen to ignore the substantial swathes of military language, coined in two World Wars, that feature so largely in Eric Partridge's *DSUE*. Likewise, I have preferred to overlook the 'public school' and 'university' vocabularies, both collected in books by Morris Marples, that seemed to me too parochial, however fascinating. A similar fate has befallen the language of a variety of occupations, all of which I would see as jargon, pure and simple. I have, on the other hand, included campus terminology wherever used, since it is hardly restricted to the university environs and spills over into the 'normal' slang of many young people. As for criminal slang or 'cant', I have included the more common terms, many of which have been popularized through television or film, but passed over the more detailed material; the nicknames of given safes, say, or the precise mechanics of selling 'from the back of a lorry' are too specific to be anything but jargon.

Cant also calls for one major exception. The first slang collections are to be found in the 16th century and as far as they are concerned, cant is simply all we have. It seems impossible that slang did not extend as widely through society then as it does today, but those early slang collections, more glossaries than dictionaries, concentrate purely on the villain's vocabulary, the language of the wandering, criminal beggars who thronged through Britain. That the other, general slang, existed, must be accepted, but at four centuries distance, we have no choice but to depend on what has been preserved. Nothing else was then collected;

perhaps it failed to find a lexicographical sponsor. Thus, desirous of going back as far as records permit, one has no choice but to include this early cant here.

One debatable area, which to my knowledge has never before received, so substantial a coverage in a general slang dictionary, is drugs. This too could be marginalized as jargon, but with literally millions of drug consumers using some subset of this large vocabulary I felt that drugs, just as was the military fifty years ago, is a topic too closely linked to contemporary society and especially to the slang-using part of it, to be ignored.

The line between slang and colloquialism, the casual language of everyday speech, is simply too close to draw with any facility. Slang slips unnoticed across that border, and while one dictionary is happy to label the distinction as it sees it, alternative lexicons may take quite the opposite viewpoint, and use their labels accordingly. Thus this dictionary contains a number of words that may be categorized by some as colloquial; I make no excuses for their presence. Certain entries have not merely moved into colloquialism but have joined standard English. As far as possible I have noted this where relevant, explaining at what stage the word progressed from slang to greater respectability.

Etymology

Slang lexicography is the collecting of the slang vocabulary and the placing of it in dictionaries, but it is not quite that simple. The nature of the vocabulary being what it is, it cannot be constrained by the same rules as govern the 'respectable' lexis of mainstream dictionary-making. For the purposes of intelligibility I have attempted to corral its more extreme vagaries, but certain idiosyncrasies have to be acknowledged. I note the problem of dating below, but slang, especially in its etymology, the explanation of the formation and roots (both linguistic and social/historical) of a word, as often plays with its basic materials as simply uses them.

In many of the etymologies that follow, the reader will have to allow for a lateral rather than a linear link between the headword and the material that underpins it. But slang is often less than forthcoming about its origins. In many cases, indeed too many as I am the first to accept, I have been forced to essay an etymology, noted thus by a '?', preferring to offer what I hope is a feasible and probable link rather than surrendering to that blank admission of failure, 'ety. unknown'.

In this I may on occasion have blundered, but I hope that, bereft of more concrete background, I have at least entered upon the right track. It is my belief that one of the greatest pleasures of a dictionary should be the 'stories' behind the words; never more so in slang dictionaries, where the search for accurate spelling, the primary impetus of mainstream dictionary use, plays a secondary role to that for definitions and roots. Thus I have tried my best to come up as accurately and informatively as I can with those same 'stories'.

A large proportion of the entries depend on standard English words – slang either extends the standard usage or gives it a figurative or jocular twist. I have taken this to be self evident and have not noted it, so where an entry does not contain an etymology, it can be assumed that this is the case.

Dating

The dating of slang is perhaps the most problematic aspect of its collection. While it would be possible (had space not precluded the insertion of such examples) to provide a good range of citations for 19th- and 20th-century terminology, once one moves further backwards into history, one's choices are severely limited and the lexicographer is forced to cannibalize predecessors, taking an appearance in these earlier dictionaries as the only available proof of a word's usage. The problem, even when dealing with more recent terminology, is compounded by the nature of the slang vocabulary. All language is by its nature spoken, but slang often stays in the mouth and off the page (or for that matter the film or TV screen or any other form of medium) for far longer than does standard English. Indeed, there is an argument, embarrassing and frustrating for the slang collector, that by the time slang has made it into some form of permanence, it's already out of date. A little harsh perhaps, and much of what follows has surprising longevity, but another point to underline slang's resistance to mainstream linguistic norms. Typically too, the concept of a 'first use' is even more debatable than it might be for a mainstream term. I regret the fact, but given this situation I have too often been forced to assume a wider date range than may really be the case. More important, however, is the effect of such imprecision on etymology. Logically one links words on a chronological basis; a word coined in, say, 1790 can generally be set down as the creator of one coined a decade later; slang, if the collector adheres strictly to such dates as are available, often rejects that basic rule and readers will find that some words appear to have come from others that, according to my dates, actually emerged after that for which they are supposedly the root. I have tried to note this where possible, but it is to be borne in mind throughout.

Geography

I have included slang terms not merely from the UK, but also from the United States, Canada, the anglophone islands of the Caribbean, Ireland (North and South), South Africa, Australia and New Zealand – in other words the main countries to have learned their English, of whatever sort, through their one-time status as British colonies. I have on the whole resisted modern India, which some might see as a possible qualifier, since Indian English, that legacy of the Raj, seems to give way to the many indigenous languages of the post-independence country when it requires slang. I have, however, included a number of Raj-era entries, since these would primarily have been spoken by White Englishmen and women seconded to the subcontinent.

When checking an entry it should be assumed that I am looking first for the original use and in this the default language and usage area – thus bearing no label – is English English and the UK; if I can isolate it elsewhere, I have labelled accordingly. English may be the mother tongue, but many words and phrases remain permanent orphans. Obviously many terms are used in England and America, the Antipodes and so on; I have not, however, attempted to list every relevant country if the default stands. As will be seen, dialect features in many etymologies, and it is my belief that a large amount of slang was generated simply by the arrival of country-dwellers in the new towns and cities of the industrial era. Their local usage came with them, but, deprived of its nurturing environment, lost its roots. No longer dialect, an essentially rural phenomenon, and certainly not qualified for standard English, it became slang, the language of the city. When possible I have identified the source of the given dialect, but where this has not been done, it must be assumed that it was used either all across England (and possibly Scotland, Wales and Ireland too) or in too many and too disparate areas to list them all.

Sources

The nature of lexicography, there is little point in denying, bears within it a necessary strand of plagiarism. Like standard English, slang, however fecund and inventive, does not reinvent itself from the ground up each time a new lexicographer sets fingers to database. While there have appeared, naturally, a wide range of glossaries, usually pertaining to criminal language, the hard core of slang dictionaries runs to perhaps 25 major titles, starting with the 16th-century glossarist Robert Copland, and moving on to this book. And like mainstream English, there are certain way-stations, after which one sees effective repetition until the next major dictionary appears. And while standard English can call on a wide range of literary productions from which to draw citations and usage guidance, slang has been relatively rarely recorded; not merely in the earliest days of collection, the mid-16th century, but right up until the last fifty years.

And when it did appear in these early days, typically in the early 17th-century plays of Thomas Dekker and Thomas Middleton, or their successors, authors of the Restoration comedies, it is too often in the form of a virtual glossary, a litany of cant or slang terms all in a single scene, rather than as a natural part of the dialogue. The material, fortunately, grows ever-more accessible, but it is not until the post-war era that slang has found a regular place in books, films, television programmes and the like. Thus, especially for the earliest material, one is thrown willy-nilly onto the mercies of such 16th-century glossarists as Robert Copland, Thomas Harman and Robert Greene. Indeed the list of canting, i.e. professional criminal, terms that they assembled remained pretty much unaltered until the efforts of the otherwise anonymous 'B.E. Gent.' in the *New Dictionary of the Canting Crew* (*c*.1698) brought a certain element of 'civilian', i.e. non-criminal, slang into his collection. B.E. dominated the 18th century, until in 1785 a new collector laid down his marker. *The Classical Dictionary of the Vulgar Tongue* by Captain Francis Grose, the slang equivalent of his near-contemporary Samuel Johnson, lasted unrivalled, and running to more than five expanded, re-edited or subsequently pirated editions, until his work was supplanted in turn by the publisher, bookseller and part-time pornographer John Camden Hotten, publishing his *Slang Dictionary* in 1859. Thirty years on, slang received not one but two multi-volumed dictionaries:

first that of Barrère and Leland (1889) and then John Farmer's and W.E. Henley's seven-volume (eight if one adds Farmer's *Vocabularia Amatoria*) *Slang and Its Analogues*, which gave the world of slang lexicography what the magisterial *New* (later *Oxford*) *English Dictionary* did for the mainstream. And 40 years later Farmer and Henley provided the backbone of Eric Partridge's own *Dictionary of Slang and Unconventional English* (1937).

Given the pre-eminence of America in today's slang vocabularies – Partridge may have been able to talk of unconventional English and mean that and only that; modern slang collectors have no such option – it may seem odd that there existed only one major 19th-century American slang dictionary: the *Vocabulum* (1859) by New York City's one-time police chief George Matsell; itself little more than yet another revision of Grose, or more properly the version of Grose edited in 1823 by the sporting journalist Pierce Egan. But slang is a city language and even at mid-century, America remained a primarily rural society. As that changed, and American cities became the world's greatest urban centres, so too did the generation of slang. The importance of that slang can be seen today in the on-going *Historical Dictionary of American Slang*, edited by Jonathan Lighter. But Lighter's work, while undoubtedly the best, is only the latest. American slang has been collected by a wide variety of lexicographers, among them Hyman Goldin, David Maurer, and Harold Wentworth and Stuart Berg Flexner, whose *Dictionary of American Slang* was for 30 years the standing authority.

As for other English-speaking countries, specific slang collections have been relatively rare. Australia's first dictionary of any sort was a slang one, the thrice-transported (and thrice-escaped) convict James Hardy Vaux's *Vocabulary of the Flash Language* (1819), offered as an appendix to his memoirs. There have been a number of glossaries of criminal slang since then, but the main collector of Antipodean slang remains Sidney J. Baker, who wrote extensively on both Australian and New Zealand slang in the 1940s and produced a dictionary for each country. For the vocabularies of South Africa and the West Indies I have checked among other sources a number of general dictionaries, truffling out the slang from the wider lexicons there displayed.

Where I have benefited hugely is the ever-increasing presence of slang, right across the media, whether old – books and magazines, intermediate – film and television, or up to date – records, tapes and CDs, graphic novels or the Internet. My reading has been substantially augmented by all these sources, and the sources on which I have been able to draw are wide-ranging indeed. It is to my great regret that I can but list them in the Bibliography. Even more regrettable is the fact that I have been unable, despite my initial hopes, to offer citations for every term. But space has militated against such inclusion. There is no doubt that citations are vital in a properly historical dictionary and had it been possible it might, as seen superbly in Jonathan Lighter's effort, have put this dictionary on a par with any such work. But at the same time, as seen less satisfyingly in Lighter's work – only two volumes of which have appeared in the last four years – it would have undermined what I wish it most to be: an accessible, useable work of reference. I had no desire to see my efforts appearing over so long a period. Time and size both conspire against citations, at least for a one-volume work of the chronological spread that I have chosen, and I opted for immediacy and, as far as I can, linguistic comprehensiveness.

Insult and offence

The nature of slang is often, indeed almost invariably, rebarbative. Even its congratulations are mitigated by a certain edge. Its nature is to cause offence, to mock, to scorn, to savage, to dismay. It is no comforter. Whether geared for racial or national insult, describing human interactions, noting intelligence, or more usually lack of it, listing parts of the body, delineating the excesses of drink and drugs, or parading the vocabulary of a criminal underworld, it is often pertinent but rarely complimentary. Thus the nature of the beast. It would hardly be slang were it otherwise. And this, in itself, causes no problems. Those, as ever, emerge in the details.

Writing in 1937, and indeed in several subsequent editions, Partridge might have found himself unwilling to spell out such terms as fuck, cunt or shit, all proscribed by the current standards of 'taste' (and indeed by his own admitted squeamishness as regarded such language), but when it came to insults, however vile, he had no problems: a nigger was a Black person; a kike, a Jew; a wog, a brown foreigner. The 'dirty words' might finally appear in full in the 1970 edition but, as for the insults, unmodified by any reference as to their possible offensiveness, they would remain part of his diction-

ary for the rest of his life. This is not, I stress, to impugn Partridge, or the ranks of his predecessors who similarly found themselves unphased by racism but aghast at 'obscenity', as a bigot. Such an attitude was a given of contemporary culture. One may deplore it, but the dictionary-maker's task is to display language, not moralize upon it. To describe, not proscribe. Sixty years on and the social background against which I operate has reversed the situation. I can and do spell out anything, but as for racial slurs, like the *OED*, which began inserting notes as to 'offensiveness' with its first postwar Supplement (1972), I prefer to offer some form of label, usually the phrase 'a derog.[atory] term for…'. The omission of such terms, as many US dictionaries are now considering, would be anathema, serving nothing but the diminution of the dictionary. I see no reason to leave them unadorned and unqualified, even if those who most need reminding of such qualifications are least likely to acknowledge them. So far, then, so good. But if race can be qualified, then why, it might be asked, should other groups – homosexuals, the disabled, the fat, the thin, the tall, the short, the stupid, the sexually active – all of whom get their fair share of invective, not claim equivalent status? Everyone's ass is up for grabs, remarked Lenny Bruce, but in the 'victim culture' of the 1990s everyone's 'ass' seems up for special treatment. I have chosen, and am quite satisfied with my choice, to resist such suggestions. Slang is as it is and what it is is largely cruel. So be it. It would be easier, were one to succumb to these politically correct sirens, to mark those terms that are not 'derog.' rather than those that are.

In conclusion

It is the duty of the lexicographer to amass the language and offer it for perusal. It is not a task that can be complete, nor ever completed. The idea of 'fixing' the language was abandoned by Dr Johnson in 1755, and his submission to the realities of an ever-expanding vocabulary has set the style for all major English dictionaries ever since. The same goes undoubtedly for slang, the creation of which is a non-stop process. The slang lexicographer can chase the booming vocabulary and even catch a good proportion, but it remains elusive. Any help would be cheerfully received. I remain open to suggestion.

Jonathon Green AUGUST 1998

The Major Slang Dictionaries 1500–2000

This short overview by no means represents a listing of every slang dictionary written since slang collection began in England, *c*.1535. The intention is merely to offer some of the main examples, with emphasis on what might be called the primary 'way-stations' in the development of anglophone slang lexicography. For those who wish to consult a detailed, scholarly treatment of the subject, I recommend Julie Coleman's *History of Cant and Slang Dictionaries* (OUP, 2004, 2005, further vols. TBA). I have also dealt at much greater length with the topic than is possible here in my own *Chasing the Sun: Dictionary-makers and the Dictionaries They Made* (Cape, 1996).

English slang lexicography falls into three periods. The 'canting' or criminal slang dictionaries of the 16th to 18th centuries, the 'vulgar tongue' works of the late 18th to mid-19th, and the 'modern' productions that have appeared since.

I. Canting

The collection of 'cant', properly the jargon of the mendicant criminal beggars of Tudor and Stuart England, echoes the near-contemporary 'beggar-books' of Europe: designed to alert the law-abiding public to the existence of such beggars – 'the canting crew' – listing their occupational types and offering a small glossary of their language. The word cant comes from Latin *cantare*, to sing, and refers to the sing-song plaints of contemporary beggars. The first such work was Robert Copland's *Hye Way to the Spytell House* (*c*.1535). In the form of a verse dialogue between the Coplan, a printer who once worked with Caxton, and the porter of the Spytell House (a charity hospital assumed to be Bart's in London), Copland notes and the Porter describes the various categories of beggars and thieves, as well as their tricks and frauds. There is no glossary as such, but some 36 terms are defined in the text.

Two similar and expanded works followed. In 1561 John Awdeley, another printer, published *The Fraternitie of Vagabondes*. The brief (nine-page) work, offering 48 headwords, falls into three parts: the first deals with rural villains, the second with their urban cousins and the third is Awdeley's list of 'the xxv. Orders of Knaues, otherwyse called a Quartern of Knaues'.

The most influential 16th-century slang work appears *c*.1566: Thomas Harman's *Caveat for Common Cursetours*. Harman, a magistrate, produced a consciously didactic work, designed to introduce the reader to 'the leud lousey language of these lewtering [loitering] luskes [idlers] and lasy lorrels [blackguards] where with they bye and sell the common people as they pass through the country. Whych language they terme Peddelars Frenche.' There are 24 small essays, each dealing with a different rank of villain, plus a list of some 114 terms. These are very briefly defined, usually with a single synonym. The work concludes with a list of contemporary beggars, e.g. 'Harry Smyth, he driueleth when he speaketh', and dialogue written in cant and translated into English.

Harman's vocabulary would remain the core of several subsequent glossaries, with a succession of 'rogue pamphlets' appearing over the next two centuries. Among these are *The Bellman of London* and *Lanthorne and Candlelight* (both 1608) by the playwright Thomas Dekker, who also included much canting vocabulary in his 1611 play, *The Roaring Girl*, co-written with Thomas Middleton; and *Martin Mark-All, beadle of Bridewell* by Samuel Rowlands (or Rid), in 1610. Others include Richard Head's *The Canting Academy, or the Devil's Cabinet opened* (1673) and John Shirley's *Triumph of Wit* (1688). Another pair of early 17th-century playwrights, Beaumont and Fletcher, were equally keen to parade their knowledge of cant in their play *Beggar's Bush* (1622).

While Harman can be seen as a sociological researcher, and Dekker (at least in his prose works) and his peers as informative reformers, the 'coney-catching' pamphlets of playwright Robert Greene are nakedly sensational. The first such pamphlet, *A Notable Discouery of Coosnage* [cozenage, or trickery] *Now daily practised by sundry lewd persons called Connie-Catchers* [confidence tricksters] *and Cross-biters* [swindlers] appeared in 1591. Five sequels followed by 1592. Greene gleefully peddles his down-market sensationalism, larded with new canting terms – the vocabularies of the various branches of confidence trickery – and supposedly first-hand anecdote, but carefully quarantined with pious horror. In one pamphlet, *The Defence of Connycatching* by 'Cuthbert Conny-catcher', he even attacks himself.

With *A New Dictionary of the Terms ancient and modern of the Canting Crew*, by the anonymous B.E., Gent. [i.e. 'gentleman'] (*c.*1698), there emerges the first major development in slang lexicography since Harman. It is the first ever stand-alone 'slang dictionary', rather than an appended glossary. The title emphasizes canting but B.E.'s vocabulary, some 4000 words, adds general slang, colloquialisms and a variety of non-criminal jargons to the core material. There are other innovations: for some entries, however few, he offers citations and etymologies, there are a number of cross-references and he adopts usage labels.

Like Harman, B.E. would be 'honoured' by his plagiarists. These include Captain Alexander Smith, whose *Thieves' New Canting Dictionary*, in his *History of the Lives and Robberies of the Most Notorious Highwaymen* (1719), is unashamedly derivative. Similarly the anonymously written *New Canting Dictionary* (1725) is no more than an adaptation. The glossary attached to the oft-reprinted *Life of the self-styled gypsy king Bamfylde Moore Carew* (1750 et seq.) is similarly sourced. And it is B.E. (embellished by the *New Canting Dictionary* which it follows almost word-for-word) whose word-list provides the basis of the 'Collection of Canting Words' included in Bailey's *Universal Etymological English Dictionary* (1737).

II. Vulgar tongue

The 18th century did not merely produce adaptations of B.E. Among other works, all offering glossaries, are *Hell Upon Earth* (1703), *The Memoirs of the right villainous John Hall* (1708), *The Amorous Gallant's Tongue*, by 'G.L.' (1710 et seq.), *The Regulator* (1718) by Claude Hitchens, Daniel Defoe's *Street Robberies Considered* (1728), James Dalton's *Genuine Narrative of Street Robberies Considered* (1728), the confessional *Discoveries of John Poulter* (1753), and George Parker's *View of Society in High and Low Life* (1781) and *Life's Painter of Variegated Characters* (1789). All these trade upon the 'glamour' of criminality and the author's retailing to the innocent but interested consumer of its specialist language, a phenomenon that has by no means vanished in modern use, whether on the printed page or online.

In 1785 the next way-station in slang collection arrives: *The Classical Dictionary of the Vulgar Tongue*, by the antiquary and former militia officer Captain Francis Grose, who was both a friend of Robert Burns and an acquaintance of Samuel Johnson. A second, substantially augmented edition appeared in 1788, followed by a third in 1796. The pirated *Lexicon Balatronicum* ('by a member of the Whip Club, assisted by Hell-Fire Dick') was effectively the fourth in 1811, while the fifth was edited by the boxing journalist Pierce Egan in 1823. In his 4000 headwords Grose incorporates his main predecessors but expands much further into general slang, his 'vulgar tongue'. Grose now set the pattern for the next century. One other dictionary appeared in 1823, *A Dictionary of the Turf, the Ring, the Chase, the Pit, of Bon Ton and the Varieties of Life*. Its author was 'Jon Bee' (properly John Badcock), who had already challenged Egan's bestselling chronicle of *Life in London* (1821), in which appear the originals of every subsequent 'Tom and Jerry' (to wit 'Corinthian Tom', the London sophisticate, and his rural friend, up to see the urban sights, Jerry Hawthorn), with his own hugely derivative *Real Life in London* (1821). Badcock's book is far more verbose than Egan, but lexicographically it is more curiosity than linguistic tool.

Four more noteworthy dictionaries appear by 1900. The first, in 1857, is the brief *Vulgar Tongue* by 'Ducange Anglicus'. It comprises a pair of glossaries, the first collected by the author, the second from a report presented to the Government in 1839. In addition there is 'The Leary Man', a flash song, and a tailor's handbill written in slang, with a translation into standard English on the reverse. It is the first to offer rhyming slang, for all that this style of slanging, even today seen by many as the essence of the whole slang vocabulary, had actually emerged around 1815.

In 1859 the first of the six editions (variously expanded) of John Camden Hotten's *Dictionary of Modern Slang, Cant and Vulgar Words*, latterly *The Slang Dictionary*, appeared. Hotten was variously a bookseller/publisher, a pirate of such American 'stars' as Mark Twain, and a cultivator of his 'flower garden', books of flagellant pornography. The dictionary has lists of rhyming slang and of backslang, both prefaced by a brief history and discussion. There is, for the first time, a 'Bibliography of Slang and Cant,' listing some 120 titles, plus his own critical comments on each. Hotten stresses that this is above all a dictionary of 'modern Slang – a list of colloquial words and phrases in present use – whether of ancient or modern formation'. He omits obsolete terms and has opted, unlike Grose, to exclude 'filthy and obscene words', although he acknowledges their prevalence in street talk. He touches on jargon, without describing it as such, and thus deals with the terminology of the *beau monde*, politics, the army and navy, the church, the law, literature and the theatre. He includes a list of slang terms for money, one for oaths, one for drunkenness and also deals with the language of shopkeepers and workmen.

Hotten was the slang dictionary until 1890 (and Chatto & Windus, who bought up his list on his death, continued to publish the book until World War One). His pre-eminence was somewhat breached in 1889 by *The Dictionary of Slang, Jargon and Cant* by Albert Barrère and C.G. Leland. However, this two-volume work was barely published when it was displaced by the seven volumes of John Farmer and W.E. Henley's *Slang and Its Analogues* (1890–1904, revised edn of vol. 1 only, 1909). Farmer, who combined slang researches with writings on spiritualism, and Henley, then one of Britain's leading poets, took slang lexicography into a new dimension. The book adopted the same 'historical' method as the contemporaneous *New English Dictionary*. All but a few headwords come with a number of citations, some 100,000 in all, set out as in a standard English dictionary, to illustrate usage and nuance. These quotes take in 'the whole period of English literature from the earliest down to the present time' and are arranged as far as possible from 'first use' to current use. As well as citations there are, wherever possible, foreign synonyms for the slang terms. English synonymy is also paramount: those listed at monosyllable (i.e. the vagina), for instance, run to 13 columns, while those at greens (i.e. sexual intercourse) run to seven. There are errors, typically in the citations, where dates and even the quotes themselves may have fallen foul of the sheer volume of the undertaking (and the fact that a succession of printers, prudishly discomfited by the content, abruptly refused to continue with the work), but the overall achievement of Farmer and Henley far outweighs such slips.

III. Modernity

To list every dictionary of 20th- and 21st-century slang is impossible. The range, from massively researched multi-volumed 'historical' dictionaries, to fly-by-night glossaries posted on the Internet, defies cataloguing. Nor is it possible to restrict 'English' slang to England. While the last slang lexicographer to dominate his field, Eric Partridge, could entitle his book (based originally on Farmer and Henley whose rights were owned by his publisher) the *Dictionary of Slang and Unconventional English* (1937 et seq.) and mean just that, such exclusivity would now be foolhardy. In dictionaries as in the vocabulary, American slang has taken over, and must take equal prominence with its transatlantic forbear. Similarly Australian slang, exemplified in the mid-20th-century work of Sidney J. Baker, has an important presence, even if Baker drew too heavily on such late 19th-century efforts as the *Australian* and the *Sydney Slang Dictionaries*, which themselves drew on both UK and US sources, rather than offering home-grown Australianisms. The mass media, the Internet, the role of English, or certainly Englishes, as a world language mean that its slang is equally multi-headed and its dictionaries reflect the fact.

Partridge, as mentioned, dominated much of the 20th century. As well as his 'pure' slang dictionary, he wrote a *Dictionary of the Underworld* and books on the military slangs of both World Wars. His is perhaps a flawed canon, his lexicographical method was less than wholly scrupulous, his inability to keep personal comment out of his definitions less than useful, his etymologizing sometimes tendentious, but his body of work can be said to have maintained the momentum of slang lexicography through the mid-20th century. He has that rare accolade: like Webster his name became an eponym. The last edition of the *DSUE* appeared in 1984; an Americanized edition, from 1945 onwards, will appear in 2005 edited by Tom Dalzell. Partridge's immediate successor, Jonathon Green, published the single-volume *Cassell's Dictionary of Slang* in 1998; a multi-volume 'historical' expansion is due in 2007.

IV. America

Slang is an urban phenomenon. Modern America seems quintessentially urban; 19th-century America was not. Thus the century saw only one major slang dictionary: the *Vocabulum* (1859) by the New York chief of police, G.W. Matsell. (Its only possible predecessor is a short glossary appended by Edward Judson to his *Mysteries and Miseries of New York* in 1848.) Much of his vocabulary seems taken wholesale from Egan's Grose, although there are a number of genuine localisms. Nonetheless, there were no contenders: Matsell remains an American pioneer. The 20th century hosted an explosion of US slang lexica. Many of these, such as Jackson and Hellyer's *Vocabulary of Criminal Slang* (1914), Godfrey Irwin's *American Tramp and Underworld Slang* (1931), Hyman E Goldin's *Dictionary of American Underworld Lingo* (1950), or the wide-ranging specialist work of David Maurer,

published in *American Speech* and elsewhere, point up the wide variety of US criminal slang. More general works include Maurice H. Weseen's *Dictionary of American Slang* (1934), Berrey and Van den Bark's *American Thesaurus of Slang* (1942, 1952), Harold Wentworth and Stuart Berg Flexner's *Dictionary of American Slang* (1960, 1975) and pre-eminently Jonathan Lighter's multi-volume work in progress, *The Historical Dictionary of American Slang* (1994 et seq.). Specialist works abound, especially as regard such sources of slang as the campus, African-American speech, drugs and war. Among these are Connie Eble's series of *Campus Slang* glossaries (1972 et seq.), the works of Edith A. Folb (*Runnin' Down Some Lines*, 1980) and Geneva Smitherman (*Black Talk*, 1994), Richard A. Spears (*The Slang and Jargon of Drink and Drugs*, 1986) and Gregory C. Clark (*Words of the Vietnam War*, 1990).

Today's anglophone slang is international, English-language rather than English. And its sources, including dictionaries, are increasingly so, as the Internet gains influence and online reference searches replace the traditional printed works. The upcoming crop of multi-volume lexica may signify the end of a half-millennium era. A search for 'slang dictionary' brings up 75,000 hits on Google: slang collection, one might suggest, has barely begun.

Jonathon Green AUGUST 2005

Acknowledgements

Acknowledgements for the first edition

This book has been five years in the making, and if one adds on my own production of slang dictionaries and allied works, the amassing of the vocabulary here displayed has been in progress since I first began collecting slang around 1980. Like the majority, if not every slang lexicographer who has preceded me, I am, and am proud to be a one-man band. To that end, as it is traditional to declaim, the vices as well as the virtues of the book will have to be laid at my door. But to suggest that the creation of this dictionary was a solo effort in every aspect would be not merely hubristic but quite simply wrong. There are a number of people both living and dead, to whom I am indebted, and I would like to make due acknowledgement here.

The profession of lexicography is, inevitably, a plagiaristic one, a linguistic Pacman that moves on, gobbling up its predecessors as it goes. In an ideal world such an admission would be unnecessary, but the language does not renew itself from scratch, arising fresh and untouched, so as to serve each new dictionary afresh. Modern English has been expanding for nearly a millennium, and Old and Middle English, its roots, for a millennium more. Thus one's primary acknowledgement must be to the slang collectors of the 16th century onwards, best-known among them Robert Copland, Thomas Harman, the otherwise anonymous B.E., Francis Grose, John Camden Hotten, Albert Barrère and Charles Leland, John Farmer and W.E. Henley, George Matsell and Jonathan Lighter. And above all, and most personally Eric Partridge, the exemplar of the breed and the arbiter of modern slang lexicographers, whose own works, first encountered decades ago, convinced me that here was a subject to which it might be worth devoting oneself.

On a more immediate level, I would like to thank my sub-editors-cum-proofreaders: Christine Cowley, Jessica Feinstein, Gill Francis, Lucy Hollingsworth, Alyson McGaw, Sam Merrell and Laura Wedgeworth. Without their efforts this would have been a lesser work. Such acknowledgement must also go to Gordon Galsworthy, whose typesetting skills are displayed on every page. And if absorption of old texts was necessary, then Karen Thomson, the country's leading dictionary dealer, has made it possible for me to read some of them in the earliest editions. I would also pay tribute to Richard Short, who assisted me with some of the most back-breaking of the work, as on occasion did my sons, Lucien and Gabriel.

Loath though I am to enter the realms of sentimentality, I am at a loss how else to render my indebtedness to Lydia Darbyshire, sub-editor-in-chief, and Sarah Chatwin at Cassell, who has masterminded the ever more complex compilation of the final manuscript. No-one could have been more tolerant of my failings, both lexicographical and personal than these two. No-one could have made a sometimes onerous task so palatable. Deprived of better words, I am enormously grateful to them both.

It is to my great regret that my editor Nigel Wilcockson left Cassell before publication. His role has been ably filled by Richard Milbank, who has taken on a publishing *fait accompli* with enormous sympathy, but for five years Nigel walked the same path as did I, offering encouragement, advice, endless good humour and support. In commissioning this dictionary he gave me the opportunity to fulfil my greatest professional desire, and I hope, with its publication, that I have justified his faith.

I must also thank, in his much-regretted absence, my late uncle Ezra 'Jack' Morris. The declaration that 'this would not have been possible without…' is a tired one, but incontrovertibly true in this case. His unexpected generosity has made it possible for me to have attained most writers' dream: to work on a major project without the need for additional employment. I wish that he could see the finished product.

Finally and with respect transcending all other acknowledgements, I must thank Susan Ford, my partner. Not only has she worked on large sections of the manuscript herself, but she has lived with it and with me throughout the book's gestation. How much this has meant is not for comment here. In many ways this is as much her book as it is mine and for that reason, as well as for so many others, I dedicate it to her.

Acknowledgements for the second edition

This second edition of *Cassell's Dictionary of Slang* is as much a by-product of my on-going researches for the multi-volume work 'on historical principles' which will follow, as it is a simple extension of its single-volume predecessor. To that end this book is equally indebted to the skills, expertise and generosity, both professional and personal, that I have been offered by a wide range of individuals throughout the continuing process of making the big dictionary. Space, inevitably, precludes greater detail but for now, in addition to everyone who was involved in the original volume, I wish to thank:

My part-time researchers Nasir Ahmad, Jeremy Noel-Todd, Richard Short, and in Australia, Jared Boorer. The copy-editors and proofreaders for the second edition: Alice Grandison, James Greenan, Patrick Heenan and David Pickering. My professional colleagues and personal friends: Tom Dalzell and Jesse Sheidlower, Peter Gilliver, Patrick Hanks, Julie Coleman, and slang collector *sans pareil* Madeline Kripke. The members of the American Dialect Society who contribute to the online ADS-L, notably Sam Clements, Gerald Cohen, Barry Popik, Fred Shapiro, George Thompson and Ben Zimmer. Michael Quinion of World Wide Words, Nick Groom at Bristol University. Dan Franklin, Jonathan Meades, Andrew Payne and Rowan Pelling. David Wilcockson and George Millous for computer expertise. Felix Dennis for making his New York apartment available and Karen Durbin for her hospitality in that city.

Richard Milbank, whose involvement with its predecessor was necessarily limited but nonetheless much valued, was kind enough to commission this second edition and has been with it from day one. I trust it proves worth the wait.

Sarah Chatwin, no longer of Cassell, has, if it were possible, contributed even more to the book, whether in her five years of research or in her more recent role as editor-in-chief of the second edition. As ever, I am in her debt.

Susie Ford, inter much alia the primary researcher of the multi-volume book, shares, if anything, an even greater proportion of the credit for this one than she notched up for the original volume.

The publishers would also like to thank Librios for their provision of database software.

How To Use *Cassell's Dictionary of Slang*

The entry Each entry in *Cassell's Dictionary of Slang* begins with the headword in bold type. The headword is immediately followed by the part of speech in italics, always includes the date of use in square brackets and may include an italic usage label in round brackets. Any variant spellings or alternative forms are indicated in bold within brackets, following the word *also*. Etymologies are placed at the end of the entry in square brackets.

Organization of entries Entries are arranged in alphabetical order on a letter-by-letter basis. Entries identical in spelling are ordered according to their part of speech, in the sequence noun, adjective, verb, adverb, phrase, exclamation, prefix, suffix, infix, pronoun, preposition, conjunction. Where the noun or verb etc has more than one distinct meaning, these are divided up or homographed according to etymology. Within the parts of speech, each homograph is given a number in superscript, for example, **dog** *n.*[1], **dog** *n.*[2], **dog** *n.*[3] etc, followed by **dog** *v.*[1], **dog** *v.*[2]. The sequence of all homographs is chronological, according to the first usage of each entry.

Where an entry or a distinct homograph has several different shades of meaning, these are given sense numbers in bold. The numbered senses may have their own dates, labels or variant spellings, or alternatively if one or all of these applies to all senses of the entry, it will be placed before the first numbered sense. Sense numbers are also ordered according to chronological first appearance.

Dating Where a date appears in the form [18C] or [19C] it indicates that the usage period of the term covers the whole century. The + sign indicates that a term is still in use, as does the label [2000s] which indicates a recent and current slang expression. Dating is based primarily on when a term, or the sense of a term, began to be used, but also takes into consideration the length

of its usage, so for example the reader might find **1** [18C] … ; **2** [mid-18C+] … ; **3** [late 18C–early 19C] … , where the second entry is still in use and the third is not, but the second originated earlier than the third.

Labels Usage labels are in italics within round brackets, usually following the date label. These indicate either the geographical usage of a term, for example (*W.I.*), or the social/cultural usage, for example (*teen*). A list of abbreviations used in the dictionary appears on p.xix. The non-geographical usage labels should be self-explanatory, for instance the use of (*juv.*) as juvenile, to suggest pre-teenage children's usage, as distinct from (*teen*); however, some of the labels are included in the list of abbreviations with brief glossaries attached.

Cross-references A word or expression which appears elsewhere in the dictionary is marked as a cross-reference, in small capital letters. Cross-references occur mainly in the etymologies, in cases where the origin of one slang expression resides wholly or partly in another slang term. For example, the entry **nabbing cheat** has the etymology [NAB *v.*[1] (2) + CHEAT n. (3)] with the bracketed numbers referring to the specific sense numbers.

Cross-references also appear in round brackets following 'cf.', which refers the reader to other entries for comparison. Often where there is a cross-reference to one headword, that headword may contain a larger collection of comparative references. These larger lists comprise groups of related synonyms, collected only for the most commonly occurring types of expression.

A second type of cross-reference directs readers from one spelling of a particular term to the main spelling under which the term is listed, for example **ampster** *see under* AMSTER. Terms may be listed under both spellings, so these are more directional pointers than direct cross-references, for example, **asshole** *see also under* ARSEHOLE and its combs. [combinations].

Abbreviations

adj.	adjective	interrog.	interrogative	RAF	Royal Air Force
adv.	adverb	Ital.	Italian	redup.	reduplication
Afk.	Afrikaans	Jam.	Jamaica	ref.	reference
Anglo-Ind.	Anglo-Indian	Jap.	Japanese	rhy. sl.	rhyming slang
Antg.	Antigua	joc.	jocular	RN	Royal Navy
approx.	approximate/approximately	journ.	journalistic	Rom.	Romany
AS	Anglo-Saxon	juv.	juvenile use (pre-teenage)	Rus.	Russian
attrib.	attributively	Lat.	Latin	S.Afr.	South African
Aus.	Australian	Ling. Fr.	Lingua Franca	S.Afr.E.	South African English
backform.	backformation	lit.	literal/literally	S.Afr.Du.	South African Dutch
backsl.	backslang	masc.	masculine	St Lu.	St Lucia
Baha.	Bahamas	MDu.	Middle Dutch	SAmE	Standard American English
Bdos	Barbados	ME	Middle English	SAusE	Standard Australian English
C	century	Med.	Medieval	Scot.	Scottish
camp gay	stereotypically effeminate	Mex.	Mexican	SE	Standard English
Can.	Canadian	MHG	Middle High German	SF	science fiction
Carib.E.	Caribbean English	milit.	military	sfx	suffix
cit.	citation	mispron.	mispronunciation	sing.	singular
colloq.	colloquial	mis-sp.	mis-spelling	Skrt	Sanskrit
comb.	combination	MLG	Middle Low German	sl.	slang
Da.	Danish	n.	noun	SNZE	Standard New Zealand English
derog.	derogatory	naut.	nautical	society	upper- and middle-class use
dial.	dialect	Norw.	Norwegian	Sp.	Spanish
dict.	dictionary	N.Z.	New Zealand	sp.	spelling
dimin.	diminutive	obs.	obsolete	spec.	specifically
Dmnca	Dominica	occas.	occasionally	subseq.	subsequent/subsequently
Du.	Dutch	OE	Old English	Sw.	Swedish
edn	edition	OF	Old French	synon.	synonym/synonymous
esp.	especially	OHG	Old High German	Tob.	Tobago
ety.	etymology	ON	Old Norse	trad.	traditional/traditionally
euph.	euphemism/euphemistic	onomat.	onomatopoeia/onomatopoeic	Trin.	Trinidad
excl.	exclamation	orig.	originally	Turk.	Turkish
ext.	extension/extended	pej.	pejorative	UKVI	UK Virgin Islands
f.	from	Pers.	Persian	Und.	Underworld (criminal
fem.	feminine	phr.	phrase		cant, *see* Introduction)
fig.	figurative/figuratively	pfx	prefix	US	United States
form.	formation	pl.	plural	US Hisp.	US Hispanic
Fr.	French	Port.	Portuguese	USVI	US Virgin Islands
Ger.	German	poss.	possibly	usu.	usually
Gk	Greek	P.R.	Puerto Rico	v.	verb
Guyn.	Guyana	prev.	previous headword	var.	variation/variant
Heb.	Hebrew	prob.	probably	vol.	volume
Hind.	Hindustani	prep.	preposition	W.I.	West Indies
Icel.	Icelandic	pron.	pronunciation	WW1	World War One
imper.	imperative	publ.	published	WW2	World War Two
Ind.	Indian	pvb	proverb/proverbial	Yid.	Yiddish
				Yorks.	Yorkshire

Short Forms of Reference

Please refer to The Major Slang Dictionaries 1500–2000 on p.xii, for further information.

Allsopp — Richard Allsopp, *Dictionary of Caribbean English Usage* (1996)

AND — W. S. Ramson, ed., *Australian National Dictionary* (1989)

Bee — Jon Bee, *A Dictionary of the Turf, The Ring, The Chase, etc* (1823)

B.E. — B.E., Gent.[leman], *Dictionary of the Canting Crew* (c.1698)

B&L — Albert Barrère & C.G. Leland, *The Dictionary of Slang, Jargon and Cant* (1889–90)

Burley — Dan Burley's *Original Handbook of Harlem Jive* (1944)

DARE — F. Cassidy, Joan Houston Hall, eds., *Dictionary of American Regional English* (1994 et seq.)

DNZE — H.W. Orsman, ed., *Dictionary of New Zealand English* (1997)

DSAE — Penny Silva, ed., *Dictionary of South African English* (1996)

DSUE — Eric Partridge, *Dictionary of Slang and Unconventional English* (1937–84, 8 edns)

DU — Eric Partridge, *Dictionary of the Underworld* (1949, 1961)

EDD — Joseph Wright, *English Dialect Dictionary* (1905, 6 vols.)

Egan's Grose — Pierce Egan, *Grose's Classical Dictionary of the Vulgar Tongue* (1823)

E.P. — Eric Partridge (*see DSUE* and *DU* above)

F&H — John Farmer & W.E. Henley, *Slang and Its Analogues* (1890–1904)

Grose — Francis Grose, *The Classical Dictionary of the Vulgar Tongue* (1785, 1788, 1796)

Harman — Thomas Harman, *Caveat for Common Cursetours* (c.1566)

HDAS — Jonathan Lighter, *The Historical Dictionary of American Slang* (1994 et seq.)

Hotten — John Camden Hotten, *A Dictionary of Modern Slang, Cant and Vulgar Words* (1859, 1860), then as *The Slang Dictionary* (1864, 1867, 1870, 1873)

Lex. Bal. — *Lexicon Balatronicum* (1811)

Matsell — George W. Matsell, *Vocabulum* (1859)

Nares — Robert Nares, *Nares' Glossary* (1822)

OED — John Simpson, Edmund Weiner, eds., *The Oxford English Dictionary* (online edition)

Share — Bernard Share, *Slanguage: a Dictionary of Irish Slang* (1997)

Vaux — Noel Maclachlan, ed., *The Memoirs of James Hardy Vaux* (1812, reprinted 1964)

Ware — J. Redding Ware, *Passing English of the Victorian Era* (1909)

Williams — Gordon Williams, *A Dictionary of Sexual Language and Imagery in Shakespearean and Stuart Literature* (1994, 3 vols.)

Y&B — Henry Yule & A.C. Burnell, *Hobson-Jobson, a Glossary of Anglo-Indian Words and Phrases* (1886)

A

A *n.* [1920s+] (*US*) a Model-*A* Ford automobile. [abbr.]

a *n.*[1] **1** [20C+] (*W.I., Guyn.*) a general term of dislike. **2** [1940s+] (*US*) used as a euph. for ASS n. (5), e.g. *haul a, bet your fat a.* [abbr. ARSE n.[1]/ASS n.]

a *n.*[2] [1960s+] (*drugs*) amphetamine (cf. AIMIES n.; AMP n.; AMPHETS n.; BAM n.[2]; BATHTUB SPEED n.; B-BOMB n.; BEAUTY n.[3]; BENZ n.; BILL n.[4]; BILLY n.[7]; BILLY WHIZ n.; BLACK AND TANS n.; BLACK AND WHITE n.[5]; BLACK BEAUTY n.; BLACKBIRD n.[3]; BLACK BOMBER n.; BLACK CADILLAC n.; BLACKJACK n.[3]; BLACK MOLLIES n.; BLACK WIDOW n.; BLANCA n.; BLUE n.[9]; BLUES n.[2]; BOLT n.[5]; BOMBER n.[2]; BOMBIDO n.; BOMBITA n.; BOTTLES n.; BRAIN-BURNERS n.; BRAIN TICKLERS n.; BROWN BOMBER n.[1]; BROWNIES n.; BROWNS n.[3]; BUMBLEBEES n.; CHRISTINA n.; COASTS TO COASTS n.; CO-PILOT n.; CRANK n.[4]; CROSSROADS n.; CROSS TOPS n.; CRYSTAL n.; DEBS n.; DEX n.; DIET PILLS n.; DISCO POWDER n.; DOOB n.[2]; DOUBLECROSS n.; DRIVERS n.[2]; EYE-OPENER n.[1]; FAST n.; FIVES n.[2]; FOOTBALLS n.; FORWARDS n.; GERMAN MARCHING PILLS n.; GO n.[5]; GO PILL n.; GREEN DRAGONS n.; GREEN HORNET n.[2]; GREENIES n.[2]; HALLOO-WACH n.; HEAD DRUGS n.; HEARTS n.; HELPERS n.; HORS D'OEUVRES n.[1]; HORSE HEADS n.; JAM n.[6]; JAM CECIL n.; JOLLY BEANS n.; JUNK n.[5]; L.A. n.; L.A. TURNABOUTS n.; LEAPER n.; LID-PROPPERS n.; LIFT PILL n.; LIGHTNING n.[2]; LOU REED n.; MACKA n.; MARATHONS n.; MEXICAN JUMPING BEANS n.; MINIBENNIE n.; MOLLIES n.; MONSTER n.[2]; MORNING SHOT n.; NUGGETS n.[3]; OLLY n.; ORANGES n.; PEP-'EM-UPS n.; PEP (PILL) n.; P.H. n.; PHET n.; PINK CHAMPAGNE n.; POWDER n.[2]; PULVER n.; PURPLE n.; PURPLE HEARTS n.; RAMRAIDER n.[2]; RED DEVILS n.; RHYTHM n.; RIPPERS n.; ROAD DOPE n.; ROSA n.; ROSES n.[2]; ROUSER n.[2]; SNAP n.[3]; SNOW n.[2]; SPARKLE PLENTY n.; SPARKLER n.[2]; SPECKLED BIRDS n.; SPEED n.[2]; SPEEDBALL n.[1]; SPLASH n.[4]; SPLIVINS n.; STRAWBERRIES n.; SULPH n.; SULPHATE n.; SWEETS n.[2]; TENS n.; THRUSTERS n.; TOFFEE WHIZZ n.; TOMBSTONE n.[3]; TRUCK-DRIVERS n.; TURKEY n.[5]; TURNABOUT n.[2]; UPPER n.[2]; WAKE-AMINE n.; WAKE-UP n.[3]; WATER n.[2]; WEST COAST TURNAROUNDS n.; WHITE n.[3]; WHITE CROSS n.; WHITES n.[4]; WHIZ n.[7]; WIDOW n.[2]; YIPPEE BEANS n.; YIP-YAP DRUG n.; ZOOM n.[3]). [abbr.]

a *n.*[3] [1960s+] (*drugs*) LSD, i.e. d-lycergic acid diethylamide-25 (cf. ACID n.[3]; ALICE n.[2]; ANIMAL n.[4]; BARRELS n.; BATTERY ACID n.; BEAST n.[4]; BLACK ACID n.; BLUE ACID n.; BLUE BARRELS n.; BLUE CHAIRS n.; BLUE HEAVEN n.; BLUE MICRODOT n.; BLUE MOONS n.; BLUE STAR n.; BLUE VIALS n.; BROWN BOMBER n.[1]; BROWN DOTS n.; BURNOUT n.; CHIEF n.[2]; CHOCOLATE CHIPS n.; CHRISTMAS TREE n.[1]; 'CID n.; CLEAR LIGHT n.; COFFEE n.; CONTACT LENS n.; CRACKERS n.[3]; CUBE n.[3]; CUPCAKES n.[2]; DEEDA n.; DOMES n.; DOTS n.[2]; FLASH n.[7]; FLAT BLUES n.; GHOST n.[1]; GRAPE PARFAIT n.; GREEN DRAGONS n.; GREEN WEDGE n.; HAWAIIAN SUNSHINE n.; HAWK n.[4]; HAZE n.; HEAVENLY BLUE n.; INSTANT ZEN n.; L n.[3]; L.B.J. n.; LIME ACID n.; LIQUID n.; LUCKY DIP n.; LUCY IN THE SKY WITH DIAMONDS n.; MELLOW YELLOW n.[2]; MICKEY MOUSE n.[4]; MICRODOT n.; MIGHTY QUINN n.; ONE WAY n.; ORANGE n.[2]; OWSLEY ACID n.; PAPER ACID n.; PAPER MUSHROOMS n.; PEACE n.[1]; PEACE TABLETS n.; PEARLY GATES n.[2]; PENGUIN n.[2]; PEPPERMINT SWIRL n.; PINK OWSLEY n.; PINK WEDGES n.; PURE LOVE n.; PURPLE n.; PURPLE BARRELS n.; PURPLE HAZE n.; PURPLE OHM n.; QUICKSILVER n.; RAINBOW n.[3]; ROYAL BLUES n.; SACRAMENT n.; SANDOZ n.; SKY BLUE n.[1]; SLIPPERY-DIP n.[1]; SMEARS n.; STRAWBERRY DIP n.; STRAWBERRY FIELDS n.; SUGAR n.[6]; SUGAR CUBES n.[2]; SUNSHINE n.[3]; SWEET PEA n.[1]; TRAVEL AGENT n.; TWENTY-FIVE n.[1]; VITAMIN A n.; WEDDING BELLS n.; WEDGE n.[4]; WHITE DUST n.; WHITE LIGHTNING n.; WINDOWPANE n.[1]; YELLOW DIMPLES n.; YELLOW SUNSHINE n.; ZEN n.). [abbr. ACID n.[3]; a powerful, synthetic hallucinogen, based on ergot and discovered in 1943 by Dr Albert Hofmann of Sandoz Laboratories, Basel, and massively popularized in the 1960s by Dr Timothy Leary (1920–96), Ken Kesey (b.1935) and his Merry Pranksters, rock groups and the 'alternative society']

a! *excl.* [1950s+] (*US Black*) absolutely! yes! certainly! [abbr. FUCKING-A! excl. (1)]

-a *sfx* [20C+] used to denote a colloq. or sl. pron. of: **1** have, e.g. *coulda, musta, shoulda, woulda.* **2** to, e.g. *gonna, gotta, oughta, wanna.* **3** of, e.g. CUPPA n.[1], KINDA/KINDER adv., LOTSA n., LOTTA n. [pron.]

aachibombo *n.* [1940s+] (*W.I.*) a codfish fritter. [W.I. *aachi,* codfish + BUMBO n.[2] (2), lit. 'codfish-arse']

aai-aai *n. see* AI-AI n.

a and b *n.* [1920s] (*US*) assault *and* battery. [abbr.]

aap *n.* [1940s+] (*S.Afr.*) a cannabis cigarette. [Afk. *aap,* an ape or monkey]

aardvark *n.* [1960s+] (*US*) a simpleton, a dullard, an oaf. [anthropomorphic use of SE; note the character *Aardvark* in Joseph Heller's *Catch-22* (1961), a cheery, bumbling oaf]

aaron, the *n.* **1** [17C–19C] a criminal, esp. a gang leader. **2** [19C] a cadger. [the biblical *Aaron,* Judaism's first high priest]

aaron's rod *n.* [19C; 1980s+] the penis. [punning on ROD n.[1] (1), f. Num. 17:8: 'Behold, the rod of Aaron...was budded, and brought forth buds, and bloomed blossoms and yielded almonds']

aasbed *n.* [1950s] (*W.I.*) a rough bed. [? ARSE n.[1] (1) + SE *bed*]

aataclaps *n.* [1990s+] (*W.I.*) a disaster, a calamity. [? SE *clap* of thunder or *collapse*]

A.B. *n.*[1] **1** [1980s] fools as a group, lit. *Asshole Brigade.* **2** [1990s+] (*US prison*) Aryan Brotherhood, the White supremacist organization that unites many White convicts during (and after) their time in jail (cf. A.C. n.; A.W. n.). **3** [1990s+] (*Aus. prison*) Aryan Breed; the Australian version of (2). [abbr.]

A.B. *n.*[2] [1980s] (*N.Z.*) the menstrual period. [abbr. *Annie Brown,* on the model of menstruation = a visiting woman]

a.b. *n.* (*also* **ab**) [1930s+] (*US drugs*) an *ab*cess that develops after injecting with an unsterile needle or an unsterile water/narcotic solution. [abbr.]

ab *n.*[1] [19C+] (*Aus.*) an *Ab*original; the predecessor of the modern ABO n.[1]. [abbr.]

ab *n.*[2] [1960s+] an *ab*dominal muscle, usu. in the context of a flat stomach. [abbr.]

abaa *adj.* [1900s] **1** silly. **2** bad, e.g. *abaa cove,* a bad man. [ety. unknown; ? 'baaing' of a sheep]

abactor *n.* (*also* **abacter**) [mid-17C–early 19C] a dishonest drover or shepherd who connives at stealing the cattle he is guarding. [Lat. *abigere*, to drive away]

abaddon *n.* [19C] a thief turned informer. [punning on *a bad 'un/Abaddon*, 'the angel of the bottomless pit', Rev. 9:11]

abaft the wheel-house *phr.* **1** [late 19C] (*US*) just below the small of the back; thus euph. for the buttocks. **2** [1900s] crazy. [naval imagery, *abaft*, behind, towards the stern]

abandannad *n.* [mid-late 19C] a thief who specializes in stealing bandanna handkerchiefs. [SE *abandoned* (boy) + *bandanna*]

abandoned habits *n.* [late 19C] the riding dress of the up-market courtesans who frequented Rotten Row in London's Hyde Park. [pun on their SE *abandoned habits*, i.e. immorality + SE *riding habit*, their costume]

abareskin *adj.* [1960s] (*US camp gay*) embarrassing. [joc. mispron. and ref. to SE *bare skin*]

abbess *n.* (*also* **lady abbess, mother abbess**) [late 17C–19C] a brothel-keeper, a madame, 'of the highflyer sort' (cf. ABBOT n.; ABBOT ON THE CROSS n.; CONVENT n.; COVENT GARDEN ABBESS n.; COVENT GARDEN NUNNERY n.; CROZIERED ABBOT n.; NUN n.; NUNNERY n.; PROVINCIAL n.; SEMINARY n.; TEMPLE n.). [ironic use of SE]

abbey-lubber *n.* [mid-16C–early 18C] a lazy monk; a reproachful name in regular use after the Reformation. [SE *abbey* + *lubber*, f. OF *lobeor*, a swindler, a parasite; the word is the origin of the naut. sl. *land-lubber*]

abbot *n.* [late 19C] a brothel-keeper's husband or lover. [the male counterpart of the ABBESS n.]

abbot on the cross *n.* [19C] a pimp (cf. APPLE-MONGER n.; APPLE SQUIRE n.; APRON SQUIRE n.; BELLSWAGGER n.; BLOKE n.; BLUDGEONER n.; BLUDGER n.[2]; BOUNCER n.[2]; BROKER n.[1]; BROTHER OF THE GUSSET n.; BULLY n.[1]; BULLY-HACK n.; CAPTAIN n.[1]; CASH CARRIER n.; COCK-BAWD n.; COCK-PIMP n.; C.P. n.; CROZIERED ABBOT n.; CUNT-PENSIONER n.; DONA JACK n.; DRAB-DRIVER n.; FAGGOT-MASTER n.; FAKER n.; FANCY COVE n.; FLASHMAN n.; GAMESTER n.; GAP-STOPPER n.; HACKNEY n.; HAYMARKET HECTOR n.; HOLER n.; JOCKUM-GAGGER n.; KIDDY n.[1]; LED CAPTAIN n.; MACKEREL n.; MUTTON-TUGGER n.; PENSIONER (TO THE PETTICOAT) n.; PENSIONER OF THE PLACKET n.; PETTICOAT MERCHANT n.; PIMP WHISK n.; PINCH-BOTTOM n.; PINCH-BUTTOCK n.; PINCH-CUNT n.; PIPPIN-SQUIRE n.; POUNCE-SHICER n.; POUNCEY n.; PUNK-MASTER n.; RUMPER n.; SCOUT n.[1]; SETTER n.[1]; SHADOW n.; SMELL-SMOCK n.; SMOCK MERCHANT n.; SMOCK PENSIONER n.; SPLIT n.[5]; SQUIRE OF THE BODY n.; SQUIRE OF THE PETTICOAT n.; SQUIRE OF THE PLACKET n.; STALLION n.; STICK SLINGER n.; STRIKER n.[1]; SUNDAY MAN n.[2]; TOWN BULL n.; TOWN TRAP n.; TUG-MUTTON n.; TURNBULL STREET ROGUE n.; VICTUALLER n.; WHISKIN n.; WHORE-EATER n.). [the male counterpart of the ABBESS n. + ON THE CROSS phr.]

Abbott's priory *n.* (*also* **Abbott's park**) [early–mid-19C] the King's Bench prison, also known as Abbott's Lodge; thus *Abbott's teeth*, the spikes that topped the prison wall (cf. BAR L n.; BATE'S FARM n.; BAY, THE n.; BENCH, THE n.; BIG L n.; BIG Q n.; BURDON'S HOTEL n.; CASTIEAU'S HOTEL n.; CRUM, THE n.; DOWNS, THE n.; EL, THE n.; ELLENBOROUGH'S LODGE n.; FARRINGDON HOTEL n.; FRESHWATER BAY n.; GATE, THE n.; HALF-WAY HOUSE n.; HOLLOWAY CASTLE n.; HORN, THE n.; HORSE, THE n.; HOTEL DE GARVIE n.; ISLAND, THE n.; JOY, THE n.; KING'S COLLEGE n.; KING'S HEAD INN (IN NEWGATE STREET), THE n.; LUD'S BULWARK n.; LUD'S UNLUCKY GATE n.; MACGORREY'S HOTEL n.; MALABAR HILTON n.; MODEL, THE n.; MOOR, THE n.; NAVY OFFICE n.; NEWGATE n.[1]; NEWMAN'S (COLLEGE) n.; OLD DOSS, THE n.; OLD NASK n.; OLD START, THE n.; PENT, THE n.; PINK PALACE, THE n.; POINT, THE n.[1]; Q n.[1]; QUENTIN n.; RASHERHOUSE n.; ROCK, THE n.; ROW, THE n.; SAN Q n.; SCRUBS, THE n.; SIBERIA n.; SPIKE PARK n.; SPIKES, THE n.; START, THE n.; STEEL, THE n.; SUN CITY n.; TOMBS, THE n.; WALL CITY n.; WHIT, THE n.; WHIT'S PALACE n.; WHITTINGTON PRIORY n.; WHITTINGTON('S) COLLEGE n.; WORKS, THE n.). [Sir Charles

Abbott (1762–1832), Lord Chief Justice (1818–32). The King's Bench prison was generically the Lodge or the *Priory*, and its 'given' name varied according to the current Lord Chief Justice; thus before 1818 'Abbott' had been 'Ellenborough', f. the previous office-holder]

ABC *n.*[1] [1920s] (*Irish*) scorch marks on one's legs. [? play on *ABC* bread company, i.e. one's legs have been toasted]

ABC *n.*[2] [1990s+] (*Aus.*) Australian-born Chinese. [abbr.]

ABC *n.*[3] *see* AMERICAN BUSINESS COLLEGE n.

a.b.c. *n.*[1] [late 17C; 19C] the vagina. [like *ABC*, it is the beginning, although of life rather than the alphabet]

a.b.c. *n.*[2] *see* ACE BOON COON n.

abdabs *n.* (*also* **habdabs**) [1940s+] **1** nervous anxiety; thus SCREAMING ABDABS n. **2** empty chatter, nonsense; thus in phr. *come the (old) abdabs* or *give someone the (old) abdabs*, to fool someone. [? echoic of the spluttering, hesitant speech of one who is thus afflicted]

abdar *n.* [19C] (*Anglo-Ind.*) a teetotaller. [Urdu *abdar*, the man in charge of the water, thus 'water-carrier', who was the head servant in 19C Anglo-Ind. society]

abdicate *v.* [1940s+] (*gay*) to leave a public lavatory in which one is soliciting, to avoid interrogation by its attendant or a policeman. [pun on SE *abdicate the throne* and THRONE n./QUEEN n.[2] (1)]

abdicated *adj.* [1940s+] (*gay*) ordered out of the public lavatory where one is looking for sex. [ABDICATE v.]

Abdul *n.* **1** [1910s–20s] (*also* **Abdullah**) a derog. term for an Afghan. **2** [1910s–40s] (*Aus.*) a derog. term for a Turkish soldier. **3** [1980s+] (*US*) a derog. term for an Arab (cf. AYRAB n.; CAMEL-CHASER n.; CAMEL-DRIVER n.; CAMEL-FUCKER n.; CAMELHEAD n.; CAMEL JOCKEY n.; DUNE COON n.; GREASER n.[1]; HANDKERCHIEF-HEAD n.[2]; HANKIE-HEAD n.; JOHNNIE n.[4]; RAG-HEAD n.[1]; RUG PEDDLER n.; SAND-COON n.; SAND-HOPPER n.; SAND-JOCKEY n.; SAND NIGGER n.; SAND TOAD n.; SAND WOG n.; TOWEL-HEAD n.). [stereotypical 'Arab' name]

Abe *n.*[1] (*also* **abe**) [19C+] a derog. term for a Jew (cf. ABIE n.; ABIE KABIBBLE n.; COHEN n.; GOLDBERG n.; HEBE n.; HYMIE n.; IKE n.; IKEY n.[1]; IKEY-MO n.; IZZY n.; MOCKIE n.; SOLLY n.; SOLOMON ISAAC n.). [abbr. of proper name, *Abraham*, the biblical patriarch]

Abe *n.*[2] **1** [1940s–60s] (*US*) a $5 bill (cf. ABE'S CABE n.; ABRAHAM LINCOLN n.; ABRAHAM NEWLAND n.; ALEXANDER HAMILTON n.[1]; BEN FRANKLIN n.; BIG GEORGE n.; BRADBURY n.; BROWN ABE n.; DEAD PRESIDENT n.; DEAD WHITEBOY n.; GEORGE n.[3]; GEORGE WASHINGTON n.[2]; GROVER n.; HAMILTON n.; HENRY HASE n.; HER MAJESTY'S PICTURES n.; JACKSON n.; KING'S PICTURES n.; LAWFUL PICTURE n.; LINCOLN n.; LOUIE n.; MARSHALL n.; OLD HICKORY n.; PICTURE n.[3]; PICTURE OF ABE (LINCOLN) n.; PICTURES OF THE QUEEN n.; PORTRAIT n.[1]; PORTRAIT OF MADISON n.; QUEEN'S PICTURES n.; RED 'ARRY n.; SIMOLEON n.; UNCLE SAM'S I.O.U. n.). **2** [1950s+] (*US drugs*) $5 worth of drugs. [ABRAHAM LINCOLN n.]

abear *v.* [late 19C; 1940s–70s] to abide, to tolerate. [OE *abearan*, to bear, to carry; thence to dial.; 1940s–70s use is US Black]

Aberdeen cutlet *n.* [19C] a dried haddock. [the Aberdeen fishing trade]

Aberdeen(s) *n.* [20C+] bean(s). [rhy. sl.]

Abergavenny *n.* [19C] a penny. [rhy. sl.; ult. *Abergavenny*, a town in Wales]

Abe's cabe *n.* [1980s+] (*drugs*) a $5 bill. [ABE n.[2] (1) + redup.]

a.b.f. *n.* [1910s+] the last drink of a session. [abbr. *absolutely bloody final drink*]

a.b.h. *n.* [2000s] a beating. [abbr. SE/legal term *actual bodily harm*, physical harm deliberately inflicted, but less serious than *grievous bodily harm*]

Abie *n.* **1** [1910s+] (*also* **Aby**) a Jew (cf. ABE n.[1]). **2** [1940s] (*US Black*) a tailor. [ABE n.[1]; (2) trad. linking of Jews and tailoring]

Abie Kabibble *n.* [1910s–30s] (*US*) a Jew (cf. ABE n.[1]). [var. on US Yid. *ish kabibble*, who cares, don't worry; prob. ult. synon. Yid.

nish gefidlt. Adopted by the vaudeville star Fanny Brice (1891–1951), the term was picked up by America's 'dean of cartoonists', Harry Hershfield, who in 1917 launched a character called Abie the Agent, based on one *Abie Kabibble*. Highly successful, the strip lasted until 1932. The term was further popularized by a swing trumpeter who adopted the name Ish Kabibble and started performing as a comic. Note also The Marx Bros. character 'Abe Kabiddle', in *The Cocoanuts* (1928)]

abigail *n*. **1** [17C–1900s] a lady's maid. **2** [1950s+] (*camp gay*) an ageing, conservative homosexual (cf. AGGIE n.²; AGNES n.; ANGIE n.; ANNIE n.; BETTY n.²; BRUCE n.; CHARLENE n.; CHARLIE n.¹⁰; CYRIL (SNEER) n.; DAISY n.²; DOROTHY'S FRIEND n.; ESTHER (THE QUEEN) n.; ETHEL n.; FRIEND OF OSCAR n.; GEORGETTE n.; GERTIE n.; HAIRY MARY n.¹; JANE n.²; JESSIE n.¹; JOAN OF ARC n.²; JOCELYN n.; JODY n.; JOEY n.⁶; LILY n.⁵; MARGERY n.; MARY n.²; MARY ANN n.¹; MAUD n.; MISS FITCH n.; MISS IT n.; MISS MOLLY n.; MISS MORALES n.; MISS NANCY n.; MISS THING n.; MOLL n.¹; MOLLY n.¹; MORRIE n.²; NANCE n.; NANCY n.²; NANCY BOY n.; NANCY DAWSON n.; NELLIE n.; NELLIE (DEANS) n.; NOLA n.; OSCAR n.¹; ST MARY n.; SHEENA n.; ZANE n.¹). [a character in Francis Beaumont and John Fletcher's play *The Scornful Lady* (*c*.1613), although she was poss. so named in allusion to the expression 'thine handmaid' used in the Bible by Abigail the Carmelitess, 1 Sam. 25:24–31]

abishag *n*. [19C] the bastard child of a woman who has been seduced and abandoned by a married man. [Heb., lit. 'the mother's error']

able and cable *phr*. [1950s] (*US Black*) ready and willing. [SE *able* + redup.]

able Grable *n*. [1940s] (*US teen*) an attractive woman (cf. READY HEDY n.). [SE *able* + US film star Betty *Grable* (1916–73)]

able to crawl under a snake's belly *phr*. [1920s+] (*orig. Aus.*) a phr. used to describe a person who acts immorally and without the least ethics, sometimes ext. as *able to crawl under a snake's belly with a top hat/with stilts on*.

able to eat an apple through a knot hole *phr*. (*also able to eat an apple through a paling fence, …a picket fence, …wire-netting, able to eat a corn on the cob…, …a slice of watermelon…, …pumpkin…*) [20C+] (*US*) a phr. used of one who has buck teeth.

able to kick the eye out of a mosquito *phr*. [late 19C–1920s] (*orig. US*) a phr. used to describe a person who is supremely competent.

abo *n*.¹ [20C+] (*Aus.*) an *Abo*riginal. [abbr.; ? ult. abbr. of the column 'Aboriginalities', launched in the Sydney *Bulletin*, 15 October 1887 (of which one regular writer signed himself 'Abo'); *AND* suggests it was current orally somewhat earlier; the SE *Aborigine* and *Aboriginal* are found in 1829 cits., while the pl. *aborigines* is found in 1803; note RMC Duntroon use *aboed*, drunk]

abo *n*.² *see* ABOLIAR n.

aboard *adv*. [19C–1940s] (*orig. US*) in one's stomach, esp. of drink; thus *get aboard*, to be drunk.

aboliar *n*. (*also abo*) [1900s–30s] (*Aus.*) an expert on Aborigine and bush customs and folktales. [ABO n.¹ + SE *liar*]

A-bomb *n*. (*US drugs*) **1** [1960s+] a combination of marijuana or hashish with opium or another narcotic (cf. ATOM BOMB n.; B-40 n.; BAZOOKA n.¹; BAZUCA n.; BOMB n.⁴). **2** [1990s+] phencyclidine mixed with formaldehyde. [the supposedly 'explosive' effects]

A-bomb juice *n*. [1940s+] (*US*) illicitly distilled alcohol. [its 'explosive' effects]

abort *v*. [1970s+] (*US gay*) to defecate immediately after anal intercourse. [black humour]

abortion *n*. [late 18C+] an all-purpose denigration of a person, an object or an enterprise.

about east *adv*. [mid-19C] (*US*) properly, regularly, as it should be. [? sailing use]

about half *phr*. [1960s] feeling well, relatively happy. [i.e. half-way between good and bad]

about it *phr*. [2000s] (*US Black*) totally committed.

about one's speed *phr*. *see* SPEED n.¹ (1).

about right *phr*.¹ [19C+] drunk; one of a number of sl. terms referring to positive aspects of drinking (cf. ABOVE PAR phr.; AFLOAT adj.; ALTOGETHERY adj.; AT REST phr.; BALMY adj.; BREEZY adj.¹; BRIGHT IN THE EYE phr.; BUOYANT adj.; BUZZING adj.; CHEERY adj.; CHIPPER adj.; CHIRPING MERRY adj.; CLEAR adj.¹; COMFORTABLE adj.; COSY adj.; ELECTRIFIED adj.; EXALTED adj.; FEEL GOOD v.; FEELING NO PAIN phr.; FEELING RIGHT ROYAL phr.; FETTLED adj.; FINE adj.¹; FIRED UP adj.; FRESH adj.¹; GAY adj.²; GEED-UP adj.²; GLAD adj.¹; GLORIOUS adj.; GOOD HUMOUR, BE IN A v.; HAPPY adj.; HEARTY adj.; INSPIRED adj.; JOLLY adj.²; JUST NICELY phr.; KEYED adj.; LIT (UP) adj.; LOOKING LIVELY phr.; MAXED adj.; MAXED OUT adj.; MAXY adj.; MELLOW adj.; MIRACULOUS adj.; NICE adj.¹; NICELY(, THANK YOU) phr.; PERKED adj.; PERTISH adj.; PLEASANT adj.; REFRESHED adj.; RIGHT adj.²; RIPE adj.¹; SALUBRIOUS adj.; SNUG adj.; SPIFFED adj.; STOKED adj.; SWEET adj.⁴; WARM adj.¹; WELL AWAY phr.; WELL UNDER WAY phr.). [the inference is that the sober state is 'wrong']

about right *phr*.² [mid-19C+] correct. [ext. of SE; the implication is of a slightly grudging admission]

about right *adv*. [mid-19C–1900s] to the best extent possible.

about that *phr*. [1990s+] (*US campus*) in agreement with.

above board *phr*. **1** [early 17C+] open, honest. **2** [mid-17C–early 18C] in a sexual context, maintaining an undisguised relationship; thus antonym *under board*. [the image is of card-players keeping their hands in clear view above the table and thus resisting any temptation to cheat]

above board *adv*. [mid-19C+] openly, honestly. [ABOVE BOARD phr. (1)]

above one's bend *phr*. [mid-19C] (*US*) beyond one's abilities. [the image is of an object beyond one's grasp; or ? above, i.e. beyond, the bend of the river on which one lives]

above oneself *phr*. [20C+] over-confident, pushy, esp. of someone who is usually more self-effacing; usu. as GET ABOVE ONESELF v.

above par *phr*. **1** [mid-19C] (*UK Und.*) well-off. **2** [late 19C] in good spirits or health. **3** [1930s] mildly drunk (cf. ABOUT RIGHT phr.¹). [Stock Exchange jargon *par*, face value]

above snakes *phr*. [mid-19C] (*US*) **1** tall. **2** above the ground. ['a snake's eye view' of life above ground]

above the odds *phr*. *see* OVER THE ODDS phr.

A-box *n*. [1990s+] (*US campus*) someone in an unpleasant mood. [abbr. ATTITUDE n. + SE *box*]

abrac *n*. [early–mid-19C] learning. [either SE *Arabic* or abbr. SE *abracadabra*]

abraham *see also under* ABRAM and its combs.

abraham *n*.¹ [19C] the penis (cf. BIG FOOT JOE n.; DR JOHNSON n.; DON CYPRIANO n.; FATHER ABRAHAM n.; HANGING JOHNNY n.; HERMAN (THE ONE-EYED GERMAN) n.; JACK n.³; JACKIE ROBINSON n.; JACK ROBINSON n.; JACOB n.¹; JAKEY n.¹; JERRY n.⁹; JIMMY n.⁵; JOHN n.⁹; JOHN HENRY n.²; JOHNNIE n.⁵; JOHNSON n.¹; JOHN THOMAS n.; JOHN WILLIE n.; JONES n.²; JULIUS CAESAR n.¹; KENNEDY n.; LITTLE DAVY n.; MAN THOMAS n.; MASTER JOHN GOODFELLOW n.; MASTER REYNARD n.; MR TOM n.¹; NEBUCHADNEZZAR n.¹; OLD ADAM n.; OLD BILL n.²; OLD BLIND BOB n.; OSCAR n.; PETER n.⁴; RODNEY n.²; ST PETER n.; SIR JOHN n.; SIR MARTIN WAGSTAFFE n.; TIMOTHY-TOOL n.; TOM n.²; UNCLE JOHN n.; UNCLE THOMAS n.; WILLIAM n.²; WYATT EARP n.¹). [*Abraham*, the biblical patriarch, i.e. the role of the penis in procreation]

abraham *n*.² *see* ABRAHAM-MAN n.

abraham *v*. [1990s+] to sham, esp. to avoid something by feigning illness. [rhy. sl., but note SHAM ABRAM v. (1)]

abraham-cove *n*. *see* ABRAHAM-MAN n.

abrahamer *n*. (*also abramer*) [late 18C–early 19C] a tramp. [ext. of ABRAHAM n.²/ABRAM n.]

abraham grains *n.* [late 19C–1900s] a publican who brews his own beer. [generic use of proper name *Abraham* + SE *grains*]

Abraham Lincoln *n.* [1950s–60s] (*US, esp. Black*) a $5 bill (cf. ABE n.²). [the face of *Abraham Lincoln* (1809–65), 16th president of the US, printed on $5 bills]

abraham-man *n.* (*also* **abraham, abraham-cove**) [mid-16C–mid-19C; 1930s] a wandering beggar, adopting tattered clothing and posing as a madman. [? the *Abraham* Ward of the Hospital of St Mary of Bethlehem, London, in which the insane patients were housed. The hospital, known popularly as Bedlam, allowed certain inmates to go begging on a number of fixed days each year; the *abram-man* posed as one of these licensed beggars. Note the parable of the beggar in Luke 16:19–31; Ribton-Turner, *A History of Vagrants* (1887), suggests Gaelic/Erse *bramanach*, a noisy fellow; + SE *man*/COVE n. (1)]

Abraham Newland *n.* [late 18C–early 19C] a banknote; thus *sham Abraham Newland*, to forge banknotes (cf. ABE n.²). [proper name of *Abraham Newland*, chief cashier of the bank of England (1778–1807)]

Abrahampstead *n.* [1970s+] Hampstead in north London. [play on the Jewish name *Abraham* + SE *Hampstead*, trad. an area with a large Jewish population]

abraham's balsam *n.* [18C] the gallows. [SE *Abraham's balm*, the chaste tree (*Vitex agnus-castus*), but presumably punning on *Abraham's bosom*, the abode of the dead]

abraham's bosom *n.* [19C+] the vagina; thus *be in Abraham's bosom* or *take a turn in Abraham's bosom*, to have sexual intercourse. [punning on the biblical use of *abraham's bosom* meaning the 'abode of the dead', e.g. at Luke 16:22: 'The beggar died, and was carried by the angels into Abraham's bosom.' In both SE and sl. defs. the implication is of 'lying on']

abraham's willing *n.* [mid-19C–1900s] a shilling (5p). [rhy. sl.]

abram *n.* [17C–mid-19C] (*UK Und.*) a wandering beggar, adopting tattered clothing and posing as a madman; thus MAUND ABRAM v. (cf. CANTING CREW n.). [abbr. ABRAM-MAN n.]

abram *adj.* **1** [mid-16C–mid-17C] insane, crazy. **2** [mid-17C–mid-19C] (*UK Und.*) naked. [ABRAM n.]

abram *v.* [mid-19C] to malinger, to fake illness. [? naut. *abram*, a malingerer; or ? rhy. sl. = *sham*]

abramer *n. see* ABRAHAMER n.

abram-man *n.* (*also* **abram-cove, abram-mort**) **1** [17C–19C] a wandering beggar, adopting tattered clothing and posing as a madman. **2** [late 18C–mid-19C] a thief specializing in pocket-books. [var. on ABRAHAM-MAN n. + COVE n. (1)/MORT n.]

abram-sham *n.* [late 19C] the practice of travelling the country posing as a madman. [ABRAM SHAM v.]

abram sham *v.* (*also* **abraham sham**) [early–mid-19C] of a beggar, to travel the country posing as a madman, to fake illness. [ABRAM n./ABRAHAM n.² + SE *sham*]

abram suit *n.* (*also* **abraham suit**) [19C] working as a writer of begging letters, the pursuit of many small-time confidence tricksters at the time. [ABRAM n./ABRAHAM n.² + SE *suit*, a petition]

abram work *n.* (*also* **abraham work**) [late 19C] any form of spurious occupation, esp. some form of confidence trick. [ABRAM n./ABRAHAM n.² + SE *work*]

abridgements *n.* [mid-19C] knee-breeches. [they are 'abridged' or cut off at the knee]

abroad *adj.* **1** [late 18C–mid-19C] of convicts, transported to a penal colony. **2** [19C] in error, confused; thus *all abroad*, wide of the mark. **3** [mid-19C] of convicts, transported to a penal colony.

abroaded *adj.* **1** [mid–late 19C] (*UK society*) living in exile somewhere other than the UK. **2** [mid–late 19C] transported to a penal colony. **3** [late 19C–1920s] imprisoned.

abscotchalater *n.* [late 19C] (*US*) one who runs away. [var. pron. of ABSQUATULATE v. (1)]

absentee *n.* [mid-19C] (*Aus.*) a convict. [? because he is absent from everyday life]

absent-minded beggar *n.* [late 19C–1900s] a soldier. [title of poem (1899) by Rudyard Kipling, celebrating the British soldier]

abso *n.* [1900s] a definite winner, usu. in a sporting context. [abbr. SE *absolute*]

absoballylutely *adv.* (*also* **absobloominglutely**) [1910s+] an intense version of absolutely, very much indeed. [SE *absolutely* + BALLY adj./BLOOMING adj.² (2) as infix]

absobloodylutely *adv.* [1930s+] an intense version of absolutely, very much indeed. [SE *absolutely* + BLOODY adj.¹ (3)]

absofuckinglutely *adv.* [1910s+] very much so indeed, without the slightest doubt; also as excl. of affirmation. [SE *absolutely* + FUCKING adj. (4), coined by WW1 troops]

absogoddamlutely *adv.* [1960s+] (*US*) absolutely. [SE *absolutely* + GOD-DAMN adj. (3)]

absolutely! *excl.* [20C+] yes! indeed!

absolutely not! *excl.* [20C+] not a hope! not a chance!

absotively *adv.* [1910s+] (*US*) without a doubt, irrefutably. [comb. of SE *absolutely* + *positively*; inverse of POSILUTELY adv.]

absquattle *v.* [mid-19C] (*orig. US*) of a person or animal, to leave, to run away, to abscond. [var. on ABSQUATULATE v. (1)]

absquatulate *v.* (*also* **absquotulate, obsquatulate**) [19C] (*orig. US*) **1** (*also* **absquat**) of people or animals, to leave, to run away, to abscond. **2** of an object, to separate, to break away from. [cod Lat. based on SE *abscond* + *squat* + sfx. *-ulate*; note John Mitchell Bonnell, 'A manual of the art of prose composition: for the use of colleges and schools' (1867): 'absquatulate – to remove one's residence away; as if squat were a Latin root, from which were formed *squatulare* and *absquatulare*']

abstain from beans *v.* [1920s] to desist from politics. [Plutarch (AD 46?–AD *c*.120), *Of the Training of Children*, 'Abstain from beans; that is, keep out of public offices, for anciently the choice of the officers of state was made by beans']

abstractionist *n.* [mid-19C] (*US*) a pickpocket. [SE *abstract*, to remove]

abstropelous *adj.* [early 18C–mid-19C] aggressively resistant to control or restraint. [corruption of SE *obstreperous*]

a-buck *n.* [1980s+] (*US gay*) lying on one's back with one's legs over one's head to enable both anal intercourse and kissing.

Aby *n. see* ABIE n. (1).

abyss *n.* [1980s+] (*US gay*) a large anus that has been frequently used for anal intercourse.

Abyssinia *phr.* [1930s+] (*orig. US*) goodbye. [punning on 'I'll be seeing you']

Abyssinian polo *n.* [1920s+] (*US*) the game of craps dice (cf. AFRICAN BILLIARDS n.; AFRICAN DOMINOES n.; AFRICAN GOLF n.; AFRICAN PILLS n.; AFRICAN POOL n.; CONGO CROQUET n.; INDOOR GOLF n.; LEAPING DOMINOES n.; MISSISSIPPI MARBLES n.; NIGGER GOLF n.). [stereotyping of craps as a Black ('Abyssinian') person's favourite game]

A.C. *n.* [2000s] (*US prison*) Aryan Circle, a White supremacist prison gang (cf. A.B. n.¹; A.W. n.). [abbr.]

ac *n.* [1990s+] (*US Black*) the Acura Legend, a popular automobile. [abbr.]

a.c.a.b. *phr.* [1940s+] *all coppers are bastards*. [abbr.; a popular tattoo in the UK, esp. among Hell's Angels and other 'outlaw' groups]

academician *n.* **1** [early 19C] a prisoner. **2** [mid–late 19C] a prostitute. [punning use of SE + ACADEMY n. (4)/ACADEMY n. (1)]

academy *n.* **1** [early 17C–19C] a brothel, one of a number of contemporary terms based on brothel = school (cf. BOARDING SCHOOL n.; CAVAULTING SCHOOL n.; COLLEGE n.; DANCING ACADEMY n.; FINISHING ACADEMY n.; LADIES' COLLEGE n.; PUSHING SCHOOL n.; RIDING ACADEMY n.; SCHOOL OF VENUS n.; SEMINARY n.; TOPPING SCHOOL n.). **2** [early 18C] a casino. **3** [mid-18C] a lunatic asylum. **4** [early 19C–1950s] a prison; used in combs. (cf. ADKINS'S

ACADEMY n.; CAMPBELL'S ACADEMY n.; FLOATING ACADEMY n.).
5 [late 19C–1900s] a billiard room. [joc. uses of SE]

Acapulco (gold) n. [1960s+] (*orig. US drugs*) a high-strength grade of marijuana (cf. ACAPULCO RED n.; AFGHAN n.; AFRICAN n.[1]; AFRICAN BLACK n.; AFRICAN BUSH n.; ANGOLA (BLACK) n.; BELYANDO SPRUE n.; BLUE DE HUE n.; CAMBODIAN RED n.; CAMBODIAN TRIP n.; CANADIAN BLACK n.; CHICAGO BLACK n.; COLOMBIAN n.; COLUMBUS BLACK n.; CONGO (BUSH) n.; DURBAN POISON n.; FUMO D'ANGOLA n.; HAWAIIAN n.; INDIAN HAY n.; INDO n.; INDONESIA n.; KAFFIR TOBACCO n.; KENTUCKY BLUE n.; KIWI GREEN n.; LUMBO n.; MALAWI GRASS n.; MAUI WOWIE n.; MEXICAN BROWN n.; MEXICAN BUSH n.; MEXICAN COMMERCIAL n.; MEXICAN GREEN n.; MEXICAN RED n.; MONTEZUMA GOLD n.; NAM BLACK n.; NEW YORK CITY SILVER n.; PANAMA CUT n.; SANTA MARTA (GOLD) n.; TEXAS TEA n.; THAI (STICK) n.; ZACATECAS PURPLE n.). [the drug derives in and around *Acapulco* de Juárez in Guerrero state on the west coast of Mexico]

Acapulco red n. [1960s+] (*drugs*) marijuana. [a less potent form of ACAPULCO (GOLD) n.]

acca n.[1] (*also* acker) [1970s+] (*Aus.*) **1** an academic, esp. one who trades on the proliferation of current, if ephemeral, intellectual fads. **2** quotidian, jargon-laden academic writing. [abbr. + a pun on OCKER n. (4)]

acca n.[2] (*also* ack, acker) [1980s+] (*Aus.*) acne spots. [abbr.]

acceleration n. [late 19C] (*UK tramp*) starvation; thus phr. *die of acceleration*. [? it speeds up the imminence of death]

accident n. [20C+] an illegitimate child. [euph.]

accidental n. [1930s] (*US prison*) an inmate convicted for a social crime.

accommodate v. [early 19C] to work as a prostitute; thus *accommodation beauty*, a prostitute. [backform. f. ACCOMMODATION HOUSE n. (1)]

accommodation house n. **1** [18C–1930s] a brothel (cf. BADGER-CRIB n.; BADGER HOUSE n.; BARRELHOUSE n.; BAT HOUSE n.[2]; BED-HOUSE n.; BOARDING HOUSE n.; BOOGIE HOUSE n.; CALL HOUSE n.; CAN HOUSE n.; CASE HOUSE n.; CAT-HOUSE n.; CIRCUS HOUSE n.; COUPLING HOUSE n.; CREEP HOUSE n.; CRIB HOUSE n.; CUNICULARY WAREHOUSE n.; DOLL HOUSE n.[2]; FAIRY HOUSE n.; FANCY HOUSE n.; FAST HOUSE n.; FLASH HOUSE n.; FRANZY HOUSE n.; GARDEN HOUSE n.[1]; GAY HOUSE n.; GOAT HOUSE n.; GRINDING-HOUSE n.[2]; HOOK HOUSE n.; HOUSE n.[1]; HOUSE OF CIVIL RECEPTION n.; HOUSE OF CONVENIENCY n.; HOUSE OF DELIGHT n.; HOUSE OF PROFESSION n.; HOUSE OF RESORT n.; HOUSE OF SALE n.; HOUSE OF STATE n.; HUMP HOUSE n.; IRISH CLUBHOUSE n.; JAZZ HOUSE n.; JOY HOUSE n.; LEANING HOUSE n.; LEAPING HOUSE n.; LONG HOUSE n.; MEAT HOUSE n.; MOLL HOUSE n.; MOLLYHOUSE n.; MOT-HOUSE n.; NANNY HOUSE n.; NAUGHTY-HOUSE n.; NOOKIE HOUSE n.; NOTCH HOUSE n.; NUGGING HOUSE n.; OCCUPYING HOUSE n.; PARLOR HOUSE n.; PEG-HOUSE n.[2]; PUNCH HOUSE n.; SHOWHOUSE n.; SLAUGHTERHOUSE n.[1]; SPORT-HOUSE n.; SPORTING HOUSE n.; TRICK HOUSE n.; TRUGGING HOUSE n.; VAULTING HOUSE n.). **2** [late 19C] a 'hotel' where rooms can be hired for short times by lovers or prostitutes and their clients. [SE *accommodation house*, a lodging house; such places, like their description, may have begun as respectable buildings but soon changed their use]

accordion n. [1960s] (*US gay*) a penis that is substantially larger than expected when erect (cf. BAGPIPE n.[2]; BANJO (STRING) n.; BLUE-VEINED PICCOLO n.; BLUE-VEINED TRUMPET n.; CHANTER-PIPE n.; FIDDLE n.[1]; FIDDLE-BOW n.; FLUTE n.[2]; LIVING FLUTE n.; LUTE n.[1]; OBOE n.; PICCOLO n.[1]; PINK OBOE n.; PINK TRUMPET n.; SILENT FLUTE n.; SKIN FLUTE n.; SPUNK TRUMPET n.; TROUSER TRUMPET n.; WHISTLE n.[2]). [the physical resemblance to the instrument]

account executive n. [1960s–80s] (*US*) a pimp working for high-class prostitutes.

accoutrements n. [19C+] the male genitals. [SE *accoutrements*, apparel, outfit, equipment]

AC/DC adj. [1930s+] **1** bisexual. **2** (*gay*) ambivalent as to taking an active or passive role in a relationship. [the opposite varieties (alternating and direct) of electrical current]

ace n.[1] (*also* ace of hearts) **1** [late 16C–1900s] the vagina. **2** [17C–early 18C] the penis.

ace n.[2] **1** [late 19C–1940s] (*US*) an important, influential person. **2** [late 19C+] (*orig. US*) something or someone of high quality or held in high esteem. **3** [late 19C+] (*orig. US*) (*also* ace of clubs) an expert. **4** [1910s+] (*orig. US*) an outstanding person, whether in character or qualifications. **5** [1940s+] (*US Black*) a very close friend, an admired figure. **6** [1950s+] something useful, important. **7** [1950s+] a term of (intimate) address. **8** [1960s] (*US campus*) used sarcastically, a fool, a clumsy person. **9** [1970s] a professional killer. [the superiority of SE *ace*, in cards]

ace n.[3] **1** [late 19C+] (*US*) $1; $1's worth (cf. ACE-NOTE n.; ACE-SPOT n.). **2** [1910s] (*US*) a single example. **3** [1920s+] (*US Und.*) a 1-year jail sentence. **4** [1950s–60] (*UK Und.*) £1. **5** [1960s] (*US gambling*) the 1-spot on a die. **6** [1970s+] (*US gambling*) $100. [SE *ace*, 1 (at dice, in cards)]

ace n.[4] **1** [1930s+] (*US drugs*) a single pill of amphetamine, barbiturate or tranquillizer (cf. PILL n.[4]). **2** [1970s+] (*US drugs*) marijuana, a marijuana cigarette. **3** [1970s+] (*US drugs*) phencyclidine (PCP), a dangerous hallucinogenic based on animal (pig) tranquillizer (cf. A.D. n.[3]; ALIAMBA n.; ANGEL DUST n.; ANGEL HAIR n.; ANGEL PUKE n.; ANIMAL TRANQ n.; AURORA BOREALIS n.; BLACK WHACK n.; BOAT n.[4]; BOLT n.[5]; BUSH n.[5]; BUSY BEE n.[2]; BUTT NAKED n.; BUZZ n.[4]; CADILLAC n.; CANNABINOL n.; C.J. n.; COSMOS n.; CRAZY COKE n.; CRYSTAL n.; CRYSTAL JOINT n.; D n.[6]; DEATH WISH n.; DETROIT PINK n.; DEVIL'S DUST n.[2]; D.O.A. n.; DUMMY DUST n.; DUST n.[5]; ELEPHANT n.[4]; ELEPHANT TRANQUILLIZER n.; EMBALMING FLUID n.; ENERGIZER n.; FAIRY DUST n.; FLAKES n.; FUEL n.; GOOD n.[2]; GOON n.[2]; GORILLA BISCUITS n.; GREEN n.[3]; GREEN LEAVES n.; GREEN TEA n.; HERMS n.; HOG n.[9]; HORSE TRANQUILLIZER n.; KAPS n.; KILLER n.[3]; KILLER WEED n.; KOOLS n.; L.B.J. n.; LOG n.[2]; MAD DOG n.[1]; MADMAN n.; MAGIC (DUST) n.; MISSILE n.; MIST n.; MONKEY DUST n.; NEW ACID n.; NEW MAGIC n.; OIL n.[3]; OZONE n.[2]; P n.[3]; PARSLEY n.[3]; PAZ n.; PCP n.; PEACE n.[1]; PEACE PILLS n.; PEACE WEED n.; PEEP n.[3]; POLVO n.; PUFFY n.[1]; ROCKET FUEL n.; SCUFFLE n.[2]; SHEETS n.; SHERM n.; SNORTS n.; SOMA n.; SPORES n.; SQUEEZE n.[9]; STARDUST n.; STEAM n.[1]; S.T.P. n.; SUPERGRASS n.[1]; SUPER JOINT n.; SURFER n.[2]; T n.[2]; TAC n.; T-BUZZ n.; TEA n.[2]; THC n.; TIC n.; TISH n.; TRANK n.; WATER n.[2]; WHITE DUST n.; WOBBLE n.[2]; WOLF n.[4]; WORM n.[5]; ZOMBIE (WEED) n.; ZOOM n.[3]; ZOOTIE n.[1]). **4** [2000s] (*US prison*) a puff on a cigarette. [SE *ace*, 1 (at dice, in cards)]

ace n.[5] [1940s–50s] (*US*) a detective. [ACE adj.]

ace n.[6] [1960s+] (*US campus*) the grade A (cf. BAKER n.[3]; BANG n.[10]; BOMB n.[1]; BULLET n.[4]; CAT n.[15]; DIGGER n.[7]; DOG n.[15]; EAGLE n.[3]; FLAG n.[9]; FLASH n.[8]; FLUNK n.[1]; FROG n.[4]; HOOK n.[6]; ZIP n.[1]). [ACE adj. + the initial letter]

ace n.[7] see ACE (OF SPADES) n.

ace adj. (*also* acey) [1930s+] (*orig. US*) best, excellent, expert, wonderful. [ACE n.[2] (2)]

ace v.[1] **1** [1920s+] (*US*) to survive, esp. to survive intensive police interrogation. **2** [1920s+] (*US*) to manipulate someone, esp. through flattery or deception. **3** [1950s] (*US*) to lead. **4** [1950s+] (*orig. US campus*) (*also* ace out) to do well, to succeed, e.g. in an examination. **5** [1950s+] to outwit. **6** [1960s+] to kill. [the supremacy of the SE *ace* in cards]

ace v.[2] [1940s+] (*US*) to move or drive fast. [ACE adj.]

ace! excl. [1980s+] an excl. of satisfaction. [ACE adj.]

ace boon coon n. (*also* a.b.c., ace boom boom, ace coon poon, ace spoon coon) [1960s+] (*orig. US Black*) one's best and most trustworthy friend. [ACE adj. + BOON COON n. + joc. vars.]

ace boy n. (*also* ace buddy) [1950s+] (*US campus*) one's best friend. [ACE adj. + SE *boy*/BUDDY n. (1)]

ace cool n. (*also* ace kool) [1980s+] (*US Black*) a very close friend. [var. on ACE COON n. + COOL adj.[1] (6)]

ace coon *n.* [1960s+] (*US Black*) **1** a best friend. **2** an important person. [ACE adj. + COON n. (7)/abbr. ACE BOON COON n.]

ace coon poon *n. see* ACE BOON COON n.

ace-deuce *n.*[1] (*also* **acey-deucey**) [20C+] (*US/W.I.*) a best friend. [lit. '1-2']

ace-deuce *n.*[2] (*also* **acey-deucey**) [1920s+] (*US Black*) 3, esp. in craps dice. [in craps throwing 3 means one 'craps out' and loses one's money]

ace-deuce *n.*[3] (*also* **acey-deucey**) [1920s+] (*US*) a panic attack, a fit of nerves, a sudden fit of temper. [ACE-DEUCE n.[2]]

ace-deuce *adj.* [1970s] **1** at an angle. **2** (*US*) bisexual. [pron. of SE *AC/DC* or AC/DC adj. (1)]

ace-flat *adj.* [1940s] (*US*) excellent, first-rate. [ACE adj. + SE *flat*, absolute, downright, unqualified]

ace gear *n.* [1960s+] (*US gay*) a sexually talented homosexual, capable of both active and passive roles. [ACE adj. + GEAR n.[3]]

ace hi *n.* [1950s] (*US Black*) a sophisticated, aware person. [ACE-HIGH adj.]

ace-high *adj.* (*also* **aces-high**) [late 19C+] (*US*) valued or esteemed highly. [poker imagery]

ace in *v.* **1** [1920s–30s] (*US tramp*) to curry favour successfully. **2** [1930s–70s] (*US Und.*) to interfere, to become involved with.

ace in the hole *n.* [20C+] (*orig. US*) a hidden asset. [poker use, the 'hole card' is that which is kept face down on the table]

ace it *v.* [1950s+] (*US*) to make a perfect score on a school or college test. [ACE v.[1] (4)]

ace kool *n. see* ACE COOL n.

ace lane *n.* [1940s] (*US Black*) a husband. [ACE adj. + LANE n. (3)]

ace-lover *n.* [1940s] (*US Black, mainly Southern/Midwest*) one's most important lover, the most important member of the opposite sex one knows, e.g. a husband, a pimp, a boyfriend. [ACE adj. + SE *lover*]

aceman *n.* [1950s] (*US teen*) the leader of a teen street gang. [ACE adj. + SE *man*]

ace-note *n.* [1920s–60s] (*US*) a $1 bill. [ACE n.[3] (1) + SE *note*]

ace of clubs *n.*[1] *see* ACE n.[2] (3).

ace of clubs *n.*[2] *see* BLACK ACE n.

ace of hearts *n. see* ACE n.[1].

ace (of spades) *n.* [1940s+] a Black person; sometime derog. but often as used by Blacks themselves to designate a friend. [ACE n.[2] (2) + SPADE n.]

ace of spades *n.*[1] [19C+] (*US Und.*) a widow. [the blackness of the clothing and the suit of cards]

ace of spades *n.*[2] [late 19C+] the female genital area (cf. ACE OF TRUMPS n.; BLACK ACE n.). [supposed resemblance to the shape of pubic hair]

ace of spades *n.*[3] [1940s] (*US Und.*) an admirable person. [ACE n.[2] (2) + card-playing imagery]

ace of trumps *n.* [early 18C] the female genital area (cf. ACE OF SPADES n.[2]; BLACK ACE n.). [a trump card 'defeats' everything]

ace-one *adj.* [1960s] (*US Black*) very best. [ACE adj. + A-1 adj. (1)]

ace out *v.*[1] [1950s+] to defeat, to take something away. [poker jargon *ace*, the highest card, which beats any others]

ace out *v.*[2] *see* ACE v.[1] (4).

ace queen *n.* [1970s] (*US gay/prison*) a very effeminate prison homosexual. [ACE adj. + QUEEN n.[2] (1)]

aces *adj.* (*also* **aces up**) [20C+] (*US*) of both people and objects, wonderful, excellent, well-respected; thus *you're aces!* [poker imagery + ACE n.[2] (2)]

aces high *n.* [1930s+] (*orig. US prison*) an inmate popular among his peers. [ACE-HIGH adj.]

aces-high *adj. see* ACE-HIGH adj.

ace spoon coon *n. see* ACE BOON COON n.

ace-spot *n.* [1910s–20s] (*US*) a $1 bill. [ACE n.[3] (1) + -SPOT sfx (2)]

aces up *adj. see* ACES adj.

ace up one's sleeve *n.* [1910s+] (*orig. US*) a hidden advantage, not to be revealed until a suitable moment. [poker use, but with

suggestions of underhand methods, rather than careful, but still legal, planning]

acey *adj. see* ACE adj.

acey-deucey *see under* ACE-DEUCE.

acey-deucey *adj.*[1] [20C+] of a friend, close, intimate. [ACE-DEUCE n.[1]]

acey-deucey *adj.*[2] [1970s+] **1** (*US Black*) complex, unstable, neither one thing nor the other. **2** (*gay*) bisexual. [ACE-DEUCE adj.]

acher *see under* ACRE.

acid *n.*[1] [20C+] (*W.I.*) rum; thus *fire the acid*, to drink rum. [joc. allusion to its strength]

acid *n.*[2] [1910s+] cheek; thus COME THE (OLD) ACID v. [SE *acid tongue*]

acid *n.*[3] [1960s+] (*drugs*) LSD, i.e. d-lycergic *acid* diethylamide-25 (cf. A n.[3]). [abbr.]

acid *n.*[4] [1980s] (*drugs*) MDMA (cf. ECSTASY n.). [orig. and primarily used for LSD (*see* ACID n.[3]), acid emerged as a nickname for another hallucinogen (albeit with a very different chemistry) in the late 1980s]

acid *n.*[5] [1990s+] (*W.I./UK Black teen*) a special unit of the Jamaican police force, especially feared because of their severe tactics. [? SE *acid*, possible use in torture; or ? ACID n.[2]]

acid cap *n.* [1990s+] a tablet or capsule of LSD. [ACID n.[3] + CAP n.[4] (2)]

acid casualty *n.* **1** [1960s+] one whose brain is deemed to have suffered from an excess of hallucinogens. **2** [1980s+] the victim of an excess of MDMA. [ACID n.[3]/ACID n.[4] + SE *casualty*]

acid drop *n.* (*also* **acidulated tablet**) [1920s] a pound, a sovereign. [the shapes]

acid freak *n.* [1960s–70s] (*drugs*) a regular user of LSD. [ACID n.[3] + FREAK sfx]

acid-head *n.* [1960s+] (*drugs*) a regular user of LSD. [ACID n.[3] + -HEAD sfx (3)]

acid house party *n.* [1980s–90s] an illegal party, often held in a large building, such as a warehouse, and often outside the big cities, where thousands of young people pay for their entertainment and, allegedly, consume MDMA and other illegal drugs. [ACID n.[4] + HOUSE n.[2] + SE *party*; post-early 1990s usage is historical]

acid pad *n.* [1960s] (*US drugs*) a place where LSD is consumed. [ACID n.[3] + PAD n.[2] (2)]

acid rapper *n.* [1960s+] (*drugs*) one who takes extra-large doses of LSD. [ACID n.[3] + fig. use of RAPPER n.[4] (1)]

acid rock *n.* (*also* **freak rock**) [1960s+] a musical style allegedly influenced by, and purporting to recreate the sensations of, LSD and similar psychedelics; orig. in 1960s but underwent a minor revival in 1980s. [ACID n.[3] + SE *rock*]

acid test *n.* [1960s] a party. [ACID n.[3] + SE *test*; a pun on SE, accentuated by the contemporary slogan *Can you pass the acid test?* as a form of initiatory challenge. The original 'acid test' party, held in a San Francisco dancehall, where participants took LSD, many for the first time, was arranged by Ken Kesey's Merry Pranksters group and can be seen as the birth of widespread consumption of LSD]

acid trip *n.* [1960s+] **1** a dose of LSD. **2** the experience, often characterized as a 'journey', of taking a hallucinogenic drug, esp. LSD. [ACID n.[3] + TRIP n.[4] (1)]

acidulated tablet *n. see* ACID DROP n.

ack *n. see* ACCA n.[2].

ackamarackus *n.* (*also* **ackamaraka, ackamaracker**) [1930s–50s] a fraudulent tale, a tall story, nonsense; usu. in phr. *old ackamarackus*. [cod Lat.]

ackamaraka *n.* (*also* **ackamaracker, ackermaracker**) [1920s+] tea. [? an exaggerated, intensified play or even rhy. sl. on CHA n.[1]]

acker *n.* (*also* **akka**) [1910s+] (*orig. milit.*) money, whether change or notes, often found in pl.; also as *ackerage*, the bill. [Arab. *akka*, 1 piastre; imported by returning British soldiers post-WW1]

acker *see also under* ACCA.

Acker Bilk *n.* [1980s] (*Aus.*) milk. [rhy. sl.; ult. US musician *Acker Bilk* (b. 1929)]

acker fortis *n. see* AGGIE FORTIS *n.*

ackermaracker *n. see* ACKAMARAKA *n.*

ackie fortis *n. see* AGGIE FORTIS *n.*

ackman *n. see* ARK-MAN *n.*

acknickulous *adj.* [1980s+] (*US Black/teen*) wonderful, marvellous. [? SE *acknowledged* + *ridiculous* + *marvellous*]

acknowledge the corn *v.* (*also* **acknowledge the malt, own the corn**) [early 19C–1950s] (*orig. US*) to admit an error. [? in a horse-stealing case in a Western state, the defendant, accused of stealing 4 horses and 4 feeds of corn, declared *I acknowledge the corn* but denied the actual horse-stealing. 'Legend says he was lynched in spite of the admission' (Ware)]

ack-ruff *n.* (*also* **ack pirate, ack ruffian**) [mid-19C] a river thief. [var. on ARK-RUFF *n.*]

acky *n.* [1930s+] (*UK Und.*) aqua fortis, nitric acid when used to test for gold. [abbr.]

acorn *n.* **1** [1920s] (*US*) the head. **2** [1970s+] (*US gay*) the glans penis. [supposed resemblance]

acorn calf *n.* [19C+] (*US*) of humans and animals, a runt, a weakling. [Western US belief that a cow that ate too many acorns produced weak offspring]

acorn-cracker *n.* [1900s–40s] (*US*) an uncouth rural person (cf. APPLE-KNOCKER n.; APPLE-PICKER n.; APPLE-SHAKER n.; APPLE-SQUEEZER n.; BAMA CHUKKER n.; BACON-SLICER n.; BERRY PICKER n.; BRIAR-BREAKER n.; BULL-DRIVER n.; CARROT-CRUNCHER n.; CHAW-BACON n.; CHERRY-PICKER n.¹; CLOVER-KICKER n.; CORNCRACKER n.; CORNHUSKER n.; CORNTHRASHER n.; COW JOCKEY n.; FARMER n.²; GOAT ROPER n.; GULLY-JUMPER n.; HAWBUCK n.; HAYFOOT n.; HAY-PITCHER n.; HAY-POUNDER n.; HOG-RUBBER n.; MOSS-JUMPER n.; NOSE PICKER n.; PEAPICKER n.; PLOW JOCKEY n.; POSSUM-EATER n.; PUDDLEJUMPER n.; PUMPKIN-ROLLER n.; RAILSPLITTER n.; RABBIT-CHOKER n.; SQUIRREL-SHOOTER n.; STUMP-JUMPER n.; SWEDE-BASHER n.; TURNIP-SNAGGER n.; WHOP-STRAW n.). [SE *acorn* + SE *crack/ cracker* n.³ (1); such individuals allegedly eat acorns]

acorns *n.* [1970s] (*US*) the testicles (cf. APPLES n.¹; APRICOTS n.; BERRIES n.¹; COCONUTS n.¹; CONKERS n.; DINGLEBERRY n.; EGGS n.¹; EGGS IN THE BASKET n.; GOOBER n.²; GOOSEBERRIES n.; GRAPES n.¹; JINGLEBERRY n.; LOVE APPLES n.; LOVE SPUDS n.; MEAT AND TWO VEG n.; NUTMEGS n.; NUTS n.²; PLUMS n.; SCALLOPED POTATOES n.; ONIONS n.; OYSTERS n.). [resemblance]

acre *n.*¹ (*also* **acher**) [1960s+] (*Aus.*) the buttocks. [SE *acre*, a large area]

acre *n.*² (*also* **acher**) [1960s+] the testicles. [? physical proximity to ACRE n.¹]

acre (of corn) *n.* [1930s–50s] (*Aus./US*) a prison sentence, cited variously as 1 month, 12 months or simply 'plenty'; thus phr. used of a recidivist, *there's corn growing for some*. [the use of corn is a ref. to hominy, a staple of Aus. prison food, the idea being that one will eat that much corn during the sentence]

acres *n.* [late 18C–mid-19C] a coward. [the character of Bob *Acres*, in R.B. Sheridan's *The Rivals* (1775), whose 'courage always oozed out of his finger ends']

acrobat *n.* [1950s–60s] (*W.I.*) a fool. [? he 'falls over' himself]

across *adv.* [1900s] (*US*) Great Britain. [*across* the Atlantic]

across lots *phr.* (*also* **cross lots**) (*US*) **1** [early 19C] via a short cut; thus GO TO HELL ACROSS LOTS! excl. **2** [mid-19C–1900s] accelerated, using fig. 'short cuts'. [SE *lot*, a piece of land set aside for building or for cultivation or pasturage]

acrylic *adj.* [20C+] (*US campus*) superficial, hard, difficult to tolerate. [the *hardness* of acrylic paint]

act *n.* **1** [late 19C+] (*orig. US*) a routine, a way of behaving, a

performance. **2** [1940s] (*US Und.*) cross-examination of a prisoner. **3** [1940s–50s] (*Aus.*) pretended illness or ill-temper.

act as if one's knickers were on fire *v.* [1960s+] to panic, to behave hysterically.

act-ass *n.* [1970s] (*US*) one who sees themself as cleverer than they really are. [SE *act* + -ASS sfx]

action *n.* **1** [mid-19C+] sexual ability, lit. the erotic 'action' of the hips or pelvis. **2** [late 19C+] sexual intercourse or similar activity. **3** [late 19C+] (*US*) financial transactions, esp. bets and wagers. **4** [1920s+] (*orig. US Black*) what is going on; thus a situation or state of affairs, anything exciting, current, interesting, depending on the context, e.g. the chance for sex, a musical performance, a night's gambling, often used in the greeting, *Where's/what's the action?* **5** [1950s–60s] the potential client for a prostitute, the victim of a confidence trick etc. **6** [1950s–60s] (*US*) one's choice, one's preference. **7** [1960s] the effects of a drug. **8** [1960s] (*US*) a revolver. **9** [1960s+] (*drugs*) the current availability of drugs and the best place to obtain them. **10** [1960s+] (*orig. US Black*) a woman. **11** [1960s–70s] manipulations, activities, esp. when illegal or corrupt. **12** [1970s+] (*US Black*) a look, a smile, a verbal response. **13** [1990s+] (*Aus. prison*) homosexuality. [all fig. uses of SE; note Shakespeare's use of *action* (and *activity*) as sexual intercourse]

action *sfx* [1940s+] (*US campus*) a combining form denoting activity, e.g. *dope action*, *babe action* (cf. BACK-DOOR ACTION n.; GUM ACTION n.; LIP ACTION n.; TAB ACTION n.).

action on a solid half traction *phr.* (*also* **action on the...**) [1940s–70s] (*US Black, mainly Harlem*) ready for anything. [ACTION n. (4)]

action piece *n.*¹ [1960s] (*US Black*) a woman. [ACTION n. (2) + PIECE n.¹ (1)]

action piece *n.*² [1960s] (*US Black*) a pistol, a revolver, a shotgun. [ACTION n. (8) + PIECE n.³ (1)]

active citizens *n.* [early 19C] lice, fleas. [play on SE]

act like one's shit don't stink *v.* (*also* **act like one's shit don't smell, ...like shit wouldn't melt in one's mouth, think one's shit doesn't stink**) [1960s+] (*orig. US*) to behave affectedly and in an arrogant manner. [E.P. claims that *think one's shit doesn't stink* dates back to 'later C.19' but offers no proof]

act one's butt off *v. see* WORK ONE'S BUTT OFF *v.*

actor *n.* [1940s+] (*US Black*) anyone out to deceive or to project a phoney image, a con-man or liar.

actorine *n.* [late 19C–1930s] (*US*) an actress. [SE *actor* + fem. sfx *-ine*]

act possum *v.* [mid-19C+] to play dead, lit. and fig. [var. on PLAY POSSUM v. (1)]

actress *n.* [1950s–70s] (*US camp gay*) an egocentric show-off, but amusing and witty nonetheless. [camp feminization]

act the angora *v.* [20C+] (*Aus.*) to play the fool (cf. ACT THE HOG v.; ACT THE JINNIT v.; ACT THE MAGGOT v.; ACT THE NIGGER v.; ACT THE PRICK v.; ARSE AROUND v.; ASS ABOUT v.; BALLOCKS ABOUT v.; CLOWN (AROUND) v.; FUCKARSE v.; HUMBUG ABOUT v.; JACK ACT v.; JESTER v.; JUNKET AROUND v.; MUCK UP v.; PLAY THE ARSE v.; PLAY THE GIDDY GOAT v.; PLAY THE JACK v.; PLAY THE NANNY GOAT v.; PLAY THE WAG v.; SEEK OTHERS AND LOSE ONESELF v.). [the SE *angora* goat, thus a laboured pun on ACT THE GOAT v.]

act the goat *v.* [late 19C+] to behave foolishly (cf. ACT THE ANGORA v.). [the assumption is that the animal is naturally foolish]

act the hog *v.* (*also* **play the monkey**) [1900s–40s] to play the fool (cf. ACT THE ANGORA v.). [the assumption is that animals are naturally foolish]

act the jinnit *v.* [20C+] (*Irish*) to play the fool, to act irrationally (cf. ACT THE ANGORA v.). [SE *act* + JINNIT n.¹, i.e. ASS n. (1)]

act the linnet *v.* [20C+] (*Irish*) to flirt. [SE *linnet*, a songbird]

act the maggot *v.* [1950s+] (*Irish*) to play the fool, to clown (cf. ACT THE ANGORA v.). [SE *act* + MAGGOT n.¹ (1)]

act the mohawk v. [1960s] (*Irish*) to misbehave. [SE *act* + ? MOHOCK n.]

act the nigger v. [mid-19C+] **1** (*US*) a derog. term meaning to play the fool (cf. ACT THE ANGORA v.). **2** (*US Black*) to act in a manner White racists expect of Black people, i.e. foolish, subservient, clownish. [SE *act* + NIGGER n.¹ (1)]

act the prick v. [1980s+] to behave foolishly (cf. ACT THE ANGORA v.). [SE *act* + PRICK n. (3)]

act the wet dog v. [late 19C] (*US*) to make a fuss, to complain. [the annoyance of a wet dog shaking its fur]

actual, the n. [mid-19C+] money (cf. ALL-POWERFUL n.; BALLAST n.²; BALSAM n.; BRAD n.¹; CHARMS n.²; COLE n.; CORKS n.¹; CORN n.¹; CORN IN EGYPT n.; FEATHERS n.¹; GRAIN n.; HORSE-NAILS n.; NECESSARY n.; NEEDFUL n.; POSSIBLES n.; POWER n.; PUTTY n.¹; RIVETS n.; SALVE n.; WHAT IT TAKES n.; WHEREWITH n.). [as in SE, where 'the actual' is opposed to 'the idea'; the sense here is of concrete, hard cash]

act-up adj. [2000s] (*UK Black/teen*) aggressive. [ACT UP v. (2)]

act up v. [20C+] **1** to make a fuss in order to attract attention to oneself. **2** to cause (someone) trouble.

act your age! excl. (*also* be your age!) [1920s+] (*orig. US*) a term of contempt, based on condemning someone who the speaker considers is acting childishly; also ext. as *act your age, not your shoe size!*

a.d. n.¹ [late 19C–1900s] (*UK society*) a drink. [orig. used on dance cards to disguise a preference for *a*lcohol over *d*ancing; partners' names were also abbreviated]

a.d. n.² (*also* ad, add) [1930s+] (*US drugs*) a drug addict. [reversed abbr., in order to avoid confusion with the law's DA, a district attorney; also simple abbr. of SE *addict*]

a.d. n.³ [1970s+] phencyclidine (cf. ACE n.⁴). [ety. unknown]

a.d. v. [1990s+] (*US campus*) to leave. [abbr. AUDI (5000) v.]

ad n. **1** [mid-19C+] an *ad*vertisement. **2** [1970s] (*US gay*) a graffito offering sexual services, as found on a public lavatory wall. [abbr.]

ad adj. [20C+] pertaining to *ad*vertising; thus *adman, ad exec, ad agency*. [abbr.]

adad! excl. [mid-17C–mid-18C] God! (cf. ADOD! excl.; AGAD! excl.; ECOD! excl.; EGAD! excl.). [DAD n.¹]

Ada from Decatur n. (*also* Decatur, eighter (from) Decatur, little Ada) [1910s+] (*US gambling*) the point of 8 in craps dice (cf. ADA ROSS n.; BAD NEWS n.; BIG BEN n.; BIG DICK n.; BOXCARS n.; CAPTAIN HICKS n.; DANGLE ROLL n.; EASY SIX n.; EIGHTY DAYS n.; FEVER (IN THE SOUTH) n.; FIN n.²; FIVE IN THE SOUTH n.; HEAVEN-ELEVEN n.; HOBO'S DELIGHT (ON A RAINY NIGHT) n.; JIMMY HIX n.; JOE n.; JOE COTTON n.; LITTLE BRITCHES n.; LITTLE DICK n.; LITTLE FOUR n.; LITTLE JOE n.; LITTLE JOSIE n.; MAMA'S BOOTS n.; MANNA FROM HEAVEN n.¹; MIDNIGHT n.¹; NINA WITH HER HAIR DOWN n.; NINETY DAYS n.; PHOEBE n.¹; PUPPY PAWS n.; QUININE n.; SNAKE EYES n.²; SQUARE PAIR n.; TWO BAD BOYS FROM ILLINOIS n.). [pun on *eighter* + proper name *Decatur*, Alabama or Texas]

Adam n. [mid-19C+] used in a variety of phr. indicating a very long time ago, e.g. WHEN ADAM WAS AN OAKUM BOY phr. [use of the first man, *Adam*, as a generic for a very long time ago]

adam n.¹ **1** [late 16C–early 19C] a bailiff, a sergeant. **2** [late 17C–19C] (*UK Und.*) a fence, a criminal receiver. **3** [mid-19C] (*UK Und.*) a thief's accomplice. **4** [late 19C] a foreman. **5** [1940s] (*US Und.*) a prison warder. [the biblical *Adam*, the first man]

adam n.² [1950s–70s] (*camp gay*) one's first (paid) sexual partner. [biblical]

adam n.³ [1980s+] MDMA (cf. ECSTASY n.). [the letters + ref. to the primal intensity of the drug experience]

adam v. [mid–late 18C] to marry. [the biblical 'first couple']

Adam and Eve n.¹ [late 19C+] (*orig. US short order*) 2 poached or fried eggs; thus *Adam and Eve on a raft*, 2 poached eggs on toast; *Adam and Eve on a raft and wreck 'em*, 2 scrambled eggs on toast. [the similarity is suggested by the fact that there are two

eggs, they are alone and 'naked'; note the army use *adam and eve wrecked*, scrambled eggs]

Adam and Eve n.² [1980s] (*Aus.*) a sleeve. [rhy. sl.]

Adam (and Eve) v. **1** [1910s+] to believe; often in the interrog. phr. *would you Adam and Eve it?* **2** [1930s+] to leave. [rhy. sl.]

Adam and Eve v. [late 17C+] to have sexual intercourse. [the first act thereof in the biblical Garden of Eden]

Adam and Eve ball n. [1920s+] an early dancing party to which the guests are invited until midnight only. [when they are, as it were, ejected from (social) Eden]

Adam and Eve's p.j.s n. [1960s+] (*US*) nudity. [P.J.'s n. (2); US version of ADAM AND EVE'S TOGS n.]

Adam and Eve's togs n. [late 19C+] nudity. [TOGS n. (1); Adam and Eve's initial nakedness in Eden]

Adam's ale n. (*also* Adam's beverage, Adam's wine) [late 15C+] water. [the biblical *Adam* to whom alcohol was unknown; 'the only drink of our first parents' (*OED*)]

Adam's arm n. [1940s] (*US*) a shovel, a spade. [the biblical *Adam* who only had his arm to dig with]

Adam's arsenal n. [late 19C] the penis. [biblical *Adam*, who had no weaponry + *arsenal*; it is 'loaded' with semen]

Adam's beverage n. see ADAM'S ALE n.

Adam's off-ox n. [late 19C+] a slow, stubborn person. [SE *Adam*, generic for man + OFF-OX n.]

Adam's own (altar) n. [late 19C] the vagina; one of many literary euphs., usu. positive (cf. ALTAR OF HYMEN n.; ALTAR OF PLEASURE n.; BOWER (OF BLISS) n.; CAVE OF HARMONY n.; CHAPEL (OF EASE) n.; CORNUCOPIA n.; CROWN OF SENSE n.; CUPID'S ALLEY n.; CYPRIAN ARBOUR n.; CYPRIAN CAVE n.; FLOWER OF CHIVALRY n.; FOUNTAIN OF LOVE n.; FRUITFUL VINE n.; GARDEN OF EDEN n.; GARDEN OF PLEASURE n.; GATE OF HORN n.; GATE OF LIFE n.; GENTLEMAN'S PLEASURE-GARDEN n.; HARBOUR (OF HOPE) n.; HOGSTYE OF VENUS n.; HOLE OF CONTENT n.; HOLE OF HOLES n.; HYPOGASTRIAN CRANNY n.; LADY FLOWER n.; LAMP OF LOVE n.; LIFE'S DAINTY n.; LOCK OF (ALL) LOCKS n.; LOVE'S HARBOUR n.; LOVE'S PARADISE n.; MILKY WAY (TO BLISS) n.; MINE OF PLEASURE n.; MOUTH OF NATURE n.; NATURE'S TREASURY n.; NATURE'S TUFTED TREASURE n.; PALACE OF PLEASURE n.; PLEASURE BOAT n.; PRIVY PARADISE n.; SEAT OF PLEASURE n.; TREASURE OF LOVE n.; VENUS'S GLOVE n.; VENUS'S HIGHWAY n.). [the biblical *Adam*]

Adam's p.j.s n. [1970s] (*US gay*) nudity. [gay version of ADAM AND EVE'S P.J.S n.]

Adam's slippers n. [1900s] (*US*) barefoot. [the biblical *Adam* who was orig. naked]

Adam's whip n. [1950s] (*US*) the penis. [the biblical *Adam* who had no other weaponry]

Adam's wine n. see ADAM'S ALE n.

adam tiler n. (*also* adam tyler) **1** [late 17C–mid-19C] a pickpocket's assistant. **2** [early 18C–mid-19C] a criminal receiver. [? SE *Adam*, generic for man + Ger. *Teile*, a share or slice]

Ada Ross n. [1940s+] (*US*) the 8 point in craps dice; also ext. as *Ada Ross the stable boss/hoss*. [var. on ADA FROM DECATUR n.]

add n. see A.D. n.².

add a nail to one's coffin v. (*also* add a peg to one's coffin, drive a nail/peg into one's coffin) [mid-19C] to drink heavily. [pun on the sealing of a coffin + the pegs that once marked off alcoholic measures in a tankard]

added to the list phr. [late 19C+] castrated. [turf jargon; *the list* was of geldings in training]

addition n. [early 18C] make-up, cosmetics. [an addition to one's natural complexion]

addle-cove n. [mid-19C] (*US*) a fool. [SE *addle*, to confuse + COVE n. (1); the sl. synon. of *addle-pate* or *addle-head*. E.P. claims late 18C but offers no proof; not in Grose, Egan, Hotten]

addled adj. [late 17C+] drunk; one of a number of synons. denoting the drunkard's confusion (cf. BAMBOOZLED adj.; BEMUSED (WITH BEER) adj.; BEWITCHED adj.; BLITHERED adj.; BLOTTO adj.;

BONKERS adj.; BRAINED adj.; CABBAGED adj.; COMATOSE adj.; COMBOOZELATED adj.; DITHERED adj.; DIZZY adj.[1]; DOODLE-ALLY adj.; DOOLALLY adj.; DOPEY adj.[1]; FAR GONE adj.; FLAKED adj.; FLAKERS adj.; FLAKO adj.; FLOOZLED adj.; FLUMMOXED adj.[2]; FLUSTERED adj.; FLUTHERED adj.; FOG-BOUND adj.; FOGGED adj.; FOGGY adj.; FOGMATIC adj.; FOO adj.; FOOZLED adj.; FRAZZLED adj.; FUDDLED adj.; FUZZY adj.; GAGA adj.; GONZO adj.[2]; GOOFED (UP) adj.; GOOFY adj.; GRONKED adj.; HALF-GONE adj.; HALF-THERE adj.; HAVE A GUEST IN THE ATTIC v.; HAZY adj.; JIGGERED adj.[1]; KNACKERED adj.; LOOPY adj.; MINDFUCKED adj.; MIZZLED adj.; MOONY adj.; MUDDLED adj.; MUDDY-HEADED adj.; MUZZY adj.; NON COMPOS adj.; NOT ALL THERE phr.; NUMB adj.; OBFUSCATED adj.; ODDISH adj.; OFF ONE'S BEAN phr.; OFF ONE'S HEAD phr.; OFF ONE'S NOB phr.; OFF ONE'S NUT phr.; OFF THE NAIL phr.; OFF THE RESERVATION phr.; OUT OF CONTROL adj.; OUT OF ONE'S GOURD phr.; OUT OF ONE'S HEAD phr.; PIXILLATED adj.; POEGAAI adj.; POGGLED adj.; POTTY adj.; RAGGED adj.; RAMMY adj.[1]; RATTLED adj.; RATTY adj.[1]; RETARDED adj.; SCATTERED adj.[1]; SCHIZZED adj.; SCREWNOODLEOUS adj.; SCREWY adj.[1]; SHOOK adj.; SLEEPY adj.[2]; STUNNED adj.; STUPID adj.; TIRED adj.[1]; TIRED AND EMOTIONAL adj.; WAZZED adj.; WEARY adj.; WIPED OUT adj.; WOLLIED adj.; WOOLLY adj.[1]; ZONED adj.). [SE *addle-pated*, stupid]

addle-plot n. [late 17C–early 19C] a spoilsport who 'addles' the 'plots' or plans of others.

add rot it! *excl. see* OD ROT IT! excl.

add up v. [1930s+] **1** to make sense, to work out as expected, esp. in phrs. *it all adds up*, *it doesn't add up*. **2** (*also* **add up to**) to amount to, to signify.

adept n. [18C] **1** a conjuror. **2** a pickpocket. **3** an alchemist. [Lat. *adeptus*, skilled in; a Med. alchemist who had attained 'the great secret' was entitled *adeptus*, completely skilled (in all the secrets of his art)]

adidas phr. [1990s+] *all day I dream about sex.* [abbr.; pun on brandname of sports shoes]

adios amoebas phr. [1980s+] (*US campus*) a farewell. [a pun on the more common *adios amigos*, popularized by the 1950s TV series *The Cisco Kid*]

Adirondack steak n. [1950s] (*US*) venison. [SE *Adirondack* + *steak*; the Adirondacks area is generally regarded as impoverished]

adjective adj. (*also* **adjectival**) [late 19C–1900s] (*mainly Aus.*) euph. for BLOODY adj.[1] (1). [note BLOODY adj.[1] (1) is so widespread in Australia that it is termed 'the great Australian adjective']

Adkins's academy n. [early–mid-19C] a London house of correction, named after its governor. [*Adkins* + ACADEMY n. (4)]

ad lib n. [1920s+] (*orig. US*) a pointed, provocative or sarcastic comment. [SE *adlib*, to extemporize; ult. Lat. *ad libitum*, as much as one desires]

Admiral Browning n. [20C+] (*orig. naut.*) human excrement (cf. BRONZE n.[2]; BROWNIE n.[4]; BROWN STUFF n.[2]; BROWN TROUT n.; DOG CHOCOLATE n.; FUDGE n.[2]; FUDGE BABY n.; MUD n.[5]; NIGGER PANCAKE n.). [facetious use of SE *admiral* + BROWN n.[3] (1)]

admiral of the blue n. [early 18C–mid-19C] a publican, an innkeeper. [his blue apron]

admiral of the narrow seas n. [mid-17C–mid-19C] a drunkard who vomits over his neighbour at table. [facetious use of SE *admiral* + *narrow seas*, the British Channel/the Irish Sea]

admiral of the red n. [mid-19C] a heavy drinker. [the drunkard's red nose/face]

admiral of the red, white and blue n. [19C] an over-dressed, flashy beadle or other minor, uniformed official. [the over-elaborate uniforms]

admiral of the white n. [mid-19C–1900s] a coward. [white is the colour of cowardice]

adobe adj. [19C+] (*US*) a generic, and in sl. use derog., term meaning Mexican, hence generic for second-rate, inferior in

combs. below. [Sp. *adobe*, sun-dried mud or clay, widely used as a building material in Mexico]

adobe dollar n. [20C+] (*US*) a Mexican peso. [ADOBE adj. + SE *dollar*]

adobe maker n. [1960s] (*US*) a derog. term for a Mexican or Mexican-American. [ADOBE adj. + SE *maker*]

adod! *excl.* [late 17C–18C] God! (cf. ADAD! excl.). [DOD n.[1]]

adonee n. [mid-16C–19C] (*UK Und.*) God. [Heb. *adonai*, the Lord, God]

adonis n. **1** [early 17C+] a very attractive male. **2** [late 19C–1900s] (*Aus.*) in ironic use, a male admirer, a lover. [Greek god *Adonis*, known for his outstanding beauty]

adonize v. [mid-18C–mid-19C] of a man, to adorn oneself. [ADONIS n. (1)]

Adrian (Quist) adj. [1970s+] (*Aus.*) drunk (cf. BOOED AND HISSED adj.; BRAHMS AND LISZT adj.; BULLAPHANTS adj.; CUDDLE AND KISSED adj.; ELEPHANT'S (TRUNK) adj.; HIT AND MISSED adj.; JOHN BULL adj.; KISKY adj.; LILLIAN GISHED adj.; LLOYD'S (LIST) adj.; LORD AND MASTERED adj.; MOLLY (THE MONK) adj.; NEWTON AND RIDLEY adj.; OLIVER TWIST adj.; SALT adj.[2]; SALT JUNK adj.; SALVATION ARMY adj.; SCHINDLER'S LIST adj.; VON-BLINKED adj.; WALLY THE MONK adj.). [rhy. sl. = PISSED adj.[1]; ult. the Aus. tennis player *Adrian Quist* (1913–91)]

adrift adj. **1** [17C] harmless. **2** [late 18C+] missing. **3** [20C+] confused. [SE naut. term; orig. in navy use]

ads n. [late 17C–mid-19C] God's; thus in various excl., e.g. *adsbleed*, *adsbud*, God's blood; *adsflesh*, God's flesh; *adsheart*, God's heart; *ads(heart's) wounds*, God's (heart's) wounds; *adslife*, *ads my life*, God's life; *adslidikins*, *adso*, God's oath, ADZOOKS! excl.

advertise v. **1** [1930s+] (*orig. US*) to show off, to act in an exhibitionist manner (and thus draw un-needed attention to oneself). **2** [1950s+] (*gay*) to dress in a sexually provocative manner. **3** [1970s] (*camp gay*) to pluck and paint one's eyebrows. [play on SE]

advertisement conveyancer n. [late 19C] a sandwich-man. [the euph. term (PC long before its time) was coined by W.E. Gladstone (1809–98) and duly mocked by London society]

advertising bar n. [1960s+] (*US gay*) a bar frequented by male prostitutes and their clients. [ADVERTISE v. (2) + SE *bar*]

advertising club n. [1950s] (*US gay*) a men's washroom. [ADVERTISE v. (2) + SE *club*]

advertising pilgrim n. see PILGRIM n.[2].

adzooks! *excl.* [late 17C–mid-19C] a mildly blasphemous oath. [ADS n.; lit. 'God's hooks']

aerated adj. (*also* **aeriated**, **airyated**) [1930s+] over-excited, angry.

aerial pingpong n. [1960s+] (*Aus.*) Australian Rules football. [mainly used in New South Wales to tease the fans, who are mainly in Victoria]

aeroplane n. [1930s+] (*Aus.*) a bow tie. [? resemblance to a propeller]

aeroplane blonde n. [1990s+] a woman with dyed blonde hair. [pun on SE *black box*/BOX n.[1] (1), i.e. her pubic hair is still black]

aeroplane skirt n. (*also* **aeroplane dress**, **airplane dress/skirt**) [2000s] a skirt with a long slit reaching the groin. [it reaches the COCK PIT n. (1)]

af n. (*also* **aff**) [1960s+] (*S.Afr.*) a derog. term for an African; thus *aftax*, a Black-owned taxi (usu. an old, American-made car). [abbr.]

affair n.[1] **1** [mid-16C–19C] the penis (cf. CONCERN n.). **2** [mid-18C+] the vagina. [SE *affair*, a thing]

affair n.[2] [1970s–80s] (*gay*) one's current lover. [SE *affair*, a sexual relationship]

affidavit man n. [late 17C–early 19C] a professional witness who, with pay, will swear to anything. [SE *affidavit*, a sworn statement that can be used in evidence]

affie n.[1] [1990s+] *afternoon.* [abbr.]

affie n.[2] [2000s] a derog. term for a Black person. [abbr. SE *African*]

affigraphy *n. see* AFFYGRAPHY n.

afflicke *n. see* FLICK n.[1] ety.

afflicted *adj.* [late 17C–early 18C] drunk; one of a number of synons. meaning defective or ill (cf. BENT OUT OF SHAPE adj.; BLIND adj.[1]; BLUE-BLIND (PARALYTIC) adj.; COCKED adj.; CRONK adj.; CROOKED adj.[1]; CROPSICK adj.; FAINT adj.; FEVERISH adj.; GUTTERED adj.; HOT adj.[3]; HURTING adj.; ILLING adj.; INVERTEBRATED adj.; LAME adj.; PALATIC adj.; PARALYSED adj.; PARALYTIC adj.; PARO adj.; PODGY adj.; POGY adj.; POTSICK adj.; SKEW-WHIFF adj.; SLEWED adj.; SQUIFFY adj.; STONY BLIND adj.; TIPPLY adj.; TOP-HEAVY adj.; TWEAKED adj.; TWISTED adj.[2]; ZIGZAGGED adj.).

afflictions *n.* [mid-19C–1900s] (*orig. drapers*) mourning clothes; thus *mitigated afflictions*, half-mourning.

affygraphy *n.* (*also* **affigraphy**) [mid-19C–1900s] an exact match, usu. as *to an affygraphy*. [SE *autograph* + ? *affidavit*]

Afghan *n.* (*also* **Afghani**) [1960s+] (*drugs*) Afghan hashish (cf. ASH n.; BANG n.[5]; BAR n.[4]; BLACK n.[3]; BLACK AND BLONDE n.; BLACK PAK n.; BLACK RUSSIAN n.; BLOCK n.[7]; BLUE CHEESE n.; BROWN n.[4]; BUTTY n.[3]; CHARAS n.; CHOCOLATE (STUFF) n.; DOUBLE ZERO n.[1]; GOLD SEAL n.; GOMA DE MOTO n.; HASH n.[2]; HASHY n.; HEESH n.; JACK FLASH n.; JIBB n.; JOHNNY CASH n.; KIF n.; LEB n.[1]; NEP n.; POTTED BUSH n.; PUCK n.[3]; PUTTY n.[2]; RED SEAL n.; ROCK n.[3]; ROCKY n.[1]; SOLES n.; TEMPLE BALLS n.).

afghan *n.* [1960s] (*US gay*) a middle-aged gay man, who sometimes cross-dresses. [SE *afghan*, a coarse-woven afghan shawl; such a man might need one]

afkop *n.* [20C+] (*S.Afr.*) an ageing prostitute. [Afk. *afkop*, no head; such women supposedly hide their unalluring faces beneath the bedclothes]

afloat *adj.* [early 19C+] drunk (cf. ABOUT RIGHT phr.[1]).

a.f.o. *phr.* [1990s+] exhausted by sexual excess. [abbr. *all fucked out*; FUCK v.[1]]

Africa *n.* [late 19C–1930s] (*US*) anywhere mainly populated or used by the Black community. [neg. stereotyping]

African *n.*[1] [1940s+] **1** (*Aus.*) (*also* **African nigger**) a tailor-made, rather than hand-rolled, cigarette. **2** (*US drugs*) marijuana (cf. ACAPULCO (GOLD) n.). [? as smoked by Black people]

African *n.*[2] (*also* **North Carolina**) [mid-19C–1920s] (*US*) one's temper; usu. as *get one's African up*, to lose one's temper; *get someone's African up*, to annoy someone. [racial stereotyping]

African *adj.* [20C+] (*US*) a derog. generic word, used alone or in several combs. below to mean stupid, slow, unskilled or a number of other similar pej. stereotypes attached to Black people, whether Africans or Afro-Americans.

African ape *n.* [1960s] (*US*) a derog. term for a Black person (cf. ALLIGATOR BAIT n.[2]; APE n.; BLACK APE n.; BLACKBELLY n.; BONGO n.[1]; BONGO LIPS n.; COCONUT HEAD n.[1]; CONGO n.[2]; COOLIE n.[1]; COTTON-PICKER n.; HOTNOT n.; HOTTENTOT n.; JUNGLE n.[2]; JUNGLE BUNNY n.; KAFFIR n.[1]; MONKEY n.[1]; ORANGUTAN n.; PORCH MONKEY n.; RASTUS n.; ROCK APE n.; SAMBO n.[1]; SORGHUM n.; SPEARCHUCKER n.; STRAIGHT OUT OF THE TREES phr.; ZULU n.).

African billiards *n.* [1910s–60s] (*US*) the game of craps dice (cf. ABYSSINIAN POLO n.).

African black *n.* (*also* **black African**) [1970s–80s] (*drugs*) marijuana (cf. ACAPULCO (GOLD) n.). [SE *African* + *black*, its origin and colour]

African bush *n.* [1970s] (*drugs*) cannabis (cf. ACAPULCO (GOLD) n.; BITCHWEED n.; BOBO BUSH n.; BROCCOLI n.; BUD n.[4]; BUDLIES n.; BUDULARS n.; BUMBUD n.; BUSH n.[5]; BUTTER FLOWER n.; CABBAGE n.[5]; CHRISTMAS TREE n.[1]; COLLIE n.[1]; COMPELLANCE WEED n.; CONGO (BUSH) n.; CORN n.[1]; CRYING WEED n.; CRYSTAL BUD n.; DITCHWEED n.; DORADILLA n.; DRAG WEED n.; ELECTRIC LETTUCE n.; FIR n.; FLOWER TOPS n.; GIGGLEWEED n.; GOLDEN LEAF n.; GRASS n.[5]; GREEN n.[3]; GREENBUD n.; GREENERY n.; GREEN GODDESS n.; GREENS n.[4]; GREEN STUFF n.[1]; GREEN TEA n.; GREENY n.[2]; HAPPY GRASS n.; HAPPY HERB n.; HAY n.[3]; HEMP n.; HERB n.[2]; HERBAL n.; HERBALZ n.; HOLY HERB n.; HOT HAY n.; HUCKLEBERRY n.[3]; INDIAN HAY n.; JOY HEMP n.; JOY WEED n.; KILLER WEED n.; KIWI GREEN n.; LAUGHING GRASS n.; LAUGHING WEED n.; LEAF n.[1]; LIPTON'S n.; LOCOWEED n.; LONG GREEN n.; LOVE WEED n.; LUMBER n.[4]; MALAWI GRASS n.; MARJORAM n.; MEXICAN BUSH n.; MEXICAN GREEN n.; MUD BUD n.; NOBLE WEED n.; PARSLEY n.[3]; PISSY WEED n.; RAGWEED n.; RAILROAD WEED n.; RED BUD n.; REEFER WEED n.; RIGHTEOUS BUSH n.; SALAD n.; SASSAFRAS n.[2]; SENSIMILLIA n.; STINK WEED n.; SUCKER WEED n.; SUGAR WEED n.; SUPERGRASS n.[1]; T n.[1]; TEA n.[2]; TEXAS TEA n.; TREE OF KNOWLEDGE n.; TREES n.; VIPER'S WEED n.; VITAMIN T n.; WEED n.[1]; WHEAT n.[2]; WISDOM-WEED n.; YERBA n.). [SE *African* + BUSH n.[5] (1)]

African dominoes *n.* (*also* **African bones**) [1920s–60s] (*US*) the game of craps dice (cf. ABYSSINIAN POLO n.).

African dust *n.* [1950s] (*US*) gold. [the gold-mines of South Africa; the equation of money = DUST n.[2] is presumably coincidental]

African engineering *n.* (*also* **Afro engineering**) [1970s] (*US*) shoddy, second-rate workmanship.

African golf *n.* [1910s+] (*US*) the game of craps dice; thus *African golfer*, a crap-shooter (cf. ABYSSINIAN POLO n.).

African golf ball *n.* **1** [1920s–70s] (*US*) a die, usu. in pl. **2** [1970s+] (*US Black*) a watermelon.

African grape *n.* [1970s+] (*US Black*) a watermelon.

African harp *n.* [1930s] (*US*) a banjo.

African lager *n.* [20C+] Guinness stout. [apart from its creamy head, the drink is virtually black]

African nigger *n. see* AFRICAN n.[1] (1).

African (people's) time *n.* [1960s+] (*orig. S.Afr.*) unpunctuality, flexible time, a general disregard for time-keeping (cf. ALASKA TIME n.; BLACK PEOPLE'S TIME n.; BLACKTIME n.; B.M.T. n.; B.P.T. n.; BRAZILIAN TIME n.; COLORED PEOPLE'S TIME n.; C.P.T. n.; HAWAIIAN TIME n.; INDIAN TIME n.; ITALIAN MEAN TIME n.; JEWISH (STANDARD) TIME n.; MAORI TIME n.; MEXICAN TIME n.; NAVAJO TIME n.; PORTUGUESE TIME n.; SPANISH TIME n.; TINKER'S TIME n.). [racial stereotyping]

African pills *n.* [1910s] (*US*) the game of craps dice (cf. ABYSSINIAN POLO n.).

African plum *n.* [1960s–70s] (*US Black*) a watermelon.

African pool *n.* [1910s] (*US*) the game of craps dice (cf. ABYSSINIAN POLO n.).

African queen *n.* [1970s] (*gay*) **1** a Black homosexual male. **2** a White homosexual male who prefers Black partners. [SE *African* + QUEEN n.[2] (1)/QUEEN sfx (2)]

African skyscraper *n.* [1950s+] (*US*) a giraffe.

African toothache *n.* [1950s–60s] (*US*) venereal disease.

African woodbine *n.* [1940s+] (*drugs*) marijuana cigarette (cf. ALLIGATOR CIGARETTE n.; HAPPY CIGARETTE n.; J n.; JIGABOO (CIG) n.; JOINT n.[5]; LIGHT-UP n.; MEXICAN CIGARETTE n.; NO-BRAND CIGARETTE n.; OFF-BRAND CIGARETTE n.; ONE-SKINNER n.; PANATELLA n.; ROLL-UP n.[2]; SMOKE n.[3]; SMOKE WAGON n.[2]; SPARK n.[2]; STICKY n.[2]; TWIST n.[7]). [Wills' *Woodbines*, popular, cheap UK cigarettes]

Africa speaks *n.* [1940s–50s] (*Aus./N.Z.*) strong liquor imported f. South Africa.

Africky *adj.* [early 17C–1900s] African. [the term is descriptive and, unlike AFRICAN adj., there is no specific pej. other than that inevitably pertaining to anything Black]

Afriks *n.* (*also* **Afrix**) [1970s+] (*S.Afr.*) English-speaking children's use for Afrikaans as a school lesson. [abbr.]

afro *n.*[1] [1930s–70s] an English or American person of African descent, a Black person. [abbr.]

afro *n.*[2] (*also* **'fro**) [1930s; 1960s+] (*orig. US Black*) Black (occas. White) hairstyle in which normally short, curly hair is allowed to grow out in a bush around the head, supposedly in the style of one's African forebears; thus *afroed*, *afro-style*, wearing an Afro hairstyle. [abbr.]

afro *v.* (*also* **'fro**) [1970s+] (*orig. US*) to grow one's hair into an AFRO n.[2] hairstyle.

Afro engineering *n. see* AFRICAN ENGINEERING n.

afromobile *n.* **1** [1900s–10s] (*US*) a 3-wheeled vehicle used to convey tourists in Palm Beach, Florida; the drivers are invariably Black. **2** [1970s+] (*US Black*) any fashionable automobile, e.g. a BMW, Lexus, Mercedes. [SE *Afro* = SE *African* + *automobile*; (1) implies subservience, (2) success]

afro set *n.* [1970s–80s] (*US Black*) anywhere that Blacks use for talking or acting in furtherance of their own social and political betterment. [AFRO n.[1] + SET n.[1]]

aft *n.* [20C+] *aft*ernoon. [abbr.]

aft *adj.* [1970s+] (*US gay*) of a homosexual male, active (cf. FORE adj.). [naut. imagery]

aftax *n. see* AF n.

after *n.* [1900s–40s] (*Aus./US*) *aft*ernoon. [abbr.]

afterbirth *n.* [1960s+] (*US/UK/W.I.*) a general term of abuse.

after-dark *n.* [late 19C] a (bookmaker's) clerk. [rhy. sl.]

after davy *n.* [mid-19C] an affidavit. [mispron.]

after-dinner man *n. see* AFTERNOON MAN n.

after-dinner mint *n.* (*also* **minter**) [1980s] (*Aus.*) a woman who is willing to swap sex for material favours (but not cash).

After Eight Mint *adj.* [1990s+] penniless. [rhy. sl. = SKINT adj.; ult. the mint confectionery *After Eights*]

after hair *phr.* [late 19C] in pursuit of women for sexual purposes. [SE *after* + HAIR n.[1] (2)]

after-hours *n.* [1950s+] (*US*) an *after-hours* bar, club or restaurant. [abbr.]

afternoon *n.* [1990s+] (*W.I., Bdos/Guyn.*) the buttocks, esp. when large and female. [? naut. *aft*, the 'behind' of a boat + play on SE *afternoon*]

afternoon delight *n.* [1970s+] sex in the afternoon.

afternoon farmer *n.* **1** [mid–late 19C] one who wastes time rather than busying themselves with proper work. **2** [1930s] (*US drugs*) an ext. of (1) in the context of opium. [thus they get down to work only in the afternoon]

afternoonified *adj.* [late 19C–1900s] smart, chic. [the regular afternoon calls made on each other by society ladies]

afternoon man *n.* (*also* **after-dinner man**) [early 17C+] a tippler, a drunkard. [note the use as Anthony Powell's book title, *Afternoon Men* (1931)]

afters *n.* **1** [20C+] pudding, dessert. **2** [1930s+] after-hours drinking in a public house.

afterthought *n.* [1910s+] the youngest child of a family, conceived long after its siblings.

after you with the po, Jane *phr.* [late 19C–1920s] a ref. to the need to take turns in using an outdoor privy; transferred in joc. usage to indoor facilities. [PO n.]

afto *n.* (*also* **arfto**) [1930s+] (*Aus./N.Z.*) *aft*ernoon. [abbr. + -O sfx (4)]

afty *n.* [1990s+] the *aft*ernoon. [abbr.]

ag *see also under* AGG.

ag *n.* (*also* **aggie**) [1910s+] **1** (*US*) (*also* **ag coll**) an *ag*ricultural *coll*ege. **2** (*US*) an agricultural student. **3** (*US*) a country bumpkin. **4** agriculture. [abbr.]

ag *adj.* [1990s+] (*US campus*) **1** angry, annoyed, irritated. **2** crazy, fun. [abbr. SE *aggravated* but note AGG v.]

ag! *excl.* [1930s+] (*S.Afr.*) a general excl., esp. of pleasure, irritation or exasperation; usu. with *man* or *sis*; also used to preface a reply to a question one finds hard to answer, e.g. *Ag, I don't really know*, or to denote a sense of resignation, *Ag, I'll have some more pap then*. [Afk. *ach*, a general excl.]

agad! *excl.* [mid-18C] a euph. excl. meaning *God!* (cf. ADAD! excl.). [GAD n.[1]]

against *adj.* [late 19C–1960s] (*drugs*) addicted to or under the influence of a drug, usu. opium or heroin.

against the pluck *phr.* [late 18C–early 19C] reluctantly, 'against the grain'. [SE *against* + PLUCK n.[1] (1)]

agate *n.* **1** [late 16C–early 17C] a very small person. **2** [1960s+] (*US*) a small penis. [the carving of tiny figures into the semi-precious stone *agate*]

agate, the *n. see* GLASSY (ALLEY), THE n.

agates *n.* (*also* **aggots**) [1940s+] (*US*) the testicles; thus *agate-cracker*, a demanding task; *get one's agates cracked*, of a man, to have sexual intercourse (cf. BAUBLES n.; CRIG n.; CROWN JEWELS n.; DIAMONDS n.; MARBLES n.[3]; PEBBLES n.[1]; ROCKS n.[4]; LADY'S JEWELS n.; STONE n.[1]). [SE *agate*, a semi-precious stone]

A-gay *n. see* A-LIST GAY n.

ag coll *n. see* AG n. (1).

-age *sfx* [1940s+] (*mainly US campus*) a sfx used to form an abstract n.; e.g. *rainage*, a situation in which it is raining; *babage*, attractive young women. [adoption of SE use as a sfx for abstract nouns, names of persons or verbs expressing action]

agent *n.* [1960s] (*US Black*) any police officer. [an agent properly works only for the FBI and is not, as such, a police officer]

agfay *n.* [1940s–70s] a male homosexual. [cod Lat. *agfay* = FAG n.[5] (1)]

agg *n.* (*also* **ag**) [1980s+] problems, trouble, annoyance. [abbr. SE *aggravation*]

agg *v.* (*also* **ag**) [1980s+] to annoy, to upset. [abbr. SE *aggravate*]

aggerawator *n.* (*also* **haggerawator**) [mid-19C–1900s] a favoured costermongers' hairstyle, consisting of a well-greased lock of hair twisted and pointing either at the corner of an eye or at an ear. [? its 'aggravation' of admiring glances]

aggie *n.*[1] (*also* **aggey**) [1960s+] (*US prison*) a long-handled hoe. [SE *agricultural implement*]

aggie *n.*[2] [1980s+] (*US gay*) a homosexual sailor (cf. ABIGAIL n.). [? generic use of the female name]

aggie *n.*[3] *see* AG n.

aggie fortis *n.* (*also* **acker fortis, ackie fortis, agur forty**) [mid-19C] (*US*) very strong drink, usu. alcoholic but sometimes coffee. [Lat. *aqua fortis*, strong water, an alternative name for nitric acid]

aggots *n. see* AGATES n.

aggranoy *v.* (*also* **agronoy**) [late 19C+] to irritate, to annoy. [SE *aggravate* + *annoy*]

aggravation *n.*[1] [1910s] a station. [rhy. sl.]

aggravation *n.*[2] [1960s+] **1** (*orig. UK police/Und.*) the difficulties that both sides of the professional law make for each other. **2** violence, quarrels, unpleasantness in general.

aggro *n.* (*also* **agro**) [1960s+] **1** problems, trouble. **2** violence, typically as enjoyed by skinheads, esp. at football matches, beating up Asians etc. **3** an aggressive attitude. **4** any form of problems, difficulties, harassment. **5** (*Aus.*) an aggressive person. [abbr. SE *aggravation* + -O sfx (3)]

aggro *adj.* [1990s+] (*orig. US campus*) hot-headed, wild, unpredictable. [AGGRO n.]

aggrovoke *v.* (*also* **agrovoke**) [1920s+] (*Aus.*) to annoy, to irritate. [SE *aggravate* + *provoke*]

agility *n.* [19C] a euph. for the vagina; thus *show one's agility*, for a woman inadvertently to reveal her vagina.

aginner *n.* [20C+] (*Irish*) one who automatically takes an oppositional stance, usu. out of envy or spite. [dial. *agin*, against]

agitate the catgut *v. see* CATGUT-SCRAPER n.

agitate the gravel *v.* [1940s–60s] (*US*) to leave.

agitator *n.* [mid–late 19C] a bell-pull, a door-knocker.

agnes *n.* [1960s+] (*US gay*) a term of address used to one who is presumed to be a fellow homosexual (cf. ABIGAIL n.). [use of female proper name]

agonies *n.* [1970s+] (*drugs*) the pain of withdrawal from narcotic drug use.

agonizer *n.* [late 19C] (*UK society*) one who makes intense efforts to gain a specific effect.

agony *n.*[1] **1** [mid-19C+] problems, difficulties; thus *put on the agony*, to complain, to moan (the implication is that the problems are not wholly genuine) and thus to exaggerate. **2** [1900s–50s] (*orig. US*) style, fashion. **3** [1980s+] (*W.I./UK Black teen*) the sensations felt during sex, notably popularized by the reggae singer Pinchers in a dancehall song of the same name.

agony *n.*[2] *see* YELLOW AGONY n. (1).

agony aunt *n.* [1970s+] a problem-solving (usu. female) columnist of newspapers and magazines to whom the lovelorn and generally wretched can write and their letters will be answered in print or privately; thus the male equivalent, *agony uncle*. [the first *OED* cit. is 1975, but it refers, in a biography of the prototype Evelyn Home, to 'the "agony aunties" [of] the 'thirties'; note AGONY COLUMN n. (2) dates from 1950s]

agony box *n.* (*US*) **1** [1900s] a piano. **2** [1920s] a record player, a phonograph. **3** [1940s–60s] a radio. **4** [2000s] a ukelele. [the effect these objects supposedly have on listeners]

agony column *n.* **1** [late 19C] the section of a newspaper dedicated to special advertisements, particularly those for missing relatives or friends, and thus filled with personal agony. **2** [1950s+] a regular newspaper or magazine feature containing readers' questions about personal problems with replies from a (usu. female) columnist.

agony in red *n.* [late 19C] a vermilion costume. [a satire on the aesthetic movement of the early 1880s when paintings were described in musical terms, e.g. 'a symphony in amber', 'a nocturne in silver-grey']

agony pipe *n.* [1930s] (*US*) a clarinet.

agony uncle *n. see* AGONY AUNT n.

A-grade *adj. see* GRADE A adj.

agreeable rattle *n.* [late 18C–mid-19C] a chattering, but not unpleasant, young man. [he 'rattles along']

agreeable ruts of life *n.* [late 19C] the vagina (cf. ALCOVE n.; ARBOUR n.; BATCAVE n.[2]; BELLY DALE n.; BELLY DINGLE n.; BIRD'S NEST n.[1]; BREACH n.; CANYON n.; CHASM n.; CHINK n.[2]; CLEFT (OF FLESH) n.; COD TRENCH n.; CRACK n.[6]; CRANNY n.[1]; CREVICE n.; CRINKUM-CRANKUM n.; CONY-BURROW n.; CUNNY WARREN n.; CUPID'S ALLEY n.; CYPRIAN ARBOUR n.; CYPRIAN CAVE n.; DIMPLE n.; DITCH n.[1]; DRAIN n.[2]; FURROW n.; GAP n.[1]; GAPE (OVER THE GARTER) n.; GASH n.[1]; GOLDFINCH'S NEST n.; GROOVE n.[1]; GROTTO n.; GULF n.; GUTTER n.[1]; HARBOUR (OF HOPE) n.; HYPOGASTRIAN CRANNY n.; LAMB-PIT n.; LOVE NEST n.; LOVE'S HARBOUR n.; NEST n.[1]; NEST IN THE BUSH n.; NICK n.[2]; NICK IN THE NOTCH n.; NOTCH n.[1]; PHOENIX NEST n.; PLACKET n.; QUARRY n.; RATTLESNAKE CANYON n.; SLASH n.[4]; SLICE n.[1]; SLICE OF LIFE n.; SLIT n.[1]; SLOT n.[2]; SLOUGH n.[2]; SLUICE n.; SPAM CHASM n.; SPLIT n.[3]; SPLIT APRICOT n.; SPLIT BEAVER n.; SPLIT FIG n.; SPLIT MUTTON n.; SPORTSMAN'S GAP n.; STENCH-TRENCH n.; TRENCH n.[1]; TUNNEL (OF LOVE) n.; VELVET TUNNEL n.; WAYSIDE DITCH n.). [pun on SE *rut*, meaning both to have sexual intercourse and a cleft or furrow]

agricultural studies *n.* [1990s+] (*US campus*) the cultivation of home-grown marijuana.

agro *n. see* AGGRO n.

agronoy *v. see* AGGRANOY v.

aground *adj.* [late 18C–19C] ruined, at a loss. [naut. imagery]

agrovoke *v. see* AGGROVOKE v.

agteros *n.* [late 19C+] (*S.Afr.*) a plodder, a dawdler, one who lags behind. [Du. *achter*, behind + *os*, ox]

agua! *excl.* [1990s+] (*US prison*) an excl. of warning: an officer is making his rounds. [? link to Sp. *agua*, water]

ague-faced *adj.* [1910s] (*US*) twitchy. [SE *ague*, a malarial fever usu. intensified by severe chills (the sufferer is likely to shake in its throes) + SE *faced*]

agur forty *n. see* AGGIE FORTIS n.

a.h. *n.* [1910s–60s] (*US*) a euph. abbr. of ASSHOLE n.[1] (1); thus *in the pig's a.h.*, in very great trouble. [abbr.]

ah-ah *n.* [1920s–30s] (*US Black*) a fool. [onomat. grunting noise]

ah cabbage *n.* [1900s] (*Aus.*) a nickname for a Chinese immi-grant (cf. AH SIN n.; CABBAGE JOHN n.; CANARY n.[9]; CHIMPUNG n.;

CHINA BOY n.; CHINEE n.; CHING n.[1]; CHINK n.; CHINKO n.; CHINO n.; CHOPSTICK n.; CHOP SUEY n.; CHOW n.; CHOW-CHOW n.; DINGBAT n.[9]; HEATHEN CHINEE n.; JOHN n.[3]; JOHN CHINAMAN n.; JOSS n.; KITCHEN SINK n.; KWANG n.; LAUNDRYMAN n.; MONGOLIAN n.; MONK n.[1]; MONKEY n.[1]; MUSHE n.; MUSTARD n.[2]; NYAM DOG n.; PADDY n.; PAT n.; PIGTAIL n.[4]; PONG n.[2]; RICE-BELLY n.[2]; RICE-EATER n.; RICE-PICKER n.; SQUEEZE-EYE n.; STINKER n.[1]; TIDDLEYWINK n.[2]; VEGETABLE JOHN n.; WEE WILLIE WINKY n.; WIDOW'S WINK n.; YAP n.[3]; YELLOW AGONY n.; YELLOW BELLY n.[3]; YELLOW FACE n.; YELLOW FISH n.; YELLOWHAMMER n.[3]). [cod-Chinese name *Ah* + SE *cabbage*; many Chinese sold vegetables from a cart]

a-head *n.* [1960s+] **1** a regular or excessive amphetamine user. **2** a regular or excessive user of LSD. [A n.[2]/A n.[3] + -HEAD sfx (3)]

a-hole *n.* [1940s+] (*US*) a euph. abbr. of ASSHOLE n.[1] (cf. AIRHOLE n.; ARSEHOLE n.; BATTY-HOLE n.; BLOWHOLE n.; BUMHOLE n.; BUNGHOLE n.[1]; BUTTHOLE n.; CORNHOLE n.; GOOSEHOLE n.; GROPEHOLE n.[1]; HOLE n.[1]; MANHOLE n.[1]; MUCKHOLE n.; POO-HOLE n.; PORTHOLE n.; SHITHOLE n.; STINK-HOLE BAY n.; TOUCH-HOLE n.).

a-hole buddy *n. see* ASSHOLE BUDDY n. (1).

-aholic *sfx* (*also* **-oholic**) [1960s+] (*orig. US*) a widely used sfx indicating one who indulges excessively; thus *chocoholic*, one who cannot stop consuming chocolate; *bookoholic*, an obsessive reader etc. [on pattern of SE *alcoholic*]

ah-pen-yen *n. see* PEN YEN n.

ah sin *n.* [late 19C] (*Aus.*) a generic term for a Chinese person (cf. AH CABBAGE n.). [their language]

ai-ai *n.* (*also* **aai-aai**) [1960s+] (*S.Afr.*) methylated spirits or absolute alcohol, as drunk by alcoholics. [Zulu *hhayi*, no, or pron. of A.A., absolute *a*lcohol]

aich *phr.* [1990s+] (*US campus*) a version of A-IGHT phr., denoting more muted approval.

AIDS for grades *n.* [1980s+] (*US campus*) the course Biology 40, 'AIDS and Other Sexually Transmitted Diseases'.

a.i.f. *adj.* [1960s+] (*Aus.*) deaf. [rhy. sl.; ult. *A.I.F.*, the Australian Imperial Forces]

a-ight *phr.* (*also* **ight**) [1990s+] (*US Black/campus*) all right. [elision of SE]

aikies! *excl.* [1930s+] (*US*) that's mine! I want to do that! I want a share! a child's term used to claim the whole or an equal part of an object; the negative response to the cry is *no aikies*, no shares. [dial. pron. of SE *equal* or the 18C Yorks. dial. *hake*, to hanker or gape after]

aikona! *excl.* [1950s+] (*S.Afr.*) never! absolutely not! [Nguni *hayikhona*, no]

aim Archie at the Armitage *v.* [1970s] (*Aus.*) to urinate (cf. POINT PERCY AT THE PORCELAIN v.).

aimie *n. see* AMY n.

aimies *n.* [1970s+] (*drugs*) **1** amphetamine (cf. A n.[2]). **2** amyl nitrite (cf. AMIES n.; AMY n.; AMYL n.; AROMA n.; BANANA SPLITS n.; BOLT n.[5]; BULLET n.[5]; CRACKERS n.[5]; HARDWARE n.; JOY JUICE n.; LOCKER ROOM n.; OZ n.; PEARLS n.[1]; POOR MAN'S COCAINE n.; POPPER n.[3]; QUICKSILVER n.; RICE CRISPIES n.; RUSH n.[3]; SNAP n.[3]; SNAPPERS n.[2]; SNIFF n.; WHITEOUT n.). [abbr.]

aim up *v.* [1990s+] (*Aus.*) to have an erection.

ainoch *n.* [late 19C+] (*tinker*) a thing. [Shelta]

ain't down with *phr.* [1980s+] (*US Black/campus*) used when referring to a situation one does not particularly like, e.g. *I ain't down with this idea!* [DOWN WITH adj. (3)]

ain't got no tale *phr.* (*also* **have no tale**) [1940s] (*US Black campus*) feeling bad.

ain't holding no air *phr.* [1970s+] (*US Black*) unimpressive, lacking credibility, lacking the basic knowledge required to take care of oneself within the ghetto. [one's ego/image is deflated]

ain'ting *adj. see* HAIN'TING adj.

ain't it a treat *n.* [late 19C–1910s] a street. [rhy. sl.]

ain't it (the truth) *phr.* [1920s+] (*US Black*) an expression of affirmation.

ain't life a grin *phr.* [1970s] (*US campus*) a cynical expression of misfortune.

ain't long enough *phr.* [1970s+] (*US Black*) of money, not enough, insufficient. [fig. use of SE + ref. to LONG GREEN n. (1)]

ain't nothing to it *phr.* [1970s+] (*US Black*) everything is simple, there are no problems; usu. in answer to question 'How are you doing?'

ain't nowhere *phr.* [1940s] (*US Black campus*) I'm not doing anything.

ain't saying nothing *phr.* [1970s] (*US Black*) a phr. indicating that the subject is of no importance.

ain't shit *phr.* [1950s+] (*US Black*) used of a person or object that is useless, worthless or of absolutely no value. [SHIT n.³ (3)]

ain't that it *phr.* (*also* **ain't that shit, ain't it the truth**) [1970s+] (*US Black*) isn't that right. [SE + SHIT n.⁴]

air *n.* [mid-19C–1980s] (*US*) nonsense, rubbish, empty chatter. [abbr. HOT AIR n.]

air *v.* **1** [1910s–40s] (*US*) to dismiss, to jilt. **2** [1970s] to leave. [GIVE SOMEONE THE AIR v.]

air bags *n.* [1940s+] (*US Black/Harlem*) the lungs.

airball *n.* [1980s+] (*US*) an idiot, a fool, someone who has nothing but air, and no brains, in their head (cf. AIRHEAD n.; BALLOON-BRAIN n.; BALLOON-HEAD n.; BUBBLEHEAD n.; CORKHEAD n.; COTTONHEAD n.; FEATHERHEAD n.; HELIUM-BRAIN n.; HOLLOWHEAD n.; LIGHT-HEAD n.¹).

air biscuit *n.* [1980s+] an extremely malodorous fart or bad vomity smell.

air-brain *n. see* AIRHEAD n. (1).

air-condition *v.* [1930s+] (*orig. US*) to fill full of holes, often by shooting; thus *air-conditioned*, full of holes, e.g. *air-conditioned socks.* [pun on SE]

air dance *n.* [1920s+] (*US prison*) a hanging. [ironic use of SE]

airedale *n.* **1** [1920s] (*US*) an unattractive man. **2** [1920s–40s] (*US*) a fool, a worthless person, a pest (cf. APEHEAD n.; ASS n.; BATBRAIN n.; BEAR'S ASS n.; BEETLEBRAIN n.; BEETLE-HEAD n.; BIRDBRAIN n.; BULLFINCH n.¹; BUNNY n.³; BUSH BUNNY n.; CALF n.¹; CALF'S HEAD n.; CHICKENBRAIN n.; CHICKENHEAD n.¹; CHOOCH n.¹; CHOOK n.; CLAM n.²; CODFISH n.; COD'S HEAD n.; CUCKOO n.¹; DINGBAT n.⁹; DONKEY n.¹; DUCK n.⁴; DUMB BUNNY n.; FISH n.⁶; FLAT FISH n.; GIDDY GOAT n.¹; GOAT n.¹; GOOSE n.¹; GOOSEHEAD n.; GULL-FINCH n.; HORSE'S ASS n.; JACK THE BEAR n.; LAMB n.; MOKE n.¹; MOUSEBRAIN n.; MULE n.¹; MULLET n.¹; PRAWN n.; PRAWNHEAD n.; PRAWN-HEADED MULLET n.; SHEEP'S HEAD n.; WOMBAT n.¹; WOODCOCK n.¹; WOOD DUCK n.; YARD DOG n.). **3** [1930s] (*US Und.*) a trustworthy friend. **4** [1930s–40s] (*US Und.*) a guard or watchman. **5** [1940s] (*US Und.*) one who runs errands for bootleggers or drug sellers. **6** [1950s] (*US*) an unattractive woman. **7** [1960s+] (*US*) a drifter, a tramp. [horseracing jargon *airedale*, a worthless racehorse]

air express *n.* [1980s] (*US gay*) sexual intercourse with an airline steward.

airey *n. see* AIRY n.¹.

air guitar *n.* [1980s+] the non-existent (or at best cardboard cut-out) 'guitar' that is 'played' by fans of heavy metal rock bands; occas. ext. to other 'instruments'.

airhead *n.* **1** [1970s+] (*US, orig. teen*) (*also* **air-brain**) an idiot, a fool, someone who has nothing but air, and no brains, in their head (cf. AIRBALL n.). **2** [1990s+] (*US campus*) an intelligent person. **3** [2000s] (*drugs*) a marijuana user. [SE *air/*AIR n. + -HEAD sfx (1)/ -HEAD sfx (3)]

airheaded *adj.* [1980s] (*US*) stupid (cf. AMOEBA-BRAINED adj.; BALD-HEADED adj.⁴; BEEF-WITTED adj.; BISCUIT-HEADED adj.; BLOCK-HEAD adj.; BLOCKHEADED adj.; BONEHEADED adj.; BUBBLEHEADED adj.; BULLET-HEADED adj.; BULLHEADED adj.; BURRHEADED adj.; CHOWDER-HEADED adj.; CHUCKLEHEADED adj.; CLOD-SKULLED adj.; CLOTH-HEADED adj.; COTTON-HEADED adj.; CULVER-HEADED adj.; DAFFY-HEADED adj.; DUFFLE-HEADED adj.; DUNDERHEADED adj.; FAT-

HEADED adj.; FUCKHEADED adj.; GOOSE-HEADED adj.; HAMMER-HEADED adj.; HEN-HEADED adj.; HULVER-HEADED adj.; IRONHEADED adj.; JOLTER-HEADED adj.; JUGHEADED adj.; KNOT-HEADED adj.; KNUCKLEHEADED adj.; LEATHER-HEADED adj.; LIGHTHEADED adj.; LUNKHEADED adj.; MALLETHEADED adj.; MEATHEADED adj.; MUDDLE-HEADED adj.; MUD-HEADED adj.; MULE-HEADED adj.; MULLETHEADED adj.; MUSH-HEADED adj.; MUTTON-HEADED adj.; NAILHEADED adj.; PINHEAD adj.; PUDDING-HEADED adj.; PUMPKIN-HEADED adj.; SAP-HEADED adj.; SQUAREHEAD adj.; SQUAREHEADED adj.; SUET-HEADED adj.; THICK-HEADED adj.; TOTTY-HEADED adj.). [AIRHEAD n. (1)]

air Hebrews *n.* (*also* **Hebrew hoppers**) [1960s+] (*US campus*) sandals. [? a pun on the popular make of athletic shoes, Air Jordans, and ref. to the biblical Hebrews crossing the River Jordan]

airhole *n.* [1920s; 1980s] (*US*) a euph. for ASSHOLE n.¹ (1) (cf. A-HOLE n.).

air hook *n.* [1950s] (*US*) the nose. [its shape]

airish *adj.*¹ (*orig. US Black*) **1** [1940s+] affected, inclined to put on airs. **2** [1960s] effeminate. [SE *to put on airs*]

airish *adj.*² [1950s+] (*orig. US Black*) chilly, windy. [SE (*cold*) *air*]

air it out *v.* [1960s+] (*US*) to expend energy.

airlock *v.* [20C+] (*Ulster*) to stop in one's tracks.

airlocked *adj.* [20C+] (*Ulster*) drunk. [AIRLOCK v.]

air loft *n.* [1930s] (*US Und.*) a warning to run away; thus in phr. *take the air loft*, to make an escape after a warning.

airly *adv. see* AIRY adj.¹.

airmail *n.* **1** [1950s+] (*UK/US*) garbage (and, in prison, human waste) that is thrown out of windows, esp. in tenements and prison, instead of being taken to dustbins, loaded into disposal chutes etc. **2** [2000s] (*US*) a stone or similar heavy weight dropped from a freeway overpass, building roof etc. [pun]

air-man-chair *n.* [late 19C–1900s] (*music hall*) the chairman or master of ceremonies. [jumbled SE]

air off oneself *v.* [20C+] (*W.I.*) to show off one's own superior status at others' expense. [SE *to put on airs*]

air one's dirty linen *v. see* WASH ONE'S DIRTY LINEN v.

air one's heels *v.* [mid-19C–1900s] to loiter about, to dawdle. [SE *air, to take the air*]

air one's lungs *v.* **1** [1910s–40s] (*US*) to complain, to swear, to curse. **2** [1960s] to argue or talk at length. [SE *air, to expose to the air/to give expression to*]

air one's paunch *v.* (*US, mainly Western*) **1** [1920s] to boast, to brag. **2** [1930s–40s] to vomit. [SE *air, to give expression to*]

air one's pores *v.* [1900s–30s] to be naked. [SE *air, to expose to the air*]

air one's tonsils *v.* [1960s] (*US*) to talk emptily. [SE *air, to give expression to*]

air out *v.* [1940s] (*US, orig. Black*) **1** to go for a walk. **2** to leave. [SE *air, to take the air*]

air out one's mouth on *v.* [20C+] (*W.I.*) to speak aggressively or abusively. [SE *air, to expose to the air + air, to give expression to*]

air pie and a walk around *n.* [late 19C–1930s] a clerk's lunch, i.e. no food.

airplane dress/skirt *n. see* AEROPLANE SKIRT n.

air pudding *n.* (*also* **wind pudding**) [mid-19C–1920s] (*US*) nothing, esp. nothing to eat.

air raid *n.* [1980s+] (*Aus. prison*) continuous talk.

air raider *n.* [1960s–80s] (*Aus.*) **1** an argumentative female. **2** any talkative person. [the noisiness of the SE *air raid*]

airs *n.* [1990s+] (*US teen*) state-of-the-art, high-priced trainers. [Nike *Air Jordan* trainer, particularly prized *c.*1990]

airs and graces *n.* **1** [late 19C+] faces. **2** [1910s–50s] (*also* **pair of braces**) (*Epsom*) horseraces. **3** [1920s+] braces. [rhy. sl.]

air the dairy *v.* [19C] of a woman, to reveal her naked breasts. [SE *air, to expose to the air + DAIRY n.*¹]

airtight *adj.* **1** [late 19C+] (*US*) complete, unassailable. **2** [1920s] (*US*) attractive. **3** [1940s] (*US Und.*) of a town or city, absolutely safe for criminal activities since the authorities have been fully and comprehensively paid off. **4** [1970s] extremely mean. **5** [1970s+] (*US gay*) in sexual contexts, having every body orifice filled.

airtights *n.* [late 19C–1930s] (*US, Western*) tinned foods.

Air Wear *n.* [1990s+] (*UK juv.*) an aggressive young person. [large, heavy 'Air Wear' boots made by Dr. Martens]

airy *n.*[1] (*also* **airey**) [mid-19C+] the 'area' of a house, adjacent to the basement steps. [pron.]

airy *n.*[2] [1970s+] a ventilator in a prison cell. [SE *air*]

airy *adj.*[1] [late 18C+] (*US*) inclined to pretentiousness or putting on airs; thus **airly**, pretentiously. [SE *to put on airs*]

airy *adj.*[2] [mid-19C+] (*Irish*) mentally unbalanced, fey. [Ir. *aerach*, eerie, haunted]

airyated *adj. see* AERATED *adj.*

airy-fairies *n.* [1930s] large feet. [joc. reverse of AIRY-FAIRY *adj.*]

airy-fairy *adj.* [1920s+] insubstantial, trivial, of minimal importance.

aitch *n. see* H *n.*[2].

a.j. *n.* [1980s+] (*US Black*) Armani jeans. [abbr.]

ajax *n.*[1] [late 16C–17C] a lavatory. [a pun on 'a jakes', a lavatory appears in Shakespeare's *King Lear* (1605–6), and in *The Metamorphosis of Ajax* (1596) by Sir John Harington (*c.*1561–1612), a plea for the introduction of the water-closet, the supposed coarseness of which so displeased Queen Elizabeth I that its author was temporarily banned from Court]

ajax *n.*[2] [1990s+] tax, esp. the tax disc displayed on a car windscreen. [rhy. sl.]

AK *n.* [1970s+] (*US Black*) the AK-47 automatic or semi-automatic assault weapon. [abbr.; the Chinese-made *AK-47* was the preferred weapon of the world's guerrilla fighters and has found its way to America's urban battlefields via mail-order purchases and illicit gun supplies]

a.k. *n.*[1] [1920s+] (*US, orig. theatre*) an old fogey. [abbr. Yid. *alter kocker*, old shit]

a.k. *n.*[2] [1930s+] (*US*) a toady. [abbr. ARSE-KISSER *n.*]

a.k. *v.* [1930s–70s] (*US*) to curry favour with, to toady to. [A.K. *n.*[2]]

a.k.a. *n.* [1950s+] (*orig. US Und.*) an alias, a false name. [abbr. SE phr. *a.k.a.* = *also known as*]

Akerman's hotel *n.* [late 18C–mid-19C] Newgate. [the name of a celebrated gaoler, *c.*1787]

akimbo *adj.* [1940s] (*UK society*) arrogant, stand-offish. [SE *arms akimbo*, standing with one's hands on hips, elbows pointed outwards; note Grose (1785): 'a kimbaw, vulgarly pronounced a kimbo [...] an insolent bullying attitude' (cf. KIMBAW *v.*)]

akimbo *v.* [1940s] (*US Black/Southern*) to saunter, esp. with one's hands in pockets or on the hips. [for ety. *see* AKIMBO *adj.*]

akip *adj.* [1950s–70s] asleep. [KIP *n.*[1] (4)]

akka *n. see* ACKER *n.*

ala *n.* [1990s+] the buttocks, the behind (cf. ANKER OF RUM *n.*; APRIL IN PARIS *n.*; ARISTOTLE *n.*; ARRIS *n.*; BEER AND SARSE *n.*; BOTTLE *n.*[2]; BOTTLE AND GLASS *n.*; BUBBLE GUM *n.*[3]; BULLI PASS *n.*; DAILY (MAIL) *n.*; DATE *n.*[3]; DEAF AND DUMB *n.*[2]; FIFE AND DRUM *n.*; KHYBER (PASS) *n.*; KINGDOM COME *n.*; LOOKING GLASS *n.*[2]; NOOK AND CRANNY *n.*; PIPE AND DRUM *n.*; PLASTER OF PARIS *n.*; PRUNE AND PLUM *n.*; QUEEN MUM *n.*; RUMDADUM *n.*; TATE *n.*; TOM (THUMB) *n.*). [rhy. sl.; *alabaster* = PLASTER OF PARIS *n.*]

Alabama *n.* [20C+] (*US Black*) **1** a native of that US state. **2** a generic term for poverty, rural backwardness, based on the neg. image of the state and used in combs. below.

Alabama kleenex *n.* [1960s] (*US*) toilet paper or absorbent kitchen paper. [ALABAMA *n.* (2) + proprietary name *Kleenex* tissues]

Alabama lie detector *n.* [1940s–60s] (*orig. US Black*) a police baton.

Alabama marbles *n.* [1910s–20s] (*US*) dice.

Alabama wool *n.* [1940s–80s] (*US*) cotton clothing.

alacompain *n.* (*also* **allacompain**) [mid-19C] rain. [perversion of rhy. sl. based on 'all complain']

Alan Border *adj.* [2000s] of events, behaviour or people, unacceptable, excessive, in bad taste. [rhy. sl. = OUT OF ORDER phr. (2); ult. Aus. cricketer *Alan Border* (b.1955)]

Alan Ladd *adj.* [1990s+] sad. [rhy. sl.; ult. film star US *Alan Ladd* (1913–64)]

Alan Whickers *n.* (*also* **alans**) [1960s+] knickers. [rhy. sl.; ult. British TV personality *Alan Whicker* (b.1925)]

alarm clock *n.* **1** [1920s] (*US*) a worrier, a nag. **2** [1920s–40s] (*US campus*) a chaperon(e). **3** [1940s] (*US Black*) a college professor. [someone who keeps one, in real or fig. uses, from 'falling asleep']

Alaska time *n.* [1970s] (*US*) unpunctuality (cf. AFRICAN (PEOPLE'S) TIME *n.*). [neg. image of the natives of the state]

Alaska turkey *n.* [19C–1940s] (*US*) a salmon. [the local salmon trade]

Albany beef *n.* [late 18C–1900s] (*US*) Hudson River sturgeon. [the one-time easy availability of sturgeon in the Hudson River near Albany, NY]

albertine *n.* [late 19C] an adroit, calculating, business-like mistress. [the character *Albertine* in Alexander Dumas fils' novel *Un Père Prodigue* (1859)]

Albertopolis *n.* [mid-19C] Kensington Gore, London SW7, site of the Royal Albert Hall and the Albert Memorial. [proper name of Queen Victoria's husband, Prince *Albert* of Saxe-Coburg-Gotha (1819–61) + sfx *-opolis*]

Alberts *n.* (*also* **Prince Alberts, Prince Alfreds, royal alberts**) (*Aus.*) **1** [late 19C] dress trousers. **2** [late 19C+] strips of cloth, usu. calico, rubbed with suet to cut down chafing and used as a substitute for socks, usu. by tramps. **3** [1930s] rough, lace-up boots. [proper name *Prince Albert* (1819–61), consort of Queen Victoria. The use came from the myth that Albert, before his marriage, was so poor that he was forced to use foot-bindings instead of proper socks]

Al Capone *n.* [1980s+] (*Aus./N.Z.*) the telephone. [rhy. sl.; ult. the Chicago gang-boss Alphonse 'Al' Capone (1899–1947)]

Al Capone ride *n.* [1970s+] (*US Black*) any old car, both the original Capone-era models and more recent ones, that lacks the most up-to-date gimmicks and accessories and is thus *de facto* 'old fashioned'. [*Al Capone* (for ety. *see* AL CAPONE *n.*) + RIDE *n.*[2] (1)]

alchy/alci *n. see* ALKY *n.*

alco *n. see* ALKO *n.*

alcoholiday *n.* [1900s] a bank holiday, may appear only in *The Sporting Times*. [SE *alcohol* + *holiday*, the alcohol drunk on a bank holiday]

alcove *n.* [late 17C] the vagina (cf. AGREEABLE RUTS OF LIFE *n.*).

alderman *n.*[1] **1** [late 18C–mid-19C] a turkey, esp. one roasted and served with sausages. **2** [mid-19C] a long smoking pipe; thus *broken alderman*, a short pipe. **3** [mid–late 19C] half-a-crown, 2s 6d (12½p). **4** [late 19C–1940s] a paunch; thus *adj. aldermanic*, portly. [the image of a paunchy, pipe-smoking, wealthy administrator of the City of London]

alderman *n.*[2] [late 19C–1950s] a large crowbar (cf. CITIZEN *n.*[1]; GENTLEMAN *n.*; LORD MAYOR *n.*[1]).

alderman double-slang'd *n.* [late 18C] a turkey garlanded with sausages. [ALDERMAN *n.*[1] (1) + SLANG *v.*[2]; the 'chains' are of sausages]

alderman in chains *n.* [19C–1900s] a turkey garlanded with sausages. [ALDERMAN *n.*[1] (1) + SE *chains* (of sausages); 'from the appearance of the City fathers, generally portly – becoming more so when carrying their chains of office over their powerful bust' (Ware); note Jonson (1621): 'Two roosted Sheriffs came whole to the bord [...] theire Chaines like sausages hung about 'em']

alderman Lushington *n. see* LUSHINGTON *n.*

alderman's nail *n.* [19C+] an animal's tail. [rhy. sl.]

alderman's pace *n.* [17C] a steady, careful pace, as befits an official with a fine sense of his own importance.

Aldershot ladies *n.* [1940s+] **1** the number 4. **2** (*darts*) double 4. **3** (*bingo or lotto*) 44 (cf. ALL THE BEANS n.; ALL THE STEPS n.; ALL THE TWOS n.; BABY'S DONE IT n.; BANG ON THE DRUM n.; BED AND BREAKFAST n.; BEING POOR n.; BLIND TWENTY n.; BOY'S FAVOURITE n.; BRIGHTON LINE n.; BUCKLE MY SHOE n.; BURLINGTON BERTIE n.[1]; BUTTERED BUN n.[3]; CHOPSTICKS n.; CLICKETY-CLICK n.; COCK AND HEN n.; CONNAUGHT RANGERS n.; COUPLE OF DUCKS n.; CRUTCH n.[2]; DAD AT THE DOOR n.; DANNY LA RUE n.; DIANA DORS n.; DINKY-DOO n.; DIRTY GERTIE n.; DIRTY OLD JEW n.; DIRTY WHORE n.; DOCTOR n.[6]; DOOR-TO-DOOR n.; DOWNING STREET n.; GARDEN GATE n.[2]; GERTY LEE n.; GOD'S IN HEAVEN n.; HALF-A-CROWN n.; HALF-A-TON n.; HALF-WAY HOUSE n.; HARRY TATE n.; HEINZ n.; HOLE IN MY SHOE n.; HORN OF PLENTY n.; HOUSE IN A STATE n.; JOYNSON-HICKS n.; KELLY'S EYE n.; KEY OF THE DOOR n.; KNOCK AT THE DOOR, A n.; LEGS ELEVEN n.; LITTLE JIMMY n.; LUCKY FOR SOME n.; ME AND YOU n.; MONKEY'S COUSIN n.; MOUTH IS SORE n.; NEVER BEEN KISSED n.; OLD-AGE PENSION n.; ONE FAT LADY n.; OPEN THE DOOR n.; POMPEY WHORE n.; RUGBY TEAM n.; SHINY TEN n.; SNAKE EYES n.[2]; SPEED LIMIT n.; STOP WORK n.; TOP OF THE HOUSE n.; TWO FAT LADIES n.; TWO LITTLE CRUTCHES n.; TWO (LITTLE) DUCKS n.; UNCLE BEN n.[1]; UNLUCKY FOR SOME n.; UP A TREE n.; WAS SHE WORTH IT? n.; WILSON'S DEN n.; YOU AND ME n.). [punning/rhyming on 2 4s = 2 whores; Aldershot is an 'army town' in the UK]

Aldgate pump *n. see* BILL ON THE PUMP AT ALDGATE n.

alec *n.* (*also* **aleck**) [1940s+] (*Aus.*) a fool or simpleton, a confidence man's victim. [? SMART ALEC(K) n. without the epithet]

alecan *n.* [late 19C–1910s] a heavy drinker.

alecie *n.* (*also* **alecy**) [late 16C] mental aberration, due to ale-drinking, intoxication. [lit. 'ale-cy', on pattern of SE *luna-cy*]

aleck *n.*[1] [1900s–30s] (*orig. US*) an unpleasant, conceited, smug person. [abbr. SMART ALEC(K) n.]

aleck *n.*[2] *see* ALEC n.

alecy *n. see* ALECIE n.

ale-draper *n.* (*also* **draper**) [late 16C–early 19C] an alehouse-keeper. [SE *ale* + *draper*, seller]

aled up *adj.* [1930s+] drunk on beer (cf. ALKIED adj.; BARRELLED adj.; BEVVIED (UP) adj.; BOOZED adj.; BOOZED UP adj.; BOOZY adj.; BOTTLED adj.[2]; BREWED adj.; BUDGY adj.; BUNG adj.[1]; BUNGY adj.; CANNED adj.[1]; CHATEAUED adj.; COGUEY adj.; CORKED adj.; CORK-SCREWED adj.; CORKY adj.; CORNED adj.; CUP-SHAKEN adj.; CUPSHOT adj.; DRINKY adj.; FORTEYED adj.; GAGED adj.; GINNED UP adj.[1]; GRAPESHOT adj.; HAVE CORNS IN THE HEAD v.; HAVE IN (SOME) LIQUOR v.; HAVE ONE'S BARREL FULL v.; HAVE ONE'S POTS ON v.; IN ONE'S ALE phr.; IN ONE'S CUPS phr.; IN ONE'S POTS phr.; JARRED adj.[1]; JUG-BITTEN adj.; JUGGED adj.; JUG-STEAMED adj.; JUICED adj.[1]; KALIED adj.; LIQUORED (UP) adj.; LUSH adj.[1]; LUSHED UP adj.; LUSHY adj.[1]; MALTED adj.; MALTY adj.; PIPED adj.[1]; POT-SHAKEN adj.; POT-SHOT adj.; POTTED (OUT) adj.[2]; SAP-HAPPY adj.; SAUCED (UP) adj.; SCOTCHED UP adj.; SHERBET(T)Y adj.; SNOOTERED adj.; SOUPED UP adj.; TANGLED adj.; TEED UP adj.; TIDDLED adj.; TIDDLY adj.; TIPPLY adj.; TITLEY adj.; TOOTED adj.; WINED adj.; WINEY adj.).

ale-knight *n.* [late 16C–mid-17C] a drunkard, a drinking companion. [SE *ale* + KNIGHT n. (1)]

alemnoch *n.* [18C–19C] (*tinker*) milk. [Shelta]

ale-spinner *n.* [19C] a brewer, a publican. [SE *ale* + *spinner*, in sense of a general manufacturer]

alexander *n.* [1900s] (*US*) a certainty. [ALEXANDER HAMILTON n.[2]; i.e. something one would put one's name to]

alexander *v.* [late 17C–early 18C] (*Anglo-Irish*) to hang someone. [proper name Sir Jerome *Alexander*, a hanging judge, active in Ireland 1660–74]

Alexander Graham Bell *n.* [1980s+] (*Aus. prison*) a cell. [rhy. sl.]

Alexander Hamilton *n.*[1] [1960s] (*US*) $10 bill (cf. ABE n.[2]). [the picture of the US politician, *Alexander Hamilton* (1757–1804), printed on the notes]

Alexander Hamilton *n.*[2] [1960s] (*US*) one's signature. [for ety. *see* ALEXANDER HAMILTON n.[1]; a confusion with JOHN HANCOCK n.]

Alexandra limp *n.* (*also* **Alexandra step**) [late 19C] (*UK society*) a manner of walking taken up by fashionable society as a deliberate tribute to the way in which Princess Alexandra (1844–1925), then Princess of Wales, walked *c.*1870. ['The name given an erstwhile fit of semi-imbecility on the part of...a crowd of limping, petticoated toadies' (F&H)]

alf *n.* [1960s+] (*Aus.*) the unsophisticated, nationalistic, basic Aus. male; more recently overtaken by OCKER n. (2). [abbr. proper name *Alfred*]

alfalfa *n.* (*US*) **1** [late 19C–1930s] a beard, whiskers. **2** [1900s–30s] the countryside (as opposed to the town/city). **3** [1910s] a bed. **4** [1910s+] money (cf. APPLE n.[5]; BANANAS n.[3]; BENTON'S MINT DROPS n.; BUNCE n.; CABBAGE n.[8]; CABBAGE LEAF n.[2]; COLIANDER (SEED) n.; CORIANDER (SEED) n.; EVERGREEN n.; FOLDING GREEN n.; GRAPES n.[2]; GREEN n.[2]; GREEN BOYS n.; GREENERY n.; GREENIE n.[2]; GREEN ONE n.[1]; GREEN SHIT n.; GREEN STAMP n.; GREEN THUMB n.; KALE (SEED) n.; LEAF n.[2]; LEAN GREEN n.; LETTUCE n.[1]; LONG GREEN n.; MINT n.[1]; MINT LEAF n.[1]; MINT SAUCE n.; PLANTAIN LEAF n.; SPINACH n.[3]). **5** [1920s–50s] dried spinach or other dehydrated vegetables. **6** [1930s–40s] tobacco. **7** [1930s–60s] nonsense, rubbish. [SE *alfalfa*, a form of Lucerne grass, used for fodder]

alfalfa *adj.* [1910s–60s] (*US*) rustic, slow, peasant-like. [ALFALFA n. (2)]

alf a mo *n.* (*also* **arf a mo**) [1910s] **1** a cigarette, esp. when it proves hard to keep alight. **2** (*Aus.*) a small moustache. [(1) Cockney pron. of SE *half a moment*; (2) SE *half* + MO n.[1] (1)]

Alf Garnett *n.* [1990s+] the hair. [rhy. sl. = BARNET n.; ult. the character *Alf Garnett* in the 1960s BBC-TV sitcom *Till Death Us Do Part*]

alfired *adj. see* ALL-FIRED adj.

'alfpenny bumper *n.* [late 19C–1900s] a halfpenny omnibus fare. [the passengers are bumped up and down]

'alfpenny dip *n.* [mid-19C+] a ship. [rhy. sl.]

alfred david *n.* (*also* **alfred davy**, **alfy**) [mid-19C–1910s] an affidavit. [pron.]

Alfred (the Great) *n.* [1990s+] weight. [rhy. sl.]

Algie *n.* (*also* **Algernon**, **Algy**) [late 19C–1930s] a generic name for any young male aristocrat. [proper name *Algernon*, seen as typically upper-class]

Ali *n.* [20C+] 'inevitable' nickname for any man surnamed Barber. [story of '*Ali* Baba and the 40 Thieves']

aliamba *n.* [1980s+] phencyclidine (cf. ACE n.[4]). [ety. unknown; ? Sp.]

alias *adj.* [1950s+] (*W.I.*) dangerous, violent. [ALIAS MAN n.]

alias man *n.* (*also* **alias**) [1950s+] (*W.I., orig. Und.*) a cheat, a hypocrite, anyone unethical. [SE *alias*, another name, an assumed name]

alibi *n.* [1910s+] an excuse. [weakened form of SE]

alibi ike *n.* [1910s+] (*US*) one who never takes the blame and invariably has a quick excuse for their faults and failings. ['Alibi Ike' (1915), the title of a short story by Ring Lardner (1885–1933), featuring a fictional baseball player]

alibi (up) *v.* **1** [1910s+] to provide an excuse for. **2** [1920s+] to make an excuse.

ali-button *v.* [1990s+] (*W.I.*) to be made a fool of by somebody. [ety. unknown]

Alice, The *n.* [late 19C+] (*Aus.*) the town of Alice Springs. [abbr.]

alice *n.*[1] [1970s] (*camp gay*) the police. [ALICE BLUE (GOWN) n.]

alice *n.*[2] [1970s+] (*drugs*) LSD (cf. A n.[3]). [L.S. – i.e. LSD; but note the autobiographical novel *Go Ask Alice*, about a 15-year-old's drug habits, and the Jefferson Airplane song 'White Rabbit' (1967), with its drug-orientated lyrics, esp. 'Go ask Alice, when she's 10ft tall'; both refs. go back to Lewis Carroll's *Alice's Adventures in Wonderland* (1866), which was seized on by the hippies for its supposed drug refs.]

Alice Blue (gown) *n.* (*also* **Miss Alice**) [1930s+] (*US gay*) the police. [ult. f. song 'My Sweet Little Alice Blue Gown' by McCarthy & Tierney (1918); thus ref. to the blue uniform]

Alice B Toklas (brownie) *n.* [1960s+] (*drugs*) a marijuana brownie. [proper name *Alice B Toklas* (1877–1967), lifetime companion to Gertrude Stein, who in her eponymous cookbook gave a recipe for this drug-based sweetmeat]

a-licker *n.* [1990s+] (*US*) a toady, a sycophant. [abbr. ARSE-LICKER n. (1)]

ali oop *n.* [1990s+] excrement (cf. BOB AND HIT n.; BRACE AND BIT n.; BRAD (PITT) n.; DOUGLAS HURD n.; EARTHA (KITT) n.; EDGAR BRITT n.; GAME OF NAP n.; GEORGE THE THIRD n.; HENRY III n.; HORSE AND TRAP n.; LEMON CURD n.; MACARONI n.[4]; MAN-TRAP n.[2]; MOCKINGBIRD n.; MY WORD n.; PONY (AND TRAP) n.; RICHARD (THE THIRD) n.; TOM TIT n.; WILLIAM n.[3]; WILLIAM THE THIRD n.). [rhy. sl. = POOP n.[2] (2)]

A-list gay *n.* (*also* **A-gay**) [1990s+] the homosexual elite. [SE *A-list*, a metaphorical list of the highest status celebrities]

alive *adj.*[1] **1** [mid–late 19C] knowledgeable, aware, esp. of a criminal scheme. **2** [1930s–40s] (*US Und.*) well-off, wealthy.

alive *adj.*[2] [1950s] (*UK Und.*) attached to a burglar alarm. [SE *alive*, charged with electric current]

aliveo *adj.* [late 19C–1930s] alert, active. [abbr. ALL ALIVO adj.]

alive or dead *n.* [20C+] the head. [rhy. sl.]

alkali *n.* [20C+] (*US*) a veteran of the West. [ALKALIED adj.]

alkalied *adj.* [mid–19C+] (*US*) experienced at living in the West. [the alkali-dense streams from which humans and cattle were forced to drink]

alkee stiff *n. see* ALKY STIFF n.

alki/alkie *n. see* ALKY n.

alkied *adj.* [1930s+] drunk (cf. ALED UP adj.). [SE *alcohol*]

alkie's itch *n.* [1940s–50s] (*Aus./US*) the twitching and nervousness that are seen in an advanced alcoholic. [ALKY n. (2) + SE *itch*]

alki stiff *n. see* ALKY STIFF n.

alko *n.* (*also* **alco**) [1980s+] an alcoholic. [abbr.]

alky *n.* (*also* **alchy, alki, alkie**) (*US*) **1** [mid–19C+] *alc*ohol. **2** [1920s+] (*also* **alci**) an *alc*oholic, a drunk. [abbr. + sfx *-y*]

alky *adj.* [1930s+] alcoholic. [ALKY n. (2)]

alky-cooker *n.* [1930s–40s] (*US*) **1** one who is employed in the illegal distillation of whisky. **2** an illegal still. [ALKY n. (1) + SE *cooker*, a cook/a stove]

alky stiff *n.* (*also* **alkee stiff, alki stiff**) [late 19C–1930s] (*US*) an alcoholic tramp. [ALKY n. (2) + STIFF n.[2] (4)]

alky up *v.* [1930s] (*US tramp*) to drink, to get drunk. [ALKY n. (1)]

all *adv.*[1] **1** [mid–19C+] used to intensify an adj., meaning very, e.g. *all fucked-up*. **2** [1920s+] used to intensify an oath or obscenity, e.g. DAMN-ALL n., FUCK-ALL n., SOD-ALL n.

all *adv.*[2] [1980s+] (*orig. US campus*) when retelling a story, with the v. *to be* to denote something said or done, often describing an attitude or a pose, sometimes used with an accompanying gesture, e.g. *She was all shouting and I was all 'No way!'*.

all about *phr.* [1980s+] (*US campus*) the subject of one's interest or desire or that which matters in a given situation; also used as a general intensifier, e.g. *I'm all about baseball.*

all about trout *phr.* [1960s] on the lookout (for an advantageous opportunity). [rhy. sl.]

all a-cock *phr.* [late 19C–1900s] defeated, overthrown. [? KNOCK INTO A COCKED HAT v. or f. cockfighting jargon *all a-kick*, defeated (the cock's legs kick in its death-agony)]

allacompain *n. see* ALACOMPAIN n.

all afloat *n.* [mid–19C] a coat. [rhy. sl.]

all alive *n.* [1940s] the number 5. [rhy. sl.]

all alivo *adj.* (*also* **all alive-o**) [mid–19C+] alert, active. [SE + -o sfx (6)]

all a-mort *adj.* [late 18C–mid-19C] shocked, surprised and thus rendered motionless. [Fr. *mort*, dead]

all and all *n.* [1980s] (*UK Black*) everyone. [pattern of I AND I pron.]

all-and-all *n.*[1] [1970s] (*US*) one's wife. [SE *and all*, and everything else and everything connected to; ? Scot. phr. 'wooed and married and all']

all-and-all *n.*[2] [1970s] (*US*) one's best suit of clothes. [? 'all (dressed up) and all']

all around my hat *phr.* (*also* **all round my hat**) [mid–19C–1920s] all over, completely. [? ballad 'All around my hat I wears a green willow']

all around the pig's arse there is pork *phr.* [1980s] (*N.Z.*) a phr. of resignation, acceptance.

all a-treat *phr.* [1900s] excellent, wonderful, sometimes used ironically to mean a mild disaster. [SE *all + a- + treat*, something highly enjoyable]

all at sea *phr.* [late 19C+] **1** (*also* **at sea, deep sea**) confused. **2** drunk. [losing one's bearings]

all balls (and bang-me-arse) *n.* [1940s+] nonsense. [the ext. is post-1940s]

all B and B *phr.* [1940s] a phr. used of a well-built, sexy woman. [abbr. all *b*osom and *b*ottom]

all beer and skittles *phr.* (*also* **all sheok and quoits**) [mid–19C+] pleasure, enjoyment, hedonism; also as neg., i.e. *not all...*

all behind in Melbourne *phr.* [1940s+] (*Aus.*) fat, heavy-buttocked. [pun on BEHIND n. (1)/SE *behind*]

all behind like barney's bull *phr.* [1940s+] (*Aus./N.Z.*) **1** late, delayed. **2** overweight. [pun; note BARNEY'S BULL n.]

all behind like the cow's tail *phr.* [20C+] (*Irish*) late. [pun]

all Betty *phr.* [early 19C] finished, 'done for'. [var. on ALL DICKY (WITH) phr.]

all bum *adj.* [mid–late 19C] of a woman, wearing a noticeably large bustle (a stuffed pad that emphasized the rear of the dress). [SE *all* + BUM n.[1] (1)]

all cock and ribs like a musterer's dog *phr.* [1970s+] (*Aus./N.Z.*) a phr. used of a very thin person. [COCK n.[2] (1) + ribs + N.Z.E. *musterer*, a shepherd]

all cop and no blue *phr.* [late 19C] a phr. used of a mean person or attitude, lit. 'all take and no give'.

all day *n.* **1** [late 19C] the end of one's life. **2** [1970s+] (*US Und.*) a life sentence.

all day, all night, just like New York *phr.* [1930s] (*US Black*) fashionable, sophisticated.

all day and a night *n.* [2000s] (*US prison*) a life sentence without the opportunity of parole. [ALL DAY n. (2)]

all day from a quarter *phr.* [1970s+] (*US Und.*) a sentence of 25 years to life. [ALL DAY n. (2) + QUARTER n.[1] (3)]

all dicky (with) *phr.* (*also* **all dickey (with)**) [late 18C–mid-19C] all over, ruined, finished, 'all up with'. [SE *all* + fig. use of DICKY adj.[1] (1)]

all dolled up like a barber's cat *phr.* [mid–late 19C] (*Can.*) dressed in the height of fashion.

alleluia lass *n.* [late 19C–1900s] a young Salvation Army woman. [SE *alleluia*, praise the Lord + *lass*]

allergic *adj.* [1930s+] (*orig. US*) sensitive to, usu. with hostile overtones, e.g. *Sorry, but I'm absolutely allergic to Tories.*

allerickstix *adv.* [late 19C; 1980s] (*US*) all right, satisfactorily. [Ger. *alles richtig*, all right]

alleviator *n.* [mid–19C–1940s] a drink, esp. in a 'medicinal' context. [ext. use of SE; i.e. it 'alleviates' one's feelings; 20C use is Aus. only]

alley *n.*[1] [mid–late 19C] the vagina; one of a number of terms equating the vagina with a road or path (cf. BLIND ALLEY n.; COCK ALLEY n.; COCK LANE n.; COVERED WAY n.; CROOKED WAY n.; CUNNY

ALLEY n.; CUPID'S ALLEY n.; DEAD-END STREET n.; HIGHWAY n.; JOY TRAIL n.; LEATHER LANE n.; LONG LANE n.; MAIN AVENUE n.; MUCH-TRAVELLED HIGHWAY n.; RED LANE n.; ROAD n.¹; ROAD TO A CHRISTENING n.; SMOCK ALLEY n.; SPAM ALLEY n.; SPEW ALLEY n.; TURNPIKE n.; VENUS'S HIGHWAY n.).

alley n.² [late 19C–1900s] a go-between. [? Fr. *aller*, to go]

alley n.³ [1920s] (*US Und.*) a place where illicit beer is brewed. [ext. of SE use]

alley n.⁴ 1 [1960s+] (*US Black*) a hospital corridor. 2 [1990s+] (*US Und.*) the open area outside a row of cells. [(1) is northeastern urban use, the image is of poor people crowding the hospitals as they do their own slums]

alley adj. (*also* **ally**) [1990s+] (*US campus*) second-rate. [the negative stereotyping of a racial ghetto]

alley apple n.¹ (*also* **alley lily**, **alley rifle**) [1910s+] (*US*) a brick or stone when used as a missile. [generic use of SE *alley*, the unsavoury area of a town or city + pun on SE *apple/lily/rifle*]

alley apple n.² [1950s+] (*US*) horse manure, excrement (cf. BARKER'S EGG n.; HORSE APPLE n.; ROAD APPLE n.). [SE *alley* + APPLE n.¹]

alley bat n. [late 19C–1930s] (*US*) a promiscuous woman, a prostitute; also used as a general term of abuse. [SE *alley*, the unsavoury area of a town + BAT n.¹]

alley cat n. [1930s+] (*US*) 1 a promiscuous woman. 2 a prostitute (cf. BABOON n.; BADGER n.¹; BAR-FLY n.; BAR-HOG n.²; BIRD n.¹; BIRD OF THE GAME n.¹; BITCH n.¹; CANARY n.¹; CAT n.¹; CHICKEN n.³; CONY n.¹; COW n.¹; CROW n.⁹; CUCKOO n.³; DICKY-BIRD n.¹; DOE n.¹; DOG n.³; DUCK n.¹; EWE-MUTTON n.; FISH n.¹; Fleet Street DOVE n.; FLESH-FLY n.; FRESH FISH n.; GREEN GOOSE n.; GUINEA BIRD n.¹; GUINEA HEN n.; HARE n.; HEDGE-BIRD TRULL n.; HEN n.¹; HEN OF THE GAME n.; HOBBY HORSE n.²; HORSE n.¹⁰; HORSE-LEECH n.²; JAY n.²; KITTIE n.; LIONESS n.; LONE DUCK n.; LOOSE FISH n.; LOT LIZARD n.; MACKEREL n.; MONKEY n.²; MOUSE n.¹; NAG n.¹; NAUGHTY DICKY-BIRD n.; NIGHTBIRD n.; NIGHTHAWK n.; NIGHTINGALE n.²; OWL n.; OYSTER n.¹; PARTRIDGE n.; PIG n.¹; PIG MEAT n.; PLOVER n.; PONY n.⁶; PUSS n.¹; QUAIL n.; RABBIT n.¹; RABBIT PIE n.; RACEHORSE n.²; SARDINE n.; SCATE n.¹; SHRIMP n.²; SOILED DOVE n.; SPARROW n.¹; SQUIRREL n.¹; STILL SOW n.; TABBY n.; THOROUGHBRED n.; TIGER n.⁴; WASP n.¹; WET HEN n.; WREN n.). 3 an illegitimate child. 4 a street urchin. 5 a womanizer. 6 a nightwatchman.

alley cat v. [1960s+] (*US*) of a woman, to act in an overtly promiscuous manner. [ALLEY CAT n. (1)]

alley-cleaner n. [1950s] (*US*) a riot gun, usu. a shotgun with a wide blast and thus used to disperse a mob. [the breadth of the shot 'cleans out' those standing across a narrow alley]

alley lily n. *see* ALLEY APPLE n.¹.

alley rat n. (*US*) 1 [1910s–50s] a particularly unpleasant, villainous and impoverished person. 2 [1930s] a pimp, esp. one involved in cheating a prostitute's clients. [SE *alley*, the unsavoury area of a town + RAT n.² (1)]

alley rifle n. *see* ALLEY APPLE n.¹.

alley up v. [1940s] (*Aus.*) to pay one's share. [SE *alley*, a marble; lit. 'to hand over one's marble']

alley-waiter n. [late 19C–1950s] (*US*) an elevator or lift. [play on the SE, with added overtones of the narrowness of an alley and the elevator car, and of a dumb-waiter]

alley way n. 1 [1910s] (*US*) the throat, in the context of drinking. 2 [1950s] (*US gay*) the anus (cf. BOSCO BOULEVARD n.; BOURNEVILLE BOULEVARD n.; BOVRIL BYPASS n.; BULLI PASS n.; CANYON n.; CHOCOLATE CANYON n.; CHOCOLATE HIGHWAY n.; CHOCOLATE RUNWAY n.; CHUFTER CHUTE n.; CHUTE n.²; DIRT-CHUTE n.; DIRT ROAD n.²; DIRT TRACK n.; FLUE n.¹; FUDGE TUNNEL n.; GRAND CANYON n.; HEINIE HIGHWAY n.; KHYBER (PASS) n.; MUSTARD ROAD n.; POOH CHUTE n.; POOP-CHUTE n.; ROAD LESS TRAVELLED n.; ROCKY ROAD n.; SHIT-CHUTE n.; SLOPCHUTE n.; TAN TRACK n.; TUNNEL n.; USED FOOD TUBE n.; USED FRUIT CHUTE n.).

alley-whipped adj. [2000s] (*US*) unpaid (or robbed of one's pay)

despite having done the work required. [the image of the hapless worker being taken out into an alley and beaten when money is requested]

all-fired adj. (*also* **alfired**) [mid-19C+] (*US*) extreme. [euph. for HELL-FIRED adj.]

all-fired adv. [mid-19C+] (*US*) extremely, very much; thus *all-firedly*, particularly, excessively. [ALL-FIRED adj.]

all forlorn n. [1960s+] a state of sexual excitement. [rhy. sl. = HORN n.² (2)]

all fruits ripe phr. 1 [1980s+] (*W.I./UK Black teen*) everything is fine, OK, all right, fit, all systems are go. 2 [1990s+] a phr. meaning all women are potential sexual partners. [image of a bumper harvest; popularized by reggae singer Junior Reid (b.1968) in a song of the same name (1992)]

all gas and gaiters phr. 1 [mid-19C+] satisfactory, as desired. 2 [1920s+] nonsense, rubbish, pomposity, bombast. [GAS n.¹ (1) + SE *gaiters*; image of a pompous, sermonizing bishop]

all get out phr. (*also* **as get out**) [mid-19C+] (*US*) a general intensifier, very much, to a great extent; usu. prefixed by *as* or *like*.

all girls together phr. *see* GIRLS TOGETHER phr.

all gong and no dinner phr. [1970s+] all talk but no action. [in an era when a gong was rung to announce the imminence of dinner]

all good phr. [1990s+] (*US Black teen*) everything is fine. [ext. of SE use]

All Hallows n. [late 16C] (*UK Und.*) the tolling place, presumably the place where the theft actually takes place, as described by those working as horse-stealers. [poss. an ironic reflection on orig. meaning of *All Hallows*, all holy men or all martyrs; the martyrs in question being those who are duped]

all h and b phr. *see* ALL HOT AND BOTHERED phr. (2).

all harbour phr. *see* HARBOUR LIGHT phr.

all-heeled adj. *see* WELL-HEELED adj.¹.

all holiday at Peckham phr. [late 18C–mid-19C] 1 all over, finished, hopeless. 2 lacking in food. [SE *holiday*, i.e. no work + pun on PECK v.¹ + *ham*, eat(ing) ham]

all honey or all turd with them phr. [late 18C–mid-19C] said of those whose relationship fluctuates violently, meaning that they are either the closest of friends or the deepest of enemies. [antithesis of SE *honey* + TURD n. (1)]

all-hot n. [mid-19C] 1 a baked potato, as sold in the street. 2 a seller of baked potatoes. [the street cry]

all hot and bothered phr. [1920s+] 1 flustered, maniacally nervous. 2 (*also* **all h and b**) sexually excited/frustrated. [ext. of SE use]

all hunk adj. [mid-19C–1940s] (*US*) satisfactory, fine. [fig. use of Du. *hunk*, home, e.g. a place of safety or security, as used in juv. games]

allicholy adj. [late 16C–mid-18C] maudlin, esp. through drink. [SE *ale* + *melancholy*; used by Shakespeare in *Two Gentlemen of Verona* (1591)]

Allied Irish n. [1990s+] (*Irish*) an act of masturbation. [rhy. sl.; *Allied Irish Bank* = WANK n.¹ (1)]

alligator n.¹ 1 [early–mid-19C] a singer who opens his mouth wide. 2 [mid–late 19C] a herring. 3 [late 19C] a shoe of which the upper and the sole have become separated. 4 [mid-19C+] (*Aus./US*) a horse. 5 [1910s–70s] (*US*) a chatterbox, a 'big mouth'. [the amphibian's gaping jaw]

alligator n.² [late 19C+] (*US*) a native of Florida. [the state's indigenous animal]

alligator n.³ 1 [20C+] (*US*) any sexually aggressive male. 2 [1930s–50s] a person, usu. non-Black, who listens to and appreciates jazz, but does not play; orig. dismissive. 3 [1950s] (*US Black*) a White jazz musician. 4 [1950s] (*US teen*) any person, irrespective of musical taste. [the jazz musicians' ref. to someone who 'swallowed up' everything on offer, ? coined by Louis Armstrong (1901–71) to describe White musicians who pirated the original ideas created by their Black peers; 'We'd call them alligators...because they were the guys who came to swallow everything we had to learn']

alligator *adv.* [1950s+] later. [rhy. sl.; note SEE YOU LATER ALLIGATOR phr.]

alligator! *excl.* [1950s+] see you later. [rhy. sl. = LATER! excl.; abbr. SEE YOU LATER ALLIGATOR phr.]

alligator bait *n.*[1] [1900s–60s] (*US*) any inedible food, esp. liver. [the practice in early 20C US construction camps of letting bull's liver rot before cooking it; the meat was thus tenderized, but simultaneously rendered too foul for any human to eat]

alligator bait *n.*[2] **1** [1900s–60s] a Black person, usu. a child (cf. AFRICAN APE n.; BIF n.; BLACKBELLY n.; BOOGER n.[3]; BOOGIE n.[2]; BOOT n.[2]; BOOTHEAD n.; BOY n.[5]; BRILLOHEAD n.; COON n.; COON JIGGER n.; CROW n.[3]; CUFFY n.; DINKY n.[1]; GAR n.[1]; GENERIC n.; GOLLY n.[1]; GOON n.[1]; GROE n.; GROID n.; HAMFAT n.[1]; HUNKY n.; JAP n.; JIG n.[5]; JIGABOO n.; JIGGER n.[11]; JIGWALKER n.; JIM n.; JIM CROW adj.; JIM FISH n.; JIT n.[3]; JONG n.[1]; MUNT n.; NAGAH n.; NIG n.[2]; NIG-BO n.; NIGGER n.[1]; OOGIE n.; SCRUB n.; SEEDY (BOY) n.; SHAKE n.[3]; SHOKE n.; SPOOK n.[1]; SQUASHO n.; WOG n.[1]; YANTA n.; ZIG n.). **2** [1940s] (*US*) a derog. term for a Black native of Florida. [image of racist Whites lynching Blacks and tossing them to the alligators and f. the practice of Southern Whites, who found it amusing to threaten such children with 'throwing them to the alligators']

alligator bait *n.*[3] [1910s–50s] (*US*) a worthless, unpleasant person, of any race.

alligator bull *n.* [1940s] (*Aus.*) nonsense, rubbish. [SE *alligator* (of which there are none in Aus.) + BULL n.[11] (1)]

alligator cigarette *n.* [1940s] (*US drugs*) a marijuana cigarette (cf. AFRICAN WOODBINE n.). [ALLIGATOR n.[3] (2) + SE *cigarette*]

alligator (horse) *n.* (*US*) **1** [19C] a tough man. **2** [mid-19C–1940s] a worthless, unpleasant person. [the animals' characteristics, and usu. used of a Kentucky frontiersman]

Alligatorland *n.* [late 19C] (*Aus.*) Queensland. [ALLIGATOR n.[1] (4) + SE *land*]

alligator mouth *n.* [1950s+] (*US*) a boaster, a braggart, someone with an inclination to boast or brag but insufficient courage to back up their words; such a person is usu. described in the ext. phr. (*he's got*) *an alligator mouth and a hummingbird/canary ass*. [like the amphibian, the mouth is always yawning open]

alligator skin *n. see* FROG n.[3] (1).

all in *phr.* **1** [late 19C+] exhausted, utterly tired, beaten. **2** [20C+] of an object, run-down, dilapidated. **3** [1900s–20s] penniless. **4** [1920s] (*Aus.*) dead. **5** [1950s] drunk. [SE *all in*, everyone (thus every thing/faculty/emotion) included]

all in a bust *phr.* [1910s–20s] very excited. [BUST n.[3] (1)]

all in my eye *phr. see* ALL MY EYE phr.

all in my eye and Betty *phr. see* ALL MY EYE AND BETTY MARTIN phr.

all in one *n.* [1970s–80s] an orgy. [the 'person' or 'orifice' is unstated + ? ref. to carnival jargon *ten in one*, a sideshow that offers 10 performers, often freaks]

all in print *phr.* [late 18C–early 19C] neat, exact, set in place.

all jake *phr.* [1910s+] (*US*) right, OK, satisfactory. [JAKE adj.[1] (2)]

all jaw (like a sheep's head) *phr.* [late 19C–1910s] overly talkative, said of a chatterbox. [pun on JAW n. (1)/SE *jaw*]

all keyhole *n.* [mid-19C–1930s] alcohol, a drink; thus *be all keyhole*, to be drunk. [pun]

all kinds of *adv.* [late 19C+] (*US*) extremely, a great deal of. [ext. of SE use]

all know *adj.* [late 19C] bookish, like a bookworm. [KNOW-ALL n.]

all laired up *phr. see* LAIRED UP phr.

all leather *adj.* **1** [19C+] of an object, excellent, first-rate. **2** [1920s] of a person, dependable, trustworthy. [the toughness and durability of leather]

all lit up *phr.* [1930s+] (*drugs*) under the influence of drugs. [LIT (UP) adj. (4)]

all mockered up *phr. see* MOCKERED UP adj.

all mops and brooms *phr. see* MOPS AND BROOMS phr.

all mouth and trousers *phr.* (*also* **all mouth, all mouth and no trousers**) [1960s+] all talk and no action, a phr. used of a braggart, a fake. [MOUTH n.[1] (3) + SE *trousers*; i.e. a pushy sexual bravado]

all my eye *phr.* (*also* **all his/your eye, (all) in my eye**) [early 18C+] utter, absolute nonsense, humbug.

all my eye and Betty Martin *phr.* (*also* **all in my eye and Betty, that's my eye (and Betty Martin)**) [late 18C+] utter, absolute nonsense. [ext. of ALL MY EYE phr.; *Betty Martin* herself continues to be a source of controversy. E.P. suspects that she was a late 18C London character and that no record of her exists other than this catchphrase. Bee and Hotten (1860) refer to the alleged Lat. prayer, *Ora pro mihi, beate Martine* ('Pray for me blessed Martin'), i.e. St Martin of Tours, the patron saint of publicans and reformed drunkards. It has yet to be found in any version of the liturgy. Writing in 1914, Dr L.A. Waddell suggests another Latinism, *O mihi Britomartis* ('O bring help to me, Britomartis'), referring to the tutelary goddess of Crete. More likely is the idea, proposed in Charles Lee's *Memoirs* (1805), that there had once been 'an abandoned woman called Grace', who, in the late 18C, married a Mr Martin. She became notorious as *Betty Martin*, and *all my eye* was apparently among her favourite phrs. A northern version of the phr. has *Peggy Martin*]

all my eye and (my) elbow *phr.* [late 19C–1900s] nonsense. [ALL MY EYE phr.+ SE *elbow*]

all my eye and my grandmother *phr.* [late 19C] nonsense. [ALL MY EYE phr. + SE *grandmother*]

all my eye and Tommy *phr.* [19C] nonsense. [masc. var. on ALL MY EYE AND BETTY MARTIN phr.]

all nations *n.* **1** [late 18C–early 19C] a mixture of drinks assembled from the dregs of bottles and glasses. **2** [19C] a coat of many colours or covered in patches. [SE phr. *flags of all nations*]

all-nighter *n.* **1** [mid-19C+] anything that lasts all night, whether work or entertainment; thus *all-night house*, a bar which is open all night. **2** [late 19C+] (*also* **all-night man**) a prostitute's client who pays for a whole night's sex. **3** [1930s+] spec. an all-night concert or dance. **4** [1960s+] (*orig. US campus*) working all night before an examination; thus PULL AN ALL-NIGHTER v. **5** [1980s] (*US*) an establishment, e.g. a resturant, that stays open all night. [ext. use of SE]

all-night man *n.* [early–mid-19C] a body-snatcher, a 'resurrectionist'. [ext. use of SE; i.e. he is working all night]

allo *adj.* [mid–late 19C] all. [pidgin; the *-o* sfx makes up for the lack of a final 'l' in Chinese speech]

all of a doodah *phr.* (*also* **all of a do-da**) [1910s+] in a fluster, in a state, very agitated. [DOODAH n.[1]]

all of a flare *phr.* [mid–late 19C] in a clumsy, incompetent manner. [FLARE n.]

all of a heap *adv.* [mid-18C+] suddenly, in a profound manner.

all of a tiswas *phr.* (*also* **all of a tizwas, all of a tizzy**) [1940s+] (*orig. RAF*) utterly confused, very excited. [? SE 'it is, it was', the image is of confusion or TIZZY n.[2]; note *Tiswas*, UK's children's light entertainment TV programme in 1970s]

all of a wonk *phr.* [1910s] jumpy, nervous, tense, in a state. [WONKY adj.]

all of it *n.* [1950s–70s] (*US prison*) a life sentence.

all one's natural *phr.* [late 19C+] all one's life. [abbr. SE phr. *all one's natural born days*]

all one's puff *phr.* [1920s+] all one's life. [PUFF n.[1] (3)]

all on one side like Lord Thomond's cocks *phr.* [late 18C–early 19C] used of a group of people who appear to be united but are, in fact, more likely to quarrel. [18C anecdote of *Lord Thomond's* (1769–1855) Irish cock-feeder, who foolishly confined a number of his lordship's cocks, due to fight the next day for a considerable sum, all in the same room. Stereotyped for the story as a stupid Irishman, he supposedly believed that since they were all 'on the same side', they would not squabble. He was wrong, and the valuable cocks destroyed each other]

all on top *phr.*[1] [1920s+] that's a lie, that is not so. [the statement is 'on top' of the facts]

all-originals *adj.* [1920s+] (*US Black*) Black people only; thus *all-originals scene*, a Blacks-only party etc. [ORIGINAL n.]

all-out *n.* [1960s] (*US campus*) an act of sexual intercourse.

all out *adj.* [20C+] exhausted.

all outdoors *phr.* [early 19C+] (*US*) the whole world, also used fig. to mean a lot; often used as a general intensifier, as in *big as all outdoors, tall as all outdoors*. [the 'big skies' and wide prairies of the US West]

all-over *n.* **1** [mid-19C] a feeling of unease or illness that extends throughout one's body. **2** [20C+] (*US*) a generalized intensive for either best or worst, as in *all-over wonderful, all-over crazy*. **3** [1910s] (*US*) a thorough inspection, a lengthy visual assessment. [16C SE *all over*, complete, to the full extent]

all over *phr.*[1] [early–late 19C] dead. [SE *all over*, finished]

all over *phr.*[2] [1920s+] absorbed in, obsessed by; thus *all over oneself*, extremely self-satisfied.

all over *phr.*[3] **1** [1950s+] pursuing (in a non-sexual manner). **2** [1950s+] making physical/sexual advances, often when not desired. **3** [1980s] (*US campus*) in control of. **4** [2000s] attacking verbally. [SE *all over*, to display great affection; note CLIMB ALL OVER v.]

all over bar the shouting *phr.* (*also* **all over but the cheering/shouting**) [mid-19C+] a foregone conclusion; often preceded by *it's…* [the 'shouting' being applause]

all-overish *adj.* **1** [mid-19C+] feeling slightly unwell, usu. as a preliminary to a full-blown attack of some illness; thus *all-overishness*, the sensation of feeling unwell. **2** [late 19C–1910s] (*also* **all over alike**) sexually excited. [ALL OVER *phr.*[1] + sfx *-ish*]

all over oneself *phr.* [1920s] (*orig. milit.*) absorbed in oneself, pleased with oneself.

all-overs *n.* **1** [late 19C] feelings of irritation. **2** [late 19C–1940s] nervous or apprehensive feelings. [ALL-OVER n. (1)]

all over the board *phr.* [1960s–70s] eccentric, unstable.

all over the joint *phr.* [1950s] (*US*) everywhere. [SE *all over* + JOINT n.[4] (3)]

all over the place like a mad woman's shit *phr.* (*also* **all over the place like a mad woman's breakfast, …knitting, …lunchbox**) [1950s+] (*Aus.*) confused, extremely messy.

all over the road like Brown's cows *phr.* [1980s] (*N.Z.*) in chaos, out of order. [? *Brown* as a generic name for a farmer or ? f. the colour of the cows]

all over the shop *phr.* **1** [late 19C] in chaos, in a mess. **2** [late 19C+] everywhere, esp. in phr. *knock all over the shop*, to beat severely. [(1) is SE 20C+]

all pills! *excl.* [late 19C+] rubbish! nonsense! [PILLS n.[1] (1); i.e. BALLOCKS! excl. (1)]

all piss and wind *phr.* (*also* **all wind (and piss)**, **full of shit and sticks**) [20C+] a phr. used of a braggart, all talk and no action. [fig. use of SE *wind* + PISS n. (1)/SHIT n.[1] (1) + SE *sticks*]

all piss and wind like the barber's dog *phr.* (*also* **all piddle/piss and wind like the barber's cat**) [1940s+] (*Aus./N.Z.*) **1** a phr. used to describe a very thin person. **2** a phr. used of a blusterer, a braggart. [see prev.]

all pissed up and nothing to show *phr.* [1910s–60s] a general phr. of discontent, based on the premise that one has drunk away one's wages and there's nothing left to show for a week's work. [PISSED *adj.*[1]; working-class var. on 'all dressed up and nowhere to go']

all-points *n.* [1960s] a general alert, a search for a missing person (cf. A.P.B. n.). [fig. use of police jargon, *all points bulletin*]

all points bulletin *n.* [1960s+] (*US campus*) a plea for help, with work, emotions and so on (cf. A.P.B. n.). [fig. use of police jargon]

all-powerful *n.* [1900s] (*Aus.*) money (cf. ACTUAL, THE n.).

all prick and breeches *phr.* [1920s+] all talk and no action, a phr. used of a braggart, a fake. [PRICK n. (2) + SE *breeches*]

all prick and ribs like a drover's dog *phr.* (*also* **all prick and ribs like a shearer's dog, …like a swaggie's dog**) [1960s+] (*Aus.*) lean and eager.

all pricks and no pence *phr.* [1920s] all talk and no action, a phr. used of a braggart, a fake. [PRICK n. (2) + SE *pence*]

all quiet *n.* [1990s+] the vagina (cf. BERKELEY (HUNT) n.; BIRCHINGTON HUNT n.; BOB AND HIT n.; DILLYPOT n.; DROPKICK AND PUNT n.; GASP AND GRUNT n.; GLUEPOT n.[2]; GRUMBLE (AND GRUNT) n.; JACK AN' DANNY n.; JAMES HUNT n.; MUST-I-HOLLER n.; ORPHAN ANNIE n.; ROGER HUNT n.; SHARP AND BLUNT n.; SIR BERKELEY n.; SOUTH POLE n.; TONY HATCH n.; TREASURE HUNT n.). [rhy. sl.; *all quiet on the Western Front* = CUNT n.[1] (1); ult. title of novel (1928) by Erich Maria Remarque]

all ribs and dick like a robber's dog *phr.* [1990s+] (*Aus.*) very thin. [SE *ribs* + DICK n.[4] (1); note computer jargon *ribs 'n' dick*: a budget with no fat, as in 'We've got ribs 'n' dick and we're supposed to find 20K for memory upgrades' in G. Branwyn, *HardWired* (1997)]

all ricky *adv.* [1940s] (*US*) satisfactorily, easily. [? SE *all right*]

all right *adj.* **1** [late 19C+] an equivocal term of measured praise, acceptable, passing muster. **2** [1900s–50s] in criminal terms, trustworthy.

all right? *phr.* **1** [1960s+] a general phr. of greeting; a question mark is assumed; often answered by 'all right' or 'not so bad'. **2** [1990s+] a coded query: do you need any drugs?

all right! *excl.* [19C+] yes indeed! I agree! [SE 20C+]

allrightnik *n.* (*also* **alrightnik**) [1910s+] (*US*) one who has succeeded, one who has raised himself from immigrant poverty to material success, esp. of New York Jews; thus *Allrightnik's Row*, Riverside Drive, home at one time of many successful Jews. [SE *all right* + -NIK sfx but the proper ety. is in Yid. *olraytnik*, an upstart, a parvenu]

all-rounder *n.* **1** [mid-19C] a collar that meets at the front, a style fashionable at the time. **2** [1930s] (*US Und.*) a clergyman who wears a 'Roman collar'.

all round my hat *phr. see* ALL AROUND MY HAT *phr.*

alls *n.* [mid-19C–1900s] a drink consisting of the dregs collected from the overflow of the pouring taps, the ends of spirit bottles and similar leavings, which was sold cheap in gin shops, esp. to women. [ALL NATIONS n. (1)/ALL SORTS n./SE *all the dregs/left-overs*; note late 19C wine merchant's *omnes*, i.e. Lat. all mixtures of odds and ends of various wines]

all sails set *phr.* [mid-19C] (*US*) drunk.

allsbay *n.* [1930s–40s] nonsense, rubbish. [cod Lat. = BALLS n.[2]]

all serene *phr.* (*also* **all sereno**) [mid-19C+] all in order, satisfactory. [Sp. *sereno*, the 'equivalent to the *English* "all's well"', a counter-sign of sentinels, supposed to have been acquired by some filibusters (pirates) who were imprisoned in Cuba, and liberated by the intercession of the British ambassador' (Hotten, 1867); E.P. prefers Gibraltar to Cuba as the passage through which the term entered English]

all set *phr.* **1** [late 18C+] of a villain, ready for any criminal undertaking. **2** [mid-19C+] ready, prepared. [ext. of SE use]

all sheok and quoits *phr. see* ALL BEER AND SKITTLES *phr.*

all shot *phr.* [late 19C+] (*orig. milit.*) exhausted, worn-out, finished. [SE *all shot to pieces*]

all Sir Garnet *phr.* (*also* **all sigarneo, all sigarno, all Sir Garny**) [late 19C+] all in order, everything as it should be. [a ref. to the military successes of *Sir Garnet* (later Lord) Wolseley (1833–1923), whose reputation was further enhanced by his efforts to improve the lot of the private soldier; the phr. was popularized through Gilbert & Sullivan's *Pirates of Penzance* (1879), when actor George Grossmith made himself up as Wolseley to sing the song 'I am the very model of a modern Major-General', and the phrase became a sl. term of the time for 'all correct']

all sorts n. [early–mid-19C] a drink consisting of the dregs collected from the overflow of the pouring taps, the ends of spirit bottles and similar leavings; it was sold cheaply in gin-shops, particularly to women. [ext. of SE use]

allspice n. [mid-19C–1900s] a grocer. [as, *inter alia*, a purveyor of SE *allspice*, the aromatic spice]

all's snug phr. [early 18C–early 19C] all is quiet. [SE *snug*, comfortable]

all stations n. [2000s] (*Aus.*) an Alsatian dog. [rhy. sl. or joc. mispron.]

all talk and no cider phr. [19C] (*US*) all theory and no practice, all proposals and no concrete results. [supposedly orig. at a party in Buck County, PA, which had been arranged to enjoy a particularly good barrel of cider; a political argument began and emotions became so heated that half the guests left, claiming that the 'party' had been merely an excuse to wrangle, rather than drink]

all tan and teeth phr. [2000s] (*UK gay*) used of a gay man who is superficially attractive but lacks greater depth.

all that n. [1920s+] a euph. for physical sex in its various aspects. [abbr. euph. SE *all that sort of thing*]

all that and a bag of chips phr. [1990s+] (*US teen*) something or someone considered absolutely excellent. [ALL THAT (AND THEN SOME) phr. (3); note that *chips* in the US are crisps in the UK]

all that (and then some) phr. 1 [1910s] just as described. 2 [1960s+] of an object, excellent, wonderful. 3 [1980s+] (*orig. US teen*) of a person, in possession of all good qualities; thus *one thinks one is all that*, to overestimate oneself. 4 [1990s+] conceited. [SE phr. *and all that, and all the rest of it*]

all that jazz n. (*also* **all that razz**) [1950s+] (*orig. US*) that sort of thing, usu. following a list of proper nouns *...and all that jazz*. [JAZZ n.[2] (1)]

all the beans n. [20C+] (*bingo*) the number 57 (cf. ALDERSHOT LADIES n.). [Heinz *57* Varieties, of which baked beans are the best known]

all the fat is in the fire phr. *see* FAT IS IN THE FIRE, THE phr.

all the go phr. [late 18C+] fashionable. [GO n.[2] (1)]

all there (and a ha'porth over) phr. 1 [mid-late 19C] honest, reliable. 2 [mid-19C] fashionable, well-dressed. 3 [late 19C+] as desired, satisfactory. 4 [late 19C+] smart, aware. 5 [late 19C+] sane, in one's right mind.

all there but the most of you phr. [mid-19C–1940s] having sexual intercourse. [*all* is the genitals, the *most* is the rest of the body]

all the steps n. [20C+] (*bingo*) the number 39 (cf. ALDERSHOT LADIES n.). [the WW1 thriller *The Thirty Nine Steps* (1915) by John Buchan]

all the ton phr. [late 18C] smart, fashionable.

all the twos n. [20C+] (*bingo*) the number 22; thus *all the threes*, 33, *all the fours*, 44, up to *all the nines*, 99 (cf. ALDERSHOT LADIES n.).

all the way adv. [1910s+] completely.

all the way phr. 1 [1950s+] (*US*) of a hamburger, occas. hot dog, with a full complement of condiments and garnishes; similarly used of other dishes on a menu, i.e. served as written, without 'holding' or substituting any item. 2 [1980s] (*N.Z.*) on a prostitute's 'menu', full intercourse.

all the way live phr. [1970s+] (*US Black*) anyone or anything considered exceptionally lively, exciting, desirable. [ALL THE WAY adv. + LIVE adj. (2)]

all the way there phr. [mid–late 19C] honest, reliable. [ext. of ALL THERE (AND A HA'PORTH OVER) phr. (1)]

all the world and his wife n. (*also* **all the world and his**

dog) [early 18C+] absolutely everyone. [the 'dog' usage is mainly Aus.]

all the world to a china orange phr. (*also* **all the world to a penny roll**) [19C] the longest possible odds, an absolute certainty (cf. BET A POUND TO A PINCH OF SHIT v.; CHELSEA COLLEGE TO A SENTRY-BOX phr.; DOLLARS TO BUTTONS phr.; DOLLARS TO DOUGHNUTS phr.; GUINEA TO A GOOSEBERRY n.; LOMBARD STREET TO A CHINA ORANGE phr.; LONDON TO A BRICK phr.; POMPEY'S PILLAR TO A STICK OF SEALING-WAX phr.; YORK MINSTER TO A BRASS FARTHING phr.).

all the year round n. [1920s+] (*Aus.*) a 12-month prison sentence.

all-time adj. [1940s+] (*US*) greatest, very best, most memorable on record. [abbr. SE *in all of time*]

all-timer n. [1970s+] the supreme example of, the greatest version. [ALL-TIME adj.]

all tits and teeth phr. [1910s+] a woman who capitalizes on her physical charms, esp. her smile and (presumably large) breasts, to make up for the lack of more subtle attractions; sometimes ext. by *...like a third-row chorus-girl*.

all to buggery phr. [20C+] unsatisfactory, mixed up, useless (cf. BUGGERY n.). [SE *buggery* + BUGGER UP v.]

all to cock phr. [20C+] unsatisfactory, mixed up, useless. [COCK n.[5] (2)]

all to heck phr. [1950s] (*US*) a general intensifier. [SE *all* + HECK n.]

all to hell phr. (*also* **gone to hell**) [19C+] 1 financially ruined. 2 wasted. 3 in chaos. 4 worn-out. 5 utterly destroyed.

all to pieces adv. [late 18C–1940s] (*also* **all to muck**) completely, utterly, to the furthest extent. [for ety. *see* ALL TO PIECES phr.]

all to pieces phr. [early 17C+] exhausted, collapsed, bankrupt. [fig. use of SE; *to* substituted for SE *in*]

all tore up/torn up phr. *see* TORE UP adj.

all to smash phr. 1 [mid-18C+] (*also* **into smash, all to shivers**) physically collapsed. 2 [mid-19C+] bankrupted, utterly destroyed; usu. in phr. *go all to smash*.

all to thunder adv. [late 19C] (*US*) completely, comprehensively.

all up phr. [late 18C+] ruined, finished, defeated; doomed, about to die; esp. in phr. ALL UP WITH phr. [SE *up*, used to indicate completion, as a synon. with SE *over/finished*]

all up in phr. [1990s+] 1 (*US campus*) sexually involved (with). 2 (*US teen*) interfering.

all up in here phr. [1970s] (*US Black*) a phr. indicating the importance of a given place or situation.

all up in the koolaid phr. [1990s+] (*US Black/campus/teen*) knowing what is going on; aware of the facts; thus phr. *all up in the koolaid without knowing the flavor*, ignorant, unaware, used to tell off an inquisitive person. [*Kool-Aid*, a popular US soft drink]

all up the country with, be v. [late 19C–1930s] to be the ruin of, to be death for. [ext. of ALL UP WITH phr.]

all up with phr. [late 18C+] 1 of a person, doomed, about to die; defeated, bankrupt. 2 of an object or plan, ruined, pointless, destroyed, finished. [ext. of ALL UP phr.]

all washed up phr. *see* WASHED UP adj.[1].

all wet phr. [1920s+] 1 (*orig. Aus.*) silly, foolish. 2 (*orig. US Black*) useless, worthless, wrong. [WET adj.[3]]

all wind (and piss) phr. *see* ALL PISS AND WIND phr.

all woke up phr. [1960s] (*US*) aware, knowledgeable.

all wool phr. [mid-19C–1900s] (*Aus./US*) excellent, first-class. [WOOL n.[1]]

all wrong phr. [1910s] (*Aus.*) drunk.

ally n. [2000s] an Alsatian dog. [abbr. + sfx -*y*]

ally adj. *see* ALLEY adj.

ally-beg n. [18C–19C] a comfortable bed. [? according to B&L, Gaelic *aille*, pleasant + *beg*, little (place); thus a pleasant little place]

alma gray *n.* [1940s+] (*Aus.*) a 3-penny piece. [rhy. sl. = TRAY n. (1); ult. 'Little' *Alma Gray*, a music hall star *c.*1900]

almanack *n.* [late 19C–1900s] the vagina. [? it brings one good fortune]

almighty *adj.* [early 19C+] mighty, great.

almighty *adv.* [early 19C] exceedingly, greatly, very.

almond *n.* [late 19C+] the penis (cf. ARTFUL DODGER n.; BLACK AND DECKER n.; BOB AND DICK n.; BRIGHTON ROCK n.; DICKERY n.; DICKORY DOCK n.; EIGHT-DAY CLOCK n.; GOOD SHIP VENUS n.; GRANDFATHER n.²; GRUESOME AND GORY n.; HACKNEY WICK n.; HAMPTON ROCK n.; HAMPTON (WICK) n.; JOLSON STORY n.; KISS-ME-QUICK n.²; MAD MICK n.; MARQUIS OF LORNE n.; MARS AND VENUS n.; MICKEY ROURKE n.; MR COOL n.¹; MOBY (DICK) n.; MYSTIC MEG n.; PADLOCK n.; PAT AND MICK n.; PICCALILLI n.; POGO STICK n.; STICK OF ROCK n.; STORMY DICK n.; THIN AND THICK n.; THREE-CARD TRICK n.; TOWER DOCK n.; UNCLE BOB n.¹; UNCLE DICK n.; WHIPPIT QUICK n.; WILLY WONKA n.). [rhy. sl.; *almond rock* = COCK n.² (1)]

almond rock *n.* [1970s] a frock. [rhy. sl.]

almond rocks *n.* (*also* **almonds**) [1910s+] socks. [rhy. sl.]

almshouse *adj.* [1980s+] (*W.I./UK Black*) of behaviour or attitude, negative; thus *almshouse business*, violence.

aloft *adj.* [late 18C+] dead; thus *go aloft*, to die. [i.e. gone up to heaven]

-alorum *sfx* (*also* **-alorium**) [late 19C+] a fake Lat. sfx used to create joc. emphasis from a n., e.g. *scorchalorum, crapalorium*. [? on pattern of SE *cockalorum*]

alpha and omega *n.* [19C] the vagina. [SE *alpha and omega*, 'the beginning and the end...of the divine being' (*OED*)]

alphabet *n.* [2000s] (*US prison*) an extremely long sentence. [pun on SE *sentence*, i.e. a 'sentence' so long that it cannot be characterized by numbers]

Alphabet City *n.* [1980s+] (*US*) Avenues A, B, C and D (and the relevant cross-streets) on New York City's Lower East Side. [the initial letters]

alphabet-slinger *n.* [1960s] (*US*) a schoolteacher. [SE *alphabet* + SLINGER n.¹ (2)]

alpha geek *n.* [1990s+] (*US campus*) one who is exceptionally well versed in (computer) technology. [SE *alpha male* + GEEK n.¹ (7)]

alpha powder *n.* [1950s] (*US drugs*) any powdered narcotic. [ety. unknown]

alphonse *n.*¹ [late 19C] a gigolo. [the character in the play *Monsieur Alphonse* (1873) by Alexander Dumas fils]

alphonse *n.*² [1940s+] (*UK Und.*) a pimp, a ponce (cf. BLUE MOON n.; CANDLE (AND) SCONCE n.; CHARLIE RONCE n.; DIDDLY-DONCE n.; DISH RAN AWAY WITH THE SPOON n.; EGG AND SPOON n.; FISH AND SHRIMP n.; JOE BONCE n.; MACGIMP n.; RONSON n.¹; SILVER SPOON n.; SILVERY MOON n.; TERRY TOON n.). [rhy. sl.; however, note Farmer, *Vocabula Amatoria* (1896): 'Alphonse, a prostitute's bully']

already *adv.* [19C+] **1** as used by Pennsylvania Germans, previously, before, ago. **2** as used by Yid. speakers and those wishing to indicate Yid. speech rhythms, an intensifier indicating immediacy, even exasperation, e.g. *So tell me, already*. [both terms are ult. rooted in the Ger. *schon*, already, yet, so far; in these uses (1) is Penn. Ger. *schun* and (2) Yid. *shoyn*]

alrightnik *n. see* ALLRIGHTNIK n.

Alsatia *n.* [late 16C–mid-19C] **1** the criminal 'no-man's-land' of contemporary London; divided into Higher Alsatia (Whitefriars in the City) and Lower Alsatia (around the Mint in Southwark). **2** in fig. use, any no-man's land. [named for *Alsace-Lorraine*, the marginal, disputed border area between France and Germany. Higher Alsatia, its earlier manifestation, was once the lands of the Whitefriars Monastery, extending from The Temple to Whitefriars Street and from Fleet Street to the Thames. After the Dissolution of the Monasteries (1536–9) the area went downhill, and, as allowed by Elizabeth I (r.1558–1603) and James I (r.1603–25), its inhabitants claimed exemption from jurisdiction of the City of London. As such, the area became a centre of corruption, a refuge for villains, debtors, cheats and gamesters and a no-man's-land for the law. The privileges were abolished in 1697, but it was decades before the old habits died out]

alsatian *adj.* [late 17C–18C] criminal, roguish. [ALSATIA n.]

Alsatians *n.* [18C–19C] members of London's criminal underworld. [ALSATIA n.]

alsatia phrase *n.* [early–mid-17C] terms from slang or criminal jargon. [ALSATIA n. + SE *phrase*]

also-ran *n.* [late 19C+] (*orig. Aus.*) a useless person, a failure, an irrelevance. [horseracing use]

altamel *n.* (*also* **altemal**) [late 17C–mid-19C] a financial summary or account produced without detail and demanded as a lump sum. [18C Du. *altemal*, wholly, all at once]

altar *n.* (*also* **altar room**) [1920s+] the lavatory (cf. BANK n.³; CHAMBER OF COMMERCE n.; CHAPEL (OF EASE) n.; CLOSET OF EASE n.; CRAPPING CASTLE n.; FEDERAL BUILDING n.; FIRST NATIONAL BANK n.; LIBRARY n.²; LITTLE BARN n.; PRIVY COUNCIL n.; SCRAPING CASTLE n.; TEMPLE n.; THRONE n.; UPSTAIRS n.²; YARD n.²).

altar of hymen *n.* (*also* **altar of love, altar of venus**) [late 16C+] the vagina (cf. ADAM'S OWN (ALTAR) n.). [SE *altar* + *Hymen*, the Greek god of marriage/*hymen*, the virginal membrane]

altar of pleasure *n.* [19C] the vagina (cf. ADAM'S OWN (ALTAR) n.). [a literary euph.]

altar room *n. see* ALTAR n.

altemal *n. see* ALTAMEL n.

alter *n.* [1950s] (*US drugs*) an opium pipe. [? it alters one's perceptions]

alter kacker *n.* (*also* **alter cocker, alter kocker**) [1920s+] (*US*) old fool, old fogey (cf. NUDNIK n.; PUTZ n.; SCHLEMAZEL n.; SCHLEMBO n.; SCHLEMIEL n.; SCHLONG n.; SCHLUB n.; SCHMO n.; SCHMUCK n.; SCHNOOK n.; YUTZ n.). [Yid. *alter kocker*, old shit. A facetious 'bilingual' version is *alter coyote*]

alter one's tune *v. see* CHANGE ONE'S TUNE v.

alter someone's dial-plate *v.* [early 19C] to disfigure someone's face. [SE *alter* + DIAL-PLATE n.]

altham *n.* [16C] (*UK Und.*) the wife or female companion of a mendicant villain. [E.P. sees this as ? root of AUTEM n.; if so, such a link would require a pun of the ALTAR OF HYMEN n. type]

altogether, the *n.* [late 19C+] nudity, esp. in phr. *in the altogether*, naked. ['altogether naked/nude'; coined by George Du Maurier in his novel *Trilby* (1894): 'I have sat for the "altogether" to several other people']

altogethery *adj.* [early 19C–1930s] (*UK society*) tipsy, drunk (cf. ABOUT RIGHT phr.¹). [SE *altogether*, completely, utterly (drunk) + sfx -*y*]

altumal *n.* [early–mid-18C] sailor's slang, naut. jargon. [Lat. *altum mare*, the deep sea]

alum, the *n.* [late 19C] (*US*) the ideal, exactly what one desires. [? phr. *à la mode*]

alvin *n.* [1940s+] (*US*) a yokel, an unsophisticated dweller in a small-town or rural settlement (cf. ARKY n.; BOBO-JOHNNY n.; CLEM n.¹; CLYDE n.¹; ELMER n.; GOMER n.²; GOMER PYLE n.; GULLY-JUMPER n.; HICK n.¹; HIRAM n.; HOB n.; HODGE n.; IKE n.; JAAP n.; JACK n.¹⁵; JAKE n.¹; JASPER n.; JEETER n.; JEFF n.; JEFF DAVIS n.; JEFFER n.; JEHU n.²; JOHNNY n.¹; JOHNNY RAW n.; JOSH n.; RALPH n.¹; REUBEN n.; ROGER n.⁴; RUBE n.¹; RUFUS n.²). [a 'typically' rural name]

alvo *adj.* [1990s+] (*US campus*) excellent, wonderful. [ety. unknown]

'Am *n.* [1990s+] (*US*) a Trans-*Am* automobile. [abbr.]

a.m. *n.* (*also* **ayem**) [late 18C+] the morning; the very early hours after midnight. [colloq. version of SE *a.m.*, ante meridiem, used in chronological notation]

amadáin/amadan/amadaun *n. see* OMADHAUN *n.*

amateur *n.*[1] (*also* E.A., **enthusiastic amateur**) [1910s+] a promiscuous young woman; thus [1920s+] (*orig. US*) *lose one's amateur standing/status*, to move into the world of professional, full-time prostitution. [the term depends on the assumption that for women any sex before marriage is tantamount to unpaid prostitution]

amateur *n.*[2] [1930s–40s] (*UK Und.*) a professional criminal who has not been in trouble with the police.

amateur hour *n.* [1950s] (*US Und.*) in the context of bank-robbing, noon, when banks expected to be robbed.

amateur night *n.* (*also* **amateur hour**) [1930s+] (*orig. US*) an exhibition of more than usual ineptitude, esp. by one who is supposedly more competent. [orig. theatrical use, when on special nights amateur hopefuls were encouraged to 'try their stuff' on a real stage]

amazon *n.* (*US campus*) **1** [1960s] an attractive, sexy woman. **2** [1960s] a very tall or muscular person of either sex. **3** [1990s+] (*US Black*) a masculine lesbian.

ambassador *n.* [1920s; 2000s] (*US*) the penis. [it 'presents its credentials' to the vagina]

ambassador of Morocco *n.* [early 19C] a shoemaker. [pun on Morocco leather]

amber *n.* (*US*) **1** [1910s–30s] (*also* **ambeer, ambier**) tobacco juice. **2** [1940s+] beer, usu. as *the amber*. [the colour]

amber fluid *n.* (*also* **amber beverage, …brew, …liquid**) **1** [mid-19C+] (*Aus.*) beer; thus *amber transfusion*, a drink of beer. **2** [1970s] whisky. [its colour]

ambidexter *n.* **1** [16C–18C] (*gambling*) a house player. **2** [17C–18C] (*also* **ambodexter**) a corrupt lawyer who takes fees from both plaintiff and defendant. [SE *ambidextrous*, in both cases the subject is seen as 'playing with both hands']

ambidextrous *adj.* [1930s+] a euph. for bisexual. [SE *ambidextrous*, capable of using both hands equally well]

ambier *n. see* AMBER *n.* (1).

ambisextrous *adj.* [1920s+] (*US*) bisexual (cf. AMBIDEXTROUS *adj.*). [pun on SE *ambidextrous*/SE *sex*]

ambo *n.* [1960s+] (*Aus./S. Afr.*) **1** an *amb*ulance. **2** an *amb*ulance officer. [abbr. + -O sfx (4)]

ambodexter *n. see* AMBIDEXTER *n.* (2).

ambs-ace *n.* **1** [late 14C–18C] nothing, next to nothing. **2** [early 16C–18C] bad luck, misfortune, worthlessness. **3** [late 17C–19C] (*also* **ames-ace**) in phr. *within ambs-ace of*, within an ace of, very close to. [SE *ambs-ace*, double ace or both aces; thus the lowest possible throw in dice]

ambulance-chaser *n.* [late 19C+] a lawyer who specializes in representing the victims of street and other accidents; to whom he offers his services – often appearing at the victim's hospital bed to promise a substantial claim – which are accepted while the victim is still too shocked to make proper and rational arrangements.

ambulance-chasing *n.* [1940s+] of a lawyer, specializing in representing the victims of street and other accidents; also used of journalists in the context of pursuing stories. [AMBULANCE-CHASER *n.*]

ameche *n.* [1930s–50s] (*Can./US*) a telephone. [proper name of actor Don *Ameche* (1908–93), who portrayed the telephone's inventor, Alexander Graham Bell, in a 1939 biopic]

amen-bawler *n.* [19C] a parson, a preacher. [SE *amen*, as a generic for prayers + SE *bawler*, one who shouts]

amen bench *n.* (*also* **amen corner**) [late 19C–1940s] (*US Black*) the front seats in a church, on either side of the pulpit; thus those who occupy them, i.e. the most devout members of the congregation. [the seats of the most enthusiastic con-gregants, who punctuate the prayer and sermon with cries of *Amen!*]

amen-curler *n.* [18C–early 19C] a parish clerk. [? SE *amen* + *curler*, one who writhes about; thus the clerk, wishing to demonstrate his piety]

amener *n.* [late 19C–1900s] a devout Anglican. [in allusion to their frequent use of *amen*]

amen-preacher *n.* [early 19C+] (*W.I.*) the carrion crow. [its black plumage, and the dislike felt by many West Indians for the White missionaries who preached at them]

amen-snorter *n.* [late 19C+] (*mainly Aus.*) a parson.

amen theatre royal *n.* [late 19C] a church. [? the innate theatricality of religious services]

amen-wallah *n.* [19C+] the chaplain's clerk. [SE *amen* + WALLAH *n.* (1)]

American *n.* [1980s] (*US*) sexual intercourse whereby the man reaches orgasm in a body roll with a woman, rather than in full penetration.

American business college *n.* (*also* **ABC**) [1940s+] (*US Black*) a liquor store. [initials, which are also those of the *A*lcoholic *B*everage *C*ommission]

American card *n.* [1930s] an erotic picture postcard.

American culture *n.* [1960s+] sexual intercourse in the face-to-face 'missionary position'. [the supposed blandness of Middle American lifestyles]

American lad *n.* [20C+] (*Irish*) unpopular fatty bacon, imported from the US. [SE *American* + LAD *n.*[1] (1)]

American trombone *n.* [1990s+] group sex between 1 woman and 2 men; the woman simultaneously fellates 1 man while being taken from the rear by the other.

American workhouse *n.* [1910s–30s] Park Lane Hotel, London. [its many American guests; it is, of course, far from a 'workhouse']

Amerika *n.* (*also* **Amerikkka**) [1970s+] (*orig. US*) America, viewed as the embodiment and headquarters of a right-wing, establish-ment-controlled, quasi-fascist conspiracy by the revolutionaries of the period. [the initials of the *Ku Klux Klan*, although note standard Ger. *Amerika*, America; an identification with Germany, however, still implied fascism/or Nazism]

ames-ace *n. see* AMBS-ACE *n.* (3).

amesjay *n.* [1930s] a sovereign. [backsl. = JAMES *n.*[3]]

a.m.f. *phr.* [1960s+] goodbye, that's it, it's all over. [euph. abbr. of *adios motherfucker*; itself occas. euph. as *adios my friend*]

AM/FM *adj.* [1980s+] bisexual. [the 2 varieties of radio frequency]

amiable *adj.* [mid-19C] (*US*) stupid.

amidships *adj.* [1910s+] in the stomach, in the solar plexus, usu. relating to a blow. [naut.]

amies *n.* (*also* **amys**) [1960s+] *am*yl nitrite (cf. AIMIES *n.*). [abbr.]

amigo *n.* [late 19C] (*US*) an (affectionate) term of address. [Sp. *amigo*, friend]

Aminadab *n.* (*also* **Aminidab**) [early 17C–early 19C] a Quaker. [a 'typical' Quaker name; 'from old comedies' (Hotten, 1867)]

Amish golf *n.* [1960s] (*US*) croquet. [SE *Amish*, a strict sect of the Mennonite church in the US + SE *golf*; the theory is that the Amish are especial fans of the game]

ammo *n.* **1** [1910s+] *amm*unition. **2** [2000s] (*US Und.*) money. [(1) abbr. + -O sfx (3); (2) fig. use of (1)]

ammunition *n.* **1** [late 17C–mid-19C] semen. **2** [19C+] lavatory paper. **3** [1920s–40s] (*US*) food, esp. as given out by the Salvation Army and similar institutions. **4** [1940s+] a tampon or sanitary towel.

ammunition leg *n.* [late 19C] a wooden leg. [SE *ammunition*, as supplied to soldiers]

ammunition wife *n.* [early–mid-19C] a prostitute. [such a woman, like fired ammunition, was HOT *adj.*[1] (1)]

amoeba-brained *adj.* [1960s+] (*US*) very stupid (cf. AIRHEADED *adj.*; B.B.-BRAINED *adj.*; BEEF-WITTED *adj.*; CHICKEN-BRAINED *adj.*; CLAY-BRAINED *adj.*; CLODBRAINED *adj.*; CLOD-SKULLED *adj.*; CORK-BRAINED *adj.*; CRACKBRAINED *adj.*; DUR-BRAINED *adj.*; FISH-BRAINED *adj.*; FUZZ-BRAINED *adj.*; JELLO-BRAINED *adj.*; JINGLE-BRAINED *adj.*;

LAMEBRAIN adj.; MUSH-BRAINED adj.; PEABRAINED adj.; PUTTY-BRAINED adj.; SHIT-BRAINED adj.). [the tiny size]

amos and andy n.[1] **1** [1940s–50s] brandy. **2** [1990s+] shandy. [rhy. sl.; the *Amos and Andy* radio show was highly popular in the US in the 1930s–40s; it featured 2 White actors, Freeman Gosden (1899–1982) and Charles Correll (1890–1972), faking it as 'dumb but happy darkies', and as such was one of the last interpretations of the old 'minstrel show']

amos and andy n.[2] [1960s] (*US Black campus*) a man who takes advantage of a woman. [see prev.]

amourette n. [early 19C–1910s] a trifling, short-lived love affair. [Fr. *amourette*, little love affair]

amp n. **1** [1950s+] (*drugs*) ampoule. **2** [1960s+] an *amp*lifier. **3** [1970s+] (*US drugs*) *amp*hetamine (cf. A n.[2]). **4** [2000s+] (*US drugs*) marijuana dipped in formaldehyde, sometimes laced with phencyclidine. [abbr.; (1), (3) and (4) play on the effects of the drugs]

amp adj. [1990s+] (*US Black*) stirred up, very emotional. [abbr. SE *amplified*]

amp down v. [1990s+] (*US campus*) to calm down, to talk quietly. [AMP adj.]

amped adj. [1970s+] (*US*) **1** high on drugs or caffeine; thus in fig. use, nervous. **2** ready, enthusiastic. [SE *amplified*; there may also be a subtler link to an AMP n. (1) of methedrine]

amped-out adj. [1970s+] (*drugs*) suffering exhaustion after using amphetamine. [AMPED adj. (1) + AMP n. (3)]

ampersand n. [mid-18C–19C] the buttocks. [the fact that in late 19C nursery alphabets the symbol was usu. printed after ('behind') the 26 letters + the suitably curving shape of the &]

amphets n. [1960s+] *amphet*amines (cf. A n.[2]). [abbr.]

amp joint n. [1980s+] (*drugs*) a marijuana cigarette laced with some form of narcotic. [AMP n. (4) + JOINT n.[5] (3)]

amp out v. [1990s+] (*US*) to act in a highly neurotic, tense manner. [AMPED adj. (1)]

ampster *see under* AMSTER.

amputate one's mahogany v. (*also* **amputate one's timber**) [mid–late 19C] to run away. [synon. for CUT (ONE'S) STICK(S) v. (1)]

amscray v. (*also* **amscra**) [1930s+] (*orig. US*) to leave quickly, to run off. [cod Lat. = *scram*]

amster n. (*also* **ampster, amsterdam**) [1940s+] (*Aus.*) one who works outside a carnival, sideshow, strip club etc, touting the pleasures inside and pulling in the customers. [rhy. sl.; *Amsterdam* = RAM n.[3]]

amster v. (*also* **ampster**) [1940s+] to work outside a carnival, sideshow, strip club etc, touting the pleasures inside and pulling in the customers. [AMSTER n.]

AMT n. [1960s+] (*US drugs*) dimethytriptamine. [? abbr.]

amulet n. [19C] the vagina. [SE *amulet*, a charm against evil]

amuse v. [18C–mid-19C] (*UK Und.*) to fool shopkeepers and other tradesmen in order to cheat or rob them. [for ety. *see* AMUSER n.]

amuser n. [mid-18C–mid-19C] (*UK Und.*) one who throws dust (sometimes snuff or pepper) in his victim's eyes and then runs off; a companion then appears and, while ostensibly offering his sympathy, picks the victim's pockets. [pun on SE *amuse*, to beguile with entertaining tales or to 'throw dust in one's eyes']

amy n. (*also* **aimie**) [1960s–70s] (*drugs*) *amy*l nitrite (cf. AIMIES n.). [abbr.]

amy-john n. [1960s–80s] a lesbian (cf. CHARLIE n.[10]; ELLEN n.; JASPER n.; JUDY n.[1]; LESLIE n.; MARGE n.; MARY JANE n.[1]; NELLIE n.; OLD TOM n.[2]; PERCY n.[1]; TOM n.[3]; WINNIE n.[1]). [play on SE *Amazon* + the comb. of male and female names]

amyl n. [1900s; 1960s+] (*drugs*) *amyl* nitrite (cf. AIMIES n.). [abbr.]

amyl queen n. [1970s] (*US gay*) a gay man who enjoys sniffing amyl nitrite, which is supposed to enhance male orgasm. [AMYL n. + QUEEN n.[2] (1)/QUEEN sfx (2)]

amys n. *see* AMIES n.

anabaptist n. [late 18C–early 19C] a pickpocket who, having been caught in the act, is 'baptized' by being placed beneath a pump or dumped into a pond. [pun on SE *Anabaptist*, an early 16C German Protestant sect, typified by the re-baptism of all members; ult. f. Gk *anabaptismos*, baptize over again]

anaconda n. [1990s+] a mixture of strong beer and rough cider or scrumpy. [var. on SNAKEBITE n. (3)]

anal astronaut n. [1990s+] a male homosexual (cf. ANAL BUCANEER n.; ANAL CRUSADER n.; ARSE BANDIT n.; ARSEHOLE BANDIT n.; ARSE JOCKEY n.; ARSE-SHAGGER n.; ASS BOY n.; ASS BURGLAR n.; ASS PIRATE n.; ASS RAIDER n.; BACK-DOOR COMMANDO n.; BACK-DOOR KICKER n.; BATTY BWOY n.; BATTYMAN n.; BATTY MONKEY n.; B.B. n.[1]; B-BOY n.; B-BWOY n.; BOOTIE-BUSTER n.; BOOTY BANDIT n.; BOOTY-BUFFER n.; BOTTOM BANDIT n.; BOTTY-BASHER n.; BROWN ARTIST n.; BUGGER-BANDIT n.; BUM BANDIT n.; BUM-BANGER n.; BUM BOY n.; BUM BUDDY n.; BUM CHUM n.; BUM-FAKER n.; BUM-JUMPER n.; BUM PLUMBER n.; BUM-PUNCHER n.; BUM-ROBBER n.; BUN BOY n.; BUTT BOY n.; BUTT PIRATE n.; BUTT RIDER n.; BUTT-RUSTLER n.; BUTT SLUT n.; CACKPIPE COSMONAUT n.; DATE PUNCHER n.; DOUGHNUT MAKER n.; DOUGHNUT POKER n.; DOUGHNUT-PUNCHER n.; EYE DOCTOR n.; FRECKLE-PUNCHER n.; HOOP STRETCHER n.; HULA RAIDER n.; JACKSY JOCKEY n.; KEISTER BANDIT n.; NAVIGATOR OF THE WINDWARD PASSAGE n.; REAR-ADMIRAL n.; REAREND LOADER n.; REAR (SEAT) GUNNER n.; RECTAL RANGER n.; RING MASTER n.; RING RAIDER n.; RUMP RANGER n.).

anal bucaneer n. [1980s+] (*US gay*) a homosexual man (cf. ANAL ASTRONAUT n.).

anal crusader n. [1990s+] (*UK juv.*) a male homosexual (cf. ANAL ASTRONAUT n.).

analken v. [late 19C] (*tinker*) to wash. [Shelta]

analt v. [late 19C] (*tinker*) to sweep. [Shelta]

anarchists n. [1910s–40s] (*Aus.*) non-safety matches. [they are 'likely to explode']

anarcho n. [1990s+] an *anarch*ist. [abbr. + -O sfx (4)]

anatomy n. [mid-19C–1900s] a very thin, emaciated person. [SE *anatomy*, a skeleton; used by Shakespeare in *Comedy of Errors* (1590)]

anca n. [late 19C] a man. [Gk *aner*, a man]

anchor n.[1] [mid-19C–1950s] (*orig. US*) a pick-axe. [resemblance]

anchor n.[2] [1910s+] (*US Und.*) a reprieve, a temporary suspension of a sentence.

anchor n.[3] [1940s–50s] (*US Und.*) a stickpin; thus *anchor and prop*, a stickpin with a safety catch that anchors it to the tie.

anchor n.[4] [1950s] (*US Black*) one's home, one's address.

anchor n.[5] [1990s+] (*Aus. juv.*) a younger relation or other small child who 'cramps one's style' and social life.

anchor v. **1** [late 19C–1970s] (*US*) to stop for a while, to settle. **2** [1920s–50s] to grant a stay of execution. [naut. imagery]

anchor (and chain) n. [1940s] (*US*) one's wife. [derog. stereotype of a wife as the restraint on male freedoms]

anchored adj. [1940s] (*US*) married.

anchors n. [1930s+] brakes; thus *drop the anchors, slam on the anchors*, put on the brakes. [naut. imagery]

ancient Chinese secret n. [1980s+] (*US Black teen*) a non-committal response used when one is asked how one managed a task. [appears to have begin with 1986 TV advert for Calgon washing powder, recalled in personal email 23 Apr. 2002: 'The Calgon in the Chinese Laundromat: Woman comes in and asks how the cleaner gets her laundry so fresh. He laughs and says "Ancient Chinese Secret". The woman in the back says "We need more Calgon" and the customer says "Ancient Chinese secret huh????" and the proprietor smiles embarassingly (very cheesy)']

ancient dutch n. *see* OLD DUTCH n.

and a coffee phr. [1970s] (*Can. prison*) the last day of one's sentence, one has breakfast but is released before the other meals; usu. as *x days and a coffee*.

and a half phr. [mid-19C+] a general intensifier, e.g. *a cunt and* *a half*, a very unpleasant person indeed, *a party and a half*, a really good party.

and a merry Christmas to you too *phr.* [1920s] a dismissive, disparaging phr. that implies quite the opposite of its SE meaning.

and did he marry poor blind Nell? *phr.* [1910s+] a phr. used to imply one's disbelief in the previous statement. [play on the clichéd conventions of popular fiction]

Andes candy *n.* [1990s+] (*US drugs*) cocaine (cf. BOLIVIAN MARCHING POWDER n.; INCA MESSAGE n.; MORNINGSIDE SPEED n.; PERUVIAN n.²). [the South American origins of cocaine + CANDY n.⁴ (2)]

and how! *excl.* [mid-19C+] (*orig. US*) a general excl. of agreement or approval, placed at the end of a sentence. [synon. Ger. *und wie!*]

and no bottles *phr.* [late 19C] without a doubt.

and no chips *phr.* [late 19C] and no mistake.

and no error *phr. see* AND NO MISTAKE (ABOUT IT) phr.

and no flies *phr.* [mid-19C] a general intensifier, no doubt or hesitation about it. [the image is of flies settling on something that is fig. 'off']

and no larks *phr. see* NO LARKING ABOUT phr.

and no messing about *phr.* [1930s+] a general intensifier, no doubt whatsoever.

and no mistake (about it) *phr.* (*also* **and no error, with no error**) [early 19C+] a general intensifier, certainly, without any doubt.

and no pickles *phr. see* PICKLES n.¹.

andramartins *n.* (*also* **andremartins**) [20C+] (*Irish*) horseplay, fooling around. [? anecdotal]

andrew *n.¹* [late 17C–early 18C] a servant, a lazy fellow. [? SE merry-*Andrew*, a buffoon, an entertainer]

andrew *n.²* [mid-19C+] **1** the Royal Navy. **2** a government department or authority. [proper name of Lieutenant ANDREW MILLAR n.; note also Shakespeare *The Merchant of Venice* (1598): 'But I should think of shallows and of flats, And see my wealthy Andrew dock'd in sands'; although cited as 'ship, esp. of war' in the *OED*, the capital may simply imply the name of a given ship]

Andrew Millar *n.* (*also* **Andrew Millar's lugger, Andrew Miller, Andrew Miller's lugger**) [19C] a man o'war. [generally accepted as a ref. to a contemporary RN Lieutenant (*see* ANDREW n.²); a negative alternative suggests the name of a (then) well-known member of a press gang]

Andrex fart *n.* [1990s+] a silent, smelly breaking of wind that lasts for quite some time. [the contemporary *Andrex* advertising slogan 'soft, strong and very long', finally replaced in 2004]

and shit *phr.* [1960s+] (*orig. US Black*) a general abstract term, usu. thrown in at the end of a sentence, in the style of YOU KNOW phr. [SHIT n.⁶; var. on AND STUFF phr.]

and stuff *phr.* [late 17C+] meaningless addition to the end of a sentence, the implication is that the 'stuff' is essentially meaningless, irrelevant.

and the horse you rode in on *phr.* [1970s+] (*US*) a dismissive, antagonistic phr.; the pfx FUCK YOU! excl. can be actually spoken or just implied. [Wild West imagery]

and then some! *excl.* (*also* **and then plenty!**) [20C+] (*orig. US*) a rejoinder to the last speaker, that's not all of it either! [E.P. suggests an origin in 18C Scot. 'and some']

and thing *phr.* [1970s+] (*UK Black*) and so on, used as a non-specific punctuation at the end of a sentence. [usu. heard as *an' t'ing*]

andy cain *n.* [20C+] rain. [rhy. sl.]

Andy Capp *n.* [1960s+] (*Aus.*) an act of defecation (cf. BANANA (SPLIT) n.; BARRY WHITE n.; BIG HIT n.¹; BRAD (PITT) n.; DANNY LA RUE n.; EARTHA (KITT) n.; EDGAR BRITT n.; EGON (RONAY) n.; GLADYS n.; HARD HIT n.; MACARONI n.⁴; PONY (AND TRAP) n.; SHEFFIELD HANDICAP n.; TOM TIT n.; TWO-BOB BIT n.; WILLIAM n.³).

[rhy. sl.; *Andy Capp* is a well-known strip cartoon character, created in 1956 by Reg Smythe for the *Daily Mirror*]

Andy Gump *n.* [1960s–70s] (*US*) a conspicuously receding chin; a notably prominent chin. [the eponymous cartoon character created by Sidney Smith in 1917; he was virtually chinless; in southwest US the banded sand snake, with its deeply countersunk jaw, is an *andy gump* snake]

Andy McGinn *n.* [1930s+] the chin. [rhy. sl.]

Andy McNish *n.* [20C+] fish. [rhy. sl.]

Andy McNoon *n.* [1910s] (*Aus.*) an utter fool. [Arab. *inta machnoon*, 'a damned fool']

Andy Maguire *n.* [20C+] (*Aus.*) a fire. [rhy. sl.]

and you (too)! *excl.* [1910s+] a dismissive, antagonistic excl., a general admonition to anyone listening after one has made a pronouncement to someone. [i.e. 'and that means you (too)']

Andy Pandy *n.* [2000s] brandy. [rhy. sl.; ult. the children's puppet *Andy Pandy*, featured on the TV programme *Watch with Mother* (1950s–70s)]

andy up *v. see* ANTE (UP) v. (1).

angel *n.¹* **1** [mid-17C–19C] (*also* **fallen angel**) a prostitute. **2** [mid-19C–1940s] a young woman, esp. a pretty one; also in direct address. **3** [1920s+] an older homosexual man, usu. one who supports a younger lover. **4** [1930s] a sandwichboard-man. **5** [1930s–60s] (*US tramp*) a passive homosexual, a tramp's young homosexual companion. **6** [1970s] (*US gay/prison*) a victim of sexual aggression. [the original spec. coinage applied only to those prostitutes whose beat ran near the Angel public house in Islington, north London]

angel *n.²* **1** [late 19C+] (*US Und.*) the prospective victim of a swindle or confidence trick. **2** [late 19C+] the financial backer of an enterprise or scheme, esp. one who puts up money for a theatrical production. **3** [1960s] (*US prison/Und.*) the rich backer of a large-scale crime. [the positive characteristics, including innocence, attributed to an SE *angel*]

angel *n.³ see* RABBI n.

angel *v.* [1920s–40s] to use one's money to back an enterprise, esp. a theatrical production. [ANGEL n.² (2)]

angel cake (and wine) *n.* (*also* **angel food cake (and wine)**) [1940s+] (*US Und./prison*) bread (and water). [joc. use of SE]

angel drink *n.* [1980s+] a wine made from marijuana. [it sends the drinker 'to heaven']

angel dust *n.* (*drugs*) **1** [1960s+] anything smokeable, e.g. tobacco, marijuana, parsley, mixed with phencyclidine. **2** [1970s] a mixture of cocaine, heroin and morphine, which can be smoked or injected. **3** [1970s] finely chopped marijuana. **4** [1970s+] phencyclidine (cf. ACE n.⁴).

angel factory *n.* [1930s+] (*US*) a seminary. [the assumption being that its products, priests, are guaranteed entry to heaven]

angel food *n.¹* [1920s–50s] (*US tramp*) preaching as experienced in a mission. [the sermon is the 'price' of the free meal]

angel food *n.²* [1960s] (*US gay*) an air force serviceman. [as a flier he reaches heaven, as a potential conquest he is someone one can EAT v.³ (1)]

angel food cake (and wine) *n. see* ANGEL CAKE (AND WINE) n.

angel hair *n.* [1970s+] (*drugs*) phencyclidine (cf. ACE n.⁴). [var. on ANGEL DUST n. (4)]

angelic *n.* (*also* **angelica**) [early–mid-19C] an unmarried young woman. [SE *angel* + proper name]

angelical *n. see* NALGA DE ANGEL n.

angelina *n.* **1** [1930s+] (*camp gay*) a young homosexual man, the partner of an older one. **2** [1940s–50s] a weakling, an effeminate person, esp. a homosexual. [ANGEL n.¹ (5) + fem. sfx *-ina*]

angelina sorority *n.* [1940s] (*camp gay*) the world of young homosexual men. [ANGELINA n. (1) + sfx *-ina* + camp use of the usu. all-woman SE *sorority*]

angel kisses *n.* [20C+] freckles. [the myth that freckles are a sign of angelic affection]

angel liquor *n.* [1940s] (*US Black*) a sweet, fortified wine. [California use; a pun on SE *angelica*; angelica liquor (angelica mixed with water) was orig. seen as a preventative against poison and the plague]

angel-maker *n.*[1] [late 19C–1900s] a baby-farmer, a woman who took in (usu. illegitimate) babies on the pretext of bringing them up in return for a fee. [the frequency of infant mortality among 'farmed' babies]

angel-maker *n.*[2] **1** [late 19C+] an abortionist. **2** [1930s+] anything, usu. a weapon or a defective piece of military hardware (ship, plane), that causes death. [euph. phr. 'join the angels']

angel off *v.* [1960s] to rob a drug dealer's customers immediately after they have bought their supplies. [? the ease of the robbery is like robbing an angel]

angel puke *n.* [1970s] (*US drugs*) phencyclidine (cf. ACE n.[4]). [var. on ANGEL DUST n. (4)]

angel puss *n.* [1940s+] (*US*) a pretty young woman, often used as an affectionate term of address. [SE *angel* + PUSS n.[3] (1)]

angels *n.* [2000s] (*drugs*) **1** amytal. **2** sodium crystals. **3** alkyl nitrites. [the concept of flying HIGH adj.[1] (2)]

angel's food *n.* [late 16C–early 17C] strong ale. [i.e. nectar]

angel's kiss *n.* [20C+] (*Aus.*) an act of urination (cf. BANGERS (AND MASH) n.; BUBBLE AND SQUEAK n.[2]; CHRISTOPHER LEE n.; COMICAL CHRIS n.; COUSIN SIS n.; CUDDLE AND KISS n.; FRAZER NASH n.; GERRY RIDDLE n.; GOODNIGHT KISS n.; GYPSY'S (KISS) n.; HI-DIDDLE-DIDDLE n.; HIT AND MISS n.; JACK DEE n.; JACKIE (DASH) n.; J. CARROLL NAISH n.; JIMMY RIDDLE n.; JOHNNY BLISS n.; JOHNNY CASH n.; LEMON TEA n.; NELSON (RIDDLE) n.; PETERS AND LEE n.; PIE AND MASH n.; PIG IN THE MIDDLE n.; RATTLE AND HISS n.; RIDDLE-ME-REE n.; ROBERT E. n.; SAMMY LEE n.; SNAKE'S (HISS) n.; SOUTHEND-ON-SEA n.; THAT AND THIS n.; TROPICAL FISH n.; VICTORY V n.; YOU AND ME n.). [rhy. sl. = PISS n. (2)]

angel's oil *n. see* OIL OF ANGELS n.

angel's teat *n. see* ANGEL TEAT n.

angel's tit *n.* [1980s+] (*US*) a cocktail made by pouring heavy cream onto dark crème de cacao and floating a cherry (the nipple) on top of that. [SE *angel* + TIT n.[3] (1)]

angel suit *n.* [late 19C] a 'combination' suit, offering a coat and waistcoat made in one, with the trousers buttoned onto it. [? similar to a 1-piece burial shroud in which one 'ascends to heaven']

angel teat *n.* (*also* **angel's teat**) [1940s–70s] (*US*) notably mellow whisky. [stillers' jargon, a mellowed whisky with a rich bouquet]

angel together *n.* [late 19C–1910s] (*mainly W.I.*) a drunkard. [ety. unknown]

angel wings *n.* [2000s] (*US drugs*) caladium. [it gets you HIGH adj.[1] (2)]

angel with a dirty face *n.* [1930s–60s] a covert, undeclared male homosexual. [ANGEL n.[1] (5) + joc. use of SE; note film *Angels with Dirty Faces* (1938)]

angie *n.* [1970s] (*US gay*) a general form of address (cf. ABIGAIL n.). [proper name + ? SE *angel*/ANGEL n.[1] (5)]

angle *n.* [20C+] (*orig. US*) any plan that should benefit its maker, an exploitable gimmick, an ulterior motive; thus *get an angle on*, to work out the optimum way of doing something; PLAY THE ANGLES v. [? the calculation of angles necessary to play a winning game of pool, snooker or billiards]

angle *v.* [20C+] (*US*) to scheme; to obtain by planning. [ANGLE n.]

angled up *adj.* [1900s–70s] (*US Black/Southern*) confused, mixed up. [SE *angled*, askew, out of kilter]

angle for farthings *v.* [late 18C–early 19C] to dangle a cap, box or other makeshift container from a prison window into the street below in the hope of picking up alms from kind-hearted passers-by.

angler *n.* (*UK Und.*) **1** [late 16C–19C; 1970s+] (*also* **anglero, starrer**) a thief who uses a pole with a hook at one end to 'fish'

items from open windows, unguarded market stalls, passing carts etc (cf. CANTING CREW n.). **2** [early 18C] a pickpocket. **3** [late 18C–early 19C] a petty thief, working in the street and always on the lookout for opportunities to commit small larcenies. **4** [late 18C–mid-19C] (*UK/US Und.*) a confidence trickster. [fishing imagery]

angle-shooter *n.* [1940s+] (*US*) a schemer, a plotter. [ANGLE n. + SE *shooter*]

Anglican inch *n.* [late 19C] the short, square whiskers affected by members of the Broad Church or liberal wing of the Church of England. [coined by the High Church ritualists]

angling-cove *n.* [late 18C–19C] a receiver of stolen goods. [ANGLER n. + COVE n. (1); i.e. 'one who fishes in troubled waters']

anglo *n.* [1940s+] (*orig. US*) anyone of ostensibly Anglo-Saxon appearance; i.e. a White person. [SE *Anglo-*, English]

anglo *adj.* [1960s+] (*US*) White, or pertaining to White lifestyle/culture. [ANGLO n.]

Angola (black) *n.* [1980s+] (*drugs*) marijuana (cf. ACAPULCO (GOLD) n.). [its origin (and colour)]

angry boy *n.* [late 16C–early 17C] a rake, a young man about town, a 'blood'. [SE *angry*, troublesome, vexatious, annoying + *boy*]

anguagela *n.* [late 19C–1900s] language. [transposition]

Angus Armanasco *n.* [1980s] (*Aus.*) a lavatory (cf. BANANA FRITTER n.; CAPTAIN'S LOG n.; DON'T BE FUNNY n.; FRANK ZAPPA n.; GENE TUNNEY n.; HOUSE OF WAX n.; ILIE NASTASE n.; KERMIT THE FROG n.; LEMON AND DASH n.; MRS CHANT'S n.; RAG AND BONE n.; ROSIE O'GRADY'S n.; SAVOURY RISSOLE n.; SNAKE'S (HISS) n.; TEX RITTER n.; THELMA (RITTER) n.). [rhy. sl. = BRASCO n.; ult. Aus. racehorse trainer *Angus Armanasco* (b.1907)]

animal *n.*[1] **1** [18C+] a general derog. description of a man, esp. a braggart. **2** [1910s] (*US campus*) a woman, esp. a promiscuous one. **3** [1910s+] a policeman (cf. BANDOG n.; BEAGLE n.[3]; BEAR n.[7]; BEAST n.[5]; BEAST-BOY n.; BEASTMAN n.; BEETLE n.[2]; BLOODHOUND n.; BLUEBIRD n.[1]; BLUEBOTTLE n.; BULL n.[10]; BULLADEEN n.; BULLDOG n.[1]; BUSY BEE n.[1]; BUZZARD n.[1]; CRAB n.[1]; DOG n.[3]; DOG-DRIVER n.; FROG n.[1]; GRUNTER n.[3]; HOG n.[5]; HORNET n.; JOHN BLUEBOTTLE n.; LAND-SHARK n.; LOBSTER n.[1]; LOCUST n.[1]; NIT n.[1]; OINKER n.; PIG n.[3]; PORKER n.[4]; RAW LOBSTER n.; ROACH n.[1]; SIDEWALK SNAIL n.; SNAKE n.[2]; SPARROW COP n.; SWINE-EATER n.; TUNNEL RAT n.; UNBOILED LOBSTER n.; WOODPECKER n.[2]; WORM n.[2]). **4** [1920s+] (*orig. US*) a physically strong man, a 'tough guy', a hired thug. **5** [1940s] (*US Black campus*) (*also* **simple animal**) a young college woman. **6** [1940s+] (*orig. Aus.*) an unpleasant person. **7** [1940s+] (*orig. US*) a passionate sexual partner. **8** [1950s+] a wild, crazy person. **9** [1960s] (*US campus*) a male student seen as sexually unsophisticated by his female peers. **10** [1970s] (*US campus*) an athlete. **11** [1990s+] a psychopath.

animal *n.*[2] [late 19C–1900s] a public house, whose sign shows a lion, bull, bear or other creature. [the original animal was the Elephant and Castle in south London]

animal *n.*[3] [1900s] (*US*) a word-for-word translation used by US students studying foreign languages (cf. BICYCLE n.; BOHN n.; CRIB n.[3]; CRIBSHEET n.; HOBBY n.; HORSE n.[6]; JACK n.[23]; PLUG n.[3]; PONY n.[3]; TROT n.[3]). [var. on HORSE n.[6] or PONY n.[3]]

animal *n.*[4] [1970s+] (*drugs*) LSD (cf. A n.[3]). [? it makes some users behave wildly]

animal *adj.* [2000s] (*UK teen*) good, excellent.

animal *sfx* [1980s+] (*US campus*) combining form indicating one who does something excessively, e.g. *party animal*. [SE *party* + ANIMAL n.[1] (8)]

animal cracker *n.* [1920s+] (*US*) an eccentric. [pun on CRACKERS adj. + ref. to Nabisco's Barnum's Animals, biscuits first marketed in 1904]

animal house *n.* (*also* **animal farm/zoo**) [1960s+] (*US campus*) a fraternity house that is generally rated the least efficient, the most degenerate and, overall, the one to avoid. [the phr. gained international popularity with the release of the film *Animal House* (1978), starring John Belushi]

animal tranq *n.* (*also* **animal trank**) [1970s+] (*drugs*) phencyclidine (cf. ACE n.[4]). [in non-recreational use, an animal tranquillizer]

aniseed Robin *n.* (*also* **anniseed Robin**) [late 17C–mid-18C] a hermaphrodite; latterly generic for a prostitute. [one *Robin*, a real-life aniseed-water seller (d.1651 and briefly married to the highwayman John Cottingham, executed 1685), noted by Pepys as a hermaphrodite and well known as such in mid-17C literature; a then popular song was entitled 'Aniseed Robin' *or* 'Cuckolds All in a Row']

ank *n. see* HANK n.[3].

anker of rum *n.* [1920s] the buttocks, the posterior (cf. ALA n.). [rhy. sl. = BUM n.[1] (1); ult. *anker*, 'A measure of wine and spirits, used in Holland, North Germany, Denmark, Sweden, and Russia. It varies in different countries; that of Rotterdam, formerly also used in England, contains 10 old wine gallons or $8^1/_3$ imperial gallons' (*OED*)]

ankle *n.*[1] [1940s] (*US*) a young woman. [metonymy]

ankle *n.*[2] [1990s+] an extremely obnoxious person.

ankle *v.* (*also* **ankle around**) (*orig. US*) **1** [1920s] to dance. **2** [1920s+] to walk. **3** [1980s] to leave, to walk away from.

ankle-beater *n.* [19C] a boy who drives cattle from the market to the slaughterer. [to avoid damaging the flesh, he would hit only the animals' ankles]

ankle-biter *n.*[1] [1920s] tight trousers, as worn by hussars.

ankle-biter *n.*[2] [1950s+] (*orig. US*) a small child. [it crawls around at ankle-height]

ankle express *n.* [1910s+] (*US*) transportation by foot, walking. [ironic use of SE]

ankle-grabber *n.* [1980s+] (*US campus*) a homosexual.

ankle-spring warehouse *n.* [late 18C] (*Anglo-Irish*) the stocks. [var. on SPRING ANKLE WAREHOUSE n. (1)]

ann *n.* [1970s+] a derog. term for a White woman; thus by ext. a Black woman who apes her White sisters. [abbr. MISS ANN n.]

Anna Maria *n.* (*also* **ave Maria**) [late 19C+] a domestic fire (cf. AUNT MARIA n.[2]). [rhy. sl.; note pron. Mar-eye-a]

Anna May Wong *n.* [1920s+] a stink, a smell. [rhy. sl. = PONG n.[1]; ult. Chinese-American film star *Anna May Wong* (1905–61)]

Anne's fan *n. see* QUEEN ANNE'S FAN n.

annie *n.* [1950s–60s] an effeminate male homosexual (cf. ABIGAIL n.). [use of female proper name]

Annie Laurie *n.* [1940s] a bus conductress. [*Annie Laurie* (1682–1764); her grandson Alexander Fergusson of Craigdarroch was the hero of Robert Burns's poem 'The Whistle'; thus *whistler*, another WW2 synon. for a conductress]

annie louise *n.* [20C+] (*Aus.*) cheese. [rhy. sl.]

annie no-rattle *n.* [20C+] (*Ulster*) one who waits until a conversation is over to put in their own opinion. [proper name *Annie* + SE *no* + *rattle*]

Annie Oakley *n.* **1** [1910s+] (*US*) a free pass, orig. to a circus, but latterly to the theatre. **2** [1940s] (*US Und.*) a pardon or discharge certificate given to a convict. [the markswoman *Annie Oakley* (Phoebe Ann Mozee Butler, 1860–1926); the holes punched in such tickets supposedly resembled the aces out of which Ms Oakley would shoot the pips]

Annie Oakley *v.* [1910s+] (*US*) to punch an admission ticket, thus rendering it free. [for ety. *see* ANNIE OAKLEY n.]

annie's room *phr.* [1910s+] (*Aus.*) a phr. used when one does not know the answer to the question 'Where is…?' [orig. milit.]

annie up *v. see* ANTE (UP) v. (1).

annihilated *adj.* [1970s+] (*orig. US campus*) extremely drunk or intoxicated by a drug (cf. ATOMIZED adj.; BALLOCKED adj.; BANGED UP TO THE EYES phr.; BANG-UP adj.; BASHED adj.; BASTED adj.; BATTERED adj.; BIFFED adj.; BLASTED adj.[2]; BLIGHTED adj.; BLITZED adj.; BLITZKRIEGED adj.; BLOWN (OUT) adj.; BLOWN UP adj.; BOMBED adj.; BOXED adj.; BRUISED adj.; BURIED adj.[2]; BUSHWHACKED adj.[1]; BUSTED adj.[1]; BUTTERED adj.[3]; BUTTWHIPPED adj.; CANED adj.; CLOBBERED adj.; CONKED adj.[2]; CREAMED adj.; CROAKED adj.; CROCKED adj.; DAMAGED adj.; DEADO adj.; DEAD TO THE (WIDE) WORLD phr.; DERAILED adj.; DONE OVER adj.[2]; DONE UP adj.[1]; FLOORED adj.; FRACTURED adj.; FUCKED UP adj.; GOOSED adj.; HAMMERED adj.; HOSED adj.; KNOCKED UP adj.; K.O.'ED adj.; LAID OUT adj.[1]; LAMBASTED adj.; MANGLED adj.; MASHED adj.; MAULED adj.; MORTAL adj.[2]; MORTALLIOUS adj.; MULLAHED adj.; MULVATHERED adj.; PLASTERED adj.[2]; PLOUGHED adj.; PULVERIZED adj.; PUMMELED adj.; PUSHED adj.[2]; RAKED adj.; RUINED adj.; SHELLACKED adj.; SHELLED adj.; SLAMMED adj.[2]; SLAUGHTERED adj.; SLUGGED adj.; SMASHED adj.; SMUCKERED adj.; SNOCKERED adj.; SQUASHED adj.; STONKERED adj.; STUFFED adj.[1]; SWATTLED adj.; TOASTED adj.; TORE UP adj.; TOTALLED (OUT) adj.; TRASHED(-OUT) adj.; WASTED adj.; WELLIED n.; WHIPPED adj.[1]; WHOOPED adj.; WRECKED adj.).

anniseed Robin *n. see* ANISEED ROBIN n.

anno domini *n.* [late 19C+] old age and its deleterious effects, esp. on physical prowess. [Lat. *anno domini*, in the year of Our Lord]

annual *n.*[1] **1** [late 19C–1900s] an annual holiday. **2** [1940s] (*Aus.*) a bath.

annual *n.*[2] [1900s] (*Aus.*) a year's jail sentence.

anodyne necklace *n.* [late 18C–early 19C] the hangman's noose. [ironic use of SE, such a necklace was orig. a form of medicinal amulet and based on the original definition of *anodyne* as soothing pain, in this context that of a mis-spent life; thus the phr. is a pun on 'painkiller']

anointed *adj.* [mid-18C–19C] used to intensify a n., e.g. an *anointed rascal*, a very definite rascal. [ext. of SE *anointed*, consecrated king or queen]

anoint (with birchen salve) *v.* [late 16C–1940s] to beat, to thrash. [ironic use of SE]

anoint with oil of hazel *v. see* HAZEL OIL n.

anonyma *n.* [mid–late 19C] a courtesan, a high-class prostitute. [Lat. *anonyma*, an unknown woman]

anorak *n.* [1980s+] **1** anyone outside a peer group who thus fails to fit in with 'the gang', esp. a studious individual who eschews drink, drugs and similar teen pleasures. **2** an obsessive, typically as regards computing (in an earlier age their interest would have been trainspotting). [SE *anorak*, a style of short coat, orig. worn by Greenland Inuits, that is seen as typifying such figures]

another clean shirt ought to see you out *phr.* [1930s+] (*N.Z.*) you look very ill, i.e. you look as if you'll soon be dead.

another county heard from *phr.* [1930s+] (*Can.*) a remark made when one of a group breaks wind. [joc. use of SE phr. usu. used of election results]

another day, another dollar *phr.* [1910s+] (*orig. US*) **1** a phr. of relief used at the end of the working day. **2** a phr. used to point up the tedium of daily existence.

another day up the Queen's arse *phr.* [1980s+] (*Aus. prison*) a day of one's sentence completed (cf. HER MAJESTY'S CARRIAGE n.; HER MAJESTY'S SCHOOL FOR HEAVY NEEDLEWORK n.; HIS MAJESTY'S BAD BARGAIN n.; KING'S COLLEGE n.; KING'S HEAD INN (IN NEWGATE STREET), THE n.; PARTAKE OF HIS MAJESTY'S HOSPITALITY v.). [SE + ARSE n.[1] (1)]

another one for the van *phr.* [1920s+] another person's gone mad. [the 'van' being that which conveys the sufferer to a psychiatric institution]

another push and you'd have been a nigger *phr.* (*also* **another push and you'd have been a Chink**) [20C+] a general insult; the implication (in this context a slur) is that one's mother was happy to have sex with all races. [SE + NIGGER n.[1] (1)/CHINK n. (1)]

answer the last muster *v.* (*also* **answer the last roll-call**) [1930s] to die. [milit. imagery]

answer the last round-up v. [1930s] to die. [Western cowboy imagery]

ant-brained adj. [1990s+] small-minded, petty.

ante n. [late 19C+] (orig. US) money in hand, cash. [Lat. ante, before, in this case, before one plays or bets]

anteater n. 1 [1970s] a man with a circumcised penis. 2 [1980s+] (US gay) an erect penis (cf. BALD-HEADED MOUSE n.; BIRD n.[8]; BIRDIE n.[1]; BLACKBIRD n.[2]; BLACKSNAKE n.; CAT n.[2]; CHUTNEY FERRET n.; COCK n.[2]; COCK ROBIN n.[2]; CUCKOO n.[2]; DEAD RABBIT n.[2]; DICKY-BIRD n.[1]; DINOSAUR n.[2]; DONKEY n.[2]; DONKEY DICK n.[2]; DRAGON n.[4]; EARTHWORM n.; EEL n.[1]; FANNY RAT n.; FERRET n.[2]; GOOSE'S NECK n.[1]; HOG n.[6]; HOGGER n.[4]; HOGLEG n.; HORSECOCK n.[2]; HORSE'S HANDBRAKE n.; IRISH HORSE n.; JACKRABBIT n.[3]; JIMMY DOG n.; LIVE RABBIT n.; LIZARD n.[3]; LOBSTER n.[4]; MAGGOT n.[2]; MARIBOU STORK n.; MOLE n.[1]; MONKEY n.[10]; MONKEY SPANNER n.; MOUSE n.[2]; MUD SNAKE n.; ONE-EYED TROUSER-SNAKE n.; ONE-EYED (WONDER) WORM n.; ONE-EYED ZIPPER FISH n.; PANT-WORM n.; PUPPY n.[2]; PYJAMA PYTHON n.; ROBIN n.[1]; SHRIMP n.[1]; SNAKE n.[3]; STALLION n.; TOAD n.[2]; TROUBLE MONKEY n.; TROUSER TROUT n.; WEASEL n.[3]; WHITE OWL n.; ZIPPERFISH n.).

ante-up n. [late 19C–1950s] (Aus.) the game of poker. [the necessity to ante up (place a preliminary bet) to indicate that one is playing a round]

ante (up) v. [mid-19C+] 1 (also andy up, annie up) to pay out money in advance; the vars. are simply folk misprons. 2 (Aus.) to surrender (something), to hand over, thus to pay one's dues. 3 in fig. use, to explain oneself. [poker use, each player must ante up (f. Lat. ante, before) a specified sum in order to enter each successive hand dealt during the game]

Anthea (Turner) n. [1990s+] any job or plan that pays well, almost invariably criminal. [rhy. sl. = EARNER n.; ult. UK TV personality Anthea Turner (b.1960)]

anthony n. (also tantony, tantany) [mid-16C–mid-19C] the runt of the litter, the favourite or smallest pig in the litter. [SE St Anthony's pig; St Anthony is the patron of swine-herds and is always represented as accompanied by a pig; also Berkshire dial. t'anthony, the smallest pig in a litter]

anthony cuffin n. [19C] a man who has knock-knees. [CUFF ANTHONY v.]

anti n. [late 18C–19C] an objector, a rebel, a dissenter, one who rejects the social status quo. [Lat. anti, against; 20C+ use is SE]

antidote n. [late 17C–early 18C] a very plain woman. [ext. of SE use, i.e. an 'antidote against attraction']

antifogmatic n. (also fog-cutter) [late 18C–19C] an alcoholic drink taken (ostensibly) to counteract the effects of cold and damp. [SE antidote/ante, against + fog + sfx -matic, a sfx used to indicate a mechanical device]

antifreeze n. 1 [1920s+] alcohol, esp. cheap and as drunk by tramps and alcoholics. 2 [1970s+] (drugs) heroin. [ext. of SE use, i.e. both refer to their supposed prophylactic powers against cold]

anti-lunch n. [19C] an appetizer, a drink taken before lunch. [either the drink is seen as counteracting one's appetite or the sp. should be ante-]

antipodean adj. [mid-17C; late 19C–1900s] in a mess, chaotic. [the Antipodes are 'the world turned upside down']

antipodes n. 1 [early–mid-19C] the buttocks. 2 [mid-19C–1920s] the vagina (cf. BOTANY BAY n.[2]; CAPE HORN n.; CAPE OF GOOD HOPE n.[1]; COCKSHIRE n.; EXETER HALL n.; GEOGRAPHY n.[1]; GREAT DIVIDE, THE n.; HAIRYFORDSHIRE n.; HOLLOWAY n.; JACK STRAW'S CASTLE n.; LEATHER LANE n.; MARBLE ARCH n.[1]; MIDLANDS n.; NETHERLANDS n.; SHOOTER'S HILL n.; SOUTH POLE n.; UPPER HOLLOWAY n.). [SE Antipodes, Australia and thus, f. UK perspective, 'the bottom of the world']

antique dealer n. [1970s+] (US gay) a young man who courts elderly, wealthy men.

ant-killer n. [mid-19C] (US) 1 a large foot, a large, heavy shoe. 2 by metonymy, a man who has or wears one.

an't please the pigs phr. [late 17C–19C] (? orig. Irish) if circumstances permit. [? SE pixies; Ware prefers pyx, the vessel in which the host or consecrated bread of the sacrament is reserved, thus making it a synon. for 'God willing', or 'please God'; also note Gentleman's Magazine, 1790: 'the suggestion is that the "pigs" were the scholars of St Anthony's School in Threadneedle St, so named by their rivals at St Paul's School, with reference to the story of St Anthony preaching to pigs and always having a pig at his side; the phr. thus emerged as a derisive ref. to the rival establishment']

ants n.[1] (US) 1 [1930s–40s] restlessness, anxiety. 2 [1940s–60s] sexual enthusiasm. [HAVE ANTS IN ONE'S PANTS v.]

ants n.[2] [1950s] (W.I./UK Black) a parasite. [SE ant, spoken as ants in Carib.E.]

ants v. [1950s] (W.I./UK Black) to live as a parasite. [ANTS n.[2]]

ant's pants n. [20C+] (Aus.) the height of fashion.

ant-stomper n. (also ants-masher) [1960s–70s] (US) 1 a large foot, a large, heavy shoe. 2 by metonymy, a man who has or wears one.

antsy adj. [1950s+] twitchy, nervous. [ANTS n.[1] + sfx -y]

anty n. [1910s–20s] (Aus.) sugar. [ants were frequently to be found in the sugar]

A-number-one n.[1] [1920s–30s] (US) oneself. [both parts indicate 'the first'; note A-1 n.]

A-number-one n.[2] see A-1 n.

anus bandit n. see ARSE BANDIT n.

anvil chorus n. [late 19C–1970s] (orig. US) carping, negative criticism. [the 'Anvil Chorus', featured in Verdi's opera Il Trovatore (1853)]

anxious adj. [1940s–70s] (US Black) good, enjoyable, admirable, pleasant. [on bad = good model]

anxious meeting n. [late 19C–1910s] (orig. US) the gathering, after a revivalist meeting, of those earnest souls who are 'anxious for salvation'; thus anxious mourner, a member of such a gathering.

any n. [late 19C+] sexual pleasures; usu. as get any (see GET SOME v.); thus GETTING ANY (LATELY)? phr. [CUNT n.[1] (1); PUSSY n. (2) etc are assumed]

any adv. see SOME adv.

any cop phr. see NO COP phr.

any dog's bottom? phr. [1930s+] (Aus.) a phr. used to enquire if someone is any use. [ety. unknown; ? canine habit of sniffing at their fellows]

any God's quantity n. [late 19C–1930s] many, a good number.

any how adj. [late 19C+] disorganized, messy.

any how adv. [mid-19C–1920s] indifferently, carelessly.

any old adj. [late 19C+] (orig. US) anything, whatever, a general term of vagueness, e.g. any old way, any old job.

any old thing n. [late 19C+] (US) any thing whatsoever. [ANY OLD adj. + SE thing]

any racket n. [mid-19C–1900s] a penny faggot. [rhy. sl.]

anything adj. [2000s] (UK teen) rude.

anything in trousers n. [late 19C+] a man, any man; usu. in phrs. like she'd/she'll fuck/go for/have anything in trousers, said of a woman who is considered sexually omnivorous and indiscriminate in her choice of partners (cf. ANYTHING ON TWO LEGS n.).

anything on two legs n. (also anything in a skirt, anything with a hole (in it)) [late 19C+] a woman, any woman; usu. in phrs. like he'd/he'll fuck/screw/shag anything…, said of a man who is considered sexually omnivorous and indiscriminate in his choice of sexual partners (cf. ANYTHING IN TROUSERS n.).

anyways! excl. [1920s+] (US campus) a dismissive excl.

any Wee Georgie? phr. [1920s+] any good? [rhy. sl.; Wee Georgie Wood = good; Wood was a popular music-hall entertainer in 1920s–30s]

anywhere adv. [1940s+] 1 (drugs) possessing drugs, as in question are you anywhere? 2 psychologically secure.

Anzac Day dinner *n.* [1930s] (*N.Z.*) a meal, usu. lunch, that is mainly (if not entirely) composed of alcohol. [*Anzac Day*, a public holiday held on 25 April (the anniversary of the Gallipoli landing in 1915) in Australia and New Zealand in memory of the nations' war dead]

A-OK! *excl.* (*also* **A-okay!**) [1950s+] intensifier of OK! excl., all's well, everything's absolutely fine. [A-1 adj. (1) + OK! excl.; originated in spaceflight jargon and spread to the wider public after the broadcast of the Mercury flight of Commander Alan Shepard (1923–98) on 5 May 1961]

A-OK *adj.* (*also* **A-okay**) [1950s+] satisfactory, fine, good.

A-1 *n.* (*also* **A-number-one, A No. 1**) [mid-19C+] someone or something first-class, the best, the favourite. [A-1 adj. (1)]

A-1 *adj.* (*also* **A-number-one, a-1, a-one**) [early 19C+] **1** (*also* **A1 copper bottomed, A1 and no mistake, letter A number 1**) excellent, perfect, first-class, in prime condition. **2** extreme, supreme, in both negative and positive contexts. [insurance jargon *A1*, the top rating given to a ship at the insurers Lloyds of London]

A-1 *adv.* **1** [late 19C+] excellently, in the best way. **2** [2000s] totally, completely. [A-1 adj.]

A-1-er *n.* [late 19C] an exceptional person, an aristocrat. [A-1 adj. (1) + sfx -*er*]

a over k *phr. see* ARSE OVER KITE *phr.*

a over t *phr.* [1980s+] head-over-heels, usu. as *go a over t.* [abbr. ARSE OVER TIT phr.]

apache *n.*[1] **1** [1930s] a lesbian. **2** [1980s] (*US gay*) (*also* **commanche**) a man who uses cosmetics. [the wearing of 'warpaint' by Apaches and other Native Americans]

apache *n.*[2] **1** [1990s+] an act of sexual intercourse without the use of a condom. **2** [2000s] (*Irish*) a joyrider. [pun on the Apache Indian style of riding bareback + BAREBACK adv.]

apartment to let *n.* (*also* **house to let, tenements to let**) **1** [mid-17C–early 19C] the vagina. **2** [18C] a widow. **3** [18C–19C] a widow's weeds. [a widow becomes 'vacant' for new (male) 'occupation']

apartment to let *phr.* (*also* **attic to let, apartments to let**) [mid-19C+] unhinged, insane, crazy. [the image is of a certain emptiness in the 'upper storey']

a.p.b. *n.* [1960s+] (*US police*) a general alert, a search for a missing person (cf. ALL-POINTS n.; ALL POINTS BULLETIN n.). [abbr. *all points bulletin*, a general alert broadcast to all officers and vehicles]

APC *n.* [1980s] (*Aus.*) a quick wash of 'important' areas of the body. [abbr. *a*rmpits and *c*rotch]

apcray *n.* [1930s+] (*US*) nonsense, rubbish. [cod Lat. = CRAP n.[3] (3)]

ape *n.* **1** [mid-16C+] a general pej., the implication being of stupidity and lumbering size. **2** [mid-19C+] (*orig. US*) (*also* **apeman**) a derog. term for a Black person (cf. AFRICAN APE n.). **3** [1920s+] a thug, a hoodlum. [a derog. use of *ape*, as fool, is found in Chaucer]

ape *adj.* **1** [1910s] (*US campus*) drunk. **2** [1920s] a generic term meaning aggressive and dangerous. [SE *ape*]

ape *v.* [1940s+] (*US*) to lose control, to act in a wild manner.

ape drape *n. see* MULLET n.[2].

ape-face *n.* [1980s] (*US*) an ugly, thuggish person.

apehangers *n.* (*also* **monkey-hangers**) [1960s+] (*orig. US*) high, extra-long motorcycle handlebars, favoured by outlaw riders such as Hell's Angels. [when riding with such equipment one's arms dangle forward like those of an ape]

apehead *n.* [mid-19C+] (*US*) a fool, an idiot (cf. AIREDALE n.). [SE *ape* + -HEAD sfx (1)]

ape-leader *n.* [mid-17C–mid-19C] an old lady. [LEAD APES IN HELL v.]

apeman *n. see* APE n. (2).

ape oil *n.* [1940s] (*US*) liquor. [? SE *ape*/it makes the drinker GO APE v. although this predates]

ape out *v.* [1960s] (*US*) to lose control, to act in a wild manner. [ext. of APE v.]

apeshit *adj.* **1** [1950s+] (*orig. US Black*) berserk, mad, crazy, extremely upset; esp. in phr. *go apeshit*; also as *apeshit for*, crazy for. **2** [1980s] (*US campus*) drunk. [SE *ape*/APE adj.]

apey *adj.* [1950s+] (*US*) crazy, unstable (cf. BATS adj.; BUG adj.; COCK-SPARROW adj.; CRAZY AS A BEDBUG phr.; CUCKOO adj.; DINGBATS adj.; DING-BATTY adj.; DOGSHIT adj.; FUNNY-BUNNY adj.; MAGGOTY adj.; RATS IN THE ATTIC phr.; SQUIRRELY adj.). [SE *ape*/APE adj. + sfx -*y*]

aphrodisiacal tennis court *n.* [17C] the vagina. [euph. coined by Britain's first translator of Rabelais, the Scot Sir Thomas Urquhart (1611–60)]

Apollo play *n.* [1940s–70s] (*US Black*) putting on an act. [the *Apollo* Theater, 125 St, Harlem]

apostle *n.* [1930s] (*US Und.*) a pellet of opium prepared for smoking (cf. APOSTLE n.; AUNTIE n.[4]; AUNTIE EMMA n.; BALOT n.; BIG O n.; BLACK n.[3]; BLACK PILL n.; BLACK STUFF n.; BROWN n.[4]; BROWN STUFF n.[1]; CANDY n.[4]; CHANDU n.; CHINESE MOLASSES n.; CHINESE TOBACCO n.; CHOCOLATE (STUFF) n.; COOLIE MUD n.; CRUZ n.; DOPIUM n.; DOVER'S POWDER n.; DREAM n.[4]; DREAM GUM n.; DREAMS n.; DREAM WAX n.; EASING POWDER n.; FI-DO-NIE n.; FIREPLUG n.[2]; FOON n.; GEE n.[6]; GOD'S (OWN) MEDICINE n.; G.O.M. n.[2]; GOMA n.; GONG n.[2]; GONGER n.; GORIC n.; GOW n.[1]; GREASE n.[2]; GREAT TOBACCO n.; GUM n.[3]; GUNPOWDER n.[3]; HIGH HAT n.[1]; HOCUS n.[2]; HOP n.[2]; LEAF n.[1]; LI-YUEN n.; MIDNIGHT OIL n.; MONKEY DUST n.; MUD n.[3]; O n.; OUPA JUICE n.; PEKOE n.; PELLICLE n.; PEN YEN n.; PILL n.[4]; POPPY n.[1]; POX n.[2]; QUILL n.[3]; ROCK n.[3]; SKAMAS n.; SKEE n.[2]; TAR n.[3]; TWANG n.[2]; WHITE STUFF n.; WYOMING KETCHUP n.; YEN n.[1]; YEN POK n.; YEN POX n.; YEN-SHEE n.).

Apostle's Grove *n.* [mid-19C–1910s] St John's Wood, London NW8. [pun. The area was well known for its up-market courtesans and 'kept women']

apostle's pinch *n.* [20C+] a pinch on the buttocks. [? fig. link to APOSTLE'S GROVE n.]

apostrophe *n.* [1910s] (*Aus.*) an obscenity.

apothecaries' Latin *n.* [mid-16C–early 19C] the mangled Latin used by apothecaries.

apothecary's bill *n.* [late 18C–early 19C] a substantial bill. [stereotyping of an apothecary as grasping]

appetizer *n.* [1970s+] (*US gay*) the first sexual partner of many encounters in the same day.

applause *n.* [1990s+] (*US Black*) gonorrhoea. [pun on CLAP n.]

Apple *n.* **1** [1930s–40s] (*US Black*) Harlem, New York City. **2** [1940s] (*US Black*) a large Northern city. **3** [1940s–50s] the earth, the universe. **4** [1940s+] (*orig. US jazz*) New York City. [abbr. BIG APPLE n.]

apple *n.*[1] [early 19C–1920s] (*US*) manure (cf. ALLEY APPLE n.[2]). [supposed resemblance]

apple *n.*[2] **1** [late 19C+] (*US*) a person. **2** [1950s] (*US Und.*) (*also* **big apple**) an important person. [(1) the image of apple in 'one rotten apple']

apple *n.*[3] [1920s+] a foolish person, a 'sucker'. [? the innocent wholesomeness of the fruit]

apple *n.*[4] [1960s] the head. [supposed resemblance]

apple *n.*[5] [1960s–70s] (*US Black*) money (cf. ALFALFA n.). [presumably a green variety]

apple *n.*[6] [1970s+] (*US Black*) the vagina (cf. BIT OF JAM n.; BONNE-BOUCHE n.; BREAD n.[2]; BREAD BOX n.; BREAD PAN n.; BUTTER n.[4]; CABBAGE n.[7]; CAKE n.[3]; CAKES n.[1]; CHERRY PIE n.; CRUMPET n.[2]; DOUGHNUT n.[2]; ESKIMO PIE n.; FIG n.[1]; FLITTER n.; FUR DOUGHNUT n.; GOLDEN DOUGHNUT n.; GROCERIES n.[2]; HAIR PIE n.; HAIRY DOUGHNUT n.; HO CAKE n.; HONEYPOT n.[1]; JAM n.[3]; JAMPOT n.[2]; JELLY n.[1]; JELLY BAG n.; JELLY BOX n.; LEMON n.[6]; LOLLIPOP n.[2]; MEDLAR (TREE) n.; MOSSY DOUGHNUT n.; MUFFIN n.[4]; MUSHROOM n.[2]; MUSTARD POT n.[1]; ORANGE n.[1]; PANCAKE n.[1]; PEACHES n.[1]; PEANUT BUTTER PUSSY n.; PIE n.[1]; PINEAPPLE n.[1]; PLUM TREE n.[1];

PUDDING-PIE n.; SPLIT APRICOT n.; SPLIT FIG n.; SUGAR BASIN n.; SUGAR-SCOOP n.; TOMATO n.). [note 17C SE *apple*, a woman and/or her virginity (see Williams Vol. 1 28–9); it can also be something to EAT v.³ (1)]

apple n.⁷ [1970s+] a derog. term for a Native American who is condemned as insufficiently nationalistic (cf. BANANA n.²; BOUNTY (BAR) n.; CHOC-ICE n.; COCONUT n.⁴; COOKIE n.⁴; FUDGSICLE n.; OREO (COOKIE) n.). [such a person is 'red on the outside but white within']

apple n.⁸ [1980s] (*drugs*) anyone who does not use drugs. [drug-specific ext. of APPLE n.³]

apple n.⁹ [1980s] (*drugs*) any pill capsule coloured red (cf. PILL n.⁴). [resemblance to the fruit]

apple n.¹⁰ [1990s+] (*UK prison*) the situation, the facts. [rhy. sl.; *apple core* = SCORE n.² (1)]

apple n.¹¹ *see* BIG APPLE n.¹.

apple and pears n. *see* APPLES (AND PEARS) n. (1).

apple and pip v. **1** [late 19C+] to sip. **2** [1960s+] to urinate (cf. DICKY DIDDLE v.; HI-DIDDLE-DIDDLE v.; PAT CASH v.; RIP VAN WINKLE v.; ZORBA v.). [rhy. sl.; (2) = SIP v.¹]

apple-blossom two-step n. [1960s+] diarrhoea, often contracted on a foreign holiday (cf. AZTEC HOP n.; BOOT-HILL TWO-STEP n.; COW'S COURANT n.; CRAB-APPLE TWO-STEP n.; FAR EAST TWO-STEP n.; GREEN APPLE QUICKSTEP n.; GRINGO GALLOP n.; JERRY-GO-NIMBLE n.; QUICK STEP n.; SOUR-APPLE QUICKSTEP n.; THOROUGH-GO-NIMBLE n.; WHERRY-GO-NIMBLE n.). [one of many sl. terms for diarrhoea that pun words for dancing/movement (i.e. SE *trot*) on TROTS, THE n.²]

apple-cart n. [late 18C+] the human body. [pun on the SE, a *cart* for carrying *apples*; there is no connection, despite appearances and a ref. in Bee, to the joc. SE phr. *upset the applecart*, which refers directly to the SE. However, the phr. *down with his apple-cart!*, knock or throw him down! (Grose 1788, *Lex. Bal.*, Hotten 1867), seems to suggest a human rather than a vegetable image]

apple core n. [1950s+] £20 (cf. AYRTON (SENNA) n.; BEEHIVE n.²; CHERRY-PICKER n.⁵). [rhy. sl. = SCORE n.¹]

apple-core v. [2000s] to seduce. [rhy. sl. = SCORE v.² (2)]

apple cucumber n. [1990s+] (*Aus. Und.*) an ext. ploy to kill or capture one's target by using a friend to get close to the target's friend, which will eventually bring the target into view.

apple-dumpling shop n. [late 18C–1920s] the female breasts.

apple fritter n. [1920s+] bitter beer. [rhy. sl.]

apple fritter adj. [2000s] emotionally bitter. [rhy. sl.]

apple-guard n. [late 19C] (*UK Und.*) a scarf and tie. [it protects the adam's apple]

applehead n. [1940s–50s] (*US*) a fool (cf. BANANA BENDER n.; BANANAHEAD n.; BAPHEAD n.; BEANBRAIN n.; BEAN-HEAD n.; BEEF-HEAD n.; BUTTERBRAIN n.; BUTTERHEAD n.; CABBAGE-HEAD n.; CAKE n.¹; CHEESE n.⁴; CHEESEHEAD n.; CHOWDER-HEAD n.; COCONUT HEAD n.²; CRUMPET n.⁴; DILL PICKLE n.; DOUGHNUT n.³; DOUGHNUT-HEAD n.; EGG n.¹; EGGHEAD n.¹; EGGO n.; GELLYHEAD n.; GOOSEBERRY n.¹; GOULASH n.; HAMHEAD n.; HANS WURST n.; LEMON n.²; MACARONI n.¹; MEATBRAIN n.; MELON n.¹; MELONHEAD n.; MUTTON-HEAD n.; ONION n.²; PEABRAIN n.; PIE-CAN n.; PIE-EATER n.; PIG SCONCE n.; PIG-WIDGEON n.; POPCORN n.²; PORK n.²; POTATO-HEAD n.; PRUNE n.²; PUD n.³; PUDDING-HEAD n.; PUMPKIN n.¹; PUMPKIN HEAD n.; QUINCE n.; RAISIN-BRAIN n.; SQUASH n.; TART n.¹; TOMATO n.; WILLIE LUNCHMEAT n.). [APPLE n.³ + -HEAD sfx (1)]

applejack n.¹ [1950s–60s] (*US Black*) a generic name for a dance, esp. the contemporary vogue style.

applejack n.² [1970s] (*US Black*) a large-brimmed, oversized hat in a 1930s–40s style. [ext. of APPLE n.⁴]

applejack n.³ [1980s+] (*drugs*) crack cocaine (cf. BOB HOPE n.; MERRY MAC n.). [rhy. sl. = CRACK n.¹³]

apple-john n. [late 16C–early 17C] a foolish and prob. impotent old man. [SE *apple-john*, a kind of apple said to keep for

2 years and to have reached perfection when shrivelled and withered]

apple knock v. [1940s] to act the yokel, to behave in an unsophisticated manner. [APPLE-KNOCKER n. (1)]

apple-knocker n. **1** [1910s+] (*US*) a rural, unsophisticated person (cf. ACORN-CRACKER n.). **2** [1920s+] (*US tramp*) an apple picker. **3** [1930s–40s] a fool. [SE *apple* + *knocker*, one who hits apples from trees; the image is of an unsophisticated rural person]

apple-monger n. [18C] a pimp (cf. ABBOT ON THE CROSS n.). [play on SE *apple-monger*, a dealer in fruit, i.e. 'ripe' females]

apple-peeler n. [mid-19C; 1970s] a knife. [the term was revived by Citizens' Band radio users]

apple-picker n. [1910s+] (*US*) a fool, an unsophisticated person, a country person (cf. ACORN-CRACKER n.). [var. on APPLE-KNOCKER n.; their stereotyped occupation]

apple pie n.¹ **1** [1930s] (*US Und.*) an eye. **2** [1940s+] the sky. [rhy. sl.]

apple pie n.² [1950s] (*US prison*) a pretty, young (prison) homosexual.

apple pie adj. [20C+] (*US*) neat, tidy, perfect. [abbr. APPLE-PIE ORDER n.]

apple-pie order n. [late 18C+] neatness, tidiness. [ety. unknown. Such suggestions that exist include a corruption of *cap à pie* (Fr. head to foot), the arrangement of the ingredients of an apple pie as they are laid neatly in a dish, and a corruption of *alpha-beta*, esp. as in the nursery rhyme that runs 'A ate it, B bit it, C cut it, D divided it...'. Perhaps the most acceptable is that proposed in Brewer, *Dict. of Phrase and Fable* (15th edn, 1995): f. Fr. *nappe plié*, folded linen, which may also give the practical joker's 'apple-pie bed']

apple-pips n. [20C+] the lips. [rhy. sl.]

apple polish v. (*also* **apple shine**) [1930s+] to curry favour, to toady. [backform. f. APPLE-POLISHER n.]

apple-polisher n. (*also* **apple-pusher, apple-shiner, apple-washer**) [1920s+] (*mainly US*) a toady, a sycophant. [the image suggests that the apple being polished is that presented to the teacher by the class goody-goody]

apples n.¹ **1** [17C+] the female breasts (cf. AVOCADOS n.; BAPS n.; BUNS n.; CAKES n.¹; CASABAS n.; CHESTNUTS n.; COCONUTS n.¹; CUPCAKES n.¹; DINGLEBERRIES n.; DUMPLINGS n.; FRIED EGGS n.²; GOODIES n.; GRAPEFRUIT n.; GRAPES n.¹; GROCERIES n.²; JUJUBES n.; LEMONS n.; LOLLIES n.). **2** [19C+] the testicles (cf. ACORNS n.). [the rounded shape; (1) has survived but became more a euph. than sl. by 20C+]

apples n.² [1990s+] (*drugs*) MDMA (cf. ECSTASY n.). [the image of an apple stamped on some MDMA pills]

apples adj. [1940s+] (*Aus./N.Z.*) satisfactory, as required; esp. in phr. *she'll be apples*, it will be fine. [APPLES AND SPICE adj.; although primarily associated with Aus., the term is also used by residents of Brooklyn, New York, in which usage it derives f. APPLE-PIE ORDER n.]

apples (and pears) n. (*also* **peaches and pears**) **1** [mid-19C+] (*also* **apple and pears**) stairs. **2** [1970s] (*UK Und.*) fig., an appearance in court; the stairs here are those of the Old Bailey. [rhy. sl.; note the children's chorus, sung for a skipping game: 'I don't want your apples, / I don't want your pears, / I don't want your sixpence/ To kiss me on the stairs'; (1) note earliest mid-19C usage is of *apple and pears*]

apples and rice adj. [1940s+] nice, usu. ironic. [rhy. sl.]

apples and spice adj. [1940s+] (*Aus.*) satisfactory (cf. APPLES adj.). [rhy. sl. = SE *nice*]

apple sauce n.¹ [late 19C+] (*US*) nonsense, balderdash, banal or out-of-date comments. [old joke, poss. orig. in minstrel shows, based on the problem of dividing equally 11 apples among 12 people/horses, the answer being that one makes apple sauce; hugely popular in 1920s, but note George Rector *The Girl from Rector's* (1927): 'There is an expression today sweeping America which I heard Corse Payton use *twenty-five years ago* [itals. added] [...] That expression is apple sauce']

apple sauce *n.*[2] [1920s+] (*orig. US*) flattery, insincere talk, cheek, impudence. [the old boarding-house trick of serving an excess of cheaply produced apple sauce to mask the deficiencies in the portions and quality of other food]

apple sauce *n.*[3] [1960s] (*US*) anything easy. [? fig. use of APPLE SAUCE n.[1], i.e. nonsensically easy]

apple sauce *n.*[4] [2000s] (*Aus.*) a horse. [rhy. sl.]

apple sauce *v.* [1960s] (*US*) to take advantage of, to flatter. [APPLE SAUCE n.[2]]

apple sauce! *excl.* [late 19C+] (*US*) rubbish! piffle! [APPLE SAUCE n.[1]]

appleseed *n. see* HAYSEED n.

apple-shaker *n.* [mid–late 19C] (*US*) a rural, unsophisticated person (cf. ACORN-CRACKER n.).

apple shine *see under* APPLE POLISH.

apple-squeezer *n.* [1930s] (*US*) a rural, unsophisticated person (cf. ACORN-CRACKER n.).

apple squire *n.* [16C–19C] **1** a pimp (cf. ABBOT ON THE CROSS n.). **2** a kept man. [although cits. predate this, poss. f. APPLES n.[1] or 17C SE *apple*, a woman and/or her virginity (see Williams, Vol. 1 28–9) + SE *squire*, mocking the esquire or the 'country squire']

apple tart *n.* (*also* **lemon tart**) [20C+] (*Aus./Irish*) a breaking of wind; also v., e.g. *he apple tarted*. [rhy. sl. = FART n. (1)]

Appleton talking *phr.* (*also* **Fernandez talking**) [20C+] (*W.I.*) used of one who is drunk and talking nonsensically or aggressively. [the brandnames of 2 popular rums, distilled in, respectively, Jam. and Trin.]

apple up *v.* [1960s] (*US*) to toady, to curry favour. [the image of handing up an apple to a teacher]

apple-washer *n. see* APPLE-POLISHER n.

apply a crimp *v. see* PUT A CRIMP INTO v.

apply lawyer foot *phr.* [1950s] (*W.I.*) to run away. [the image is of a foot that, like a lawyer, helps one 'get away']

apply lip gloss *v.* [1980s+] of a woman, to masturbate (cf. BEAT THE BEAVER v.; BRUSH THE BEAVER v.; BUTTER THE MUFFIN v.; CLAP ONE'S CLIT v.; CLOUT ONE'S COOKIE v.; CLUB THE CLAM v.; DO THE TWO-FINGERED SHUFFLE v.; DRILL FOR OIL v.; FINGER FUCK v.; FLICK THE BEAN v.; FLICK THE SWITCH v.; FLOSS THE CAT v.; GLAZE THE DONUT v.; GREASE THE GASH v.; HIT THE SLIT v.; HOSE ONE'S HOLE v.; JENNY OFF v.; JILL OFF v.; LIGHT THE CANDLE v.; PET ONE'S PUSSYCAT v.; PET THE POODLE v.; PLAY STINKY PINKY v.; PLAY TIDDLYWINKS v.; POKE ONE'S PUSSY v.; SLAM THE CLAM v.; SLING ONE'S JELLY v.; STIR IT UP v.; STIR ONE'S STEW v.; THUMB v.; WAZ v.). [the image of vaginal secretions coating the labia]

appo *n.* [1990s+] an *app*lication form (for a job). [abbr. + -O sfx (3)]

appy *n.* [1980s+] (*S.Afr.*) an *app*rentice. [abbr. + sfx -*y*]

apricock water *n.* **1** [early 18C] apricot ale. **2** [early–mid-18C] gin. [16C–18C sp. of SE *apricot*]

apricot (and peach) *n.* [1990s+] the beach. [rhy. sl.]

apricots *n.* [1960s–80s] (*Aus.*) the testicles (cf. ACORNS n.). [the shape]

April fool copper *n.* **1** [1950s] (*US Und.*) a small-town policeman; a private detective; a badly dressed policeman. **2** [1990s+] (*US prison*) a prison guard. [COPPER n.[3] (1)]

April fools *n.* **1** [late 19C+] tools; usu. implements for burglary. **2** [20C+] stool(s) (for sitting). **3** [1930s+] football pools. [rhy. sl.]

April gentleman *n.* [late 16C] a newly married man. [the popularity of spring weddings]

April in Paris *n.* [2000s] the buttocks, the behind (cf. ALA n.). [rhy. sl. = ARRIS n. (2)]

April showers *n.* [20C+] flowers. [rhy. sl.]

apron *n.*[1] [1920s] a wife, a woman, esp. when used generically.

apron *n.*[2] [1920s–50s] (*US*) a bartender (cf. APRONER n.). [metonymy; i.e. the garment he or she wears]

apron and gaiters *n.* (*also* **gaiters**) [late 19C–1910s] a bishop, a dean. [metonymy, i.e. his vestments]

aproneer *n.* **1** [mid-17C] a Roundhead. **2** [mid-17C–early 18C] a shopkeeper. [the aristocratic Cavaliers made this contemptuous link between 'trade' (symbolized by a worker's *apron*) and their parliamentary rivals]

aproner *n.* (*also* **apron-man**) [early–mid-17C] a bartender (cf. APRON n.[2]). [his usu. blue SE *apron*]

apron husband *n.* [early 17C] a man who is seen as involving himself excessively in his wife's business. [metonymy of SE *apron* = wife + SE *husband*]

apron preacher *n.* [mid-17C] a lay preacher.

apron-rogue *n.* [mid-17C] a labourer, an artisan. [a play on SE synon. *apron-man*]

apron squire *n.* [late 16C] a pimp (cf. ABBOT ON THE CROSS n.). [metonymy of SE *apron* = woman + SE *squire*/SQUIRE n.[1] (1)]

apron-stringed *adj.* [1950s] of a man, henpecked by a woman.

apron-string hold *n.* (*also* **apron-string tenure**) [late 17C–early 19C] an estate that a man holds only during the lifetime of his wife.

apron-up *adj.* [late 18C–19C] pregnant. [the use of an *apron* to hide a pregnancy, also f. the inevitable raising of the apron's profile as the foetus grows]

apron-washings *n.* [1900s] porter. [image of a brewery worker wringing out his beer-soaked *apron*]

aqua *n.* [mid-19C–1960s] water. [Ital. *acqua*; Ling. Fr. *akwa*]

aqua lung *n.* [1980s+] (*US drugs*) a long pipe for smoking marijuana, which is placed in a bucket of water to cool the smoke. [SE *aqua lung*, 'a portable diving apparatus consisting of containers of compressed air...which feed air automatically through a valve and mouthpiece to the diver as he requires it' (*OED*)]

A.R. *n.* [1970s] (*Can. Und.*) an armed robbery. [abbr.]

arab *n.*[1] **1** [mid-19C–1900s] (*US*) any wild or excitable looking person. **2** [mid-19C+] a street urchin. **3** [1930s–40s] (*US*) a street peddler. [orig. 'Arab of the streets' or 'city Arab' f. the trad. nomadic and derog. stereotype of Middle Eastern Arabs]

arab *n.*[2] [20C+] (*US*) a derog. term for a Jew (cf. BAGEL n.[1]; BAGEL BENDER n.; CAMEL-DRIVER n.; CHRIST-KILLER n.[1]; JEW BABY n.; JEW BOY n.; JEWISH PRINCE n.; JEWISH PRINCESS n.; JIGGER n.[13]; KIKE n.; LOX JOCK n.; MOTZER n.[1]; NOODLE SOUP DRINKER n.; OI YOI YOI n.; OVEN-DODGER n.; PORKER n.[2]; PORKY n.[1]; RED SEA PEDESTRIAN n.; SCHNOINK n.; SHEENY n.[1]; WHITE NIGGER n.; YEHUDI n.; YID n.[1]; YIDDISHER n.; YIDDLE n.). [ARAB n.[1] (3) + a ref. to Jewish and Arabic Semitic origins; coined by *Variety* magazine writer Jack Conway *c.*1925]

arab *n.*[3] [1950s] (*US*) a street bookmaker, an illicit bookmaker. [ARAB n.[1] (3)]

arab *v.*[1] [20C+] (*US*) to sell or peddle on the streets. [ARAB n.[1] (3) + negative racial stereotype]

arab *v.*[2] [1950s] (*US*) to work as a street bookmaker. [ARAB n.[3]]

arabber *n.* (*also* **ayraba**) **1** [20C+] a street urchin. **2** [1940s+] a peddler. [ARAB n.[1]]

arab's knees *n.* [2000s] (*Irish*) keys. [rhy. sl.]

-arama *sfx see* -ORAMA sfx.

arbor vitae *n.* [18C–19C] the penis. [Lat. *arbor vitae*, the tree of life]

arbour *n.* [late 19C] the vagina (cf. AGREEABLE RUTS OF LIFE n.). [SE *arbour*, a shady retreat]

Arby's *phr.* [2000s] (*US Black*) a derog. description of a sexually experienced woman. [*Arby's* fast food franchise, purveyors of roast beef sandwiches, thus play on MEAT n. (3)]

Arch, the *n.* [1950s+] Marble *Arch*, London W1. [abbr.]

Archbishop Laud n. [1960s] fraud. [rhy. sl.; the term (used in Cook, *The Crust on its Uppers*, 1962) may, like a number of similar cits., be a nonce-word; ult. William *Laud* (1573–1645), Archbishop of Canterbury]

arch-cove n. [mid-late 19C] (*UK Und.*) the leader of a gang of thieves. [SE pfx *arch-*, principal + COVE n. (1)]

arch-dell n. [early 18C–early 19C] (*UK Und.*) the woman accomplice of a criminal gang-leader. [SE pfx *arch-*, principal + DELL n. (1)]

arch-doxy n. [early 18C–early 19C] (*UK Und.*) the woman accomplice of a gang-leader. [SE pfx *arch-*, principal + DOXY n. (1)]

arch-duke n. [late 18C–early 19C] a comical or eccentric person. [? a specific archduke. E.P. suggests the Duke in Shakespeare's *Measure for Measure* (1604), who is 'certainly eccentric enough to serve as an archetype']

archer n. [1990s+] £2000. [the sum of £2000 was the disputed payment which formed the basis of the libel case brought in 1987 against the *Daily Star* newspaper by the writer Jeffrey *Archer* (now Lord Archer, b.1940)]

archer up n. [late 19C] a certainty. [the champion jockey Fred *Archer* (1857–86) and thus phr. 'Archer is up in the saddle', which, to betting men, more than likely meant a winning horse]

arch-gonnof n. [mid-late 19C] (*UK Und.*) the leader of a gang of thieves. [SE pfx *arch-*, principal + GONNOF n. (2)]

archie n. (*also* **archy**) [late 19C] (*Aus.*) a young station-hand, prob. a well-connected young man out from the UK. [proper name, seen as upper-class]

architorture n. [1990s+] (*US campus*) a course in *archi*tecture. [perversion of SE; abbr. + SE *torture*]

archives n. [1990s+] (*US campus*) a thing of the past, used in phr. *I'm archives*, goodbye, I'm leaving.

arch-rogue n. **1** [early 17C–18C] the leader of a gang of thieves. **2** [mid-17C–19C] a confirmed villain. [SE pfx *arch-*, principal + ROGUE n.[1]]

archy n. *see* ARCHIE n.

arctic adj. [1980s] (*US campus*) of a person, emotionally chilly, very distant. [SE *arctic* conditions, extremely cold]

arctic explorer n. [1940s+] (*US drugs*) a user of cocaine. [pun on SNOW n.[2] (1)]

ard n. [17C–early 19C] (*UK Und.*) the foot. [? related to the Nordic *ard*, plough, a term used in archaeology to describe the style of plough in use during the Bronze Age; note E.P. rejects this use]

ard adj. [late 18C–early 19C] hot. [Fr. *ardent*, passionate, eager]

ardent n. [mid-late 19C] (*orig. US*) spirits. [SE *ardent* spirits]

area n. **1** [19C] pubic hair. **2** [1970s+] (*US campus*) the genitals. [euph. abbr. SE *pubic area*, genital area]

area code n. [2000s] (*US campus*) a promiscuous female. [rap artist, Ludacris, with his song 'Area Codes' (2001), including the line 'I've got hoes, in different area codes']

area-sneak n. (*also* **area diver**, **...lurker**, **...slum**) [19C–1930s] a thief who specializes in robbing basements. [SE *area*, the small sunken court adjacent to the basement of a house + SNEAK n.[1] (2)]

arer adv. [late 19C–1900s] more so, to any greater extent. [a fake 'comparative' of SE *are*, e.g. 'We *are*, and what's more, we can't be any arer' (Ware)]

are you kidding? phr. [1940s+] you can't be serious, surely you're joking. [KID (AROUND) v. (2)]

are you prepared? phr. (*also* **are you ready?**) [1960s+] (*orig. US gay*) a phr. implying amazement or shock, both approving and disapproving.

are your boots laced? phr. [1930s–40s] (*US Black*) a general query as to the state of affairs; is everything in order? are you ready? do you understand?

are you saving it for the worms? phr. [1940s+] (*orig. US*) addressed to a supposed virgin, this phr. is intended to shame or bluster her into intercourse. [SE *worm's meat*, a corpse]

arf n. [late 19C] *a*fternoon. [abbr./pron.]

arf a mo n. *see* ALF A MO n.

arfto n. *see* AFTO n.

arfy-darfy, the n. [1960s] (*US tramp*) the road, in the context of a tramp; often as *on the arfy-darfy*. [? a nonce coinage by Nelson Algren (1909–81); ? SE *artful dodger*]

arge n. [1940s–50s] silver. [abbr. SE *argent*, silver]

argee n. (*also* **argee whiskey, r.g.**) [mid-19C] (*US*) inferior whisky. [abbr. ROTGUT n. (3)]

Argie n. [1980s+] an *Arg*entinian. [abbr. + sfx *-ie*; coined in 1982 by Britain's *Sun* newspaper, as part of its jingoistic approach to the Falklands War (1982)]

argle-bargle n. (*also* **argol-bargol, argy-bargle**) [early 19C+] an argument. [ARGLE-BARGLE V.]

argle-bargle v. (*also* **argol-bargol**) [early 19C+] to have an argument. [abbr. SE *argue* + redup. or + ? *haggle*; note *argle*, 16C to dispute, 19C to bandy words]

Argo n. [1950s] an *Arg*entinian. [abbr. + *-o* sfx (3)]

argue the toss v. [1910s–20s] to argue long and loud. [the tossing of a coin; later use is SE]

argufy v. [mid-18C–1980s] to argue; also *argufication, argufier*, an argument. [SE *argue*]

argy-bargle n. *see* ARGLE-BARGLE n.

argy-bargy n. (*also* **argie-bargie, arging and barging**) [late 19C+] (*orig. Scot.*) argument, confusion, confrontation. [ARGY-BARGY V.]

argy-bargy v. [late 19C+] to argue. [abbr. SE *argue* + redup.; note earlier ARGLE-BARGLE V.]

ari/aris n. *see* ARRIS n.

-arina/-arino sfx *see* -ERINO sfx.

aristippus n. **1** [early 17C–18C] Canary wine. **2** [late 17C–18C] a diet drink, made of sarsparilla, cinchona bark and other ingredients, available at certain coffee houses. [proper name *Aristippus* (c.435–366BC), Greek philosopher and founder of the rigorously hedonistic Cyreneiac school of philosophy]

aristo n. [mid-19C+] an *aristo*crat. [abbr.]

aristotle n. **1** [late 19C+] a bottle. **2** [1910s+] courage. **3** [1950s+] the buttocks, the behind (cf. ALA n.). [rhy. sl.; (2) = BOTTLE n.[2] (2); (3) = BOTTLE AND GLASS n. (1) = ARSE n.[1] (1)]

arithmetic bug n. [1910s+] (*US*) a louse. [so-called because 'they added to our troubles, subtracted from our pleasures, divided our attention and multiplied like -ll' (W. Carter, *Devil Dog*, 1920)]

Arizona n. [1940s+] (*US short order*) buttermilk. [the belief that anyone who orders buttermilk (rather than liquor) ought to be in Arizona for their health]

Arizona adj. [20C+] (*US*) a generic derog. term, usu. used in a variety of combs. below. [the stereotyping of the state and its natives as poor and backward]

Arizona canary n. (*also* **Arizona nightingale**) [1930s–60s] a donkey or mule (cf. COLORADO MOCKINGBIRD n.; DESERT CANARY n.; MOUNTAIN CANARY n.; ROCKY MOUNTAIN CANARY n.). [CANARY n.[10]]

Arizona cloudburst n. [1960s] (*US*) a sandstorm.

Arizona paint job n. [1960s] (*US*) no paint at all.

Arizona perfume n. [1940s–60s] (*US prison/Und.*) gas, as inhaled in the prison gas chamber. [the popularity of the death penalty in the state]

Arizona tenor n. [1940s–70s] (*US*) a victim of tuberculosis who coughs deeply and often; the dry Arizona climate was seen as good for the lungs.

ark n. **1** [1950s] (*US*) a low bar-room, a 'dive'; thus (*US Black*) a dancehall. **2** [1960s–80s] a car. [? fig. use of Noah's *Ark*, i.e. a refuge from the hostile world]

ark and wins n. (also **ark and winns**) [late 17C–early 19C] (UK Und.) a sculler, a rowing boat. [SE ark + ? WIN n., i.e. the cost of its hire]

Arkansas adj. (also **arkansaw**) [20C+] (US) a generic derog. term, usu. used in a variety of combs. below. [the stereotyping of the state and its natives as poor, dishonest and backward]

Arkansas asphalt n. [1960s] (US) logs laid side by side to form a 'corduroy' road. [orig. logging jargon]

Arkansas chicken n. [20C+] (US) salt pork.

Arkansas credit card n. [1970s+] (US) a piece of hose used to syphon petrol from another car into the tank of one's own. [ironic use of SE]

Arkansas fire extinguisher n. [1960s] (US) a chamberpot.

Arkansas lizard n. [1910s–30s] (US) a flea, a louse.

Arkansas special n. (also **Arkansas traveller**) [1950s–60s] (US) a little-used railway branchline. [ARKANSAS adj. + train jargon special/traveller]

Arkansas T-bone n. [1960s] (US) bacon.

Arkansas toothpick n. (also **Missouri toothpick**) [mid-19C+] (US) a large knife, similar to a Bowie knife. [ARKANSAS adj./ MISSOURI adj. + SE toothpick]

Arkansas traveller n. see ARKANSAS SPECIAL n.

Arkansas wedding cake n. [1950s] (US) corn bread. [plain corn bread is the antithesis of a rich wedding cake]

arkansaw adj. see ARKANSAS adj.

arkansaw v. [1950s] (US) 1 to cheat, to take advantage of. 2 to shoot in an unsportsmanlike manner, whether targeting animals or humans. 3 to share expenses, esp. of a meal. [ARKANSAS adj.]

ark-floater n. [late 19C] a veteran actor. [Noah's Ark (synon. for antiquity) + theatre jargon floats, footlights]

Arkie n. see ARKY n.

ark-man n. (also **ackman**) [early 18C] (UK Und.) a river thief, who specializes in robbing river traffic. [SE ark, a ship or boat]

ark-pirate n. [late 18C–mid-19C] (UK Und.) a river thief. [var. on ARK-MAN n.]

ark-ruff n. (also **ark-ruffian**) [18C–19C] (UK Und.) a river thief. [var. on ARK-MAN n.]

Arky n. (also **Arkie**) [1920s+] (US) a (usu. White, usu. poor) native of Arkansas, ext. use to any yokel (cf. ALVIN n.). [abbr.]

arky adj. [late 19C–1940s] (US) old-fashioned, out-of-date. [SE Noah's Ark, back to which the things in question may supposedly date, although there may also be a link to SE archaic]

arkymalarkey n. [1930s] (US) nonsense. [ACKAMARACKUS n.]

arm n.[1] 1 [20C+] the penis (cf. BABY'S ARM n.; BEST LEG OF THREE n.; BLACKLEG n.[3]; HOGLEG n.; LIKE A BABY'S ARM WITH AN APPLE IN ITS FIST phr.; LOVE ARM n.; MIDDLE LEG n.; PENSIONER'S LEG n.; PORK LEG n.; SHORT-ARM INSPECTION n.; THIRD LEG n.). 2 [1970s] an erection, sexual stimulation. [it, too, sticks out from the body]

arm n.[2] 1 [1930s–50s] (US Und.) the act of robbing someone by choking them from behind and thus rendering them immobile; thus arm-man, one who robs in this way. 2 [1960s] influence, power. 3 [1990s+] (UK Black) an armed robbery.

arm n.[3] [1960s+] (S.Afr. drugs) a measure of cannabis, approx. the size of a maize cob and weighing about 2kg (4.25lb).

arm v. see PUT THE ARM ON v. (1).

armbreaker n. [1990s+] especially energetic masturbation.

arm candy n. [1990s+] a pretty woman whose role is merely to adorn the arm of her male companion (cf. BRAIN CANDY n.; EYE CANDY n.; MIND CANDY n.).

armed for bear phr. [1960s+] very heavily armed, lit. and fig. [hunting jargon, the killing of bears requires a large weapon]

armful n. 1 [late 17C] a wife. 2 [20C+] (Aus.) a plump woman. 3 [1940s] (US) an attractive woman.

arm man n. see STRONG-ARM MAN n.

armor n. [1990s+] (US campus) the female body. [the male 'wears' it]

armoured cow n. [1940s–50s] tinned corned beef.

armour float n. see I'M AFLOAT n. (2).

armpiece n. [1990s+] a companion, i.e. one who is 'on one's arm'.

armpit n. [1960s+] 1 (orig. US) the least appetizing, poorest, most run-down and potentially dangerous area of a city or town; often as armpit of the nation/universe (cf. ARSEHOLE n.). 2 (orig. US) used similarly of a place, e.g. a nightclub or café. 3 (US campus) an unpleasant individual. [the link of the SE armpit with dirt and smell]

arm-props n. [early–mid-19C] crutches.

arms and legs n. [late 19C+] weak beer or tea, i.e. a drink that has 'no body'.

armshouse n. [1990s+] (UK Black/teen) armed gang warfare.

armstrong adj. [20C+] used to describe anything that is operated by hand rather than by machinery. [SE arm + strong]

armstrong heater n. [1930s] (US) one's arms, when embracing a loved one. [ARMSTRONG adj. + SE heater]

arm up v. [1980s+] (Aus. prison) to arm oneself.

army n. [1930s] (US Und.) an armless beggar. [SE arm + sfx -y]

army and navy n. [1910s+] gravy. [rhy. sl.]

army brat n. [1930s+] (orig. US) the son, or more usu. daughter, of a commissioned officer.

army game n. [late 19C+] (US) 1 poker, chuck-a-luck, FIND THE LADY n. or any other gambling game played outside the casino in army camps and similar establishments. 2 trickery, deceit, passing responsibility onto others. [the popularity of chuck-a-luck among US Civil War soldiers. The hit 1950s British Army-based sitcom, The Army Game, may have reflected (2), but more likely refers to 17C SE game, dodges, tricks + an ironic use of game as 'life, way of doing things']

army Latin n. [mid-19C] (US) obscene language. [typically that used by irascible drill sergeants]

army rocks n. [1910s+] socks. [rhy. sl.; orig. grey woollen Army socks]

army strawberries n. [1940s] (US milit.) prunes.

army style n. [1960s+] (US gay) oral sex followed by beating up the fellator, presumably to prove one's 'masculinity'. [ironic use of SE]

archy n. [1920s–30s] (US Black) one who puts on airs. [? corruption of SE aren't you, e.g. 'aren't you the one', 'aren't you the big shot' etc]

arnold n. (also **Mr Arnold**) [1970s+] (W.I.) pork. [ety. unknown]

aroma n. (also **aroma of man, aroma of men**) [1970s+] (drugs) amyl nitrite (cf. AIMIES n.). [amyl nitrite, used in medicine to stimulate the heart and recreationally to enhance the moment of orgasm, has a strong 'rotten banana' smell]

-aroo sfx see -EROO sfx.

-aroon/-arooney/-aroonie/-arootie sfx see -EROONIE sfx.

around the... see also ROUND THE...

around the horn phr. [1930s+] (US) having experienced unpleasant treatment. [? ref. to a voyage 'around Cape Horn', a notably rough journey]

around the way adj. [1980s+] (W.I./UK Black teen) from the neighbourhood.

around-the-way girl n. [1990s+] (US Black) a young woman from the neighbourhood or ghetto; a casual girlfriend rather than a steady one. [AROUND THE WAY adj. + SE girl]

around the world n. (also **around the horn, around the universe**) [1930s+] licking and sucking the partner's body, including the genitals and sometimes the anus; thus half-way around the world, fellatio and anilingus. [the tongue 'travels' around the body; usu. used by a prostitute as part of the 'menu' of paid services she can offer]

array v. [late 15C–16C] to discomfit, to thrash, to drub. [SE *array*, to dress, thus to 'dress down']

arrers n. [1990s+] the game of darts. [Cockneyfied pron. of SE *arrows*, i.e. the darts]

arrest v. [1980s+] (*US campus*) to accuse another of dressing unfashionably, usu. behind their back. [FASHION ARREST n.]

arrested by the bailiff of marshland phr. [late 17C–19C] stricken with ague. [ague, a malarial fever, can be caused by damp conditions]

arrested by the white serjeant phr. [late 18C–mid-19C] said of a man who has been fetched out of the tavern by his wife.

'arrico veins n. [late 19C–1900s] varicose veins. [mispron. + ? a pun on Fr. *haricot verts*, green beans]

'Arriet n. see 'ARRY n.

arris n. (*also* **ari, aris, arry, harris**) **1** [late 19C+] a bottle. **2** [1950s+] the buttocks, the behind (cf. ALA n.). [rhy. sl; abbr. ARISTOTLE n.]

arrive at the end of the sentimental journey v. [late 19C–1910s] of a man, to have sexual intercourse; one of many euph. terms for sexual intercourse (cf. DO A KINDNESS v.; DO A THING v.; DO IT v.[1]; GINICOMTWIG v.; GO BIRDS-NESTING v.; HANDLE v.; HAVE A BIT OF FUN (WITH) v.; KISS v.[1]; MAKE BABIES v.; PLUCK A ROSE v.; PUT THE DEVIL INTO HELL v.; SLEEP WITH v.; SPORT v.[1]; STAY WITH v.[1]). [literary euph.; the conclusion of Laurence Sterne's *Sentimental Journey* (1768), in which the narrator obviously retires to bed with a chambermaid]

arrow n. [late 19C+] a dart; thus *the arrows game*, darts.

'Arry n. [late 19C–1920s] the typical Cockney man, usu. a costermonger; thus the female equivalent *'Arriet*; thus *'arryish*, typical of a costermonger. [popular proper name]

arry n. see ARRIS n.

'arrydom n. [late 19C–1900s] the world of the typical Cockney costermonger. ['ARRY n. + sfx -*dom*, position, condition]

'arry's worrier n. [late 19C–1900s] a concertina. ['ARRY n. + SE *worrier*]

arsapeek adj. [1910s] (*Aus.*) upside down. [ARSE n.[1] (1)]

arse see also under ASS and its combs.

arse n.[1] **1** [late 14C+] the buttocks, the anus (cf. ASS n.). **2** [16C+] (in a sexual context) the vagina; occas. the penis. **3** [early 17C+] of an object, the rear. **4** [mid-18C+] used generically to mean one's person, one's body. **5** [1930s+] an unpleasant person, esp. a fool, an idiot; thus *make an arse of oneself*, to act stupidly (cf. ASS n.; ASSHOLE n.[1]; BUNGHOLE n.[1]; BUTT n.[1]; DATE n.[3]; POON n.[1]; PRAT n.[1]; RAAS n.; RINGPIECE n.; SHITHOLE n.; SHITTER n.[2]). **6** [1930s+] (*Aus.*) a worthless, unpleasant place. **7** [1930s+] (*orig. US/Aus.*) sexual conquests; thus generic for a woman when viewed purely as a sex object, often as *a piece/bit of arse* (cf. PIECE OF ASS n.). [SE at coinage, it gradually moved into sl. Its sources include a variety of words found in several Teutonic and Scandinavian languages. The nearest relation is the German *arsch*, and there are definite links back to the Greek *orros* and *orsos*. In English it dates at least to 1000, when it is spelt *ars, ears* or *ars*. The modern sp. appears *c*.1300. Once rendered taboo, *arse* was to be resisted in polite conversation and printed only after the exclusion of crucial consonants, typically by Grose, who prefers *a–e* to the full-blown word. It remained off-limits, at least in print, until 1930, when Frederic Manning used it in full in his memoir of WW1, *Her Privates We* (itself a slightly bawdy pun). Since then the word has become relatively acceptable, and such phrs. as ARSE ABOUT v.[1] or NOT KNOW ONE'S ARSE FROM ONE'S ELBOW v., while not yet SE, are as much colloq. as sl. That said, *arse/ass*, remains one of those 'filthy words' cited in 1978 by the US Federal Communications Commission as indecent, if not actually obscene. (2) note Love (ed.), *Works of John Wilmot Earl of Rochester* (1999): '"Arses" is used by metonymy for "vaginas" as is usual in Restoration verse when the rhyme is with "tarses"'. Note the US spelling ASS n. (although this appears increasingly in the UK in the late 1990s) is often synon., but it should be noted that Shakespeare opts for *ass*, often in a punning context, on several occasions. In combs., both spellings have been included at the same headword, unless usage is nation-specific, where the relevant sp. has been used]

arse n.[2] **1** [1940s+] (*orig. Aus.*) cheek, effrontery. **2** [1990s+] luck. **3** [2000s] courage. [fig. use of ARSE n.[1] (1)]

arse n.[3] [1950s+] (*Aus.*) dismissal from a job; thus *give the arse*, to dismiss; *get the (big) arse*, to be dismissed. [fig. use of ARSE n.[1] (1)]

arse, the n. (*also* **ass, the**) [1930s+] (*UK/US*) used as a general intensifier, e.g. SCREW THE ARSE OFF v. [ARSE n.[1] (1)/ASS n. (2)]

arse v.[1] [1950s+] to reverse a vehicle. [ARSE n.[1] (3)]

arse v.[2] [1990s+] to drink, to consume. [ARSE n.[1] (1) as a catch-all term]

arse about v.[1] **1** [mid-17C; 1920s+] to waste time. **2** [1940s+] to fool around. [ASS n. (1); note also SE *ass*, to act the ass, to behave like a donkey. The orig. ety. undoubtedly refers to the animal, thus fool, but the sense, as born out by the sp., refers to ARSE n.[1] (5), although significantly predates it (cf. ASS ABOUT v.)]

arse about v.[2] [late 18C–early 19C] to turn round. [ARSE n.[1] (1)]

arse about face phr. [late 19C+] back-to-front, in confusion. [ARSE n.[1] (1) + SE *about face*]

arseache n. (*also* **assache**) **1** [1950s+] (*Aus./US*) a general insult. **2** [1990s+] a bad temper. [ARSE n.[1] (1) + SE *ache*]

arse-alight n. [1940s] a German WW2 V-2 rocket. [ARSE n.[1] (1) + SE *alight*, i.e. flames come out of its behind]

arse around v. [20C+] to mess about, to play the fool, waste time (cf. ACT THE ANGORA v.). [var. on ARSE ABOUT v.[1]]

arse backwards phr. (*also* **ass backward(s)**) [late 19C+] (*UK/US*) back-to-front, thus fig. in a mess, chaotic. [ARSE n.[1] (1)/ASS n. + SE *backwards*]

arse bandit n. (*also* **anus bandit, arse-bender, ass-bandit, bandit**) [1960s+] (*UK/US*) a homosexual male; thus *arse-banditry*, homosexuality (cf. ANAL ASTRONAUT n.). [ARSE n.[1] (1)/ASS n. (2) + BANDIT sfx (2)]

arse banditry n. [2000s] homosexuality, homosexual activities. [ARSE BANDIT n.]

arse-cabbage n. [1990s+] haemorrhoids. [ARSE n.[1] (1) + SE *cabbage*; f. the site and the physical appearance]

arse-cooler n. [mid–late 19C] a bustle on a woman's dress. [ARSE n.[1] (1)+ SE *cooler*]

arse crawl v. [late 19C+] to toady to, to act as a sycophant; thus *arse-crawler*, a sycophant. [ARSE n.[1] (1) + SE *crawl*]

arse-creep v. (*also* **creep up someone's arse**) [1940s+] to toady to. [ARSE n.[1] (1) + CREEP v. (1)]

arsed adj. **1** [1980s+] bothered, concerned, e.g. *I can't be arsed to do it.* **2** [2000s] fed up. [ARSE n.[1] (1)]

-arsed sfx[1] [mid-16C+] describing someone's ARSE n.[1] (1), often describing shape or size, e.g. *bare-arsed, big-arsed, broad-arsed*. [ARSE n.[1] (1); the initial cit., before any use of arse became sl., is in Abbot Aelfric's *Glossary*, *c*.1000, as trans. of the Lat. *tergosus*]

-arsed sfx[2] see -ASSED sfx.

arsed up adj. (*also* **assed up**) [1930s+] (*UK/US*) confused, mixed up; the mildest of such synons. as BUGGERED UP adj. (1). [ARSE n.[1] (1)/ASS n. (2) + SE *up*]

arse-end n. (*also* **ass-end**) (*UK/US*) **1** [1930s+] the end, the rear end, the buttocks (cf. BACK n.[1]; BACK BOTTIE n.; BACK DOOR n.; BACK-DOOR TRUMPET n.; BACK ENTRANCE n.; BACK EYE n.; BACKLAND n.; BACK-PORCH n.; BACKSLICE n.; BACKSLIT n.; BACK TOTTIE n.; BACKYARD n.; BEHIND n.; BUSINESS END n.; END n.[1]; GATES n.[2]; HIND n.; HINDSIDE n.; REAR n.[1]; REAR END n.; SOUTH END n.; TRADESMAN'S ENTRANCE n.; WORKMAN'S ENTRANCE n.). **2** [1940s+] the least desirable piece of. **3** [1940s+] a very unappealing place; esp. in phr. *the arse-end of the universe, arse-end of nowhere*.

4 [1950s+] of a place, the worst, most unhospitable area. [ARSE n.[1]/ASS n. + SE *end*]

arse-grapes *n.* (*also* **bottom grapes**) [1990s+] haemorrhoids, piles. [ARSE n.[1] (1)/SE *bottom* + SE *grapes*]

arsehole *see also under* ASSHOLE and its combs.

arsehole *n.* **1** [mid-16C+] the anus (cf. A-HOLE n.). **2** [1930s+] (*orig US*) a general derog. term. **3** [1930s+] (*orig. US*) the least appetizing, poorest, most run-down and potentially dangerous area of a city or town or place (cf. ARMPIT n.; ASSHOLE OF THE UNIVERSE n.). **4** [1940s+] (*also* **arsehold**) the end, the back of anything. **5** [2000s] courage. [ARSE n.[1] (1) + SE *hole*; note Wright, *Volume of Vocabularies* (1857), citing 14C AS/Lat. vocab., *Arcehoole, podex*; note US sp. ASSHOLE n.[1], particularly for orig. usage of (2) and (4)]

arsehole *adj.* (*also* **arseholing, arsoles**) [1930s+] a general adj. of derision (cf. ASSHOLE adj.). [ARSEHOLE n. (2)]

arsehole *v.* [1960s+] (*Aus.*) to dismiss, to get rid of. [ARSEHOLE n. (1)]

arsehole bandit *n.* [1960s+] a homosexual male (cf. ANAL ASTRONAUT n.) (cf. ASSHOLE BANDIT n.). [ARSEHOLE n. (1) + BANDIT sfx (2); ext. of ARSE BANDIT n.]

arsehole crawl *v.* (*also* **arsehole creep**) [late 19C+] to grovel unashamedly, to play the sycophant. [ext. of ARSE CRAWL v./ARSE-CREEP v.]

arsehole-crawler *n.* (*also* **arsehole-creeper, arsel-creeper**) [late 19C+] a sycophant; thus a general term of abuse. [ARSEHOLE CRAWL v.]

arseholed *adj.* [1940s+] very drunk (cf. ASS ON BACKWARDS phr.; BANGED UP TO THE EYES phr.; BLUE-EYED adj.[1]; BOSS-EYED adj.; BRIGHT IN THE EYE phr.; BUG-EYED adj.; BUNG-EYED adj.; COCK-EYED adj.[1]; CROSS-EYED adj.; CUT OVER THE HEAD adj.; CUNTED adj.[2]; EYES SET AT EIGHT IN THE MORNING phr.; EYES SET IN ONE'S HEAD phr.; FACED adj.[1]; FORTEYED adj.; FUCKFACED adj.; FULL TO THE GILLS phr.; GEE-EYED adj.; GOGGLE-EYED adj.; HAVE GLASS EYES v.; HAVE ONE'S EYES OPENED v.; HAVE THE SUN IN ONE'S EYES v.; HOT-HEADED adj.; ICED TO THE EYEBROWS phr.; KNEE-WALKING adj.; LEGLESS adj.; LOOP-LEGGED adj.; MOON-EYED adj.; MUDDY-HEADED adj.; NODDY-HEADED adj.; OFF ONE'S HEAD phr.; ORY-EYED adj.; OUT OF ONE'S HEAD phr.; OUT OF ONE'S TITS phr.; OWL-EYED adj.; PIE-EYED adj.; PINK AROUND THE GILLS phr.; PISSED AS ARSEHOLES phr.; PISSED TO THE EYEBALLS phr.; PISSY-ARSED adj.; PISSY-EYED adj.; POPEYED adj.; POT-EYED adj.; RAT-ARSED adj.; SHITFACED adj.[2]; SQUIFFY-EYED adj.; STEWED TO THE GILLS phr.; TANGLE-LEGGED adj.; TITTED adj.; TOTTY-HEADED adj.; WALL-EYED adj.). [PISSED AS ARSEHOLES phr.]

arsehole lucky *adj.* [1950s+] extremely fortunate.

arsehole-perisher *n.* [1900s] a short jacket. [ARSEHOLE n. (1) + SE *perish*, to suffer the cold]

arsehole polisher *n.* [1970s] a sycophant, a toady. [ARSEHOLE n. (1) + SE *polish*]

arseholes! *excl.* [late 19C+] rubbish! nonsense! [ARSEHOLE n. (1)]

arseholes to breakfast time *phr.* (*also* **arsehole to breakfast table**) [late 19C+] very unsatisfactory, totally confused, very chaotic.

arseholey *adj.* **1** [late 19C+] sycophantic. **2** [1990s+] a general derog. epithet. [ARSEHOLE-CRAWLER n.]

arseholing *adj. see* ARSEHOLE adj.

arseholishness *n.* [2000s] behaving in a foolish manner. [ARSEHOLE n. (2)]

arse it *v.* (*also* **ass it**) [1970s+] (*UK/US*) to leave, to exit (cf. ARSE OFF v.; ARSE OUT v.[1]). [ARSE n.[1] (1)/ASS n. (2); on model of BUS (IT) v.]

arse jockey *n.* [1990s+] (*UK juv.*) a male homosexual (cf. ANAL ASTRONAUT n.). [ARSE n.[1] (1) + SE *jockey*/JOCKEY n.[3] (2)]

arse-kiss *v.* (*also* **ass-kiss**) [1940s+] (*UK/US*) to toady; usu. as *arse-/ass-kissing*, sycophancy. [backform. f. ARSE-KISSER n.]

arse-kisser *n.* (*also* **ass-kisser**) [mid-18C; 1940s+] (*UK/US*) a sycophant, a toady, one who curries favour. [ARSE n.[1] (1)/ASS n. (2) + SE *kisser*]

arse-kissing *adj.* (*also* **ass-kissing, butt-kissing**) [1940s+] (*UK/US*) toadying, begging, supplicatory. [ARSE-KISS v.]

arsel-creeper *n. see* ARSEHOLE-CRAWLER n.

arse-lick *n.* (*also* **ass-lick**) [1970s+] (*orig. US*) a toady, a sycophant, a groveller. [ARSE-LICK v.]

arse-lick *v.* (*also* **ass-lick**) [1910s+] (*UK/US*) to toady, to be sycophantic (towards); thus *arse-/ass-licking*, sycophancy, grovelling. [ARSE n.[1] (1)/ASS n. (2) + SE *lick*]

arse-licker *n.* (*also* **ass-licker**) **1** [1930s+] (*UK/US*) a toady, a sycophant. **2** [1980s+] (*UK/US*) an anilinguist. [ARSE-LICK v.]

arse-licking *adj.* (*also* **ass-licking, butt-licking**) **1** [1930s+] extremely servile, grovelling. **2** [2000s] (*also* **arselick**) exaggerated. [ARSE-LICK v.]

arselins coup *n.* [19C] sexual intercourse; thus in phr. *get an arselins coup*, of a woman, to have sexual intercourse. [ARSE n.[1] (1) + sfx *-ling*, implying direction + SE *coup*, fall; thus lit. 'falling backwards']

arsenal *n.*[1] [1950s] **1** (*US drugs*) a supply of narcotics concealed in the rectum (usu. in some form of metal containter). **2** any stock of drugs in one's possession. [(1) play on SE *arsenal*/ARSE n.[1] (1); (2) f. (1)]

arsenal *n.*[2] [1990s+] the genitals.

Arsenal are at home *phr.* [2000s] used by a (N. London) woman to indicate that she is having a period. [the red-and-white strip worn by Arsenal Football Club, Highbury, N5, London]

arseness *n.* [20C+] (*W.I., Trin./Tob.*) wilful stupidity. [ARSE n.[1] (5) + sfx *-ness*, state or condition]

arsenuts *n.* [1990s+] (*UK juv.*) faecal matter found clinging to the anal hairs and buttock cleft. [ARSE n.[1] (1) + SE *nuts*]

arse off *v.* [late 19C+] to leave quickly (cf. ARSE IT v.; ARSE OUT v.[1]). [ARSE n.[1] (1) + SE *off*]

arse on backwards *phr.* (*also* **ass on backwards**) [20C+] back-to-front, confused. [ARSE n.[1] (1) + SE *backwards*]

arse-opener *n.* [late 19C+] the penis (cf. ARSE WEDGE n.; ASS-BREAKER n.; AUGER n.; BEARD-SPLITTER n.; BEAVER CLEAVER n.; BITCH HAMMER n.; BORE n.[2]; BUSH-BEATER n.; BUSHWHACKER n.[2]; CHERRY-SPLITTER n.; CLEAT n.; COCK HAMMER n.; COCK-OPENER n.; CRACK-HUNTER n.; CRANNY-HUNTER n.; CROWBAR n.; CUNT-BUSTER n.; EYE-OPENER n.[2]; GUTHAMMER n.; GUT-WRENCH n.; HAIR-DIVIDER n.; KIDNEY-BUSTER n.; KIDNEY-PRODDER n.; KIDNEY-SCRAPER n.; KIDNEY-WIPER n.; LIVER-DISTURBER n.; LUNG-DISTURBER n.; MARROWBONE AND CLEAVER n.; MEAT-CLEAVER n.; RUMP-SPLITTER n.; SHIT-STABBER n.; SPLIT MUTTON n.; TICKLER n.[4]; TONSIL-TICKLER n.; WEDGE n.[2]; WOMB-BEATER n.). [ARSE n.[1] (2) + SE *opener*]

arse out *v.*[1] [late 19C+] to leave quickly (cf. ARSE IT v.; ARSE OFF v.). [ARSE n.[1] (1) + SE *out*]

arse out *v.*[2] [1950s+] to dismiss from a job. [ARSE n.[3] + SE *out*]

arse over apex *phr.* [1920s+] head-over-heels. [ARSE n.[1] (1) + SE *apex*]

arse over appetite *phr.* (*also* **ass over appetite**) [1930s+] head-over-heels. [ARSE n.[1] (1)/ASS n. (2) + SE *appetite*]

arse over elbow *phr. see* ARSE OVER TIT phr.

arse over head *phr.* [1920s+] head-over-heels. [ARSE n.[1] (1) + SE *head*]

arse over header *n.* [20C+] (*Aus.*) the varsovienne, a dance of ? French origin, resembling some of the Polish national dances. [rhy. sl.; ult. Fr. *Varsovien*, f. *Varsovie*, Warsaw]

arse over kettle *phr. see* ARSE OVER TEAKETTLE phr.

arse over kick *phr.* [1920s+] (*Irish*) head over heels. [ARSE n.[1] (1) + SE *kick*]

arse over kite *phr.* (*also* **a over k**) [1960s+] (*N.Z.*) head-over-heels. [ARSE n.[1] (1) + northern UK dial. *kite*, the stomach]

arse over teakettle *phr.* (*also* **arse/ass over kettle, ass over**

teakettle) [1940s+] head-over-heels. [ARSE n.¹ (1)/ASS n. (2) + SE teakettle]

arse over tip phr. [1920s+] head-over-heels. [euph. for ARSE OVER TIT phr.]

arse over tit phr. (also arse/ass over elbow, ass over tit) [1910s+] head-over-heels. [ARSE n.¹ (1)/ASS n. (2) + TIT n.³ (1)/SE elbow/abbr.]

arse over turkey phr. [late 19C–1920s] head-over-heels. [ARSE n.¹ (1) + SE turkey]

arse-paper n. (also ass-paper) [1930s+] (N.Z./US) lavatory paper. [ARSE n.¹ (1) + SE paper]

arsepapered adj. [1980s] (Aus.) ignored. [half-rhy. sl.]

arsepiece n. [1990s+] a general term of derision. [ARSE n.¹ (1) + SE piece]

arse poker n. [1980s] anal intercourse. [ARSE n.¹ (1) + play on SE poker = game/phallic implement]

arser n. [20C+] (orig. hunting/riding) a fall on one's behind. [ARSE n.¹ (1)]

arse rugs n. [1900s] trousers. [ARSE n.¹ (1) + SE rug, a coarse material used as a cloak]

arse-shagger n. [1990s+] a male homosexual; a sodomite (cf. ANAL ASTRONAUT n.). [ARSE n.¹ (1) + SHAGGER n.¹ (1)]

arse-splitting adj. [2000s] a general intensifier: extreme, very great. [fig. use of ARSE n.¹ (1) + SE splitting]

arse-stabber n. [1990s+] a sodomite. [ARSE n.¹ (1) + SE stabber; note synon. RMC Duntroon (Aus.) arse pumper, arse reamer, arse rimmer]

arse-strings n. [late 16C] a metaphorical part of the body, holding the buttocks in place. [ARSE n.¹ (1) + SE strings]

arse up v. [20C+] to ruin, to make a mess of; thus intensified as arse up with care. [ARSE AROUND v.]

arse-up phr. (also arse-up-to-teacup) [20C+] head-over-heels.

arse upwards adj. 1 [17C+] lucky, fortunate, often as rise/raise arse upwards, to be lucky; thus [19C] pun on Mr R. Suppards, a very lucky man. 2 [1990s+] easily. [ARSE n.¹ (1) + SE upwards; getting up from a fall in this manner was believed to be lucky]

arse wedge n. [late 19C] the penis (cf. ARSE-OPENER n.). [ARSE n.¹ (2) + SE wedge]

arse-wise adj. [20C+] absurd, ludicrous, wrong, a generic negative. [ARSE n.¹ (1) + SE wise]

arse-worm n. [late 17C–early 18C] a small or short person. [ARSE n.¹ (1) + SE worm]

arsey adj.¹ (also arsie, arsy) [1950s+] (Aus.) lucky, occas. as arsey, a lucky person. [TIN-ARSED adj.]

arsey adj.² [2000s] stupid. [ARSE n.¹ (5)]

arsey-boo phr. [1980s] (N.Z.) in a state of chaos, wrong. [ARSE n.¹ (1) + sfx -y + ? BUGGERED adj.²]

arsey-tarsey v. [1910s–20s] (Aus.) to fall upside down. [ARSE n.¹ (1) + sfx -y + redup.]

arsey-tarsey phr. [1980s] (N.Z.) in a mess, incoherent. [ARSEY-TARSEY v.]

arsey-turvey phr. [mid-19C; 1930s] (US) upside down. [ARSE n.¹ (1) + SE topsy turvy]

arsey-varsey phr. (also arsey-versey, arsy-versy) 1 [mid-16C+] upside down, topsy-turvy, back-to-front. 2 [late 16C+] head-over-heels, usu. in phr. fall arsey-varsey, fall head-over-heels. 3 [mid-17C–early 18C] contrary, perverse, preposterous. [ARSE n.¹ (1) + sfx -y + redup.; on model of SE vice-versa. Prior use was SE]

arsie adj. see ARSEY adj.¹.

ars musica n. [late 18C–19C] the anus, esp. when it breaks wind. [pun on ARSE n.¹ (1)/Lat. ars musica, the musical art + pun on BUMFIDDLE n. (2)]

arsoles adj. see ARSEHOLE adj.

arson v. [1970s–80s] (UK Black) to set alight.

arsy see under ARSEY and its combs.

art n. [1980s–90s] (US campus) a thing of the past, used in

phr. I'm art, goodbye, I'm leaving. [the image is of an 'old master']

artesian n. [late 19C–1910s] (Aus.) beer brewed in Australia. [orig. a very popular beer brewed with water from a well-known artesian well at Sale, Gippsland, Victoria]

art fag n. [1990s+] (US campus) one who is overly affected, pretentious or 'arty'. [SE art + FAG n.⁵; however, there is no need for the target actually to be gay, the term merely reflects the time-honoured, philistine association of the arts with effeminacy]

artful as a (whole) wagon-load of monkeys phr. see CUNNING AS A (WHOLE) WAGON-LOAD OF MONKEYS phr.

artful dodger n. 1 [mid-19C+] a lodger. 2 [2000s] a penis (cf. ALMOND n.). [rhy. sl.; the original Artful Dodger appears in Charles Dickens's Oliver Twist (1838); (1) the 'artful' here implies the lodger's trad. interest in his landlady; (2) = TODGER n.]

artful fox n. [late 19C–1900s] a box in the theatre. [rhy. sl.]

arthur n. [1970s] a bank. [abbr. J. ARTHUR (RANK) n. (1)]

arthur bliss n. see JOHNNY BLISS n.

Arthur Guinness talk n. see UNCLE ARTHUR n.

Arthur Murray n. see RUBY (MURRAY) n.

Arthur Power n. [2000s] (Irish) a shower. [rhy. sl.]

Arthurs n. see UNCLE ARTHUR n.

artical adj. [1950s+] (W.I./UK Black teen) bonafide, genuine, sincere, respected. [var. on HORTICAL adj.]

artichoke n. 1 [17C–19C] a debauched old woman. 2 [1990s+] the vagina (cf. CABBAGE n.⁷). [like the vegetable, such a woman is supposedly spiky on the outside but still tasty within]

artichoke and an oyster n. see HAVE A HEARTY-CHOKE FOR BREAKFAST v.

artichoke (ripe) v. [mid–late 19C] to smoke (a pipe). [rhy. sl.]

article n. 1 [late 18C+] a general pej. description of any person, often as sarcastic pretty article. 2 [early 19C+] a woman. 3 [early 19C+] the vagina (cf. BLACK THING n.; CONUNDRUM n.; DOODLE-DO n.; DOWN BELOW n.¹; DOWN THERE n.; ET-CAETERA n.; GIZMO n.; HEY-NONNY-NO n.; INEFFABLE, THE n.; JIGGUMBOB n.; JUSTUM n.; KNACK n.; KNICK-KNACK n.¹; NAME IT NOT, THE n.; NICK-NACK n.¹; NONNY NO n.; NONSUCH n.; OLD THING n.³; PLACE, THE n.; STUFF n.⁶; THAT THERE n.; THAT THING n.; THING n.²; THINGY n.; TRINKET n.; UNIT n.; VADE-MECUM n.; WHAT'S ITS NAME n.; WHIM-WHAM n.; YOU KNOW WHAT n.; YOU KNOW WHERE n.). 4 [mid-19C] the penis. 5 [mid-19C+] (Irish/US) a creature. 6 [mid-19C+] a euph. for a chamberpot.

article of virtue n. [mid-19C–1910s] a virgin. [pun on Fr. objet de vertu, a curio, an antique]

articles n. 1 [late 18C–mid-19C] breeches, trousers. 2 [early 19C] a brace of pistols. 3 [late 19C] the genitals. [euph.]

artillery n.¹ 1 [19C+] (US) personal weaponry. 2 [1930s+] (US drugs) equipment for injecting drugs. 3 [1980s+] (Aus. prison) cutlery, which when metal doubled as weaponry. [(2) plays on SHOT n.⁶ (2)]

artillery n.² (also field artillery) (US) 1 [1920s] the female breasts. 2 [1970s] the attractive female figure. [image of a woman as a rival in 'the sex war'; note also 17C use of artillery to mean sexual 'equipment']

artillery n.³ [1930s+] (US) beans. [beans, trad. and physiologically, are equated with the breaking of wind and are thus empowered with 'shooting' ability]

artilleryman n. [late 19C–1910s] a drunkard. [the 'explosiveness' of his talk and actions]

artist n. 1 [mid-19C+] (US Und./Irish) an adroit rogue, usu. a pickpocket, sneak-thief or confidence trickster. 2 [late 19C] (US Und.) a skilful card-sharp.

artist sfx [late 19C+] (orig. US) a generic term for a person, esp. when cited as an expert or devotee of an activity; in combs. (cf. BACK-DOOR ARTIST n.; BACKSIDE ARTIST n.; BANG ARTIST n.; BASH

ARTIST n.; BEAT ARTIST n.; BILGE ARTIST n.; BLUFF ARTIST n.; BOOZE ARTIST n.; BROWN ARTIST n.; BULL ARTIST n.; BULLSHIT ARTIST n.; BUM CHECK ARTIST n.; BUNCO ARTIST n.; BURN ARTIST n.; CHIV ARTIST n.; CLIP ARTIST n.; COCK ARTIST n.; COMPO ARTIST n.; CON-ARTIST n.; CRAP ARTIST n.; FACE ARTIST n.; FAIR-PLAY ARTIST n.; FANG ARTIST n.[1]; FANG ARTIST n.[2]; FAST-BUCK ARTIST n.; FINGER ARTIST n.; GAB-ARTIST n.; GRANDSTAND-ARTIST n.; GROG ARTIST n.; GUMSHOE ARTIST n.; GUN ARTIST n.; GYP ARTIST n.; HEIST ARTIST n.; HOLD-OUT ARTIST n.; JEFF ARTIST n.; JIVE ARTIST n.; KNOB ARTIST n.; LEGSHAKE ARTIST n.; MAKE-OUT ARTIST n.; MIX-UP ARTIST n.; MOUTH ARTIST n.; NECKLACE ARTIST n.; NEEDLE ARTIST n.; PIGEON ARTIST n.; PIGSKIN ARTIST n.; PIN ARTIST n.; PISS ARTIST n.; PUFF ARTIST n.; PUNCH-OUT ARTIST n.; PUT-ON ARTIST n.; RAPE ARTIST n.; RIP-OFF ARTIST n.; SACK ARTIST n.; SHAFT ARTIST n.; SHAG ARTIST n.; SHAKE ARTIST n.; SHORT CON ARTIST n.; SKID ARTIST n.; SKIN ARTIST n.; SOAPBOX ARTIST n.; TAKE-ARTIST n.; TAKE-OFF ARTIST n.; TRAPEZE ARTIST n.; WIND-UP ARTIST n.). [note ARTIST n. (1), the mid-19C US Und. use, a skilful pickpocket or thief]

artiste n. [1980s+] (US gay) an especially competent fellator. [the final 'e' reflects both theatrical use and feminization]

artsy-craftsy adj. [1960s+] pretentious, humourless, self-opinionated. [the Arts and Crafts Exhibition Society, founded in London in 1888, but more generally an attack on the perceived failings of those condemned as 'artistic']

artsy-fartsy adj. [1960s+] pretentious; occas. as a n., a preten-tious person. [var. on ARTY-FARTY adj.]

arty adj. [20C+] pretentious.

arty-(and-)crafty adj. [1950s+] pretentious, humourless. [for ety. see ARTSY-CRAFTSY adj.]

arty-farty adj. (also arty-tarty) [1950s+] pretentious, overly intellectual or artistic, exhibiting superficial form and little positive content etc. [SE art + redup./FART n. (2)]

arty roller n. (also arty rolla) [1910s+] (Aus.) a collar. [rhy. sl.]

arvie n. [1970s+] (S.Afr.) the afternoon, often as this arvie, this afternoon. [abbr./pron.]

arvo n. (also avvo) [1930s+] (mainly Aus.) 1 afternoon. 2 afternoon tea. [abbr./pron. SE + -o sfx (4)]

as a bastard phr. (also as a beast, as a cunt) [1970s+] a general intensifier, usu. with adj. (cf. LIKE A BASTARD adv.). [BASTARD n. (1)/SE beast/CUNT n.[2] (1)]

as a bitch phr. [1950s+] a general intensifier.

as (all) hell phr. [20C+] a general intensifier, very, extremely.

as arse adv. (also as ass, as balls) [20C+] (W.I./US) a general intensifier, e.g. cold as arse. [ARSE n.[1] (1)/ASS n. (2)/BALLS n.[1] (1)]

as buggery adv. [1940s+] a general intensifier, e.g. hot as buggery. [SE buggery]

Ascot races n. [20C+] 1 the horseraces. 2 braces (US: suspenders). [rhy. sl.; usu. as 'ascots']

as dead as barney's bull phr. [mid-19C] completely worthless. [BARNEY'S BULL n.]

asexual adj. [1980s+] (US campus) uninterested in sex. [var. on SE asexual, sexless]

as fuck adv. [1970s+] a general intensifier, the coarse synon. for 'as anything'. [FUCK n.[5]]

as get out phr. see ALL GET OUT phr.

as good as ever twanged phr. [late 16C–early 17C] as good as possible. [TWANG v.[1]]

as good as you would desire to piss on phr. (also ...to piss upon) [late 17C–early 19C] excellent, first-rate.

ash n. [1990s+] (UK Black) hashish (cf. AFGHAN n.). [London pron. of HASH n.[2]]

ash v. [1990s+] to drop cigarette or cannabis cigarette ash onto the floor.

ash beans and long oats n. (also oats) [mid-19C] a beating, a flogging. [SE ash(plant), a walking-stick]

ashcan n.[1] 1 [1910s+] (US) an unpleasant person. 2 [1930s] the

buttocks. 3 [1930s] the vagina. [SE ashcan; (2) and (3) note CAN n.[1]]

ashcan n.[2] [1950s+] (US) 1 a small but powerful firecracker, its explosive effects intensified by the layer of tinfoil in which it is wrapped. 2 a car. [US Navy ashcan, a depth charge]

ashcan v. [1930s+] (US) to discard, to throw away. [i.e. to throw in the SAmE ashcan]

ash-cat n.[1] [mid-late 19C] (US) a dirty, dishevelled child; thus a general insult irrespective of age. [UK dial. ashcat, anyone, usu. a child, who sits near the fire, poking at the ashes]

ash-cat n.[2] [mid-19C–1900s] (US) a thin, wasted, ragged Black person. [the tendency of Black flesh tones, when unhealthy, to seem grey]

ash-cat sam n. [mid-19C–1900s] a sooty, dirty individual, esp. a child. [ASH-CAT n.[1] + generic use of proper name Sam]

as hell phr. see AS (ALL) HELL phr.

ash-faced adj. [1900s] (US) having a light complexion, applied to light-skinned Blacks. [the 'grey' skin tone]

as high as Gilderoy phr. see HIGHER THAN GILDEROY'S KITE phr.

ash-spots n. (US Black) 1 [1970s] goose pimples. 2 [2000s] lighter spots that appear on one's arms and legs when one gets cold. [the lighter colour compared to the Black skin tone]

ashy adj. [20C+] (US Black) pale, ashen-faced. [i.e. 'pale' Black]

Asia Minor n.[1] [late 19C] Belgravia, London. [ext. of SE; f. the wealthy Jews who bought houses there]

Asia Minor n.[2] [late 19C–1910s; 2000s] Kensington and Bayswater, London. [early use f. the large population of retired Indian civil servants; modern use refers to the Asian population, whether transient or immigrant]

Asian moll n. see JAP MOLL n.

asiatic n. [1940s+] (US) a crazy person. [ASIATIC adj.]

asiatic adj. [1940s+] (US) insane, crazy. [coined by the US Marines whose experiences beneath the Asian sun had driven some of them mad]

asinico n. (also asinego) [early 17C–early 19C] a fool, a simpleton. [Sp. asinico, a small donkey]

as Irish as Paddy's Murphy's pig phr. (also as Irish as Patrick Murphy's pig) [late 19C+] quintessentially Irish.

ask n. [1980s+] (Aus.) the cost, the asking price. [abbr.]

ask another! excl. see ASK (ME) ANOTHER! excl.

ask bogy! excl. [late 18C–early 19C] go to hell! [SE bogy/boggard, a goblin]

ask cheeks near Cunnyborough phr. [mid-18C–mid-19C] a dismissive retort, used by women only, equivalent to ASK MY ARSE! excl. [CONY-BURROW n. (2)]

asker n. 1 [mid-19C+] a beggar. 2 [1960s+] one who demands a lot of money, usu. of a corrupt policeman demanding large bribes. [SE ask]

askew n. see SKEW n.[1] ety.

ask for a piece of wife v. [20C+] (W.I.) to ask a woman to whom one is not married for sex; thus give wife, to permit such an adulterous affair.

ask for it v. [20C+] to act in such manner that unpleasant consequences will (almost) inevitably follow, to 'ask for trouble'. ['it' being trouble]

ask for the ring v. [1950s+] to perform anal intercourse (cf. ASSFUCK v.; BACKDOOR v.[1]; BACKSCULL v.; BACKSCUTTLE v.[2]; BAG v.[7]; BEND SOME HAM v.; BROWN v.[3]; BROWN-HOLE v.; BUFF v.[2]; BUFU v.; BUST A CAP v.; BUST SOME BOOTY v.; BUTTFUCK v.; BUY THE RING v.; COAT v.; CORNHOLE v.; CRUISE THE CHOCOLATE FREEWAY v.; DIG A DITCH v.; DIP IN THE FUDGE POT v.; DOGFUCK v.; DO IT UP BROWN v.; DOT THE 'I' v.; DRILL FOR MARMITE v.; DRILL FOR VEGEMITE v.; DROP ANCHOR IN THE BUM BAY v.; FREAK FUCK v.; GET SOME BOOTY v.; GET SOME BROWN (SUGAR) v.; GET SOME DUKE v.; GOOSE v.[3]; GO UP THE OLD DIRT ROAD v.; GREASE AND LEASE v.; JOG v.[2]; JUNGLE UP v.; KEISTER STAB v.; LEATHER v.[2]; MOON v.[2]; PACK MUD v.; PACK PEANUT BUTTER v.; PLUG v.[1]; POGUE v.; POP IT IN THE TOASTER v.; PRAT FOR v.;

PUNCH IT v.[2]; PUNK v.[2]; PUNK (OUT) v.; PUSH SHIT UPHILL v.; RECTIFY v.; RIDE THE DECK v.; RIDE THE TAN TRACK v.; RUMP v.; SADDLE UP v.; SHIT-FUCK v.; SHIT-STAB v.; SHOOT IN THE TAIL v.; SHOOT SOMEONE'S STAR v.; STICK ONE'S DUCK IN THE MUD v.; SWIVE v.; TAKE IT UP THE ASS v.; TAKE ON SOME BACKS v.; TAKE THE HERSHEY HIGHWAY v.; THREAD v.; THROW A BUTTONHOLE ON v.; TOM-FUCK v.; TRIM SOMEONE'S RIM v.; WHITEWASH SOMEONE'S KIDNEYS v.). [RING n.[1] (2) + pun on wedding preparations]

ask (me) another! *excl.* [late 19C+] a riposte to one who has just recited a riddle or a dated or unfunny joke.

ask me one on sport *phr.* [1990s+] used to deflect a question to which the speaker does not know the answer. [a knowledge of sport being seen as the least 'intellectual' of attainments]

ask my arse! *excl.* (*also* **ask my ass!**) [late 18C+] a coarse and evasive response, go to hell! [ARSE n.[1] (1)/ASS n. (2)]

ask my aunt! *excl.* [late 19C] (*US*) go to hell! [euph. for ASK MY ARSE! excl.]

ask-no-questions *n.* [1950s] (*Aus.*) a euph. for ARSE n.[1] (1).

asleep at the switch, be *v.* [late 19C+] (*US*) to be inattentive, not concentrating on a task. [railroad jargon 'switch', the points lever]

asleep at the wheel, be *v.* [20C+] to be inattentive, not concentrating on a task. [motoring imagery]

as long as one's arm *phr.* (*also* **as long as a rainy Sunday**) [mid-17C+] extensive, substantial.

as many faces as a churchyard clock *phr.* [20C+] a phr. used of anyone seen as duplicitous or unreliable. [church clocks can have faces on all 4 sides of a rectangular tower]

as mim as old Betty Martin at a funeral, be *v.* [early 19C] to be walking in a prim, orderly manner. [dial. *mim*, affectedly modest, demure, primly silent or quiet; the term is imitative of pursed lips. Whether this is the same *Betty Martin* as ALL MY EYE AND BETTY MARTIN phr. is unknown]

as much fun as a... *phr.* [20C+] in a variety of similes, all meaning no fun whatsoever, including *as much fun as a wet blanket/Sunday*.

as much use as a... *phr.* [late 19C+] in a variety of similes, all meaning no use whatsoever, including [late 19C+] *as much use as my arse*; [20C+] *as much use as a (sick) headache*; [1970s+] *as much use as a chocolate teapot*.

as muck *adv.* [late 19C+] extremely, utterly; either following a pej. adj., e.g. *as sick as muck*, or implying one, e.g. *as rich as muck*.

asoc *n.* (*also* **asocial**) [1990s+] (*US Und.*) a child molester. [sociological jargon 'antagonistic to society or social order' + SE *asocial*, inconsiderate of or hostile to other people]

asparagus *n.* [1990s+] (*Aus. racing*) one who is full of ideas on the day's races and suggestions as to possible winners. [pun on racing tips/*asparagus* tips]

aspect *n.* [late 19C–1900s] an amorous glance. [Ital. *aspetto!* look!]

asphalt arab *n.* [1950s] (*US*) a city person, as nicknamed by a country dweller. [SE *asphalt* + ARAB n.[1] (2)]

aspinall *n.* [late 19C–1900s] enamel. [*Aspinall*, the inventor and manufacturer of a variety of oxidized enamel paint]

as popular as a pork chop at a Jewish wedding *phr. see* LIKE A PORK CHOP AT A JEWISH WEDDING phr.

as popular as a turd in the fruit salad *phr.* [1990s+] (*Aus.*) extremely unpopular. [TURD n. (1)]

aspro *n. see* ASS PRO n.

ass *see also under* ARSE and its combs.

ass *n.* **1** [early 16C+] an unpleasant person, esp. a fool, idiot (cf. AIREDALE n.; ARSE n.[1]). **2** [mid-16C; mid-18C+] (*orig. US*) the buttocks; the anus (cf. ARSE n.[1]). **3** [mid-19C+] (*US*) (in a sexual context) the vagina; occas. the penis. **4** [1930s+] (*orig. US/Aus.*) sexual conquests; thus generic for a woman when viewed purely as a sex object, often as PIECE OF ASS n. (1). **5** [1930s+] (*US*) used

generically to mean one's person, one's body. **6** [1960s+] (*US*) of an object, the rear. **7** [1980s+] (*US*) an unpleasant or disgusting object. **8** [1990s+] (*US drugs*) the last, and thus least potent puff on a marijuana cigarette or pipe. **9** [2000s] (*US*) mentality, character, personality. [(1) SE *ass*, a donkey; subseq. defs. *see* ARSE n.[1]; (2) note this US sp. appears increasingly in the UK in the late 1990s+]

ass, the *n.[1]* (*also* **arse, the**) [1960s+] (*orig. US*) a bad temper; esp. in phr. *have/get (a case of) the ass*, to be angry. [fig. use of ARSE n.[1] (1)/ASS n. (2)]

ass, the *n.[2]* [1980s+] (*US campus/gay*) something unpleasant, a disappointment. [ASS n. (7)]

-ass *sfx* [1930s+] (*mainly US Black*) used to form generally negative (but increasingly positive too) adj. and occas. nouns, e.g. BITCH-ASS adj.; CANDY-ASS n.[1]; DRAG-ASS adj. [ARSE n.[1] (1)/ASS n. (2)]

ass about *v.* [late 19C–1930s] to play the fool (cf. ACT THE ANGORA v.). [SE *ass*, donkey/ASS n. (1); note ARSE ABOUT v.[1], although the homonymity with US *ass* and UK *arse* is coincidental]

ass around *v.* [1950s] (*US*) to wander around (in a foolish manner). [ASS n. (1)]

assassin *n.[1]* [late 19C] (*UK Und.*) a term of abuse.

assassin *n.[2]* [1900s–10s] an ornamental bow worn at a woman's breast. [it 'kills' her admirers]

ass backward(s) *phr. see* ARSE BACKWARDS phr.

ass-bad *adj. see* BAD-ASS adj.

ass bandit *n.* [1950s+] (*US*) a womanizer, a playboy. [ASS n. (4) + SE *bandit*]

ass-belly *n.* [1970s+] (*US*) a grotesquely fat person. [ASS n. (2) + SE *belly*; the similarity of the 2 fleshy protuberances]

ass betting *n.* [2000s] (*US prison*) gambling without the means of paying back one's losses. [play on BET ONE'S (SWEET) ASS v.]

ass-bite *n.* [1970s] (*US*) a very unpopular person. [ASS BITE v.]

ass bite *v.* [1970s] (*US*) usu. of an employer, to harass, to nag. [ASS n. (2) + SE *bite*]

ass blow *v.* [1960s+] (*US gay*) to perform anilingus (cf. AUSTRALIAN n.). [ASS n. (2) + BLOW v.[2] (3)]

assbone *n.* [1970s+] (*US*) the buttocks; also as coccyx in phr. *break one's assbone*. [ASS n. (2) + SE *bone*]

ass boy *n.* [1980s] (*US*) a male homosexual (cf. ANAL ASTRONAUT n.). [ASS n. (2) + SE *boy*]

ass-breaker *n.* (*US*) **1** [1950s] a difficult, boring or exasperating job, problem or situation. **2** [1950s+] a dive in which the diver lands stomach down on the water, rather than cutting through it (cf. ASS-BUSTER n.; ASS-RIPPER n.; BACK-BUSTER n.; BELLIER n.; BELLY-BUSTER n.; BELLYFLOP n.; BELLY-WASHER n.[2]; BELLY-WHOPPER n.). **3** [1960s] a nag, a dominating woman, one who destroys the self-confidence of a man. **4** [2000s] a thug. **5** [2000s] the penis (cf. ARSE-OPENER n.). [fig. use of ASS n. (2) + SE *breaker*]

ass-bucket *n.* [1950s] (*US*) an unpopular or unimportant person. [ASS n. (2) + SE *bucket*]

assbulb *n.* [2000s] (*US Black*) a lazy person. [ASS n. (2) + ? SE *lightbulb*]

ass burglar *n.* [1970s+] (*US*) a male homosexual (cf. ANAL ASTRONAUT n.). [ASS n. (2) + SE *burglar*; var. on TURD-BURGLAR n.]

ass business *n.* [1980s+] (*US gay*) male homosexual prostitution. [ASS n. (2) + BUSINESS n.[2] (3)]

ass-buster *n.* **1** [1950s] (*US*) a dive in which a swimmer jumps, holds their nose and hits the water buttocks-first, the aim, and the result, being to make a big splash (cf. ASS-BREAKER n.). **2** [1970s] an outstanding person. **3** [2000s] a fall. **4** [2000s] something challenging. [ASS n. (2) + BUSTER n.[5]]

ass-busting *adj.* (*US*) **1** [1970s] exhausting, tiring. **2** [2000s] remarkable, amazing. [BUST ONE'S ASS v. (1)]

ass-chewing *n.* [1950s+] (*orig. US milit.*) a scolding, a serious reprimand. [ASS n. (2) + SE *chew*]

ass-deep *adj.* (*also* **tits deep**) [1950s+] (*US*) **1** very deep; usu. in such phr. as ASS DEEP TO A TALL MOOSE phr. **2** totally involved with, with an excessive amount of. [ASS n. (2)/TIT n.³ (1) + SE *deep*; lit. deep enough to reach one's buttocks or breasts]

ass deep to a tall moose *phr.* [1970s] very deep, often used of water or snow. [fig. use of ASS-DEEP adj.+ SE *tall moose*]

ass-dragging *adj.* [1990s+] (*US*) run-down, worn-out. [ASS n. (2) + SE *drag*]

-assed *sfx* (*also* -arsed) [1940s+] (*orig. US*) a general intensifier, e.g. NELLY-ASSED adj. [ext. of -ASS sfx; but note earlier HALF-ASSED adj.]

assed out *adj.* [1980s+] (*US Black*) **1** defeated, out of luck, impoverished. **2** dead, killed. [fig. use of ASS n. (2)]

ass-end-backwards *phr.* (*also* **ass-end up**) [1960s+] in confusion, back-to-front, upside down; thus defeated. [ASS n. (2) + SE *end + backwards/up*]

ass-end of nowhere *n.* [1920s+] (*US*) nowhere, a very out-of-the-way place. [fig. use of ASS n. (2) + SE *end + nowhere*]

ass-end-to *phr.* [late 19C–1950s] (*US*) in confusion. [ASS n. (2) + SE *end + to*]

ass-end up *phr. see* ASS-END-BACKWARDS *phr.*

assface *n.* [1990s+] (*US campus*) an unpleasant, stupid person. [ASS n. (2) + SE *face*]

ass-fault *n.* [1990s+] (*US campus*) **1** the crease between one's buttocks. **2** extreme stupidity. [ASS n. (2) + SE *fault*, a crevice]

ass-frontwards *adj.* [1960s] head-over-heels. [ASS n. (2) + SE *frontwards*]

assfuck *n.* (*US*) **1** [1940s+] an act of anal intercourse. **2** [1970s] an instance of cruel victimization. **3** [1990s+] an all-purpose derog. term of address. [(1) ASSFUCK v.; (2) and (3) f. (1)]

assfuck *v.* [1940s+] (*US*) to have anal intercourse (cf. ASK FOR THE RING v.). [ARSE n.¹ (1)/ASS n. (2) + FUCK v.¹]

ass-fucker *n.* [1940s+] (*US*) one who has anal sex, the implication is usu. a male homosexual. [ASSFUCK v.]

assfucking *n.* [1940s+] (*US*) anal intercourse. [ASSFUCK v.]

ass games *n.* [1980s+] (*US gay*) a variety of homosexual practices, including anal intercourse and sado-masochism. [ASS n. (2)]

ass gasket *n.* [1990s+] (*US campus*) the paper protector that is placed over a lavatory seat to indicate its sanitized state. [ASS n. (2) + SE *gasket*, a thin, flat ring used as a seal between 2 surfaces]

ass-grabbing *adj.* (*US*) **1** [1960s] irritating. **2** [1970s] (*also* **butt-grabbing**) good, exciting. [ASS n. (2) + SE *grabbing*]

ass hammer *n.* [1960s+] (*US campus*) a motorcycle. [ASS n. (2) + SE *hammer*; the battering one receives from its seat on one's own]

asshat *n.* [2000s] (*US*) a fool. [var. on ASSHEAD n.]

asshead *n.* [16C–early 17C; 1940s+] a fool (cf. ASSHOLE n.¹; BEAR'S ASS n.; CRAZY-ASS n.; DUMB-ASS n.; HORSE'S ASS n.; JERK-ASS n.). [ASS n. (1)/ASS n. (2) + -HEAD sfx (1); 1940s+ use US]

assheaded *adj.* [16C–early 17C] foolish (cf. ASSHOLE n.¹; BEAR'S ASS n.; CRAZY-ASS n.; DUMB-ASS n.; HORSE'S ASS n.; JERK-ASS n.). [ASS-HEAD n.]

ass-high to a tall Indian *phr.* (*also* **hip-high to a tall Indian, knee-high to a tall Indian**) [late 19C+] (*US*) an unspecified measure of height, usu. not very tall. [ASS n. (2)]

as shit *adv.* (*also* **as shite**) [1960s+] a general intensifer, e.g. *mad as shit*. [SHIT n.¹ (1)/SHITE n. (1)]

asshole *see also under* ARSEHOLE *and its combs.*

asshole *n.¹* (*US*) **1** [mid-19C+] the anus (cf. A-HOLE n.). **2** [mid-19C+] the least appetizing, poorest, most run-down and poss. dangerous area of a city or town or place. **3** [1930s+] a fool, a derog. description of a subject (cf. ARSE n.¹; ASSHEAD n.). **4** [1970s+] a general term of address. [ASS n. (2) + HOLE n.¹ (1); note UK sp. ARSEHOLE n.]

asshole *n.²* see ASSHOLE BUDDY n. (1).

asshole *adj.* [1930s+] (*US*) a general negative description, unpleasant, worthless, stupid, obnoxious etc (cf. ARSEHOLE adj.). [ASSHOLE n.¹ (3)]

asshole *v.* [1940s] (*US*) to grovel, to beg, to toady. [ASSHOLE n.¹ (3)]

asshole around *v.* [1950s+] (*US*) to idle, to loiter, to waste time. [ASSHOLE n.¹ (3)]

asshole bandit *n.* [1950s+] **1** (*US*) a derog. term for a male homosexual (cf. ARSEHOLE BANDIT n.). **2** (*US gay*) an anilinguist. **3** (*US gay*) in anal intercourse, the active partner. [ASSHOLE n.¹ (1)]

asshole-breath *n.* [1960s+] (*US*) a term of contempt. [ASSHOLE n.¹ (3)]

asshole buddy *n.* **1** [1940s+] (*US*) (*also* **a-hole buddy, asshole**) an extremely close friend. **2** [1950s+] (*US gay*) normally heterosexual men who, deprived for whatever reason of women, enjoy anal intercourse, both as an active or passive partner. [ASSHOLE n.¹ (1)/A-HOLE n. + BUDDY n. (1)]

asshole-deep *adj.* [1960s+] (*US*) extremely deep. [ext. of ASS-DEEP adj. (1)]

asshole of the universe *n.* (*also* **asshole of creation, ...the world, arsehole of the universe, bunghole..., dunghill...**) [late 17C; mid-19C+] (*UK/US*) applied to anywhere considered especially unpleasant, usu. hot and in the Third World by a Western expatriate. [ARSEHOLE n. (3)/ASSHOLE n.¹ (2)/BUNGHOLE n.¹/SE *dunghill* (late 17C); note description of Holland as 'the Buttock of the world, full of veins and blood, but no bones in't' in *A Brief Character of the Low Countries* (1660) and Primo Levi's ref. to Auschwitz as *anus mundi*, a Lat. synon.]

assholingest *adj.* [1970s] (*US*) the notional superlative of ASSHOLE adj.

ass-hound *n.* **1** [1940s] (*US*) a womanizer, a 'skirt chaser'. **2** [1980s+] (*US gay*) one who enjoys anal intercourse and is primarily sexually attracted by the buttocks. [ASS n. (4)/ASS n. (4) + HOUND sfx]

assig *n.* [late 17C–early 19C] an *assignation*. [abbr.]

assist *n.* [1990s+] **1** back-up, usu. in the form of physical power. **2** the person drawn in to provide this back-up. [sporting imagery]

asskash *n.* [1950s] (*US drugs*) a supply of narcotics, concealed in the rectum, usu. in a metal container. [ASS n. (2) + SE *cache*]

ass-keister *v. see* KEISTER v. (1).

ass-kick *n.* [1970s+] (*US*) **1** a very demanding task. **2** a punishment, a beating. [fig. use of KICK ASS v.]

ass-kicker *n.¹* [1960s+] (*US*) a shoe, esp. a man's pointed shoe. [SE *kick* + ASS n. (2)]

ass-kicker *n.²* **1** [1960s+] (*orig. US*) (*also* **arse-kicker**) an aggressive, domineering person, a bully. **2** [1970s] (*US*) of a place, unpleasant, challenging. **3** [1970s+] (*orig. US*) an amusing, successful, exciting person. [ARSE n.¹ (1)/ASS n. (2) + SE *kicker*]

ass-kicking *n.* (*also* **behind-kicking**) [1930s+] (*US*) a beating. [KICK ASS v.]

ass-kicking *adj.* (*US*) **1** [1960s+] in fig. use, a general intensifier, extremely, very much, powerfully. **2** [1970s+] vicious, thuggish. [ASS-KICKING n.]

assload *n.* [mid-19C; 1950s+] (*US*) an excess. [ASS n. (2) + SE *load*]

ass-man *n.* **1** [1950s+] (*UK/US*) (*also* **arse-man**) a man who finds a woman's buttocks her most alluring feature (cf. BUM MAN n.; LEG MAN n.²; TIT MAN n.). **2** [1960s+] (*UK/US*) (*also* **arse-man**) a successful seducer. **3** [1970s+] (*US gay*) a man who is primarily attracted to the buttocks and enjoys anal intercourse. [(1) ARSE n.¹ (1)/ASS n. (2); (2) ARSE n.¹ (7)/ASS n. (4); (3) ASS n. (2) + SE *man*, an expert or specialist in something or one who favours a specified product]

ass-master *n.* [1990s+] (*US campus*) a general term of abuse. [ASS n. (2) + SE *master*]

associates *n.* [1980s+] (*US Black*) friends.

ass-off *n.* [1960s+] (*US campus*) a time-waster. [ASS n. (1)]

ass off *phr.* [1940s+] (*US*) a general intensifier. [ASS n. (5)]

ass on backwards *phr.* [2000s] drunk (cf. ARSEHOLED adj.). [ARSE ON BACKWARDS phr.]

ass out *n.* [2000s] (*US prison*) an inmate who has neither advantages nor respect. [ASS n. (1)]

ass-out *adj. see* ASSED OUT adj.

ass out *v.* **1** [1990s+] (*US Black*) to rush away. **2** [1990s+] (*US campus*) to make a fool of oneself. **3** [2000s] (*US campus*) to go to sleep. [fig. uses of var. defs. of ASS n.]

ass pack *n.* [1950s+] (*US*) a small pouch-like bag strapped around the wearer's waist. [ASS n. (2) + SE *pack*]

ass peddler *n.* (*also* **butt peddler**) [1940s+] (*US*) anyone who sells their body as a prostitute, male or female (cf. BANGTAIL n.[1]; BEAVE n.; COIN COLLECTOR n.; COMMERCIAL n.[2]; COMMERCIAL QUEER n.; COMMODITY n.; CRACK SALESMAN n.; DICK PEDDLER n.; GOLD-DIGGER n.; GREENGROCER n.; HIP-PEDDLER n.; HUSTLER n.; HUSTLING BROAD n.; MALE-HUSTLER n.; MEAT-MERCHANT n.; MERCHANDISE n.; MUFF MERCHANT n.; NIGHT TRADER n.; NOCKTRESS n.; PEDDLER n.; PIECE OF TRADE n.; PINTLE-MERCHANT n.; PLIER n.; PRESENTERER n.; PURSE-FINDER n.; RECEIVER GENERAL n.; RENT n.[2]; RENT BOY n.; RENTER n.; SALES LADY n.; STUD-HUSTLER n.; TAIL-TRADER n.; TRADE n.; TRADER n.; TRADING DAME n.; TRAFFIC n.; TWAT-SELLER n.). [ASS n. (2)/ASS n. (3) + SE *peddler*]

ass pirate *n.* [1980s+] (*US*) a male homosexual (cf. ANAL ASTRONAUT n.). [var. on ARSE BANDIT n.; note synon. RMC Duntroon (Aus.) *poo pirate*]

ass-poots *n.* [1960s] (*US*) beans. [ASS n. (2) + POOT n.[2] (1), the propensity of beans to cause an excess of breaking wind]

ass pro *n.* (*also* **aspro, asspro**) [1960s+] (*Aus./US*) a male homosexual prostitute. [ASS n. (2) + abbr. SE *prostitute/professional*; despite the apparent simplicity of the ety., Hancock, 'Shelta and Polari' (1984) suggests Ling. Fr. *aspro*, money]

ass queen *n.* [1980s+] (*US gay*) one whose primary area of sexual interest is the buttocks. [ASS n. (2) + QUEEN n.[2] (1)/QUEEN sfx (2)]

ass raider *n.* [1980s+] **1** (*US*) a male homosexual (cf. ANAL ASTRONAUT n.). **2** (*US gay*) the active partner in anal intercourse. [ASS n. (2) + SE *raid*]

ass-ripper *n.* **1** [1950s+] (*US*) a dive in which a swimmer jumps, holds his nose and hits the water buttocks-first; the aim – and the result – is to make a big splash (cf. ASS-BREAKER n.). **2** [1960s] (*US campus*) a difficult course or examination. [ASS n. (2) + SE *rip*]

ass-scratcher *n.* (*US*) **1** [1930s] a loafer, an idler. **2** [1990s+] something that makes one think. [ASS n. (2) + SE *scratcher*; one who simply sits around, scratching his buttocks]

ass-side-before *phr.* [1960s] head-over-heels, in confusion. [ASS n. (2) + SE *side* + *before*]

ass-sucker *n.* [late 19C; 1960s+] (*US*) a sycophant, a toady. [ASS n. (2) + SE *sucker*]

ass-tickler *n.* [1970s] (*US*) something amusing. [ASS n. (2) + TICKLE v.[1]]

ass-tight *adj.* [1960s] (*US*) **1** of things, very tight. **2** in fig. use, very efficient. **3** of friends, very intimate. [ASS n. (2) + SE *tight*]

ass-to-elbow *adj.* [1980s] (*US*) extremely crowded. [ASS n. (2) + SE *elbow*]

ass-ugly *adj.* [1990s+] (*US*) very unattractive. [i.e. looking like an ASS n. (2)]

ass up *v.* [2000s] (*US Black*) to take drugs, to get intoxicated on drugs. [fig. use of ASS n. (2)]

ass up to *v.* [1970s] (*US*) to toady to, to curry favour. [ASS n. (2)]

ass watcher *n.* [1950s–70s] (*US gay*) one who walks the streets looking for a potential sexual partner. [ASS n. (2) + SE *watcher*]

ass-waxing *n.* [1960s+] (*US*) a thrashing, a beating. [backform. f. WAX SOMEONE'S ASS v.]

assways *adv.* (*also* **arseways, ass-to and every whichaway**) [1930s+] (*orig. US*) skew-whiff, back-to-front. [ASS n. (2)]

ass-whipped *adj.* [1970s+] (*US*) completely and utterly exhausted. [ASS n. (2) + SE *whipped*]

ass-whipping *n.* (*also* **ass-whupping**) (*orig. US*) **1** [1950s+] a particularly savage beating. **2** [1990s+] in fig. use, any form of non-physical punishment. [ASS n. (2) + SE *whipping/*WHUP v.]

ass-wipe *n.* (*also* **arse-wipe, wipe**) (*UK/US*) **1** [mid-16C; 1950s+] (*also* **ass-wiper**) lavatory paper. **2** [1950s+] a general term of abuse, occas. affectionate use between friends; thus one who is *not worth wiping one's ass on*. **3** [1980s+] any worthless piece of paper, e.g. a parking ticket, a newspaper. [ARSE n.[1] (1)/ASS n. (2) + SE *wipe*]

ass-wiper *n.* **1** [1920s+] (*also* **arsewiper**) a sycophant, a toady. **2** [1960s] (*drugs*) a severe heroin addiction. **3** [1960s+] something extremely difficult, demanding. [ARSE n.[1] (1)/ASS n. (2) + SE *wipe*]

assy *adj.* **1** [1980s+] (*US gay*) malicious, sarcastic. **2** [2000s] (*US Black*) insignificant, second-rate, unimportant. [fig. use of ASS n. (1)]

assy-fussy *adj.* [1970s] (*US*) back-to-front. [ASS n. (2) + assonance/initial letter]

astard-ba *n.* [1930s] a bastard. [semi-backsl.]

aste *n.* [early 17C] (*UK Und.*) money. [? Ital. *asta*, auction]

asterisk *n.* [1900s] (*Aus.*) a euph. for any unspecified obscenity. [the * that takes the place of the printed letter; on pattern of BLANKY adj. or DASHED adj.]

as the actress said to the bishop *phr.* (*also* **as the bishop said to the actress**) [1930s+] a phr. used after a remark, turning what may have been a perfectly innocent comment into a sexual innuendo, e.g. Pull it out and we'll see how long it is...as the actress said to the bishop; occas. simply as a playful remark. [the supposed immorality of actresses]

Aston Villa *n.* [1990s+] **1** a pillow. **2** a pillar. [rhy. sl.; Cockney pron. of *Villa*; ult. UK football team *Aston Villa*]

Astorbilt *n.* (*also* **Mr Astorbilt, Mrs Astorbilt**) (*US*) **1** [late 19C+] one who considers themselves a cut above their peers. **2** [20C+] one who dresses ostentatiously. **3** [1920s+] a member of high society. [names *Astor* + *Vanderbilt*, 2 of America's wealthiest families]

astorperious *adj.* [1930s+] (*US*) arrogant, haughty. [*Astor* (see prev.) + SE *imperious*]

Astor's pet horse *n.* (*also* **Astor's pet poodle**) (*US*) **1** [1930s+] an over-made-up or overdressed woman. **2** [1960s+] an arrogant, haughty person. [joc. use of proper name *Astor* (see ASTORBILT n.) + SE *pet horse*]

astronomer *n.* [mid-19C] a horse that holds its head high. [it is always staring at the sky]

astro travel *n.* [1970s] (*US drugs*) imaginary space travel while under the influence of a psychedelic or psychotropic drug.

as useless as a pork chop/slice of bacon at a Jewish wedding *phr. see* LIKE A PORK CHOP AT A JEWISH WEDDING phr.

as winking *adv. see* LIKE WINKING adv.

at a rate of knots *adv.* [late 19C+] very fast. [naut. use]

at ballarat *phr.* [1990s+] (*Aus.*) having an erection. [joc. use of proper name *Ballarat*, the last stop on the railway line from Melbourne]

at bat *adj.* [late 19C+] (*orig. US*) **1** involved in, occupied by. **2** taking one's turn. [baseball use; the UK use reflects cricket]

at Bushey Park *phr.* (*also* **in Bushey Park**) [early 19C] poor, impoverished. [BUSHED adj.[1]]

atch *v.* [1920s] (*UK tramp*) to arrest. [cod Lat. for SE *catch*]

atchker *v.* [1910s–20s] (*UK tramp*) to arrest. [cod Lat. for SE *catch*]

ate-the-bolts *n.* [20C+] (*Ulster*) one who is a glutton for work.

ate up *adj. see* EAT UP adj.

ate-your-bun *n.* [1990s+] (*Irish*) a general term of abuse.

at full belt *adv.* [1960s] at full speed. [BELT v.[1]]

at half-mast *phr.* [1940s+] in a partially lowered position, used esp. of trousers or a partial erection of the penis; thus, *at quarter-mast*.

athanasian wench *n.* [late 18C–early 19C] a promiscuous young woman, a prostitute. [a pun on the *Athanasian* Creed, which begins with the words, 'quicumque vult', i.e. QUICUMQUE VULT n.]

atheneum *n.* [late 19C–1900s] the penis. [? the *Athenaeum* Club, London, which might be seen as the fount of all wisdom]

Athenian *n.* [1970s+] (*gay*) a pederast. [stereotyped link between homosexuality and Greece]

at her last prayers *phr.* [late 17C–early 19C] a phr. used to typify an old maid.

-ati *sfx* [1990s+] a sfx used to denote a given group, as defined by the n., e.g. *glitterati*, *rockerati*. [on patten of SE *literati*]

at it *phr.* **1** [late 16C+] indulging in sexual intercourse. **2** [early 17C+] fighting, lit. or fig. **3** [18C+] involved in something illegal or bad. **4** [19C–1900s] kissing and cuddling. **5** [mid-19C] drinking heavily. **6** [late 19C+] involved in an argument, emotionally moved. **7** [1920s+] teasing, provoking. [SE *at* + IT n.[1] (1)/SE *it*, i.e. a crime]

atkins *n.* [late 19C–1920s] a generic term for a typical private solider in the British army. [abbr. TOMMY ATKINS n. (1)]

Atlantic ranger *n.* [late 19C] a herring. [its breeding grounds]

atlas *n.* [1980s] (*US prison*) **1** a very strong prisoner. **2** a prisoner who attempts to carry out everything unaided. [ult. the mythical *Atlas* who held up the earth in his hands, but note US strong man Charles *Atlas* (1894–1972)]

atmos *n.* [1990s+] (*orig. US teen*) atmosphere or ambience, used in a positive fashion. [abbr.]

at number one London *phr.* [mid-19C–1900s] of a woman, to be menstruating. [ety. unknown; 'Number One London' is trad. Apsley House, former home of the Duke of Wellington, at Hyde Park Corner]

at nurse *phr.* [late 18C–early 19C] for a person to be in the hands of (dishonest) trustees.

atom bomb *n.* [1960s+] (*US drugs*) **1** a combination of marijuana or hashish with opium or heroin (cf. A-BOMB n.). **2** a combination of cannabis and cocaine. [play on SE *atomic bomb*, intensified by BOMB n.[4]]

atom-bombo *n.* [1940s+] (*Aus.*) strong, cheap wine. [SE *atomic bomb*]

atomic atmosphere *n.* [1980s+] (*US campus*) the stink created by someone's having recently broken wind.

atomized *adj.* [1950s] (*US*) drunk (cf. ANNIHILATED adj.).

atomy *n.* [late 16C–19C] a small, thin or deformed person. [SE *anatomy*]

atop Mt Shasta *phr.* (*also* **from Mount Shasta**) [1930s–50s] (*US drugs*) addicted to narcotics. [*Mt. Shasta*, an extinct volcano in N. California; ? the image of the addict as one whose strength has vanished]

at outs *phr. see* ON THE OUTS phr. (2).

at quarter-mast *phr. see* AT HALF-MAST phr.

at rest *phr.* [19C] tipsy, drunk (cf. ABOUT RIGHT phr.[1]).

at rug *phr.* [early–mid-19C] asleep, in bed. [SE *rug*]

at sea *phr. see* ALL AT SEA phr. (1).

atshitshi *n.* [1980s+] (*drugs*) marijuana. [ety. unknown]

at someone's titty *phr. see* ON SOMEONE'S TITTY phr.

at sparrow crow *phr.* [1940s] (*Aus.*) at dawn. [euph. for AT SPARROW'S FART phr.]

at sparrow's fart *phr.* [late 19C+] at dawn, early in the morning; usu. *up at...* [the dawn chorus; note synon. use by British Army in North Africa during WW2, *crow-pee*]

at Staines *phr.* [early 19C] in financial difficulties (cf. AT THE BUSH phr.). [the Bush Inn at *Staines*, ? a popular refuge for London debtors]

attaboy *n.* [1930s+] (*US*) a statement of congratulation. [ATTABOY! excl.]

attaboy! *excl.* (*also* **attababes! attababy! attagirl! thattaboy!**) [20C+] (*orig. US*) a general excl. of admiration and encouragement. [? phr. 'that's the boy' etc or 'at her, boy' (E.P.), where 'her' is neuter. Note US milit./police jargon *attaboy*, a commendation;

Fraser & Gibbons, *Soldier & Sailor Words & Phrases* (1925), suggests it is 'American slang used by players and lookers on at Base-ball matches']

attack *n.* [early 19C] the moment of starting a meal or dish.

attack *v.* [mid-19C] to begin, to address oneself to, e.g. *attack that beef*.

attack of the week's end *n.* (*also* **attack of the month's end**) [late 19C–1910s] the poverty that comes after one's weekly or monthly wages have run out.

attagirl! *excl. see* ATTABOY! excl.

attensh *n.* [1930s] *attention*. [abbr.]

at the Bush *phr.* [early 19C] in financial difficulties (cf. AT STAINES phr.). [the *Bush* Inn at Staines, ? a popular refuge for London debtors]

at the death *phr.* [20C+] in the end, in conclusion. [SE *death*, termination, finality]

at the micks *phr.* (*also* **at the mix**) [1960s+] causing trouble. [pun on MIX v.[1] + ? ref. to MICK n.[1] (1), a (rowdy) Irishman]

at (the) outs *phr.* [late 19C–1930s] arguing or angry with someone.

at the outside *phr.* [mid-19C+] at the limit, to the fullest extent.

at the pinch *phr.* [late 18C–early 19C] working as a thief, esp. petty theft from shops carried out during a purchase, giving short change or passing counterfeit money in exchange for goods. [PINCH v. (2)]

at the races *phr.* [20C+] working as a street-walker. [? her euph. to prying acquaintances]

at the school of placebo, be *v.* (*also* **go to the school of placebo**) [mid-14C–17C] to be a toady or sycophant. [SE *placebo*, the Vespers for the Dead, ult. Lat. *placebo*, I shall please]

at the sign of the horn *phr.* [late 17C–early 19C] suffering cuckoldry. [HORN n.[1] (1) + image of a fake tavern sign]

at the top of the house *phr.* [late 17C–mid-19C] very angry.

attic *n.* **1** [early 19C+] (*orig. boxing*) the head; thus HAVE A GUEST IN THE ATTIC n. **2** [late 19C] the vagina.

attic to let *phr. see* APARTMENT TO LET phr.

attitude *n.* (*also* **'tude**) [late 19C; 1960s+] one's whole posture towards society, its rules and one's own place among them. [early use appears to refer to problems between individuals; in modern use the assumption is that an attitude is hostile to the prevailing establishment status quo, although it may well fit happily into the complementary rebellious teenage standpoint. Thus the rap band NWA, Niggers With Attitude. The meaning shifted slightly f. 1970s–80s, negative, antisocial, to 1990s+, haughty, pretentious]

attitude! *excl.* [1980s+] a comment made to a person who is seen as displaying ATTITUDE n.

attitude adjustment *n.* [2000s] (*US prison*) the administration of mood-altering drugs to a prisoner seen as disruptive; the physical subjugation of such a prisoner. [euph.]

Attleborough *n.* [mid–late 19C] (*US*) cheap or sham jewellery. [? the town of its manufacture]

attorney *n.* [early 19C] a grilled and devilled goose or turkey drumstick. [legal jargon *devil*, a lawyer working free for another lawyer]

attract *v.* [late 19C–1930s] to steal, to pilfer. [ironic euph.]

Auckland Park *n.* [1980s+] (*S.Afr.*) the South African Broadcasting Corporation (SABC). [by metonymy, *Auckland Park* is the Johannesburg suburb where the SABC headquarters is situated]

auctioneer *n.* [mid-19C–1920s] (*orig. boxing*) the fist. [it 'knocks things down'; the orig. auctioneer was that of prize-fighter Tom Sayers (*fl.*1845–60)]

Audi (5000) *v.* (*also* **audi**) [1990s+] (*US teen*) to rush away, to run off, to escape. [pron. of OUTIE phr. as *Audi*, an upscale automobile (the Audi 5000 is a favoured model)]

Audi (5000) *phr.* (*also* **5000, outtie 5000**) [1990s+] (*US*

Black/teen) a general phr. of farewell, goodbye, see you, I'm off etc. [AUDI (5000) v.]

audition the finger puppets v. (*also* **audition the hand puppet**) [1990s+] to masturbate (cf. DO THE (FIVE-)KNUCKLE SHUFFLE (ON THE OLD PISS PUMP) v.; DO THE TWO-FINGERED SHUFFLE v.; FINGER FUCK v.; GIVE ONESELF A LOW FIVE v.; HAND GALLOP v.; HAND JIG v.; HAND JIVE v.; HAND JOB v.; HAND SHANDY n.; PLAY A LITTLE FIVE-ON-ONE v.; RIDE THE HANDCAR v.; RUN ONE'S HAND UP THE FLAGPOLE v.; SHAKE HANDS WITH THE GOVERNOR v.; SHAKE HANDS WITH THE UNEMPLOYED v.; SHAKE HANDS WITH THE WIFE'S BEST FRIEND v.; TAKE MATTERS INTO ONE'S OWN HANDS v.; TAKE ONESELF IN HAND v.).

auger n. **1** [late 17C; 20C+] the penis; thus *auger-hole*, the vagina (cf. ARSE-OPENER n.). **2** [1980s] (*US campus*) an excessively hard worker. [SE *auger*, a tool for boring]

augur n. [late 19C] (*US*) a bore, an excessive talker. [a pun on SE *auger*, a bore; note SE *augur*, a prophet]

August ham n. [1920s–30s] (*US Black*) a watermelon. [the month of ripening + the pinkness of both foodstuffs]

auld kirker n. *see* KIRKER n.

Auld Reikle n. *see* OLD REEKIE n.

aunt n.[1] **1** [17C–1970s] a prostitute. **2** [17C+] (*also* **auntie**) a procuress, a madame. **3** [mid-19C–1940s] (*US*) (*also* **auntie**) an old Black woman, used by both Blacks and Whites. [note synon. Yid. *mume*, lit. 'aunt']

aunt n.[2] [20C+] (*US*) menstruation; usu. in such phrs. *as Aunt Flo is visiting, my red-headed aunt has arrived, Aunt Jody's come with her suitcase* etc. [euph.]

aunt n.[3] *see* AUNTIE n.[2] (1).

aunt, the n. *see* MY AUNT n.

Aunt Betsy's cookie store n. [1990s+] (*US campus*) Alcoholic Beverage Control store. [initial letters]

Aunt Fanny n. [1940s+] used to express negation or disbelief, e.g. *tell that to my Aunt Fanny; Agree? My Aunt Fanny*. [joc. use of proper name + an added emphasis from FANNY n.[1]]

Aunt Flo n. (*also* **Flo**) [1950s+] (*US*) menstruation. [euph.; AUNT n.[2] + pun on SE *flow*]

Aunt Hagar('s children) n. [1930s–40s] (*US Black*) the Black race. [Gen. 21:9, *Hagar* the Egyptian, the wife of Abraham and the mother of Ishmael]

Aunt Hazel n. *see* HAZEL n.

auntie n.[1] (*also* **aunty**) [mid-19C+] the lavatory; thus *go to visit aunty* (cf. DO ONE'S BUSINESS v.; GO TO MARY'S ROOM v.; MOTHER JONES n.; MRS CHANT'S n.; MRS JONES n.; MRS MURPHY n.; MY AUNT n.; NEIGHBOUR JONES n.; SEE MRS MURRAY v.; UNCLE n.[1]; VISIT MISS MURPHY v.; VISIT MISS WHITE v.; VISIT SIR HARRY v.; WIDOW JONES n.). [euph.]

auntie n.[2] **1** [1920s+] (*US gay*) (*also* **aunt, tante**) an ageing male homosexual (cf. AUNT MAME n.; AUNT MATHILDA n.; DADDY n.; DADDY-O n.; DAUGHTER n.; GRANDMA n.[2]; HUSBAND n.[1]; MADAM n.[1]; MAMA n.; MOTHER n.[1]; MOTHER GA-GA n.; MOTHER PARKER n.; MOTHER SUPERIOR n.[1]; NEPHEW n.). **2** [1940s+] an ageing female, occas. male prostitute. **3** [1960s] a male 'madam'.

auntie n.[3] **1** [1940s+] the British Broadcasting Corporation, orig. used by independent TV companies, but now general. **2** [1950s+] (*Aus.*) the Australian Broadcasting Commission (ABC). [in both cases the implication is of prissiness, paternalism, reticence and trad. conservatism]

auntie n.[4] [1950s+] (*drugs*) opium (cf. APOSTLE n.). [? link to AUNT NORA n.]

auntie n.[5] *see* AUNT n.[1].

Auntie Ella n. (*also* **Cousin Ella**) [20C+] an umbrella. [rhy. sl.]

Auntie Emma n. (*drugs*) **1** [1970s] morphine (cf. BARMECIDE n.; BIRDIE POWDER n.; CECIL n.[1]; CUBE n.[1]; DREAM n.[4]; DREAMER n.; DUST n.[5]; DYNAMITE n.[2]; EMSEL n.; FIRST LINE n.; FOOLISH POWDER n.; GOD'S (OWN) MEDICINE n.; G.O.M. n.[2]; GOW n.[1]; HAPPY DUST n.; HAPPY POWDER n.; HEAVEN DUST n.; HOCUS n.[2]; HOP n.[2]; HOWS

n.; ICE-CREAM n.[1]; JOY DUST n.; JOY FLAKES n.; JOY POWDER n.; M n.[1]; MARGIE n.; MARY n.[3]; MAYO n.; MISS EMMA n.; MISS MORPH n.; MOJO n.[2]; MONKEY n.[12]; MONKEY MEDICINE n.; M.S. n.; NOSE POWDER n.; NUMBER 13 n.; RED CROSS n.; SHIT n.[5]; SLUMBER PARTY n.; SNOW n.[2]; STUFF n.[3]; SUGAR n.[6]; SWEET JESUS n.; SWEET MORPHEUS n.; SWEET STUFF n.; UNKIE n.[1]; WHITE n.[3]; WHITE CROSS n.; WHITE SILK n.; WHITE STUFF n.; WITCH, THE n.). **2** [1980s+] opium (cf. APOSTLE n.). [(1) initial *M*]

Auntie Flora n. [20C+] (*W.I., Antg./St Lu.*) the floor; *knock/take Auntie Flora*, to sleep on the floor. [partial rhy. sl.]

Auntie Jane n. [1970s] (*Irish*) menstruation, a period. [AUNT n.[2] + proper name]

auntie-man n. (*also* **antiman**) [1940s+] (*W.I.*) an effeminate man. [AUNTIE n.[2] + SE *man*]

Auntie Meg n. [20C+] (*Aus.*) a keg (of beer). [rhy. sl.]

Aunt(ie) Nelly n. [20C+] the belly. [rhy. sl.]

auntie's ruin n. [1900s–60s] a disreputable, untrustworthy, seedy man. [the type of Lothario who might charm a spinster aunt]

Aunt Jane n.[1] [1920s] (*US*) the town of Tijuana, Mexico. [lit. trans. of Sp. *tía*, aunt + *juana*, Jane]

Aunt Jane n.[2] [1960s–70s] (*US Black*) **1** a subservient, obsequious Black woman. **2** a Black woman whose world is defined by spiritual rather than secular values; a regular church-goer and religious believer. [generic use of proper name]

Aunt Jemima n. [1920s+] (*US Black*) a subservient, obsequious Black woman, the female version of UNCLE TOM n. (1); an early fast-food chain, Aunt Jemima's Kitchen, featuring pictures of a stereotype 'Black Mammy' existed in the 1960s (cf. AUNT THOMASINA n.). [generic use of proper name; Aunt Jemima was a stock figure of the black songster tradition and she entered popular iconography and pancake mythology through a song, 'Old Aunt Jemima', written and first performed in 1875 by the black minstrel Billy Kersands, who, it has been suggested, adapted it from an actual slave song of the antebellum work-fields. In the fall of 1889, it was heard by Chris Rutt, a man in search of a name for his new self-rising pancake mix. Ruff sold out his Aunt Jemima pancake mix to the R.T. Davis Milling Company which brought Aunt Jemima to life in the person of one Nancy Green, a domestic cook. (Adapted from Tosches, *Where Dead Voices Gather*, 2001)]

Aunt Lilian visiting phr. (*also* **Aunt Minnie is visiting**) [1960s] (*US campus*) menstruating. [AUNT n.[2] + proper name]

Aunt Mame n. [1970s+] (*US gay*) an older male homosexual (cf. AUNTIE n.[2]). [the 1958 movie *Auntie Mame*, starring Rosalind Russell as an eccentric, rich aunt]

Aunt Maria n.[1] [late 19C–1900s] the female genitals. [? AUNT MARIA n.[2], i.e. they get 'hot']

Aunt Maria n.[2] [20C+] a fire (cf. ANNA MARIA n.). [rhy. sl.; note pron. Mar-eye-a]

Aunt Mary n.[1] **1** [mid-19C+] a Black woman who is a regular church-goer and religious believer. **2** [1970s] a downtrodden, subservient Black woman. [generic use of proper name]

Aunt Mary n.[2] [1950s+] (*drugs*) marijuana (cf. BENNY MASON n.; DONA JUANITA n.; DON JEM n.; HOUDINI n.[2]; JANE n.[3]; JOHNSON n.[4]; JUANITA n.; LUCY n.[2]; MAHARISHEE n.; MARGIE n.; MARIGOLD n.[2]; MARY AND JOHNNY n.; MARY ANN n.[3]; MARY JANE n.[2]; MARY WARNER n.; MARY WEAVER n.; MEG n.[2]; MR WARNER n.; M.J. n.; NIXON n.; ROSA MARIA n.; SWEET LUCY n.). [abbr. *marijuana*]

Aunt Mathilda n. [1970s+] (*US gay*) a middle-aged male homosexual (cf. AUNTIE n.[2]).

Aunt Minnie is visiting phr. *see* AUNT LILIAN VISITING phr.

Aunt Nora n. [1950s+] (*drugs*) cocaine (cf. BERNICE n.; BERNIE n.; BERNIE'S FLAKES n.; C n.[2]; CARRIE (NATION) n.; CECIL n.[2]; CHARLES n.[2]; CHARLIE n.[9]; CHARLIE BLOW n.; CHARLOTTE n.; CHAS n.; CHOLLY n.[2]; CORINNE n.; COUSIN CHARLIE n.; JANE n.[3]; LITTLE JOE (IN THE SNOW) n.; MARY JANE n.[2]; OLD MADGE n.[2]; PEDRO n.[2]; SCOTTY n.[1];

VITAMIN C n.). [ety. unknown; ? proper name or ? N of *Nora* and *ne* of cocaine; note cocaine is a 'feminine' drug, see GIRL n.²]

aunt pollys *n*. [2000s] (*US Black*) very small testicles. [ety. unknown]

Aunt Rose *n*. [1990s+] (*US*) menstruation. [AUNT n.² + proper name/colour]

Aunt Sally *n*. **1** [early 19C–1960s] (*US Black*) (*also* **Sal, Sally**) a subservient Black woman, happy to curry favour with Whites at the price of her autonomy. **2** [late 19C+] a scapegoat, often unfairly so. [SE *Aunt Sally*, 'a game much in vogue at fairs and races, in which the figure of a woman's head with a pipe in its mouth is set up, and the player, throwing sticks from a certain distance, aims at breaking the pipe' (*OED*). According to Ware, the original Aunt Sally was a black-faced doll, popular in early 19C London; its face also served as the shop-sign for a second-hand clothiers. The doll, in turn, came from Black Sal, a character created by Pierce Egan in *Life in London* (1821)]

Aunt Sam *n. see* UNCLE SAM n.¹.

Aunt Thomasina *n*. (*also* **Aunt Tom, Madame Thomasina**) [1960s+] (*orig. US Black*) a subservient, obsequious Black woman (cf. AUNT JEMIMA n.). [female var. on UNCLE TOM n. (1)]

aunt tillies *n*. [1940s] (*US*) an old-fashioned woman's nightgown. [the image of *Tillie* as an old-fashioned name, accentuated by pfx *Aunt*]

aunty *n. see* AUNTIE n.¹.

aurev *phr*. [1920s] goodbye. [abbr. Fr. *au revoir*]

aurium *n*. [mid-16C] (*UK Und.*) a wandering beggar posing as some type of priest. [? Lat. *aurius*, an ear, i.e. that which hears confession]

aurora borealis *n*. [1980s+] (*US drugs*) phencyclidine (cf. ACE n.⁴). [SE *aurora borealis*, the 'northern lights', lit. northern dawn, but note NORTHERN LIGHTS n.]

Aussie *n*. [1910s+] **1** *Australia*. **2** an *Australian*. [abbr.]

Aussie *adj*. [1910s+] Australian. [AUSSIE n. (2)]

Aussie kiss *n*. [2000s] (*Irish*) cunnilingus (cf. DOWNTOWN n.¹; GET DOWN v.³; GO DOWN v.⁶; GO DOWNSTAIRS FOR BREAKFAST v.; GO SOUTH v.²; GO UNDER THE HOUSE v.). [play on *down under*, i.e. the vagina/DOWN UNDER n. (1)]

Australian *n*. [1970s+] (*US gay*) **1** anilingus (cf. ASS BLOW v.; BOTTLE v.³; BROWN JOB n.²; BROWN OUT v.; BROWN WINGS n.; CLEAN UP THE KITCHEN v.; EAT v.³; EAT JAM v.; EAT OUT v.²; FELCH v.; GO SOUTH v.²; REAM JOB n.; RIM v.²; RIM JOB n.; ROSELEAF v.; TONGUE LASH v.; TONGUE SANDWICH n.; TOSSED SALAD n.; TOSS SALAD v.; WHITEWASH v.³). **2** an anilinguist. [punning on SE *down under/* DOWN UNDER n. (1)]

Australian active *n*. [1980s+] (*US gay*) the partner who performs anilingus; thus *Australian passive*, the one who receives. [AUSTRALIAN n. + SE *active/passive*]

Australian flag *n*. [late 19C–1910s] a shirt tail, protruding between the trousers and waistcoat. [like Australia, it is DOWN UNDER n./SE *down under*]

Australian salute *n*. [1970s+] (*Aus.*) a characteristic Aus. gesture of brushing away flies from one's face.

autem *n*. [mid-16C–mid-19C] (*UK Und.*) a church. [? SE *anthem* or ? Yid. *a'tume*, a forbidden church, although the Yid. may be a later coinage. Bee suggests Lat. *auditio*; E.P. opts for ALTHAM n. and a further theory suggests Fr. *autel*, an altar (note Fr. Und. *entonne*, church) and the SE *altar* may indeed be the actual root]

autem-bawler *n*. (*also* **autem-bawley**) [early 18C–mid-19C] a parson. [AUTEM n. + SE *bawl*, to shout]

autem-cackler *n*. (*also* **anthem-cackler**) [early 18C–19C] a dissenter, spec. a Puritan. [AUTEM n./SE *anthem* + SE *cackle*, to talk]

autem cackle tub *n*. **1** [early 18C–mid-19C] a conventicle or dissenters' meeting house. **2** [late 18C–mid-19C] a pulpit. [AUTEM-CACKLER n. + CACKLE TUB n.]

autem-cove *n*. **1** [mid-18C] (*UK Und.*) a married man. **2** [mid-19C] a preacher, a parson. [AUTEM n. + COVE n. (1)]

autem-dipper *n*. [17C–mid-19C] an Anabaptist. [AUTEM n. + the *dipping* of baptism]

autem-diver *n*. (*also* **anthem diver**) [early 18C–mid-19C] **1** a pickpocket specializing in the robbery of church congregations. **2** a churchwarden or other petty official charged with responsibility for distributing alms to the poor; their charges regarded them as little more than licensed robbers. [AUTEM n./SE *anthem* + DIVER n. (2)]

autem-gogler *n*. (*also* **autem-goggler**) [early 18C–mid-19C] (*UK Und.*) a fortune-teller, a conjuror. [AUTEM n. + GOGGLER n. (2)]

autem jet *n*. [early 18C–mid-19C] a parson. [AUTEM n. + SE *jet*, black, i.e. the black clerical gown]

autem mort *n*. (*also* **autem mot/mott**) [mid-16C–mid-19C] (*UK Und.*) a mistress, as in a woman who cohabits with a man, or accompanies a mendicant villain on his travels and in his crimes (cf. CANTING CREW n.). [AUTEM n. + MORT n., lit. a 'married woman', although there may never have been a ceremony. 'Shee is a wyfe married at the church and they be as chaste as a cowe, which gooeth to bull every month, with what bull she careth not' (Harman)]

autem prickear *n*. [early 18C–mid-19C] a dissenter, spec. a Puritan. [AUTEM n. + SE *prick-ear*, skullcap]

autem quaver *n*. [early 18C–mid-19C] a Quaker; thus *autem quaver tub*, a Quaker meeting house. [AUTEM n. + SE *quaver*, to shiver or tremble; Quakers 'tremble' at the word of the Lord]

autem sneak *n*. [early 19C] the robbery of churches or chapels. [AUTEM n. + SNEAK n.¹ (1)]

author *n*. [1980s+] (*US drugs*) an addict or doctor who writes illegal prescriptions for drug users.

auto *n*. [1980s+] (*US drugs*) a device consisting of an aquarium pump and an oxygen mask used to smoke cannabis. [SE *automatic*]

autograph *n*. [1950s] (*US drugs*) a narcotic injection. [it is 'written' in blood]

automobile *n. see* PONY n.³.

automobubble *n*. [20C+] (*US*) an automobile. [joc. mispron.]

autumn *n*. [mid-19C] death by hanging. [play on GO OFF WITH THE FALL OF THE LEAF v.]

auxiliary *n*. [1970s+] (*US gay*) the male genitals.

av *n*. [late 19C–1910s] (*US*) an avenue. [abbr.]

avachat *n*. [1980s] (*Aus.*) a chatterer. [rhy. sl.]

avast! *excl*. [late 17C–1920s] stop (what one is doing)! [naut. jargon *avast*, stop; ult. f. Du. *hou'vast*, *houd vast*, hold fast]

'ave a Jew boy's *n*. [1910s+] weight. [Cockney mispron. of SE *avoirdupois*]

ave Maria *n. see* ANNA MARIA n.

Avenoodles *n*. (*also* **Fifth Avenoodles**) [mid–late 19C] (*US*) the élite residents of New York City. [proper name Fifth Avenue, pron. 'avenoo' + SE *noodle*, a fool]

Avenue, the *n*. [1910s–50s] (*US*) Broadway, New York City.

avenue-tank *n*. [1940s] (*US Black/Harlem*) the double-decker buses on New York's Fifth Avenue route.

average bear, the *n*. [1980s+] (*US*) an average person. [the TV cartoon *Yogi Bear*, whose catchphrase was 'smarter than the average bear']

avo *n*. [1980s+] (*Aus./N.Z./S.Afr.*) an avocado pear. [abbr.]

avocados *n*. [1930s+] (*US*) the female breasts (cf. APPLES n.¹). [their shape]

avoirdupois-man *n*. [18C–early 19C] a thief of brass weights from shop counters; his profession was known as the *avoirdupois lay*. [*avoirdupois*, the standard system of weights used in the UK before metrication; it covered all goods except precious metals, precious stones and medicines]

avuncular adj. [mid-19C–1920s] (with ref. to) a pawnbroker; thus *avuncularism*, forced to use a pawnbroker. [play on UNCLE n.[1] (1)]

avvy n. (also **avvie**) [1990s+] the afternoon. [abbr.]

A.W. n. [2000s] (US prison) Aryan Warrior, a White supremacist prison gang (cf. A.B. n.[1]; A.C. n.). [abbr.]

awake adj. (also **a wake-up**) [early 19C+] aware, understanding, acquainted with, usu. of a (criminal) scheme.

awash adj. [1940s+] drunk.

away adj.[1] [late 19C+] **1** in prison; spec. (in London) any prison outside London. **2** (UK prison/police) escaped, from prison or police cells. **3** dead.

away adj.[2] **1** [1960s+] emotionally satisfied, usu. when intoxicated with drugs or drink. **2** [1990s+] successful, as in a seduction.

away adv. **1** [mid-19C+] straightaway, forthwith, directly, without hesitation or delay, esp. in imper., e.g. *fire away*, start talking, 'say your piece'; *right away*, at once, immediately. **2** [1900s] (US) as an intensifier, exceedingly.

away and claw mould on yourself! excl. [20C+] (Ulster) a general excl. of dismissal.

awayday girl n. [1990s+] a prostitute who lives outside London and commutes in to pick up clients in the metropolis (cf. BANKSIDE LADY n.; BATTERY GIRL n.; B-GIRL n.; BUSINESS GIRL n.; CALL-GIRL n.; COME-ON GIRL n.; CROSS-GIRL n.; FANCY GIRL n.; FANCY WOMAN n.; FANDANGO GIRL n.; FLASH GIRL n.[1]; FLY-GIRL n.; FRENCH GIRL n.; GIRL n.[1]; GOOD GIRL n.; JITNEY GIRL n.; JOY GIRL n.; ONE-WAY GIRL n.; PARLOR GIRL n.; PARTY GIRL n.; SHORT-TIME GIRL n.; SHUTTER-GIRL n.; TEN O'CLOCK GIRL n.; THREE-WAY GIRL n.; WORKING GIRL n.). [the cheap-rate 'away-day' train fares on which they depended]

away from home phr. [1990s+] of a (sexual) relationship, illicit, adulterous. [sports imagery]

away laughing phr. see LAUGHING adj.

away on a hack phr. (also **away in a hack**) [1930s+] (Irish) lucky, successful. [SE *hack*, a horse]

away to fuck! excl. (also **away to hell!**) [20C+] (mainly Scot./Irish) a general dismissive excl.

away to the fritz phr. see ON THE FRITZ phr. (3).

away to the hills phr. [20C+] (Irish) mentally unbalanced.

away with the band phr. [20C+] (Ulster) drunk.

away with the fairies phr. [20C+] (orig. Irish) **1** mentally unbalanced. **2** out of this world. [fig. uses of SE]

awerdenty n. [mid-19C+] (US) strong drink, often whisky, brandy. [Sp. *aguardiente*, strong water, thus brandy (*aguardiente* is more like a Spanish form of Italian *grappa* or French *marc*]

awesome adj. **1** [1920s+] (also **awes**) impressive, enormous, frightening. **2** [1970s+] (orig. US teen) wonderful, excellent, the best. [weak use of SE; the term gained a new currency, especial among the pre-teens, with the popularity c.1990 of the cartoon/film heroes Teenage Mutant Ninja Turtles, in which it featured heavily]

awesome! excl. [1980s+] an excl. used to indicate that something is very good. [AWESOME adj. (2)]

awfu adj. [1990s+] (US campus) unpleasant. [abbr. SE *awful*]

awful n. [mid–late 19C] a 'blood-and-thunder' romance, a 'penny dreadful'.

awful adj.[1] [19C] a general negative intensifier, orig. frightful, very ugly, monstrous. [SE by late 19C]

awful adj.[2] [late 19C+] excellent, first-rate. [AWFUL adj.[1]; an early version of the bad = good model that underpins such latterday sl. terms as BAD adj. (2)]

awful adv. [19C] awfully, very, extremely. [AWFUL adj.[1]]

awful doom n. [1900s] (Aus.) room, i.e. space. [rhy. sl.]

a-wiper n. [1960s] (US) a sycophant, a toady. [abbr. ASS-WIPER n. (1)]

'Awkins n. see HAWKINS n.[2].

awkward adj. [late 19C–1910s] pregnant.

awkward as a Chow on a bike phr. [1920s+] (Aus.) extremely clumsy, uncoordinated. [CHOW n.; the apparently unlikely pairing of Chinese immigrants and bicycles]

awl n. [17C] the penis. [SE *awl*, a tool for making holes in leather]

awning over the toy shop n. [1990s+] (Aus.) a male beer belly. [appearance; the *toy shop* is the genitals]

A.W.O.L. n. [1910s+] (US) a deserter. [A.W.O.L. adj.]

A.W.O.L. adj. (also **a.w.l.**) **1** [1910s+] (orig. milit.) absent without leave; also fig. use. **2** [1980s] *amour without love*, used by habituees of singles bars to denote their brief (strictly sexual) entanglements. [abbr.; coined during US Civil War, c.1863]

A word n. [1980s+] (US gay) AIDS. [on model of the 'F' word as a euph. for FUCK v.[1]]

awright! excl. [1960s+] that's good, I feel great etc. [phonetic trans. of US pron. of *all right* as a greeting or excl.]

awse adj. [1980s+] (US) wonderful, perfect, first-rate. [abbr. AWESOME adj. (2)]

ax n.[1] **1** [late 19C+] (US Und./Black) a knife, esp. a switchblade. **2** [1920s–40s] (US prison/UK Und.) a razor.

ax n.[2] [1910s–70s] (US) the penis; thus *axman*, a womanizer, a sexual athlete (cf. BATTERING PIECE n.; BAYONET n.; BAZOOKA n.[1]; BEEF BAYONET n.; BLADE n.[1]; BLOODHAMMER n.; BLUDGEON n.; BODKIN n.[1]; BOW n.; BROKEN ARROW n.; CANNON n.[1]; CLAM SPEAR n.; CULTY-GUN n.; CUTLASS n.; CUTTY GUN n.; DAGGER n.[1]; DINGBAT n.[10]; DRILL n.; FIXED BAYONET n.; GAFF n.[4]; GRISTLE HAMMER n.; GUIDED MISSILE n.; GUN n.[1]; HAMMER n.[1]; HAMMER-HANDLE n.; HAMMERHEAD n.[2]; HARPOON n.; HEAT-SEEKING (MOISTURE) MISSILE n.; IRON n.[1]; JACKHAMMER n.; JIZZ ROCKET n.; LAMB CANNON n.; LANCE n.; LANCE OF LOVE n.; LILAC LOVE LANCE n.; LOADED GUN n.; LOVE DART n.; LOVE GUN n.; LOVE TORPEDO n.; LOVE TRUNCHEON n.; MEAT AXE n.[2]; MEAT LANCE n.; MUSKET n.; MUTTON DAGGER n.; MUTTON GUN n.; MUTTON MUSKET n.; PEACEMAKER n.[1]; PEASHOOTER n.[2]; PIKE n.[1]; PINK TORPEDO n.; PISTOL n.[1]; POCKET ROCKET n.[2]; POLL AXE n.; PORK SWORD n.; PORRIDGE GUN n.; PORTABLE POCKET ROCKET n.; RAMROD n.; RED-HOT POKER n.; ROD n.[1]; ROGERING IRON n.; SENSITIVE TRUNCHEON n.; SHOOTING IRON n.; SLAUGHTERING-KNIFE n.; SPAM JAVELIN n.; SPUNKHAMMER n.; STICKY SPUD GUN n.; SWORD n.; TRIGGER n.[2]; WACKER n.; WALLOPER n.[1]; WATER PISTOL n.; WEAPON n.[1]; WHAMMER n.).

ax n.[3] (also **axe**) [1950s+] **1** (US Black) any musical instrument, esp. guitar. **2** ext. as any form of 'tool' with which one works, i.e. a typewriter. [orig. Black jazz use, when the instrument was more likely a saxophone or trumpet; the saxophone supposedly resembles an axe]

axe n. (also **ax**) [1910s+] dismissal, an act of dismissal.

axe v. (also **ax**) [1920s+] to close down, to terminate; to dismiss, esp. of businesses, jobs.

axe up v. [1980s] (Aus.) to share. [i.e. to cut up, to divide]

axe wound n. [1990s+] the vagina. [AX n.[2] + SE *wound*; note RMC Duntroon (Aus.) synon. *axe chop*, sexual intercourse from the male point of view, and *axe wank*, female masturbation; note Cleland, *Memoirs of a Woman of Pleasure* (1748–9): 'His hands convulsively squeez'd, opened, press'd together again the lips and sides of that deep flesh-wound']

axholder n. [late 19C+] (US) the hand.

axis n. [19C] the vagina, one of several terms noting the organ's bodily centrality (cf. CENTRAL CUT n.; CENTRE OF ATTRACTION n.; CENTRE OF BLISS n.; CENTRIQUE PART n.; MIDDLE CUT n.; MIDDLE KINGDOM n.; MIDLANDS n.).

axle n. [1930s–50s] the buttocks. [play on its position/ARSEHOLE n. (1)]

axle grease n. **1** [late 19C–1940s] (orig. Aus.) (also **pin-grease**) butter. **2** [20C+] semen. **3** [1920s+] (Aus.) (also **axle**) money. **4** [1930s+] a thick application used for one's hair.

axman n.[1] (also **axe man**) **1** [late 19C+] (orig. US Black) one who carries or wields a knife. **2** [1920s–40s] (US prison) a barber. [AX n.[1] + SE *man*]

axman *n.*[2] [1970s+] (*orig. US Black*) a musician, esp. a guitarist. [AX n.[3] (1) + SE *man*]

axman *n.*[3] *see* AX n.[2]

ayem *n. see* A.M. n.

Aylesbury (Duck) *n.* [1990s+] anything at all, nothing, i.e. euph. for a FUCK n.[4] [rhy. sl.]

Aylesbury'ed *adj.* [1990s+] exhausted. [rhy. sl.; *Aylesbury ducked* = FUCKED adj.[1] (2)]

a-yo! *excl.* [1990s+] a greeting. [? YO! excl. (2)]

Ayrab *n.* (*also* **A-rab**) [1940s+] (*US*) a derog. term for an Arab (cf. ABDUL n.). [deliberate mispron. and popularized in song 'Ahab the Ayrab' (1962) by Ray Stevens. While usu. used of Arabs or Muslim believers, occas. used by European Jews (Ashkenazis) of Eastern and North African Jews (Sephardis)]

ayraba *n. see* ARABBER n.

ayrton (senna) *n.* [1990s+] £10, a £10 note (cf. BIG BEN n.; COCK AND HEN n.; LOST AND FOUND n.; TONY BENN n.). [rhy. sl. = TENNER n. (1); ult. champion racing driver Ayrton Senna (1960–94)]

Aztec hop *n.* (*also* **Aztec two-step**) [1950s+] diarrhoea (cf. APPLE-BLOSSOM TWO-STEP n.; AZTEC REVENGE n.; BOMBAY BOTTOM n.; CURSE OF THE PHAROAHS n.; DELHI BELLY n.; FAR EAST TWO-STEP n.; GIs n.; GRINGO GALLOP n.; GYPPY TUMMY n.; HONG KONG DOG n.; MEXICALI REVENGE n.; MEXICAN FOXTROT n.; MEXICAN TOOTHACHE n.; MEXICAN TWO-STEP n.; MONTEZUMA'S REVENGE n.; RANGOON RUNS n.; SINGAPORE TUMMY n.; SPANISH TUMMY n.; TOURISTAS n.; TURKEY TROT n.; WOG GUT n.). [its supposed provenance in Mexico + pun on SE *trot*/TROTS, THE n.[2]]

Aztec revenge *n.* [2000s] diarrhoea (cf. AZTEC HOP n.). [see prev.]

azure *adj. see* BLUE adj.[3]

B

B *n.*[1] (*also* **bee**) [1950s+] (*drugs*) Benzedrine; thus *B-head*, a user of Benzedrine. [abbr.]

B *n.*[2] [1960s] (*Aus*) an MGB, the 'B' model of the MG sports car. [abbr.]

B *n.*[3] (*also* **bee**) [1960s+] (*drugs*) enough marijuana to fill a matchbox. [abbr. SE *box*]

B *n.*[4] [1970s–80s] (*US Black*) a Cadillac *Brougham*. [abbr.]

B *n.*[5] [1990s+] (*US Black*) a woman. [abbr. BITCH *n.*[1] (1)]

B *n.*[6] [1990s+] (*US Black*) a term of address, to either sex. [abbr. BLOOD *n.*[5] (3)]

b *n.*[1] [mid-19C] a bug. [abbr.]

b *n.*[2] **1** [late 19C] a kiss. **2** [1920s+] (*also* **bee**) a bastard. **3** [1940s] (*Aus.*) a bugger. [abbr.; (1) SE *buss*]

b *n.*[3] [1900s] a policeman. [abbr. BLUE *n.*[3] (2)]

b *n.*[4] [1960s] nonsense, rubbish. [abbr. BALLOCKS *n.*[2] (2)]

b *n.*[5] *see* BLUNT *n.*[3] (1).

b *adj.* (*also* **bee**) [1920s+] a euph. for BLOODY *adj.*[1] (1); thus also *bee aitch*, bloody hell, *bee eff*, bloody fool. [abbr.]

B-40 *n.* [1980s+] (*drugs*) a cigar laced with marijuana and dipped in malt liquor (cf. A-BOMB *n.*). [the bomber plane *B-40*, i.e. its effects]

b.a. *n.*[1] [1950s+] (*W.I., Guyn.*) a general term of great dislike. [abbr. SE *big* + ARSE *n.*[1] (5)]

b.a. *n.*[2] [1950s+] absolutely nothing. [abbr. BUGGER-ALL *n.*]

b.a. *n.*[3] *see* BULLSHIT ARTIST *n.*

b.a. *adj.* [1960s+] (*US*) naked. [abbr. BARE-ASS *adj.* (1)]

b.a. *v.* [1970s–80s] (*US campus, Calif.*) to expose one's buttocks for the purpose of evoking shock and/or amusement. [abbr. BARE-ASS *v.*]

baa cheat *n.* [early 18C] a sheep. [a sheep's *baa* + CHEAT *n.* (1)]

baa-lamb *n.*[1] [20C+] anyone mild, pleasing, amicable; often used by women of malleable men. [nursery use *baa-lamb*, a lamb]

baa-lamb *n.*[2] [20C+] a tram. [rhy. sl.]

baa-lamb *n.*[3] [1910s+] a euph. for BASTARD *n.* (1). [assonance]

baana *n.* [20C+] (*W.I., USVI*) the buttocks. [echoic of the 'bang' as one sits down]

baarie *n.* (*also* **bari, barry**) [1970s] (*S.Afr.*) a fool, one who has newly arrived at a township from the countryside. [Zulu sl. *ubari*, a bumpkin, an unsophisticated person]

bab *n.*[1] (*Aus./N.Z.*) **1** [1910s–60s] a cook. **2** [1920s+] a criminal. [rhy. sl.; abbr. BABBLER *n.*[1]]

bab *n.*[2] [1970s+] (*W.I.*) a policeman. [abbr. BABYLON *n.*[1] (2)]

baba *v.* [20C+] (*W.I.*) to dribble. [Sp. *baba*, spittle, slaver]

babalaas *n.* (*also* **babalazi, babelaas, bubblejas**) [1940s+] (*S.Afr*) a hangover; thus *babalaas/babalaased*, suffering from a hangover; *babalaasdop*, a drink taken to alleviate the hangover, the 'hair of the dog'. [Zulu *i-babalazi*, the after-effects of a drinking-bout]

babalonian *n. see* BABE-A-LONIAN *n.*

babania *n. see* BABONYA *n.*

babarton/babaton *n. see* BARBERTON *n.*

babbie-shop *n.* (*also* **babi-shop, bobbyshop**) [1970s+] (*S.Afr.*) an Indian-owned store. [Hind. *babu*, a gentleman, Mr; used derog. in Raj period for an Indian clerk + SE *shop*]

babbitt *n.* [1920s+] (*US*) a self-opinionated, self-satisfied small-town bourgeois, with all the prejudices of such a figure; thus n. *Babbitry*. [George F *Babbitt*, the hero of Sinclair Lewis's novel *Babbitt* (1922); *babbitt* appears itself to be a symbolic concoction of *babble* and *rabbit*, summarizing its bearer's qualities]

-babble *sfx* [1980s+] used to denote a variety of pretentious or incomprehensible jargon, e.g. *ecobabble*, *technobabble*. [on model of the slightly earlier PSYCHOBABBLE *n.*; ult. SE *babble*]

babbler *n.*[1] (*also* **babbling brook**) (*Aus./N.Z.*) **1** [20C+] a cook, esp. in an institution, mining camp or farm. **2** [1920s+] a criminal, a villain. [rhy. sl.; *babbling brook* = (1) SE *cook*; (2) CROOK *n.*[2] (2)]

babbler *n.*[2] [1930s] (*US campus*) a mediocrity, an unlikeable person. [? SE *babble*]

babe *n.* (*orig. US*) **1** [1910s+] a girl, girlfriend or young woman, esp. if attractive; thus *babe alert*, a warning to other men to note the approach of an attractive woman. **2** [1910s+] a form of address, irrespective of sex, e.g. *Where you goin', babe?* **3** [1910s+] (*also* **the babes**) something excellent, desirable. **4** [1980s+] used congratulatorily, a person of either sex (although still usu. female). **5** [1980s+] (*US campus*) an unpleasant woman. [the term entered sl. *c.*1915, waned somewhat after 1950 but gained a new lease of life, and began to refer to either sex, in the late 1980s; (2) Jim Thompson, *South of Heaven* (1967), has a cit. with a 1920s context]

babe-a-lonian *n.* (*also* **babalonian**) [1990s+] (*US campus*) a good-looking woman. [BABYLON *n.*[2]]

babe in the wood *n.* [late 17C–early 19C] one who is imprisoned in the stocks or pillory. [SE *babe* + the wooden construction of the stocks/pillory + pun on the title of the folktale]

babelaas *n. see* BABALAAS *n.*

babe lair *n.* [1990s+] (*US*) an apartment used by a man for the seduction of women. [BABE *n.* (1) + SE *lair*; coined in the skit (and later film) 'Wayne's World' on US TV *Saturday Night Live*, the major contemporary popularizer of the word *babe*]

babelicious *adj.* [1990s+] of a woman, very beautiful, very sexy. [BABE *n.* (1) + -LICIOUS sfx]

babe magnet *n.* (*also* **poontang magnet, shag magnet**) [1980s+] a man who is (or an object which makes a man) irresistibly alluring to a woman. [BABE *n.* (1)/POONTANG *n.* (3)/SHAG *n.*[1] (1) + MAGNET sfx]

babe of grace *n.* [early–mid-19C] one who looks 'holier-than-thou' but is not. [lit. 'child of grace']

baberton *n. see* BARBERTON *n.*

Babe Ruth *n.* [1970s–80s] (*N.Z. prison*) the truth. [rhy. sl.; ult. US baseball star George Herman *'Babe' Ruth* (1895–1948)]

babes *n.* [1930s+] a term of affection or simply of address between either sex. [BABE *n.* (2)]

babes, the *n. see* BABE *n.* (3).

babette *n.* [1970s+] (*US gay*) a very youthful-looking homosexual male. [BABE n. (1) + SE fem. sfx *-ette*]

babies *n.* [1980s+] (*US gay*) semen. [the fertilizing role of semen]

babi-shop *n. see* BABBIE-SHOP n.

babonya *n.* (*also* **babania**) [1970s+] (*US drugs*) drugs in general, spec. heroin. [Sicilian dial. *babonya*, the (bubonic) plague]

baboo *n. see* BABU n.

baboon *n.* **1** [early 16C+] a thug, a ruffian, a ne'er-do-well; thus *baboonish*, foolish. **2** [1930s] (*US Und.*) a very hard-working prostitute (cf. ALLEY CAT n.). [SE; like *ape*/APE n. (1), the *baboon* is stereotyped as an aggressive, thuggish creature]

baboon-faced *adj.* (*also* **baboon-visaged**) [1940s+] very ugly. [SE *baboon*]

babu *n.* (*also* **babu-man, baboo**) [20C+] (*W.I.*) **1** an old East Indian man, usu. bearded and poor. **2** an ugly old man. **3** an imaginary figure, ugly and old, conjured up to frighten children. [Hind. *babu*, a term of respect (Mr, Esquire) or an educated man]

baby *n.*[1] [19C] in cards, the Jack. [the Jack as the 'baby' of the King and Queen]

baby *n.*[2] **1** [mid-19C+] a bottle or glass of liquor; thus *kiss the baby*, to take a drink; *the baby is born*, there is enough money to buy a bottle. **2** [mid-19C+] a small or half-sized bottle, whether of spirits or a non-alcoholic drink, orig. soda water; thus *baby and nurse*, a small bottle of soda water with twopennyworth of spirits. **3** [1930s] (*US*) a glass of milk.

baby *n.*[3] **1** [mid-19C+] (*orig. US*) a person, often a woman. **2** [late 19C+] (*orig. US*) a person, occas. an object or an animal, of one's affection. **3** [late 19C+] (*US, mainly Black*) a term of affection or general address between people of any sex. **4** [20C+] (*US*) a person, often self-referential as in *this baby*. **5** [1900s–30s] (*US*) an object of excellence. **6** [1920s+] (*orig. US*) an otherwise unnamed item or object, esp. used of automobiles, weapons and machinery. **7** [1920s+] (*orig. US*) one's special interest or responsibility, usu. with the possessive pronoun, e.g. *it's my baby*. **8** [1960s+] (*US gay*) an under-age/teenage boy. **9** [1970s] (*US*) an attractive young woman.

baby *n.*[4] [1960s+] (*drugs*) marijuana. [BABY n.[3] (2), as a term of affection for the drug]

baby *adj.* [late 19C+] small.

baby-ass *adj.* [1990s+] (*US Black*) childish. [SE *baby* + -ASS sfx]

baby Benz *n.* [1980s+] (*US Black*) the Mercedes Benz model 190E, which is small and sporty. [BABY adj. + BENZ n.]

baby bhang *n.* [1980s] (*drugs*) marijuana. [BABY adj. + BHANG n.; the implication is of inferior potency]

baby-blues *n.*[1] (*also* **icy-blues**) (*orig. US*) human eyes, irrespective of their actual colour. [SE *baby-blue*, a light shade of blue, often associated with a baby's eyes; the implication is of candour and innocence]

baby-blues *n.*[2] [1950s] (*US*) a policeman (cf. BLACKJACK n.[4]; BLUE n.[3]; BLUEBELLY n.; BLUEBIRD n.[1]; BLUEBOTTLE n.; BLUE BOY n.[2]; BLUE CAP n.[2]; BLUECOAT n.; BLUE DEVIL n.[1]; BLUE HEELER n.; BLUEJACKET n.[1]; BLUE LAMP (BOY) n.; BLUE LIGHT n.[2]; BLUE MEANIE n.; BLUESUIT n.; BLUEY n.[1]; BOYS IN BLUE n.; BRASS BUTTONS n.; BROWN BOMBER n.[1]; BUTTONS n.[1]; CLOTHES n.; GENTLEMAN IN BLUE n.; GREEN BEAN n.[2]; GREEN HORNET n.; GREY GHOST n.; JOHN BLUEBOTTLE n.; KHAKI n.[4]; RAW LOBSTER n.; SKY n.[2]; SUIT n.[4]; UNBOILED LOBSTER n.[1]; UNIFORM n.; WOODPECKER n.[2]). [play on SE *baby-blues*/BLUES n.[2] (1)]

baby bonus *n.* [1940s+] (*Aus./Can.*) a family allowance.

baby bouillon *n. see* BABY GRAVY n.

baby buggy *n.* [1970s+] (*US gay*) a convertible sports car. [play on SE]

baby bumpers *n.* [1960s+] the female breasts. [SE *baby* + *bumper*, a railway buffer]

baby buster *n.* [1980s+] one who was born in the period after the *baby boom* that followed WW2, thus one born during a baby bust. [on analogy of the *boom* and *bust* of economic jargon]

baby butch *n.* [1960s+] (*US gay*) a young, boyish lesbian. [BABY adj. + BUTCH n.[4] (3)]

baby button *n.* [1960s+] the navel. [the umbilical cord, connecting baby to mother]

babycakes *n.* (*also* **cakes, cakie**) [1960s+] (*US*) **1** a term of affection between friends (cf. CAKE n.[5]). **2** a (pretty) young woman or a handsome young man. [SE *baby* + *cake*; so intimate a friend is 'good enough to eat']

baby-catcher *n.* (*US*) **1** [1930s–70s] a midwife. **2** [1960s–70s] a doctor.

baby chick farm *n.* [1950s] (*US Black*) 'the locations or towns where the girls look fine from a young age on' (Durst, *The Jives of Dr Hepcat*, 1953). [SE *baby* + pun on SE *chick*/CHICK n.[4] (2) + *farm*]

baby child *n.* (*US Black*) **1** [1920s+] a baby; a child. **2** [1970s+] a younger, less respected or less experienced individual. **3** [1970s+] an immature person.

baby chute *n.* [1990s+] the vagina (cf. BABY-MAKER n.; BATH OF BIRTH n.; BRAT-GETTING PLACE n.; CERTIFICATE OF BIRTH n.; GENERATING PLACE n.; INSTRUMENT (OF GENERATION) n.; NURSERY n.).

baby crew *n.* [1980s+] the junior member of a hooligan gang. [BABY adj. + CREW n. (3)]

baby crockett *n.* [1970s+] (*camp gay*) a fake cowboy. [proper name of *Davy Crockett* (1786–1836), the 19C Western hero, whose adventures were fictionalized in the 1950s US TV series]

baby-daddy *n. see* BABY-FATHER n.

baby-doll *n.* **1** [20C+] (*US*) a girl, a woman, esp. when attractive. **2** [20C+] a direct term of address. **3** [1920s] a success. **4** [1980s+] (*US gay*) an attractive male. [SE *baby* + DOLL n.[1] (5)]

baby dolls *n.* [1940s] (*US*) a style of high-heeled women's shoes.

baby-dreads *n.* [1990s+] (*US Black*) a short version of the braided hair worn by Rastafarians. [BABY adj. + DREAD n.[2] (5)]

baby dyke *n.* [1970s+] (*US gay*) a young, inexperienced lesbian. [BABY adj. + DYKE n.]

baby factory *n.* [1990s+] (*US Black*) a woman who has had a large number of children.

baby-farmer *n.* [20C+] an older person, usu. a woman, who prefers affairs with people much younger than themselves. [play on SE *baby-farmer*, one who reared orphan children, often in atrocious conditions]

baby-father *n.* (*also* **baby-daddy, baby-poppa**) [1970s+] (*UK/US Black, orig. W.I.*) a boyfriend, esp. the father of one's child although not one's legal husband.

baby-fetcher *n.* [1910s+] the penis (cf. BABY-MAKER n.; BRAT-GETTER n.; CHILD-GETTER n.; INSTRUMENT (OF GENERATION) n.).

baby fluid *n.* [1930s] (*US*) semen (cf. BABY GRAVY n.; COCK JUICE n.; COME-JUICE n.; DOG WATER n.; FRENCH-FRIED ICE WATER n.; FRUIT JUICE n.; JIZZWATER n.; JUICE n.[2]; JUNGLE JUICE n.; LETCH-WATER n.; LOVE JUICE n.; MONKEY-JUICE n.; PUD WATER n.; RINSE n.[1]; SPAM JUICE n.; SPUD JUICE n.[2]; SPUDWATER n.; WATER OF LIFE n.).

baby gangster *n.* [2000s] (*US Black/teen*) a gang member who has yet to commit a murder.

baby gravy *n.* (*also* **baby bouillon**) [1990s+] semen (cf. BALLOCK GRAVY n.; BATTER n.[1]; BEEF GRAVY n.; BEER n.; BOLLOCK YOGHURT n.; BUTTER n.[1]; COCK SAUCE n.; COCOA n.[2]; CREAM n.[1]; CREAMED BEEF n.; CUSTARD n.; DUCK BUTTER n.; EGG-WHITE n.; FISH n.[10]; FRENCH DRESSING n.; FRENCH-FRIED ICE-CREAM n.; FRENCH-FRIED ICE WATER n.; FRUIT JUICE n.; FUCKSAUCE n.; GNAT BUTTER n.; GORILLA MILK n.; GRAVY n.[1]; HONEY n.[2]; HOT MILK n.; ICE-CREAM n.[2]; JAM n.[7]; JELLY n.[1]; LIVING SAUCE n.; LOVE CUSTARD n.; MELTED BUTTER n.[1]; MILK n.[1]; MILT n.; NAD-JAM n.; NECTAR n.; NUT-BUTTER n.; OYSTER n.[2]; PINEAPPLE CHUNK n.; PUDDING n.[1]; PUD WATER n.; ROE n.; SAUCE n.[2]; SOUL SAUCE n.; SPANISH RICE n.; SPUD JUICE n.[2]; SPUDWATER n.; STARCH n.; SUGAR n.[4]; VINEGAR n.[2]; WHIPPED CREAM n.). [SE *baby* + SE *gravy*/GRAVY n.[1] (2)/SE *bouillon*]

baby in the boat *n.* [1930s] the clitoris; thus *kiss the baby in the boat*, to perform cunnilingus (cf. BALD MAN IN A BOAT n.; BEAN n.[4]; BELL n.[1]; BOY IN THE BOAT n.; BUTTON n.[1]; CHUNKY SHRIMP n.; COCK PIT n.; DICK n.[8]; DINGLEBERRY n.; DOT n.[2]; FUN-BUTTON n.; JOY BUTTON n.; LITTLE MAN (IN THE BOAT) n.; LITTLE PLOUGHMAN n.; LITTLE SHAME TONGUE n.; LOVE BUTTON n.; LULLO-BUMP n.; NUTS n.[2]; SKIPPER n.[5]; TASTE BUD n.).

baby in the bushes *n.* [1970s+] (*US*) an illegitimate child. [such a baby is trad. conceived and/or delivered in the bushes]

baby jane *n.* [1990s+] (*US*) a child or underage female prostitute (cf. BLACK MARIA n.[2]; BROWN BESSIE n.; CHARLIE n.[10]; COLUMBINE n.; COUSIN BETTY n.; DOLL TEARSHEET n.; DOLLY n.[1]; DOLLY BOY n.; GERTIE n.; JACK n.[12]; JACK'S DELIGHT n.; JACK-WHORE n.; JUDE n.; JUDY n.[1]; KATE n.[1]; KELSEY n.; KITTIE n.; MADAM VAN n.; MADGE HOWLET n.; MAGGIE n.[1]; MAID MARIAN n.; MAUD n.; MOLL n.[1]; MOLLY n.[1]; NANNY n.[1]; POLL n.[2]; POLLY n.[1]; RITA n.; SUSAN SALIVA n.; TOM n.[7]; TOMMY n.[6]). [SE *baby* + generic use of proper name]

baby Jesus, the *n. see* BEJAZUS, THE n.

baby-kisser *n.* [1940s+] (*US Black*) a politician. [the campaigning politician's propensity to believe that the babies encountered enjoy being kissed by a total stranger]

baby life *n.* [1950s+] (*US prison*) the maximum sentence that prisoners must serve (6 years, 4 months) before a parole board is bound to consider their case for the first time. [BABY adj. + LIFE n. (1)]

Babylon *n.*[1] **1** [mid-19C+] the hedonistic, exciting world of the city, as opposed to the quietness of the countryside; spec. London. **2** [1940s+] (*orig. W.I., then UK/US Black*) the police; prison warder. **3** [1950s+] a generic term for White Western society. **4** [1970s+] any oppression or the forces that oppress the Black (esp. Rastafarian) man. **5** [1970s+] anyone perceived as putting material gains before spiritual ones. [*Babylon*, the ancient capital of Mesopotamia and used fig. to imply sinful luxury, esp. by the Church of Rome. In Rastafarian iconography Babylon is opposed to Zion – the promised land of Africa, esp. Ethiopia]

Babylon *n.*[2] [1980s+] anywhere that attractive women are supposed to congregate or, mythically, are supposed to have their origin. [BABE n. (1); pron. *Babe-y-lon*]

Babylon House *n.* [2000s] a police station. [BABYLON n.[1]]

Babylon-land *n.* [1970s+] (*W.I.*) any country, typically a materialist Western state, seen by Rastafarians as corrupt and materialistic. [BABYLON n.[1] (3) + SE *land*]

baby-maker *n.* **1** [late 19C–1900s] (*also* **lady-maker**) the penis (cf. BABY-FETCHER n.). **2** [late 19C–1900s] the vagina (cf. BABY CHUTE n.). **3** [1960s] a sexually powerful man. **4** (*also* **BM**) [1970s+] (*S.Afr. gay*) a heterosexual. [the procreative function of the organ]

baby-mother *n.* (*also* **baby momma, baby mamma**) [1980s+] (*orig. UK Black*) a girlfriend, spec. the woman who has one's baby but with whom one may not actually live.

baby-o *n.* [1960s] a general term of address, usu. to a woman. [BABY n.[3] (3) + -O sfx (1)]

baby paps *n.* (*also* **baby's pap**) [mid-19C–1910s] caps. [rhy. sl.; ? resemblance of a cap to the breast]

baby paste *n.* [1970s+] (*US gay*) semen.

baby poppa *n. see* BABY-FATHER n.

baby pro *n.* [1970s+] (*US*) **1** a prostitute under the age of legal consent. **2** the profession of child prostitution. [SE *baby* + *pro*(*stitute*)]

baby-rape *n.* [1960s+] (*US*) statutory rape. [SE *baby-rape*, paedophilia]

baby-raper *n.* [1950s+] (*US*) **1** a man who commits statutory rape. **2** a general derog. term of abuse; thus *baby-raping*, of a person, despicable, disgusting. [BABY-RAPE n.]

baby's arm *n.* [1960s+] the penis, esp. when large (cf. ARM n.[1]). [resemblance]

baby's cries *n.* [1920s+] the eyes. [rhy. sl.]

baby's done it *n.* [1940s+] (*bingo*) the number 2 (cf. ALDERSHOT LADIES n.). [a pun on NUMBER TWO n.[1] (1)]

baby's head *n.* [1910s–60s] steak and kidney pudding. [the supposed resemblance, presumably that of the smooth suet pastry top rather than the meat and gravy it contains]

babysit *v.* **1** [1960s+] (*drugs*) to take care of someone either under the influence of a drug (esp. the hallucinogenic LSD) or, more often, recovering from an unpleasant, drug-induced experience. **2** [1980s+] to monitor progress, to take care of, to watch over.

babysitter *n.* **1** [20C+] (*Can.*) a prison officer. **2** [1980s] (*US drugs*) someone who hides drugs temporarily during importation from one country or area to another. [ironic use of SE]

baby-skull *n.* [1900s] (*US campus*) an apple dumpling. [the supposed resemblance]

baby's leg *n.* [late 19C+] meat loaf, jam roly-poly. [the supposed resemblance]

baby-snatcher *n.* [1920s+] (*US*) an obstetrician. [ironic use of SE *baby-snatcher*, a kidnapper]

baby-snatching *n.* [1920s+] of either sex, marrying or having an affair with someone much younger than oneself; thus *baby-snatcher*, one who marries a noticeably younger partner.

baby('s) pap *n. see* BABY PAPS n.

baby's pram *n.* [20C+] jam. [rhy. sl.]

baby's public house *n.* [late 19C–1900s] the female breasts.

bacca *n.* (*also* **baccer, bacco, baccy, backee, backer**) [late 17C+] tobacco. [abbr.]

bacca-box *n.* (*also* **baccy-box**) [1900s–20s] **1** the mouth. **2** the nose. [BACCA n. + SE *box*; (2) presumably f. snuff rather than tobacco]

bacca-pipes *n.* [mid–late 19C] whiskers curled in small, close ringlets. [BACCA n. + SE *pipe*; the similarity to a type of *tobacco-pipe*]

baccare! *excl.* [mid-16C–mid-17C] go back! [cod Lat.]

baccer *n. see* BACCA n.

bacchus marsh *n.* [1990s+] (*Aus.*) a semi-erect penis. [*Bacchus Marsh*, a town half-way between Melbourne and Ballarat]

bacco *n. see* BACCA n.

baccy *see under* BACCA and its combs.

baccy stick *n.* [late 19C] (*US*) the human leg. [tobacco was orig. sold in short twists a few inches long]

bach *n.*[1] (*also* **bache, batch**) [mid-19C–1940s] (*US*) a *bach*elor; thus *old bach*, a confirmed bachelor. [abbr.]

bach *n.*[2] [1920s+] (*N.Z.*) **1** a farm-worker's cottage. **2** a weekend cottage. [i.e. a *bach*elor pad]

bachelor's baby *n.* [mid-19C+] an illegitimate child.

bachelor's buttons *n.* [late 16C–17C] a foetus, presumably of an illegitimate child. [? SE phr. *wear bachelor's buttons*, to be unmarried]

bachelor's fare *n.* (*also* **batchelor's fare**) [late 18C–early 19C] bread and cheese and kisses.

bachelor's son *n.* (*also* **batchelor's son**) [late 17C–18C] an illegitimate child. [euph.]

bachelor's wife *n.* [1950s+] (*US*) a metal plunger with a long wooden handle, used for washing clothes in a tub. [the implement performs the stereotypically wifely chore]

bachie *n.* [20C+] (*W.I.*) a room or any small place kept by a man for solo living or for conducting love affairs away from the family home; thus *live bachie*, to live alone. [abbr. SE *bachelor*]

bach (it) *v.* [late 19C+] (*orig. US*) to live by oneself. [BACH n.[1]]

back *n.*[1] **1** [20C+] a painful or 'bad' back. **2** [1980s] the anus (cf. ARSE-END n.). **3** [1990s+] (*US Black*) the posterior, the buttocks; thus *baby's got back*, used to remark favourably on a woman's posterior. [note the 17C use of a strong *back* to imply a woman's sexual strength]

back *n.*[2] [1960s] a dollar bill. [abbr. GREENBACK n.[2] (1)]

back *n.*[3] [1980s] (*US drugs*) *back*-up, help. [abbr.]

back *adj.*[1] [1930s–50s] (*US Black*) well-established, traditional, tried and tested. [abbr. WAY BACK *adj.*]

back *adj.*[2] [1940s+] (*US*) served and drunk alongside or together with an alcoholic drink, usu. as an order to the barman, e.g. *Scotch with soda back.*

back *v.* [mid–late 17C] to have sexual intercourse. [SE *back*, to cover or to copulate]

back *adv.* [1940s+] (*US Black*) really, very much, completely.

back-a-bush *adj.* [20C+] (*W.I., Jam.*) far away, deep in the countryside, in the 'back of beyond'.

back-ah-yard *n.* 1 [1930s] (*US*) a poor area of the city. 2 [1960s+] (*W.I.*) the Caribbean. 3 [1960s+] (*W.I.*) home. [SE *back* + SE *yard*, garden]

back alley *n.* [late 19C+] (*US Black*) the main street of an otherwise run-down or red-light area. [a term of approval, *back alley* is another variety of the Black reversal of White values]

back-alley deal *n.* [late 19C+] (*US Black*) a deal between one unsuspecting victim and the person who intends on and succeeds in cheating them.

back-and-belly *n.*[1] [1950s] (*W.I.*) a hypocrite, an untrustworthy person. [dial. *back and belly*, a double-edged machete, which can cut with either edge and is thus 'two-faced']

back-and-belly *n.*[2] [1950s] (*W.I.*) a very thin person. [for ety. see BACK-AND-BELLY *n.*[1]]

back and fill *v.* (*Aus./US*) 1 [mid-19C+] to vacillate. 2 [1940s+] to charm a potential victim before subjecting them to a confidence trick. [SE *back and fill*, to go backwards and forwards; thus the trickster bemuses the victim with a lengthy, convoluted patter]

back-and-front *n.* [1950s] (*W.I.*) a hypocrite. [var. on BACK-AND-BELLY *n.*[1]]

back-and-neck *n.* [20C+] (*W.I., St Kitts*) a very thin person. [the back and neck of a chicken, the cheapest portion available and one that is almost devoid of meat]

back-assward *adj.* (*also* **back-asswards**) [1940s+] (*US*) confused, muddled, backwards (cf. BASS-ACKWARDS *adj.*). [joc. reversal of ASS BACKWARD(S) *phr.* emphasizing the meaning]

back a tail *v.* [1960s+] (*Aus.*) to sodomize. [SE *back*, to mount from behind + TAIL *n.*[2] (1)]

backbeat *n.* [1970s] (*US Black*) 1 an underlying theme or quality. 2 one's heartbeat. [jazz use *backbeat*, a secondary beat that underlies the main theme]

backbeat of the trey thirty *phr.* [1940s] (*US Black/Harlem*) the third day of the month.

back bottie *n.* [1980s] (*Aus.*) the anus (cf. ARSE-END *n.*). [on pattern of FRONT BOTTOM *n.*]

back-buster *n.* [1960s+] (*US*) a dive in which one lands flat on the water (cf. ASS-BREAKER *n.*).

backcap *n.* [late 19C+] (*US*) 1 an insult based on attacking the subject's family. 2 a sharp or witty reply, as offered in the ritual name-calling known as the dozens. [it 'caps' the previous statement]

backcap *v.* (*US*) 1 [late 19C+] to insult someone by disparaging their family. 2 [late 19C–1900s] to speak evil of someone, so as to spoil their game. [BACKCAP *n.*]

backchat *n.*[1] [20C+] cheek, impudence, malicious gossip. [SE *back* + *chat*; ? orig. milit. use]

backchat *n.*[2] [1930s] (*UK Und.*) the back door.

backchat *v.* [1910s+] (*Aus.*) to answer back. [BACKCHAT *n.*[1]]

back-cheat *n.* [early 18C–early 19C] (*UK Und.*) a cloak. [SE *back* + CHEAT *n.* (1), lit. 'back thing']

backclap *v.* [late 19C] to insult someone or disparage something. [SE *back* + 14C SE *clap*, to talk loudly, chatter]

back door *n.* 1 [late 16C+] (*also* **back way**) the anus; thus *go up the back door*, to have heterosexual anal intercourse (cf. ARSE-END *n.*). 2 [mid-19C] (*also* **back premises**) the vagina. [pun on SE]

back-door *adj.* [1920s+] (*US Black*) devious, cunning, untrustworthy, usu. in combs., e.g. BACK-DOOR ARTIST *n.* [*back door*, while often referring to the anus in White use, almost always means underhand or secretive for Blacks]

backdoor *v.*[1] [early 18C; 1960s+] to subject to anal intercourse (cf. ASK FOR THE RING *v.*). 2 [1960s] to accuse, to inform. [BACK DOOR *n.*]

backdoor *v.*[2] [1980s+] (*Aus. prison*) for one prisoner – just released – to cuckold one who remains imprisoned. [BACK-DOOR MAN *n.*[1]]

back-door action *n.* 1 [1940s+] sodomy. 2 [1970s+] (*US*) adultery (cf. BACK-DOOR MAN *n.*[1]). [BACK DOOR *n.* (1)/SE *back-door* + ACTION *sfx*]

back-door artist *n.* [1940s–60s] (*US Black/drugs*) a drug addict who preys on fellow addicts for money or drugs. [BACK-DOOR *adj.* + ARTIST *sfx*]

back-door commando *n.* (*also* **back-door merchant**) [1990s+] a male homosexual (cf. ANAL ASTRONAUT *n.*). [BACK DOOR *n.* (1) + SE *commando*/MERCHANT *n.*]

back-dooring *n.* [1980s] (*US*) adultery. [BACK-DOOR ACTION *n.* (2)]

backdoor jive *n.* [1940s] (*US Black*) (inside) information. [BACK-DOOR *adj.* + JIVE *n.*[1] (3)]

back-door kicker *n.* [1990s+] a male homosexual (cf. ANAL ASTRONAUT *n.*). [BACK DOOR *n.* (1) + SE *kicker*]

back-door man *n.*[1] (*also* **backdoor merchant**) [1920s+] (*orig. US Black*) an adulterer (cf. BACK-DOOR ACTION *n.*). [he comes in 'through the back door']

back-door man *n.*[2] [1960s+] one who practises anal intercourse; in homosexual anal sex, the active partner. [BACK DOOR *n.* (1) + SE *man*; note synon. RMC Duntroon (Aus.) *man at the back door*]

back-door merchant *n. see* BACK-DOOR COMMANDO *n.*

back-door parole *n.* [1930s+] (*US prison*) 1 dying in prison before one's sentence is over (cf. BACK-GATE PAROLE *n.*). 2 parole. [SE *back-door*, clandestine + *parole*; the remains of those who die in prison are taken out surreptitiously and buried in the prison cemetery]

back-door trot *n.* (*also* **back-door trots**) 1 [19C+] diarrhoea. 2 [1950s+] over-frequent urination. [BACK DOOR *n.* (1)/SE *backdoor* that leads to the privy + SE *trot*/TROTS, THE *n.*[2]]

back-door trumpet *n.* [mid-19C+] the anus (cf. ARSE-END *n.*). [BACK DOOR *n.* (1) + SE *trumpet*; the 'tune' it plays is, of course, a FART *n.* (1)]

back-door work *n.* [late 19C+] anal intercourse, sodomy. [BACK DOOR *n.* (1) + SE *work*]

back double *n.* [late 19C+] a back street. [SE *back* + *double*, a twist or turn]

backed *adj.*[1] [late 17C–early 19C] dead. [either f. lying on one's *back*, or, according to B.E. and then Grose (1785), f. being supported on the *backs* of those who carry one's coffin; SE *backed*, supported at the back, underpins the latter ety.]

backed *adj.*[2] [1990s+] (*US campus*) intoxicated by marijuana. [one is 'knocked back/on one's back' by the strength]

backed-up *adj.* [late 19C+] (*US*) constipated. [SE *backed up* (usu. of water or of traffic), having met an obstruction in the flow]

backee *n. see* BACCA *n.*

back-end-to *adj.* [1920s+] (*US*) in confusion.

back entrance *n.* (*also* **back gate**) [late 19C+] the anus (cf. ARSE-END *n.*).

backer *n.*[1] [1990s+] (*UK/Irish juv.*) a lift on the back of a bicycle. [one is on the 'back seat']

backer *n.*[2] *see* BACCA *n.*

back eye *n.* [1960s+] 1 the anus (cf. ARSE-END *n.*). 2 anal intercourse. [SE *back* + EYE *sfx*]

backfire *v.* [1970s+] to break wind; also, in fig. use, to speak abusively. [SE *backfire*, for an internal-combustion engine to ignite prematurely; such ignition causes a loud explosion]

back forty *n.* [1950s+] (*US*) an out-of-the-way, usu. barren, piece of land. [SE *back*, out of the way + *forty*, a plot of 40 acres (16 hectares)]

backgammoner *n.* [early–mid-19C] a sodomite, one who practises anal intercourse. [pun on SE]

backgammon-player *n.* [mid-17C–19C] a sodomite. [pun on SE + SE *gammon*, the bottom piece of a flitch of bacon, including the hind leg]

back gate *n. see* BACK ENTRANCE *n.*

back-gate parole *n.* (*also* back-gate commute, ...discharge, ...exit, south-gate discharge) [1920s+] (*US prison*) an inmate's death in prison (cf. BACK-DOOR PAROLE *n.*). [dead prisoners are taken out through the back gate of the prison and buried without ceremony]

back-hairing *n.* [1900s] fighting among women. [such fights often involve the pulling of the long hair at the back of a woman's head]

back-hand *v.*[1] [mid-19C–1900s] to drink more than one's share. [BACK-HANDER *n.* (2)]

back-hand *v.*[2] [1960s+] to give a bribe. [BACK-HANDER *n.* (4)]

backhand drive *v.* [1940s+] (*US gay*) to poke someone between the buttocks.

back-hander *n.* **1** [early 19C] a slap or blow in the face with the back of the hand. **2** [mid–late 19C] a drink taken out of turn or an extra drink taken while the decanter circulates. **3** [mid-19C+] in fig. use, a comment that is underhand. **4** [1910s+] a bribe, a payoff for services rendered. [all are given with or out of the back of the hand]

backhouse *n.* (*also* back-house) [late 16C; 20C+] a privy (cf. BOGHOUSE *n.*; BOG-SHOP *n.*; CALIFORNIA HOUSE *n.*; CARSEY *n.*; CASE *n.*[3]; COFFEE-HOUSE *n.*; COFFEE-SHOP *n.*[1]; COTTAGE *n.*; CRAPHOUSE *n.*; CRAPPING CASA *n.*; CRAPPING KEN *n.*; DOLLAR HOUSE *n.*; DOLL HOUSE *n.*[1]; DUNNAKEN *n.*; DUNNIGAN *n.*; GARDEN HOUSE *n.*[2]; GONG HOUSE *n.*; GREENHOUSE *n.*[1]; HONEY HOUSE *n.*; HOUSE OF COMMONS *n.*; HOUSE OF EASEMENT *n.*; HOUSE OF OFFICE *n.*; HOUSE OF WAX *n.*; IVY COTTAGE *n.*; JAKEHOUSE *n.*; JOHNNY HOUSE *n.*; LEAKHOUSE *n.*; LITTLE HOUSE *n.*; NECESSARY HOUSE *n.*; PARLIAMENT (HOUSE) *n.*; PETTY HOUSE *n.*; PISSHOUSE *n.*; SHITHOUSE *n.*; SHOUSE *n.*; SNAKE'S HOUSE *n.*; STATE HOUSE *n.*). [its position behind the house; 20C+ use is US]

back in one's cart *v.* [1910s–20s] (*Aus.*) to butt in, to ask for more.

back in the day(s) *phr.* [1990s+] (*orig. US Black teen*) a synon. for 'once upon a time'.

back in the saddle (again) *phr.* [1950s–70s] (*US*) menstruating. [SE phr. *back in the saddle*, getting back to a regular routine; ? milit. or cowboy use]

back in the woods *phr.* [1960s+] (*US*) unsophisticated, gauche. [the stereotype of those who live there]

backitive *n.* [1990s+] (*W.I.*) collateral, in the form of money or contacts. [something/someone that 'backs one up']

back-jaw *n.* [1950s+] (*US Black*) an insolent reply. [BACK-JAW *v.*]

back-jaw *v.* [1920s+] (*US Black*) to answer back rudely. [SE *back* + JAW *v.*[1] (1)]

back-jump *n.*[1] [19C] a back window, spec. a prison window. [SE *back* + JUMP *n.*[1] (3); presumably from the robber or villain jumping out through the window]

back-jump *n.*[2] [1950s+] (*US Black*) anal intercourse, either hetero- or homosexual. [SE *back* + JUMP *n.*[3] (1)]

back-jump *v.* [late 19C] to enter a house by a back entrance, either a door or window; thus *back-jumper*, a thief who enters houses via a back door or window. [BACK-JUMP *n.*[1]]

back-land *n.* [late 17C–mid-19C] (*W.I.*) the buttocks (cf. ARSE-END *n.*). [pun on SE]

backlip *n.* [1950s–70s] (*US*) cheek, insolence.

backlip *v.* [1950s] (*US*) to cheek, to speak insolently to. [SE *back* + LIP *n.*[1] (1)]

backlog *n.* [1960s] (*US*) a wife. [17C SE *backlog*, a large log that

rests at the back of the fire and provides steady heat as its burns. As she lies in bed, a wife provides a similar function]

backmark *n.* [1950s+] (*US Black/prison*) **1** an undesirable characteristic. **2** an informer, esp. in prison. [SE *back* + *mark*; in both senses the image is of secrecy and deliberate concealment]

back number *n.* [late 19C+] an irrelevant person, a 'has-been', a person or thing that is behind the times, out-of-date or useless; also used of a former lover, now discarded. [the previous and thus 'dead' editions of newspapers]

back-number *adj.* [late 19C+] old-fashioned, out-of-date. [BACK NUMBER *n.*]

back-number *v.* [1900s] to discard. [BACK NUMBER *n.*]

back of beyond *n.* [early 19C+] anywhere considered by the speaker as inaccessible, outside the purlieus of acceptable life. ['civilization' is implied]

back of Bourke *n.* (*also* back of Burke, Back o' Sunset, other side of Bourke, out back o' sunset) [20C+] a long way away, a place far away; also used as a phr. meaning far far away. [proper name *Bourke*, a town in the extreme west of New South Wales/SE *sunset*]

back off! *excl.* [1950s+] (*orig. US Black*) go away! stop bothering me!

back off Jackson! *excl.* [1990s+] (*US teen*) calm down! [BACK OFF! *excl.* + JACKSON *n.*]

back off the boards *v.* (*also* back off the earth) [1910s+] (*US*) to surpass. [SE *back*, to push away, to cause to retreat]

back of God speed *phr.* (*also* behind God speed) [20C+] (*Irish*) very far away. [SE *God speed*, farewell]

back of my hand (and the sole of my foot) *phr.* [late 19C+] (*Irish/Scot.*) a phr. implying contempt and rejection. [the object of the rejection will get a slap or a kick]

back of the hand down *n.* [late 19C–1900s] bribery. [BACK-HANDER *n.*]

back of the neck *n.* [1940s] (*Irish*) a distasteful person. [? i.e. unwashed]

back of the net! *excl.* [1980s] **1** a drinking toast, an encouragement to drink or eat. **2** an excl. meaning wonderful! perfect! [football jargon, meaning the ball has entered the net and a goal has been scored]

back one out *v.* [1990s+] to defecate (cf. CURL ONE OFF *v.*; PINCH ONE OFF *v.*; SNAP ONE OFF *v.*; THROTTLE ONE *v.*).

back one's fist *v.* [1990s+] (*W.I.*) to masturbate.

Back o' Sunset *n. see* BACK OF BOURKE *n.*

back-out *n.*[1] [19C] (*US*) cowardice, the act of withdrawal.

back-out *n.*[2] [1970s] (*W.I.*) a woman's dress cut very low in the back.

back out *v.* [early–mid-19C] to retreat. [horseracing jargon *back out*, to bring a horse backwards out of a stall]

back-pedal! *excl.* [1910s–20s] an excl. calling for restraint, steady on! hold it! [SE *back-pedal*, to backtrack, to take a comment back; ult. cycling imagery]

back-porch *n.* [1950+] (*US*) the buttocks (cf. ARSE-END *n.*).

back premises *n. see* BACK DOOR *n.* (2).

backra *n.* (*also* buccra, buckra, buckrah) (*W.I./US Black*) **1** [late 18C+] a master, a boss. **2** [late 18C+] a White man; thus *buckra-nigger*, a 'White man's negro' or subservient Black; *buckra-bittle*, buckra victuals or White man's food. **3** [19C] white as a colour, e.g. *buckra yam*, a white yam. **4** [1920s] one who, while Black, moves in White society and sees themself as the White man's equal. [Black patois of Surinam *bakra*, master. This in turn was based on Efik (the language of the Calabar coast) *mba*, all + *kara* to encompass, get round, to master (a subject); thus *mbakara*, *makara*, a White man, a European, with a parallel meaning of a demon, a powerful and superior being (cf. OFAY *n.*). Note the popular (if erroneous) ety. *back raw*; the White man was known for his beatings]

backra fire *n.* [20C+] (*W.I.*) electricity. [BACKRA *n.* (2) + SE *fire*]

backra johnny n. [19C+] (W.I.) **1** a poor White. **2** a light-skinned Black person. [BACKRA n. (2) + JOHNNIE n.² (1)]

backraman n. [late 18C+] (W.I.) a master, a boss. [BACKRA n. (1) + SE man]

backra nigger n. [19C+] (W.I.) a light-skinned person and, as such, one who is despised. [BACKRA n. (3) + NIGGER n.¹ (1)]

backra pickney n. [19C+] (W.I.) **1** a White child. **2** a light-skinned mixed-race child. [BACKRA n. (3) + W.I. pron. of PICCANINNY n.]

back roll v. [1980s+] (drugs) to roll a joint so that only 1 layer of paper surrounds the mix.

backroom boy n. [1990s+] (UK gay) one who enjoys the semi-public sex of the (often dark) back rooms in gay clubs. [SE back room + boy; + play on SE backroom boys, the unsung experts of any organization]

back-row hopper n. [late 19C–1900s] a scrounger who frequents taverns in the hope of finding someone willing to buy them a drink. [theatrical imagery]

backs n. [1960s+] (US campus/gay/prison) the buttocks (cf. ARSE-END n.).

back sass v. [1910s+] (US) to answer back rudely; thus back-sasser, a cheeky person. [SE back + SASS n.]

back-scratcher n. [late 19C+] (US) a sycophant, a toady.

backscull v. [1970s] to have anal intercourse (cf. ASK FOR THE RING v.).

backscuttle n. [late 19C+] **1** heterosexual anal intercourse. **2** sodomy performed by homosexuals; thus do a back scuttle, to have sex from the rear, to sodomize. [BACKSCUTTLE v.²]

backscuttle v.¹ [late 19C+] (UK Und.) to leave or enter a house from the back way. [SE back + scuttle, to bore a hole (in order to sink a ship)]

backscuttle v.² [late 19C+] **1** to have homosexual or heterosexual anal intercourse (cf. ASK FOR THE RING v.). **2** to have heterosexual intercourse in the rear-entry position. [for ety. see BACKSCUTTLE v.¹]

backscuttler n. [1930s+] (Aus.) a sodomite. [BACKSCUTTLE v.²; although v. works for both hetero- and homosexual intercourse, the n., apparently found only in Aus., refers only to homosexuals]

backseat driver n.¹ [1920s+] (orig. US) anyone who offers unwanted advice to the person who is actually in charge of, or at least performing, the task for which the advice is given. [motoring imagery]

backseat driver n.² [1960s+] a lazy person, a shirker. [rhy. sl. = SKIVER n.]

backshee n. see BAKSHEESH n.

backshee adj. see BUCKSHEE adj. (1).

backsheesh n. see BAKSHEESH n.

backshot n. [1950s+] (UK Black) anal intercourse. [i.e. to shoot in the back]

backside artist n. [1980s+] (US gay) a male homosexual who enjoys anal intercourse. [SE backside + ARTIST sfx]

backside of nowhere n. [1960s+] (US) nowhere, a very out-of-the-way place. [SE backside + SE nowhere]

backsiding n. [1990s+] (W.I.) a severe thrashing. [SE backside]

backslack n. [1900s–50s] (US) cheek, insolence. [SE back + SLACK n.¹ (1)]

back slammer cutout n. [1940s] (US Black) (premature) death. [SE back + SLAMMER n.² (2) + CUT OUT v.⁴; play on BACK-DOOR PAROLE n. (1)]

backslang it v. [early 19C–1900s] **1** to leave by the back door, thus to leave surreptitiously, quietly. **2** to make a deliberate detour to avoid meeting a certain person or persons. **3** (Aus.) to request lodgings from strangers as one travels through the back country. **4** to enter a house from the back way. [? link to BACK SLUM n.; the term predates the linguistic variety of backsl., while there seems to be no link to SLANG n.¹ itself; ? link to SLING ONE'S HOOK v.² (1)]

backslice n. [1980s] of a man or woman, the anus (cf. ARSE-END n.). [SE back + SLICE n.¹ (1)]

backsliding n. (also **bestial backsliding**) [17C] sexual intercourse in the rear-entry position.

backslit n. [1980s] of a man or woman, the anus (cf. ARSE-END n.). [SE back + SLIT n.¹ (1)]

back slum n. [19C] (UK Und.) the back entrance to a building, the back door or window. [SE back + SLUM n.¹ (1)]

back slums n. [19C] areas or streets known for a high proportion of criminal residents. [later SE for very poor slums]

backsman n. [mid-19C] (US) a burglar. [? one who goes in the back way; however, G. A. Thompson (personal correspondence) suggests 'a mistake or typo for "Cracksman"']

back someone out v. [mid-19C+] (US) to challenge, to face down. [SE back, to cause to retreat]

back someone's play v. [1970s] (US) to support one's own statement or action or back up those of another person. [gambling jargon]

backstage adj. [1970s+] (US gay) **1** uncouth, rude. **2** genuine, unpretentious.

back-staircase n. [mid–late 19C] a bustle on a dress.

backstall n. (UK Und.) **1** [19C] a member of a garrotting gang who keeps watch and provides physical assistance to the actual garrotter if necessary. **2** [19C–1900s] a thief's accomplice. [SE back + STALL n.¹ (2)]

backstop n. **1** [1940s+] (Aus.) a supporter, an accomplice, someone who can be relied on. **2** [1950s+] (US Und.) in a pickpocket team, the one who works directly behind the victim. [(1) cricket jargon backstop, a fielder who stands behind the wicket-keeper to stop any balls the keeper may have missed; (2) baseball jargon backstop, the catcher]

back-street wife n. [1930s] (US) a mistress.

backswing n. [1950s+] (US gay) a position for homosexual anal intercourse where the passive partner lies on his stomach, presenting buttocks to his partner.

back-talk n. (also **backtalk**) [mid-19C+] cheek, impertinence; thus imper. no back-talk, that's it, there's no more to be said. [Ulster dial. backtalk, to answer back rudely]

back-talk v. [1920s+] to cheek, to be impudent. [BACK-TALK n.]

back-talking n. [1960s+] (US) gossip, cheek, impertinence. [BACK-TALK v.]

back the barber v. [1950s] (Aus.) to interfere, to butt in.

back the barrow v. [1910s] (Aus.) to interfere, to butt in.

back the breeze v. [1950s] (US) to chatter, to gossip. [the enthusiasm of one's speech fig. makes the wind reverse direction]

back-timber n. [mid-17C] clothing.

back time n. [1950s+] (US Und.) time spent in prison awaiting sentencing.

back-to-back adj. [1980s+] (US Black) **1** affectionate, friendly, intimate. **2** of a person, outstanding, superb.

back to back adv. [1970s–80s] (US Black) to the greatest possible extent, comprehensively, fully.

back tottie n. [1980s] (Aus.) of a woman, occas. a man, the anus (cf. ARSE-END n.; FRONT TOTTIE n.). [SE back + TOTTIE n.² (2)]

backtrack v. [1950s+] (drugs) to withdraw the plunger of the syringe, before an injection into the vein, to make sure that the needle is in a vein by sucking up some blood.

back-up n.¹ [1920s+] (Aus.) a second helping of food, thus as v., to take a second helping. [SE back-up, support, help]

back-up n.² [1960s+] (Aus.) multiple rape of a woman. [BACK UP v.⁵]

back-up n.³ [1980s+] **1** (Aus./N.Z.) retaliation, revenge. **2** (Aus. prison) one who can be relied on for support, e.g. in a fight. [BACK UP v.⁷]

back up v.¹ **1** [20C+] to go away, to retreat, to stop talking, esp. as imper. **2** [1910s] (US) to back down.

back up v.[2] [1920s+] (*Aus.*) to take a second helping of food. [BACK-UP n.[1]]

back up v.[3] (*drugs*) **1** [1930s] to refuse to sell drugs on the premise that the purchaser might be an informer or undercover policeman. **2** [1960s+] to pump the hypodermic so that blood comes into the tube, mixing with the drug/water solution before shooting it back into the vein. [SE *back up*, to reverse (either the movement of the plunger or the decision to sell drugs)]

back up v.[4] [1930s+] (*drugs*) to distend the vein during drug taking, thus making it easier to insert the needle. [? SE *put one's back up*; the distension of the vein raises it above the surrounding flesh]

back up v.[5] [1960s+] (*Aus./US*) to have serial sex with a woman. [SE *back up*, to form a queue]

back up v.[6] [1970s–80s] (*N.Z. prison*) to reoffend, to repeat.

back up v.[7] [1980s+] (*Aus./N.Z.*) to take revenge, esp. when in a gang. [SE *back up*, to support]

back up off my tip (for the simple fact you on it like a gnat) *phr.* [2000s] (*US Black teen*) stop annoying me, go away. [BACK-UP v.[1] (1) + TIP n.[7]]

back-up pills n. [1910s+] aphrodisiacs. [they supposedly SE *back up* one's potency or make seduction easier]

backwards n. **1** [1960s+] a depressant. **2** [1970s] the state of mind specific to taking a barbiturate. **3** [1990s+] an unpleasant experience while using LSD.

backward skid n. *see* FRONT-WHEEL SKID n.

backward thinking n. [1980s] (*US Black*) confused, muddled thinking.

backwash n. **1** [1900s–30s] (*US*) insolent talk, cheek, nonsensical talk. **2** [1990s+] liquid that flows back into a bottle, poss. after being in one's mouth when one drinks straight from it. [SE *backwash*, the motion of a receding wave]

back water v. [1950s+] (*US*) to retract a statement, to back down from a position; thus *take back water*, to back down, to accept defeat. [naut. jargon *back water*, to reverse a boat]

back way n. *see* BACK DOOR n. (1).

back-wheel skid n. *see* FRONT-WHEEL SKID n.

backy n. [1900s–60s] (*US*) a privy. [abbr. BACKHOUSE n.]

backyard n. [1960s+] (*US*) the buttocks, esp. in the context of anal intercourse (cf. ARSE-END n.).

backyard adj. [1910s+] (*orig. Aus.*) small, trivial, insignificant, esp. of business conducted from one's own home.

backyard cousin n. (*also* **backyard relation**) [1930s+] (*US*) a relation, poss. an illegitimate child, of whom the speaker is not proud. [BACKYARD adj. + SE *cousin/relation*]

backyard trots n. [1960s–70s] (*US*) diarrhoea. [TROTS, THE n.[2]; also one 'trots' through the backyard on the way to the privy]

bacon n.[1] **1** [late 16C–17C] human flesh, a human being. **2** [late 16C–17C] a rustic, a clown (cf. BACON-BONCE n.[1]). **3** [17C] the genitals. **4** [1910s–20s] the penis (cf. BACON BAZOOKA n.; BALONEY n.[2]; BEEF n.[1]; BEEF BAYONET n.; BEEF INJECTION n.; BLACK PUDDING n.; BLIND MEAT n.; BLUE-VEINED STEAK n.; BLUE-VEIN SALAMI n.; BOLOGNA n.; BUTCHER n.[1]; CRIMSON CHITTERLING n.; DANGLEPORK n.; DARK MEAT n.; DEAD MEAT n.; HAIRY SAUSAGE n.; HAM n.[5]; HAMBONE n.[3]; HAM HOWITZER n.; HOT DOG n.[1]; JEWISH CORNED BEEF n.; JUNGLE MEAT n.; KNOCKWURST n.; LIVE SAUSAGE n.; LOVESTEAK n.; MEAT n.; MEAT INJECTION n.; MUTTON n.[3]; OSCAR n.; PIECE OF MEAT n.; PORK n.[2]; PORK LEG n.; PORK SWORD n.; RAW MEAT n.; ROUND STEAK n.; SALAMI n.; SAUSAGE n.[1]; SCHNITZEL n.; SMALL MEAT n.; SNATCH SALAMI n.; SPAM n.; SPAMJAGGER n.; SPAM JAVELIN n.; SPAM SCEPTRE n.; TUBESTEAK n.; TUBESTEAK OF LOVE n.; WEENIE n.[1]; WHITE MEAT n.). **5** [1990s+] (*US campus*) a woman. [SE *bacon*; (2) the role of *bacon* as the staple meat of peasant England]

bacon n.[2] **1** [1900s–40s] money. **2** [1990s+] (*US Black*) the good life, material success. [SE *bacon*; the rich fattiness of the meat as a metaphor for wealth]

bacon n.[3] [1970s+] the police. [ext. of PIG n.[3] (1)]

bacon and eggs n. [1940s+] (*orig. Aus.*) legs. [rhy. sl.]

bacon bazooka n. [1990s+] the penis. [BACON n.[1] (4) + BAZOOKA n.[1] (4)]

bacon-bonce n.[1] **1** [20C+] one who is partially bald. **2** [1940s+] the brain. **3** [1950s] (*UK juv.*) the face. **4** [1950s+] a dullard, a simpleton, a yokel (cf. BACON n.[1]). [SE *bacon* + BONCE n. (1); lit. 'pig-head']

bacon-bonce n.[2] [1990s+] a child molester. [rhy. sl. = NONCE n.[1] (1)]

bacon-face n. [19C] a term of abuse. [BACON-FACED adj.]

bacon-faced adj. [early 17C–19C] fat-faced, heavily jowled. [SE *bacon* + *faced*]

bacon fed adj. [late 16C–early 19C] fat, greasy. [the qualities of the cooked pig]

bacon hole n. [1940s+] the mouth.

bacon-picker n. [mid-17C] a glutton.

bacon (rind) adj. [1990s+] blind. [rhy. sl.]

bacon sandwich n. [1990s+] the vagina; one of a number of terms that equate the vagina with raw meat (cf. BADLY PACKED KEBAB n.; BEEF n.[1]; BIT OF MEAT n.; BIT OF MUTTON n.; BIT OF PORK n.; BIT ON A FORK n.; BUTCHER'S SHOP n.[1]; CAT'S MEAT n.[2]; CLUB SANDWICH n.; DARK MEAT n.; FURBURGER n.; FUZZBURGER n.; HAMBURGER SHOT n.; MEAT n.; MEAT MARKET n.[2]; MUTTON n.[1]; PRIME CUT n.; RENKING MEAT n.; SPLIT MUTTON n.). [coarse fig. use of SE]

bacon-slicer n. [mid-17C] a rustic, a yokel (cf. ACORN-CRACKER n.). [the occupation]

bacon strips n. [1990s+] the labia majora (cf. BEEF CURTAINS n.; BUM BACON n.; KNICKER BACON n.; MEAT CURTAINS n.; MUTTONFLAPS n.; STEAK DRAPES n.; SUSHI TACO n.; VERTICAL BACON SANDWICH n.).

bad n. [1990s+] (*US campus*) fault; thus MY BAD phr.[1].

bad adj. **1** [20C+] (*orig. US Black*) good, exciting; the implication being that the individual/object so defined is bad in establishment eyes and thus good in those of any outlaw/criminal, drug or other minority culture, esp. in Black use; thus comparative *badder*, superlative BADDEST adj. **2** [20C+] (*orig. US Black*) dangerous, aggressive. **3** [1900s] (*US Und.*) dangerous, un-suborned, thus honest. **4** [1990s+] (*US*) sexy, provocative. [note Ger. *schlecht*, bad, orig. meant good; also 19C Aus. convict jargon *bad fellow*, a convict who cooperates with the authorities; *good fellow*, one who maintains intra-convict solidarity; Smitherman, *Black Talk* (1994), suggests Mandingo *a ka nyi ko-jugu*, it is good, badly, i.e. so good that it is bad]

bad adv. [1930s] (*US*) a general intensifier, very, extremely.

bad actor n. **1** [late 19C+] an unpleasant individual, an aggressive trouble-maker; thus *bad-acting*, troublemaking. **2** [1910s–20s] a vicious or unbroken horse.

bad-ass n. (*also* **badass**) **1** [1950s+] (*US*) an unpleasant, aggressive individual. **2** [1970s+] (*US*) a tough, admirable individual. **3** [1970s+] (*US Black*) an untrustworthy male. [BAD-ASS adj.]

bad-ass adj. (*also* **ass-bad, badass, bad-assed**) (*orig. US Black*) **1** [1950s+] tough, aggressive, frightening. **2** [1970s+] formidable, admirable, first-rate. [SE *bad*/BAD adj. + -ASS sfx; given the use of *bad*, the term is as much congratulatory as not]

bad ass v. [1970s+] (*US*) to bully, to behave like a thug. [BAD-ASS n. (1)]

bad-ass nigger n. (*also* **bad man**) [1980s+] (*US Black*) an aggressive, tough Black man who rejects the constraints and humiliation of the role the White authorities have selected for him; thus *bad-ass bitch*, the female equivalent. [BAD-ASS adj. (1) + NIGGER n.[1] (1)]

bad bongos n. [1970s] (*US campus*) a situation in which things do not go as desired/required. [? assonance]

bad boy n. **1** [1920s+] (*US*) a tearaway, a young criminal. **2** [1950s] (*US Black*) a general term of approval, referring both to individuals and to objects. **3** [1950s+] (*US Black/W.I., Guyn.*) in positive version of (1), a Black who rejects the second-class role offered by the dominant White society. **4** [2000s] (*US*) anything considered impressive. [BAD adj. + SE *boy*; (2) and (4) f. (3)]

bad-boy *adj.* [1980s] (*US Black*) attractive, well-dressed. [BAD BOY n. (2)]

bad break *n.* [late 19C+] (*orig. US*) a stroke of bad luck. [SE *bad* + BREAK n.¹ (1)]

bad-breath *v.* [1970s] (*US*) to inform on, to speak ill of.

bad bundle *n.* [1970s+] (*drugs*) inferior-quality heroin. [SE *bad* + BUNDLE n.⁴ (1)]

bad bwoy *n.* (*also* **bad bwai**) [1970s+] (*W.I./UK Black teen*) a villain, a criminal, a rebellious young male. [W.I. pron. of BAD BOY n. (3); given the bad = good model it is not necessarily pej.]

bad case of the tins *n.* (*US gay*) **1** [1930s+] a state of fear, esp. of being raped. **2** [1980s+] (*temporary*) impotence. [ety. unknown; ? TIN-CAN n.]

bad cess to you! *excl.* (*also* **good cess to you!**) [mid-19C+] (*orig. Irish*) bad (or good) luck to you! [? abbr. SE *success* (OED); Ware suggests dial. *cess*, a piece of turf; thus 'may you live in a good/bad place'; E.P. prefers *cess*, assessment; thus 'may you suffer a good/bad (tax) assessment']

bad count *n.* [1980s] (*US Und.*) **1** an unfair decision. **2** a short measure of drugs. [boxing jargon *bad count*, a count that is too long or too short]

bad crowd *n.* [late 19C–1900s] (*US*) an unpleasant, untrustworthy person. [as a group, use is SE]

baddest *adj.* [1930s+] (*US Black*) very best, supreme. [the superlative of BAD adj. (2)]

baddie *n.* (*also* **baddy**) **1** [1900s] (*Aus.*) an immoral person. **2** [1930s+] an unpleasant person, spec. a criminal. **3** [1940s+] in film or TV melodramas, the stereotyped villain who must, and will, be vanquished (cf. GOODIE n.¹). **4** [1960s] (*US campus*) a difficult course. [nursery use of SE *bad*]

baddiwad *n.* [1960s+] (*US teen*) something that is bad. [BADDIE n. (2) + redup.; coined by Anthony Burgess in *A Clockwork Orange* (1962)]

bad dog *n.* [1940s+] (*Aus.*) a bad debt. [unpaid, it won't 'lie down']

bad-doing *adj.* [1960s+] (*US Black*) first-rate, excellent, superior. [BAD adj. (2) + SE *doing*]

bad dough *n. see* BAD PAPER n. (1).

baddy *n. see* BADDIE n.

bade *v.* [1990s+] (*W.I.*) to make lots of money, usu. in gambling. [? BAD adj. (2)]

bad egg *n.* (*orig. US*) **1** [mid-19C+] (*also* **rotten egg**) a rogue, a villain. **2** [mid-19C+] a worthless speculation. **3** [1920s] a tough man. [SE *bad* + EGG n.¹ (1)]

Baden-Powell *n.* **1** [late 19C–1960s] a trowel. **2** [20C+] (*Aus.*) a towel. [rhy. sl.; ult. Robert *Baden-Powell* (1857–1941), the founder of the Boy Scouts]

badered *adj.* [1980s+] drunk. [LEGLESS adj. (1); ult. the RAF's 'legless ace' Sir Douglas *Bader* (1910–82), immortalized in the film *Reach for the Sky* (1956)]

bad-eye *n.*¹ [late 19C] (*US*) cheap, home-distilled whisky. [? var. on RED-EYE n.¹; + ? it may render the drinker blind]

bad-eye *n.*² [late 19C+] (*orig. US Black*) a threatening glance, a threat, the evil eye; the person staring in this way. [? Mandingo *nyejugu*; unlike many Black uses of *bad*, this uses the SE *bad*, evil, rather than BAD adj. (2)]

bad-eye *v.* [1950s+] (*US Black/P.R.*) to stare down. [BAD-EYE n.²]

bad face *n.* [1960s] (*US Black*) an unpleasant, disagreeable person.

bad fall *n.* [1910s+] (*US Und.*) an arrest and charge from which one cannot escape, despite attempting to intimidate or bribe the plaintiff or a prosecution witness. [SE *bad* + FALL n. (1)]

bad-food *n.* [20C+] (*W.I.*) food that supposedly contains 'magic' ingredients that will influence a man to choose a particular woman.

bad form *n.* [late 19C+] (*orig. UK society*) anything socially unacceptable. [horseracing use *form*, the state of a horse's health etc]

badge *n.*¹ [18C–mid-19C] (*UK Und.*) **1** a brand used as a judicial punishment. **2** one who has been thus branded.

badge *n.*² [1920s+] **1** (*US prison*) a warder, a guard, anyone in authority. **2** (*US*) a policeman (cf. GOLD-BADGE MAN n.; GOLDEN BOY n.; GOLD STAR n.; OUR FRIEND WITH THE TALKING BROOCH n.; PRIVATE STAR n.; RUSTY GUN n.; SHIELD n.; TINNER n.; TIN RIBS n.; TIN SHIELD n.; TIN STAR n.). [the wearer's badge of office]

badge *n.*³ *see* BADGER n.¹ (3).

badge *v.* [1960s+] (*US*) to show one's badge (typically that of a police department) to gain (free) admission.

badge-cove *n.* [early 18C–mid-19C] one who draws a pension from their parish; they are distinguished by a special badge. [SE *badge* + COVE n. (1); *badge* in this case meaning an official document or licence; an Und. version of SE *badge-man*, a licensed beggar or almsman]

badge man *n.* [1940s–50s] (*US prison*) an inmate who identifies with the authorities rather than his peers. [the *badge* of the person in charge]

badger *n.*¹ (*UK Und.*) **1** [early 18C–mid-19C] a thief who specializes in robbery on the riverbank, after which he murders the victim and disposes of the corpse in the water. **2** [mid-19C+] a thief who rifles the pockets of a man who is currently engaged with his accomplice, a prostitute. **3** [mid-19C–1940s] (*also* **badge**) (*US*) a prostitute, esp. one who participates in a scheme to rob her clients (cf. ALLEY CAT n.). [SE *badger*, an animal which is both nocturnal and carnivorous; the prostitute/thief also 'devour' their victims after dark]

badger *n.*² [19C] (*US*) a chamberpot; thus *badger fight, pulling the badger*, a practical joke whereby an innocent is lured into a hoax fight between a dog and a badger but ends up being splashed by the contents of a chamberpot.

badger *n.*³ [early 19C+] (*US*) an old man. [? the ill-temper of the animal]

badger *n.*⁴ [mid-19C+] (*US*) the nickname of the natives or inhabitants of Wisconsin. [the early Wisconsin lead-miners (*badgers*) who lived in subterranean diggings alongside the seams of lead they were mining; for detailed discussion see R.H. Thornton, *An American Glossary*, I 32–3 (1912)]

badger *n.*⁵ [1990s+] **1** (*US*) an unattractive woman; thus *badger set*, anywhere that such women can take advantage of men. **2** (*orig. US*) the female genital area. **3** (*US*) a male homosexual. **4** (*US*) an attractive woman or generic for attractive women in general. [less 'aggressive' versions of BADGER n.¹ (3)]

badger *n.*⁶ *see* BADGER GAME n. (1).

badger *v.* [late 19C+] of a prostitute, to steal from a client; thus n. *badgering*. [BADGER n.¹ (3)]

badger-bill *n.* [1940s+] (*W.I.*) a hypocrite, a 'two-faced', untrustworthy person. [dial. *badger-bill*, a double-edged machete]

badger-box *n.* [late 19C] (*Aus.*) 'a roughly-constructed dwelling' (Morris).

badger-crib *n.* [mid-19C–1900s] a brothel that specializes in robbing its clients (cf. ACCOMMODATION HOUSE n.; BAWDY KEN n.; BOFF JOINT n.; CAB JOINT n.; CARSEY n.; CASA n.¹; CASE n.³; CASEO n.; CASER n.⁴; CHIPPIE JOINT n.; CREEP JOINT n.; CREEP PAD n.; CRIB n.¹; CRIB JOINT n.; DOSSING CRIB n.; DRUM n.³; FLASH DRUM n.; FLASH KEN n.; GRIND JOINT n.²; JAZZ JOINT n.; JOINT n.⁴; MOLL CRIB n.; MOT-CASE n.; PANEL CRIB n.; PEGGING-CRIB n.; RIB JOINT n.¹; RUM KEN n.; SMUGGLING-KEN n.; SNOOZING KEN n.; TOUCH CRIB n.; WAPPING KEN n.). [BADGER GAME n. + CRIB n.¹ (2)]

badger game *n.* [mid-19C+] (*orig. US*) **1** (*also* **badger**) the ensnaring of a client by a woman, often a prostitute, and his subseq. robbery, either by the woman herself or more often by her pimp, posing as an 'outraged boyfriend'; the man often emerged, while the pair were *in flagrante*, from a hidden door or panel in the bedroom wall; thus *badger game worker*, one who practises this swindle; BADGER MAN n. **2** in ext. use, to perform a confidence trick based on exploiting the victim's interest in a woman. [BADGER n.¹ + SE *game*, scheme, intrigue]

badger-gassing n. [1990s+] (*UK juv.*) an especially foul-smelling breaking of wind.

badger house n. [mid-19C–1900s] (*US*) an establishment, often a brothel, where the client is robbed (cf. ACCOMMODATION HOUSE n.). [BADGER GAME n. (1) + HOUSE n.¹ (1)]

badger-legged adj. [mid-17C–early 18C] used of a person with one leg shorter than the other. [the erroneous belief that badgers are similarly equipped]

badger man n. [mid-19C+] (*Aus.*) the accomplice of a prostitute who tricks her clients. [BADGER GAME n. (1) + SE *man*]

badger moll n. [mid-19C+] (*US*) a woman, often a prostitute, who tricks her client. [BADGER GAME n. (1) + MOLL n.¹ (1)]

badger worker n. [mid-19C–1940s] (*US*) the accomplice of a prostitute who tricks her clients. [BADGER GAME n. (1) + SE *worker*/WORKER n.¹ (1)]

bad go n. (*drugs*) **1** [1950–70s] a short or disappointing measure of drugs. **2** [1980s+] a bad reaction to a drug. [SE *bad* + (1) GO n.¹ (3); (2) GO n.³ (1)]

bad guy n. [1940s+] (*orig. US*) in film or TV melodramas, the stereotyped villain. [SE *bad* + *guy*]

bad hair n. [1920s+] (*US Black/W.I.*) a Black person's naturally kinky hair, thus *bad-haired*. [BAD adj. (1) + SE *hair*]

bad halfpenny n. **1** [early 19C] any errand or task that proves pointless. **2** [mid-19C–1910s] an unpleasant, untrustworthy person (cf. BAD PENNY n.).

bad hat n. [early 19C–1950s] a rogue, an untrustworthy person. [according to Charles Mackay's *Memoirs of Extraordinary Popular Delusions* (1841) f. a London election in the borough of Southwark, *c.*1838, in which one of the candidates was well known as a hat-maker. As he campaigned he would single out any voter whose hat fell beneath the highest standards and declare: 'What a shocking bad hat you have got, call at my warehouse and you shall have a new one.' On the day of the election, as he gave his final speech, his opponents urged a hostile crowd to drown him out by chanting: 'What a shocking bad hat!' The phr. caught on and, first in its entirety and subseq. in its abbr. form, entered popular sl. It survived through the 19C and gradually declined through the first half of the 20C. An alternative ety. attributes the phr. to the Duke of Wellington, who on his first visit to the Peers' Gallery of the House of Commons remarked, on looking down on the members of the Reform Parliament: 'I never saw so many shocking bad hats in my life'; but note Egan, *Book of Sports* (1832): 'I will allow those blackguard little boys again to insult me with the prevailing, foolish, unmeaning phrase of "What a shocking bad hat you have got!" if ever they lay hold of me more']

bad-head n. **1** [20C+] (*W.I.*) a tearaway, a young criminal. **2** [1960s] (*US*) a very unattractive face.

bad in the head adj. [1980s+] (*US Black*) **1** eccentric, out of control. **2** unhappy.

bad iron n. [mid-19C–1910s] bad luck, a failure, a disaster. [ety. unknown]

bad john n. **1** [1960s–70s] (*W.I./UK Black*) a tearaway, a young criminal; thus *badjohnism*, criminality; *play bad-john*, to act like a hooligan (although not actually to be one). **2** [1970s] (*UK Black*) a gangster, an important criminal. [SE *bad* + JOHN n.¹ (1)]

bad lad n. *see* LAD, THE n.

bad lamps n. [1960s+] (*US gay*) dark glasses. [SE *bad* + *lamp*/LAMPS n.¹]

bad lands n. [late 19C+] (*US*) **1** the slum area of a city (orig. coined for that in Chicago). **2** any dangerous area. [ironic use of SE *badlands*, arid, barren areas of the Western US]

bad lot n. [mid-19C+] an unpleasant, untrustworthy person. [auction house jargon *bad lot*, one that will not sell]

badly done adj. [20C+] (*Ulster*) embarrassed. [SE *badly* + DO v.² (1)]

badly packed kebab n. [2000s] the vagina (cf. BACON SANDWICH n.).

Bad Man n. (*also* **Bad Man Below**) [20C+] (*US Black*) the Devil.

bad man n. *see* BAD-ASS NIGGER n.

bad medicine n. [mid-19C+] (*orig. US*) something or someone sinister or ill-fated. [the SE use of *medicine* to translate terms used in a variety of native American languages meaning a fetish, spell or charm; note use of 'bad juju' and 'juju-man' in the spy novels of John le Carré (b.1931)]

bad-mind n. [20C+] (*W.I.*) malice, spite, animosity.

bad-minded adj. [20C+] (*W.I.*) envious, nasty, wishing someone ill. [BAD-MIND n.]

badminton n. [mid-19C] **1** claret cup. **2** blood (cf. BORDEAUX n.; CARMINE n.; CLARET n.; CRANBERRY SAUCE n.; DUTCH PINK n.; GRAVY n.¹; JUICE n.²; KETCHUP n.; LIQUID ROUGE n.; PORT WINE n.; RED GRAVY n.; RED INK n.¹; RED STUFF n.¹; ROSY, THE n.¹; RUBY n.¹). [the iced cup, made of claret, sugar, spice and cucumber peel, was invented at *Badminton*, the country seat of the Duke of Beaufort; the term was extended to boxing jargon where it meant blood (cf. CLARET n.)]

badmouth n. (*orig. US Black/W.I.*) **1** [1960s+] a curse, a spell; often in phr. *put the bad mouth on.* **2** [1970s+] malicious gossip. **3** [1980s+] one who talks maliciously or argumentatively. [BADMOUTH v.]

badmouth adj. [1970s+] malicious, defamatory. [BADMOUTH n. (2)]

badmouth v. [1940s+] **1** to attack verbally, to slander. **2** to beat someone in an argument or verbal contest. [SE but note Mandingo *dajugu*, bad mouth]

badness n. [1980s+] (*US/W.I./UK Black teen*) **1** delinquent or unruly behaviour, often just for the sake of it. **2** on bad = good model, a state of excellence, admirability. [(1) SE *bad*; (2) BAD adj. (1)]

bad news n. (*orig. US*) **1** [1910s+] the bill, usu. in a café or restaurant. **2** [1910s+] an unattractive, unpleasant person or thing. **3** [1920s+] a shotgun or revolver. **4** [1930s] one's death, usu. in phr. *hear the bad news*, to be killed. **5** [1930s+] the losing throw of 3 in craps dice (cf. ADA FROM DECATUR n.). **6** [1940s+] an unpleasant situation, difficulties, trouble. **7** [1940s+] a troublesome, threatening person. **8** [1960s] a pessimist.

bad news adj. [1960s+] (*orig. US*) unpleasant, threatening. [BAD NEWS n. (2)]

bad news wagon n. [1970s] a police car. [BAD NEWS n. (6)]

bad nigger n. **1** [20C+] (*US Black*) a violent, amoral Black person (as viewed positively by his Black peers). **2** [1910s] (*Aus.*) an Aborigine who refuses to cooperate with the authorities. **3** [1920s+] (*US Black*) a Black who rejects the second-class role offered by the dominant White society. [BAD adj. (1) + NIGGER n.¹ (1)]

bad paper n. **1** [1910s+] (*also* **bad dough**) any form of fraudulent documents, counterfeit money or similar written or printed frauds or forgeries. **2** [1960s+] an IOU that will not be paid by the debtor. **3** [1990s+] (*US prison*) a negative report on a prisoner. [SE *bad* + PAPER n.¹]

bad-pay adj. [20C+] (*W.I.*) extremely slow to pay debts or any money that is owed and expected.

bad penny n. (*also* **bad shilling**) [mid-19C+] an unpleasant, untrustworthy person (cf. BAD HALFPENNY n.).

bad place in the road n. (*also* **bad spot in the road, narrow place in the road, spot in the road**) [1930s–60s] (*US*) an out-of-the-way, unimportant place or settlement.

bad poker n. [1920s] (*US Und.*) a mistake, a foolish move.

bad rags n. [1960s–70s] (*US Black*) one's best, most fashionable clothes. [BAD adj. (1) + RAGS n. (1)]

bad rap n. 1 [1940s+] (US) a serious criminal charge. 2 [1960s+] the state of being criticized unfairly. 3 [1970s+] an unfair criminal charge or sentence. 4 [1970s+] a sentence of 20 years or more. [SE *bad* + RAP n.⁴]

bad rap v. [1960s+] (orig. US) to malign, to criticize unfairly. [BAD RAP n. (2)]

bad scene n. 1 [1950s+] an unpleasant situation; on the bad = good model, *it's a really bad scene* could be a term of approval. 2 [1960s] an unpleasant or unpopular person. [SE *bad*/BAD adj. (1) + SCENE n. (1); (2) f. (1)]

bad scran n. (also **bad scram, bad scrant**) [mid-19C+] (orig. Anglo-Irish) bad luck; usu. as phr. *bad scran to*. [SE *bad* + SCRAN n.]

bad shag n. [late 18C–early 19C] an unsatisfactory lover; usu. in phr. *he is but bad shag*. [SE *bad* + SHAG n.¹ (1); note SHAG n.¹ (4), used later 20C+ in phrs. like 'a good shag', 'a bad shag']

bad shilling n.¹ 1 [late 19C] one's last shilling. 2 [late 19C–1930s] (Aus.) a remittance man.

bad shilling n.² see BAD PENNY n.

bad shit n.¹ [1960s+] worse than average problems. [SE *bad* + SHIT n.³ (2)]

bad shit n.² [1960s+] better than average marijuana. [BAD adj. (1) + SHIT n.⁵ (2)]

bad shot n. [mid-19C+] a poor guess. [SE *bad* + SHOT n.⁵ (1)]

bad show! excl. [20C+] a general excl. of disappointment or disapproval.

bad siddown n. [20C+] (W.I., Jam.) poor behaviour in public, disregard of other people's feelings. [SE *bad sit-down*; the image is of a prostitute lazing around on a street corner; also note Krio (Sierra Leone Creole) *bad sidom*, a woman sitting so as to expose her genitals]

bad smash n. [20C+] counterfeit coins. [SE *bad* + SMASH n.²]

bad spot in the road n. see BAD PLACE IN THE ROAD n.

bad steer n. see BUM STEER n.

badster n. [1920s+] (Aus.) a villain, a morally bad person. [SE *bad* + sfx. *-ster*]

bad stuff n. see GOOD STUFF n. (2).

bad talk n. [1960s–70s] (US Black) 1 conversation or writing that considers and/or urges revolutionary attitudes and actions; such talk is *bad* both in White eyes and as the prerogative of Blacks. 2 a form of ritual name-calling, based on insulting one's target's family. 3 any form of abusive, negative speech. [SE *bad*/BAD adj. (1) + SE *talk*]

bad time n. [1970s] (US Und.) a prison sentence that causes the subject, who cannot acclimatize, a great deal of suffering. [SE *bad* + TIME n.¹]

bad-time v. [1960s] (US) to be sexually unfaithful to one's partner.

bad trip n. [1960s+] 1 (drugs) a bad or frightening experience while taking psychedelic drugs. 2 ext. as any sort of unpleasant or unnerving experience. [SE *bad* + TRIP n.⁴ (1)]

bad trot n. (Aus.) 1 [20C+] an unfair situation or result. 2 [1920s+] a run of bad luck. [SE *bad* + TROT n.² (4)]

bad 'un n. 1 [mid–late 19C] (UK Und.) a counterfeit coin. 2 [mid-19C+] a rogue, an untrustworthy person. [lit. 'a bad one']

baduzi n. [2000s] (US Black) the smell of sexual intercourse. [BOOTY n. (1) + DICK n.⁴ (1) + PUSSY n. (2)]

bad weave n. [1970s+] (US Black) one's best clothes. [BAD adj. (1) + WEAVE n.² (1)]

bafan adj. [1950s+] (W.I. Rasta) clumsy, awkward; thus *bafang*, a child who has not learned to walk for its first 2–7 years. [synon. Twi *bafan*]

baffin n. see BIFFIN n.².

bafflegab n. [1950s+] (US) (deliberately) unintelligible jargon, esp. as used for the purposes of obfuscation by politicians, civil servants, bureaucrats, businessmen etc. [SE *baffle* + GAB n. (3); coined May 1952, by the assistant general counsel of the US Chamber of Commerce, Milton Smith: 'I decided we needed a new and catchy word to describe the utter incom-

prehensibility, ambiguity, verbosity and complexity of govern-ment regulations']

bafoon n. (also **puffoon**) [20C+] (W.I.) a stench, esp. a fart. [echoic]

bag n.¹ 1 [mid-16C+] the scrotum (cf. BALL-BAG n.). 2 [early 17C] the vagina; one of many terms that refer to the vagina as a receptacle, usu. for semen or the penis (cf. BASKET n.¹; BEEHIVE n.¹; BOX n.¹; BREAD BOX n.; BREAD PAN n.; BUCKET n.³; BUTTER-BOAT n.; BUTTERBOX n.³; CANISTER n.¹; CALDRON n.; CAN n.¹; CASE n.²; CHUFF-BOX n.; CLOSET n.¹; COAL BIN n.¹; COCK ALLEY n.; COCK HALL n.; COCK-HOLDER n.; COCK INN n.; COCK LANE n.; COCK-LOCKER n.; COCKLOFT n.; COCK PIT n.; COCKSHIRE n.; COD TRENCH n.; CORNER CUPBOARD n.; CRADLE n.; CREAM-JUG n.; DOODLE-CASE n.; DOODLE-SACK n.¹; EEL POT n.; FLESHPOT n.; FLOWERPOT n.; FURRY LETTERBOX n.; FUZZY CUP n.; GLUEPOT n.²; GREASEBOX n.; HAIRY CUP n.; HIVE n.; HONEYPOT n.¹; ICEBOX n.³; INKWELL n.; JAMPOT n.²; JELLY BAG n.; JELLY BOX n.; JEWEL BOX n.; JOY BOX n.; KENNEL n.¹; KETTLE n.¹; KEYHOLE n.; KIPPER BOX n.; LOBSTER-POT n.; LOVE GLOVE n.; LOVE'S CABINET n.; LUCKY BAG n.; MELTING POT n.; MILKER n.¹; MILKING PAIL n.; MILK JUG n.¹; MIRACULOUS PITCHER (THAT HOLDS WATER WITH THE MOUTH DOWN) n.; MOLE-CATCHER n.; MONEYBOX n.; MOUSEHOLE n.; MUSTARD POT n.¹; NEEDLECASE n.; NETTLE BED n.; NICHE COCK n.; OYSTER-CATCHER n.; PENCIL-SHARPENER n.; PIGEONHOLE n.; PIN-BOX n.; PIN-CASE n.; PIN-CUSHION n.; PINK VELVET SAUSAGE WALLET n.; PINTLE-CASE n.; PITCHER n.¹; POT n.³; POUCH n.; PRICK-HOLDER n.; PRICK HOLE n.; PURSE n.; RECEPTACLE n.; SACK n.¹; SASSY BOX n.; SATCHEL n.; SCABBARD n.; SECOND-HAND GLOVE n.; SHAG-BAG n.; SHAKE-BAG n.¹; SHELL n.; SHOT-LOCKER n.; SNAKE GULLY n.; SNAKEPIT n.; SNATCH-BOX n.; SNOT-LOCKER n.; SPUNK-POT n.; STEWPOT n.; STINKPOT n.; TOOLBOX n.¹; TOOL CHEST n.; VELVET-LINED MEAT GRINDER n.; VENUS'S GLOVE n.). 3 [late 17C+] the womb. 4 [1940s] the stomach.

bag n.² 1 [mid-19C] (UK Und.) the act and proceeds of pick-pocketing; thus *bring a bag off*, to pick pockets (successfully). 2 [20C+] (Aus.) any form of gain, lit. or fig. 3 [1920s+] (US Und.) the proceeds of any illegal activity, e.g. unauthorized bookmaking; thus *have the bag on*, to work as a bookmaker. [the lit. *bag* of money]

bag n.³ [mid-19C–1900s] (UK Und.) a purse.

bag n.⁴ 1 [late 19C+] (US) a promiscuous woman, a prostitute (cf. BAGEROO n.; COMMON SEWER n.; GARBAGE CAN n.; SHAG-BAG n.; SHAKE-BAG n.¹; WHOREBAG n.). 2 [1920s+] (orig. US) an unattractive woman, esp. as *old bag*. 3 [1930s+] a homosexual man, esp. an unattractive and/or passive one.

bag n.⁵ [1910s–20s] (Aus.) a meal, a 'feed', or a drinking session.

bag n.⁶ [1920s] (US prison) a strait jacket, used for punishment.

bag n.⁷ [1920s+] (US) a contraceptive sheath; thus *bagged up*, wearing a contraceptive. [SE *bag*, a receptacle]

bag n.⁸ [1920s+] (US/Aus.) a suit of clothes. [rhy. sl.; *bag of fruit* = suit]

bag n.⁹ [1940s+] 1 a state of drunkenness or intoxication; usu. in IN THE BAG phr.³ (1). 2 a hangover.

bag n.¹⁰ [1940s+] (US campus) a despised person, an outsider. [the sort of person who 'brings their lunch in a bag']

bag n.¹¹ (orig. US drugs) 1 [1950s+] a measure of narcotics, typically sold as a NICKEL BAG n. or a DIME BAG n. 2 [1950s+] a store of drugs, as carried by a dealer. 3 [1960s+] a balloon containg heroin, thus through metonymy, the drug heroin. 4 [1980s+] a ¼oz (7g) measure of a drug, usu. marijuana. [the glassine bags into which the drugs are divided]

bag n.¹² [1960s] a form of bludgeon made from several socks inside each other, filled with sand packed round a solid, ball-shaped object. [abbr. SE *sandbag*]

bag n.¹³ [1960s+] (US) a bed, esp. in phr. *bag it*, *hit the bag*, go to bed, go to sleep. [? an old mattress being a *bag* of feathers or straw]

bag n.[14] [1960s+] (orig. US Black) **1** taste, disposition, attitude, occupation, preference, way of life; thus *get one's own bag going*, to pursue one's own interests. **2** one's preferred drug. [used in 1930s to refer to an actual *bag* used to hold bootleg liquor and in 1950s to that which held narcotics, bag took on its abstract (and still current) meaning in the 1960s; Gold, *A Jazz Lexicon* (1964), suggests link to SE *bag of tricks*]

bag n.[15] *see* FRATTY-BAGGER n.

bag, the n. [late 19C+] (*Glasgow*) money.

bag v.[1] **1** [19C+] to shoot (to kill), of animals and humans. **2** [1910s+] to hit, to knock out. **3** [1990s+] (*Aus.*) to wound, to beat.

bag v.[2] **1** [early 19C+] to seize, to catch, to arrest. **2** [mid-19C+] to steal, to rob. **3** [mid-19C+] to gain, to secure possession of, to win for oneself (esp. after repeated efforts). **4** [1910s+] to claim. **5** [1990s+] to get something non-material. [ext. uses of SE *bag*, to place in a bag]

bag v.[3] **1** [mid-late 19C] to dismiss. **2** [1960s+] to stop doing something, to dismiss an idea or plan; thus BAG THAT! excl.

bag v.[4] [1950s+] (*Aus./US*) to denigrate, to criticize; thus *bagger*, a negative critic. [dial. *bag*, to dismiss, to jilt/ext. BAG v.[1]]

bag v.[5] [1950s+] (*US Black*) to swallow semen or vaginal fluid during oral intercourse. [SE *bag*, a receptacle, in this case the mouth]

bag v.[6] (*also* **bag up**) [1960s+] (*drugs*) to divide bulk purchases of drugs into smaller quantities for dealing. [BAG n.[11]]

bag v.[7] **1** [1960s+] (*US, mainly campus/teen*) of a man, to seduce, to have sexual intercourse. **2** [1970s+] (*US gay*) to have homosexual anal intercourse (cf. ASK FOR THE RING v.). [BAG n.[1]]

bag v.[8] [1960s+] (*US*) to classify, to put into categories. [BAG n.[14] (1)]

bag v.[9] [1960s+] (*US drugs*) to inhale glue or a similarly intoxicating substance. [the glue is poured into a paper or polythene *bag*, from which the fumes are sucked into one's mouth]

bag v.[10] [1960s+] (*US*) to make a mess of, to fail at, to botch.

bag v.[11] (*US campus*) **1** [1960s+] to neglect, to stop, to disregard. **2** [1980s+] to throw away; to give up. [one tosses things into 'a bag']

bag v.[12] (*US campus*) **1** [1960s+] to miss a class or examination, to give up a course of study. **2** [1980s+] to break a date, to 'stand someone up'. [ext. BAG v.[11]]

bag v.[13] [1970s] (*US*) to wear. [the image of 'getting into a bag']

bag v.[14] [1980s+] **1** (*US*) to hide something unpleasant from the speaker's sight, e.g. *bag that, it's gross!* (cf. BAG ONE'S HEAD v.). **2** (*US campus*) to kidnap, esp. as part of a fraternity prank. [SE *bag*, a receptacle, in which the distasteful matter or the victim of the kidnapping is hidden]

bag v.[15] *see* BAG (IT) v.

-bag sfx [1910s+] used in comb. with another term, usu. a n., to describe a contemptible, despised person, when of a woman, often with implications of promiscuity (cf. -BALL sfx; BARFBAG n.; CRAP-BAG n.; DIRTBAG n.; DOSS-BAG n.; DOUCHEBAG n.; FUCKBAG n.; GAB-BAG n.; GEE BAG n.; HAIRBAG n.; HO-BAG n.; HORRORBAG n.; HOSEBAG n.; JITBAG n.; JIZZBAG n.; MINGE BAG n.; PUS-BAG n.; RATBAG n.; SCRUFF-BAG n.; SCUMBAG n.; SCUZZBAG n.; SHAG-BAG n.; SHITBAG n.; SLAGBAG n.; SLEAZEBAG n.; SLIMEBAG n.; SLY-BAG n.; SNOTBAG n.; SPUNK-BAG n.; TOSS-BAG n.; WANK-BAG n.; WHOREBAG n.). [SE *bag*/BAG n.[7]; the implication is of being a receptacle for something, most usu. sperm; note also BAG n.[4]/BAG n.[10] (cf. earlier HAYBAG n.; SHAG-BAG n.)]

bagadga n. (*also* **bagaga, bagada**) [1960s+] (*Ling. Fr./Polari*) the penis. [Ital. *baggagio*, baggage]

bagaga v. [1960s] (*US*) of a man, to have sexual intercourse; one of a number of sl. terms relating to anatomy (cf. BALL v.[2]; BALLOCK v.[2]; BONE v.[1]; BONE DOWN v.; BUTTOCK v.; COCK v.[1]; COCK IT v.; DICK v.[2]; DOODLE v.[2]; DORK v.; JOCK v.[1]; KNOB v.[1]; NOB v.[3]; PIN v.[1]; PRONG v.; QUIFF v.[1]; QUIM v.; ROD v.; SNAKE v.[3]; STIFF v.[4]). [BAGADGA n.]

bag and bottle n. [mid-late 17C] food and drink.

bag-blind adj. [20C+] (*W.I.*) socially contemptible, very low-class, slum-dwelling. [Bdos *bag-blind*, a rudimentary window blind made of a jute sack used for sugar, flour etc]

bag bride n. [1990s+] (*drugs*) a prostitute who is addicted to crack cocaine. [BAG n.[11] + ironic use of SE *bride*]

bag-carrier n. [1900s] (*Aus.*) a bookmaker. [the *bag* in which he keeps his cash]

bag-chasing adj. [1970s] obsessed by obtaining narcotic drugs. [BAG n.[11] + SE *chasing*]

bag dude n. [1970s] (*US Black*) a drug dealer. [BAG n.[11] (2) + DUDE n. (1)]

bagel n.[1] **1** [1950s+] (*US*) (*also* **Jew bagel**) a Jew (cf. ARAB n.[2]). **2** [1980s+] (*S.Afr.*) a spoilt, wealthy, upper-class (Jewish) young man. [Yid. *bagel*, a style of doughnut-shaped bread roll popular among Jews]

bagel n.[2] [1970s+] (*US sporting*) a score of zero; thus *bagel job*, a defeat in which the losers fail to score. [the circular shape of the *bagel* with its O-shaped hole]

bagel v. [1990s+] (*US sporting*) to achieve a score of zero. [BAGEL n.[2]]

bagel baby n. [1950s+] (*US*) a young middle-class Jewish woman, active in liberal causes. [SE *bagel*/BAGEL n.[1] (1) + BABY n.[3] (1)]

bagel bender n. [1970s+] (*US*) a Jew (cf. ARAB n.[2]). [SE *bagel* + *bender*]

bageroo n. [1930s] (*US*) a prostitute. [BAG n.[4] (1) + -EROO sfx]

baggage n.[1] [16C-17C] **1** a worthless man. **2** rubbish, nonsense.

baggage n.[2] [late 16C+] a woman, esp. one considered immoral or sexually autonomous. [the image of woman as a man's burden or encumbrance; the initial use is often synon. with a camp-follower (a woman who follows the military) but by 17C is more commonly found as a comb., e.g. *saucy baggage*, *sly baggage* and as such is relatively affectionate; however, there may also be links to Fr. *bagasse*, a prostitute, a wanton]

baggage n.[3] [1900s-30s] a woman due to be sent to South America in the White slave trade. [ext. of SE]

baggage n.[4] [1970s+] (*US gay*) the male genitals.

baggage bouncer n. *see* BAGGAGE SMASHER n.

baggage-box n. (*also* **baggage-boy**) [1940s+] (*US*) a homosexual prostitute who offers active sex to clients, i.e. as well as the usual passive participation in sodomy, he will play the active sodomizer and also offer fellatio. [? BAGGAGE n.[2] + SE *box*/*boy*]

baggage-man n. [early 18C] (*UK Und.*) the member of a pickpocketing team who is handed the booty and then runs off with it. [pun on SE]

baggage-room n. [mid-19C] (*US*) the stomach.

baggage smasher n. (*also* **baggage bouncer**) [mid-19C+] (*US*) **1** a railway porter. **2** one who steals unguarded luggage from railway stations. **3** a clumsy person. **4** a coarse, brutal person.

bagged adj.[1] (orig. *US*) **1** [mid-19C+] arrested, caught. **2** [1920s+] fooled, tricked. **3** [1970s+] as *bagged up*, in one's cell. [BAG v.[2] (1); ult. SE *bag*, a game-bag, in which dead and thus captive birds are placed]

bagged adj.[2] (*US*) **1** [1940s+] of sporting contests, when the outcome has been rendered certain by underhand or illicit means. **2** [1970s] easy, simple, no problem. **3** [1970s] made amenable by a bribe. [IN THE BAG phr.[1]]

bagged adj.[3] [1950s+] drunk. [printers' jargon *bag*, a pot of beer and the phr. *put one's head in a bag*, to be drunk]

bagged out adj. [1980s+] (*US*) style-less, shabby, run-down. [a supposed resemblance to a BAG LADY n.[1]]

bagged up adj.[1] *see* BAG n.[7].

bagged up adj.[2] *see* BAGGED adj.[1] (3).

bagger n.[1] (*also* **bag-thief**) [late 19C-1900s] a thief who specializes in stealing rings. [? Fr. *bague*, a ring]

bagger n.[2] [1980s+] a clumsy person. [one who should be put in a bag or have a bag placed over their head]

bagger *n.*[3] [1990s+] (*UK teen*) one who breaks an appointment. [BAG *v.*[12] (2)]

bagger *n.*[4] *see* FRATTY-BAGGER n.

baggie *n.*[1] [1970s+] (*US*) a contraceptive sheath. [BAG n.[7]]

baggie *n.*[2] (*also* **Baggie**) [1970s+] (*drugs*) a small plastic bag used popularly for holding small amounts of marijuana or powdered drugs. [SE *bag*, a receptacle + trademark *Baggies*, a branded form of plastic sandwich bag]

baggie bags *n.* [1980s+] (*drugs*) plastic food bags used for holding small amounts of marijuana. [ext. of BAGGIE n.[2]]

baggies *n.* [1960s+] (*orig. surfing*) **1** loose-fitting 'boxer-shorts'-style of swimming trunks. **2** loose-fitting baggy trousers. [SE *baggy*]

bagging *n.*[1] [1900s] (*Aus.*) clothing.

bagging *n.*[2] [1960s] (*US campus*) drinking. [BAG n.[9] (1)]

bagging *n.*[3] (*also* **doing the bag**) [1990s+] (*drugs*) using an inhalant for 'recreational' purposes. [BAG v.[9]; the pouring of the inhalant into a bag before use]

baggins *n.* [2000s] (*US Black*) a woman with whom one has had sex. [ext. of BAG n.[4] (1)]

baggy *n.* [1990s+] (*W.I.*) women's underwear.

baggy *adj.* [1960s] (*US*) of a woman, slatternly, unattractive. [BAG n.[4] (1)]

baggyarse *n.* (*also* **baggy**) [1980s+] (*Aus. prison*) the lowest rank of prison officer. [SE *baggy* + ARSE n.[1] (1); their stereotypically ill-fitting, new uniforms]

baghead *n.* [2000s] (*drugs*) a heroin addict. [BAG n.[11] (3) + -HEAD sfx (3)]

bag-ho *n.* [2000s] (*US Black*) an extremely unattractive woman. [BAG n.[4] (1) + HO n.[1] (3)]

bag (it) *v.* [1970s] (*US campus/teen*) to bring one's lunch in a paper bag. [Yorks. dial. *bag out*, for a farm-worker to bring their packed lunch to the fields]

bag it *v.* **1** [late 19C+] (*US*) (*also* **bag school**) to play truant. **2** [1960s] (*US*) to fake illness to get out of work. **3** [1960s+] (*US*) to disregard, to give up; thus imper. *bag it*, go away!, forget it! **4** [1960s+] (*US campus*) to be quiet, usu. as imper. **5** [1970s] (*US*) to go to sleep. [SE *bag*, a satchel or BAG n.[3]; note milit. jargon *bag it*, to malinger]

bag it! *excl. see* BAG THAT! excl.

bag job *n.*[1] [1960s] (*US campus*) an unpleasant person. [SE *bag* + JOB n.[6] (1), i.e. one who deserves a *bag* over their head]

bag job *n.*[2] (*also* **black bag job**) [1970s] (*US*) 'an illegal search of a suspect's property by agents of the Federal Bureau of Investigation, esp. for the purpose of copying or stealing incriminating documents etc' (*OED*). [SE *bag* + JOB n.[4]; the black bin-bags used to remove objects]

bag lady *n.*[1] [1960s+] a woman who acts as a go-between, carrying money, esp. in the form of bribes or illicit pay-offs, between 2 parties.

bag lady *n.*[2] [1960s+] (*orig. US*) a female derelict, usu. sleeping rough or in shelters, often an alcoholic or meths drinker, whose most cherished possessions are the numbers of (to an outsider) junk-filled shopping bags, which festoon her as she walks and which never leave her side. [abbr. shopping *bag lady*. Coined for such women living on the streets of New York City]

bagman *n.*[1] (*also* **bag man, bagsman**) **1** [mid-18C+] a commercial traveller. **2** [late 19C] (*UK*) a street dealer of second-hand clothes. **3** [1910s+] (*Aus.*) a tramp who travels on horseback; thus *bagman's leg*, the loss of a leg through falling under rolling stock; *bagman's union*, the brotherhood of travellers. [SE *bag*, whether of samples or possessions]

bagman *n.*[2] (*also* **bag man**) **1** [20C+] (*Aus./US*) one who collects or administers the collection of money obtained by various criminal activities. **2** [1950s+] (*orig. US*) a messenger, a go-between, esp. one who conveys a bribe from the one who offers it to the one who accepts. **3** [1960s+] (*orig. US*) a major narcotics dealer, i.e. one who has 'the bag'. **4** [1970s] (*Aus. Und.*) in a shoplifting

team, the person who actually takes the targeted object. **5** [2000s] (*orig. US*) fig. use of (2), an employee, a menial, esp. one who takes the blame for the decisions and activities of their employer. [SE *bag* + *man*, lit. one who carries a bag; Funk's *Standard Dict.* (1928) suggests 'one to whom graft is paid', but this is not sustained elsewhere]

bagman's gazette, the *n.* [1910s+] (*Aus.*) gossip and rumour, reified as an imaginary 'newspaper'. [BAGMAN n.[1] (3) + SE *gazette*]

bag of beer *n.* (*also* **bag o' beer**) [late 19C–1900s] a quart pot of beer, holding a mixture of porter and ale. [? joc. use of SE; note Fraser & Gibbons, *Soldier & Sailor Words & Phrases* (1925): 'Bag Of, A: Sufficiency, Plenty; e.g. A Bag of Beer']

bag of bones *n.*[1] (*also* **bone-bag, bone-heap, bundle of bones, stack of bones**) [mid-19C+] a noticeably thin person, or horse (cf. BAREBONES n.; BONE n.[6]; BONE-IN-A-VALLEY n.; BONES n.[1]; BONEYARD n.[1]; DRY-BONE n.).

bag of bones *n.*[2] [1980s] (*US Black*) marijuana cigarettes. [SE *bag* + BONE n.[11] (1)]

bag of coke *n.* **1** [20C+] sexual intercourse. **2** [1940s+] (*Aus.*) a man, a fellow. [rhy. sl.; (1) = POKE n.[1] (1); (2) = BLOKE n.]

bag of crap *n. see* BAG OF SHIT n.

bag-off *adj.* [1990s+] pertaining to pairing off, forming relationships. [BAG OFF v.]

bag off *v.* [1980s+] to pair off, to form a relationship; to pick up a sexual partner. [? SE *put in a bag*, lumped together]

bag of flour *n.* [1980s+] a shower (bathroom or rain). [rhy. sl.]

bag of fruit *n.* (*also* **bowl of fruit, box..., tin...**) [1920s+] (*Aus./N.Z./S.Afr.*) a suit. [rhy. sl.]

bag of guts *n.* [late 19C–1970s] (*US*) a fat person.

bag of jello *n. see* JELLO-BRAIN n.

bag of lead *n.* [1980s+] (*Aus. prison*) a bed. [rhy. sl.]

bag of mystery *n. see* BAGS OF MYSTERY n.

bag of nails *n.* [mid-19C–1940s] (*Aus./US*) chaos, disorder. [joc. pron. of SE *bacchanals* + the disorder of such a bagful]

bag of nuts *n.* [1910s] something exceptional.

bag of sand *n.* [1990s+] 1000, usu £1000. [rhy. sl. =GRAND n.[1]]

bag of shells *n.* [1950s+] (*Aus.*) a trifle, an unimportant object.

bag of shit *n.* (*also* **sack of shit, bag of crap**) [1940s+] a general term of abuse. [SE *bag/sack* + SHIT n.[1] (1)/CRAP n.[3] (1)]

bag of shit tied up with string *n.* [1950s+] a derog. personal description; usu. as *he looks like a...*

bag of smacked twats *n.* [1990s+] a general derog. description of an unattractive woman. [TWAT n. (1)]

bag of snakes *n.*[1] [1910s–50s] (*Aus.*) a drooping female breast. [such a bag is mis-shapen, lumpy, soft]

bag of snakes *n.*[2] [1950s+] (*Can.*) a lively, sexy young woman. [the liveliness of such a bag]

bag of tricks *n.* **1** [mid-19C+] whatever one needs. **2** [mid–late 19C] the penis. **3** [late 19C] the vagina. [SE *bag of tricks*, a clever or dextrous device]

bag of tripe *n.* [mid-19C+] an unpleasant person. [SE *bag* + TRIPE n.[2]]

bag of wind *n.* [19C+] a talkative person.

bag of yeast *n.* [1960s+] (*Aus.*) a priest. [rhy. sl.]

bag on *v.* [1980s+] (*US campus*) **1** to criticize, usu. wittily. **2** to complain. [BAG v.[4]]

bag one's head *v.* [mid-19C+] (*US*) to give in, to back off, to admit defeat. [lit. 'put one's head in a bag']

bag onto *v.* [1940s] (*US*) to notice, to pay attention to, often as imper. *bag onto that*, take a look at that. [fig. use of BAG v.[2] (1)]

bag o' wank *n.* [1990s+] a general term of abuse. [SE *bag* + WANK n.[1]]

bag-o-wire *n.* [1950s+] (*W.I. Rasta*) a betrayer. [i.e. if one grasps a bag of (barbed) wire one will get hurt]

bagpipe *n.*[1] **1** [early 17C–1910s] a long-winded, monotonous speaker. **2** [1940s] (*US Black*) a vacuum cleaner.

bagpipe *n.*[2] [17C–early 18C] the penis (cf. ACCORDION n.).

bagpipes *n.* [mid-19C] (*US*) the lungs.

bagpiping *n.* [late 18C+] intercourse under the armpit, generally a homosexual practice. [the required posture may be seen as resembling a piper at work]

bag-puncher/-punching *n. see* PUNCH THE BAG v.

bags *n.*[1] **1** [mid-18C+] (*US gay*) the testicles. **2** [1930s+] (*US*) the female breasts (cf. BALLOONS n.; BEE-STINGS n.; BELLS n.[3]; BOMBERS n.; BOMBS n.; BONGOS n.; BUMP n.[3]; CUPID'S KETTLEDRUMS n.; EYES n.[1]; FLESHY BAGPIPES n.; FUNBAGS n.; GLOBES n.; GUNS n.; HOOTER n.[3]; HOWITZER n.; JIBS n.[1]; LAMPS n.[2]; LUMPS n.[2]; MARACAS n.[1]; MOSQUITO BITES n.; MOUNTAINS n.; NUBBIES n.; PUPPIES n.[2]; ROCKETS n.; WHEELS n.[3]). **3** [1930s+] (*Irish*) a despised person. **4** [1960s+] (*Irish*) a mess, also in phr. *make bags of*, to make a mess of.

bags *n.*[2] [mid-19C+] trousers. [? BUMBAGS n.]

bags *v. see* BAGSY v.

bag school *v. see* BAG IT v. (1).

bags I! *excl.* (*also* **bags! bagsy!**) [20C+] (*UK juv.*) that's mine! I want to do that! [BAG v.[2] (3); an allied formula, mainly in preparatory schools, is *quis?* (Lat. who?) to offer an object, to which the responses are *ego!* (Lat. I) if one wishes to make a claim, or *baggy/bags I no par* (no part) if one wishes to be excluded]

bag-slinger *n.* [1930s] (*US*) a street-walker. [the trad. street prostitute carried a large bag; SLINGER n.[1] (2)]

bagsman *n. see* BAGMAN n.[1].

bags (of) *n.* [mid-19C; 1910s+] many, a great deal. [sporting jargon *bag*, the day's kill + a lit. *bagful*; the sl. use was popularized in WW1]

bags of mystery *n.* (*also* **bag of mystery, mysteries, mystery, mystery bags**) [mid-19C+] sausages or saveloys. [their dubious constituents; note RN use *mystery torpedoes, links of love*; British Army use *spotted mystery*]

bag some rays *v.* [1980s+] (*US*) to sunbathe, to get a suntan (cf. CATCH SOME RAYS v.). [BAG v.[2] + RAYS n.]

bag-swinger *n.* (*Aus.*) **1** [1930s+] a bookmaker. **2** [1950s–60s] a street-walker, a prostitute. [their essential equipment]

bagsy *adj.* [1920s–30s] (*Glasgow*) shapeless, lumpy. [ext. of SE *baggy*]

bagsy *v.* (*also* **bags**) [1940s+] to claim. [BAGS I! excl.]

bagsy! *excl. see* BAGS I! excl.

bag that! *excl.* (*also* **bag it!**) [1960s+] (*US*) forget it! [SE *bag*, to put in a bag/BAG v.[3] (2)]

bag-thief *n. see* BAGGER n.[1].

bag up *v.*[1] [1980s+] (*UK/US Black/W.I. teen*) to be caught or arrested by the police. [BAG v.[2] (1)]

bag up *v.*[2] [1990s+] (*UK/US Black/W.I. teen*) to laugh very hard at something. [? to fold up like a SE *bag*]

bag up *v.*[3] *see* BAG v.[6].

bag woman *n.* [1960s+] (*US*) a female go-between, taking money (usu. bribes or other illicit pay-offs) between 2 parties. [the female version of BAGMAN n.[2] (2)]

bag your face! *excl.* [1980s+] (*orig. US*) a general dismissive excl. [BAG v.[14]; var. on GO BAG YOUR HEAD! excl.]

bag z's *v.* (*also* **bag zeds, pick up z's**) [1960s+] (*US campus*) to nap, to sleep. [BAG v.[2] + Z n.[1]]

BAH *n.* [2000s] (*US Black*) a derog. description of a woman. [abbr. BITCH-ASS adj. + HO n.[1] (2)]

bah! *excl.* [early 17C+] an excl. of contempt. [somewhat defunct in general use, but taken up in 1990s by US teenagers]

bahakas *n.* (*also* **bahookey**) [1990s+] (*US*) buttocks, behind. [ety. unknown; ? var. on BAZOOKAS n.]

bahama mama *n.* [1980s+] (*US Black*) a fat, unattractive 'Black Mammy' stereotype, supposedly typical of the West Indies. [proper name *Bahamas* + SE *Mama*]

bah-fungoo! *excl.* (*also* **fungoo!**) [1940s+] (*US*) an excl. of contempt or dismissal. [Ital. *va t f'an culo*, 'go fuck yourself in the ass']

bahookey *n. see* BAHAKAS n.

bahtyman *n. see* BATTYMAN n.

bail *n.* [2000s] credit. [fig. use of SE *bail*, temporary release from prison in exchnage for securities]

bail *v.* **1** [1940s] (*US Black*) to enjoy oneself. **2** [1970s+] (*US campus*) to leave. **3** [1980s+] to play truant; also in non-school/college context. **4** [1980s+] to terminate a relationship, to break up; to abandon in a non-sexual sense. **5** [1990s+] to run. **6** [1990s+] to throw away. **7** [2000s] to back down, to abandon a promised act. [SE *bail out*, to escape from an airplane cockpit]

Bailey, the *n.* **1** [mid-19C+] the Central Criminal Court, London; generally known as the Old *Bailey*. **2** [late 19C] (*Aus.*) prison in general. [abbr. (2) f. (1)]

bailiff of marsham *n.* [17C] the ague or malarial fever; thus *arrested by the bailiff of marsham*, stricken with the fever. [such a fever sprang from the mosquitoes and poisoned air of the damp and stagnant marshlands]

bail on *v.* (*US teen*) **1** [1960s+] to oppress, to give a hard time to, to trouble. **2** [1980s] to break a date. **3** [1990s+] to leave someone. [? SE *bale*, torment, sorrow, misery, or dial. *baleise*, to beat, to thrash, to flog]

bail-out *n.* [1990s+] (*US*) an evasion, an escape. [BAIL OUT v. (1)]

bail out *v.* **1** [late 19C+] (*orig. US*) to leave in a hurry, to run off, to escape from a difficult situation. **2** [1940s] (*Aus.*) to lock out. **3** [1970s] to go mad. **4** [1980s] (*US*) to die. **5** [1980s+] (*US*) to abandon, to terminate a relationship. [orig. milit. use]

bail someone out *v.* [1970s+] (*orig. US*) to rescue someone.

bail up *v.* [mid-19C+] **1** (*Aus.*) to trap, to corner; the orig. use was to describe the 'stand and deliver' tactics of late 19C bushrangers. **2** (*Aus.*) to stop someone in the street for a chat. **3** to arrest. **4** to rob. [SE *bail*, a bar or frame used to confine an animal, esp. a cow when milking; (1) the term flourished during the bushrangers' heyday, although it is still occas. used, either of animals or of the victims of criminals]

bail up! *excl.* [mid-19C–1910s] (*orig. Aus.*) stop! the bushrangers' equivalent to the UK highwayman's 'Stand and deliver!' [adopted in UK from BAIL UP v. (1)]

bain *n.* [1910s] (*W.I.*) the buttocks; esp. in dismissive excl. *yo' bain!* [ety. unknown]

baister *n. see* BASTER n.[1].

bait *n.*[1] **1** [mid–late 19C] (*US*) one's intended prey or victim. **2** [1930s+] an attractive man or woman used to lure a victim into a con-game or a mugging. **3** [1970s+] (*US gay*) an undercover policeman, used for entrapment of homosexuals. [SE *bait*, a lure]

bait *n.*[2] (*also* **bate**) **1** [late 19C+] (*also* **batey**) a temper, a tantrum. **2** [1950s] any form of mood, no anger implied. [16C *bait*, to be snarling and snapping, like a dog endeavouring to break its chain and attack a persecutor; orig. juv. use, esp. in preparatory and public schools and carried over by former pupils into their adult lives]

bait *n.*[3] **1** [1930s+] an individual who is likely to get into trouble or face unwanted attention; esp. as sfx *-bait*, e.g. JAILBAIT n. **2** [1960s+] (*US*) an effeminate man who receives unwanted sexual attention from homosexual men. [SE *bait*, a lure]

bait *n.*[4] [1980s+] (*US Black*) a woman with noticeable body odour. [the rotting meat or fish that is often used as a hunter's *bait*]

bait layer *n.* [1980s] (*N.Z.*) a station cook; latterly used for an army cook. [UK north. dial. *bait*, food + SE *lay out* (i.e. on a table)]

bait the hook *v.* [1970s+] (*US gay*) to have sexual intercourse. [angling imagery]

Bajan spree *n.* [20C+] (*W.I., Trin.*) a small, spontaneous party. [SE *Bajan*, a native of Barbados + SPREE n.[1]]

baje *n.* (*also* **bajee, bajie**) [20C+] (*W.I.*) a Bajan, a native of Barbados. [abbr.]

bake *n.*[1] [1910s] **1** (*Irish*) an agitated state, poss. irritated. **2** anything bad. **3** the head. [(2) and (3) WW1 use]

bake *n.*[2] **1** [1970s] (*Aus. Und.*) a negative description, as given in court by a policeman who wishes to ensure that the defendant gets a long sentence; thus *no-bake*, a good or neutral description. **2** [1990s+] an interrogation. [play on ROAST v. (3)/ROAST v. (5)]

bake *n.*³ *see* HOMEBAKE n.

bake *n.*⁴ *see* BEAK n.² (2).

bake *v.*¹ [1950s–60s] (*US drugs*) to prepare an injection of a narcotic by heating the powder and water mixture.

bake *v.*² [1950s+] (*US prison*) to execute in the electric chair. [blackly humorous use of SE]

bake *v.*³ [1980s+] (*Aus. prison*) to reprimand; to criticize severely. [play on ROAST v.]

bake *v.*⁴ *see* HOMEBAKE v.

bakebrain *n.* (*also* **bakehead**) [1940s] (*US*) a fool, an idiot (cf. BALLOON-BRAIN n.; BATBRAIN n.; BEANBRAIN n.; BEETLEBRAIN n.; BIRDBRAIN n.; BUTTERBRAIN n.; CHICKENBRAIN n.; CRACKBRAIN n.; DICKBRAIN n.; DILLBRAIN n.; DORKBRAIN n.; DUR-BRAIN n.; FUCKBRAIN n.; GUMBRAIN n.; JINGLE-BRAINS n.; LAMEBRAIN n.; MEATBRAIN n.; MOUSEBRAIN n.; OUNCE-BRAIN n.; PEABRAIN n.; PIMPLE BRAIN n.; RAISIN-BRAIN n.; SLIVER-BRAIN n.; SQUAREBRAIN n.; WETBRAIN n.). [SE *bake* + sfx *-brain/-HEAD* sfx (1); here the image is of hardness]

bake break *n.* [1980s+] (*US drugs*) a break from work during which one smokes a pipe, e.g. of marijuana or of crack cocaine. [one 'bakes' the ROCK n.³ in order to smoke it]

baked *adj.* **1** [late 18C–1900s] (*also* **baked up**) exhausted. **2** [late 19C; 1980s] (*also* **baked up**) sun-burned or very tanned. **3** [1980s+] (*US*) under the influence of marijuana. **4** [1980s+] (*US campus*) drunk. **5** [2000s] intoxicated by cannabis.

baked bean *n.*¹ [1990s+] (*Aus.*) a male homosexual. [rhy. sl. = QUEEN n.² (1)]

baked bean *n.*² [2000s] a sexual encounter. [rhy. sl. = SCENE n. (6)]

baked dinner *n.* [late 19C–1900s] (*UK Und.*) bread. [used to fool new arrivals at a prison who assume such a dinner will be somewhat more extensive]

baked potato *n. see* FRIED POTATO n.

baked up *adj. see* BAKED adj.

baked wind *n.* [1900s–20s] (*US*) nonsense, rubbish. [var. on HOT AIR n.]

bakehead *n. see* BAKEBRAIN n.

bake it *v.* [late 19C+] to refrain from visiting the lavatory, however desperate the need to defecate. [the excreta remain in the 'oven' of one's intestines]

bake one *v.* [1990s+] to defer defecation, however urgently one requires it. [var. on BAKE IT v.]

bake potatoes *v.* [1930s+] (*US gay*) to have anal intercourse.

baker *n.*¹ [late 19C] (*US Und.*) an idler. [mistranslation of LOAFER n. (2)]

baker *n.*² [1950s] (*US Und.*) the electric chair. [BAKE v.²]

baker *n.*³ [1960s] (*US campus*) the grade B (cf. ACE n.⁶). [initial letter]

baker-kneed *adj.* **1** [17C–19C] knock-kneed. **2** [mid-17C] effeminate. [(1) knock-knees are a physical problem supposedly characteristic of a baker's job; (2) in folk myth knock-knees are one of the 'proofs' of effeminacy]

baker-legged *adj.* **1** [17C–mid-18C] knock-kneed. **2** [17C–18C] effeminate. [var. on BAKER-KNEED adj.]

baker's dozen *n.*¹ [20C+] a cousin. [rhy. sl.]

baker's dozen *n.*² [1970s+] (*US gay*) a group of attractive young men.

baker's yeast *n.* [1980s] (*Aus.*) a priest. [rhy. sl.]

bakery goods *n.* [1960s+] (*US gay*) the buttocks, the anus; thus phr. *the baker's is closed*, sex is not available (cf. BISCUITS n.; BUN n.²; BUN-BUN n.; BUNS n.; CAKES n.¹; CRUMPET n.²; CUPCAKES n.¹; DOUGHNUT n.²; DOUGHY n.²; ENGLISH MUFFINS n.; HOT BUNS n.; JAMPOT n.³; JAM ROLL n.; POUNDCAKE n.; SWEETCAKES n.; SWEETCHEEKS n.; SWISS-ROLL n.; TROUSER CAKES n.).

bake sale *n.* [1980s+] (*US drugs*) a session of smoking crack cocaine. [play on SAmE phr.]

bake someone's bread *v.* [late 14C] to kill, to 'do for'.

bakgat *adj.* [1960s+] (*S.Afr.*) splendid, first-rate, 'posh'. [? Afk. *bak*, fine + *gat*, hole (anus)]

bakgat! *excl.* [1960s+] (*S.Afr.*) an excl. of approval, pleasure etc. [BAKGAT adj.]

bakhara *n. see* BUCKAROO n.

baking pot *n. see* MELTING POT n.

bakkie *n.* [1960s+] (*S.Afr.*) a light truck, a pick-up, a 4×4 vehicle. [Afk. *bak*, a container + dimin. sfx *-ie*]

bakore *n.* [1970s+] (*S.Afr.*) large, protruding ears. [Afk. *bak*, a bowl + *ore*, ears]

baksheesh *n.* (*also* **backshee, backsheesh, buckshee, bucksheech, buckshish**) **1** [mid-19C+] a gratuity, a tip. **2** [1910s+] something free, a 'perk'. [Pers. *bakhshish*, present, ult. f. *bakhshi-dan*, to give. Given the stereotyping of the 'Oriental merchant' or the Third World beggar, the implication tends to be slightly pej.]

baksheesh *adj.* [1910s] (*Aus.*) convenient, easy, undemanding. [BAKSHEESH n. (2)]

baksheesh *v.* (*also* **buckshish**) [late 19C+] to give a tip.

baksheesh *adv.* [1910s] (*Aus.*) for free. [BAKSHEESH n. (2)]

bala *n.*¹ [early–mid-19C] coarse or senseless talk. [Cornish *bal*, loud talking]

bala *n.*² [1990s+] a *bala*clava. [abbr.]

balaclava *n.* [mid-19C] a full beard. [the beards worn by many soldiers who had returned from the rigours of the Crimean War of 1854–6]

balaclava *v.* [20C+] to have sexual intercourse. [rhy. sl. = CHARVER v. (1)]

balahack *n.* (*also* **ballyhack, ballywack, ballywrack**) [mid-19C–1920s] a euph. for *hell*; thus combs. *all to ballyhack*, *go to ballyhack*. [? Irish *baile*, a town + HECK n.]

balahack *v.* (*US*) **1** [late 19C+] to confuse, to blunder. **2** [1930s+] to impose upon. **3** [1930s+] to beat severely. [BALAHACK n.]

balahu *n.* [1940s+] (*W.I.*) a noisy, boisterous person. [BALLYHOO n.]

balance *v.* [1940s–50s] (*Aus.*) to swindle.

balangas *n.* [1980s+] (*US*) the female breasts. [P.R. Sp.]

balcony *n.* [1940s+] (*Aus./US*) the female breasts, esp. as thrust up and forward in the brassieres of the 1940s–50s.

bald brigade *n. see* BALD-HEADED ROW n.

balderdash *n.* **1** [16C–18C] any adulterated or mixed drink, typically milk and beer, beer and wine, brandy and mineral water, which, while duly consumed, was generally considered unpleasant. **2** [late 17C–18C] obscenity. **3** [early 19C] (*Anglo-Irish*) a fool. [like the SE meaning of 'nonsense', which is the sole 20C+ survivor, f. 16C *balderdash*, frothy water. The origin appears to be Scand., whether in Da. *balder*, noise or clatter, Norw. *bjaldra*, to speak indistinctly, or Icel. *baldras*, to make a clatter. *Dash* comes f. Da. *daske*, to slap or flap; thus *dask*, a slap. The Welsh *baldorddus*, noisy, f. *baldordd*, idle, noisy talk, chatter, may also play a role. An alternative ety. has been suggested (and backed up by a 16C ref. to 'barbers balderdash') as coming from the froth and foam made by barbers in *dashing* their *balls* (spherical pieces of soap) backwards and forwards in hot water]

baldface dish *n.* [19C] (*US*) a plain white china plate. [its lack of ornamentation]

baldfaced shirt *n.* [late 19C–1960s] (*US*) a dress shirt with a starched front. [SE *baldfaced cattle*, Herefords, which have white faces]

baldfaced stag *n.* [mid-19C] a bald man. [play on SE]

baldface (whisky) *n.* (*also* **baldface juice, ballface (whisky)**) [early 19C+] (*US*) cheap, potent whisky. [? the *baldfaced hornet*, which has a notable sting + SE *whisky*]

baldhead *n.* **1** [late 19C+] (*orig. US*) an old man. **2** [1970s+] (*W.I.*) a member of the Rastafarian cult who does not, however, sport the characteristic beard and dreadlocks (cf. CLEAN-FACED MAN n.). **3** [1970s+] (*also* **ballhead**) (*W.I.*) a White person. **4** [1970s+] (*also* **ballhead**) (*W.I.*) a non-Rastafarian Black person. **5** [1980s] (*UK Black*) (*also* **ballhead**) a bald person. **6** [1980s+] (*N.Z., Maori*) (*also* **ballhead**) an outsider. [SE *bald/ball-head*, a head shaped like a ball; thus the person who has one. In Rastafarian use most Whites, however hirsute, may be considered to be *ballheads*, in comparison with the Rastaman and his flowing dreadlocks]

bald-headed *adj.*[1] [mid-19C+] totally unprepared, utterly spontaneous. [the image of one who rushes out without even pausing to put on a hat]

bald-headed *adj.*[2] [late 19C+] (*US Black*) deliberately deceptive, underhand, e.g. *a bald-headed lie*. [one who makes no effort to mask their bald head]

bald-headed *adj.*[3] [1930s+] (*US*) bare, hairless, shining white.

bald-headed *adj.*[4] [1940s] (*US Black*) stupid, foolish (cf. AIRHEADED adj.). [such a person has nothing 'on top']

bald-headed *adv.* [mid-19C+] precipitately, esp. in phr. *go (at) it/something baldheaded, go bald-headed at/for/into*, to put all one's efforts into, to commit oneself wholly, to attack without care or thought – and totally disregard the possible consequences. [BALD-HEADED adj.[1]]

bald-headed bandit *n.* (*also* **bald-headed bastard, ...sailor**) [1920s+] the penis (cf. BALD-HEADED HERMIT n.).

bald-headed butter *n.* [late 19C–1900s] a portion of butter in which there are no hairs. [the pre-industrial era of butter manufacture]

bald-headed department *n. see* BALD-HEADED ROW n.

bald-headed hermit *n.* (*also* **bald-headed friar, baldpate friar**) [mid-17C–19C] the penis, esp. an uncircumcised penis (cf. BALD-HEADED BANDIT n.; BLIND COCK n.; BLIND MEAT n.; CAVALIER n.; CLIPDICK n.; TURTLENECK (SWEATER) n.). [the monk's bald tonsure and the *glans penis* which, in uncircumcised men, 'hides away' beneath the foreskin]

bald-headed lump *n.* [1930s] (*US tramp*) a parcel of food containing only the basics, with no 'sweets' such as cake or pie. [SE *baldheaded*, i.e. nothing 'on' the food]

bald-headed mouse *n.* [1980s] (*US gay*) the erect penis (cf. ANTEATER n.).

bald-headed row *n.* (*also* **bald brigade, bald-headed department**) [1900s–20s] the men, stereotyped as old, who take the front row of a burlesque or similar show. [BALDHEAD n. (1) + SE *row*/BRIGADE n./SE *department*]

bald-headed sailor *n. see* BALD-HEADED BANDIT n.

baldie *n.* (*also* **baldy**) **1** [mid-19C+] (*orig. US*) a bald man; thus used as a nickname for one who is bald. **2** [late 19C–1940s] an old man. [abbr.]

bald man in a boat *n.* [20C+] the clitoris (cf. BABY IN THE BOAT n.).

baldober *n.* (*also* **baldover, baldower**) [late 19C–1900s] (*UK Und.*) a boss, a leader, a spokesperson. [Ger. Und., ult. Heb. *baal*, a master + *dovor*, a word]

bald-rib *n.* [early 17C] a thin, bony person. [SE *bald-rib*, 'A joint of pork cut from nearer the rump than the spare-rib, so called "because the bones thereof are made bald and bare of flesh" (Minsheu)' (*OED*)]

bald-tyre bandit *n.* [1970s+] (*UK Und.*) a traffic police officer. [SE *bald-tyre* +BANDIT sfx (1); such police are considered less competent or important than their criminal-catching peers]

balductum *n.* [late 16C–early 17C] nonsense, rubbish. [SE *balductum*, a posset, hot milk curdled with ale or wine]

balductum *adj.* [late 16C–early 17C] nonsensical, rubbish. [BALDUCTUM n.]

baldwin *n.* [1990s+] (*US campus*) an attractive person. [the collective fame and attractiveness of the *Baldwin* brothers, all Hollywood actors, namely Alec Baldwin (b.1958), Daniel Baldwin (b.1960), William Baldwin (b.1963) and Stephen Baldwin (b.1966)]

baldy *n. see* BALDIE n.

bale *n.* [1960s+] (*drugs*) marijuana. [SE *bale*, a (wrapped) bundle; note Landy (1971) states 'seventy-five to 500 pounds of marijuana']

bale of goods *n. see* PIECE OF GOODS n. (2).

bale of hay *n.* (*also* **bale of straw**) **1** [late 19C] (*US short order*) corned beef and cabbage. **2** [1920s+] (*orig. US theatre*) a White woman, esp. a blonde. **3** [1930s] (*US*) a strawberry ice-cream. [SE *bale + hay/straw/*STRAW n.[1]]

bale of straw *n.* [2000s] a state of nakedness. [rhy. sl. = IN THE RAW phr.]

bales of briquettes *n.* [1970s+] (*Irish*) platform-soled shoes. [resemblance]

Balkan tap *n.* [20C+] madness. [on pattern of DOOLALLY TAP n.; proper name *Balkans* + *tap*, sunstroke; the term evolved to characterize the growing, happy indolence that took over men involved in the Macedonian campaign in WW1]

ball *n.*[1] (*US*) **1** [mid-18C–1910s] a bullet. **2** [late 19C–1920s] a silver dollar. [? its circularity]

ball *n.*[2] [mid-19C] (*UK Und.*) a prison ration, 170g (6oz) of meat. [? the resemblance of the lump of meat]

ball *n.*[3] [mid-19C+] (*orig. US*) a shot of liquor, esp. in phrs. *a beer and a ball*, a beer and a shot of whisky; *ball joint*, a bar. [BALL OF FIRE n.[1]]

ball *n.*[4] [20C+] **1** a walk. **2** a talk. [abbr. BALL OF CHALK n.]

ball *n.*[5] [1910s–30s] a small package of a narcotic or other drug. [the drug package is rolled into a ball]

ball *n.*[6] **1** [1910s+] (*US*) base*ball*. **2** [1980s+] (*orig. US Black*) basket*ball*. [abbr.]

ball *n.*[7] **1** [1930s+] (*orig. US Black*) a party, a celebration; a riotously extravagant good time. **2** [1950s] (*US drugs*) a feeling of well-being, a 'high', from a drug. **3** [1960s] an orgy. **4** [1970s+] a delightful person.

ball *n.*[8] (*orig. US*) **1** [1940s+] sexual intercourse. **2** [1970s] one who has or offers sexual intercourse. [BALL v.[2]]

ball *n.*[9] [1990s+] (*US*) a stupid or silly person; used as a response to an unintelligent action, as a sarcastic response to a foolish remark or as an observation of another's character (or lack thereof). [BALLS n.[1] (1)]

ball *v.*[1] [1940s+] (*orig. US Black*) to have a good time, to enjoy oneself. [BALL n.[7] (1)]

ball *v.*[2] [1950s+] to have sexual intercourse (cf. BAGAGA v.). [BALLS n.[1] (1) but note SE *ball*, a dance and combs. at DANCE v.[1]]

ball *v.*[3] [1980s+] (*US Black*) to play basketball. [BALL n.[6] (2)]

ball *v.*[4] *see* BALL OF CHALK v.

ball *v.*[5] *see* BALL (OUT) v.

-ball *sfx* [20C+] used in comb. with another term, usu. a n., to describe a contemptible, despised person, when of a woman, often with implications of promiscuity (cf. -BAG sfx; CHEESEBALL n.; CORNBALL n.; CRUDBALL n.; DIRTBALL n.; FRUITBALL n.; FUCKBALL n.; GOOFBALL n.[2]; GREASEBALL n.; JELLY BALL n.; NUTBALL n.; ODDBALL n.; SCREWBALL n.; SCUMBALL n.; SCUZZBALL n.; SHITBALL n.; SLUDGEBALL n.; SOURBALL n.). [SE *ball*, i.e. a 'ball of...']

balla *n. see* BALLER n. (1).

ballad *n.* **1** [1950s] (*W.I./UK Black*) a story, usu. long and complicated. **2** [1970s+] (*US gay*) an excuse.

ballad-basket *n.* [mid-18C–19C] a street-singer.

ballahoo *adj.* [20C+] (*W.I.*) noisy, boisterous, obstreperous. [BALLYHOO n.]

ball and bat *n.* [1900s–20s] a hat. [rhy. sl.]

ball and chain *n.* **1** [1920s+] (*orig. US Black*) one's wife or regular girlfriend; thus *ball-and-chained*, married. **2** [1940s] (*US Und.*) a tramp's younger male companion. [SE *ball and chain*, a device that secured convicts during 19C]

ball and chalk *see under* BALL OF CHALK.

ballarag *v. see* BALLYRAG *v.*

ballarat *n.*[1] [1980s+] (*Aus. prison*) a homosexual. [rhy. sl. = CAT n.[13] (1)]

ballarat *n.*[2] *see* AT BALLARAT *phr.*

ballarat lantern *n.* [late 19C–1940s] (*Aus./N.Z.*) a candle stuck in the neck of a bottle, the bottom of which has been knocked off. [proper name *Ballarat* + SE *lantern*; a necessity in pre-electrified days]

Ballarat passive *n.* [1980s] (*Aus.*) a male homosexual. [BALLARAT n.[1]]

ballast *n.*[1] [early 19C–1930s] heavy food. [SE *ballast*, seen as 'stuffing' a ship and thus a stomach]

ballast *n.*[2] **1** [mid-19C–1940s] money (cf. ACTUAL, THE n.). **2** [1900s] (*US*) a gun. [SE *ballast*, i.e. it helps one stay 'afloat' and 'on an even keel']

ball-bag *n.* **1** [late 19C+] the scrotum (cf. BAG n.[1]; BO-JACK n.; BOLLOCKBAG n.; BOZACK n.; DADDY-BAG n.; GRAND BAG n.; NADBAG n.; NUTSACK n.; PURSE n.; RAISIN BAG n.; SACK O' NUTS n.; TADPOLE CARRIER n.). **2** [1960s] (*US*) a jockstrap. [BALLS n.[1] (1) + BAG n.[1] (1)]

ball-breaker *n.* (*orig. US*) **1** [1950s+] a difficult, boring or exasperating job, problem or situation. **2** [1950s+] a person who sets difficult work or problems, a hard taskmaster. **3** [1970s] a tease. **4** [1970s] a thug. **5** [1970s] a weapon. **6** [1970s+] (*also* **ball-lopper**) a dominating woman, one who destroys the self-confidence of a man. [BALLS n.[1] (1) + SE *breaker*]

ball-breaking *n.* (*also* **ball-busting**) [1940s+] (*orig. US*) harassment. [BALL-BREAKER n./BALL-BUSTER n. in all senses]

ball-breaking *adj.* (*also* **ball-busting**) **1** [1940s+] (*orig. US*) acting as a hard taskmaster or dominating woman. **2** [1970s] very irritating. **3** [1980s] physically demanding, exhausting. [BALL-BREAKER n./BALL-BUSTER n.]

ball-buster *n.* **1** [20C+] (*US Und.*) a thief who grabs his victim by the testicles while his accomplice takes his wallet. **2** [1940s+] (*orig. US*) a nagging woman. **3** [1950s–60s] (*US campus*) a notably hard course or examination. **4** [1950s+] any overbearingly unpleasant person or circumstances. **5** [1960s+] any thing or person seen as extraordinary or outstanding. **6** [1980s+] (*also* **buster**) a tease. [BALLS n.[1] (1) + SE *buster*; but note Yid. *baleboosteh*, a bossy woman, lit. 'mistress of the house']

ball-clanker *n.* [1960s] (*US*) a man who boasts, prob. groundlessly, of his sexual prowess. [BALLS n.[1] (1) + SE *clanker*]

ball-crusher *n.* **1** [1970s+] a dominating woman who 'emasculates' her partner, usu. a husband. **2** [1980s+] a sexually voracious woman who exhausts her partner's virility. [BALLS n.[1] (1) + SE *crush*]

ball-cutter *n.* [1960s+] (*US*) a nagging, domineering or demanding woman. [BALLS n.[1] (1) + SE *cutter*]

balled-up *adj.* [late 19C+] confused, mixed up, in a mess. [BALLS v. (1); note Willard (1896): 'To come to a standstill after making spasmodic and somewhat erratic efforts — as a horse does when snow gathers in balls upon its hoofs']

baller *n.* [1990s+] **1** (*US Black*) (*also* **balla, bawla**) one who is extremely rich, esp. from the profits of criminality. **2** (*US campus*) one who enjoys playing sport, esp. basketball. **3** (*US campus*) an attractive person. [? HAVE A BALL v.; the term is used esp. by the Los Angeles gang the Bloods; *balla/bawla* are consciously 'wrong' spellings, designed to emphasize the 'outlaw' status of such individuals]

baller blocker *n.* [2000s] (*US Black*) a person who stops one from succeeding. [BALLER n. (1) + SE *blocker*]

ballface *n.* [mid–late 19C] (*US Black*) a White person. [? BALLFACE (WHISKY) n.]

ball-faced *adj.* [1990s+] a general term of derision, lit. 'testicle-faced'. [BALLS n.[1] (1) + SE *-faced*]

ballface (whisky) *n. see* BALDFACE (WHISKY) n.

ballgame *n.* (*also* **ball game, ball-game**) [1930s+] (*orig. US*) a state of affairs, a situation; esp. in phr. *different/whole new ball game*, a radically new situation (to which one will be forced to adapt). [SE *ball-game*, a sporting event, esp. a baseball game]

ball gown *n.* [1970s+] (*US camp gay*) a man's suit.

ball-gusted *adj.* [mid-19C] (*US*) disgusted, appalled. [BALLY adj. + SE *disgusted*]

ballhead *n. see* BALDHEAD n.

ballhop *n.* [1970s+] (*Irish*) a rumour, an unsupported theory, a lie; thus *ballhopper*, a rumour-monger. [Gaelic sport]

balling *n.*[1] **1** [1930s+] (*orig. US Black*) having fun. **2** [1990s+] (*US Black*) enriching oneself by selling drugs (usu. crack cocaine). **3** [2000s] (*US drugs*) carrying a package of contraband cocaine by placing it in the vagina. **4** [2000s] showing off, flaunting one's possessions. [BALL v.[1]; ? (2) and 4) fig. use; ? (3) f. (2) or the SE *ball* that is hidden]

balling *n.*[2] [1960s+] (*orig. US Black*) having sexual intercourse. [BALL v.[2]]

balling *n.*[3] [1990s+] (*US Black*) excelling in the playing of basketball. [BALL n.[6] (2)]

balling *adj.* [1950s–60s] (*US*) excellent, wonderful, first-rate; usu. as *balling chick*, an attractive girl or woman. [BALLING n.[1] (1)]

ballistics *n.* [1990s+] (*US Black*) the facts, information, usu. in rap lyrics. [SE *ballistics* + implication of *statistics*]

ball it off *v.* [mid-19C] (*US*) to travel at speed. [the rolling of a ball]

ball it up *v.* [1950s–60s] (*US*) to celebrate in an uproarious manner. [BALL v.[1]]

ball-less *adj.* [1950s+] weak, emasculated; thus *ball-less wonder*, an especially weak individual. [BALLS n.[1] (1) + sfx *-less*]

ball-lopper *n. see* BALL-BREAKER n. (6).

ball lump *n.* [1920s–50s] (*US tramp*) a parcel of food given to tramp. [resemblance]

ball naked *adj.* [1960s+] (*US*) utterly naked. [abbr. BALLOCK NAKED adj.]

ballock *n.* (*also* **bollock**) **1** [late 17C+] a testicle; usu. in pl. (*see* BALLOCKS n.[1]). **2** [1940s+] a general term of abuse (cf. BALLOCKS n.[2]). [OE *beallucas*, itself Teut. root *ball-*; *ballock(s)* meant testicle(s) f. 11C but remained SE until late 17C; it appears in Bailey's *Universal Etymological English Dictionary* in all edns f. 1721–1800 but was not included in Samuel Johnson's *Dictionary*, which drew heavily on Bailey's word-list, in 1755; one must thus assume that the word was passing then from polite use; it was definitely slang by 1800 and appears as such in Grose (1796) although, oddly, in neither Grose (1785), Hotten nor F&H]

ballock *v.*[1] (*also* **bollock, bullock**) [mid-18C–mid-19C] (*US*) to grab by the genitals when fighting. [BALLOCK n. (1)]

ballock *v.*[2] [late 19C] to have sexual intercourse (cf. BAGAGA v.). [BALLOCK n. (1)]

ballock *v.*[3] (*also* **ballocks, bollock, bollocks**) [1930s+] to reprimand, to tell off. [fig. use of BALLOCK n. (1)]

ballocked *adj.* [1980s+] very drunk (cf. ANNIHILATED adj.). [fig. use of BALLOCK v.[2], i.e. FUCKED UP adj. (12)]

ballockeering *adj.* [mid-17C] lusty. [BALLOCK n. (1); however, a note on the translation claims: 'M. Le Duchat says, and proves it, that *couilleaux* only means *cucullated*, i.e. hooded monkish sort of rabbins […] not at all alluding to the *scrotum* (*couillon* in French)']

ballock gravy *n.* [2000s] semen (cf. BABY GRAVY n.). [BALLOCK n. (1) + GRAVY n.[1] (2)]

ballocking *n.*[1] [late 19C] sexual intercourse. [BALLOCK v.[2]]

ballocking *n.*[2] (*also* **bollocking, bolly**) [1940s+] a severe telling off, a scolding. [BALLOCK v.[3]]

ballock naked *adj.* (*also* **ballocky naked, bollicky…, bollock…, bollocks…, bollocky…, bollocky**) [1930s+] totally naked, thus revealing one's genitals; also used of women. [BALLOCK n. (1) + SE *naked*]

ballocks *n.*[1] (*also* **ballyx, bollix, bollocks, bollox, bollux**)

1 [late 17C+] testicles. **2** [1930s+] a mess; thus *make a ballocks of.* **3** [1990s+] used in phr. as intensifier, e.g. *laugh one's ballocks off.* [BALLOCK n.]

ballocks n.² (*also* **bollix, bollocks, bollox**) **1** [late 18C–early 19C] a parson. **2** [1910s+] (*also* **bollixing**) rubbish, nonsense (cf. BALLS n.²). **3** [1910s+] a person in a state of confusion, who is talking (2). **4** [1910s+] a fool, an incompetent (cf. BALLOCK n.; BASTICLES n.; SATCHEL n.; SCROTE n.). **5** [1920s+] a person, often used affectionately. **6** [1940s+] (*orig. Irish*) (*also* **bolix, bullox**) an unpleasant person; esp. with adj., e.g. *right old bollix, little ballocks.* **7** [1990s+] used as a direct, pej. term of address. [fig. use of BALLOCKS n.¹ (1); or ? (2) developed f. (1) on the premise that sermonizing is, *de facto,* nonsense]

ballocks n.³ (*also* **bollocks**) [1980s+] courage, vigour.

ballocks n.⁴ *see* DOG'S BALLOCKS n. (2).

ballocks v.¹ *see* BALLOCK v.³.

ballocks v.² *see* BALLOCKS (UP) v.

ballocks! *excl.* (*also* **bollix! bollocks! bollox!**) **1** [late 17C+] rubbish! nonsense! **2** [1950s+] as an excl. of derision. **3** [1980s+] a general excl. of annoyance, frustration. [BALLOCKS n.¹ (1); but modern use tends to emphasize BALLOCKS n.² (2)]

ballocks about v. (*also* **ballocks around, bollocks about/around**) [1950s+] **1** to mess about, to play the fool (cf. ACT THE ANGORA v.). **2** to infuriate, to waste someone's time, to be indecisive. [BALLOCKS (UP) v.]

ballocksed (up) adj. (*also* **bollixed (up), bollocksed (up), bolloxed (up)**)) **1** [1930s+] ruined, messed up, thwarted, in a muddle. **2** [2000s] drunk (cf. ANNIHILATED adj.). [BALLOCKS (UP) v. (1)]

ballocks in brackets n. [20C+] a bow-legged man. [BALLOCKS n.¹ (1); visual appearance]

ballocks (up) v. (*also* **bollix (up), bollocks (up), bollox (up), bollux (up)**) [1930s+] **1** (*orig. Aus.*) to ruin, to make a mess of. **2** to waste time, to fiddle with. [BALLOCKS n.¹ (2)]

ballocks worker n. [1950s] any overbearingly unpleasant person or circumstance. [BALLOCKS n.¹ (1) + SE *worker*]

ballocky naked adj. *see* BALLOCK NAKED adj.

ball of chalk n. (*also* **ball and chalk**) [20C+] a walk. [rhy. sl.]

ball of chalk v. (*also* **ball, ball and chalk, bowl of chalk, lump of chalk**) [20C+] **1** to talk. **2** to walk. [rhy. sl.]

ball of dirt n. [late 19C] (*US*) the earth. [fig. use of SE + ? rhy. sl.]

ball off v.¹ [late 19C] (*US*) to treat to a drink. [BALL n.³]

ball off v.² [1950s+] to masturbate; one of many such verbs that use 'off' (cf. BEAT OFF v.²; BRING OFF BY HAND v.; BRING ONESELF OFF v.; DO ONESELF (OFF) v.; DUB OFF v.; FLIP OFF v.¹; FLIP ONESELF OFF v.; FREAK OFF v.; FRIG OFF v.; GET OFF v.⁵; JACK OFF v.¹; JAG OFF v.; JENNY OFF v.; JERK OFF v.¹; JILL OFF v.; PLAY ONESELF OFF v.; POUND OFF v.; PULL OFF v.³; PUMP OFF v.; RUB OFF v.; RUN OFF v.²; SCREW OFF v.; SNAP ONE OFF v.; STROKE v.¹; TOSS (OFF) v.¹; WANK OFF v.; WHACK OFF v.¹; WHIP OFF v.²; WORK (ONESELF) OFF v.; YANK OFF v.). [BALLS n.¹ (1) / BALL v.²]

ball of fire n.¹ [18C–19C] a glass of brandy. [the effect of the liquor]

ball of fire n.² [20C+] **1** an individual known for their energy, resourcefulness or drive. **2** (*US*) a fast vehicle. **3** an excellent thing, idea.

ball of lead n. [1900s–20s] the head. [rhy. sl.]

ball of muscle n. [1930s+] (*Aus.*) an energetic, lively person.

ball of twine n. [20C+] (*Aus.*) a railway line. [rhy. sl.]

ball of wax n. [19C] a shoemaker. [the wax used in shoe-making]

ball of yarn n. [1940s–60s] (*US*) the female genitals. [19C Anglo-Irish bawdy folk-song, e.g. the lyric 'Keep both hands on your little ball of yarn']

balloon n.¹ (*US*) **1** [late 18C] a security certificate issued by the Confederation (the original 13 colonies that seceded from Britain).

2 [1970s+] $1. **3** [1970s+] (*gambling*) $10. [(1) ? the certificates were less than substantial]

balloon n.² [20C+] (*Ulster*) a garrulous person. [they are 'full of hot air']

balloon n.³ [1920s–30s] (*US*) a bedroll; thus in phr. *carrying the balloon,* looking for work. [the supposed resemblance]

balloon n.⁴ **1** [1950s+] a condom. **2** [1960s+] (*drugs*) a condom that is used to carry heroin, cocaine or any other powdered narcotic drug. **3** [2000s] (*drugs*) a heroin supplier. [portions of heroin are often sold in a contraceptive, tied off at the end]

balloon v.¹ [late 18C] (*UK Und.*) for a pickpocket to mingle with the crowds watching the launch of the then new manned balloons.

balloon v.² [1960s+] (*drugs*) to package narcotic drugs for distribution and sale. [BALLOON n.⁴ (2)]

balloon-brain n. [1940s+] (*US*) a fool, a simpleton (cf. AIRBALL n.; BAKEBRAIN n.). [SE *balloon* + sfx -*brain*; the image is of emptiness or hot air]

balloon (car) n. [20C+] the saloon bar of a public house. [rhy. sl.]

balloon-head n. [1930s+] (*US*) a fool, a simpleton (cf. AIRBALL n.). [SE *balloon* + -HEAD sfx (1)]

balloon it v. [1920s–30s] (*US*) to pack up one's bedroll and set off travelling. [BALLOON n.³]

balloon juice n.¹ [late 19C+] **1** soda water; thus *balloon juice lowerer,* a teetotaller, who only drinks or 'lowers' soda water. **2** ginger beer. **3** (*W.I., Bdos/Guyn.*) any form of sweet, colourful fizzy drink. [? gaseous nature of soda-water; contemp. use is W.I. only]

balloon juice n.² [1900s–60s] (*US*) nonsense, rubbish, empty chatter (cf. BALLOON SOUP n.). [SE *balloon* + *juice,* i.e. HOT AIR n.]

balloon-knot bandit n. [1990s+] a male homosexual. [BALLOON n.⁴ (1) +SE *knot* +BANDIT sfx (2); the knotting of the condom post-intercourse]

balloon room n. [1940s–50s] (*US Black*) a place where people gather to smoke marijuana. [like the SE *balloon,* marijuana smokers get HIGH adj.¹ (2)]

balloon room without a parachute n. [1950s–70s] (*US Black*) a disappointment, a let-down, esp. a place where one has been promised a smoke of marijuana but which, in fact, offers no supply. [BALLOON ROOM n.]

balloons n. [1940s+] conspicuously large female breasts (cf. BAGS n.¹).

balloon soup n. [1920s–30s] (*US*) nonsense, empty chatter (cf. BALLOON JUICE n.²). [i.e. HOT AIR n.]

ballot n. *see* BALOT n.

ball (out) v. [1930s+] to travel at high speed, to leave. [abbr. BALL THE JACK v. (1)]

ball out v. *see* BAWL (OUT) v.

ballow v. [19C+] (*US*) to lay claim to. [Lancashire dial. *ballow, balla,* I claim]

ball-park adj. (*also* **in the (right) ball-park**) [1950s+] (*orig. US*) of a figure, approximate, rough, estimated, esp. in phr. *ball-park figure.* [SE *ball-park,* a baseball stadium, i.e. the rough estimate of the number of fans watching a sporting event]

balls n.¹ **1** [16C+] the testicles (cf. BOBBLES n.¹; BULLETS n.¹; BUM-BALLS n.; CHUCKIES n.; CUBES n.²; GLOBES n.; GOOLIES n.; LOVE GRENADES n.; MARACAS n.²; NUGGETS n.²; ORBS n.). **2** [17C; 1950s–60s] (*US*) the female breasts (cf. BAGS n.¹). **3** [mid-19C+] a blunder, an error. **4** [late 19C+] courage, bravery; supposedly quintessential male qualities, but now as often applied to women. **5** [1950s+] substance, power, strength. **6** [1960s+] effrontery, gall, audacity. **7** [2000s] (*US Black*) something excellent, wonderful; one's preference. [the shape; (6) is on bad = good model]

balls n.² [20C+] rubbish, nonsense (cf. BALLOCKS n.²). [fig. use of BALLS n.¹ (1)]

balls n.³ [1930s–40s] (*orig. US*) nothing, e.g. 'What kind of a tip do I get?' 'Balls.' [fig. use of BALLS n.¹ (1)]

balls *n.*[4] [1950s+] a synon. with ARSE *n.*[1] (4), e.g. *work one's balls off, put one's balls on the line.*

balls, the *n.* [1930s+] (*US*) a superlative, either good or bad according to context. [BALLS *n.*[1] (1); their importance to a man]

balls *adj.* [1980s+] (*US*) tough, masculine, courageous. [BALLS *n.*[1] (4)]

balls *v.* **1** [late 19C+] to make a mess of. **2** [1990s+] to secrete near one's genitals. [(1) BALLS *n.*[1] (3); (2) BALLS *n.*[1] (1)]

balls! *excl.* [late 19C+] **1** (*also* **bawls!**) rubbish! nonsense! **2** an excl. of disappointment. [BALLS *n.*[2]]

balls-ache *v.* [20C+] to nag, to whinge; thus *balls-aching*, nagging, demanding. [BALLS *n.*[1] (1) + SE *ache*, on model of BELLYACHE *v.*]

balls and all *phr.* [20C+] (*orig. US*) everything, totally, completely. [BALLS *n.*[1] (1)]

balls-ass *adj.* [1960s+] (*US*) tough, masculine, courageous. [BALLS *n.*[1] (4) +-ASS sfx]

balls-ass naked *adj. see* BALLS NAKED *adj.*

balls, bees and buggery! *excl.* [late 19C+] a general excl. [BALLS! *excl.* (2) + BUGGERY! *excl.* + assonance]

ballsed-up *adj.* [1940s+] in chaos, in a mess, ruined. [BALLS UP *v.*]

ballsie *adj. see* BALLSY *adj.* (2).

ball slap *v.* [1990s+] of a man, to have sexual intercourse (cf. BELLY BUMP *v.*). [BALLS *n.*[1] (1) + SE *slap*]

balls naked *adj.* (*also* **balls-ass naked**) (*Can./US*) stark naked. [BALLS *n.*[1] (1) (+ -ASS sfx) + SE *naked*]

ball someone's brains out *v. see* FUCK SOMEONE'S BRAINS OUT *v.*

balls out *adv.* [1940s+] at full tilt, absolutely committed, all out. [BALLS *n.*[1] (1); the implication is that one is willing to risk injuring the genitals]

balls, picnics and parties! *excl.* [1920s+] a general excl. [euph. + punning on SE *balls*, dances and BALLS *n.*[1] (1)]

balls to —! *phr.* (*also* **balls with —!**) [1930s+] a dismissive phr. aimed at people, objects or circumstances; thus *balls to you! balls to that!* [BALLS *n.*[1] (1)/BALLS! *excl.* (1)]

balls-to-the-wall *adj.* **1** [1960s+] all-out, at maximum speed, with one's greatest effort. **2** [2000s] (*US campus*) drinking with the intention of getting drunk. [BALLS! *excl.* (1) + SE *wall*; a coarse version of SE *back(s) to the wall*]

balls to the walls *phr.* [1970s+] (*US campus*) said of a tense or frantic time or situation that requires the ability to fight back, eg. *From now until Christmas it's balls to the walls.* [BALLS-TO-THE-WALL *adj.* (1)]

balls-to-the-wind *adv.* [1980s+] (*US*) at top speed. [BALLS *n.*[1] (1) + SE *wind*]

balls-up *n.* [1910s+] (*orig. milit.*) a blunder, an error. [BALLS *n.*[1] (3)]

balls up *v.* [1910s+] to make a mess of, to ruin, to blunder, to make a mistake. [BALLS-UP *n.*; var. on BALL UP *v.*]

balls with —! *excl. see* BALLS TO —! *phr.*

ballsy *adj.* **1** [1930s+] absurd, ridiculous. **2** [1960s+] (*also* **ballsie**) tough, masculine, courageous. [BALLS *n.*[1] (4) + sfx -*y*]

ball-tearer *n.* **1** [1950s+] (*orig. US*) usu. of a woman, esp. a wife, a nag. **2** [1960s+] (*Aus.*) a physically demanding task. **3** [1970s] (*Aus.*) a violent person. **4** [1970s+] anything spectacular or notably impressive. **5** [1980s] (*Aus.*) a major problem, an exasperation. [BALLS *n.*[1] (1) + SE *tearer*]

ball the jack *v.* **1** [1910s+] (*US*) to drive very fast, to work very hard. **2** [1910s+] (*US Black*) to perform an energetic dance to a backing of hand claps. **3** [1910s+] to enjoy a riotous party. **4** [1920s] to risk everything on a single throw. **5** [1920s] to be the last straw. **6** [1920s+] (*US Black*) to have sexual intercourse. **7** [1950s] to move in a noticeable manner. [SAmE phr. *high-ball*, the railway man's hand signal to set a train in motion + *jack*, an orig. US Black term for a locomotive, abbr. of SE *jackass*, a donkey that, like the locomotive, works very hard; used first in

the lumberjack jargon *ball the jack*, of a logging train, to go very fast; thence to general railroad jargon and after that mainstream sl.]

ballum rancum *n.* (*also* **ballum rankum, ballum ranorum, balum rancum**) [late 17C–19C] an orgy, lit. a dance at which all concerned 'dance in their *birthday* suits' (Grose, 1796). [BALLS *n.*[1] (1) + pun on SE *ball*, a dance + *rank*, rancid; D. Cassidy on *American Dialect Society-List* (Internet, 2003) suggests Irish *Ball iomrá na gcumainn*: the place everyone is talking about]

ball-up *n.* [20C+] (*US*) a mess, a confusion. [BALL UP *v.*]

ball up *v.* (*US*) **1** [mid-19C+] to become confused, muddled. **2** [late 19C+] to muddle, to err, to blunder, to make a mistake, to entangle oneself with; thus *balled up*, confused, eccentric. **3** [1910s+] to ruin, to make a mess of, to clog up, to confuse, to botch. [BALLS *n.*[1] (3); var. on BALLS UP *v.*]

bally *adj.* [mid-19C+] a general negative adj., a euph. for BLOODY *adj.*[1].

bally *adv.* [mid-19C+] a general negative intensifier, very, exceedingly, a euph. for BLOODY *adv.*

Ballygobackwards *n.* [1990s+] (*Irish*) an urban nickname for what is seen as a typical rural town. [Irish *baile*, a town + SE *go backwards*]

ballyhack *n. see* BALAHACK *n.*

ballyhoo *n.* [20C+] rubbish, nonsense, empty praise, fuss and bother. [carnival and fairground jargon *ballyhoo*, a barker's speech or a performance given outside the actual attraction, both aimed at touting the attraction itself. The ety. remains obscure; some of the theories, as cited in Mencken, *The American Language* (3rd edn, 1936), include f. Gaelic *bailinghadh*, collect (pron. *ballyhoo*), because the predominantly Irish fairground touts of the mid-19C shouted 'Bailinghadh anois!' ('Collection now!') when they passed the hat for payment; f. the cod Arabic cry *b'Allah hoo*, 'through God it is', used by the 'dervishes' in the Oriental Village sited at the Chicago World's Fair of 1893; a comb. of SE *ballet* + *whoop*. Note 19C naut. jargon *ballyhoo of blazes*, a term of contempt for an unpopular vessel]

ballyhoo *v.* **1** [20C+] (*orig. US*) to publicize to excess, often when the product cannot live up to the manufactured image; thus *ballyhooer*, a promoter, a publicist. **2** to talk nonsense. [BALLYHOO *n.*]

ballyhooly *n.* **1** [late 19C+] (*Irish*) bad trouble. **2** [1910s–20s] rubbish, nonsense. **3** [1940s] noise, commotion, crying. [note music-hall use *Ballyhooly truth*, a lie; the Cork village of *Ballyhooly*, near Fermoy, notable for its faction fights + BALLYHOO *n.*]

ballyrag *v.* (*also* **ballarag**) [mid-19C+] (*orig. Irish*) to bully, to pressurize, to scold. [var. on BULLYRAG *v.*]

ballywack/ballywrack *n. see* BALAHACK *n.*

ballyx *n. see* BALLOCKS *n.*[1].

balm *n.* [mid-19C+] a lie. [SE *balm*, 'a healing, soothing, or softly restorative, agency or influence' (OED)]

balmedest balm *n.* [late 19C–1900s] the ultimate in soothing. [SE *balm*]

balm of Gilead *n.* [late 19C] (*US*) **1** money. **2** illicitly distilled whisky. [the phr. 'Is there no balm in Gilead?' Jer. 8:22, meaning 'is there no remedy or consolation?'; both money and whisky provide a much-needed consolation for life's problems]

balmy *n.* **1** [1940s] a prison wing for disturbed inmates. **2** [1940s–50s] a mad or eccentric person. [BARMY *adj.*]

balmy, the *n.* [mid–late 19C] sleep; thus phr. *have a dose of the balmy*, to sleep. [Note *balmy slumbers* (Shakespeare, *Othello* II.ii)]

balmy *adj.* **1** [mid–late 19C] drunk (cf. ABOUT RIGHT phr.[1]). **2** [mid-19C+] insane, eccentric. [SE *balm*, soothing but pun on BARMY *adj.*]

balmy breeze *n.* [1960s+] cheese. [rhy. sl.]

baloney *n.*[1] (*also* **boloney**) [late 19C+] (*orig. US*) **1** nonsense, rubbish, humbug. **2** a worthless, stupid person. [? *Bologna* sausage; the *OED* rejects the connection as 'conjectural', but note Adams

(*Western Words*, 1968): 'Bologna bulls, animals of inferior quality whose meat is used to make Bologna sausage'. E.P. offers Rom. *peloné*, testicles; thus BALLS n.² or BALLOCKS n.² (2)]

baloney *n.*² (*also* **baloney pony**) [1940s+] (*orig. US*) the penis; thus *have a baloney colonic*, to have anal intercourse (cf. BACON n.¹). [the *Bologna* sausage, transformed in US to *baloney*]

baloney! *excl.* (*also* **boloney!**) [1920s+] (*orig. US*) nonsense! [BALONEY n.¹ (1)]

baloney bender *n.* [1930s] (*US*) one who talks nonsense, an idiot. [BALONEY n.¹ (1)]

baloney pony *n. see* BALONEY n.².

baloobas *n. see* BAZOOKAS n.

balooey *n.* [20C+] (*orig. US*) **1** nonsense, rubbish. **2** a worthless, stupid person. [BALONEY n.¹ + SE excl. *pooh*!]

balot *n.* (*also* **ballot**) [1970s] (*US drugs*) opium; occas. heroin (cf. APOSTLE n.). [Sp. *balota*, a small ball (usu. used in voting, thus a 'ballot'); presumably the shape of pellets of opium]

balsam *n.* [late 17C–1900s] money (cf. ACTUAL, THE n.). [SE *balsam*, a soothing, healing unguent; it 'heals' financial pains]

Balt *n.* (*also* **Baltie**) [1940s+] (*Aus.*) any European refugee or immigrant. [the mistaken belief that all such people came from the Baltic states]

baltic *adj.* [1990s+] (*US*) cold; usu. in phr. *it's bloody baltic*. [the low temperatures of the Baltic Sea]

Balto *n.* (*also* **Balt**) [mid-19C+] (*US*) *Balt*imore, Maryland. [abbr.]

baluba *n.* [1960s+] (*Irish*) a general term of abuse. [the *Baluba* tribe in Katanga, the former Belgian Congo; coined by Irish soldiers serving with the UN in the early 1960s who stereotyped the Baluba as notably savage]

balum rancum *n. see* BALLUM RANCUM n.

bam *n.*¹ **1** [18C–19C] a hoax. **2** [late 19C] a beggar who fakes physical ills. [BAM v.¹]

bam *n.*² (*drugs*) **1** [1950s+] (*also* **bamalam**) low-grade marijuana. **2** [1960s+] amphetamine (cf. A n.²). **3** [1970s+] a barbiturate/amphetamine mix (cf. BLUEY n.⁴; FRENCH BLUE n.). [Mex. *bombita*, a little bomb + SE *bam!* echoic of an explosion]

bam *n.*³ [1950s+] (*orig. US Black*) a girlfriend, a steady date. [Ital. *bambina*]

bam *n.*⁴ [1990s+] a violent person. [onomat.]

bam *v.*¹ [18C–19C] to hoax. [abbr. BAMBOOZLE v. (1)]

bam *v.*² [20C+] to hit. [echoic]

bam! *excl.* [1910s+] echoic of a sudden sound or action.

Bama *n.* **1** [1920s+] (*also* **'Bam**) Ala*bama*. **2** [1940s+] (*US Black*) a generic term for the South and things Southern; thus an implication of rural naïvety. **3** [1970s+] (*also* **bamma, bammer**) (*US Black*) someone or something considered unacceptable or odd. [abbr. *Alabama*, the archetypal southern state]

bama *adj.* (*also* **bamma, bammy**) [1920s+] unsophisticated, out of style, foolish. [BAMA n.]

bama chukker *n.* [1940s+] (*US Black*) a poor southern rural White (cf. ACORN-CRACKER n.). [BAMA n. (2) + SAmE *chucker*, one who husks corncobs]

bamalam *n. see* BAM n.² (1).

bamba *n.*¹ [1980s+] (*UK Black*) the vagina, used as a general term of abuse (cf. BERKELEY (HUNT) n.; BLURT n.; COOZE n.; CUNT n.²; DILLYPOT n.; DITCH n.¹; DOOS n.; POES n.; POON n.¹; PRAT n.¹; PUD n.³; PUM-PUM n.²; TWAT n.; VAG n.²). [BUM n.¹ (2)]

bamba *n.*² *see* BAMBALACHA n.

bambache *n.* [late 19C–1920s] (*US Black*) a riotous, wild party. [Sp.]

bamb(a)claat *n.* (*also* **bambclaht**) (*UK Black*) a sanitary towel, thus a term of abuse. [BAMBA n.¹ + Jam. *claat* or *cloth*]

bambalacha *n.* (*also* **bamba**) [1950s+] (*drugs*) marijuana; thus *bambalacha rancher/rambler*, a marijuana smoker. [Sp.]

bam-bam *n.*¹ [20C+] (*W.I.*) the buttocks, the posterior. [echoic of the buttocks' slap onto a solid surface]

bam-bam *n.*² [2000s] (*US prison*) a psychiatric ward or psychiatric

patient. [BAM! excl., i.e. they beat their heads against the wall]

bambclaat/bambclaht *n. see* BAMB(A)CLAAT n.

bamber *n.*¹ [1980s] an intellectual. [ult. UK author and broadcaster *Bamber* Gascoigne (b.1935), who hosted the BBC quiz show *University Challenge* 1962–87]

bamber *n.*² [1980s+] (*US drugs*) second-rate marijuana. [? BAMBALACHA n.]

Bambi effect *n.* [1950s+] (*gay*) the turning of a young (otherwise homosexual) man's fancy to (heterosexual) love. [the parting of the youthful Bambi and his erstwhile pal Thumper in the Disney film *Bambi* (1942)]

bamblusterate *v.* (*also* **bamblustercate**) [19C] to hoax or confuse in a noisy manner. [BAM v.¹ + SE *bluster*]

bamboo *n.* **1** [1920s–60s] (*US Und.*) an opium pipe; an opium addict; thus *suck (the) bamboo*, to smoke opium. **2** [1970s] (*W.I.*) the penis.

bamboo *adj.* **1** [1930s–60s] used of a Westerner who has 'gone native' while stationed in the Far East. **2** [1950s–60s] eccentric, mad. [a very common plant in the area; (2) f. (1)]

bamboo baksheesh *n.* [mid-19C] a tip that is accompanied by a blow. [SE *bamboo* + BAKSHEESH n. (1); the demands for baksheesh were seen as so irritating by White people in the East that the overly importuning natives, while receiving their money, were made to pay for it]

bamboo chow-chow *n.* [mid–late 19C] a thrashing. [pidgin use]

bambooing *n.* [mid-19C] a thrashing, a whipping. [the *bamboo* cane employed]

bamboo puffer *n.* [late 19C–1950s] (*US drugs*) an opium smoker. [BAMBOO n. (1) + SE *puffer*]

bamboo-wedding *n.* [20C+] (*W.I.*) a wedding according to Hindu rites; thus *marry under bamboo*. [the *bamboo* tent set up for the ceremony]

bamboozlable *adj.* [late 19C+] gullible. [BAMBOOZLE v. (1)]

bamboozle *v.* **1** [early 18C+] (*also* **bamboxter**) to hoax, to trick, to confuse; thus *adj.*, *bamboozling, bamboozlingly*; *n.*, *bamboozli-fication* (cf. BAMFOOZLE v.; BEDOOZLE v.; BOOZLE v.; BUMFUZZLE v.; FOOZLE v.; FOOZLED adj.; JARGOOZLE v.; RUMFOOZELED adj.; SKYFOOZLE v.). **2** [early 19C] to abuse, to libel. [prob. Und. origin, although no proof exists; (1) appears in an article by Swift in *Tatler* no. 230 in 1710, as an illustration of 'the continual Corruption of our English Tongue', along with such new sl. terms as BANTER n. (cited by E.P. as a poss. root); BUBBLE v.¹; BULLY n.¹; MOB n.² (1); PUT n.¹ (1); SHAM n.¹. Hotten (1860) suggests that it might have emerged in late 17C (Jonathan Swift thought so) and that it was ult. 'a term derived from the *Gipsies*']

bamboozled *adj.* **1** [early 18C+] (*also* **bumfoozled**) confused. **2** [mid-19C] (*US*) cheated. **3** [mid-19C] (*US*) drunk (cf. ADDLED adj.). **4** [1950s] (*US drugs*) intoxicated by a drug. [BAMBOOZLE v.]

bamboozler *n.* [early 18C+] a trickster. [BAMBOOZLE v. (1)]

bambosh *n.* [mid-19C] deceptive humbug. [BAMBOOZLE v. (1) + BOSH n.¹]

bamboxter *v. see* BAMBOOZLE v. (1).

bamfoozle *v.* [mid-19C+] (*US*) to trick, to hoax. [var. on BAMBOOZLE v. (1)]

bamfoozled *adj.* [mid-19C] (*US*) a euph. for DAMNED adj., e.g. *I'll be bamfoozled*.

bam, in yo face! *excl.* [1990s+] (*US teen*) an excl. of triumph, of victory in an argument. [BAM! excl. + IN SOMEONE'S FACE phr.]

bamma *n. see* BAMA n. (3).

bamma *adj. see* BAMA adj.

bammaed up *adj.* [1980s] (*US campus*) extremely unattractive. [BAMA adj.]

bammer *n.*¹ [1990s+] (*US drugs*) second-rate marijuana. [BAMMIES n.]

bammer *n.*² *see* BAMA n. (3).

bammer *adj.* [1990s+] (*US Black teen*) bad, fake. [? BAMA adj.]

bammer-boat *n.* [20C+] (*W.I., Guyn.*) a small boat used for smuggling; thus *bammer-boy*, one who uses such a boat for smuggling. [SE *bum-boat*, a small boat used to ferry provisions out to moored ships]

bammies *n.* [1950s+] (*US drugs*) second-rate marijuana. [? BAMA adj.]

bammy *adj. see* BAMA adj.

bamo! *excl.* [1940s+] (*W.I.*) let's go! [Sp. *vamos!* let's go!]

bamp *n.* [1990s+] (*UK juv.*) a general term of abuse.

bampot *n. see* BARMPOT n.

bamsie *n.* (*also* **bamsee, bamsey**) [20C+] (*W.I.*) the buttocks, the posterior. [BUM n.[1] (1)]

bamsie-fly *n.* [20C+] (*W.I.*) a persistent nuisance. [BAMSIE n. + SE *fly*]

bamsie-man *n.* [20C+] (*W.I.*) an effeminate man. [BAMSIE n. + SE *man*]

bamsquabbled *adj. see* BUMSQUABBLED adj.

ban *n.* [19C] (*Anglo-Irish*) a Lord Lieutenant of Ireland. [? pun on SE *ban*, a curse, or *ban*, a proclamation; note Slav. *ban*, lord, master]

Banana *adj.* (*also* **banana**) [1950s+] (*S.Afr.*) referring to the province of Natal, now KwaZulu-Natal; thus *Banana Republic*, *banana country*, *Bananaland*, *Bananalander* etc. [the province's main crop]

banana *n.*[1] **1** [1910s+] (*US*) a stupid or worthless person, a simpleton. **2** [1980s] (*US campus*) a bad thing. [? the fruit is SOFT adj. (1) + YELLOW adj.[1] (1)]

banana *n.*[2] **1** [1910s+] (*also* **green banana**) the penis (cf. BEAN n.[4]; CARROT n.[1]; CUCUMBER n.[2]; HARICOT n.[1]; MUSHROOM n.[4]; OKRA n.; PLUM TREE n.[1]; POPERIN PEAR n.; RADISH n.; STRING BEAN n.; TUMMY BANANA n.). **2** [1940s+] (*US Black*) (*also* **bananaskin**) a light-skinned Black person, esp. an attractive woman. **3** [1960s+] a derog. term for an Asian who has chosen to adopt White, Western values (cf. APPLE n.[7]). [the colour and/or shape of the fruit; (2) YELLOW adj.[2] (1); (3) the person is 'yellow outside but white inside']

banana *n.*[3] [1930s–40s] (*US Und.*) a homosexual. [like the SE *banana* he is a BENT adj. (5) FRUIT n.[2] (2)]

banana *n.*[4] **1** [1950s] (*Aus.*) a £1 note. **2** [1960s+] $1. [it is 'sweet and acceptable']

banana *n.*[5] [1980s] a tube used for snorting cocaine. [? its shape]

banana bender *n.* **1** [1960s+] (*Aus.*) a Queenslander. **2** [1990s+] as a stereotyping of (1), a fool (cf. APPLEHEAD n.). [the state's major crop]

Banana boy *n.* [1960s+] a boy from one of Dr Barnardo's homes for orphaned and deprived children; thus female equivalent *Banana girl*. [joc. mispron. of *Barnardo*]

banana boy *n.* [1950s+] (*S.Afr.*) a resident or native of Natal. [BANANA adj.]

banana cake *n.* [1970s+] (*US*) an eccentric. [var. on FRUITCAKE n.[1]]

Banana City *n.* **1** [late 19C+] (*Aus.*) Brisbane, Queensland. **2** [1970s+] (*S.Afr.*) Durban. [on model of BANANALAND n.]

banana factory *n.* [1980s+] (*US campus*) a hectic, horrible or futile situation. [? BANANAS adj. + SE *factory*]

banana-farm *n.* [1960s+] a psychiatric institution in a tropical or semi-tropical country. [BANANAS adj./SE *bananas* + FUNNY FARM n.]

banana fritter *n.* [1990s+] a lavatory (cf. ANGUS ARMANASCO n.). [rhy. sl. = SHITTER n.[1] (4)]

Banana girl *n. see* BANANA BOY n.

bananahead *n.* [1940s+] (*US*) a simpleton, a fool (cf. APPLEHEAD n.). [BANANA n.[1] (1) + -HEAD sfx (1)]

banana-jockey *n.* [20C+] (*W.I., Gren.*) one who gets a free ride from the country by climbing onto a banana lorry heading for town. [SE *banana* + JOCKEY n.[3] (2)]

Bananaland *n.* [late 19C+] (*Aus.*) Queensland; thus *Bananalander*, *Banana-eater*, a native of Queensland. [the banana crop produced there]

banana man *n.* [mid-19C+] (*Aus.*) an inhabitant of Queensland. [BANANALAND n.]

banana-nose *n.* [1910s+] (*US*) a long or hooked nose; thus used as a nickname or epithet. [resemblance]

banana oil *n.* [1920s+] (*US*) nonsense, insincere or hypocritical talk. [the supposed smoothness of the fig. oil]

banana peddler *n.* (*also* **banana pusher**) [1910s] (*US*) an Italian immigrant. [the trade in which some immigrants worked]

bananas *n.*[1] [1920s+] (*US*) nonsense; also as excl. [abbr. BANANA OIL n.]

bananas *n.*[2] [1970s+] a corrupt policeman. [coined during the 1970s investigation of London's Special Patrol Group, declared to be 'yellow, bent and hanging around in bunches']

bananas *n.*[3] [1990s+] money in general (cf. ALFALFA n.; BEANS n.[1]; BERRIES n.[2]; CANARY n.[5]; COCONUT n.[2]; GRAPES n.[2]; POTATO n.[4]). [colour + pattern of money = pl. fruits/vegetables]

bananas *adj.* **1** [1930s+] of a person, crazy, eccentric (cf. FRUITCAKE adj.; FRUITY adj.[2]; NUTTY adj.[2]; OFF ONE'S CAKE phr.; OFF ONE'S NANA phr.). **2** [1930s+] homosexual. **3** [1990s+] of an object, crazy, unbelievable. [? one's mind or in (2) sexuality is 'bent out of shape']

bananaskin *n. see* BANANA n.[2] (2).

banana (split) *n.* [1990s+] an act of defecation (cf. ANDY CAPP n.). [rhy. sl. = SHIT n.[1] (3)]

banana splits *n.* [1960s+] (*drugs*) amyl nitrite (cf. AIMIES n.). [the drug's odour of 'rotten bananas']

banana (splits) *n.* [1990s+] diarrhoea (cf. EARTHA (KITT) n.; EDGAR BRITT n.; JIMMY BRITTS n.; NICKER BITS n.; SAINT MORITZ n.; THREEPENNY BITS n.; TOMMY GUNS n.; TOM TITS n.; TREY-BITS n.; TWO-BOB BIT n.; WILLIAM PITTS n.; ZACHARY SCOTTS n.; ZASU PITTS n.). [rhy. sl. = SHITS, the n. (1)]

banbury *n.* [late 19C+] a promiscuous woman (cf. BARBER'S CHAIR n.; BARRACK HACK n.; BICYCLE n.; BIKE n.; BOBTAIL n.[1]; CATTLE n.; EASY RIDER n.[1]; FERRY n.; GARRISON HACK n.; HACK n.[1]; HACKNEY n.; HOBBY HORSE n.[2]; HORSEMAN n.[1]; NAG n.[1]; OMNIBUS n.; PONY n.[6]; PUBLIC LEDGER n.; RACEHORSE n.[2]; SADDLEBAG n.; SCHOOL BIKE n.; THOROUGHBRED n.; THOROUGHFARE n.; TOWN BIKE n.; WAGON n.[2]). [the supposed link between *Banbury* cakes and JAM TART n. (2); also the nursery rhyme 'Ride a cock-horse to Banbury Cross']

Banbury-blood *n.* [17C] a Puritan; thus a hypocrite. [SE *Banbury*, the Oxfordshire town, once a centre of highly enthusiastic Puritanism + BLOOD n.[1]]

Banbury story *n.* (*also* **story of a cock and a bull, tale...**) [late 17C–1910s] nonsense, foolish chatter. [nursery rhyme 'Ride a cock-horse to Banbury Cross'; the sl. ref. is presumably punning on 'cock' (as in 'cock and bull'), since the rhyme itself refers either to the destruction of Banbury Cross by Puritan zealots, a ride taken by Queen Elizabeth I or the need for an extra 'coach' horse to ascend the steep hills on the London–Banbury journey, rather than any particular garrulousness on behalf of the natives of the town]

banchoot *n.* (*also* **beteechoot**) [late 18C+] (*Anglo-Ind.*) a coarse insult, which carries far greater weight in India than in the UK. [Hind. *ban*, sister or *betee*, daughter + *choad*, a male copulator; thus lit. 'sister-/daughter-fucker']

banco *see under* BUNCO and its combs.

band *n.* **1** [1920s–60s] (*US Black*) a woman. **2** [1940s+] (*Aus./US*) a prostitute. [? SE *bantam* (hen)]

banda *n.* [1990s+] (*US Black*) a poor, ghetto child. [? SE *abandoned*]

Band-Aid *n.* [1960s+] (*orig. US milit.*) a doctor. [brandname *Band-Aid*; the US equivalent of the UK Elastoplast]

Band-Aid liberal *n.* [1980s+] a half-hearted liberal, whose beliefs can be easily compromised; such an individual would rather place a Band-Aid on an issue and cover it up than dig into the roots and deal with it. [brandname *Band-Aid*; the US equivalent of the UK Elastoplast + SE *liberal*. Note the Band-Aid rock concerts of 1982, which themselves punned on the name *Band-Aid* + SE *band* + *aid*]

bandalu *adj*. [1990s+] (*W.I.*) crooked, illicit; thus a *bandulu bizness*, a racket, a swindle. [ety. unknown]

bandbox *n*. (*US Und.*) **1** [late 17C; 1930s+] a country workhouse or local prison. **2** [1940s–50s] a prison from which it is easy to escape. [SE *bandbox*, a fragile structure or one in which space is restricted]

b & d *n*. (*also* b/d) [1960s+] *b*ondage and *d*iscipline, a sexual 'speciality'. [abbr.]

b and e *n*. (*also* B and E, B&E) [1960s+] (*orig. US police*) *b*reaking *and e*ntering. [abbr.]

b and e *v*. (*also* B and E, B&E) [1960s+] (*US Und./police*) to break and enter.

banded *adj*. [19C] hungry. [? the tightening of the band or belt around one's diminishing waist]

bander *n*. *see* BAND OF HOPE *n*.[2].

bandhouse *n*. [1900s–60s] (*US Und.*) a workhouse or prison (cf. BIG HOUSE n.; BIRDHOUSE n.; BLACK HOUSE n.; BLOCKHOUSE n.; BOARDING HOUSE n.; BUGHOUSE n.; DOGHOUSE n.; FLOPHOUSE n.; GLASSHOUSE n.[1]; HEN HOUSE n.[2]; HOUSE n.[1]; HOUSE OF D n.; HOUSE OF MANY SLAMMERS n.; HOUSE THAT JACK BUILT n.[1]; IRON HOUSE n.; JUGHOUSE n.; LITTLE HOUSE n.; LOUSE HOUSE n.; MADHOUSE n.; PEG-HOUSE n.[2]; PLAYHOUSE n.; RASHERHOUSE n.; RATHOUSE n.; RESTHOUSE n.; SKOOKUM HOUSE n.; SORORITY HOUSE n.; SPRING ANKLE WAREHOUSE n.; STONE HOUSE n.). [? dial. *band*, a rope or fastening]

bandicoot *v*. [late 19C+] (*Aus.*) to steal potatoes from the fields by removing the potatoes from the soil and carefully replacing the plant on which they grow; thus *bandicooter*. [SE *bandicoot*, a small marsupial known for its burrowing]

band in the box *n*. [1940s+] venereal disease. [rhy. sl. = POX n.[1] (2)]

bandit *n*.[1] [1960s+] (*US*) a coin-operated gaming machine, a fruit machine. [abbr. ONE-ARMED BANDIT n.]

bandit *n*.[2] [1970s] (*US*) an attractive woman.

bandit *n*.[3] *see* ARSE BANDIT n.

bandit *sfx* **1** [1950s+] a villain, often used in combs. as a generic for a criminal practising a speciality. **2** [1960s+] in combs., a homosexual (cf. ARSE BANDIT n.; ARSEHOLE BANDIT n.; BALLOON-KNOT BANDIT n.; BLUE-ARSED BANDIT n.; BOMB BANDIT n.; BOOTY BANDIT n.; BOTTOM BANDIT n.; BUGGER-BANDIT n.; BUM BANDIT n.; CHOCOLATE BANDIT n.; KEISTER BANDIT n.; PISSHOLE BANDIT n.; SHORT-ARM BANDIT n.; TROUSER BANDIT n.). **3** [1990s+] an obsessive, a user. [ironic use of SE *bandit*]

band moll *n*. [1960s] (*Aus./US*) a woman who associates herself with rock or jazz bands, offering her body for a share in their celebrity. [SE *band* + MOLL n.[1] (1)]

band of hope *n*.[1] [mid-19C] (*Aus.*) lemonade. [the *Band of Hope*, formed 1847, was a temperance society]

band of hope *n*.[2] (*also* bander) [20C+] (*Aus.*) soap. [rhy. sl.; ult. *see* BAND OF HOPE n.[1]]

bandog *n*. **1** [17C–19C] a bailiff or bailiff's assistant. **2** [late 18C] a bandbox. **3** [19C] a policeman (cf. ANIMAL n.[1]). **4** [early 19C] a ruffian. [SE *band*, chain + *dog*. Orig. a large guard-dog, the term re-entered SE in the 1980s to describe a cross-breed of Neapolitan mastiffs and US pit bull terriers; poss. further link to SE *dog*, to pursue, thus note Ned Ward, *Hudibras Redivivus* (1705–7): 'young Drunkards reeling, Bayliffs dogging']

bandook *n*. (*also* bundook) [late 19C–1940s] (*orig. Anglo-Ind.*) a musket, a rifle, a crossbow. ['*Bunduk* was a name applied by the Arabs to filberts (as some allege) because they came from Venice (*Banadik*, ? f. Ger. *Venedig*). The name was transferred to the nut-like pellets shot from crossbows and thence the crossbows or arblasts were called bundooks, f. *kaus al-bundook*, pellet bow.

From crossbows the name was transferred again to fire arms' (Y&B)]

bandore *n*. [late 17C–18C] a widow's head-dress, worn to signify her mourning state. [Fr. *bandeau*]

bandowzer *n*. [early–mid-19C] a heavy blow. [ety. unknown; ? var. on FERRICADOUZER n. (1)]

b & p *n*. [late 19C–1900s] an effeminate young man (cf. BEANPEA n.). [a case involving 2 such youths, Boulton and Park, known only, so taboo was the thought of homosexuality, by their initials *B and P*]

B-and-Q *n*. [1990s+] (*US drugs*) a mixture of *b*onita and *q*uinine sold as counterfeit heroin. [abbr.; ult. punning on the DIY superstore *B&Q*]

band rat *n*. [1940s–60s] a woman who associates herself with musicians, usu. offering sex in return for proxy celebrity. [SE *band* + RAT sfx]

b and s *n*. [mid-19C+] brandy *and* *s*oda; occas. [late 19C] reversed as *s and b*. [abbr.]

bandulu *n*. [20C+] (*W.I. Rasta*) a bandit, a criminal, one who lives by guile. [ety. unknown; ? link to Fr. *bandeau*, a headscarf, i.e. worn here as a mask]

bandy *n*.[1] [19C] a silver sixpence. [SE *bandy*; the easy bending of the thin silver]

bandy *n*.[2] [1990s+] (*US teen/campus*) a dedicated member of a marching band; esp. one whose social life is limited to fellow musicians.

bane, the *n*. [late 19C–1910s] brandy. [SE *bane*, that which causes ruin; on model of BLUE RUIN n.]

bang *n*.[1] **1** [16C+] a blow, a hit, as aimed at and received by a person. **2** [1940s+] (*US Und.*) (*also* banger) a criminal charge. [ON *banga*, to hammer]

bang *n*.[2] **1** [late 17C–18C] a pelvic thrust during intercourse. **2** [18C+] an act of sexual intercourse, used in both hetero- and homosexual contexts. **3** [1930s+] (*Aus.*) a brothel. **4** [1940s+] (*also* bangee) a man or woman as a sexual performer, e.g. *he/she's a great bang*. **5** [1990s+] (*US Black gang*) a multiple rape, an orgy. **6** [2000s] (*US teen*) a party, with overtones of (5). [(3) thus according to Baker, *Australian Slang* (1941) but note Simes, *A Dict. of Australian Underworld Slang* (1993): 'the sense is not recorded by other writers or dictionaries']

bang *n*.[3] **1** [mid–late 19C] a lie; thus *bang word*, a curse word, an oath. **2** [1930s] (*US Und.*) information.

bang *n*.[4] [20C+] (*US*) a crowd of people. [ext. of SHEBANG n.]

bang *n*.[5] (*also* bhang) [1930s+] cannabis, esp. in the form of hashish (cf. AFGHAN n.). [Urdu *bhang*, Indian hemp (*Cannabis indica*); the term appears in Eng. in mid-16C but its use was simply as an exotic foreign word until the 1930s when, as *bang*, it was incorporated into popular sl., a process that was accelerated by returnees from the Hippie Trail of the 1960s; *bhang* itself remains primarily a technical term, used to describe cannabis as produced and consumed in India and Pakistan]

bang *n*.[6] (*also* bang in the arm) [1920s+] (*drugs*) a single injection of a narcotic drug, e.g. *a bang of cocaine*. [the force used to push the needle into one's flesh + the instantly pleasurable sensation that the drug creates + play on SHOT n.[6] (2). Note the erroneous sp. *bhang*, which is cited in the *OED* (1922) and leads that dictionary to assume it is a 'revived' version of the proper use of *bhang*, as a synon. for Indian cannabis (cf. BANG n.[5])]

bang *n*.[7] [1920s+] **1** (*orig. US*) a thrill, often in the context of drug use; thus GET A BANG (OUT OF) v. **2** energy. [SE *bang*, a hit, a knock; thus a stimulus]

bang *n*.[8] [1930s–60s] (*US*) **1** luck, fortune, situation; thus *bad bang*, bad luck, an unfortunate situation; *big bang*, a thrill. **2** a handsome man.

bang *n*.[9] [1940s+] (*US*) a try, an attempt, usu. in phr. *take a bang (at)*, to have a try, to make an attempt.

bang n.[10] [1960s] (US campus) a grade of B; thus bang and a half, a grade of B+ (cf. ACE n.[6]). [initial letter]

bang n.[11] [1980s+] (US) a murder. [BANG v.[3]]

bang adj.[1] **1** [early–mid-19C] smart, alert. **2** [1920s–50s] (US) exciting. [abbr. BANG-UP adj. (2)]

bang adj.[2] [mid-19C+] (S.Afr.) scared; thus bangbroek, a coward; bangbroek, cowardly. [Afk. bang, scared + broek, trousers]

bang v.[1] **1** [late 16C+] to hit, to thump. **2** [18C+] to copulate with; like many sl. terms involving sex, this implies an aggression irrespective of any affection; usu. of men, but occas. of women (cf. BASH v.[1]; BASTE v.; BATTER v.; BEAT WITH AN UGLY STICK v.; BELT v.[1]; BIFF v.[1]; BOFF v.[1]; BONG v.[1]; BONK v.[1]; BOP v.[1]; BULK v.; BUMBASTE v.; BUM-FEAGUE v.; BUSHWHACK v.; CANE v.; CHARGE v.[1]; CHOP v.[10]; CLIP v.[1]; CLUB v.; CRUNCH v.; CUT v.[7]; DECK v.[3]; DOCK v.[1]; DRILL v.[1]; DRIVE v.[1]; DUFF v.[2]; FEAGUE v.; FEEZE v.; FIRK v.; FLIMP v.; FLOG v.[1]; FOIN v.; GASH v.; GOOSE v.[3]; GO THROUGH v.[2]; GUN v.[2]; HAMMER v.[1]; HIT v.[1]; IMPALE v.; JAB v.[2]; JACK UP v.[6]; JAG v.[2]; JOB v.[1]; JOUNCE v.; JUKE v.[2]; JUMP v.[1]; KICK v.[11]; KICK IT v.[5]; KILL v.[4]; KNOB v.[1]; KNOCK v.[1]; LANCE v.; LASH v.[2]; MASH v.[2]; MESS v.; MUSS v.; NAIL v.; NICK v.[2]; NIP v.[1]; PEG v.[5]; PERFORATE v.; PIN v.[1]; PIP v.[1]; PLANK v.; PLONK v.; PLUG v.[1]; POKE v.; POP v.[1]; POUND v.[2]; PRANG v.; PUNCH v.; RIP INTO v.; SCRAG v.; SCREW v.[2]; SHAFT v.; SHAG v.[1]; SHAKE v.[1]; SHANGHAI v.; SHOOT v.[1]; SHOVE v.[1]; SLAM v.[1]; SMOKE v.[2]; SNABBLE v.; SOCK IT TO v.; SPEAR THE BEARDED CLAM v.; SPEAR THE HAIRY DOUGHNUT v.; SPIKE v.[3]; SPIT v.[1]; SPLIT v.[1]; STAB v.; STICK IT INTO v.; STICK IT ON v.[2]; STITCH v.; STUFF v.[1]; SWINGE v.; SWITCH v.; TEW v.; THUMP v.; TONK v.; TORPEDO v.[2]; TOUZLE v.; TOWZE v.; TRAMPLE v.; TRIM v.; TROUNCE v.; TUMP v.; WALLOP v.; WALLOP IT IN v.; WAX v.[2]; WAX ASS v.; WHACK IT IN v.; WHIP IT IN v.; WHOMP v.; WHOP IT UP v.). **3** [late 19C] to dismiss from a job. **4** [late 19C+] to impress. **5** [1940s] (US) to masturbate; one of many terms for the v. that relate to hitting (cf. BANG THE BISHOP v.). **6** [1950s+] to have sexual intercourse. **7** [1960s] to thrill. **8** [1990s+] (US) to inflict, to 'hit with'.

bang v.[2] **1** [mid-18C–1910s] to surpass; esp. in phr. bang bob-tail, bang everything etc. **2** [1990s+] (US Black) to make an impact. [Cumbrian dial.]

bang v.[3] (also bang off) [early 19C+] (US) to kill by shooting. [noise of the weapon]

bang v.[4] [1900s] (US Und.) to rob, to steal.

bang v.[5] **1** [1920s+] (drugs) to inject heroin. **2** [1950s+] to throw back a drink. **3** [1960s] to inject someone with heroin. [BANG n.[7] (1)]

bang v.[6] [1960s+] (US) to make a turn while driving; thus bang a U-ie, to make a U-turn etc, also fig.

bang v.[7] **1** [1980s+] to be a member of a gang. **2** [1990s+] (orig. US Black) to fight, to kill. [abbr. GANGBANG v. (3)]

bang adv. **1** [early 19C+] absolutely, directly, e.g. bang in trouble. **2** very, extremely. [SE bang, a sudden action or shock]

bang a hanger v. [1920s+] to steal a purse. [BANG v.[4] + HANGER n.]

bang and biff n. [1930s+] syphilis. [rhy. sl. = SYPH n.]

bang a pitcher v. [17C] to empty a pot of beer. [BANG v.[1] (1) + SE pitcher; one bangs the emptied pitcher on the table]

bangarang n. [1970s+] (W.I.) hubbub, uproar, disorder. [BANG n.[1] (1) + echoic redup.]

bangarang adj. [1940s+] (W.I.) worthless, good-for-nothing. [BANG n.[1] (1) + echoic redup.]

bang a reefer v. [1950s] to smoke marijuana. [BANG v.[5] (1) + REEFER n.[2] (1)]

bang around v. [20C+] **1** of a person, to make one's presence felt, with little practical result. **2** of an item, a situation, to linger, without coming to a conclusion. [SE bang around, to make noise]

bang artist n. [1960s] (US gay) an active male homosexual. [BANG n.[2] (2) + ARTIST sfx]

bang away v. see BANG ON v.

bang back v. see KNOCK BACK v.[2].

bang Banagher v. see BEAT BANAGHAN v.

bang-beggar n. [mid–late 19C] (mainly Scot.) a constable. [BANG v.[1] (1) + SE beggar; their ill-treatment of tramps]

bang-bellied adj. [1940s+] (W.I.) having a large paunch. [dial. bang-belly, a swollen abdomen, whether of a malnourished child or a pregnant woman]

bang-belly n. [20C+] (W.I.) a starving child. [BANG v.[1] (1) + SE belly; the child hits its stomach to indicate its hunger]

bange n. [mid-19C+] (Aus.) a rest, a sleep. [dial. benge, to lounge, to laze about; note New Eng. dial. bange, to idle about, to take advantage of another's hospitality]

bange v. [late 19C] (Aus.) to rest, to sleep. [BANGE n.]

banged to rights adj. see BANG TO RIGHTS adj.

banged up adj.[1] [20C+] **1** (orig. UK Und.) (also **banged away**) locked up in one's cell; thus, generically, in prison. **2** in fig. use, trapped. **3** of a building or place, locked up. [SE bang; the cell door is lit. banged shut]

banged up adj.[2] [20C+] **1** of people, beaten up, injured. **2** of objects, broken, battered, esp. of a car with notable damage to the panel-work. [BANG v.[1] (1)]

banged up adj.[3] [1920s+] (drugs) under the influence of a drug. [BANG n.[6]]

banged up to the eyes phr. [mid-19C–1920s] very drunk (cf. ANNIHILATED adj.; ARSEHOLED adj.). [fig. use of BANGED UP adj.[2] (1)]

bangee n. see BANG n.[2] (4).

banger n.[1] **1** [mid-17C–19C] a notable lie. **2** [mid-17C–19C] a person who lies. **3** [early 19C] something excellent. **4** [early 19C] something large. [fig. use of BANG v.[1] (1)]

banger n.[2] [late 19C+] (Aus.) a morning coat. [play on CLAW-HAMMER n. (1)]

banger n.[3] [20C+] the penis. [BANG v.[1] (2); but note BANGER n.[4]; like a sausage it 'spits' when it is put in the OVEN n. (1)]

banger n.[4] [1910s+] (orig. Aus.) a sausage. [? its propensity to explode if cooked without initial pricking of the skin]

banger n.[5] [1930s–40s] (US) $1. [one 'bangs it down' on a counter or table]

banger n.[6] [1950s+] one who hits (hard). [BANG v.[1] (1)]

banger n.[7] [1950s+] (drugs) **1** a hypodermic syringe. **2** one who injects narcotics. [BANG v.[5] (1)]

banger n.[8] [1960s] one who copulates. [BANG v.[1] (2)]

banger n.[9] [1960s+] **1** a dilapidated motorcar. **2** in fig. use, anything or anyone worn-out and run-down. **3** a cylinder, usu. in comb. four-banger, six-banger. **4** an automobile engine. [the sound of an ill-tuned, ageing engine]

banger n.[10] [1990s+] (US Black) a gang member. [abbr. GANGBANGER n. (1)]

banger n.[11] [2000s] (US Black/prison) any form of knife. [BANG v.[1] (1)]

banger n.[12] see BANG n.[1] (2).

bangers n. [1980s+] (Irish) the testicles (cf. BOJANGLES n.; CHIMES n.; CLANKERS n.; CLAPPERS n.[1]; CLINKERS n.[2]; CLOCK-WEIGHTS n.; CRACKERS n.[6]; DANGLERS n.; DANGLY-BITS n.; DING-DONGS n.[2]; DUSTERS n.; FRICK AND FRACK n.; GONGS n.; HANGERS n.; KNOCKERS n.[2]; POUNDERS n.; SWINGERS n.; TUMBLERS n.; WHIRLIGIGS n.). [BANG v.[1] (1), i.e. they bang together]

bangers (and mash) n. [1970s+] an act of urination (cf. ANGEL'S KISS n.). [rhy. sl. = SLASH n.[3] (1)]

bangers and red lead n. [1920s+] tinned sausages and tomato sauce. [BANGER n.[4] + naut. sl. red lead, tomato ketchup or tinned tomatoes]

bang heads v. [1960s] (US) to fight.

banging n. [1980s+] **1** (US) sexual intercourse. **2** (US Black) indulging in multiple rape or, if the woman is willing, in an orgy. **3** fighting, living the life of a gangsta. [abbr. GANG-BANGING n.[1]/GANG-BANGING n.[2]]

banging adj. **1** [late 18C] big, great in size. **2** [1990s+] (orig. US

Black) popular. **3** [1990s+] a general term of admiration, excellent, first-rate, wonderful. [BANG adv.]

banging-shop *n.* [1930s+] (*US*) a brothel (cf. BLACKSMITH'S SHOP n.; BUMSHOP n.; BUTTOCKING SHOP n.; BUTTONHOLE FACTORY n.; CAKE SHOP n.; CAT-SHOP n.; DOLL SHOP n.; FISH MARKET n.; FLESH MARKET n.; GIRL-SHOP n.; GREENGROCERY n.¹; HARDWARE SHOP n.; HOOK SHOP n.; KIP SHOP n.¹; KNOCKING-SHOP n.; KNOCK SHOP n.; MOLL SHOP n.; NANNY-SHOP n.; POISON SHOP n.; RUB-A-TUG SHOP n.; SHOP n.¹; SMOCK SHOP n.; WARM SHOP n.]. [BANG n.² (2) + SE *shop*/SHOP n.¹ (1); note synon. US milit. jargon *bang house*]

bang in the arm *n.* see BANG n.⁶.

bang it *v.* [1970s+] (*US gay*) to achieve orgasm.

bangle *v.* [1990s+] to arrest. [SE *bangle*, i.e. a handcuff]

bang like a hammer on a nail *v.* (*also* **bang like a rattlesnake on a nail**) [1950s+] (*orig. Aus.*) to rate as an enthusiastic sexual performer. [BANG v.¹ (2)]

bang like a shithouse door (in a gale) *v.* (*also* **bang like a buggered tappet, bang like a dunny door (in a gale)**) [1960s+] (*orig. Aus.*) to rate as an enthusiastic sexual performer; usu. said by men of women. [BANG v.¹ (2) + SHITHOUSE n. (2) + SE *door*]

bang off *v.*¹ [2000s+] to ejaculate. [BANG v.¹ (2)]

bang off *v.*² see BANG v.³.

bang off *adv.* [1920s+] immediately. [ext. BANG adv. (1)]

bang of the latch *n.* [20C+] (*Irish*) one final drink after 'time' has been called. [i.e. before the pub door is latched for the night]

bang on *v.* (*also* **bang away**) [1940s+] to talk repetitiously and tediously. [SE *bang*; the noise of one's monologue]

bang on *adv.* [1940s+] exactly right, extremely apposite, excellent. [BANG adv.; orig. RAF jargon *bang on the target*]

bang on the drum *n.* [1940s+] (*bingo*) the number 71 (cf. ALDERSHOT LADIES n.). [rhy. sl.]

bangotcher *n.* [1950s+] (*Aus.*) a Western film. [shouts of *Bang! I've got you!*]

bang out *adj.* see BANG-UP adj. (2).

bang out *v.*¹ [19C+] to rush away, to leave quickly. [SE *bang*, make a noise]

bang out *v.*² [1940s+] (*UK prison*) to lock up a cell door. [var. on BANG UP v.² (2)]

bang out *v.*³ [1970s] (*US prison*) to murder or beat up. [BANG v.¹ (1)]

bang out *v.*⁴ see KNOCK OUT v.¹.

bang outfit *n.* see OUTFIT n.³ (2).

bang-pitcher *n.* [mid–late 17C] a drunkard. [BANG v.¹ (1) + SE *pitcher*; the thumping of a tankard on the table]

bang shoot, the *n.* see WHOLE BANG SHOOT, THE n.

bang-slap *adv.* see SLAP-BANG adv.

bang someone's ear *v.* [1950s+] (*US*) to talk incessantly (and tediously). [var. on BANG ON v.]

bangster *n.*¹ **1** [mid-16C–18C] a boaster, a braggart. **2** [late 16C] a bully. [BANG v.¹ + -STER sfx]

bangster *n.*² [1910s+] (*US drugs*) a narcotics addict. [BANG v.⁵ (1) + -STER sfx]

bang-stick *n.* [1970s+] any form of firearm.

bang-straw *n.* [late 18C] a farm-worker, esp. a thresher. [metonymy]

bangtail *n.*¹ (*also* **bang-tail**) [late 17C+] a prostitute (cf. ASS PEDDLER n.; BELLY-PIECE n.¹; BIT OF MUTTON n.; BUN n.²; BUTTOCK n.; COOKIE n.¹; COOZE n.; CRACK n.⁶; DEAD MEAT n.; DOWNY BIT n.; FLASHTAIL n.; GASH n.¹; LACED MUTTON n.; MOT n.; MUFF n.¹; MUFF MERCHANT n.; MUTTON n.¹; NOTCH n.¹; NOTCH MOLL n.; OPEN-ARSE n.²; RUMP n.; RUMPER n.; SPLIT-ARSE MECHANIC n.; STALE MUTTON n.; STINGTAIL n.; TACKLE n.¹; TAIL n.²; TAIL-TRADER n.; TAIL-WORKER n.; TICKLE-TAIL n.; TICKLE-TAIL FUNCTION n.; TOY n.¹; TWAT-SELLER n.; WAGTAIL n.). [BANG v.¹ (2) + TAIL n.² (3); 20C+ US Black use]

bangtail *n.*² [mid-19C+] (*Aus./US*) a horse, spec. any animal which has its tail cropped square; thus (*Aus.*) *bang-tail muster*, a round-up of cattle during which the tuft at the end of the tail is cut straight across as the cattle are counted; thus *bang-tailed*, cut square. [SE *bang*, to cut (the front hair) square across, so that it ends abruptly]

bangtail *v.* [1940s+] (*US*) to hurry. [SE *bang* + TAIL n.² (1)]

bang the banjo *v.* [1970s] (*US*) to masturbate (cf. BANG THE BISHOP v.). [BANG v.¹ (5) + assonance]

bang the bishop *v.* (*also* **bash the bishop, bash the priest, batter the bishop, beat the bishop, flog the bishop, murder the bishop**) [late 19C+] to masturbate; one of many terms for the v. that relate to hitting (cf. BANG v.¹; BANG THE BANJO v.; BASH THE CANDLE v.; BASH THE STICK v.; BEAT ONE'S DUMMY v.; BEAT ONE'S HOG v.; BEAT ONE'S MEAT v.; BEAT THE DOG v.; BEAT THE PUP v.; BEAT THE STICK v.; BELT IT v.; BELT ONE'S BATTER v.; BELT ONE'S HOG v.; BLUDGEON THE BEEFSTEAK v.; BOFF v.; BOP ONE'S BALONEY v.; BOP ONE'S RICHARD v.; BOP THE BISHOP v.; BOX THE BOZACK v.; BOX THE JESUIT AND GET COCKROACHES v.; CONK THE CARDINAL v.; CUFF THE CARROT v.; CUFF THE DUMMY v.; FLOG v.¹; FLOG ONE'S DOGGIN v.; FLOG ONE'S DONG v.; FLOG ONE'S DONKEY v.; FLOG ONE'S MUTTON v.; FLOG THE DOG v.; FLOG THE (FINLESS) DOLPHIN v.; FLOG THE HOG v.; HAVE A BEAT v.; HIT A LICK v.; HIT IT v.³; KNOCK ONE OUT v.; KNOCK THE TOP OFF v.; MASH v.¹; POUND OFF v.; POUND ONE'S MEAT v.; POUND ONE'S PORK v.; POUND ONE'S PUD v.; SLAM THE HAM v.; SLAM THE HAMMER v.; SLAP IT v.; SLAP THE MONKEY v.; SLAP THE SALAMI v.; SPANK v.²; SPANK... v.; SPANK THE MONKEY v.; THRAP v.; WHACK v.¹; WHACK IT v.; WHACK OFF v.¹; WHACK THE ONE-EYED WORM v.). [ety. unknown, although E.P. suggests a resemblance of the penis to a bishop's mitre or to the *bishop* in a trad. designed 'Staunton' chess set; however, simple assonance is equally likely]

bang the bush *v.* [mid-19C] (*US*) to surpass everything. [BANG v.² (1) + SE *bush*]

bang the gong *v.* [late 19C–1940s] (*US drugs*) to smoke opium. [BANG v.¹ (1) + GONG n.² (1) + pun]

bang through the elephant *v.* [19C] to plumb the depths of dissipation. [BANG adv. + ? ELEPHANT'S (TRUNK) adj.]

bang to rights *adj.* (*also* **banged to rights**) [20C+] (*orig. US, esp. Und.*) caught in the act, caught red-handed. [BANG adv. + SE *to rights*, fairly, according to the law]

bang-up *n.*¹ **1** [19C] a dandy, a fashionable man. **2** [mid-19C] (*Anglo-Irish/US*) an overcoat with a cape and high collar. [BANG-UP adj. (2)]

bang-up *n.*² [1950s+] (*UK prison*) **1** imprisonment within one's cell, without association or exercise. **2** the shutting of a cell door (at the end of the prison day). [BANG UP v.² (2)]

bang-up *adj.* **1** [early 19C] drunk (cf. ANNIHILATED adj.). **2** [early 19C+] (*also* **bang out**) first-rate, excellent, fashionable, stylish; often as *bang up to the mark* or *bang up to dick*. **3** [mid-19C] (*US*) impoverished, penniless. **4** [mid-19C] (*US*) finished. [onomat./ BANG adv. but note Fr. *bien*, well or good as excl.]

bang up *v.*¹ [1920s+] to inject a narcotic drug. [BANG v.⁵ (1) + SE *up*]

bang up *v.*² **1** [1930s+] (*UK prison*) to imprison. **2** [1940s+] (*UK prison*) to lock a prisoner in a cell. **3** [1950s+] (*UK prison*) to be locked up in a cell. **4** [1980s+] (*Aus. prison*) to alert a prison officer by banging on one's cell door. [the banging of the cell door]

bang up *v.*³ [1980s+] to injure. [BANG v.¹ (1)]

bang up *adv.* [early 19C+] completely, very much so, directly. [ext. BANG adv. (1)]

bang up against *adj.* (*also* **bung up against**) [19C+] very close. [BANG adv. (1)/BUNG adv. + SE *up against*]

bang-up prime *adj.* [19C] absolutely excellent. [BANG UP adv. + SE *prime*]

bang wagon *n.* [1960s] (*US*) an ambulance. [it carries those who have 'had a bang']

bang water *n.* [1920s+] (*Can.*) petrol. [the sound of a car's engine + SE *water*]

bang wattle gum *v. see* BEAT BANAGHAN v.

bang-word *n.* [late 19C–1900s] a highly expressive word, a 'swear-word'.

banjax *v.* (*also* **bandjax**) [1920s+] to batter, to destroy, to ruin, to get in the way of. [usu. in Irish use; f. ? Dublin sl.]

banjaxed *adj.* [1930s+] broken, ruined, smashed up. [BANJAX v.]

banjo *n.*[1] **1** [mid-19C–1900s] a bedpan. **2** [late 19C+] (*orig. Aus.*) a shoulder of mutton. **3** [late 19C+] (*orig. Aus.*) a shovel; thus *banjo and anchor*, a shovel and pick; *banjo-swinger*, manual labourer. **4** [late 19C+] (*Aus./US*) a frying pan. **5** [1990s+] a piece of excrement. [the shape]

banjo *n.*[2] [1920s] (*US*) an eye. [backform. f. BANJO-EYES n.]

banjo *v.* [1970s+] **1** to force a door or window. **2** (*orig. milit.*) to hit, to beat up, to defeat. [BANJO n.[1] (3)]

banjoey *n.* [late 19C–1900s] a banjo-player. [SE *banjo* + *joey*, a clown, supposedly coined by the banjo-playing Prince of Wales, later Edward VII (r.1901–10)]

banjo-eyes *n.* [1900s–70s] (*US*) one who has large, wide-open eyes; thus *banjo-eyed*. [SE *banjo*; the round, white drumskin on the instrument]

banjo (string) *n.* [1990s+] the frenum, i.e. the ridge of skin connecting the foreskin to the base of the 'bell end' of the penis (cf. ACCORDION n.). [? resemblance]

banjy boy *n.* [1990s+] (*US Black*) a gay male who dresses as if he were part of the heterosexual hip-hop culture. [? BUM BOY n. (1)/BATTY BWOY n.]

Bank, the *n.* [mid-19C] (*UK Und.*) Mill*bank* Pentitentiary. [abbr.; built according to Jeremy Bentham's ideas on prison reform, outlined in his pamphlet *The Panopticon or Inspection House*, the prison opened in 1821. A gloomy, labyrinthine place, with a reputation for disease and poor conditions, it was shut in 1891]

bank *n.*[1] [19C] the vagina, esp. when seen as a means of making money; one of a number of terms pointing up the commercial potential of the vagina (cf. BOODLE n.[4]; BREADWINNER n.; BUDGET n.; CUSTOM HOUSE n.; CUSTOM HOUSE GOODS n.; EVE'S CUSTOM HOUSE n.; EXCHEQUER n.; HAIRY-BANK n.; IRISH FORTUNE n.; MONEY n.[1]; MONEYBOX n.; MONEY MACHINE n.; MONEY-MAKER n.; MONEY POCKET n.; MONEY-SPINNER n.; POCKET-BOOK n.; PURSE n.; RECEIPT OF CUSTOM n.; TILL n.; WARE n.).

bank *n.*[2] [20C+] (*Aus./US Black/campus*) money, one's fortune. [SE *bankroll*]

bank *n.*[3] [1900s–40s] (*US Black*) the lavatory; esp. *visit the bank, take a trip to the bank* (cf. ALTAR n.). [euph.]

bank *n.*[4] [1930s] (*US prison*) a shot of a narcotic. [BANG n.[6]]

bank *v.*[1] [19C+] (*UK Und.*) **1** to steal. **2** to hide away in a safe place. **3** to go fair shares.

bank *v.*[2] [1990s+] (*US*) to attack. [BANG v.[1] (1)]

bank *v.*[3] *see* BANKROLL v.

bank bandit pills *n.* [1960s+] (*drugs*) depressants. [their calming effect, suitable for use during a robbery]

banker *n.*[1] [early 17C; 1910s+] a 'respectable' figure who holds the profits of crime for a thief, one who holds money for a drug dealer (in case of their arrest) etc. [SE *bank*; 1910s+ use US Und.]

banker *n.*[2] [late 19C+] (*orig. gambling*) a sure thing, something or someone on which one can depend, a safe bet (fig. and lit.). [SE *banker*, one who runs a bank; such figures are supposedly dependable and trustworthy]

banker chapel ho *n.* [late 19C–1900s] Whitechapel in east London; by ext. coarse or vulgar language. [cod Ital. *bianca capella*, white chapel + excl. *ho!*]

bank-man *n.* [1900s] (*US Und.*) a bank robber.

bank of Dunlop *n.* [1990s+] a fig. 'bank' on which 'rubber' cheques are drawn. [brandname *Dunlop*, manufacturer of rubber tyres]

bank off *v.* [1950s+] (*US prison*) to place an inmate in the punishment cells. [similarity of the punishment block to a bank vault]

bank on *v.* [late 19C+] to take for granted, to assume as a certainty; thus phr. (*you can*) *take that to the bank*, that's a promise, you can be sure. [gambling jargon *bet the bank*, to commit oneself completely]

bank-rag *n.* [mid-19C] (*US*) a banknote (cf. BILL n.[2]; BIT OF STIFF n.[1]; BLANKET n.[1]; BRIEF n.[2]; CRACKLE n.; CRINKLE n.; CRINKLER n.; CRISP n.; CRISP ONE n.; FLIMSY n.; FOLDING n.; FOLDING GREEN n.; LIL n.[1]; MINT LEAF n.[1]; NOTE n.[1]; PAPER n.[1]; PLASTER n.[1]; RAG n.[1]; RUM SCREEN n.; SCREEN n.[1]; SCREEVE n.; SHEET n.; SHINPLASTER n.; SOFT MONEY n.; SOFT STUFF n.; STIFF n.[3]; WALLPAPER n.; WHITE MONEY n.). [SE *bank* + RAG n.[1] (3)]

bankroll *v.* (*also* **bank**) **1** [1920s+] (*orig. US*) to provide financial backing for a project, legal or otherwise. **2** [1940s] (*US Und.*) to take a victim's money in a confidence trick where the victim is allowed to win and lose, but always loses more than he wins. [SE *bankroll*, a roll of banknotes]

bankroller *n.* (*also* **bankroll, bankroll guy, bankroll man**) [1930s+] (*orig. US*) one who provides financial backing for a project, legal or otherwise. [BANKROLL v.]

bankrupt cart *n.* [late 18C–early 19C] a 1-horse chaise. ['said to be so called by a Lord Chief Justice, from their being so frequently used on Sunday jaunts by extravagant shopkeepers and tradesmen' (Grose, 1796)]

Bankside lady *n.* [17C] a prostitute (cf. AWAYDAY GIRL n.; FANCY WOMAN n.; GAY LADY n.; LADY n.[1]; LADYBIRD n.; LADY OF PLEASURE n.; LADY OF THE LAKE n.; LAKER LADY n.; NIGHTGOWN LADY n.; PERFECT LADY n.; PLEASURE-LADY n.; SALES LADY n.; SPORTING LADY n.). [*Bankside*, on the south bank of the Thames at Southwark, the centre of London prostitution during the 17C]

banneger *n.* [1950s] (*US*) a hard blow (with the fist). [? link to BEAT BANAGHAN v./BANGER n.[6]]

banner *n.*[1] [18C] pubic hair. [? SE *banner*, a flag; in this context the 'flag' displayed by the genitals]

banner *n.*[2] [1920s–30s] (*US tramp*) a bedroll. [one unfurls it]

banner *n.*[3] [1930s–40s] (*US prison*) a report citing a violation of prison regulations.

bans *n.* [20C+] (*W.I. Rasta*) a whole lot, a great deal. [? SE a *bunch of*]

bant *v.* [mid-19C–1920s] (*US*) to diet. [proper name William Banting (1797–1878), a fashionable undertaker who reduced his own weight through dieting and a tight-laced corset]

bantam *n.* **1** [late 19C–1920s] a lover, a womanizer. **2** [1930s–50s] (*US Black*) (*also* **banter**) a young woman. [SE *bantam*, a small variety of domestic fowl; note WW2 US Black milit. jargon *banta issue*, a Black female soldier]

banter *n.* [late 17C–18C] good-humoured nonsense or teasing. [cited by B.E. *c.*1700, the term was one of those, along with BAMBOOZLE v. (1), MOB n.[2] (1) and PUT n.[1] (1), attacked by Swift in *Tatler* no. 230 in 1710 and inspired his proposals to reform the language; despite his condemnation of the term as 'first borrowed from the bullies in White Friars, then fell among the footmen' and as an 'Alsatia phrase' it had joined SE by 1800]

banter *v.*[1] [late 17C–18C] to tease good-humouredly. [BANTER n.; SE by 1900]

banter *v.*[2] [mid-19C+] (*US/Irish*) to challenge. [strong version of BANTER v.[1]]

banter play built on a coke frame *n. see* COKE FRAME n.

bantling *n.* **1** [mid-16C–mid-19C] a child; also in fig. use, something weak or unformed. **2** [18C; 1980s] an illegitimate child. [Ger. *Bänkling*, bastard, ult. SE *bank*, bench; thus 'a child begotten on a bench, and not in the marriage-bed' (Webster, 1864)]

banton *v.* [1990s+] (*W.I.*) to pose as a superior person. [? link to Jam. dancehall star Buju *Banton* (b.1973)]

Bantu beer *n.* [1960s+] (*S.Afr.*) a drink made from fermented prickly pears and honey. [SE *Bantu*, a derog. generic for a Black African + *beer*]

banty *adj.* [late 19C+] saucy, impudent. [northern dial. *banty*, a small conceited person]

Banyan day *n.* **1** [mid-18C–1900s] Saturday, or any day of the week without work, and thus money. **2** [1930s–40s] (*Aus.*) Friday. [orig. naut. use, a day on which sailors ate no meat; ult. *Banian*, a Hindu merchant (Gujerati *vaniyo*, man of the trading caste), which caste trad. abstained from meat]

banzai *n.* [1900s–30s] a spree. [BANZAI! excl.]

banzai! *excl.* [20C+] a general excl. of exultation, excitement. [Jap. *banzai*, hurrah!, lit. 'let him (the Emperor) live ten thousand years!']

banzaimobile *n.* [1970s] a Japanese-made motorcycle. [BANZAI! excl. + -MOBILE sfx]

b.a.p. *n.* [1980s+] (*US*) an upwardly mobile Black achiever, usu. from the Black middle class. [abbr. *Black American prince/princess*]

baphead *n.* [2000s] (*UK teen*) a fool (cf. APPLEHEAD n.). [? SE *bap*, a soft, flat bread roll + -HEAD sfx (1)]

bappo *n.* [1920s+] (*Aus.*) a Baptist. [abbr. + -o sfx (4)]

baps *n.* [1980s+] (*orig. Ulster*) the female breasts (cf. APPLES n.[1]). [SE *bap*, a small (soft) bread roll]

bapsouse *v.* [1900s–50s] (*US*) **1** to baptize. **2** in fig. use, to start off a new machine. [SE *baptize* + *souse*, immerse]

baptist *n.* [early–mid-19C] a pickpocket who has been caught and ducked or 'baptized'. [pun on SE *Baptists*, who immerse new converts in water]

baptize *v.* [17C+] to dilute wine or alcohol. [i.e. to 'immerse in water']

baptized *adj.* **1** [17C–early 19C] of alcohol, usu. spirits, watered down. **2** [1930s–50s] (*Aus.*) drowned. [BAPTIZE v.]

bar *n.*[1] [mid-16C–mid-17C] (*UK Und.*) a kind of false die, on which certain numbers are prevented from turning up. [SE *bar*, a solid object of which one pair of sides is longer than the other]

bar *n.*[2] **1** [late 19C+] £1 sterling, orig. a sovereign; thus HALF-A-BAR n. **2** [1920s+] (*Irish*) a shilling (5p). [SE *bar*, a standard of weight or a denomination of a currency, esp. as used by 18C merchants in trading with Africans who exchanged their goods for a set number of iron bars; or ? Rom. *bauro*, heavy, big]

bar *n.*[3] (*also* **bar-up**) [20C+] the (usu. erect) penis; thus HAVE A BAR ON v. [its rigidity]

bar *n.*[4] (*drugs*) **1** [1960s+] cannabis, usu. as 1oz of hashish; thus in multiples that refer to ounce-weights, e.g. a *nine-bar*, 9oz (cf. AFGHAN n.). **2** [2000s] 1oz of heroin. [the shape of a typical lump of the drug]

bar *n.*[5] [1970s] (*US gay*) any public area, such as a park or beach, that is frequented by gay men looking for sex. [? on the basis of a SE *bar* being a popular site for such activities]

bar *v.*[1] **1** [early 19C+] of actions, to reject unequivocally. **2** [1910s+] (*Aus*) of people, to dislike intensely. [? 17C *bar*, to take exception to + dicing and 2-up jargon *bar*, to declare a throw void]

bar *v.*[2] *see* IRON BAR v.

Bara *n.* [1970s+] (*S.Afr.*) Baragwanath Hospital, Soweto. [abbr.]

barb *n.*[1] [1900s–20s] (*US campus*) a student who is not a member of a Greek-letter fraternity. [play on SE *barbarian*, to ancient Greeks, one who is not a Greek]

barb *n.*[2] (*also* **barbie**) [1960s+] (*drugs*) any of the hypnotic drugs derived from *barb*ituric acid. [abbr.]

barb *v.*[1] [mid-19C] (*US*) to *barber*, to cut hair. [abbr.; note SE *barb*, to clip, e.g. a hedge or a coin]

barb *v.*[2] *see* BARBER v.[1] (1).

barbadoes *v.* [mid-17C–mid-19C] (*Irish*) to transport to the West Indies. [proper name *Barbados*; after the Drogheda massacre of 1655, Oliver Cromwell transported many Irish people as an added punishment]

Barbary Coast *n.* [mid-19C–1940s] the red-light area of a city, esp. as frequented by sailors on leave. [16C proper name *Barbary Coast*, the countries of the northern coast of Africa; as a sl. term the phr. has applied specifically to the San Francisco waterfront

before the 1906 earthquake, Water Street, New York City, and part of Elizabeth Street, Sydney (from Campbell Street to Devonshire Street) during WW2; E.P. cites late 17C–early 19C *Little Barbary*, Wapping, home of the Ratcliff Highway, once London's tough port area]

barbecue *n.*[1] **1** [1920s] (*US*) a savage fight. **2** [1990s+] (*US prison*) the murder of a fellow-inmate by tossing a Molotov cocktail or petrol bomb into their cell. [SE *barbecue*, the roasting of a whole animal over an open fire]

barbecue *n.*[2] [1920s–60s] (*US Black*) an attractive woman, esp. one who enjoys or offers oral sex. [? such a woman is a 'hot piece of meat'; ? a precursor of modern SPIT ROAST n.]

barbecue *v.* **1** [1970s] (*US prison*) to electrocute; also to beat up severely. **2** [2000s] (*US Black/drugs*) to smoke marijuana.

barbed wire *n.*[1] (*also* **barbed drink**, **barbwire**) [1930s+] (*US*) strong whisky or brandy. [it 'tears you up']

barbed wire *n.*[2] [1990s+] (*Aus.*) Castlemaine XXXX lager. [the appearance of the xxxx]

barber *n.*[1] [late 16C–mid-17C] a prostitute diseased with syphilis. [? plays on the role of a barber as a primitive surgeon (who might treat syphilis), as well as the red-striped barber's pole (i.e. bloody and phallic), and the fact that his shaving water/her vagina is *hot*/HOT adj.[3] (1)]

barber *n.*[2] [early 19C] (*Can./US*) a bitterly cold wind. [it appears to 'cut' one's exposed face]

barber *n.*[3] [late 19C–1930s] (*Aus.*) a shearer. [they 'shave' sheep]

barber *n.*[4] [1920s+] (*US, esp. sporting*) a tediously talkative person. [the trad. loquacious *barber*, underpinned by US commentator Walter 'Red' Barber (1908–92)]

barber *n.*[5] **1** [1920s+] (*Aus.*) a hotel manager or owner. **2** [1920s+] (*UK Und.*) a thief who steals from hotel guest rooms. **3** [1930s] (*US Und.*) a pimp. [a pun on SE *barber*, who gives customers a trim/TRIM v. (4)]

barber *n.*[6] [1930s+] (*Aus.*) a tramp. [? BARBER'S CAT n.[1] (1), i.e. he is undernourished and thin]

barber *v.*[1] **1** [late 16C] (*also* **barb**) to clip the edges of gold coins. **2** [mid-19C] (*UK Und.*) to cheat. **3** [mid-19C+] (*orig. UK Und.*) to rob, to steal; thus *hotel barber*, a thief who specializes in robbing hotel guests. [a pun on SE *barber*, who gives customers a trim/TRIM v. (4)]

barber *v.*[2] [late 19C–1930s] (*Aus.*) to shear. [BARBER n.[3]]

barber *v.*[3] [1910s+] (*US*) to gossip, to chatter; thus *barbering*, conversation. [the supposed predilection of *barbers* for chattering on at their captive customers]

barber a joint *v.* [20C+] (*UK Und.*) to rob a bedroom while its occupant is sleeping. [BARBER v.[1] (3) + JOINT n.[4] (3)]

barbered broads *n.* [1950s] (*Aus.*) cards that have been shaved down one side to facilitate cheating. [SE *barber*, who gives customers a 'trim']

barber's block *n.* **1** [early 19C+] the head. **2** [late 19C–1920s] an overdressed man. [ext. of SE *barber's block*, the wooden 'head' on which a barber placed a wig]

barber's breakfast *n.* [1960s+] (*N.Z.*) a cough or dry retch, a glass of water and a cigarette (cf. BUSHMAN'S BREAKFAST n.; COCKNEY BREAKFAST n.; COWBOY'S BREAKFAST n.; DINGO'S BREAKFAST n.; DROVER'S BREAKFAST n.; DUCK'S BREAKFAST n.; JOCKEY'S BREAKFAST n.; KENTUCKY BREAKFAST n.; MEXICAN BREAKFAST n.; POMMY'S BREAKFAST n.; SPITALFIELDS' BREAKFAST n.). [N.Z.E. *barber*, a shearer]

barber's cat *n.*[1] **1** [mid–late 19C] a sickly, malnourished person. **2** [1930s] (*drugs*) an emaciated opium addict. [the lack of edible scraps at a barber's shop. 'An expression too coarse to print' (Hotten, 1867); Ware suggests corruption of *bare brisket*]

barber's cat *n.*[2] [1910s–50s] a gossip, a chatterer; one who prefers talk to action. [phr. *like the barber's cat – all wind and piss*]

barber's chair *n.* [early 16C–mid-19C] a promiscuous woman;

a prostitute (cf. BANBURY n.). [abbr. of phr. *common as a barber's chair*, which can be used by all-comers]

barber's clerk *n*. [mid–late 19C] an ignoramus; an overdressed man. [negative stereotyping]

barber's delight *n*. [late 19C–1930s] (*Aus.*) a silk shirt. [BARBER n.[3], i.e. it is not wool]

barber's knock *n*. [early–mid-19C] a double-knock, the first hard, the second far softer.

barber's pole *n*. [1990s+] a penis streaked with blood after intercourse with a menstruating woman. [the red-and-white-striped pole trad. signifiying a barber's shop; punning on POLE n.]

barber's sign *n*. [late 18C–early 19C] the penis and testicles. [the red-and-white-striped pole trad. signifiying a barber's shop; 'a standing pole and two wash-balls' (Grose, 1796). Note SE *wash-ball*, a ball of soap, often used for shaving]

barberton *n*. (*also* **babarton, babaton, baberton**) [1940s+] (*S.Afr.*) an illicit liquor (Blacks were not allowed to buy 'White man's liquor' before 1962), composed of bread, malt, sugar, yeast and warm water; thus *Barberton queen*, a brewer/seller of the drink. [proper name *Barberton*, a town in the East Transvaal]

barbie *n*.[1] [1990s+] (*US gay*) a feminine homosexual who prefers to dress in woman's clothing. [for ety. *see* BARBIE (DOLL) n.]

barbie *n*.[2] [1980s+] (*orig. Aus.*) a *barbe*cue. [abbr.]

barbie *n*.[3] *see* BARB n.[2].

Barbie (Doll) *n*. [1970s+] (*orig. US*) a super-conformist, conventionally attractive woman. [the name of a blue-eyed, blonde-haired designer-labelled plastic doll, created in 1959 for little girls and apparently a role-model for some of their elder sisters]

barbit *n*. [1980s] a *barbi*turate (cf. BAM n.[2]; BARBS n.; BLOCKBUSTER n.[1]; BLOCKERS n.; BLUE n.[9]; BLUE ANGEL n.; BLUE BANDS n.; BLUE BULLETS n.; BLUE DOLLS n.; BLUE DRAGONS n.; BLUE HEAVEN n.; BOMB n.[4]; BOMBER n.[2]; DEBS n.; DOWN n.[5]; DOWNER n.[5]; FENDER-BENDER n.; FLATHEADS n.; GANGSTER PILLS n.; G.B. n.[3]; GOOF n.[2]; GOOFBALL n.[1]; GOOF PILL n.; GORILLA PILLS n.; GREEN DRAGONS n.; GROUNDER n.[1]; GUMDROP n.[2]; HORS D'OEUVRES n.[1]; IDIOT PILLS n.; JIBLET n.; KING KONG PILLS n.; MARSHMALLOW n.[2]; MEXICAN JUMPING BEANS n.; MEXICAN RED n.; NEBBIE n.; NEMBIE n.; NEMISH n.; PEANUT n.[2]; PINK LADY n.; PINKS n.; PURPLE HEARTS n.; RAINBOW n.[3]; RED AND BLUE n.; RED BIRDS n.; RED BULLETS n.; RED DEVILS n.; RED JACKETS n.; REDS n.[3]; SLEEPER n.[3]; SLOW-EM-UPS n.; SOFTBALLS n.; SOPOR n.; STOPPERS n.; STUMBLERS n.; TOOIES n.). [abbr.]

barbs *n*. (*drugs*) **1** [1960s+] barbiturates (cf. BARBIT n.). **2** [1980s+] cocaine. [(2) is a misreading of (1)]

bar-bummer *n*. [1900s–20s] (*Aus.*) one who spends their time in bars. [SE bar + BUMMER n.[3] (1)]

barbwire *n*. *see* BARBED WIRE n.[1].

barb wire deal *n*. [1950s] (*US*) a difficult situation. [SE *barbed wire* + *deal*]

Barclay (and) Perkins *n*. [mid-19C–1900s] beer, stout. [the London brewers *Barclay, Perkins* & Co]

Barclay's (bank) *n*. (*also* **Midland (bank)**) [1930s+] masturbation. [rhy. sl. = WANK n.[1] (1)]

Barcoo *n*.[1] [late 19C] (*Aus.*) language heavily peppered with obscenities. [proper name *Barcoo*, a region of Queensland where, presumably, such speech was frequent]

Barcoo *n*.[2] [late 19C–1900s] (*Aus.*) bouts of vomiting caused by the ingestion of fly-polluted food. [abbr. *Barcoo sickness*]

Barcoo Bill *n*. [1910s] (*Aus.*) a generic term for a bushman. [*Barco* + generic use of proper name *Bill*]

Barcoo rot *n*. (*also* **kennedy rot**) [late 19C+] (*Aus.*) a form of scurvy. [*Barcoo* + SE *rot*, a putrescent, wasting disease]

Barcoo salute *n*. (*also* **Queensland salute**) [late 19C+] (*Aus.*) a characteristic Aus. gesture of brushing flies away from one's face. [*Barcoo/Queensland* + SE *salute*]

Barcoo sandwich *n*. [1960s+] (*Aus.*) **1** a curlew between 2 sheets

of bark. **2** a goanna between 2 sheets of bark. **3** a double rum between 2 beers. [*Barcoo* + SE *sandwich*]

Barcoo shout *n*. [1910s] (*Aus*) 3 drinks for half-a-crown (12.5p), a bargain at a time when drinks were usu. a shilling (5p) each. [*Barcoo* + SHOUT n.[1] (1)]

Barcoo spew *n*. (*also* **Barcoo vomit**) [late 19C+] (*Aus.*) severe vomiting brought on by drinking bad water and often accompanied by attacks of dysentery. [*Barcoo* + SE *spew/vomit*]

bardache *n*. (*also* **bardash**) [mid-16C–early 18C] a male homosexual. [SE *bardash*, a catamite; ult. ? f. Arabic *bardaj*, a slave]

bardache *v*. (*also* **bardash**) [mid-16C–17C] to sodomize, to perform anal intercourse. [BARDACHE n.]

bardacious *adj*. [1900s–30s] excellent, wonderful, the very best. [var. on BODACIOUS adj. (1)]

bar-dog *n*. [late 19C–1970s] (*US, Western*) a bartender; thus *bardogging*, tending bar. [SE *bar* + *dog*(*sbody*), a worker, a drudge; note SE *sea-dog* for model]

bardolph *n*. [early 19C] a red nose, the result of excessive drinking; thus *Bardolph-faced*, having a red nose. [*Bardolph*, a character in Shakespeare's *Henry V* (1598–9)]

bare *adj*. [2000s] (*UK Black teen*) many, lots of.

bare-arsed *adj*. (*also* **bare-assed**) [mid-16C+] naked; also in fig. use, lacking means or supplies. [SE *bare* + -ARSED sfx[1]/-ASSED sfx]

bare-ass *adj*. (*also* **bare-assed**) **1** [1930s+] naked; also in fig. use, bereft, lacking. **2** [1960s] in fig. use, naïve. **3** [1970s] (*US Und.*) of a burglar, not wearing any gloves (to prevent identification). [SE *bare* + ARSE n.[1] (1)/-ASS sfx; (2) the image is of a bare-bottomed infant]

bare-ass *v*. [1970s–80s] to pose naked, to strip. [BARE-ASS adj. (1)]

bareback *adv*. [1950s+] of having sexual intercourse, unprotected, without using a contraceptive sheath; thus *bareback riding*, having unprotected sex; *bareback rider*, a man who has sex without a condom. [the nakedness of the penis; note RIDE v.[1] (1)]

barebacking *n*. [1990s+] hetero- or homosexual intercourse without the use of a condom. [BAREBACK adv.]

bare-balls *adj*. [1960s] (*US*) completely naked. [SE *bare* +BALLS n.[1] (1)]

barebones *n*. [late 16C; 1910s] a thin person (cf. BAG OF BONES n.[1]).

bare-brisket *n*. [19C–1900s] a thin person. [SE *bare* + BRISKET n.[1]]

bare-bum *n*. [20C+] (*Aus.*) a dinner jacket. [SE *bare* +BUM n.[1] (1); the jacket is short, as opposed to a tailcoat]

bared *adj*. [mid-19C–1900s] shaved. [SE *bare*, to denude]

barefoot *adj*. (*also* **barefooted**) (*US*) **1** [mid-19C+] of an alcoholic drink, undiluted, 'straight'. **2** [mid-19C+] of tea or coffee, without milk/cream or sugar. **3** [1950s] cornbread made without eggs or fat.

barelegged *adj*. [early 18C] (*US*) of an alcoholic drink, undiluted.

bares *n*. [1960s–70s] (*US*) the *bare* hands. [abbr.]

barf *n*. [1960s+] **1** (*orig. US*) vomit; thus fig. something disgusting. **2** (*US*) any form of repulsive food. **3** (*US campus*) an ugly girl. [BARF v.]

barf *v*. **1** [1940s+] (*mainly US campus*) to vomit (cf. BARK v.[2]; BISON v.; BOAG v.; BOKE v.; BOOT v.[9]; BUICK v.; BURK v.[2]; BURP v.; CALF v.; CALL THE DOGS v.; CALVE v.; CARK v.; CHIRP v.; COUGH v.; COUGH UP v.; CROAK v.[4]; EARL v.; FLOB v.; FRED v.; GAWK v.[2]; HACK v.[7]; HARRY v.; HONK v.[1]; HOOK v.[11]; HOOP v.[2]; OOK v.; PERK v.; RALPH v.; SPIT UP v.; WHOOPS v.; WOOF v.[3]; YACK v.; YANK v.[2]; YAWP v.; YODEL v.; YUCK v.; YUCK UP v.; YUKE v.; ZUKE v.). **2** [1960s] (*US campus*) as *barf on*, in fig. use, to be treated unfairly. [echoic]

barf! *excl*. (*also* **barfaroo!**) [1970s+] (*US*) that's disgusting! don't make me sick! [BARF n.]

barf around *v*. [1960s] (*US campus*) to waste time. [fig. use of BARF v.]

barfbag *n*. [1960s+] (*US*) **1** an air-sickness bag, as provided on air flights. **2** a general term of abuse. [BARF n. (1) + SE *bag/*-BAG sfx]

barf city *n.* [1940s+] (*US teen*) anything particularly unpleasant. [BARF n. (1) + CITY sfx]

barfer *n.* [1940s] (*US*) a disgusting, worthless person. [BARF n. (1)]

bar-fly *n.* **1** [20C+] (*orig. US*) the habitual occupier of a bar, day in, day out. **2** [1950s+] a prostitute who works from a bar; a woman frequenting bars to pick up men (cf. ALLEY CAT n.). [ext. of SE use, one who 'buzzes around' a bar]

bar-fly *v.* [1950s] (*US*) to habitually frequent bars. [BAR-FLY n. (1)]

barf me out! *excl.* [1980s+] (*US*) an excl. indicating absolute disapproval. [BARF! excl.]

barf on a board *n.* [1960s+] (*US*) chipped creamed beef on toast. [BARF n. (1); note synon. US milit. jargon 'shit on a shingle']

barf someone out *v.* [1980s+] (*US*) to disgust, to revolt; thus *barfed out*, disgusted. [BARF n. (1)]

barfulous *adj.* [1980s+] (*US campus*) repellent, disgusting. [BARF n. (1); orig. computing use]

barfy *adj.* (*US campus/teen*) **1** [1950s+] nauseating, repulsive. **2** [1960s] feeling ill. [BARF n. (1) + sfx *-y*]

bargain basement *n.* [1940s–70s] anywhere sex partners can be found easily, thus a cheap prostitute. [joc. use of SE *bargain basement*, the bargain department of a large store]

barge *n.*[1] **1** [mid-19C] a large (old) woman. **2** [1950s+] (*US*) a large foot. **3** [1960s+] a particularly large vagina. **4** [1960s+] (*US Black*) a large car, esp. a Cadillac. [SE *barge*; barges are generally large and unwieldy vessels]

barge *n.*[2] [late 19C–1900s] an imitation (padded) breast. ['from their likeness to the wide prow of canal-barges' (Ware)]

barge *n.*[3] **1** [late 19C–1940s] an argument, a dispute. **2** [20C+] (*Irish*) a cantankerous, argumentative woman. [BARGE v.[1]]

barge *v.*[1] [mid-19C+] to abuse, to attack verbally, to 'slang'; thus *barge the point*, to argue, to dispute. [? SE *bargee*, a bargeman, an occupation known for its 'colourful' language, or Scot. *bargle*, to squabble; 20C+ use mainly Irish]

barge *v.*[2] *see* BARGE (IN) v.

barge-arse *n.* [mid-19C–1900s; 1990s+] one who has fat buttocks. [SE *barge* + ARSE n.[1] (1)]

barge at *v.* [late 19C+] to argue aggressively. [BARGE v.[1]]

bargee *n.* [late 19C+] a general insult, the inference is a loud-mouthed, objectionable individual; also in affectionate use. [stereotyping of SE *bargee*, a bargeman]

barge (in) *v.* (*also* **barge**) [late 19C+] to interrupt rudely, to push one's way in. [SE *barge*, a flat-bottomed canal- or river-boat, esp. its clumsy motions]

bar golf *n.* [1980s+] (*US campus*) the practice of going from bar to bar drinking. [play on a round of golf/a round of drinks]

bar handles *n.* [1960s] an excess of fat around one's stomach, a 'spare tyre' (cf. HANDLES n.; LOVE HANDLES n.). [SE *bar* + *handle*; the fat has developed after too many trips to the bar]

bar-hog *n.*[1] [1930s] (*US*) a heavy drinker who spends most of their time in the bar. [SE *bar* + joc. use of *hog*]

bar-hog *n.*[2] [1960s] (*US*) a part-time prostitute, who frequents bars and uses them as a base for soliciting (cf. ALLEY CAT n.). [SE *bar* + HOG n.[7] (1)]

bar-hop *n.* [1900s–30s; 2000s] (*US*) a bartender. [they 'hop' around the bar]

bar-hop *v.* [1950s+] (*US*) to go from bar to bar, drinking and investigating the social possibilities; thus *barhopper*, one who bar-hops; *barhop*, the act of moving from bar to bar. [SE *bar* + HOP v.[1] (7)]

barhound *n.* [1920s;1990s+] the habitual occupier of a bar. [SE *bar* + HOUND sfx]

bari *n. see* BAARIE n.

bark *n.*[1] **1** [mid-18C–19C; 1940s–60s] the human skin; thus *take*

the bark off, to beat, to thrash. **2** [mid-19C; 1920s] any skin, or animal hide. [SE *bark*, the outer surface of a tree; coined *c.*1750 but all 20C use is US Black]

bark *n.*[2] [late 18C–19C] an Irish person; thus *Barkshire*, Ireland. [various northern dials.; ? f. image of a noisy Irish person shouting or 'barking']

bark *n.*[3] **1** [1920s] (*US*) bragging. **2** [1990s+] (*US campus*) a lie, a 'tall tale'.

bark *n.*[4] [1990s+] (*Aus.*) an act of vomiting. [echoic]

bark *v.*[1] **1** [mid-18C+] to flagellate. **2** [late 19C+] to hurt by breaking the skin. [BARK n.[1] (1)]

bark *v.*[2] **1** [19C] to cough. **2** [early 19C+] to tout a shop or attraction; to work as a costermonger's assistant. **3** [late 19C] (*UK Und.*) to inform. **4** [late 19C–1940s] to make a loud, sudden noise, esp. that of firing a handgun. **5** [1950s+] to hurt. **6** [1960s] (*US*) to boast, to brag. **7** [1990s+] (*Aus.*) to vomit (cf. BARK v.). **8** [1990s+] (*US campus*) to lie. [all fig. uses of SE]

bark and growl *n.* [late 19C+] a trowel. [rhy. sl.]

barker *n.*[1] **1** [late 15C–17C; 19C] a thug, esp. one who offers verbal, but perhaps not physical, aggression. **2** [late 17C+] a shop tout, esp. the tout who stands outside a second-hand clothes shop attempting to lure customers within. **3** [late 18C+] a pistol. **4** [19C] one who coughs. **5** [early–mid-19C] a tout who lures victims into mock auctions or corrupt casinos. **6** [mid-19C] a costermonger's assistant. **7** [mid-19C+] an employee of a saloon or similar place of recreational entertainment who lures in passers-by from the street. **8** [1900s–40s] (*US*) an auctioneer. [SE *bark*, to shout loudly; (1) 19C use is US; (2) 20C+ use is mainly US]

barker *n.*[2] [1910s] a sausage. [a ref. to the once popular song 'Oh vare and oh vare is my leedle vee dog/Oh vare, oh vare is he gone?']

barkers *n.* **1** [1920s–50s] (*US Und.*) shoes. **2** [1940s–50s] (*US Black*) tight, painful shoes. [tight shoes hurt one's feet, which therefore 'bark' with pain]

barker's *adj.* [1930s–50s] naked, nude. [rhy. sl. = STARKERS adj.[1]; ult. *Barker's*, a large department store in High Street Kensington, London]

barker's egg *n.* [1980s+] (*orig. Aus.*) dog excrement, esp. when very old; thus *barker's nest*, a pile of dog excrement (cf. ALLEY APPLE n.[2]). [SE *barker*, a dog + *egg*]

barking *adj.* [1900s; 1960s+] absolutely crazy, highly eccentric; usu. as *barking mad*. [? the image of a rabid dog or a madman howling at the moon]

barking dogs *n.* [1930s–70s] (*US*) aching or sore feet. [a pun on SE; note DOGS n.[1] (1)]

barking iron *n.* [late 18C–mid-19C] a pistol, usu. in pl. [the noise]

barking spider *n.* **1** [1980s+] (*US campus*) the audible breaking of wind. **2** [1990s+] the anus. [the resemblance + the noise of defection or farting; ult. the Aus. *barking spider*, which produces and barking or whistling noise]

bark up the wrong tree *v.* (*also* **bark up the wrong creek, jump the wrong stump**) [early 19C+] (*orig. US*) to make a mistake, to misdirect one's efforts. [the image of a dog chasing a racoon into a tree]

barkwell and holdfast *n.* [mid-19C] (*US*) someone who will back their words with deeds; a tough fighter. [pvb 'Brag's a good dog, but Holdfast is better']

Bar L *n.* [1980s+] (*Scot.*) *Bar*linnie prison, Glasgow (cf. ABBOTT'S PRIORY n.). [abbr. of name, but note the poss. pun on use of *Bar* in many brands used by US ranchers to distinguish their cattle, e.g. Bar X, Bar Y (in which the bar is a horizontal line drawn beneath the letter); Bar L thus offers a suggestion of the Wild West, in this case of Scotland]

barley *n.*[1] (*also* **barley juice, ...pop, ...water, ...wine**) [early 17C+] beer. [SE *barley* (+ JUICE n.[3] (1)/POP n.[2] (1)/SE *water/wine*); late 19C+ use is US Midwest/Black/campus]

barley n.[2] [1990s+] cocaine (cf. BIG BLOKE n.[2]; BILLIE HOKE n.; BOB MARLEY n.; NICKA LAUDA n.; OATS n.[2]; PATSY CLINE n.; SALVADOR DALI n.; WHISTLE (AND FLUTE) n.; YOU-KNOW n.[2]). [rhy. sl.; *oats and barley* = CHARLIE n.[9] (1)]

barley v. [1960s] (*Aus.*) to stop doing something when asked. [? dial. *barley!*, a call for a temporary truce in wrestling, linked by *EDD* to Fr. *bailler*, to give, to grant, to yield over; note also naut. *belay*, stop]

barley-break n. [17C] sexual play. ['An old country game [...] originally played by six persons (three of each sex) in couples; one couple, being left in a middle den termed 'hell,' had to catch the others, who were allowed to separate or 'break' when hard pressed, and thus to change partners, but had when caught to take their turn as catchers' (*OED*)]

barleybree n. [late 18C–19C] (*Scot.*) strong ale. [SE *barley* + 15C *bree*, broth or juice in which anything has been boiled or marinated]

barleybroth n. [late 16C–19C] strong ale. [SE *barley* + *broth*]

barleybun gentleman n. [mid-16C] a rich gentleman who prefers to live poorly. [SE *barleybun*, a plain bun made with barley + *gentleman*]

barley juice/pop/water/wine n. *see* BARLEY n.[1].

Barlinnie drumstick n. [1930s+] (*Glasgow*) a lead pipe studded with nails. [Scotland's high-security *Barlinnie* prison, where the carrier of such a weapon might end up]

barmaid's blush n.[1] [20C+] (*Aus.*) a flush, as in poker. [rhy. sl.]

barmaid's blush n.[2] **1** [1910s–70s] (*Aus.*) ginger beer/rum and raspberry cordial. **2** [1940s] port and lemon.

barmecide n. [1950s] (*US drugs*) morphine; thus *barmecided*, addicted to or under the influence of morphine (cf. AUNTIE EMMA n.). [SE *Barmecide*, 'Patronymic of a family of princes ruling at Bagdad just before Haroun-al-Raschid, concerning one of whom the story is told in the Arabian Nights, that he put a succession of empty dishes before a beggar, pretending that they contained a sumptuous repast—a fiction which the beggar humorously accepted. Hence, one who offers imaginary food or illusory benefits' (*OED*); thus the image of morphine-induced fantasies]

barmpot n. (*also* **bampot**) [1910s+] an eccentric. [BARMY adj. + -POT sfx]

barmy adj. [mid-19C+] insane, eccentric; thus *put on the barmy stick*, to feign insanity; (*UK Und.*) *barmies*, those categorized as weak-minded. [dial. *barm*, yeast; thus frothing like fermenting yeast; note also the lunatic asylum in Barming, Kent]

barn n.[1] [late 19C–1900s] a public ballroom. [Highbury *Barn*, north London, site of one of the last such venues]

barn n.[2] (*also* **barn door**) [1920s; 1960s+] (*US*) the trouser fly.

Barnaby Rudge n. [20C+] a judge. [rhy. sl.; ult. the proper name coined by Charles Dickens as the title of his novel, 1841]

barnacle n.[1] **1** [late 16C] (*UK Und.*) that member of a team of swindlers who poses as an independent individual, ostensibly having no knowledge of his new companions but keenly ready to befriend the victim, often pretending to be drunk. **2** [late 16C] (*UK Und.*) one who speaks through their nose. **3** [17C] (*UK Und.*) one who pays too close an attendance, a hanger-on. **4** [early 17C] (*UK Und.*) a decoy swindler, a swindler's assistant. **5** [1920s–30s] (*US tramp*) one who persists at something. [all f. 14C SE *barnacle*, a type of pincer used to restrain recalcitrant horses; thus an instrument of torture for humans, which in turn must come from the shellfish that clings to ships' bottoms. The image in all cases is of clinging tight]

barnacle n.[2] [late 17C–early 19C] **1** a good job or quick profit easily obtained. **2** a tip given to a groom at a horse sale. [the recipient 'sticks onto' both]

barnacle n.[3] [1950s] (*US Und.*) a woman. [she 'clings' to a man]

barnacled adj. [late 17C–18C] wearing spectacles. [BARNACLES n. (1)]

barnacles n. **1** [mid-16C–1910s] spectacles, eye-glasses. **2** [late

17C+] (*UK Und.*) fetters, irons; latterly handcuffs. [like the SE *barnacle*, a horse's bit, they pinch the nose or wrist]

barnard n. [mid-16C–early 17C] (*UK Und.*) that member of a team of swindlers who poses as an independent individual, ostensibly having no knowledge of his new companions but keenly ready to befriend the victim and often pretending to be drunk. [SE *berner*, one who waits with a relay of hounds to intercept a hunted animal]

barnard's law n. [mid-16C–early 17C] (*UK Und.*) a form of card-sharping in which a team of 4 con-men fleece a victim. [BARNARD n. + LAW n.[1]]

barnburner n. [1930s+] (*US*) **1** a huge and resounding success. **2** a very stylish, classy woman. **3** an expert, a highly competent person. [(1) ? f. a party so riotously enjoyable that one ends up by burning down the barn in which it is held; note Mathews, *Dict. Americanisms* (1951): '*Barnburner*, A member of a faction of the democratic party in N.Y. State (*c*.1840–50) so zealous for reforms that they would "burn the barn to get rid of the rats"']

barnburners n. [1970s] (*Can.*) the Royal Canadian Mounted Police. [the burning down by the RCMP, in 1976, of a barn in rural Quebec which was being used as a meeting place for French-Canadian separatists]

barn dance n. [1950s+] (*Aus./N.Z.*) pedestrians rushing across a 'buzz crossing', in which one 'buzzes' a button to change the traffic light. [SE + ref. to Traffic Commissioner *Barnes*, inventor of the buzz crossing, first seen in New York City]

barn door n. *see* BARN n.[2].

barn door is open, the phr. (*also* **the barn gate is open**) [1920s; 1960s+] (*orig. US*) a phr. used to warn a man that his trouser-fly is undone (cf. COW BARN IS OPEN, THE phr.). [BARN DOOR n.]

barndoor savage n. [late 19C–1940s] a rustic, a yokel.

barner n. [mid-19C–1900s] a fashionable young working-class man of north London. [BARN n.[1]; Highbury Barn, a lavish pleasure-garden and entertainment centre, flourished as a 'nothern Cremorne' from 1835–71 when escalating rowdiness finally cost the owner his licence]

barneries n. [late 19C–1900s] the Adelphi Stores, in the Strand, London WC2. [Miss *Barnes*, the proprietress]

barnet n. [mid-19C+] hair. [abbr. BARNET FAIR n.]

barnet cut n. [1940s–50s] a haircut, esp. in prison; those who received this cut were presumed to be serving a short sentence. [BARNET n. + SE *cut*]

barnet fair n. (*also* **barney fair**) [mid-19C+] the hair. [rhy. sl.; the actual Barnet Fair fl. 16C–18C as the country's major horse fair; so important was the town's position on a main northbound thoroughfare that it became known as 'the town of inns']

barney n.[1] **1** [mid-19C] (*US campus*) a bad recitation. **2** [mid-19C–1930s] (*UK Und.*) a fake fight, arranged by criminals to distract a potential victim's attention. **3** [late 19C] (*US*) a hoax. **4** [late 19C+] humbug, cheating, fraud, esp. of a 'fixed' sporting event. **5** [1900s–50s] a tease. [? the holding of dubious sporting events, e.g. bare-knuckle boxing, in or behind the *barn*, and thus a fig. use of BARNEY n.[3] (1). However, E.P., quoting Apperson, refers to the phr. *come, come, that's Barney Castle*, a response to anyone making a particularly specious excuse. This in turn, it is claimed, refers to the Catholic earls' Northern Rising of 1569, when Barnard Castle was held by Sir George Bowes who refused, despite many challenges, to leave his fortifications and engage in battle. The 'Rising in the North' certainly created the Durham dial. *Barnard Castle*, a coward, taken from the jibe 'A coward, a coward, o' Barney castle/Dare na come out to fight a battle']

barney n.[2] **1** [mid-19C; 1980s+] (*US campus*) an unsophisticated person, one who is not part of currently approved fashions or attitudes. **2** [1970s] (*US Black*) the penis; thus *put barney in the VCR*, to have sexual intercourse. **3** [1990s+] (*US campus*) an attractive man. [plays on the proper name *Barney Rubble*, a character in the TV cartoon (and latterly the film) *The Flintstones*, thus believed by college students. But note mid-19C cit. based on ? negative stereotyping of Irish immigrants, thus BARNEY n.[3]]

barney n.[3] **1** [mid-19C+] an enjoyable social occasion, a rowdy party. **2** [mid-19C+] an argument, a discussion, a suggestion. **3** [mid–late 19C] a crowd of people. **4** [late 19C+] a fight; also as *bit of (a) barney*. **5** [1900s–30s] (*UK Und.*) a fake fight, arranged by criminals to distract a potential victim's attention. [proper name *Barney*, associated with the Irish and their stereotyped aggression (cf. PADDY n.[3])]

barney n.[4] [20C+] (*Irish*) one's head, mind; usu. in phr. *don't bother your barney*. [? BARNET n.]

barney adj. [late 19C] unfair, crooked (esp. by pre-arrangement). [BARNEY n.[1] (4)]

barney v.[1] **1** [mid-19C] (*UK Und.*) to avoid responsibilities; to 'get out of'; to give up on. **2** [late 19C] (*Aus./N.Z.*) to fight, to argue; also *barney over*. [BARNEY n.[3]]

barney v.[2] [20C+] to cheat, to act unfairly. [BARNEY n.[1] (4)]

barney clapper n. *see* BONNY-CLAPPER n.

barney dillon n. [1930s+] (*Irish/Scot.*) a shilling (5p). [rhy. sl.]

barney maguire n. [20C+] (*Aus./US*) a fire. [rhy. sl.]

barney moke n. [1940s–70s] a pocket. [rhy. sl. = POKE n.[2] (2)]

Barney (Rubble) n. [1980s+] trouble. [rhy. sl.; the proper name *Barney Rubble*, a character in the TV cartoon (and latterly the film) *The Flintstones*]

barney's bull n. [1950s] (*Aus./N.Z.*) **1** a worthless person or thing (cf. ALL BEHIND LIKE BARNEY'S BULL phr.; AS DEAD AS BARNEY'S BULL phr.; LIKE BARNEY'S BULL phr.). **2** nonsense, rubbish. [? long-lost anecdotal ref.; E.P. suggests poss. corruption of *Boanerges*]

barn gate is open, the phr. *see* BARN DOOR IS OPEN, THE phr.

barnstormers n. **1** [mid–late 19C] groups of actors who tour the country specializing in plays that will appeal to their rustic audiences; their improvised stages were often set up in barns. **2** [1920s] (*US*) itinerant flyers who travelled the country putting on flying and aerobatic displays. [SE *barn* + *storm*, to attack]

Barnwell ague n. [mid-17C–early 19C] gonorrhoea. [proper name *Barnwell*, a brothel district or f. joc. 'burn well' + SE *ague*; note Hall, *College Words and Customs* (1856): 'Barnwell. At Cambridge, Eng., a place of resort for characters of bad report'; note Cambridge University decree 1675: 'Hereafter no scholar whatsoever [...] upon any pretence whatsoever, shall go into any house of bad report in Barnewell, on pain [...] of being expelled from the university']

Barnyard n. [1960s+] (*US campus*) Barnard College.

barnyard golf n. [1920s–40s] (*US*) pitching horseshoes.

barnyard pimp n. [1940s+] (*US prison*) fried chicken. [the role of the cockerel]

barnyard preacher n. (*also* **barn preacher**) [early 19C+] (*US*) an unprofessional or part-time lay preacher.

barnyard savage n. [1900s–50s] (*US*) a loutish country yokel.

bar of soap n. [1940s+] drugs. [rhy. sl. = DOPE n.[1] (6)]

baron n. (*also* **tobacco baron**) **1** [1910s+] (*UK/US Und.*) a major criminal. **2** [1940s+] (*UK prison*) an influential convict within a prison, esp. one who trades in tobacco or drugs. **3** [1950s] anyone who has money.

baron v. [1940s+] (*UK prison*) to control the traffic in tobacco or drugs, the primary prison commodities. [BARON n. (2)]

baronet n. [mid-18C] a sirloin of beef. [play on SE *baron of beef*]

Baron George n. [late 19C] a fat man. [South London use; f. George Parkes, a portly theatrical landlord, nicknamed *Baron George*]

barossa n. [1980s+] (*Aus.*) a woman. [*Barossa* Pearl, a sweet white wine]

bar polisher n. [1940s–60s] (*orig. US Black*) a hard drinker.

barprop n. [1980s] (*US*) the habitual occupier of a bar. [SE *bar* + *prop*, support]

barrack n. [late 19C+] (*Aus.*) banter, chat.

barrack v. [late 19C+] (*Aus.*) **1** to support a team or individual in a sporting context; thus *barracker*, a supporter; thus to support or promote anything or anyone. **2** to back up a confidence trickster. **3** to tease. [Northern Ireland dial. *barrack*, to brag, to be boastful of one's fighting powers; unlike SE use, no antagonism is implied, other than the usual partisanship; E.P., via a correspondent in 1944, offers an alternative ety., 'from the rough teams that used to play football on the vacant land near the Victoria barracks (in Melbourne)'; such players were known as *barrackers*]

barrack hack n. [late 19C] **1** a prostitute (cf. BANBURY n.). **2** a woman who regularly attends military balls. [SE *barrack hack*, a horse available to any soldier in a barracks; like the animal, the human is available to anyone who wishes to 'ride']

barrack-room lawyer n. (*also* **barrack lawyer, guardhouse lawyer**) [1910s+] any amateur, esp. in the services or in prison, who considers himself more expert in the law, esp. Queen's Regulations or prison rules, than any professional and who will offer services, often to their detriment, to others.

barracuda n. **1** [1930s+] (*US*) a violent, aggressive criminal. **2** [1950s+] (*US*) a domineering, argumentative person. **3** [1960s] (*US*) a predatory homosexual, desperate to obtain a desired partner no matter what it takes. **4** [1970s+] (*US*) a sexual enthusiast, esp. female. **5** [1980s] (*US campus*) a nasty woman. [SE *barracuda*, a large and voracious fish (*Sphyraena barracuda*) of the perch family]

barrakin n. *see* BARRIKIN n. (1).

barred adj. [mid-16C–mid-18C; 1950s] (*UK Und.*) referring to a type of false or 'barred' dice, with one of the sides fractionally longer than the others so that they will not easily lie on certain sides; such dice might be *barred sice-aces* (6-1), *barred cater-treys* (4-3) etc. [SE *bar*, a piece of material that is long in proportion to its thickness. Although the last *OED* cit. is in 1753, when the term has been trimmed to *barr dice*, and E.P. dates it 16C–17C, Aus. use, with the same meaning, persists in mid-20C]

barrel n.[1] [late 19C–1900s] (*orig. US*) a large amount, usu. of money. [SE *barrel of money*]

barrel n.[2] [late 19C–1920s] (*US*) a political 'slush' fund. [PORK BARREL n.]

barrel n.[3] [1940s+] a fat person. [resemblance]

barrel v.[1] [1930s–60s] (*US tramp*) to drink, usu. to excess.

barrel v.[2] **1** [1930s+] (*orig. US*) to charge along, to move swiftly. **2** [1960s+] (*Aus.*) to knock down, to hit, esp. as a result of a tackle in football. **3** [1970s] (*Aus.*) to kill. [SE *barrel into*, to crash in at speed, like a barrel rolling downhill]

barrel-ass n. [1940s] (*US*) a fat person. [SE *barrel*/BARREL n.[3] + ASS n. (2)/-ASS sfx]

barrel-ass v. [1960s+] (*US*) to rush headlong, to charge at; to drive fast. [SE *barrel into* + ASS n. (2)]

barrel-boarder n. (*also* **barrel dosser, barrel-house stiff, barrel stiff**) [late 19C–1960s] (*US*) an ageing, impoverished, alcoholic tramp who frequents low saloons. [BARRELHOUSE n. + SE *boarder*/DOSSER n. (1)/STIFF n.[2] (4)]

barrel fever n. [late 18C] drunkenness; thus delirium tremens.

barrelhouse n. (*also* **barrel-house**) [late 19C–1940s] (*US*) a brothel or cheap saloon (cf. ACCOMMODATION HOUSE n.). [the barrels of beer available in such places]

barrelhouse adj. (*also* **barrel-house**) [late 19C+] (*US, orig. jazz*) of both music and places, rough, tough, unpretentious music that started off in the repertoire of the musicians who played for cheap saloons. [BARRELHOUSE n.]

barrelhouse v. (*also* **barrel-house**) **1** [1910s–40s] (*US*) to frequent a cheap saloon or brothel. **2** [1930s–60s] (*US Black*) to look for sexual partners, to have sexual intercourse. **3** [1950s] (*US*) to drive very fast. [BARRELHOUSE n.]

barrel-house stiff n. *see* BARREL-BOARDER n.

barrelled *adj.* (*also* **barrelled up**) [1910s–60s] (*US*) drunk (cf. ALED UP adj.).

barrel of fat *n.* [20C+] (*Aus.*) a hat. [rhy. sl.]

barrel of treacle *n.* [late 19C–1900s] love, esp. the outward signs of being in love. [the fig. sticky sweetness thereof]

barrels *n.* [1970s+] (*drugs*) LSD (cf. A n.³). [the shape of some LSD capsules]

barrel stiff *n.* *see* BARREL-BOARDER n.

barrel-wash *n.* [1980s] (*Can.*) illicitly distilled liquor.

barren Joey *n.* [1940s] (*Aus.*) a prostitute. [SE *barren* + ? SAusE *joey*, a young kangaroo; she 'jumps around' but has no children]

barrier *n.* [1910s] (*Aus.*) a bar. [it stands between the customer and the alcohol]

Barrier reef *n.* [1980s] (*Aus.*) teeth. [rhy. sl.]

barrikin *n.* **1** [mid-19C] (*also* **barrakin**) unintelligible language. **2** [mid-19C] a hawker's sales patter. **3** [late 19C] chatter. [Fr. *baragouin*, an incomprehensible or alien language, itself f. Breton *bara*, bread + *gwîn*, wine or *gwenn*, white, referring to the astonishment of Breton soldiers at the sight of white bread (Roulin in *Littré Supp.*) and thus transferred to describe bizarre, unintelligible speech]

barrister's *n.* [late 19C–1900s] (*UK Und.*) the nickname of a thieves' coffeehouse, popular at the time. [the host's name]

barrow *n.* (*Aus.*) **1** [1940s] a police van. **2** [1950s+] a second-hand motorcar.

barrow *v.* [mid-19C–1910s] to take home a drunkard who is reclining or passed out in a wheel-barrow.

barrow-bunter *n.* [mid-18C] a female costermonger. [SE *barrow* + BUNTER n. (1)]

barrow-man *n.* [early–mid 19C] a man under sentence of transportation. [the employment of such convicts, awaiting their ship in prison, in wheeling around barrows full of earth]

barrows *n.* [1990s+] (*W.I.*) a loan, esp. of money. [SE *borrows*]

barrow-tram *n.* [late 19C] a clumsy, ungainly person. [SE *barrow-tram*, the shaft of a barrow]

barry *n.* *see* BAARIE n.

barry *adj.*¹ [20C+] lovely, sweet, excellent. [Rom. *baro*, big, important]

barry *adj.*² [1990s+] (*Scot. juv.*) embarrassing.

Barry Crocker *n.* [1990s+] (*Aus.*) a shocker, something bad. [rhy. sl.; ult. Aus. entertainer/film actor *Barry Crocker* (b.1935)]

Barry White *n.* [2000s] an act of defecation (cf. ANDY CAPP n.). [rhy. sl. = SHITE n. (2); ult. US soul singer *Barry White* (1944–2003)]

barse *n.* **1** [1960s] (*US campus*) a consistent blunderer. **2** [1990s+] the perineum, i.e. the portion of flesh between the underside of the testes and the anus. [BALLS n.¹ (1) + ARSE n.¹ (1)]

barsterd *n.* *see* BASTARD n. (1).

bar steward *n.* [1920s+] a euph. for bastard. [joc. pron. of SE]

barstool jockey *n.* [1980s] (*US*) the habitual occupier of a bar. [SE *barstool* + JOCKEY n.³ (2)]

bart *n.* (*also* **barty**) [late 19C–1940s] (*Aus.*) a woman. [ety. unknown; ? rhy. sl. = TART n.¹ (1)]

bar that! *excl.* [mid-19C] stop! be quiet! [BAR v.¹ (1)]

bar the bubble *v.* [late 18C–early 19C] to make an exception against the general rule. [SE *bar*, except + play on BUBBLE n.¹ (1)]

bartholomew baby *n.* [late 17C–mid-19C] one who is dressed in tawdry finery. [the dolls sold at the annual Bartholomew Fair, which flourished 1133–1855, when it was suppressed and its grounds replaced by the Smithfield Meat Market]

bartholomew (boar) pig *n.* [16C–17C] a fat man. [SE *Bartholomew pig*, roast pork sold at Bartholomew Fair (see prev.)]

bartholomew doll *n.* [late 18C–early 19C] an overdressed, vulgar woman. [the bright, tawdry dolls sold at Bartholomew Fair]

barty *n.* *see* BART n.

bar-up *n.* *see* BAR n.³.

bar up *v.* [1980s] (*Aus.*) to achieve an erection. [BAR n.³]

bas *n.* [1920s+] *bas*tard. [abbr.]

base *n.* (*drugs*) **1** [1960s+] morphine base, from which heroin is processed. **2** [1970s+] cocaine. **3** [1970s+] coca paste, from which cocaine is processed. **4** [1980s+] (*also* **base-rock**) crack cocaine (cf. BAZOOKA n.¹; BLOW n.⁶; BLUE n.⁹; BOB n.⁶; BOBO n.²; BOMB n.⁴; BONECRUSHER n.²; BOULDER n.; BREAKFAST OF CHAMPIONS n.; BUMP n.⁴; CAKES n.¹; CANDY n.¹; CAP n.⁴; CAVVY n.; CHALK n.⁴; CHEESE n.⁸; CHEMICAL n.; CLOUD n.¹; CLOUD NINE n.; COKE n.¹; COOKIE n.³; CRACK n.¹³; CRACKOLA n.; CRANK n.⁴; CREAMY n.¹; DEVIL, THE n.; DEVIL'S DANDRUFF n.; DICE n.²; DIME n.²; DIP n.¹⁰; D.O.A. n.; EYE-OPENER n.¹; FIFTY-ONE n.; FISH SCALES n.; FLAKE n.¹; FREEBASE n.; GOLD n.²; GRAVEL n.; GRIT n.⁶; HAIL n.; HAMBURGER HELPER n.; HANDBALL n.²; HARDBALL n.²; HUBBA n.²; HYDRO n.; ICE-CREAM n.¹; JELLY BEANS n.; JOHNSON n.⁴; KIBBLES & BITS n.; KOKOMO n.; LIDO n.; LIGHTNING n.²; NUGGETS n.³; ONE-FIFTY-ONE n.; PAPER n.²; PEBBLES n.²; PEE-WEE n.; PONY n.⁷; PRODUCT n.; RAW n.¹; READY (ROCK) n.; READYWASH n.; RED CAPS n.; ROCK n.³; ROCKS n.⁵; ROCKY n.; ROX n.; SCOTTY n.¹; SHIT n.⁵; SLAB n.³; SMOKE n.³; SNOW n.²; SNOWFLAKE n.¹; SNOW TOKE n.; STONE n.¹; SUPERCHARGE n.; SUPERCLOUD n.; TEETH n.; TWEAKS n.; TWIG n.³; ULTIMATE n.; WASH n.⁴; WASHED ROCK n.; WASH-ROCK n.; WHITE n.³; YALE n.; YEYO n.). [(2–4) abbr. FREEBASE n. (1), although this itself refers not to crack, but to base cocaine, the enjoyment of which predated crack and appealed, through its high price and complex paraphernalia, to a higher social group than the often impoverished crack-users; (4) + ROCK n.³ (4)]

base *v.*¹ (*orig. US Black*) **1** to disparage, to criticize, to humiliate another person. **2** to argue. [SE *debase*]

base *v.*² [1980s+] (*drugs*) **1** to smoke cocaine. **2** to intensify the effect of cocaine by heating it in combination with ether or other chemicals before inhaling. [abbr. FREEBASE v.]

baseball *adj.* [late 19C–1900s] (*US*) small, insignificant. [the small size of the baseball]

baseburner *n.* [late 19C] (*US*) the buttocks. [SE *base-burner*, 'a sheet-iron stove for burning anthracite coal, which is only fed at the top, while the fire is confined to the base, or lower part of the stove' (Bartlett, *Dict. Americanisms*, 1877)]

base crazies *n.* [1980s+] (*drugs*) the psychosis that can overtake regular consumers of crack cocaine, typically manifested in a feverish desire to find and consume every last granule of the drug. [BASE n. (4) + SE *crazy*]

based out *adj.* [2000s] (*drugs*) overcome by the effects of excessive smoking of crack cocaine. [BASE v.²]

base-freak *n.* [1990s+] (*drugs*) a smoker of crack cocaine. [BASE n. (4) + FREAK sfx]

base gallery *n.* [1980s+] (*drugs*) a place where users of crack cocaine gather to consume their drug (cf. BASING GALLERY n.). [BASE n. (4) + SE *gallery*]

base-head *n.* (*drugs*) **1** [1970s+] one who smokes cocaine. **2** [1980s+] a regular consumer of crack cocaine. [BASE n. (4) + -HEAD sfx (3)]

basehouse *n.* [1980s+] (*drugs*) a place where users gather to consume crack cocaine. [BASE n. (4) + SE *house*]

basengro *n.* [1900s–10s] (*UK tramp*) a shepherd. [Rom.]

base on *v.* [1980s+] (*US campus*) to criticize. [SE *debase*]

base out *v.* [20C+] (*W.I.*) to sit around, to hang about with friends or family, watching the passing world and occasionally commenting upon it. [SE *base*, i.e. the posterior]

baser *n.* [1980s+] (*US drugs*) one who uses crack cocaine. [BASE v.²/BASE n. (4)]

base rock *n.* *see* BASE n. (4).

base walloper *n.* [1940s+] (*Aus./N.Z. milit.*) a clerk. [influenced by WALLAH n.]

bash *n.*¹ **1** [late 19C–1930s] a judicial flogging; thus *9 months and a bash*, a sentence of 9 months' imprisonment and a flogging. **2** [1940s] a fight. **3** [1950s] (*Aus.*) brutality, harsh treatment.

bash n.[2] [1930s+] **1** (US Und.) any form of exploit, e.g. a robbery. **2** a puff on a cigarette. **3** sexual intercourse. **4** a party. **5** an attempt, a try, esp. as phr. *give it/have a bash (at)*. **6** a thrill of pleasure. [SE *bash*, a heavy blow]

bash n.[3] [1970s+] (*drugs*) marijuana. [? misprint for BUSH n.[5] (1)]

bash n.[4] *see* BASHER n.[2].

bash, the n. [1930s+] the world of street prostitution; thus ON THE BASH phr. (2). [BASH v.[2] (2)]

bash v.[1] **1** [late 16C+] (*also* **bash off**) to hit, to batter (with the fist). **2** [mid–late 19C] (*UK prison*) to flog as a judicial punishment. **3** [1910s] (*Aus.*) to dismiss from employment. **4** [1960s+] to have sexual intercourse (cf. BANG v.[1]). [Sw. *basa*, to baste, whip, flog, lash, or Da. *baske*, to beat, strike, cudgel; but poss. onomat.]

bash v.[2] **1** [1910s+] (*Aus.*) (*also* **bash it, give it a bash, have a bash**) to drink heavily; thus ON THE BASH phr. (1). **2** [1930s+] to work as a prostitute; thus BASH, THE n. **3** [1970s+] (*US*) to berate, to criticize, to abuse, esp. in sfx form -*bashing*, e.g. POMMIE-BASHING n. [fig. use of BASH v.[1] (1)]

bash v.[3] [1950s+] to make an attempt. [BASH n.[2] (5)]

bash artist n. [1980s+] a violent individual. [BASH v.[1] (1) + ARTIST sfx]

bash Christ out of v. [1970s] (*Aus.*) to beat severely. [BASH v.[1] (1)]

bashed adj. [1960s+] (*US campus*) drunk (cf. ANNIHILATED adj.). [BASH v.[2] (1)]

basher n.[1] **1** [mid-19C+] a professional fighter (and as such used as a professional nickname). **2** [mid-19C+] a thug. **3** [1940s] (*UK Und.*) the member of a smash-and-grab team who breaks the shop window. **4** [1980s+] (*Aus. prison*) a notably violent prison officer. [BASH v.[1] (1)]

basher n.[2] (*also* **bash**) [1980s+] a makeshift shelter. [milit. jargon *basha*, a shelter made of bamboo and attap (a type of palm frond used for thatching), which was common in Southeast Asia. More recently it has been found among the homeless denizens of London's CARDBOARD CITY n. or the protesters at the women's camp at Greenham Common, Berkshire]

-basher sfx [1940s+] (*orig. milit.*) a person, usu. in. comb. with a defining n., implying an occupation of job.

bashi-bazouk n. [mid-19C+] a ruffian, a hooligan, a thug. [Turk. *Bashi-Bazouk*, lit. 'one whose head is turned'; in 19C a mercenary soldier, fighting for the Turks and known for his bloodthirsty excesses; in WW1 sailors' nickname for a Royal Marine]

bashing n.[1] **1** [late 19C+] a beating; also in fig. use (cf. FAG-BASHING n.; GAY-BASHING n.; PADDY-BASHING n.; PAKI-BASHING n.; POOFTER-BASHING n.; QUEER-BASHING n.). **2** [1970s+] verbal aggression, from severe criticism to affectionate teasing. [BASH v.[1] (1)/BASH v.[2] (3)]

bashing n.[2] [1920s+] masturbation. [fig. use of BASH v.[1] (1)]

bashing n.[3] [1930s+] prostitution. [BASH v.[2] (2)]

bashing-in n. (*also* **bashing-out**) [late 19C] the flogging administered to prisoners on their arrival in prison or immediately before their release. [BASH v.[1] (2)]

bash into v. [1920s+] to meet by chance. [fig. use of BASH v.[1] (1)]

bash it v. *see* BASH v.[2] (1).

bash it up you phr. [1940s+] (*Aus.*) go away, leave me in peace. [BASH v.[1] (1)]

bashment n. [1990s+] (*W.I./US Black/US campus*) an amazing thing. [fig. use of BASH v.[1] (1)]

bash off v. *see* BASH v.[1] (1).

bash on v. [1940s+] (*orig. milit.*) to persist, to keep making an effort. [BASH v.[1] (1)]

bash out v. [1950s+] **1** to produce with only minimal care, esp. of writing. **2** to do, to perform. [BASH v.[1] (1)]

bash someone's ear v. *see* EARBASH v.

bash the beat v. (*also* **do the beat**) [1970s+] (*Aus. gay*) to frequent an area in search of a sexual partner. [BASH v.[1] (1)/SE *do* + BEAT n.[1] (1)]

bash the bishop v. *see* BANG THE BISHOP v.

bash the candle v. [1990s+] to masturbate (cf. BANG THE BISHOP v.). [BASH v.[1] (1) + SE *candle* as phallic image]

bash the living Moses out of v. (*also* **give Moses**) [mid-19C+] to beat severely; thus *catch Moses*, to receive a severe beating or punishment. [BASH v.[1] (1)]

bash the priest v. *see* BANG THE BISHOP v.

bash the spine v. [1940s+] (*Aus.*) to idle, to waste time, to loaf around. [BASH v.[1] (1) + SE *spine*]

bash the stick v. [1950s+] (*Aus.*) to masturbate (cf. BANG THE BISHOP v.). [BASH v.[1] (1) + STICK n.[1] (1)]

bash up v. **1** [1920s+] (*mainly UK juv.*) to beat up, to thrash. **2** [1940s] (*N.Z.*) to make, to create. **3** [1960s] to hurt. [ext. of BASH v.[1] (1)]

bashy adj. [1990s+] amazing, wonderful, a general term of admiration.

basic adj. [1970s+] unexciting, unexceptional, uneventful.

basie n. [1990s+] a *base*ball bat. [abbr. + sfx -*ie*]

basil n. [late 16C–19C] an iron fetter worn on one leg only. [? SE *basilisk*, a large cannon, generally made of brass, and throwing a shot weighing about 90kg (200lb)]

basinful n. **1** [1930s] a look (at). **2** [1930s+] an excessive amount, more than enough; usu. in phr. *I've had a basinful of*. [SE *basinful*, the contents of a basin; ? (1) f. (2)]

basing n. [1980s+] (*drugs*) using crack cocaine. [BASE v.[2]/BASE n. (4)]

basing gallery n. [1980s+] (*drugs*) a place where crack cocaine users gather to consume their drug (cf. BASE GALLERY n.). [BASING n. + SE *gallery*; on model of SHOOTING GALLERY n. (2)]

basin of gravy n. [1950s+] a baby. [rhy. sl.]

baskerville n. [1970s+] (*Aus.*) an informer. [pun on Arthur Conan Doyle's *The Hound of the Baskervilles* (1902)]

basket n.[1] **1** [late 19C+] the stomach. **2** [1940s+] (*gay*) (*also* **basketful of meat, basketwork**) the male genitals; the bulge caused by their display in tight trousers. **3** [2000s] the vagina (cf. BAG n.[1]).

basket n.[2] [1930s+] a euph. for BASTARD n. (1). [pron.]

basket! excl. [late 18C–early 19C] an excl. directed at those who are unable or unwilling to pay their gambling debts. [from the practice at 18C cockpits whereby such debtors were placed in a *basket*, suspended above the pit until the fights ended]

basket case n. **1** [1910s+] a disabled person, whether mentally or physically. **2** [1950s+] one who is incapable of tackling a situation. **3** [1960s] in fig. use, something extremely shocking, moving etc. **4** [1970s+] one who behaves in a notably eccentric manner. [orig. WW1 milit. use, a quadriplegic, who, bereft of all 4 limbs, is carried around in a basket]

basket days n. [1960s–70s] (*US gay*) a spell of fine weather, permitting one to wear light clothes that reveal one's genitals. [BASKET n.[1] (2) + SE *days*]

basketed adj. [late 18C–19C] abandoned, ignored, misunderstood, confused. [BASKET! excl.]

basketeer v. [1940s–70s] (*gay*) to wander the streets gazing at male genitals; this can provide some men with adequate satisfaction, others may simply be sizing up the available talent for later developments; also as n. [BASKET n.[1] (2); coined by the homosexual community, the term is now occas. applied to women]

basketful of meat n. *see* BASKET n.[1] (2).

basket lunch n. (*also* **lunch**) [1950s+] (*mainly gay*) fellatio (cf. BOX LUNCH n.; DOG'S DINNER n.; CHEW v.[1]; CHOW DOWN v.; EAT v.[3]; EAT IT v.[1]; EAT SAUSAGE v.; GNAW THE BONE v.; GNAW THE 'NANA v.; GOBBLE n.; GOBBLE v.[1]; GOBBLEDYGOO n.; GOBBLE THE GOO v.; HAVE A CHICKEN DINNER v.; KNOB-GOBBLING n.; KOWTOW CHOW n.; MUNCH v.[1]; MUNCHING THE TRUNCHEON n.; MUNCH THE TRUNCH v.; NIBBLE v.[2]; NOSH n.; NOSH v.; PICKLE-CHUGGING n.; SCARF v.; SCOFF v.; SPAM SUPPER n.; TURKEY GOBBLE n.; WOOF IT v.). [BASKET n.[1] (2) + SE *lunch*]

basket-maker *n.* [late 18C–19C] the vagina; thus a woman in a sexual context. [BASKET-MAKING n.]

basket-making *n.* [late 17C–early 19C] sexual intercourse. ['making feet for children's stockings' (Grose, 1785)]

basket man *n.* [1930s] (*US Und.*) a graft collector for a criminal gang.

basket of oranges *n.* [late 19C–1900s] (*orig. Aus.*) an attractive woman. [fig. use of mining jargon *basket of oranges*, nuggets of gold, as discovered in the gold fields]

basket party *n.* [1970s+] (*US gay*) a man with large genitals. [BASKET n.¹ (2) + SE *party*]

basket picnic *n.* [1940s–70s] (*gay*) staring at other men's genitals while wandering the streets. [BASKET n.¹ (2) + SE *picnic*]

basket-watch *v.* (*also* **basket-shop**) [1940s–70s] (*gay*) to wander the streets gazing at male genitals; thus *basket-watcher*. [BASKET n.¹ (2) + SE *watch*]

basket weaver *n.* [1960s–70s] (*US gay*) one who wears tight trousers for sexual display; thus *basket-weaving*, wearing tight trousers. [BASKET n.¹ (2) + SE *weaver*]

basketwork *n. see* BASKET n.¹ (2).

bass *n.*¹ [1960s–70s] (*Scot.gang*) a term of abuse. [abbr. BASTARD n. (1)]

bass *n.*² [1970s] (*US campus*) a large glass of liquor, a fifth of a gallon. [the use of sizes of fish to define sizes of glass]

bass *v.* [1990s+] (*US Black*) to argue loudly. [ety. unknown; ? the loudness of the *bass* in music]

bassa-bassa *n.* [20C+] (*W.I.*) trouble, a fuss, a noisy argument. [Yoruba *basa-basa*, nonsense]

bass-ackwards *adj.* (*also* **backasswards**) [mid-19C; 1930s+] back-to-front; thus fig. a mess, chaos (cf. BACK-ASSWARD adj.). [joc. reversal of ASS BACKWARD(s) phr. emphasizing the meaning]

bass and flinders *n.* [1960s+] (*Aus.*) windows. [rhy. sl.; Aus. pron. 'winders'; ult. Aus. explorers George *Bass* (1771–1803) + Matthew *Flinders* (1774–1814)]

bastard *n.* **1** [late 16C+] (*also* **barsterd**) a contemptible, objectionable person; thus LIKE A BASTARD adv. **2** [1910s+] (*orig. Aus.*) a general term for a man, a person or any form of creature or thing; not esp. derog., e.g. *lucky bastard*. **3** [1910s+] (*orig. Aus.*) a term of man-to-man affection. **4** [1920s+] an admirable person, creature or object. **5** [1930s+] (*orig. Aus.*) a situation, a circumstance, usu. a problematic one; also used of a person or situation or place. **6** [1930s+] an object.

bastard *adj.* **1** [1920s+] a general intensifier, carrying the same pej. imagery as BASTARD n. (1). **2** [2000s] as an infix.

bastard-faced *adj.* [1950s] a general term of abuse. [BASTARD n. (1) + SE *faced*]

bastarding *adj.* (*also* **bastering**) [1940s+] a general intensifer, a modified version of FUCKING adj. [BASTARD n. (1)]

bastardly *adj.* [1910s+] a negative intensifier. [BASTARD n. (1)]

bastardly gullion *n.* [late 18C–early 19C] a bastard's bastard. [SE *bastardly* + Lancashire dial. *gullion*, a mean worthless wretch]

bastard well *adv.* [1920s–50s] extremely, very much. [BASTARD adj. (1)]

baste *v.* **1** [late 19C] of a man, to have sexual intercourse (cf. BANG v.¹). **2** [1950s+] (*US Black*) to attack or ridicule someone behind their back. [SE *baste*, to beat, to thrash]

basted *adj.* [1920s+] drunk; one of a number of terms that equate drunkenness with suffering violence; many of the terms can also apply to the effects of drugs (cf. ANNIHILATED adj.). [fig. use of SE *baste*, to beat, to thrash]

baster *n.*¹ (*also* **baister**) [late 19C+] (*US*) something notably large of its type; often as *old baster*. [? BASTARD n. (1) or ? (less likely) the large roast that needs substantial *basting* in the oven]

baster *n.*² [1920s–40s] (*Aus./US*) a house thief.

bastering *adj. see* BASTARDING adj.

baste someone's coat *v.* (*also* **baste someone's jacket**) [16C–18C] to thrash, to beat severely. [ext. of SE *baste*, to beat]

basticles *n.* [1990s+] a general term of annoyance, abuse etc (cf. BALLOCKS n.²). [SE *bastard* + *testicles*]

bastille *n.* **1** [late 18C–early 19C] Coldbath Fields prison in London. **2** [19C] a workhouse. **3** [mid-19C] a tramps' lodging house. **4** [mid-19C+] (*US*) any prison. **5** [1960s] a police station. [Fr. *bastille*, a fortified tower, and esp. the main Paris prison, built in 14C, the destruction of which in 1789 triggered the French Revolution; note *Bastille by the Bay*, coined by San Francisco columnist Herb Caen for San Quentin prison]

basuco *n.* (*also* **bazuko**) [1980s+] (*drugs*) coca paste, part of the process that produces cocaine, mixed with a variety of impure and poss. toxic substances, e.g. leaded gasoline, kerosene, sulphuric acid and potassium permanganate; smoking *basuco* as a 'cigarette' (mixing basuco either with tobacco or marijuana) is common in cocaine-producing countries. [Colombian Sp., + ? links to Sp. *bazucar*, to shake violently or *basura*, waste, rubbish; a parallel ety. suggests the SE *bazooka*, with a ref. to the drug's 'explosive' effect]

B.A.T. *n.* [2000s] (*US Black*) unfashionable footwear. [*busted-ass toes*]

bat *n.*¹ [early 17C+] a prostitute or promiscuous woman. [like the creatures, they appear at night]

bat *n.*² **1** [early 19C+] a hard blow. **2** [late 19C–1930s] a thug, a 'hard man'. **3** [1920s] (*US*) a complaint or a comment. **4** [1960s] (*US prison*) a trial. [SE *bat*, to hit; note in (1) 14C–17C *bat*, a hard blow with a club or staff]

bat *n.*³ **1** [mid-19C] (*UK Und.*) a prison sentence. **2** [mid-19C+] (*orig. US*) a spree, a binge; thus ON A BAT phr.; ON THE BAT phr.¹. **3** [late 19C+] a pace, a speed, a stroke. **4** [1920s–30s] the price. **5** [1940s] (*US Black*) a job. [dial. *bat*, a stroke, a pace]

bat *n.*⁴ **1** [late 19C+] (*orig. US*) a foolish, worthless person. **2** [1930s+] an unattractive woman, often old. **3** [1930s+] a quarrelsome, unpleasant woman. **4** [1960s+] (*US gay*) a male homosexual. [SE *bat*, the animal]

bat *n.*⁵ [20C+] in pl., insanity, esp. manifested in a drinker's delirium tremens. [BATTY adj.¹, although it could be a result of a BAT n.³ (2)]

bat *n.*⁶ **1** [1930s+] (*Aus.*) a riding-whip. **2** [1930s] (*US prison*) a whip used for discipline. [SE *bat*, a stick, used as a weapon]

bat *n.*⁷ [1930s+] (*US/Aus.*) the penis; thus (*Aus.*) *go off the bat*, to masturbate; *bat and balls*, the penis and testicles; *batter*, a man with a large penis; one of number of terms equating the penis with a stick or rod (cf. BLOW STICK n.; BROOM-HANDLE n.; BROOMSTICK n.¹; CLOTHES-PROP n.¹; CLUB n.; COPPER-STICK n.; CREAMSTICK n.; DIPSTICK n.; DRUMSTICK n.; FESCUE n.; FIDDLESTICK n.¹; FIDDLING-STICK n.; FUCKPOLE n.; FUCKSTICK n.; GIGGLESTICK n.¹; GUNSTICK n.; GUTSTICK n.; HANDSTAFF n.; JAPSTICK n.; JOLLY STICK n.; JOYSTICK n.¹; LIGHTNING ROD n.; LIQUORICE STICK n.; LOVE STAFF n.; LOVE STICK n.; MOON STICK n.; MORNING WOOD n.; NIGHT STICK n.¹; NIMROD n.¹; PASSION STICK n.; PIKESTAFF n.; PILGRIM'S STAFF n.; POGO STICK n.; POKING-STICK n.; POLE n.; RAMROD n.; ROD n.¹; ROLLING-PIN n.; SHIT-STICK n.; SHOOTING STICK n.; (STAFF OF LIFE) n.; STAFF OF LOVE n.; STICK n.¹; STUMP n.¹; SUGAR-STICK n.; TOOTLING STICK n.; TRAPSTICK n.; VEINY BANG-STICK n.; VINEGAR STICK n.; WHITE-STAFF n.; WIGGLESTICK n.; WOOD n.⁴; WOODEN SPOON n.²; WOODIE n.²; WRIGGLING POLE n.). [SE *bat*, a stick, a stout piece of wood]

bat *n.*⁸ [1970s+] a marijuana or hashish cigarette (cf. AFRICAN WOODBINE n.; DOPE STICK n.; DREAM STICK n.; GANGSTER STICK n.; GIGGLESTICK n.²; HOP STICK n.; HOT STICK n.; JIVE STICK n.; JOYSTICK n.²; KICK STICK n.; PIMP STICK n.¹; STICK n.⁹; STICK OF GAGE n.; TEA-STICK n.). [pun on STICK n.⁹ (3)]

bat *n.*⁹ *see* GOLDBRICK n. (1).

bat *adj.* [1960s+] (*US campus*) good, attractive. [BAD adj. (1)]

bat *v.*¹ (*orig. US*) **1** [mid-19C+] to hit. **2** [late 19C–1900s] to overcome, to beat. **3** [late 19C+] to wander (aimlessly) around; usu. in BAT AROUND v. **4** [1900s] (*US campus*) to earn a grade.

5 [1900s] (*US*) to drink. **6** [1930s] (*US*) to substitute. **7** [1950s] to complain. [(1) is SE to mid-19C]

bat *v.*[2] [1910s–20s] (*US*) to act, to conduct oneself.

bat and ball *n.* [20C+] (*Aus.*) a wall. [rhy. sl.]

bat and ball *v.* [1980s+] (*Aus.*) to leave, to depart. [rhy. sl. = STALL *v.*[3] (3)]

bat and bowl *v.* [1950s+] to be bisexual. [cricket imagery, *batting* and *bowling* are the 2 antithetical positions in the game]

bat around *v.* [late 19C+] (*US*) to idle, to waste one's time; to wander (aimlessly). [ext. of BAT *v.*[1] (3)]

bat-ass *v.* [1980s+] (*US*) to move at top speed. [(*like a*) *bat* (*out of hell*) + -ASS sfx]

bat-bat *n.* [20C+] (*W.I. juv.*) the buttocks, the posterior. [SE *butt*(ocks)]

bat-boy *n.* [1970s+] (*US gay*) a hitchhiker who allows a homosexual driver to fellate him in exchange for a ride. [BAT *n.*[7] + SE *boy*]

batbrain *n.* (*also* **bathead**) [1940s+] (*US*) a fool or a crazy person; thus **batbrained**, stupid, crazy (cf. AIREDALE *n.*; BAKEBRAIN *n.*). [SE *bat*, a piece of wood + sfx. *-brain*]

bat carrier *n.* [1930s+] (*US prison*) a police informer. [ety. unknown; ? baseball]

batcave *n.*[1] [late 19C] (*US*) a police station and/or its cells.

batcave *n.*[2] [1970s+] **1** (*gay*) the anus. **2** the vagina (cf. AGREEABLE RUTS OF LIFE *n.*). [the *Batman* comics and films, in which the *batcave*, dark, subterranean and mysterious, is the headquarters where Batman (and Robin) keep their car, their hi-tech weapons and other crime-fighting material; also note BAT *n.*[7], although this is a primarily heterosexual term]

batcave *v.* [1980s+] (*US campus*) to sleep. [for ety. *see* BATCAVE *n.*[2] (i.e. Batman's HQ as a place of rest)]

batch *n.*[1] [late 18C–early 19C; 1950s] a quantity of liquor; thus a heavy night's drinking. [SE *batch*, a quantity, a number; in this case of bottles or glasses]

batch *n.*[2] *see* BACH *n.*[1].

batch *v.* (*also* **bach**) [late 19C+] (*Aus./US*) to live by oneself; the inference is obviously of a male, but occas. also a female. [SE *bachelor*]

batchelor *see also under* BACHELOR combs.

batcher *n.* [20C+] (*Aus.*) one who lives alone. [BATCH *v.*]

batch up *v.* [1960s] (*US*) of a man and woman, to cohabit. [i.e. the couple make themselves into a SE *batch*, a quantity]

batchy *adj.* [late 19C+] silly, stupid. [? BATTY *adj.*[1]]

batcrap *n. see* BATSHIT *n.*

bate *n. see* BAIT *n.*[2].

Bates *n. see* MR BATES *n.*

Bate's Farm *n.* (*also* **Bate's Garden, Charley Bates' Farm/Garden**) [mid–late 19C] Cold Bath Fields prison, in Farringdon, London, *fl.* 1794–1877, and known for its severity; thus *feed the chickens on Charley Bate's farm*, to be sentenced to the treadmill (cf. ABBOTT'S PRIORY *n.*). [the name of a well-known warder]

bate up *n.* [20C+] an act of sexual intercourse. [? 16C SE *bate*, an argument]

batey *n. see* BAIT *n.*[2] (1).

bat for *v.* [1920s+] to offer one's support. [baseball imagery]

bat for the other side *v.* (*also* **bat for the other team**) [1990s+] to be a homosexual. [cricket/baseball imagery]

bat-fowler *n.* [late 16C–early 17C] a swindler, a sharper. [SE *bat-fowl*, to catch birds at night by dazzling them with a light and knocking them down or netting them]

bat-fowling *n.* **1** [late 16C–early 17C] (*UK Und.*) swindling, hoaxing. **2** [17C] looking for sex. [BAT-FOWLER *n.*]

bath *n.* [late 19C] (*Aus.*) a glass of beer.

bath bun *n.* **1** [1950s+] a son. **2** [1970s+] the sun. [rhy. sl.]

bathead *n. see* BATBRAIN *n.*

bathers *n.* [20C+] (*orig. Aus.*) a bathing costume. [abbr. SE]

bat hide *n.* (*also* **batwing**) [late 19C–1920s] (*US*) paper money, esp. a \$1 bill (cf. BEAR-SKIN *n.*[2]; BUTTER SKIN *n.*; COONSKIN *n.*; DOESKIN *n.*; EEL SKIN *n.*[1]; FROG *n.*[3]; SKIN *n.*[8]; TOADSKIN *n.*). [? thinness of the paper money; var. on SKIN *n.*[8]]

bath of birth *n.* [19C] the vagina (cf. BABY CHUTE *n.*). [lit. euph. coined by US writer Walt Whitman (1819–92)]

bat house *n.*[1] [1900s–60s] (*US tramp*) a psychiatric institution. [BATS *adj.* + SE *house*]

bat house *n.*[2] [20C+] (*Aus.*) a brothel (cf. ACCOMMODATION HOUSE *n.*). [BAT *n.*[1] + HOUSE *n.*[1] (1)]

bat-house *adj.* [20C+] mad, crazy, insane. [BATS *adj.* + SE *house*]

bathsheba *n.* [1970s+] (*US gay*) one who frequents gay bathhouses. [SE *baths* + pun on the biblical queen *Bathsheba*/QUEEN *n.*[2] (1)]

bathtub hooch *n.* (*also* **bathtub slop**) [1930s+] (*US*) illicitly distilled alcohol, esp. in the Prohibition era. [SE *bathtub*, the place it was made + HOOCH *n.*[1] (1)]

bathtub scum *n.* [1980s+] (*US campus*) an unpleasant person. [play on SE]

bathtub speed *n.* [1960s+] (*drugs*) methcathinone, a form of amphetamine that produces a more intense and longer lasting 'high' than does cocaine (cf. A *n.*[2]). [artificial amphetamine, on pattern of BATHTUB HOOCH *n.*, i.e. home-produced liquor]

bati *n.* (*also* **batti, batty**) [1980s+] (*W.I./UK Black*) the buttocks. [abbr./pron. of SE]

batman *n.* **1** [1980s] (*Aus.*) a man with a large penis. **2** [1980s+] (*Aus. prison*) an onanist. [BAT *n.*[7] + sfx *-man*]

bat material *n.* [1980s+] (*Aus. prison*) pornography. [BAT *n.*[7] + SE *material*]

batmobile *v.* [1990s+] (*orig. US*) to put up one's defences. [the Batmobile, in the *Batman* movies, which has a mechanical shield]

batner *n.* (*also* **battener, battner**) [late 17C–early 19C] an ox. [16C SE *batten*, for an animal to put on weight]

bato *n.* [1970s+] **1** (*US Black*) any Mexican, Puerto Rican or other Latin person (cf. BIG HAT *n.*[2]; BORDER BROTHERS *n.*; CHICO *n.*[2]; CHOLITA *n.*; CHOLO *n.*; CHUC *n.*; CHULO *n.*; CREAM *n.*[2]; DAGO *n.*; FELIPE *n.*; GOLD-TOOTH *n.*; GREASEBALL *n.*; GREASE GUT *n.*; GREASER *n.*[1]; HICK *n.*[1]; ISLAND NIGGER *n.*; JOSÉ *n.*; LUBRICATOR *n.*; MARINE TIGER *n.*; NIGGERICAN *n.*; OILER *n.*[2]; PACHUCO *n.*; PANCHO *n.*; PARAKEET *n.*; PINEAPPLE *n.*[6]; RICAN *n.*; SMOKE *n.*[6]; SPIC *n.*; TIGER *n.*[10]; TOMATO-PICKER *n.*; WETBACK *n.*; YELLOW BELLY *n.*[2]). **2** (*US Hisp.*) a general term of address. [Sp. *bato*, a guy, a bloke, a dude]

bato loco *n.* (*also* **vato loco**) [1970s+] (*US Hisp.*) an affectionate nickname for a fellow Spanish-American, usu. a gang member with a reputation for extra violence, poise, courage and other attributes of street life. [BATO *n.*/VATO *n.* + Sp. *loco*, lit. 'crazy dude']

bat oneself out *v.* [1940s] (*US*) to work oneself to exhaustion. [BAT *v.*[2]]

bat one's mouth *v.* [1920s] (*US*) to talk. [BAT *v.*[1] (1) + SE *mouth*]

bats *n.* [mid-19C–1920s] a pair of bad boots. [? they are no more comfortable than walking on a pair of flat *bats*]

bats *adj.* [20C+] crazy, insane, eccentric (cf. APEY *adj.*; BAT-HOUSE *adj.*; BATSHIT *adj.*; BATSO *adj.*; BATTY *adj.*[1]). [HAVE BATS IN THE BELFRY *v.*]

bat's balls *n.* [1960s] (*US*) the very best, the ultimate. [var. on CAT'S WHISKERS *n.*]

batshit *n.* (*also* **batcrap**) (*US*) **1** [1940s+] lies, nonsense, rubbish. **2** [1960s–70s] an insane person. [play on BULLSHIT *n.* (2); (2) BATS *adj.* + APESHIT *adj.* (1)]

batshit *adj.* [1960s+] insane, crazy; often in phr. *go batshit*, to become insane, to act crazily (cf. BATS *adj.*). [BATSHIT *n.* (2)]

batshit *v.* [1960s–70s] (*US*) **1** to tell lies, to tease, to confuse with false information. **2** to gossip, to chatter inconsequentially. [BATSHIT *n.* (1)]

batso *adj.* [1970s+] (*US*) crazy, eccentric. [BATS *adj.* +-O sfx (3)]

bat someone's ear *v.* [1940s] (*US*) to pester, to nag. [BAT *v.*[1] (1) + SE *ear*]

batsucker *n.* [2000s] (*Aus.*) fellator or fellatrix. [BAT n.[7] + SE *sucker*]

batt *n.* [mid-19C] a shoe. [Polari]

batta-foot *n.* [1990s+] (*W.I.*) an unexceptional individual.

battalion *n.* [18C] (*UK Und.*) a criminal gang. [but note E.P. in *DU*: 'I doubt this definition and this classification']

batted out *adj.* [1930s+] (*US Und.*) arrested. [baseball imagery]

battener *n. see* BATNER n.

batter *n.*[1] **1** [early 19C] flattery. **2** [20C+] semen (cf. BABY GRAVY n.). [SE *batter*, a form of paste]

batter *n.*[2] [mid-19C] wear and tear, stress and strain; thus *can't stand the batter*, not up to the stress. [SE *batter*, to hit]

batter *n.*[3] [mid-19C+] a drinking spree. [ext. of BAT n.[3] (2)]

batter *n.*[4] [late 19C] (*US*) money (cf. BREAD n.[1]; BREADFRUIT n.; CAKE n.[2]; COOKIE n.[3]; CORNCAKE n.; CRACKER n.[10]; CRUMBS n.; DOUGH n.[1]; GINGERBREAD n.[1]; LONG BREAD n.; MOTSER n.). [pun on DOUGH n.[1] (1)/SE *batter*]

batter *v.* **1** [mid-18C+] of a man, to have sexual intercourse (cf. BANG v.[1]). **2** [late 19C+] (*US*) to beg; thus phr. *on the batter*, living as a beggar. **3** [1930s+] of a woman or homosexual man, to work as a (street) prostitute. [fig. use of BAT v.[1] (1); (2) refers to a beggar 'battering' on a door]

battered *adj.* [mid-19C+] drunk (cf. ANNIHILATED adj.). [BATTER n.[3]]

battered bully *n.* [late 17C–early 18C] 'an old well-cudgell'd and bruis'd huffing fellow' (B.E.). [SE *battered* + BULLY n.[1] (1)]

batter-fang *v.* (*also* **batty-fang**) [mid-17C–19C] to hit; thus n., a violent person; *batty-fanging, batty-fagging*, a beating. [SE *batter* + *fang*, to seize, to attack]

battering piece *n.* (*also* **battering ram**) [mid-18C–19C] the penis (cf. AX n.[2]). [SE *battering piece*, a heavy cannon specially designed for besieging and destroying fortifications]

battering ram *n.* [1920s–30s] a formidable (older) woman.

Battersea'd *adj.* [mid-18C] to have one's penis treated for venereal disease. [the curative herbs that grew in the market-gardens of Battersea]

batter the bishop *v. see* BANG THE BISHOP v.

batter through *v.* [late 19C+] to struggle on.

battery *n.* [1990s+] (*W.I.*) a man who uses a performance-enhancing drug during intercourse. [he 'charges his battery']

battery *v.* **1** [mid-late 19C] (*Ling. Fr./Polari*) to knock, to strike; thus *battery carsey*, to knock on a door. **2** [1990s+] (*W.I.*) for 2 or more men to have sex with the same woman. [Ital. *battere*, to hit]

battery acid *n.* **1** [1940s] (*US milit.*) coffee. **2** [1940s] (*US milit.*) synthetic lemon juice. **3** [1970s+] (*drugs*) LSD (cf. A n.[3]). [(1) and (2) play on SE; (3) on ACID n.[3]]

battery girl *n.* [1960s–70s] a prostitute who works as one of a group and who is paid in food and drugs and 'pocket-money' (cf. AWAYDAY GIRL n.). [SE *battery*, a collection of similar objects grouped together + SE *girl*]

bat the breeze *v.* [1930s+] (*orig. Aus./US milit.*) to chatter, to gossip (cf. BREEZE PUNCHER n.). [BAT v.[1] (1) + SE *breeze*]

bat them out *v.* [1920s] (*US*) to gossip, to chatter. [fig. use of BAT v.[1] (1)]

batti *n. see* BATI n.

battie-boy *n. see* BATTY BWOY n.

batting practice *n.* [1990s+] (*US campus*) frequenting a succession of bars with the intention of getting drunk. [joc. use of baseball jargon]

battle *n.* [1930s–40s] (*US Black/Harlem*) a very unattractive woman. [abbr. BATTLE AXE n.[1] (1)]

battle *v.* **1** [late 19C+] (*Aus.*) (*also* **battle it out**) to struggle for a livelihood, to work in a low-paid job; both imply some self-congratulation. **2** [late 19C+] (*Aus.*) of a tramp, to subsist between periods of employment. **3** [late 19C+] (*Aus.*) to subsist by making small bets at the racetrack. **4** [late 19C+] (*Aus.*) to work as a

prostitute; thus ON THE BATTLE phr. **5** [1990s+] (*W.I./UK Black teen*) to compete, usu. in freestyle rapping, sometimes in breakdancing. [SE *battle*, to struggle]

battle and cruiser *n. see* BATTLE-CRUISER n.[2].

battle axe *n.*[1] (*also* **battle-ax**) **1** [late 19C+] (*orig. US*) a formidable (older) woman. **2** [1930s] (*US campus*) a fat young woman. **3** [1930s] (*US Und.*) a female vagrant. **4** [1980s] (*US campus*) an ex-girlfriend; usu. as *old battle-ax*.

battle axe *n.*[2] [1930s] (*US Black*) a trumpet. [ext. of AX n.[3] (1)]

battle-cruiser *n.*[1] **1** [1910s+] a tough and aggressive (older) woman. **2** [1970s+] (1) as applied to a lesbian.

battle-cruiser *n.*[2] (*also* **battle and cruiser, battleship and cruiser**) [1930s+] a public house. [rhy. sl. = BOOZER n. (2)]

battle-hammed *adj.* [1930s–40s] (*US Black*) mis-shapen about the hips. [SE *hams*, thighs, which 'battle' against each other as one walks]

battle it out *v. see* BATTLE v. (1).

battle of the Nile *n.* [mid-19C–1900s] a hat. [rhy. sl. = TILE n.; ult. the *Battle of the Nile* (1 August 1798), where Nelson defeated Napoleon's fleet, thus wrecking the French expedition to Egypt]

battle of Waterloo *n.* **1** [1900s–50s] a stew. **2** [1940s] a queue. [rhy. sl.; ult. the *Battle of Waterloo* (18 June 1815), between Britain and France]

battle one's butt off *v. see* WORK ONE'S BUTT OFF v.

battler *n.* **1** [late 19C+] (*Aus.*) one who uses natural, rather than social or economic, advantages to pursue the struggle for existence and is seen as brave in doing so. **2** [late 19C+] a prostitute. **3** [1900s] a formidable or domineering woman. **4** [1920s] a thug, a violent gangster. **5** [1980s+] a small-time race-course bettor. [BATTLE v. (1)]

battle-royal *n.* [late 17C–1930s] a serious quarrel, an impassioned argument. [SE *battle-royal*, any battle in which a king leads his forces; also f. cockpit jargon, a cockfight in which a number of cocks fight until only 1 remains alive]

battleship *n.* (*US*) **1** [late 19C+] a formidable or domineering woman, a tough, large and aggressive (older) woman. **2** [1910s–40s] a large, heavy shoe. **3** [1910s+] the foot. **4** [1940s+] a shapely young woman; thus *built like a brick battleship*, having a very shapely figure. **5** [1980s] a large car.

battleship and cruiser *n. see* BATTLE-CRUISER n.[2].

battle the bones *v.* [mid-19C] to play at dice. [SE *battle*, to fight + BONES n.[1] (1)]

battle the purple-helmeted warrior *v.* [1980s+] to masturbate.

battle the rattler *v.* [1920s+] (*Aus.*) to travel on the railways without paying. [BATTLE v. (1) + RATTLER n.[1] (3)]

battle the subs *v.* [1920s+] (*Aus.*) to sell goods door-to-door in the suburbs. [BATTLE v. (1) + SE sub(urb)s]

battle wagon *n.* **1** [1910s+] (*US*) a warship. **2** [1920s–30s] (*US tramp*) a wagon carrying coal. **3** [1920s–40s] (*US Und.*) a police patrol wagon or car. **4** [1940s] (*US*) a homosexual man. **5** [1950s] a large car. [(3) note Liverpool, UK *battle taxi*, a police Land Rover]

battling-stick *n.* [mid-19C] (*US Black*) **1** a stick used to beat slaves. **2** a stick used for stirring clothes as they boiled in the laundry. [SE *batter*, to beat + *stick*]

battner *n. see* BATNER n.

batts *n. see* BOTS n. (3).

batty *n.*[1] [mid-late 19C] wages, tips. [Anglo-Ind. *batta*, an extra allowance given to troops or public servants while serving in the field or on a variety of special postings; also subsistence money given to prisoners, witnesses etc. The payment to soldiers, orig. restricted to field service, became recognized as a regular perk of Indian service, irrespective of the posting. The word comes from Hind. *bhata*, ult. f. *bhat*, an advance without interest made to a ploughman or *bat*, a pack-saddle (as used in the field)]

batty *n.*[2] *see* BATI n.

batty *adj.*[1] [20C+] insane, crazy, eccentric (cf. BATS adj.). [either

HAVE BATS IN THE BELFRY v. or f. the proper name Fitzherbert *Batty*, a 19C barrister whose certification as mad in 1839 caused much interest, although the time lag is significant]

batty *adj.*[2] [2000s] (*UK teen*) homosexual. [BATI n.]

batty bwoy *n.* (*also* **battie-boy, batty boy**) [1990s+] (*W.I./UK Black teen*) a homosexual; thus a term of abuse (cf. ANAL ASTRONAUT n.). [BATI n. + Carib. pron. of SE *boy*; var. on BATTYMAN n.]

batty-fang *v. see* BATTER-FANG v.

batty-hole *n.* [20C+] (*W.I.*) the anus (cf. A-HOLE n.). [BATI n. + SE *hole*]

battyman *n.* (*also* **bahtyman**) **1** [1950s+] (*W.I.*) a homosexual (cf. ANAL ASTRONAUT n.). **2** [1980s+] (*UK Black/teen*) a term of abuse for an unpopular individual. [BATI n. + SE *man*]

batty monkey *n.* [1990s+] (*W.I./UK Black*) a homosexual man (cf. ANAL ASTRONAUT n.). [BATI n. + SE *monkey*]

batty paper *n.* [20C+] (*W.I./UK Black*) lavatory paper. [BATI n. + SE *paper*]

batty rider *n.* [1990s+] (*W.I./UK Black teen*) a type of skimpy, cut-off shorts worn so tight that they 'ride' up and expose the sides of the wearer's bottom. [BATI n. + SE *rider*]

batty-wax *n.* [20C+] (*W.I.*) a stupid, gullible person. [BATI n. + SE *wax*, i.e. excrement]

batwank *n.* [1990s+] nonsense, rubbish; something that wastes one's time. [SE *bat* + WANK n.[1] (4)]

batwing *n.*[1] **1** [1930s] (*US*) (*also* **bat-wing chaps**) cowboy trousers. **2** [1940s] (*US*) a swinging door, e.g. in a saloon; thus usu. in pl. **3** [1940s] (*US*) a bow-tie. **4** [1970s] (*US*) a half-pint flask of liquor, esp. bootleg liquor. **5** [1990s+] (*orig. US*) an upper arm that is flabby or old and so hangs down, usu. in pl. [resemblance; plus (5) f. BATWING adj. (2)]

batwing *n.*[2] *see* BAT HIDE n.

batwing *adj.* **1** [1980s+] of a jumper, with sleeves that hang loose under the upper arm. **2** [1990s+] thus of a person's upper arms, flabby or old so that the skin hangs loose. [resemblance]

bat-wing chaps *n. see* BATWING n.[1] (1).

baubee *n.* (*also* **bawbee**) **1** [early 17C+] a halfpenny or penny. **2** [mid-19C–1900s] money in general. **3** [1900s] (*US*) a worthless trifle. [Scot. *bawbee*, a coin equivalent in value to an Eng. halfpenny; despite the useful similarity to SE *bauble*, a trinket and Fr. *bas billon*, mixed metal, the term appears to come f. the proper name of a 16C mint-master, the laird of *Sillebawby*]

bauble *n.* [late 16C–18C] the penis (cf. CHINGUS n.; DICKY-DOODLE n.; DIDDLYWHACKER n.; DILLER n.; DILLY n.[4]; DILLYWHACKER n.; DING n.[3]; DING-DONG n.[4]; DINGER n.[7]; DINGLE n.[1]; DINGUS n.; DINGWALLACE n.; DITTY n.[2]; DOJIGGER n.; DOODLE n.[2]; DOODLE-DO n.; DOOVER n.; FLIM-FLAM n.[2]; GIMMICK n.; GIZMO n.; HICKEY n.[2]; KNACK n.; KNICK-KNACK n.[1]; THING n.[2]; THINGUMMY n.; THINGY n.; TRIFLE n.; TRINKET n.; TYROOGER n.; WHANGDOODLE n.[2]; WHAT-NOT n.; WHAT'S ITS NAME n.; WHIM-WHAM n.; WHOOZIS n.; YOU KNOW WHAT n.). [SE *bauble*, a plaything/a showy trinket]

baubles *n.* (*also* **bawbels, bawbles, baws**) [mid-18C–19C] the testicles (cf. AGATES n.). [SE *bauble*, a plaything/a showy trinket]

baudrons *n.* (*also* **baudrans**) [mid-17C–early 19C] (*Scot.*) a pet name for a cat. [? Scot. Gaelic *beadrach*, a playful girl]

baudy knight *n. see* BAWDY BACHELOR n.

b.a.v. *n.* [1980s] (*US campus*) a person who has not had sexual intercourse for a long time. [abbr. BORN-AGAIN VIRGIN n.]

bawbee *n. see* BAUBEE n.

bawbels/bawbles *n. see* BAUBLES n.

bawcock *n.* [late 16C–early 17C] a fine fellow. [Fr. *beau coq*, lit. 'a fine cock', although Nares, citing Shakespearian use, prefers *boy cock*, i.e. a young cock; the term was briefly resuscitated by the 19C historical novelist Harrison Ainsworth in *Constable of the Tower* (1862)]

bawd physic *n.* (*also* **bawdy-physic**) [mid–late 16C] an insubordinate servant. [lit. 'a lewd, vulgar doctor']

bawdy bachelor *n.* (*also* **baudy knight**) [late 17C] a bachelor who has no intention of altering his status.

bawdy banquet *n.* [mid-16C] whoremongering. [sex as food]

bawdy basket *n.* [mid-16C–18C] (*UK Und.*) a female beggar who sells obscene literature, as well as pins, ballads and other goods (cf. CANTING CREW n.). [one of the 23 ranks of professional mendicant villains, as listed in a number of contemporary glossaries]

bawdy-house bottle *n.* [late 17C–early 18C] **1** a particularly small bottle. **2** the very last bottle of a drinking session. [such bottles were designed to be sold at *bawdy houses* (brothels), where they offered the owner yet another means of fleecing clients. Grose (1785) notes that of these frauds this 'is one of the least reprehensible; the less they give a man of their infernal beverages, the kinder they behave']

bawdy-house glass *n.* [early 19C] a small glass.

bawdy ken *n.* (*also* **bawdyken, bodikin**) [early–mid-19C] a brothel (cf. BADGER-CRIB n.). [SE *bawdy* + KEN n.[1] (1)]

bawdy physic *n. see* BAWD PHYSIC n.

bawker *n.* [late 16C] one who cheats at bowls. [SE *balker*, one who hinders deliberately]

bawl *v.*[1] [20C+] (*W.I./UK Black*) **1** to complain about one's problems, esp. financial. **2** to exclaim from shock, disbelief or surprise. **3** to confess. [SE *bawl*, to cry]

bawl *v.*[2] [1930s] to suck; to swallow. [ety. unknown]

bawl *v.*[3] *see* BAWL (OUT) v.

bawla *n. see* BALLER n. (1).

bawling out *n.* [20C+] a reprimand, a telling-off. [BAWL (OUT) v. (1)]

bawl off *v.* [1940s+] (*Irish*) to attack verbally, to scold severely. [var. on BAWL (OUT) v. (1)]

bawl-out *n.*[1] **1** [mid-19C] (*UK Und.*) anything that creates suspicions in a watcher/listener. **2** [1910s+] (*US*) a criticism, an accusation, a scolding. [BAWL (OUT) v. (1)]

bawl-out *n.*[2] [1990s+] (*W.I.*) something visually exciting. [it makes one SE *bawl out*]

bawl (out) *v.* (*also* **ball out**) [mid-19C+] (*orig. US*) **1** to scold, to reprimand, to criticize; all such attacks are delivered in a loud voice. **2** to announce oneself, to reveal something. [SE *bawl*, to shout at the top of one's voice, orig. to howl like a dog]

bawls! *excl. see* BALLS! excl. (1).

bawly-ike *n.* [1930s–50s] (*US*) a complainer, a whinger. [SE *bawl* + IKE n. (1)]

baws *n. see* BAUBLES n.

Bay, the *n.* **1** [early–mid-19C] (*Aus.*) Botany *Bay*. **2** [early 19C+] (*S.Afr.*) Port Elizabeth. **3** [mid-19C] (*Can.*) the Hudson's *Bay* Company or one of its stores. **4** [1920s] (*US Und.*) San Quentin prison, California (cf. ABBOTT's PRIORY n.). **5** [1940s+] (*Aus.*) the State Penitentiary, Long *Bay*, New South Wales. **6** [1950s] (*Aus.*) Sandy *Bay* prison. [abbr.; (2) overlooks Algoa Bay, (4) San Francisco Bay]

Bay City *n.* [1950s] (*US*) the city of San Francisco, California. [the San Francisco Bay on which the city stands; however, the fictitious (and massively corrupt) *Bay City* created by Raymond Chandler (1888–1959), is generally seen to be Oakland, California]

bay fever *n.* [early–mid-19C] the shamming of illness by convicts, in an attempt to avoid transportation to Botany Bay, New South Wales. [BAY, THE n. (1) + SE *fever*]

bay front *n. see* BAY WINDOW n. (1).

bay horse *n.* [1950s–60s] (*US tramp*) bay rum, a hair tonic; thus *bay horse jockey*, a drinker of bay rum.

bayonet *n.* **1** [19C] the penis (cf. AX n.[2]). **2** [1950s] (*US drugs*) a hypodermic syringe or needle.

bayoo *n.* [mid–late 19C] (*US Black*) an unpopular, unappealing person, 'a man of whom Quashie thinks very little, "a low down mean cuss"' (Farmer, *Americanisms Old New*, 1889). [? BOYO n.[1] (2)]

Bays, the n. see BAZE, THE n.

Bay State n. [1930s+] (US drugs) a hypodermic syringe. [proprietary name]

Bay Street boys n. [20C+] (W.I., Baha.) the White mercantile élite who control the Bahamas. [the business centre of Bay Street, Nassau]

Bayswater captain n. [1900s] a layabout, a sponger. [so many of them chose Bayswater, London, as a residence, as it was cheap but within reasonable distance of the West End and Mayfair]

bay window n. **1** [mid–late 19C] (also **bay front**) the stomach of a pregnant woman. **2** [mid-19C+] a man's fat stomach; thus the fat man himself.

baz n. [2000s] (Irish) pubic hair. [ety. unknown]

bazaar n.[1] [mid-19C] a shop, a shop counter. [Pers. bazar, a market; thence to Hind.]

bazaar n.[2] [late 19C] the vagina, considered as an economic adjunct.

bazaar n.[3] [late 19C–1910s] a bar in a public house. [rhy. sl.]

bazaared adj. [late 19C–1900s] (UK society) cheated, robbed, over-charged. ['the extortion practised by remorseless, smiling English ladies at bazaars' (Ware)]

Baze, the n. (also **the Baize, the Bays**) [1940s–60s] Bayswater Road, London W2. [abbr./pron.; before the Street Offences Act 1959, Bayswater Road was one of London's centres of street prostitution, seen as slightly less classy than its rivals Piccadilly and, even smarter, Mayfair]

bazel n. [early 19C] (UK Und.) stolen cloth. [SE embezzle]

bazongas n. (also **bazonkas, bazoongas, bazungas**) [1970s+] the female breasts (cf. BAZOOKAS n.; BAZOOM n.; BAZOOMBAS n.; BUZZY n.; CAJOOBLIES n.; CHALUBBIES n.; GARBONZAS n.; GAZONGAS n.; JABONGOES n.; KAHOONAS n.; ZOOMER n.; ZOOMS n.). [SE bosom]

bazonkas adj. [1970s+] (US) crazy. [SE berserk + BONKERS adj. (2)/BANANAS adj. (1)]

bazoo n.[1] (US) **1** [late 19C+] mouth. **2** [1910s] an orator. [Du. bazu(in), a trumpet]

bazoo n.[2] (also **bazzonus**) [1900s–20s] (US) a lout; a fool. [? BAZOO n.[1](1), i.e. the unchecked noisiness]

bazooka n.[1] **1** [1910s] a metaphorical, fictional part of the body. **2** [1950s] the buttocks. **3** [1950s] the head, the mind, with implications of stupidity. **4** [1950s+] the penis (cf. AX n.[2]). **5** [1980s+] (US Black) an especially large and potent marijuana cigarette, laced with cocaine (cf. A-BOMB n.). **6** [1990s+] (drugs) cocaine, crack cocaine (cf. BASE n.). **7** [2000s] (US drugs) a cigarette that mixes coca paste and tobacco. [all f. the anti-tank rocket launcher, first used in WW2; like BAZOO n.[1] the term may stem f. the Du. bazu(in), a trumpet, in this case f. the shape; (7) note BASUCO n.]

bazooka n.[2] [1940s–50s] a fool. [? SE bazooka, on principle that it 'sounds funny'; or ? BAZOO n.[2]]

bazooka adj. see BAZOOKAS adj.

bazooka v. [1990s+] (US drugs) to smoke a piece of crack cocaine. [BAZOOKA n.[1] (6)]

bazookas n. (also **baloobas**) [1960s+] the female breasts; thus bit of bazooka, petting, i.e. touching the breasts (and perhaps other parts of the body), but stopping short of penetration (cf. BAZONGAS n.). [play on SE bosom]

bazookas adj. (also **bazooka**) [1970s+] (US) crazy. [SE berserk]

bazoom n. (also **bozoom**) [1920s+] the female breast; usu. pl. (cf. BAZONGAS n.). [joc. pron. of SE bosom]

bazoombas n. (also **bazoomas**) [1980s+] (US) the female breasts (cf. BAZONGAS n.).

bazoongas n. see BAZONGAS n.

bazooz n. [1960s] (US) the nose. [BAZOO n.[1]/Du. bazu(in), a trumpet]

bazuca n. [1980s+] (US Black) a large and potent marijuana cigarette, laced with cocaine (cf. A-BOMB n.). [mis-sp. of BAZOOKA n.[1] (5)]

bazuco n. (also **bazuca**) [1980s+] (drugs) the oily substance in freebase cocaine. [Sp. bazuco, base]

bazuko n. see BASUCO n.

bazungas n. see BAZONGAS n.

bazz n. [1980s] (Aus.) an average, unintelligent male. [Barry 'Bazza' McKenzie, created by Barry Humphries]

bazzard n. see BUZZARD n.[1] (7).

bazzer n. [2000s] (Irish) a haircut. [? BAZ n.]

bazzonus n. see BAZOO n.[2].

B.B. n. see BITCH'S BASTARD n.

b.b. n.[1] [20C+] a male homosexual (cf. ANAL ASTRONAUT n.). [abbr. BUM BOY n. (1)]

b.b. n.[2] [1910s–70s] (US) a bedbug. [abbr.]

b-ball n. [1960s] (US Black) basketball. [abbr.]

b-ball v. [1990s+] (US Black) to play basketball. [B-BALL n.]

B.B.B. crop n. [1940s] (UK prison) a very short haircut. [Bad Borstal Boy + SE crop]

b.b.-brained adj. [1960s] (US) stupid (cf. AMOEBA-BRAINED adj.). [the minuscule size of a b.b. shot, 'an air gun pellet having a diameter of approximately 0.45 or 0.56 cm (0.177 or 0.22 inches), used esp. by young people' (OED)]

b.b. head n. [1980s] (US Black) **1** a young man with a tight-curled, 'knotty' head. **2** an unattractive woman, esp. one with short, fuzzy, nappy hair. [the supposed resemblance to a b.b. shot (see prev.), 'an air gun pellet having a diameter of approximately 0.45 or 0.56 cm (0.177 or 0.22 inches), used esp. by young people' (OED)]

b.b.l. n. [1920s] (US) a great deal. [? bloody big lot]

b-bomb n. **1** [1960s+] (US drugs) amphetamine (cf. A n.[2]). **2** [2000s] MDMA (cf. ECSTASY n.). [the explosive effects; (1) abbr. Benzedrine + ? var. on A-BOMB n.]

B-boy n. [1970s+] (orig. US Black) a Black male teenager, focused on RAP n.[5] music and the ghetto street lifestyle. [coined in 1975 to describe those who followed DJ Kool Herc of the Hevalo Club in New York; generally accepted as abbr. beat-boy]

b-boy n. [1980s+] (US gay) a passive male homosexual, poss. a male prostitute (cf. ANAL ASTRONAUT n.).

B-broad n. see B-GIRL n. (2).

BB's n. [1940s] (US Black/campus) a clever person, a teacher. [abbr. SE big brains]

BB stacker n. [1960s] **1** (US) a fool. **2** (US teen) a woman with large breasts. [US army jargon BB stacker, one who loads machine-gun belts]

b-bwoy n. [1990s+] (W.I.) a male homosexual (cf. ANAL ASTRONAUT n.). [abbr. BATTY BWOY n.]

b.c. n. [1960s+] (US Black) contraception, usu. contraceptive pills. [abbr. birth control]

b.c. adj. [late 19C–1900s] extremely old. [chronological notation BC, before Christ]

b.d. n. see BULL-DYKE n.

b-drink n. [1930s–60s] (US) a drink that resembles whisky (and charged as such) but is in fact cold tea; served to the female companion of a man, or homosexual customer, who has entered a club in the hope of sex; thus b-drinker/bee-drinker, the woman, or man, who consumes such drinks. [B-GIRL n. (1), i.e. the sort of drink she consumes]

b.d.t. n. (also **b.d.t.'s**) [20C+] (US) **1** diarrhoea. **2** over-frequent urination. [abbr. BACK-DOOR TROT n.]

b.d.v. n. [1930s] (UK tramp) a cigarette stub, picked up in the street. [abbr. bend down Virginia]

b-e v. [1970s] to commit the crime of breaking and entry. [B AND E n.]

beach bitch n. [1970s+] (US gay) one who frequents holiday resorts and beaches looking for sex. [SE beach + BITCH n.[1] (17)]

beach bum n. (also **beach rat**) [1950s+] (Aus./US) a person, usu. a teenager, who hangs around the beach all day and surfs. [SE beach + BUM n.[3] (1)/RAT sfx]

beach bunny *n.* [1960s+] a young woman who frequents the world of surfing, but does not herself surf. [SE *beach* + BUNNY n.¹ (2)]

beach-cadger *n.* [mid-19C–1910s] a beggar who favours seaside resorts, and poses as a sailor. [SE *beach* + CADGER n. (1)]

beachcomber *n.*¹ **1** [late 19C] an idler. **2** [1910s–50s] (*Can.*) a White man living with an Inuit woman. **3** [1920s–30s] (*US tramp*) a tramp who frequents docks and waterfront areas. **4** [1950s] (*Aus.*) one who walks the streets in the hope of picking up a woman; thus *beach-combing*, *combing*. [SE *beachcomber*, a settler in the Pacific islands, living by pearl-fishing and other means]

beachcomber *n.*² [1990s+] a male homosexual. [pun on *log*/LOG n.⁴; the beachcomber pushes logs; the homosexual is a LOG-PUSHER n.]

beached *adj.*¹ [late 19C+] (*orig. RN*) unemployed, impoverished. [ext. of SE; one is living as an impoverished beachcomber]

beached *adj.*² [1990s+] (*US teen*) **1** absolutely exhausted. **2** stranded, abandoned. [the imagery of a beached whale]

beach rat *n. see* BEACH BUM n.

beacon *n.* [late 19C] a red nose.

bead *n.* [19C] a glass of spirits. [SE *bead*, a bubble found in spirits or wine]

bead-counter *n.* [early 19C] a clergyman; an overtly religious person; a recluse. [the rosary beads of Roman Catholics]

beadie *v. see* BEADY v.

bead-jiggler *n.* (*also* **bead-mumbler**) [1960s] (*US*) a Roman Catholic, esp. a priest. [the use of a rosary]

beadle *n.*¹ [early 19C] (*UK Und.*) anyone who wears a long, blue overcoat (the uniform of a parish *beadle*).

beadle *n.*² [late 19C–1900s] (*US*) an inhabitant of the state of Virginia. [? their serious, beadle-like demeanour]

bead-mumbler *n. see* BEAD-JIGGLER n.

bead-puller *n.* [20C+] (*US*) a Roman Catholic. [SE *rosary beads*]

beads *n.*¹ **1** [1930s] (*US Und.*) morphine tablets. **2** [1940s] (*UK Und.*) diamonds. **3** [1970s] (*US*) the eyes. [shape]

beads *n.*² [1960s+] (*US gay*) one's inner awareness of being homosexual, a metaphorical string of beads worn by all male homosexuals. Always in phrs. such as DROP ONE'S BEADS v.; IN THE BEADS phr.; MY BEADS! excl.; RATTLE ONE'S BEADS v.; READ SOMEONE'S BEADS v.; WRECK SOMONE'S BEADS v.

bead-twirler *n.* [1990s+] a derog. term for a Roman Cathloic. [the use of rosary beads]

beady *n.* [1970s+] (*US*) an eye. [SE phr. *beady* (*little*) *eye*]

beady *v.* (*also* **beadie**) [1990s+] to see, to look at. [BEADY n.]

beagle *n.*¹ [early 17C] a prostitute.

beagle *n.*² [mid-19C] (*US*) a native of Virginia. [the popularity of fox-hunting in the state]

beagle *n.*³ [1920s–30s] **1** (*US*) a nose. **2** (*US Und.*) a policeman; a detective (cf. ANIMAL n.¹; BULL n.¹⁰; CINDER BULL n.; DOG n.³; EAGLE EYE n.; ELEPHANT EARS n.; FERRET n.³; MOUSER n.³; SCISSORBILL n.; SHARK n.¹; STAG n.¹; WEASEL n.¹; YARD BULL n.). [the dog's sniffing abilities]

beagle *n.*⁴ [1920s+] (*US Und.*) a sausage, esp. a 'hot dog'. [pun]

beagle *n.*⁵ [1940s–50s] (*US*) a (usu. unattractive) young woman. [DOG n.³ (2)]

beagle *v.*¹ [1960s–70s] to pick pockets. [the dog's 'sniffing-out' qualities]

beagle *v.*² [1990s+] to leave. [? SE *beetle off*]

be a grape on *v. see* HAVE A GRAPE ON v.

beak *n.*¹ **1** [mid-18C+] a judge, a magistrate. **2** [19C] a sheriff's officer, a policeman. **3** [1910s+] a schoolmaster. [Hotten (1859) + Ware suggest OE *beag*, a necklace worn as a badge of office, but (1) more likely f. HARMAN n.]

beak *n.*² **1** [mid-19C+] the nose; thus *beaky*, possessing a large nose. **2** [mid-19C+] (*also* **bake**) the mouth or face. **3** [late 19C–1900s] the penis. **4** [2000s] (*drugs*) (*also* **beek**) cocaine. [SE *beak* of a bird; (4) f. (1)]

beak *v.*¹ [late 16C–early 17C] to beg. [like a bird, the beggar 'pecks around']

beak *v.*² [late 19C] to bring an offender before a magistrate. [BEAK n.¹ (1)]

beaker *n.*¹ [early 18C–mid-19C] (*UK Und.*) a silver tankard.

beaker *n.*² [mid-19C] (*UK Und.*) a fowl, a chicken. [SE *beak*]

beaker-hauler *n.* [19C] a poultry thief who hawks booty from door to door. [BEAKER n.² + SE *haul*]

beak-gander *n.* [late 19C] a senior judge. [BEAK n.¹ (1) + SE *gander*, a foolish (old) man]

beak-hunter *n.* (*also* **beaker-hunter**) [mid-19C–1900s] a poultry-thief; thus *beak-hunting*, poultry-stealing. [SE *beak*/BEAKER n.² + *hunter*]

beak-o! *excl.* [1980s+] (*Aus. prison*) an excl. used to upbraid one who is staring. [BEAK n.² (1), i.e. they are 'nosey']

beak off *v.* [20C+] (*Ulster*) to truant. [synon. Scot. *bake*]

beak-runner *n.* [late 18C] (*UK Und.*) an officer of the law, lit. 'a runner for the magistrate'. [BEAK n.¹ (1) + SE *runner*]

beaksman *n.* [early–mid-19C] a policeman; a police-office clerk. [BEAK n.¹ (1) + SE *man*]

beaky *adj.* [2000s] nosy, inquisitive. [BEAK n.² (1)]

beaky lady/man *n.* [20C+] (*Ulster*) a truancy officer. [BEAK OFF v.]

beals *n.* [1990s+] a fool, an idiot, an unsophisticated person. [ety. unknown; ? slightly pathetic fictional character *Ian Beale* in BBC TV soap opera *EastEnders*]

beam *n.*¹ [early 19C+] the buttocks, the hips (cf. BEAM-ENDS n.).

beam *n.*² [1940s] (*US Black*) the sun. [abbr. SE *sunbeam*; Burley actually writes 'bean' (see BEAN n.⁷) but Major, *Juba to Jive: A Dict. of Afro-American Slang* (1994), suggests it is a misprint for this]

beam *v.*¹ [1940s+] (*US Black*) **1** (*also* **beam on**) to look at, to stare. **2** in fig. use, to ascertain what is happening. [obs. SE *beam*, to shed light upon]

beam *v.*² [1990s+] (*US juv.*) of a girl's nipples, to be erect. [? play on HEADLIGHTS n. (3)]

beamed *adv.* [1970s] (*US*) staring at, focused on. [BEAM v.¹ (1)]

beam-ends *n.* [early 19C+] the buttocks; often as *on one's beam-ends*, fallen over (cf. BEAM n.¹). [naut. *beam ends*, the ends of a ship's lateral beams, if these touch the water, the ship is on the verge of capsizing]

Beamer *n.* (*also* **Bee Em, bimaz, bimmer**) [1980s+] (*orig. US*) a BMW motorcar. [pron. of initials; more elliptical refs. are found on a variety of RAP n.⁵ songs to specific BMW models, e.g. 325i, 735i, 740i, 750iL, 850i]

beamer *n.*¹ **1** [late 19C+] a smile. **2** [1950s+] a blush. [SE *beam*, to smile broadly]

beamer *n.*² [1980s+] (*drugs*) a user of crack cocaine. [? the triple-beam scales used in weighing drugs and/or *Star Trek* line, BEAM ME UP, SCOTTY! excl. (2)]

beaming *n.* [1980s+] (*US Black*) using drugs, esp. crack cocaine. [BEAMER n.²]

beam me up, Scotty *n.* [1980s+] (*drugs*) a mixture of phencyclidine and cocaine, thus phrs. *talk to Scotty*, *high off Scotty*, *see Scotty*, to be under the influence of the drug. [BEAM ME UP, SCOTTY! excl. (2)]

beam me up, Scotty! *excl.* **1** [1970s] (*US campus*) an expression of the desire to be elsewhere. **2** [1980s+] (*drugs*) usu. of crack cocaine, give me some drugs! [the TV series *Star Trek* (from 1966), in which Captain Kirk's injunction to the chief engineer, *Scotty*, became a trademark catchphrase; (2) i.e. get me HIGH adj.¹ (2)]

beam on *v. see* BEAM v.¹ (1).

beam out *v.* [1980s+] (*US campus*) to daydream. [BEAM v.¹ (1) + *out*, i.e to stare into the middle distance]

beam-up *n.* [1980s+] (*US Black/drugs*) the effects of smoking crack. [BEAM UP v.]

beam up *v.* [1970s+] (*US Black/teen*) to become intoxicated through drug-taking. [BEAM ME UP, SCOTTY! excl. (1)]

beamy *adj.*[1] [20C+] (*US*) of a person, broad, wide, overweight; thus *broad in the beam*. [naut. jargon *beam*, the width of a ship]

beamy *adj.*[2] 1 [1950s] (*US Black*) wonderful, a play on CRAZY adj. (2). 2 [1960s] (*US*) eccentric, crazy. [OFF (THE) BEAM phr.; (1) is bad = good model]

bean *n.*[1] 1 [mid-17C; late 19C+] money, irrespective of the coin; *not a bean*, absolutely nothing (cf. BEANS n.[1]). 2 [19C] a sovereign, a guinea; thus HALF-A-BEAN n. 3 [20C+] (*US*) (*also* green bean) a dollar; thus HALF-A-BEAN n. 4 [1900s] (*US*) a dollar bill, of any denomination. 5 [1960s] (*US*) $100. 6 [1960s+] a poker chip.

bean *n.*[2] 1 [mid-19C+] a general term of affectionate address. 2 [1910s+] (*US*) a foolish or unpleasant person. [abbr. *beanstalk* or *beanpole* or f. BEAN-TOSSER n.]

bean *n.*[3] [late 19C] (*US*) a foolish, silly notion. [? corruption of 'bee in one's bonnet']

bean *n.*[4] 1 [late 19C+] the penis (cf. BANANA n.[2]). 2 [1940s–50s] (*US*) the hymen; thus *cop a bean*, to deflower, to have sexual intercourse. 3 [1990s+] the clitoris (cf. BABY IN THE BOAT n.).

bean *n.*[5] (*also* beano) [20C+] the head.

bean *n.*[6] (*US Black/drugs*) 1 [1920s] a package of a drug. 2 [1960s+] usu. in pl., any form of tablet, esp. Benzedrine; thus *beaned up*, under the influence of Benzedrine (cf. PILL n.[4]). [resemblance]

bean *n.*[7] [1940s–70s] (*US Black*) the sun. [note comment at BEAM n.[2]]

bean *n.*[8] [1940s+] (*US*) a Mexican, any Spanish-American (cf. BEANBAG n.; BEAN BANDIT n.; BEAN DIP n.; BEAN-EATER n.; BEANER n.[3]; BEANO n.[2]; BURRITO n.; CHILE n.; CHILE-BELLY n.; CHILE-CHOKER n.; CHILE-EATER n.; CHILE-HEAD n.; CHOKE n.[2]; FRIJOLE-EATER n.; FRITO n.; PEPPER BELLY n.; PEPPER GUT n.; PINTO BEAN n.; RICE-AND-BEAN n.; TACO n.; TACO-EATER n.; TACO-HEAD n.; TOSTADO n.). [stereotyping of the Mexican diet]

bean *v.* [1910s+] (*orig. US*) to hit on the head. [BEAN n.[5]]

beanbag *n.* [1970s] (*US*) a Mexican. [ext. of BEAN n.[8]]

bean bandit *n.* [1950s–60s] (*US*) a Mexican. [BEAN n.[8] + SE *bandit*]

beanbelly *n.*[1] (*also* bean-belly) [mid-17C–19C] a native of Leicestershire, UK. [that county's production of beans]

beanbelly *n.*[2] (*also* bean-belly) [1960s+] (*US*) a pot belly. [the general 'inflationary' effect of eating lentils etc]

beanbrain *n.* [1950s+] (*US*) a fool (cf. APPLEHEAD n.; BAKEBRAIN n.). [the implication is of minimal size]

bean-choker *n.* [1980s+] (*US*) a Spanish-American. [SE *bean*, the stereotypical Hispanic food + *choker*]

bean-count *v.* [1990s+] (*US campus*) to stare at breasts. [? erect nipples]

bean counter *n.* [1970s+] (*US*) anyone who deals with financial matters, esp. an accountant or statistician.

bean-date *n. see* JELLY-DATE n.

bean dip *n.* [1990s+] (*US*) a derog. term for a Mexican. [play on BEAN n.[8]/SE *bean*]

bean-eater *n.* (*US*) 1 [late 19C+] an inhabitant of Boston, Massachusetts; thus *bean-eating*, Bostonian in manner (cf. BEAN-SHOOTER n.[2]; BEAN TOWN n.). 2 [1910s+] a derog. term for a Mexican (cf. BEAN n.[8]). [the supposed preference of Bostonians and Mexicans for beans]

beaner *n.*[1] [late 19C–1900s] a scolding, a telling-off. [GIVE SOMEONE BEANS v. (1)]

beaner *n.*[2] [1910s–70s] (*US*) something excellent. [? Fr. *bien*]

beaner *n.*[3] [1960s+] (*US*) 1 a Mexican; thus *beaner shoes*, huaraches (leather-thonged sandals, orig. worn by Mexican Indians); *beaner wagon*, an old, dilapidated car typically driven by Mexican immigrants (cf. BEAN n.[8]). 2 a Cuban or other Latin-American. [stereotyping; beans are seen as a staple of the Hispanic immigrant diet]

beaner *adj.* [1960s+] (*US*) Mexican, pertaining to Mexican culture. [BEANER n.[3] (1)]

beanery *n.* 1 [late 19C+] (*US*) a cheap restaurant, orig. one that specialized in beans. 2 [1900s–20s] (*US*) a boarding house.

bean 3 [1940s–60s] (*US prison*) a prison; a prison dining room. [SE *beans*, seen as part of the staple menu]

beanery *adj.* [1950s] (*US*) small, insignificant. [? the size of SE *beans* or the cheapness of a BEANERY n. (1)]

beanfeast *n.* (*also* bean feed) [mid-19C+] any form of festivity or celebration; thus *bean-feaster*. [SE *beanfeast*, an annual dinner given by employers to their workers; in its original form beans were a featured dish]

bean flicker *n.* [1990s+] a lesbian (cf. BUMPER n.[5]; CRACK SNAKER n.; DONUT-BUMPER n.; FINGER ARTIST n.; FUZZ BUMPER n.; LADY-LOVER n.; PUSSY BUMPER n.; PUSSY QUEER n.). [BEAN n.[4] (3) + SE *flicker*]

bean foundry *n.* [1900s] (*US*) a cheap restaurant.

bean-head *n.* 1 [1910s+] (*US*) a fool (cf. APPLEHEAD n.). 2 [1950s] someone with a crew-cut hairstyle. [BEAN n.[2] (2)/SE *bean*+ -HEAD sfx (1)/SE *head*]

bean house *n.* [1970s+] (*US*) a cheap restaurant; thus in phr. *bean house bull*, extravagant stories, 'tall tales'.

beanie *n.*[1] 1 [1900s; 1940s+] (*orig. US*) a small, tight-fitting cap, similar to a large skull-cap; thus *propeller-beanie*, such a cap with a small propeller affixed to its top. 2 [1950s] a blackjack, a cosh. 3 [1970s] (*US*) a slingshot. [BEAN n.[5] + dimin. sfx *-ie*]

beanie *n.*[2] [1960s] (*US*) a pot belly. [it is filled with/created by beans]

beanie *n.*[3] [1990s+] (*UK teen*) an attractive young woman. [? she is 'keen as a bean']

bean-jacks *n.* [1930s+] (*Irish*) a female public convenience. [Irish *bean*, a woman +JAKES n.]

bean juice *n.* [1970s+] (*US gay*) oily sweat exuded from the anus or liquid found around the anus of one who constantly breaks wind. [the stereotypical result of eating beans]

bean man *n.* [1960s] (*drugs*) a seller of any type of drugs in pill form. [BEAN n.[6] (2) + SE *man*/MAN, THE n. (3)]

beanmobile *n.* [1980s+] (*US*) a 'lowrider' automobile, as customized and driven by Mexican/Puerto Rican teenagers and gang members. [BEAN n.[8] + -MOBILE sfx]

bean money *n.* [1960s] (*US*) subsistence. [just enough to buy a meal of beans]

beano *n.*[1] 1 [late 19C–1910s] a commotion, a fight. 2 [late 19C+] a party, a celebration. [BEANFEAST n.; this abbr. orig. used by printers, who usu. called it a *goose* or *wayzgoose*]

beano *n.*[2] [1970s+] a derog. term for a Mexican (cf. BEAN n.[8]). [BEAN n.[8] + -O sfx (1)]

beano *n.*[3] *see* BEAN n.[5].

bean oil *n.* [1970s+] (*US gay*) hair oil, esp. when used to lubricate the penis before sex. [BEAN n.[4] (1) + SE (*hair*) *oil*]

beanpea *n.* [late 19C–1900s] an effeminate young man (cf. B & P n.). [a case involving 2 such youths, known only, so taboo was the thought of homosexuality, by their initials *B and P*, i.e. Boulton and Park]

beanpole *n.* [mid-19C+] a tall, thin person (cf. BEANSTALK n.[1]).

bean queen *n.* [1970s+] (*US gay*) 1 a non-Hispanic person who prefers Hispanic partners for sex. 2 a Hispanic DRAG QUEEN n. (1). [BEAN n.[8] + QUEEN n.[2] (1)/QUEEN sfx (2)]

beanraker *n.* [1900s] (*Aus.*) one who is good at amassing money. [BEAN n.[1] (1) + RAKE (IT) IN v.]

beans *n.*[1] [mid-19C+] money (cf. BANANAS n.[3]). [Fr. *biens*, property; but note BEAN n.[1] (1)]

beans *n.*[2] [late 19C] a disappointment, a punishment. [backform. f. GIVE SOMEONE BEANS v. (1)]

beans *n.*[3] (*also* bean time) [1940s+] (*US*) 1 food. 2 a mealtime.

beans! *excl.* 1 [1910s–20s] (*US*) a mild excl. of surprise, disbelief etc. 2 [1950s+] (*US, mainly juv.*) a claim, esp. a claim of first rights to something.

bean-shooter *n.*[1] (*US*) 1 [1910s] a catapult or slingshot. 2 [1930s+] a gun.

bean-shooter n.[2] [1920s] (*US*) an native of Boston, Mass. [var. on BEAN-EATER n. (1)]

beanstalk n.[1] [1950s–70s] (*US*) a tall person (cf. BEANPOLE n.).

beanstalk n.[2] [1980s+] (*Aus. prison*) talk, chatter. [rhy. sl.; ult. fairy tale *Jack and the Beanstalk*]

bean time n. *see* BEANS n.[3].

bean-tosser n. [19C] the penis. [? shape]

Bean Town n. [late 19C+] (*US*) Boston, Massachusetts. [the supposed local staple]

bean town n. [20C+] (*US*) that part of a town in which the poor or the immigrants live, such immigrants are stereotypically, but not invariably, Hispanics. [BEAN n.[8] + the equation of a mainly bean diet with poverty]

bean wagon n. [1940s–50s] (*US*) a cheap restaurant, esp. one that has been converted from a disused railway car. [BEANERY n. (1) + SE *wagon*]

beany n. [1940s–60s] (*US*) a catapult. [abbr. BEAN-SHOOTER n.[1]]

beany adj. [1910s] (*US*) eccentric. [OFF ONE'S BEAN phr.]

Bear, the n. *see* JACK THE BEAR n.

bear n.[1] **1** [late 17C+] a gruff, irritable person; amplified in phr. *a bear with a sore head*. **2** [1910s+] (*US*) someone who overworks their employees or students, a hard taskmaster/mistress; esp. in phr. *a bear for*. **3** [1940s+] (*US Black*) a particularly ugly person, whether male or female (cf. BOOGER BEAR n.). **4** [1980s] a grasping person, a miser. **5** [1990s+] (*US*) a hairy, beefy homosexual male. [perceived ursine characteristics]

bear n.[2] [early 18C+] a Russian; thus *the Bear*, Russia in general. [the Russian 'national animal']

bear n.[3] [mid-18C+] the pupil of a private tutor. [the tutor is seen as 'leading' a pupil, esp. on the 'Grand Tour' of cultural/social Europe, like a keeper with a tame bear]

bear n.[4] **1** [20C+] (*US*) an expert, an adept. **2** [1900s–20s] (*US*) an exciting or otherwise exceptional example; an excellent, admirable person. **3** [1910s–30s] (*US*) an attractive (young) woman; usu. in phr. *She's a bear*. **4** [1960s] (*US campus*) a well-dressed man. **5** [1970s] (*US gay*) sex as a compulsion. [the strength and power of the animal]

bear n.[5] **1** [20C+] (*US*) sunstroke. **2** [1920s+] (*US Black*) a misfortune, an unfortunate situation, a feeling of depression. **3** [1950s] (*US prison*) solitary confinement. **4** [1950s] (*US Black*) an overcoat. **5** [1960s–70s] (*US campus*) any difficult course or circumstance relating to college work. **6** [1970s] (*US Black*) an unpleasant lifestyle. [the animal's negative characteristics]

bear n.[6] [1950s–70s] (*US*) the vulva. [it is furry and it 'bites']

bear n.[7] [1970s+] (*US*) a policeman; thus *bear in the air*, a police helicopter (cf. ANIMAL n.[1]). [US Forest Service's mascot *Smokey the Bear*]

bear, the n. [1940s–60s] (*US Black*) poverty, misery. [BEAR n.[5] (2)]

bear a bob v. [18C–early 19C] to lend a hand. [SE *bear a bob*, join in a chorus]

bear a hand v. [late 18C–1930s] to hurry up, to make haste.

bear cat n. (*US*) **1** [1900s–40s] something excellent, first-rate. **2** [1920s+] an aggressive or forceful person; one of great energy or ability. [BEAR n.[4] (2)/SE *bearcat*]

beard n.[1] **1** [16C+] female pubic hair. **2** [1920s+] a bearded man; thus, by stereotyping, a beatnik, intellectual. **3** [1970s] (*US*) a Hasidic Jew.

beard n.[2] **1** [1950s] in betting, one who bets on behalf of a racehorse trainer — who is not supposed to do so on his own runner. **2** [1950s+] a friend who acts as a 'cover', usu. for extra-marital affairs. **3** [1960s+] (*US gay/lesbian*) a man who poses as the husband or lover of a lesbian, in order to disguise her real sexual preference. **4** [1960s+] (*US gay/lesbian*) a woman who poses as the wife or lover of a homosexual man, in order to disguise his real sexual preference. **5** [1990s+] a disguise; something or someone who encourages misdirection. [gambling jargon *beard*,

a go-between who places bets for another person; thus protecting their identity]

beard v. **1** [1950s+] to act as a 'cover' for a friend, usu. in extra-marital affairs. **2** [1960s+] (*US gay/lesbian*) of a man, to pretend to be the husband or lover of a lesbian, to disguise her real sexual preference. **3** [1960s+] (*US gay/lesbian*) of a woman, to pose as the wife or lover of a homosexual man, to disguise his real sexual preference. [BEARD n.[2]]

beard! excl. [1990s+] (*UK juv.*) an excl. of disbelief or scepticism.

bearded clam n. [1960s+] the vagina; one of several terms linking the organ to fish (cf. BEARDED OYSTER n.; BIT OF FISH n.; BIT OF SKATE n.; CLAM n.[1]; COOTER n.[1]; DAMP n.; FISH n.[1]; FISH MARKET n.; FISH MITTEN n.; FISHPOND n.; FISH TANK n.[1]; FREE-FISHERY n.; FUZZY LAP FLOUNDER n.; HAIRY CLAM n.; HIRSUTE OYSTER n.; KIPPER n.[4]; KIPPER BOX n.; LING n.; LOBSTER-POT n.; OLD LING n.; OYSTER n.[1]; PERIWINKLE n.; RED SNAPPER n.; SHELL n.; SNAPPER n.[7]; SNAPPING TURTLE (PUSS) n.; TENCH n.[2]; TROUT n.[1]; TUNA (FISH) n.; WHELK n.). [BEARD n.[1] (1) + CLAM n.[1] (2)]

bearded lady n. (*also* bearded taco) [1960s+] the vagina. [BEARD n.[1] (1) + joc. use of SE]

bearded oyster n. [1910s+] the vagina (cf. BEARDED CLAM n.). [BEARD n.[1] (1) + OYSTER n.[1] (1)]

bearded weirdie n. *see* WEIRDIE n. (1).

beardie n. **1** [1900s–10s] (*Aus.*) a member of a body of South-cottians (believers in the teaching of Joanna Southcott (1750–1814), who announced herself as the woman spoken of in Rev. 12), followers of the local prophet John Wroe (1782–1863), who called themselves Christian Israelites. **2** [1940s+] (*orig. Aus.*) a bearded person. **3** [1960s] (*N.Z.*) a dog.

beard-jammer n. [1920s–60s] (*US*) a pimp. [BEARD n.[1] (1) + SE *jammer*]

beardless wonder n. [1950s] (*US*) an incompetent or foolish person.

beard-man n. [1960s] (*W.I.*) a Rastafarian. [his appearance]

beard ride n. [1980s] (*US*) cunnilingus (cf. BUSH DINNER n.[2]; DIPPING IN THE BUSH n.; DIVE IN THE BUSHES v.; EAT A FURBURGER v.; EAT HAIR PIE v.; FURBURGER n.; FUZZBURGER n.; HAIR PIE n.; HAVE A MOUSTACHE v.; MOUSTACHE n.; MOUSTACHE RIDE n.; MUFF v.[2]; MUFF JOB n.; MUNCH THE CARPET v.; SIP AT THE FUZZY CUP v.; SIP FROM THE HAIRY TEACUP v.; WEAR THE BEARD v.). [BEARD n.[1] (1) + RIDE n.[1] (1)]

beard-splitter n. **1** [late 17C–early 19C] a seducer, a sexual athlete. **2** [19C] the penis (cf. ARSE-OPENER n.). [BEARD n.[1] (1) + SE *splitter*]

bearer-up n. **1** [mid–late 19C] a decoy who induces victims to play with card cheats. **2** [late 19C] (*UK Und.*) a pimp who robs his prostitute's client. [BEAR UP v.; K. Chesney, in *Victorian Undwerworld* (1970) suggests a 'bully who robs men decoyed by woman accomplice' but no Dict. supports this def.]

bear fight n. [mid-19C] (*UK society*) a play fight, a bit of 'rough-and-tumble'.

bear-garden n. [late 17C–early 18C] the vagina.

bear-garden (discourse) n. [late 17C–early 19C] coarse language, vulgarity. [SE *bear garden*, orig. a venue for bear-baiting, latterly any scene of rowdy behaviour]

bear-garden jaw n. [late 18C–early 19C] coarse language. [BEAR-GARDEN (DISCOURSE) n. + JAW n. (1)]

be-argued adj. (*also* beargered) [mid-19C–1900s] drunk. [SE *argumentative*]

bearings n. [1940s] (*Aus.*) the stomach. [SE *bearing*, that part of a machine that supports a shaft or axle]

bear-leader n. [mid-18C–19C] a travelling tutor, thus by ext. an expert who teaches by example. [the nickname for the tutors of the 18C who ferried their aristocratic pupils around the 'Grand Tour' of Europe]

bear meat n. [1970s] (*US*) an easy target. [the size of a SE *bear*]

bear party *n.* [mid-19C] an all-male party, esp. on the night preceding the wedding of one of the men.

bear's ass *n.* **1** [1960s] (*US campus*) a fool, an ignoramus (cf. AIREDALE n.; ASSHEAD n.). **2** [1990s+] (*US*) a harsh taskmaster. [SE *bear*/BEAR n.¹ (2) + ASS n. (2)]

bear sign *n.* [1900s] (*US*) a doughnut. [cowboy/trapper jargon *bear sign*, bear droppings; a doughnut has a similar shape]

bear-skin *n.*¹ [late 16C; mid-18C] hair, latterly pubic hair. [resemblance]

bear-skin *n.*² [early 18C] (*UK Und.*) money (cf. BAT HIDE n.). [furs as a trading commodity]

bear's paw *n.* [20C+] a saw. [rhy. sl.]

bear story *n.* [mid-19C–1950s] (*US*) a 'tall story', an exaggerated story. [the wildly overblown stories told by bear-trappers and other woodsmen to credulous listeners]

bear trap *n.* [19C+] (*US*) a difficult situation.

bear-trapper's hat *n.* [1990s+] a large, hairy vagina, esp. one that is dark in colour.

bear-up *n.* [late 19C–1900s] (*Aus.*) the pursuit of a woman. [SE *bear-up*, a hold-up]

bear up *v.* [early 19C] to help in the commission of a swindle or fraud. [SE *bear up*, to support]

bear with a sore head *n. see* BEAR n.¹ (1).

beasel *n.* [1920s+] (*US*) a young woman; thus *beasel hound*, a man who pursues women. [? SE *besom*]

beast *n.*¹ [mid-18C+] an unpopular or unpleasant person.

beast *n.*² [late 19C–1900s] a bicycle. [synon. with SE *beast*, a horse]

beast *n.*³ [1950s+] **1** (*US, mainly campus*) a young woman, esp. an unattractive but sexually voracious one. **2** (*US, mainly campus*) any unattractive young woman. **3** (*US/W.I.*) a girlfriend viewed in a sexual context, esp. when she has another established relationship already.

beast *n.*⁴ (*drugs*) **1** [1950s+] heroin; thus heroin addiction. **2** [1960s+] LSD (cf. A n.³). [? their unpredictable effects]

beast *n.*⁵ **1** [1960s+] (*orig. US Black*) a White person. **2** [1970s+] (*W.I./UK Black teen*) (*also* **beast, the**) the police or any authoritarian figure, someone who represents the real or perceived oppressors. **3** [1980s+] (*Aus. prison*) a prison officer. [(1) coined by Black Nationalists in the 1960s; it lapsed thereafter but reappeared among rebellious youths in the 1990s]

beast *n.*⁶ [1980s+] (*UK prison*) a child molester, a sexual offender. [SE *beast*, a brutal, very unpleasant person]

beast *n.*⁷ [1980s+] cheap beer.

beast, the *n. see* BEAST n.⁵ (2).

beast *adj.* **1** [1950s+] (*W.I.*) a general intensifier, both positive and negative. **2** [1970s+] White; pertaining to White culture. [survival of schoolboy intensifier *beastly*, very good, very bad]

beast *v.* [1980s+] to molest a child. [BEAST n.⁶]

beast-boy *n.* (*also* **beast-bwoy**) [1990s+] (*UK Black*) a policeman (cf. ANIMAL n.¹). [BEAST n.⁵ + SE *boy*]

beast-lick *n.* [1940s+] (*W.I.*) a harsh, heavy blow, such as might be given to an animal. [SE *beast* + *lick*, a blow]

beastly *adj.* **1** [late 16C+] unpleasant, distasteful. **2** [1950s] (*US Black*) excellent, wonderful, very enjoyable. [(2) on bad = good model]

beastly *adv.* [19C–1920s] (*UK society*) exceedingly, excessively, very. [BEASTLY adj. (1)]

beastman *n.* [1970s+] (*UK Black*) a policeman (cf. ANIMAL n.¹). [BEAST n.⁵ (2)]

beastmaster *n.* [1980s+] (*US campus*) a man who consistently dates unattractive women. [BEAST n.³ (2) + SE *master*; note the similarly titled 'sword and sorcery' film of the period]

beastness *n.* [20C+] (*W.I.*) male promiscuity. [SE *beastliness*]

beast of a *phr.* [late 19C+] applied to anything seen as unpleasant.

beast wagon *n.* [1980s] (*UK Black*) a police van. [BEAST n.⁵ (2) + SE *wagon*]

beasty *n. see* BHEESTIE n.

beasty *adj.*¹ [1980s+] (*US campus*) disgusting, repellent, unattractive. [BEAST n.¹]

beasty *adj.*² [1990s+] (*UK juv.*) a general term of approbation, congratulation. [on bad = good model]

beat *n.*¹ **1** [late 18C+] (*orig. UK Und.*) a street or streets as walked by a prostitute. **2** [early 19C+] (*orig. UK Und.*) one's own area of activity or operation. **3** [mid-19C] (*UK Und.*) an area in which a pickpocket works. **4** [1940s+] (*Aus.*) the area patrolled by a sheep or cattle musterer. **5** [1950s–60s] (*US prison*) the area in which a criminal gang operates, thanks to bribing a local politician/police department. [SE *beat the bounds*]

beat *n.*² **1** [mid-19C–1900s] (*US*) an outstanding person, one who defeats all rivals. **2** [mid-19C–1910s] an outstanding object, an incomparable circumstance. [SE *beat*, to overcome; note WW1 milit. *my beat*, my girlfriend]

beat *n.*³ **1** [mid-19C–1930s] (*US*) an unreliable person, esp. one who fails to pay their debts. **2** [mid-19C–1960s] a swindler, a confidence trickster; thus ON THE BEAT phr. **3** [mid-19C–1960s] a loafer, a layabout, a sponger. **4** [1930s] (*US Und.*) a swindle. **5** [1950s+] (*orig. US*) (*also* **beatster**) a beatnik. [i.e. they 'beat' the rules of society]

beat *n.*⁴ [mid-19C–1950s] (*US*) an escape, usu. from prison. [BEAT IT v.]

beat *n.*⁵ [20C+] (*US*) information.

beat *n.*⁶ **1** [1970s] a prostitute's client who likes to be beaten, often bringing his own equipment with him. **2** [1970s+] (*US gay*) a homophobic thug. [SE *beat*, to hit]

beat *adj.* **1** [19C+] of a person, exhausted, tired out, emotionally and physically (cf. BEAT OUT adj.). **2** [mid-19C–1930s] (*US*) amazed, astonished, at a loss. **3** [1930s+] depressed, emotionally raw; esp. in phr. [1950s+] *beat generation*. **4** [1930s+] of a thing, worn-out, no longer fashionable. **5** [1930s+] (*orig. US Black*) of people, out of funds. **6** [1940s–50s] (*US drugs*) adulterated. **7** [1940s+] (*US*) useless, worthless; boring. **8** [1940s+] (*orig. US*) disillusioned, sad, world-weary. **9** [1950s] (*US drugs*) of an addict, craving for a dose of a drug. **10** [1980s] (*US campus*) bad, depressing. **11** [1980s+] (*US campus*) very ugly. **12** [1980s+] (*US campus*) stupid, weak, ineffectual. [SE *beaten*]

beat *v.*¹ **1** [mid-19C+] (*US*) to steal from, to defraud, to rob; often as BEAT SOMEONE FOR v. **2** [mid-19C+] (*orig. US*) to defeat intellectually, to baffle, to confuse; usu. as *beats me*, esp. BEATS ME! excl. (cf. HAVE ONE BEAT v.). **3** [late 19C–1930s] to leave quickly. **4** [late 19C+] of a criminal, to get away with a crime; of a lawyer, to defend a client successfully. **5** [20C+] (*US*) to escape from prison. **6** [1910s+] (*US*) to escape punishment. **7** [1940s+] (*US Black*) (*also* **beat up on**) of a man, to have heterosexual intercourse.

beat *v.*² *see* BEAT OFF v.² (1).

beat about the bush *v.* (*also* **beat around the bush, bush-beat, go about the bush**) [late 16C+] to avoid a topic, to fail deliberately to come to the point. [hunting imagery]

beat a dje *v.* [20C+] (*W.I., Gren.*) to be in the mood for a physical or verbal confrontation, esp. one that will last for several days. [SE *beat* + Fr. *guerre*, war]

beat akeybo *v.* [mid-19C] to be confusing; thus *he beats akeybo*, he acts in an extreme manner; *akeybo beats the Devil*, something is extremely confusing. [ety. unknown; note Norfolk dial. *acabo, akeybo*, used in phr. *that would puzzle acabo*]

beat all *v.* (*also* **beat all holler, beat all hollow, beat all nature**) [late 18C+] to surpass in every way; often in phr. *don't that beat all*.

beat all cockfight *v.* [20C+] (*W.I.*) to be unbelievable, unheard of, utterly ridiculous.

beat all to sticks *v.* (*also* **knock all to sticks**) [mid-19C] to thrash, to beat severely. [SE *knock to pieces*]

beat a rap v. **1** [1920s+] to be found not guilty in a court (cf. BEAT THE RAP v.). **2** [1940s] (US) in non-judicial context, to extricate oneself from difficult circumstances. [SE beat + RAP n.⁴ (6)/RAP n.⁴ (9)]

beat around the bush v. see BEAT ABOUT THE BUSH v.

beat artist n. [1980s+] (US Black) one who sells poor-quality or fake drugs. [BEAT v.¹ (1) + ARTIST sfx]

beat-ass adj.¹ [2000s] (US) excellent, outstanding. [SE beat + ASS n. (5)]

beat-ass adj.² [2000s] (US) second-rate. [BEAT adj. (4) + -ASS sfx]

beat ass v. [1940s+] (US) to leave, to depart. [BEAT v.¹ (3) + ASS n. (5)]

beat a trick v. [1970s+] (US Und.) of a prostitute, to rob a client. [BEAT v.¹ (1) + TRICK n.¹ (3)]

beat Banaghan v. (also **bang Banagher, bang wattle gum, beat Bannagher**) [late 18C+] (orig. Irish) to tell fabulous, fantastic tales, often ext. by and Banagher beat the Devil. [? name of a real story-teller who is surpassed by the current talker; f. the town of Banagher, a notorious 'rotten borough'. To 'beat it' would be to surpass any extreme]

beat basher n. [1950s] (UK juv.) a policeman. [BEAT n.¹ (2) + BASH v.¹ (1)]

beat bobtail v. [late 19C–1950s] (US) to surpass in every way. [? euph. for beat the devil, but also ? link to the 'bob-tailed nag' of Stephen Foster's song 'Camptown Races' (1850)]

beatbox n. [1980s+] (orig. US) **1** an electronic drum machine. **2** a large, portable tape deck. [SE beat, rhythm + BOX n.⁵ (7)]

beat brown v. see DO BROWN v. (1).

beat cheeks v. [1990s+] (US) to leave (at speed). [BEAT v.¹ (3) + SE cheeks; var. on BEAT ASS v.]

beat-down n. [1980s+] (US Black) a fight, a beating. [BEAT DOWN v.]

beat down v. [1980s+] (US Black) to fight, to beat up, to defeat severely. [ext. of SE]

beat-'em-up n. [1990s+] an action film or computer game.

beaten-out adv. [mid-19C] impoverished. [BEAT adj. (1)]

beater n.¹ [late 16C–early 17C] (UK Und.) one who lures a victim into a crooked game of cards or dice. [SE beater, one who drives game towards the guns; the imagery reflects the world of hunting (cf. BIRD n.³; BUSH n.¹; VERSER n.)]

beater n.² **1** [mid–late 19C] (US) a person or thing that beats or surpasses others. **2** [1980s+] a beaten-up vehicle.

beater n.³ [1930s+] one who refuses to pay their debts; a swindler. [DEADBEAT n. (5) or BEAT v.¹ (1)]

beater n.⁴ [1940s] (US Black/Harlem) cash; money. [? money 'beats' one's problems]

beater-cases n. [18C–mid-19C] (UK Und.) shoes. [DEW-BEATERS n. (2) + SE case]

beaters n. [mid–late 19C] (US) shoes, boots. [DEW-BEATERS n. (2)]

beat feet v. see BEAT (THE) FEET v.

beat for v. **1** [1940s–60s] to be short of, usu. money. **2** [1960s] to be deprived of. [BEAT adj. (5)]

beat for the yolk phr. [1940s] (US Black/Harlem) short of cash, temporarily impoverished. [BEAT adj. (5) + SE yolk]

beat generation n. see BEAT adj. (3).

beat hell v. [mid-19C+] to surpass, to exceed in expectation, to surprise; often as if this don't beat hell (cf. BEAT (THE) HELL OUT OF v.; TO BEAT HELL phr.).

beat hell out of v. see BEAT (THE) HELL OUT OF v.

beat him so his hide won't hold hay v. see HIDE WON'T HOLD HAY phr.

beat hollow v. see HOLLOW adv.

beat into fits v. (also **beat out of fits**) [mid-19C+] to defeat or surpass completely.

beat it v. [20C+] (US) to travel or leave in a hurry; often as imper. beat it!; also ext. as beat it while the beating's/going's good. [SE beat a path]

beat it on the hoof v. [late 17C–mid-18C] to walk on foot. [SE beat a path + HOOF n. (1)]

beat liquor v. [20C+] (W.I.) to drink heavily. [SE beat, to hit]

beatmeat n. [1980s] (US gay) masturbation; the post-ejaculatory penis. [BEAT ONE'S MEAT v. (1)]

beat-nuts n. [1970s] (US) an obsessive masturbator. [SE beat/BEAT ONE'S MEAT v. (1) + NUTS n.² (1), i.e. var. on NUMBNUTS n.]

beat-off n. [1970s] **1** (US) an act of masturbation. **2** (US campus) an unpleasant person. [backform. f. BEAT OFF v.² (1)]

beat off v.¹ [1920s] (US Und.) to rob, to break into. [BEAT v.¹ (1)]

beat off v.² [1960s+] (US) **1** (also **beat**) to masturbate (cf. BALL OFF v.²). **2** to masturbate another person. **3** in fig. use, to waste time, to loaf around. [SE beat/BEAT ONE'S MEAT v. (1) + COME OFF v.¹]

beat one's bird v. see BIRD n.⁸ (1).

beat one's chops v. see BEAT (UP) ONE'S GUMS v.

beat one's dummy v. (also **beat the dummy, flog one's dummy**) [1930s+] to masturbate (cf. BANG THE BISHOP v.). [SE beat/flog/whip + DUMMY n.³; note BEAT OFF v.² (1)]

beat one's gums v. see BEAT (UP) ONE'S GUMS v.

beat one's hog v. [1970s+] to masturbate (cf. BANG THE BISHOP v.; BEAT THE BEAVER v.; BEAT THE DOG v.; BEAT THE PUP v.; BELT ONE'S HOG v.; BLEED THE LIZARD v.; BRUSH THE BEAVER v.; BURP THE WORM v.; CHOKE THE CHICKEN v.; CLUB THE CLAM v.; COME ONE'S TURKEY v.; DRAIN THE MONSTER v.; FEED THE DUCKS v.; FEED THE PIGEONS v.; FLOG ONE'S DOGGIN v.; FLOG ONE'S DONKEY v.; FLOG THE DOG v.; FLOG THE (FINLESS) DOLPHIN v.; FLOG THE HOG v.; FLOSS THE CAT v.; FREE THE TADPOLES v.; FREE WILLY v.; GALLOP ONE'S ANTELOPE v.; GALLOP THE (OLD) LIZARD v.; HACK THE HOG v.; HAVE A CONVERSATION WITH THE ONE-EYED TROUSER SNAKE v.; HUG THE HOG v.; LOPE ONE'S MULE v.; MILK THE LIZARD v.; PET ONE'S PUSSYCAT v.; PET THE POODLE v.; POKE ONE'S PUSSY v.; SIPHON THE PYTHON v.; SLAM THE CLAM v.; SLAP THE MONKEY v.; SNAKE v.³; SPANK THE MONKEY v.; SPERM THE WORM v.; STRANGLE THE GOOSE v.; TAKE ONE'S SNAKE FOR A GALLOP v.; TUG ONE'S SLUG v.; WALK ONE'S FERRET v.; WHACK THE ONE-EYED WORM v.; WHIP THE BALONEY PONY v.). [SE beat/BEAT OFF v.² (1) + HOG n.⁶]

beat one's little brother v. see LITTLE BROTHER n. (1).

beat one's meat v. [1940s+] (orig. US) **1** (also **flog one's meat**) to masturbate; also fig. and in phr. GO BEAT YOUR MEAT! excl. (cf. BANG THE BISHOP v.; BLUDGEON THE BEEFSTEAK v.; BOB ONE'S BALONEY v.; BOP ONE'S BALONEY v.; BUFF THE BANANA v.; BUTTER THE MUFFIN v.; CHURN BUTTER v.; CLEAR THE CUSTARD v.; CLOUT ONE'S COOKIE v.; COME ONE'S MUTTON v.; CREAM ONE'S BEEF v.; CREAM THE CHEESE v.; CUFF THE CARROT v.; FLOG ONE'S MUTTON v.; GLAZE THE DONUT v.; HAM SHANK v.; HAND SHANDY n.; HOLD THE SAUSAGE HOSTAGE v.; JACK THE CORN v.; JERK ONE'S GHERKIN v.; JERK ONE'S JELLY v.; JUICE ONE'S FRUIT v.; JUICE THE PLUM v.; PADDLE THE PICKLE v.; PEEL THE BANANA v.; POUND ONE'S MEAT v.; POUND ONE'S PORK v.; POUND ONE'S PUD v.; PULL ONE'S PUD v.; PUMP ONE'S PICKLE v.; SHUCK THE CORN v.; SLAM THE HAM v.; SLAP THE SALAMI v.; SLING ONE'S JELLY v.; TICKLE ONE'S PICKLE v.; WAX ONE'S CARROT v.; WHIP THE BALONEY PONY v.; YANK ONE'S MEAT v.). **2** to brag, to boast. [SE beat/BEAT OFF v.² (1) + MEAT n. (2)]

beat (one's) skin v. [1940s] (US Black/Harlem) to applaud, to clap.

beat one's way v. [late 19C–1960s] (US) to make one's way by employing illegal means, e.g. cheating, swindling, sponging. [SE beat one's way, to cut a path]

beat out adj. [mid-18C+] (US) exhausted, emotionally stressed (cf. BEAT adj.).

beat out (of) v. [mid-19C+] (US) **1** to cheat, to defraud. **2** to overcome, to beat a rival.

beat out of fits v. see BEAT INTO FITS v.

beat pad n. [1930s–50s] (US drugs) a place where drugs are consumed. [SE beat(nik) + PAD n.² (2)]

beat-pounder *n.* [20C+] a policeman (cf. BEETLE-CRUSHER n.; BLUDGER n.[2]; BODY-SNATCHER n.; CATCHER n.[1]; CLODHOPPER n.; COLLAR n.[2]; CRIME-BUSTER n.; CRUSHER n.[2]; CUDDLE-COOK n.; DOOR-BASHER n.; DOOR SHAKER n.; FINGER n.[3]; FOOTSLOGGER n.; GABBER n.[2]; GRAB n.; HEAD KNOCKER n.; HEAVY n.[1]; HEAVY-FOOT n.; HOONCHASER n.; KILLJOY n.; MUTTON-SHUNTER n.; NAB n.[2]; NABMAN n.; NAILER n.[2]; NIPPER n.[1]; PADDLER n.[2]; PAVEMENT POUNDER n.; PEACEMAKER n.[2]; PEEPER n.; PINCHER n.[1]; PINNER n.[1]; POUNDER n.; PUSSYFOOT n.; RABBIT-PIE SHIFTER n.; REELER n.[1]; ROPER n.; SCUFFER n.; SHADOW n.; SHAGGER n.[2]; SHOULDER-TAPPER n.; SKULL-BUSTER n.; SLAPMAN n.; SNATCHER n.; SNOOP n.[1]; SNOOPER n.; SPOTTER n.[1]; STICKER-LICKER n.; STOP n.[1]; STOPPER n.; WAL n.; WALLOPER n.[1]). [SE *beat*/BEAT n.[1] (2) + SE *pound*]

beats me! *excl.* (*also* **beats all!**) [mid-19C+] a general excl. of incomprehension, 'I just can't understand it'. [BEAT v.[1] (2)]

beat someone for *v.* [1950s+] to take a person's money, whether it is offered or not, to rob or trick someone out of their money. [BEAT v.[1] (1)]

beat someone out of *v.* [mid-19C+] (*orig. US*) to cheat, to steal from, to defraud. [BEAT v.[1] (1)]

beat someone's arse/ass *v. see* BUST SOMEONE'S ASS v.

beat someone's jock off *v. see* KNOCK SOMEONE'S JOCK OFF v.

beat someone's time *v.* **1** [mid–late 19C] (*US*) to confuse, to confound. **2** [1930s–50s] (*US Black/campus*) to cheat or be cheated in a love affair. [BEAT v.[1] + SE *time*]

beat someone to the gun *v.* (*also* **beat to the wheel**) [1920s–30s] (*US*) to start first, to do something before somebody else. [sporting imagery]

beat someone to the punch *v.* [1960s+] (*orig. US Black*) **1** to arrive at a destination sooner than another person. **2** to appreciate or understand something faster than another person. [boxing imagery]

beatster *n. see* BEAT n.[3] (5).

beat tar *v.* (*also* **slap tar**) [20C+] (*W.I., Bdos*) to walk around. [SE *beat* + *tar*, by metonymy the pavement]

beat the bags off *v.* [1920s–40s] to overcome totally. [SE *beat* + BAGS n.[2]]

beat the band *v.* [late 19C+] (*orig. US*) to surpass comprehensively, esp. in excl. *that beats the band!* that's beyond rival/compare!

beat the beaver *v.* [1970s+] of a woman, to masturbate (cf. APPLY LIP GLOSS v.; BEAT ONE'S HOG v.). [BEAT OFF v.[2] (1) + BEAVER n.[5] (1)]

beat the bishop *v. see* BANG THE BISHOP v.

beat the boards *v.* [1940s] (*US Black*) to (tap)dance.

beat the booby *v.* [late 18C–early 19C] to beat one's hands against one's sides to get warm on a cold day. [pun on SE *booby*, a large, slow-flying bird/*booby*, a fool]

beat the books *v.* [1940s+] (*US/W.I.*) to work very hard.

beat the breeze *v.* [1940s+] (*US*) to chatter, to gossip. [SE *beat* + SE *breeze*/BREEZE n.[2] (3)]

beat the bricks *v.* [1920s+] (*US*) to walk the streets, esp. when in search of work.

beat the bugs *v.* [mid-19C–1910s] to surpass any contender. [SE *beat*]

beat the bush *v.* [late 16C] (*UK Und.*) to ensnare a victim. [hunting jargon *beat the bush*, to beat the undergrowth to drive out game]

beat-the-bush *adj.* [early 19C] non-committal, evasive. [BEAT ABOUT THE BUSH v.]

beat the cars *v.* [19C] (*US*) to surpass in every way. [SE *beat* + *street cars*]

beat the crap out of *v. see* KNOCK THE CRAP OUT OF v.

beat the cunt out of *v.* [1980s] (*UK*) to beat severely. [CUNT n.[4]; var. on BEAT THE CRAP OUT OF v.]

beat the daylights out of *v. see* BEAT THE (LIVING) DAYLIGHTS OUT OF v.

beat the dog *v.* [1930s+] to masturbate (cf. BANG THE BISHOP v.; BEAT ONE'S HOG v.). [BEAT OFF v.[2] (1) + DOG n.[4] (1)]

beat the dummy *v. see* BEAT ONE'S DUMMY v.

beat the Dutch *v.* [mid-18C+] to do something outstanding; thus *that beats the Dutch*, describing something that is otherwise barely credible. [the Dutch as a national enemy and commercial rival]

beat (the) feet *v.* (*US campus*) **1** [1940s+] to leave, to depart. **2** [1970s] to hurry.

beat the freight *v.* [1930s] (*Can.*) to steal a ride on a freight train.

beat the gong *v.* [1930s–60s] (*drugs*) to smoke opium. [SE *beat* + GONG n.[2] (2)]

beat the goose *v.* [late 19C] to strike one's hands under the armpits to warm them. [the movement supposedly resembles a goose in flight]

beat the gun *v. see* JUMP THE GUN v.

beat the hay *v. see* HIT THE HAY v. (2).

beat (the) hell out of *v.* (*orig. US*) **1** [1920s+] to beat severely. **2** [1960s+] to amaze, to confound. [SE *beat* + HELL, THE phr.[1] (2); (2) BEAT HELL v.]

beat the hoof *v.* [late 17C–early 19C] to walk. [SE *beat* + HOOF n. (1)]

beat the hound out of *v.* [1940s+] (*US*) to thrash severely. [SE *beat*, hit + SE *hound*, cussedness, stubbornness]

beat the Jews *v.* [mid-19C–1960s] to surpass any contender. [SE *beat*, surpass + *Jews*; i.e. the stereotype of Jewish ambition/ deviousness]

beat the lard out of *v.* (*also* **beat the meal out of**) [mid-19C+] (*Irish*) to beat, to thrash. [SE *beat* + LARD n. (3)/SE *meal*]

beat the (living) daylights out of *v.* (*also* **beat the lights out of, knock the daylight(s) out of**) [mid-19C+] to beat severely; occas. as *eternal/everlasting daylights*. [SE *beat*/knock + DAYLIGHTS n. (2)]

beat the (living) piss out of *v.* [1930s+] (*orig. US*) to beat severely. [SE *beat* + PISS, THE n.]

beat the priest *v.* [20C+] (*W.I., Gren.*) to commit a major crime and act brazenly in acknowledging it without any form of shame or sorrow. [SE *beat*, defeat + negative image of clerical hypocrisy]

beat the pup *v.* [1940s–50s] (*US*) to masturbate (cf. BANG THE BISHOP v.; BEAT ONE'S HOG v.). [BEAT OFF v.[2] (1) + PUPPY n.[2] (1)]

beat the rap *v.* [1920s+] (*US*) to be found innocent of a charge in court (cf. BEAT A RAP v.). [SE *beat* + RAP n.[4] (9)]

beat the road *v.* [late 19C] (*US*) to travel by train without paying. [BEAT v.[1] (1) + (*rail*)*road*]

beat the rocks *v.* [1940s] (*US Black*) to walk the streets. [esp. used in the context of walking the streets in search of employment]

beat the sheets *v.* (*also* **press the sheets**) [1950s+] to sleep deeply.

beat the shit(e) out of *v.* [1930s+] (*orig. US*) **1** to beat severely. **2** to improve upon, to be superior to, to surpass. **3** to confuse completely. [SE *beat* + SHIT, THE n.[2]/SHITE n. (5)]

beat the starter *v.* (*also* **cheat the starter**) [1910s+] to have a child out of wedlock, to become pregnant before one's wedding (cf. JUMP THE GUN v.). [sporting imagery; in a false start a competitor will set off before the starting pistol has been fired]

beat the stick *v.* [1990s+] to masturbate (cf. BANG THE BISHOP v.). [BEAT OFF v.[2] (1) + STICK n.[1] (1)]

beat the tar out of *v.* (*also* **whale the tar out of**) [20C+] (*US*) to beat someone up very badly. [fig. use of SE *tar* = essence, 'daylights']

beat the tracks *v.* [20C+] (*Aus.*) to walk a long way, usu. over rough country. [SE *beat*, hit/BEAT IT v. + *tracks*]

beattie and babs *n.* [1930s+] body lice. [rhy. sl. = CRAB n.[2]]

beat to snuff *v.* [early 19C–1920s] to defeat comprehensively. [SE *beat*, defeat + *snuff*, powdered tobacco; thus lit. 'to reduce to powder']

beat to the socks *adv.* (*also* **beat to the heels**) [1930s–50s] (*US Black*) tired out, utterly exhausted. [BEAT adj. (1) + SE *socks/heels*; the image is of a long, fruitless trudge that has worn out one's shoes/socks]

beat-up *adj.* **1** [mid-19C+] (*US*) exhausted. **2** [1930s+] (*US*) dilapidated, run-down, ageing. **3** [1980s+] (*US campus*) wrong, bad.

beat up *v.* **1** [20C+] (*orig. US*) to nag, harass. **2** [1910s] to promote, to encourage. [fig. use of SE *beat up*, to attack]

beat up on *v. see* BEAT v.¹ (7).

beat (up) one's gums *v.* (*also* **beat (up) one's chops**) [1930s+] (*US*) **1** to chatter, to talk, esp. in an irritating manner (cf. GUM BEAT v.). **2** to talk in a melodramatic manner. **3** to eat. [SE *beat* + SE *gums*/CHOPS n.¹ (1)]

beat up (the quarters of) *v.* [late 19C] (*UK society*) to call upon unceremoniously. [SE *beat up*, to visit, to tour + SE *quarters*, dwelling-place, home; SE use is to arouse, to disturb]

beat with an ugly stick *v.* **1** [1960s+] (*Aus./US*) to be made unattractive; often used as a supposed reason for one's lack of good looks, e.g. *he was beat with an ugly stick*. **2** [1980s+] (*US campus*) of a man, to have sexual intercourse (cf. BANG v.¹).

beau *n.* [1980s+] (*US campus*) **1** a stupid or clumsy person. **2** a boyfriend. [SE *beau*, a suitor, a sweetheart]

beau-catcher *n.* [mid-19C–1920s] a lock of hair equivalent to the modern *kiss-curl*. [SE *beau* + *catcher*; such a lock was calculated to ensnare young men. The term did not survive the 19C in the UK but lasted until the 1920s or beyond in the US. 'In olden times this was called a *lovelock*, when it was the mark at which all the Puritan and ranting preachers levelled their pulpit pop-guns, loaded with sharp and virulent abuse' (Hotten, 1867)]

beaucoup *n.* (*also* **beaucoups, boocoo, bookoo, boo-koos, booku, buckoo, buku**) [1910s+] (*orig. Aus./US*) a large quantity of, a lot of (cf. BOKO adj.¹). [Fr. *beaucoup*, many; despite this early origin, the term was properly popularized during the Vietnam War, when it was picked up by GIs as part of the recently used French/Vietnamese pidgin and usu. pron. 'boo-coo']

beaucoup *adj.* (*also* **beaucoups**) [1920s+] (*US*) excellent, first-rate. [BEAUCOUP n.]

beaucoup *adv.* (*also* **bocoo, boocoo, boo-koos, buku**) [1910s+] (*orig. US/Aus.*) very (much), extremely, used as a general intensifier. [Fr. *beaucoup*, very much/BEAUCOUP n.]

beau-dollar *n.* (*also* **bo-dollar**) [1940s+] (*US Black*) a silver dollar. [SE *beau*, a dandy, the presumption being that the dandy carried a good supply of such coins. Other suggestions include abbr. HOBO n.² (1) or SE *boat* or *boar* (the hog seen as a desirable commodity), corruption of SE *Boer* (a supposed lucky piece carried by British soldiers during the Boer Wars (1880–1, 1899–1902)]

beauhunk *n.* [1980s+] (*US campus*) **1** a boyfriend. **2** a sexy-looking young man. [BEAU n. (2)/Fr. *beau*, attractive + HUNK n.¹ (6) + pun on derog. BOHUNK n.]

beau-nasty *n.* [late 18C–early 19C] a well-dressed, but ill-kempt and grubby dandy. [SE *beau* + *nasty*]

beauns *n.* [1970s+] (*US gay*) the buttocks. [SE *beau* + BUNS n. (2)]

beaut *n.*¹ (*also* **bute**) [mid-19C+] (*orig US*) **1** a beautiful person or thing. **2** a splendid example of a type (human or not). **3** ironic uses of (1) and (2). [abbr. SE; coined in US, but most common use is Aus.]

beaut *n.*² [1990s+] (*UK juv.*) **1** a cigarette. **2** a magic mushroom.

beaut *adj.* [1940s+] (*Aus.*) an all-purpose term of admiration. [abbr. SE *beautiful*/BEAUTY adj.]

beaut! *excl.* [1950s+] (*Aus./N.Z.*) an all-purpose positive excl., e.g. *you beaut!* [abbr. BEAUTY! excl.]

beautiful *adj.* [mid-19C+] (*orig. US*) **1** pleasing, admirable. **2** happy, satisfied. **3** clever, shrewd, also used ironically.

beautiful *adv.* [mid-19C+] well, perfectly. [BEAUTIFUL adj. (1)]

beau-trap *n.* **1** [late 17C–mid-19C] a confidence trickster, esp. a card-sharp. **2** [late 18C–early 19C] a badly laid paving stone that traps water beneath it and, when it is stepped on, squirts that water onto the dandy's finery. [SE *beau*, a suitor, a sweetheart + *trap*]

beauty *n.*¹ **1** [19C] the vagina. **2** [1960s+] (*US gay*) (*also* **beautocks, beauts**) the buttocks. [(1) one of the relatively congratulatory terms; (2) pron. as well as praise]

beauty *n.*² [early 19C+] **1** an admirable person or creature. **2** in ironic use, any person, admirable, attractive or otherwise. **3** a thing, usu. with positive overtones.

beauty *n.*³ [1960s] Biphetamine, a strong amphetamine (cf. A n.²). [abbr. BLACK BEAUTY n.]

beauty *adj.* [1940s+] (*Aus.*) a general term of admiration. [abbr. SE *beautiful*]

beauty! *excl.* [1940s+] (*Aus./UK*) excellent! a general excl. of approval; often pron. *bewdy!* [BEAUTY adj.]

beauty mark *n.* (*also* **beauty spot**) [mid-19C+] (*US*) **1** one's face. **2** a scar. [joc. use of SE]

beauty spot *n.* [18C–19C] the vagina; one of a number of terms linking the female genital area with nature (cf. BELLE-CHOSE n.; BELLY DALE n.; BOWER (OF BLISS) n.; DAISY n.³; EVERGREENS n.; FLOWER OF CHIVALRY n.; FLOWERPOT n.; FRONT GARDEN n.; FRUITFUL VINE n.; GARDEN n.; GARDEN OF EDEN n.; GARDEN OF PLEASURE n.; GENTLEMAN'S PLEASURE-GARDEN n.; GREEN MEADOW n.; HIDDEN FOREST n.; LADY FLOWER n.; MEDLAR (TREE) n.; MIRACULOUS CAIRN n.; MOSSY DOUGHNUT n.; MOUTH OF NATURE n.; NATURE n.; NATURE'S TREASURY n.; NATURE'S TUFTED TREASURE n.; NEST IN THE BUSH n.; NETTLE BED n.; ORCHARD n.; PARSLEY BED n.; PLUM TREE n.¹; PUMP DALE n.; ROSE n.¹; SHADY SPRING n.; TEAZLE n.).

beav *n.* [1980s+] (*US campus*) a name that indicates that the referent is acting like a little brother. [US TV show *Leave It To Beaver*]

beave *n.* [1950s] a prostitute (cf. ASS PEDDLER n.). [abbr. BEAVER n.⁵ (1)]

beaver *n.*¹ [17C+] a hat of any sort. [abbr. SE *beaver hat*; note Ned Ward, *The London Spy* (1699): 'What are those Eagle-look'd Fellows, in their Narrow Brim'd White Beavers'; but note SE *beaver/bever*, that part of a helmet which when let down covers the face]

beaver *n.*² [mid-18C] (*UK Und*) butter. [ety. unknown; ? link to dial. *bever*, refreshment, i.e. bread and *butter*]

beaver *n.*³ [mid-19C; 1940s] (*US*) money. [use of *beaver* pelts as a mode of exchange]

beaver *n.*⁴ **1** [1910s–60s] a bearded man. **2** [1910s+] a beard; thus *beavered*, bearded. [thus the early 20C street game in which children would compete to be the first to spot a bearded man and signify their success by shouting *beaver!*]

beaver *n.*⁵ (*orig. US*) **1** [1920s+] female pubic hair, the vagina, esp. in commercial pornography use; thus *beaver book*, a porno-graphic book; *beaver film*, a pornographic film etc. **2** [1960s+] a woman. [the supposed similarity between the beaver's coat and the pubic hair]

beaver book *n.* [2000s] (*US*) a pornographic book or magazine, esp. those featuring the open vagina. [BEAVER n.⁵ (1)]

beaver cleaver *n.* [1990s+] the penis (cf. ARSE-OPENER n.). [BEAVER n.⁵ (1) + SE *cleaver*]

beaver patrol *n.*¹ [1960s+] a group of young men looking for suitable female company. [BEAVER n.⁵ (1) + SE *patrol*]

beaver patrol *n.*² [1970s] a group or team of enthusiastic (young) workers. [EAGER BEAVER n.]

beaver shooter *n.* [1960s–70s] a peeping Tom, a voyeur. [BEAVER n.⁵ (1) + SE *shooter/shoot a glance*]

beaver shot *n.* [1970s+] (*US*) **1** a close-up photograph of, or camera-angle on, the female genitals; used in commercial pornography. **2** a chance glimpse (by a man) of the same area. [BEAVER n.⁵ (1) + SE *shot*]

beaver-tail *n.*[1] [mid-19C] a hairstyle, popular *c.*1860–70, whereby middle-class women wore their hair in a net, which then fell onto their shoulders. [the similarity of 'the shape of the netted hair to a beaver's flat and comparatively shapeless tail' (Ware)]

beaver-tail *n.*[2] [1970s+] (*US*) a cosh, a sap. [the similarity in shape]

Beavis *n.* [1990s+] (*US campus*) one who fails to prove acceptable to social norms. [the TV cartoon *Beavis and Butthead*, featuring a pair of socially inadequate teenagers]

beazle *n.* [1930s] (*US campus*) an unappealing person. [? 16C SE *beazler*, a drunkard, a sot]

be back *adj.* [2000s] (*US Black*) warning, e.g. *be back lights*, warning lights. [idea of 'keeping back' from the danger]

bebee *n.* (*also* **beebee**) **1** [mid-19C] a woman, a lady. **2** [late 19C] a prostitute; a female bed-mate. [Hind. *bibi*, a lady]

bebop *v.* **1** [1950s–60s] (*US*) to fight, esp. as one of a street gang; thus *bebopper*, a juvenile delinquent. **2** [1970s+] to walk in an arrogant, 'cocky' manner. [(1) BOP v. (1); (2) BOP v. (3); pun on SE *bebop*, a style of jazz/dancing]

bebop glasses *n.* [1940s] (*US Black*) a then-fashionable style of dark glasses, with notably thick frames as well as blackened lenses. [SE *bebop*, the style of jazz played in 1940s by such musicians as Charlie Parker, Kenny Clarke and Bud Powell, as well as Dizzy Gillespie; the glasses were popularized by these stars, esp. Gillespie]

bebopper *n.* (*also* **bopper**) **1** [1940s+] (*orig. US Black/jazz*) one who dances to bebop tunes. **2** [1940s+] (*orig. US Black/jazz*) (*also* **bopster**) a musician who plays in the bop style. **3** [1960s] (*US*) a juvenile delinquent. **4** [1980s+] (*US Black*) (*also* **beebopper**) an inexperienced, naïve and, on those grounds, unpopular person. [the SE *bebop* jazz craze, new and sophisticated in 1940s, but archaic by 1980s]

beck *n.*[1] [late 17C–mid-19C] (*UK Und.*) a constable. [abbr. *harman-beck* (see HARMAN n.)]

beck *n.*[2] [1980s+] a well-off, middle-class Jewish teenager or young person, orig. just girls, usu. from north London, often collectively as *becks*. [abbr. girl's name *Rebecca*; ? also *Becks* beer, their supposedly favoured drink]

become a landowner *v. see* LANDED ESTATE n.

bed *n.* [1940s+] the world of sex; sexual intercourse. [metonymy]

bed *v.* [late 18C+] to seduce, to have sexual intercourse with. [abbr. SE *take to bed*; note mid-16C–mid-18C SE *bed*, to take (a wife) to bed, e.g. in D'Urfey, *Pills to Purge Melancholy* (1719–20): 'Lastly brought her here, / To court her for his Dear; / To Wed and Bed'; also in non-marital sense: 'Each Hour I long to bed thee: / But if confin'd, / Sould scare believ't a Joy']

bedad! *excl.* [early 18C+] (*Irish*) by God! [SE *by* + DAD n.[1]]

bedamned *adv. see* DAMNED adv.

bed and breakfast *n.* [1940s+] (*bingo*) the number 26 (cf. ALDERSHOT LADIES n.). [2s 6d (12½p), at one time the going rate for a B&B establishment]

bed athlete *n.* (*also* **bed-bounder, bedroom athlete**) [1940s+] (*orig. US*) a promiscuous person.

bedbait *n.* [1930s+] (*US*) an underage sexual partner; they can be of either sex although most often a teenage girl. [SE *bed* + BAIT n.[3] (1); var. on JAILBAIT n. (2)]

bedbug *n.*[1] [1930s–60s] (*US Black*) an unpleasant and/or insignificant person. [identification]

bedbug *n.*[2] [1940s] (*US Black*) a Black Pullman porter. [SE *bedbug*; among their other duties the porters turned back beds for their (mainly White) passengers]

bedbug alley *n.* (*also* **bedbug row**) [1920s–50s] (*US*) the poorest area of a town. [the supposed infestation of *bedbugs*]

bedder *n.* [late 19C–1900s] a bedroom. [SE *bed* + -ER sfx]

beddies *n.* (*also* **beddie**) [1960s–70s] bed, in the context of a place for sex.

beddy *n.* [1980s+] (*US campus*) an attractive, sexually available young woman. [SE *bed* + sfx *-y*; but note BETTY n.[4]]

beddy-bye *n.* [20C+] bedtime; *go beddy-bye*, to go to sleep. [a conscious use of a usu. juv. term]

bed-faggot *n.* (*also* **bed-fagot**) [mid-19C] a prostitute. [SE *bed* + FAGGOT n.[2] (2)]

bed-fellow *n.* [late 19C] **1** the vagina. **2** the penis. [pun]

Bedfordshire *n.* [mid-17C+] bed; thus *Bedfordshire woman*, a prostitute; *go up the wooden hill to Bedfordshire*, to go to bed. [SE *bed* + sfx *-shire*; ult. real UK county *Bedfordshire*]

bedhop *v.* [1960s+] to live a sexually promiscuous life; thus *n. bedhopping*.

bed-house *n.* **1** [mid-19C] (*US*) a 'short-time' hotel. **2** [1920s+] (*US Black*) a brothel (cf. ACCOMMODATION HOUSE n.). [SE *bed* + HOUSE n.[1] (1)]

Bedlam beggar *n.* [17C–early 19C] a wandering beggar, adopting tattered clothing and posing as a madman. [the *Bedlam* (Bethlehem) Hospital]

bedonderd *adj.* (*also* **bedonnerd**) [1960s+] (*S.Afr.*) crazy. [Du. *bedonderd*, mad]

bedoozle *v.* [mid-late 19C; 2000s] (*US*) to confuse; thus *bedoozling*, astounding, amazing. [? SE *bedazzle* + BAMBOOZLE v. (1)]

bed-presser *n.* **1** [late 16C+] a whoremonger, a womanizer. **2** [late 16C+] a dull and heavy man. **3** [19C] a prostitute.

bedroom athlete *n. see* BED ATHLETE n.

bedroom eyes *n.* [1910s+] a look in the eyes that invites the person on whom it is focused towards seduction.

bedroom furniture *n. see* PIECE OF FURNITURE n.

bed-sit *n.* (*also* **bed-sitter, bedsit**) [1960s+] a single room in a house, available for renting. [abbr. *bed-sitting* room]

bedstead relation *n.* [1960s] (*US*) in-laws, relations by marriage. [SE *bedstead*, occupied by the married couple]

bee *see also under* B *or* B.

bee *n.*[1] **1** [1900s–20s] (*US*) ambition. **2** [1950s–60s] drug addiction. **3** [1950s–60s] (*US Black*) an idea. [the image is of 'stinging', in (2) with pain, in (1) and (3) as a jolt of inspiration; but note phr. *bee in one's bonnet*]

bee *n.*[2] [1990s+] (*US*) a frisbee, a game of fris*bee*. [abbr.]

beeatch *n. see* BIATCH n.

Beeb, the *n.* [1960s+] the British Broadcasting Corporation (BBC). [pron. of the *BB*(C)]

beebee *n. see* BEBEE n.

beebopper *n. see* BEBOPPER n. (4).

Beecham's pill *n.* **1** [1920s–30s] a bill; in pl. any form of sign (i.e. a handbill) denoting one's qualifications for begging (e.g. 'blind', 'ex-soldier' etc). **2** [950s+] (*Aus.*) a fool, a simpleton (cf. BEERY BUFF n.; BERK n.; BERKELEY (HUNT) n.; CHARLIE n.[6]; CHARLIE SMIRKE n.; DOLLYPOT n.; DOLLYPOT n.; EGG AND SPOON n.; HAMPTON (WICK) n.; HARRY HUGGINS n.; HEARTHRUG n.; HORSE'S RUG n.; JACK (AND JILL) n.; J. ARTHUR (RANK) n.; JOE ERK n.; JOE (HUNT) n.; KISS-ME-QUICK n.[2]; KIT-KAT n.; LITTLE BROWN JUG n.; LUMP AND BUMP n.; LUMP OF SCHOOL n.; MILK JUG n.[2]; MUFFIN n.[1]; NOAH'S (ARK) n.; PAPER HAT n.; STEAMER n.[3]; STEAM TUG n.; STONE JUG n.[2]; THIRTY-FIRST OF MAY n.; TIN HAT n.[2]; TOBY JUG n.; TOM TUG n.[1]; TOP HAT n.[1]; TRILBY HAT n.; TWELVE-INCH RULE n.; TWO-FOOT RULE n.; WILLY WONKA n.). **3** [1950s+] a still (photograph). **4** [1970s+] a will. [rhy. sl.; (2) = DILL n.]

Beecham's (pills) *n.* [late 19C+] **1** the testicles. **2** in fig. use, nonsense. [despite E.P., as echoed by *Maledicta* IV (1980), more likely a play on PILLS n.[1] (1)/*Beecham's Pills*, the popular UK medicine than rhy. sl. (on *testi-cles*)]

bee-cup *n.* [1970s+] (*US gay*) large pectorals. [play on brassiere size 'B-cup']

Bee Em *n. see* BEAMER n.

beef *n.*[1] **1** [17C+] (*also* **beef-steak**) the penis (cf. BACON n.[1]). **2** [17C–18C] the vagina (cf. BACON SANDWICH n.). **3** [late 18C+] human flesh. **4** [mid-19C+] (*orig. US*) physical strength, power, muscles. **5** [late 19C] used in Clare Market, a provisions market in London WC2, to describe cat's meat. **6** [20C+] (*W.I., Jam.*) (*also* **piece of beef**) a sexually appealing man or woman. **7** [1920s+] (*US*) (*also* **piece of beef**) a well-built male; used by both heterosexuals and homosexuals. [(6) note Shakespearian use in *Henry IV Part 1* 'O, my sweet beefe, I must still be good Angell to thee']

beef *n.*² **1** [late 19C–1950s] (*US tramp*) an act of betrayal to the authorities. **2** [late 19C+] (*US*) a complaint, a problem, an altercation; thus *what's your/the beef*, what's your/the problem?; *make a beef*, to complain, to make a fuss. **3** [late 19C+] (*US campus*) a mistake; thus *make a beef*, to err, to blunder. **4** [1920s–80s] (*US Und.*) a crime under investigation. **5** [1920s+] a criminal charge. **6** [1940s+] (*US Black*) statement, conversation, line of talk. **7** [1950s+] (*US Und.*) a discussion, chatter. **8** [1960s] (*US Und.*) an arrest. **9** [1960s] (*US Und.*) a criminal act. **10** [1960s–70s] (*US*) a (usu. hotel or restaurant) bill. **11** [1960s–70s] (*US prison*) a jail sentence. **12** [1960s+] (*US prison*) a disciplinary charge. **13** [1980s] (*US campus*) facts, information. **14** [2000s] (*UK Black*) general aggression, an atmosphere of violence. [BEEF v.¹]

beef *n.*³ [1940s–50s] (*US*) liquor. [? BEEF n.¹ (4)]

beef *v.*¹ **1** [early–mid-19C] to raise a hue and cry. **2** [mid-19C] to raise an alarm (but not over a crime). **3** [mid-19C–1910s] (*orig. theatre*) to shout. **4** [mid-19C+] to complain. **5** [late 19C] (*US*) to bully. **6** [late 19C–1960s] (*US tramp*) to give someone away, to betray to the authorities, to own up. **7** [late 19C+] (*US*) to argue. **8** [20C+] (*US*) to talk loudly (esp. to no real purpose). **9** [1900s] (*US*) to waste time. **10** [1900s–10s] (*US*) to blunder, to make a mistake. **11** [1910s–50s] to say, to declare. **12** [1970s] (*US prison*) to charge with a crime. **13** [2000s] (*US Black*) to have a problem with (someone). [CRY (HOT) BEEF v.]

beef *v.*² **1** [late 19C] (*US*) to shoot dead. **2** [1900s–50s] (*orig. US*) to knock (someone) down. **3** [1940s+] to engage in sexual intercourse. [agricultural jargon *beef*, to slaughter an ox]

beef *v.*³ *see* BEEF UP v. (1).

beef! *excl. see* HOT BEEF! excl.

beef and *n.* [late 19C] (*US*) an order of corned beef and beans.

beef and ham *n.* **1** [1940s] (*also* **plate of ham**) a tram (cf. TROLLEY AND TRAM n.). **2** [1950s–70s] a pram. [rhy. sl.]

beef-a-roni *n.* [1980s+] (*US campus*) a sexy man. [play on BEEFCAKE n. (2) + popular US fast-food]

beef baby *n.* [2000s] (*US Black*) a child fathered by a gangster who is living temporarily with a girlfriend or mistress while hiding from the authorities.

beef-bag *n.* [mid-19C–1930s] (*Aus.*) a shirt. [BEEF n.¹ (3) + SE *bag*]

beef bayonet *n.* [1960s+] the penis (cf. AX n.²; BACON n.¹). [play on SE, but note BEEF n.¹ (1)]

beefcake *n.* (*orig. US*) **1** [1940s+] a male pin-up. **2** [1950s+] any attractive, muscular man. **3** [1970s] male sex-appeal. **4** [1970s] as a term of address. [on model of CHEESECAKE n.¹]

Beef City *n.* [1940s] a situation where one is complaining. [BEEF n.² (2)+ CITY sfx]

beef curtains *n.* (*also* **roast beef curtains**) [1980s+] (*orig. US*) the labia majora (cf. BACON STRIPS n.; CURTAINS n.²; DEW-FLAPS n.; MEAT CURTAINS n.; STEAK DRAPES n.). [BEEF n.¹ (2) + SE *curtains*]

beefeater *n.*¹ [17C; 20C+] (*US*) an Englishman or woman. [SE *beefeater*, a Yeoman of the Guard, one of London's tourist icons]

beefeater *n.*² [1900s–10s] (*US*) a cattle rustler or poacher. [his 'appetite' for cattle]

beefer *n.* [late 19C–1960s] **1** (*US*) a whinger, a complainer. **2** (*US tramp*) an informer. [BEEF v.¹ (4)/BEEF v.¹ (6)]

beef gravy *n.* [1980s+] (*US gay*) semen (cf. BABY GRAVY n.). [BEEF n.¹ (1) + SE *gravy*/GRAVY n.¹ (2)]

beef-head *n.* **1** [late 18C–early 19C] a fool, a simpleton (cf. APPLEHEAD n.). **2** [19C] (*US*) a Texan, a cowboy. **3** [1980s] (*UK Black*) a skinhead, usu. synon. with a member of a right-wing/racist party. [SE *beef* + -HEAD sfx (1)]

beef-headed *adj.* [mid-19C+] (*US*) stupid, foolish (cf. APPLEHEAD n.; BEEF-WITTED adj.). [BEEF-HEAD n. (1)]

beef-heart *n.* **1** [1910s–70s] a bean. **2** [1950s+] a fart. [(1) loose rhy. sl. and the presumed effect; (2) true rhy. sl.]

beef injection *n.* (*also* **hot beef injection/incision**) [1980s+] (*orig. US*) **1** sexual intercourse; thus *slip one the hot beef*, to have sexual intercourse from the male point of view. **2** a penis (cf. BACON n.¹). [BEEF n.¹ (1) + SE *injection/incision*]

beef it *v.* [19C] to eat heartily. [SE *beef*, as a symbol of the ultimate in consumption]

beef it out *v.* [1900s–20s] (*Aus.*) to call or sing, occas. to play, loudly and enthusiastically. [BEEF v.¹ (8)]

beefo *adj.* [1950s] well-built, muscled, physically solid. [BEEF n.¹ (4) + -o sfx]

beefsteak eye *n.* [1950s–70s] (*US*) a black eye. [the practice of putting raw steak on a black eye]

beef torpedo *n.* [2000s] (*US*) the penis. [BEEF n.¹ (1) + TORPEDO n.³]

beef to the heel *n.* [late 19C–1920s] a bulky, heavy-set woman, usu. of a countrywoman. [BEEF TO THE HEEL(S) adj.]

beef to the heel(s) *adj.* [20C+] bulky, brawny, stocky, esp. of thick, strong legs or thick female ankles. [BEEF n.¹ (3)]

beef trust *n.* [1940s+] (*US*) an obese person, a group of obese people. [BEEF n.¹ (3)/ironic use of SE *beef trust*, a conglomerate of beef producers/processors; orig. late 19C carnival use, created by showman W.B. 'Billy' Watson, who thus named his sideshow of grotesquely overweight women]

beef tube *n.* [1950s] (*orig. US*) the penis. [SE *beef*/BEEF n.¹ (1) + SE *tube*]

beef-tugging *n.* [late 19C–1900s] (*London*) eating at City cafés and restaurants. [SE; the indigestibility of the tough meat served there]

beef up *v.* [1940s+] **1** (*also* **beef**) to strengthen, to improve. **2** to put on weight and/or muscles. [i.e. to add SE *beef*/BEEF n.¹ (4)]

beef-witted *adj.* [early 17C] stupid, simple (cf. AIRHEADED adj.; AMOEBA-BRAINED adj.; BEEF-HEADED adj.; BIRD-WITTED adj.; DIM-WITTED adj.; NIMWIT adj.; NITWITTED adj.). [SE *beef* + sfx -*witted*; used by Shakespeare in 1606, the term resurfaced briefly in late 19C, describing 'this British bull-neckedness, this British beef-wittedness']

beefy *adj.* **1** [mid-19C] lucky. **2** [mid-19C+] well-built, muscled, stolid. **3** [mid-19C+] thick, usu. of a woman's ankles or wrists. **4** [1910s+] fleshy, overweight. [BEEF n.¹ (3) + sfx -*y*]

bee-gum *n.* **1** [late 19C–1930s] (*US*) a top hat. **2** [1960s] a hairstyle in which a woman piles her hair on the top of her head. [Southern dial. *bee-gum*, a hollow tree or log used as a beehive]

bee-gum hat *n.* [late 19C] (*US*) a tall hat. [for ety. *see* prev.]

beehive *n.*¹ [late 19C–1930s] the vagina (cf. BAG n.¹). [the implication is of honey rather than stings]

beehive *n.*² **1** [1920s+] the number 5. **2** [1960s+] a £5 note (cf. DEEP-SEA DIVER n.²; HALF-A-COCK n.; JACK n.⁴; JACK'S (ALIVE) n.; LADY GODIVA n.; LINCOLN'S INN n.; NUNNY-BUNNY n.; SCUBA (DIVER) n.; SKY-DIVER n.; TINY TIM n.). [rhy. sl.]

beek *n. see* BEAK n.¹ (4).

beel *n.* [1950s] (*W.I., USVI*) a motorcar. [abbr. SE *automobile*]

bee-luther-hatchee *n. see* B LUTHER HATCHETT n.

beemer *n. see* BEAMER n.

been *adj. see* BENE adj.

been there *phr.* **1** [mid-19C+] (*orig. US*) a dismissive phr. used to imply that one has already experienced the so-called 'novelty' of which another person is speaking. **2** [late 19C+] a remark passed by a man on seeing a passing woman with whom (he claims) he has slept.

been there, done that *phr.* [1990s+] used to summarize the assumed youthful ennui of the 1990s; voiced when offered some new stimulus and often ext. with *...got the T-shirt*. [ext. of BEEN THERE phr.; the phr. was adopted in soft-drink advertising of the mid-1990s; the ref. to the *T-shirt* underpins the marketing that accompanies any new cultural phenomenon, esp. mainstream films]

been to see Captain Bates? *phr.* [late 19C] a greeting to a person one knows or suspects has been in prison. [proper name of *Captain Bates*, a well-known London prison governor (cf. BATE'S FARM n.)]

been to three county fairs and a goat-fucking *phr.* (*also* **...and a goat-roping**) [1970s+] (*US, mainly Southern*) a phr. implying one's astonishment (i.e. one has had many, varied experiences, but never one such as this).

beeper *n.* [1980s+] a personal pager.

beeper boy *n.* [1980s+] (*US*) a drug dealer. [from the use of the BEEPER n. in the pre-mobile phone era]

beer *n.* [1960s+] (*US Black/campus*) semen (cf. BABY GRAVY n.).

beer *v.* **1** [late 18C+] to get drunk on beer. **2** [late 19C+] to give someone a beer, usu. in imper. *beer me!* **3** [1910s] to spend one's money on beer. [(1) mid-19C+ use is Aus.]

beer and sarse *n.* [1980s] (*Aus.*) the buttocks (cf. ALA n.). [rhy. sl. = ARSE n.¹ (1); ult. SARSE n.]

beer barn *n.* *see* BOOZE BARN n.

beer barrel *n.* **1** [19C] the stomach. **2** [1940s] a beer drunkard. **3** [1940s+] (*orig. US*) a (beer-drinker's) paunch. **4** [1950s] a fat person.

beer-boep *n.* *see* BOEP n.

beer bong *n.* [1980s] (*US campus*) a device consisting of a funnel attached to a tube, which facilitates the speedier drinking of beer; thus *do a beer bong*, to drink beer through such a device. [SE *beer* + BONG n.¹]

beer-bottle *n.* [late 19C–1900s] a stout, red-faced man. [metonymy]

beer bottle beat *n.* [1970s] (*US*) a client who likes to be beaten by a prostitute who is wielding a beer bottle.

beer bust *n.* [1960s+] (*US*) a drinking party that concentrates on beer. [SE *beer* + BUST n.³ (1)]

beer-buzzer *n.* [late 19C] (*US*) one who frequents saloons in the hope of cadging free beer. [SE *beer* + BUZZ v.³ (3)]

beer-chewer *n.* (*also* **beer-guzzler, ...-sparrer, ...-sucker**) [late 19C+] (*Aus.*) a heavy drinker of beer.

Beer City *n.* (*also* **Beer Town**) [1970s] (*US*) Milwaukee, Wisconsin. [famous for its breweries]

beer-crawl *n.* [20C+] a leisurely progress from public house to public house, drinking 1 or more beers in each. [SE *beer* + CRAWL n. (2)]

beer-eater *n.* [late 19C–1910s] a heavy drinker. [note P.G. Wodehouse: 'It was my uncle George who discovered that alcohol was a food well in advance of modern medical thought' (*The Inimitable Jeeves*, 1923)]

beered up *adj.* [1930s+] (*orig. US*) drunk on beer.

beer goggle *v.* [1980s+] (*US campus*) to find someone attractive because of the influence of alcohol. [BEER GOGGLES n./SE *beer* + GOGGLE (AT) v.]

beer goggles *n.* [1980s+] (*US campus*) blurred vision that follows an excess of (beer) drinking; such vision has the added effect of making hitherto unexciting individuals appear sexually alluring.

beer goitre *n.* [1980s] (*N.Z.*) a beer belly.

beer gut *n.* [1950s+] a paunch, a beer belly.

beer-guzzler *n.* *see* BEER-CHEWER n.

beerhead *n.* (*US*) **1** [1940s] a German. **2** [1970s] a beer drunkard. [SE *beer* + -HEAD sfx (2)/-HEAD sfx (3)]

beer-jerker *n.*¹ [1930s] (*US*) a drunkard. [SE *beer* + JERKER n.¹ (2)]

beer-jerker *n.*² (*also* **beer-slinger, beer-yanker**) [mid-19C+] a bartender who draws beer in a saloon. [SE *beer* + JERKER n.¹ (3)/SLINGER n.¹ (1)/YANK v.¹ (1)]

beer joint *n.* [1920s+] (*US*) a saloon or bar serving primarily beer. [SE *beer* + JOINT n.⁴ (3)]

beer-jugger *n.* [late 19C–1900s] (*US*) a barmaid.

beer keg *n.* *see* KEG n.¹.

beer mill *n.* [late 19C] a saloon that sells beer. [on pattern of GIN-MILL n. (1)]

beer muscle *n.* [1930s–40s] (*US*) a pot belly, engendered by excessive beer-drinking. [the 'muscle' is in fact fat]

beer-o! *excl.* [late 19C] a cry raised by workers when one of their number commits a blunder that has to be paid for by buying their fellows a round of drink. [SE *beer* + -O sfx (7)]

beerocracy *n.* [late 19C] the world of brewers and publicans. [SE *beer* + *aristocracy*]

beer-off *n.* [1930s–70s] an off-licence, a liquor store.

beer pot *n.* [1980s+] a fat stomach caused by a steady intake of beer. [SE *beer* + POT n.⁹]

beer scooter *n.* [1990s+] the process, when very drunk, of making one's way home without knowing what form of transport was employed.

beer-slinger *n.*¹ [mid–late 19C] a regular beer-drinker. [they 'sling it down']

beer-slinger *n.*² *see* BEER-JERKER n.².

beer-sparrer/-sucker *n.* *see* BEER-CHEWER n.

beer's talking *phr.* *see* IT'S THE BEER TALKING phr.

beer street *n.* [late 19C–1900s] the mouth or throat. [fig. street name; note William Hogarth's celebrated engraving of 1751]

beer-swiper *n.* [1910s] (*Aus.*) a drunkard. [SE *beer* + SWIPE v.¹]

beer token *n.* [1990s+] money. [the assumed primacy of alcohol in making a claim on one's wages]

Beer Town *n.* *see* BEER CITY n.

beer-trap *n.* [late 19C–1930s] the mouth. [SE *beer* + SE *trap*/TRAP n.³]

beer-up *n.* [1910s+] (*Aus.*) a riotous, drunken party. [BEER UP v. (2)]

beer up *v.* [late 19C+] **1** to give someone money for beer. **2** to get drunk.

beery *adj.* **1** [mid-19C+] drunk, tipsy. **2** [late 19C] (*US*) of emotions, songs etc, induced by drink.

beer-yanker *n.* *see* BEER-JERKER n.².

beery buff *n.* [20C+] a fool (cf. BEECHAM'S PILL n.). [rhy. sl. = MUFF n.² (1)]

bees (and honey) *n.* (*also* **beesum**) [late 19C+] money (cf. BREAD AND HONEY n.; BROMLEY (BY BOW) n.; BUGS BUNNY n.; CHARLEY ROLLAR n.; COD'S ROE n.; COW AND CALF n.; COW'S (CALF) n.; DOT AND DASH n.; EASTER BUNNY n.¹; GENE TUNNEY n.; HONEY n.⁴; JEMMY O'GOBLIN n.; KANGA n.¹; LOLLY n.⁴; NELSON EDDIES n.; ORANGE SQUASH n.; OSCAR (ASCHE) n.; OXFORD (SCHOLAR) n.; PIE AND MASH n.; POLLY n.⁴; POT OF HONEY n.; ROGAN GOSH n.; SAUCEPAN LID n.; SCREAM AND HOLLAR n.; SHIRT (AND) COLLAR n.; SHOWER BATH n.; SUGAR n.¹; SUGAR AND HONEY n.; TOM (AND FUNNY) n.; TOOT n.²). [rhy. sl.]

bee's knees *n.* (*also* **bee's nuts, pig's scream, sparrow's chirp, turkey's elbow**) [20C+] (*orig. US*) **1** a superior person, or someone who poses as such. **2** the best.

bees'n *n.* [2000s] (*US Black*) an act of relaxation. [SE *be*, v.]

bee-stings *n.* [1960s+] (*orig. US*) small female breasts (cf. BAGS n.¹). [supposedly comparable size]

beesum *n.* *see* BEES (AND HONEY) n.

beeswax *n.*¹ **1** [mid-19C] second-rate, soft cheese. **2** [mid–late 19C] a bore, usu. as *old beeswax*. [(1) is 'full of holes'; (2) puns on SE *bore*, a hole]

beeswax *n.*² **1** [1930s+] (*US*) business; often as *none of your beeswax*. **2** [2000s] flattery, nonsense. [joc. solipsism]

bees wingers *n.* [1960s+] the fingers. [rhy. sl.]

beetle *n.*¹ [1910s–60s] (*US*) an eccentric, a madman, an obsessive fan. [a type of BUG n.⁵ (2)]

beetle *n.*² **1** [1910s+] a horse. **2** [1930s–60s] a young woman, esp. one who dresses in flashy clothes. **3** [1950s] (*UK juv.*) a policeman (cf. ANIMAL n.¹). [ety. unknown; ? she 'beetles' around]

beetle bait *n.* [1940s] (*Aus.*) treacle or golden syrup.

beetle bonnet *n. see* HERBIE'S BONNET *n.*

beetlebrain *n.* (*also* **beetlebrow, gnatbrain**) [17C+] a fool (cf. AIREDALE *n.*; BAKEBRAIN *n.*). [SE *beetle*, an instrument used in various industrial applications to drive, wedge, flatten or ram, used in combs. to imply dullness, heaviness or stupidity + sfx *-brain*]

beetle-case *n.* [mid–late 19C] a large boot or shoe.

beetle-crusher *n.* [mid-19C+] **1** the foot. **2** (*also* **grasshopper crusher**) a shoe, esp. a large, heavy boot, often as worn by labourers, the police or the army. **3** (*UK juv.*) a policeman (cf. BEAT-POUNDER *n.*). **4** a horse with large feet.

beetle fat *n.* [1950s] (*UK juv.*) bubble gum.

beetle-head *n.* [16C–18C; 1940s–50s] a fool; *beetle-headed*, stupid (cf. AIREDALE *n.*). [SE *beetle* + -HEAD sfx (1); 1940s–50s use US]

beetle off *v.* [1920s+] (*orig. RAF*) to leave, to wander off; thus *beetle in, beetle up*, to arrive. [the orig. image was of flying directly (as a beetle flies) back to base]

beetle's blood *n.* [1920s–30s] (*Anglo-Irish*) stout beer. [the *beetle*, like the beer, is black]

beetle-squasher *n.* [mid-19C] the foot; a shoe.

beetle-sticker *n.* [mid–late 19C] an entomologist. [the mounting of specimens]

beetroot mug *n.* [late 19C–1910s] a red face. [MUG n.[1] (2); ? coined by Charles Ross, creator, *c.*1867, of the comic character Ally Sloper, a dissipated-looking old man with a red and swollen nose. Poss. the orig. of SE phr. *red as a beetroot*]

beevos *n.* [1970s] (*US campus*) beer. [BEVVY n. (1)]

beeze *n.* [1940s] the penis. [ety. unknown; ? obs. SE *bezel*, a cutting tool]

beezer *n.*[1] **1** [20C+] (*orig. US boxing*) the nose. **2** [1910s+] (*orig. US*) the head, the face.

beezer *n.*[2] [1910s+] something or someone excellent; the best example. [ety. unknown]

beezer *n.*[3] [1920s–40s] a 'fellow', a 'chap'. [? BUGGER n.[1] (1) + GEEZER n.[1] (1)]

beezer *adj.* [1930s+] very attractive, excellent. [BEEZER n.[2]]

bef *adj.* [1940s+] (*W.I.*) stupid, useless. [? Scot. *beff*, a fool, a stupid person]

be farts and cell partners *n.* [2000s] (*US prison*) a meal of beans and frankfurters. [assonance; *beans* make you fart while frankfurters are their 'partners' in the tin]

befogged *adj. see* FOGGED *adj.* (1).

befok *adj.* [1970s+] (*S.Afr.*) **1** of people, unhappy, lacking in good sense, crazy, exhausted. **2** of objects, ruined, spoiled, out of order. [Afk. *befok*, FUCKED *adj.*[1]]

befoozeled *adj. see* FOOZLED *adj.* (3).

before Abe *n.* [1940s] (*US Black/Harlem*) **1** the era of slavery; the period before Emancipation. **2** in fig. use, work, a regular job. [for Afro-Americans any time before 1 January 1863, when President *Abraham* Lincoln signed the Emancipation Proclamation; (2) plays on SLAVE n. (2)]

before Abe jive *n.* [1940s] (*US Black/Harlem*) hard, thankless work. [BEFORE ABE n. (2) + JIVE n.[1] (4)]

before day creep *n.* [1920s–40s] (*US Black*) a surreptitious late-night or early-morning visit to one's lover. [SE *before day*(*break*) + CREEP v. (4)]

before one can say Jack Robinson *phr.* (*also* **before one can say Jack Robertson, before one could say Jack Robinson, while one could…, quicker than you can…**) [late 18C+] instantly, at once, very quickly. [there is no specific *Jack Robinson*; perhaps it was a minor tongue-twister]

before one was dry behind the ears *phr. see* WET BEHIND THE EARS *phr.*

before you could say winking *phr. see* LIKE WINKING *adv.*

beg act *n.* [1940s] (*US Black/Harlem*) an attempt to obtain money.

begad! *excl.* [mid-18C+] a mild, if once blasphemous oath, lit. 'by God!' [GAD n.[1]]

beg for a piece *v.* (*also* **chase a piece, get…, look for…**) [20C+] (*W.I.*) to pursue a woman for sex. [SE *beg/chase/get/look for* + PIECE n.[1] (1)]

beggar *n.* [mid-19C+] **1** a man, a person, used both negatively, e.g. *a nasty-looking beggar*, and positively or affectionately, e.g. *you're a funny beggar*. **2** a thing, an object, a creature.

beggar boy's (ass) *n.* **1** [late 19C+] money. **2** [1930s+] Bass ale. [note this is the UK SE *ass*, donkey, not ASS n. or ARSE n.[1]]

beggared *adj.* [mid-19C+] a euph. for BUGGERED adj.[1]; thus *I'll be beggared if…*

beggar (for) *n.* (*also* **beggar to**) [mid-19C+] an exemplar, an enthusiast, one who is keen on, e.g. *a beggar for work, a beggar to argue*. [they lit. *beg for* the subject]

beggar-maker *n.* [late 18C–early 19C] a publican. [their depriving people of money]

beggar my neighbour *phr.* [1920s+] visiting the labour exchange/unemployment office to draw unemployment benefit. [rhy. sl. = *on the labour*]

beggars *n.* [19C–1900s] in card-playing, the numbered cards, marked 2–10. [they are inferior to the 'court' cards]

beggar's benison! *excl.* [late 18C–early 19C] a popular toast before drinking. [SE *beggar* + *benison*, blessing, i.e. MAY YOUR PRICK AND PURSE NEVER FAIL YOU! excl.]

beggar's bolts *n.* [late 16C] stones. [SE *beggar* + *bolt*, an arrow; thus a projectile]

beggar's bullets *n.* [late 18C] stones. [poverty deprives the beggar of an actual weapon]

beggar's lagging *n.* [1940s–50s] (*UK prison*) a sentence of 90 days' imprisonment, commonly that meted out for vagrancy. [SE *beggar* + LAGGING n. (2)]

beggar's plush *n.* [late 17C] corduroy, cotton velvet. [SE *beggar* + *plush*, a kind of cloth having a nap longer and softer than that of velvet; used for rich garments, e.g. footmen's liveries]

beggar's velvet *n.* [mid-19C] particles of lint and similar household dirt that gather behind or beneath sofas, tables or beds (often following the shaking of an eiderdown).

beggar to *n. see* BEGGAR (FOR) *n.*

begger off *v. see* BUGGER OFF *v.*

begging *adj.* [2000s] (*UK Black*) aspiring, envious, e.g. *begging Black*, used of White people attempting to emulate a Black lifestyle, also of envy of another's ability, possession, appearance etc.

begging for it *phr.* [1950s+] a male comment on a woman who, supposedly if not actually, is inflamed with lust (cf. GAGGING FOR adj.). [SE *beg* + *it*/IT n.[1] (1)]

begin on *v.* (*also* **begin upon**) [early–mid-19C] (*orig. US*) to attack verbally.

begonia *n.* [1970s+] (*US Black gay*) a term for a fellow Black homosexual. [identification of homosexuality with flowers/shrubs]

be good *phr.* [20C+] a joc. phr. used on parting; often ext. by *if you can't be good, be careful!*, which in itself can be ext. by *if you can't be careful, buy a pram!*

begorra! *excl.* (*also* **begor! begorry!**) [mid-17C+] by God! not invariably Irish but the clichéd expletive of each and every stage Irishman yet created.

begosh! *excl. see* BY GOSH! *excl.*

begum *n.* [mid-19C–1900s] (*Anglo-Ind.*) a rich widow. [Urdu *begam*, a queen, princess, or lady of high rank]

beg up a storm *v. see* TALK UP A STORM *v.*

beg your pardon *n.* [late 19C] a garden. [rhy. sl.]

behave foundry *n.* [1900s] (*US*) a prison.

behave local *v.* [20C+] (*W.I.*) to act in a crude, unsophisticated manner. [SE *behave* + *local*, rough, of inferior quality]

behavish *adj.* [1980s+] (*US Black*) badly behaved. [SE *behave* + sfx *-ish*, of the nature or character of]

behind *n.* **1** [mid-16C+] the buttocks, the posterior (cf. ARSE-END n.). **2** [late 19C+] anthropomorphically, the back of an object, e.g. a car, a bus; thus *adv.*, working as a bus conductor.

behind *adv.* **1** [1930s+] (*orig. US*) involved with, concerned about, believing in. **2** [1950s+] (*US Black*) as a result of, as a consequence of, in reference to. **3** [1960s+] (*orig. US*) in full understanding of. **4** [1970s] (*orig. US*) excited by, obsessed with.

behind a dime *phr.* [1980s+] (*US*) to any extent, under any circumstances; usu. in phr. *I wouldn't trust (someone) behind a dime*. [SAmE *dime*, the tiny 10-cent coin; i.e. there is no way such a person can 'hide']

behindativeness *n.* [late 19C] a large dress-pannier, fashionably affixed to a lady's dress *c.*1888. [SE *behind*/BEHIND n. (2) + sfx *-ative*, tending to point out]

behind God Speed *phr. see* BACK OF GOD SPEED phr.

behind-kicking *n. see* ASS-KICKING n.

behind like a slave-driver *phr.* (*also* **behind like a tak-tak**) [20C+] (*W.I.*) begging, harassing, pressurizing. [the *tak-tak* or *acoushi* ant, a fierce pest]

behind one's door *phr.* [1950s+] (*UK prison*) locked up in solitary confinement; also as an order, *behind your doors*, 'get into your cells'.

behind oneself *phr.* [late 19C] out-of-date, out-of-fashion, not up with the latest situation. [SE *behind*, backward]

behind the behind *n.* [1930s] sodomy. [SE *behind* + BEHIND n. (1)]

behind the eight ball *phr.* [1930s+] (*orig. US*) in trouble, in a difficult situation. [pool imagery]

behind the parade *phr.* [1920s+] (*orig. US Black*) old-fashioned, passé.

behind the ramp *phr.* [1980s] a phr. used of anyone in authority, esp. a police officer or prison warder. [the *ramp* implies some form of desk]

behind the scales *phr.* (*also* **behind the scale**) [1980s+] (*US Black*) at a drug seller's place of business, thus in general the weighing and selling of the drug. [drugs are bought in bulk then weighed out in smaller measures for sale; the image is of a small shopkeeper behind the counter]

behind the walls *phr.* (*also* **inside the walls**) [20C+] (*US Und.*) in prison.

behind with the rent *phr.* [2000s] homosexual. [pun on BEHIND n. (1) + RENT n.² + rhy. sl. = BENT adj. (5)]

beige *n.* [1940s+] (*US Black*) a light-skinned Black person. [SE *beige*, yellowish-grey]

beige *adj.* [1980s+] (*US*) deeply tedious, very bland. [the perceived blandness of the colour *beige*]

beige frame *n.* [1950s] (*US Black*) 'smooth brown skinned girls, girls with heavy tan' (Durst, *The Jives of Dr Hepcat*, 1953). [BEIGE n. + FRAME n.¹ (1)]

beiging *n.* [1980s+] (*drugs*) a process that alters the colour of cocaine to light brown, thus making it appear purer than it actually is. [SE *beige*]

be-in *n.* [1960s] (*orig. US*) a gathering of young people, usu. hippies, for mutual admiration, smoking cannabis and listening to music. [play on SE *be in* (*touch*)/*being*; taken from the original *Human Be-in* at Golden Gate Park, San Francisco, 1967; the *-in* sfx ext. to include *fuck-in, smoke-in, love-in, sit-in* etc]

being poor *n.* [1960s] (*bingo*) the number 4 (cf. ALDERSHOT LADIES n.). [rhy. sl.]

bejabers, the *n.* (*also* **the bejabbers**) [1950s+] a euph. for HELL, THE phr.¹ (2), the essence, the 'life', e.g. *beat the bejabers out of.* [BEJABERS! excl.]

bejabers! *excl.* (*also* **bejabbers!**) [late 18C+] a mild excl., lit. BY JESUS! excl.

bejazus, the *n.* (*also* **the baby Jesus, the bejasus, the bejeesus, the bejeezus, the bejesus, the bejeysus, the bloody Jesus, the Jesus, the living Jesus, the plazazus**) [20C+] the

life, the 'daylights'; esp. in phr. *beat/kick/knock the bejazus out of.* [BEJAZUS! excl.]

bejazus! *excl.* [late 19C+] a mild excl., lit. BY JESUS! excl.

bejesus *adj.* [late 19C+] (*US*) a general intensifier, esp. with implications of assurance, arrogance. [BEJAZUS! excl.]

bejeysus, the *n. see* BEJAZUS, THE n.

belagot *n.* [1940s+] (*W.I.*) a large iron pot, used for cooking cow-tripes after butchering. [dial *belagot*, tripes; lit. *belly-gut*]

belch *n.*¹ **1** [late 17C–mid-19C] second-rate beer. **2** [late 17C–mid-19C] malt liquor. **3** [1930s] (*US*) a drunken vagrant. [the effects of the beer]

belch *n.*² [late 19C–1960s] (*US*) a noisy complaint. [SE *belch*, an eructation]

belch *v.* [20C+] (*US*) **1** to complain; thus *belcher*, a whinger. **2** to inform on. [BELCH n.²]

belcher *n.*¹ **1** [early–mid-19C] (*also* **belcher fogle**) a coster-monger's handkerchief, usu. blue with white or occas. yellow spots. **2** [mid-19C] a thick ring. [the boxer Jim *Belcher* (d.1811), whose preferred adornments these were; since the 19C a *belcher* can be any spotted handkerchief]

belcher *n.*² [mid–late 19C] orig. showman's use, a dedicated beer-drinker. [BELCH n.¹ (1)]

belcher *n.*³ [1900s–60s] (*US Und.*) **1** an informer. **2** a complainant. [BELCH v.]

belcher fogle *n. see* BELCHER n.¹ (1).

belfa *n.* (*also* **bellfa, bilfa**) [late 17C–early 18C] a prostitute. [? Fr. *belle*, beautiful]

belfry *n.* [20C+] the head. [backform. f. HAVE BATS IN THE BELFRY v.]

Belgie *n.* [1910s+] a *Belg*ian. [abbr.; note a single early 17C SE use]

believer *n.* [1920s+] (*US*) a gullible person, one who will believe whatever they are told; thus *make a believer* (*out of*), to convince.

bell *n.*¹ **1** [late 16C] the penis. **2** [1980s+] the clitoris (cf. BABY IN THE BOAT n.).

bell *n.*² [19C+] o'clock, usu. in pl., e.g. *eight bells*, 8 o'clock. [naut. use; a bell was struck to indicate the change in the day's watches]

bell *n.*³ [mid-19C] a song.

bell *n.*⁴ [1960s] (*US Black*) personal notoriety, reputation. [the image of a *bell* around a cat's neck, announcing its imminent arrival]

bell *n.*⁵ [1970s] (*US*) **1** a hotel doorman. **2** a bellboy. [? abbr. *bell captain*]

bell *n.*⁶ *see* BELL END n.

bell *n.*⁷ *see* BUTTON n.¹ (3).

bell *n.*⁸ *see* GIVE SOMEONE A BELL v.

bell *v.* (*also* **bell up**) [1970s+] to call on the telephone. [backform. f. GIVE SOMEONE A BELL v.]

bell-bastard *n.* [late 19C] the bastard child of a bastard mother. [? pfx *bel*, indicating relationship, as used in SE *belfader, beldame*, grandfather, grandmother]

bell cow *n.* [19C] (*US*) a leader, a boss. [rural *bell cow*, the lead cow or ox, which wears a bell and is the herd leader]

belle *n.* [1930s+] (*gay*) a good-looking, young homosexual man. [Fr. *belle*, a beautiful woman]

belle-chose *n.* [late 14C] a lit. euph. for the vagina (cf. BEAUTY SPOT n.). [Fr. *belle chose*, a beautiful thing; coined by Geoffrey Chaucer (*c.*1345–1400)]

belled up *adj.* [1970s] in possession of a burglar alarm.

bell end *n.* (*also* **bell, bell ender**) **1** [1980s+] the tip of the penis. **2** [1990s+] a general term of abuse (cf. CHOAD n.; DONGER n.¹; HANG-OUT n.²; KNOB n.¹; NUDGER n.; PECKER n.²; PLONKER n.; SCHNITZEL n.). [the shape]

beller *n.* [1970s] (*US*) a loud laugh. [it 'rings out']

beller-croaker *adj.* [mid–late 19C] noticeably beautiful, outstandingly attractive. [Fr. *belle à croquer*, beautiful enough to command desire]

bellers *n. see* BELLOWS n. (1).

bellfa n. see BELFA n.

bellhop n. (also **bellhopper**) [20C+] (US) a hotel doorman, a bell-boy. [they 'hop to it' when the desk clerk rings the bell]

bellibone n. [1910s–20s] a well-dressed young woman. [Fr. belle et bonne, beautiful and good]

bellier n. **1** [early 19C] a punch to the belly. **2** [1920s] a 'belly-flop' dive (cf. ASS-BREAKER n.). [lit. 'belly-er']

bellies in blue n. see BOYS IN BLUE n.

bellies to the bar! excl. see BELLY UP adj.[2] (2).

belling n. [late 19C] the head of the penis. [the shape of a bell]

bellman n. [1970s+] (UK Und.) the criminal specialist who silences electronic alarm systems.

bellower n. [late 18C–early 19C] a town crier. [SE bellow, to shout loudly]

bellows n. **1** [early 17C–1920s] (also **bellers**) the lungs. **2** [late 18C] the male genitals. [SE bellows, 'an instrument or machine constructed to furnish a strong blast of air' (OED); (1) 20C use mainly US]

bellowsed adj.[1] [mid-19C] out of breath. [BELLOWS n. (1)]

bellowsed adj.[2] [mid-19C] transported as a convict. [? 'blown away' (across the sea) or see BELLOWSER n.[2]]

bellowser n.[1] [early 19C] a punch in the stomach, a 'blow in the wind'; thus bellowsing, winding in order to kill. [BELLOWS n. (1)]

bellowser n.[2] [early–mid-19C] (Aus./UK Und.) a sentence of lifetime transportation; thus knap/nap a bellowser, to be transported for life. [such a sentence 'takes one's breath away']

bellows to mend phr. [late 18C–1910s] used to describe a broken-winded horse or human. [play on SE phr./BELLOWS n. (1)]

bell-ringer n. [1930s–60s] (US) a great success. [the fairground attraction in which one proves one's strength by hammering on a spring and, if successful, ringing a bell]

bell ringers n. [20C+] the fingers. [rhy. sl.]

bell rope n.[1] [mid-19C] a fashionable hairstyle in which men wore their hair twisted into 2 ropes, on each side of the face. [pun, such a hairstyle is designed to 'draw the belles']

bell rope n.[2] [1960s–70s] (US) the penis. [it gets 'pulled']

bells n.[1] [1940s–50s] (US Black) an expression of approval; in phrs. that rings my bells, I hear bells. [? abbr. wedding bells, or phr. you ring my bell]

bells n.[2] [1940s+] bell-bottomed trousers. [abbr.]

bells n.[3] [1970s] the female breasts (cf. BAGS n.[1]). [supposed resemblance]

bells n.[4] see BELL n.[2].

bells! excl. [1920s+] (orig. US Black) a general excl. of alarm, anger, surprise. [abbr. HELL'S BELLS! excl.]

bells and whistles n. [1960s+] (orig. US) embellishments, gimmicks, esp. used in advertising copy to 'talk up' a product that, bereft of such add-ons, would have little to offer over its peers.

bellswagger n. (also **belswagger**) **1** [late 16C–mid-18C] a womanizer, a pimp (cf. ABBOT ON THE CROSS n.). **2** [late 16C–early 19C] a noisy braggart, a bully. [one who 'swaggers his belly'; Nares cites one 'St. Belswagger of Mims' but cannot offer any information on 'the history of this canonised person']

bell the cat v. [18C] to undertake something dangerous. [the nursery tale; SE f. 1800]

bell-topped adj. [late 19C+] describing a penis that is larger at the top than it is at the base. [the shape]

bell-topper n. [mid-19C–1940s] (Aus./N.Z.) a top hat. [SE bell + TOPPER n.[3] (2)]

bell tower n. [1990s+] the shaft of the penis. [play on BELL END n.]

bell up v. see BELL v.

bell-wether n. **1** [mid-15C–mid-18C] the leader of a mob. **2** [mid-15C–19C] a very noisy man. [SE bell-wether, the leading sheep of a flock, on whose neck a bell is hung]

belly n.[1] [1920s–60s] (US) bravery, courage. [var. on GUTS n.[2] (1)]

belly n.[2] see BELLY LAUGH n. (2).

belly-ache n. [mid-19C+] a stomach-ache. [SE 16C–early 19C]

bellyache n. [1930s+] a complaint, a moan, whingeing. [BELLYACHE v.; note WW1 Aus. milit. belly-ache, a fatal wound]

bellyache v. [late 19C+] to complain, to moan. [play on SE]

belly-acher n. [1930s+] a whinger, a whiner. [BELLYACHE v.]

bellyaching n. [1920s+] complaining, whingeing. [BELLYACHE v.]

belly and back adv. [20C+] (W.I., Guyn.) utterly, completely, ruthlessly. [lit. 'on both sides']

belly-bachelor n. [20C+] (Irish) a man whose amorous pursuits are determined by the income of each potential women. [a rich wife will help pay the food bills]

belly-band n. [late 19C–1920s] a wide belt, a corset. [SE belly-band, the strap that passes round the belly of a horse in harness]

belly-bomber n. [1980s+] (US) a hamburger, esp. when particularly greasy.

belly-booster adv. see BELLYFLOP adv.

belly-bottom concrete n. [1950s+] (W.I.) a very large, round boiled dumpling. [its weight and consistency]

belly-bound adj. [17C–19C] usu. of horses, constipated. [SE belly + bound, constipated]

belly bristles n. [19C] pubic hair.

belly bump v. **1** [late 19C+] (also **belly bust**) to have sexual intercourse; one of a number of terms relating to the proximity of bits of the anatomy during the act (cf. BALL SLAP v.; BUMP BELLIES v.; BUMP FUZZ v.; BUMP PUSSIES v.; BUMP UGLIES v.; DO A BIT OF GIBLET PIE v.; DO A JUMBLE-GIBLETS v.; DO A PLASTER OF WARM GUTS v.; GO BELLY-BUMPING v.; GO TAIL-TICKLING v.; GO TUMMY TICKLING v.; JOIN GIBLETS v.; JOIN PAUNCHES v.; NAIL TWO WAMES TOGETHER v.; PLAY AT BELLY-TO-BELLY v.; RUB BELLIES v.; WRIGGLE NAVELS v.). **2** [1910s] (US) to slide downhill, face-down on a sledge. [for (1) note the saucily punning ballad 'The Maiden's Choice' (1755) 'And the tune that he plays is called belly pat']

belly-bump adv. see BELLYFLOP adv.

belly bumper n. [19C] a womanizer, a promiscuous man. [BELLY BUMP v. (1)]

belly-bumper adv. see BELLYFLOP adv.

belly burglar n. (also **belly robber**) [20C+] (Can./US) a cook or steward. [orig. milit. jargon, f. the trad. meanness of cooks]

belly bust v. see BELLY BUMP v. (1).

belly-buster n. **1** [20C+] (Aus./US) (also **belly-smacker**) a dive that knocks the wind from the diver (cf. ASS-BREAKER n.). **2** [1960s+] a belly-laugh. **3** [1980s+] (US) a large hero sandwich or 'submarine'. **4** [1980s+] (US) a very funny joke. [SE belly + BURSTER n.[4]]

belly-buster adv. see BELLYFLOP adv.

belly button n. [mid-19C+] (esp. juv.) the navel; thus my belly button is playing hell with my backbone, I am very hungry.

belly cheat n. (also **belly chete**) **1** [mid-16C–mid-19C] (UK Und.) an apron. **2** [early 17C] food. **3** [early 19C] padding worn by a woman in the hope of counterfeiting pregnancy. [SE belly + (1) and (2) CHEAT n. (1), lit. 'stomach thing'; (3) SE cheat]

belly cheater n. [1910s+] (US) a cook.

belly chere n. (also **belly cheer**) [mid-16C–mid-17C] food; thus belly-cheering, eating and drinking.

belly chete n. see BELLY CHEAT n.

belly dale n. [late 19C] the vagina (cf. AGREEABLE RUTS OF LIFE n.; BEAUTY SPOT n.). [SE belly + dale, a (river) valley]

belly dingle n. [late 19C] the vagina (cf. AGREEABLE RUTS OF LIFE n.). [SE belly + dingle, a wooded hollow, a deep narrow cleft between hills]

belly entrance n. [late 19C] the vagina; one of a number of terms relating to an entrance (cf. ENTRANCE n.; FORECASTER n.; FORECASTLE n.; FORE-COURT n.; FOREDECK n.; FOREGUT n.; FORE-HATCH n.; FORE-ROOM n.; FOREWOMAN n.; FRONT ATTIC n.; FRONT

BOTTOM n.; FRONT BUM n.; FRONT ENTRANCE n.; FRONT GARDEN n.; FRONT GUT n.; FRONT PARLOUR n.; FRONT ROOM n.; FRONT WINDOW n.; GATE OF HORN n.; GATE OF LIFE n.; GUT ENTRANCE n.; IVORY GATE n.; UNDER-ENTRANCE n.; WATER-GATE n.; WAY-IN n.].

belly fiddle n. [1900s–40s] (US Black) a guitar. [the normal fiddle or violin is held beneath the chin, while the guitar is strapped across the stomach]

belly-flapper adv. see BELLYFLOP adv.

bellyflop n. (also belly-flopper, belly-thumper) [1920s+] a dive in which one lands flat on the belly (and, in extreme circumstances, winds oneself), rather than cutting through the water; also used fig. (cf. ASS-BREAKER n.).

bellyflop v. [1920s+] to throw oneself down, to collapse; to fail badly. [fig. use of BELLYFLOP n.]

bellyflop adv. (also belly-booster, belly-bump, belly-bumper, belly-buster, belly-flapper, belly-gut) [20C+] (US) of sliding down a hill on a sledge, face-downwards.

belly-flopper n. see BELLYFLOP n.

belly-fucker n. [1970s+] (US gay) 1 a homosexual man attracted to men with taut stomachs. 2 a homosexual man who achieves ejaculation by rubbing his penis on his partner's stomach. [SE belly + FUCK v.[1]]

bellyful n.[1] (also bellyfull) [late 14C+] a sufficiency (the implication is of 'more than enough'), whether of food or drink or something else which the subject has lost patience with/interest in through repetition; often as have a bellyful of. [ext. of SE use; rendered colloq. only because belly itself is considered coarse]

bellyful n.[2] [mid-17C–1920s] a thrashing. [one has a bellyful of pain]

belly full and behind drunk phr. [20C+] (W.I.) immobile, incapable of movement after a large meal and a good deal to drink. [BEHIND n. (1)]

belly furniture n. [mid-17C] food. [SE belly + furniture; that with which something is stocked or filled; contents]

belly-go-firster n. (also belly-go-fister, belly-go-fuster) [early–mid-19C] a blow to the stomach, esp. one given with no warning, or at the start of a fight.

belly grease n. [1930s] (US) hard liquor. [lit. 'stomach-fat']

belly-grunting n. [1920s+] (Aus.) a bad stomach-ache. [one 'grunts' with pain]

belly gun n. [1920s+] (orig. US) a small gun that is most effective when fired at short range, esp. when aimed at a victim's abdomen. [such a gun can be tucked into one's waistband and/or pressed against the victim's waist]

belly-gut n. [mid-16C–mid-18C] a greedy, lazy person. [the greediness is implied in the redup., lit. 'stomach-stomach']

belly-gut adv. see BELLYFLOP adv.

belly habit n. [1940s+] (drugs) pains in the stomach that may accompany withdrawal from continued heroin use. [SE belly + HABIT n. (3)]

belly laugh n. [1920s+] 1 (also belly-shaking laugh) a deep, sonorous laugh. 2 (also belly) a joke. [it appears to come from deep in the stomach]

belly-paunch n. [mid-16C–17C] a glutton. [var. on BELLY-GUT n.]

belly-piece n.[1] [17C] a prostitute, a mistress (cf. BANGTAIL n.[1]). [SE belly + piece; but note PIECE n.[1] (1)]

belly-piece n.[2] [17C–18C] an apron. [SE belly + piece]

belly-plea. n. [18C] a plea, offered by a female criminal facing the death sentence, that since she is pregnant, the law should spare her unborn child's life; thus plead one's belly, to make such an entreaty.

belly queen n. [1960s+] (US gay) 1 a homosexual man who enjoys face-to-face intercourse, usu. between the partner's thighs. 2 one who rubs his penis on his partner's stomach to produce ejaculation. 3 one who only likes partners with flat, hard stomachs. [SE belly + QUEEN n.[2] (1)/QUEEN sfx (2)]

belly robber n. see BELLY BURGLAR n.

belly-robbing adj. [1920s] (US tramp) cheating, extortionate. [the assumption that one's money is needed for food]

belly rub n. [1920s+] (US) a dance. [BELLY RUB v.]

belly rub v. [1920s+] (US) to dance close to one's partner.

belly ruffian n. (also ruffian) [late 17C–19C] the penis. [affectionate play on SE]

belly-shaking laugh n. see BELLY LAUGH n. (1).

belly-smacker n. see BELLY-BUSTER n. (1).

belly-thumper n. see BELLYFLOP n.

belly-timber n. (also tummy-timber) [early 17C–19C] food. [SE belly + timber, the 'stuff' of which a person is made]

belly up adj.[1] [17C–1900s] of a woman, pregnant. [the shape of her stomach]

belly up adj.[2] 1 [1920s+] failed, finished, esp. bankrupt; usu. prefaced by go. 2 [1930s+] dead. 3 [1970s+] drunk. [resembling a dead fish]

belly up v. [1980s+] (US) to die. [BELLY UP adj.[2] (2)]

belly up! excl. (also bellies to the bar! belly up to the bar!) [1920s–30s] (Can./US) the drinks are on the house! [BELLY UP TO v.]

belly up to v. [20C+] to move straight towards, to approach directly. [the pushing forward of one's stomach]

belly vengeance n. [mid-19C] weak, sour beer, often the cause of stomach upsets; thus the stomach upset itself (cf. SCREW-BELLY n.). [East Anglian dial. bellywengins]

belly wash n.[1] (US) 1 [late 19C–1960s] a soft drink. 2 [1900s–30s] a weak or bad alcoholic drink. 3 [1930s–40s] soup. [SE belly + wash, kitchen swill, liquid food for animals]

belly wash n.[2] [late 19C+] (US) nonsense. [fig. use of BELLY WASH n.[1]]

belly-washer n.[1] [20C+] (US) 1 a soft drink. 2 wine. [BELLY WASH n.[1]]

belly-washer n.[2] [1960s–70s] (US) a dive in which one lands flat on the belly (and, in extreme circumstances, winds oneself), rather than cutting through the water (cf. ASS-BREAKER n.).

belly whiskers n. [late 19C] female pubic hair.

belly-whopper n. [1910s+] (US) a dive, usu. into water, but also onto the ground (cf. ASS-BREAKER n.). [SE belly + WHOP! excl.]

belly-woman n. [1950s+] (W.I.) 1 an unmarried pregnant woman. 2 in fig. use, a cutlass with a rounded blade.

belonger n. [1990s+] a person of African descent living in the West Indies. [? the value of African roots to a perceived sense of Blackness]

belong to Greater London v. [late 19C] to be well known in the metropolis. [a play on SE Greater London, the suburbs immediately surrounding the capital and included with the central districts when assessing its population]

below Nathaniel phr. [late 19C–1910s] even further down than hell. [Nathaniel, Satan (Ware) or f. rhy. sl. Nathaniel = hell (E.P.)]

below par adj. 1 [19C+] unwell, emotionally low. 2 [1900s] less than successful. 3 [1920s] of less than average intelligence. [Stock Exchange jargon below par, at a discount]

below the belt phr. [late 19C] underhand, illegal, cheating. [boxing use, which declares such blows as foul; 20C+ use is SE]

below the mahogany phr. [20C+] drunk. [the MAHOGANY n.[2] (2), beneath which the drinker has slipped]

bel-shangle n. [late 16C–early 17C] a fool. [? SE bell-jangler; a fool capering with cap and bells]

belswagger n. see BELLSWAGGER n.

belt n.[1] 1 [mid-19C+] a blow, a hit, a punch. 2 [1930s+] (drugs) the immediate effect of a drug, usu. one that has been injected. 3 [1930s+] a thrill. 4 [1940s–60s] an act of sexual intercourse. 5 [1950s] (Aus.) a prostitute. 6 [1950s] a sexually appealing woman. 7 [1950s] (US) a try, an attempt. [(1) BELT v.[1] (1); subseq. defs. all fig. uses of (1)]

belt n.[2] (orig. US) 1 [1920s+] a drink of, a swig or swallow of, e.g.

a belt of coffee. **2** [1940s–60s] a measure of marijuana or any other drug. [BELT v.¹ (2)]

belt v.¹ **1** [early 19C+] (*also* **belt up**) to hit (with a fist), to flog, to thrash. **2** [mid-19C+] to drink heavily, esp. straight from the bottle. **3** [late 19C+] (*also* **belt along**) to rush, to hurry. **4** [1960s] to trounce, to defeat soundly. **5** [1960s+] of a man, to have sexual intercourse (cf. BANG v.¹). [(1) f. to hit with a belt; subseq. defs. all fig. uses of (1)]

belt v.² *see* BELT (IT) v.

belt down v. [20C+] to rain very hard. [BELT v.¹ (1)]

belter n.¹ [1900s] a prostitute. [? BELT n.¹ (1)/BELT n.¹ (4)]

belter n.² [1950s+] **1** an admirable, exciting, or exceptional person. **2** something exceptional, exciting, amusing etc. [northern dial. *belter*, a heavy blow or series of blows]

belter n.³ [1950s+] **1** a boisterous, energetic singer. **2** a loud, emotional and melodramatic song. [BELT (IT) v.]

Belteshazzar's off-ox n. [mid-19C+] a headstrong person. [also see Dan. 4:8–27, in which Daniel, also known as Belteshazzar, foretells Nebuchadnezzar's decline into a state of ox-like stupidity]

belting n. [19C+] a beating. [BELT v.¹ (1)]

belting adj. [1950s+] excellent, very good of its type. [fig. use of BELT v.¹ (1)]

beltinker n. [late 19C] a beating, a thrashing. [? BELT v.¹ (1), i.e. a *belting*]

belt (it) v. (*also* **belt it out**) [1950s+] to sing loudly and enthusiastically. [BELT v.¹ (1); 'it' is the song]

belt it v. **1** [1940s+] to masturbate (cf. BANG THE BISHOP v.). **2** [1970s] to drive exceptionally fast. [ext. of BELT v.¹ (1)/BELT v.¹ (3)]

belt of the crozier n. [1990s+] a reprimand from the Church, spec. from a bishop. [BELT n.¹ (1) + SE *crozier*]

belt one's batter v. [1900s–40s] **1** to copulate with a woman. **2** to masturbate (cf. BANG THE BISHOP v.). [BELT v.¹ (1) + BATTER n.¹ (1)]

belt one's hog v. [1960s+] (*US*) to masturbate (cf. BANG THE BISHOP v.; BEAT ONE'S HOG v.). [BELT v.¹ (1) + HOG n.⁶]

belt out v. **1** [1910s] (*Aus.*) to create, to gain, to make. **2** [1910s+] (*orig. Aus.*) to sing lustily; to broadcast noisily. **3** [1930s] (*US*) to eat heartily. **4** [1940s+] (*US*) to knock down, to destroy. **5** [1960s+] (*US*) to murder. [fig. uses of BELT v.¹ (1)]

belt someone's arse/ass v. *see* KICK SOMEONE'S ASS v.

belt the bottle v. [1930s+] (*orig. US*) to drink heavily. [BELT v.¹ (2) + SE *bottle*]

belt the grape v. [1930s+] to drink heavily. [BELT v.¹ (2) + SE *grape*]

belt-up n. [1960s] a fight. [BELT v.¹ (1)]

belt up v.¹ [1930s+] (*orig. RAF*) to be quiet, esp. in excl. *belt up!* shut up! [one wraps a fig. 'belt' around one's mouth]

belt up v.² *see* BELT v.¹ (1).

belty adv. [1950s] (*UK prison*) enthusiastically. [? fig. use of BELT v.¹ (1)]

be lucky phr. [1930s+] (*mainly London*) goodbye.

beluthahatchie n. *see* B LUTHER HATCHETT n.

belvidere n. [late 19C–1900s] a good-looking man. [the statue of the Apollo *Belvedere*]

belyando spew n. [late 19C–1940s] (*Aus.*) a rural sickness, mainly in Queensland. [*Belyando* River, in central Queensland + SE *spew*, vomit]

belyando sprue n. [1970s+] (*Aus. drugs*) marijuana (cf. ACAPULCO (GOLD) n.). [a popular 'home-grown' crop in the *Belyando* River area of Queensland]

b.e.m. n. [1950s+] (*orig. US*) bug-eyed monster/monsters; a popular category of SF writing and described as such by fans. [abbr.]

bembe n. [20C+] (*W.I.*) a bully, a large, strong person of either sex. [? *bam-boy* or Sp. *bemba*, a Black person's thick lips or *Bemba*, a Central African people]

be missing! excl. [1920s+] (*US*) go away! [a phr. first used by Chicago mobster Spike O'Donnell in rejecting the overtures/threats of Al Capone (1899–1947); but note Schele de Vere, *Americanisms* (1872): 'Missing, to be found, denotes, in Western parlance, to be absent, or to run away']

bemused (with beer) adj. [mid-18C–19C] drunk (cf. ADDLED adj.).

be my guest phr. (*also* **be my Georgie Best**) [1950s+] (*orig. US*) a phr. of encouragement (esp. in response to a request to borrow something), go ahead, feel free, help yourself. [i.e. 'make yourself at home'; the rhy. sl. version rhymes on the celebrated UK footballer, *George Best* (b.1946)]

ben n.¹ [late 17C–mid-19C] (*UK Und.*) a simpleton, a fool (cf. ALVIN n.; BLIND FREDDIE n.; CHARLIE n.⁶; DAN n.²; ISAAC n.; JACK n.¹; JEMMY n.¹; JUDY n.²; NEDDY n.¹; NED FOOL n.; NELLIE n.; PATSY n.; RALPH SPOONER n.; RIGHT CHARLIE n.; SAM n.¹; SAMMY (SOFT) n.; SILLY BILLY n.; SILLY WILLY n.; TOM CONEY n.; TOM-DOODLE n.; TOM-FARTHING n.). [? link to BENE adj.; thus 'good fellow']

ben n.² **1** [early 19C–1900s] (*orig. theatre*) a benefit, i.e. 'a theatrical performance the receipts from which are given to a particular actor, the playwright, or some other person connected with the theatre' (*OED*). **2** [1900s] benefit. [abbr.]

ben n.³ [late 19C] (*UK society*) a lie. [Ital. pvb *se non e vero, e ben trovato*, 'even if it is not true, it is a happy invention'; this was anglicized as *benjamin trovato*, a lie, then shorted to *ben trovato*, *ben tro* and finally *ben*]

ben n.⁴ [late 19C–1930s] a coat, a waistcoat. [abbr. BENJAMIN n.¹]

ben adj. *see* BENE adj.

benbouse n. (*also* **bene bowse**) [mid-16C–18C] (*UK Und.*) the best beer. [BENE adj. + BOUSE n.]

ben-bowsy adj. [early 17C] drunk. [BENBOUSE n.]

Ben Cartwright n. [2000s] nonsense, rubbish. [rhy. sl.; ult. fictional character *Ben Cartwright* from US TV's *Bonanza* (ran 1959–73) = SHITE n. (3)]

Bench, the n. [early 19C] the King's Bench prison (cf. ABBOTT'S PRIORY n.). [abbr.]

bench v.¹ [1920s] (*US*) to sleep on a public bench.

bench v.² [1990s+] (*US Black*) to criticize. [sporting imagery, i.e. sending a badly performing player to sit on the substitutes' bench]

bencher n. **1** [late 19C+] (*US*) any idle or ineffectual person. **2** [1930s] (*US Und.*) one who visits opium dens, but only to observe, not smoke. [BENCH-WARMER n.¹]

bench-flopper n. *see* BENCH-WARMER n.².

bench-legged n. [1900s] (*US*) of people, but more usu. of dogs, bow-legged. [legs that could straddle a bench]

bench-man n. [1960s] (*US Und.*) a judge. [the SE *bench* on which they sit + *man*]

bench-points n. [late 19C–1900s] physical advantages. [used of people but f. dog and cat shows where the animals are placed on a bench for judging]

bench-warmer n.¹ [late 19C+] (*US*) **1** any idle or ineffectual person. **2** a substitute in a sports team.

bench-warmer n.² (*also* **bench-flopper**) [1910s–40s] (*US*) a tramp, a vagrant. [the proliferation of tramps sleeping on the benches of city streets and parks]

ben cove n. [17C–18C] a good fellow, a friend. [BENE adj. + COVE n. (1)]

ben cull n. *see* BENE CULL n.

bend n.¹ [late 19C–1910s] a waistcoat. [? it 'bends' around the stomach]

bend n.² [late 19C+] a drunken spree. [abbr. BENDER n.² (1)]

bend n.³ **1** [20C+] (*Anglo-Irish*) an appointment, a rendezvous. **2** [1950s] a tip-off, information; as in phr. *give the bend*. [? SE *bond/bind*; (1) E.P. suggests the bow given when greeting somebody]

bend n.⁴ [1960s] an experience created by a hallucinogenic drug. [BEND v.³]

bend *n.*[5] [1990s+] (*US Black*) a prostitute. [? BEND OVER (FOR) v.]

bend *v.*[1] [mid-18C] to drink hard. [? SE *bend*, to apply oneself, to pull or strain]

bend *v.*[2] **1** [1920s+] to allow oneself to be corrupted. **2** [1930s] (*US Und.*) to steal. **3** [1930s+] (*also* **bend backwards**) to pervert, to corrupt, to commit some form of fraudulent manoeuvre, esp. as in losing a race deliberately, bribing a policeman or a sporting competitor. **4** [1980s+] (*US*) to kill. [ext. of SE; i.e. to *bend* the rules]

bend *v.*[3] [1930s+] (*US drugs*) to betray the effects of a given drug. [BENT adj. (1)]

bend down for *v.* [late 19C+] to consent to buggery.

bend-down plaza *n.* [20C+] (*W.I., Jam.*) a row of roadside peddlers, specializing in items that are hard to get in shops, because of import restrictions. [the customers have to *bend down* + sarcastic use of *Plaza*, often used as the name of a shopping mall]

bended knees *n.* [1950s+] cheese. [rhy. sl.]

bender *n.*[1] **1** [late 18C–1930s] a sixpence (2½p). **2** [early–mid-19C] a shilling (5p). [the ease with which the thin metal could be bent; 'Bender [...] takes its name from the form, the usual shape of the old coin, which were bent, twice, adversely, presenting the appearance at the edge of the letter (*s*)' (Bee)]

bender *n.*[2] **1** [19C+] a bout of riotous drinking, often lasting several days and including random acts of excess, violence etc; thus mostly as ON A BENDER phr. (1). **2** [mid-late 19C] (*US*) a rampage. **3** [mid-19C–1910s] anything exceptional, astounding. **4** [1930s+] (*drugs*) a drug party or bout of excessive drug taking; usu. as ON A BENDER phr. (3). [the image of a drunkard (or drug user) as unsteady on their feet, or ? f. an image of bending a bow or elbow. Note naut. jargon *benjo*, a spree, f. Ital./Ling. Fr. *buen giorno*, a good day]

bender *n.*[3] **1** [mid-19C–1940s] the arm. **2** [mid-19C–1940s] the elbow (cf. OVER THE BENDER phr.). **3** [mid-19C+] the leg. **4** [1940s–50s] the knee. [the physical function of a joint; (3) lapsed in mainstream sl. by 1900 but adopted by US Blacks *c.*1940]

bender *n.*[4] **1** [1930s] (*US Und.*) a thief, a cheat. **2** [1930s+] a stolen car. **3** [2000s] a robbery. [BENT adj. (4)]

bender *n.*[5] **1** [1940s+] a male homosexual. **2** [1990s+] (*mainly UK juv.*) a term of abuse for an unpopular individual. [(1) note *Guild Dict. of Homosexual Terms* (1965): '*bender*: A homosexual who submits to passive anal intercourse']

bender *n.*[6] [1980s] (*UK Und.*) a suspended prison sentence. [rhy. sl. = *suspender*]

bender! *excl.* [early 19C] nonsense! humbug! rubbish! [ety. unknown; note WW1 RN *bender*, a yarn, a tale]

bendigo *n.* [mid-19C] a rough fur cap. [the professional name of William Thompson (1811–89), the Nottingham prize-fighter who fought as *Bendigo* and ended his days as an evangelical preacher]

bending and bowing *phr.* [1930s–50s] (*US drugs*) experiencing the effects of a drug, esp. heroin. [BEND v.[3]]

bending edger *n.* [1960s–70s] (*UK prison*) a boy who submits to homosexual advances, esp. from members of staff in an approved school. [BENDER n.[5] (1)]

bend of the filbert *n.* [18C] a bow of the head, a nod. [SE *bend* + pun on SE *filbert*, a nut (cf. FILBERT n.[1])]

bend one's back *v.* [1920s–30s] (*Aus./US*) to work hard.

bend one's elbow *v.* (*also* **bend the elbow**) [20C+] to have a drink (cf. CROOK THE ELBOW v.). [the physical action of tipping up a glass]

bend over backwards *v.* (*also* **fall over backwards, lean...**) [1920s+] to go out of one's way to do something, usu. altruistically.

bend over (for) *v.* [1950s+] **1** to submit to, to lay oneself open; the image is of submitting to buggery, but the popular use is less specific. **2** to sodomize. **3** to get into difficulties, to be put at a disadvantage; also as excl. *bend over!* you're bothering me! **4** to make a confession to the police.

bend some ham *v.* [1980s+] (*US gay*) to have anal intercourse (cf. ASK FOR THE RING v.). [SE *bend* + *hams*, the buttocks]

bend the elbow *v. see* BEND ONE'S ELBOW v.

bend the habit *v. see* HABIT n. (1).

bend up *v.* [1990s+] (*UK prison*) to beat up. [the bending up of the arms behind the back prior to separating the fighters]

bene *adj.* (*also* **been, ben, bien**) [mid-16C–mid-19C] (*UK Und.*) good; it can also be conjugated as *benar*, better and *benat*, best. [Lat. *bonus* and Fr. *bon*, good]

bene bouse *n.* (*also* **bene bowse**) [17C–18C] drink, lit. 'good liquor'; thus *bene-bowsy*, tipsy (with good drink). [BENE adj. + BOUSE n. (1)]

bene cove *n.* (*also* **bene cofe**) [early 17C–mid-19C] (*UK Und.*) a friend, lit. 'a good fellow', thus a fellow criminal. [BENE adj. + COVE n. (1)]

bene cull *n.* (*also* **ben cull**) [19C] a good fellow, a friend. [BENE adj. + CULL n.[1] (4)]

bene darkmans *phr.* [mid-16C–mid-19C] (*UK Und.*) goodnight. [BENE adj. + DARKMANS n.; E.P. (in *DU*) suggests 'ca. 1560 or even earlier. Not dictionaried, however, until 1698 (B.E.)']

benedict *n.* (*also* **benedick**) [19C–1910s] a married man, esp. a newly married man or a formerly confirmed bachelor who changes his mind. [Shakespeare's character *Benedict* in *Much Ado About Nothing* (1599)]

beneek/beneekte *n. see* BENEUKT adj.

bene-feaker *n.* (*also* **bene-faker, ben-faker, ben-feaker**) [late 17C–19C] a counterfeiter, initially of documents, later of money. [BENE adj. + FAKER n. (1); lit. 'good-maker']

bene-feaker of gybes *n.* [late 17C–mid-19C] (*UK Und.*) a forger of passes and similar documents. [BENE-FEAKER n. + GYBE n.]

bene mort *n.* (*also* **bien mort**) [17C–mid-19C] a pretty woman. [BENE adj. + MORT n.]

beneship *n.* (*also* **benship**) [mid-16C–17C] something that is very good. [BENE adj.; the term moved into SE by 18C, when Bailey's *Universal Etymological English Dictionary* (1721 et seq.) defined *beenship*, worship, goodness. Note Carew, *The History of Bampfylde Moore Carew* (1750), who defines 'beenship rat' as 'goodnight' in his list of Scot. gypsy terms]

beneshiply *adv.* **1** [17C] excellently. **2** [late 18C–early 19C] worshipfully. [BENESHIP n. + sfx *-ly*]

beneukt *adj.* (*also* **beneek, beneekte**) [1960s+] (*S.Afr.*) **1** contrary, impossible. **2** bad-tempered, insane. [Du. *neuk*, to deceive, to push]

benevolence *n.* [early 18C] (*UK society*) doing good for others in the hope that one will receive equal good in return; often as a euph. for sexual intercourse. ['Ostentation and fear united, with hopes of retaliation in kind hereafter' (Bee)]

ben-faker/-feaker *n. see* BENE-FEAKER n.

ben-flake *n.* [mid-19C] a cheap beefsteak, 'used at a slap-bang, i.e. a low cook-shop or eating house' (Ducange Anglicus, *The Vulgar Tongue*, 1857). [rhy. sl.]

Ben Franklin *n.* (*also* **benjamin, Benjamin Franklin, Benny (Franklin), Franklin, Mr Franklin**) [1930s+] (*US*) a $100 bill (cf. ABE n.[2]). [the portrait of *Benjamin Franklin* (1706–90), one of America's Founding Fathers, printed on the notes]

Bengal blanket *n.* [19C] (*Anglo-Ind.*) the sun, a blue sky. [the good weather that 'blankets' Bengal]

bengal lancers *n.* [1930s–40s] (*Aus.*) razor gangs. [pun on SE *Bengal Lancers*, an Indian Army regiment]

benies *n.* (*also* **bennies**) [1940s+] (*US campus*) *ben*efits, spec. those of the GI Bill that puts US service veterans through college for free; thus ext. as food. [abbr.]

benish *adj. see* BENNISH adj.

benjamin *n.*[1] [early–mid-19C] a coat. [? the name of a tailor;

according to Hotten (1874), an acknowledgement of the many (Jewish) tailors thus named]

benjamin n.[2] *see* BEN FRANKLIN n.

Benjamin Franklin n. *see* BEN FRANKLIN n.

benjamins n. [1990s+] (*US Black*) money, esp. a $100 bill. [BEN FRANKLIN n.]

benji n. [1980s+] a $100 bill. [BEN FRANKLIN n.]

benjy n. (*also* **benjie**) [19C] a coat. [abbr. BENJAMIN n.[1]]

bennie(s) n. *see* BENNY n.[3].

bennish adj. (*also* **benish**) [late 17C–18C] foolish. [BEN n.[1]]

benny n.[1] **1** [mid-19C–1940s] (*orig. US naut.*) a straw hat. **2** [20C+] (*US*) (*also* **binny**) an overcoat.

benny n.[2] **1** [1920s+] (*US*) a person, a fellow. **2** [1930s+] a male homosexual; thus *steam bath benny*, a male homosexual who frequents steam baths. [? generic use of proper name]

benny n.[3] (*also* **bennie, bennies**) [1940s+] (*orig. US drugs*) Benzedrine; thus *benny-head*, a Benzedrine user. [abbr.]

benny n.[4] [1980s] **1** as used by the British Army, an inhabitant of the Falkland Islands. **2** anyone seen as an unsophisticated peasant. [a derog. ref. derived from an intellectually deficient rural character in the UK TV soap opera *Crossroads*]

Benny (Franklin) n. *see* BEN FRANKLIN n.

Benny Hill n. [1990s+] **1** a drill. **2** a till, a cash register. **3** a contraceptive pill. [rhy. sl.; ult. UK comedian *Benny Hill* (1925–92)]

benny mason n. (*also* **Mr Mason**) [1990s+] (*US campus*) particularly strong marijuana (cf. AUNT MARY n.[2]). [such marijuana was kept sealed in *Mason* jars]

benny worker n. [1920s–40s] (*US Und.*) a pickpocket or shoplifter who disguises their hands under an overcoat. [BENNY n.[1] (2) + WORKER n.[1] (1)]

beno n. [1950s+] the period of menstruation and thus, for many couples, no sex. ['there'll *be no* fun']

bens n. *see* BENZ n.

benship n. *see* BENESHIP n.

bent n. (*also* **bent-shot**) [1950s+] a homosexual. [BENT adj. (5)]

bent adj. **1** [mid-19C+] intoxicated by liquor or [1930s+] drugs. **2** [1910s] spoiled, ruined. **3** [1910s+] criminal, corrupt. **4** [1930s+] illegal, stolen. **5** [1950s+] sexually eccentric, esp. homosexual. **6** [1960s+] impoverished, penniless. **7** [1960s+] (*orig. US*) eccentric, acting oddly, behaving in a strange manner. **8** [1960s+] (*US*) angry, excited, usu. in phr. BENT OUT OF SHAPE adj. [all fig. uses of SE, +pun on BROKE adj.[1]]

bent as a butcher's hook phr. (*also* **bent as a bootlace**) [1950s–70s] extremely corrupt, highly criminal. [an intensified form of BENT adj. (3)]

bent as a nine-bob note phr. (*also* **bent as a forty-eight pence piece**) [1960s+] **1** of a person, dishonest. **2** of an object, stolen. **3** homosexual. [BENT adj. (3)/BENT adj. (5) + NINE-BOB NOTE n.]

bent as a two-bob watch phr. [1980s] (*Aus.*) extremely corrupt. [BENT adj. (3); the extreme cheapness of the watch]

bent copper n. [1910s+] a corrupt policeman. [BENT adj. (3) + COPPER n.[3] (1); pun on SE]

Benton's mint drops n. (*also* **Bentons**) [early–mid-19C] (*US*) gold coins; thus *mint drops*, money (cf. ALFALFA n.). [proper name Thomas Hart *Benton* (1792–1858), campaigner for a gold currency in US; the synon. sweet, a sugar-plum flavoured with peppermint + pun on MINT n.[1] (2)]

bent out of shape adj. [1960s+] **1** intoxicated by a drug, esp. cannabis or LSD, or extremely drunk (cf. AFFLICTED adj.). **2** very angry. **3** socially inept, embarrassing. [BENT adj. (1)/BENT adj. (8) + pun on SE]

bent screw n. [1940s+] (*UK prison*) a corrupt prison warder. [BENT adj. (3) + SCREW n.[2] (3) + pun on SE]

bent-shot n. *see* BENT n.

bent up adj. [late 19C] (*US*) infatuated, obsessively in love. [BENT adj. (7) + ? pun on MASHED (ON) adj. (1)]

bent wrist n. *see* LIMP WRIST n. (1).

Benz n. [1950s+] a Mercedes *Benz* automobile. [abbr.]

benz n. (*also* **bens, benzie**) **1** [1940s+] (*drugs*) amphetamine (cf. A n.[2]). **2** [2000s] MDMA (cf. ECSTASY n.). [abbr. *Benzedrine* + pun on Benz n., which also 'makes one go fast']

benzed adj. [1950s] under the influence of Benzedrine. [BENZ n.]

benzine n. **1** [mid-19C–1900s] (*US*) cheap 'rotgut' whisky; thus *hit the benzine can, maul the benzine*, to drink whisky to excess; *benzinery*, a saloon. **2** [20C+] (*W.I., Guyn./Trin.*) a form of unlicensed and very potent rum distilled secretly in the countryside. [SE *benzine*, petroleum ether]

benzine buggy n. (*also* **gasoline buggy/go-cart**) [1900s–20s] (*US*) an automobile. [SE *benzine* + BUGGY n.[1] (1)]

benzo n.[1] [1980s+] (*US Black*) a Mercedes *Benz* automobile. [abbr.]

benzo n.[2] [1990s+] (*drugs*) Benzodiopate. [abbr.]

be off (with you)! excl. [late 19C+] go away!

beong n. [mid-19C–1900s] 1 shilling (5p). [Polari *bianco*, white; the shilling is a 'silver' coin]

be out! excl. [1990s+] (*US Black*) a general excl. of encouragement, enjoy yourself!, have fun!

Berdoo n. (*also* **San Bardoo/Berdoo**) [20C+] (*US*) San Bernardino, California. [abbr.]

bere adj. [1990s+] (*UK Black*) of people or things, first-rate, excellent.

bereavement lurk n. [mid–late 19C] a form of begging that depends on attracting sympathy for the fact that one's wife has supposedly just died. [SE *bereavement* + LURK n. (1)]

berg n. *see* BURG n.[1].

bergie n. [1970s] (*S.Afr.*) a vagrant living on the slopes of Table Mountain, Cape Town. [Afk. *berg*, mountain]

bergoo n. *see* BURGOO n.

berick v. [1980s+] (*US drugs*) to smoke an outsized marijuana pipe (2m (6ft) or longer). [ety. unknown]

berk n. (*also* **burk, burke**) [1930s+] a fool, an incompetent (cf. BEECHAM'S PILL n.). [abbr. BERKELEY (HUNT) n. (2)]

berk adj. [1980s+] stupid. [BERK n.]

Berkeley (hunt) n. (*also* **Berkshire Hunt, Burlington Hunt**) **1** [late 19C+] the vagina (cf. ALL QUIET n.). **2** [1930s+] a fool, an incompetent (cf. BAMBA n.[1]; BEECHAM'S PILL n.). **3** [1930s+] sexual intercourse. [rhy. sl. = CUNT n.[1] (1)/CUNT n.[2] (1)]

berkeleys n. [late 19C] the female breasts. [Rom. *berk*, breast]

berkish adj. [1930s] stupid, foolish. [BERK n.]

berko adj. [1960s+] (*Aus.*) berserk; in weakened form, temporarily out of control. [abbr. SE *beserk* + -O sfx (5)]

Berkshire hog n. [1950s+] (*W.I.*) **1** an ugly person. **2** a very dark-complexioned Black man. [SE *Berkshire hog*, a large, dark-skinned pig]

Berkshire hunt n. *see* BERKELEY (HUNT) n.

berley n. (*also* **burley**) [1940s+] (*Aus.*) nonsense, humbug. [? SE *berley*, ground bait/BURLEY n.[1]]

Bermondsey banger n. [late 19C–1900s] 'a society leader among the South London tanneries. He must frequent "the Star", be prepared to hold his own and fight at all times for his social belt' (Ware). [*Bermondsey*, an area of south London + *banger*, one who both 'bangs' his fellows physically, and makes a 'bang' in society]

Bermudas n. [early 17C–18C] certain areas of London that were considered safe havens for criminals and debtors. [proper name *Bermuda Islands*, where certain well-connected debtors fled to avoid their creditors. London's *Bermudas* were either the alleys and passageways running near Drury Lane, Covent Garden, and/or the Mint in Southwark]

bernice n. (*also* **bernies**) [late 19C+] (*US drugs*) cocaine in crystal form (cf. AUNT NORA n.). ['Possibly the term is based on *burnies*, referring to crystals of cocaine added to a tobacco cigarette and smoked' Spears, *Slang and Jargon of Drugs and Drink* (1986); note cocaine is a 'feminine' drug, *see* GIRL n.[2]]

bernie *n.* [late 19C+] (*US drugs*) cocaine (cf. AUNT NORA *n.*). [BERNICE *n.*]

bernie's flakes *n.* [1950s+] (*drugs*) cocaine (cf. AUNT NORA *n.*). [BERNIE *n.* + SE *flake*]

berries *n.*[1] **1** [1910s] (*US*) beans. **2** [1950s+] the testicles (cf. ACORNS *n.*). **3** [1970s+] (*US Black*) a woman's nipples. [resemblance]

berries *n.*[2] [1910s–40s] dollars, money (cf. BANANAS *n.*[3]).

berries *n.*[3] [1970s+] (*US Black*) wine. [its basic component]

berries, the *n.* [20C+] (*US*) **1** the best, the superlative. **2** as a negative, the ultimate, the last straw. [fig. use of SE; but note Scot. *to be no the berry*, to be a bad character]

berry *n.*[1] **1** [late 19C] (*US*) an easy opponent, anyone seen as 'soft'. **2** [1910s–40s] (*US*) $1, usu. in pl. **3** [1930s] (*US*) a person. **4** [1930s] a £1 note. **5** [1930s] (*US Und.*) an attractive woman. **6** [1950s+] (*US*) a testicle, usu. in pl. see BERRIES *n.*[1] (2). [(3) Williams notes a number of 17C sexual riddles in which a *berry* represents the penis]

berry *n.*[2] [1920s] (*US drugs*) a capsule of a powdered drug, e.g. heroin (cf. PILL *n.*[4]).

berry *n.*[3] [1990s+] **1** one who is into bizarre, 'kinky' sex. **2** one who cannot get a partner. **3** (*US Black*) a girl who barters sex for drugs (usu. crack cocaine). [STRAWBERRY *n.*[2] (2)]

berry *n.*[4] *see* CONY-BURROW *n.* (1).

berry picker *n.* [20C+] (*US*) a rural person, a country dweller (cf. ACORN-CRACKER *n.*).

bertha *n.* (*also* **big bertha**) **1** [1920s–40s; 1980s+] (*US*) a fat person. **2** [1970s+] (*US camp gay*) a nickname for any tall, heavy-set man, esp. if effeminate. [WW1 Ger. gun, *Big Bertha*, a 42cm (16½in) mortar; ult. the proper name Frau *Bertha* Krupp von Bohlen und Halbach (1886–1957), the owner of the Krupp steelworks in Germany]

bertiss *n.* [1940s+] (*W.I.*) the buttocks. [ety. unknown]

beserko *n.* [1980s+] (*US*) an unstable, eccentric person. [SE *beserk* + -o sfx (2)]

beside the book *adj.* [late 17C] utterly mistaken. [SE *beside*, in addition, over and above + *book*, in the sense of an authority, a book of rules; 18C+ use is SE]

beside the lighter *phr.* [late 17C–18C] in a poor condition. [? SE *lighter*, a boat used to transport goods/passengers to and from a vessel that has to be moored in deeper water]

besognio *n.* (*also* **besogno, besonio, bisognio**) [late 16C–early 17C] a greedy beggar, a worthless person. [Ital. *bisogno*, need, want; also a newly levied, untrained and unblooded soldier]

bespattered *adj.* [1910s–20s] a euph. for BLOODY *adj.*[1] (1).

bess *n.*[1] **1** [17C–19C] (*UK Und.*) a short iron bar, used to break open doors, force locks etc. **2** [early 19C] a picklock. [BETTY *n.*[1]]

bess *n.*[2] [early 18C–mid-19C] a firelock or musket. [abbr. BROWN BESS *n.*]

bessie *n.* [late 19C] (*US*) a blackjack, a club.

Bess of Bedlam *n.* [mid-19C] a lunatic vagrant. [SE *Bess*, generic female name + *Bedlam* (the Bethlehem Hospital for the insane)]

bessy *n.* [19C+] (*W.I.*) a busybody, a gossip. [dial. *bessy*, an ill-mannered woman or girl; ? linked to BESS OF BEDLAM *n.*]

best *n.*[1] [late 17C; late 19C] a popular toast, abbr. of *to the best cunt in Christendom*.

best *n.*[2] [1960s] pornography featuring bestiality. [abbr.]

best *v.* [mid-19C+] **1** to get the better of. **2** to cheat. [orig. dial.]

best boy *n.* [1900s–10s] (*orig. US*) a sweetheart, a boyfriend, a husband. [on model of BEST GIRL *n.*]

best-built *adj.* [1970s] describing a woman with a voluptuous figure. [SE/BUILT *adj.* (1); lit. built in the best way possible]

bested *adj.* [mid-19C+] defeated, defrauded. [BEST *v.*]

bester *n.* **1** [mid-19C] a villain who is equally happy to use physical force or verbal deceits to extract money from victims. **2** [mid-19C] (*UK Und.*) a criminal who deceives his peers. **3** [20C+] (*Aus.*) a fraudulent bookmaker. [phr. *get the best of*]

best girl *n.* [late 19C+] (*orig. US*) a sweetheart, a girlfriend, a wife (cf. BEST BOY *n.*).

best in Christendom *n.* [late 17C–18C] the vagina. [popularized by John Wilmot, Earl of Rochester (1647–80), who was also responsible for the synon. BULL'S EYE *n.*[1]; CROWN OF SENSE *n.*; KENNEL *n.*[1]; TARGET *n.*[1]]

best leg of three *n.* [late 19C–1900s] the penis (cf. ARM *n.*[1]).

best of a charley *n.* [early 19C] upsetting a watchman in his box, a popular 'game' among upper-class rowdies. [CHARLEY *n.*[1] (1)]

best (of it), the *n.* [early 19C+] an advantage.

best part *n.* [late 16C–early 17C] the vagina. [coined by John Donne (1572–1631)]

bet! *excl.* **1** [1980s+] (*US campus*) a response to an event that is totally unexpected but greatly appreciated, e.g. *Class is cancelled today? Bet!* **2** [1990s+] (*US*) a general excl. of affirmation or agreement. [YOU BET! excl.]

bet a fat man *v.* [1930s+] (*US Black*) to assure or to believe with absolute confidence. [? the fig. size of one's wager]

bet a pound to a pinch of shit *v.* (*also* **bet a pound to a pinch of poop**) [1940s+] a statement denoting the speaker's absolute confidence, whether in a real bet or merely a point of view (cf. ALL THE WORLD TO A CHINA ORANGE *phr.*). [SHIT *n.*[1] (1)/POOP *n.*[2] (2)]

betcha! *excl.* (*also* **betcher!**) [1920s+] (*orig. US*) a general excl. of affirmation or agreement. [elision of SE *bet you*]

beteechoot *n. see* BANCHOOT *n.*

bethel the city *v.* [early–mid-18C] **1** to be a poor host. **2** to eat in chop-houses. [proper name of Slingsby *Bethel* (1617–97) who, with Henry Cornish, was elected Sheriff of London in 1680; according to the historian Roger North, Bethel 'used to walk about more like a corncutter than sheriff of London. He kept no house, but lived upon chops, whence it is proverbial for not feasting "to Bethel the city"' (*Examen*, 1740)]

bethlehemites *n.* [late 18C] (*UK Und.*) carol-singers. [the staple topic of most carols]

Bethlehem steel *n.* [1980s+] (*US Black*) a boastful description of the rigidity of one's erect penis. [play on the name of the US steel manufacturer]

bet like the Watsons *v.* [1940s–70s] (*Aus.*) to bet heavily. [the *Watson Brothers* (fl.1880s–1910s). They were legendary punters but their background is unknown; poss. born in Bendigo, Victoria, they have been variously cited as Sydney hoteliers and outback shearers in New South Wales]

betoger *n.* [1970s+] (*S.Afr.*) a political demonstrator. [Afk. *betoog*, demonstrate]

bet one's balls *v.* [1940s–60s] (*Aus.*) to be very certain. [SE *bet* + BALLS *n.*[1] (1)]

bet one's boots *v.* (*also* **bet one's socks, gamble one's socks**) [mid-19C+] (*orig. US*) to be certain, to wager everything in total confidence. [betting one's boots in a US frontier state would be a very serious bet]

bet one's bottom dollar *v.* (*also* **bet one's bottom ace, bet one's last dollar, stake one's bottom dollar**) [mid-19C+] to be absolutely certain. [SE *bottom dollar*, one's very last one; such certainty encourages a wager of one's complete assets]

bet one's buttons *v.* (*also* **bet one's braces, …hat, …shirt, wager one's beaver**) [mid-17C; mid-19C+] to bet all one's money, to go the limit, to commit oneself unreservedly to something.

bet one's head to a China orange *v.* [mid-19C] to be very certain.

bet one's last dollar *v. see* BET ONE'S BOTTOM DOLLAR *v.*

bet one's neck *v.* [1920s] (*US*) to be absolutely sure, to commit oneself unreservedly.

bet one's shirt *v. see* BET ONE'S BUTTONS *v.*

bet one's socks *v. see* BET ONE'S BOOTS *v.*

bet one's (sweet) ass v. [1940s+] to be absolutely certain about a suggested course of action. [SE *bet* + ASS n. (2)]

bet one's (sweet) life v. [mid-19C+] to be absolutely sure, to commit oneself unreservedly.

bet on the blue v. (*also* bet on the Mary Lou) [1920s+] (*Aus.*) to bet on credit. [var. on BLUE n.[7], i.e. a piece of paper, in this case an I.O.U; ? *Mary Lou* = rhy. sl.]

bet on the wrong side of the post v. [late 18C–early 19C] to make a losing bet. [SE *winning post*]

betsy n. (*also* Betsey Jane, old betsy) [mid-19C–1960s] (*US*) a gun, thence a pistol. [abbr. BROWN BESS n.]

better v. [early–mid-19C] (*UK Und.*) to relock a door. [BETTY n.[1]]

better half n. [late 16C+] one's wife or partner, usu. in joc. use (cf. BITTER HALF n.; INFERIOR HALF n.).

better than a kick in the ass (with a frozen foot) phr. (*also* better than a kick in the arse) [1960s+] (*Can./US*) said of a situation that could be worse than it actually is.

better than a poke in the eye with a blunt stick phr. (*also* ...with a burnt stick) [late 19C+] said of a situation that could be worse than it actually is.

better than a slap in the belly with a wet fish phr. [1930s+] (*orig. US*) said of a situation that could be worse than it actually is.

better than a thump on the back with a stone phr. [late 18C–early 19C] said of a situation that could be worse than it actually is.

better than smashing your leg phr. [mid-19C] said of a situation that could be worse than it actually is.

better-than-thou adj. *see* HOLIER-THAN-THOU adj.

bet the farm v. [1940s+] (*US*) lit. and fig., to bet unreservedly.

betty n.[1] **1** [mid-17C–mid-19C] (*UK Und.*) a short iron bar, used to break open doors, force locks etc. **2** [late 17C–early 19C] a small flask, used to hold wine. **3** [18C+] a skeleton key, a picklock. [fig. use of proper name]

betty n.[2] **1** [late 17C+] a homosexual man (cf. ABIGAIL n.). **2** [19C] a man who takes on a woman's household duties. **3** [1970s+] (*S.Afr. gay*) a light-skinned Black man. [fig. use of proper name; note Scot./US dial. *jenny(-woman)*, a man who meddles in or assists in a woman's housework; and 17C *Bettyland*, esp. in pamphlet *Erotopolis, The Present State of Betty-Land*, in which the term stands for (1) the female body, (2) the lowlife areas of London and (3) human sexuality; in it one finds 'Rutland' and the great city of 'Pego', the 'centre of the whole (i.e. hole = vagina) Empire']

betty n.[3] **1** [mid-19C] (*US, Southern*) a cowhide whip. **2** [20C+] a chamberpot. **3** [20C+] (*Irish*) a fireguard. **4** [20C+] a schoolteacher. [dimin. of SE *Elizabeth*; the implication, in all cases, is of domesticity]

betty n.[4] [1970s+] (*US campus*) a pretty young woman. [proper name + the character *Betty* in the *Flintstones* TV cartoon]

betty v. [early 19C] (*UK Und.*) to pick a lock or to relock a lock after committing a robbery so as to avoid detection. [BETTY n.[1] (3)]

Betty Bupe n. [1990s+] (*US drugs*) *Bup*renex, *Bup*renorphine, a narcotic painkiller. [abbr. + play on cartoon character *Betty Boop*]

betty coed n. [1960s+] (*US*) a generic for a wholesome, middle-class sorority girl. [song 'Betty Coed' (Paul Fogarty and Rudy Vallee, 1930) and film *Betty Co-Ed* (1947)]

Betty Grable n. [1950s+] **1** a sable fur coat. **2** (*Aus.*) a table. [rhy. sl.; ult. film star and WW2 pin-up *Betty Grable* (1916–73)]

betty lea n. (*also* betty lee) [1940s+] tea. [rhy. sl.]

betty rub! excl. [1980s+] (*US campus*) a phr. used by one man to another, meaning 'you're going to get lucky with her'. [BETTY n.[4]]

betty swallocks n. [1990s+] itching, uncomfortable testicles. [joc. reversal of 'sweaty BALLOCKS n.[1] (1)']

betwattled adj. [late 18C–early 19C] bewildered, confused. [orig. dial.]

between jobs n. [20C+] (*US*) a small cigar. [? analogous with the brandname of a small cigar 'Between the Acts' (launched 1948); travelling salesmen could smoke them between their calls]

between the two Ws phr. [mid-19C] infected with venereal disease. [SHOT BETWEEN WIND AND WATER phr.]

between you and me and jack mum phr. *see* JACK MUM n.

betwixt and between phr. [19C] undecided, uncertain, 'neither one thing nor the other'.

bet your ass! excl. (*also* bet your arse/buns!) [1950s+] **1** an excl. of enthusiastic agreement, you're absolutely right! **2** an excl. of dismissal or disbelief, you must be joking! [BET ONE'S (SWEET) ASS v.]

bet your (sweet) life! excl. [mid-19C+] (*orig. US*) an excl. of dismissal, you must be joking! [BET ONE'S (SWEET) LIFE v.]

Beulah n. [1970s+] (*US Black gay*) a Black homosexual. [a stereotypical, if old-fashioned Black female name]

be up off me! excl. [2000s] (*US Black*) go away! leave me alone!

bev n. (*also* bevarly) [mid-19C+] alcohol, esp. beer; thus a drink. [abbr. SE *beverage* or BEVVY n.]

beverage n. [late 17C–early 19C] money for drink, demanded of anyone wearing a new suit of clothes; thus in general use, a tip. [SE, though similar to Fr. *pourboire*, a tip, lit. 'in order to drink']

bevvied (up) adj. [1960s+] drunk (cf. ALED UP adj.). [BEVVY v.]

bevvy n. (*also* bevy) **1** [late 19C+] alcohol, esp. beer; thus *bevvy-casey, bevvy-ken*, a beer-house, a public house; *bevvy-homey*, a drunkard (lit. 'beer-man'); *on the bevvy*, a drinking session. **2** [1930s+] a drink. **3** [1960s] a (drunken) party. [Lat. *bibere*, to drink. Note East Anglia dial. *bever*, a 4 o'clock halt on the road for drink; Eton/Winchester *bevers*, afternoon tea; Charterhouse *bevor*, a wedge of bread eaten between dinner and supper]

bevvy v. [late 19C+] to drink. [BEVVY n. (1)]

bevvy omee n. [20C+] (*Ling. Fr./Polari*) a drunkard. [BEVVY n. (1) + OMEE n. (3)]

bevvy up n. [1960s] a drinking session. [BEVVY UP v.]

bevvy up v. [1940s+] to drink heavily. [BEVVY v.]

bevy n. *see* BEVVY n.

beware n. [mid-19C] anything one can drink. [Polari]

bewdy! excl. *see* BEAUTY! excl.

bewer n. *see* BUER n.

bewitched adj. [early 17C–early 18C] drunk (cf. ADDLED adj.).

bex adj. [20C+] (*W.I. Rasta*) angry. [SE *vex, vexed*]

bexandebs n. [18C–19C] young Jewish women from the ghetto area of Wentworth Street, London E1. [common Jewish names, Rebecca (*becks*) and Deborah (*debs*)]

Bexley Heath n. [late 19C+] the teeth. [rhy. sl.; ult. UK town]

beyond the beyonds n. [1910s+] (*Anglo-Irish*) the furthest, the absolute limit.

beyond the breakers phr. [1900s] (*US*) beyond limits. [sea imagery]

beyond the rabbit-proof fence phr. [late 19C+] (*Aus.*) in the wilds, at the back of beyond, the edge of 'civilization'; also in fig. use. [the rabbit-proof fencing erected in Aus. to protect crops]

be your age! excl. *see* ACT YOUR AGE! excl.

bezabor n. [mid-19C] (*US*) a strange, eccentric person. [SE *bizarre* + SAmE *neighbor*]

bezark n. [1920s–40s] (*US*) an eccentric or unpleasant person. [? SE *berserk*]

bezesus n. (*also* bezusus) [1930s] (*US*) circumstances, situation. [BEJAZUS, THE n.]

bezoomy adj. [1990s+] (*US teen*) angry. [SE *berserk* + *zoom*; coined by Anthony Burgess in *A Clockwork Orange* (1962)]

bezzazz n. *see* BIZZAZ n.

bezzie n. [1990s+] one's *best* friend. [BEZZIE adj.]

bezzie adj. [1990s+] best, as in best friend. [abbr.]

bezzler n. [1900s] (*US*) a self-important person. [Lancashire dial. *bezzler*, something large]

b.f. *n.* **1** [late 19C+] (*orig. US*) a bloody fool. **2** [1920s+] (*US campus*) a boy friend. **3** [1930s] (*US Und.*) a pimp. **4** [1970s+] (*US gay/lesbian*) in a lesbian couple, the 'male'. [abbr.]

b.f. *v. see* BUTTFUCK *v.*

b.f.d. *phr.* [1960s+] (*US*) so what! I should care less! [abbr. *big fucking deal*/euph. *big fat deal*]

b.f.e. *n.* (*also* **b.f.a.**) [1980s+] (*US campus*) somewhere very far away. [abbr. *butt fucking Egypt*/*butt fucking Africa* (*see* BUMFUCK, EGYPT *n.*)]

b flat *n.* [mid-19C–1900s] a bedbug. [B n.¹ + FLAT-BACK n.]

b.g. *n.* [1980s+] (*orig. US Black/teen*) baby gangster, one who is a member of a gang, but has yet to shoot or kill anyone. [abbr.]

b-girl *n.* (*US*) **1** [1930s–60s] a dancehall hostess whose primary job is not to dance but to promote liquor sales to the clientele. **2** [1930s+] (*orig. US*) (*also* **B-broad**) a part-time prostitute, who frequents bars and uses them as a base for soliciting; thus *B-case*, a charge of soliciting (cf. AWAYDAY GIRL n.). **3** [1960s] (*US gay*) the homosexual equivalent of (2). **4** [1980s+] (*US Black*) the female equivalent of the B-BOY n. [abbr. *bar-girl* or (Trimble, *5,000 Adult Sex Words & Phrases*, 1966) *business-girl*]

b.h. *n.* [late 19C–1930s] a bank holiday. [abbr.]

bhang *n. see* BANG n.⁵

bhangramuffin *n.* [1990s+] (*UK Asian*) the Asian equivalent of the W.I./UK Black RAGAMUFFIN n. (3). [*bhangra*, a form of popular music developed in the UK Asian community and blending Asian folk + Western dance music]

bheestie *n.* (*also* **beasty**) [late 18C–mid-19C] (*Anglo-Ind.*) a water carrier. [Persian *bihishti*, water-carrier (lit. 'person of paradise')]

bhong *n. see* BONG n.¹

bhowji *n.* [20C+] (*W.I.*) an elderly East Indian woman. [Hind. *bhaabii*, one's elder brother's wife]

b'hoy *n.* **1** [mid-19C+] (*orig. US*) a 'lad', a young rowdy, esp. those found around the Bowery, New York City (cf. G'HAL n.). **2** [late 19C+] an Irishman. [Irish pron. of SE *boy*]

bhuttu *n.* (*also* **bhutto, buhtuh**) [20C+] (*W.I. Rasta*) an uncouth, out-of-fashion, uncultured person. [ety. unknown]

Bi *n.* [1930s] (*US Und.*) a Buick. [abbr.]

bi *n.* [1960s+] a bisexual person. [BI adj.]

bi *adj.* (*also* **by**) [1930s+] *bi*sexual. [abbr.]

bianc *n.* (*also* **bionc, bionk**) [mid–late 19C] a shilling (5p). [Ital. *bianco*, white = silver]

bianca capellas *n.* [late 19C–1900s] White Chapel cigars. [a heavy-handed Ital. pun]

biatch *n.* (*also* **beeatch**) [1990s+] (*US Black/teen*) vars. on BITCH n.¹; can be used to refer to a male or a female, a friend or an enemy etc; also as an excl. [deliberately exaggerated pron.]

bib-all-night *n.* [early 17C] a heavy drinker. [SE *bib*, to drink + *all night*]

bib and bub *n.* [20C+] (*Aus.*) a tub; thus *have a bib and bub*, take a bath. [rhy. sl.]

bibbing *n.* [1970s+] (*US gay*) augmenting sexual activity with extra items or preparatory actions. [? SE *bib*, applied pre-eating]

bibble chunks *n.* [1990s+] the female breasts. [ety. unknown]

bibbling *adj.* [1900s] (*Irish*) drunken. [SE *bib*, to drink]

bibe *n.* [1930s+] (*Anglo-Irish*) a bringer of bad luck; an unpleasant person. [? Irish word]

bible *n.*¹ [late 18C] (*UK Und.*) a large piece of lead, stripped from a roof. [the supposed resemblance to the dimensions of a large Bible]

bible *n.*² **1** [19C+] absolute authority, the truth; thus *torah*, a 'Judaized' equivalent, based on the Heb. *Torah*, the Old Testament. **2** [1940s+] (*US*) any authoritative book, catalogue, reference work, listing, varying as to the context. [the myth that religious superstitions attain to superior truthfulness]

bible *n.*³ [mid-19C+] a peddler's box of pins, needles and other items of haberdashery. [? its dimensions are those of a small bible]

bible *n.*⁴ [mid-19C+] (*US*) a book of cigarette papers. [he 'relies' on it]

bibleback *n.* [mid-19C+] a sanctimonious, 'holier-than-thou' person; thus a missionary or proselytizer.

bible-backed *adj.* (*US*) **1** [mid-19C–1910s] of a person, round-shouldered and hump-backed. **2** [1940s+] sanctimonious, oppressively pious; esp. a Protestant who is conspicuously anti-Catholic. [BIBLEBACK n.; the image in (1) is that the self-proclaimedly pious should have such a bearing]

bible-banger *n.* **1** [19C] (*also* **bible-sharp**) a clergyman, a preacher. **2** [1940s+] (*Aus./N.Z./US campus*) a religious fanatic.

bible-basher *n.* (*also* **bible-buster**) [20C+] (*orig. Aus.*) a clergyman; a religious fanatic; thus *bible-bash*, to act in an overly pious fashion.

bible-beater *n.* [1970s+] (*US campus*) an evangelizing, fundamentalist Christian.

bible-belter *n.* [1920s+] a native of those (mainly southern) US states where fundamentalist Christianity dominates social mores. [SE *Bible Belt*]

bible-buster *n. see* BIBLE-BASHER n.

bible-carrier *n.* [mid-19C] a streetseller of songs who offers the sheet-music but does not give a performance to encourage sales.

bible mill *n.* [late 19C–1900s] a public house. [SE *bible* + *mill*, the noise therein reminiscent of a church full of praying congregants]

bible-pounder *n.* [late 19C+] a clergyman, a preacher.

bible-puncher *n.* [20C+] (*orig. milit.*) a religious person, usu. one who wishes to thrust their beliefs on any who will listen and many who would rather not; thus *bible-punching*, giving a sermon.

bible-ranter *n.* [1920s–30s] (*US*) a clergyman, a preacher.

bible salesman *n.* [1970s] (*US prison*) a Protestant preacher.

bible-sharp *n. see* BIBLE-BANGER n. (1).

bible-thumper *n.* **1** [late 19C+] (*also* **god-thumper**) a notably religious person, esp. a clergyman; thus *bible-thumping*, fanatical preaching. **2** [1980s+] a street preacher. **3** [1990s+] (*US prison*) an inmate who adopts religious beliefs during their sentence, whether genuinely or as a way of dealing with prison life. [one who thumps the Bible in order to underline the points they are expounding, often in a sermon]

bible-walloper *n.* [20C+] (*US*) a clergyman, a preacher.

bicarb *n.* [1920s+] *bicarb*onate of soda. [abbr.]

biccie *see under* BIKKIE.

bice *n.* (*also* **byce**) [20C+] 2, thus £2 or a 2-year sentence. [Fr. *bis*, twice]

bicho *n.* [1960s+] (*US, orig. Hisp.*) the penis. [synon. Sp. sl.]

bickies *n. see* BIKKIES n.

bicycle *n.* **1** [1900s] (*US campus*) a translation of a text, classical or otherwise, for the illegitimate use of students (cf. ANIMAL n.³). **2** [1940s+] a prostitute, a promiscuous woman (cf. BANBURY n.). **3** [1960s–70s] a bisexual. [all pun on SE *ride*]

bicycle bum *n.* [1920s+] (*Aus.*) a seasonal worker, cycling between jobs. [SE *bicycle* + BUM n.³ (1)]

bid *n.*¹ [1900s] (*US campus*) a young girl. [abbr. BIDDY n.² (1)]

bid *n.*² [1960s+] (*US Black*) a prison sentence. [var. pron. of BIT n.⁵]

bid *n.*³ [2000s] an old person. [non-gender-specific use of BIDDY n.² (4)]

bidaciously *adv. see* BODACIOUSLY adv. (1).

biddie *n.* [1940s] (*US Black*) a young girl; thus *little biddie/biddie baby*, a small girl, a small woman. [BIDDY n.² (1)]

bid-dims *n.* [20C+] (*W.I.*) a young man's trousers that are too short and narrow. [onomat. *bid-dim*, the sound of a rifle shot; such trousers supposedly resemble a rifle barrel]

biddy *n.*¹ **1** [17C–19C] a chicken. **2** [1930s+] (*US*) an egg. [dial.]

biddy *n.*² **1** [17C+] any woman, esp. an Irish female servant. **2** [late 18C+] a young woman. **3** [1900s] (*US*) a policeman. **4** [1940s+] (*US*) an old woman, usu. irritating, interfering; usu. as *old*

biddy. 5 [1980s+] (*US Black*) a teenage girl. [*Biddy*, a nickname for the popular Irish name Bridget]

biddy *n.*[3] *see* RED BIDDY n.

biddy-peck *v.* [20C+] (*US*) to nag mildly. [play on BIDDY n.[1] (1)/BIDDY n.[2] (1) + SE *peck*; i.e. var. on HENPECK v.]

bidgee *n.* [1920s+] (*Aus.*) an alcoholic's drink, consisting primarily of methylated spirits. [*Murrumbidgee River*, Australia]

biding *n.* [mid-18C] (*UK Und.*) wherever thieves divide their booty.

bidstand *n.* (*also* **bid-stand, bid stand**) [late 16C–17C] a highwayman. [he 'bids' victims 'stand and deliver']

bien *adj. see* BENE adj.

bienly *adv.* [18C–early 19C] very well, excellently. [Fr. *bien*, well]

bien mort *n. see* BENE MORT n.

BIF *n.* [1990s+] (*UK*) a derog. term for a Black man (cf. ALLIGATOR BAIT n.[2]). [*black ignorant fucker* (FUCKER n. (3))]

bif *v. see* BIFF v.[1].

biff *n.*[1] (*orig. US*) **1** [late 19C+] a blow, a slap, a punch; also in fig. use; thus (*Aus.*) *biff merchant*, a thug; *go the biff*, to fight. **2** [1910s] energy, spirit, 'zip'. [Scot. *beff*, a blow, a buffet; (1) *HDAS* has a mid-19C cit., but it appears to be a general echoic use rather than a specific use as a n.]

biff *n.*[2] [1930s+] (*US campus*) an unattractive, stupid and/or promiscuous woman. [abbr. BIFFER n.]

biff *n.*[3] [2000s] a fool. [? one who has suffered a BIFF n.[1] (1) on the head or one who has a *beef* brain or head]

biff *v.*[1] (*also* **bif**) **1** [late 19C] to rebuff, to reject, to leave without an answer. **2** [late 19C+] to hit. **3** [late 19C+] to kill, to murder. **4** [late 19C+] (*Aus.*) to throw; to throw out. **5** [1940s] of a weapon, to fire. **6** [1970s+] (*S.Afr. juv.*) to ejaculate. **7** [1980s+] (*US campus*) to fail (an examination), to fall causing embarrassment. **8** [1990s+] (*orig. US*) to have sexual intercourse (cf. BANG v.[1]). [BIFF n.[1] (1)]

biff *v.*[2] **1** [1920s+] to go, to move, to proceed; usu. in comb. with a prep. e.g. *biff off, biff around*. **2** [1980s] (*US campus*) to visit the lavatory. [(1) appears to be a nonce-word coined/used by P.G. Wodehouse]

biff *adv.* [20C+] (*orig. US*) used with *go* to mean 'with a violent blow', e.g. *the brick went biff through the plate-glass window*. [echoic]

biffa *n.* [1990s+] (*UK juv.*) a fat person. [BIFFA adj.]

biffa *adj.* [1990s+] (*UK juv.*) ugly. [comic character *Biffo* the Bear]

biffed *adj.* [1920s] (*US*) drunk (cf. ANNIHILATED adj.). [BIFF v.[1] (2); cognate with other terms equating drunkenness with suffering a blow]

biffer *n.* [1930s+] (*US Black*) an unpleasant, unattractive and/or promiscuous woman. [? BIFF v.[1] (2)]

biffin *n.*[1] [late 19C] an intimate friend. [affectionate use of dial. *biffin*, a variety of cooking apple, cultivated especially in Norfolk]

biffin *n.*[2] (*also* **baffin, biffon**) [1990s+] **1** (*also* **biffin bridge**) the perineum, that area between the scrotum and anus or the vagina and anus. **2** sweat secreted in this area during intercourse. [fig. use of BIFF v.[1] (2), i.e. one is *biffing* against it during intercourse]

biff merchant *n. see* BIFF n.[1] (1).

biffo *n.* [1990s+] (*Aus.*) a fight; the sport of wrestling. [BIFF n.[1] (1) + -o sfx (4)]

biffon *n. see* BIFFIN n.[2].

biffs *n.* [1920s+] (*Aus. juv.*) a beating, a caning. [BIFF n.[1] (1)]

biffy *n.* **1** [1930s+] (*US*) a privy, an outdoor lavatory. **2** [1940s+] (*Can./US*) an indoor lavatory; thus *go biffy*, to visit the lavatory. **3** [1980s] (*Can./US campus*) a portable lavatory. [? milit. jargon *bivvy*, a small shelter, ult. SE *bivouac*]

biffy *adj.* [20C+] drunk. [? BEVVY n. or a play on SQUIFFY adj. (1)]

biftah *n.* [1980s+] (*drugs*) cannabis or a cannabis cigarette. [ety. unknown; ? link to BIFF n.[1] (1), i.e. one takes a hit/HIT n.[3] (5)]

big *n.* [1940s+] (*US*) a superior person or one who claims to be.

big *adj.*[1] [late 16C–mid-18C; 1950s] pregnant. [SE *big*]

big *adj.*[2] **1** [late 19C] (*orig. US*) excellent, wonderful. **2** [late 19C+]

important. **3** [20C+] (*orig. US*) generous, magnanimous; usu. in phr. *that's big of you*. **4** [1920s+] successful, popular.

big *adj.*[3] **1** [late 19C+] (*US*) used of large amounts of money. **2** [1980s] large quantities of. **3** [1990s+] (*drugs*) large quantities of.

big *v.* [1930s+] (*US/W.I.*) to make pregnant. [biblical *big with child*]

big *adv.* **1** [late 17C; mid-19C+] notably, conspicuously, e.g. *win big, go over big*. **2** [mid-19C+] to a great extent. [orig. US, other than one-off 17C cit. in (1)]

Big A *n.*[1] **1** [1970s+] (*US*) Amarillo, Texas (cf. BIG B n.; BIG D n.; BIG M n.; BIG T n.; BIG V n.). **2** [1970s+] (*US*) Atlanta, Georgia. **3** [1980s+] (*US*) New York. **4** [1980s+] (*Aus.*) Australia. [abbr.; (3) BIG APPLE n.]

Big A *n.*[2] [1980s+] (*US*) Acquired Immuno-Deficiency Syndrome (AIDS). [on model of BIG C n. (2); BIG H n. (2)]

big a *n.* [1950s+] (*Aus.*) a brush-off, rejection, dismissal (from a job). [the *big arse* (ARSE n.[3])]

big-able *adj.* [20C+] (*W.I.*) massive, frighteningly huge.

big alley *n.* [1930s] (*orig. US tramp*) the main street.

big and bulky *n.* [1900s] (*Aus.*) a horse-drawn carriage. [rhy. sl. = SE *sulky*]

big-and-plenty *adj.* (*also* **big and so-so**) [20C+] (*W.I., Gren.*) fat and clumsy, and of low quality (used of people and things, e.g. vegetables).

Big Apple *n.* [1920s+] New York City. [in the *New Yorker*, 6 August 1984, Charles Gillett, the president of the New York Convention & Visitors Bureau, Inc., spoke on the value of the image of New York as the 'Big Apple'. It was his organization that plucked the term from the jazz lingo of the 1920s. The phr. in the jazz world, he said, had been playing 'the Big Stem in the Big Apple', the Big Stem being Broadway. For an exhaustive study see Cohen (ed.), *Studies in Slang* III (1993) and IV (1995)]

big apple *n.*[1] (*also* **apple**) [1960s+] (*orig. US Black*) a large-brimmed, oversized hat, in 1930s–40s style. [? APPLE-KNOCKER n. (1), such a hat being similar to those worn by a farm-worker to keep off the sun; or ? f. the size, fig. resembling that of the BIG APPLE n.]

big apple *n.*[2] *see* APPLE n.[2] (2).

big ass *n.* [1950s–60s] (*US*) a superior person or one who claims to be so. [SE *big* + ASS n. (1)]

big-ass *adj.* (*also* **big-assed**) (*US*) **1** [1940s+] big (in size). **2** [1950s+] important, powerful, self-opinionated. [SE *big* + ASS n. (2)/BIG ASS n.; the supposed crushing power of such massive buttocks]

big-ass *v.* [1980s+] (*US Southwest*) to make a fool of. [SE *big* + ASS n. (1)]

big-assedly *adv.* [1960s] (*US*) aggressively. [BIG-ASS adj. (2)]

big auger *n.* [mid-19C+] (*US, mainly Western*) an important person, a boss. [SE *big* + *auger*, a tool that bores holes; thus one who makes 'a big impression']

Big B *n.* [1970s] (*US*) Baltimore, Maryland (cf. BIG A n.[1]). [abbr.]

big bag *n.* [1960s+] (*drugs*) **1** heroin. **2** a large wholesale quantity of narcotics. [SE *big*, important + BAG n.[11] (1)/BAG n.[11] (3)]

big ballocks *n.* [1950s] a self-important man. [SE *big* + fig. use of BALLOCKS n.[1] (1)]

big banana *n.* (*US/Aus.*) **1** [1960s+] a superior person or one who claims to be. **2** [1980s+] the most important thing, the crux of a matter. [on model of BIG CHEESE n. + showbiz *top banana*, the star comedian]

big bean *n.* [1940s] (*US Black*) the sun. [SE *big* + BEAN n.[7]]

big-bellied *adj. see* FULL IN THE BELLY phr.

big-belly *adj.* [1920s+] (*W.I.*) greedy.

big Ben *n.* [1960s+] (*US gambling*) the point of 10 in craps dice (cf. ADA FROM DECATUR n.). [rhy. sl.; var. on BIG DICK n. (1)]

big ben *n.* **1** [1930s+] the number 10. **2** [1950s] 10 shillings. **3** [1950s+] £10 (cf. AYRTON (SENNA) n.). [rhy. sl.; *Big Ben* is the name of the bell in the clock tower St Stephen's Tower, the tallest tower of the Houses of Parliament, London]

big bertha *n. see* BERTHA *n.*

big bill *n.* [1930s] (*US Und.*) $1000. [SE *big* + *bill*; punning on proper name]

big bit *n.* [1940s+] (*US Und.*) a long prison sentence. [SE *big* + BIT n.[5]]

big bitch *n.* (*also* bitch) [1960s+] (*US prison*) a conviction under any crime that carries a mandatory life sentence; or a sentence so long that it is an equivalent; thus *put the bitch on*, to file charges against a criminal as a habitual offender. [SE *big* + BITCH n.[1] (6)]

big blink *n.* [1970s–80s] death. [var. on BIG SLEEP n.]

big bloke *n.*[1] [1910s] (*Aus.*) a boss, a superior. [SE *big* + BLOKE n.]

big bloke *n.*[2] [1930s+] (*drugs*) cocaine (cf. BARLEY n.[2]). [rhy. sl. = COKE n.[1] (1)]

big blow *n.* [20C+] (*Aus./US*) a hurricane. [SE *big* + SAusE *blow*, a storm]

big board *n.* [20C+] the New York Stock Exchange. [SE *board*, a board at the Stock Exchange on which share prices are displayed]

big boat *n.* [1910s+] a large, trad. American car, esp. a large station wagon. [SE *big* + BOAT n.[1] (3)]

big bob *n.* [late 19C] an aristocrat, a notable person.

big bopper *n.* [1980s+] (*US*) a superior person or one who claims to be. [SE *big* + BOPPER n.[1], lit. 'big hitter']

big boss, the *n.* [1920s+] (*US*) God. [joc. cod-intimacy]

big bout yah *adj.* [1980s+] (*W.I.*) of a person, important. [lit. ' big (i.e. important) about you']

big boy *n.*[1] **1** [1910s+] (*US*) a general term of address, sometimes sincere, often ironic. **2** [1920s+] (*US*) a superior person or one who claims to be. **3** [1920s+] (*US Und.*) (*also* **big fellow**) the head of an organized crime syndicate or some equivalent figure. **4** [1920s+] (*US Black*) a foolish, reckless, devil-may-care young man, a loveable idiot. **5** [1960s] (*US*) God.

big boy *n.*[2] **1** [1940s] (*US*) a $100 bill. **2** [1970s] (*US*) a shotgun. [? milit. *big boy*, a large, heavy or impressive piece of equipment or weaponry]

big brother *n.* [1960s] (*US gay*) the penis.

big brown eyes *n.* (*also* **big brownies, brown eyes**) [1930s–80s] attractive female breasts. [heavy-handed euph. based on colour of aureole]

big brown ones *n.* [1990s+] (*drugs*) MDMA (cf. ECSTASY n.). [the capsules in which the drug is sold]

big-buck *adj.* [1990s+] (*US Black*) expensive. [BIG BUCKS n.]

big bucks *n.* (*also* **big buck**) [1950s+] (*orig. US*) a large amount of money, esp. as earned by performers or stolen by criminals, or as a large, but non-specific price. [SE *big*/BIG adj.[3] (1) + BUCK n.[3] (3)]

big bug *n.* [19C+] (*orig. US*) an important person, an aristocrat, esp. someone who considers themself to be important and acts accordingly. [SE *big* + BUG n.[1] (1)]

big burg *n.* **1** [1910s–40s] (*US*) (*also* **main burg**) New York City. **2** [1920s] any city. [SE *big* + BURG n.[1]]

big butt *n.* [1910s–50s] (*US*) an important person. [SE *big* + BUTT n.[1] (3)]

Big C *n.* **1** [1950s+] (*drugs*) cocaine (cf. BIG D n.; BIG H n.; BIG M n.; BIG O n.). **2** [1960s+] (*also* **ca**) cancer; the horror disease (*pace* AIDS) of the 20th century which, as the supreme threat to life, cannot be named in full without a shudder (cf. BIG A n.[2]). **3** [2000s] cirrhosis of the liver. [abbr.]

big casino *n.* (*US*) **1** [late 19C+] an important person (cf. LITTLE CASINO n.). **2** [1900s] a large person. **3** [1920s+] the best, the ultimate, the most important. **4** [1930s+] anything terminal, fatal, esp. a disease, e.g. cancer; also syphilis. [the big wins and big losses involved]

big casino *adv.* [1990s+] (*US*) in an important, committed manner. [BIG CASINO n. (3)]

big cheese *n.* [20C+] (*orig. US*) an important person, an influential figure, a boss in a situation or job.

big chief *n.* **1** [1930s+] an important or the most important man. **2** [1950s] God. **3** [1960s] (*drugs*) mescaline.

big cigar *n.* [1920s] (*US Black*) a self-important person. [the stereotyped smoking habits of such figures]

big-cock *adj.* [1960s–70s] (*US*) enormous, outsized. [SE *big* + COCK n.[2] (1)]

big cog *n.* [2000s] an important or self-important person. [play on BIG WHEEL n.]

big coin *n.* [1990s+] (*US teen*) a large amount of money. [SE *big*/BIG adj.[3] (1) + COIN n.]

big con *n.* [1940s+] (*orig. US Und.*) any major confidence trick, the keynote of which is that the victim is persuaded to send for (usu. large sums of) money, rather than merely defrauding him/her of what they may have in their possession. [SE *big* + CON n.[1] (7)]

big cough *n.* [1920s–30s] (*US Und.*) a bomb. [the noise]

Big D *n.* (*US*) **1** [1960s+] the nickname of a variety of suitably initialled US cities, e.g. Dallas, Texas; Detroit, Michigan; Denver, Colorado (cf. BIG A n.[1]). **2** [1950s+] (*drugs*) dilaudid (cf. BIG C n.). **3** [1960s] (*drugs*) LSD. **4** [1970s+] death. [abbr.]

big daddy *n.* (*also* **big dad, big papa**) **1** [1940s+] (*US Black*) (*also* **big poppa**) any influential Black man aged 30 plus, a power in his own community. **2** [1950s–60s] (*mainly US Black*) one's grandfather. **3** [1950s–70s] (*US*) a male lover, a sweetheart. **4** [1960s] (*US*) a pimp (cf. DADDY n.; OLD MAN n.[1]; PAPA n.; PUFF DADDY n.; SWING DADDY n.). **5** [1960s+] (*orig. US*) an important person. **6** [1960s+] (*US*) the most important of its kind (not necessarily a human being). **7** [1970s] heroin (cf. BOY n.[7]; HARRY n.[2]; HENRY n.[2]; HIM n.[1]; JOHN n.[16]; MISTER n.[2]). **8** [1970s+] (*US gay*) the 'masculine' member of a homosexual couple. [fig. uses of SE]

big daddy pot *n.* [1960s+] (*W.I.*) a large iron pot, used for cooking cow-tripes after butchering. [BIG DADDY n. (6) + SE *pot*]

big day *n.* [1930s–50s] (*US prison*) visiting day.

big deal *n.* [1940s+] (*orig. US*) **1** an important person. **2** (*also* **hot deal**) anything that is considered important to the speaker; often ironic; thus NO BIG DEAL phr. [SE *big* + DEAL n.[1] (7)]

big deal *adj.* [1960s+] important, urgent, impressive etc. [BIG DEAL n. (2)]

big deal *v.* (*US*) **1** [1940s] to get what one wants by clever, forceful negotiation. **2** [1960s] to aggrandize, to magnify the importance of. [BIG DEAL n.]

big deal! *excl.* [1950s+] (*orig. US*) a dismissive, sarcastic phr., what's important about that? why bother me? [BIG DEAL n. (2)]

big dealer *n.* [1940s–70s] (*US*) an important person. [BIG DEAL n. (1)]

big deuce *n.* [1980s+] (*US teen*) WW2. [SE *big* + *deuce*, 2]

big Dick *n.* **1** [late 19C+] (*US gambling*) the point of 10 in craps dice; usu. ext. as *big Dick from Boston* (cf. ADA FROM DECATUR n.). **2** [1930s] (*US prison*) a 10-year jail sentence. **3** [1960s+] an important person; also attrib. [SE *big* + generic use of proper name/DICK n.[4]]

big dick from Boston *n.* [1930s+] (*US gay*) a loud-mouthed, boorish tourist, one who is puritanical at home but up for anything away from it. [punning on BIG DICK n.; generic use of proper name/DICK n.[4] (1)]

big dime *n.* [1920s+] (*US, mainly gambling*) a sum of $1000 or $10,000. [BIG adj.[3] (1) + DIME n.[1] (3)]

big dish *n.* [1940s] (*Aus.*) a big win; thus *go for the big dish*, to place a large bet, to gamble heavily.

big ditch *n.* (*US*) **1** [19C] the Erie Canal. **2** [mid-19C+] the Atlantic Ocean (cf. BIG DRINK n.; BIG FERRY n.; BIG MOIST n.; BIG POND n.; DITCH n.[2]; DUB, THE n.; DUCKPOND n.; POND, THE n.; PUDDLE n.; WATER, THE n.). **3** [1910s–60s] the Panama Canal. [DITCH n.[2]; joc. deliberate understatement]

big do *n.* [1900s–20s] (*US Black*) any notable event. [var. on BIG DOING n. (1)]

big dog *n.* **1** [mid-19C+] (*US*) an important person; thus *Big Dog Upstairs*, God. **2** [late 19C] a thug; a BOUNCER n.² (5). **3** [1990s+] a term of address to a friend.

big dog of the tanyard *n.* [mid–late 19C] an important person, the most important person. [fig. use of SE ? a fierce dog kept in a tanyard]

big dog with the brass collar *n.* [mid–late 19C] an important person, esp. in a business context.

big doing *n.* (*also* **big doings**) (*US*) **1** [20C+] any notable event, esp. a party or celebration. **2** [1900s–20s] a boaster, a braggart. [SE *big* + *doing*, what is being done]

big doing *adj.* [20C+] (*US*) conceited, self-opinionated, snobbish. [SE *big* (*things*) + *doing*, performing]

big dome *n. see* DOUBLE DOME n.

big-dome *adj.* [1950s] intellectual. [BIG DOME n.]

big drink *n.* [mid-19C+] (*US*) **1** the Mississippi River. **2** the ocean, esp. the Atlantic or Pacific Ocean (cf. BIG DITCH n.). [DRINK n.¹; joc. deliberate understatement]

big-dubs *n.* [20C+] (*W.I.*) a large and good-humoured man. [Carib.E. *big-dubs*, a large, polished marble]

big dude *n.* [1960s] (*US*) an important person. [SE *big* + DUDE n. (7)]

big Dutchman *n.* [late 19C+] (*US*) a general term of disparagement. [SE *big* + DUTCHMAN n., lit. 'German'/'foreigner', here used as a general pej.]

Big Easy, the *n.* [1970s+] (*US*) New Orleans, Louisiana. [? coined by James Conaway as the title of his novel *The Big Easy* (1970), later a popular film (1986); presumably f. the stereotype of its free-and-easy lifestyle]

big enchilada *n.* [1970s+] (*US*) an important person. [very popular during the Watergate Scandal (1973–4) when the White House tapes used it variously to describe corrupt personnel]

big end of *n.* [late 19C–1940s] (*orig. US*) the majority, the larger share (of loot); thus *big end of a month*, 3 weeks.

big end of the horn *n. see* LITTLE END OF THE HORN n.

big enough to choke a cow *phr.* (*also* **big enough to choke an elephant, …a horse, …an ox**) [late 19C+] (*US*) of a bankroll, extremely big.

big eye *n.* (*US*) **1** [19C+] avarice, greed; thus *have the big eye (for)*, to covet. **2** [1930s+] a stare, esp. when hostile or curious. **3** [1960s–70s] a television.

big eye *v.* **1** [20C+] to act greedily. **2** [1920s] (*US*) to stare at amorously. **3** [1930s+] to look at fixedly, to stare at. [BIG EYE n.]

big eyes *n.* [1930s–50s] (*US*) police officers engaged in surveillance duties. [BIG EYE n. (2)]

big eyes (for) *phr.* [1950s–60s] (*US Black*) happy, esp. meaning 'I am happy for you/about it'. [BIG EYE n. (1)]

big-feeler *n.* [1960s–70s] (*US*) an arrogant, self-important person. [BIG-FEELING adj.]

big-feeling *adj.* [late 19C+] haughty, conceited. [one who feels themself *big*]

big fellow *n. see* BIG BOY n.¹ (3).

big ferry *n.* [mid-19C] (*US*) the Atlantic Ocean (cf. BIG DITCH n.).

big figure *n.* [mid-19C] (*US*) a large scale; thus *do something on the big figure, go the big figure*, to do something on a large scale. [SE *big* + *figure*; a number, a sum]

big finger *n.* [1910s] (*US*) the senior figure.

big fish *n.* (*US*) **1** [early 19C+] an important, powerful person. **2** [mid-19C–1950s] an important event, undertaking etc. [SE *big* + FISH n.³]

big foe *n. see* BIG FOUR n.

Big Fog *n.* [1900s] (*Aus.*) London. [play on BIG SMOKE n. (1)]

big foot country *n.* [1940s–70s] (*US Black*) the southern United

States. [? the population 'walks tall'; note legendary 'Bigfoot', a monstrous creature allegedly found in California]

big foot Joe *n.* [1960s] the penis (cf. ABRAHAM n.¹). [? nickname]

big four *n.* (*also* **big foe**) [1920s; 1980s+] (*US Black*) tough, élite (often physically large) detectives, dealing with organized crime and similar areas; such police officers match their wide powers with indiscriminate physical violence and the general belief (in modern use) that all members of the Black community are *de facto* criminals. [the old practice of manning all police vehicles with 4 officers]

big gates *n.* [late 19C+] (*UK Und.*) a prison. [metonymy]

bigged *adj.* [1940s–50s] (*US Black*) pregnant. [BIG v.]

big George *n.* [1940s] (*US*) a self-important person. [SE *big* + generic use of proper name]

big george *n.* [1940s+] (*US*) a quarter, 25 cents (cf. ABE n.²). [SE *big*, used ironically + GEORGE n.³]

bigger thomas *n.* [1960s] (*US Black*) a rebellious Black man, one who refuses to abide by White society's rules and struggles against them. [proper name of *Bigger Thomas*, the hero of Richard Wright's novel *Native Son* (1940)]

biggerty *see under* BIGGITY.

biggest toad in the puddle *n.* [mid-19C–1910s] (*US*) a leader, a chief, the most important person in a situation. [fig.]

biggety *see under* BIGGITY.

biggie *n.* (*also* **biggy**) **1** [1920s+] (*orig. US*) anything or anyone large, important, successful, esp. used in entertainment industries. **2** [1950s+] (*W.I.*) a 750ml (26fl oz) bottle of rum. **3** [1970s] (*US prison*) the prison authorities. **4** [1990s+] £1000. [SE *big* + sfx *-ie/-y*]

biggins *n.*¹ (*also* **biggs**) [1990s+] (*UK juv.*) something unimportant, also used as an expression of dismissal. [BIG DEAL n. (2)]

biggins *n.*² (*also* **biggs**) [1990s+] (*UK juv.*) dark sweat marks appearing under the armpits of one's shirt or jacket. [*On Safari*, a UK TV children's show presented by Christopher *Biggins*, particularly those episodes in which 'he presented the (by most long forgotten) show in which he was in a "pretend" jungle but would sweat like a horse. This made his shirt darker in several malodorous places!' (*Online Dict. of Playground Slang*, 2001)]

big girl's blouse *n.* (*also* **girl's blouse**) [1960s+] a weakling, an ineffectual person; usu. found as *You big girl's blouse!*; also attrib. [the phr., now widespread, originated like the similarly deracinated GOBSMACKED adj. in the north of the UK]

biggitive *adj.* [20C+] (*W.I.*) bumptious, pushy, showing off; thus *biggitive with yourself*, self-satisfied. [var. on BIGGITY adj.]

biggity *adj.* (*also* **biggerty, biggety, bigotty**) [late 19C+] (*orig. US Black*) haughty, conceited, bumptious. [SE *big*]

biggity *adv.* (*also* **biggerty, biggety**) [1930s+] (*orig. US Black*) in a haughty manner. [BIGGITY adj.]

Big Green *n.*¹ [1930s+] (*US campus*) a nickname for Dartmouth College. [the college colour]

Big Green *n.*² [1990s+] (*US*) California's Environmental Protection Act (1990). [SE *big* on pattern of SAmE *big steel* etc, a generic word for a whole industry + *green*, relevant to ecology/conservationism]

biggs *see under* BIGGINS.

big gun *n.* **1** [mid-19C+] (*orig. US*) an important person. **2** [1900s] (*US Und.*) a leading thief.

big guy *n.* (*US*) **1** [20C+] anyone important or considered as such, e.g. a gang boss. **2** [1920s+] (*also* **big man**) God, Christ. **3** [1980s] a friend; thus a joc. form of address.

biggy *n.*¹ [1950s+] (*W.I.*) a man who is both tall and lazy. [SE *big*]

biggy *n.*² *see* BIGGIE n.

Big H *n.* **1** [1950s+] (*drugs*) heroin (cf. BIG C n.; BIG HARRY n.; CHINESE H n.; H n.²; HACHE n.; HARRY n.²; HAZEL n.; H CAPS n.; HELEN n.; HENRY n.²; HORSE n.⁸; VITAMIN H n.). **2** [1980s+] a heart attack (cf. BIG A n.²). [initial letters]

big Harry n. [1960s+] (drugs) heroin (cf. BIG H n.). [initial letters]

big hat n.[1] (US) 1 [1940s+] an important person. 2 [1960s+] a policeman or state trooper. [the headgear worn as part of many US police uniforms]

big hat n.[2] [1970s] (US) a Mexican (cf. BATO n.). [the clichéd large Mexican hat]

big head n.[1] 1 [mid-19C–1900s] (US) conceit, self-importance. 2 [mid-19C+] a conceited or arrogant person. 3 [1930s] (US) an important person. 4 [1930s–70s] a successful person. 5 [1940s] (US prison) the warden. 6 [1970s–80s] (UK Black/drugs) a large cannabis cigarette. 7 [2000s] an intellectual.

big head n.[2] see HEAD n.[12].

big-headed adj. (also **big-head**) [1920s+] arrogant, conceited. [BIG HEAD n.[1] (2)]

big hen's biddy n. [1930s] (US Black) a coward, a weakling.

big hit n.[1] [1950s+] (Aus.) an act of defecation (cf. ANDY CAPP n.). [rhy. sl. = SHIT n.[1] (3)]

big hit n.[2] [1970s] (US prison) a long term of imprisonment, usu. 3 years or more. [ironic use of SE big + hit, a success]

big house n. 1 [mid-19C] the workhouse. 2 [1900s] a theatre. 3 [1910s+] (US Und.) (also **big stir**) prison, esp. San Quentin prison, sometimes ext. as big house up the river or (S.Afr. Und.) Pretoria Central prison (cf. BANDHOUSE n.). 4 [1950s+] any large, forbidding institution, esp. a psychiatric institution.

big house nigger n. [1950s] (US Black) any proud, arrogant person. [SE big + HOUSE NIGGER n.]

big huey, the n. [1970s–80s] (N.Z. prison) a long sentence. [play on SE long/Louisiana governor Huey P. Long (1893–1935)]

bigified adj. [1960s+] (US) haughty, conceited. [SE big + sfx -ified]

big Ike n. [1900s–10s] (US) an important person. [SE big + IKE n. (2)]

big I, little you n. [1960s–70s] (US) an important person.

big Injun n. (also **big Indian**) [late 19C–1900s] (US) an important person (cf. GREAT WHITE CHIEF n.). [SE big + INJUN n./INDIAN n.[1] (2)]

big (it up) v. [1980s+] (W.I./UK Black teen) to aggrandize, to embellish, to praise, to extol. [SE big]

big J n. [1970s+] (US gay) simultaneously fellating and sodomizing one's partner. [? big job]

big jab n. (also **doctorate in applied chemistry, stainless steel ride**) [2000s] (US prison) a lethal injection, used in executions. [SE big + JAB n.[2] (1)]

big job n.[1] [mid-19C] (US) murder, assassination; thus do the big job, to kill. [euph.]

big job n.[2] [1930s] anything notably large of its type, e.g. an automobile. [SE big + JOB n.[4]]

big jobs n. [1940s+] (orig. US juv.) excreta; thus do big jobs, to defecate. [euph.]

big John n. [1970s+] (US Black) the police. [SE big + JOHN n.[4]]

big joint n. see BIG STORE n.

big juice n. [1960s–70s] (US Black) a White gang-boss. [SE big + JUICE n.[1] (4)]

big jump n. [1910s] (US) death; usu. in phr. put someone over the big jump.

big juta, little juta, all same price phr. [20C+] (W.I.) anything goes, irrespective of size or quality; usu. used of a country person who lacks the city dweller's standards of choice. [Hind. juutaa, a shoe, and orig. used of shoes]

big kahuna, the n. see KAHUNA n.

Big L n. [1970s] (US prison) Leavenworth prison, Kansas (cf. ABBOTT'S PRIORY n.).

big L n. [1980s+] 1 (US) love. 2 (US campus) a person who is a failure. 3 (UK prison) a life sentence. [abbr.; (2) LOSER n. (1)]

big league n. [20C+] (US) an important or influential situation or position. [sporting imagery]

big-league adj. [1910s+] (US) important, substantial, powerful. [BIG LEAGUE n.]

big-leaguer n. 1 [1910s–40s] an important person. 2 [1920s] an important thing. 3 [1950s] a major criminal. 4 [1950s–60s] a resourceful person who can handle any situation. [BIG LEAGUE n.]

big leg adj. [1970s+] (US) sexy. [SE big +LEG n.[7] (3)]

big legs n. [1970s–80s] a big spender. [? who has trousers with big pockets]

big licks n. [mid-late 19C] (US/Aus.) hard work; usu. as put in big licks or go in/on big licks, to make a great effort. [SE big + lick, a blow; note Aus. racing jargon go for the big lick, to bet heavily]

big lump n. [2000s] (UK prison) a long sentence.

Big M n. 1 [1950s+] £1 million. 2 [1950s+] (drugs) morphine (cf. BIG C n.). 3 [1960s] marriage. 4 [1970s] Memphis, Tennessee (cf. BIG A n.[1]). [initial letters]

big Mac n. [1990s+] (UK Und.) an Ingram Mac-10 machine pistol. [abbr.]

big mac n. [1990s+] dismissal from a job. [rhy. sl. = SACK, THE n.; ult. the McDonald's hamburger Big Mac]

big Magilla n. [2000s] (US) an important, influential person. [play on the Magilla Gorilla show/GORILLA n.[1] (5); but note Yid. gantz megillah, a whole rigmarole]

big mama n.[1] [1940s+] (US Black) one's grandmother. [cognate with BIG DADDY n. (2)]

big mama n.[2] 1 [1970s+] anything notably large, substantial. 2 [1990s+] (US) the ocean. [SE big + MAMA n. (3)]

Big Man n. [1900s–30s] (US Und.) the Pinkerton Detective Agency.

big man n.[1] 1 [late 19C+] any form of superior person, esp. in a criminal context. 2 [1910s+] (drugs) a dealer, esp. a major dealer, selling bulk quantities of drugs. 3 [1970s] (US Black) a gallon of wine.

big man n.[2] see BIG GUY n. (2).

big meadow n. [1930s] (US Und.) prison.

big medicine n. 1 [late 19C; 1980s] (US) an important or influential person or thing. 2 [1910s+] (US) something or someone dangerous. [(2) BAD MEDICINE n.]

big mitt n. [1900s–40s] (US Und.) a form of swindling involving the use of a stacked hand while playing poker. [SE big + MITT n. (2)]

big mitt man n. [1930s–40s] (US Und.) a confidence trickster. [BIG MITT n.]

big moist n. [1940s] (US Black) the Atlantic Ocean (cf. BIG DITCH n.).

big moment n. [1920s–60s] (Irish/US) the person with whom one is infatuated.

bigmouth n. [late 19C+] (orig. US) 1 a braggart, a boaster. 2 an informer, a tell-tale. 3 empty boasting, showing off. [BIG-MOUTHED adj.]

bigmouth v. [1960s+] (US) to brag (about). [BIGMOUTH n. (1)]

big-mouthed adj. (also **bigmouth**) 1 [17C+] boastful, self-aggrandizing. 2 [late 19C] noisy.

big mover n. [1950s+] (Aus.) one who is a consistent success, e.g. as a womanizer. [SE big + MOVER n. (1)]

big mucky-muck n. see HIGH MUCK-A-MUCK n.

bignaduo n. [1910s+] (W.I.) a boaster, a bumptious person, a show-off, one who puts on airs. [lit. 'big as a door']

big nickel n. [1920s+] (US, mainly gambling) a sum of $500 or $5000. [BIG adj.[3] (1) + NICKEL n. (6)]

big nigger n. [20C+] (US) in poker, a game in which the high spade splits the pot. [the blackness of the spade suit]

big nigger in charge n. see HEAD NIGGER IN CHARGE n.

big noise n. 1 [mid-19C; 1950s] (US) trouble, disturbance. 2 [20C+] (orig. US) an important, powerful person.

bignose n. [20C+] a derog. name for a Jew (cf. CLIP n.[4]; CLIP-DICK n.; CURLY-WURLY n.; EAGLE BEAK n.; HOOK n.[8]; HOOKEY n.; HOOKNOSE n.; HOOKY n.[3]; LONG-NOSE n.; SHONK n.; WEEPER n.[1]).

big note n. [1990s+] £100, a £100 note. [SE big + NOTE n.[1] (1)]

big-note v. [1940s+] (Aus.) to boast, usu. as big-note oneself, to inflate one's achievements. [SE big + note, paper money, currency]

big note man n. [1950s] (Aus.) a rich man.

big noter n. [1960s+] (Aus.) a show-off, a braggart. [BIG-NOTE v.]

big number n.[1] [mid-19C–1900s] a brothel. [the outsize numbers painted on brothel doors in Paris]

big number n.[2] 1 [1940s–60s] (US) an important person. 2 [1950s] (US prison) one who poses as more important in the outside world than they really are. [SE big + NUMBER n.[1] (2)]

Big O n. 1 [1950s+] (drugs) opium (cf. APOSTLE n.; BIG C n.). 2 [1960s+] an orgasm. 3 [1980s] (US campus) a person with no personality. [initial letter/zero]

big — -o, the phr. [1980s+] (orig. US) used of landmark birthdays, e.g. those that mark another decade, e.g. big three-o, big four-o etc.

big old time n. see HIGH (OLD) TIME n.

big one n. 1 [mid-19C+] £100, £1000. 2 [mid-19C+] (US) $100, $1000. 3 [1900s–50s] (US Und.) a major and extremely lucrative coup. 4 [1960s+] (US) $1 million. 5 [1970s+] a large – unspecified – amount of money. 6 [1970s+] (US) $1.

big one, the n. 1 [1950s+] a major operation. 2 [1950s+] (US) WW2. 3 [1960s] (US) death. 4 [1980s+] (orig. US) a major disaster that hasn't happened yet, esp. California's long-awaited major earthquake or a nuclear war.

Big Orange n. [1980s+] (US) Los Angeles, California. [on model of BIG APPLE n.; the ref. is to the state's orange groves]

big order n. see TALL ORDER n.

bigotty adj. see BIGGITY adj.

big papa n. see BIG DADDY n.

big paper n. (also tall paper) [1990s+] (US Black) a great deal of money. [BIG adj.[3] (1)/TALL adj.[2] (3) + PAPER n.[1] (2)]

big parade, the n. [1920s–50s] (US) WW1. [the title of the film The Big Parade (1925), screenplay by Laurence Stallings, although the phr. is never used in the film itself]

big pasture n. [20C+] (US) a prison. [as used by cowboys and other Westerners]

big people n. [mid-19C+] important, influential people.

big pond n. [mid-19C+] (orig. US) the Atlantic Ocean (cf. BIG DITCH n.). [SE big + POND, THE n. (1); joc. deliberate understatement]

big poppa n. see BIG DADDY n. (1).

big pot n. (also great pot) [late 19C+] a leader, an important person. [? SE potentate; which was also Oxford jargon in 1850s to mean a don or a prominent undergraduate]

big potato n.[1] [late 19C+] an important person.

big potato n.[2] [1980s+] (US) Moscow. [on model of BIG APPLE n./BIG ORANGE n.; potatoes are the main constituent of vodka]

big puddle n. see PUDDLE n.

Big Q n. [2000s] (US Und.) San Quentin prison (cf. ABBOTT'S PRIORY n.).

big razzoo n. [1930s+] a gesture of extreme contempt or scorn. [SE big + RAZZ n.[1] (1)]

Big Red n. [1940s+] (US campus) Cornell University. [the college colour]

Big Red with the long green stem n. [1940s–50s] (US Black) Seventh Avenue, between 130th Street and 150th Street, the centre of Harlem nightlife. [BIG APPLE n. + LONG GREEN n. (1) + MAIN STEM, THE n. (2)]

Big Rock n. see ROCK, THE n. (2).

big rock n. [1960s] (US) a prison. [SE big + ROCK n.[6]]

big rod n. 1 [1920s+] (US) an important person. 2 [1940s] (US Und.) a machine gun.

big school n. [1920s–60s] (US tramp) a state prison (cf. BOARDING SCHOOL n.; CITY COLLEGE n.; FINISHING SCHOOL n.; GLADIATOR SCHOOL n.; GRAYSTONE COLLEGE n.; KING'S COLLEGE n.; LITTLE SCHOOL n.; NEWMAN'S (COLLEGE) n.; ROCK COLLEGE n.; SCHOOL n.[2]; STATE COLLEGE n.; WHITTINGTON('S) COLLEGE n.). [as compared to LITTLE SCHOOL n.]

big screech n. [1910s] (US) an important person.

big screw n. [1920s–30s] (US prison) the Deputy Warden. [SE big + SCREW n.[2] (3)]

big shit n. (US) 1 [1930s+] an important person or one who claims to be. 2 [2000s] serious business. [SE big + SHIT n.[2] (1)/SHIT n.[4]]

big-shit adj. [1960s] (US) self-important. [BIG SHIT n. (1)]

big-shit adv. [1990s+] (US) to a great extent. [BIG SHIT n. (2)]

big shit! excl. 1 [1910s+] a response suggesting that someone is a BIG SHOT n., in phr. big shot, big shit! 2 [1960s+] (US campus) an excl. of agreement or a dismissive, sarcastic excl. [BIG SHIT n. (1)/SE big + SHIT n.[3] (4)]

big shot n. (also shot, top shot) [1920s+] (orig. US) a superior person or one who claims to be?; also as a term of address. [the term began as a positive ref. to a major criminal, but by 1930s it was mainly used ironically and implied that the individual in question was rather too pleased with themself. Note dial. queer shot, an odd fellow, a strange 'customer'; great shot mid-19C, an important person]

big-shot adj. [1920s+] (orig. US) superior, important, powerful or posing as such (esp. in the criminal milieu). [BIG SHOT n.]

big shot v. (also bigshot) [1950s+] (US) to show off, to act like an important person. [BIG SHOT n.]

big show n. 1 [20C+] (US) an important person. 2 [1910s] an important situation. [SE big + show(-off)]

big six n. [1950s+] (US prison) the prison riot squad; thus big six talk, empty, if aggressive, talk. [? there are 6 officers; the high number 6 in dice]

big sleep n. [1930s+] (orig. US) death. [coined by Raymond Chandler as title of his book The Big Sleep (1939), although HDAS suggests (without confirmatory cits.) that he 'gave currency' to the term]

Big Smoke n. 1 [late 19C+] London. 2 [late 19C+] any town or city. 3 [late 19C+] (Aus.) Sydney. 4 [late 19C+] (Aus.) Melbourne. 5 [1930s+] Pittsburgh, Pennsylvania. 6 [1980s+] (Irish) Dublin. [the pollution and general dirt associated with a major city. OED suggests orig. Aus. trans. of Aboriginal toom-virran, big-smoke]

big smoke n. [1900s–30s] (US) an important person.

Big Snarl n. (also Big Stoush) [1910s+] (Aus.) WW1, orig. used by ex-soldiers. [SE big + snarl/STOUSH n. (1)]

big spender n. [1940s+] a spendthrift, one who flashes their money around; esp. in phr. last of the big spenders, used ironically to mock a cheapskate or someone who is spending a great deal of money that they patently cannot afford. [usu. slightly derog., the implication being that any such 'spender' will also be a SUCKER n.[3] (1)]

big spit n. (also long spit) [1950s+] (Aus.) the act of vomiting; thus GO FOR THE BIG SPIT v.

big spuds n. [1930s] (US tramp) those in authority. [lit. 'big potatoes'; joc. antonym of SMALL POTATOES n. (1)]

big squash n. [1910s–60s] an important person or someone who think they are. [BIG SQUEEZE n. + ? on pattern of BIG CHEESE n., SE squash, the vegetable]

big squeeze n. [20C+] (US) an important person. [SE big + SQUEEZE n.[7] (1)]

big stick n.[1] [20C+] (orig. US) 1 an important person. 2 a figure of authority, esp. a policeman or foreman. 3 fig. authority, violence. [? their real or fig. truncheon or similar badge of office/chastisement. Note Theodore Roosevelt's dictum: 'Speak softly and carry a big stick']

big stick n.[2] [1930s] (US) dynamite.

big stiff n. [20C+] (orig. US) a general term of abuse, a fool. [SE big + STIFF n.[2] (5)]

big store n. (also big joint) [20C+] (US Und.) a fake casino or broker's office, in which victims are subjected to an elaborate large-scale swindle. [note Maurer, The Big Con (1940): ' The big store An establishment against which big-con men play their victims. For the wire and the pay-off, it is set up like a poolroom which takes race bets. For the rag, it is set up to resemble a broker's office. Stores are set up with a careful attention to detail which makes them seem bona fide. After each play, the store is taken down and all equipment stored away']

Big Stoush n. see BIG SNARL n.

big stuff n. **1** [late 19C] a strong, violent person. **2** [1910s–60s] (US) a term of address, usu. slightly derog. **3** [1910s+] (orig. US) an important or self-important person. **4** [1920s+] (US) a major criminal. **5** [1950s–60s] an important situation, esp. with criminal overtones. **6** [1950s+] (US) a large amount of money. [milit. jargon big stuff, heavy artillery shells]

big stunt n. [1910s] WW1. [SE big + STUNT n.]

big style adv. see BIG TIME adv.

big swing n. [1960s+] (US) the prison gallows. [SE big + SE swing/SWING v.¹ (1)]

Big T n. [1970s] (US) **1** Tucson, Arizona (cf. BIG A n.¹). **2** Tampa, Florida. [abbr.]

big talk n. [mid-19C+] boasting, braggartry, verbal self-aggrandizement.

big talk v. [1950s+] (US) to show off, to try to impress. [BIG TALK n.]

big talker n. [20C+] one who boasts, a braggart. [BIG TALK n.]

big thing n. **1** [mid-19C] (US Und.) a large amount of plunder. **2** [mid-19C+] anything important, noteworthy; often as a negative phr. NO BIG THING phr. **3** [1980s] (US drugs) 1kg of cocaine.

big thing, the n. [20C+] a generous, magnanimous act; often as do the big thing, make a generous gesture.

big ticket (item) n. [1940s+] (US) something that is expensive, requiring a considerable financial outlay. [the high-priced ticket placed on expensive retail goods in a shop]

big time n.¹ **1** [mid-19C–1950s] (US) an exciting, enjoyable time. **2** [20C+] success, fame, power; thus get big time, to put on airs and graces. **3** [1920s+] an important person or a powerful, impressive thing, esp. in ironic use. **4** [1950s+] a form of address, whether or not ironic. [theatrical use, vaudeville theatres with top-line acts and thus only 2 (long) shows per day, the opposite of 'small time', which featured shorter acts]

big time n.² [1930s+] (US prison) a lengthy sentence, of 3 or more years. [SE big + TIME n.¹]

big-time adj. (also **bigtime**) **1** [1910s+] (orig. US) (also **big-timey**) of a person, important, successful, powerful. **2** [1920s+] of a situation, very great. **3** [1930s+] desperate, urgent, forceful. [BIG TIME n.¹]

big time v. [1940s+] **1** (orig. US) to act in a self-important manner. **2** (US Black) to live well. [BIG TIME n.¹]

big time adv. (also **big style**) [1950s+] (orig. US Black/prison) very much, completely, absolutely, e.g. she loves him big time. [BIG TIME n.¹ (3)]

big timer n. **1** [1920s+] (orig. US) an important person, a major criminal. **2** [1970s] (US prison) one who is serving a long sentence. [BIG-TIME adj. (1)/TIME n.¹]

big-timey adj. see BIG-TIME adj. (1).

big toast n. [1950s] (US Black) an outstanding person.

big top n. [1920s+] (US Und.) prison, esp. the main cellblock.

big toter n. [1970s] (US) a shotgun. [SE big + tote, to carry]

big town n. [20C+] (US) **1** New York City. **2** any city, esp. Chicago.

bigtown adj. [1940s–50s] (US Black) sophisticated, successful, influential. [BIG TOWN n., i.e. urban]

big track n. see FAST TRACK n.

big-tree adj. [1940s+] (W.I.) violent, bullying, gangsterish. [BIG-TREE BOY n.]

big-tree boy n. (also **big-tree man**) [1910s+] (W.I.) an idler, a semi-gangster, esp. if idling near a large banyan tree in Victoria Park, Kingston, Jamaica.

big twist n. [1930s+] (Aus.) a cause for celebration, a great success. [SE big + 'twist of fate']

Big Two, the n. [1950s+] (US) WW2.

big-up n. [1990s+] a positive reference to, a promotion of. [BIG UP v. (2)]

big up adj. [1970s+] (W.I.) important; of a person, socially or otherwise powerful; of an object, powerful, fashionable. [SE big; note BIG UP v.]

big up v. [1990s+] (UK Black/W.I.) **1** to act in a proud, self-confident matter. **2** to promote, to boost, to praise. **3** to greet friends, to pay tribute to something or someone big or important, e.g. Big up the dancehall crew dem, seen, come again.

Big V n. [1970s] (US) Las Vegas, Nevada (cf. BIG A n.¹). [abbr.]

big vegetable n. [1910s] (orig. US) an important person, an influential figure, the boss. [var. on BIG CHEESE n.]

big water n. see WATER, THE n. (3).

big wheel n. (also **wheel**) [1930s+] (orig. US) an important, influential person, esp. in business. [the image of a smooth-running, powerful machine]

big white chief n. see GREAT WHITE CHIEF n.

big white telephone n. [1970s+] the lavatory. [TELEPHONE n.²]

big whoop! excl. [1980s+] (US) a dismissive, sarcastic phr., what's important about that? [SE whoop, a cry (of exultation, triumph); a var. on BIG DEAL! excl.]

bigwig n. (also **big wig**) [early 18C+] a powerful, important person, often a politician or bureaucrat. [SE big + wig]

big willie n. [1990s+] (US Black) a sophisticated, successful urban Black male. [SE big + generic use of proper name; + ? WILLIE n.⁵; 'the Big Willie...is...the strong, silent type...an old-school romantic (and) a savvy businessman...a free thinker, fluent with modern technology. He is fearless, vigilant and innovative.' Vibe magazine, September 1996]

big willie adj. [1990s+] (US Black) important, influential, powerful. [BIG WILLIE n.]

Big Wind n. (also **Big Windy**) [1940s+] (US) Chicago, Illinois. [var. on WINDY CITY n.]

big works n. [1910s] (US) an important person. [SE big + WORKS, THE n. (2)]

big X, the n. [1980s+] (US campus) one's menstrual period. [marked on a calendar with an X]

big yard n. **1** [1940s+] (W.I.) a prison. **2** [1970s] (US prison) a prison recreation area. [SE big + yard, the exercise area of a prison]

bijou adj. [1960s+] small and pretty, usu. in combs. with a n. + the sfx -ette, e.g. I'll have just a bijou drinkette, 'just a little' drink. [Fr.]

bike n. **1** [1940s+] a promiscuous woman (cf. BANBURY n.). **2** [1960s] an act of sexual intercourse. [pun on SE ride/RIDE v.¹ (1)]

bike it v. [1980s] to leave.

biker n. **1** [late 19C] a cyclist. **2** [1960s+] (orig. US) a motorcycle rider, usu. a member of an outlaw motorcycle gang; also attrib. **3** [1980s] a 'biker movie', devoted to the fictionalized exploits of outlaw motrcyclists. [SE (motor)bike]

biker's coffee n. [2000s] (US drugs) a mix of coffee and methamphetamine. [BIKER n. (2) + SE coffee]

bikie n. (also **bikey**) [1960s+] (Aus./N.Z.) an 'outlaw' motorcyclist, e.g. a Hell's Angel. [var. on BIKER n. (2)]

bikini burger n. [1990s+] wisps of pubic hair protruding from a bikini. [SE bikini + FURBURGER n.]

bikkie n. (also **biccie**) [1980s+] **1** a biscuit, often in pl. **2** (Aus. drugs) a biscuit cooked with a dose of hashish. [dimin. of SE biscuit]

bikkies n. (also **biccies, bickies**) [1960s+] (Aus.) money; thus big bikkies, a large amount of money. [BIKKIE n. (1); thus the roundness of coins]

bil n. [late 17C–mid-18C] (UK Und.) a sword. [abbr. of BILBO n. (1)]

bilayutee pawnee *n.* [late 19C] (*Anglo-Ind.*) soda water. [Arab. *wildayat*, kingdom, province, then Hind. *bilayuti*, Europe + *panee/pawnee*, water]

bilbo *n.* (*also* **bilboa**) **1** [late 17C–mid-19C] (*UK Und.*) a ruffian's sword; thus *bilbo's the word*, it's time for swords, i.e. fighting. **2** [18C–early 19C] iron ankle shackles, also called 'iron-garters'. **3** [late 18C–early 19C] in pl., the stocks. [SE *bilbo, bilboa*, a high-quality sword, imported from Bilbao in Spain; Williams includes *bilbo* among the sword synons. used for penis]

bilbo *v.* [mid-18C] (*UK Und.*) to place in shackles or irons. [BILBO n. (2)]

bilfa *n. see* BELFA n.

bilge *n.* [20C+] nonsense, rubbish. [abbr. BILGEWATER n. (2)]

bilge artist *n.* [1920s+] (*Aus.*) a braggart, one given to boasting. [BILGE n. + ARTIST sfx]

bilgewater *n.* **1** [late 19C] thin beer; thus any thin, tasteless drink, alcoholic or otherwise. **2** [late 19C+] (*mainly UK juv.*) nonsense, rubbish, piffle. **3** [1920s] urine. [SE *bilgewater*, the foul water that collects in a vessel's bilges]

bilingual *adj.* **1** [1980s+] (*orig. US gay*) describing one who licks and sucks both the anus and penis of his partner. **2** [1960s] (*US*) describing one who enjoys oral sex with both men and women, a bisexual fan of oral intercourse. [pun on SE]

biljim *n. see* BILLJIM n.

bilk *n.* **1** [mid-17C–mid-18C] an empty, meaningless statement. **2** [late 17C–mid-18C] a hoax, an act of cheating. **3** [mid-19C] (*US*) a disappointment. **4** [mid-19C+] (*US Und.*) a swindler or cheat. **5** [1940s] (*US*) a form of swindle worked on a brothel madam. [cribbage jargon *balk*, to spoil an adversary's score in their crib]

bilk *adj.* [mid-18C] wrong, misleading, meaningless. [BILK n. (2)]

bilk *v.* **1** [mid-17C+] (*UK Und.*) to cheat, to swindle. **2** [19C] to evade payments, esp. of a prostitute's client. [BILK n. (2)]

bilker *n.* [early 18C–1940s] one who habitually cheats, esp. in refusing to pay a bill, e.g. a cabman's fare. [BILK v.]

bilk the blues *v.* [mid-19C] to evade capture by the police. [BILK v. + BLUE n.³ (2)]

bilk the schoolmaster *v.* [early 19C] to get knowledge without paying for it, e.g. the experience that comes with living one's life. [BILK v. + SE *schoolmaster*]

Bill *n.¹* **1** [late 19C–1910s] used to address an otherwise unknown male. **2** [1960s–70s] (*US camp gay*) a 'masculine' male homosexual, a term of address to such a person, particularly used ironically.

Bill *n.²* [1900s] (*Aus.*) a generic for an Aus. soldier.

Bill *n.³ see* OLD BILL n.

Bill, the *n.* [1960s+] the police. [abbr. OLD BILL n.]

bill *n.¹* **1** [mid-17C] the penis. **2** [early–mid-19C+] (*US*) the nose.

bill *n.²* [20C+] **1** any banknote (cf. BANK-RAG n.). **2** $1, a $1 bill. **3** $10. **4** $20. **5** (*also* **one bill**) $100. [abbr. SE *dollar bill*]

bill *n.³* [1910s] (*US*) a divorce. [abbr. SE *bill of divorce*]

bill *n.⁴* [2000s] amphetamine (sulphate) (cf. A n.²). [abbr. BILLY WHIZ n. (1)]

bill *n.⁵ see* BILL (OF GOODS) n.

bill *v.* [1910s–40s] (*US*) to divorce. [BILL n.³]

billabonger *n.* [late 19C–1950s] (*Aus.*) a vagrant. [SE *billabong*, a dry watercourse, in which such men took shelter and slept]

billet *n.* [19C+] an appointment, a job; thus (*Aus.*) *billet-hunter*, a job-seeker. [SE *billet*, a place in which a soldier is billeted; a soldier's lodging or quarters]

billiard ball *n.* **1** [17C] a testicle, usu. in pl.; esp. in phr. *billiard balls and stick*, the testicles (and penis). **2** [19C] the head (presumably of a bald person).

billied *adj.* [1950s] (*US drugs*) addicted to cocaine. [BILLIE HOKE n.]

billie hoke *n.* [1950s+] (*drugs*) cocaine (cf. BARLEY n.²). [rhy. sl. = COKE n.¹ (1)]

billies *n.* (*also* **billys**) [1980s] (*US teen*) money. [dimin. of BILL n.² (1)]

bill in *v.* [1930s] to butt in, to interrupt. [BILL n.¹(2)]

Billingsgate pheasant *n.* [late 19C–1900s] a red herring (the fish). [*Billingsgate*, London's wholesale fish market]

billjim *n.* (*also* **biljim**) **1** [1900s–10s] (*Aus.*) the typical Australian male. **2** [1910s] used in WW1 for an Aus. soldier. [the proper names *Bill + Jim*; (2) a synthetic var., *billzac* (SE bill + ANZAC) was created by the Aus. press during WW1, but never spread beyond their own columns]

bill-o! *excl.* [20C+] (*UK juv.*) a cry of warning. [SE (*watch out*) *below!*]

bill (of goods) *n.* (*also* **bill**) [20C+] (*orig. US*) false promises, a hoax, theories that are not followed up by practice; thus *sell one a bill of goods*, to persuade (someone) to accept something undesirable, to swindle someone. [SE *bill of goods*, a consignment of merchandise]

bill of sale *n.* **1** [17C] a widow's peak. **2** [18C–mid-19C] a widow's weeds. [? a widow is 'back on the (marriage) market']

bill on the pump at Aldgate *n.* (*also* **Aldgate pump, draft on the pump at Aldgate, draught…**) [mid-18C–19C] a bad bill of exchange. [SE *bill/draft*, a written order for the payment of money + proper name *Aldgate Pump*, near junction of Fenchurch Street and Leadenhall Street in London; the pump was a City institution, but hardly a safe financial one]

bill-poster *n.* [1930s–40s] (*US Und.*) a forger, a counterfeiter, a passer of bad cheques.

bill shop *n.* [1960s+] a police station. [BILL, THE n. + SE *shop*]

bill skinner *n.* [2000s] (*Irish*) dinner. [rhy. sl.]

bill (up) *v.* [1980s+] (*drugs*) to roll up a cannabis cigarette. [UK Black pron. of BUILD v. (1)]

bill-wagon *n. see* WAGON n.¹.

Billy *n. see* KING BILLY n.

billy *n.¹* [mid-19C] the vagina. [? a play on the *billycock* hat, a low-crowned felt hat]

billy *n.²* **1** [mid-19C] a short iron crowbar, used by criminals. **2** [mid–late 19C] (*UK Und.*) stolen metal. **3** [mid-19C+] (*orig. US*) (*also* **bill**) a policeman's wooden club (orig. untanned cowhide, covered in wool), now SE?. **4** [mid-19C+] a form of blackjack, usu.'loaded' with lead. **5** [1980s] (*US Black*) the police. **6** [2000s] (*US prison*) a White man.

billy *n.³* [mid-19C] a silk handkerchief, worn by London costermongers. [? King *William* IV, in whose reign (1830–37) the practice began. The silk handkerchief was a central part of costermonger fashion, often apeing that of the prize-ring, where fancy handkerchiefs were an essential trademark of certain fighters. As Mayhew, *London Labour and the London Poor* (1861–2), notes: 'The costermonger…prides himself most of all upon his neckerchief and boots. Men, women, boys and girls all have a passion for these articles. The man who does not wear his silk neckerchief/his "King's-man" as it is called – is known to be in desperate circumstances, the implication being that it has gone to supply the morning's stock money']

billy *n.⁴* [mid-19C–1930s] (*Aus.*) a billycock hat. [SE *billycock*, a low crowned felt hat; ult. f. *bully-cocked*, used 1721, prob. meaning 'cocked after the fashion of the bullies' or street thugs of the period]

billy *n.⁵* (*also* **billy-maria**) [20C+] (*US*) a hillbilly, a rustic fool. [abbr.]

billy *n.⁶* [1960s] (*US*) a policeman (cf. BILLY BOY n.; BILLY MAN n.; BOBBY n.; BOBBY PEELER n.; BRENDA n.²; CHARLIE GOON n.; DICK n.⁶; JACK n.¹⁹; JENNY DARBY n.; JOE n.²; JOEY n.²; JOHN n.⁴; JOHN BLUEBOTTLE n.; JOHN DUNN n.²; JOHN ELBOW n.; JOHN HOP n.; JOHN LAW n.; JOHNNIE NAB n.; JOHNNY n.²; JOHNNY DARBY n.; JOHNNY GALLAGHER n.; JOHNNY LAW n.; JOHN Q LAW n.; MUG JOHN n.; O'MALLEY n.; PADDY n.; PENELOPE n.; PETER JAY n.; ROBERT n.²;

SHAMUS n.; UNCLE BILL n.; UNCLE BOB n.[1]; WATER-BOBBY n.). [BILLY n.[2] (3)]

billy n.[7] [1990s+] (*drugs*) amphetamine (cf. A n.[2]). [abbr. BILLY WHIZ n. (1)]

billy, the n. [1910s] someone or something excellent, admirable. [ety. unknown]

Billy Bad-Ass n. (*also* **Billy Joe Bad-Ass**) [1970s+] (*orig. US*) usu. in ironic use, anyone who sets themselves up as tough, aggressive. [generic name *Billy (Joe)* + BAD-ASS n. (1)]

billy barlow n.[1] [mid-19C] a fool. [*Billy Barlow*, a real-life street clown, fl.1840 around the East End of London. 'Billy was a real person, semi-idiotic, and, though in dirt and rags, fancied himself a swell of the first water. Occasionally he came out with real witticisms [...] and died in Whitechapel Workhouse' (Hotten, 1864)]

billy barlow n.[2] [20C+] (*US*) a large pocket knife with folding blades. [? brandname]

billy-be-damned n. (*also* **billy bedam**) **1** [mid-19C+] (*US*) a euph. for *hell*, usu. in comparative phrs. used to indicate absoluteness, e.g. *dead as billy-be-damned, blacker than billy-be-damned*. **2** [late 19C+] (*also* **billy-be-blowed**) an ext. of DAMNED adj. [? orig. a euph. for the Devil or SE *hell*]

billy born drunk n. [late 19C–1900s] a drunkard all one's life. [proper name *Billy* + quasi-nickname *Born-Drunk*]

billy boy n. [1960s] (*US*) a policeman (cf. BILLY n.[6]). [BILLY n.[2] (3) + SE *boy*]

Billy Bunter n. [2000s+] a member of the public, a customer. [rhy. sl. = PUNTER n.[1] (4); ult. the fictional schoolboy *Billy Bunter*, created by Frank Richards]

billy button n.[1] [mid–late 19C] mutton. [rhy. sl.]

billy button n.[2] [20C+] (*W.I.*) a gullible fool, esp. one who performs a job of work without first making sure that they will be paid. [joc. use of 'proper name' + ? rhy. sl. = (gets) nothing]

billy buzman n. [19C] a pickpocket who specializes in stealing silk handkerchiefs. [BILLY n.[3] + BUZMAN n.]

billy-cart n. [1950s+] (*Aus./N.Z.*) a child's homemade 'go-kart'. [abbr. SE *billy-goat cart*]

billycock n. [mid–late 19C] a hat with a low crown; primarily worn by carters, it was also popular among the clergy; thus *billycock gang*, the clergy as a group. [? *bully-cocked*, 'cocked after the fashion of the bullies']

billy d juice n. [1990s+] (*US Black/teen*) Colt .45 malt liquor. [proper name *Billy D* + JUICE n.[3] (1)]

billy-fencer n. [mid-19C] a marine store owner. [? BILLY n.[2] (2) + -FENCER sfx]

billy-fencing shop n. [mid–late 19C] a shop that specializes in buying stolen precious metals. [BILLY-FENCER n. + SE *shop*]

billy goat n.[1] **1** [mid-19C–1930s] (*orig. US*) a lecher. **2** [1910s] (*orig. US*) a bad-tempered man. [the goat's supposed characteristics]

billy goat n.[2] [late 19C] a bearded man. [the goat's 'beard'; thus SE *goatee*]

billy goat n.[3] [1980s+] **1** a coat. **2** the throat. [rhy. sl.; var. on NANNY (GOAT) n.]

billy goat v. [1930s–60s] (*orig. US*) to philander. [the image of the goat as the epitome of lechery]

billy-goat alley n. (*also* **billy-goat hill**) [1930s+] (*US*) the poorest section of a town. [? the denizens keeping goats or, since such areas are associated with various social excesses, f. their 'goatishness']

billy gorman n. [late 19C] a foreman or ganger. [rhy. sl.]

Billy Harran's dog n. [20C+] (*Irish*) a time-server, one who befriends whoever they happen to be with. [anecdotal]

billy hell n. (*US*) **1** [19C] a fantasy place that epitomizes the ultimate in bleakness and desolation; usu. in comparative phr. for intensification, e.g. *meaner than..., hot as...* **2** [late 19C+] the essence, the 'daylights', e.g. *knock the billy hell out of*.

billy-hunting n. [mid-19C] **1** trading in old (poss. stolen) metal. **2** stealing handkerchiefs. [BILLY n.[2] (2)/BILLY n.[3] + SE *hunting*]

billy-jack adj. [1980s] (*US Black*) unsophisticated, from the back woods. [the title of a 1971 film featuring a raw country-boy]

Billy Joe Bad-Ass n. see BILLY BAD-ASS n.

billy knife n. [20C+] (*US*) a large pocket knife. [abbr. BILLY BARLOW n.[2]]

billy liar n. [1990s+] a tyre. [rhy. sl.; ult. book *Billy Liar* (1959) by Keith Waterhouse and the subseq. film (1963)]

billy lid n. [1980s+] (*Aus.*) a child (cf. BINLID n.[2]; DIXIE LID n.; SAUCEPAN LID n.; TEAPOT (LID) n.; TIN LID n.). [rhy. sl. = KID n.[1] (1)]

billy man n. [1960s] a policeman (cf. BILLY n.[6]). [ext. of BILLY n.[2] (3)]

billy-maria n. see BILLY n.[5].

billy muggins n. [1910s+] (*Aus.*) a fool. [generic use of proper name + MUGGINS n.[1] (1)]

billy-my-nag n. see BOB-MY-NAG n.

billy-noodle n. [late 19C+] (*US/Aus.*) a man who firmly believes, all evidence to the contrary notwithstanding, that no woman can resist his charms. [SE *billy*, generic for a man + NOODLE n.[1] (2); US use is 19C; Aus. is 20C+]

billy-o n. **1** [20C+] (*also* **billy-oh**) a euph. for *hell*, thus trouble, punishment. **2** [1910s] nonsense, rubbish. [? proper name *billy* + -O sfx (7)]

Billy Prescott n. see CHARLIE PRESCOTT n.

billys n. see BILLIES n.

Billy the Kid n. [1920s–30s] a very orthodox Jew (cf. BOX OF GLUE n.; BUCKLE MY SHOE n.; CISCO KID n.; FIFTEEN AND TWO n.; FIVE TO TWO n.; FOUR BY TWO n.; FRONT-WHEEL SKID n.; HALF PAST TWO n.; KANGAROO n.[3]; KANKER n.; NON-SKID n.[2]; POT OF GLUE n.; PULL-THROUGH n.; QUARTER TO TWO n.; SARAH SOO n.; SAUCEPAN LID n.; SLIPPERY (SID) n.; TEAPOT (LID) n.; TEN TO TWO n.; TIN LID n.). [rhy. sl. = YID n.[1]; plus the wearing of large, black, wide-brimmed hat seen as similar to a cowboy hat; ult. the legendary cowboy *Billy the Kid* (b. c.1859)]

billy turniptop n. [late 19C–1900s] an agricultural labourer. [generic use of proper name + joc. use of SE; Ware suggests that it is 'probably an outgrowth of TOMMY ATKINS n. (1)']

Billy Whiz n. (*also* **whizz**) [1990s+] (*UK drugs*) **1** amphetamine (cf. A n.[2]). **2** a mixture of heroin and cocaine. [*Billy Whizz*, a character in a children's comic; as his name suggests, he moves fast]

Billy Wright adj. [1990s+] a general negative: useless, disgusting, repellent. [rhy. sl.; ult. UK footballer *Billy Wright* (1924–94)]

biltong curtain n. [1970s–80s] (*S.Afr.*) a joc. name for the borders of pre-independence South Africa. [SE *biltong*, salted, wind-dried meat, a S.Afr. national foodstuff + a pun on SE *iron curtain*]

Bim n. [late 19C+] a Bajan, a native of Barbados; thus *Bimshire*, Barbados. [from Igbo *bem*, my house, home, household, folk, fellows + ? Yoruba *ebi mi*, my folk/relative; many Igbo slaves were taken to Barbados]

bim n.[1] [1950s–70s] (*US Black*) a policeman. [ety. unknown; ? abbr. BIMBO n. (2)]

bim n.[2] see BIMBO n.

bim adv. [late 18C–mid-19C] echoic of a sudden act, esp. of one object hitting another.

bimaz n. see BEAMER n.

bimbette n. [1980s+] a junior or aspirant 'good-time girl'. [BIMBO n. (5) + SE fem. sfx -*ette*]

bimbo n. **1** [1910s–40s] (*orig. US*) (*also* **bim**) a man, usu. young. **2** [1920s–50s] (*US*) a thug. **3** [1920s+] (*Ling. Fr./Polari*) a dupe, an insignificant person. **4** [1920s+] (*orig. US*) (*also* **bim, bimb, bimby**) a woman. **5** [1980s+] an unintelligent, but attractive, young man or woman. [the earliest use of *bimbo* is found c.1900 in America, where it was synon. with 'bozo' to mean a man, prob. unintelligent. A parallel use was that to mean 'baby', abbr. from the Italian *bambino*. By the 1920s the word meant young woman, often a prostitute; simultaneously it meant a tramp's companion, poss. gay. The writer Jack Conway (of *Variety* magazine) used it spec. to mean a 'dumb girl'. *Bimbo* gained a new currency during the 1980s when it came to describe a young woman, usu. something of a gold-digger and indulged as such by rich and/or powerful older men and the media to whom they tell or sell their tales. The original 1980s bimbo was a 'model', Fiona Wright, who delighted the press with revelations of her relationship with Sir Ralph Halpern, a millionaire businessman]

bimbo *adj.*[1] [1960s+] stupid, foolish. [BIMBO n. (3)]

bimbo *adj.*[2] [2000s] (*US*) pertaining to (attractive) young women. [BIMBO n. (5)]

Bimi *n.* [1970s] (*US*) a West Indian. [BIM n.]

Bimi *adj.* [1970s] (*US*) West Indian. [BIMI n.]

bimmer *n. see* BEAMER n.

bimp *n.* [1920s] (*UK tramp*) 1 shilling (5p). [BEONG n.]

bimp *v.* [1960s+] to spy, esp. as a sexual voyeur. [ety. unknown]

bimps *n.* [1970s] (*US campus*) French fried potatoes. [ety. unknown]

Bimshire *n. see* BIM n.

bin *n.* 1 [mid-19C+] a pocket. 2 [late 19C] an unpleasant or run-down place. 3 [1900s] (*US*) a safe. 4 [1930s+] a psychiatric institution. 5 [1970s–80s] a police or prison cell. 6 [1990s+] a prison.

bin *v.* 1 [1940s+] to throw away, to discard. 2 [1960s+] to commit to a psychiatric institution. [abbr. SE *throws in the bin*; (2) BIN n. (4)]

binco *n.* [mid-19C] (*Ling. Fr./Polari*) a kerosene flare. [Ital. *bianco*, white]

bind *n.* 1 [mid-19C+] a difficult situation, a predicament. 2 [1930s+] a bore, a nuisance. [such problems 'tie one up']

bind *v.* [1920s+] (*orig. RAF*) 1 to bore intensely. 2 to complain, to scold. [poss. the most commonly used of all RAF sl.; thus the celebrated BBC radio comedy programme of the late 1940s, *Much Binding in the Marsh*]

binder *n.*[1] 1 [late 19C–1900s] an egg. 2 [late 19C+] (*N.Z.*) a good, filling meal; thus *go a binder*, to eat a meal. 3 [20C+] a piece of bread and cheese. [all f. their 'binding' or costive properties]

binder *n.*[2] [late 19C–1950s] 1 a last drink. 2 one who orders a drink in a public house after 'last orders'. [? it 'binds' its predecessors together]

binder *n.*[3] [1920s+] 1 (*orig. RAF*) a bore. 2 a habitual complainer. [BIND v.]

binderjuice *n.* [2000s] (*US Black*) vaginal secretions (cf. BITCH BUTTER n.; BOOTY JUICE n.; CLAM CHOWDER n.; CLAMJAM n.; COME n.; COME-JUICE n.; COOZE n.; CREAM n.[1]; CROTCH CHEESE n.; CROTCH OIL n.; DROOL n.; FANNY BATTER n.; FLAP SNOT n.; FRENCH DIP n.; GOOSE-GREASE n.; GRAVY n.[1]; GREASE n.[3]; HONEY n.[2]; JAM n.[7]; JUICE n.[2]; JUNGLE JUICE n.; LETCHWATER n.; LOVE JUICE n.; MILK n.[1]; OIL n.[1]; POONTANG JUICE n.; PUSSY JUICE n.; SAUCE n.[2]).

binders *n.* [1940s–60s] brakes; thus *jump on the binders*, to put on the brakes; *hit the binders!* brake! [their tightening on a moving wheel]

binding *adj. see* BLINDING adj.[2].

bindle *n.* 1 [late 19C+] (*US*) a bundle containing clothes and possessions, esp. a bedding-roll carried by a tramp. 2 [1920s] any other bundle or package. 3 [1920s+] (*drugs*) a small measure of narcotics, wrapped in a folded square of paper (cf. BUNDLE n.[4]). [Ger. *Bündel*, a package]

bindle bo *n. see* BINDLE STIFF n.

bindle-boy *n.* [1930s–50s] (*US gay*) the young companion of a homosexual tramp. [BINDLE n. (1) + SE *boy*]

bindle bum *n. see* BINDLE STIFF n.

bindle Kate *n.* [1950s] (*US drugs*) a female narcotics addict. [BINDLE n. (3) + generic female name]

bindle-man *n.* [late 19C+] (*US*) a tramp. [BINDLE n. (1) + SE *man*]

bindle punk *n.* [1930s] (*US*) a tramp. [BINDLE n. (1) + PUNK n.[1] (3)]

bindle stiff *n.* (*also* **bindle bo, bindle bum, bundle stiff, bundle stiff willie**) (*US*) 1 [late 19C+] a tramp, spec. one carrying a bedroll; formerly a migrant worker. 2 [1920s–60s] an unimportant man. [BINDLE n. (1) + STIFF n.[2] (4)/BO n.[2] (1)/BUM n.[3] (1)]

bine *n.* (*Aus.*) 1 [20C+] an English immigrant. 2 [1940s] an English soldier. [from the popular cigarette brand, Wills Wood*bines*]

bines *n.* [1950s] spectacles. [BINS n.[2] (1)]

bing *n.*[1] [1930s+] (*US Und.*) solitary confinement. [ety. unknown; image of one being thrown into a cell and landing 'bing!']

bing *n.*[2] [1930s+] (*drugs*) enough of a drug for a single injection. [BING v.[2]]

bing *n.*[3] [1990s+] (*US Black/campus*) money.

bing *v.*[1] [mid-16C+] (*UK Und.*) to go. [? Rom.; Walter Scott resurrected it for his literary romances of the period in the early 19C]

bing *v.*[2] [20C+] to hit. [echoic]

bingaloo *adj.* [late 19C–1920s] (*US*) stupid.

bing a waste *v.* (*also* **bing avast**) [mid-16C–18C; 1920s] (*UK Und.*) to go away, to depart. [the *OED* suggests a poss. gypsy root but offers no elaboration + SE *waste*, wasteland, desert or f. 16C SE *aways*, away; Carew, *The History of Bampfylde Moore Carew* (1750), has *bing feck you*, devil take you, and *bing lee ma*, devil miss me as 'gypsy language']

bing-bang *n.* [1910s–20s] a repeated heavy thump or a continued banging noise. [echoic]

bing-bongs *n.* [1990s+] the female breasts. [the idea of them knocking together]

binge *n.* 1 [late 19C+] (*also* **binge-up**) excessive consumption, usu. of drink and (latterly) drugs. 2 [1920s+] in weak use, any form of party or outing. 3 [1920s+] a situation. 4 [1950s] a campaign. [dial.]

binge *v.* 1 [mid-19C+] to drink heavily. 2 [1990s+] (*drugs*) to indulge in a continuous period of crack cocaine use; thus *binging*, using crack cocaine for long periods; also used of cocaine in general. [BINGE n. (1)]

binged *adj.* (*also* **binged up, binjed up**) [20C+] drunk. [BINGE v. (1)]

bingee *n. see* BINGY n.

binge-up *n. see* BINGE n. (1).

binge up *v.* [1910s] to cheer someone up, to enliven. [ext. of BINGE v. (1)]

bingey *n.*[1] [late 19C] (*Anglo-Irish*) the penis. [? dial. *bing*, a heap, a pile or *bing*, to hit]

bingey *n.*[2] *see* BINGY n.

binghi *n.* (*also* **Binghi**) [1900s–50s] (*Aus./N.Z.*) an aboriginal or Native Australian. [Dharuk *binghi*, a brother]

bingie *n. see* BINGY n.

bingle *n.*[1] [1940s+] (*Aus.*) 1 a fight. 2 a collision, a crash. [? echoic *bing*, the sound of a collision; c.1900 baseball use *bingle*, a blow, a hit (of the ball)]

bingle *n.*[2] [1950s+] (*US drugs*) 1 a large supply of narcotics. 2 a drug seller. [var. on BINDLE n. (3)]

bingo *n.*[1] [late 17C–19C] brandy or any hard liquor. [? *B* for brandy + Yorks. dial. *stingo*, strong ale (*OED*) or SE *binge* (E.P.)]

bingo *n.*[2] 1 [late 17C–19C] a drinking bout. 2 [1950s+] (*Can./US prison*) a riot. [ext. of BINGO n.[1]; (2) ext. of (1)]

bingo *n.*[3] 1 [1900s–20s] a hard blow. 2 [1930s–50s] (*US drugs*) a narcotic injection. [? misuse of baseball jargon *bingle*, a hit for a single]

bingo *n.*[4] [1960s] (*US*) a woman. [mispron. of BIMBO n. (4)]

bingo *adj.* [early 19C] (*UK Und.*) of a face, red (through alcohol, esp. brandy). [BINGO n.[1]]

bingo *v.* [1980s+] (*drugs*) to inject a drug. [BINGO n.[3] (2)]

bingo! *excl.* **1** [20C+] (*also* **bingorino! zingo!**) an excl. used to imply a moment's surprise, excitement, suddenness etc, e.g. *There I was, walking along, then bingo! a cat fell on my head.* **2** [1920s+] an excl. used to imply success, esp. of a sighting of something or somebody. [echoic of SE *bing!* a thump; in a flash]

bingo-bag *n.* [1990s+] (*W.I.*) underwear. [? briefs as opposed to G-strings, thongs etc]

bingo-boy *n.* **1** [late 17C–19C] a male lover of brandy (cf. BINGO-MORT n.). **2** [1940s] (*US gang*) a drunk. [BINGO n.[1] + SE *boy*]

bingo-club *n.* [late 17C–mid-18C] a set of rakes whose favourite tipple is brandy. [BINGO n.[1]]

bingoed *adj.* [1920s+] (*UK society*) drunk. [BINGO n.[1]]

bingo-mort *n.* (*also* **bingo-mott**) [early 18C–19C] a female lover of brandy (cf. BINGO-BOY n.). [BINGO n.[1] + MORT n.]

bingorino! *excl. see* BINGO! excl. (1).

bingo wings *n.* [1990s+] flabby upper arms. [the image of an old lady waving her arm to signal a 'full house' in a bingo hall; but also var. on BATWING n.[1] (5)]

bing room *n.* [1920s–50s] (*US drugs*) a room where narcotics users gather to take drugs. [BING v.[2], i.e. a SHOOTING GALLERY n.]

bings *n.* [20C+] (*Irish/Scot.*) lots of, a large amount.

bingy *n.* (*also* **bingee, bingey, bingie, binjy**) [mid-19C–1920s] (*Aus./N.Z.*) the stomach. [Dharuk *bingy*, the stomach]

binjed up *adj. see* BINGED adj.

binjy *n. see* BINGY n.

binky *n.[1]* **1** [1910s] (*US*) any small mechanical object. **2** [1950s] (*drugs*) (*also* **bopper**) a needle used for injecting narcotic drugs, most often a disposable needle that is prescribed to a diabetic. [(1) ? SE *dinky*; (2) BING n.[2]]

binky *n.[2]* [1960s] (*US*) the buttocks. [? Scot. *bink*, a bench]

binlid *n.[1]* [1990s+] (*Ulster*) a fool. [fig. use of abbr. of SE *dustbin lid*; (2) rhy. sl.]

binlid *n.[2]* [2000s] a child (cf. BILLY LID n.). [rhy. sl. = KID n.[1] (1)]

binned *adj.* [late 19C] hanged. [proper name Bartholomew *Binns*, the London hangman in 1883]

Binnie Hale *n.* [1940s+] a tale, i.e. a 'tall story' or confidence trickster's 'line'. [rhy. sl.; ult. UK actress *Binnie Hale* (1899–1984)]

binnie one *n.* [1980s] (*Aus. juv.*) urination. [BUSINESS n.[3] + NUMBER ONE n.[4] (1)]

binnie two *n.* [1980s] (*Aus. juv.*) defecation. [BUSINESS n.[3] + NUMBER TWO n.[1] (1)]

binns *n. see* BINS n.[2].

binny *n. see* BENNY n.[1] (2).

binos *n.* [2000s] (*US*) binoculars. [abbr.]

bins *n.[1]* [1930s+] a pair of trousers. [BIN n. (1), i.e. the pockets that they contain]

bins *n.[2]* (*also* **binns**) [1930s+] **1** glasses, spectacles. **2** binoculars. **3** the eyes. [abbr. SE *binoculars*]

bint *n.* (*also* **binty**) **1** [1910s+] a young woman; thus *lush bint*, a very good-looking woman; *go binting*, to go on leave. **2** [1950s] (*Aus.*) a general term of abuse. [Arabic *bint*, daughter; thus a woman who has yet to bear a child; noted in 1855 by the explorer Richard Burton (1821–90), the term gained fuller currency during WW1 and WW2, when it was adopted by Allied servicemen; note WW1 milit. *the bint*, the man who plays a female role in a milit. concert party]

bio *n.[1]* [1910s+] (*S.Afr.*) the cinema. [Afk. *bioscope*, a cinema; obs. elsewhere, the term remains current in South Africa]

bio *n.[2]* [1940s+] a biography. [abbr.]

biockey *n.* [mid–late 19C] (*Anglo-Ital.*) money. [Ital. *baiocchi*, lit. 'browns', thus cf. BROWN n.[2]]

biog *n.* [1930s+] (*orig. US*) a biography. [abbr.]

biolinging *n.* [2000s] (*US Black/teen*) writing and singing hip-hop lyrics in 2 languages, i.e. Spanish and English. [SE *bilingual*]

bionc *n. see* BIANC n.

bionic *adj.* [1970s+] **1** exceptional, outstandingly gifted. **2** extreme, beyond the limit. [SE *bionic*, 'having or being an artificial, esp. electromechanical, device that replaces part of the body; having ordinary human capabilities increased (as if) by the aid of such devices' (*OED*); coined 1963 but popularized by the 1970s TV series *Six-Million Dollar Man*, starring actor Lee Majors]

bionk *n. see* BIANC n.

bioscope *n.* [1910s] a drink of brandy. [SE *bioscope*, a cinema; the more one drinks the more 'moving pictures' one sees]

bip *v.[1] see* BIPE v.

bip *v.[2] see* BIP (INTO) v.

bip *adv.* [mid-19C+] echoic of the sound of an object hitting/being hit suddenly.

bip-bam-thank-you-ma'am *n.* [20C+] quick, spontaneous intercourse, with the implication that only the man will achieve pleasure. [BIP adv. + BAM! excl.]

bipe *n.* [1960s+] (*US*) a bisexual. [? joc. use of SE *bipolar*]

bipe *v.* (*also* **bip, scallybip**) [1960s–70s] (*US prison*) to break into and rob houses while the occupants are asleep; thus *bipper/ scallybipper*, a thief who specializes in this.

bip (into) *v.* [1970s+] (*US campus*) to hit. [echoic]

bippy *n.* [1960s+] (*orig. US*) a synon. for ASS n. (2), esp. in phr. *you can bet your* (*sweet*) *bippy.* [coined on NBC-TV's *Rowan and Martin's Laugh-In, c.1967*]

birch broom *n.* [mid-19C–1960s] a room. [rhy. sl.]

Birchington hunt *n.* [1930s+] the vagina (cf. ALL QUIET n.). [rhy. sl.; var. on BERKELEY (HUNT) n. (1) + ? overtones of sado-masochism]

bird *n.[1]* **1** [mid-16C–17C; 1950s+] a prostitute, a promiscuous woman (cf. ALLEY CAT n.). **2** [mid-19C+] a young woman, a girlfriend. **3** [late 19C] (*US*) an attractive (young) woman. **4** [1920s+] (*US*) a male homosexual. **5** [1950s–70s] (*US Black*) an experienced, tough female prostitute. **6** [1960s] used in sing. as a generic term for all women.

bird *n.[2]* **1** [mid-16C+] (*also* **birdie**) a person, a man, a 'bloke'. **2** [mid-19C] (*US*) a dissolute or degenerate person, 'a fast man, woman or horse' (R.H. Thornton, *An American Glossary*, 1912); often ext. as *perfect bird*. **3** [1910s] (*US*) an animal. **4** [1930s] (*US tramp*) an outsider, a conventional person. **5** [1970s] (*US*) an eccentric.

bird *n.[3]* (*orig. UK Und.*) **1** [late 16C+] a confidence trickster's victim. **2** [17C+] a prisoner; thus *a bird has flown*, a prisoner has escaped. [(1) the imagery reflects the world of hunting (cf. BEATER n.[1]); (2) note WW1 RN *bird*, a man continually in trouble]

bird *n.[4]* [mid-19C] a Black slave. [abbr. BLACKBIRD n.[1] (1)]

bird *n.[5]* **1** [early 19C+] (*US*) a loud, derisive noise, imitative of a fart; esp. in phr. GIVE (SOMEONE) THE BIRD v. **2** [20C+] one who deserves ridicule. **3** [1920s+] any form of ridicule or derision. [echoic of a harsh bird-call]

bird *n.[6]* [mid–late 19C] (*US*) $1. [the American eagle engraved upon it]

bird *n.[7]* **1** [late 19C] (*US*) something unpleasant. **2** [late 19C–1900s] (*US campus*) a term of reproach. **3** [late 19C] (*also* **dicky-bird**) something or someone excellent or admirable.

bird *n.[8]* **1** [late 19C+] (*mainly US*) the penis; thus *beat/jerk one's bird*, to masturbate; *get one's bird in a splint*, to get into (painful) difficulties; *eat/gobble/swallow someone's bird*, to fellate; *how's your bird?* a phr. of greeting; *not on your bird!* in no way! impossible! (cf. ANTEATER n.). **2** [1960s–70s] (*US*) the vagina; thus *bird-washing*, mutual cunnilingus (cf. BLACK CAT WITH ITS THROAT CUT n.; BUN n.[2]; BUNNY n.[1]; CAT'S MEAT n.[2]; CATTY-CAT n.; CHAT n.[2]; CONY n.[1]; CUNNY WARREN n.; DOG n.[4]; KITTEN n.[2]; KITTY n.[2]; MALKIN n.; MUFF n.[1]; PEANUT BUTTER PUSSY n.; POOZLE n.; PUSS n.[1]; PUSSY n.; PUSSYCAT n.; PUSSY HOLE n.; ROUGH MALKIN n.; SNAPPING TURTLE (PUSS) n.; SQUIRREL n.[2].) **3** [1970s] (*US gay*) fellatio.

bird *n.*[9] [1900s] (*Aus.*) one who has been dismissed from a job. [? one has to 'fly away']

bird *n.*[10] **1** [1920s+] a prison sentence; thus *birded* (*up*), imprisoned; *in bird*, in prison; *do bird*, serve a sentence; *first bird*, one's first prison sentence. **2** [1930s–40s] previous convictions. **3** [1950s–60s] in fig. use, any form of constraint, responsibility. [abbr. BIRDLIME n.[2]]

bird *n.*[11] [1930s+] (*mainly US*) an aircraft, esp. a helicopter, spacecraft, missile etc.

bird *n.*[12] **1** [1960s–70s] (*US*) the Thunder*bird*, a motorcar. **2** [1990s+] (*US Black*) Thunder*bird* wine. [abbr.]

bird *n.*[13] [1960s+] (*US*) an obscene gesture of dismissal, mockery; usu. as FLIP THE BIRD v. or SHOOT THE BIRD v. [ext. of BIRD n.[5] (1)]

bird *n.*[14] [1970s+] the mind, sanity; thus *lose one's bird*, to go mad; *out of one's bird*, crazy, mad. [ety. unknown]

bird *adj.* [late 19C] (*US campus*) wonderful, first-rate, admirable. [BIRD n.[7] (3)]

bird *v.*[1] [late 16C–early 17C] to rob, to steal, to search for plunder. [BIRD n.[3]]

bird *v.*[2] [1940s–60s] (*US*) to talk nonsense; usu. in interrog. *you ain't just (a)-birding?* [BIRD TURD v.]

bird *v.*[3] *see* FLIP THE BIRD v.

birdbath *n.* [1970s] the vagina. [BIRD n.[8] (1) + SE *bath*]

birdbrain *n.* [1940s+] a fool; thus *bird-brained*, stupid (cf. AIREDALE n.; BAKEBRAIN n.). [SE *bird* + sfx *-brain*]

birdcage *n.*[1] **1** [mid–late 19C] a bustle on a woman's dress. **2** [mid-19C–1900s] a 4-wheeled cab. **3** [late 19C–1950s] (*US*) a prison cell, spec. the condemned cell into which a prisoner is transferred from DEATH ROW n. for the last few days prior to his execution. **4** [1900s–60s] a dormitory for women students. **5** [1920s–40s] (*US*) a brothel (cf. BULLPEN n.; BULLRING CAMP n.; CAT FLAT n.; CAT-HOUSE n.; CAT-SHOP n.; CAT WAGON n.; CHICKEN RANCH n.; CIRCUS HOUSE n.; CONY-BURROW n.; COWBAY n.; COWYARD n.; CUNNY WARREN n.; FISH MARKET n.; GOOSEBERRY RANCH n.; GOOSING RANCH n.; GOOSING SLUM n.; HEIFER DEN n.; HEN-COOP n.; HOG RANCH n.; PHEASANTRY n.; ROOKERY n.; SNAKEPIT n.; WARREN n.[1]; ZOO n.[1]). **6** [1930s–60s] (*US*) an elevator with an openwork sliding metal gate. **7** [1940s–50s] a sleeping cubicle in a flophouse, separated from its neighbours by a 'wall' of chicken wire. **8** [1970s–80s] (*N.Z. prison*) the exercise yard. [resemblance; note WW1 milit. *birdcage*, a holding cage near the front lines for prisoners of war, prior to their transfer to a proper prison camp]

birdcage *n.*[2] [1960s–70s] (*US gay*) the anus. [BIRD n.[8] (1) + SE *cage*]

birdcage hype *n.* [1930s–50s] (*US drugs*) the lowest class of heroin addict. [? BIRDCAGE n.[1] (7) + HYPE n.[2] (2); note Maurer, 'Language of the Underworld Narcotic Addict' Pt.2 (1938): 'Probably so-called because this type of addict often lives in a *bird-cage* or *bird-cage joint*, a very cheap lodging house with chicken-wire netting separating the small sleeping compartments. Transients who live in these establishments are called *bird-cage stiffs*. There is also a saying that when an underworld addict is down and out, "he has a bird cage on one foot and a boxing glove on the other" – a humorous var. of "a boot on one foot and a shoe on the other"']

bird circuit *n.* [1960s–70s] (*US gay*) the touring of gay bars in a succession of cities. [BIRD n.[8] (1) + SE *circuit*]

bird colonel *n.* [1940s+] (*US*) a full colonel in the US marines; thus *make bird*, to gain this promotion; *light bird*, a lieutenant-colonel. [the silver eagles affixed to the uniform's shoulders denote the rank]

birdcrap *n.* [1970s] (*US*) nonsense, rubbish. [SE *bird* + CRAP n.[3] (1)/CRAP n.[3] (3)]

bird division *n.* [1950s] (*US*) US Airforce.

bird dog *n.* **1** [20C+] a receiver of stolen goods. **2** [1920s–40s] a persistent, tenacious person. **3** [1930s] (*US Und.*) a contact man for stock and bond thieves. **4** [1930s+] one who lures victims into

positions of vulnerability. **5** [1940s–70s] (*US campus/teen*) a young man, bereft of a partner of his own, who attempts to steal a woman from someone else. **6** [1950s+] an assistant, esp. in police or journalism. **7** [1950s+] a watcher, an observer. [SE *bird dog*, a retriever, which fetches things]

bird dog *v.*[1] [1940s+] **1** (*US, mainly teen*) to steal another person's girlfriend, to break up a school or college romance. **2** (*US*) to pimp for, to solicit for another person. **3** (*US*) to hang around in the hope of making a pick-up, either for sex or commercial gain. **4** (*US*) to spend more time away from home than staying in with one's family. [BIRD DOG n. (5)]

bird dog *v.*[2] [1950s+] (*US*) **1** to observe, to lie in wait. **2** to follow. **3** to watch over, to protect. **4** to eavesdrop. [BIRD DOG n. (7)]

bird dogger *n.* [1960s] (*US*) one who tries overly hard to gain acceptance or approval. [SE *bird dog*, a retriever, which is seen as especially keen to please]

bird eater *n.* [1960s–70s] (*US*) a finicky eater. [SE phr. *eat like a bird*]

birder *n.* [late 19C] (*Aus.*) a slave-trader. [abbr. SE *blackbirder*, a slaver]

bird-happy *adj.* [1970s] (*UK prison*) emotionally affected by a (long) prison sentence. [BIRD n.[10] (1) + -HAPPY sfx (1)]

birdhouse *n.* **1** [1940s] (*US*) a prison (cf. BANDHOUSE n.). **2** [1950s] (*US drugs*) a place where one can purchase narcotics. [puns on (1) BIRD n.[10] (1)/(2) BIRD'S EYE n.[2] (2) + SE *house*]

birdie *n.*[1] [20C+] the penis (cf. ANTEATER n.). [ext. of BIRD n.[8] (1)]

birdie *n.*[2] [1930s+] an effeminate male. [BIRD n.[1] (4); note 14C–16C SE *bird*, a young man]

birdie *n.*[3] [1990s+] (*Irish*) a kiss. [play on PECK n.[2]]

birdie *n.*[4] *see* BIRD n.[2] (1).

birdie powder *n.* [1940s+] (*drugs*) **1** heroin. **2** morphine (cf. AUNTIE EMMA n.). **3** cocaine (cf. BOLIVIAN MARCHING POWDER n.; BOUNCING POWDER n.; CHALK n.[4]; DUST n.[5]; FAIRY POWDER n.; FOOLISH POWDER n.; FRISKY POWDER n.; GIGGLE DUST n.; GOLD DUST n.; GUNPOWDER n.[3]; HAPPY DUST n.; HAPPY POWDER n.; HEAVEN DUST n.; JAZZ TALC n.; JOY DUST n.; JOY POWDER n.; LOPPY DUST n.; MARCHING POWDER n.; NOSE POWDER n.; PIMP (DUST) n.; POWDER n.[2]; POWDERED DIAMONDS n.; SHERBET n.; SHOWBIZ SHERBET n.; STARDUST n.; SUGAR n.[6]; WACKY DUST n.). [? BIRD'S EYE n.[2] (2) or joc. use of SE *birdseed*]

bird in a gilded cage *n.* [1970s+] (*US gay*) a man's crotch in a pair of expensive trousers. [BIRD n.[8] (1)]

birdlime *n.*[1] [18C–early 19C] a thief (cf. FINGERS ARE MADE OF LIME-TWIGS phr.; LIME-FINGERED adj.; LIME-TWIG n.). [SE *bird-lime*, a sticky substance spread on twigs so that birds may be caught; the ref. is to the thief's 'sticky fingers']

birdlime *n.*[2] (*also* bird's lime) [mid-19C+] **1** prison sentence. **2** the time, e.g. *what's the birdlime?* [rhy. sl. = TIME n.[1]]

birdlime *adj.* [late 18C] larcenous, thieving. [BIRDLIME n.[1]]

bird never flew on one wing, a *phr.* [20C+] a phr. used as a formula for accepting a second drink (and pretending that one is doing so more from duty than pleasure).

bird of passage *n.* [1940s] a tramp, a vagrant.

bird of the game *n.*[1] [17C] a prostitute (cf. ALLEY CAT n.). [BIRD n.[1] (1) + GAME n.[1] (3)]

bird of the game *n.*[2] [mid-19C] a womanizer. [BIRD n.[2] (2) + GAME n.[1] (1)]

bird of the night *n. see* NIGHTBIRD n.

birds *n.* [1980s+] (*drugs*) amobarbitol, Amytal. [they make one 'fly']

birdseed *n.*[1] [1910s] chocolates or other sweets. [play on the attraction of SE *birdseed* to a BIRD n.[1] (4)]

birdseed *n.*[2] [1930s–60s] (*US*) **1** rubbish, nonsense. **2** any breakfast cereal seen as resembling birdseed.

bird's eye *n.*[1] [mid-17C–19C] a handkerchief. [resemblance of the pattern]

bird's eye *n.*[2] (*also* birdseye) **1** [mid-19C–1900s] tobacco.

2 [1930s+] (*drugs*) a small amount of narcotics. **3** [1950s] (*drugs*) a weak injection of narcotics. [(1) proprietary name; (2) and (3) resemblance: a bird's eye is small; note Maurer, 'Lang. of the Underworld Narcotic Addict' Pt.1 (1936): 'Probably so called from the constriction of the pupils and glassy appearance of the addict's eyes immediately after injection']

bird's eye fogle *n.* [mid-19C] a silk handkerchief with a 'bird's-eye' pattern. [BIRD'S EYE n.[1] + FOGLE n.]

bird's eye wipe *n.* [mid-19C] any spotted silk handkerchief, as sported by fashionable costermongers. [BIRD'S EYE n.[1] + WIPE n.[3] (1)]

birdshit *n.* **1** [1960s] (*US*) a term of contempt. **2** [1970s] (*US*) nonsense, rubbish. [SE *bird* + SHIT n.[1] (1)/SHIT n.[1] (2)/SHIT n.[3] (4)]

bird's lime *n. see* BIRDLIME n.[2].

bird's nest *n.*[1] **1** [late 16C–mid-18C] (*female*) pubic hair. **2** [late 18C] the vagina (cf. AGREEABLE RUTS OF LIFE n.). **3** [1970s] (*gay*) a hairy chest; of a woman, the breasts. **4** [1970s+] (*US gay*) visible pubic hair extending from the crotch to the navel. [SE *bird*/BIRD n.[1] + SE *nest*/NEST n.[1]]

bird's nest *n.*[2] [1930s–60s] (*US Und.*) somewhere worth robbing. [the image of a nest filled with eggs]

bird's-nester *n.* [late 18C] a promiscuous man, a womanizer. [BIRD'S NEST n.[1] (2)]

birds of a feather *n.* [17C–18C] members of the same gang. [pvb 'birds of a feather flock together']

bird taker *n.* **1** [1930s–40s] a sodomite. **2** [1950s] the vagina. **3** [1970s+] (*US gay*) a male prostitute. [BIRD n.[8] (1) + SE *taker*]

bird turd *n.* [1950s–70s] (*US*) **1** nothing, an insignificant amount. **2** an insignificant, worthless person. [SE *bird* + TURD n.]

bird turd *v.* [1940s+] (*US*) to talk nonsense; esp. in interrog. phr. *you ain't just (a-)bird-turding?* [BIRD TURD n., assumed but uncited earlier]

bird (up) *v.* [2000s] to pursue women for sex. [BIRD n.[1] (2)]

bird-washing *n. see* BIRD n.[8] (2).

bird-witted *adj.* [17C–18C; 1930s] foolish, scatter-brained, gullible (cf. BEEF-WITTED adj.).

birdwood *n.* [1940s] (*US*) **1** (*drugs*) marijuana, a marijuana cigarette. **2** a cigarette. [ety. unknown]

birk *n.* [mid-19C] a house. [backsl. = CRIB n.[1] (1)]

Birkenstock buddy *n.* [1990s+] (*US campus*) an environmentalist. [the *Birkenstock* shoe, popular among such individuals + BUDDY n. (1)]

birl *n.* [late 19C+] (*Scot.*) a twist or turn. [dial. *birl*, a rapid twist or turn]

Birmingham screwdriver *n.* (*also* **Brummagem screwdriver**) [20C+] a hammer. [SE *Birmingham*/BRUMMAGEM n. (2); the supposed oafishness of the Birmingham worker who would rather hammer in a screw than use the correct tool; despite normal racial stereotypes (and their supposed jobs) a US usage *Yiddish screwdriver* has been noted c.1939]

birthday suit *n.* [late 17C+] the naked body; usu. in phr. *in one's birthday suit*. [the state in which one emerges from the womb; note also a probable pun by Rochester c.1673: 'Nay looks, and lives, and loves by Rote, / In an old tawdrey Birth-Day-Coat' — in which a 'birthday coat' is properly a coat worn at court on occasion of a royal birthday]

bis *n. see* BISCUIT n.[3] (2).

biscoe *n. see* BRASCO n.

biscuit *n.*[1] [mid-19C+] a young woman; thus *cold biscuit*, an unappealing young woman. [her being 'sweet' and/or 'good enough to eat'; Williams offers examples of *biscuit* as a sexual organ, citing the appearance of biscuits as 17C 'brothel-fare']

biscuit *n.*[2] **1** [late 19C–1930s] (*US*) a watch. **2** [1930s+] the face, the head. **3** [1980s+] a record. [the resemblance of these round objects]

biscuit *n.*[3] **1** [1930s] (*US Black*) a penis. **2** [1930s+] (*US*) (*also* **bis**) a pistol, a handgun. [? one 'snaps' it]

biscuit *n.*[4] [1930s–40s] (*US Black*) a pillow. [resemblance; note WW1 UK milit. use *biscuit*, a coir-fibre mattress]

biscuit *n.*[5] [1960s–80s] (*US*) a woman's hairstyle in which the hair is done up in a small knot, usu. favoured by elderly women with thinning hair. [a pun on SE *biscuit*, a small bun]

biscuit *n.*[6] (*drugs*) **1** [1970s] a tablet of methadone. **2** [1980s+] 50 rocks of crack cocaine. **3** [1990s+] a tablet of MDMA (cf. ECSTASY n.). [the shape]

biscuit *n.*[7] [1980s] (*US campus*) a gullible person.

biscuit *n.*[8] [1980s+] (*US Black*) a type of shoe worn for comfort rather than style and favoured by older people.

biscuit *n.*[9] [1990s+] (*US Black*) a cowardly man. [euph. for BITCH n.[1] (5)]

biscuit and beer *v.* [late 19C–1900s] to swindle a gullible dupe by betting them a biscuit against a glass of beer; one will, of course, win.

biscuit-arsed *adj.* [1990s+] (*Scot.*) self-pitying.

biscuit beggar *n.* [1960s] (*US*) a Native American. [? their poverty]

biscuit city *n.* [1980s] something one desires, the absolute best thing or situation?. [colloq. phr. *take the biscuit* + CITY sfx]

biscuit-eater *n.* (*US*) **1** [1950s–70s] a euph. for BITCH n.[1] (1); esp. in phr. *son of a biscuit-eater*, a worthless person. **2** [1960s–70s] (*also* **biscuit-hound**) a worthless dog. [such a dog will eat biscuits provided by its owner but will not forage for its own food]

biscuit factory *n.* [1900s–50s] Reading jail. [it was sited next to the Huntley & Palmer's biscuit factory; thus the *Biscuit Men*, the Reading football team]

biscuit-headed *adj.* [mid-19C] (*US*) foolish (cf. AIRHEADED adj.).

biscuit hooks *n.* [1930s–60s] (*US*) the hands. [SE *biscuit* + SE *hooks*/HOOK n.[1] (1)]

biscuit-hound *n. see* BISCUIT-EATER n. (2).

biscuit nibbler *n.* [mid-19C] a young person.

biscuit-roller *n.* [1930s+] (*US Black*) a (usu. female) lover. [BISCUITS n.]

biscuits *n.* [1940s+] (*orig. US Black*) the buttocks; thus *biscuit-bandit*, an active male homosexual (cf. BAKERY GOODS n.). [the roundness]

biscuits and cheese *n.* [1940s+] the knees. [rhy. sl.]

biscuit shooter *n.* **1** [late 19C–1960s] a waiter or waitress. **2** [1900s] (*US milit.*) a female servant working for an army officer. **3** [1910s–30s] (*US*) a cook. [SE *biscuit* + *shoot*, to throw violently]

biscuit snatcher *n.* [1950s] (*US Black*) a hand; in pl. the fingers.

bish *n.* [1950s] (*UK juv.*) a stupid mistake or situation. [ety. unknown]

bish *v.*[1] [1940s] (*Aus./N.Z.*) to throw. [var. on BIFF v.[1] (4)]

bish *v.*[2] [1950s] (*UK juv.*) to spoil, to blunder. [BISH n.]

bishop *n.*[1] [late 16C–mid-17C] a fly that is burnt in a candle flame. [BISHOP v.[1]]

bishop *n.*[2] [early 18C–19C] a mixture of wine and water, topped off by a roasted orange. [a clergyman's favourite]

bishop *n.*[3] **1** [late 18C] a bustle. **2** [late 18C–early 19C] a large condom. **3** [19C–1900s] a chamberpot. **4** [late 19C+] (*US Black/campus*) the penis. **5** [1940s] (*UK Und.*) a folding jemmy. [the size/rotundity]

bishop *n.*[4] [mid–late 19C] a broken signpost. [mild anti-clericalism: it neither points the way nor travels it]

bishop *n.*[5] [1950s–70s] a private detective. [he 'searches out sin']

bishop *v.*[1] [early 16C–mid-19C] to burn, to let burn. [pvb 'the bishop hath played the cook' or 'the bishop has put his foot into the pot']

bishop *v.*[2] [early 18C–19C] to use any form of trickery, esp. the burning of marks into the teeth, in order to reduce the appearance of a horse's age. [a man called *Bishop* who specialized in such frauds]

bishop *v.*[3] [early 19C] (*UK Und.*) to change the markings on a stolen watch to facilitate its resale. [pun on SE *bishop*, to administer the rite of confirmation]

bishop v.[4] [mid-19C] to murder by drowning. [the murderer *Bishop*, who in Bethnal Green in 1831 drowned a boy in order to sell the body for dissection]

Bishop Barker n. [mid-19C–1910s] (*Aus.*) a drinking glass of the largest size. [Frederick *Barker* (1808–82), Anglican Bishop of Sydney; the bishop was a teetotaller, but he was extremely tall]

bishop's finger n. [mid-19C] a signpost. [BISHOP n.[4] + SE *finger(-post)*]

bishop's nose n. *see* PARSON'S NOSE n.

bisognio n. *see* BESOGNIO n.

bisom n. [20C+] (*Aus.*) an undisciplined child. [SE *besom*, a witch]

bison v. [1980s+] (*US campus*) to vomit (cf. BARF v.). [echoic]

bit n.[1] **1** [mid-16C–1960s] money. **2** [late 17C–19C] the silver coin of the lowest denomination. **3** [early 18C–mid-19C] (*UK Und.*) a purse. **4** [early 19C+] (*US*) 12.5 cents; but usu. in phr. *two bits*, 25 cents; FOUR BITS n.; *six bits*, 75 cents; LONG BIT n.[1]; SHORT BIT n.[1]. **5** [mid-19C–1960s] any low-denomination coin, e.g. *threepenny bit*, *fourpenny bit*. **6** [late 19C–1900s] (*US Und.*) a bribe, e.g. as offered by a thief to a policeman. **7** [late 19C–1950s] (*US Und.*) a share of the profit from a theft. **8** [1910s+] a wager, an investment, an insurance premium.

bit n.[2] **1** [17C; mid-19C+] a young woman. **2** [17C–19C] a euph. for the vagina. **3** [1950s] (*gay*) a young man.

bit n.[3] [17C+] sexual intercourse; usu. in combs. (cf. BIT, THE n.; BIT OF BRUSH n.; BIT OF BUM n.; BIT OF CUFF n.; BIT OF FISH n.; BIT OF FRUIT n.; BIT OF HAIR n.; BIT OF KEG n.; BIT OF MEAT n.; BIT OF MUTTON n.; BIT OF OLD n.; BIT OF SLAP AND TICKLE n.; BIT OF SNUG n.; BIT OF TAIL n.; BIT OF THIS AND THAT n.; BIT OF TICKLE n.; BIT OF TIT n.; BIT OF UNDER n.; DO A BIT v.; DO A BIT OF BUSINESS v.; DO A BIT OF COCK-FIGHTING v.; DO A BIT OF FLAT v.; DO A BIT OF GIBLET PIE v.; DO A BIT OF (LADIES') TAILORING v.; DO A BIT OF SKIRT v.; DO A BIT OF STUFF v.; GET A BIT v.[2]; HAVE A BIT OF BEEF v.; HAVE A BIT OF BUM v.; HAVE A BIT OF CAULIFLOWER v.; HAVE A BIT OF COCK v.; HAVE A BIT OF CUNT v.; HAVE A BIT OF CURLY GREENS v.; HAVE A BIT OF FISH (ON A FORK) v.; HAVE A BIT OF GUTSTICK v.; HAVE A BIT OF JAM v.; HAVE A BIT OF MEAT v.; HAVE A BIT OF MUTTON v.; HAVE A BIT OF PORK v.; HAVE A BIT OF QUIMSY v.; HAVE A BIT OF ROUGH v.; HAVE A BIT OF SHARP AND BLUNT v.; HAVE A BIT OF SPLIT MUTTON v.; HAVE A BIT OF SUGAR STICK v.; HAVE A BIT OF SUMMER CABBAGE v.).

bit n.[4] [mid-19C+] a short time, a brief period, usu. as *for a bit*.

bit n.[5] [mid-19C+] (*UK/US Und.*) a prison sentence of any length; thus *one-year bit*, *two-year bit* etc; thus *do a bit*, to serve a sentence. [ext. of BIT n.[4]]

bit n.[6] [20C+] (*Aus. Und.*) a jemmy, a crowbar. [SE *bit*, a biting or cutting tool]

bit n.[7] [1930s+] (*Ulster*) a worker's or schoolchild's packed lunch. [abbr. SE *a bit to eat*]

bit n.[8] [1950s+] (*orig. US jazz*) **1** any well-defined action, plan, series of events or attitudes, usu. but not necessarily, of short duration. **2** one's attitude, personality or way of life. **3** the role that one assumes in a situation or in life, e.g. *the college-boy bit*, *the hippie bit*. [theatrical jargon *bit*, a role]

bit n.[9] [2000s] (*UK Und.*) a drug in pill form, e.g. ecstasy or amphetamine (cf. PILL n.[4]).

bit, the n. [1990s+] (*Irish*) sexual intercourse (cf. BIT n.[3]). [euph.]

bit adj.[1] [late 17C–19C] robbed, cheated, outwitted. [BITE v.]

bit adj.[2] [1990s+] (*US Black*) fallen in love.

bit by the brewer's dog adj. (*also* **bit by a barnmouse**) [1930s–40s] (*US*) drunk.

bitch n.[1] **1** [early 17C+] a derog. term for a woman, usu. judged an unpleasant one. **2** [18C+] a general derog. term of address to a woman, or a female creature. **3** [18C+] a prostitute (cf. ALLEY CAT n.). **4** [18C+] (*orig. US*) something or someone considered extraordinary or surprising. **5** [mid-18C+] a derog. term for a weak or subservient man; thus as a term of address. **6** [mid-18C+]

anything unpleasant, difficult, problematic, 'the devil', e.g. *that's the bitch of it*. **7** [mid-18C+] (*UK/W.I.*) a general derog. term for a man. **8** [early 19C] (*UK campus*) one who plays host at a tea-party. **9** [early 19C+] an otherwise unspecified object or creature. **10** [mid-19C+] the queen in playing cards or in chess. **11** [1910s+] (*W.I./UK/US Black teen*) a person, neither necessarily negative nor aimed solely at women, nor used solely by men. **12** [1920s+] (*US gay/prison*) (*also* **bitchy**) an effeminate male, supposedly the 'passive' partner in a homosexual couple; a male prostitute. **13** [1920s+] (*orig. US*) an exceptionally skilled person. **14** [1950s+] one who complains or makes (what are perceived as) unfairly negative comments, irrespective of gender. **15** [1950s+] (*Can. prison*) a habitual criminal. **16** [1950s+] (*US prison*) a homosexual. **17** [1960s] (*gay*) a fellow homosexual, usu. a friend. **18** [1970s+] (*US Black*) a girlfriend. **19** [1990s+] a large amount of money. **20** [1990s+] (*US Black*) a thing. **21** [1990s+] a subservient person, a servant. **22** [1990s+] (*gay*) a submissive lesbian. [*bitch* as derog. sl. dates to early 17C, before which it was SE. By 18C it was seen, according to Grose (1785), as 'the most offensive appellation that can be given to an English woman, even more provoking than that of whore', and he cites the 'Billingsgate' rejoinder: 'I may be a whore, but can't be a bitch.' The original use implied disapproval of the woman's sexuality, i.e. *bitch in heat*; today's use focuses on her personality]

bitch n.[2] [late 19C–1950s] (*US, Western*) an improvised lamp made of a twist of rag in a container of grease (cf. SLUT LAMP n.). [ety. unknown]

bitch n.[3] [1940s+] (*orig. US*) a complaint. [BITCH v.[2] (3); note also BITCH n.[1] (14)]

bitch n.[4] [1980s+] (*US drugs*) one who knowingly dispenses unpleasantly adulterated varieties of marijuana. [BITCH n.[1] (7) + BITCHWEED n.]

bitch n.[5] [1980s+] (*orig. US campus*) the middle seat in a car. [BITCH n.[1] (1), i.e. where a woman would sit]

bitch n.[6] *see* BIG BITCH n.

bitch adj.[1] [1970s+] (*US Black*) weak, with implications of effeminacy. [BITCH n.[1] (5)]

bitch adj.[2] *see* BITCHING adj. (1).

bitch v.[1] **1** [late 16C+] to go whoring. **2** [18C; 1950s+] to act in a promiscuous manner. [BITCH n.[1] (1)]

bitch v.[2] **1** [early 18C; 1910s+] (*orig. US*) to complain. **2** [late 18C–mid-19C] (*UK Und.*) to give in, esp. through cowardice. **3** [early 19C+] to spoil, to ruin. **4** [1920s–60s] (*US*) to cheat, to swindle. **5** [1930s+] to treat badly. **6** [1950s+] (*orig. US*) to criticize, to attack verbally, to nag. [all imply that the subject is acting like various defs. of BITCH n.[1]]

bitch v.[3] [early–mid-19C] (*UK campus*) to drink tea. [BITCH n.[1] (8)]

bitch and moan v. [1960s+] (*orig. US*) to complain all the time. [ext. of BITCH v.[2] (1)]

bitch-ass adj. [1950s+] (*US Black*) a general pej. [BITCH n.[1] (1)/BITCH n.[1] (7) + -ASS sfx]

bitch-ass nigga n. [1990s+] (*US Black teen*) a general term of Black-on-Black abuse, lit. a Black person who complains. [BITCH-ASS adj. + NIGGA n.]

bitch-bag n. [2000s] (*Irish*) the testicles. [? BITCH v.[1] + BAG n.[1] (1)]

bitch bath n. [1940s–50s] (*US*) a 'bath' in which the usual water is replaced by an application of cosmetics, masking the dirt rather than removing it. [BITCH n.[1] (1) + SE *bath*]

bitch booby n. [late 18C] a rough, unsophisticated country woman; 'military term' (Grose, 1785). [BITCH n.[1] (1) + BOOBY n.[1]]

bitch box n. [1940s+] (*US*) **1** a small box into which employees of a business can put their complaints/suggestions. **2** a public address system; a loudspeaker. [BITCH v.[2] (1) + SE *box*]

bitch boy n. [1990s+] (*US campus*) **1** an idiot, a general term of abuse to a man. **2** used as a term of affectionate address between male friends. [BITCH n.[1] (5) + SE *boy*]

bitch butter *n.* [1970s] (*US Black*) vaginal secretions (cf. BINDERJUICE n.). [BITCH n.¹ (1) + BUTTER n.¹ (1)]

bitched, buggered and bewildered *phr. see* FUCKED UP AND FAR FROM HOME phr.

bitched off *adj.* [1950s] (*US*) furious. [BITCH v.² (3)]

bitched (up) *adj.* **1** [early 19C+] ruined, spoilt. **2** [1910s+] confused. **3** [1960s–70s] (*US*) angry. [BITCH v.² (3)]

bitchen *adj. see* BITCHING adj. (2).

bitcher *n.* [1960s+] a complainer, a whinger. [BITCH v.² (1)]

bitchery *n.* [1920s] (*US gay*) a bar frequented by homosexuals. [BITCH n.¹ (12)]

Bitches' Heaven *n.* [1920s] (*US tramp*) Boston. [allegedly f. the numerous cheap prostitutes (BITCH n.¹ (3))]

bitch fight *n.* [1960s] (*US gay*) an argument between 2 homosexual men. [BITCH n.¹ (17)]

bitch-fou *adj.* [late 18C] (*Scot.*) very drunk. [FOU adj.¹, lit. 'full as a bitch', the 'bitch' here being a pregnant female dog]

bitch hammer *n.* [2000s] the penis (cf. ARSE-OPENER n.). [BITCH n.¹ (1) + SE *hammer*/HAMMER n.¹ (1)]

bitch-happy *adj.* [2000s] (*US*) grateful. [grateful as a BITCH n.¹ (1)]

bitchin *adj. see* BITCHING adj.

bitchin! *excl.* (*also* **bitchen! bitching!**) [1950s+] (*US, esp. surfer*) wonderful! great! subseq. adopted by teen girls of 1980s California. [BITCHING adj. (2)]

bitching *n.* [1920s+] (*US*) arguing, complaining, nagging. [BITCH v.² (1)]

bitching *adj.* (*also* **bitchin**) **1** [mid-19C+] (*orig. Aus.*) (*also* **bitch**) an intense pej., a euph. for BLOODY adj.¹ (1). **2** [1950s+] (*also* **bitchen**) excellent, wonderful. [(1) BITCH n.¹ (1)/BITCH n.¹ (6); (2) on bad = good model or ? BITCH n.¹ (4)]

bitching party *n. see* BITCH PARTY n.

bitching session *n. see* BITCH SESSION n.

bitchin twitchin! *excl.* [1960s+] a superlative form of BITCHIN! excl. [redup./assonance]

bitch-kitty *n.* [1940s+] (*US*) something extraordinary, esp. extraordinarily hard to achieve. [BITCH n.¹ (4) + ? SE *kitty*]

bitch-kitty *adj.* [1960s] (*US*) extraordinary, exceptional, extreme. [BITCH-KITTY n.]

bitch lick *n.* [1980s+] (*W.I./UK Black*) a devastating blow. [? the sort of SE *lick* one gives a BITCH n.¹ (1)]

bitch off *v.* [1970s] (*US campus*) to annoy, to irritate. [BITCH v.² (6)]

bitch-on-wheels *n.* [1940s] (*US*) an extreme example, someone or something infinitely superior. [BITCH n.¹ (4)]

bitch out *v.* [1980s+] (*US campus*) to tell someone off. [BITCH v.² (6)]

bitch party *n.* (*also* **bitching party**) **1** [early 19C] (*orig. UK campus*) a tea party. **2** [late 19C+] a party composed solely of women guests. [(1) BITCH n.¹ (8); (2) BITCH n.¹ (1) + SE *party*]

bitch's bastard *n.* (*also* **B.B.**) [1930s+] (*UK prison*) a severe, poss. violent warder. [SE *bitch*, i.e. a female dog + BASTARD n. (1)]

bitch's blind *n.* [1970s+] (*US gay*) a homosexual or bisexual man's heterosexual wife. [BITCH n.¹ (17) + BLIND n.¹ (1)]

bitch's Christmas *n.* [1960s] (*US gay*) Halloween. [BITCH n.¹ (17); f. the mostly gay parades prevalent in US at this time]

bitch session *n.* (*also* **bitching session**) [1940s+] (*orig. US milit.*) a conversation in which one airs one's complaints. [BITCH v.² (1) + SE *session*]

bitch slap *n.* [1990s+] **1** (*US Black*) the killing of a woman. **2** (*US prison*) a slap rather than a punch with the clenched fist; the implication is that the victim isn't 'man enough' to deliver a proper blow. [BITCH SLAP v.; (1) ironic reversal of BITCH SLAP v. (1)]

bitch slap *v.* [1990s+] (*orig. US Black*) **1** of a woman, to hit a man, usu. her male partner. **2** of a woman or gay man, to harangue somebody. **3** of a man, to hit somebody in an 'effeminate' way

(i.e. to slap rather than punch with the clenched fist; the implication is that the victim isn't 'man enough' to deliver a proper blow). **4** to hit, irrespective of gender or style. [BITCH n.¹ (1)/BITCH n.¹ (12) + SE *slap*]

bitch-squeak *n.* [1950s] (*US*) a tell-tale, garrulous woman. [BITCH n.¹ (1) + SE *squeaK*]

bitch's wine *n.* [mid–late 19C] champagne. [BITCH n.¹ (1) + SE *wine*; ? supposedly preferred by women drinkers]

bitch the pot *v. see* STAND BITCH v. (2).

bitch up *v.*¹ [late 19C+] to make a mess of things, to make a mistake. [BITCH v.² (3)]

bitch up *v.*² [2000s] (*US prison*) to surrender, to act in a cowardly manner. [BITCH n.¹ (12)]

Bitchville *n.* [1990s+] (*US*) a notional state of cowardice. [BITCH n.¹ (5) + -VILLE sfx¹]

bitch water *n.* [1940s] (*US*) cologne. [BITCH n.¹ (1) + SE *water*]

bitchweed *n.* [1980s+] (*US drugs*) adulterated, contaminated, inferior or otherwise 'bad' marijuana (cf. AFRICAN BUSH n.). [BITCH n.¹ (6) + WEED n.¹ (4)]

bitch wheel *n.* [1950s] (*W.I.*) a large, round boiled dumpling. [? BITCH n.¹ or W.I. pron. of SE *big* + shape (of a wheel)]

bitchy *n. see* BITCH n.¹ (12).

bitchy *adj.* (*also* **bitch**) **1** [1920s+] (*orig. US*) sexually provocative, sexually appealing. **2** [1940s+] malicious, sarcastic. **3** [1940s+] (*US*) difficult. [BITCH n.¹ (1)/BITCH n.¹ (6)]

bit cull *n.* [mid-19C] (*UK Und.*) a coiner. [BIT n.¹ (1) + CULL n.¹ (4)]

bite *n.*¹ **1** [late 16C] a sum of money. **2** [late 17C–19C] a cheat, a confidence trickster. **3** [18C–1920s] a hoax, a confidence trick, a fraud. **4** [18C+] (*UK Und.*) that which is cadged; thus *a good bite*, a complaisant victim. **5** [mid-18C+] (*Aus.*) a cadger. **6** [1900s] (*US*) a share of profits. **7** [1910s+] (*orig. Aus.*) an attempt to obtain a loan. **8** [1930s+] (*Aus.*) an act of begging. **9** [1950s+] (*US*) the price, the cost, esp. when the item is expensive. **10** [1970s] (*US*) an unpleasant surprise or experience; abbr. of *bite in the ass*. **11** [1970s+] a bribe.

bite *n.*² [17C+] the vagina, 'secreta ( ) mulierum'; one of many words that suggest that the vagina is a threat to men (cf. CATCH 'EM (ALL) ALIVE-O n.; CLAP-TRAP n.²; COCK-TRAP n.; EEL-SKINNER n.; FIRES OF HELL n.; FLY-CAGE n.; FOOL TRAP n.; MANGLE n.¹; MAN-TRAP n.¹; MOLE-CATCHER n.; MOUSETRAP n.¹; NUMBER NIP n.; RED SNAPPER n.; SNAPPER n.⁷; SNAPPING TURTLE (PUSS) n.; SNATCH n.¹; SPERM SUCKER n.; STAFF BREAKER n.; SUCK AND SWALLOW n.; SUCKER n.²; VACUUM n.; VELVET-LINED MEAT GRINDER n.). [SE *bite* or Anglo-Saxon *byht*, the fork of the legs; 20C+ use mainly US Black]

bite *n.*³ [late 19C] a person from Yorkshire. [abbr. YORKSHIRE BITE n.]

bite *n.*⁴ [1910s] (*Aus.*) a measure or 'shot' of hard liquor. [its fig. effect on the drinker]

bite *v.* **1** [late 16C–mid-19C] to rob, to steal. **2** [17C+] to 'fall for', to 'take the bait'. **3** [17C+] to worry, to annoy, to irritate; often ext. as *bite someone's ass*, *bite someone's britches*; thus *what's biting you?* **4** [mid-17C–1920s] to cheat, to deceive; thus *bitten*, deceived, hoaxed. **5** [late 18C–early 19C] to overreach, to impose. **6** [late 19C+] (*Aus./US*) to cadge or borrow from, usu. money; thus *bitten out*, subjected to as much begging and cadging as a person or place will tolerate. **7** [1910s+] to be objectionable, distasteful, unpleasant; thus as n., a disparaging person. **8** [1940s] to pressurize, to blackmail. **9** [1960s+] (*US*) to ask for money, esp. when one has no real intention of repaying it. **10** [1970s+] (*US Black*) in rap music, to plagiarize lyrics from other people; thus *biting*, copying another artist. **11** [1980s+] (*US campus*) to copy, e.g. a suit of clothes.

bite! *excl.* [early–mid-18C] tricked you! caught you! [BITE v. (4)]

bite a blow *v.* [late 17C–early 18C] to accomplish a major theft. [BITE v. (1) + SE *blow*, a hit]

bite-and-blow *n.* [20C+] (*W.I.*) successful deceit, emollient hypocrisy. [dial. *bite-and-blow*, to blow a cool breath on a place before biting it and thus (theoretically) minimizing the pain]

bite-etite *n.* (*also* **bitytite**) [late 19C–1900s] hunger, appetite. [SE *bite* + *appetite*]

bite feathers *v.* [1960s] (*US gay*) to lie on one's stomach. [the image of the passive partner in sodomy biting the pillow]

bite it *v.* (*US*) **1** [1960s+] to die. **2** [2000s] to trip, to fall. [abbr. BITE THE DUST V.]

bite it! *excl.* [1940s+] (*US*) a phr. of aggressive dismissal. [SE *bite*, 'it' is the penis or posterior (cf. BITE MY ASS! excl.)]

bite (it) off *phr.* [mid-19C+] (*US*) to restrain oneself, to stop talking. [i.e. bite one's tongue off]

bite me! *excl.* [1980s+] (*US campus*) a general derog./dismissive excl. [BITE MY ASS! excl.]

bite moose! *excl.* [1980s+] (*US*) an excl. of dismissal. [? euph. of BITE MY ASS! excl.]

bite my ass! *excl.* (*also* **bite my arse!**) [1950s+] (*orig. US*) a general excl. of contempt or dismissal.

bite on *v.* [1980s+] (*US campus*) to imitate. [BITE V. (10)]

bite one's bait *v.* [1970s] (*US*) to pause before making too precipitate a decision. [SE *bite* + 16C *bait*, food; the image is of 'chewing over' the topic]

bite one's grannam *v.* (*also* **bite one's grandam**) [mid–late 17C] to become very drunk. [SE *bite* + *grannam*, corn, the basic constituent of some spirits]

bite one's lips *v.* [1950s+] (*drugs*) to smoke marijuana. [? one's intoxicated state leads to such injury]

bite one's nails *v.* [1960s–70s] (*US gay*) for a homosexual man to use mutually recognizable coded gestures to indicate his interest in someone.

bite one's name in *v.* [mid-19C] to drink heavily. [ety. unknown]

bite one's thumb at *v.* (*also* **bite one's thumb to**) [late 16C–1900s] to make a gesture of contempt or of threat. [the gesturer extends the thumb and clicks its nail forward on the front teeth]

bite (on) the bridle *v.* [14C–early 19C] to be in reduced circumstances, to be impoverished. [SE *bite on the bridle*, to champ at the bit, like a restless horse]

bite (on) the bullet *v.* (*also* **bite on the bullet**) **1** [late 19C+] to suffer in silence. **2** [1910s+] to do what is necessary, however unappealing. [the placing of a bullet between the teeth of wounded soldiers or sailors when they were undergoing surgery in pre-anaesthesia days]

bite on the nail *v.* [1940s] (*US*) to suffer in silence.

biter *n.*[1] **1** [late 17C–early 18C] a card-sharp. **2** [late 17C–mid-19C] a confidence trickster. **3** [1950s+] (*Aus.*) a cadger. **4** [1980s+] (*US*) an unpleasant, contemptible person. [BITE V.]

biter *n.*[2] [late 18C] a lascivious woman. [BITE n.[2]]

biter *n.*[3] [1940s] (*US*) of an animal, the mouth.

biter *n.*[4] [1980s+] (*US Black*) a plagiarist, esp. in rap/hip-hop. [BITE v. (10)]

biter of peters *n.* (*also* **biter of peeters**) [late 18C–early 19C] (*UK Und.*) one who specializes in stealing trunks and boxes from the back of stage-coaches or carts. [BITE THE PETER v.]

biters *n.* [1940s] (*US*) teeth.

bites and scratches *n. see* CUTS AND SCRATCHES n.

bite someone's ass/britches *v. see* BITE V. (3).

bite someone's crank *v.* [1960s+] to fellate. [SE *bite* + CRANK n.[5] (1)]

bite someone's ear *v.* (*also* **bite someone's lug**) [mid-19C+] **1** to nag, to importune. **2** to borrow money. [BITE v. (3)/BITE v. (6) + SE *ear*; (1) orig. a phr. of endearment]

bite someone's head off *v.* [late 18C] to attack verbally, esp. in response to an ostensibly mild statement.

bite someone's name *v.* [1920s+] (*Aus.*) to eat a meal for which someone else has paid. [the payer has fig. 'signed' for the food]

bite someone's nose off *v.* [late 19C+] to attack verbally.

bite the bag *v.* **1** [1950s+] (*US*) to be very unsatisfactory; esp. in imper. (*go*) *bite the bag!* an excl. of dismissal, disapproval or contempt. **2** [1970s] (*US campus*) to be quiet, usu. as imper. [SE *bite* + ? BAG n.[1] (1)]

bite the big one *v.* [1970s+] (*US*) **1** to be distasteful, unpleasant, second-rate. **2** to die, to suffer harm. [SE *bite* + 'the big one' = (1) the penis; (2) any serious injury or harm]

bite the bone *v.* [1970s+] (*US teen*) to be disgusting, unpleasant, second-rate. [SE *bite* + ? BONE n.[1] (1)]

bite the bridle *v. see* BITE (ON) THE BRIDLE v.

bite the bullet *v. see* BITE (ON) THE BULLET v.

bite the dust *v.* **1** [mid-19C] to fall over. **2** [mid-19C+] to die. **3** [late 19C+] (*Aus./US*) to be defeated, to be prevailed over. [US Wild West cliché]

bite the hairy banana *v.* [1960s] to be unpleasant, to cause annoyance, to be distasteful.

bite the hand that feeds one *v.* [20C+] to injure a benefactor, to act ungratefully. [the image is of an ungrateful horse or dog]

bite the ice! *excl.* [1970s+] (*US teen*) an excl. of dismissal, 'go to hell!' [the pain of chewing ice]

bite the peter *v.* [late 17C–19C] to steal suitcases or portmanteaux. [BITE V. (1) + PETER n.[2] (1)]

bite the roger *v.* [18C] to steal a portmanteau. [BITE V. (1) + ROGER n.[3]]

bite the root *v.* [1980s] to be third-rate. [image of root as something 'low']

bite this! *excl.* [1980s+] (*US*) a general derog. excl.

bite your bum! *excl.* (*also* **bite your backside!**) [1950s+] (*Aus./N.Z.*) an excl. of contemptuous dismissal.

bit faker *n.* [19C] (*UK Und.*) a coiner, a counterfeiter; thus *bit-faking*, counterfeiting, coining. [BIT n.[1] (1) + FAKER n. (2)]

bit for the finger *n.* [19C] sexual fondling.

bities *n.* [1990s+] (*Aus.*) a general term for biting insects. [SE *bite*]

biting dog *n.* [1950s] (*US gay*) the anal sphincter in the context of intercourse.

bit M *phr.* [1980s] eccentric. [SE *mad*]

bit-maker *n.* [early–late 19C] (*UK Und.*) a coiner, a counterfeiter. [BIT n.[1] (1) + SE *maker*]

bit of (a) *n.* **1** [early 19C+] a good example of, a specimen of, e.g. *bit of a horseman*, BIT OF A LAD n. **2** [late 19C+] (*UK/Aus.*) a young person, as in *bit of a girl*. [SE *bit*; (2) BIT n.[2] (1)]

bit of a groat *n.* [early 18C] a woman, seen in a sexual context.

bit of a lad *n.* [1930s+] a cheeky, self-possessed youth who 'fancies himself'. [BIT OF (A) n. (1) + SE *lad*]

bit of all right, a *phr.* (*also* **a little bit of all right**) **1** [late 19C+] an attractive person, usu. a young woman. **2** [20C+] anything good and advantageous, esp. a pleasant surprise.

bit of bazooka *n. see* BAZOOKAS n.

bit of beef *n.* [late 19C–1900s] a quid of tobacco, less than a pipeful. [? tobacco's use as an appetite suppressant]

bit of blink *n.* [late 19C–1900s] drink. [rhy. sl.]

bit of blood *n.* **1** [early 19C] a dandy. **2** [early–mid-19C] a spirited, mettlesome horse. [SE *bit* + *blood*, pedigree; (1) f. (2)]

bit of both *n.* [1990s+] bisexuality, a taste for sex with men and women.

bit of braille *n.* (*Aus.*) **1** [1930s+] a racing tip. **2** [1940s+] a tip-off. **3** [1940s+] sexual groping. [SE *bit* + *Braille*, the alphabet for the blind; the image of 'feeling something out']

bit of brown *n.* **1** [17C] copulation. **2** [late 19C+] sodomy. [SE *bit* + (1) the *brown* pubic hair; (2) BROWN n.[3] (2)]

bit of brush *n.* [1950s] sexual intercourse; thus a young woman, viewed purely as a sexual object (cf. BIT n.[3]). [SE *bit* + BRUSH n.[3] (2)]

bit of bull *n.* [19C] beef.

bit of bum *n.* [late 19C+] sexual gratification, whether homo- or heterosexual (cf. BIT n.[3]). [SE *bit* + BUM n.[1]]

bit of calico *n. see* CALICO n.

bit of cavalry *n.* [early–mid-19C] a horse. [SE *bit* + *cavalry*, horses]

bit of crackling *n.* [20C+] **1** an attractive woman. **2** an attractive man. [SE *bit* + CRACKLING n.]

bit of crumb *n.* [late 19C] a plump, attractive woman. [SE *bit* + CRUMB n.[1] (1)]

bit of cuff *n.* [late 19C–1900s] a young woman, regarded as a sex object; thus sexual intercourse (cf. BIT n.[3]). [SE *bit* + (*off the*) *cuff*, i.e. spontaneous sex, or SE *cuff*, a blow; thus one of the wide range of terms that equate sex with violence]

bit of drapery *n. see* DRAPERY MISS n.

bit of ebony *n.* [mid-19C+] a Black woman, viewed as a sex object. [SE *bit* + EBONY n. (1)]

bit of fat *n.* [mid-19C+] an unexpected advantage. [SE *fat*, of a profitable occupation]

bit of fish *n.* [mid-19C–1900s] **1** the vagina (cf. BEARDED CLAM n.). **2** sexual intercourse (cf. BIT n.[3]). [SE *bit* + FISH n.[1] (1)]

bit of fluff *n.* **1** [20C+] an attractive, but otherwise unexceptional woman; occas. a young man. **2** [1980s] any thing or person considered insignificant or ineffectual. [SE *bit* + FLUFF n.[1] (2)/SE *fluff*]

bit of frock *n.* [late 19C–1910s] an attarctive (young) woman. [SE *frock*]

bit of fruit *n.* [1940s] sexual intercourse (cf. BIT n.[3]). [FRUIT n.[2] (1)]

bit of gig *n.* [early 19C] a spree, a bit of fun. [SE *bit* + *gig*, merriment, fun]

bit of goods *n.* [mid-19C+] a young woman.

bit of goose *n.* [1930s] a piece of good fortune.

bit of grease *n.* [late 19C–1900s] (*Anglo-Ind.*) a stout, smiling Hindu woman. [E.P. stresses 'non-derogatory', although that assessment may vary according to one's viewpoint]

bit of grey *n.* [late 19C–1900s] an elderly person who is recruited to attend weddings or funerals and by their presence add a degree of solemnity to the proceedings. [SE *bit* + *grey* (hair); note 1990s+ business jargon *grey matter*, an older person recruited to a young firm to give it some gravitas]

bit of hair *n.* [late 19C+] sexual intercourse; thus *get/have a bit of hair* (cf. BIT n.[3]). [SE *bit* + HAIR n.[1] (2)]

bit of hard *n.* (*also* **bit of stiff**) [late 19C] an erection. [SE *bit* + HARD n.[3]/STIFF n.[1]]

bit of haw-haw *n.* [late 19C–1900s] a fop, a dandy. [SE *bit* + *haw-haw*, echoic of an aristocratic drawl]

bit of heliotrope *n.* [1900s] (*Aus.*) a girlfriend. [SE *heliotrope*, a flower]

bit of hollow *n.* [early 19C] an item of poultry, e.g. a duck, a turkey. [the cavities that can be stuffed]

bit of jam *n.* **1** [late 19C] the vagina (cf. APPLE n.[6]). **2** [late 19C–1900s] an attractive woman. [SE *bit* + JAM n.[3]]

bit of keg *n.* [late 19C] sexual intercourse (cf. BIT n.[3]). [abbr. SE *kegmeg* or *cagmag*, rotten meat or a tough old goose]

bit of meat *n.* [early 18C+] **1** the vagina (cf. BACON SANDWICH n.). **2** sexual intercourse (cf. BIT n.[3]). **3** a woman considered as nothing more than a sex object. [SE *bit* + MEAT n. (1)]

bit of melon *n.* [1900s] (*Aus.*) an attractive woman.

bit of mess *n.* [1950s+] (*UK Und.*) a prostitute's male lover, who is neither ponce nor client. [? affectionate nickname]

bit of muslin *n.* (*also* **piece of fine linen, piece of muslin**) [19C–1950s] a young woman. [SE *bit* + *muslin*, a cloth used for dress-making, thus metonymy]

bit of mutton *n.* [19C] **1** a woman, esp. a prostitute (cf. BANGTAIL n.[1]). **2** sexual intercourse (cf. BIT n.[3]). **3** the vagina (cf. BACON SANDWICH n.). [SE *bit* + MUTTON n.[1]]

bit of nifty *n. see* NIFTY n.

bit of no good *n.* [1940s+] a good deal of harm; usu. in phr. *do oneself a bit of no good*.

bit of nonsense *n.* **1** [20C+] (*UK society*) a mistress. **2** [1950s+] any form of villainy, esp. when easily accomplished.

bit of old *n.* [1990s+] sexual intercourse (cf. BIT n.[3]). [euph.]

bit of pooh *n.* [late 19C–1900s] flattery, esp. in the context of courtship. [SE *bit* + *pooh!* nonsense!]

bit of pork *n.* [18C–1900s] the vagina (cf. BACON SANDWICH n.). [SE *bit* + PORK n.[1] (1)]

bit of posh *n.* [1970s+] an attractive young woman who is also considered intelligent or upper-class. [var. on BIT OF ROUGH n.[2]]

bit of prairie *n.* [late 19C–1900s] a momentary lull in the flow of traffic down the Strand, then London's busiest street. [SE *bit* + *prairie*, an open space]

bit of raspberry *n.* [late 19C–1900s] an attractive woman (cf. REAL RASPBERRY JAM n.).

bit of red *n.*[1] [18C–19C] a soldier. [his uniform]

bit of red *n.*[2] [late 19C] vaginal intercourse. [as opposed to BIT OF BROWN n. (2)]

bit of ring *n.* [1930s+] anal intercourse. [SE *bit* + RING n.[1] (2)]

bit of rough *n.*[1] [mid-19C+] the vagina. [its rubbing against the penis]

bit of rough *n.*[2] [20C+] a lover, orig. female but from mid-20C male, from a lower class and tougher background than their partner. [SE *rough*]

bit of scarlet *n.* [mid-19C] an oath. [? the use of the word BLOODY adj.[1] (1)]

bit of skate *n.* [late 19C+] the vagina (cf. BEARDED CLAM n.).

bit of skirt *n.* [late 19C+] a woman; thus DO A BIT OF SKIRT v. [SE *bit* + SKIRT n. (1)]

bit of slap and tickle *n.* **1** [1910s+] sexual foreplay, necking. **2** [1950s+] sexual intercourse; thus *have a bit of slap and tickle*, to have sexual intercourse (cf. BIT n.[3]). [in trad. stereotyping, he tickles, she slaps]

bit of snug *n.* [late 19C] **1** sexual intercourse (cf. BIT n.[3]). **2** the penis. [SE *bit* + SNUG v.[1]]

bit of soap *n. see* SOAP n.[4].

bit of Spanish *n.* [18C] (*UK Und.*) a natural wig, made from human rather than animal hair. [? use of long, dark Spanish tresses in wigs]

bit of stick *n.* [1980s+] £5. [ety. unknown]

bit of stiff *n.*[1] [mid-19C–1900s] money as notes or bills of exchange; thus *do/take a/the bit of stiff*, to accept a post-dated cheque or promissory note (cf. BANK-RAG n.). [SE *bit* + STIFF n.[3] (3)]

bit of stiff *n.*[2] *see* BIT OF HARD n.

bit of stuff *n.* **1** [mid-18C+] (*also* **lump of stuff**) a young woman, usu. attractive and often out, enjoying herself. **2** [early 19C] an overdressed man, an over-confident man. **3** [early 19C] a prize-fighter. **4** [mid-19C] an admirable person. **5** [1900s] (*Aus.*) a horse. **6** [1940s] (*Irish*) a tough, aggressive young man. [SE *bit* + *stuff*, material]

bit of tail *n.* [1920s+] sexual intercourse (cf. BIT n.[3]). [SE *bit* + TAIL n.[2] (6)]

bit of the other *n. see* OTHER, THE n.

bit of this and that *n.* [1970s–80s] (*N.Z.*) sexual intercourse (cf. BIT n.[3]). [euph.]

bit of tickle *n.* [1920s+] **1** a woman, regarded as a sex object. **2** sexual intercourse (cf. BIT n.[3]). [abbr. BIT OF SLAP AND TICKLE n. although chronology suggests the other way around]

bit of tit *n.* [1920s+] **1** a woman regarded as a sex object. **2** sexual intercourse (cf. BIT n.[3]). [SE *bit* + TIT n.[3] (1)]

bit of tripe *n.* [late 19C] one's wife. [? rhy. sl.]

bit of under *n.* [1930s–50s] sexual intercourse (cf. BIT n.[3]). [SE *bit* + UNDER n.]

bit on a fork *n.* [mid-19C+] the vagina (cf. BACON SANDWICH n.). [BIT n.[2] + pun on SE phr./SE *fork*, crotch]

bit on the cuff *adj.* [1930s+] (*Aus./N.Z.*) excessive, severe, 'over the top'. [rhy. sl. = BIT ROUGH, A phr.]

bit on the side *n.* [1920s+] **1** an affair; a lover other than one's regular partner (married or otherwise). **2** an act of sexual intercourse with someone other than your partner. [on the 'side' of the marital 'straight and narrow']

bit previous, a *phr. see* PREVIOUS adj.

bit rough, a *phr.* [1940s+] (*Aus.*) unreasonable, unfair.

bits *n.* [1990s+] the genitals.

bits and bats *n.* [20C+] (*UK Und.*) knick-knacks, items of jewellery. [Yorks. dial. *bits and bats*, bits and pieces]

bits and bobs *n.* [1950s+] bits and pieces. [Midlands dial.]

bitser *n. see* BITZA n.

bit swift, a *n.* [1970s+] (*UK police/Und.*) the taking of unfair advantage, usu. the complaint is made by the villain against the arresting officer. [SE *bit* adj. + SWIFT adj. (5)]

bitten by a barn-mouse *phr.* (*also* **bitten by a barn weasel**) [mid-17C–early 19C] drunk. [? the *barn-mouse* consumes barley, from which beer is brewed]

bitten by the tavern bitch *phr.* [17C–18C] drunk.

bitter-ender *n.* [mid-19C+] a diehard, one who does not give up until the *bitter end*.

bitter-gatter *n.* [late 19C] a mixed drink of beer and gin. [SE *bitter* (ale) + GATTER n. (2)]

bitter half *n.* [late 19C+] one's wife, occas. one's husband. [ironic pun on BETTER HALF n.]

bitter mouth *n.* [1930s–40s] negative, cynical speech. [rare and mainly southern; talk that 'leaves a bad taste in one's mouth']

bit to go with *n.* [late 19C–1900s] (*orig. US*) generosity. [? parting comment, 'Here's a bit to go with']

bit turner-out *n.* [early–mid-19C] a counterfeiter. [BIT n.[1] (1) + SE *turn-out*, to make]

bitty *n.*[1] [late 19C–1900s] a skeleton key. [SE *bit*, a small piece (of something mechanical)]

bitty *n.*[2] [1990s+] (*US Black*) a young woman. [var. on BIDDY n.[2] (2)]

bitty *adj.* [20C+] tiny, small, insignificant, often preceded by 'little'. [dimin. of SE *bit*]

Bitumen, the *n. see* TRACK, THE n.

bitumen blonde *n.* (*also* **charcoal blonde**) [1930s–50s] (*Aus.*) a derog. name for an Aborigine woman. [SE *bitumen*, black asphalt/*charcoal* + *blonde*]

bitytite *n. see* BITE-ETITE n.

bitza *n.* (*also* **bitser**) (*Aus.*) **1** [1920s+] a contraption made of a selection of disparate bits and pieces. **2** [1930s+] a mongrel dog; by ext. any 'mongrel'. [SE *bits and pieces*]

bivvy *n.* [mid–late 19C] alcohol, esp. beer. [Lat. *bibere*, to drink (cf. BEVVY n.)]

biz *n.*[1] **1** [mid–19C+] (*orig. US*) business. **2** [1910s+] a situation, with no actual 'business' attached. [abbr.]

biz *n.*[2] [1930s+] (*drugs*) **1** the kit (eye-dropper, needle, spoon etc) used by a narcotics addict for injections. **2** a bag or portion of drugs; thus *in biz*, working as a drug dealer. [abbr. (1) BUSINESS n.[5] (1); (2) SE *business*]

biz, the *n.* [late 19C+] the real thing (and to be respected as such). [BIZ n.[1] (1)]

bizalls *n.* [2000s] (*US Black*) the testicles. [BALLS n.[1] (1) + *iz* used as an infix]

bizarro *n.* [1980s] a strange, eccentric person. [BIZARRO adj.]

bizarro *adj.* [1970s+] (*US teen*) weird, eccentric. [SE *bizarre* + -o sfx (3), but note *Bizarro*, a character in *Superman* comics]

biznai *n.* (*also* **bizney**) [late 19C–1920s] business, happenings, events, circumstances. [abbr.]

biznatch *n.* (*also* **bizatch**) [1990s+] (*US Black*) vars. on BITCH n.[1]; can be used to refer to a male or a female, a friend or an enemy etc.

bizzaz *n.* (*also* **bezzazz**) [1910s+] (*US*) style, glamour. [? PIZZAZZ n. (2) + ? BUSINESS, THE n. (1)]

bizzie *n. see* BUSY n.

bizzo *n.* [1950s+] (*Aus.*) business. [abbr. SE *business* + -o sfx (4)]

bizzy *n. see* BUSY n.

b.j. *n.* (*also* **b-j, bee jay**) [1940s+] (*US*) fellatio. [abbr. BLOW JOB n. (1)]

B-job *n.* [1970s] (*US*) fellatio. [abbr. BLOW JOB n. (1)]

b-joint *n.* [1950s+] (*US*) a bar that employs women whose primary job is not to dance but to promote liquor sales to the clientele. [B-GIRL n. (1) + JOINT n.[4] (3)]

B.K. *n.*[1] [1990s+] (*US Black*) Burger King. [abbr.]

B.K. *n.*[2] [1990s+] (*US prison*) 'Blood Killer', as used by the Crips gang to threaten their rival Bloods.

b.k. *n. see* BROWNIE KING n.

blab *n.* **1** [mid-16C+] a tell-tale. **2** [mid-19C+] talk. [*Blab* and its v. forms *blab* and, apparently, *blabber* are the first sl. terms relating to speech and can be found as such in the 16C. Their history, however, is somewhat older. There is even, according to the *OED*, a question whether what appears to be an obvious link even exists. *Blab*, then spelt *blabbe* and meaning a 'chatterer', occurs in Chaucer *c.*1374; *blab*, meaning simply 'chatter' or 'loose talk', can be found in *The Tale of Beryn* (*c.*1400), but then promptly vanishes until the 16C, when it is augmented by a v. form, *blab*, to chatter (1535). This, in turn, creates a n., *blabber*, a chatterer. However, the v. *blabber* predates all these; it occurs in *Piers Ploughman* (1362) and, with its n. *blabberer*, is common in the works of John Wyclif (1330–84). Thus, however tempting it may seem, one cannot simply assume that *blab* is a 14C abbr. of *blabber*. Instead, the *OED* suggests, it is related to the n. *labbe*, a revealer of secrets, in Chaucer, and the v. *labbe* in *Piers Ploughman* and to *labbyng*, open-mouthed. It can also be linked to the Old Dutch *labben*, to chatter. Thus *blab/blabbe* might be a mixture of *labbe* and *blabber*; but might also simply be onomat.]

blab *v.* **1** [mid-16C+] to talk; thus *blab it out*, to hurry and finish talking. **2** [late 16C; mid-19C] to inform on. **3** [late 16C+] to confess, to reveal, to tell about. [BLAB n.]

blabber *n.* **1** [1920s] a newspaper. **2** [1940s–70s] the mouth. [BLAB v. (1)]

blabberguts *n.* [1910s] (*US*) a gossip. [SE *blabber* (see ety. BLAB n.) + -GUTS sfx]

blabbermouth *n.* (*also* **blabmouth**) [1920s+] a gossip, an indiscreet talker. [SE *blabber*/BLAB n. + SE *mouth*]

blabbermouth *adj.* (*also* **blabmouth**) [1940s] indiscreet, gossiping. [BLABBERMOUTH n.]

blabberskite *n.* [2000s] a voluble, boastful speaker. [SE *blabber* (see ety. BLAB n.) + BLATHERSKITE n. (1)]

blabfest *n.* (*also* **talkfest**) [late 19C+] (*US*) a gathering where those involved devote themselves to talking, esp. unashamed gossip. [BLAB n. (2)/SE *talk* + -FEST sfx]

blabmouth *see under* BLABBERMOUTH.

blab sheet *n.* [1940s–60s] (*orig. US Black*) a newspaper. [BLAB v. (3) + SHEET n. (1)]

blabs in labs *n.* [1970s+] (*US campus*) a course in linguistics, the 'labs' are language laboratories. [BLAB n. (2) + SE *lab*(oratory)]

black *n.*[1] (*also* **black parts**) [mid–late 17C] the female genitals. [the darkness of the HOLE n.[1] (2)]

black *n.*[2] **1** [early–mid-19C] a *black*guard. **2** [1920s+] a *black*mailer. **3** [1920s+] blackmail; thus PUT THE BLACK ON v. **4** [1940s+] the *black* market; thus *on the black*, engaged in the black market. [abbr.]

black *n.*[3] **1** [1930s–40s] (*US Black*) the night, night-time. **2** [1940s+] (*drugs*) opium (cf. APOSTLE n.). **3** [1960s+] (*drugs*) a generic term for hashish, esp. varieties that are very dark khaki (cf. AFGHAN n.). **4** [2000s] (*drugs*) heroin; esp. black tar heroin (cf. BLACK STUFF n.; BLACK TAR n.; BLANCO n.; BROWN n.[4]; BROWN POWDER n.; BROWN RHINE n.; BROWN STUFF n.[1]; BROWN SUGAR n.; CHOCOLATE ROCK n.; CHOCOLATE (STUFF) n.; DARK BROWN SHIT n.; DOG FOOD n.[4]; GOLD n.[2]; GOLD DUST n.; GOLDEN GIRL n.[2]; GREEN DRAGONS n.; HAZEL n.; OLD LADY WHITE n.; RED CHICKEN n.; RED

ROCK n.; SNOW n.[2]; SNOW POWDER AND ROCKS n.; TAR n.[3]; TOOTSIE ROLL n.[2]; WHITE n.[3]; WHITE BAG n.; WHITE CROSS n.; WHITE DYNAMITE n.; WHITE GIRL n.; WHITE HORSE n.[3]; WHITE LADY n.[2]; WHITE SERPENT n.; WHITE SHIT n.; WHITE STUFF n.; YELLOW JESUS n.). [colour]

black n.[4] [1940s+] (orig. milit.) a mistake, a serious error. [SE black mark]

black n.[5] [1980s] (US campus) incomprehensible course material. [one is 'in the dark']

black n.[6] [1980s+] (US Black) a form of address, e.g. Whassup, Black? [abbr. SE black man]

black adj. **1** [mid-19C+] depressed, sullen, irritable. **2** [1970s+] (Irish) crowded. [(1) SE in 18C; a black mood; (2) 'black with people']

black v. **1** [late 19C] (UK Und.) to colour one's face black with burnt cork, as a 'nigger minstrel'. **2** [1920s+] to blackmail. [abbr.]

black ace n. (also ace of clubs) [mid-17C] the female genital area (cf. ACE OF SPADES n.[2]; ACE OF TRUMPS n.). [? the colour and shape of the pubic hair]

black acid n. [1970s+] (drugs) **1** LSD (cf. A n.[3]). **2** LSD and phencyclidine. [? packaging/the negative image + ACID n.[3]]

black act n.[1] [mid–late 19C] (US) the profession of undertaking. [var. on BLACK ART n.[2]]

black act n.[2] see BLACK ART n.[1].

black African n. see AFRICAN BLACK n.

black and blonde n. [1980s+] (Aus. prison) hashish (cf. AFGHAN n.).

Black and Decker n. [1990s+] the penis (cf. ALMOND n.). [rhy. sl. = PECKER n.[2]; ult. Black and Decker, the brand of DIY tools, thus also punning on TOOL n.[1] (1)]

black and tan n.[1] **1** [mid-19C] (US Black) the Southern states. **2** [mid–late 19C] (US) a mulatto, a person of mixed race. **3** [1930s–40s] a mixture of dark and light-skinned Black people. [the violence meted out to the Black population]

black and tan n.[2] [late 19C+] a drink composed of porter and ale or stout and ale. [the respective colours of the porter/stout (black) and ale (tan)]

black-and-tan adj. [late 19C+] (US) **1** referring to the mixing of Blacks and Whites, e.g. BLACK-AND-TAN CLUB n. **2** mixed-race.

black-and-tan club n. (also black-and-tan joint, ...parlour, ...resort) [1920s–60s] (US) **1** a place where both Blacks and Whites can meet and mingle. **2** a place patronized by African Americans. [BLACK-AND-TAN adj. (1) + SE club; Smitherman, Black Talk (1994), suggests (2) on the basis of African American skin tones rather than the greater division between the 2 races]

black and tans n. [1960s] (drugs) capsules of the amphetamine Durophet (cf. A n.[2]). [the colours of the capsule]

black and white n.[1] **1** [mid-19C] handwriting. **2** [1970s] a document. [SE down in black and white, in writing]

black and white n.[2] [late 19C–1900s; 1990s+] (UK Und.) night. [rhy. sl.]

black and white n.[3] [1920s–30s] (UK tramp) tea and sugar. [the colours]

black and white n.[4] (also blackandwhite, black-and-white) (US) **1** [1950s+] a police car painted black and white. **2** [1960s–70s] a policeman.

black and white n.[5] [1960s+] (drugs) **1** a black and white capsule, esp. Biphetamine, Dilantin/Phenobarbitol mix. **2** a 12.5mg capsule of the amphetamine Durophet (cf. A n.[2]). [the colours of the capsule]

black and white minstrel n. see MINSTREL n.

black and white work n. [early 19C] writing. [BLACK AND WHITE n.[1] (1)]

black ankle n. [late 19C–1930s] (US) a person of mixed race; usu. Black, Indian and White. [var. on DOMINICKER n. (2)]

black annie n. **1** [20C+] a police or prison van. **2** [1930s–60s] (US prison) (also **black aunty**) a whip, used for punishments. [the colour + generic use of proper name]

black ape n. [1920s] (US) a derog. term for a Black person (cf. AFRICAN APE n.).

black army n. [1920s] the female underworld. [? their chosen clothing, their sinister image; note Aus. black army, a flock of crows]

black arse n. [late 17C–early 19C] a kettle, esp. in phr. the pot calls the kettle black arse. [SE black + ARSE n.[1] (3); both utensils have been discoloured by the flame; this is the same phr. as the modern one; but the final vulgarism has been quietly dropped]

black art n.[1] (also **black act**) [late 16C–mid-19C] (UK Und.) lock-picking. [SE black art, magic or necromancy; thus ext. to a criminal activity that required 'devilish ability']

black art n.[2] [mid-19C+] the profession of undertaking. [the role of black in a funeral]

blackas n. see BLACKERS n. (1).

black as a bull's backside phr. (also **black as a bear's asshole**, ...a dago's armpits, ...a nigger's hide, ...the inside of a Taranaki cow) [20C+] (Aus./N.Z.) extremely black, usu. of darkness. [SE bull + backside/bear + ASSHOLE n.[1] (1)/DAGO n. (1) + SE armpit/NIGGER n.[1] (1) + HIDE n.[1] (1)/SE inside + cow + Taranaki, an area of the South Island, with many dairy herds]

black as a musterer's billy phr. [1940s] (N.Z.) extremely black, usu. of darkness. [SE musterer + billy, a kettle black with use]

black as a yard up a stove-pipe phr. [1930s] (US) extremely black, usu. of darkness.

black as Natoby's ass phr. [1970s] (US) very Black in skin tone, dark-skinned. [? anecdotal]

black as Newgate phr. (also **dark as Newgate**) [early 19C] **1** of an expression, frowning, glowering. **2** of a garment, dirty. [Newgate, 19C London's main convict prison and the site of many executions; its reputation was fig. black]

black as Newgate knocker phr. (also **dark as Newgate knocker**) **1** [late 19C] of a night, very dark. **2** [1980s] very dirty. [for ety. see prev.]

black ass n. [1940s–80s] (US) a state of depression or disgust; thus black-assed, depressed, disgusted. [SE black + ASS n. (5)]

black-ass adj. **1** [1960s+] (US) intensifying extension of Black; dark-complexioned. **2** [1970s+] (US) as a negative intensifier, total, extreme. [(1) SE black + -ASS sfx; (2) BLACK ASS n.]

black-assed peas n. [1940s+] (US Black) soul food, esp. black-eyed peas. [the colouring of the legume; ult. ASS n. (2)]

black as the ace of spades phr. [19C+] very Black, usu. of people rather than objects.

black as the hinges of hell phr. [19C+] (US) very Black, usu. of people rather than objects.

black as the inside of a Taranaki cow phr. see BLACK AS A BULL'S BACKSIDE phr.

black aunty n. see BLACK ANNIE n. (2).

black backra n. [1950s+] (W.I.) a respected Black man. [SE black + BACKRA n. (1)]

black bagging n. [20C+] (US) the genitals of Black women, seen collectively, i.e. for sexual exploitation. [SE black + BAG n.[1] (2)]

black-bagging n. [late 19C] setting off dynamite bombs. [dynamite was carried in black bags and deposited at railway stations and other targets]

black bag job n. see BAG JOB n.[2].

black ball n. see BLACKBIRD n.[1] (6).

blackball v. [mid-18C–early 19C] to exclude a person, esp. from a club or other closed group. [SE f. 1830s; the placing of black balls in a ballot box; depending on the rules, a majority or even 1 black ball rendered a candidate ineligible for membership]

black beauty n. **1** [1960s+] (US drugs) Biphetamine, a strong amphetamine (cf. A n.[2]). **2** [2000s] a depressant. [the colour of the capsules; ult. Anna Sewell's novel Black Beauty (1877)]

black beetle *n.* [mid–late 19C] a constable in the Thames River police. [? his uniform]

black beetles *n.* [early–mid-19C] the proletariat. [a derog. view of the scurrying, indistinguishable masses]

black beezer *n.* [1910s+] a Black person's face. [SE *black* + BEEZER n.[1] (2)]

blackbelly *n.* [1940s–50s] (*US*) a derog. term for a Black person (cf. AFRICAN APE n.; ALLIGATOR BAIT n.[2]; BLACKBIRD n.[1]; CHARCOAL n.; CHIMNEY CHOPS n.; CHOCO n.[2]; CHOCOLATE n.[1]; CHOCOLATE BABY n.; CHOCOLATE BAR n.; CHOCOLATE BUNNY n.; CHOCOLATE DROP n.; CLOUD n.[3]; COAL n.[1]; COAL BIN n.[2]; COAL MINE n.; COAL-SCUTTLER n.; COCOA n.[1]; DARK n.[2]; DARK CLOUD n.; DARKIE n.[1]; DAY AND MARTIN n.; EIGHTBALL n.[1]; INK n.[2]; INKBUG n.; INKSPOT n.; MOLESKIN n.; MUD FLAP n.[1]; RAISIN n.; SCUTTLE n.; SHADE n.[2]; SHADOW n.; SHIT-SKIN n.; SMOKE n.[6]; SMOKED YANKEE n.; SMOKY n.; SMUDGE n.[2]; SMUT-BUTT n.; SOOTY n.; STOVE LID n.; SUNBURNED IRISHMAN n.; TAR BABY n.; TOUCH OF THE TARBRUSH phr.).

black belt *n.* [1920s+] (*US*) that part of a larger urban area in which the Black community lives, the Black ghetto. [SE *black* + *belt*, a zone or district]

blackberry *n.* [mid-19C; 1980s+] (*US*) a Black person. [pun on the SE fruit]

blackberry swagger *n.* [mid-19C–1900s] a hawker of shoelaces, tapes and similar small items. [? the black colour of the laces + *swagger*, one who carries a 'swag' or pack]

black bess *n.* **1** [early 18C–mid-19C] a firelock or musket. **2** [late 19C] the vagina. **3** [late 19C] (*Aus. Und.*) a prison van. [SE *black* + generic use of proper name]

black betsey *n.* (*also* **black betty**) [20C+] a police van. [var. on BLACK ANNIE n. (1)]

black betty *n.* [mid-18C–19C] (*US*) liquor, esp. a bottle that is circulated among the guests at a wedding party; tradition demands that everyone, irrespective of age, must *kiss black betty*, i.e. take a swig from the bottle. [SE *black* + *betty*, a pear-shaped bottle, covered with straw and often used to contain olive oil; properly known as a *Florence flask*]

blackbird *n.*[1] **1** [mid–late 19C] a slave *en route* from the place of capture to their destination; thus *blackbird-catcher*, a slaver or slave ship; BLACKBIRDER n. **2** [mid-19C–1900s] (*Aus.*) an Aborigine; thus *blackbird shooting*, the killing for 'sport' of Aborigines by White settlers. **3** [mid-19C–1910s] a Melanesian; thus *blackbird-catching, blackbird-hunting*. **4** [late 19C+] a derog. term for a Black person (cf. BLACKBELLY n.). **5** [1900s] (*US*) a Black child. **6** [1960s+] (*US Black*) (*also* **black ball**) a dark-complexioned Black person.

blackbird *n.*[2] [1940s+] (*US*) a penis (cf. ANTEATER n.).

blackbird *n.*[3] [1970s+] (*drugs*) a strong (20mg) capsule of amphetamine (cf. A n.[2]). [the colour of the capsules]

blackbird and thrush *v.* [late 19C] to clean one's boots or shoes. [rhy. sl. = *brush*]

blackbirder *n.* [late 19C] a man (or ship) working in the Pacific slave trade, a slave-trader. [BLACKBIRD n.[1] (1)]

blackbirding *n.* [late 19C–1930s] the slave trade, esp. between the Pacific Islands and the Queensland sugar plantations in Australia. [BLACKBIRD n.[1] (1)]

black bomber *n.* [1960s+] (*drugs*) a strong (20mg) capsule of amphetamine, coloured black (cf. A n.[2]). [packaging + BOMBER n.[2]]

black boogaloo *n.* [1960s–70s] (*US Black*) a feeling of blackness. [name of a dance popular in 1960s]

black bottle *n.* [1910s–60s] (*US*) any poisonous drink, esp. knockout drops. [SE, the use of *black* carries overtones of death, but presumably the term is also a descendant of 19C 'black drop', a dark-coloured medicine, mainly composed of opium, plus vinegar and spices. It was widely believed by 20C tramps that such a drink was administered to men in charity wards whose resulting death saved the administration the trouble of caring for them]

black bottom *n.* [1910s+] that part of a larger urban area in which the Black community lives. [SE *black* + BOTTOM n.[3]]

black box *n.* (*also* **black knob**) [late 17C–mid-19C] (*UK Und.*) a lawyer. [the *black*-painted deed *boxes*]

black boy *n.* [mid-19C] a parson, a clergyman. [his vestments]

black bracelets *n. see* BRACELETS n.

black buggy *n.* [1960s] a hearse. [SE *black* + *buggy*]

black cadillac *n.* [1970s+] (*US drugs*) amphetamine (cf. A n.[2]). [colour of capsules + fig. ref. to the quality of the car]

black cap *n.* [late 19C] (*UK Und.*) a thief who befriends a servant girl in order to gain her trust and access to her master's house.

black cattle *n.* **1** [18C] clergymen as a group; thus *black cattle show*, a gathering of clergymen. **2** [late 18C–early 19C] lice. [the colour, either of the insect or the vestments]

black cat with its throat cut *n.* [1950s+] the vagina and female pubic hair (cf. BIRD n.[8]). [CAT n.[3] (1) + resemblance]

black cloud *n.* [1930s] (*US*) a group of Black people.

black coat *n.* **1** [early 17C–1900s] a clergyman, a parson. **2** [1920s+] (*Aus.*) a waiter. **3** [1930s–60s] (*US*) an undertaker. [the trad. clothing]

black cove dubber *n.* [early–mid-19C] (*UK Und.*) a gaoler, a turnkey. [SE black + COVE n. (1) + DUB v.[1] (1)]

black cow *n.* [1910s–50s] (*US teen/campus*) **1** chocolate milk shake. **2** root beer (and milk). [SE *black* + COW n.[5] (1)]

black diamond *n.* [mid-19C] a person whose tough exterior hides a 'heart of gold'.

black diamonds *n.* [mid-19C] **1** (*also* **dusty diamonds**) coal. **2** a coal heaver. [the value of the mineral, if only to the mine-owners]

black dog *n.*[1] [mid-17C–early 18C] a counterfeit silver coin, e.g. a shilling. [use of SE *black* as a generic negative, evil, sinister, illicit etc + ? DOG n.[6]]

black dog *n.*[2] **1** [early 19C+] a fit of depression or ill humour. **2** [1930s] delirium tremens. [the most celebrated of such depressions was that suffered by the former prime minister Sir Winston Churchill]

black domina *n.* [2000s] (*drugs*) a strong type of marijuana (cf. ACAPULCO (GOLD) n.; AFGHAN n.; BLACK GANJA n.; BLACK GOLD n.; BLACK GUNGEON n.; BLACK GUNION n.; BLACK MO n.; BLUE MOONS n.; BLUE SKY BLOND n.; GOLD n.[2]; GOLDEN LEAF n.; GREEN n.[3]; GREENBUD n.; GREEN GODDESS n.; GREEN STUFF n.[1]; GREEN TEA n.; GREENY n.[2]; LONG GREEN n.; MARIGOLD n.[2]; PURPLE HAZE n.; RED BUD n.; RED CROSS n.; RED DIRT n.; SILVER PEARL n.; WHITE WIDOW n.).

black drop *n.* [early 19C] (*Anglo-Irish*) port wine. [its dark colour + DROP (OF THE CREATURE) n.]

black duck *n.*[1] [mid-18C–19C] a Native American Indian. [SE *black duck*, any dark duck, e.g. mallard, redleg; like the birds, the Native Americans were considered prey by the 18C colonists]

black duck *n.*[2] [1990s+] (*Aus.*) Swan lager. [the logo]

black dust *n.* [1980s] (*US Black*) an extremely dark-skinned person.

blackee *n. see* BLACKIE n.[1].

blackers *n.* **1** [1930s+] (*also* **blackas**) blackberries. **2** [1940s] champagne and Guinness, mixed. [*black* velvet + -ER sfx]

blackey *n. see* BLACKIE n.[1].

black eye *n.* [mid-18C+] a bad reputation, a blow to one's reputation.

black eye *v.* [1900s] to criticize. [BLACK EYE n.]

black-eyed susan *n.* [mid–late 19C] (*US, Texas*) a revolver. [? the black 'eye' of the barrel]

black fay *n.* [1960s] (*US Black*) a Black person considered subservient to Whites. [SE *black* + FAY n.]

blackfellows' act *n.* (*also* **dog act**) [1920s+] (*Aus.*) a government order than can be used by publicans to discipline or bar drunkards. [SAusE *blackfellow* (now derog.), a Native Australian]

blackfellow's game *n.* [1940s] (*Aus.*) the game of euchre. [for ety. *see* prev.; its popularity among Native Australians]

black fever *n. see* JUNGLE FEVER *n.* (1).

black fly *n.* [late 18C–mid-19C] a parson. ['the greatest drawback on the farmer is the black fly, i.e. the parson who takes a tithe of the harvest' (Grose, 1796)]

Blackford block *n.* (*also* **Blackford swell, Blackford toff**) [late 19C–1900s] a sporadically well-dressed man. [the London clothes-hire firm of *Blackford's* + SE *block*; the wooden head on which wigs were displayed/SWELL *n.* (1)/TOFF *n.* (3)]

blackfriars! *excl.* [mid–late 19C] (*US Und.*) a shout of warning, 'someone's coming, let's run for it!' [? the black uniform of various authorities, reminiscent of the black-garbed Dominicans]

black gang *n.* [1920s–30s] villains who prey upon other villains, esp. on racecourse confidence tricksters, 'find-the-lady' men, fairground showmen and the like. [BLACK *n.*[2] (3) + SE *gang*; such villains blackmail their peers for a share of their profits]

black ganja *n.* [1970s+] (*drugs*) dark-coloured marijuana (cf. BLACK DOMINA *n.*). [SE *black* + GANJA *n.*]

black gentleman *n. see* BLACK MAN *n.*

blackgin *n. see* GIN *n.*[1] (1).

black gold *n.* **1** [1960s] Black women in general, as sex objects. **2** [1980s+] (*drugs*) high-potency marijuana (cf. BLACK DOMINA *n.*). [(1) SE; (2) BLACK *n.*[3] (3) + ACAPULCO (GOLD) *n.*]

blackguard *n.* **1** [mid-17C] a shabby, dirty individual. **2** [late 18C] (*US*) a foul-mouthed person, a slanderer. ['a term said to be derived from a number of dirty tattered and roguish boys, who attended at the horse guards [...] in St James's Park, to black the boots and shoes of the soldiers, or to do any other dirty offices, these were nick-named the black guards' (Grose, 1785)]

blackguard *v.* [mid-19C+] to swear at, to curse (someone); thus *blackguarding*, talking obscenely. [BLACKGUARD *n.* (2)]

blackguardly *adj.* [late 19C] shabby, dirty. [BLACKGUARD *n.* (1)]

black gungeon *n.* [1960s+] (*drugs*) an especially potent form of marijuana (cf. BLACK DOMINA *n.*). [SE *black* + GANJA *n.*]

black gunion *n.* [1960s+] (*drugs*) marijuana (cf. BLACK DOMINA *n.*). [SE *black* + GUNGEON *n.*]

black hash *n.* [1980s+] (*drugs*) hashish that has been mixed with opium during its manufacture. [SE *black* + HASH *n.*[2]; opium is black, thus darkening the usu. khaki-coloured hashish]

black hat *n.*[1] [mid–late 19C] (*Aus.*) a newly arrived immigrant. [he would still wear his black, citified hat in the bush]

black hat *n.*[2] [1970s+] (*US*) a villain, a BADDIE *n.* (3). [the trad. means of identifying a villain in films]

blackhead *n.* [1970s–80s] (*UK Black*) a Black person.

Black Hole *n.* [late 19C–1930s] Cheltenham. [the large number of ex-Indian Army or Indian Civil Service officers who retired there; the ref. is to the *Black Hole* of Calcutta (1756)]

black hole *n.*[1] [19C] the vagina; one of a number of terms that equate the vagina with hell or any similar dark, threatening place (cf. BORE *n.*[2]; BOTTOMLESS PIT *n.*; BUGGLE-BO *n.*; BUNGHOLE *n.*[1]; CELLAR *n.*[1]; COCK PIT *n.*; DARK HOLE *n.*; FIRE *n.*[2]; FIRELOCK *n.*; FIRES OF HELL *n.*; FORGE *n.*; FUCKHOLE *n.*; FURRY HOLE *n.*; GLORY HOLE *n.*[2]; GULLY (HOLE) *n.*; HELL *n.*[1]; HOLE *n.*[1]; HOLE OF CONTENT *n.*; HOLE OF HOLES *n.*; INKWELL *n.*; JOY HOLE *n.*; KEYHOLE *n.*; LAMB-PIT *n.*; LOVE HOLE *n.*; MANHOLE *n.*[1]; MARK OF THE BEAST *n.*; MAW *n.*; MOLLY'S HOLE *n.*; MOUSEHOLE *n.*; MUCKHOLE *n.*; OVEN *n.*; PASSION PIT *n.*; PEEHOLE *n.*; PIGEONHOLE *n.*; PIT *n.*[1]; PIT HOLE *n.*; POKE-HOLE *n.*; POLE HOLE *n.*; PORTHOLE *n.*; PRICK HOLE *n.*; PUSSY HOLE *n.*; QUEEN OF HOLES *n.*; SECOND HOLE FROM THE BACK OF THE NECK *n.*; SNAKEPIT *n.*; SOCKET *n.*; SPITFIRE *n.*; TOUCH-HOLE *n.*; UNDERWORLD *n.*; WHIRLPIT *n.*).

black hole *n.*[2] [early 19C+] **1** (*US prison*) the (underground) punishment cells in a prison. **2** a police or prison cell. **3** any room set aside for punishment, e.g. in a workhouse or orphanage. [orig. UK milit.]

black house *n.* [mid-19C] **1** a prison (cf. BANDHOUSE *n.*). **2** any place of business where the employees are exploited by long hours and low wages. [SE *black*, evil + *house*]

blackie *n.*[1] (*also* **blackee, blackey, blacky**) [18C+] a Black person; also attrib. [SE *black* + sfx *-ie/-y*; the sfx ensures the term's negative, patronizing implication]

blackie *n.*[2] [1950s] (*US gang*) a *black*jack. [abbr. + sfx *-ie*]

blackie-white *n.* (*also* **blacky-white**) [1930s–40s] (*Anglo-Ind.*) a half-caste. [BLACKIE *n.*[1] + SE *white*]

Black Indies *n.* [late 17C–mid-19C] Newcastle upon Tyne, in its role as a centre of coal-mining. [the Indies, whether East or West, were the sources of great mercantile wealth; *black* implies the area's mines]

blacking *n.* [2000s] (*UK juv.*) a male initiation ceremony whereby a boy has his genitals covered in black shoe polish.

black Irish *n.* [20C+] (*US*) **1** a person with a terrible temper. **2** a working-class Irish person, typically an unsophisticated new immigrant. **3** an Irish Protestant. **4** a former slave, who took their surname from an Irish owner. [SE *black Irish*, an Irish person with notably Mediterranean features – dark hair and eyes – but with no overtones of ill temper. One theory suggests that the original 'black Irish' were the descendants of mixed marriages between the Irish and the shipwrecked sailors of the Spanish Armada, cast ashore in 1588]

black-is-white *adv.* [20C+] (*W.I.*) thoroughly, comprehensively, without restraint. [i.e. one will argue that 'black is white']

black ivory *n.* [late 19C] Black slaves. [their value]

Black Jack *n.* [early 19C] the Recorder of London. [the nickname of Sir John Sylvester, the Common Sergeant of London *c.*1810]

black jack *n.*[1] **1** [late 16C–mid-19C] a leather jug used for drinking, coated with tar on its exterior. **2** [late 19C] a type of suitcase or portmanteau. **3** [late 19C–1900s] (*Aus.*) a tin pot used for boiling tea. [SE *black* + *jack*, a vessel for liquor (either for holding it or for drinking from); orig. and usu. of waxed leather coated outside with tar or pitch]

black jack *n.*[2] [mid-19C+] the ace of spades. [SE *black* + generic use of proper name]

black jack *n.*[3] **1** [1900s] some form of poison. **2** [1930s] (*US tramp*) a purgative. [? nickname]

black jack *n.*[4] **1** [1940s+] (*US gay*) a Black man's penis. **2** [1950s+] (*US*) a Black woman's genitals. [SE *black* + JACK *n.*[3]]

blackjack *n.*[1] **1** [mid–late 19C] (*US*) rum sweetened with molasses. **2** [late 19C+] (*US*) very strong black coffee, usu. sweetened with molasses. **3** [20C+] (*Aus.*) treacle. **4** [20C+] (*US*) illegally distilled whisky. [SE *black*, the colour of the drinks/treacle + JACK *n.*[16]]

blackjack *n.*[2] [1920s] (*US*) a thug. [his weapon]

blackjack *n.*[3] [1960s] (*US drugs*) amphetamine (cf. A *n.*[2]). [colour of the capsules]

blackjack *n.*[4] [1970s+] (*S.Afr.*) a Black municipal policeman (cf. BABY-BLUES *n.*[2]). [his uniform colour + ? his weaponry]

black job *n.* [mid–late 19C] a funeral.

black jock *n.* **1** [late 18C] pubic hair. **2** [late 19C] (*also* **brown jock, grey jock**) the vagina. [SE *black* + JOCK *n.*[1] (1)]

black joint *n.* [1920s] (*US Black/Harlem*) any Black night-club catering specifically to White 'tourists'. [SE *black* + JOINT *n.*[4] (3)]

black joke *n.* (*also* **coal-black joke**) [mid-18C+] the female genitals. [contemporary popular song, *The Harlot Unmasked* (*c.*1735) the chorus of which ran, 'Her black joke and belly so white'; Williams notes that 'the C18 saw numerous songs circulating to the tune '*Black Joke*''; E.P. suggests 'something to be cracked']

black justice *n.* [1960s+] (*US Black*) Black self-determination as opposed to White justice, which Black radicals experience only as a prejudiced farce.

black knob *n. see* BLACK BOX *n.*

black label *n.* [1980s+] (*Aus. prison*) illicit home-fermented liquor. [play on proprietary Johnnie Walker *Black Label* whisky]

blackleg *n.*[1] **1** [late 18C–1910s] a racecourse swindler. **2** [late 18C–1910s] (*also* **blackshanks**) any swindler; thus *blacklegging*, *black-leggery*, swindling. **3** [19C] a professional gambler or layer of odds. **4** [late 19C] (*US*) a fashionable dandy. **5** [1930s–50s] (*US Und.*) a professional criminal. [? SE *game-cocks*, which have black legs, or f. the black boots such swindlers always wore; another suggestion notes a pun on ROOK n.[1]/SE *rook*, a bird that also has black legs]

blackleg *n.*[2] [mid-19C+] a strike-breaker. [ety unknown; ? link to Scot. *blackleg*, a go-between (usu. in love-affairs, but fig. between bosses and workers]

blackleg *n.*[3] [20C+] a Black man's penis (cf. ARM n.[1]). [SE *black* + the idea of it being a 'leg']

blackleg *n.*[4] [1910s] (*US*) strong black coffee.

blackleg *v.* [late 19C+] to work as a strike-breaker. [BLACKLEG n.[2]]

black man *n.* (*also* **black gentleman**) [17C+] the Devil. [the Devil, personifying evil, is naturally black]

black man kissed her *n.* [1910s; 1950s+] a sister. [rhy. sl.]

black maria *n.*[1] (*also* **black mariah**) **1** [mid-19C+] (*orig. US*) a prison van for conveying prisoners. **2** [mid-19C+] (*orig. US*) a hearse. **3** [1980s] (*orig. US*) an ambulance. [SE *black*, the colour of the van, but the ety. of *maria* is unknown; suggestions include an abbr. of *married*, i.e. 2 or more prisoners chained together; a play on the *-ria* of Queen Victoria's name (which fails in the face of its origins in the US, although *V.R.* was inscribed on the British vans) and Brewer's suggestion in *Dict. of Phrase and Fable* (1894) of a derivation f. one Maria Lee, a Black madam of Boston, Massachusetts, who was so large and fearsome that she was regularly called upon by the local police to help them arrest and take criminals to prison. According to F&H, themselves citing 'a writer on slang', the term was coined *c.*1838 in Philadelphia, although the *OED* first use is 1847 (usefully for Brewer from a Boston newspaper) and E.P. notes Joseph Neal's story *The Prison Van, or, The Black Maria* (1844)]

black maria *n.*[2] [20C+] **1** a Black woman's genitals. **2** a Black prostitute (cf. BABY JANE n.). [SE *black* + generic use of proper name]

black meat *n.* [20C+] **1** a Black woman's genitals. **2** a Black woman. [SE *black* + MEAT n. (1)]

black mo *n.* (*also* **black moat, black mote**) [1970s+] (*drugs*) **1** a particularly potent variety of marijuana, with notably dark colouring (cf. BLACK DOMINA n.). **2** marijuana mixed with honey. [SE *black* + MO n.[4]/MOTA n.]

black mollies *n.* [1970s] (*US drugs*) amphetamines (cf. A n.[2]). [SE *black* + MOLLIES n.]

black Monday *n.* **1** [mid-18C–early 19C] the first day back at school after the holidays. **2** [mid-19C] the day on which a death sentence is carried out. [SE *black* as generic for bad, evil, depressing]

black mote *n. see* BLACK MO n.

black mouth *n.*[1] [mid-17C] a slanderer. [SE *black*, malicious, evil + *mouth*]

black mouth *n.*[2] [20C+] a Black woman's genitals.

blackmouth *n.* [20C+] (*Ulster*) a Presbyterian.

black mouth *adj.* [17C–19C] slanderous, malicious. [BLACK MOUTH n.[1]]

black mummer *n.* [early 19C] an unshaven person.

black muns *n.* [17C–18C] hoods and scarves made of lutestring (a glossy silk fabric) or alamode (a thin, light, glossy black silk). [SE *black* + MUNS n.[1] (1)]

black neb *n.* [20C+] (*Ulster*) a Presbyterian. [SE *black* + NEB n.[1] (3)]

black nigger *n.* [19C–1950s] (*US Black*) a derog. term of address used between Black men. [SE *black* + NIGGER n.[1] (1)]

black nigger in charge *n. see* HEAD NIGGER IN CHARGE n.

black oil *n.* [1970s–80s] (*US drugs*) hashish oil (cf. CHERRY LEB n.; OIL n.[3]; RED OIL n.; SOIL n.).

black ointment *n.* [mid-19C] (*UK Und.*) a piece of raw meat. [its use as a cure for black eyes]

black-on-black *n.* [1940s+] (*US Black*) a car with black paintwork and all-black interior upholstery and fittings.

blackout *n.*[1] (*also* **black-out**) **1** [1940s] (*US Black*) a very dark-skinned person. **2** [1940s+] (*S.Afr./US*) black coffee. [pun on SE]

blackout *n.*[2] (*also* **black-out**) [1990s+] (*US*) a restaurant or store taken over and controlled by a group of (young) African Americans (who then leave without paying for the food or goods). [the image of the young Blacks 'taking out' the goods]

black out *v.* [1940s] (*US Und.*) to murder; to assassinate.

black out with *adj.* [1920s+] (*Irish*) hostile towards.

black Pak *n.* [1960s+] (*drugs*) a variety of hashish produced in Pakistan (cf. AFGHAN n.). [its dark colour + PAK n. (1)]

black parts *n. see* BLACK n.[1].

black pencil *n.* [1970s] a Black man's penis (cf. FLESH PENCIL n.; PEN n.[1]; PENCIL n.; PENCIL DICK n.; QUILL n.[1]). [SE *black* + PENCIL n. (2); play on SE]

black people's time *n.* [1960s+] (*US/UK Black*) unpunctuality, lateness (cf. AFRICAN (PEOPLE'S) TIME n.). [joc. use of derog. racial stereotyping]

black-pepper brain *n.* (*also* **black-pepper grains**) [1960s+] (*W.I.*) very short hair, growing close to the scalp in small balls of fluff. [resemblance to black peppercorns]

black peter *n.* [1930s+] (*Aus.*) a cell for solitary confinement. [SE *black* + PETER n.[2] (5)]

black pill *n.* (*also* **green pill**) [20C+] (*drugs*) an opium pill (cf. APOSTLE n.). [the colour of the drug; opium is rolled into a PILL n.[4] (1) for smoking]

black pimp *n.* [1930s–40s] (*US Black/Southern*) a telephone that is hooked into a party line and thus offers its user free calls. [the image of a pimp endlessly making calls + the colour of early telephones]

blackplate *n.* [1940s+] soul food. [a pun on the US restaurant dish, the 'blue plate special', and the trad. *Black* person's food]

black pot *n.* [late 16C–early 19C] a drunkard. [SE *black pot*, a beer mug]

Black Power dance *n.* (*also* **power dance**) [1960s] (*US Black*) **1** looting. **2** fighting back against White oppression. [SE *Black Power* + ironic use of *dance*]

black Protestant *n.* (*also* **black Prod**) [1960s+] (*US*) **1** a derog. term used by Catholics to describe a violently anti-Catholic Protestant. **2** a non-practising Protestant. [SE *black* as generic for Protestant, on model of 'scarlet' for Catholicism + *Protestant*/PROD n.]

black pudding *n.* [mid-19C+] a Black man's penis (cf. BACON n.[1]). [SE *black* + PUDDING n.[1] (4)]

black ring *n.* [19C] the vagina. [SE *black* + RING n.[1] (1)]

black rot, the *n.* [mid-19C] (*US*) a fit of intense depression. [it 'rots one's brain']

black Russian *n.* [1980s+] (*drugs*) cannabis resin, hashish, esp. when mixed with opium (cf. AFGHAN n.). [? ref. to the supposedly chic cigarette brand]

black sal *n.* (*also* **black sukey**) [mid-19C–1900s] a kettle. [SE *black* + *sal*, abbr. Sally/*sukey*, abbr. Susan; ? ref. to the nursery rhyme 'Polly Put the Kettle On' ('Sukey take it off again'); but note E.P.'s suggestion Welsh Gipsy *sukar*, to hum, to whisper]

blackshanks *n. see* BLACKLEG n.[1] (2).

black sheep *n.* **1** [late 18C–19C] a 'bad lot', a badly behaved, disappointing or otherwise 'alien' individual, standing out from a crowd of conforming or well-behaved people. **2** [early 19C] a clergyman. **3** [mid–late 19C] a strike-breaker.

black sheep *v.* [20C+] (*US*) to take advantage of another person's temporary disability or absence to steal their job. [BLACK SHEEP n. (3)]

black-shoe adj. [1950s] (US campus) formal, sober. [the formality of such footwear]

black-silk barge n. [late 19C–1900s] (UK society) a stout woman who ought to avoid dances. [her *black silk* clothes, chosen to minimize her bulk, fail to offset her *barge*-like proportions]

blacksmith n. 1 [late 19C+] (Aus.) a cook on an outback station, usu. derog. 2 [1920s–40s] (US Und.) a safe-breaker. [the hammers, chisels and similar tools common to both occupations]

blacksmith v. [1930s] (US Und.) to break into a safe. [BLACKSMITH n. (2)]

blacksmith's daughter n. [mid-19C] a key, a lock and key, a padlock. [? ref. to a chastity belt]

blacksmith's shop n. [20C+] a brothel run by a Black madam and presumably featuring a number of Black prostitutes (cf. BANGING-SHOP n.). [play on SE/SHOP n.[1] (1) + ? HAMMA n./HAMMER MAN n.[1]]

blacksnake n. [1930s+] (US Black) a Black penis (cf. ANTEATER n.). [SE *black* + SNAKE n.[3]]

blacksnake v. [19C] (US) to whip, to punish. [SE *black snake*, a long braided whip, used by mule-drivers and teamsters]

blacksock v. [1990s+] (US) to perform in a pornographic movie. [the stereotypical cheap pornographic movie, in which the male actors, otherwise naked, often keep on their socks]

black spice racket n. [early 19C] to rob chimney sweeps of their soot. [appearance + RACKET n.[1] (1)]

blacksploitation n. *see* BLAXPLOITATION n.

black spy, the n. [late 17C–mid-19C] the Devil; ext. as a derog. term of address.

blackstick n. [1930s–60s] (orig. US Black) a clarinet.

black strap n. 1 [late 18C+] poor-quality liquor, esp. port wine. 2 [1920s] a variety of chewing tobacco. 3 [1920s–60s] (US) very strong black coffee. [SE *black strap*, molasses, and thus referring to its excessive sweetness]

black stuff n. (drugs) 1 [1930s+] opium; thus *shovelling the black stuff*, addicted to opium (cf. APOSTLE n.). 2 [1960s+] stout, esp. Guinness. 3 [2000s] heroin (cf. BLACK n.[3]). [STUFF n.[3] (2); opium is black; the ref. to heroin, usu. brown or white, is based on its relation to opium]

black stump n. [1950s+] (Aus.) a symbolic marker that divides the known or 'civilized' world from the unknown wastelands beyond; usu. in phr. *this side of the black stump, beyond the black stump*; also fig. *beyond the black stump*, insane, eccentric. [SE *black* + *stump*, a free-standing post or pillar]

black sukey n. *see* BLACK SAL n.

black tar n. [1980s+] (drugs) heroin processed in Mexico (cf. BLACK n.[3]). [SE *black* + TAR n.[3]]

black taxi n. [1980s] (Aus.) an official limousine that ferries government members etc to and from houses, appointments and the like.

black teapot n. [late 19C] a Black footman. [? his duties include pouring tea]

black thing n. [mid-18C] the vagina (cf. ARTICLE n.). [euph.]

black 360 degrees adj. [1960s+] (US Black) intensely and specifically Black in personality and consciousness. [360° describes a complete circle, thus totality]

blacktime n. [1990s+] (UK/US Black) unpunctuality (cf. AFRICAN (PEOPLE'S) TIME n.). [negative stereotyping]

black top n. [1920s] (US tramp) a tent used for the projection of films.

blacktop n. 1 [1930s+] (US) a minor road, a back road. 2 [1990s+] an asphalt playground. [its black asphalt surface]

black town n. [late 19C+] that part of a larger urban area in which the Black community lives.

black up v. [1950s+] (W.I.) to get drunk. [one is 'blind' drunk]

black up adv. [1940s+] (W.I.) in a very drunken manner. [BLACK UP v.]

black velvet n. 1 [late 19C+] (Aus./N.Z.) any dark-skinned woman; thus a *bit of black velvet*; occas. of men. 2 [1930s+] a mixture of stout and champagne. 3 [1960s] (US) a Black woman's genitals. [fig. use of SE, based on the colour and smoothness, whether of skin or the drink]

black wagon n. (US) 1 [mid-19C+] a hearse. 2 [late 19C] a police car.

Blackwall Tunnel n. [20C+] a ship's funnel. [rhy. sl.]

black wash n. [1940s+] (W.I.) coffee. [SE *black* + WASH n.[1]]

black water n. [mid-19C–1960s] (US, Western) weak black coffee.

black whack n. [1980s+] (drugs) phencyclidine (cf. ACE n.[4]). [SE *black* + WHACK n.[1] (1)]

black widow n. [1970s] (drugs) any black capsule that contains amphetamine (cf. A n.[2]). [the packaging]

black-work n. [mid-19C] funeral arrangements, undertaking. [the pre-eminent role of black in funerary arrangements]

blacky n. *see* BLACKIE n.[1].

blacky-white n. *see* BLACKIE-WHITE n.

bladder n.[1] [late 16C–19C] a talkative, long-winded and thus boring person. [SE *bladder of wind*]

bladder n.[2] (also **blatter**) [1900s–60s] (US) a newspaper. [Ger. *Blatt*, leaf and therefore newspaper]

bladder n.[3] [1930s] (US Und.) an unattractive and/or ageing prostitute.

bladdered adj. [1990s+] drunk. [play on GET A SKINFUL v.]

bladder of fat n. [1900s–10s] a hat. [rhy. sl.]

bladder of lard n.[1] 1 [mid-late 19C] a bald-headed man. 2 [mid-19C+] a fat man. [derog. comparisons]

bladder of lard n.[2] 1 [20C+] a playing card. 2 [1910s] a card as used in the game of bingo. 3 [1920s–50s] Scotland Yard, former headquarters of the Metropolitan Police. [rhy. sl.]

bladderscat n. [1960s] (US) nonsense, rubbish, foolish talk; an untrustworthy person. [var. on BLATHERSKITE n.]

bladdy adj. (also **bleddy**) [1940s+] (S.Afr./W.I.) a general expletive, the local pron. of the UK BLOODY adj.[1] (1).

blade n.[1] [17C–19C] the penis (cf. AX n.[2]).

blade n.[2] 1 [17C+] a 'sharp fellow'. 2 [18C–19C] a man. 3 [1910s] (Scot./US) one's wife, usu. *old blade*, or girlfriend. 4 [1980s] (US Black) a Cadillac. 5 [1990s+] an expert, a connoisseur, a wise man or one posing as such. [SHARP adj.]

blade n.[3] [late 19C+] (US) any knife, esp. a switchblade. [SE *blade*, a sharp weapon]

blade n.[4] [1980s+] (Ulster) 1 a showily or bizarrely dressed woman. 2 a cantankerous, verbally abusive woman. 3 a 'difficult' child. [they are all 'sharp']

blade v.[1] [early 19C] to act as a roisterer, a 'sharp' man or woman. [BLADE n.[2] (1)]

blade v.[2] [1980s+] (US campus) to get rid of. [? SE *blade*, a sharp weapon; thus the offending item is 'cut out' of one's life]

blade v.[3] [1980s+] (Aus./US Und.) to stab, to slash with a sharp/bladed weapon. [BLADE n.[3]]

blades n. [1980s+] (US drugs) smoking hashish by placing a piece on a knife blade and then exposing it to a flame, e.g. *let's do some blades*.

blades of meat n. *see* PLATES (OF MEAT) n.

bladhunk n. [18C–19C] (tinker) a prison. [Shelta]

blag n. 1 [late 19C+] robbery, often with violence, esp. of a bank or post office. 2 [1920s+] bag-snatching, watch-stealing. 3 [1930s+] a wages' snatch. 4 [1940s+] (orig. UK Und.) a persuasive if lying story. [? SE *blackguard*]

blag v. 1 [late 19C+] (orig. UK Und.) (also **blague**) to steal. 2 [1940s+] to deceive, to hoax. 3 [1950s] to be rude or cheeky. 4 [1960s+] to persuade, esp. as in *blag in (to)*, to talk one's way into a party, concert etc. 5 [1970s+] to obtain for free. 6 [2000s] to pretend. [BLAG n.]

blagger n. 1 [1930s+] a thief, esp. a bank robber. 2 [1990s+] a smooth talker, a persuasive person. 3 [2000s] a sponger. [BLAG v.]

blagging *n.* [20C+] (*UK Und./police*) **1** a robbery. **2** violence, in the course of a robbery. [BLAG v. (1)]

blag merchant *n.* [1950s+] a pay-roll robber. [BLAG n. (3) + MERCHANT n.]

blague *v. see* BLAG v. (1).

blah *n.*[1] [1910s+] **1** (*orig. US*) pompous, banal verbosity; also nonsense. **2** a fool, an idiot. [? BLAH v. (2) or ? Ger. *Blech*, nonsense or onomat.]

blah *n.*[2] [1950s+] (*S.Afr.*) brother. [pron.]

blah *adj.* **1** [1920s] (*US*) insane, crazy. **2** [1920s+] (*orig. US*) insincere, verbose, pompous. **3** [1920s+] wonky, wrong. **4** [1930s+] very drunk. **5** [1960s+] blasé, uninterested, non-committal. **6** [1990s+] banal, clichéd. [BLAH v.]

blah *v.* **1** [1920s] to chatter, to gossip. **2** [1960s+] to speak in an insincere, pompous manner; thus intensified as *blah-blah-blah*. [onomat.]

blah! *excl.* [2000s] (*US campus*) an excl. of boredom or resignation. [BLAH n.[1] (1)]

blah, blah, blah *phr.* **1** [1910s+] (*also* **blah, blah, blah**) a phr. used to imply that a statement is meaningless or nonsense, albeit delivered in the most serious of tones. **2** [1940s+] (*Aus./US*) as a synon. for etcetera, 'and so on'. **3** [1960s] an otherwise unidentified object. [BLAH n.[1]]

blahs, the *n.* [1960s+] (*Aus./US*) depression, despondency, low condition. [? BLAH n.[1]]

blam *v.* [1970s+] to do something that generates noise. [echoic]

blame *adj.* (*also* **blamed, blamedest, blarmed**) [mid-19C+] (*US*) a euph. for DAMN adj./DAMNED adj.

blame *v.* [mid-19C+] (*US*) a euph. for DAMN v., used in mild excls.

blame *adv.* (*also* **blamed**) [mid-19C–1900s] confoundedly, exceedingly. [BLAME adj.]

blamed/blamedest *adj. see* BLAME adj.

blame it! *excl.* [early 19C–1930s] a euph. for DAMMIT! excl. [BLAME adj.]

blamentation! *excl.* (*also* **blamenation!**) [mid-19C] (*US*) a mild expletive; a euph. for DAMNATION! excl. [BLAME adj.]

blamps *n.* [1990s+] large breasts. [? SE *big* + HEADLAMPS n.[2]]

blanca *n.* [1950s–60s] (*US drugs*) **1** amphetamine (cf. A n.[2]). **2** cocaine (cf. COCONUT n.[3]; DAMA BLANCA n.; DR WHITE n.; FROST n.[2]; GOLD DUST n.; GOLDEN GIRL n.[2]; GREEN GOLD n.; LADY SNOW n.[2]; LITTLE JOE (IN THE SNOW) n.; OLD LADY WHITE n.; PARADISE (WHITE) n.; SNOW n.[1]; SNOWFLAKE n.[1]; SNOW WHITE n.; TEETH n.; WHITE n.[3]; WHITE BRICK n.; WHITE CROSS n.; WHITE GIRL n.; WHITE HORSE n.[3]; WHITE LADY n.[2]; WHITE MOSQUITOES n.; WHITE SHIT n.; WHITE STUFF n.). [Sp. *blanca*, white]

blanched *adj.* (*also* **blanshed**) [1960s+] (*US Black*) ruined either physically or socially. [pun on SE *blanched*, whitened + *blanch*, to turn white with fear, embarrassment]

blanco *n.* **1** [1960s+] (*US Black*) a White person. **2** [1970s+] (*drugs*) heroin (cf. BLACK n.[3]). [Sp. *blanco*, white; some varieties of heroin are white, rather than the usual brown]

blandander *v.* **1** [late 19C–1910s] to cajole, to offer blandishments. **2** [late 19C+] to talk nonsense. [SE *blandish*/BLETHER v. and/or BLARNEY v. (1)]

blank *n.* **1** [mid-19C+] a euph. for a variety of obscenities, e.g. BUGGER n.[1], SHIT n.[2], BASTARD n. etc. **2** [1950s–70s] (*US prison*) an aspirin. **3** [1950s+] (*orig. prison*) a rejection, esp. of a parole application. **4** [1960s] a halt, a stop. **5** [1960s] a fault, a bad characteristic. **6** [1960s] a bad or insignificant, worthless person. **7** [1960s+] (*drugs*) any powder sold as a narcotic but absolutely without effect; thus generic for second-rate drugs. [(1) for ety. *see* BLANK adj.]

blank *adj.* (*also* **blanked, blanking**) [mid-19C+] a euph. for DAMN adj./DAMNED adj. (or FUCKING adj.). [lit. the 'blank space' that replaces the unuttered oath]

blank *v.*[1] [late 19C] (*Aus.*) to curse, to swear at. [for ety. *see* BLANK adj.]

blank *v.*[2] **1** [1970s+] to ignore. **2** [1990s+] to wipe out, to reject. **3** [1990s+] to overlook. [SE *blank out*, to erase; note baseball jargon *blank*, to retire a team without letting them score]

blankard *n.* [20C+] (*Aus.*) a bastard. [BLANK n. (1) + SE (*bast*)*ard*]

blanked *adj. see* BLANK adj.

blanker *n.* [1900s–10s] (*Aus.*) a euph. for BUGGER n.[1]. [BLANK n. (1)]

blanket *n.*[1] [mid-19C] (*US*) a currency note; thus money in general (cf. BANK-RAG n.). [it offers its holder comfort]

blanket *n.*[2] [late 19C+] (*S.Afr.*) a peasant, an unsophisticated African; thus in synon. combs. *blanket-boy, blanket-kaffir*; thus *blanket-vote*, the collective Black vote. [the trad. blankets that such individuals wear; note 19C US *blanket brave, blanket Indian*, 'an Indian of a low cultural level [...] a semi-civilized Indian' (Mathews, *Dict. Americanisms*, 1951)]

blanket *n.*[3] [1920s–30s] **1** (*US tramp*) an overcoat, which regularly doubles as a blanket. **2** (*US tramp*) a newspaper (which is often used as a makeshift blanket). **3** (*US Und.*) a bulletproof vest. **4** (*US tramp*) a griddlecake or pancake.

blanket *n.*[4] **1** [1920s–40s] a cigarette paper; thus *tumblings and blankets*, tobacco and papers. **2** [1960s] (*US campus*) a cigarette. **3** [1980s+] (*drugs*) a marijuana cigarette. [the shape; (2) may be an error]

blanket-ass *n.* (*also* **blanket-head**) [1950s+] (*US*) a Native American (cf. BLANKET-BUCK n.). [SE *blanket*, used as adj. to denote Native American +ASS n. (5)/-HEAD sfx (2); blankets are supposedly inseparable from Indians]

Blanket Bay *n.* [late 18C–1900s] (*Aus./US*) bed (cf. BLANKET FAIR n.).

blanket-buck *n.* [20C+] (*US*) a Native American (cf. BLANKET-ASS n.). [SE *blanket* + BUCK n.[1] (5)]

blanket drill *n.* (*orig. milit.*) **1** [1920s+] masturbation. **2** [1960s] sexual intercourse. [note milit. jargon *blanket drill*, sleep]

blanket fair *n.* [late 19C] bed (cf. BLANKET BAY n.). [the orig. *Blanket Fair* was the name given to that held on the Thames during the great frost of 1683–4]

blanket-head *n. see* BLANKET-ASS n.

blanket hornpipe *n.* [early 19C] sexual intercourse (cf. DANCE v.[1]).

blanket job *n.* **1** [1930s–60s] (*US prison*) homosexual gang-rape: the victim's head is placed beneath a blanket while he is assaulted. **2** [1980s] (*UK Und.*) a form of gangland execution whereby the victim is tricked into hiding beneath a blanket – and then shot dead. **3** [1980s] (*also* **blanket treatment**) a beating given by prison officers.

blanket muster *n. see* TARPAULIN MUSTER n.

blanket party *n.* **1** [1930s] (*US*) sexual intercourse. **2** [1970s+] (*US prison*) the murder of a fellow prisoner by tossing a blanket over the head and then bludgeoning or stabbing them to death. **3** [1970s+] an initiation rite whereby a new prisoner is forcibly smothered in a blanket, then beaten up or gang-raped by their fellows; similarly applied to teen gang initiations. **4** [1970s+] (*N.Z./US prison*) a beating, an attack, where the victim is first covered with a blanket so they are unable to identify their attacker(s). [ironic use of SE]

blanket stiff *n.* [late 19C+] (*US*) a tramp, esp. a Western tramp. [SE *blanket*, a bedroll + STIFF n.[2] (4)]

blanket treatment *n. see* BLANKET JOB n. (3).

blankety *adj.* [mid-19C+] a general term of condemnation. [var. on BLANK adj.]

blankety-blank *phr.* (*also* **blinkety-blankety**) [late 19C+] a general term of condemnation, which is found in all parts of speech, e.g. *you blankety-blank!* or *that blankety-blank, no-good so-and-so* or *don't you blankety-blank me!* [a euph. in which the words indicate 2 blanks, for presumed obscenities, on the page]

blankey *adj. see* BLANKY adj.

blanking *adj. see* BLANK adj.

blank out v. **1** [1950s+] to render unconscious. **2** [2000s] to become (temporarily) unconscious.

blanks n. [late 19C–1910s] (*Anglo-Ind.*) White people. [Fr. *blanc*, white; Y&B offers only a single cit. from 1718 and states 'we know not if anywhere else in English']

blank up v. [1980s+] (*US Black*) to trick, to murder. [to render one's victim 'blank']

blanky adj. (*also* **blankey**) [late 19C+] a euph. for BLOODY adj.[1], DAMNED adj. (2) or a similar negative intensifier. [BLANK adj.]

blanny n. [1920s–50s] (*US*) flattery. [SE *blandishment*/BLARNEY n.]

blanny v. [1960s] (*US*) to flatter. [BLANNY n.]

blanshed adj. *see* BLANCHED adj.

blaps n. [1960s+] (*S.Afr.*) a gaucherie, a blunder. [Afk. *blaps*, a blunder, a howler, a 'blooper']

blap up v. [1980s] (*UK Black*) to deceive by talking fast. [echoic of the fast speech]

blar v. [1990s+] (*W.I.*) to show off. [? BLAH n.[1] (1)]

blarey-eyed adj. [1970s] (*US Black*) a general insult. [? SE *bleary-eyed*/US Southern *blare-eyed*, heaving bulging eyes]

blarge v. [1970s] (*Ulster*) to do anything unceremoniously and loudly. [SE *blunder* + *barge*]

blaring cheat n. *see* BLEATING CHEAT n.

blarmed adj. *see* BLAME adj.

blarney n. [late 18C+] nonsense, charming but empty chatter; also as excl. [*Blarney*, a village near Cork in Ireland. Within the castle is an inscribed stone, which is hard to approach, and the popular belief is that anyone who kisses this 'Blarney stone' will ever after be gifted with a persuasive, plausible tongue; note Bartlett, *Dict. Americanisms* (1848): 'Dr. Jamieson doubts the Irish origin of this word, and adopts the French etymon *baliverne*, a lie, a fib, gull; also, a babbling, idle discourse']

blarney v. **1** [late 18C+] to flatter, to talk nonsense; thus *blarneyed*, flattered, cajoled. **2** [late 19C] (*US Und.*) to pick locks. [BLARNEY n.]

blarney boy n. [1950s] one who is charming, but whose words are nonsensical and empty. [BLARNEY n. + SE *boy*]

blarsted adj. *see* BLASTED adj.[1].

blart n. [1990s+] **1** (*also* **blit**) the vagina. **2** a generic for women, considered as sexual objects. [? BLART v.; *blit* references SLIT n.[1] (1)]

blart v. [late 19C+] to talk wildly, noisily. [dial. *blart*, to howl]

blase adj. [early–mid-19C] exhausted by enjoyment, weary and disgusted with it, used up. [SE f. 1860s; Fr. *blasé*, exhausted by pleasure; the word was popularized by a French farce *L'homme blasé*, which was staged (*c.*1840) in 2 versions. In the second of these a character was called Blasé; the modern use to mean 'supercilious' dates f. 1930s]

blast n.[1] **1** [late 19C+] a severe reprimand, a verbal attack. **2** [1950s–60s] a telephone call. **3** [1950s–70s] (*US prison*) a false rumour. **4** [1960s] (*US*) a lie. [ext. use of SE; (1) BLAST v.[1] (3)]

blast n.[2] [1920s–50s] an armed (bank) robbery.

blast n.[3] **1** [1940s+] (*drugs*) an injection or inhalation of a narcotic drug and the immediate effect. **2** [1950s+] (*US*) a drink of liquor. **3** [1950s+] a thrill, a very good time. **4** [1950s+] a wild, uproarious party. **5** [1970s] something funny, amusing. **6** [1970s+] (*orig. US*) a puff of a marijuana cigarette; the effect thereof. **7** [1990s+] an admirable person. **8** [1990s+] (*US Black*) a song. **9** [1990s+] a smoke of a crack pipe. [BLAST v.[4]]

blast n.[4] [1950s–70s] a DAMN n. [BLAST! excl.]

blast v.[1] [mid-18C+] a euph. for DAMN v., used in mild excls. **2** [late 18C+] to swear, to curse. **3** [mid-19C+] to scold, to criticize, to vilify. **4** [1940s+] to complain. [lit. 'blast to hell']

blast v.[2] **1** [1920s+] (*orig. US*) to shoot a gun. **2** [1930s–70s] (*orig. US*) to shoot or kill someone with a gun. **3** [1930s+] (*orig. US*) to defeat heavily. **4** [1960s] (*US Black*) to do something well. **5** [1960s] (*US campus*) to fail an examination or test. **6** [1980s] (*UK Black*) to beat up. [SE *blast*, to blow violently]

blast v.[3] **1** [1930s] to leave. **2** [1930s] to give up trying. **3** [1970s+] to move fast. [SE *blast off*]

blast v.[4] **1** [1940s+] (*drugs*) to smoke a marijuana or hashish cigarette. **2** [1950s–60s] (*US*) to go completely mad (esp. under the influence of drugs). **3** [1950s+] to take narcotics. **4** [1980s] to give someone an injection. **5** [1980s+] (*drugs*) to smoke crack cocaine. [the immediate effect of the drug on one's brain, but ult. early 16C Scot. *blast*, a smoke of tobacco]

blast v.[5] **1** [1960s] (*US*) to play music passionately. **2** [1970s] (*US*) to drive fast. **3** [1990s+] (*orig. US Black/teen*) to play a record (loudly).

blast v.[6] *see* BURN v.[1].

blast! excl. [20C+] a mild. excl., a euph. for DAMN! excl. [BLAST v.[1] (1)]

blast a joint v. [1950s+] (*drugs*) to smoke marijuana. [BLAST v.[4] (1) + JOINT n.[5] (3)]

blast a roach v. [1950s+] (*drugs*) to inhale deeply on a marijuana cigarette. [BLAST v.[4] (1) + ROACH n.[2] (2)]

blast a stick v. [1960s+] (*drugs*) to smoke marijuana. [BLAST v.[4] (1) + STICK n.[9] (3)]

blasted adj.[1] (*also* **blarsted**) **1** [late 17C+] a euph. for DAMNED adj. **2** [1980s+] as an infix. [abbr. SE *God blasted*]

blasted adj.[2] [1930s+] very drunk or heavily intoxicated by a drug (cf. ANNIHILATED adj.). [fig. use of SE *blast*]

blasted brimstone n. [late 18C] (*UK Und.*) a prostitute. [SE *blasted*, cursed + BRIMSTONE n. (1)]

blasted fellow n. [mid-18C–early 19C] a complete villain. [SE *blasted*, cursed + *fellow*]

blaster n.[1] (*US Und.*) **1** [1910s–30s] a safe-blower. **2** [1930s–60s] a thug or gangster who is armed. **3** [1930s+] a pistol, a revolver, a shotgun. [(1) SE *blast*; (2) and (3) BLAST v.[2] (1)]

blaster n.[2] [1980s+] a large, portable cassette recorder/player. [abbr. GHETTOBLASTER n.]

blast from the past n. (*also* **blast from one's past**) [1960s+] (*orig. US*) anything that, or anyone who, causes nostalgia, esp. a piece of music, a popular song or an old friend.

blastiferous adj. [1900s] (*Aus.*) a synon. for BLASTED adj.[1] (1).

blasting party n. [1950s–70s] (*orig. US Black*) a party where the guests smoke marijuana (in favour of drinking). [BLAST v.[4] (1) + SE *party*]

blast my eyes! excl. *see* DAMN MY EYES! excl.

blast my old boots! excl. *see* FUCK MY OLD BOOTS! excl.

blast-off n. [1960s] (*US*) **1** an orgasm. **2** a thrill, a very good time.

blast off v. **1** [1950s+] (*US*) to leave; often as an imper. **2** [1960s] (*US drugs*) to experience a drug and thus get HIGH adj.[1] (2). **3** [1990s+] (*US*) to have an orgasm.

blast party n. [1950s–60s] (*US Black*) a gathering of marijuana smokers. [BLAST v.[4] + SE *party*]

blast the lid off v. *see* BLOW THE LID OFF v. (1).

blast your eyes! excl. *see* DAMN MY EYES! excl.

blat n. [1930s+] (*US*) a newspaper. [Ger. *Blatt*, leaf; thus newspaper]

blat v. **1** [18C–1910s] to talk wildly or loudly. **2** [20C+] (*US*) to talk at length (and with no real importance). [SE *blat*, bleating or shrill sound]

blatant adv. [1990s+] (*UK Black*) a general intensifier, definitely, undoubtedly, very much so. [SE *blatant*, glaringly or defiantly conspicuous]

blater n. **1** [18C–mid-19C] a sheep. **2** [18C–19C] a calf. [? SE *bleat*]

blather *see also under* BLETHER.

blatherskite n. **1** [mid-16C; mid-19C+] (*also* **bletherskate**, **bletherskite**) a voluble, boastful speaker. **2** [early 19C+] (*also* **blatherumskite**, **bletherumskite**) rubbish, foolish talk. [BLETHER v. and SE *skate*, to slide over]

blatherskite adj. [late 18C–19C] noisy, boastful. [BLATHERSKITE n. (1)]

blatherskite v. [late 19C] to boast, to talk nonsense. [BLATHER-SKITE n. (2)]

blatherskite! excl. (also **bletherskate! bletherskite!**) [1900s] nonsense! [BLATHERSKITE n. (2)]

blatherumskite n. see BLATHERSKITE n. (2).

-blatt sfx [1980s+] (US campus) a sfx of familiarity or endearment added to nouns.

blatter n.[1] [20C+] an attack, a blow. [BLATTER v.]

blatter n.[2] see BLADDER n.[2].

blatter v. [late 19C+] to hit, to attack. [Scot. blatter, to rush with clattering noise]

blaw n. [1990s+] (Scot. drugs) cannabis. [Scot. var. on BLOW n.[6] (7)]

blaxican n. [2000s] (US Black) one who is of mixed Black and Mexican blood. [SE Black + Mexican]

blaxploitation n. (also **blacksploitation**) [1970s+] (orig. US) the use of Black actors in a (usu. low-budget) film featuring a plot filled with sex and violence and peopled by stereotypes (pimps, prostitutes, drug dealers etc). [SE Black + exploitation]

blaze v.[1] [1980s+] (US campus) to leave. [SE blaze the trail]

blaze v.[2] [1990s+] (orig. US Black/drugs) **1** to smoke marijuana. **2** to light a cannabis cigarette.

blaze v.[3] [1990s+] (US campus) to have sexual intercourse.

blaze away v. [mid-19C+] to work at anything with enthusiasm and energy. [SE blaze, to burn with the fervour of devotion, excitement, or passion + blaze away, to fire a weapon rapidly]

blazed adj. [1990s+] (drugs) intoxicated by a drug. [SE blazed, inflamed]

blaze on v. [1980s+] (US Black) to attack or knock down without warning. [? SE blaze away/out, to fire continuously]

blazer n. (US) **1** [mid-late 19C] someone or something exceptional of their type. **2** [1900s–30s] a hoax, a lie, a cheating trick; thus run a blazer, to deceive, to trick. [SE blazer, anything that blazes or shines; thus in (2) it dazzles the victim]

blazers n. [late 19C] spectacles. [the reflection of the sun in their lenses]

blazes n. **1** [early 19C+] a euph. for hell in various phrs., e.g. GO TO BLAZES! excl.; WHAT THE BLAZES! excl. **2** [mid-19C] the guts, the innards, the 'stuffing'. [the trad. fires of hell]

blazes! excl. [mid-19C+] a euph. for HELL! excl.

blazes, Kate! excl. [20C+] (Irish) a general excl. of surprise, annoyance etc. [BLAZES! excl. + generic use of proper name]

blaze up v. [2000s] (drugs) to light a marijuana or hashish cigarette.

blazing adj. **1** [mid-19C+] (orig. US) a general intensifier, esp. in phr. blazing row, a vicious argument. **2** [1980s+] (US) first-rate, excellent. **3** [1990s+] (US Black/teen) of a woman, extremely attractive.

blazing adv. [mid-19C] (US) very good, very well.

bleach v. [mid-19C–1900s] (US campus) to miss a class or other meeting, e.g. morning chapel. [? play on SE blank out]

bleached mort n. [late 18C] a woman with a pale complexion. [SE bleached + MORT n.]

bleacher n. (also **bleecher**) **1** [late 18C–mid-19C] a woman, usu. pej. **2** [1930s] (Glasgow) a maidservant. [her job is bleaching clothes]

bleachification n. [1990s+] (US) the gentrification of former working-class blocks. [SE bleach, a whitening agent; such blocks were often Black or Puerto Rican; their new, richer owners will be White]

bleak adj. [mid-late 19C] (US) attractive, handsome; thus bleak-mort, a pretty young woman. [? SE bleak, pale, wan]

bleary adj. (also **bleary-eyed**) [20C+] drunk. [SE bleary, short-sighted]

bleat n. **1** [20C+] a (feeble) complaint. **2** [1900s] talk, statements. **3** [1930s–40s] (US) an act of informing, a revelation. **4** [1950s] (UK prison) a petition to the Home Secretary for reduction or repeal of one's sentence. [the weak chance of success is underlined by the allusion to the sound of a sheep]

bleat v. **1** [mid-19C+] (orig. milit.) to complain, to whinge. **2** [20C+] to inform on someone. [(1) mid-16C–mid-19C use SE]

bleater n.[1] [early 17C–early 19C] (UK Und.) one who is tricked by a confidence trickster. [SE bleater, a lamb (to the slaughter)]

bleater n.[2] [mid-17C] (UK Und.) a sheep.

bleater n.[3] **1** [1920s] a weakling, a whinger. **2** [1940s] (US Und.) an informer. [BLEAT v.]

bleating cheat n. (also **blaring cheat, bleating chete**) [mid-16C–19C] (UK Und.) a sheep. [SE bleat + CHEAT n. (1)]

bleating cull n. [18C–early 19C] a sheep-stealer. [BLEATER n.[2] + CULL n.[1] (4)]

bleating prig n. [18C–early 19C] sheep-stealing. [BLEATER n.[2] + PRIG n.[1] (1); note BLEATING RIG n.]

bleating rig n. [late 18C–early 19C] (UK Und.) sheep-stealing. [BLEATER n.[2] + RIG n.[2] (2)]

bleddy adj. see BLADDY adj.

bleecher n. see BLEACHER n.

bleed n.[1] [late 19C–1900s] blood; usu. in phr. she'll have his bleed, used of a woman's forthcoming attack on her husband.

bleed n.[2] [1970s+] (US Black) a Black person. [BLOOD n.[5] (1)]

bleed v.[1] **1** [mid-17C+] to extort money from; thus bleeder, one who extorts money. **2** [mid-17C+] (UK Und.) to part with one's money without complaint, to submit oneself to extortion. **3** [1960s] (US) to take advantage of. [SE bleed dry]

bleed v.[2] [1960s–70s] (US) to sweat profusely.

bleeder n.[1] **1** [early 19C] a spur, usu. pl. **2** [mid-19C] (US) a knife, when used as a weapon. [SE bleed, to draw blood]

bleeder n.[2] [mid-19C] (UK Und.) a lie.

bleeder n.[3] [late 19C] a sovereign. [one 'bleeds' money to creditors]

bleeder n.[4] **1** [late 19C+] a person (occas. an animal) or thing, usu. but not invariably with derog. implications. **2** [1900s] a generic term for a working-class East Ender. [lit. one who draws blood]

bleeding adj. **1** [mid-19C+] a general negative adj., a euph. for BLOODY adj.[1] (1); also as intensifier, bleeding hell etc. **2** [1930s+] as an infix.

bleeding cully n. (also **bleeding cull**) [18C–early 19C] a gullible victim, one who parts cheerfully with their money. [BLEED v.[1] (2) + CULLY n. (1)/CULL n.[1] (2)]

bleeding dirt n. [1940s–70s] (gay) extorting money from homosexuals. [BLEED v.[1] (1) + DIRT n.[2] (4)]

bleeding new adj. [late 18C] fresh, new. [the image of fish, which bleed only when they are fresh]

bleeding Nora! excl. see FUCKING NORA! excl.

bleed like a (stuck) pig v. [17C+] to bleed heavily, to lose a good deal of blood.

bleed one's turkey v. [1920s+] to urinate (cf. BLEED THE LIVER v.; DRAIN ONE'S RADIATOR v.; DRAIN THE DRAGON v.; DRAIN THE LILY v.; DRAIN THE (MAIN) VEIN v.; DRAW OFF v.[2]; LEAK v.[1]; EMPTY THE ANACONDA v.; SIPHON THE PYTHON v.; STRAIN OFF v.; STRAIN ONE'S GREENS v.; STRAIN THE POTATOES v.; TAKE A LEAK v.; TAP A KIDNEY v.). [SE bleed + SE turkey/? TURKEY NECK n.]

bleed the liver v. [1920s+] to urinate (cf. BLEED ONE'S TURKEY v.).

bleed the lizard v. [1990s+] to masturbate (cf. BEAT ONE'S HOG v.). [SE bleed + LIZARD n.[3]]

bleed white v. [20C+] to submit to excessive extortion, thus draining every drop of money/blood.

bleedy adj. see BLOODY adj.[1].

bleep n. [1970s+] a euph. substitute for various taboo terms, e.g. SHIT n.[1] in phr. beat the bleep out of. [the electronic 'bleeping' out of supposed obscenities on radio and TV; the modern equivalent of BLANK n.]

bleep v. [1970s+] a euph. substitute for various taboo terms, e.g. FUCK! excl. in *bleep you!* [for ety. *see* prev.]

bleeping adj. [1970s+] a euph. for various taboo words, e.g. FUCKING adj. (1). [for ety. *see* BLEEP n.]

blem n. [1960s] (*US campus*) a spot, a pimple. [abbr. SE *blemish*]

blemm v. [1980s+] (*Irish*) to rush, to move at speed. [ety. unknown]

blemmed up adj. [1920s] (*Irish*) smartly or fashionably dressed. [ety. unknown; ? BLEMM v.]

blend n. [1990s+] (*drugs*) marijuana. [? a mixture of several varieties of the drug]

blend v. [20C+] (*US*) **1** to marry. **2** to have sexual intercourse.

blender n. [1990s+] (*W.I.*) an aggressive person. [the image of a food *blender* chopping and whirling ingredients together]

blenker v. [mid-19C] (*US*) to plunder. [Brigadier-General Louis *Blenker* (1812–63), whose troops, starving for lack of proper rations, plundered civilian homes near Warrenton, Virginia in April 1862]

blenz n. [2000s] (*US Black*) an attractive woman. [ety. unknown]

blerry adj. [1920s+] (*S.Afr.*) a general expletive, the local pron. of the UK BLOODY adj.[1]. [Afk. pron.]

bleskop n. [1960s+] (*S.Afr.*) **1** a bald-headed person. **2** a bald head. [Afk. *bles*, bald + *kop*, head]

bless v.[1] [early 19C] to curse someone, to reprimand, to scold. [ironic reversal of usual SE use]

bless v.[2] [1960s+] (*US Black*) to have sexual intercourse.

blessed adj. [19C+] a joc. euph. for DAMNED adj. (1).

bless in v. [2000s] (*US prison*) to beat up a new member of a gang as an initiation rite.

blessing n. **1** [late 18C–mid-19C] a small quantity over and above the stated measure, given to a customer by a stall-holder or shopkeeper. **2** [late 19C] (*Irish*) a tip, a hand-out. [14C SE *blessing*, a present; note Devon dial. *blessing*, an extra handful of produce thrown in as a bonus to an order, and also the belief, common to many religions, that those who give charity are blessed]

bless me! excl. [18C+] a mild excl. [abbr. *Lord bless me!*, but note BLESS ONESELF v.]

bless my buttocks! excl. [1960s] (*US*) a mild euph., poss. for KISS MY ARSE! excl.

bless my heart! excl. (*also* bless my eye-balls!, …eyesight!, …lucky stars!, …stars!) [mid-18C+] a mild excl.

bless my soul n. [1980s] (*Aus.*) unemployment benefit (cf. COB O' COAL n.; CON AND COAL n.; HORSE AND FOAL n.; JAM ROLL n.; KID CREOLE n.; NAT KING COLE n.; OLD KING COLE n.; ROCK AND ROLL n.; SAUSAGE ROLL n.; STRUM AND STROLL n.; TOILET ROLL n.). [rhy. sl. = SE *dole*]

bless oneself v. [17C–18C] to curse. [SE *bless oneself*, to say 'God bless me!']

bless someone out v. [1990s+] (*US Black*) to curse someone. [BLESS v.[1]]

bless the world with one's heels v. [mid-16C] to be hanged. [? the feet twitching in the air could be likened to making the sign of the cross]

blether n. (*also* blethers) **1** [late 18C+] (*also* blather) nonsense. **2** [late 19C–1920s] one who talks nonsense. **3** [1920s] foolish talkativeness. **4** [2000s] a chat. [ME *blather*, nonsense; thus Scot. *blether*, Irish *bladar*, flattery]

blether v. (*also* blather) [late 18C+] to talk nonsense, continually and at length. [BLETHER n. (1)]

blethering n. (*also* blething, blathering) [mid-19C+] talking nonsense. [BLETHER n.]

blethers n. *see* BLETHER n.

bletherskate/bletherskite *see under* BLATHERSKITE.

bletherumskite n. *see* BLATHERSKITE n. (2).

blething n. *see* BLETHERING n.

blew v.[1] **1** [mid-19C] to end a relationship. **2** [mid-19C+] to waste, usu. money; thus *blew one's screw*, to spend all one's wages at once (cf. BLUE v.[2]). [BLOW v.[5] (1)]

blew v.[2] [mid-late 19C] to inform on, to betray. [BLOW v.[1] (2)]

blewed adj. *see* BLUED adj.[1].

blew in one's red 'un v. [late 19C] to pawn one's watch and spend the money thus realized on drink. [BLEW v.[1] (2)/BLUE v.[2] (3) + RED 'UN n.[1] (1)]

blew it v. [mid-19C–1920s] to betray a fellow villain to the police. [BLEW v.[2]]

blew one's screw v. *see* BLEW v.[1] (2).

blew out adj. *see* BLOWN (OUT) adj.

blews n. *see* BLUES n.[1].

blick adj. [2000s] (*UK teen*) unpleasant, unattractive. [echoic for the sound of disgust, i.e. *blech!*]

bliff n. [1990s+] the vagina. [ety. unknown]

bliff mag n. [1990s+] a pornographic magazine. [BLIFF n. + colloq. SE *mag*, a magazine]

bligh n. [1980s+] (*W.I./UK Black teen*) a chance, an opportunity, an opening. [ety. unknown]

blighted adj. (*also* blighting) **1** [late 19C+] a euph. for BLOODY adj.[1] (1). **2** [1910s–40s] very drunk or heavily intoxicated by a drug (cf. ANNIHILATED adj.).

blighter n. [late 19C+] **1** a living creature, usu. human but also animal, usu. derog. **2** an object, usu. dismissive. [lit. one who *blights* their surroundings but ? also a euph. for BUGGER n.[1]; later 20C+ use is usu. ironic, with images of such actors as Terry-Thomas (1911–90) or Leslie Phillips (b.1924); Ware has theatrical use as 'an actor of evil omen', synon. with JONAH n.]

Blighty n. [1910s+] (*orig. Ind. Army*) **1** England. **2** (*also* Blighty one, Blighty wound) a wound gained during WW1 that was sufficiently incapacitating to ensure one's being sent home to England from the front; also used for other wars. [Hind. *bilyati* = *wilyati*, foreign, esp. European; ult. f. Arabic *wilayat*, an inhabited country, a foreign country; *bilyati* was used in a variety of contexts, the best known being *bilyati panee*, 'European water', i.e. soda water]

Blighty adj. [1910s+] English, pertaining to English lifestyle/culture. [BLIGHTY n.]

blikkeys n. [1990s+] (*drugs*) fake crack cocaine that has been manufactured from flakes of soap powder. [ety. unknown]

Blikkiesdorp n. (*S.Afr.*) **1** [1950s+] (*also* Blikkiesbaai, Blikkiesfontein, Overblikkiesberg) a fictitious town, used to personify an insignificant, small town. **2** [1960s+] a slum, a shanty-town. [Afk. *blikkie*, little tin + *dorp*, town]

Blikoor n. [late 19C+] (*S.Afr.*) a derog. term for an inhabitant of the Orange Free State. [Afk. *blik*, tin + *oor*, an ear]

blim n. [1990s+] (*drugs*) **1** a small piece of hashish, not really sufficient to make a full-strength 3-paper cigarette, but enough for perhaps a weak one or a single-skin effort. **2** the residue in a pipe used for smoking hashish. [ety. unknown]

blimey n. [1910s–30s] (*US*) a Briton. [pun on LIMEY n. (1) and the British use of BLIMEY! excl.]

blimey! excl. (*also* blime!) [late 19C+] an excl. denoting surprise or disbelief. [oath 'God blind me!']

blimey O'Reilly! excl. [1920s+] a general excl., presumed to be an intensifier of BLIMEY! excl. [assonant ext. of BLIMEY! excl.]

blimin adj. [1980s] (*N.Z.*) a mild expletive. [pron. of BLOOMING adj.[2] (1)]

blimp n.[1] **1** [1920s–60s] a promiscuous young woman. **2** [1930s+] a backward-looking, ultra-conservative figure, orig. a military man, terrified of progress and determined to do anything to prevent it. **3** [1930s+] a very fat person. [the fictitious *Colonel Blimp*, the personification of (1), invented by the cartoonist and caricaturist David Low (1891–1963) (his rotund shape echoed the WW1 'blimp', a small airship orig. consisting of a gas-bag – note GASBAG n. – with the fuselage of an aeroplane slung underneath). Already widespread, the term and the image became even more popular with the Powell/Pressburger film *The Life and Death of Col. Blimp* (1943)]

blimp *n.*[2] [1960s+] a glance, a look, also as v., to glance.

blimp boat *n.* [1980s+] (*US campus*) a very fat person. [BLIMP n.[1] (3) + SE *boat*]

blimpish *adj.* [1930s+] conservative, hidebound, stick-in-the-mud. [BLIMP n.[1] (2)]

blimpo *n.* [1930s+] (*US*) a very fat person. [BLIMP n.[1] (3) + -O sfx (1)]

blimp out *v.* [1970s+] (*US campus*) **1** to eat voraciously. **2** to become grossly fat. [BLIMP n.[1] (3)]

blimpy *adj.* [1990s+] (*US*) fat. [BLIMP n.[1] (3)]

blind *n.*[1] **1** [late 18C+] an excuse, a pretence. **2** [early 19C; 1950s–70s] a deceptive person. **3** [20C+] (*US Und.*) a supposedly legitimate business which in fact masks a criminal one. [SE *blind*, any means or place of concealment]

blind *n.*[2] [late 19C] night-time; thus *do a blind*, to do a MOONLIGHT FLIT n.

blind *n.*[3] **1** [late 19C] an order to leave a town (presumably on the railroad). **2** [late 19C–1960s] (*US tramp*) (*also* **blind baggage, blind car**) a baggage car that has no door at the end leading to the inside; thus it cannot be accessed while the train is in motion; thus *blind baggage tourist*, one who travels on such cars; *beat the blind, jump the blind*, to ride in such a car. [SE *blind*, i.e. it has no windows; (1) f. (2)]

blind *n.*[4] [1920s] (*US campus*) an evening out with someone whom one has never met.

blind *n.*[5] [2000s] (*US prison*) an area in which prisoners cannot be watched by officers.

blind *n.*[6] *see* BLINDER n.[3] (1).

blind *adj.*[1] (*also* **blinded**) **1** [early 17C+] (*orig. UK Und.*) extremely drunk (cf. AFFLICTED adj.) (cf. BLIND DRUNK adj.). **2** [1950s+] (*orig. Und.*) intoxicated from drug use. [so drunk one cannot see]

blind *adj.*[2] **1** [late 19C+] (*also* **blinded**) complete, utter. **2** [20C+] (*bingo*) describing the round numbers, e.g. BLIND TWENTY n. **3** [1930s+] a negative intensifier, e.g. *not a blind bit of use, not a blind word, not take a blind bit of notice*. [(2) the '0' represents the blindness]

blind *adj.*[3] [1920s+] (*gay*) uncircumcised.

blind *adj.*[4] [1990s+] (*S.Afr. juv.*) unfortunate, unlucky.

blind *v.*[1] **1** [mid-19C] to cheat. **2** [1900s] (*US campus*) to answer all the questions one is posed by an instructor, esp. when one has done no actual preparation. [SE *blind*, to conceal]

blind *v.*[2] [late 19C+] to swear. [euph. for such words as BLOODY adj.[1] and BLEEDING adj.]

blind *v.*[3] [1910s–40s] (*US campus*) to expose another's ignorance. [? one 'blinds' them with one's own knowledge]

blind *v.*[4] [1920s–50s] to drive very fast and without noticing anyone else on the road.

blind *adv.*[1] [late 19C+] utterly, completely. [devoid of any external modification]

blind *adv.*[2] [1930s] (*US tramp*) in a closed baggage car. [BLIND n.[3] (2)]

blind alley *n.* **1** [late 19C] the vagina (cf. ALLEY n.[1]). **2** [late 19C+] an unlicensed drinking house.

blind as Chloe *phr. see* DRUNK AS CHLOE phr.

blind-baggage *n. see* BLIND n.[3] (2).

blind billy's bargain *n.* [late 19C+] a 'bargain' that is, in fact, no bargain at all, since one is unable to impose one's own conditions on the person with whom one is dealing. [*Blind Billy*, a former Limerick hangman; the soon-to-be-hanged person was in no position to bargain]

blind both eyes *phr.* [late 19C] of eggs, fried on both sides, 'turned over'.

blind boy *n.* [late 17C] the penis. [SE]

blind car *n. see* BLIND n.[3] (2).

blind charley *n.* [mid-19C] (*US*) a lamp-post. [SE *blind* + CHARLEY n.[1] (1)]

blind cheeks *n.* [early 17C–19C] the posterior; thus *kiss/buss blind cheeks!*, a euph. for KISS MY ARSE! excl. [the shape of the 'nether cheeks']

blind cobbler's thumb *n.* [1990s+] a derog. description of the face of an unattractive woman; usu. in phr. *face like a blind cobbler's thumb*. [? covered in pockmarks, resembling needle-pricks]

blind cock *n.* [1980s+] (*US gay*) an uncircumcised penis (cf. BALD-HEADED HERMIT n.). [BLIND adj.[3] + COCK n.[2] (1)]

blind Cupid *n.* **1** [late 18C–early 19C] an ugly blind man. **2** [early 19C] the buttocks. [*Cupid*, the god of love, is often painted as blind]

blind date *n.* [1920s+] (*orig. US*) an evening out with someone whom one has never met but who will be introduced by a mutual friend. [SE *blind* + DATE n.[1] (2)]

blind dragon *n.* [1920s–30s] (*UK society*) a chaperon(e). [SE *blind* + *dragon*, a fierce old woman; she casts a 'blind eye' on her charge's frolics]

blind drunk *adj.* [mid–late 19C] extremely drunk. [SE in 20C]

blinded *adj.*[1] *see* BLIND adj.[1].

blinded *adj.*[2] *see* BLIND adj.[2] (1).

blinder *n.*[1] [late 19C] a blow to the eye.

blinder *n.*[2] **1** [20C+] a cheap, bad cigar; mostly in pl. **2** [1930s] a Woodbine cigarette (the cheapest available brand); mostly in pl. [ext. of SE use; ? the smoke or the smell gets in one's eyes]

blinder *n.*[3] **1** [1910s+] (*also* **blind**) a drunken spree, a binge; thus phr. *on a blinder/blind*, on a drinking spree. **2** [1950s] an intoxicating cocktail. [BLIND adj.[1] (1)]

blinder *n.*[4] [1960s+] a hard and exciting sporting encounter; esp. as to *play a blinder*. [one is *blinded* by the quality of the game]

blind eye *n.* **1** [late 18C–1900s] the buttocks. **2** [late 19C] the vagina; thus *get a shove in the blind eye/wink at the blind eye*, to have sexual intercourse. **3** [1970s] (*US gay*) the anus. [coarsely joc. use of SE; (3) EYE sfx]

blind fart *n.* [late 19C+] a noiseless but very malodorous breaking of wind.

blindfolded lady with the scales *n.* [1940s–50s] (*US Black*) justice, as a concept rather than as a product of the legal system. [the trad. image of justice, seen in statues, illustrations etc]

blind Freddie *n.* [1940s+] (*Aus.*) an imaginary figure seen as representing the lowest denominator of incompetence; thus used in phr. such as *blind Freddie could see that; wouldn't fool blind Freddie* (cf. BEN n.[1]). [some commentators have posited a real-life 'blind Freddie' – a blind beggar in the streets of Sydney in the 1920s – but no one has yet properly identified him; note personal correspondence from P.K. Lynch 7/10/00: 'mebbe Sir Frederick Pottinger, Bt, who got into financial trouble in the Coldstream Guards and enlisted as a trooper in the NSW Mounted Police, which hunted bushrangers. Was famed for closing his eyes before loosing off his pistol after miscreants — who more or less inevitably "bounding, rode away". Accidentally shot himself while boarding a coach in Springwood, NSW in 1865.']

blind harper *n.* [late 17C–mid-19C] a beggar who fakes blindness, distracting attention from the disguise by playing a harp or fiddle.

blind hookey *n.* [mid-19C–1900s] madness, foolishness, a leap in the dark. [proper name *Blind Hookey*, a card-game in which 5 cards are dealt face down. The dealer takes the centre card and, if that is the highest, wins all the bets; if it is the lowest, the dealer pays all 4]

blind inches *n.* [late 19C] the measurement of the different lengths of one's penis when erect or flaccid. [one does not see the extra length when the penis is flaccid]

blinding *n.* [1940s] swearing, using profanities. [BLIND v.[2]]

blinding *adj.*[1] [1930s+] wonderful, terrific, perfect etc. [? so intense as to render one blind]

blinding *adj.*[2] (*also* **binding**) [1940s+] a euph. for BLOODY *adj.*[1] (1).

blind jam *n.* [1930s] (*US Und.*) an arrest without a specific charge. [fig. use of SE *blind*, i.e one cannot 'see' a charge + JAM *n.*[4] (1)]

blindman's buff *n.* [1960s+] snuff. [rhy. sl.]

blind man's holiday *n.* 1 [late 16C–1900s] night-time. 2 [late 17C–early 18C] nightfall, dusk. [once night falls there is nothing – in a pre-street-light world – for a blind man to see]

blind meat *n.* [1920s+] (*US gay*) an uncircumcised penis (cf. BACON *n.*[1]; BALD-HEADED HERMIT *n.*). [SE *blind* + MEAT *n.* (2)]

blind mullet *n.* [1980s] (*Aus.*) a piece of excrement (cf. BROWN TROUT *n.*). [rhy. sl.]

blindo *n.*[1] [mid-19C–1900s] a drunken spree. [BLINDO *adj.* + -O *sfx* (4)]

blindo *n.*[2] [20C+] (*UK tramp*) a sixpence (2½p).

blindo *adj.* (*also* **blind-o**, **blindoe**) [mid-19C–1920s] tipsy. [BLIND *adj.*[1] (1) + -O *sfx* (3)]

blind O'Reilly! *excl.* [1910s+] 1 a general excl. of surprise, excitement etc. 2 used as an intensifier. [*O'Reilly* was apparently a real person, poss. a trade-unionist on the Liverpool docks]

blind pig *n.* (*also* **pig**) 1 [late 19C+] (*US*) an unlicensed drinking house, a speakeasy, an 'after-hours' bar. 2 [late 19C+] the whisky served in such an establishment. 3 [1970s] a variety of cocktail. [? the typical architecture of the earliest of such bars, a blank façade bereft of windows and with only a small peep-hole in its door. Alternatively f. the practice of disguising the bar as an exhibition of natural freaks; G. A. Thompson (personal correspondence) notes a 'widely publicised case written up in *N.Y. Gazette & General Advertiser*, Sept. 15, and *N.Y. Commercial Advertiser*, 14 Sept. in 1838 where a man in Dedham, Mass. "took out a regular license for the exhibition of a 'striped pig'"; he paints a pig appropriately, charges "four pence hapenny" admission, gives a drink of liquor for free']

blind-pigger *n.* [late 19C+] (*US*) the proprietor of an illicit drinking establishment. [BLIND PIG *n.* (1)]

blind robin *n.* [mid-19C+] (*US*) a smoked herring. [the red herring and the robin's red breast]

blinds *n.* [1920s–30s] (*US tramp*) the false door at the end of carriages, thus places between the carriages where a hobo can hide while riding on a passenger train.

blindside *v.* (*orig. US*) 1 [20C+] to take by surprise. 2 [1920s+] to take advantage of. [US football jargon *blindside*, to attack or strike (an opponent) on the side on which the view is obstructed]

blind staggers *n. see* STAGGERS *n.*

blind tiger *n.* (*also* **tiger**) (*US*) 1 [late 19C+] an unlicensed drinking house. 2 [1900s] illicit whisky. 3 [1920s] the owner of an illicit bar. [ety. unknown; var. on BLIND PIG *n.*]

blind to the wide *phr. see* DEAD TO THE (WIDE) WORLD *phr.*

blind twenty *n.* [20C+] (*bingo*) the number 20; also multiples of 10 up to 80, thus *blind thirty*, *blind forty* etc (cf. ALDERSHOT LADIES *n.*). [BLIND *adj.*[2] (2)]

bling *n.* (*also* **bling-bling**) [1990s+] money, ostentatious jewellery and personal items. [MTV News (online) 30/4/03: 'The term, which is used to describe diamonds, jewelry and all forms of showy style, was coined by New Orleans rap family Cash Money Millionaires back in the late '90s and started gaining national awareness with a song titled "Bling Bling" by Cash Money artist BG.']

bling-bling *adj.* [1990s+] (*orig. US Black*) showy, indicative of conspicuous consumption. [BLING *n.*]

bling-bling *v.* [2000s] (*orig. US Black*) to demonstrate one's material wealth. [BLING *n.*]

blinger *n.* [1940s–60s] (*US*) the extreme example of a type or situation. [SE *blink* or echoic *bling*, used for something that hits one with a sudden thump]

blinging *adj.* [2000s] (*US Black*) showy, ostentatious. [BLING *n.*]

Blinglish *n.* [2000s] (*UK Black/teen*) Jamaican patois as adopted by White English youth. [BLING *n.* + SE *English*]

blink *n.*[1] 1 [early–mid-19C] a light. 2 [late 19C] (*US*) a look, a glance. 3 [late 19C–1930s] (*UK Und.*) a pair of spectacles. 4 [20C+] (*orig. US tramp*) (*also* **blinkie**, **blinky**) a blind person, a one-eyed person. 5 [1900s–30s] (*US*) an eye.

blink *n.*[2] [late 19C–1900s] a drink. [abbr. BIT OF BLINK *n.*]

blink *n.*[3] [1910s+] (*Aus.*) a cigarette butt. [smoking it causes one to blink because of the smoke entering the eyes]

blink *v.* 1 [mid-19C+] to ignore, deny. 2 [late 19C] (*US*) to drink. 3 [late 19C–1920s] (*US*) to see. 4 [1910s] (*Irish*) to bewitch, to spoil.

blinked out *adj.* [20C+] malfunctioning, out of order. [ON THE BLINK *phr.*[1] (1)]

blinker *n.* 1 [late 18C] (*UK Und.*) a wink. 2 [19C] a hard blow in the eye. 3 [mid-19C+] (*orig. US*) a black eye. 4 [late 19C] a man, a fellow. 5 [1970s] a camera. 6 [1970s+] (*US Und.*) a police surveillance helicopter. 7 [1980s] (*US*) a quadriplegic.

blinkers *n.* 1 [late 18C+] the eyes, occas. sing. 2 [mid-19C–1970s] eyeglasses, spectacles.

blinkety-blankety *phr. see* BLANKETY-BLANK *phr.*

blink-fencer *n.* [mid–late 19C] a seller of spectacles. [BLINKERS *n.* (2) + -FENCER *sfx*]

blinkie *n. see* BLINK *n.*[1] (4).

blinking *adj.* [20C+] a mild pej. [euph. for BLOOMING *adj.*[2] (1)]

blinko *n.* [late 19C] an 'amateur night' at the local public house. [? one blinks at the mediocrity of it all]

blinko *adv.* [1950s+] (*US*) very, to an extreme extent; always with *drunk*. [one blinks to clear one's drunken vision]

blink-pickings *n.* [1910s+] (*Aus.*) cigarette stubs, picked up from the gutter and either relit or recombined in a new hand-rolled cigarette. [BLINK *n.*[3] + SE *pickings*]

blinks *n.* 1 [17C+] a nickname for one who blinks all the time. 2 [mid-19C] the eyes. 3 [mid-19C] a pair of spectacles.

blinky *n. see* BLINK *n.*[1] (4).

blinky *adj.* [1900s] (*US*) obscure, opaque.

blinky bill *n.* [1980s] (*Aus.*) a fool. [rhy. sl. = DILL *n.*]

blip *n.*[1] [late 19C–1970s] a blow. [onomat. for a small, short, sharp sound, underpinned by milit. jargon *blip*, a small elongated mark projected on a radar screen, itself ref. to the 'bleeping' noise of radar]

blip *n.*[2] 1 [20C+] a temporary hiatus. 2 [1940s+] (*US Black*) a surprise, a sudden disappointment. [for ety. *see* prev.]

blip *n.*[3] [1930s–50s] (*US Black*) a cent, a nickel. [ext. of BLIP *n.*[1]; accentuating the smallness of the sound and the coin]

blip *n.*[4] [1930s–60s] (*US Black*) something excellent. [ety. unknown]

blip *n.*[5] [2000s] (*US Black*) one's emotional 'territory'. [ety. unknown]

blip *adj.* [1930s–60s] (*US Black*) fine, good. [BLIP *n.*[4]]

blip *v.* [1930s+] (*orig. milit.*) to open and close the throttle; thus revving a car engine while the clutch is disengaged. [orig. WW1 use, applied. spec. to aeroplanes]

blip (off) *v.* (*orig. US*) 1 [1920s–30s] to hit hard, to shoot. 2 [1920s+] to kill, to murder. [BLIP *n.*[1]]

blirt *n.* [1950s+] (*Irish*) a general term of abuse, loudmouth. [Scot. *blirt*, a storm of wind and rain]

blissed out *adj.* [1970s+] experiencing a state of (usu. drug- or meditation-induced) ecstasy. [BLISS OUT *v.*]

blissout *n.* [1970s+] a state of (usu. drug- or meditation-induced) ecstasy. [BLISS OUT *v.*]

bliss out *v.* [1970s+] to experience a state of (usu. drug- or meditation-induced) ecstasy. [according to *HDAS* coined/introduced by followers of Maharaj Ji, *c.*1972]

blister *n.*[1] 1 [early 19C–1960s] an offensive or argumentative person, usu. *old blister*; also used affectionately. 2 [20C+] an unattractive or promiscuous woman. [the unpleasantness of the physical blister]

blister *n.*[2] [mid-19C–1940s] a legal summons. [something one 'sticks to' the victim; in 20C use the summons results from *scorching*, i.e. exceeding the speed limit (*see* SCORCH v. (1))]

blister *n.*[3] (*also* **poultice**) [1900s–50s] (*Aus.*) a mortgage. [? the cost of the mortgage 'scorches' one's pocket]

blister *n.*[4] [1930s] (*US Und.*) a tramp who deliberately creates scars and sores on the limbs by the application of acid or alkalis, in order to attract more sympathy and thus money.

blister *n.*[5] *see* SKIN-AND-BLISTER n.

blister *v.* **1** [late 19C–1900s] to punish, to fine, to hurt; also as excl. *blister them! blister me!* **2** [1900s–30s] for a policeman to take one's name in connection with an offence. **3** [1900s–30s] to be summoned or punished for an offence. **4** [1940s+] to attack verbally. [BLISTER n.[2]]

blistered *n.* [mid-19C+] a euph. for DAMNED adj. (1).

blistering *adj.* [20C+] a general expletive, used as a euph. for a variety of taboo synons. [the heat of one's language raises blisters]

blit *n. see* BLART n. (1).

blither *n.* [1910s] nonsense. [BLITHER v.]

blither *v.* [mid-19C+] to talk nonsense. [BLETHER v.]

blithered *adj.* [1910s+] (*Aus.*) very drunk (cf. ADDLED adj.). [BLITHER v., i.e. the inarticulacy of the very drunk]

blitherer *n.*[1] [20C+] a silly fool. [BLITHER v.]

blitherer *n.*[2] [1910s] (*Aus.*) an exemplar. [ety. unknown]

blithering *n.* [late 19C+] talking nonsense, babbling on. [BLITHER v.]

blithering *adj.* [late 19C+] absolute, complete; esp. in phr. *blithering idiot, blithering fool* etc. [BLITHERING n.]

blithero *adv.* [1950s] (*Irish*) extremely. [BLITHERING adj.]

blitter *v.* [20C+] (*Ulster*) to break wind; thus n., a fart. [Scot. *blitter*, to rattle]

blittered *adj.* [2000s] overcome by a given drug. [? BLITHERED adj. or OBLITERATED adj.]

blitz *v.*[1] [1900s] (*US campus*) to absent oneself from a recitation.

blitz *v.*[2] **1** [1940s] to scold. **2** [1940s+] (*orig. US*) to defeat comprehensively, to crush, to overcome, to destroy. **3** [1940s+] to stun, to amaze. **4** [1940s+] to arrive or leave quickly, to appear. **5** [1960s+] to saturate with an advertising campaign or similar form of wide-spectrum information. **6** [1970s+] (*US campus*) to perform well (in an examination). **7** [1980s] (*UK Und.*) to break into a premises for burglary. [Ger. *Blitzkrieg*, lightning war]

blitzed *adj.* **1** [1960s+] drunk or experiencing the effects of a drug (cf. ANNIHILATED adj.). **2** [1970s] absolutely exhausted, emotionally drained. [BLITZ v.[2] (2)]

blitz it *v.* [1940s] (*S.Afr. campus*) to hurry, to 'get a move on'. [BLITZ v.[2] (4)]

blitzkrieged *adj.* [1970s+] (*US campus*) drunk or experiencing the effects of a drug (cf. ANNIHILATED adj.). [Ger. *Blitzkrieg*, lightning war]

blivet *n.* (*also* **blivit**) [1940s+] (*US, orig. Aus. milit.*) **1** something useless, unnecessary, annoying (popularly defined as '10 pounds of shit in a 5-pound bag'). **2** a fat or unpleasant person or thing. **3** a distasteful job or situation. ['the expression arose among American flyers in New Guinea and is of Australian origin' (*HDAS*)]

blixen-bus *n.* [1910s–20s] (*US*) an automobile. [Ger. *Blitzen*, lightning + SE *bus*]

blizzard *n.*[1] (*US*) **1** [19C] a hard blow. **2** [19C] a stinging remark, esp. to end an argument or as a parting shot. **3** [mid-19C] a large fire. **4** [mid–late 19C] a rifle shot or volley of shots. **5** [late 19C] a drink of alcohol, a 'bracer'. [dial. *blizzer*, a heavy blow + SE *blizzard*]

blizzard *n.*[2] [1970s] (*US campus*) an unpleasant or unpopular person. [? play on BLOWHARD n.[1]]

blizzard *n.*[3] [1990s+] (*drugs*) a cloudy white substance seen in a crack cocaine pipe.

blizzard *v.* [mid-19C] (*US*) to let off a volley of shots.

blizzard-dodger *n.* [1930s] (*US*) a tramp who travels south in the winter to avoid the cold weather.

bloak *n. see* BLOKE n.

bloan *n. see* BLOWEN n. (1).

bloat *n.* (*US*) **1** [mid-19C] a worthless, conceited individual. **2** [mid-19C–1920s] a drunkard.

bloated *adj.* [1910s] (*US*) drunk. [BLOAT n. (2)]

bloater *n.* **1** [late 19C] a general term of affectionate address. **2** [late 19C] a self-opinionated person. **3** [late 19C+] a fat person. [abbr. *Yarmouth bloater*; when the fish is first smoked it swells up conspicuously, although it then shrinks as it cools]

blob *n.*[1] **1** [20C+] (*mainly Aus.*) an insignificant person. **2** [1960s] (*US campus*) an ugly or offensive person. **3** [1960s+] a fat person.

blob *n.*[2] [1990s+] a condom.

blob *n.*[3] *see* ON THE BLOB phr.[1].

blob *v.*[1] [mid-19C] **1** to talk indiscreetly. **2** (*Aus./UK Und.*) to beg by delivering some form of speechifying or patter. [var. on BLAB v. (1)]

blob *v.*[2] [1900s–60s] (*US*) to make a mistake. [? a *blob* of ink that mars an otherwise faultless piece of handwriting]

blobbermouth *n.* [1930s+] an indiscreet talker. [BLOB v.[1] (1) + SE *mouth*]

blob off *v.* [2000s] to ejaculate. [the SE *blobs* of semen]

block *n.*[1] **1** [mid-16C–18C] a fool, an idiot. **2** [17C+] the head; usu. in phr. KNOCK SOMEONE'S BLOCK OFF v.

block *n.*[2] [late 19C–1900s] (*Scot. Und.*) a policeman. [? BLOCK n.[1] or ? a hard-hearted person]

block *n.*[3] [20C+] (*UK prison*) the punishment cells; the maximum security cells. [abbr. SE *punishment block*]

block *n.*[4] **1** [1910s+] (*Aus./US Und.*) a watch. **2** [1970s] (*Can. prison*) a cigarette lighter. [? shape]

block *n.*[5] [1920s+] an act of sexual intercourse. [PUT THE BLOCKS TO v.]

block *n.*[6] [1930s] (*US Und.*) 7 days in jail. [SE *block*, an amount of time]

block *n.*[7] **1** [1930s–40s] (*US drugs*) a cube of morphine. **2** [1970s+] (*drugs*) compressed hashish or marijuana (cf. AFGHAN n.). [? packaging or the cubic shape]

block *n.*[8] *see* PUT THE BLOCK ON v.

block *v.*[1] [mid-19C] to stand a drink. [SE phr. *put one on the block*]

block *v.*[2] **1** [late 19C–1900s] to loiter, to 'hang around'. **2** [1930s+] (*Aus.*) to deceive, to get the better of. **3** [1970s+] (*N.Z.*) to gang-rape; thus *on the block*, of a woman, about to be subjected to gang-rape. **4** [1970s+] (*US Black*) to ruin another man's sexual activities by stealing his woman, interrupting his seduction etc; thus COP, LOCK AND BLOCK v. [SE *block*, to bar the way; (3) + ? implication of SE *block*, a group, a collection]

block *v.*[3] [late 19C–1940s] to have sexual intercourse. [abbr. PUT THE BLOCKS TO v.]

blockade *n.* [mid-19C–1940s] (*US*) illicitly distilled whisky; thus *blockader*, a distiller. [the need to defeat the customs blockade to sell it]

blockade *v.* [late 19C–1940s] (*US*) to distil illicit liquor. [SE *blockade*, a barrier, in this case against whisky-runners]

block a hat *v.* [mid-19C] to knock someone's hat over their eyes.

block-and-block *adj.* [early–mid-18C] (*US*) very drunk. [Lincolnshire dial. *blocker*, extreme drunkenness]

block and fall *n.* [1920s–40s] (*US Und.*) very strong, and prob. adulterated, liquor (cf. BLOCK AND TACKLE n.[2]). [SE *block* + *fall*, i.e. 'you'd get a shock, walk a block and fall in the gutter' (Sante, *Low Life*, 1991)]

block and fall joint *n.* [1920s–40s] (*US*) a tavern, catering mainly to Black people, in which one would most likely be given some form of knockout drop in one's drink and then be robbed. [BLOCK AND FALL n. + JOINT n.⁴ (3)]

block and slang n. [1910s–40s] (*US Und.*) a gold watch and chain. [BLOCK n.⁴ (1) + SLANG n.² (2)]

block and tackle n.¹ [late 19C–1940s] (*orig. Aus.*) a watch and chain. [BLOCK n.⁴ (1) + TACKLE n.²]

block and tackle n.² [1930s+] (*US*) a very strong drink (cf. BLOCK AND FALL n.). [i.e. 'you have one, walk one block and you're ready to tackle anyone']

block and tackle n.³ [1930s+] handcuffs. [rhy. sl. = SE *shackle*]

block a quiet pub v. *see* PUB n. (1).

block boy n. **1** [1970s] (*US Black*) a 'corner-boy'. **2** [1990s+] a gay man who dresses as if he were part of the heterosexual hip-hop culture. [he looks as if he were someone 'off the block']

blockbust v. [1950s+] to be the first Black family to move into a formerly all-White inner city area. [SE *block* + BUST v.¹ (1)]

blockbuster n.¹ **1** [1940s+] a very hard blow, in lit. or fig. use. **2** [1940s+] anything enormous, gigantic; often used of a best-selling novel, film, TV series etc. **3** [1940s+] an intoxicating drink. **4** [1950s+] (*drugs*) a barbiturate (cf. BARBIT n.). [BLOCK n.¹ (2) + BUST v.¹ (1)]

blockbuster n.² **1** [1950s] the first Black family to move into a formerly all-White inner city area. **2** [1960s+] the first White family to move back into an inner city area, driving out the poor minority tenants and starting the process of gentrification. [BLOCKBUST v.]

blockbusting n. [1980s+] (*US Black*) an attack by one gang who move out of their own territory to invade that of another. [SE *block* + BUST v.¹ (1)]

blocked adj. (*also* **blocked up, block up**) [1950s+] drunk or intoxicated with a drug, usu. cannabis or barbiturates. [rational thought processes are impeded]

blockee n. *see* BLOCKIE n.

blocker n. [1970s] (*US*) a hanger-on. [SE *block*, a barrier; such a person will not 'get out of the way']

blockers n. [1980s+] (*drugs*) barbiturates (cf. BARBIT n.). [abbr. BLOCKBUSTER n.¹ (4)]

block game n. (*also* **the peeks**) [1940s] (*US Und.*) a variety of the 'shell game' employing small boxes.

blockhead n.¹ [mid-16C+] a fool, a simpleton, an idiot. [SE *block*, a lump of wood + -HEAD sfx (1)]

blockhead n.² [1980s+] (*drugs*) a dedicated user of cannabis. [BLOCK n.⁷ (2) + -HEAD sfx (3)]

blockhead adj. (*also* **blockheadly**) [early 18C] stupid, foolish (cf. AIRHEADED adj.). [BLOCKHEAD n.¹]

blockheaded adj. [20C+] stupid (cf. AIRHEADED adj.). [BLOCKHEAD n.¹]

blockhouse n. [17C–18C] (*UK Und.*) a prison (cf. BANDHOUSE n.). [SE *blockhouse*, a small fort or defensive wooden enclosure]

blockie n. (*also* **blockee, blocky**) [1940s+] (*Aus.*) a blocker, one who occupies a small block of rural or semi-rural land. [SAusE *block*, a parcel of land on which settlers could build or farm]

blocking n. [1970s+] (*N.Z.*) gang-rape. [BLOCK v.² (3)]

blockish adj. [late 16C–mid-19C] stupid; thus *blockishness*, stupidity. [SE *block*, a barrier + sfx -*ish*]

Block Island turkey n. [mid–late 19C] (*US*) salt cod. [proper name of *Block Island*, Connecticut]

Blockite n. *see* DO THE BLOCK v. (1).

block of ice n. [2000s] dice. [rhy. sl.]

block ornament n. [mid–late 19C] an eccentric-looking person. [SE *block ornament*, a small piece of meat displayed on a butcher's block]

block up adj. *see* BLOCKED adj.

blocky n. *see* BLOCKIE n.

blodger n. *see* BLUDGER n.² (4).

bloke n. [mid-19C+] **1** (*also* **bloak**) a man; thus a *proper bloke*, a man who accords with the cultural standards of the speaker;

blokery, the masculine world; *blokeish*, adj. **2** (*UK Und.*) the owner, the master. **3** (*US Und.*) a detective, police-officer or minor judge. **4** (*Aus.*) a person in authority or of superior status. **5** (*UK juv./teen*) a hard worker. **6** a public house or tavern landlord. **7** a lover, a boyfriend. **8** (*Aus. Und.*) a pimp (cf. ABBOT ON THE CROSS n.). **9** (*US*) (*also* **bloak**) a fool. **10** as a term of address. [either Shelta or Rom., although there is also a case for the Du. *blok*, a fool]

bloke, the n. [mid-19C–1920s] (*UK Und.*) a judge; similarly used of the Captain in a naval context.

bloker n. [1950s] (*US drugs*) a cocaine addict. [BIG BLOKE n.²]

bloke with the jasey n. *see* JASEY n.

blokie n. (*also* **blokey**) **1** [late 19C+] (*US*) a man. **2** [1900s–20s] as a term of address. [BLOKE n.]

blonde n. [1970s+] (*drugs*) marijuana. [a light-coloured variety]

blonde and sweet n. [1940s+] (*US*) coffee with cream and sugar. [pun on SE]

blondie n. (*also* **blondy**) [late 19C+] **1** a blonde person, usu. a woman (cf. DARKIE n.¹). **2** (*US Black*) a White woman (irrespective of hair colour). **3** a nickname or term of intimate address to anyone with blond(e) hair. [SE *blonde*]

blone n. [19C+] (*Irish/Scot.*) a woman. [BLOWEN n. (1)]

blonk n. [1980s+] (*Aus. prison*) a fool. [? echoic of a solid object, i.e. the fool's head, hitting something hard]

blood n.¹ [mid-16C–19C] a rake, a roisterer, an aristocratic rowdy; also attrib. [SE *blood*, either in the sense of the seat of the emotions or in that of breeding]

blood n.² **1** [mid-19C+] a cheap 'blood-and-thunder' magazine, the precursor of 20C comics and even the bloodier computer games. **2** [1900s] (*US campus*) a perfect recitation. **3** [1920s] (*US Und.*) a killer.

blood n.³ [late 19C–1900s] a wallflower. [the colour]

blood n.⁴ **1** [1910s–40s] (*US*) ketchup, tomato sauce. **2** [1950s–70s] (*US Black*) wine. [the colour]

blood n.⁵ [1960s+] **1** (*US/UK Black*) a (fellow) Black person. **2** (*US Black*) a young Black man. **3** (*US/UK Black*) a term of address to a fellow Black; by ext. a general term of address used by any race. **4** (*UK Black*) a blood relation. **5** (*US campus*) a friend. [abbr. SE *blood brother*]

blood adj. [mid-19C; 1910s] hearty, rakish. [BLOOD n.¹]

blood v. **1** [mid-19C–1900s] to deprive of money. **2** [20C+] (*Aus.*) to cause to bleed. [(1) BLEED v.¹ (1); (2) SE *blood*]

blood adv. [1990s+] (*Aus./US*) completely, utterly. [SE phr. 'blood is thicker than water']

blood and guts alderman n. [19C] a fat, pompous man.

blood and 'ounds! excl. (*also* **blood and ouns!**) [mid-16C–1950s] a mild oath. [lit. 'blood and wounds!', i.e. of Christ]

blood ball n. [late 19C–1900s] an annual butchers' ball. [the butchers' sanguineous trade]

blood blister n. [20C+] (*Aus.*) a sister. [rhy. sl.]

blood box n. [1970s+] (*Aus./US*) an ambulance.

blood bucket n. [1960s] (*US*) a notably tough saloon or bar. [var. on BLOODY BUCKET n. (1)]

blood claat n. (*also* **blood claht, ...clot, ...cloth**) [1950s+] (*orig. and mainly W.I./UK Black*) a highly derog. description of another person. [Jam. pron. of SE *blood cloth*, a sanitary towel]

bloodclaat adj. [1970s+] a general derog. intensifier. [BLOOD CLAAT n.]

blood factory n. [2000s] a hospital.

bloodfire! excl. [1990s+] (*UK/US Black*) an excl. of greeting to a fellow Black person. [BLOOD n.⁵ (3)]

bloodhammer n. [2000s] the penis (cf. AX n.²).

bloodhound n. [early 19C+] **1** one who perjures themself for money. **2** a policeman (cf. ANIMAL n.¹). [reverse anthropomorphism]

blood house n. [1950s+] (*Aus./N.Z.*) a public house with a reputation for violence.

blood in, blood out *phr.* [1990s+] (*US Und.*) a ritual phr. meaning that to join a prison or street gang you must kill, and that you may leave it (other than finishing your sentence) only by being killed yourself.

blood medicine *n.* [late 19C] (*US*) alcohol. ['a tonic']

blood oath! *excl.* (*also* **bloody oath!**) [mid-19C+] (*Aus.*) a general expression of agreement.

blood or beer! *excl.* [late 19C–1900s] a street challenge, albeit usu. joc., i.e. 'will you fight or buy a round?'

blood red *n.* [2000s] fellatio (cf. CHOCKA(-BLOCK) v.; DIVINE BROWN n.; PLATE v.¹; PLATE OF HAM n.¹; RUBBER DUCK n.¹; SLICE OF HAM n.). [rhy. sl. = HEAD n.¹⁰]

blood-red fancy *n.* [mid-19C] a crimson handkerchief, as worn by costermongers. [SE *blood-red* + *fancy handkerchief*]

blood sports *n.* [1990s+] performing cunnilingus on a menstruating woman.

blood's worth bottling *phr. see* BOTTLING adj.

blood tub *n.* [mid–late 19C] **1** a thug, a tough, a street gangster. **2** a theatre presenting lurid melodrama. **3** in fig. use, a dangerous place or situation. [the *Blood Tubs*, a Baltimore street gang, who allegedly earned their name from having 'on an election day, dipped an obnoxious German's head in a tub of warm blood, and then sent him running through the town' (Farmer, *Americanisms Old New*, 1889)]

blood wagon *n.* [1930s+] an ambulance.

blood-worm *n.* [mid-19C–1900s] a sausage, esp. a black pudding. [its main ingredient and its appearance]

bloody *n.* [1980s+] (*US campus*) a bloody Mary, a drink of which the chief constituents are vodka and tomato juice. [abbr.]

bloody *adj.*¹ (*also* **bleedy**) **1** [late 18C+] a general negative adj., abominable or terrible; esp. in the UK and Aus., where it is so widespread as to be termed 'the great Australian adjective'. **2** [early 19C+] usu. of a person or experience, unpleasant. **3** [20C+] as an infix, e.g. ABSOBLOODYLUTELY adv., *not bloody likely* etc. [BLOODY adv.; Grose wrote in 1796 of how popular *bloody* was among the contemporary London underworld. There is no doubt that, along with the transported felons of the period, it made its way to the penal colonies of Botany Bay. Fifty years later it was well-established. In his book *Travels in New South Wales* (1847), Alexander Marjoribanks noted the prevalence of the word, claiming that he had heard a bullock-driver use it 27 times in 15 minutes, a rate of speech, he then calculated, that over a 50-year period would produce some 18,200,000 repetitions of the 'disgusting word'. The Sydney *Bulletin* called it 'the Australian adjective' in its edition of 18 August 1894, explaining that 'it is more used, and used more exclusively by Australians, than by any other allegedly civilized nation'. The term gained its final sanctification as the 'Great Australian Adjective' when W.T. Goodge used it as the title for one of the poems he included in his *Hits! Skits! and Jingles!* (1899)]

bloody *adj.*² [mid-19C] rakish. [BLOOD n.¹]

bloody *adv.* (*also* **bloodyful**) [late 17C+] a general negative intensifier, very, exceedingly, abominably or desperately. [SE *blood*. As E.P. states: 'There is no need for ingenious etymologies, the idea of blood suffices.' There are also no links to theology, nor to the term *'sblood* (God's blood). In addition, declare F&H in their definition: 'In passing it may be mentioned that there is no ground for attributing its derivation to "By'r Our Lady".' Like other so-called 'obscenities' or 'Anglo-Saxon words', *bloody* has experienced a fluctuating position as regards usage. As the *OED* put it in 1887, it has been 'in general colloquial use from the Restoration to c.175? Now constantly in the mouths of the lowest classes, but by respectable people considered "a horrid word", on a par with obscene or profane language, and usually printed in the newspapers as b--y.' The latter proscription has largely vanished. When *bloody* does crop up in the press it tends to be in direct, quoted speech and is printed in full, but the term,

in the UK at least, has yet to enter 'polite' society. As to its ety., the *OED* links it to the preoccupations of the 'bloods' or aristocratic rowdies of the end of the 17C and beginning of the 18C (cf. BLOOD n.¹). Thus the phr. 'bloody drunk' meant 'as drunk as a blood'. Its associations with bloodshed and murder (typically a *bloody battle*) 'have recommended it to the rough classes as a word that appeals to their imagination' and the *OED* goes on to compare its late 19C popularity with other 'impressive or graphic intensives, seen in the use of jolly, awfully, terribly, devilish, deuced, damned, ripping, rattling, thumping, stunning, thundering etc']

bloody back *n.* [late 18C–mid-19C] a soldier. [his scarlet jacket; ? extra ref. to the frequent floggings of army discipline]

bloody bucket *n.* (*also* **bucket of blood, tub of blood**) (*US*) **1** [late 19C+] a notably tough saloon or bar. **2** [1920s] a speakeasy. **3** [1920s+] a cocktail made up of vodka and tomato juice, a 'bloody Mary'. **4** [1960s] a tough area of a town or city, orig. that which surrounded a local rough tavern. [the original 19C *Bucket of Blood*, Shorty Young's tavern in Havre, Montana; its reputation spread and the term became generic for similar establishments; but note ref. to 18C 'a dwelling in Water Lane, off Fleet Street, known as "Blood Bowl house" [...] where there seldom passed a month without the commission of a murder' (in Peter Ackroyd's *London*, 2000)]

bloody flag is out *phr.* [late 17C–early 19C] drunk. [orig. in Shakespeare's *Henry V* (1598–9): 'Stand for your own; unwind your bloody flag'; ult. the aggressiveness that so often accompanies heavy drinking]

bloodyful *adv. see* BLOODY adv.

bloody jemmy *n.* [early 19C–1910s] an uncooked sheep's head. [SE *bloody* + JEMMY n.¹ (2)]

bloody Jesus, the *n. see* BEJAZUS, THE n.

bloody mary *n.* [1940s+] (*US*) a menstruating woman, used by a woman of herself, e.g. *I'm bloody mary today*. [pun on Mary I of England (1516–58), known popularly as *Bloody Mary* for her vindictive attacks on Protestantism]

bloody Monday *n.* [late 17C–18C] the last day of the school term, on which holidays begin and on which punishments are trad. given out. [thus the episode in Rudyard Kipling's *Stalky and Co.* (1899) when the headmaster canes the entire school before sending them home]

bloody monthlies *n.* [20C+] menstruation, usu. male use. [male irritation puns BLOODY adj.¹ (1) and SE *bloody*; thus the joc. def. 'a bloody waste of fucking time']

bloody murder *n. see* BLUE MURDER n.

bloody Nora! *excl.* [2000s] an excl. of displeasure. [BLOODY adj.¹ (1) + generic use of proper name]

bloody oath! *excl. see* BLOOD OATH! excl.

blooey! *excl.* (*also* **blooie!**) (*orig. US*) **1** [1910s+] an excl. used to mimic the sound of an explosion. **2** [1920s] an excl. used to denote failure, collapse. [echoic]

bloomer *n.*¹ **1** [late 19C+] (*orig. Aus.*) an error, a slip; thus *go/make a bloomer*, *come a bloomer*. **2** [20C+] a complete failure, a disaster. **3** [1910s] (*US*) a fraud. **4** [1910s] (*US*) a joke; thus *pull a bloomer*, make a joke. **5** [1910s–50s] (*US Und.*) a safe that proves to be empty. [BLOOMING adj.² (1) + SE *error*]

bloomer *n.*² [late 19C] a good-looking woman. [SE *bloom*]

bloomer *n.*³ [1900s] (*Aus./Can.*) a newly arrived immigrant. [they *bloom* in their new circumstances]

blooming *adj.*¹ [late 19C] (*US campus*) excellent.

blooming *adj.*² [late 19C+] a euph. for BLOODY adj.¹ (1), e.g. *blooming error*, a major mistake. **2** [20C+] as an infix. [popularized by the music-hall star Alfred 'The Great' Vance in the 1880s]

blooming shoot, the *n.* [late 19C] absolutely everything, 'the lot'. [BLOOMING adj.² (1) + WHOLE BANG SHOOT, THE n.]

blooming six foot of tripe *n.* [late 19C] a large policeman. [BLOOMING adj.² (1) + joc. use of SE]

bloop n. 1 [1950s+] a euph. substitute for various taboo terms. 2 [1960s+] (orig. US) an embarrassing verbal error, often delivered by a public figure or someone in authority to their own detriment. [BLOOPER n. (2)]

bloop v. [1950s] (US) to hit, to punch. [backform. f. BLOOPER n. (1)]

blooper n. 1 [1940s] (US) a swinging blow. 2 [1940s+] (orig. US) an embarrassing verbal error, often delivered by a public or authority figure to their own detriment. [? BLAB v. (3) + oops! or ? baseball blooper, 'a soggy fly to an unoccupied spot behind the backs of the infielders', NY Times (1937)]

blooter n. (also **bloot**) [late 19C+] (Ulster/US Black) a coarse, stupid peasant (cf. BOOBY n.¹; BUNGO n.; GAWIE n.; GAWK n.; GILLY n.; GOOF n.¹; JAY n.³; JAYBIRD n.¹; JAYHAWK n.; JAYHAWKER n.; JOSKIN n.; SCHLUB n.). [Scot. bluiter, a rough, clumsy fellow]

blooter v. [2000s] (Scot.) to hit. [Scot. blouter, a blast of wind]

blootered adj. (also **bloothered, bluthered**) [1970s+] drunk. [Scot. blout, of liquids, to boil over]

blooterer n. [20C+] a scourge, a persecutor. [? BLOOTER n. or Scot. blouter, a blast of wind]

blosh v. [2000s] to ejaculate (cf. BLURT v.; CHUNK v.¹; JET ONE'S JUICE v.; MELT v.; SKEET v.²; SLIME v.²; SPAFF v.; SPEW v.; SPEW ONE'S GOO v.; SPIT v.¹; SPLATTER ONE'S BATTER v.; SPLOOGE v.; SPOOGE v.; SPRECK UP v.; SPUFF v.; SQUIRT (OFF) v.; SQUIRT ONE'S JUICE v.).

bloss n. 1 [17C–early 19C] a beggar's female companion. 2 [late 17C–early 19C] (UK Und.) a thief. 3 [late 17C–early 19C] (UK Und.) a prostitute. [BLOWSE n.]

blossom n.¹ [mid-late 19C] a strait-laced or jealous person. [ety. unknown]

blossom n.² [1950s] (Aus.) the female genital area. [positive connotations, esp. child-bearing]

blossom-top n. [mid-late 19C] (US) a red-headed or red-faced person. [SE blossom, presumably a red one + top]

blot n.¹ [1920s–70s] an unpleasant person. [a fig. 'blot on the landscape']

blot n.² [1940s+] (Aus.) the anus, the buttocks.

blot n.³ [1950s] (US Und.) the criminal underworld.

blot n.⁴ [1960s+] (drugs) a dose of LSD on paper. [abbr. BLOTTER n.² (3)]

blotch n. [1950s+] (mainly UK juv.) blotting-paper.

blotch v. [1980s+] (US campus) to emit a small amount of liquid at the same time as breaking wind; thus blotcher, a liquid-emitting FART n. that stains one's underwear. [SE blotch, a wet patch]

blotcher n. [1980s] (US campus) a fart that also emits a small amount of fecal liquid. [BLOTCH v.]

blot one's copybook v. [1910s+] to make an error, practical or behavioural.

blotter n.¹ [1910s–50s] (US) a drunkard with a seemingly infinite capacity for alcohol. [play on SOAK n.¹ (1)]

blotter n.² 1 [1950s+] (drugs) a small piece of cotton through which a drug solution is filtered as it is drawn into a needle. 2 [1950s+] (drugs) any drugs that are retrieved by soaking or boiling such a cloth. 3 [1960s+] (drugs) a dose of LSD carried on a small square of blotting-paper; the paper and the drug it has absorbed are consumed together. 4 [1990s+] (UK Black) a drug dealer.

blot the scrip v. [mid-17C–early 19C] (UK Und.) to put into writing; thus blot the scrip and jark it, to sign a contract. [SE blot + scrip, a scrap of paper, a few lines of writing]

blotto adj. (orig. US) 1 [1910s+] very drunk (cf. ADDLED adj.). 2 [1920s+] of people, exhausted, confused, dazed, unconscious. 3 [1930s] absolutely forgotten. 4 [1980s+] intoxicated by a drug. [? one's mind having blotted out reality, or one's body blotted up the alcohol]

blou n. (also **die blou**) [20C+] (S.Afr.) methylated spirits, as used by alcoholics. [Afk. blou, blue, the colour of meths]

blou adj. [1940s+] (S.Afr. drugs) intoxicated by a drug. [BLOU n.]

bloubaadjie n. [1970s] (S.Afr.) 1 a habitual criminal serving an indeterminate sentence. 2 an indeterminate prison sentence of 9–15 years. 3 a provincial traffic officer. [Afk. blou, blue + baadjie, badge]

blougat n. [1960s+] (S.Afr.) a national serviceman or woman who has completed half his training. [Afk. blou, blue + gat, anus (arse)]

bloupak n. [1980s+] (S.Afr.) an auxiliary police officer (used in those areas where the police wear blue uniforms). [Afk. blou, blue + pakke, suit]

blouperd n. [1980s+] (S.Afr.) methylated spirits. [BLOU n. + perd, horse; one who 'rides' it]

blouse n. (also **blouze**) 1 [late 16C–early 18C] a slatternly woman, a prostitute. 2 [1930s+] (also **blouser**) a derog. term for a woman. [BLOWSE n.; (2) may simply refer to SE blouse]

blouse v. [1920s] (US) to leave. [? BLOW v.⁶ (3)]

blouse and skirt! excl. [1970s–80s] (UK Black) a mild excl., usu. as what the…, who the… etc.

blouser n. see BLOUSE n. (2).

blouser v. [late 19C–1900s] to cover up, to hide. [Fr. blouse, a jacket; thus to cover with one's jacket, to secrete. Ware suggests that the use is xenophobic, such a jacket would 'cover over an honest Englishman's waistcoat']

bloutrein n. (also **blue train**) [1980s+] (S.Afr.) methylated spirits. [the Blue Train, a luxury passenger train running between Cape Town and Pretoria; the implication being that those who drink meths take the 'fast train' to death]

blouwzola n. see BLOWSER n.¹.

blouzabella n. (also **blowsabella**) [late 18C–early 19C] a slattern. [BLOWSE n. + Ital. bella, a good-looking slattern]

blouzalinda n. [late 18C–mid-19C] a slattern. [BLOWSE n. + Sp. linda, beautiful]

blouze n. see BLOUSE n.

bloviate v. [mid-late 19C] (US) to talk loudly or aggressively. [? SE blow + sfx -ate, to 'blow off steam']

blow n.¹ 1 [mid-17C] sexual intercourse. 2 [early 19C] a prostitute. [(1) SE blow, on sex = violence pattern; (2) BLOWEN n. (1)]

blow n.² 1 [early 19C–1940s] (orig. US) a celebration, a party, a spree. 2 [mid-19C] (US campus) a reveller, a party-goer. 3 [1910s+] a breath of fresh air; esp. in phr. get a blow.

blow n.³ 1 [mid-19C–1900s] (US) a betrayal, the passing of information, esp. to the authorities. 2 [1910s] (Aus.) boasting. 3 [1970s] (US) the import or essence of one's conversation.

blow n.⁴ [mid-19C+] (Aus./US) a rest, a break from work, a period of relaxation. [the image of a horse or human blowing out breath]

blow n.⁵ [late 19C–1900s] a shilling (5p). [ety. unknown]

blow n.⁶ (drugs) 1 [1900s] (US) a smoke of opium. 2 [1930s] a cigarette or a puff on a cigarette. 3 [1950s+] a snort or sniff of cocaine. 4 [1960s+] cocaine (cf. NOSE n.³; NOSE CANDY n.; NOSE POWDER n.; SNEEZE n.; SNIFF n.; SNORT n.; TOOT n.¹; WHIFF n.). 5 [1980s] (N.Z.) the act of sniffing glue; usu. in phr. have a blow, to sniff glue. 6 [1980s+] a puff on a marijuana cigarette or pipe. 7 [1990s+] cannabis. 8 [1990s+] crack cocaine (cf. BASE n.). 9 [1990s+] a puff on a crack cocaine pipe. [BLOW v.⁴]

blow n.⁷ [1910s–20s] a synon. for a DAMN n. [BLOW! excl.¹ (2)]

blow n.⁸ [1920s–60s] (US) a pistol. [SE blow, to explode]

blow n.⁹ [1950s+] the act of playing music.

blow n.¹⁰ [1960s] (US Black) of a pimp, the loss of one of his prostitutes. [BLOW v.⁵ (4)]

blow n.¹¹ [1960s+] (drugs) 1 a shot of heroin that misses the vein. 2 a small portion of heroin, inhaled rather than injected. [(1) BLOW A SHOT v.; (2) BLOW v.⁴ (3)]

blow n.¹² see BLOWHARD n.²

blow n.¹³ see BLOW JOB n. (1).

blow, the n. [1960s] (US) a form of confidence trick in which the victim is convinced that it is possible to raise the denomination on notes, e.g. from $10 to $100.

blow *v.*[1] **1** [15C+] to speak angrily. **2** [late 16C+] to inform on, to betray, to expose, to reveal (evidence of wrong-doing, espionage etc); ext. as *blow the works* (cf. BLOW UPON v.). **3** [mid-18C; 1970s+] to sing. **4** [late 18C+] (*also* **blow off**) to boast, to brag. **5** [early 19C] to destroy someone's reputation. **6** [mid-19C] to tease aggressively. **7** [mid-19C+] to inform, to confess. **8** [1910s+] (*US*) to become, e.g. *blow chilly*, to be stand-offish. **9** [1920s+] (*US Black*) to talk (nonsense), to talk insincerely. **10** [1940s+] (*US Und.*) to realize.

blow *v.*[2] **1** [17C] to bring to orgasm. **2** [mid-17C+] to reach orgasm (cf. BLOW OFF v.[2]; BLOW (ONE'S) COOKIES v.; BLOW ONE'S CORK v.; BLOW ONE'S DUST v.; BLOW ONE'S HUMP v.; BLOW ONE'S JUICE v.; BLOW ONE'S LOAD v.; BLOW ONE'S LOT v.; BLOW ONE'S MUCK v.; BLOW ONE'S TUBES v.; BLOW ONE'S WAD v.[2]). **3** [1930s+] (*also* **blow off**) to fellate; occas. to perform cunnilingus (cf. BLOW JOB n.; BLOW SOMEONE'S HEAD v.; BLOW SOMEONE'S GLASS v.; BLOW SOMEONE'S PIPE v.; BLOW SOMEONE'S WHISTLE v.; BLOW SOME TUNES v.; BLOW THE BEEF BUGLE v.; BLOW THE SKIN FLUTE v.; FLUTE v.[2]; HUFFLE v.; HUM n.[7]; HUM v.[5]; HUM JOB n.; HUMMER n.[9]; MEAT WHISTLE n.; PIPE v.[4]; PIPEJOB n.; PLAY A TUNE (ON THE ONE-HOLED FLUTE) v.; PLAY THE FLUTE v.[1]; PLAY THE PINK OBOE v.; PLAY THE SKIN FLUTE v.; ROCK SOMEONE'S MIC v.; TALK TO THE MIKE v.). **4** [1970s+] (*US campus*) to have sexual intercourse. [SE *blow*, to explode; (3) the appearance of the physical act]

blow *v.*[3] **1** [mid-17C] to break wind. **2** [1960s+] to vomit (cf. BRING UP v.[1]; CHUCK v.[1]; DISH IT v.; FLASH v.[6]; HEAVE v.[2]; HURL v.; LOSE v.; LOSE IT v.; PUT v.; THROW v.[1]; THROW UP v.[1]; TOSS v.[2]; UNSPIT v.; UNSWALLOW v.; UPCHUCK v.). **3** [1970s] to defecate.

blow *v.*[4] **1** [mid-19C+] to smoke, orig. in a pipe. **2** [20C+] to smoke marijuana, usu. in combs. with a n., e.g. BLOW GAGE n. **3** [1910s+] (*US drugs*) to inhale a narcotic, usu. heroin or cocaine. **4** [1960s+] (*also* **blow off**) to inject a narcotic. **5** [2000s] to smoke crack cocaine.

blow *v.*[5] **1** [mid-19C+] to squander, to waste, esp. of money, opportunity, a relationship etc (cf. BLEW v.[1]; BLUE v.[2]). **2** [late 19C+] to treat to a meal, to food and/or drink; usu. as *blow someone to*. **3** [20C+] to spend. **4** [1960s–70s] (*US*) of a pimp, to lose a prostitute from one's STABLE n. (2).

blow *v.*[6] **1** [late 19C] (*US*) to go round with, to associate with. **2** [late 19C–1900s] (*US*) to leave behind, to depart from. **3** [late 19C+] (*US*) (*also* **blow it**) to depart at speed, to walk away quickly; usu. in phrs., e.g. *blow the joint*, *blow the scene*, *blow the town*; thus imper. *go blow!* go away! **4** [1930s–50s] (*US prison*) to escape from prison. **5** [1960s] (*US*) to drive through a red traffic light or similar traffic sign.

blow *v.*[7] **1** [late 19C+] to ruin, to upset, to destroy, to lose. **2** [20C+] to botch, to bungle, to lose (a contest or game); esp. as *blow it*. **3** [20C+] to crack under emotional or other pressure, to explode emotionally. **4** [20C+] of people, to reject, to abandon. **5** [1900s] of a situation, to give up on. **6** [1910s] (*US Und.*) to discover that something is missing. **7** [1910s+] (*orig. US*) to miss, e.g. a train, an appointment. **8** [1920s–60s] (*US*) to dismiss from a job, to break off a love affair. **9** [1960s+] (*US*) to fail. **10** [1970s+] of a situation or experience, to be unpleasant, pointless, useless.

blow *v.*[8] **1** [1940s+] (*orig. US Black*) to play music. **2** [1950s–60s] (*US*) to create, to 'whip up'. **3** [1950s+] (*US Black*) to talk enthusiastically and fluently. **4** [1950s+] (*US Black*) to perform on any 'instrument', e.g. a writer's word processor etc. **5** [1960s] (*US campus*) to toady to, to act the sycophant. **6** [1980s] (*US campus*) to sing well. [the lit. and fig. blowing and playing of various wind instruments]

blow *v.*[9] [1970s] to come to an end. [abbr. SE *blow over*]

blow! *excl.*[1] **1** [18C+] a dismissive excl., a synon. for TO HELL WITH —! excl. **2** [19C+] a euph. for DAMN! excl.

blow! *excl.*[2] [1930s+] go away! [BLOW v.[6] (3)]

blow a cloud *v.* **1** [19C+] to smoke a tobacco pipe or cigar.

2 [1930s] (*also* **cock a cloud**) to smoke opium; thus *cloud-blower*, an opium smoker.

blow a cork *v. see* BLOW ONE'S CORK v. (3).

blow a fuse *v.* **1** [1920s+] to explode (usu. with rage). **2** [1950s–60s] of a plan, to go disastrously wrong.

blow a fuse! *excl.* [1960s+] (*Scot.*) go away!

blow a gasket *v.* (*also* **blow one's gasket**, ...**one's gauge**, **bust a gasket**) [1940s+] to explode with rage, to go crazy.

blow a gut *v.* [1950s+] (*US Black*) to explode with laughter. [var. on BUST A GUT v. (2)]

blow air *v.* [1950s] to waste time.

blow-all *n. see* BUGGER-ALL n.

blow a raspberry *v. see* RASPBERRY n.[1] (1).

blow a shot *v.* (*also* **blow it**) [1930s+] (*drugs*) to blunder when injecting oneself or someone else and miss the vein, wasting the narcotic in the skin. [BLOW v.[7] (2) + SHOT n.[6] (2); note also BLOW v.[4] (4)]

blow ass *v.* (*also* **swing ass**) [1980s+] (*US*) to walk fast, to run off. [BLOW v.[6] (3)/SWING v.[6] + ASS n. (5)]

blow at *v.* [1980s+] (*US campus*) to became annoyed with, to attack verbally. [BLOW v.[1] (1)]

blow a valve *v.* (*also* **blow a tube**) [1950s+] (*US*) to explode with rage.

blow a vein *v.* [1980s] (*US*) to have an apoplectic fit (and die of it). [SE *blow*, to explode + *vein*]

blowback *n.*[2] [2000s] the spray of blood, bones, tissue etc from the victim of a shooting.

blowback *n.*[1] [1980s+] (*drugs*) an exhalation of cannabis smoke into another's mouth (cf. SHOTGUN n.[3]). [SE *blow back*]

blow back *v.* [1920s–30s] (*US*) to return stolen goods, to pay back money. [BLOW v.[5] (3)]

blowbag *n.* [1920s+] (*Aus.*) a loud-mouthed braggart. [BLOW v.[1] (4) + WINDBAG n. (1)]

blow black *v.* (*also* **blow change**) [1980s] (*US Black*) to talk about and/or initiate Black activism, social change, revolution and any similar form of racial advancement. [BLOW v.[1] (4) + SE *black*/(political or social) *change*]

blow-boy *n.* [1930s+] (*US*) a male homosexual (cf. BONE-EATER n.). [BLOW v.[2] (3) + SE *boy*]

blowcaine *n.* [1980s+] crack cocaine diluted with powdered cocaine. [BLOW n.[6] (4) + SE *cocaine* + play on SE *procaine*, *novocaine* etc]

blow card *n.* [1910s–50s] (*US Und.*) **1** a final or useless playing card. **2** in fig. use, any final or useless thing. [? BLOW OFF n.[2] + SE *card*]

blow change *v.*[1] [20C+] to squander one's money. [BLOW v.[5] (1) + SE *change*]

blow change *v.*[2] *see* BLOW BLACK v.

blow charlie *v.* [1960s–70s] (*drugs*) to take cocaine. [BLOW v.[4] (3) + CHARLIE n.[9] (1)]

blow choice *n.* [2000s] (*US campus*) a socially unacceptable or stupid person. [? BLOW v.[7] (10)]

blow chow *v.* [1960s+] (*US*) to vomit (cf. BLOW DOUGHNUTS v.; BLOW (ONE'S) COOKIES v.; BLOW ONE'S GROCERIES v.; BLOW ONE'S LUNCH v.; CHUCK ONE'S BISCUITS v.; FLIP ONE'S COOKIES v.; FLOAT AN AIR BISCUIT v.; LOSE A DINNER v.; LOSE A MEAL v.; LOSE ONE'S DOUGHNUTS v.; LOSE ONE'S LUNCH v.; PARK A CUSTARD v.; POP ONE'S COOKIES v.; SHOOT ONE'S COOKIES v.; SPEW ONE'S GUTS v.; SPILL ONE'S BREAKFAST v.; SPILL ONE'S GUTS v.; SPIT BEEF v.; THROW ONE'S COOKIES v.; TOSS A REVERSE LUNCH v.; TOSS ONE'S COOKIES v.; TOSS ONE'S LOLLIES v.). [BLOW v.[3] (2) + CHOW n.[1] (2)]

blow chunks *v.* (*also* **blow grits**, **spew chunks**) **1** [1960s+] to vomit. **2** [1990s+] in fig. use, of a thing, to be terrible or unpleasant. [BLOW v.[3] (2) + SE *chunks* (of food)]

blow coke *v.* [1920s+] (*drugs*) to inhale cocaine; thus *coke blower*, a cocaine sniffer. [BLOW v.[4] (3) + COKE n.[1] (1)]

blow dinner *v. see* BLOW ONE'S LUNCH v.

blow domes v. [1990s+] (US) to amaze, to astound. [SE blow, to explode + DOME n. (1)]

blow doughnuts v. (also blow donuts, throw donuts) [1970s+] (US campus) to vomit or regurgitate (cf. BLOW CHOW v.). [BLOW v.³ (2)/SE throw+ SE doughnut/SAmE donut]

blow down v. 1 [mid-19C+] (US) to kill with a firearm, to shoot dead. 2 [1930s] (US Und.) to modify, to soften. 3 [1960s] (US) to defeat comprehensively, to overwhelm. 4 [1980s+] (US) to pass at high speed.

blow down someone's ear v. [1930s+] to whisper, esp. to whisper information (accurate or otherwise) that is intended to persuade the hearer to do what one wishes (cf. BLOW IN SOMEONE'S EAR v.).

blow down someone's lug v. [1950s] (Aus.) to nag at. [SE blow down + LUG n.¹]

blowed adj.¹ [mid-19C+] used as a euph. for DAMNED adj. in general mild oaths of surprise, shock or annoyance.

blowed adj.² see BLOWN (OUT) adj. (2).

blowed! excl. see I'LL BE BLOWED! excl.

blowed-in-the-glass adj. (also blowed-in-the-bottle, blown-in-the-bottle/-glass) [late 19C+] (orig. US) genuine, authentic, trustworthy. [early glass-blowing often trapped bubbles in the finished object]

blowed-in-the-glass (stiff) n. (also blowed-in-the-bottle, blown-in-the-glass stiff) [late 19C–1940s] (US tramp) an elite tramp. [BLOWED-IN-THE-GLASS adj. + STIFF n.² (4)]

blowen n. 1 [late 17C+] (also bloan) a woman, spec. a prostitute. 2 [late 18C–early 19C] (UK Und.) the pretend wife of a shoplifter. 3 [mid-19C] a mistress. [according to George Borrow f. Rom. beluñi, 'a sister in debauchery'. Hotten (1867) notes Ger. Bluhen, bloom, and Buhlen, sweetheart, but adds 'the street term…may mean one whose reputation has been blown on, or damaged' (cf. BLOW ON v./BLOW v.¹ (5))]

blowen of the ken n. [late 18C] a landlady, a 'mistress of the house'. [BLOWEN n. (1) + KEN n.¹ (1)]

blowen spenie n. [late 18C] (US Und.) a thief's female companion. [BLOWEN n. (2) + ? link to UK dial. spean, the teat of a female animal]

blower n.¹ [late 17C–19C] (UK Und.) a woman, spec. a prostitute; the antonym of JOMER n. [? Rom./Polari]

blower n.² [early 19C] a pipe.

blower n.³ 1 [mid-19C–1920s] a braggart. 2 [1990s+] an annoying person. [BLOW v.¹ (4)]

blower n.⁴ [late 19C–1920s] (US Und.) a safe-breaker.

blower n.⁵ [1920s+] a telephone. [following on f. the earlier 'speaking tubes' down which one had to blow to alert the other person; note bookmaker jargon blower, the betting shop public address system that broadcasts races, odds and results]

blower n.⁶ [1940s–50s] (US Black) a handkerchief. [SE blow (one's nose)]

blower n.⁷ [1940s+] (W.I.) a spendthrift. [BLOW v.⁵ (1)]

blower n.⁸ [1970s] (US) a shotgun. [SE blow, to explode, underpinned by BLOW (SOMEONE) AWAY v. (1); BLOW DOWN v. (1)]

blow fiend n. [1990s+] (US drugs) a cocaine addict. [BLOW n.⁶ (4) + FIEND n.² (1)]

blow fire v. [1980s+] (US Black) to do anything well and keenly, esp. dancing, musicianship etc. [ext. of BLOW v.⁸ (1)]

blowfish n. [2000s] an insignificant, unpleasant person. [SE blowfish, a puffer, a saltwater fish that is ordinarily thrown away by fishermen]

blowfly n. 1 [late 19C+] (Aus.) an officious person; thus blowflyism, officiousness, 'red tape'. 2 [20C+] (US) a boaster. [SE blowfly/BLOW v.¹ (4) + SE fly]

blow foam v. [late 19C] (US) to drink beer.

blow for v. [1950s] (US) to be keen on, to be eager for. [? one's heavy breathing]

blow gage v. (also blow gauge) [1940s+] (orig. US Black) to smoke marijuana. [BLOW v.⁴ (2) + GAGE n.²]

blow great guns v. [19C+] 1 to blow a violent storm. 2 to make a great fuss about something. [SE blow/BLOW v.¹ + GREAT GUNS adv.]

blow grits v. see BLOW CHUNKS v.

blow g's v. see BLOW ONE'S GROCERIES v.

blow-gun n.¹ [mid-19C; 1960s] (US) a braggart. [SE/BLOW v.¹ (4)]

blow-gun n.² [1930s–40s] (US Und.) a short-barrelled shot-gun; a pistol with a large barrel. [SE/BLOW (SOMEONE) AWAY v. (1)]

blowhard n.¹ [early 19C–1920s] (orig. US) a boaster, a loud and egocentric talker?. [BLOW v.¹ (4) + SE hard; subseq. use is SE]

blowhard n.² (also blow) [1990s+] (Irish) methylated spirits.

blowhard adj. [1910s+] (US) boastful, self-aggrandizing. [BLOWHARD n.¹]

blow heavy v. [1980s+] (US Black) to talk seriously of a con-textually vital matter. [BLOW v.¹ + HEAVY adv. (3); jazz imagery]

blowhole n. 1 [1920s+] (Aus.) a talkative person. 2 [1940s–50s] (US) the mouth. 3 [1940s+] (US) the anus (cf. A-HOLE n.). [pun on SE but for (1) and (2) note BLOW v.¹]

blow hot and cold v. [mid-16C–19C] to vacillate. [subseq. use is SE]

blowie n. (also blowy) [1910s+] (Aus./N.Z.) a blowfly. [abbr. + sfx -ie/-y]

blow-in n. [1920s+] (Aus./Irish/US) a stranger, a newcomer, someone who has 'blown in', esp. one who is not yet accepted by the locals. [BLOW IN v.¹]

blow in v.¹ (also blow along, …down, …into, …over, …up) [late 19C+] to arrive unexpectedly and casually; thus what's this blown in, who's this?, a usu. unfriendly ref. to a new arrival. [image of being wafted by a chance breeze]

blow in v.² (US) 1 [late 19C] to obtain. 2 [late 19C+] to squander, to waste, usu. of money. [ext. of BLOW v.⁵ (1); (1) is perhaps misuse]

blow in v.³ [1960s] (US) to hit, to beat up.

blow in a bowl v. [early 16C] to be a habitual drunkard. [synon. with late 19C+ HIT THE BOOZE v.]

blowing n.¹ [late 17C–mid-19C] (UK Und.) a woman, spec. a prostitute. [BLOWEN n. (1)]

blowing n.² [mid-19C] (US) a state of drunkenness. [ety. unknown]

blowing n.³ 1 [mid-19C+] boasting, aggrandizing. 2 [late 19C] telling off, reprimanding. [(1) BLOW v.¹ (4); (2) BLOW v.¹ (1)]

blowing-up n. [early 19C–1900s] a scolding. [BLOW UP v.¹ (5)]

blow in one's pipe v. [mid-19C–1910s] to spend one's money. [BLOW v.⁵ (1)/play on SE]

blow in someone's ear v. [1970s+] to whisper (cf. BLOW DOWN SOMEONE'S EAR v.).

blow it v.¹ see BLOW v.⁶ (3).

blow it v.² see BLOW v.⁷ (2).

blow it v.³ see BLOW A SHOT v.

blow it! excl. [early 19C+] a mild excl. of annoyance, a euph. for a variety of 'stronger' synons.

blow it off v. see BLOW OFF v.¹ (5).

blow it out v. see BLOW OUT v.¹ (3).

blow it out of one's ass v. [1970s] (US) to squander foolishly; to make a foolhardy mistake. [BLOW v.⁵ (1)]

blow it out your ass! excl. (also blow it! blow it out!) [1940s+] (orig. US milit.) a general excl. of derision, contempt or dismissal of the previous speaker's statement. [SE blow + ASS n. (2)]

blow jaw v. [1980s] (US) to smoke marijuana. [BLOW v.⁴ (2) + stressed pron. of SE (mari)jua(na)]

blow job n. 1 [1930s+] (orig. US) (also blow, job) fellatio (cf. BLOW v.²). 2 [1960s] (US campus) in fig. use, an act of sycophancy. 3 [1960s+] (orig. US) (also blow job artist) a fellator or fellatrix.

4 [1970s] (*US campus*) an unpleasant experience or situation.
5 [1990s+] (*US Black*) cunnilingus. [BLOW v.² (3) + JOB n.⁴]

blow me! *excl.* (*also* **blow me pink! blow me tight! blow me up!**) [late 18C+] an excl. of surprise, denial or dismissal. [earlier use f. BLOW! excl.¹; later use f. BLOW v.² (3)]

blow me down! *excl.* [1930s+] a mild expletive.

blow monkey *n.* [1990s+] (*drugs*) a regular or excessive user of cocaine. [BLOW n.⁶ (4) + MONKEY n.¹² (3)]

blow mud *v.* [1990s+] to defecate loudly. [coarse use of SE]

blow my dickey! *excl.* [early 19C–1920s] a general excl. of surprise, amazement etc.

blow-my-skull(-off) *n.* [mid-19C] (*Aus.*) an alcoholic drink that mixes wine, opium, cayenne pepper and rum, popular at the gold diggings; an alternative recipe mixes boiling water, sugar, lime or lemon juice, porter, rum and brandy. [SE *blow* + *skull*]

blow my wig! *excl.* [early–mid-19C] a mild excl.

blown *adj.* (*also* **blown up, blown upon**) [late 17C+] revealed. [abbr. SE *blown open*/BLOW v.¹ (2)]

blown (away) *adj. see* BLOWN (OUT) adj.

blown-in-the-bottle/-glass *see under* BLOWED-IN-THE-GLASS.

blown (out) *adj.* (*also* **blown away**) **1** [mid-19C+] shocked, exhausted, overcome. **2** [1970s+] (*US campus*) (*also* **blowed**) drunk, under the influence of a drug (cf. ANNIHILATED adj.). **3** [1980s+] (*US campus*) crazy, insane. **4** [1990s+] dishevelled. [SE *blow*, to explode]

blown up *adj.* [1970s+] (*US*) drunk or overindulging in drugs (cf. ANNIHILATED adj.). [SE *blow*, to explode + ? image of a bloated drunkard]

blown up/upon *adj. see* BLOWN adj.

blow off *n.*¹ **1** [mid-19C–1950s] (*US*) an emotional outburst, a sudden fight or argument, a sensational piece of news. **2** [late 19C+] a party, a celebration. **3** [1950s+] a braggart. [BLOW v.¹]

blow off *n.*² **1** [1900s–10s] the end, the climax, esp. a decisive conclusion, an absolute end. **2** [1910s–50s] the very last tolerable happening in a series, 'the last straw'. **3** [1920s] (*US Und.*) the act of commiting a robbery or burglary. **4** [1920s+] (*US Und.*) the final stage of a confidence game, when the victim, now robbed, is quickly sent on his way. [SE *blow*, to explode.BLOW v.⁶ (2)]

blow off *n.*³ [1930s] (*US Und.*) a jail-break. [BLOW v.⁶ (4)]

blow off *n.*⁴ **1** [1960s+] (*US campus*) a lazy person, a 'layabout'. **2** [1970s+] (*US teen*) anything considered exceptionally easy. [SE *blow*, to blow something away with a puff of air]

blow off *v.*¹ **1** [mid-19C] (*US*) to stop, to cease. **2** [1910s] (*US*) of events, to develop, to happen. **3** [1940s+] (*US*) to get rid of, esp. (*US Und.*) in the concluding stages of a con-game. **4** [1950s] (*US Und.*) to interrupt criminals during a crime. **5** [1960s+] (*US*) (*also* **blow it off**) to ignore, to make little of. **6** [1960s+] (*US campus*) to fail an examination. **7** [1980s] (*US*) to kill. **8** [1980s+] (*US*) to reject a sexual advance. **9** [1980s+] to terminate a relationship, to jilt someone by not turning up. [SE *blow*, explode]

blow off *v.*² **1** [late 19C+] to release pent-up emotion. **2** [1910s+] to get angry (with). **3** [1970s+] (*US gay*) to achieve orgasm (cf. BLOW v.²). [BLOW OFF n.¹ (1)/BLOW OFF STEAM v.]

blow off *v.*³ [late 19C+] (*orig. US*) to treat. [BLOW v.⁵ (2)]

blow off *v.*⁴ [20C+] (*orig. naut.*) to break wind. [SE *blow*, explode]

blow off *v.*⁵ [1980s+] (*US campus*) to play truant. [BLOW v.⁷ (7)]

blow off *v.*⁶ [1990s+] (*US*) to make a turn.

blow off *v.*⁷ *see* BLOW v.¹ (4).

blow off *v.*⁸ *see* BLOW v.² (3).

blow off *v.*⁹ *see* BLOW v.⁴ (4).

blow off! *excl.* [1910s+] (*Aus.*) a excl. of dismissal. [BLOW v.⁶ (3)]

blow off (at) one's mouth *v.* (*also* **blow off at the head**) [1940s+] to talk loudly or aggressively, to boast. [BLOW OFF v.² (1) + SE *mouth*]

blow (off) one's bazoo *v.* [late 19C–1940s] (*US*) to boast. [BLOW v.¹ (4) + BAZOO n.¹ (1)]

blow (off on) the groundsills *v.* (*also* **...the groundsels**) [late 17C–18C] (*UK Und.*) to have sexual intercourse while lying on the floor. [SE *blow* + *groundsills/groundsels*, the foundation or lowest part of any structure, i.e. one's panting breath is exhaled at ground level]

blow off steam *v.* (*also* **get off steam, let off steam/wind, shoot off steam**) [early 19C+] to release one's (pent-up) emotions, to become angry or noisy and excited.

blow (off) the loose corn(s) *v.* [late 17C–early 18C] to have sexual intercourse. [the image is of sex in a barn, one's panting blows away loose corn]

blowoh! *excl.* [1980s] (*UK Black*) a term of surprise and shock, 'wow!' or 'isn't *that* incredible!' [? BLOW ME! excl. +SE *wow!*]

blow on *v.* [mid-19C+] (*US*) **1** to attack verbally. **2** to betray. [BLOW v.¹]

blow one out *v.* [1900s–30s] (*orig. milit.*) to make a rude noise in someone's direction. ['one' is a RASPBERRY n.¹ (1)]

blow one's bags (out) *v.* (*also* **blow one's bag out**) [1910s+] (*Aus.*) to boast. [BLOW v.¹ (4)]

blow one's barrel *v.* [1940s] (*US*) to lose control. [the barrel is that of a gun]

blow one's bazoo *v. see* BLOW (OFF) ONE'S BAZOO v.

blow one's cap *v. see* BLOW ONE'S TOP v.¹.

blow (one's) cookies *v.* **1** [1960s+] to vomit (cf. BLOW CHOW v.). **2** [1990s+] to reach orgasm. [(1) BLOW v.³ (2)/SE *blow* + *cookies* = food consumed/(2) plays on (1) + BLOW v.² (2)]

blow one's cool *v.* [1960s+] **1** to lose control, to become nervous or angry. **2** to ruin one's image, to discomfit, to make a fool of oneself. [BLOW v.⁵ (1) + COOL n.² (1)]

blow one's copper *v.* [1930s+] (*US prison*) to lose the reduction in sentence that would otherwise accrue for good conduct; thus *hold one's copper*, to maintain good conduct. [BLOW v.⁵ (1)/SE *hold* + COPPER n.³ (3)]

blow one's cork *v.* [1920s+] (*US*) **1** to go mad. **2** to lose one's temper. **3** (*also* **blow a cork**) to become excited. **4** to achieve orgasm. [SE *blow*, to explode/BLOW v.² (2)]

blow one's dust *v.* [1960s–70s] to masturbate, to ejaculate. [BLOW v.² (2) + SE *dust*]

blow oneself out *v.* [early–mid-19C] to binge. [BLOW v.⁵ (2)]

blow one's gasket/gauge *v. see* BLOW A GASKET v.

blow one's gob off *v.* (*also* **blow one's gab off**) [1910s] to lose one's temper. [SE *blow*, to explode + GOB n.¹ (1)/GAB n. (1)]

blow one's gourd *v.* (*also* **flip one's gourd, lose...**) [1970s+] (*orig. US*) to lose emotional control. [SE *blow*, to explode/FLIP v.⁴ (2)/SE *lose* + GOURD n.² (1)]

blow one's groceries *v.* (*also* **blow g's, lose one's groceries**) [1970s+] (*US campus*) to vomit (cf. BLOW CHOW v.). [BLOW v.³ (2)/LOSE v. (1) + SE *groceries*]

blow one's head (off) *v. see* BLOW ONE'S MIND v.

blow one's horn *v.*¹ [early 18C] to be a cuckold, to be cuckolded. [play on SE/HORN n.¹ (1)]

blow one's horn *v.*² (*US*) **1** [mid–late 19C] to speak or sing out of turn. **2** [late 19C+] (*also* **toot one's horn**) to brag, to boast. [play on SE/BLOW v.¹ (4)]

blow one's horn *v.*³ [20C+] (*US*) to break wind. [play on SE/BLOW v.³ (1)]

blow one's hump *v.* [1950s+] **1** (*US*) to achieve orgasm. **2** (*drugs*) to become intoxicated on a drug, usu. marijuana (cf. GO OVER THE HUMP v.). [BLOW v.² (2)/BLOW v.⁴ (2) + SE *hump*]

blow one's jets *v.* [1940s–60s] (*orig. US Black*) to get angry or annoyed.

blow one's juice *v.* [1990s+] to reach orgasm. [BLOW v.² (2) + JUICE n.² (1)]

blow one's lid *v.* [1920s+] to go mad, to lose emotional control. [SE *blow*, explode + LID n.¹ (2)]

blow one's load *v.* [1990s+] usu. of a man, to ejaculate, to come to orgasm. [BLOW v.² (2) + LOAD n.⁵ (2)]

blow one's lot v. [1940s+] (Aus.) to come to orgasm, to ejaculate. [BLOW v.² (2) + SE lot]

blow one's lump v. see LUMP n.³.

blow one's lumps v. [1930s–40s] (US Black) **1** to play very energetically. **2** to act in the desired manner. [BLOW v.⁸]

blow one's lunch v. (also **blow dinner**) [1950s+] (US) to vomit (cf. BLOW CHOW v.). [BLOW v.³ (2) + LUNCH n.² (2)]

blow one's mind v. **1** [1950s+] (orig. US drugs) (also **blow one's head**, **blow one's skull**) to become intoxicated by a drug. **2** [1960s+] (also **blow one's head (off)**) to shock, to surprise, to amaze; thus *mind-blown*, emotionally shattered. **3** [1960s+] to become mad. **4** [1960s+] to drive someone mad, to destroy someone's powers of reasoning. [SE blow, explode + mind/head/skull]

blow one's muck v. [1990s+] of a man, to ejaculate, to reach orgasm. [BLOW v.² (2) + MUCK n.⁴]

blow one's nose v. [1950s] (US) to inform, to talk to. [pun on SE/BLOW v.¹ (2); note NOSE n.¹ (1)]

blow one's pipes v. [1970s+] (US teen) to make a loud noise through a car's exhaust pipe by suddenly pressing down on the accelerator.

blow one's roof v.¹ [1940s+] (US) to act hysterically, to act irrationally, to lose one's temper. [SE blow, explode/BLOW v.¹ (1) + ROOF n. (2); var. on HIT THE ROOF v.]

blow one's roof v.² (also **blow one's top**) [1950s+] (drugs) to smoke cannabis. [BLOW v.⁴ (2)/SE blow, to explode + SE roof/ROOF n. (2)/TOP n.¹]

blow one's shoes v. [20C+] (US) to lose control, to lose one's composure. [BLOW v.¹ (1) + SE shoes]

blow one's skull v. see BLOW ONE'S MIND v. (1).

blow one's snoot off v. [1910s–30s] (US) to reprimand, to criticize harshly. [SE blow + SNOOT n. (1)]

blow one's stack v. [1940s+] (US) to lose control, to lose one's temper. [the image of a release of smoke through a smoke-stack]

blow one's top v.¹ (also **blow one's cap**, **...topper**) **1** [1920s+] (orig. US) to lose one's sanity. **2** [1930s] (US tramp) to commit suicide, esp. by shooting. **3** [1930s+] (orig. US) to express intense emotion, to become very excited. **4** [1930s+] (orig. US) to lose one's temper, to become violent. **5** [1940s–50s] (US Black) to talk too much. [SE blow, explode + TOP n.¹/SE cap/TOPPER n.³ (1); the image is of a volcano]

blow one's top v.² see BLOW ONE'S ROOF v.².

blow one's tubes v. [1990s+] of a man, to achieve orgasm. [the image is of a submarine, but note BLOW v.² (2) + TUBE n.¹ (1)]

blow one's wad v.¹ [1940s+] (US) to spend all one's money. [BLOW v.⁵ (1) + WAD n.¹ (1)]

blow one's wad v.² [1990s+] (US) **1** to ejaculate. **2** to indicate surprise or excitement. **3** to speak one's mind. [SE blow, to explode/lit. + fig. uses of BLOW v.² (2) + WAD n.⁶]

blow one's wig v. **1** [1930s–40s] (US Black) (also **fracture one's wig**) to feel excited, enthusiastic or furious. **2** [1950s] to lose one's mind. [SE blow, explode + WIG n.³ (1)]

blow-out n.¹ **1** [early 19C+] a binge of eating, drinking and debauchery, later usage includes drug-taking; also in fig. use. **2** [early 19C+] a party. **3** [late 19C+] a good time, an exciting event. **4** [early 19C–1930s] (US) a brawl, a noisy argument. **5** [1900s] an organized dance, held in a dancehall and frequented by working-class young people.

blow-out n.² [1960s–70s] (US Black/campus) a very large 'Afro' hairstyle; a hairstyle in which one's natural tight curls or kinks are blown out with a hairdryer.

blow-out n.³ [1980s+] a comprehensive defeat. [jazz use; when 2 bands staged a competition, the winner was said to blow its rival out of the house; thus the defeat itself was a blow-out; note RMC Duntroon (Aus.) blowout, an academic failure]

blow out v.¹ **1** [early 19C+] to eat and/or drink to excess. **2** [mid-

19C] to treat. **3** [1970s+] (US campus) (also **blow it out**) to have a spree. [SE blow out, to expand, but note BLOW v.⁵]

blow out v.² **1** [mid-19C+] (orig. US) to murder, to kill. **2** [1900s] to spend all one's funds. **3** [1910s+] (orig. US) to reject, to break a promise, to neglect a rendezvous etc. **4** [1940s] (US) to die. **5** [1960s–70s] (US) to destroy, to spoil. **6** [1970s+] (US) to collapse, to malfunction.

blow out v.³ [late 19C–1900s] to steal.

blow out v.⁴ **1** [1970s+] (US campus) to shock, to embarrass. **2** [1970s+] (orig. US) to astound, to amaze. **3** [1980s] (US campus) to tell off, to criticize. [BLOW v.¹]

blow out (of) v. (also **blow out of**) **1** [20C+] to leave, to depart from a place. **2** [1980s+] to send away, to reject. [BLOW v.⁶ (3)]

blow out someone's lamp v. (also **blow out someone's light**) [20C+] (US/Aus.) to murder, to kill.

blow out the afterglow v. [1930s–40s] (US Black) to turn out the lights. [many Blacks moved from candles and oil lamps to electricity only in the 1930s–40s]

blow out the kite v. [mid–late 19C] to have a full stomach. [the food makes one's stomach expand like the 'belly' of a kite in the wind]

blowpipe n. [1920s+] (US) a rifle.

blowsabella n. see BLOUZABELLA n.

blowse n. (also **blowsy**, **blowz**, **blowze**) [mid-16C–1900s] a slatternly woman, a prostitute. [? link to Du. blos, blush. Bailey's Universal Etymological English Dictionary (1721 et seq.) defines it as: 'a fat, red-faced, bloted wench, or one whose head is dressed like a slattern']

blowse v. [1980s+] (drugs) to sniff glue; usu. as blowsing, glue-sniffing. [? Northumberland dial. blow, to breathe; but note BIG GIRL'S BLOUSE n., the image is of the stupidity of this form of drug-taking]

blowsed-up adj. [1980s+] (drugs) intoxicated after sniffing glue. [BLOWSE v.]

blowser n.¹ (also **blouwzola**) [1920s+] a slatternly woman. [BLOWSE n.]

blowser n.² [1980s+] (drugs) a glue-sniffer. [BLOWSE v.]

blowsing n. see BLOWSE v.

blow sky high v. [mid-19C+] (orig. US) **1** (also **give sky-high**, **sky-high**) to scold, to reprimand. **2** to destroy, to ruin. **3** to collapse, to come to ruins. [SE blow up]

blow smoke v.¹ **1** [mid-19C+] to confuse, to mystify through speech. **2** [1930s+] (US) to boast, to brag; to flatter. [SE blow + SMOKE n.² (1)]

blow smoke v.² [1980s+] (drugs) **1** to inhale cocaine. **2** to smoke crack cocaine. **3** (US campus) to smoke marijuana. [BLOW v.⁴ + SMOKE n.³ (3)]

blow smoke up someone's ass v. [1950s+] to confuse, to tell lies to. [intensification of BLOW SMOKE v.¹ (1) + ASS n. (2)]

blow snot-rockets v. [1990s+] (US campus) to blow one's nose without the use of a tissue, by blocking one nostril and blowing hard through the other nostril. [SNOT n.¹ (1)]

blow snow v. [1950s–70s] (drugs) to inhale cocaine. [BLOW v.⁴ (3) + SNOW n.² (1)]

blow some dirt v. see DIRT n.² (5).

blow (someone) away v. **1** [1910s+] (orig. US Black) to shoot dead. **2** [1960s+] to defeat decisively. **3** [1960s+] to make intoxicated with a drug or drink. **4** [1970s+] (orig. US teen) to impress, to bowl over, to astound. **5** [1980s] (US Black) to defeat verbally. **6** [1980s+] to kill. [ext. of SE use + Southern dial. use or jazz use, for 2 bands to engage in an on-stage competition, the winner was deemed to have blown away its rival]

blow someone down v.¹ [1930s–40s] to kill, to murder someone. [var. on BLOW (SOMEONE) AWAY v. (1)]

blow someone down v.² [1950s] (US) to reject a sexual advance.

blow someone out v. **1** [1960s+] to exhaust. **2** [1970s] to shock.

3 [1970s+] to ignore, to dismiss, to reject; for one of a couple to abandon the relationship.

blow someone out of the water *v.* [1950s+] (*orig. US*) to defeat comprehensively, to overwhelm.

blow someone's act *v.* (*also* **blow the act**) [1970s+] (*US*) to ruin, to spoil, to interfere. [BLOW *v.*^{7} (1) + SE *act*]

blow someone's back off *v.* [1980s] of a man, to have sexual intercourse.

blow someone's cover *v. see* PULL SOMEONE'S COVER(s) v.

blow someone's glass *v.* [1970s+] to perform fellatio on a man. [BLOW *v.*^{2} (3) + GLASS n.^{4}]

blow someone's head *v.* [1970s+] (*US*) to fellate. [BLOW *v.*^{2} (3) + HEAD n.^{7} (1)]

blow someone's lights *v.* [1910s+] to knock unconscious; to kill.

blow someone's pipe *v.* (*also* **blow the pipe**) [1910s] (*US*) to fellate. [SE *blow*, inflate/BLOW *v.*^{2} (3) + PIPE n.^{2} (1)]

blow someone's stack *v.* [1960s] to make someone lose their temper. [BLOW ONE'S STACK v.]

blow someone's whistle *v.* [1970s] (*US gay*) to fellate. [BLOW *v.*^{2} (3) + WHISTLE n.^{2} (2)]

blow someone to *v. see* BLOW v.^{5} (2).

blow some tunes *v.* **1** [1980s+] (*US Black*) to perform cunnilingus. **2** [2000s] (*US*) to fellate in hetero- or homosexual contexts. [joc. use of BLOW *v.*^{2} (3) + SE *tunes*]

blow stake *n.* [1930s] money that one risks on a bet. [BLOW *v.*^{5} (1) + SE *stake*]

blow steam *v.* [1950s] (*US*) to chatter aimlessly and pointlessly.

blow stick *n.* [1960s+] the penis (cf. BAT n.^{7}). [BLOW *v.*^{2} (3) + STICK n.^{1} (1)]

blowsy *n. see* BLOWSE n.

blow the act *v. see* BLOW SOMEONE'S ACT v.

blow the beef bugle *v.* [1960s] to fellate. [SE *blow*/BLOW *v.*^{2} (3)]

blow the coals *v.* [late 17C–18C] to stir up trouble between 2 parties. [fig. use of SE]

blow the doors off *v.* [1960s+] (*orig. US*) to drive at high speed past another car.

blow the duke *v.* [1960s–70s] to make a complete mess of something. [BLOW *v.*^{7} (2) + fig. use of DUKE n.^{3} (3)]

blow the froth (off) *v.* [1910s–30s] (*Aus.*) to drink beer; thus to celebrate, to have a good time.

blow the froth off! *excl.* [1910s] (*Aus.*) a dismissive excl., stop being silly! [BLOW THE FROTH (OFF) v., the idea is of removing the superfluous]

blow the gab *v.* [late 18C–early 19C] to betray a secret, to inform against. [BLOW *v.*^{1} (2) + SE *gab*, speech, conversation]

blow the gaff *v.* **1** [early 19C+] to reveal a secret, esp. a hoax or deception. **2** [late 19C+] (*US*) to make a mess of, to bungle. [BLOW *v.*^{1} (2)/BLOW *v.*^{7} (1) + ? PENNY GAFF n.; thus fig. to give away the plot of a show]

blow the gap *v.* [early 19C] to inform on, to betray. [var. on BLOW THE GAB v.]

blow the gig *v.* [1950s–60s] (*orig. US Black*) **1** to lose a job. **2** to resign from a job. [BLOW *v.*^{7} (1) + GIG n.^{5} (4)]

blow the groundsills *v. see* BLOW (OFF ON) THE GROUNDSILLS v.

blow the head off *v.* [1960s] (*US gay*) to ejaculate large amounts of semen while being fellated. [BLOW *v.*^{2} (2)/SE *blow*, to explode + HEAD n.^{7} (1)/HEAD n.^{10}/SE *head*]

blow the lid off *v.* [1920s+] (*also* **blast the lid off**) to reveal, to uncover, esp. a scandal involving those 'in high places'. **2** [1970s] to unleash a great deal of trouble.

blow the loose corn(s) *v. see* BLOW (OFF) THE LOOSE CORN(s) v.

blow the pipe *v. see* BLOW SOMEONE'S PIPE v.

blow the show *v.* (*also* **blow the scene**) [1960s+] (*orig. US*) to ruin the entire situation, to miss an opportunity to do or gain something. [BLOW *v.*^{7} (1) + SHOW n.^{1} (1)/SCENE n. (1)]

blow the skin flute *v.* [1940s+] to fellate. [BLOW *v.*^{2} (3) + SKIN FLUTE n.]

blow the sky *v.* [1940s] (*US Black*) to lose one's mind; to become unconscious, to pass out drunk.

blow the socks off *v.*^{1} [1960s+] to bring to orgasm.

blow the socks off *v.*^{2} *see* KNOCK THE SOCKS OFF v. (3).

blow the whistle on *v.* **1** [1920s+] to bring to an end. **2** [1930s+] to inform against someone. [sporting imagery of a referee]

blow the works *v. see* BLOW v.^{1} (2).

blow this popsicle stand *v.* (*also* **blow this garage**, **blow this taco stand**) [1960s+] (*US campus*) to leave, esp. somewhere one dislikes or pretends to dislike. [BLOW *v.*^{6} (3) + generic use of SE *popsicle stand*]

blow-through *n.* [1940s–50s] an act of sexual intercourse. [SE *blow through*, the process of blowing steam through the cylinder of an engine etc to clear it of air]

blow through *v.* [1950s+] (*Aus.*) to leave, to run off; esp. as excl. *blow through!* go away! [BLOW *v.*^{6} (3) + SE *through*]

blowtop *n.* [1930s+] (*US Black*) **1** a violent, unstable person. **2** a jazz muscian, esp. a first-rate performer. [BLOW ONE'S TOP v.^{1}]

blowtorch *n.* [1940s] (*US*) the penis.

blow-up *n.*^{1} **1** [late 18C–19C] a revelation, a discovery, esp. the embarrassment or confusion that follows such a revelation. **2** [late 18C+] a short-lived but emotional quarrel, a fit of temper. **3** [19C] a financial collapse. **4** [mid-19C–1910s] a scolding, a telling off. **5** [1920s] (*US Und.*) a rumour. [SE *blow up*, to explode]

blow-up *n.*^{2} [1960s–70s] (*US Black*) a natural hairstyle, cut short.

blow-up *n.*^{3} [1980s+] (*drugs*) crack cocaine cut with lidocaine to increase the size, weight and street value. [SE *blow up*, to inflate]

blow up *v.*^{1} **1** [early 17C–1930s] to ruin, to thrash severely. **2** [late 17C–early 19C] to ruin financially. **3** [mid-18C] to discredit. **4** [late 18C] to reveal. **5** [19C+] to tell off, to reprimand. **6** [early 19C] (*US*) to make pregnant. **7** [early 19C+] to lose control, to lose patience, to become enraged. **8** [late 19C+] (*US*) to overpraise; to aggrandize. **9** [20C+] to break down, of people (usu. athletes), animals (racehorses, greyhounds), schemes or plans and machinery. **10** [1970s] (*US*) to shoot. **11** [1990s+] (*US Black*) to use to excess. **12** [2000s] (*US Black*) to raid, to invade.

blow up *v.*^{2} [late 19C+] (*orig. US*) **1** to sound a whistle as a signal, e.g. at the end of a working day. **2** to wake up, to start work.

blow up *v.*^{3} **1** [1910s] (*Aus.*) to hail, to call out to. **2** [2000s] (*US campus*) of a mobile phone, to ring.

blow up *v.*^{4} **1** [1980s] (*US Black*) to inherit a legacy. **2** [1980s+] (*orig. US Black*) to achieve great success, esp. after a time of struggle and obscurity. **3** [1990s+] (*US Black*) to rush around. **4** [1990s+] (*US*) to make money quickly from selling drugs.

blow up a storm *v.* **1** (*orig. US*) to play music with great energy and enthusiasm. **2** to make a fuss. [SE/BLOW v.^{8}]

blow upon *v.* **1** [15C–19C] to inform against, to betray. **2** [17C–19C] to discredit, to defame. [BLOW *v.*^{1} (2)/SE *blow*, to breathe; thus to use the breath in speaking + *upon*]

blow wise *v.* [late 19C+] (*US*) **1** to see where one's own interests lie. **2** to understand. [BLOW *v.*^{1} (8) + WISE adj. (1)]

blow with a French faggot-stick *n.* (*also* **blow with a French cowl-staff**, **...a Naples cowl-staff**) [17C–early 19C] the loss of one's nose through syphilis; thus *knocked with French faggot-stick*, referring to those who are thus injured. [FRENCH adj. (1)]

blowy *n. see* BLOWIE n.

blow your horn if you don't sell fish *phr.* [1900s] (*US*) a phr. used when someone blows their nose noisily. [? punning on a contemporary car sticker/HORN n.^{4} (1)]

blow your mind roulette *n.* [1960s] (*US Black/drugs*) a drug-based game whereby the participants toss a variety of unspecified pills onto a table and then take whatever they fancy and wait to discover what the effects will be. [BLOW ONE'S MIND v. (1) + SE *Russian roulette*]

blowz/blowze n. *see* BLOWSE n.

blow z's v. [1960s+] (*US*) **1** to sleep. **2** to snore. [SE *blow* + z n.[1]]

blub v. [mid-19C+] (*mainly UK juv.*) to cry, to burst into tears. [abbr. SE *blubber*]

blubber n.[1] [late 18C] (*UK Und.*) the mouth. [BLAB n.]

blubber n.[2] **1** [late 18C] (*orig. US Und.*) the female breasts; thus SPORT BLUBBER v. **2** [late 18C+] fatness, obesity. [SE *blubber*, fat]

blubber n.[3] [late 19C] (*Aus.*) a jellyfish.

blubberass n. [1970s+] (*US*) a grossly fat person. [SE *blubber* + -ASS sfx]

blubberation n. [1910s] weeping. [BLUB v. + SE sfx *-eration*]

blubber-belly n. [19C] a very fat person. [SE *blubber* + *belly*]

blubber-butt n. [1950s+] (*orig. US*) a grossly fat person. [SE *blubber* + BUTT n.[1] (2)]

blubbered adj. [2000s] intoxicated by drink and/or drugs. [one's muscles turn to *blubber*]

blubber-gut n. (*also* **blubber-guts**) [1940s+] (*US*) a grossly fat person. [SE *blubber* + *guts*]

blubber-head n. (*also* **blubber-noddle**) [late 18C–1950s] a fool; thus *blubber-headed*, foolish. [SE *blubber* + -HEAD sfx (1)/NODDLE n. (1)]

blubber-mouth n. (*also* **blubber mush**) (*US*) **1** [early–mid-19C; 1950s] one whose face has heavy jowls. **2** [1930s] one who cries readily. [SE *blubber* + *mouth*/MUSH n.[2]]

blucher n. [late 19C–1900s] an 'outsider' cab that is forbidden to enter the London railway termini. [proper name of Field-Marshal von *Blücher* (1742–1819). According to the Social Science Review (vol. I, 1864), the cabs were 'named after the Prussian Field Marshal who arrived on the field of Waterloo only to do the work that chanced to be undone']

bludge n. [1940s+] (*Aus.*) **1** a period of idleness. **2** an imposition. **3** an act of scrounging. **4** an easy job, a sinecure. [BLUDGE v.]

bludge v. (*Aus.*) **1** [late 19C+] to evade one's responsibilities. **2** [1900s–10s] to live on the earnings of a prostitute. **3** [1940s+] to loaf about, to idle; thus adj. *bludging*. **4** [1940s+] to cadge, to scrounge; also as *bludge in*, to gatecrash; thus ON THE BLUDGE phr. [backform. f. BLUDGER n.[2]]

bludgeon n. [late 19C] the penis (cf. AX n.[2]).

bludgeon business n. [mid-19C] robbery with violence.

bludgeoner n. [mid-19C] **1** a pimp (cf. ABBOT ON THE CROSS n.). **2** a tough man employed to keep order at a brothel. **3** (*US Und.*) the man who plays the 'outraged husband' in the BADGER GAME n.

bludgeon the beefsteak v. [1980s+] to masturbate (cf. BANG THE BISHOP v.). [var. on BEAT ONE'S MEAT v.]

bludger n.[1] [mid-19C+] (*mainly Aus.*) a thief who is as willing to use violence as not. [? SE *bludgeoner*; thus ult. *bludgeon*]

bludger n.[2] (*Aus.*) **1** [late 19C+] a pimp (cf. ABBOT ON THE CROSS n.). **2** [20C+] a general term of abuse, usu. implying that the person in question lives off the efforts and money of others. **3** [1910s+] a white-collar worker (from the point of view of a manual labourer, who sees such work as idling). **4** [1940s] (*also* **blodger**) an idler, a lazy person or creature. **5** [1940s+] (*Aus. Und.*) a policeman (cf. BEAT-POUNDER n.). **6** [1950s+] one who does not contribute their fair share. [SE *bludgeoner*; note RMC Duntroon (Aus.) *bludger*, a civilian]

bludget n. [1920s–40s] (*Aus./US*) a female thief. [BLUDGER n.[1] + SE fem. sfx *-et(te)*]

blue n.[1] **1** [late 18C–19C] an intellectual woman. **2** [mid-19C–1900s] (*US campus*) a puritanical, strait-laced student. [abbr. SE *blue-stocking*, a term that originated *c*.1750 when a coterie of intellectual ladies – Mrs Montague, Mrs Vesey and Mrs Ord – set out to replace London society's trad. post-dinner pursuits (card-playing) with more cerebral amusements. Formal dress was no longer required and among those who attended their soirées was Benjamin Stillingfleet, who habitually wore grey or blue worsted, instead of black silk, stockings. Admiral Boscawen, a staunch traditionalist, labelled these events 'the Blue Stocking Society'; the ladies were called Blue Stockingers, then Blue Stocking Ladies and finally Blue Stockings; note also 17C *blue*, used after the Restoration of Charles II in 1660 to denote any diehard Puritan who disapproved of the new moral freedoms]

blue n.[2] **1** [19C+] (*US Black*) a dark-complexioned Black person (cf. BLUESKIN n.[2]). **2** [20C+] (*S.Afr.*) methylated spirits. **3** [1930s] (*US*) a blue poker chip. **4** [1950s+] a £5 note. [colour; in (1) note 18C–19C Louisiana dial. *blue*, a mix of Indian, Black and White, as well as Allen, *The Language of Ethnic Conflict* (1983): '*Die Blaue*, which Mencken, *The American Language* (3rd edn, 1936), says was used for black servants by German residents of Baltimore in the 1880s; they changed it to *die Schwarze* when the blacks caught on']

blue n.[3] **1** [mid-19C–1900s] a blue-uniformed soldier. **2** [mid-19C+] a policeman; the police (cf. BABY-BLUES n.[2]). **3** [1930s+] (*US prison*) a prison inmate. [the colour of the uniform]

blue n.[4] **1** [mid-19C+] a 'smutty' anecdote, a piece of pornography. **2** [late 19C] an obscene or libidinous anecdote. [BLUE adj.[3]]

blue n.[5] **1** [1900s–10s] the sea. **2** [1940s–50s] (*US Black*) the sky.

blue n.[6] [1900s–30s] a drinking binge, a spree. [BLUE v.[2] (2)]

blue n.[7] [1910s+] (*Aus./N.Z.*) a summons; also used in milit. context, a 'write-up'. [the colour of the paper on which it is printed; note Lawson (1899): 'His character was pretty bad just then, so there was a piece of blue paper cut for him']

blue n.[8] [1940s+] (*Aus./N.Z.*) **1** a blunder, a mistake. **2** a brawl, a quarrel; thus *send off the blue*, to start a fight. **3** a serious complaint, an objection; thus BUNG ON A BLUE v.; thus *wear the blue*, to take the blame. [abbr. BLOOMER n.[1]]

blue n.[9] (*drugs*) **1** [1960s+] usu. in pl., an amphetamine (cf. A n.[2]). **2** [1960s+] a barbiturate (cf. BARBIT n.). **3** [1970s] (*UK prison*) (*also* **double blue**) an amphetamine-barbiturate mixture. **4** [1980s+] crack cocaine (cf. BASE n.). [(1) the colour of the pills; (2) ? misreading]

blue n.[10] [1990s+] (*drugs*) a blue Rizla paper, used for rolling cannabis cigarettes or to wrap small amounts of cocaine.

blue n.[11] *see* BLUE RUIN n. (1).

blue n.[12] *see* BLUES n.[1].

blue n.[13] *see* BLUEY n.[1] (4).

blue adj.[1] **1** [late 17C+] miserable, depressed. **2** [early 18C–1960s] confused, terrified, disappointed. **3** [mid-19C+] (*orig. US*) a general intensifier, e.g. BLUE MURDER n., *scared blue*. **4** [mid-19C+] unpromising, discouraging.

blue adj.[2] **1** [early 19C+] (*US/Aus.*) drunk. **2** [1940s+] (*S.Afr.*) under the influence of marijuana. [? '*blue in the face*'; (1) appears in the early 19C US, lasts until the mid-century then re-emerges in Aus. by the early 20C]

blue adj.[3] (*also* **azure**) [early 19C+] coarse, obscene, pornographic; thus *blue film*, *blue movie*. [? BLUEGOWN n.; ? the Fr. *Bibliothèque bleue*, 'a series of books of questionable character' (F&H) or ? the opposite of BROWN adj.[2]]

blue adj.[4] [mid-19C] of a woman, intellectual; thus (*US campus*) excessively hard-working, overly dedicated. [BLUE n.[1]]

blue adj.[5] [late 19C+] a euph. for BLOODY adj.[1] (1).

blue adj.[6] [1920s+] Black, as in skin colour (cf. BLUEBLACK adj.). [BLUE n.[2] (1)]

blue adj.[7] [1990s+] (*US gay*) homosexual. [? BLUE adj.[3] or ? the trad. colour of clothing for baby boys]

blue v.[1] [early 18C] to blush. [the colouring (actually dark red) of one's complexion]

blue v.[2] **1** [late 19C] to make a blunder, to be a mistake. **2** [mid-19C+] of money, to squander (cf. BLEW v.[1]). **3** [mid–late 19C] (*also* **blue in**) to pawn. [BLOW v.[5] (1)/BLOW v.[7] (1)]

blue v.[3] [1960s+] (*Aus.*) **1** to argue, to fight. **2** to reprimand, to swear at. **3** to boast. [BLUE n.[8] (2)]

blue about the gills *phr. see* GREEN ABOUT THE GILLS *phr.*

blue acid *n.* [1960s+] (*drugs*) LSD (cf. A n.³). [SE *blue* + ACID n.³; the colour of a capsule]

blue-and-white *n.* [1970s+] (*US*) **1** a police car, painted in those colours (e.g. in New York City or Washington, DC). **2** a policeman in such a police car.

blue angel *n.* [1970s+] (*drugs*) a barbiturate (cf. BARBIT n.). [the drugs come in blue capsules]

blue-apron *n.* [late 17C–mid-19C] a tradesman. [his 'uniform']

blue around the gills *phr. see* GREEN ABOUT THE GILLS *phr.*

blue-arsed bandit *n.* [1990s+] a homosexual male. [BLUE adj.⁷ + ARSE n.¹ (1) + BANDIT sfx (2); ext. of ARSE BANDIT n.]

blue-backs *n.* (*also* **bluebacks**) **1** [mid–late 19C] (*US*) money issued by the Confederate States of America (cf. BROWN-BACK n.; GREENBACK n.²; YELLOW-BACK n.¹). **2** [late 19C] (*S.Afr.*) money issued briefly by the Orange Free State. [its colour]

blue balls *n.* **1** [1910s+] a feeling of intense sexual frustration; thus *have blue balls*, of a man, to be very sexually frustrated. **2** [1920s+] a venereal bubo. **3** [1920s+] (*US*) gonorrhoea. [SE *blue* + BALLS n.¹ (1)]

blue bands *n.* [1960s+] (*drugs*) barbiturates (cf. BARBIT n.). [packaging]

blue barrels *n.* [1970s+] (*drugs*) LSD (cf. A n.³). [packaging]

blue-bellied *adj.* (*US*) **1** [mid-19C–1910s] in the South, pertaining to a Northerner, esp. a New Englander. **2** [1920s] of a person, despicable, repellent. **3** [1920s] a derog. term for a policeman. [BLUEBELLY n.]

bluebelly *n.* (*US*) **1** [early 19C+] a Northerner, a Yankee, esp. a Northern soldier during the Civil War (1861–5). **2** [mid–late 19C] a pretentious, self-opinionated person. **3** [late 19C+] a policeman (cf. BABY-BLUES n.²). [the uniforms of (1) the Northern troops, (3) the police); (2) f. (1)]

blueberry (hill) *n.* [1960s+] the police. [rhy. sl. = OLD BILL n.]

blueberry pie *n.* [1960s+] (*US gay*) a sailor. [the blue uniform + something one can EAT v.³ (1)]

blue billy *n.*¹ [mid–late 19C] a blue handkerchief with white spots, worn and used in prize fights. [SE *blue* + BILLY n.³; 'Before a set to it is common to take it from the neck and tie it round the leg as a garter, or round the waist to "keep it in the wind"' (Hotten, 1867). The *blue billy* made its way to New York where it was defined in a detective manual (*c.*1870) as 'a strange handkerchief']

blue billy *n.*² [late 19C] refuse ammoniacal lime from gas factories. [the colour]

bluebird *n.*¹ **1** [mid-19C] (*US Southern*) a Northern, Unionist soldier. **2** [1910s–60s] (*US*) a policeman (cf. ANIMAL n.¹; BABY-BLUES n.²). [the colour of the uniform]

bluebird *n.*² [1930s–70s] (*Aus./US*) a police car, a police wagon. [the colour of the Buicks and later Fords that fulfilled the role]

bluebird *n.*³ [1960s+] (*drugs*) a capsule of sodium amytal. [packaging]

bluebird *n.*⁴ [1990s+] (*US Black teen*) something annoying or worrying. [BLUE adj.¹ (4)]

blue bit *n.* **1** [late 18C] (*US Und.*) counterfeit money. **2** [1980s+] (*Aus. prison*) a A$10 note. [BIT n.¹]

blueblack *adj.* [late 19C+] (*US Black*) of skin colour, so dark it seems to have tints of blue (cf. BLUE adj.⁶).

blue blanket *n.* **1** [late 18C–19C] the sky. **2** [mid-19C] a rough coat made of coarse pilot-cloth (an indigo cloth used for ship officers' greatcoats).

blue-blasted *adj.* [mid-19C] (*US*) a euph. for DAMNED adj. (1).

blue blazes *n.* (*also* **blue blaizes**) [19C+] a euph. for *hell*, usu. in phrs., e.g. *hot as blue blazes*, *go blue blazes*. [SE *blue* + BLAZES n. (1); nothing more than alliteration although note BLUE adj.⁵]

blue-blinded *adj.* [1910s] (*Aus.*) utterly overcome. [BLUE-BLIND (PARALYTIC) adj.]

blue-blind (paralytic) *adj.* [1900s–10s] (*Aus.*) extremely drunk (cf. AFFLICTED adj.). [BLUE adj.² (1) + BLIND DRUNK adj.]

blue boar *n.* [late 18C–19C] a venereal bubo. [? the notorious *Blue Boar* tavern in London, sited on the corner of Oxford Street and Tottenham Court Road, next to the St Giles rookery and thus a centre of lowlife]

blue board *n.* [20C+] a venereal bubo. [ext. of BLUE BOAR n.]

blue bomber *n.* [1970s] (*US drugs*) valium. [the colour of the pill or capsule]

blue boots *n.* [1950s] (*US*) depression. [BLUE adj.¹ (1) + alliteration]

bluebottle *n.* **1** [late 16C–early 17C] a beadle. **2** [mid-19C+] a policeman (cf. ANIMAL n.¹; BABY-BLUES n.²).

blue boy *n.*¹ [late 18C–19C] a venereal bubo. [var. on BLUE BOAR n.]

blue boy *n.*² (*also* **blueboy**) [late 19C+] a policeman, a police car (cf. BABY-BLUES n.²). [the uniform]

blue boy *n.*³ [1950s] (*US Black*) a Black male. [? the BLUE adj.⁶ tone of very dark skin + ? the emotional overtones of BLUE adj.¹ (1)]

blue brick *n.* [1980s] (*UK Und.*) a prison. [BLUE adj.¹ (1) + SE *brick*, i.e. the walls]

blue broadway *n.* [1940s] (*US Black/Harlem*) Heaven. [the *blue sky* + image of *Broadway*, New York, then in its prime, as an earthly version of paradise]

blue bullets *n.* [1960s+] barbiturates (cf. BARBIT n.). [packaging]

blue butter *n.* [mid-19C–1900s] an ointment used for the treatment of venereal sores. [the mercury on which it was based]

blue cap *n.*¹ [late 16C–early 18C] a Scotsman. [metonymy]

blue cap *n.*² [1930s] a policeman (cf. BABY-BLUES n.²).

blue cent *n. see* RED CENT n.

blue chairs *n.* [1980s+] (*drugs*) LSD (cf. A n.³). [ety. unknown; ? mispron. of BLUE CHEER n.]

blue-cheek *n.* [mid-19C] a style for facial hair whereby all whiskers were shaved off, leaving the cheek 'blue'.

blue cheer *n.* [1960s] (*US drugs*) a capsule of LSD cut with Methedrine or some other form of 'speed'. [the laundry detergent *Blue Cheer* and/or the rock band of the same name]

blue cheese *n.* [1950s–70s] (*US drugs*) hashish (cf. AFGHAN n.). [? its consistency]

blue-chin *n.* [20C+] (*Aus.*) an actor. [the fact that not shaving can make one's chin look blue and actors tend to shave for the evening performance rather than in the morning]

blue-chinned *adj.* [1900s] unshaven, usu. of actors. [BLUE-CHIN n.]

blue clouds *n.* [1970s+] (*drugs*) amobarbital sodium. [packaging]

bluecoat *n.* **1** [late 16C–18C] a servant who wore a blue coat, a servant's coat. **2** [late 16C–1930s] one who wears a blue coat, spec. a beadle in the 16C and later a blue-coated soldier, sailor or policeman. **3** [17C+] (*US*) a policeman (cf. BABY-BLUES n.²). **4** [mid-19C] (*US, Southern*) a Northern, Unionist soldier. **5** [1940s+] (*S.Afr.*) (*also* **bluejacket**) an habitual criminal serving an indeterminate sentence; thus an indeterminate sentence of 9–15 years.

blued *adj.*¹ (*also* **blewed**) [mid-19C] drunk. [BLUE adj.² (1)]

blued *adj.*² [mid–late 19C] depressed. [BLUE adj.¹ (1)]

blue damn *n.* [late 19C–1900s] an oath. [BLUE adj.³ + SE *damn*]

blue dangers *n.* [1960s+] (*US Und.*) **1** marked police cars (when painted blue, as in New York City). **2** blue-uniformed police officers. [the colour of the vehicle or uniform]

blue de hue *n.* [1970s] (*drugs*) marijuana from Vietnam (cf. ACAPULCO (GOLD) n.). [assonance; Hue ('Hoo-ay') is a major city in Vietnam]

blue devil *n.*¹ [mid-19C] **1** (*US*) a servant. **2** (*UK/US Und.*) a policeman (cf. BABY-BLUES n.²). [the blue uniform]

blue devil *n.*² [1960s–70s] (*drugs*) a depressant, esp. Phenobarbitone (luminal), amobarbital. [packaging]

blue devils *n.*[1] **1** [18C+] a fit of depression; thus *in the blues*. **2** [19C+] delirium tremens; thus *in the blues*. [BLUE adj.[1] (1) feelings that 'bedevil' the sufferer; ? (2) the 'blue devils' the drunkard supposedly sees]

blue devils *n.*[2] [19C] the police. [the blue uniform + derog. use of SE]

blue dolls *n.* [1960s] (*drugs*) barbiturates (cf. BARBIT n.). [SE *blue* + DOLL n.[2]]

blue dragons *n.* [1970s] (*US drugs*) barbiturates (cf. BARBIT n.).

blue duck *n.* **1** [late 19C+] (*Aus.*) a lost cause, a failure. **2** [1980s] (*N.Z.*) a (baseless) rumour. [DEAD DUCK n. (1)]

blue-eyed *adj.*[1] [mid-19C] (*US campus*) drunk (cf. ARSEHOLED adj.). [BLUE adj.[2] (1)]

blue-eyed *adj.*[2] [20C+] (*US*) a euph. for DAMNED adj. [note BLUE adj.[5]]

blue-eyed boy *n.* (*also* **blue eyes**) [1910s–30s] a special favourite. [SE f. 1930s]

blue-eyed soul *n.* [1960s+] (*orig. US Black*) **1** the characteristic of emotional sensitivity (i.e. 'soul') applied to White people. **2** a style of popular music in which White performers performed soul songs, usu. the province of Black performers; most popular in 1960s. [SE *blue-eyed*, i.e. shorthand for White + *soul music*]

blue-eyed soul brother/sister *n.* [1970s+] (*US Black*) any White who is accepted as genuinely friendly towards Blacks. [BLUE-EYED SOUL n. (1) + SOUL BROTHER n./SOUL SISTER n.]

blue eyes *n. see* BLUE-EYED BOY n.

blue fear *n.* [late 19C] very great fear. [BLUE adj.[1] (3) + SE *fear*]

blue flag *n.* [late 18C–early 19C] a publican. [their blue apron]

blue foot *n.* [1970s–80s] (*UK Black*) a prostitute. [? she is cold from standing in the street]

blue funk *n.* [mid-19C+] abject terror, utter cowardice, complete misery; thus *blue-funked*, utterly terrified. [BLUE adj.[1] (3) + FUNK n.[2] (1); +? the colour of the terrified individual's skin, which turns a leaden blue-grey]

blue goose *n.* (*US*) **1** [1920s–30s] the general convict cage at a prison camp. **2** [1960s] a small, run-down café or bar. **3** [1950s] an establishment where liquor is sold illegally. [? LIKE SHIT THROUGH A GOOSE adv.]

blue goose *v.* [1970s] (*US Black*) to engage in sexual affairs. [GOOSE v.[3] (7)]

bluegown *n.* [late 16C–early 17C] a prostitute. [metonymy; prostitutes confined in a house of correction wore a blue dress as their uniform]

bluegrass *v.* [1950s–60s] (*US drugs*) to commit a drug user to the Lexington Federal Narcotics Hospital in Lexington, Kentucky. [the *Bluegrass State*, the nickname of Kentucky]

blue gum *n.*[1] (*US*) **1** [mid-19C+] (*also* **bluegum moke, bluegum terror**) a Black person, seen by the (White) speaker as especially malevolent; the belief was that their bite is supposedly poisonous. **2** [1930s+] a very dark Black person. **3** [1970s] a person of mixed Indian, White and Black ancestry. [the bluish gums that many Blacks have]

blue gum *n.*[2] [20C+] (*US*) bootleg whisky. [ety. unknown]

bluehair *n.* (*also* **bluehaired**) [1980s+] (*US campus*) an old person, usu. female. [the bluish tint that old ladies sometimes have put into their otherwise grey hair]

bluehead *n.* [mid-19C] (*US*) strong and illicitly distilled whisky. [? it has a bluish tinge]

blue heaven *n.* (*drugs*) **1** [1950s+] amytal barbiturate (cf. BARBIT n.). **2** [1960s+] LSD (cf. A n.[3]). **3** [1980s+] alkyl nitrates. [colour of capsule/tablet + play on the popular song 'My Blue Heaven' (1927)]

blue heeler *n.* (*Aus.*) **1** [1980s] a can of Foster's lager. **2** [1990s+] a policeman (cf. BABY-BLUES n.[2]). [SAusE *blue heeler*, a cattle dog; the Foster's can is predominantly blue]

blue hen's chicken *n.* **1** [late 18C+] a resident of the state of Delaware. **2** [late 18C+] (*US*) a spirited, plucky person, a good fighter. **3** [20C+] a dominant, aggressive and very short-tempered person, esp. a woman. **4** [20C+] an important person or one who poses as such. [SE *blue hen*, a hen supposed to breed first-rate fighting cocks; the US state of Delaware is known as 'the Blue Hen State']

blue horrors *n.* [late 19C–1900s] delirium tremens. [HORRORS, THE n. (2)]

blue in *v. see* BLUE v.[2] (3).

bluejacket *n.*[1] **1** [early 19C–1910s] a sailor. **2** [mid-19C] (*US*) a Northern, Unionist soldier. **3** [mid-19C] (*US*) an abolitionist. **4** [mid-19C+] a policeman (cf. BABY-BLUES n.[2]). **5** [late 19C] a coastguard. [the uniform]

bluejacket *n.*[2] *see* BLUECOAT n. (5).

bluejay *n.* [1950s] (*US drugs*) a capsule of sodium amytal. [the colour]

blue-jeans femme *n. see* LOW FEMME n.

blue Jews *n.* [1970s] (*US gay*) a pair of blue denim Levis, usu. tight. [the trad. colour + play on stereotypical Jewish names: Levi-Strauss]

blue john *n.* (*US*) **1** [mid-19C+] skimmed milk. **2** [1900s] sour or nearly sour milk. [such milk has a slightly blue tinge]

blue johnny *n.* [mid-19C] (*US*) a Northern, Unionist soldier. [his uniform + generic use of proper name]

blue lamp (boy) *n.* [1900s–50s] (*UK juv.*) a policeman (cf. BABY-BLUES n.[2]). [the *blue lamp* that hung outside UK police stations; note 1949 movie *The Blue Lamp*]

blue light *n.*[1] **1** [19C] (*US*) a pious, sanctimonious individual. **2** [mid-late 19C] (*US campus*) a student who informs on other students to the authorities. [SE *blue laws*, severely puritanical laws enacted in New England; or ? the blue light that signifies a police station; note WW1 Aus. milit. *blue light*, 'a prophylactic establishment'; note US *blue light*, one who opposed the War of 1812]

blue light *n.*[2] **1** [1930s+] a police car. **2** [2000s] (*US*) a policeman (cf. BABY-BLUES n.[2]). [the rotating/flashing blue lights on top of police cars; (2) f. (1)]

blue light *n.*[3] [1940s+] (*W.I.*) an obscenity, a swearword, a coarse, vulgar expression. [? BLUE adj.[3]]

blue-light (clinic) *n.* [20C+] (*Aus.*) a venereal disease clinic. [its 'signpost']

blue lightning *n.* [mid-19C] (*US, Western*) a revolver, a 6-gun. [the flash when a bullet is fired]

blue-light special *n.*[1] [1990s+] (*US Black*) a policeman. [SE *blue lights* on police cars + play on *blue-plate special*]

blue-light special *n.*[2] [1990s+] (*US Black*) a cheap, low-quality retail item. [play on SE *blueplate special* + ? implication of illegality thus the BLUE LIGHT n.[2] might be interested]

blue me! *excl.* [1900s] (*Aus.*) a general excl.of emphasis. [var. on BLOW ME! excl.]

blue meanie *n.* [1960s–70s] a policeman; thus the establishment in general (cf. BABY-BLUES n.[2]). [*Blue Meanies*, the 'villains' of the animated film *Yellow Submarine* (1968), featuring The Beatles]

blue-metal *v.* [late 19C–1940s] (*Aus.*) to throw pieces of stone, esp. in a street-fight. [SE *blue metal*, small pieces of stone, used in street-fights]

blue microdot *n.* (*also* **blue mist**) [1970s+] (*drugs*) LSD (cf. A n.[3]). [SE *blue* + MICRODOT n./MIST n.]

blue mollies *n. see* MOLLIES n.

blue Monday *n.* **1** [mid-19C–1920s] a Monday taken off work and dedicated to self-indulgence. **2** [1960s] a start-of-the-week feeling of depression that follows a weekend of pleasurable excess. [BLUE adj.[2] (1)/BLUE adj.[1] (1) + SE *Monday*]

blue moon *n.* **1** [20C+] a spoon. **2** [1970s+] (*Aus.*) a pimp (cf. ALPHONSE n.[2]). [rhy. sl.; (2) = HOON n. (1)]

blue moon *v.* [late 19C–1930s] to romance, to 'chat up'. [rhy. sl. = SPOON v.[1]]

blue moons n. [1960s+] (US drugs) **1** (also **blue sage**) a variety of marijuana (cf. BLACK DOMINA n.). **2** LSD (cf. A n.³). [colour]

blue mouldies n. see BLUES n.¹.

blue murder n. (also **bloody murder**) [mid-19C+] cries of terror, horror, alarm; usu. in phrs. cry blue murder; SCREAM BLUE MURDER v. [BLUE adj.¹ (3) + SE murder]

bluenose n.¹ (US) **1** [late 18C+] a Canadian, esp. a resident of Nova Scotia. **2** [mid-19C] a Northerner, esp. a New Englander. **3** [late 19C+] a dedicated, fanatical puritan, almost invariably a teetotaller. **4** [1920s+] someone who sees themself as superior to their neighbours. [SE bluenose, a variety of potato native to Nova Scotia, but note late 17C Scot. bluenose, a Scot. Presbyterian and the stereotyped New England Yankee, seen as BLUE-NOSED adj. (3), thus the northern nose is blue with chilly disapproval]

bluenose n.² [1960s] (US) a sycophant, a toady. [analogous with BROWN NOSE n.]

bluenose v. [1960s] (US campus) to toady. [BLUENOSE n.²]

blue-nosed adj. (orig. US) **1** [early 19C+] pertaining to being a Nova Scotian. **2** [mid-19C+] pertaining to being a New Englander. **3** [mid-19C+] rigidly, repressively puritan. [BLUENOSE n.¹]

bluenoser n. (US) **1** [mid-19C–1930s] a Canadian. **2** [1970s] a fanatical puritan. [BLUENOSE n.¹]

blue ocean n. [1980s+] (S.Afr.) methylated spirits. [colour]

blue o'clock in the morning n. [late 19C–1900s] the last minutes of proper night-time, when darkness is gradually giving way to dawn. [rhy. sl. = two o'clock in the morning]

blue one n. [1950s] (Irish) a £10 note. [colour]

blue paper n. see BLUEY n.¹ (3).

blue-pencil v. **1** [late 19C+] to censor, to edit by cutting; thus as n. blue pencil, the act of censorship; thus fig. get the blue pencil, to be verbally abused. **2** [1900s] in ext. use, to bring to a conclusion. [the trad. colour of the editor's pencil]

blue pig n. [1950s+] (US) **1** an unlicensed drinking house, a speakeasy, an 'after-hours' bar. **2** the whisky served in such an establishment. [BLUE GOOSE n. (3) + BLIND PIG n. (1)]

blue pigeon n. [late 18C–19C] (UK Und.) **1** a thief who specializes in stealing the lead from roofs. **2** (also **pigeon**) small offcuts of lead or similar materials, taken from the job in hand and sold off as perks by plumbers. [like an avian pigeon, the thief 'perches' on a church roof]

blue pigeon flyer n. (also **blue pigeon filer**) [mid-19C] a stealer of lead from the roofs of buildings; such a thief poses as a journeyman glazier, plumber or other workman who gets to the roof, strips off the lead and hides it (often by wrapping it round the body) before leaving the house. [ext. of BLUE PIGEON n. (1)]

blue pill n. [mid–late 19C] (US) a bullet. [SE blue, lead + SE pill/PILL n.¹ (3)]

blue plum n. (also **blue plumb**) [late 18C–early 19C] a bullet; thus give someone a taste of plum, to wound or kill with a bullet; thus surfeited with a blue plumb, wounded by gunfire. [SE blue + plumb, a small piece of lead + pun on the fruit]

blue ribbon n. [early 19C] gin. [SE blue ribbon, a blue ribbon worn as a badge of honour; thus referring to the quality of the best gin]

blue ribboner n. (also **blue ribbon army, blue ribbonite**) [late 19C–1910s] a teetotaller, a total abstainer. [the blue ribbons such individuals wore to proclaim their drink-free status. A Blue Ribbon Army was instituted in 1882, but the Army and its ribbons had virtually vanished by 1896]

blue ribbon fakers n. [late 19C–1900s] a teetotaller, a total abstainer. [SE blue ribbon + FAKER n. (5)]

blue room n. **1** [1920s+] (US Und.) a punishment cell. **2** [1950s+] (Aus.) an interrogation room in a police station. [its lack of light + once incarcerated there, one feels BLUE adj.¹ (1)]

blue ruin n. **1** [19C–1900s] (also **blue**) gin, esp. second-rate gin (cf. MOTHER'S (RUIN) n.). **2** [mid-19C] (US) a strong kind of

applejack, peach brandy or whisky. [BLUE TAPE n./BLUE RIBBON n. etc + SE ruin; i.e. its effects]

blues n.¹ (also **blews, blue, blue mouldies**) [mid-18C+] misery, depression, unhappiness. [orig. general, White use, despite assumption that the term was created/patented by US Blacks. The OED's first cit. is from a letter by the actor David Garrick (11 July 1741): 'I am far from being quite well, tho not troubled wth ye Blews as I have been']

blues n.² [late 19C+] (Aus.) the police. **2** [1960s+] amphetamines (cf. A n.²). **3** [1980s+] (Aus. prison) prison officers; thus used as adj. to refer to staff activity, e.g. blue talk, prison officer conversations etc. [the colour of the uniform or the pills]

blues n.³ **1** [1910s+] (Aus.) a blue uniform. **2** [1940s] any trousers. **3** [1940s] police uniform. **4** [1960s+] (US prison) prison uniform. **5** [1970s] (US) a sailor's trousers. **6** [1970s] (US) blue eyes, esp. as baby-blues. **7** [1970s+] (US) blue jeans. [colour]

blues n.⁴ [1970s+] (W.I.) a shebeen, an illegal drinking club or a party where drink is sold without a licence. [? BLUE n.⁶]

blue sage n. see BLUE MOONS n. (1).

blueshirt n.¹ [1920s+] (Aus) **1** a farmer or estate owner. **2** a lazy worker, a slacker.

blueshirt n.² [1930s] (Irish) a member of the Fine Gael party, thus anyone espousing right-wing views. [the Blueshirts, a 1930s Irish fascist movement, named for their uniform]

blueskin n.¹ (US) **1** [late 18C] a keen supporter of the American Revolution. **2** [mid-19C] a Northern, Unionist soldier. [uniforms]

blueskin n.² **1** [late 18C–early 19C] the offspring of a White man and a Black woman, a mulatto. **2** [early–mid-19C] a Black person (cf. BLUE n.²). **3** [late 19C] the penis. [skin tone]

blueskin n.³ **1** [late 18C–1900s] (US, mainly campus) a puritan, a repressive moralist. **2** [mid–late 19C] a Presbyterian. [the repressive 'blue laws' passed in New England; i.e. their demeanour; reinforced by BLUE n.¹ (2)]

blue sky n.¹ [1940s–80s] (S.Afr.) the Cinderella prison in Boksburg. [? the view]

blue sky n.² (also **sky**) [1980s+] (US drugs) heroin. [? BLUE SKY v. (1), i.e. the dreaminess produced by the drug; or ? simply it gets one HIGH adj.¹ (2)]

blue sky v. [1950s+] (US) **1** to wonder about things in an unrestrained manner, preferring pleasurable fantasy to tedious fact. **2** to talk unrestrainedly, in a speculative manner; thus [1970s] blue-skyer, blue-sky artist, one who speculates freely, with little basis in fact. [one is day-dreaming, fig. gazing at the sky]

blue sky blond n. [1980s+] (drugs) high-potency marijuana from Colombia (cf. BLACK DOMINA n.). [the light colour of the leaves]

blue star n. [1980s+] (drugs) a variety of LSD, emblazoned with a blue star symbol (cf. A n.³).

blue-steel n. [1940s–60s] (US) a pistol. [its manufacture]

blue stocking n. [19C–1920s] (US) a puritan, esp. a Presbyterian. [SE blue stocking (see BLUE n.¹) and/or the repressive 'blue laws' passed in New England]

bluestone n. [late 19C–1940s] the very lowest-quality gin or whisky. [SE bluestone, copper sulphate or vitriol]

bluesuit n. [1950s] (US) a uniformed policeman (cf. BABY-BLUES n.²). [the uniform]

blue tape n. [late 18C–mid-19C] gin, esp. second-rate gin. [SE blue + TAPE n.]

blue tips n. [1970s+] (drugs) a depressant. [packaging of the capsule]

bluetit n. see TIT n.³ (6).

blue-tongue n. [1900s–50s] (Aus.) a roustabout, an itinerant labourer. [SE blue-tongue, an Aus. lizard of the genus Tiliqua, belonging to the family Scincidae; the ref. is to the sleepiness of such lizards]

blue train n. see BLOUTREIN n.

Blue 'Un, the *n.* [late 19C–1900s] the *Winning Post*, a sporting newspaper. [so named to distinguish it from the PINK 'UN, THE *n.* (1) and the BROWN 'UN, THE *n.*]

blue vein *n.* (*also* **blue veiner**) **1** [1970s] an erection. **2** [1980s+] (*Aus. prison*) the penis. [the vein that runs up the penis]

blue-veined custard chucker *n.* [1990s+] the penis. [BLUE VEIN *n.* + CUSTARD *n.* + SE *chucker*]

blue-veined havana *n.* [1990s+] penis; thus *smoke the blue-veined havana*, to fellate someone. [BLUE VEIN *n.* + SE *Havana* (cigar) + SMOKE v.⁸]

blue-veined junket pump *n.* (*also* **blue-veined porridge gun**, **...yoghurt gun**, **purple-helmeted junket gun**) [1980s+] the penis. [BLUE VEIN *n.*/SE *purple helmet* + SE *junket*/PORRIDGE GUN *n.*/*yoghurt* + *pump*/*gun*; note synon. RMC Duntroon (Aus.) *(purple-headed) junket pumper*]

blue-veined piccolo *n.* [1990s+] the penis (cf. ACCORDION *n.*). [BLUE VEIN *n.* + SE *piccolo*]

blue-veined root-on *n.* [1990s+] an erection. [BLUE VEIN *n.* + ROOT-ON *n.*]

blue-veined steak *n.* [1980s+] the penis (cf. BACON *n.*¹). [BLUE VEIN *n.* + SE *steak*]

blue-veined trumpet *n.* [1980s+] the penis (cf. ACCORDION *n.*). [BLUE VEIN *n.* + SE *trumpet*]

blue veiner *n. see* BLUE VEIN *n.*

blue-vein salami *n.* [1990s+] the penis, usu. in the context of fellatio (cf. BACON *n.*¹). [BLUE VEIN *n.* + SALAMI *n.*]

blue velvet *n.* [1960s–70s] (*drugs*) a mixture of an antihistamine and paregoric. [the 'smoothness' of its effects]

blue vials *n.* [1980s+] (*drugs*) LSD (cf. A *n.*³). [packaging]

blue whistler *n.* [mid–late 19C] (*US*) a bullet. [the *blue* lead in the bullet and the noise it makes; note the Civil War-era cannon named 'The Blue Whistler', used at the battle of Val Verde, NM]

bluey *n.*¹ **1** [mid-19C] a policeman (cf. BABY-BLUES *n.*²). **2** [mid-19C+] (*UK Und.*) lead. **3** [20C+] (*Aus./N.Z.*) (*also* **blue paper**) a summons, a traffic ticket. **4** [20C+] (*orig. Aus.*) (*also* **blue**) a red-headed person. **5** [1910s] (*Aus.*) a blue-tongued lizard. **6** [1910s+] (*Aus.*) a blue heeler, an Australian cattle dog. **7** [1990s+] a £5 note. **8** [1990s+] (*Aus.*) a can of Foster's lager. **9** [1990s+] (*Aus. prison*) a police warrant. [all SE *blue* + sfx -*y*]

bluey *n.*² [late 19C+] (*Aus.*) **1** a pack. **2** any form of luggage. [the trad. blue blanket that covered a pack]

bluey *n.*³ [20C+] a drinker of methylated spirits. [SE *blue*, the colour of meths + sfx -*y*]

bluey *n.*⁴ [1970s] (*UK prison/drugs*) any form of amphetamine-barbiturate mixture (cf. BAM *n.*²).

bluey *n.*⁵ [1990s+] a pornographic film. [BLUE *adj.*³]

bluey-cracking *n.* [mid-19C] stealing lead from the roofs of buildings. [BLUEY *n.*¹ (2) + CRACK v.³ (3)]

bluey-hunter *n.* [mid-19C] a thief who specializes in stealing lead from the roofs of houses and other buildings. [BLUEY *n.*¹ (2) + SE *hunter*]

bluff *n.*¹ **1** [mid-19C+] an excuse, a pretence. **2** [late 19C–1910s] deception. **3** [late 19C+] (*US*) an impostor, a deceiver, one who bluffs. [BLUFF v.]

bluff *n.*² [1950s+] a female homosexual who can alternate between active/passive roles. [BUTCH *n.*⁴ (1) + FLUFF *n.*¹ (3)]

bluff *v.* [late 18C–19C] to confuse, to mislead or deter by a show of confidence or superiority; to fob off. [20C use is SE/poker jargon: 'To impose upon (an opponent) as to the value of one's hand of cards, by betting heavily upon it, speaking or gesticulating or otherwise acting in such a way as to make believe that it is stronger than it is, so as to induce him to "throw up" his cards and lose his stake, rather than run the risk of betting against the bluffer' (*OED*); ult. a late 17C Und. term + ? link to SE *bluff*, a blinker for a horse]

bluff artist *n.* [1930s] an insincere person, a confidence trickster. [BLUFF v. + ARTIST sfx]

bluff as bull beef *phr. see* LOOK LIKE BULL-BEEF v.

bluff cuffs with the solid senders *n.* [1940s] (*US Black*) trousers with large, ballooning turn-ups.

bluffer *n.*¹ **1** [late 17C–mid-19C] (*UK Und.*) an innkeeper. **2** [1900s] (*US*) the landlord of a hotel. [? their 'bluff' manners, whether using *bluff* as hearty or as in setting out to deceive]

bluffer *n.*² [20C+] one who relies on an assumed manner to get away with lies. [BLUFF v.]

bluff-stakes *n.* [1910s] (*Aus.*) a deceitful attempt to influence someone else's conduct. [BLUFF v. + SE *stakes*]

bluff the rats *v.* [1910s–20s] to spread panic. [BLUFF v. + SE *rats*; they will thus 'leave a sinking ship']

blug *n.* [late 19C] (*US campus*) a stylish, socially admirable individual.

bluggy *adj.* [mid–19C–1920s] (*US*) a deliberate mispron. (as if one were drunk or otherwise verbally impaired) of BLOODY *adj.*¹.

blumpies *n.* [2000s] (*US Black*) female-to-male fellatio, while the man is seated on the toilet. [? SE *bump*]

blunderbuss *n.*¹ (*also* **blunderbust**) [late 17C–1960s] a fool, a clumsy, noisy fellow. [20C use is US. SE *blunderbuss*, a short gun with a large bore; its unwieldy clumsiness and inaccuracy are transferred to the human version]

blunderbuss *n.*² [1930s] (*US prison*) a sawn-off shotgun.

blunderbuss *n.*³ [1940s+] (*US*) any large motor vehicle that handles badly. [pun on SE *blunder bus*]

blunderhead *n.* (*also* **blunderkin**) [late 16C+] a fool. [SE *blunder* + -HEAD sfx (1)]

Blundstones *n.* [20C+] (*Aus.*) elastic-sided boots. [the proprietary name]

blunk *adj.* [1960s–70s] (*drugs*) intoxicated. [? BLOTTO *adj.* (1) or ? BLIND *adj.*¹ (1)+ SE *drunk*]

blunt *n.*¹ [18C–1910s] money, esp. cash in hand; thus *unblunted*, impoverished. [? Fr. *blond*, yellow, using as in other sl. terms the colour of the coin to denote its name; or ? f. SE *blunt*, referring to the edge of unmilled coins, or ?, least feasibly, f. Mr John *Blunt*, chief architect of the South Sea Bubble financial scandal of 1720]

blunt *n.*² [1980s] (*US drugs*) a hypodermic needle.

blunt *n.*³ [1980s+] (*orig. US drugs*) **1** (*also* **b**) a marijuana cigarette made of buds rolled in a tobacco leaf, taken from the wrapper of a Phillies Blunt cigar; thus the cigar itself (cf. PHILLY *n.*; VEGA *n.*). **2** marijuana. [note the cigar can be of any brand and can contain crack cocaine as well as marijuana; a version of the *blunt* is also sealed with a layer of honey]

blunt *n.*⁴ [1980s+] (*drugs*) any drug available in a blunt-ended capsule (cf. PILL *n.*⁴).

blunted *adj.* [mid-19C] (*US Und.*) supplied with money. [BLUNT *n.*¹]

blunted (up) *adj.* (*also* **blunted out**) [1980s+] (*drugs*) under the influence of a marijuana/cannabis cigarette. [BLUNT *n.*³]

blunt ken *n.* [mid-19C] (*US Und.*) a bank. [BLUNT *n.*¹ + KEN *n.*¹ (1)]

blunt magazine *n.* [early–mid-19C] a bank. [BLUNT *n.*¹ + SE *magazine*, a warehouse]

bluppy *n. see* BUPPIE *n.*

blur-an-ages/-ouns! *excl. see* TARE AN' AGES! *excl.*

blurb *n.* [20C+] (*orig. US*) **1** a brief piece of promotional material, typically as printed on the back of books. **2** promotional talk. **3** a short newspaper story. [coined 1907 by the US humorist Gelett Burgess (1866–1951), after designing a humorous bookplate (to be given away at a booksellers' dinner), which featured an attractive young woman (lifted from an advertisement for tooth powder or health tonic and suitably embellished by Burgess) whom he christened 'Miss Belinda Blurb']

blurb *v.* [1920s+] (*orig. US*) to promote. [BLURB *n.*]

blurry *adj.* [late 19C+] slurred mispron. of BLOODY *adj.*¹.

blurt *n.* [1990s+] the vagina; thus, a general term of abuse (cf.

BAMBA n.[1]). [? an anatomic var. on BLOT n.[2]; ? pun on 17C *blurt*, a constable, and CUNT n.[1] (1)/CUNT n.[2] (1)]

blurt *v.* [2000s] to ejaculate (cf. BLOSH v.). [play of SE *blurt out*]

blurt! *excl.* [early 17C] a general excl. of disdain. [SE *blurt*, to make a contemptuous puffing gesture with the lips, to puff in scorn]

blurter *n.* **1** [1960s+] the anus, the buttocks. **2** [2000s] a fart. [BLOT n.[2]/SE *blurt out*]

blushing *adj.* [1900s–30s] a euph. for BLOODY adj.[1].

blush like a black dog *v.* (*also* **blush like a blue dog**) [late 16C–early 19C] not to blush at all. [16C–17C = *black*; subseq. use is *blue*; a black/blue dog will not turn pink]

bluthered *adj. see* BLOOTERED adj.

B Luther Hatchett *n.* (*also* **bee-luther-hatchee, beluthahatchie**) [1920s–40s] (*US Black*) the ultimate in far-away, unpleasant places, the 'back of beyond'. [nonsense words]

bly *n.*[1] [1930s] (*UK Und.*) an oxyacetylene blowlamp, as used by safe-crackers. [SE *blow* + oxy]

bly *n.*[2] [1950s+] (*W.I. Rasta*) a chance. [? SE (*proba*)*bly*, (*possi*)*bly*]

bly-hunka *n.* (*also* **bly-hunker**) [19C] (*UK tramp*) a horse. [? Shelta]

BM *n.* [1990s+] a *BMW* car. [abbr.]

b.m. *n.*[1] [1920s–80s] (*gay*) a heterosexual person. [abbr. *baby maker*]

b.m. *n.*[2] [1960s+] **1** a visit to the lavatory. **2** a piece of excrement. [abbr. *bowel movement*]

b.m. *v.* [1960s+] to defecate. [B.M. n.[2] (1)]

b-m *n.* [1940s] (*gay*) a heterosexual man, i.e. *bloody masculine*.

b.m.o.c. *n.* (*also* **b.w.o.c.**) [1930s+] (*US campus*) a socially prominent, important person in the context of student life. [abbr. *big man/woman on campus*]

b-more ho *n.* [2000s] (*US Black*) a female who looks attractive from a distance, but not close-up. [abbr. *block* or *more* + HO n.[1] (4)]

b.m.t. *n.* [1990s+] unpunctuality (cf. AFRICAN (PEOPLE'S) TIME n.). [abbr. *Black Man's Time*, thus negative racial stereotyping]

b.m.t. *phr.* [1990s+] (*US Black*) a phr. designed to affirm one's authority, masculinity etc and thus reinforce one's argument. [abbr. *Black man talking*]

b.m.w. *n.* **1** [1980s+] the BMW motorcar, esp. popular as a status symbol and as a target for theft. **2** [1990s+] (*US Black*) a Black man who is working. [abbr. There are various 'translations' of *BMW*, 'Black man's wheels', 'Black man's wagon', 'Bob Marley and the Wailers', 'break my windows'. The actual name comes from that of the German manufacturer, *Bayerische Motor Werke*; (2) is apparently based on the 'luxury' of finding a job if Black]

b.n.i.c. *n. see* H.N.I.C. n.

b.o. *n.* [1930s+] **1** (*orig. US*) body odour; thus *b.o. juice*. **2** (*US campus*) deodorant. [abbr.; invented and widely popularized by the Lifebuoy soap advertising campaign *c.*1930]

b.o. *phr.* **1** [1950s+] go way, leave me alone. **2** [1990s+] (*US campus*) a general threat. [abbr. BUGGER OFF! excl./SE *beat on*]

bo *n.*[1] (*also* **boh**) [early 19C+] a fellow, a man, a friend, often as form of address, e.g. *Hey, bo*. [SE *boy*]

bo *n.*[2] **1** [late 19C+] (*Aus./US*) a vagrant, a tramp; also attrib.; thus ON THE BO phr. **2** [1960s+] (*US*) a tramp's young homosexual companion, thus a young, effeminate male homosexual. [abbr. HOBO n.[2] (1)]

bo *n.*[3] [1950s] (*US campus*) a bohemian. [abbr.]

bo *n.*[4] [1970s+] (*US drugs*) Colombian marijuana. [abbr. Colom*bo*]

bo *v.*[1] [1910s–20s] (*US*) to live as a tramp. [BO n.[2] (1)]

bo *v.*[2] [2000s] (*US Black*) to act like a fool. [? BO n.[1]/BO n.[2] (1) but note BOING-BOING n.]

boag *v.* [1980s+] (*US campus*) to vomit (cf. BARF v.). [BOGUE n.[2]]

boak *see under* BOKE.

boang *n. see* BOONG n.

boar *n.*[1] [mid-18C] (*UK Und.*) a shilling. [play on HOG n.[1] (1)]

boar *n.*[2] [1950s+] (*W.I.*) a straight cutlass with a hooked end. [? resemblance to a boar's tusks]

board *n.*[1] [early–mid-18C] a shilling (5p). [var. on BORD n.]

board *n.*[2] [20C+] (*UK tramp*) a picture sold in the street. [it is painted on a *board*]

board *n.*[3] [1970s] (*US*) the human leg. [? it gives one support]

board *v.*[1] **1** [early 17C] to woo a woman as a preliminary to love-making. **2** [early 17C–mid-19C] to have sexual intercourse.

board *v.*[2] [1930s–40s] (*US Black*) to eat. [SE *board*, a table, esp. one spread with food]

board a land carrack *v.* (*also* **board a ship in the bows**) [early 17C; early 19C] of a man, to have sexual intercourse. [BOARD v.[1] + fig. use of SE *land-carrack*, a coasting vessel]

board and plank *n.* [20C+] an American. [rhy. sl. = YANK n. (1)]

board a ship in the bows *v. see* BOARD A LAND CARRACK v.

boarding house *n.* **1** [mid-late 19C] (*US*) a brothel (cf. ACCOMMODATION HOUSE n.). **2** [mid-19C+] a prison (cf. BANDHOUSE n.; BOARDING SCHOOL n.; BURDON'S HOTEL n.; CASTIEAU'S HOTEL n.; CROSS-BAR HOTEL n.; CROWBAR HOTEL n.; ELLENBOROUGH'S LODGE n.; FAMILY HOTEL n.; FARRINGDON HOTEL n.; FREE HOTEL n.; GREEN-LIGHT HOTEL n.; GRAYBAR HOTEL n.; HARD-ROCK HOTEL n.; HOTEL n.; HOTEL CROWBAR n.; HOTEL DE GARVIE n.; KING'S HEAD INN (IN NEWGATE STREET), THE n.; MACGORREY'S HOTEL n.; MALABAR HILTON n.; SHERIFF'S HOTEL n.; SPIKE HOTEL n.; STONE HOTEL n.; TEETOTAL HOTEL n.; WINDSOR GROUP HOTEL n.). [note *the boarding house*, the old nickname for New York City's Tombs prison]

boarding-house reach *n.* [1900s–30s] (*US*) reaching rudely across the table to grab what one wants, rather than asking for it to be passed; also in fig. use, a snatch or grab. [the presumed selfishness of boarding-house guests, each of whom attempts to corral the most food for themself]

boarding scholar *n.* [late 17C–early 18C] (*UK Und.*) a prisoner.

boarding school *n.* **1** [late 17C–19C] a prison (cf. BIG SCHOOL n.; BOARDING HOUSE n.). **2** [late 18C] a brothel (cf. ACADEMY n.). [ironic use of SE]

board lodger *n.* [mid-19C] a prostitute who gives the owner of the brothel a share of her income in exchange for board and lodging.

boardman *n.* [mid-19C] 'men who take a stand on the curb of a public thoroughfare, and deliver prepared speeches to effect a sale of any articles they have to vend' (Hotten, 1859). [he augmented his pitch by displaying a board to which were affixed coloured pictures]

board of green cloth *n.* **1** [late 18C–mid-19C] a billiard table. **2** [19C] a card-table. [the green baize that covers it]

boards *n.* [1920s+] playing cards. [the material of which they are made]

boardsman *n.* [1970s] (*UK Und.*) one who plays the '3-card trick'. [BOARDS n. + SE *man*]

board stiff *n.* [1900s–40s] (*US*) a 'sandwich man'.

boar pussy *n.* [1950s+] (*US prison*) homosexual anal intercourse. [SE *boar*, generic for a male animal + PUSSY n. (2)]

boar's nest *n.* [late 19C+] (*US*) **1** anywhere, orig. a logging or mining camp, where only men live or only men are admitted. **2** an untidy room or house. [SE *boar* + *nest*; note the bar in the TV series *The Dukes of Hazzard*, set in America's bootlegging country, which was named the Boar's Nest, although it appeared to entertain women customers]

boasie *n.* (*also* **boasy**) [1950s+] (*W.I.*) **1** a show-off, a boaster. **2** a flashily dressed person. [BOASIE adj.]

boasie *adj.* (*also* **boasify, boasy, bosy**) [1930s+] (*W.I.*) proud, boastful, showy. [SE *boastful* and/or Yoruba *bosi*, proud and ostentatious]

boasy-naked *n.* [1950s+] (*W.I.*) a shameless show-off. [BOASIE adj. + SE *naked*]

boat _n._[1] **1** [late 18C+] (_US Black_) the vagina. **2** [1910s–30s] (_US_) an airplane. **3** [1910s+] (_US_) a Cadillac or any other large car?. **4** [1920s] (_US Und._) a freight car used to transport bootleg beer. **5** [1950s+] (_US_) a large foot. **6** [1950s+] (_US_) a large shoe or boot. [the size and supposed resemblance]

boat _n._[2] **1** [late 19C] (_UK tramp_) a jail sentence of 20 years or a life sentence; thus GET THE BOAT _v.; in the boat,_ sentenced to penal servitude. **2** [20C+] (_US Und._) transportation from one prison to another; the mode of transport is irrelevant. [BOAT _v._]

boat _n._[3] [1940s+] the face. [abbr. BOATRACE _n._[2]]

boat _n._[4] [1980s+] (_drugs_) **1** a cannabis cigarette (cf. BOMB _n._[4]). **2** phencyclidine (cf. ACE _n._[4]). [? one 'sails away']

boat _v._ (_UK Und._) **1** [mid–late 19C; 1990s+] to transport a convict. **2** [mid-19C–1900s] to sentence to penal servitude. [the ships that transported the convicts to Australia]

b.o.a.t. _n._ [1980s+] a semi-professional prostitute whose clients tend to be wealthy and whose payments are often less obvious than mere cash. [abbr. _bordering on a tart_]

boat and oar _n._ (_also_ **broken oar**) [1930s+] a prostitute (cf. BRASS (NAIL) _n._; CHAMPAGNE GLASS _n._; FORTY-FOUR _n._[2]; JANE SHORE _n._; JODRELL (BANK) _n._; KEWPIE _n._; MALLEE ROOT _n._; RORY (O'MOORE) _n._; SIX AND FOUR _n._; SLOOP OF WAR _n._; SWINGING DOOR _n._; TUG O' WAR _n._; TWO BY FOUR _n._). [rhy. sl. = _whore_]

boated _adj._ [mid–late 19C] sentenced to a long term in prison. [BOAT _v._ (2)]

boat-jumper _n._ [1980s+] (_US_) a recently arrived immigrant. [the pej. image of immigrants as stowaways who have to avoid immigration procedures by jumping from boat to dock]

boatrace _n._[1] [1910s+] (_US_) any form of 'fixed' sporting contest. [orig. horseracing jargon only; the winner 'sails in']

boatrace _n._[2] [1940s+] the face. [rhy. sl.]

boat ride _n._ [1960s] (_US_) a pleasant, undemanding task. [one 'sails' through it]

boat rider _n._ [1930s–40s] (_US Und._) a professional gambler who works the transatlantic liners.

boats, the _n._ [mid-19C] the penal hulks, moored on the Thames.

BOB _n._ (_also_ **b.o.b.**) [1990s+] (_US Black_) a derog. description of an unattractive female, lit. _big old bitch_.

Bob _n._[1] [18C] a generic term for man, on lines of such equally common names as Jack, Tom etc.

Bob _n._[2] [19C+] a euph. for _God,_ esp. in phrs. S'ELP ME (BOB)! excl. and NO SIREE (BOB)! (cf. COCK _n._[1]; COD _n._[1]; COKK _n._; DAD _n._[1]; DAG _n._[2]; DOD _n._[1]; DOG _n._[1]; GAD _n._[1]; GAR _n._[1]; GAW _n._; GED _n._; GODFREY _n._; GOG _n._; GOM _n._[1]; GOR _n._; GORRY _n._; GOSH _n._; GUINEA _n._[2]; GUM _n._[2]; GUY _n._[4]; HANNAH _n._; JOVE _n._; OD _n._[1]; UD _n._).

bob _n._[1] [mid-17C–18C] (_Can._) an act of sexual intercourse. [BOB _v._[2]]

bob _n._[2] [late 17C–mid-19C; 1920s–30s] a shoplifter's assistant, to whom the stolen goods are quickly passed by the actual lifter; 20C use refers to any shoplifter.

bob _n._[3] [18C] gin. [BOBSTICK _n._ (2), i.e. a shilling's worth of gin]

bob _n._[4] **1** [late 18C+] a shilling (5p). **2** [mid-19C+] money in general. **3** [1930s+] (_US_) $1. [BOBSTICK _n._]

bob _n._[5] [mid-19C] (_Aus._) 50 strokes of the lash (cf. BULL _n._[5]; CANARY _n._[4]; TESTER _n._[1]). [BOB _n._[4] (1); different numbers of lashes were named for different values of coin]

bob _n._[6] [1980s+] (_drugs_) **1** crack cocaine (cf. BASE _n._). **2** a marijuana cigarette. [abbr. BOBO _n._[2]]

bob _n._[7] [1990s+] (_US prison_) an effeminate male homosexual. [_bend over backwards_]

bob _n._[8] _see_ BOBTAIL _n._[3].

bob _n._[9] _see_ RUM BOB _n._ (3).

bob _adj._ [late 17C–mid-19C] (_UK Und._) **1** pleasant, satisfactory; usu. in phr. _all is bob._ **2** lively, cheery (cf. BOBBISH _adj._). [? SE _bob v.,_ i.e. to 'bob up and down' with good humour and energy]

bob _v._[1] **1** [late 17C–early 19C] (_UK Und._) to cheat, to deceive; thus

bobbed, cheated. **2** [late 18C] thrashed, beaten. [OF _bober,_ to deceive. SE to late 17C and found as such in Shakespeare]

bob _v._[2] [late 16C–18C] of a man, to have sexual intercourse. [SE _bob,_ a light, tapping blow or _bob,_ to move up and down; there may be a pun on SE _bob,_ to cut an animal's tail/TAIL _n._[2] (3)]

bob _v._[3] [1940s] to act in a nervous manner. [SE _bob_ (up and down)]

bob _v._[4] _see_ RALPH _v._

bob! _excl._ [mid–late 19C] (_UK society_) stop! enough! esp. as response to the drink pourer's request 'Say when?'.

bob and dick _n._ [1970s] the penis (cf. ALMOND _n._). [rhy. sl. = PRICK _n._ (2)]

bob and dick _adj._ [1970s+] sick, esp. after drinking. [rhy. sl.]

bob and hit _n._ **1** [late 19C] the vagina (cf. ALL QUIET _n._). **2** [1990s+] excrement (cf. ALI OOP _n._). [rhy. sl. = (1) PIT _n._[1] (1); (2) SHIT _n._[1] (1)]

bob and hit _v._ [1990s+] to defecate (cf. JOHNNY TAPP _v._; TOMTIT _v._). [rhy. sl. = SHIT _v._[1] (1)]

bob and weave _v._ [1920s+] to avoid direct action, whether confrontation, explanation, aggression etc. [boxing imagery]

bob a nob _phr._ [early 19C+] 1 shilling for each person, used when estimating the cost of meals, outings, tickets etc. [BOB _n._[4] (1) + NOB _n._[1] (1)]

bob around _v._ [mid-19C] to move quickly from place to place. [note Mathews, _Dict. Americanisms_ (1951): 'The popularity, and possibly the origin of this expression may have been occasioned by a popular song "Bobbing Around" sung by Stephen C. Masseet, a minstrel, in California mining camps during the fifties']

bobbasheely _n._ (_also_ **bobashilly**) [19C+] (_US_) a friend. [Choctaw _itibapishili,_ my brother]

bobbasheely _v._ [1930s+] (_US_) to saunter, to move in a friendly fashion, to mix with. [BOBBASHEELY _n._]

bobbe mayse _n. see_ BUBBE MAYSE _n._

bobber _n._[1] [mid–late 19C] a friend, a chum, a fellow worker. [Shropshire dial. _bobber,_ a term of friendly greeting, e.g. 'Hello bobber']

bobber _n._[2] [1940s–60s] (_Aus_) a female breast (cf. BOUNCERS _n._; HANGERS _n._; HEAVER _n._[1]; JIGGLER _n._; KNOCKERS _n._[2]; MASHERS _n._[2]; PANTERS _n._; POINTERS _n._; SHIRT-STRETCHER _n._; SWINGERS _n._; TREMBLERS _n._[1]; WALLOPIES _n._; WHAMDANGLERS _n._; WOBBLERS _n._). [? BUBBIES _n._ or ? it bobs up and down]

bobbers _n._ [1940s+] (_Aus._) the corks that are worn around the rim of a hat to keep away the flies. [SE _bob v._; their movement]

bobbery _n._ (_also_ **bobberie**) **1** [late 18C+] an argument, a disturbance. **2** [1910s] (_also_ **bobberee**) a hoax or trick, esp. if illegal. [Hind. _Bap re!_ O father!, a common excl. of surprise or grief. A popular term, apparently coined _c._1816 in the Raj, it had spread to such widely separated areas as East Anglia and Aus. by the mid-century. Note Anglo-Ind. hunting use _bobbery pack,_ a mongrel, mixed pack of hounds]

bobbie _n. see_ BOBBY _n._

bobbing _n._ [2000s] (_US Black_) a state of inactivity or unconsciousness. [? the _bobbing_ of one's lethargic head]

bobbins _n._ [1990s+] nonsense, rubbish; also used as a general negative. [Lancashire dial. _bobbin-winding,_ a term of disparagement or ridicule; + ? euph. for BALLOCKS _n._[2] (2)]

bobbish _adj._ (_also_ **bobborous**) [18C+] healthy, in good spirits, cheery. [BOB _adj._]

bobbishly _adv._ [19C] healthily, cheerily, often used as a farewell in letters; thus TOLBOBBISHLY adv. [BOBBISH _adj._]

bobble _n._ [1920s] (_US_) a mess, an error, a confusion.

bobble _v._ **1** [mid-17C–early 18C] to swindle, to cheat. **2** [1940s] (_US Und._) to excite a victim's suspicions, esp. when passing them short change. [(1) could be a misprint or misreading for BUBBLE _v._[1]; E.P. cites a correspondent who found 'an "indignant gentleman captain" writing to the Navy Board' _c._1688 and using the word, even though the SE _bobble,_ to bob up and down, was not found until 1812]

bobbles *n.* **1** [late 19C] the testicles (cf. BALLS n.[1]). **2** [20C+] (*US Black*) gaudy, flashy, ostentatious jewellery. [SE *baubles*]

bobborous *adj. see* BOBBISH adj.

bobby *n.* (*also* **bobbie**) **1** [mid-19C+] a British or Aus. policeman (cf. BILLY n.[6]). **2** [20C+] (*US*) an Englishman. **3** [1980s+] (*Aus. prison*) a prison officer. [Sir Robert Peel (1788–1850), who established the force in the 19C. 'The term is, however, older. The official square-keeper, who is always armed with a cane to drive away idle and disorderly urchins, has, time out of mind, been called by said urchins *Bobby the Beadle*. Bobby is also an old English word for striking, or hitting, a quality not unknown to policemen' (Hotten, 1860)]

bobby atkins *n.* [1900s–10s] a private soldier. [var. on TOMMY ATKINS n. (1)]

bobby-dangler *n.* [1930s+] (*Can.*) the penis. [play on BOBBY-DAZZLER n. + SE *dangle*]

bobby-dazzler *n.* (*also* **dickey dazzler, mickey dazzler**) [late 19C+] anything or anyone seen as exceptional, wonderful. [? intensification of dial. *bobby*, smartly dressed, in high spirits (cf. BOBBISH adj.) + SE *dazzler*]

bobby martin *n.* [20C+] (*Aus.*) a carton. [rhy. sl.]

Bobby Moore *n.* [1960s+] a door. [rhy. sl.; ult. UK footballer *Bobby Moore* (1941–93)]

bobby peeler *n.* [mid–late 19C] a policeman (cf. BILLY n.[6]). [Sir *Robert Peel* (for ety. *see* BOBBY n.)]

bobby rocks *n.* [20C+] (*Aus.*) a pair of socks. [rhy. sl.]

bobby's helmet *n.* (*also* **bobby's hat**) [1930s+] the glans penis. [BOBBY n. (1) + SE *helmet/hat*; the shape of the 'bell end']

bobbyshop *n. see* BABBIE-SHOP n.

bobby's labourers *n.* [late 19C] volunteers who joined up as special constables during the Fenian scares of the 1860s. [BOBBY n. (1) + SE *labourer*]

bobby soxer *n.* (*also* **bobby sox**) [1940s+] (*US*) a teenage girl wearing bobby-socks; thus adj. *bobbysox*, girlish. [orig. describing the fans of Frank Sinatra in 1940s and thus teenage girls of the late 1940s–50s who enjoyed pop music and its ancillary pleasures]

bobby-twister *n.* [late 19C] a thug who will stop at nothing, even killing a policeman. [BOBBY n. (1) + SE *twist*]

Bob Cryer *n.* [2000s] a liar. [rhy. sl.; ult. UK politician *Bob Cryer* (1934–94)]

bob cull *n.* [late 17C–18C] (*UK Und.*) a pleasant, good-natured person. [BOB adj. + CULL n.[1] (2)]

bob, harry and dick *adj.* [late 19C–1900s] sick, usu. from drinking. [rhy. sl.]

bob hop *n.* [1980s] (*N.Z.*) a dance. [BOB n.[4] + HOP n.[1] (3)]

Bob Hope *n.* **1** [1960s+] (*Aus.*) soap. **2** [1960s+] (*drugs*) cannabis (cf. JACK FLASH n.; JOHNNY CASH n.; OLLY n.; ROPE n.[3]; SOAP n.[7]). **3** [1990s+] (*drugs*) crack cocaine (cf. APPLEJACK n.). [rhy. sl.; (2) = DOPE n.[1] (6); (3) = COKE n.[1] (4); ult. the comedian and film star *Bob Hope* (1903–2003)]

bob in *n.* (*Aus./N.Z.*) **1** [late 19C+] the payment of a shilling (5p) into a common pot, esp. as used for buying drinks. **2** [1940s] (*Aus.*) a dicing game in which all players contribute a shilling (5p); the winner then buys the round of drinks. [BOB n.[4] (1) + SE *in*]

bob it *v.* [mid-19C] to abandon, to give up. [BOB! excl.]

bob ken *n.* (*UK Und.*) **1** [late 17C–early 19C] a house considered worth robbing. **2** [late 18C–early 19C] a house occupied by thieves. [BOB adj. + KEN n.[1] (1)]

bobkhes *n.* (*also* **bopkes, bubbkis, bubkhes, bubkis, bupkes, bupkis, buppkes**) [20C+] **1** an absurd idea, an insulting sum, price or proposition. **2** nothing (in sense of a return, a reward), esp. in show business use. [Yid. *bobkhes*, goat droppings/Yid. *bupkes*, beans]

Bob Marley *n.* [2000s] cocaine (cf. BARLEY n.[2]). [rhy. sl. = CHARLIE n.[9] (1); ult. the Jamaican Reggae musician *Bob Marley* (1945–81)]

bob-my-nag *n.* (*also* **billy-my-nag**) [late 19C] the penis. [NAG n.[2]]

bob my pal *n.* [mid–late 19C] a girl. [rhy. sl. = GAL n. (1)]

bobo *n.[1]* **1** [1940s+] a fool (cf. BOZO n.[1]; DILDO n.; DIMBO n.; DIMMO n.[3]; DOZO n.; DUBBO n.; DUMBO n.; DUMMO n.; EGGO n.; EL DORKO n.; GADSO n.; GARBONZO n.; IGNO n.; IMBO n.; IMBY n. JAZZBO n.; JUMBO n.[1]; MACO n.[2]; MONGO n.[1]; REMO n.; SCHLEMBO n.; STUPO n.; THICKO n.). **2** [2000s] a generic insult, an fat, ugly oaf. **3** [2000s] a *bourgeois bohemian*. **4** [2000s] (*US Black*) a generic term for a White man. [? Sp. *bobón*, a clumsy simpleton or popular children's entertainer, *Bobo* the Clown or Sp. *bobo*, stupid; (3) also abbr.]

bobo *n.[2]* (*drugs*) **1** [1950s+] marijuana. **2** [1990s+] crack cocaine (cf. BASE n.). [(1) abbr. BOBO BUSH n.; (2) ? BOBO n.[1] (4), i.e. its whiteness]

bobo *adj.* [1980s+] (*US Black/campus*) drunk or intoxicated with a drug. [? BOBO n.[1] (1) or ? BOBO n.[2]]

bobo bush *n.* [1930s+] (*drugs*) marijuana (cf. AFRICAN BUSH n.). [? BOBO n.[1] (1) + BUSH n.[5] (1)]

bo-bo jockey *n.* [1950s] (*US drugs*) a cannabis smoker. [BOBO n.[2] (1) + JOCKEY n.[3] (8)]

bobo-johnny *n.* [20C+] (*W.I.*) **1** a bogeyman, an imaginary monster conjured up to frighten naughty children. **2** a peasant, an unsophisticated country person (cf. ALVIN n.). [? Yoruba *buburu*, bad, evil + JOHNNIE n.[2] (1)]

bobol *n.* [1920s+] (*W.I.*) fraud and corruption, practised by senior figures in government, business or any position of power; thus *make/run a bobol*, to organize a fraud; *bobol(ize)*, to steal a company's or the public's funds; *bobolism*, large-scale corruption; *bobolist*, a fraudster. [? Fr. Creole *Vaval*, a masque king of the St Lucia carnival, symbolically thrown into the sea on Ash Wednesday. Orig., in the 1920s, the term became associated with corrupt 'speculators' trading between Martinique and St Lucia and thence to the larger world of fraud. Note Earl Lovelace's *The Dragon Can't Dance* 221: 'Bobolee was a sort of effigy of Judas, fellars got an old jacket and old pants and stuffed it up with straw to beat on Good Friday, and all the boys with big sticks beating it and running behind it, crying: "Beat! Beat! Beat the bobolee!"']

bobolition *n.* [early–mid-19C] (*US*) abolition.

bob on *v.* [1920s–30s] (*orig. milit.*) to await anxiously. [SE *bob* v.; the image of a cork bobbing on choppy water]

bob one's baloney *v.* [1990s+] to masturbate (cf. BEAT ONE'S MEAT v.). [SE *bob*, move up and down/BOP v. (1) + BALONEY n.[2]]

bob powell *n.* [20C+] (*Aus.*) a towel. [rhy. sl.; ? ult. US composer *Bob Powell* (b.1961)]

bobsey twins *n.* [1950s–80s] (*US camp gay*) the police, when working as a pair. [the children's adventure story *The Bobbsey Twins*, created 1904 by 'Laure Lee Hope' (Edward Stratemeyer) + ref. to UK BOBBY n. (1)]

bob squash *n.* [20C+] **1** a wash. **2** a public convenience; thus *work the bob*, for a pickpocket to rob jackets and coats that have been hung up while people wash their hands. [rhy. sl.]

bobstay *n.* [late 18C–early 19C] the frenum or ligament of the penis. [naut. jargon *bobstay*, a rope that holds down the bowsprit of a ship, counteracting the upward force of the foremast stays]

bobstick *n.* [late 18C–mid-19C] **1** a shilling (5p). **2** a shilling's worth. [ety. unknown]

bob's your uncle *phr.* [20C+] everything will be absolutely fine, there is nothing to worry about; sometimes prefixed by *and*. [according to A.J. Langguth, *Saki* (1981), f. the apparently nepotistic choice by Tory leader Robert Cecil of his nephew Arthur Balfour as Chief Secretary for Ireland in 1900, a decision that was both surprising and unpopular]

bobtail *n.[1]* (*also* **bob-tail, bob tail**) **1** [early 17C] an unpleasant person. **2** [mid-17C–early 19C] an impotent man, a eunuch. **3** [mid-17C–mid-19C] a prostitute (cf. BANBURY n.). [pun on SE *bobtail*, a horse or dog with its tail cut short; thus in (1) a *cur*, (3)

SE *bob*, go up and down + TAIL n.[2] (3) + a horse is also good for a RIDE n.[1] (1)]

bobtail n.[2] **1** [early 19C] a dandy. **2** [late 19C] a waiter. [the wide skirts of his coat]

bobtail n.[3] (*also* **bob**) [1900s] (*US milit.*) a dishonourable discharge; the soldier thus discharged.

bobtail adj. [19C+] (*US*) worthless. [poker jargon *bobtail flush*, *bobtail straight*, hands that have only 3 of the 5 cards required to make them bettable]

bobtail (car) n. **1** [late 19C] (*US*) 'a small tram-car horsed by a single animal, and on which the only official is a driver, whose office it is to collect fares and generally perform the duties of conductor in addition to his own' (Farmer, *Americanisms Old New*, 1889). **2** [1920s–30s] (*US tramp*) a short local freight train. [SE *bobtail*, a horse's tail that has been docked or cut short]

bob up v. [late 19C+] to appear (unexpectedly).

bob-wire n. [1910s–30s] (*US*) barbed wire. [pron.]

Boche n. (*also* **Bosche**) [1910s+] **1** a German, esp. a German soldier. **2** the German language. [post-WW1 use is historical; f. Fr. *caboche*, head, or *Alboche*, a modification of *Allemand*, German; Fraser & Gibbons, *Soldier & Sailor Words & Phrases* (1925), suggest a root 'about 1860, as low-class Parisian slang, meaning "bad lot"'; and that the transfer to a description of Germans came after the Franco-Prussian War of 1870–1 when the enemy was still 'les Prussiens']

bock n. [1960s] (*US*) a Bohemian, a Czech. [Ger. *Bock*, he-goat, or SE *bock*, a sweetish dark beer, originating in Germany (as *Eimbockbier*), brewed in winter to be drunk in spring]

boco n. [1940s–50s] (*UK juv.*) the head. [var. on BOKO n.]

bocoo adv. see BEAUCOUP adv.

bod n. **1** [1930s+] a corpse. **2** [1950s+] a person, a 'body'; often in comb. with adj. to denote a job, e.g. *legal bod*, a lawyer. **3** [1960s+] the human body, esp. as an object for sexual intercourse, e.g. *give out bod*, make oneself available for sex. **4** [1960s+] (*US campus*) a physically attractive person of the opposite sex. **5** [1980s] the chassis or body of a vehicle. [SE *body*; (2) the *OED* offers cits. for 1788, 1813 but suggests that, while still meaning 'a person', they may in fact abbr. Scot. *bodach*, a peasant, a churl, rather than *body*]

bod adj. [1960s+] (*US campus*) outstanding, exceptional. [abbr. BODACIOUS adj. (1)]

bodach n. [1920s] a general term of abuse. [Irish/Scopt. *bodach*, a churl or lout]

bodacious adj. (*also* **bodashes**, **bowdacious**) **1** [mid-19C+] (*orig. US*) excellent, wonderful, very enjoyable. **2** [mid-19C+] (*US*) audacious, unceremonious, insolent. **3** [1930s+] (*US campus*) of a young woman, attractive, esp. possessed of large breasts. **4** [1970s+] (*orig. US*) exciting, impressive. [SE *bold* + *audacious*. Coined in the 19C, the term was 'relaunched' on 1970s Citizen's Band radio and popularized with the release of the hit teen film *Bill and Ted's Excellent Adventure* (1989). Major, *Juba to Jive: A Dict. of Afro-American Slang* (1994), suggests earlier US Black use, and root in Bantu *botesha*, grand, big]

bodaciously adv. (*US*) **1** [mid-19C+] (*also* **bidaciously**) impressively, entirely. **2** [1930s+] extremely, very. [BODACIOUS adj.]

bodacious tatas n. [1980s+] (*US campus*) large breasts. [BODACIOUS adj. (3) + TA-TAS n.[2]]

bodaggle n. [1970s] (*US*) a masculine lesbian. [BULL-DAGGER n.]

bodashes adj. see BODACIOUS adj.

boddy n. [1980s] (*Aus.*) a *bodice*. [abbr. + sfx -*y*]

bodelicious adj. [1990s+] (*US*) excellent, first-rate. [BODACIOUS adj. (1) + -LICIOUS sfx]

bodge n. see BODGIE n. (1).

bodger n. [1940s+] (*Aus.*) anything or anyone second-rate, fake or otherwise worthless. [SE *bodge*, to mend badly, to patch up]

bodger adj. [1940s+] (*Aus.*) **1** fraudulent, second-rate, worthless. **2** of names, assumed, false. [BODGER n.]

bodgie n. **1** [1950s+] (*also* **bodgie-boy**, **bodge**) the equivalent of a Teddy boy (cf. WIDGIE n.). **2** [1960s+] (*Aus.*) anything worthless; thus *pull a bodgie*, to pose as something one is not. **3** [1980s] a misfit, a person who does not fit in. **4** [1980s] a loafer. [BODGER n.; f. the post-war black market in American-made cloth and attempts by crooked salesmen to pass off inferior cloth as this; when young men started using US accents in order to aggrandize themselves were termed *bodgies*, a fig. ref. to the cloth. Note McGill, *Dict. of Kiwi Slang* (1988): 'Origins various: English word "bodge", to patch or mend clumsily; "bodger", WWII slang for a worthless person; US teen slang "bodgie" for young male jitterbug with long and curly hair and too large sports jacket; E.P. guesses distortion of "boysies" for boys'; (1) post-1960s use historical]

bodgie adj. **1** [1940s+] (*Aus.*) fake, counterfeit. **2** [1980s] of a job, unprofessional; thus v. *bodgie up*. [BODGER adj.]

bodice-ripper n. [1980s+] a historical novel (or film), with a greater than usual emphasis on sex, esp. the seduction or even rape of the heroine. [the period costumes and their fate]

bo-dick n. see BO-JACK n.

bodikin n. see BAWDY KEN n.

bodini n. (*also* **budini**) [1960s+] (*US*) the penis. [Ital. *bodino*, blood sausage]

bodkin n.[1] [17C–19C] the penis (cf. AX n.[2]). [SE *bodkin*, a large needle or small dagger, esp. a large needle-shaped instrument with a blunt, knobbed point]

bodkin n.[2] [mid-17C–mid-19C] a person who is wedged between 2 others, esp. when there is room for only the original couple; thus *sit bodkin* or *ride bodkin*, for a coach passenger to ride wedged between 2 people when there is not room for a 3rd person. [SE *bodkin*, a long, thin object, usu. a pin; the earliest cognate use is in John Ford's *The Fancies* (1638) when it refers to the person squashed between 2 others in the same bed]

bo-dollar n. see BEAU-DOLLAR n.

body n. **1** [late 17C+] (*UK Und.*) a person, esp. a suspect or wanted criminal or one who is to be 'framed' for a crime; thus [1960s+] *give someone a body*, to inform, to betray the names of one's criminal associates, usu. as an exhortation, *Go on, John, give us a body (and we'll be kinder to you)*. **2** [mid-19C–1960s] (*US*) a generic term for women, esp. as sex objects. **3** [1960s] (*US*) sexual intercourse. **4** [1960s] (*US campus*) an athlete.

body v. [early 19C] to hit someone in the body; thus *bodier*, a body-blow.

body and breeches adv. [late 19C–1900s] (*US*) completely, wholly.

body bag n. **1** [early–mid-19C] an undershirt, a vest. **2** [mid-19C] a shirt. **3** [1990s+] a condom.

body-binder n. [early 19C] (*orig. boxing*) a waistcoat or a broad belt.

body cheese n. see CHEESE n.[2] (2).

body come down v. [1990s+] (*W.I.*) to lose a significant amount of weight.

body companion n. [mid-19C] (*US*) a louse.

body count n. [1970s+] (*US*) those people who are present. [Vietnam war jargon *body count*, the number of dead enemy bodies counted after a battle/operation]

body-cover n. [mid-late 19C] (*US Und.*) an overcoat.

body exchange n. [1960s–70s] (*US*) anywhere that people can meet in the hope of finding a new sexual partner, e.g. a singles bar, a party.

body guard n. [mid-19C] (*US*) a louse.

body lover n. **1** [1940s–60s] a homosexual who prefers rubbing and fondling a body to anal penetration or fellatio. **2** [1960s] a homosexual who derives sexual pleasure from body-builders.

body of divinity bound in black calf n. [mid-18C–early 19C] a parson. [a description usu. attached to a Bible]

body-pop v. (also **pop**) [1980s+] (orig. US) to break-dance.

body-popper n. [1980s+] (orig. US) a break-dancer. [BODY-POP v.]

body queen n. [1960s+] (gay) one who looks primarily for partners who specialize in body-building. [SE body + QUEEN n.² (1)/QUEEN SFX (2)]

body shop n.¹ [1970s+] (US) anywhere that people can meet in the hope of finding a new sexual partner. [the implication is that one can 'buy' a new partner]

body shop n.² **1** [1970s+] (US) a morgue, a cemetery. **2** [1990s+] (US Black) a hospital. [a play on the SE, which, as referenced in (2), refers to the 'mending' of automobiles]

body-slangs n. [early 19C] body irons. [SE body + SLANG n.² (1)]

body-snatcher n. (orig. US) **1** [late 18C–mid-19C] a bailiff. **2** [late 18C–mid-19C] a cat-stealer. **3** [early–mid-19C] a resurrectionist. **4** [mid-19C] a cabman. **5** [mid-19C–1930s] a policeman (cf. BEAT-POUNDER n.). **6** [late 19C–1930s] a promiscuous, 'forward' woman, esp. a prostitute. **7** [late 19C+] an undertaker. **8** [1910s] a doctor. [ext. use of SE; (3) SE after mid-19C; note WW1 Aus. milit. body-snatcher, a member of a raiding party, the aim of which was to bring back prisoners; UK milit. body-snatcher, a sniper]

body wax n. (also **wax**) [late 19C+] human excrement. [? play on SE ear wax]

boep n. (also **beer-boep**) [1970s+] (S.Afr.) a paunch, a beer belly. [Afk. boepens, a paunch]

boer n. [1960s+] (S.Afr. Und.) any member of the S.Afr. security forces, whether in the services, the police force or the prison department. [Du. boer, a farmer, and among various fig. uses a pej. name for an Afrikaner]

boer baroque n. [1980s] (S.Afr.) vulgar, if expensive, interior decoration. [SE Boer + baroque, 'a florid style of architectural decoration, which arose in Italy in the late Renaissance and became prevalent in Europe during the 18th century' (OED)]

boere-kugel n. see KUGEL n.

boeretroos n. [20C+] (S.Afr.) strong, flavoursome black coffee. [Afk., lit. 'Boer's solace']

boers n. [late 19C] (S.Afr.) S.Afr. whisky or brandy, distilled in the colony. [Du. boer, a farmer and thus an Afrikaner]

boesman n. [1950s+] (S.Afr.) a derog. term of address to an Indian or Coloured person. [Afk. boesman, bushman]

boet n. (also **boetie, boeta**) (S.Afr.) **1** [mid-19C+] a brother, usu. the eldest or favourite. **2** [20C+] a friendly mode of address between Whites. **3** [1970s] a pej. nickname for a Black male employee. **4** [1970s+] a political fellow-traveller. **5** [1970s+] an Afrikaner or any overly aggressive, macho male. [Afk. boet, brother]

boetie-boetie adj. [1950s–70s] (S.Afr.) overly friendly, using flattery with an ulterior motive, sycophantic. [BOET n. (1)]

boette n. [1920s] (US tramp) a female tramp. [BO n.² (1) + SE fem. sfx -ette]

b.o.f. n. [2000s] a tedious, conventional, killjoy older person. [abbr. boring old fart (FART n. (2))]

boff n.¹ (orig. US) **1** [1920s–60s] a strong blow. **2** [1930s+] an act of sexual intercourse. **3** [1990s+] a person seen as a sex object, a potential person to have sexual intercourse with. [SE buff, a blow, stroke, buffet]

boff n.² [1940s+] orig. entertainment use, a laugh, a joke. [BOFFO adj.]

boff n.³ [1990s+] (UK juv.) a child who is considered too keen on work, a 'teacher's pet'. [? SE boffin]

boff v. (orig. US) **1** [1920s+] to hit, to assault. **2** [1930s+] to copulate with (cf. BANG v.¹). **3** [1930s+] to masturbate (cf. BANG THE BISHOP v.; CHUG v.²; CLAW v.; DIDDLE v.¹; FLIP v.²; FLOG v.¹; FRIG v.; GRIND v.¹; HANDLE v.; JACK v.³; JACKAL v.; JERK v.⁴; JOSTLE v.; LARK v.; LEVY v.; MASH v.¹; MESS v.; MILK v.²; PULL v.⁷; RINSE v.¹; RUCK v.; SEW v.; SHABBA v.; SHAG v.¹; SHAKE v.¹; SHANK v.³; SNAKE v.³; SPANK v.²; STROKE v.¹; STROP v.²; STRUM v.; THRAP v.; TONK v.; TUG v.; WANK

v.; WAZ v.; WHACK v.¹). **4** [1950s] to lose out, to lose money, to cause someone to lose their money. **5** [1960s] to fail, to blunder, to make a mistake. **6** [1960s] (US campus) to caress sexually, to 'neck'. [BOFF n.¹]

boffer n. **1** [1930s+] a masturbator. **2** [1970s+] (US) one who has sexual intercourse. [BOFF v.]

boffin n. [1940s+] any form of scientific expert, orig. those RAF scientists who were working on radar. [ety. unknown; although, according to Robert Watson-Watt (1892–1973), the inventor of radar, the term 'has something to do with an obsolete type of aircraft called the Baffin, something to do with that odd bird, the Puffin' (Three Steps to Victory, 1957)]

boff joint n. [1930s] a brothel (cf. BADGER-CRIB n.). [BOFF v. (2) + JOINT n.⁴ (3)]

boffo n.¹ [1920s+] (US) $1. [ety. unknown]

boffo n.² (also **boppo**) [1930s–60s] (US prison) a year (in jail). [? BOFF v. (1)/BOP v. (1)]

boffo n.³ [1960s+] a big laugh, a very funny joke. [BOFFO adj.]

boffo adj. [1940s+] (US) superb, magnificent, excellent, usu. show business use. [fig. use of BOFF v. (1) + -o sfx (7)]

boffo! excl. [1940s+] (US) an excl. indicating suddenness, abruptness. [BOFFO adj.]

boffola n. **1** [1940s+] (orig. US) a laugh, esp. a loud 'belly laugh', usu. show business use. **2** [1950s] (US) a success, usu. show business use. [BOFFO adj. + -OLA sfx]

bog n.¹ (also **bogs**) [late 18C+] a lavatory; thus [early 19C] go to bog, to use the lavatory. [BOGHOUSE n.; 'a low word, scarcely found in literature, however common in coarse colloquial language' (OED)]

bog n.² [1980s] (Aus.) a racist term aimed at any non-White individual.

bog v.¹ **1** [16C] to defile with excrement. **2** [16C; late 19C] to defecate. **3** [1960s+] to make a mess of. **4** [1990s+] to look dirty, unkempt. [defined by the OED, which offers no cits., as 'bog, intr. To exonerate the bowels; also trans. to defile with excrement' and as 'a low word, scarcely found in literature, however common in coarse colloquial language'; note also SE bog, to be enmired in a bog]

bog v.² [1960s+] to wet the end of a cigarette while smoking it. [SE bog, a marsh]

bog v.³ [1990s+] (UK juv.) to stare at someone in (what is seen as) an aggressive manner.

bogan n. [1980s+] (Aus./N.Z.) **1** an uncouth person. **2** one who is mindlessly conventional. **3** a social misfit. [ety. unknown; ? link to BODGIE n. (3)]

bog Arab n. [1990s+] a derog. term for an Irish person (cf. BOGGER n.¹; BOGHOPPER n.; BOGLANDER n.; BOG-RAT n.; BOGTROTTER n.; BOG-WOG n.; CHAW-MOUTH n.; CHINAMAN n.²; DEAR JOY n.; DONKEY n.¹; DONOVAN n.¹; FLANNEL MOUTH n.; GAS-HOUSE MICK n.; GREEN NIGGER n.; HARP n.¹; POTATO-EATER n.; SHAMROCK n.; SPUD n.²; TEA CADDY n.; THATCHED HEAD n.; WHITE WOG n.). [SE bog + ARAB n.¹; racial stereotyping]

bogart n. [1950s+] (US Black) a bully; thus pull a bogart, to act tough; jump bogart, to become aggressive. [Humphrey Bogart (1899–1957), whose roles often portrayed a gangster or tough-guy]

bogart v. (also **bogard**) **1** [1950s+] (orig. US Black) to act aggressively, in a bullying manner. **2** [1960s+] to retain something selfishly, esp. to monopolize or smoke too much of a cannabis cigarette (cf. BOGART A JOINT v.). **3** [1970s+] to waste time, to play around. **4** [1990s+] (US campus) to leave. **5** [1990s+] (US teen) to steal. **6** [2000s] (US campus) to take something with someone else's knowledge but without their approval. [BOGART n.]

bogart adv. [1960s] (US) aggressively, unrestrainedly. [BOGART v. (1)]

bogart a joint v. **1** [1960s+] to salivate on a cannabis cigarette. **2** [1960s+] (drugs) to take more than one's fair share of a cannabis cigarette. **3** [1970s+] (*US campus*) to steal, to take an unfair share. [BOGART v. (2) + JOINT n.[5] (3); the legend fact of Humphrey *Bogart*'s alleged greediness in this area and the sl. it generated was popularized in the film *Easy Rider* (1969)]

bogblocker *n.* [1980s+] a general term to denote anything particularly unpleasant. [BOG n.[1] + SE *blocker*; the image is of some obstruction, prob. faecal, blocking a lavatory]

bogbrush *n.* [1960s+] a lavatory brush. [BOG n.[1] + SE *brush*]

bog bumf *n.* [20C+] lavatory paper. [BOG n.[1] + BUMF n. (2)]

bogel *v.* [1990s+] (*US campus*) to do nothing. [? BOGLE n.]

bogey *n.*[1] (*also* **bogie, bogy**) **1** [mid-19C+] a landlord. **2** [1920s] an informer. **3** [1920s+] a policeman, a detective. [BOGIE n.[1]; play on this devilishness]

bogey *n.*[2] (*also* **bogie**) (*Aus.*) **1** [mid-19C+] a bathe, a wash. **2** [1940s] a bathing-place, a bath. [? Aboriginal]

bogey *n.*[3] (*also* **bogie, bogy**) [1930s+] **1** a piece of dried mucus. **2** a nickname given to a man with prominent, wide nostrils. [? SE *boggy*, soft, spongy; thus the consistency of such pieces of mucus]

bogey *n.*[4] [1940s–50s] (*US*) a Black person. [BOOGIE n.[2] (1)]

bogey *n.*[5] *see* BOGIE n.[1].

bogey *adj. see* BOGUS adj. (1).

bogey *v.*[1] [mid-19C+] (*Aus.*) to bathe; thus *bogying*, bathing. [BOGEY n.[2] (1)]

bogey *v.*[2] [1980s+] (*US*) to act greedily, esp. in consumption of drugs. [BOGART v. (2)]

bog-eyed *adj.* [1940s+] having tired eyes, the result of too little sleep or too much alcohol. [one's eyes seem 'muddy']

bogey up *v. see* BOGGY UP v.

bogger *n.*[1] [20C+] a derog. term for an Irish person (cf. BOG ARAB n.). [SE *bog*, the supposed orig. dwelling-place of many immigrants]

bogger *n.*[2] *see* BUGGER n.[1] (1).

boggeral *n.* (*also* **boggerall, bokkerol**) [1960s+] (*S.Afr.*) nothing at all. [pron. of BUGGER-ALL n.]

boggering *adj. see* BUGGERING adj.

boggie bear *n. see* BOOGER BEAR n.

boggie up *v. see* BOGGY UP v.

boggin' *adj.* **1** [1950s+] of a film, X-rated. **2** [1960s+] (*Scot.*) dirty, smelly, horrible, a general term for anything unpleasant. [SE *bog*]

boggins *n.* [mid-19C–1920s] (*Aus.*) plenty, a great deal. [*AND* states 'ety unknown' but ? BOG IN v.]

boggle *n.* [mid-19C] a mess, a mistake, an error. [BOGGLE v. (1)]

boggle *v.* **1** [mid-17C–1950s] to blunder, to do something very badly. **2** [late 18C+] to amaze, to confuse, to disorientate. [SE *boggle*, to fumble; (2) popularized by General Alexander Haig's celebrated remark 'It boggles the mind']

boggled *adj.* [1990s+] confused, disorientated. [BOGGLE v. (2)]

boggle-de-botch *n.* (*also* **boggledybotch**) [mid-19C] a mess, a blunder, a bungling. [BOGGLE n. + SE *botch*, a mess, an error]

boggler *v.* [early 19C] a prostitute, a promiscuous woman. [SE *boggler*, a fumbler]

boggling *n.* [early 19C] (*US*) hesitating unnecessarily, delaying, finding something difficult. [? BOGGLE v. (2)]

boggy up *v.* (*also* **bogey up, boggie up**) [1940s+] to turn informer. [BOGEY n.[1] (2)]

boghopper *n.* [20C+] **1** a derog. term for an Irish person (cf. BOG ARAB n.). **2** (*US*) a peasant, an unsophisticated rural person (cf. BOGMAN n.; BOGTROTTER n.; CLOD n.[1]; CLOD-BUSTER n.; CLOD-CRUSHER n.; CLODHOPPER n.; CLOD-JUMPER n.; CLOD-KNOCKER n.; CLOD-MASHER n.; CLOUTED-SHOE n.; CLUMPERTON n.; HIGH-SHOE n.; HOBNAIL n.; PUNCH CLOD n.; SHITKICKER n.; SOD-BUSTER n.). [SE *bog* + *hopper*; (1) racial stereotyping]

boghouse *n.* [mid-17C+] a lavatory, a privy (cf. BACKHOUSE n.). [BOG v.[1] + SE *house*]

bogie *see also under* BOGEY.

bogie *n.*[1] (*also* **bogey**) [mid-19C+] the Devil; thus OLD BOGEY n.

bogie *n.*[2] [2000s] (*US Black*) a cigarette. [? BOGART v. (2)]

bogie house *n.* [late 19C+] (*Aus.*) a bathroom. [BOGEY n.[2] + SE *house*]

bog-in *n.* [1910s+] (*Aus.*) a heavy meal. [BOG IN v. (1)]

bog in *v.* (*also* **bog into**) (*orig. Aus.*) **1** [late 19C+] to eat heartily. **2** [late 19C+] to work hard, to do anything energetically; thus as imper. **3** [1910s] to interfere in. **4** [1910s+] to get started. **5** [1910s+] to not stand on ceremony. [? SE *bog*, the image is of 'getting stuck in']

bogish *adj.* (*also* **boguish**) [1930s–40s] (*US Black*) fake, spurious. [var. on BOGUS adj. (2)]

boglander *n.* [late 17C+] an Irishman (cf. BOG ARAB n.). [SE *bog* + *land*]

bog Latin *n.* **1** [late 18C+] fake Latin. **2** [1940s+] tinkers' Gaelic. [the term is found as synon. with SE *shelta*, a form of jargon used by tinkers, which is based on Gaelic and rendered further incomprehensible to non-adepts by the inversion or arbitrary alteration of initial consonants]

bogle *n.* [1990s+] (*W.I./UK/US Black teen*) a dance originated by Jamaican Gerald Levy in 1991 and popularized in song by artists such as Buju Banton. [its main characteristic is bending the body backwards]

bogman *n.* **1** [late 19C] (*UK prison*) a prisoner working outdoors. **2** [1940s+] (*Irish*) (*also* **bog person**) a general term of abuse, presuming rural origins and general backwardness (cf. BOGHOPPER n.).

bog off *v.* [1950s+] (*orig. RAF*) to go away, usu. as a dismissive excl. *bog off!* [BOG n.[1]; euph. for FUCK OFF! excl. (1); ult. var. on BUGGER OFF v.]

bog-oranges *n.* [19C] potatoes. [SE *bog*/BOGLANDER n. + SE *oranges*; racial stereotyping, the main constituent of the Irish diet is supposedly potatoes]

bog-ordinary *adj. see* BOG-STANDARD adj.

bog person *n. see* BOGMAN n. (2).

bog queen *n.* [1960s+] (*UK gay*) a homosexual man who frequents public toilets for sex. [BOG n.[1] + QUEEN n.[2] (1)/QUEEN SFX (2)]

bog-rat *n.* [20C+] an Irish person (cf. BOG ARAB n.). [SE *bog* + *rat*; racial stereotyping]

bogroll *n.* [20C+] lavatory paper. [BOG n.[1] + SE *roll*]

bogs *n. see* BOG n.[1].

bog-shop *n.* [mid-19C–1900s] an outside lavatory (cf. BACKHOUSE n.). [BOG n.[1] + SE *shop*]

bog-standard *adj.* (*also* **bog-ordinary**) [1980s+] average. [despite assumed link to BOG n.[1] the *OED* suggests ultimate ety. in *box-standard*, 'motoring, engineering, and other technical contexts: in standard manufactured form, unmodified; (hence) basic, unexceptional']

bogtrotter *n.* **1** [mid-17C+] a derog. term for an Irish person; thus *adj.*, *bogtrotting* (cf. BOG ARAB n.). **2** [mid-19C+] a peasant, a yokel (cf. BOGHOPPER n.). [lit. 'one who runs through the bogs'; thus those who live among the peat bogs of Ireland; racial stereotyping. B.E. states that the orig. use was 'Scotch or North Country Moss-troopers or High-Way Men'. Camden, *Britannia* (1605) used the term to describe the inhabitants of the 'debatable' borders between Scotland and England]

bogue *n.*[1] [19C] (*US*) a native of Florida. [Choctaw *bog*, a stream or creek; thus the swamps that typify the topography of southern Florida]

bogue *n.*[2] [1960s+] (*US drugs*) the sickness that follows an addict's withdrawal from regular narcotic use. [ety. unknown; ? BOGUS adj.; Smitherson suggests Hausa *boko*, bad, fake]

bogue *n.*[3] [1970s] (*US*) a stupid, unpleasant person. [BOGUS adj. (1)]

bogue *adj.*[1] **1** [1950s+] (*US teen*) fake, unsophisticated, naïve. **2** [1960s+] (*US campus/teen*) disgusting, unappealing. [BOGUS adj.]

bogue *adj.*[2] [1960s–70s] (*US drugs*) suffering from narcotic withdrawal symptoms. [BOGUE n.[2]]

bogue v. [1980s] (*US campus*) to bring down, to subdue. [BOGUE n.²]

boguey adj. (*also* **boogy**) [1970s] (*US drugs*) suffering from heroin withdrawal. [BOGUE n.²]

boguish adj. *see* BOGISH adj.

bogus n. **1** [early–mid-19C] (*US*) a machine used to produce counterfeit money. **2** [early 19C+] counterfeit money. **3** [20C+] (*US*) a fake, a spurious imitation. **4** [1970s–80s] (*UK Black*) a lie, a 'story'. [note *OED*: 'Dr S. Willard, of Chicago...quotes from the Painesville (Ohio) *Telegraph* of July 6 and Nov. 2, 1827, the word bogus as a n. applied to an apparatus for coining false money. Mr Eber D. Howe, who was then editor of that paper, describes in his *Autobiography* (1878) the discovery of such a piece of mechanism in the hands of a gang of coiners at Painesville, in May 1827; it was a mysterious-looking object, and some one in the crowd styled it a "bogus", a designation adopted in the succeeding numbers of the paper. Dr Willard considers this to have been short for "tantrabogus", a word familiar to him from his childhood, and which in his father's time was commonly applied in Vermont to any ill-looking object. He points out that "tantarabobs" is given in Halliwell, *Dict. of Archaic and Provincial Words* (1847), as a Devonshire word for the devil; bogus seems thus to be related to bogy etc'. Farmer, *Americanisms Old New* (1889), posits an Italian swindler called Borghese, working across the southwest US distributing fictitious notes, cheques etc, *c*.1837; this surname was gradually changed to Borges and thence bogus. The writer J.R. Lowell, also cited by Farmer, opted for Fr. *bagasse*, the refuse of sugar-cane after the juice was extracted]

bogus adj. [mid-19C+] **1** (*also* **bogey**) a general term of disapproval, unpleasant, undesirable, untrustworthy, unfair. **2** (*also* **bogy**) fake, spurious. **3** (*US campus*) great, excellent. **4** (*US campus*) pretentious, pointless, stupid. [BOGUS n.]

bogus v. [1990s+] (*US*) to fool, hoodwink. [BOGUS adj. (2)]

bogus beef n. [1930s+] (*US Black*) a groundless complaint. [BOGUS adj. (2) + BEEF n.² (2)]

bogwash n. [1990s+] (*UK juv.*) an initiation rite whereby the victim has their head pushed into a lavatory pan which is then flushed. [BOG n.¹ + SE *wash*]

bog-wog n. [1990s+] a derog. term for an Irish person (cf. BOG ARAB n.; WHITE WOG n.). [SE *bog* + WOG n.¹ (3); racial stereotyping]

bogy *see also under* BOGEY.

bogy adj. *see* BOGUS adj. (2).

boh n. *see* BO n.¹.

bohak/bohawk n. *see* BOHUNK n.

bohee n. *see* GEORGE BOHEE n.

boheize n. [2000s] (*US Black*) a house. [ety. unknown; ? BO n.¹ + pron. SE *house*]

boheme n. (*also* **bohem, bohemian, bohim**) [1980s+] (*US campus*) one who identifies with the 1960s. [SE *Bohemian*, an artist, literary person or actor, who leads a free, vagabond or irregular life, despising accepted conventions]

Bohemie n. [1960s] (*US*) a Czech or Slavic immigrant. [SE *Bohemian*, i.e. Czechoslovakian]

bohn n. (*US campus*) **1** [mid-19C] a translation of a text, classical or otherwise, for the illegitimate use of students (cf. ANIMAL n.³). **2** [late 19C–1900s] a studious person. [*Bohn*'s Classical Library; but reinforced by BONE v.³]

bohn v. [1900s] to work hard. [BOHN n. (2)]

boho n.¹ [1920s–30s] (*US*) a Czech immigrant. [abbr. SE *Bohemian*, a Czechoslovakian]

boho n.² **1** [1960s+] a cultural non-conformist, a bohemian. **2** [1980s+] (*US campus*) in ironic, teasing use, one who identifies with the 1960s. [abbr. SE *Bohemian*, a literary/social 'vagabond']

boho adj. [1960s+] (*orig. US*) bohemian. [BOHO n.² (1)]

bohunk n. (*also* **bohak, bohawk**) [20C+] (*US*) **1** a Slav immigrant f. Eastern Europe. **2** an oafish, dull, if muscular person. **3** a second-rate person. **4** an East European language. **5** in pl., as a term of address, the equivalent of 'my boys'. [SE *Bohemian* + *Hungarian*]

bohunk adj. [20C+] (*US*) Slavic. [BOHUNK n. (1)]

bohunkus n. (*also* **bohunky**) [1920s+] (*US*) the buttocks, thus fig. oneself, e.g. in phr. *get your bohunkus out of here!* [BOHUNK n. (2) + ? echoic of buttocks slapping onto a hard seat]

boil n. [17C] the alarm.

boil v. **1** [late 16C–early 17C] to find out, to unmask, to betray. **2** [mid-19C–1930s] (*US*) to rush along. **3** [late 19C+] to be angry; thus *boiled up, boiling up*, angry. **4** [1950s] (*US*) to annoy, to infuriate.

boil and pus n. [1980s] (*Aus.*) an omnibus. [rhy. sl.]

boil down v. [late 19C] (*US Black*) to correct or rebuke.

boiled n. [19C–1910s] *boiled* beef, *boiled* mutton or *boiled* potatoes. [abbr.]

boiled adj. **1** [late 19C+] (*also* **boiled as an owl**) drunk. **2** [1920s+] angry, furious.

boiled dinner n. [1940s] (*US*) an Irishman. [culinary stereotyping]

boiled dog n. [1910s+] (*Aus./N.Z.*) snobbery, stand-offishness, 'side'. [? SE *boiled shirt* + DOG n.⁵ (1)]

boiled lobster n. [late 19C–1900s] a soldier. [LOBSTER n.¹ (1); cooked lobsters turn red/pink]

boiled-owlish adj. [late 19C] having a washed-out complexion with staring, sleepy eyes, the result of working all night. [but note DRUNK AS A BOILED OWL phr.]

boiled rag n. (*also* **boiled linen**) [mid-19C–1910s] (*Aus./US*) a starched dress shirt. [joc. var. on BOILED SHIRT n.]

boiled shirt n. (*also* **biled shirt**) **1** [mid-19C+] a starched dress shirt. **2** [1970s] (*US*) a respectably dressed man. [earlier use can denote, in US, simply a white shirt; such shirts were lit. boiled in the wash to remove the starch but note BALDFACED SHIRT n.]

boiled stuff n. [early 17C] prostitutes, viewed collectively. [used by Shakespeare in *Cymbeline* (1610); the ref. is to the sweating tubs, used to treat venereal diseases]

boiler n.¹ [late 19C–1960s] (*US*) the stomach. [play on SE]

boiler n.² **1** [20C+] (*US*) a tobacco pipe. **2** [1910s–50s] (*US*) an automobile; thus *on the hot boiler*, stealing automobiles. **3** [1920s–30s] (*US Und.*) an illegal still or its minder. **4** [1930s] (*US drugs*) a spoon used to heat the mixture of water and powdered narcotic prior to an injection. **5** [1950s+] (*Aus. prison*) any form of homemade device used to heat water. [the steam or smoke that they all produce]

boiler n.³ [1960s+] **1** an old woman, without any remaining sexual appeal; often as *old boiler*. **2** a woman, usu. an unattractive one. **3** (*US*) a quarrelsome, irascible person. [the old, tough birds used as boiling chickens]

boiler acid n. (*also* **boiler compound**) [1940s–60s] (*US*) extremely unpleasant-tasting coffee.

boiler factory n. [1920s] (*US*) an unappealing young person.

boilerhouse n. [2000s] one's wife. [rhy. sl. = SE *spouse*]

boilermaker n. **1** [1920s+] a 50/50 mix of mild and brown ale. **2** [1940s–50s] (*US*) beer with a whisky chaser, the US working man's trad. drink. [? the preferred drink of a SE *boilermaker*, or strong enough to clean a boiler. Subseq. use of (2) is SE]

boilerplate n. [20C+] (*US*) clichéd writing; thus ext. to any banal creation. [legal and journ. jargon *boilerplate*, standard practice used by lawyers (the regular clauses in any contract) or the media (the basic syndicated wire-service stories used throughout the US newspaper system)]

boiler-plated adj. [late 19C+] (*US*) absolutely dependable and consistent. [SE *boiler-plate*, the iron used in the manufacture of boilers]

boiler-room n. [1930s+] (*US*) any room full of noisy, energetic activity, e.g. a political campaign headquarters, a newspaper cityroom, a room used by illegal bookmakers, stock swindlers or confidence tricksters.

boiling n.[1] [early–mid-17C] a betrayal, an unmasking. [BOIL v. (1)]

boiling n.[2] [mid-19C+] absolutely everything or everybody. [abbr. WHOLE BOILING LOT, THE n.]

boiling adj. **1** [mid-19C+] (US campus) angry. **2** [late 19C] (US) drunk. [BOILED adj./BOIL v. (3)]

boiling-out n. [20C+] (US) a scolding, a telling-off. [BOIL v. (3)]

boilo n. [1930s] (US) hot, illicit whisky. [SE boil + -o sfx (1)]

boil off the stomach v. [1970s] (US) to vomit copiously.

boil one's cabbage twice v. (also **chew one's cabbage twice, sell...**) [late 19C+] (US) to repeat oneself.

boil one's lobster v. [late 18C–early 19C] for a clergyman to become a soldier. [SE lobster/LOBSTER n.[1] (1); the unboiled lobster is blue-black, thus resembling a clergyman's black garb; the boiled lobster turns red, recalling the soldier's scarlet uniform]

boil-out n. [1940s–50s] (US drugs) total abstention from narcotics in the hope of achieving complete withdrawal.

boilover n. [late 19C+] (Aus.) in sport, spec. horseracing, an upset, the failure of a favourite to win.

boil-pricker n. [1960s–70s] (US) a pointed shoe. [SE boil, a pustule + pricker]

boil someone's cabbage v. [1920s] (US) of a man, to have sexual intercourse. [SE boil + CABBAGE n.[7] (1)]

boil the billy v. [1950s+] (Aus.) to make a cup of tea. [an actual 'billy' (trad. associated with cooking in the open) need not be used; the term can be applied to a kettle]

boil-up n.[1] **1** [1920s–30s] (Aus./US/N.Z. tramp) a period during which tramps rest from the road, wash and repair clothes, have a meal and do similar 'housekeeping'. **2** [1980s] (Aus. prison) the illicit making of tea. [the SE boiling of the water for the clothes/tea]

boil-up n.[2] [1940s] (Aus.) an argument. [one's temper boils up (and over)]

boil up v. [1920s–30s] (Aus./US/N.Z. tramp) to rest from the road, in order to wash and repair clothes etc. [BOIL-UP n.[1] (1)]

boing v. [1990s+] (US) to kill, to shoot dead. [? BONK v.[1] (1)]

boing-boing n. [1960s+] (US) a tourist. [SE boing, the sound of elastic snapping back; the image is of the head twanging backwards and forwards as its owner gazes at the big city sights]

boink v. [1980+] (US) to have intercourse with. [BONK v.[1] (2)]

bo-ink-um n. [19C] guts, stamina, endurance. [ety. unknown]

boja n. [1950s] (W.I.) an untrustworthy person. [? BUDGE n.[1] (1) or ? BODGER n. or ? SE botcher]

bo-jack n. (also **bo-dick**) [1970s+] (US Black) **1** a form of address to a male. **2** the scrotum, the penis (cf. BALL-BAG n.). [BO n.[1] + (1) JACK n.[6]/DICK n.[1]; (2) JACK n.[3] (1)/DICK n.[4] (1)]

bojangles n. [2000s] (US Black) the testicles (cf. BANGERS n.). [the idea of the testicles 'jangling' against each other; ult. the song 'Mr Bojangles']

bojie n. see BOOJEE n.

bok n. (S.Afr.) **1** [1950s] a young woman, a girlfriend. **2** [1970s+] an enthusiast; thus bok for, 'up for', game for. **3** [1970s+] a hero, a masculine or athletic male. [Afk. bok, a 'flame', a beau]

bokbaard n. (also **bokbaardjie**) [1910s+] (S.Afr.) a goatee beard. [Afk. bok, a goat + baard, a beard]

bokdrol n. [1970s] (S.Afr.) **1** a chocolate-covered peanut. **2** anything, e.g. a hairstyle, that resembles a pile of goat droppings. [Afk. bok, goat + drol, dropping]

boke n.[1] [mid-19C–1960s] (US) the nose. [BOKO n. (1)]

boke n.[2] (also **boak**) [1930s+] (Ulster) vomit. [BOKE v.]

boke v. (also **boak, bowk**) [1930s+] to vomit (cf. BARF v.). [synon. Scot.; ult OE bealcan, to belch, 'throw up']

bok for adj. see BOK n. (2).

bokin-a-smowl n. [1980s+] (US drugs) smoking a pipe or other container filled with cannabis. [joc. reversal]

bokkerol n. see BOGGERAL n.

bokkie n. [1950s+] (S.Afr.) **1** an affectionate form of address, esp. to women. **2** a girlfriend. [Afk. bok, a kid (antelope, goat etc) + dimin. sfx -ie]

boko n. (also **koboko**) **1** [mid-19C+] the nose. **2** [late 19C] a person. **3** [1900s] (Aus.) a person or animal blind in 1 eye; thus boko-eyed, half-blind. [(1) ? BEAK n.[2] (1) and/or COCONUT n.[1]; Ware suggests an alternative ety.: the clown Joseph Grimaldi's (1779–1837) trademark tapping of his nose with the comment, C'est beaucoup, that's plenty]

boko adj.[1] [late 19C] too much, excessive (cf. BEAUCOUP n.). [Fr. beaucoup]

boko adj.[2] [1950s] (UK juv.) penniless, broke.

boko-smasher n. [late 19C–1900s] a thug. [BOKO n. (1) + SE smasher, lit. 'nose-smasher']

bokum n. see BUNKUM n.

bola adj. [1990s+] (US campus) a general term of approval. [? college sports cheer boola-boola]

boldacious adj. [1980s] (US Black) excessive behaviour (over-aggressive, arrogant, unrestrained etc) that is inappropriate for a situation. [SE bold + BODACIOUS adj. (2)]

bold as a miller's shirt phr. [late 18C–early 19C] very bold. [pvb 'bold as a miller's shirt, which every days takes a rogue by the collar']

bold as brass adj. [late 18C+] arrogant, impudent, outspoken, shameless. [var. on SE brazen]

boldface adj. **1** [late 17C–early 18C] brazen, impudent. **2** [20C+] (W.I./UK Black) capable of petty crime.

boldrumptious adj. [late 19C–1900s] presumptuous. [SE bold + presumptuous]

bold thing, the n. [1980s+] (Irish) sexual intercourse.

boldyke n. see BULL-DYKE n.

bolicky adj. see BOLLACKING adj.

Bolivian marching powder n. (also **Bolivian brain food, Bolivian flake**) [1970s+] (drugs) cocaine (cf. ANDES CANDY n.; BIRDIE POWDER n.). [Bolivia, like Colombia, is a major source of cocaine]

bolix adj. see BALLOCKS n.[2] (6).

bollacking adj. (also **bolicky**) [1970s] (Irish) a coarse intensive. [BALLOCKS n.[1] (1)]

bollemakiesie adv. [1920s+] (S.Afr.) head-over-heels. [Afk. bollemakiesie, a somersault]

bollicking adv. [1920s] (US) a general intensifier, e.g. bollicking great, bollicking awful. [BALLOCK n. (1)]

bollicky adj. [1960s+] (Aus.) naked. [BALLOCK n. (1)]

bollicky bare-ass adj. [1990s+] absolutely naked. [BOLLICKY adj. + BARE-ASS adj. (1)]

bollicky bill adj. [late 19C+] naked. [BALLOCK n. (1); Bollicky Bill (the Sailor), a character in a coarse late 19C song]

bollicky naked adj. see BALLOCK NAKED adj.

Bollinger bolshevik n. [1980s+] a liberal, one who preaches socialism but espouses a capitalist lifestyle, the intensity of whose pronouncements on social problems is in direct proportion to their ability to escape their existence (cf. CADILLAC COMMIE n.; CHAMPAGNE SOCIALIST n.; LIMOUSINE LIBERAL n.; PARLOUR PINK n.). [Bollinger champagne + Bolshevik]

bollix see under BALLOCKS and its combs.

bollock see also under BALLOCK and its combs.

bollock n. [1970s+] (UK society) a ball (i.e. a party). [pun on BALLOCK n. (1)]

bollock-all n. see FUCK-ALL n.

bollockbag n. [1990s+] the scrotum, container of testicles (cf. BALL-BAG n.). [BALLOCK n. (1) + SE bag/BAG n.[1] (1)]

bollockbrain n. [1960s+] a general term of abuse. [BALLOCK n. (1) + sfx -brain]

bollockchops n. [1990s+] a derog. term of address. [BALLOCK n. (1) + CHOPS n.[1] (1)]

bollocko adj. [1950s+] naked. [BALLOCK NAKED adj. + -o sfx (7)]

bollocks see also under BALLOCKS and its combs.

bollocks *n. see* DOG'S BALLOCKS n. (2).

bollock snot *n.* [2000s] semen (cf. COCK PUKE n.; COCK SNOT n.; GLUE n.[1]; GOO n.[1]; GOO-GOO n.[3]; JOLLOP n.[2]; KNOB SNOT n.; LATHER n.[1]; LUMP n.[3]; OIL n.[1]; OINTMENT n.[2]; PASTE n.[1]; PECKER SNOT n.; SLIME n.[1]; SPEW n.; SPLOOGE n.; SPOO n.; SPOOCH n.; SPOOGE n.; SPUME n.; STICKY n.[1]; TALLOW n.). [BALLOCK n. (1)+ SNOT n.[1] (4)]

bollock yoghurt *n.* [1990s+] semen (cf. BABY GRAVY n.). [BALLOCK n. (1) + SE *yoghurt*]

bollo-loco *n.* [1970s] (*US/P.R.*) a promiscuous woman or girl. [Sp., lit. 'crazy chick']

bollox see also under BALLOCKS and its combs.

bollox up *v.* [1930s] (*US*) to go. [fig. use of BALLOCK n. (1)]

bollux see under BALLOCKS and its combs.

Bolly *n.* [1980s+] *Boll*inger champagne. [abbr. + sfx -*y*]

bolly *n. see* BALLOCKING n.[2].

bolly-eyed *adj.* [1990s+] having unfocused eyes. [? Yorks. dial. *boll*, left-handed]

bolo *adj.*[1] [1940s–50s] incorrectly aligned. [? milit. use *Bolo*, a spy (ult. one *Bolo Pasha*, executed for treason in 1918) or abbr. *Bolshevik*, i.e. fig. something that 'is not straight'; note Vietnamera US Army *bolo*, to ruin or fail deliberately]

bolo *adj.*[2] [1940s+] (*W.I.*) hard. [ety. unknown]

bologna *n.* [1940s+] a penis (cf. BACON n.[1]). [Bologna SAUSAGE n.[1] (1)]

boloney see under BALONEY.

bolshie *n.* (*also* **bolshy**) [1910s+] **1** a Bolshevik. **2** in weak use of (1), a left-winger, a socialist. **3** an unconventional person (as judged by a conservative), an opponent of the status quo. [abbr. Rus. *Bolshevik*, the majority; 'a member of that part of the Russian Social-Democratic Party which took Lenin's side in the split that followed the second Congress of the party in 1903, seized power in the "October" Revolution of 1917, and was subsequently renamed the (Russian) Communist Party' (*OED*)]

bolshie *adj.* (*also* **bolshy**) **1** [1910s+] uncooperative, obstructive, subversive. **2** [1930s+] left-wing. [BOLSHIE n.]

bolshiness *n.* [1970s+] rebelliousness, anti-authoritarianism. [BOLSHIE adj. (1)]

bolt *n.*[1] [19C+] a swift departure. [BOLT v. (1)]

bolt *n.*[2] [mid-19C] the throat. [? SE *bolt*, to swallow hastily, to gulp down whole]

bolt *n.*[3] **1** [mid-19C–1900s] (*US campus*) the act of deliberately missing a class or meeting. **2** [mid-19C–1900s] (*US campus*) the cancellation of a class or meeting. **3** [late 19C–1910s] (*Aus./UK*) an act of running away, of absenting oneself, an escape from prison. [BOLT v.]

bolt *n.*[4] [1980s] (*US campus*) a very handsome man.

bolt *n.*[5] [1980s+] (*drugs*) **1** phencyclidine (cf. ACE n.[4]). **2** isobutyl nitrite (cf. AIMIES n.). **3** amphetamine (cf. A n.[2]). [tradename for amyl nitrite]

bolt *v.* **1** [late 17C–19C] to leave, to run off. **2** [early 18C] to rush. **3** [mid-19C–1900s] (*US campus*) to cut a class. **4** [mid-19C+] of a man or usu. a woman, to run off with a lover. **5** [mid-19C+] to leave one's spouse, to jilt someone. **6** [late 19C+] (*Aus. prison*) (*also* **do the bolt**) to escape from prison. **7** [1990s+] (*US campus*) to defecate in one's pants. [use of SE *bolt*, a missile, as an image of moving at speed; (1) 20C+ use is SE]

bolter *n.*[1] (*also* **bolter of the Mint, bolter of Whitefriars**) [late 17C–18C] (*UK Und.*) 'one that doth but peep out of Whitefriars, and retire again like a rabbit out of his hole' (Shadwell, *The Squire of Alsatia*, 1688). [SE *bolter*, a fugitive from justice. *Whitefriars*, near St Paul's Cathedral, and the *Mint*, near Southwark, were both well-known refuges for 17C–18C villains]

bolter *n.*[2] **1** [early 19C] (*Aus.*) a person once serving a sentence of transportation who absconds and remains free long enough (7 years) to be given an official pardon in the newspaper. **2** [early 19C+] one who flees their obligations and responsibilities; thus

esp. a woman who runs away from her husband, home and family. **3** [mid-19C] (*Aus.*) a bushranger. [SE *bolt*, to run off, esp. used of horses and, as such, suitable for the upper/upper-middle class milieu in which it is used; (2) the *locus classicus* is in Nancy Mitford's novel *The Pursuit of Love* (1945), where an errant figure is known simply as 'The Bolter']

bolter's chance *n.* [1940s+] (*Aus.*) an outside chance; thus *not have a bolter's chance*, to have no chance at all. [BOLTER n.[2] (1)]

bolt from the blue *n.* [late 19C] anything wholly unexpected, usu. unpleasant. [the image is of a thunderbolt; 20C+ use SE]

bolt-in-tun *v.* [early 19C] to run off, to escape; found in such deliberately oblique phrs. as *he's gone to bolt-in-tun* or *the bolt-in-tun is concerned*. [var. on BOLT v.; *Bolt-in-Tun*, a well-known London inn]

B.O.L.T.O.P. *phr.* [1940s+] *better on lips than on paper*, written over an 'X' (signifying a kiss) on a love letter or envelope (cf. B.U.R.M.A. phr.; E.G.Y.P.T. phr.; F.U.J.I.A.M.A. phr.; H.O.L.L.A.N.D. phr.; I.L.U.V.M. phr.; I.T.A.L.Y. phr.; L.Y.K.A.H. phr.; N.O.R.W.I.C.H. phr.; P.O.L.O. phr.; S.W.A.L.K. phr.). [abbr.]

bolts-and-nuts *adj. see* NUTS-AND-BOLTS adj.[1].

boltsprit *n.* [late 17C–early 18C] the nose; thus *break one's boltsprit*, to lose one's nose as a result of syphilis. [SE *bowsprit*, a large spar extending from the stem of a vessel, to which the foremast stays are fastened]

bolt the moon *v. see* SHOOT THE MOON v.[1].

bolus *n.* [late 18C–1960s] an apothecary; a doctor. [SE *bolus*, a large pill, part of their stock-in-trade]

boman *n.* (*UK Und.*) **1** [17C–18C] a gallant, a sweetheart. **2** [late 18C–early 19C] a thief. [? Fr. *beau*, good-looking + SE *man*]

boman *adj.* [early 18C] (*UK Und.*) safe. [? E.P. suggests fig. use of BOMAN n.]

bomb *n.*[1] **1** [1910s+] (*US*) a surprise event, a sensational development. **2** [1950s] (*US*) a very sexy woman. **3** [1950s+] a large sum of money; often in MAKE A BOMB n. **4** [1950s+] (*orig. UK theatre*) a major success. **5** [1960s] (*US campus*) the grade of B (cf. ACE n.[6]). **6** [1960s+] (*orig. US theatre*) a disaster, a flop. **7** [1960s+] (*US campus*) a difficult examination. **8** [1970s+] (*US*) a hard blow (with a fist).

bomb *n.*[2] [1930s–40s] (*US prison*) an egg, usu. boiled.

bomb *n.*[3] **1** [1950s–70s] (*US*) a fast car or motorcycle. **2** [1950s+] (*orig. Aus./N.Z./US*) a dilapidated, run-down old car. **3** [1970s] (*US prison*) a roll of burning toilet paper, used to heat water or food. **4** [1980s+] (*Aus./N.Z. prison*) an illicit gadget used to heat water (for brewing tea etc).

bomb *n.*[4] (*drugs*) **1** [1950s+] a very large and potent cannabis cigarette (cf. A-BOMB n.; BOAT n.[4]; BOMBER n.[2]; CHRONIC n.; CLIMB n.[2]; CRIPPLE n.[2]; CRYING WEED n.; DREAM n.[4]; DYNAMITE n.[2]; GIGGLE-STICK n.[2]; GIGGLEWEED n.; GOOD GIGGLES n.; HAPPY CIGARETTE n.; HAPPY GAS n.; HAPPY GRASS n.; HAPPY HERB n.; HAPPY STICKS n.; HAZE n.; JOY n.; JOY HEMP n.; JOY SMOKE n.; JOYSTICK n.[2]; JOY WEED n.; LAUGHING GRASS n.; LAUGHING WEED n.; LOC n.[1]; LOCO n.; LOCOWEED n.; LOVE WEED n.; OOH-WEE n.; PARACHUTE n.[2]; POCKET ROCKET n.[1]; PURPLE HAZE n.; ROCKET n.[2]; SPUTNIK n.; STRATOCRUISER n.; TORPEDO n.[2]). **2** [1960s] (*Aus.*) an illegal stimulant given to a racing animal. **3** [1960s–70s] heroin of well-above-average purity. **4** [1960s+] any form of pill containing sleep-inducing or depressant drugs (cf. BARBIT n.). **5** [1980s+] crack cocaine (cf. BASE n.). **6** [1990s+] (*US*) a package of drugs. **7** [2000s] amphetamine, mixed into a drink and swallowed.

bomb, the *n.* (*also* **da bomb, the bombness**) [1960s+] (*US Black/campus*) the best, the ultimate.

bomb *adj.* [1970s+] very good, excellent, best. [BOMB, THE n.]

bomb *v.*[1] **1** [1940s+] (*Aus.*) to dope a horse. **2** [1960s+] (*US*) to hit hard. **3** [1970s] (*US*) to criticize harshly. **4** [1980s+] (*orig. US Black*) to spray-paint a subway or railway car, a building or similar space with graffiti.

bomb *v.*[2] **1** [1960s] (*US campus*) to get the grade 'B' on a test or examination. **2** [1960s+] (*US*) to fail, to do badly; also BOMB OUT v. **3** [1970s] (*US*) (*also* **bomb off**) of machinery or other equipment, to break down, to malfunction. **4** [1990s+] of an experience, to be bad or disappointing. [BOMB n.[1]]

bomb *v.*[3] **1** [1960s+] to move, esp. to drive fast; usu. as *bomb along*, *bomb around*, *bomb down* (the road), *bomb off*, to rush around (aimlessly). **2** [1970s] to work hard at something.

bomb *v.*[4] **1** [1970s+] (*US campus*) to get very drunk. **2** [2000s] (*drugs*) to consume a drug, e.g. amphetamine.

Bombay bloomers *n.* [1970s] (*Aus.*) baggy shorts. [? orig. worn by servicemen in India]

Bombay bottom *n.* [1990s+] (*Aus.*) an attack of diarrhoea, occasioned by food poisoning (cf. AZTEC HOP n.).

Bombay fornicator *n.* [20C+] (*Anglo-Ind.*) a wickerwork chair with arms and an extended footrest. [presumably long enough to double as a bed]

bombazine *n. see* BUMBAZINE n.

bomb bandit *n.* [1990s+] a homosexual. [var. on BUM BANDIT n.]

bomb-diggety *adj.* [1990s+] (*US Black*) a general term of approval. [BOMB, THE n. + HOT DIGGETY (DOG)! excl.]

bombed *adj.* **1** [1950s+] (*orig. US*) drunk (cf. ANNIHILATED adj.). **2** [1960s–70s] (*US campus*) marked down on an examination. **3** [1960s+] (*orig. US*) intoxicated by a drug. **4** [1970s] (*US campus*) generally unwell.

bombed out *adj.*[1] **1** [1950s+] overcome by an excess of alcohol or drugs. **2** [1950s+] exhausted. **3** [1960s] driven mad. [BOMBED adj.]

bombed out *adj.*[2] [1990s+] (*Irish*) jilted, sent on one's away, rejected. [BOMB OUT v. (4)]

bomber *n.*[1] [1940s] (*UK Und.*) a safe-breaker who uses explosives.

bomber *n.*[2] (*drugs*) **1** [1940s+] a very large and potent cannabis cigarette (cf. BOMB n.[4]). **2** [1960s+] a barbiturate or an amphetamine (cf. A n.[2]; BARBIT n.). [resemblance]

bomber *n.*[3] [1980s+] (*US teen*) a loud breaking of wind.

bombers *n.* [1970s] (*US*) the female breasts (cf. BAGS n.[1]).

bombhead *n.*[1] [1960s] a happy-go-lucky, eccentric person. [BOMB v.[3] (1) + -HEAD sfx (1)]

bombhead *n.*[2] [1990s+] the head of the penis. [? resemblance to the shape of the explosive]

bombido *n.* (*also* **bombida**) [1960s+] (*drugs*) **1** injectable amphetamine (cf. A n.[2]). **2** heroin, esp. when mixed with cocaine. **3** a form of depressant. [Sp. *bombido*, a little bomb]

bombita *n.* (*also* **bombida**) [1960s+] (*drugs*) **1** amphetamine (cf. A n.[2]). **2** methamphetamine, a compound 'designer drug' made from ingredients easily extracted from over-the-counter drugs (cf. BOO n.[4]; CHALK n.[1]; CHRISTINA n.; COOL SMOKE n.; CRINGE n.; CRINK n.; GLASS n.[5]; ICE n.[6]; LEMON DROP n.; METH n.[1]; POOR MAN'S COCAINE n.; QUILL n.[2]; REDNECK COCAINE n.; ROCK n.[3]; ROCK CRANK n.; SHABU n.; SKETCH n.[3]). **3** a mix of heroin and cocaine. **4** a depressant. [Sp. *bombita*, a little bomb]

bombness, the *n. see* BOMB, THE n.

bombo *see also under* BUMBO and its combs.

bombo *n.* [1940s+] (*Aus.*) cheap wine, methylated spirits or a combination of both. [SE *bomb* + -O sfx (4); it 'knocks one out'. Note SE *bumbo*, 'A liquor composed of rum, sugar, water and nutmeg' (*OED*)]

bomb off *v. see* BOMB v.[2] (3).

bomb out *v.* **1** [1960s+] (*Aus./US campus*) to perform poorly, esp. in an examination. **2** [1970s] (*US*) to fail to make an expected appearance. **3** [1980s] to die, esp. from a drug overdose. **4** [1990s+] to get rid of, to terminate a relationship. **5** [1990s+] to become extremely intoxicated. [BOMB v.[2]]

bomb-proof *adj.* [mid-19C+] (*orig. US milit.*) untouchable, absolutely secure and safe. [ext. of SE]

bombs *n.* [1960s–70s] (*US*) the female breasts (cf. BAGS n.[1]).

bombshell *n.* **1** [late 19C+] a shock, a surprise, usu. unpleasant. **2** [1910s+] (*orig. US*) a very sexy woman, esp. as *blonde bombshell*.

bombsville *n.* [1960s+] any kind of failure in life. [BOMB v.[2] (2) + -VILLE sfx[1]]

bommy-knocker *n. see* DONGER-KNOCKER n.

bona *n.*[1] [mid–late 19C] a woman. [Ital. *buona*, a good woman]

bona *n.*[2] *see* BONEY n.[1].

bona *adj.* (*also* **bonar, boner**) [mid-19C+] (*Ling. Fr./Polari*) good, pleasant, agreeable. [Ital. *buono*, good]

bona fide *n.* [1910s–50s] (*Irish*) **1** a genuine traveller, as defined by the WW1 Defence of the Realm Act, which allowed anyone who had genuinely travelled 3 miles to be served drink at any hour of the day or night; thus phr. *do the bona fide*, to travel the requisite distance in order to indulge in after-hours drinking. **2** one who was enjoying such extending drinking time. **3** the premises that provide such a drink. [Lat. *bona fide*, in good faith; the act was amended to restrict the drinking to 2 hours after closing time (10pm) and 3 miles beyond the city limits; it was abolished on 4 July 1960]

bona fide *adj.* [20C+] (*Aus.*) terrified. [rhy. sl.]

bonanza *n.* [late 19C+] (*orig. US*) good luck, esp. in quantity and unexpected. [Sp. *bonanza*, good weather, prosperity; orig. applied to wealth taken from the silver mines of the Comstock lode in US]

bona omee *n.* (*also* **bona homey**) [1960s] (*camp gay*) a pleasant person, lit. a 'good man'. [BONA adj. + OMEE n. (3)]

bonar *adj. see* BONA adj.

bona roba *n.* [late 16C–19C] a prostitute. [Ital. *bona roba*, a fine dress]

bonaroo *adj.* (*also* **bonarue, bonneroo, bonny-roo**) [1920s+] (*US prison*) excellent, first-rate. [Cajun; thus ult. Fr. *bon*, good]

bonarooed *adj.* (*also* **bonerooed**) [1970s+] **1** (*US prison*) dressed in one's best clothes. **2** of a place, smartened up, embellished. [BONAROO adj.]

bonaroos *n.* (*also* **boneroos**) [1970s+] (*US prison*) one's best clothes. [BONAROOED adj. (1)]

bonarue *adj. see* BONAROO adj.

bona vardering *adj. see* VARDA v.

bonbons *n.* [1970s+] (*US gay*) **1** erogenous zones on the male body. **2** anal virginity. **3** common sense. [Fr. *bonbons*, sweets]

bonce *n.* **1** [late 19C+] (*also* **bonse**) the head. **2** [1910s+] a hat. [SE *bonce*, a large marble]

bondage *n.* [1940s] (*US Black/Harlem*) debts.

bonds *n.* [1960s+] (*US*) the clothes with which a pimp bedecks his working women. [since his money has paid for them, this 'binds' the women to him]

bone *n.*[1] **1** [mid-17C+] the penis; thus *put the bone to*, to have sexual intercourse (cf. BONE PHONE n.; BONER n.[4]; FUN BONE n.; HAMBONE n.[3]; JIGGLING BONE n.; JOY BONE n.; LOVE BONE n.; MAIN BONE n.; SPUNKBONE n.; WISHBONE n.). **2** [1910s+] (*also* **bone-on**) the erect penis. **3** [1960s] the fig. bone that makes a penis erect and potent.

bone *n.*[2] [mid–late 19C] a subscriber's ticket for the opera. [Fr. *abonnement*, a subscription. Note the small ivory disc, also called a *bone*, issued by theatre managers to favoured friends and acquaintances]

bone *n.*[3] [late 19C] (*US campus*) a very hard-working student. [BONE v.[3]]

bone *n.*[4] **1** [late 19C] (*Aus.*) £1 sterling. **2** [late 19C] a bribe. **3** [late 19C+] (*US*) $1. [SE *throw one a bone*]

bone *n.*[5] [1910s–40s] (*US*) a fool, a dullard, an idiot. [BONEHEADED adj.]

bone *n.*[6] **1** [late 19C] a thin man (cf. BAG OF BONES n.[1]). **2** [1910s+] (*US Black*) a thin woman.

bone *n.*[7] [1920s] (*US, Western*) a horse.

bone *n.*[8] **1** [1930s] (*US Und.*) a Black person. **2** [1940s] (*US Black*) a person of mixed race, esp. Anglo-Irish-Black. [BONES n.¹ (1); they are also 'black and white']

bone n.⁹ [1940s] (*US*) something annoying or irritating. [SE *bone in one's throat*]

bone n.¹⁰ [1950s+] (*orig. US Black/jazz*) a trom*bone*. [abbr.]

bone n.¹¹ **1** [1970s+] (*US drugs*) a cannabis cigarette (cf. CARROT n.²; CONE n.²; FAT ONE n.²; FATTY n.; FINGER n.⁵; HOOTER n.⁷; LINE n.⁴; LOG n.²; NAIL n.³; NOSECONE n.; PIN n.¹; PIN JOINT n.; PINNER n.³; SAUSAGE n.³; THUMB n.; TOOTHPICK n.¹; Tootsie ROLL n.²; TORCH n.; TROMPIE n.; TUSKEE n.; TWIG n.³). **2** [1990s+] (*US Black/drugs*) a cigarette that mixes tobacco and crack cocaine. **3** [1990s+] (*US drugs*) (a $50 piece of) crack cocaine. **4** [2000s] (*US prison*) a cigarette. [the whiteness of the cigarette/crack cocaine]

bone n.¹² [1980s+] (*W.I./UK/US Black teen*) one's essence, one's core, one's soul (cf. BONE adv.).

bone n.¹³ *see* BONES n.¹.

bone adj.¹ **1** [mid-19C] good. **2** [1970s] (*US Und.*) complete, absolute. [Ital. *buono*/Fr. *bon*, good]

bone adj.² (*US*) **1** [1910s] stupid, incompetent. **2** [1990s+] bad, false. [BONE n.⁵]

bone v.¹ **1** [late 17C; 1980s+] to have sexual intercourse (cf. BAGAGA v.). **2** [1970s+] to sodomize; also in fig. use. [BONE n.¹ (1)]

bone v.² **1** [late 17C–1940s] to rob, to steal; thus *bone the fence*, to find out where goods have been hidden by a receiver and then steal them. **2** [late 17C+] (*UK Und.*) to arrest, to seize; thus *boned*, arrested, captured. **3** [19C+] (*UK Und.*) to interrogate. **4** [mid-19C] (*US*) to betray, to inform against. **5** [mid-19C–1920s] (*US*) to beg for, to raise money for a cause. **6** [1900s] (*US campus*) to charge with. **7** [1900s] (*US*) to annoy, to infuriate. **8** [1900s] (*US*) to look for and find. **9** [1900s–40s] to nag, to pester, e.g. for an unpaid debt. **10** [1930s] (*US*) to solicit, to proposition. **11** [1980s] (*US teen*) to victimize, to treat unfairly. [? the image of a dog finding and/or worrying a bone]

bone v.³ (*also* **bone up (on)**) [mid-19C+] (*orig. US*) to learn, to revise, to study hard. [? SE *bone*, to polish or *Bohn* translations of the classics, the latter underpinned by BOHN n.]

bone v.⁴ [mid-19C+] (*US, orig. milit.*) to work hard; also ext. as *bone down*, *bone in*, *bone through* etc. [? the use of a flat bone surface to polish one's boots to a shine]

bone v.⁵ [20C+] (*Aus.*) to jinx, to bring bad luck to. [SAusE *point a bone*, an Aborigine practice]

bone v.⁶ (*also* **bone up**) [1980s+] to drive fast. [? BONE adj.¹]

bone adv. [1930s+] (*US Black*) thoroughly, completely (cf. BONE n.¹²). [SE *bone*, i.e. to one's very depths]

bone-ache n. (*also* **bone-ague**) [16C–mid-17C] venereal disease. [the side-effects of syphilis]

bone-bag n. *see* BAG OF BONES n.¹.

bone-baster n. [late 16C–mid-17C] a cudgel. [SE *bone* + SE *baste*]

bone-bender n.¹ (*also* **bone-breaker, ...-butcher, ...-carpenter, ...-chiseller**) [late 19C+] (*US*) a surgeon (cf. BONEJUGGLER n.; BONES n.¹; CROSS-BONES n.; SAWBONES n.).

bone-bender n.² *see* BONECRUSHER n.¹ (2).

bone box n.¹ **1** [late 18C–mid-19C] the mouth. **2** [1940s] the head.

bone box n.² **1** [late 19C–1940s] (*US*) a coffin. **2** [1970s] (*US*) an ambulance. **3** [1970s] (*US prison*) a hearse.

bone-breaker n. [late 19C–1910s] fever, ague. [the aches it induces in the bones]

bone-breaker/-butcher/-carpenter n. *see* BONE-BENDER n.¹.

bone carrier n. [1910s+] (*US*) a gossip, a rumour-monger. [CARRY A BONE v.]

bone cart n. [1910s] (*Aus.*) an ambulance.

bone-chiseller n. *see* BONE-BENDER n.¹.

bone-cleaner n. [late 19C–1900s] a domestic servant. [SE *bones*, objects made of ivory + *cleaner*]

bonecrusher n.¹ **1** [late 19C] (*sporting*) a large-calibre sporting rifle, used on large game. **2** [1940s–60s] (*also* **bone-bender, bone-cracker**) (*US*) a wrestler. **3** [1960s–70s] (*US*) a person who shakes hands forcefully. **4** [1970s+] (*US prison*) a large knife. **5** [2000s] a prison guard who uses physical force. [its effects]

bonecrusher n.² [1990s+] (*US drugs*) **1** a near-overdose in which the user feels as if the injection they have just taken is crushing their bones. **2** painful withdrawal symptoms. **3** crack cocaine (cf. BASE n.).

boned adj.¹ [1930s+] tipsy. [the image of a *boned* carcass, reduced to flabby, floppy meat]

boned adj.² [1960s–70s] hit hard on the head. [the *bone* is that of the battered skull]

bone dance n. [1980s+] (*US campus*) sexual intercourse; thus *do the bone (dance)*, to have sexual intercourse. [BONE n.¹ (1)]

bone-dome n. [1930s+] a protective helmet, initially for flyers, latterly [1950s+] motorcyclists and [1980s+] cyclists. [SE *bone* + *dome*, i.e. the protection + the shape]

boned out adj.¹ **1** [1990s+] (*US Black*) exhausted, esp. of a man who has just had sex. **2** [2000s] (*US gang*) having retreated from a confrontation. [BONE v.⁴]

boned out adj.² [1990s+] (*US Black*) out of money. [BONE n.⁴ (3)]

bone down v. [1970s+] (*US*) to have sexual intercourse (cf. BAGAGA v.). [BONE n.¹ (1)]

boned turkey n. [mid-19C] (*US*) a dish of hash.

bone-eater n. [2000s] (*US Black*) a male homosexual (cf. BLOW-BOY n.; BONE SMUGGLER n.; BONE-STROKER n.; BUGLEBOY n.; COCK-KNOCKER n.; COCKSUCKER n.; DICKHOUND n.; DICKY-LICKER n.; DINNER MASHER n.; FLUTER n.²; GOOBER-GRABBER n.²; JAM FAG n.; KNOB ARTIST n.; KNOB JOCKEY n.; LUNCHBOX LANCER n.; MAN-EATER n.; MUZZLER n.³; NUDGER n.; PEE-PEE n.¹; PETER-EATER n.; PICKLE KISSER n.; POLE PLEASER n.; POLE SITTER n.; SAUSAGE JOCKEY n.; SAUSAGE SMUGGLER n.; SEMEN DEMON n.; SENOR-EATER n.; SHORE DINNER n.; SKIN-DIVER n.; SPERM BURPER n.; SPUNKBONE JOCKEY n.; SUCKER n.⁶; SWEETCORN SHINER n.; SWORD-FIGHTER n.; TOOTLE MERCHANT n.; TROUSER BANDIT n.; TUBESTEAK TARZAN n.). [BONE n.¹ (1) + EAT v.³ (1)]

bone factory n.¹ **1** [1950s] (*US Und.*) a hospital (cf. BONE-HOUSE n.; BONEYARD n.¹). **2** [2000s] (*US*) an old people's home.

bone factory n.² *see* BONE ORCHARD n.

bone-gobbler n. *see* GOBBLER n.² (3).

bone-grubber n. [mid-19C] a scavenger who specializes in collecting old bones and selling them to rag-shops or to the bone-grinders. [SE *bone* + *grubber*]

bonehead n.¹ **1** [20C+] (*orig. US*) a fool, a dullard, an idiot. **2** [1920s–60s] a stubborn person. [BONEHEADED adj.; Moore, *Lexicon of Cadet Language* (1993), suggests an alternative link to BONE n.¹ (1) on pattern of DICKHEAD n.]

bonehead n.² [1910s+] a stupid error. [backform. f. BONEHEAD PLAY n., itself from BONEHEAD n.¹ (1)]

bonehead n.³ [1940s+] a bald person. [the head is shaved to the bone]

bonehead n.⁴ [1990s+] a user of crack cocaine. [BONE n.¹¹ (3) + -HEAD sfx (3)]

boneheaded adj. (*also* **bonehead**) [mid-19C+] stupid (cf. AIRHEADED adj.). [SE *bone* + -HEAD sfx (1); the image is of the hardness of bone]

bonehead English n. [1920s+] (*US campus*) a remedial course in elementary English composition. [BONEHEAD n.¹ (1) + SE *English*]

bonehead play n. [20C+] (*US*) an elementary, obvious error or mistake; thus *pull a bonehead play*, to make an elementary error. [BONEHEAD n.¹ (1) + PLAY n.¹ (2); note *locus classicus* the 'bonehead play' committed by Giants' 19-year-old Fred Merkle rookie substitute in the Giants vs. Cubs game on 23 September 1908; the term was coined by the NY press which headlined 'Merkle's Bonehead Play']

bone-heap n. *see* BAG OF BONES n.¹.

bone-hider n. [late 19C] (*Aus.*) an undertaker.

bone hog n. [1990s+] (US) a dedicated and enthusiastic fellatrix. [BONE n.¹ (1) + SE hog]

bone-house n. **1** [late 18C–19C] a coffin. **2** [19C] the human body. **3** [early–mid-19C] a house or vault in which the bones of the dead are piled up, a charnel-house. **4** [1940s–60s] (US Und.) a hospital (cf. BONE FACTORY n.¹). [SE bone + house]

bone-in-a-valley n. [1950s+] (W.I.) a thin person (cf. BAG OF BONES n.¹). [BONE n.¹ (2)]

bonejuggler n. [1970s–80s] (UK Black) a doctor (cf. BONE-BENDER n.¹).

bone-on n. see BONE n.¹ (2).

bone orchard n. (also **bone factory**) [mid-19C+] (US) a cemetery (cf. BONEYARD n.¹).

bone out v. [1990s+] (US Black) to run away, to leave fast. [? BONE v.⁶ + ? move one's bones]

bone phone n. [20C+] (US) the penis. [BONE n.¹ (1) + SE phone]

bone-picker n.¹ [late 18C–mid-19C] a footman. [the poor standard of the meals, often based on left-overs, that were given to servants]

bone-picker n.² [mid-19C–1900s] a scavenger, a rag and bone man.

bone-polisher n.¹ [early–mid-19C] a footman; any servant. [ext. of SE use; the bones or ivory objects that require cleaning]

bone-polisher n.² **1** [mid-19C] the cat-o'-nine-tails or the man who wields it. **2** [1920s–30s] (US tramp) a (vicious) dog. [(1) the 'polishing' of the malefactor's bones; (2) the bones are those of animals, or of the victims the dog attacks]

bone queen n. [1970s+] (US gay) a fellator. [BONE n.¹ (1) + QUEEN n.² (1)/QUEEN SFX (2)]

boner n.¹ [19C] a hard blow.

boner n.² (US campus) **1** [late 19C+] a hard worker. **2** [1960s] a difficult examination. [BONE v.³]

boner n.³ [1910s+] (US) a serious mistake; thus pull a bone(r), to make a mistake. [BONEHEAD n.²]

boner n.⁴ **1** [1950s+] an erection. **2** [1980s+] the penis (cf. BONE n.¹). **3** [1990s+] (Aus.) of a man, one who has sexual intercourse; thus mad boner, an especially keen FUCKER n. (1). **4** [1990s+] (Aus.) a general term of abuse, on pattern of FUCKER n. (3). **5** [2000s] (US) in fig. use of (1), an obsession. [BONE n.¹ (1)]

boner adj. see BONA adj.

bone-riding n. [2000s] having sexual intercourse, whether vaginal or anal. [BONE n.¹ (1) + RIDE v.¹ (1)]

bonerific adj. [2000s] (US Black) very attractive (cf. COOLARIFIC adj.; FABURRIFIC adj.). [BONAROO adj./BONER n.⁴ (1) + SE terrific]

boner nochy phr. [late 19C] (Ling. Fr./Polari) good night. [Ital. buona notte, good night]

bonerooed adj. see BONAROOED adj.

boneroos n. see BONAROOS n.

bones n.¹ **1** [late 14C+] dice, esp. in imper. roll them bones. **2** [19C] the human teeth. **3** [mid-19C] (US) gambling chips; occas. in sing. **4** [late 19C] a surgeon (cf. BONE-BENDER n.¹). **5** [late 19C+] dominoes; occas. in sing. **6** [1900s] (US campus) a skeleton. **7** [1960s–70s] (US) a thin person (cf. BAG OF BONES n.¹). [ext. of SE use; the use of bone/ivory, note dice were orig. made of bone]

bones n.² [20C+] (US) a Black person. [? old vaudeville cross-talk act in which 1 speaker was Mr Bones]

bones n.³ [1990s+] (US prison) a gang tattoo.

bone-setter n.¹ [early–mid-17C] an impassioned lover. [he crushes his partner's bones in his passionate embrace]

bone-setter n.² **1** [mid-18C–early 19C] a horse that gives its rider an uncomfortable journey. **2** [early–mid-19C] a hackney coach. [SE bone-setter, a surgeon]

bone-setter n.³ [early 19C] (US) a surprise, i.e. a jolt. [it shakes one's bones]

bone-shaker n. **1** [late 19C+] an early model of bicycle, with solid rather than rubber tyres; thus later use implies any old or run-down bicycle. **2** [20C+] a decrepit vehicle with, inter alia, inadequate springs, thus jolting its passengers.

boneshop n. [late 19C–1900s] the workhouse. [the paucity of the provisions]

bone smuggler n. [1990s+] **1** a male homosexual (cf. BONE-EATER n.). **2** a male homosexual who dresses in female clothes; a DRAG QUEEN n. (1). [BONE n.¹ (1); (1) it is 'smuggled' into the anus; (2) it is 'smuggled' behind the female clothes]

bone-stroker n. [1990s+] **1** a masturbator. **2** a male homosexual (cf. BONE-EATER n.). [BONE n.¹ (1) + SE stroker]

bone the fence v. see BONE v.² (1).

bonetop n. [1960s] (US) a fool, a dullard. [SE bone + TOP n.¹]

bone up v.¹ [1910s] (US) to pay off a debt. [BONE n.⁴ (3)]

bone up v.² [2000s] of the penis, to become erect. [BONE n.¹ (2)]

bone up v.³ see BONE v.⁶.

bone up (on) v. see BONE v.³.

boney n.¹ (also **bona**) [20C+] (Ulster) a bonfire, esp. one lit on 12 July, Orangeman's Day. [abbr. SE; ult. bone-fire]

boney n.² (also **bonie**) [1970s+] (S.Afr.) **1** a bicycle. **2** a motorcycle. [BONE-SHAKER n.]

boney adj. [1990s+] (UK Black) honest, sincere. [SE bona fide]

boneyard n.¹ **1** [19C] a very thin or emaciated person or animal (cf. BAG OF BONES n.¹). **2** [mid-19C+] a cemetery (cf. BONE ORCHARD n.). **3** [1930s] (US tramp) a hospital, esp. in the context of a post-mortem examination (cf. BONE FACTORY n.¹). [SE bone; (4) BONE v.¹ (1)]

boneyard n.² [2000s] (US prison) the family or conjugal visiting area. [BONE v.¹ (1)]

bonfire n. [1910s–40s] (orig. milit.) a cigarette, a cigarette stub. [post WW1 use is US Black]

bong n.¹ (also **bhong**) [1970s+] (US drugs) a kind of bowl-shaped water-pipe used for smoking cannabis (the specifics vary as to the maker); thus (Aus.) bongineering, bongology, the construction of such pipes. [Thai baung, lit. 'cylindrical wooden tube']

bong n.² [1990s+] (UK juv.) an eccentric. [? echoic of the supposed noise of tapping an empty head]

bong n.³ see BUNG n.¹.

bong adj. [1960s–70s] (US) excellent. [Fr. bon, good]

bong v.¹ **1** [1940s+] (US/N.Z.) to hit. **2** [1960s] (US campus) to reject someone for membership in a fraternity, club etc. **3** [1990s+] to have sexual intercourse (cf. BANG v.¹). [var. on BONK v.¹]

bong v.² see BONG (ON) v.

bong! excl. [1930s+] a term used to suggest the sound of a blow or a sudden noise. [onomat.]

bongo n.¹ [1940s+] (orig. US) a derog. term for a Black person?; thus bongo-bongo land, a Third World/African country (cf. AFRICAN APE n.). [Bongo, seen as a stereotypically 'African' name]

bongo n.² [1980s+] (Aus. drugs) a kind of bowl-shaped water-pipe used for smoking cannabis. [BONG n.¹]

bongo adj. [1950s–70s] (US) crazy, eccentric. [BONKERS adj. (2)]

bongo-bongo land n. see BONGO n.¹.

bongo lips n. [1990s+] (US) a derog. term for a Black person (cf. AFRICAN APE n.; BRILLOHEAD n.). [BONGO n.¹ + the image of thick lips]

bong (on) v. [1970s+] (drugs) to smoke cannabis through a BONG n.¹. [BONG n.¹]

bongos n. [1980s+] (US) the female breasts (cf. BAGS n.¹). [they resemble bongo drums or they 'bong' up and down]

bong swat n. [1980s+] (US drugs) an inhalation of a pipeful of cannabis. [BONG n.¹ + SE swat, a hit (i.e. HIT n.³ (5))]

bong tong n. [late 19C–1910s] (Aus./US) the social élite and their lifestyle and manners, used ironically. [a deliberate deflatory mispron. of Fr. bon ton, good taste, good breeding]

bongy adj. see BUNGY adj.

bonie n. see BONEY n.².

boniface n. [early 18C–1910s] a public house landlord, in US a hotelier. [Boniface, the jovial innkeeper in George Farquhar's The

Beaux' Stratagem (1707); however, the term does not appear in print for a century)

bonified *adj.* [1970s–80s] (*US Black*) competent, qualified, being the right man for job. [? Fr. *bon*, good + sfx *-ified* or pron. of Lat. *bona fide*, genuine, lit. 'in good faith']

boning *n.* [1980s+] (*US campus*) sexual intercourse. [BONE v.[1] (1)]

bonings *n.* [early 19C] (*UK Und.*) stolen goods. [BONE v.[2] (1)]

bonita *n.* (*drugs*) **1** [1960s+] milk sugar, commonly used to adulterate heroin. **2** [2000s] heroin. [Sp., lit. 'good little girl'; (2) may be misreading of (1)]

bonk *n.* **1** [1930s+] an abrupt, heavy sound, a thump. **2** [1970s+] sexual intercourse. **3** [1970s+] a blow, esp. on top of the head. **4** [1980s] an erection. **5** [1990s+] usu. of a woman, one who is available for sex. [echoic/BONK v.[1]; the theory that (2) is backsl. for KNOB v.[1] (2) should be rejected]

bonk *adj. see* BONKERS adj.

bonk *v.[1]* **1** [1930s+] to hit (esp. on the head). **2** [1970s+] to have sexual intercourse (cf. BANG v.[1]). **3** [1990s+] (*US campus*) to break down, to wear out. [echoic + note WW1 milit. use *bonk*, to shell]

bonk *v.[2] see* BUNK v.[5] (2).

bonk! *excl.* **1** [1980s] (*US campus*) (*also* **bonk it!**) a negative expression of disapproval or disagreement. **2** [1990s+] (*US teen*) used after a statement to emphasize one's feeling that it is unbelievable or fantastic. [BONK v.[1] (2), i.e. euph. for FUCK! excl./FUCK IT! excl.]

bonkers *adj.* (*also* **bonk, bonks**) **1** [1930s] mildly drunk (cf. ADDLED adj.). **2** [1940s+] (*orig. RN*) stupid, insane, eccentric, esp. in phrs. *drive bonkers, go bonkers*. [BONK n. (1), i.e. the result of a fig. blow to the head/brain]

bonking *n.* [1980s+] sexual intercourse. [BONK v.[1] (2)]

bonking *adj.* [1970s] a general intensifier. [BONK v.[1] (2), i.e. euph. for FUCKING adj. (1)]

bonk it! *excl. see* BONK! excl. (1).

bonk-on *n.* [1980s+] an erection. [BONK n. (4)]

bonks *adj. see* BONKERS adj.

bonne-bouche *n.* [late 19C] the vagina (cf. APPLE n.[6]). [Fr. *bonne bouche*, a 'pleasant taste', anglicized as a 'tasty morsel']

bonneroo *adj. see* BONAROO adj.

bonnet *n.[1]* **1** [mid–late 19C] a gambling cheat who poses as a normal player, thus luring the victim to join the game, but who, as the play proceeds, begins cheating in favour of the bank or house. **2** [early 19C] a pretext or pretence, esp. as the legitimate job behind which a thief hides their true occupation, e.g. a newspaper seller or porter. **3** [mid-19C] a sham bidder at auctions who works to drive up the price. **4** [late 19C] one who encourages sales for a street vendor by praising the goods. [fig. use of BONNET v. (2) although (2) predates it]

bonnet *n.[2]* (*also* **cap**) [late 19C] a woman. [metonymy]

bonnet *n.[3]* [late 19C] a thug. [BONNET v. (1)]

bonnet *v.* **1** [mid-19C–1930s] to pull or crush a person's hat over their eyes, thus temporarily blinding them. **2** [mid–late 19C] to cheat. [(2) f. (1)]

bonnet-builder *n.* [mid–late 19C] a milliner.

bonnet flipper *n.* [1950s] (*US Black*) a person, e.g. a performer, who excites people's emotions. [SE *bonnet* as metonym for the head + FLIP v.[4] (2)]

bonnet for *v.* [early 19C] to back up someone in their claims, to provide an alibi for someone. [BONNET n.[1] (2)]

bonnets so blue *n.* [mid-19C] (*Irish*) stew. [rhy. sl.]

bonnetter *n.* **1** [mid-19C] a cheat's accomplice, who lures victims into the game. **2** [mid-19C–1900s] a smashing blow on one's hat. [BONNET v.]

bonnibel *n.* [early 17C] an attractive woman. [Fr. *bonne et belle*, good and beautiful]

bonnie Brillo *n.* [1980s+] (*US campus*) one who is obsessively neat and tidy. [proper name *Bonnie*, with implications of domestic cheeriness + brandname *Brillo*, the scouring pad]

bonny-baller *n.* [mid–late 17C] a male sexual predator. [? his pursuit of a BONNIBEL n.]

bonny-clapper *n.* (*also* **barney clapper, bonny clabbe, ...clabber, ...clabo, bonnyclaber, bony-clabber, clabber**) [17C+] sour buttermilk.

bonny fair *n.* [20C+] (*US*) the hair. [rhy. sl.]

bonny-roo *adj. see* BONAROO adj.

bonny-throw *n.* [late 18C] (*US Und.*) the highway; thus *bonny-lay*, highway robbery.

bono *adj.* [mid–late 19C] (*Ling. Fr./Polari*) good. [Ital. *buono*, good]

bono Johnny *n.* [late 19C–1900s] an Englishman. [Chinese pidgin, 'a good John Bull']

bono omee *n.* [mid-19C–1950s] a husband. [BONO adj. + OMEE n. (3)]

bonse *n. see* BONCE n. (1).

bonsella *n.* [1940s+] (*S.Afr.*) a present, a gratuity, a 'perk'. [Zulu *ibhanselo*, a small present or *bansela*, thanks in a tangible form]

bonser *adj. see* BONZER adj.

bont *adj.* [1970s+] (*S.Afr.*) gaudy, lurid, colourful. [Du. *bonte*, gaudy]

bontoger *adj.* (*also* **bontogeriro, bontoser, bonziorie**) [20C+] (*Aus.*) good; occas. as adv. extremely, very. [var. on BONTOSHER n.]

bontosher *n.* [1900s–50s] (*Aus.*) a term of the highest praise. [Fr. *bon toujours*, good all the time]

bonus! *excl.* [1980s+] (*US campus*) excellent! wonderful! first-class! [SE *bonus*, something extra, but note BONA adj.]

bony-clabber *n. see* BONNY-CLAPPER n.

bonza *see also under* BONZER.

bonzarina *n.* (*also* **bonzerina**) [1900s–50s] (*Aus.*) a notably beautiful woman. [BONZER n. (2) + fem. sfx *-arina/-erina*]

bonzer *n.* [20C+] (*Aus.*) **1** a good thing. **2** (*also* **bonza**) an admirable person. [BONZER adj.]

bonzer *adj.* (*also* **bonser, bonza, bonzerino**) [20C+] (*Aus./N.Z.*) good. [mongrel mixture of Fr. *bon*, good + SE *bonanza* + BONTOGER adj.]

bonzer *adv.* [1960s–70s] (*Aus.*) very well, very, extremely. [BONZER adj.]

bonzerina *n. see* BONZARINA n.

bonzerino *adj. see* BONZER adj.

bonziorie *adj. see* BONTOGER adj.

bonzo *adj.* **1** [1950s] (*UK Und.*) skilful. **2** [1980s+] eccentric, crazy. [? the UK 1920s cartoon puppy *Bonzo* or 1951 film *Bedtime for Bonzo* (a chimp)]

boo *n.[1]* [late 19C] (*US*) money. [abbr. BOODLE n.[1] (3)]

boo *n.[2]* [1900s] (*US*) nasal mucus. [abbr. BOOGER n.[1] (1)]

boo *n.[3]* **1** [1930s–50s] (*US Black*) a bad scare, a serious fright. **2** [1970s] a ghostwriter. [SE *boo!*, an excl. designed to surprise/frighten someone]

boo *n.[4]* (*drugs*) **1** [1950s+] (*also* **bu**) marijuana. **2** [2000s] methamphetamine (cf. BOMBITA n.). [abbr. JABOOBY n.]

boo *n.[5]* [1990s+] (*US Black*) **1** a child. **2** a sweetheart, a loved one, a close friend. [? BABY n.[3] (3); ? BOOTY n.]

boo *n.[6]* [1990s+] (*W.I.*) an idiot, a fool. [? abbr. BOOBY n.[1]]

boo *adj.* [1950s] (*US teen*) excellent. [? BOO n.[4] (1), on model of DOPE n.[1] (6)/DOPE adj.[2] (2)]

boo *v.* [mid-19C] to speak or write in a mawkishly romantic manner. [BOOHOO v. (1)]

boo! *excl.* [early 19C] nonsense!

booai *n.* (*also* **booay**) [20C+] (*N.Z.*) the backwoods, remote rural areas; thus *up the booai*, totally confused, absolutely wrong. [? Maori *puhoi*, dull, slow or *Puhoi*, a failed mid-19C utopian settlement]

boob *n.[1]* [20C+] **1** (*orig. Aus.*) a prison, orig. milit. use; thus (*Aus./N.Z.*) BOOB BLUE n.; BOOB CAT n.; *boob dot*, a small blue dot tattooed beneath the eye, indicating a spell in borstal or prison; *boob gear*, prison uniform; BOOB HAPPY adj.; BOOBHEAD n.; BOOB

RAT n.; *boob talk*, prison jargon; *boob tat*, a prison tattoo; *boob tea*, weak, prison-brewed tea; *boob weed*, prison-issue tobacco; *do boob*, to serve time in prison. **2** (*US*) a police station, esp. the police cells, a local or city prison. [BOOBY-HATCH n. (1); note WW1 milit. use for detention cells]

boob *n.*[2] **1** [20C+] (*orig. US*) a fool, an idiot. **2** [1900s–40s] (*US*) an inmate of a psychiatric institution. **3** [1930s] (*US tramp*) an innocent, a potential victim of a thief. **4** [1940s+] an error, a blunder. [abbr. BOOBY n.[1]]

boob *n.*[3] [1940s+] (*orig. US*) **1** a female breast, usu. in pl. (cf. BOOBIES n.). **2** in pl., the chest of a fat male. [BUBS n.[1]; (1) since 1970s one of the terms esp. favoured by women]

boob *adj.* [20C+] (*Aus.*) inferior, second-rate. [BOOB n.[2] (1)]

boob *v.* [1910s+] to make a mistake, to blunder. [BOOB n.[2] (1)/BOOB n.[2] (4)]

boobatch *n.* [1930s–40s] (*US*) an old Polish immigrant. [? Polish = grandfather]

boob blue *n.* [1980s] (*N.Z. prison*) alcohol made from Brasso metal polish. [BOOB n.[1] (1) + BLUE n.[2] (2)]

boob box *n.* (*also* **booby box**) [1960s] (*US*) a psychiatric institution; also attrib. [BOOB n.[2] (1)/BOOBY n.[1] + SE *box*/BOX n.[2] (2)]

boob cat *n.* [1980s+] (*Aus. prison*) a prisoner who suspends his usual heterosexuality for a homosexual life while in jail. [BOOB n.[1] (1) + CAT n.[13] (1)]

booberkin *n.* [late 17C] a fool, a simpleton. [BOOBY n.[1] + dimin. sfx -*kin*]

boob happy *adj.* [1980s+] (*Aus. prison*) institutionalized, no longer able to survive outside the prison environment. [BOOB n.[1] (1) + -HAPPY sfx (1)]

boobhead *n.* [1960s+] (*Aus.*) a prisoner, esp. an influential or tough prisoner. [BOOB n.[1] (1) + -HEAD sfx (1)]

boobies *n.* [1930s+] (*orig. US*) the female breasts; occas. in sing. (cf. BOOB n.[3]). [BUBS n.[1]]

boobish *adj. see* BOOBY adj.[1]

boob job *n.* (*also* **tit job**) [1980s+] cosmetic/plastic surgery on the breast, usu. for enlarging with some form of implant. [BOOB n.[3] (1)/ TIT n.[3] (1) + JOB n.[4]]

Boob McNutt *n.* [1930s–60s] (*US*) a fool, a simpleton. [BOOB n.[2] (1) + NUT n.[4] (1); ult. f. *Boob McNutt*, a strip cartoon character (running 1915–34) created by Rube Goldberg]

booboisie *n.* [1920s+] (*US*) respectable fools, considered as a class in their own right; a synon. for modern 'Middle America'. [BOOB n.[2] (1) + *bourgeoisie*. Coined by H.L. Mencken as part of a list of words describing 'the victims of the Depression, then current' and published in the Baltimore *Evening Sun* on 15 February 1922 in a list of 50 similar terms, including *boobariat, booberati, boobarian*]

boo-boo *n.*[1] [1900s] (*US*) a joke. [ety. unknown]

boo-boo *n.*[2] [1900s–20s] (*US*) $1. [abbr. + redup. BOODLE n.[1] (3)]

boo-boo *n.*[3] **1** [1950s] (*US*) usu. in pl., the testicles. **2** [1970s] (*US gay*) an erection. [? Yid. *bulba*, potato. Major, *Juba to Jive: A Dict. of Afro-American Slang* (1994), suggests link to Bantu *mbubu*]

boo-boo *n.*[4] **1** [1950s+] (*also* **bubu**) (*orig. US*) a blunder, usu. embarrassing. **2** [2000s] something unpleasant, an unacceptable situation. [BOOB n.[2] (4)]

boo-boo *n.*[5] [1950s+] (*US*) a minor scar or bruise, an acne spot etc. [BOOB v. + redup.]

boo-boo *n.*[6] (*also* **booby**) [1980s] (*Aus.*) nasal mucus.

boo-boo *n.*[7] [1990s+] (*US*) the buttocks, the posterior. [abbr. SE *buttocks*]

boo-boo *adj.* [1990s+] (*US campus*) bad, second-rate. [BOO-BOO n.[4]]

boo-boo *v.* [1950s+] (*orig. US*) to blunder, to make a mistake. [BOOB v. + redup.]

boo-boos *n.*[1] [1990s+] (*US*) a Black person. [? BOOB n.[2] (1)]

boo-boos *n.*[2] *see* BOO-BOO n.[3] (1).

boob play *n.* [1930s+] a foolish action, an error, a blunder. [BOOB n.[2] (1) + PLAY n.[1] (2)]

boob rat *n.* [1950s] (*Aus. Und.*) a prisoner, esp. a recidivist. [BOOB n.[1] (1) + RAT n.[2] (6)]

boobs *n. see* BOOB n.[3].

boob trap *n.* [1920s–60s] (*US*) a nightclub or similar place of entertainment where gullible customers are defrauded of cash. [BOOB n.[2] (1) + SE *trap*]

boob-tube *n.*[1] [1960s+] (*orig. US*) television, thus *boob tuber*, one who watches television a lot. [BOOB n.[2] (1) + TUBE n.[3] (2)]

boob-tube *n.*[2] [1970s+] a woman's tight, strapless top, usu. of knitted or elasticated fabric. [BOOB n.[3] (1) + SE *tube*]

boobus *n.* [1990s+] (*US Black, Los Angeles*) small breasts. [BOOB n.[3] (1)]

booby *n.*[1] [early 17C+] a fool, an idiot, a peasant (cf. BITCH BOOBY n.; BLOOTER n.; DOG BOOBY n.). [? Sp. *bobo*, a fool]

booby *n.*[2] [1910s–50s] (*US*) a cell, a lock-up. [BOOBY-HUTCH n.[2]]

booby *n.*[3] *see* BOOBIES n.

booby *n.*[4] *see* BOO-BOO n.[6].

booby *adj.*[1] (*also* **boobish**) [late 17C+] stupid, foolish. [BOOBY n.[1]]

booby *adj.*[2] [1990s+] (*US*) having big breasts; thus by stereotyping, promiscuous. [BOOB n.[3] (1)]

booby-hatch *n.* **1** [mid-19C–1960s] (*orig. US*) a prison, a police station, a police patrol wagon. **2** [late 19C+] (*also* **booby-box**) a lunatic asylum. [BOOBY n.[1] + SE *hatch*, hutch, underpinned by the well-known asylum at Colney Hatch near London, opened in 1851]

booby-house *n.* [late 19C–1940s] (*US*) a lunatic asylum. [BOOBY n.[1] + SE *house*]

booby-hutch *n.*[1] [late 18C–early 19C] **1** a 1-horse chaise, thus any clumsy carriage. **2** a leather bottle. [BOOBY n.[1] + SE *hutch*; (2) plays on the idea of the bottle, full of liquor, 'ensnaring' the fool]

booby-hutch *n.*[2] **1** [late 19C] (*US*) a police station. **2** [1920s–30s] (*UK Und.*) a cell. **3** [1940s] a lunatic asylum. [BOOBY n.[1] + SE *hutch*. Note milit. use *booby hutch*, a dugout; *boobies' hutch*, a tolerated if unofficial bar in a barracks, which is open after the canteen shuts]

booby-wagon *n.* [1920s–60s] (*US*) the vehicle in which arrested people are transported to the local police station or prison. [BOOBY n.[2] + SE *wagon*]

booch *n.* (*also* **boogh**) [20C+] (*Ulster*) a heavy blow, a slap, a punch, a thump. [echoic]

boochie *n. see* BOOJEE n.

boocoo *see under* BEAUCOUP.

boocoodles *n.* (*also* **bookoodles**) [20C+] (*US*) many, a good deal. [Fr. *beaucoup*, many + OODLES n.]

booda *n.* [1990s+] (*US Black gang*) a large, cannabis-impregnated cookie or biscuit. [pron. of BUDDHA n.]

boodgeree! *excl.* [late 19C+] (*Aus. pidgin*) a general excl. of approval, pleasure. [Dharuk *bujari*, good]

boodle *n.*[1] **1** [early 17C–19C] (*orig. US*) a crowd or collection of people or things; usu. in phr. *the whole boodle*. **2** [early 19C–1920s] (*US*) counterfeit money. **3** [mid-19C+] booty, money, esp. money that has been acquired illegally or through corruption. **4** [mid-19C+] (*US Und.*) a fake bankroll, i.e. a bill of large denomination wrapped around a roll of smaller bills (or even paper). **5** [late 19C–1950s] a large amount of money. **6** [late 19C–1970s] a roll of banknotes. **7** [1930s] (*US prison*) a bribe extracted from prisoners by the warders or 'trusties'. **8** [1960s] (*US campus*) a parcel of food, usu. sweets or snacks, sent to a student. **9** [1960s] (*US drugs*) a packet of narcotics. **10** [1960s+] (*US Und.*) anything sent to a prisoner from the outside world, not necessarily money. **11** [1970s] working capital. [either Du. *boedel*, household effects, and thus one's personal estate, or Scot. *bodle*, a small coin worth 2 Scot. pence (or ⅙ of an English one) and as such usu. glossed as 'worthless'. (3) is the most common modern meaning, which has developed primarily in the US; note West Point *boodle*, contraband edibles, sweets etc]

boodle *n.*[2] [mid-19C] a fool. [? link to NOODLE n.[1]; ? Devon dial. *buddled*, drunk]

boodle *n.*[3] [1930s–60s] (*US tramp*) a jail where a tramp lives during the cold winter months.

boodle *n.*[4] [1980s] (*US*) the vagina (cf. BANK n.[1]). [BOOTY n. (1), but note image of the vagina as a commercially useful commodity (cf. BOODLE n.[1])]

boodle *adj.* [late 19C] (*US*) corrupt. [BOODLE n.[1]]

boodle *v.*[1] [late 19C–1900s] (*US*) to engage in corruption, to bribe. [BOODLE n.[1] (3)]

boodle *v.*[2] [1940s–70s] (*US campus*) to pet, to neck. [SE *bundle*, of an engaged couple, to sleep together, but fully clothed]

boodle bag *n.* (*US*) **1** [1920s] loot, as contained in a bag. **2** [1920s+] a purse, a small money-pouch, usu. worn around the neck; later ext. to any small bag. **3** [2000s] a 'goodie bag' with free gifts, promotional material etc, as given way by a company, e.g. at a press launch. [BOODLE n.[1] + SE *bag*]

boodle buyer *n.* [1940s] (*UK Und.*) a criminal receiver who specializes in large items. [BOODLE n.[1] (5)]

boodler *n.* (*Aus./US*) **1** [late 19C–1900s] a swindler, specializing in passing counterfeit notes. **2** [late 19C–1960s] (*also* **boodle**) a corrupt politician. [BOODLE n.[1]]

boody *see under* BOOTY and its combs.

booed and hissed *adj.* [1980s] drunk (cf. ADRIAN (QUIST) adj.). [rhy. sl. = PISSED adj.[1]]

boof *n.* [2000s] (*US prison*) contraband hidden in the rectum. [ety. unknown]

boofa *n.* (*also* **boofer**) [1970s+] (*US*) a fool, an incompetent. [BOOFHEAD n. (1) or pron. BUTTFUCKER n.]

boofed (out) *adj.* [1980s+] (*US campus*) puffed out, usu. of hair. [SE *bouffant*]

booferbox *n.* [1980s+] (*orig. US*) a large radio/tape recorder/stereo particularly popular among ghetto youths. [*boof*, echoic of the heavy bass notes emerging from the machine + SE *box*/BOX n.[5] (7)]

boofhead *n.* [1940s+] (*orig. Aus.*) **1** a fool, an idiot, a simpleton. **2** a person or animal having a large head. [Lincolnshire dial.]

boofter *n. see* POOFTER n. (1).

boog *n.* [1940s+] **1** (*US*) a Black person. **2** (*Aus.*) an Aborigine. [abbr. BOOGIE n.[2]]

boog *adj.* [1940s+] (*US*) Black, in racial terms. [BOOG n.]

boog *v.*[1] [1930s] (*US Black*) to irritate, to annoy. [although the logical root is BUG v.[2] (2), this term appears to predate that]

boog *v.*[2] [1940s+] (*US Black*) to enjoy oneself, to 'party', to dance. [BOOGIE v. (1)]

booga bear *n. see* BOOGER BEAR n.

boogalee *n. see* BOOGERLEE n.

boogaloo *n.* [1970s–80s] (*US*) a Black person. [BOOGIE n.[2] + SE *boogaloo*]

boogaloo *adj.* [1970s–80s] (*US*) pertaining to Blacks, racially Black. [BOOGALOO n.]

boogaloo *v.* [1960s+] (*orig. US Black*) **1** to dance. **2** to fool around. [SE *boogaloo*, a dance step of the 1960s]

boogar *n. see* BOOGER n.[3].

boo-gee *n. see* GEE n.[7]

booger *n.*[1] **1** [late 19C+] (*US*) (*also* **bugger**) a piece of nasal mucus. **2** [1980s+] (*also* **boogersnot**) a general term of abuse. [SE *bugger*]

booger *n.*[2] **1** [20C+] a person, animal or object with no derog. implications. **2** [1910s+] (*US Black*) anything unpleasant, burdensome, difficult. **3** [1930s+] (*US Black*) on bad = good model, something excellent, someone admirable. **4** [1950s+] (*US, Southern*) sexual intercourse with a woman. **5** [1960s] the female genitals. **6** [1960s+] (*US campus*) an unpleasant person. **7** [1980s+] (*US campus*) an extremely unattractive woman. [BUGGER n.[1]]

booger *n.*[3] (*also* **boogar**) [1970s+] (*US*) a derog. term for a Black person (cf. ALLIGATOR BAIT n.[2]). [var. on BOOGIE n.[2]]

booger *v.*[1] [late 19C+] (*US, Western*) to shy, to panic, usu. of an animal; thus **boogery** adj. [such panicking is supposedly the effect of a SE *booger*, a ghost, a hobgoblin]

booger *v.*[2] [20C+] (*US*) to sodomize. [SE *bugger*]

booger bear *n.* (*also* **boogie bear, booga bear, buger-bear**) [1940s+] (*US Black*) **1** a notably ugly person. **2** any difficult situation or unpleasant thing. [BOOGER n.[2] (2) + BEAR n.[1] (3); note US regional use *booger bear*, a hobgoblin used to frighten children]

boogerboo *n.* [1940s–60s] (*US Black*) an unpleasant situation or person. [BOOGER BEAR n.]

boogerboo *v.* [1940s–60s] (*US Black*) to behave in an unpleasant manner, to be insincere. [BOOGERBOO n.]

booger hook *n.* [2000s] (*US Black*) a punch delivered when one's opponent is not expecting it. [BOOGER n.[2] (2) + SE *hook*]

boogering *adj.* (*also* **booging**) [1960s] (*US*) damned, in the sense of irritating, infuriating. [BUGGERING adj.]

boogerlee *n.* (*also* **boogalee**) **1** [1960s] a person of mixed Black and White ancestry. **2** [1960s+] (*US*) a Cajun (a person of French descent in Louisiana). [? BOOGIE n.[2] + ? proper name *Stagolee*; ? var. on BOOGALOO n.]

boogerman *n.* [1940s] (*US*) a policeman. [SE *bogeyman*]

booger off *v. see* BUGGER OFF v.

boogers *n.* [1970s] (*W.I.*) in pl., trainers. [? BOOGER n.[1] (1)]

boogersnot *n. see* BOOGER n.[1] (2).

booger sugar *n. see* SUGAR n.[6] (2).

booger wagon *n.* [1960s] a prison van. [BOOGERMAN n. + SE *wagon*]

boogery *adj.* (*also* **buggery**) [20C+] (*US*) **1** frightened, frightening; thus *boogery-eyed*, wide-eyed. **2** unpleasant, malicious. [(1) BOOGER v.[1]; (2) BOOGER n.[2] (2)]

booget *n.* [mid-16C–mid-17C] (*UK Und.*) an itinerant tinker's basket. [SE *budget*, a pouch, bag, wallet, usu. of leather]

boogey *n. see* BOOGIE n.[2].

boogh *n. see* BOOCH n.

boogie *n.*[1] [late 19C+] (*US*) a piece of nasal mucus. [BOOGER n.[1] (1)]

boogie *n.*[2] (*also* **boogey, boogy**) [1920s+] **1** (*US*) a derog. term for a Black person (cf. ALLIGATOR BAIT n.[2]). **2** (*US Black*) a neutral or non-derog. term for a fellow Black person. [SE *bogey* or US dial. *boogerman*, bogeyman]

boogie *n.*[3] **1** [1930s+] (*US Black*) the vagina. **2** [1940s–60s] (*US Black*) sexual intercourse. **3** [1950s] (*US Black*) a sexually promiscuous person. **4** [1960s] (*US Black*) syphilis. **5** [1960s+] (*orig. US Black*) a good time, a party. **6** [1980s] (*orig. US Black*) energy. **7** [1990s+] (*US drugs*) marijuana, esp. when more than usu. strong. [BOOGIE v., despite date of (1)]

boogie *n.*[4] *see* BOOGIE HOUSE n. (1).

boogie *adj.* [1930s+] (*US*) Black, Afro-American. [BOOGIE n.[2]]

boogie *v.* (*orig. US Black*) **1** [1940s+] to enjoy oneself, to have a party, a good time; thus excl. *boogie down!* let's have fun! **2** [1940s+] (*also* **get one's boogies on**) to dance, often energetically. **3** [1940s+] to have sexual intercourse. **4** [1970s+] to go, to move, to do something quickly. [SE *boogie-woogie*, a form of jazz-based dance]

boogie board *n.* [1980s+] (*orig. Aus.*) a cut-down, half-sized surfboard. [BOOGIE v. (2) + SE *board*]

boogie box *n.* [1980s+] a large, portable cassette/tape player. [BOOGIE v. (2) + SE *box*/BOX n.[5] (7), but given initial association of such players with African-Americans, note poss. racist implications of 'boogie']

boogie house *n.* (*also* **boogie joint**) **1** [1920s–40s] (*US prison*) (*also* **boogie**) the prison hospital. **2** [1930s–70s] (*US Black*) a brothel (cf. ACCOMMODATION HOUSE n.). [BOOGIE v. (1) + HOUSE n.[1] (1)/JOINT n.[4] (3)]

boogie-joogie *n.* (*also* **boogie-joogy**) (*US Black*) **1** [1950s] boogie-woogie music. **2** [1970s] trickery, deceit. [BOOGIE v. (1) + redup./JUKE n.¹/JUKE n.²]

boogie-joogie v. (*also* **boogie-joogy**) [1960s] to enjoy oneself, to have a good time, to lead a hedonistic lifestyle. [BOOGIE v. (1) + JUKE v.³ (2)]

boogie town n. [1990s+] (*US*) the Black section of a town or city. [BOOGIE adj. + SE *town*]

boogie-woogie n. [1940s+] **1** (*US*) an emotional outburst. **2** (*US, Southern*) secondary syphilis. [fig. uses of SE *boogie-woogie* music]

boogie-woogie v. (*US Black*) [1930s] to enjoy oneself. **2** [1930s+] to leave, to depart. [fig. use of SE *boogie-woogie*, a form of jazz-based dance]

booging adj. *see* BOOGERING adj.

boogity-boogity adv. [1940s] (*US Black*) quickly. [BOOKITY-BOOK v.]

boogler n. [1960s] (*US Black*) a regular party-goer. [BOOGIE v. (1)]

boogooyagga n. [1940s+] (*W.I.*) a good-for-nothing person; also adj., worthless.

boogy n. *see* BOOGIE n.².

boogy adj.¹ [1960s+] suspicious, dubious, untrustworthy. [? BOGIE n.¹ or ? fig. use of BOGUEY adj.]

boogy adj.² *see* BOGUEY adj.

boo-hog n. *see* HOG n.⁷ (1).

boohonged adj. [1990s+] (*US campus*) drunk. [? BEER BONG n.]

boo-hoo n. [late 19C–1960s] whingeing, complaining. [BOOHOO v. (2)]

boohoo v. [mid-19C+] (*orig. US*) **1** to cry, to weep, to burst into tears. **2** to whinge, to complain; thus *boohooism*, nagging. [echoic]

boohoo! excl. [1930s+] a sarcastic excl. implying that one is shedding (utterly unfelt) tears at a given comment or event. [BOOHOO v. (1)]

booitjie n. *see* BOYKIE n.

boojee n. (*also* **bojie, boochie, boojie, boojum, boojy, bourgie, buzhie**) [1970s+] (*orig. US Black*) a bourgeois, middle-class and thus law-abiding Black (equally applicable to Whites). [abbr. SE *bourgeois*, middle-class]

boojee adj. (*also* **bojie, boojum, boojy, bourgie, buji**) [1970s+] bourgeois, middle-class. [BOOJEE n.]

boojie n. [1930s] (*US drugs*) a marijuana cigarette. [? BOO n.⁴ (1)]

boojum n.¹ [late 19C] a person, esp. a moralist. [from Lewis Carroll's poem 'The Hunting of the Snark' (1876), with its last line 'For the Snark *was* a Boojum, you see']

boojum n.² [2000s] (*US*) the vagina, in a sexual context. [? var. on BOOTY n. (1)]

boojum/boojy *see under* BOOJEE.

Book, the n. [1960s+] (*US Black*) the oral tradition that forms the basis of Black pimping.

book n.¹ **1** [19C+] a magazine, a periodical; mainly illiterate use. **2** [1950s+] (*US Black*) a pimp's supply of the names and addresses of clients.

book n.² **1** [mid-19C+] a bet. **2** [mid-19C+] a *book*maker's business. **3** [late 19C+] (*Aus./US*) a *book*maker; also attrib. [abbr.]

book n.³ **1** [20C+] (*Irish*) a class in primary school. **2** [1970s] (*US campus*) a study period. [the role of reading]

book n.⁴ (*orig. US prison*) **1** [20C+] the maximum sentence for a given crime. **2** [1920s–60s] a 1-year jail sentence. **3** [1920s+] (*also* **book of F.N.O.**) a life sentence; thus *bookman*, one serving a life sentence. **4** [1940s] in non-criminal contexts, any form of severe punishment. [a fig. *book* of punishments and/or broken rules; (3) abbr. SE *from now on*]

book n.⁵ [1960s] (*US campus*) an assiduous, hard worker. [BOOK v.³ (2)]

book v.¹ **1** [mid-19C] to take a private bet, which is written down in one's betting *book*. **2** [mid-19C+] to wager outside a sporting context. **3** [late 19C] to pay out bets. **4** [late 19C+] to work as a bookmaker; to take bets. [BOOK n.²]

book v.² **1** [mid-19C+] to arrest, to write down in a police charge

book. **2** [1970s] to note, to understand. [(1) one's name etc is written into a record book (now a computer)]

book v.³ [1960s+] (*US campus*) **1** to look at, to examine. **2** (*also* **book ass, book it, book tits**) to study assiduously. [SE *book*; (2) + ASS n. (5)/TIT n.³ (1) used reflexively]

book v.⁴ [1970s] (*US Black*) to fight.

book v.⁵ (*also* **book it**) [1970s+] (*US campus*) to leave, to go fast. [BOOKITY-BOOK v.]

book ass v. *see* BOOK v.³ (2).

book-beater n. [1940s] (*US teen*) a hard worker (at school). [BEAT THE BOOKS v.]

bookbinder's wife n. [late 18C–19C] the vagina. [play on 'her' occupation 'manufacturing in sheets']

book bluffing n. [mid-19C] (*US Und.*) a form of swindling whereby one offers an expensive book to the buyer, but actually hands over a cheap one, which has been substituted during the packing process.

booked adj.¹ **1** [19C] (*orig. boxing*) destined, fated, caught, disposed of. **2** [20C+] (*US*) fatally ill; thus *booked for kingdom come*. **3** [1930s] (*UK Und.*) insane. [? having *booked* one's space in the graveyard or 'set down in the book of history' (Bee)]

booked adj.² [1990s+] (*US campus*) ugly. [? BOOG adj.]

booker n. [1960s] (*US campus*) an assiduous worker. [BOOK v.³ (2)]

bookful n. [1920s+] (*US Und.*) a life sentence. [BOOK n.⁴ (3)]

bookie n. **1** [late 19C+] (*also* **booky**) (*orig. Aus.*) a *book*maker; also attrib., pertaining to bookmaking. **2** [1920s+] a bookmaker's establishment; usu. as *bookie's*. [abbr.]

bookie joint n. (*also* **bookie mill**) [1940s+] (*US*) a bookmaker's office. [BOOKIE n. (1) + JOINT n.⁴ (3)/SE *mill*, used to mean a place of work/activity]

booking n. [1990s+] (*US Und./police*) an arrest. [BOOK v.² (1)]

book it v.¹ *see* BOOK v.³ (2).

book it v.² *see* BOOK v.⁵.

bookity-book v. [late 19C–1930s] (*US Black*) to run fast, to move quickly. [? echoic of the sound of shoes slapping on the ground]

book-keeper n. [late 18C–early 19C] one who fails to return borrowed books. [pun]

book of many pages n. [1940s] (*US Black*) a dictionary.

book of the four kings, the n. *see* HISTORY OF THE FOUR KINGS, THE n.

bookoo *see also under* BEAUCOUP.

bookoo v. [1930s–60s] (*US Black*) to talk loudly and aggressively. [Fr. *beaucoup*, very much, thus very much noise]

bookoodles n. *see* BOOCOODLES n.

book-pad v. [late 17C–mid-18C] to plagiarize. [SE *book* + model of FOOTPAD n.]

bookra n. (*also* **bukra**) [1910s–40s] (*Aus./N.Z.*) tomorrow. [Arabic]

book rat n. [late 19C] (*US*) an obsessive reader, a bookworm. [they 'chew up' books]

bookrunner n. [1980s+] (*Aus. prison*) a prisoner on day release for educational purposes. [the prisoner uses books to 'escape']

books n.¹ [early 18C–1910s] a pack of playing cards; thus *plant the books*, to stack a deck of cards ready for cheating. [abbr. DEVIL'S BOOKS n., i.e. the pious identification of gambling with sin]

books n.² [2000s] (*US prison*) a prisoner's cash account, used for the canteen, postage stamps etc.

Booksellers' Row n. [mid-19C] Holywell Street, London WC2. [a deliberate euph. since the 'books' sold in Holywell Street, before it was knocked down for the Aldwych development, were strictly pornographic]

book-sharp n. [late 19C] (*US, Western*) an intellectual. [SE *book* + SHARP n.¹ (2)]

book smart adj. [1980s+] (*US campus*) academically high-flying, but low on common sense and social skills.

book the joint v. [1970s+] (*US teen*) to look over a place, to check its amenities. [BOOK v.³ (1) + JOINT n.⁴ (3)]

book tits v. see BOOK v.³ (2).

booku n. see BEAUCOUP n.

book up v. [1960s+] (US) to study assiduously. [SE]

bookworm n. [1940s] (US Und.) a shoplifter who specializes in stealing rare books. [play on SE]

booky n.¹ [mid-19C] a bouquet. [mispron.]

booky n.² see BOOKIE n. (1).

boola-boola n. [1930s+] (US campus) 1 college chauvinism; also ext. to any form of in-group self-congratulation. 2 a male college member. [college sports cheer boola-boola]

boolhipper n. [1970s+] (US Black) a leather coat. [ety. unknown; ? link to BULLY n.¹ (3)]

boom n.¹ [late 19C–1960s] (US) a positive endorsement, a 'plug'. [BOOM v.¹ (2)]

boom n.² 1 [1940s+] (drugs) marijuana; thus boom-boy, a marijuana smoker, (S.Afr.) boom-skuif, boomstop, a marijuana cigarette. 2 [1950s–60s] heroin and/or the sensation of intoxication by heroin. [Afk. boom, a tree or ? BOO n.⁴ (1)]

boom adj. [1990s+] excellent, very best. [BOOM v.¹ (2)]

boom v.¹ (US) 1 [early 19C] to hurry. 2 [late 19C–1950s] to promote, to extol. 3 [20C+] to live as a transient worker. [naut. jargon boom, for a sailing ship to reach top speed (the wind-filled sails 'boom' with the movement). (2) is SE since 1960s]

boom v.² see BOOM-BOOM v. (2).

boom! excl. 1 [1950s+] (also boom-boom) an echoic excl. used to imply suddenness, of a statement, an action etc, e.g. I came out of the shop and boom! there he was. 2 [1980s+] (US Black) a general excl. of agreement. [onomat. sound of an explosion]

boom-boom n.¹ 1 [1910s+] (US juv.) a soldier. 2 [1940s] (US Black campus) a cowboy film. 3 [1940s+] (US Black) a pistol, rifle or shotgun. [the sound of a shot]

boom-boom n.² [1960s+] (US juv.) excrement. [? echoic of defecation]

boom-boom n.³ [1960s+] (US) sexual intercourse; thus boom-boom girl, a prostitute; boom-boom parlor, a brothel.

boom-boom v. 1 [1930s] to reach orgasm. 2 [1960s+] (US) (also boom) to have sexual intercourse. [(1) echoic of an explosion; (2) BOOM-BOOM n.³]

boombox n. (also boomer) [1980s+] a large, portable cassette/CD/radio player. [ext. of SE; i.e. its reverberating bass]

boomer n.¹ (Aus./US) 1 [mid-19C+] a gross lie. 2 [late 19C+] anything considered exceptionally large or strong. 3 [late 19C+] something considered successful or popular. [SAusE boomah, a large kangaroo; note RMC Duntroon (Aus.) boomer, a general term of approval or enthusiasm]

boomer n.² 1 [late 19C–1950s] a boom town. 2 [late 19C+] (US) an enthusiast, esp. one who promotes or pushes a new enterprise. [BOOM v.¹ (2)]

boomer n.³ 1 [late 19C+] (US) a transient worker, a migrant; thus boomer reporter, a journalist who works on papers all over the country, never keeping any particular job for too long. 2 [1920s–30s] (US Und.) a transient thief, one who works in a particular town for a short while, then moves on. [SE boom, an economic upswing; the US boomers moved from one boom oil camp to the next during the 1920s–30s]

boomer n.⁴ [1960s+] 1 (US) a thunderstorm, a thunder-cloud. 2 (US surfing) a huge wave. 3 (US) in fig. use, something impressive. [the noise of thunder]

boomer n.⁵ [1980s+] (orig. US) a member of the 'baby-boom' generation (born in the late 1940s). [abbr. SE phr. baby boomer]

boomer n.⁶ see BOOMBOX n.

boomerang n. 1 [late 19C+] (US Und.) an unpleasant or undesired result, a COMEBACK n.¹ (2). 2 [1950s] (Aus.) something, esp. a book, that one wishes to have returned. [SE boomerang, which comes back to its thrower]

boomerang v. 1 [1940s] to bring unpleasant consequences. 2 [1990s+] (US Und.) to return to prison almost immediately on finishing the last sentence. [SE boomerang which, after one has thrown it, returns]

boomerang cheque n. [1950s–60s] (Aus.) a 'bouncing' cheque, which is not honoured and is 'returned to drawer'. [SE boomerang + cheque]

booming adj. 1 [mid-19C+] (Aus.) large. 2 [late 19C] grand. 3 [late 19C+] successful, flourishing. 4 [1990s+] (US Black) good-looking. 5 [1990s+] (US campus) excellent, worthy of approval. [SE boom, to advance keenly, to prosper]

boom! pow! bam! excl. [1990s+] (US Black teen) an excl. used to place emphasis in one's conversation. [orig. in comic books; ext. of BOOM! excl. (1)]

boomster n. [late 19C] (orig. US) a speculator. [SE boom, an economic upturn]

boon n.¹ [1950s] (US Black) $1. [? BONE n.⁴ (3)]

boon n.² [1960s+] (US Black) 1 a close friend. 2 a Black person. [? SE boon companion or Fr. bon, good + poss. link to BONE n.⁸ (1)]

boon v. [1990s+] to drive cross-country. [BOONDOCKS n.]

boon coon n. [1950s+] (US Black) a close companion. [SE boon (companion) + COON n. (7)]

boondock adj. [1950s+] (US) rural. [BOONDOCKS n.]

boondock v. [1960s+] (US campus) to neck, to pet or make love in an automobile. [BOONDOCKS n., i.e. a secluded rural spot suitable for love-making]

boondocker n. (also docker) [1960s+] (US campus) a picnic held in the woods where students can drink, play around, neck etc. [BOONDOCKS n.]

boondockers n. [1940s+] (US) a pair of strong shoes suitable for rough use. [BOONDOCKS n.]

boondocks n. [1940s+] (US) rough country, jungle, an isolated or wild region; in fig. use, an isolated unappealing place. [Tagalog bundock, a mountain; orig. used by US milit. (esp. US Marine Corps) to mean the field, the bush, the jungle, anywhere the troops operate that is not designated a firebase, a basecamp or occupied by civilians]

boondoggle n. [1930s+] (US) a waste of time, of money, of energy, esp. used by US government for a project that is considered wasteful of tax dollars; thus moondoggle, any form of lunar exploration judged to be a waste of public money. [according to the term's coiner, Robert Marshall: '"Boon doggles" is simply a term applied back in the pioneer days to what we call gadgets today.' The term also referred to the braided leather lanyard worn by scouts (a woggle in the UK) and earlier still to the cowboy term for making saddle trappings out of odds and ends of available leather, something they did when there was no proper work. The 1940s edn of Brewer, Dict. of Phrase and Fable notes the Scot. boondoggle, a marble given as gift and for which one has not had to make any effort – that ety. has been dropped from the 1995 edn]

boondoggle v. [1930s+] to waste time; thus boondoggler, a loafer, a time waster; boondoggling, time-wasting. [BOONDOGGLE n.]

booner n. [1970s+] (US) a Black person. [BOON COON n. + ? overtones of BOONDOCKS n., i.e. rural stupidity]

boong n. (also boang, bung) [mid-19C+] (Aus.) 1 a derog. term for an Aborigine; also attrib. 2 (also boonga) a native of Papua New Guinea. 3 any non-White person. [Wemba boong, a human being, a man]

boongie n. [2000s] (US prison) a prison officer. [ety. unknown]

boong moll n. 1 [1930s+] (Aus.) a prostitute who prefers Aborigine clients. 2 [1960s–70s] a passive male homosexual. 3 [1960s–70s] (US gay) a Black person. [BOONG n. + MOLL n.¹ (1); ? (2) refers to sexual exploitation of female Aborigines]

boongy bungee n. see BOONGIE BUNGEE n.

boonie n.¹ 1 [1950s+] a peasant, a country person (cf. BRUSH APE n.; BRUSH HOG n.; BUSH APE n.; BUSH HOG n.; BUSH RAT n.; BUSH-SCRUBBER n.¹; BUSHY n.¹; COUNTRY BOOKIE n.; COUNTRY COKES n.; COUNTRY CRACKER n.; COUNTRY HICK n.; COUNTRY JERK n.; COUNTRY

JOHNNY n.; COUNTRY PUT n.; CULCHIE n.; HILLJACK n.; WOOD HICK n.). **2** [1950s+] an outdoor lavatory. **3** [1960s–70s] a picnic held in the woods; thus *go on a boonie*, to go on a picnic in which sex is likely to be involved. [BOONDOCKS n.]

boonie *n.*[2] [1970s+] (*US*) a Black person. [BOONER n.]

boonie *adj.* [1960s+] (*US*) pertaining to the countryside or country culture. [BOONIE n.[1]]

boonie rat *n.* [1960s–70s] (*US, orig. milit.*) a US combat infantryman in Vietnam. [BOONIES n. + SE *rat*]

boonies *n.* [1950s+] (*US campus*) rural areas, the countryside (not necessarily rough or unpleasant). [BOONDOCKS n.]

boop *v. see* BOP v.

boopety *adj.* [20C+] (*US*) arrogant, self-important. [UPPITY adj. (1)]

boops *n.* [1970s+] (*W.I., Jam.*) a wealthy lover. [? POPS n. (3)]

boopsie *n.* [1970s+] (*W.I.*) a woman who enjoys the favours (material and otherwise) of her wealthy lover. [BOOPS n. + sfx *-ie*; note POPSIE n.[2]]

boorde *n. see* BORD n.

boose *see also under* BOUSE and its combs.

booser *n. see* BOOZER n. (1).

boosey *adj. see* BOOZEY adj.

booshwa/booshwah *n. see* BUSHWA n.

boosle *v. see* BOOZLE v.

boost *n.*[1] [mid-19C+] a statement of praise. [BOOST v.[1]]

boost *n.*[2] (*US Und./police*) **1** [1930s+] a robbery, usu. shoplifting. **2** [2000s] a stolen vehicle. [BOOST v.[2]]

boost *v.*[1] [early 19C+] (*US*) to praise, to extol, esp. one's own town or city; thus *booster*, one who makes such promotions; *give the boost*, to praise.

boost *v.*[2] [20C+] (*US Und.*) to steal, esp. to shoplift. [SE *boost*, to lift, to push, to hoist]

boost *v.*[3] [1930s] (*US*) to attack. [? BUST v.[1] (4)]

boost *v.*[4] [1980s+] (*US campus*) to seduce, to have sexual intercourse with. [ext. of BOOST v.[1]]

boost *v.*[5] [1990s+] (*Scot. juv.*) to leave. [ety. unknown]

boost and shoot *v.* [1960s+] (*drugs*) to steal to support a drug habit. [BOOST v.[2] + SHOOT v.[7] (1)]

booster *n.*[1] [20C+] (*US Und.*) **1** a shoplifter, esp. when on a large and professional scale; thus *booster fold*, a way of carrying stolen goods so as to render them invisible to store detectives; *booster box*, a package that looks sealed but enables a shoplifter to secrete stolen goods. **2** [1940s+] a thief. [BOOST v.[2]]

booster *n.*[2] [20C+] (*US*) **1** a house player in a casino who entices genuine players to bet (and usu. lose) their money. **2** any form of confederate working with a confidence trickster. [BOOST v.[2]]

booster *n.*[3] [1960s] (*US*) something exceptional of its type. [BOOST v.[1]]

booster *n.*[4] [1990s+] (*W.I.*) an aphrodisiac. [SE *boost*, to lift]

boosting *n.* (*US Und.*) **1** [1920s+] shoplifting. **2** [1960s+] theft in general. [BOOST v.[2]]

boosting bloomers *n.* (*also* **booster bloomers, booster drawers, booster skirt**) [1940s+] (*US Und.*) underwear that has been specially adapted for secreting items that have been shoplifted. [BOOSTING n. (1)/BOOSTER n.[1] (1) + SE *bloomers/drawers/skirt*]

boosting mob *n.* [1900s–20s] (*US Und.*) a gang of pickpockets. [BOOST v.[2]]

boost-up boy *n.* [1960s] (*UK Und.*) a thief. [BOOST v.[2]]

boosy *n. see* BUZZY n.

boosy *adj. see* BOUSY adj.

boot *n.*[1] [late 19C–1910s] (*US campus*) a toady, a sycophant. [abbr. BOOTLICKER n.]

boot *n.*[2] **1** [1910s+] (*US milit.*) any new recruit in the US armed forces; thus *boot camp*, basic training camp; *boot second lieutenant*, a newly commissioned second lieutenant. **2** [1950s+] (*US/UK Black*) a fellow Black (usu. derog.). **3** [1950s+] (*US*) a derog. term

for a Black person (cf. ALLIGATOR BAIT n.[2]). **4** [1950s+] a woman, the implication is of unattractiveness; thus often as *old boot*. **5** [1990s+] (*Can.*) a woman whose overt promiscuity renders her unattractive. [SE *boot*, the orig. ref. was to the leggings worn by recruits to the US Navy during training]

boot *n.*[3] [1920s–40s] (*US*) a *boot*legger. [abbr.]

boot *n.*[4] **1** [1930s+] (*US*) a thrill; thus *boot in the ass*, a thrill, a jolt of pleasure. **2** [1990s+] (*drugs*) a dose of a given drug. [fig. uses of SE *boot*, a kick; (1) + ASS n. (2)]

boot *n.*[5] **1** [1950s+] an automobile tyre. **2** [1970s+] (*US/W.I.*) a condom; thus *have one's boots on*, to use a condom. (2).

boot, the *n.* **1** [late 19C+] ejection, dismissal, defeat in all cases, esp. when sudden and ruthless; thus *get the boot*, to be thrown out, both of a place or one's employment; GIVE SOMEONE THE BOOT v. (1). **2** [late 19C+] an act of kicking; usu. in GIVE SOMEONE THE BOOT v. (2).

boot *v.*[1] **1** [mid-19C+] (*also* **boot up**) to kick, usu. in a fight. **2** [mid-19C+] to eject, to 'kick out'. **3** [1910s] (*US*) to dismiss, to ignore.

boot *v.*[2] **1** [20C+] (*US*) (*also* **boot it**) to walk or run away. **2** [1940s–50s] (*US Black/teen*) to drive a car (at speed).

boot *v.*[3] [1900s–10s] (*US campus*) to toady to. [BOOT n.[1]]

boot *v.*[4] [1920s–30s] (*US*) to bootleg. [BOOT n.[3]]

boot *v.*[5] [1920s–50s] (*US Black*) to give, to hand over. [SE *boot*, to share (booty)]

boot *v.*[6] **1** [1940s] (*US Black*) to introduce. **2** [1940s–50s] (*US Black*) to become aware. **3** [1940s–50s] (*US Black*) to inform, to explain. **4** [1960s–70s] (*US*) to disparage, to criticize.

boot *v.*[7] [1940s+] (*US, orig. sporting*) to blunder, to make a mistake. [lit. to reach for a ball but kick it rather than hold it]

boot *v.*[8] [1950s+] (*drugs*) **1** (*also* **kick**) to inject a drug in stages, drawing the heroin/blood mixture up into the syringe/eyedropper, then injecting, then repeating the process several times; usu. as BOOTING n.[3]. **2** in ext. use, to smoke or sniff heroin or crack cocaine. [(1) ? this 'pumping' action supposedly intensifies the KICK n.[5] (1) that accompanies the injection; or ? BOOT v.[1] (1), i.e. the visual resemblance to the act of repeatedly kicking]

boot *v.*[9] [1970s+] (*US campus*) to vomit (cf. BARF v.). [? echoic]

boot and shoe *n.* (*also* **boot and shoe fiend**) [1930s–50s] (*US drugs*) the lowest class of narcotics user. [such an addict has pawned even his shoes in order to buy narcotics]

boot-and-shoe booster *n. see* SNATCH-AND-GRAB BOOSTER n.

boot around *v.* [1930s] to kick, usu. in a fight. [BOOT v.[1] (1)]

boot boy *n.* [1970s+] a skinhead. [the heavy boots that make up part of their 'uniform']

boot camp *n. see* BOOT n.[2] (1).

boot-catcher *n.* [late 18C–early 19C] the servant whose task it is to help guests off with and to clean their boots on arrival at an inn.

bootchkey *n.* (*also* **butchski**) [1920s+] (*US*) a Czech immigrant. [Czech *pockej*, wait, used by Czech youngsters while playing games and thus adopted as generic by early Eastern European immigrants to US]

boot-eater *n.* [late 19C] a juror who would rather 'eat their boots' than find anyone guilty.

booted *adj.* [1940s+] (*drugs*) under the influence of (narcotic) drugs. [BOOT v.[8] despite chronology of cits.]

booted (on) *adj.* [1940s+] (*US Black*) aware, knowledgeable, smart. [BOOT v.[6]; note Burley: 'The fellow who is "hipped" or "hepped" is common indeed. But the one who is "booted" is a unique individual [...] To be hipped one has to have his boots on. The tighter the boots are laced, the more hipped the wearer is supposed to be']

booter *n.*[1] [1900s] (*US campus*) a toady, a sycophant. [BOOT v.[3]]

booter *n.*[2] [1920s–40s] (*US*) a bootlegger. [BOOT v.[4]]

booter *n.*[3] [1990s+] (*US drugs*) cocaine. [BOOT v.[8] (2)]

bootfaced *adj.* [1930s+] gloomy, miserable-looking. [naut. jargon *have a sea-boot face*, to look unhappy]

boothale *v.* [late 16C–early 17C] to rob, to steal. [SE *booty* + *hale*, haul]

boot-haler *n.* [17C] a highwayman. [BOOTHALE v.]

boothead *n.* [1980s+] (*US*) a derog. term for a Black person (cf. ALLIGATOR BAIT n.²). [BOOT n.² (3) + -HEAD sfx (2)]

booth-heaver *n. see* HEAVE A BOUGH v.

boot hill *n.* (*US*) **1** [19C] a cemetery. **2** [20C+] a prison cemetery. [orig. Western *Boot Hill*, in Dodge City, the cemetery set aside for those who died 'with their boots on', i.e. in a gunfight]

boot-hill two-step *n.* [1960s] (*US*) diarrhoea (cf. APPLE-BLOSSOM TWO-STEP n.). [SE *boot-heel* + *two-step*; pun on SE *trot*/TROTS, THE n.²]

bootie *n.* [1920s–30s] (*US*) a *boot*legger. [abbr.]

bootie *adj. see* BOOTSIE adj.

bootie-buster *n.* [1980s] (*US*) a male homosexual (cf. ANAL ASTRONAUT n.). [BOOTY n. (2) + BUST v.¹ (4)]

bootilitious *adj. see* BOOTYLICIOUS adj.

boot in *v.* [1920s] (*US*) to urge, to force. [SE *boot*, to kick]

booting *n.*¹ [1920s–30s] (*US Black*) having sexual intercourse. [BOOTY n. (1)]

booting *n.*² [1930s] bootlegging. [abbr.]

booting *n.*³ [1960s] (*drugs*) enjoying the immediate effects of a narcotic injection by injecting heroin a little by little. [BOOT v.⁸ (1)]

boot in the ass *n. see* BOOT n.⁴ (1).

boot it *v. see* BOOT v.² (1).

bootjack *n.* [mid-19C] (*US campus*) a fool. [SE *bootjack*, an inanimate object used for pulling off boots]

bootjack *adj.* [1960s] stolen. [BOOTJACK v.]

bootjack *v.* [1930s+] to steal. [SE *bootjack*, the image of removing something, i.e. from its owner]

bootkisser *n.* [1960s] a sycophant, a toady.

bootleg *n.* **1** [late 19C+] (*orig. US*) illicit liquor, usu. whisky (other than during US Prohibition). **2** [1900s–20s] (*US*) adulterated coffee, usu. mixed with chicory. **3** [1920s–30s] (*US Black*) a bootlegger. **4** [1950s+] (*orig. US*) a bootleg or pirated record, tape or video etc. **5** [1990s+] (*US teen*) anything or anyone considered pitiful, embarrassing, second-rate etc. **6** [2000s] a song that is a mix of 2 completely different songs spliced into a single track. [the orig. practice of carrying the illicit liquor hidden in one's boot-legs]

bootleg *adj.* (*orig. US*) **1** [late 19C+] of liquor, illegally transported, smuggled or distilled. **2** [late 19C+] fake, counterfeit. **3** [1920s+] illegal in general. **4** [2000s] (*US teen*) in fig. use, second-rate. [BOOTLEG v.]

bootleg *v.* **1** [late 19C+] to smuggle, to transport illegally (generally, but not invariably, of liquor). **2** [1920s–30s] to manufacture and sell illegal liquor. **3** [1940s] to sell cheaply. **4** [1960s+] to make an illegal copy of music, video etc. [BOOTLEG n.; later use of (2) is SE]

bootlegger *n.* [late 19C–1930s] (*orig. US*) a smuggler or manufacturer of illicit liquor; thus *bootlegger turn*, a handbrake turn (performed to avoid an on-coming car full of revenue officers or police)?. [BOOTLEG v.; 1940s+ use is SE and covers the pirating of records, tapes, computer games etc]

bootlick *n.* [mid–19C+] (*orig. US*) a cowardly, obsequious person, a toady, one who curries favour. [BOOTLICK v.]

bootlick *v.* [mid–19C+] (*orig. US*) to toady, to curry favour; thus *boot-licking*, sycophantic. [SE]

bootlicker *n.* [mid–19C+] (*orig. US*) a cowardly, obsequious person, a toady, one who curries favour. [BOOTLICK v.]

boot lip *n.* [20C+] (*US*) a Black person. [BOOT n.² (3) + SE *lip*]

boot out *v.* [late 19C+] to eject, to dismiss. [ext. of BOOT v.¹ (2)]

boot polish *n.* [1950s] (*UK Und.*) blackmail. ['colour']

boots *n.*¹ [early 17C; mid-19C+] a fellow, a person; usu. in combs. e.g. CLEVER BOOTS n.; SMARTY-BOOTS n. (1). [? metonymy]

boots *n.*² **1** [late 18C–19C] the servant assigned to the cleaning of boots and other odd jobs. **2** [late 18C–early 19C] the youngest member, i.e. of a regiment, a club etc. [abbr. BOOT-CATCHER n.; (1) 20C+ use is SE; note Grose (1785) cites only (2)]

boots *n.*³ [1960s] (*US Black*) a fellow Black person, sometimes derog. [BOOT n.² (2)]

boots and all *phr.* [mid-19C; 1940s+] (*Aus./N.Z.*) absolutely, completely, with no reservations.

boots and socks *n.* [20C+] (*Aus./UK*) venereal disease. [rhy. sl. = POX n.¹ (2)]

bootsie *adj.* (*also* **bootie**, **bootsey**, **bootsy**) [1990s+] (*US Black teen*) bad, phoney, inferior, second-rate. [? BOOTLEG adj.]

boot-snitch *n.* [1940s] (*US Black/Harlem*) **1** an informer, a tell-tale. **2** a dictionary. [BOOT v.⁶ (3) + SNITCH n.¹ (3)]

bootstrap *v.* [1950s+] (*orig. US*) to improve one's lot in life by one's own efforts. [phr. *pull oneself up by one's bootstraps*. Note computer jargon *boot(strap)*, to start the machine]

bootsy *adj. see* BOOTSIE adj.

boot the gong (around) *v. see* KICK THE GONG AROUND v.¹.

boot up *v.*¹ **1** [1950s–60s] (*US drugs*) to use a drink or drug to improve one's feelings, e.g. to inject heroin, to drink wine. **2** [1970s+] (*US Black*) to get ready for a fight. **3** [1990s+] (*UK drugs*) to take a narcotic. [BOOT v.⁸/SE *boot*, to lift]

boot up *v.*² [1970s+] (*US Black*) to put on a condom. [BOOT n.⁵ (2)]

boot up *v.*³ *see* BOOT v.¹ (1).

booty *n.* (*also* **boody**) [1920s+] (*US Black*) **1** the vagina; thus by metonymy woman, esp. as a sex-object and generic for sex (whether with a man or a woman). **2** the buttocks, the rectum; thus BOOTY BANDIT n.; *booty-struck*, obsessively lecherous. **3** a generic term for the body, thus a person. [SE *body*; note BUTT n.¹]

booty *adj.* [1990s+] (*US/UK Black/W.I.*) **1** weak. **2** second-rate, inferior. **3** gullible. [? fig. use of BOOTY n. (2) as a negative in the same way as ARSE n.¹ is used]

booty *v.* [17C–18C] to cheat, to play falsely. [PLAY BOOTY v.]

booty bandit *n.* **1** [20C+] (*US*) (*also* **boody bandit**) a homo-sexual male (cf. ANAL ASTRONAUT n.). **2** a heterosexual man who aggressively gropes or rubs up against women. [BOOTY n. + BANDIT sfx (2)]

booty banditry *n.* [1990s+] (*US*) male homosexual rape. [BOOTY BANDIT n. (1)]

booty-buffer *n.* [1990s+] a male homosexual; a heterosexual who enjoys anal intercourse (cf. ANAL ASTRONAUT n.). [BOOTY n. (2) + SE *buffer*, one who polishes]

booty call *n.* (*also* **boody call**) [1990s+] (*orig. US Black teen*) **1** a late-night rendezvous. **2** a person used for casual sex. [BOOTY n. (1) + SE *call*]

booty drought *n.* [1980s+] (*US Black/campus*) a lack of sex. [BOOTY n. (1) + SE *drought*/DROUGHT n. (2)]

booty-fellow *n.* [mid-16C; 19C] one who takes a share of the booty. [SE *booty* + *fellow*]

booty-funk *adj.* [1990s+] (*US campus*) unattractive. [BOOTY n. (2) + FUNK n.¹ (3), lit. 'stinky-arse']

booty-ho *n.* [2000s] (*US Black*) a female one dislikes as a person but finds exciting sexually. [BOOTY n. (1) + HO n.¹ (8)]

booty juice *n.* [2000s] (*US Black*) a mix of sweat and vaginal juices (cf. BINDERJUICE n.). [BOOTY n. (1) + JUICE n.² (1)]

bootylicious *adj.* (*also* **boodylicious**, **bootilitious**) [1990s+] **1** (*US Black*) second-rate, inferior. **2** (*Black*) a general term of approval, wonderful, attractive, sexy. [playing on BOOTY adj. + -LICIOUS sfx to make negative version of BODELICIOUS adj.; (2) BOOTY n. (1)]

booveroo *n.* [1900s] (*Aus.*) a layabout, a LARRIKIN n. [? Lincolnshire dial. *boof*, a clumsy fellow]

boo-ya *adj.* [1990s+] (*W.I./UK/US Black teen*) totally wonderful, incredibly fine. [? hip-hop group the *Boo-Ya Tribe*; ? abbr. BOOYAKA adj.]

booya! *excl.* (*also* **booyah!**) (*US Black/campus*) **1** [1980s+] a term used to indicate suddenness or surprise. **2** [1990s+] an echoic term used to imitate the sound of a shotgun being fired. **3** [2000s] an excl. denoting 'I told you so!' [SE excl. *boo!* + *yah*]

booyaka *adj.* [1990s+] (*W.I./UK/US Black teen*) totally wonderful, incredibly fine. [BOOYAKA! excl.]

booyaka! *excl.* [1990s+] **1** (*W.I./UK Black teen*) an excl. of delight, pleasure, made by using the mouth to simulate gun shots fired in celebration or appreciation of something. **2** (*orig. W.I., Jam.*) an excl. representing gunshots, a gunfight. [? echoic]

booze *n.* **1** [early 17C+] (*also* **booz, bouze, bues**) alcohol, a drink; for earlier uses *see* BOUSE n. (1). **2** [mid-18C+] a drinking spree. **3** [late 19C–1910s] a (glass of) drink. [the orig. sp./pron. is BOUSE n. but it was superseded by *booze* in the early 17C]

booze *v.* (*also* **booze it, bouze, buse**) [early 17C+] to drink. [the orig. sp./pron. is BOUSE v. but it was superseded by *booze* in the early 17C]

booze artist *n.* [1920s+] (*orig. Aus.*) a drunkard. [BOOZE n. (1) + ARTIST sfx]

booze balloon *n.* [1970s+] (*N.Z.*) a fat stomach that has resulted from sustained heavy drinking. [BOOZE n. (1) + SE *balloon*]

booze barn *n.* (*also* **beer barn**) [1970s+] (*N.Z.*) anywhere dedicated to the large-scale and rapid service of alcohol. [BOOZE n. (1) + SE *barn*]

booze bazaar *n.* [late 19C–1900s] (*US*) a bar. [BOOZE n. (1) + SE *bazaar*]

booze belly *n.* [1960s–70s] (*US*) a fat stomach that has resulted from excessive drinking. [BOOZE n. (1) + SE *belly*]

booze bus *n.* [1990s+] (*Aus.*) a police van used for random breath tests (for excess alcohol). [BOOZE n. (1) + SE *bus*]

booze-capper *n.* [1900s–10s] a woman who works in a bar to persuade customers to drink more than they wish or should. [BOOZE n. (1) + CAPPER n.^{1} (2)]

booze-casa *n.* [mid-19C] a public house, a tavern. [BOOZE n. (1) + CASA n.^{1}]

booze clerk *n.* [late 19C–1920s] (*US*) a bartender. [BOOZE n. (1) + SE *clerk*]

booze crib *n.* (*also* **booze joint, ...mill**) [mid-19C–1930s] (*UK/US Und.*) a bar, a tavern, any drinking establishment. [BOOZE n. (1) + CRIB n.^{1} (2)/JOINT n.^{4} (3)/SE *mill*, a place of activity, work]

boozed *adj.* [mid-18C+] drunk (cf. ALED UP adj.; BOUSED adj.). [BOOZE n. (1)]

boozed up *adj.* (*also* **boozed-out**) [late 19C+] drunk (cf. ALED UP adj.). [BOOZE UP v. (2)]

booze emporium *n. see* BOOZORIUM n.

booze factory *n.* (*also* **rum factory**) [late 19C–1900s] (*US*) a bar. [BOOZE n. (1)/SE *rum* + *factory*]

booze-fencer *n.* [late 19C–1900s] a licensed victualler. [BOOZE n. (1) + -FENCER sfx]

boozefest *n.* [1930s–60s] (*US*) a drunken party. [BOOZE n. (1) + -FEST sfx]

booze fight *n.* [1940s+] (*orig. US Black*) a drinking spree. [BOOZE n. (1) + fig. use of SE *fight*]

booze-fighter *n.* **1** [20C+] (*Aus./US*) (*also* **booze killer**) a drunkard. **2** [1920s–60s] (*US*) a narcotics addict (in the context of using alcohol to counter withdrawal symptoms). [BOOZE n. (1) + SE *fighter*/SE *killer*]

booze-fighting *adj.* [1900s–40s] rowdy, regularly drinking, drunk. [BOOZE-FIGHTER n. (1)]

booze foundry *n.* [1930s] (*US*) a saloon. [BOOZE n. (1) + SE *foundry*]

boozegob *n.* [1930s] (*US*) a drunkard. [BOOZE n. (1) + GOB n.^{1} (1)]

booze-head *n.* (*also* **booze freak**) [1960s–70s] (*US*) a drunkard. [BOOZE n. (1) + -HEAD sfx (3)/FREAK sfx]

booze-hoister *n.* **1** [1910s–20s] (*US*) a prodigious drinker. **2** [1930s] a bartender. [BOOZE n. (1) + SE *hoister*]

booze hound *n.* [1910s+] (*US*) a dedicated drinker. [BOOZE n. (1) + HOUND sfx]

booze it *v. see* BOOZE v.

booze it up *v. see* BOOZE UP v. (2).

booze joint *n. see* BOOZE CRIB n.

booze ken *n. see* BOUSING-KEN n. (1).

booze killer *n. see* BOOZE-FIGHTER n. (1).

boozelum *n. see* BOOZEROO n.

booze mill *n. see* BOOZE CRIB n.

boozen-ken *n. see* BOUSING-KEN n. (1).

boozeologist *n.* [1900s] (*US*) a bartender. [BOOZE n. (1) + sfx -*ologist*, a student of professor of a given 'ology']

booze-pusher *n.* [late 19C–1900s] a licensed victualler. [BOOZE n. (1) + PUSH v.^{2} (1)]

boozer *n.* **1** [late 18C+] (*also* **booser**) a drunkard. **2** [late 19C+] (*also* **oozer**) a public house or bar. [BOOZE n. (1)]

boozeroo *n.* (*also* **boozelum**) [1940s+] (*N.Z.*) **1** a drinking spree. **2** a public house. [BOOZE n. (1) + -EROO sfx/-*elum*]

booze-rooster *n.* [1960s] (*N.Z.*) a heavy drinker. [play on BOOZEROO n.]

booze runner *n.* [1920s–30s] (*US Und.*) a transporter/smuggler of illegal alcohol; the vehicle or vessel used for such transport; thus *booze run*, the act of smuggling. [BOOZE n. (1) + RUNNER n.^{1} (3)]

boozery *n.* [1910s–50s] (*US*) a drinking place. [BOOZE n. (1) + sfx -*ery*]

booze-shunter *n.* [late 19C–1900s] a beer drinker. [BOOZE n. (1) + SE *shunter*; coined by railwaymen working for the Southern Region]

booze-stupe *n.* [1950s] (*US*) an alcoholic. [BOOZE n. (1) + STUPE n.; lit. 'drink-fool']

booze-up *n.* [late 19C+] a drinking party, a heavy drinking session. [BOOZE UP v. (2)]

booze up *v.* **1** [late 19C–1910s] (*Aus.*) to make someone else drink or drunk. **2** [1910s] (*also* **booze it up**) to drink, to get drunk. [BOOZE n.]

boozey *adj.* (*also* **boosey**) [late 18C+] drunken. [BOOZE n. (1)]

boozician *n.* [1940s+] (*Aus./US*) a heavy drinker, a drunkard. [BOOZE n. (1) + sfx -*ician*, on pattern of SE *physician, mortician* etc]

boozing *n.* (*also* **bousing, busing**) [mid-17C+] drinking. [BOOZE v./BOUSE v.]

boozing-can/-crib/-ken *n. see* BOUSING-KEN n.

boozington *n.* (*also* **Mr Boozington**) [mid-19C–1910s] (*Aus.*) a drunkard. [BOOZE n. (1) + sfx -*ington*]

boozle *n.* [1940s–60s] sexual intercourse. [? fig. use of BOOZLE v./BAMBOOZLE v. (1), i.e. a confusion of bodies]

boozle *v.* (*also* **boosle**) [late 18C] to confuse, to outwit. [abbr. BAMBOOZLE v. (1)]

boozorium *n.* (*also* **booze emporium**) [20C+] (*Can./US*) a bar-room, esp. in a hotel. [BOOZE n. (1) + sfx -*orium*/*emporium*]

boozy *n.* [1920s+] (*Anglo-Irish*) a drunkard. [BOOZE n. (1) + sfx -*y*]

boozy *adj.* **1** [late 17C+] (*also* **bouzy**) drunk, drunken (cf. ALED UP adj.; BOUSY adj.). **2** [1930s+] redolent of alcohol. [BOOZE n. (1) + sfx -*y*]

bop *n.*^{1} **1** [1930s+] (*orig. US*) a blow. **2** [1950s–60s] (*US*) a member of a teen street gang. **3** [1950s–60s] (*US*) a fight between teen street gangs. **4** [1950s+] (*orig. US*) a dance. **5** [1960s] (*Scot.*) a hairstyle copied from that of Elvis Presley. **6** [1970s+] (*drugs*) an injection of a narcotic drug, the taking or immediate effect of any drug, e.g. a puff on a cannabis cigarette. **7** [1990s+] (*US Black*) a bouncing style of walking, a stride. [BOP v.]

bop *n.*^{2} [1970s] (*US Black drugs*) a drug in pill form; thus *drop a bop*, to take a drug (cf. PILL n.^{4}). [play on HIT n.^{3} (6)/BOP n.^{1} (1)]

bop *n.*^{3} [1970s+] (*US Black*) foolish talk, prattle, nonsense. [abbr. REBOP n.]

bop *n.*[4] [1980s+] (*S.Afr.*) the former Republic of *Bop*huthatswana, one of the Black 'homelands' with its territory surrounded by the Transvaal and Orange Free State. [abbr.; *Bophuthatswana* = lit. 'gathering of the Tswana']

bop *v.* (*also* **boop**) **1** [1920s+] (*orig. US*) to hit. **2** [1930s+] (*orig. US*) to kill. **3** [1950s+] (*orig. US*) to walk in a carefree, bouncy way. **4** [1950s+] (*US*) to fight (with a weapon). **5** [1950s+] (*orig. US*) to dance. **6** [1970s+] (*US*) to have sexual intercourse (cf. BANG v.[1]). **7** [1980s] (*orig. US*) to be exciting. **8** [1980s] (*orig. US*) to ride, i.e. a bicycle or car. **9** [1990s+] (*orig. US*) to look for someone to seduce. [Kentish dial. *bop*, to throw anything down with a resounding noise; ult. onomat.]

bop! *excl.* [1940s] a general excl. of surprise or suddenness. [BOP v. (1)]

bop around *v.* [1960s+] to keep moving, to wander about rather than stay put; to visit briefly. [BOP v. (3)]

bo-peep *n.* **1** [early 17C–early 19C] a person who hides themself in order to spy on others. **2** [late 19C+] sleep. **3** [1940s+] a look, a 'peep'; often in phr. *go for a bo-peep*. **4** [1960s+] (*US gay*) the eyes. **5** [1980s+] (*US gay*) dark glasses. [nursery rhyme *Little Bo Peep* compounded by rhy. sl. in (2) and (3)]

bo-peep *v.* [late 19C+] to sleep. [rhy. sl.; ult. nursery rhyme *Little Bo Peep*]

bop it up *v.* [1950s] (*US teen*) to enjoy oneself, to go out on a spree. [BOP v. (5)]

bopkes *n. see* BOBKHES n.

bop one's baloney *v.* [1970s+] to masturbate (cf. BANG THE BISHOP v.; BEAT ONE'S MEAT v.). [BOP v. (1) + BALONEY n.[2]]

bop one's richard *v.* [1990s+] to masturbate (cf. BANG THE BISHOP v.). [BOP v. (1) + SE *Richard*, i.e. DICK n.[4] (1)]

bop out *v.* [20C+] (*US*) to faint. [BOP v. (1); the image is of being knocked over]

bopper *n.*[1] [1950s–60s] (*US*) a gang fighter. [BOP v. (4)]

bopper *n.*[2] [1970s] a young girl, usu. in very early teens, with a predilection for rock music and the boys who play it. [abbr. TEENYBOPPER n. (1)]

bopper *n.*[3] [1990s+] a person looking for sex all the time. [BOP v. (6)/BOP v. (9)]

bopper *n.*[4] *see* BEBOPPER n.

bopper *n.*[5] *see* BINKY n.[1] (2).

boppers *n.* [1960s–70s] (*US campus*) boots, shoes. [echoic of the noise of one's footsteps]

bopping club *n.* [1950s] (*US*) a street gang that has regular fights with opponents. [BOP v. (4)]

bopping gang *n.* [1950s] (*US*) a street gang with active fighters. [BOP v. (4)]

boppy *adj.* [1940s+] jolly, cheery, upbeat. [jazz use, *bop* music]

bopster *n. see* BEBOPPER n. (2).

bop the bishop *v.* [1990s+] to masturbate. [BOP v. (1); var. on BANG THE BISHOP v.]

bop up *v.* [1970s–80s] (*N.Z. prison*) to improve the tailoring of prison-issue clothing; thus *bopped-up*, enhanced. [fig. use of BOP v. (1), cognate with KNOCK UP v.[3] (1)]

bora *n.* [1990s+] (*UK Black*) a knife. [? SE *borer*]

borac *n. see* BORAK n.

borachio *n. see* BORRACHIO n.

boracic *see under* BORASS.

boracic (lint) *adj.* (*also* **brassic, brassick, brassic lint**) [1940s+] out of funds, impoverished, pron. 'brassic'. [rhy. sl. = SKINT adj.]

borak *n.* (*also* **borac, borack, borax**) [mid-19C+] (*Aus./N.Z.*) nonsense, humbug, chaff, banter. [Wathawurung *burag*, no, not, via Aus. pidgin *borak*, used to express negation]

borarco *n. see* BORRACHIO n.

borass *n.* (*also* **boracic, boress**) [1950s+] (*US campus*) a trick, a prank, a hoax. [? fig. use of BORAX n.[1] or ? *bore ass*]

borass *v.* (*also* **boracic, boress**) [1950s–70s] (*US campus*) to hoax, to play tricks. [BORASS n.]

borax *n.*[1] [1920s+] (*US*) **1** rubbish, lies, exaggeration. **2** shoddy, cheap manufactured goods. [SE *borax*, cheap and shoddy material, esp. as peddled by immigrant Jews; supposedly orig. in the practice of a maker of borax (acid borate of sodium) soap offering coupons for cheap furniture]

borax *n.*[2] *see* BORAK n.

bord *n.* (*also* **boorde, borde**) [mid-16C–early 19C] a shilling (5p). [SE *bord*, shield]

bordeaux *n.* [mid-19C–1900s] blood (cf. BADMINTON n.). [SE *bordeaux*, a variety of red wine]

bordens *n.* [1940s–70s] (*US*) the female breasts; also ext. as *borden's and elsie's*; *bordens and bowman*; one of many sl. terms for breasts relating to their role as milk-giving (cf. BUBBIES n.; CHI-CHI n.[1]; CREAM JUGS n.; DAIRY n.[1]; DAIRY ARRANGEMENTS n.; DINNERS n.; DUGS n.; ELDERS n.; FEEDING BOTTLES n.; FUCK UDDERS n.; JUGS n.; LUNCHCOUNTER n.; MILK BAR n.[1]; MILK BOTTLES n.; MILK CAN n.; MILKERS n.; MILK FACTORIES n.; MILK ROUTE n.; MILK SHAKES n.; MILK SHOP n.; MILK WAGON n.; MILKY WAY (TO BLISS) n.; NATURE'S FOUNTS n.; NINNY JUGS n.; NORKS n.; PAPS n.[1]; TIT n.[3]; TITTY n.[1]; UDDERS n.). [the firm *Borden's*, producers of milk and dairy products; *elsie* presumably refers to a 'typical' name for a cow]

border brothers *n.* [2000s] (*US prison*) Mexicans (cf. BATO n.).

border reef *n.* [1980s] (*Aus.*) the teeth. [rhy. sl.]

borders *n.* (*also* **border reds**) [1970s+] (*drugs*) non-proprietary capsules of barbiturate powder sold on the black market. [their container, a capsule with a red border as well as the implication that they have been made up on the US/Mexico border]

bore *n.*[1] [mid-18C] the equivalent of Fr. *ennui*, a feeling of world-weariness, the equivalent of Eng. *spleen*; thus *French bore*, one who feels or at least affects indifference to all things and people. **2** [late 18C–early 19C] a tedious person or thing, a nuisance. **3** [early 19C] (*US*) a trick, a hoax. [*OED* states ety. unknown. ? f. SE *bore*, to drill into, but this fails to account for sense (1), from which (2) and (3) presumably stem. E.P. suggests poss. link to *boar*, an uncouth, ignorant person, but this still ignores (1), which lasted as sl. no later than the 1760s. Grose (1785) notes that (2) and (3) were very fashionable *c.*1780 and then vanished. 'Not so, burly Grose,' says Hotten in 1859, 'the term is still in favour and as piquant and expressive as ever.' However, although Hotten includes it, the word was by then virtually, if not actually, SE]

bore *n.*[2] **1** [mid-19C] the penis (cf. ARSE-OPENER n.). **2** [mid-19C–1940s] the vagina (cf. BLACK HOLE n.[1]). [SE *bore*, (1) an auger/(2) a hole, a crevice or cranny]

bore *v.*[1] [early 17C–early 19C] to tease, to mock, to humiliate. [SE *bore*, to drill a hole; 19C use primarily US]

bore *v.*[2] [mid-17C+] to have sexual intercourse, whether hetero- or homosexual. [SE *bore*, to drill a hole]

bore *v.*[3] **1** [mid-18C–mid-19C] to impose one's views, opinions or simply presence upon those who find them tedious and irritating. **2** [late 18C–mid-19C] to irritate, to annoy. [(1) SE from mid-19C]

bore *v.*[4] [mid-19C–1950s] (*US*) to shoot a hole in. [note 17C SE *bore*, to run through with a sword]

bore a hole in *v.* [mid-19C] (*US*) to shoot. [ext. of BORE v.[4]]

bored for the simples *adj.* [1920s–30s] (*US*) a phr. meaning 'cured of one's foolishness', e.g. *he ought to be bored for the simples*, he is a fool. [var. on CUT FOR THE SIMPLES adj.; SE *bore*, to make a hole + dial. *simples*, simple-mindedness; + ? a ref. to trepanning]

bore it up *v.* [1940s+] (*Aus.*) to attack viciously or energetically; also in fig. use. [SE *bore*, to pierce, stab, run through with a weapon; to wound]

bore rigid *v.* [1970s+] to bore very much. [BORE v.[3] (1) + SE *rigid*; later var. on BORE STIFF v.]

bore someone a new one *v.* [1950s] (*US*) to attack savagely, either physically or verbally. ['one' is an ASSHOLE n.¹ (1); thus var. on TEAR SOMEONE A NEW ASS(HOLE) v.]

bore someone's ear v. [late 18C–19C] to bore (as a talker). [BORE v.³ (1) + pun; note OED *bore (someone's) ears*, to consign to perpetual slavery (allusion to Exod. 21:6)]

boress see under BORASS.

bore stiff v. [20C+] (*orig. US*) to bore completely (cf. BORE RIGID v.). [BORE v.³ (1) + SE *stiff*, corpse-like; one is rendered virtually dead by tedium]

bore the pants off v. (*also* bore the arse off, ...knickers off) [1930s+] to bore completely and totally. [BORE v.³ (1) + PANTS, THE n./ARSE, THE n./SE *knickers*]

boretto-man n. [late 17C] a male homosexual. [SE *bore* + Ital. dimin. sfx *-etto*; i.e. 'a little borer']

bore up v. [1980s+] (*UK Black*) to fight, to assault. [SE *bore*, to drill a hole]

Boris n. [1980s] a generic derog. term for a Russian. [proper name]

boris bold adj. [2000s] cold. [rhy. sl.]

born (a bit) tired adj. [late 19C–1940s] a sarcastic description of a congenitally lazy person, e.g. *you have to forgive him, he was born tired*.

born-again n. [1990s+] (*US campus*) a fundamentalist Christian. [SE *born-again*, adj., after John 3:3: 'Except a man be born again, he cannot see the kingdom of God']

born-again virgin n. [1980s+] a celibate person, whether homosexual or heterosexual, through choice or otherwise (cf. B.A.V. n.).

born and bred n. [2000s] a bed. [rhy. sl.]

born on Wednesday looking both ways for Sunday phr. (*also* born in the middle of the week...) [mid-19C+] (*US*) cross-eyed.

born tired adj. see BORN (A BIT) TIRED adj.

born under a threepenny halfpenny planet phr. [17C–19C] a phr. said of a complete failure; usu. ext. by ...*never to be worth a groat*.

born with burned feet phr. [1970s] (*US*) illegitimate.

'Boro n. [1970s+] (*US*) a Marlboro cigarette. [abbr.]

boro-onions n. [early–mid-19C] (*Cockney*) inhabitants of Southwark, London SE1. [*Boro(ugh)nians*; ult. *Borough*, an area of London]

borrachio n. (*also* borachio, borarco, borracho) 1 [17C–19C] a drunkard. 2 [late 17C] a skin for holding wine. [Sp. *borracho*, a drunkard, drunk]

borrak v. see POKE (THE) BORAK v.

borrow v. [early 19C+] (*US Und.*) to steal. [ironic use of SE]

borrow and beg n. [20C+] an egg. [rhy. sl.]

borstal mark n. (*also* borstal spot) [1990s+] (*UK prison/Und.*) a blue dot tattooed on the face, the mark of a spell in borstal.

b.o.s. n. [1990s+] (*US/P.R. gang*) a beating on sight. [abbr.]

bosbefok adj. see BOSSIE adj.

bosca/boscar adj. see BOSKER adj.

Bosche n. see BOCHE n.

'boscis n. see PROBOSCIS n.

bosco n. [1920s–70s] (*US*) a foolish, unimportant person. [? BOSKY adj. but note ety. for GEEK n.¹]

bosco boulevard n. [1980s+] (*US gay*) the anus (cf. ALLEY WAY n.). [? SE *bosky*, dark and wooded]

bosh n.¹ [mid-18C+] nonsense, rubbish. [Turk. *bosh*, empty, worthless. The term gained enormous popularity from the success of James Morier's novel *Ayesha* (1834), a bestseller, esp. in the Standard Novels edn of 1846]

bosh n.² [mid-19C–1930s] a fiddle; *bosh-faker, bosh-killer, boshman*, a fiddle-player. [Rom. *bosh*, to fiddle, to crow]

bosh n.³ [late 19C–1900s] margarine or any other substitute (e.g. the short-lived *butterine*) for butter. [abbr. *bosch butter*, artificial butter manufactured at 'Hertogenbosch' or 'Bosch' (Bois-le-duc) in Holland; ? reinforced by BOSH n.¹]

bosh v. [late 19C] 1 to spoil, to render useless. 2 (*also* bosh up) to cause trouble for, to irritate. 3 to apply liberally (used of paint, plaster etc). [BOSH n.¹]

bosh! excl.¹ [mid-19C+] rubbish! nonsense! [BOSH n.¹]

bosh! excl.² [1990s+] an echoic term used to imply suddenness of action.

bosher n. [1910s–30s] one who talks nonsense. [BOSH n.¹]

boshey adj. see BOSHY adj.

bosh-shot n. [1930s–50s] a bad shot, an unsuccessful attempt. [BOSH v. (1) + SE *shot*]

boshta n. (*also* boshter) [1900s–10s] (*Aus.*) something or someone outstanding. [BOSHTA adj. (1)]

boshta adj. (*also* boshter) 1 [20C+] (*Aus.*) good. 2 [1910s] on good terms with, popular. [? SE *bonanza* or ? BOSKER adj.]

boshta adv. [1910s] (*Aus.*) excellently, very well. [BOSHTA adj.]

bosh up v.¹ [late 19C–1920s] to go bankrupt. [BOSH v.]

bosh up v.² see BOSH v. (2).

boshy adj. (*also* boshey) [mid-18C+] foolish, nonsensical. [BOSH n.¹]

bosie v. [1970s+] (*W.I., Trin.*) to beat extremely hard, so as to bend the victim double. [W.I. *bosie*, a hunchback; ? link to Aus. cricket jargon *bosie*, a googly or 'wrong 'un'; it 'bends' across the pitch]

boskage of Venus n. [late 19C] female pubic hair. [SE *boskage*, a thicket, grove, woody undergrowth]

bos-ken n. (*also* bosken) [19C] a farmhouse. [Lat. *bos*, OX + KEN n.¹ (1)]

bosker adj. (*also* bosca, boscar) [20C+] (*Aus./N.Z.*) good. [var. on BONZER adj.]

boskiness n. [late 19C] drunkenness. [BOSKY adj. + sfx *-ness*]

bosky adj. (*also* bosko) [early 18C–1930s] drunk. [? SE *bosky*, wooded, bushy; thus one's vision is obscured and one's feet may stumble]

bos-man n. (*also* bosman) [mid-19C] a farmer. [Lat. *bos*, ox]

bosom buddy n. [1960s] (*US campus*) a male homosexual.

bosom friend n. 1 [18C+] (*also* bosom chum) a louse. 2 [19C] alcoholic drink. 3 [20C+] (*US*) a pack of money kept for security inside a woman's brassiere while she is travelling. [play on *bosom friend*, an especially intimate friend]

boss n.¹ [late 16C–mid-17C] a fat woman. [SE *boss*, a swelling or protuberance]

boss n.² 1 [mid-17C+] (*orig. US*) (*also* bosshead) the master (or mistress), the manager, the 'guvnor'. 2 [mid-19C+] (*US*) an exceptional person. 3 [mid-19C+] (*orig. US*) a term of address, esp. to a man whose name one does not know. 4 [late 19C+] a 'criminal mastermind'. 5 [1930s] (*UK prison*) a prison governor. 6 [1950s+] (*US prison*) a prison warder. [Du. *baas*, master, in which form it first appeared in the American colonies in mid-17C. The term did not arrive in the UK until the mid-19C and has always been sl. or colloq.]

boss n.³ [late 19C] a view, a sight of. [? BOSS-EYE n., i.e. a 'squint' at]

boss n.⁴ [2000s] (*US Black*) female-to-male fellatio. [the dominant role of the male BOSS n.² (1)]

Boss, the n. [20C+] (*orig. US*) God. [BOSS n.² (1); the use of sl. to 'humanize' the Deity]

boss adj. 1 [mid-19C+] (*orig. US*) best, ultimate. 2 [mid-19C+] (*orig. US*) excellent, wonderful; also intensified as *boss like hot sauce*. 3 [mid-19C+] (*orig. US*) superior, important, influential. 4 [late 19C] (*Aus.*) of criminals, very dangerous. 5 [late 19C] (*US*) arrogant, overbearing. 6 [1960s] dedicated, obsessed with. 7 [2000s] important, meaningful. [BOSS n.² (1)]

boss v. [mid-19C+] 1 (*also* boss about, boss around) of a person, to domineer, to order about. 2 of an object, to dominate, to take control of. 3 to make a mess of, to spoil. [BOSS n.² (1); (1) is SE in 20C+]

boss adv. [1970s+] (*US*) splendidly, excellently, perfectly. [BOSS adj. (2)]

boss bitch n. [1960s] (*US Black*) the senior member of a pimp's STABLE n. (2) of prostitutes. [BOSS n.² (1) + BITCH n.¹ (11)]

boss-boy n. [20C+] (*S.Afr.*) a Black foreman or overseer in charge of subordinate Black workers. [BOSS n.² (1) + S.Afr. derog. *boy*, an African, usu. a servant or labourer]

Boss Charlie n. (*also* **Boss Charley**) [20C+] (*US Black*) a White man, esp. in authority (cf. MR CHARLIE n.). [BOSS n.² (1) + generic use of proper name *Charlie*]

boss cocky n. [late 19C+] **1** (*Aus.*) a farmer who employs labour and still works. **2** (*Aus.*) a person in authority. **3** (*Aus./N.Z.*) the overseer of a shearing-shed. [BOSS n.² (1) + COCKY n.² (1)]

boss con n. *see* CON BOSS n.

boss dog n. [20C+] **1** (*US*) an important person or one who poses as such. **2** (*US prison*) a prison rapist, one who exploits weaker prisoners, esp. sexually. [BOSS n.² (1) + SE *dog*]

bossers n. [late 19C–1900s] spectacles. [? BOSS-EYED adj.]

boss-eye n. [late 19C+] one who squints or has an injured eye. [BOSS-EYED adj. (1)]

boss-eyed adj. **1** [mid-19C+] squinting. **2** [1950s] tipsy, drunk (cf. ARSEHOLED adj.). [BOSS v. (3) + SE *eyed*]

bossgame n. [1970s] (*US Black*) an important person, usu. in ironic use. [BOSS n.² (1)]

bosshead n. *see* BOSS n.² (1).

bossie adj. (*also* **bosbefok**) [1970s+] (*S.Afr., orig. milit.*) used to indicate that someone has gone mad through exposure to tropical heat and life in the bush, lit. 'bush-fucked'. [Afk. *bos*, bush + *befok*, FUCKED adj.¹ (2)]

boss lady n. **1** [1920s+] a female superior. **2** [1950s+] (*US*) (*also* **boss-woman**) a wife who dominates her husband. [BOSS n.² (1) + SE *lady/woman*]

boss-man n. **1** [19C] (*US*) the overseer, foreman, employer, chief prison guard etc, anyone in authority. **2** [1970s+] (*US gay*) the 'masculine' member of a homosexual couple. [BOSS n.² (1) + SE *man*]

boss nigger in charge n. *see* HEAD NIGGER IN CHARGE n.

boss player n. [1960s] (*US Black*) a thoroughly experienced, professional, worldly-wise pimp who may even transcend pimping for superior occupations; the term can be applied to any admirable figure outside the pimp milieu (cf. CANDYMAN n.; HOE JOCKEY n.; LONG-SHOE n.; MACK DADDY n.; PIMP WHISK n.; PROMOTED PIMP n.; STAR n.²). [BOSS adj. (3) + PLAYER n.¹ (3)]

boss's royal n. *see* ROYAL n.³.

boss the show v. (*also* **boss the shebang**) [late 19C] to take charge of events. [BOSS v. (1) + SHOW n.¹ (1)/SHEBANG n. (5)]

boss trick n. [1960s+] in prostitution, a good customer. [BOSS adj. (2) + TRICK n.¹ (3)]

boss up v. [20C+] (*S.Afr.*) **1** to manage a house, to organize the servants. **2** to work hard. [BOSS v. (1)]

boss up! excl. [late 19C+] (*S.Afr.*) take care! look out! [calque f. Cape Du. *pas op!* look out!]

boss-woman n. *see* BOSS LADY n. (2).

bossy n. [1930s] (*US tramp*) beef; thus *bossy in a bowl*, beef stew. [Lat. *bos*, ox]

bossy adj. [late 19C+] (*orig. US*) officious, domineering. [BOSS n.² (1) + sfx -*y*]

bossy-boots n. [20C+] (*mainly UK juv.*) an officious, domineering person. [BOSSY adj. + BOOTS n.¹; on model of SMARTY-BOOTS n.]

bosta n. (*W.I.*) **1** [1940s+] a tough, chewy sweet. **2** [1950s] a sandal made from recycled tyres. [proper name of the populist politician Sir Alexander *Bustamente* (1884–1977), seen as tough]

bosthoon n. (*also* **bostoom, bostoon**) [mid-19C–1960s] (*Irish*) a fool. [Irish *bastún*, lout]

Boston strawberries n. [late 19C+] (*US*) baked beans. [the city's stereotyped dish. The other stereotype is meanness; thus railroad use *Boston quarter*, a nickel or dime tip]

Boston woodcock n. [1930s+] (*US*) pork and beans. [analogous with SE *Scotch woodcock*, hard-boiled eggs chopped up, mixed with anchovy sauce, and then laid on slices of hot buttered toast. The foodstuffs here are staples of the Boston area]

bostoom/bostoon n. *see* BOSTHOON n.

bosy adj. *see* BOASIE adj.

bot n.¹ **1** [late 19C] (*Aus.*) a scheme, a plot, a plan. **2** [1910s+] (*Aus./N.Z.*) (*also* **bott**) a cadger, a scrounger, a hanger-on; thus *on the bot*, cadging. **3** [1940s+] (*N.Z.*) a germ; thus *have the bot*, to feel unwell or irritable; *how are the bots biting?* a phr. of greeting. [fig. use of SE *botfly* (*see* BOTFLY n.)]

bot n.² [late 19C+] a *bott*le. [abbr.]

bot n.³ **1** [1920s+] the buttocks. **2** [1990s+] (*also* **bott**) an act of homosexual anal intercourse. [abbr. SE *bottom*]

bot v. (*Aus./N.Z.*) **1** [1910s] to impose oneself. **2** [1930s+] to scrounge; thus *cold botting*, knocking on a stranger's front door and asking for food. [BOT n.¹ (2); (2) note salesman's jargon *cold call*, to arrive without a prior appointment in the hope of making a sale]

bot about v. [1920s+] (*Aus./N.Z.*) to wander restlessly from place to place. [BOT v. (2)]

botanical excursion n. [mid-19C] transportation to New South Wales. [a pun on the penal colony at *Botany Bay*]

Botany Bay n.¹ [late 18C–19C] penal servitude. [Australia's earliest convict settlement was at *Botany Bay*, New South Wales]

Botany Bay n.² [late 19C] the vagina (cf. ANTIPODES n.). [the penal colony of *Botany Bay* was 'down under']

Botany Bay v. (*also* **do a Botany**) [20C+] (*Aus.*) to run away. [rhy. sl.]

Botany Bay coat-of-arms n. [early–mid-19C] (*Aus.*) a broken nose and black eyes. [the violence that was prevalent at the convict settlement]

Botany Bay dozen n. [late 18C–mid-19C] (*Aus. Und.*) a punishment of 25 lashes.

Botany Bay fever n. [early–mid-19C] transportation to New South Wales.

Botany beer party n. [late 19C] a party at which there is no form of intoxicating liquor. [brandname of *Botany beer*, which was declared after a court case in 1883 not to be real beer]

botch n.¹ (*also* **botcher**) [late 18C–early 19C] a tailor. [abbr. SE *botcher*, one who repairs or patches; also note SE *bodger* and dial. *botch*, a cobbler]

botch n.² [1960s] (*US*) gonorrhoea. [SE *botch*, an eruptive sore, an ulcer, a plague-spot, thus Deut. 28:27 'The Lord will smite thee with the botch of Egypt, and with the emerods, and with the scab, and with the itch, whereof thou canst not be healed']

botch v. [1990s+] (*US campus*) to ignore. [? 'not watch' or ? SE *botch*]

botfly n. (*Aus.*) **1** [20C+] an unpleasant, troublesome, interfering person. **2** [1940s+] a scrounger. [SE *botfly*, an insect of the genus *Oestrus*; its eggs produce the parasitical worm or maggot, the bot]

Botha's babes n. [1970s+] (*S.Afr.*) members of the South African Army Women's College at George, Cape Province. [name of President P.W. *Botha* (b.1916), who established the corps in 1971; they were also known in Afk. as *soldoedie*, 'soldier lass']

both ends of the busk! excl. [late 18C–early 19C] a toast before drinking (cf. MILK AND WATER! excl.). [SE *busk*, a corset, spec. its stiffening/supporting whalebone or other agent; the top would support the breasts, the bottom be near the vagina, the parts of the body that are being celebrated in this toast]

bother n. [mid-19C+] trouble, difficulties; thus *in bother*, in trouble.

bother! excl. [early 19C+] a mild excl. [Anglo-Irish but no spec. root found; ? corruption of *pother*, disturbance]

botherate v. [20C+] (*US Black*) to annoy, to menace, to threaten. [SE *bother*, to annoy + sfx -*ate*]

botheration n. [late 18C+] annoyance, irritation. [SE *bother*; late 19C+ use is mainly US Black]

botheration! *excl.* [19C+] a mild excl. of annoyance that precludes anything more lurid and thus taboo.

bother boy *n.* [1970s] a youth dedicated to fighting, usu. a skinhead. [BOTHER n. + SE *boy*]

bothered up *adj.* [1920s+] flustered, maniacally nervous, sometimes through the suppression of lust.

bothering *n.* [late 18C] a loud fuss, a commotion.

botherment *n.* [mid-19C] annoyance, irritation. [SE *bother* + sfx *-ment*]

bother one's soul-case *v. see* BURST ONE'S SOUL-CASE v.

both hands *n.* [1930s–60s] (*US Und.*) a sentence of 10 years. [the 10 fingers thereon]

both-side *adj.* [20C+] (*W.I., Trin.*) deceitful, hypocritical. [one who speaks out of 'both sides' of their mouth]

both ways *adj.* [1960s+] bisexual. [SWING BOTH WAYS v.]

both ways from the ace *phr.* (*also* **both ways from the jack, forty/fifty ways from the ace**) [1910s–20s] (*US*) in every way, completely. [card-playing imagery]

bots *n.* **1** [16C–17C] syphilis. **2** [late 16C–mid-17C] a general oath. **3** [late 18C–19C] (*also* **batts, botts**) a general sense of physical unease. **4** [1900s] (*US*) depression. [SE *bots*, a disease of horses caused by infestation of botfly larvae in the digestive tract]

botsie *n.* [20C+] (*W.I.*) the posterior, the buttocks. [SE *bottom*]

bott *n.*[1] *see* BOT n.[1] (2).

bott *n.*[2] *see* BOT n.[3] (2).

bott *v.* [1990s+] to sodomize. [abbr. SE *bottom*]

bottee *n.* [1990s+] a passive homosexual, one who is sodomized. [BOTT v.]

botter *n.* [1990s+] a male homosexual; spec. an active sodomizer. [BOTT v.]

bottie *n.* (*also* **botty**) [mid-19C+] (*UK juv.*) a baby's or small child's buttocks. [abbr. SE *bottom*]

bottle *n.*[1] [early 18C] the penis. [the supposed resemblance]

bottle *n.*[2] **1** [1900s–30s] (*UK Und.*) the hip pocket (which is near the buttocks); thus ON THE BOTTLE phr. (1). **2** [1910s+] courage, bravery; thus *has your bottle fallen out?* are you afraid? **3** [1940s] a severe reprimand. **4** [1950s+] the buttocks, the posterior; thus ON THE BOTTLE phr. (2) (cf. ALA n.). **5** [2000s] a person, usu. in a derog. sense. [abbr. BOTTLE AND GLASS n.; which, in turn, plays on 18C SE *bottom*, character for (3)]

bottle *n.*[3] **1** [late 19C–1930s] a share of money. **2** [1960s+] £2. [BOTTLE v.[2]]

bottle *v.*[1] [20C+] to hit someone (in the face) with a broken bottle.

bottle *v.*[2] [1920s+] to collect money from a busker's audience; thus *bottling*, collecting money from the audience, 'passing round the hat'. [ext. use of SE *bottle* as a general container]

bottle *v.*[3] [1950s+] **1** of a man, to have sexual intercourse. **2** to sodomize. **3** (*gay*) to lick the anus, to perform anilingus (cf. AUSTRALIAN n.). **4** (*UK prison*) of a prisoner, to hide drugs etc by wrapping in plastic and inserting up the anus. [BOTTLE n.[2] (4)]

bottle *v.*[4] [1970s] to stink, to smell badly. [? rhy. sl.; *bottle of drink* = stink]

bottle-ache *n.* [mid-19C–1900s] delirium tremens.

bottle and glass *n.* **1** [1910s+] the buttocks, the anus (cf. ALA n.; CHORUS AND VERSE n.; COUNCIL GRITTER n.; DATE n.[3]; DEAF AND DUMB n.[2]; ELEPHANT (AND CASTLE) n.; GARY GLITTER n.; JAM ROLL n.; KHYBER (PASS) n.; LIGHT AND BITTER n.; LONDON TAXI n.; MERRY OLD SOUL n.; NORTH POLE n.; PEARLY KING n.; RONSON n.[2]; ROY CASTLE n.; SOUTH POLE n.; SPAM FRITTER n.; SWISS-ROLL n.; THELMA (RITTER) n.; WINDSOR CASTLE n.). **2** [1950s+] courage, bravery, 'spirit'. [rhy. sl. = ARSE n.[1] (1); for semantics *see* BOTTLE n.[2]]

bottle (and stopper) *n.* [1910s+] (*US*) a policeman (cf. CLODHOPPER n.; CLUB AND STICK n.; GINGER-POP n.; GRASSHOPPER n.[3]; GREASY (MOP) n.; HAMMER AND SAW n.; HOT SCONE n.; JOE GOSS n.; JOHN HOP n.; LEMON (DROP) n.; LOLLIPOP n.[3]; PORK CHOP n.[1]; SCONE n.[1]; SLOP n.[3]; SPINNING TOP n.; STRING AND TOP n.). [rhy. sl. = COPPER n.[3] (1)]

bottle-arse *n.* [mid-16C; late 19C–1910s] a person with notably broad buttocks; thus *bottle-arsed*. [SE *bottle* + ARSE n.[1] (1), i.e resemblance; but note printers' jargon *bottle-arsed*, worn type that is thicker at one end than the other]

bottle baby *n.* [1920s+] (*orig. US*) an alcoholic tramp who has become insane and whose mental age is that of an infant. [pun on SE *bottle baby*, an infant fed by bottle rather than by breast]

bottle blonde *n.* **1** [20C+] a woman with dyed hair. **2** [2000s] (*Aus.*) a stupid individual. [the *bottle* the hair dye comes from; (2) f. (1)]

bottle-boy *n.* [1930s–40s] (*US*) a drunkard, an alcoholic.

bottled *adj.*[1] **1** [19C] arrested, caught. **2** [late 19C–1910s] stuck in one place, halted. [BOTTLE UP v.; (2) note Ware's suggestion that it refers to the trapping by the US Navy of the Spanish fleet in Santiago in 1898]

bottled *adj.*[2] (*also* **bottled out**) [1920s–60s] drunk (cf. ALED UP adj.).

bottled earthquake *n.* [mid–late 19C] a strong alcoholic drink (cf. EARTHQUAKE n.).

bottled in the barn *n.* [1940s–50s] (*US*) illicitly distilled whisky. [pun on SE *bottled in bond*, bottled and then held in a Customs warehouse until the appropriate duty is paid]

bottled out *adj. see* BOTTLED adj.[2].

bottled up *adj.* [late 19C] fully occupied, unable to take on any new commitments. [SE *bottled up*, contained in a bottle]

bottlegreen and lousy *adj.* [1950s+] (*Aus.*) utterly down-and-out. [one's complexion and the state of one's body]

bottlehead *n.* [mid-17C–mid-19C] **1** a fool; thus *bottle-headed*, foolish. **2** a drunkard. [SE *bottle* + -HEAD sfx (1)/-HEAD sfx (3); their brains are fuddled by alcohol, whether lit. or fig.]

bottle-ho *see under* BOTTLE-O.

bottle-holder *n.* [mid-18C–19C] a supporter, an assistant; thus *bottle-holding*, assistance, support. [boxing use, where the fighter's 'second' holds a bottle of water]

bottle hound *n.* [1960s+] (*US*) an alcoholic, a heavy drinker. [SE *bottle* + HOUND sfx]

bottle it *v.*[1] [late 19C+] (*orig. US*) to be quiet, to shut up; usu. in imper. [SE *bottle it up*]

bottle it *v.*[2] [1950s+] to back down, to act in a cowardly manner. [BOTTLE n.[2] (2)]

bottle juggler *v.* [1910s] (*US*) a barperson.

bottleneck *n.* [1970s+] (*S.Afr. drugs*) a mixture of tobacco and marijuana (sometimes with other forms of drugs) packed into the neck of a broken bottle, which serves as a pipe and through which it is smoked.

bottle-nose *n.* (*also* **bottlenozzle**) [early 17C; mid-19C–1920s] one who has a large, prominent nose. [its shape + the implication of drunkenness]

bottlenosed *adj.* **1** [mid-16C–early 17C; mid-19C+] large-nosed. **2** [18C–mid-19C] drunk. **3** [1920s] thus Jewish, in a stereotypical, derog. context. [BOTTLE-NOSE n.]

bottle-o *n.* (*Aus./N.Z.*) **1** [1900s–60s] (*also* **bottle-ho, bottle-oh**) a collector and seller of used bottles; also of 'rags and bones'. **2** [1990s+] a liquor store. [SE *bottle* + -O sfx (4)]

bottle-o *adj.* (*also* **bottle-ho**) [1900s] (*Aus.*) pertaining to the collectors and sellers of used bottles. [BOTTLE-O n. (1)]

bottle of beer *n.* [20C+] the ear. [rhy. sl.]

bottle of cola *n.* (*also* **bottle of Kola**) [1910s–40s] a bowler hat. [rhy. sl.; *Kola* was a bottled drink made by R. White and sold in London]

bottle of fizz *phr.* [1930s+] (*UK Und.*) working as a pickpocket. [rhy. sl. = ON THE WHIZ phr.]

bottle of sauce *n.* [late 19C+] a horse. [rhy. sl.]

bottle of scent *adj.* [1990s+] of a man, homosexual, effeminate. [rhy. sl. = BENT adj. (5)]

bottle of scotch *n.* [19C] a watch, spec. one of the

cheap Waterbury watches, produced since 1884 in Waterbury, Connecticut. [rhy. sl.]

bottle of spruce n.[1] **1** [mid-19C–1900s] 2 pence. **2** [1930s–40s] (US gambling) 2. [rhy. sl. = DEUCE n.[1] but note BOTTLE OF SPRUCE n.[2]]

bottle of spruce n.[2] [19C–1900s] zero, nothing; thus *I don't care a bottle of spruce.* [proper name of *Spruce* Beer, a weak, cheap and thus essentially valueless commodity; its price was 2d]

bottle of water n. **1** [1930s+] a daughter. **2** [1990s+] (drugs) a quarter (of an ounce). [rhy. sl.]

bottle of wine n. [1990s+] a judicial fine. [rhy. sl.]

bottle-oh n. see BOTTLE-O n. (1).

bottle opener n. [1970s] (US gay) an active male homosexual. [BOTTLE n.[2] (4)]

bottle out v. [1970s+] to be a coward, to run away, to back down from a challenge. [BOTTLE n.[2] (2)]

bottler n.[1] **1** [mid-19C+] (Aus./N.Z.) anyone or anything outstanding, either in a positive or negative manner, usu. congratulatory, e.g. *you little bottler.* **2** [1930s] (US Und.) a prostitute. **3** [1930s+] a sodomite. **4** [1940s+] a coward, someone who 'bottles out'. **5** [1940s+] (N.Z.) a 'hard case', a thug; usu. as *bloody bottler.* [BOTTLE n.[2] (2)/BOTTLE n.[2] (4); (1) and (4) the positive/negative division is between one who has 'bottle' and one who 'bottles out']

bottler n.[2] [1920s+] one who 'passes round the hat', e.g. after a busker's performance. [BOTTLE v.[2]]

bottles n. [1980s+] (drugs) **1** crack cocaine vials. **2** amphetamines (cf. A n.[2]). [the containers in which the drug is sold]

bottles of booze n. [1940s–50s] (US) shoes. [rhy. sl.; ult. BOOZE n. (1)]

bottle tipper n. [1940s–60s] (US) a drunkard.

bottle tokes n. [1980s+] (US drugs) a method of smoking hashish where a small hole is made in a bottle (usu. a beer bottle), then a cigarette with a small chunk of hashish on the tip is inserted in the hole. [SE *bottle* + TOKE n.[2] (1)]

bottletop n.[1] [20C+] a gain, a benefit, something good. [rhy. sl. = COP n.[2] (2)]

bottletop n.[2] [1950s] (N.Z.) a policeman's helmet. [resemblance + ref. to BLUEBOTTLE n. (2)]

bottle up v. [late 19C–1940s] to abandon an argument, to 'call it quits'. [SE *bottle up*, to repress]

bottle up and go v. [1930s–40s] (US Black) to leave, esp. after an unpleasant disagreement. [BOTTLE IT v.[1]]

bottle wash n. [late 19C+] nonsense, rubbish. [i.e. the dregs washed out of a bottle]

bottley adj. [2000s] nervous. [BOTTLE OUT v./LOSE ONE'S BOTTLE v.]

bottling adj. [20C+] (Aus.) excellent, first-class; also note approving/congratulatory phr. *his/her/your blood's worth bottling.* [BOTTLER n.[1] (1)]

bottom n.[1] **1** [mid-17C] capital, (financial) resources. **2** [late 17C–mid-19C] stamina, endurance, 'grit'. [sporting jargon; note 17C–18C phr. *stand on one's own bottom*, to act independently, to act for oneself]

bottom n.[2] [early 19C] (US) a (fast) runner. [? SE *bottom*, 'the part of a boot or shoe below the uppers; the sole, heel, and shank' (OED)]

bottom n.[3] [mid-19C+] (US Black) the Black area of a town. [such areas were often on low-lying land, near a river]

bottom n.[4] [1970s+] in sado-masochistic sex, a passive or masochistic person. [as opposed to a TOP n.[3]]

bottom adj. [late 18C–mid-19C] courageous, full of stamina and endurance. [BOTTOM n.[1] (2)]

bottom v. **1** [20C+] (US campus) to finish off a drink, to empty a glass. **2** [1900s–30s] (Aus.) to bet all one's money. [one reaches the *bottom*]

bottom baby n. see BOTTOM WOMAN n. (1).

bottom bandit n. (also **botty burglar**) [1990s+] a male homosexual (cf. ANAL ASTRONAUT n.). [SE *bottom* + BANDIT sfx (2)]

bottom bitch n. see BOTTOM WOMAN n. (1).

bottom burp n. [1980s+] a fart. [SE *bottom* + BURP n.; generally juv. but popularized on BBC TV's 1980s comedy *The Young Ones*]

bottom dealer n. [1930s+] (US) a swindler, a cheat. [card imagery; lit. one who deals from the bottom of the pack]

bottom feeder n. [1970s+] (US teen) **1** a despicable, unpleasant person. **2** one who has yet to make their mark, a 'wannabe'. **3** a social outcast. **4** a gossip, esp. a trader in malevolent and harmful stories. [SE *bottom-feeder*, a fish that feeds off the sea- or riverbed]

bottom grapes n. see ARSE-GRAPES n.

bottom ho/lady n. see BOTTOM WOMAN n. (1).

bottomless pit n. [late 18C–19C] the vagina (cf. BLACK HOLE n.[1]).

bottom line n. **1** [1980s+] the end result, the final assessment. **2** [1990s+] something steady, reliable. [SE *bottom line*, the final profit/loss figure on an account]

bottom line v. [1980s+] (orig. US) to sum up, to speak succinctly. [BOTTOM LINE n.]

bottom man n. [1970s+] the submissive partner in a homosexual sado-masochistic couple. [metaphorically rather than always physically 'on the bottom']

bottom of a woman's tu quoque n. [late 18C–early 19C] the crown of a woman's head. [presumably TU QUOQUE n., although anatomically bizarre]

bottom rib n. [1970s] (US Black) a wife. [supposedly the rib taken from Adam and used in the creation of woman]

bottom road n. [1930s] (UK tramp) a road leading from London to the South Coast. [the 'bottom' of the UK]

bottoms n. [20C+] (US Black) the least pleasant, the poorest part of a ghetto or inner-city area. [lit. the physically low-lying areas of a town]

bottoms up! excl. [20C+] (orig. RN) a popular toast before drinking. [the *bottoms* are those of the glasses as the drinks are emptied into the drinkers' mouths]

bottom-wetter n. [late 19C+] **1** sexual intercourse, from the point of view of a woman. **2** a penis. [vaginal secretions and semen]

bottom woman n. [1960s+] (US Black) **1** (also **bottom baby**, ...**bitch**, ...**ho**, ...**lady**) the most reliable and experienced of a pimp's STABLE n. (2) of prostitutes. **2** one's (attractive) girlfriend. [SE *bottom*, a foundation]

botts n. see BOTS n. (3).

botty n. see BOTTIE n.

botty adj. [mid-19C] conceited, swaggering. [orig. stable use]

botty-basher n. [1990s+] (UK juv.) a male homosexual (cf. ANAL ASTRONAUT n.). [BOTTIE n. + BASH v.[1] (4)]

botty burglar n. see BOTTOM BANDIT n.

botty burp n. [1990s+] the breaking of wind. [BOTTIE n. + SE *burp*]

boudoir bandicoot n. [1980s] (Aus.) a promiscuous male. [var. on LOUNGE LIZARD n. (1)]

bouffer n. see BUFE n.

bought it adj. [1940s+] killed, usu. in battle. [BUY THE FARM v.]

bougie adj. (also **bougy**) [1970s+] taking on the attitudes and lifestyle of the middle classes. [SE *bourgeois*]

boulder n. **1** [late 19C–1900s] (US) a diamond. **2** [1980s+] (drugs) a generic term for crack cocaine; spec. $20 worth of crack cocaine (cf. BASE n.). [play on ROCK n.[2] (1)/ROCK n.[3] (4)]

bouldered adj. [1980s+] (Aus. drugs) very heavily intoxicated by a drug, usu. cannabis. [pun on STONED (OUT) adj. (2)]

boulder-holder n. (also **over-the-shoulder-boulder-holder**) **1** [1950s+] (Aus./US) a brassiere (cf. SHOULDER BOULDERS n.). **2** [2000s] a tank-top.

boulevard boy n. [1970s+] (US, Los Angeles) a male homosexual prostitute who works Sunset or Hollywood Boulevard (cf. BOULEVARD JUNKIE n.).

boulevard cowboy n. [1940s+] (US) a taxi-driver, esp. a reckless driver whose driving style is uninhibited by the presence of other drivers, let alone pedestrians.

boulevard junkie n. [1980s] (US, Los Angeles) a drug user who frequents Sunset or Hollywood Boulevard (cf. BOULEVARD BOY n.). JUNKIE n. (2)]

boulevard westerner n. [1940s+] (US) a reckless taxi-driver. [var. on BOULEVARD COWBOY n.]

bouman n. [1910s+] (Irish) a friend, a 'pal'. [ety. unknown; ? BOMAN n. (1)]

bounce n.[1] 1 [late 17C] a braggart, a swaggerer. 2 [18C–1920s] a boast, a self-aggrandizing lie. 3 [early 18C–1980s] (orig. Aus.) cheek, impudence, arrogance. 4 [early–mid-19C] a well-dressed braggart and/or swindler. 5 [late 19C+] energy.

bounce n.[2] 1 [mid-19C] (UK Und.) a confidence trick, a swindle. 2 [1930s–60s] (US Und.) arrest and subseq. trial. 3 [1970s] (UK Und.) fiddling and dishonest practice (adjusting invoices, stealing stock etc) by retail shop employees.

bounce n.[3] [late 19C] cherry brandy. [? its effects]

bounce n.[4] [late 19C] (US) a trip, a journey. [the state of the roads/vehicles]

bounce n.[5] (also **bouncy-bouncy**) [1960s+] an act of sexual intercourse.

bounce n.[6] [1960s] a rejection, e.g. of a book proposal. [BOUNCE, THE n.]

bounce n.[7] [2000s] (US) a commission.

bounce n.[8] see BUNCE n.

bounce, the n. (also **the grand bounce**) [late 19C+] (US) ejection, esp. from a saloon or bar; usu. in GET THE BOUNCE v. or GIVE SOMEONE THE BOUNCE v.

bounce v.[1] 1 [16C–17C; 1960s+] of a man, to have sexual intercourse. 2 [mid-17C–1920s] (US) to persuade, to influence by flattery. 3 [late 17C+] to boast, to brag, to bully, to scold, to intimidate. 4 [mid-18C–mid-19C] to lie. 5 [late 18C+] to refuse admission or to throw out of a party, a place of entertainment etc. 6 [early 19C–1900s] to rob, to cheat. 7 [late 19C] to avoid, to get rid of a person. 8 [late 19C+] to dismiss, usu. from a job. 9 [late 19C+] (US) to reject, esp. of a proposal of marriage. 10 [late 19C+] (US Black/teen) to leave. 11 [20C+] to escape arrest/prosecution while posing as a respectable person. 12 [1900s–30s] (US campus) to be sent down from college, to be sent out of class. 13 [1910s] (US) to punch. 14 [1910s] (Aus.) to move someone forcibly. 15 [1910s–30s] (US) (also **bounce off**) to kill. 16 [1920s] (US) to attack, esp. from an ambush. 17 [1920s–40s] to beat up. 18 [1930s] (UK Und.) to assault, using a piece of lead concealed in a sock. 19 [1930s+] (US) to treat, to pay for, to ply with drink. 20 [1950s+] (US teen/Und.) to move, to go. 21 [1960s+] to work as a BOUNCER n.[2] (5) in a bar etc. 22 [1980s] (US police) to arrest and interrogate; to pressurize. [1960s+ use of (1) is Aus.]

bounce v.[2] 1 [early 19C] to put oneself in debt, e.g. making a bet or ordering a drink, knowing that one has no funds. 2 [1900s] (Aus.) to lose money. 3 [1920s–50s] to pay a cheque, knowing that one has insufficient funds in one's bank account. 4 [1930s–50s] of a bank, to refuse to honour a cheque, marking it 'return to drawer'. [(3) and (4) SE since 1960s]

bounceable adj. (also **bouncible**) [mid-19C] prone to boasting or showing off. [BOUNCE v.[1] (3) + sfx -able/-ible]

bounce a car v. [2000s] (US prison) to borrow a fellow inmate's radio. [ety. unknown]

bounce for v. [1970s] (US) to agree, to hand over without payment. [ext. of BOUNCE v.[1]]

bounceful adj. [mid-19C] arrogant, domineering. [BOUNCE n.[1] (3) + sfx -ful]

bounce in v. [1940s] (US) to appear in an aggressive manner.

bounce it off v. [mid-17C–mid-18C] to drink heartily.

bounce off v. see BOUNCE v.[1] (15).

bouncer n.[1] [late 16C; mid-19C] (US) something or someone exceptionally large.

bouncer n.[2] 1 [late 17C–early 19C] (UK Und.) a swaggerer, a blusterer, a bully. 2 [mid-18C–mid-19C] a liar. 3 [late 18C–1900s] an unashamed lie. 4 [mid–late 19C] (UK Und.) a thief who steals from shops, often while distracting the merchant's attention with his argumentative bargaining. 5 [mid-19C+] (orig. US) a large, tough man employed to keep order in premises, often a pub, club, concert hall etc. 6 [late 19C] (UK Und.) a sharp, a cheat. 7 [late 19C] (UK Und.) a pimp, esp. one who practises the MURPHY GAME n.[1] (cf. ABBOT ON THE CROSS n.). 8 [late 19C] (UK Und.) a thug who, allied with a male street prostitute, blackmails homosexuals. [BOUNCE v.[1]]

bouncer n.[3] [mid-late 19C] (US) a social climber. [SE bounce, to rebound; the social climber rebounds from any number of rebuffs, secure in the overwhelming power of money]

bouncer n.[4] [1930s+] (US Und.) a bad cheque. [BOUNCE v.[2]]

bounce refrigerators v. [1990s+] (US campus) to have sexual intercourse. [var. on BUMP UGLIES v.]

bounceroo n. [1930s–40s] (US) ejection, dismissal. [BOUNCE, THE n. + -EROO sfx]

bouncers n. [1950s+] female breasts (cf. BOBBER n.[2]).

bounce the ball v. 1 [1910s–20s] (Aus.) to assert oneself. 2 [1920s+] (N.Z.) to assess public opinion. [(2) from the habit of rugby players testing the bounce of a ball prior to drop-kicking it off]

bouncible adj. see BOUNCEABLE adj.

bouncing n.[1] [late 19C] a severe scolding; also as adj. [BOUNCE v.[1] (3)]

bouncing n.[2] [1980s] (US) going out on a spree, to enjoy oneself. [BOUNCE v.[1] (19)]

bouncing adj. [late 16C–17C] big, lusty, energetic. [SE f. 1700]

bouncing ben n. [mid-19C–1920s] an intellectual, a learned person. [? a sceptical view of learning, i.e. a BEN n.[1] who 'bounces' with their own self-importance]

bouncing buffer n. [early–mid-19C] a beggar. [London dial. bouncer, a professional beggar + BUFFER n.[4] (2)]

bouncing cheat n. [18C] (UK Und.) a bottle. [SE bounce + CHEAT n. (1); the bottle 'bounces' as the cork is drawn]

bouncing paper n. [1940s] (US Und.) bad cheques. [BOUNCE v.[2] + PAPER n.[1] (1)]

bouncing powder n. [1930s+] (drugs) cocaine (cf. BIRDIE POWDER n.). [the effect it has on its temporarily enlivened users]

bouncy-bouncy n. see BOUNCE n.[5]

bouncy in one's deuce of benders adj. (also **bouncy in one's brace of dukes**) [1900s–40s] (US Black) subservient to White people. [lit. bouncing up and down on one's legs, 'bowing and scraping']

bounder n.[1] [early 19C; 1960s] (US) a severe blow. [SE bound, to leap]

bounder n.[2] [mid-19C] a 4-wheeled cab. [the 'bounding' motion as the cab runs along uneven roads]

bounder n.[3] 1 [late 19C+] one who is considered socially unacceptable or ill-mannered; thus adj. bounderish. 2 [1900s] a person, with no derog. overtones. [orig. university use, one who 'bounds' about; but note B&L: 'one who is beyond the boundary of good fellowship.' The individual so branded may not be intrinsically ill-mannered, but has been declared so by the prevailing standards of his fellows; post-1930s use usu. ironic or historic]

bounder v. [19C] (US) to scrub or wash thoroughly. [SE bound, to jump, i.e. the energy expended]

bounetter n. [mid-19C] a confidence trickster, esp. one who makes a living telling fortunes. [? BONNETTER n. (1)]

boung see under BUNG and its combs.

boungie bungee *n.* (*also* **boongy bungee**) [20C+] (*W.I.*) the buttocks, the posterior. [var. on BUM n.[1] (1)]

bounty (bar) *n.* [1970s+] (*UK Black*) a Black man or woman who is 'black on the outside but white inside' (cf. APPLE n.[7]). [the *Bounty bar*, a popular sweet, made of chocolate-covered flaked coconut, thus CHOCOLATE n.[1] (3)]

bourgie *see under* BOOJEE.

bourke-street *adj.* [1940s] (*Aus.*) citified. [the financial centre of *Bourke Street*, Sydney]

Bourneville boulevard *n.* [1990s+] the anus; one of a number of sl. terms relating to the colour (cf. ALLEY WAY n.; BOVRIL BYPASS n.; BRONZE n.[2]; BROWN n.[3]; BROWN EYE n.; BROWNIE n.[4]; BROWN PIPE n.; BROWN STAR n.; CHOC-BOX n.; CHOCOLATE CANYON n.; CHOCOLATE HIGHWAY n.; CHOCOLATE RUNWAY n.; CHOCOLATE STARFISH n.; DIRT BOX n.; DIRT-CHUTE n.; DIRT ROAD n.[2]; DIRT TRACK n.; FUDGEPOT n.; FUDGE TUNNEL n.; HERSHEY HIGHWAY n.; MUSTARD POT n.[1]; MUSTARD ROAD n.; ROCKY ROAD n.; VEGEMITE VALLEY n.). [*Bourneville* chocolate, a popular dark chocolate/CHOCOLATE adj. (2)]

bouse *n.* **1** [mid-16C–1910s] (*UK Und.*) (*also* **boose, bowse**) drink; thus *ben bouse*, good drink; for later uses *see* BOOZE n. (1). **2** [late 17C] a toast. [Du. *buizen* or Ger. *bausen*, to drink to excess. The *OED*'s first use is *c*.1300, but this may be only the drinking vessel, not its contents; the Du. term too is rooted in *buise*, a large drinking vessel. Although *bouse* can be found in ME, its popularity came with its Und. usage]

bouse *v.* (*also* **boose, bowse, bowze**) [mid-16C–18C] (*UK Und.*) to drink (cf. BOOZE v.). [BOUSE n.]

boused *adj.* (*also* **boosed, bowzed**) [mid-18C–1920s] drunk (cf. ALED UP adj.; BOOZED adj.). [BOUSE v.]

boushwa/boushwah *n. see* BUSHWA n.

bousing-ken *n.* **1** [mid-16C–1930s] (*UK Und.*) (*also* **boosing-ken, booze ken, boozen-ken, boozing-can/-crib/-ken, bouseing-ken, bowse-ken, bowsing-crib/-Inn/-ken, bowzing-ken**) an ale-house; latterly a public house. **2** [mid-19C] (*UK Und.*) (*also* **boozing-ken**) a coffee-house. [BOUSE v./BOOZE v. + KEN n.[1]/CRIB n.[1]]

bousy *n. see* BOWSIE n.

bousy *adj.* (*also* **boosy, bowsy**) [early 16C–19C] (*UK Und.*) drunken, looking drunk. [BOUSE n. + sfx -y]

bout it *adj.* [1990s+] an all-purpose adj., covering variously one's knowledge, willingness, availability, self-assuredness etc.

bout it! *excl.* [1990s+] (*US juv.*) **1** a verbal challenge, deliberately intended to start a fight. **2** what are you doing? [SE phr. what are you going to do *about it*?]

bouze *see under* BOOZE.

bouzzie *n. see* BOWSIE n.

Bovril *n.* [1930s–50s] (*Aus.*) a general term of dismissal, abuse, rubbish, nonsense, anything unimpressive. [? a play on BULLSHIT n.; in Aus./UK Bovril is a beef extract-based spread, often taken as a hot drink]

Bovril bypass *n.* [1990s+] the anus (cf. ALLEY WAY n.; BOURNEVILLE BOULEVARD n.). [for ety. *see* BOVRIL n.; the association of the anus with the colour brown]

bovver *n.* [1960s+] fighting, disturbance, esp. that caused by skinhead youths. [Cockney pron. of BOTHER n.]

bovver boots *n.* [1970s+] high-laced boots preferred as footwear by skinhead youths, usu. merchandised under the brandname Dr Martins. [BOVVER n. + SE *boots*]

bovver boy *n.* [1960s–70s] a hooligan, usu. a SKINHEAD n. (3), and quite likely a football fan and member of the right-wing National Front; his female equivalent was a *bovver bird*. [BOVVER n. + SE *boy*/BIRD n.[1] (2)]

bow *n.* [mid-16C–19C] the penis (cf. AX n.[2]). [it shoots 'arrows', presumably of desire]

bow *v.* [1990s+] (*W.I.*) to perform oral sex, presumably female to male.

bow and arrow *n.[1]* [late 19C+] **1** a sparrow. **2** a costermonger's barrow. **3** a *chara*banc, a coach. [rhy. sl. + (1) ref. to poem 'Who Killed Cock Robin?']

bow and arrow *n.[2]* [1930s–40s] (*US*) a Native American. [the stereotypical weaponry]

bow and quiver *n.* [20C+] the liver, as a human organ rather than as edible offal. [rhy. sl.]

bow-cat *n.* [1990s+] (*W.I.*) a heterosexual man who performs cunnilingus. [BOW v. + CAT n.[11] (4)]

bow-catcher *n.* [mid-19C] a lock of hair equivalent to the modern kiss-curl. [var. on BEAU-CATCHER n.]

bowdacious *adj. see* BODACIOUS adj.

bow down *v.* [2000s] (*US Black*) to act subserviently, to acknowledge one's inferiority.

bowel baby *n.* [1990s+] (*US*) a general term of abuse.

bowel off *v.* [1950s] (*US*) to have an attack of diarrhoea.

bower *n.* **1** [mid-19C] (*UK Und.*) as *the Bower*, Newgate prison. **2** [20C+] (*Aus.*) a prison. [ironic uses of SE *bower*, a shady grove]

bower-bird *n.* [1920s+] (*Aus.*) **1** a petty thief. **2** a scavenger of waste and similar trifles. [SE *bower-bird*, one of several Aus. birds of the starling family, which build bowers or 'runs' and adorn them with feathers, bones, shells etc; (1) reinforced by BOWER n. (2)]

bower bird *v.* [1920s+] (*Aus.*) to hang around, to scavenge. [BOWER-BIRD n. (2)]

bower (of bliss) *n.* [late 18C–19C] the vagina (cf. ADAM'S OWN (ALTAR) n.; BEAUTY SPOT n.). [SE *bower of bliss*, 'a vague poetic word for an idealized abode, not realized in any actual dwelling' (*OED*)]

bowery *adj.* [1900s–60s] pertaining to tramps and hobos, thus impoverished, poor. [the *Bowery*, the downtown section of 3rd Avenue in New York, the trad. home of the city's down-and-outs]

bowhead *n.* [1980s+] (*US campus*) a young woman who pays a good deal of attention to her looks, dress and general image; she is assumed to be foolish, at best. [SE *bow* + -HEAD sfx (1); lit. a woman with bows in her hair; the image is of a 'nice little girl']

bowk *v. see* BOKE v.

bowl *n.* (*drugs*) **1** [1930s+] an opium pipe. **2** [1970s+] a pipe used for smoking marijuana; thus a pipeful of marijuana. **3** [1990s+] a pipe of crack cocaine.

bowlas *n.* [mid–late 19C] round tarts made of sugar, apple and bread, sold in the streets. [Anglo-Ind. *bowla*, a portmanteau; ult. f. Hind. *baola*]

bowlegged *adj.* [1990s+] (*US prison*) **1** concurrent, referring to a prison sentence. **2** consecutive, referring to a prison sentence.

bowler *n.[1]* [1950s] (*US drugs*) an opium smoker. [BOWL n. (1)]

bowler *n.[2]* **1** [1970s+] (*Irish*) a dog, usu. a mongrel. **2** [2000s] by ext. of (1), an ugly person. [SE *bawl*, i.e. bark]

bowler-hatted *adj.* [1910s+] dismissed, retired. [milit. use *bowler-hatted*, retired from active service (and thus from wearing a uniform) and given a desk job in Whitehall, where the trad. civil service 'uniform' featured a bowler]

bowles *n.* [mid-19C–1900s] shoes. [? the shape]

bowl from the pavilion end *v.* [1990s+] to be a homosexual. [cricket imagery; no especial gay relevance to the *pavilion end* (the name of the other end will differ as to the ground, e.g. that at Lords is the 'Nursery End' which could be seen as bearing its own poss. paedophile overtones), other than (prob. coincidentally) that the pavilion is likely to contain the lavatories]

bowl me the time *v.* [1950s–80s] (*S.Afr.*, *orig. milit.*) what's the time? [SE *bowl*, to deliver (a ball)]

bowl of chalk *v. see* BALL OF CHALK v.

bowl off *v.* [mid-19C] to die. [SE *bowl*, to ride along on wheels]

bowl of jelly *n.* (*also* **can of jelly**) [1930s+] (*US*) a notably fat person.

bowl of soup *n. see* CUP OF TEA n. (3).

bowl out v. **1** [early–mid-19C] to kill. **2** [early 19C+] to find out; to be found out. **3** [mid-19C] to die. **4** [mid-19C+] to defeat, to overcome, to get the better of. [cricket imagery]

bowl-over n. [20C+] (Aus.) a fight, a brawl. [BOWL OVER v. (2)]

bowl over v. [mid-19C+] **1** to astonish, to surprise. **2** to defeat, also fig. use. [cricket imagery]

bow low v. [1970s] (US gay) to leave, esp. for one's own benefit.

bowl the hoop n. [mid-19C] soup. [rhy. sl.]

bowman n. [early 19C] (UK Und.) a thief. [abbr. BOWMAN-PRIG n.]

bowman adj. [late 17C–early 18C] excellent, first-rate; thus all's bowman, all's safe, everything is in order. [? Fr. beau, good-looking]

bowman ken n. [late 17C–early 19C] (UK Und.) **1** a house considered worth robbing. **2** a house occupied by thieves. [BOWMAN adj./BOWMAN-PRIG n. + KEN n.¹ (1)]

bowman-prig n. (also **boman-prig**) [early 18C] a first-rate thief. [BOWMAN adj. + PRIG n.¹ (1)]

bow-out n. [1940s] a resignation. [BOW OUT v.]

bow out v. [20C+] to retreat or withdraw, to resign.

bowse see under BOUSE and its combs.

bowser n.¹ [1950s–60s] (N.Z.) a petrol garage, also selling food and drink. [SE bowser, a portable fuel container]

bowser n.² **1** [1960s+] a generic term for any species of dog. **2** [1980s] (US campus) an ugly woman. **3** [2000s] (Irish) a troublesome character. [the once-common dog name]

bowser bag n. [1960s+] (US) a bag provided by some restaurants for customers to take home left-overs, ostensibly for later consumption by a pet dog. [BOWSER n.² (1) + SE bag]

bowsie n. (also **bousy, bouzzie, bowsey, bowsy**) (Irish) **1** [late 19C+] a general term of abuse. **2** [20C+] a street urchin, a lout. [Share suggests Ger. böse, evil, unpleasant, introduced by the German troops of William III at end of 17C]

bow-sow n. [1930s–50s] (US drugs) narcotics. [Chinese or 'cod' Chinese]

bowsprit n. **1** [18C–19C] the nose. **2** [mid-18C+] the penis, esp, when erect. [SE bowsprit, 'a large spar or boom running out from the stem of a vessel, to which (and the jib-boom and flying jib-boom, which extend beyond it) the foremast stays are fastened' (OED)]

bowsprit in parenthesis n. [mid-19C] (US) a nose that has been pulled, presumably during a fight or argument. [BOWSPRIT n. (1) + SE in parenthesis, a digression, an interlude]

bowsy n. see BOWSIE n.

bowsy adj. see BOUSY adj.

bow the crumpet v. [1930s+] (Aus.) to plead guilty. [SE bow + CRUMPET n.¹; one nods 'yes' when asked to plead]

bow-tie n.¹ [1940s] (N.Z.) a married woman's lover, a 'fancy-man'. [the image of the smooth, bow-tied Lothario]

bow-tie n.² [1950s] (US) a lesbian; thus bow-tie club, bow-tie party.

bow to the porcelain god(dess) v. see KISS THE PORCELAIN GOD(DESS) v.

bow-window n. [mid–late 19C] a large, protruding stomach; thus adj. bow-windowed.

bow-wow n.¹ **1** [late 18C–19C] (US) a native of Boston, Massachusetts. **2** [late 18C+] (mainly UK juv.) a dog. **3** [mid-19C] (also **bow-wow coat**) a heavy, shaggy greatcoat, popular among fans of the Prize Ring. **4** [1900s–30s] (US) a sausage. **5** [1960s+] an ugly woman. **6** [1990s+] (Aus.) an unattractive person. [(1) and (3)–(6) play on (2)]

bow-wow n.² **1** [19C] nonsense. **2** [early 19C; 1940s–60s] (UK/US Black) a gun. **3** [mid–late 19C] (mainly Ind.) a lover. [the noises, the pistol 'barks', the lover 'yaps']

bow-wow mutton n. [late 18C–19C] dog's flesh; rotten meat. [BOW-WOW n.¹ (2) + SE mutton]

bow-wow shop n. [18C] a second-hand clothes shop in London's Monmouth Street, the city's old-clothes centre at the

time. [BOW-WOW n.¹ (2) + SE shop; 'so called because the servant barks and the master bites' (Grose, 1788)]

bowyer n. [late 18C] one who exaggerates, who tells implausible, if grandiose, tales. [SE phr. draw the long bow, to exaggerate]

bowze v. see under BOUSE and its combs.

box n.¹ **1** [mid-16C+] the vagina; thus a generic term for a woman (cf. BAG n.¹). **2** [1930s–50s] (US) the mouth. **3** [1940s+] (US gay) the male genitals; thus the bulge of genitals in tight trousers. **4** [1950s–70s] (US Black) the buttocks, the anus. **5** [1960s] (US Black) sexual intercourse. [(2) note ref. in Ned Ward, The London Spy (1698) to 'a box that has neither lid nor bottom to it']

box n.² **1** [early 17C; mid-19C+] a coffin. **2** [19C+] a prison, a prison cell. **3** [late 19C] (US campus) a pulpit. **4** [20C+] a safe (esp. an old-fashioned model). **5** [1910s+] the witness box; thus (Aus.) jump in the box, to turn Queen's evidence; also fig. use. **6** [1930s] (US) a cash till. **7** [1950s+] (US Und.) a punishment cell.

box n.³ **1** [late 17C] a small drinking house or tavern. **2** [mid-18C–mid-19C] a house, spec. a lodging house. **3** [20C+] a nightclub. **4** [1940s] (US Black) a room; an apartment. [Fr. boîte, lodging house or restaurant, latterly a nightclub]

box n.⁴ [late 19C–1940s] (Aus.) a blunder, a mix-up, a mess. [fig. use of farming jargon box, to mix up 2 herds or flocks by mistake]

box n.⁵ **1** [1910s+] (US) a piano; thus bang the box, play the piano. **2** [1910s+] a radio, a record player. **3** [1920s+] (US) (also **hell-box**) an accordion. **4** [1920s+] (orig. US Black) a guitar, a fiddle, a banjo. **5** [1940s+] (US) a jukebox. **6** [1960s+] television; thus on the box, on television. **7** [1960s+] a tape-recorder, stereo system, cassette tape deck. **8** [1980s] (UK Black) a speaker-cabinet for a sound system.

box n.⁶ [1960s+] (US prison) a measure of marijuana, orig. that which filled a matchbox.

box n.⁷ [1970s] (US) a refrigerator. [abbr. SE icebox]

box n.⁸ [1970s] (US Black) one's personal style. [synon. of BAG n.¹⁴]

box n.⁹ [1970s] (US prison) a carton of cigarettes, the equivalent of $15 in a barter economy.

box n.¹⁰ [1970s+] the brain, the head. [abbr. BRAINBOX n.¹]

box v. [1920s+] (Aus./N.Z.) to make a blunder, to mix something up; spec. of cards, to shuffle. [BOX n.⁴]

box-about n. [1950s] (W.I.) **1** a man who is an idler, a loafer. **2** a trollop, a promiscuous woman, esp. when she has a number of children, each by a different father. [SE box about, to sail up and down, often changing the direction; ult. ? f. boxing the compass]

box about v. [20C+] to move from place to place without any steady job. [to carry one's boxes, i.e. possessions, around; but see BOX-ABOUT n.]

box a charley v. [early–mid-19C] to turn over a watchman in his box. [SE box + CHARLEY n.¹ (1)]

box-ankled adj. [late 19C+] (US) having legs so made that the ankle-bones knock together.

box around v. [1950s] (W.I.) to move from place to place without any steady job. [BOX ABOUT v.]

box-bag n. [1990s+] (US prison) the amount of marijuana that can be purchased in exchange for a carton of cigarettes (worth approx. $10).

box-beater n. [1910s–40s] (US) a piano-player. [BOX n.⁵ (1) + beater]

box-busting n. [1950s] (US Und.) safe-cracking. [BOX n.² (4)]

boxcar n. **1** [1950s–70s] (US) usu. in pl., a large foot or shoe. **2** [1970s] a large, clumsy person. **3** [1970s] (US Und.) a prison punishment cell. **4** [1970s] (US prison) a cell. [SE boxcar, a large closed-in railway goods wagon]

boxcar number n. [1930s–50s] (US Und.) a large amount; a long prison sentence.

boxcars n. [20C+] (gambling) **1** the point of 12 in craps dice (cf. ADA FROM DECATUR n.). **2** in fig. use, bad luck. [the resemblance of the 2 '6's side-by-side to a railway wagon; 12 is a losing throw]

box city adj. [1980s+] (US) dead. [BOX n.² (1) + CITY sfx]

box clever *v.* [1910s+] to carry out any enterprise smartly and efficiently. [boxing imagery]

boxed *adj.* (*US*) 1 [1930s+] drunk or overcome by drugs (cf. ANNIHILATED adj.). 2 [1960s+] dead. [? OUT OF ONE'S BOX phr. or ? BOX n.² (1), i.e. one is effectively 'dead']

boxed-up *adj.* (*also* **boxed**) 1 [mid-19C; 1980s+] in prison. 2 [late 19C+] (*Aus.*) confused, muddled, upset. [(1) BOX n.² (2); (2) farming jargon *box* (*see* BOX n.⁴)]

boxer *n.*¹ 1 [late 19C] (*Aus.*) a low-crowned felt hat. 2 [late 19C–1900s] a tall hat, a top hat. [the shape]

boxer *n.*² [1910s+] (*Aus.*) 1 in the game of two-up the person who takes charge of the apparatus and of the money staked by the main bettors. 2 a commission paid to (1). [SE *box*]

boxer *n.*³ [1920s–30s] (*US tramp*) a boxcar.

boxer *n.*⁴ [1930s] (*US Und.*) a safe-cracker. [BOX n.² (4)]

box fire *n.* [1940s] (*US Black/Harlem*) a cigarette or cigar (stub).

box-getter *n.* [1930s] (*UK Und.*) one who steals from tills. [BOX n.² (6) + SE *getter*]

box Harry *v.* [early 19C–1900s] 1 to take lunch and tea at the same time. 2 to go without a meal. 3 to take things as they are. [northern dial.; thus Lancashire *Boxharry week*, 'the blank week between payweeks when the workmen lived on credit or starved' (*EDD*). Bee suggests that 'confined truants, at school, without fire, fought or boxed an old figure nicknamed 'Harry', which hung up in their prison/to keep heat'. B&L suggest that it means 'box or fight the devil', i.e. OLD HARRY n. (1)]

box hat *n.* [late 19C] a silk top hat. [orig. dial.]

boxhead *n.* 1 [20C+] a fool, a simpleton; thus *box-headed*, stupid. 2 [1920s–40s] (*US*) a Scandinavian. [SE *box* + -HEAD sfx (1)/-HEAD sfx (2); (2) var. on SQUAREHEAD n.² (2)]

boxies *n.* [2000s] boxer-shorts. [abbr.]

box-irons *n.* [late 18C–mid-19C] shoes. [SE *box-iron*, a smoothing iron with a cavity to contain some form of heating]

box-it *n.* [1980s] a drink composed of wine and cider, consumed by alcoholics. [? the use of cheap boxed rather than bottled wine]

box (it) about *v.* [late 17C–early 18C] to drink briskly. [SE *box*, to fight with the fists; thus to 'hit (the drink) hard'; 19C use is SE]

box job *n.* [1930s+] (*US*) breaking open a safe. [BOX n.² (4) + JOB n.³ (1)]

box-lobby puppy *n.* [late 18C–early 19C] a would-be man of fashion, with ambition, but lacking income; thus *box-lobby lounger*, one who frequents this area. [SE *box lobby*, the area outside a theatre's boxes, patronized by the fashionable and would-be fashionable + SE *puppy*]

box lunch *n.* [1960s+] 1 cunnilingus (cf. BUSH DINNER n.²; CHEW v.¹; CHOW BOX v.; CHOW DOWN v.; DINE AT THE Y v.; EAT v.³; EAT IT v.¹; EAT A FURBURGER v.; EAT AT THE Y v.; EAT HAIR PIE v.; EAT OUT v.²; EAT PIE v.; EAT PUSSY v.; FISH v.³; FISH-QUEEN v.; FRESS v.; FURBURGER n.; FUZZBURGER n.; GASH-EATER n.; GO DOWN FOR THE GRAVY v.; GO DOWNSTAIRS FOR BREAKFAST v.; GO FISH v.; GO FOR A TACO v.; HAIR PIE n.; HAM-ON-HAM n.; HAVE LUNCH DOWNTOWN v.; HUNT THE ANCHOVY v.; KIPPER FEAST n.; LUNCH n.³; LUNCH AT THE LAZY Y v.; MUNCH v.¹; MUNCH THE CARPET v.; NIBBLE v.²; NOSH v.; PUSSY-EATING n.; SACK LUNCH n.; SIP AT THE FUZZY CUP v.; SIP FROM THE HAIRY TEACUP v.). 2 fellatio (cf. BASKET LUNCH n.). [BOX n.¹ + LUNCH n.³/SE *lunch*]

boxman *n.* [mid-19C; 20C+] (*US Und.*) a safe-cracker. [BOX n.² (4) + SE *man*]

box of birds, be a *v.* (*also* **be a box of fluffy ducks**) [1940s+] (*Aus./N.Z./UK*) to be very cheerful.

box of dominoes *n.* 1 [mid-19C] the mouth, the teeth. 2 [late 19C–1920s] a piano. [orig. dominoes were made of ivory]

box of fives *n. see* BUNCH OF FIVES n.

box of fluffy ducks *n. see* BOX OF BIRDS, BE A v.

box of fruit *n. see* BAG OF FRUIT n.

box of glue *n.* [1920s–60s] (*US*) a Jew (cf. BILLY THE KID n.). [rhy. sl.]

box of ivories *n.* [mid-19C] the mouth.

box of minutes *n.* [mid-19C] a watch; a watch-maker's shop.

box of rocks *n.* [1980s] (*US*) a fool. [phr. *dumb as a box of rocks*]

box of sharks *n.* [1950s+] (*Can.*) used when one wishes to express surprise or shock, e.g. *she nearly had a box of sharks.*

box of toys *n.* [20C+] noise. [rhy. sl.]

box of tricks *n.* 1 [mid-19C+] whatever one needs, the best. 2 [late 19C+] a tool-box. 3 [1930s] the genitals. 4 [1930s] a crafty person. 5 [1960s] the cinema. [(5) rhy. sl. = FLICKS n.]

box-on *n.* [1910s+] (*Aus.*) a fight. [BOX ON v.]

box on *v.* [1910s+] (*Aus.*) to keep going, to persevere; thus *box on with*, to fight with, to punch. [the boxing referee's command *box on!* after a brief stoppage in the fight]

box one's mumps *v.* [early 19C] to walk off, to leave.

box out of the ring *v.* [1970s+] (*Aus./N.Z.*) to have an affair, to have extra-marital sex. [boxing imagery]

box rustler *n.* [late 19C–1920s] (*US, Western*) a chorus-girl who followed her performance by mixing with the patrons in their boxes, promoting the sale of drinks (and, when desired, offering herself as a part-time prostitute. [SE *box* + *rustler*, a cattle-thief]

box screw *n.* [1930s–40s] (*US Und.*) a bank guard. [BOX n.² (4) + SCREW n.² (3)]

box slugger *n.* [1970s] (*US Und.*) a safe-breaker. [BOX n.² (4) + weak form of SLUGGER n. (1)]

box the bozack *v.* [1990s+] to masturbate (cf. BANG THE BISHOP v.). [SE *box* + BOZACK n.]

box the compass *v.* [mid-18C–1940s] to answer all possible questions, to adapt oneself to a wide variety of circumstances. [naut. jargon *box the compass*, to name the points of the compass, either backwards or in random order]

box the Jesuit and get cockroaches *v.* [mid-18C–early 19C] to masturbate (cf. BANG THE BISHOP v.). [pun on SE *cockroaches* + the stereotyping of Jesuits as alien and repellent beings. Like many terms for 'masturbate' this one relies on an image of using violence against the penis, i.e. *box*, to hit]

box the tonsils *v.* [1980s+] to kiss with the tongue, to French kiss.

box the watch *v.* [mid-19C] to overturn someone, e.g. a watchman, in a sentry or similar box.

box the wine bin *v.* [early–mid-19C] to leave the table after drinking only moderately. [SE *box*, to put in a box]

box time *n.* [1990s+] (*US prison*) time spent in solitary confinement.

box tosser *n.* [1960s–70s] a sexually enthusiastic woman. [BOX n.¹ (1) + SE *toss*]

box unseen *n.* [early 17C] the vagina. [BOX n.¹ (1)]

box-up *n.* [1910s+] a quandary, a state of confusion. [farming jargon *box*, the mixing up of different flocks of sheep]

box up *v.* [1950s] to have a relationship with. [? BOX n.² (2)]

box work *n.* [1970s] (*US Und.*) the physical act of safe-breaking. [BOX WORKER n.]

box worker *n.* [1940s–50s] (*US Und.*) a safe-breaker. [BOX n.² (4) + WORKER n.¹ (1)]

boy *n.*¹ 1 [early 19C] a sovereign (£1 sterling). 2 [20C+] (*US*) a dollar bill of any denomination. [abbr. YELLOW BOY n.¹]

boy *n.*² [mid-19C] a hump on a person's back; thus *him and his boy*, a hunchback. [the hunchback is seen as carrying a small child]

boy *n.*³ [late 19C–1900s] (*US*) a generic term for an unspecified object.

boy *n.*⁴ [late 19C–1910s] champagne. [allegedly f. Edward VII's habit of merely saying 'Boy!' to an attendant page who automatically brought him a glass of champagne. Note Binstead & Wells, *A Pink 'Un and a Pelican* (1898): 'The young bucks of the present day, by the way, generally allude to a bottle of champagne erroneously as "the Boy," in evident ignorance of the origin of the term, which is as follows: At a shooting party of His Royal Highness's, the guns were followed at a distance by a lad who wheeled a barrow-load of champagne, packed in ice. The weather was intensely close and muggy, and whenever anybody felt inclined for a drink he called out "Boy!" to the youth in attendance; the frequency with which this happened leading to the adoption of the term. It does not follow, however, that everybody who uses the word nowadays was out shooting that day with the Prince']

boy *n.*[5] **1** [1920s] (*US Black*) a friend or neighbour, a person in one's group or gang. **2** [1940s+] (*US*) a derog. term of address to a Black man (cf. ALLIGATOR BAIT n.[2]). **3** [1970s] (*US Black*) a low-status gang member. **4** [1970s+] a 'character', a 'card'. [abbr. HOMEBOY n. (3)]

boy *n.*[6] **1** [1930s+] (*gay*) a male prostitute. **2** [1950s+] (*US prison*) a gay prison inmate, esp. the passive partner in a relationship with an otherwise heterosexual convict. **3** [1990s+] (*US gay*) in sado-masochistic sex, the passive or subservient partner.

boy *n.*[7] (*drugs*) **1** [1950s+] heroin (cf. BIG DADDY n.). **2** [1980s+] cocaine. [the image of heroin as a 'masculine' drug, i.e. one that 'knocks you down', rather than cocaine or GIRL n.[2] (1), the injecting of which gives a sexual thrill (although heroin, too, has that effect on some users); (2) may be a misreading]

boy, the *n.*[1] [mid-19C+] the penis. [its innate masculinity]

boy, the *n.*[2] [mid-19C+] someone important, or posing as such; thus phr. *I'm the boy*, I am the right person for the job.

boy *v.* [2000s] (*UK teen*) to tease.

boy! *excl.* (*also* **boy-oh-boy!**) [late 19C+] (*orig. US*) a general excl. of excitement, pleasure, surprise, amazement.

boy and girl *n.* [1950s] (*US drugs*) heroin. [BOY n.[7] (1) and GIRL n.[2] (2)]

boy-ass *n.* [1940s+] a boy who exists simply as a sex object for his homosexual partners. [SE *boy* + ASS n. (2)]

boy bar *n.* [2000s] (*US*) a bar primarily used by male homosexuals.

boy-buster *n.* [1940s–50s] (*Aus.*) a man, esp. a prisoner, who specializes in seducing young men. [SE *boy* + BUST v.[1] (7)]

boychick *n.* (*also* **boychik**) [1950s+] a general term of affection between males; a man who acts like a child. [SE *boy* + Yid. dimin. sfx *-tschik*]

boydyke *n.* [1990s+] (*US gay*) a boyish 'masculine' lesbian. [SE *boy* + DYKE n.]

boy-farm *n.* [late 19C–1900s] a school; thus *boy-farmer*, a school-teacher.

boyfriend *n.* [1950s] (*US*) a term of address between men, rarely affectionate.

boy-girl *n.*[1] (*also* **boy-gal**) [1950s+] a homosexual (cf. GAL-BOY n.; GIRL-BOY n.; GIRLYBOY n.; HALF A MAN n.; HESH n.; HE-SHE n.; HIMMER n.; IN-BETWEEN n.; OMEE-POLONE n.; SHE-HE n.; SHE-MALE n.; SHE-MAN n.; SHIM n.[3]; THIRD SEXER n.; WOMAN-MAN n.).

boy-girl *n.*[2] [1980s+] (*US drugs*) a mixture of heroin and cocaine, usu. as an injection but sometimes inhaled. [BOY n.[7] (1) + GIRL n.[2] (1)]

boygul *n.* [1980s+] (*US gay*) an effeminate youth. [Yid. *bagel*, a soft, circular doughnut-like bread (i.e. resemblance to a vagina) + BOY-GIRL n.[1]]

boy howdy! *excl.* [1920s+] (*US*) a mild excl. [BOY! excl. + HOWDY DOODY! excl.]

boy in blue *n.*[1] [1930s–40s] (*Irish*) a stew. [rhy. sl.]

boy in blue *n.*[2] *see* BOYS IN BLUE n.

boy in the boat *n.* [1910s+] the clitoris (cf. BABY IN THE BOAT n.).

boy Jones, the *n.* [mid 19C–1900s] a teller of secrets. [one *Jones*, a chimney sweep, who, *c.*1840, while cleaning the chimneys at Buckingham Palace, fell into an empty hearth and supposedly overheard Queen Victoria and Prince Albert talking of state secrets]

boykie *n.* (*also* **booitjie, boytjie**) (*S.Afr.*) **1** [1970s–80s] an African male servant. **2** [1970s+] a general affectionate term for a male, fellow, chap, 'bloke'. **3** [1970s+] an exceptionally clever person. [SE *boy* + Afk. sfx *-kie*]

boy-meets-girl *adj.* [1940s+] stereotypically romantic, esp. as in the plots of popular films or books.

boyo *n.*[1] **1** [mid-19C+] a term of address, usu. Welsh, Irish or clichéd. **2** [late 19C+] (*also* **boyoh**) a man, sometimes used of an object. [SE *boy* + -o sfx (1)]

boyo *n.*[2] [late 19C+] the penis. [ext. of BOY, THE n.[1]]

boy of the Holy Ground *n.* [early 19C] a thug, a hoodlum. [SE *boy* + HOLY GROUND n.]

boy of the slang *n. see* SLANG-BOY n.

boyoh *n. see* BOYO n.[1] (2).

boy-oh-boy! *excl. see* BOY! excl.

boy racer *n.* [1990s+] a daredevil young car-driver; the term implies disdain for such puerile antics. [note motorcycle jargon *boy racer*, Model 7R AJS racing motorcycle, manufactured for the mass market in 1948]

boys *n.* [1930s+] individuals conforming to a specific job description, e.g. the *software boys*, the *public relations boys*.

boys, the *n.* **1** [early 19C+] one's (male) social circle; one's companions or 'gang'. **2** [early 19C+] (*orig. US*) a criminal or violent gang, esp. the hangers-on of a corrupt politician. **3** [20C+] (*US*) the police. **4** [20C+] criminals in general, esp. the thieves and swindlers who frequented race-courses or dog-tracks in the 1920s–50s. **5** [1920s+] the employees or hangers-on of a particular world, e.g. advertising or boxing. **6** [1920s+] (*Irish*) Republican revolutionaries, esp. when fleeing capture. **7** [1950s] (*UK/W.I.*) the immigrant W.I. community. **8** [1950s+] the US Mafia. **9** [1960s+] (*US campus*) the male homosexual community.

boys-a-boys! *excl.* (*also* **boys-o-boys!**) [20C+] (*Irish*) a general excl. of amazement, disbelief.

boys and girls *n.* [1920s+] (*orig. US*) a general term of address, in fact the audience may be all male or all female.

boys blue *n. see* BOYS IN BLUE n.

boy's favourite *n.* [1950s+] (*bingo*) the number 16 (cf. ALDERSHOT LADIES n.). [16 is the age of consent in the UK]

boy's gaol *n.* [1980s+] (*Aus. prison*) a prison which abounds in petty rules.

boysie *n.* [20C+] a general term of address to a male. [SE *boy* + dimin. sfx *-ie*]

boys in blue *n.* (*also* **bellies in blue, boys blue, men in blue**) [late 19C+] the police; occas. in sing. (cf. BABY-BLUES n.[2]). [note 1920s UK *boys in blue*, permanently disabled ex-servicemen, some 7000 of whom were inmates of hospitals in Greater London area and wore a blue uniform; early use meant the RN]

boy's meat *n.* (*also* **maid's meat, servant's meat**) [1930s+] (*S.Afr.*) cheap cuts of meat that are cooked for the servants' meals. [S.Afr.E. *boy, maid*, the male and female servant]

boys-o-boys! *excl. see* BOYS-A-BOYS! excl.

boys on ice *n.* [late 19C] lice. [rhy. sl.]

Boystown *n.* [1960s+] (*gay*) the predominantly gay neighbourhood of West Hollywood. [pun on *Boys' Town*, a celebrated home for delinquent boys]

boystown sound *n.* [1970s–80s] music popular in gay discos. [BOYSTOWN n. + SE *sound* + play on popular musical descriptions, e.g. the Liverpool sound, the Motown sound]

boy stuff *n.* [1990s+] (*US*) gay sex.

boytjie *n. see* BOYKIE n.

boy toy *n.*[1] [1950s] (*US gay*) the penis.

boy toy *n.*[2] *see* TOY BOY n.

boy with the boots *n.* [late 19C+] (*Anglo-Irish*) the joker in a pack of cards. [the use of the card as a trump, 'booting' other cards]

bozack n. (also **'zack**) [1990s+] (orig. US Black teen) the scrotum, the penis (cf. BALL-BAG n.). [ety. unknown; ? Black pron. of BALLS n.¹ (1) + sfx -ack]

bozark n. [1920s] (US) a stupid girl.

bozo n.¹ [1910s+] (orig. US) **1** a person, a fellow, a man; there is a slight overtone of clownishness. **2** a form of address. **3** a fool, an idiot (cf. BOBO n.¹). **4** a tough person, a thug. [? Sp. term meaning the light beard of adolescence or ? Sp. bozal, simple, stupid, or ? US fairground use BO n.² (1) or ? Ital. bozzo, a cuckold, a bastard]

bozo n.² [1950s+] (drugs) 1oz (28g) of heroin. [abbr. oz, an ounce]

bozo adj. **1** [1940s+] crazy, eccentric. **2** [1980s+] stupid, with implications of thuggishness. [(1) BOZO n.¹ (3); (2) BOZO n.¹ (4)]

bozoom n. see BAZOOM n.

b.p. n. [1970s] (US) a child prostitute. [abbr. BABY PRO n. (1)]

b.p.o.m. n. [1950s–70s] (gay) a large penis. [abbr. big piece of meat/MEAT n. (2)]

b.p.t. n. [1990s+] unpunctuality (cf. AFRICAN (PEOPLE'S) TIME n.). [abbr. BLACK PEOPLE'S TIME n.]

b.q. n. see BROWNIE QUEEN n.

b.r. n. [1910s–70s] (US) a bankroll. [abbr.]

bra n.¹ (also **bras**) [1910s+] a brassiere. [abbr.]

bra n.² **1** [1950s+] (S Afr.) brother, esp. as a pfx to a given name, e.g. Bra Victor. **2** [1950s+] (S.Afr./US) (also **brah**) an informal term of address to another person (whether male or female). **3** [1970s+] an important, influential person, 'one of the boys'. **4** [1980s] 'a Black man who is acknowledged to be particularly STREETWISE adj. and adept at making the most of urban life, while remaining part of working-class Black society' (DSAE). [abbr. SE brother]

braa n. [1950s+] (W.I. Rasta) brother, as a term of address. [pron.]

braata n. [1910s+] (W.I.) a little extra, like the 13th biscuit in a baker's dozen, or an extra helping of food; in musical shows it has come to be the encore. [Mex. Sp. barata, cheap]

brace n.¹ [late 19C] a drink taken as a pick-me-up, a 'bracer'. [SE bracer, a nerve tonic]

brace n.² [late 19C–1900s] (US) any form of gambling game in which there is concealed cheating (cf. BRACE GAME n.; BRACE ROOM n.). [SE brace, to bluster, to domineer]

brace n.³ see BRACE (TAVERN) n.

brace v. **1** [late 19C] (US gambling) to cheat. **2** [late 19C+] (US) to demand, esp. money. **3** [20C+] to question, usu. of police. **4** [20C+] to face up to, to shake up, to grab. **5** [1910s–30s] (US Und.) to corrupt, to bribe, to intimidate. **6** [1910s+] to accost, to solicit. [? 15C SE brace, to bluster, esp. in phr. face and brace]

brace and bit n. **1** [1980s+] (Aus. drugs/prison) the equipment (a needle, a spoon, a dropper) required for injecting narcotics. **2** [2000s] excrement (cf. ALI OOP n.). [rhy. sl.; (1) = FIT n.²; (2) = SHIT n.¹ (1)]

brace and bits n. [1920s] female breasts (cf. BRADFORD CITIES n.; BRADLEYS n.; BRISTOL BITS n.; BRISTOL CITY n.; CABMAN'S RESTS n.; CATS AND KITTIES n.; CHARLIES n.¹; CHARLIE WHEELER n.; EARTHA (KITT) n.; FAINTING FITS n.; GEORGIE BEST n.; JERSEY (CITY) n.; LEWIS AND WHITTY n.; MAE WEST n.; MANCHESTER CITIES n.; MARY ELLENS n.; MODS AND ROCKERS n.; MOONLIGHT FLITS n.; RACKS (OF MEAT) n.; TALE OF TWO CITIES n.; THOUSAND PITIES n.; THREEPENNY BITS n.; THRUPS n.¹; TOWNS AND CITIES n.; TREY-BITS n.; TWO-BOB BIT n.; WALTER MITTY n.; WOOLY WEST n.). [rhy. sl. + pun on SE brace, a pair]

braced game n. see BRACE GAME n.

brace-face n. [1990s+] (UK juv.) an insult aimed at one who wears a corrective brace on their teeth.

brace game n. (also **braced game**) **1** [late 19C–1940s] (US) any form of gambling game in which there is concealed cheating; thus brace dealer, a crooked dealer. **2** [1900s–40s] any fraudulent scheme. [BRACE n.² + SE game]

brace house n. see SKINNING HOUSE n.

bracelets n. (also **black bracelets**) [mid-17C+] (orig. UK Und.) handcuffs.

brace of broads n. [1940s] (US Black) one's shoulders. [SE brace, a pair + BROAD n.³]

brace of hookers n. [1940s] (US Black) one's arms. [SE brace + ext. of HOOK n.¹ (1)]

brace of horned cows n. [1940s] (US Black) a pair of aching feet.

brace of shakes, a n. see TWO SHAKES phr.

bracer n. [early 19C+] (orig. US) an alcoholic drink, esp. as a 'pick-me-up'. [SE bracer, a nerve tonic]

brace room n. [late 19C] (US Und.) a gambling house where all games are invariably corrupt. [BRACE n.² + SE room]

bracers n. [1920s–30s] (US tramp) the legs.

brace (tavern) n. [late 18C–early 19C] a room in the southeast corner of the King's Bench prison, London, where prisoners can buy beer. [its 'barmen', a pair or brace of brothers surnamed Partridge]

brace up v. [mid–late 19C] to pawn stolen goods. [? Fr. argot braser des faffes, to forge documents]

brace-up-'tomach n. [1970s] (W.I.) a woman with larger-than-average breasts. [SE brace up, to firm up + stomach]

bracket n. [1950s+] an unspecified part of the body, presumably the nose; thus usu. in phr. a punch up the bracket. [the resemblance]

bracket-face n. [late 17C–1910s] a person with an ugly face.

bracket-mug n. [mid–late 19C] a person with an ugly face. [SE bracket + MUG n.¹ (2)]

bracmard n. [mid-17C] the penis. [Fr. braquemard, a short broad sword]

Brad n.¹ see BRADBURY n.

Brad n.² see BRAD (PITT) n.

brad n.¹ **1** [19C] a halfpenny, a cent. **2** [early 19C–1910s] in pl., cash money; thus TIP THE BRADS v. (cf. ACTUAL, THE n.). [? f. SE brad, a shoemaker's rivet]

brad n.² [mid-19C] (US Und.) a burglar's tool, a saw.

brad n.³ [1910s] a cigarette. [play on COFFIN NAIL n.² (1) and SE nail/brad, a rivet]

bradarax! excl. (also **bragadap!**) [1990s+] (W.I.) echoic, onomat. words representing the sound of an object or objects crashing to the floor, gunfire or other sudden noises.

Bradbury n. (also **Brad, John Bradbury**) [1910s–50s] a banknote (cf. ABE n.²). [proper name of Sir John Bradbury, secretary to the Treasury c.1915]

brad-faking n. [mid-19C] playing at cards. [BRAD n.¹ (2) + FAKE v.¹ (2)]

Bradford cities n. [1990s+] breasts (cf. BRACE AND BITS n.). [rhy. sl.]

bradleys n. [1990s+] **1** the female breasts (cf. BRACE AND BITS n.). **2** (Irish) armpits. [rhy. sl. brad(ley) pitts = (1) TIT n.³ (1); (2) SE armpit; ult. US film star Brad Pitt (b.1964)]

Brad (Pitt) n. [1990s+] **1** excrement, also in fig. use (cf. ALI OOP n.). **2** an act of defecation (cf. ANDY CAPP n.). [rhy. sl. = SHIT n.¹; ult. US film star Brad Pitt (b.1964)]

brads n. see BRAD n.¹ (2).

bradshaw n. [late 19C–1900s] a precise person, one who is good at figures. [Bradshaw's Railway Guide, the comprehensive Victorian timetable, founded by George Bradshaw (1801–53) and publ. 1839–61]

bradys n. [1990s+] (US Black) young, middle-class, suburban Whites; thus **brady**, typically conservative. [the type of character portrayed in the 1960s TV series The Brady Bunch]

brag n.¹ (also **brag-boy**) [late 16C–18C] a swaggering braggart. [abbr. SE; 19C+ use is SE]

brag n.² [early 19C] a moneylender. [note Egan, Life in London (1821): 'Logic termed these persons Brags, in consequence of their repeatedly advertising to render embarrassed individuals assistance, yet making them pay well for it']

brag adj. [19C–1900s] (US) first-rate, out of the ordinary, notable. [SE brag, to boast; thus worth boasting about]

bragadap! *excl. see* BRADARAX! excl.

brag-boy *n. see* BRAG n.[1].

braggadocio *n.* [mid-19C] a sentence of 3 months' imprisonment given to a known thief or regular offender. [SE *braggadocio*, an empty, idle boast or boaster; thus the professional thief's boast that they will never be caught]

braggadocious *adj.* [1940s+] (*US*) arrogant, loud-mouthed; thus *braggadociousness*, arrogance.

brag it out with a card of ten *v.* (*also* **face it out with a card of ten**) [mid-16C] to brazen out a situation. [the image of bluffing in a card-game, in which 10 is only an average card]

brah *n.*[1] *see* BRA n.[2] (2).

brah *n.*[2] *see* BRO n.[1] (2).

brahma *n. see* BRAMA n.

Brahma bull *n.* [1980s+] (*Aus. prison*) an act of masturbation. [rhy. sl. = PULL v.[7]]

Brahms and Liszt *adj.* (*also* **Mozart and Liszt**) [1920s+] drunk (cf. ADRIAN (QUIST) adj.). [rhy. sl. = PISSED adj.[1]; ult. composers Johannes *Brahms* (1833–97)/Wolfgang Amadeus *Mozart* (1756–91) + Franz *Liszt* (1811–86)]

brain *n.*[1] **1** [mid-19C+] (*orig. US*) a planner, an 'ideas man', a mastermind, often in a criminal context, i.e. someone who plans a bank raid but does not participate in the actual action; often found in fiction as *The Brain* or *Brains* (cf. BRAINS n.). **2** [1910s+] (*orig. US*) an intellectual, an intelligent person, esp. as one who is unpleasantly, anti-socially intellectual. **3** [1940s] (*US Und.*) (*also* **brainbox**) the combination of a safe. **4** [1980s] (*US campus*) in ironic reversal, a stupid person.

brain *n.*[2] [1990s+] (*US*) fellatio (cf. DOME-SHOT v.; FACE n.[2]; FACE-FUCK v.; FACE-FUCKING n.; FACE PUSSY n.; GET HEAD v.; GIVE HEAD v.; HEAD n.[10]; HEAD v.[2]; HEAD JOB n.; SKULL n.[7]; SKULL v.[2]; SKULL-BUGGERY n.; SKULL FUCK n.; SKULL JOB n.; WHIP SOME SKULL ON v.). [var. on HEAD n.[10]]

brain *v.* **1** [mid-17C; early 19C+] to hit on the head (and knock out); thus *brained*, hit very hard on the head; also in fig. use. **2** [1940s–60s] to ponder, to think about. [note 14C–19C SE *brain*, to kill by dashing out the brains of]

brain barrel *n. see* BRAIN BUCKET n. (1).

brainbox *n.*[1] **1** [late 18C+] (*also* **brain receptacle, brain-case**) the head, the skull. **2** [1910s+] the mind. **3** [1950s] (*US*) a crash helmet. **4** [1950s+] a clever person.

brainbox *n.*[2] *see* BRAIN n.[1] (3).

brain bucket *n.* **1** [mid-19C–1910s] (*US*) (*also* **brain barrel**) the head, the skull. **2** [1950s+] (*UK juv.*) a protective helmet, whatever its use.

brain-burners *n.* [1970s] (*US drugs/gay*) amphetamines when taken intravenously (cf. A n.[2]).

brain burp *n.* [1990s+] (*US campus*) a random thought (cf. BRAIN FART n.). [SE *brain* + BURP n., i.e. its spontaneity]

brain candy *n.* [1990s+] anything superficially attractive but intellectually undemanding (cf. ARM CANDY n.). [on model of EYE CANDY n.]

brain-canister *n.* [mid–19C+] the head.

brain capsule *n.* [1900s] (*US*) a cigarette. [the supposedly stimulating properties of nicotine]

brain-case *n. see* BRAINBOX n.[1] (1).

brainchild *n.* **1** [1940s+] an idea, an inspiration. **2** [1960s+] (*US*) a very intelligent person.

brain college *n.* [late 19C] (*US*) a lunatic asylum. [ironic use]

brain damage *n.* **1** [1990s+] beer. **2** [2000s+] (*drugs*) heroin. [the supposed effects]

brain-dead *adj.* [1980s+] utterly stupid, completely inept. [SE *brain-dead*, used of one who, while still technically alive, is in a persistent vegetative state]

brain drain *n.* [1960s+] the emigration of highly qualified people, generally scientists and academics, from Britain in search of more prestigious jobs, better facilities for research and higher salaries.

brain drainer *n.* [1960s] (*Aus.*) a university.

brained *adj.* [1990s+] **1** emotionally exhausted. **2** drunk (cf. ADDLED adj.).

brain fart *n.* [1980s+] (*orig. US campus*) **1** a nonsensical idea (cf. BRAIN BURP n.). **2** a loss of memory. [SE *brain* + FART n. (1)]

brainfart *v.* [1990s+] (*US campus*) to have a temporary loss of memory. [BRAIN FART n. (2)]

brainfart! *excl.* [1980s] (*orig. US campus*) a general excl. implying that the speaker has lost the thread, forgotten what they were talking about, made a major mental error and all in all lost the power of rational speech and thought. [BRAIN FART n.]

brain guy *n.* [1930s–40s] (*US*) the planner behind a criminal gang. [BRAIN n.[1] (1) + GUY n.[2] (1)]

brainiac *n.* [1980s+] a really clever person. [SE *brain* + *maniac*]

brainless wonder *n.* [1920s] (*US*) a fool, a scatter-brained person; a stupid thing. [SE *brainless* + *wonder*, an outstanding specimen of something + ? play on a carnival attraction, the 'Boneless Wonder']

braino *n.* [1980s+] (*US*) a very clever person. [BRAIN n.[1] (2) + -O sfx (1)]

brainpan *n.* **1** [late 15C+] the human head. **2** [17C+] the mind. [SE *brain-pan*, that which contains the brain, the skull]

brain-pot *n.* [mid-19C] the skull, the head.

brain receptacle *n. see* BRAINBOX n.[1] (1).

brains *n.* [1910s+] (*orig. US*) the head of a criminal gang, often as *the brains*; also in non-criminal use (cf. BRAIN n.[1]). [note UK police jargon *the brains*, the CID or plain-clothes detective department, usu. ironic]

brainstem *n.* [1980s] (*US campus*) an eccentric. [SE *brainstem*, 'the central trunk of the brain upon which the cerebrum and cerebellum are set, and which continues downwards to form the spinal cord' (*OED*)]

brainstorm *n.* [20C+] (*orig. US*) **1** a nervous breakdown, a physical or emotional collapse. **2** a sudden inspiration or bright idea. [ext. of SE use; (1) popularized by the murder trial of society architect Harry Thaw in 1907–8, during which his lawyer claimed he had suffered a 'brain storm']

brain tablet *n.* [1930s] (*US*) a cigarette.

brain ticklers *n.* [1960s+] (*drugs*) amphetamines (cf. A n.[2]). [amphetamine accelerates the activity of the central nervous system and thence the brain]

brainwave *n.* [late 19C+] a sudden inspiration or bright idea.

brake lurk *n. see* BREAK LURK n.

brakie *n.* (*also* **brakey, braky**) [late 19C+] (*US tramp*) a railroad brakeman. [abbr. + sfx *-ie/-ey/-y*]

brama *n.* (*also* **brahma, bramah, bramma**) [1910s+] **1** a pretty woman. **2** anything good, enjoyable, attractive. [Skrt *Brahma*, the supreme God of post-Vedic Hindu mythology]

bran *n.* [mid-19C] a loaf. [one of its constituents]

Branch, the *n.* [1970s+] used in various UK and one-time Commonwealth countries to denote the Special Branch, that department of the national police force that deals with 'subversion'.

branch out *v.* [1920s+] (*Aus.*) to become very fat. [SE *branch out*, to expand]

brand *v.* [1920s–50s] (*Scot. gang*) to slash with a razor; thus to scar.

brand-fire new *adj.* (*also* **bran-fire new**) [early 19C+] (*US*) absolutely new.

brand X *n.* [1970s+] (*US Black*) marijuana; a marijuana cigarette. [joc. play on the drug's illegality]

brandy *n.* (*also* **brandy-coatee, brandy-coortee**) [late 19C] (*Anglo-Ind.*) a coat, a raincoat. [Hind. *barani*, a cloak (+ SE *coat*/Hind. *kurta*, a form of knee-length shirt, worn outside the trousers)]

brandy and fashoda *n*. [late 19C–1900s] (*UK society*) brandy and soda. [play on SE based on the *Fashoda Incident* of 1898, when French and British forces clashed in the Sudan following the battle of Omdurman]

brandy blossom *n*. (*also* **brandy-nose**) [late 19C] a red-pimpled nose, the result of excessive drinking of brandy.

brandy-coatee/-coortee *n*. *see* BRANDY n.

brandy-face *n*. [late 17C–mid-19C] a drunkard; thus *brandy-faced*, red-faced. [the effects of consistent over-drinking]

brandy is Latin for pig and goose *phr*. [mid-18C–19C] a phr. used to apologize for drinking brandy after eating either pig or goose. [pun on Lat. *anser*, a goose/SE *answer*]

brandy-nose *n*. *see* BRANDY BLOSSOM n.

brandy-pawnee *n*. [19C] (*Anglo-Ind.*) brandy and water. [SE *brandy* + Hind. *pani*, water]

brandy-shunter *n*. [late 19C–1900s] a heavy drinker of brandy. [SE *brandy* + *shunter*, a mover]

brandy snap *n*.[1] [1920s+] (*Aus.*) a scab on one's face. [its resemblance to a SE *brandy snap*, a very thin gingerbread biscuit]

brandy snap *n*.[2] [1940s+] (*US*) a slap. [rhy. sl.]

bran-faced *adj*. [late 18C–early 19C] freckled. [SE *bran*, the husk of a cereal after grinding + sfx *–faced*]

bran-fire new *adj*. *see* BRAND-FIRE NEW adj.

brangle *v*. [18C] to have sexual intercourse. [SE *brangle*, to shake, to dance]

brannigan *n*. (*US*) **1** [late 19C+] a drunken spree; thus ON A BRANNIGAN *phr*. **2** [1940s+] (*also* **branigan**) a fight, a violent argument. **3** [1970s] a farce, a fiasco. [? proper name, but more likely f. stereotype of the fighting Irish drunk/Jim 'Lugs' *Brannigan*, a popular Dublin policeman renowned for dealing with street fights in a fair manner in 1920s–30s]

bran up *v*. [1920s] (*US*) to eat. [SE *bran*]

brary *n*. [1960s+] (*US campus*) the library; thus *brary dog*, someone who studies in the library; v. *brary*, to attend the library. [clipping]

bras *n*. *see* BRA n.[1]

brasco *n*. (*also* **biscoe, brascoe**) [1960s+] (*Aus.*) a lavatory. ['where the brass knobs go']

brass *n*.[1] [16C+] (*also* **brassey**) money; esp. as in Northern phr. *where there's muck there's brass* and similar homilies (cf. FAMILY JEWELS n.; FAMILY PLATE n.; GLISTENER n.; GLITTER n.; HARLEQUIN n.; IRON n.[2]; METAL n.[1]; MUMPER'S BRASS n.; PEWTER n.; QUARTZ n.; RAINBOW n.[1]; SHEEN n.[1]; SHINE n.[1]; SHINERS n.[1]; SHINNIES n.; SHINO n.; SHINY, THE n.; SPANGLE n.). **2** [20C+] (*W.I.*) a penny. **3** [1920s] any genuine jewellery. **4** [1920s–60s] (*US Und.*) a fake 'gold' ring; thus *shove the brass*, to peddle fake jewellery. **5** [1970s] (*US prison*) currency used in jail.

brass *n*.[2] [late 16C+] audacity, gall, cheek. [the image of SE *brass* as a measure of hardness and thus insensibility]

brass *n*.[3] **1** [late 19C+] a senior officer in the police, a prison or the armed services. **2** [1940s+] any variety of senior official, e.g. a politician. [abbr. BRASS HAT n.]

brass *n*.[4] (*also* **brasses, brassies**) [1930s+] (*US Black*) brass knuckles.

brass *n*.[5] *see* BRASS (NAIL) n.

brass *adj*.[1] [1950s–60s] fashionable, chic. [as preferred by the BRASS n.[3] or those of similar social status]

brass *adj*.[2] [1950s+] out of cash, impoverished. [abbr. BORACIC (LINT) adj., pron. 'brassic']

brass *v*. [1930s+] (*Aus.*) to defraud, to trick. [Und. *brass*, a fraudulent betting 'system'; ult. BRASS n.[1] (1)]

brass along *v*. [1910s+] to go through life cheerfully, without much regard for the feelings of others. [BRASS n.[2]]

brass ankle *n*. [1920s–60s] a person of mixed race. ['My father thinks that the term originated in the neighborhood of Monck's Corner, South Carolina, where the descendants of a Portuguese colony who had intermarried with Negroes and afterwards married largely within their own group were noted for their brass bracelets and anklets' (*AS*, XVIII, 1943)]

brass ass *n*.[1] [1950s–70s] (*US*) a general term of abuse.

brass ass *n*.[2] [1970s+] (*US*) insolence; thus *brass-assed*, insolent. [SE *brass*/BRASS n.[2] + ASS n. (2) (cf. SE *brazen*)]

brass balls *n*. (*also* **steel balls**) [1960s+] **1** anything severely challenging, esp. in a 'masculine' context. **2** courage, 'guts'; thus *brass-balled*, courageous, tough. **3** cheek, effrontery. [SE *brass*/BRASS n.[2] + BALLS n.[1] (1)]

brass balls *adv*. [1990s+] in a tough, courageous manner. [BRASS BALLS n. (2)]

brass band *n*. [20C+] the hand. [rhy. sl.]

brass band with a leader *n*. [late 19C] (*US*) pork and beans; thus *brass band without a leader*, beans without the pork.

brass bonce *n*. [1950s] (*UK juv.*) a policeman. [? the helmet]

brass button *n*. [mid-19C–1930s] (*US*) a soldier, esp. an officer (cf. BRASS BUTTONS n.). [metonymy]

brass buttons *n*. (*also* **brass button**) [1900s–60s] (*US*) a policeman (cf. BABY-BLUES n.[2]). [metonymy]

brass down *v*. [1900s] to pay money owed. [BRASS n.[1] (1)]

brassed (off) *adj*. [1940s+] irritated, fed up, annoyed. [BRASS OFF v.]

brasser *n*. [1960s+] (*Irish*) a slut, a prostitute; also used affectionately. [ext. of BRASS (NAIL) n.]

brasses *n*. *see* BRASS n.[4]

brassey *n*.[1] [1920s] **1** a policeman. **2** an informer. [metonymy; (2) f. (1)]

brassey *n*.[2] *see* BRASS n.[1] (1).

brass-face *n*. [late 16C; early 19C+] an impudent person. [SE *brass*/BRASS n.[2] + SE *face*]

brass-faced *adj*. (*also* **brassface, brass-visaged**) [late 16C; early 19C+] impudent. [BRASS-FACE n.]

brass farthing *n*. (*also* **brass fart**) [mid-17C–mid-19C] something of the utmost insignificance; usu. in phr. *I don't give a brass farthing*. [mid-19C+ use is SE]

brass guts *n*. [1940s+] **1** cheek, insolence. **2** courage, nerve. [SE *brass*/BRASS n.[2] + SE *guts*]

brass hat *n*. [late 19C+] a senior officer in the police or services; thus *brass-hatted*. [the gold braid or similar adornment on their caps, itself known as SCRAMBLED EGGS n.[1]]

brass-head *n*. [1950s] **1** (*US*) a fool. **2** (*W.I.*) a Black person who has a reddish tint to their hair – the result of a diet lacking sufficient protein. [SE *brass* + -HEAD sfx (1)/SE *head*; (1) the hardness; (2) the colour]

brass-house *n*. [2000s] a brothel (cf. ACCOMMODATION HOUSE n.). [BRASS (NAIL) n. + HOUSE n.[1] (1)]

brassic/brassick/brassic lint *adj*. *see* BORACIC (LINT) adj.

brassie *n*. [1960s–70s] (*Aus.*) a brassiere. [abbr.]

brassies *n*. *see* BRASS n.[4]

brass it out *v*. *see* BRASS OUT v.

brass-knocker *n*. [late 19C–1900s] (*UK tramp*) left-over food, scraps. [if a house boasts a brass knocker it is likely that the owners are wealthy enough to give away their left-overs. Note Y&B *brass-knocker*: 'a term applied to a *réchauffé* or serving up again of yesterday's dinner or supper; a piece of Anglo-Indian slang it is supposed to be a corruption of (Hind.) *basi khana*, stale food']

brass man *n*. [1930s+] **1** (*Aus.*) a confidence trickster. **2** (*US Und.*) a politician or one who has influence among politicians. [BRASS n.[2]/BRASS n.[3] + SE *man*]

brass monkey *n*. [1980s+] (*US*) an alcoholic concoction available in liquor stores. [? brandname]

brass monkey *adj*. [late 19C+] (*orig. US*) extremely cold in temperature; often as *brass monkey weather*. [COLD ENOUGH TO FREEZE THE BALLS OFF A BRASS MONKEY phr.]

brass-mounted *adj*. [late 19C] (*US*) a general intensifier, e.g. *I don't give a brass-mounted cuss*.

brass (nail) *n.* (*also* **brass-nob**) [1930s+] a prostitute (cf. BOAT AND OAR n.). [rhy. sl. = TAIL n.² (4)]

brass neck *n.* [1960s+] impudence, audacity; often in phr. *have a brass neck.* [SE *brass* + *neck*, i.e. able to STICK ONE'S NECK OUT v. without risk of hurting it because it's as tough as brass; but note BRASS n.² + NECK n.² (1)]

brass-neck *adj.* (*also* **brass-necked**) [20C+] (*orig. milit.*) shameless, impudent. [BRASS NECK n.]

brass-nob *n. see* BRASS (NAIL) n.

brass nuts *n.* [1940s+] (*US prison*) a senior prison officer. [BRASS n.³ + NUTS n.² (1)]

brass off *v.* [1920s+] (*orig. naut.*) to tell off, to scold, to grumble. [? the primary activity of the BRASS n.³ (1)]

brass out *v.* (*also* **brass it out**) [1950s+] to bluff, bluster or brazen one's way out of a situation. [BRASS n.²]

brass peddler *n.* [1920s–40s] (*US tramp*) a tramp that sells fake gold jewellery. [BRASS n.¹ (4) + SE *peddler*]

brass-plater *n.* [1920s] a professional man. [one who advertises their place of work by the *brass plate* placed at its doorway, e.g. a consultant, a lawyer. Note mid-19C coal trade jargon *brass-plate merchant*, a second-rate coal retailer]

brass pounder *n.* [1930s] (*US tramp*) a telegraph operator. [the brass key of the telegraph]

brass rail *n.* [1920s–40s] (*US*) a bar; thus *brass railer*, one who frequents bars. [metonymy]

brass tacks *n.* [late 19C+] (*orig. US*) the facts, as in the central issues or heart of a matter; usu. in phr. GET DOWN TO (BRASS) TACKS v. [rhy. sl.; virtually SE]

brass up *v.* [late 19C+] to hand over money; to pay a debt. [BRASS n.¹ (1)]

brass-visaged *adj. see* BRASS-FACED adj.

brass wig *n.* [1940s] (*US Black*) a senior officer of the police or armed services. [var. on BRASS HAT n.]

brassy *adj.* **1** [mid-16C–18C] impudent, shameless. **2** [20C+] of a woman, showy, flashy, ostentatious; implies a superficial bright hardness, but also possible prostitution. **3** [1910s] wealthy, rich. [(1) and (2) BRASS n.²; (3) BRASS n.¹ (1) + sfx -*y*]

brat *n.* [1930s+] (*US prison*) the young partner of a prison homosexual. [SE *brat*, a child]

brat-getter *n.* [19C] the penis (cf. BABY-FETCHER n.). [SE *brat* + *get*, to procreate]

brat-getting place *n.* [19C] the vagina (cf. BABY CHUTE n.).

brat pack *n.* [1980s+] any selection of successful young hopefuls, novelists, chefs etc. [the mid-1980s *brat pack* of youthful Hollywood up-and-comers; itself coined on model of the Hollywood's *Holmby Hills Rat Pack*, a coterie of film stars and singers led by Humphrey Bogart in the 1950s]

brattery *n.* [late 18C–mid-19C] a nursery. [SE *brat*]

bratty *adj.* [1960s+] (*orig. US*) of a child or adolescent, spoiled, badly-behaved; of an adult, immature, given to behaving like a spoiled child. [SE *brat*]

brat-whacker *n. see* KID-WALLOPER n.

brave *n.* [late 16C–17C] a thug, a hired assassin. [BRAVO n.]

brave and bold *adj.* [20C+] cold. [rhy. sl.]

bravo *n.* [late 16C–mid-18C] a hired killer, a thug. [Ital. *bravo*, brave]

braw *n.* [2000s] (*US teen*) a friend or close acquaintance. [SE *brother*]

brawl *n.* [1920s–50s] a riotous, noisy party.

brawny-buttock *n.* [early 18C] a general term of abuse, presumably aimed at a large or fat person.

Brazilian time *n.* [1960s+] unpunctuality (cf. AFRICAN (PEOPLE'S) TIME n.). [derog. stereotyping]

breach *n.* [late 16C–19C] the vagina (cf. AGREEABLE RUTS OF LIFE n.).

breached *adj. see* BREECHED adj.

bread *n.*¹ **1** [late 18C–19C] employment, a means of earning money; thus *out of bread*, unemployed. **2** [1930s+] (*also* **breads**) money (cf. BATTER n.⁴). [(1) Yid. *broyt*, money, but note E.P. suggestion rhy. sl. BREAD AND HONEY n. although this significantly predates; (2) something one might eat but also basic to life, as is bread]

bread *n.*² (*orig. US Black*) **1** [late 19C–1960s] the vagina; esp. in the context of cunnilingus (cf. APPLE n.⁶). **2** [1930s] the penis. [? the 'staff of life' or, if seen as a generator of money, BREAD n.¹ (1)]

bread and bread *n.* [1960s+] a homosexual couple; thus *bread and bread don't make a sandwich*, the reply given by one effeminate gay man when partnered with another; a parallel phr. is 'I'm a pouf, not a lesbian'.

bread and butter *n.*¹ (*also* **bread and dripping**) **1** [mid-18C+] one's basic income and the work that provides it. **2** [mid-19C] one's personal life, a matter in which someone may interfere. [the foodstuffs as staples; (2) early e.g. of 20C+ BUSINESS n.¹ (5)]

bread and butter *n.*² **1** [late 19C+] the gutter. **2** [1980s] (*Aus.*) a stutter. **3** [1990s+] an eccentric or mad person (cf. KEITH MOON n.; MAN IN THE MOON n.³; MICKEY ROONEY n.; POUND OF BUTTER n.). **4** [1990s+] a golf putter. [rhy. sl.; (2) = NUTTER n.¹]

bread-and-butter *adj.* **1** [19C] childish, juvenile, esp. schoolgirlish. **2** [mid-19C+] plain. **3** [20C+] basic, fundamental, quotidian. [the blandness of the food]

bread and butter fashion *n.* [late 18C–early 19C] sexual intercourse. [the proximity of the *bread* and *butter*, which 'lie on' each other]

bread and butter john *n.* [1940s] (*US Und.*) a tramp who begs from house to house. [SE *bread and butter* + JOHN n.⁶]

bread and butter letter *n.* [20C+] a letter of thanks sent to one's host shortly after having enjoyed the hospitality. [note journ. jargon *bread and butter column*, a column fuelled in the main by press agent hand-outs and similar varieties of free publicity for those who send it to the writer; such a column harms no one, 'butters up' a variety of individuals and keeps the writer off the breadline]

bread-and-butter teeth *n.* [20C+] buck teeth. [large and white, they resemble slices of bread and butter]

bread and butter warehouse *n.* [late 18C] Ranelagh Gardens in Chelsea, London, which was built as a pleasure garden in 1741, but gradually fell into disrepute and was shut down in 1803; it is now part of the gardens of the Chelsea Hospital. [? the teas served in its tea rooms or BREAD AND BUTTER FASHION n.]

bread and cheese *n.* **1** [late 19C] the knees. **2** [late 19C–1960s] a sneeze. [rhy. sl.]

bread and cheese *adj.* [17C–18C; mid-19C–1900s] ordinary, run-of-the-mill, unexceptional. [the quotidian edibles]

bread and cheese *v.* [late 19C+] to sneeze. [BREAD AND CHEESE n.]

bread and dripping *n. see* BREAD AND BUTTER n.¹.

bread and honey *n.* [1950s+] money (cf. BEES (AND HONEY) n.). [rhy. sl.]

bread and jam *n.* [20C+] a tram. [rhy. sl.]

bread and lard *adj.* [20C+] hard. [rhy. sl.]

bread and pullet *n.* [late 19C–1910s] bread with no butter, jam or other additive. [SE *bread* + pun on SE *pull it*]

bread and scrape *n.* [mid-19C+] a piece of bread barely covered in a thin layer or *scrape* of butter or meat dripping.

bread and skip *n.* [20C+] (*US*) an inadequate meal. [e.g. 'bread and molasses, and skip the molasses']

bread and with it *n.* [mid-19C] a light meal, i.e. bread and something else with it.

bread-bag *n.* [mid-19C] the stomach.

breadbasket *n.* [mid-18C+] (*orig. boxing*) the stomach. [boxing jargon]

bread box *n.* **1** [1910s–30s] (*US*) the stomach. **2** [1940s] (*US Und.*) a safe that can be opened easily. **3** [1960s] the vagina (cf. APPLE n.[6]; BAG n.[1]). **4** [2000s] (*US*) a small car. [(2), (3) and (4) supposed resemblance, i.e. a small container]

bread-cutter *n.* (*also* **bread-grinder**) [1960s–70s] (*US*) a tooth.

breadearner *n.* [early 19C] (*Irish*) a knife, as used by a shoeblack.

breadfruit *n.* [1940s] (*US Black*) a $10 bill (cf. BATTER n.[4]).

breadfruit swapper *n.* [20C+] (*W.I., Bdos*) a very poor person. [such a person is forced to barter rather than pay for goods]

bread-grinder *n. see* BREAD-CUTTER n.

breadhead *n.* [1960s+] an individual who is interested primarily in acquiring money. [BREAD n.[1] (2) + -HEAD sfx (4); coined during the anti-money 1960s]

bread hooks *n.* [1910s+] (*US*) the hands. [SE *bread* + SE *hooks*/HOOK n.[1] (1)]

bread knife *n.* [2000s] one's wife. [rhy. sl.]

bread pan *n.* [1930s] (*US Black*) the vagina (cf. APPLE n.[6]; BAG n.[1]). [BREAD n.[2] (2) + SE *pan*]

bread room *n.* [mid-18C–mid 19C] the stomach.

breads *n. see* BREAD n.[1] (2).

breadsnapper *n.* (*also* **breadsnatcher**) [late 19C+] (*Scot./Irish/US*) a child. [lit. 'a child who can eat their weight in groceries']

breadsnatchers *n.* [1960s] (*US*) the hands.

bread stasher *n.* [1940s–60s] (*orig. US Black*) a working man. [BREAD n.[1] + STASH v.[1] (2)]

breadsville *n.* [1940s–60s] (*US*) a bank. [BREAD n.[1] (2) + -VILLE sfx[1]]

bread trap *n.* [late 19C–1920s] (*US*) the mouth. [SE *bread* + SE *trap*/TRAP n.[3]]

breadwinner *n.* **1** [mid-19C] (*UK Und.*) a knife. **2** [late 19C] the vagina (cf. BANK n.[1]). [(2) the vagina viewed as a commercial commodity]

break *n.[1]* **1** [early 19C+] (*orig. US*) a piece of luck, usu. good, but note BAD BREAK n. **2** [late 19C–1930s] (*US*) an error, a mistake. **3** [1920s+] (*orig. US*) a piece of special treatment, kindness, fair treatment.

break *n.[2]* **1** [mid-19C+] (*orig. US*) an escape, from prison or custody; often in MAKE A BREAK v.; thus *do a break*, to run off, to depart. **2** [1920s] (*UK Und.*) a building with 2 entrances/exits, used by con-men to disappear from their victim or pursuer.

break *n.[3]* [late 19C] (*UK Und.*) a collection taken to give money to a prisoner either awaiting trial or recently discharged.

break *n.[4]* [1900s–60s] a remark, poss. in bad taste. [a play on CRACK n.[11] (1)]

break *n.[5]* [1910s+] (*US*) a break-in, a robbery.

break *v.[1]* **1** [early 18C; late 19C+] to render impoverished. **2** [late 18C; 1900s] to become impoverished. **3** [1940s+] (*Aus.*) to cost, e.g. *that'll break (for)* $5.

break *v.[2]* (*US*) **1** [mid-19C+] of people, to rush off, to leave suddenly; to escape from prison. **2** [late 19C+] (*also* **break down**) of things, events, to turn out, to transpire, to develop. **3** [1930s] to conduct oneself. **4** [1930s+] to reveal, to promote, to publicize, usu. in a media context. [SE *break away/break down*]

break *v.[3]* [late 19C–1900s] to cut, to ignore deliberately, to snub. [SE *break away (from)*]

break *v.[4]* [late 19C+] to give change for a note or large-denomination coin.

break *v.[5]* [20C+] (*Ulster*) to embarrass. [? to make blood 'break out' in a blush]

break *v.[6]* [1960s] (*US prison*) to ask for or receive leniency for a violation. [BREAK n.[1]]

break *v.[7] see* BREAK UP v. (4).

break a bit off *v.* [20C+] to have sexual intercourse; the idea that the erect penis 'breaks' following orgasm (cf. BREAK IT OFF v.; KNOCK A PIECE v.; PUT IT IN AND BREAK IT v.; RIP OFF A PIECE v.; SAW OFF A CHUNK v.; TEAR OFF A PIECE v.). [? the equation of sex and violence]

break a bottle in an empty sack *v.* [late 18C–early 19C] to make a cheating bet. [a sack that is empty cannot contain a bottle]

break a breath *v. see* BREAK ON v. (2).

break a drum *v.* [mid-19C] (*UK Und.*) to burgle a house. [SE *break (in)* + DRUM n.[3] (6)]

break a gut *v. see* BUST A GUT v.

break a leg *v.* **1** [1900s–30s] (*US*) to be arrested. **2** [1910s–50s] (*orig. US*) to hurry.

break a leg! *excl.* [1950s+] usu. to an actor, good luck! [theatrical superstition outlaws the actual phr. 'good luck'; note Ger. *Hals-und Beinbruch* (May you break your neck and leg)]

break a pudding *v.* [20C+] (*Irish*) to belch. [the result of one's eating]

break-ass *adv.* [1960s] (*US*) at top speed. [SE *break* + -ASS sfx]

break-away *n.* [late 19C+] (*Aus./N.Z.*) **1** (*also* **break-in, break-out**) a bout of madness or drunkenness. **2** a person who has been 'broken', whether mentally or physically.

break bad *v.* **1** [1960s+] (*US Black*) to become angry or aggressive. **2** [1980s] (*US campus*) to perform well. [BREAK v.[2] (3) + SE *bad*]

break camp *v.* [1970s+] (*US campus*) to hurry; to leave.

breakdown *n.[1]* [mid-18C–1900s] (*Aus.*) a measure of liquor. [a bottle 'breaks down' into several such measures]

breakdown *n.[2]* [1940s+] (*US Und.*) an explanation.

breakdown *n.[3]* [1990s+] (*US Black*) a shotgun. [such weapons can be 'broken' between the barrel and the stock]

break down *v.[1]* **1** [20C+] (*N.Z.*) to make lighter. **2** [1980s] (*US campus*) to relax. [SE *breakdown*, to dismantle]

break down *v.[2]* [1930s] (*orig. US Black*) to be better than.

break down *v.[3] see* BREAK v.[2] (2).

break down *v.[4] see* BREAK (IT) DOWN v.

breakdowns *n.* [1990s+] (*drugs*) a $40 piece of crack cocaine sold for $20. [the dealer 'breaks down' the price]

breaker *n.[1]* **1** [late 19C] a safe-breaker who relies on picklocks and similar skills rather than on explosives. **2** [1900s–60s] a burglar. [SE *break in*]

breaker *n.[2]* [1970s] a Citizen's Band radio enthusiast. [the code-word *breaker*, signifying one's desire to join a conversation]

breakfast of champions *n.* [1990s+] **1** the labia. **2** mutual oral-genital stimulation. **3** (*US drugs*) crack cocaine (cf. BASE n.). [pun on the slogan for US breakfast cereal, Wheaties, long celebrated as the *breakfast of champions*]

breakfast pipe *n.* [mid-19C] (*US*) the gullet.

breakfast uptown *n.* [1940s–60s] (*orig. US Black*) a night in jail.

break for tall timber *v. see* TAKE TO THE (TALL) TIMBER v.

break ill *v.* [1980s] (*US Black*) to make a mistake, to take the wrong course of action. [BREAK v.[2] (3) + ILL adj. (2)]

break-in *n. see* BREAK-AWAY n. (1).

break in *v.* **1** [1910s+] (*Aus.*) to deflower. **2** [1970s+] (*US gay/prison*) to forcibly initiate a new inmate into homosexuality.

breaking *n.[1]* [20C+] *breaking* and entering. [abbr.]

breaking *n.[2]* [1980s] (*US Black*) becoming obsessive, going to extremes. [one 'breaks out' of the status quo]

breaking *n.[3]* [1980s+] (*US*) a dance style originating in New York's South Bronx, in which dancers spin, whirl and twist, pivoting on heads, elbows, knees etc, usu. performed to HIP-HOP n. or RAP n.[5] music. [abbr. SE *break dancing*]

breaking up of the spell *n.* [19C] the end of the nightly performance at the Theatres-Royal, London; as the crowds disperse pickpockets move among them looking for valuables. [SPELLKEN n. (1)]

break it big *v.* [1950s] (*Aus.*) to win heavily, esp. when gambling.

break (it) down *v.* [1920s+] (*US Black*) to explain, to put the listener right.

break it down *v.[1]* [1930s+] (*US Black*) to get excited, to become emotional. [ext. of SE *break down*, to become distraught]

break it down *v.[2]* [1930s+] (*Aus.*) to give in, to desist; to act reasonably. [SE *break down*, to dismantle]

break it off *v.* **1** [20C+] (*US*) to wound or hurt verbally. **2** [20C+]

(*US Black*) to have sexual intercourse (cf. BREAK A BIT OFF v.).
3 [1940s–60s] (*US Black*) to stop talking.

break it off in v. [late 19C+] (*US*) to treat or hurt badly. [the image is of some form of knife]

break it up! *excl.* [1930s+] a general admonition to stop what one is doing, e.g. to move on, to break up a meeting (of several people or a couple).

break luck v. *see* BREAK (ONE'S) LUCK v.

break lurk n. (*also* **brake lurk**) [mid-19C] (*UK Und.*) a fraudulent begging letter, claiming a broken limb or ribs. [SE *break* + LURK n. (1)]

break me off a piece *phr.* [1980s+] (*orig. US Black*) I want some, give me some.

break night v. [1960s+] (*US*) to stay up all night partying, talking etc. [one 'breaks through' the night + ref. to the SE *break of day*]

break-o'-day drum n. [late 19C] an all-night tavern. [SE *break-o'-day*, dawn + DRUM n.³ (7)]

break off v.¹ **1** [1910s] (*US drugs*) to stop taking a narcotic drug. **2** [2000s] (*US Black*) to disengage oneself from a confrontation.

break off v.² [1990s+] (*US Black/campus*) **1** to share, esp. to share one's pleasures. **2** to pay. [i.e. *breaking off* a small piece of hashish and offering it as a gift]

break off one's math v. [2000s] (*US Black*) to give out one's telephone number.

break on v. [1930s+] (*US Black*) **1** to denigrate someone behind their back. **2** (*also* **break a breath**) to humiliate someone in public. [one 'breaks' their image]

break one's ankle v. (*also* **sprain one's ankle**) [late 18C+] to be seduced, to become pregnant out of wedlock (cf. BREAK ONE'S LEG (ABOVE THE KNEE) v.; MAKE A TRIP v.). [euph.; 18C–19C UK, 20C+ mainly in US]

break one's arm v. [1960s–70s] (*US*) to boast. [the idea of breaking one's arm while patting oneself on the back]

break one's arrow v. [early 17C] of a man, to come to orgasm, to ejaculate. [the 'arrrow', i.e. a rigid penis, is thus 'broken']

break one's arse/ass v. *see* BUST ONE'S ASS v.

break one's back v. **1** [mid-19C+] to stretch beyond one's limits, esp. financially, to become bankrupt. **2** [1900s] (*Aus.*) to become excessively worried or emotional.

break one's balls v. (*also* **bust one's balls**) [1960s+] (*orig. US*) **1** to make a great effort, to work very hard, esp. at a physically demanding task (cf. BREAK SOMEONE'S BALLS v.). **2** to meet with disaster. [SE *break/*BUST v.¹ (4) + BALLS n.¹ (1)]

break one's cherry v. *see* LOSE ONE'S CHERRY v.

break one's chops v. [1970s] to talk incessantly. [var. on BREAK SOMEONE'S CHOPS v.]

break one's duck v. [1980s+] (*W.I.*) to have an initial experience, usu. sexual. [cricket imagery]

break one's gall v. [late 18C–early 19C] (*UK Und.*) to cheer up, esp. of one who has just arrived in prison and is still suitably dejected. [SE *break* + *gall*, bitterness]

break one's hump v. [1930s+] (*US*) to make a special effort (cf. BREAK SOMEONE'S HUMP v.).

break one's leg v. *see* BREAKYLEG n.¹.

break one's leg (above the knee) v. (*also* **break one's toe**) **1** [late 17C+] to become pregnant out of wedlock (cf. BREAK ONE'S ANKLE v.). **2** [19C] of a womanizing man, to become father to a child, whether one wishes to or not. **3** [late 19C–1940s] of a young woman, to lose one's virginity, to be seduced.

break (one's) luck v. **1** [1930s+] of a prostitute, to encounter the first customer of the day. **2** [1960s] in general use, to have a piece of good fortune.

break one's neck v. **1** [1910s+] to need to urinate urgently. **2** [1930s+] to make a special effort.

break one's neck for v. (*also* **break one's neck after**) [late 19C+] to yearn for, to be desperate for.

break one's (own) neck v. [1960s–70s] (*US*) to get married.

[? the weight of matrimonial responsibilities that form a yoke across one's neck]

break one's shins against Covent Garden rails v. [late 18C] to catch venereal disease. [Covent Garden, London, being a centre of prostitution]

break one's shit string v. [1960s+] (*US gay*) to have violent anal intercourse. [instead of excrement, there is blood]

break one's tail v. *see* BUST ONE'S ASS v.

break one's toe v. *see* BREAK ONE'S LEG (ABOVE THE KNEE) v.

break-out n. *see* BREAK-AWAY n.

break out v.¹ **1** [mid–late 19C] (*US*) to appear. **2** [1950s+] (*US Black*) to leave.

break out v.² **1** [mid-19C+] to break open a package and remove its contents; to get an article or articles from a place of storage. **2** [late 19C] (*US tramp*) to have just become a tramp. **3** [1960s+] to free someone, e.g. from prison.

break out v.³ (*also* **break over**) [1920s+] to become socially or sexually wild.

break out into assholes v. [1970s+] (*US*) to become terrified. [SE *break out* + ASSHOLE n.¹ (1); a play on SE *break out into a rash* etc]

break out with v. (*also* **bust out with**) [1980s+] (*US Black/campus*) **1** to do, say or wear something surprising or exciting. **2** to produce something unexpected and/or suddenly.

breaks n.¹ [1910s] (*US Und.*) any crowded area, e.g. a theatre exit, which offers opportunities to a pickpocket. [BREAKS n.²]

breaks n.² [1910s+] (*orig. US/baseball*) luck, chance, opportunities, either *good breaks* or *bad breaks*. [SE *break (in the road)*]

break shins v. [late 17C–19C] to borrow money, esp. during an emergency, when one is forced to run from person to person in the hope of a loan. [Rus. tradition of beating the shins of those who refuse to pay their debts]

break someone down v. [1990s+] (*US prison*) to turn a fellow inmate into a homosexual.

break someone in half v. [2000s] (*UK Black*) of a man, to have sexual intercourse in an extremely (and deliberately) violent manner.

break someone in two v. [20C+] to beat someone up badly, to break their bones.

break someone off some v. [1990s+] (*US Black*) to give, esp. to hand over drugs.

break someone's arse/ass v. *see* BUST SOMEONE'S ASS v.

break someone's balls v. (*also* **bust someone's balls**) [1950s+] (*orig. US*) **1** to complain, to nag. **2** to attack, to persecute, to harass. **3** to force someone to work hard (cf. BREAK ONE'S BALLS v.). **4** to meet with disaster. [SE *break/*BUST v.¹ (4) + BALLS n.¹ (1)]

break someone's chops v. **1** [1950s] to make a great fuss about something to someone, to nag. **2** [1950s+] to tease, to attack verbally. **3** [1970s+] to infuriate. [SE *break* + CHOPS n.¹ (1)/CHOPS n.¹ (3)]

break someone's face v.¹ (*also* **break someone's head, change someone's face, rearrange...**) [late 19C+] (*US*) to beat someone up.

break someone's face v.² **1** [1970s] (*US gay*) to startle, to surprise. **2** [1990s+] (*US Black*) to hurt someone's feelings. [BREAK SOMEONE'S FACE v.¹]

break someone's hole v. [1970s] (*US*) to beat up. [SE *break* + HOLE n.¹ (1)]

break someone's hump v. [1950s+] (*US*) to harass, to persecute, to cause problems for (cf. BREAK ONE'S HUMP v.).

break someone's rass v. *see* BUST SOMEONE'S ASS v.

break-teeth words n. [late 18C–early 19C] words that are considered hard to pronounce, long and incomprehensible words.

break the neck of v. [late 19C] to commence, to set events in motions. [synon. of SE *break the back of*]

break the needle v. (*US drugs*) **1** [1940s] to use up all the available drugs. **2** [1950s–70s] to attempt to end one's addiction to narcotics. [the *needle* being a hypodermic syringe]

break the pale *v.* [late 16C–early 17C] to commit adultery. [SE *pale*, a limit, boundary; a restriction; a defence, a safeguard]

break the sound barrier *v.* [1960s] (*Can.*) to break wind. [a pun on SE]

break to the set *v.* [1950s+] (*US Black*) to move to or arrive at a gathering. [BREAK v.² (1) + SET n.¹ (3)]

break-up *n.* [1920s+] (*Aus.*) anyone or anything considered highly amusing or risible. [BREAK UP v. (2)]

break up *v.* **1** [late 19C–1930s] (*US*) to make someone very upset, to make someone ill with tension, to cause someone to cry. **2** [late 19C+] (*orig. US*) to cause someone to laugh heartily. **3** [20C+] (*US*) to act hysterically, to act irrationally. **4** [1920s+] (*also* **break**) to collapse in laughter.

break water *v.* (*also* **bust water**) [1990s+] (*W.I.*) of a man, to reach orgasm.

break weak *v.* [20C+] (*US*) to act in a cowardly manner. [BREAK v.² (3) + SE *weak*]

break wide *v.* [20C+] (*US Black*) **1** to lose interest. **2** to leave in a hurry. [(1) BREAK v.² (3); (2) BREAK v.² (1) + SE *wide*]

breakyleg *n.*¹ [mid-19C] strong drink, esp. whisky; thus *break one's leg*, to become badly drunk. [the concept is an old one. Hotten (1860) notes that 'in the ancient Egyptian language the determinative character in the hieroglyphic verb 'to be drunk' has the significant form of the leg of man being amputated'; note also dial. phr. 'been to Bungay fair and broken both his legs', to be drunk]

breakyleg *n.*² (*also* **breaky**) [mid-19C] a shilling (5p). [ety. unknown; ? the price of BREAKYLEG n.¹]

break yourself *phr.* [2000s] (*US Black*) listen up, wake up (lit. or fig.).

bream *n.* [1970s] (*US*) a half-pint (300ml) of liquor. [the use of different sizes of fish to denote varying sizes of glass; note a similar form of ranking used by British Rail freight wagons, which were labelled *trout, perch, whale* etc]

breast fleet *n.* [late 18C–early 19C] Roman Catholics, seen as a group. [the beating of their breasts during certain prayers]

breast-plate *n.* [late 19C] (*US*) a tie that masks a dirty shirt.

breast (up to) *v.* [20C+] (*Aus.*) to accost; thus *breast the bar*, to walk up to a bar to order a drink.

breastworks *n.* [early 19C+] the female breasts. [pun on SE]

breath-and-britches *n.* **1** [1920s–30s; 2000s] (*US Black*) a ne'er-do-well, an untrustworthy, disreputable man. **2** [2000s] a very thin person. [breath that smells of liquor and britches that are constantly being dropped at another woman's bedside]

breathe down someone's neck *v.* **1** [1930s+] to be physically close. **2** [1940s+] to be in hot pursuit or in competition.

breathe natural gas *v.* [1940s–60s] (*orig. US Black*) to be aware, alert, knowledgeable.

breather *n.*¹ [mid-19C] (*US*) something superlative. [? it makes one draw a breath in awe]

breather *n.*² **1** [1910s] a lung. **2** [1940s+] one who makes a phone call, saying nothing and merely breathing, usu. for sexual pleasure. **3** [1970s] the nose.

breathe someone's air *v.* [1990s+] (*US prison*) to get on someone's nerves, to invade someone's privacy.

bredren *n.* (*also* **bredrin**) [1990s+] (*W.I./UK Black*) a friend. [SE *brethren* + biblical overtones of Rastafarian *bredren*]

bree *n.* [1930s–70s] (*US Black/Harlem*) a young woman. [ety. unknown]

breech *n.* [1900s–20s] (*US Und.*) a trouser pocket. [the cits. are inconsistent as to the front or back pockets, although usage may simply have reversed over time]

breech *v.* [1930s] (*UK Und.*) to steal from someone's trousers.

breeched *adj.* (*also* **breached**) [19C] (*UK Und.*) financially well-off, materially comfortable. [having money in one's breeches;

Egan, *Book of Sports* (1832) further defines *well-breeched* as 'a cant phrase for persons who possess all the comforts of life — i.e., who have lots of money']

breech hook *n. see* HOOK n.¹ (2).

breechloader *n.* [1910s] one who is sodomized, usu. a male homosexual. [pun on SE *breechloader*, a firearm loaded at the back of the bore + *breech*, the anus]

breechy *adj.* [20C+] (*US*) of a woman, immoral. [dial. *breachy*, of cattle, liable to break through the pasture fence]

breed *n.* [late 19C+] (*orig. US*) a half-*breed*, a derog. term for a Native American. [abbr.]

breed *v.* **1** [1970s+] (*W.I.*) to impregnate. **2** [1990s+] (*US campus*) to have sexual intercourse.

breed a black eye (for oneself) *v.* [1960s] (*US*) to stir up trouble for oneself.

breed a scab (on one's nose) *v.* [20C+] (*US*) to stir up trouble for oneself. [someone is likely to punch your nose]

breeded up *adj.* [2000s] (*UK Black*) pregnant. [BREED v.]

breeder *n.*¹ [1930s] (*US Und.*) a master criminal.

breeder *n.*² **1** [1980s] (*US campus*) one who is in a steady relationship. **2** [1980s+] (*gay*) a heterosexual, esp. one who favours child-rearing. **3** [1990s+] (*gay*) a married homosexual who produces children. [note Shakespeare *III Henry IV* II i: 'You love the breeder (i.e. a child-bearing woman) better than the male']

breeder-belt *n.* [1990s+] (*Aus. gay*) the suburbs. [BREEDER n.² (2)]

breeding-cage *n.* [late 19C] a matrimonial bed.

breef *n.* [mid-19C] (*UK Und.*) a pack of cards used by cheats, the edges have been minutely trimmed to indicate the high cards. [var. on BRIEF n.¹]

breeker *n. see* BREKER n.

breeze *n.*¹ [late 18C–1940s] an argument, a disturbance, a quarrel; thus *have a breeze in one's breech*, to be disturbed, confused. [dial. *breeze*, a gadfly]

breeze *n.*² **1** [late 19C–1950s] a rumour, a scandal. **2** [1910s] (*US Und.*) a confidence trickster's patter. **3** [1930s+] (*US*) empty chatter. **4** [2000s] (*US campus*) something of no importance.

breeze *n.*³ [1910s+] (*Aus./W.I.*) freedom; thus *give me breeze, give it a breeze*, leave me in peace, give me some room (cf. BREEZE v.¹. [like the wind, it cannot be controlled]

breeze *n.*⁴ **1** [1920s+] anything easy, simple, no problems; usu. as phr. *it's a breeze*. **2** [1930s–40s] (*US Black*) a great extent, a large amount. [one simply 'blows' through it]

breeze *n.*⁵ [1950s+] (*W.I.*) small change, anything less than a shilling. [ety. unknown; ? it is as insubstantial as a SE *breeze*]

breeze *n.*⁶ **1** [1960s+] (*US Black/campus*) a person, esp. as a greeting, 'Breeze!' **2** [2000s] (*US campus*) a non-committal, sarcastic response. [COOL BREEZE n./COOL BREEZE! excl.]

breeze *n.*⁷ [1970s+] (*US Black*) a relaxed person; a smart, fashionable person. [the positive image of SE *breeze*]

breeze *v.*¹ (*US*) **1** [late 19C+] (*also* **fan the breeze**) to escape from an institution. **2** [20C+] to appear, to arrive, usu. in comb. with a prep., e.g. BREEZE IN v. (1). **3** [1910s+] to go fast. **4** [1910s+] (*also* **cop a breeze**) to leave; to go away; thus (US) *breeze off*, go away, leave me alone; (*W.I.*) *breeze me a bit*, go away, leave me in peace, (*W.I.*) *breeze me ase* (ears), shut up, be quiet (cf. BREEZE n.³).

breeze *v.*² (*also* **breeze in, breeze it, breeze through**) [20C+] (*Aus.*) to do something easily. [BREEZE n.⁴ (1)]

breeze *v.*³ [1910s–30s] (*US tramp*) to deceive with chat, to chatter. [BREEZE n.²]

breeze in *v.* **1** [20C+] to arrive, esp. unexpectedly. **2** [1970s+] (*also* **breeze into**) to enter, esp. without invitation. [BREEZE v.¹ (2)]

breeze in/it *v. see* BREEZE v.².

breeze it *v.* [1950s] (*US*) to stay calm, to relax. [? SE *breeze*]

breeze me ase *phr. see* BREEZE v.¹ (4).

breeze off *phr. see* BREEZE v.¹ (4).

breeze puncher *n.* [1910s+] (*US*) an excessive talker (cf. BAT THE BREEZE v.).

breezer *n.*[1] [1920s–50s] (*US*) an open-topped car.

breezer *n.*[2] [1970s+] (*Aus.*) the act of breaking wind. [like the breeze it is 'wind']

breezer *n.*[3] [2000s] (*US campus*) an unpopular, second-rate person. [BREEZE n.[2] (4)]

breezer to sneezer *phr.* (*also* sneezer to breezer) [late 19C+] (*Aus.*) from nose to tail. [SE *breezer* + SNEEZER n.[1] (4)]

breeze through *v. see* BREEZE v.[2].

breeze-up *n.* [1910s] (*Aus.*) fear. [play on GET THE BREEZE UP v.]

breezing *n.* [mid-19C] (*US*) a scolding, a telling-off. [BACK THE BREEZE v.]

breezy *n.* [2000s] (*US teen*) a young woman, presumably attractive. [BREEZY adj.[1] (4)]

breezy *adj.*[1] **1** [mid-19C] (*US*) drunk (cf. ABOUT RIGHT phr.[1]). **2** [late 19C+] bright and cheery, sometimes too loud and bumptious. **3** [1990s+] (*UK Black*) of a place, smart, fashionable. **4** [2000s] (*US Black*) of a woman, attractive.

breezy *adj.*[2] [20C+] (*Aus.*) short-tempered. [SE *blow up*, lose one's temper]

breezy *adj.*[3] [1910s+] frightened, fearful. [GET THE BREEZE UP v.]

breezy *adj.*[4] [1960s] (*US campus*) easy, simple. [BREEZE n.[4] (1)]

breezy bertie *n.* [1920s] a brash, self-confident, insensitive young man. [BREEZY adj.[1] (2) + generic name]

brek *n. see* BREKKIE n.

breker *n.* (*also* breeker) [1970s+] (*S.Afr.*) **1** a tough, macho man, a fighter. **2** a motorcycle rider dressed in the classic 'leathers', jeans, boots etc. [Afk. *breek*, to break]

brekker *n.* (*also* brekkers) [late 19C+] breakfast. [SE *break(fast)* + -ER sfx]

brekkie *n.* (*also* brek, brekky) **1** [1920s+] breakfast. **2** [1980s] (*UK prison*) breakfast as the last meal before release from prison. [abbr. SE *breakfast* + sfx -ie/-y]

brekky bong *v.* [1980s+] (*Aus. drugs*) to smoke cannabis as soon as one wakes up. [BREKKIE n. (1) + BONG (ON) v.]

bremmalow *n.* [2000s] (*US Black*) an unattractive female. [ety. unknown]

brenda *n.*[1] [1980s] (*gay*) a conventional person.

brenda *n.*[2] (*also* brenda bracelets, Brenda Star(r)) [1980s] (*camp gay*) a policeman (cf. BILLY n.[6]). [joc. assonance, but note BRENDA n.[1] (+ BRACELETS n./proper name Brenda Starr (*see* BRENDA STARR n.))]

Brenda Frickers *n.* [1990s+] knickers. [rhy. sl.; ult. Irish character actress *Brenda Fricker* (b.1944)]

Brenda Starr *n.* [1970s] (*US camp gay*) a journalist. [the eponymous strip cartoon created by Dale Messick for the *Chicago Tribune* in 1940 but still running]

brer *n.* [late 19C+] (*UK Black*) a fellow Black person. [pron. of SE *brother*]

br'er nancy *n.* [20C+] (*W.I.*) an untrustworthy, cunning person. [br'er, brother + *Anansie*, the folk-tale hero, who escapes trouble through lying]

brethren of the brush *n. see* BROTHER OF THE BRUSH n.

brevet wife *n.* [late 19C] a woman with whom a man cohabits but to whom he is not legally married. [SE *brevet*, a nominal rank that confers extra authority but no extra pay]

brew *n.*[1] **1** [late 19C–1920s] a meal including tea. **2** [late 19C+] a pot or drink of tea. **3** [20C+] (*orig. US*) (*also* brewster) beer, ale, esp. (*UK*) Carlsberg Special Brew, very strong canned beer. **4** [1900s] (*US*) any form of homemade concoction. **5** [1910s+] (*US*) a pot or cup of coffee; thus *cup of brew*, one's preference. **6** [1960s] homemade wine. **7** [1970s+] (*Can./US/N.Z. prison*) (*also* homebrew) illicitly brewed alcohol. [(1) f. (2)]

brew *n.*[2] *see* BUROO n.

brew *v.* [1950s+] (*drugs*) to prepare heroin for injection by heating with water in a spoon or bottle cap.

brew dog *n.* [1980s+] (*US campus*) **1** (a bottle of) beer. **2** (*also* brew dogger) a heavy beer drinker. [BREW n.[1] (3) + DOG n.[11]]

brewed *adj.* [1980s] (*US campus*) drunk (cf. ALED UP adj.). [BREW n.[1] (3)]

brewer's asthma *n.* [1950s+] (*Aus./N.Z.*) **1** shortness of breath. **2** (*also* brewer's croup) a very bad hangover. [play on SE *brewer's asthma*, a disease that is caused by malt contamination]

brewer's dog *n. see* BREWER'S HORSE n.

brewer's droop *n.* [1960s+] (*orig. Aus.*) temporary impotence due to the effects of alcohol on the erectile tissue.

brewer's fizzle *n.* [early 18C] beer, ale.

brewer's goitre *n.* [1950s+] (*Aus.*) a beer belly. [SE *goitre*, a swelling on the neck]

brewer's horse *n.* (*also* brewer's dog) [late 16C–17C] a drunkard, a state of drunkenness; thus *drive the brewer's horse*, to be drunk; i.e. one who has fig. been 'bitten by the brewer's horse']

brewery *n.* [1950s+] (*drugs*) a place to buy and smoke opium. [BREW v.]

brewha *n.* (*also* brewhaha) [1980s+] (*US campus*) a can or drink of beer. [puns on BREW n.[1] (3) + SE *brouhaha*]

brewhound *n.* [1980s+] (*US campus*) a regular drunkard (but not an actual alcoholic). [BREW n.[1] (3) + HOUND sfx]

brew house *n.* [1980s] (*US Black*) a liquor store. [BREW n.[1] (3) + SE *house*; orig. SE *brewhouse*, a brewery]

brewising the bed *phr.* (*also* bruising the bed) [late 18C] fouling one's bed. [supposed similarity of the mess to SE *brewis*, a broth made from beef and vegetables or the fat scum from the pot in which salt beef has been boiled]

brewski *n.* (*also* brewsky) [1980s+] (*US campus*) a can or drink of beer. [BREW n.[1] (3) + -SKI sfx]

brewster *n. see* BREW n.[1] (3).

brewstered *adj.* [2000s] very well-off. [BREWSTER'S n.]

Brewster's *n.* [2000s] a large amount of money. [the film *Brewster's Millions* (1985)]

brew-up *n.* [1940s+] **1** the making of tea. **2** a pause in one's activities to allow tea to be made. **3** a meal, including tea. **4** (*Aus. prison*) illicit liquor, made in prison. [BREW UP v.; (2)–(4) f. (1)]

brew up *v.* [1940s+] to make tea.

brew with hops *v.* [1950s] (*US drugs*) to inject (a solution of) opium into the median cephalic vein.

Brian Clough *adj.* [2000s] rough. [rhy. sl.; ult. UK football player and manager *Brian Clough* (1935–2004)]

Brian O'Flynn *n.* [20C+] gin. [rhy. sl.; var. on BRIAN (O'LINN) n.]

Brian (O'Linn) *n.* (*also* brian, Brian O'Lynn, bryan o' lin) [mid-19C+] gin. [rhy. sl.]

briar *n.* (*US Und.*) **1** [early-mid-19C] a burglar's tool, a file, a saw. **2** [1920s–50s] a hacksaw blade.

briar-breaker *n.* (*also* briar-hopper, brier-breaker/-hopper) [1930s+] (*US, mainly Midwest*) a rustic, a peasant, an unsophisticated person (cf. ACORN-CRACKER n.).

briar patch *n.* [1960s] (*US*) (female) pubic hair.

briar-root *n.* [late 19C] an ill-shaped, battered nose. [resemblance to a SE *briar-root pipe*]

brick *n.*[1] [mid-19C] (*Aus.*) a gang member; thus *brickism*, the philosophy of joining and acting in a gang. [? ironic use of BRICK n.[3] (1)/SE *brick*]

brick *n.*[2] [mid–late 19C] (*US*) a punishment, performed by bringing someone's knees close up to the chin and lashing their arms tightly to the knees. [the body becomes 'brick-shaped']

brick *n.*[3] **1** [mid-19C+] a reliable, kind, selfless person. **2** [late 19C] (*US campus*) courage, spirit, 'pluck'. **3** [late 19C] as *my brick*, a term of friendly address. [the solidity of the object]

brick *n.*[4] **1** [1910s+] (*Aus.*) a £10 or $10 note. **2** [1980s+] (*Aus. prison*) a 10-pound weight. **3** [1990s+] (*Aus.*) a 10-year prison sentence. [the colour (red) of the Aus. note; (2) and (3) f. (1)]

brick *n.*[5] **1** [1910s–20s] a fool. **2** [1960s+] (*US campus*) a mess, a failure. [SE *brick*/DROP A BRICK v.]

brick *n.*[6] **1** [1950s+] (*US prison*) a carton of cigarettes. **2** [1960s+] (*drugs*) a block of marijuana; usu. 1kg (2.2lb). **3** [1970s+] (*drugs*) 1kg (2.2lb) of heroin. **4** [1970s+] (*US drugs*) 1kg (2.2lb) of cocaine or crack cocaine. **5** [1980s+] (*US*) a brick-shaped package. **6** [1990s+] a large piece of excrement. [the shape]

brick *n.*[7] *see* BRICKHOUSE n.[2] (1).

brick *adj.* [2000s] (*US Black*) of weather, cold. [? cold as a SE *brick*]

brick *v.*[1] **1** [1920s] (*US Und.*) to throw a brick through a shop window in order to steal the contents. **2** [1960s] (*US*) to throw bricks, esp. at the police, the National Guard or any other form of authority against whom one is demonstrating.

brick *v.*[2] (*also* **bricker**) [1960s–70s] to steal, to filch, to cheat. [note bus-drivers' jargon *make a brick*, to defraud London transport]

brick *v.*[3] [1980s+] (*US campus*) to fail, to receive a failing grade, to perform badly in one's work. [DROP A BRICK v. (1)]

brick *v.*[4] [1980s+] (*Aus. prison*) to use concocted evidence to have a person imprisoned. [? SE *brick up*]

brick *v.*[5] *see* BRICK (IT) v.

bricked *adj.* [late 16C–mid-17C] smartly dressed. [? SE *breeched*]

bricker *v. see* BRICK v.[2].

brickfielder *n.* [mid-19C+] (*Aus.*) **1** in Sydney, a sudden squally wind, bringing relief at the end of a hot day (although sometimes accompanied by a dust-storm. **2** a hot, dusty wind that blows over parts of northern Australia. **3** a nuisance. [orig. a thick cloud of dust brought over Sydney, New South Wales, by a south wind from neighbouring sandhills (called the 'brickfields')]

brick gum *n.* (*drugs*) **1** [1930s–50s] a block of unprocessed opium. **2** [1980s+] heroin. [SE *brick* + GUM n.[3]]

brickhouse *n.*[1] [1900s] (*US milit.*) a psychiatric institution. ['probably derived from the kind of building in which is housed the general hospital for insane soldiers at Washington, D.C.' (M'Govern, *Sarjint Larry an' Frinds*, 1906)]

brickhouse *n.*[2] [1970s+] (*US Black/campus*) **1** (*also* **brick**) an attractive woman. **2** (*also* **house**) a woman with a large chest. [BUILT LIKE A BRICK SHITHOUSE phr.]

brickie *n.* (*also* **bricky**) [late 19C+] a *brick*layer. [abbr. + sfx *-ie/-y*]

brickish *adj.* [mid-19C] a general term of approbation; thus *brickishness*, the quality of being good-hearted or *brickish*. [BRICK n.[3] (1)]

brick (it) *v.* [1990s+] to be terrified, to be very nervous. [SHIT A BRICK v. (2)]

bricklayer *n.* [late 19C] a clergyman. [? SE *rubrick layer*, but F&H note, first, the medieval church official the *operarius*, the workman 'on whom devolved the charge of repairing and maintaining the sacred fabric' of a church or cathedral; and, second, the line in Ephesians that compares such early Christians as St Paul to 'master-builders' whose greatest 'building' is the Church]

brick-presser *n.* [1920s–30s] (*US Black*) a tramp, a vagrant. [PRESS THE BRICKS v.]

bricks *n.* [1930s+] **1** the city streets, esp. seen f. a prison cell. **2** the urban environment in general. **3** a street prostitute's beat. [metonymy]

bricks and mortar *n.*[1] **1** [late 19C+] a house, a building, property in general, esp. as the image of a secure investment. **2** [1960s] (*US*) school books. [metonymy]

bricks and mortar *n.*[2] [20C+] a daughter. [rhy. sl.]

bricktop *n.* [mid-19C+] (*US*) a red-headed person. [the redness of typical bricks]

bricky *n. see* BRICKIE n.

bricky *adj.*[1] [mid–late 19C] plucky, courageous. [BRICK n.[3] (1)]

bricky *adj.*[2] [mid–late 19C] tipsy. [HAVE A BRICK IN ONE'S HAT v.]

bridal chamber *n.* [1930s] (*US tramp*) a very cheap lodging house.

bridal suite *n.* [1970s+] (*N.Z. prison*) a 2-man cell. [it is seen as encouraging prison homosexuality]

briddy *n.* [1990s+] (*US Black*) a woman. [? proper name *Bridy*, i.e. Bridget, or SE *bride*]

bride *n.* **1** [late 19C–1930s] a prostitute. **2** [1910s+] a woman, esp. a girlfriend.

bride and groom *n.*[1] **1** [late 19C–1960s] a broom. **2** [20C+] a room. [rhy. sl.]

bride and groom *n.*[2] [1920s+] (*orig. US short order*) 2 poached or fried eggs.

bridge *n.* **1** [1920s+] (*N.Z.*) a glance, a look. **2** [1920s+] (*Aus.*) an introduction. **3** [1930s+] (*Aus.*) a plausible excuse. [differing senses of SE *bridge a gap*]

bridge *v.*[1] [19C] (*UK Und.*) **1** to double-cross, to betray (a confidence). **2** in gambling to deceive one's backer by deliberately losing the game. [the image is of 2 confederates getting together to throw a 3rd party from a (metaphorical) bridge]

bridge *v.*[2] (*also* **bring up**) [1930s+] (*drugs*) to ready a vein for injection, by making it swell out of the surrounding flesh.

bridge *v.*[3] **1** [1960s] (*Aus.*) to look at something. **2** [1980s+] (*Aus. prison*) to show off; to gesture as if threatening a fight.

bridge and tunnel (people) *n.* [1980s+] (*US*) used by Manhattanites to describe those who live in the outer boroughs (Queens, Brooklyn, Long Island) or New Jersey and travel to Manhattan via the Holland Tunnel (New Jersey) or over the East Side bridges.

bridget *n.* [mid-19C–1920s] (*Aus./US*) a servant girl. [proper name *Bridget*, a popular Irish name and thus common among the Irish maids of New York]

bridget *v.* [mid-19C–1900s] (*orig. US*) to obtain money from servant girls by false pretences. [BRIDGET n.; Ware notes that the late 19C Fenians commonly used such servants to 'launder' their otherwise illicit funds]

bridle-cull *n.* [early 18C–mid-19C] (*UK Und.*) a highwayman. [SE *bridle* + CULL n.[1] (4)]

bridle-string *n.* (*also* **bridle**) [mid-17C–18C] the frenum or ligament of the penis. [it is attached to the 'head' of the penis]

brief *n.*[1] [late 17C–mid-19C] a pack of doctored playing cards; the edges have been carefully trimmed to indicate, to the cheat, which cards are high. [Ger. *Briefe*, a playing card]

brief *n.*[2] **1** [mid-19C] a raffle ticket. **2** [mid-19C–1920s] a pawnbroker's ticket. **3** [mid-19C+] a ticket in general (bus, tube etc); thus *brief-puncher*, ticket collector; *brief-jigger*, ticket office. **4** [late 19C] any form of false document, typically a reference or recommendation. **5** [late 19C–1910s] a betting slip. **6** [late 19C+] (*UK Und.*) a note or letter. **7** [late 19C+] a licence. **8** [20C+] (*Anglo-Irish*) a banknote (cf. BANK-RAG n.). **9** [1930s] (*UK Und.*) a revoked parole. **10** [1930s+] a barrister, whose legal commissions are their briefs. **11** [1940s+] a (stolen) cheque. **12** [1960s] (*Aus.*) a union card; a letter on official paper. **13** [1960s+] (*UK police*) a warrant to arrest or search. [Lat. *breve*, a letter or note; ult. f. *brevis*, short]

brief *adj.* [late 19C] (*US Black*) elegant, well-dressed, smart. [i.e. 'no frills']

briefcase brigade *n.* [1980s+] (*Aus. prison*) civilian staff members, with overtones of 'do-gooding'. [SE *briefcase* + BRIGADE n.]

brief-jigger/-puncher *n. see* BRIEF n.[2] (3).

brief-snatcher *n.* [late 19C] a pickpocket who specializes in stealing from members of a racecourse crowd. [BRIEF n.[2] (5) + SE *snatcher*]

brier-breaker/-hopper *n. see* BRIAR-BREAKER n.

brierpatch child *n.* [1950s–60s] (*US*) an illegitimate child. [the image of a brierpatch as being secluded and thus safe for an illegitimate delivery/illicit encounter; note US dial. *lap child*, the youngest child, still confined to their mother's lap, a spoiled child; *yard child*, a child old enough to play in the yard]

briffen *n.* [1920s+] a woman. [? Liverpool tramps' use *briffen*, bread and dripping]

brig *n.* [mid-19C+] (*orig. US naut.*) a prison; a police station. [orig.

sited between the 2 forward guns on the starboard side of the gun-deck]

brig v. [1920s–50s] (US milit.) to imprison. [BRIG n.]

brigade n. [mid-19C+] any collection of supposedly like-minded individuals, e.g. DIRTY MAC BRIGADE n., GREEN WELLY BRIGADE n.

briggity adj. (also **brigity**) [late 19C–1920s] (US) arrogant, self-opinionated. [BIGGITY adj., but ? link to SE brag, to boast]

brigg's rest n. [20C+] a vest. [rhy. sl.]

brigh n. [mid–late 19C] (UK Und.) a trouser pocket; thus brighful, a pocketful.

Brigham Young n. [2000s] the tongue. [rhy. sl.; ult. Mormon founder Brigham Young (1801–77)]

bright n.[1] [20C+] (US Black) a light-skinned Black person.

bright n.[2] [1930s–70s] (US Black) a day, daylight, morning. [note poetic use of 13C–19C SE bright, brightness, light]

bright n.[3] see BRIGHT BOY n.

bright adj. [1990s+] (W.I.) daring, precocious. [SE bright, clever]

bright and frisky n. [1940s–60s] whisky. [rhy. sl.]

bright boy n. (also **bright**) [1910s–30s] (orig. US) often used ironically, a clever person, a 'know-it-all'. [SE bright, clever]

bright disease n. [1950s] (US Black) knowing too much. [SE bright, clever]

brightening n. [1930s–40s] (US Black) dawn, morning. [BRIGHT n.[2]]

bright eyes n. **1** [1930s–60s] (US prison) a lookout. **2** [1960s] (US campus) used ironically, an incompetent, a blunder.

bright in the eye phr. [late 19C–1920s] tipsy, drunk (cf. ABOUT RIGHT phr.[1]; ARSEHOLED adj.).

Brighton line n. [20C+] (bingo) the number 9 (cf. ALDERSHOT LADIES n.). [rhy. sl.]

Brighton pier adj. (also **Chelsea pier**) **1** [mid-19C+] peculiar, strange. **2** [1950s+] homosexual. [rhy. sl. = SE queer/QUEER adj.[1] (3); ult. the piers in Brighton, on the south coast of England or Chelsea, London]

Brighton pier v. [1990s+] to leave, to run off. [rhy. sl. = SE disappear]

Brighton rock n. **1** [1940s+] the penis (cf. ALMOND n.). **2** [1990s+] a courtroom dock. [rhy. sl.; (1) = COCK n.[2] (1); ult. the sticks of rock sold in Brighton, England (from which Graham Greene's novel Brighton Rock (1938) also takes its name)]

brights n. **1** [1960s] (US) headlights. **2** [1970s] (US Black) the eyes.

bright-skin n. [1930s+] (US Black) a light-skinned Black or White person.

bright spark n. [20C+] a lively, energetic person, but often used ironically as a derog. term.

bright specimen n. [late 19C] a term, based on irony, for a lively, energetic person.

brigity adj. see BRIGGITY adj.

brill adj. (also **brillo**) [1970s+] wonderful, excellent. [abbr. SE brilliant]

brill! excl. (also **brillo!**) [1980s+] wonderful! excellent! [BRILL adj.]

brilli adj. [1940s–60s] (gay) effeminately sentimental. [BRILLIANT n.]

brilliant n. [1940s–60s] (gay) an obviously, exaggeratedly homosexual man. [SE brilliant, having showy good qualities]

brilliant adj. [early 19C; 1940s+] (US campus) excellent, worthy of admiration.

brilliant (stark-naked) n. [early–mid-19C] raw, undiluted gin. [it shines in the glass]

brillo see also under BRILL.

brillo n. see BRILLOHEAD n.

brillohead n. (also **brillo**) [1980s+] **1** a derog. term for a Black person (cf. AFRICAN APE n.; ALLIGATOR BAIT n.[2]; BONGO LIPS n.; COCONUT HEAD n.[1]; CURLYHEAD n.; KINK n.[2]; PINK-TONGUE n.; RUGHEAD n.; SHAD MOUTH n.; SHINE n.[4]; VELCRO HEAD n.). **2** (orig.

US campus) a person with very coarse hair. [resemblance to the coarse texture of a Brillo pad, a scourer]

brillo pad n. [2000s] (Irish) a sanitary towel. [resemblance; ult. brandname Brillo pad, a scourer]

brim n.[1] **1** [late 17C–1910s] an abandoned or promiscuous woman. **2** [late 18C–19C] (also **brimmer**) a termagant. [abbr. SE brimstone/BRIMSTONE n.; in both cases she is 'hot']

brim n.[2] **1** [1960s–80s] (US Black) a hat. **2** [1990s+] the flesh at the base of one's glans penis.

brim v. [late 17C–early 18C] of a man, to have sexual intercourse. [dial. brim, of a boar, to have intercourse with a sow]

brimmer n.[1] **1** [mid-17C–early 18C] a broad-brimmed hat. **2** [mid-17C–19C] a brimming glass.

brimmer n.[2] see BRIM n.[1] (2).

brimstone n. **1** [late 17C–18C] a prostitute. **2** [early–mid-19C] a termagant. [SE brimstone, sulphur, i.e. 'hot stuff']

brimstone buster n. (also **brimstone peddler**) [19C] (US) a ranting preacher. [SE brimstone, hellfire + BUST v.[1]/SE peddle]

brindle n. [1900s–50s] (Aus.) a half-caste; also attrib. [SE brindled, usu. of an animal, streaked]

brindle v. [1950s+] (W.I. Rasta) to be angry. [? SE bridle, to draw back resentfully, to exhibit an offended air]

brine/briney n. see BRINY n.

bring v. **1** [early 19C] to steal. **2** [20C+] to get or be given a prison sentence. [euph.]

bring-and-carry n. see CARRY-GO-BRING-COME n.

bring ass to get ass v. [1950s+] (US) to take a risk in order to make a gain. [fig. use of ASS n. (2)]

bringdown n. **1** [1930s+] (orig. US) anything depressing, either a person or a situation. **2** [1960s] (drugs) as ext. of (1), any social force militating against the drug user's desire to attain nirvana. [BRING DOWN v.[1]]

bringdown adj. [1970s] (US) depressing. [BRINGDOWN n. (1)]

bring down v.[1] **1** [1930s+] (orig. US Black) to depress. **2** [1940s+] to bring the experience of a drug to an (abrupt) end. **3** [1980s] to calm down. [SE bring + DOWN adj.[2] (1); but note US Black phr. bring down my love on me, make me happy]

bring down v.[2] **1** [1950s] (US prison) to earn a prison sentence. **2** [1970s+] (US) to have someone sent to prison; to arrest.

bring down the house v. see BRING THE HOUSE DOWN v.

bring drama v. [1990s+] (US campus) to be very serious.

bringer n. see BRINJER n.

bring-go-bring-come n. see CARRY-GO-BRING-COME n.

bring guts to a bear v. see CARRY GUTS TO A BEAR v.

bring in v. [1990s+] (UK Black) **1** to be included in a proposition or plan. **2** to receive a share of the profits.

bring it all back home v. [1980s+] (US campus) to go out and have a good time.

bring it away v. [20C+] to effect an abortion. ['it' being the foetus]

bring (it) off v. [early 18C–mid-19C] (UK Und.) to steal, to pickpocket.

bringle v. [1990s+] (W.I.) to be annoyed or angry. [? SE bridle]

bring mud v. [1920s] (US Black) to let down, to disappoint.

bring off v.[1] [late 17C; 20C+] to bring to orgasm. [E.P. suggests 'probably since 16C' (as he does for BRING ON v.) but offers no cit. or further proof; nor is there any ref. in a dictionary (slang or standard) before his own although HDAS offers a 1675 cit.]

bring off v.[2] see BRING (IT) OFF v.

bring off by hand v. [early 19C+] to masturbate (someone else) (cf. BALL OFF v.[2]). [BRING OFF v.[1] + SE hand]

bring on v. [20C+] to excite sexually. [see comment in ety. of BRING OFF v.[1]]

bring one's arse to an anchor v. see BRING ONE TO AN ANCHOR v.

bring oneself off v. [1960s+] to masturbate (cf. BALL OFF v.[2]). [BRING OFF v.[1]]

bring one's hogs to a fair market v. (also ...to a fine market) [17C–19C] to be particularly successful in one's business; also fig. and ironic; thus the opposite *sell one's pigs in a bad market*, to do badly.

bring one's Jonah on v. [20C+] (*W.I.*) to attack verbally, to vilify. [naut. sl. *Jonah*, a person who personifies bad luck; such individuals were sometimes tossed overboard, esp. in a storm, to placate the elements; ult. the biblical prophet *Jonah*, who, while supposedly 'fleeing the Lord', was similarly tossed overboard and swallowed by 'a great fish', presumably a whale]

bring one's ring up v. [1970s+] to vomit violently. [ety. unknown]

bring one to an anchor v. (also **bring one's arse to an anchor**) [late 18C–mid-19C] to sit down. [naut. imagery]

bring on the china v. [1900s–30s] to bring to orgasm. [BRING ON v. + ? rhy. sl. but with what or ? pun on SE *China root*, a once-popular medicinal plant]

bring on your bears phr. [late 19C] (*US*) a challenge, 'do your worst'. [SE *bear*, a rough, uncouth person]

bring out v. **1** [late 19C] (*UK Und.*) for a senior criminal to initiate a young beginner. **2** [1940s–50s] (*US Black*) to introduce a hitherto ignorant or naïve person to a faster, more sophisticated lifestyle. **3** [1940s+] (*US gay*) to introduce someone to the homosexual lifestyle; to recruit a male prostitute.

bring pinnock to pannock v. [mid-16C–early 17C] to bring to grief, to cause to be ruined, to bring something to nothing. [? dial. but none of the extant dial. meanings of *pinnock* – a small bridge or a drain or culvert, the hedge-sparrow or the blue titmouse, a sticky red clay, mixed with small stones – is relevant (*pannock* seems to be redup.); or ? the change from 'i' to 'a' could be said to 'ruin' the word, but seems insufficient]

bring someone to their milk v. [mid-19C] (*US*) to subdue someone, to bring someone to their senses, to make them accept authority; also *come to one's milk*, to come to one's senses. [? the image of a baby quieteening when given its milk; ? a stubborn calf that refuses to drink but gives in when overwhelmed by hunger]

bring someone up v. [1970s+] (*US Black*) **1** to criticize, to tell off. **2** to explain. [SE *bring up short* + mid-19C SE *bring up*, to bring into the presence of authority or for examination]

bring the house down v. (also **bring down the house**) [mid-18C+] to delight, to gain overall approval. [theatrical imagery]

bring the noise! excl. (*US Black*) **1** [1970s+] play music! **2** [1990s+] turn up the volume!

bring to light v. [early 19C] of a thief, to produce stolen property in order to claim a reward or quash a prosecution.

bring undone v. [1980s+] (*Aus. prison*) to wreck someone's plans.

bring up v.[1] [early 18C+] to vomit (cf. BLOW v.[3]). [the contents of one's stomach]

bring up v.[2] *see* BRIDGE v.[2].

bring up by hand v. [late 19C] to achieve an erection. [pun]

brinjer n. (also **bringer**) [mid-19C–1900s] (*US*) something exceptional. [? Scot. *breenger*, a formidable foe, ult. f. *breenge*, to rush forward recklessly]

brink v. [1950s–70s] (*US drugs*) to buy narcotics.

brinks n. [1960s+] (*W.I. Rasta*) a title given to a man who is supplying a woman with money. [SE *brings* (the money) or ? the firm of *Brinksmat* Security, used to transport large sums of cash]

briny n. (also **brine, briney**) [mid-19C+] the sea, the seaside; thus *do the briny*, to go to the seaside. [SE *brine* + sfx *-y*; i.e. its saltiness]

briny adj. [1940s] (*US Black*) in a bad mood, angry. [? play on SALTY adj. (3)]

Bris n. (also **Brissie**) [1940s+] (*Aus.*) *Bris*bane, the capital of Queensland. [abbr.]

brisby n. [1910s–20s] a net or lace curtain used to cover the lower part of a (sash) window. [SE *brise-bise*, f. Fr. *brise-bise*, windbreaker]

brisk adj. [18C–1900s] cheery, sprightly, lively. [SE *brisk*, sharp or smart in regard to movement]

brisk about v. (also **brisk up**) [mid-19C] to enliven, to animate.

brisket n.[1] [late 18C+] the human chest. [SE *brisket*, the breast of an animal]

brisket n.[2] [1950s–60s] (*US drugs*) a small pack of narcotics. [ety. unknown]

brisket-beater n. [late 18C–mid-19C] a Roman Catholic. [BRISKET n.[1] + SE *beater*]

brisket-cut n. [early 19C] a blow to the chest. [BRISKET n.[1] + SE *cut*, a blow]

briskets n. [20C+] the female breasts. [BRISKET n.[1]]

brisk up v. *see* BRISK ABOUT v.

Brissie n. *see* BRIS n.

bristles n. [mid-16C–early 19C] (*UK Und.*) dice whose weight has been altered by having bristles forced into them.

Bristol n. [mid-19C–1900s] a visiting card. [SE *Bristol-board*, a type of pasteboard with a smooth surface, popular for printing such cards]

Bristol bits n. (also **Bristols**) [1960s+] the female breasts (cf. BRACE AND BITS n.). [rhy. sl. = TIT n.[3] (1)]

Bristol City n. [20C+] a female breast; usu. in pl. (cf. BRACE AND BITS n.). [rhy. sl. = TITTY n.[1] (1)]

Bristol hog n. [late 18C–mid-19C] a native of Bristol.

Bristol man n. [early–mid-19C] a villain, a rogue. [such figures would often drift towards Bristol, presumably, as a major port, conducive to villainy]

Bristol milk n. [17C–18C] sherry, esp. rich, sweet sherry. [now a trademark of Harvey's, the Bristol sherry importers]

Bristols n. *see* BRISTOL BITS n.

Bristol stone n. [late 17C] sham diamonds. [SE *Bristol stone*, a kind of transparent rock-crystal found in the Clifton limestone near Bristol, Avon, resembling the diamond in brilliancy]

Brit n. [20C+] a *Brit*on. [abbr.]

Brit, the n. [late 19C–1900s] the *Brit*annia Theatre, Hoxton, London E1. [abbr.]

Brit adj. [1950s+] *Brit*ish. [abbr.]

britannia n. [1950s] (*Aus.*) a double-headed penny used in the game of two-up. [the engraving of Britannia on the reverse of pre-decimalization pennies]

britannia metal n. **1** [19C] the erect penis. **2** [1980s] something fake, sham. [SE *britannia metal*, an alloy of tin and regulus of antimony, resembling silver in appearance; users of (1) ignored the underlying negative implications]

British champagne n. (also **British champaigne**) [early 19C] porter, dark ale. [a tribute to the quality of the beer or a sneer at the lack of home-grown wines]

British navy n. [1980s] (*Aus.*) gravy. [rhy. sl.]

British roarer n. [late 19C–1900s] the lion that appears alongside the unicorn on the British national coat of arms.

Britney Spears n. [2000s] beer(s). [rhy. sl.; ult. US pop star *Britney Spears* (b.1981)]

brits n. *see* BRITTS n.

Britsville n. [1970s] (*Aus.*) England, esp. London. [BRIT n. + -VILLE sfx[1]]

Britts n. (also **brits**) [1940s+] (*Aus.*) terror; thus *have the Brits up*, to be terrified. [JIMMY BRITTS n. (2)]

Brixton riot n. [2000s] a diet. [rhy. sl.; ult. the predominantly Black area of *Brixton*, south London, where riots occurred in 1981, 1985 and 1995]

Brixton suitcase n. (also **Brixton briefcase, suitcase**) [1970s–80s] (*UK Black*) a large stereo tape recorder-cum-radio carried by youths (cf. THIRD-WORLD BRIEFCASE n.). [the predominantly Black area of Brixton, south London]

bro n.[1] **1** [mid-18C+] (*later use mainly US Black*) a brother, whether lit. or fig. **2** [1920s+] (*mainly US Black*) (also **brah, broh, bruh**) a term of address to a male, esp. between fellow Blacks. **3** [1960s] a

Black male. [abbr. SE *brother*/BROTHER n.; (1) note public school use for lit. *brother* only]

bro *n.*[2] [1990s+] (*US Black*) a heavy, steel-toecapped shoe, favoured by street gangs. [abbr. BROGAN n./fig. use of BRO n.[1] (1)]

bro *n.*[3] *see* BUROO n.

broad *n.*[1] **1** [17C–19C] a sovereign, a 20-shilling coin. **2** [1970s+] a credit or similar card. [BROADS n. + (1) ? its size]

broad *n.*[2] **1** [1910s] (*US Und.*) a female confederate. **2** [1910s+] (*orig. US*) a prostitute. **3** [1910s+] (*orig. US*) a woman; the implication is of promiscuity. **4** [1940s+] (*US prison*) (*also* **broad boy, broadski**) an effeminate male homosexual, often a prostitute. **5** [1940s+] (*US Black/campus*) (*also* **brodie**) an attractive woman. **6** [1970s+] (*US gay*) the buttocks. [? link to the shapeliness of a woman's shoulders (cf. BROAD n.[3]); Gold, *A Jazz Lexicon* (1964), also suggests link to SE *broad-minded*; note also Jackson & Hellyer, *Vocabulary of Criminal Slang* (1914): 'Broad is derived from the far-fetched metaphor for "meal ticket," signifying a female provider for a pimp, from the fanciful correspondence of a meal ticket to a railroad or other ticket, which latter originally was exclusively used by "gonifs" to indicate "broad" or a conductor's hat check']

broad *n.*[3] [1940s] (*US Black*) the human shoulder.

broad *n.*[4] *see* BROADS n. (1).

broad *adj.* **1** [mid-19C–1900s] knowing, alert, 'on the ball'; if not actually criminal then willing and able to bend the rules. **2** [1990s+] (*W.I.*) physically large; socially important. [var. on WIDE adj. (1)]

broad and shallow *n.* [mid-19C] the 'Broad Church'. [*Broad Church* members of the Church of England, 'who take its formularies and doctrines in a broad or liberal sense and hold that the church should be comprehensive and tolerant' (*OED*)]

broad-arsed *adj.* [late 19C+] having wide hips. [SE *broad* + -ARSED sfx[1]]

broad boy *n. see* BROAD n.[2] (4).

broadbrim *n.* **1** [early 18C–mid-19C] a Quaker; thus *broad-brimmed*, sedate. **2** [mid–late 19C] a quiet, sedate old man, irrespective of religion. [the broad-brimmed hats adopted by many members of the Society of Friends]

broadbrow *n.* [1920s] a person of wide tastes and interests.

broadcast *v.* [1920s+] to talk loudly and aggressively; also as a n.

broad cove *n.* [early 19C] a card-sharp. [BROADS n. (1) + COVE n. (1)]

broad faker *n.* [late 19C–1900s] a card-player, usu. a cheat. [BROADS n. (1) + FAKER n. (1)]

broad-faking *n.* **1** [mid-19C] card-playing, esp. with a tinge of illegality/cheating. **2** [late 19C] the 3-card trick. [BROAD FAKER n. + sfx *-ing*]

broad-fencer *n.* [mid-19C] (*UK Und.*) a peddler of lists of racing tips (known as 'correct cards') at horseraces. [BROADS n. (1) + -FENCER sfx]

broad gang *n.* [1900s] a group running a 3-card trick. [BROADS n. (1) + SE *gang*]

broad-gauge lady *n.* [late 19C] a woman with wide hips. [a pun on her breadth, and a ref. to the *broad-gauge* railway tracks, 7ft (1m) wide, which were abandoned when British railways were standardized at 4ft 8½in (44m) in the 1890s]

broadie *n.* [1930s+] (*US*) a woman; the inference is of promiscuity if not actual prostitution. [BROAD n.[2] (3)]

broad in the beam *adj.* [late 19C+] fat, overweight, esp. around the hips and buttocks. [naut. jargon]

broad joint *n.* [1900s] the place where a 3-card trick swindle is set up. [BROADS n. (1) + JOINT n.[4] (2)]

broadman *n. see* BROADSMAN n.

broad mob *n.* [late 19C+] a gang of card-sharps. [BROADS n. (1) + MOB n.[2] (3)]

broad-pitcher *n.* [mid–late 19C] (*UK Und.*) a street criminal who works the 3-card trick. [BROADS n. (2) + PITCHER n.[3] (2)]

broad-player *n.* **1** [early–mid-19C] an expert card-player. **2** [late 19C+] a card-sharp. [BROADS n. (1) + SE *player*]

broads *n.* **1** [mid-18C+] playing cards; occas. in sing. **2** [late 19C+] the 3-card trick. **3** [1920s+] money. **4** [1970s] any form of documentation, e.g. identification papers, ration book, driving licence etc. [? the 'breadth' of the piece of card; but note George Parker, *Life's Painter* (1789), 'who are continually looking out for flats in order to do upon them the broads', implying a play on FLAT n.[2] (1), although note also FLAT n.[1] (1), i.e. dice]

broadski *n. see* BROAD n.[2] (4).

broadsman *n.* (*also* **broadman**) [mid-19C+] a card-sharp. [BROADS n. (1) + SE *man*]

broad spieler *n.* [1910s] (*US Und.*) the conductor of the 3-card trick. [BROADS n. (2) + SPIELER n. (1)]

broad tosser *n.* [1920s+] (*US*) a card-sharp. [BROADS n. (1) + SE *tosser*]

Broadway *n.* [2000s] (*US prison*) an area in the prison where inmates can come and go freely. [*Broadway*, New York City's entertainment centre]

Broadway battleship *n.* [1910s] (*orig. US Black*) a New York City streetcar.

Broadway hello *n.* [1930s] (*US Und.*) a friendly greeting that prefaces a homicidal attack.

Broadway joe *n.* (*also* **Broadway boy**) [late 19C+] (*US*) a well-dressed idler, living off his wits and, when possible, gullible women. [*Broadway*, New York City's entertainment centre + JOE n.[1] (2)/the proper name]

broad worker *n.* [1940s] (*UK Und.*) a card-sharp. [BROADS n. (1) + WORKER n.[1] (1)]

broady *n.* [mid–late 19C] **1** cloth. **2** (*UK Und.*) anything considered worth stealing. [SE *broadcloth*, 'fine, plain-wove, dressed, double width, black cloth, used chiefly for men's garments' (*OED*)]

broady-worker *n.* [mid-19C–1910s] (*UK Und.*) a criminal who sells third-rate cloth as the finest material or stolen goods as legitimate. [BROADY n. + SE *worker*/WORKER n.[1] (1)]

broccoli *n.* [1980s+] **1** (*drugs*) marijuana (cf. AFRICAN BUSH n.). **2** (*US*) pubic hair. [supposed similarity to the green vegetable]

brodie *n.* (*US*) **1** [late 19C+] a jump, a leap, a dive. **2** [1910s+] long odds, a chance. **3** [1930s–50s] (*drugs*) any form of faked illness, usu. some kind of fit, whereby a user attempts to get narcotics from a doctor. **4** [1930s–60s] an error, a failure. **5** [1950s+] a tight turn; a spin made by a skidding vehicle. [for ety. *see* TAKE A BRODIE v.]

brodie *v.* (*US*) **1** [1920s] to take a chance. **2** [1930s+] to blunder, to fail. **3** [1960s] of a vehicle, to spin, to skid. [BRODIE n.]

broer *n.* [1970s+] (*S.Afr.*) **1** brother. **2** one's best friend. [abbr. Afk. *broeder*, brother]

brogan *n.* [mid-19C+] (*US*) a shoe, esp. a stout, coarse shoe (often as issued to US prisoners). [Irish and Gaelic *brógan*, dimin. of *bróg*, shoe]

broganeer *n.* (*also* **broganier**) [late 18C–early 19C] one who has a noticeable Irish accent. [SE *brogue*, the Irish accent]

broggy *n.* [2000s] (*Aus.*) a skid mark on the road; thus *do a broggy*, to skid and produce a mark. [misreading of BRODIE n. (5)]

broh *n. see* BRO n.[1] (2).

broiler *n.* **1** [1900s–20s] (*US*) a small chorus-girl. **2** [1900s] any woman. [pun on SE *broiler* (chicken)]

broke *adj.*[1] [mid-16C+] out of funds, impoverished, poor. [orig. image was of creditors physically 'breaking' a debtor]

broke *adj.*[2] [1990s+] (*US campus*) **1** intoxicated from marijuana. **2** of an experience, intense, extreme.

broke *adj.*[3] *see* BROKEN adj.[2].

broke-ass *adj.* [1990s+] out of funds, impoverished, poor. [BROKE adj.[1] + -ASS sfx]

broke-dick *adj.* [1960s+] (*US*) worthless, useless. [SE *broke* + DICK n.[4] (1), i.e. impotent]

broke for *adv.* [1940s–50s] (*Aus.*) in great need of, desperate for; esp. in phr. *broke for a feed*, very hungry. [fig. use of BROKE adj.[1]]

broken *adj.*[1] [mid-17C–mid-18C] out of funds, impoverished, poor. [BROKE adj.[1]]

broken *adj.*[2] (*also* **broke**) [1990s+] (*US Black*) very unattractive.

broken alderman *n. see* ALDERMAN n.[1] (2).

broken arms *n.* [1910s] (*US*) left-over food. [? pun on SE *broken victuals*, when *victuals*, usu. food, takes its secondary 17C meaning of weapons or military 'arms']

broken arrow *n.* [1940s] (*US*) a malfunctioning penis; thus an impotent male (cf. AX n.[2]).

broken arse *n.* [1980s+] (*N.Z. prison*) a prisoner who sides with the authorities and thus ranks lowest in the prisoners' hierarchy. [SE *broken* + ARSE n.[1] (5)]

broken brigade *n.* [late 19C–1900s] (*UK society*) aristocratic younger sons, impoverished through the inequalities of primogeniture, who are forced to live on their wits. [SE *broken*/BROKEN adj.[1] + BRIGADE n.]

broken heart *n.* [1990s+] breaking wind. [rhy. sl. = FART n. (1)]

broken hill *n.* [1940s–50s] (*Aus.*) any silver coin. [proper name *Broken Hill*, a major Aus. silver mining area]

broken-kneed *adj.* [late 18C] bankrupt.

broken-legged *adj.* [17C–1910s] seduced, deflowered. [BREAK ONE'S LEG (ABOVE THE KNEE) v. (3)]

broken mug *n.* [1940s] (*US*) a hug. [rhy. sl.]

broken oar *n. see* BOAT AND OAR n.

broken packet of biscuits, be a *v.* [1990s+] (*Aus.*) to live a life that looks good to outsiders but is really filled with problems. [the crumbs are invisible through the outer wrapping]

broken up *adj. see* BROKE UP adj.

broken wrist *n. see* LIMP WRIST n. (1).

broker *n.*[1] [mid-18C] a pimp (cf. ABBOT ON THE CROSS n.). [SE *broker*, a retailer of commodities, a middleman]

broker *n.*[2] [late 19C+] (*orig. Aus.*) someone who is usu. having financial problems, a poor person. [BROKE adj.[1] + pun on SE *broker*]

broker *n.*[3] (*drugs*) 1 [1930s+] a go-between in a drug deal, or in any illegal transaction. 2 [2000s] a heavy drug user.

brokered *adj.* [late 19C] having had one's possessions removed by law. [SE phr. *have the brokers in* + ? pun on BROKE adj.[1]]

broke to the wide *phr.* (*also* **broke to the world**) [1900s–10s] absolutely penniless. [BROKE adj.[1] + TO THE WIDE adv.]

broke up *adj.* (*also* **broken up**) [late 19C+] (*orig. US*) 1 injured, hurt. 2 depressed, badly upset. 3 touched, affected. [suffering from a 'broken heart']

brokie *n.* [1950s] (*Aus.*) one who has no money. [BROKE adj.[1] + sfx *-ie*]

brolly *n.* [mid-19C+] (*orig. UK teen/campus*) an umbrella. [abbr.]

broly *adj.* [1990s+] (*US Black*) friendly. [BRO n.[1] (1) + *-ly*, i.e. SE *brotherly*]

brom *v.* [1970s+] (*S.Afr.*) to complain. [Afk. *brom*, growl]

bromide *n.* [1900s–60s] (*US*) 1 a person whose thoughts and conversation are conventional and commonplace; a dull, boring person. 2 a commonplace saying, a trite remark, a soothing statement; thus *bromidic*, commonplace; *bromidically*, conventionally. [SE *bromide*, a dose of potassium bromide taken as a sedative]

Bromigham *n. see* BRUMMAGEM n.

Bromley (by Bow) *n.* [1990s+] money (cf. BEES (AND HONEY) n.). [rhy. sl. = DOUGH n.[1] (1); ult. area of east London]

Brommagem *adj. see* BRUMMAGEM adj.

bromo *n. see* NEXUS n.

Brompton cocktail *n.* [1960s+] a drug 'cocktail' of a variety of strong painkillers mixed with alcohol, supposedly created for terminally ill patients at the Brompton Hospital, London.

bronco *n.* (*also* **bronc, broncho**) 1 [1920s] (*US Und.*) a term of address to a man. 2 [1930s+] (*US gay*) a young man, a novice in the gay world and thus somewhat rough; thus *bronco-buster*, an older man who favours sex with young/underage boys. 3 [1950s–60s] (*US prison*) (*also* **bronc, bronk**) the effeminate companion/lover of a 'masculine' prison homosexual. [SE *bronco*, an unbroken horse]

bronco *adj.* (*also* **broncho**) [mid-19C–1940s] (*US*) wild, untameable. [Sp. *bronco*, rough, esp. as applied to an untamed or half-tamed horse]

bronk *n. see* BRONCO n. (3).

bronstrops *n.* [17C] a procuress. [SE *bawdstrot*, a pander or procuress]

Bronx *n.* [1980s+] (*Aus. prison*) that area of the prison reserved for intractable prisoners. [its reputation as a particularly tough borough of New York City]

Bronx cheer *n.* [1920s+] (*orig. US*) a loud, derisive noise, imitative of a fart. [the uncouth manners of the *Bronx*, New York City]

Bronx cheer *v.* [1940s+] (*US*) to make a noise like a BRONX CHEER n. [BRONX CHEER n.]

Bronx Indian *n.* [1940s] (*US*) a Jew (cf. BROOKLYN INDIAN n.). [the once-large Jewish population of the *Bronx*, New York City + pun on *Indian*, a 'Native' American]

bronze *n.*[1] [mid-19C] self-confidence, arrogance, cheek. [var. on BRASS n.[2]]

bronze *n.*[2] (*also* **bronza, bronzer, bronzo**) 1 [1950s+] (*Aus.*) the anus, the posterior; thus *ugly as a hatful of bronzas*, very ugly (cf. BOURNEVILLE BOULEVARD n.). 2 [1980s] excrement (cf. ADMIRAL BROWNING n.). [its colour]

bronze *v.* [early 19C] to impose upon, to cheat. [play on DO UP BROWN v.]

bronze figure *n.* [20C+] a kipper. [rhy. sl.]

bronze john *n.* [mid-19C] (*US*) yellow fever. [play on YELLOW JACK n.[1]]

bronzer *n. see* BRONZE n.[2].

bronze up *v.* [1980s+] (*Aus. prison*) to register a 'dirty protest' by smearing one's cell walls with faeces. [BRONZE n.[2] (2)]

bronzewing *n.* [20C+] (*Aus.*) 1 a member of the working class. 2 a half-caste Native Australian. [the colour of the *bronzewing* pigeon]

bronzo *n. see* BRONZE n.[2].

broo *n. see* BUROO n.

broody *adj.* 1 [late 19C+] contemplative, (sullenly) meditative, feeling depressed or moody. 2 [20C+] of a woman, feeling a maternal desire to have a(nother) baby. [SE *broody*, of a hen, sitting on her eggs]

Brooklyn Indian *n.* [20C+] (*US*) a Jew (cf. BRONX INDIAN n.). [*Brooklyn*, New York City, home to many Jews + pun. on *Indian*, a 'Native' American]

brooks *n.*[1] [1900s–10s] (*S.Afr.*) trousers. [Du. *broeks*, breeches]

brooks *n.*[2] [1970s] (*US Black*) an expensive, esp. silk, shirt. [New York City's up-market clothiers *Brooks* Brothers]

Brooksey boy *n.* [1920s] (*US*) a smart dresser. [New York City's up-market clothiers *Brooks* Brothers]

Brooks of Sheffield *n.* [mid–late 19C] nobody, a nameless person. [Charles Dickens's *David Copperfield* (1850) in which the villainous Mr Murdstone initially uses the name instead of David's own]

broom *n.*[1] [late 19C] 1 pubic hair. 2 the female genitals. [synon. with BRUSH n.[2] (1); note early 17C *broom*, a horse's tail]

broom *n.*[2] [late 19C–1900s] a would-be dandy, one who fails in his ambitions. [mispron. of *brum*, abbr. BRUMMAGEM n. (7)]

broom *n.*[3] [1940s] (*US Black*) a cigar. [SE *broomstick*]

broom *n.*[4] [1940s–70s] (*US Black*) an act of walking, of movement; thus *knock a broom*, to walk away. [BROOM (IT) v. + ? play on DUST v.[2] (1)]

broom *v. see* BROOM (IT) v.

Broomface *n.* [1950s] (*US*) the federal government. [the figure of a bearded UNCLE SAM n.[1]]

broom-handle *n.* [late 19C] the erect penis (cf. BAT n.[7]).

broomhilda *n.* [1980s+] (*US campus*) a short, unattractive woman. [a US comic strip character, itself a pun on the Wagnerian heroine *Brünhilde*]

broomie *n.* (*also* **broom-tail**) [late 19C+] (*orig. US*) a mustang (esp. a mare) with a short bushy tail. [SE *broom*, a horse's tail]

broom (it) *v.* [late 18C+] to disappear quickly. [the image of sweeping away; orig. UK use faded but was revived by US Blacks, esp. in Harlem]

broomstick *n.*[1] [19C] the penis (cf. BAT n.[7]).

broomstick *n.*[2] [early 19C] a person who puts up fraudulent bail. [BROOMSTICK BAIL n.]

broomstick *n.*[3] [late 19C–1900s] (*Can.*) a gun or rifle. [it 'cleans up']

broomstick bail *n.* [late 17C–early 19C] fraudulent bail. [play on legal jargon *straw bail*, insufficient bail; broomsticks were often made with straw brushes]

broom-tail *n. see* BROOMIE n.

broom to the slammer that fronts the drape crib *v.* [1940s] (*US Black*) to walk over to the clothes closet. [BROOM (IT) v.+ SLAMMER n.[2] (2) + SE *front* + DRAPE n. (1) + CRIB n.[1] (1)]

Broomtown *n.* [1990s+] (*US*) an area of town inhabited mainly by White people only. [ety. unknown]

brooze *v. see* BROWSE v.

brophys, the *n.* [1950s+] (*Irish*) venereal disease. [joc. nickname for the supposed insects, relations of body lice or crabs, which allegedly carried the disease]

broseley *n.* [mid-19C] a pipe; esp. in phr. *cock a broseley*, to smoke a pipe. [proper name *Broseley*, Shropshire, famous for its 'churchwarden' pipes]

broth *n.* [1970s] (*US campus*) *broth*er. [abbr.]

brothel *n.* [1950s+] (*Aus.*) an extremely untidy place or room. [fig. use of SE]

brothel creepers *n.* (*also* **creepers, corridor creepers**) [1950s+] suede shoes, often in lurid colours, with extra thick rubber soles, esp. popular among rock 'n' roll fans of the 1950s (and in 1980s revival). [CREEPERS n.[1] (2); orig. 1940s service use, referring, first, to officers' suede shoes and then to a form of 'desert boot' issued during WW2]

brothel stompers *n.* [1970s+] (*US campus*) suede shoes. [var. on BROTHEL CREEPERS n., although these 'respectable' versions have no great thickness of sole]

brother *n.* 1 [late 19C+] a general form of address to an unnamed male or to oneself. 2 [1910s+] a Black male; thus BROTHERS, THE n. 3 [1920s+] (*mainly US Black*) a form of address to a (fellow) Black male. 4 [1970s+] (*Black*) a non-Black male accepted in the Black community.

brother and sister *n.* [1980s+] a blister. [rhy. sl.]

brother blade *n. see* BROTHER (OF THE) BLADE n.

brother bung *n. see* BROTHER (OF THE) BUNG n.

brother chip *n.* 1 [19C] a carpenter (cf. CHIPPIE n.[3]; CHIPS n.[1]). 2 [19C] a fellow professional of any sort. [BROTHER (OF THE)... n. + SE *chips* of wood; (2) f. (1)]

brother hod *n.* (*also* **hod**) [late 18C–early 19C] a bricklayer's mate or labourer (cf. KNIGHT OF THE HOD n.). [BROTHER (OF THE)... n. + the SE *hod* they carry]

brother in black *n.* [1930s–40s] (*US Black*) a form of address to a fellow Black man; a Black man; thus *sister in black*, a Black woman.

brother-in-law *n.* [1930s–40s] (*US Und.*) a pimp running 2 street prostitutes (cf. CORRAL n.; FAMILY n.[1]; FLOCK n.; HOE TRAIN n.; HORSE n.[10]; ORPHAN n.; OUTLAW n.; SISTER-IN-LAW n.; STABLE n.; STABLE-BOSS n.; STABLE SISTER n.; STRING (OF PONIES) n.; WIFE n.[2]).

brother-in-law *v.* [1920s] (*US*) to pursue clandestinely the wife or girlfriend of another man.

brotherman *n.* (*also* **brother man**) [1970s+] (*US Black*) a form of address to a fellow Black man. [ext. BROTHER n. (3)]

brother (of the)... *n.* [mid-17C–1900s] a phr. used of members of various professions, a member of, a practitioner of; always constructed with a n. denoting, lit. or fig., the occupation (cf. BROTHER CHIP n.; BROTHER HOD n.; BROTHER (OF THE) BLADE n.; BROTHER OF THE BOLUS n.; BROTHER OF THE BRUSH n.; BROTHER OF THE BUNCH OF FIVES n.;BROTHER (OF THE) BUNG n.; BROTHER OF THE BUSKIN n.; BROTHER OF THE COIF n.; BROTHER OF THE GUSSET n.; BROTHER (OF THE) QUILL n.; BROTHER OF THE STRING n.; BROTHER (OF THE) WHIP n.; KNIGHT OF THE... n.).

brother (of the) blade *n.* 1 [mid-17C–19C] a swordsman, a fellow soldier. 2 [mid-18C–19C] a fellow member of the same profession or occupation. [BROTHER (OF THE)... n. + SE *blade*; (2) f. (1)]

brother of the bolus *n.* [mid-19C] (*US*) a physician. [BROTHER (OF THE)... n. + SE *bolus*, a large pill]

brother of the brush *n.* (*also* **brethren of the brush, son of the brush**) 1 [late 17C–1900s] an artist. 2 [19C] a house painter. [BROTHER (OF THE)... n. + SE *brush*]

brother of the bunch of fives *n.* [mid-19C] a prize-fighter, a professional boxer. [BROTHER (OF THE)... n. + BUNCH OF FIVES n.]

brother (of the) bung *n.* [mid-18C–1900s] a publican, an innkeeper. [BROTHER (OF THE)... n. + SE *bung*/BUNG n.[3]]

brother of the buskin *n.* [late 18C] a musician. [BROTHER (OF THE)... n. + SE *buskin*]

brother of the coif *n.* [late 18C] a barrister. [BROTHER (OF THE)... n. + SE *coif*, a coiffed wig, part of his 'uniform']

brother of the gusset *n.* (*also* **knight..., squire...**) [late 17C–19C] a pimp, a procurer (cf. ABBOT ON THE CROSS n.). [BROTHER (OF THE)... n./KNIGHT OF THE... n./SQUIRE n.[1] (1) + GUSSET n.]

brother of the quill *n.* [late 17C–19C] a writer, an author (cf. GENTLEMAN OF THE QUILL n.; KNIGHT OF THE QUILL n.). [BROTHER (OF THE)... n. + SE *quill*]

brother of the string *n.* [late 17C–19C] a musician. [BROTHER (OF THE)... n. + SE *string*]

brother (of the) whip *n.* [late 18C–mid-19C] a coachman. [BROTHER (OF THE)... n. + SE *whip*]

brother round mouth *n.* [early 19C] the anus. [its 'speech' is a FART n. (1)]

brothers, the *n.* [1960s+] (*orig. US Black*) 1 Black people, orig. in 1960s Black radical use, now used by both Black and White speakers with only residual political overtones. 2 one's intimates, one's close friends. [BROTHER n. (2)/SE *brother*]

brothers and sisters *n.* [1920s–30s] (*US*) whiskers. [rhy. sl.]

brother starling *n.* [late 17C–19C] one who shares a friend's mistress. [SE *brother* + *starling*; ? the characteristics of the bird]

brother-where-are-you? *n.* (*also* **brother-where-art-thou**) [1920s] a drunkard. [his being 'blind' drunk]

brother whip *n. see* BROTHER (OF THE) WHIP n.

broth of a boy *n.* (*also* **broth of a lad**) [late 17C; 19C+] (*orig. Irish*) the essence of what a young man should be, a downright good fellow. [the image of broth being the distilled essence and 'goodness' of the meat]

brougham *n.* [1980s+] (*US Black*) an elegant, expensive and prized motorcar. [the smart 19C carriages named for Lord Henry *Brougham* (1778–1868)]

brought *adj.* [1940s] (*US Black*) depressed. [abbr. BROUGHT DOWN adj.]

brought down *adj.* [1940s+] depressed, esp. after a period of elation. [BRING DOWN v.[1] (1)]

broughtonian *n.* [late 18C–early 19C] a boxer; thus *Broughton's mark*, the pit of the stomach. [proper name Jack *Broughton*, 'Captain of the Boxers', inventor of the first prototype 'muffler' or boxing glove, writer of 'Broughton's Rules' (which lasted 1743–1838) and champion of England 1730–5]

brought out *adj.* [1950s+] (*gay*) initiated into the homosexual lifestyle. [BRING OUT v. (3)]

brought to the basket *phr. see* GO TO THE BASKET v.

brought-upsy n. [1990s+] (*W.I.*) upbringing.

brov n. *see* BRUV n.

Brow(, the) n. [1970s+] (*S.Afr.*) Hillbrow, a densely populated, tough, high-rise suburb of Johannesburg. [abbr.]

brown n.[1] **1** [19C] porter, stout. **2** [mid-19C] brandy. **3** [late 19C–1910s] 2 pennyworth of whisky, esp. as sold in Mooney's Tavern in the Strand, London WC2. **4** [1920s–30s] (*US Und.*) whisky. **5** [1950s+] brown ale. [the colour]

brown n.[2] **1** [early 19C–1930s] a halfpenny; a penny. **2** [1980s] (*UK Black*) a £10 note. [the colour of the 'copper' coin or the note]

brown n.[3] **1** [late 19C+] (*also* **round brown**) the anus (cf. BOURNEVILLE BOULEVARD n.). **2** [late 19C+] sodomy, anal intercourse. **3** [1960s+] (*gay*) the dominant partner in anal sex. [the colour]

brown n.[4] **1** [1900s] (*drugs*) opium (cf. APOSTLE n.). **2** [1960s+] (*drugs*) heroin (cf. BLACK n.[3]). **3** [1960s+] (*drugs*) hashish (cf. AFGHAN n.). **4** [1990s+] a cigarette. **5** [2000s] (*US drugs*) by ext. from (2), a Mexican. [the colour]

brown n.[5] [1900s] (*Aus.*) an admirable person.

brown n.[6] [1910s+] (*US Black*) a young, brown-skinned person, esp. as a boy- or girlfriend.

brown adj.[1] [early 19C–1910s] alert, aware. [BROWN v.[1](1)]

brown adj.[2] [mid-19C; 1950s] worthy, earnest, totally devoid of any *double entendre* or 'smut'. [the brown clothes popular among the sedulously pure Quakers]

brown adj.[3] [1930s+] used in combs. to imply homosexuality. [BROWN n.[3] (2)]

brown v.[1] **1** [19C+] (*orig. US*) to understand. **2** [mid-19C] to do perfectly. **3** [mid-19C–1920s] to get the better of, to surpass. [DO BROWN v. (1)]

brown v.[2] [1920s] (*US*) used in a number of semi-euph. excl., e.g. *I'll be browned! brown me!* [? BROWN n.[3] (2), thus synon. with BUGGER v.[1]]

brown v.[3] (*also* **do a brown**) [1930s+] (*orig. US*) to perform anal intercourse, to sodomize (cf. ASK FOR THE RING v.). [BROWN n.[3] (1)]

brown v.[4] *see* BROWN (UP) v.

brown abe n. [1930s–60s] (*US Black*) a cent; thus *brown Abes and buffalo heads*, small change, cents and nickels (cf. ABE n.[2]). [President *Abraham* Lincoln's head is on the cent, a *buffalo head* is on the nickel]

brown ankle n. [1970s+] (*N.Z. prison*) a sycophant, a toady. [he has crawled so far 'up the arse' of the authorities that only his ankles are visible]

brown artist n. [1950s+] a male homosexual who takes the active role in anal intercourse (cf. ANAL ASTRONAUT n.; BROWN BOMBER n.[3]; BROWN DIRT COWBOY n.; BROWN-HATTER n.; BROWNIE n.[4]; BROWNIE KING n.; CHOCOLATE BANDIT n.; CHOCOLATE PUNCHER n.; CHOCOLATE RUNWAY PILOT n.; CHOCOLATE SPEEDWAY RIDER n.; CHUTNEY FARMER n.; CHUTNEY FERRET n.; COCOA-SHUNTER n.; DIRT-TAMPER n.; DUNG-PUNCHER n.; FUDGE-NUDGER n.; FUDGE-PACKER n.; HAEMORRHOID HITMAN n.; HITCHHIKER ON THE HERSHEY HIGHWAY n.; LOG-CABIN RAIDER n.; LOG-PUSHER n.; MARMITE DRILLER n.; MUD-PACKER n.; PEANUT PACKER n.; PEANUT-PACKER n.; POO-PACKER n.; POO PERCOLATOR n.; POO-PIPE PIRATE n.; POO PIRATE n.; POO-STABBER n.; PRUNE-PUSHER n.; PUTTY PUSHER n.; SHIT-STABBER n.; TAN-TRACKER n.; TURD-BURGLAR n.; TURD-PACKER n.; TURD-PUNCHER n.; VISITOR TO VEGEMITE VALLEY n.). [BROWN adj.[3]+ ARTIST sfx]

brown-back n. [1920s–70s] a 10-shilling note (cf. BLUE-BACKS n.). [its colour; the brown 10-shilling notes were issued in 1928 and superseded by the 50p piece after decimalization in 1971; from 1940 until 1948 the notes were mauve rather than brown]

brownbag v. [1960s+] (*US*) **1** to drink liquor from a bottle 'hidden' in the (brown-paper) bag in which it is bought from the liquor store and which is necessary in US states where drinking in the street is illegal. **2** to take one's own supply of alcohol to a restaurant. **3** to take a packed lunch to work or school.

brownbagger n. **1** [1950s] (*US campus*) an excessively hard-working student. **2** [1960s+] (*US*) one who takes a packed lunch to school or work. [BROWNBAG v.; note 1950s USAF jargon *brown-bagger*, a married man; in (1) the *brown bag* contains books rather than lunch]

brown berry n. [1960s] (*US gay*) a virgin anus. [BROWN adj.[3] + SE *berry*, i.e. it is ready to be 'picked']

brown bess n. (*also* **brown bessie, brown betsy**) [late 18C–1900s] a firelock or musket, otherwise known as the 'soldier's best friend'; thus MARRY BROWN BESS v. [the brown walnut stock, although there may be links to Du. *bus* or Ger. *Busche*, a gun barrel]

brown bess adv. (*also* **brown bessie**) [mid-19C] yes. [rhy. sl.]

brown bessie n. [mid-17C] a prostitute (cf. BABY JANE n.).

brown Betty n. [1960s] (*US gay*) a Black man. [SE *brown* plus generic/assonant female name]

brown bomber n.[1] **1** [1940s–70s] (*also* **brown bomb**) a laxative pill. **2** [1950s+] (*Aus., Sydney*) a parking policeman (cf. BABY-BLUES n.[2]). **3** [1960s] (*drugs*) a strong (20mg) capsule of amphetamine, usu. coloured brown (cf. A n.[2]). **4** [2000s] LSD (cf. A n.[3]). [the colour of the uniform, pill or capsule]

brown bomber n.[2] [1950s+] (*N.Z.*) DB (Dominion Breweries) brown ale.

brown bomber n.[3] [1990s+] a male homosexual; a sodomite (cf. BROWN ARTIST n.). [BROWN adj.[3] + SE *bomber*]

brown bread adj.[1] [early 17C] utter, complete.

brown bread adj.[2] [1960s+] dead. [rhy. sl.]

brown bucket n. *see* BUCKET n.[3] (2).

brown creatures n. [mid-19C–1920s] bronchitis. [joc. mispron.; note milit. use *Bill Harris*, bilharzia, *Corporal Forbes*, cholera morbus]

brown dirt cowboy n. [1970s+] a male homosexual (cf. BROWN ARTIST n.). [BROWN adj.[3] + SE *dirt* + *cowboy*]

brown diver n. [2000s] (*US Black*) a male homosexual. [BROWN adj.[3] + SE *diver*]

brown dots n. [1970s+] (*drugs*) LSD (cf. A n.[3]). [its packaging]

browned off adj. [1930s+] (*orig. milit.*) irritated, annoyed. [accumulation of brown rust on fatigued or worn-out metal; but note the various uses of BROWN v.[3] in the context of sodomy]

browned up adj. [1930s–40s] irritated, annoyed. [var. on BROWNED OFF adj.]

browner n. [1980s] (*Can. teen*) a Black person. [BROWN n.[6]]

brown eye n. **1** [1950s+] the anus (cf. BOURNEVILLE BOULEVARD n.). **2** [1980s+] anal intercourse; thus *do the brown eye express, get some brown/tight eye*, to sodomize. [play on SE; BROWN n.[3] + EYE sfx]

brown-eye v. **1** [1940s+] (*US*) to sodomize. **2** [1990s+] (*Aus.*) to drop one's trousers and underwear and reveal one's naked buttocks to anyone who is watching, a mainly juv. prank. [BROWN EYE n. (1)]

brown eyes n. *see* BIG BROWN EYES n.

brown family n. (*also* **browning family**) [1930s+] a generally obs. generic term for homosexuals, referring to the predilection for anal intercourse. [BROWN adj.[3]/BROWNING n.[1] + SE *family*]

brown flight n. [1980s+] (*N.Z.*) the removal from predominantly Maori schools of the children of Pacific islanders, fearful of supposedly low standards.

brown gargle n. [1950s+] (*Irish*) stout. [SE *brown* + GARGLE n. (1)]

brown george n. **1** [17C–early 19C] bread. **2** [mid-17C–18C] a hard, coarse biscuit. **3** [early–mid-19C] a brown wig. **4** [mid-late19C] an earthenware jug. [ety. unknown; cf. naut. jargon *negroes' heads*, brown loaves eaten on board ship]

brown hat n. [late 19C+] a cat. [rhy. sl.]

brown-hatter n. (*also* **brown hat, hatter**) [1910s+] (*orig. RN*) a male homosexual, usu. one who takes the active role in anal intercourse (cf. BROWN ARTIST n.). [? a jibe at a long-dead gay fashion or the coarse image of an excrement-coated meatus]

brown highway n. see CHOCOLATE HIGHWAY n.

brown-hole v. [1980s+] (US gay) to have anal intercourse (cf. ASK FOR THE RING v.). [BROWN v.³ + HOLE n.¹ (1)]

brownie n.¹ **1** [early 19C–1950s] (orig. UK Und.) a penny; a halfpenny. **2** [1920s–50s] (US Black) a cent. [the colour]

brownie n.² **1** [mid-19C+] (Aus./N.Z./US) (also **browny**) a brown-skinned person, an Asian; spec. (Aus.) an Aborgine, a Japanese; (N.Z.) a Maori (cf. BUDDHAHEAD n.; CAMEL RIDER n.; CHARLIE n.⁷; CHINK n.; CHINKI-CHONK n.; CHOKE n.²; CHOPSTICK n.; COOLIE n.¹; DINK n.²; FISH-HEAD n.¹; FLANGEHEAD n.; GINK n.¹; GOO-GOO n.¹; GOOK n.²; GOW n.⁴; HORRIE n.; MR MOTO n.; MONKEY n.¹; MOON-FACE n.; MUSTARD n.²; NIG n.²; NIG-NOG n.²; NIP n.; NOGGY n.; NUPRIN n.; PAKI n.; PIE-FACE n.²; PING n.; PLATE-FACE n.; POWER POINT n.; RICE-EATER n.; RICE MAN n.; RICER n.; SLANT n.⁴; SLIT n.²; SLOPE n.²; SQUINT-EYE n.; SUSHI NIGGER n.; TIGHT EYES n.; WOG n.¹; YELLOW NIGGER n.; YELLOW PERIL n.; ZIPPERHEAD n.). **2** [late 19C+] (Aus.) a cake made of flour, fat and sugar, and filled with raisins or currants. **3** [20C+] a shot of whisky.

brownie n.³ [late 19C] usu. in pl., a small, cheap cigarette. [the maker's name Brown's]

brownie n.⁴ **1** [1920s+] (Aus./US) the anus, the buttocks (cf. BOURNEVILLE BOULEVARD n.). **2** [1940s+] a homosexual, esp. the passive partner in anal intercourse (cf. BROWN ARTIST n.; BROWNIE KING n.; BROWNIE QUEEN n.). **3** [1970s] the vagina; thus hawk one's brownie, to work as a prostitute. **4** [1990s+] a piece of excrement (cf. ADMIRAL BROWNING n.). [BROWN n.³]

brownie n.⁵ [1920s] (US Und.) a child. [? BROWN n.² (1); ? BROWN n.³ (1)]

brownie n.⁶ [1920s–50s] (US Und.) a machine gun. [the Browning machine gun]

brownie n.⁷ [1960s+] (US) a small (usu. chocolate) cake impregnated with hashish or marijuana. [brownie, a trad. US cake]

brownie arcade n. [1940s] (US Black/Harlem) an amusement arcade. [the slot-machines that take 1 cent or a BROWNIE n.¹ (2)]

brownie king n. (also **b.k.**) [1970s] (US gay) a male homosexual who takes the active role in anal intercourse (cf. BROWN ARTIST n.). [BROWNIE n.⁴ (1) + antonym of BROWNIE QUEEN n.]

brownie point n. [1950s+] a notional 'award' for good behaviour, in effect a sarcastic and backhanded compliment for any perceived sycophancy. [links have been made to the Brownies, the junior form of the Girl Guides, and to BROWN-NOSE v.; recent reearch suggests that its origin may also lie in wartime American food rationing, in which ration points in various colours were required to make food purchases: red and brown ones, for example, referred to meats and fats. There are many refs. in wartime newspapers to 'brown points']

brownie queen n. (also **b.q.**, **browning queen/sister**) [1940s+] a male homosexual who is the passive partner in anal intercourse (cf. BROWN ARTIST n.; BROWNIE KING n.). [BROWNIE n.⁴ (2) + QUEEN n.² (1)/QUEEN SFX (2)]

brownies n. [1960s+] (US drugs) amphetamines (cf. A n.²). [the colour of the pill or capsule]

brownie (up) v. [1960s+] to act the toady, to be a sycophant. [ext. of BROWN (UP) v. + ref. to BROWNIE POINT n.]

browning n.¹ [late 19C] anal intercourse. [BROWN v.³/BROWN n.³]

browning n.² [1980s+] (W.I.) a light-skinned Black woman.

browning family n. see BROWN FAMILY n.

browning queen/sister n. see BROWNIE QUEEN n.

browning sisters n. [1930s+] homosexuals in general. [BROWNING n.¹ + SE sisters]

brown job n.¹ [1960s+] flattery, empty praise. [BROWN-NOSE v.]

brown job n.² [1960s+] (gay) anilingus (cf. AUSTRALIAN n.). [BROWN adj.³ + JOB n.⁴]

brown jock n. see BLACK JOCK n. (2).

brown joe v. [1940s+] (Aus.) to know; thus brown joe, in the know. [rhy. sl.]

brown joe adv. [mid-19C] no. [rhy. sl.]

brown madam n. [late 18C–19C] the vagina.

brown man n. [1950s+] (W.I.) **1** a light-skinned Black man. **2** a prosperous Black man. [(2) the belief that light skin is best]

brown meat n. [late 19C+] (US) a Black woman considered as a sex object. [SE brown + MEAT n. (7)]

brown nose n. (also **brown snout**) [1930s+] (orig. US milit.) a toady, a sycophant; thus have a brown nose, to be a sycophant; also attrib. [BROWN-NOSE v.]

brown-nose v. [1910s+] (orig. US milit.) to play the sycophant, to curry favour, to toady. [SE brown + SE nose, one achieves this coloration by 'kissing arse']

brown-noser n. [1950s+] (orig. US milit.) anyone who pays excessive court to authority, at school, in work etc. [BROWN-NOSE v.]

brown off v. **1** [1930s+] to annoy, to irritate. **2** [1950s] (US) to blunder, to make a mistake. **3** [1960s] (US campus) to reject a request for a date. [(1) backform. f. BROWNED OFF adj.; subseq. defs. f. (1)]

brown-out n. [1990s+] (US) a boycott organized by US Latino groups.

brown out v. [1980s+] (US gay) to perform anilingus (cf. AUSTRALIAN n.). [BROWN v.³]

brown paper n. [1930s+] a trick, a pursuit, a profession, a 'game'. [rhy. sl. = CAPER n.²]

brown paper men n. [mid-19C] the poorest class of gamblers. [? their wagering in pence, i.e. BROWN n.² (1)]

brown pipe n. [1990s+] the anus; thus brown pipe engineer, a male homosexual, a sodomite (cf. BOURNEVILLE BOULEVARD n.).

brown polish n. [late 19C–1900s] (orig. US) **1** a Black person. **2** a mulatto.

brown powder n. [1950s+] (drugs) heroin (cf. BLACK n.³). [Mexican heroin, and some other varieties, is brown rather than the usual white]

brown rhine n. [1950s] (drugs) heroin (cf. BLACK n.³). [SE brown/BROWN POWDER n. + RHINE n.]

browns n.¹ [early 19C] (UK Und.) counterfeit halfpennies. [BROWN n.² (1)]

browns n.² [late 19C] (US) hot cakes.

browns n.³ [1960s+] (US drugs) amphetamines (cf. A n.²).

brown salve! excl. [mid-19C] used as a rejoinder, meaning 'I understand'; the expression combines a degree of surprise at what has been said with, ultimately, comprehension of what it means. [ety. unknown]

brown sheet n. [1970s–80s] (UK Black) a £10 note. [SE brown, i.e. its colour + SHEET n. (2)]

brown shell n. [late 19C] an onion.

brown shower n. [1990s+] (US) an act of defecation for sexual purposes. [on pattern of GOLDEN SHOWER n.]

brownskin n. [late 19C+] (US Black) a light-skinned Black person.

brownskin adj. [mid-19C; 1920s+] (US Black) used of a light-skinned Black person.

brown snout n. see BROWN NOSE n.

brown star n. (also **pink starfish**, **starfish**) [1990s+] the anus (cf. BOURNEVILLE BOULEVARD n.). [resemblance]

brownstone adj. [mid-19C–1900s] (US) pertaining to the upper or upper-middle classes. [SE brownstone, a type of New York City house, built 1850–80, fronted with brownstone and favoured by this section of society]

brownstone front n.¹ [mid-19C–1900s] (US) an aristocrat, a member of the upper classes. [their brownstone houses]

brownstone front n.² [late 19C] (US short order) **1** corned beef hash. **2** steak. [play on prev.]

brownstoner n. [mid–late 19C] (US) a member of the upper-middle or mercantile class; thus *brownstone club*, a private club; *brownstone vote*, the political stance of the upper-middle class. [SE *brownstone*, a type of New York City house, built 1850–80, fronted with brownstone and favoured by this section of society]

brown stuff *n.*[1] **1** [1900s] (*Aus./US*) whisky. **2** [1930s–40s] (*US drugs*) opium (cf. APOSTLE n.). **3** [1970s] (*US drugs*) Mexican heroin (cf. BLACK n.[3]). [SE *brown* + STUFF n.[3]; the colour]

brown stuff *n.*[2] [1950s+] excrement, also used fig. (cf. ADMIRAL BROWNING n.). [the colour]

brown sugar *n.* **1** [1930s+] (*orig. US Black*) an attractive Black woman. **2** [1970s+] (*drugs*) heroin (cf. BLACK n.[3]) **3** [1970s+] (*drugs*) low-grade or adulterated heroin. **4** [1980s+] sexual intercourse with a Black person. [the colour; the Black use of (1) crossed over into White vocabulary with the success of the Rolling Stones' song of the same name in 1971; the drug use was a spin-off from this]

brown suit! *excl.* [mid-19C] no chance! [? the transgression of some contemporary fashion norm]

brown tommy *n.* [late 18C–19C] brown bread. [SE *brown* + TOMMY n.[1] (1)]

brown tongue *v.* [1930s+] to toady, to curry favour. [var. on BROWN-NOSE v.]

brown-tonguer *n.* (*also* **brown-tongue**) [20C+] a toady, a sycophant. [BROWN TONGUE v.]

Browntown *n.* [1950s+] (*US*) the Black area of a town or city.

brown trout *n.* [1990s+] excrement; thus *fish for brown trout*, to have anal intercourse (cf. ADMIRAL BROWNING n.; BLIND MULLET n.). [it 'swims' in the lavatory bowl]

Brown 'Un, the *n.* [late 19C–1900s] the *Sportsman*, a sporting newspaper. [the colour of the newsprint (cf. BLUE 'UN, THE n.)]

brown (up) *v.* [1960s+] to act the toady, to be a sycophant (cf. BROWNIE (UP) v.). [abbr. BROWN-NOSE v.]

brown velvet *n.* [1930s] (*N.Z*) a derog. term for a Maori woman, esp. when seen simply as a sex object.

brown wings *n.* [1950s+] (*orig. Hell's Angels*) heterosexual anilingus or anal intercourse (cf. AUSTRALIAN n.). [BROWN adj.[3] + the 'wings' awarded to a qualified fighter pilot]

browny *n. see* BROWNIE n.[2] (1).

browse *v.* (*also* **brooze, bruise, bruze**) [late 19C–1900s] (*Aus./US*) to loaf around, to wander idly, to dawdle. [SE *browse*, of cattle, to nibble on twigs or buds; ult. f. 16C *browse*, a bud, a young shoot]

browsing and sluicing *n.* [late 19C; 1920s+] eating and drinking. [coined and most commonly used by P.G. Wodehouse (1881–1975), but echoed by many of his fans; earlier 1885 cit. refers to cannibalism]

brr rabbit *v.* [1970s] (*US campus*) to complain about the cold. [SE *brr*, an echoic acknowledgement of cold weather + pun on the character *Brer Rabbit*, the creation of Joel Chandler Harris (1848–1908)]

brr-y *adj.* [1970s] (*US Black*) chilly, cold. [SE *brr* + sfx *-y*]

bruce *n.* **1** [1940s–70s] (*gay*) a term of address among male homosexuals (cf. ABIGAIL n.). **2** [1980s+] (*US campus*) a male who thinks he is suave and sophisticated but is not. [*Bruce* is seen as a 'typical' gay name; ? its potential, in camp usage, for being lisped; ? the relationship betwen Batman, i.e. *Bruce* Wayne and his 'ward' Robin (Dick Grayson)]

Bruce Lees *n.* [2000s] erect female nipples. [Kung Fu champion and movie star *Bruce Lee* (1941–73), i.e. a SE *hard* + NIP n. (1)/NIP n.[5]]

bruffam *n.* [late 19C–1900s] a small, closed carriage, properly known as a *brougham*, pron. 'broom' and named after Lord *Brougham*. [deliberate mispron. of the SE, pretending that the 'gh' is pron. 'ff' as in 'enough']

bruh *n. see* BRO n.[1] (2).

bruise *v. see* BROWSE v.

bruised *adj.* [mid-19C] (*US*) drunk (cf. ANNIHILATED adj.). [euph.]

bruiser *n.* **1** [mid-18C+] a boxer, a prize-fighter. **2** [early 19C] one who performs strongly (although not necessarily aggressively). **3** [mid-19C+] any form of thug who prefers to express himself with his fists. **4** [late 19C] a pimp. **5** [1960s–70s] (*US*) a black eye. [SE *bruise*]

bruising *n.* [mid-18C–1900s] boxing; any form of fighting with the fists; thus *bruising match*, a boxing fight; *bruising shop*, a boxers' training gym. [SE *bruise*]

bruising the bed *phr. see* BREWISING THE BED phr.

bruisy *adj.* [1940s+] (*US Und.*) powerfully built, physically aggressive. [BRUISER n.]

Brum *n.* [mid-19C+] **1** Birmingham. **2** a Birmingham accent. **3** a resident of Birmingham. [abbr. BRUMMAGEM n.]

brum *n.*[1] **1** [late 18C–1910s] money. **2** [late 18C–1910s] a counterfeit coin. **3** [late 19C+] something inferior. **4** [1910s–20s] (*Aus./US*) cheap goods. [BRUM n. (1); the reputation of Birmingham as a centre of cheap mass production; (1) refers to the copper coins struck in 19C by Boulton & Watt at their works in Birmingham]

brum *n.*[2] [1920s] (*US*) a prostitute. [? BRUM adj., i.e. she is an 'inferior' form of woman; or ? var. on BRIM n.[1] (1)]

brum *adj.* [late 19C+] (*mainly Aus.*) second-rate; fake, counterfeit, of inferior make. [BRUM n.[1]]

brumbie *n.* (*also* **brumby**) [late 19C–1930s] (*Aus.*) an ill-bred, uncouth individual. [SAusE *brumbie*, a wild or half-tamed horse]

brumbie *adj.* (*also* **brumby**) [late 19C–1930s] (*Aus.*) worn-out, ill-bred, uncouth. [SAusE *brumbie*, a wild or half-tamed horse]

brumby bull *n.* [late 19C+] (*Aus.*) a remittance man. [BRUMBIE adj. + SE *bull*]

Brummagem *n.* (*also* **Bromigham**) **1** [late 17C–mid-19C] a counterfeit coin. **2** [late 17C+] the city of Birmingham. **3** [late 17C+] the Birmingham accent. **4** [late 17C+] an inhabitant of, or person from, Birmingham. **5** [mid-19C] (*also* **Brummagen**) anything fake or inferior in make. **6** [mid-19C] a spur. **7** [late 19C] a second-rate person. [neg. stereotyping of Birmingham]

Brummagem *adj.* (*also* **Brommagem**) **1** [mid-17C+] cheap, second-rate, fake. **2** pertaining to Birmingham, i.e. of an accent or native. [BRUMMAGEM n.; although in (1) a cit. predates it]

Brummagem button *n.* **1** [early–mid-17C] a shilling, poss. a counterfeit one. **2** [mid-19C+] a native of Birmingham. [BRUMMAGEM adj.(1)/BRUMMAGEM n. (4) + SE *button*]

Brummagem conscience *n.* [late 17C] a very bad conscience. [BRUMMAGEM adj. (1)+ SE *conscience*]

Brummagem groats *n.* [late 17C–mid-19C] counterfeit coins manufactured in Birmingham. [BRUMMAGEM adj. (1)+ SE *groats*]

Brummagem protestants *n.* [late 17C] Whigs or Dissenters. [BRUMMAGEM adj. (1)+ SE *protestant*]

Brummagem screwdriver *n. see* BIRMINGHAM SCREWDRIVER n.

Brummagem wine *n.* [late 17C] any adulterated or mixed drink. [BRUMMAGEM adj. (1)+ SE *wine*]

Brummagen *n. see* BRUMMAGEM n. (5).

Brummie/brummie *see under* BRUMMY or BRUMMY.

brummish *adj.* [19C] counterfeit, second-rate. [abbr. BRUMMAGEM adj.]

Brummy *n.* (*also* **Brummie**) [mid-19C+] a native of Birmingham. [BRUMMAGEM n. (4)]

Brummy *adj.* (*also* **Brummie**) [1940s+] pertaining to Birmingham, i.e. of an accent or native. [BRUMMAGEM n.]

brummy *n.* (*also* **brummie**) [1920s+] a counterfeit coin. [BRUMMAGEM n. (1)]

brummy *adj.* (*also* **brummie**) [20C+] second-rate, tawdry, counterfeit. [BRUMMAGEM adj.]

brums *n.* [1910s+] (*Aus.*) cheap, if showy clothes. [BRUM adj.]

brunette *n.* (*US*) **1** [late 19C–1930s] a Black person. **2** [1940s] a Native American.

Bruno n. [1970s+] (US campus) Brown University. [proper name Bruno, 'brown one']

brunser n. [1930s+] (US) **1** (also **brunster**) a homosexual, esp. a catamite or tramp's young homosexual companion. **2** a general derog. term for an unappealing person. [? BROWN n.³]

brush n.¹ **1** [late 17C–1920s] a hasty exit. **2** [mid-18C] one who rushes off. [BRUSH v.¹]

brush n.² **1** [late 18C; 1930s+] pubic hair. **2** [20C+] (Aus./N.Z.) a young woman, a generic term for women. **3** [20C+] (US) (also **brusher**) a moustache or other facial hair. [SE brush, undergrowth]

brush n.³ **1** [late 18C–mid-19C] the penis. **2** [late 18C+] (also **dab/daub of the brush**) sexual intercourse, usu. heterosexual, occas. homosexual. **3** [1940s+] (N.Z./Aus.) a woman who is sexually available. [the penis brushes against the vagina]

brush n.⁴ [late 18C–19C] a house-painter. [his basic tool]

brush n.⁵ **1** [late 19C–1900s] a small glass, made of an inverted cone fixed to a thick stem, which is used for drinking drams of whisky or other spirits. **2** [1910s–30s] a drink of whisky. [the supposed resemblance of the glass's shape to that of a house-painter's brush]

brush n.⁶ see BRUSH-OFF n.

brush v.¹ (also **brush off**) [late 17C–19C] (UK Und.) to rush off, to run away. [SE brush, to rush into with force or collision; ult. Fr. brosser, to dash through dense underwood]

brush v.² [1940s–60s] (US Black) **1** to defeat, to overcome; to beat up. **2** to ignore. [BRUSH OFF v.¹]

brush and lope v. [late 18C–early 19C] to leave in a hurry. [BRUSH v.¹ + SE lope]

brush ape n. [1920s–60s] (US) a hillbilly, a peasant (cf. BOONIE n.¹; BRUSH HOG n.). [SE brush, undergrowth, small branches + APE n. (1)]

brush-by n. see BRUSH-OFF n.

brush colt n. [1940s+] (US) an illegitimate child. [SE brush colt, a horse that has not been deliberately bred]

brush elbows v. see RUB ELBOWS (WITH) v.

brusher n.¹ [late 17C–mid-19C] a very full glass. [? its contents brush against the rim or BRUSH n.⁵]

brusher n.² [19C+] a schoolmaster. [abbr. BUM-BRUSHER n.]

brusher n.³ [late 19C] (Aus.) a 'bloke', a 'chap'. [dial. brusher, a lively, active boy]

brusher n.⁴ see BRUSH n.² (3).

brusheroo n. see BRUSH-OFF n.

brush hog n. (also **brush Yankee**) [1950s] (US) a farmer, an unsophisticated rustic (cf. BOONIE n.¹). [var. on BRUSH APE n.]

brush mouth n. [1940s] (US Black) a sip of whisky. [BRUSH n.⁵ (2) + SE mouth]

brush-off n. (also **brush, brusheroo, brush-by**) [early 18C+] a snub, an act of rejection; thus GIVE SOMEONE THE BRUSH(-OFF) v. [SE brush, to sweep, as with a brush; the image of brushing specks of dirt from one's clothes]

brush off v.¹ **1** [early 19C+] to ignore, to treat contemptuously, to dismiss. **2** [1940s] (US Und.) to murder. [BRUSH-OFF n.]

brush off v.² see BRUSH v.¹.

brush one's teeth v. [1970s+] **1** (US gay) to perform fellatio. **2** (US Black) to perform cunnilingus. [pun on SE + the proximity of one's SE teeth + BRUSH n.² (1)]

brush someone's coat v. [mid-16C–early 18C] to thrash someone, to beat someone up.

brush someone's teeth v. [1970s] (US) to hit someone in the face. [pun on SE]

brush the beaver v. [1990s+] of a woman, to masturbate (cf. APPLY LIP GLOSS v.; BEAT ONE'S HOG v.). [SE brush + BEAVER n.⁵ (1)]

brush-up n. [1910s+] (US) a scuffle, a skirmish. [SE brush, a collision]

brush up a flat v. [mid-19C] to flatter a gullible person. [SE brush, to clean by brushing + FLAT n.² (1)]

brush with a man v. [late 18C–early 19C] to have a fight. [SE brush, to collide with]

brush with a woman n. [late 18C–early 19C] to have sexual intercourse. [SE brush, to collide with]

brush Yankee n. see BRUSH HOG n.

Brussels n. [1920s–30s] a 3-month prison sentence. [SE Brussels carpet/CARPET n.² (1)]

brussel sprout n. **1** [1910s+] a Boy Scout. **2** [1980s+] (Aus.) a lout. **3** [2000s] an affectionate term of address. [rhy. sl.; (3) = OLD SCOUT n.]

brutal adj. **1** [mid-19C+] (Irish) terrible. **2** [1920s+] (orig. US) very good, first-rate. **3** [1960s+] (orig. US campus) hard, difficult, horrible, a general negative. [ext. of SE use; (2) on bad = good model]

brutally adv. [1990s+] (US teen) completely, utterly. [BRUTAL adj. (2)]

brute n. **1** [late 17C+] a general term used to imply the size or effect of the object and the distaste of the speaker; usu. in phr. a brute of a... **2** [1980s+] (Aus. prison) an erection.

brutus n. [1980s+] (US campus) a mean, ugly person. [SE brute 'Latinized' by sfx -us; + ref. to Shakespeare's Julius Caesar and the character Brutus and the phr. 'Et tu Brute?']

bruv n. (also **brov**) [1980s+] a brother, esp. as a form of address to a friend (or actual sibling).

bruz n. (also **bruzz**) [1950s+] (US Black) an affectionate term of address. [SE brother]

bruze v. see BROWSE v.

bruzz n. see BRUZ n.

bry n. [late 19C–1900s] gin. [BRIAN (O'LINN) n.]

bryan o' lin n. see BRIAN (O'LINN) n.

Bryant and May n. [1920s+] a light ale. [pun on SE lights, i.e. the matches produced by the Bryant and May company]

Bryant and Mays n. [1900s–10s] stays (a form of light underbodice that preceded the corset). [rhy. sl.; see prev.]

Bryant and May's chuckaway n. [late 19C–1900s] a woman working at Bryant and May's match factory. [pun on CHUCKAWAY n., with a grim ref. to the disposability of those who worked at this dirty, dangerous task]

b.s. n. [1910s+] (orig. US) rubbish, nonsense. [abbr. BULLSHIT n.; note synon. WW1 Aus. milit beer esses, based on signalman's pron. of b.s.]

b.s. (around) v. [20C+] (orig. US) to talk nonsense, to prevaricate. [B.S. n.]

b.s. artist n. see BULLSHIT ARTIST n.

b.s.-er n. [1960s] (US campus) a time-waster. [B.S.(AROUND) v./abbr. BULLSHITTER n. (1)]

b.s.h.s n. [1970s+] the female breasts. [abbr. the joc. notional administrative measure, British Standard Handfuls, a pun on the BSI, British Standards Institution]

b.t.m. n. [mid-19C; 1910s+] the buttocks. [euph. abbr. SE bottom]

b.t.o. n. [1940s+] (US campus) one who schemes successfully to get their own way. [abbr. big time operator]

BTs n. [1970s] (US) barbiturates. [abbr.]

b.u. n. [1930s] (US campus) sexual drive or desire. [abbr. biological urge]

bu n. see BOO n.⁴ (1).

bub n.¹ (also **bubb**) [mid-17C–19C] drink, esp. strong beer. [Lat. bibere, to drink]

bub n.² [late 17C] the victim of a fraud or hoax. [abbr. BUBBLE n.¹ (1)]

bub n.³ **1** [19C+] (US) a brother. **2** [early 19C+] (US) a boy, esp. when used as a derog. form of address, implying youth, insignificance etc. **3** [1980s+] (US campus) a person devoid of redeeming qualities. [SE bubby, a little boy]

bub n.⁴ see BUBBLY n.

bub n.⁵ see BUBS n.¹.

bub v.¹ [17C–19C] to drink. [BUB n.¹]

bub *v.*² [early 18C–early 19C] **1** to cheat. **2** to bribe. [BUB n.²]

bub and grub *n. see* GRUB AND BUB n.

bubb *n. see* BUB n.¹.

bubba *n.* **1** [19C+] (*US*) a brother. **2** [20C+] (*Aus./US Black*) (*also* **bubbo**) a baby, a young child. **3** [1940s+] (*US*) a generic term for an uneducated Southern male. **4** [1980s+] a general term of address to an unnamed male. **5** [2000s] a fat man. [? pron. by a (younger) sibling]

bubbalah *n. see* BUBELE n.

bubbed *adj.* [19C] drunk. [BUB v.¹]

bubbeleh *n. see* BUBELE n.

bubbelizer *n.* [20C+] (*Ulster*) a stammerer. [their 'bu-bu-bu' stammering]

bubbe mayse *n.* (*also* **bobbe mayse, bubeh miseh**) [20C+] an old wife's tale. [Yid. *Bovo Mayse*, the Story of Bovo (or Buovo), an early 16C narrative poem written in Italy and translated into Yiddish by the scholar Elijah Bochur. Its unlikely tales, featuring the hero Bovo, were meant as satire. When rewritten in 19C prose it was corrupted as *bubbe mayse*, lit. 'a grandmother's story', since only a gullible old lady was presumed to believe the stories as they stood]

bubber *n.*¹ **1** [mid-17C–early 19C] a heavy drinker. **2** [late 17C–early 19C] a drinking bowl. **3** [late 17C–mid-19C] a thief who steals from taverns. [BUB v.¹]

bubber *n.*² [mid-19C] (*US*) an old woman with large, pendulous breasts. [BUBS n.¹]

bubbery *n.* [early 19C] noise, rowdiness. [BUB v.¹; i.e. the behaviour of the drinkers]

bubbie *n. see* BUBBY n.¹.

bubbies *n.* [late 17C+] the female breasts; occas. in sing. (cf. BORDENS n.). [either f. Lat. *bibere*, to drink, or poss. – in the way that some claim that SE *pap* is onomat., stemming from the infant's sucking lips – from the hungry child's cries of 'Bub, bub!']

bubbing *n.* [late 17C] drinking; thus *bubbing-house*, *bubbing-school*, a tavern. [BUB v.¹]

bubbing *adj.* [late 17C] drunken. [BUB v.¹]

bubbkis *n. see* BOBKHES n.

bubble *n.*¹ **1** [late 17C–19C] a victim, one who is ripe for being fooled. **2** [18C–1920s] a sham or otherwise dubious company; thus any dubious scheme. [the schemes so proposed are as insubstantial, if as superficially shiny, as a soap bubble; the (linguistic) archetype is the *South Sea Bubble* of 1721; BUBBLE v.¹]

bubble *n.*² **1** [1900s–70s] (*orig. US*) any automobile. **2** [1960s] a small (3-wheeled) automobile, briefly popular in early 1960s. [abbr. AUTOMOBUBBLE n.]

bubble *n.*³ (*also* **old bubble**) [1930s+] one's wife. [rhy. sl. = TROUBLE AND STRIFE n. (1)]

bubble *n.*⁴ [1940s–60s] (*US*) the female breast. [? BUB v.¹ or ? abbr. BUBS n.¹ or ? resemblance]

bubble *n.*⁵ [1950s+] a Greek. [abbr. BUBBLE AND SQUEAK n.² (2); note the intensified *archbubble*, although this is poss. a nonce-coinage in Cook, *The Crust on its Uppers* (1962)]

bubble *n.*⁶ [1960s] (*drugs*) a small, oval swelling on the skin caused by a careless injection of heroin.

bubble *n.*⁷ *see* BUBBLE-TOP n. (1).

bubble *v.*¹ [mid-17C–19C] to cheat, to hoax, to swindle; thus *bubbleable*, gullible. [the insubstantiality of a SE *bubble* (cf. ety. at BAMBOOZLE v.)]

bubble *v.*² [20C+] (*orig. Aus.*) to be in high spirits. **2** [1990s+] (*US Black*) to improve one's situation, to make money; thus BUBBLING n.². [SE *bubble up*]

bubble *v.*³ [1900s–30s] (*US*) to drive a car. [BUBBLE n.² (1)]

bubble *v.*⁴ [1960s] (*US drugs*) to miss the vein when performing a hypodermic injection; the surrounding skin 'bubbles' up. [BUBBLE n.⁶]

bubble *v.*⁵ *see* BUBBLE (UP) v.

bubble and squeak *n.*¹ (*also* **bubbles and squeaks**) [late 18C–19C; 1930s–40s] (left-over) beef and cabbage and/or potatoes fried up together; occas. fish and potatoes. [the noise of the cooking; subseq. use is SE and almost always potatoes and cabbage]

bubble and squeak *n.*² **1** [late 19C+] a magistrate. **2** [20C+] a Greek. **3** [1910s+] a schoolmaster. **4** [1970s+] a week. **5** [2000s] (*Aus.*) an act of urination (cf. ANGEL'S KISS n.). [rhy. sl.; (1) = BEAK n.¹ (1); (3) = BEAK n.¹ (3); (5) = LEAK n.² (1)]

bubble (and squeak) *v.* [20C+] to speak, esp. to inform to the police. [rhy. sl.]

bubble and squeak *adv.* [early–mid-19C] vigorously. [the noise and action that gives BUBBLE AND SQUEAK n.¹ its name]

bubble around *v.* [late 19C] to make a harsh verbal attack on someone. [fig. use of SE *blow bubbles*]

bubble-bow *n.* [early–mid-18C] a woman's tweezer-case. [BUBBLE v.¹ + SE *beau*, lit. 'beau-fooler']

bubblebrain *n. see* BUBBLEHEAD n.

bubble buff *n.* [17C–early 18C] a bailiff. [BUBBLE v.¹ + BUFF n.² (1)]

bubblebutt *n.* [1970s+] (*US campus*) **1** large, protruding, rounded buttocks. **2** the person who has such a physique. [SE *bubble* + BUTT n.¹ (2)]

bubbled *adv.* [mid-19C+] betrayed, informed against. [BUBBLE v.¹]

bubble dancing *n.* [1940s] (*US*) washing up. [SE *soap bubbles* + pun on SE *bubble-dancer*, a woman who dances, wearing nothing but strategically placed balloons]

bubble gum *n.*¹ [1960s+] **1** (*orig. music business*) catchy, simplistic pop music aimed specifically at the pre-pubescent and early teenage girl market, all, allegedly, prime consumers of SE *bubble-gum*; by ext. anything considered frivolous, banal, unimaginative; also attrib. **2** nonsense.

bubble gum *n.*² [1980s] (*US campus*) a policeman.

bubble gum *n.*³ [1990s+] the buttocks, the behind (cf. ALA n.). [rhy. sl. = BUM n.¹ (1)]

bubble-gum machine *n.* **1** [1960s+] (*US*) (*also* **bubble**) the flashing lights on top of a police car (cf. BUBBLE-TOP n.). **2** [1970s] (*US*) the police car itself. **3** [1970s+] (*US gay*) a condom vending machine, as found in a men's public lavatory. [resemblance]

bubble-gummer *n.* [1960s+] a girl aged 10–14, also an adolescent boy. [BUBBLE GUM n.¹ (1)]

bubblehead *n.* (*also* **bubblebrain**) [1950s+] (*US*) a foolish, careless person, with a brain full of air (cf. AIRBALL n.). [SE *bubble* + -HEAD sfx (1)]

bubbleheaded *adj.* [1970s] silly, foolish (cf. AIRHEADED adj.). [BUBBLEHEAD n.]

bubblejas *n. see* BABALAAS n.

bubble juice *n. see* BUBBLY n.

bubble-man *n.* [mid-19C] one who promotes fraudulent companies. [BUBBLE n.¹ (2) + SE *man*]

bubbler *n.*¹ [18C] a swindler. [BUBBLE v.¹]

bubbler *n.*² [1970s+] (*Aus.*) a school drinking fountain.

bubbles *n. see* BUBBLY n.

bubbles and squeaks *n.*¹ [1950s] Greeks and Cypriots seen collectively. [BUBBLE n.⁵/BUBBLE AND SQUEAK n.² (2) + pun on BUBBLE AND SQUEAK n.¹, i.e. the noise of their dispute]

bubbles and squeaks *n.*² *see* BUBBLE AND SQUEAK n.¹.

bubble-top *n.* [1960s+] (*US*) (*also* **bubble**) **1** the flashing lights on top of a police car (cf. BUBBLE-GUM MACHINE n.). **2** (*US*) the police car itself. **3** (*US campus*) a girl with a bouffant hairdo. [resemblance]

bubble (up) *v.* [1980s+] to inform, to betray. [abbr. BUBBLE (AND SQUEAK) v. or PUT THE BUBBLE IN v.]

bubble water *n. see* BUBBLY n.

bubbling *n.*¹ [late 17C–early 18C] (an act of) cheating, hoaxing, swindling. [BUBBLE v.¹]

bubbling n.[2] [1990s+] (*US Black teen*) rising up, coming up, emerging vigorously. [BUBBLE v.[2]]

bubbly n. (*also* **bub, bubble juice, bubbles, bubble water**) [20C+] champagne. [note WW1 RN *bubbly*, rum]

bubbly jock n. **1** [late 18C–1920s] a turkey. **2** [mid–late 19C] a foolish braggart. **3** [late 19C] an excessive talker. [rhy. sl. = SE *turkey cock*; (2) implies a turkey's characteristics, strutting and making too much noise. Note milit. jargon the *Bubbly Jocks*, the Royal Scots Greys, whose rival regiments equate them with the farmyard bird]

bubbo n. *see* BUBBA n. (2).

bubbs n. *see* BUBS n.[1].

bubby n.[1] (*also* **bubbie**) [mid-19C+] a friendly term of address. [BUB n.[3] (2) + BUDDY n. (1)]

bubby n.[2] *see* BUBBIES n.

bube n. (*also* **bubo**) [late 16C–1920s] venereal disease, esp. syphilis. [SE *bubo*, an inflamed swelling or abscess, one of the possible signs of venereal disease]

bubeh miseh n. *see* BUBBE MAYSE n.

bubele n. (*also* **bubbalah, bubbeleh, bubeleh**) [20C+] a general affectionate term of address. [Yid. *bubele*, little grandmother]

bubkhes/bubkis n. *see* BOBKHES n.

bubo n. *see* BUBE n.

bubonic adj. [1990s+] extreme, notably powerful. [SE *bubonic plague* which devastated Europe during the 14C Black Death]

bubs n.[1] (*also* **bubbs**) [early 19C+] a female breast; occas. in sing. [abbr. BUBBIES n.]

bubs n.[2] [1960s+] (*Aus.*) kindergarten. [SE *babies*]

bubu n.[1] [1950s+] (*W.I. Rasta*) a fool. [? BOOB n.[2] (1)]

bubu n.[2] *see* BOO-BOO n.[4] (1).

buccaneer n. [1990s+] a male homosexual. [rhy. sl. = QUEER n. (4)]

buck n.[1] **1** [late 16C–mid-19C] a cuckold. **2** [early 17C–18C] a bold, daring person of either sex. **3** [late 17C+] a bold, dashing man, a roisterer; thus *cut a buck*, to show off. **4** [mid-18C] (*US*) a peasant, a rural person (cf. BUCKWHEAT n.). **5** [late 18C–mid-19C] as *my buck*, an affectionate term of address. **6** [mid-19C–1920s] a dandy. **7** [mid-19C–1960s] a small dealer who works for a more powerful master. **8** [mid-19C] (*US/Aus./N.Z.*) a man, esp. Indian or Black, esp. as *buck nigger* or *buck blacky* when it becomes derog. unless used by Blacks. **9** [1900s–40s] (*Aus.*) a foreman. **10** [1900s–60s] (*US prison*) a priest, esp. as a prison chaplain. **11** [1910s+] (*Aus.*) spirit, energy. **12** [1920s+] (*orig. Liverpool*) (*also* **buckess**) a tearaway, a young, aggressive criminal. **13** [2000s] (*UK juv.*) an extremely attractive person of either sex. [all fig. uses of SE *buck*, the he-goat or male deer. The strength and sexuality of the male animal underpins the stereotypical (8) in particular. (2) is also abbr. of *buck-a-dandy*, a fop, but note Ware, who suggests a root in SE *buckram*, a stiffening fabric used by such dandies in the full-skirted coats of the 18C]

buck n.[2] [mid–late 19C] an unlicensed cab-driver. [cabman's jargon *buck*, a fraudulent passenger used by an unlicensed London cabbie, who could get near a theatre or restaurant in the Strand only if he appeared to be bringing a fare; thus a reasonably respectable young man would be picked up, driven a few yards and then dropped]

buck n.[3] **1** [mid-19C+] (*US*) $1; $10. **2** [late 19C] a sixpence, usu. preceded by a number of shillings, e.g. *six and a buck*, 6s 6d. **3** [1920s+] (*US*) money, usu. in pl., irrespective of quantity (although the image is usu. of a quantity). **4** [1960s+] (*US*) $100; thus *half-buck*, $50. **5** [1970s+] (*Aus.*) A$1. **6** [1970s+] (*S.Afr.*) a rand. **7** [1980s+] (*US*) 100 of anything, not merely money. [orig. abbr. SE *buckskin*, an item used for barter in 19C America]

buck n.[4] [late 19C–1940s] talk, conversation, esp. when garrulous or irritating. [Hind. *bak*, speech, talk]

buck n.[5] [1910s] (*US Und.*) a prison. [ety. unknown]

buck n.[6] **1** [1910s+] (*Aus./N.Z.*) a try, an attempt; thus *give it a*

buck or *have a buck*, to have a try at something. **2** [1960s] (*US prison*) a strike. [SE *buck* v.]

buck n.[7] [1930s+] (*US prison*) homemade alcohol. [? it 'bucks you up']

buck n.[8] [1940s] (*Irish*) tuberculosis. [it was a 'galloping' disease]

buck adj.[1] **1** [late 18C+] tough, virile, aggressive. **2** [mid-19C] (*US campus*) excellent, first-rate. [BUCK n.[1]]

buck adj.[2] *see* BUCKSHEE adj.

buck v.[1] [early 17C+] to have sexual intercourse. [orig. used of rabbits; late 19C+ use is usu. US]

buck v.[2] **1** [mid-19C–1930s] (*US*) to bet (against) in a game of chance. **2** [mid-19C+] to protest, to object, to show irritation. **3** [late 19C–1920s] (*US*) to desire, to work towards, to aim for. **4** [late 19C+] to avoid, to resist, to oppose oneself to; thus *buck the system*, to fight against the status quo. **5** [1980s] (*US campus*) to miss a class. **6** [1990s+] (*US campus*) to intimidate. **7** [1990s+] (*US Black/teen*) to shoot a weapon. **8** [1990s+] (*drugs*) to steal someone's money. [SE *buck*, to oppose, to come up against]

buck v.[3] **1** [late 19C–1900s] to talk, to chatter; thus *buck-stick*, a chatterer. **2** [late 19C–1940s] to swagger, to talk big or bumptiously, to brag. [synon. Hind. *bakna, bukh*]

buck v.[4] **1** [late 19C+] to move, to run. **2** [1910s] (*US*) (*also* **buck in**) to make an effort. **3** [1990s+] (*W.I.*) to meet up with someone.

buck v.[5] (*US*) **1** [1960s+] (*also* **buck-slip**) to pass, to give. **2** [1990s+] to shoot.

buck v.[6] (*W.I.*) **1** [1970s] to stub (one's toe). **2** [1990s+] to butt with the forehead.

buck v.[7] *see* BUCK (THE TIGER) v.

buck adv. [1990s+] (*US Black*) utterly, totally, completely. [BUCK adj.[1]]

buck a bull off the bridge v. [1910s–40s] (*US*) to perform wonders, to achieve anything one wants.

buck against v. [late 19C–1920s] (*orig. US*) to oppose vehemently and determinedly. [the image of a bucking, uncontrolled horse/BUCK v.[2] (4)]

buck-and-a-half n. [1960s+] (*US*) $150. [BUCK n.[3] (4) + SE *half*]

buckaroo n. (*also* **bakhara**) **1** [17C+] (*US Black*) a poor person, of any race. **2** [early 19C+] a cowboy or cattle-driver. **3** [1920s+] a lively young man. **4** [1930s+] a man, a fellow. [Sp. *vaquero*, cowboy, cow hand]

buck-assed adj. [1940s] (*US*) simple, unadorned, lit. 'naked'.

buck bail n. [late 18C–early 19C] (*UK Und.*) bail put up by one member of a gang for another.

buck bathing n. [1930s] (*US*) nude bathing. [BUCK NAKED adj.]

buck blacky n. *see* BUCK n.[1] (8).

buck-buck! excl. [1990s+] (*US Black teen*) the onomat. noise of a gun being fired.

bucked adj. [20C+] made to feel better, cheered, encouraged. [BUCK UP v.[2]]

bucked (out) adj. (*also* **bucked out**) [1980s+] (*Irish*) finished, 'done for'. [? euph. for FUCKED adj.[1]]

buckee n. *see* BUCKY n.[2].

buckeen n. [late 18C–early 19C] a bully. [Anglo-Irish *buckeen*, a younger son of the impoverished Anglo-Irish aristocracy. The term apes the better-known *squireen*, a petty landowner]

bucker n.[1] [mid-19C+] (*US*) a gambler. [BUCK (THE TIGER) v.]

bucker n.[2] [late 19C–1900s] (*US*) a rebel, one who refuses to follow the party line. [BUCK v.[2] (4)]

bucker n.[3] (*US*) **1** [1930s–70s] a cowboy. **2** [1960s] a toady, one who curries favour for self-advancement.

bucker n.[4] [1980s] (*US*) $1. [BUCK n.[3] (1)]

buckeroo n. [1940s+] (*US*) $1. [BUCK n.[3] (1) + -EROO sfx]

buckess n. *see* BUCK n.[1] (12).

bucket n.[1] [mid-19C–1910s] (*UK Und.*) a glass.

bucket n.[2] [late 19C; 1930s+] (*Can./US Und.*) a county or local prison; thus *drop in the bucket*, to put in prison (cf. BUCKET AND PAIL n.; COW'S LICK n.; FILLET OF VEAL n.; HOKEY n.[1]; JOE GURR n.; MOBY (DICK) n.; SHOVEL (AND PICK) n.; SORROWFUL TALE n.). [rhy. sl. *bucket and pail* = jail]

bucket n.[3] **1** [late 19C; 1990s+] the vagina, esp. when large or loose (cf. BAG n.[1]). **2** [1930s+] (*US*) (*also* **brown bucket**) the anus, the buttocks; thus *paint the bucket*, to have anal intercourse.

bucket n.[4] [1910s] any form of motor vehicle, boat or aeroplane that has become run-down and dilapidated. [predates both RUST BUCKET n. (2) or BUCKET OF BOLTS n.]

bucket n.[5] **1** [1950s–60s] (*US*) a plump woman, an unattractive woman. **2** [1990s+] (*US campus*) an incompetent, clumsy person. [(1) resemblance. (2) BUCKETHEAD n. (1)]

bucket n.[6] [1990s+] (*US*) in basketball, a scoring shot. [the *bucket/basket*]

bucket n.[7] *see* BUCKET (BONG) n.

bucket v. **1** [19C] (*UK Und.*) to deceive, to cheat, to swindle, to ruin, esp. to rob an accomplice of their share of a robbery; thus *bucketer*, one who does this. **2** [1970s+] (*Aus.*) to disdain, to denigrate, to despise. ['To bucket a person is synonymous with putting him in the well' (Vaux)]

bucket about v. [1920s] to move backwards/forwards/from side to side, to oscillate. [? image of a bucket floating on water]

bucket afloat n. (*also* **bucket and float**) [mid–late 19C; 1910s] a coat. [rhy. sl.]

bucket and pail n. (*also* **lard and pail, mop and pail**) [1930s+] prison (cf. BUCKET n.[2]). [rhy. sl. = jail]

bucket (bong) n. [1990s+] (*Aus./US drugs*) a form of gravity pipe for smoking marijuana, made with a 2-litre (3½-pint) plastic bottle and a bucket. [SE *bucket* + BONG n.[1]]

bucket boy n. (*also* **bucket queen**) [1970s+] (*US gay*) a passive partner in anal intercourse. [BUCKET n.[3] (2) + SE *boy*/QUEEN n.[2] (1)]

bucket broad n. [1940s–70s] (*US Und.*) a prostitute who permits anal intercourse. [BUCKET n.[3] (2) + BROAD n.[2] (2)]

bucket cunt n. (*also* **bucket fanny**) [1990s+] a large vagina. [coarsely joc. use of sl./BUCKET n.[3] (1) + CUNT n.[1] (1)/FANNY n.[1] (1)]

bucket (down) v. [1920s+] to rain very heavily. [as if poured from a *bucket*]

bucket gaff n. (*also* **bucket job**) [1960s–70s] (*UK Und.*) a fraudulent company. [BUCKET v. (1) + GAFF n.[1] (10)/SE *job*]

buckethead n. **1** [20C+] (*US*) a fool, a simpleton; thus *bucket-headed*, stupid. **2** [1990s+] (*US Black*) a woman, esp. a fellatrix. [SE *bucket* + -HEAD sfx (1)]

bucket house n. *see* BUCKET SHOP n.[1].

bucketing n. [mid-19C–1910s] a hard task, which one performs only when coerced. [the effort involved in a laborious task, e.g. filling a bath, using only a bucket or bailing out a boat]

bucket job n. *see* BUCKET GAFF n.

bucketmouth n. [1970s] (*US*) **1** a chatterer. **2** one who habitually uses 'bad language'. [SE *bucket* + sfx -*mouth*]

bucket of blood n.[1] [1940s] (*US Und.*) tomato ketchup.

bucket of blood n.[2] *see* BLOODY BUCKET n.

bucket of blubber n. *see* BUCKET OF LARD n.

bucket of bolts n. [1940s+] (*US*) a broken-down motor vehicle. [BUCKET n.[4] + SE *bolts*]

bucket of dirt n. *see* DICKY (DIRT) n.

bucket of lard n. (*also* **bucket of blubber, pail of lard**) [1920s+] a very fat person.

bucket of puss n. [1990s+] (*US*) a person to be pitied and despised.

bucket of shit n. *see* CROCK OF SHIT n.

bucket of smashed crabs n. [1990s+] a general derog. description of an unattractive woman.

bucket of snots n. [2000s] (*Irish*) an unattractive person. [SE *bucket* + SNOT n.[1] (1)]

bucket of worms n. [1970s+] (*US*) an unpleasant, complex and unappetizing situation. [var. on CAN OF WORMS n.]

bucket queen n. *see* BUCKET BOY n.

buckets n. [early 19C] boots or shoes.

bucket shop n.[1] (*also* **bucket house**) [mid–late 19C] a gin-mill, a low-class liquor-shop. [SE *bucket*, the container used for mixing/drinking]

bucket shop n.[2] (*orig. US*) **1** [late 19C+] an unauthorized office used orig. for smaller gambling transactions in grain, and subseq. ext. to offices for other types of gambling and betting on the markets, stocks etc. **2** [1980s+] a cut-price travel agent, specializing in long-haul air flights. ['The market authority in Chicago, called the Board of Trade, would not allow a deal in "options" of less than 5,000 bushels of grain. In order to catch men of small means, what was called the "Open Board of Trade" commenced business in an alley under the regular Board of Trade Rooms. There was an elevator to carry the members of the board to their rooms, and occasionally a member, if trade was slack, would call out, "I'll send down and get a bucketful pretty soon," referring to the speculators in the "Open Board of Trade" below' (*Leeds Mercury*, December 1886)]

bucket shopper n. [1920s–30s] (*US Und.*) one who operates (from) an unauthorized office used for gambling and betting on the markets, stocks etc. [BUCKET SHOP n.[2] (1)]

buckeye n.[1] (*US*) **1** [early 19C+] (*also* **buckey, bucky**) an inhabitant of Ohio. **2** [early 19C+] a rustic or country person (cf. BUCKWHEAT n.). **3** [mid-19C–1900s] an inferior person or thing, esp. one of no value, poor quality or cheap (but often showy). [(1) the *buckeye* tree (*Aesculus glabra*, the American horse chestnut), which flourishes in the state and is featured on its flag; (3) the poor quality of that tree's wood + ? poor reputation of Ohioans]

buckeye n.[2] [mid-19C; 1950s+] (*US*) rotgut whisky. [the addition of *buckeye* nuts to the liquor during its production]

buckeye n.[3] [late 19C–1940s] (*US*) a small place of business, esp. one found in a slum area, spec. a cigar factory. [specific use of BUCKEYE n.[1] (3)]

buck-eyed adj. [mid-19C+] (*US Black*) having eyes considered out of the ordinary, cross-eyed, squinting, protruding etc. [SE *buck*, to project]

buck face n. (*also* **buck's face, buck's head**) [early 17C–early 19C] a cuckold. [BUCK n.[1] (1)]

buck fever n. [late 19C+] (*S.Afr./US*) nervousness in the face of an unknown or new situation that may render one incapable of action. [hunting jargon *buck fever*, the nerves felt by inexperienced hunters faced with the game they have been pursuing; they get so excited they fail to shoot]

buck-fifty n. [1990s+] (*US prison*) a razor-slash that runs either over the top of the skull or from ear to ear. [play on BUCK n.[3] (4)-*fifty*, i.e. $150]

buck-fitch n. [late 17C–early 19C] (*UK Und.*) an ageing lecher, an old roué. [SE *buck-fitch*, a male polecat]

buck for v. [late 19C+] (*orig. milit.*) to struggle towards, to act energetically in one's own interest. [SE *buck*, to come up against]

buckhead n. [1990s+] (*UK juv.*) a person with buck teeth.

buckhorse n. [mid–late 19C] a blow on the ear. [the pugilist *Buckhorse* (real name John Smith) who, for a small charge, allowed people to hit him hard on the side of the head]

Buck House n. [1910s+] *Buc*kingham Palace, London home of the British royal family. [abbr.]

buckijit n. [20C+] (*Irish*) a very great fool. [BUCKING adj. + EEJIT n.]

buck in v. *see* BUCK v.[4] (2).

bucking adj. [late 19C+] (*Irish*) a general intensifier. [BUCK adj.[1]]

Buckinger's boot n. [late 18C–19C] the vagina. [proper name of Matthew *Buchinger*, b.1674 in Germany and known as 'The Little man of Nuremberg'. He was only 29" tall and born limbless, 'notwithstanding which he drew coats of arms very neatly and could write the Lord's Prayer within the compass of one shilling, he was married to a tall handsome woman, and traversed the country, shewing himself for money' (Grose, 1796). He was also a master dice manipulator. For him, a boot could fit only his THIRD LEG n.]

bucking horse n. [1910s] (*Aus.*) a sovereign (£1).

bucking match n. [late 19C] (*US Black*) a fight in which each combatant uses only their head. [animal imagery]

buck into v. [late 19C–1900s] (*US*) to encounter; to become involved in.

buckish *adj.*[1] [late 18C–early 19C] acting like a BUCK n.[1] (3).

buckish *adj.*[2] [1900s–10s] in high spirits. [BUCK UP v.[2] + sfx -*ish*]

buckle n.[1] [early 19C] a fetter, usu. in pl. [ext. of SE use]

buckle n.[2] [late 19C–1900s] (*Aus.*) a positive or cheerful state, condition, mood. [SE *buckle*, to apply oneself vigorously]

buckle n.[3] see BUCKLE MY SHOE n.

buckle v. **1** [late 16C–mid-19C] to be married. **2** [mid-17C–1900s] to marry, to become a mistress. **3** [mid-19C+] to arrest; usu. as *buckled*. **4** [mid-19C] to understand. **5** [1970s+] (*US*) to argue, to fight. [SE *buckle*, to join. (2) E.P. suggests 20C Aus. use, but it is in neither *AND* nor *DNZE*]

buckle-beggar n. [early 18C–mid-19C] a clergyman who performs irregular marriages. [BUCKLE v. (2) + SE *beggar*]

buckle-bosom n. [early 17C] a constable, a catchpoll. [SE *buckle*, to grapple, to engage/BUCKLE v. (3) + *bosom*]

bucklebury n. [1910s–20s] a euph. for SE *buggery*. [play on name of the Berkshire town]

buckled *adj.* [1920s+] (*Irish*) drunk.

buckle down v. (*also* buckle to) [18C+] (*orig. US*) to set to work, to apply oneself vigorously. [ext. of SE *buckle*, to apply oneself vigorously]

buckle-hammed n. [early 17C] having crooked legs. [SE *buckle*, to warp, to bend, to crumple + HAMS n. (1)]

buckle my shoe n. (*also* buckle) **1** [1910s–60s] a Jew (cf. BILLY THE KID n.). **2** [1940s+] (*bingo*) the number 2 (cf. ALDERSHOT LADIES n.). [rhy. sl.]

buckler n. [late 16C–mid-17C] the vagina. [SE *buckler*, a small round shield; play on SWORD n.]

buckle to v. see BUCKLE DOWN v.

Buckley's n. (*also* Buckley's chance, Buckley's show) [late 19C+] (*Aus./N.Z.*) no chance at all. [? proper name of *William Buckley* (1780–1856), an escaped convict who spent 32 years living with Aborigines in South Victoria; or pun on name of defunct firm of *Buckley and Nunn* (founded by Mars Buckley and Crumpton Nunn in 1851) therefore one has 2 chances 'Buckley and Nunn', i.e. none; see *Ozwords* (October 2000), journal of the *AND* centre, for a full discussion]

buck-load n. [19C] (*US*) a large measure of liquor. [BUCK n.[1] (1) + SE *load* or play on SHOT n.[6] (1), i.e. *buck-shot*]

buck naked *adj.* [mid-19C; 1920s+] (*orig. US*) (*also* bucked) naked. [? corruption of BUTT n.[1] (2) + SE *naked*]

buck nigger n. see BUCK n.[1] (8).

buck night n. (*also* buck's night) [1910s+] (*Aus.*) a party for men only (cf. STAG NIGHT n.). [BUCK n.[1] (3) + SE *night*]

bucko n.[1] **1** [late 19C+] a bully, a blustering swaggerer. **2** [late 19C+] a general term of address, e.g. *my bucko*. **3** [1910s+] (*Irish*) a spirited young man. [BUCK n.[1] + -o sfx (1), thence naut. jargon *bucko*, an overbearing ship's officer, who enforces his will through (threats of) violence, usu. as *bucko mate*]

bucko n.[2] [1980s+] (*US*) $1. [BUCK n.[3] (1)]

bucko *adj.* [late 19C+] aggressive, overbearing, domineering. [BUCKO n.[1] (1)]

buck off v. [1990s+] (*US Black*) to murder, to kill. [BUCK v.[2] (7)]

buck of the first head n. [late 18C–early 19C] a celebrated debauchee, whose excesses outpace those of his peers. [BUCK n.[1] (3) + SE *first head*, primacy]

buckoo n. see BEAUCOUP n.

buck out v. [1920s–60s] (*US, Western*) to die; also in fig. use. [equine imagery]

buck party n. [late 19C–1950s] (*Aus./US*) a party for men only. [BUCK n.[1] (3) + SE *party*]

buck-passer n. see PASS THE BUCK v. (1).

buck private n. [late 19C+] (*US milit.*) a private soldier who is trying for promotion; thus occas. other ranks in a similar position, e.g. *buck colonel*, a colonel who wishes to be a general. [BUCK FOR v.]

buckra n. see BACKRA n.

Buck Rogers n. [1980s+] (*Aus. prison*) the ignition of anal wind. [? the idea of a space-ship blasting off; ult. the fictional space hero *Buck Rogers*]

Buck Rogers time n. [2000s] (*US prison*) a parole date that is set far into the future. [note US Army WWII *Buck Rogers gun*, an M-3 light machine gun; the fictional space hero *Buck Rogers* operates several centuries in the future]

bucks n. see BUCK n.[3] (3).

buck's face/head n. see BUCK FACE n.

buckshee *adj.* (*also* buck) **1** [1910s+] (*also* backshee) free, gratis. **2** [1930s] (*US Und.*) released from jail. **3** [1940s] obtained irregularly. [BAKSHEESH n./Pers. *baksheesh*, a gift, a present; thus a tip; picked up by Middle East and Ind. Imperial troops and thus brought to the West]

buckshee/bucksheech n. see BAKSHEESH n.

buckshine n. [mid-19C+] a native of Tennessee. [ety. unknown]

buckshish see under BAKSHEESH.

buck-sick *adj.* [20C+] (*W.I.*) tired of a boring, but still vital task. [BUCK *adj.*[1] (1) + SE *sick*]

buckskin n. **1** [late 18C–early 19C] an American soldier, fighting in the Revolutionary War. **2** [mid-19C+] a native of Virginia. [SE *buckskin*, leather (garments) made from the skin of a buck]

buck-slip v. see BUCK v.[5] (1).

buck's night n. see BUCK NIGHT n.

buckteen n. [mid-18C] (*UK Und.*) shoplifting. [ety. unknown]

buck the horse v. [20C+] (*UK Und.*) to deliberately cause trouble in prison by refusing to accept discipline. [SE/BUCK v.[2] (4)]

buck the saw v. [1960s] (*US Black*) to overcome a challenge, to triumph despite heavy odds. [BUCK v.[2] (4) + pun on *bucksaw*, a heavy form of frame-saw used with a buck or sawing-frame]

buck (the tiger) v. [mid-19C+] (*US*) **1** to play the game of faro; thus fig. *buck against the tiger*, to face overwhelming odds. **2** to gamble. [BUCK v.[2] (4) + TIGER n.[3]]

bucktown n. [1990s+] (*US Black*) Brooklyn, New York City. [BUCK n.[1] (3)/BUCK n.[1] (8); note US regional (Ohio) *bucktown*, the rough part of town]

buck-up n.[1] **1** [1900s] (*Aus.*) alcohol, esp. beer. **2** [1910s] encouragement, cheering up. **3** [1950s+] (*W.I.*) a social gathering, for no specific purpose other than enjoyment. [BUCK UP v.[2]]

buck-up n.[2] [late 19C] (*US*) buckwheat cakes.

buck up v.[1] [early–mid-19C] to dress oneself up. [BUCK n.[1] (3)]

buck up v.[2] [mid-19C+] **1** to encourage, to cheer someone up. **2** to cheer (oneself) up. **3** to improve. [orig. Winchester Coll. jargon; ult. SE *buck*, to boost]

buck up! *excl.* [mid-19C+] **1** cheer up! **2** hurry up! **3** come on! improve yourself! put more effort in! [BUCK UP v.[2]]

buck up to v. [19C] (*US*) to make advances, to court. [? BUCK v.[3] (1)]

buck up (with) v. (*also* buck up on) [1920s+] (*UK Black*) to challenge, to encounter; to meet. [BUCK v.[2] (4)]

buckwheat n. **1** [mid-19C+] (*US*) (*also* buckwheater) a naïve peasant, a gullible country person (cf. ACORN-CRACKER n.; BUCK n.[1]; BUCKEYE n.[1]; COB n.[2]; CORNBALL n.; CORNCOB n.; CORNCOBBER n.; CORNCRACKER n.; CORNFED n.[2]; CORNPONE n.; EAR OF CORN n.; GOOBER n.[2]; HAYSEED n.; JUNIPER n.[1]; QUANDONG n.; SWEDE n.[2]; WHEAT n.[1]). **2** [1930s+] (*US Black*) a light-skinned Black person. [SE *buckwheat*, the cereal grain *Fagopyrum esculentum*, used as cattle-feed in Europe, but cooked for humans in the US; the foodstuff (and thus the term) was popularized by the Black child actor William 'Buckwheat' Thomas, who appeared in the 1930s *Our Gang* series of Saturday morning films]

buckwheat crop *n.* [1960s] (*US*) a marriage that takes place when the bride is already pregnant. [*buckwheat* ripens faster than other grains]

buck-whyling *n.* [1990s+] (*US Black*) chatting, engaging in general conversation. [BUCK n.¹ (8) + SE *while away* (time)]

buck-wild *adj.* [1940s+] (*US Black*) insane, crazy; extreme, intense, desperate. [the state of a *buck* during the rutting season]

buck-wilding *n.* [1990s+] (*US Black*) intense activity, usu. sexual or violent. [BUCK-WILD adj.]

bucky *n.¹* [mid-19C] (*US*) a general term of address to a male. [BUCK n.¹ (3) + sfx -*y*]

bucky *n.²* (*also* **buckee**) [1990s+] (*W.I. Rasta/UK Black*) a gun, usu homemade. [SE *buck* v. + sfx -*y*]

bucky *n.³ see* BUCKEYE n.¹ (1).

bud *n.¹* [17C; mid-19C+] a general nickname or term of address for a brother or eldest son, any boy or man, or a close friend. [abbr. BUDDY n. but note 17C use here]

bud *n.²* **1** [late 19C] (*orig. US*) a young, pubescent girl. **2** [late 19C–1920s] a debutante. **3** [1900s–20s] a young, immature man. **4** [1970s+] (*US gay*) a homosexual teenager. [SE *bud*, a flower that is yet to be fully opened + phr. *bud of promise*]

bud *n.³* [1930s+] (*US*) a nipple.

bud *n.⁴* (*also* **buds**) [1980s+] (*orig. US drugs*) **1** cannabis (cf. AFRICAN BUSH n.). **2** that part of the cannabis plant that is smoked. [SE *bud*]

budded out *adj.* [1990s+] (*US campus*) intoxicated by marijuana. [BUD n.⁴]

buddha *n.* (*also* **buda**) [1980s+] (*drugs*) **1** a potent form of marijuana. **2** a mix of marijuana and crack cocaine. **3** marijuana spiked with opium. [its Oriental origins]

buddha *adj.* [1990s+] (*US campus*) excellent, worthy of admiration. [BUDDHA n.; ult. the Buddha, *fl.* 5C BC]

buddha belly *n.* [1970s+] (*US*) a very fat person. [the trad. statues of the *Buddha*, resplendent with a huge stomach]

buddhahead *n.* [1940s+] (*US*) **1** an Oriental or Asian person (cf. BROWNIE n.²). **2** a Japanese-American (cf. CARPET NAP n.; GUINEA n.; JAP n.; JAPPY n.; KATONK n.; MICRO-CHIP n.; MR MOTO n.; MONKEY n.¹; NIP n.; ORANGE PIP n.²; PONG n.²; RAT TRAP n.; SKIBBY n.; SKIVVY n.¹; YELLOW BELLY n.³; YELLOWTAIL n.). [SE *Buddha* + -HEAD sfx (2); (2) their less assimilated lifestyle, pidgin English and similarly 'unsophisticated' ways]

buddha monk *n.* [2000s] (*US Black*) an habitual marijuana smoker. [BUDDHA n. (1) + SE *monk*]

buddha sticks *n.* [1970s+] (*drugs*) marijuana grown in Thailand, which is sold wrapped around small, satay sticks. [SE *Buddha/*BUDDHA n. + SE *sticks*]

buddhist priest! *excl.* [1970s] (*US*) a euph. for JESUS (CHRIST)! excl.

buddie *see also under* BUDDY.

buddley *n.* [20C+] (*Ulster*) **1** a fat person. **2** a sausage. [Irish *bodalach*, a large, ungainly young person]

buddy *n.* **1** [mid-19C+] (*also* **buddyroo**) (*orig. US*) a friend, an acquaintance (cf. BUD n.¹). **2** [mid-19C+] (*orig. US*) a form of address. **3** [1970s+] (*W.I./UK Black teen*) a sexual partner. **4** [1990s+] (*US/W.I.*) the penis. **5** [1990s+] (*W.I./UK Black teen*) the body. [SE *brother* or dial. *butty*; itself ult. obs. SE *booty*, sharing]

buddy *adj.¹* [1950s] (*Aus.*) a euph. for BLOODY adj.¹.

buddy *adj.²* [1950s–60s] (*Aus./US*) friendly. [BUDDY n. (1)]

buddy *adj.³* (*also* **buddie**) [1990s+] (*US Black*) referring to something that appears fine at first, but is actually a cheap imitation, a knock-off, rip-off or fake, e.g. *Get that buddy shit out of here*. [? *Buddies*, a brand of shoe that looks fashionable but is reputed to fall apart very quickly]

buddy *v.* (*also* **buddy up, buddy with**) (*orig. US*) **1** [1910s+] to become friendly, to live or travel as friends. **2** [1950s+] to ingratiate oneself, to curry favour with someone. [BUDDY n. (1)]

buddy-boy *n.* [1950s+] (*orig. US*) a friend, usu. in a negative or ironic use; esp. as a term of address. [BUDDY n. (1)]

buddy-buddy *n.* (*also* **buddie-buddie**) [1940s+] (*US*) a close friend. [redup. BUDDY n. (1)]

buddy-buddy *adj.* [1940s+] exceptionally and overtly friendly, prob. insincerely so. [BUDDY-BUDDY n.]

buddy-buddy *v.* [1940s+] (*orig. US milit.*) to befriend. [BUDDY-BUDDY n.]

buddy-buddy *adv.* [1950s+] (*orig. US*) in a friendly manner. [BUDDY-BUDDY n.]

buddy-fuck *n.* [2000s] (*US gay*) **1** a sexual partner, but not a steady lover. **2** an act of hedonistic, non-committed sex. [BUDDY-FUCK v.²]

buddy-fuck *v.¹* [1960s+] (*US, mainly milit./campus*) to impose on, betray or otherwise inconvenience a friend; thus *buddy-fucker*, *buddy-fucking* (cf. BUTTFUCK v.). [BUDDY n. (1) + FUCK v.² (1)]

buddy-fuck *v.²* [2000s] (*US gay*) to have intercourse with a friend rather than a lover. [BUDDY n. (1) + FUCK v.¹]

buddy-gee *n.* (*also* **buddy-ghee**) [1930s–60s] (*US Black*) a friend. [BUDDY n. (1) + GEE n.³ (1)]

buddy-o *n.* (*also* **buddy-roe**) [1940s+] (*US*) an affectionate or ironic term of address. [BUDDY n. (2) + -O sfx (1)]

buddyroo *n. see* BUDDY n. (1).

buddyseat *n.* [1940s+] the pillion seat on a motorcycle. [BUDDY n. (1) + SE *seat*]

buddy sex *n.* [2000s] (*US gay*) hedonistic sexual intercourse without commitment. [BUDDY n. (1) + SE *sex*]

buddy up/with *v. see* BUDDY v.

budge *n.¹* (*also* **budgie**) [late 17C–19C] **1** a sneak-thief, esp. one who specializes in entering houses and taking furs, cloaks and coats. **2** the criminal speciality of sneak-thieving. [SE *budge*, a kind of fur, consisting of lamb's skin with the wool dressed outwards]

budge *n.²* [19C–1900s] liquor. [BUB n.¹]

budge *v.¹* [17C–19C] to leave. [SE *budge*, to move]

budge *v.²* [early 19C] to drink. [BUB v.¹]

budge *v.³* [mid-19C] to inform. [SE *budge*, to move against, to act in hostility to]

budge a beak *v.* [early 17C] to run away (from the law). [SE *budge* + HARMAN n.; note this predates BEAK n.¹ (1)]

budge and snudge *n.* [late 17C–mid-18C] (*UK Und.*) a housebreaker and their accomplice. [BUDGE n.¹ (1) + SNUDGE n.; note the 1950s British TV sitcom *Bootsie and Snudge*, based on the misadventures of 2 army friends]

budge kain *n.* [19C] (*Scot.*) a public house, a tavern. [BUDGE n.² + KEN n.¹]

budger *n.* [early 19C] (*UK Und.*) a drunkard. [BUDGE v.²]

budget *n.* [late 19C] the vagina (cf. BANK n.¹). [SE *budget*, a pouch, bag, wallet, usu. of leather]

budget *adj.* [1980s+] (*US campus/UK juv.*) a general negative, applied to people or objects, inferior, second-rate, stupid.

budgey *adj. see* BUDGY adj.

budgie *n.¹* **1** [1930s+] a *budgerigar*. **2** [1960s+] (*UK Und.*) a talkative person, esp. in police use, a minor informer. [abbr. SE *budgerigar*, a popular cage bird, which can be taught to speak; thus RAF jargon (*paraffin*) *budgie*, a helicopter, presumably the source of the Duchess of York's storybook creation]

budgie *n.² see* BUDGE n.¹.

budging ken *n.* (*also* **budging crib**) [early–mid-19C] a public house, a tavern; thus *cove of the budging-ken*, a landlord. [BUDGE v.² + KEN n.¹]

budgy *adj.* (*also* **budgey**) [mid-19C–1910s] drunk (cf. ALED UP adj.). [BUDGE n.²]

budhead *n.* [1970s+] (*US Black*) a beer drinker. [brandname *Budweiser* beer + -HEAD sfx (3)]

budini n. see BODINI n.

budion n. [20C+] (Ulster) a small penis. [Irish boidín, the penis]

budiquette n. [1980s+] (US drugs) the etiquette the governs the smoking of marijuana. [BUD n.⁴ + SE (et)iquette]

budli-budli n. [20C+] **1** sodomy. **2** a male homosexual. [Urdu badli, change, used in late 19C as Raj sl. for a locum tenens and in 20C+ Indian vernacular as a temporary employee]

budlies n. [1980s+] (drugs) cannabis or the part of the cannabis that is smoked (cf. AFRICAN BUSH n.). [BUD n.⁴]

budman n. [1980s+] (US campus) a marijuana dealer. [BUD n.⁴ + SE man]

budmash n. [late 19C–1910s] (orig. Ind. army) a villain, a rascal. [Hind. badmash, a rascal]

buds n.¹ [1980s+] (drugs) alkyl nitrates. [ety. unknown; ? link to BUD n.⁴]

buds n.² see BUD n.⁴.

bud-sack n. [1980s+] (US) a container for marijuana. [BUD n.⁴ + SE sack]

buducie n. [2000s] (US Black) a rank, sharp odour, the result of sexual intercourse. [abbr. of BUTT n.¹ (2) + DICK n.⁴ (1) + PUSSY n. (2)]

budulars n. [1980s+] (drugs) cannabis or the part of the cannabis that is smoked (cf. AFRICAN BUSH n.). [BUD n.⁴]

buel n. [1980s+] (US campus) food. [SE body + fuel]

buel v. [1980s+] (US campus) to eat voraciously. [BUEL n.]

Buenos Aires n. [late 19C] Royal Crescent, Margate; thus go/take the road to Buenos Aires, to start working as a prostitute. [the number of street prostitutes in that part of Margate; Buenos Aires was seen as a centre of White slavery]

buer n. (also bewer, buor, bure) [late 19C+] (orig. tramp) a woman, esp. one seen as sexually appealing and/or of loose character. [? Shelta]

bues n. see BOOZE n. (1).

buf adj. [1980s+] (US teen) of a man, attractive. [? SE beautiful/beautiful fellow or BUFF adj.²]

bufe n. (also bouffer, bufa, bufer, buff, buffer) [mid-16C–19C] (UK Und.) a dog. [echoic of a bark; Ribton-Turner, A History of Vagrants (1887), suggests Welsh bwch, a buck, a male animal]

bufe nabber n. (also buff-knapper, buffer-nabber/-napper) [late 16C–mid-19C] a dog stealer. [BUFE n. + NAPPER n.¹ (1)/NABBER n. (1)]

bufer n. see BUFE n.

buff n.¹ [17C+] the bare skin; usu. as in (the) buff, naked. [the colour of 'white' flesh]

buff n.² **1** [mid-17C–18C] a man, a person. **2** [20C+] (Irish) a country-dweller, a naïve person. **3** [20C+] (Irish) a self-important person. [BUFF n.¹]

buff n.³ [1930s+] an enthusiast, a (knowledgeable) fan. [The Buffs, men or boys who follow firemen and the fires they fight; f. the buff uniforms worn by volunteer firemen in New York City. The term gradually expanded to take in any (amateur) enthusiast, e.g. film buff, sports buff]

buff n.⁴ see BUFE n.

buff adj.¹ [17C+] naked. [BUFF n.¹]

buff adj.² [1980s+] strong, muscular, healthy, good-looking. [BUFFED adj. (2)]

buff v.¹ **1** [mid-18C] to swear to, to testify; thus, to brazen out; to inform against. **2** [1990s+] (US drugs) to manipulate, to con, to threaten. [? SE buff, to 'polish' the truth]

buff v.² **1** [1970s+] (US gay) to have anal intercourse (cf. ASK FOR THE RING v.). **2** [1990s+] to perform oral sex. [SE buff, to polish]

buffa n. see BUFFER n.⁴.

buffalo n.¹ **1** [mid-19C] (US) during the Civil War, a looter. **2** [mid-19C] (US) a Southerner who does not support the Confederacy. **3** [mid-19C; 1940s+] (orig. US, later W.I.) a large, stupid person. **4** [20C+] (US Und.) a Black man. **5** [1960s] (US) a fat woman.

buffalo n.² (also buffalohead) [1920s–70s] (US) a nickel (5 cents). [the picture of a buffalo head on the reverse of the coin]

buffalo v. [late 19C+] (US) to overawe, to frighten, to confuse, to pressurize. [the size and strength of the animal]

buffaloed adj. [1900s–50s] (orig. US) coerced, fooled, crushed. [BUFFALO v.]

buffalohead n. see BUFFALO n.²

buffalo navigator n. [1930s–40s] (Aus.) a bullock-driver.

buffalo piss n. [1970s+] (US) weak beer (cf. GNAT'S PISS n.; HORSE PISS n.; MONKEY PISS n.; PANTHER PISS n.; PIDDLE n.; PISS n.; RAT'S PISS n.; SHARK'S PISS n.; SHEEP'S PISS n.).

buffalo soldier n. [mid-19C+] (US) a Black soldier fighting in the US Army. [so called by the Native Americans who compared their hair to that of the matted hair between a buffalo's horns]

buffarilla n. (also bufferilla) [1960s+] (US campus) a plump, homely young woman. [SE buffalo + gorilla]

buff-ball n. [late 19C] a dance attended by prostitutes; thus, de facto, an orgy. [guests are soon in the BUFF n.¹]

buff boy n. [1970s] a male homosexual prostitute or passive partner in anal intercourse. [BUFF adj.¹ + boy]

buff-coat n. [mid–late 17C] a soldier. [the buff-coloured uniform; later use SE]

buffed adj. **1** [19C] drunk. **2** [1950s+] well-muscled. [SE buffed up, polished; (1) via alcohol; (2) via workout sessions at a gym]

buffer see also under BUFE and its combs.

buffer n.¹ [early 19C] a pistol. [BUFE n., i.e. the 'bark']

buffer n.² (UK Und.) **1** [late 17C–mid-19C] a villain who kills healthy horses and sells the skins. **2** [mid-18C–mid-19C] a villain. [BUFF n.¹, i.e. the skin; note Bee: 'The term Buffer takes its derivation from a custom which at one time prevailed of carrying Bandanas, sarsnets, French stockings, and silk of various kinds, next the shirts of the sellers; so that upon making a sale, they were obliged to undress in order to come at the goods, or in other words, to strip to the skin or buff it']

buffer n.³ [mid-18C–mid-19C] one who swears false oaths for a fee. [BUFF v.¹ (1)]

buffer n.⁴ (also buffa) **1** [mid-18C+] a genial old fool, a description more affectionate than critical; thus often as old buffer. **2** [mid-18C+] a fool, used with a degree of contempt. **3** [late 18C–early 19C] an inn-keeper. **4** [mid-19C] a tradesman. [Fr. bouffard, a fool or clown]

buffer n.⁵ [late 18C–19C] a boxer; a fighter. [SE buff, a blow]

buffer n.⁶ [1990s+] (drugs) **1** a user of crack cocaine. **2** one who offers oral sex in return for cocaine. [SE buffer, a substance used in the manufacture of CRACK n.¹³; (2) note BUFF v.² (2)]

bufferilla n. see BUFFARILLA n.

buffer-lurking n. (also tike-lurking) [mid-19C] (UK Und.) stealing dogs. [BUFE n./SE tike, a dog + LURKING n. (1)]

buffers n. [late 19C+] the female breasts.

buffer's nab n. [late 17C–early 18C] (UK Und.) **1** a counterfeit seal, shaped like a dog's head, used to give spurious authenticity to counterfeit documents. **2** a fake pass. [BUFE n. + NAB n.¹ (1)]

buffet n. (also buffet flat) [1920s–60s] (US, mainly Black) an establishment that sells illicitly distilled liquor, esp. a private house that does so. [Fr. buffet, a sideboard or corner cupboard; thus the food/drink found there]

buffing n. [1990s+] female masturbation. [SE buff, to polish]

buffing the dog n. [late 18C–mid-19C] killing a stolen dog that has not been advertised for (and that can thus be sold back to its owner). The skin is sold and the flesh used for dog's-meat. [BUFF n.¹, i.e. the skin]

buff it v. [mid-19C] to go naked. [BUFF n.¹]

buff it out v. [1970s] (US drugs) to adulterate a drug. [? SE buff up or the addition of some form of buffer]

buffity adj. [1950s+] (W.I.) fat, clumsy and stupid. [dial. buffo, unwieldy; ult. Ewe bofaa, broad and thick]

buff-knapper n. see BUFE NABBER n.

buffle n. [late 16C–early 19C] a fool; thus *buffling*, foolish. [Fr. *buffle*, a buffalo]

buffle v. [early 18C] to fool. [BUFFLE n.]

bufflehead n. [mid-17C–19C] a fool. [BUFFLE n. + -HEAD sfx (1). An alternative ety. suggests Du. *buffel*, blockhead]

buffleheaded adj. [late 17C–19C] stupid, foolish. [BUFFLE-HEAD n.]

buffling adj. *see* BUFFLE n.

buff the banana v. (*also* **buff one's helmet**) [1980s+] to masturbate (cf. BEAT ONE'S MEAT v.; BUFF THE BISHOP v.; CLEAN ONE'S RIFLE v.; CLEAN SOMEONE'S PIPE v.; POLISH... v.; SHINE ONE'S POLE v.; STROKE v.¹; STROKE v.¹; STROKE ONE'S OAR v.; VARNISH ONE'S POLE v.; VARNISH THE FLAGPOLE v.; WAX ONE'S CARROT v.; WAX THE BUICK v.). [SE *buff*, to polish + BANANA n.² (1)/HELMET n. (1)]

buff the bishop v. (*also* **polish the bishop**) [1990s+] to masturbate (cf. BUFF THE BANANA v.). [SE *buff*, to polish + *bishop*; var. on BANG THE BISHOP v.]

buff to one's work v. [early–mid-19C] to strip off preparatory to starting a fist-fight. [BUFF n.¹]

buff to the stuff v. [late 19C] (*UK Und.*) to claim that stolen property is one's own. [BUFF v.¹ (1)]

buffugly adj. [2000s] (*US Black*) extremely unattractive. [abbr. BUTT n.¹ (2) + FUCKING adj. (1) + SE *ugly*]

buffy n.¹ [mid-19C] a genial old fool. [var. on BUFFER n.⁴ (1)]

buffy n.² [1980s+] a muscular woman or girl. [BUFF adj.²; reinforced by TV show, *Buffy the Vampire Slayer*]

buffy adj. [mid-19C–1920s] drunk. [? BEVVY n. (1) or Fr. *bouffé*, bloated]

buft n. [late 16C] (*UK Und.*) 1 a decoy. 2 a thief; thus *buftrap*, a thief-catcher. [SE *buff*, to puff out; (2) note E.P. (in *DU*) prefers 'harlot's protector', although the rest of the list are all synon. for 'thief']

buftie (boy) n. (*also* **bufty (boy)**) [1990s+] (*Scot.*) a male homosexual. [? BUTTFUCKER n. (1)]

bufu n. [1980s+] (*orig. US*) a male homosexual. [abbr. BUTTFUCKER n. (1) on model of MOFO n.]

bufu v. [1980s] (*US*) to have anal intercourse (cf. ASK FOR THE RING v.). [BUFU n.]

bufu-bufu adj. [1940s+] (*W.I.*) fat, swollen, blubbery, too big, clumsy or lumbering. [Twi *bufoo*, swollen + Ewa *bofaa*, broad and thick]

bug n.¹ 1 [mid-16C+] a person, esp. one who puts on airs; thus *bug's words*, boasting language. 2 [1960s] (*US campus*) an insignificant person, an irritating person. [ult. f. *bug*, an object of fear, a hobgoblin]

bug n.² [mid-18C] a man who incites homosexuals to join him in illegal pleasures. [? SE *bugger*]

bug n.³ [late 18C–early 19C] (*Anglo-Irish*) an Englishman. [the belief that English settlers imported insects to Ireland in mid-18C]

bug n.⁴ 1 [mid-19C–1920s] a breast-pin. 2 [late 19C–1930s] (*US gambling*) any device that aids cheating. 3 [late 19C+] (*US*) a small object of any kind. 4 [1910s–30s] (*Can.*) an old car rebuilt as a HOT-ROD n. 5 [1910s+] (*US*) a small car, esp. the Volkswagen Beetle. 6 [1920s] identification, suspicion; i.e. fig. use of (8) or (9). 7 [1920s–40s] (*US*) a telegraph transmission key. 8 [1920s–50s] (*US*) a makeshift lantern or flashlight. 9 [1920s+] (*US Und.*) a burglar alarm. 10 [1930s] (*US Und.*) a time clock. 11 [1940s+] (*orig. US*) any form of electronic surveillance gadget. 12 [1960s] (*US Black*) a trick. 13 [1960s+] (*Can./US prison*) a homemade water heater for making coffee. [the size of a SE *bug*, an insect, usu. a beetle or similar]

bug n.⁵ 1 [mid-19C–1920s] dishonesty; esp. in phr. PUT THE BUG ON v. 2 [mid-19C+] (*orig. US*) an enthusiast, a fan, a devotee; thus *bugess*, a female fan. 3 [late 19C+] an obsession; often in combs.,

e.g. *travel bug*, a desire to go travelling. 4 [20C+] an insane, unstable person. 5 [20C+] an idea; thus *put a bug in someone's ear*, to inspire. 6 [1900s] (*US*) a fool. 7 [1950s] (*US Und.*) a prostitute's client. 8 [1950s] (*US*) a (left-wing) 'soapbox' orator. 9 [1960s–70s] a cheat, an unreliable person. 10 [2000s] (*US prison*) a fight. [all f. concept of an invasive insect]

bug n.⁶ (*orig. US*) 1 [mid-19C+] a microbe, a germ. 2 [1910s+] (*drugs*) a side effect of an excessive consumption of amphetamine or amphetamine-type drugs, whereby the sufferer believes insects are living beneath their skin and scratches desperately in order to remove them; usu. as *cocaine bug, crank/speed bugs*. 3 [1920s+] an illness, a disease (cf. BUG, THE n.). 4 [1940s] usu. in pl., crabs, body lice. [? SE *bug*, an object of terror; although *OED* questions the link]

bug n.⁷ [late 19C–1900s] a wallflower. [? a 'fly' on the wall]

bug n.⁸ 1 [late 19C+] (*orig. US*) a defect, a problem in any form of machine (including computers and their software). 2 [1930s+] any form of error or delay.

bug n.⁹ (*US*) 1 [20C+] a promiscuous woman. 2 [1980s] the vagina. [? derog. association of a woman with an insect or ? dismissive, f. the size]

bug n.¹⁰ [1910s–30s] (*US Und.*) an open sore on the arm which is kept from healing and used to enhance one's efforts at begging; also used by prisoners to get into the prison hospital.

bug, the n. (*US*) 1 [1940s–50s] tuberculosis. 2 [1950s] malaria. 3 [1990s+] AIDS. [BUG n.⁶ (3)]

bug adj. [1900s–10s] (*US*) mad, crazy, obsessed with (cf. APEY adj.; BUGGED adj.¹; BUGGED OUT adj.; BUGGY adj.²; BUGHOUSE adj.¹; BUGS adj.; BUGSHIT adj.). [BUG n.⁵ (4)]

bug v.¹ 1 [late 18C–19C] to bribe (a policeman or, earlier, a bailiff). 2 [early 19C] to hand over, to give; often as BUG OVER v. 3 [late 19C] to obtain by underhand or illegal means. [(1) 19C use is mainly US]

bug v.² 1 [mid-19C; 1960s] to ruin, to destroy. 2 [1940s+] to annoy, to irritate. 3 [1940s+] (*also* **bug up**) to pressurize, to nag. 4 [1950s+] to scare, to unnerve. 5 [1980s+] (*US*) to be tense, nervous, depressed. 6 [2000s] (*US Black*) to fight. [i.e. to act like a SE *bug*, an insect]

bug v.³ 1 [20C+] (*US*) to walk slowly, lethargically. 2 [1970s] (*US Black*) to terminate one's interest in something/someone. [the pace of the insect]

bug v.⁴ [1910s+] to tap a telephone or to install any form of electronic surveillance. [although this use predates BUG n.⁴ (11) by 20 years, it remains the logical if anomalous link]

bug v.⁵ [1930s] 1 (*US Und.*) to have an open, unhealed sore on one's arm, to enhance one's efforts at begging. 2 (*US drugs*) to inject one's arm with something that will produce a large and unpleasant-looking swelling; the intention is to obtain a shot of narcotic from a doctor. [BUG n.¹⁰]

bug v.⁶ 1 [1930s+] (*orig. US*) to be insane or to act as if one is. 2 [1940s+] (*orig. US*) to confine someone in a psychiatric institution. 3 [1950s] (*US prison*) to subject a prisoner to a psychiatric examination. 4 [1960s+] (*US*) to be shocked, appalled. 5 [1990s+] (*US drugs*) to experience hallucinations from drug use. [BUG n.⁵ (4)]

bug v.⁷ [1950s] (*US*) to see, to notice. [BUG-EYE v.]

bug v.⁸ [1980s+] (*US*) in rap music, to do something impressive in a performance. [fig. use of BUG v.⁶ (1)]

bug adv. [late 19C–1900s] (*US*) madly, crazily. [BUG n.⁵ (4)]

buga n. [1970s] (*US gay*) a heterosexual. [Sp. *buga*/SE *boogieman*]

bugaboo n.¹ 1 [19C] a bailiff, a sheriff's officer. 2 [20C+] (*US Black*) a pesterer, a nuisance, esp. in a sexual context. 3 [1900s–10s] (*US*) a fuss, a commotion. [SE *bugaboo*, a bogeyman, someone or something of whom one is scared]

bugaboo n.² [1910s+] (*W.I.*) nasal mucus, esp. when dry. [dial. *boggle* + *bug*, mucus; but note SE *bugaboo*, a bogeyman/BOGEY n.³ (1)]

bug and flea *n.* [1960s+] (a cup of) tea. [rhy. sl.]

bugbear *n.* [late 17C] the female pubic area. [the darkness, both lit. and fig., of the pubic hair]

bug bomb *n.* [1940s+] (*US*) an aerosol insecticide. [SE *bug* + *bomb*]

bug cell *n.* [1940s] (*US prison*) a padded cell. [BUG n.⁵ (4) + SE *cell*]

bug chaser *n.* [1990s+] one who aims deliberately to become infected with HIV/AIDS. [BUG, THE n. (3) + SE *chaser*]

bug club *n.* [1920s] (*US*) a psychiatric institution. [BUG n.⁵ (4) + SE *club*]

bug doctor *n.* (*also* **bug doc**) [1930s+] any form of expert dealing with mental problems, a psychoanalyst, a psychologist etc. [BUG n.⁵ (4) + SE *doctor*]

bug-eater *n.* [19C] (*US*) **1** an inhabitant of Nebraska. **2** an unimportant or worthless person. [ext. uses of SE; (1) the poverty-stricken appearance of the inhabitants; at some stage of the 19C the state was overrun by locusts (bugs) and a serious attempt was made to persuade the impoverished country-people to adopt them as a diet]

buger-bear *n. see* BOOGER BEAR n.

bugess *n. see* BUG n.⁵ (2).

bug-eye *n.* [20C+] **1** one who has round or bulging eyes. **2** a round or bulging eye. [BUG-EYED adj. (1)]

bug-eye *v.* [1950s–60s] (*US*) to stare. [BUG-EYE n.]

bug-eyed *adj.* **1** [late 19C+] cross-eyed. **2** [20C+] drunk or intoxicated by drugs (cf. ARSEHOLED adj.). **3** [1920s+] amazed, astounded. **4** [1940s+] showing signs of insanity. [(1) one's eyes are popping like those of some insects; subseq. defs. f. (1)]

bugfucker *n.* [1970s] (*US*) a man with an extremely small penis. [SE *bug*, an insect + FUCKER n. (1)]

bugged *adj.*¹ **1** [1940s+] infuriated, angry. **2** [1940s+] (*also* **bugged up**) of a person or situation, crazy, insane, mentally unstable (cf. BUG adj.). **3** [1960s] frightened. **4** [1990s+] (*US Black/drugs*) experiencing a sense of paranoia after smoking strong marijuana or crack cocaine. **5** [2000s] fashionably weird. [HAVE BUGS (IN THE HEAD) v.]

bugged *adj.*² [1970s+] (*drugs*) covered with sores and abscesses from repeated use of non-sterile needles. [BUG v.⁵ (2)]

bugged on *adj.* [1940s–50s] (*US Black*) obsessed with, very enthusiastic about. [BUG n.⁵ (3)]

bugged out *adj.* [1950s+] (*US*) bizarre, eccentric (cf. BUG adj.). [ext. of BUGGED adj.¹ (2)]

bugged up *adj.*¹ [late 19C–1930s] (*US*) dressed up. [BUG n.¹ (1) + ? ref. to BUG n.⁴ (1)]

bugged up *adj.*² *see* BUGGED adj.¹ (2).

bugger *n.*¹ **1** [early 18C+] (*also* **bogger**) a person, usu. a man, a 'bloke'; esp. as *silly bugger, daft bugger* etc, none of which is necessarily pej. **2** [mid-19C+] a thing, or creature, with no special connotations. **3** [1910s+] something unpleasant or undesirable, a great nuisance; thus *a bugger to...* **4** [1980s+] (*S.Afr.*) a dedicatedly masculine male, whose lack of sensitivity is more than compensated for in his enthusiasm for all forms of sport. [SE *bugger*, a sodomite; a trans. of 14C Fr. *bougre*, ult. Lat. *Bulgarus*, a Bulgarian, a name given to a sect of heretics who came from Bulgaria in the 11C. The term was transferred to the Albigensian heretics, who it was believed were largely homosexual. Despite appearances, the term remains SE, although the *OED*, *c*.1900, states that 'in decent use only as a legal term'. Its verbal and comb. uses are, however, sl., as are the n. uses cited here]

bugger *n.*² [mid-19C] (*US Und.*) a pickpocket. [BUG n.⁴ (1)]

bugger *n.*³ [1920s+] a semi-euph. synon. for DAMN n.

bugger *n.*⁴ [1980s+] (*drugs*) Mexican black tar heroin. [BOOGER n.¹ (1), i.e. its texture]

bugger *n.*⁵ *see* BOOGER n.¹ (1).

bugger *v.*¹ [late 18C+] a semi-euph. synon. for DAMN v., used in excls.; thus to curse. [SE *bugger*, to sodomize]

bugger *v.*² [1920s+] to make a mess of. [ext. of SE *bugger*]

bugger! *excl.* [20C+] a synon. for DAMN! excl.

bugger about *v.* (*also* **bugger around**) [1920s+] **1** to wander around. **2** to mess about with something. **3** to waste time, to stall, to be unhelpful. **4** to make someone's life miserable or difficult in some way. [BUGGER v.²]

bugger-all *n.* (*also* **blow-all, sweet bugger-all**) [1920s+] absolutely nothing; also as adv., absolutely no...

buggerama! *excl.* [1980s] (*N.Z.*) an excl. of annoyance. [BUGGER! excl. + -ORAMA sfx]

buggeranto *n.* [late 17C–early 18C] a male homosexual. [SE *bugger* + 'Spanish' sfx *-anto*; note character in Rochester *Sodom* (1684):'Buggeranthes Generall of the Army']

bugger around *v. see* BUGGER ABOUT v.

bugger around on *v.* [1970s+] (*Can.*) to commit adultery, to be unfaithful. [ext. of BUGGER ABOUT v. (4)]

bugger-bandit *n.* [2000s] a male homosexual (cf. ANAL ASTRONAUT n.). [SE *bugger* + BANDIT sfx (2)]

bugger-chick *n.* [1980s+] (*S.Afr.*) 'the compliant girlfriend of an aggressively masculine man' (*DSAE*). [BUGGER n.¹ (4) + CHICK n.⁴ (3)]

buggered *adj.*¹ [mid-19C+] a synon. for DAMNED adj. [BUGGER v.¹]

buggered *adj.*² [1940s+] **1** exhausted. **2** of machinery, not working; of a person, confused. **3** defeated, destroyed. [BUGGER v.²]

buggered for the want of an Irish King *phr. see* IRISH KING n.

buggered if I know *phr.* [1940s+] a phr. in answer to a question, stating one's absolute ignorance. [BUGGERED adj.¹]

buggered up *adj.* **1** [mid-19C+] of objects, broken, out of order. **2** [1910s+] of people, physically beaten or hurt; exhausted. **3** [1910s+] of plans, ideas, schemes, ruined, aborted. [BUGGER UP v.]

bugger for *phr.* **1** [1950s+] a phr. denoting an enthusiast, an obsessive, e.g. a *bugger for work*. **2** [1990s+] someone highly reluctant to do something. [SE *bugger* + (1) var. on BUG n.⁵ (2)]

buggering *adj.* (*also* **boggering**) [late 17C+] a general negative adj. [BUGGER v.¹ although predates it]

bugger it! *excl.* [1940s+] an excl. of annoyance, esp. when an inanimate object or a previously determined plan of action fails to function as required. [BUGGER! excl.]

buggerize about *n.* [1940s+] (*Aus.*) **1** to wander around. **2** to mess about with something. **3** to waste time, to stall, to be unhelpful. **4** to make someone's life miserable or difficult in some way. [var. on BUGGER ABOUT v.]

buggerlug *v.* [late 19C] to waste time on trivial activities. [BUGGER ABOUT v. (3) + ?]

bugger-lugger *n.* **1** [late 19C] one who wastes time on trivial activities. **2** [1920s] in fig. use, a factory hand. [BUGGERLUG v.]

buggerlugs *n.* [late 19C+] (*orig. RN*) **1** a general term of (affectionate) address, usu. among men. **2** brushed back 'wings' of hair (cf. BUGGER'S GRIPS n.). [SE *bugger* + LUG n.¹; lit. 'sodomite ears']

bugger me! *excl.* [1950s+] a general excl. of surprise, annoyance, alarm. [BUGGER v.¹]

bugger me dead! *excl.* [1980s+] (*Aus.*) a general excl. of surprise, annoyance, alarm. [ext. of BUGGER ME! excl.]

bugger off *v.* (*also* **begger off, booger off**) [1920s+] to go away; esp. as BUGGER OFF! excl. [SE *bugger*, i.e. synon with FUCK OFF v. (1)]

bugger off! *excl.* [1920s+] go away! leave me alone! a general excl. of dismissal or disbelief in an idea or statement. [BUGGER OFF v.]

buggeroo *n.* [1940s+] an eccentric person, a 'character'. [BUGGER n.¹ (1) + -EROO sfx + ? pun on BUCKEROO n.]

bugger's grips *n.* [20C+] (*orig. RN*) the brushed back 'wings' of hair that adorn the temples of many upper-class Englishmen. Coarse rumour imputes these as the handholds for those who are positioning such partners ready for anal penetration (cf. BUGGERLUGS n.). [SE *bugger* + *grips*. Note tailor's jargon *bugger-bafflers*, the side vents on a man's jacket]

bugger's woods *n*. [1970s] an out-of-the-way place, an unimportant place. [SAmE *boogerman*, bogeyman; he is supposed to live there]

bugger that for a game of soldiers! *excl*. *see* FUCK THAT FOR A GAME OF SOLDIERS! excl.

bugger-up *n*. [1990s+] a blunder, a mistake. [BUGGER UP v.]

bugger up *v*. [1920s+] **1** to make a mess of, to blunder. **2** to hurt, to injure, lit. or fig. [BUGGER v.²; note Papua New Guinea Tok Pisin *bagarap*, used as all-purpose neg., e.g. no good, broken]

buggery *n*. [1980s+] (*Aus.*) a difficult time, problems. [backf. f. ALL TO BUGGERY phr.]

buggery *adj*. *see* BOOGERY adj.

buggery! *excl*. [1970s+] an excl. of annoyance.

bugger you! *excl*. [20C+] a vehement excl. expressing personal antagonism. [BUGGER v.¹]

bugging *n*.¹ [late 17C–mid-19C] the taking of bribes by bailiffs and other court officials. [? backform. f. BUG THE WRIT n.]

bugging *n*.² [1910s+] the tapping of a telephone, or other forms of electronic surveillance. [BUG v.⁴]

bugging *n*.³ [1980s+] **1** (*US*) going crazy, suffering mental stress. **2** (*US campus*) relaxing. **3** (*US campus*) acting in a foolish manner. **4** (*US campus*) asking someone to do something silly or foolish. **5** (*US teen*) feeling stupid. [BUG v.²]

bugging *adj*. **1** [1940s–50s] (*US*) a euph. for FUCKING adj. **2** [1990s+] (*US campus*) in error, annoyed. [BUG v.²]

buggins *n*. [late 19C] a fool. [a generic term for a 'foolish' name]

buggins' turn *n*. [20C+] a sinecure that comes to all members of a committee, board of directors etc, as long as they remain members of that group and, in due course, inevitably take their turn at a task; the antithesis of promotion by merit. [proper name *Buggins*, used as a stereotype for a time-serving mediocrity]

buggle-bo *n*. (*also* **bugle-bow**) [17C] the vagina (cf. BLACK HOLE n.¹). [SE *bogle*, a demon, usu. black]

buggy *n*.¹ **1** [20C+] (*orig. US*) (*also* **gas buggy**) a car; thus *buggy bandit*, a car thief or one who uses a getaway car after a robbery. **2** [1910s–40s] (*US*) a wheelbarrow. [the orig. SE *gasoline buggy*. The earlier *buggy* was a light 1-horse (sometimes 2-horse) vehicle, for 1 or 2 people; it is cited as slang in Grose (1785) and Hotten (1859 et al.)]

buggy *n*.² [1930s] (*US drugs*) a makeshift 'syringe' used by a narcotics addict.

buggy *adj*.¹ [19C+] infested with any sort of bug: lice, bedbugs etc. [SE *bug*]

buggy *adj*.² [late 19C+] (*US*) lit. or fig., unstable, insane (cf. BUG adj.). [BUG n.⁵ (4)]

buggy *adj*.³ [1930s] (*US*) pertaining to jazz fans. [BUG n.⁵ (2)]

buggy bandit *n*. *see* BUGGY n.¹ (1).

buggy bin *n*. [1940s] (*US*) a psychiatric institution. [BUGGY adj.² + BIN n. (4)]

bugher *n*. (*also* **bughar**) [mid-17C–18C] (*UK Und.*) a (little, yelping) dog. [echoic of its bark; var. on BUFE n.]

bughouse *n*. **1** [mid-19C+] (*US*) a vermin-infested lodging house (latterly hotel). **2** [late 19C+] a hospital, esp. a lunatic asylum; thus *bughouse fable*, an exaggerated story; *bug ward*, *bughouse ward*, a psychiatric ward; also attrib. **3** [1900s–10s] (*US*) nonsense, rubbish. **4** [1920s–30s] (*US*) a prison (cf. BANDHOUSE n.). **5** [1920s+] (*orig. S.Afr.*) a run-down, dirty, third-rate cinema. [SE *bug*/BUG n.⁵ (4) + *house*]

bughouse *adj*.¹ [late 19C+] (*US*) insane, crazy (cf. BUG adj.). [BUGHOUSE n. (2); Flynt, *Tramping with Tramps* (1900) attributes the coinage to the tramp Boston Mary who believed she had 'bugs' crawling in her brain]

bughouse *adj*.² [1910s–30s] (*Aus.*) second-rate. [BUGHOUSE n. (1)]

bughouse square *n*. [1920s–60s] (*US*) any centre of urban life, typically Union Square, New York City, or Washington Square, Chicago, where tramps, vagrants, the more or less deranged and any other eccentrics gather. [BUGHOUSE adj.¹ + SE *square*]

bug-hunter *n*.¹ [late 18C–early 19C] an upholsterer. [SE *bug*; they dislodge the insects as they repair the furniture]

bug-hunter *n*.² [mid–late 19C] a street thief who specializes in snatching (drunken) men's jewellery; thus *bug-hunting*, robbing or cheating drunks, esp. after dark. [BUG n.⁴ (1) + SE *hunter*; also a pun on schoolboy *bug-hunter*, a naturalist]

bug-hunter *n*.³ [late 19C+] an entomologist. [SE]

bug hut *n*. [1930s+] a tawdry, run-down cinema. [var. on FLEAPIT n./BUGHOUSE n. (5)]

bug hutch *n*. [1910s] a small hut or sleeping place.

bug in one's ear *n*. [20C+] (*US*) **1** a friendly warning. **2** rumour, gossip. [fig. use of SE *bug*]

bug juice *n*. **1** [mid-19C+] (*Can./US*) (*also* **bug poison**) illicitly distilled whisky; thus any form of alcohol, esp. cheap and appealing to alcoholics. **2** [late 19C+] (*Can./US*) a soft drink. **3** [1940s–50s] (*US Und.*) knockout drops. **4** [1940s+] (*UK prison*) a sedative drug used for controlling violent or non-cooperative prisoners. **5** [1940s+] (*Can./US*) petrol. **6** [1940s+] (*Can./US*) a mix of saliva and tobacco juice that forms the residue or 'dottle' in a pipe. **7** [1940s+] (*Can./US*) insecticide. [BUG n.⁵ (4); (7) SE *bug* + SE *juice*/JUICE n.³. Orig. the Schlechter whisky drunk by the Pennsylvania Dutch, cheap and second-rate; subseq. a generic for any bad whisky; note 1930s Annapolis jargon *bug juice*, meat gravy]

bugle *n*.¹ **1** [early 19C+] the nose; thus *blow one's bugle*, blow one's nose; ON THE BUGLE phr. **2** [late 19C] a loud voice. **3** [1990s+] (*drugs*) cocaine. **4** [2000s] an act of inhaling cocaine.

bugle *n*.² [1980s+] (*Irish*) an erection. [play on HORN n.² (3)]

bugle-bow *n*. *see* BUGGLE-BO n.

bugleboy *n*. [1960s] (*US gay*) a passive male homosexual (cf. BONE-EATER n.). [one *blows*/BLOW v.² (3) a *bugle*/BUGLE n.²]

bugle duster *n*. [1960s+] a handkerchief. [BUGLE n.¹ (1) + SE *duster*]

bugly *adj*. *see* BUTT-UGLY adj.

bug man *n*. [1960s] one who plants and conducts clandestine surveillance with electronic equipment. [BUG n.⁴ (11) + SE *man*]

bug off *v*. [1950s+] to leave, esp. as BUG OFF! excl. [abbr. BUGGER OFF v.]

bug off! *excl*. [1950s+] a euph. for BUGGER OFF! excl. [BUG OFF v.]

bugology *n*. [mid-19C+] (*US campus*) biology, entomology; thus *bugologist*, an entomologist. [SE *bug* + sfx -*ology*]

bug on *v*. [1990s+] (*US teen*) to aggravate. [BUG v.² (2)]

bugout *n*. [1990s+] (*US campus*) someone who acts in a silly or comic way. [BUG OUT v.² (1)]

bug out *v*.¹ **1** [1950s+] (*US*) to leave, to run away. **2** [1970] to default on one's duties. [BUG v.³]

bug out *v*.² **1** [1950s+] to go insane, to lose emotional control; thus *bug out on*, to attack in a psychotic rage. **2** [1950s+] to drive mad, lit. or fig. **3** [1970s+] to subject to psychotherapy. **4** [1990s+] to lose one's temper. **5** [1990s+] (*US drugs*) to experience temporary hallucinations while intoxicated from drug use. **6** [1990s+] (*US campus*) to experience pleasure. **7** [1990s+] to act in an excited manner, to be astonished. [BUG v.⁶]

bug over *v*. [19C] (*UK Und.*) to hand over. [BUG v.¹ (2) + SE *over*]

bug poison *n*. *see* BUG JUICE n. (1).

bug rake *n*. [1930s+] a comb. [SE *bug* + *rake*]

bugs *n*. *see* BUG n.⁶ (4).

bugs *adj*. [20C+] (*orig. US*) crazy, eccentric; also occas. *bugs*, insanity; thus *bugs on*, crazy about, obsessed by (cf. BUG adj.). [HAVE BUGS (IN THE HEAD) v.]

bug's age *n*. [1930s] (*US*) a very long time. [SE *bug* + *age*]

bugs and fleas *n*. [1930s–40s] (*US*) the knees. [rhy. sl.]

Bugs Bunny *n.* [1950s+] (*orig. Aus.*) money (cf. BEES (AND HONEY) n.). [rhy. sl., ult. f. Warner Bros. character *Bugs Bunny*, created 1940]

bugshit *adj.* [1970s+] (*US*) crazy, eccentric (cf. BUG *adj.*). [BUGS *adj.* + DIPSHIT *adj.* (1)]

bugster *n.* [1920s–50s] (*US Und.*) a night watchman. [ety. unknown]

bug's words *n. see* BUG *n.*[1] (1).

bug test *n.* [1930s–50s] (*US prison*) an intelligence test. [BUG *n.*[5] (4) + SE *test*]

bug the writ *v.* [late 17C–19C] of a bailiff or other court officer, to postpone handing out a writ, having been given a suitable bribe. [BUG *v.*[1] (1) + SE *writ*]

bug trap *n.* (*US*) **1** [1920s] a verminous lodging house. **2** [1960s] a bed. [SE (*bed*) *bug* + *trap*]

bugturd *n. see* TURD *n.* (2).

bug up *v.*[1] [1940s] (*US*) to ruin, to spoil. [abbr. BUGGER UP *v.*]

bug up *v.*[2] **1** [1940s] (*US drugs*) to experience the effects of smoking marijuana. **2** [1940s+] to make nervous, to confuse, to excite. **3** [1960s] to go crazy. [BUG *v.*[6] (1)]

bug up *v.*[3] *see* BUG *v.*[2] (3).

buguyaga *n.* [1950s+] (*W.I. Rasta*) a sloppy, dirty person, e.g. a vagrant. [SE *bugaboo*/Carib.E. *bugo-bugo*, rough and crusty + Ewe *yakayaka*, slovenly ? + Hausa *buguzunzumi*, a big, fat, sloppy person]

buguyaga *adj.* [1990s+] (*W.I.*) of behaviour, coarse, uncouth. [BUGUYAGA *n.*]

bug-walk *n.* **1** [mid-19C–1900s] a bed. **2** [late 19C–1910s] the parting of the hair. **3** [late 19C] (*Aus*) a small road. [SE *bug* + *walk*. Note milit. jargon *bug-run*, a parting]

bug ward *n.* [1900s] (*US*) a psychiatric institution. [BUG *n.*[5] (4) + SE *ward*]

buhtuh *n. see* BHUTTU *n.*

buick *v.* (*also* **call buicks**) [1970s+] (*US*) to vomit (cf. BARF *v.*). [echoic]

build *n.* [mid–late 19C] the cut or style of one's clothes.

build *v.* **1** [late 19C+] (*orig. Aus.*) to prepare, food, drink, a cannabis cigarette etc. **2** [1930s] (*US Und.*) to ceate confidence or apparent friendship, for the sake of enticing a victim.

build a sconce *v.* [mid-17C–early 18C] to run up a large bill at a tavern or inn, esp. when one has no intention of paying it. [Oxford University jargon *sconce*, a fine of a tankard of ale imposed by undergraduates on each other for various small misdemeanours. Note the *OED* prefers to link the phr. to SE *sconce*, a small fort or earthwork, but this lacks any drinking ref.]

build a spliff *v.* [1980s+] to roll a cannabis cigarette. [BUILD *v.* (1) + SPLIFF *n.* (1)]

builder's bum *n.* (*also* **brickie's bum, builder's crack, plumber's crack**) [1990s+] the crevice between the buttocks that is revealed when one bends forward and, if wearing low-cut trousers, the waist is forced downwards; orig. of male builders but now used generally. [SE *builder* + BUM *n.*[1] (1)]

builder-upper *n.* [1930s+] (*orig. US*) a promoter, a publicity man, a morale booster.

build pigpens *v.* [1950s] (*US*) to deceive, esp. for a merchant to cheat a customer. [the practice of woodcutters who pile the wood on their carts in the shape of a pigpen; thus making the pile, which is hollow, appear larger than it is]

build the biscuits *v.* [1900s] (*US cowboy*) to prepare a meal when travelling.

build the fence *v.* [20C+] (*US*) to marry, usu. after the bride is already pregnant. [phr. *plant the corn before you build the fence*, to act prematurely]

build time *v.* [1960s] (*US prison/Und.*) to serve a jail sentence. [SE *build* + TIME *n.*[1]]

build-up *n.* [1920s+] (*orig. US*) preparation, esp. an accumulation

of favourable publicity designed to popularize a person, product etc.

build up *v.* **1** [1900s] (*orig. UK Und.*) to dress up in one's best clothes in order to present a respectable, if fraudulent, image. **2** [1970s+] (*drugs*) to roll a cannabis cigarette. [(2) BUILD *v.* (1)]

built *adj.* **1** [1930s+] (*US*) of a woman, attractive and with a noticeably good figure. **2** [1960s+] (*US campus*) of a man (or woman), well muscled; if man, poss. referring spec. to his penis.

built like a brick shithouse *phr.* (*also* **built like a brick slaughter house, stacked like a brick backhouse**) [1910s+] (*orig. US*) describing a very strong, muscled man or woman, who resembles a solid edifice, often euphemized as 'schoolhouse', 'outhouse' etc; also (*Aus.*) **built like a brick dunny**. [SE *built*/BUILT *adj.*/STACKED *adj.*[1] (3) + *brick* + SHITHOUSE *n.* (2)/SE *slaughter house*/BACKHOUSE *n.*]

built like a tripod *phr.* [1990s+] (*US*) having a large penis. [SE *built*/BUILT *adj.* (2); the image is of a THIRD LEG *n.*]

buji *adj. see* BOOJEE *adj.*

bujok *adj.* [1930s] a term of disdain. [? Polish]

buke *v.* [20C+] (*US*) to sodomize. [abbr. SE *rebuke*, the image is one of punishment]

bukra *n. see* BOOKRA *n.*

buku *see under* BEAUCOUP.

bul *n. see* BULL *n.*[10] (1).

bulchin *n.* (*also* **bulkin, bull chin**) **1** [early-mid-17C] a term of contempt to any male. **2** [17C–early 19C] a term of endearment to a child, usu. a chubby one. [SE *bulchin*, a bull-calf]

bulge *n.* [mid-19C+] (*US*) an advantage; esp. in HAVE THE BULGE ON *v.* [SE *bulge*, a protuberance]

bulge *v.* [mid-19C] (*US*) to make someone rush off. [lit. to push someone out]

bulger *n.* [mid-19C] something very important of its type. [SE *bulge*, a protuberance]

bulger *adj.* [mid-19C+] large. [BULGER *n.*]

bulk *n.* (*also* **bulker**) [mid-17C–mid-19C] (*UK Und.*) a thief's, esp. a pickpocket's, accomplice who jostles the victim while their pocket is picked. [? SE *bulk*, a large lump; thus the image of this human 'lump' pushing one around]

bulk *adj.* [1970s+] (*Aus.*) many, lots. [? SE *bulk buying*]

bulk *v.* **1** [late 17C] of a prostitute, to have sexual intercourse (cf. BANG *v.*[1]). **2** [late 17C–1920s] (*UK Und.*) to push; to jostle when picking a pocket.

bulk and file *n.* [late 17C–18C] (*UK Und.*) a pickpocket and their assistant, albeit in reverse order (*see* ety.); one jostles the victim, the other picks the pocket. [BULK *n.* + FILE *n.* (2)]

bulker *n.*[1] [late 16C–early 19C] a poor prostitute who is forced to sleep in the streets; thus *bulk-begotten*, said of the child of a prostitute. [SE *bulk*, a heap, on which she lies]

bulker *n.*[2] *see* BULK *n.*

bulkin *n. see* BULCHIN *n.*

bulk-monger *n.* [18C] a prostitute who consorts with thieves, esp. pickpockets. [BULK *n.* + sfx *-monger*]

bulky *n.* **1** [19C; 1930s] a policeman, a prison guard; thus *bulkie ken*, a police station. **2** [1920s+] (*Ulster*) a member of the Royal Ulster Constabulary; thus the *bulkies*, the RUC. [SE *bulky*, sizeable + ? 17C def. as pompous, self-important; (1) + KEN *n.*[1] (1)]

Bull *n. see* JOHN BULL *n.*

bull *n.*[1] **1** [late 16C+] a womanizer, a successful philanderer. **2** [1930s+] an aggressively masculine lesbian (cf. BULL BITCH *n.*[2]; BULL-DAGGER *n.*; BULLDICKER *n.*; BULL-DYKE *n.*). **3** [1950s+] (*orig. US*) (*also* **bull queer**) a macho male homosexual. **4** [1990s+] (*W.I.*) (*also* **buller, buller-man**) a male homosexual. [the image of the animal]

bull *n.*[2] (*also* **bull-calf**) [mid-17C–1940s] a blunder, an error; a self-contradictory proposition, esp. that which is made by an Irishman. [Grose (1785) posits an eponym, one Obadiah *Bull*, 'a blundering lawyer of London, who lived in the reign of Henry

VII', but he appears to have no actual substance. The link to Ireland is simply another e.g. of derog. stereotyping; the term's uses predate any such link by many years]

bull n.[3] [late 17C–early 19C] false hair, worn by a woman (cf. BULL-HEAD n.[2]; BULL-TOUR n.). [? its resemblance to the hair between a bull's horns]

bull n.[4] **1** [late 18C–1910s] 5 shillings, a crown; thus HALF-A-BULL n. **2** [1910s] a counterfeit coin. [BULL'S EYE n.[2] (1)]

bull n.[5] [mid-19C] (Aus.) 75 strokes of the lash (cf. BOB n.[5]). [BULL n.[4] (1); different numbers of lashes were named for different values of coin]

bull n.[6] [mid-19C] (US) a railway locomotive (cf. BULLGINE n.). [i.e. its strength]

bull n.[7] (US) **1** [mid-19C] an ox. **2** [1920s–30s] a 'buffalo' nickel (cf. BULL-HEAD n.[3]). [(2) the engraving on the coin]

bull n.[8] [mid-19C+] any form of prison meat. [orig. UK but by 20C mainly US]

bull n.[9] [late 19C–1940s] a second brew of tea, the once-used leaves are left in the pot and a new kettleful of boiling water poured over them. [SE bull, a drink made by putting water into an empty spirit cask, or over a sugar-mat, to catch some of the flavour]

bull n.[10] [late 19C+] **1** (orig. US) (also **bul**) a policeman?; thus (US tramp) bull buster, one who is obsessed with assaulting the police; fresh bull, a policeman who cannot be bribed; wise bull, a detective (cf. ANIMAL n.[1]). **2** (US) a detective (cf. BEAGLE n.[3]). **3** (US Und.) a veteran, a long-term convict. **4** a railroad security guard. **5** (US prison) a prison warder. [Ger. sl. Bulle, policeman or poss. Sp. sl. bul, policeman; (1) orig. US but Aus./UK Black use late 20C+]

bull n.[11] **1** [late 19C+] (orig. US) lies, flattery, insincere talk of any kind. **2** [1940s+] (orig. milit.) unnecessary routine or discipline; thus bulled-up, dressed according to the strictest military regulations. [euph. abbr. of BULLSHIT n. although cits. here predate]

bull n.[12] [1930s–40s] (US gay/prison) any form of note, letter etc. [abbr. SE bulletin]

bull n.[13] **1** [1930s+] in poker, an ace. **2** [1990s+] (drugs) 1g of pure cocaine. [BULLET n.[1]]

bull n.[14] [1950s+] (Aus.) a casual wharf labourer who is given preferential treatment by the foreman; thus bull system, employment practices on the docks whereby the men line up for work every morning and the foremen pick them for a day's work. [? SE bull, i.e. a comparison of strength]

bull n.[15] **1** [1960s–70s] (US campus) an academically successful person. **2** [1980s] a self-assured, poised person. [? reverse anthropomorphism]

bull adj. **1** [mid-19C–1940s] (US) large, powerful, authoritative. **2** [1940s+] (US gay) of a lesbian or male homosexual, masculine, aggressive. [the image of the animal]

bull v.[1] **1** [16C–17C] to mock, to tease. **2** [17C–19C] to cheat, to defraud. **3** [18C+] of a man, to have sexual intercourse. **4** [late 19C+] (US) to act violently, aggressively. **5** [1900s–50s] to cow, to intimidate. **6** [1910s] (US campus) to act clumsily. **7** [1920s] (US Und.) to deceive for the purposes of swindling. [SE bully]

bull v.[2] [early 19C+] (Aus.) to adulterate, to weaken; thus bulled grog, diluted liquor. [note RN jargon bull the barrel/cask, to pour water into an empty rum barrel; the resulting (weakly alcoholic) liquid can be drunk]

bull v.[3] [mid-19C–1930s] (US campus) to fail an examination. [BULL n.[2]]

bull v.[4] **1** [mid-19C+] (Aus.) to brag, to boast; thus bulldocia, boasting. **2** [20C+] to deceive, to tell lies. **3** [20C+] (US) to chat, to gossip. [the aggressive energy of the SE bull, reinforced by BULL n.[11] (1)]

bull v.[5] [1980s+] (W.I.) to bugger, to pursue a homosexual sex-life. [the animal's image as a stud]

bull! excl. [1920s+] nonsense! [BULL n.[11] (1)]

bulladeen n. [1960s] (US Black) a policeman (cf. ANIMAL n.[1]). [BULL n.[10]]

bullamakanka n. (also **bullabananka**, **bullamanka**, **willamakanka**) [1950s+] (Aus.) an imaginary place, supposedly far from civilization. [? Fiji bullamacow, bullybeef]

bull and cow n. (also **pantomime cow**) **1** [mid-19C–1970s] a row, an argument. **2** [20C+] a loud noise. [rhy. sl.; (2) f. (1)]

bull-ants n. [1920s–30s] (Aus.) trousers. [rhy. sl. = PANTS n.[1] (2)]

bullaphants adj. [20C+] (Irish) drunk (cf. ADRIAN (QUIST) adj.). [var. on ELEPHANT'S (TRUNK) adj.]

bull artist n. [1910s+] a braggart, a boaster, one who lies or deceives. [BULL n.[11] (1) + ARTIST sfx]

bull-beef n. [late 16C–19C] meat, esp. beef.

bull-beef adj. [late 18C–early 19C] fierce, intolerant, macho. [? BULL-BEEF n.]

bull bitch n.[1] [1930s–50s] (US) something or someone unimaginably bad. [BULL adj. (1) + BITCH n.[1] (6)]

bull bitch n.[2] [1960s+] (US) a lesbian (cf. BULL n.[1]). [BULL adj. (2) + BITCH n.[1] (1)]

bull-bucka n. (also **bull-bucker**) [1940s+] (W.I.) a thug, a bully, an aggressive man. [SE bull + 18C US dial. buck, to butt; thus one who thinks he is strong enough to butt a bull or ? BULL adj. (1) + BACKRA n.]

bull buster n. see BULL n.[10].

bull butter n. [late 19C–1940s] (US) margarine. [its innate fakeness + coarse ref. to bull semen]

bull-calf n.[1] [late 16C–19C] a great, hulking, undisciplined oaf.

bull-calf n.[2] see BULL n.[2].

bull camp n. [late 19C–1930s] (US) a camp of outdoor workers, e.g. on an oil pipeline. [image of SE bull as 'male' or BULL adj. (1)]

bull chin n. see BULCHIN n.

bull come n. (also **bull gism**) [1920s] cream gravy. [SE bull + COME n. (2)/JISM n. (2)]

bull con n. [late 19C+] (US) specious, deceitful talk. [BULL adj. (1)/BULL n.[11] (1) + CON n.[1] (7)]

bull cook n. [1900s–70s] (US tramp) a chef's assistant, an odd-job man.

bullcorn n. [1960s+] (US) nonsense, rubbish. [euph. for BULLSHIT n. (1)/BULL CON n.]

bullcrap n. [1950s+] any form of specious talk, nonsense, rubbish, lies, flattery; also as a dismissive excl. [var. on BULLSHIT n. (1) + CRAP n.[3] (3)]

bull-dagger n. (also **bull-dag**, **dagger**) [1920s+] a masculine lesbian; thus bull-dagging, engaging in lesbian sex (cf. BULL n.[1]). [BULL-DYKE n.]

bulldicker n. [1960s+] (US gay) a masculine lesbian, spec. who uses her clitoris to mimic the penis as in heterosexual intercourse (cf. BULL n.[1]). [BULL adj. (2) + DICK n.[4] (1); play on BULL-DYKE n.]

bull dicky n. (also **bull dinky**) [1940s+] (US) any form of specious talk, nonsense, rubbish, lies, flattery. [BULL n.[11] (1) + DICKY n.[5]/DINGUS n. (2)]

bull-dike see also under BULL-DYKE.

bull dinky n. see BULL DICKY n.

bulldocia n. see BULL v.[4] (1).

bulldog n.[1] **1** [late 17C–19C] a sheriff's officer. **2** [early 19C] (US) a watchman. **3** [late 19C–1940s] (US) a policeman (cf. ANIMAL n.[1]). **4** [1970s] (US prison) a bully, a tough aggressive man. [note Oxbridge jargon bulldog, an assistant to the Proctors, those dons charged with maintaining university discipline]

bulldog n.[2] [18C–1940s] a pistol. [it 'growls']

bulldog n.[3] [early 19C] a sugar-loaf. [? both are squat, solid shapes]

bulldog adj. [20C+] **1** large and potentially violent and/or threatening. **2** uncompromising, indomitable. [anthropomorphism]

bulldog v. **1** [1930s–60s] (US Und.) to destroy, to wear down.

2 [1920s–50s] (*US*) to brag, to exaggerate, to lie. **3** [1960s+] (*US Und.*) to harass, whether verbally or physically.

bulldogger *n.* [1990s+] (*US Black*) a violent person. [BULLDOG v. (3)]

bulldose *n.* (*also* **bulldoze**) [mid–late 19C] (*US*) a severe flogging. [a *dose* of the *bull*-whip]

bulldose *v.* (*also* **bulldoze**) **1** [late 19C] to flog, to beat severely. **2** [late 19C+] to intimidate, to coerce, to force through violence; thus *bulldozing*, an act of violent coercion. [BULLDOSE n.]

bulldoser *n.* (*also* **bulldozer**) (*US*) **1** [late 19C] a large pistol. **2** [late 19C+] a bully, a thug. **3** [1950s] a domineering woman. [BULLDOSE v.]

bull-dragging *adj.* [20C+] (*Irish*) tedious, laborious.

bull-driver *n.* [1900s] (*US*) a peasant, a farmer (cf. ACORN-CRACKER n.).

bull durham! *excl.* [1920s–30s] (*US*) nonsense! [ext. of BULL! excl.; ult. brandname of rolling tobacco]

bulldust *n.* [1920s+] (*Aus.*) a euph. for BULLSHIT n.; thus *bulldust artist*; *bullduster*. [note DUST n.³ (1)]

bulldust *v.* [1960s+] (*Aus.*) to lie, to fabricate. [BULLDUST n.]

bull-dyke *n.* (*also* **B.D.**, **boldyke**, **bull-dike**, **bull-diker**, **bull-dyker**) [20C+] (*orig. US*) a masculine lesbian, usu. an unpleasant, excessively man-hating one (cf. BULL n.¹). [SE *bull*/BULL adj. (2) + ? DYKE n. (*see* ety. for more comments)]

bull-dyking *n.* (*also* **bull-diking**) [1920s+] indulging in lesbian sex. [BULL-DYKE n.]

bulled-up *adj. see* BULL n.¹¹ (2).

buller(-man) *n. see* BULL n.¹ (4).

bullet *n.*¹ **1** [early 19C+] in poker, an ace; esp. in phr. *two bullets and a bragger*, 2 aces and a knave or 9; thus, in the card-game brag, a winning hand. **2** [late 19C–1970s] (*US*) \$1; in pl., money in general. **3** [1950s] a French franc. **4** [1960s+] (*US prison*) a 1-year sentence. **5** [1970s+] (*drugs*) (*also* **bullethead**) a single capsule of a drug, usu. a barbiturate (cf. PILL n.⁴); often in pl. **6** [1970s+] (*N.Z. drugs*) a portion of cannabis wrapped in silver foil. [the image is of a single bullet]

bullet *n.*² **1** [mid-19C+] a notice of dismissal; thus GET THE BULLET v.; GIVE SOMEONE THE BULLET v.; SHAKE THE BULLET (AT) v. **2** [1960s–70s] (*US*) an ejaculation of semen; thus *shoot bullets*, to ejaculate. [(2) note Shakespeare *Henry IV Pt II*: 'Do you discharge upon mine hostess? — I will discharge upon her, Sir John, with two bullets'; here the ref. is primarily to the testicles]

bullet *n.*³ [late 19C] (*US*) a doughnut.

bullet *n.*⁴ [1970s+] (*US campus*) the grade of B (cf. ACE n.⁶). [initial letter]

bullet *n.*⁵ [1980s+] (*drugs*) **1** isobutyl nitrite. **2** (*N.Z.*) cooking foil, as used in heating and smoking heroin, or measuring cannabis. **3** (*US gay*) amyl nitrite (cf. AIMIES n.). [ety. unknown; ? its effect]

bullethead *n. see* BULLET n.¹ (5).

bullet-head *n.* **1** [18C–mid-19C] a fool, a dullard. **2** [1950s–80s] someone with a crew-cut hairstyle. [(1) BULLET-HEADED adj.; (2) the hardness of the projectile]

bullet-headed *adj.* [late 17C+] foolish, stupid (cf. AIRHEADED adj.). [SE *bullet* + -HEAD sfx (1); the hardness of the projectile]

bullet house *n.* (*also* **tinny house**) [1990s+] (*N.Z. drugs*) a house or flat used for cannabis dealing. [BULLET n.⁵ (2)/TINNIE n.² (2) + SE *house*]

bullet-proof *adj.* **1** [1920s+] immune, irrefutable. **2** [1940s–60s] (*orig. US Black*) very drunk.

bullets *n.*¹ **1** [late 16C; 19C] the testicles (cf. BALLS n.¹). **2** [1910s+] beans. **3** [1950s–60s] peas. **4** [1980s+] (*Aus. drugs/prison*) marijuana that has been compressed around thin sticks. [the shape]

bullets *n.*² *see* BULLET n.¹ (5).

bullfeathers *n.* [20C+] (*US*) rubbish, nonsense (cf. GOOFER FEATHERS n.; HORSEFEATHERS n.; KANGAROO FEATHERS n.). [BULLSHIT n. + SE *feathers*; note adverts for Washington hamburger grill

Bullfeathers 'When Teddy Roosevelt was hungry, he'd grumble, "Oh, bullfeathers"']

bullfest *n.* [1910s–40s] a group, usu. of men, sitting around gossiping. [BULL n.¹¹ (1) + sfx -FEST sfx]

bull fiddle *n.* **1** [late 19C; 1930s+] (*US*) the double-bass. **2** [20C+] a stringed instrument made from a tin can; thus *bull-fiddle voice*, a deep bass voice. [SE *bull*/BULL adj. (1) + SE *fiddle*]

bullfighter *n.* [1930s] (*US tramp*) an empty passenger coach, either when standing in the yards or attached to a freight train.

bullfinch *n.*¹ [late 16C–mid-17C] a fool, a simpleton (cf. AIREDALE n.). [? the bird's willingness to be trained to sing]

bullfinch *n.*² [early 19C] a sovereign.

bull-flesh *n.* [late 19C] swagger, boastfulness, arrogance. [the innate bulkiness of the animal]

bull-fodder *n.* [1910s+] (*orig. Aus.*) rubbish, nonsense, lies. [euph. for BULLSHIT n. (1)]

bullfrog *n. see* FROG n. (2).

bull fuck *n.* [1910s+] (*US/Can.*) **1** cream gravy (cf. GRAVY n.¹). **2** custard. **3** stew thickened with flour. [SE *bull* + fig. use of FUCK n.² (1)]

bull gang *n.* **1** [20C+] (*US*) a team of manual labourers. **2** [1950s+] (*W.I.*) plantation labourers who perform odd jobs. **3** [1970s] (*Can./US prison*) a gang of hardened, dangerous prisoners, used for manual labour. [SE *bull*/BULL adj. (1) + *gang*]

bullgine *n.* [mid-19C] (*US*) a railway locomotive (cf. BULL n.⁶). [SE *bull*/BULL adj. (1) + SE (*en*)*gine*]

bull gism *n. see* BULL COME n.

bull-goose *n.* [1950s+] (*US*) the leader, the boss. [SE *bull-goose*, the goose which maintains order among the rest of the flock]

bull gravy *n.* [1940s+] (*US*) cream gravy. [GRAVY n.¹ (2), i.e. var. on BULL FUCK n. (1)]

bull-head *n.*¹ [early 17C–1940s] a fool. [SE *bull* + -HEAD sfx (1); the stolidity of a bull]

bull-head *n.*² [late 17C] a mass of curled or frizzled hair worn over the forehead by a woman (cf. BULL n.³). [the resemblance of the style to a bull's matted 'forelocks']

bull-head *n.*³ [1940s] (*US*) a 'buffalo' nickel (cf. BULL n.⁷). [it carried a bull's head on one face]

bullhead clap *n.* (*also* **bullheaded clap**) [1940s+] (*US*) extremely severe gonorrhoea. [SE *bullhead* used as an intensifier + CLAP n.]

bullheaded *adj.* [mid-17C+] foolish, stubborn (cf. AIRHEADED adj.). [BULL-HEAD n.¹]

bullhead luck *n.* [late 19C] very good luck. [SE *bullhead* used as an intensifier + SE *luck*]

bull hockey *n.* [1960s+] (*US*) any form of specious talk, lies, flattery, insincerity, nonsense etc. [SE *bull* + HOCKIE n. (2)]

bull horrors *n.*¹ [1920s–30s] (*US tramp*) an irrational fear of the police. [BULL n.¹⁰ + HORRORS, THE n.]

bull horrors *n.*² **1** [1930s–50s] (*US*) severe delirium tremens; usu. caused by drink, sometimes by cocaine. **2** [1970s] (*US drugs*) the after-effects of excessive cocaine use. [BULL adj. (1) + HORRORS, THE n.]

bullicky *n. see* BULLOCKY n.

bulling *n.* [1910s–60s] (*orig. US Black*) something that is good, admirable, impressive. [? BULL adj.]

Bulli Pass *n.* [1990s+] (*Aus.*) the anus, the buttocks (cf. ALA n.; ALLEY WAY n.). [rhy. sl. = ARSE n.¹ (1); ult. *Bulli Pass*, NSW, Australia]

bullish *adj.* [late 19C+] enthusiastic, keen. [Stock Exchange jargon *bull*, one who trades on the premise of a rising market]

bullissimo *adj.* [mid-19C] (*US*) extremely good, absolutely excellent. [BULLY adj.¹ + 'Ital.' sfx -*issimo*]

bullivant *n.* [late 19C–1930s] a large, clumsy person. [SE *bull* + *elephant*]

bull-jive *n.* [1960s+] (*US*) **1** teasing, abuse. **2** nonsense, empty chatter. [BULL-JIVE v.]

bull-jive v. [1940s+] (*US Black*) to tease, to hoax. [BULL n.[11] (1) + JIVE v.[1] (2)]

Bull Land n. [1910s] (*Aus.*) England; Britain. [JOHN BULL n. + SE *land*]

bull luck n. [late 19C–1910s] (*US*) very good luck. [BULL adj. (1) + SE *luck*]

bull manure n. *see* BULLSHIT n. (2).

bull merchant n. [1910s–50s] (*Aus./US*) one who speaks insincerely. [BULL n.[11] (1) + MERCHANT n.]

bull money n. [late 19C] money handed over to a potentially blackmailing discoverer by someone who has been caught *in flagrante delicto* in the open air. [BULL v.[1] (3) + SE *money*]

bull moose n.[1] [1920s–50s] (*US*) the leader, the boss.

bull moose n.[2] [1960s] (*US*) 5 cents, a nickel (cf. BULL n.[7]). [the 'buffalo' nickel carried a bull's head on one face]

bull moose n.[3] *see* MOOSE n.[1].

bull muffin n. [1980s] (*US*) specious talk, nonsense, rubbish, insincerity. [BULL n.[11] (1) + MEADOW MUFFIN n., i.e. BULLSHIT n. (1)]

bullo n. [1930s+] (*Aus./US*) nonsense, rubbish. [BULLSHIT n. (1) + -O sfx (4)]

bullock n. [19C+] (*Aus.*) a countryman, a bushman.

bullock v.[1] 1 [early 18C–1900s] to bully, to intimidate. 2 [mid–late 19C] (*Aus.*) to perform heavy manual labour. 3 [late 19C+] (*Aus.*) to push through.

bullock v.[2] *see* BALLOCK v.[1].

bullocker n. [1920s+] (*Aus.*) 1 a bullock-driver. 2 a foreman, a boss.

bullockese n. *see* BULLOCKY n. (2).

bullock-puncher n. [mid-19C+] (*Aus.*) a bullock-driver; thus *bullock-punching*. [on model of US *cow-puncher*]

bullock's blood n. [1920s–70s] a mixture of strong beer and rum.

bullock's eye n. [19C] port. [the colour]

bullock's heart n. [late 19C] the breaking of wind. [rhy. sl. = FART n.]

bullock's (horn) n. [mid-19C–1980s] pawn. [rhy. sl.]

bullock('s horn) v. [mid-19C–1960s] to pawn. [rhy. sl.]

bullock's liver n. [late 19C+] a river. [rhy. sl.]

bullock wagon n. [1920s+] (*Aus.*) nonsense, rubbish. [ext. of BULL n.[11] (1)]

bullocky n. (*also* **bullicky**) [late 19C+] (*Aus./N.Z.*) 1 a bullock-driver. 2 (*also* **bullockese**) the language or jargon of bullock-drivers; the inference being of a preponderance of obscenities and oaths.

bullocky's delight n. (*also* **bullocky's joy**) [20C+] (*Aus.*) treacle, golden syrup (cf. COCKY'S DELIGHT n.). [BULLOCKY n. (1) + SE *delight/joy*]

bull of the woods n. [late 19C+] (*US*) the boss, the leader, or someone who poses as such. [logging jargon *bull of the woods*, the foreman]

bullox n. *see* BALLOCKS n.[2] (6).

bull party n. [late 19C–1900s] a men-only party. [SE *bull* + *party*]

bullpen n. 1 [early 19C+] (*orig. UK Und.*) a holding cell surrounded by steel mesh or an open 'cage' made of steel bars (orig. of wooden bars). 2 [mid-19C–1930s] (*US*) a small house or room used by a prostitute; thus a cheap brothel (cf. BIRDCAGE n.[1]). 3 [late 19C+] (*US police*) the holding cage in a precinct house. 4 [20C+] (*US*) any type of enclosed waiting area. 5 [20C+] (*US*) the dock in a courtroom. 6 [1910s+] (*US*) a prison exercise yard or internal association area. 7 [1920s–30s] (*US prison*) a punishment cell. 8 [1930s+] (*US*) any enclosure (college dormitory, factory changing room etc) where a group of men associate, gossip etc.

bull piss n. [1910s+] (*US*) very low-quality, cheap liquor. [SE *bull* + PISS n. (1)]

bull point n. [mid-19C+] (*US*) a point of advantage or superiority. [the image of a bull's strength]

bull pucky n. (*also* **bull puckey**) [1970s+] (*US*) any form of specious talk, insincerity, flattery, lies. [SE *bull* + PUCKEY n.; i.e. var. on BULLSHIT n. (1)]

bull-puncher n. (*also* **bullock-puncher, puncher**) [late 19C+] 1 (*Aus.*) a bullock-driver. 2 (*US*) the driver of an ox-team.

bull pup n. [mid–late 19C] (*US*) a pistol. [it 'barks' or 'growls']

bull-pusher n. [late 19C] (*US*) the driver of an ox-team.

bull queer n. *see* BULL n.[1] (3).

bullrag v. *see* BULLYRAG v.

bull-riding n. [2000s] (*US Black*) sexual intercourse in the rear-entry position.

bull-ring n. 1 [mid-19C–1940s] (*US Und.*) severe interrogation of a prisoner, the 'third degree'. 2 [1910s+] a military training ground. 3 [1920s–30s] (*US prison*) a prison exercise yard or an open space used for punishments. [ext. of SE. use; (2) orig. that sited at Étaples, northern France, the British Army training centre during WW1]

bullring camp n. [1950s+] (*US gay*) a male homosexual (or more rarely heterosexual) brothel; in weaker form, anywhere frequented by virile 'masculine' men (cf. BIRDCAGE n.[1]).

bull-roar n. [1970s+] (*US*) any form of specious talk, insincerity, flattery, lies. [euph. for BULLSHIT n. (1)]

bulls n. [1940s+] (*Aus./US*) any form of specious talk, insincerity, flattery, lies. [euph. for BULLSHIT n. (1)]

bull's aunts n. [1940s] (*US*) trousers. [rhy. sl. = PANTS n.[1] (2); note US pron.]

bull scare n. [1940s–60s] (*US Black*) an aggressive, menacing manner that is no more than a bluff. [BULLSHIT n. (1) + SE *scare*]

bull-screw n. *see* SCREW n.[2] (3).

bull session n. (*also* **bullshit session**) 1 [1910s+] (*US*) usu. of men, a period of sitting around, gossiping. 2 [1940s–50s] (*US Black/teen*) police interrogation. [SE *bull*, as a generic for male/BULL n.[11] (1)/BULLSHIT n. (1) + SE *session*; (2) plays on BULL n.[10]]

bull's eye n.[1] [late 17C] the vagina (cf. BEST IN CHRISTENDOM n.). [joc. euph. coined by John Wilmot, Earl of Rochester (1647–80)]

bull's eye n.[2] 1 [late 17C–19C] a crown or 5-shilling (25p) piece (cf. BULL n.[4]). 2 [early 19C–1950s] a large, round sweet. 3 [mid-19C] a bull's-eye lantern. 4 [mid–late 19C] a thick, old-fashioned watch. [? the size and shape; (2) later use is SE]

bull's-eye day n. [1920s+] (*Irish*) Wednesday, the day on which British Army pensions are disbursed. [one scores a financial *bull's eye*]

bullsh n. (*also* **bulsh**) [1910s+] (*Aus.*) rubbish, nonsense. [abbr. BULLSHIT n.]

bullsh v. *see* BULLSHIT v.

bull-shiner n. [1920s] (*US*) a policeman's truncheon. [? the shininess of the wood; or ? the BULL n.[10] gives one a SHINER n.[1] (6)]

bullshipper n. [1930s+] a braggart, a liar. [euph. for BULLSHITTER n. (1)]

bullshit n. 1 [20C+] nonsense, lies. 2 [1910s+] (*also* **bull manure**) rubbish, anything second-rate or useless. 3 [1920s+] an object or task that is seen as annoying, irritating or 'nonsense'. 4 [1970s] an argument. 5 [1970s] (*US drugs*) marijuana. [fig. use of SE *bull* + SHIT n.[1] (1), i.e. 'bull dung']

bullshit adj.[1] 1 [1940s+] nonsensical, absurd, pointless. 2 [1960s+] second-rate, inferior. [BULLSHIT n.]

bullshit adj.[2] [1980s+] (*US campus*) 1 very angry, furious. 2 drunk, intoxicated by a drug. [fig. uses of BULLSHIT n.]

bullshit v. (*also* **bullsh**) 1 [1920s+] to gossip, to chatter inconsequentially. 2 [1940s+] (*also* **bullshit on**) to tell lies, to tease, to confuse with false information. 3 [1960s+] (*also* **bullshit around**) to play around, to waste time. [BULLSHIT n.]

bullshit! excl. [1940s+] (*orig. US*) rubbish! nonsense! [BULLSHIT n. (1)]

bullshit artist n. (*also* **b.a., b.s. artist, bullshit thrower**)

[1940s+] anyone with a good line of persuasive, if insincere patter. [BULLSHIT n. (1) + ARTIST sfx]

bullshit on v. see BULLSHIT v. (2).

bullshit session n. see BULL SESSION n.

bullshitter n. (also **bulsh**, **bullshit**) **1** [1920s+] a braggart, a liar. **2** [1940s+] the mouth. [BULLSHIT n. (1)]

bullshit thrower n. see BULLSHIT ARTIST n.

bullshitty adj. [1940s] useless, nonsensical, absurd. [BULLSHIT adj.[1]]

bull shooter n. [1920s–60s] (US) a braggart, a liar. [BULL n.[11] (1) + SE shooter]

bull simple adj. [1930s–60s] (US tramp) frightened of the police. [BULL n.[10] + SE simple]

bullskate v. [1940s–60s] (US Black) to boast, to brag. [var. on BULLSHIT v. (+ ? SKATE v.[1])]

bull slinger n. [1930s+] (US) a braggart, a liar. [BULL n.[11] (1) + SE slinger]

bull's look n. [1960s] (Irish) a hostile glare.

bullstuff n. [1980s] (US) nonsense. [euph. for BULLSHIT n. (1)]

bull-sugar n. [1960s–70s] nonsense, rubbish. [SE bull + SUGAR n.[3] (1), i.e. var. on BULLSHIT n. (1)]

bull's wool n.[1] **1** [20C+] (Aus.) a young man with a mop of bushy hair. **2** [1900s–40s] second-hand, cheap or homemade clothes. **3** [1930s–60s] (US Black) stolen clothes. [UK milit. bull's wool, coarse woollen cloth or yarn]

bull's wool n.[2] [1920s+] (Aus./N.Z.) any form of specious talk, lies, insincerity, rubbish. [euph. for BULLSHIT n. (1)]

bull the tea v. [20C+] (N.Z.) to add soda to tea, which makes it more potent. [BULL v.[2] + SE tea]

bull thrower n. [1910s–60s] (US) a braggart, a liar. [BULL n.[11] (1) + SE thrower]

bull-tour n. [early 18C] a mass of curled or frizzled hair worn over the forehead by a woman (cf. BULL n.[3]). [var. on BULL-HEAD n.[2]]

bull trap n. (also **bully trap**) **1** [19C] (US Und.) one who impersonates an official in order to extort money. **2** [1930s+] (Aus.) a villain who impersonates a policeman and preys on couples in lover's lanes, extorting money from those who should not, for whatever reason, be there. [active and passive uses of BULL n.[10] + SE trap]

bullwash n. [1980s] (US) any form of specious talk, lies, nonsense, insincerity. [BULLSHIT n. + ? var. on BUSHWA n. (1)]

bull-week n. see CALF-WEEK n.

bullwhack v. [mid–late 19C] (US) to drive an ox-team. [SE bull + WHACK v.[1] (1)]

bullwhacker n. [mid-19C–1950s] (Aus./US) an ox-driver. [BULLWHACK v. + SAmE bullwhacker, the ox-driver's whip]

bull-wool adj. [1920s+] (US campus) second-rate, inferior. [BULL'S WOOL n.[1] (2)]

bully n.[1] **1** [late 16C–1930s] a good fellow, a companion. **2** [mid-17C–1900s] a thug hired for purposes of violence or intimidation. **3** [mid-17C+] a pimp, a procurer (cf. ABBOT ON THE CROSS n.). **4** [late 17C–mid-19C] a braggart, a boaster. **5** [mid-18C] a prostitute's client. [? Du. boel, a lover of either sex; (1) post-18C use is mainly US (cf. ety. at BAMBOOZLE v.)]

bully n.[2] [20C+] bully beef (pickled or tinned beef). [Fr. boeuf boulli, boiled beef]

bully n.[3] [20C+] (Aus.) the Sydney Bulletin, a popular news magazine. [abbr.]

bully adj.[1] [late 17C+] (orig. UK, mainly US) excellent, first-rate. [BULLY n.[1] (1)]

bully adj.[2] [18C] aggressive, tough. [BULLY n.[1] (2)]

bully v. [18C] to act as a hired thug. [BULLY n.[1] (2)]

bully adv. [mid-19C–1910s] very well. [BULLY adj.[1]]

bully! excl. [mid-19C–1910s] excellent! [BULLY adj.[1]]

bully back n. [early 17C–early 19C] a man hired by a brothel to act as a bouncer, strong-arm man, occasional lover or 'husband'

of the madam or one of the prostitutes and a generally intimidating presence. [BULLY n.[1] (2) (although 1 cit. here predates it) + SE back, to support, to back up]

bully back v. [late 18C] to be employed by a brothel as a bouncer or to be a generally intimidatory presence. [BULLY BACK n.]

bully beef n. [1950s+] (UK prison) a chief officer. [rhy. sl.]

bully-buck n. [18C] a thug who deliberately starts fights between others, so as to rob them in the confusion. [BULLY n.[1] (2) + BUCK n.[1] (3)]

bully-cock n. [late 18C–early 19C] one who deliberately encourages quarrels so as to rob those who are engaged in the argument. [BULLY n.[1] (2) + fig. use SE cock]

bully-fake n. [late 19C–1910s] a piece of luck. [BULLY adj.[1] + FAKE n.[1]]

bully-fake adj. [late 19C] lucky, advantageous. [BULLY-FAKE n.]

bully-fop n. [late 17C–18C] a brainless chatterer, a talkative bore. [BULLY n.[1] (1) + SE fop]

bully for —! excl. [late 18C+] (orig. US) well done! congratulations!, usu. ironic/sarcastic use. [BULLY adj.[1]]

bully-hack n. [early 18C] a pimp (cf. ABBOT ON THE CROSS n.). [BULLY n.[1] (3) + HACKNEY n. (2)]

bully-hector n. see HECTOR n.[1].

bully huff n. (also **bully huff-cap**) [late 17C–early 19C] one who poses as a prostitute's husband and then defrauds her client of his money by threats of violence or blackmail. [BULLY n.[1] (2)/BULLY n.[1] (3)/? BULLY n.[1] (5) + HUFF n.[1] (1)]

bullying n. [early 18C] pimping. [BULLY n.[1] (3)]

bullyrag v. (also **bullrag**) [late 18C+] to bully, to pressurize, to taunt; to cheat out of by intimidation; also n. [BULLY n.[1] (2) + RAG v.[1] (1)]

bullyragging n. [late 19C] scolding. [BULLYRAG v.]

bully-rock n. (also **bully-rook**) **1** [late 17C–18C] a boon companion. **2** [mid-17C–early 18C] a hired thug. [BULLY n.[1] (1)/BULLY n.[1] (2) + SE rock/ROOK n.[1] (1)]

bully-ruffian n. (also **bully-ruffin**) **1** [mid-17C] the penis. **2** [mid-17C–18C] a highwayman who runs contrary to popular fantasies of gentlemanly robbers by shouting and swearing at his victims, in order to intimidate them further. [BULLY n.[1] (2) + SE ruffian]

bully-swagger n. [early 19C] a ruffianly braggart. [BULLY n.[1] (2) + SE swagger]

bully trap n.[1] (UK Und.) **1** [late 17C–18C] a card-sharp, a cheat. **2** [late 18C–early 19C] a mild-looking man, whose lack of overt aggression fools thugs into thinking that they can take advantage of him. [active and passive uses of BULLY n.[1] (2) + SE trap]

bully trap n.[2] see BULL TRAP n. (1).

bully-woolies n. [1960s–70s] (US) long underwear. [BULL'S WOOL n.[1] (2)]

bulrush n. [1990s+] a paintbrush. [rhy. sl.]

bulsh n.[1] see BULLSH n.

bulsh n.[2] see BULLSHITTER n.

bum n.[1] **1** [16C+] (also **bumm**, **bumb**) the posterior, the buttocks, the anus. **2** [17C–18C] in a sexual context, the vagina. **3** [late 17C+] in a sexual context, the anus as a target for sodomy. [orig. ME; echoic of the smack of one's backside hitting a flat surface, and as such coined as early as 1386. The word is also allied to a variety of terms meaning protuberance or swelling, typically bump]

bum n.[2] [mid-17C–1900s] a bailiff. [? SE bound, bailiff (Blackstone, Commentaries, 1768); or ? physical proximity of the bailiff to those being arrested (Hotten, 1867); or ? abbr. SE bum-bailiff, 'a bailliff of the meanest kind' (Johnson, Dictionary, 1755)]

bum n.[3] **1** [mid-19C+] (US) a tramp, a vagrant. **2** [20C+] (US) a term of abuse for anyone unpleasant?; thus make a bum of, to make someone look a fool. **3** [20C+] (boxing) a poor, incompetent fighter; similarly used of a racehorse. **4** [1900s] (US Und.) a travelling thief. **5** [1910s] (US) a worldly, promiscuous man.

6 [1910s–20s] an incompetent sportsman (other than a boxer). **7** [1920s–50s] something worthless or unsatisfactory. **8** [1920s+] a general term of address, as often affectionate as hostile. **9** [1920s+] (*US*) a promiscuous woman. **10** [1920s+] (*US*) a fan or obsessive, usu. of a specified sport, e.g. *scuba bum, surf bum*. **11** [1930s] (*US Und.*) an experienced criminal. **12** [1940s+] a semi-professional athlete who makes a living training others rather than entering high-grade competitions, e.g. *tennis bum, ski bum, surf bum*. [abbr. BUMMER n.³ (2); subseq. defs. developments of (1); (5) and (9) pun on SE *tramp*/TRAMP n. (1)]

bum *n.*⁴ [late 19C–1930s] a spree; thus *on a bum*, on a spree. [BUM v.⁵ (1)]

bum *adj.* **1** [mid-19C+] (*orig. US*) useless, second-rate, poor, inferior, dirty, ragged; thus *bum for*, bad for one, e.g. one's health. **2** [late 19C+] fake, counterfeit. **3** [20C+] slightly ill, under the weather. **4** [20C+] (*US*) injured; malfunctioning. **5** [20C+] (*US*) (*also* **bummin'**) depressed. **6** [20C+] unfair; esp. in *bum beef*, an unfair charge or arrest. **7** [1930s+] of food, stale, bad, 'off'. **8** [1960s] (*US*) aggressive, threatening. [BUM n.³ (1)]

bum *v.*¹ **1** [late 17C–18C] to arrest. **2** [19C] to serve with a summons. [BUM n.²]

bum *v.*² **1** [early 19C] to act noisily. **2** [20C+] to boast, to brag; thus *bum up*, to praise, to promote; *bumming*, boastful. [Irish *bommanach*, bragging, boastful]

bum *v.*³ [early 19C+] (*Irish/Scot./US*) to set the bailiffs on. [BUM n.²]

bum *v.*⁴ **1** [mid-19C+] (*also* **bum around, bum out**) to wander around. **2** [mid-19C+] to beg; thus *bum a fag*, ask for a cigarette. **3** [mid-19C+] (*also* **bum around**) to act lazily, to do nothing positive. **4** [1980s] (*US Black*) to steal someone's lover. **5** [1980s] (*US Black*) to cheat, to rob. **6** [1990s+] (*US campus*) to dress in a casual manner. [BUM n.³]

bum *v.*⁵ **1** [late 19C–1940s] (*US campus*) to go out on a spree. **2** [1910s–30s] to play truant. [ext. of BUM v.⁴ (1)]

bum *v.*⁶ [1970s+] to sodomize. [BUM n.¹ (1)]

bum *v.*⁷ [1980s+] (*US campus*) to feel depressed. [BUM adj. (5)/BUMMER n.⁴ (3)]

bum *adv.* [late 19C] badly, incompetently. [BUM adj. (1)]

bum! *excl.* [1940s+] an excl. of derision or annoyance. [BUM n.¹ (1)]

bum and stroke *n.* [2000s] a glass of rum and Coca-Cola. [rhy. sl.; *bum* = rum; *stroke* = Coke]

bum a ride *v.* [late 19C+] (*US*) to get a free ride. [BUM v.⁴ (2)]

bum around *v. see* BUM v.⁴.

bumb *n. see* BUM n.¹ (1).

bumba *n.* (*also* **bumpa**) [20C+] (*US Black*) the buttocks. [BUM n.¹ (1); but ? note BUMBO n.² (2)]

bum bacon *n.* [1990s+] the labia (cf. BACON STRIPS n.). [BUM n.¹ (1) + SE *bacon*]

bum bag *n.* (*also* **butt pack**) [1950s+] (*orig. skiing*) a small bag or pouch, secured to a belt and worn around the waist (cf. FANNY PACK n.). [BUM n.¹ (1) + SE *bag*]

bumbags *n.* [mid-19C–1950s] trousers. [BUM n.¹ (1) + SE *bags*]

bum-balls *n.* [19C] the testicles (cf. BALLS n.¹). [BUM n.¹ (1) + SE *balls*]

bum bandit *n.* [1960s+] a homosexual male (cf. ANAL ASTRONAUT n.; BUN BANDIT n.). [BUM n.¹ (1) + BANDIT sfx (2)]

bum-banger *n.* [1940s] (*Aus.*) **1** a short jacket, just covering the buttocks. **2** a male homosexual (cf. ANAL ASTRONAUT n.). [BUM n.¹ (1) + SE *banger*]

bum-bass *n.* [late 18C–19C] a 'cello.

bumbaste *v.* **1** [mid-16C–early 18C] to beat hard on the buttocks; also in fig. use. **2** [mid-17C–19C] to have sexual intercourse, esp. in the 'rear position' (cf. BANG v.¹). **3** [18C–19C] to beat, to assault. [BUM n.¹ (1) + SE *baste*, to thrash]

bumbazine *n.* (*also* **bombazine**) [mid-19C] (*US*) the buttocks. [? pun on BUM n.¹ (1) + SE *bombasine*, 'a twilled or corded dress-

material, composed of silk and worsted; sometimes also of cotton and worsted, or of worsted alone. In black the material is much used in mourning' (*OED*); note Walt Kelly's short-lived cartoon strip *Bumbazine and Albert*, featuring a young Black boy who talks to animals, created in 1943 and a precursor to *Pogo*]

bum-beating *n.* [early 17C] jostling. [BUM n.¹ (1) + SE *beating*]

bum beef *n. see* BUM adj. (6).

bum-beefed *adj.* [1930s–60s] (*US Und.*) arrested on false charges, esp. after evidence (typically drugs) has been placed on the defendant. [BUM adj. (6) + BEEF n.² (5)]

bumbee work *n.* [20C+] (*Ulster*) nonsense. [SE *bumble-bee* and its 'buzz']

bumbershoot *n.* (*also* **bumberella**) [19C+] (*US*) an umbrella. [joc. corruption; ? it 'shoots' up]

bum-bitch *n.* [1990s+] (*US Black*) a derog. term for a young street girl. [BUM n.³ (1)+ BITCH n.¹ (1)]

bumble *n.*¹ [mid-19C] a beadle; thus *bumble-crew, bumbledom*, a collective name for corporations, vestries and other official bodies. [*Mr Bumble* in Charles Dickens's *Oliver Twist* (1838)]

bumble *n.*² [2000s] nonsense, empty chatter. [16C SE *bumble*, a humming noise]

bumble *v.* [late 17C] to have sexual intercourse. [ext. of SE use + ? ref. to 'the birds and the bees'/BUM n.¹ (2)]

bumblebee *n.*¹ **1** [1930s+] a male lover. **2** [1960s] (*US Black*) the vagina; thus also a female lover. [ety. unknown]

bumblebee *n.*² **1** [1940s] (*US Und.*) a $1 bill (cf. CANARY n.⁵). **2** [1960s] (*US campus*) a commercially published subject outline. [ety. unknown]

bumblebee *n.*³ **1** [1960s+] (*Aus.*) a knee. **2** [1990s+] a tree. **3** [2000s] venereal disease, VD. [rhy. sl.]

bumblebee *adj.* [20C+] (*US*) of a crop, one that has become dried up and stunted. [the crop has become so low that the saying has it that the bees can lie on their backs sucking the juice from the flowers or plants]

bumblebees *n.* [1970s+] (*drugs*) amphetamines (cf. A n.²). [? striped capsules of certain brands of the drug or f. their 'sting']

bumblebee whisky *n.* [mid-19C+] (*US*) especially potent whisky. [it 'stings']

bumble-footed *adj.* [mid-19C] club-footed.

bumblefuck *n.* [1980s+] (*US campus*) anywhere categorized as very far away. [var. on BUMFUCK n.]

bumble-puppy *n.* [mid-19C+] amateurish whist, and latterly bridge, the level typically played in family or friendly games. [SE *bumble-puppy*, an early form of bagatelle, usu. played in public houses, in which stone balls are rolled down a sloping board, which is pierced with numbered holes. This is based on an older 16C game, usu. played by women, *troule-in-madame* or *troll-madam*]

bum-bluff *n. see* BUM-FLUFF n.¹.

bumbo *n.*¹ **1** [mid-18C–19C] a drink composed of brandy, sugar and water. **2** [1910s+] (*Aus.*) cheap (fortified) wine. [ety. unknown; ? (2) underpinned by BUM n.³ (1), its usual drinker]

bumbo *n.*² (*also* **bombo**) **1** [late 18C+] (*also* **bombo-red**) the vagina. **2** [1960s] the buttocks, the anus. [BUM n.¹, but note Efik *mbumbu*, rotten, putrefied, decomposed; orig. W.I. use, where the term is also used to mean SE *alligator*; thus suggesting poss. *vagina dentata* imagery]

bumbo! *excl.* [1980s] (*W.I.*) an excl. of surprise, shock, annoyance. [BUMBO n.² (2)]

bum-boat *n.* **1** [late 17C] a scavenger's boat, used to pick up the debris of shipping disasters. **2** [mid-18C–1940s] a boat that brought provisions from land out to larger vessels anchored offshore; thus as a term of affectionate ridicule between sailors; latterly, a boat used by hawkers selling goods to passengers on large ships. [BUM n.¹ (1) + SE *boat*; the original role of such vessels was to collect human and other waste from boats at anchor; they also carried out vegetables etc to sell on board]

bumbo-claat *n.* (*also* **bombo-claat, bombo-cloth, bumbo-cloth**) [1950s+] (*W.I.*) **1** a sanitary towel. **2** a highly derog. term of abuse. **3** a euph for FUCK, THE n. [BUMBO n.² (2) + SE *cloth*]

bumbole *adj.* [1920s] (*US Black*) a general swear word. [BUMBOLE excl.]

bumbole! *excl.* [1920s] (*US Black*) an expletive. [? BUMHOLE n.]

bum-boozer *n.* [late 19C–1920s] a drunkard. [BUM n.³ (1) + BOOZER n. (1)]

bumbosity *n.* (*also* **bombosity**) [1930s+] (*US*) the buttocks. [artificial ext. of BUM n.¹ (1)]

bum boy *n.* **1** [19C+] a male homosexual (cf. ANAL ASTRONAUT n.). **2** [20C+] anyone regularly saddled with dirty jobs. **3** [20C+] a toady, a sycophant. **4** [1990s+] (*mainly UK juv.*) a term of abuse, irrespective of sexuality, for an unpopular individual. [BUM n.¹ (1) + SE *boy*; (4) on pattern of GAY adj.⁴]

bum bread (on) *n.* [1980s] (*US prison*) to berate a fellow inmate.

bum-brusher *n.* [18C–19C] a schoolmaster. [BUM n.¹ (1) + SE *brush*, to thrash; note WW1 Aus. milit. *bumbrusher*, an officer's servant]

bumbud *n.* [1990s+] (*US Black teen*) marijuana, a marijuana cigarette (cf. AFRICAN BUSH n.). [BUD n.⁴]

bum buddy *n.* [1990s+] a homosexual (cf. ANAL ASTRONAUT n.). [BUM n.¹ (1) + BUDDY n. (1)]

bum-burn *n.* [1990s+] (*UK juv.*) pain during defecation, the result of eating an excess of over-spiced food. [BUM n.¹ (1) + SE *burn*]

bum card *n.* [mid-16C–early 17C] (*gambling*) a marked card. [fig. use of BUM n.¹ (1) + SE *card*]

bum-charter *n.* [early 19C] (*UK Und.*) prison bread soaked in hot water. [ety. unknown]

bumchat *v.* [1950s+] (*orig. W.I.*) to make statements to a woman with the sole intention of seducing her. [BUM n.¹ (2) + SE *chat*]

bum check artist *n.* [1940s–50s] (*US Und.*) one who passes bad cheques. [BUM adj. (2) + SAmE *check* + ARTIST sfx]

bum chum *n.* **1** [1970s] (*orig. Aus.*) an intimate friend. **2** [1990s+] a male homosexual (cf. ANAL ASTRONAUT n.). [BUM n.¹ (1) + CHUM n.¹ (1)]

bum clink *n.* [mid–late 19C] bad or second-rate beer. [Midlands dial.]

Bum Court *n.* [mid–late 16C] the Ecclesiastical Court. [? BUM n.¹ (1); its members spent much time sitting down]

bum-crack *n.¹ see* CRACK n.².

bum-crack *n.² see* CRACK n.⁶ (4).

bum-crawler *n.* [1930s] a toady, a sycophant. [BUM n.¹ (1) + SE *crawl*]

bum-creeper *n.* **1** [mid-17C–19C] one who walks with their back noticeably bent. **2** [1910s+] a sycophant. [BUM n.¹ (1) + SE *creeper*]

bum-curtain *n.* [19C] a jacket. [BUM n.¹ (1) + SE *curtain*]

bum deal *n.* [20C+] (*orig. US*) a poor bargain, a mistaken agreement. [BUM adj. (1) + SE *deal*]

bum-drops *n.* [1930s] hen's eggs. [BUM n.¹ (1) + SE *drops*]

bumf *n.* (*also* **bumph, bumpf, bunf**) [late 19C+] **1** paperwork, paper. **2** lavatory paper. **3** scrap paper. [abbr. BUM-FODDER n. (1)]

bumface *n.* [1940s+] (*mainly UK juv.*) a general term of disdain. [BUM n.¹ (1) + SE *face*]

bumfaced *adj.* [1940s] (*mainly UK juv.*) stupid, foolish, a general term of abuse. [BUMFACE n.]

bum factory *n.* [1920s–30s] (*US*) **1** a cheap hostel. **2** a mission. [BUM n.³ (1) + SE *factory*]

bum-fake *v.* [late 19C] to have sexual intercourse; thus GO BUM-FAKING v. [BUM n.¹ (1) + FAKE v.¹ (2)]

bum-faker *n.* **1** [18C] a womanizer, a promiscuous man. **2** [late 19C] a male homosexual (cf. ANAL ASTRONAUT n.). [BUM-FAKE v.]

bum-feague *v.* (*also* **bumfeagle, bum-feg**) [late 16C–early 17C] **1** to thrash, to beat severely. **2** to have sexual intercourse (cf. BANG v.¹). [BUM n.¹ (1) + SE *feague*/FEAGUE v.]

bumfest *n.* [1990s+] a homosexual orgy. [BUM n.¹ (3) + -FEST sfx]

bumfiddle *n.* **1** [late 17C–early 18C] the vagina. **2** [early 18C] the anus, esp. when it breaks wind. [BUM n.¹ (1) + SE *fiddle*]

bum fiddle *v.* [17C–early 18C] **1** to have sexual intercourse. **2** to harm, to attack. [BUM n.¹ (1) + SE *fiddle*]

bum-fighter *n.* [early 18C] a womanizer, a whoremonger. [BUM n.¹ (2) + SE *fighter*]

bum finger *n.* [1940s–50s] (*US prison/Und.*) **1** a false accusation. **2** an unfair jail sentence. [BUM adj. (6) + FINGER v.² (3)]

bum-finger *v.* [1960s] (*US Und*) **1** to make a false accusation against someone. **2** to send to jail unfairly. [BUM FINGER n.]

bum-firker *n.* [late 17C–early 18C] a sodomite. [BUM n.¹ (3) + FIRK v.]

bum-firking *n.* [late 17C] sodomizing. [BUM-FIRKER n.]

bum-fluff *n.¹* (*also* **bum-bluff**) **1** [late 19C+] the very light growth of hair on the face of a boy who is on the verge of needing to shave; also attrib. **2** [1940s+] (*Aus.*) empty talk, nonsense. **3** [1990s+] pubic hair. **4** [2000s] a term of abuse. [BUM n.¹ (1) + SE *fluff*]

bum-fluff *n.² see* BUM-FODDER n. (1).

bumflummux *v.* [mid-19C] (*US*) to confound, to confuse. [BUM n.¹ (1) + FLUMMOX v.¹ (4)]

bum-fodder *n.* **1** [mid-17C+] (*also* **bum fluff, tail fodder**) lavatory paper. **2** [mid-17C–mid-18C] trashy literature, only good for use as (1). **3** [1900s–10s] (*US*) tabloid newspapers. [BUM n.¹ (1) + SE *fodder*]

bumfoolery *n.* [2000s] homosexuality, homosexual activity. [BUM n.¹ (1) + SE *tomfoolery*]

bumfoozle *v. see* BUMFUZZLE v.

bum-freezer *n.* **1** [1930s+] a short jacket that stops short of covering the buttocks, orig. describing an Eton jacket, latterly the 'Italian' styles of the 1950s and thence any short (men's) jacket. **2** [2000s] used of a very short skirt. [BUM n.¹ (1) + SE *freezer*]

bumfuck *n.* **1** [1970s+] (*US*) an extremely unpleasant person. **2** [1970s+] (*Aus.*) an extremely tedious task, i.e. a PAIN IN THE ARSE n. (2). **3** [1970s+] (*US gay*) a sexually inadequate partner. **4** [1980s] anal intercourse. [BUMFUCK v. (1)]

bumfuck *adj.* [1970s+] third-rate, nondescript. [BUMFUCK n.]

bumfuck *v.* (*orig. US*) **1** [mid-19C+] to sodomize. **2** [20C+] to massage the prostate as a way of diagnosing and treating gonorrhoea. [BUM n.¹ (1) + FUCK v.¹]

Bumfuck, Egypt *n.* (*also* **bumfuck, Africa; buttfucking Africa; buttfucking Egypt; east buttfuck; Egypt**) [1970s+] (*US milit./campus*) a very distant place. [BUMFUCK adj.; orig. US milit. jargon]

bumfucker *n.* [2000s] a sodomite; a pederast. [BUMFUCK v. (1)]

bumfuddled *adj.* (*also* **bunfungered**) [20C+] (*US*) confused, mixed up. [BAMBOOZLED adj. (1)]

bumfuzzle *v.* (*also* **bumfoozle, dumfoozle**) [20C+] (*US*) to hoax, to trick, to confuse. [BAMBOOZLE v. (1)]

bum gang *n.* [1920s] (*US prison*) the prisoners who perform the most unpleasant tasks.

bum gravy *n.* [2000s] diarrhoea. [BUM n.¹ (1) + SE *gravy*]

bum-gut *n.* [mid-17C; 1920s] the anus. [BUM n.¹ (1) + SE *gut*]

bumhole *n.* **1** [mid-19C+] the anus (cf. A-HOLE n.). **2** [1960s+] a despicable person. [BUM n.¹ (1)+ SE *hole*]

bumhole *adj.* [1950s+] second-rate, inferior. [BUMHOLE n.]

bum-jerker *n.* [early–mid-19C] a schoolmaster. [BUM n.¹ (1) + SE *jerk*, to hit]

bum juice *n.* [1990s+] sweat that gathers between the buttocks. [BUM n.¹ (1) + SE *juice*]

bum-jumper *n.* [1990s+] a male homosexual (cf. ANAL ASTRONAUT n.). [BUM n.¹ (1) + JUMP v.¹ (1)]

bum kick *v.* [1960s+] (*US*) to depress, to annoy; thus *bumkicked*, depressed, irritated. [BUM KICKS n.]

bum kicks *n.* (*also* **bumkick**) [1940s–60s] (*US*) an unpleasant experience. [BUM adj. (1) + KICKS n.³]

bumkin *n.* [mid-17C–18C] the buttocks. [BUM n.[1] (1) + dimin. sfx -*kin*]

bum-labour *n.* [early 18C] prostitution. [BUM n.[1] (2) + SE *labour*]

bum-licker *n.* [1930s+] a toady, a sycophant. [BUM n.[1] (1) + SE *licker*]

bumly *adj.*[1] [20C+] (*US*) depressed. [BUM adj. (5)]

bumly *adj.*[2] [1990s+] pertaining to the world, lifestyle, or image of a tramp or hobo. [BUM n.[3] (1)]

bumm *n. see* BUM n.[1] (1).

bum man *n.* [1950s+] a heterosexual man who finds a woman's buttocks her most alluring feature (cf. ASS-MAN n.). [BUM n.[1] (1)]

bummaree *n.* **1** [late 18C–19C] a middle-man, esp. at Billingsgate fish market. **2** [late 19C–1900s] a *bain-Marie* or double-boiler. [joc. mispron.]

bummed *adj.*[1] [late 18C] arrested. [BUM n.[2]]

bummed *adj.*[2] **1** [20C+] drunk or intoxicated with drugs. **2** [1970s+] depressed, miserable. **3** [1970s+] angry. [BUM adj.]

bummed out *adj.* [1970s+] **1** suffering from an unpleasant drug experience. **2** drunk. **3** depressed, miserable. **4** disappointed, feeling 'put upon' by others. **5** angry. **6** not working, broken, dilapidated. **7** (*US campus*) casually dressed. [ext. of BUMMED adj.[2]]

bummer *n.*[1] (*also* **bummy**) [mid-17C–early 19C] a bum-bailiff. [BUM n.[2]]

bummer *n.*[2] [mid-19C] (*US campus*) a 'fast' young man. [? BUMMER n.[3]]

bummer *n.*[3] **1** [mid-19C–1910s] (*orig. US*) a scrounger. **2** [mid-19C–1940s] (*US/Aus.*) a tramp, a vagrant. **3** [late 19C] a commercial traveller. [the precursor of BUM n.[3] (1); note Schele de Vere, *Americanisms* (1872): 'he is, far more likely, descended from the German *Bummler*, a man who goes about without aim and purpose, and lives on the fruits of other people's labor']

bummer *n.*[4] **1** [mid-19C+] an unpleasant, unpopular or depressing person. **2** [1960s+] (*drugs*) an unpleasant drug experience, esp. while using LSD or any other hallucinogenic. **3** [1960s+] (*also* **el bummero**) any unpleasant experience, depressing circumstances. **4** [1960s+] (*US campus*) a hard examination. **5** [1970s+] a failure or bad idea. [BUM adj. (1); (2) spec. BUM TRIP n.; orig. Hell's Angels use for a bad crash, see Tom Wolfe, *The Electric Kool-Aid Acid Test* (1968): 'Bummer was the Angels' term for a bad trip on a motorcycle and very quckly it became the hip world's term for a bad trip on LSD'; note 19C racing jargon *bummer*, a bad gambling loss]

bummer *n.*[5] (*also* **bummer-boy**) [1960s+] (*gay*) a sodomite. [BUM n.[1] (1)]

bummer *adj.* [1970s] (*US*) depressing. [BUMMER n.[4] (3)]

bummer! *excl.* [1960s+] (*orig. US*) an excl. of annoyance, disgust, disappointment, commiseration. [BUMMER n.[4] (3)]

bummer-boy *n. see* BUMMER n.[5].

bummie *n. see* BUMMY n.[1].

bummin' *adj. see* BUM adj. (5).

bumming *n.* **1** [mid-19C] (*US campus*) living as an idler or loafer. **2** [mid–late 19C] (*US*) living as a vagrant tramp or hobo. **3** [1990s+] (*US campus*) relaxing. **4** [1990s+] (*US teen*) dressing unfashionably. [BUM v.[4] (1)]

bumming *adj. see* BUM v.[2] (2).

bumm-shot *n.* [1990s+] (*W.I.*) something very bad. [BUM adj. (1)/BUM n.[1] (1) + SHOT n.[5] (1)]

bummy *n.*[1] (*also* **bummie**) [1940s+] (*US*) an alcoholic tramp. [BUM n.[3] (1) + RUMMY n.[1] (2)]

bummy *n.*[2] *see* BUMMER n.[1].

bummy *adj.* **1** [late 19C+] useless, second-rate, inferior. **2** [1980s+] ragged, poor, reminiscent of a vagrant. [BUM adj. (1)/BUM n.[3] (1)]

bum-numbing *adj.* [1970s+] infinitely tedious, usu. applied to work of some sort. [BUM n.[1] (1) + SE *numbing*; the image is of sitting so long that one loses sensation in the buttocks]

bum out *v.*[1] [1960s+] **1** (*US*) to disappoint, to depress. **2** (*US*) to be

disappointed, to be depressed. **3** (*US campus*) to fail a test. [BUM adj. (1)]

bum out *v.*[2] *see* BUM v.[4] (1).

bump *n.*[1] (*orig. US*) **1** [1920s+] the action of thrusting forward the abdomen or hips, as in a dance; thus *bumper*, a striptease artist who performs this action. **2** [1970s+] spontaneous, cursory sexual intercourse. [SE *bump*/BUMP v.[1] (1)]

bump *n.*[2] **1** [1940s] dismissal, 'the sack'. **2** [1940s–50s] (*US*) a raise, a promotion. [ext. use of SE *bump*, a blow]

bump *n.*[3] [1950s] (*US*) the female breast, usu. in pl. (cf. BAGS n.[1]).

bump *n.*[4] (*drugs*) **1** [1980s] a draw on a cannabis cigarette. **2** [1980s+] an inhalation of cocaine, usu. small. **3** [1990s+] crack cocaine (cf. BASE n.). **4** [1990s+] a piece of crack cocaine, ready for smoking, or crushed up into a 'line' for inhaling. **5** [1990s+] fake crack cocaine. **6** [1990s+] 1 dose ($20) of ketamine. [play on HIT n.[3]]

bump *v.*[1] **1** [mid-17C–18C; 1960s+] (*US campus*) to have sexual intercourse. **2** [1930s+] (*US*) to impregnate. **3** [1980s] (*W.I., Baha.*) to work as a prostitute.

bump *v.*[2] **1** [late 19C] (*US*) to terminate a relationship. **2** [20C+] to dismiss an employee, or someone from a team. **3** [1920s+] a prison sentence. **4** [1940s+] (*also* **bump up**) to increase, i.e. a prison sentence. **4** [1940s+] (*also* **bump up**) to increase wages or, in gambling use, a bet. **5** [1940s+] to move someone up or down a queue, appointment calendar etc. **6** [1960s+] in air travel, to move up one or more classes, while still travelling on one's original ticket, usu. in passive. **7** [1960s+] to promote.

bump *v.*[3] **1** [late 19C+] (*Aus./US*) (*also* **bump someone's head**) to get the better of, to outdo, to deceive. **2** [late 19C+] (*orig. Aus.*) to meet, to accost; thus *how (are) you bumping?* a general phr. of greeting. **3** [1910s+] to beat up. **4** [1940s] to fight successfully, to defeat.

bump *v.*[4] [1910s+] **1** to kill, to murder. **2** to shoot dead. [BUMP OFF v.]

bump *v.*[5] [1970s] (*US*) to dance. [SE *bump and grind*]

bump *v.*[6] [1990s+] (*US Black*) to create, to produce.

bump *v.*[7] [1990s+] (*US Black*) to steal. [synon. of CLOUT v.[2] (1)/HIT v.[1] (1)]

bump *v.*[8] [1990s+] to boost one's intoxication (by taking more drugs).

bump *v.*[9] [2000s] of music, a record, to play.

bumpa *n. see* BUMBA n.

bump across *v.* [20C+] (*Aus.*) to meet by accident. [var. on SE *bump into*]

bump along *v.* [1900s] (*Aus.*) to appear, to arrive.

bump and grab *v.* [1990s+] (*US Black*) to drive deliberately into someone's car with the intention of stopping and then robbing them. [on model of SE *smash and grab*]

bump bellies *v.* [20C+] (*US*) to have sexual intercourse (cf. BELLY BUMP v.).

bumper *n.*[1] **1** [late 17C–19C] a full glass, esp. when raised in a toast; also as v., to make a toast. **2** [mid-19C+] anything unusually large or plentiful. **3** [20C+] (*W.I.*) a drunkard, a habitual drinker, esp. of rum. [the bumping of glasses in the toast or f. SE *bumping*, huge, great. Popular ety. suggests a supposed Fr. toast, *au bon père*, to the good father, i.e. the pope]

bumper *n.*[2] **1** [late 19C] (*US*) a trunk. **2** [20C+] (*US/W.I.*) the buttocks. [ext. of BUM n.[1] (1) + echoic of the buttocks hitting a hard surface; (2) ? play on KEISTER n. (1)/KEISTER n. (7)]

bumper *n.*[3] [late 19C+] (*Aus./N.Z.*) a cigarette butt; thus *bumper-dashing*, *bumper-shooting*, picking up cigarette butts from the street. [BUTT n.[2] (1) + SE *stump*]

bumper *n.*[4] [1930s–40s] (*US*) 5 cents, a nickel. [ety unknown; ? they bump together in the pocket/one bumps it down on the table]

bumper *n.*[5] [1940s+] a masculine lesbian (cf. BEAN FLICKER n.). [BUMP PUSSIES v. (1) + ext. of SE use, i.e. her aggressiveness]

bumper n.[6] [1990s+] (Irish) an amateur flat race. [? contestants may fall off with a bump or bump each other's horses]

bumper n.[7] [2000s] (UK drugs) a portion of a drug, e.g. a 'line' of cocaine. [it 'bumps up' one's energy]

bumper adj. [mid-19C+] especially large, especially abundant. [BUMPER n.[1] (2)]

bumper v. [1960s+] (Aus.) to construct a cigarette from cigarette ends. [BUMPER n.[3]]

bumper head n. [1990s+] (US) one who performs oral sex. [the head 'bumps' on the partner's body]

bum-perisher n. (also **bum-shaver, bum-starver**) [late 19C+] a short jacket. [BUM n.[1] (1) + SE shaver; the implication is of failing to warm, cover or reach the buttocks, but note PERISHER n.[1] and SHAVER n.[3]]

bumper-jumper n. [1970s] (US) a driver who stays too close to the vehicle immediately in front, a 'tail-gater'.

bumper kit n. [1990s+] (US Black) a woman's posterior or buttocks. [BUMPER n.[2] (2) + SE kit]

bumpers n. [1940s+] the female breasts.

bumper-shooter n. [1940s+] (Aus.) a picker-up of discarded cigarette ends; thus bumper-shooting, bumper-sniping, following this practice. [BUMPER n.[3] + SE shooter; note Aus. army sl. bumper-sniping, a punishment that requires the defaulter to pick up cigarette ends]

bumper to bumper phr. [1970s+] (US lesbian) of lesbians, vagina to vagina, said of dancing or sexual intercourse. [BUMP PUSSIES v. (1); note BUMPER n.[5]]

bumper-up n. 1 [20C+] a dockyard labourer. 2 [1920s+] (Aus.) a pickpocket's assistant. 3 [1920s+] (Aus.) a handyman who works for a prostitute. 4 [1920s+] (Aus.) a general term for an absolute incompetent.

bumper-upper n. [1920s+] (Aus.) a handyman who works for a prostitute; thus derog. phr. he couldn't get a job as a bumper-upper in a brothel. [ext. of BUMPER-UP n. (3)]

bump fuzz v. [1980s+] (US campus) to have sexual intercourse (cf. BELLY BUMP v.). [SE bump + FUZZ n.[2] (1)]

bump gums v. see BUMP (ONE'S) GUMS v.

bump heads v. [1950s] (US) 1 to clash (physically or otherwise), to argue, to debate. 2 in fig. use, to encounter.

bumpie n. see BUPPIE n.

bumping n.[1] [1980s+] (US Black teen) the sound of a car stereo. [the 'bumps' come from the thud of the bass, which will be turned up high]

bumping n.[2] [1990s+] (US Black) having an uproariously good time.

bumping adj. 1 [late 19C–1900s] large. 2 [1980s] (US campus) stylish, attractive. 3 [1980s+] (US Black/campus) exhilarating. [fig. uses of SE bump, to hit, to thump]

bump into v. [20C+] (orig. US) to meet by accident, to encounter.

bump iron v. (also **drive iron**) [1990s+] (US prison) to work out with body-building weights.

bum plumber n. [1990s+] a male homosexual, a sodomite (cf. ANAL ASTRONAUT n.). [BUM n.[1] (1) + SE plumber]

bump man n. [1930s–40s] (US) a pickpocket. [he 'bumps into' his victims]

bump nasties v. see BUMP UGLIES v.

bump(-off) n. 1 [1920s–60s] (orig. US) a murder; thus bump-off guy, a killer. 2 [1930s] the end of something, typically criminal activity.

bump off v. 1 [20C+] (orig. US) to murder; thus bump oneself off, to commit suicide. 2 [1910s+] to dismiss, to get rid of. 3 [1920s] to wound. 4 [1920s] (US Und.) to raid. 5 [1920s–50s] to die. [SE bump, to push]

bump (one's) gums v. (also **run one's gums**) [20C+] (orig. US Black) to argue, to talk excessively.

bump pussies v. 1 [1940s+] (gay) of lesbians or male homo-sexuals, to have sexual intercourse (cf. BELLY BUMP v.). 2 [1960s–

70s] of male homosexuals, to find themselves too sexually similar (both passive, both active) to have satisfactory sex. [SE bump + PUSSY n. (2); the use of a 'vagina' word accentuates the effeminacy]

bumps n.[1] 1 [1900s] (US) hard treatment. 2 [1960s–70s] (US Black) a rash, esp. on the face.

bumps n.[2] [1960s] (US) an affectionate name for one's grandfather. [? juv. mispron.]

bumpsie adj. (also **bumpsy, bumsie**) [early–mid-17C] drunk. [? liable to 'bump' into people or to fall over with a 'bump']

bump someone's head v. see BUMP v.[3] (1).

bump start n. [1970s+] a violent gesture or action (whether physical or metaphorical). [BUMP START v.]

bump start v. [1970s+] to make a violent gesture or action. [SE]

bump-stick n. [late 19C–1910s] a police truncheon.

bumpsy adj. see BUMPSIE adj.

bump that! excl. [1980s] (US campus) an excl. of dismissal. [BUMP v.[2]]

bumptious adj. 1 [19C+] offensively self-assertive. 2 [late 19C–1920s] (US Black) short-tempered. [SE bump + sfx -ious on pattern of fractious, mendacious etc]

bump titties v. [1990s+] (US Black) to fight. [SE bump + TITTY n.[1] (1)]

bump uglies v. (also **bump nasties**) [1990s+] (US Black/teen) to have sexual intercourse (cf. BELLY BUMP v.). [SE bump + ugly/nasty (bodies)]

bum-puncher n. [1980s+] (Aus.) a homosexual (cf. ANAL ASTRONAUT n.). [BUM n.[1] (1) + SE puncher]

bum punching n. [1980s+] (Aus.) (homosexual) anal intercourse. [note synon. RMC Duntroon (Aus.) poo debting, poo pushing]

bump up v. see BUMP v.[2] (4).

bumpy n. [1960s] (US) the buttocks. [ext. of BUM n.[1] (1) + the physical 'bump' of the buttocks]

bumpy adj. [1990s+] homosexual. [BUMPY n.]

bum-ranger n. [18C] a womanizer, a promiscuous man. [BUM n.[1] (1) + RANGE v. (1)]

bum rap n. (orig. US) 1 [1920s+] a false accusation or an unfair sentence. 2 [1940s+] a misfortune, an unfair action. 3 [1950s+] harsh (and poss. unfair) criticism. 4 [1970s] a bad reputation. [BUM adj. + RAP n.[4]]

bum rap v. 1 [1940s+] to convict or accuse falsely. 2 [1950s+] to slander, to attack verbally, to catcall. [BUM RAP n.]

bum-robber n. [20C+] a male homosexual (cf. ANAL ASTRONAUT n.). [BUM n.[1] (1). + SE robber]

bum-roll n. [17C] a bustle. [BUM n.[1] (1) + SE roll; the shape]

bumrush n. [1980s+] (US Black) 1 a police raid. 2 a stampede, esp. of a crowd wanting to get into a rock concert or film show (usu. without tickets and dependent on force of numbers to overwhelm the security guards). [BUMRUSH v.]

bumrush v. 1 [1930s+] (orig. US) to eject. 2 [1980s+] (orig. US Black) to attack, to destroy through violence. 3 [1980s+] (orig. US Black) to get in (to a concert, a club) without having to pay. 4 [1980s+] (orig. US Black) to move as a crowd, using numbers to gain access. 5 [1980s+] (US campus) to be overlooked, rejected. 6 [1980s+] (US) to pursue. 7 [1990s+] (US) to run off fast; to escape, e.g. from a police raid. [BUM'S RUSH n.]

bum-shaver n.[1] [18C] a womanizer, a promiscuous man. [BUM n.[1] (2) + SHAVER n.[1] (1)/SHAVER n.[2] (2)]

bum-shaver n.[2] see BUM-PERISHER n.

bumshop n. [mid-19C–1900s] 1 a brothel (cf. BANGING-SHOP n.). 2 the vagina. [BUM n.[1] (2) + SE shop]

bumsie adj. see BUMPSIE adj.

bumsky adj. [1910s] (US) second-rate, inferior. [BUM adj. (1) + -SKI sfx]

bum soup n. [1990s+] diarrhoea. [BUM n.[1] (1) + SE soup]

bumsquabbled adj. (also **bamsquabbled**) [mid-19C] (US) discomfited, defeated; confused. [ety. unknown]

bum's rush *n.* (*also* **rush**) [20C+] (*orig. US Und.*) **1** a rejection. **2** forcible movement. **3** (*also* **fool's rush**) forcible ejection, esp. from a bar or club, esp. as *get* or *give the bum's rush*. [BUM n.³ (1) + SE *rush*, a sudden onslaught; the origin of the phr. came in the saloons of late 19C New York where vagrants and other hungry people attempted to take advantage of the sometimes sumptuous free lunch counters, which were meant for drinkers only]

bum-starver *n. see* BUM-PERISHER n.

bum steer *n.* (*also* **bad steer**) [20C+] (*US*) **1** a piece of bad advice or misinformation. **2** a mistake, the wrong direction. [BUM adj. (1)/SE *bad* + SE *steer*]

bumsuck *v.* [1930s+] to toady to, to act the sycophant. [BUM n.¹ (1) + SE *suck*]

bum-sucker *n.* [mid-19C; 1940s+] a sycophant, a crawler. [BUMSUCK v.]

bumswiggled *adj.* (*also* **bumswizzled**) [19C+] confounded, ruined. [ety. unknown; ? BAMBOOZLED adj. (1)]

bum tags *n.* [20C+] deposits of faecal matter in the hairs around a badly cleaned anus. [BUM n.¹ (1) + SE *tag*]

bum-tickler *n.* **1** [18C] a womanizer, a promiscuous man. **2** [late 19C] the penis. [BUM n.¹ (2) + SE *tickler*]

bum-trap *n.* [mid-18C–early 19C] a bailiff or bailiff's assistant. [BUM n.² + TRAP n.²]

bum trip *n.* [1960s+] **1** an unpleasant experience while under the influence of drugs. **2** in fig. use, any bad situation or experience. **3** (*US campus*) an uninteresting or lazy person. [BUM adj. (1) + TRIP n.⁴]

bum up *v. see* BUM v.² (2).

bum van *n.* [1980s+] (*Aus. prison*) the van that transports prisoners to prison. [BUM n.³ (1) + SE *van*]

bum wad *n.* [1940s] (*US*) lavatory paper. [BUM n.¹ (1) + SE *wad*]

bum-warmer *n.* [1940s] a long suit jacket, covering the buttocks. [on model of BUM-FREEZER n.]

bum-worker *n.* [18C] a womanizer, a promiscuous man. [BUM n.¹ (2) + SE *worker*]

bun *n.¹* **1** [late 16C–19C] a squirrel. **2** [late 18C–19C] a rabbit. [dial.]

bun *n.²* **1** [mid-17C+] pubic hair; thus the vagina (cf. BIRD n.⁸). **2** [late 19C] a young woman (with no pej. links). **3** [20C+] the buttocks (cf. BAKERY GOODS n.). **4** [1930s] (*Scot.*) a prostitute (cf. BANGTAIL n.¹). **5** [1980s] an attractive woman, one who is 'good enough to eat'. [(1) BUN n.¹ (2); (4) ? 16C north. dial. *bun*, the tail of a hare]

bun *n.³* **1** [late 19C+] a state of drunkenness; esp. as HAVE A BUN ON v. **2** [1900s] (*US*) a state of weeping. **3** [1910s] (*US*) a fit of laughter. [? links to Worcestershire dial. *bun*, a bung or cork or Angus dial. *bun*, a large cask]

bun *n.⁴* (*also* **bun hat**) [1910s+] (*N.Z.*) a bowler hat. [resemblance]

bun *n.⁵* [1980s+] (*drugs*) a quantity of cannabis resin, either 1kg or 5kg. [? its resemblance to a SE *bun*]

bun *v.¹* [1990s+] (*US Black*) to have sexual intercourse. [? BUN n.¹ (2), i.e. the notoriously sex-driven SE *bunny-rabbit*]

bun *v.²* [1990s+] (*orig. UK Black*) to smoke cannabis or crack cocaine. [pron. of BURN v.³ (2)]

bun bandit *n.* [1960s] (*US gay*) one who performs the active role in anal intercourse. [BUN n.² (3) + BANDIT sfx (2); var. on BUM BANDIT n.]

bun boy *n.* [1950s+] a homosexual (cf. ANAL ASTRONAUT n.). [BUN n.² (3) + SE *boy*]

bun-bun *n.* [1970s+] (*US gay*) the buttocks (cf. BAKERY GOODS n.). [redup. of BUN n.² (3)]

bunce *n.* (*also* **bounce, bunse, bunts**) [18C+] money (esp. for nothing); thus extras, bonuses, profits (cf. ALFALFA n.). [coster jargon *bunts*, second-rate apples, which were sold off cheap or even given away to market boys, who could in turn sell them at a small profit. Hotten (1867) adds 'money obtained by giving light weight, &c.'. Bunts were further divided into *fair bunts* and

unfair bunts, depending on whether or not the coster was aware of his boy's tricks]

bunce *v.* [20C+] (*costermonger*) to overcharge. [BUNCE n.]

buncer *n.* **1** [mid-19C+] a salesperson who works for a commission. **2** [20C+] (*costermonger*) one who overcharges the customers. [BUNCE n.]

bunce up *v.* [20C+] (*Ulster*) to pool resources. [BUNCE n.]

bunch *n.* **1** [late 17C+] a group; usu. in phrs. *best of the bunch*; *best of a bad bunch*. **2** [20C+] a quantity.

bunch *v.* [20C+] (*US*) to leave a job, to leave something unfinished. [BUNK (OFF) v. (1)]

bunch! *excl.* [1900s] (*US campus*) nonsense! rubbish! [? abbr. *bunch of* BULLSHIT n. (1)]

bunched *adj.* [1970s+] (*Irish*) exhausted.

bunch of charms *n.* [1900s] a pretty young woman.

bunch of dog's meat *n.* [mid-19C] a squalling baby. [its fate if it does not stop whingeing]

bunch of fives *v.* (*also* **box of fives, bunch of five/ivories**) [19C+] the hand, usu. when clenched in a fist; thus a punch; occas. in phr. *chuck up the bunch of fives*, to die. [the 5 fingers]

bunch of grapes *n.* **1** [1910s] (*Aus.*) in cards, the suit of clubs. **2** [1930s] (*US*) jailor's keys. [resemblance]

bunch of ivories *n. see* BUNCH OF FIVES n.

bunch of onions *n.* [mid-19C] a watch and seals.

bunch of rags *n.* [1910s–60s] (*US*) a young woman, esp. a prostitute.

bunch punch *n.* [1970s+] (*orig. US campus*) group sex in which a number of men have sex with one woman. [BUNCH PUNCH v.]

bunch punch *v.* [1970s+] (*orig. US campus*) to have group sex, usu. a gang-rape. [BUNCH n. (1) + PUNCH v. (1)]

bunchy *n.* [1940s+] (*W.I.*) the buttocks. [BUM n.¹ (1) + ? 14C SE *bunchy*, swelling]

bunchy *adj.* [20C+] (*US*) chubby. [14C SE *bunchy*, swelling]

bunco *n.* (*also* **banco, bunko**) (*orig. US Und.*) **1** [late 19C–1920s] a swindler. **2** [late 19C+] fraud, a dishonest gambling game. **3** [1910s+] deceit, flattery, empty nonsense. **4** [1960s+] a police squad devoted to combating confidence tricksters. [Sp. *banca*, a card-game similar to monte]

bunco *adj.* (*also* **bunko**) (*orig. US Und.*) **1** [late 19C+] pertaining to swindlers and confidence tricksters. **2** [20C+] deceptive, fraudulent. [BUNCO n. (2)]

bunco *v.* (*also* **bunko**) [late 19C+] (*orig. US Und.*) to swindle, to defraud. [BUNCO n. (2)]

bunco artist *n.* (*also* **bunko artist**) [20C+] (*orig. US Und.*) a confidence trickster. [BUNCO n. (2) + ARTIST sfx]

bunco game *n.* (*also* **bunk game, bunko game**) (*orig. US Und.*) **1** [late 19C–1970s] a generic term for swindling, confidence trickery. **2** [1900s–20s] any form of 'fixed' gambling game. [BUNCO n. (2) + SE *game*]

bunco man *n.* (*also* **banco man, bunk, bunko man**) [late 19C–1950s] (*orig. US Und.*) a swindler, a confidence trickster. [BUNCO n. (2) + SE *man*; Asbury, *The Gangs of Chicago* (1940) differentiates: 'the [confidence man] operated all kinds of swindles, while the bunko man specialized in playing banco, sometimes called bunko, which was an adaptation of the old English game of eight-dice cloth']

buncombe *n. see* BUNKUM n.

buncombe *adj.* [mid-19C] (*US*) nonsensical. [BUNKUM n.]

bunco squad *n.* (*also* **bunco people, bunko people**) [1940s+] (*US police/Und.*) a special squad devoted to combating confidence tricksters. [BUNCO n. (1) + SE *squad*]

bunco-steerer *n.* (*also* **banco-steerer, bunko-steerer**) [late 19C+] (*orig. US Und.*) that member of a confidence trickster gang whose task is to entrap the victim into the current swindle. [BUNCO n. (2) + STEERER n. (1)]

bunco-steering *n.* [late 19C–1940s] (*orig. US Und.*) confidence trickery. [BUNCO-STEERER n.]

bundabust *n.* (*also* **bundobust**) [late 19C–1950s] (*orig. Ind. army*) **1** discipline, regulations. **2** arrangements. **3** a revenue settlement. [Hind. *band-o-bast*, tying and binding]

bunder *n.* [late 19C–1930s] (*Anglo-Chinese*) any supposedly remarkable piece of information that turns out to be no more than a false rumour. [Hind. *band*, an artificial embankment or quay, esp. the Shangai *Bund*, the city's main (pre-revolutionary) commercial centre]

bundie *n.* [20C+] (*Irish*) a child's buttocks. [BUN n.² (3)]

bundle *n.*¹ **1** [mid-17C+] a large amount of something; of drugs, a prescribed amount. **2** [late 19C+] a large amount of money. **3** [20C+] loot, plunder. **4** [1930s+] (*US prison*) a long prison sentence.

bundle *n.*² [mid-18C–1950s] a woman, esp. a fat one; one's wife thus (*US*) a girlfriend, a female companion. [19C use of is generally derog.; 20C use is neutral]

bundle *n.*³ **1** [1930s+] a fight. **2** [1990s+] sexual intercourse. [the participants have been 'bundled' together; (2) note 18C–19C SE *bundle*, to sleep in one's clothes on the same bed or couch with]

bundle *n.*⁴ **1** [1960s+] (*drugs*) a package of 25 $5 bags of heroin. **2** [1990s+] (*US Black/drugs*) a portion of crack cocaine or marijuana or any kind of drug available on sale. [BINDLE n.]

bundle *v.* **1** [late 18C–1940s] to have sexual intercourse. **2** [early 19C] to pass something over. **3** [1930s] (*US tramp*) to steal, esp. when a degree of physical violence is involved. **4** [1930s+] to fight. [SE *bundle* (*together*), i.e., the proximity of the bodies, whether sexual or violent]

bundle! *excl.* [1990s+] (*UK juv.*) a shout that signifies that a fight is taking place. [BUNDLE n.³ (1)]

bundle-bum *n.* [1920s–30s] (*US tramp*) the lowest grade of tramp. [SE *bundle* + BUM n.³ (1)]

bundle connection *n.* [1990s+] (*US drugs*) a mid-level drug dealer, working between bulk wholesalers and street-level retailers. [BUNDLE n.⁴ (1) + CONNECTION n. (2)]

bundle of bones *n. see* BAG OF BONES n.¹.

bundle off *v.* [19C–1900s] to send away in a hurry. [fig. use of SE; subseq. use is SE]

bundle of socks *n.* [late 19C+] (*Aus.*) the head. [rhy. sl. = THINKBOX n.]

bundle of ten *n.* [1910s] a packet of 10 cigarettes.

bundle stiff (willie) *n. see* BINDLE STIFF n.

bundletail *n.* [late 17C–early 18C] a short, fat, squat woman. [SE *bundle* + TAIL n.² (3)]

bundle that would trip a white wings *n.* [1900s] (*US*) a very large amount of money. [BUNDLE n.¹ (2)]

bundobust *n. see* BUNDABUST n.

bundook *n. see* BANDOOK n.

bundu-bashing *n.* [1970s+] (*S.Afr.*) travelling through wild or near-impenetrable rough country. [S.Afr.E. *bundu*, 'the back of beyond' + SE *bash*]

bun-duster *n.* [1920s] (*US*) an effete young man who attends smart tea parties and charms old ladies. [SE *bun* + DUST OFF v.¹, i.e. he finishes off the buns]

bundy *n.* [1970s+] (*Aus.*) Bundaberg rum. [abbr. of the proprietary name of a brand of rum, ult. f. the town in Queensland]

bundy off *v.* [1990s+] (*Aus. prison*) to die, esp. of a drug overdose. [fig. use of PUNCH THE BUNDY v. and thus synon. with PUNCH THE CLOCK v. (3)]

bun feast *n.* [late 19C–1900s] a third-rate feast, where even the buns are not enough to make one full. [ext. of SE use but ? ironic ref. to BEANFEAST n.]

bunfight *n.* [late 19C+] a tea party, esp. with the image of children struggling for sticky buns. [SE *bun* + *fight*]

bunfungered *adj. see* BUMFUDDLED adj.

bung *n.*¹ (*also* **boung, bong**) **1** [mid-16C–mid-19C] (*UK Und.*) a purse. **2** [late 16C–mid-18C] a pocket. **3** [late 16C–mid-19C] a

cut-purse. **4** [1950s+] a bribe. **5** [1990s+] a loan. [Frisian *pung*, purse]

bung *n.*² **1** [late 16C+] (*also* **bung head**) a general insult. **2** [late 18C+] the anus. **3** [1950s–60s] (*US*) the buttocks. **4** [1960s] (*US*) the vagina. [SE *bung*; note Welsh *bwng*, an orifice]

bung *n.*³ **1** [mid-19C–1900s] a brewer; a brewery. **2** [mid-19C–1910s] an inn-keeper or publican; thus the *bung ball*, an annual publican's dance. **3** [late 19C–1950s] beer. **4** [1910s] (*Aus.*) a generic term for breweries and their interests. [SE *bung*, the stopper of a barrel of beer]

bung *n.*⁴ [mid-19C+] (*US*) a lump, a swelling. [SE *bung up*, to bruise, to beat]

bung *n.*⁵ [late 19C] (*Aus.*) eviction.

bung *n.*⁶ [late 19C–1910s] (*UK juv.*) a lie. [ety. unknown; ? BUNG v. (3), i.e. it 'throws away' the truth]

bung *n.*⁷ **1** [late 19C+] a blow; esp. in phr. *bung in the eye*, a blow in the eye. **2** [20C+] a black eye. [dial., ult. echoic]

bung *n.*⁸ (*also* **bunghole, bungy**) [1910s+] (*Aus., orig. milit.*) cheese. [its costive effects, i.e. it makes you BUNGED UP adj.² (1)]

bung *n.*⁹ [1980s+] (*US drugs*) a bowl-shaped water-pipe used for smoking marijuana. [var. on BONG n.¹]

bung *n.*¹⁰ *see* BOONG n.

bung *adj.*¹ [19C] (*Scot.*) drunk (cf. ALED UP adj.). [BUNG n.³/fig. use of BUNG v. (1), i.e. to be 'hit' by drunkenness]

bung *adj.*² [1900s] (*Aus.*) impoverished; bankrupt. [? BUNG n.⁵]

bung *v.* **1** [early 19C+] to hit, to punch, esp. in the eye. **2** [mid–late 19C] to lie, to deceive by lying. **3** [mid-19C+] to pass, to throw, usu. energetically or aggressively. **4** [mid-19C+] to hand over, to give quickly; esp. in imper., e.g. *bung this round to Fred*. **5** [late 19C+] to hand out money, often to bet or to bribe. **6** [20C+] to place (inside). **7** [1910s+] of speech, to give, e.g. *bung someone the word*. **8** [1940s+] (*also* **bung out**) to get rid of, to dispose of. **9** [1950s+] (*UK Und./police*) to bribe or to pay protection money. [echoic of tossing an article with some violence]

bung *adv.* [mid-19C+] precisely, accurately; usu. as *bung in*; *bung on*. [BANG adv. (1)]

bungality *n.* [mid-19C] (*Aus.*) stupidity. [ety. unknown]

bungalow (bill) *n.* [late 19C+] a man who is either not very intelligent ('nothing up top') or endowed with large genitals ('it's all down below'). [pun]

bungaree/bungary *n. see* BUNGERY n.

bungdung *n.* [1920s+] (*Aus.*) a large firecracker. [? BANDOOK n.]

bunged *adj.* [1930s+] (*S.Afr.*) tipsy. [BUNG n.³ (3)]

bunged up *adj.*¹ **1** [early 19C–1910s] of the eyes, blackened. **2** [mid-19C+] (*Aus./US*) hurt, injured. [var. on SE *banged up* + note BUNG n.⁷]

bunged up *adj.*² **1** [late 19C+] stuffy, blocked, esp. of one's nose during 'flu or a cold, or of constipation. **2** [1900s] (*US*) second-rate, broken down. **3** [1910s+] (*US*) injured. **4** [1930s] (*Aus*) in a bad way, hopeless. **5** [1980s] squashed, creased, pushed together uncomfortably. [SE *bung*, to enclose]

bungee *adj.* [1990s+] (*US campus*) extremely. [SE *bungee jumping*, an 'extreme sport']

bunger *n.*¹ (*Aus.*) **1** [late 19C] a cannon. **2** [1900s] an outstanding example. [BUNG v. (3)]

bunger *n.*² [1900s–40s] (*US*) a black eye. [BUNG n.⁷ (2)]

bunger *n.*³ [1960s] **1** (*US*) the anus. **2** a male homosexual. [BUNGHOLE n.¹ (2)/BUNG n.² (2)]

bungery *n.* (*also* **bungaree, bungary**) [late 19C–1900s] a tavern, a public house; thus *Bohemian bungery*, a public house frequented by (impecunious) writers and artists. [SE *bung*, the stopper of a beer-barrel/BUNG n.³]

bung-eye *n.* (*also* **bungy-eye**) [late 19C+] (*Aus.*) an eye infection caused by flies. [BUNGED UP adj.¹ (2) + SE *eye*]

bung-eyed *adj.* **1** [early–mid-19C] drunk (cf. ARSEHOLED adj.). **2** [1960s+] cross-eyed. [the volume of liquor 'bungs up' one's vision; but note SE *bung*, a stopper (for a cask)]

bung eyes *n.* [1960s–70s] (*US*) protruding eyes. [BUNG v. (1) + SE *eyes*]

bung-fodder *n.* [late 19C+] (*US*) lavatory paper. [BUNG n.² (2) + SE *fodder*]

bungfoodle *v.* [1900s] (*Aus.*) to deceive, to 'mess around'. [? BAMBOOZLE v. (1)]

bungfunger *v.* [mid-19C] (*US*) to confuse. [? BAMBOOZLE v. (1)]

bung head *n. see* BUNG n.² (1).

bung ho *adj.* [1950s] proper, right, good. [BUNG HO! excl. (1)]

bung ho! *excl.* **1** [1920s+] a toast before drinking. **2** [1930s–40s] goodbye. [SE *bung* or BUNG v. (3); i.e. one 'throws' the drunk down]

bunghole *n.*¹ **1** [early 17C; late 19C–1900s] (*US*) the vagina (cf. BLACK HOLE n.¹). **2** [early 17C+] the anus, the rectum (cf. A-HOLE n.). **3** [mid-17C] in fig. use of (2), something that stinks. **4** [20C+] (*Aus.*) the mouth. **5** [1960s+] (*US campus*) a term of abuse (cf. ARSE n.¹). [SE *bung* + *hole*]

bunghole *n.² see* BUNG n.⁸.

bunghole *v.* **1** [1930s+] to sodomize. **2** [1950s] (*US drugs*) to inject narcotics. [(1) BUNGHOLE n.¹ (2); (2) Spears, *Slang and Jargon of Drugs and Drink* (1986), suggests 'probably nonce' but the term plays on the equation of narcotics and excrement, see SHIT n.⁵]

bunghole buddy *n.* [1940s] (*US*) a very close friend. [BUNGHOLE n.¹ (2) + BUDDY n. (1); var. on ASSHOLE BUDDY n. (1)]

bungi *n.* (*also* **bungie, bungy**) [1980s+] (*S.Afr.*) a 'drop-out', a HIPPIE n.² (3). [Hind. *bhang*, cannabis or Ndebele *im-banje*, marijuana. Coined at Rhodes University, Grahamstown]

bungie-bird *n.* [late 16C] a Franciscan friar. [name *Friar Bungay*, as in Robert Greene's *Friar Bacon and Friar Bongay* (acted 1594)]

bungie-boy *n.* [1990s+] (*US gay*) a homosexual or bisexual male who maintains a heterosexual appearance. [ety. unknown]

bung it (in) *n.* [1920s+] gin. [rhy. sl.]

bung it (in) *v.* [late 19C] to gamble at a casino.

bung it on *v.* [1940s+] (*Aus./N.Z.*) **1** to act affectedly, to strike poses, to assume an accent. **2** to overcharge. **3** to assert pressure. **4** to exaggerate, to act temperamentally. [BUNG v. (3)]

bung-juice *n.* [late 19C] beer, stout. [SE *bung* + *juice*]

bungle *n.* [1990s+] (*W.I.*) someone who performs oral sex on a woman. [elided pron. of BUNGHOLE n.¹ (1)]

bungler *n.* [late 16C–early 18C] an impotent husband; thus *bungling*, sexually inadequate if not actually impotent. [SE *bungler*, an unskilful worker]

bung-nip *v. see* NIP A BUNG v.

bung-nipper *n.* (*also* **boung-napper, boung-nipper, bung napper**) [mid-17C–mid-19C] (*UK Und.*) a cut-purse; a pickpocket. [BUNG n.¹ (1) + NIPPER n.¹ (1)]

bungo *n.* [20C+] (*W.I., Jam.*) a crude, boorish, ignorant Black person, a country bumpkin (cf. BLOOTER n.). [? Hausa *bungu*, a nincompoop, a country bumpkin]

bungo *v.* [1980s] (*US campus*) to mistreat severely, to inflict injury on. [BUNGO n. but ? BANJO v. (2)/BUNG v. (1)]

bungo-bessy *n.* [1940s+] (*W.I.*) **1** an interfering busybody. **2** a boorish low-class woman. [BUNGO n. + BESSY n.]

bung off *v.* [20C+] to leave. [fig. use of BUNG v. (4)]

bung on *v.* [1960s+] **1** to put on a garment, to get dressed, usu. in comb. with an article of clothing, e.g. *bung on a jacket*. **2** to organize, to arrange. **3** to perform an action. [BUNG v. (3)]

bung on a blue *v.* (*also* **put a blue on, put on a blue, stack on a blue**) [1950s+] (*Aus.*) to make a fuss, to create a disturbance, to raise an issue. [BUNG v. (3)/SE *put*/*stack* + BLUE n.⁸ (2)/BLUE n.⁸ (3)]

bung on an act *v.* [1920s+] (*Aus.*) **1** to lose one's temper and deliver a stream of obscenities/oaths. **2** (*also* **bung on a turn**) to make trouble. [BUNG v. (3) + SE *act*]

bung one on *v.* [1950s+] to hit. [BUNG v. (3); 'one' is a blow or punch]

bung one's eye *v.* **1** [late 18C–19C] to drink a dram, to drink

heartily, to get drunk. **2** [1910s] (*US*) a drinking toast. [lit. to drink until one's eyes are *bunged*, closed]

bung on side *v.* (*also* **bung on swerve**) [1950s+] (*Aus.*) to show off. [BUNG v. (3) + SIDE n.¹/SE *swerve* + pun on billiards/snooker use]

bung on the bull *v.* [1940s+] (*Aus.*) to show off, to act in a pretentious manner. [BUNG v. (3) + BULL n.¹¹ (1)]

bungo-talk *n.* [1940s+] (*W.I.*) illiterate speech, the lowest level of uncultivated Jamaican speech. [BUNGO n. + SE *talk*]

bungo-toughy *n.* [1940s+] (*W.I., Guyn.*) a little child who eats or behaves like a hooligan. [BUNGO n.. + TOUGHIE n.]

bung (out) *v.* [mid-19C–1910s] (*US*) to protrude, to stick out. [fig. use of BUNG v. (3)]

bung out *v.*¹ [1900s] (*N.Z.*) to die. [BUNG v. (3)]

bung out *v.*² *see* BUNG v. (8).

bung-starter *n.* [late 19C–1930s] (*US*) a bartender. [SE *bung-starter*, an implement used to remove the bungs from casks of beer]

bungs up *adj.* [1970s] (*US*) very drunk, rolling drunk. [naut. jargon *bungs up*, a vessel that is rolling in a heavy sea to such an extent that the *bungs* in her planking are visible]

bung up *v.* **1** [19C+] to stop up. **2** [early 19C+] to close someone's eye with a punch or for the eye to close after a punch. **3** [late 19C] to impregnate. [SE *bung*; (1) SE before 19C]

bung up against *adj. see* BANG UP AGAINST adj.

bung upwards *adv.* [late 18C–early 19C] lying on one's stomach. [BUNG n.² (2) + SE *upwards*]

bungwad *n.* (*US*) **1** [1920s] lavatory paper. **2** [1990s+] a general insult. [BUNG n.² (2) + SE *wad*/-WAD sfx]

bungy *n.*¹ *see* BUNG n.⁸.

bungy *n.*² *see* BUNGI n.

bungy *adj.* (*also* **bongy**) [mid-18C–mid-19C] drunk (cf. ALED UP adj.). [SE *bung*]

bungy-eye *n. see* BUNG-EYE n.

bun hat *n. see* BUN n.⁴.

bunhouse *n.*¹ [1940s] (*UK Und.*) public relief. [the distribution of free buns]

bunhouse *n.*² [2000s] a brothel. [? BUN n.²]

bunion derby *n.* [1920s; 1990s+] (*US*) a cross-country marathon. [SE *bunion* + *The Derby*, a well-known horse race in the UK and as the Kentucky Derby in the US]

bunji *n.* [1980s+] (*Aus.*) a White man, often old and impoverished, who pursues Aboriginal women for sex. [Goreng Goreng *banji*, friend + SE *man*]

bun joint *n.* [late 19C] (*US*) a coffeehouse. [SE *bun* + JOINT n.⁴ (3)]

bunk *n.*¹ (*also* **the bunk**) **1** [20C+] (*orig. US*) rubbish, nonsense; thus *bunky*, nonsensical; *put the bunk*, to talk nonsense. **2** [1900s] a foolish person. **3** [1920s] (*US tramp*) good manners. [abbr. BUNKUM n.]

bunk *n.*² [1910s+] (*US*) **1** a Slav immigrant from Eastern Europe. **2** an oafish, dull, if muscular, person.

bunk *n.*³ **1** [1940s] (*US Und.*) synthetic liquor. **2** [1980s+] (*drugs*) fake cocaine. [ext./specific uses of BUNK n.¹ (1)]

bunk *n.*⁴ *see* BUNCO MAN n.

bunk *n.*⁵ *see* DO A BUNK v.

bunk, the *n. see* BUNK n.¹.

bunk *adj.* [20C+] **1** bad, second-rate, inferior; infuriating. **2** fake, counterfeit. **3** unsophisticated, unfashionable, ugly. [BUNK n.¹ (1)]

bunk *v.*¹ **1** [mid-19C+] to escape, to run off (under pressure). **2** [late 19C+] to leave, to be off (of one's own volition). **3** [1920s] to rush. [Lincolnshire dial. *bunk*, to run away, to make off]

bunk *v.*² (*also* **bunk down, bunk up**) **1** [mid-19C+] (*orig. US*) to sleep; esp. in the context of a shared prison cell, service dormitory etc. **2** [1900s–10s] in fig. use, to asssociate with. **3** [1900s–40s] to lie down. [SE *bunk*, a bed]

bunk v.[3] **1** [mid-19C+] to talk nonsense, to fool someone. **2** [1900s] to overcome completely, lit. to reduce to 'nonsense'. [BUNK n.[1] (1)]

bunk v.[4] [1920s+] (US) to hide, to conceal.

bunk v.[5] **1** [1950s] (Aus.) to give someone a lift on one's bicycle crossbar (cf. DINK n.[5]; DINK v.; DONK n.[1]; DOUBLER n.[2]; DOUBLE-BANK v.). **2** [1980s+] (also **bonk**) to travel without a fare, to get in (e.g. to a cinema) without a ticket. [BUNK UP v.[1]]

bunk! excl. [1910s+] (orig. US) nonsense! [BUNK n.[1] (1)]

bunk down v. see BUNK v.[2].

bunked adj. [1900s] (US) abandoned, deserted, esp. by one owing money.

bunker n.[1] [mid-19C] beer. [? a fig. coal bunker at which one 'fuels up' or Ling. Fr. bona acqua, good water]

bunker n.[2] [1930s] a sodomite; thus BUNKER-SHY n. [euph. for SE bugger; however, Irwin, American Tramp and Und. Slang (1931), suggests a ref. to a sailor's bunk, wherein seaboard homosexuality takes place]

bunkered adj. [late 19C+] in difficulties. [golfing imagery]

bunker-shy n. [1920s+] (orig. US prison/tramp) a young man, orig. a prisoner, frightened of being forced into homosexual sex. [BUNKER n.[2] + SE shy]

bunkey n. see BUNKIE n. (1).

bunk game n. see BUNCO GAME n.

bunk habit n. (also **bunk yen**) **1** [late 19C–1930s] (US drugs) the act of frequenting an opium den, too poor to buy one's own drugs but in the hope that someone else will offer a treat or simply to inhale the airborne fumes. **2** [1930s–60s] (US drugs) the desire to sleep excessively, resulting from one's addiction to narcotics. [SE bunk, a rudimentary bed as used by a smoker + yen, desire/HABIT n.]

bunkie n. **1** [mid-19C+] (US milit./campus/prison) (also **bunkey**, **bunky**) a room-mate. **2** [1970s+] (US) a general term of address, usu. condescending. [US army use bunkie, a bunkmate; thus a friend]

bunk into v. [20C+] (US) **1** to meet by accident. **2** to knock against. [BUMP INTO v.]

bunk it v. [mid-19C+] (US) **1** to sleep in a bunk (rather than a proper bed). **2** to sleep in any rough, makeshift manner. [SE bunk]

bunko see under BUNCO and its combs.

bunk (off) v. **1** [late 19C+] to leave. **2** [1970s+] to play truant. **3** [1990s+] to avoid one's responsibilities, esp. work. [BUNK v.[1]]

bunk out v. [1970s+] (Irish) to play truant. [var. on BUNK (OFF) v. (2)]

bunk over v. [20C+] to go across. [BUNK v.[1] (2)]

bunks v. [1950s+] (W.I. Rasta) to knock or bump against; thus bunks mi res, catch my rest, take a nap. [SE bounce]

bunk sheet n. [1920s–30s] (US) a sensational newspaper. [BUNK n.[1] (1) + SHEET n. (1)]

bunkshooter n. [1910s–20s] (US) a preacher. [BUNK n.[1] (1) + SHOOT v.[1] (4)]

bunkum n. (also **buncombe**, **bokum**) [19C+] (orig. US) nonsense, rubbish, flattery. [proper name of Buncombe County in North Carolina. The word emerged during the debate on the 'Missouri Question' in 1821 when Felix Walker, the member from this district, rose to speak. Although the debate was due to end and members begged him to sit down, he refused, explaining that his constituents expected it, and that he was bund 'to make a speech for Buncombe'. The term stuck, first as buncombe, then bunkum, then, as abbr. by the satirist George Ade, BUNK n.[1] (1). An alternative ety. links it to the gambling dice game banco or bunco, the cheating at which soon made it a synon. for fraud]

bunkum adj. [19C] (US) excellent, first-rate, esp. of food. [? link to Fr. bon, good]

bunkum town n. (also **bunkumville**) [1900s] (US) that area of the town where the poor live. [BUNKUM n. + SE town/-VILLE sfx[1]]

bunk up n.[1] [20C+] (orig. Aus.) help, assistance. [BUNK UP v.[1]]

bunk up n.[2] [1930s+] (orig. UK services) an act of sexual intercourse. [SE bunk]

bunk up v.[1] [20C+] to help, esp. in climbing up or over an obstacle, when one person either lets the other stand on their back or links their hands to make a 'stirrup' into which the climber can put one foot and boost themself upwards.

bunk up v.[2] [1930s–40s] (US gay) to have male homosexual intercourse.

bunk up v.[3] see BUNK v.[2].

bunky n. see BUNKIE n. (1).

bunky adj. see BUNK n.[1] (1).

bunk yen n. see BUNK HABIT n.

bunk you! excl. [1980s+] (US campus) a euph. for FUCK YOU! excl.

bun merchant n. [1960s] (US gay) a male prostitute specializing in taking a passive role. [BUN n.[2] (3) + MERCHANT n.]

bunned adj. [1900s–30s] (US) drunk. [BUN n.[3] (1)]

bunnick (up) v. [late 19C–1910s] to beat, to ruin, to dispose of, to 'put paid' to. [? BUNKERED adj./BUNK v.[1]]

bunny n.[1] **1** [17C+] the vagina (cf. BIRD n.[8]). **2** [18C; 1930s+] a sexually attractive young woman. **3** [20C+] (US Black) a promiscuous woman, whose habits emulate the preoccupations of rabbits. **4** [1920s+] (US) a male or female homosexual prostitute. **5** [1920s+] a sanitary towel. **6** [1930s+] (US) the buttocks. [? 16C north. dial. bun, the tail of a hare (cf. BUN n.[2]); also abbr. SE bunny, the stereotypically 'sexy' rabbit]

bunny n.[2] **1** [late 17C] a rabbit. **2** [20C+] a poor player of a sport. **3** [1950s+] rabbit fur, as used for making garments; thus the garments themselves. [SE bunny, an affectionate name for both rabbits and squirrels; (1) subseq. use is SE]

bunny n.[3] **1** [1920s+] (orig. US/Aus.) a fool, a simpleton (cf. AIREDALE n.). **2** [2000s] (US Black) a weakling. [SE bunny; i.e. the supposed stupidity of a rabbit]

bunny n.[4] **1** [1950s–60s] a talkative person. **2** [1950s+] a chat, a conversation. [RABBIT n.[10]]

bunny n.[5] see RABBIT n.[7].

bunny v. [1950s+] to talk, to chat with. [RABBIT (AND PORK) v.]

bunny boiler n. [1990s+] an unstable woman. [from a scene in the film Fatal Attraction (1987)]

bunny boy n. [1940s+] (S.Afr.) a male homosexual. [SE bunny + boy]

bunny chow n. [1950s+] (S.Afr.) vegetarian curry sold as a take-away in a hollowed-out half-loaf of bread (cf. CURRY BUNNY n.). [Hind. bania, a caste of merchants, thus generic for a Gujerati businessman, who followed a vegetarian diet and for whom a café-owner orig. created the dish]

bunny-hugger n. [1990s+] an environmentalist, esp. an anti-blood sport campaigner.

bun over brisket phr. [1900s] (Aus.) head-over-heels. [BUN n.[2] (3) + BRISKET n.[1]]

bun-puncher n. (also **bun-strangler**) [1910s–30s] a teetotaller; thus bun-punching, teetotal.

bun-rush n. see BUN-STRUGGLE n.

buns n. **1** [1950s+] a woman's breasts (cf. APPLES n.[1]). **2** [1960s+] the buttocks; thus (US gay) burn some buns or split some buns, to have sexual intercourse (cf. BAKERY GOODS n.). **3** [1980s+] in fig. use, one's body, oneself. [joc. resemblance to the food-stuffs]

bunse n. see BUNCE n.

bunsen burner n. [1990s+] any job or plan that pays well, almost invariably criminal. [rhy. sl. = EARNER n.]

bunser n. [20C+] (Irish) a pet name for a child. ['a (little) bun']

bun-strangler n. see BUN-PUNCHER n.

bun-struggle n. (also **bun-rush**, **muffin-struggle**, **tea-scramble**) [late 19C–1950s] a tea party. [var. on BUN-WORRY n. (1)]

bunt n. **1** [late 17C–early 19C] an apron. **2** [early 19C; 1970s+]

the buttocks. [SE *bunt*, the part of a fishing net that forms a bag or pouch; 1970s+ use of (2) is US gay]

bunt *v.* [late 18C] to jostle against, to knock. [dial. *bunt*, to push, to butt]

bunter *n.* **1** [18C–mid-19C] (*UK Und.*) a woman who scavenges for rags in the street. **2** [18C–mid-19C] (*UK Und.*) (*also* **bunt**) a poor, poss. thieving, prostitute. **3** [mid-19C] (*UK Und.*) a prostitute who hires lodgings, uses them for a short time then leaves without paying her rent. **4** [late 19C–1900s] (*UK Und.*) 'a woman thief of the lowest possible kind' (Ware). **5** [20C+] a man who fails in almost everything he does. **6** [1970s+] (*US gay*) an effeminate homosexual. [ety. unknown; ? link to BUNT n. (1)]

bunter's tea *n.* [early–mid-18C] strong liquor, usu. gin. [BUNTER n. (1) + SE *tea*]

bunting sticks *n.* [1930s] legs.

bunting time *n.* [late 17C–18C] summer. [fig. use of BUNT v., i.e. to have sexual intercourse]

buntling *n.* [late 17C–mid-19C] (*UK Und.*) a petticoat; thus *haul up the main buntlings*, to pull up a woman's petticoats. [BUNT n. (1), lit. a 'small apron.']

bun-trap *n.* [20C+] the mouth. [SE *bun* + SE *trap*/TRAP n.³]

bunts *n. see* BUNCE n.

bunty *n.* [1920s+] an affectionate term for a small, middle-aged person. [Scot./Irish *bunty*, short and squat]

bununus *n.* [1940s] (*W.I.*) a term of endearment applied to a person or object. [? Sp. *bueno*, good; ? Fr. *bon à nous*, good to us]

bununus *adj.* [1940s] (*W.I.*) a general term of approval, pretty, wonderful, glorious, fantastic. [BUNUNUS n.]

bun up *n.* [1980s+] (*Aus. prison*) homosexual gang-rape. [BUNS n. (2)]

bun wagon *n.* [1980s+] (*Aus.*) a police van. [? SE *bun* or ? BUNS n. (2)]

bun-worry *n.* **1** [late 19C–1900s] (*orig. milit.*) a tea party. **2** [late 19C+] (*Aus./N.Z.*) a general jollification. [SE *bun* + *worry*, to bite at like a dog]

bunyip *n.* [mid-19C+] (*Aus., Sydney*) an impostor, a pretender. [SE *bunyip*, 'the Aboriginal name of a fabulous monster inhabiting the rushy swamps and lagoons in the interior of Australia' (OED)]

buor *n. see* BUER n.

buoyant *adj.* [20C+] drunk; thus *buoyantly*, drunkenly (cf. ABOUT RIGHT phr.¹). [play on SE]

bup *n. see* BUPPER n.

bupkes/bupkis *n. see* BOBKHES n.

bupper *n.* (*also* **bup, buppie, buppies, bups, bupsie**) [late 19C–1900s] (*mainly UK juv.*) bread and butter. [elision/mispron.]

buppie *n.* (*also* **bumpie, buppy, bluppy**) [1980+] (*orig. US*) a Black upwardly mobile young professional. [SE *Black* + YUPPIE n.]

buppkes *n. see* BOBKHES n.

bups/bupsie *n. see* BUPPER n.

burble *v.* [late 19C+] to chatter pleasantly, thus *burbler*, a chatty person. [? linked to Ital. *borbogliare*, to make a rumbling or grumbling noise, Port. *borbulhar* + Sp. *borbollar* but coined by Lewis Carroll in *Through the Looking-Glass* (1871) in which the Jabberwock 'came whiffling through the tulgey wood,/And burbled as it came!']

burdetts *n.* [19C] boots. [rhy. sl. on *Burdett Coutts*, the bankers]

Burdon's hotel *n.* [mid-19C] Whitecross Street prison, London (cf. ABBOTT'S PRIORY n.; BOARDING HOUSE n.). [proper name of Mr *Burdon*, a one-time governor]

bure *n. see* BUER n.

burerk *n. see* BURICK n.

burg *n.*¹ (*also* **berg, burgh**) [mid-19C+] (*US*) a town, a city. [Lat. *burgus*, thence Ger. *Burg*, a town (orig. a walled town)]

burg *n.*² [1980s] (*S.Afr.*) a fool, an idiot, an unpleasant person. [BERK n.]

burg *n.*³ [1980s+] (*Aus./US Black gang*) a burglary; thus *burg merchant*, a burglar; thus DO A BURG v. [abbr.]

burgandy *n. see* CLARET n.

burgers *n.* [1990s+] (*drugs*) MDMA; usu. as *brown burgers, white burgers* (cf. ECSTASY n.).

burger (with cheese) *n.* (*also* **double burger (with cheese), triple burger with cheese**) [1980s+] (*US campus*) a sexy/very sexy/very, very sexy woman. [she's 'very good to eat'; a savoury version of the usual identification of pretty women with sweet-meats or cakes]

burgess of the... *n. see* KNIGHT OF THE... n.

burgew *n. see* BURGOO n.

burgh *n. see* BURG n.¹.

burglar *n.* **1** [late 19C–1960s] (*US*) a swindler, a bribe-taker. **2** [1920s+] a sodomite. **3** [1980s+] a security prison officer. [play on SE; (2) euph. for SE *bugger* and implication of 'breaking in'; note WW1 milit. *burglars*, Bulgarians]

burglar alarm *n.* [1990s+] the human arm. [rhy. sl.]

burglar cop *n.* (*also* **burglar copper**) [1900s–50s] (*US Und.*) a corrupt policeman. [SE *burglar* + COP n.¹ (1)/COPPER n.³ (1)]

burglar hole *n.* [1970s+] (*US*) a peephole in a front door. [through which one can espy potential robbers]

burgle *v.* [1960s+] to sodomize. [BURGLAR n. (2)]

Burgoo *adj.* [late 19C] (*Aus.*) pertaining to Scotland or the Scots; by ext. the Presbyterian church. [BURGOO n., seen as a Scottish staple]

burgoo *n.* (*also* **bergoo, burgew**) [mid-19C+] stew or porridge. [Arabic *burgul*, cooked, parched and cracked wheat. Orig. an 18C thick oatmeal gruel, consumed by seamen; also known as *loblolly*, a soup or stew made with a variety of meat and vegetables, often eaten at outdoor feasts in the US, esp. in Kentucky]

burick *n.* (*also* **burerk**) **1** [19C] a prostitute. **2** [mid–late 19C] a wife. **3** [mid–late 19C] a flashily dressed woman. [Rom. *burk*, breast or Scot. *bure*, a loose woman]

buried *adj.*¹ (*US Und.*) **1** [20C+] put in prison for a non-specific length of time. **2** [1930s–40s] held incommunicado. **3** [1930s+] serving a life sentence or a very long sentence.

buried *adj.*² [1920s] (*orig. US Black*) extremely drunk (cf. ANNIHILATED adj.).

burk *n. see* BERK n.

burk *v.*¹ [late 19C–1910s] (*orig. N.Z.*) to avoid work. [? rhy. sl. *burk* = SE *shirk* or f. SE *burk*, to smother, to 'hush up'. Both are ult. f. *burke*, to strangle (named after the early 19C 'resurrectionists' or grave-robbers *Burke* and Hare (*see* BURKE v.)]

burk *v.*² [1960s] (*US*) **1** to vomit (cf. BARF v.). **2** to break wind. [? onomat.]

burk *v.*³ *see* BURKE v. (2).

burke *n. see* BERK n.

burke *v.* **1** [mid-19C] to murder; thus *burking*, murdering to provide bodies for dissection. **2** [late 19C+] (*also* **burk**) to suppress, to cover up. [proper name of the Edinburgh criminal William *Burke* (1792–1829) who, along with his partner William Hare (1790–c.1860), murdered people in order to sell their corpses to the medical school for surgical dissection. Burke was hanged; Hare, who turned King's evidence, escaped the noose]

burker *n.* [early–mid-19C] a 'resurrectionist' or body-snatcher, esp. for the purpose of selling the corpse to a hospital's anatomy department (in an era when the dissection of human corpses was still illegal). [the early 19C 'resurrectionists' or grave-robbers *Burke* and Hare (*see* BURKE v.)]

Burketown mosquito net *n.* [1960s+] (*Aus.*) a bottle of rum and a cow-dung fire. [proper name of the outback town of *Burketown*, Queensland]

burking *n. see* BURKE v. (1).

burley *n.*¹ (*also* **burly**) [20C+] (*US*) a *burle*sque show, a striptease show. [abbr. BURLYCUE n.]

burley *n.*² *see* BERLEY n.

burleycue/burley-que *n. see* BURLYCUE n.

Burlington Bertie n.[1] [20C+] (bingo) the number 30 (cf. ALDERSHOT LADIES n.). [rhy. sl.; ult. BURLINGTON BERTIE n.[2]]

Burlington Bertie n.[2] [1900s–30s] a dandyish, overdressed young man, very conscious of (and pleased with) his appearance. [the music-hall song 'Burlington Bertie from Bow', sung by Vesta Tilley c.1908]

Burlington hunt n. see BERKELEY (HUNT) n.

burly n.[1] [1910s–30s] (US tramp) an able-bodied, aggressive tramp or burglar. [SE burly]

burly n.[2] see BURLEY n.[1].

burlycue n. (also **burleycue, burley-que**) [20C+] (US) a burlesque show. [pron.]

B.U.R.M.A. phr. [late 19C+] a lover's acronym, be undressed, ready, my angel, written on envelopes of love letters (cf. B.O.L.T.O.P. phr.). [abbr.]

burn n.[1] **1** [late 19C+] (US) a joke, a prank. **2** [1960s+] (orig. US) a fraud, a confidence trick; thus the sale of bad or fake drugs. **3** [1960s+] (US) a major disappointment. **4** [1990s+] (W.I.) an act of infidelity. [the victim 'gets their fingers burned']

burn n.[2] [20C+] (US) a love-bite. [resemblance to a burn scar]

burn n.[3] [1940s+] (orig. Und.) tobaccco; a smoke, a cigarette; thus (Aus.) twist a burn, roll a cigarette.

burn n.[4] [1940s+] fast-driving in an automobile. [BURN v.[4] (1)]

burn n.[5] [1950s] (US) a permanent wave hairstyle. [it is 'burned' into the hair]

burn n.[6] [1950s] (US Und.) execution in the electric chair. [BURN v.[5] (3)]

burn n.[7] (also **burnie**) [1970s+] (US) a sideburn. [abbr.]

burn n.[8] [1980s+] a hard stare.

burn n.[9] [1990s+] importance, relevance, pertinence.

burn v.[1] (also **blast**) [late 14C+] to infect with a venereal disease. [20C+ use is mainly US Black]

burn v.[2] **1** [mid-19C] (US Und.) to work as a BURNER n.[1] (2). **2** [20C+] (orig. US) to fail, to go wrong. **3** [20C+] to annoy, to infuriate, to embarrass. **4** [1920s] (also **burn up**) to cheat (esp. at cards), to defraud (cf. BURN THE KEN v.; BURN THE TOWN v. for earlier uses). **5** [1920s+] to rob, to steal. **6** [1920s+] (also **take a burn**) to become angry. **7** [1930s+] (US Black) to defeat. **8** [1940s] to be sexually aroused, available. **9** [1950s+] to fail to pay a debt, meet an obligation. **10** [1950s+] (drugs) to sell cut or second-rate drugs, or simply to take a buyer's money and vanish without delivering the promised drugs; as burn for a stash, to steal a dealer's cache of drugs. **11** [1960s] to experience elation from the effects of an injected drug. **12** [1960s] (US drugs) to steal a fellow user's drugs. **13** [1960s–70s] to betray sexually. **14** [1960s+] to recognize. **15** [1960s+] to arrest. **16** [1960s+] to write a disciplinary report. **17** [1960s–70s] (US Black) to do something well. **18** [1970s] to dismiss an employee, to jilt a lover. **19** [1970s–80s] (US campus) (also **burn for**) to focus on a given goal. **20** [1970s–80s] (drugs) to betray a drug user to the authorities. **21** [1970s+] (campus) to grade harshly. **22** [1970s+] (US Und.) to pass dud cheques. **23** [1980s] (drugs) to overdose.

burn v.[3] **1** [20C+] (US) to smoke a cigarette. **2** [1960s+] (drugs) to smoke a cannabis cigarette. **3** [1990s+] (UK Black/drugs) to smoke a cigarette laced with crack cocaine.

burn v.[4] (orig. US) **1** [20C+] to drive a vehicle, usu. car or motorcycle, fast. **2** [1940s+] (also **burn one's soles**) to go fast, to leave at high speed. [SE burn up the road]

burn v.[5] **1** [1910s+] (orig. US) to be punished, to get into trouble. **2** [1920s+] (orig. US) to punish; ext. as BURN SOMEONE'S EARS v. **3** [1920s+] (orig. US) to execute or be executed in the electric chair; thus burning party, judicial execution. **4** [1930s+] (orig. US) (also **burn up**) to shoot dead. **5** [1930s+] to kill, to murder. **6** [1960s+] (orig. US) to attack, verbally or physically. **7** [1960s] (US campus) to turn down a request for a date. **8** [1980s+] (US) to cause trouble for someone.

burn v.[6] **1** [1960s+] (US Black) to prepare food, to cook, esp. to cook well. **2** [1980s] (Aus.) to have a barbecue.

burn v.[7] [1970s] (US Black) to improvise; orig. in music, but latterly in any context.

burn v.[8] **1** [1970s+] (US) to photocopy. **2** [2000s] (orig. computing) to record (information/music) onto a writable CD-Rom. [the heating involved in the process]

burn! excl. [1980s+] (US campus) a triumphant or gloating excl. used after successfully insulting or verbally attacking someone. [BURN v.[2] (6)]

burn artist n. [1960s+] a con-man, a cheat, esp. in the drug world, where they will either sell second-rate drugs or take a buyer's money and vanish without delivering the goods. [BURN v.[2] (10) + ARTIST sfx]

burn bad powder v. [1910s–20s] to break wind. [the stench]

burn coal v. (US) **1** [1940s+] of a White person, to have sex with a Black person. **2** [1990s+] to have a lesbian or heterosexual relationship.

burn-crust n. [mid-18C–early 19C] a baker.

burn down v. **1** [1930s–60s] to shoot, to kill. **2** [1950s] to overdo, to use to excess. **3** [1960s+] to attack, verbally or physically. [BURN v.[5]]

burndt adj. see BURNT adj.[1] (3).

burned adj.[1] (also **burnt**) [mid-17C–early 19C; 1930s–40s] infected with venereal disease. [BURN v.[1]; thus 18C naval joke, to be sent out a sacrifice and come home a burnt offering, to be sent off to fight for the Navy, but to return carrying venereal disease; 1930s–40s use appears to be US only]

burned adj.[2] (also **burnt**) **1** [1930s+] (US) cheated or robbed of any commodity or possession. **2** [1930s+] (US) treated badly, taken advantage of. **3** [1960s+] (drugs) sold bad, adulterated or fake drugs. **4** [1990s+] (US prison) in trouble, out of luck. [BURN v.[2]]

burned (at) adj. [1940s+] annoyed (with). [BURN v.[2] (6)]

burned out adj.[1] (also **burnt out**) **1** [1920s+] (also **burned**) exhausted, worn out. **2** [1930s+] (drugs) used of a vein that has collapsed due to an excess of injections. **3** [1950s+] having had too much drink and/or drugs, which have taken their toll both physically and esp. mentally. **4** [1960s] (drugs) used of a drug dealer who has been noted by the police. **5** [1960s+] bored with, tired of, exhausted by; usu. as burned out on. [SE burned, burnt, of a fire, out, extinct, used up]

burned out adj.[2] (also **burnt out**) [1990s+] (Irish) annoyed, irritated. [var. on BURNED (AT) adj.]

burned up adj. [1920s+] (orig. US) **1** very excited. **2** extremely angry. [BURN v.[2] (6)]

burner n.[1] **1** [18C] a card-sharp, a swindler. **2** [mid-19C] (US Und.) a confidence trickster who told the victim a story – often simply asking him to change a banknote – that resulted in the production of their wallet; the burner then snatched it and ran off. **3** [1970s] (US Black) a thief. [BURN v.[2]]

burner n.[2] **1** [early 19C] venereal disease. **2** [late 19C] a sharp blow or punch. **3** [1920s–60s; 1980s+] (US Black) a pistol. **4** [1940s] (US) a cheap cigar. **5** [1940s] (US) a pipe. **6** [1950s] an exceptional person. **7** [1990s+] (US teen) fast sexual intercourse. [all fig./ext. uses of SE burn]

burner n.[3] [1940s+] (UK/US Und.) an expert in the use of an oxy-acetylene torch.

burner n.[4] [1970s] (US gay) a cigarette.

burner n.[5] [1990s+] (US Black/teen) a large piece of graffiti, usu. involving many colours. [one 'burns' it onto the wall and/or it glows with colour]

burner n.[6] [1990s+] (US Black/teen) a cellular telephone that is being used illegally. [BURN v.[2] (5)]

burner n.[7] see GREASE-BURNER n.

burners on high adj. [1990s+] (US campus) being in a state of sexual excitement. [SE (*after*)-*burner*, an auxiliary burner fitted to the exhaust pipe of a jet engine to increase its thrust]

burnese *n.* (*also* **burneys, crowns**) [1910s+] (*drugs*) cocaine. [BURNIE n.^{1}]

burn for *v. see* BURN v.^{2} (19).

burn for a stash *v. see* BURN v.^{2} (10).

burnie *n.*^{1} [late 19C–1920s] (*US drugs*) cocaine; orig. a proprietary mix of snuff and cocaine, designed as a catarrh medicine and inhaled through a glass and rubber tube. [BERNICE n.]

burnie *n.*^{2} **1** [1940s] (*US drugs*) a (half-smoked) marijuana cigarette. **2** [1980s] (*US juv.*) a pre-adolescent who smokes, drinks and uses drugs. [SE *burn*]

burnie *n.*^{3} [1990s+] a tyre mark. [BURN RUBBER V. (1)]

burnie *n.*^{4} *see* BURN n.^{7}.

burnie blower *n.* (*also* **burny blower**) [late 19C] (*US drugs*) a cocaine user. [BURNIE n.^{1} + BLOW v.^{4} (1)]

burning *adj.*^{1} [mid-19C+] a euph. for BLOODY adj.^{1}.

burning *adj.*^{2} [1960s] (*orig. US Black*) a general term of approval, wonderful, excellent.

burning-down habit *n.* [1950s+] an extremely heavy addiction to narcotics. [SE *burning down* + HABIT n. (3)]

burning party *n. see* BURN v.^{5} (3).

burning shame *n.* [late 18C–early 19C] **1** a form of sexual 'game', whereby 'a lighted candle [is] stuck into the parts of a woman, certainly not intended by nature for a candlestick' (Grose, 1796). **2** a nightwatchman placed at the door of a brothel, holding a lantern, even in daylight, to deter people from wandering in and out. [puns]

burn it blue *v.* [early 18C] to act outrageously, poss. by speaking very coarsely. [SE *burn* + image of 'turn the air blue' (cf. BLUE adj.^{3})]

burn it out/up *v. see* BURN UP v.^{2}.

burn leather *v.* [1930s–40s] (*orig. US Black*) to dance; to move fast.

burn my breeches! *excl.* [early 19C] a general excl.

burn my clothes! *excl.* [1930s] (*US*) a general excl.

burn off *v.* [1980s+] to accelerate past another driver. [BURN v.^{4} (1)]

burn on *v.* [1980s+] (*US*) to insult. [BURN v.^{2} (3)]

burn one *v.*^{1} [1930s] (*US*) a glass of malted milk.

burn one *v.*^{2} [1960s+] (*drugs*) to smoke cannabis. [BURN v.^{3} (2)]

burn one's collar *v.* [1940s] (*US*) to get very angry. [GET HOT UNDER THE COLLAR v.]

burn one's foot *v.* (*US*) **1** [1920s] to hurry. **2** [1960s] to become pregnant.

burn one's poker *v.* (*also* **burn one's tail**) [19C–1900s] to catch a venereal disease. [fig. use of SE + BURN v.^{1}]

burn one's shoulder *v.* [mid-18C] to be drunk. [? the burn comes from a fire or ? by falling on the stove]

burn one's soles *v. see* BURN v.^{4} (2).

burnout *n.* **1** [1960s+] (*drugs*) a heavy user of drugs. **2** [1970s+] the situation of having exhausted one's capabilities (whether through sheer hard work or through drink and/or drugged excess), being no longer able to function efficiently at a job or discipline. **3** [1980s] a collapse, esp. when sudden. **4** [1980s] (*US*) a burned-out building. **5** [1990s+] (*UK prison*) the setting on fire of a despised prisoner's cell. **6** [1990s+] (*US campus*) LSD (cf. A n.^{3}). **7** [1990s+] spinning the rear wheels of a car without moving, thus causing a cloud of smoke. [BURN OUT v.; orig. 1940s *burnout*, the sudden loss of power in a jet or rocket engine]

burn out *v.* **1** [early 19C] (*US Und.*) to be arrested as a result of a tip-off or an informer. **2** [1910s+] (*also* **burn up**) to become mentally or physically exhausted. **3** [1950s] to die, from over-work, exhaustion. **4** [1950s+] (*US*) to suffer a setback or failure. **5** [1960s] to become bored. **6** [1960s] to use up or exhaust a source for stolen goods. **7** [1960s] (*US campus*) to do well. **8** [1990s+] to stop or give up suddenly. [fig. uses of SE]

burn paper *v.* [1970s] (*US Und.*) to pass counterfeit cheques, money orders or other financial instruments. [BURN v.^{2} (22) + PAPER n.^{1} (1)]

burn powder *v.* [late 18C; 1920s] (*US*) to fire a gun.

burn rubber *v.* (*also* **get rubber, smoke rubber**) **1** [1930s+] to drive a car very fast, esp. when accelerating from a standing start. **2** [1940s–60s] (*orig. US Black*) to have sexual intercourse. [the smoking tyres that accompany acceleration; (2) fig. use of (1)]

burn rubber! *excl.* [2000s] (*US prison*) go away! leave me alone! [BURN RUBBER V. (1)]

burn smoke *v.* [1970s] (*US*) to go very fast.

burn someone's ears *v.* (*also* **burn someone's ass**) [1950s–60s] (*US*) to reprimand severely. [BURN v.^{5} (2) + SE *ears*/ASS n. (5)]

burn someone's goat *v.* [1940s] (*US*) to infuriate, to annoy. [BURN v.^{2} (3) + var. on GET SOMEONE'S GOAT v. (1)]

burnt *adj.*^{1} (*US campus*) **1** [1960s+] disappointed, betrayed, esp. sexually. **2** [1980s] emotionally drained. **3** [1980s] (*also* **burndt**) embarrassed. **4** [1980s+] (*also* **burnt out**) physically exhausted. [BURN OUT v.]

burnt *adj.*^{2} [1980s+] (*US teen*) terrible, hopeless. [BURNED OUT adj.^{1}]

burnt *adj.*^{3} *see* BURNED adj.^{1}.

burnt *adj.*^{4} *see* BURNED adj.^{2}.

burnt (cinder) *n.* (*also* **red hot cinder**) [1910s+] a window. [rhy. sl. = window (Cockney pron. winder)]

burn the breeze *v. see* BUST THE BREEZE v.

burn the grass *v.* [1940s–50s] (*Aus.*) to urinate in the open air (cf. DO AN AGRICULTURAL v.; DO A RURAL v.; GO CATCH A HORSE v.; GO LOOK AT THE CROPS v.; KILL A SNAKE v.; LOOK AT THE WALL v.; LOOK UPON A HEDGE v.; SPLASH THE BOOTS v.; WATER THE FLOWERS v.). [the destructive effect of urine on grass]

burn the ken *v.* [early 18C–early 19C] to stay at an inn, then leave without paying one's bill. [BURN v.^{2} (4), although chronologically much earlier + KEN n.^{1}]

burn the Thames *v.* [late 18C] to accomplish a noteworthy feat. [var. on SET THE THAMES ON FIRE v.; note synon. US regional use *burn up someone's millpond*]

burn the town *v.* [late 17C–18C] of servicemen, to leave a town without paying for one's board and lodging. [BURN v.^{2} (4), although chronologically much earlier + SE *town*]

burn the water *v.* [early–mid-19C] to spear salmon by torchlight. [late 19C+ use is SE]

burn the wind *v. see* BUST THE BREEZE v.

burnt offering *n.* [late 19C+] a joking description of any food that has been burned on the stove.

burnt out *adj.*^{1} *see* BURNED OUT adj.^{1}.

burnt out *adj.*^{2} *see* BURNED OUT adj.^{2}.

burnt out *adj.*^{3} *see* BURNT adj.^{1} (4).

burn-up *n.* [1950s+] fast riding of a motorcycle, esp. used by outlaw bike riders, Rockers etc. [BURN UP v.^{2}]

burn up *v.*^{1} **1** [late 19C] (*orig. US*) to criticize severely. **2** [late 19C+] (*orig. US*) to annoy, to irritate. **3** [late 19C+] (*orig. US*) to cut a swathe through. **4** [1920s–60s] (*orig. US*) to excite. **5** [1920s+] (*orig. US*) to outdo, to surpass. **6** [1920s+] (*orig. US*) to become annoyed, esp. underpinned by embarrassment. **7** [1930s] (*US tramp*) to betray one's partner to the police. [BURN v.^{2}]

burn up *v.*^{2} (*also* **burn it up, burn it out**) [1920s+] to ride fast on a motorcycle, car or other machine.

burn up *v.*^{3} **1** [1930s+] to draw attention to. **2** [1970s] to be under intense police pressure.

burn up *v.*^{4} *see* BURN v.^{2} (4).

burn up *v.*^{5} *see* BURN v.^{5} (4).

burn up *v.*^{6} *see* BURN OUT v. (2).

burn wheels *v.* [1960s+] to drive a car very fast. [one's smoking wheels]

burn with a low blue flame *v.* [1920s+] to be extremely drunk. [the image of lighting the alcohol fumes pouring from one's mouth]

burny blower *n. see* BURNIE BLOWER n.

burn you! *excl.* [late 19C–1920s] go to hell! [earlier dial. use; i.e. burn in the fires of hell]

buroo *n.* (*also* **brew, bro, broo**) [1920s+] (*Ulster/Scot.*) unemployment office, Labour exchange; thus *on the buroo*, unemployed and collecting benefits; an unemployed person. [Scot. pron. of SE *bureau*]

burp *n.* [1920s+] a belch. [echoic]

burp *v.* **1** [1930s–70s] (*US*) to speak in a cheery or arrogant manner. **2** [1930s+] (*orig. US*) to belch. **3** [1960s+] (*Aus.*) (*also* **burp a rainbow**) to vomit (cf. BARF v.). [echoic]

burp a chirp *v.* [1950s] (*US Black*) to sing. [BURP v. (2) + SE *chirp*; assonance]

burpgun *n.* [1950s+] (*US*) an automatic rifle. [BURP v. (2) + SE *gun*]

burp the worm *v.* (*also* **burp the snake**) [1990s+] to masturbate (cf. BEAT ONE'S HOG v.). [BURP v. (2) + WORM n.¹, i.e. play on *burp the baby*]

burr *n.* [16C–early 19C] a hanger-on, one who 'clings'. [SE *burr*, a plant-head that clings to clothes etc]

burra *adj.* [late 19C] (*Anglo-Ind.*) great, large; thus *burra sahib*, a great man; *burra khana*, a banquet; *burra mem*, a great lady; *burra beebee*, a lady who claims precedence at social gatherings. [Hind. *burra*, great]

burrhead *n.* [20C+] (*US*) **1** a Black person. **2** a fool. [SE *burr*, a rough file + -HEAD sfx (2), i.e. the tightly curled Black hair; (2) -HEAD sfx (1)]

burrheaded *adj.* **1** [1920s+] (*US*) having the tight, curly hair typical of Black people. **2** [1940s] (*US*) stupid (cf. AIRHEADED adj.). [BURRHEAD n.]

burrito *n.* **1** [1980s] (*US*) a derog. term for anyone of Latin or Spanish-American descent (cf. BEAN n.⁸). **2** [1980s+] (*US campus*) the penis (cf. ENCHILADA n.; TACO (BELL) n.). [Mex. *burrito*, a maize-flour tortilla rolled around a savoury filling]

burrow *n.¹* [1960s+] (*Aus.*) a pocket.

burrow *n.²* *see* CONY-BURROW n. (1).

burry *n.* [1910s+] (*Aus.*) an Aborigine. [? pron. of *Aborigine*]

burst *n.¹* [mid-late 19C] (*UK Und.*) a burglary (cf. BUST n.²). [SE *burst*, the act of bursting, breaking open]

burst *n.²* [mid-19C–1910s] a spree, a party with much eating and excessive drinking; thus ON THE BURST phr. [SE *burst*, a sudden flurry of activity; 20C use mainly Aus.]

burst *v.¹* **1** [mid-19C] (*US campus*) to fail an examination. **2** [late 19C–1900s] to spend one's money lavishly, to go out on a spree. **3** [late 19C+] to beat up, usu. as a threat *I'll burst him!*

burst *v.²* *see* BUST v.¹ (1).

burst *v.³* *see* BUST v.² (1).

burst a blood-vessel *v.* (*also* **bust a blood-vessel**) [20C+] to lose one's temper, to lose emotional control.

burster *n.¹* (*also* **buster**) [19C] a loaf of bread; thus as *twopenny burster*, a twopenny loaf. [SE *burst*, i.e. it fills one's stomach]

burster *n.²* [mid-19C] (*UK Und.*) a burglar (cf. BUSTER n.²). [BUST v.¹ (1)]

burster *n.³* [mid-19C] **1** an exhausting physical effort. **2** anything of notable size or otherwise remarkable nature (cf. BUSTER n.¹).

burster *n.⁴* (*also* **buster**) **1** [mid-19C] (*orig. boxing*) a heavy fall that could end a fight. **2** [mid-late 19C] a fall from a horse; thus *come a buster*, to fall from one's horse. **3** [1900s] (*Aus.*) in fig. use, 'a cropper'. [one 'bursts' oneself]

burster *n.⁵* *see* BUSTER n.³.

burst him!/her! *excl.* [late 19C] an excl. of annoyance, confound him! the hell with her! etc.

burst in someone's crust *v.* (*also* **bust in someone's crust, cave in…**) [mid-19C–1910s] (*US*) **1** to hit hard enough to break the skin. **2** to suffer a knock or injury that breaks the skin.

burst me bagpipes! *excl.* [1990s+] (*US Black teen*) an excl. of surprise, astonishment, annoyance etc.

burst one's boiler *v.* (*also* **bust one's boiler**) (*orig. US*) **1** [mid-19C] to come to grief, to get into trouble. **2** [mid-19C] to lose one's temper. **3** [mid-late 19C] to lose emotional control. **4** [mid-19C–1940s] (*also* **burst one's boilers**) to overexert oneself physically. [fig. uses of SE]

burst one's soul-case *v.* (*also* **bother one's soul-case, rack…, wear out…, work out…**) [late 19C+] (*W.I.*) to wear oneself out with hard work. [SE *burst/bother/rack/wear out/work out* + SOUL-CASE n.]

burst one's stay-lace *v.* [late 19C] to become over-excited or over-emotional. [SE *stay*, the precursor of the corset]

burst-up *n. see* BUST-UP n.¹ (2).

burton *n.* [1960s–70s] a male prostitute. [rhy. sl.; *Burton-on-Trent* = RENT n.²; ult. UK town]

Burton-on-Trent *n.* [1930s+] the rent. [rhy. sl.; ult. the UK town]

bury *v.* **1** [late 19C–1900s] (*US*) to eat heartily. **2** [20C+] (*orig. US*) to condemn to a long spell in prison. **3** [1900s–30s] (*US prison*) to betray, to inform on. **4** [1900s–50s] (*US*) to hide. **5** [1930s+] (*orig. US*) to kill, to murder. **6** [1950s–80s] (*N.Z./US prison*) to place in solitary confinement. **7** [1970s+] (*orig. US*) to cause serious trouble for. **8** [1990s+] (*orig. US*) to complain to, to be annoyed with. [all fig. uses of SE]

bury a moll *v.* [mid-19C] to run away from one's mistress. [SE *bury* + MOLL n.¹ (1)]

bury a quaker *v.* [mid-19C] to defecate. [SE *bury* + QUAKER n.]

bury ground *n. see* BURY PATCH n.

burying face *n.* [late 19C–1900s] a miserable face. [an expression suitable for a funeral]

bury it *v.* [mid-19C+] of a man, to have sexual intercourse; one of a number of terms relating to the penis in the act (cf. BURY OLD FAGIN v.; BURY ONE'S BONE v.; BURY THE BALDY FELLA v.; BURY THE BRISKET v.; DIP ONE'S WICK v.; DIP THE DAGGER v.; DIP THE SCHNITZEL v.; EXERCISE THE FERRET v.; FLESH (IT) v.; FLESH ONE'S WILL v.; GET IT WET v.; GET ONE'S BANANA PEELED v.; GET ONE'S DIPPER WET v.; GET ONE'S LANCE WAXED v.; GIVE HARD FOR SOFT v.; GIVE IT TO v.¹; GIVE SOMEONE A BONE v.; GIVE SOMEONE SOME (MEAT) v.; GIVE THE DOG A BONE v.; GREASE THE WEASEL v.; HANG ONE'S BUGLE IN AN INVISIBLE BALDRICK v.; HIDE THE BALONEY v.; HIDE THE SALAMI v.; HIDE THE SAUSAGE v.; HIDE THE WEENIE v.; INTRODUCE CHARLEY v.; JOCKUM CLOY v.; LAY (SOME) PIPE v.; LAY THE ROD v.; LOWER THE BOOM (ON) v.; MOISTEN ONE'S WICK v.; PARK THE PINK CADILLAC v.; PLAY COMRADE WOBBLY HIDES HIS HELMET v.; PLAY HIDE THE SALAMI v.; POP IT IN v.; POUND ONE'S MEAT v.; PUT IT IN AND BREAK IT v.; PUT IT UP v.; PUT THE MEAT TO v.; PUT THE WOOD TO v.; SHARPEN ONE'S PENCIL v.; SINK THE LITTLE MAN IN THE BOAT v.; SINK THE SAUSAGE v.; SINK THE SOLDIER v.; SIPHON THE PYTHON v.; SKIN THE LIVE RABBIT v.; SLIP IN DAINTIE DAVIE v.; SLIP INTO v.; SLIP IT TO v.; SLIP SOMEONE THE FISH v.; SOCK IT TO v.; SQUEEZE ONE'S LEMON v.; STICK ONE'S DUCK IN THE MUD v.; STROP ONE'S BEAK v.; TALLOW UP ONE'S POLE v.; THROW THE DAGGER v.; THROW THE HARPOON IN(TO) v.; TIP THE LONG 'UN v.; TOSS IT TO v.; WALLOP IT IN v.; WHACK IT IN v.; WHIP IT ON SOMEONE v.¹; WHOP IT UP v.).

bury old fagin *v.* [1950s] of a man, to have sexual intercourse (cf. BURY IT v.). [SE *bury* + FAGAN n.]

bury one's bone *v.* (*also* **bury one's beef**) [1970s+] (*US Black*) of a man, to have sexual intercourse (cf. BURY IT v.). [SE *bury* + BONE n.¹ (1)]

bury one's bone in the back garden *v.* (*also* **bury one's bone in the back yard**) [1990s+] to sodomize. [BURY ONE'S BONE v. + pun on SE]

bury patch *n.* (*also* **bury ground**) [1960s–70s] (*US*) a cemetery. [dial. *bury*, to be buried]

bury the baldy fella *v.* [1980s+] (*Irish*) to achieve vaginal penetration, thus to have sexual intercourse (cf. BURY IT v.).

bury the brisket v. [1950s+] (US) of a man, to have sexual intercourse (cf. BURY IT v.).

bury the hatchet v. (also **bury the tomahawk**) [mid-18C+] to make up one's differences; thus [late 19C+] *dig up* or *take up the hatchet*, to renew hostilities. [the *hatchet* as a symbol of hostility; 20C+ use is SE]

bury the landlady v. [late 19C] to leave one's lodgings without paying the rent.

bus n.[1] [late 19C–1900s] a dowdy dress. [such a garment is only worth wearing for a trip on public transport]

bus n.[2] 1 [1910s] a boat. 2 [1910s+] an aeroplane. 3 [1910s+] an automobile, a truck etc, esp. a large one. 4 [1920s–40s] a motorcycle, a motorcycle and side-car. 5 [1930s] (US) an elevator, a lift. 6 [1980s] (US campus) a fat woman. [all exts. of SE (omni)bus]

bus v.[1] (also **bust**) [1990s+] (US Black) to have fun, to enjoy oneself. [abbr. BUST A GUT v. (2)]

bus v.[2] see BUS (IT) v.

bus! excl. [mid–late 19C] enough! stop! [Hind. bas, stop]

bus and tram n. [20C+] jam. [rhy. sl.]

bus-bellied ben n. [late 19C–1900s] an alderman. [his stomach has the dimensions of an omnibus; hence the rhyme 'Bus-bellied Ben/Eats enough for ten']

busby n. [late 19C] 1 pubic hair. 2 the vagina. [SE busby, the tall fur cap as worn by various regiments of the British army]

bus driver n. [1990s+] (US juv.) a superior player, use. in '1-on-1' games, e.g. basketball. [the player 'takes the opponent to school']

buse v. see BOOZE v.

buser n. see BUSSER n.[2].

Bush, the n. [1930s+] Shepherds *Bush*, London W12. [abbr.]

bush n.[1] [late 16C–early 17C] (UK Und.) the place where thieves defraud their victim. [the imagery reflects the world of hunting (cf. BEATER n.[1])]

bush n.[2] 1 [17C+] the pubic hair of either sex. 2 [20C+] (Aus./US) a moustache, a beard. 3 [1960s–70s] (Aus.) a young woman, seen in a purely sexual context. 4 [1970s] a hairstyle in which normally short, curly black hair is allowed to grow out around the head.

bush n.[3] [late 19C] the cat-o'-nine-tails. [resemblance]

bush n.[4] 1 [1910s] (US) the countryside, the small towns. 2 [1930s+] (Aus.) the suburbs.

bush n.[5] 1 [1930s+] (drugs) marijuana (cf. AFRICAN BUSH n.). 2 [1980s] (W.I.) second-rate marijuana. 3 [1980s+] cocaine. 4 [2000s] phencyclidine (cf. ACE n.[4]). [(1) and (3) are both plants]

bush n.[6] [1960s] (US) an important person or one who likes to pose as such. [? SE bourgeois]

bush adj.[1] 1 [late 19C+] uncivilized, inferior, rough-and-ready, esp. in combs., e.g. *bush justice*, *bush education*. 2 [1910s+] (US) second-rate, unsophisticated, amateur. 3 [1960s] (US campus) easy. 4 [1960s] (US campus) uninhibited, crazy. [SE bush, the rough, uncultivated countryside; note RMC Duntroon (Aus.) *bush pig*, a very ugly woman or one who, while not otherwise attractive, is sufficiently promiscuous/available for relieving the male's sexual needs]

bush adj.[2] [1990s+] (W.I.) of a woman, well-groomed.

bush v.[1] [mid-19C+] (US) to exhaust, to tire out. [backform. f. BUSHED adj.[2] (1)]

bush v.[2] [1930s–70s] to trick, to lie (to). [BUSHWA n. (1)]

bush v.[3] [1940s+] (orig. US) to ambush, to mug. [abbr. BUSHWHACK v. (1)]

bush v.[4] [1980s+] (US) to act in a second-rate manner. [backform. f. BUSHER n.]

bush ape n. [1940s] 1 (Aus./US) a peasant (cf. BOONIE n.[1]). 2 (Aus.) a rural worker. 3 (Aus.) an itinerant fruit-picker, usu. in Queensland.

bush bacon n. [20C+] (US) a rabbit.

bush baptist n. [20C+] (mainly Aus./N.Z.) one who either has no religion or belongs to a dubious sub-cult. [BUSH adj.[1] (1) + SE baptist]

bush-bashing n. [1960s+] (Aus.) travelling in the bush, either on foot or in a 4-wheeled off-road vehicle.

bush-beat v. see BEAT ABOUT THE BUSH v.

bush-beater n. [mid-17C–19C] the penis (cf. ARSE-OPENER n.). [BUSH n.[2] (1) + SE beater + pun on BEAT ABOUT THE BUSH v.]

bushbitch n. [1980s+] (US) an ugly woman. [SE bush + BITCH n.[1] (1)]

bush boogie n. [1990s+] (US) a Black person. [SE bush + BOOGIE n.[2] (1)]

bush bunny n. [1930s+] (Aus.) a gullible fool (cf. AIREDALE n.). [SE bush + BUNNY n.[3] (1)]

bush-buzzer n. [1980s] (Aus.) a vibrator. [BUSH n.[2] (1) + SE buzzer]

bush carpenter n. [20C+] (Aus.) a second-rate carpenter. [BUSH adj.[1] (1) + SE carpenter]

bush college n. (also **bush university**) [1970s+] (S.Afr.) a derog. description (by Black students) of a segregated, Blacks-only college or university. [BUSH adj.[1] (1)]

bush-cove n. [early 19C] a gypsy. [SE bush +COVE n. (1); their sleeping under hedges]

bush dinner n.[1] [late 19C+] (Aus.) a damper (a form of unleavened cake, baked in the ashes), mutton and tea; thus BUSHMAN'S HOT DINNER n. [SE bush + dinner]

bush dinner n.[2] [1960s+] (US) cunnilingus (cf. BEARD RIDE n.; BOX LUNCH n.). [BUSH n.[2] (1) + SE dinner]

bushed adj.[1] [early–mid-19C] (UK Und./Aus.) poor, impoverished. [SE bush]

bushed adj.[2] 1 [mid-19C+] (orig. US) exhausted, tired out, as if one had been wandering, lost, through the woods. 2 [mid-19C+] (Aus.) disorientated, lost (either lit. in the bush or generally so); thus fig. 'lost' (for ideas, words etc). 3 [1910s] (Aus.) drunk. [SE bush]

bushed on adj. [late 19C] very pleased with.

bushel and peck n. [late 19C+] the neck. [rhy. sl.]

bushel bubby n. [late 18C–early 19C] a woman with large breasts. [SE bushel, a dry measure + BUBBIES n.]

bushel-cunted adj. [late 17C–19C] having a large vagina. [SE bushel, a measure of volume; thus a large quantity + CUNT n.[1] (1)]

bushel of coke n. [20C+] a man. [rhy. sl. = BLOKE n. (1)]

bushel of tits n. [1970s] (US) a woman with large breasts. [SE bushel + TIT n.[3] (1)]

busher n. [1910s+] (US) an amateur, an unsophisticated person. [BUSH adj.[1] (2)]

Bushey Park see under BUSHY PARK.

bush-faking n. [late 19C] sexual intercourse. [BUSH n.[2] (1) + FAKE v.[1] (2)]

bushfire blonde n. [1940s+] (Aus.) a red-headed woman. [the flames of the bushfire]

bush-head n.[1] [1940s] (US) a person with bushy hair.

bush-head n.[2] [1950s–70s] (Aus.) a naïve, unsophisticated person, a peasant. [BUSH adj.[1] (1) + -HEAD sfx (1)]

bush hog n. [1980s] (US) a peasant (cf. BOONIE n.[1]). [SE]

bushie see also under BUSHY.

bushie n. [20C+] (W.I.) a form of unlicensed and very potent rum distilled secretly in the countryside. [SE bush + sfx -ie]

bush lawyer n. [early 19C+] (Aus.) one who claims to 'lay down the law', but has no real authority to do so. [SE bush + lawyer]

bush league n. [1910s+] anywhere considered second-rate, out-of-the-way. [baseball imagery]

bush league adj. 1 [20C+] (US) amateur, unprofessional, unsophisticated; thus *bushleaguer*, a person who is a failure. 2 [1980s] (US campus) unfair, stupid, inadequate. [baseball jargon *bush leagues*, second-rate teams, leagues and thus players]

bushman's bible n. [late 19C+] (Aus.) the Sydney *Bulletin*. [SE bushman, one who lives in the bush or outback + Bible. The magazine always backed the interest of those living outside the big cities]

bushman's breakfast n. [late 19C+] (Aus.) a cough and a look around, or any other minimal 'breakfast' (cf. BARBER'S BREAKFAST n.). [the lack of 'civilized' amenities in the bush]

bushman's clock n. [mid-19C+] (Aus.) a kookaburra or laughing jackass. [its sounds punctuate the day]

bushman's friend n. **1** [late 19C+] (S.Afr.) a large bush-cutting knife. **2** [1980s] (N.Z.) any large-leafed plant that can be used as lavatory 'paper'.

bushman's hot dinner n. [1940s+] (Aus./N.Z.) a damper and mustard (cf. BUSH DINNER n.¹).

bush parole n. (also **bush pass**) [1920s+] (orig. US prison) an escape. [SE bush + parole/pass]

bush patrol n.¹ [1950s+] (US prison) an escape.

bush patrol n.² [1960s] (US) **1** sexual foreplay. **2** sexual intercourse. [BUSH n.² (1) + SE patrol]

bushpig n. [1980s+] **1** (US campus) an extremely ugly woman. **2** (Aus.) a general insult, irrespective of sex. **3** (Aus. prison) a female prison officer. [(1) note acronym c.1986 T.T.B.B.R: 'turn that bush pig round', used when a woman thus described enters a public house]

bush radio n. (also **bush wireless, jail wireless**) [1930s+] (orig. Aus.) a network of gossip and rumour that brings news, often inaccurate, before the official sources (cf. BUSH TELEGRAPH n.).

bushranger n. **1** [mid-19C] (UK Und.) a low-class prostitute. **2** [1940s+] (Aus.) a petty swindler, one who takes advantage of another. **3** [1950s] (Aus.) a dubious business enterprise that exploits rather than serves its customers. [weak use of SE bush-ranger, a highwayman]

bush rat n. [1930s–40s] (US) a peasant, a hillbilly (cf. BOONIE n.¹).

bush-scrubber n.¹ [late 19C] (Aus.) a boor, a bumpkin (cf. BOONIE n.¹). [SE bush + SAusE scrubber, one who lives in the scrub]

bush-scrubber n.² [1940s+] a rural prostitute. [SE bush + SCRUBBER n.² (1); plays on BUSH-SCRUBBER n.¹]

bush-tail adj. [20C+] (Aus.) cunning, deceptive. [image of an animal vanishing into the bush]

bush telegraph n. (orig. Aus.) **1** [mid–late 19C] a member of a bushranging gang whose task is to keep his colleagues informed of the whereabouts of potential victims or efforts to capture them. **2** [mid-19C+] (also **bush telegram**) a network of gossip and rumour that brings news, often inaccurate, before the official sources (cf. BUSH RADIO n.).

bush university n. see BUSH COLLEGE n.

bush up v. [1940s–50s] (Aus.) to confuse, to baffle. [BUSH v.²]

bushwa n. (also **booshwa, booshwah, boushwa, boushwah, bushwah, bushwash**) **1** [20C+] nonsense, lies. **2** [1920s] a pretentious, arrogant person. **3** [1940s] a yokel. **4** [1940s] (US Und.) an outsider who dislikes criminals. [(1) BULLSHIT n. (1) although slightly predates; ? link to Can. bois de vache, buffalo dung; (2) Can. bourgeois, the head voyageur of a trading post or expedition]

bush week n. [1940s+] (Aus.) a fig. 'week' when dubious deals may be proposed and confidence tricks carried out; usu. in phr. What do you think this is? Bush Week?, used to fend off what is considered a dubious suggestion. [the image of the rural 'bush' dwellers coming innocently to town]

bushwhack n. [1930s+] an ambush, a hijack; an assassination. [backform. f. BUSHWHACK v. (1)]

bushwhack v. **1** [19C+] (orig. US) to ambush, to attack without warning; lit. and fig. **2** [late 19C] (US) to seek out, to discover surreptitiously. **3** [late 19C] (US) to hide. **4** [1910s] to borrow without permission; the theory is that such items will, eventually be returned, but the term (and the action) is virtually synon. with stealing. **5** [1910s–40s] (US campus) to have sexual intercourse in a field or wood (cf. BANG v.¹). **6** [1920s] (US) to beat up. **7** [1950s–70s] (US campus) to spy and sneak up on courting couples in automobiles. **8** [1980s] to trick, to deceive. [SE bush-

whack, to live in the backwoods. Those settlers who did so were doubtless versed in moving quietly through the woods in pursuit of prey. Note Schele de Vere, Americanisms (1872): 'Originally it was a harmless word, denoting simply the process of propelling a boat by pulling the bushes on the edges of the stream, or of beating them down with a scythe or a cudgel in order to open a way through a thicket']

bushwhacked adj.¹ [1960s] (orig. US) very drunk (cf. ANNIHILATED adj.). [fig. use of BUSHWHACK v. (1)]

bushwhacked adj.² [2000s] ambushed, hijacked. [BUSHWHACK v. (1)]

bushwhacker n.¹ **1** [19C] (US) an illegitimate child. **2** [19C+] (Aus./US) one who lives far from urban 'civilization'. **3** [mid-19C] (orig. US) an ambusher, an attacker. [BUSHWHACK v. (1)]

bushwhacker n.² [late 19C] the penis (cf. ARSE-OPENER n.). [BUSH n.² (1) + WHACK v.¹ (1)]

bushwhacker n.³ [1950s] (US drugs) a marijuana smoker. [BUSH n.⁵ (1) + fig. use of WHACK v.¹ (1)]

bushwhacker adj. [2000s] uncivilized. [BUSHWHACKER n.¹ (2)]

bush wireless n. see BUSH RADIO n.

bushy n.¹ (also **bushie**) **1** [late 19C+] (Aus./W.I.) one who lives in the country (cf. BOONIE n.¹). **2** [1980s] (S.Afr.) a half-caste. [SE bush]

bushy n.² (also **bushie**) [1980s] (Aus.) a very ugly woman. [abbr. BUSHPIG n. (1)]

bushy adj. [late 19C+] (Aus./W.I.) unsophisticated, countrified. [BUSHY n.¹ (1)]

Bushy Park n.¹ (also **Bushey Park**) [late 18C–19C] female pubic hair; thus take a turn at Bushy Park, of a man, to have sexual intercourse. [BUSH n.² (1) + pun on the place Bushey Park, Middlesex, UK]

Bushy Park n.² (also **Bushey Park**) [mid-19C–1960s] fun, a joke. [rhy. sl. = LARK n.¹ (2); ult. the place Bushey Park, Middlesex, UK]

business n.¹ **1** [17C; late 19C+] (UK Und.) criminal activity; thus do a bit of business, to commit a crime. **2** [mid-17C–mid-19C] a vague description of unspecified mechanical/material objects. **3** [18C+] a (difficult) situation; usu. defined by a n./adj; often as look like business, of a person or situation, to look serious or threatening. **4** [mid-18C+] a murder, an assassination; usu. as DO THE BUSINESS v. (2); occas. as get the business. **5** [20C+] a matter in which someone may interfere; thus mind one's own business, to keep out of other people's affairs.

business n.² **1** [17C+] sexual intercourse, irrespective of sexuality; thus do the business, to have sexual intercourse. **2** [early 18C; mid-19C+] a prostitute's euph. for intercourse. **3** [1900s–60s] (US) prostitution as a trade or act. **4** [1920s] (US) a woman. **5** [1940s] the fly buttons or zip. **6** [1940s+] (orig. US) the male or female genitals. **7** [1950s] (US Und.) an effeminate/passive male homosexual.

business n.³ [mid-19C+] a euph. term for faeces or urine; esp. in DO ONE'S BUSINESS v.

business n.⁴ (US) **1** [1930s–40s] intense interrogation, 'the third degree'. **2** [1940s+] complaints, verbal criticism.

business n.⁵ [1930s+] **1** (drugs) the equipment used to take opium and, latterly, heroin. **2** (US prison) a weapon.

business, the n. [late 19C+] **1** the best, the peak of excellence; often found as do the business. **2** cheating, fraud, deception.

business v. [1930s+] (orig. US Black) to be concerned with, to be interested in; thus got the business, to be able to put someone down. [lit. SE do business (with)]

business boy n. [1970s+] a homosexual male prostitute (cf. BUSINESS GIRL n.). [BUSINESS n.² (2) + SE boy]

business end n. **1** [late 19C+] that part (practical or metaphorical) that really matters; thus (US) the business end of a tin tack, the point. **2** [1970s] the anus (cf. ARSE-END n.). [BUSINESS, THE n. (1), i.e. the end that 'does the business']

business girl *n.* [1920s+] a prostitute (cf. AWAYDAY GIRL n.; BUSINESS BOY n.). [BUSINESS n.² (2) + SE *girl*]

businessman's trip *n.* (*also* **businessman's lunchtime high, businessman's special**) [1960s+] (*drugs*) dimethyltryptamine. [unlike the 8-hour duration of a 'normal' LSD TRIP n.⁴ (1), this vastly intensified experience lasts only a few minutes, leaving the user free to get on with other things]

busing *n.* [20C+] (*W.I.*) verbal violence, using obscene and aggressive language. [SE *abuse* v.]

bus (it) *v.* [mid-19C+] to travel by bus; thus similar *tram it*, to travel by tram.

busk *v.* **1** [mid-19C] to sell obscene songs and books in the street or in public houses. **2** [mid-19C] to sell goods to a retailer. **3** [mid-19C+] to work as a street performer. [? naut. jargon *busk*, to cruise the seas, esp. as a pirate; ult. Ital. *buscare*, to filch, to prowl]

busker *n.* [mid-19C–1950s] one who sings, plays or otherwise entertains in public houses or, latterly, on the street, typically alongside a cinema queue. [BUSK v. (3); SE after mid-20C]

busk it *v.* [2000s] to act or speak in a nonchalant manner. [fig. use of BUSK v. (3)]

busman *n. see* BUSTMAN n.

busnacking *n.* (*also* **buznacking, buzznacking**) **1** [mid-19C] waiting around, wasting time. **2** [late 19C–1900s] prying, interfering, 'butting in'. **3** [1900s] acting in an excessively fussy, officious manner. [dial. *buzz*, to move around in an agitated manner + dial. *knack*, to talk in an affected manner; ? link to SE *nag*; note naut. jargon *busk*, to tack about]

bus-napper *n.* (*also* **buz-napper**) **1** [late 18C–early 19C] (*UK Und.*) a constable. **2** [late 18C–mid-19C] a young pickpocket. **3** [20C+] (*Aus.*) a policeman. [BUZZ n.² (2) + NAB v.¹; lit. 'pickpocket-taker']

bus-napper's academy *n.* (*also* **buz-napper's academy**) [late 18C–mid-19C] a school for thieves. [BUS-NAPPER n. (2) + SE *academy*]

bus-napper's kinchin *n.* [18C] a watchman. [BUS-NAPPER n. (1) + KINCHIN n. (1), lit. a 'constable's child']

bus ride *n.* [2000s] (*US prison*) a court appearance, to which one is conveyed by bus.

buss *v.* **1** [mid-18C] (*UK Und.*) to steal. **2** [mid-19C+] (*US*) to court. [SE *buss*, a kiss]

buss a lime *v.* [1950s+] (*W.I.*) to enjoy a spontaneous social gathering. [BUST v.⁸ + LIME n.¹]

buss arse *v.* [20C+] (*W.I.*) to beat, to thrash. [BUST v.¹ (4) + ARSE n.¹ (1)]

buss beggar *n.* **1** [17C–19C] an ageing prostitute. **2** [late 18C–early 19C] an aged roué whose enthusiasm for sexual encounters is matched only by the unwillingness of the young and pretty to offer them. [SE *buss*, a kiss + SE *beggar*; in both cases the subject is 'begging for a kiss']

buss-belt *n.* [1960s+] (*W.I.*) a very fat man. [SE *burst belt*]

buss blind cheeks! *excl. see* BLIND CHEEKS n.

buss cove *n.* [mid-19C] a bus ticket collector. [SE *bus* + COVE n. (1)]

buss cunu *v.* [20C+] (*W.I.*) to have sexual intercourse. [BUST v.¹ (4) + CONY n.¹ (2)]

buss dirt *v.* [20C+] (*W.I.*) to make the fastest exit possible. [BUST v.¹ (4) + SE *dirt*]

busser *n.¹* [mid-19C] (*US*) the mouth. [SE *buss*, to kiss]

busser *n.²* (*also* **buser**) [late 19C–1900s] a bus horse.

bussie *n.* (*also* **bussy**) [1940s–80s] (*US*) a bus worker.

buss me rass! *excl.* [1940s+] (*W.I.*) a dismissive excl., lit. KISS MY ARSE! excl. [SE *buss* + RAAS n. (1)]

bussy *n. see* BUSSIE n.

bust *n.¹* **1** [mid-19C+] (*US*) an absolute failure, esp. an embarrassing one or a misjudgement. **2** [late 19C–1900s; 1960s] (*US campus*) failure in one's examinations; a hard examination. **3** [20C+] (*orig. US*) (*also* **busting**) a financial collapse. **4** [20C+]

a demotion. **5** [1930s] (*US tramp*) a serious mistake; a piece of very bad luck. **6** [1940s] (*US*) a piece of false information. **7** [1980s+] (*US campus*) fault, as in *my bust*. **8** [1990s+] (*US Black gang*) a coward, a weakling. [dial. var. on SE *burst*]

bust *n.²* **1** [mid-19C+] a burglary; thus *do a bust*, to break into a house (cf. BURST n.¹). **2** [1930s+] (*also* **bust-up**) a police raid, esp. on drug users or dealers. **3** [1950s+] (*US Black*) the police. **4** [1950s+] (*orig. US*) an arrest; a criminal charge. [dial. var. on SE *burst*; (1) 20C+ use Aus.]

bust *n.³* (*also* **bust-up**) **1** [mid-19C+] (*orig. US*) a drinking party, a spree, a celebration; thus ON A BUST phr.². **2** [1980s] (*US campus*) an exciting, good experience or event. [SE *burst*, a frolic, a spree]

bust *n.⁴* [1920s+] a blow, a punch. [BUST v.¹ (4)]

bust *n.⁵* [1960s] (*US Black*) an orgasm. [BUST v.³ (4)]

bust *adj.* [mid-19C+] **1** (*also* **busted**) impoverished, out of funds. **2** bankrupt, subject to financial collapse. **3** broken.

bust *v.¹* **1** [late 18C+] (*also* **burst**) to intrude, to break into. **2** [mid-19C+] to kill, to murder. **3** [late 19C+] to raid. **4** [late 19C+] to hit. **5** [20C+] to fight. **6** [1930s] to defeat. **7** [1940s+] to rape, to deflower (forcibly). **8** [1940s+] to arrest, esp. on a drugs charge. **9** [1960s–70s] (*US*) to catch someone out. **10** [1990s+] to discipline, e.g. at work.

bust *v.²* **1** [early 19C+] (*US*) (*also* **burst**) to cause to go bankrupt, to ruin. **2** [mid-19C+] (*orig. US*) (*also* **bust up**) to come to financial ruin, to go bankrupt. **3** [mid-19C+] to inform against. **4** [late 19C+] to reduce in rank, to demote. **5** [1920s] (*US*) to get the better of, to 'put one over'. **6** [1950s] to 'break', as in journalistic stories. [ext. uses of BUST v.¹]

bust *v.³* **1** [mid-19C] to go on a spree. **2** [mid-19C+] (*orig. US*) (*also* **bust along, bust by**) to go very fast. **3** [late 19C+] to explode with rage and pent-up emotion. **4** [1960s+] (*US Black*) to ejaculate, esp. prematurely (cf. BUST A NUT v.; BUST A SHOT v.; BUST ONE'S KICKS OFF v.; BUST SOMEONE OUT v.). **5** [1980s] (*UK Black*) to launch, e.g. a new song. [var. on SE *burst*]

bust *v.⁴* [mid-19C–1930s] a euph. for DAMN v., used in mild excls.

bust *v.⁵* (*US campus*) **1** [mid-19C–1970s] to fail an examination. **2** [1950s+] to do well, esp. in a test, to receive a good grade, e.g. *he busted an A in Math*. **3** [1960s+] of a college professor, to fail a student. [fig. use of BUST v.²]

bust *v.⁶* (*also* **bust up**) **1** [late 19C+] (*Aus.*) to waste money, usu. on drink. **2** [late 19C+] to have a major quarrel, to end a love-affair, to divorce. **3** [1920s+] (*orig. US*) to break down in laughter. **4** [1930s] to make someone depressed. **5** [1980s+] (*US*) to make someone else laugh. [ext. uses of BUST v.¹]

bust *v.⁷* [1930s] (*US*) to appear, to arrive.

bust *v.⁸* [1950s+] (*US Black*) an all-purpose v. of action, to do, to happen.

bust *v.⁹* [1980s+] (*US Black*) to pay attention, to notice, to listen to. [fig. use of BUST v.¹]

bust *v.¹⁰ see* BUS v.¹.

bust *v.¹¹ see* BUST OUT v.⁵ (1).

bust! *excl.* [1900s] a euph. for DAMN! excl. [BUST v.⁴]

busta *n.* [1990s+] (*US Black teen*) **1** a fake person, a weak individual, a general derog. term. **2** an informer, a person who tattle-tales. [BUSTER n.¹ (8)]

busta backbone *n.* [1950s] (*W.I.*) a tough sugar candy, extremely hard to chew. [the effort of chewing it will *bust one's backbone*]

bust a blood-vessel *v. see* BURST A BLOOD-VESSEL v.

busta brown *n. see* BUSTER BROWN n.

bust a cap *v.* (*also* **bust caps**) **1** [1930s+] (*US*) to fire a bullet/bullets. **2** [1950s–60s] (*drugs*) to inject a shot of heroin (which comes in capsule form). **3** [1970s+] (*US gay*) in fig. use of (1), to have aggressive, fast anal intercourse (cf. ASK FOR THE RING v.). [BUST v.¹ (4) + CAP n.²/CAP n.⁴ (1)]

bust a cherry *v.* [1940s+] **1** to deflower. **2** to be deflowered; to lose one's virginity. **3** in fig. use, to experience something new. [BUST v.¹ (7) + CHERRY n.¹ (1)]

bust a frog! *excl.* [mid-19C–1930s] (*Cockney*) a mild excl.

bust a gasket *v. see* BLOW A GASKET v.

bust a grape *v.* [1970s+] (*US Black/prison*) **1** to engage in any form of hard, productive work. **2** to lose emotional control; to hit someone. [BUST v.[1] (4) + SE *grape*; var. on BUST A GUT v.]

bust a gun *v.* [1980s] (*UK Black*) to fire a gun. [var. on BUST A CAP v. (1)]

bust a gusset *v.* [20C+] (*US*) to break down with laughter, to lose control, to make a superlative effort. [SE; the straining so hard that the seams of one's clothes split]

bust a gut *v.* (*also* **bust one's gut, break a gut, rupture...**) [1910s+] **1** to work very hard (cf. SPLIT A GUT v.). **2** to strain oneself (esp. by laughing). **3** (*US*) to be overcome with emotion, e.g. rage, delight etc. **4** to beat someone up. [SE *bust/break/rupture* + SE *gut*]

bust a light *v. see* JUMP v.[5].

bust along *v. see* BUST v.[3] (2).

bust a move *v.* [1980s+] (*orig. US Black*) **1** to make a physical move. **2** to make a serious effort, to take action. **3** to snub. [BUST v.[8] + SE *move*/MOVE n.]

bust a nut *v.* (*also* **bust one's nut**) [1930s+] (*orig. US*) **1** to reach orgasm. **2** (*also* **bust one's nuts**) to work hard, to strain oneself. **3** to have sexual intercourse. **4** to masturbate. [SE *bust*/BUST v.[3] (4) + NUT n.[9] (1)/NUTS n.[2] (1); (2) var. on BUST A GUT v. (1)]

bust a rhyme *v. see* BUST RHYMES v.

bust around *v.* [1940s] (*US*) to fight with, to attack. [BUST v.[1] (4)]

bust a shot *v.* (*US/UK Black*) [1970s+] **1** usu. of a man, to reach orgasm. **2** [2000s] to shoot someone. **3** [2000s] to deal drugs. [BUST v.[3] (4)/BUST v.[8] + SHOT n.[2]/SE *shot*/SHOT n.[6] (2)]

bust-ass *adj.* [1980s+] (*US*) a general derog. term. [SE *bust* + -ASS sfx]

bust ass *v.* [1960s+] **1** (*US*) to travel very fast. **2** (*US*) to work very hard. **3** (*US Black*) to do well, succeed. [SE *bust* + ASS n. (5)]

bust a sweat *v.* [1980s+] (*US Black*) to be sexually excited. [BUST v.[8] + SE *sweat*]

bust by *v. see* BUST v.[3] (2).

bust caps *v. see* BUST A CAP v.

bust-down *n.* [2000s] (*US Black*) a share of a cigarette. [SE *bust*]

busted *adj.*[1] (*also* **busted up**) **1** [mid-19C+] dead. **2** [20C+] broken. **3** [20C+] exhausted. **4** [1920s+] depressed, in pain. **5** [1950s+] drunk (cf. ANNIHILATED adj.). **6** [1990s+] (*US Black*) ugly, unattractive. [SE *bust*/BUST v.[1]]

busted *adj.*[2] **1** [20C+] caught out, in a non-criminal context. **2** [1910s+] (*US*) (*also* **busted out**) expelled, thrown out, esp. from an institutional job; reduced in rank. **3** [1940s+] (*orig. US*) arrested, esp. on drug charges. [BUST v.[1]; (2) BUST v.[2] (4)]

busted *adj.*[3] [2000s] (*US campus*) wrong. [fig. use of BUST v.[1]]

busted out *adj. see* BUSTED adj.[2] (2).

busted up *adj.*[1] *see* BUSTED adj.[1].

busted up *adj.*[2] *see* BUSTED (OUT) adj.

buster *n.*[1] **1** [mid-19C] a 'roistering blade'. **2** [mid-late 19C] a dandy. **3** [mid-19C+] a large or full-grown child. **4** [mid-19C+] something or someone exceptional of its or their type (cf. BURSTER n.[3]). **5** [late 19C] as spec. use of (3), the teenage Bavarian giantess, who appeared in London music-halls under the name 'Maid Marian' and after a brief but successful career died before she reached the age of 20. **6** [late 19C] a substantial meal. **7** [1900s–20s] (*US Und.*) one who fights. **8** [1990s+] (*US Black gang*) a loser, a failure, a coward, a general derog. term (cf. BUSTA n.). [fig. uses of BUST v.[1]]

buster *n.*[2] **1** [mid-late 19C] a house-breaker (cf. BURSTER n.[2]).

2 [1900s] a thief, usu. with an identifying n. **3** [1900s–40s] (*US Und.*) a house-breaker's crowbar. **4** [1940s] (*US Und.*) a policeman's truncheon. **5** [1950s] (*US Und.*) one who breaks into premises and destroys the contents, while not actually stealing anything - the aim is to persuade the owner to pay 'protection' money. **6** [1950s+] (*Can.*) a shoplifter. [BUST v.[1]]

buster *n.*[3] (*also* **burster**) [mid-19C–1920s] a spree; thus *in for a buster*, keen to go out on a spree; as *rare buster*, implying at high speed. [BUST n.[3] (1)]

buster *n.*[4] **1** [mid-19C+] a person, often an old and cantankerous one; thus *old buster*, a general term of (affectionate) address. **2** [1920s+] (*US*) a general term of address to any otherwise unnamed male. **3** [2000s] (*US prison*) a term for Northern Mexicans used by Southern Mexicans. [BUSTER n.[1]]

buster *n.*[5] **1** [late 19C+] an exhausting physical effort. **2** a heavy fall. **3** a battle, a fight; a blow. [BUST v.[1] (4)]

buster *n.*[6] [1970s] (*US*) a motor vehicle that gives one a bumpy and painful ride. [abbr. KIDNEY-BUSTER n. (2)]

buster *n.*[7] [1990s+] (*US Black*) an informer. [BUST v.[2] (3)]

buster *n.*[8] *see* BALL-BUSTER n. (6).

buster *n.*[9] *see* BURSTER n.[1].

buster *n.*[10] *see* BURSTER n.[4].

buster brown *n.* (*also* **busta brown**) [1990s+] (*US Black*) a hanger-on. [ext. of BUSTER n.[1] (8)/BUSTA n. (1)]

buster-in *n.* [1930s] (*US*) a house-breaker. [BUST IN v. (1)]

busters *n.*[1] [1960s–70s] (*US Black*) pleasure, enjoyment, 'kicks'. [ext. of BUST n.[3] (1)]

busters *n.*[2] [1990s+] (*US Black*) the police. [BUST v.[1] (8)]

bust fresh *v.* [1980s+] (*US teen*) to look one's best, usu. coupled to a specific event, such as a party, an anniversary, a festival. [BUST v.[8] + FRESH adj.[3] (2)]

busthead *n.* **1** [mid-19C+] (*US*) strong whisky, or gin, esp. when illegally distilled (cf. BUSTSKULL n.). **2** [1960s] (*US tramp*) a drunk. [SE *bust* + *head*]

bus therapy *n.* [2000s] (*US prison*) moving prisoners from one institution to another to ensure their isolation from lawyers, family etc.

bust in *v.* (*also* **bust through**) **1** [late 19C+] (*US*) to enter, with overtones of speed, aggressiveness etc. **2** [1920s–50s] to interfere, to 'butt in'. **3** [1950s] to gatecrash a party. [BUST v.[1]]

busting *n.*[1] [2000s] (*US teen*) doing something skilfully. [BUST v.[8]]

busting *n.*[2] *see* BUST n.[1] (3).

busting *adj.*[1] [mid-19C–1920s] **1** (*US*) very large. **2** very happy. [BUSTER n.[1] (4)]

busting *adj.*[2] [1950s+] desperate. [SE *bursting*]

busting out *phr.* (*also* **busting loose**) [1990s+] (*US Black*) looking good, attractive, well-dressed, successful etc, feeling good. [fig. use of BUST v.[8]]

bust in someone's crust *v. see* BURST IN SOMEONE'S CRUST v.

bust in the ass *v.* [1950s] (*US*) to kick, to harm; lit. and fig. uses. [SE *bust*/BUST v.[1] (4) + ASS n. (2)]

bust it! *excl.* [1920s] (*US*) be quiet!

bustle *n.*[1] [early–mid-19C] money; thus *on the bustle*, cadging a loan. [SE *bustle*, stir, fuss, tumult; 'If a man is worth a thousand pounds, 'tis *blunt*; if as much money be collected in various sums, 'tis *bustle*' (Bee)]

bustle *n.*[2] [1920s–70s] (*US*) the buttocks, the posterior. [SE *bustle*, a 'dress-improver', a small pad or wire framework that accentuates the back of the dress]

bustle, the *n.* [late 19C] (*UK Und*) an act of pickpocketing in which a young woman asks the proposed victim of the crime for the time, pretends to stumble against him, so that her accomplice can protest to the man, while the woman effects the theft.

bustle *v.*[1] [mid-19C+] to confuse, to perplex. [ext. use of SE *bustle*, to stir, to rouse]

bustle *v.*[2] [late 19C] (*UK Und*) to pickpocket. [BUSTLE, THE n.]

bustle-punching n. (also **bustle-pinching, bustle-rub-bing**) [1960s+] (UK police) the action of the frotteur, using the anonymity of a dense crowd to rub one's penis against the nearby buttocks of defenceless women. [BUSTLE n.² + SE punch/pinch/rub]

bustler n. [1910s] (Aus.) a notably hard worker in a shearing shed.

bust loose v. [1920s+] (US) 1 to commence, to start happening. 2 to break free from constraints. 3 to escape from an institution. [SE bust, break + SE loose]

bust-maker n. [late 19C] a seducer, a womanizer. [SE bust, the female breasts, i.e. the increased size of a pregnant woman's breasts]

bustman n. (also **busman**) [1940s+] (Aus.) a burglar, a house-breaker. [BUST n.² (1) + SE man]

bust my boiler! excl. (also **bust my biler!**) [1910s] an excl. of surprise or annoyance. [BURST ONE'S BOILER v.]

bust on v. 1 [1960s] (US) to hit, to attack. 2 [1960s+] (US) to criticize. 3 [1990s+] (US Black) to inform against someone. [BUST v.¹ (4)/BUST v.² (3)]

bust one's ass v. (also **break one's arse, ...ass, ...tail, bust one's arse, ...buns, ...butt, ...pants**) (orig. US) 1 [1930s+] to work extremely hard, to put in a great effort (cf. BUST SOMEONE'S ASS v.). 2 [1940s+] to get injured (esp. in a car or similar crash). [SE bust + ARSE n.¹ (4)/ASS n. (5)]

bust one's balls v. see BREAK ONE'S BALLS v.

bust one's bananas v. [1970s] (US) to work to the limits of one's ability and strength. [SE bust + SE bananas]

bust one's boiler v. see BURST ONE'S BOILER v.

bust one's buns/butt v. see BUST ONE'S ASS v.

bust one's buttons v. (also **pop one's buttons**) 1 [1950s+] (US) to strain oneself physically or emotionally. 2 [1960s+] to swell with pride. [SE burst/pop; the real or fig. bursting out of one's clothing]

bust one's chops v. [1950s+] (US) 1 to talk incessantly. 2 to work hard. 3 to make a great fuss about something?. [SE bust + CHOPS n.¹ (1)/CHOPS n.¹ (3)]

bust one's conk v. [1930s–40s] (US Black) 1 to work very hard. 2 to show one's happiness in an emotional outburst. 3 to go mad. [SE bust+ CONK n.¹ (4)]

bust one's gut v. see BUST A GUT v.

bust one's hump v. [1950s+] (US) to work very hard. [SE bust + fig. use of SE hump, a humped back]

bust one's kicks off v. [1960s] (US) to reach orgasm. [fig. use of SE bust/BUST v.³ (4) + KICK n.⁵ (1)]

bust one's nut(s) v. see BUST A NUT v.

bust one's pants v. see BUST ONE'S ASS v.

bust one's vest v. [1940s–50s] (US Black) to be generous, to display one's munificence. [the image of a chest swelling]

bust open v. [1950s] (US) to distress, to make unhappy. [SE bust + open]

bust-out n.¹ [20C+] an enormous feast. [BUST n.³ (1) + SE out]

bust-out n.² 1 [1930s+] (US) an escape, esp. from prison. 2 [1960s+] (US) failure, ruin, a 'smash-up'. [S?]

bust-out n.³ [1950s–70s] crooked dice.

bust-out adj.¹ [1950s+] (US) an intensifying adj., extreme, tremendous, great, obvious, simple. [SE bust + SE out]

bust-out adj.² 1 [1950s+] illegal, esp. of dice. 2 [1950s+] of a place or machine, e.g. a car, run-down. 3 [1970s+] (US) of a person, impoverished (cf. BUSTED (OUT) adj.). [BUST adj. (1) + SE out/BUST OUT v.⁵]

bust out v.¹ [mid-19C; 1990s+] (orig. US) to betray secrets. [BUST v.² (3)]

bust out v.² 1 [mid-19C+] (orig. US) to escape, usu. from prison. 2 [1940s+] (orig. US) to run off, to leave. 3 [1990s+] (W.I.) in fig. use, to be successful. 4 [1990s+] (US) to help someone else escape from prison. [SE bust]

bust out v.³ [late 19C; 1990s+] (US Black) to laugh. [SE burst/bust out laughing]

bust out v.⁴ [late 19C+] to do, to perform, to make happen.

bust out v.⁵ 1 [1930s+] (US campus) (also **bust**) to expel a student. 2 [1960s+] (US) to ruin financially, esp. through gambling. 3 [1960s+] to ruin, to destroy. 4 [1970s] to dismiss from a job. 5 [1990s+] to go bankrupt. [BUST v.² + SE out]

bust out v.⁶ [1960s+] (US Black/P.R.) to deflower. [ext. of BUST v.¹ (7)]

bust out v.⁷ [1990s+] to shout at someone, to tell someone off.

bust-out joint n. [1930s–50s] an illegal gambling establishment. [BUST-OUT adj.² (1) + JOINT n.⁴ (3)]

bust-out man n. [1960s] (US Und.) a house gambler who cheats the bettors at a casino. [BUST-OUT adj.² (1) + SE man]

bust out with v. see BREAK OUT WITH v.

bust rhymes v. (also **bust a rhyme, bust rhythms**) [1980s+] (orig. US Black) to work as a RAP n.⁵ music DJ n. or M.C. n. (2). [BUST v.⁸ + SE rhymes/rhythms]

bustskull n. [mid-19C+] (US) strong whisky, esp. when illegally distilled (cf. BUSTHEAD n.; POPSKULL n.; SWELLHEAD n.²). [SE bust + SE skull]

bust slugs v. [1990s+] to fire a gun. [BUST v.¹ (4) + SE slug]

bust some booty v. [1980s+] (US Black) 1 to perform sexual intercourse. 2 to perform anal intercourse (cf. ASK FOR THE RING v.). [SE bust/fig. use of BUST v.¹ (4) + BOOTY n.]

bust someone out v. [1980s+] (US Black) of a man, to have sexual intercourse with someone, to bring someone to orgasm. [SE bust/BUST v.³ (4)]

bust someone's ass v. (also **beat someone's arse, ...ass, break someone's arse, ...ass, ...rass, bust someone's arse**) 1 [1930s+] (orig. US) to beat up, to attack physically (cf. BUST ONE'S ASS v.). 2 [1960s+] (US) to harass, to nag, to annoy. 3 [1970s] (US) to arrest. 4 [2000s] (US) to sodomize. [SE bust/BUST v.¹ (4) + ARSE n.¹ (4)/ASS n. (5)/RAAS n. (1)]

bust someone's balls v. see BREAK SOMEONE'S BALLS v.

bust someone's horns v. [1980s+] (US) to goad, to annoy someone. [var. on BUST SOMEONE'S ASS v. (2)]

bust someone's hump v. [1970s+] (US) to harass, to annoy, to persecute. [BUST SOMEONE'S ASS v. (2)]

bust some z's v. (also **cut (some) z's, hit some z's**) [1960s+] (US) to have a nap; to sleep. [z n.¹]

bust suds v. [1950s+] (US Black) to work as a washer-up. [BUST v.⁸ + SE suds]

bust the breeze v. (also **burn the breeze/wind**) [late 19C+] (US) to go fast, orig. on horseback. [fig. uses of SE bust/burn + breeze]

bust the mainline v. see HIT THE MAINLINE v.

bust this! excl. [1980s+] (orig. US Black) now look here! pay attention! [BUST v.⁸]

bust through v. see BUST IN v.

bust-up n.¹ 1 [mid-19C+] (US) an explosion, lit. or fig. 2 [mid-19C+] (also **burst-up**) a serious quarrel or argument, a fight. 3 [late 19C] a day off. 4 [20C+] a collapse, either emotional or financial. [SE bust, to break; spec. related to (2) BUST v.⁶ (2); (3) BUST v.³ (1); (4) BUST v.² (2)]

bust-up n.² see BUST n.² (2).

bust-up n.³ see BUST n.³.

bust up v.¹ 1 [20C+] to stop something, e.g. a fight, happening. 2 [1920s+] to conclude, e.g. an evening out or a party. [SE bust, to break (up)]

bust up v.² [1960s+] to beat someone up, to hurt someone in a fight (cf. BUST-UP n.¹). [BUST v.¹ (4) + SE up]

bust up v.³ see BUST v.² (2).

bust up v.⁴ see BUST v.⁶.

bust water v. see BREAK WATER v.

busty adj. [1910s+] of a female, having large breasts; often in combs., e.g. busty beauty. [SE bust, the female breasts]

busy n. (*also* **bizzie, bizzy, busybody**) [20C+] a policeman, spec. a CID officer, a detective. [SE *busybody*; their rushing around, unlike a uniformed officer, who plods along a set beat]

busy adj. [1970s] interfering, 'nosy'.

busy as a one-armed paper-hanger phr. (*also ...a bird dog, ...a one-armed bill-poster, ...a one-armed milker, ...a one-legged man in an ass-kicking contest, ...a one-legged tap-dancer*) [20C+] (*orig. Aus./US*) extremely busy; often ext. by *with hives* or *with an itch*.

busy bee n.[1] [1950s] (*UK juv.*) a policeman (cf. ANIMAL n.[1]). [ext. of BUSY n.]

busy bee n.[2] [1970s+] (*drugs*) phencyclidine (cf. ACE n.[4]). [rhy. sl. = PCP n.]

busybody n. *see* BUSY n.

busy-lickum n. [1990s+] (*W.I.*) **1** a gossip, a tattle-tale. **2** gossip. [fig. use of SE *busy* + *lick*, to hit]

busy-sack n. [mid-19C–1900s] a carpet-bag. [? SE *business*]

but adv. **1** [mid-19C; 1930s+] (*orig. Aus.*) used (mainly) at the end of sentences to give added emphasis, 'no doubt about it', 'absolutely'; e.g. *He's a nice bloke, but.* **2** [1930s+] (*US*) used as an intensifier, e.g. *but crazy, but cool*; BUT GOOD phr.

butch n.[1] [mid-19C] (*US*) a butcher's knife. [abbr.]

butch n.[2] [1910s] (*Aus.*) a doctor. [abbr. SE *butcher*]

butch n.[3] [1910s+] a vendor, a seller of sweets etc. [abbr. BUTCHER n.[5]]

butch n.[4] **1** [1930s+] (*orig. US*) a nickname for a tough man, e.g. the hero of Damon Runyon's short story 'Butch Minds the Baby' (1930); also a nickname for a large, tough woman (not a lesbian). **2** [1940s] (*US milit.*) a commanding officer. **3** [1940s+] (*orig. US*) a masculine lesbian. **4** [1940s+] (*orig. US*) a short, 'macho' haircut (used for either gender). **5** [1950s+] (*orig. US*) a masculine male homosexual. **6** [1990s+] (*Aus. teen*) a promiscuous young woman. [SE *butcher*, a 'man of blood', a violent person]

butch adj. **1** [1930s+] (*orig. US gay*) studiously masculine, of male or female homosexuals. **2** [1940s+] (*orig. US*) heterosexual. **3** [1940s+] of a woman (irrespective of sexuality), masculine, aggressive. **4** [1960s+] (*orig. US*) tough, manly. [BUTCH n.[4]]

butcha n. [mid-19C] (*Anglo-Ind.*) a child. [Hind. *butcha*, a child]

butch-broad n. [1960s] a masculine lesbian. [BUTCH adj. (1) + BROAD n.[2] (3)]

butch down (on) v. [1980s] (*US*) to act in a physically aggressive manner. [BUTCH n.[4] (1)]

butcher n.[1] [19C] the penis (cf. BACON n.[1]; BUTCHER'S SHOP n.[1]).

butcher n.[2] **1** [mid-19C] (*US*) a butcher's knife. **2** [mid-19C+] (*US*) a surgeon, a doctor, esp. an inefficient surgeon. **3** [1910s+] (*Aus./US*) a barber, esp. a second-rate barber, who cuts people when shaving them. **4** [1920s–40s] (*US prison*) the chief warder. **5** [1940s+] (*US*) a bungler, an incompetent, irrespective of profession. **6** [1950s+] one who practises cosmetic work. [SE *butcher*, the image is of hacking the meat to pieces]

butcher n.[3] [mid-19C+] in playing cards, a king. [his warlike image or joc. ref. to the SE occupation]

butcher n.[4] [late 19C–1900s] stout. [a pun on the SE description of the stereotypically rotund butcher]

butcher n.[5] [late 19C+] (*US*) a seller of sweets, fruit, soft drinks etc, working typically in a cinema or a railway train. [ety. unknown; ? *butcher* as generic for a salesman]

butcher n.[6] [late 19C+] (*Aus.*) **1** a glass of beer, orig. ⅔ pint, later around ½ pint. **2** a 6fl oz (170ml) glass. [? the popularity of beer among butchers, but note BUTCHER n.[4];thus a pun]

butcher v.[1] [mid-19C] a euph. for DAMN v.; used in mild excls. (cf. BUTCHERING adj.).

butcher v.[2] [1970s+] (*US gay*) to deflower a young man.

butcher v.[3] [1990s+] to look at, to stare. [BUTCHER'S (HOOK) n.]

butcher boy n. [1930s] (*US gay*) a male homosexual who has intercourse with a lesbian. [ext. of BUTCH n.[4] (3)]

butchering adj. [mid-19C+] a euph. for BLOODY adj.[1] (cf. BUTCHER v.[1]).

butcher knife n. [1960s+] (*US gay*) the penis. [note synon. 17C euph. *slaughter-knife*]

butcher's n.[1] [late 19C] noon. [Polari]

butcher's n.[2] *see* BUTCHER'S (HOOK) n.

butcher's adj. *see* BUTCHER'S (HOOK) adj.

butcher's canary n. [1930s+] (*Aus.*) a blowfly. [such insects are often found in butcher's shops]

butcher's cart n. *see* BUTCHER WAGON n.

butcher's dog n. [late 18C–early 19C] a married man. [the *butcher's dog* can 'lie by the beef without touching it']

butcher's hoof n. [1990s+] (*Aus.*) a male homosexual. [rhy. sl. = POOF n. (1)]

butcher's (hook) n. (*also* **butcher's look**) [1910s+] a look, a glance; thus HAVE A BUTCHER'S (AT) v. [rhy. sl.]

butcher's (hook) adj. (*Aus.*) **1** [20C+] ill, sick. **2** [1910s+] angry, annoyed; thus *go butcher's hook*, lose one's temper (with). [rhy. sl. = CROOK adj. (3)]

butcher's meat n. [late 18C] meat bought on credit. [it remains the butcher's property, if only in theory, until fully paid for]

butcher's mourning n. [mid-19C] a white hat with a black band. [the normal mourning hat was black, but butchers apparently disliked the colour]

butcher's picnic n. [1960s+] (*Aus.*) a noisy party or other occasion that lacks decorum. [stereotype of the rumbustious butcher]

butcher's shop n.[1] [19C] the vagina (cf. BACON SANDWICH n.). [the image of 'raw meat' + BUTCHER n.[1]]

butcher's shop n.[2] **1** [1930s] the execution shed within a prison. **2** [1960s] (*orig. US Black*) a hospital.

butcher wagon n. (*also* **butcher's cart**) [late 19C+] (*US prison*) an ambulance.

butchilinity n. [1990s+] (*US gay*) of a male homosexual or lesbian, the quality of being masculine. [BUTCH n.[4] (3)/BUTCH n.[4] (5) + SE *masculinity*]

butch in v. [2000s] (*US prison*) to force a fellow prisoner to give oral sex in return for favours, protection etc. [BUTCH n.[4] (5)]

butch (it up) v. [1960s+] (*US gay*) of a homosexual male, to accentuate a spurious masculinity in order to hide one's actual homosexuality; of a lesbian, to accentuate one's 'maleness'. [BUTCH adj. (1)]

butch number n. (*also* **butch queen**) [1960s+] a 'masculine' male homosexual; usu. in question, e.g. *who's that butch number over there?* [BUTCH adj. (1) + NUMBER n.[1] (3)/QUEEN n.[2] (1)]

butchski n. *see* BOOTCHKEY n.

butchy adj. [1950s+] (*US*) usu. of a woman, masculine-looking, looking like a masculine lesbian. [BUTCH adj. (1)]

but good phr. [1950s+] (*orig. US*) very much so, extremely. [BUT adv. (2) + SE *good*]

but hey! excl. [1990s+] (*US*) used as an affectionate acknowledgement or emphasis, esp. when the previous comments have been negative. [abbr. 'But hey, what does it really matter...']

butler's grace n. [early 17C] no financial reward, a thank-you but no money.

butt n.[1] **1** [mid-18C] the vagina. **2** [19C+] the buttocks, the posterior. **3** [late 19C–50s] (*US*) a fool, an unpleasant person (cf. ARSE n.[1]). **4** [1910s+] a generic for one's body, oneself. **5** [1940s+] (*US prison/Und.*) the final portion of one's sentence. **6** [1970s] (*US campus*) a woman. [note (2) precedes (1) but is SE before 19C]

butt n.[2] **1** [mid-19C+] a cigarette or cigar end. **2** [20C+] a cigarette. **3** [1900s] (*US milit.*) in fig. use of (1), a short time. [ext. of BUTT n.[1] (2)]

butt n.[3] *see* BUTTY n.[1].

butt adj. [1990s+] (*US Black/campus*) second-rate, inferior. [BUTT n.[1] (2)]

butt v. [1940s–50s] (*US*) **1** to pass someone a cigarette. **2** to crush out a cigarette. [BUTT n.[2]]

butt adv. [1980s+] (*US campus*) a general intensifier, very, very much, extremely, incredibly, truly. [BUTT n.[1] (2), seen as something physically powerful]

butta/buttah *see under* BUTTER.

butt-ass adv. [1980s+] (*US*) very. [BUTT adv. + -ASS sfx]

butt-bang *see under* BUTTFUCK.

butt boy n. [1980s+] (*US campus*) **1** a homosexual male (cf. ANAL ASTRONAUT n.). **2** in fig. use, a weakling, a subservient figure. **3** a stupid, inept youth. [BUTT n.[1] (2) + SE *boy*]

buttbreath n. [1990s+] (*US*) a general term of abuse. [BUTT n.[1] (2) + SE *breath*; lit. one whose breath smells like faeces]

butt buddy n. [1990s+] a very close friend. [BUTT n.[1] (2) + BUDDY n. (1)]

butt-chuckler n. [1990s+] a masturbator; thus a general term of abusive address. [BUTT n.[1] (2) + pun on SE *chuck*, to toss]

butt-crazy adv. [1990s+] (*US teen*) utterly, completely. [BUTT adv. + SE *crazy*]

butt darts n. [1990s+] (*UK juv.*) anal intercourse. [BUTT n.[1] (2) + SE *darts*]

butt down v. [20C+] (*W.I., Guyn.*) to ignore, to cut dead, to pass by rudely. [SE *butt* v.]

butteker n. [late 18C–19C] a shop. [Ital. *bottega*; Rom. *butteka*]

butt-end n. *see* FAG END n.

butter n.[1] **1** [late 17C+] semen; thus *buttery*, semen-filled (cf. BABY GRAVY n.). **2** [1920s] (*US*) nitroglycerine. [resemblance]

butter n.[2] [early 19C+] flattery, unctuousness.

butter n.[3] [1980s+] (*US Black*) the buttocks. [ext. of BUTT n.[1] (2)]

butter n.[4] [1980s+] (*US Black*) **1** the vagina (cf. APPLE n.[6]). **2** a woman, esp. when sexually active. **3** an attractive man. [SE *butter*, i.e. its smoothness]

butter n.[5] (*also* **butta, buttah**) [1990s+] **1** (*orig. US Black/teen*) a general term of approval, the best, the most fashionable, attractive etc; thus *like butter/butta*, well-executed or performed smoothly or well. **2** (*W.I.*) any easily achieved thing, something requiring no effort. [BUTTER adj.[2]]

butter adj.[1] (*also* **butters**) **1** [1970s] (*US*) naïve, spoilt, foolish. **2** [1980s+] (*orig. US campus*) of an object or person, unfashionable, unsophisticated. **3** [1990s+] (*orig. US campus*) of a woman, unattractive. [play on CHEESY adj.[2]; ? note BHUTTU n.]

butter adj.[2] (*also* **butta, buttah**) [1990s+] (*orig. US Black/teen*) a general term of approval, attractive, excellent etc. ['smooth as butter']

butter v. **1** [late 17C–18C] (*gambling*) to increase one's wager. **2** [18C+] to flatter; thus to disguise with euphemism, flattery etc. **3** [19C] to whip, to thrash.

butter a bun v. [1950s+] (*US*) to have sexual intercourse. [SE *butter* + BUN n.[2] (1)]

butter-and-egg v. [1930s] (*US*) to act or pose as a wealthy provincial businessman or farmer. [BUTTER-AND-EGG MAN n.]

butter-and-egg man n. (*also* **butter-and-egger**) [1920s–60s] (*US*) a prosperous farmer or small-town leading citizen who comes to the big city and poses embarrassingly as a playboy. [the dairy products such men often sold. The term was popularized by the nightclub owner Marie Louise 'Texas' Guinan (1884–1933), otherwise celebrated for her invariable greeting, 'Hello sucker!' Columnist Walter Winchell attributed the term to master of ceremonies Harry Richman, while the original 'butter-and-egg man' was supposedly 'Uncle Sam' Balcon, a New York provisioner. The term was further popularized first by Louis Armstrong's song 'The Butter-and-Egg Man' (1924) and by George S. Kaufman's similarly named play of 1925]

butter-and-eggs trot n. [late 18C] a short jog-trot. [based on the way market women make their way, carrying butter and eggs, into the weekly market]

butter baby n. [1980s+] (*US Black*) **1** a woman, often a mulatto,

who is considered sexy. **2** a woman with large breasts and buttocks. [SE *butter* + BABY n.[3] (1); one of a variety of sl. terms equating women with food + ? early use of BUTTER adj.[2]]

butterbag n. [mid-17C] a Dutchman (cf. BUTTERBOX n.[1]). [stereotype of Dutch as butter-makers]

butterball n. [1940s+] an overweight or plump young person; also as adj. [SE *butter-ball*, a moulded ball of butter]

butter bean teeth n. [1960s–70s] buck teeth. [resemblance to the large white beans]

butter-boat n. [19C] the vagina (cf. BAG n.[1]). [BUTTER n.[1] (1) + SE *boat* + pun on SE *butter-boat*, a vessel in which one serves melted butter]

butterbox n.[1] **1** [early 17C–mid-19C] a Dutchman (cf. BUTTERBAG n.). **2** [mid-19C] a German. [Dutch butter production and consumption]

butterbox n.[2] **1** [late 17C] a fop. **2** [1960s+] an effeminate male; also attrib. [the 'softness' of butter]

butterbox n.[3] [early 18C] the vagina (cf. BAG n.[1]). [BUTTER n.[1] (1) + SE *box*; Nares perhaps prudishly, prefers the def. 'a woman's breast' ? but Rawson (1989) notes that F&H also include that def. (although they may be merely echoing Nares)]

butterbrain n. [1970s+] (*US*) a fool (cf. APPLEHEAD n.; BAKEBRAIN n.). [BUTTERFINGERS n. + sfx *-brain*]

buttercup n. **1** [late 19C–1920s] a pet name for a child. **2** [1920s] (*US*) a young boy. **3** [1930s–40s] an effeminate male homosexual. **4** [1960s] (*US*) a pretty young girl.

buttered adj.[1] **1** [mid–late 19C] (*US*) whipped, flogged. **2** [late 19C] subjected to sexual intercourse. [(1) BUTTER v. (3); (2) ext. use/BUTTER n.[1] (1)]

buttered adj.[2] [1940s+] (*US Black*) well-turned-out, elegant. [SE *butter* + sfx *-ed*, i.e. smooth]

buttered adj.[3] [1990s+] drunk (cf. ANNIHILATED adj.). [? fig. use of BUTTER v. (3)]

buttered bread adj. [1990s+] dead. [rhy. sl.]

buttered bun n.[1] **1** [mid-17C+] (*also* **buttered scone**) a woman who has had intercourse with one man and is about to repeat this immediately with a new partner; thus *have/do/go in on the buttered bun/scone*, of a man, to take second place in a bout of serial intercourse. **2** [late 17C+] a mistress, a prostitute. [play on SE + BUTTER n.[1] (1) +BUN n.[2] (1)]

buttered bun n.[2] [early 18C] a country fool, a rustic simpleton.

buttered bun n.[3] (*also* **buttered scone**) [1940s+] (*bingo*) the number 1 (cf. ALDERSHOT LADIES n.). [rhy. sl.]

butterface n. [2000s] (*US Black*) a female whose body is very attractive, but who has an unattractive face. [pron. 'but her face']

butterfingers n. (*also* **butter-thumbs**) [mid-19C+] (*mainly UK juv.*) one who lets things slip through their fingers; thus adj. *butter-fingered*.

butter flap n. [mid-19C] **1** a trap or light carriage. **2** a cap. [rhy. sl.]

butterflies (in one's stomach) n. [1940s] nerves, apprehension, tension. [the 'fluttering' sensation of adrenalin]

butter flower n. [1970s+] (*drugs*) marijuana (cf. AFRICAN BUSH n.). [? the smooth cannabis resin is the *butter*, the leaves the *flower*]

butterfly n.[1] **1** [late 19C–1940s] an effeminate weakling. **2** [20C+] (*US*) an overdressed, flashy person. **3** [1930s–40s] (*orig. US Black*) an attractive young woman. **4** [1940s–60s] (*US campus*) a flirt. **5** [1950s–60s] (*also* **butterfly boy**) an effeminate male homosexual. **6** [1980s] (*US gay*) a Black homosexual. **7** [1990s+] (*US Und.*) a new, young and attractive prisoner, characterized as being potentially appealing to prison homosexuals. [the perceived qualities of the insect; + ? (3) ref. to Black actress Thelma 'Butterfly' McQueen (1911–95) who played a weeping maid in *Gone with the Wind* (1939)]

butterfly n.[2] [1920s–30s] (*US*) a worthless cheque; thus *butterfly man*, one who passed such cheques. [it flutters away]

butterfly n.[3] see FLOATER n.[6].

butterfly n.[4] see IRON BUTTERFLY n.

butterfly adj. [1900s] of clothes, gaudy, tasteless, flashy. [BUTTERFLY n.[1] (2)]

butterfly boy n. see BUTTERFLY n.[1] (5).

butterfly kiss n. [late 19C+] a 'kiss' made by caressing someone's skin by fluttering one's eyelashes.

butterhead n. 1 [1940s] (US Black) a Black person who, for whatever reason, is considered an embarrassment to their race. 2 [1950s+] (US) (also **butter gills**) a fool; thus **butterheaded**, foolish (cf. APPLEHEAD n.). [BUTTERFINGERS n. + -HEAD sfx (1)]

butterinsky n. see BUTTINSKI n.

butter-knife n. [19C] the penis. [BUTTER n.[1] (1) + SE knife]

buttermilk bottom n. [1920s+] (US Black) the Black area of town. [the stereotyped link between buttermilk and Black appetites; the term was coined for the Black section of Atlanta, Georgia, but spread to many towns and cities in the Southern states]

butter money n. see EGG MONEY n.

buttermouth n. [mid-16C–19C] a Dutchman. [nationalist stereotyping]

butter mouth v. [1990s+] (US Black) to flatter. [BUTTER UP v.]

butternut n. [mid–late 19C] (US) a Northern supporter of the Confederacy during the US Civil War. [the brown Confederate uniforms (worn in the West and which preceded their grey ones) which were dyed with the juice of the butternut]

butter out v. see BUTTER UP v.

butter pecan n. [1990s+] (US Black teen) an attractive Puerto Rican/Latino woman. [SE butter pecan ice-cream, which is light brown and sweet]

butter-print n. [17C–early 18C] a baby, a child, esp. when illegitimate.

butters adj. see BUTTER adj.[1].

butter skin n. [1930s+] (US) money (cf. BAT HIDE n.). [SE butter + SKIN n.[8]]

butter teeth n. [17C+] (US) buck teeth. [var. on BREAD-AND-BUTTER TEETH n. or BUTTER BEAN TEETH n.]

butter the fish v. [1920s] to win at cards. [ety. unknown; culinary imagery]

butter the muffin v. [1990s+] of a woman, to masturbate (cf. APPLY LIP GLOSS v.; BEAT ONE'S MEAT v.). [MUFFIN n.[4] (4); the vaginal juices represent the butter]

butter-thumbs n. see BUTTERFINGERS n.

butter up v. (also **butter out**) [early 19C+] to flatter, to ingratiate oneself; thus buttering up, excessive flattery. [ext. of BUTTER v. (2)]

butter-weight n. [early 18C] a good measure. [SE butter-weight, 18oz (510g) or more to the pound, when the normal equivalent is 16oz (450g)]

butter-whore n. [late 16C–18C] an ill-tempered woman who sells butter.

butter wrapper n. [late 19C] (Aus.) a newspaper.

buttery adj.[1] [mid-19C] susceptible to flattery. [BUTTER v. (2)]

buttery adj.[2] [1990s+] (US campus) bad. [BUTTER adj.[1] (2)]

buttery adj.[3] [2000s] (US Black) first-rate, excellent. [BUTTER adj.[2]]

buttface n. [1970s+] (US) a general term of contempt with the implication of unattractiveness. [BUTT n.[1] (2) + SE face]

butt fiend n. [1960s] (US) a heavy smoker. [BUTT n.[2] (2) + SE fiend]

buttfuck n. 1 [1970s+] an act of anal intercourse. 2 [1980s+] a tedious piece of work, i.e. PAIN IN THE ARSE n. (2). 3 [1980s+] a disaster, a piece of victimization. [lit. and fig. uses of BUTTFUCK v. (1)]

buttfuck v. (also **b.f.**, **butt-bang**) 1 [1960s+] (US) to subject to anal intercourse; thus derog. adj. buttfucking (cf. ASK FOR THE RING v.). 2 [1970s+] in fig. use, to treat unfairly, to cheat, to deceive (cf. BUDDY-FUCK v.[1]). [BUTT n.[1] (2) + FUCK v.[1]]

buttfucker n. (US) 1 [1960s+] (also **butt-banger**) one who indulges in anal intercourse. 2 [1970s+] a bully. [BUTTFUCK v.]

buttfucking Africa/Egypt n. see BUMFUCK, EGYPT n.

buttfuck motel n. [1990s+] (US) prison. [BUTTFUCK n. (1) + SE motel; i.e. the frequency of sodomy in US prisons]

butt-girl n. [1980s] (US) a woman used to run errands, e.g. for a fashion photographer. [? fig. use of BUTT n.[1] (2), i.e. she has a menial status, or SE butt, a target (of derision)]

butt-grabbing adj. see ASS-GRABBING adj. (2).

butthead n. [1980s+] (US) a stupid or obnoxious person; thus adj. buttheaded. [BUTT n.[1] (2) + -HEAD sfx (1); a term hugely popularized since the early 1990s in MTV's semi-animated series Beavis and Butthead]

butthole n. (US) 1 [1950s+] the anus (cf. A-HOLE n.). 2 [1960s+] a term of contempt. 3 [1990s+] anal intercourse. [BUTT n.[1] (2) + SE hole]

butthook n. [1980s] (US) a lout. [? play on SE buttock]

buttie n. see BUTTY n.[1].

buttiken n. [mid–late 19C] a shop. [? Fr. boutique + KEN n.[1] (1)]

butt-in n. [20C+] (US) 1 concern, affair; usu. in a negative phr. none of one's butt-in. 2 a meddler, one who interferes. [BUTT IN v. (1)]

butt in v. (also **butt into**) [20C+] (orig. US) 1 to interfere, to make a nuisance of oneself. 2 to arrive. [SE butt, to strike or push (with the head or horns)]

buttinski n. (also **buttinsky**, **butterinsky**) [20C+] (orig. US) one who intrudes, interferes. [BUTT-IN n. (2) + -SKI sfx]

butt-kicker n. [1980s+] (US) an outstanding performer at a pursuit. [BUTT n.[1] (2) + SE kicker]

butt-kicking adj. [1980s+] (US) 1 outstanding. 2 strong, powerful, aggressive. [BUTT-KICKER n.]

butt-kissing adj. see ARSE-KISSING adj.

buttlick n. [1980s+] (US campus) 1 a fool (cf. BUTTMUNCH n.; BUTT PLUG n.). 2 a toady. [BUTT n.[1] (2) + SE lick]

butt-licking adj. see ARSE-LICKING adj.

buttload n. [1980s+] (US campus) a large quantity; often in pl. [fig. use of BUTT n.[1] (2)/BUTT adv. + SE load]

buttly adj. see BUTT-UGLY adj.

buttmunch n. [1990s+] a fool (cf. BUTTLICK n.). [BUTT n.[1] (2) + SE munch]

butt naked n. [1980s+] (drugs) phencyclidine (cf. ACE n.[4]). [ety. unknown; ? it strips away one's inhibitions]

buttock n. (also **buttocks**) [mid-16C–early 19C] (UK Und.) a prostitute, esp. one who dispenses her favours for free (cf. BANG-TAIL n.[1]). [metonymy]

buttock v. [mid-18C] to have sexual intercourse (cf. BAGAGA v.). [BUTTOCK n.]

buttock and file n. [late 17C–19C] a prostitute who doubles as a pickpocket. [BUTTOCK n. + FILE n. (2); Ware and others define it as 'a shoplifter' but E.P. (DU) rejects this as erroneous]

buttock and tongue n. [late 17C–early 19C] a shrewish woman. [BUTTOCK n. + SE tongue]

buttock and trimmings n. [late 18C–early 19C] an Irish wager, a rump of beef and a dozen of claret.

buttock and twang n. 1 [late 17C–early 19C] a prostitute who does not double as a pickpocket. 2 [18C] a robbery executed by a prostitute who lures a customer, picked up in a tavern, into a dark alley where she picks his pocket and her male accomplice knocks down the victim so that both can escape. [BUTTOCK n. + TWANG n.[1] (2)]

buttock-ball n. 1 [late 17C–early 18C] a dance at which the chief aim is to find sexual partners, the equivalent of a MEAT MARKET n.[1]. 2 [late 18C–early 19C] sexual intercourse. [BUTTOCK n. + SE ball; the 'Buttock Ball in St Giles', held weekly and described by Ned Ward, A Compleat and Humorous Account of all the Remarkable Clubs and Societies (1709) as 'this School of Venus' and a 'Diabolical Academy', is attended by 'a mottl'd Diversity of

Rakes, Beaus, grave Hypocrites, and Apprentices; Pimps, Bullies, Stallions, Valets, Butlers, and disguis'd Livery-Men; Thieves, Gamesters, Sweetners, Town Traps and Highwaymen; Procurers, Punks, Cooks, Jades and Chambermaids; damn'd filing Whores, sill Sows and Fireships; lewd Widows, wicked Wives and whorish Daughters; these Larded, by Chance, with here and there, a maid, but the fewest of that Sport of any.' Ward suggests that the first such dance was held 'by the Cole-Yard Gateway into *Drury-Lane*', then a centre of prostitution, c.1670]

buttock-banqueting *n.* [mid-16C–mid-17C] working as a prostitute. [BUTTOCK n. + SE *banqueting*]

buttock broker *n.* [late 17C–early 19C] a brothel-keeper. [BUTTOCK n. + SE *broker*]

buttocking *adj.* [late 17C–mid-18C] promiscuous, whorish. [BUTTOCK n.]

buttocking shop *n.* [early 19C] a brothel (cf. BANGING-SHOP n.). [BUTTOCK v. + SE *shop*/SHOP n.¹ (1)]

buttock jig *n. see* DANCE v.¹.

buttock mail *n.* [mid-16C–early 19C] a fine imposed for fornication. [BUTTOCK n. + SE *mail*, payment, tax]

buttock penance *n.* [early 18C] a caning or thrashing at school.

buttocks *n. see* BUTTOCK n.

button *n.¹* 1 [late 17C] the penis. 2 [19C+] a baby's penis. 3 [20C+] (*also* **bell**) the clitoris (cf. BABY IN THE BOAT n.). 4 [1910s+] the chin, esp. in phr. *on the button*, a blow square on the chin and thus in fig. use. 5 [1920s–70s] (*US*) a male or female nipple; occas. of an animal, e.g. a pig. [shape and/or size of SE *button*]

button *n.²* [mid-18C–19C] any form of illicit decoy, esp. the 3-card trick. [? fig. use of SE *button*, something small and worthless]

button *n.³* 1 [late 18C–mid-19C] a counterfeit shilling. 2 [19C] a shilling (5p). 3 [mid-19C] (*also* **shiny button**) any coin. 4 [1940s] (*US Black/campus*) money. 5 [1950s] (*US Und.*) in pl., derisively small amounts, e.g. of money, stolen goods etc.

button *n.⁴* [1910s] (*US*) a bright, cheeky person.

button *n.⁵* [1940s+] (*US Und.*) a lookout. [? BUTTON MAN n.]

button *n.⁶* [1950s] (*US gang*) a switchblade knife. [the *button* that must be pressed to extend the blade]

button *n.⁷* 1 [1960s] (*drugs*) a capsule containing heroin or opium (cf. PILL n.⁴). 2 [1960s+] (*drugs*) mescaline; peyote; often in pl. 3 [1960s+] (*S.Afr. drugs*) a Mandrax (methaqualone) tablet; thus *button-kop* (lit. 'button-head'), a regular Mandrax user. [(2) mescaline is synthesized from peyote SE *buttons*]

button *n.⁸* [1960s+] (*US Und.*) the status of being in a US Mafia 'family'; thus *earn a button*, to be made a member of the Mafia.

button *n. see* BUTTONS n.¹ (2).

button *v.* 1 [mid-19C+] (*UK Und.*) to act as a confidence trickster's accomplice, a decoy. 2 [1910s] of a trick, a ploy, to work. 3 [1990s+] (*US prison*) to keep a lookout. [BUTTON n.²; (3) BUTTON n.⁵]

button B *adj.* [1930s–50s] penniless. [the old payphones, where one could push *button B* in the hope of redeeming some other caller's forgotten change]

button-boy *n.* [late 19C+] a (hotel) page. [his button-adorned uniform]

button-bung *n.* [17C] a button thief. [SE *button* + BUNG n.¹ (3)]

button-buster *n.* [1940s–60s] (*orig. US Black*) a braggart, a boaster. [the image is of a chest swollen with pride]

button-down *adj.* (*also* **buttoned down**) [1950s+] (*orig. US*) conforming, holding establishment, conservative values (cf. BUTTONED UP adj.). [the button-down collared shirts from Brooks Brothers (New York) that are the uniform of the US business establishment]

buttoned *adj.* [1940s] in order, sorted out, arranged successfully. [abbr. BUTTONED UP adj. (2)]

buttoned up *adj.* 1 [1930s+] silent. 2 [1940s+] all prepared,

sorted satisfactorily. 3 [1950s+] repressed (cf. BUTTON-DOWN adj.). 4 [1980s] emotionally balanced. [all fig. uses of SE]

buttoner *n.* (*Aus./UK Und.*) 1 [mid-19C] a decoy. 2 [mid-19C+] the member of a gang running a game of the 3-card trick who persuades passers-by to bet on the inevitably fraudulent game. 3 [late 19C] in ext. use, referring to any crooked businessman. [BUTTON n.²]

button finger *n.* [1990s+] the finger used by a woman to masturbate herself or her partner. [BUTTON n.¹ (3) + SE *finger*; pun on BUTTERFINGERS n.]

button guy *n. see* BUTTON MAN n.

buttonhole *n.* 1 [mid-18C–19C] the vagina (cf. BLACK HOLE n.¹). 2 [1940s–50s] a woman.

buttonhole cousin *n.* (*also* **buttonhole connection, buttonhole relation**) [20C+] (*US*) a distant relation (e.g. a third or fourth cousin), a family friend. [ety. unknown; ? one SE *buttonholes* them and claims a relationship]

buttonhole factory *n.* [19C] a brothel (cf. BANGING-SHOP n.). [BUTTONHOLE n. (1) + SE *factory*]

buttonhole worker *n.* [19C] 1 the penis. 2 a womanizer, a promiscuous man; thus *buttonhole working*, sexual intercourse. [BUTTONHOLE n. (1) + SE *worker*]

button it *v. see* BUTTON ONE'S LIP v.

button jock *n.* [1980s+] anyone who operates a console. [SE *button* + JOCK n.³]

button-kop *n. see* BUTTON n.⁷ (3).

button loose *phr. see* BUTTON SHORT, A phr.

button lurk *n.* [1910s] (*Aus.*) a trick played on a naïve woman by a man, bent on intercourse, who removes a button from his coat and promises that it will serve adequately as a contraceptive pessary. [SE *button* + LURK n. (3)]

button man *n.* (*also* **button guy**) [1960s+] (*US*) a member of the Mafia. [BUTTON n.⁸]

button missing *phr. see* BUTTON SHORT, A phr.

button music *n.* [2000s] HOUSE n.² music. [it is played on machines, with buttons, rather than live instruments]

button one's lip *v.* (*also* **button it, button one's chin, …face, …gabber, …gob, …lipper, …mouth, …nose, …trap**) [20C+] to be quiet, to stop talking; thus *keep one's lip buttoned*, to keep quiet (cf. BUTTON SOMEONE'S LIP v.). [SE *button* + SE *lip/chin/face*/GABBER n.¹/GOB n.¹ (1)/*lipper/mouth/nose/*TRAP n.³]

button on to *v.* [1900s–10s] to grab hold of someone before forcing oneself on their company, whether they like it or not. [the grabbing of the jacket buttons]

buttons *n.¹* 1 [mid-19C+] a page-boy, a doorman. 2 [late 19C+] a policeman, occas. in sing. (cf. BABY-BLUES n.²). [their uniforms]

buttons *n.²* [mid-19C+] brains, native wit; esp. in phrs. *doesn't have all his buttons, doesn't have a full row of buttons, has a few buttons missing, not to have (got) all one's buttons on, to be a button short, have lost one's buttons,* to not be very intelligent; *have all one's buttons done up,* to be smart, to be aware, 'on the ball'.

buttons *n.³ see* BUTTON n.⁷.

buttons and bows *n.* [20C+] (*Aus.*) toes. [rhy. sl.]

button short, a *phr.* (*also* **button loose, button missing**) [20C+] eccentric, one of many phrs. implying the subject is 'not all there'. [var. on NOT ALL THERE phr.]

button someone's lip *v.* [1950s+] to make someone keep quiet. [BUTTON ONE'S LIP v.]

button up *v.* 1 [mid-19C+] to be quiet. 2 [20C+] (*US*) (*also* **button up the day**) to quit work for the day. 3 [1900s] (*Aus.*) of a person, to keep hold of their money. 4 [1930s] (*US prison*) to place in solitary confinement. 5 [1950s–60s] to close, to shut down, to withhold information. [fig. uses of SE; orig. US stockbroker jargon]

butt out *v.* [20C+] 1 to leave. 2 (*W.I.*) to emerge, to come out of a passage or hidden place. [BUTT n.¹ (2) + SE *out*; (2) + ? SE *butt*, v.]

butt out! *excl.* [1960s+] go away! leave me alone! [BUTT OUT v. (1)]

butt peddler *n. see* ASS PEDDLER n.

butt pirate *n.* [1980s+] (*US*) a homosexual male (cf. ANAL ASTRONAUT n.). [BUTT n.¹ (2) + SE *pirate*]

butt plug *n.* (*orig. US*) **1** [1980s+] a plug, usu. rubber, inserted in the anus during sexual activity. **2** [1990s+] a fool (cf. BUTTLICK n.). [BUTT n.¹ (2) + SE *plug*]

butt-plunger *n.* **1** [1970s+] (*US*) a man who inserts a dildo into his own anus then walks around naked while a prostitute looks on. **2** [2000s] (*US gay*) the penis (cf. CHINK-STOPPER n.; COCK SOCKET n.; CORK n.³; CUNT PLUGGER n.; CUNT-STOPPER n.; GAP-STOPPER n.; GOBSTOPPER n.; PLUG-TAIL n.). [BUTT n.¹ (2) + SE *plunger*]

butt-puckered *adj.* [1970s] (*US*) scared. [BUTT n.¹ (2) + SE *pucker*; the supposed need to tighten the anus in the face of involuntary, fear-generated defecation]

butt pussy *n.* [20C+] (*US*) the anus, usu. in a gay context. [BUTT n.¹ (2) + PUSSY n. (2)]

butt rider *n.* [1990s+] (*US juv.*) a male homosexual (cf. ANAL ASTRONAUT n.). [BUTT n.¹ (2) + RIDE v.¹ (1)]

butt-rustler *n.* [2000s] (*US*) a male homosexual (cf. ANAL ASTRONAUT n.). [BUTT n.¹ (2) + SE *rustler*]

butt slut *n.* [1990s+] (*orig. US*) **1** a homosexual male, usu. taking a passive role (cf. ANAL ASTRONAUT n.). **2** a woman who prefers anal to vaginal intercourse. [BUTT n.¹ (2) + SE *slut*/SLUT n. (3)]

butts on! *excl.* **1** [1930s+] (*US*) a cry that calls for the right to smoke the last few puffs of another smoker's cigarette. **2** [1970s+] (*Irish*) a cry to claim someone's apple core.

butt-sprung *adj.* [1930s–40s] (*US Black*) of a garment, ill-fitting, esp. around the buttocks. [BUTT n.¹ (2) + SE *slung*]

butt-suck *v.* [1970s+] (*US*) to toady. [BUTT n.¹ (2) + SE *suck*]

butt-ugly *adj.* (*also* **bugly, buttly**) [1980s+] **1** (*US*) very ugly. **2** (*US*) a general derog. term. [BUTT n.¹ (2) + SE *ugly*]

butt-wad *n.* [1990s+] (*US*) lavatory paper. [BUTT n.¹ (2) + SE *wad*]

buttwhip *v.* [1970s] (*US Black*) to spank, usu. a child; thus *buttwhipping*, a spanking. [BUTT n.¹ (2)+ SE *whip*]

buttwhipped *adj.* [1990s+] drunk (cf. ANNIHILATED adj.). [fig. use of BUTTWHIP v.]

buttwipe *n.* (*US*) **1** [1970s] lavatory paper. **2** [1990s+] a term of abuse. [BUTT n.¹ (2) + SE *wipe*]

buttwooping *n.* [1970s] (*US Black*) a spanking. [BUTTWHIP v.]

butty *n.*¹ (*also* **butt, buttie**) [mid-19C+] (*mainly UK northern*) a friend, a 'mate'. [orig. dial.]

butty *n.*² [20C+] (*mainly UK northern*) a sandwich; thus *jam butty, chip butty* etc. [SE *butter(ed bread)*]

butty *n.*³ [1980s+] (*Aus. drugs/prison*) hashish (cf. AFGHAN n.). [? BUTT n.²]

butty *adj.* [20C+] (*Irish*) short. [BUTT n.¹ (2)]

buvare *n.* [mid–late 19C] a drink. [Polari]

Buxton bloaters *n.* [late 19C–1900s] overweight invalids, wheeling around in bath chairs while they take the medicinal waters. [proper name *Buxton* + SE *bloat(ed)*]

Buxton limp *n.* [late 19C–1900s] the hobbling walk affected by invalids taking the waters. [the popular medicinal springs at *Buxton*, Derbyshire]

buy *n.* [1930s+] (*drugs*) **1** the purchase of a drug. **2** money required to purchase a quantity of drugs.

buy *v.* **1** [1910s+] (*also* **buy into**) to accept, to believe; often in phr. *I'll buy that*, I can accept that; *do you think he'll buy it? do you think he'll be persuaded?* **2** [1930s+] (*orig. US*) to cause, to make happen, to bring upon oneself.

buy a brush *v.* [late 17C–mid-19C] to run away. [SE *buy* + BRUSH n.¹ (1)]

buy a drink *v.* [1940s] (*US*) to pour a drink.

buy a salad *v.* [1990s+] (*W.I.*) to be rendered stupid.

buy a ticket *v.* (*US*) **1** [late 19C+] to die. **2** [1970s] to trust, to

tolerate, to accept someone's statements. **3** [1980s] to call someone's bluff.

buy a woof ticket *v.* (*also* **buy a wolf ticket**) [1980s+] (*US Black*) to capitulate to verbal intimidation. [WOOF v.¹]

buyer *n.* [20C+] (*UK Und./police*) a receiver of stolen goods.

buy into *v. see* BUY v.

buy it *v.* **1** [early 19C; 1920s+] to suffer a mishap, esp. to die or be badly hurt. **2** [1920s+] of an inanimate object, to be broken or destroyed. [(1) a single cit. exists for 1825, but nothing follows for a century; WW1 use is abbr. *buy a packet*]

buy new shoes *v.* [1920s–50s] (*US Und.*) to jump bail.

buy one's boots in Crooked Lane and one's stockings in Bandy-legged Walk *v.* [late 18C–early 19C] to have bandy legs.

buy on the never tick *v.* [1920s] to buy on credit. [SE *buy* + NEVER-NEVER (LAND) n.; TICK n.³ (1)]

buy out *v.* [1950s] (*US*) to escape, to avoid a predicament.

buy someone a hat *v.* [1910s+] (*US*) to bribe someone. [euph.]

buy someone's thirst *v.* [late 19C] (*orig. US*) to pay for someone's drink.

buy the baby (new) shoes *v.* [20C+] (*US*) to act in a purposeful manner.

buy the big one *v.* [1980s] (*US*) to die. [BIG ONE, THE n. (3)]

buy the dick *v.* [1960s–70s] (*US*) to get into trouble; to die. [SE *buy* + fig. use of DICK n.⁴ (1)]

buy the farm *v.* [1950s+] to die. [orig. US Air Force use: 'Jet pilots say that when a jet crashes on a farm the farmer usually sues the government for damage done to his farm by the crash, and the amount demanded is always more than enough to pay off the mortgage and then buy the farm outright. Since this type of crash (i.e. in a jet fighter) is nearly always fatal to the pilot, the pilot pays for the farm with his life' (Leo F. Engler, 'A Glossary of Air Force Slang', *American Speech* XXX:2, in *HDAS*)]

buy the rabbit(s) *v.* [early 19C–1930s] (*orig. US*) to conclude a deal unfavourably, to do badly. [a rabbit is presumably the lesser bargain in this hypothetical deal; note 16C pvb 'who will change a rabbit for a rat?']

buy the ring *v.* [1980s+] to perform anal intercourse (cf. ASK FOR THE RING v.). [SE *buy* + RING n.¹ (2); pun on wedding preparations]

buy the sack *v.* [early 18C–early 19C] to get drunk. [SE *sack*, a variety of white wine imported f. Spain and the Canaries]

buy the wad *v.* [1960s] (*US*) to suffer whatever is worst. [SE *buy* + WAD n.¹ (2)]

buy-up *n.* [1980s] (*Aus. prison*) a prisoner's weekly allowance and the purchases they make.

buz *n. see* BUZZ n.².

buz *v.*¹ (*also* **buzz**) [early 18C–19C] to drain a glass or bottle; occas. to share the last bottle of wine equally among all drinkers, when there is not enough for a whole glass each. [? BOOZE v.]

buz *v.*² *see* BUZZ v.³.

buz-bloak *n.* [mid-19C] (*UK Und.*) a pickpocket who specializes in loose cash and purses (as opposed to jewellery or handkerchiefs). [BUZZ n.² (3) + BLOKE n. (1)]

buz-cove *n.* [early 19C] (*UK Und.*) a pickpocket. [BUZZ n.² (3) + COVE n. (1)]

buz-faker *n.* [19C] a pickpocket, esp. one who makes the victims drunk before robbing them. [BUZZ n.² (3) + FAKER n.; given the victim is a drunkard]

buz-faking *n.* (*also* **buzz-faking**) [mid–late 19C] picking pockets. [BUZZ n.² (3) + FAKE v.¹ (3)]

buz-gloak *n.* (*also* **buzz-gloak**) [19C] (*UK Und.*) a pickpocket. [BUZZ n.² (3) + GLOAK n.]

buzhie *n. see* BOOJEE n.

buz-knacker *n.* (*also* **buzz-knacker**) [mid-19C] a trainer of young pickpockets. [BUZZ n.² (2) + SE *knacker*, a harness maker and (?) a maker of small (harness-related) articles]

buzman *n.* (*also* **buzzman**) [late 18C–mid-19C] (*UK Und.*) a pickpocket. [BUZZ n.² (3) + SE *man*]

buznacking *n. see* BUSNACKING n.

buz-napper *see under* BUS-NAPPER and its combs.

buz-wig *n.* [mid-19C] a pompous fool.

buzwuz *n.* [late 19C] nonsense. [echoic]

buzz *n.*¹ **1** [17C+] chatter, conversation. **2** [1910s+] a rumour. **3** [1920s+] a telephone call; usu. as GIVE SOMEONE A BUZZ v.¹ **4** [1930s] (*US Und.*) an exploratory conversation. **5** [1930s] (*US Und.*) a warning. **6** [1930s+] (*US*) a call on an intercom. **7** [1970s] nonsense. [BUZZ v.¹; note WW1 UK army *buzzer*, a signaller]

buzz *n.*² (*also* **buz**) **1** [early 18C] a thief. **2** [early 18C–mid-19C] a pickpocket. **3** [late 18C–mid-19C] the picking of pockets. **4** [1950s] (*US Und.*) purse-snatching.

buzz *n.*³ **1** [mid-19C; 1930s+] (*orig. US*) a (usu.) pleasant sensation from drinking. **2** [late 19C+] (*orig. US*) a thrill, a feeling of excitement. **3** [1930s+] the immediate response to taking a drug, esp. barbiturates or cannabis. **4** [1970s+] any form of sensation, good or bad. [ext. of SE; i.e. a sense of heightened emotion]

buzz *n.*⁴ [1970s] (*drugs*) phencyclidine (cf. ACE n.⁴). [BUZZ n.³ (3)]

buzz *n.*⁵ [1980s+] (*US*) a close haircut, given with clippers. [the noise of the clippers]

buzz *v.*¹ **1** [late 16C+] to talk about, to gossip, to promote a rumour. **2** [late 19C] (*US*) to scold, to tell off. [SE *buzz*, echoic of the bee]

buzz *v.*² [18C+] to make a move, to go, to arrive, to leave, to depart; usu. in comb. with a prep.

buzz *v.*³ (*also* **buz**) **1** [late 18C+] to pick pockets. **2** [late 19C] in fig. use, to cheat. **3** [1910s–20s] (*Aus./US tramp*) to beg. **4** [1950s] (*US Und.*) to work as a purse-snatcher. [BUZZ n.²]

buzz *v.*⁴ **1** [mid-19C–1960s] (*US*) to question, to interview. **2** [mid-19C+] (*US*) to flirt with. **3** [1900s] to talk. **4** [1910s+] to telephone or to use an intercom. **5** [1910s–20s] (*Aus./US tramp*) to solicit hand-outs. **6** [1950s–60s] (*US*) to irritate. [ext. of BUZZ v.¹]

buzz *v.*⁵ [late 19C+] to throw (hard). [echoic]

buzz *v.*⁶ **1** [1920s+] to happen. **2** [1950s] to make, to prepare, to put on. **3** [1950s+] to become lively, energetic, esp. of the atmosphere at a party or the performance of a rock band.

buzz *v.*⁷ [1940s–60s] (*US Black*) to kiss. [SE *buss*, to kiss]

buzz *v.*⁸ **1** [1960s+] (*orig. US*) to experience a drug pleasurably. **2** [1960s+] (*US teen*) to drive around town in one's car, looking for amusement. **3** [1960s+] (*teen*) to become excited. **4** [1960s+] to swoop on, in an aircraft or vehicle. **5** [2000s] (*US*) to fail to stop at a red traffic light. [BUZZ n.³]

buzz *v.*⁹ *see* BUZ v.¹.

buzza *v.* [late 18C] to challenge someone to empty what remains of a bottle into their glass and then to drink it all down. [? BUZZ v.¹ + SE *all*]

buzzard *n.*¹ **1** [late 16C–19C] a weak, foolish person, a gullible dupe; thus adj. *buzzardly*. **2** [19C+] an old and unattractive person; often as *old buzzard*. **3** [mid-19C+] (*US*) a native of the state of Georgia. **4** [1900s] (*US*) a filthy child. **5** [1900s] (*US milit.*) an honourable discharge. **6** [1900s–40s] (*US*) a worthless horse. **7** [1910s] (*US Und.*) (*also* **bazzard**) a policeman (cf. ANIMAL n.¹). **8** [1910s–30s] (*US tramp*) a second-rate thief; one who preys on women. **9** [1910s–30s] (*US Und.*) a beggar, the lowest form of tramp. **10** [1950s–60s] an animal, a creature. **11** [1980s] an unattractive woman. [all fig. uses of SE; note RMC Duntroon (Aus.) *buzzard*, a woman, often with connotations of the predatory]

buzzard *n.*² [late 19C] (*US*) a silver dollar. [the eagle inscribed on it]

buzzard-bait *n.* [mid-19C+] (*US*) **1** a corpse abandoned in the open. **2** a person fated for death or otherwise doomed. **3** a scraggy old horse.

buzzard-meat *n.* [late 19C–1930s] (*US*) **1** a corpse abandoned in the open. **2** a person fated for death or otherwise doomed.

buzzard roost *n.* (*also* **buzzard's roost**) **1** [late 19C–1940s] (*US*) (*also* **buzzard's row**) a run-down or disreputable place. **2** [1920s–40s] (*US, Southern*) the top gallery in a theatre, usu. reserved for Blacks. [the slaughterhouse area, where buzzards gathered to eat the discarded entrails]

buzz around like a blue-arsed fly *v.* (*also* **run around like a blue-arsed fly**) [late 19C+] to be excessively busy, often to the detriment of others, to rush around headlong (cf. LIKE A BLUE-ARSED BABOON adv.).

buzz bomb *n.* **1** [1940s] (*US*) any sort of strong cocktail. **2** [1980s+] (*US drugs*) nitrous oxide. [BUZZ n.³ + SE *bomb*/BOMB n.⁴ + pun on SE *buzz-bomb*, a flying bomb]

buzz-box *n.* [1920s–30s] an automobile. [SE *buzz*, the sound of the engine + SE *box*]

buzz buggy *n.* [1910s–40s] (*US*) an automobile, esp. a cheap one. [SE *buzz*, the sound of the engine + BUGGY n.¹ (1)]

buzz cruncher *n.* (*also* **buzz crusher**, **buzz stripper**) [1980s+] (*US campus*) a person or thing that destroys a feeling of euphoria, a spoilsport (cf. RAPE SOMEONE'S BUZZ v.). [BUZZ n.³ + SE *crunch/crush/strip*]

buzzed *adj.* [1950s+] **1** mildly drunk, tipsy. **2** mildly intoxicated by a drug. **3** excited. [BUZZ n.³]

buzzed out *n.* [1980s+] (*US drugs*) asleep or in a stupor from taking so many drugs or so much of a drug. [BUZZ n.³]

buzzer *n.*¹ **1** [early 19C+] a pickpocket. **2** [late 19C] (*UK Und.*) a confidence trickster who fools a shopkeeper into parting with a gold sovereign using sleight of hand and some hidden wax. [BUZZ v.³]

buzzer *n.*² [late 19C–1900s] any form of car. [the noise it makes]

buzzer *n.*³ [1910s+] (*US*) a police or private detective's badge. [the officer SE *buzzes* it in one's face; Irwin, *American Tramp and Und. Slang* (1931), suggests a link to BUZZ v.¹ (2)]

buzzer *n.*⁴ [1990s+] a male homosexual. [? he *buzzes* around]

buzz-faking *n. see* BUZ-FAKING n.

buzz-gloak *n. see* BUZ-GLOAK n.

buzzie *n.* [2000s] (*Irish*) a traveller. [the dilapidated *buses* which some travellers use]

buzzies *n. see* BUZZY n.

buzz in *v.* [1930s] to arrive, to enter. [antonym of BUZZ OFF v. (1)]

buzzing *n.* (*also* **buzzing lay**, **fly-buzzing**) [19C+] stealing, esp. picking pockets. [BUZZ v.³ (1) (+ LAY n.⁴ (1)/FLY n.²)]

buzzing *adj.* **1** [1920s+] exciting, active. **2** [2000s] (*US campus*) drunk (cf. ABOUT RIGHT phr.¹). [BUZZ n.³]

buzz it *v.* [1950s] (*US*) to relax, to stay calm. [BUZZ n.³]

buzzkill *n.* (*also* **buzzstomp**) [1980s+] (*US campus*) **1** an unpleasant experience or event. **2** an unpleasant person, esp. one who ruins a hitherto enjoyable time. [BUZZ n.³ + SE *kill/stomp*]

buzzkill! *excl.* (*also* **buzzstomp!**) [1980s+] (*US campus*) a general. excl. of disappointment and irritation, e.g. too bad! that's awful! [BUZZKILL n.]

buzz-knacker *n. see* BUZ-KNACKER n.

buzzman *n.*¹ [mid-19C–1950s] (*US Und.*) an informer. [BUZZ n.¹ (1) + sfx *-man*]

buzzman *n.*² *see* BUZMAN n.

buzznacking *n. see* BUSNACKING n.

buzz off *v.* **1** [20C+] to leave, to depart. **2** [1940s] (*US campus*) to be quiet; often as imper. **3** [1960s] in fig. use of (1), to die. [BUZZ v.² + ext. of SE; i.e. image of busy bees]

buzz off! *excl.* **1** [20C+] go away! **2** [1910s] in fig. use, don't make me laugh!, shut up!, don't talk nonsense! [BUZZ OFF v.]

buzzstomp *see under* BUZZKILL.

buzz wagon *n.* [1900s–60s] an automobile. [the noise]

buzzy *n.* (*also* **boosy**) [1970s+] a female breast; usu. in pl. as *buzzies* (cf. BAZONGAS n.). [SE *bosom*]

buzzy *adj.*¹ [mid-18C] tipsy. [BOUSY adj.]

buzzy *adj.*[2] [late 19C–1930s] crazy, eccentric. [? 'bees in one's bonnet']

buzzy *adj.*[3] [2000s] thrilling. [BUZZ n.[3]]

buzzy house *n.* [1900s] (*US*) a lunatic asylum. [BUZZY adj.[2] + SE *house*]

b.v.h. *n.* [1990s+] the penis. [abbr. *blue veined hooligan*]

bwai *n. see* BWOY n.

B-way *n.* (*also* B'way) [mid-19C+] (*US*) Broadway, New York City. [abbr.]

b.w.o.c. *n. see* B.M.O.C. n.

bwoy *n.* (*also* **bwai**) [1950s+] (*W.I./UK Black*) a boy. [W.I. pron. of SE *boy*]

bwoy! *excl.* (*also* **bwai!**) [1990s+] (*W.I./UK Black*) **1** a general excl. of excitement, pleasure. **2** a general excl. of surprise, disdain. [BWOY n./BOY! excl.]

by *adj. see* BI adj.

by *prep.* [1920s+] in one's opinion, as far as one is concerned, e.g. *by me, by you, by us.* [? Yid. form., e.g. *by me it's OK*]

by a considerable/damn/darn/darned/durn sight *phr. see* BY A LONG SIGHT phr.

by a jugful *phr.* [early 19C+] (*US*) by a great deal, 'by a long chalk', usu. in negative.

by all that's blue! *excl.* [mid-19C] a mild excl. or oath. [Fr. *parbleu!* lit. 'by (a) blue (thing)!'; ? ult. BLUE adj.[1] (3)]

by a long chalk *phr.* (*also* **by long chalks**) [mid-19C+] by a long way, often in negative phr. *not by a long chalk.* [use of *chalk* in scoring points, e.g. in billiards, darts]

by a long shot *phr.* [mid-19C+] (*orig. US*) by a good distance, by a considerable amount; usu. as a negative, e.g. *too fast by a long shot* or *not by a long shot*, in no way at all, by an extremely unlikely chance. [SE *long* + SHOT n.[5] (1)]

by a long sight *phr.* (*also* **by a considerable sight, by a damn sight, by a darn(ed) sight, by a durn sight**) [early 19C+] (*US*) by a long way, by a good deal, usu. as a negative phr. *not by a...* [SIGHT n.[2]]

by a street *phr.* [20C+] by a long way.

by-blow *n.* (*also* **bye-blow**) [late 16C–early 19C] a bastard (cf. BY-CHOP n.; BY-SCAPE n.). [SE *by-blow*, anything that happens, usu. unfortunate, in parallel to the main thrust of one's life or intentions. Ware also suggests Fr. *bibelot*, a rare, precious small *objet d'art*. SE f. 1800]

by Cain! *excl.* [early–mid-19C] (*US*) a mild, euph. oath, *by hell!*

byce *n. see* BICE n.

by chalks *phr.* [late 19C–1910s] (*Aus.*) by a long way; often in negative phr. *not by chalks.* [abbr. BY A LONG CHALK phr.]

by-chop *n.* [17C; 1990s+] a bastard. [var. on BY-BLOW n.]

by Christ! *excl. see* CHRIST! excl.

by Christchurch! *excl.* [1940s+] (*N.Z./UK*) a oath, a euph./pun on BY CHRIST! excl. [using the towns of *Christchurch*, found in both countries]

by Christopher! *excl. see* CHRISTOPHER! excl.

by crackey! *excl.* [late 19C+] a euph. for BY CHRIST! excl.

by crimus! *excl. see* CRIMAST! excl.

by cripes! *excl. see* CRIPES! excl.

by dash! *excl. see* DASH! excl.

bye-blow *n. see* BY-BLOW n.

bye-bye(s) *n.* [mid-19C+] sleep, unconsciousness; esp. in phr. *go to bye-bye(s)*, to go to sleep. [earlier nursery use *bye-bye*, sleep]

bye-drink *n.* [mid-18C–19C] an alcoholic drink, taken other than at mealtimes. [SE *bye and/the bye*]

by George! *excl.* (*also* George!) [late 17C+] a euph. excl. for BY JESUS! excl. or JESUS (CHRIST)! excl.

by ghost! *excl.* [1960s] (*Aus.*) a general excl.

by gigs! *excl.* [mid-16C–17C] a mild euph. for BY JESUS! excl.

by ginger! *excl.* [mid-19C–1930s] (*US*) a mild euph. for BY JESUS! excl.

by Gis! *excl. see* BY JIS! excl.

by-god *adv.* [late 19C+] (*US*) a general intensifier, e.g. *the by-god worst thing ever.*

by god's dines! *excl.* [late 16C–early 17C] a mild oath. [? 14C SE *dignesse*, dignity]

by goles! *excl.* [early 18C–early 19C] a euph. for *by God!*

by golly! *excl.* (*also* **by goley, by gollies**) [mid-19C+] a mild euph. for *by God!*

by good gravy! *excl. see* BY GRAVY! excl.

by gorry! *excl.* (*also* **by gor!**) [mid-19C+] (*orig. US*) a euph. for *by God!*

by gosh! *excl.* (*also* **begosh!**) [mid-18C+] a mild euph. for *by God!* [GOSH n.]

by grabs! *excl.* [late 19C+] (*US*) a euph. for *by God!*

by granny! *excl. see* MY GRANNY! excl. (2).

by gravy! *excl.* (*also* **by good gravy!**) [mid-19C+] (*US*) a mild oath. [euph. for *by God!*]

by guess and by God *phr.* [1930s+] by sheer luck.

by guess and by godfrey *phr.* [1900s] taking a course of action or movement without any real plan. [naut. use; to steer 'at hazard without a set course or without the guidance of landmarks' (*OED*)]

by guess and by golly *phr.* (*also* **by guess and by gosh**) [late 19C+] (*US*) haphazardly, without a planned direction, completely at random.

by gum! *excl.* (*also* **gum!**) [19C+] a euph. for *(by) God!* [GUM n.[2]]

by half! *excl.* [late 17C+] an emphatic intensifier.

by heck! *excl. see* HECK! excl.

by hokey! *excl.* (*also* **by hoky-poky! by hooky! by the hokey! by the hoky-poky!**) [19C+] (*US*) a mild excl. [? euph. for *hell!* or f. SE *hocus-pocus*]

by Jackson! *excl.* [mid–late 19C+] a mild oath, a euph. for BY JESUS! excl.

by Jesus! *excl. see* JESUS (CHRIST)! excl.

by-Jesus *n.* [1940s] the guts, the stuffing, the 'daylights'.

by jimminy! *excl.* (*also* **by Jim! by Jimmy!**) [early 19C+] a mild oath, a euph. for BY JESUS! excl.

by jing! *excl.* [19C–1900s] a mild oath, a euph. for BY JESUS! excl.

by jingo! *excl.* [late 17C+] a euph. for BY JESUS! excl.; intensified as *by the living jingo!* [euph. for BY JESUS! excl. but ? note St Gingoulph (Hotten, 1867); Ribton-Turner, *A History of Vagrants* (1887), suggests a Rom. root via Basque *Jinkoa*, God (lit. 'he who is on high'), adopted by the gypsies of northern Spain and southern France; it may also have been imported by soldiers from those areas who served in Edward I's conquest of Wales in 1284]

by jinks! *excl.* [mid-19C+] a general excl., a euph. for BY JESUS! excl.

by Jis! *excl.* (*also* **by Gis!**) [16C–17C] a euph. for BY JESUS! excl.

by Joe! *excl.* [mid-19C–1940s] (*US*) a mild oath, a euph. for BY JESUS! excl. but note BY JOVE! excl.

by Jove! *excl.* [late 16C+] by God!

by Jupiter! *excl. see* JUPITER! excl.

byke *n.* [1990s+] (*US gay*) a bisexual woman. [BI adj. + DYKE n.]

Byker tea-cake *n.* [1990s+] a headbutt. [*Byker*, a tough area of Newcastle]

by long chalks *phr. see* BY A LONG CHALK phr.

by my cadaver! *excl.* [late 19C–1900s] (*Cockney*) a mild oath.

by my figgins! *excl.* (*also* **by my fig!**) [mid-17C–mid-19C] a general excl. of astonishment or emphasis. [? SE *faith* + ? dimin. sfx *-kins*]

by my hood! *excl.* [late 14C–16C] a mild oath or excl.

by my sowkins! *excl.* [1900s] (*Aus.*) an excl. of assertion.

b.y.o. *phr.* [1960s+] (*Aus./US*) bring your own, refers to bringing drinks to a party or an unlicensed restaurant; thus in ext. use. [abbr.]

b.y.o.b. *phr.* [1950s+] (*Aus./US*) bring your own bottle or booze. [abbr. SE/BOOZE n. (1)]

b.y.o.g. *phr.* [1960s+] (*Aus.*) *bring your own grog.* [abbr. SE/GROG n.[1] (1)]

b.y.o.l. *phr.* [1960s+] (*Aus./US*) *bring your own liquor.* [the abbr. has been ext. to include such usages as *bring your own lunch, bring your own laptop* etc]

by one's lonely *phr. see* ON ONE'S LONELY phr.

by-scape *n.* [mid-17C] a bastard (cf. BY-BLOW n.). [SE *by-,* aside + abbr. *escape*]

b.y.t. *phr.* [2000s] *bright young things.* [abbr.; the orig. *bright young people/things* flourished in the 1920s–30s]

by the balls *phr.* [1910s+] (*orig. US*) at one's mercy; usu. in *phr. have someone by the balls.* [BALLS n.[1] (1); thus the celebrated Vietnam-era motto, 'if you have them by the balls, their hearts and minds will follow', which mocked the official instruction to win over the 'hearts and minds' of the Vietnamese]

by the clock *phr.* [1910s] (*US*) absolutely, definitely. [the regularity of time-keeping]

by the cringe! *excl.* [1980s] a euph for BY CHRIST! excl.

by the good Katty! *excl.* [late 19C] (*UK, northern*) a mild oath, *by the good* (*St*) *Catherine!*

by the great horn spoon! *excl.* (*also* **by the great anchor!**) [mid-19C+] (*mainly US*) a mild excl; a euph. for *by God!*

by the hokey! *excl. see* BY HOKEY! excl.

by the holy! *excl.* [19C–1900s] a general excl. of surprise, excitement, alarm etc.

by the holy poker (and the tumbling Tom)! *excl.* (*also by* the holy iron! by the holy poker of hell!) [19C–1920s] a general oath. ['Irish' (Hotten, 1860)]

by the Lord Harry! *excl.* [late 17C–1940s] a mild oath.

by the mouse-foot! *excl.* [mid-16C–17C] a mild excl.

by the new time *adv.* [1910s+] very quickly. [Irish *the new time,* popular name for daylight-saving time]

by the piper (that played before Moses)! *excl.* (*also* **by the piper that shook the Giant's Causeway**) [19C] a mild excl.

by the powers of Moll Doyle! *excl.* (*also* **by the powers of Moll Kelly!**) [early 19C+] (*Irish*) a mild oath. [for ety. *see* GIVE SOMEONE MOLL DOYLE v.]

by the sacred stars and stripes! *excl.* [late 19C] (*US*) an excl. of surprise. [the 'sanctity' of the US flag]

by the throat *phr.* [1940s+] (*Aus.*) to have the situation under control; usu. as *have it by the throat* or *have* (*got*) *the game by the throat.*

by this hat! *excl.* [late 16C] a general excl.

by way of Cheapside *phr.* [late 18C–early 19C] on the cheap, at a bargain price; often as *come at it by way of Cheapside* or *come home by way of Cheapside.* [pun on proper name *Cheapside,* a well-known street in the City of London. This name comes from AS *chepe,* a market, a place of buying and selling; although directly linked, the adj. use, meaning low in price, does not emerge until the early 16C]

b'zillion *n. see* ZILLION n.

C

C *n.*[1] **1** [mid-16C] 100. **2** [mid-19C+] (*US*) $100 (cf. L *n.*[1]; V *n.*[1]; X *n.*[1]). [SE *century*; Roman numerals]

C *n.*[2] (*also* **the C, cee**) **1** [1920s+] (*drugs*) cocaine (cf. AUNT NORA *n.*). **2** [1990s+] methcathinone. [abbr.]

C *n.*[3] *see* CUNT *n.*[1] (1).

C-3 *adj.* [1910s–30s] third-rate, inadequate, inferior. [play on A-1 *adj.* (1) with the third letter of the alphabet]

c.a. *n.* [1950s] (*US*) a county attorney. [abbr.]

ca *n. see* BIG C *n.* (2).

ca- *pfx see* KER- pfx and its combs.

caad *v. see* CARD *v.*[1].

cab *n.*[1] [mid-17C–early 18C] a Cavalier. [? Sp. *Caballero* or abbr. SE]

cab *n.*[2] (*also* **cabb**) [18C+] *cab*bage. [abbr.]

cab *n.*[3] [early–mid-19C] a brothel. [? SE *cabin* or *cabal*, a group that associates secretly and, by implication, for illegal or subversive activities]

cab *n.*[4] [mid-19C–1910s] a cheat, a 'crib'. [abbr. CABBAGE *n.*[4]]

cab *v.*[1] **1** [early 19C+] (*also* **cab it**) to travel by cab; 20C+ use usu. *cab it.* **2** [1980s+] to drive a cab; thus *cabbing*, working as a cab-driver. [SE *cab*, which, despite Hotten (1860), may 'smack of slang' but is not]

cab *v.*[2] [late 19C] to cheat, to pilfer. [CAB *n.*[4]]

caballo *n.* (*also* **kabayo**) [1960s+] (*drugs*) heroin. [pun on Sp. *caballo*, a horse/HORSE *n.*[8]]

cabba-cabba *adj.* [1990s+] (*W.I.*) rough, vulgar, badly dressed. [ety. unknown]

Cabbage, the *n.* [late 19C] the Savoy Theatre, London. [pun on SE *Savoy cabbage*]

cabbage *n.*[1] **1** [mid-17C–19C] small off-cuts of material, taken from the job in hand and sold off as perks by tailors. **2** [late 17C–18C; 1930s] (*also* **cabbage-eater, cabbage-monger**) a tailor. [? corruption of 17C SE *garbage/carbage*, shreds and patches used as padding; predated by *hell* or *eye*: 'From the first, when taxed with their knavery, they equivocally swear, that if they have taken any they wish they may find it in *hell*! or, alluding to the second protest, that what they have over and above is not more than they could put in their *eye*. Now generally termed *cabbage*' (Hindley, *The Old Book Collector's Miscellany*, 1871–3)]

cabbage *n.*[2] [late 17C–early 18C] a form of hairdressing resembling a chignon, popular at this time. [resemblance]

cabbage *n.*[3] [mid-18C; 1930s] a person, a fellow, a chap (cf. CAULIFLOWER *n.*[3]). [Fr. *choux*, lit. 'cabbage', used as a term of endearment]

cabbage *n.*[4] [mid–late 19C] a 'crib' or other form of cheat used by schoolchildren. [? CABBAGE *n.*[1] (1), tailors' scraps, thus 'padding'; ? OF *cabuse*, imposture, trick; *cabuser*, to deceive, to cheat; also OF *cabas*, cheating, theft; Fr. *cabasser*, to pack up, to cheat, to steal; *cabasseur*, deceiver, thief; 'but evidence is wanting' (*OED*)]

cabbage *n.*[5] (*also* **spinach**) **1** [mid-19C+] a cheap, inferior cigar. **2** [mid-19C+] (*US*) tobacco. **3** [1980s+] (*N.Z. drugs*) low-grade marijuana (cf. AFRICAN BUSH *n.*). [its supposedly being made of *cabbage* rather than tobacco or marijuana leaves]

cabbage *n.*[6] [late 19C] (*Aus.*) a native or inhabitant of Victoria. [CABBAGE GARDEN *n.*]

cabbage *n.*[7] **1** [late 19C+] the vagina; one of a number of terms that equates the vagina with a vegetable (cf. APPLE *n.*[6]; ARTICHOKE *n.*; CABBAGE PATCH *n.*[1]; CAULIFLOWER *n.*[1]; EVERGREENS *n.*; GREENGROCERY *n.*[2]; GREEN MEADOW *n.*; GROCERIES *n.*[2]; MUSHROOM *n.*[2]). **2** [1940s+] a girl, a young woman. [? a play on GREENS *n.*[2]]

cabbage *n.*[8] [20C+] **1** (*orig. US*) cash, banknotes (cf. ALFALFA *n.*). **2** (*S.Afr.*) a 10-rand banknote. [the colour of the notes]

cabbage *v.*[1] [mid–late 19C] to use a 'crib'. [CABBAGE *n.*[4]]

cabbage *v.*[2] **1** [18C–1940s] to steal, to pilfer. **2** [mid-19C–1900s] (*US*) to grab. **3** [late 19C] to plagiarize. [CABBAGE *n.*[1] (1)]

cabbage *v.*[3] **1** [1980s+] (*N.Z. drugs*) to smoke second-rate marijuana. **2** [2000s+] to be intoxicated by drugs or drink. [(1) suggests that the equally green drug has all the potency of the vegetable; (2) adds image of the cabbage as a VEGETABLE *adj.*]

cabbage-contractor *n.* [19C] a tailor. [CABBAGE *n.*[1] (1)]

cabbaged *adj.* [1990s+] **1** absolutely exhausted, metaphorically brain-dead from overwork. **2** rendered imbecilic. **3** drunk or drugged (cf. ADDLED *adj.*). [one has become a 'vegetable' (cf. VEGETABLE *adj.*)]

cabbage-eater *n.*[1] [20C+] (*US*) **1** a German. **2** a Russian. [racial stereotyping: both nationalities are allegedly devoted consumers of cabbage]

cabbage-eater *n.*[2] *see* CABBAGE *n.*[1] (2).

cabbage field/garden *n. see* CABBAGE PATCH *n.*[1].

cabbage garden *n.* (*also* **cabbage patch, cabbage state**) [late 19C–1950s] (*Aus.*) Victoria; thus *cabbage gardener, cabbage patcher, cabbage stater*, a native of Victoria (cf. CABBAGE *n.*[6]). [the state crop]

cabbage-gelder *n.* [mid-19C–1900s] a gardener, a greengrocer. [joc. image of one who gelds or 'castrates', i.e. cuts, the stalks of cabbages]

cabbage hat *n. see* CABBAGE-TREE HAT *n.*

cabbage-head *n.* **1** [late 17C+] a fool, a stupid person (cf. APPLEHEAD *n.*). **2** [mid-19C+] (*US*) a Dutch or German person. **3** [2000s] (*US drugs*) one who will try any drug. [SE *cabbage* + -HEAD sfx (1)/-HEAD sfx (2)/-HEAD sfx (3); the shape and the supposed 'vegetable' matter of which the fool's brain is composed. Such a person is considered 'green']

cabbage John *n.* [1900s] (*Aus.*) a Chinese vegetable seller (cf. AH CABBAGE *n.*). [SE *cabbage* + JOHN *n.*[3]]

cabbage leaf *n.*[1] (*also* **cabbage roll**) [mid-19C–1910s] (*US*) a poor-quality cigar; thus the joc. query *Who's smoking cabbage leaves?* [the quality of the tobacco]

cabbage leaf *n.*[2] (*also* **cabbage leaves**) [1930s–60s] (*US*) money, banknotes (cf. ALFALFA *n.*). [ext. of CABBAGE *n.*[8] (1)]

cabbage-monger *n. see* CABBAGE *n.*[1] (2).

cabbage patch n.[1] (*also* **cabbage field/garden**) [late 19C] the vagina (cf. CABBAGE n.[7]). [pun on GREENS n.[2]]

cabbage patch n.[2] [late 19C–1910s] (*US*) a thing or place of little importance. [the size of such a patch in one's garden and the commonness of the vegetable]

cabbage patch n.[3] *see* CABBAGE GARDEN n.

cabbage plant n. [early 19C] an umbrella. [resemblance]

cabbager n.[1] [19C–1900s] a tailor. [CABBAGE n.[1] (1)]

cabbager n.[2] *see* CABBAGITE n.

cabbage roll n. *see* CABBAGE LEAF n.[1].

cabbage state n. *see* CABBAGE GARDEN n.

cabbage stumps n. [late 19C] the legs. [supposedly reminiscent of cut-off cabbage stalks]

cabbage town n. [20C+] (*US*) **1** the German immigrant section of a town. **2** the poor area of a town. [racial stereotyping: the Germans' taste for *Sauerkraut* or pickled cabbage]

cabbage tree v. [1940s] (*US*) to flee. [rhy. sl.]

cabbage-tree hat n. (*also* **cabbage hat**) [1940s+] (*Aus./US*) an informer. [rhy. sl. = RAT n.[2] (3)]

cabbage-tree mob n. [mid-19C] (*Aus.*) a class of layabout, typified by the wearing of a *cabbage-tree hat* (a hat made of woven cabbage-tree or cabbage-palm leaves).

cabbagio perfumo n. [late 19C+] a cheap cigar (cf. FLOR DI CABBAGIO n.). [cod Spanish meaning 'a perfumed cabbage'; mocking the Spanish/Cuban origin of the best cigars and their names]

cabbagite n. (*also* **cabbager**) [mid-19C] (*Aus.*) a layabout. [CABBAGE-TREE MOB n.]

cabber n. [20C+] (*Ulster*) a ring of dirt around the neck, a 'tide-mark'. [dial. *cab*, to clog with dirt]

cabbie n. (*also* **cabby**) [mid-19C+] a cab-driver. [SE *cab* + sfx -*ie/-y*]

cabeza n. [mid-19C+] (*US, Southwest*) the head. [synon. Sp.]

cabin fever n. [1910s+] lassitude, restlessness or irritability as a result of being confined in too small a space, with no variety in companions or occupations. [coined for those suffering on long sea voyages]

cab it v. *see* CAB v.[1] (1).

cab joint n. [1930s+] (*orig. US*) **1** a brothel (cf. BADGER-CRIB n.). **2** a nightclub to which patrons would be steered, were they to request such a place, by a complaisant cab-driver. [SE *cab* + JOINT n.[4] (3), but note CAB n.[3]]

cable n. [mid-18C; 1990s+] (*US*) the penis.

cabman's rests n. (*also* **rests**) [late 19C–1920s] the female breasts (cf. BRACE AND BITS n.). [rhy. sl.]

cab mat n. [late 19C] **1** a prostitute. **2** the vagina. [CAB n.[3] + SE *mat*, i.e. something one 'lies on']

cab moll n. [mid–late 19C] (*orig. US*) a prostitute who works either lit. in cabs and trains or, poss., from or at a brothel. [SE *cab*/CAB n.[3] + MOLL n.[1] (2)]

caboodle n. (*also* **calaboodle, capoodle**) [mid-19C+] a large mixed-up collection of objects or people; usu. in phr. WHOLE KIT AND CABOODLE, THE n. [? KER- pfx + BOODLE n.[1] (1)]

caboose n.[1] **1** [19C+] (*US*) a person who continually follows along behind, a hanger-on. **2** [20C+] (*US*) the buttocks, the behind. **3** [1920s] (*US*) a slow-witted person. **4** [1950s] (*US*) the last child in a family. **5** [1960s] (*US campus*) the last man in a session of group sex. [for ety. *see* CABOOSE n.[2]; SAmE *caboose* as adopted in the American West to mean the cow-hide container stretched across the rear of the chuck wagon, which, when full, hangs down behind the wagon. Thence it was used by the railroads to mean a wagon (usu. attached to a freight train) in which the crew could eat, sleep and cook. (4) also puns on SE *papoose*]

caboose n.[2] (*US*) **1** [mid-19C–1940s] a cubby-hole, a small room. **2** [mid-19C+] any form of place or room. **3** [mid-19C+] a prison. **4** [1950s] in fig. use, penury, poor living circumstances. [Du.

kabuis, a cook's galley; briefly used in 18C/19C UK naval jargon to mean a galley, but thereafter appears only in US]

caboose v.[1] [late 19C–1930s] (*US*) to imprison. [CABOOSE n.[2] (3)]

caboose v.[2] [2000s] (*US*) to sodomize. [CABOOSE n.[1] (2)]

cab rank n. [1950s+] a bank. [rhy. sl.]

cab-ranker n. [1920s] a cheap cigar. [punning on SE *cab(bage)* + *rank*, offensively smelly]

caca n. (*also* **ca-ca, ka-ka, kaka**) **1** [late 19C+] excrement; also used fig. **2** [1960s+] (*US drugs*) heroin; esp. when inferior, bogus or adulterated (cf. CRAP n.[7]; CROWN CRAP n.; DARK BROWN SHIT n.; DIRT n.[4]; DRECK n.; JUNK n.[5]; MUD n.[3]; POISON n.[3]; SCHMUTZ n.; SEWER n.[2]; SHIT n.[5]; STUFF n.[3]; WHITE SHIT n.). **3** [1970s] (*US*) nonsense, rubbish. [Sp. *caca*, excrement; (2) = SHIT n.[5] (1); (3) = SHIT n.[3] (4)]

caca v. (*also* **make caca**) [20C+] to defecate (cf. CACK v.[1]; CRAP v.[2]; DUKIE v.; DUMP v.[2]; KAK v.; LUMP v.[5]; MESS v.; POO v.; POOP v.[2]; POO-POO v.[2]; POOT v.; SCUMBER v.; SCUMMER v.; SHIT v.[1]; SHITE v.). [CACA n. (1)]

caca! *excl.* [1970s] an excl. of negation or anger. [CACA n. (3)]

cacada n. [20C+] (*W.I.*) a little food or a very small amount of money, typically used to appease a beggar. [CACA n. (1) + Fr. *dents*, teeth. Either no more food than would slightly dirty the teeth or bits of food that remain between the teeth after eating]

cacafuego n. [early 17C–early 19C] a braggart, a noisy bully. [Port. *cagar*, to excrete + Sp. *fuego*, fire, lit. 'shit-fire'. Also the name of a Spanish galleon taken by Sir Francis Drake in 1577]

cack n.[1] [late 19C–1900s] (*US*) a small child. [? CACK n.[2] (1) or SE *cackle*]

cack n.[2] (*also* **cak, kak**) **1** [late 19C+] excrement; also used fig. **2** [1970s+] (*Irish*) a general term of abuse. **3** [1990s+] rubbish, dirt, filth. **4** [1990s+] nonsense, rubbish. [15C–16C SE *cack*, to void excrement, itself linked to synon. Lat. *cacare* and OE *cachús*, a latrine]

cack n.[3] **1** [1900s–50s] (*US Black*) a respected person, an important figure in the community. **2** [1960s] (*US campus*) a good-looking woman. [CACK v.[2] (2)]

cack n.[4] [1990s+] (*Aus*) **1** a laugh. **2** someone who has a good sense of humour. [SE *cackle*]

cack adj. (*also* **cak**) [1990s+] a general negative, disgusting, loathsome etc. [CACK n.[2] (1)]

cack v.[1] [late 18C+] to defecate (cf. CACA v.). [16C–early 18C SE *cack*, to excrete]

cack v.[2] **1** [late 19C+] to fall asleep. **2** [1900s–40s] (*US Black*) to boast, to brag, esp. of one's good fortune. **3** [1900s–40s] (*US Black*) to kill. **4** [1960s] (*US*) to amaze. [CACKLE v. (1)]

cack v.[3] [1990s+] (*Aus./US*) to joke, to (have a) laugh. [CACK n.[4]]

cack-broad n. (*also* **cackle-broad**) [1940s] (*US Black*) one who flaunts their wealth, esp. a nouveau riche woman. [CACK v.[2] (2)/CACKLE v. (1) + BROAD n.[2] (3)]

cacked adj. [1990s+] (*US teen*) messed up. [CACK v.[1]]

cacker n. [1990s+] (*US*) a blunderer, one who makes a mess, lit. and fig. [CACK v.[1]]

cack-hand n. [2000s] a clumsy, awkward person. [backform. f. CACK-HANDED adj.]

cack-handed adj. [mid-19C+] clumsy, awkward. [? CACK v.[1]; note Fr. *mains de merde*, awkward, butter-fingered, lit. 'shit-hands'; note dial. *cack-handed*, left-handed]

cackie n. *see* CACKY n.

cackle n.[1] [late 17C+] empty chatter, foolish talk. [CACKLE v. (1)]

cackle n.[2] [1930s–60s] (*US*) an egg. [SE *cackle*, the sound made by a hen]

cackle v. **1** [late 16C+] to talk, to chatter, to prattle. **2** [late 17C+] (*UK Und.*) to reveal secrets through indiscreet talk, to inform. [SE *cackle*, the sound made by a hen]

cackleberry n. [20C+] (*Aus./US*) an egg (cf. CACKLE FRUIT n.). [SE *cackle*, the noise of a hen + SE *berry*]

cacklebird *n.* [1960s+] (*US*) a hen. [SE *cackle*, the noise of a hen + SE *bird*]

cackle-bladder *n.* [1930s–50s] (*US Und.*) a small bladder of chicken blood held in the mouth and used by criminals to counterfeit the coughing up of blood.

cackle factory *n.* [1950s] (*US*) a psychiatric institution. [CACKLE v. (1) + SE *factory*]

cackle fruit *n.* (*also* **cackle jelly**) [20C+] an egg (cf. CACKLEBERRY n.). [SE *cackle*, the noise of a hen + SE *fruit*]

cackle one's fat *v.* [1940s+] to brag, to boast. [CACKLE v. (2) + SE *fat*, abundance, wealth]

cackler *n.*[1] **1** [15C–19C] a tale-teller, one who talks 'out of turn'. **2** [20C+] (*US*) an office worker, a clerk. [the image, when in a group, of a flock of hens; (2) note Irwin, *American Tramp and Und. Slang* (1931): 'Cackler.- [...] A white collar worker; this name originated by the I.W.W., who have had a hard time interesting this class of worker in their movement, and who say a clerk or office worker will talk, 'cackle,' all day and do nothing to improve his condition']

cackler *n.*[2] **1** [17C–18C] a hen. **2** [1930s–60s] (*US Und.*) an egg. [the noise made by a hen]

cacklers' ken *n.* [18C–early 19C] (*UK Und.*) a hen roost. [CACKLER n.[2] (1) + KEN n.[1] (1)]

cackle tub *n.* [mid-19C–1900s] a pulpit. [CACKLE v. (1) + TUB n.[1] (2)]

cackling-cheat *n.* (*also* **cackling-chete**) [mid-16C–early 19C] (*UK Und.*) a cock, a capon. [SE *cackle* + CHEAT n. (1)]

cackling-cove *n.* [mid–late 19C] (*UK tramp*) an actor. [SE *cackle* + COVE n. (1). 'The cadger seeing no difference between observing Shakespeare and whining floridly for pence' (Ware)]

cackling fart *n.* [17C–18C] an egg. [CACKLER n.[2] (1) + fig. use of FART n. (1)]

cacknacker *n. see* COCK-KNOCKER n.

cacko *adj.* [1960s] (*Aus.*) extremely drunk. [fig. use of CACK n.[2] (1) + -O sfx (5)]

cack on *v.* [1990s+] (*UK juv.*) to reprimand. [fig. use of CACK v.[1]]

cack one's pants *v. see* SHIT ONE'S PANTS v.

cackpipe *n.* [1990s+] the anus, the rectum. [CACK n.[2] (1) + SE *pipe*]

cackpipe cosmonaut *n.* [1990s+] a male homosexual (cf. ANAL ASTRONAUT n.). [CACKPIPE n.]

cacks *n.* [1920s] children's shoes. [Cumberland dial.]

cacky *n.* (*also* **cackie**) [late 19C+] human excrement. [CACK n.[2] (1) + sfx -ie/-y]

cacky *adj.* **1** [late 19C+] covered in excrement. **2** [1970s+] in fig. use, disgusting, second-rate. [CACK n.[2] (1)]

cactus *n.* [1960s+] (*drugs*) mescaline, peyote. [its origin in the peyote cactus; SE *mescaline*, properly the alkaloid 3,4,5-trimethoxyphenethylamine, is the active ingredient of the peyote cactus]

cactus *adj.* [1940s+] (*Aus.*) ruined, useless, finished, dead. [? pun on CACK n.[2] (1)]

cactus buttons *n.* [1960s+] (*drugs*) mescaline. [CACTUS n. + BUTTON n.[2] (2)]

cactus juice *n.*[1] [1960s+] tequila or mescal. [the origin of tequila/mescal in distilling the fermented sap of a maguey (*Agave tequilana*)]

cactus juice *n.*[2] [1970s] (*US*) mescaline. [CACTUS n. + SE *juice*; pun on CACTUS JUICE n.[1]]

Cad *n.* **1** [1920s+] (*orig. US*) a Cadillac. **2** [1970s–80s] (*US Black*) in fig. use, an attractive woman. [abbr.]

cad *n.*[1] **1** [late 18C–mid-19C] a passenger taken on board by a coachman for his own profit. **2** [late 18C–mid-19C] a coachman's assistant. **3** [early 19C+] a poorly behaved, ill-mannered lout; thus artists' jargon *cad-catcher*, pictures painted to attract the undiscriminating; *caddish*, adj. **4** [mid-19C] a lowly rated assistant. **5** [mid-19C] a messenger boy. **6** [mid–late 19C] an omnibus conductor. **7** [mid-19C–1910s] (*US campus*) an academy or prep school student. [SE *cadee*, *caddie*, a cadet; thence Eton and Oxford jargon *cad*, a townsman, the implication being that such a figure could not be 'a gentleman', and late 19C *cad-mad*, the excesses of a nouveau-riche undergraduate; cf. the cognate but somewhat later BOUNDER n.[3] (1)]

cad *n.*[2] [1930s+] (*drugs*) 1oz (28g) of a narcotic. [abbr. CADILLAC n. (1)]

cad *n.*[3] *see* CADGER n. (1).

cadator *n.* [late 17C–early 18C] a confidence trickster, esp. one posing as a 'gentleman fallen on hard times'. [Lat. *cado*, I fall]

cadaver *n.* [late 19C–1900s] (*orig. US*) a bankrupt. [SE *cadaver*, a corpse]

cadaver cadet *n.* [1980s+] a necrophile. [SE *cadaver*, a corpse + *cadet*]

cadazy *adj.* [1980s] (*UK Black*) mad, crazy. [SE *crazy* + infix *mad*]

Cadbury canal *n.* (*also* **Cadbury alley**, **Cadbury channel**) [1990s+] the rectal passage. [play on *Cadbury*, the major UK chocolate manufacturer/CHOCOLATE adj. (2), used in combs. relating to homosexual anal intercourse]

Cadbury's canal boat cruiser *n.* [1990s+] a male homosexual. [CADBURY CANAL n. + ref. to CRUISE v.[1] (5)]

Cadbury's canal engineer *n.* [1990s+] a male homosexual. [CADBURY CANAL n. + SE *engineer*]

Cadbury snack *n.* [2000s] one's back. [rhy. sl.]

caddee *n.* [early–mid-19C] **1** a thief's assistant. **2** a person who frequents tavern yards and persuades customers to patronize another inn, for which they are paid by its landlord. **3** a passer-on of counterfeit money. [CAD n.[1]]

caddie *n.* (*also* **caddy**) [late 19C+] (*orig. Aus.*) a hat; a slouch hat. [? CADY n. (1)]

Caddy *n.* (*also* **Caddie**) [1920s+] (*US*) a Cadillac. [abbr. + sfx -ie/-y]

cadet *n.*[1] **1** [late 17C–early 18C] a junior in the East India Company. **2** [19C] a street thug. **3** [1900s–40s] (*US*) a pimp. [the essential image of a loafer and an idler persists as the meanings develop]

cadet *n.*[2] [1940s–70s] (*drugs*) a novice user of drugs.

cadet *n.*[3] *see* SPACE CADET n. (3).

cadge, the *n.* **1** [early–mid-19C] the profession or act of begging; thus *do a cadge* or *on the cadge*, to exist by begging. **2** [1930s] (*Glasgow*) a message. [CADGE v. (1)]

cadge *v.* **1** [late 18C+] orig. to wander the country as a beggar; thence to beg (from). **2** [20C+] (*Ulster*) to hawk, esp. poteen or illicit whisky. **3** [1980s] to steal. [? SE *cadge*, a pannier, as used by beggars; ? ult. f. Fr. *cacher*, to hide away. 20C+ use was more colloq. than sl.]

cadge-cloak *n.* (*also* **cadge-gloak**) [early 19C] (*UK Und.*) a beggar. [CADGE v. (1) + GLOAK n., lit. 'a wandering fellow']

cadger *n.* **1** [late 18C+] (*also* **cad**) a beggar. **2** [mid–late 19C] (*UK Und.*) a shoplifter-cum-beggar; also used for the lowest rank of pickpocket. **3** [mid-19C+] a genteel 'sponger'. **4** [late 19C] anyone in a service industry, e.g. a waiter, cab-driver, who solicits for tips. **5** [20C+] (*Ulster*) a hawker, esp. one who sells poteen or illicit whisky. [CADGE v. (1)]

cadging *n.* [early 19C+] begging; thus *cadging-bag*, a bag in which to put one's profits; *cadging-face*, an expression designed to elicit sympathy; *grub-cadging*, begging house to house for food. [CADGE v. (1)]

cadgy *adj.* (*also* **cagy**) [late 19C+] (*US*) sexually adventurous. [18C Scot. *caigie* and Suffolk dial. *kedge*, cheerful, wanton, sportive]

cadi *n. see* CADY n.

Cadillac *n.* [1990s+] (*US prison*) **1** coffee with cream and sugar. **2** something considered the best. **3** a vacant cell. **4** a line used for transferring articles, e.g. a pack of cigarettes, from one cell to another. **5** an easy job within the prison. [the *Cadillac* car as (1) and (2) a 'good thing', (3) a space, (4) and (5) a var. on CAR n.]

cadillac n. (*US drugs*) **1** [1930s+] a 1oz (28g) packet of a powdered drug. **2** [1950s+] any powdered, thus usu. narcotic, drug. **3** [1970s+] phencyclidine (cf. ACE n.[4]). [expensive drugs equated with an expensive car]

Cadillac commie n. [1990s+] (*US*) a liberal, one who preaches socialism but espouses a capitalist lifestyle (cf. BOLLINGER BOLSHEVIK n.). [the *Cadillac* car is trad. antipathetic to left-wing ideology]

cads on castors n. [late 19C–1900s] cyclists. [CAD n.[1] (3) + SE *castor*]

cady n. (*also* **cadi**) **1** [mid-19C+] a hat (cf. KADI n.). **2** [1920s+] (*N.Z.*) a straw hat. [Scot. *cadie*, a cap]

caesaration! excl. [late 19C] (*US*) a mild oath. [proper name Julius *Caesar* + sfx *-ation*, on pattern of BOTHERATION! excl.]

caf n. (*also* **caff, kayf, caffy**) [1920s+] a corruption of café, usu. a cheap and cheerful one.

café au lait n. [1920s+] (*US Black*) a light-skinned Black woman. [Fr. *café au lait*, coffee with milk, i.e. the colour of this beverage; orig. coined to describe the women chosen for the chorus line of Harlem's Cotton Club; thus ? pun on SE *café*]

café au lait adj. [1940s+] of a Black person, light-skinned. [CAFÉ AU LAIT n.]

café de move-on n. [1920s+] (*S.Afr.*) a small mobile canteen catering for workers at their place of work. [S.Afr.E. *café*, a convenience store + the need for the canteen to 'move on' when the authorities arrive. The whole phr. is a play on a notional upmarket *Café de...*]

cafeteria n. [1980s+] (*US gay*) anywhere that plays host to repeated oral sex, e.g. a public lavatory or bath-house. [one goes there to EAT v.[3] (1)]

caff n. see CAF n.

caffan n. see CASSAN n.

caffer n. (*also* **kaffir**) [mid–late 19C] a convict who has been transported to New South Wales and subseq. escaped. [? link to Yorks. dial. *caff*, to break a bargain, to curtail a journey, or *caffle*, to argue]

caffler n. [late 19C+] (*Irish*) a contemptible person; often cheeky and foolish. [dial. *caffler*, a quarrelsome person]

caffling n. [late 19C+] (*Irish*) idle chatter, gossip. [CAFFLER n.]

caffy n. see CAF n.

caflugalty n. (*also* **cafugelty**) [1910s–30s] (*US*) a row, an argument. [? KERFUFFLE n.]

cafone n. see GAVONE n.

caf up v. [1980s+] (*US campus*) to ingest caffeine, usu. in the form of coffee, to promote one's energy. [SE *caffeine*]

cag n. (*also* **kagg**) [19C] sulkiness, ill humour. [dial./RN jargon *cag*, an argument]

cag v. (*also* **keg**) [early–mid-19C] to irritate, to annoy; thus *caggy*, ill-natured; *cagged*, irritated, angry. [dial.]

cage n. **1** [late 16C+] a prison. **2** [mid-19C] a dress-improver or bustle. **3** [late 19C] a bed. **4** [1900s] (*US*) a hat. **5** [1920s–30s] (*US tramp*) a cubicle within a tramp's lodging house. **6** [1930s+] (*US*) an elevator, a lift. **7** [1930s+] (*US Und.*) a holding cell in a police station or jail. **8** [1960s+] (*US*) an automobile. **9** [1970s+] (*US gay*) a depressing room or apartment. [all fig. uses of SE; (1) SE in earlier use; Hindley, *The Life and Times of James Catnach* (1878), glosses (1) as 'the round-house']

caged adj. [1940s] (*US*) drunk. [? the drunkard is fit to be SE *caged*]

cage of ivories n. [mid-19C] a set of good teeth. [SE *cage* + IVORY n. (1); the teeth represent the 'bars']

cagey adj. **1** [late 19C+] (*also* **cagy**) non-committal, reticent, wary. **2** [1920s+] cunning, crafty. **3** [1950s] sexually exciting. [SE *cage*; the image of a caged animal, gazing suspiciously at human onlookers]

cagged/caggy adj. see CAG v.

cagmag n. **1** [late 18C–1920s] refuse, rubbish, odds and ends. **2** [late 19C–1920s] gossip, tittle-tattle. [dial. *cag-mag*, an old goose, not fit for eating (according to Grose (1796), such geese were dumped on the undiscriminating London market), an inferior breed of sheep, a disreputable old woman, anything valueless or second-rate. Hotten's (1864) suggestion – a corruption of the Gk *kakos mageiros*, a bad cook, and used as such in university sl. – must be rejected]

cagmag adj. [mid-19C] second-rate, inferior, 'rubbishy'. [CAGMAG n. (1)]

cagy adj.[1] see CADGY adj.

cagy adj.[2] see CAGEY adj. (1).

cahoonas n. see KAHOONAS n.

cahoot v. [mid–late 19C; 1940s] (*US*) to act in partnership. [backform. f. IN CAHOOTS (WITH) phr.]

cahoots adv. see IN CAHOOTS (WITH) phr.

cain and abel n. (*also* **Cain and Able**) [mid-19C+] a table. [rhy. sl.]

caine n. [1980s+] (*drugs*) **1** co*caine*. **2** crack co*caine*. [abbr.]

cainsham smoke n. [late 17C–early 18C] the tears of a man who is beaten by his wife. [? a lost story pertaining to *Keynsham*, near Bristol, UK]

caj adj. see CAS adj.

cajooblies n. [1990s+] the female breasts (cf. BAZONGAS n.).

cajun n. see COJONES n.

cak see under CACK.

cake n.[1] **1** [late 18C–19C] (*also* **cakey**) a fool (cf. APPLEHEAD n.). **2** [early 19C; 1920s–30s] (*US, esp. gang*) a dandy, a fop; youths who wore stylish wide-bottomed trousers. [the 'softness' of the unintelligent head or ? the 'tastiness' of the person]

cake n.[2] **1** [20C+] (*Aus.*) a gold nugget. **2** [1960s] (*US Black*) (*also* **cakes**) money (cf. BATTER n.[4]). [ext. of BREAD n.[1] (2)]

cake n.[3] **1** [1900s–60s] (*orig. Aus.*) a prostitute. **2** [1940s–60s] (*US Black*) an attractive woman. **3** [1950s+] (*US Black*) the vagina (cf. APPLE n.[6]). [one of a number of words that equate attractive young women with sweetmeats]

cake n.[4] [1950s] (*US drugs/prison*) drugs smuggled into a prison or hospital.

cake n.[5] (*also* **cakes**) **1** [1960s+] (*US*) a term of affection between friends (cf. BABYCAKES n.). **2** [1980s] (*US campus*) a weak person. [(1) so intimate a friend is 'good enough to eat']

cake, the n. [1900s–20s] (*US*) a (self-appointedly) admirable person.

cake adj.[1] [1960s+] (*US campus*) easy, simple; thus *cake*, an easy course/test. [PIECE OF CAKE n.]

cake adj.[2] see CAKEY adj.

cake and wine n. [1920s] (*US prison*) bread and water.

cake basket n. [1920s] (*US*) a limousine.

cake boy n. [1970s+] (*US gay*) a male homosexual; thus *Navy cake*, a homosexual sailor. [one who is both SOFT adj. (3) and good enough to EAT v.[3] (1)]

cake cutter n. [1940s+] (*orig. US Black*) one who short-changes a customer.

caked adj.[1] **1** [1900s] on good (amatory) terms. **2** [1940s+] (*also* **caked up**) well-supplied with, spec. well-off. [CAKE n.[2] (2)]

caked adj.[2] [1990s+] (*US campus*) drunk. [? fig. use of CACK v.[1]]

cake-date n. see JELLY-DATE n.

caked up adj. see CAKED adj.[1] (2).

cake-eater n. [1910s+] (*US*) **1** a self-indulgent or effeminate young man. **2** an effete young man who attends smart tea parties and charms old ladies. **3** any wealthy young man, a playboy. **4** as a joc./affectionate term of address.

cakehole n. **1** [1940s+] the mouth; often in phr. *shut your cakehole* (cf. PIE HOLE n.). **2** [2000s] (*Irish*) the anus.

cake is dough phr. [mid-16C+] one's project has failed, one's plans have not worked out. [the image is of a cake mixture failing to rise in the oven]

cake out v. [1920s–30s] (*US*) to dress in a rakish manner. [CAKE n.[1] (2)]

cakes *n.*[1] **1** [1950s+] (*orig. US*) the female breasts (cf. APPLES n.[1]). **2** [1970s] (*US*) the buttocks (cf. BAKERY GOODS n.). **3** [1980s+] (*US Black*) the vagina (cf. APPLE n.[6]). **4** [1990s+] (*drugs*) round discs of crack cocaine (cf. BASE n.). [all fig. use of the size and shape of a SE *cake*]

cakes *n.*[2] *see* BABYCAKES n.

cakes *n.*[3] *see* CAKE n.[2] (2).

cakes *n.*[4] *see* CAKE n.[5].

cakes-and-coffee *adj.* [1900s–30s] (*US*) basic, fundamental.

cake shop *n.* [1950s–60s] (*Aus.*) a brothel (cf. BANGING-SHOP n.). [CAKE n.[3] (1)+ SE *shop*/SHOP n.[1] (1)]

cakewalk *n.* **1** [late 19C+] anything considered very easy. **2** [1900s] (*Aus.*) something excellent. **3** [1930s] money that has been obtained without effort. [SE *cakewalk*, a dance in which the contestants (usu. US Black) promenade around a cake placed in the centre of the dance-floor; those who perform the fanciest steps lit. 'take the cake'. Orig. as WW1 milit. jargon, an attack or raid that met with little or no opposition]

cakewalk *v.* [1930s] (*US*) to succeed without problems. [CAKEWALK n. (1)]

cakey *n. see* CAKE n.[1] (1).

cakey *adj.* (*also* **cake**) [late 19C+] stupid, foolish, 'soft'. [CAKE n.[1] (1)]

cakey-pannum fencer *n.* [mid-19C] a street-seller of pastries. [SE *cake* + PANNAM n. (1) + -FENCER sfx]

cakie *n. see* BABYCAKES n.

cakpants *n.* [2000s] a general term of abuse, the implication is that the subject is a coward, who soils their underwear through fear. [CACK n.[2] (1) + SE *pants*]

Cal *n.* **1** [late 19C] (*Anglo-Ind.*) *Cal*cutta. **2** [late 19C+] (*US*) *Cal*ifornia. [abbr.]

cal *n.* [mid-19C] a hangman. [abbr. of proper name Thomas *Cal*craft (*fl.*1860), a hangman]

calabash *n.*[1] [early 18C–19C] the human head. [Persian *kharbuz*, or *kharbuza*, melon or watermelon; ult. Arabic *khirbiz*, melon, or *kirbiz*, pumpkin or gourd]

calabash *n.*[2] (*also* **calibash**) [mid–late 19C] (*Aus.*) a promissory note or IOU. [the image is of the essential worthlessness of such notes, which were no more valid as money than had they been written on a *calabash* or gourd-shell (*see* CALABASH n.[1])]

calabash cover *n.* [late 19C] (*US*) a hat. [CALABASH n.[1]]

calaboodle *n. see* CABOODLE n.

calaboose *n.* (*also* **calabozo**) [late 18C+] (*orig. US*) a prison. [Sp. *calabozo*, jail]

calaboose *v.* [mid-19C] (*US*) to imprison. [CALABOOSE n.]

calamity-howler *n.* (*also* **calamity-shouter**) [late 19C–1940s] (*US*) a prophet of doom; thus *calamity howl*, a statement of extreme pessimism.

calamity jane *n.* [20C+] (*US*) a nagging woman, a pessimist, a worrier. [the markswoman Martha Jane Canary Burke (1852–1903), known as *Calamity Jane* for the effect her 6-guns had on those who opposed her]

calathumpian *n.* [1910s+] one who claims an imaginary religion. [ety. unknown; ? SE *calamity* + *thump* + play on CALLITHUMPIAN n.]

calculate *v.* [early–mid-19C] (*US*) to think, to opine.

calcutta *n.* [1990s+] butter. [rhy. sl.; ult. city in India]

caldee *v.* (*also* **caldees, chaldee**) [mid–late 17C] to trick, to swindle. [? SE *Chaldee*, an astrologer]

caldron *n.* [19C] the vagina (cf. BAG n.[1]). [SE *cauldron*]

caleb quotum *n.* (*also* **Caleb Quotem**) [mid–late 19C] **1** a parish clerk. **2** a jack of all trades. [proper name of a character in the play *The Wags of Windsor*]

calebs *n.* [mid-19C] (*US Und.*) a burglar's device for unlocking doors. [? anecdotal, from an actual robber called Caleb and his preferred implement]

caledonia *n.* [1920s–50s] (*US Black*) a Black woman who refuses to accept the trad. role into which her birth is supposed to have thrust her. [? a book ? play ? song]

calendar *n.* (*US Und.*) **1** [1920s+] a year spent in prison. **2** [1940s] a case awaiting trial. [abbr. SE *calendar year*]

calf *n.*[1] **1** [mid-16C–1920s] (*also* **veal**) a fool, a simpleton; thus *calfy*, uncoordinated (cf. AIREDALE n.). **2** [20C+] (*US*) a coward. [dial. Note the UK comedian Steve Coogan's 1990s character Paul *Calf*, a loutish, stupid, hedonistic Mancunian]

calf *n.*[2] [1940s] (*US Black*) a Cadillac. [? initial letter]

calf *n.*[3] *see* ESSEX CALF n.

calf *v.* [1960s] (*US*) to vomit (cf. BARF v.). [? echoic]

calf-clingers *n.* [mid-19C] very tight-fitting trousers.

calf-lolly *n.* [mid–late 17C] an idle simpleton. [CALF n.[1] (1) + dial. *lolly*, a fool, an idler]

calf's head *n.* **1** [17C–early 19C] a fool (cf. AIREDALE n.). **2** [19C] a white-faced man with a large head. [CALF n.[1] (1)]

calfskin fiddle *n.* [late 18C–early 19C] a drum. [its calfskin head]

calf-slobber *n.* **1** [1920s+] (*US*) a meringue topping for pastry; thus fig. [1980s+] nothing whatsoever, e.g. *that's just calf-slobber to me.* **2** [2000s] foam on a glass of beer. [dial. *calf-slobber*, the saliva that forms around a calf's mouth]

calf-sticking *n.* [mid-19C–1910s] (*UK Und.*) pretending that perfectly normal goods have supposedly been stolen; a greater price can thus be asked, since some customers like the idea of obtaining stolen goods. [CALF n.[1] (1) + STICK v.[1] (1)]

calf-week *n.* (*also* **bull-week, cow-week**) [mid-19C] the 3 weeks immediately before Christmas, characterized in shops and factories by an increasingly heavy workload. [the cattle names imply stolid labouring]

Cali *n.* [1930s+] the state of *Cali*fornia. [abbr.]

Cali *adj.* [1990s+] *Cali*fornian. [CALI n.]

calibash *n. see* CALABASH n.[2].

calico *n.* (*also* **calic**) [mid-19C–1940s] (*US*) a woman; thus *calico fever*, the desire to pursue women; *new calico*, a young woman; *old calico*, an old woman; *calico queen*, a prostitute; *bit of calico*, sexual groping. [SE *calico*, a cloth, somewhat coarser than muslin, from which women's dresses were often made. There may also be links to Scot. *cailliach*, an old woman, *calik*, a gossip and *callack*, a young woman]

calico *adj.* [early 18C–mid-19C; 1950s] thin, wasted. [the thinness of the cloth]

calico *v.* [19C] (*US*) to court women, to associate with women. [CALICO n.]

calico ball *n.* (*also* **calico hop**) [mid-19C–1930s] (*US*) a cheap, popular public dance. [the *calico* (rather than silk or satin) dresses worn by the women]

calico muster *n. see* TARPAULIN MUSTER n.

calicot *n.* [late 19C–1900s] a 'counter-jumper'. [Fr. *calicot*, a draper's assistant, though sl. use is the same]

California *n.* [mid-19C] money, esp. a gold piece. [the *California* Gold Rush of the 1840s]

California banknote *n.* (*also* **California shinplaster**) [mid-19C] (*US*) an animal hide, which was used as money in early 19C California. [replaced by coins and notes subseq. to the 1849 Gold Rush]

California bankroll *n.* (*also* **California roll, Kansas City (bank)roll, Philadelphia..., Philly...**) [1940s+] (*US Black/ gambling*) a show bankroll in which 1 large-denomination note is exhibited on the outside, concealing a quantity of small bills; thus *California roller*, one who carries such a 'bankroll' (cf. CHICAGO BANKROLL n. FLASH ROLL n.; GAMBLER'S ROLL n.; GANGSTA ROLL n.; GLORY ROLL n.; MEXICAN BANKROLL n.; MICHIGAN ROLL n.; MISSOURI BANKROLL n.; NIGGER'S BANKROLL n.; NIGGER'S BANKROLL n.; POCKET ROLL n.). [SE *bankroll*/ROLL n.[2]; a general slur on various states depending on a speaker's prejudice]

California bible *n.* (*also* **California prayerbook**) [mid-19C+] (*US*) a deck of cards. [the stereotyped sinfulness of California]

California blanket *n.* (*also* **Tucson blanket**) [1920s–40s] (*US*) newspapers, when used by tramps as a substitute for blankets. [SE *California* + SE *blanket*/BLANKET n.³ (2)]

California collar *n.* [19C] (*US*) a noose, used for hangings. [the numbers of vigilantes to be found in California, most of whom favoured hanging first and ascertaining guilt later]

California cornflakes *n.* [1970s+] (*drugs*) cocaine. [joc. play on the breakfast cereal's slogan: it's 'good for you each morning']

California house *n.* [1970s] (*US*) an outside privy (cf. BACKHOUSE n.). [? the good weather in California, which permits an outdoor lifestyle]

California moccasins *n.* [1920s–60s] (*US*) makeshift 'socks' made from sacks or similar rags. [as worn by impoverished tramps who travelled to and then in California]

Californian *n.* [mid–late 19C] a dried red herring. [the association of the red i.e. gold colour, with the *Californian* Gold Rush]

California overshoes *n.* [19C] (*US*) makeshift 'socks' made by wrapping the feet in sacks, often flour sacks, over which boots can then be put on. [as used by tramps and/or unsuccessful gold prospectors]

California prayerbook *n. see* CALIFORNIA BIBLE n.

California roll *n. see* CALIFORNIA BANKROLL n.

California shinplaster *n. see* CALIFORNIA BANKNOTE n.

California socks *n.* [1900s–60s] (*US*) makeshift 'socks' made from sacks or other rags.

California stop *n.* (*also* **Hollywood stop**) [1970s+] (*US*) of a motorist, running a stop sign. [stereotyped Californians are seen as contemptuous of the law]

California sunshine *n.* [1970s+] (*drugs*) LSD. [*California* + SUNSHINE n.³]

California toothpick *n.* [mid-19C] (*US*) a large knife.

caliwampus *adj. see* CATAWAMPUS adj.

call *n.¹* [1960s–70s] **1** the first feelings that follow drinking an alcoholic drink. **2** (*drugs*) the immediate response to an injection of a drug. [a pun on the religious use of *call*, a summons to a higher spirituality]

call *n.² see* SHOUT n.¹ (2).

call *v.¹* **1** [mid-18C+] to beg. **2** [late 19C+] to blame. [fig. uses of SE]

call *v.²* [1920s+] (*US*) to challenge. [poker jargon]

call *v.³* [1980s] (*Aus.*) to vomit. [abbr. CALL FOR HUGHIE v./CALL FOR RALPH v.]

call *v.⁴ see* CALL (OUT) v.

call a cop *v.* [1990s+] to stop. [rhy. sl.]

call a go *v.* [mid-19C] **1** of a street-seller, to move on. **2** to give up.

callan park *n.* [20C+] (*Aus.*) a psychiatric institution. [the name of a psychiatric hospital in Sydney, used to represent any such hospital]

call apartment *n. see* CALL FLAT n.

Callard & Bowsers *n.* [1960s+] trousers. [rhy. sl.; ult. a firm of confectioners]

call a spade a (bloody) shovel *v.* [1910s+] to speak aggressively or vehemently. [a play on the usu. phr. *call a spade a spade*]

callawampus *adj.* [1940s+] (*W.I.*) big, fine, stout, grand. [CATAWAMPUS adj.]

call-boy *n.* [1960s+] a male prostitute who can be hired on the phone. [a male CALL-GIRL n. (2)]

call buicks *v. see* BUICK v.

call Charles *v.* (*also* **call dinosaurs, call Earl, call seals**) [1970s+] (*Aus./US*) to vomit (cf. CALL FOR HERB v.; CALL FOR HUGHIE v.; CALL FOR RALPH v.; CRY HUGHIE v.; CALL THE DOGS v.; EARL v.; FRED v.; HARRY v.; HOLLER NEW YORK v.; RALPH v.; SHOUT FOR RUTH v.; SPEAK WELSH v.). [onomat. for the sound of vomiting, i.e. one is calling out the name/word when one vomits]

call copper *v.* (*also* **scream copper**) [1930s+] (*UK Und.*) to inform the police (cf. HOLLER COPPER v.; TURN COPPER v.). [SE *call* + COPPER n.³ (1)]

call-dog *n.* [1940s+] (*W.I.*) a fish too small for human consumption. [one *calls the dog* to eat it]

calldown *n.* [late 19C–1950s] (*US*) a telling-off, a scolding.

call down *v.* [late 19C+] to scold, to reprimand.

calle *n.* [mid-17C–mid-19C] (*UK Und.*) a cloak. [SE *caul*, a (net) bag, usu. for the hair]

call Earl *v. see* CALL CHARLES v.

callet *n.* [early 16C–18C] a prostitute, a promiscuous woman. [? Fr. *cailette*, a fool, lit. 'a small quail'; Fr. *calotte*, a skullcap; Gaelic *caille*, a girl; Nares suggests that 'it is more likely to have been derived from the personage of [...] Callot, Kit. The fair, or perhaps more properly the brown associate of one Giles Hathr. They are supposed to have been the first couple of English persons who took up the occupation of gipsies']

Calley, the *n. see* CALLY, THE n. (2).

call flat *n.* (*also* **call apartment**) [1910s–40s] (*US*) a brothel. [var. on CALL HOUSE n.]

call for Herb *v.* [1960s+] (*Aus.*) to vomit (cf. CALL CHARLES v.). [echoic]

call for Hughie *v.* (*also* **call for Bill**) [1960s+] (*UK society*) to vomit (cf. CALL CHARLES v.). [onomat.]

call for Ralph *v.* (*also* **call Ralph**) [1960s+] to vomit (cf. CALL CHARLES v.). [onomat.]

call full-mouth *v.* (*also* **call raw**) [20C+] (*W.I.*) to address an elder or senior person without using Mr, Mrs or Miss. [FULLMOUTH adj./CALL *raw*; i.e. 'uncooked' by good manners]

call-girl *n.* (*also* **call girl**) **1** [late 19C+] a woman who works in a brothel. **2** [1930s+] (*orig. US*) (*also* **call Mom**) a prostitute who advertises her services through an agency, through the (print) media, in telephone kiosks etc and visits a client in his own home or hotel room (cf. AWAYDAY GIRL n.). [SE *call*, to make a telephone call + GIRL n.¹ (1)]

call hogs *v.* [1910s–60s] (*US*) to snore. [the noise]

call house *n.* **1** [late 19C+] a brothel to which men can come without making any prior appointment (cf. ACCOMMODATION HOUSE n.). **2** [1910s+] a hetero- or homosexual brothel to which women or men are summoned by telephone after they have been selected, via some form of visual 'menu', by the male clientele; thus *call trade*, prostitution arranged on this basis. [SE *call* (*on*), to visit + HOUSE n.¹ (1)]

callibisters *n.* [16C–17C] the vagina. [*callistris*, the penis]

callibogus *n.* [late 18C–19C] (*US*) a mixture of rum and spruce beer. [ety. unknown]

callie *n.¹ see* CALLY n.

callie *n.² see* COLLIE n.¹.

calling card *n.* **1** [1920s–40s] (*US Und.*) fingerprints. **2** [1980s] (*Irish*) a euph. for excrement. [one leaves one's calling card]

call in one's marker *v.* (*also* **call in a marker, ...someone's marker**) [1970s+] (*US*) to demand repayment of a favour. [fig. use of MARKER n.² (1)]

call in someone's chips *v.* [late 19C] (*US*) to challenge, to call someone's bluff. [poker imagery]

call it a day *v.* [mid-19C+] **1** (*also* **call it a go, ...a night**) to stop, to go no further, to express satisfaction with progress or acceptance that one cannot improve a position. **2** to die. [? cribbage jargon *call a go*, to change one's tactics, to give in]

call it george *v.* (*also* **call it wally**) [20C+] (*W.I.*) to agree that a matter is concluded, to bring something to an end, e.g. a day's work. [joc. generic use of proper names]

callithumpian *n.* (*also* **callithump**) [mid-19C+] (*US*) a band or member of a band that makes discordant so-called 'music' by playing a number of instruments, either in an unlikely combination or conjured up from unlikely objects, such as washboards, tin kettles etc. [ety. unknown, ? link to SE *thump*]

call it quits *v.* [20C+] to die.

call it wally v. see CALL IT GEORGE v.

call joint n. [1930s–40s] (US) a brothel. [SE call (on) + JOINT n.[4] (3)]

call Mom n. see CALL-GIRL n. (2).

call off all bets v. [1940s–50s] (US Black) to die. [poker imagery]

call on the carpet v. **1** [1960s] (US) to reprimand, to scold. **2** [1990s+] (US prison) to challenge another speaker to justify his remarks, whether hostile, gossiping or whatever. [ON THE CARPET phr.[2]]

call (out) v. **1** [late 19C+] to challenge to a fight. **2** [1990s+] (US campus) to embarrass. [early 19C SE call out, challenge to a duel]

call out v. [1920s] (US Und.) to use a stolen cheque.

call Ralph v. see CALL FOR RALPH v.

call raw v. see CALL FULL-MOUTH v.

call seals v. see CALL CHARLES v.

call someone out of their name v. [1900s–40s] (US Black) to insult through name-calling.

call someone's card v. [1980s] (US) to call someone's bluff. [poker imagery]

call someone's game v. [1980s+] (US) to call someone's bluff, to challenge. [poker imagery]

call someone's hand v. [mid-19C–1950s] (US) to issue a challenge, to call someone's bluff. [poker imagery]

call the coin v. [1950s+] (US) to call 'heads or tails' when a coin is tossed.

call the dogs v. [1990s+] (US campus) to vomit (cf. BARF v.; CALL CHARLES v.). [one's 'barking' noises]

call the game in v. [1910s+] (Aus./N.Z.) to abandon one's efforts, to admit defeat. [lit. to bring a game, e.g. of rugby, to an end]

call the knock v. [2000s] to track down, to apprehend and arrest. [SE knock on the door]

call the shots v. (also **call the plays**) [1930s+] to dictate a course of action, to say what should happen. [dice gambling]

call the turn v. [late 19C+] (US) to predict accurately. [gambling use, calling the next turn of the wheel in the game of faro]

Cally n. [1930s+] (US) California. [abbr.]

Cally, the n. [late 19C+] (UK, London) **1** the Caledonian Market, London N1. **2** (also **the Calley**) the Caledonian Road. [abbr.]

cally n. (also **callie**) [1910s–30s] (US tramp) **1** a prison. **2** a police station. [abbr. CALABOOSE n.]

Caló n. [1940s+] (US) Chicano street sl., linked to Mexican and gypsy patois. [abbr. SE California, to which the sl. is unique]

calonkus n. [late 19C+] (Aus.) a fool. [? echoic of the 'kalonk' of hitting one's head with a palm or fist]

caloop v. [20C+] (US) to go courting, to kiss and cuddle. [? KER- pfx + SE loop, to encircle (with one's arms)]

calp n. see KELP n.[1].

calve v. [mid-19C] (US) to vomit (cf. BARF v.). [echoic]

calves gone to grass phr. [late 18C–19C] denoting someone who has noticeably thin legs; thus joc. remark: 'veal will be cheap, calves fall' on noticing a man whose calves fall away. [a pun]

Calvin Klein n. **1** [1990s+] a judicial fine. **2** [1990s+] wine. **3** [2000s] 9. [rhy. sl.; ult. US clothes designer Calvin Klein (b.1942)]

Cam n. (also **Cam red**) [1970s+] Cambodian marijuana, usu. very strong. [abbr.]

cam n. see CAMI n.

camac n. [19C] (Irish) anything that is over-complex or over-expensive to achieve its essentially simple purpose. [clergymen Ryan and Camac, hanged for counterfeiting at Wexford in the early 19C]

camarada de aquella n. [1960s+] (US) a general term of high praise. [Sp., lit. 'a number-one guy', 'a real down dude']

Camberwell death trap n. [late 19C–1900s] the Surrey Canal. [the drownings that occurred there]

Cambodian red n. (also **Cam red**) [1960s+] (drugs) a slightly reddish variety of marijuana grown in Cambodia (cf. ACAPULCO (GOLD) n.).

Cambodian trip n. (also **Cam trip**) [1960s+] (drugs) a very potent, almost hallucinogenic, variety of marijuana (cf. ACAPULCO (GOLD) n.). [TRIP n.[4] (2)]

cambra n. (also **komra**) [18C+] a dog. [Shelta]

Cambridge fortune n. [late 17C–early 19C] a woman who has no fortune of her own and must rely for attraction on her personal charms alone. [punning on 2 staples of the Cambridgeshire countryside, the term is defined by Grose (1785) as 'a wind-mill and a water-mill', i.e. she can talk and urinate but that is all]

Cambridge nightingale n. (also **Cambridgeshire night-ingale**) [late 19C] a frog (cf. CAPE NIGHTINGALE n.; DUTCH NIGHTINGALE n.; FEN NIGHTINGALE n.; IRISH NIGHTINGALE n.). [the large numbers of croaking frogs found in the marshy Fens]

Cambridge oak n. (also **Cambridgeshire oak**) [late 18C–early 19C] a willow. [the frequency of willows in that county]

Cambridgeshire camel n. [late 17C–18C] a native or established resident of Cambridgeshire. [the stilt-walkers once found in the Fens]

Cambridgeshire nightingale n. see CAMBRIDGE NIGHTINGALE n.

Cambridgeshire oak n. see CAMBRIDGE OAK n.

Camden Town n. [mid-19C–1910s] a halfpenny. [rhy. sl. = BROWN n.[2] (1); ult. area of London, NW1]

camel n.[1] [mid-19C–1910s] (S.Afr.) a giraffe. [joc. substitution; both have prominent necks]

camel n.[2] [late 19C] (US) a bustle or 'dress-improver'. [the camel's and the bustle's 'hump']

camel n.[3] [1990s+] (Aus. prison) a prisoner who neglects personal hygiene. [the stereotyping of the animal as dirty]

camel-breath adj. [1960s] a general derog. adj.

camel-chaser n. [1960s+] (orig. US) a derog. term for a Syrian or an Indian (from India) or any form of Arab from the Middle East (cf. ABDUL n.). [SE camel, as stereotype + chaser]

camel-driver n. **1** [1920s] (US) a Jew (cf. ARAB n.[2]). **2** [1960s+] an Arab, a native of the Middle East (cf. ABDUL n.). [(1) the inference is of Middle Eastern origins rather than professional stereotyping]

camel-dung n. [20C+] a derog. name for unpleasant-tasting cigarettes, orig. made from Egyptian tobacco.

camel-fucker n. [1960s+] (US) a derog. term for an Arab, a native of the Middle East (cf. ABDUL n.). [SE camel, as stereotype + FUCKER n. (1)]

camelhead n. [2000s] (US) a derog. term for an Arab, a native of the Middle East (cf. ABDUL n.). [SE camel, as stereotype + -HEAD sfx (2)]

camel jockey n. (also **camel-jock**) [1960s+] (US) a derog. term for an Arab, a native of the Middle East (cf. ABDUL n.). [SE camel, as stereotype + SE jockey/JOCKEY n.[3] (2)/JOCK n.[2] (1)]

camel-puncher n. [1910s] (Aus.) a camel-driver. [SE camel + var. on BULL-PUNCHER n.]

camel rider n. [1930s] (US Und.) an Asian (cf. BROWNIE n.[2]). [SE camel, as stereotype + rider]

camel's complaint n. [late 19C–1920s] depression. [pun on the HUMP n.[1]]

camel toe n. (also **camel's foot, camel toes**) [1990s+] (orig. US) the vulva as seen through a tight pair of jeans or trousers. [supposed resemblance]

cameo cut n. [1980s–90s] (US Black) a short-cropped Black haircut, pioneered by the hip-hop culture. [as popularized by the lead singer of Cameo, Larry Blackmon; note cameo cut, the name of a technique for decorative glass-cutting]

camera obscura n. [late 19C–1900s] (US) the buttocks, the anus. [pun on Lat. camera obscura, a dark place]

camerer cuss n. [1910s–30s] a London bus. [rhy. sl.; the clockmakers Camerer Cuss was founded in 1788]

camesa *n.* (*also* **kemesa**) [mid-17C–19C] a shirt. [Sp. *camisa*, a shirt]

cami *n.* (*also* **cam, cammy**) [20C+] **1** a *cami*sole or underbodice. **2** *cami*-knickers. [abbr.]

cami-knicks *n.* [1930s+] an undergarment that combines camisole and knickers. [abbr. SE *cami-knickers*]

Camilla Parker (Bowles) *n.* [1990s+] a *Rolls Royce* car. [rhy. sl.; ult. *Camilla Parker Bowles* (b.1949), Duchess of Cornwall, wife of the Prince of Wales)

camisole *n.* [1930s–50s] (*US prison*) a strait-jacket.

camister *n.* [mid-19C] (*UK Und.*) a clergyman, a preacher. [SE *camis*, a surplice + CAMESA n.]

cammie *n.* (*also* **camo**) [1970s+] (*orig. US milit.*) *camo*uflage (uniform). [abbr. + sfx -*ie*/-o sfx (6)]

cammie *adj.* (*also* **cammy, camo**) [1970s+] (*orig. US milit.*) of uniforms, *camo*uflage. [CAMMIE n.]

cammy *n. see* CAMI n.

camouflage cocktail *n.* [1930s] (*US Black*) a cocktail designed to hide the poor-quality liquor of the Prohibition era.

Camp, the *n.* **1** [late 18C–early 19C] (*Aus.*) Sydney. **2** [mid-19C] (*Aus.*) Hobart. **3** [20C+] the area outside Port Stanley in the Falkland Islands.

camp *n.*[1] [mid-19C+] (*Aus.*) a short rest, a lie-down; thus *have a camp, go to camp*, to take a rest.

camp *n.*[2] (*orig. US*) **1** [1920s+] an effeminate male homosexual. **2** [1920s+] (*also* **camping**) flamboyance, overt exhibitionism; thus a flamboyant person (of either sex). **3** [1930s–40s] a gathering place for male homosexuals. [CAMP adj. (1)]

camp *adj.* [mid-19C+] **1** (*also* **campish, camping**) effeminate, affected, exaggerated; the general image is that of limp-wristed homosexuality. **2** strange, though amusing. **3** stylish. ['Actions and gestures of exaggerated emphasis. Probably from the French. Used chiefly by persons of exceptional want of character. "How very camp he is."' (Ware). Anthony Burgess suggests a link to SE *camp*, a military base, mining or railroad camp, in which, as in a prison, a lack of women might lead to homosexuality and where effeminate men would act deliberately in this manner to attract admirers. He also notes the availability, in London, of soldiers from the city barracks, willing to indulge gay men-about-town]

camp *v.*[1] (*Aus.*) **1** [mid-19C+] to rest, to lie down. **2** [late 19C] to die. [CAMP n.[1]]

camp *v.*[2] **1** [1920s+] to act ostentatiously and outrageously in a homosexual manner, although by no means restricted – verbally or physically – to the gay world. **2** [2000s] (*UK juv.*) to act in an exaggeratedly 'gay' manner in order to humiliate a boy who is or is believed to be homosexual. [CAMP adj.]

camp *adv.* [1970s+] (*US gay*) in an effeminate, affected, exaggerated manner.

camp about *v.* (*also* **camp around, camp it up**) **1** [1920s+] of a man, to act in a deliberate and exaggeratedly effeminate manner; used of effeminate male homosexuals and those who, maliciously or otherwise, are attempting to mimic them. **2** to be witty, whimsical, amusing. **3** to render something 'camp'. [ext. of CAMP v.[2]]

campaign coat *n.* [mid-17C–early 18C] a tattered old coat, worn by beggars to excite sympathy in passers-by. [orig. a milit. uniform, then in civilian tailoring a style of coat that resembled milit. uniform; as worn by a beggar such a coat was supposed to present the image of an old soldier down on his luck]

camp as a row of (pink chiffon) tents *phr.* [1950s+] of a male homosexual, extremely, ostentatiously effeminate. [pun on SE *camp*/CAMP adj. (1)]

camp as Chloe *phr.* [1950s–60s] of a man or a male homosexual, extremely affected, effeminate. [CAMP adj. (1) + ? the same Chloe as inspired DRUNK AS CHLOE phr.]

Campbell's academy *n.* [late 18C–early 19C] the hulks, or floating prisons, sited in ships moored in the Thames Estuary.

[*Campbell*, the name of the first director of such prisons + ACADEMY n. (4)]

camp candlestick *n.* [late 18C–early 19C] an empty bottle. [the use of such an empty bottle as a candlestick in army camps etc]

camp dog *n.* [1920s–40s] (*US tramp*) one who runs errands and does small jobs for his fellow tramps.

camp down *v.* [late 19C] (*Aus.*) **1** to go to bed. **2** to die. [CAMP v.[1]]

camped *adj.* [late 19C] (*Aus.*) exhausted. [CAMP n.[1] (1)]

camper *n.*[1] [1960s+] (*US gay*) a young boyish lesbian. [CAMP adj. (1)]

camper *n.*[2] [1970s+] (*US*) a person, an individual; usu. as HAPPY CAMPER n. [the studied jollity of a holiday *camp*]

campfire girl *n.* [1970s+] (*US camp gay*) a soldier. [play on CAMP adj. (1)]

camphor and moth *n.* [1930s] (*UK tramp*) broth. [rhy. sl.]

camping *n. see* CAMP n.[2] (2).

camping/campish *adj. see* CAMP adj. (1).

camp it off *v.* [1970s+] (*US gay*) to shrug off an insult. [CAMP v.[2] (1)]

camp it up *v. see* CAMP ABOUT v.

camp meat *n.* [20C+] (*US*) deer that has been illegally shot by poachers. [i.e. *meat* obtained by those in a *camp*, rather than on a farm]

camposity *n.* [1950s] the world and culture of male homosexuals. [CAMP adj. (1)]

camp strawberries *n.* [1940s] (*US tramp*) beans, a staple of tramp meals.

campy *adj.* **1** [1930s+] ostentatious, affected, effeminate. **2** [1970s+] (*US Black*) extremely close-knit, happy, cheerful and free-spirited to the point of infuriating one's companions. [CAMP adj. (1)]

Cam red *n. see* CAMBODIAN RED n.

Cam trip *n. see* CAMBODIAN TRIP n.

can *n.*[1] **1** [17C+] the vagina (cf. BAG n.[1]). **2** [1910s+] (*US*) the buttocks, the anus; thus used as a euph. for ASS n. (2) in various senses, e.g. *pain in the can, flatter the can off* etc. **3** [1910s+] (*US*) the human head. **4** [1910s+] the mouth. [SE *can*, a container]

can *n.*[2] [mid-19C] (*US*) $1. [ety. unknown]

can *n.*[3] **1** [late 19C] a small room, e.g. in a hotel. **2** [20C+] (*US*) a water closet, a lavatory. **3** [1910s+] a prison, a police station lock-up. **4** [1920s] (*US Und.*) a still. **5** [1920s+] (*US Und.*) a safe. **6** [1930s] (*US Und.*) a bank. [SE *can*, a container]

can *n.*[4] [late 19C] a barman; thus *touch the can*, to pay for a round of drinks. [he fills the beer cans for his customers]

can *n.*[5] (*drugs*) **1** [late 19C–1920s] a 5oz (140g) container of opium. **2** [1930s] a 1oz (28g) container of opium. **3** [1930s–50s] 1oz (28g) of morphine. **4** [1950s+] approx. 1oz (28g) of marijuana. **5** [1980s] (*Aus.*) a phial of morphine, sufficient for a single injection. [a (notional) can into which the drug is measured out]

can *n.*[6] [1900s–20s] a pocket.

can *n.*[7] [1910s–20s] (*US*) a bomb; thus *can-maker*, a bomb-maker.

can *n.*[8] [1920s+] (*US*) a dilapidated, run-down, malfunctioning vehicle. [SE *tin-can*]

can *v.*[1] [20C+] to stop doing something; esp. in imper., e.g. *can that noise!* (cf. CAN IT v.). [fig. 'place it in a can']

can *v.*[2] [20C+] (*orig. US*) to reject, to abandon, to discard, to dismiss from a job, to throw out, to ignore. [toss out on one's CAN n.[1] (2)]

can *v.*[3] [1910s+] (*US*) to put in prison. [CAN n.[3] (3)]

can *v.*[4] [1940s–70s] (*US*) to have anal sex with. [CAN n.[1] (2)]

can *v.*[5] [1960s] (*US Black/drugs*) to package heroin for sale. [? link to CAN n.[5]]

Canadian *adj.* [1970s–80s] (*US gay*) uncircumcised. [the preponderance of circumcised men in the US]

Canadian bacon *n.* [1970s+] (*US gay*) an uncircumcised penis. [CANADIAN adj. + BACON n.[1] (4); play on foodstuff]

Canadian black *n.* [1960s+] (*drugs*) marijuana (cf. ACAPULCO (GOLD) n.). [the country of origin + the dark green colouring]

Canadian caper *n.* [1960s] (*Aus.*) a paper. [rhy. sl.]

canadoe *n.* [early 17C] a drink. [? SE *can* + Fr. *d'eau*, of water]

can a duck swim? *phr.* (*also* **will a fish swim?**) [mid-19C+] a phr. used to emphasize one's absolute agreement; thus *can a duck whistle?*, a sarcastic rejoinder.

Canaka *n. see* KANAKA n.[1].

canal boat *n.*[1] (*also* **canal-barge**) [1920s–70s] (*US*) a large foot or shoe. [supposed resemblance]

canal boat *n.*[2] [1960s+] the Totalizator. [rhy. sl. + TOTE, THE n. (1)]

canaller *n.* [mid–late 19C] (*orig. US*) **1** a canal boat. **2** one who lives on a canal boat.

canamo *n.* [1970s+] (*US drugs*) marijuana. [Sp. *cañamo*, a reed]

canappa *n.* [1930s] (*drugs*) marijuana. [Sp. ?]

canaries *n.* [1930s+] bananas. [SE *canary* yellow]

Canarsie whitefish *n. see* CONEY ISLAND WHITEFISH n.

canary *n.*[1] (*also* **canary-bird**) **1** [17C] the vagina. **2** [18C–early 19C] a mistress. **3** [18C–early 19C] a prostitute (cf. ALLEY CAT n.). **4** [mid-19C] a thief's female accomplice. **5** [1940s+] (*Aus.*) a woman. [? the gaudy colouring of her clothes and/or SE *canary*, a small fluttering bird; Henke, *Gutter Life and Language* (1988), suggests that 'fairies' appear only at night]

canary *n.*[2] **1** [19C+] (*Aus./US*) a convict. **2** [late 19C] (*UK prison*) a prisoner who been caught in an escape attempt. **3** [late 19C] a convict's yellow jacket. [the yellow uniforms that they wore and their being 'caged'; poss. reinforced by earlier CANARY-BIRD n.[1] although that image referred to the cage and not the colour]

canary *n.*[3] [early 19C] a yellow silk handkerchief, as worn by a costermonger.

canary *n.*[4] [mid-19C] (*Aus.*) 100 strokes of the lash (cf. BOB n.[5]). [CANARY n.[5] (1); the term plays on the monetary value signifying the number of strokes]

canary *n.*[5] **1** [mid-19C–1900s] a guinea; a sovereign; a gold coin (cf. BANANAS n.[3]; BUMBLEBEE n.[2]; DELOG n.; GELT n.; GILT n.[1]; GINGERBREAD n.[1]; GOLD n.[1]; GOREE n.; NUGGETS n.[1]; OCHRE n.; OLD MR GORY n.; RED n.[2]; REDGE n.; RED ROGUE n.; RED STUFF n.[2]; RED 'UN n.[1]; RIDGE n.; YELLOW n.[2]; YELLOW-BACK n.[1]; YELLOW BIRD n.; YELLOW BOY n.[1]; YELLOW JACKET n.[3]; YELLOW KELTER n.; YELLOW STUFF n.). **2** [late 19C] a half-sovereign (50p). [the colour of the gold coin]

canary *n.*[6] **1** [late 19C] (*US*) a woman. **2** [late 19C–1900s] (*US campus*) a female student at a mixed college. **3** [late 19C+] (*US*) a chorus-singer placed in the gallery from where they urge on the rest of the audience. **4** [20C+] a female singer, usu. fronting a band. **5** [1920s+] (*UK/US/S.Afr. Und.*) an informer. **6** [1930s] (*US Und.*) a loquacious person, a chatterer. **7** [1930s–50s] a singer, irrespective of gender. [SE *canary*, a popular songbird; + ? inference of cowardice since the canary is 'yellow']

canary *n.*[7] [late 19C–1900s] a form on which one signs a promise to make a donation to the Salvation Army; a charity subscription. [the yellow paper used by the Salvationists, whose colours were red and yellow. The nickname came from William Booth (1829–1912) himself. Ware notes that red paper was more expensive]

canary *n.*[8] [late 19C–1900s] an ornament worn at the hip. ['in true descent from the cod-piece, though not so glaring in its declaration' (Ware)]

canary *n.*[9] **1** [late 19C–1910s] (*Aus./N.Z.*) a Chinese immigrant (cf. AH CABBAGE n.). **2** [1940s] (*US Black*) a mulatto girl. [the *yellow* stereotype; (2) YELLOW adj.[2] (1)]

canary *n.*[10] [late 19C+] (*US*) a mule; usu. in comb. with a geographical name (cf. ARIZONA CANARY n.). [the noise of its braying, the antithesis of the song of a mellifluous bird]

canary *n.*[11] [1900s] (*US campus*) a cigarette. [? a specific brand with yellow packaging]

canary *n.*[12] [1980s+] (*Irish*) a fright. [ety. unknown]

canary *v.* [1930s–40s] (*US*) **1** to work as a band vocalist; to sing. **2** of a criminal, to confess; to turn state's evidence. [CANARY n.[6] (4)/CANARY n.[6] (5)]

canary-bird *n.*[1] [17C–mid-19C] **1** a prisoner. **2** a young villain. [the cage in which the prisoner is kept, or the young villain will end up; (2) has an added inference of his smartness of dress]

canary-bird *n.*[2] [late 17C–mid-19C] a guinea or gold coin. [ext. of CANARY n.[5] (1)]

canary-bird *n.*[3] *see* CANARY n.[1].

canary hatch *n.* [1960s] (*US*) a psychiatric institution. [var. on BOOBY-HATCH n. (2)]

canary kid *n.* [1940s] (*US Und.*) a weakling; a coward. [YELLOW adj.[3] (1)]

canasta *n.* [1950s–70s] the male or female genitals; thus (*US gay*) *play canasta*, to ogle other men's crotches. [the card-game, ult. f. Sp. *canasta*, a basket; thus pun on BASKET n.[1] (2)]

canat *n. see* KINAT n.

cancelled stamp *n.* [1920s] (*US*) a shy person.

cancelled stick *n.* [1960s+] (*drugs*) a marijuana cigarette. [? SE *cancel*, i.e. it 'cancels' you out + STICK n.[9] (3); pun on CANCER STICK n.]

cancel someone out *v.* [1990s+] to murder someone.

cancel someone's ticket *v.* [1960s+] to murder, to assassinate.

cancer *n.* [1970s+] (*US*) severe rust on an automobile.

cancer alley *n.* [1980s+] (*US*) the industrial area of a city. [the polluting factories may well issue carcinogens into the atmosphere]

cancer stick *n.* (*also* **cancer pill**) [1950s+] a cigarette. [the proven link between tobacco and lung cancer; note Jap. use of *cancer stick*, a mobile telephone, referring to the belief that the phones can irradiate the user]

C&A *adj.* [1950s–60s] homosexual. [rhy. sl. = GAY adj.[1] (3); ult. *C&A*, a chain of clothing stores in the UK]

C and B *v. see* COAT AND BADGE v.

C and E man *n.* [1960s] (*US*) someone who attends church only rarely. [Christmas and Easter; the festivals that attract the irregular attender]

C and H *n.* [1960s+] (*US Black*) a mixture of cocaine and heroin. [C n.[2] (1) + H n.[2] (1); also pun on brandname of *C & H* cane sugar]

candle *v.*[1] [late 19C] to check carefully. [SE *candle*, to test an egg's freshness by holding it to a candle flame]

candle *v.*[2] [1930s] to make angry, to annoy. [var. on BURN v.[2] (3)]

candle (and) sconce *n.* [1940s+] a pimp, a ponce (cf. ALPHONSE n.[2]). [rhy. sl.]

candle-basher *n.* [late 19C–1960s] a spinster. [the candle's use as a dildo]

candle eater *n.* [1920s–30s] (*US tramp*) a Russian. [? their poverty]

candle sconce *n. see* CANDLE (AND) SCONCE n.

candle shop *n.* [late 19C] a Roman Catholic church. [the many candles that burn in one]

candlesperm *n.* [1920s+] (*US Black*) melted wax from a candle, which drips down into globular beadlets. [resemblance to drops of semen/sperm; Major, *Juba to Jive: A Dict. of Afro-American Slang* (1994), defines it as a 'voodoo term']

candlestick *n.*[1] [mid-17C; late 19C] the vagina. [a place into which the phallic 'candle' is inserted]

candlestick *n.*[2] **1** [mid-19C] a fountain, spec. one in Trafalgar Square, London WC2. **2** [20C+] (*Irish*) a drop of mucus running from the nose. [the running of water or mucus supposedly resembles that of wax]

candlesticks *n.* [late 18C–early 19C] small, bad or untunable bells. [? the impossibility of getting a clear note when striking a candlestick]

C and M *n*. [1950s+] (*drugs*) a cocaine and morphine mixture. [C n.² (1) + M n. (1)]

can-do *adj*. [20C+] (*orig. US*) positive, enthusiastic, aggressive. [affirmative phr. *I can do it*]

can do *phr*. [20C+] it is possible, it is within my power; thus NO CAN DO phr.

candy *n*.¹ [late 19C+] (*US*) something admirable.

candy *n*.² **1** [20C+] (*US*) money. **2** [1920s–40s] (*US Und*.) jewellery.

candy *n*.³ **1** [1920s+] (*orig. US Black*) sex as an abstract; thus spec. sexual intercourse. **2** [1930s+] a sexually desirable person of either sex. **3** [1950s+] (*gay*) the passive partner in anal intercourse. **4** [1950s+] (*US gay*) a pretty, young homosexual boy. **5** [1960s] (*US teen*) a weakling.

candy *n*.⁴ **1** [1930s] (*US drugs*) opium (cf. APOSTLE n.). **2** [1930s+] (*drugs*) cocaine. **3** [1960s+] (*drugs*) any drug, esp. in capsule form (cf. PILL n.⁴). **4** [1980s+] (*US Black/drugs*) heroin. **5** [2000s] (*US drugs*) crack cocaine (cf. BASE n.). [SAmE *candy*, sweets; i.e. an adult 'sweet'; + abbr. NOSE CANDY n.]

candy *n*.⁵ [2000s] (*US Black*) the decoration or customization of an automobile.

candy, the *n*. [1900s] (*US*) something excellent, admirable, desirable.

candy *adj*.¹ [mid-18C–early 19C] (*mainly Anglo-Irish*) drunk. [ety. unknown; ? link to SE *can*, a container for liquids]

candy *adj*.² [late 19C] (*US Und*.) of dice, transparent.

candy *adj*.³ **1** [1900s; 1990s+] (*US campus*) excellent, worthy of admiration. **2** [1930s+] (*US*) of a job or any other activity, e.g. a crime, easy, undemanding, 'soft'. [SAmE *candy*, sweets]

candy *adj*.⁴ [1910s+] (*US*) of a person, soft, weak, effeminate. [abbr. CANDY-ASS adj.]

candy-ass *n*.¹ [1960s+] a coward, a weakling, an over-sensitive person. [CANDY-ASS adj.]

candy-ass *n*.² [1960s+] (*US camp gay*) **1** an attractive young man, thus a term of abuse by non-gays. **2** a sweet, sexy young woman. [CANDY n.³ (2) + -ASS sfx]

candy-ass *adj*. [1950s+] (*US*) **1** (*also* **candy-assed**) of a person, weak, ineffectual. **2** of a job, examination etc, insufficiently challenging, too easy. [SE *candy*/CANDY adj.³/CANDY adj.⁴ + -ASS sfx]

candy-bag *n*. (*also* **candy boy**) [1920s+] (*Aus*.) a handyman who works for a prostitute. [CANDY n.³ (1) + BAGMAN n.² (1)/SE *boy*]

candy bar *n*. [1950s] (*US drugs*) a place where cocaine is sold. [CANDY n.⁴ (2) + SE *bar*]

candy-bar punk *n*. [1960s] (*US prison*) a prisoner who has become a passive homosexual while in prison. [the gifts or payments of candy bars that he receives for his services]

candy boy *n*.¹ [1900s] (*US*) a boyfriend, a beloved male. [SAmE *candy* + SE *boy*]

candy boy *n*.² *see* CANDY-BAG n.

candy-butt *n*. [1970s+] (*US Black*) a young, inexperienced male. [SAmE *candy* + BUTT n.¹ (4); var. on CANDY-ASS n.¹]

candy C *n*. [1950s–70s] (*drugs*) cocaine. [SAmE *candy*/CANDY n.⁴ (2) + C n.² (1)]

candy cane *n*.¹ [late 19C–1970s] (*US*) the penis. [like the synon. sweet, it can be sucked]

candy cane *n*.² [1980s+] (*US Black*) cocaine, whether as powder or crack. [SAmE *candy*/CANDY n.⁴ (2) + (*co*)*caine* + play on SE]

candy cock *n*. [1910s] (*US*) a well-behaved, pleasant person; the inference is of softness. [SAmE *candy* + COCK n.² (1)]

candy fiend *n*. [1950s] (*US drugs*) a cocaine addict. [CANDY n.⁴ (2) + FIEND n.² (1)]

candy-flip *v*. [1990s+] (*US drugs*) to mix or sequence LSD and MDMA; thus *candy-flipping*.

candy kid *n*. **1** [1900s–40s] (*US*) a successful womanizer. **2** [1900s–50s] (*US*) a well-behaved, pleasant person. **3** [1900s–50s] (*US*) a weakling, a mother's boy, a favoured child. **4** [1910s–40s]

(*US*) a dandy, a fashionably dressed person. **5** [1940s–50s] (*Aus*.) a jack-of-all-trades employed by a brothel. [SAmE *candy* + KID n.¹ (4)]

candy-leg *n*. [1920s–40s] (*US campus*) a rich student who is also attractive to women.

candy maker *n*. [1960s] (*US*) a male homosexual who masturbates (but does not fellate) a partner, then swallows the resultant semen.

candyman *n*. **1** [1910s–30s] (*US*) a dandy. **2** [1920s+] (*US Black*) a woman's male partner or (illicit) lover. **3** [1960s+] (*drugs*) a drug dealer. **4** [1980s] (*US Black*) a pimp (cf. BOSS PLAYER n.; CUTTER n.¹; EASTMAN n.; EASY RIDER n.¹; FAGGOTER n.; GORILLA PIMP n.; ICEBERG SLIM n.; LOWRIDER n.¹; MACK n.¹; MACK MAN n.; MAIN MAN n.¹; PLAYER n.¹; PUFF DADDY n.; SWEETBACK (MAN) n.; SWEETMAN n.; SWEET WILLIE n.; SWING DADDY n.; WELFARE PIMP n.). [the 'sweetness' of SAmE *candy*]

candy rock *n*. [1990s+] (*Aus. drugs*) cocaine hydrochloride. [CANDY n.⁴ (2) + ROCK n.³ (3)]

candystriper *n*. [1960s+] (*US*) a volunteer nurse's aide; thus *candystripe*, to work as such an aide. [the usu. red and white striped uniform]

candy team *n*. [1930s] (*US*) the preferred team of mules. [CANDY adj.³ (1)]

candy wagon *n*. **1** [1920s+] (*US*) a buggy. **2** [1940s+] a light truck.

cane *n*.¹ **1** [20C+] (*UK Und*.) a short house-breaker's crowbar. **2** [1930s] a bassoon. [resemblance]

cane *n*.² [1980s+] (*US Black*) cocaine, whether as powder or crack. [abbr. CANDY CANE n.²]

cane *v*. **1** [1910s+] to defeat, to treat harshly. **2** [1940s] (*also* **cane it**) to attack, esp. fig., e.g. to drink heartily, to take a large amount of drugs. **3** [1960s+] to have sexual intercourse (cf. BANG v.¹). **4** [1990s+] (*also* **cane it**) to hurry, to rush. **5** [1990s+] (*also* **cane it**) to do something in an aggressive, urgent manner, e.g. a robbery. **6** [1990s+] (*also* **cane it**) to make a lot of money. **7** [1990s+] (*UK juv*.) to be seriously reprimanded. [fig. uses of SE]

caned *adj*. [1980s+] **1** (*drugs*) extremely intoxicated by a drug, usu. cannabis. **2** very drunk (cf. ANNIHILATED adj.). [the equation of the effects of drink/drugs with suffering violence/CANE v. (2)]

cane nigger *n*. [late 19C] a cheerful person. [SE (*sugar*)*cane* + NIGGER n.¹ (1), i.e. stereotyped image of a cane field worker]

cane oil *n*. [1970s] (*W.I.*) rum. [SE *cane oil*, liquor of the sugar-cane]

cane toad *n*. [1990s+] (*Aus*.) a rich old man. [SE *cane toad*, the large toad, *bufo marinus*]

canetta *n*. [1970s+] (*US gay*) the buttocks. [CAN n.¹ (2) + sfx *-etta*]

can house *n*. [20C+] (*US, mainly Chicago*) a brothel (cf. ACCOMMODATION HOUSE n.). [CAN n.¹ (1) + HOUSE n.¹ (1)]

caning *n*. [1940s+] the act of consuming enthusiastically. [CANE v. (2)]

canister *n*.¹ (*also* **cannister**) **1** [late 18C] the vagina (cf. BAG n.¹). **2** [late 18C+] the head. **3** [late 19C] a hat. **4** [1900s–30s] (*US*) a watch. **5** [1900s–50s] (*US Und*.) a revolver. **6** [1910s–50s] (*US Und*.) a jail. **7** [1920s] (*US Und*.) a lookout. **8** [1930s–50s] (*US*) a safe or bank vault. [all fig. uses of SE *canister*, a container]

canister *n*.² [late 19C–1900s] a clergyman. [SE *camis*, a surplice + CAMESA n.]

canister-cap *n*. [mid-19C] a hat. [CANISTER n.¹ (2) + SE *cap*]

canister set *n*. [1970s+] (*US gay*) the buttocks. [CAN n.¹ (2)]

can it *v*. [20C+] (*orig. US*) **1** to stop, esp. to stop talking; usu. in excl. *can it!*, shut up! **2** to reject or give up. [ext. of CAN v.¹]

cank *n*. [mid-17C–early 19C] (*UK Und*.) a dumb person. [? ironic reverse of dial. *cank*, a gossip, a chatterer]

cank *adj*. [mid-17C–early 19C] (*UK Und*.) dumb. [CANK n.]

canker *n*. *see* KANKER n.

cankywampus *adj*. *see* CATAWAMPUS adj.

can moocher *n*. *see* TOMATO-CAN VAG n.

cannabinol *n.* [1970s] (*US drugs*) phencyclidine (cf. ACE n.[4]). [misreading of SE *cannabinol*, the active constituent of cannabis]

Cannacker *n. see* CANUCK n.

cannakin *n. see* CANNIKEN n.[1].

canned *adj.*[1] (*also* **canned up**) [1910s+] drunk (cf. ALED UP adj.). [SE *can*, a container for liquids]

canned *adj.*[2] [1920s] (*US*) of writing or information, rote, pre-packaged, 'boilerplate'. [the idea that comes in a SE *can*]

canned cattle *n.* [1930s] (*US prison*) corned beef.

canned cow *n.* [20C+] (*US*) condensed milk. [SE *canned* + COW n.[5] (1)]

canned fruit *n. see* FRUIT n.[2] (2).

canned goods *n.* [1910s–70s] (*US*) a virgin of either sex, usu. female; the genitalia of such a person. [pun on SE *can*/CAN n.[1] (1) + the image of a sealed tin]

canned heat *n.* [1910s–60s] (*US*) a form of crude alcohol, intended for heating purposes but drunk, as is methylated spirits, by down-and-out alcoholics who can afford nothing better; thus *canned heater*, *canned-heat stiff*, one who drinks such alcohol.

canned sativa *n.* [1980s+] (*drugs*) cannabis. [pun on Lat. *Cannabis sativa* + ? drug use of CANNED adj.[1]]

canned stuff *n.* [1930s–50s] (*US drugs*) commercially packaged opium. [SE *canned* + STUFF n.[3] (2)]

canned up *adj. see* CANNED adj.[1].

canned willie *n.* [1900s–10s] (*US*) corned beef.

canner *n.* [late 19C–1910s] (*US*) a scraggy cow or other animal fit only for the lower end of the canned meat market.

cannery *n.* [1910s+] (*US prison*) a prison. [ext. of CAN n.[3] (3)]

cannibal *n.*[1] [17C] a notably harsh bargainer or grasping tradesman. [a pun on SE *cannibal*, one who 'eats' his fellow human beings]

cannibal *n.*[2] **1** [1920s–30s] (*US tramp*) an older homosexual tramp who travels with a young boy. **2** [1960s+] (*US Black*) one who indulges in oral sex. [pun on SE *eat*/EAT v.[3] (1)]

cannie *n.* **1** [1940s] a *cannib*al. **2** [1990s+] (*Scot.*) a *can*teen, usu. institutional. [abbr.]

canniken *n.*[1] (*also* **cannakin, cannikin**) [17C–early 19C] (*UK Und.*) the plague. [? SE *canker*]

canniken *n.*[2] (*also* **cannikin**) [late 17C–mid-19C] a small can. [SE *can* + dimin. sfx *-ikin*; B.E. notes 'among the Dutch'; Hotten (1859) suggests 'similar to pannikin']

cannister *n. see* CANISTER n.[1].

Cannock *n. see* CANUCK n.

cannon *n.*[1] **1** [20C+] (*US*) a gun, esp. a large one; thus a gun barrel. **2** [1910s–30s] (*US*) a hired gunman. **3** [1950s] (*US drugs*) a hypodermic syringe. **4** [1960s+] (*US*) the penis (cf. AX n.[2]). **5** [1970s] (*US*) a pimp. [(3) is play on GUN n.[1] (3)]

cannon *n.*[2] [20C+] **1** the act of pickpocketing. **2** the act of pickpocketing. [GUN n.[6] (3); note Irwin, *American Tramp and Und. Slang* (1931): 'No doubt from the Yiddish, "gonoph," a thief, which became "gon" and then "gun" and so to its present form. In the argot, "cannon", "rod", "gun", "gat", "heater" and "torch" are all used to designate a revolver or pistol, but cannon is the only word of the group used synonymously with "gun" as a derivative of the root word, "gonov," a thief']

cannon *adj.* (*also* **canon, cannoned**) [mid-19C–1940s] drunk. [SE *cannon*; i.e. one has been knocked down]

cannon *v.* [1920s–40s] (*US Und.*) to work as a pickpocket. [CANNON n.[2] (1)]

cannon and khaki *n. see* KHAKI n.[1].

cannonball *n.*[1] [late 19C] (*US short order*) crullers.

cannonball *n.*[2] [late 19C–1960s] (*US tramp*) an express train.

cannonball *n.*[3] [1920s–50s] (*US Und.*) a smaller safe that is held within a larger one.

cannonball *n.*[4] [1920s–60s] (*US Und.*) a message out of jail sent by a convict.

cannonball *n.*[5] [1940s–60s] (*US*) a superior person or one who claims to be so.

cannonball *n.*[6] [1950s–70s] (*US drugs*) a mixed injection, e.g. of heroin and cocaine or morphine and cocaine.

cannonballs *n.* [late 19C] the testicles. [the shape]

cannoned *adj. see* CANNON adj.

cannon mob *n.* [20C+] a pickpocketing gang. [CANNON n.[2] (1) + MOB n.[2] (3)]

cannot look at *phr.* [late 19C+] a phr. meaning bears no comparison, cannot equal, has no chance of competing with.

Cannuck *n. see* CANUCK n.

canoe *n.*[1] [20C+] a shoe. [rhy. sl.]

canoe *n.*[2] [1930s+] (*US*) a large car.

canoe *n.*[3] [1960s–80s] the vagina. [the supposed resemblance of the vagina to the elongated oval shape of a canoe]

canoe *v.*[1] (*also* **john canoo**) [mid-19C; 1920s–50s] to cuddle, to caress sexually. [CANOODLE v.]

canoe *v.*[2] [1980s+] of a cigarette or cannabis cigarette, to burn down on top or one side rather than evenly. [the burned side presumably resembles the hollowed portion of a canoe]

canoe inspection *n.* [1960s–70s] (*US*) a medical inspection of the female genitals. [CANOE n.[3]]

canoevre *n.* [early–mid-19C] an attempt at swindling or a similarly dubious enterprise. [? link to SE *manoeuvre*]

can of beans *n. see* CAN OF WORMS n.

can of Coke *n.* [1990s+] a joke. [rhy. sl.]

can of jelly *n. see* BOWL OF JELLY n.

can of oil *n.* (*also* **canov**) [20C+] a boil. [rhy. sl.]

can of piss *n.* [2000s] (*Irish*) a term of abuse.

can of worms *n.* (*also* **can of beans, …peas**) [1940s+] (*orig. US*) an unpleasant, complex and unappetizing situation, thus phr. *open a can of worms*.

canon *adj. see* CANNON adj.

canoneer *n.* [mid–late 17C] an interpreter of ecclesiastical canons, a canonist.

canoodle *v.* (*also* **conoodle**) [mid-19C+] (*orig. US*) to cuddle, to caress sexually; thus *canoodler*, one who is devoted to giving or getting such caresses; *canoodlism*, love-making. [ety. unknown but presumably linked to SE *cuddle*]

can opener *n.*[1] [1910s–60s] **1** (*UK/US Und.*) any tool used for the breaking open of a safe, when explosives would lead to discovery. **2** (*UK/US Und.*) (*also* **can shooter**) a safe-breaker. **3** (*US*) a saber. [CAN n.[3] (5) + SE *opener*]

can opener *n.*[2] [1910s–40s] (*US*) a cook.

canov *n. see* CAN OF OIL n.

can racket *n.* [late 19C] (*US*) a party devoted to drinking beer. [SE *can* + RACKET n.[2]]

cans *n.* [1950s+] (*US*) the female breasts. [? cans of milk or just resemblance]

can shooter *n. see* CAN OPENER n.[1] (2).

cant *n.*[1] [mid-16C+] the language of the world of professional thieves and itinerant criminal beggars; the term echoes the whining tones in which they 'chant' for alms. [Lat. *cantare*, to sing. The term originates in conventional 12C society as a pej. description of church services that were condemned as substituting rote mouthings for real devotion. It was this use that led to the application of the term to, and adoption by, criminal beggars. SE *cant*, while obviously linked, is generally seen as relating to a pair of 17C Presbyterian ministers, Andrew *Cant* and his son Alexander. In a number of 18C/19C works, e.g. Johnson, *Dictionary* (1755), *cant* is used as synon. for SE *slang*]

cant *n.*[2] [mid-19C] (*UK tramp*) food. [SE *cant*, to toss or throw; thus that which one 'cants' down one's throat]

cant *n.*[3] [mid-19C] **1** a blow. **2** a gift. [SE *cant*, a throw; (2) the gift is 'thrown' to the recipient]

cant *v.*[1] (*UK Und.*) **1** [mid-16C–19C] to speak, to talk, esp. underworld slang. **2** [early 17C] to beg for alms. [CANT n.[1]]

cant *v.*[2] [mid-18C–early 19C] to drink, to swallow. [SE *decant*]

Cantab. *n.* **1** [mid-18C–mid-19C] a member (usu. an undergraduate) of Cambridge University. **2** [mid-19C] a member (usu. an undergraduate) of Harvard University in Cambridge, Mass. [abbr. of Lat. *Cantabrigiensis*, of Cambridge University]

cantankerous *adj.* [late 18C–19C] irritable, ill-tempered, quick to become angry. [SE in 20C; ? f. ME *contak*, quarrelling, argument]

can't be bad *phr.* [1960s+] a general phr. of approval.

canteen *n.* [early 19C+] (*S.Afr.*) a public house, a tavern; thus *canteen-keeper*, a publican. [? orig. milit. use]

canter *n.* [mid-16C–19C] a professional thief or criminal mendicant. [CANT *v.*[1] (1)]

canterbury *n.* [late 17C] a pace between a trot and gallop. [abbr. SE *Canterbury trot*; the pace, which is the root of SE *canter*, is supposedly that adopted by the Canterbury pilgrims as they rode on their way to the cathedral]

Canterbury story *n.* (*also* **Canterbury tale**) [mid-16C–early 19C] a long, elaborate and ultimately tedious story. [the tales told by pilgrims on the way to Canterbury, and esp. f. the title of Chaucer's *Canterbury Tales* (c.1387)]

canter gloak *n.* [late 18C–mid-19C] (*UK Und.*) **1** a parson. **2** a liar. [SE *cant* + GLOAK *n.*]

can't find one's arse with both hands *phr.* (*also* ...with two hands, **can't find one's ass with both/two hands**) [20C+] **1** very drunk. **2** absolutely confused, totally incompetent. [ARSE *n.*[1] (1)/ASS *n.* (2)]

can't — for toffee *phr.* [late 19C+] said of a particularly incompetent person; 'it' varies as to context.

can't go no further, just like a bear's brother *phr.* [1940s] (*US Black*) miserable, out of sorts, dejected.

can't hit a lick *phr.* [1920s–30s] (*US Black*) used of an inability to succeed in a given aim, esp. that of making money either legally or otherwise. [SE *hit* + LICK *n.*[1] (3); musical imagery]

canticle *n.* [late 18C–mid-19C] a parish clerk. [SE *canticle*, a hymn used during church services. The clerk trad. led the congregation in singing]

canting *n.* [mid-16C–mid-19C] thieves' jargon. [CANT *v.*[1] (1)]

canting crew *n.* (*also* **canting tribe**) [mid-16C–19C] the world of professional thieves and criminal mendicants. [CANT *v.*[1] (1) + CREW *n.* (1)/SE *tribe*. The 'official' *canting crew*, as delineated by Grose (1785), encompassed 23 orders. Men (in descending order of status): RUFFLER *n.*; UPRIGHT MAN *n.*; HOOKER *n.*[1] or ANGLER *n.*; ROGUE *n.*[1]; WILD ROGUE *n.*; PRIGGER (OF PRANCERS) *n.*; PALLIARD *n.*; FRATER *n.*; JARKMAN *n.* or PATRICO *n.*; FRESHWATER MARINER *n.* or WHIP-JACK *n.*; DOMMERER *n.*; DRUNKEN TINKER *n.*; SWADDLER *n.*; ABRAM *n.*. Women: DEMANDER FOR GLIMMER *n.*; BAWDY BASKET *n.*; MORT *n.*; AUTEM MORT *n.*; WALKING MORT *n.*; DOXY *n.*; DELL *n.*; KINCHIN MORT *n.* However, such lists vary, e.g. that in the *New Canting Dict.* (1725) runs to 64 'job descriptions']

can't keep still *n.* *see* NEVER STAND STILL *n.*

cant of dobbin *n.* [late 18C–early 19C] a roll of ribbon. [SE *cant*, a share, a portion + ? dial. *dobbin*, a form of weaving machine, or *dobbie*, worsted]

cant of togs *n.* [mid-19C] a (charitable) gift of clothes. [CANT *n.*[3] (2) + TOGS *n.* (1)]

can't say 'naval intelligencer' *phr.* (*also* **can't say national intelligencer**) [late 19C+] (*US*) very drunk.

can't see a hole in a (forty-foot) ladder *phr.* [mid-19C+] very drunk.

can't see someone's arse for dust *phr.* [late 19C+] a phr. used to describe a speedy departure. [ARSE *n.*[1] (1)]

can't see through a ladder *phr.* [mid-19C+] **1** (*also* **too drunk to see through a ladder**) extremely drunk. **2** very stupid (cf. COULD FUCK UP A WET DREAM *phr.*; COULDN'T SEE THE ROAD TO THE DUNNY IF IT HAD RED FLAGS ON IT *phr.*; CRUISING WITH ONE'S LIGHTS ON (DIM) *phr.*; LIKE A ROPE-DANCER'S POLE WITH LEAD AT BOTH ENDS *phr.*; LOOKS LIKE HE WOULDN'T PISS IF HIS PANTS WERE ON FIRE, HE *phr.*; NOT ENOUGH SENSE TO POUR PISS OUT OF A BOOT *phr.*; NOT GO THREE ROUNDS WITH A REVOLVING DOOR *phr.*; NOT IN THE RACE *phr.*; NOT KNOW IF ONE'S ARSE WAS ON FIRE *v.*; NOT KNOW ONE'S ARSE FROM A HOLE IN THE GROUND *v.*; NOT KNOW ONE'S ARSE FROM ONE'S ELBOW *v.*; NOT KNOW ONE'S BUTT FROM A GOURD *v.*; NOT KNOW WHETHER TO SHIT OR GO BLIND *v.*; SHE WOULDN'T KNOW IF SOMEONE WAS UP HER *phr.*).

can't shit a shitter *phr.* (*also* **don't bullshit a bullshitter, don't shit a shitter**) [1950s+] a phr. meaning you can't fool someone who deals in fooling others. [SHIT *v.*[3] (1)/BULLSHIT *v.* (2) + SHITTER *n.*[2] /BULLSHITTER *n.* (1)]

can't speak threepenny bit *phr.* [late 19C] speechless, struck dumb. [? image of *threepenny bit* as an insignificant sum]

can't take a trick *phr.* [1940s+] (*Aus.*) consistently unlucky. [card-game imagery]

can't touch the sides *phr.* [1970s+] a coarse joke referring to a large, and thus loose, vagina or anus, used by both hetero- and homosexuals.

canty *adj.*[1] [mid-19C+] (*Irish*) pleasant, cheerful; neat, thorough. [Low Ger. *kant*, lively, cheerful]

canty *adj.*[2] [1920s+] (*Aus.*) unpleasant, ill-tempered. [SE *cantankerous*]

Canuck *n.* (*also* **Cannacker, Cannock, Cannuck, Canucker, Kanacka, Kanaka, Kanuck, Kanuk, Knuck**) [mid-19C+] (*US*) a derog. term for a Canadian, esp. a French Canadian. [Can. Fr. *canaque*, f. Hawaiian *kanaka*, a man or simply *Can(ada)* + *(chin)ook*. The term supposedly orig. in the Maine lumber camps; as regards derog. status, note email to *American Dialect Society-List* (Internet, 4 August 1999): "Canuck" is not in the least offensive, as Canadian linguists and lay folk have told me. Note the hockey team, the Vancouver Canucks']

Canuck *adj.* [mid-19C+] (*US*) Canadian. [CANUCK *n.*]

canvas *n.* **1** [19C] the human skin. **2** [1940s+] (*US Und.*) a straitjacket.

canvas muster *n.* *see* TARPAULIN MUSTER *n.*

canyon *n.* **1** [1930s+] the vagina (cf. AGREEABLE RUTS OF LIFE *n.*). **2** [1980s+] the anus (cf. ALLEY WAY *n.*).

can you beat it? *phr.* (*also* **can you beat that?**) [mid-19C+] (*orig. US*) a phr. used to express surprise or amazement.

can you dig it? *phr.* [1960s+] (*US Black*) a rhetorical phr. seeking affirmation as a response. [DIG *v.*[5] (4)]

can you keep one down? *phr.* [1910s] (*Aus.*) an invitation to drink.

can you see green in my eyes? *phr.* [mid-19C+] do you think I'm lying?

can you tie that? *excl.* (*also* **can you tie him/it?**) [late 19C–1930s] (*US*) an excl. of surprise or amazement, would you believe it? [SE *tie*, to equal, thus lit. 'can you equal that?']

cap *n.*[1] [mid-19C+] (*orig. and mainly US*) *cap*tain. [abbr.; Ware cites some UK use but *cap'n* is more common]

cap *n.*[2] [mid-19C+] (*US*) a bullet, a shot.

cap *n.*[3] [late 19C+] (*US Und.*) the act of ensnaring a victim into a confidence game. [CAPPER *n.*[1] (1)]

cap *n.*[4] **1** [1920s+] (*drugs*) a capsule containing a narcotic, usu. heroin (cf. PILL *n.*[4]). **2** [1960s+] (*drugs*) a capsule of LSD. **3** [1980s+] (*drugs*) crack cocaine (cf. BASE *n.*[1]). **4** [1990s+] (*US prison*) a measure of marijuana, as much as can be fitted into a small cap, e.g. of a toothpaste tube or a container of chapstick. [abbr.]

cap *n.*[5] (*orig. US Black*) **1** [1940s+] a rejoinder. **2** [1960s] an insult aimed at someone's family; used as part of a ritualized interchange. [CAP (ON) *v.*]

cap *n.*[6] (*US Black*) **1** [1950s+] the mind. **2** [1990s+] the top of the head, the cranium. [they 'cap' the body]

cap *n.*[7] [1960s–70s] (*US Black*) the mouth, esp. as used in oral-genital sex; thus *give (someone) some cap*, to fellate, to perform cunnilingus. [CAP *n.*[6]; strained parallel to HEAD *n.*[10]]

cap *n.*[8] *see* BONNET *n.*[2].

cap *n.*[9] *see* CAPPER *n.*[1].

cap *v.*[1] **1** [late 16C–early 17C] to arrest (for debt). **2** [mid-19C] (*UK Und.*) to take, to grab hold of. [abbr. SE *capture*]

cap *v.*[2] [late 17C–early 19C] (*UK Und.*) to swear an oath. [Lat. *capias*, you may take, a term used in a variety of legal writs, e.g. *capias ad respondendum*, to enforce attendance at court, and *capias ad satisfaciendum*, after judgement, to imprison the defendant until the plaintiff's claim is satisfied]

cap *v.*[3] [early 19C] (*US Und.*) to give satisfaction. [? SE *capitulate* or doff one's *cap*]

cap *v.*[4] [early 19C+] to act as a confederate in a gambling game. [20C+ use mainly US]

cap *v.*[5] (*drugs*) **1** [1940s+] to transfer bulk drugs (in powder form) into capsules for sale. **2** [1950s–60s] to be given drugs for free. [CAP *n.*[4] (1)]

cap *v.*[6] [1970s] to shoot a person in the knee or leg as a form of punishment. [abbr. SE *kneecap*]

cap *v.*[7] [1970s+] (*orig. US Black*) **1** to fire a gun; thus *capping*, gunfire. **2** to kill, to murder, to shoot dead. [CAP *n.*[2]]

cap *v.*[8] [1990s+] (*US campus*) to punch someone in the face. [CAP *n.*[6]/CAP *n.*[7]]

cap *v.*[9] *see* CAP (ON) *v.*

cap acquaintance *n.* [late 18C–early 19C] a slight or passing acquaintance. [a person one knows well enough to raise one's cap to when passing in the street, but not to speak to properly]

Cape Ann turkey *n.* [mid-19C–1940s] (*US*) salt cod. [SE *Cape Ann*, a cape in northern Massachusetts]

Cape Cod turkey *n.* **1** [mid-19C–1960s] (*US*) salt cod; a codfish dinner. **2** [20C+] corned (salt) beef and cabbage. [SE *Cape Cod* in Massachusetts]

capeesh? *phr.* [1950s+] (*US*) do you understand? [Ital. *capisce*, do you understand?]

cape horn *n.* [late 19C] the vagina (cf. ANTIPODES *n.*). [pun on HORN *n.*[2] (1)]

cape kelly *n.* [1950s] (*Aus.*) the stomach. [rhy. sl. = SE *belly*]

capella *n.* [19C] an overcoat. [Lat. *cappella*, little cloak or cape, ult. f. *cappella* or cloak of St Martin, preserved by the Frankish kings as a sacred relic, carried into battle and used to give sanctity to oaths. The name was then applied to the sanctuary in which the relic was preserved under the care of its *cappellani* (chaplains), and thence to any sanctuary containing holy relics and thus to any place used for worship, other than a church, the earlier name for which was *oratorium*, the oratory]

Cape nightingale *n.* [late 19C+] (*S.Afr.*) a frog (cf. CAMBRIDGE NIGHTINGALE *n.*).

cape of good hope *n.*[1] [19C] the vagina (cf. ANTIPODES *n.*). [the pleasure it offers plus its position near the 'bottom' of the globe]

cape of good hope *n.*[2] [20C+] soap. [rhy. sl.]

caper *n.*[1] [mid-19C] a chorister. [the SE *cape* that is part of their uniform]

caper *n.*[2] **1** [mid-19C+] a dodge, a trick. **2** [mid-19C+] a situation, an event. **3** [late 19C+] (*mainly US*) an occupation, a job. **4** [late 19C+] the proper course of action; esp. ext. as *the proper caper*, the right thing to do. **5** [1920s+] a large-scale crime, usu. involving a great deal of elaborate planning and aimed at very large sums of money, expensive pieces of jewellery etc. The supposed lack of violence in such enterprises lent them a somewhat jokey air. **6** [1920s+] a crime, irrespective of scale. **7** [1950s+] a scheme. [SE *caper*, a frisky movement]

caper *v.*[1] [late 18C–mid-19C] to be hanged. [SE *caper*, to dance or leap in a frolicsome manner]

caper *v.*[2] [1960s+] to commit a crime; esp. as a profesional thief. [CAPER *n.*[2] (6)]

caperdewsie *n.* [early–mid-17C] stocks; prison. [pron. of CAPPADOCHIO *n.*]

caper juice *n.* [19C] whisky. [a sufficiency or an excess causes one to 'cut capers']

caper merchant *n.* [late 18C–mid-19C] a dancing master. [SE *caper* + MERCHANT *n.*]

Cape smoke *n.* [early 19C+] whisky or rough, strong brandy distilled in South Africa. [Swahili *moshi*, banana liquor, lit. smoke, steam, soot, lamp-black]

capey *n.* (*also* **capie**) [1940s+] (*S.Afr.*) a Cape Coloured, a member of the Coloured population group of the Cape Province, esp. of the Western Province of the Cape; thus *capeytaal*, 'capey language', the argot spoken by some Coloureds, a patois of Afrikaans, English and Xhosa.

capital g's *n.* [2000s] (*US Black*) the testicles. [? SE *gonads*]

capital K *n.* [1940s+] (*W.I.*) knock-knees. [the approx. shape]

capitation drugget *n.* [late 17C] cheap, second-rate fabric. [SE *drugget*, a coarse woollen material used mainly for floorcoverings or tablecloths + SE *capitation*, a tax that was levied on the fabric]

cap'n *n.* [mid-19C+] captain. [abbr.]

cap'n toke *n.* [1980s+] (*US campus*) a marijuana smoker. [CAP'N *n.* + TOKE *n.*[2]; the honorary rank of Captain is a HIPPIE *n.*[2] (3) term used *inter alia* for Jerry Garcia (1942–95) of the Grateful Dead, known as 'Captain Trips']

capo *n.* [1950s+] **1** (*US Und.*) a senior figure in the US Mafia; thus *capo di tutti capi*, the supreme 'boss of bosses'. **2** (*UK Und.*) a senior gangster. **3** in fig. use, anybody or thing that is 'in charge'. [Ital. *caporegime*]

cap (on) *v.* **1** [20C+] to make a smart rejoinder. **2** [20C+] to lie. **3** [1900s] to brag about, to aggrandize. **4** [1950s] to dumfound, to render silent. **5** [1960s] (*US*) to entice a victim into a swindle. **6** [1960s+] (*US Black*) to insult someone, esp. by disparaging their family. [early 19C dial. *cap*, to surpass, to outdo]

capon *n.*[1] [17C–early 19C] a eunuch; an impotent man. [SE *capon*, a castrated cock]

capon *n.*[2] [mid-17C–early 19C] **1** used for a variety of fish, e.g. a red herring, a sole, a dried haddock. **2** a bloater. [the cheap herring as a substitute for the more expensive SE *capon*]

capon *n.*[3] [1940s–60s] a young homosexual man, sometimes but not invariably a prostitute. [SE *capon*, a castrated cock; the ref. is to CHICKEN *n.*[4] (4) rather than to any sexual malfunction]

cap one's arm *v.* [1960s] (*US drugs*) to take an injection of a narcotic. [CAP *n.*[4] (1)]

cap one's lucky *v.* [20C+] (*Aus.*) to run off, to leave at speed. [SE *cap*, to protect + *lucky*; i.e. to take advantage of one's opportunity to run away]

capoodle *n.* *see* CABOODLE *n.*

capot me! *excl.* [mid-18C] a general excl. [piquet jargon, *capot*, to score a capot against, to win all the tricks from. In this context 'to score off']

cap out *v.* [1960s] (*US Black*) to go to sleep. [CAP *n.*[6]]

cappadochio *n.* [early 17C] the stocks; prison. [? the country of *Cappadocia*, the ruler of which, according to Horace (65–8BC), was rich in slaves but lacked cash. This ety., backed by Nares, is dismissed as 'far-fetched' by the *OED*]

capped *adj.*[1] [1930s+] outdone, defeated. [CAP (ON) *v.* (1)]

capped *adj.*[2] [1970s+] (*US*) shot dead. [CAP *v.*[7] (2)]

capper *n.*[1] **1** [mid-18C+] (*also* **cap**) a confederate in a gambling game who poses as another gambler but actually works to swindle the genuine participants; similarly used in confidence tricks. **2** [late 19C+] (*US*) an employee of a casino, brothel, strip-club etc, who points a potential client towards the variety of self-indulgence they seek. **3** [1900s–20s] (*US*) a shop tout. [(1) such a confederate is always able to SE *cap*, surpass everyone else's bet; (2) and (3) are ext. use of (1)]

capper *n.*[2] **1** [1920s+] anything seen as terminal, 'the last straw'.

2 [1960s+] an anecdote that steals the limelight from a previous anecdote, a punchline. [CAP (ON) v.]

capperclaw v. see CLAPPERCLAW v.

capping n. [1960s+] (US Black) the ritual exchange of verbal insults. [CAP (ON) v. (6)]

capricornified adj. [late 18C] cuckolded. [proper name of the constellation and sign of the zodiac Capricorn, the He-Goat; thus one who has been made to 'wear the HORNS n.']

capron hardy n. [mid-15C–mid-16C] an impudent fellow. [Fr. capron hardi, lit. 'bold hood']

caps n. (drugs) **1** [1960s+] heroin. **2** [1960s+] psilocybin/psilocin. **3** [1980s+] crack cocaine. [CAP n.⁴ (1)]

cap-sick adj. [early 17C] drunk or mentally confused. [fig. use of SE cap + sick]

capsize v. **1** [late 18C–early 19C] to fall over when drunk. **2** [late 18C+] to overturn.

captain n.¹ **1** [16C–mid-19C] a pimp (cf. ABBOT ON THE CROSS n.). **2** [late 17C–19C] a successful highwayman. **3** [mid-18C] a thug employed to keep order in a gaming house. **4** [late 18C–mid-19C; 1930s] the leader of a criminal gang. **5** [mid–late 19C] (Aus.) a successful bushranger. **6** [20C+] (S.Afr.) the third most important member of a prison gang.

captain n.² [late 16C+] a general term of address. [note 20C+ RMC Duntroon (Aus.) Captain Cadbury, a male homosexual, although as noted by Moore, Lexicon of Cadet Language (1993), the link is more properly to modern comic book 'superheroes', e.g. Captain America]

captain n.³ [mid-18C–early 19C] money; thus the captain is not at home, I have no money. [a ref. to money's importance]

captain n.⁴ **1** [1910s–20s] (US Und.) a susceptible person. **2** [1920s+] (Aus./US) (also **skipper**) someone who has money to spend, and uses it on the assembled company.

Captain Armstrong n. (also **Johnny Armstrong**) [mid–late 19C] a corrupt jockey. [CAPTAIN n.² + SE armstrong, he uses his 'strong arms' to rein in his horse]

Captain Bligh n. [1990s+] a pie. [rhy. sl.; ult. Captain William Bligh (1754–1817) of HMS Bounty]

Captain Bloods n. [20C+] (Aus.) potatoes. [rhy. sl. = SPUD n.² (1); ult. the Irish adventurer Captain Thomas Blood (1618–80), best-known for a failed attempt to steal the British Crown Jewels in 1671]

Captain Bluff n. (also **Captain Bluster**) [late17C–18C] a bully, a braggart. [CAPTAIN n.¹ + SE bluff/bluster]

Captain Bounce n. [18C] a bully, a braggart. [CAPTAIN n.¹ + SE bounce]

Captain Cash n. [1950s+] (Aus.) that member of a group who, recently or temporarily well-off, is expected to buy drinks for the rest. [SE captain +SE cash]

Captain Cheddar n. [1980s+] (US campus) an unattractive, 'cheesy' male. [SE captain + SE cheddar (cheese)]

Captain Cook n.¹ (also **Captain Cooker, cooker**) [late 19C] (Aus./N.Z.) a pig, esp. one which is run-down or ill-kempt. [proper name of Captain James Cook (1728–79), the explorer who introduced pigs to New Zealand]

Captain Cook n.² **1** [late 19C–1960s] a book. **2** [1940s+] (Aus./N.Z./US) a look. **3** [1980s+] a hook, i.e. a punch. [rhy. sl.; ult. navigator and explorer Captain James Cook (1728–79)]

Captain Cook adj. [1950s] (Aus.) ill, sick. [rhy. sl. = CROOK adj. (3); ult. Captain James Cook (1728–79)]

Captain Cooker n. see CAPTAIN COOK n.¹.

Captain Copperthorne's crew n. [late 18C] (orig. naut.) a group or team without a stated hierarchy, where everyone concerned wishes to lead. [? the inadequacies of some long-vanished officer]

Captain Crank n. [18C–early 19C] the leader of a band of highwaymen. [CAPTAIN n.¹ (2) + ? pun SE crank, that which is crooked]

Captain Flashman n. [mid-19C] (UK Und.) a blusterer, a coward. [CAPTAIN n.¹ + FLASHMAN n.]

Captain Grand n. [18C–19C] a haughty, blustering man. [CAPTAIN n.¹ + SE grand]

Captain Grimes n. [1980s] The Times newspaper. [rhy. sl. + ? ref. to Evelyn Waugh's Captain Grimes, the raffish schoolmaster of Decline and Fall (1928)]

Captain Hackum n. [late 17C–early 19C] a bully, a braggart. [CAPTAIN n.¹ + SE hack them]

Captain Hicks n. [1930s–40s] in craps dice, the point of 6 made with a pair of 3s (cf. ADA FROM DECATUR n.). [rhy. sl.; var. on JIMMY HIX n. (1)]

Captain Hook n. **1** [1990s+] a look, a glance. **2** [2000s] a book. [rhy. sl.; ult. the character Captain Hook in J.M. Barrie's Peter Pan (1904)]

Captain Hook v. [1990s+] to look. [rhy. sl.]

Captain Huff n. [late 17C–18C] a braggart, a bully, a thug. [CAPTAIN n.¹ + HUFF n.¹]

captain is at home phr. (also **captain is come**) [late 18C–mid-19C] a euph. phr. used to indicate that a woman is menstruating. [play on Gk catamenia, monthly + elision of SE captain + home/come]

Captain Kettle v. [late 19C–1930s] to settle (after some energetic dispute). [rhy. sl.; ult. the character Captain Kettle, created by Cutliffe Hyne, who appeared in stories publ. 1893–1938]

Captain Kirk n. [1990s+] a Turk. [rhy. sl.; ult. the fictional Captain James T. Kirk, master of the Starship Enterprise in the cult TV series Star Trek]

captain lieutenant n. [late 18C–early 19C] the flesh of an old calf. [thus meat that is neither quite veal nor yet proper beef. In milit. jargon a captain lieutenant has the rank of the former but remains on the pay of the latter]

captain of the chocolate runway n. see CHOCOLATE RUNWAY PILOT n.

Captain Podd n. [late 18C–early 19C] a puppeteer. [the proper name of Captain Podd, a celebrated puppeteer of the period]

Captain Queer-nabs n. [late 17C–mid-19C] a shabby, ill-dressed person. [CAPTAIN n.¹ + QUEER NAB n.]

Captain Quiz n. [18C] a mocker. [CAPTAIN n.¹ + SE quiz, to mock, to make fun of]

Captain Save-a-ho n. [1990s+] (US Black teen) a man who lavishes attentions and gifts on a woman; his aim is seduction, but despite his expensive efforts he is rarely successful. [CAPTAIN n.¹ + SE save a + HO n.¹ (5)]

Captain Sharp n. [early 17C–19C] **1** a card-sharp, a cheat. **2** a hired thug used to police corrupt gambling games. [CAPTAIN n.¹ + SHARP n.¹ (1)]

captain's log n. [1990s+] a lavatory (cf. ANGUS ARMANASCO n.). [rhy. sl.; captain's log = BOG n.¹; presumably linked to the cult TV series Star Trek, each episode of which began with the intonation 'Captain's Log, Stardate...']

Captain Standish n. [18C] the penis. [SE captain + SE stand, he 'stands erect']

captain tober n. [mid-19C] (UK Und.) a leading highwayman. [CAPTAIN n.¹ (2) + TOBY n.² (2)]

Captain Tom n. **1** [late 17C–early 19C] the leader of a mob. **2** [late 18C–early 19C] the mob itself. [CAPTAIN n.¹ + TOM n.¹ (1)]

capture n. [1910s+] (UK Und.) an arrest and conviction for a crime; thus get a capture, to be arrested.

capture v. [1980s+] (UK Und.) to arrest.

capture the bishop v. [1990s+] to masturbate. [var. on BANG THE BISHOP v.]

capture the crumb v. see TAKE THE CAKE v.

capture the pickled biscuit v. [late 19C–1940s] (Aus.) to beat all rivals, esp. with the implication that the person, event etc is even more startling or appalling than might have been expected. [ext. of colloq. phr. take the biscuit]

capun n. [1990s+] (US prison) one who has been sentenced to death. [abbr. capital punishment]

cap up v. [1960s+] (drugs) to transfer bulk drugs (in powder form) into capsules for sale. [ext. of CAP v.⁵ (1)]

capurtle n. [1950s+] a woman seen as a sex object. [? SE capital, excellent, first-class]

caput adj. [1910s+] finished, over, ruined etc. [Ger. kaputt, done for; also milit. use as 'stolen' during WW1]

car n. (US prison) **1** [1970s+] a group of inmates who associate to run money-making schemes, dominate other prisoners, and otherwise 'rule' the institution. **2** [1990s+] a group of prisoners who pool their supply of drugs. **3** [1990s+] a line used for transferring articles, e.g. a pack of cigarettes, from one cell to another. [the image of the prisoners driving/sitting in the same car]

caramel clone n. [2000s] (US Black) a light-skinned Black person.

caramel sundae n. [1990s+] (US Black teen) an attractive, sexy, medium- to light-skinned Black woman.

caravan n. **1** [late 17C] a coach travelling from the provinces to London. **2** [late 17C–early 19C] (UK Und.) a large sum of money, esp. when seen by thieves as potential booty. **3** [late 17C–early 19C] the victim of financial fraud. **4** [early 19C] a police van, a 'black maria'. **5** [mid-19C] a railway train. **6** [mid-19C] a railway 'special' taking London boxing fans to a fight held outside the capital. [SE caravan, a procession of merchants, travelling together for mutual safety, usu. as found in the Middle or Far East]

caravan v.¹ [1910s–20s] to have a picnic. [the SE caravan or procession of vehicles that convey the picnickers]

caravan v.² [1980s+] (US teen) to drive (stolen) cars in groups and to perform a variety of elaborate manoeuvres on the street. [SE caravan, a procession of merchants]

caravansera n. [mid-19C] a railway station. [caravanserai, a form of Oriental coaching inn where the merchant caravans could find food and shelter; ult. Per. karwan, caravan + sara, palace]

carb n. [1940s+] (orig. US) a carburettor. [abbr.]

carbine v. [late 19C] (US, Western) to cheat, to victimize. [SE carbine, a short musket, presumably used by the villain]

carbo n. (also **carb**) [1970s+] (orig. US) carbohydrates, or a meal or food that contains a high percentage of carbohydrate. [abbr. + -o sfx (6)]

carbo-load v. [1990s+] (US campus) to drink beer. [SE carbo-load, to ingest carbohydrates (of which beer contains many)]

carbonado v. [late 16C–17C] to cut, to slash, to hack. [Sp. carbonado, to score meat before grilling or broiling it]

carbon copy n. [1990s+] (US Black) **1** an imitator, someone who yearns to emulate their hero or heroine. **2** someone who resembles their parents.

carbuncle face n. [late 17C–18C] a face covered in boils and pimples. [SE carbuncle, an inflamed abscess + face]

carburettor n. **1** [1910s] the heart. **2** [1980s+] (drugs) a water pipe, used for smoking cannabis or crack cocaine. [fig. uses of SE]

carby n. [1950s+] (Aus.) a carburettor. [abbr. + sfx -y]

card n.¹ [mid-18C–mid-19C] a device, an expedient; thus one's best card, the best plan, the ideal way of acting. [SURE CARD n.]

card n.² **1** [late 18C; 1940s+] a joker, a clown. **2** [mid-19C+] a character, a noticeable person, a likeable eccentric. **3** [mid-19C+] an attraction, a 'drawing card'. **4** [1940s] (US) an amusing thing or circumstance. **5** [1970s] a fool. [? one who stands out from the 'pack']

card n.³ (US drugs) **1** [1900s–40s] pieces of opium weighed out onto a (playing) card; the usual ration of prepared opium used in a single smokng session. **2** [1920s–30s] a means of selling opium in which pills of the drug are stuck to the bottom of a playing card.

card, the n. [mid-19C] the correct thing. [abbr. SE invitation card/card of admission]

card v.¹ (also **caad**) [20C+] (W.I./UK Black teen) to jeer jokingly or mock someone about some event, their appearance or situation. [Scot. card, to scold, to tell off]

card v.² [1950s+] (W.I. Rasta) to fool someone. [? CARD n.² (5) or ? CARD v.¹]

card v.³ [1970s+] (US campus) to request proof of age (in a bar) by producing an identification card.

cardboard box n. [1970s+] venereal disease. [rhy. sl. = POX n.¹ (2)]

cardboard city n. [1980s+] the cardboard box 'homes' that are used as shelter by the homeless. [the original Cardboard City was situated on London's South Bank, but increasing homelessness has meant that the term now applies to any such gathering]

card-carrying adj. (also **card-holding**) [1950s+] (US) genuine, dependable, the 'real thing'. [the orig. application of the phr. to Communists, who carried their Party card]

card-cony-catching n. (also **card-coney-catching**) [mid-16C–18C] trickery, cheating, usu. with cards. [SE card + CONY-CATCHING n.]

carder n. [mid-19C] (UK Und.) a professional card-player.

card-holding adj. see CARD-CARRYING adj.

cardinal n.¹ [mid-18C–19C] a lady's cloak. [resemblance to a cardinal's cloak]

cardinal n.² [mid-19C+] mulled red wine. [it is red, as are a cardinal's outer vestments]

cardinal n.³ [late 19C–1910s] a shoeblack. [ety. unknown; ? use of a red cloth]

cardinal is at home phr. (also **cardinal is come**) [late 18C] a euph. phr. used to indicate that a woman is menstruating. [the red of a cardinal's vestments and that of menstrual blood]

card mechanic n. see MECHANIC n. (3).

care! excl. [2000s] (US campus) a sarcastic retort, demonstrating a lack of interest. [i.e. SE like I care!]

care a hoot v. see GIVE A HOOT v.

care a toss v. see GIVE A TOSS v.

career boy n. [1970s+] a male homosexual prostitute. [play on SE career girl]

care factor zero phr. [1990s+] (US teen) a phr. indicating indifference, I really couldn't care less. [the use of SE factor as a measure of sunblock strength]

careless talk n. [1940s+] a stick of chalk, usu. as used by darts players for scoring. [rhy. sl.; the ref. is to the WW2 posters with the legend 'Careless talk costs lives']

care package n. [1960s+] (US campus/teen) a package of 'supplies' sent to a student or solo teenager by a parent. [the US CARE package, a package of goods distributed by CARE, the Cooperative for Assistance and Relief Everywhere, to the poor citizens of foreign countries]

care two hoots v. see GIVE A HOOT v.

carga n. [1960s+] (US prison/Hisp.) heroin. [Sp. = charge, i.e. CHARGE n.²]

cargo n.¹ [early 17C] a person. [ety. unknown. Despite the apparent logic of relating this to CARGO n.², i.e. a person as a fig. burden or load, this use precedes the adoption of the Sp. word into SE, and there is no evidence of Sp. cargo being used in this way]

cargo n.² **1** [late 17C–18C] a large sum of money. **2** [mid-18C] a thief's or pickpocket's takings. **3** [1990s+] (W.I./UK Black teen) a heavy gold chain and medallion sported as an outward (sometimes pretentious) show of wealth. [SE cargo, freight carried on a ship; ult. Sp. cargo, loading, carga, freight]

cargo! excl. [early 17C] a general excl. [? euph. for CHRIST! excl.; or ? corruption of Italian corragio! courage!]

carhop n. (US) **1** [1930s+] a waiter or waitress who serves customers in their parked cars. **2** [1970s+] a street prostitute (of either sex) who has sex in clients' cars. [i.e. one who hops between cars]

carhop v. (*US*) **1** [1930s+] to work as a waiter or waitress, serving customers in their parked cars. **2** [1970s+] to work as a street prostitute, having sex with clients who drive up in their cars. **3** [1990s+] to steal from parked cars. [CARHOP n.]

Caribee Islands n. [late 18C] certain areas of London that were considered safe havens for criminals and debtors. [SE *Caribbean Islands*, symbolizing far distance from any authority]

car-jack v. [1990s+] (*US*) to hijack an automobile or rob its driver.

car-jacker n. [1990s+] (*US*) one who hijacks an automobile or robs its driver. [CAR-JACK v.]

car-jacking n. [1990s+] (*US*) hijacking an automobile or robbing its driver. [CAR-JACK v.]

car-jockey n. [1950s+] (*US*) a carpark or garage attendant. [SE *car* + JOCKEY n.[3] (2)]

cark n. [1970s] (*US*) the penis. [COCK n.[2] (1)]

cark v. (*also* **kark**) [1970s+] (*orig. Aus.*) **1** to die; often as *cark it*. **2** of machinery, to break down. **3** to vomit (cf. BARF v.). [dial. *cark* or *kark*, to caw like a crow; thus the association is with a carrion bird]

carked adj. [1970s] (*Aus.*) ruined, destroyed, exhausted. [CARK v./dial. *cark*, care, sorrow, anxiety]

carl comedian n. [1970s+] (*US campus*) a dismissive term for a raconteur whose jokes and stories fail to make the desired impact. [ironic use of SE *comedian* + assonant proper name]

carleycue n. (*also* **carlique, curlicue**) [late 19C–1910s] (*Irish*) anything small or of little value. [ext. of SE *curlicue*]

carlotta n. [1940s–60s] (*camp gay*) **1** a heterosexual who interferes in the gay world, either as a homophobe or as a 'tourist'. **2** a popular 'camp' name. [the effeminization used by the camp gay world]

carl rosa n. [1960s+] a poser, anyone pretending to be something that they are not; thus the *old carl rosa*, a fraud. [rhy. sl.; ult. the popular *Carl Rosa* Operatic Society, founded in London in 1875]

carmes n. (*also* **carnes**) [mid-19C–1900s] flattery. [Rom.]

carmine n. [19C] blood (cf. BADMINTON n.). [SE *carmine*, red or crimson pigment obtained from cochineal]

carn! excl. [1980s] (*N.Z.*) hurry up! [Antipodean pron. of SE *come on!*]

carnal n. (*also* **carnales**) [1970s+] (*US Hisp.*) someone from one's own social group, a friend from the same neighbourhood. [Sp. *carnal*, flesh]

carnal-trap n. [mid-17C–19C] the vagina. [coined by Sir Thomas Urquhart (1611–60) for his translation of Rabelais]

carnapper n. [1950s+] (*orig. US*) one who steals a car for joy-riding (rather than for resale), and then dumps it or returns it to the place from where it was taken. [play on SE *kidnapper*; modern use esp. Filipino]

carne n. [1980s+] (*drugs*) heroin. [Sp. *carne*, meat; the image is of the drug's strength]

carnes n. see CARMES n.

carney n.[1] [early 19C–1920s] **1** soft, hypocritical talk; thus *come the old carney*, to flatter. **2** a smooth talker; thus *carneying*, smooth talking, flattery. [Yorks. dial. *carney*, cajolery, flattery. Despite the poss. link to CARNEY n.[3], this use precedes it by a century; ult. ety. unknown]

carney n.[2] (*also* **carnie**) [late 19C+] (*Aus.*) a lizard. [Wemba *gaani*, any of the lizards used in the Aboriginal diet, e.g. the Jew lizard, lace lizard etc]

carney n.[3] (*also* **carny**) [1930s+] (*US*) **1** a carnival worker. **2** (*also* **carnie**) a carnival, a fair. [abbr.]

carney adj. (*also* **carny**) **1** [1910s+] sly, artful. **2** [1930s+] (*US*) pertaining to the carnival or carnival workers. [lit. pertaining to a carnival; thus a negative stereotype]

carney v. (*also* **carny**) [early 19C+] to wheedle, to flatter; thus *carneying*, in a wheedling manner. [CARNEY n.[1] (1); there is no link to later US CARNEY n.[3], for all that the carney is likely to

employ wheedling tones to encourage patrons to spend their money]

carnie see also under CARNEY.

carnie n.[1] (*also* **carny**) (*N.Z.*) **1** [1960s+] an under-age girl seen as a sex object. **2** [1980s+] a young person living on the streets. [SE *carnal knowledge*]

carnie n.[2] [1990s+] a carnation. [abbr. + sfx -*ie*]

carnish n. [mid-19C] (*UK Und.*) meat; thus (*northern Und.*) *carnish-ken*, a thieves' eating-house; *cove of the carnish-ken*, the owner of such a place. [Ital. *carne*, meat. Imported via Ling. Fr.]

carny see under CARNEY.

carny n. see CARNIE n.[1].

carob v. [19C] (*UK tramp*) to cut. [Shelta]

Carolina racehorse n. [mid-19C] (*US*) a razorback hog. [joc. ref. to the prevalence of the animal in North and South Carolina]

caroline n. [mid–late 19C] (*Irish*) a style of tall hat. [? anecdotal]

carol singer n. [1930s+] (*Aus., Brisbane*) a police car with a loudspeaker.

caroon n. (*also* **carroon**) [mid–late 19C] a crown or 5 shillings (25p). [Ital. *corona*, a crown]

carp n. [1900s–30s] (*US*) a whinger, a complainer. [SE *carp*, to find fault with, to reprehend, to take exception to]

carpark n. [1950s+] (*UK Und.*) an informer. [rhy. sl. = NARK n.[1] (1)]

carpenter's dream n. [1970s+] an available woman. [pun, i.e. 'flat as a board and easy to screw'/SCREW v.[1] (1)]

carpet n.[1] [late 19C+] the grass, the ground. [early use sporting, e.g. cricket and baseball; also in UK/US air forces]

carpet n.[2] (*also* **carpeting**) **1** [20C+] (*UK prison*) a 3-month sentence. **2** [1940s+] £3, £30. [rhy. sl. CARPET-BAG n. = DRAG n.[4]; or ? f. the earlier assumption that prison workshops took just 90 days to produce a particular type of regulation-size carpet. But note No. 77, *Mark of Broad Arrow* (1903): 'Your "Auto-leyne" cares little about a "drag" (three months), a sixer (a "carpet" it is generally called), or a "stretch"'; however, note Michael Quinion, *World Wide Words* (Internet, 6 May 2000): 'I suspect No 77 made a mistake, since "carpet" came about as the result of a bit of rhyming slang: "carpet-bag" = "drag", implying that the two words have always meant the same thing']

carpet n.[3] [1920s+] (*Aus.*) £1. [ety. unknown; ? misprint of CARPET n.[2] (2)]

carpet n.[4] [1980s+] the female pubic hair; used only in terms relating to cunnilingus (and thus lesbians), e.g. MUNCH THE CARPET v. (cf. CARPET-BITER n.).

carpet, the n. [1960s] (*US Black*) a confidence trick practised by a street criminal.

carpet v. (*also* **mat**) [mid-19C+] to reprimand, esp. in the context of a superior telling off an employee; thus *carpeting*, a telling-off. [ON THE CARPET phr.[2]]

carpet-bag n. [20C+] (*UK Und.*) a 3-month sentence. [ext. of CARPET n.[2] (1)/rhy. sl. = DRAG n.[4]]

carpetbag v. [1930s] (*US campus*) **1** to attempt to make a good impression, usu. on one's teachers, by pretending to have an all-consuming interest in a given subject. **2** to deceive. [SE *carpet-bagger*, a derog. description applied, after the US Civil War (1861–5), to immigrants from the Northern into the Southern states, whose 'property qualification' consisted merely of the contents of the carpet-bag they had brought with them. Hence, applied to all Northerners who went South and tried, by a variety of deceitful tricks, to obtain political influence, esp. by claiming an interest in local areas of which, in fact, they had no real knowledge]

carpet-biter n. **1** [1940s+] someone who becomes so enraged that they start chewing the carpet. **2** [1990s+] a lesbian (cf. CARPET-MUNCHER n.; CAT-LAPPER n.; CHUFF MUNCHER n.; CLAM SMACKER n.; CUNT-SUCKER n.; FANNY NOSHER n.; GAP-LAPPER n.; GUSSET-NUZZLER n.; LEG-LICKER n.; LOVER UNDER THE LAP n.; MUFF-DIVER n.;

MUFFER n.[1]; MUFF-MUNCHER n.; SUCKER n.[6]; TOP-DIVER n.). [(1) ? the myth that Adolf Hitler was prone to such hysterical rages; (2) var. on CARPET-MUNCHER n.]

carpet bushman n. [1910s] (Aus.) a businessman who owns land in the outback but rarely visits.

carpet captain/champion n. see CARPET KNIGHT n. (1).

carpet-cleaning n. [1990s+] cunnilingus. [CARPET n.[4] + SE clean]

carpet dance n. [late 19C–1900s] (UK society) a dance for close friends, held in one's drawing room. [unlike a larger dance, held in a ballroom with a properly sprung floor, the boards are kept covered]

carpeting n. see CARPET n.[2].

carpet joint n. [1930s+] (US) an up-market nightclub. [SE carpet + JOINT n.[4] (3)]

carpet knight n. [late 16C–19C] 1 (also carpet captain, ...champion, ...lover, ...monger, ...squire, ...warrior) a man whose 'knightly exploits' concentrate on the boudoir rather than the battlefield. 2 a man who frequents drawing rooms rather than places of work. [orig. a soldier who was dubbed knight at court (thus kneeling on a carpet) rather than in the chaos of a battlefield]

carpet lecture n. [1910s] (Aus.) an official reprimand. [ON THE CARPET phr.[2]]

carpet-muncher n. (also carpet-licker, rug-muncher) [1980s+] (orig. US campus) 1 a lesbian (cf. CARPET-BITER n.). 2 a person who performs cunnilingus. [CARPET n.[4] + MUNCH v.[1] (2)]

carpet-munching n. [1980s+] cunnilingus. [CARPET-MUNCHER n.]

carpet nap n. [1980s] (Aus.) a Japanese person (cf. BUDDHAHEAD n.). [rhy. sl. = JAP n.]

carpet patrol n. [1980s+] (drugs) smokers of crack cocaine who search the floor for any grains of the drug they may have dropped.

carpet rat n. [1970s+] (US) a small child.

carpet road n. [late 17C–early 18C] a smooth, well-maintained road.

carpet squire n. see CARPET KNIGHT n. (1).

carpet-swab n. [mid-19C] a carpet-bag.

carpet trade n. [late 16C] sexual dalliance. [i.e. 'the occupations and amusements of the chamber or boudoir' (OED); such rooms would be carpeted]

carpet walker n. [1930s–70s] (US drugs) a narcotics addict. [? the addict is normally comatose rather than frenetically ambulant]

carpet warrior n. see CARPET KNIGHT n. (1).

carpy adj. [1940s–50s] (UK prison) locked away in one's cell at night. [Lat. carpe diem, 'make the most of the day']

carra n. (also carrer) [1920s+] (Aus.) a caravan. [abbr.]

carriage drag n. [late 19C] (UK tramp) a jail sentence of 1 week. [DRAG n.[4] + ? image of those who ride in carriages getting an easier life, even in prison]

carriage trade n. [1940s+] the upper classes, usu. used ironically. [a hangover f. earlier divisions of transport. Note mid-19C SE carriage company, those who own their own carriage(s); thus the wealthy or upper classes]

carried adj. [late 19C–1900s] married. [rhy. sl.]

carried story n. [20C+] (Ulster) a piece of gossip, a rumour. [it is carried from person to person]

carrie (nation) n. [1950s+] (drugs) cocaine (cf. AUNT NORA n.). [initial letter + proper name; ult. Carrie Nation (1847–1911), the US temperance campaigner]

carrier n. 1 [18C–1910s] that member of a criminal gang who either carries information between gang members or carries away the proceeds of a robbery, of pickpocketing etc. 2 [mid-18C] a thigh. 3 [1950s–70s] (US drugs) a distributor of drugs.

carrier-pigeon n. [late 18C–mid-19C] one who specializes in swindling lottery office-keepers.

car-ringing n. [1950s+] the practice of altering a car for the purposes of using it as a getaway vehicle, hold-up van etc or for reselling it to an unsuspecting customer. [SE car + RING v.[1] (11)]

carrion n. 1 [late 14C–early 19C] the human body. 2 [17C–mid-18C] a prostitute; thus carrion-flogger, a pimp. [SE carrion, used derog. to denote the body and thus a human being]

carrion-case n. [mid-19C] a shirt. [the shirt's enclosing of the CARRION n. (1)]

carrion-crow man n. [20C+] (W.I., Guyn.) a man who canvasses business for an undertaker following a death. [SE carrion-crow, a species of crow that feeds on dead flesh]

carrion-flogger n. [late 17C–early 18C] a coachman.

carrion-hunter n. [late 18C–mid-19C] 1 a promiscuous woman. 2 an undertaker. [both supposedly search for bodies, whether warm or cold]

carrion-row n. [early 18C] a place where one buys second-rate meat. [SE carrion + row, a street + pun on SE carrion-crow]

carriwitchet n. [late 18C–1900s] a hoaxing, puzzling question. [ety. unknown; ? link to SE witch]

carroon n. see CAROON n.

carrot n.[1] [mid-16C+] the penis; thus CUFF THE CARROT v. (cf. BANANA n.[2].). [its shape, also f. the consumption of carrots by rabbits or coneys; also note correspondence from John Geipel (7 June 2000) 'I [have] identified a cluster of obviously related words, many of them vulgar or taboo, all based on the Romani word kar (literally, "thorn","spike" or "prickle" – the original Sanskrit meaning) applied to the penis. The word has long been in circulation in impolite Spanish, as caralo, in the original Romani, anatomical sense; this, in turn, has given rise to such expressions as the exclamations: caray, carape, the universal Hispanic caramba and the euphemistic caracoles (literally: "snails"). Other derivative forms are: No importa un carajo (it doesn't matter a bit), Ni carajo (nothing at all), the Mexican Que carajo quieres? (What the hell do you want?), caralote (idiot, nut-case); de caralo (spendid) and vete al caralo (go to hell). The dimin. carajillo (little prick) refers to the mug of coffee with a slug of brandy, taken to kick-start a cold winter's day']

carrot n.[2] 1 [mid-18C–19C] a large bundle of tobacco. 2 [1980s+] (drugs) a very large cannabis cigarette packed to the brim and generally the size of an average garden carrot (cf. BONE n.[11]). [note the Camberwell carrot, an extra-large cannabis cigarette, coined in the film Withnail & I (1986)]

carrot-cruncher n. [1960s+] a countryman, a peasant, esp. a visitor to London from the provinces and the countryside (cf. ACORN-CRACKER n.). [the equation of root vegetables and country-dwellers]

carrothead n. [mid-19C+] (US) a red-headed person; thus carrot-headed.

carrot-pated adj. [late 17C–early 19C] having red hair.

carrots n. [late 17C+] a red-headed person, red hair in general. [the colour of the vegetable. Ware declares that 'it has not in origin anything to do with "carrots"', preferring an association with Judas Iscariot, trad. seen as a red-head]

carrot-top n. [20C+] a red-headed person.

carrot-topped adj. (also carrot-top) [20C+] having red hair.

carrotty adj. (also carroty, carroty-headed, carrotty-pated) [18C+] having red hair. [CARROTS n.]

carrucha n. [1970s+] (US) a broken-down old car. [Sp.]

carry n. (US drugs) 1 [1930s–50s] enough of a drug to provide a given period of euphoria. 2 [1960s] the amount of drugs that one is carrying at any given moment, esp. when stored for an emergency. [CARRY v. (1)]

carry v. 1 [1930s] (US drugs) for a supply of drugs to suffice an addict for a given period of time. 2 [1930s+] (orig. US) to carry money, to be in the money. 3 [1930s+] (orig. US) to carry a weapon, e.g. a gun or knife. 4 [1940s+] (orig. US drugs) to carry drugs. 5 [1980s+] (Aus. prison) to smuggle or hold contraband. [ext. uses of SE]

carry a bone v. [1910s] (US) to gossip, to spread rumours. [pvb 'a dog that will bring you a bone will carry one away']

carry a broom at the masthead v. [early 19C] to work as a prostitute. [the naval tradition of hoisting a broom to signify that a ship has been sold]

carry a case v. [20C+] (US Und.) to be out on bail. [pun on SE case, bag/case, impending trial]

carry a chip on one's shoulder v. (also **have a chip on one's shoulder**) [mid-19C+] (orig. US) to bear a grudge against the world at large; thus a chip on one's shoulder, a grudge or display of defiance or ill-humour, a sense of inferiority characterized by a quickness to take offence. [the trad. 19C US way of offering a challenge to fight was to place a chip of wood on one's shoulder – most US homes had a pile of wood for fuel – and challenge someone to knock it off; thus to go around with such a chip meant one challenged the whole world]

carry a flag v. [1930s+] (US tramp) to travel under an assumed name or alias.

carry a torch v. (also **carry the torch**) [1930s+] (orig. US) to mourn a dead love affair, to feel love without its being returned; thus torch-carrier, one who is suffering such pain. [the 'light of love' is still burning, albeit unreciprocated]

carry both ends of the log v. [1920s+] (Aus.) to take all the work on oneself (despite there being others equally qualified in attendance).

carry-come-and-bring-come n. see CARRY-GO-BRING-COME n.

carry corn v. [mid-19C–1900s] to behave well when successful, i.e. to be a modest winner, to restrain oneself despite gaining power or money. [Yorks. dial.]

carry dog v. [mid-19C+] to put on airs. [var. on PUT ON DOG v. (1)]

carry-go-bring-come n. (also **bring-and-carry, bring-go-bring-come, carry-come-and-bring-come**) [1940s+] (W.I.) 1 a gossip, a tattle-tale. 2 gossip. [the sequence of events]

carry guts to a bear v. (also **bring guts to a bear, pack..., tote...**) [late 17C+] to perform an extremely distasteful or absolutely basic task, usu. implying inadequacy or stupidity; thus he's not fit to..., he hasn't enough/the brains to...

carrying n. [1960s+] 1 in possession of illicit drugs. 2 in possession of a gun (cf. PACKING n.[2]). 3 in possession of sufficient cash to buy a round of drinks. [CARRY v.]

carrying a load adj. [20C+] drunk. [LOAD n.[2]]

carrying-on n. (also **carryings on**) [mid-17C; mid-19C+] any form of conspicuous behaviour, e.g. making a fuss, flirting ostentatiously. [SE carry on, to do, to act/CARRY ON v.]

carry in one's heart v. [1940s–50s] (S.Afr.) to bear a grudge in the hope of getting eventual revenge.

carry-knave n. [mid-17C] a coach. [Nares, misintepreting 'knave' and extrapolating backwards to the 'carry', suggests a def. of 'cheap prostitute'; Williams dismisses this]

carry Matilda v. [late 19C+] (Aus.) to go on the tramp, carrying one's pack. [SE carry + MATILDA n.]

carry me out (and bury me decently)! excl. [late 18C–1930s] a general excl. of disbelief and displeasure. [play on Lat. nunc dimittis, 'Now let thy servant depart...', the first words of the Song of Simeon in Luke 2:29; bolstered by images of prize- and cockfighting]

carry milk-pails v. [mid-19C] of a man, to walk with a woman on each arm. [the image of a milkmaid with her yoke and 2 pails]

carry no coals v. [late 16C–17C] to show oneself proof against swindling or insults. [reverse of SE phr. carry coals to do dirty or degrading work, thus to accept insults]

carry-on n. [late 19C+] 1 a commotion, an exciting event, a disturbance, fuss, excitement; usu. in phrs. what a carry-on!; a right/real carry-on. 2 activity, with no excesses implied. [CARRY ON v.]

carry on v. 1 [mid-19C+] to make a fuss. 2 [mid-19C+] to behave in an obstreperous or ostentatious manner. 3 [mid-19C+] (orig. US) to flirt. 4 [late 19C+] to have an adulterous or additional (if unmarried) relationship, usu. as carry on with.

carry one's arse v. (also **carry one's ass**) [1970s+] (US/W.I., Bdos/Trin.) to leave, to run off. [SE carry + ARSE n.[1] (4)/ASS n. (5)]

carry one's own weight v. [1950s+] (US) 1 to take responsibility for one's actions. 2 to have influence. [ext. of CARRY WEIGHT v. (2)]

carry one's tail v. [20C+] (W.I.) to leave, to run off. [SE carry + TAIL n.[2] (1)]

carry on proper v. [late 19C+] to behave properly. [SE carry on, to do, to act + PROPER adv. (2)]

carry on top ropes v. see SWAY AWAY ON ALL TOP ROPES v.

carry-over n. [late 19C–1940s] a hangover that lingers on. [SE carry-over, something remaining or transferred from one period to the next]

carry someone's ass v. [1990s+] to beat someone. [ASS n. (2)]

carry the baby v. see HOLD THE BABY v.

carry the banner v. (also **carry the stick, pack the banner**) (US) 1 [late 19C+] to walk the streets as a tramp. 2 [1920s–30s] to sleep rough, esp. of the thousands of homeless children who were forced to sleep in the New York streets. 3 [1930s] to live as a tramp. [? the carrying of banners at left-wing protest marches, many of which focused on the plight of the poor or homeless; PACK v.[1] (1)]

carry the cag v. [early 19C] to be easily irritated, to lack a sense of humour, esp. as regards jokes against oneself. [SE carry + CAG n.]

carry the can (for) v. (also **carry the can back, ...for**) [1920s+] (orig. naut.) to take the blame for someone, to do someone's 'dirty work', esp. in phr. left carrying the can.

carry the cosh v. [late 19C–1940s] (UK Und.) working as a pimp. [SE carry + COSH n. (1); the general def. develops from the earlier (late 19C) practice of the pimp ambushing and robbing the prostitute's client]

carry the drum v. [1940s] (Aus.) to work slowly (in a shearing shed). [? the image of a drummer beating slowly, as in a funeral procession]

carry the keg v. [early 19C] to be easily annoyed, to be unable to take a joke. [pun on SE keg/CAG n.]

carry the mail v.[1] [1920s–70s] (US) 1 to go fast. 2 to take responsibility for a difficult task. [the reputation of the US postal service for overcoming any object in order to deliver the mail]

carry the mail v.[2] [1940s–50s] (Aus.) to stand a round of drinks. [the 'delivery' of the drinks]

carry the stick v. see CARRY THE BANNER v.

carry the stockwhip v. [1930s+] (Aus., Northern Territories) of a wife, to dominate her husband.

carry the torch v. see CARRY A TORCH v.

carry the war into Africa v. [mid-19C] (US) to act aggressively, to go over to the attack. [the Roman attack on Carthage in 256BC]

carry weight v. [1930s+] 1 to be depressed. 2 to take responsibility or to take the blame (cf. CARRY ONE'S OWN WEIGHT v.). [WEIGHT n.[1]]

carry your hip! excl. [20C+] (W.I.) get out! go away! [SE hip, euph. for the buttocks, the backside]

carser n. see CASA n.[1].

carsey n. (orig. Polari) 1 [mid-19C] a brothel (cf. BADGER-CRIB n.). 2 [mid-19C] a thieves' den. 3 [mid–late 19C] a public house. 4 [late 19C+] (also **carsi, cawsy, karsey, karzee, karzey, karzi, karzie, karzy, kazi, kharzi, khazi**) a lavatory (cf. BACKHOUSE n.). 5 [late 19C+] a house. 6 [late 19C+] (also **carsi, cawsy, karsey, karzee, karzey, karzi, karzie, karzy, kazi, kharzi, khazi**) any messy or otherwise unappealing place. [CASE n.[3]/Ital. casa, house]

cart n.[1] [late 16C–1900s] the gallows. [the cart that took the prisoner from prison to the gallows, esp. from Newgate to Tyburn]

cart *n.*² [mid-19C] a racecourse.

cart *n.*³ [mid-late 19C] the carapace of a crab. [resemblance; orig. Norfolk dial.]

cart *n.*⁴ [1950s] (*US*) a *cart*on. [abbr.]

cart *v.* **1** [late 16C-early 19C] 'the punishment formerly indicted on bawds, who were placed in a tumbrel or cart, and led through a town, that their persons might be known' (Grose, 1785). **2** [mid-19C+] to carry, to drag; thus *cart away, cart out* etc.

carted *adj. see* IN THE CART phr. (2).

cart-grease *n.* **1** [late 19C+] rancid butter. **2** [late 19C+] butter. **3** [20C+] margarine.

cartloads *n.* (*also* **cartload**) [late 16C-mid-19C] many, a great quantity, esp. of a desirable commodity.

cartnapper *n.* [1950s+] a person who steals supermarket trolleys. [SE *cart* + NAPPER *n.*¹ (1)]

cartocracy *n.* [late 19C-1900s] (*UK society*) those rich enough to afford a dog-cart. [SE *cart* + (*arist*)*ocracy*]

cartoon *n.* [1920s+] a fool, an absurd person. [metonymy]

cart out with *v.* [late 19C+] to court, to 'go out with'. [SE *cart*]

carts *n.*¹ [mid-late 19C] a pair of shoes. [? echoic of the sound of a labourer's heavy, boot-clad step, or CART *n.*³]

carts *n.*² [1980s+] (*Polari*) the male genitals. [CATSO *n.* (2)]

cartso *n. see* CATSO *n.*

cartucho *n.* [1950s+] (*drugs*) a package of marijuana cigarettes. [? Sp. *cartucho*, a small box]

cartwheel *n.*¹ **1** [mid-late 19C] a crown or 5-shilling (25p) piece. **2** [late 19C+] (*Can./US*) a silver dollar. [the shape; used in WW1 Aus. milit. for a 5-franc piece]

cartwheel *n.*² [late 19C] a broad hint. [a cartwheel is too large to be ignored]

cartwheel *n.*³ [1900s-40s] (*Aus.*) a round damper marked with a cross. [the resemblance to spokes on a wheel]

cartwheel *n.*⁴ **1** [1930s] (*US drugs*) a fake heroin withdrawal spasm. **2** [1960s-70s] (*drugs*) a drug in pill form, usu. amphetamine or Benzedrine; often in pl.

carty *adj.* [mid-late 19C] of a horse, like a carthorse, whether in build or breed.

cartzo *n. see* CATSO *n.*

carve *v.* (*US*) **1** [late 19C+] to attack (and cut) with a bladed weapon. **2** [late 19C+] to destroy, to annihilate completely, esp. in a financial or business context. **3** [1940s] to thrill, to excite. [Williams notes use of *carve*, to enjoy sexually]

carve a slice *v.* **1** [late 18C; 20C+] to have sexual intercourse. **2** [2000s] to take a portion of the profits.

carved out of wood *adj.* [1950s+] stupid.

carver *n.* [1900s-30s] (*US*) a knife when used as a weapon. [CARVE *v.* (1) + SE *carver*, a carving knife]

carver and gilder *n.* [early 19C] a match-maker. [ironic use of SE; the elite professions are reduced to sl. in the lowly context of match-making]

carve someone's knob *v.* [1950s] (*US Black*) to explain, to make understand. [SE *carve* + KNOB *n.*¹ (1)]

carve someone up *v.* [1970s+] for a driver, to force another out of the way through aggressive (and potentially dangerous) driving. [ext. of CARVE UP *v.*]

carve-up *n.* **1** [1930s] a legacy, i.e. one's share of a will. **2** [1930s+] any situation in which one feels oneself unfairly deprived of a desired aim or object. **3** [1930s+] a knife or razor-slashing. **4** [1940s] a war. **5** [1940s+] (*UK Und.*) a share-out of loot, profits etc. **6** [1950s] an upset, a fuss. **7** [1960s] an error, a mistake. [CARVE UP *v.*]

carve up *v.* **1** [late 19C+] (*orig. US*) to destroy, to annihilate completely, esp. in a financial or business context. **2** [1920s+] to attack (and cut) with a razor, a knife or other bladed weapon, also in fig. use. **3** [1930s+] to swindle, to cheat. **4** [1930s+] (*UK Und.*) to share out booty, profits etc. [fig. uses of SE]

carve up scores *v.* [1930s] (*US*) to reminisce with an old friend. [SE *carve up*/CARVE UP *v.* (4) + SCORE *n.*² (1)]

carvie *n.* (*also* **carving china**) [1940s-50s] (*UK prison*) one who helps share or divide up a ration of tobacco; a prisoner may take on a regular 'carvie' for periods of his sentence; thus a trusted friend. [SE *carve up*/CARVE UP *v.* (4) (+ CHINA (PLATE) *n.*)]

carving contest *n. see* CUTTING CONTEST *n.*

carving knife *n.* [1910s] one's wife. [rhy. sl.]

carwash *n.* [1970s+] (*US gay*) sexual intercourse in a car.

cas *adj.* (*also* **caj, cazh, kasj**) [1980s+] a term of general approval for anything favoured, e.g. a close friend, an item of clothing, a rock band, a given activity. [pron. 'cazz'; abbr. CASUAL *adj.*]

ca-sa *n.* (*also* **ca. sa.**) [late 18C-mid-19C] a writ of *capias ad satisfaciendum*, after judgement, to imprison the defendant until the plaintiff's claim is satisfied. [abbr.]

casa *n.*¹ (*also* **carser, casey, cassey**) [late 17C+] a house, a brothel (cf. BADGER-CRIB *n.*). [Ital./Sp. *casa*, a house]

casa *n.*² [1940s+] (*Aus.*) a ladies' man. [abbr. proper name Giovanni Casanova (1725–98), the eponym for a sexually successful man]

casaba *n.* [1950s+] (*US*) the head. [SE *cassava*, 'A plant, called also by its Brazilian name Manioc [...] two varieties (or species) of which are extensively cultivated in the West Indies and tropical America, as also in Africa, for their fleshy tuberous roots, which yield the greatest portion of the daily food of the natives of tropical America' (*OED*)]

casabas *n.* [1930s+] (*US*) the female breasts (cf. APPLES *n.*¹). [SE *casaba*, a large fruit]

cascade *n.* [late 19C+] (*Aus.*) beer. [orig. Tasmanian use, f. the *Cascade Brewing Company* of Hobart; ult. f. the *cascade* of water that was used for brewing]

cascade *v.* [mid-17C+] a euph. for to vomit. [from the visual imagery]

case *n.*¹ [17C; mid-19C+] (*US*) a situation; usu. in phrs., e.g. *have a bad case of the brokes*, to be poor.

case *n.*² (*also* **kaze**) [17C-mid-18C] the vagina (cf. BAG *n.*¹). [SE *case*, a container (for the penis)]

case *n.*³ **1** [17C-1900s] a house. **2** [late 17C-mid-19C] a shop, a warehouse. **3** [late 17C-1970s] a brothel, esp. those sited in the Haymarket, London in mid-late 19C (cf. BADGER-CRIB *n.*). **4** [mid-19C] a lavatory (cf. BACKHOUSE *n.*). [Ital. *casa*, house]

case *n.*⁴ **1** [mid-19C] (*US*) a doomed person. **2** [mid-19C] (*US*) an exceptional person. **3** [mid-19C+] a ne'er-do-well, a dubious character. **4** [mid-19C+] a person, irrespective of status, morals etc., although the usage, usu. denoted by an adj., tends to be dismissive. **5** [1980s] (*Aus.*) a nymphomaniac. [personification of SE *case*, a condition, a state]

case *n.*⁵ **1** [mid-late 19C] a counterfeit crown (5 shillings/25p); thus HALF-A-CASE *n.* **2** [mid-19C+] (*US*) (*also* **case note**) a dollar; thus usu. with a number, e.g. *5 cases/5-case note*, 5$. **3** [1930s] (*US Und.*) one's last dollar. [? Fr. *caisse*, cash or CASER *n.*¹]

case *n.*⁶ **1** [mid-19C+] (*orig. US*) an infatuation, a love affair; thus an adulterous affair. **2** [1970s] a pair of lovers. [CASE *n.*¹]

case *n.*⁷ [mid-19C+] (*orig. US*) an eccentric person; esp. as *rum case*, or in phr. *you are a case*. [? a suitable *case* for the police courts]

case *n.*⁸ **1** [20C+] (*US Und.*) the charge or crime for which one is tried and poss. convicted. **2** [2000s] (*US prison*) punishment for breaking prison rules. [ext. of SE *case*, the actual judicial proceedings]

case *n.*⁹ [1930s+] a surveillance, a look around. [CASE *v.*¹ (1)]

case *adj.* [1900s-50s] (*US*) usu. of money, the last available; spare; thus CASE DOUGH *n.* [? it has been kept in a case or similar receptacle; ? abbr. SE *just in case*; ? CASE *n.*⁵ (2)]

case *v.*¹ **1** [1910s+] (*orig. US*) (*also* **case out**) to look over, to appraise, esp. before a robbery. **2** [1940s-50s] (*UK prison*) to discipline, to put on report. **3** [2000s] (*US Black*) to steal; to exchange money for a higher denomination. [orig. faro jargon *case*, to watch carefully]

case *v.*[2] [1920s–30s] (*UK Und.*) to delay, to spoil, to cause to be postponed. [? to put aside in a fig. *case*]

case *v.*[3] [1970s] (*US Black*) **1** to joke about. **2** to tell off, to scold. [ext. of CASE v.[1] (2)]

cased *adj.*[1] [1940s–50s] (*UK Und.*) charged with an offence. [CASE n.[8] (1)]

cased *adj.*[2] [1950s+] (*S.Afr.*) infatuated with, having a relationship with. [CASE n.[6] (1)]

case dough *n.* (*also* **case dime, …dollar, …note**) [1900s–60s] (*US prison/gambling*) limited money, one's last available funds. [CASE adj. + DOUGH n.[1] (1)/SE *dime/dollar/note*]

cased up *adj.*[1] [1930s+] living with. [GO CASE v.]

cased up *adj.*[2] [1930s] (*US Und.*) imprisoned. [CASE n.[8] (1)]

case-fro *n.* (*also* **case-froe, case-frow, case-vrow**) [late 17C–early 19C] a prostitute, esp. one who works in a brothel. [CASE n.[3] (3) + Ger. *Frau*/Du. *vrow*, a woman]

case house *n.* [1910s–60s] a brothel. [CASE n.[3] (3) + HOUSE n.[1] (1)]

case it around *v.* [1980s] (*US teen*) **1** to check a place or situation. **2** to move onto a new activity. [CASE v.[1] (1)]

case-keeper *n.* [1930s] a brothel-owner. [CASE n.[3] (3)]

case note *n.*[1] *see* CASE n.[5] (2).

case note *n.*[2] *see* CASE DOUGH n.

caseo *n.* [1930s+] **1** a brothel (cf. BADGER-CRIB n.). **2** the hiring of a prostitute for a whole night. **3** a prostitute who hires out for a whole night. **4** in fig. ext., a party or situation involving women behaving 'improperly'. [CASE n.[3] (3)]

case of crabs *n.* [late 19C] a failure. [CASE n.[1] + ? rowing jargon *catch a crab*, to miss a stroke]

case off *v. see* CASE OUT v.[1].

case of pickles *n.* [19C–1910s] a serious problem. [CASE n.[1] + IN A PICKLE phr. (1)]

case of stump *n.* [late 19C] poverty, pennilessness. [CASE n.[1] + STUMPED (UP) adj. (1)]

case of the brokes *n.* [1920s] a state of being penniless. [CASE n.[1] + BROKE adj.[1]]

case of the reds *phr.* [1960s+] (*US teen*) a state of irritation at the world. [CASE n.[1] + ? MEAN REDS n.]

case o' pistles *n.* [20C+] (*Ulster*) the buttocks. [lit. 'a case of pistols'; ? ref. to SE *pizzle*, a bull's penis]

case out *v.*[1] (*also* **case off**) [1940s] (*US*) to leave, to go away.

case out *v.*[2] [1940s–60s] (*US*) to join forces for any undertaking. [ext. of CASE v.[1] (2)]

case out *v.*[3] *see* CASE v.[1] (1).

caser *n.*[1] **1** [early 19C–1950s] 5 shillings (25p). **2** [1900s–30s] (*US*) $1. **3** [1940s–50s] (*Aus.*) a 5-year prison sentence. [Yid. *kesef*, silver; thus the silver 5-shilling piece, and the US dollar, then worth 5 shillings (25p)]

caser *n.*[2] [1940s–50s] (*UK prison*) a prison officer notorious for excessive discipline. [CASE v.[1] (2)]

caser *n.*[3] [1940s+] one who inspects a property before burglary. [CASE v.[1] (1)]

caser *n.*[4] [1950s+] a brothel (cf. BADGER-CRIB n.). [CASE n.[3] (3)]

caser *n.*[5] [2000s] (*Aus.*) an unattractive woman. [one would have to drink a case er [i.e. 'of'] beer before making love to them]

case-ranging *n.* [1920s] the inspection of a property with the intention of robbing it. [CASE n.[3] (1) + SE *range*, to look over, to survey]

case the joint *v.* (*also* **case the gaff/job**) [1910s+] to survey a house, shop etc, with a view to subseq. robbing it. [CASE v.[1] (1) + JOINT n.[4] (2)/GAFF n.[1] (8)/JOB n.[3] (1)]

case-vrow *n. see* CASE-FRO n.

casey *n.*[1] (*also* **cassey**) [19C] cheese. [CASSAN n.]

casey *n.*[2] *see* CASA n.[1].

casey *n.*[3] *see* K.C. n.

casey brown *n.* (*also* **k.c. brown**) [1930s] (*US Black*) a mythical figure endowed with the ability to fight for Black rights and against racism. [an artificial proper name *Casey* or *K.C. Brown*]

casey jones *n.* (*US*) **1** [1930s+] a train-driver, a locomotive engineer. **2** [1940s+] a railway train. [the legendary locomotive engineer John Luther *Jones* (1864–1900); his nickname came from the town of Cayce, pron. *Casey*, Kentucky, his fame from his death, attempting to avoid the crash that killed him, which was later immortalised in a poem by Wallace Stevens, an engine wiper]

cash *n.* [late 17C–early 19C] cheese. [CASSAN n.]

cash *v.*[1] **1** [mid-19C+] (*US*) to lend or give money. **2** [1950s] to pass counterfeit money.

cash *v.*[2] (*US*) **1** [1900s] to quit, to give up one's efforts. **2** [1930s] to die. [abbr. CASH IN ONE'S CHIPS v.]

cash and carry *v.* [late 19C+] to marry; thus *cash and carried*, married. [rhy. sl.]

cash-ass *n.* [1970s+] (*gay*) a male prostitute who pretends not to be until promised cash. [SE *cash* + -ASS sfx; a pun on SE *cautious*]

cash carrier *n.* [late 19C] a pimp (cf. ABBOT ON THE CROSS n.).

cashed *adj.* **1** [20C+] (*US campus*) physically, mentally or economically exhausted. **2** [1940s] (*US*) dead. **3** [1980s+] (*drugs*) used of a marijuana bowl or pipe that contains nothing but ash. **4** [2000s] to have had a sufficiency. [? CASH IN ONE'S CHIPS v.]

cashed up *adj.* [1930s+] (*Aus./N.Z.*) wealthy, well-off, albeit temporarily.

cash-in *n.* [1920s] (*US*) the end, i.e. death. [CASH IN v. (1)]

cash in *v.* (*orig. US*) **1** [late 19C+] to die. **2** [late 19C+] to settle up one's accounts or debts, esp. in card-playing. **3** [1920s+] to make a profit, to exploit; often as *cash in on*. **4** [1930s] to stop arguing or prevaricating, to confess. **5** [1960s] to give up.

cash (in) one's checks *v.* (*also* **cash one's last check**) [late 19C+] (*orig. US*) to die (cf. CASH IN ONE'S CHIPS v.; GET ONE'S CHECKS v.; HAND IN ONE'S CHECKS v.; HAND IN ONE'S CHIPS v.; HAVE (HAD) ONE'S CHIPS v.; PASS IN ONE'S CHECKS v.; PASS IN ONE'S CHIPS v.; SEND IN ONE'S CHECKS v.). [fig. use of CASH IN v. (2) + SE *checks*, gambling chips]

cash in one's chips *v.* **1** [late 19C] (*US*) to change one's way of life. **2** [late 19C] (*US*) to give oneself up. **3** [late 19C+] (*orig. US*) (*also* **cash in one's stack**) to die (cf. CASH (IN) ONE'S CHECKS v.). **4** [late 19C+] to kill. **5** [1950s] to be 'over', finished. **6** [1960s+] to commit suicide. [gambling jargon; the action one takes on leaving a game, assuming one still has some chips in hand]

cash in the food stamps of love *v.* [1970s+] (*US Black*) to accept a less than ideal sexual partner through one's needs or frustration.

cashish *n.* [2000s] money. [SE *cash* + *hashish* (as a desirable/valuable commodity)]

cashmere *n.* [1960s] (*US Black*) a sweater, irrespective of the material.

cashola *n.* [1950s+] (*US*) cash. [SE *cash* + -OLA sfx; on the pattern of PAYOLA n.]

cash on delivery *n.* [late 19C] (*US*) codfish. [play on abbr. *C.O.D.*/SE *cod*]

cash one's checks *v. see* CASH (IN) ONE'S CHECKS v.

cash one's last check *v. see* CASH (IN) ONE'S CHECKS v.

cash one's pistol *v.* [late 19C] (*US, Western*) to rob a bank at gunpoint. [joc. image of presenting a pistol at the counter rather than a cheque]

cash out *v.* [1960s] **1** to die. **2** to kill oneself. **3** to murder, to kill.

cash up *v.* **1** [19C] to pay up, to pay over; thus to pay one's debts. **2** [1950s+] (*Aus.*) to earn money. **3** [1970s] (*US campus*) to work out.

casian *n.* [1990s+] (*UK Black*) a policeman. [? pron. of SE *catch* + *man*]

casing *n.* [1920s+] (*orig. US*) the assessment of a place or person to calculate how vulnerable it is or they are to robbery. [CASE v.[1] (1)]

cask *n.* **1** [mid-19C] 'fashionable Slang for a brougham, or other private carriage' (Hotten, 1859). **2** [1930s] (*US Und.*) a taxi. [SE *cask*, 'a wooden vessel of cylindrical form' (*OED*)]

casket nail *n.* (*also* **casket tack**) [1960s] (*US*) a cigarette. [var. on COFFIN NAIL n.² (1)]

Caspar (Milquetoast) *n.* (*also* **Casper Milktoast**, …**Milque-toast, Milquetoast, Mr…**) [1930s+] a cowardly, weak person. [the central character in the cartoon 'The Timid Soul' created by H.T. Webster, first publ. in *New York World*, May 1924]

casper *n.* [1980s] (*US Black*) a particularly light-skinned Black person. [1950s cartoon character *Casper the Friendly Ghost*, who is white]

cassan *n.* (*also* **caffan, cass, cassam, cassin, cassom, casson, casum, casun, caz, cosan**) [mid-16C–mid-19C] (*UK Und.*) cheese. [Rom. *cas*, cheese; cf. SE *casein*, the milk ingredient that is the basis of cheese; caffan is a misprint, due to confusion with the 'long s'; Hotten (1859) notes that this has been 'ridiculously inserted']

cass-cass *adj.* [20C+] (*W.I.*) untidy, disreputable, inferior, low-class. [Twi *kasakasa*, very thin, *akasakasa*, a dispute]

cassey *n.¹ see* CASA n.¹.

cassey *n.² see* CASEY n.¹.

cassin/cassom/casson *n. see* CASSAN n.

casspir *n.* [1980s+] (*S.Afr.*) an armoured vehicle used by the South African police and army, usu. in the context of keeping order in the townships. [anagram of *CSIR*, Council for Scientific & Industrial Research + *SAP*, South African Police]

cast *adj.* [1930s–40s] (*Irish/N.Z.*) drunk. [? pun on SE *cast down*]

cast a net *v.* [20C+] (*Aus.*) to have a bet. [rhy. sl.]

castell *v.* [early 17C] to look, to see. [? SE *castle*, from the battlements of which one can get a long-range view]

caster *n.¹* [mid-16C–mid-19C] (*UK Und.*) a cloak. [ety. unknown, but F&H suggests a link to CASTOR n.]

caster *n.²* [mid-19C+] anything or anyone that has been rejected or cast aside. [SE *cast off*. Note milit. jargon *caster*, a horse considered no longer fit for the cavalry or horse artillery and sold at public auction]

caster *n.³* [late 19C] (*US*) a testicle. [? SE *castor*, a small wheel used to make furniture mobile]

castieau's hotel *n.* [mid-19C] (*Aus.*) a prison (cf. ABBOTT'S PRIORY n.; BOARDING HOUSE n.). [the name of its one-time governor]

casting *n.* [mid-19C] (*US*) a coin; thus **castings**, cash. [SE *cast*, to form molten metal into a shape with a mould]

cast-iron and double-bolted *adj.* [late 19C+] extremely strong. [fig. use of engineering terminology]

cast-iron horrors *n.* [1900s–20s] (*Anglo-Irish*) delirium tremens. [SE *cast-iron*, 'hard-and-fast', unyielding + HORRORS, THE n. (2)]

Castle, the *n. see* HOLLOWAY CASTLE n.

castle *n.* [1940s+] (*US Black*) one's house, one's home. [on model of the cliché, *an Englishman's home is his castle*]

Castle Catholics *n.* [early 19C–1920s] Irish Catholics who rejected nationalism, preferring to curry favour with and ape the lifestyle of the ruling British. [Dublin *Castle*, the seat of British rule]

Castle hack *n.* [1900s–10s] (*Irish*) an informer. [Dublin *Castle* (*see* CASTLE CATHOLICS n.) + HACK n.¹ (2)]

castle rag *n.* [mid-19C] (*UK Und.*) 4 pence. [rhy. sl. = FLAG n.¹ (1)]

cast nasturtiums *v.* [20C+] a joc. mispron. of SE *cast aspersions*.

cast one's cap *v.* [late 16C–17C] to be indifferent, to abandon as lost. [pvb 'cast one's cap at the wind']

cast one's skin *v.* **1** [mid-19C] to strip oneself naked. **2** [late 19C] (*UK society*) to rejuvenate oneself. [animal imagery]

castor *n.* [mid-17C–19C] a hat; thus *demi-castor*, 'an inferior quality of beaver's fur, or a mixture of beaver's and other fur' (*OED*). [14C *castor*, a beaver. Such hats were made of beaver fur or, as was increasingly the case, of rabbit, disguised to look as if they were beaver]

castor *adj.* [1940s+] (*Aus.*) excellent, admirable, first-rate; thus *be on the castor with*, to be popular with. [? SE *castor sugar*; thus parallel to SWEET adj.¹ (2); Simes, *A Dict. of Australian Underworld Slang* (1993), prefers the old criminal sign of tugging one's hat or CASTOR n. to indicate 'all clear', used fig. in the non-criminal world]

Castro clone *n.* [1970s+] (*US gay*) a popular variety of post-gay-liberation stereotype, often posing as a lumberjack with checked flannel shirt, Levis, heavy boots etc. [*Castro* Street, San Francisco, known as The Castro, and the centre of the gay community + CLONE n. (2)]

cast the calf *v.* (*also* **cast the wanes, slip the calf**) [mid-17C–mid-19C] of a woman, to undergo an abortion. [ext. of SE use, ref. to cows (+ ? SE *wain*, a wagon or ? SE *wean*, a child)]

cast the house out of the windows *v.* [mid-16C–19C] to make a great deal of noise or disturbance in one's house.

cast the net *v.* [1970s+] (*US*) of a pimp, to employ an experienced prostitute to lure a new woman into joining his team.

cast the wanes *v. see* CAST THE CALF v.

cast up *v.* [late 19C+] (*Ulster*) to bear a grudge, to remind someone of their failings. [abbr./play on SE *cast up accounts*, to make a reckoning]

cast up one's accounts *v.* (*also* **cast up one's reckoning**) **1** [late 16C–19C] to vomit (cf. THROW UP ONE'S ACCOUNTS v.). **2** [late 17C–mid-18C] to be drunk, and so likely to vomit. [play on SE *cast up accounts*, to make a reckoning]

casual *n.¹* **1** [19C] a casual pauper. **2** [mid-19C+] a part-time labourer or other employee. **3** [late 19C+] the casual ward in a hospital. [SE *casual*, non-essential or, in the case of paupers, only temporarily needy]

casual *n.²* [1980s+] **1** a working-class youth who dresses in the designer-labelled clothing of their society peers but whose accent and lifestyle remains resolutely proletarian. **2** a football hooligan who adopts such a style. [SE *casual clothing*]

casual *adj.* **1** [1950s+] (*US campus*) acceptable, satisfactory. **2** [1970s] clever, witty. **3** [1980s] not worth becoming upset about. [SE *casual*; note 19C use *casual*, not to be depended on, uncertain, 'happy-go-lucky'; thus another e.g. of the bad = good model]

casualty *n.* [late 19C–1900s] a black eye.

casualty *adj.* [mid–late 19C] casual; thus *casualty-boy*, a boy who hires himself out to a costermonger or market greengrocer.

casum/casun *n. see* CASSAN n.

cat *n.¹* **1** [15C–18C;1940s+] (*also* **kat, painted cat**) a prostitute (cf. ALLEY CAT n.). **2** [17C+] a woman, esp. a spiteful and malicious one; thus *old cat*, an unpleasant, gossiping old woman. **3** [18C+] a gossip. **4** [late 19C] a drunken, violent prostitute. **5** [1900s] (*US Und.*) one who researches potential robberies, plans them and poss. works as a lookout. **6** [1910s+] a sexually attractive woman. **7** [1920s–30s] (*US*) an itinerant worker. **8** [1920s–40s] (*US prison*) an informer. [a variety of supposedly feline qualities; 1940s+ use of (1) is US Black]

cat *n.²* [17C] the penis; esp. in phr. *a bit for one's cat*, sexual intercourse (cf. ANTEATER n.). [abbr. CATSO n. or ? the pecrceived lecherousness of a SE tom*cat*]

cat *n.³* **1** [late 17C+] female pubic hair and genitals; thus *cat-lapper*, one who performs cunnilingus. **2** [mid-19C] a ladies' muff; thus *free a cat*, to steal a muff. **3** [1970s+] (*US gay*) a lesbian. [(2) fig. use of (1)]

cat *n.⁴* [late 18C–early 19C] the cat-o'-nine-tails; thus *get the cat*, to be given a judicial whipping, and the right-wingers' litany of *bring back the cat*. [abbr.; later use is SE]

cat *n.⁵* [early–mid-19C] a quart pot (cf. CHICKEN n.⁵; HEN n.²). [a large KITTEN n.¹ (a quart is 2 pints)]

cat *n.⁶* **1** [mid-19C+] a person, as needed in a given situation, e.g.

she's never going to be their kind of cat. **2** [1920s–30s] an animal, not a cat.

cat *n.*[7] [late 19C] a native of Cheshire. [phr. to 'grin like a Cheshire cat', as immortalized in Lewis Carroll's *Alice in Wonderland* (1866)]

cat *n.*[8] [1900s] (*Aus.*) a business syndicate. [abbr.]

cat *n.*[9] [1900s–30s] (*US tramp*) a semi-criminal vagrant. [abbr. GAYCAT n.]

cat *n.*[10] **1** [1910s+] (*orig. US*) Caterpillar tractor; thus a tractor of any make. **2** [1980s+] (*US Black*) a Cadillac. [abbr.]

cat *n.*[11] **1** [1920s+] a jazz musician. **2** [1920s+] (*US Black*) a smartly dressed, fashion-conscious man, thus a 'sharp cat'. **3** [1930s] a jazz fan. **4** [1930s+] a person, usu. male (like so many initially Black terms, adopted by beatniks and then hippies). **5** [1980s+] a user of crack cocaine. [? ALLIGATOR n.[3]; abbr. to gator, gate, *cat*; Gold, *A Jazz Lexicon* (1964), suggests 'most. prob. shortened form of general and Negro slang TOMCAT n.[2] (1)']

cat *n.*[12] **1** [1930s+] (*US*) (*also* **cat walker**) a cat burglar. **2** [2000s] a narcotics user. [(1) abbr.; (2) f. (1), i.e. the surreptitious style of a drug addict in public]

cat *n.*[13] **1** [1950s+] (*Aus.*) a passive male homosexual; thus *cats' gaol*, a prison where the majority of inmates are homosexual/transsexual; *cats' yard*, an area where gay or otherwise vulnerable prisoners can be segregated. **2** [1970s+] (*UK prison*) a weakling. **3** [1970s+] (*Aus. sporting*) a player who cannot take the rough-and-tumble of the game. [(1) ? SE *catamite*, a boy kept for homosexual purposes; but note PUSSY n. (9)/PUSSY n. (10)]

cat *n.*[14] [1960s] (*US*) illicitly distilled whisky. [abbr. WILDCAT n.[2] (1)]

cat *n.*[15] [1960s] (*US campus*) the grade C (cf. ACE n.[6]). [initial letter]

cat *n.*[16] [1990s+] (*drugs*) methcathinone. [abbr.]

cat *n.*[17] *see* KITTY n.[3].

cat *adj.* **1** [20C+] (*Irish*) terrible, shocking, unpleasant, rough. **2** [1980s] (*US campus*) likeable, approved of. [Irish *cat marbh*, mischief, calamity, or abbr. of SE *catastrophe*; (2) on bad = good model]

cat *v.*[1] [1940s–70s] (*US gang*) to talk, to gossip. [CAT n.[1] (3)]

cat *v.*[2] [1950s–70s] (*US teen/gang*) to loaf about. [the indolence of the SE *cat*]

cat *v.*[3] *see* CAT AROUND v. (1).

cat *v.*[4] *see* CAT (UP) v.

catalogue queen *n.* [1960s+] (*US gay*) a homosexual man who uses physique and body-building magazines as masturbatory pornography. [SE *catalogue* + QUEEN n.[2] (1)/QUEEN sfx (2)]

catamaran *n.* **1** [late 18C–19C] an old scraggy woman, a disagreeable harridan. **2** [mid-19C] a run-down horse. [pun on CAT n.[1] (2) + poss. pun on orig. SE *catamaran*, a fireship. But note also CAT O'MOUNTAIN n. (1)]

catamaran trick *n.* [early 19C] a practical joke. [? early 19C SE *catamaran*, an ill-tempered person]

cat and dog life *n.* [19C+] an unhappy marriage, in which the partners fight like cat and dog.

cat and kitten hunter *n.* [mid-19C] (*UK Und.*) 'those who purloin pewter quart and pint pots from the top of area railings'. [CAT n.[5] + KITTEN n.[1]]

cat and kitten hunting *n.* (*also* **cat and kitten sneaking**) [mid-19C] (*UK Und.*) the stealing of pint and quart pots from public houses. [CAT n.[5] + KITTEN n.[1]]

cat and kitten rig *n.* [early 19C] (*UK Und.*) the stealing of pint and quart pots from public houses. [CAT n.[5] + KITTEN n.[1] + RIG n.[2] (2)]

cat and mouse *n.* [mid-19C+] a house. [rhy. sl.]

Cat-and-Mouse Act *n.* [1910s] the nickname for the Prisoners (Temporary Discharge for Ill-health) Act of 1913 to enable (suffragette) hunger-strikers to be released temporarily (and thus defuse public outrage at their treatment and their own desire for well-publicized martyrdom).

cataract *n.* [mid-19C] a large, many-layered black cravat, used to

show off one's stick-pin and similar jewellery; such an item was especially favoured by 19C commercial travellers. [SE *cataract*, a waterfall; it 'flows' down the wearer's chest]

cat around *v.* **1** [20C+] (*orig. US*) (*also* **cat**) to search for a sexual partner. **2** [1910s+] (*orig. US*) to be sexually unfaithful. **3** [1930s+] (*orig. US*) to wander about purposelessly. **4** [1940s] (*US Black*) to ask questions. [the perceived lecherousness of the SE *tomcat* (cf. TOM CAT v.)]

catarumpus *n.* [mid-19C] (*US*) a riot, a commotion, a rumpus. [? CATAWAMPUS adj. (3)]

catawampus *n.* **1** [mid–late 19C] a biting, stinging insect. **2** [mid-19C–1930s] (*US*) a peculiar or remarkable thing or person. [CATAWAMPUS adj.]

catawampus *adj.* (*also* **caliwampus, cankywampus, cattywampus**) (*US*) [mid-19C–1930s] **1** fierce, pitiless. **2** ill-tempered, crotchety. **3** askew. **4** out of order, wrong. [ety. unknown; ? SE *cater-/catty-cornered*, diagonal]

catawampus *v.* (*US*) **1** [mid-19C–1900s] to confuse, to confound. **2** [mid-19C–1900s] to injure, to harm. **3** [1900s] to move in a diagonal line. [CATAWAMPUS adj.]

catawampus! *excl.* [19C] (*US*) a general excl., often as *Great catawampus!* [SE *catawampus*, a hobgoblin or imaginary demon; in turn ? f. 17C *catamount*, a panther]

catawampusly *adv.* (*also* **catawamptiously**) [mid-19C–1900s] (*US*) fiercely. [CATAWAMPUS adj.]

cat bar *n.* (*also* **cat's bar**) [1950s–80s] (*N.Z.*) a bar set aside for women and their escorts (cf. CAT-PARTY n.). [CAT n.[1] (2) + SE *bar*]

catbird *n.* [20C+] (*US*) **1** a mischievous or cunning person. **2** a person of authority or power. [the SE *catbird (Dumatella carolinensis)* is so-called f. its habit of harassing cats; thus trans. to the human *catbird*'s dealings with fellow humans]

catbird *adj.* [mid-19C] (*US*) perfect, ideal. [ety. unknown; predates CATBIRD n. (2)]

catbird seat *n.* [1940s+] a privileged or advantageous position. [SE *catbird (Dumatella carolinensis)*/CATBIRD n. (2) + *seat*. The catbird takes up a high, exposed position to deliver its song. The image is of a cat looking down on a targeted bird. Orig. a term used by a poker opponent of the sportscaster Red Barber (1908–92) and popularized first by him and latterly by a James Thurber story, 'The Catbird Seat' (1942)]

catch *n.*[1] **1** [mid-18C+] one who is seen as matrimonially desirable; often in phrs. *a good catch; no catch.* **2** [1900s–10s] anything desirable. **3** [1960s+] (*US Black*) a woman, esp. a woman recruited into prostitution. **4** [1960s+] (*US Black*) the number of clients a prostitute has serviced within a given time.

catch *n.*[2] [mid-19C] (*UK Und.*) a thief's booty, a stolen item.

catch *v.*[1] **1** [late 19C+] to grasp the meaning, often in negative, e.g. *I didn't quite catch...* **2** [late 19C+] to find out, to discover. **3** [1920s+] of a show or other type of entertainment, to listen to, to watch, to attend. **4** [1960s+] to notice, to appreciate.

catch *v.*[2] **1** [late 19C+] to ensnare a victim in a confidence trick or crooked gambling game. **2** [20C+] to obtain, to get, to come into possession of a given item, lit. or fig. **3** [1960s] (*US prison*) to make a good impression. **4** [1960s+] (*also* **catch action**) to seduce. **5** [1960s+] (*US Black*) of a pimp, to persuade a woman (whether a prostitute or not) to start working for him; thus *catching*, seducing a woman into prostitution. **6** [1970s] (*US Black*) to work as a prostitute.

catch *v.*[3] [late 19C+] to become pregnant.

catch *v.*[4] [1920s+] to obtain, to get; both lit. and fig.

catch *v.*[5] [1940s+] (*orig. US*) to have a casual social encounter with.

catch *v.*[6] [1960s+] to take the passive role in (usu. homosexual) sexual intercourse. [baseball imagery (as opposed to 'throw')]

catch a buzz *v.* [1970s+] **1** to start experiencing the (pleasurable) effects of alcohol or a given drug. **2** (*lesbian*) to masturbate with an electric vibrator. [CATCH v.² (2) + BUZZ n.³; (2) puns on (1)/SE *buzz*, the sound of the machine]

catch (a) cold v. [late 18C+] **1** to get into trouble, poss. through impetuousness. **2** to lose out financially, poss. after purchasing a supposed 'bargain', which proves to be otherwise.

catch action n. [1960s] (*US Black*) young women, typically runaways who have just arrived in the big city and are vulnerable to being recruited as prostitutes. [CATCH n.¹ (3) + ACTION n. (10)]

catch action v. see CATCH v.² (4).

catch a face v. see THROW ON A FACE v.

catch a few z's v. see CATCH (SOME) z's v.

catch a flatline v. see FLATLINE v.

catch a fox v. [late 17C–18C] to be very drunk; thus *caught a fox*, drunk. [FOX v.¹ (2)]

catch a glad v. [20C+] (*W.I.*) to experience an outburst of spontaneous joy. [CATCH v.² (2) + SE *glad*(ness)]

catch a horse v. [20C+] (*Aus.*) to urinate. [euph.]

catch air v. **1** [1920s–70s] (*US Black*) to leave quickly, to rush off. **2** [1950s] (*US*) to take a break. [CATCH v.² (2) + SE *air*]

catch a load of v. [1920s+] (*US*) to catch sight of. [CATCH v.² (2) + var. on GET A LOAD OF v.]

catch and kill one's own v. [1970s+] (*Aus.*) to look after oneself, to sort out one's own problems without outside aid. [the image of the self-sufficient dweller in the outback]

catch an oyster v. [19C] of a woman, to have sexual intercourse (cf. DO A BOTTOM-WETTER v.; DO A TUMBLE v.¹; DO A WET BOTTOM v.; DO A WET 'UN v.; DRAW A CORK v.²; DROP 'EM v.; FEED ONE'S PUSSY v.; GET SHOT IN THE TAIL v.; GET SOME ROD v.; GET SOME SWEET v.; GIVE A HOT POULTICE FOR THE IRISH TOOTHACHE v.; GIVE JUICE FOR JELLY v.; GIVE MUTTON FOR BEEF v.; GO STAR-GAZING (ON ONE'S BACK) v.; GO TO BUCK v.; HAVE A BIT OF GOOSE'S NECK v.; HAVE A BIT OF GUTSTICK v.; HAVE A BIT OF SUGAR STICK v.; HAVE A LIVE SAUSAGE FOR SUPPER v.; LIGHT THE LAMP v.; LOOK AT THE CEILING v.; LOSE THE MATCH AND POCKET THE STAKES v.; OPEN UP v.¹; PRAY WITH ONE'S KNEES UPWARDS v.; RIDE THE PONY v.; SEE THE STARS LYING UPON ONE'S BACK v.; SLIP IT ABOUT v.; STAND THE PUSH v.; SUCK THE SUGAR-STICK v.; TAKE IN AND DO FOR v.; TAKE IN BEEF v.; TAKE THE STARCH OUT OF v.; THROW (SOME) ASS v.; TURN UP v.¹; TURN UP ONE'S TAIL v.; WIND ONE'S CLOCK v.). [OYSTER n.² (2)]

catchar n. [1970s] (*W.I.*) one who attempts to interfere maliciously in a couple's love affair; thus one who talks out of turn, who does not 'mind their own business'. [Bhojpuri *khachchar*, lit. 'mule' and thus used as a term of abuse]

catch arse v. [20C+] (*W.I.*) to find it hard to make enough money to live. [SE *catch* + fig. use of ARSE n.¹ (1)]

catch a square v. [2000s] (*US prison*) to prepare to fight. [the corners in a boxing ring]

catch a tartar v. [late 17C+] to encounter an apparent victim or weakling who turns out to be much stronger than suspected. [TARTAR n. (3)]

catch a vap v. (*also* **catch a vapse**) [20C+] (*W.I.*) to be suddenly inspired to do something, to do something on the spur of the moment. [VAP n. (2)]

catch-bet n. [mid-19C] a bet made with the intention of ensnaring a gullible punter.

catch cold v. see CATCH (A) COLD v.

catch colt n. [20C+] (*US*) an illegitimate child. [dial. *catch colt*, a colt that was bred unintentionally]

catch copper v. [16C] to come to harm, to suffer grief. [ety. unknown]

catch 'em-alive n. [mid-19C] **1** a trap. **2** a tooth-comb.

catch 'em alive oh! excl. [mid-19C] a popular, if meaningless, catchphrase.

catch 'em (all) alive-o n. **1** [mid-19C] the vagina; one of a number of terms equating it with a threat to the penis; thus a prostitute (cf. BITE n.²). **2** [mid-19C] a fly-paper. **3** [mid-19C–1900s] a small comb.

catcher n.¹ [mid-19C] (*US*) a watchman, a policeman (cf. BEAT-POUNDER n.).

catcher n.² [1960s+] one who plays the passive role during sexual intercourse; this can relate to homosexual, sado-masochistic or 'straight' heterosexual intercourse. [CATCH v.⁶]

catcher n.³ see FLAT-CATCHER n.¹ (2).

catcher n.⁴ see STASH CATCHER n.

catcher's mitt n. [1980s+] (*US*) a contraceptive diaphragm. [SE *catch*, i.e. semen + baseball imagery]

catch-fart n. [late 17C–19C] a footman (cf. FART-CATCHER n.). [SE *catch* + FART n. (1), i.e. his being forced to walk closely behind his master or mistress]

catch flack v. (*also* **catch flak**, **get flack/flak**) [1960s+] (*US*) to receive criticism, to face verbal attacks. [SE *catch/get* + FLAK n. (3)]

catch fleas for someone v. [19C–1910s] to have sexual intercourse with someone. [the image of monkeys removing each other's fleas]

catch France v. [1920s+] (*W.I.*) to find it hard to make enough money to live. [SE *catch* + FRANCE n.]

catch heat v. [1970s+] (*US*) to get into trouble.

catch hell v. (*also* **cop hell**, **get hell**) **1** [mid-19C+] (*orig. US*) to get into trouble, to suffer a telling-off. **2** [1920s+] to suffer. **3** [1920s+] (*W.I./US*) to find it hard to make enough money to live, to subsist, to suffer great hardship.

catching n. see CATCH v.² (5).

catching harvest n. [late 17C–mid-19C] (*UK Und.*) a bad time for highway robbery since heavy traffic is likely to impede a safe getaway. [SE *catching harvest*, unpredictable, unsettled weather + a pun on SE *catch*, implying that the highwayman may get caught]

catching the bird phr. [1930s+] (*Aus.*) picking up a woman while driving one's car and then persuading her to agree to sex. [SE *catch* + BIRD n.¹ (2)]

catch it v. [1960s–70s] (*US gay*) to fellate. [i.e. 'catch it' (the penis) in one's mouth but note CATCH v.⁶]

catch it (hot) v. **1** [mid-19C+] to be severely reprimanded, punished or beaten. **2** [1950s–60s] to be shot. [euph. for CATCH HELL v.]

catch jesse v. see GIVE (SOMEONE) JESSE v.

catch me (at it)! excl. [mid-19C–1930s] a defiant excl. implying that one will never be caught.

catch Moses v. see BASH THE LIVING MOSES OUT OF v.

catch nennen v. (*also* **catch royal**, **catch skin**, **catch tail**) [20C+] (*W.I., Trin.*) to find it hard to make enough money to live. [SE *catch* + fig. uses of NENNEN n./ROYAL n.²/SE *skin*/TAIL n.² (1)]

catch on v. see CATCH ON (TO) v.

catch one's balls in a wringer v. (*also* **catch oneself in a wringer**, **catch one's tit in a wringer**) [1970s+] to find oneself in trouble, in an unpleasant situation. [the most famous use was during the Watergate affair (1972) when US Attorney General John Mitchell suggested that if Katherine Graham, proprietor of the *Washington Post*, were to permit the printing of revelations on White House involvement, she would 'catch her big fat tit in a wringer']

catch one's death (of cold) v. (*also* **catch a death**, **get one's death**, **take one's death**) [early 18C+] to catch a (bad) cold.

catch oneself on v. [1980s+] (*Irish*) to come to one's senses. [CATCH ON v. (2)]

catch one's length v. [20C+] (*W.I.*) to settle down, to understand what must be done. [lit. to estimate the size of the problem]

catch one's lunch v. [1960s+] (*US*) to be defeated so comprehensively as to feel physically sick.

catch one's tit in a wringer v. see CATCH ONE'S BALLS IN A WRINGER v.

catch on the fly v. [1920s–30s] (*US tramp*) to board a moving (freight) train. [SE *catch* + ON THE FLY adv.¹ (3)]

catch on the hop v. (also **catch on the h.o.p.**, **get on the hop/h.o.p.**) [mid-19C+] to catch unawares. [SE *catch* + ON THE HOP phr.[1] (2)]

catch on the non-plus v. [late 19C] to catch unawares.

catch on (to) v. [late 19C+] (orig. US) **1** to attach or fix oneself to, to join on, to catch hold of. **2** to understand, to become aware of. **3** to become popular or fashionable.

catch out v. [1970s+] **1** (US tramp) to leave by train. **2** (US prison) to move, to leave an area quickly. [i.e. to *catch* a train *out* of town]

catchpenny n. **1** [early 19C–1900s] a pamphlet or broadsheet sold in the streets and detailing a lurid, if imaginary, murder. **2** [mid-19C] a cheap theatre or music hall. [SE *catchpenny* adj., designed for sales rather than quality]

catchpole n. [late 17C–18C] a sergeant or bailiff, esp. one who arrests for debt. [Lat. *cacepollus*, chicken catcher, dating from a period when debts were paid in kind as well as cash]

catchpole rapparee n. [early 18C] a constable. [CATCHPOLE n. + SE *rapparee*, a bandit, a robber]

catch rapid v. [1980s+] (Irish) to catch in the act.

catch royal v. see CATCH NENNEN v.

catch rubber v. see PEEL RUBBER v.

catch shit v. (orig. US) **1** [1950s+] to be scolded or told off, to get into trouble. **2** [1960s+] to suffer physical harm. **3** [1980s+] to impress; usu. in phr. *didn't catch shit*, didn't impress. [SE *catch* + SHIT n.[3] (2)]

catch skin v. see CATCH NENNEN v.

catch someone bending v. [20C+] to catch someone at a disadvantage.

catch someone napping v. (also **take someone napping**) [19C] to take someone by surprise, to catch someone off their guard. [20C+ use is SE]

catch someone with their pants down v. [1930s+] (orig. US) caught in a state of embarrassing unpreparedness, caught red-handed; often in 'lit.' use of sexual infidelities.

catch some rays v. (also **catch sun**) [1960s+] to sunbathe (cf. BAG SOME RAYS v.). [CATCH v.[2] (2) + RAYS n./SE *sun*]

catch some rays phr. [2000s] (US teen) goodbye, a feasible alternative farewell in sun-drenched California. [CATCH SOME RAYS v.]

catch (some) z's v. (also **catch a few z's**) [1960s+] (US) to have a nap. [CATCH v.[2] (2) + z n.[1]]

catch sun v. see CATCH SOME RAYS v.

catch tail v. see CATCH NENNEN v.

catch the chain v. [20C+] (US Und.) to move from a local jail to a proper prison. [the chain that links the prisoners together during their journey]

catch the owl v. [late 18C–early 19C] to play a trick on an innocent countryman, who is decoyed into a barn under the pretext of catching an owl; when he enters, a bucket of water is poured upon his head.

catch the stifles v. see NAB THE STIFLES v.

catch under the pinny v. [1900s–30s] of a man, to have sexual intercourse with a woman, to seduce. [SE *catch* + SE *pinny*, abbr. SE *pinafore*]

catch up v. [1930s+] (drugs) to withdraw from drug addiction. [one 'catches up' with life. The image of addiction is one of suspended animation]

catch vapors v. [1990s+] (US campus) to become jealous.

catch wise v. [1930s–70s] (US) to understand, to grasp. [CATCH ON (TO) v. (2) + WISE UP v. (2)]

catch wood v. [1980s+] (US) **1** to get an erection. **2** in fig. use, to become extremely excited. [CATCH v.[2] (2) + WOOD n.[4] (2)]

catchy adj. **1** [early 19C] attractive, esp. when seen as 'cheaply' so. **2** [mid-19C] tending to take an undue advantage. [SE *catch*]

catch you (later) phr. [1950s+] (orig. US Black) goodbye. [CATCH v.[5]]

catch you on the flip flop phr. [1970s+] (US campus) goodbye. [CATCH v.[5] + SE *flip-flop*, a reversal, lit. a somersault]

catch z's v. see CATCH (SOME) z's v.

cat clothes n. [1950s] (orig. US Black) fashionable clothing as favoured by jazz fans. [CAT n.[11] (2) + SE *clothes*]

cat couldn't scratch it phr. (also **one a cat couldn't scratch**) [1960s+] (US) a phr. used of an especially hard penile erection.

cat cuff n. [20C+] (US) a bluff.

cat-eating-shit grin n. see SHIT-EATING GRIN n.

caterpillar n.[1] **1** [late 16C–18C] a ne'er-do-well, one who lives on his wits and others' gullibility. **2** [mid-18C–early 19C] a soldier. [SE *caterpillar*, a rapacious person]

caterpillar n.[2] [mid-late 19C] a girls' school. [? the girls will emerge as adult 'butterflies']

caterpillar n.[3] [20C+] (Aus.) a drunkard. [the drunkard crawls, caterpillar-like, from pub to pub or along the floor]

caterpillar n.[4] [1930s] a slow horse. [its speed]

caterpillar v. [mid-19C–1900s] (US) to leave quietly. [SE *caterpillar*, which it moves slowly/quietly]

caterpillar's raincoat n. (also **caterpillar coat**) [1970s–80s] (UK Black) a condom. [? i.e. a cocoon]

caterpillar's spats n. see CAT'S PYJAMAS n.

cater-trey n. [mid-16C–early 19C] (UK Und.) dice or crooked dice. [*cater*, 4 + *trey*, 3; ult. Fr. *quatre* + *trois*]

caterwaul v. **1** [mid-16C–19C] to indulge in sexual foreplay; to have sexual intercourse. **2** [mid-16C–early 19C] to wander the streets at night, looking for excitement, esp. sexual conquests. [SE *caterwaul*, to make a noise like rutting cats]

catever n. (also **kerteever**, **kerterver**) [mid-19C] **1** a strange affair. **2** an eccentric person. [Ital. *cattivo*, bad]

catever adj. (also **cateva**, **kerteever**, **kerterver**) [mid-19C–1900s] odd, strange, bad.

cat-eye n.[1] [20C+] (W.I.) a Black (or other non-European) person with cat-like grey-green irises in their eyes.

cat-eye n.[2] [1970s] (US) a late-night work shift.

catface n. [1950s–70s] (US) a wrinkle in one's clothing. [fanciful resemblance; note timber jargon *catface*, a mark in a piece of lumber-wood]

cat-fart about v. (also **cat-fart around**) [1950s–60s] to act in a fussy manner. [SE *cat* + FART ABOUT v.]

cat fight n. [1950s+] a fight between 2 (or more) women. [CAT n.[1] (2) + SE *fight*]

catfish n. [mid-19C–1910s] (US) an unpleasant person. [the unattractiveness of the SE *catfish*]

catfish! excl. [1940s–50s] a mild oath, e.g. *suffering catfish!*

Catfish Row n. [20C+] (US) an area of a town in which the Black population live. [SE *catfish*, supposedly a staple of a Black person's diet]

cat-fit n. [1900s–30s] (US) a tantrum. [reverse anthropomorphism]

catflap n. [1990s+] **1** the anus. **2** a bisexual person. [(2) it swings both ways]

cat flat n. [1940s] (US Und.) a brothel (cf. BIRDCAGE n.[1]). [CAT n.[1] (1) + SE *flat*]

cat food n. [1960s–70s] (US Black) sexual intercourse. [CAT n.[3] (1) + SE *food*]

cat-foot v. [20C+] (US) to move stealthily. [var. on PUSSYFOOT (AROUND) v.]

cat-foot adv. [1900s] stealthily. [CAT-FOOT v.]

cat-footed adj. [1930s] stealthy. [CAT-FOOT v.]

catgut n. [20C+] (US) cheap whisky. [var. on ROTGUT n. (3)]

catgut-scraper n. (also **catgut-teaser**, **catgut-tickler**, **catgut-squeezer**) [early 17C–1940s] a fiddler or violinist; as *agitate the catgut*, to play the fiddle. [the *catgut* violin strings]

catharpin fashion n. [late 17C–early 19C] 'when People in Company Drink cross, and not round about from the Right to the Left according to the Sun's motion' (B.E.). [? Gk *kata*, across + *pinein*, to drink; or naut. jargon *cat-harpings*, 'the ropes or (now more generally) iron cramps that serve to brace in the shrouds of the lower-masts behind their respective yards, so as to tighten the shrouds and also give more room to draw the yards in when the ship is close-hauled' (*OED*)]

cathead *n.* [1950s] (*US*) a fool. [SE *cathead*, a large biscuit eaten in the US; he or she has no more brains than a biscuit]

catheads *n.* [early 19C] the female breasts. [SE *cathead*, a large biscuit eaten in the US; thus the breast's roundness reflects that of the foodstuff; however, the term predates US use. E.P. cites 18C naut. jargon *cathead*, 'a beam projecting almost horizontally at each side of the bows of a ship, for raising the anchor from the surface of the water to the deck without touching the bows, and for carrying the anchor on its stock-end when suspended outside the ship's side' (*OED*). But other than there being a pair of *catheads*, it is hard to see any more concrete a link]

cathedral *adj.* [late 17C–18C] antique, ancient, out-of-date. [the antiquity of the great *cathedrals*]

catherine hayes *n.* [mid–late 19C] (*Aus.*) a drink made of claret, sugar and nutmeg/orange. [proper name *Catherine Hayes*; E.P. suggests an 'Irish singer so popular in Australia', but given slang's love of crime, note *Catherine Hayes* (1690–1725), who murdered her lover following a drinking bout]

catherine wheel *n.* [late 19C] the vagina.

cathleen mavoureen system *n.* *see* KATHLEEN MAVOURNEEN SYSTEM n.

cat-house *n.* [1910s+] (*US*) a brothel (cf. ACCOMMODATION HOUSE n.; BIRDCAGE n.¹). [CAT n.¹ (1) + HOUSE n.¹ (1)]

cat in a sack *n.* [1960s–70s] (*US*) something to suspect or be wary of; thus *buy a cat in a sack*, to buy something that one has not actually inspected.

cat in the pan *n.* [mid-16C–mid-19C] a traitor, one who changes sides to advance their self-interest; thus *turn cat in the pan*, to inform, to betray, to change sides. [phr. *turn the cat in the pan*, 'to reverse the order of things so dextrously as to make them appear the very opposite of what they really are' (*OED*) and/or ? *cate* (lit. a culinary 'dainty' and here used as *cake*) *in the pan*, a pancake, which must be turned if it is to be cooked]

catish *adj.* [19C] (*US*) elegant, stylish. [the popular idea of the sinuously elegant feline]

Cat-J *n.* [2000s] (*US prison*) a prisoner considered mentally unstable. [abbr. *Category J*]

cat-lap *n.* **1** [late 18C–19C] tea or coffee. **2** [19C] any form of weak drink, including watered-down alcohol. **3** [19C] milk. [SE *cat* + LAP n.² (4)/SE *lap*, to drink]

cat-lapper *n.* [1960s] (*US*) a (lesbian) cunnilinguist (cf. CARPET-BITER n.). [CAT n.³ (1) + SE *lapper*]

cat-lick *n.* [1930s] a casual, perfunctory wash. [the phr. is supposedly reminiscent of a cat, although, in fact, cats are punctilious in their self-cleansing]

cat-licker *n.* (*also* **cat lick**) [1920s+] (*US*) a Roman Catholic (cf. CATTLE DOG n.¹; CATTLE TICKS n.). [mispron. of SE *Catholic*]

cat-man *n.* [1940s–60s] (*US Black*) a cat burglar. [CAT n.¹² (1) + SE *man*]

cat-meat pusher *n.* [late 19C–1900s] a street-seller of cooked horsemeat, presumably as petfood.

cat melodeon *adj.* (*also* **cat melodium**) [20C+] appalling, disastrous. [? CAT adj. (1) + the supposed tendency of accordion (*melodeon*) players to fluff their notes]

cat-nap *n.* [2000s] (*US prison*) a relatively short sentence. [SE *catnap*, a short sleep]

catnip *n.* [1950s+] (*drugs*) inferior or fake marijuana. [the US name for UK *catmint*; gullible buyers might well be sold bags of catnip (*Nepeta cataria*) or 50% catnip and 50% marijuana. Note Burroughs, *The Naked Lunch* (1959): 'Catnip smells like marijuana when it burns. Frequently passed on the incautious or uninstructed']

catnip *v.* [1950s–60s] (*US drugs*) to sell second-rate marijuana. [CATNIP n.]

catolla *n.* [early 19C] a noisy, foolish person, esp. one who makes foolish bets. [ety. unknown; ? Ital./Sp.; note Egan, *Book of Sports* (1832): 'This phrase is a recently *coined* one, and may be termed a new reading for the old *flash* terms of "*a precious sam — a spooney — a muff — a flat — a go-alonger*, &c." or in plain English, a *fool*. The original catolla (the name of a man who was in the habit of using the *Castle* [i.e. the Castle Tavern, Holborn, a celebrated sporting inn] was distinguished for his *mar-plot* qualities and stupid bets. Also in offering wagers, that when called upon to cover, it generally turned out that he had no *blunt* to stake. Catolla, from proving too annoying, was ultimately *laughed out*; but unfortunately his family are very numerous, and still continue to furnish amusement for [...] frequenters of the *Castle Tavern*']

cat o'mountain *n.* **1** [17C] a high-spirited prostitute or promiscuous woman. **2** [mid–late 19C] (*US*) a shrew. [SE *catamount*, a cougar or panther]

cat o'nine *n.* [1950s+] (*W.I.*) severe punishment, a beating. [SE *cat o'nine tails*]

cat on testy dodge *n.* [late 19C] a genteel female beggar who asks for money at people's houses, often backing her request with a (fake) testimonial from a charity. [CAT n.¹ (2) + TESTER n.¹ (1) + DODGE n. (1)]

cat on the peek port *n.* [1940s] (*US Black*) a lookout man. [CAT n.¹¹ (4) + PEEK n.]

cat (out) *v.* [1940s+] (*US Black*) to wander the streets aimlessly, to stay out all night, to hide away.

cat-party *n.* (*also* **cats' party**) [late 19C+] a party consisting of women only (cf. CAT BAR n.). [CAT n.¹ (2) + SE *party*]

cat piss *n.* *see* CAT'S PEE n.

cat road *n.* [1930s–40s] (*US*) a back road. [a cat's nocturnal wanderings]

cat's *n.* [1920s+] **1** anything exceptional, superlative. **2** a superior person, or someone who poses as such. [abbr. CAT'S PYJAMAS n.]

cats and kitties *n.* [1930s+] (*US*) the female breasts (cf. BRACE AND BITS n.). [rhy. sl. = TITTY n.¹ (1)]

cats and mice *n.* [20C+] (*Aus.*) dice. [rhy. sl.]

cat's ass *n.*¹ [1940s+] (*US campus*) the bruise left by a love bite, usu. on the neck. [SE *cat* + ASS n. (2), i.e. supposed resemblance]

cat's ass *n.*² (*also* **cat's arse**) [1960s+] (*US/Can.*) **1** anything exceptional or superlative. **2** a superior person or someone who poses as such. [SE *cat* + ASS n. (2)/ARSE n.¹ (1)]

cat's ass *adj.* [1970s+] (*US*) excellent, first-rate. [CAT'S ASS n.² (1)]

cat's balls *n.* [1960s] (*US*) **1** anything exceptional, superlative. **2** a superior person, or someone who poses as such. [SE *cat's* + BALLS n.¹ (1)]

cat's bar *n.* *see* CAT BAR n.

cat's cuffs *n.* *see* CAT'S PYJAMAS n.

cat sense *n.* [1930s–40s] (*US Black*) common sense, intelligence.

cat's face *n.* [1940s+] in cards, the ace. [rhy. sl.]

cat's foot *n.* [late 17C] a dupe. [for ety. *see* CAT'S PAW n.]

cat-shag *v.* [1940s–70s] (*Aus.*) to fool around. [SE *cat* + SHAG v.¹ (2)]

cat's head *n.* [mid-18C] (*UK*) a halfpenny roll of bread.

cat's head cut open *n.* [19C] the labia minora. [supposed resemblance]

cat shit *n.* *see* TURTLE SHIT n. (1).

cat-shop *n.* (*also* **cats'-nest**) [1930s–50s] (*US*) a brothel (cf. BANGING-SHOP n.; BIRDCAGE n.¹). [CAT n.¹ (1) + SHOP n.¹ (1)/SHOP n.¹ (1)/SE *nest*]

cat-skin *n.*¹ [mid-19C] a second-rate silk hat.

cat-skin *n.*² [1970s+] (*Irish*) the outer crust or end of a loaf of bread.

cat's kittens *n.* [1920s] (*US*) anything or anyone exceptional, superlative. [var. on CAT'S PYJAMAS n.]

cat's meat *n.*¹ **1** [early–mid-19C] the human lungs. **2** [late 19C+]

(mainly UK juv.) a meat pie. [the lungs and similar animal intestines are used for cat's and dog's meat]

cat's meat *n.*[2] [19C] the vagina (cf. BACON SANDWICH *n.*; BIRD *n.*[8]).

cat's meat *n.*[3] [1960s] *(N.Z.)* something easy to achieve or endure.

cat's-meat gaff *n.* [1960s–80s] a hospital, usu. gynaecological. [CAT'S MEAT *n.*[2] + GAFF *n.*[1] (8)]

cat's meat shop *n.* [mid-19C] *(UK Und.)* a restaurant.

cat-smellers *n.* [mid-19C] *(US)* facial hair, whiskers. [a cat uses its whiskers as an extra sense]

cat's meow *n. (also* **cat's miaou, cat's miaow, cat's tonsillitis)** [1920s+] *(Aus./US)* **1** anything exceptional or superlative. **2** a superior person or someone who poses as such. [SE *cat* + *meow*; var. on CAT'S WHISKERS *n.*]

cat's milk *n.* [1940s–60s] *(UK Und.)* silk. [rhy. sl.]

cat's mitts *n.* [1910s] *(US)* **1** anything exceptional, superlative. **2** a superior person, or someone who poses as such. [abbr. SE *cat's mittens*; euph. var. on CAT'S NUTS *n.*]

cat's mother, the *n.* [1950s+] a response to the question 'Who are you?' when that question is considered impertinent or over-intrusive. [? the (middle-class) admonition to a child talking of 'she', when describing a woman, who ought to be 'Mrs X' or 'Miss Y': *'who is she? the cat's mother?'*]

cat-sneaking *n.* [late 19C] the stealing of pewter tankards from public houses. [CAT *n.*[5] + SNEAK *v.*[1] (1)]

cat's nightgown *n. see* CAT'S PYJAMAS *n.*

cat's nouns! *excl. (also* **nouns!)** [mid-16C–18C] a mild, blasphemous oath, lit. 'God's wounds'.

cat's nuts *n.* [1910s+] *(US)* **1** anything exceptional, superlative. **2** a superior person or someone who poses as such. [SE *cat's* + NUTS *n.*[2] (1); early var. on CAT'S WHISKERS *n.*]

catso *n. (also* **cartso, cartzo, cazzo)** **1** [late 16C–early 17C] a rogue or rascal. **2** [17C+] the penis. [Ital. *cazzo*, the penis, lit. 'thrust']

catso! *excl. (also* **catzo!)** [late 16C–mid-18C] a general excl. of annoyance, surprise etc. [CATSO *n.*]

cat's pajamas *n. see* CAT'S PYJAMAS *n.*

cats' party *n. see* CAT-PARTY *n.*

cat's paw *n.* [mid-17C–19C] a dupe (cf. CAT'S FOOT *n.*). [the softness of the animal's paw + the fable of the monkey and the cat, latterly the fox and the cat. The pair were cooking potatoes in hot ashes and when they were cooked the fox grabbed the cat's paw and used it to extract the hot potatoes – thus the implication is of using another to perform one's own work. The term became SE in 20C+]

cat's pee *n. (also* **cat piss)** [20C+] any form of weak alcoholic drink. [SE *cat* + PEE *n.*[1] (1)/PISS *n.* (1)]

cat spraddle *v.* [20C+] *(W.I.)* **1** to fall spreadeagled on the ground. **2** to beat severely. [dial. *spraddle*, to sprawl + ? SE *spreadeagle*; the image is of a falling cat]

cat's prick *n.* [1990s+] *(UK juv.)* the elongated end of a burning cigarette, caused by its being shared and smoked fast. [SE *cat* + PRICK *n.* (2)]

cat's pyjamas *n. (also* **cat's cuffs, …nightgown, …pajamas, caterpillar's spats, kitten's vest)** [1920s+] *(orig. US)* **1** anything exceptional, superlative. **2** used sarcastically, a joke, a 'laugh'. **3** a superior person or someone who poses as such. [coined, like many other similar terms, by the US sportwriter T.A. 'Tad' Dorgan (1877–1929)]

cat sticks *n.* [late 18C–19C] very thin legs. [SE *catstick*, a stick or bat used in games of tip-cat or trap-ball]

cat's tonsillitis *n. see* CAT'S MEOW *n.*

cat's water *n.* [19C] gin. [? ref. to the taste being like urine]

cat's whiskers *n. (also* **clam's cuticle/garters, crocodile's adenoids, elephant's fallen arches, frog's eyebrows, lily's whiskers, owl's bowels, oyster's eye-tooth, pig's whiskers, sandfly's garters, snake's eyebrows, …hips, …toenail)** [1920s+] **1** anything exceptional, superlative. **2** a superior person or someone who poses as such. [var. on CAT'S PYJAMAS *n.*; later use is mainly Aus.]

catter *n.* [1910s–30s] *(US Und.)* a tramp who rides the platforms of passenger or freight cars, the tender of an engine and similar spaces. [SE *cat*, the image of the animal clinging to some perilous perch]

cat that cracks the whip *n.* [1940s] *(US Black)* a playboy. [CAT *n.*[11] (4)]

cattie *n. (also* **catty)** [late 19C+] *(UK juv.)* a catapult. [abbr.]

catting *n.*[1] [late 17C+] looking for female company and/ or conquests. [SE *tomcat*, a stereotypically libidinous animal; obs. in the UK by the early 19C; 20C+ use is US Black (cf. CAT AROUND *v.*)]

catting *n.*[2] [late 18C+] vomiting. [abbr. CAT (UP) *v.*]

catting *n.*[3] [1980s+] *(US Black)* a style of walking, characterized by a slight dip in the stride, adopted by young urban Black men. [CAT *n.*[11] (2)]

cattle *n.* **1** [late 16C–18C] a collective *n.* for prostitutes (cf. BANBURY *n.*). **2** [late 16C+] people, sometimes contemptible. [(1) note SE *cattle*, horses, which are, like prostitutes, 'ridden']

cattle *v. see* CATTLE (TRUCK) *v.*

cattle-banger *n. see* COW-BANGER *n.*

cattle dog *n.*[1] [20C+] *(N.Z., mainly juv.)* a derog. name for a Roman Catholic (cf. CAT-LICKER *n.*). [mispron. of SE *Catholic*]

cattle dog *n.*[2] [20C+] *(Aus.)* a catalogue. [rhy. sl./mispron.]

cattle-duffer *n.* [mid-19C+] *(Aus.)* a cattle thief. [SE *cattle* + DUFFER *n.*[1]]

cattle-duffing *n.* [late 19C+] *(Aus.)* cattle thieving. [CATTLE-DUFFER *n.*]

cattle eater *n.* [late 19C] *(US)* a cattle thief.

cattle puncher *n. see* COW-PUNCHER *n.*

cattle racket *n.* [mid-late 19C] *(Aus.)* any form of organized swindle. [originating in a large-scale cattle-rustling racket in New South Wales during the 1840s]

cattle ramp *adj.* [1980s] *(Aus.)* effeminate, homosexual. [rhy. sl. = CAMP *adj.* (1)]

cattle stiff *n.* [1910s–20s] *(US tramp)* a cowboy. [SE *cattle* + STIFF *n.*[2] (7)]

cattle ticks *n.* [20C+] *(Aus.)* Catholics (cf. CAT-LICKER *n.*). [rhy. sl./mispron.]

cattle train *n.* [1940s–50s] *(US Black)* a Cadillac. [the name + the size of the car]

cattle (truck) *v.* [20C+] to copulate, also fig.; thus *cattled*, ruined, hurt, destroyed, beaten etc. [rhy. sl. = FUCK *v.*[1]]

catty *n.*[1] [1950s+] *(Irish)* a Catholic. [abbr.]

catty *n.*[2] *see* CATTIE *n.*

catty-cat *n.* [1970s+] *(US Black)* **1** the vagina (cf. BIRD *n.*[8]). **2** sexual intercourse. [redup. of CAT *n.*[3] (1)]

cattywampus *adj. see* CATAWAMPUS *adj.*

cat-up *n. (also* **cat work)** [1930s–40s] *(US Und.)* robbery of itinerant workers at gunpoint; thus *cat-up man, cat worker*, one who commits such robberies. [CAT UP *v.*[1] (1)]

cat (up) *v.* [late 18C+] to vomit; thus fig. *cat with laughter*, to laugh 'until one is sick'. [? abbr. SE *cataract*, i.e. the waterfall effect, but cf. JERK THE CAT *v.*; WHIP THE CAT *v.*[2] (2); 20C+ use mainly US]

cat up *v.*[1] [1920s–30s] *(US Und.)* **1** to hold up an itinerant worker at gunpoint. **2** to rob by stealth. [? GAT *n.*[1] (1)]

cat up *v.*[2] [1950s] *(US)* to hide away, esp. from the police. [the elusiveness of a cat]

cat wagon *n.* *(US)* **1** [19C–1960s] a travelling brothel (cf. BIRDCAGE *n.*[1]). **2** [1970s] a van used to take prostitutes to prison. [CAT *n.*[1] (1). Found in many US rural areas before the anti-'White slavery' legislation of 1910; the women travelled in and worked from a horse-drawn covered wagon, following the cattle trails or visiting cowboys out on the range]

cat walk *n.* [1960s+] (*US Black*) a strutting style of walking, intended to emphasize one's pride, independence and masculinity. [CAT n.[11] (2)]

cat walker *n. see* CAT n.[12] (1).

catwanker *n.* [1990s+] a general term of derision. [SE *cat* + WANKER n.; lit. a 'cat-masturbater']

cat-whipper *n.* [20C+] (*Aus.*) one who whinges over their misfortunes. [WHIP THE CAT v.[3] (3)]

cat work/worker *n. see* CAT-UP n.

catzerie *n.* [late 16C] roguery. [CATSO n. (1)]

Cauc *n.* [1980s] (*US*) a Caucasian, i.e. a White person. [abbr.]

caudge-pawed *adj.* [late 17C–18C] left-handed. [var. on CAW-PAWED adj.]

caudle of hempseed *n.* [17C] the hangman's noose. [pun on SE *caudle*, a gruel spiced with wine or ale and given to the sick, and esp. to women in labour; thus the noose is ironically also a form of 'painkiller']

caught holding one's dick *phr.* [20C+] (*US*) to be caught in an embarrassing or generally disadvantageous situation. [SE *caught holding* + DICK n.[4] (1)]

caught in a snowstorm *adj.* **1** [1930s] experiencing the hallucinations that accompany an overdose of morphine. **2** [1930s–50s] (*US drugs*) under the influence of cocaine. [SNOW n.[2]]

caught (out) *adj.* [mid-19C+] pregnant.

caught short *adj.* **1** [1950s+] desperate to visit a lavatory as soon as possible. **2** [1950s+] of a woman, surprised by menstruation starting, beyond reach of tampons, sanitary towels etc. **3** [1950s+] in an emergency or unforseen situation. **4** [1960s] (*US*) a euph. for expecting a child out of wedlock. [(1) later var. on TAKEN SHORT adj.; subseq. defs. f. (1)]

caught with one's breeches down *phr.* (*also* **caught with one's britches down**) [mid-19C+] to be caught unprepared, usu. in flagrante.

caught with one's trousers down *phr.* (*also* **caught with one's pants down**) [1930s+] surprised in an embarrassing position or, on a metaphorical level, caught without adequate defences or preparation.

caught with rem-in-re *phr.* [mid-17C] caught having sexual intercourse. [fake legalese, lit. 'caught with thing in thing'; Williams: 'A tr. of the Latin is used in a churchwarden's court testimony to the effect that proof of adultery requires seeing "the thing in the thing".']

cauldron *n.* [mid-17C–early 18C] the vagina. [euph.]

cauli *n.* (*also* **caulie, collie**) [late 19C+] a *cauliflower*. [abbr.]

cauliflower *n.*[1] **1** [late 18C–19C] the vagina; thus *do a bit of cauliflower, eat cauliflower*, to have sexual intercourse (cf. CABBAGE n.[7]). **2** [1990s+] sexual intercourse. ['A woman, who was giving evidence in a case wherein it was necessary to express those parts, made use of the term cauliflower, for which the judge on the bench, a peevish old fellow, reproved her, saying she might as well call it an artichoke. Not so, my lord, replied she, for an artichoke has a bottom, but a **** and a cauliflower have none' (Grose, 1785)]

cauliflower *n.*[2] [late 18C–early 19C] **1** a large white wig 'such as is commonly worn by the dignified clergy, and was formerly by physicians' (Grose, 1785). **2** one who wears powder in their hair.

cauliflower *n.*[3] [mid-19C] (*US*) a person, a fellow (cf. CABBAGE n.[3]). [? Fr. *choux*, cabbage, used as a term of affection]

cauliflower *n.*[4] [late 19C+] the foaming top of a newly-poured glass of beer. [its whiteness]

cauliflower *n.*[5] [20C+] a 'cauliflower ear', the sign of a boxer whose ears have taken too many punches to retain their original shape.

cauliflower *n.*[6] [1970s] (*US*) cowardice, fear. [? its white 'heart'; or rhy. sl. *cauliflower ear* = fear]

cauliflower cock *n.* [2000s] (*US Black*) a dildo. [? the use of vegetables as dildos, although not presumably a cauliflower]

caulk *v.* [mid-19C] **1** to have sexual intercourse. **2** to have a surreptitious nap. [either SE *caulk*, to fill, to stuff, or ME *cauk*, for a male bird to tread the female; note 1930s Annapolis jargon *caulk off*, to sleep]

caulked *adj.* [19C] (*US*) exhausted. [naut. jargon *caulk*, to lie down on a soft plank, to sleep with one's clothes on; thus the sailor, rather than the usual pitch or oakum, was fig. 'stopping up the cracks' in the deck]

caulker *n.* **1** [19C] the last drink of an evening. **2** [19C] an exceptionally amusing story, which 'cannot be topped'. **3** mid–late 19C] a lie. [early version of CORKER n.[2]; ult. either a mis-sp. or f. naut. jargon *caulk*, to stop up the seams of a ship to 'keep out the wet']

caulk off *v.* [late 19C–1930s] to idle, to waste time on the job. [WW1 RN *caulk*, a nap, a short sleep]

'cause *prep. see* 'COS prep.

cause whore *n.* [1990s+] a voluble proselytizer for modish, leftish causes, often but not necessarily female.

caution *n.* [mid-19C+] **1** a 'character', an eccentric, a 'difficult' person, sometimes ext. as *a caution to snakes*. **2** anything staggering or alarming. [i.e. one with whom caution must be exercised]

caution sign *n.* [1970s+] (*US Black*) anyone who dresses in an excessively gaudy and vulgar manner, with many clashing bright colours. [image of bright red 'Stop' signs etc]

cavalier *n.* [20C+] (*orig.* RN, *now mainly UK teen*) an uncircumcised penis; thus the boy/man who has one (cf. BALD-HEADED HERMIT n.). [the antonym of ROUNDHEAD n.[2]]

cavalry curate *n.* [late 19C–1910s] a curate who rides (a horse) rather than walks round his parish.

cavault *v.* [late 17C–mid-19C] to have sexual intercourse; one of a number of words equating sex with horseriding. [Ling. Fr. *cavolta*, riding]

cavaulting school *n.* [late 17C–early 19C] a brothel (cf. ACADEMY n.). [CAVAULT v.]

cave *n.*[1] **1** [1920s–40s] (*US Und.*) a hiding place. **2** [1920s–50s] (*US prison*) a cell. **3** [1930s–40s] (*US Black*) one's room, one's home, one's dwelling place.

cave *n.*[2] (*also* **cave bitch, …boy**) [1990s+] (*US Black*) a White person. [the belief that the early cave-dwellers were all White, as Black Africans lived on the plains]

cave *v.* [mid-19C+] (*chiefly US*) **1** to give in, to yield to pressure from above, to break down, to give way, to collapse. **2** to die.

cave! *excl.* [mid-19C+] (*UK juv.*) look out! [Lat. *cave*, beware; pron. 'kay-vee']

cave bitch/boy *n. see* CAVE n.[2].

cave-dweller *n.* (*US*) **1** [late 19C] one who lives in the cellar of a slum tenement. **2** [late 19C–1930s] a member of the old New York aristocracy. [such aristocrats still lived in the dark, old mansions their families had built earlier in the century]

cave in *v.* **1** [early 19C+] (*orig. US*) to give in, to yield to pressure from above, to break down, to give way, to collapse. **2** [1980s] (*N.Z.*) to defecate.

cave in someone's crust *v. see* BURST IN SOMEONE'S CRUST v.

cave-man *n.* [20C+] an ostentatiously macho male, a 'he-man'; thus *cave-man stuff*, a rough form of wooing or love-making, reminiscent of the clichéd cave-man who (at least in cartoons) drags his woman around by her hair.

Cave of Harmony *n.* [mid-19C] the Cider Cellars or Evans's supper rooms and singing saloon in London.

cave of harmony *n.* [mid-19C] the vagina (cf. ADAM'S OWN (ALTAR) n.).

cave out *v.* [late 19C] (*orig. US*) to come to an end. [mining jargon *cave out*, the metal casing at the end of a tunnel]

cavern *n.* [1900s] (*Aus.*) the mouth.

cavey *n. see* CAVY n.

cavi *n. see* CAVVY n.

cavi *adj.* [1990s+] (*US Black*) first-class, excellent, materially successful. [abbr. SE *caviar* as a symbol of luxury and wealth]

caviar *n.* (*also* **caviare**) [late 19C–1920s] a passage of printed text that has been erased by a (Russian) censor. [the criss-cross pattern of white lines and black diamonds which was stamped over the offending material, and which, given its Russian provenance, could be seen as resembling caviar]

cavite all star *n.* [1970s] (*drugs*) marijuana. [*Cavite*, a former US naval base in Manila Bay]

cavvy *n.* (*also* **cavi**) [1990s+] **1** marijuana. **2** crack cocaine (cf. BASE n.). [? SE *caviar*; the ref. is presumably to its cost and quality rather than to its fishiness]

cavvy *adj. see* CAVI adj.

cavy *n.* (*also* **cavey**) [mid-17C] a Cavalier. [abbr.]

caw-handed *adj.* [late 17C–early 19C] clumsy, awkward. [Oxfordshire dial. *caw*, a fool and *cawing*, awkward]

caw-pawed *adj.* [late 18C–early 19C] clumsy, awkward. [for ety. *see* CAW-HANDED adj.]

cawsy *n. see* CARSEY n.

caxon *n.* [late 18C–early 19C] an old, worn-out wig. [? from the surname *Caxon*]

cayac *n.* [20C+] (*W.I., Gren.*) a country bumpkin. [generic use of *Cayac*, a native of the island of Carriacou]

cayuse *n.* (*US*) **1** [mid-19C+] (*also* **cayouse**) an Indian pony. **2** [mid-19C+] any (inferior) horse. **3** [1900s–20s] a worthless person. ['The wild horse of Oregon, named for the Cayuse Indians, an equestrian people [...]. The name is now commonly used by the northern cowboy to refer to any horse. At first the term was used for the western horse, to set it apart from a horse brought overland from the East. In later years the name came to be applied as a term of contempt to any scrubby, under-sized horse.' Francis Haines, *Western Horseman*, Vol. II No. 2 (March–April 1937)]

caz *n. see* CASSAN n.

caze *n.* [late 19C–1910s] the female genitals. [? misreading of Ital. *cazzo*, the penis]

cazh *adj. see* CAS adj.

cazzo *n. see* CATSO n.

c.b. *v. see* COCK BLOCK v.

c.b. *phr.* [1970s+] cock and *balls*. [abbr. used in sado-masochism contact advertisements to advertise 'cock and balls torture']

c.c. *n.*[1] **1** [1930s+] (*US prison*) the condemned cells. **2** [1950s] one who is awaiting execution on a capital charge. **3** [1970s] (*US prison*) concurrent sentences. [abbr. (1) condemned to capital punishment]

c.c. *n.*[2] [1980s] (*US drugs*) a dealer's sample of cocaine, given away to enlist new customers. [SE *calling card*]

c.c.m. *phr.* [1990s+] (*US Black*) cold cash *money*. [abbr.]

c.c.w. *phr.* [1980s+] (*US police/Und.*) carrying a concealed weapon. [abbr.]

cease *v.* [1920s–50s] (*US Black*) to die. [abbr. SE *decease*]

cecil *n.*[1] [1930s–40s] (*US drugs*) morphine (cf. AUNTIE EMMA n.). [Spears, *Slang and Jargon of Drugs and Drink* (1986), suggests a play on *M. sul.*, morphine sulphate]

cecil *n.*[2] [1930s] (*US prison*) cocaine (cf. AUNT NORA n.). [initial letter; note US pron. *seesul*]

Cecil Gee *n.* [1990s+] the human knee. [rhy. sl.; ult. the *Cecil Gee* chain of men's tailoring shops]

cedar *n.* [1930s+] (*Aus.*) a fool. [SE *cedar*, i.e. a 'wooden' head]

cedar (pencil) *n.* [mid-19C+] (*US Und.*) a cheap pencil. [the cedar wood of which it is made; such pencils are usu. unpainted and cheap to purchase]

cee *n. see* C n.[2].

celeb *n.* [1910s+] (*orig. US*) a celebrity. [abbr.]

celebrity fucker *n.* [1960s+] (*orig. US*) anyone who courts the famous with the hope of enjoying some proxy fame. [SE *celebrity* + FUCKER n. (1)]

celestial *adj.*[1] [mid-late 19C] used of a turned-up nose. [SE *celestial*, heavenly, such a nose 'points to the heavens']

celestial *adj.*[2] [mid-19C–1910s] pertaining to Chinese people or culture. [SE *celestial empire*, a trans. of one of the names for China]

cell *v.* [20C+] (*UK/US prison*) **1** (*also* **cell up**) to share a cell with. **2** to have one's cell, e.g. *where does he cell?* [the OED cites 2 16C uses, but they apply to a monk's not a prisoner's cell]

cellar *n.*[1] (*also* **cellarage, cellar-door**) [17C–19C] the vagina (cf. BLACK HOLE n.[1]).

cellar *n.*[2] [late 19C] a shoe, a boot; usu. in pl. [its 'low' position on the body]

cellar cordial *n.* [1900s] (*Aus.*) alcohol.

cellar-door *n. see* CELLAR n.[1].

cellar-flap *n.* [mid-late 19C] a tap dance. [rhy. sl.; the image is also of a dance performed on a space no larger than the trap-door leading to a cellar]

cellar-flap *v.* [20C+] to borrow. [rhy. sl. = TAP v.[3] (2)]

cellar smeller *n.* (*also* **cellar sniffer**) [1920s] (*US*) **1** a Prohibition agent or temperance campaigner. **2** a young man who is always on hand for free liquor.

cell gangster *n.* (*also* **cell warrior**) [2000s] (*US prison*) one who poses as tough while in their cell but follows orders elsewhere.

cellie *n.* (*also* **celly**) **1** [1970s+] (*US prison*) a cellmate. **2** [2000s] (*US*) ext. to general, non-prison use, a friend. [abbr. + sfx -*ie*/-*y*]

cellier *n.* [late 17C] an outright lie. [proper name Elizabeth *Cellier*, implicated, with her partner Thomas Dangerfield, in the Meal Tub Plot of 1679; this plot, which accused various prominent Roman Catholics of treason, hinged on papers supposedly hidden beneath Mrs Cellier's meal tub. It collapsed when Dangerfield was imprisoned for perjury and Cellier was sent to the pillory]

cells *n.* [late 19C+] a (brief) term of imprisonment. [SE phr. *night(s) in the cells*]

cell task *n.* [1940s–50s] (*UK prison*) a pin-up picture. [ironic ref. to the official *cell tasks* set prisoners. The pin-up's real-life incarnation would obviously make a preferable 'task' to any set by the authorities]

celluloid *n.* [1910s] (*Aus.*) money. [it 'burns' easily]

cell up *v. see* CELL v. (1).

cell warrior *n. see* CELL GANGSTER n.

celly *n.*[1] [1990s+] (*US*) a mobile phone. [abbr. SAmE *cellphone*]

celly *n.*[2] *see* CELLIE n.

cement *n.* **1** [1930s] (*US drugs*) any form of illegally merchandised narcotics. **2** [1970s+] (*Aus.*) any form of diarrhoea cure, such as kaolin (and morphine), which depends for its efficacy on 'hardening' the contents of the stomach.

cement city *n.* [1970s] (*US*) a cemetery.

cement-head *n.* [1940s+] (*US teen*) a gullible, conventional person. [SE *cement* + -HEAD sfx (1)]

cement kimono *n.* (*also* **cement overcoat, cement overshoes**) [1950s+] (*US Und.*) a method of disposing of a corpse by placing it inside a barrel filled with wet cement and tossing the resultant lump into a river.

cement-mixer *n.*[1] (*US*) **1** [1910s+] a rickety, broken-down vehicle. **2** [1930s+] a dance. **3** [1960s] a striptease artist (or prostitute who offers a strip as part of her services). [its movement + (2) ? it is a *mixer* that *cements* relationships]

cement-mixer *n.*[2] [1960s] (*US*) an overweight, aggressive woman. [resemblance]

cement overcoat/overshoes *n. see* CEMENT KIMONO n.

cemetery *n.* [1990s+] (*W.I.*) a term of abuse for a woman suspected of having had an abortion.

cent *n.* [1960s–70s] (*US Black*) **1** $1 (cf. DIME n.[1]; DIME NOTE n.; DIMES, THE n.; DIMMY n.; DOUBLE DIME n.; NICK n.[5]; NICKEL n.[1]; NICKEL NOTE n.; RED CENT n.; THIN DIME n.). **2** $100.

centerfield v. [1930s] (US) to perform cunnilingus. [the 'centrality' of the vagina to the female body]

center lead n. [1920s] (US) the forehead. [rhy. sl.]

centerman n. [20C+] (Can./US prison) a prisoner who toadies to the guards. [prison use center, the guards' 'office' in a prison wing]

centipees n. [late 18C–early 19C] a tailor of soldiers' clothing. [synon. milit. use sancipees; ult. sank, to work as a menial servant in a dining room]

cent-per-cent n. (also **cent-per-center, shent-per-shent, shent-per-shenter**) [late 17C–1910s] a usurer; also attrib. [his graspingness; he takes back 100% interest for every £100 loaned; 'shent-per-shent/-shenter' is 'mock' Yid. pron. due to the stereotype of Jews being moneylenders]

central sfx [1990s+] (US) a fig. 'place' that acts as an intensifier to a n. (cf. CITY sfx.).

central cut n. (also **central furrow, central office, cut**) [mid-18C–19C] the vagina (cf. AXIS n.).

centre half n. [1990s+] a scarf. [rhy. sl.; ult. a position in football]

centre of attraction n. [mid-18C–19C] the vagina (cf. AXIS n.).

centre of bliss n. [late 19C] the vagina (cf. AXIS n.).

centrique part n. [19C] the vagina (cf. AXIS n.). [coined by John Donne]

century n. 1 [mid-19C+] $100 or £100. 2 [1900s–50s] the number 100. [16C SE century, a group of 100 things]

century v. [1910s–20s] (US) to save up $100, to make $100, esp. through gambling. [CENTURY n. (1)]

century note n. [1900s–40s] (US) a $100 bill. [CENTURY n. (1)]

cereb n. [1970s+] (US campus) one who works exceptionally hard. [SE cerebral]

cert n. [late 19C+] 1 a definite winner, usu. in a sporting context. 2 a certainty. [SE certainty]

cert adv. [late 19C–1930s] certainly.

certificate of birth n. [19C] the vagina, one of the few terms that deal with the vagina in its procreative rather than sexual role (cf. BABY CHUTE n.).

cess n. see SESS n.

C file n. [2000s] (US prison) the central file of information held on each prisoner. [abbr.]

c.f.m. adj. [1980s+] (US) sexually suggestive; thus c.f.m. shoes, c.f.m. dress etc (cf. COME-FUCK-ME'S n.; FUCK-ME adj.). [abbr. come fuck me]

c.h. n. [late 19C] conquering hero, usu. used ironically. [abbr.; ult. the frequent playing, subseq. to the Egyptian War (1882), of the tune 'See the Conquering Hero Comes']

cha n.[1] (also **chah, chai, char**) [20C+] tea. [Mandarin ch'a, tea]

cha n.[2] [1980s+] (drugs) cocaine. [abbr. CHARLIE n.[9] (1)]

chaar ou n. (also **char ou**) [1970s+] (S.Afr.) an Indian. [? Hind. chaar admi, people in general + Afk. ou, a person]

chaben n. (also **chabin, shabeen**) [20C+] (W.I.) a person of mixed African/European descent; such people have pale brown skin, coarse reddish hair and, sometimes, freckles and greyish eyes. [Fr. chabins, sheep bred in Bery, with thick, long hair. Such sheep were once seen as a sheep/goat cross, and the term, exported to Dominica, was used as a synon. for 'half-breed']

chabobs n. [1960s] (US) the female breasts. [? KER- pfx + BOOB n.[3] (1); note CHORB n.]

cha-cha n. [1950s+] (US Black) sexual intercourse. [SE cha-cha, a popular ballroom dance]

cha-cha adj. [1960s–80s] (US) fashionable or smart, esp. when pertaining to homosexuals. [var. on CHI-CHI adj. (1)]

cha-cha v. [1950s+] (US Black) to have sexual intercourse. [CHA-CHA n.]

chacha queen n. [1980s+] (US gay) a Hispanic male homosexual. [chacha, the dance used as a generic for Spanish-American + QUEEN n.[2] (1)]

cha-ching! excl. [1990s+] (US teen) an excl. used to signify that something or someone has made one happy. [echoic of the sound of a cash register and popularized by the film Wayne's World (1992); it can still be used in the context of money, but refers more commonly to general pleasures, esp. a passing pretty woman]

chachundar n. [20C+] (W.I.) used by those of Indian descent to describe an East Indian woman who has a close friendship or even a child with a Black man. [Hind. chhachuudar, a mole or shrew]

chad n. (also **Mr Chad**) [1940s+] a chalked-up, cartoon-style picture of a rudimentary human head 'looking over' an equally basic brick wall plus the slogan Wot, no —. [ety. unknown]

chafe v. [late 17C–mid-19C] to beat, to thrash; thus chafed, beaten. [SE chafe, to warm, to heat]

chafe-litter n. [mid-16C–early 17C] (UK Und.) an impudent, cheeky person. [lit. 'rub-bed']

chafer n. see COCKCHAFER n. (3).

chafer v. see CHARVER v. (1).

chaff n.[1] [mid-17C+] banter, badinage or ridicule. [CHAFF v. (1)]

chaff n.[2] [1930s+] (Aus.) money (cf. CHALK n.[1]; CRAP n.[1]; DIRT n.[1]; DROSS n.; DUST n.[2]; FILTHY, THE n.; GREEN SHIT n.; JUNK n.[3]; MUCK n.[1]; RUBBISH n.; SAND n.; SHIT n.[7]; SHUCKS n.; TRASH n.[1]). [SE chaff, husks of corn after threshing]

chaff v. 1 [mid-17C+] to banter, to tease, usu. gently; thus chaff down a peeler, to tease a policeman; (UK campus) chaff a cad, for an undergraduate to insult a townsman. 2 [1960s+] (S.Afr.) to give someone something, to tell someone something. 3 [1970s+] (S.Afr.) to flirt, to approach sexually, to 'get fresh'. [SE chafe, to rub]

chaff-cutter n.[1] [mid-19C] 1 a malicious talker, a slanderer. 2 gossip, slander. 3 a wit. [CHAFF v. (1)]

chaff-cutter n.[2] [1940s–50s] (Aus.) a typewriter. [SE chaff-cutter, a machine that cuts chaff for fodder, i.e. the noise of the keys]

chaffer n.[1] [late 16C] a sexual partner; the image is of promiscuity.

chaffer n.[2] 1 [19C] the throat. 2 [early 19C–1910s] one who banters or teases, a teaser. 3 [mid-19C] the tongue; the mouth. [CHAFF v. (1)]

chaffer v.[1] [mid–late 19C] to banter, to tease; to chatter; thus chaffering, bantering, chattering. [ext. of CHAFF v. (1)]

chaffer v.[2] see CHARVER v. (1).

chaffing n. [early 19C+] teasing, bantering. [CHAFF v. (1)]

chaffing-box n. (also **chaffing-closet**) [mid-19C] the mouth. [CHAFF v. (1) + SE box/closet]

chaffing-crib n. [19C] a man's private room, where he receives and entertains his friends. [CHAFF v. (1) + CRIB n.[1] (1)]

chaffy adj. [19C] jolly, bantering, light-hearted. [CHAFF v. (1)]

chah/chai n. see CHA n.[1].

chai n. (also **chi, chie, chy**) [mid-19C+] (UK Und./tramp) a woman. [Rom.]

chain and crank n. (also **pedal and crank**) [20C+] 1 a bank. 2 (Irish) an act of masturbation. [rhy. sl.; (2) = WANK n.[1] (1)]

chain and locket n. [20C+] a pocket. [rhy. sl.]

chained lightning n. see CHAIN LIGHTNING n.[2].

chain gang n.[1] [late 19C+] 1 the Lord Mayor and Lady Mayoress of London. 2 married men. [actual and metaphorical 'chains of office']

chain gang n.[2] 1 [1950s] (US teen) a group of students walking to class. 2 [1970s] (US gay) a circle of 3 or more people, hetero- or homosexual, all linked physically in mutual sex acts. [pun on SE]

chain (it) up! excl. [mid-19C–1920s] shut up! be quiet! [fig. use of phr. chain that dog up]

chain jerk n. [1930s+] (US) joint masturbation, often in competition, by a group of boys, poss. sitting in a circle; also as v. [SE chain + JERK-OFF n. (1)]

chain lightning n.[1] [mid-19C] (*US*) misery, punishment, hell. [the fiery torments of hell]

chain lightning n.[2] (*also* **chained lightning**) [mid-19C–1930s] **1** (*orig. US*) strong, if cheap, whisky. **2** potato spirit. [SE *chain lightning*, lightning that moves rapidly in a forked or zigzag course. The image is of the immediacy and strength of the whisky's effect. (2) 'Potato spirit, import from Germany. Filthy mess – poisonous to a degree. Smuggled mainly' (Ware)]

chain lightning n.[3] [late 19C–1920s] an exceptionally able person. [the 'spark']

chain man n. [1930s] (*US tramp*) a thief or pickpcket who specializes in taking watches.

chains, the n. [late 19C–1900s] (*S.Afr.*) the Johannesburg Stock Exchange. [the chains that closed off a portion of Simmonds Street so that dealers could conduct their business. 'The Chains' lasted from 1887 to 1902, being replaced by a new Stock Exchange building in 1903]

chain up! excl. see CHAIN (IT) UP! excl.

chain up a pup v. [1900s–20s] (*Aus.*) to get drinks on credit. [DOG n.[10] (2)]

chair, the n. (*also* **wire chair**) **1** [late 19C+] (*orig. US*) the electric chair. **2** [1950s] the chair in which a prisoner condemned to the gas chamber sits.

chairbacker n. [1950s+] (*US, Southern*) an unprofessional, part-time lay preacher. [the chair that such a preacher carries with him for use as an impromptu pulpit]

chair days n. [late 19C–1900s] (*UK society*) old age. [when one is confined to a chair]

chair-pounder n. [1910s] (*US*) an office worker. [he or she spends the day sitting down]

chair-warmer n. [late 19C+] a supernumerary, one who is there but does nothing, an observer. [theatrical jargon *chair-warmer*, 'a lady whose talent is comprised in her physical charms, and who can neither sing, dance, nor act' (Ware)]

chaka-chaka adj. **1** [1950s+] (*W.I. Rasta*) messy, disorderly, untidy. **2** [1980s+] (*W.I./UK Black teen*) untidy or unkempt. [Ewe *tsáka*, to mix, be mixed]

chal n. [19C+] a man. [Rom.]

chaldee v. see CALDEE v.

chal droch n. [18C–19C] (*tinker*) a knife. [Shelta]

chale! excl. [1950s+] (*US*) an excl. implying dismissal, no! [Sp.]

chalfonts n. [1970s+] haemorrhoids. [rhy. sl. *Chalfont St Giles* = SE *piles*; ult. village in Buckinghamshire, UK]

chalice n. (*also* **chalewa**) [1950s+] a pipe used for smoking marijuana, which, when used by Rastafarians, takes on a sacred and ritualistic role; thus the 'religious' name.

chalk n.[1] [late 18C–early 19C] (*US*) a quarter dollar, 25 cents (cf. CHAFF n.[2]).

chalk n.[2] [mid-19C] a scar or scratch. [CHALK v.[1]]

chalk n.[3] **1** [1920s+] (*US*) milk or cream. **2** [1940s–80s] (*US Black*) a White person. [the colour]

chalk n.[4] (*US drugs*) **1** [1960s+] methamphetamine, Benzedrine, Methedrine (cf. BOMBITA n.). **2** [1960s+] cocaine (cf. BIRDIE POWDER n.). **3** [1970s] methadone. **4** [1990s+] crack cocaine (cf. BASE n.). [the white colour; (3) may be an error, confusing the abbr. 'meth' used for (1)]

chalk n.[5] see CHALK (FARM) n.

chalk, the n. [mid–late 19C] (*US*) **1** the fashion. **2** the absolute truth. [? the use of *chalk* by a teacher]

chalk adj. [late 19C+] spurious, unknown, incompetent. [the use of chalk to mark up the names of new jockeys on the telegraph board at a racetrack; those of established riders are painted]

chalk v.[1] [late 18C–19C] (*UK Und.*) to slash or cut someone's face. [resemblance to a chalk mark]

chalk v.[2] [mid-19C] (*US*) to charge for. [SE *chalk up*]

chalk v.[3] **1** [1920s–30s] (*US tramp*) to arrest, albeit without a specific charge. **2** [1950s] (*US Black*) to take note of.

chalk v.[4] [1980s+] (*drugs*) **1** to lighten the colour of cocaine in order to make it appear more pure; thus *chalking*, chemically altering the colour of cocaine so it looks white. **2** to cut cocaine into lines for snorting. [SE *chalk*; (1) the ingredient used; (2) 'chalk up']

chalk against v. [late 19C] to bear a grudge against. [the chalking up of one's debts on a piece of wood by shopkeepers, publicans etc]

chalk and talk n. (*also* **chalk-and-talker**) [1920s+] (*Aus.*) a schoolteacher, esp. an old-fashioned, trad. teacher; also used of any form of trainer.

chalk boulder n. [1920s] (*US*) a shoulder. [rhy. sl.]

chalk down v. see CHALK OUT v. (2).

chalk eater n. [1930s–60s] (*US gambling*) a gambler who prefers betting on short-priced favourites. [the chalking of odds on a bookmaker's slate]

chalked up adj. (*US drugs*) **1** [1930s] a narcotic that has been adulterated with milk of magnesia. **2** [1950s+] under the influence of cocaine. [the whiteness of cocaine]

chalker n.[1] [late 18C–early 19C] an Irish thug, the equivalent of a London MOHOCK n., who specializes in roaming the streets and slashing the face of any unfortunate victim; thus *chalking*, carrying out this species of urban terrorism or 'amusement' as Grose (1785) grimly notes it. [CHALK v.[1] + ironic use of SE *chalk*, to draw a line]

chalker n.[2] [mid-19C] a London milkman. [his supposed watering down of milk with chalky water]

chalker n.[3] [1990s+] (*US campus*) an extremely obese person. [to measure their girth one has to reach as far round as far as poss., make a chalk mark, and repeat around the other side]

chalk (farm) n. **1** [mid-19C+] an arm. **2** [1920s+] harm. [rhy. sl.; ult. *Chalk Farm*, London NW1]

chalk farm n. [mid-19C] **1** credit at a public house. **2** a duel. [(1) SE *chalk*; (2) ? CHALK v.[1]; ult. *Chalk Farm*, London NW1]

chalk head n. [mid-19C] **1** one who is good at calculating figures. **2** a waiter. [calculation with chalk on a slate; (2) is specific ext. of (1)]

chalkie n. **1** [1940s+] (*Aus.*) (*also* **chalky**) a schoolteacher. **2** [1990s+] (*Irish*) a pavement artist. [both wield chalk]

chalkies n. [mid-19C] (*US*) the teeth. [the whiteness]

chalk it up! excl. [1910s–20s] look at that! [fig. use of *chalk it up*, make a note]

chalk marquis n. [late 19C–1900s] a spurious marquis. [CHALK adj. + SE *marquis*]

chalk off v.[1] [mid-19C] (*US*) to leave. [WALK ONE'S CHALKS v.]

chalk off v.[2] [mid-19C–1910s] to look at closely. [one stares at a metaphorical chalk mark]

chalk one's hat v. [19C] to travel for free, orig. and esp. in railroad use. [the custom of the conductor placing a white mark or ticket on the headgear of the passenger]

chalk out v. **1** [17C–19C] to describe clearly, to give directions. **2** [mid-19C] (*also* **chalk down**) to plan. **3** [1940s] to die. **4** [1940s+] (*US*) (*also* **chalk off**) to murder, to kill. [the drawing of a line with chalk; in (4) that drawn around the corpse]

chalks n. [mid-19C] the legs. [ety. unknown]

Chalk Sunday n. [20C+] (*Irish*) the first Sunday in Lent. [the backs of those still unmarried on that day were marked with chalk]

chalky n. see CHALKIE n. (1).

chalubbies n. [1970s] (*US*) the female breasts (cf. BAZONGAS n.). [JABONGOES n. + BUBBIES n.]

cham n. (*also* **chammy**) [mid-19C–1930s] *cham*pagne. [abbr.]

cham v. [mid–late 19C] to drink *cham*pagne. [CHAM n.]

chamber lye n. [mid-17C–early 19C] urine standing in a chamberpot. [play on SE *chamber(pot)* + *lye/lie*; note late 19C–early 20C Southern US Black use *chamber lye*, urine sprinkled around a garden to keep wandering deer away]

chamber music *n.* [late 19C+] the sound of a chamberpot being used. [pun]

chamber of commerce *n.* [1900s–40s] (*US Black/campus*) a lavatory (cf. ALTAR n.). [SE *chamber*, a lavatory + pun on DO ONE'S BUSINESS v.]

chamber of horrors *n.*[1] [19C] sausages. [the supposedly dubious contents]

chamber of horrors *n.*[2] [late 19C] the Peeresses' Gallery at the House of Lords. ['its being railed round as if it contained objectionable or repulsive inmates' (B&L)]

chameleon diet *n.* [late 17C–early 18C] a poor diet. [? SE *chameleon*, an inconstant or variable person]

chamming *n.* [mid–late 19C] drinking champagne (to excess). [CHAM v.]

chammy *n. see* CHAM n.

champ *n.*[1] [late 19C] appetite. [SE *champ*, to eat, to chew]

champ *n.*[2] **1** [1910s+] an excellent, first-rate person, often as a form of address. **2** [1990s+] (*US campus*) in stronger var. of (1), one who does things to excess. [SE *champion*]

champ *n.*[3] [1960s–70s] (*drugs*) a drug user who refuses to reveal their sources to the police. [CHAMPION adj.]

champ *adj.* [1930s+] (*US*) first-rate. [CHAMP n.[2] (1)]

Champagne Charlie *n.* **1** [mid–late 19C] a devotee of champagne. **2** [late 19C+] a debauchee, a dissipated man. [the song 'Champagne Charlie is My Name' by H.J. Whymark and Alfred Lee was written in 1867 and was a hit on both sides of the Atlantic. The original *Champagne Charlie* was a wine-merchant who was very free with gifts of his stock]

champagne coupons *n.* [1950s] money.

champagne glass *n.* [1990s+] a prostitute (cf. BOAT AND OAR n.). [rhy. sl. = BRASS (NAIL) n.]

champagner *n.* [late 19C–1900s] a fashionable prostitute. [her consumption of this expensive drink]

champagne shoulders *n.* [late 19C] (*UK society*) sloping shoulders. [resembling a champagne bottle]

champagne socialist *n.* (*also* **sushi socialist**) [1990s+] one who preaches socialism but espouses a capitalist lifestyle (cf. BOLLINGER BOLSHEVIK n.).

champagne trick *n.* [1990s+] a particularly wealthy or generous client for a prostitute. [fig. use of *champagne* + TRICK n.[1] (3)]

champagne weather *n.* [late 19C] (*UK society*) bad weather. [ironic or ? one needs a glass of *champagne* to cheer oneself up]

champaigne country *n.* [early–mid-19C] self-indulgence in eating and drinking. [SE *champagne* as a metaphor for luxury]

champers *n.* (*also* **shampers**) [1950s+] *champ*agne. [abbr. SE *champagne* + -ER sfx]

champion *n.* [1900s] the penis.

champion *adj.* [late 19C+] (*mainly northern*) first-rate, excellent.

champion *adv.* [late 19C+] (*mainly northern*) excellently, perfectly.

champion slump of 1897 *n.* [late 19C] the motorcar. [London's motor manufacturers staged a great procession of their products on Lord Mayor's Day, 1897. The aim was to launch the new mode of transport with a great fanfare but, as the term implies, it failed – at least initially]

champy *n.* [late 19C] (*US*) *champ*agne. [abbr. + sfx -*y*]

chance child *n.* [mid-19C] an illegitimate child (cf. COME-BY-CHANCE (CHILD) n.).

chance it *v.* (*also* **chance her**) [early 19C+] to take risks, to gamble. [ext. of SE *chance*]

chance one's arm *v.* (*also* **chance one's mitt**) [late 19C+] to take risks. [SE *chance* + *arm*/MITT n. (3); ? orig. tailors' jargon, but according to Share, the ref. is to a 1492 feud between the Butlers and the Fitzgeralds. The Earl of Kildare, the leading Fitzgerald, cut a hole in the door of St Patrick's Cathedral in Dublin and thrust in his arm, hoping that it would be grabbed rather than cut off. Thus it was, and the feud ended]

chancer *n.* **1** [late 19C+] anyone who risks their luck, usu.

foolishly, although the over-riding image is of their 'getting away with it'. **2** [1990s+] a bet, a wager. [CHANCE IT v.]

chance would be a fine thing *phr.* [20C+] a phr. used of anything that seems absolutely unlikely.

chancy *adj.* **1** [18C] lucky. **2** [19C+] untrustworthy, undependable. **3** [1980s+] (*Irish*) good-looking. [SE *chance*, which can be fortunate or otherwise]

C.H. & D. *phr.* [1930s] (*US tramp*) a phr. declaring one's need for food and shelter. [abbr. cold, *h*ungry and *d*ry + play on the initials of the *C*incinnati, *H*amilton and *D*ayton Railroad]

chandelier *n.* [1970s–80s] (*N.Z. prison*) an ear. [rhy. sl.]

chandler-ken *n.* [early 19C] a chandler's shop, selling general provisions, groceries etc. [SE *chandler* + KEN n.[1] (1)]

chandu *n.* [1910s–20s] (*drugs*) Chinese opium prepared for smoking (cf. APOSTLE n.). [? synon. Malay]

chaney-eyed *adj.* [late 19C] **1** small-eyed; thus like a China doll. **2** one-eyed; rarely, glassy-eyed. [? *chaney* = China, as in chinaware or porcelain; china being the original material used for 'glass' eyes]

chang-chang *v.* [20C+] (*W.I., Gren.*) to cut a man or boy's hair in an amateurish, raggedy manner. [? echoic of the sound of the barber's scissors]

change *n.*[1] [early 19C+] something given or taken in return, usu. in phrs., e.g. GIVE SOMEONE CHANGE v.; NOT GET ANY CHANGE OUT OF v.

change *n.*[2] **1** [mid-19C+] (*orig. US Black*) money, whether in notes or coins; often as *piece of change*. **2** [1940s+] in fig. use, any insignificant, unquantifiable amount, not necessarily monetary. **3** [1950s] (*US Black*) a game of dice. **4** [1970s+] (*US prison*) in a jail sentence, any period of time less than a whole year.

change, the *n.* [1940s+] the menopause; also used joc. of a man. [euph. SE *the change of life*]

change black dog for monkey *v.* [1920s+] (*W.I.*) to get nothing from a deal, to remain as poor as one already was. [one is still left with a useless animal]

change channels *v.* (*also* **change the channel**) **1** [1950s+] (*US*) to change the subject of conversation or one's line of thought; often as imper. **2** [1970s] to find a new relationship. [TV imagery]

change-machine *n.* (*also* **change-register**) [1970s+] (*US gay*) the buttocks. [their role in commercial sex]

change one's breath *v.* [late 19C–1900s] (*US*) to drink alcohol.

change one's copy *v.* [early 17C] to alter one's opinions or statements, esp. to go back on what one has previously said (cf. CHANGE ONE'S NOTE v.; CHANGE ONE'S SONG v.; CHANGE ONE'S TUNE v.).

change one's luck *v.* **1** [1960s–70s] (*US*) for a White person to have sex with a Black person (esp. for the first time). **2** [1970s+] (*US gay*) to perform homosexual sex for the first time.

change one's note *v.* [late 17C+] to alter one's opinions or statements, esp. to go back on what one has previously said (cf. CHANGE ONE'S COPY v.). [musical imagery]

change one's song *v.* [mid-17C–early 19C] to alter one's opinions or statements (cf. CHANGE ONE'S COPY v.). [musical imagery; var. on next]

change one's tune *v.* (*also* **alter one's tune**) [late 16C+] to alter one's opinions or statements, esp. to go back on what one has previously said (cf. CHANGE ONE'S COPY v.). [musical imagery]

change-register *n. see* CHANGE-MACHINE n.

changes *n.* [1950s+] (*orig. US Black*) any alteration in one's mental or emotional state; usu. as *go through changes*, to undergo such an alteration or *put/take someone through changes*, to alter someone else. [jazz use *changes*, a chord sequence, thence adopted by hippies/drug users/New Agers in the late 1960s+]

change someone's face *v. see* BREAK SOMEONE'S FACE v.[1].

change teams *v.* [1990s+] to reverse one's sexuality.

change the channel *v. see* CHANGE CHANNELS v.

change the record! *excl. see* PUT ANOTHER RECORD ON! excl.

changie *n.* [2000s] a changing room. [abbr. + sfx *-ie*]

chank *v.* [19C] (*US*) to eat noisily, to chew loudly. [? SE *champ* or echoic]

channel fleet *n.* [20C+] (*Irish*) a street. [rhy. sl.]

channel (line) *n.* [1930s+] (*drugs*) the vein into which a drug is injected.

Channel Nine *n.* [1980s] (*Aus.*) wine. [rhy. sl.; ult. Aus. TV channel]

channel swimmer *n.* [1950s–70s] (*drugs*) one who injects heroin. [CHANNEL (LINE) n. + pun]

chant *n.* (*also* **chaunt**) (*UK Und.*) 1 [mid-18C–early 19C] a newspaper advertisement; an account of a robbery. 2 [late 18C–19C] a song. 3 [early 19C] any form of marking, on silver, linen etc. 4 [early–mid 19C] one's name (and address); thus *tip someone a queer chant*, to give a false name, esp. to a tradesman one wishes to defraud. 5 [mid-19C] sheet music, a printed ballad with its lyrics. [CHANT v./fig. uses of SE *chant*, to sing]

chant *v.* (*also* **chaunt**) 1 [mid-17C–1930s] (*orig. UK Und.*) to sing, esp. to sing for money in the street; to sing to sell one's wares. 2 [mid-18C] (*UK Und.*) to count up. 3 [late 18C–early 19C] (*UK Und.*) to publish an account in a newspaper. 4 [19C] (*UK Und.*) to sell a horse fraudulently. 5 [early 19C] (*UK Und.*) to mark one's personal possessions with an identifying name. 6 [mid-19C] (*US*) to talk (about), to talk persuasively. 7 [late 19C–1900s] to swear. 8 [1930s] (*UK tramp*) to sing for alms. 9 [1980s] (*UK Black*) to speechify in the street. [CHANT n./fig. uses of SE *chant*, to sing]

chant down *v.* [1980s] (*W.I.*) to criticize.

chanted *adj.* (*also* **chaunted**) [early–mid 19C] 1 famous, celebrated, lit. 'sung'. 2 (*UK Und.*) of a stolen article, to have the theft announced in public (by a town crier or similar figure). 3 of one's property, marked, identified as one's own. [CHANT v.]

chanter *n.* (*also* **chaunter**) 1 [early 18C–1930s] a seller and singer of street ballads. 2 [mid-19C–1920s] (*also* **chanterer**) a crooked horse dealer, also of dogs. [CHANT v. (1)/CHANT v. (4)]

chanter cull *n. see* CHAUNTER CULL n.

chanter-pipe *n.* (*also* **chanter**) [mid-18C–mid-19C] the penis (cf. ACCORDION n.). [SE *chanter* = Irish bagpipes]

chanticleer *n.* [mid–late 19C] the penis. [a pun on COCK n.² (1); the cock in the fable of Reynard the Fox is thus named; Williams notes its use as synon. for a lecher]

chanting *n.* (*also* **chaunting**) [19C–1930s] 1 the selling of a poor horse by concealing its defects and 'crying up' its good ones. 2 street-singing. [CHANT v. (4)/CHANT v. (1)]

chanting ken *n.* [late 19C–1900s] a music hall. [CHANT v. (1) + KEN n.¹ (1)]

chanting slum *n.* [mid-19C] a music hall. [CHANT v. (1) + SLUM n.¹ (1)]

chant the poker *v.* [19C] to exaggerate; thus *don't chant the poker*, don't exaggerate. [CHANT v. (6) + ety. unknown; note POKER TALK n.]

chap *n.* 1 [18C+] a man or boy, esp. in sense of 'one of us' (cf. ONE OF THE CHAPS n.). 2 [late 19C] a male sweetheart. 3 [late 19C] a sailor. 4 [late 19C+] an otherwise unspecified object. 5 [1920s+] (*Irish*) the hero, the leading man in a film. [abbr. of late 16C SE *chapman*, a customer and, as such, relates to COVE n. (1). An alternative ety., however, links it to the Rom. *chavo* or *chavi*, a child, and thus places it as the antecedent of the 19C use. Todd (revised edn of *Johnson's Dictionary*, 1818) notes 'it usually designates a person of whom a contemptuous opinion is entertained', but the *OED* adds 'it is now merely familiar and non-dignified, being chiefly applied to a young man']

chap, a *n. see* FELLOW, A n.

chap *v.*¹ [1920s–30s] to *chap*eron. [abbr.]

chap *v.*² [1990s+] to be unsatisfactory, to be bad. [? SE *chap*, to crack open, to cause fissures]

Chapel, the *n.* [mid–late 19C] White*chapel*, east London. [abbr.]

chapel *n. see* CHAPEL (OF EASE) n.

chapel hat pegs *n.* [20C+] erect female nipples; usu. in phr. *stand/standing up like chapel hat pegs*.

chapel (of ease) *n.* 1 [late 16C–19C] the vagina (cf. ADAM'S OWN (ALTAR) n.). 2 [17C–mid-19C] a privy, a lavatory (cf. ALTAR n.). [play on SE]

chapel of little ease *n.* [late 19C] a police station. [SE *little-ease*, 'a place in which there is little ease for him who occupies it. A narrow place of confinement; spec. the name of a dungeon in the Tower of London, and of an ancient place of punishment for unruly apprentices at the Guildhall, London. Also, the pillory or stocks' (*OED*) + play on CHAPEL (OF EASE) n.]

chapp *n.* [2000s] (*US Black*) a child. [ety. unknown]

chapped *adj.* (*also* **chapt**) [late 17C–1900s] thirsty. [SE *chapped*, cracked, dried out]

chapper *n.*¹ [late 19C] the mouth. [? SE *chaps*, the mouth, the jaws]

chapper *n.*² [20C+] (*UK Und.*) a policeman. [? Yid.]

chapper *v.* [late 19C–1900s] to drink. [CHAPPER n.¹]

chappie *n.* (*also* **chappy**) 1 [early 19C+] a person, esp. a close friend. 2 [mid-19C+] a term of address to a friend. 3 [late 19C+] a man about town; often as *cheeky chappie/chappy*. [CHAP n. (1)]

chappy *adj.* [late 17C–mid-18C] talkative. [SE *chaps*, the mouth, the jaws]

chaps *n. see* CHOPS n.¹ (1).

chaps, the *n.* [1980s] (*Aus.*) the police. [CHAP n. (1)]

chap someone's ass *v.* [1960s] (*US*) to annoy, to irritate. [SE *chap*, to crack the skin + ASS n. (5)]

chapt *adj. see* CHAPPED adj.

char *n.*¹ [mid-18C+] a charwoman. [note orig. 18C *char*, to do odd jobs; B.E. (1698): '*Chare-woman*, Underdrudges, or taskers, assistants to Servantmaids'. The modern synon. *charlady* began as late 19C joc. but now, like *tea-lady*, *cleaning-lady* etc is almost SE; note Nares: 'chare or chare-work. Task-work, or any labour [...] *Chare-woman* is still used, for one hired to work by the day']

char *n.*² *see* CHA n.¹.

char *v.* 1 [late 18C] to solicit, to work as a prostitute. 2 [mid-19C+] to work as a cleaner, usu. in a private house. [CHAR n.¹]

chara *n.* (*also* **sharrer, sharry**) [1920s–60s] a *chara*banc, a coach. [abbr.]

character *n.* 1 [mid-18C+] an eccentric or otherwise distinctive person. 2 [20C+] (*orig. US*) a person. 3 [1960s+] (*US Und.*) a professional criminal; also attrib. [(1) abbr. SE *odd character*]

character academy *n.* [mid-19C] (*UK Und.*) a place where unemployed (and poss. previously dismissed) servants concoct spurious references or 'characters'.

charactered *adj.* [early 18C–early 19C] (*UK Und.*) branded on the hand. [SE *character*, a brand, a stamp]

charas *n.* (*also* **churus**) [1920s+] (*drugs*) hashish (cf. AFGHAN n.). [Hind. *charas*, hashish]

charcoal *n.* [20C+] (*US*) 1 a derog. term for a Black person; thus *charcoal blossom*, a young Black woman; *charcoal lily*, a very dark Black boy; *charcoal bandit*, a Black criminal (cf. BLACKBELLY n.). 2 as used by a Black person, thus not derog.

charcoal blonde *n. see* BITUMEN BLONDE n.

charcoal tart *n.* [20C+] (*Aus.*) a thin, unleavened loaf baked in the embers.

charge *n.*¹ [20C+] (*Irish*) 1 a loud-mouthed woman. 2 a lazy, loutish person. [Anglo-Norman *kark*, a burden]

charge *n.*² 1 [1920s+] the effect of a given drug. 2 [1920s+] an injection of a narcotic drug. 3 [1940s+] drugs in general, spec. marijuana. 4 [1950s+] a thrill, a feeling of excitement or satisfaction; thus *get a charge out of*. 5 [1980s] (*Aus.*) a glass of liquor, esp. spirits. 6 [2000s] a feeling of amusement. [SE *charge*, an accumulation of electricity, but note 1877 Mrs Frank Leslie, *California*: 'The tiny "charge" [of opium] constituting one pipe-full is soon exhausted, and holding the last whiff as long as

possible, the smoker prepares another, and another and yet
another']

charge v.[1] **1** [late 16C–mid-17C; 1960s] of a man, to have sexual
intercourse (cf. BANG v.[1]). **2** [late 19C] (US) to have a riotously
good time. **3** [1930s+] (US) to hold up (a bank) at gunpoint.
4 [1960s] (US) to arouse sexually. [SE *charge*, to attack]

charge v.[2] (*drugs*) **1** [1930s] to use narcotic drugs. **2** [1930s–60s] to
smoke marijuana. [CHARGE n.[2]]

charged (up) *adj*. [1920s+] **1** intoxicated by alcohol; thus *half-
charged*, tipsy. **2** intoxicated by drugs, esp. cannabis. **3** emotionally
tense, irrespective of the stimulus. [CHARGE n.[2]]

charge like a wounded bull v. [1990s+] (*orig. Aus.*) to ask
for a large amount of money; to render a substantial bill.

charger n. [1900s] the penis.

charge someone off v. [1960s] (US) **1** to end a relationship.
2 to ignore someone one knows well. [SE *charge at*, i.e. to push
someone away]

charging n. [1970s+] (US Black) an instance of outwitting, insult
or verbal humiliation. [SE *charge*, to command, to exhort
authoritatively]

Charing Cross n. (*also* **chair and cross**) [mid-19C+] a horse.
[rhy. sl.; note Cockney pron. 'crorss'; ult. *Charing Cross*, London
WC1, best known for its railway station and Charing Cross Rd,
home of many booksellers]

chariot n. **1** [mid–late 19C] an omnibus. **2** [20C+] a motorcar.

chariot-buzzer n. [mid-19C] a pickpocket who specializes in
the passengers of an omnibus; thus *chariot-buzzing*. [CHARIOT n. (1)
+ BUZZER n.[1] (1)]

charity n. **1** [1920s+] (US/Aus.) an amateur prostitute or a
professional who undercuts her peers (cf. CHARITY n.), usu. by
'giving it away free' (cf. CHARITY ASS n.; CHARITY CUNT n.; CHARITY
DAME n.; CHARITY GIRL n.; CHARITY GOODS n.; CHARITY MOLL n.;
CHARITY WORKER n.; FOR-FREE n.; FREEBIE n.; FREE-FOR-ALL n.;
FREELANCE n.). **2** [1970s] (Aus. gay) a promiscuous man, one who
'gives it away for free'.

charity ass n. [1920s–50s] a woman who 'gives it away'; thus
sexual intercourse for which no payment is expected (cf. CHARITY
n.). [SE *charity* + ASS n. (4)]

charity bob n. [late 19C–1900s] a form of quick curtsy peculiar
to charity-school girls.

charity case n. [1960s+] an older sexual partner whose needs
are gratified by a younger man or woman out of kindness rather
than desire.

charity cunt n. [1910s; 2000s] (US) a promiscuous woman who
'gives it away for free' (cf. CHARITY n.). [SE *charity* + CUNT n.[1] (3)]

charity dame n. [1930s+] (Aus.) a promiscuous woman who
'gives it away for free' (cf. CHARITY n.). [SE *charity* + DAME n.]

charity fuck n. (*also* **pity fuck**) [1960s+] an act of sexual
intercourse engaged in out of pity (cf. MERCY FUCK n.). [SE *charity*
+ FUCK n.[1] (1)]

charity girl n. [1920s+] (US) a promiscuous woman who 'gives
it away for free' (cf. CHARITY n.).

charity goods n. [1970s+] (US gay) a male prostitute who gives
sex but does not get paid (cf. CHARITY n.).

charity moll n. [1940s+] (Aus.) an amateur prostitute, or a
professional who undercuts her peers (cf. CHARITY n.). [SE *charity*
+ MOLL n.[1] (2)]

charity stuff n. **1** [1950s+] (US) a promiscuous woman
who 'gives it away for free' (cf. CHARITY n.). **2** [1970s+] (US
gay) a male prostitute who gives sex but does not get paid (cf.
CHARITY n.).

charity worker n. [1940s+] (US) a promiscuous woman who
'gives it away for free' (cf. CHARITY n.).

Charlene n. [1970s] **1** (US Black) a White woman, esp. one who
is in a position of authority over Blacks. **2** (US gay) a popular
camp nickname for a homosexual man (cf. ABIGAIL n.). [(1) fem.
dimin. MR CHARLIE n.; (2) female name as generic]

Charles n. *see* CHARLIE n.

charles n.[1] [1920s+] (US Black) a derog. term for a White man.
[BOSS CHARLIE n.]

charles n.[2] [1960s+] (*drugs*) cocaine (cf. AUNT NORA n.). [initial
letter]

charles brady n. *see* CHARLEY BRADY n.

Charles Dance n. [1990s+] a chance. [rhy. sl.; ult. the British
actor and film star *Charles Dance* (b.1946)]

charles james n. [late 19C+] **1** a theatrical box. **2** (*hunting*) a
fox. [rhy. sl.; ult. politician *Charles James* Fox (1749–1806)]

Charley n. *see* CHARLIE n.

charley *see also under* CHARLIE and its combs.

charley n.[1] (*also* **charlie**) **1** [late 17C; 19C] a watchman, a
beadle. **2** [mid-19C] a gold watch. [punning cant; supposedly linked
to the improvement of the London watch system by Charles I,
but no use of the word for 150 years afterwards is recorded;
(2) pun on (1)]

charley n.[2] (*also* **charlie, cholly**) [1920s–70s] (US Black) a dollar
bill.

charley n.[3] (*also* **charlie**) [1960s] (US) the penis.

charley n.[4] (*also* **charlie**) [1960s+] (US Black) a derog. term for
a White man. [BOSS CHARLIE n.]

charley n.[5] *see* CHARLEY (HORSE) n.

Charley Bate's Farm/Garden n. *see* BATE'S FARM n.

charley beck n. [1940s] (US) a forged cheque. [rhy. sl.]

charley brady n. (*also* **charles brady**) [late 19C–1960s] a hat.
[rhy. sl. = CADY n. (1)]

charley chalk n. [1940s] (US) talk. [rhy. sl.]

Charley Dilke n. (*also* **Charlie Dilke**) [20C+] milk. [rhy. sl.;
ult. radical politician Sir *Charles Dilke* (1843–1911)]

charley frisky n. [mid-19C–1900s] whisky. [rhy. sl.]

charley (horse) n. (*also* **horse**) [late 19C+] (*orig. US*) a cramp
or sudden stiffness in the leg; thus *charley-horsed*, suffering from
such a problem. [orig. baseball use *c*.1886]

charley howard n. [1920s+] a coward; thus TURN CHARLIE v.
[rhy. sl.; poss. based on Tennyson 'The Revenge': 'Then sware
Lord Thomas Howard: "'Fore God I am no coward"'; however,
note CHARLIE adj. (2)]

charley-ken n. [early 19C] (UK Und.) a watchman's box. [CHARLEY
n.[1] (1) + KEN n.[1] (1)]

charley lancaster n. [mid-19C] a handkerchief. [rhy. sl.
= Cockney pron. 'handkercher']

charley-man n. [late 17C–mid-19C] a watchman, a beadle.
[CHARLEY n.[1] (1)]

charley mason n. (*also* **stone mason**) **1** [20C+] a basin.
2 [1960s+] a try, a go, an attempt. [rhy. sl.; (2) = 'basinful']

charley-pitcher n. (*also* **charlie-pitcher**) [mid-19C] **1** a
gambler. **2** (UK Und.) one who runs a 3-card trick card-game.
[? OE *ceorl* or SE *churl*, a peasant; however, *charley* may simply be
a generic term for the peasant to whom he 'pitches the tale', or a
euph. for the derisive *churl*]

charley pope n. [1910s] soap. [rhy. sl.]

Charley Pride n. (*also* **Charlie Pride**) [2000s] a ride. [rhy. sl.; ult.
African-American country and western musician *Charley Pride*
(b.1938)]

charley randy n. [mid-19C–1900s] brandy. [rhy. sl.]

charley rocks n. *see* SIDNEY ROCKS n.

charley rollar n. [1920s–40s] (US) a dollar (cf. BEES (AND HONEY)
n.). [rhy. sl.]

charley roller n. *see* TOMMY ROLLER n.

Charley's aunt! *excl*. [1910s] an excl. of amusement.

charley's fiddle n. [early–mid-19C] a watchman's rattle.
[CHARLEY n.[1] (1) + FIDDLE n.[4]]

charley sheard n. [1970s+] a beard. [rhy. sl.]

charley skinner n. [mid-19C–1900s] dinner. [rhy. sl.]

charley-wag v. [1900s] to play truant. [PLAY THE CHARLEY
WAG v.]

Charlie *n.* (*also* **Charles, Charley, Mr Charles**) [1960s–70s] (*US, orig. milit.*) a member of the Viet Cong. [initial letters; post-1973 use is historical]

charlie *see also under* CHARLEY and its combs.

charlie *n.*[1] [early 19C+] (*orig. US*) a generic term for a person, usu. a man.

charlie *n.*[2] **1** [mid-19C] a small, pointed beard. **2** [1920s] (*US*) a moustachioed male. [that worn by King *Charles I* (r.1625–49)]

charlie *n.*[3] [mid-late 19C] a fox. [CHARLES JAMES n. (2)]

charlie *n.*[4] [mid-19C+] a hunchback. [Lancashire dial.; who supposedly carried his 'little brother Charlie' on his back. Note army jargon *charlie*, a pack]

charlie *n.*[5] (*also* **charley**) [1920s] a chamberpot.

charlie *n.*[6] [1920s+] a fool; esp. as RIGHT CHARLIE n. (cf. BEECHAM'S PILL n.; BEN n.[1]). [rhy. sl. *charlie hunt* = CUNT n.[2] (1); given the popularity of the term among otherwise 'clean' radio and TV comedians, one must assume they (and their audiences) are ignorant of the ety.]

charlie *n.*[7] [1930s] (*US*) an Asian man (cf. BROWNIE n.[2]). [the fictional Chinese detective *Charlie Chan*, created in 1925 by Earl Derr Biggers]

charlie *n.*[8] [1930s+] a ponce, a pimp. [abbr. CHARLIE RONCE n.]

charlie *n.*[9] (*also* **charley**) (*drugs*) **1** [1930s+] cocaine (cf. AUNT NORA n.). **2** [1990s+] a heavy user of cocaine. [the same initial letter but note cocaine is white and MR CHARLIE n. means a White man]

charlie *n.*[10] [1940s+] (*Aus.*) **1** a woman. **2** a prostitute (cf. BABY JANE n.). **3** a lesbian (cf. AMY-JOHN n.). **4** a male homosexual (cf. ABIGAIL n.). [CHARLIE WHEELER n. (1); Simes, *A Dict. of Australian Underworld Slang* (1993), adds: '"Charlie" was an old Eng. name for nightwatchman: this may be the origin' (cf. CHARLEY n.[1])]

charlie *n.*[11] [1960s] (*US campus*) menstruation.

charlie *n.*[12] [1990s+] (*UK juv.*) a brick; thus *half-charlie*, a half-brick.

charlie *adj.* **1** [early 19C+] wary. **2** [1930s+] frightened, cowardly. [CHARLEY n.[1] (1)/CHARLEY HOWARD n.]

charlie blow *n.* [1970s] (*US drugs*) cocaine (cf. AUNT NORA n.). [CHARLIE n.[9] (1) + BLOW n.[6] (4)]

charlie-boy *n.* [late 19C–1910s] (*US*) an effeminate young man. [CHARLIE adj.]

charlie britt *n.* [1940s+] (*Aus.*) a fit. [rhy. sl.; ? fig. use of JIMMY BRITTS n.]

charlie chap *n.* [1910s] (*Aus.*) a moustache resembling that worn (in character) by *Charlie Chap*lin. [abbr.; ult. film star *Charlie Chaplin* (1889–1977)]

Charlie Chaplain *n.* [1980s+] (*Aus. prison*) a prison chaplain. [rhy. sl./pun; ult. film star *Charlie Chaplin* (1889–1977)]

charlie chase *n.* [20C+] (*Aus.*) a race; thus *not in the charlie*, not worthy of consideration, i.e. NOT IN THE RACE phr. [rhy. sl.]

Charlie Chester *n.* [1990s+] (*UK juv.*) a child molester. [rhy. sl.; ult. UK comedian *Charlie Chester* (b.1914)]

Charlie Clore *n.* [1960s] the ground, 'the floor'. [rhy. sl.; ult. property developer *Sir Charles Clore* (1904–79)]

charlie coke *n.* (*also* **charlie cocaine**) [1930s+] (*US drugs*) a cocaine addict. [CHARLIE n.[9] (1) + COKE n.[1]/SE *cocaine*]

Charlie Cooke *n.* [1990s+] a look, a glance. [rhy. sl.; ult. UK footballer *Charlie Cooke* (b.1942)]

charlie cotton *n. see* COTTON n.[1] (1).

charlied *adj.* [1990s+] experiencing the effects of cocaine. [CHARLIE n.[9] (1)]

Charlie Drake *n.* **1** [1960s–70s] a brake (on a car). **2** [1990s+] a break (for tea etc). [rhy. sl.; ult. UK comedian *Charlie Drake* (b.1925)]

charlie freer *n.* [late 19C–1980s] beer. [rhy. sl.]

charlie goon *n.* (*also* **charlie goons**) [1960s] (*US Black*) a policeman, the police (cf. BILLY n.[6]). [MR CHARLIE n. + GOON n.[1] (4)]

charlie horner *n. see* JOHNNY HORNER n.

charlie irvine *n.* [1970s+] (*US Black*) the police. [? *criminal investigator*]

charlie nebs *n.* [1960s] (*US Black*) the police. [MR CHARLIE n. + SE *neb*, a beak, although *neb* may be mispron. for NAB n.[2] (1)]

charlie-on-the-spot *n.* [19C–1940s] (*US*) a reliable or punctual person (cf. JOHNNY-ON-THE-SPOT n.). [CHARLIE n.[1] + SE *spot*]

charlie potatoes *n.* [2000s] a rich and powerful person. [CHARLIE n.[1] + POTATO n.[4]]

Charlie Prescott *n.* (*also* **Billy Prescott, Charley Prescott, Colonel Prescott, Jimmy Prescott, John Prescott, prescott**) [mid-19C–1960s] a waistcoat. [rhy. sl.; ? anecdotal]

charlie rawler *n.* [1920s–40s] (*US*) a collar. [rhy. sl.]

charlie ronce *n.* (*also* **harry ronce, joe ronce, johnny ronce**) [1930s+] a ponce, a pimp (cf. ALPHONSE n.[2]). [rhy. sl.]

charlie rousers *n. see* JOHNNY ROWSERS n.

charlies *n.*[1] (*also* **charleys**) [mid-19C+] the female breasts (cf. BRACE AND BITS n.). [? Aus. rhy. sl. CHARLIE WHEELER n. = sheila n. (1) = a woman, and thus her distinguishing characteristics. Ware attributes the term to the predilection of King Charles II (r.1660–85) for décolletage, which would seem fanciful but for the date, which well precedes CHARLIE WHEELER n.. E.P. suggests Rom. *chara*, to touch, to meddle with]

charlies *n.*[2] [1960s] the testicles. [? CHARLIES n.[1]]

charlie's dead *phr.* [1950s+] (*UK juv.*) a warning to a woman that her slip is showing (cf. COTTON IS LOW phr.; JOHN IS DEAD phr.; MONDAY COMES BEFORE SUNDAY phr.; MRS WHITE IS OUT OF JAIL phr.; P.H.D. phr.; THERE'S A LETTER IN THE POST OFFICE phr.).

Charlie Smirke *n.* [1970s+] a fool (cf. BEECHAM'S PILL n.). [rhy. sl. = BERK n.; ult. UK jockey *Charlie Smirke* who, in 1922–53, claimed 3 Derbies and the St Leger among other successes]

charlie taylor *n.* [1930s–50s] (*US, Southwest*) syrup or molasses into which bacon or ham fat has been poured. [? anecdotal]

Charlie Wheeler *n.* [1940s+] (*Aus.*) **1** a woman. **2** in pl., the female breasts (cf. BRACE AND BITS n.). [rhy. sl. = sheila n. (1); ult. proper name *Charles Wheeler* (1881–1977), a painter specializing in nudes]

charlie whitehouse *n.* [20C+] (*US*) a chamberpot. [ext. of CHARLIE n.[5], the whiteness of the porcelain utensil]

Charlie Wood *n. see* MR WOOD n.

charlotte *n.* [1960s–70s] (*US drugs*) cocaine (cf. AUNT NORA n.). ['feminized' version of CHARLIE n.[9] (1); note cocaine is a 'feminine' drug, see GIRL n.[2]]

charm *n.*[1] [late 16C–mid-19C] a picklock. [it 'charms' locks open]

charm *n.*[2] *see* CHARMS n.[1] (2).

charm *v.* [1960s+] (*US Black*) to 'chat up'.

charmboat *n. see* DREAMBOAT n. (1).

charm bracelet *n.* [1970s+] (*US gay*) a metaphorical list of one's lovers, a 'little black book'.

charmer *n.*[1] [18C+] an attractive young woman.

charmer *n.*[2] [1900s] the penis.

charming! *excl.* [1960s+] an excl. used as a response to a statement that the speaker feels to be rude, crude or otherwise unacceptable, sometimes as *charming, I'm sure!*

charming mottle *n.* [late 19C–1940s] (*Aus.*) a bottle. [rhy. sl.]

charming wife *n.* [1910s+] a knife. [rhy. sl.]

charm-pot *n.* [2000s] (*US*) a charmer, also used ironically. [SE *charm* + -POT sfx]

charms *n.*[1] **1** [18C+] the female breasts; esp. in phr. *flash one's charms*, to reveal one's breasts. **2** [early 18C; late 19C+] (*also* **charm**) the male genitals. [euph.]

charms *n.*[2] [late 19C] (*US*) money (cf. ACTUAL, THE n.). [the effect of money on otherwise intractable situations]

char ou *n. see* CHAAR OU n.

charper *v.* [mid-19C+] (*Ling. Fr./Polari*) to search. [Ital. *cercare*, to seek; for an alternative ety. *see* ety. at CHARVER v.]

charpering carsey *n.* [late 19C] (*Ling. Fr./Polari*) a police station. [CHARPER V. + CARSEY n. (5)]

charpering omi *n.* [late 19C] (*Ling. Fr./Polari*) a policeman. [CHARPER V. + OMEE n. (3)]

charra *n.* [1970s+] (*S.Afr.*) a derog. term of address to an Indian. [CHAAR OU n.]

charrshom *n.* (*also* **chershom**) [18C+] (*tinker*) a crown, a 5-shilling (25p) coin. [Shelta]

chart *n.* [1900s] (*US*) the face.

chart *v.* [1960s] (*US*) to commit to memory, to comprehend.

charter the bar *v.* (*also* **charter the grocery**) [late 19C–1930s] to buy drinks for everyone in a bar or public house. [SE *charter*, to hire]

charver *n.* (*also* **charva**, **charve**) [late 19C+] sexual intercourse; thus *bona palone for a charver*, an 'easy lay', a 'good-time girl' (lit. 'a good girl for a fuck'). [CHARVER V. (1)]

charver *v.* (*also* **charva**) **1** [mid-17C; late 19C+] (*also* **chafer**, **chaffer**, **chauver**) to have sexual intercourse. **2** [late 19C+] (*costermonger*) to ruin, to spoil or interfere in another's business, i.e. to FUCK V.² (1). [note Polari etymologist W.S. Wilcox in a letter 25/11/99: 'Partridge derives *charva* and *charper* from Romany *chava* (touch) and Italian *cercare* respectively, but I think the centuries-old Italian slang word *chiavare* (fuck) and *chiappare* (catch, seize) are far more likely candidates, both in meaning and in form. Compare *scarper* from *scappare*. Regarding the chi- becoming (ts)-, this is the standard reflex in Genoese dialect, where *chiavare* becomes *ciavâ*']

charvered *adj.* [1930s+] ruined, wrecked, exhausted. [CHARVER V. (2)]

charvering donna *n.* (*also* **charvering dona**, **...doner**, **chauvering dona**, **...doner**, **...donna**) [late 19C] (*Ling. Fr./Polari*) a prostitute. [CHARVER V. (1) + DONA n. (1)]

charvering omee *n.* [mid-19C] (*Ling. Fr./Polari*) a policeman. [CHARVER V. (2) + OMEE n. (3); var. on CHARPERING OMI n.]

char wallah *n.* (*also* **lemonade wallah**, **pop wallah**) [1910s–30s] a teetotaller. [CHA n.¹ + WALLAH n. (1)]

chas *n.* [2000s] cocaine (cf. AUNT NORA n.). [Chas = abbr. of proper name *Charlie*, thus for CHARLIE n.⁹ (1)]

chase *n.* [1990s+] (*drugs*) the act of smoking heroin. [CHASE V.² (1)]

chase *v.*¹ **1** [late 19C] (*US tramp*) to escort, to travel with. **2** [late 19C–1950s] (*US*) (*also* **chase oneself**) to run off, to leave; esp. in imper. (*go*) *chase yourself!* go away!; thus *get the chase*, to be ejected or chased away. **3** [20C+] (*US*) (*also* **chase around**) to pursue women, esp. as an adulterer; also of homosexuals, to pursue other men.

chase *v.*² [1970s+] (*drugs*) **1** to smoke heroin. **2** to smoke cocaine. **3** to smoke marijuana. [abbr. CHASE THE DRAGON v. (1); ? (2) and (3) misuse, as phr. strictly refers to heroin]

chase a cow *v. see* CHASE (UP) A COW v.

chase a piece *v. see* BEG FOR A PIECE v.

chase around *v. see* CHASE V.¹ (3).

chase cheers *v.* [1930s+] (*Aus.*) to curry favour with the masses; thus *cheer-chaser*, a toady to popular opinion; *cheer-chasing*, taking a deliberately populist stand.

chase oneself *v. see* CHASE V.¹ (2).

chaser *n.*¹ **1** [late 19C+] (*orig. US*) a glass of water, soda or beer taken after a shot of spirits, usu. to dilute the impact; from late 1980s onwards generally the other way around, a strong spirit that is taken after drinking a pint of beer to increase the impact, usu. *whisky chaser*. **2** [20C+] similarly used of foods. **3** [1900s] a final touch, e.g. when getting dressed up. **4** [1900s] in fig. use of (1), anything 'lesser' that follows. **5** [1980s] (*drugs*) a dilutant. [1940s+ use of (1) is SE]

chaser *n.*² **1** [1900s] one who runs errands. **2** [1910s+] (*mainly US*) a womanizer. **3** [1950s] a promiscuous woman. **4** [1960s] in homosexual use of (2), a predatory older homosexual. **5** [1990s+] (*US prison*) a prison officer who is in charge of chain gangs or escape recovery teams. [(2) note SE *woman-chaser*]

chaser *n.*³ [1990s+] (*drugs*) a frequent user of crack cocaine. [CHASE V.² (2)/SE *chase*, i.e. to be addicted]

chase the bag *v.* [1960s+] (*drugs*) to seek out supplies and/or to be addicted to heroin. [SE *chase* + BAG n.¹¹ (1)]

chase the can *v.* [late 19C–1940s] to drink freely at a bar.

chase the dragon *v.* **1** [1960s+] (*drugs*) to smoke heroin, sucking up the smoke of the drug, which is burned on a piece of kitchen foil. The heated heroin liquefies and flows across the paper, gradually giving off smoke, which is sucked into the smoker's lungs by a tube, also usu. made of kitchen foil. **2** [2000s] (*US prison*) to look for a supply of heroin. [SE *chase*, i.e. the smoke + *dragon*, which underlines the Oriental origin of much of the heroin found in the UK]

chase the hares *v.* [20C+] to chase women. [a pun on HAIR n.¹ (2)]

chase the (penny) weight *v.* [1910s–70s] (*Aus.*) to prospect for gold.

chase the sun(set) *v.* [1910s–50s] (*Aus.*) to live as a tramp.

chase-up *n.* [1940s–60s] a car chase.

chase up *v.* [1950s+] **1** to pursue (a matter or person) vigorously with a specific intent, esp. after an earlier unsatisfactory response. **2** to make efforts to find or obtain quickly.

chase (up) a cow *v.* (*also* **hunt up a cow**, **move a cow**) [1950s] (*Aus.*) for an amorous couple to search out a secluded spot in the bush in order to have sexual intercourse. [the ideal patch would have been one used by a sleeping cow, i.e. pre-warmed]

chase yourself! *excl. see* CHASE V.¹ (2).

chasing *n.* [1980s+] (*drugs*) the act of smoking heroin. [CHASE V.² (1)]

chasm *n.* [19C] the vagina (cf. AGREEABLE RUTS OF LIFE n.).

chasse *n.* [mid-19C–1910s] a cup of coffee that accompanies a shot of spirits, usu. whisky; a liqueur taken after or with coffee. [abbr. Fr. *chasse-café*, lit. 'chase-coffee']

chasse *v.* [mid-19C] (*UK society*) to dismiss, to send away. [SE *chassé*, a gliding step, in a quadrille and other dances; it gives the illusion of walking]

chassis *n.* (*also* **chassy**) [1930s+] **1** the female figure; thus CLASSY CHASSIS n. **2** the male body. [automobile imagery]

chat *n.*¹ **1** [mid-16C–18C] the gallows. **2** [early 19C] (*Scot. Und.*) a seal. **3** [mid–late 19C] a thing, an object. **4** [late 19C] a criminal 'job' or undertaking. **5** [late 19C–1930s] a house, esp. one picked for burglary. [CHEAT n.]

chat *n.*² **1** [18C] a cat. **2** [19C+] the vagina (cf. BIRD n.⁸). [Fr. *chat*, cat]

chat *n.*³ **1** [early 19C–1910s] cheek, impudence. **2** [early 19C–1920s] the truth, the apposite thing, the subject under discussion. **3** [1910s+] verbal skills, fluency, articulacy, the ability to charm a victim with words alone. **4** [1950s+] terminology, a special language, jargon. [SE *chat*, a conversation, a discussion]

chat *n.*⁴ **1** [1930s–50s] (*Irish*) methylated spirits, as drunk by alcoholics. **2** [1960s+] (*Aus.*) a general insult, usu. aimed at an old man, esp. an alcoholic. [its effects; (2) f. (1) but note CHATS n.², i.e. a LOUSE n.]

chat *n.*⁵ [1950s] (*W.I.*) a male gossip. [CHAT-CHAT v.]

chat *n.*⁶ *see* CHATS n.²

chat *v.*¹ **1** [late 19C+] (*also* **chat up**) to attempt the first, verbal stages of seduction. **2** [20C+] (*also* **chat up**) to gossip, to talk familiarly. **3** [1950s] to trick verbally, to 'con', to persuade. **4** [1950s+] (*also* **chat up**) in fig. use of (1), in non-sexual contexts. **5** [1970s+] to interview. **6** [1990s+] (*UK Black*) to sing rap lyrics. [fig. uses of SE; Williams gives 17C examples of SE *chat* used as a euph. for sexual intercourse, e.g. Pepys, *Diary*, 11 August 1663, '[The king] hath a chat now and then of Mrs. Stewart']

chat *v.*² [1910s–20s] to search for lice. [CHATS n.²]

chat-bags n. [1910s] (*Aus.*) underwear. [CHATS n.² + BAGS n.²; the infestation of lice during WW1]

chat-chat v. [1950s+] (*W.I.*) to gossip. [SE *chat* + redup.]

chat down v. [1950s+] (*W.I.*) to make one's first advances to a young woman or man in the hope of eventual sexual conquest. [var. on CHAT v.¹ (1)]

chateau cardboard n. [1980s+] (*Aus./S.Afr.*) wine sold in 2.5- or 5-litre (4½-/9-pint) containers, placed in a cardboard box. [play on Fr. *chateau*; the labels on bottles of Bordeaux wine always indicate the *chateau* at which they are produced]

chateaued adj. [1980s+] (*UK society*) very drunk on wine (cf. ALED UP adj.). [puns on SE *shattered* and Fr. *chateau*]

chates n.¹ see CHATS n.¹.

chates n.² see CHEATS n.².

chatham and dover v. [1900s] to stop, to cease. [rhy. sl. = SE *give over*]

chat 'n' chew n. [1940s–60s] (*orig. US Black*) a restaurant, a café.

chats n.¹ (*also* **chates**, **chatts**) [mid-16C–mid-19C] (*UK Und.*) the gallows. [CHEAT n.]

chats n.² (*also* **chatts**, **chits**) [late 17C+] (*orig. UK Und.*) lice; occas. in sing. [SE *chattels*, moveable property, typically livestock, 'lice being the chief livestock of beggars, gypsies, and the rest of the canting crew' (Grose, 1785); 20C+ use mainly Aus.]

chats n.³ [1960s] excessive verbosity, caused by nerves, fear, shock etc.

chat someone's name v. [1950s+] (*W.I., Jam.*) to gossip maliciously about an absent third party. [CHAT v.¹ (2)]

chatta n. [late 19C] an umbrella. [Skrt *chhatra*, an umbrella]

chatter-basket n. (*also* **chatter-bags**, **chatter-bladder**, **chatter-bones**, **chatter-cart**) [late 18C–1910s] a small, noisy child.

chatterbox n. **1** [mid-19C] (*US*) the mouth. **2** [1930s–40s] a record player. **3** [1940s] a telephone. **4** [1940s] a car radio; thus *chatterbox and fish pole*, a radio and aerial. **5** [1940s–50s] a machine gun. **6** [1950s] (*US Und.*) a typewriter. **7** [1960s] a walkie-talkie. [despite Grose (1785) and *Lex. Bal.*, *chatterbox*, a habitual chatterer is SE: a 'contemptuous or playful name' (*OED*)]

chatter-broth n. [late 18C–early 19C] tea. [the stereotypical chattering women supposed to gather around the tea-table]

chatter-cart n. see CHATTER-BASKET n.

chatterer n. (*also* **chattering**) [early 19C] a blow to the mouth that makes the recipient's teeth chatter. [fig. use of SE and pun on *shattering*]

chatterers n. [19C] the teeth.

chattergun n. [1930s+] a machinegun or sub-machinegun. [its noise]

chattering n. see CHATTERER n.

chattering box n. [early 18C] a pulpit.

chattermag n. **1** [mid-late 19C] a gossip, a chatterbox. **2** [late 19C] chatter, gossip. [SE *chatter* + MAG n.² (1)]

chattermag v. [1900s] to chatter. [CHATTERMAG n.]

chattery n. [early 19C] (*UK Und.*) one or more linen articles. [? CHATS n.², as they are easily infested by lice]

chattey adj. see CHATTY adj.

chattry-feeder n. (*also* **chatty-feeder**) [mid-19C] (*UK prison*) a spoon. [? it *feeds* that which *chatters*, i.e. the mouth]

chatts see also under CHATS.

chatts n. [mid-19C] dice. [they 'chatter' as they hit the table]

chatty n.¹ [mid-18C–1950s] a pot. [Tamil *shatti*, Telegu *chatti*, a pot; orig. Anglo-Ind. but spread across the British Empire]

chatty n.² [19C] a filthy man. [CHATTY adj.]

chatty adj. (*also* **chattey**) [mid-18C–1940s] lousy, infested; thus *chatty doss*, a louse-infested bed; *chatty dosser*, a louse-ridden tramp. [CHATS n.²]

chatty-chatty n. [1950s+] (*W.I.*) a habitual gossip. [SE *chatty*, talkative + redup.]

chatty-feeder n. see CHATTRY-FEEDER n.

chat-up n.¹ [1910s–20s] a search for lice. [CHAT v.²]

chat-up n.² [1960s+] the first, verbal stages of seduction; thus *chat-up line*, the words used. [CHAT v.¹ (1)]

chat up v. see CHAT v.¹.

chauki n. see CHOKEY n.

chauncy adj. [2000s] (*US Black*) unattractive. [ety. unknown]

chaunt see also under CHANT and its combs.

chaunter cove n. [mid-late 19C] a journalist, a reporter. [CHANT v. (3) + COVE n. (1)]

chaunter cull n. (*also* **chanter-cull**) [late 18C–19C] (*UK Und.*) a composer of ballads, broadsides and similar productions for the use of street singers and versifiers. [CHANTER n. (1) + CULL n.¹ (4)]

chaunter upon the leer n. [late 18C–19C] an advertiser. [CHAUNT UPON THE LEER v.]

chaunt-fencer n. [mid-19C] a seller of sheet music and ballad lyrics, 'last dying speeches' (on the gallows) and similar broadsides. [CHANT n. (5) + -FENCER sfx]

chaunting-cove n. [19C] a dishonest horse-dealer. [CHANT v. (4) +COVE n. (1)]

chaunting-lay n. [mid-late 19C] street-singing. [CHANT v. (1) + LAY n.⁴ (1)]

chaunt the play v. [mid-late 19C] (*UK Und.*) to explain the criminal lifestyle and methods. [fig. use of CHANT v. (1)]

chaunt upon the leer v. [late 18C] to advertise, to publicize, to write up in the press. [CHANT v. (3) + LEER n.]

chauver v. see CHARVER v. (1).

chauverer-cove n. (*also* **chauvering-cove**) [mid-19C] a womanizer, a promiscuous man. [CHARVER v. (1) + COVE n. (1)]

chauvering dona/doner/donna n. see CHARVERING DONNA n.

chauvering moll n. [mid-late 19C] a prostitute. [CHARVER v. (1) + MOLL n.¹ (2)]

chav n. [2000s] a vulgar, loud, working-class person; although not exclusively male there is a fem. var. *chavette*. [CHAVY n. (1); alternative suggested etys. include the town of *Chatham* in Kent, a home to such people, and the 1990s+ Northeast term *charver/charva*, a young, usu. male, version of the above]

chavala n. [1970s+] (*US*) **1** a woman. **2** a dismissive term for a man, suggesting that he is weak and effeminate. [Sp. *chava*, a girl]

chavy n. (*also* **chavey**, **chavvie**, **chavvy**) **1** [mid-19C+] (*Polari*) a child. **2** [late 19C+] a form of address to a man, e.g. *wotcher chavvy*. [Rom. *chavi*, a child]

chaw n.¹ **1** [mid-late 19C] a yokel. **2** [1910s–40s] (*US*) an Irish immigrant. **3** [1970s] (*US campus*) a handsome man. [? dial. *chaw*, chew, as in chewing tobacco]

chaw n.² **1** [mid-late 19C] (*US campus*) a trick, a prank. **2** [late 19C–1920s] a conversation. [fig. uses of dial. *chaw*, to chew]

chaw v. **1** [mid-late 19C] to kill. **2** [mid-19C–1900s] (*US campus*) to trick, to hoax. **3** [mid-19C–1920s] (*US*) (*also* **chaw up**) to mangle, to get the better of, to humiliate, to surpass, to destroy; thus CHAWED (UP) adj. **4** [late 19C–1900s] (*US*) used in oaths, e.g. *chaw me up if…* **5** [1980s] to arrest. [fig. uses of dial. *chaw*, to chew]

chaw-bacon n. [early 19C+] a rustic, a peasant; thus a fool; also attrib. (cf. ACORN-CRACKER n.). [SE *chew bacon*]

chawed (up) adj. [mid-19C–1960s] embarrassed, humiliated, defeated (cf. CHEWED adj.). [CHAW v. (3)]

chaw-mouth n. [late 19C+] (*US*) a talkative person; thus a derog. term for an Irishman (cf. BOG ARAB n.). [*chaw* = SE *chew* + *mouth*; the noisy talker 'chews on' his words; + the alleged talkativeness of the Irish]

chawry goods n. [1980s] stolen property. [CHAW v. (5)]

chaws n. [mid-19C] sexual intercourse. [? CHARVER v. or a var. on copulation/aggression link, thus dial. *chaw*, to chew]

chaw up v. see CHAW v. (3).

chay n. (*also* **chay-cart**, **shay**) [mid-18C–1910s] a chaise or light carriage. [pron. 'shay']

chazerai *n.* [20C+] **1** a 'pigsty', a mess. **2** junk, rubbish, nonsense. [Yid./Heb. *chazer*, a pig]

chazerai *adj.* [20C+] cheap, worthless, rubbishy. [CHAZERAI n. (2)]

chbye *phr.* [1980s+] (*US campus*) goodbye. [joc. mispron.]

C-head *n.* [1980s+] (*drugs*) a cocaine user. [C n.² (1) + -HEAD sfx (3)]

cheap *adj.* **1** [mid-19C–1920s] out of sorts, feeling ill. **2** [late 19C–1930s] (*US Black*) dishonest. **3** [late 19C+] mean, miserly, grasping. **4** [late 19C+] (*also* **cheapshit**) unpleasant, cruel. **5** [2000s] (*US campus*) embarrassed.

cheap and nasty *n.* [1930s] (*Aus.*) a meat pasty. [rhy. sl.]

cheap as dirt *adj.* (*also* **dirt-cheap**) [early 19C+] extremely cheap.

cheap-ass *adj.* [1960s+] (*US*) cheap, inferior, second-rate. [SE *cheap* + -ASS sfx]

cheap charlie *n.* **1** [late 19C–1900s] (*US*) a candy store. **2** [1960s] one who accepts the second-rate, either through poverty or lack of taste. **3** [1960s+] a mean person (cf. CHEAP JOHN n.²). [SE *cheap*/CHEAP adj. (3) + CHARLIE n.¹]

cheapie *n.* **1** [1930s+] anything, e.g. a film or play, produced on a low budget. **2** [1940s+] anything or anyone of little value or poor quality. **3** [1970s+] (*orig. US*) a mean person. [SE *cheap* + sfx -*ie*]

cheap john *n.¹* **1** [mid-19C+] (*US*) a pawnbroker. **2** [mid-19C+] (*US*) a pawnshop. **3** [mid-19C+] (*also* **cheap jack**, **cheap johnny**) a shop or person selling cheap goods. **4** [1960s] (*US*) a seedy brothel or bar. [SE *cheap* + JOHN n.¹ (1)/JACK n.²/JOHNNIE n.² (1)]

cheap john *n.²* (*also* **short john**) [late 19C+] a mean, miserly person (cf. CHEAP CHARLIE n.). [CHEAP adj. (3)/SE *short* + JOHN n.¹ (1)]

cheap john *adj.* [late 19C–1900s] of goods, cheap, in poor taste. [CHEAP JOHN n.¹ (3)]

cheap john *v.* [mid–late 19C] to sell cheap goods. [CHEAP JOHN n.¹ (3)]

cheap johnny *n. see* CHEAP JOHN n.¹ (3).

cheapo *n.* **1** [1910s+] a mean person. **2** [1970s+] something that is produced cheaply. [SE *cheap* + -o sfx (2)]

cheapo *adj.* (*also* **cheapo-cheapo**) [1970s+] cheap, produced cheaply; thus often also of inferior quality. [SE *cheap* + -o sfx (3) (+ redup.)]

cheapshit *adj. see* CHEAP adj. (4).

cheap shot *n.* [1960s+] (*US*) a wounding, sneering remark; thus *cheap-shot artist*, one who habitually makes such remarks. [SE *cheap*, in sense of (i) costing little effort, (ii) being vulgar, in poor taste + SHOT n.³ (1)]

cheap-shot *adj.* [1960s+] sneering, denigrating. [CHEAP SHOT n.]

cheap shotter *n.* [1970s+] (*US*) one who makes wounding, cruel remarks. [CHEAP SHOT n.]

cheapskate *n.* [late 19C+] (*orig. US*) **1** an unpleasant person. **2** (*also* **short skate**) a mean, ungenerous person. [SE *cheap*/*short* + SKATE n. (4); orig. 'cheap skate', later use is 1 word]

cheapskate *adj.* [20C+] **1** (*orig. US*) mean, stingy. **2** second-rate. [CHEAPSKATE n.]

cheap-trick *adj.* [1960s] pertaining to the poorer of a prostitute's clients. [SE *cheap* + TRICK n.¹ (3)]

cheapwad *n.* [1970s+] (*US*) a mean, ungenerous person. [SE *cheap* + -WAD sfx]

cheat *n.* (*also* **chete**) **1** [mid-16C–mid-18C] a thing, usu. in combs. (cf. BAA CHEAT n.; BACK-CHEAT n.; BELLY CHEAT n.; BLEATING CHEAT n.; BOUNCING CHEAT n.; CACKLING-CHEAT n.; FAMBLING-CHEAT n.; GRUNTING-CHEAT n.; HANGING CHEAT n.; LOWING CHEAT n.; LULLABY-CHEAT n.; MUFFLING-CHEAT n.; MUZZLING CHEAT n.; NABBING CHEAT n.; NAB CHEAT n.; NUBBING CHEAT n.; PRATING-CHEAT n.; PRATTLING-CHEAT n.; QUACKING CHEAT n.; QUAKING CHEAT n.; SMELLING-CHEAT n.; TOPPING CHEAT n.; TRUNDLING-

CHEAT n.; WHIDDING CHEAT n.). **2** [mid-16C–mid-18C] a stolen thing. **3** [17C–mid-18C] (*also* **cheats**) the gallows (cf. CHATS n.¹). [AS *chete*, a thing; (3) note Lawson (1907) describing the gallows at Darlinghurst Goal: 'Prisoners have walked under, and even glanced up at, it […] without ever guessing, or thinking to guess, what the Thing was']

cheater *n.¹* **1** [1910s+] an adulterer. **2** [1920s] (*US*) an act of adultery. **3** [1940s] a condom. **4** [1940s+] anything that makes a task simpler, provides safety, gives one advantage etc. [fig. uses of SE]

cheater *n.² see* CHEATOR n.

cheaters *n.¹* **1** [mid-16C–early 17C; 1930s] crooked dice. **2** [1930s+] (*US tramp*) marked cards.

cheaters *n.²* (*also* **cheeters**) **1** [20C+] (*orig. US*) (*also* **eye cheaters**) glasses, spectacles, esp. dark glasses; thus *smoke cheaters*, dark glasses. **2** [1910s–70s] close-fitting men's underpants, usu. with elastic legbands. **3** [1940s+] pads which are placed in a brassiere to suggest a fuller breast. **4** [1950s+] (*orig. US*) false teeth. [they help the eyes/genitals/breasts/teeth *cheat* their own inadequacies]

cheating law *n.* [mid-16C–early 17C] (*UK Und.*) crooked dice play or card-sharping. [SE *cheating* + LAW n.¹]

cheating-stick *n. see* CHEAT-STICK n.

cheat (on) *v.* [1920s+] (*orig. US*) to betray one's partner or spouse; thus to commit adultery.

cheator *n.* (*also* **cheater**) [mid-16C–mid-17C] (*UK Und.*) one who plays with crooked dice. [SE *cheat*]

cheats *n.¹* [late 16C–early 17C] money won by dice cheats.

cheats *n.²* (*also* **chates**) **1** [late 17C] an ostentatious, fur-backed waistcoat. **2** [late 17C–early 19C] sham sleeves, cuffs or wristbands, used to mask an otherwise dirty shirt.

cheats *n.³ see* CHEAT n. (3).

cheat sheet *n.* [1950s+] (*US campus*) notes smuggled into an examination.

cheat-stick *n.* (*also* **cheating-stick**) [1930s–50s] (*US campus*) a slide-rule.

cheat the starter *v. see* BEAT THE STARTER v.

cheat the worms *v.* [mid–late 19C] to recover from a serious illness. [the worms are those encountered in the grave]

cheba *n. see* CHIBA n.² (1).

chebs *n.* [1990s+] the female breasts. [CHABOBS n.]

checaco/chechaco *n. see* CHEECHAKO n.

che-che *n.* (*also* **chi-chi**) [20C+] (*W.I.*) **1** a poor White person (cf. CHEE-CHEE n.). **2** a person with a light complexion and freckles. **3** a cowardly, ugly boy. [clipping of FRENCHIE n.¹ (5) or RED CHENKE n.]

check *n.¹* (*US*) **1** [mid-19C–1910s] money, cash. **2** [1920s–60s] $1. [SE *check*, a counter]

check *n.²* (*US drugs*) **1** [1920s–70s] a measure of a drug, usu. 1oz (28g) in a folded packet. **2** [1980s+] one's personal supply of drugs. [SAmE *check*, a token, a ticket]

check *v.¹* **1** [1920s+] (*orig. US*) to look over, to inspect. **2** [1970s+] (*orig. US Black*) to visit, to call in on someone. **3** [1970s+] (*orig. US*) to criticize, to attack verbally. **4** [1990s+] (*orig. US*) to assess, to envisage. **5** [1990s+] (*US prison*) to fight.

check *v.²* (*also* **check to**) **1** [1960s+] (*orig. US*) to meet, to chat with; esp. in phr. CHECK YOU (LATER) phr. **2** [1970s+] (*W.I./UK Black teen*) to strike up or to have a (usu. sexual) relationship with someone; thus *checking*, having a relationship.

check! *excl.* [1920s+] (*orig. US*) a general excl. of affirmation, OK, that's right, everything's in order. [SAmE *check*, to tick a box]

check a trap *v.* (*also* **check one's trap**) [1990s+] (*US Black*) **1** to monitor a given situation, to oversee one's business, esp. when it is illicit. **2** to spend time with a lover, esp. one with whom one is having an affair. [play on SE *check one's trap*, but note CHECK v.¹ (1)/CHECK v.² (2)]

check 'em *phr.* [2000s] (*US Black*) to apologise for or acknowledge a foolish remark or action. [CHECK ONESELF v. + 'them' is one's testicles]

checker, the n. [mid-19C–1910s] (US) the ideal, the very thing. [that which *checks* everything else]

checkerboard n. (US) **1** [1920s+] a work crew or work gang composed of Black and White people. **2** [1960s] a place or neighbourhood where both Black and White people live or congregate.

check for v. [1990s+] (W.I./UK Black teen) **1** to hate or dislike someone or something, to avoid, to resist becoming involved with. **2** to like, to be involved with. [CHECK v.² (2)]

check in v. **1** [20C+] (US) (*also* **cheque in**) check in to die. **2** [1960s] (US) (*also* **check it in**) to go to bed. **3** [1970s+] (US) to say hello. **4** [1990s+] (UK/US Und.) to move from the general prison population into protective solitary confinement. [SE *check in*, to register (i.e. at a hotel)]

check it in phr. [1990s+] (US Black) an imper. used by a mugger to his or her victim, when demanding that they hand over money, valuables etc. [SE *check in*, the idea of checking possessions into a left-luggage locker]

check it out v. [1980s+] (US campus) to look for a partner for romance or sex. [CHECK OUT v.² (1)]

check it to v. [1930s+] (US) to say goodbye. [CHECK v.² (1)]

check off v. [2000s+] (US prison) to request protective custody. [CHECK IN v. (4)]

check oneself v. [1960s+] (US) to compose oneself, to 'get a grip'; usu. as excl. *check yourself!* (cf. CHECK 'EM phr.). [SE *check*, to stop]

check one's hat v. *see* GET ONE'S HAT v.

check one's nerves v. [1940s] (US Black) to take a grip on oneself, to control one's emotions. [SE *check*, to stop + *nerves*]

check one's trap v. *see* CHECK A TRAP v.

checkout n.¹ [1950s+] (orig. US) an interrogatory or investigatory glance. [CHECK OUT v.² (1)]

checkout n.² [1990s+] (US prison) an inmate who kills themself while in prison. [CHECK OUT v.¹ (3)]

check out v.¹ **1** [1920s+] (orig. US) to die. **2** [1920s+] (orig. US) to leave. **3** [1970s] to kill. [SE *check out*, to sign out of a hotel, office etc]

check out v.² **1** [1950s+] (orig. US) to look over, to sum up; esp. as excl. *check this out!* **2** [1950s+] (orig. US) to work out, to fit in. **3** [1970s] (W.I.) for a young man, to date a woman regularly and/or visit her home. **4** [1970s+] to visit, to call in on someone. **5** [1980s] to believe, to accept. **6** [1980s+] to take note of. [ext. of CHECK v.¹]

check, please phr. [1970s] (US Black) a phr. indicating the conclusion of a meeting. [SAmE *check*, a bill]

checks! excl. [1960s+] (US, mainly juv.) a claim, esp. a claim of first rights to something.

check someone's chin v. [1990s+] (US Black teen) to hit on the jaw; such a blow is a CHIN CHECK n. [CHECK v.¹ (5)]

check someone's oil v. **1** [1930s+] (US) to have sexual intercourse. **2** [1990s+] to masturbate someone. [euph. but note OIL n.¹]

check the war! excl. [1940s] (US Black) stop fighting! [SE *check*, to stop, to cease + *war*]

check to v. *see* CHECK v.².

check up on v. [1930s+] to eye in a sexual manner.

check you (later) phr. [1970s+] (orig. US Black/campus) goodbye, see you later. [CHECK v.² (1)]

check you on the flip side phr. (*also* **check you on the flip flop**) [1970s] (US campus) goodbye. [CHECK v.² (1)]

check yourself! excl. *see* CHECK ONESELF v.

cheddar n.¹ [1990s+] (US campus) someone who is socially unacceptable, who does not fit in. [CHEESY adj.² (5)]

cheddar n.² [1990s+] (US) money. [CHEESE n.¹]

cheder n. [1970s] (UK Und.) a prison cell. [Yid. *cheder*, a small room, a study; usu. used as a schoolroom for the teaching of religion]

cheeb n. [1990s+] (US drugs) marijuana. [abbr. CHIBA n.² (1)]

cheeba n. *see* CHIBA n.² (1).

cheechako n. (*also* **checaco, chechaco, cheechaker, cheechalko**) [late 19C–1960s] a newcomer, a novice, esp. a newly arrived immigrant in the mining districts of northwest North America. [Chinook jargon *chee*, new + *chako*, to come; thus 'newcomer']

chee-chee n. (*also* **chi-chi**) [mid-19C+] a derog. term for a half-caste or Eurasian (the child of an English father and Indian mother) (cf. CHE-CHE n.). [? south Indian excl. *chi!*, fie! nonsense! or ? onomat. representation of the accent. Y&B note, however: 'there are many well-educated East Indians who are quite free from this mincing accent'. Ironically, the accent appears to have been that expressly taught at the convents and Christian Brothers' schools set up by the Raj to educate the children of such unions. Note Du. *lip-lap*, the equivalent term for Dutch-Javans]

chee-chee adj. (*also* **chi-chi, shee-shee**) [mid-19C–1960s] having the characteristics of the Eurasian stereotype, esp. the supposed mincing accent; thus pretentious, affected or smart, stylish. [CHEE-CHEE n.]

cheek n.¹ [mid-19C] a share, a portion.

cheek n.² [mid-19C+] **1** verbal insolence. **2** audacity, impudence; esp. in phr. *have the cheek (to)*, to dare, to have the nerve (to do something). [the movement of the *cheeks* when speaking]

cheek v.¹ [mid-19C+] to address in an impudent or insolent manner. [CHEEK n.² (1)]

cheek v.² [1990s+] (drugs) to smuggle or hide drugs by placing them in the rectum or mouth. [SE *cheek*, either of the face, or synon. with buttocks]

cheekiness n. [mid-19C+] audacity, effrontery, impudence. [CHEEK n.²]

cheekish adj. [mid-19C] impudent. [CHEEK n.²]

cheek it (out) v. [mid–late 19C] to face down, to brazen out. [CHEEK v.¹]

cheeks n.¹ [mid-17C+] the posterior, the buttocks. [the OED cites a one-off use in 1660, but the term is then lost (at least from print) until Bee in 1823 and resurfaces again only in James Joyce's *Ulysses* (1922)]

cheeks n.² [mid-19C] an imaginary person; thus CHEEKS! excl. [note synon. 19C naut. jargon *Cheeks the Marine*; ult. CHEEKS n.¹]

cheeks! excl. [mid–late 19C] a coarse and insulting retort to a question. [CHEEKS n.², i.e. ASK MY ARSE! excl.]

cheeks and ears n. [early 17C] a form of head-dress, briefly in fashion. [? it covered them all]

cheeky adj. [mid-19C+] impudent, esp. in the context of a younger person failing to respect their elder. [CHEEK n.² (2)]

cheeky-arsed adj. [20C+] rude, impudent. [CHEEKY adj. + -ASSED sfx]

cheeky chappie/chappy n. *see* CHAPPIE n. (3).

cheeky possum n. [1930s+] (Aus.) an impudent (young) person. [CHEEKY adj. + POSSUM n. (3)]

cheena n. [1990s+] (US teen) a woman. [coined by Anthony Burgess in *A Clockwork Orange* (1962); ult. Rus. *zhenshina*, a woman]

cheeo n. [1970s+] (drugs) marijuana seeds, which are chewed. [SE *chew*]

cheep n. [late 19C+] a sound, a noise, esp. of complaint; usu. in phr. *not a cheep out of*, not a sound from. [SE *cheep*, a faint, shrill sound, esp. of a young bird]

cheep v. [1900s–20s] to complain, to inform on. [CHEEP n.]

cheer-chaser n. *see* CHASE CHEERS v.

cheerer n. [19C] a revivifying glass of alcohol. [late 18C Scot. use]

cheerful earful n. [1940s+] (US) unpleasant news. [ironic]

cheerful giver n. [20C+] the human liver. [rhy. sl.]

cheeri *phr.* [1930s+] (*N.Z.*) goodbye. [CHEERIO phr.]

cheeribye *phr.* (*also* **cheerybye, cheery-pip**) [1930s+] goodbye. [CHEERIO phr.]

cheerio *n.* [1950s+] (*N.Z.*) a small sausage, like a frankfurter. [? *cheers*, a toast. These sausages are the sort that would be served as a snack with drinks]

cheerio *adj.* **1** [1910s–30s] cheerful, merry. **2** [1930s+] (*S.Afr.*) tipsy, slightly drunk. [CHEERS! excl. (1), the toast that precedes that drunkenness]

cheerio *phr.* [1910s+] **1** goodbye. **2** a popular toast before drinking. **3** hello. [? link to Ital. *ciao*, goodbye or CHEERS! excl. + -O sfx (7)]

cheerioski *phr.* [1920s–30s] goodbye. [CHEERIO phr. (1) + -SKI sfx]

cheers! *excl.* **1** [1910s+] one of the most common toasts before drinking. **2** [1910s+] thank-you. **3** [1920s+] an excl. of approval. **4** [1940s+] goodbye. [(4) ? link to Ital. *ciao*, goodbye]

cheery *adj.* **1** [17C] excellent, first-rate. **2** [18C+] drunk (cf. ABOUT RIGHT phr.[1]).

cheerybye/cheery-pip *phr. see* CHEERIBYE phr.

cheese *n.*[1] [mid-19C+] (*US teen*) money. [? the yellow colour or ? play on BREAD n.[1] (2) although this predates it]

cheese *n.*[2] **1** [mid-19C+] the smegma that accumulates around the uncircumcised penis or, occas., the unwashed labia. **2** [1920s+] (*US*) (*also* **body cheese**) secretions found between the toes. [resemblance and smell of over-ripe cheese]

cheese *n.*[3] [late 19C–1910s] (*US*) one's affair, one's concern. [ety. unknown]

cheese *n.*[4] **1** [late 19C+] an unpleasant, incompetent, stupid person; usu. ext. as *big cheese, old cheese, piece of cheese, plate of cheese, poor cheese* etc. **2** [late 19C+] as (1) but used joc./ affectionately. **3** [1900s] (*US*) a fool (cf. APPLEHEAD n.). **4** [1950s] (*US*) nonsense; thus phr. *no cheese*, no bad thing, something 'not to be sniffed at'. **5** [1980s+] (*US campus*) something out of date. **6** [1980s+] (*US campus*) someone or something unattractive, unappealing, undesirable. [CHEESY adj.[2]]

cheese *n.*[5] **1** [1910s+] (*Aus.*) one's girlfriend or wife. **2** [1950s–70s] (*US campus*) a young woman; thus *check the cheese*, watch women pass by. **3** [1960s+] an attractive young man or woman. [CHEESE AND KISSES n.; (2) + CHECK v.[1] (1)]

cheese *n.*[6] [1960s] a smile. [CHEESE v.[3]]

cheese *n.*[7] [1970s] (*US*) a light-skinned Black person. [the yellowish colour of many cheeses]

cheese *n.*[8] [1990s+] (*drugs*) crack cocaine (cf. BASE n.). [? the colour]

cheese *n.*[9] *see* CHEESEBOX n. (2).

cheese, the *n.* **1** [early 19C–1960s] (*also* **the real cheese**) the best (of a given type or style), the superlative (cf. CHESHIRE, THE n.; STILTON, THE n.). **2** [mid-19C–1920s] just what is wanted. **3** [late 19C–1920s] an admirable person; esp. as *the real cheese*. **4** [20C+] an important or influential person, the boss. [Persian and Urdu *chiz*, thing. 'The expression used to be common among Anglo-Indians, e.g. "My new Arab is the real *chiz*", i.e. the real thing' (Y&B). Note Charles Kingsley's punning nonce-word *casein*, the real thing, f. SE *casein*, the basic ingredient of cheese]

cheese *adj. see* CHEESY adj.[3].

cheese *v.*[1] **1** [early 19C–1960s] (*also* **cheese it**) to stop, to leave off; thus CHEESE IT! excl. **2** [early 19C; 1980s] (*US campus*) to go, to wander in a casual manner. **3** [late 19C] (*US*) to disregard, to ignore. **4** [2000s] (*US Black*) to treat badly. [? SE *cease* or f. pvb 'after cheese (at the end of a meal) comes nothing']

cheese *v.*[2] [late 19C] (*US*) to pilfer. [ety. unknown]

cheese *v.*[3] [1930s+] (*orig. UK public school*) to smile. [the photographer's demand that one 'say "cheese"' to produce a smile]

cheese *v.*[4] **1** [1940s+] to break wind. **2** [1950s+] to ejaculate. **3** [1980s+] (*US campus*) to vomit. [(1) the smell; (2) and (3) ext. uses of (1)]

cheese *v.*[5] [1970s] (*US*) to play up to, to toady to. [CHEESE-EATER n. (1)]

cheese! *excl.* [1900s–50s] (*US*) a euph. for JESUS! excl.

cheese and bread! *excl. see* CHEESE ON! excl.[1].

cheese and crackers *n.* [1990s+] the testicles (cf. CHRISTMAS CRACKERS n.; COBBLERS n.; COFFEE STALLS n.; CREAM CRACKERS n.; FUN AND FROLICS n.; GENERAL SMUTS n.; HAW MAWS n.; HENRY HALLS n.; JACKSON POLLOCKS n.; KEN DODDS n.; MARACAS n.[2]; MARBLE HALLS n.; MAX WALLS n.; NIAGARA FALLS n.; NICK BUTTS n.; NOBBY HALLS n.; NUTCRACKERS n.[3]; ORCHESTRA n.; SALADA CRACKERS n.; TOM DOOLIES n.; TOMMY ROLLOCKS n.; TOWNS n.; WENTWORTH FALLS n.). [rhy. sl. = KNACKERS n.]

cheese and crackers! *excl.* [1940s+] (*US*) a euph. for JESUS (CHRIST)! excl.

cheese and crust! *excl.* [mid-19C–1920s] a euph. for JESUS (CHRIST)! excl. [pron.]

cheese and kisses *n.* [20C+] one's wife. [rhy. sl. =SE *Missus*. Now mainly Aus. and usu. abbr. to CHEESE n.[5] (1)]

cheeseball *n.* [1990s+] (*US campus*) someone or something unattractive, unappealing, undesirable or not attuned to group standards. [SE *cheeseball*, a recipe/product made from cheese; ult. CHEESY adj.[2] (5) + -BALL sfx]

cheesebox *n.* **1** [1930s–50s] (*US*) a run-down, dilapidated vehicle. **2** [1980s] (*US campus*) a computer; thus *cheese*, software. **3** [1990s+] the head, the mind. [supposed resemblance]

cheesecake *n.*[1] **1** [mid–late 17C] a prostitute. **2** [1930s+] (*orig. US*) pin-up pictures; thus *cheese-caker*, a photographer who specializes in pin-up shots. **3** [1930s+] (*orig. US*) a pin-up girl, a sexy woman. [? the photographer's call for the woman to 'say "cheese"' (cf. CHEESE v.[3]) or f. common equation of foods with attractive women]

cheesecake *n.*[2] [2000s] (*US Black*) a White homosexual. [the colour but why homosexual?]

cheese-cutter *n.* **1** [mid-19C] an aquiline nose. **2** [late 19C+] a large, square peak on a cap; thus a flat cloth cap. **3** [1960s] the penis. [resemblance to a cheese knife]

cheese-cutters *n.* [mid-19C] bandy legs.

cheesed *adj. see* CHEESED (OFF) adj.

cheese dagger *n.* (*also* **cheese scraper, cheese slicer**) [1900s–60s] (*US*) a knife. [note US milit. use *cheese-knife*, a sword]

cheesedick *n.* [1980s+] (*US*) an obnoxious person (cf. CHEESE DONG n.). [CHEESE n.[4] (1)/CHEESE n.[2] (1) + DICK n.[4] (1)/DICK n.[4] (6)]

cheesed (off) *adj.* (*also* **cheesed**) [1940s+] miserable, annoyed, fed up. [? euph. for PISSED OFF adj.; earlier Liverpool excl. *cheese off!*, go away! stop irritating me!]

cheese dong *n.* [1980s+] (*US campus*) a stupid, unpleasant person (cf. CHEESEDICK n.). [CHEESE n.[4] (1)/CHEESE n.[2] (1) + DONG n.[1]]

cheese-eater *n.* **1** [late 19C+] (*US*) a toady, a sycophant. **2** [1950s+] (*US*) an informer. **3** [2000s] (*US Black*) a subservient Black person who courts White affection. [equation of *cheese* with RAT n.[2]; note Urquhart, *The Complete Works of Rabelais* (1653): 'He chargeth the defendant, that he was a botcher, cheese-eater, and trimmer of man's flesh embalmed', where the term is a general derog.]

cheese grater *n.* [1990s+] a waiter. [rhy. sl.]

cheesehead *n.* **1** [1910s+] (*US*) an idiot, a fool; also attrib. (cf. APPLEHEAD n.). **2** [1960s+] (*US teen*) a general pej. term, esp. directed at an overly emotional or dramatic person.

cheese it *v. see* CHEESE v.[1] (1).

cheese it! *excl.* **1** [early 19C+] (*also* **cheese on!**) stop it! **2** [early 19C+] be quiet! **3** [mid-19C] (*UK Und.*) be off! run away! [CHEESE v.[1] (1)]

cheeseman *n.* (*US campus*) **1** [1970s] a womanizer. **2** [1980s+] a socially inept person. [(1) CHEESE n.[5] (3); (2) CHEESE n.[4] (6)]

cheese off *v.*[1] [1950s+] to annoy. [backform. f. CHEESED (OFF) adj.]

cheese off v.² [1980s+] (*US campus*) to beg from. [to get cheese off someone]

cheese on! excl.¹ (*also* **cheese and bread! cheese on bread!**) [20C+] (*W.I., Bdos*) a euph. for JESUS (CHRIST)! excl. (cf. CHEESE AND CRUST! excl.).

cheese on! excl.² see CHEESE IT! excl. (1).

cheeser n.¹ **1** [19C] a burp. **2** [early 19C] a strong-smelling fart. **3** [late 19C] a chestnut. **4** [1960s–70s] a person who has smelly feet. [all supposedly smell like ripe cheese]

cheeser n.² **1** [1970s] (*US gang*) a traitor. **2** [1990s+] (*US campus*) one who is not attuned to the prevailing group standards. **3** [1990s+] one who is constantly asking to borrow things, usu. without having much to offer in return. [CHEESE n.⁴ (1)/CHEESE n.⁴ (6)]

cheese ridge n. [1990s+] the part of the penis between the glans and the shaft. [CHEESE n.² (1) + SE *ridge*]

cheeses, the n. [1940s] the 'utility' mark, made of 2 capital Cs, meaning 'civilian clothing' plus the date of manufacture. [initial letter + resemblance to wedges of cheese]

cheese scraper/slicer n. see CHEESE DAGGER n.

cheese-toaster n. **1** [late 18C–1910s] a sword. **2** [1910s] a bayonet. [in an era before grills, one skewered the lump of cheese and held it to the fire]

cheese tube n. [1990s+] the urethra. [CHEESE n.² (1)]

cheese whiz n. (*also* **cheez whiz**) [1980s+] (*US campus*) **1** someone who mistakenly thinks that they are impressive. **2** something out of date. [CHEESE n.⁴ (6)/CHEESE n.⁴ (5) + pun on the name of a proprietary US cheese spread]

cheesy adj.¹ (*also* **cheezy**) [mid-19C] fine or showy. [CHEESE, THE n. (1)]

cheesy adj.² (*also* **cheezy**) **1** [mid-19C+] outdated, unfashionable, cheap and nasty. **2** [late 19C+] unwell, peaky. **3** [late 19C+] smelly, esp. [1930s+] (*gay*) of a foreskin, smegma-coated. **4** [1950s] (*US teen*) disloyal. **5** [1970s+] socially unacceptable. [lit. or fig. smelling of ripe cheese]

cheesy adj.³ (*also* **cheese, cheezy**) [late 19C+] false, hypocritical. [the 'say "cheese"' ritual for the summoning up of instant false smiles for the camera]

cheesy head n. [1990s+] a penis that has not been cleansed of smegma. [CHEESE n.² (1) + HEAD n.⁷ (1)]

cheesy kiss n. [20C+] (*Aus.*) a miss, esp. a missed catch at cricket. [rhy. sl.]

cheesy quaver n. [2000s] **1** a favour. **2** a raver. [rhy. sl., ult. *Quavers*, a brand of cheesy snack]

cheesy rider n. **1** [1960s–70s] a sycophant. **2** [1990s+] (*US prison*) an informer. [pun on film title *Easy Rider* (1969) + spec. use of CHEESY adj.² (cf. CHEESE-EATER n.)]

cheesy, sleazy, greasy phr. [1980s+] (*US campus*) used of a woman seen as promiscuous. [CHEESY adj.² (5) + SLEAZY adj. (1) + SE *greasy*]

cheeters n. see CHEATERS n.².

cheever n. (*also* **cheeva**) [1990s+] (*drugs*) marijuana. [pron. of CHIVA n./CHIBA n.² (1)]

cheez whiz n. see CHEESE WHIZ n.

cheezy see under CHEESY.

chef n. **1** [1910s–60s] (*US drugs*) one who prepares the pipes in an opium den. **2** [1920s] (*US Und.*) one who runs a illicit still. **3** [1930s] (*US prison*) the executioner in charge of the electric chair. **4** [1940s] opium ashes, residue. **5** [1990s+] one who cooks crack cocaine.

chef v. [1910s–50s] (*US drugs*) to prepare opium for smoking. [CHEF n. (1)]

chefeneer n. [20C+] (*Irish*) a small cupboard-cum-sideboard, often used to hold one's best plates etc. [Fr. *chiffonier*, 'a piece of furniture with drawers in which women put away their needlework, cuttings of cloth, etc', Littré, *Dictionnaire* (1863–72)]

chello! excl. [1980s+] (*US campus*) a greeting. [joc. mispron. or ? link to Ital. *ciao*, hello/goodbye]

Chelsea bun n. [1990s+] **1** one's son. **2** the sun. [rhy. sl.; ult. the cake]

Chelsea College to a sentry-box phr. (*also* **Chelsea Hospital to a sentry-box**) [19C] the longest possible odds (cf. ALL THE WORLD TO A CHINA ORANGE phr.). [*Chelsea College*, the second London Polytechnic, was founded in 1891; it orig. contained the Chelsea Art School. *Chelsea Hospital* is the home for UK veterans and, as such, might have something to do with the proximity of the 'sentry-box' in this term]

Chelsea pier adj. see BRIGHTON PIER adj.

Chelsea smile n. [1970s+] a knife slash that runs from the corner of the mouth up and across the cheek (cf. GLASGOW KISS n.; GORBALS KISS n.). [such cuts are inflicted on rival supporters by knives wielded by the more violent section of the fans of *Chelsea* Football Club]

Cheltenham (gold) adj. [1950s+] cold. [rhy. sl.; ult. *Cheltenham Gold Cup*]

chemical n. **1** [1930s+] bad or adulterated narcotics. **2** [1950s+] any chemical drug, as opposed to marijuana etc; often in pl. **3** [1980s+] (*Aus. prison*) in pl., toiletries, shampoo etc. **4** [1980s+] (*drugs*) crack cocaine (cf. BASE n.). [their manufacture]

chemical head n. [1930s+] (*US Black*) hair that has been straightened through the application of a special mixture.

chemise-lifter n. **1** [1960s+] a male homosexual. **2** [1990s+] a lesbian (cf. SKIRT-LIFTER n.). [(1) ? a nonce-coinage by the Aus. writer and comedian Barry Humphries (b.1934), playing on the widely used synon. SHIRTLIFTER n.; (2) offers the 'female' *chemise* vs. the 'male' *shirt*]

chemisery n. [1980s+] (*US campus*) chemistry. [play on SE *misery*]

chemist n. [20C+] **1** one who runs an illicit distillery. **2** (*W.I.*) an abortionist.

chemist bill n. [mid-19C+] (*W.I.*) a deceitful, hypocritical person. [dial. *chemist's bill*, a 2-edged machete; ult. f. an apothecary's knife, which 'cuts on both sides']

chemistry n. [1990s+] (*US drugs*) the manufacture of drugs, e.g. LSD, crack cocaine, phencyclidine, with common household items and chemicals often stolen from the local hospital or pharmacy. [CHEMICAL n. (2)]

chemmed-up adv. [2000s] under the influence of drugs. [CHEMICAL n. (2)]

chemozzle n. see SHEMOZZLE n.

chepemans n. [16C] (*UK Und.*) Cheapside Market. [*Chepe*, Cheapside + -MANS sfx. Cheapside, ult. f. OE *ceap* or *chepe*, market, was medieval London's main market, flourishing until Henry III (r.1216–72) decided to diversify food-selling into other areas]

chepooka n. [1960s+] (*US teen*) nonsense. [coined by Anthony Burgess in *A Clockwork Orange* (1962); ult. Rus. *chyepookha*, nonsense]

cheque-book farmer n. [1920s+] (*S.Afr.*) a farmer who is not primarily dependent on agriculture for his income. [he pays the farm's expenses from other income, rather than from the produce of the farm itself]

cheque-busting n. (*also* **cheque-bursting**) [1910s–40s] (*Aus.*) going on a spending spree; thus *cheque-buster/burster*, one who does this. [SE *cheque*, the lump-sum payment given to a rural worker at the end of his season-long contract]

chequed up adj. [20C+] (*Aus.*) one who is well-supplied with money. [for ety. see CHEQUE-BUSTING n.]

cheque in v. see CHECK IN v. (1).

cheque-man n. [late 19C+] (*Aus.*) a spendthrift, one who spends his season's wages in a single glorious spree. [for ety. see CHEQUE-BUSTING n.]

cheque-proud adj. [late 19C–1910s] (*N.Z.*) recently paid, and keen to start spending. [for ety. see CHEQUE-BUSTING n.]

Chequer Inn (in Newgate Street), the *n. see* KING'S HEAD INN (IN NEWGATE STREET), THE n.

cher *adj.* [1960s] (*US campus*) attractive. [abbr. CHERRY adj. (8); ult. CHERRY adj. (1)]

cheri *n.* [mid-19C] a charming woman. [Madame Montigny, an actress at the Gymnase in Paris who appeared under the stage name of Rose *Cheri*. 'A singularly pure woman and an angelic actress. Used by upper-class gentlemen to describe their mistresses' (Ware)]

chermozzle *n. see* SHEMOZZLE n.

cherrie *n.* [1960s+] (*S.Afr.*) a woman, a girlfriend. [var. on CHERRY n.¹ (8)]

cherries *n.*¹ [20C+] (*US*) the female nipples. [resemblance]

cherries *n.*² [1950s–80s] greyhound racing tracks. [rhy. sl.; CHERRY HOG n. = DOGS, THE n.]

cherry *n.*¹ **1** [1920s+] (*orig. US*) a female virgin; thus BUST A CHERRY v.; *pluck a cherry*, to deflower. **2** [1920s+] (*gay*) an anal virgin; anal virginity. **3** [1920s+] a male virgin; thus *harvest the cherries*, to take a youth and deprive him of his virginity. **4** [1930s+] (*orig. US*) the hymen, i.e. one's virginity; thus LOSE ONE'S CHERRY v. **5** [1950s+] (*US*) an old car in near-mint condition. **6** [1950s+] (*orig. US milit.*) a novice, e.g. a fresh troop, one who has yet to be 'blooded' in combat, or a prisoner serving their first jail sentence. **7** [1960s–70s] in fig. use, the state of being without sex for some time. **8** [1960s+] (*S.Afr.*) a woman, a girlfriend. **9** [1990s+] the penis. [SE *cherry*, the image is of ripeness; Williams offers examples of *cherry* in sexual contexts, but none refers to virginity, instead they play on the supposed similarity of the black cherry and female pubic hair, or on cherry *stones* and STONE n.¹ (1)]

cherry *n.*² **1** [1930s+] a love bite, usu. on the neck. **2** [1940s+] (*US*) the still-glowing stub of a cigarette. **3** [1980s+] a blush. [resemblance]

cherry *n.*³ [1960s] an annoying individual. [ext. of CHERRY n.¹ (6)]

cherry *n.*⁴ [1960s+] (*US*) the red revolving light on top of a police car; thus CHERRY-TOP n.

cherry *adj.* **1** [1920s+] (*US*) virgin, virginal. **2** [1920s+] of people, in good health. **3** [1950s+] of goods etc, in mint condition, brand-new. **4** [1950s+] (*orig. milit.*) inexperienced, new, untested. **5** [1960s+] innocent, naïve. **6** [1960s+] devoid of any form of recording equipment. **7** [1970s] of a given experience or action, the very first, initiating; thus *cherry kicks*, the first injection after a former drugs user is freed from prison. **8** [1980s+] (*US campus*) very attractive. [CHERRY n.¹]

cherry *v.* [1980s+] to blush. [CHERRY n.² (3)]

cherry *adv.* [2000s] very. [joc. pron.]

cherry ace *n.* [1940s–60s] the face. [rhy. sl.]

cherry blossom kiss *n.* [1990s+] the act of performing oral sex on a woman during her menstrual period. [the colour of blood]

cherry-bomb muffler *n. see* MEXICAN MUFFLER n.

cherry-bounce *n.* **1** [late 17C–19C] cherry brandy. **2** [mid-18C] brandy mixed with sugar. [its effects]

cherry-boy *n.* [1970s+] (*US*) a male virgin. [CHERRY adj. (1)]

cherry-bust *n.* [1970s] (*US*) the act of losing one's virginity, applicable to both sexes. [CHERRY n.¹ (4)+ BUST v.¹ (7)]

cherry-buster *n.* [1950s+] (*US*) a (young) man who specializes in deflowering virgins. [CHERRY n.¹ (1) + BUST v.¹ (7)]

cherry-case *n.* [late 19C] (*Aus.*) a coffin. [made of cherry-wood, or stained a (black) cherry colour]

cherry-colour *adj.* [mid-19C] red or black. [the term is most used in a cheating trick with cards, in which the trickster bets an innocent victim that he can accurately predict the colour of the next card to appear. Since cherries are both red and black, as are cards, he cannot lose; *see* next]

cherry-coloured *adj.* [late 18C–19C] coloured black or red. [the usual assumption is red, but black cherries are equally common; thus a *cherry-coloured cat*, a black cat (Grose 1785); *see* prev.]

cherry farm *n.* [1960s–70s] (*US*) a prison that houses first-offenders. [CHERRY n.¹ (6) + SE *farm*, a prison]

cherry flips *n.* [1920s] the lips. [rhy. sl.]

cherryhead *n.* [2000s] (*US Black*) a male who pretends to a level of sophistication he does not have. [CHERRY n.¹ (6)]

cherry hog *n.* [20C+] a dog, usu. a greyhound. [rhy. sl. = DOGS, THE n.]

cherry Leb *n.* [1970s–80s] (*US drugs*) hashish oil (cf. BLACK OIL n.). [the black colour + LEB n.¹]

cherry-merry *n.* [mid-19C] a present of money. [? given when one is/or is rendering someone CHERRY-MERRY adj.]

cherry-merry *adj.* [late 18C] cheerful, merry, esp. after drinking. [? the *cherry-red* colour of wine + SE *merry*]

cherry-merry bamboo *n.* [mid-19C] (*Anglo-Ind.*) a beating. [ironic use of CHERRY-MERRY n., in this case as an unwanted gift + SE *bamboo* (*cane*)]

cherry-nose *n.* [1940s] (*S.Afr.*) sherry. [SE *sherry* + the effect of excess sherry consumption on the complexion]

cherry oggs *n.* [1920s+] greyhound racing. [rhy. sl. = DOGS, THE n.]

cherry out *v.* [1980s+] (*US*) to make as good as new. [CHERRY adj. (3)]

cherry-picker *n.*¹ [1920s–40s] a yokel, a peasant (cf. ACORN-CRACKER n.). [a typical rural occupation]

cherry-picker *n.*² [1930s] (*US*) a large, hooked nose. [such a nose is supposedly big enough to hang over a branch as a hook while one picks cherries from the tree]

cherry-picker *n.*³ [1960s] (*US*) a pointed shoe.

cherry-picker *n.*⁴ [1960s+] a seducer of virgins. [CHERRY n.¹ (1)]

cherry-picker *n.*⁵ [1970s+] £1 (cf. COW'S LICKER n.; FIDDLEY(-DID) n.; HOLE IN THE GROUND n.; JOHN DUNN n.¹; LOST AND FOUND n.; MERRY-GO-ROUND n.¹; PENCIL, OPEN, LOST AND FOUND n.; TEAPOT (LID) n.). [rhy. sl. = NICKER n.² (1)]

cherry pie *n.* **1** [late 19C+] a virgin. **2** [late 19C+] a woman. **3** [20C+] the vagina, esp. if the woman is menstruating (cf. APPLE n.⁶). [CHERRY n.¹ (1) + SE *pie*; (3) refers to the colour of blood]

cherry-pipe *n.* [late 19C] a woman. [rhy. sl. =CHERRY-RIPE n.²]

cherrypop *v.* [1950s+] (*orig. US*) to seduce and deflower virgins, usu. women. [POP A CHERRY v.]

cherry prick *n.* [20C+] a male virgin. [CHERRY adj. (1) + PRICK n. (2)]

cherry red *n.* [1990s+] the head. [rhy. sl.]

cherry reds *n.* [1960s+] Dr. Martens boots, as worn as part of the skinhead uniform (cf. DOCS n.). [the colour of a particular style]

cherry-ripe *n.*¹ **1** [late 18C–early 19C] a Bow Street Runner. **2** [mid-19C] a footman dressed in red plush. [their uniforms]

cherry-ripe *n.*² [mid–late 19C] (*UK Und.*) a woman. [SE *cherry* + SE *ripe*, the implication is of virginity, albeit temporary, although this predates CHERRY n.¹ (1)]

cherry-ripe *n.*³ **1** [mid-19C+] a pipe. **2** [20C+] nonsense. [rhy. sl.; (2) = TRIPE n.²]

cherry-splitter *n.* [19C–1960s] the penis (cf. ARSE-OPENER n.). [CHERRY n.¹ (4) + SE *splitter*]

cherry tart *n. see* RASPBERRY TART n.

cherry-top *n.* [1970s+] (*US*) **1** a police car with a red light on its roof. **2** a policeman. **3** the red light itself. [CHERRY n.⁴]

cherry tree *n.* [1980s+] a very tall virgin. [CHERRY n.¹ (1) + TREE n.²]

chershom *n. see* CHARRSHOM n.

cherubim *n.* **1** [late 18C] a whingeing child. **2** [mid-19C+] a choirboy. [joc. ref. to the line 'To Thee cherubim and seraphim continually do cry' in the *Te Deum*; a similar pun is seen in Ned Ward, *The London Spy* (1699), describing a prostitute as a 'cherubimical lass'; (2) adds the choirboy's supposedly angelic persona]

Cheshire, the *n.* [late 19C–1900s] the best, the ideal. [play on CHEESE, THE n. (1)]

chesky *n.* [20C+] (*US*) a derog. term for a Czech immigrant. [Czech *czezki*, pron. 'chesky']

chest *adj.* [1900s] of a person, puffed-up, self-satisfied; thus *get chest*, to look for a fight.

chester *n.* **1** [1940s] (*US Und.*) a second-rate criminal. **2** [1990s+] (*US campus*) a socially inept person. [? CHESTER (THE) MOLESTER n.]

Chester (the) Molester *n.* [1980s+] (*US campus/Und.*) a child abuser, a sex criminal.

chest flesh *n.* [1990s+] the female breasts.

chestily *adv.* (*also* **chesty**) [late 19C–1940s] arrogantly, in a conceited way. [CHESTY adj. (1)]

chestnut *n.* [late 19C+] (*orig. US*) **1** an old, much-repeated joke that has long-since lost any real humour. **2** any anecdote (not necessarily true) that is often repeated. **3** anything once popular, now hackneyed and unfashionable. **4** a scheme, a trick. [the term emerged *c.*1880 but appears to have originated in the play *Broken Sword* (1816) by W. Dimond. The relevant passage reads: 'Zavior: When suddenly from the thick boughs of a cork tree. / Pablo: (Jumping up.) A chestnut, Captain, a chestnut. Captain, this is the twenty-seventh time I have heard you relate this story, and you invariably said, a chestnut, till now']

chestnut *v.* [1900s] to come out with an oft-repeated anecdote, homily or joke. [CHESTNUT n.]

chestnuts *n.* [1950s–70s] the female breasts (cf. APPLES n.[1]). [pun on SE *chest* + *nuts*/NUTS n.[2] (1)]

chest-plaster *n.* [late 19C] a flat cravat that covers the shirt-front between the coat and the throat. [it 'bandages' the sometimes less than spotless shirt-front]

chest-pounder *n.* [1930s] (*US*) a Roman Catholic. [the ritual tapping of the chest that accompanies statements of *Mea culpa*]

chest puppy *n.* [1990s+] (*Aus.*) the female breast. [? 1960s description of film star Elizabeth Taylor (b.1932) as 'two small dogs fighting under a mink rug']

chesty *adj.* **1** [19C+] (*US*) arrogant, conceited. **2** [20C+] pugnacious, aggressive. **3** [1930s+] prone to suffer from infections of the chest. **4** [1950s+] of a woman, having prominent breasts; thus as term of address. [all SE *chest*; note US milit. hero 'Chesty' Pullar]

chesty *adv. see* CHESTILY adv.

chete *n. see* CHEAT n.

Chev *n. see* CHEVVY n.

chev *n. see* CHIV n.[1] (1).

chevalier Atkins *n.* [late 19C–1900s] a generic term for the typical private soldier in the British army. [SE *chevalier*, a Knight + TOMMY ATKINS n. (1)]

cheveaux *n. see* SHIVOO n.

chevie *n. see* CHEVY (CHASE) n.

chev man *n. see* CHIV ARTIST n.

Chevvy *n.* (*also* **Chev, Chevvie, Chevy**) [1920s+] (*orig. US*) a *Chevrolet* automobile. [abbr.]

chevy *n.*[1] [2000s] (*US Black*) a homosexual male. [? rhy. sl; CHEVVY n. = *Chevrolet* = gay]

chevy *n.*[2] *see* CHIV n.[1] (1).

chevy (chase) *n.* (*also* **chevie, chivvy chase**) [mid-19C+] the face. [rhy. sl., ult. the proper name *Chevy Chase*, the site of a celebrated 17C border skirmish and thus the subject and title of a popular ballad; the alleged origin in US actor *Chevy Chase* (b.1943) is invalid, although it may have contributed to the term's longevity]

chew *n.* **1** [mid-19C+] a quid of chewing tobacco. **2** [20C+] (*S.Afr.*) food. **3** [1910s] (*US*) talk, shouting.

chew *v.*[1] **1** [mid-19C+] (*orig. US*) to eat. **2** [late 19C+] (*US*) (*also*

chew one's yap) to talk. **3** [20C+] (*US*) to argue, to protest. **4** [1930s+] (*US*) to fellate (cf. BASKET LUNCH n.). **5** [1940s+] to perfom cunnilingus (cf. BOX LUNCH n.). **6** [1940s+] (*US Black*) to abuse, to attack verbally or physically. **7** [1990s+] (*US campus*) to be bad, to be disappointing.

chew *v.*[2] *see* CHEW (IT) OVER v.

chewallop *adv.* [mid-19C+] when falling or hitting, hard and suddenly, also as n., a fall or dive. [var. on KERWHALLOP v.]

chew ass *v. see* CHEW (SOMEONE'S) ASS v.

chew down *v.* [1930s–60s] (*US*) to cheat financially. [joc. use of SE + ref. to JEW (DOWN) v.]

chew dust *v. see* TAKE THE DUST v.

chewed *adj.* [1940s] (*US Black*) angry, annoyed, defeated (cf. CHAWED (UP) adj.). [CHEW v.[1] (6)]

chewed-up *adj.* **1** [mid-19C+] nervous, out of sorts. **2** [1920s+] suffering from a telling-off. [SE *chew*/CHEW v.[1] (6)]

chewers *n.* [1940s] (*US Black*) teeth, real or false.

chew face *v.* [1930s+] (*US campus*) to kiss. [note *Bulletin* (Sydney) 15 October 1887 12/1: 'In the absence of her parson-bestowed spouse she gradually evolved a partiality for chewing the radiant hasher's eyebrow, and developed an undue fondness for the encirclement of her waist by his humerus, ulna and radius']

chew fish *v. see* FISH v.[3].

chewie *n.* (*also* **chewy**) [1920s+] (*orig. Aus.*) *che*wing gum; thus *chewie on your boot*, a phr. used by barrackers at football matches in an attempt to put off a place-kicker by suggesting that he has chewing gum on his boot. [abbr.]

chewing *n.* (*also* **chewings**) (*US*) **1** [20C+] food. **2** [1960s+] a telling-off, a scolding. [SE *chew*/CHEW v.[1] (6)]

chewing gum *n.* [1920s] (*US*) empty, meaningless chatter. [CHEW v.[1] (2)]

chewing gums *n.* [1990s+] (*US teen*) very tight shorts, i.e. they have to 'stretch'.

chewing match *n.* [20C+] (*US*) an argument. [CHEW v.[1] (3)]

chewings *n. see* CHEWING n.

chew into dishcloths *v.* [late 19C–1900s] (*US*) to destroy completely, to annihilate.

chew (it) over *v.* (*also* **chew, chew on, chow over**) [mid-19C+] to discuss, to consider, to ponder.

chew nails *v.* [1970s] (*US campus*) to be enraged.

chew 'n' spew *n.* **1** [1960s–80s] (*Aus.*) a cheap restaurant. **2** [1980s–90s] (*Aus. prison*) any ready-cooked meal, e.g. hamburgers, fish and chips. **3** [1980s+] (*Aus. prison*) prison food. **4** [1980s+] (*Aus. prison*) prison officers.

chew on *v.*[1] [1960s+] (*US*) to nag, to pester.

chew on *v.*[2] *see* CHEW (IT) OVER v.

chew one's bit *v.* [20C+] (*US*) **1** to be anxious or upset. **2** to argue or talk loudly. [SE *champ at the bit*, (of horses) to be restive]

chew one's cabbage twice *v. see* BOIL ONE'S CABBAGE TWICE v.

chew one's cud *v. see* CHEW THE CUD v. (1).

chew one's own tobacco *v.* (*also* **chew one's own meat**) (*US*) **1** [mid-19C–1900s] to rely on oneself. **2** [1920s] to ponder an action or opinion before committing oneself.

chew one's tobacco twice *v.* [1920s] (*US*) to be mean, to be tight-fisted.

chew one's yap *v. see* CHEW v.[1] (2).

chew on someone's ass *v. see* CHEW (SOMEONE'S) ASS v.

chew on this! *excl.* (*also* **chew on it! ...that!**) [1930s+] an obscene retort. [the ref. is to the penis]

chew out *v.* [1920s+] (*orig. US*) to tell off, to harangue. [ext. of CHEW v.[1] (6)]

chew over *v.*[1] *see* CHEW (IT) OVER v.

chew over *v.*[2] *see* CHEW UP v. (1).

chew (someone's) ass *v.* (*also* **chew on someone's ass**) [1940s+] (*US, orig. milit.*) to tell off, to berate, to criticize severely. [SE *chew* + fig. use of ASS n. (2)]

chew someone's balls off *v.* (*also* **chew someone's**

ballocks/nackers off) [1920s+] to reprimand severely. [SE *chew* + BALLS n.[1] (1)/BALLOCKS n.[1] (1)/NACKERS n.]

chew someone's ear v. (*also* **chew someone's lug**) (*Aus.*) **1** [late 19C–1900s] to cadge, to beg. **2** [late 19C+] to talk intensely. **3** [late 19C+] (*also* **chew someone's ear off, ...ear out, ...nose off**) to nag, to talk tediously at someone. [SE *chew* + *ear*/LUG n.[1]]

chew the beef v. [1940s] (*US Und.*) to complain.

chew the boot v. [1940s–50s] (*US*) to converse, to talk something over.

chew the carpet v.[1] (*also* **eat the carpet**) [1950s+] (*US*) to lose emotional control, to suffer a temper tantrum (cf. CHEW THE RUG v.).

chew the carpet v.[2] *see* MUNCH THE CARPET v.

chew the cheese v. [1980s+] (*US campus*) to vomit.

chew the cud v. **1** [17C+] (*also* **chew one's cud**) to ponder, to think something over. **2** [mid-19C–1900s] to chew tobacco; thus *cud-chewer*, one who chews tobacco.

chew-the-fat n. [1910s] a garrulous person. [CHEW THE FAT v. (1)]

chew the fat v. **1** [late 19C+] to converse, to talk something over. **2** [1910s–30s] to complain; to be resentful. [rhy. sl. = *have a chat*; but cf. similar phrs. CHEW THE CUD v.; CHEW THE GREASE v.; CHEW THE RAG v.; CHEW THE RUG v.]

chew the grease v. [1910s–20s] to talk something over.

chew the Irish bubblegum v. [1980s] to chatter foolishly, to talk nonsense.

chew the rag v. [late 19C+] (*US*) **1** to gossip, to chatter. **2** to grumble, to complain. **3** to argue, to speak irresponsibly. [RAG n.[3]; orig. use held overtones of grumbling and complaining, but this vanished by the 1920s]

chew the rug v. **1** [late 19C+] to gossip, to chatter. **2** [1970s+] (*US*) to lose emotional control, to suffer a temper tantrum (cf. CHEW THE CARPET v.[1]).

chewtobaccy n. [mid-19C–1940s] (*US Black*) chewing tobacco. [note synon. Bahamas dial. *chewbaca*]

chew up v. (*US*) **1** [mid-19C+] (*also* **chew over**) to defeat, to overcome; ext. as [1940s+] *chew up and spit out*. **2** [1910s+] to scold harshly, to reprimand severely.

chew up old touches v. [1950s] (*US*) to reminisce. [SE *chew* + TOUCH n.[1] (5)]

chew-water n. [1940s+] (*W.I.*) thin, tasteless soup. [dial. *chew-water*, left-over cooking water, thrown out for the pigs]

chewy n.[1] [1990s+] (*US Black/drugs*) a cigar or marijuana-filled cigar, rolled with cocaine powder (rather than crack). [? one chews at it as one smokes]

chewy n.[2] *see* CHEWIE n.

Chi n. [late 19C+] (*US*) **1** Chicago. **2** attrib., as a nickname for a person. [abbr.]

chi n.[1] [1980s+] (*drugs*) heroin. [abbr. CHINESE H n. or CHINA WHITE n. (1)]

chi n.[2] *see* CHAI n.

chiack *see under* CHI-IKE.

chian n. *see* CHRISTACRUTCHIAN n.

chian adj. [1990s+] (*US*) insincere, hypocritcal. [CHRISTACRUTCHIAN n.]

chib n.[1] [late 19C] the face. [var. on CHIV n.[3]]

chib n.[2] [1930s+] a knife or razor. [CHIV n.[1] (1)]

chib v. *see* CHIV v. (3).

chiba n.[1] [1970s] (*US*) an informer. [? link to CHIVA n.]

chiba n.[2] (*also* **chiba-chiba**) (*drugs*) **1** [1970s+] (*also* **cheba, cheeba**) high-potency marijuana; spec. from Colombia but used of any powerful marijuana. **2** [1990s+] heroin. [CHIVA n.]

chibbing n. *see* CHIVVING n.

chibs n. [1970s] (*US/P.R.*) the buttocks. [var. on CHIPS n.[3]]

Chic n. [1900s] (*US Und.*) Chicago. [abbr.]

Chicago atomizer n. *see* CHICAGO TYPEWRITER n.

Chicago bankroll n. (*also* **Chicago roll**) [1960s+] (*US Black/gambling*) a show bankroll in which 1 large-denomination note is exhibited on the outside, concealing a quantity of small bills; thus *California roller*, one who carries such a 'bankroll' (cf. CALIFORNIA BANKROLL n.). [SE *bankroll*/ROLL n.[2]]

Chicago black n. (*also* **Chicago green**) [1970s+] (*US drugs*) varieties of marijuana, characterized by the colour, popular (and presumably grown) in and around Chicago (cf. ACAPULCO (GOLD) n.).

Chicago chicken n. [late 19C] (*US, Western*) salt pork or bacon. [the meat-packing industry of the city]

Chicago lightning n. [1920s–30s] (*US*) gunfire. [the city's reputation as a centre of gangland warfare]

Chicago mowing machine n. [1940s] (*US Und.*) a machine gun.

Chicago overcoat n. [1930s+] (*US*) a coffin; thus, fig., death, murder. [the practice of sealing corpses in cement prior to disposing of them at sea]

Chicago piano n. [1940s+] (*US*) a Thompson sub-machinegun, which achieved notoriety as the preferred weapon of Chicago gangsters in the 1920s and later. [note WW2 RN jargon *Chicago piano*, a multiple pom-pom]

Chicago pills n. [1940s] (*US Und.*) bullets. [play on SE *pill*/PILL n.[1] (3)]

Chicago roll n. *see* CHICAGO BANKROLL n.

Chicago typewriter n. (*also* **Chicago atomizer**) [1940s+] (*US*) a Thompson sub-machinegun.

chicalean adj. [1990s+] (*US campus*) excellent, stylish, worthy of admiration. [ety. unknown. ? SE *chic*]

chice n. (*also* **chice-am-a-trice, chice-a-trice**) [mid–late 19C] (*UK tramp*) nothing; also adj., no good. [SHICE n.[1] (2)]

chicharra n. *see* CHIRA n.

chi-chi *see also under* CHEE-CHEE.

chi-chi n.[1] [1960s+] (*US*) the female breast; usu. in pl. (cf. BORDENS n.). [Jap. *chi-chi*, milk, the breast]

chi-chi n.[2] *see* CHE-CHE n.

chi-chi adj. (*also* **shishi**) **1** [1920s+] homosexual. **2** [1930s+] affected, pretentious, 'pretty-pretty'. [Fr. *chi-chi*; ? link to Rom. *chichi*, nothing]

chichibangas n. [1960s+] (*US*) the female breasts. [CHI-CHI n.[1] + BONGOS n.]

chick n.[1] [19C] (*US*) a man. [SE *chicken*, lively, perky and 'good enough to eat']

chick n.[2] [mid–late 19C] (*Anglo-Ind.*) a coin worth 4 rupees. [SE *chequeen* (Ital. *zecchino*), a Venetian coin, also known as a *sequin* and worth at various times from 7 shillings (35p) to 9 shillings 6 pence (47½p) in pre-decimalized money]

chick n.[3] [late 19C] fashionableness, smartness, chic. [mispron. Fr. *chic*]

chick n.[4] **1** [late 19C] a novice. **2** [20C+] a young woman. **3** [1940s+] a girlfriend. **4** [1940s+] a male prostitute. **5** [1950s+] (*also* **chicky**) a term of address to a (young) woman. **6** [1960s] (*US prison*) a young man, prey for prison homosexuals. [the perceived vulnerability of a SE *chicken*]

chick adj. (*orig. US*) **1** [1950s+] composed of women. **2** [1990s+] of interest to girls or women, e.g. *a chick movie, chick lit*. [CHICK n.[4] (2)]

chick! excl. (*also* **chickie! chicky!**) [1910s–60s] (*US*) a warning of the impending approach of authority – whether policeman, parent or teacher – and thus a command to stop whatever one is doing that might cause that authority to act against one. [CHICKEN n.[1], i.e. one is acting in a cowardly way]

chickabiddy n. **1** [late 18C–early 19C] a young woman. **2** [late 18C+] a chicken. **3** [late 19C] (*also* **chickaweewee**) a young man, in ironic address. [nursery use, ult. rural dial. Note BIDDY n.[1] (1)]

chickadee n. (*orig. US*) **1** [20C+] a young woman. **2** [1940s] a young man; often an ironic term of address to a man. [ext. of CHICK n.⁴ (2); ult. SAmE *chickadee*, a type of tit-mouse]

chickaleary *adj.* [mid-19C–1900s] artful, knowing; usu. as *chickaleary cove*, an artful, knowing, 'clever' fellow. [popularized by the song 'The Chickaleery Cove' by the music-hall star Alfred 'The Great Vance' Stephens (1839–88). ? f. CHEEKY adj. + LEERY adj. (1) (+ COVE n. (1))]

chickaweewee *n. see* CHICKABIDDY n. (3).

chickee *n. see* CHICKIE n.¹ (1).

chicken *n.*¹ 1 [17C+] (*also* chickie) a timid creature, a coward. 2 [late 18C+] a weak or naïve person. 3 [1930s+] (*US Black*) a sheepish, foolish grin. 4 [1950s] (*US*) cowardice. 5 [1950s+] (*orig. US teen*) a contest of nerve in which 2 cars drive either at each other or towards an obstacle or cliff edge etc – the loser or 'chicken' is the driver who turns aside or brakes first; thus any form of foolish dare-devilry or, fig., competition; note the earlier CHICKEN FIGHT n. [SE *chicken*, a stereotypically 'cowardly' creature]

chicken *n.*² 1 [mid-17C+] a term of address to a child or young woman. 2 [early 19C–1950s] a young man, often as a term of address. [SE *chick*, a term of endearment]

chicken *n.*³ 1 [18C+] a young woman, esp. [late 18C–mid-19C] a prostitute (cf. ALLEY CAT n.). 2 [20C+] (*US*) young women considered collectively; thus sexual intercourse with one. 3 [1980s] (*US Black*) an unattractive (old) woman. 4 [1980s] (*US Black*) an aggressive woman. [note the Black terms, (3) and (4) are the direct reverse of the usual White equivalents, on the good = bad model]

chicken *n.*⁴ 1 [early 19C+] an underage girl, in a sexual context. 2 [mid-19C] anything young, small or insignificant. 3 [mid-19C] (*UK*) a novice, esp. a young boxer. 4 [late 19C+] (*gay*) an underage boy, or such boys considered collectively. 5 [1940s+] a young man used as a lure (usu. to blackmail or pressurize gay men) by swindlers. 6 [1940s+] (*US Und.*) a kidnap victim. 7 [1960s+] a child who is used for paedophiliac sexual exploitation. 8 [1960s+] a young lesbian. 9 [2000s] a young heterosexual male prostitute, servicing only opposite-sex partners. [(3) note 19C US milit. jargon *chicken*, a close friend or young 'buddy']

chicken *n.*⁵ [mid-19C] a pint pot (cf. CAT n.⁵; KITTEN n.¹). [a small HEN n.²]

chicken *n.*⁶ [mid-19C] (*US*) 1 a thing, a phenomenon. 2 a person (no cowardice is implied).

chicken *n.*⁷ [1900s–40s] (*US*) bacon, sausages.

chicken *n.*⁸ *see* CHICKENSHIT n. (4).

chicken *adj.*¹ [late 18C+] (*orig. US*) petty, insignificant. [CHICKEN n.¹ (1)]

chicken *adj.*² (*also* **chicken-ass**) [1930s+] cowardly, timid. [CHICKEN n.¹ (1)]

chicken *adj.*³ [1960s+] (*gay*) underage, boyish, inexperienced. [CHICKEN n.⁴ (4)]

chicken *v.* [1930s] (*US Black*) to grin sheepishly. [CHICKEN n.¹ (3)]

chicken *adv.* [1940s+] cowardly, scared. [CHICKEN n.¹ (1)]

chicken! *excl.* [1950s+] (*orig. US*) a derisive cry, coward! [CHICKEN n.¹ (1)]

chicken and rice *adj.* [2000s] nice. [rhy. sl.]

chicken-ass *adj. see* CHICKEN adj.².

chickenbone special *n.* [1950s] (*US Black*) anything second-rate, inferior, cheap and unattractive. [the bags of home-made fried chicken taken by Southern Blacks on railroad trips. Segregation kept them from using the White-only dining cars]

chickenbrain *n.* [1910s] (*US*) a fool (cf. AIREDALE n.; BAKEBRAIN n.). [SE *chicken*/CHICKEN adj.¹ + sfx *-brain*]

chicken-brained *adj.* [1910s] stupid (cf. AMOEBA-BRAINED adj.). [CHICKENBRAIN n.]

chicken-breasted *adj.* [late 18C–early 19C] of a woman, having very small breasts.

chicken-butcher *n.*¹ [late 18C–early 19C] 1 a poulterer. 2 one who shoots very young game.

chicken-butcher *n.*² [1930s–40s] (*US campus*) a womanizer. [CHICKEN n.³ (1)]

chicken butt *phr.* [1960s] (*US Black*) nothing, no matter, forget it; used in response to the query *what's up?* [SE *chicken* + BUTT n.¹ (2); its inherent insignificance]

chicken change *n. see* CHICKENFEED n.¹ (1).

chicken-chaser *n. see* CHICKEN FANCIER n. (1).

chicken-chasing *n.* [2000s] (*US*) pursuing underage boys. [CHICKEN n.⁴ (4) + SE *chasing*]

chicken cock *n.* [1920s–30s] (*US Black*) bootleg bourbon. [US regional *chicken cock*, a cockerel]

chicken colonel *n.* [1910s+] (*US*) a full colonel in the US Army or Air Force. [the silver eagles affixed to the uniform's shoulders that denote rank]

chicken coop *n.* 1 [1900s–10s] (*US*) any small place. 2 [1940s] (*US Und.*) a women's prison. 3 [1960s] (*US*) a police car or patrol wagon. 4 [1970s] (*US*) an outside lavatory. 5 [1970s+] (*US gay*) any place that is full of young men. [play on SE/CHICKEN n.³ (1)/CHICKEN n.⁴ (4)]

chicken-crap *adj. see* CHICKENSHIT adj. (2).

chicken dinner *n.* 1 [1940s] (*US Black*) an attractive young woman. 2 [1970s–80s] (*US gay*) a young or underage boy, in the context of his being the subject of fellatio. [ext. of CHICKEN n.³ (1)/CHICKEN n.⁴ (4) + the idea of being 'good enough to eat']

chicken-eater *n.* (*US*) 1 [1950s+] an unprofessional, part-time lay preacher. 2 [1960s–70s] a Methodist. [members of the congregation would give the preacher roast chicken for his Sunday lunch]

chicken fancier *n.* (*US*) 1 [1910s] (*also* **chicken-chaser**) a womanizer. 2 [1960s] (*also* **chicken-freak**) a male homosexual who has a penchant for young boys (cf. CHICKEN-HAWK n.; CHICKEN QUEEN n.; CHICKEN RUSTLER n.). [CHICKEN n.³ (1)/CHICKEN n.⁴ (4) + SE *fancier*/*chaser*/FREAK sfx]

chickenfeed *n.*¹ 1 [mid-19C+] (*also* **chicken change**) small change. 2 [20C+] derisorily small amounts of money or anything else.

chickenfeed *n.*² [1930s] (*US*) nonsense, rubbish.

chicken fight *n.* [1930s] (*US*) a contest of nerves. [CHICKEN n.¹ (5)/CHICKEN (OUT) v.]

chicken fixings *n.* (*also* **chicken fixins**) [mid-19C–1910s] (*US*) trifles, small possessions. [SAmE *fixings*, the trimmings that accompany a roast chicken]

chicken-freak *n. see* CHICKEN FANCIER n. (2).

chicken-fucker *n.* [1950s+] (*US*) a general derog. term, often intensified by ext. *bald-headed chicken-fucker*.

chicken gizzard *n.* [mid-19C] (*US*) a coward. [CHICKEN n.¹ (1) + SE *gizzard*]

chicken-gutted *adj.* [1950s+] (*US*) cowardly. [CHICKEN n.¹ (1) + SE *gutted*]

chicken-hammed *adj.* [18C–early 19C] bandy-legged. [SE *chicken* + *ham*, the back of the thigh and buttock]

chicken-hawk *n.* (*orig. US*) 1 [1960s+] an older male homosexual with a preference for young boys (cf. CHICKEN FANCIER n.). 2 [1980s] an older man who prefers teenage girls for sex. [CHICKEN n.⁴ (4)/CHICKEN n.⁴ (1) + SE *hawk*]

chickenhead *n.*¹ (*also* **chicken's head**) (*US Black*) 1 [1960s+] an aggressive, unpleasant woman. 2 [1960s+] a stupid, immature girl. 3 [1960s+] a fool (cf. AIREDALE n.). 4 [1980s] a woman with little or no hair. 5 [1980s] a woman with unruly, unkempt hair. 6 [1990s+] a fellatrix. 7 [1990s+] a promiscuous woman. [SE *chicken*/CHICKEN n.³]

chickenhead *n.*² [1990s+] (*US teen*) 1 one who talks a lot. 2 a crack cocaine addict. [(1) the chicken's constant squawking; (2) the chicken's bobbing head as mirrored by the addict as they bend over the crack pipe stem]

chicken-heart *n.* [late 19C+] a coward. [CHICKEN-HEARTED adj.]

chicken-hearted *adj.* [late 18C+] cowardly. [CHICKEN *n.*[1] (1) + SE *hearted*]

chicken hockey *n.* [1970s] (*US*) one's fig. intestines, innards, i.e. the 'stuffing', the 'daylights'; usu. in phr. *kick/knock the chicken-hockey out of.* [SE *chicken* + HOCKIE *n.* (1)]

chicken-house *n. see* CHICKEN RANCH *n.*

chicken inspector *n.* [1920s+] (*US*) a womanizer, a lady-killer. [CHICKEN *n.*[3] (1) + SE *inspector*]

chicken-lifter *n.* [late 19C–1900s] (*US*) a chicken thief; thus any form of petty thief. [SE *chicken* + LIFT *v.*[1] (1)]

chicken-lips *n.* [2000s] (*US Black*) a White person.

chicken-liver *n.* [1930s–40s] a coward. [CHICKEN-LIVERED adj.]

chicken-livered *adj.* [late 19C+] cowardly. [CHICKEN *n.*[1] (1) + SE *liver*; note SE *lily-livered*]

chicken man *n.* **1** [early 19C] a paedophile. **2** [1980s+] (*Aus. prison*) one who has been jailed for bestiality. [CHICKEN *n.*[4] (1)/SE *chicken*]

chicken money *n.* [19C] (*US*) spending money, small change. [var. on CHICKENFEED *n.*[1] (1)]

chicken nabob *n.* [late 18C–early 19C] a merchant who has returned from India with a moderate rather than a magnificent fortune. [SE *chicken*, diminutive ('borrowed from the chicken turtle' notes Grose (1796), who defines 'moderate' as £50,000–60,000) + *nabob*, one who has returned from India with great wealth, ult. f. Urdu *nawab*, deputy governor]

chicken-neck *v.* [1990s+] (*US*) to move one's head rapidly from side to side. [the similar action of the fowl]

chicken of the sea *n.* [1970s+] (*US gay*) a young sailor. [CHICKEN *n.*[4] (4) + play on brandname of canned tuna]

chicken (out) *v.* (*also* **go chicken**) [1930s+] (*orig. US*) to be scared, to be too frightened to act, to back out. [CHICKEN *n.*[1] (1)]

chicken-perch *n.* [late 19C+] a church. [rhy. sl.]

chicken-plucking *adj.* [1960s] (*US*) a general term of abuse, second-rate, vulgar, insignificant. [euph. for MOTHERFUCKING adj. (1)]

chicken-poo-poo *adj. see* CHICKENSHIT adj. (1).

chicken pox *n.* [1960s+] (*US gay*) the urge to have sex with underage boys. [CHICKEN *n.*[4] (4) + pun on SE; there is no apparent link to POX *n.*[1]]

chicken-preacher *n.* [20C+] (*US*) an unprofessional, part-time lay preacher. [CHICKEN adj.[1] + SE *preacher* or ? abbr. *chicken-eating preacher*]

chicken queen *n.* [1960s+] (*US gay*) an older homosexual male who prefers sex with teenage boys (cf. CHICKEN FANCIER *n.*). [CHICKEN *n.*[4] (4) + QUEEN *n.*[2] (1)/QUEEN sfx (2)]

chicken ranch *n.* (*also* **chicken-house**) [1960s+] a brothel (cf. BIRDCAGE *n.*[1]). [the original mid-19C *Chicken Ranch* was at Gilbert, Texas. One ety. suggests that the clients, mainly local farmers, paid for their pleasures with chickens, but more likely is a use of CHICKEN *n.*[3]]

chicken run *n.*[1] (*also* **chickie-run**) [1950s+] a teenage virility ritual involving the driving of 2 cars at high speed towards each other, or towards a dangerous obstacle; the first one to turn aside or brake is the loser or 'chicken'. [CHICKEN *n.*[1] (5)]

chicken run *n.*[2] [1970s+] (*S.Afr.*) the flight from South Africa of (White) people, fearing for their future in a non-apartheid country. [CHICKEN *n.*[1] (1)]

chicken rustler *n.* [1970s] (*US gay*) a male homosexual who has been placed in charge of underage boys, e.g. a scoutmaster or choirmaster (cf. CHICKEN FANCIER *n.*). [CHICKEN *n.*[4] (4) + SE *rustler*]

chicken scratch *n.*[1] [1940s+] (*US Black*) a very small amount of money. [? the small impression it makes on one's expenses; or CHICKEN adj.[1] + SCRATCH *n.*[4] (4); ult. var. on CHICKENFEED *n.*[1]]

chicken scratch *n.*[2] [1950s+] **1** (*US*) illegible handwriting. **2** (*US Black*) short, tightly curled hair. [resemblance]

chicken scratch *n.*[3] [1980s+] (*drugs*) the searching on hands and knees for grains of crack cocaine that have dropped to the floor.

chicken scratching *n.* [1940s–50s] (*US Black*) an inadequate effort, a poorly done job, a lack of real commitment to a task. [the lack of real impression a chicken's scratching makes on the ground]

chicken's hash *n.* [2000s] cash. [rhy. sl.]

chicken's head *n. see* CHICKENHEAD *n.*[1].

chickenshit *n.* [1940s+] **1** (*orig. US*) a coward. **2** (*orig. US*) a contemptible, disgusting person. **3** (*orig. US*) a disgusting, unacceptable action or situation. **4** (*orig. US milit.*) (*also* **chicken**) meaningless, petty discipline. [CHICKEN *n.*[1] (1)/SE *chicken* + SHIT *n.*[1] (1); the cowardice of the person/the essential insignificance of the substance]

chickenshit *adj.* [1940s+] (*orig. US*) **1** (*also* **chicken-poo-poo**) weak. **2** (*also* **chicken-crap**) insufficient, inadequate, of poor quality. **3** cowardly, fearful. **4** petty, insignificant. [CHICKENSHIT *n.*]

chickenshit *v.* [1960s+] (*orig. US*) to act in a cowardly or otherwise distasteful manner. [CHICKENSHIT *n.*]

chickenshits, the *n.* [1950s] (*US*) diarrhoea. [SE *chicken* + SHITS, THE *n.*]

chicken snatcher *n. see* CHICKEN THIEF *n.*

chicken's neck *n.* [20C+] a cheque. [rhy. sl.]

chicken-spanking *n.* [1950s] (*US*) sexual intercourse with a chicken.

chicken thief *n.* (*also* **chicken snatcher**) [1910s–40s] (*Aus.*) a petty thief. [SE *chicken* + *thief*]

chicken tracks *n.* [late 19C+] (*US*) illegible handwriting.

chicken walk *n.* [late 19C] (*UK prison*) an exercise yard.

chickie *n.*[1] **1** [1910s+] (*orig. Aus.*) (*also* **chickee**) a young woman. **2** [1950s] (*US*) a chicken. [dimin. of CHICK *n.*[4] (2)/SE *chicken*]

chickie *n.*[2] *see* CHICKEN *n.*[1] (1).

chickie! *excl. see* CHICK! excl.

chickie-run *n. see* CHICKEN RUN *n.*[1].

chickle-a-leary chap *n.* [early–mid-19C] an artful, knowing fellow. [var. or predecessor of CHICKALEARY adj.]

chicklet *n.* (*also* **chicklette**) [1920s+] (*orig. US*) a young woman. [CHICK *n.*[4] (2) + dimin. sfx *-let(te)*]

chick magnet *n.* [1990s+] a man who is irresistibly alluring to women. [CHICK *n.*[4] (2) + MAGNET sfx]

chicko *n. see* CHICO *n.*[1].

chicky *n. see* CHICK *n.*[4] (5).

chicky! *excl. see* CHICK! excl.

chiclets *n.* [1960s+] (*US*) the teeth. [trademark *Chiclets*, a popular chewing gum; the pieces of gum resemble teeth]

chico *n.*[1] (*also* **chicko**) [1950s–60s] a child. [SE *chick*]

chico *n.*[2] [1960s+] (*US*) **1** a Mexican, esp. one considered of a lower class or mixed blood (cf. BATO *n.*). **2** a Puerto Rican, also as a term of address. **3** a Cuban. [*Chico*, a popular Mexican name, esp. during ascendancy of baseball stars Chico Cardenas, Chico Fernandez, Chico Salmon and Chico Ruiz]

chic sale *n.* [1940s+] (*US*) a privy, an outside lavatory. [proper name *Chic Sale*, 'the champion privy builder of Sangamon Co., Ill.' and best known for his book *The Specialist* (1929)]

chie *n. see* CHAI *n.*

chief *n.*[1] **1** [1920s+] a general term of address, often to an unknown person. **2** [1940s+] (*W.I.*) a potential victim of a confidence trickster, a credulous person; the term, common as a form of address, is used ironically by the con-man when he approaches the victim. **3** [1970s+] (*S.Afr.*) a form of address, either between those of the same race or by Whites to a Black whose name they do not know. **4** [1990s+] (*UK Black*) a general insult, a fool, a braggart etc. **5** [1990s+] (*US*) a stupid person. [SE *chief*, the head of a tribe; thus the stereotyping of Native Americans as stupid]

chief *n.*[2] [1960s+] (*drugs*) a hallucinogenic drug, esp. LSD or mescaline (cf. A n.[3]). [? the association of such drugs with Mexican Indians and Native Americans]

chief v. [1990s+] (UK Black) to insult. [CHIEF n.[1] (4)]

chief cook and bottle-washer n. (also **head cook and bottle-washer**) **1** [19C+] a foreman, a person in authority. **2** [20C+] a general factotum who may, in fact, carry out neither of these duties.

chief muck of the crib n. [early 19C] an important person, but within only a small field of activity. [muck is synon. with both HIGH MUCK-A-MUCK n. and LORD MUCK n. but predates both and must thus be a fig. use of colloq. muck, anything filthy, disgusting or abhorrent + CRIB n.[1] (1)]

chief out v. [1990s+] to smoke marijuana. [? CHIEF n.[2]]

chieving-lay n. see CHIVING LAY n. (1).

chiff n. see CHIV n.[1] (1).

chigger n.[1] [1990s+] (US Black) an Asian person who aspires to be a Black person and adopts a Black, spec. HIP-HOP n./RAP n.[5], lifestyle (cf. SQUIGGER n.; WIGGA n.). [SE Chinese + NIGGER n.[1] (10)]

chigger n.[2] see JIGGER n.[2] (1).

chi-ike n. (also **chiack, chi-hike, chi-yike, chyack**) [mid-19C–1910s] **1** a hearty greeting. **2** (Aus.) argument, criticism, teasing, heckling. [CHI-IKE v.; orig. costermonger use]

chi-ike v. (also **chiack, chi-hike, chi-yike, chyack**) [mid-19C+] (mainly Aus./N.Z.) **1** to tease, to fool, to deceive. **2** to shout. [echoic]

chikwa n. see CHINKER n.

child n. **1** [mid-18C–1930s] (also **lad**) a person; usu. as this child, me, myself. **2** [1980s] (US campus) a general term of address to anyone.

child-getter n. [19C] the penis (cf. BABY-FETCHER n.).

child of darkmans n. [18C] a bellman. [DARKMANS n.; var. on next]

child of darkness n. [late 17C–early 18C] (UK Und.) a bellman or nightwatchman who walked the streets at night calling out the hours.

child of the horn-thumb n. [early 17C] a cut-purse. [SE child + HORN-THUMB n.]

children n. [1980s] (UK Und.) burglars' tools. [rhy. sl. boys and girls = TWIRL n. (1)]

children in the wood n. [mid–late 19C] dice in a box.

chile n. (also **chile-bean, chili, chili-bean**) [1930s+] (US) a derog. term for a Mexican (cf. BEAN n.[8]). [see next]

chile- pfx (also **chili-**) [1910s+] (US) a pfx used to denote a Mexican or anything supposedly Mexican. [the SE chile-/chili-pepper, a stereotypically popular Mex. food]

chile-belly n. (also **chile-gut, chili-belly, chili-gut**) [1960s+] (US) a Mexican (cf. BEAN n.[8]). [CHILE- pfx + SE belly/gut]

chile-chaser n. (also **chili-chaser**) [1950s+] (US) a US border patrolman, employed to prevent Mexicans from entering the country illegally. [CHILE n. + SE chaser]

chile-choker n. (also **chili-choker**) [1950s+] **1** (US) a Mexican (cf. BEAN n.[8]). **2** (US Black, Los Angeles) a derog. term of address to a fellow Black; the premise being that they are no better than a Mexican. [CHILE- pfx + choker]

chile chump n. (also **chili-chump**) [1940s+] (US Black) a pimp who has only 1 woman working for him, an inexperienced pimp (cf. CHILE PIMP n.; CHUMP n.[1]; COFFEE-AND PIMP n.; POPCORN PIMP n.; SIMPLE PIMP n.; SWEETMAN n.). [CHILE- pfx + CHUMP n.[1] (5); the ref. is to the incompetence of small-time Mexican pimps]

chile-eater n. (also **chile-chomper, chile-picker, chili-chomper, chili-eater, chili-picker**) [20C+] (US) a Mexican (cf. BEAN n.[8]). [CHILE- pfx + SE eater]

chile-gut n. see CHILE-BELLY n.

chile-head n. (also **chili-head**) [1970s+] (US) a Mexican (cf. BEAN n.[8]). [CHILE- pfx + -HEAD sfx (2)]

chile-picker n. see CHILE-EATER n.

chile pimp n. (also **chile mack, chili mack, chili pimp**) [1960s+] (US Black) a pimp who has only 1 woman working for him; thus a second-rate pimp (cf. CHILE CHUMP n.). [CHILE- pfx + SE pimp/MACK n.[1] (1)]

chili see under CHILE and its combs.

chili v. [1940s–50s] (US Black) to ignore, to brush off. [? CHILL n.[1] (1)]

chill n.[1] **1** [20C+] (orig. US) rejection, 'the cold shoulder'; thus give someone the chill, to ignore, to snub. **2** [1940s] (US Und.) a situation where a potential victim of a con trick loses interest in the hoax. [CHILLY adj.[1] (1)]

chill n.[2] [1930s+] murder, death, assassination; occas. a severe beating that knocks someone unconscious. [the cold corpse]

chill n.[3] [1970s+] (US campus) beer. [it has been chilled]

chill n.[4] [1980s+] (US) a pose of indifference or 'coolness'. [CHILL adj. (4)]

chill adj. [1980s+] **1** (US Black) fashionable, chic, 'with it'. **2** (US Black) correct, the real thing. **3** (US Black) safe. **4** (US campus) calm, untroubled, relaxed. [CHILL OUT v.]

chill v.[1] [mid-19C] to heat up. [abbr. SE take the chill off]

chill v.[2] **1** [1930s] (US Und.) to knock out or down. **2** [1930s+] to murder, to assassinate. **3** [1980s] (US Black) to undermine someone's plans. [CHILL n.[2]]

chill v.[3] **1** [1930s+] (orig. US) to give up on, to abandon. **2** [1930s+] (US Und.) to deal with, to nullify, e.g. a criminal charge. **3** [1940s] (US Und.) for the victim of a confidence trick to lose interest. **4** [1940s+] (orig. US) to become emotionally cold or withdrawn. **5** [1940s+] (US) to tolerate, to make no fuss about, to submit to. **6** [1950s] (US Und.) to get rid of the victim once the confidence game has reached its climax and he has been robbed. [CHILL n.[1]]

chill v.[4] see CHILL (FOR) v.

chill v.[5] see CHILL (OUT) v.

chill adv. [1900s–10s] (US campus) totally, completely. [var. on COLD adv.[1] (1)]

chill phr. [1980s+] (orig. US Black) wait, stop. [CHILL (OUT) v.]

chillam n. (also **chillum**) **1** [late 18C+] (Anglo-Ind.) a pipeful of tobacco. **2** [1960s+] (orig. W.I. drugs) a pipe used for smoking marijuana. [Hind. chilam, the bowl of a hugga pipe or hookah]

chillax v. [2000s] (US campus) to wind down and relax. [CHILL (OUT) v. (1)+ SE relax]

chilled adj. [1940s–60s] (US Black/teen) standoffish, resentful. [CHILL v.[3] (4)]

chilled-off adj. [1930s+] (US) killed, murdered. [CHILL v.[2] (2)]

chilled-out adj. [1980s+] calm, relaxed. [CHILL (OUT) v. (1)]

chillers n. [20C+] (Irish) **1** jowls. **2** a double chin. [OE ceolor, the throat]

chill (for) v. [1900s–70s] (US) to ignore, to pretend to ignore. [CHILL n.[1] (1)]

chillicracker n. [1930s–50s] (Anglo-Ind.) a derog. term for a person of mixed racial descent (esp. Eurasian). [?]

chilling n. [1980s+] relaxing, acting in a 'cool' manner. [CHILL (OUT) v. (1)]

chilling adj. [1980s+] good, excellent. [CHILL (OUT) v. (1)]

chilli queen n. [2000s] (US Black) an attractive Latina. [CHILE-pfx + SE queen]

chill (out) v. **1** [1930s+] (orig. US) to calm down, to control one's emotions, to relax, to act 'cool'; often as imper. **2** [1930s+] (orig. US) to calm someone down. **3** [1980s+] (orig. US Black) to pass the time of day, to 'hang out'. **4** [1990s+] (US Black) to take a break, to pause.

chill-out adj. [1980s+] designed to create a relaxed atmosphere; thus chill-out room, a part of a nightclub where people can relax and chat rather than dance. [CHILL (OUT) v. (1)]

chill pad n. [1990s+] (US Black) one's home. [CHILL (OUT) v. (1) + PAD n.[2] (2)]

chill pill n. [1980s+] (US campus) a metaphorical 'medicine' that acts to calm one down. [CHILL (OUT) v. (1)]

chillum *n. see* CHILLAM n.

chilly *n.*[1] [1980s+] (*US campus*) a cold beer.

chilly *n.*[2] [2000s] (*US Black*) a mentholated cigarette.

chilly *adj.*[1] **1** [late 19C+] emotionless, withdrawn, detached. **2** [1990s+] cold-blooded, terrifying. [SE *chilly*, cold]

chilly *adj.*[2] **1** [1950s+] calm, relaxed; thus LAY CHILLY v.; *play it chilly*, *hang chilly*, to act in a 'cool', relaxed manner. **2** [1980s+] acceptable. **3** [1980s+] attractive, fine. **4** [2000s] skilful, competent at a given task or profession. [CHILL (OUT) v.]

chilly dog *n.* [1980s+] (*US campus*) beer.

chilly down *v.* [1980s+] (*US*) to pass the time of day, to 'hang out'. [CHILL (OUT) v. (3)]

chilly mitt *n.* [1900s+] (*US*) a rejection, a snub; usu. in phr. *get/give the chilly mitt*. [CHILLY adj.[1] (1) + MITT n. (3); var. on FROZEN MITT n.]

chilly most *n.* [1980s+] (*US Black*) a relaxed, composed person. [CHILLY adj.[2] (1) + MOST, THE n.]

chilly most *adj.* [1980s+] (*US Black/teen*) wonderful, perfect, excellent. [CHILLY MOST n.]

chime *n.* **1** [mid-19C] (*US*) false praise, empty flattery, esp. when aimed at tricking or defrauding its object. **2** [1930s–40s] (*US Black*) 1 hour. **3** [1940s] (*US Black*) the beating of one's heart. [(1) note 17C–18C *chime*, a mere empty 'jingle' of words]

chimer *n.* [1940s] (*US Black*) **1** a clock or watch. **2** the heart, which also 'ticks'. [17C SE *chimer*, one who rings bells]

chimes *n.* [1960s] (*US*) the testicles (cf. BANGERS n.). [the facetious resemblance to a pair of hanging bells]

chimmy *n.*[1] [20C+] (*Aus./W.I.*) a woman's undergarment, essentially synon. with a petticoat. [SE *chemise*]

chimmy *n.*[2] [1950s+] (*W.I.*) a chamberpot.

chimmy *n.*[3] *see* SHIMMY n.[2].

chimney *n.* **1** [mid-19C+] a heavy smoker. **2** [1920s–40s] (*US Black*) a (top) hat. **3** [1940s+] (*US Black*) the head. [(2) and (3) the chimney's position on top of the house]

chimney chops *n.* [late 18C] a derog. term for a Black person (cf. BLACKBELLY n.). [the blackness of a *chimney* + CHOPS n.[1] (1); given the continuing arguments vis-a-vis the inclusion of racial abuse in dictionaries, it is interesting, perhaps, to note that Grose (1785), in a relatively rare acknowledgement of such a problem, defines this term as 'an abusive appellation']

chimney-corner *adj.* [20C+] (*US*) unofficial, not genuine, on the basis of popular acceptance; thus *chimney-corner law*, popular opinion, saloon-bar opinion. [the image of people chatting in a chimney corner]

chimney-pot *n.* [mid–late 19C] a cylindrical black silk hat, fashionable during the latter half of the 19C. [resemblance]

chimney sweep *n.*[1] (*also* **chimney sweeper**) [mid–late 19C] a nickname for an aperient, known as 'the black dose' or 'black drop', composed mainly of opium, mixed with vinegar and spices. [its colour + the fact that it 'cleans one out']

chimney sweep *n.*[2] [late 19C] a clergyman. [his black clothing]

chimozzle *n. see* SHEMOZZLE n.

chimpung *n.* [1940s+] (*W.I.*) a derog. name for a Chinese person (cf. AH CABBAGE n.). [supposed imitation of Chinese speech]

chin *n.*[1] **1** [mid-19C+] (*also* **chin-chin**) talk, chatter, conversation. **2** [1900s] (*US*) cheek, impudence.

chin *n.*[2] [1960s–70s] (*S.Afr. township*) money. [ety. unknown; ? a local language]

chin *v.*[1] (*also* **chin-chin**) [late 19C+] (*US*) to chatter; thus *chinning*, idle conversation, chatter. [CHIN n.[1] (1)]

chin *v.*[2] [1910s+] (*orig. Glasgow*) to hit someone (on the chin).

China *n.* [late 19C+] (*UK/Cockney*) anywhere other than England (poss. even other than London) or a generic term for the place where rich people go on holiday.

china *n.*[1] [1940s–50s] (*US*) money. [ety. unknown]

china *n.*[2] (*US*) **1** [1940s+] teeth. **2** [1960s] tea, as served at a lunch counter. [SE *china*, crockery]

china *n.*[3] *see* CHINA (PLATE) n.

chinaberry *n.* [2000s] (*US Black*) sexual intercourse as a highly pleasurable experience. [ult. SAmE, *chinaberry*, a tree common in Southern states; but why?]

China boy *n.* [mid-19C+] a derog. term for a Chinese man (cf. AH CABBAGE n.).

china clippers *n.* [1950s+] (*US*) false teeth. [CHINA n.[2] (1) + pun on Pan-American Airlines 'China Clipper' flying-boat service to the Far East]

Chinaman *n.*[1] [late 19C] (*US*) a cup of tea. [SE *Chinese tea*]

Chinaman *n.*[2] [late 19C+] an Irishman (cf. BOG ARAB n.). [fig. use that implies the alienation of an immigrant]

Chinaman *n.*[3] [1900s] (*Aus.*) in dice, a 5.

Chinaman *n.*[4] [1930s+] (*US drugs*) withdrawal from a narcotic, usu. heroin; thus HAVE A CHINAMAN ON ONE'S BACK v.; thus *kill a Chinaman*, to withdraw from narcotics. [the Chinese origin of opium, the base of heroin]

Chinaman *n.*[5] [1940s–50s] (*W.I.*) a farthing. [like the stereotyped Chinese, the coin is small]

Chinaman *n.*[6] [1970s+] (*US*) one who has political influence; thus *have a Chinaman*, to have political influence. [the image of the 'wily Oriental', now derog.]

Chinaman's chance *n.* (*also* **Chinese chance**) [1910s+] (*US*) **1** no chance whatsoever, no luck. **2** the slightest possible chance, the slightest degree of chance. [orig. gold rush use, when the Chinese worked otherwise abandoned claims]

Chinaman's luck *n.* (*also* **luck of a Chow**) [1900s] (*Aus.*) good luck, with an implication of it being undeserved. [for ety. *see* prev.]

Chinaman's nightmare *n.* [1980s] (*US*) bedlam, chaos. [racial stereotyping]

Chinaman's shout *n.* [20C+] (*Aus.*) a supposed 'treat' for which everyone involved must pay. [the presumed miserliness of the Chinese]

Chinaman's trot *n.* [late 19C–1900s] (*Aus.*) a slow and steady jog.

Chinamat *n.* [1930s–50s] (*US*) a cheap Chinese restaurant. [SE *China* + (*auto*)*mat*]

china (plate) *n.* (*also* **chiner**) **1** [late 19C+] one's (best) friend; often as OLD CHINA n. **2** [1950s–70s] (*Aus.*) one's wife. [rhy. sl. = SE *mate*; (2) note Powis (1977) suggests 'particularly used to mean a highly regarded husband or wife']

China Street *n.* [early–mid-19C] Bow Street, London WC2. [its proximity to Covent Garden, then a market, and thus to 'China oranges']

China Street pig *n.* [early 19C] a Bow Street police officer. [CHINA STREET n. + PIG n.[3] (1); the large central London police station is in Bow Street, London WC2]

China white *n.* (*also* **Chinese white**) [1960s+] (*drugs*) **1** heroin, esp. when of above-average strength (cf. CHINESE BROWN n.; CHINESE H n.; CHINESE No. 3 n.; CHINESE RED n.; CHINESE ROCKS n.; MEXICAN BROWN n.; MEXICAN HORSE n.; MEXICAN MUD n.; SRI LANKAN BROWN n.; THAI WHITE n.). **2** fentanyl, a powerful synthetic narcotic. [the colour and the stereotyped linking of the East to narcotics, orig. opium, subseq. heroin]

chinch *n.*[1] **1** [mid-19C–1950s] a bedbug; thus *chinchy*, infested with bugs. **2** [1960s] a term of affection, usu. aimed at a child. [Sp. *chinche*, a bedbug]

chinch *n.*[2] [1940s–60s] (*US*) a miser (cf. CHINCHY adj.). [ME/OF/SE 14C–16C *chiche*, parsimonious, mean]

chin check *n.* [1990s+] (*US campus*) a fight, a blow to the jaw. [CHECK SOMEONE'S CHIN v.]

chin-chin *see also under* CHIN.

chin-chin! *excl.* **1** [late 18C+] a popular toast before drinking, synon. with 'Good health!' or 'Cheers!' **2** [1910s–50s] goodbye. **3** [1940s] a greeting. [Chinese *ts'ing ts'ing*, a general salutation, and as such picked up by sailors on Far East tours. A response, which has not entered the vocab., is *pa pa*]

chinch pad *n.* [1940s–50s] (*US Black tramp*) a very low standard of rooming house or hotel. [CHINCH n.¹ (1) + PAD n.² (2)]

chinchy *adj.* [1900s–60s] (*US*) miserly, mean, stingy (cf. CHINCH n.²). [SE 14C–16C SE *chinch*, a miser]

chincough *n.* [20C+] (*Irish*) **1** whooping cough. **2** a spasm of laughter or tears. [OE *cincian*, to gasp and cough]

chin curtains *n. see* LACE CURTAINS n.¹.

'chine *n.* [1950s–60s] (*US Black*) a car or motorcycle. [abbr. SE *machine*]

Chinee *n.* [mid-19C–1960s] a derog. term for a Chinese person (cf. AH CABBAGE n.). [abbr. SE *Chinese*]

Chinee *adj.* [1920s–60s] Chinese. [CHINEE n.]

chinee *n.¹* (*also* **chinee ducket**) [1930s] (*US*) a complimentary ticket. [abbr. CHINESE DUCKET n.]

chinee *n.² see* SHINE n.⁴ (1).

chiner *n. see* CHINA (PLATE) n.

Chinese *adj.* [20C+] a racial stereotype used in many combs. below to mean something slightly askew or out of kilter, physically, ethically or otherwise. [the Chinese eye-shape, plus negative stereotyping to do with the supposed cunning of the 'wily Orientals']

Chinese angle *n.* [1930s–40s] (*US*) a strange twist. [CHINESE adj.]

Chinese B *n.* [1950s+] (*US*) a grade that is marked higher than the student's work really deserved. [CHINESE adj. + the preferential treatment given to supposedly disadvantaged Oriental students in an early form of affirmative action]

Chinese brown *n.* [1970s+] (*drugs*) a form of heroin (cf. CHINA WHITE n.). [SE *Chinese* + BROWN n.⁴ (2)]

Chinese chance *n. see* CHINAMAN'S CHANCE n.

Chinese consumption *n.* [1930s+] (*Aus.*) a smoker's cough. [pun on 'wun bung lung', a 'Chinese' name]

Chinese copy *n.* [1930s+] (*US*) any copy that faithfully reproduces not just the accurate work but the mistakes too. [? the stereotype (usu. ascribed to Japan) of Oriental workmen as taking Western inventions and faithfully copying them in order to sell the cheaper reproductions back to the West]

Chinese cure *n.* [1950s–60s] (*drugs*) a form of withdrawing from a narcotic addiction: a mix of heroin and Wampole's Tonic is consumed, with the proportion of narctoic gradually reduced to zero. [? its origin]

Chinese deal *n.* [1970s+] a deal that fails to materialize. [CHINESE adj.; the negative stereotype of a Chinese businessman as one who enjoys the minutiae of bargaining but cannot be trusted to deliver the goods]

Chinese ducket *n.* [1930s] (*US*) a complimentary ticket to a theatrical or sporting event. [DUCKET n. (1); the punch-holes in such tickets supposedly resembled Chinese money]

Chinese fashion *adv.* [1960s+] used to describe having sexual intercourse, with the couple lying on their sides. [CHINESE adj.; the implication is that such a position accommodates the supposedly transverse Chinese vagina]

Chinese fire drill *n.* **1** [1940s+] bedlam, chaos. **2** [1970s–80s] (*orig. US campus*) a student game whereby a car stops at the traffic lights and all those inside jump out, run round and round the car and then jump in again before the lights change.

Chinese flush *n.* (*also* **Chinese straight**) [1940s–60s] in poker, a worthless hand, i.e. 4 cards of a flush or a straight – a proper hand requires 5. [CHINESE adj.]

Chinese H *n.* [1980s+] (*drugs*) heroin (cf. BIG H n.; CHINA WHITE n.). [SE *Chinese* + H n.² (1)]

Chinese loan *n.* [late 19C] an unattainably large sum of money.

Chinese molasses *n.* [1950s–70s] (*drugs*) opium (cf. APOSTLE n.). [the origin and consistency of opium]

Chinese needlework *n.* [1930s–50s] (*US drugs*) **1** the world of drug-dealing. **2** (*also* **embroidery**) an injection of narcotics. [the

hypodermic *needle* used for injecting heroin and the stereotyped linking of the East to narcotics, orig. opium, subseq. heroin]

Chinese No. 3 *n.* [1970s+] (*drugs*) a variety of heroin, processed in Hong Kong and imported by Chinese smugglers (cf. CHINA WHITE n.).

Chinese red *n.* [1970s+] (*drugs*) heroin (cf. CHINA WHITE n.).

Chinese rocks *n.* [1970s+] (*drugs*) heroin (cf. CHINA WHITE n.).

Chinese rot *n.* [1940s–60s] (*US*) **1** venereal disease. **2** any form of unspecified 'mystery' disease. [the 'inscrutable' East]

Chinese saxophone *n. see* SAXOPHONE n.

Chinese screwdriver *n.* [1950s+] (*Aus.*) a hammer. [CHINESE adj.; the supposed inability of the Chinese to perform simple physical tasks]

Chinese smoking *n.* [1960s] (*N.Z.*) sucking tobacco smoke through the mouth and exhaling through the nostrils. [? the smoke is reminiscent of the typical long 'Chinese' whiskers]

Chinese straight *n. see* CHINESE FLUSH n.

Chinese take-away *n.* [1970s+] (*gay*) a bar where Oriental boys or young men are available for picking up by Western men. [pun on SE]

Chinese tobacco *n.* [1920s–50s] opium (cf. APOSTLE n.). [despite the fact that Britain introduced China to opium *c.*1840, the drug and the nation have been inextricably linked ever since]

Chinese white *n. see* CHINA WHITE n.

chiney-brush *n.* [1990s+] (*W.I.*) something that enhances sexual performance. [lit. 'China brush'; ? the fineness of a brush used to paint porcelain]

chiney-royal *n. see* ROYAL n.¹ (2).

chinfest *n.* [1940s+] (*US*) any meeting at which there is a good deal of talking and gossip. [CHIN n.¹ (1) + -FEST sfx]

ching *n.¹* (*also* **ching-ching, ching-chong**) [late 19C–1900s] (*US*) a derog. term for a Chinese person (cf. AH CABBAGE n.). [common Chinese name]

ching *n.²* **1** [1970s–80s] (*S.Afr.*) money (cf. CHINK n.¹; CHINKERS n.; CLACKER n.²; CLANK n.²; CLINK n.²; CRACKLE n.²; GINGLEBOY n.; JING n.; JINGLE n.³; JINGLER n.²; JINK n.¹; RATTLE n.³; TINKLE n.). **2** [2000s] £5, a £5 note. [echoic]

ching *n.³* [1990s+] (*drugs*) cocaine. [? on pattern of later BLING n., the sparkle of a cocaine crystal]

chingao! *excl.* [1960s+] (*US*) a general phr. of shock, surprise, resignation, WHAT THE FUCK! excl. [imper. of Sp. sl. *chingar*, a synon. with FUCK v.¹]

chingazo *n.* (*also* **chingaso**) **1** [1970s+] sexual intercourse. **2** [1990s+] the boss, the leader, lit. a FUCKER n. (3). [Sp. sl. *chingar*, FUCK v.¹]

ching-ching/-chong *n. see* CHING n.¹.

ching-chong *adj.* [1970s–80s] (*UK Black*) a derog. adj. meaning Chinese, Oriental. [CHING n.¹]

chingo *n.* [1960s+] (*US*) a great deal. [Sp. sl. *chingar*, FUCK v.¹; lit. 'a fuck of a lot']

chin goods *n.* [1900s] (*US*) chatter. [CHIN n.¹ (1)]

chingus *n.* (*US*) **1** [1940s+] the penis (cf. BAUBLE n.). **2** [1980s+] any unnamed object. [DINGUS n.; (1) note Sp. sl. *chingar*, a synon. with FUCK v.¹]

'chining *n.* [1950s–60s] (*US Black*) driving an automobile. ['CHINE n.]

chin-jaw *n.* [1940s] (*US*) idle chatter. [CHIN n.¹ (1) + JAW n. (1)]

Chink *n.* (*also* **Chinkee, Chinkie, Chinky**) **1** [late 19C+] (*orig. Aus.*) (*also* **chinky-chap**) a derog. term for a Chinese person (cf. AH CABBAGE n.). **2** [1910s+] a nickname for a Chinese person or someone with Chinese features. **3** [1930s] (*orig. US*) the Chinese language. **4** [1950s+] (*orig. US*) a derog. term for any Oriental or Asian person (cf. BROWNIE n.²). [SE *China* or f. Chinese *ching-ching*, a courteous excl. (*DARE*)]

Chink *adj.* (*also* **Chinkie, Chinky**) [late 19C+] a derog. adj. meaning Chinese; thus a derog. term for Oriental in general. [CHINK n.]

chink *n.*[1] [late 16C–1950s] money; often in pl. (cf. CHING *n.*[2]). [echoic]

chink *n.*[2] [17C–19C] the vagina (cf. AGREEABLE RUTS OF LIFE *n.*).

Chinkee *n. see* CHINK *n.*

chinker *n.* (*also* **chikwa, cinqua, cinque**) [late 17C+] (*Ling. Fr./Polari*) the number 5. [Ital. *cinque*, 5]

chinkers *n.* [mid-late 19C] money, esp. as coins (cf. CHING *n.*[2]). [CHINK *n.*[1]]

chinki-chonk *n.* (*also* **chinky-chonk**) [1970s+] a derog. term for any Asian person (cf. BROWNIE *n.*[2]). [CHINK *n.* (4) + redup.]

Chinkie *see also under* CHINK.

chinkie-jog *n.* [1930s] (*Aus.*) a slow and steady jog. [CHINK *adj.*]

chink joint *n.* [1940s+] a derog. term for a cheap Chinese restaurant. [CHINK *adj.* +JOINT *n.*[4] (3)]

chinko *n.* [late 19C] (*orig. N.Z.*) a derog. term for a Chinese person (cf. AH CABBAGE *n.*). [CHINK *n.* (1) + -O *sfx* (1)]

Chink's *n.* (*also* **Chinks**) **1** [1900s] (*US*) a Chinese-owned shop. **2** [1930s+] a Chinese restaurant. **3** [1930s+] (*orig. US*) Chinese food. [CHINK *n.* (1); usu. considered derog. terms]

chinks *n.* [1930s+] (*Irish*) the 'creeps', the 'shivers'; esp. in phr. *give someone the chinks*. [dial. *chink*, a coughing fit]

chink-stick *n.* [1950s+] (*W.I.*) a rough board bed. [CHINCH *n.*[1] (1), a bedbug, with which such beds are often infested + SE *stick*, a plank of wood]

chink-stopper *n.* [late 19C] the penis (cf. BUTT-PLUNGER *n.*). [CHINK *n.*[2] + SE *stopper*, a plug]

Chinky *n.* (*also* **Chinkie**) [1980s+] **1** a Chinese restaurant. **2** (take-away) Chinese food. [CHINK *n.*; usu. considered derog. terms]

Chinky *adj. see* CHINK *adj.*

chinky *adj.*[1] [late 19C] (*Aus.*) monetary. [CHINK *n.*[1]]

chinky *adj.*[2] [1970s] (*US campus*) stingy, mean. [CHINCHY *adj.* + ref. to a SE *chink*, i.e. the tightness of one's wallet and pockets]

chinky-chap *n. see* CHINK *n.* (1).

chinky-chonk *n. see* CHINKI-CHONK *n.*

chinless wonder *n.* [1910s+] a male scion of the British upper classes; prob. wealthy, certainly well-connected, but essentially devoid of intelligence or 'character'. [his stereotyped receding chin; a firm chin supposedly indicates a 'firm' personality]

chin music *n.* **1** [early 19C+] conversation, chatter, talk, esp. defiant, aggressive, cheeky talk; thus *jerk chin music*, to gossip, to chatter; also in sports, the attempted intimidation of a rival player. **2** [1900s] (*US*) promotional copy, persuasive writing. [CHIN *n.*[1] (1) + SE *music*]

chinner *n.* [1900s–10s] (*US*) **1** an actor, a performer. **2** a garrulous, verbose person. [CHIN *v.*[1]; lit. a 'talker']

chinny *adj.* [late 19C] (*US*) talkative, garrulous. [CHIN *n.*[1] (1)]

Chino *n.* **1** [mid-19C+] a Chinese immigrant; also attrib. (cf. AH CABBAGE *n.*). **2** [1930s–50s] (*US drugs*) a Chinese drug dealer. [abbr. SE *Chinese*]

chin-prop *n.* [mid-19C] a brooch. [SE *chin* + PROP *n.*[4] (1); it sits at the top of a blouse]

chin pubes *n.* [1990s+] (*US teen*) a beard. [SE *chin* + PUBES *n.*]

chin rest *n.* [1990s+] the female perineum, considered in the context of giving a woman oral sex.

chin-scraper *n. see* SCRAPER *n.*[1] (1).

chin-splitter *n.* [1900s] (*US*) a narrow goatee beard.

chinstrap *n.*[1] [20C+] (*Ulster*) a dirty ring around an unwashed neck, a 'tide-mark'.

chinstrap *n.*[2] [1910s+] the buttocks. [thus note army jargon *on one's chinstraps*, absolutely exhausted]

chin-tearer *n.* [late 19C] a barber. [in his shaving rather than hairdressing role]

chintz *n.* [late 19C+] a bedbug. [CHINCH *n.*[1] (1)]

chintzy *adj.* (*also* **chinzy**) **1** [mid-19C+] second-rate, inferior, cheap-looking. **2** [1950s+] stingy, mean. [dial. *chincy*, mean, niggardly/CHINCHY *adj.*, ult. the CHINCH *n.*[1] (1) or *chintz*, an insect

that attacks corn or grain and when squashed has an unpleasant smell]

chin up! *excl.* [1930s+] cheer up! don't worry!

chinwag *n.* **1** [mid-19C] officious impertinence. **2** [late 19C+] a chat, a conversation.

chinwag *v.* [mid-19C+] to chat, to converse. [CHINWAG *n.*]

chinwork *n.* [1970s] (*US*) a chat, a conversation. [CHIN *n.*[1] (1)]

chip *n.*[1] [late 17C–1900s] a child. [CHIP OF THE OLD BLOCK *n.* (1)]

chip *n.*[2] **1** [mid-19C+] £1, a sovereign. **2** [late 19C–1920s] a dollar. **3** [1930s–50s] a shilling. **4** [1940s] a rupee. [? gambling *chips*. Note racing jargon *chip*, a shilling; Indian army jargon *chip*, rupee]

chip *n.*[3] [late 19C–1950s] (*US*) **1** a woman. **2** a promiscuous woman, esp. a prostitute. [abbr. CHIPPIE *n.*[1] (1)]

chip *n.*[4] [20C+] (*Aus.*) an argument; a reprimand. [CHIP *v.*[1] (3)]

chip *n.*[5] [1910s–50s] (*US Und.*) a cash register. [? CHIP *n.*[2]]

chip *n.*[6] [1950s] (*US Black*) a sip (of liquor). [SE *chip*, a small amount]

chip *n.*[7] (*drugs*) **1** [1970s+] heroin, esp. that has been diluted or 'cut'. **2** [2000s] any form of cigarette cut with phencyclidine. [CHIP *v.*[2] (3)]

chip *n.*[8] [1990s+] (*US Black teen*) a cellular/portable phone that is stolen and therefore used to make illegal and free phone calls. [the SE *microchip* that powers it]

chip *adj. see* CHIPPER *adj.*

chip *v.*[1] (*mainly Aus./N.Z.*) **1** [late 19C+] (*also* **make chip-chip**) to tease, to banter with; thus CHIPPING *n.*[1]. **2** [20C+] to interrupt, to speak impudently. **3** [20C+] (*also* **chip the lips**) to complain, to criticize. **4** [1900s] to hit. **5** [1910s] of a man, to flirt with a woman. [dial. *chip*, a tiff, a quarrel]

chip *v.*[2] **1** [late 19C+] (*US Und.*) to carry out a small crime with only minimal profits. **2** [1950s+] (*orig. US drugs*) to dabble in narcotic drug use (cf. CHIPPIE *v.*[1]). **3** [1950s+] (*US drugs*) to dilute drugs. [SE *chip*, a small amount]

chip *v.*[3] [1940s] (*US Black*) to sip one's drink. [SE *chip*, a small amount]

chip *v.*[4] [1970s+] (*orig. UK Black*) to leave, to depart, to go somewhere. [ety. unknown; ? link to UK dial. *chip*, to step down or to SE *ship out*, to leave]

chip *v.*[5] *see* CHIPPIE *v.*[2] (1).

chip at *v.* [1950s+] to quarrel with, to criticize. [ext. of CHIP *v.*[1] (3)]

chip from the old block *n. see* CHIP OF THE OLD BLOCK *n.*

chiphead *n.* [1980s+] a computer enthusiast. [SE (*silicon*) *chip* + -HEAD *sfx* (4)]

chip in *v.* (*also* **chip into, chuck in**) [mid-19C+] (*orig. US*) **1** to contribute. **2** to include in one's speaking. **3** to join in. **4** to butt in, to interrupt. [poker jargon *chip in*, to put one's gambling chips on the table to signify one's joining in the round of betting]

chip in broth *n.* [late 17C] a thing or matter of no importance, an addition that does neither good nor harm. [SE *chip*, anything unimportant, without flavour or nutrition]

chip in porridge *n.* [mid-late 19C] a thing or matter of no importance.

chip in pottage *n.* [late 17C] a thing or matter of no importance.

chip into *v. see* CHIP IN *v.*

chipmunks *n.* [2000s] bathing trunks. [rhy. sl.]

chip of the old block *n.* (*also* **chip off the old block, chip from the old block**) [mid-17C+] **1** someone who resembles their father, or reproduces the family characteristics. **2** something that resembles an original or source object. [the preferred 20C+ version is with *off*]

chip one's teeth *v.* [1940s+] (*US, orig. milit.*) to talk, esp. to excess or angrily. [one's fury fig. damages one's teeth]

chip on one's shoulder *n. see* CARRY A CHIP ON ONE'S SHOULDER *v.*

chippens *n.* [20C+] (*Irish*) money. [? SE *chippings*]

chipper *n.*[1] [19C] a cheerful, lively young man. [CHIPPER adj.]

chipper *n.*[2] [mid-19C] in boxing, a sharp blow, a jab. [SE *chip*, as a v.]

chipper *n.*[3] [late 19C] (*US Und.*) a cheat, a swindler. [? CHIP v.[2] (1)]

chipper *n.*[4] [1910s+] (*Irish/Welsh*) a fish and chip shop. [SE *chip*]

chipper *n.*[5] [1980s+] (*drugs*) an occasional user of narcotics. [CHIP v.[2] (2)]

chipper *adj.* (*also* **chip**) [mid-18C+] (*orig. US*) cheerful, lively, perhaps slightly drunk (cf. ABOUT RIGHT phr.[1]). [dial. *chipper*, a cheery song, amiable chatter]

chipper *v.* [mid-late 19C] (*US*) to cheer (someone) up. [CHIPPER adj.]

chippery *n.* [1900s–10s] a verbal exchange, an argument. [SE *chipper*, to twitter, to babble]

chippie *n.*[1] (*also* **chippy**) **1** [mid-19C+] (*orig. US*) a promiscuous young woman, a prostitute (often a part-timer or 'amateur'). **2** [1930s–40s] (*US Black*) a prostitute's dress. **3** [1940s] (*US Black*) a slim, attractive 'glamour girl'. **4** [1960s–70s] (*US gay*) a male prostitute or promiscuous gay man. [? SE *cheap* or Fr. *chipie*, a shrewish woman; note Asbury, *The Gangs of Chicago* (1940): 'in the middle of 1860 it was estimated by the [Chicago] Tribune that two thousand "chippies" plied their unholy trade in the retail business district alone']

chippie *n.*[2] **1** [late 19C–1930s] (*US*) a young person. **2** [late 19C–1970s] (*US*) a beginner, an innocent. [CHIP OF THE OLD BLOCK n. (1); or ? they have only just 'chipped in' (CHIP IN v. (3))]

chippie *n.*[3] (*also* **chippy**) [20C+] **1** a carpenter, esp. theatrical or film use (cf. BROTHER CHIP n.). **2** the 'inevitable' nickname for men surnamed *Wood* or *Carpenter*. [SE *chips* of wood; orig. RN jargon *chippy*, the ship's carpenter, *chippy chap*, a carpenter's mate]

chippie *n.*[4] (*also* **chippy**) **1** [1910s+] a fish and chip shop. **2** [1990s+] a chip shop owner. **3** [1980s] (*N.Z.*) a potato chip (fried). [abbr.]

chippie *n.*[5] (*also* **chippy, chippy user**) (*orig. US drugs*) **1** [1920s+] an occasional user of (usu. narcotic) drugs. **2** [1960s+] a limited drug addiction. [CHIPPIE v.[1]]

chippie *v.*[1] (*also* **chippy**) [1920s+] (*orig. US drugs*) to use narcotics, esp. heroin, on an irregular basis rather than habitually through addiction. [? SE *cheap* or CHIP v.[2] (1)]

chippie *v.*[2] (*also* **chippy, chippy around**) **1** [1930s+] (*also* **chip**) to be sexually unfaithful. **2** [1960s+] (*US Black*) to seduce, to be attracted to. **3** [1980s+] to act as a prostitute. [CHIPPIE n.[1]]

chippie *v.*[3] (*also* **chippy**) [1970s] to work half-heartedly. [? SE *chip away at*]

chippie-chaser *n.* (*also* **chippy-chaser**) **1** [late 19C–1930s] a well-dressed loafer who spec. pursues young shopgirls and even schoolgirls. **2** [1920s+] a devotee of prostitutes or promiscuous women; also in homosexual use. [CHIPPIE n.[1] (1) + SE *chaser*]

chippie-chasing *n.* (*also* **chippy-chasing**) [1910s+] pursuing prostitutes or promiscuous women. [CHIPPIE-CHASER n. (2)]

chippie habit *n.* (*also* **chippy habit**) [1930s+] the occasional use of a narcotic, rather than the regular use necessitated by addiction. [CHIPPIE v.[1] + HABIT n. (1)]

chippie joint *n.* (*also* **chippie house, chippy house, chippy joint**) [1920s+] (*US*) a brothel (cf. BADGER-CRIB n.). [CHIPPIE n.[1] (1) + HOUSE n.[1] (1)/JOINT n.[4] (3)]

chippified *adj.* [1950s] (*US*) of a woman, promiscuous, esp. when acting as an 'amateur' prostitute. [CHIPPIE n.[1] (1)]

chipping *n.*[1] [late 19C+] (*Aus.*) an act of teasing, being impudent or cheeky. [CHIP v.[1] (1)]

chipping *n.*[2] [1920s] the act of tipping. [CHIP n.[2]]

chipping *n.*[3] (*also* **chippying**) [1950s+] (*drugs*) the occasional use of drugs. [CHIP v.[2] (2)/CHIPPIE v.[1]]

chip potato *adv.* [1960s+] (*Aus.*) later. [rhy. sl.; pron. 'potater']

chippy *see also under* CHIPPIE *and its combs.*

chippy *adj.*[1] [late 19C–1930s] **1** hungover. **2** unwell, sick. [CHEAP adj. (1)]

chippy *adj.*[2] **1** [late 19C+] cheeky, impudent. **2** [20C+] angry, irritated. **3** [1970s+] resentful, jealous. [CARRY A CHIP ON ONE'S SHOULDER v.; usu. in middle-class use and often as a means of dismissing genuine complaints, the implication is that such 'chippiness' has no real justification other than class-based resentment; note also CHIP v.[1]]

chippy *adj.*[3] [1900s–10s] cheerful, merry. [CHIRPY adj.]

chippying *n. see* CHIPPING n.[3].

chippy's playground *n. see* PLAYGROUND n.

chippy user *n. see* CHIPPIE n.[5].

chips *n.*[1] [late 18C+] a carpenter (cf. BROTHER CHIP n.).

chips *n.*[2] [mid-19C+] (*mainly US*) money, orig. a sovereign; thus IN THE CHIPS phr.; WHEN THE CHIPS ARE DOWN phr. [SE *chip*, a counter used in a game of chance]

chips *n.*[3] [1960s+] (*US*) the buttocks. [? SE *chip*, buffalo dung]

chips and chase *n.* [1920s] (*US*) the face. [rhy. sl.]

chips (and peas) *n.* [1960s+] the knees. [rhy. sl.]

chipstick *n.* [2000s] a fool. [on the model of DIPSTICK n. (2)]

chip the lips *v. see* CHIP v.[1] (3).

chiquita *n.* (*also* **chiquita banana**) [1960s+] **1** an attractive woman. **2** a woman, usu. as a term of address. [*Chiquita*, brand of bananas; BANANA n.[2] (2)]

chira *n.* (*also* **chicharra**) [1970s+] (*drugs*) marijuana. [Sp. *chicharra*, a cicada; thus ? play on ROACH n.[2] (1)]

chirk *adj.* (*also* **chirky**) [mid-late 19C] (*US*) cheerful, happy. [SE *chirk*, chirrup; prior use New Eng. dial.]

chirk (up) *v.* [mid-19C–1930s] (*US*) to cheer up. [CHIRK adj.]

chirp *n.* **1** [1920s] (*US Und.*) an act of informing, a betrayal. **2** [1930s–70s] (*US*) a female vocalist. **3** [1940s+] (*UK Black*) meaningless chatter. [CHIRP v.]

chirp *v.* **1** [early 19C+] (*US*) to talk loudly, to interrupt. **2** [mid-19C+] to inform. **3** [1910s+] (*US*) to sing. **4** [1930s] (*US*) to provide information. **5** [1970s–80s] (*UK Black*) to talk glibly and persuasively. **6** [1980s] (*US campus*) to vomit (cf. BARF v.). **7** [1990s+] (*S.Afr.*) to tease, to taunt, to complain.

chirper *n.*[1] [mid-19C] a glass or tankard. [CHIRPING MERRY adj.]

chirper *n.*[2] **1** [late 19C] the mouth. **2** [late 19C–1950s] a singer. **3** [1930s] an informer, a gossip. [CHIRP v.]

chirper *n.*[3] *see* CHIRP n. (2).

chirpiness *n.* [mid-19C+] happiness, cheerfulness. [CHIRPY adj.]

chirping merry *adj.* [mid-17C–early 19C] cheerfully drunk; thus *chirping glass*, 'a cheerful glass, that makes the company chirp like birds in spring' (Grose, 1785); *chirping-cup*, 'a merry cup, or glass; one which makes you chirp' (Nares); also a *chirping bottle* (cf. ABOUT RIGHT phr.[1]).

chirp out *v.* (*also* **pull a chirper**) [1970s] (*US*) to accelerate one's car from a standstill so as to make the tyres screech. [SE *chirp*]

chirpy *adj.* [mid-19C+] happy, gay, cheerful. [SE *chirrup*/one *chirps* with pleasure]

chirrup *v.* **1** [19C] to chat. **2** [late 19C] to cheer or boo a music hall performer. [the response varies as to whether or not the singer has tipped the gallery]

chirrup and titter *n. see* GIGGLE AND TITTER n.

chirruper *n.* [mid-18C–mid-19C] an extra glass of alcohol. [its effect will make the drinker CHIRPING MERRY adj.]

chirrupy *adj.* [19C] cheerful. [var. on CHIRPY adj. although slightly earlier]

chis *n.* (*also* **chise**) [early 19C] (*UK tramp*) nothing; also adj., no good. [var. on CHICE n.]

chise *n.* (*also* **chis**) [early 19C] a knife (cf. CHISER n.). [var. on CHIV n.[1] (1)]

chisel *n.* **1** [mid-late 19C] a swindler. **2** [1930s+] a swindle, a deception. [CHISEL v.[1] (1)]

chisel *v.*[1] (*also* **chizzel, chizzle**) **1** [early 19C+] to cheat; thus *chisel on/chisel out of*, to defraud. **2** [1940s] (*US*) to be unfaithful.

3 [1940s–50s] to persuade. [SE *chisel*, to cut or pare down; thus 'to take a slice off' (Hotten, 1867); (2) fig. use of (1)]

chisel *v.*[2] [1920s–70s] (*US*) **1** to butt in, to intrude, to insinuate oneself, e.g. on another man's date; usu. as *chisel in*. **2** to beg.

chisel-chin *n.* [1950s–60s] (*US*) one whose lower jaw protrudes. [supposed resemblance]

chiseler *n.* (*also* **chiseller**) [1910s+] (*orig. US*) a cheat, a swindler. [CHISEL v.[1] (1)]

chiseller *n.* (*also* **chiselur, chisler, chissler**) [20C+] (*Irish*) a child. [var. on dial. *childer*, a child]

chiselly *adj.* [late 19C] (*US campus*) unpleasant. [CHISEL v.[1] (1)]

chiser *n.* (*also* **chiver**) [early–mid-19C] a knife (cf. CHISE n.). [var. on CHIV n.[1] (1)]

chit *n.* [late 18C+] a letter, a note. [CHITTY n.]

chitari *n.* [1960s+] (*drugs*) a variety of cannabis. [? Hind.]

chitchat *n.*[1] [late 17C–18C] banter, light talk. [SE *chat* + redup.; SE f. 1800]

chitchat *n.*[2] [19C] a measure of alcohol. [? enough to foster a pleasant CHITCHAT n.[1]]

chit-chat *v.* [early 19C+] to chatter, to gossip. [CHITCHAT n.[1]]

chitlin *adj.* [1920s+] (*US*) pertaining to the US South. [Black/Southern pron. of SE *chitterlings*, the intestines, usu. of pigs, considered the stereotypical food of the region]

chitlins *n.* [mid-19C+] (*US, Southern*) the bowels. [for ety. *see* CHITLIN adj.]

chitlins 101 *n.* [1960s–70s] (*US Black campus*) any form of Black Studies course. [self-mockery; the stereotyped Black love of soul food, the recipes of which often feature offal or chitlins (*see* CHITLINS n.)]

Chitlin Switch *n.* [1920s+] (*US Black*) a sterotypical small Southern town. [CHITLIN adj.]

Chi-town *n.* (*also* **Chi town**) [1920s; 1990s+] Chicago. [CHI n. (1) + SE *town*]

chits *n.*[1] [1940s–50s] (*US Black*) pig intestines. [abbr. SE *chitlins* (*see* CHITLINS n.)]

chits *n.*[2] *see* CHATS n.[2].

chitterling *n.* (*also* **chitterlin**) **1** [17C–19C] the penis. **2** [late 17C] a flaccid penis. [SE *chitterlings*, the small intestines of animals, esp. pigs]

chitterlings *n.*[1] (*also* **chitterlins**) [late 18C–19C] the bowels. [for ety. *see* CHITTERLING n.]

chitterlings *n.*[2] (*also* **chitterlins**) [early–mid-19C] shirt frills, as affected by ageing dandies. [? f. butchers' jargon *frill*, the mesentry veins, suspending the viscera from the backbone]

chitty *n.* [late 17C+] (*orig. Anglo-Ind.*) a letter, a note, any small piece of paper inscribed with writing, usu. instructions. [Hind. *chitthi*, a letter or note. Also, a certificate given to a servant or the like, a pass' (Y&B); ult. Skrt *chitra*, a spot or mark]

chitty-face *n.* **1** [early 17C–18C] a child with a pinched face or a baby-face; thus *chitty-faced*, baby-faced. **2** [early 18C] a young female prostitute. [dial. *chitty*, thin, baby-faced/SE *chit*, a child]

chiv *n.*[1] **1** [late 17C+] (*UK Und.*) (*also* **chev, chevy, chiff, chive, chivvy, chivy, skiv**) a knife. **2** [2000s] a scar (from a knife slash). [Rom. *chiv, chive*, a knife]

chiv *n.*[2] [mid-19C–1910s] (*US, Western*) a White Southerner. [SE *chivalry*; f. the South's obsession with 'honour' and 'chivalry']

chiv *n.*[3] (*also* **shif**) [1900s–10s] (*Aus.*) the face. [CHEVY (CHASE) n.]

chiv *v.* (*also* **chive**) **1** [18C–mid-19C] to cut off. **2** [early 18C–early 19C] to saw, to file. **3** [mid-18C+] (*also* **chib**) to stab, to cut with a knife. **4** [1930s] to smash a glass in someone's face and slash them with the shards. [Rom. *chiv*, to stab/CHIV n.[1] (1)]

chiva *n.* [1960s+] (*US drugs*) heroin. [synon. in US Hisp. sl. (CALÓ n.)]

chivalry *n.* [mid-19C] sexual intercourse.

chivaria *n.* [1970s+] (*US drugs*) any place where one can buy heroin. [CHIVA n.]

chiv artist *n.* (*also* **chev man, chiv man**) [1920s–50s] (*US*) an expert in using a knife. [CHIV n.[1] (1) + ARTIST sfx/SE *man*]

chive *see also under* CHIV.

chive *n. see* CHIVEY n. (2).

chive-fencer *n.* **1** [mid-19C] a street-seller of knives and cutlery. **2** [1900s] one who harbours murderers. [CHIV n.[1] (1) + -FENCER sfx]

chiver *n. see* CHISER n.

chivey *n.* **1** [late 18C–mid-19C] (*also* **chivie**) a scolding, a telling off. **2** [mid-19C] (*also* **chive**) a shout. [dial. *chevy*, to pursue, to hunt, to tease; ? ult. proper name *Chevy Chase*, the site of a celebrated border skirmish, soon memorialized in a popular 17C ballad. Also note the game *Chevy Chase*, which depends on the shouting of the word 'chive']

chivey *v.* [early 19C+] to chase around, to hunt about, to leave quickly. [dial. *chevy*, to pursue, to hunt]

chiving lay *n.* **1** [18C–early 19C] (*also* **chieving-lay**) cutting the braces of a coach (the strong leather straps that suspend the body of a coach from the springs), so that the coachman dismounts and, while his attention is distracted by the person who has done this, an accomplice plunders the boot of its contents. **2** [mid-18C] cutting off a woman's belt, thus stealing any jewellery or watches that might be attached. **3** [late 18C–early 19C] (*UK Und.*) cutting open the back of a coach to steal the large wigs worn by the passengers. [CHIV v. (1) + LAY n.[4] (1)]

chiv man *n. see* CHIV ARTIST n.

chivoo *n. see* SHIVOO n.

chiv the froe *v.* [mid-18C] (*UK Und.*) to steal from a woman by cutting round the pockets of her outer garment. [CHIV v. (1) + FROE n.[1]]

chivver *n.* [1920s+] an expert in using a knife (cf. CHIV ARTIST n.). [CHIV n.[1] (1)]

chivving *n.* (*also* **chibbing**) [20C+] a stabbing. [CHIV v. (3)]

chivvy *n.*[1] (*also* **chivy**) **1** [late 19C–1950s] the face. **2** [1920s] a general term of address, 'old chap'. **3** [1940s–50s] a moustache. [CHEVY (CHASE) n.]

chivvy *n.*[2] *see* CHIV n.[1] (1).

chivvy *v.*[1] **1** [mid-19C–1910s] to tease, to mock, to make fun of. **2** [late 19C+] to scold, to tell off. [CHIVEY n. (1)]

chivvy *v.*[2] [20C+] to slash with a knife. [ext. of CHIV v. (3)]

chivvy chase *n. see* CHEVY (CHASE) n.

chivy *n.*[1] *see* CHIV n.[1] (1).

chivy *n.*[2] *see* CHIVVY n.[1].

chivy *adj.* [late 19C] relating to the use of knives; thus *chivy duel*, a knife fight. [CHIV n.[1] (1)]

chi-yike *see under* CHI-IKE.

chiz *n.*[1] [1950s] something unpleasant, unfair, disappointing. [CHISEL n. (2) + SWIZ n.[2]]

chiz *n.*[2] *see* CHIZZER n.

chiz *adj.* (*also* **chiz-chiz**) [1950s] awful. [CHIZ n.[1]]

chizz *v.* [1940s–50s] (*UK juv.*) to cheat, to swindle. [CHISEL v.[1] (1)]

chizzel *v. see* CHISEL v.[1].

chizzer *n.* (*also* **chiz**) [1930s] a cheat, a swindler. [CHISEL v.[1] (1)]

chizzle *v. see* CHISEL v.[1].

chizzlin *n.* [2000s] (*US teen*) relaxing. [CHILLING n. (+ ? SE *sizzling*)]

choad *n.* (*also* **chode, choda**) **1** [1960s+] (*orig. US teen*) the penis; thus *choadsmoker*, a fellator or fellatrix. **2** [1980s+] a piece of excrement. **3** [1990s+] (*also* **chodelick, dickchode**) a fool, an idiot (cf. BELL END n.; COCK n.[2]; DIBBLE n.[2]; DICK n.[4]; DINK n.[2]; DIPSTICK n.; DODE n.; DORK n.; GADSO n.; HAMPTON (WICK) n.; HORSE'S HANGDOWN n.; KISS-ME-QUICK n.[2]; PANHANDLE n.[2]; PILLOCK n.[1]; PORK n.[2]; PRICK n.; PUD n.[3]; PUTZ n.; SCHLONG n.; SCHMUCK n.; WILLY WONKA n.; YOYO n.[1]; YUTZ n.). **4** [1990s+] the perineum. [? Navajo *chodis*, penis]

choak pear *n. see* CHOKE PEAR n.

choc *n.*[1] [1910s+] (*Aus.*) a soldier who is reluctant to fight. [CHOCOLATE SOLDIER n. (2)]

choc *n.*[2] *see* CHOCTAW *n.*[2].

choc-a-block *adj. see* CHOCK-A-BLOCK *adj.*

choc-box *n.* [1990s+] the anus (cf. BOURNEVILLE BOULEVARD *n.*). [play on SE/CHOCOLATE *adj.* (2) + BOX *n.*[1] (4); note RMC Duntroon (Aus.) *choc:* (1) to penetrate (someone) anally; (2) to annoy someone or to give someone a hard time]

chocha *n.* [1960s+] (*US*) **1** the vagina. **2** sexual intercourse. [Sp. *chocha,* a doddering woman]

cho-cho *n.* [2000s] (*US prison*) ice-cream and other sweets purchased from the prison canteen. [? SE *chocolate*]

choc-ice *n.* [1990s+] (*US Black*) a derog. term for a fellow Black person who may be Black racially, but whose opinions, attitudes, lifestyle and goals are all taken from White society and standards (cf. APPLE *n.*[7]). [the SE *choc-ice* is black outside but white within]

chock *adj. see* CHOCOLATE *adj.* (1).

chocka *adj. see* CHOKKA *adj.*

chock-a-block *adj.* (*also* **choc-a-block, chuck-a-block**) **1** [mid-19C+] crammed full, crammed together; thus *chockablock full.* **2** [1970s+] (*Aus.*) in fig. use, in the middle of having sexual intercourse. [naut. jargon *chockablock,* 'said of a tackle when the two blocks run close together so that they touch each other— the limit of hoisting' (*OED*); transferred to people this became naut. jargon and thence sl.]

chocka(-block) *v.* [1980s+] (*Aus. prison*) to fellate (cf. BLOOD RED *n.*). [? rhy. sl. = (get a mouthful of) COCK *n.*[2] (1)]

chock and log *n.* [20C+] (*Aus.*) a dog. [rhy. sl.]

chocker *n. see* CHOKKA *n.*

chocker *adj.*[1] [1940s+] (*orig. naut.*) fed up, disgruntled. [CHOCK-A-BLOCK *adj.* (1), i.e. with emotions]

chocker *adj.*[2] *see* CHOKKA *adj.*

chockers *n.* [late 19C+] (*costermonger*) the feet; boots. [ety. unknown; ? *chalk* = walk; ? *chockerblockers* = dockers, ? a type of shoe]

chockers (with) *adv.* [1980s+] (*Aus.*) full of. [CHOKKA *adj.*]

chocko *n. see* CHOCO *n.*[1].

chocks away! *excl.* (*also* **pull chocks!**) [1930s+] (*orig. RAF*) let's go! let's be off! [the *chocks,* orig. wood, that were positioned as 'brakes' next to aircraft wheels]

choco *n.*[1] (*also* **chocko**) [1930s+] (*Aus.*) **1** a militiaman or conscripted soldier, esp. one who was drafted into the WW2 militia but never left the country. **2** a conscientious objector. [CHOCOLATE SOLDIER *n.* (2)]

choco *n.*[2] (*also* **choko**) [1970s+] (*mainly UK middle/upper class*) a derog. term for a Black person (cf. BLACKBELLY *n.*). [abbr. CHOCOLATE *n.*[1] (1)]

chocolate *n.*[1] **1** [1920s+] (*mainly US*) a derog. term for a Black person (cf. BLACKBELLY *n.*). **2** [1920s+] (*US Black*) as used by a Black person, thus not derog.; ext. to *chocolate-to-the-bone,* a person with very dark skin. **3** [1970s+] the anus, homosexuality in general. **4** [2000s] (*US Black*) as a term of address for a fellow Black. [colour; (1) poss. link to rhy. sl. *chocolate frog* = WOG *n.*[1]. (1) According to *Maledicta* II (1978) 'especially a woman or homosexual'; all gay uses have the extra connotation of EAT *v.*[3] (1)]

chocolate *n.*[2] [1980s+] (*S.Afr. Black*) a 20-rand note. [its colour]

chocolate *n.*[3] *see* CHOCOLATE (STUFF) *n.*

chocolate *adj.* (*mainly US*) **1** [20C+] (*also* **chock**) used derog. in ref. to a Black person, unless used by a Black person when not derog.; also ext. as *chocolate-to-the-bone,* referring to very dark skin. **2** [1970s+] pertaining to the anus, to defecation and, by ext., to homosexuality. [in both cases, ext. in a variety of combs. below, f. the brownness of the chocolate]

chocolate baby *n.* [1900s] (*US*) a derog. term for a Black person (cf. BLACKBELLY *n.*). [CHOCOLATE *adj.* (1) + BABY *n.*[3] (1)]

chocolate bandit *n.* [1980s] a male homosexual (cf. BROWN ARTIST *n.*). [CHOCOLATE *adj.* (2) + BANDIT sfx (2)]

chocolate bar *n.* (*also* **chocolate chip**) [20C+] (*US*) a

derog. term for a Black person (cf. BLACKBELLY *n.*). [CHOCOLATE *adj.* (1)]

chocolate bunny *n.* [1980s] (*US*) a derog. term for a Black person (cf. BLACKBELLY *n.*). [CHOCOLATE *adj.* (1) + SE *bunny* + inference of BUNNY *n.*[3] (1)]

chocolate cake *n.* [2000s] (*US*) homosexual anal intercourse. [CHOCOLATE *adj.* (2)]

chocolate canyon *n.* [1990s+] the anus; thus *ride the chocolate canyon,* to have anal intercourse (usu. in homosexul context) (cf. ALLEY WAY *n.*; BOURNEVILLE BOULEVARD *n.*). [CHOCOLATE *adj.* (2) + CANYON *n.* (2)]

chocolate cha-cha *n.* [1980s+] (*Aus./US*) anal intercourse; thus *dance the chocolate cha-cha* (cf. ASK FOR THE RING *v.*). [CHOCOLATE *adj.* (2) + SE *cha-cha*]

chocolate chimney sweep *n.* [1990s+] one who performs anal intercourse. [CHOCOLATE *adj.* (2) + added image of 'cleaning out']

chocolate chip *n. see* CHOCOLATE BAR *n.*

chocolate chips *n.* [1970s+] (*drugs*) LSD (cf. A *n.*[3]). [a variety of LSD packaged in brown capsules/pills]

chocolate city *n.* **1** [1970s] (*US Black*) Washington, D.C. **2** [1970s+] (*US*) a Black ghetto, any concentration of Blacks. [CHOCOLATE *adj.* (1) + CITY sfx/SE *city*; coined by George Clinton (b.1940), founder of the funk bands Parliament and Funkadelic]

chocolate deluxe *n.* [1990s+] (*US Black teen*) an attractive, sexy, dark-complexioned Black woman. [SE *chocolate*/CHOCOLATE *adj.* (1); a popular brand of ice-cream]

chocolate drop *n.* [20C+] a derog. term for a Black person (cf. BLACKBELLY *n.*). [CHOCOLATE *adj.* (1)]

chocolate frog *n.* [1980s+] (*Aus.*) **1** an informer. **2** influenza. **3** an immigrant from southern Europe. [rhy. sl.; (1) = DOG *n.*[3] (7); (2) = WOG *n.*[2] (2); (3) = WOG *n.*[1] (6)]

chocolate highway *n.* (*also* **brown highway, chocolate freeway, ...speedway, ...tunnel, ...whizzway**) [1970s+] (*US*) the rectum or anus (cf. ALLEY WAY *n.*; BOURNEVILLE BOULEVARD *n.*). [CHOCOLATE *adj.* (2)/BROWN *adj.*[3] + SE *highway*/SAmE *freeway*/SE *speedway/tunnel/whizz*; note RMC Duntroon (Aus.) *chieftain of the chocolate/choccie channel,* a male homosexual [...] who engages in homosexual or heterosexual anal coition]

chocolate lover *n.* [1960s+] (*US*) one who prefers Black sexual partners, whether hetero- or homosexual. [CHOCOLATE *n.*[1] (1)]

chocolate puncher *n.* [1970s+] (*Aus.*) a male homosexual (cf. BROWN ARTIST *n.*). [CHOCOLATE *adj.* (2) + SE *punch*]

chocolate rock *n.* [1990s+] (*drugs*) **1** a dark substance that is produced in the pipe during the smoking of crack cocaine. **2** smoking crack cocaine and heroin at the same time (cf. BLACK *n.*[3]). [SE *chocolate,* brown + ROCK *n.*[3] (4)]

chocolate runway *n.* [1990s+] the anus (cf. ALLEY WAY *n.*; BOURNEVILLE BOULEVARD *n.*). [CHOCOLATE *adj.* (2) + SE *runway*]

chocolate runway pilot *n.* (*also* **captain of the chocolate runway**) [1990s+] a male homosexual (cf. BROWN ARTIST *n.*). [CHOCOLATE RUNWAY *n.* + SE *pilot*]

chocolate sandwich *n.* [1990s+] a sexual threesome involving 1 Black person and 2 White people (cf. CLUB SANDWICH *n.*; MAKE A SANDWICH *v.*; SANDWICH *n.*[2]; SAUSAGE SANDWICH *n.*). [CHOCOLATE *adj.* (1)+ SANDWICH *n.*[2]]

chocolate soldier *n.* (*Aus.*) **1** [1910s] a member of the 8th Infantry Brigade of the Australian Imperial Forces (A.I.F.) who arrived in Egypt too late to join in the Gallipoli campaign. **2** [1940s] a soldier who was drafted into the WW2 militia but never left the country. [SE *chocolate soldier,* a soldier who will not fight]

chocolate speedway *n. see* CHOCOLATE HIGHWAY *n.*

chocolate speedway rider *n.* [1990s+] a male homosexual (cf. BROWN ARTIST *n.*). [CHOCOLATE SPEEDWAY *n.*]

chocolate starfish *n.* [1990s+] the anus (cf. BOURNEVILLE BOULEVARD *n.*). [CHOCOLATE *adj.* (2) + SE *starfish*]

chocolate (stuff) *n.* (*drugs*) **1** [1950s] opium (cf. APOSTLE *n.*). **2** [1950s+] heroin, usu. that manufactured in Mexico (cf. BLACK *n.*[3]). **3** [1970s+] hashish (cf. AFGHAN *n.*). [STUFF *n.*[3] (2); the colour of the drugs]

chocolate thunder *n.* [1980s+] (*US Black*) any Black basketball player. [CHOCOLATE *adj.* (1) + SE *thunder*]

chocolate tunnel/whizzway *n. see* CHOCOLATE HIGHWAY *n.*

choco-taco *n.* [2000s] (*US Black*) a Mexican who pretends or aspires to be Black; also a Mexican who interferes with a Black person's life in some way, e.g. by sleeping with his girlfriend. [CHOCO *n.*[2] + TACO *n.* (1)]

choctaw *n.*[1] [mid-19C–1930s] (*orig. US*) an unknown, foreign or otherwise incomprehensible language. [SE *choctaw*, the language of the Choctaw, a Muskogean North American Indian people, orig. inhabiting Mississippi and Alabama]

choctaw *n.*[2] (*also* **choc**) [late 19C+] (*US*) homemade beer or whisky. [? proper name *Choctaw*; the stereotypical Native American being satisfied with inferior products]

choda/chode *n. see* CHOAD *n.*

choff *n.* [1950s–60s] food. [CHOW *n.*[1] (2) + SCOFF *n.*; Cape Du. (and orig. European Du.) term meaning a quarter of a day, and thus 1 of the 4 meals eaten in a day]

choge/chogey/choggie *n. see* CHOKE *n.*[2] (2).

choice *adj.* **1** [late 19C+] excellent, first-rate. **2** [1980s+] a general intensifier.

choice riot *n.* [late 19C–1900s] an unpleasant noise.

choice spirit *n.* [late 18C–mid-19C] a devil-may-care, selfish, drunken person. [SE *choice spirit*, a spirit of special excellence, worthy of being chosen; SE was coined by Shakespeare in *Henry VI Pt 1* (1599)]

choir bird *n. see* QUEER BIRD *n.*

choirboy *n.* **1** [1930s+] (*US Und.*) a novice thief. **2** [1940s+] (*US*) an innocent, honest person, a naïve, foolish person. **3** [1970s] (*US gay*) a novice male prostitute. **4** [1970s+] (*US*) a novice policeman. **5** [1990s+] (*US Black*) a derog. term for a Black person seen as embracing White values. [the perceived innocence of the SE *choirboy*]

choir cove *n. see* QUEER COVE *n.*

choke *n.*[1] **1** [late 19C–1920s] prison bread, which is hard to swallow and indigestible. **2** [1920s+] (*Aus.*) an act of garrotting. **3** [1940s+] a shock to the nerves; nervousness. **4** [1970s] a cigarette. **5** [1990s+] (*US campus*) marijuana. [all cause one to choke]

choke *n.*[2] [1970s+] **1** (*US*) a derog. term for a Mexican (cf. BEAN *n.*[8]). **2** (*Aus. milit*) (*also* **choge, chogey, choggie**) a derog. term for an Asian (cf. BROWNIE *n.*[2]). [(1) abbr. CHILE-CHOKER *n.* (1); (2) ety. unknown; a link seems unlikely unless as a derog. ref. to Chinese food]

choke *v.*[1] **1** [mid-19C+] (*US*) (*also* **choke in/up**) to stop talking, esp. as imper. *choke it!, choke up!* shut up (cf. CHOKE OFF *v.*). **2** [1950s+] (*N.Z./US*) to stop doing something; to turn off, e.g. a radio. **3** [1960s] (*US campus*) to reprimand or refuse; to 'shoot down'.

choke *v.*[2] [1930s+] to surprise, to shock, to disgust. [CHOKED *adj.*[1]]

choke *v.*[3] [1960s+] **1** (*US Black/campus*) to lose one's nerve when faced with pressure. **2** (*US campus*) to do badly in work that one should have found easy. [orig. sporting jargon *choke up*, to become tense and thus ineffective under pressure]

choke *v.*[4] [1960s+] (*US campus*) to smoke marijuana. [? CHOKE *n.*[1] (5)/SE *choke*]

choke a brown dog *phr.* [1980s] (*Aus.*) a general negative or condemnatory phr. used variously as to context.

choke a darkie *v.* (*also* **park a darkie, sink..., strangle...**) [1960s+] (*Aus.*) to defecate. [SE *choke* + pun on SE *dark* + sfx *-y*/DARKIE *n.*[1]]

choke and chew *n.* (*also* **choke and puke**) [1970s+] (*US*) a

roadside café, a truckstop. [SE *choke* + *chew*/*puke*; the poor quality of the food]

choke-and-rob *v. see* LOCK OFF *v.*

chokebored *adj.* [1940s+] (*US*) (of a person) thin; thus *chokebore pants*, trousers that narrow towards the bottom, esp. riding breeches. [SE *chokebore*, a shotgun of which the bore narrows towards the muzzle, keeping the shot together and increasing the effective range]

choked *adj.*[1] **1** [late 19C+] (*also* **choked off, choked up, choky**) upset, annoyed, depressed, having 'a lump in one's throat'. **2** [1940s] overcome with laughter. [SE *choke*]

choked *adj.*[2] [1990s+] (*US campus*) drunk. [one's inability to speak coherently]

choked by a hempen quinsey *phr.* [late 18C–early 19C] hanged. [SE *quinsey*, inflammation of the throat, tonsillitis; *hempen* refers to the hangman's noose]

choked down *adj.* [1970s+] (*US Black*) well-dressed (cf. CHOKED UP (TIGHT) *adj.*). [CHOKER *n.*[3] (7)]

choked off *adj. see* CHOKED *adj.*[1] (1).

choke dog *n.* **1** [early 19C] rum, grog. **2** [late 19C–1910s] cheese. [joc. ref. to the effects; note D'Urfey, *Pills to Purge Melancholy* (1719–20): 'She made such puddings would choak a Dog']

choked up *adj. see* CHOKED *adj.*[1] (1).

choked up (tight) *adj.* [1960s+] (*US Black*) formally dressed, spec. in a buttoned-up shirt (cf. CHOKED DOWN *adj.*). [CHOKER *n.*[3] (7)]

chokee *n. see* CHOKEY *n.*

choke'em arse *n.* [1900s] (*Can.*) cheese. [SE *choke* + ARSE *n.*[1] (1); its constipatory effects]

choke in *v. see* CHOKE *v.*[1] (1).

choke Kojak *v.* (*also* **strangle Kojak**) [1990s+] to masturbate. [SE *choke*/*strangle* + proper name *Kojak*, a detective played by the bald Telly Savalas (1924–94) in the eponymous 1970s US TV series (cf. BALD-HEADED HERMIT *n.*)]

choke-me *n.* [1950s] (*W.I.*) foofoo, a mixture of yams, plantains and cassava boiled and then pounded into a thick mass. [its heavy, cloying consistency]

choke off *v.* **1** [19C+] to silence in mid-flow, to stop someone from talking. **2** [mid-19C] (*UK Und.*) to arrest, to seize. **3** [mid-late 19C] to render someone uninterested (in). **4** [mid-19C+] to get rid of someone or something. **5** [mid-19C+] to halt a person's activities. **6** [late 19C] to dismiss, to ignore. **7** [late 19C] to stop one's own one's action, speech etc. **8** [1910s–20s] to reprimand. [SE *choke v.* + the use of a *choke* to force a dog to relinquish its grip]

choke one's lizard *v. see* GALLOP THE (OLD) LIZARD *v.*

choke pear *n.* (*also* **choak pear**) [late 16C–early 19C] an unanswerable objection, a reproof. [SE *choke pear*, an instrument of torture, similar in shape to the rubber gags favoured by today's sado-masochism adepts, made of an iron 'pear', which is forced into the victim's mouth. A key is turned and spikes protrude from the metal into the mouth, rendering it impossible to remove unless the mouth is cut or another key obtained. This object was itself derived f. 16C *choke pear*, an inedible, hard pear, suitable for making the drink perry, but rejected as a dessert]

choker *n.*[1] **1** [early 19C] a rebuff. **2** [mid-19C] an especially amusing story or anecdote, a lie. **3** [late 19C–1910s] an embarrassing question. **4** [1950s+] a disappointment, an annoyance. **5** [1950s+] (*Irish*) a person who fails to come up to expectations. [CHOKE *v.*[1]/SE *choke*]

choker *n.*[2] **1** [early 19C] a large quantity. **2** [1920s–30s] cheese.

choker *n.*[3] **1** [mid-19C] a garrotter. **2** [mid-19C] a cravat; thus *white-choker*, the white cravat worn by tavern waiters or mutes at a funeral and thus the waiter himself. **3** [mid-late 19C] a clergyman. **4** [mid-19C–1930s] the hangman's noose; thus the hangman. **5** [mid-19C–1960s] a high collar. **6** [late 19C–1930s] a large neckerchief, which was worn high round the throat.

7 [1900s–40s] (*US Black*) a tie. [fig. uses of SE *choker*, that which chokes]

choker *n.*[4] **1** [mid-19C+] a prison. **2** [1990s+] (*Irish*) a cell for solitary confinement.

choker *n.*[5] [1910s–40s] (*Irish*) a cigarette.

choke-rag *n.* (*also* **choke-strap**) [1940s–50s] (*US*) a necktie. [SE and its supposed effect on the (reluctant) wearer]

choker-hole *n.* [1920s–40s] (*US*) a doughnut. [the fat-saturated dough is likely to choke the eater]

chokes *n.* [1980s+] (*US drugs*) an extreme response to taking an extra-large puff on a marijuana cigarette or a pipe.

chokes and croaks *n.* [1960s+] (*US campus*) a course in first aid and safety education.

choke-strap *n. see* CHOKE-RAG n.

choke the chicken *v.* [1990s+] (*also* **choke the chook**) **1** to masturbate (cf. BEAT ONE'S HOG v.). **2** to masturbate a partner.

choke up *v.*[1] **1** [mid-18C; 20C+] to speak. **2** [20C+] (*US*) to give unwillingly, esp. to pay a long-standing debt.

choke up *v.*[2] *see* CHOKE v.[1] (1).

choke up tight *v. see* CHOKED UP (TIGHT) adj.

chokey *n.* (*also* **chauki, chokee**) [mid-19C+] **1** a prison; also in fig. use. **2** (*UK Und.*) the punishment cells. **3** imprisonment. **4** the prison punishment diet of bread and water; thus *chokey merchant*, one who is suffering such a punishment. [Hind. *chauki*, a 4-sided building or a shed, esp. a custom's house or police station and thus a lock-up]

chokey *v.* [1930s–50s] (*UK prison*) to place in the punishment cells. [CHOKEY n. (2)]

choking oyster *n.* (*also* **stopping oyster**) [late 15C–16C] a reply that silences one's opponent.

choking pie *n.* (*also* **cold pie**) [17C–early 19C] a heavy-handed practical joke played on someone who falls asleep in company; cotton is wrapped up in a tube of paper, this is then set on fire and the smoke is directed up the sleeper's nostrils.

chokka *n.* (*also* **chocker**) [mid-19C+] a man. [ety. unknown]

chokka *adj.* (*also* **chocka, chocker, chokker**) **1** [1920s+] full to the brim. **2** [1940s+] extremely dissatisfied, unhappy, 'fed up'. **3** [1990s+] (*UK juv.*) great, wonderful, excellent. [SE *choc full* or CHOCK-A-BLOCK adj.]

choko *n. see* CHOCO n.[2].

choky *adj. see* CHOKED adj.[1] (1).

cholita *n.* (*also* **chola**) [1960s+] (*US*) **1** a derog. term for a Mexican woman, esp. one considered of a lower class or mixed blood (cf. BATO n.). **2** a female member of a teen gang. [fem. CHOLO n.]

cholly *n.*[1] [1960s] (*US gay*) a prostitute's client, i.e. one who pays in dollars. [? MR CHARLIE n., the source of employment and thus money]

cholly *n.*[2] [1970s+] (*drugs*) cocaine (cf. AUNT NORA n.). [CHARLIE n.[9] (1)]

cholly *n.*[3] *see* CHARLEY n.[2].

cholly hoss *n. see* HORSE n.[4] (3).

cholo *n.* (*US*) **1** [mid-19C+] a derog. term for a Mexican or South American, esp. one considered of a lower class or mixed blood (cf. BATO n.; CHOLITA n.). **2** [1970s+] a teenage gang member. [*Cholollán*, now *Cholula*, a district of Mexico]

cholo *adj.* [1930s+] pertaining to a Mexican or Mexican culture. [CHOLO n. (1)]

chom *n. see* CHOMUS n.

chommie *n.* (*also* **tjommie**) [1940s+] (*S.Afr.*) a friend, a pal, a mate, also as a form of address. [SE *chum*]

cho-mo *n.* [1990s+] (*US Und.*) child molester. [abbr.]

chomp *n.* [1960s+] a bite, a mouthful. [SE *chomp*, to bite, to chew]

chomp *v.* [1980s+] (*US campus*) to be disgusting, unappealing, second-rate. [orig. computer jargon]

chomper *n.* [1980s+] (*US campus*) anyone or anything inferior, second-rate, unappealing. [CHOMP v.]

chompers *n.* [20C+] (*US*) teeth, either genuine or false. [SE *chomp*, to take a bite]

chomus *n.* (*also* **chom**) [1930s+] (*US*) a (private) detective. [var. on SHAMUS n. (2)]

chone *n.* [1960s] (*US*) sexual intercourse. [ety. unknown; ? abbr. ACTION n. (2)]

chong *adj.* [2000s] (*UK teen*) attractive. [ety. unknown]

chonga *n.* [2000s] (*drugs*) cocaine. [ety. unknown]

chonk *n.* [1990s+] sexual intercourse. [fig. use of CHONK v.]

chonk *v.* [1930s] (*US Und.*) to hit over the hit (with a sap). [echoic]

chonkeys *n.* [mid-19C] a form of meat pasty, sold in the streets. [ety. unknown; E.P., after Ware, suggests the proper name of a long-forgotten pieman, but note Fr. sl. *chancre*, a paunch (lit. 'ulcer') and *manger comme un chancre*, to eat heartily]

chooch *n.*[1] [1970s+] (*US*) a fool; esp. large and thuggish (cf. AIREDALE n.). [southern Ital. *ciuccio*, a donkey; thus a fool]

chooch *n.*[2] [1980s+] (*US drugs*) a stingy dealer. [? CHINCH n.[2]]

choo-choo *n. see* TRAIN n.[1].

choof *n.* [1980s+] (*Aus. drugs*) cannabis. [? SE *chuff*, to puff]

choof (off) *v.* (*also* **chuff**) [1940s+] (*Aus.*) to go, to move, to leave. [SE *chuff*, to go, usu. of a locomotive]

choogle *v.* [1960s+] (*US*) **1** to drive around. **2** in fig. use, to continue; to persist. [? *choo-choo* + *chug*, i.e. train noises]

chook *n.* (*also* **chook-chook, chookie**) (*usu. Aus./NZ*) **1** [late 19C+] a chicken. **2** [1930s] a punning nickname for anyone called Fowler or other 'chicken' surnames. **3** [1940s+] a woman. **4** [1950s+] a fool (cf. AIREDALE n.). [SE *chicken*]

chookie *n.* (*also* **chooky**) **1** [1940s+] (*Aus.*) a general term of affection. **2** [1980s] (*N.Z.*) a girlfriend; any young woman. [CHOOK n. (3)]

chook's bum *n.* [1980s] (*N.Z.*) the mouth. [CHOOK n. (1) + BUM n.[1] (1), ult. ? resemblance]

choom *n.* [1910s+] (*Aus./N.Z.*) **1** an Englishman. **2** a term of address. [northern pron. of *chum*, picked up by ANZAC forces in WW1]

choops *n.* [2000s] (*US Black*) a cigarette. [ety. unknown]

choops! *excl.* [mid-19C–1900s] (*orig. Anglo-Ind.*) be quiet! shut up! [Hind. *chuprao*, keep quiet]

choor *v.* [2000s] **1** to steal. **2** to arrest. [CHORE v.]

choose *v.* [1960s+] (*US Black*) for a prostitute to select the pimp for whom she will work; thus *choosing money*, the voluntary donation of her earnings by the prostitute to signify to her new pimp that she has chosen him.

choose off *v.* [1970s+] (*US Black*) to challenge to a fight; thus imper. *choose off!*; to fight.

choose out *v.* [1930s+] (*US*) to challenge to a fight.

choose up *v.* [1960s+] (*US prison*) for an experienced inmate to select a newcomer as a homosexual partner, whether or not the latter agrees to act as one.

choosing money *n.* [1970s+] money that a new prostitute gives her pimp on joining his STABLE n. (2). [CHOOSE v.]

chootah *adj.* [mid-19C–1940s] (*orig. Anglo-Ind.*) small, insignificant. [Urdu *chota*, small]

chop *n.*[1] **1** [late 18C–early 19C] a blow with the fist, esp. to the face. **2** [1960s+] a blow in martial arts, using the side of the hand. **3** [1990s+] (*drugs*) the chopping of cocaine into lines.

chop *n.*[2] (*also* **chop-chop**) [early 19C+] food; thus *small chop*, small items of food. [orig. W.Afr. pidgin, where colonists and Africans alike used it to describe indigenous food. It was further suggested that orig. chop meant a particular dish, 'long pig', human flesh]

chop *n.*[3] **1** [mid-19C+] (*mainly Aus.*) something to be valued or prized. **2** [late 19C] (*UK Und.*) a bargain based on exchange of goods. **3** [1910s+] (*orig. Aus.*) a share, a portion.

chop *n.*[4] [1940s+] (*orig. US*) a cut, usu. in a salary or in a price.

chop *n.*[5] [1950s–70s] (*US juv.*) an insult, a cruel remark. [CHOP v.[5] (2)]

chop n.[6] [1980s+] (*UK Black*) gold, as in chains, rings and similar jewellery. [? SE *chop*, goods bearing a mark that determines their quality]

chop v.[1] (*also* **chop up**) [mid-17C–early 19C] **1** to do something quickly. **2** [late 18C–mid-19C] to speak. [SE *chop*, to thrust or move with force or suddenness]

chop v.[2] (*also* **chop down**) **1** [mid-18C+] to kill. **2** [1920s+] (*US*) to shoot, esp. with an automatic weapon. **3** [1950s] (*US Und.*) to stab. [SE *chop*; (2) CHOPPER n.[5] (1)]

chop v.[3] [mid-19C; 1960s+] to eat. [CHOP n.[2]]

chop v.[4] [mid–late 19C] to eat a chop.

chop v.[5] **1** [late 19C–1950s] (*US*) to stop what one is doing. **2** [1950s–70s] (*US Black*) to attack someone verbally, to discredit someone, to have the last word. **3** [1970s] (*US Black*) to walk. **4** [1980s+] to dismiss from a job. [ext. of SE *chop*, to cut (off)]

chop v.[6] [1910s] (*Aus.*) **1** to share. **2** to interfere. [CHOP n.[3] (3)]

chop v.[7] [1940s–50s] to hang someone. [? the 'chopping off' of the victim's breath]

chop v.[8] [1950s+] (*orig. US*) to customize a car or motorcycle. [one 'chops' it up]

chop v.[9] [1960s+] (*drugs*) to adulterate, usu. a drug in powder form. [SE *chop*, to cut; one chops up the drug with whatever adulterant one is using]

chop v.[10] [1960s+] of a man, to have sexual intercourse (cf. BANG v.[1]).

chop by chance n. [late 17C–early 18C] a very rare or extraordinary event.

chop-chop n. see CHOP n.[2].

chop-chop v. [mid-19C+] to hurry. [CHOP-CHOP! excl.]

chop-chop adv. [mid-19C+] quickly, fast. [CHOP-CHOP v.]

chop-chop! excl. [mid-19C+] hurry up! [Chinese pidgin, orig. Chinese *k'wâi-k'wâi*]

chop-church n. (*also* **church-chopper**) [late 18C–early 19C] a corrupt dealer in benefices, the choicest of which could be sold off to the highest bidder. [SE *chop*, to barter + *church*]

chop cotton v. [1960s] (*US*) to work hard.

chop down v. see CHOP v.[2].

chop it! excl. [1950s] (*US*) stop it! forget it! [CHOP v.[5] (1)]

chop it up v. [1950s–60s] (*US*) to discuss, to talk about.

chop no hash v. [1900s] (*US*) to make no impression, to be of no importance.

chop off v. [late 19C–1930s] (*US*) to finish, to bring to a conclusion, e.g. of work. [SE *chop*, to cut]

chopped hay n. [1910s–20s] imperfectly assimilated knowledge.

chopped liver n. [1940s+] (*US*) anything seen as trivial; esp. in phr. *now that ain't chopped liver*, that is important.

chopper n.[1] **1** [late 18C–mid-19C] a blow to the face. **2** [1910s+] (*Aus.*) a blow to the back of the neck, given with the side of the hand. **3** [1940s+] the penis. [SE *chop*, to cut]

chopper n.[2] [late 19C–1900s] (*US*) a ticket-taker. [they *chop* or tear in half the tickets]

chopper n.[3] **1** [late 19C+] an open, straight-bladed razor. **2** [1990s+] (*US prison*) a stabbing weapon.

chopper n.[4] [late 19C+] a tail. [ety. unknown; ? its wagging is a chopping motion]

chopper n.[5] **1** [1920s+] (*US*) a Thompson sub-machine gun, usu. gangster use; thus *chopper squad*, a group of men carrying such guns. **2** [1920s+] (*US*) one who uses a sub-machinegun. **3** [2000s] (*US Black*) any form of gun. [it 'chops down' its targets]

chopper n.[6] [1940s+] (*Aus.*) a Roman Catholic. [abbr. ROCK-CHOPPER n.]

chopper n.[7] [1950s+] a helicopter. [the rotor blades resemble those of a food processor, i.e. they 'chop']

chopper n.[8] [1960s+] (*orig. US*) a cut-down, customized motorcycle, spec. a Harley-Davidson, preferred for speed and style by outlaw motorcycle gangs, e.g. Hell's Angels. [CHOP v.[8]]

chopper n.[9] [1980s] (*N.Z. campus*) a derog. term for a Malaysian. [ety. unknown]

chopper v. [1960s+] **1** to travel by helicopter. **2** to transport by helicopter. [CHOPPER n.[7]]

choppers n. **1** [early–mid-19C] the jaw. **2** [1940s+] the teeth; thus *china choppers*, false teeth. **3** [1960s] (*US Black*) the legs, esp. the thighs.

chopping adj. [mid-17C–early 19C] lusty, sexually forward. [SE *chopping*, vigorous, large, strapping]

chopping high adj. [1950s] (*US Black*) living well. [CHOP v.[3]]

chopping sticks n. see CHOPSTICKS n.

choppy-socky adj. see CHOP-SOCKY adj.

chops n.[1] **1** [late 16C+] (*also* **chaps**) the jaws, the mouth, the lips. **2** [late 19C] (*Aus.*) food, a meal. **3** [20C+] a synon. for ARSE n.[1] (4); esp. in phr. *freeze/sweat/work one's chops off*. **4** [1940s+] (*orig. US Black*) ability, skill, competence. [16C SE; (4) f. jazz musicians fig. ref. to the use of one's mouth and lips in playing a wind instrument]

chops n.[2] [1980s] (*UK Black*) jewellery. [ety. unknown]

chops v. [1990s+] (*UK juv.*) to be cheeky, to be verbose. [CHOPS n.[1] (1)]

chop-shop n. [1960s+] a garage where cars or motorbikes can be customized. [CHOP v.[8] + SE *shop*]

chop-socky adj. (*also* **choppy-socky**) [1970s+] (*orig. US*) used of a kung-fu film. [SE *chop*, to do a spec. martial arts move, to slice + SOCK v.[1] (1)]

chopstick n. [1940s+] (*US Black*) a derog. term for an Asian or Oriental person, esp. Chinese; also attrib. (cf. AH CABBAGE n.; BROWNIE n.[2]). [the use of chopsticks in eating Oriental food]

chopsticks n. (*also* **chopping sticks**) [1940s+] (*bingo*) the number 6 or 26 (cf. ALDERSHOT LADIES n.). [rhy. sl.]

chop suey n. [1920s+] (*US*) **1** a Chinese person (cf. AH CABBAGE n.). **2** a Chinese restaurant. **3** a person of mixed ancestry. [SE *chopped up* + *chop suey*, a dish of stir-fried meat and vegetables, created by Chinese chefs for their Western customers. Not part of Oriental cuisine, it was seen as adequate for the Western palate. The orig. Chinese is *shap suì*, mixed bits]

chop ten v. see COCK TEN v.

chop the whiners v. see WHINERS n.

chop-up n. [1910s+] (*Aus. Und.*) a division of plunder. [CHOP n.[3] (3)/SE *chop up*]

chop up v. see CHOP v.[1].

chop up the whiners v. see WHINERS n.

chop wood v. [1960s–70s] (*US*) to snore. [echoic]

chorb n. [1970s+] (*S.Afr. teen*) a spot, a pimple, acne. [? Bantu *chubaba*, a skin blemish]

chore v. (*also* **chory**) [1970s+] to steal (cf. CORE v.). [Rom. *cor/chore*, to steal; thus link to costermonger *chordy gear*, stolen goods]

chorie n. [2000s] a thief. [CHORE v.]

chorrie n. (*also* **tjorie**, **tjorrie**) [1960s+] (*S.Afr.*) a broken-down old car. [Afk. *tjor*, a crock]

chorros n. [1990s+] (*US prison/Hisp.*) a lookout. [? Sp.]

chorus and verse n. [1990s+] the anus, the rectum (cf. BOTTLE AND GLASS n.). [rhy. sl. = erse, i.e. arse]

chorus man n. [1920s] (*US*) an effeminate, poss. homosexual, man.

chory v. see CHORE v.

chosen adj. [1960s+] (*US prison*) selected, like it or not, as the homosexual lover of an older, tougher inmate. [CHOOSE UP v.]

chosen pals n. (*also* **chosen pells**) [late 18C] (*UK Und.*) highwaymen who go out robbing in pairs. [SE *choose* + Gypsy *pal*, an accomplice in crime]

chossel n. [20C+] (*W.I.*) a girlfriend. [CHOSSEL v.]

chossel v. [20C+] (*W.I.*) to start a romantic or sexual relationship. [? SE *choose* + HUSTLE v. (1)]

chota n. [1960s+] (*US*) **1** the police. **2** a police informer. [Sp.]

chotchkie n. see TCHOTCHKE n.

chote *n.* [20C+] (*W.I.*) flattery of another person or boasting about oneself; thus *give someone* (*a lot of*) *chote*, to attempt to persuade someone through such talk. [CHOTE v.]

chote *v.* [20C+] (*W.I.*) to flatter, to persuade through compliments. [Sp. *chotear*, to joke, to banter]

chounter *v.* [late 17C–18C] to talk sharply and sometimes aggressively. [either earlier form of *chunter* (as suggested by *OED*) or f. Devon dial. *chounting*, taunting, jeering, grumbling]

chouse *n.* (*also* **chowse**) **1** [mid-17C] a cheat, a swindler. **2** [mid-17C–mid-18C] a dupe, a gullible victim. **3** [early–mid-18C] a swindle, a confidence trick. [Turkish *chiaus*, *chaus*, an official messenger. The link here comes either from the fleecing in 1609 of some Turkish and Persian merchants by an agent or *chiaus* of Sir Robert Shirley (the *OED* rejects this for lack of corroborative evidence), or from the philologist Thomas Henshaw's remark that a Turkish messenger 'is little better than a fool', a dictum that he claimed was sufficient proof of an ety.]

chouse *v.* (*also* **chowse, chowze**) [mid-17C+] to trick, to defraud; often as *chouse someone out of.* [CHOUSE n. (1)]

chouser *n.* [early 18C–19C] a swindler, a confidence trickster. [CHOUSE v.]

chout *n.* [mid-19C] (*East London*) a show, an entertainment. [? SE *shout* or f. East Anglian dial. *chout*, merry-making, a frolic]

chovey *n.* [late 18C–19C] a shop; thus *ann-chovey* and *man-chovey*, the female and male shop assistant. [ety. unknown]

chovy bouncing *n.* [late 19C] (*Aus. Und.*) shoplifting. [CHOVEY n. + BOUNCE v.[1] (6)]

Chow *n.* [late 19C+] (*Aus.*) a derog. term for a Chinese person, esp. an immigrant or a descendant of one (cf. AH CABBAGE n.). [abbr. pidgin *chow-chow*, food; ult. ? the *chow* dog, eaten in China]

Chow *adj.* [1910s+] (*Aus.*) a derog. term describing a Chinese person or thing. [CHOW n.]

chow *n.*[1] **1** [mid-19C] (*UK prison*) a single 'chew' of tobacco. **2** [mid-19C+] food, esp. in an institutional setting, e.g. an army mess-hall or prison. **3** [late 19C+] a meal-time, usu. in some form of institution. **4** [1920s+] (*Aus.*) cabbage. **5** [1940s] snuff. **6** [1950s–60s] a meal. [Anglo-Chinese pidgin *chow*, a mixture (of any kind) thus food; (4) ? Fr. *choux*, cabbage]

chow *n.*[2] [late 19C–1910s] talk; thus *have plenty of chow*, to be highly loquacious. [orig. theatrical use; ult. ety. unknown; ? CHEW v.[1] (2)/JAW n. (1)]

chow *v.*[1] [mid-19C+] to eat; to *chow up*, prepare food. [CHOW n.[1] (2)]

chow *v.*[2] [late 19C] to chatter, to prattle. [CHOW n.[2]; mainly theatrical use]

chow *phr.* [1960s+] goodbye. [pron. of CIAO phr.]

chow box *v.* [1990s+] (*US*) to perform cunnilingus (cf. BOX LUNCH n.). [CHOW v.[1], i.e. EAT v.[3] + BOX n.[1] (1)]

chow cart *n. see* CHOW WAGON n.

chow-chow *n.* **1** [mid-19C–1940s] (*orig. Anglo-Chinese, later Aus./N.Z.*) food; occas. as v., to eat. **2** [mid-19C+] (*Aus.*) a derog. term for a Chinese person (cf. AH CABBAGE n.). [pidgin *chow-chow*, an edible mixture, typically of pickles or preserves, also a mixed cargo]

chowdar *n.* (*also* **chowder**) [mid-19C] a fool. [? Anglo-Chinese, but note CHOWDER-HEAD n.]

chowder-head *n.* (*also* **chowder-brain**) [mid-19C+] (*US*) a fool, a stupid person (cf. APPLEHEAD n.). [SAmE *chowder*, a fish stew + -HEAD sfx (1) but more prob. corruption of JOLTERHEAD n.]

chowder-headed *adj.* [early–mid-19C] foolish (cf. AIRHEADED adj.). [CHOWDER-HEAD n., although slightly predates]

chow down *v.* **1** [1940s+] (*US*) to eat voraciously; also as imper. *chow down*, start eating. **2** [1950s+] (*US*) to perform oral sex (cf. BASKET LUNCH n.; BOX LUNCH n.). **3** [1960s] (*US campus*) to kiss, to pet. [CHOW v.[1]]

chow for now *phr.* [1990s+] (*US campus*) goodbye. [CHOW phr. + assonance]

chow hound *n.* [1910s+] a glutton. [CHOW n.[1] (2) + HOUND sfx]

Chowland *n.* [1900s] (*Aus.*) Queensland. [CHOW n. + SE -*land*; the destination of many Chinese immigrants]

chow line *n.* [1910s+] (*US, orig. milit.*) a queue for food. [CHOW n.[1] (2) + SAmE *line*, queue]

chow out *v.* [1970s+] (*US campus*) to overeat. [CHOW v.[1]]

chow over *v. see* CHEW (IT) OVER v.

chowse *see under* CHOUSE.

chow up *v. see* CHOW v.[1].

chow wagon *n.* (*also* **chow cart**) [1940s+] (*US prison*) a trolley carrying prisoners' meals. [CHOW n.[1] (2) + SE *wagon*/*cart*]

chowze *v. see* CHOUSE v.

chrimbo *n.* (*also* **crimbo**) [1980s+] Christmas. [abbr.]

chrissie *n.*[1] [1950s+] (*Irish*) a working-class person with delusions of grandeur, esp. as shown in their dress sense. [*Chrissie*, a character in the play *Liffey Lane* (1951) by Maura Laverty]

chrissie *n.*[2] (*also* **chrissy**) [1970s+] Christmas. [abbr.]

Christ *n.* (*also* **the Christ**) [1940s+] a general abstract intensifier, implying quantity, strength etc; a synon. with FUCK, THE n., HELL, THE phr.[1] (2), SHIT, THE n.[3].

Christ! *excl.* (*also* **by Christ! my Christ!**) [late 17C+] the main blasphemous oath, which carried a good deal more resonance when religion (and thus potential blasphemy) had greater power? (cf. JESUS (CHRIST)! excl.).

christacrutchian *n.* (*also* **chian**) [1990s+] (*US*) a Bible-thumping, back-sliding hypocrite. [CHRIST ON A CRUTCH! excl.]

Christ almighty *adj.* [20C+] a general intensifier. [CHRIST ALMIGHTY! excl.]

Christ almighty! *excl.* [20C+] a common blasphemous excl.

Christ-awful *adj.* [1940s+] (*orig. US*) especially appalling. [var. on GOD-AWFUL adj.]

Christ-bitten *adj.* [1930s+] (*US*) a general derog. description e.g. *these Christ-bitten idiots*. [lit. *bitten by Christ*, i.e. fanatically religious]

christen *v.* **1** [mid-18C–19C] (*UK Und.*) to change the markings on a stolen watch to facilitate its resale. **2** [late 18C–early 19C] to water down wine or spirits; thus *christened*, adulterated. **3** [late 19C+] to carry out a practical joke in which a chamberpot is emptied over someone's head. **4** [late 19C+] to mark or otherwise damage, esp. of a dog that reveals its lack of house-training. **5** [late 19C+] to use for the first time.

christened by a baker *adj.* (*also* **christened by the baker**) [late 18C–early 19C] freckle-faced. [freckles are reminiscent of spots of brown flour]

christener *n.* [late 18C–19C] a criminal who fakes the identity marks – the 'christening' – on cheap gold and silver watches. [CHRISTEN v. (1)]

christer *n.* (*also* **christ-shouter**) [1920s+] (*US*) a derog. term for an overly religious person, esp. a proselytizing teetotaller. [orig. referring to those who belonged to US college Christian Associations of the 1920s]

Christian *n.*[1] [17C+] an overly religious person.

Christian *n.*[2] [early–mid-19C] a tradesman who is willing to give credit. [he has 'faith' in the creditor]

Christian *n.*[3] [1960s] (*US Black*) a cigar.

Christian *adj.* [19C] of things, 'decent', 'respectable' or 'presentable'.

Christian pony *n.* **1** [late 18C] a chairman of a meeting. **2** [late 18C–early 19C] a sedan chair man. **3** [mid–late 19C] (*Can.*) a handcart man. [SE *Christian*, a human being + *pony*, generic for a beast of burden]

christina *n.* (*also* **cris, cristina**) [1970s+] (*drugs*) amphetamine, methamphetamine (cf. A n.[2]; BOMBITA n.). [SE *crystal*]

Christ Jesus! *excl. see* JESUS (CHRIST)! excl.

Christ-killer *n.*[1] [mid-19C+] (*US*) a derog. term for a Jew (cf. ARAB n.[2]). [the teaching by trad. Christianity that the Jews killed Christ and should be punished accordingly]

Christ-killer n.[2] [1930s] (US) a noisy political orator. [the majority of such orators were self-proclaimed atheists]

Christless adj. [1910s+] (US) a synon. for GOD-DAMN adj. (1).

christly adj. [1910s+] (US) a general intensifier.

Christmas! excl. [20C+] a euph. for CHRIST! excl.

christmas adj. [1960s] (N.Z.) fine, admirable.

Christmas card n. [1950s+] a train guard, a military guard. [rhy. sl.]

Christmas compliments n. [late 18C–early 19C] a cough, 'kibed' (chillblained) heels and a snotty nose. [the effects of winter weather. Grose (1796) includes the synon. *Christian compliments* but it is a misprint, as can be seen by his cross-ref. to 'Christmas' at 'compliment']

Christmas crackers n. [1970s+] the testicles; thus *Christmas crackered*, utterly exhausted (cf. CHEESE AND CRACKERS n.). [rhy. sl. = KNACKERS n.; *Christmas crackered* = KNACKERED adj. (1)]

Christmas eve v. [1930s+] to believe. [rhy. sl.]

Christmas hold n. [1950s+] (Aus.) a squeeze of one's opponent's testicles. [pun on 'hand full of nuts/NUTS n.[2] (1)', in SE a popular Yuletide pleasure]

Christmas log n. [1970s] a dog. [rhy. sl.]

Christmas rolls n. [1960s–70s] (drugs) a mixture of different coloured depressant pills.

Christmas tree n.[1] (drugs) 1 [1960s+] a stimulant (Deximal spansules). 2 [1960s+] a depressant (Butabarbital, Tuinal). 3 [1980s] LSD (cf. A n.[3]). 4 [2000s] marijuana (cf. AFRICAN BUSH n.). [the multi-coloured pills are reminiscent of a Christmas tree's lights]

Christmas tree n.[2] [1980s] (US) an over-made-up or overdressed woman. [abbr. phr. *lit up like a Christmas tree*]

Christmas tree n.[3] [1990s+] the human knee. [rhy. sl.]

Christmas tree n.[4] [1990s+] (US prison) a makeshift, homemade knife. [its triangular shape, plus the serrated edges filed into the knife are supposedly reminiscent of the stereotyped Christmas pine]

Christ on a bike! excl. [1960s+] a mild excl. (cf. JESUS CHRIST ON A RAFT! excl.).

Christ on a crutch! excl. [1940s+] a mild excl.

Christ on a fire engine! excl. [1990s+] a general expression of surprise.

Christopher! excl. (also **by Christopher!**) [mid-19C+] a euph. for CHRIST! excl.

Christopher Columbus! excl. [1940s+] a euph. for CHRIST! excl. [ult. explorer and discover of America, *Christopher Columbus* (1451–1506)]

Christopher Lee n. [1990s+] an act of urination (cf. ANGEL'S KISS n.). [rhy. sl. = PEE n.[1] (2)/WEE n.; ult. UK actor *Christopher Lee* (b.1922)]

christ-shouter n. *see* CHRISTER n.

chrome n. 1 [1970s+] (US Black) a gun. 2 [1990s+] (US Black) loose change, esp. dimes, quarters and half-dollars. [(1) the *chrome* finish applied to many models of pistol/revolver; (2) the silvery colour]

chrome dome n. [1960s+] (orig. US) 1 a bald head. 2 a bald-headed person. [SE *chrome* + DOME n. (1)]

chrome-plated adj. [1950s] (US gay) dressed up in one's best or new clothes.

chromo n. [late 19C+] 1 (Aus.) (also **cromo**) a prostitute. 2 an ugly, distasteful person. 3 (US campus) something above average. [SE *chromolithograph*, a picture printed in colours from stone. Although the term is uniquely Aus., it originates in the comparison by US writer Francis Brett Harte (1836–1902) of an overdressed, over-made-up prostitute with a chromolithograph – both are colourful and flashy, but neither resembles natural beauty]

chromo adj. [late 19C+] (US) spurious, fake, counterfeit. [abbr. SE *chromolithographic* (*see* CHROMO n.)]

chronic n. (drugs) 1 [1920s–50s] a regular narcotics user. 2 [1980s+] one who smokes cannabis every day. 3 [1990s+] extra-strong marijuana (cf. BOMB n.[4]). 4 [2000s] marijuana mixed with crack cocaine. [SE *chronic*, severe, extreme; thus the extent of the habit or the drug's effects. In both cases an example of the bad = good model + ? CHRONIC adj. (1)]

chronic adj. 1 [late 19C+] extreme, usu. in a negative sense; often as phr. *something chronic*. 2 [1990s+] (orig. US drugs) of marijuana, first-rate, very strong.

chronic v. [1910s–30s] (US tramp) to beg; to investigate. [? one poses as a *chronic* invalid]

chroniced (out) adj. [1990s+] (US Black/drugs) intoxicated by very strong marijuana. [CHRONIC n. (3)]

chronicker n. (also **croniker**) 1 [1910s–30s] (US tramp) a tramp who begs food rather than money. 2 [1920s–30s] an ill-natured tramp. [CHRONIC v.]

chryssie n. [1920s+] (Aus.) a *chrys*anthemum. [abbr.]

chub n.[1] 1 [early 16C–early 19C] an inexperienced, naïve person, a fool. 2 [mid-16C–18C] a rustic simpleton; thus adj. *chubbish* (cf. BACON n.[1]). 3 [mid-19C+] a fat person; the fat on their body. 4 [late 19C] (US campus) a child, a baby. [SE *chub*, a short, squat fish; thus a pun on 'thick' or 'dense'; (1) and (2) the fish is 'easily taken' notes Grose (1785)]

chub n.[2] [19C] a Texan. [ety. unknown; ? ref. to CHUB n.[1] (3)]

chub n.[3] *see* CHUBBY n.[2].

chubb v. *see* CHUBB (UP) v.

chubbies n. [1960s–70s] (US) large and attractive female breasts.

chubbingly adj. [late 17C–early 18C] chubby.

chubbly n. [1990s+] a fat woman's breast. [SE *chubby*/CHUBBIES n.]

chubbo n. (also **chub-chub, chubo, chubo twin**) [1970s+] (US) a fat person. [CHUB n.[1] (3)]

chubbs n. [1990s+] (US Black) a fat person. [CHUB n.[1] (3)]

chubb (up) v. [1940s–80s] (UK prison) to lock up a cell for the night; thus *unchubb*, to unlock. [the proprietary name of *Chubb* locks]

chubby n.[1] [1920s] a short, squat umbrella.

chubby n.[2] (also **chub**) [1990s+] an erection. [play on CRACK A FAT v.]

chubby-chaser n. [1970s+] a man who prefers (unfashionably) plump or fat women or, if gay, men.

chubbyfat adj. [1940s–50s] (US Black) very fat, obese.

chub-chub n. *see* CHUBBO n.

chubette n. [1950s+] a fat person, usu. a young woman, but in camp gay use a boy. [CHUB n.[1] (3) + SE fem. sfx -*ette*]

chub off v. [late 19C–1900s] (US) to lose. [? CHUB n.[1] (1)]

chubo (twin) n. *see* CHUBBO n.

chuc n. (also **chuco**) [1940s+] (US) 1 a Mexican-American, esp. a member of a street gang (cf. BATO n.). 2 a pointed shoe, associated with Mexican youths. [abbr. PACHUCO n.]

Chuck n. (also **Mr Chuck**) [1960s+] (US Black) a White man. [colloq. *Chuck*, the nickname derived from Charles, thus MR CHARLIE n. (1)]

chuck n.[1] [late 16C+] a term of endearment. [dial. The term also meant a call to fowls (or pigs). It persists in 20C+ northern dial., typified by its use in the UK ITV soap opera *Coronation Street*]

chuck n.[2] 1 [mid-18C+] a toss, a throw. 2 [late 19C+] the act of rejection, usu. as *the chuck* and usu. in the context of terminating a relationship or a term of employment; thus *sling (someone) the chuck*, to end a relationship; GET THE CHUCK v.; GIVE SOMEONE THE CHUCK(-UP) v. 3 [1960s+] (Aus.) vomit. 4 [1960s+] (Aus.) an act of vomiting. 5 [1980s] (Aus.) a temper tantrum. [CHUCK v.[1]]

chuck n.[3] 1 [mid-19C–1900s] the act of eating, a mealtime. 2 [mid-19C+] food. 3 [mid-19C+] (UK prison) bread. [orig. referring to bread and ship-biscuit only, ult. ? f. *chuck*, a lump or hunk (of food)]

chuck n.[4] [late 19C+] a verdict of not guilty. [CHUCK OUT v.]

chuck n.[5] *see* CHUCK-FARTHING n.

chuck *adj.* [1960s–70s] (*US Black*) racially White. [CHUCK n.]

chuck *v.*[1] **1** [late 16C+] to throw away/down/into/over/up. **2** [mid-17C; late 19C+] to end an affair, to reject a lover. **3** [mid-19C+] to do or perform, usu. with a defining n. (often referring to a fit or similar convulsion); in many combs. below. **4** [late 19C] to eject. **5** [late 19C–1910s] to dismiss from employment. **6** [late 19C+] to give up, to abandon, to stop doing something. **7** [late 19C+] to spend extravagantly. **8** [late 19C+] (*UK Und.*) to find not guilty. **9** [late 19C+] to throw out, e.g. of a tavern. **10** [1900s] (*Aus.*) to donate money to a charitable collection. **11** [1930s] (*US*) to throw a party. **12** [1950s+] (*orig. US/Aus.*) (*also* **chuck up**) to vomit (cf. BLOW v.[3]). **13** [1990s+] (*UK juv.*) to ejaculate (cf. CHUCK ONE'S LOAD v.; CHUCK ONE'S MUCK v.). **14** [1990s+] (*drugs*) to withdraw from heroin.

chuck *v.*[2] **1** [mid-17C–18C] to have sexual intercourse. **2** [late 18C–early 19C; 1990s+] of a woman, to make sexual advances. [1990s+ use of (2) is Black. Grose (1796) suggests that the term applies to women only]

chuck *v.*[3] **1** [mid-19C] (*US*) to hit (with the fist). **2** [1990s+] (*W.I.*) to act aggressively, thuggishly.

chuck *v.*[4] (*also* **chuck up**) [mid-19C–1950s] (*UK/US Und.*) to eat. [CHUCK n.[3]]

chuck-a-block *adj. see* CHOCK-A-BLOCK adj.

chuckaboo *n.* [late 19C–1900s] a general term of endearment. [CHUCK n.[1]]

chuck a bridge *v.* (*also* **put on a bridge**) [1970s+] (*Aus.*) for a woman to reveal her underwear (inadvertently or otherwise). [SE *chuck* + *bridge*, i.e. the crotch of her knickers]

chuck a brown dog *v.* (*also* **kick a brown dog**) [20C+] (*Aus./US*) to let off steam, to get rid of tension.

chuckaby *n.* [early 17C] a general term of endearment. [CHUCK n.[1]]

chuck a charley *v.* (*also* **chuck a charlie**) [1940s+] (*Aus.*) to throw a fit. [CHUCK v.[1] (3) + CHARLIE BRITT n.]

chuck a cheesy *v.* [1990s+] (*Aus.*) to grin. [CHUCK v.[1] (3) + CHEESE n.[6]]

chuck a chest *v. see* CHUCK THE GAB v.

chuck a dummy *v.* (*also* **chuck the dummy**) [late 19C+] **1** to vomit. **2** to have a fit, esp. when only pretending. **3** to absent oneself. **4** to lose one's temper. [CHUCK v.[1] (3) + SE *dummy*, a fake; (2) orig. milit., to pretend to faint on parade in order to escape duties]

chuck a fit *v.* **1** [mid–late 19C] to fake a fit. **2** [1920s] to have a fig. fit; to lose emotional control. [CHUCK v.[1] (3) + SE *fit*]

chuck a flap *v. see* FLAP v.[1]

chuck a jolly *v.* [mid–late 19C] to praise enthusiastically, to 'talk up' inferior goods. [CHUCK v.[1] (3) + SE *jolly*; orig. used by costermongers to describe their habit of boosting the dubious virtues of some otherwise unappealing item offered on a friend's stall]

chuck a mag *v.* [mid–late 19C] (*UK Und.*) to work as a confidence trickster. [CHUCK v.[1] (3) + MAGSMAN n.[1] (3)]

chuck a mental *v.* [1980s+] (*Aus./N.Z.*) to lose one's temper. [CHUCK v.[1] (3) + MENTAL n.[2]]

chuck a mickey *v.* (*also* **throw a mickey**) [1950s+] (*Aus.*) to lose one's temper, to have a tantrum. [CHUCK v.[1] (3) + ? MICKEY n.[1] (1), i.e. negative stereotype of aggressive Irishman]

chuck an Oliver *v.* (*also* **do an Oliver**) [1980s] (*Aus.*) to ask for a second helping of food. [CHUCK v.[1] (3) + *Oliver Twist* and his request 'May I have some more?']

chuck a shoulder *v.* [late 19C–1900s] to ignore, to 'cut'. [CHUCK v.[1] (3) + SE *cold shoulder*]

chuck a sixer *v. see* THROW A SEVEN v.

chuck a slob *v.* [1950s] (*US gay*) to kiss. [CHUCK v.[1] (1) + SLOBBER n.[2]/SLOB v.]

chuck a slug *v.* (*also* **toss a slug**) [1930s] to shoot. [CHUCK v.[1] (1)/SE *toss* + SLUG n.[2] (1)]

chuck a spas *v.* (*also* **chuck a spaz**) [1990s+] (*Aus.*) to lose one's temper. [CHUCK v.[1] (3) + SPAZ n. (1)]

chuck a stall *v.* [mid-19C] (*UK Und.*) a pickpocketing technique, one member of the team walks in front of the victim, slowing him or her down while another picks the pocket. [CHUCK v.[1] (3) + STALL n.[1] (5)]

chuck a swell *v.* [1930s] to spend extravagantly. [CHUCK v.[1] (7)/CHUCK v.[1] (3) + SWELL n. (1)]

chuck a tread *v.* [late 19C–1900s] of a man, to have sexual intercourse. [CHUCK v.[1] (3) + SE *tread*, for a cock to have intercourse with a hen]

chuck a turd *v.* [19C+] to excrete. [CHUCK v.[1] (1) + TURD n. (1)]

chuckaway *n.* [late 19C–1900s] a lucifer or non-safety match. [CHUCK v.[1] (1) + *away*]

chuck a willie *v.* (*also* **chuck a willy, throw a willy**) [1940s+] (*Aus.*) to throw a fit, lit. or fig. [CHUCK v.[1] (3) + WILLIE n.[3]]

chuck a wobbler/wobbly *v. see* THROW A WOBBLY v.

chuck a wobbly *v.* (*also* **chuck a wobbler**) [1960s+] (*Aus./N.Z.*) to tell a dubious story. [CHUCK v.[1] (3) + WOBBLY n.[3]]

chuck-bread *n.* [late 19C–1900s] (*UK tramp*) waste bread that would be thrown away were it not offered to tramps. [SE]

chucked *adj.*[1] **1** [late 18C–19C] slightly drunk, tipsy (cf. ANNIHILATED adj.). **2** [mid–late 19C] disappointed, tricked. **3** [late 19C+] thrown out; acquitted. **4** [late 19C+] rejected by a lover. [CHUCK v.[1]]

chucked *adj.*[2] [early 19C] (*UK Und.*) amorous. [CHUCK v.[2] (2)]

chucker *n.* [late 19C] a public house potman. [he 'chucks' barrels around]

chucker-out *n.* [late 19C+] a staff member at pubs, dancehalls, concert-halls and similar places of public entertainment who ejects, by force if necessary, rowdy and undesirable people. [CHUCK OUT v.]

chuckey *n. see* CHUCKY n.[2].

chuck-farthing *n.* (*also* **chuck**) [late 17C–early 19C] a parish clerk. [SE *chuck-farthing*, a precursor of 20C+ pitch and toss, in which coins are first pitched at a mark, and then tossed at a hole by the player who came nearest the mark, and who wins everything that landed in the hole; used as the proper name of a character in the *Satire against Hypocrites*, cited by B.E.]

chuck habit *n.* [1930s–60s] (*US drugs*) the increase in appetite that accompanies withdrawal from narcotics. [CHUCK n.[3] (2)/CHUCK v.[1] (6) + HABIT n. (3)]

chuck horrors *n.* [1920s–60s] **1** (*US Und.*) a craving for food. **2** (*US drugs*) the craving for food or, paradoxically, the obsessive loathing of food that accompanies one's withdrawal from heroin. [CHUCK n.[3] (2)/CHUCK v.[1] (6) + HORRORS, THE n. (4)]

chuck house *n.* [1930s–60s] (*US tramp*) a restaurant; also used for the canteen in a mine or mill. [CHUCK n.[3] (2)]

chuckie *n.* [1990s+] (*W.I.*) a thug. [CHUCK v.[3] (2)]

Chuckie Armani *n.* [1980s+] (*Ulster*) the Sinn Féin leader Gerry Adams (b.1949). [the IRA slogan *tiocfaidh ár lá*, our day will come + Adams's well-known taste in upmarket tailoring]

chuckies *n.* [1960s+] testicles. [pun on BALLS n.[1] (1)/SE *balls*, which one can 'chuck'; Scot. chuckies = stones; ? + CHUCK v.[2] (1)]

chuck-in *n.*[1] [late 19C–1910s] (*Aus.*) a certainty.

chuck-in *n.*[2] [late 19C+] (*Aus.*) a voluntary subscription. [CHUCK IN v.[1]]

chuck in *v.*[1] [late 19C+] to add as a bonus, to throw in. [CHUCK v.[1] (1)]

chuck in *v.*[2] *see* CHIP IN v.

chucking-out time *n.* (*also* **chucking time**) [late 19C+] closing time at a public house; this was orig. 12.30am, before the WWI legislation limiting open hours, which made it, according to the time of day, 2.30pm (3.00pm in London) and 10.30pm (11.00pm in London). The afternoon closing time has since been abandoned. [CHUCK OUT v.]

chuck in one's alley *v. see* THROW IN ONE'S ALLEY v. (1).

chuck in one's knife and fork *v. see* LAY DOWN ONE'S KNIFE AND FORK *v.*

chuck in the towel *v.* [20C+] to give in, to surrender. [boxing imagery]

chuck it *v.* (*also* **chuck it in**, **chuck it up**) **1** [mid-19C+] to give up, esp. of a job. **2** [1960s] (*US campus*) to commit suicide. [CHUCK *v.*¹ (6)]

chuck it! *excl.* [late 19C+] stop it! [CHUCK IT *v.* (1)]

chuck it in! *excl.* (*also* **chuck it up!**) [mid-19C+] stop it! [CHUCK IT *v.* (1)]

chuck it into *v. see* THROW IT INTO *v.* (2).

chuck it out *v.* [20C+] to speak without restraint. [fig. use of CHUCK *v.*¹ (1)]

chuck it up *v. see* CHUCK IT *v.*

chuck it up! *excl. see* CHUCK IT IN! excl.

chuckle *v.* [1960s+] (*Aus.*, *Queensland*) to vomit. [ext. of CHUCK *v.*¹ (12)]

chucklehead *n.* [early 18C–19C] a dolt, a simpleton, a fool; thus the fool's head. [18C SE *chuckle*, a clumsy or stupid fellow + -HEAD sfx (1)]

chuckleheaded *adj.* [mid-18C+] foolish (cf. AIRHEADED adj.). [CHUCKLEHEAD n.]

chuck me in the gutter *n.* [20C+] (*Aus.*) butter. [rhy. sl.]

chuck mill *n.* [late 19C] (*US*) a hotel. [CHUCK n.³ (2)]

chuck off (at) *v.* [20C+] (*Aus./N.Z.*) to sneer at, to speak sarcastically; the addition of *at* implies bantering, teasing (cf. CHUCK UP (AT) v.). [fig. use of CHUCK *v.*¹ (1)]

chuck-office *n.* (*also* **chuck-hole**) [17C] the vagina, esp. in the context of the *half-crown chuck-office*, a prostitute's trick whereby she would stand on her head, exhibiting her spread vulva and clients would throw coins into the vagina. [SE *chuck-farthing*, 'a game of combined skill and chance in which coins were pitched at a mark, and then chucked or tossed at a hole by the player who came nearest the mark, and who won all that alighted in the hole' (*OED*); Priss Fotheringham, the apparent 'champion', had absorbed some 15 half-crowns (£1.87)]

chuck one's ace *v.* [1900s] (*Aus.*) to pass out. [card-playing imagery]

chuck one's biscuits *v.* [1990s+] to vomit (cf. BLOW CHOW v.). [CHUCK *v.*¹ (1)/CHUCK *v.*¹ (12)]

chuck one's fat around *v.* [late 19C] to talk loudly and stupidly. [CHUCK *v.*¹ (1)]

chuck one's hand in *v.* [late 19C+] to die. [card-playing imagery; note WW1 milit. *chuck one's hand in*, to refuse or cease to do anything]

chuck one's load *v.* [1990s+] to ejaculate. [CHUCK *v.*¹ (1)/CHUCK *v.*¹ (13) + LOAD n.⁵ (2)]

chuck one's lollies *v. see* TOSS ONE'S LOLLIES *v.*

chuck one's muck *v.* [1990s+] to ejaculate. [CHUCK *v.*¹ (1)/CHUCK *v.*¹ (13) + MUCK n.⁴]

chuck one's weight around *v.* (*also* **chuck one's weight about**) [20C+] to act in an arrogant, aggressive manner. [CHUCK *v.*¹ (1); Ware suggests orig. milit.: of 'one of the household brigades']

chuck-out *n.* **1** [late 19C+] (*N.Z.*) a dismissal (from a job). **2** [1920s+] the end of drinking time in a public house, or place of entertainment, when customers are asked to drink up and leave. [CHUCK OUT v.]

chuck out *v.* [late 19C+] **1** of people, occas. animals, to throw out, to expel physically. **2** of objects, to get rid of, to throw away. [CHUCK *v.*¹ (1)]

chuck over *v.* [late 19C+] to abandon, to dismiss, to throw over, to jilt. [CHUCK *v.*¹ (2)]

chucks *n.*¹ [1940s+] (*drugs*) the craving for food that affects a heroin addict once they have withdrawn from using the drug, which, on the whole, destroys the appetite during its regular use. [abbr. CHUCK HORRORS n.]

chucks *n.*² (*also* **Chuck T's**) [1960s+] Converse All-Star baseball boots, signed by designer *Chuck* Taylor.

chucks *n.*³ (*also* **chuka sticks**) [1970s+] the *nunchuku*, a martial arts weapon modelled on a Chinese rice flail and made of 2 hardwood sticks linked by a chain.

chucks! *excl.* [mid–late 19C] (*UK juv.*) look out!

chuck sevens *v. see* THROW A SEVEN *v.* (5).

chuck (someone) the whisper *v. see* SLING (SOMEONE) THE WHISPER *v.* (2).

chuck the dummy *n. see* CHUCK A DUMMY *v.*

chuck the gab *v.* (*also* **chuck a chest**) [1930s] to 'tell the tale' for the purposes of begging or confidence trickery; to talk eloquently and articulately. [CHUCK *v.*¹ (3) + GAB n. (2)/? SE *chest*]

chuck the seven *v. see* THROW A SEVEN *v.* (3).

Chuck T's *n. see* CHUCKS n.².

chuck-up *n.*¹ [late 19C+] (*UK Und.*) a release from prison. [CHUCK UP *v.*² (2)]

chuck-up *n.*² [1910s–40s] a cheer, encouragement. [CHUCK *v.*¹ (1); i.e. one 'throws up' the cheer]

chuck-up *adj.* [1940s+] (*W.I.*) short and stout; thus *chuck-up man*, a short, stout person. [CHUCK n.¹]

chuck up *v.*¹ [mid-19C+] to surrender. [abbr. CHUCK UP THE SPONGE v.]

chuck up *v.*² **1** [mid-19C+] to abandon, to stop an action, to dismiss, to throw over, to jilt. **2** [late 19C+] (*UK Und.*) to be released from prison. [CHUCK *v.*¹]

chuck up *v.*³ *see* CHUCK *v.*¹ (12).

chuck up *v.*⁴ *see* CHUCK *v.*⁴.

chuck up (at) *v.* [1900s] (*Aus.*) to tease aggressively (cf. CHUCK OFF (AT) v.). [fig. use of CHUCK *v.*¹ (1)]

chuck up gravel *v. see* SCRATCH GRAVEL *v.* (2).

chuck-up man *n. see* CHUCK-UP adj.

chuck up the sponge *v. see* THROW IN THE TOWEL *v.*

chuck wagon *n.* (*US*) **1** [20C+] a buffet. **2** [1950s–60s] a small restaurant or café. [cowboy jargon *chuck wagon*, the wagon that carried the provisions and cooking equipment for a ranch; ult. CHUCK n.³ (2) + SE *wagon*]

chuck wagon chicken *n.* [20C+] (*US*) bacon. [*see* prev.]

chucky *n.*¹ [18C–mid-19C] a term of endearment. [CHUCK n.¹]

chucky *n.*² (*also* **chuckey**) [late 18C–mid-19C] a chicken, a fowl.

chuck you, Farley! *excl.* [1930s+] a joc. euph. expletive, reversing FUCK YOU, CHARLEY! excl.

chuco *n. see* CHUC n.

chud *n.*¹ [1990s+] (*Aus.*) a tough, virile, well-built man. [? CHAP n. (1) + STUD n.¹ (11)]

chud *n.*² [1990s+] (*orig. Aus./N.Z.*) chewing gum. [abbr. CHUTTY n.]

chud *adj.* [1980s+] (*US campus*) disgusting, repellent. [film title *Chud* (1984), cannibalistic humanoid underground dwellers]

chuddy *n. see* CHUTTY n.

chud-nuts *n.* [1990s+] (*UK juv.*) faecal matter adhering to the anal hair.

chuff *n.*¹ **1** [mid-15C–early 17C] a generally derisive name for anyone seen as boorish, unsophisticated or rude. **2** [late 16C–mid-19C] a miser. [dial. *chuff*, surly, ill-tempered]

chuff *n.*² **1** [1940s+] the buttocks, the anus. **2** [1940s+] (*mainly Aus./northern UK*) the vagina. **3** [1960s–70s] (*US*) (*also* **chuffer**) a young, passive homosexual. **4** [1970s] (*gay*) pubic hair. [dial. *chuff*, fat, plump; (2), (3) and (4) ext. of (1)]

chuff *n.*³ [1980s+] the act of breaking wind. [CHUFF *v.*²]

chuff *n.*⁴ [1990s+] a synon. for FUCK, THE n.

chuff *adj.*¹ [mid-19C–1900s] happy, cheerful. [dial.]

chuff *adj.*² [mid-19C–1900s] rude, impudent. [CHUFF n.¹ (1)]

chuff *v.*¹ [1940s+] a euph. synon. for FUCK *v.*¹, mainly used in the north of England.

chuff *v.*² [1940s+] to break wind. [echoic/CHUFF n.² (1)]

chuff *v.*³ [1990s+] to smoke a drug, esp. marijuana. [? SE *puff*]

chuff v.[4] see CHOOF (OFF) v.

chuff adder n. [1960s] a male homosexual. [CHUFF n.[2] (1) + pun on SE *puff adder*/POOF n. (1)]

chuff-box n. [1940s+] the vagina (cf. BAG n.[1]). [CHUFF v.[1]/CHUFF n.[2] (2) + BOX n.[1] (1) or ? dial *chuff*, to cuff, to hit, as the penis 'hits' the vagina during intercourse]

chuff chum n. [1960s+] a male homosexual. [CHUFF n.[2] (1) + CHUM n.[1] (1)]

chuffchute n. see CHUFTER CHUTE n.

chuffed adj. (also **chuft**) [1950s+] **1** (orig. milit.) very pleased, delighted, happy; often *dead chuffed* or ext. to *chuffed to fuck*, *chuffed to arseholes*, *chuffed to buggery* etc. **2** annoyed, disgruntled. [16C SE *chuff*, swollen out or puffed with fat, or the muzzle of an animal]

chuffer n. see CHUFF n.[2] (3).

chuffing adj. [1990s+] a synon. for FUCKING adj. [CHUFF v.[1]]

chuff it! excl.[1] [mid-19C] used to an importuning street-seller or beggar, go away! take it away! get rid of yourself!/it! [? SHOVE OFF v.]

chuff it! excl.[2] [20C+] a euph. for FUCK IT! excl. [CHUFF v.[1]]

chuff muncher n. [1990s+] a lesbian (cf. CARPET-BITER n.). [CHUFF n.[2] (2)]

chuffy n. see CHUTTY n.

chuffy adj.[1] [late 18C+] chubby, round-faced. [dial. *chuffy*, chubby-cheeked, healthy]

chuffy adj.[2] [late 19C] surly. [CHUFF n.[1] (1)]

chuffy badge n. [1990s+] (UK juv.) a metaphorical 'badge' worn by one who is exhibiting signs of self-satisfaction. [CHUFFED adj.]

chuft adj. see CHUFFED adj.

chufter chute n. (also **chuffchute**) [2000s] the anus (cf. ALLEY WAY n.). [CHUFF n.[2] (1) + CHUTE n.[2]]

chug n. see CHUG-A-LUG n.

chug v.[1] [1950s+] **1** to drink down in a single draught, to drink quickly; thus (US campus) *chugging contest*, a drinking competition in which each contestant has to down a succession of drinks in a single swallow. **2** in fig. use, to 'swallow', to bear, to take. [CHUG-A-LUG v.]

chug v.[2] [1990s+] to masturbate (cf. BOFF v.).

chug-a-lug n. (also **chug**) [1960s–80s] a drink. [CHUG-A-LUG v.]

chug-a-lug v. (also **chuglug**) [1930s+] to down a drink. [echoic]

chugalug! excl. [1950s+] a popular drinking toast. [CHUG-A-LUG v.]

chugarrow! excl. [20C+] shut up! [milit. *chubarrow*, itself adopted f. Hind. *chuprao*, be quiet!]

chuggerhead n. (also **chugger**) [1970s] (US) a dolt, a simpleton, a fool. [var. on CHUCKLEHEAD n.]

chuglug v. see CHUG-A-LUG v.

chugs n. [1960s–70s] (US) the female breasts. [var. on JUGS n.]

chugwagon n. [1900s–20s] (US) a motorcar. [SE *chug* (along) + pun on cowboy jargon *chuck wagon*]

chuka sticks n. see CHUCKS n.[3]

chul v. [mid–late 19C] to succeed. [? Hind. *chul*, go along, hurry]

chullo! excl. [mid–late 19C] (orig. Anglo-Ind.) hurry up! move along! [Hind. *chello*, move along]

chulo n. [1990s+] (US) a Mexican-American teenage gangster (cf. BATO n.). [Sp. *chulo*, pimp; note Ana María Eccles' 'Spanish Ethnic Labels: Chulo' (2001): '"Estas o vas muy chulo" means smartly dressed (in a lower class fashion). "Eres un chulo" means a boasting, somehow despicable person. "Es un chulo" means "pimp". "Una chulada" means exaggerated, or false bravado. I always think of a "chulo madrileno" as a fellow with tight pants, a scarf around the neck and a visor type beret, dancing, clinging tightly to his partner']

chum n.[1] (also **chummy**) **1** [late 17C+] (also **chummie**) a close friend, a room-mate, a cell mate. **2** [late 18C–19C] (UK Und.) a fellow-prisoner. **3** [mid-19C+] a term of friendly address. **4** [1990s+] (UK juv.) (also **chum boy, chummer**) a male

homosexual. [(1) mid-19C+ use is SE, although Hotten (1859) includes it since it is 'in such frequent use with the lower orders that it demanded a place in this glossary']

chum n.[2] [19C] (Aus.) a new immigrant, a newcomer. [abbr. NEW CHUM n.]

chum n.[3] [late 19C] the vagina. [CHUM n.[1] (1), i.e. the 'friend' of the penis]

chum v. **1** [mid-18C+] (also **chum in**) to live with, to befriend. **2** [mid-19C–1930s] to put someone in a position of sharing accommodation. **3** [mid-19C+] (also **chum in**) to join in with. [coined by John Wesley (1703–91) in 1730, drawing on 17C SE *chum*, one who lodges in the same college rooms. Presumably f. *chamber*, poss. abbr. *chamber-fellow* or *chamber-mate*, although no proof has been discovered]

chum along with v. (also **chum up with**) **1** [late 19C+] (also **chum in with, chum around with**) to become friendly with. **2** [1910s] (UK Und.) to work as an accomplice with. [CHUM v. (1)]

chum boy n. see CHUM n.[1] (4).

chum in v. see CHUM v.

chum in with v. see CHUM ALONG WITH v. (1).

chummage n. **1** [late 18C–mid-19C] a sum of money paid by a rich prisoner to a poorer one, for which payment the latter forfeited his part of a shared cell, leaving it all to the rich prisoner and taking up a position in some communal area of the prison. **2** [late 18C–19C] a monetary forfeit, usu. 2s 6d (12½p), paid over by a new prisoner to those who have already established themselves in the prison. **3** [late 19C] in a non-custodial sense, a payment from a newcomer. [SE *chummage*, the sharing of rooms by a number of people. The rich-to-poor bribe has also been recorded as taking place at mid-19C universities]

chummer n. see CHUM n.[1] (4).

chummery n. **1** [mid-19C] friendship, friendliness. **2** [late 19C+] the sharing of rooms with a friend. [CHUM n.[1] (1)]

chummie n. see CHUM n.[1] (1).

chumming n. [late 19C] making friends. [CHUM v. (1)]

chumming up n. [mid-19C] (UK prison) the initiatory welcoming of a new prisoner, paid for by a mandatory fee of 2s 6d (12½p). [CHUMMAGE n. (2)]

chummo n. [1940s] (US) a friend, esp. as a term of address. [CHUM n.[1] + -O sfx (1)]

chummy n.[1] [mid-19C] a low-crowned hat. [it was notably comfortable and as such seen as *chummy*, or friendly, to the wearer]

chummy n.[2] [mid-19C+] a chimney sweep or his assistant. [SE *chimney* or his preferred hat, a CHUMMY n.[1]]

chummy n.[3] [1920s+] a person. [note 1940s+ police use *chummy*, a form of address from anyone to whom the policeman is talking, a suspect]

chummy n.[4] see CHUM n.[1].

chummy n.[5] see NEW CHUM n. (1).

chummy adj. (also **chummy-chummy**) [late 19C+] friendly. [CHUM n.[1] (1)]

chummy v. [1980s+] (US campus) to vomit. [CHUM THE FISH v.]

chummy adv. [late 19C] in a friendly manner. [CHUMMY adj.]

chummy-chummy adj. see CHUMMY adj.

chump n.[1] **1** [mid-19C+] the head, the face. **2** [mid-19C+] a person, esp. a regular working man; thus, in sl. terms, a fool. **3** [late 19C+] (also **chumpie**) anyone gullible, easily taken in. **4** [late 19C] a general term of address, either derog. or teasing. **5** [1970s] (US Black) a second-rate pimp, one who just makes enough money to get by (cf. CHILE CHUMP n.). **6** [1970s+] (US Black) a disloyal gang member. **7** [1990s+] (US prison) a deliberate insult, implying the subject's weakness and/or homosexuality; the spur to a fight. [18C SE *chump*, a short thick lump of wood chopped or sawn from timber]

chump n.[2] [late 19C] (UK Und.) food. [Suffolk dial. *bread and chumps*, bread and cheese; Devon dial. *chump*, to eat noisily]

chump *adj.* [20C+] (*also* **chump-ass, chumpish**) **1** stupid, gullible. **2** unsophisticated, second-rate, provincial. [CHUMP n.[1]]

chump *v.* [1920s+] **1** (*also* **chump out**) to trick, to deceive, to make a fool of someone. **2** (*US Black*) to act like a fool, to be exploited. [CHUMP n.[1] (3)]

chump change *n.* [1950s+] (*US Black*) small change, esp. a sum of money that is too small to buy anything worthwhile; also in fig. use. [CHUMP n.[1] (1) + SE *change*]

chump-change *adj.* [1970s+] second-rate, inferior, good only for fools. [CHUMP CHANGE n.]

chump down *v. see* CHUMP (SOMEONE) DOWN v.

chumpie *n.*[1] [1980s+] (*US Black/campus*) **1** something that causes happiness, joy or excitement. **2** something exceptional, outstanding. **3** a large amount. [SE *champion*]

chumpie *n.*[2] *see* CHUMP n.[1] (3).

chumpish *adj. see* CHUMP adj.

chump job *n.* [1930s+] (*US*) respectable, low-paying, regular work. [CHUMP n.[1] (1)]

chump off *v.* (*US Black*) **1** [1930s+] to act like a fool. **2** [1950s] to lose money irresponsibly. **3** [1970s+] to look down on, to disdain. **4** [1970s+] to dupe, to get the better of. **5** [1970s+] to defeat in a verbal battle. [CHUMP v. (2)]

chump of wood *adv.* [mid-19C] no good. [rhy. sl.]

chump out *v.*[1] [1960s] (*US Black*) to make a mistake, to blunder. [CHUMP n.[1]]

chump out *v.*[2] *see* CHUMP v. (1).

chumps elizas *n.* [mid-19C+] the Champs Élysées, Paris. [pron.; 'Five Pounder Tourists' (Ware)]

chump (someone) down *v.* (*also* **chump (someone) out**) [1970s+] (*US Black*) to humiliate someone. [CHUMP v. (1)]

chump squeeze *n.* [1950s–60s] (*US Black*) a punch on the arm or shoulder, its meaning varying according to context. [CHUMP n.[1] + SE *squeeze*]

chumpy *adj.* **1** [20C+] naïve, stupid, gullible. **2** [1900s–20s] (*US campus*) mean, contemptible. **3** [1960s] eccentric, odd. [CHUMP n.[1]]

chum the fish *v.* [1980s+] (*US campus*) to vomit. [SE *chum*, to throw ground-bait into the water to attract fish; var. on FEED THE FISHES v. (2)]

chum up with *v. see* CHUM ALONG WITH v.

Chunder *n. see* RAM CHUNDUR n.

chunder *n.* [1950s+] (*Aus.*) **1** an act of vomiting; thus *chunderous, chundersome*, fit to make one vomit. **2** vomit. [CHUNDER v.]

chunder *v.* [1950s+] (*orig. Aus.*) to vomit. [according to Barry Humphries (b.1934), the great popularizer of the word in his 'Barry Mackenzie' strip in *Private Eye* and on film, f. naut. shout of warning 'watch under!'; thus Humphries, *Collected Barry Mackenzie* (1988): 'Jeez I'm sorry lady — I forget to yell watch under.' He also offers rhy. sl. f. *Chunder Loo of Akim Foo* = SE *spew*. Chunder Loo featured in a long-running series of advertisements for Cobra boot polish (*c.*1910–29), drawn by Norman Lindsay (1879–1969) (and occas. by his brother Lionel) featured in the Sydney *Bulletin*. Thence it moved from public school slang to surf jargon to popular use; Moore, *Lexicon of Cadet Language* (1993), adds ? link to UK dial. *chounter/chunter/chunder*, to grumble]

chunder bunny *n.* [1980s+] (*orig. N.Z.*) one who cannot hold their liquor. [CHUNDER v. + BUNNY n.[3] (1)]

chunderous/chundersome *adj. see* CHUNDER n. (1).

chundini *n.* [1970s+] (*US gay*) the buttocks.

chung *adj.* [2000s] (*UK teen*) attractive, sexy. [ety. unknown]

chunk *n.*[1] **1** [mid-19C+] (*orig. US*) a large amount, a good deal of, esp. money. **2** [1940s–50s] (*US prison*) a long sentence. [dial. *chuck*, a lump, a large, awkwardly shaped piece]

chunk *n.*[2] [20C+] (*Can. Und.*) a handgun. [? its shape, size and weight]

chunk *v.*[1] **1** [late 19C+] (*US Black*) to discard, to throw away, to

throw. **2** [1940s–60s] (*US*) to ejaculate (cf. BLOSH v.). **3** [1950s+] (*US campus/W.I.*) to batter, to beat up, to fight. [CHUCK v.[1] (1)]

chunk *v.*[2] [1980s+] (*US campus*) to vomit. [BLOW CHUNKS v. (1)]

chunk *v.*[3] [1980s+] (*US campus*) to do badly. [echoic of 'hitting the bottom']

chunka *n.* (*also* **chunker**) [20C+] (*Aus.*) the chief. [abbr. CHUNK OF BEEF n.]

chunka beef *n. see* CHUNK OF BEEF n.

chunkery *n.* [1970s+] fatness. [SE *chunky*]

chunking *n.* [2000s] (*US prison*) throwing water or liquid matter on inmates or staff. [CHUNK v.[1] (1)]

chunk of beef *n.* (*also* **chunka beef**) [20C+] (*Aus.*) the chief, the boss. [rhy. sl.]

chunk of wood *adj.* [mid-19C] good; usu. in negative phr. *no chunk of wood*. [rhy. sl.]

chunky *n.* [1970s+] (*US drugs*) hashish. [SE *chunk*]

chunky *adj.* [1950s+] (*US Black*) used to describe attractive female buttocks.

chunky shrimp *n.* [2000s] (*UK Black*) the clitoris of a fat woman (cf. BABY IN THE BOAT n.). [supposed resemblance]

chunt *n.* [2000s] (*US campus*) an unpleasant, incompetent person. [CHUMP n.[1] (3) + CUNT n.[2] (1)]

chupidee *n.* (*also* **chupiddy, chupidie, chupidy**) [20C+] (*W.I.*) a gullible, ignorant fool; thus *chupidness* stupidity; *talk chupidness*, to talk silly nonsense. [*chupid*, local pron. of stupid]

church *n.*[1] [late 19C–1900s] a general term of endearment, e.g. *my church*, my dear.

church *n.*[2] [late 19C–1940s] (*US Und.*) a place where the identity of stolen jewellery is altered. [play on CHRISTEN v. (1)]

church *n.*[3] [1970s] (*US*) the end. [in the context of a funeral]

church a yack *v.* (*also* **church a jack**) [mid-19C–1930s] (*UK Und.*) to take the works of one watch and place them in the case of another with the aim of disguising its origins. [play on CHRISTEN v. (1) + YACK n.[1]]

church-bell *n.* [late 19C–1900s] a talkative woman.

church-called *adj.* [1920s–50s] (*US Black*) drawn to the vocation of preaching.

church-chopper *n. see* CHOP-CHURCH n.

churcher *n.* [late 19C] a threepenny piece. [the Cockney version of society's CHURCH-PIECE n.]

church is out *phr.* [1950s–60s] (*US*) everything is finished, no alternative is available. [i.e. the service is over; one has no further chance to pray]

church key *n.* [1950s+] (*US*) a can-opener. [the similarity in shape of the WW2 US forces GI can-opener and an old-fashioned key]

church mouse *n.* **1** [late 19C+] a regular attender at church. **2** [1940s–70s] (*gay*) a male homosexual who frequents crowded churches in order to fondle any potential sex partners.

church parade *n.* [late 19C–1900s] (*UK society*) the regular post-Sunday matins promenading of fashionable people.

church-piece *n.* [late 19C–1900s] (*UK society*) a threepenny piece. [it was the smallest silver coin and thus the least one could decently place in the collection plate]

churchwarden *n.* **1** [mid-19C] a clay pipe with a very long stem. **2** [1930s] (*US drugs*) a long-stemmed opium pipe. [the supposed predilection of churchwardens for such pipes]

church work *n.* [late 18C] any work that proceeds slowly. [? the time taken to build the great cathedrals or the tedium of religious services]

churchy *adj.* [mid-19C+] pious.

churchyard cough *n.* (*also* **churchyarder, graveyarder**) [late 17C+] a particularly bad cough, esp. one that is likely to lead to the sufferer's death. [both the likelihood of death and burial and the reputation of churchyards as centres of disease]

churchyard luck *n.* [late 19C–1900s] the death of one child in a large but impoverished family. [cruel but pragmatic, the loss of an extra mouth to feed is 'lucky' for the penniless parents]

churn *n.* [19C] the vagina. [it makes BUTTER n.¹ (1); Williams notes 16C use of *churning*, copulation]

churn butter *v.* [1940s] to masturbate (cf. BEAT ONE'S MEAT v.). [SE *churn* + BUTTER n.¹ (1)]

churus *n. see* CHARAS n.

chury *n.* [early 19C] a knife. [Welsh Rom. *chury*, a knife; ult. f. Hind. *chhuri*]

chute *n.*¹ [late 19C] (*US*) a cheap eating place. [the serving and quality of food in such places is compared with the tossing of rubbish down the garbage chute of a tenement block]

chute *n.*² [1970s+] (*US*) the rectum or anus; thus *go up the chute*, to have anal intercourse (cf. ALLEY WAY n.).

chutes *n.* [1930s–50s] (*US Und.*) the subway.

chutney *n.* [1970s+] sodomy. [like CHOCOLATE n.¹ (3), *chutney* is brown and thus generic for matters referring to defecation and sodomy]

chutney farmer *n.* [1990s+] a male homosexual (cf. BROWN ARTIST n.). [CHUTNEY n. + fig. use SE *farmer*]

chutney ferret *n.* **1** [1950s+] the penis (cf. ANTEATER n.). **2** [1980s+] a male homosexual, a sodomite (cf. BROWN ARTIST n.). [CHUTNEY n. + FERRET n.²]

chutty *n.* (*also* **chuddy, chuffy**) [1940s+] (*orig. Aus./N.Z.*) chewing gum. [? SE *chew*]

chutzpah *n.* (*also* **chutzpa**) [late 19C+] gall, cheek, outrageousness, audacity, bravado, nerve, courage. [Heb. *chutzpah*, insolence, audacity]

chutzpah *adj.* [late 19C] cheeky. [CHUTZPAH n.]

chy *n. see* CHAI n.

chyack *see under* CHI-IKE.

ci *n.* [2000s] (*US Black*) a cigarette. [abbr.]

ciao *phr.* [1960s+] goodbye. [Ital.]

'cid *n.* [1970s+] (*drugs*) LSD (cf. A n.³). [abbr. ACID n.³]

cider-and *n.* [18C] any form of mixed drink in which the basic constituent is cider.

cig *n.* [late 19C+] a *cig*arette, a *cig*ar. [abbr.]

cigar box *n.* **1** [19C] a violin. **2** [1970s] (*US*) a cheaply built house; thus *cigar box row*, the area of town in which the poor live. [the flimsiness of the cigar-box construction]

cigar burn *n.* [1990s+] the anus. [resemblance]

cigarette (holder) *n.* [1990s+] a shoulder. [rhy. sl.]

cigarette paper *n.* [1930s+] (*drugs*) a (small) packet of heroin. [a BINDLE n. (3) (latterly a WRAP n.⁴) of heroin (or cocaine) is approx. the size of a cigarette paper]

cigarette pimp *n.* [1950s–60s] (*US Black*) a second-rate pimp, esp. a pimp who solicits for his women (cf. CHILE CHUMP n.). [his women make no more than cigarette money]

cigarette swag *n.* [1930s–60s] (*Aus.*) a very thin pack or swag, implying poverty. [resemblance]

cigarette with no name *n. see* NO-BRAND CIGARETTE n.

cigger *n.* [1920s+] (*Aus.*) a *cig*arette. [abbr./pron.]

ciggie *n.* (*also* **ciggy**) [20C+] a *cig*arette. [abbr. + sfx *-ie*/-*y*]

ciggy-boo *n.* (*also* **ciggy-poo**) [1940s+] (*Aus./US*) a cigarette. [CIGGIE n. + sfx *-boo*/-*poo*]

cinch *n.*¹ **1** [late 19C+] (*orig. US*) (*also* **sinch, skinch**) a simple, easily attained thing, a certainty; thus *cinchy*, easy, easily attained or attainable; *cinch-looking*, apparently easy; *have the cinch on*, to place oneself in an unassailable position. **2** [1930s] (*US*) an easily seduced woman. [SE *cinch*, grip tightly; thus something one can grasp easily. Orig. f. Sp. *cincha*, a saddle girth or bellyband, adopted in US West]

cinch *n.*² (*also* **cinch-notice**) [20C+] (*US campus*) a note sent to a student warning them to work hard and generally 'get a grip'. [SE *cinch*]

cinch *adj.* [late 19C–1960s] (*US*) definite, guaranteed. [CINCH n.¹ (1)]

cinch *v.* **1** [late 19C] (*US*) to impose upon. **2** [late 19C–1910s] (*US*) to defeat, to overcome, to trounce. **3** [20C+] (*orig. US*) to guarantee, to make certain, to make conclusive. [fig. use of SE *cinch*, to make tight (orig. of a saddle); underpinned by CINCH n.¹ (1)]

cinch-notice *n. see* CINCH n.².

cinchy *adj. see* CINCH n.¹ (1).

Cinci *n.* (*also* **Cincie, Cincy**) [late 19C–1970s] (*US*) *Cinci*nnati, Ohio. [abbr.]

Cincinnati chicken *n.* (*also* **Cincinnatti turkey**) [1900s–70s] (*US*) salt pork. [contemporary identification of *Cincinnati* with pig products]

Cincinnati doubloon *n.* [mid-19C] (*US*) a penny, a cent. [proper name *Cincinnati* + SE *doubloon*, a coin worth 36 shillings; the ref. is to the reputation of Cincinnati businessmen as cheats]

Cincinnati olives *n.* [late 19C] (*US*) pigs. [for ety. *see* CINCINNATI CHICKEN n.]

Cincinnati oysters *n.* [late 19C] (*US*) pickled pigs' feet. [for ety. *see* CINCINNATI CHICKEN n.]

Cincinnati quail *n.* [late 19C] (*US*) pork or bacon, esp. fat pork. [for ety. *see* CINCINNATI CHICKEN n.]

Cincinnati turkey *n. see* CINCINNATI CHICKEN n.

Cincy *n. see* CINCI n.

cinder *n.* [mid-19C–1930s] any form of spirit (brandy, whisky etc), taken in tea, soda water or other drink; thus *put a cinder in*, to add liquor to an otherwise non-alcoholic drink. [SE *cinder*, an ember or piece of glowing coal; thus it makes the basic drink 'hot']

cinder bull *n.* [1930s+] (*US tramp*) a railroad detective (cf. BEAGLE n.³; CINDER DICK n.). [the *cinders* that lie on the tracks + BULL n.¹⁰ (2)]

cinder dick *n.* [1920s+] (*US tramp*) a railroad detective (cf. CINDER BULL n.). [the *cinders* that lie on the tracks + DICK n.⁶ (1)]

cinderella *n.* **1** [late 19C] (*UK society*) a dance that ends at midnight. **2** [1970s+] (*US gay*) an older homosexual who both looks better by candlelight and has to be home by midnight. [the fairy-tale of *Cinderella*]

cinder-garbler *n.* [late 18C–early 19C] a servant girl. [SE *cinder* + *garbler*, a sifter; the servant's morning duty of cleaning out last night's dead fires]

cinder-grifter *n.* [1920s+] (*US*) a tramp. [the *cinders* that lie on the tracks + GRIFTER n.]

cinder-shifter *n.* [1920s+] (*Aus.*) a dirt-track motorcycle racer. [such tracks are covered with dead cinders]

cinder-sifter *n.* **1** [late 19C] a hat with an open-work brim, which supposedly resembles the household tool. **2** [1920s–40s] (*US tramp*) a tramp, esp. one who uses the railroads. [SE *cinder-sifter*, a contrivance for sifting dust or ashes from cinders; (2) var. on CINDER-GRIFTER n.]

cinder trail *n.* [1920s] (*US tramp*) the railroad; the life of tramping, esp. when travelling on railroads. [the *cinders* that lie on the tracks + SE *trail*]

cinnamon stick *n.* [1940s–60s] (*gay*) the faeces-stained penis after anal intercourse. [resemblance + STICK n.¹ (1); SE *cinnamon sticks* are brown]

cinqua *n. see* CHINKER n.

cinquanter *n.*¹ [early–mid-17C] a gambler. [Fr. *cinque*, the number 5, marked on a die]

cinquanter *n.*² [early 17C–mid-18C] an old man. [Fr. *cinquante*, 50; i.e. years of age]

cinque *n. see* CHINKER n.

cinque ports *n.* [17C] the female genitals and anus. ['a group of sea-ports (originally five, whence the name) situated on the south-east coast of England [...] the five "Ports" are Hastings, Sandwich, Dover, Romney, Hithe, to which were added in very early times the "Ancient Towns" of Rye and Winchelsea' (*OED*);

the genitals are in the 'south' of the body, plus play on *port*, that which is entered]

cipher *n.* (*also* **cypher**) [1990s+] (*US Black/teen*) a circle of Black friends, a group of people, e.g. marijuana smokers, rap MCs. [ety. unknown]

cipher *v.* (*also* **cypher**) [mid-19C+] to calculate, to think out. [SE *cipher*, to work out arithmetically]

circle *n.* [1930s] (*US jazz*) a gramophone record.

circle jerk *n.* (*also* **ring jerk**) **1** [1940s+] (*orig. US*) joint masturbation, often in competition, by a group of boys or men, usu. sitting in a circle. **2** [1970s+] (*US*) chaos, a mess. **3** [1990s+] (*Can.*) a man who harasses prostitutes and their customers for fun. **4** [2000s] (*orig. US*) a pointless or inconclusive discussion by a number of people. [SE *circle* + JERK OFF v.[1]]

circle-jerk *v.* [1950s+] (*US*) of boys or men, to indulge in group masturbation; thus *circle-jerker*, one who joins a group of masturbators. [CIRCLE JERK n. (1)]

circler *n.* [1950s] (*W.I.*) a small, round, boiled dumpling. [its shape]

circle suck *n.* [1990s+] (*US*) 1 man or woman fellating a group of men. [on pattern of CIRCLE JERK n. (1)]

circling boy *n.* [early 17C] (*UK Und.*) a thug who works in a criminal gang and helps lure victims into a position where they might be robbed, with or without violence. [SE *circling*, moving around]

circs *n.* [late 19C+] *circ*umstances. [abbr.]

circuit *n. see* DIESEL THERAPY n.

circular file *n.* [1940s+] (*orig. US*) a wastepaper basket (cf. FILE v.[3]; ROUND FILE n.). [note synon. US Army *file 17*]

circumbendibus *n.* **1** [late 17C–1900s] a long and winding route. **2** [late 18C–1900s] a long and winding story. [17C cod Lat. *circum* + *bend*, bend around + Lat. ablative pl. *-ibus*]

circumference *n.* [20C+] a fat person's waist.

circus *n.* **1** [mid-19C+] (*orig. US*) a commotion, an adventure. **2** [late 19C] (*US*) a humiliating example. **3** [late 19C+] (*US*) a live sex show; thus *circus house*, the place where such exhibitions are staged. **4** [1910s] (*Aus.*) one's own affair, one's business. **5** [1930s] (*US*) a fake fit or seizure, performed in the hope of obtaining an injection of narcotics from a sympathetic doctor. **6** [1940s] (*US*) a place. **7** [1950s+] (*orig. US*) a company, group or set of people acting or performing together, esp. in sport or entertainment, e.g. the *Grand Prix circus*. **8** [1960s+] (*US*) an orgy; sexual excess. [fig. uses of SE]

circus bees *n.* (*also* **circus squirrels**) [1920s–60s] (*US tramp*) fleas, lice, crabs, bedbugs.

Circus cowboys *n.* [1960s+] young male gay prostitutes who congregate in and around Piccadilly *Circus*, London W1.

circus girl *n.* [1960s] a woman who is willing to indulge in sex shows or acts of 'perverted' sex. [CIRCUS n. (3)]

circus house *n.* [late 19C–1960s] (*US*) a brothel, esp. one featuring sex shows (cf. ACCOMMODATION HOUSE n.; BIRDCAGE n.[1]). [CIRCUS n. (3) + HOUSE n.[1] (1); such establishments originated in New Orleans and also saw the birth of jazz]

circus love *n.* [1950s+] sex shows. [CIRCUS n. (3)]

circus rider *n.* [1980s+] (*US*) one who participates in orgies. [CIRCUS n. (8) + RIDER n.[1] (1)]

circus squirrels *n. see* CIRCUS BEES n.

circus try *n.* [1940s] (*US*) a determined effort, a good try. [the supposed pluckiness of circus performers]

cirq *n.* (*also* **kirk**) [1990s+] (*UK juv.*) one who has been circumcised. [abbr.]

cisco *n.* [2000s] (*US Black/drugs*) any drink that has had phencyclidine added to it. [brandname *Cisco*, a cheap but potent wine]

Cisco Kid *n.* [1960s+] a Jew (cf. BILLY THE KID n.). [rhy. sl. = YID n.[1]; ult. *Cisco Kid*, a 1950s US TV series]

ciss *n. see* SISSY n.

cissie/cissy *see under* SISSY.

cissy *adj.* [1940s] easy, simple. [SISSY n.]

cit *n.* (*also* **citt**) [mid-17C+] a *cit*izen, spec. of London. [abbr.; the implication is of an urban dweller as opposed to a country-man or of a tradesman or shopkeeper as opposed to a gentleman. 'A pert low tradesman, a pragmatical trader' (Johnson, *Dictionary*, 1755)]

citizen *n.*[1] [mid-late 19C] (*UK Und.*) a wedge used for opening safes; thus *citizen's friend*, a smaller form of wedge (cf. ALDERMAN n.[2]). [? it 'does its duty']

citizen *n.*[2] **1** [20C+] (*US*) a person, the implication being of a respectable individual as opposed to a criminal. **2** [1910s+] a rough, poss. criminal person. **3** [1970s] (*US gay*) in specific use of (1), a heterosexual. [SE; note *citizen*, a civilian as opposed to a soldier, used by Shakespeare in *Coriolanus* (1607)]

citron *n. see* LEMON n.[1] (2).

citt *n. see* CIT n.

city *sfx* [1940s+] (*orig. US*) a general sfx meaning a place or situation, whether concrete or abstract (cf. CENTRAL sfx). [SE *city*; note Gold, *A Jazz Lexicon* (1964): 'according to jazzmen, first used by either Lester Young or Emmett Barry c. 1938']

city bug *n.* [20C+] (*US*) a city person, as seen from a farmer's point of view. [SE *city* + BUG n.[1] (1)]

city bulldog *n.* [early 18C] a constable. [SE *city* + BULLDOG n.[1] (1)]

city clag blues *n.* [1980s+] (*Aus. drugs*) the unpleasant sensation in one's mouth following excessive smoking of cannabis. [SE *city* + proprietary name, *Clag* glue + BLUES n.[1]]

city college *n.* **1** [late 18C–early 19C] Newgate prison. **2** [mid-19C–1940s] (*US*) the Tombs prison, New York City. **3** [1930s] any prison (cf. BIG SCHOOL n.). [COLLEGE n.; ironic]

city minute *n. see* NEW YORK MINUTE n.

City Road African *n.* [late 19C–1900s] a prostitute. [? the relative exoticism of the City Road, London EC1, for those who normally looked for prostitutes in the West End]

city sherry *n.* [late 19C] bitter beer.

city slicker *n.* **1** [20C+] a city person, with overtones of cunning, duplicity. **2** [2000s] (*Aus. teen*) one who wears fashionable clothes. [SE *city* + SLICKER n.]

city's light horse *n.* [1930s] a secretary who has become her employer's mistress. [such a 'light horse' is easy to mount/ MOUNT v.[3]]

city stage *n.* [18C–early 19C] the (Newgate) gallows. [the position of Newgate in the City of London; also the condemned villains' 'dance' for their audience]

city tote *n.* [1990s+] a coat. [rhy. sl.]

city-wire *n.* [17C] a fashionable lady. [use of wires in clothing and hair]

civet *n.* [18C–19C] the vagina. [the musky odour of *civet*, used in perfumes and viewed as overtly erotic; thus *civet-cat*, a general term of abuse for a women seen as too (threateningly) sexy, e.g. as used by Virginia Woolf (1882–1941) of Katherine Mansfield (1888–1923)]

civies *n. see* CIVVIES n. (1).

civilian *n.* **1** [1940s+] (*US*) an outsider, one who is not part of a given group. **2** [1970s] (*US gay*) a heterosexual.

civility money *n.* [late 18C–early 19C] a cash payment claimed by bailiffs for discharging their duty in a courteous manner.

civil rig *n.* [mid-19C] (*UK Und.*) any means of gaining money through (excessive) politeness. [SE *civil* + RIG n.[2] (2)]

civvie *n.* (*also* **civvy**, **civy**) **1** [late 19C+] a *civil*ian; thus termed by members of the forces, the prison service, police etc. **2** [1990s+] (*UK prison*) a commercially sold, 'tailor-made' cigarette. [abbr. + sfx *-ie/-y*; (1) note RMC Duntroon sp. *civie* or occas. *syph*]

civvies *n.* **1** [late 19C+] (*also* **civies**) civilian clothing, i.e. neither a uniform nor one's working clothes. **2** [1970s+] (*US gay*) badly designed clothing. [CIVVIE n. (1); note Fraser & Gibbons, *Soldier &*

Sailor Words & Phrases (1925): '"Civvies" [...] is a Service term at least 70 years old']

civvy *adj.* (*also* **civvie**) [late 19C+] civilian. [CIVVIE n. (1)]

civvy street *n.* [1940s+] the world of civilian life, usu. service use. [CIVVY adj. + SE *street*]

civy *n. see* CIVVIE n.

c.j. *n.* [1970s] (*drugs*) phencyclidine (cf. ACE n.⁴). [abbr. CRYSTAL JOINT n.]

C-jag *n.* [1940s] (*US drugs*) a cocaine binge. [C n.² (1)+ JAG n.¹ (4)]

C-jam *n.* (*also* **C-jame**) [1960s] (*drugs*) cocaine. [C n.² (1)+ JAM n.⁶ (2)]

CK-one *n.* [2000s] (*UK drugs*) cocaine and ketamine; latterly crack cocaine and ketamine. [initial letters + play on the perfume name *CK-one* made by Calvin Klein]

clabber *n.¹ see* BONNY-CLAPPER n.

clabber *n.² see* CLOBBER n.

clack *n.* **1** [late 16C+] the tongue, usu. a woman's. **2** [late 16C+] a noisy conversation. **3** [late 17C+] whining, whingeing, nagging. [SE *clack*, idle gossip. Grose (1785) links it to the clapper that regulates a water-mill and claims that the term is 'chiefly applied to women'; note WW1 milit. *clack*, gossip, rumour]

clack-box *n.* [mid–late 19C] **1** the mouth. **2** a garrulous person. [CLACK n. (1)]

clacker *n.¹* [19C] **1** the mouth. **2** the teeth. [CLACK n. (1) + the noise of the teeth rattling together; note WW1 milit. *clacker*, a chatterer, a rumourmonger]

clacker *n.²* [1900s–20s] (*US*) a dollar (cf. CHING n.²). [? the noise of the coins hitting each other or a solid object]

clacker *n.³* [1960s+] (*Aus./UK juv.*) the anus, the rectum; esp. in contemptuous/dismissive phr. *stuff it up your clacker.* [? Lat. *cloaca*, a sewer]

clackers *n.* [1930s+] false teeth. [CLACKER n.¹ (2)]

clack-loft *n.* [late 18C] a pulpit. [CLACK n. (3) + SE *loft*, a church gallery]

clad in Stafford blue *phr.* [15C] bruised from a beating. [SE *clad*, dressed + *Stafford blue*, a type of blue cloth; pun on SE *staff*]

clag *n.* [1980s+] (*Aus. prison*) porridge.

clagnut *n.* [1990s+] a small piece of excrement clinging to the anal hairs (cf. CLINKER n.⁴; DAGS n.²; DILBERRY n.; FARTLEBERRIES n.; GOOSEBERRY n.⁴; GRIBBER n.; KLINGON n.; TAGNUTS n.; WINNIT n.). [northern dial. *clag*, a sticky mass entangled in hair]

claim *n.* [20C+] (*Irish*) a woman who is picked up at a dance, usu. to have sexual intercourse.

claim *v.¹* **1** [late 19C] to steal. **2** [late 19C+] (*UK Und.*) to arrest; thus *claimed*, under arrest. **3** [2000s] to choose a victim.

claim *v.²* **1** [1970s] (*US Black*) for a prostitute to ally herself to a pimp by paying him money. **2** [1990s+] (*US Black gang*) (*also* **claim the hood**) to claim membership in a gang. [SE; (1) + var. on CHOOSE v.]

Claire Rayner *n.* [1990s+] a trainer. [rhy. sl.; ult. UK agony aunt and novelist *Claire Rayner* (b.1931)]

clam *n.¹* **1** [early 19C–1950s] the mouth. **2** [mid-19C+] (*US*) the vagina, the hymen (cf. BEARDED CLAM n.). **3** [mid-19C+] (*also* **clam-mouth**) a tight-lipped person. **4** [1900s] (*US*) a mean person; thus *tight as a clamshell*, very close-fisted. **5** [1910s+] a sneaky person. [fig. uses of SE; all open and/or shut like the bivalve]

clam *n.²* **1** [mid-19C+] (*US*) a fool, a worthless individual (cf. AIREDALE n.). **2** [1980s] a heavy blow. [its unmoving stolidity; (1) ? + phr. HAPPY AS A CLAM phr.]

clam *n.³* [late 19C+] (*US*) $1, usu. in pl. [ety. unknown; ? link to WAMPUM n., another shell = money term]

clam *n.⁴* [1970s+] a lump of phlegm. [punning var. on OYSTER n.² (1)]

clam *v.* [late 19C] (*UK Und.*) to beg. [one uses one's CLAM n.¹ (1)]

clam-act *n.* [1940s] silence, a refusal to act. [CLAM n.¹ (3)]

clambake *n.* **1** [late 19C+] a party or get-together. **2** [1930s+]

(*US*) an event, esp. one that fails to live up to the obvious efforts that have been put into its preparation. **3** [1930s+] (*US Black/jazz*) a spontaneous musical session. [plays on SE]

clambake *v.* [1980s+] (*US drugs*) to smoke marijuana in a car with the windows up.

clam-basket *n.* [early 19C] (*US*) the stomach.

clam-catcher *n.* [mid-19C–1900s] (*US*) a native or inhabitant of New Jersey. [the prevalence of clams off the state's shores]

clam chowder *n.* [2000s] (*UK Black*) vaginal secretions (cf. BINDERJUICE n.). [CLAM n.¹ (2)]

clam-diggers *n.* (*US*) **1** [20C+] the hands. **2** [1910s+] the nickname of the inhabitants of various towns in northeast US. **3** [1950s+] trousers cut off at midcalf.

clamdiving *n.* [2000s] cunnilingus (cf. DIVE v.²; DIVE A MUFF v.; DIVE FOR BLACK PEARLS v.; DIVE IN THE BUSHES v.; DIVE IN THE CANYON v.; MUFF-DIVE v.; PEARL DIVE v.²). [CLAM n.¹ (2) + DIVE v.²]

clam-headed *adj.* [late 19C] (*Aus.*) stubborn.

clamjam *n.* [1990s+] vaginal secretions (cf. BINDERJUICE n.). [CLAM n.¹ (2) + JAM n.⁷ (4)]

clam jousting *n.* [1990s+] lesbian sex. [CLAM n.¹ (2) + SE *joust*]

clam jungle *n.* [2000s] the female genitals and pubic hair. [CLAM n.¹ (2)]

clammed *adj.* [late 17C–1940s] starved. [the mouth is closed like a SE *clam*]

clammed (up) *adj.* [1930s+] silent, discreet, refusing to talk. [CLAM (UP) v. (2)]

clammer *n.* [1990s+] prison. [one is shut up like a SE *clam* + SLAMMER n.² (1)]

clam-mouth *n. see* CLAM n.¹ (3).

clammy *adj.* (*US*) **1** [late 19C–1900s] a general term of abuse. **2** [1920s] foolish, stupid. [CLAM n.² (1)]

clamp *v.* [mid-19C–1960s] (*US*) to arrest, to seize. [the *clamping* on of handcuffs]

clampers *n.* (*also* **clamps**) **1** [late 19C+] (*US*) the hands. **2** [1940s] (*US Und.*) handcuffs.

clams *n.* [1960s+] (*US*) the hands. [CLAM-DIGGERS n. (1)]

clam's cuticle/garters *n. see* CAT'S WHISKERS n.

clamshell *n.¹* **1** [early 19C+] (*US*) the mouth or, in pl., jaws or lips. **2** [1930s] (*US Und.*) the ear. [ext. of CLAM n.¹ (1); (2) supposed resemblance]

clamshell *n.²* [1920s] (*US*) a $1 coin. [CLAM n.³]

clam smacker *n.* [1990s+] (*US*) a lesbian (cf. CARPET-BITER n.). [CLAM n.¹ (2) + SMACK v.¹ (1)]

clam spear *n.* [1970s–90s] the penis (cf. AX n.²).

clamtrap *n.* [early 19C–1940s] (*US*) the mouth. [play on SE *clam* + *trap* but note CLAM n.¹ (1) + TRAP n.³]

clam (up) *v.* **1** [late 19C] to refuse food. **2** [1910s+] (*also* **do the clam**) to stop talking, to become deliberately secretive; thus *the clam-ups*, silence, a refusal to speak. [the strength with which the bivalve shuts itself tight]

clanger *n.* [1950s+] **1** a mistake, esp. a social solecism; thus intensified as *clangeroo*. **2** (*Aus.*) a lie, a shock. [the 'noise' of it 'hitting the ground']

clank *n.* (*also* **clink**) **1** [late 17C–mid-19C] (*UK Und.*) (*also* **clanker**) a silver tankard; thus RUM CLANK n. **2** [late 18C] (*UK Und.*) a silver plate. **3** [19C] (*US*) a silver dollar (cf. CHING n.²). [echoic; i.e. the tankard, plate or dollar hitting a table]

clanker *n.* [late 17C–early 19C] a gross, deliberate lie. [? the fig. 'thump' of the lie as it falls from one's mouth]

clanker-napper *n.* [late 17C–early 19C] a thief who specializes in stealing silver tankards or plates. [CLANK n. (2) + NAPPER n.¹ (1)]

clankers *n.* [1990s+] the testicles (cf. BANGERS n.). [they 'clank' together]

clanking (for) *adj.* [1990s+] (*UK juv.*) desperate for sex.

clank-napper *n.* [18C–early 19C] one who steals tankards from public houses. [CLANK n. (1) + NAPPER n.¹ (1)]

clanks n. [1980s+] (US) delirium tremens, nervousness. [? aural hallucinations; orig. USAF, *the clanks*, nervousness]

clap n. (also **claps**) [17C+] venereal disease, esp. gonorrhoea. [OF *clapoir*, bubo; thus *clapoire* or *clapier*, a place of debauchery and the illness one can contract there. The term appears as SE in late 16C but starts appearing in cant/sl. lists in late 17C; Henke, *Gutter Life and Language* (1988), quotes Cotgrave's def. (in *Dict. French and English Tongues*, 1611) of *clapier* as a rabbits' nest (as well as a name for 'old time Baudie houses'); thus a pun on SE *coney*, rabbit/CONY n.[1] (2) — a man might catch the disease from a *coney*/CONY n.[1] (3) who was working in a *clapoir*]

clap v.[1] [17C+] to infect with venereal disease. [CLAP n.]

clap v.[2] [mid-19C–1910s] to seize, to arrest. [SE *clap one's hands on*]

clap v.[3] [1950s+] (W.I. Rasta) **1** to hit, to break. **2** to stride. [SE *clap*, to strike a hard surface]

clap clinic n. [1970s+] a clinic specializing in venereal diseases. [CLAP n. + SE *clinic*]

clapdish n. see CLAP-TRAP n.[1] (1).

claperdugeon n. see CLAPPERDUDGEON n.

clap eyes on v. [late 18C+] to catch sight of.

clap in v. [late 17C–early 18C] to rush in vigorously, to push oneself forward, to arrive or leave in a decisive manner. [SE *clap (of thunder)*, i.e. the energy of one's arrival/departure]

clap it up v. [late 16C–17C] to get married.

clap of thunder n. [early–mid-19C] a glass of brandy. [play on FLASH OF LIGHTNING n.]

clap on v. [mid–late 19C] to commit oneself, to make a determined effort. [ext. SE *clap on*, to place with promptness and effect]

clap one's clit v. [1970s+] of a woman, to masturbate (cf. APPLY LIP GLOSS v.). [SE *clap*, to hit + CLIT n.]

clap on the shoulder n. [17C–early 19C] an arrest for debt; thus CLAP-SHOULDER n.

clappdogeon n. see CLAPPERDUDGEON n.

clapped adj. **1** [mid-17C+] venereally diseased. **2** [1960s+] exhausted; worn-out, useless. [CLAP n.; (2) abbr. CLAPPED OUT adj.]

clapped out adj. [1940s+] worn-out, useless, esp. of machinery, cars etc. [CLAPPED adj. (1); i.e. the deleterious effects of the CLAP n., even on things that could not poss. contract it]

clapped up adj. [1920s+] venerally diseased. [ext. of CLAPPED adj. (1)]

clapper n.[1] **1** [17C+] the tongue, esp. of a talkative person; thus *hold your clapper!* be quiet! **2** [1900s–30s] the mouth. [SE *clapper*, tongue of a bell]

clapper n.[2] **1** [mid-18C] gonorrhoea. **2** [1950s] (US) a venereally diseased person. [CLAP n.]

clapper n.[3] [1900s–40s] a hit, a blow. [SE *clap*, to strike]

clapper n.[4] [1910s–30s] a sandwich-man; thus the boards he carries. [the fig. clapping together of the boards]

clapperclaw v. (also **cappercraw**) **1** [17C–mid-19C] to claw or scratch with the open hand and nails, to beat, to thrash, to drub. **2** [late 17C–18C] of a man, to have sexual intercourse, to fondle sexually. **3** [late 17C–early 19C] to abuse verbally, to revile; thus as n. [CLAPPER n.[1] (1) + SE *claw*. The term vanished in the UK but (1) and (3) have survived in parts of the US, where they are usu. applied to women]

clapperdudgeon n. (also **claperdugeon, clappdogeon, clapperdogeon**) **1** [mid-16C–mid-19C] (UK Und.) a beggar who worked with a female companion, posing as man and wife and complete with counterfeit marriage licence; he might also deliberately poison himself with ratsbane or spearwort (arsenic) to raise impressive sores. **2** [early 18C] a general term of abuse. [SE *clapper*, hitter + *dudgeon*, the hilt of a dagger. Its origins remain a mystery, but it has been suggested that it comes from the beggar hitting his clapdish (a wooden dish with a lid, carried by lepers, beggars and mendicants generally, to give warning of their approach and to receive alms) with a dudgeon. *Clapdish* is, in turn, behind the phr. *your tongue goes like a baker's clapdish*]

clappers n.[1] [1930s+] (orig. UK milit.) the testicles (cf. BANGERS n.). [their 'clapping together']

clappers n.[2] [1960s] (US Black) an evangelical church, typified by a high degree of participation by the congregation, typically singing, hand-clapping, responding to the prayers and sermon.

clapping for credit n. [1970s+] (US campus) a music appreciation course. [one claps in time to the music]

clapping the dog n. [1990s+] stimulating a woman's genitals with one's fingers. [SE *clap* v. + DOG n.[4] (2)]

clappy adj. [1930s+] suffering from venereal disease. [CLAP n.]

claps n. see CLAP n.

clap shack n. [1940s] (US) a venereal disease clinic or hospital ward. [CLAP n. + SE *shack*]

clap-shoulder n. [17C] a bailiff or watchman. [CLAP ON THE SHOULDER n.]

clapster n. [late 19C] **1** one who suffers regularly and often from venereal disease. **2** a promiscuous man. [CLAP n. + -STER sfx]

clap-trap n.[1] **1** [19C+] (also **clapdish**) idle chatter, meaningless talk, often completely incorrect or misinformed talk; thus *claptrappy*, nonsensical; also as adj. **2** [19C+] any device used to milk an audience for applause. **3** [1960s–70s] (US Black) the mouth. [play on SE; lit. 'an artifice for attracting applause' (Bartlett, *Dict. Americanisms*, 1848)]

clap-trap n.[2] **1** [late 19C] the vagina (cf. BITE n.[2]). **2** [1980s] a brothel where one might contract venereal disease. [CLAP n. + SE *trap*; ? pun on CLAP-TRAP n.[1] (1)]

Clare Market cleavers n. [late 19C–1900s] butchers working in and around Clare Market, London WC2; thus butchers' jargon *cleavin*, boastful. [Clare Market was established in 17C, but vanished beneath the Kingsway/Aldwych developments (1900–5)]

Clare Market duck n. [late 19C–1900s] a bullock's heart stuffed with sage and onions. [for ety. see CLARE MARKET CLEAVERS n.]

clarence adj. [1910s] (US) upper-class, or affecting such airs. [generic/stereotypical use of proper name]

claret n. (also **burgundy**) [early 17C+] blood; thus [1920s] (boxing) *claret*, to draw blood from an opponent; *claret-christening*, the first blow to draw blood (cf. BADMINTON n.). [OF *claret*, clear, bright, light; orig. used to describe yellowish or light red wines from plain red or white wines. Used in UK from *c.*1600 to describe red wines of the Bordeaux vineyards only]

claret v. [early–mid-19C] (orig. boxing) to draw blood, to bleed. [CLARET n.]

claret-jug n. (also **claret-spout**) [mid-19C] the nose. [CLARET n. + pun]

clarinet-player n. [1950s] (Aus.) a fellator or fellatrix. [pun on SE; the key image is that of *blowing* (BLOW v.[2] (3))]

clarity n. [2000s] (drugs) MDMA (cf. ECSTASY n.). [its effects]

Clark Kent adj. **1** [1990s+] corrupt. **2** [2000s] homosexual. [rhy. sl.; (1) = BENT adj. (3); (2) = BENT adj. (5); ult. fr. *Clark Kent*, the comic and film character 'Superman']

clart n. **1** [20C+] (Ulster) an untidy woman. **2** [1970s+] sticky excrement; thus IN THE CLARTS phr. [dial. *clart*, viscous sticky mud or filth]

clashbag n. (also **clashbeg**) [20C+] (Ulster) a gossip, a tattle-tale. [dial. *clash*, to gossip]

clashy n. [mid-19C] (orig. Anglo-Ind.) a labourer; thus any 'low fellow'. [Urdu *khlasy*, a tent-pitcher, a surveyor's chain-man, a native sailor]

class n. **1** [mid-19C+] distinction, quality, orig. used of athletes. **2** [20C+] an upper-class or aristocratic person.

class adj. [late 19C+] (orig. US) stylish, impressive, superior.

class A n. [1990s+] (drugs) any drug, e.g. heroin, cocaine, categorized as *Class A* under the UK Dangerous Drugs Act (1971).

class act n. [1970s+] (orig. US) an impressive performance, example or instance, both lit. and metaphorically, used of things or individuals. [CLASS adj. + SE *act*]

classic *n.* [1960s+] (*orig. US campus*) anyone or anything that is regarded as out of the ordinary, eccentric; the implication is one of ironic appraisal.

classic *adj.* [1940s+] a general adj. of supreme approval, wonderful, admirable, incomparable, the best. [ext. of SE use but perhaps, given its use in sl., with a slight ref. to the *classic* horseraces]

Classo *n.* [1980s+] (*Aus. prison*) the *Class*ification Committe; the *class*ification a prisoner receives. [abbr. + -*o* sfx (4)]

class up *v.* [1980s+] (*US*) to make classy, esp. in phr. *class up one's act*, to start living in a more classy manner. [CLASS n. (1)]

classy *adj.* [late 19C+] of high or superior class, stylish, smart. [CLASS n. (1)]

classy *adv.* [late 19C+] (*US*) in a sophisticated manner. [CLASSY adj.]

classy chassis *n.* [1950s–60s] (*US*) an attractive figure, the body of a good-looking, well-built woman, thus an attractive woman. [CLASSY adj. + CHASSIS n. (1)]

clatter *n.*[1] [late 19C–1910s] (*US*) a 'time', an instance. [the fig. 'explosion' that punctuates each instance of an act]

clatter *n.*[2] [20C+] (*orig. Irish*) a blow, a beating, esp. given by a parent to a child. [CLATTER v.[1]]

clatter *n.*[3] [20C+] (*Irish*) a large number. [they knock together]

clatter *n.*[4] [1910s–50s] (*US Und.*) a police patrol wagon.

clatter *v.*[1] [20C+] to hit, to beat up. [orig. UK northern dial.]

clatter *v.*[2] [20C+] (*Irish*) to gossip (cf. CLATTERBRAIN n.). [US dial. *clatter*, idle gossip]

clatterbrain *n.* (*also* **clatterbox**) [19C] a gossip (cf. CLATTER v.[2]). [US dial. *clatter*, idle gossip, and earlier UK dial. *clatterbrains*, an idle, lazy gossip]

clatty *adj.* [1960s+] (*Scot./Irish juv.*) utterly filthy. [? CLART n. (2)]

claven *n.* [1990s+] (*US campus*) a know-it-all. [ety. unknown]

clavo *n.* 1 [1970s+] (*US prison*) a hiding place. 2 [1990s+] (*US prison*) a prisoner who is in possession of something valuable, esp. drugs. 3 [1990s+] (*US campus*) drugs. [US Hisp. sl. (CALÓ n.) *clavo*, a thief]

claw *n.*[1] 1 [early 17C+] a hand, a finger. 2 [late 19C] (*UK prison*) a blow with a whip. 3 [1910s–50s] (*US Und.*) the member of a pickpocket team who actually steals. 4 [1960s] (*US Und.*) a policeman.

claw *n.*[2] *see* CLAW-HAMMER n. (1).

claw *v.* 1 [late 16C–18C] to fondle sexually, to masturbate a partner (cf. BOFF v.). 2 [1910s] (*US Und.*) to steal; to grab. 3 [1920s–30s] (*US tramp*) to arrest.

claw-back *n.* [16C–17C] a sycophant, a toady. [they metaphorically 'claw' at one's back. Note obs. SE *claw*, to flatter, to wheedle, to cajole]

claw-buttock *n.* [mid-17C–19C] the penis.

clawed off *adj.* 1 [late 17C–18C] severely beaten or thrashed. 2 [late 18C–early 19C] suffering a severe dose of venereal disease. [CLAW OFF v./SE *claw*, to scratch]

claw-hammer *n.* 1 [mid-19C+] (*also* **claw**) a tailcoat, as worn with full evening dress; thus *claw-hammered*, wearing a tailcoat. 2 [20C+] (*Ulster*) a pig's foot. [supposed resemblance of the divided tail or foot to the tool]

claw off *v.* (*also* **have claws for breakfast**) [late 17C–early 19C] to thrash, to beat severely. [SE *claw*, to scratch; but ? pun on naut. *claw off*, to keep far enough away from the shore to avoid shipwreck]

claw one's toes *v.* [mid-15C] to indulge oneself. [the pleasure of scratching one's feet]

claw-poll *n.* [16C] a sycophant, a toady. [they metaphorically 'claw' at one's SE *poll*, hair. Note obs. SE *claw*, to flatter, to wheedle, to cajole]

claws *n.* [late 19C+] the fingers.

claw sky *v. see* GRAB SKY v.

claw-thumper *n. see* CRAW-THUMPER n. (1).

clay *n.* [late 18C–19C] a clay pipe.

clay-assed *adj.* [1960s–70s] (*US*) stupid, peasant-like (cf. DIZZY-ASS adj.; DOZEY-ARSED adj.; DUMB-ASS adj.; HORSE-ASS adj.; SILLY-ASS adj.; SOFT-ARSED adj.).

clay-brained *adj.* [late 16C; 1980s+] stupid (cf. AMOEBA-BRAINED adj.). [SE *clay*, i.e. its density + sfx -*brained*; 1980s+ use refers also to CLAY-EATER n.]

clay-eater *n.* [mid-19C+] (*US*) a poor White, esp. a native of North or South Carolina or Georgia. [the lit. eating of clay by such people in order to supplement their otherwise meagre diet]

clay puncher *n.* [late 19C] (*Aus.*) a miner.

clay-punching *n.* [1900s] (*Aus.*) working as a miner. [CLAY PUNCHER n.]

clayton's *n.* [1980s+] (*Aus.*) a myth, an illusion, a fantasy. [the advertising line for *Clayton's* non-alcoholic drink (made from African kola nuts and citrus essences): 'It's the drink I have when I'm not having a drink', written by Noel Delbridge, creative director of ad agency D'Arcy, McManus & Masius]

clean *adj.*[1] **1** [mid-19C+] (*UK Und.*) without any form of incriminating identification. **2** [mid-19C+] honest, not corrupt. **3** [late 19C–1960s] (*US*) penniless, without money. **4** [1910s+] beyond any possible suspicion, guiltless. **5** [1910s+] sober. **6** [1920s–50s] (*US Und.*) peaceful. **7** [1940s] without any conditions, no 'strings attached'. **8** [1940s+] not carrying a weapon. **9** [1940s+] (*drugs*) of a person (occas. a place), not in possession of a drug. **10** [1950s+] (*drugs*) not using any form of drug, not currently addicted. **11** [1970s+] devoid of problems. **12** [2000s] (*US Und.*) free of surveillance. [negative uses of SE *clean*, i.e. not dirty]

clean *adj.*[2] **1** [mid-19C+] (*UK Und.*) skilful, expert. **2** [1950s+] (*US Black/prison*) of a man, dressed in the height of current fashion, perfectly groomed. **3** [1960s] (*US*) first-class, excellent. **4** [1960s] (*US Black/Und.*) of a crime, well-planned. **5** [1970s+] of an object, fashionable, well-made. [positive uses of SE *clean*; (3) note 1930s+ jazz use, technically precise]

clean *v.* **1** [mid-19C–1960s] (*US tramp*) to rob (of everything). **2** [mid-19C–1970s] to beat, to overcome; thus *cleaning*, a thrashing. **3** [late 19C+] to tell off severely. **4** [late 19C+] (*orig. gambling*) to take all of an opponent's money. **5** [1900s–50s] (*US Und.*) for a pickpocket to rid him- or herself of the stolen object as soon as it has been secured. **6** [1910s+] (*US Und.*) to empty a stolen wallet or purse.

clean *adv.* **1** [late 15C+] honestly, fairly. **2** [mid-16C+] entirely, completely; thus *clean away*, escaped completely; *clean forget*, completely forget. **3** [late 19C–1900s] (*US*) in profit.

clean and ready *adj.* [1980s] (*US Black*) **1** prepared for any eventuality. **2** well-dressed, fashionable.

clean around the bend *phr.* [1920s+] utterly insane (cf. HARPIC adj.; LOOPED (UP) adj.; LOOPY adj.; OFF ONE'S LOOP phr.; ROUND THE BEND phr.; ROUND THE TWIST phr.; UP THE LOOP phr.). [CLEAN adv. (2) + ROUND THE BEND phr. + pun on advertising slogan use for the lavatory cleaner *Harpic*]

clean as a jaybird *phr.* [1930s–40s] (*US*) penniless, without money. [ext. of CLEAN adj.[1] (3)]

clean broke *adj.* [mid-19C+] absolutely penniless. [CLEAN adv. (2) + BROKE adj.[1]]

cleaned (out) *adj.* [early 19C+] bereft of money, either through gambling or some form of confidence trick or hoax. [CLEAN OUT v. (2)]

cleaner *n.* [1920s] (*US*) a successful swindler. [CLEAN OUT v. (2)]

cleaner than the board of health *phr.* [1960s–70s] (*US Black*) extremely well turned-out, dressed in the height of fashion. [play on SE *clean*/CLEAN adj.[2] (2)]

clean-faced man *n.* [1960s+] (*W.I.*) a Rastafarian who does not, however, sport the characteristic beard and dreadlocks (cf. BALDHEAD n.).

clean gone *adj.* [1920s] utterly insane. [CLEAN adv. (2) + GONE adj.³ (3)]

clean house *v.* (*US*) **1** [20C+] to sort things out once and for all, to punish, to beat. **2** [1960s] to leave (fast).

clean it up *v. see* CLEAN UP v.².

clean job *n.* [late 19C+] (*Aus./US*) a thorough or complete job; often used in the context of murder or violence; usu. as *make a clean job of (it)*.

clean one's rifle *v.* [20C+] to masturbate (cf. BUFF THE BANANA v.).

clean out *v.* **1** [19C+] to thrash. **2** [19C+] to ruin financially or materially. **3** [mid-19C+] to steal. **4** [mid-19C+] (*US*) to defeat heavily, to trounce, to 'make short work of'. **5** [mid-19C+] to do well financially. **6** [late 19C–1930s] (*US*) of a place, to smash up. **7** [late 19C+] (*gambling*) to take all of an opponent's money. **8** [1930s–60s] (*US Und.*) of police, to raid.

clean potato *n.* [19C+] (*Aus.*) anyone who is not a convict. [play on SE]

clean potato, the *n.* [late 19C–1920s] the right thing, the apposite thing.

clean queen *n.* [1960s+] (*US gay*) a gay man who combines trips to the launderette with the opportunity to look for partners. [SE *clean* adj. + QUEEN n.² (1)/QUEEN sfx (2)]

clean shirt *n.* [1940s] (*UK prison*) a beating administered by warders to a new prisoner on admission.

clean-shirt day *n.* [19C] Sunday. [the only day of the week when even the poorest wore a clean shirt]

clean shot *n.* [1920s+] a piece of good luck, a favourable opportunity. [SE *clean* + SHOT n.⁵ (1); fig. use of hunting jargon]

cleanskin *n.* (*also* **clearskin**) [1940s+] (*Aus./N.Z.*) **1** a person without a criminal record. **2** an honest person, esp. in politics. [SE *cleanskin/clearskin*, an unbranded cow]

clean skin *n. see* LILYWHITE n.³ (2).

clean sneak *n.* [1930s–40s] (*US*) a getaway (from a robbery, killing or other crime) without leaving incriminating clues. [SE *clean* + SNEAK n.¹ (3)]

clean someone's clock *v.* (*orig. US*) **1** [1940s+] to beat up severely, to destroy. **2** [1980s+] to take all someone's money, esp. during gambling. [fig. use of SE; ? link to US railroad jargon *clean the clock*, to apply the airbrakes and thus bring the train to a sudden stop; the 'clock' in question is the air gauge, which on halting, immediately registers zero and is thus 'clean']

clean someone's greens *v.* [1960s–70s] (*US*) to beat up severely. [? assonance]

clean someone's pipe *v.* (*also* **clean the pipe**) [20C+] (*US*) to perform fellatio (cf. BUFF THE BANANA v.; CLEAN SOMEONE'S RIFLE v.; HOOVER (UP) v.; KNOCK THE DUST OFF THE OLD SOMBRERO v.; POLISH n.; POLISH AND SHINE n.; POLISH (SOMEONE'S GUN) v.; POLISH THE KNOB v.; POLISH THE OLD GERMAN HELMET v.; RINSE v.¹; SHINER n.⁴; SHINE UP v.). [SE *clean* + PIPE n.² (1)]

clean someone's plow *v.* [20C+] (*US*) to thrash, to beat severely.

clean someone's rifle *v.* [1990s+] (*W.I.*) to fellate (cf. CLEAN SOMEONE'S PIPE v.). [play on SE *rifle*/GUN n.¹ (2)]

clean the board *v.* [late 19C] to eat everything that is put in front of one; thus, fig., to finish completely, to empty. [SE *clean* + *board*, a table]

clean the pipe *v. see* CLEAN SOMEONE'S PIPE v.

clean the slate *v.* [mid-19C+] lit. or fig., to pay off one's outstanding debts.

clean to the bone *phr.* (*also* **ragged to the bone**) [1950s+] (*US Black*) **1** exceptionally well-dressed. **2** handsome. [CLEAN adj.² (2)/RAGGED DOWN (HEAVY) adj. + TO THE BONE phr.]

clean-up *n.*¹ **1** [mid-19C+] (*US gambling*) the climactic round of a gambling game in which the successful gambler takes the last of his opponent's money, esp. in cheating contexts. **2** [late 19C+] (*orig. US*) a profit, an exceptional financial success; a betting coup. [CLEAN UP v.¹ (1)]

clean-up *n.*² [1970s] (*US*) an excuse, a story or an alibi used to extricate oneself from a situation or an error. [CLEAN UP v.¹ (7)]

clean up *v.*¹ (*also* **clear (up)**) **1** [mid-19C+] to do very well out of a project, esp. in gambling use. **2** [late 19C–1950s] to empty, to empty of its contents. **3** [late 19C+] to beat, to overcome. **4** [late 19C+] to make a large profit. **5** [20C+] to get rid of (hostile or alien elements). **6** [1930s] (*US*) to kill for revenge. **7** [1960s] (*US Black*) to make excuses, to create an alibi. **8** [1960s] (*US Black*) to confess, esp. to telling lies or to failure. [fig. uses of SE]

clean up *v.*² (*also* **clean it up**) [20C+] (*US Und.*) to explain; to find out information.

clean up *v.*³ **1** [1910s+] to stop drinking alcohol. **2** [1950s+] (*drugs*) (*also* **clear up**) to abandon one's drug use, either by oneself or through some form of rehabilitation. [CLEAN adj.¹ (5)/CLEAN adj.¹ (10)]

clean up on *v.* [1910s+] to deal with successfully, to take advantage of, to do well out of. [CLEAN UP v.¹ (1)]

clean up one's act *v.* [1960s+] (*orig. US*) to modify or improve one's behaviour. [SE *clean up* + ACT n. (1)]

clean up the kitchen *n.* (*also* **sweep up the kitchen**) [1930s–40s] (*US short order*) an order for hash or a hamburger.

clean up the kitchen *v.* (*also* **scrub the kitchen**) [1930s+] (*US*) to perform anilingus or cunnilingus (cf. AUSTRALIAN n.). [SE *clean up* + KITCHEN n.¹ (1)]

clean wheat *n.* [mid-19C–1900s] the best, the supreme exemplar of a type. [? wheat that has been threshed and is thus free of all impurities]

clear *adj.*¹ (*also* **in the clear**) [late 17C–19C] (*UK Und.*) very drunk (cf. ABOUT RIGHT phr.¹). [? an ironic use of SE *clear*, the drunkard's head is of course far from clear]

clear *adj.*² **1** [mid–late 19C] (*US*) pure, unadulterated. **2** [1990s+] (*US gay*) exclusively homosexual.

clear *v.*¹ *see* CLEAN UP v.¹.

clear *v.*² *see* CLEAR (OFF) v.

clear *adv.* [19C+] completely, totally.

clear as mud *phr.* [mid-19C+] **1** completely unclear. **2** (*also* **clear as ditchwater**) in ironic use, absolutely clear.

clear crystal *n.* [mid-19C–1920s] any clear spirit, e.g. gin, but also ext. to brandy or rum.

clear cut *n.* [1980s] (*US Black*) **1** stylish clothes. **2** pure drugs. [var. on SE *clean cut*]

cleared (out) *adj.* [mid–late 19C] bereft of funds, impoverished. [CLEAR OUT v. (2)]

clear field *n.* [1960s–70s] (*US*) an unimpeded opportunity, esp. for making contact with or pursuing a member of the opposite sex. [sporting imagery]

clear grit *n.* [mid–late 19C] the real thing, the genuine article; thus *be the clear grit*, to have genuine spirit or pluck. [CLEAR adj.¹ (1) + GRIT n.¹]

clear light *n.* [1970s+] (*drugs*) a variety of LSD (cf. A n.³).

clear (off) *v.* [mid-19C+] to leave, to depart; esp. as imper. *clear off!*

clear out *v.* **1** [19C+] to leave, to run away. **2** [19C+] to take all an opponent's money, to ruin financially. **3** [late 19C–1910s] to rob. [(1) to 'clear away' one's presence]

clear quill *n. see* PURE QUILL n.

clearskin *n. see* CLEANSKIN n.

clear the coop *v.* (*also* **clear the fowl-house**) [mid–late 19C] (*US*) to rush off, to vacate. [CLEAR (OFF) v. + SE *coop*]

clear the custard *v.* [1990s+] to masturbate, after a long period of continence (cf. BEAT ONE'S MEAT v.). [SE *clear* + CUSTARD n.]

clear the fowl-house *v. see* CLEAR THE COOP v.

clear up *v.*¹ *see* CLEAN UP v.¹.

clear up *v.*² *see* CLEAN UP v.³ (2).

cleat *n.* [late 19C] the penis; esp. the glans (cf. ARSE-OPENER n.). [SE *cleat*, a wedge]

cleavage queen *n.* [1970s] (*gay*) a heterosexual. [SE *cleavage* + QUEEN *n.*[2] (1)]

cleave *n. see* CLOVEN *n.*

cleave *v.* **1** [mid-17C–18C] of a woman, to behave promiscuously. **2** [18C–early 19C] of a woman, usu. a prostitute, to pose as a virgin while not being one. [SE *cleave*, to split, i.e. her legs or her supposed hymen]

cleaver *n.*[1] [18C–19C] a butcher. [his job and his tools]

cleaver *n.*[2] [late 18C–early 19C] a promiscuous woman. [CLEAVE *v.* (1)]

cleave the pin *v.* [late 16C] of a woman, to bring a man to orgasm. [archery jargon *cleave the pin*, to score a bull's-eye]

cleek *n.* [1950s] (*orig. US*) a sad, melancholy person; thus one who spoils a party. [jazz use]

cleety *adj. see* CLUTEY *adj.*

cleft *n.*[1] *see* CLIFT *n.*

cleft *n.*[2] *see* CLOVEN *n.*

cleft *adj.* [18C–early 19C] (*UK Und.*) of a woman, usu. a prostitute, posing as a virgin while not being one. [CLEAVE *v.* (2)]

cleft (of flesh) *n.* [mid-18C–19C] the vagina (cf. AGREEABLE RUTS OF LIFE *n.*).

clefty *v. see* CLIFTIE *v.*

cleg *n.* [20C+] (*Ulster*) a parasite, a hanger-on. [lit. 'a horsefly']

clem *n.*[1] **1** [late 19C] (*US*) a farmer, a peasant (cf. ALVIN *n.*). **2** [1960s] (*Irish*) a second-rate thing. [proper name *Clarence*, considered a stereotypical 'country' name]

clem *n.*[2] [late 19C+] (*US*) a fight between travelling carnival or circus people and local townspeople. [CLEM *n.*[1] (1)]

clem *v.* (*also* **do a clem**) [mid-19C–1930s] (*UK tramp*) to go hungry, to starve. [16C+ dial. *clem*, to starve, to waste from hunger; ult. f. various Teut. roots meaning 'pinch' or 'squeeze']

clencher *n. see* CLINCHER *n.*[1]

clenchpoop *n. see* CLINCHPOOP *n.*

clergyman *n.* [late 18C–19C] a chimney sweep. [the colour of both professions' clothes]

clericals *n.* [mid-19C] clerical garments (i.e. those worn by clergymen).

clerked *adj.* [late 18C–mid-19C] soothed, gulled, imposed upon. [SE *clerk*; such 'learned' figures were automatically distrusted by the illiterate masses]

clerk of the kitchen *n.* [mid–late 17C] one who goes to the tavern for food as well as drink.

clerk of the works *n.* [early–mid-19C] a minor functionary.

Cleveland *n.* [1920s] (*US*) a $1000 bill. [the head of US President Grover *Cleveland* (1837–1908), which is printed on the bill]

clever *n.* (*also* **u-clever**) [1960s+] (*S.Afr.*) a gangster, a streetwise individual. [SE + Isicamtho *uclever*]

clever *adj.* **1** [mid-18C–1900s] (*US*) good-natured, well-disposed, amiable (often too well-disposed for one's own good and thus applied to those whose intelligence is considered somewhat deficient). **2** [19C+] (*orig. Aus./N.Z.*) in good health, in order, working well etc; thus *not too clever*, a generally negative response to 'how are you?', 'how is it?' etc. **3** [19C+] skilful, adroit. **4** [mid-19C; 1970s+] fashionable. **5** [late 19C+] cunning, duplicitous. **6** [20C+] (*Ulster*) of a garment, roomy. **7** [1970s+] (*US gay*) good-looking, charming. [18C SE *clever*, 'active' rather than 'infirm', healthy]

clever boots *n.* [1930s+] a clever person, esp. one who is 'too clever for their own good'.

clever clogs *n.* [mid-19C; 1960s+] (*mainly UK juv.*) a slightly pej. description of anyone considered notably clever (often 'too clever for their own good'). [orig dial.]

clever dick *n.* (*also* **cleverpot, cleversides, cleversticks**) [late 19C+] a clever person, esp. when considered suspiciously so.

clever-dick *adj.* [1950s+] self-satisfied, too smart for one's own good. [CLEVER DICK *n.*]

clever Mike *n.* [1950s+] a bicycle. [rhy. sl. = SE *bike*]

clevvies *n.* [1970s] (*US Black*) a woman, a girl. [? SE *cloven/cleft*, i.e. ref. to the vagina]

clewner *n.* [mid-16C] a senior rank of villain: 'Sir, yet there is another company / Of the same sect, that live more subtily, / And be in manner as master wardens, / To whom these rogers obey as captains / And be named clewners, as I hear say' (Copland, *Hye way to the Spyttel House*, *c*.1535). [ety. unknown; Ribton-Turner, *A History of Vagrants* (1887), suggests Gaelic *cluainear*, a cunning fellow, a hypocrite, Erse *cluanaire*, a seducer, a flatterer, Manx *cleaynagh*, a tempter]

cleyme *n.* (*also* **clyme**) [17C–early 19C] (*UK Und.*) an artificial sore or wound, as placed on the body by a variety of mendicant villains. [ety. unknown; E.P. suggests a Cockney pron. of SE *claim*, i.e. a claim on one's pity; the *cleyme* is created by 'bruising Crowsfoot, Speerwort, and Salt together, and clapping them on the Place, which frest the Skin, then with a Linnen rag, which sticks close to it, they tear off the Skin, and strew on it a little Powder'd Arsenick, which makes it look angrily …' (B.E.)]

clica *n.* [1960s+] (*US*) a gang. [Sp. *clica*, a clique]

click *n.*[1] [late 18C–mid-19C] (*UK Und.*) a blow. [dial.]

click *n.*[2] [mid–late 19C] a robbery, a theft. [? the SE *click* of a lock]

click *n.*[3] (*also* **clique**) [mid-19C+] a clique, a gang; thus CLICK UP *v.* [SE *clique*]

click *n.*[4] [1930s–40s] the making of an acquaintance; a flirtation, a pick-up. [CLICK *v.*[3] (1)]

click *n.*[5] [1930s–50s] (*US*) a success. [CLICK *v.*[3] (2)]

click *n.*[6] *see* KLICK *n.*

click *adj.* [1930s–50s] (*US*) successful. [CLICK *v.*[3] (2)]

click *v.*[1] [late 17C–19C] (*UK Und.*) to snatch, to rob. [northern dial. *cleek*, to snatch, to clutch eagerly]

click *v.*[2] [mid-18C–early 19C] to stand at one's shop doorway and inveigle customers in. [backform. f. CLICKER *n.*[1]]

click *v.*[3] [1910s+] **1** (*also* **click with**) to get on with, to strike up a friendship with; thus *clicking* (*with*), making a successful contact, usu. with a member of the opposite sex (albeit not necessarily sexual). **2** to become proficient or successful at, to come together. **3** to work out exactly as planned. **4** for something to become clear or comprehensible, esp. after a period of puzzlement, to 'ring a bell'. **5** to be recognized. **6** (*orig. Irish*) to pick up a member of the opposite sex. **7** to be chosen or selected. [the image of a lock or similar form of machinery working as planned]

click *v.*[4] [1930s+] to become pregnant. [also used in rural Aus. of a cow]

click *v.*[5] [2000s] (*US prison*) to attack in a group. [CLICK *n.*[3]]

click! *excl.* [1930s] a general excl. of satisfaction, indicating the successful conclusion of a plan. [CLICK *v.*[3] (3)]

clicker *n.*[1] [late 17C–19C] a shopkeeper's (orig. a shoemender's) tout. [shoemaker's jargon *clicker*, a foreman shoemaker who cuts out the leather for boots and shoes, and gives it out to the workmen, or a workman who works at cutting the uppers of boots and shoes]

clicker *n.*[2] [late 18C–early 19C] the gang member deputed to divide up the spoils fairly. [CLICK *v.*[1]]

clicker *n.*[3] [early 19C] a watch.

clicker *n.*[4] **1** [early–mid-19C] (*orig. boxing jargon*) a knockout blow. **2** [1940s] (*US*) a photographer. [the noise of the blow or the camera shutter]

clicker *n.*[5] [late 19C] (*UK Und.*) a thief. [CLICK *v.*[1]]

clicker *n.*[6] [1920s] (*UK prison*) a warder. [one who 'clicks the key']

clickers *n.* [1990s+] false teeth. [the sound they make]

clicket *n.* [late 16C–early 17C] the penis. [SE *clicket*, a latch-key]

clicket *v.* [late 16C–19C] to copulate; thus *at the clicket*, having intercourse. [SE *clicket*, of the fox, to be in heat, to copulate]

clickety-click *n.* **1** [20C+] (*bingo*) the numbers 6 or 66 (cf. ALDERSHOT LADIES *n.*). **2** [2000s] (*Aus.*) a stick. [rhy. sl.]

clickety-clicks *n.* [1960s+] women's underpants. [rhy. sl. = KNICKS *n.* (2)]

click in v. [1990s+] (*US gang*) to become initiated into a gang. [CLICK n.[3]]

click it v. [1910s] to die; to be killed.

clickman toad n. [late 18C–mid-19C] **1** a watch. **2** a West Countryman. ['A West-country man, who had never seen a watch, found one on a heath near Pool, which, by the motion of the hand, and the noise of the wheels, he concluded to be a living creature of the toad kind, and, from its clicking, he named it a clickman toad' (Grose, 1785)]

click (onto) v. [1990s+] (*US Black*) to affiliate oneself to, to associate with. [CLICK v.[3] (1)]

clicks n. [2000s] (*US prison*) minutes spent on the telephone.

click up v. [1930s+] (*esp. US prison*) to join a gang, if a prison gang usu. one formed on racist lines. [CLICK n.[3]]

click with v. see CLICK v.[3] (1).

clie n. see CLY n.

cliff ape n. [1920s+] (*US*) a rough, thuggish man. [SE *cliff* + APE n. (3)]

cliff-dweller n. [late 19C–1960s] (*US*) one who lives in a skyscraper apartment block, esp. in New York City. [SE *cliff-dwellers*, a tribe of Native Americans living lit. in cliffs in the Southwest]

cliffhanger n. [1930s+] any suspenseful, threatening situation, although usu. one from which one is eventually delivered. [orig. the film description of such silent-era serials as *The Perils of Pauline* (starring Pearl White) in which the heroine, at an episode's end, was often lit. hanging from a cliff]

clift n. (*also* **cleft**) [late 19C+] (*orig. Irish*) a fool; thus with the levels of stupidity, *quarter clift*, *three-quarter clift*; thus *the two ends of a clift*, an utter fool. [? SE *cleave*, i.e. their brain has been cut in several pieces]

clift v. [mid-19C–1900s] to steal (cf. CLIFTIE v.). [? SE *cleave*, to adhere to; or ? *clift*, to split, to divide (in this case possessions from their owner)]

cliftie v. (*also* **clefty**, **clifty**) [20C+] (*Aus.*) to steal. [CLIFT v., but note Gk *klephtys*, a thief]

cligh see under CLY.

climb n.[1] [1910s+] (*UK Und.*) cat burglary; thus *at the climb*, *climbing*, working as a cat burglar.

climb n.[2] [1940s+] (*drugs*) a marijuana cigarette (cf. BOMB n.[4]). [? it makes one CLIMB UP THE WALLS v. (3) or ? play on HIGH adj.[1] (2)]

climb v. (*also* **climb on**) [late 19C+] (*US*) of a man, to have sexual intercourse; to enter a woman and commence intercourse. [Williams has several 16C/17C e.g.s of *climb* in a sexual context, usu. in phr. *climb the tree*]

climb all over v. **1** [late 19C+] to trounce, to defeat heavily. **2** [1940s+] to attack physically. **3** [1940s+] to attack verbally, to reprimand. **4** [1950s+] to maul sexually, usu. spoken by a woman of a man. [fig. use of SE; note ALL OVER phr.[3]]

climb-a-pole n. [mid-19C] (*US*) an arrogant, 'stuck-up' person; also attrib. [one climbs so as to look down on the world]

climb-down n. [late 19C+] a humiliating surrender in an argument, esp. after one has doggedly held one's own position for some time.

climber n. [20C+] (*UK Und.*) a cat burglar. [CLIMB n.[1]]

climbing Mary n. [1940s] a female window-cleaner.

climbing trees to get away from it phr. (*also* **got to swim underwater to dodge it**, **so busy I've had to put a boy/man on to help**) [1940s+] (*Aus.*) a phr. used by a man who wishes to boast of the success of his sex life; usu. in answer to a question, e.g. GETTING ANY (LATELY)? phr.

climb in on v. [late 19C] (*US*) to overcome easily, to get the better of, esp. by trickery.

climb on v. see CLIMB v.

climb someone's frame v. (*also* **climb someone's back**) (*US*) **1** [late 19C+] (*also* **climb over someone's frame**) to harass

or criticize verbally. **2** [1930s–60s] (*also* **jar/rock someone's frame**) to assault physically.

climb the golden staircase v. [late 19C] **1** (*US*) to die. **2** to fail badly.

climb the greasy pole v. [late 19C] to die.

climb the ladder v. see CLIMB THREE TREES WITH A LADDER v.

climb the mountain of piety v. [late 19C–1900s] to take possessions to the pawnshop. [the world's first government-authorized pawnbrokers, which were established in Rome and sited on the Monte di Pietà ('the mountain of piety')]

climb the six-foot ladder v. [1940s–60s] (*orig. US Black*) to die. [the trad. 6ft depth of a grave]

climb the tree by one's neck v. [1910s] (*Aus.*) to be hanged.

climb the walls v. see CLIMB UP THE WALLS v.

climb three trees with a ladder v. (*also* **climb the ladder**) [mid-16C–19C] to be hanged. [the framework of the wooden gallows]

climb up someone's ass v. [1980s] (*US*) to subject to pressure. [SE + ASS n. (2)]

climb up the walls v. (*also* **climb the walls**, **run up the walls**) **1** [1930s+] to lose one's temper, to run out of patience. **2** [1960s+] to approach insanity through nerves, irritation, tension etc. **3** [1960s+] to become highly excited.

clinah n. see CLINER n.

clinch n. **1** [mid-19C] a prison cell; thus *get the clinch*, to be locked up; *clinched*, imprisoned. **2** [20C+] a sexual embrace. [SE *clinch*/CLINCH v.]

clinch v. [late 19C–1960s] to embrace sexually. [SE *clinch*]

clinched adj. [20C+] drunk. ['in the grip' of alcohol]

clincher n.[1] (*also* **clencher**) **1** [18C+] the ultimate solution, the culmination; thus [mid-19C] in fig. use, *get the clincher*, to be imprisoned. **2** [mid-19C] an irrefutable lie. [SE *clinch*]

clincher n.[2] [1950s] (*US prison*) a smokeable cigarette end. [one has to 'clench' it between one's fingertips]

clinchpoop n. (*also* **clenchpoop**) [mid–late 16C] an ill-mannered lout, one who lacks gentlemanly breeding. [? *clincher*, the workman who clinched the bolts in ship-building, in this case of the poop]

cliner n. (*also* **clinah**) [late 19C–1940s] (*Aus./US*) a woman, a girlfriend. [ety. unknown; ? Ger. *Kleine*, little one]

clinger n. [late 19C] a woman who holds tightly to her partner during a dance.

clingy adj. [20C+] over-dependent, esp. emotionally.

clinic n. [1950s] a public house. [one visits for 'a bit of what the doctor ordered']

Clink n. [16C] a sanctuary for criminals in Southwark; the villains who frequented this area were known as CLINKERS n. [CLINK n.[1] (1)]

clink n.[1] **1** [early 16C+] (*also* **clinker**, **clinky**) a prison. **2** [late 19C] (*Aus. prison*) a leg-chain. **3** [1900s] (*US*) a police station. [either SE *clink*, to secure, to fasten securely, or onomat. noise of clinking chains; note use of *clink* as description of the RMC Duntroon (Aus.) by its cadets; also WW1 milit. *clink*, guard room]

clink n.[2] (*also* **clinkum**) **1** [late 18C+] money (cf. CHING n.[2]). **2** [mid–late 19C] (*also* **clinker**) a coin. [echoic]

clink n.[3] [mid–late 19C] bad or second-rate beer. [abbr. BUM CLINK n.]

clink n.[4] [1930s–40s] (*US Black*) a fellow Black man. [? fig. use of CLINK n.[1] (1), so many Blacks being imprisoned, or f. the colour of SE *clinker*, a grey-black ash that remains after a fire]

clink n.[5] see CLANK n.

clink v. [early 19C–1910s] (*UK Und.*) to arrest. [CLINK n.[1] (1)]

clink and clank n. [1930s–40s] (*US Und.*) a bank. [rhy. sl.]

clinker n.[1] [late 17C–mid-18C] a crafty person. [? CLINKERS n.[1] (1)]

clinker n.[2] [mid-18C–1940s] (*orig. sporting*) anything, or anyone, considered excellent, first-rate. [something that 'rings a (celebratory) bell']

clinker n.³ [mid-19C–1910s] a sharp blow. [it 'clinks' on its target]

clinker n.⁴ [mid-19C+] a piece of excrement adhering to the anus; often in pl.; thus *have clinkers in one's bum*, to act nervously or restlessly (cf. CLAGNUT n.). [? SE *cling* or *clinker*, a hardened mass]

clinker n.⁵ [1900s–30s] (US) a hard biscuit. [SE *clinker*, a very hard brick; ? since its ult. ety. is Du., as imported by Dutch immigrants]

clinker n.⁶ **1** [1930s–50s] (US) a musical discord, a fluffed note. **2** [1950s–60s] a second-rate, worthless person. **3** [1950s+] something second-rate, inferior, esp. a performance. **4** [1960s] (US) a problem, a difficulty. [orig. baseball use]

clinker n.⁷ *see* CLINK n.¹ (1).

clinker n.⁸ *see* CLINK n.² (2).

clinker n.⁹ *see* CLINKERS n.¹ (1).

Clinkers n. [16C] a collective term for the villains who inhabited the criminal sanctuary of the CLINK n. in Southwark. [CLINK n.]

clinkers n.¹ **1** [late 17C–mid-19C; 1950s] chains and fetters worn by imprisoned felons; occas. in sing. **2** [1940s] (US Und.) handcuffs. [the sound of the fetters on stone floors]

clinkers n.² [20C+] (Ulster) the testicles (cf. BANGERS n.). [they 'clink' together]

clinkers n.³ [1900s] stairs. [? the noise made when one climbs them]

clinkers n.⁴ [1970s+] bedbugs.

clinkers n.⁵ *see* CLINKER n.⁴.

clinkerum n. [19C] a prison. [CLINK n.¹ (1)]

clinking adj. (also **hell-clinking**) [mid-19C–1930s] excellent, admirable, first-rate, esp. of racehorses. [CLINKER n.²]

clink rig n. (also **clinking**) [mid-19C] (UK Und.) the stealing of tankards from taverns; thus *clink rigger*, one who steals tankards. [SE *clink*, the noise of tankards hit together + RIG n.² (2)]

clinkum n. *see* CLINK n.².

clinky n. *see* CLINK n.¹ (1).

clip n.¹ **1** [19C+] a go, a time. **2** [early 19C+] a sharp blow. [CLIP v.¹ (3)]

clip n.² **1** [mid-19C+] a rate of movement, a pace; thus *fair/good clip*, a (reasonably) high speed. **2** [mid-19C–1930s] (US) a smart, clever or lively young woman or man. **3** [1900s] (US campus) a situation. [CLIP v.²]

clip n.³ **1** [1930s–60s] (US) a theft. **2** [1960s] (US Und.) a thief or robber. [CLIP v.¹ (4)]

clip n.⁴ [1940s] a male Jew (cf. BIGNOSE n.). [abbr. CLIPDICK n. (1)]

clip n.⁵ [1990s+] (drugs) a bundle of the bottles in which crack cocaine is distributed, tied with a rubber band to facilitate carriage. [it is clipped to one's belt]

clip n.⁶ [2000s] (US) a pager. [it is clipped to one's belt]

clip n.⁷ *see* CLIP-JOINT n.

clip v.¹ **1** [16C–mid-18C] to have sexual intercourse (cf. BANG v.¹). **2** [17C] to caress. **3** [late 17C+] to hit, to tap sharply. **4** [late 19C+] (orig. US) (also **clip in**) to defraud, to steal from, to rob. **5** [1910s+] (US) to shoot, usu. dead. **6** [1940s+] (US) to place under arrest. **7** [1950s] (US drugs) to adulterate a drug. **8** [1950s+] to beat, i.e. in a card-game. **9** [1960s+] to esteem as, to reckon. [SE *clip*, to cut or snip]

clip v.² [mid-19C+] to move quickly, to run. [SE *clip*, of a bird, to fly fast]

clip artist n. [1940s–60s] (US Und.) **1** a petty thief. **2** a swindler. [CLIP v.¹ (4) + ARTIST sfx]

clip a steamer n. [1990s+] (UK juv.) to defecate. [semantically linked to TURD n. (1), with its root in SE *torn*, the image is of cutting off a piece of excrement which, in the cold, might steam with body heat]

clipdick n. [1940s+] **1** a derog. term for a male Jew (cf. BIGNOSE n.). **2** a circumcised penis (cf. BALD-HEADED HERMIT n.; JEWISH CORNED BEEF n.; JEWISH NATIONAL n.; JEW'S COMPLIMENT n.; JEW'S LANCE n.; KOSHER DILL n.; LOP COCK n.; LOW NECK AND SHORT SLEEVES n.; ONE-EYED BOY WITH HIS SHIRTSLEEVES ROLLED UP n.; ROUNDHEAD n.²). [SE *clip* + DICK n.⁴ (1); his circumcision]

clip in v. *see* CLIP v.¹ (4).

clip-joint n. (also **clip**, **clip-dive**) [1930s+] (orig. US) a club or similar place of entertainment where the customers are deliberately and systematically defrauded under the guise of charging them for their pleasure. [CLIP v.¹ (4) + JOINT n.⁴ (3)]

clip-nit n. [late 17C] a dirty ruffian. [SE *clip*, to grasp + *nit*, a louse egg]

clipped adj.¹ [1930s+] (US) shot. [CLIP v.¹ (5)]

clipped adj.² [1910s+] (US) circumcised. [SE *clip*]

clipped adj.³ [1950s] (US) out of funds.

clipped within the ring n. [late 16C–early 17C] deflowered. [SE *clip* + RING n.¹ (1)]

clipper n.¹ **1** [early 18C] (UK Und.) a cut-purse. **2** [1940s] a philanderer, a womanizer. **3** [1940s] (US) a petty thief or confidence trickster. **4** [1960s] (US Und.) a thug, a violent person. **5** [1960s+] a professional store thief. [(3) and (5) CLIP v.¹ (4), but despite the obvious synonymy, chronology makes (1) and other defs. fig. use of SE]

clipper n.² **1** [mid-19C] an attractive person, esp. a woman. **2** [mid-19C–1920s] an excellent thing. [SE *clipper*, a fast-sailing vessel, esp. the raked schooners of America and subseq. the Aus. passenger ships]

clipper n.³ [1980s+] (S.Afr.) a 100-rand note. [? Afk. *klippe*, diamonds or the need for a *paper-clip* to keep 100 rand's worth of 10-rand notes together]

clippie n. [1940s+] a bus conductress, who orig. *clipped* tickets.

clipping n. [1970s+] (UK Und.) posing as a prostitute, obtaining the money, but absconding before intercourse takes place. [CLIP v.¹ (4)]

clipping adj.¹ [mid–late 19C] of a pace, fast. [CLIP v.²]

clipping adj.² [mid-19C–1920s] excellent, first-rate. [CLIPPER n.² (2)]

clipping adv. [late 19C] excellently, ideally. [CLIPPING adj.²]

clippings of tin n. [1910s+] (Irish) a trifling, worthless quantity.

clippy n. [1990s+] a (male) hairdresser's shop, a barber's. [SE *clip* + sfx *-y*]

clip queen n. [1940s] (US gay) a male prostitute who specializes in robbing clients. [CLIP v.¹ (4) + QUEEN n.² (1)]

clips, the n. [1900s] an admirable person or thing, someone who is smart, socially successful. [CLIPPING adj.²]

clip side of big moist n. [1940s] (US Black/Harlem) Europe. [CLIP v.¹ (5) + BIG MOIST n.; Europe was at that time a battleground of WW2]

clipster n. [1940s–60s] (US) a swindler. [CLIP v.¹ (4) + -STER sfx]

clip the King's English v. [late 17C–18C] to slur one's words when drunk; thus, to be drunk. [SE *clip*, to mutilate]

clip up v. [1950s] to toss a coin.

clique n. *see* CLICK n.³.

clit n. [1950s+] the *clitoris*. [abbr.]

clit fight n. [1990s+] (US) a sexual game between 2 women. [CLIT n. + SE *fight*]

clithopper n. [1960s+] (lesbian) a promiscuous lesbian. [CLIT n.; on pattern of BEDHOP v., lit. to move or 'hop' from clitoris to clitoris]

clitlins n. [2000s] (UK Black) the vagina. [CLIT n. + SE *chitlins*, i.e. idea of 'meat' that one can EAT v.³ (1)]

clitty n. [1930s+] the *clitoris*. [abbr. + sfx *-y*]

clitty adj. *see* CLUTEY adj.

clitty litter n. [2000s] (UK Black) stains on one's underwear produced by vaginal secretions. [CLITTY n. + SE *litter*, punning on *kitty litter*, a cat's 'toilet']

cloak n. [early 18C] (UK Und.) a watch-case.

cloak-twitcher n. [early 18C–early 19C] (UK Und.) a thief specializing in the theft of cloaks.

clob *v. see* CLOBBER *v.*² (1).

clobber *n.* (*also* **clabber, klobber**) **1** [late 19C] (*UK Und.*) ? a shirt. **2** [late 19C+] clothes, esp. good-quality or conspicuous clothes. **3** [1930s+] things. [ety. unknown; ? Yid., so claimed by Ware who suggests 'Hebrew KLBR' (the Heb. has been anglicized without vowels)]

clobber *v.*¹ (*also* **klobber**) [late 19C–1900s] to dress up; thus *clobbered*, well-dressed. [CLOBBER n. (2)]

clobber *v.*² **1** [late 19C+] (*also* **clob**) to hit, to beat up, to kill; thus *clobbering*, a beating. **2** [1940s+] to defeat heavily. **3** [1950s+] to criticize, to treat harshly. **4** [1960s+] in fig. use, i.e. to accost. **5** [1990s+] to make a physical effort. [ety. unknown, ? echoic of the sound of the blow; note US Air Force Academy *clobber in*, to crash]

clobbered *adj.* [1940s+] drunk (cf. ANNIHILATED adj.). [fig. use of CLOBBER *v.*² (1)]

clobbering machine *n.* (*also* **great Kiwi clobbering machine**) [1970s+] a strain of innate conservatism found in local or national bureaucracy or government that invariably opposes change. [CLOBBER *v.*² (1) + SE *machine*]

clobber someone with *v.* [1940s+] to force an unpleasant or unwanted task or duty on someone. [CLOBBER *v.*² (1)]

clobber the kleenex *v.* (*also* **put Mr Kleenex's kids through college**) [1990s+] to masturbate. [CLOBBER *v.*² (1) + *Kleenex*, proprietary brand of paper tissues]

clobber up *v.* **1** [mid-19C] to mend or patch clothes. **2** [1900s–10s] to dress smartly. [tailor's jargon *clobber*, to renovate old garments; ? ult. cobblers' jargon *clobber*, a black paste used by cobblers to fill up and conceal cracks in the leather of boots and shoes]

clobbo *n.* [1950s] a dull, stupid person. [? CLOD n.¹ (1)]

clock *n.*¹ **1** [late 19C] a bomb; thus *got a clock*, carrying a handbag (in which the bomb is hidden). **2** [late 19C+] a watch. **3** [20C+] the face; occas. the head. **4** [20C+] a speedometer, taximeter or similar dial that has a 'face'. **5** [1940s–50s] (*US Black*) (*also* **clocker**) the heart. **6** [1950s] (*US prison*) in fig. use of (4), courage. **7** [1980s] a blow, esp. to the face. **8** [1980s] surveillance, observation. [fig. uses of SE referring either to the clock's face or its ticking; (1) note a bomb-carrier who, when stopped during the dynamite scare of the 1880s by an alert policeman, on being asked what was in his bag, replied 'A clock']

clock *n.*² [1940s–60s] (*Aus.*) a prison sentence of 12 months; thus *round the clock*, in prison for 12 months. [the 12 hours of the clock face]

clock *n.*³ *see* CLOCKER n.².

clock *v.*¹ (*also* **clock up**) **1** [late 19C+] to attain a given time or number in a race or similarly measured distance or quantity. **2** [1940s+] to record the time etc. [the clock used to measure such times]

clock *v.*² **1** [1910s+] to look at. **2** [1920s+] to see, to recognize, to notice, to watch, to understand, to work something out. **3** [1950s] (*US*) to reconnoitre, usu. of a possible crime site. **4** [1980s] (*US*) of a prostitute, to pick up a customer. [the image of checking the time on a clock]

clock *v.*³ **1** [1920s+] (*orig. Aus./N.Z.*) to hit, usu. in the face. **2** [2000s] to defeat, to beat. [CLOCK n.¹ (3)]

clock *v.*⁴ [1980s+] (*US Black*) **1** to achieve, to accomplish, to succeed. **2** to earn money. [SE *clock up*]

clock *v.*⁵ [1980s+] (*US Black*) to sell drugs, thus to make money from drug-dealing. [CLOCKER n.³, but note CLOCK *v.*⁴ (2)]

clock *v.*⁶ [2000s] (*US Black*) to lose one's temper; to become violent. [CLOCK OUT v.]

clock a daffy *v.* [20C+] (*S.Afr.*) to tell a deceitful story with the intention of tricking the hearer. [CLOCK *v.*² (2) + DAFFY n.³]

clock a grip *v.* [1990s+] (*US Black*) to make a sudden windfall of money, esp. through drug sales or some other illegal scheme. [CLOCK *v.*⁴ (2) + GRIP n.¹ (4)]

clocker *n.*¹ **1** [1900s–50s] (*US*) a handicapper, bookmaker or racing tipster who bases their information on timing the horses on their morning exercise. **2** [1940s+] (*UK Und.*) a second-hand car dealer who illegally alters a car's mileage.

clocker *n.*² (*also* **clock**) [1930s+] (*Irish*) a cockroach, a beetle. [orig. dial.]

clocker *n.*³ [1980s+] (*drugs*) a dealer of crack cocaine; thus *clocking*, working as a crack dealer. [SE *clock*, a time piece. The need for the drug and the appearances of the dealer both seem to occur at regular intervals, and these dealers are on call 'around the clock'; but note CLOCK *v.*⁴ (2)]

clocker *n.*⁴ *see* CLOCK n.¹ (5).

clockers *n.* [1940s] (*US Und.*) the eyes. [CLOCK *v.*² (1)]

clockey *n. see* CLOCKY n.

clock in *v.* [1910s+] to arrive. [SE *clock in*, to register one's arrival at work on a time-clock]

clocking *n.*¹ [1980s+] (*US Black*) saying inappropriate, tactless things, acting insanely. [CLOCK OUT v. (2)]

clocking *n.*² [1980s+] (*US Black*) working as a drug seller. [CLOCK v.⁵]

clocking paper *n.* [1980s+] (*drugs*) profits from selling drugs. [CLOCKING n.² + PAPER n.¹ (2)]

clock on to *v.* [1930s+] to recognize. [CLOCK *v.*² (2)]

clock out *v.* [1980s] **1** to die. **2** to go very crazy, to be 'out of it'. [SE *clock out*, to leave a place of employment; (2) + ? var. on WIND UP *v.*² (1)/WOUND-UP adj. (2)]

clock up *v. see* CLOCK *v.*¹.

clock-weights *n.* [19C] the testicles (cf. BANGERS n.). [they supposedly swing backwards and forwards]

clockwork *n.* (*US Black*) **1** [1940s+] (*also* **clockworks**) the human brain, the mind. **2** [2000s] the female buttocks. [(1) the mechanism that makes the clock 'work'; (2) the movement]

clocky *n.* (*also* **clockey**) [late 18C–mid-19C] a watchman. [the regularity of his rounds]

clod *n.*¹ **1** [late 16C+] a stupid person, esp. a dull-witted peasant; thus *cloddish*, stupid (cf. BOGHOPPER n.). **2** [1960s+] a rude, awkward person; thus *cloddish*, clumsy. [SE *clod*, a lump of earth or mud]

clod *n.*² [1910s] (*UK tramp*) a penny or any copper coin; usu. in pl. [rhy. sl.; CLODHOPPER n. = *copper*]

clodbrained *adj.* [1940s] (*Irish*) very stupid (cf. AMOEBA-BRAINED adj.). [CLOD n.¹ (1) + sfx -*brained*]

clod-buster *n.* [1950s+] (*US*) a rustic, a farmer (cf. BOGHOPPER n.). [lit. one who breaks up clods (of earth)]

clod-crusher *n.* [late 19C–1910s] (*US*) a rustic, a farmer (cf. BOGHOPPER n.). [note also: 'an epithet used by Americans to describe the large feet which they believe to be the characteristics of English women as compared with those of their own country' (B&L)]

cloddipole *n. see* CLODPOLL n.

cloddish *adj. see* CLOD n.¹.

cloddy *adj.* [late 19C] aristocratic-looking. [dog-fanciers' jargon *cloddy*, low to the ground, short in the back and thickset (the characteristics of the ideal bulldog)]

clodhopper *n.* **1** [late 17C+] (*orig. UK Und.*) a clumsy oaf, a boor, a dull-witted peasant. **2** [late 19C+] (*US*) a rustic, a farmer (cf. BOGHOPPER n.). **3** [late 19C+] (*also* **clodskipper**) a heavy work shoe. **4** [1930s] a street dancer, begging for cash. **5** [1960s] a large and clumsy foot. **6** [1960s+] a policeman (cf. BEAT-POUNDER n.; BOTTLE (AND STOPPER) n.). [SE *clod* + *hopper*, lit. one who hops over the clods of earth; note SE *clod-hopper*, a ploughman (cited as slang by B.E. c.1698); (6) also rhy. sl. = COPPER n.³ (1)]

clodhopper *adj.* [1930s] (*US*) rural, small-town, rustic. [CLODHOPPER n. (2)]

clodhopping *adj.* [mid-19C+] unsophisticated, rustic. [CLODHOPPER n. (1)]

clod-jumper *n.* [1910s+] (*US*) a rustic, a farmer (cf. BOGHOPPER n.). [SE *clod* + *jumper*; on model of CLODHOPPER n. (2)]

clod-knocker *n.* [1940s–70s] (*US*) a rustic, a farmer (cf. BOGHOPPER n.). [SE *clod* + *knocker*; on model of CLODHOPPER n. (2)]

clod-masher *n.* (*US/Aus.*) **1** [1910s–40s] a large foot. **2** [1910s–70s] (*also* **clod-smasher**) a heavy shoe. **3** [1940s–70s] a clumsy oaf, a rustic (cf. BOGHOPPER n.). [SE *clod* +*masher*; on model of CLODHOPPER n.]

clodpate *n.* (*also* **clotpate**) [mid-17C–mid-18C] a fool, a dullard; thus *clod-pated*, stupid (cf. PLUMP-PATE n.; SAP-PATE n.; SHALLOW PATE n.). [CLOD n.¹ (1) + SE *pate*, the head; on model of -HEAD sfx (1)]

clodpoll *n.* (*also* **cloddipole, clodpole, clotpold**) [early 17C+] a fool, an incompetent. [CLOD n.¹ (1) + SE *poll*, the head]

clods and stickings *n.* [mid-19C–1910s] gruel with dumplings.

clodskipper *n. see* CLODHOPPER n. (3).

clodskull *n.* [early 18C] a fool. [CLOD-SKULLED adj.]

clod-skulled *adj.* [late 17C–early 18C] stupid (cf. AIRHEADED adj.; AMOEBA-BRAINED adj.; BEEF-WITTED adj.; NUMBSKULLED adj.; THICK-SKULLED adj.). [CLOD n.¹ (1) + SE *skull*]

clod-smasher *n. see* CLOD-MASHER n. (2).

cloggie *adj.* [1990s+] Dutch. [the stereotyped wearing of *clogs* by the Dutch]

cloggite *n.* [1990s+] a Dutch person. [the stereotyped wearing of *clogs* by the Dutch]

clomp *n.* **1** [20C+] (*US*) (*also* **clomper**) a heavy boot or shoe. **2** [20C+] the sound of something heavy or solid hitting the ground. **3** [1960s+] (*US*) a blow. [echoic]

clompers *n.* [1960s–70s] (*US*) false teeth. [echoic]

clone *n.* [1970s+] **1** (*US*) anyone who imitates another person to a slavish extent; thus a tedious, unimportant person. **2** (*US gay*) a general description of a gay man who poses as one of a variety of super-masculine stereotypes, e.g. truck-driver, military man, cowboy etc, a style epitomized by the members of the 1970s disco group the Village People. [SE *clone*, a thing produced in imitation of, or closely resembling, another; (2) note 'Queer Slang in the Gay 90s' (1999) on *Gaymart.com*: 'In the 70's the look included a mustache, muscle shirt/flannel shirt and Levi's. The late 80's – 90's included short hair, long sideburns, white t-shirt, shorts/jeans and Doc boots with gray socks']

clone zone *n.* [1990s+] (*US gay*) somewhere that gay 'clones' associate. [CLONE n. (2)]

clonk *n.* [20C+] **1** a blow, a hit. **2** the noise of one hard object striking another. [echoic]

clonk *v.* [20C+] to hit. [CLONK n. (1)]

clonker *n. see* CLUNKER n.¹.

clootie *adj. see* CLUTEY adj.

clop *n.* (*also* **cloop**) [1940s+] (*orig. US*) a blow. [echoic]

clop *v.* [1940s+] (*orig. US*) to hit hard. [CLOP n.]

close *adj.* **1** [1900s] (*Aus.*) well-informed, knowledgeable. **2** [1950s] (*US jazz*) masterful. [? gambling phr. *play close to one's chest*]

close as God's curse to a whore's arse *adj.* [late 18C–early 19C] very close.

close as ninety-nine is to one hundred *adj.* [1930s–40s] (*US Black*) extremely close, as close as possible.

close as shirt and shitten arse *adj.* [late 18C–early 19C] extremely close.

close call *n.* [late 19C+] (*orig. US*) a very near thing. [sporting imagery]

closed swinging *n.* [1970s+] swapping parties in which only husband-and-wife partnerships take part, with no singles allowed to unbalance the situation; the opposite of OPEN SWINGING n. [SE *closed* + SWINGING n.²]

close file *n.* [mid-19C] a secretive or uncommunicative person. [SE *close* + FILE n. (5)]

close one's face *v. see* SHUT ONE'S FACE (UP) v.

close one's trap *v. see* SHUT ONE'S TRAP v.

close shave *n.* (*also* **close pinch, narrow shave, narrow squeak, near shave, near squeak**) [early 19C+] (*orig. US*) a very near thing.

closet *n.*¹ [late 17C] the vagina (cf. BAG n.¹). [euph.]

closet *n.*² [1960s+] (*orig. gay*) a metaphorical 'cupboard' in which a homosexual who is unwilling to reveal his or her sexuality is seen to live.

closet *adj.* (*also* **closeted**) [1960s+] secretive, clandestine, hidden, usu. in the context of homosexuality. [CLOSET n.²]

closet case *n.* **1** [1950s+] (*US campus*) a socially inept, unattractive person; a hard worker. **2** [1960s+] (*gay*) a homosexual who finds it difficult or impossible to admit their sexuality in public. [CLOSET adj. + CASE n.⁴ (4); note (1) predates gay use of CLOSET adj./CLOSET n.²]

closet-man *n.* [1950s+] (*W.I.*) a sanitary inspector. [SE *water closet*]

closet of ease *n.* [mid-17C] a lavatory or water closet (cf. ALTAR n.). [euph.]

close to one's belly *phr.* [1920s–40s] (*US*) almost totally impoverished, very poor.

close to the blanket *phr.* (*also* **close to the cushion**) [1900s–10s] (*US, Western*) almost totally impoverished, very poor. [gambling use, when a poker game would be played on a spread blanket; thus when one's pile of money gets smaller and smaller and 'close to the blanket']

closet queen *n.* (*also* **closet queer**) [1960s+] (*gay*) a homosexual who finds it difficult to admit his sexuality. [CLOSET adj. + QUEEN n.² (1)/QUEER n. (4); James, *America's Homosexual Underground* (1965), offers a link to (water) *closet* and suggests that the *closet queen* is one who dares not have sex at home, preferring the anonymity of public lavatories, bathhouses, parks etc]

closetry *n.* [1970s] (*gay*) the practice of a homosexual hiding their real sexuality. [CLOSET n.²]

close-up *n.* [1990s+] (*US*) a frighteningly sudden, unexpected and sometimes unwanted, kiss. [ext. of film use]

close up *v.* [late 19C] (*Aus.*) to stop talking.

close your head! *excl.* [1930s–40s] shut up! be quiet!

close your shell! *excl.* [late 19C] (*US campus*) be quiet!

closh *n.* [late 18C–early 19C] a Dutch seaman. [common Du. proper name *Klaas*, itself abbr. of *Nicolaas*]

closhy *adj.* [1910s] stupid. [CLOSH n.; thus the derog. stereotype of a slow, stolid Dutchman]

clot *n.*¹ [1940s+] **1** a fool, often used affectionately, e.g. *you silly clot*. **2** nonsense. [CLOD n.¹ (1)]

clot *n.*² [1950s+] (*W.I.*) a highly derog. description of another person. [abbr. BLOOD CLAAT n.]

cloth *n.* [late 19C] the vagina. [? play on theatre use *cloth*, the curtain which stands between the audience and the stage]

cloth, the *n.* [early 18C+] a generic term for the clergy, the world of the clergy. [their vestments]

cloth-ears *n.* [20C+] a general term of mild abuse, esp. to someone who at first seems not to have heard one's comment. [abbr. of phr. *have cloth-ears*, to be stupid, lit. to be unable to hear due to a flap-eared cap]

clothed heavy *adj.* [1970s+] (*US Black*) very well-dressed.

clothes *n.* [1970s] (*US*) a detective (cf. BABY-BLUES n.²). [abbr. SE *plain clothes*]

clotheshorse *n.* [1930s+] **1** a fashion model. **2** an exquisitely well-dressed, fashionable person, although the implication is that beyond such perfection lies little else (cf. CLOTHES-PEG n.¹).

clothesline *v.* [1980s+] (*US*) to strike someone hard across the throat, usu. using the edge of the hand. [orig. an illicit tackle in US football]

clothes-peg *n.*¹ (*also* **clothes-prop, garment-peg**) [1910s–20s] a fashionably dressed person (cf. CLOTHESHORSE n.).

clothes-peg *n.*² [1930s+] an egg. [rhy. sl.; note Franklyn, *Dict. of Rhyming Slang* (1960), claims this usage is erroneous]

clothes-pegs n.[1] [1940s] (Aus.) teeth. [resemblance]

clothes-pegs n.[2] [1940s+] the legs. [rhy. sl.]

clothes-prop n.[1] **1** [late 19C] the erect penis (cf. BAT n.[7]). **2** [1900s] a silly, empty-headed person. [see Williams for 17C fig. use of *prop*, penis]

clothes-prop n.[2] see CLOTHES-PEG n.[1].

cloth-head n. (also **felt-head**) [1920s+] a fool. [SE *cloth/felt* + -HEAD sfx (1)]

cloth-headed adj. [1920s+] foolish (cf. AIRHEADED adj.). [CLOTH-HEAD n.]

cloth market n. [late 17C–early 19C] bed. [its linen covers]

clotpate n. see CLODPATE.

clotpold n. see CLODPOLL n.

clotty n. [1960s+] (*Irish*) a general term of abuse. [ety. unknown; ? link to Yorks. dial. *cloddy*, an awkward, ill-dressed person]

clotzed adj. [1960s] (*US campus*) becoming tense and 'frozen' under pressure. [KLUTZ n.]

cloud n.[1] **1** [late 17C–early 19C] tobacco, tobacco smoke. **2** [1980s+] (*drugs*) the smoke that one inhales from a pipe of crack cocaine. **3** [1990s+] (*drugs*) the stimulating effect that follows smoking crack cocaine. **4** [1990s+] (*drugs*) crack cocaine (cf. BASE n.).

cloud n.[2] [late 19C] (*UK Und.*) an attic.

cloud n.[3] [1920s] a derog. term for a Black person, esp. a crowd of Black people (cf. BLACKBELLY n.). [play on SMOKE n.[6] (1) but note CLOUDY adj.]

cloud-blower n. see BLOW A CLOUD v. (2).

cloud chaser n. [1950s] (*US*) a pilot.

cloud nine n. **1** [1950s+] a state of bliss, sometimes drug-induced. **2** [1980s+] (*drugs*) crack cocaine (cf. BASE n.). [according to Brewer, *Dict. of Phrase and Fable* (15th edn, 1995), the term stems from the classification of clouds by the US Weather Bureau. There are 9 divisions, and number 9 is cumulonimbus, a cumulus cloud of great vertical extent, topped with shapes that resemble mountains or towers]

cloud seven n. [1950s+] a state of bliss, often drug-induced. [var. on CLOUD NINE n.; presumably less blissful, but 7 is trad. a 'lucky' number]

cloud-walker n. [1940s] (*US teen*) a good dancer.

cloudy adj. [late 17C] dark-complexioned.

clout n.[1] **1** [16C–1920s] (*UK Und.*) (also **snoot-cloot**) a cotton handkerchief. **2** [16C+] clothing. **3** [mid-17C–1950s] a sanitary towel or nappy. **4** [1990s+] the vagina. [14C SE *clout*, a piece of cloth; a handkerchief; (1) + SNOOT n. (1)]

clout n.[2] **1** [16C+] a heavy blow; thus *the clouts*, a heavy beating. **2** [1960s–70s] aggression, power. [ety. unknown; ? link to SE *clout*, a cloth, thus a 'lump' of material, thus any sort of lump; or ? link to SE *clod*. Earlier use was SE. Note WW1 Aus. milit. *clout*, a wound]

clout n.[3] [early 19C; 1920s+] (*US Und.*) an act of robbery. [CLOUT v.[2] (1)]

clout n.[4] [mid-19C; 1930s+] (*orig. US*) influence, esp. in politics. [generally assumed to have been coined *c*.1937 in Chicago and quickly disseminated across the US and thence the English-speaking world (however, note 1 cit. found in 1868). According to Safire, *Political Dict.* (1978), either f. baseball jargon *clout*, a big hit, thus one who 'packs a punch' in government; or CLOUT v.[2] (1), to steal, since in the cynical world of US politics all politicians are seen to tend to larceny]

clout n.[5] **1** [20C+] a philanderer. **2** [1930s+] (*US*) a thief, e.g. a pickpocket or shoplifter. [CLOUT v.[2] (1)]

clout n.[6] [20C+] a stupid, oafish person. [SE *clout*, a lump of earth; thus a synon. with CLOD n.[1] (1)]

clout v.[1] [16C+] to hit, to give a heavy blow to. [CLOUT n.[2] (1); earlier use was SE]

clout v.[2] **1** [20C+] (*US*) to steal; to rob; thus *clouted*, stolen. **2** [1920s–30s] (*US Und.*) to arrest. **3** [1950s] (*Aus.*) to cheat by

palming a card or cards. [CLOUT n.[1] (1) in the context of handkerchiefs being stolen, as by 18C pickpockets]

clouted adj. [1950s+] (*US*) in possession of political influence. [CLOUT n.[4]]

clouted-shoe n. (also **clouted shoon, clout-shoe**) [late 17C–early 19C] a yokel, an unsophisticated peasant (cf. BOGHOPPER n.). [SE *clouted shoe*, a shoe tipped with iron and secured with iron nails; the footwear of such individuals]

clouter n.[1] **1** [early 18C] a pickpocket whose speciality is stealing silk handkerchiefs. **2** [1950s] a thief. [CLOUT n.[1] (1)]

clouter n.[2] [1910s] a heavy blow. [CLOUT v.[1]]

clout-head n. [1990s+] a thug, a ruffian. [CLOUT v.[1] + -HEAD sfx (1)]

clouting n. [early 18C–early 19C] the stealing of handkerchiefs. [CLOUT n.[1] (1)]

clouting lay n. [late 18C–19C] (*UK Und.*) the stealing of handkerchiefs. [CLOUTING n.+ LAY n.[4] (1)]

clout one's cookie v. [1970s] (*US*) of a woman, to masturbate (cf. APPLY LIP GLOSS v.; BEAT ONE'S MEAT v.). [CLOUT v.[1] + COOCHIE n.]

clouts, the n. see CLOUT n.[2] (1).

clout-shoe n. see CLOUTED-SHOE n.

clove-hunter n. [late 19C] (*US*) a theatre patron who drinks (from a flask) during a play and then chews cloves in an attempt to disguise the smell of the liquor on their breath.

cloven n. (also **cleave, cleft**) [late 18C–early 19C] a woman, usu. a prostitute, who poses as a virgin but, in reality, is not. [SE *cloven*, split]

cloven hoofter n. [1990s+] (*Aus.*) a male homosexual. [rhy. sl. = POOFTER n. (1)]

cloven spot n. [late 17C–19C] the vagina. [one of a number of synons. coined by John Cleland for his 1749 novel *Memoirs of a Woman of Pleasure* ('Fanny Hill'), a pornographic work paradoxically without obscenities]

clover-eater n. [mid-19C] (*US*) an inhabitant of Virginia. [the diet of the very poor]

clover-kicker n. (*US*) **1** [1910s–60s] a clumsy oaf, a boor, a dull-witted peasant. **2** [1940s–60s] a rustic, a farmer (cf. ACORN-CRACKER n.). [play on SE]

clowes n. (also **clows**) [late 18C] a rogue, a villain. [CLOY n.[1]]

clown n.[1] **1** [20C+] a general term of abuse, esp. as a fool, an idiot; also used affectionately. **2** [1920s–50s] (*US Und.*) a policeman. **3** [1950s] (*US Black*) a state of having fun, one's frivolous, self-indulgent, partying side; thus *get one's clown down*, to indulge that aspect of one's character. **4** [1950s] (*US Black*) a fuss, complaining.

clown n.[2] see TOWN CLOWN n.

clown v. [1990s+] (*US Black*) to ridicule, to humiliate. [i.e. to make into a fig. clown]

clown (around) v. (also **clown about**) [late 19C+] to play the fool (cf. ACT THE ANGORA v.). [ext. of SE *clown*, to act like a clown]

clowning n. [2000s] (*US Black*) **1** fooling about. **2** doing well, being successful. [(1) CLOWN (AROUND) v.; (2) on bad = good model]

clownish adj. [17C] stupid, foolish. [SE *clown*]

clows n. see CLOWES n.

cloy n.[1] (also **cloye**) [late 18C–early 19C] (*UK Und.*) a thief, a pickpocket. [CLOY v. (2)]

cloy n.[2] see CLY n.

cloy v. (also **cloye**) (*UK Und.*) **1** [late 16C] to arrest. **2** [early 17C–mid-19C] to steal. [CLY v.]

cloyer n. [17C–18C] a pickpocket or cut-purse, spec. an experienced one who demands a share of their younger peers' profits. [? CLOY n.[1], ? CLOY v. (2) or ? SE *cloyne*, to act deceitfully or fraudulently, to cheat]

club n. **1** [mid-17C–19C] the penis (cf. BAT n.[7]). **2** [mid-late 18C] a thick pigtail, shaped like a club and worn by men and subseq.

women, which was fashionable in 1750–1800 in the UK; the term has survived in US dials. meaning *bun*.

club *v.* [19C+] to have sexual intercourse (cf. BANG v.[1]).

club and stick *n.* [1930s–40s] a policeman (cf. BOTTLE (AND STOPPER) n.). [rhy. sl. = DICK n.[6] (2); the implements are, of course, apposite]

clubbed *adj.* [1990s+] pregnant. [IN THE CLUB phr.]

clubby *n.* [1900s] (*Aus.*) a member of a club or lodge.

club Fed *n.* [1980s+] (*US*) a low-security *Fed*eral penitentiary, usu. for white-collar prisoners and offering them many privileges. [abbr. + pun on *Club Med*, the holiday firm]

club-fist *n.* [late 16C–early 17C] a thug.

club-foot *n.* 1 [1940s] (*US gay*) a slightly deformed penis. 2 [1950s] (*US*) a general term of abuse; the implication is of ungainliness. 3 [1950s–70s] (*US*) a large, clumsy foot. [SE *clubfoot*, a deformed foot]

clubhouse *n.* [1900s–40s] a police station.

club member *n. see* MEMBER n.[2] (2).

club sandwich *n.* 1 [1960s–70s] (*US campus*) a sexual threesome (cf. CHOCOLATE SANDWICH n.). 2 [1990s+] the vagina, esp. with pronounced labia (cf. BACON SANDWICH n.).

club the clam *v.* [1960s+] of a woman, to masturbate (cf. APPLY LIP GLOSS v.; BEAT ONE'S HOG v.). [SE *club* + CLAM n.[1] (2)]

cluck *n.*[1] 1 [20C+] (*orig. US*) (*also* **kluck**) a dull, stupid person (with the brains of a chicken). 2 [1960s] (*US*) an egg.

cluck *n.*[2] 1 [1900s–50s] (*orig. US*) a counterfeit coin. 2 [1970s] (*US*) a tedious situation. [fig. use of *cluck* as a dud, a second-rate object; ? (2) the 'clucking' noise one makes when irritated or bored]

cluck *n.*[3] [1940s] (*US*) a derog. term for a person with notably dark skin. [ety. unknown]

cluck *n.*[4] (*also* **clucker**) [1980s+] (*drugs*) a user of crack cocaine. [ety. unknown; ? link to CLUCK v.[2] (1), i.e. the loquacity engendered by the drug]

cluck *v.*[1] [late 19C] (*UK Und.*) to acquit. [ety. unknown]

cluck *v.*[2] (*US*) 1 [1920s+] to speak. 2 [1960s] to be cowardly and run away. 3 [2000s] to inform on. [the noise a SE *chicken* makes; (2) CHICKEN n.[1] (1)]

cluck *v.*[3] [1990s+] (*UK drugs*) 1 to crave crack cocaine. 2 to suffer withdrawal symptoms from any narcotic. [CLUCK n.[4]]

clucka *n.* [2000s] (*US Black/drugs*) a regular user of methamphetamine. [? var. on CLUCK n.[4]]

clucker *n. see* CLUCK n.[4].

cluckhead *n.*[1] [1940s+] a fool. [CLUCK n.[1] (1) + -HEAD sfx (1)]

cluckhead *n.*[2] [1990s+] (*US Black gang*) a regular user of crack cocaine. [ext. of CLUCK n.[4] + -HEAD sfx (3)]

clucky *adj.* [1940s+] (*Aus./N.Z.*) pregnant. [dial. *clucky*, used of a broody hen]

cludgie *n.* [1980s+] a lavatory. [dial. *cludgy*, sticky, wet and heavy]

clue *n.*[1] 1 [19C] (*Scot.*) the vagina. 2 [1930s+] (*Aus.*) a woman.

clue *n.*[2] [1920s+] knowledge in general, or a spec. piece of information; esp. as *not have a clue*.

clue *v.* [1950s+] (*US*) to inform, to tell. [CLUE n.[2]]

clued in *adj.* (*also* **clued**, **clued up**) [1950s+] aware. [CLUE v./CLUE (SOMEONE) IN v.]

clueful *adj.* [1980s] (*US campus*) aware, intelligent, savvy. [opposite of CLUELESS adj.]

clue in *v. see* CLUE (SOMEONE) IN v.

clue in! *excl.* [1980s] (*US campus*) pay attention! [CLUE (SOMEONE) IN v.]

clueless *adj.* [1940s+] stupid, ignorant, incompetent. [CLUE n.[2] + sfx *-less*]

clue (someone) in *v.* (*also* **clue (someone) up**) [1940s+] (*orig. US*) to explain, to inform, to make aware. [CLUE n.[2]]

cluey *adj.* [1960s+] (*Aus.*) properly informed. [CLUE v.]

clump *n.* [mid-19C+] a blow, a heavy hit. [SE *clump*, a lump, then a heavy stick]

clump *v.* [mid-19C+] to hit heavily, to thump. [CLUMP n.]

clumper *n.* 1 [mid–late 19C] a heavy-soled walking boot. 2 [mid-19C+] one who hits hard. [CLUMP v.]

clumperton *n.* [mid-16C–early 18C] a fool, a yokel (cf. BOGHOPPER n.). [fig. use of CLUMP v. on pattern of SE *simpleton*]

clumsy as a cub-bear handling his prick *phr.* [20C+] (*Can.*) very clumsy.

clumsy dick *n.* [late 19C–1920s] a very clumsy person. [SE *clumsy* + DICK n.[1] (1)]

clunge *n.* [1990s+] 1 the anus; esp. in abusive, dismissive phr. *up your clunge!* 2 the vagina. [dial. *clung*, tight shrivelled, ult. SE *cling*]

clunk *n.*[1] 1 [early 19C+] a noise, typically of a door shutting, a hard object hitting another one etc. 2 [1940s] a blow. [echoic]

clunk *n.*[2] (*Aus./US*) 1 [20C+] a man. 2 [1920s+] a fool. [LUNK n.]

clunk *v.* 1 [late 18C+] to make the sound of a cork being withdrawn from a bottle or of liquid pouring through a narrow-necked vessel or being shaken around in a half-empty vessel. 2 [1930s+] to hit, to strike, esp. on the head. [echoic]

clunker *n.*[1] (*also* **clonker**, **clunk**, **klunker**) [1940s+] 1 a worn-out, useless car. 2 anything useless, unattractive, incompetent. [? the noise it makes]

clunker *n.*[2] 1 [1950s+] a fool, a dolt, an incompetent. 2 [1970s+] (*US*) a blunder, a mistake. [CLUNK n.[2] (2)]

clunkhead *n.* [1950s+] (*US*) a fool. [CLUNK n.[2] (2) + -HEAD sfx (1)]

clush *adj.* [mid–late 19C] easy, simple. [ety. unknown]

clusterfuck *n.* 1 [1960s+] (*orig. US*) an orgy, irrespective of sexual preference. 2 [1960s+] (*orig. US*) gang-rape. 3 [1970s+] chaos. 4 [1980s+] a group of indecisive people, unable to decide what to do next. [SE *cluster* + FUCK n.[1] (1)/-FUCK sfx/FUCKUP n.]

cluster-fuck *v.* [2000s] (*US*) to confuse. [CLUSTERFUCK n. (3)]

cluster-screw *n.* [1970s] (*US*) 1 an orgy. 2 in fig. use, a chaotic situation. [SE *cluster* + SCREW n.[1] (2); a semi-bowdlerized version of CLUSTERFUCK n.]

clutch *n.*[1] 1 [late 18C] the hand. 2 [late 19C–1900s] (*UK society*) a dance (the activity, not the event). [(1) its action; (2) the physical proximity of the dancers]

clutch *n.*[2] [1970s] (*US*) a clumsy person. [KLUTZ n.]

clutch *v.* [1950s–60s] (*US campus*) to freeze up under pressure. [backform. f. CLUTCHED (UP) adj.]

clutch-buster *n.* [1940s–60s] (*orig. US Black*) one who drives a HOT-ROD n. (1). [SE *clutch* + fig. use of BUST v.[1] (4)]

clutch-butt *n.* [1960s] (*US*) sexual intercourse. [SE *clutch* + BUTT n.[1] (2)]

clutched (up) *adj.* [1950s+] (*US*) frightened, nervous, tense, awed. [the physical effects of such emotions]

clutch-fist *n.* [mid-17C] a miser.

clutch-fisted *adj.* [late 17C–18C] mean, miserly. [CLUTCH-FIST n.]

clutey *adj.* (*also* **cleety**, **clitty**, **clootie**) [late 19C+] (*Irish*) awkward. [dial. *clootie*, a left-handed person]

clutz *n. see* KLUTZ n.

cly *n.* (*also* **clie**, **cligh**, **cloy**) [mid-17C–19C] 1 money. 2 a pocket, also a purse or wallet. [? CLY v.]

cly *v.* (*also* **cligh**) [mid-16C–mid-19C] to seize, to get, to take; to steal. [poss. f. Ger. *kleien* and Du. *kleyen*, to scratch (with the nails), to claw the head; Ribton-Turner, *A History of Vagrants* (1887), suggests Erse *cloib*, a snatch]

clyde *n.*[1] [1950s+] (*orig. US Black*) an unsophisticated person, a provincial, a yokel (cf. ALVIN n.). [a stereotypical 'peasant' name]

clyde *n.*[2] [1970s] (*US*) a wide-brimmed hat, a fedora. [a style worn by '*Clyde* Barrow' (Warren Beatty) in the film *Bonnie and Clyde* (1967)]

clydesdale *n.* [1980s] (*US*) an attractive male. [? the solid dependability of the *Clydesdale* horse or the attractiveness of the *Clydesdale* terrier]

cly-faker *n.* [early–mid-19C] a pickpocket. [CLY n. (2) + FAKER n.]

clyme *n. see* CLEYME n.

clyster-pipe *n.* **1** [early 17C–early 19C] a doctor, an apothecary. **2** [late 17C–mid-19C] (*also* **glister-pipe**) the penis. [SE *clyster-pipe*, a pipe used to administer clysters, or enemas]

cly the jerk *v.* [mid-16C–early 19C] (*UK Und.*) to be whipped. [CLY v. + SE *jerk*, a stroke of the whip]

C man *n. see* CUNT MAN n.

C-note *n.* **1** [20C+] (*US*) a $100 bill. **2** [1970s] (*US prison*) a 100-year jail sentence. [C n.[1]]

C.N.R. strawberries *n.* [1970s] (*Can. prison*) prunes. [ety. unknown; ? joc. use of Canadian National Railways]

co *n.*[1] [mid-16C–18C] a man (cf. COE n.). [abbr. COVE n. (1)]

co *n.*[2] [late 19C–1920s] (*UK society*) a co-respondent (in a divorce case) (cf. CO-D n.; CO-RE n.). [abbr.]

co- *pfx see* KER- pfx and its combs.

coach *n.* [1960s] (*US drugs*) the unsmoked portion of a cannabis cigarette. [pun on ROACH n.[2] (3)]

coachee/coachey/coachie *n. see* COACHY n.

coach (it) *v.* **1** [17C+] to travel by coach. **2** [mid-19C] (*UK campus*) to prepare a candidate for an examination; to undergo such preparation. [(1) the original use was extended to motor vehicles in the 20C+]

coachman on the box *n.* [1940s+] venereal disease. [rhy. sl. = POX n.[1] (2)]

coachman's seat *n.* [late 19C] (*Aus.*) a bustle or dress improver. [? a coachman is seated behind]

coach-wheel *n.* **1** [late 18C–1960s] a 5-shilling (25p) piece, a crown. **2** [early–mid-19C] (*US*) a silver dollar. [like the SE *coach-wheel*, the crown piece was, by numismatic standards, large and round]

coachy *n.* (*also* **coachee, coachey, coachie**) [late 18C–1900s] a coachman. [on the model of SE *bargee*/CABBIE n., but note synon. Magyar *kocsi*, Bohemian *koèi*, dial. Ger. *kutsche*]

coads *n. see* COD n.[1].

coakie *n. see* COKIE n.

coal *n.*[1] **1** [1930s+] a derog. term for a dark-skinned Black person, esp. a woman; thus *load of coal*, a gathering of Black people (cf. BLACKBELLY n.). **2** [1990s+] (*Aus.*) dark 'bags' under the eyes.

coal *n.*[2] [1970s] (*US*) the lit end or glowing ash of a cigarette.

coal *n.*[3] *see* COAL (HEAVER) n.

coal *n.*[4] *see* COLE n.

coal and coke *adj.* (*also* **coals and coke**) [20C+] penniless, impoverished. [rhy. sl. = BROKE adj.[1]]

coal bin *n.*[1] [1930s] (*US Black*) the vagina (cf. BAG n.[1]).

coal bin *n.*[2] [1970s+] (*US Black*) a derog. term describing a dark-complexioned Black person (cf. BLACKBELLY n.).

coal-black joke *n. see* BLACK JOKE n.

coalbox *n.* **1** [mid-19C+] the chorus (of a song). **2** [1920s] a music hall. [? the noise of a coalbox being shaken]

coal burner *n.* [1970s+] a White man or woman who enjoys sexual relations with a Black man or woman. [COAL n.[1] (1) + SE *burner*, pun on SE]

coaley *n. see* COALIE n.

coal (heaver) *n.* (*also* **heaver**) [1910s–20s] a coin of small value, usu. a penny. [rhy. sl. = STIVER n. (1)]

coal-hole *n.* [early 19C] (*US Und.*) a cell in which drunks are imprisoned.

coalie *n.* (*also* **coaley**) **1** [early 19C+] a coal-heaver. **2** [mid-19C+] a wharf labourer who loads ships with coal. [abbr. SE; (1) post-1840s use is usu. Aus.; note naval jargon *coalie*, a stoker]

coal mine *n.* [1940s+] (*US Black*) a derog. term for a dark-complexioned Black person (cf. BLACKBELLY n.).

Coalopolis *n.* [late 19C+] (*Aus.*) Newcastle, New South Wales. [its coal mines]

coalpot *n.* [1940s] (*US Black*) a pipe.

coal sack *n.* [late 19C] a blind alley. [mispron. of *cul-de-sac*]

coals and coke *adj. see* COAL AND COKE adj.

coal-scuttle *n.*[1] [mid-19C] (*UK Und.*) the punishment cell.

coal-scuttle *n.*[2] [mid-late 19C] a poke bonnet, which it supposedly resembled. [its chief characteristic was the sides, which projected well beyond those of the face; fashionable *c.*1850]

coal-scuttle blonde *n.* [1930s–50s] (*US*) a Black woman with a blonde wig.

coal-scuttler *n.* [1900s] (*US*) a derog. term for a Black person (cf. BLACKBELLY n.).

coal-shutes *n.* [1940s+] (*US*) a very dark-complexioned Black person. [note USN *coal-chute*, a dirty hammock]

coarse Christian *n.* [20C+] (*Ulster*) a person of innate worth but poor manners, a 'rough diamond'.

coarse one *n.* [1930s–40s] (*US Und.*) a large-denomination dollar bill, esp. when used to impress a confidence man's potential victim.

Coast, the *n.* **1** [20C+] the West Coast of the US, esp. Los Angeles. **2** [1960s] the Atlantic coast, to inhabitants of the Pacific seaboard. [the Pacific Coast has been thus known since the mid-19C]

coast *v.* [1930s+] **1** (*US drugs*) to achieve the somnolent, peaceful state that follows an injection of heroin. **2** (*US drugs*) to experience the sensation that follows the use of cocaine. **3** (*US*) to relax, to act in a relaxed manner. [SE *coast*, to proceed easily; (2) Spears, *Slang and Jargon of Drugs and Drink* (1986), suggests 'a slight overdose']

coast (about) *v.* [late 19C–1940s] (*Aus.*) to live as a tramp or vagrant. [SE *coast*, to wander]

coast (a) lime *v.* [1950s] (*W.I./UK Black*) to hang around chatting and socializing. [SE *coast* + LIME n.[1]]

coaster *n.*[1] (*Aus.*) **1** [late 19C–1950s] a tramp. **2** [late 19C+] a loafer, an idler. [COAST (ABOUT) v.]

coaster *n.*[2] [1950s+] (*N.Z.*) someone who originates from or lives on the west coast of the South Island. [SE *coast*]

coast home *v.* [1930s] (*orig. US*) to win easily, usu. in a sporting context.

coast lime *v. see* COAST (A) LIME v.

coasts to coasts *n.* [1960s+] (*US drugs*) amphetamines (cf. A n.[2]). [? their use by long-distance truck-drivers]

coat *n.* [1910s+] a suspect. [COAT v. (2)]

coat *v.* **1** [20C+] to reprimand, to scold. **2** [1910s+] to arrest. **3** [1930s+] to beat up, to hit. **4** [1940s+] (*Aus.*) to ostracize. **5** [1970s] (*US gay*) to have anal intercourse (cf. ASK FOR THE RING v.). [the image of grabbing a lapel; (4) in Aus. one tugs one's own lapel as a sign that a given person is not to be trusted]

coat and badge *v.* (*also* **C and B**) [1910s+] to cadge; usu. in phrs. *on the coat and badge*, *on the C and B*, cadging. [rhy. sl.; *Doggett's Coat and Badge*, awarded to Thames watermen who, with this prize, had the right to charge higher fares in their mid-19C heyday]

coat game *n.* [1940s] (*US Und.*) theft.

coathanger *n.* [1930s+] (*Aus.*) Sydney Harbour Bridge. [the shape]

coathangers *n.* [1990s+] large and erect nipples. [play on CHAPEL HAT PEGS n.]

coating *n.* [1950s+] a scolding. [COAT v. (1)]

coat party *n.* [2000s] (*US prison*) throwing a coat over a prisoner's head prior to beating him up.

coatpuller *n.* [1980s+] (*Aus. prison*) an escapee.

coax *v.* [late 18C] to pull down the soiled or holed part of one's stocking so that it is hidden by the heel of one's shoe. [orig. use of SE *coax*, to fool, to take in, this use is apparently linked to 16C *cokes*, a simpleton, a gullible fool]

coaxyorum *n.* [1990s+] (*Irish*) **1** an opportunist. **2** a cake prepared by a putative mother-in-law to show respect to her daughter's boyfriend. [SE *coax* + 'Lat.' sfx]

cob *n.*[1] [late 17C–mid-19C] a Spanish dollar. [B.E. states 'in Ireland']

cob *n.*[2] [19C] (*US*) a farmer, a rustic (cf. BUCKWHEAT n.). [SE *corncob* + ? derog. ref. to supposed use of corncobs in the privy as a substitute for lavatory paper]

cob *n.*[3] (*UK prison*) **1** [late 19C] a punishment cell. **2** [1940s–50s] prison bread. [orig. dial. *cob*, a small roundish loaf]

cob *n.*[4] [1920s–60s] (*US*) the penis. [orig. dial.]

cob *n.*[5] [1950s–70s] (*N.Z.*) a friend, a mate. [abbr. COBBER n.[2]]

cob *n.*[6] [1970s+] (*S.Afr. drugs*) a quantity of marijuana, about the size of a corncob and sometimes packaged in maize leaves.

cob *v. see* COP v.

Cobar shower *n.* [1940s+] (*Aus.*) **1** a flower. **2** a shower of rain. **3** a dust storm. [rhy. sl.; *Cobar* is a copper-mining town in New South Wales. In the case of (2) other Aus. names can be substituted according to local geography]

cobber *n.*[1] [19C–1910s] a great lie. [naut. jargon *cob*, to hit on the buttocks with something flat]

cobber *n.*[2] (*also* **cobba**) [late 19C+] (*Aus.*) a friend, a mate. [? dial *cob*, to take a liking to someone; or ? Heb./Yid. *chaver*, a 'pal', a 'chum']

cobber *v.* (*also* **cobber up**) [1910s–60s] (*Aus./N.Z.*) to befriend; thus *cobbery*, friendly. [COBBER n.[2]]

cobber-dobber *n.* [1960s–70s] (*Aus.*) one who informs on a friend. [COBBER n.[2] + DOB (IN) v. (2)]

cobble-colter *n.* [late 17C–mid-19C] (*UK Und.*) a turkey. [*cobble* = gobble]

cobbler *n.*[1] (*Aus./N.Z.*) **1** [late 19C–1950s] the last and least willing sheep to be sheared. **2** [1900s] the last of anything. [based on an old joke, quoted in *OED*: 'In the harvest field English rustics used to say, when picking up the last sheaf, "This is what the cobbler threw at his wife." "What?" "The last."']

cobbler *n.*[2] [20C+] (*US Und.*) a forger, esp. of passports, currency and stocks and bonds. [? SE *cobble*, to put together or join roughly or clumsily]

cobblers *n.* **1** [late 19C] the past. **2** [1930s+] (*also* **cobbler's awls**, **cobblers' stalls**) the testicles (cf. CHEESE AND CRACKERS n.). **3** [1950s+] rubbish, nonsense. [rhy. sl.; (1) *cobbler's last* = past; (2) *cobbler's awls* = BALLS n.[1] (1); (3) on model of BALLOCKS n.[1] (1)/BALLOCKS n.[2] (2)]

cobblers *adj.* [1990s+] stupid, mistaken. [COBBLERS n. (3)]

cobblers! *excl.* [1950s+] **1** rubbish! nonsense! **2** an excl. of irritation. [COBBLERS n.; on model of BALLOCKS! excl.]

cobblers' awls *n. see* COBBLERS n. (2).

cobbler's knot *n.* [mid-19C] a lock of hair shaped like the figure 6 and twisted from the temple back towards the ear.

cobbler's marbles *n.* [mid-19C] Asiatic cholera. [mispron. of *cholera morbus*]

cobbler's punch *n.*[1] [late 18C–early 19C] a mixture consisting of treacle, vinegar, gin and water. [pun on the cobbler's *punch*, a fool]

cobbler's punch *n.*[2] [early 19C] urine with a cinder in it. [pun on COBBLER'S PUNCH n.[1] + COBS n.]

cobblers' stalls *n. see* COBBLERS n. (2).

cobbo *n.* [1920s+] (*Aus.*) a close friend. [COBBER n.[2] + -o sfx (4)]

cobby *n. see* CUBBY n.

cobby *adj. see* HAVE A COB ON v.

cobitis *n.* [1940s–50s] (*UK Und.*) a loathing of invariably unpleasant prison food. [COB n.[3] (2) + sfx *-itis*, usu. used of diseases]

cob o' coal *n.* [1920s–50s] unemployment benefit (cf. BLESS MY SOUL n.). [rhy. sl. = SE *dole*]

cobs *n.* [20C+] the testicles. [dial.]

cobweb-cheat *n.* [late 17C–early 18C] a swindler who can be easily found out. [SE *cobweb* + *cheat*, his swindles have no more substance than a cobweb]

cobweb-pretence *n.* [late 17C–early 18C] an inadequate ruse, a plot that can be detected easily. [SE *cobweb* + *pretence*, such ruses are utterly insubstantial]

cobweb rig *n.* [late 18C–early 19C] (*UK Und.*) a form of swindle or confidence trick. [? SE *cobweb*, a subtly woven snare + RIG n.[2] (2), despite COBWEB-CHEAT n. and COBWEB-PRETENCE n., which imply incompetence]

cocabola *n.* [1940s–50s] (*US*) a Black person. [Arawak *kakabali*, thence Sp. *cocobolo/cocobola*, the timber from any one of several species of tree of the Central American genus *Dalbergia*, or the tree itself, a dark hardwood]

Coca-Cola *n.* [1950s+] (*Aus.*) a bowler, in cricket. [rhy. sl.; ult. the soft drink brand *Coca-Cola*]

coca-cola *n.* [1990s+] (*W.I.*) a curvaceous figure. [var. on COKE FRAME n.; ult. the soft drink brand *Coca-Cola*]

cocaine bugs *n. see* BUG n.[6] (2).

coch *v.* (*UK Black*) **1** [1970s–80s] to stay, to hide out. **2** [1970s–80s] to lean on. **3** [2000s] to move without being seen. [ety. unknown]

coche *n.* [1990s+] (*US prison/Hisp.*) a prison guard. [Sp. *coche*, pig, thus PIG n.[3] (4)]

cochineal *n.* [late 19C–1900s] red wine. [SE *cochineal*, a scarlet dye]

cochore *v.* [20C+] (*W.I., Guyn.*) **1** to tell tales of others in order to curry favour with a superior. **2** to persuade, to charm, to lull into false confidence. [? SE *cajole*]

cochornis *n.* [1970s+] (*drugs*) marijuana. [? Sp.]

Cock *n.* [late 19C] (*UK Und.*) a Londoner. [abbr. *Cockney*]

cock *n.*[1] [late 14C–early 19C] a euph. for *God*, esp. used in a variety of oaths (cf. BOB n.[2]). [mispron.]

cock *n.*[2] **1** [late 16C+] (*UK/US Northern*) the penis (cf. ANTEATER n.). **2** [17C] a man as a sexual being. **3** [1920s+] (*US Black*) sexual intercourse. **4** [1960s–70s] (*US Black*) an orgasm. **5** [1960s+] a show-off, a self-promoter, a general term of abuse (cf. CHOAD n.; COCKCHAFER n.; COCK CHEESE n.; COCKFACE n.; COCKHEAD n.; COCKMUNCH n.; COCKSUCK n.). [(1) Lat. *cuccus*, the male domestic fowl; thus the term has been used for any object that resembles a cock's head. As far as its use as a sexual term is concerned, *cock* here mixes the basic image of the cock as rooster (itself a 19C US euph.) and the cock's head seen as a tap-like shape, this secondary aspect emphasized by its function in 'pouring' semen. The word remained in perfectly standard use until Queen Victoria's coronation, shortly after which it joined the ranks of the taboo. It has yet to return to the mainstream. Note that E.P. claims 'always SE but since 1830 a vulgarism' and *OED* (in late 19C) notes 'the current name among the people, but, *pudoris causa*, not admissible in polite speech or literature']

cock *n.*[3] [early 17C+] a general term of address, esp. Cockney use. [abbr. SE *Cockney*]

cock *n.*[4] **1** [mid-17C–1900s] a man, spec. a plucky fighter. **2** [late 17C–19C] an expert, an exemplar. **3** [late 18C] (*UK Und.*) one who, being hanged, dies bravely. [characteristics of the bird]

cock *n.*[5] **1** [mid-19C] a broadsheet or pamphlet, sold in the streets and relating some form of lurid and sensational incident, typically a fire, a murder or an accident. **2** [1940s+] nonsense, rubbish; often as (*load of*) *old cock*. [SE *cock and bull story* but note COOK UP v.[1] (2) + the *Cock Lane ghost*, 'which had a great run, and was a rich harvest to the running stationers' (Hotten, 1867)]

cock *n.*[6] **1** [mid-19C+] (*US, mainly Black/Southern*) the vagina. **2** [1920s+] intercourse with a woman. **3** [1970s+] (*US Southern*) a woman, viewed solely as a sexual object; thus *a piece of cock* (cf. PIECE OF ASS n.). [Fr. *coquille*, cockleshell or cowrie]

cock *n.*[7] [1970s] a man who is easy to sponge on, spec. one who buys more than his necessary share in a pub. [SE *cock*, i.e. like the bird, he enjoys showing off]

cock *adj.*[1] [mid-16C+] chief, top, most important. [SE *cockerel*]

cock *adj.*[2] [1960s+] (*US*) pornographic. [COCK n.[2] (1)]

cock *v.*[1] [17C; late 19C+] to have sexual intercourse; thus *cocking*, sexual intercourse; *cock in one's eye*, amorous (cf. BAGAGA v.). [COCK n.[2] (1)]

cock *v.*[2] [19C] to smoke. [17C SE *cock*, to place a match in the cock of a matchlock gun]

cock *v.*[3] [1930s] (*US*) to knock out. [abbr. COLD-COCK v.]

cock-a-brass *n.* [late 18C] (*UK Und.*) a member of a team of card-sharpers who diverts a disgruntled victim from pursuing them. [COCK n.[4] (1) + BRASS n.[2]]

cock a cloud *v. see* BLOW A CLOUD v. (2).

cock a deaf 'un *v.* [1920s+] to pretend to be deaf, or at least to ignore by 'not hearing' the speaker. [SE *cock*, to turn up + *deaf one*, i.e. an ear]

cock-a-doodle *n.*[1] [mid-19C] a very strengthening form of broth made with beaten eggs in brandy and water. [? play on SE *cock-a-doodle*, the noise of a cockerel]

cock-a-doodle *n.*[2] [1930s+] (*Aus.*) nonsense, rubbish. [SE *cock-a-doodle*, the noise of a cockerel, but note COCK n.[5] (2)]

cock-a-fanny *n.* [1990s+] of a man, placing his genitals between his thighs to simulate female genitals. [COCK n.[2] (1) + FANNY n.[1] (1)]

cock-a-hoop *adj.* (*also* **cock-a-whoop, cock-on-hoop**) [mid-16C–mid-19C] in high spirits, transported with joy. [ety. unknown. The *OED* cites it as a 'phrase of doubtful origin, the history of which has been further obscured by subsequent attempts, explicit or implicit, to analyse it', but offers a number of such attempts, the most interesting being that cited in Thomas Blount's *Glossographia* (1670): 'Cock-on-Hoop, our Ancestors call'd that the Cock which we call a Spigget, or perhaps they used such Cocks in their vessels, as are still retained in water-pipes. The Cock being taken out, and laid on the hoop of the vessel, they used to drink up the ale as it ran out without intermission [...] and then they were Cock-on-Hoop, i.e. at the height of mirth and jollity. A saying still retained'. SE *c.*1830 onwards]

cock-ale *n.* [mid-17C–mid-19C] a variety of beer that supposedly has aphrodisiac properties. [SE *cock-ale*, ale mixed with the jelly or minced meat of a boiled cock, besides other ingredients + a pun on COCK n.[2] (1)]

cockaleekie *adj.* [1990s+] cheeky. [rhy. sl.; ult. a type of soup]

cockalize *v.* **1** [1930s+] (*US juv.*) to humiliate/initiate a boy by smearing his penis with some substance, urinating on him, hitting his penis with a knotted handkerchief etc. **2** [1960s] (*US*) to beat, to defeat heavily. [COCK n.[2] (1)]

cock alley *n.* [late 18C–19C] the female genitals (cf. ALLEY n.[1]; BAG n.[1]). [COCK n.[2] (1)]

cock-a-loft *adj.* [late 19C] affected, pompous. [SE *cock*, to swagger, to boast + ? COCK n.[2] (1), i.e. fig. brandishing of the erect penis]

cockalorum *n.* [early 18C–19C] a self-important little man. [joc. nonce-word, but note Du. *kockeloeren*, to crow. The first *OED* cit. specifies cockalorum as 'the Marquis of Huntly, whose father, the Duke of Gordon, was called "Cock of the North"']

cockalorum *adj.* [early 18C–19C] swaggering, boastful, self-important. [COCKALORUM n.]

cockamamie *n.* (*US*) **1** [1920s+] an absurd situation, a 'nonsense'. **2** [1930s+] an absurd, eccentric person. [COCKAMAMIE adj.]

cockamamie *adj.* (*also* **cockamamy**) [1920s+] confused, ludicrous, fake, fraudulent, absurd?. [? *decalcomania*, a picture or design left on the skin as a 'transfer', from specially prepared paper, which is wetted and rubbed (popular *c.*1862–4). Rosten, *The Joys of Yiddish* (1968), suggests that the shift came because 'on the Lower East Side [...] no one knew how to spell "decalcomania"', thus note Kober, *Thunder over the Bronx* (1935): 'Then there were the "cockamanies" — painted strips of paper which the kids applied to their wrists and rubbed with spit until the image was transferred to their hand']

cock-and-breeches *n.* [early 19C] a small, sturdy boy. [COCK n.[2] (1) + SE *breeches*]

cock and hen *n.* (*also* **cockeren, cockle (and hen)**) **1** [20C+] £10 (cf. AYRTON (SENNA) n.). **2** [20C+] a pen. **3** [1910s+]

(*bingo/gambling*) the number 10 (cf. ALDERSHOT LADIES n.). **4** [1940s–50s] a 10-year jail sentence. [rhy. sl.]

cock and hen club *n.* [19C] a club that admits both men and women.

cock and pinch *n.* [mid-19C] an old-fashioned hat, favoured by dandies of the period. [the hat was *cocked* back and front and *pinched* at the sides and it was made of beaver fur]

cock artist *n.* [1990s+] a sexually sophisticated male. [COCK n.[2] (1) + ARTIST sfx]

cockasaurus *n.* [2000s] (*US Black*) a very large penis. [COCK n.[2] (1) + SE *dinosaur*]

cock a snoot (at) *v.* (*also* **cock a snook (at), concoct a snoot**) [late 19C+] to disdain, to ignore, to turn up one's nose; thus *cocking snooty*, disdainfully. [SE *cock*, to turn up + SNOOT n. (1)]

cockatoo *n.*[1] [mid-17C] the penis. [ext. of COCK n.[2] (1), punning on SE *cock/cockatoo*]

cockatoo *n.*[2] (*Aus.*) **1** [mid–late 19C] a convict serving time on Cockatoo Island. **2** [mid-19C+] a lookout for those engaged in some form of illegality. [(1) *Cockatoo* Island, Sydney, where criminals were held *c.*1870; (2) f. (1) or the noted wariness of the bird]

cockatoo *n.*[3] (*also* **cockatooer**) [mid-19C+] (*Aus./N.Z.*) a small farmer; thus *cockatoo fence*, a fence erected by such a farmer; *cockatoo's weather*, fine by day, wet at night or fine in the week, wet on Sunday. [the image of a SE *cockatoo* sitting on a fence and staring around + COCKATOO n.[2] (1), as orig. such farmers had come from Sydney to the Port Fairy area]

cockatoo *v.*[1] [late 19C] (*Aus.*) to farm on a small scale. [COCKATOO n.[3]]

cockatoo *v.*[2] [1940s+] (*Aus.*) to keep a lookout. [COCKATOO n.[2] (2)]

cockatooer *n. see* COCKATOO n.[3].

cockatrice *n.* **1** [mid-16C–mid-19C] (*also* **cock-trick**) a prostitute (cf. COCK-BAWD n.; COCKCHAFER n.; COCK-TAIL n.[1]; CONY-CATCHER n.[1]; FORESKIN HUNTER n.; FOOL TRAP n.; GOATMILKER n.; GOBBLEDYGOO n.[1]; JOHN CATCHER n.; NEEDLE WOMAN n.; NESTLECOCK n.; PINCH-PRICK n.; PINTLE-MERCHANT n.; SPERM-BUCKET n.). **2** [18C–19C] a baby. [SE *cockatrice*, a hybrid monster with head, wings and feet of a cock, terminating in a serpent with a barbed tail; (1) such a monster can kill with a mere glance + pun on COCK n.[2] (1) + fem. sfx *-trix*; (2) the monster is born from an egg. Halliwell, editor/reviser of Nares, suggests that (1) 'seems to be applied especially to a captain's concubine']

cockaty *adj.* [1990s+] (*W.I.*) affected, putting on airs.

cock-a-wax *n.* (*also* **cockowax**) **1** [late 18C–19C] a familiar term of address; esp. as *my old cock-a-wax*. **2** [early–mid-19C] (*also* **son of wax**) a cobbler, who uses wax in his work.

cock-a-whoop *adj. see* COCK-A-HOOP adj.

cock-bawd *n.* **1** [17C–19C] a procurer (cf. ABBOT ON THE CROSS n.). **2** [late 17C–early 18C] a superior prostitute (cf. COCKATRICE n.). [COCK n.[2] (1) + SE *bawd*, lit. a 'male whore']

cockbite *n.* [1960s+] (*US*) a repellent, unpopular person. [? a person who, if permitted, would bite one's penis, i.e. COCK n.[2] (1)]

cock block *n.* [2000s] (*US Black*) a woman who permits sexual intimacy but refuses intercourse. [COCK BLOCK v. (1)]

cock block *v.* (*also* **c.b.**) (*US Black*) **1** [1980s+] to ruin another man's sexual activities by stealing his woman, interrupting his seduction etc; thus *cock-blocker*, one who does this. **2** [2000s] any interference in someone's plans, efforts etc. [COCK n.[2] (1) + SE *block*]

cock book *n.* [1960s+] (*US*) pornography. [COCK n.[2] (1) + SE *book*]

cock-brain *n.* [late 16C–17C; 20C+] a foolish young man; thus *cockbrained*, foolish. [COCK n.[2] (1) + sfx *-brain*; ? a young man's trad. obsession with sex. 20C+ use is US only]

cock-broth *n.* [17C; 1930s] (*UK tramp*) any form of strong, satisfying soup.

cock-catch v. [late 19C–1900s] (*orig. milit.*) to obtain money on false pretences. [COCK n.⁵ (1)]

cockchafer n. **1** [mid-19C] a woman who permits or encourages a good deal of sexual intimacy but not intercourse (cf. COCKTEASER n.). **2** [mid-19C] a prostitute (cf. COCKATRICE n.). **3** [mid–late 19C] (*UK Und./prison*) (*also* **chafer**) a prison treadmill. **4** [late 19C] the vagina. **5** [1920s–40s] a general term of abuse. [COCK n.² (1) + SE *chafer*, that which chafes or rubs painfully]

cock cheese n. (*also* **dick cheese, knob cheese, …stilton, …yoghurt, nob stilton, prick cheese**) **1** [late 19C+] smegma. **2** [2000s] a general term of abuse. [COCK n.² (1)/DICK n.⁴ (1)/KNOB n.¹ (3)/NOB n.⁵ (1)/PRICK n. (2) + CHEESE n.² (1)]

cock collar n. [1970s] (*US Black*) the head of one's penis, esp. its base, where it joins the main shaft. [COCK n.² (1) + SE *collar*]

cock-diesel n. [1990s+] **1** (*US Black/campus*) a strong, muscular, attractive man (cf. COCKSTRONG adj.). **2** (*US gay*) a muscular male homosexual. [COCK n.² (1) + DIESEL n.²]

cock doctor n. [20C+] a venerealogist. [COCK n.² (1) + SE *doctor*]

cocked adj. [mid-18C+] (*US*) drunk (cf. AFFLICTED adj.). [SE *cocked*, askew]

cocked and ready to rock phr. (*also* **locked, cocked and ready to rock**) [1970s+] (*US Black*) completely prepared. [firearms imagery]

cocker n.¹ [late 19C+] a general term of address, usu. to a man. [COCK n.³]

cocker n.² [late 19C+] (*orig. Aus.*) a *cock*roach. [abbr. + sfx *-er*]

cocker n.³ [1920s] (*US*) a racing tipster.

cocker adj. [early 19C] calculating. [Edward *Cocker* (1631–76), an engraver and teacher, the writer of *Cocker's Arithmetic* (publ. posthumously in 1678)]

cockerel n. [mid–late 17C] the penis. [COCK n.² (1) + pun on the bird, 'a young cock' (*OED*)]

cockeren n. *see* COCK AND HEN n.

cockers-p n. [1980s] (*UK society*) a cocktail party. [elision/abbr. of SE and + -ER sfx]

cock-eye n. [mid-19C+] a squinting eye; thus as a nickname. [COCK-EYED adj.¹ (1)]

cock-eye adj. [late 19C] messy, topsy-turvy. [COCK-EYED adj.¹]

cock-eye Bob n. (*also* **cock-eye, cock-eyed Bob**) [late 19C+] (*Aus., Western*) a cyclone or thunderstorm. [COCK-EYED adj.¹ (1) + generic use of *Bob*]

cock-eyed adj.¹ **1** [mid-18C+] squinting. **2** [20C+] topsy-turvy, ludicrous, absurd. **3** [20C+] crazy, irrational, eccentric, odd. **4** [1920s+] out of true, at an angle; both lit. and fig. **5** [1920s+] very drunk (cf. ARSEHOLED adj.). [SE *cock*, to bend (a joint or limb) at an angle + *eye*]

cock-eyed adj.² [1910s+] a synon. for *confounded*, used in excl.

cock-eyed adv. [1900s] in a critical manner.

cockface n. [1960s+] (*US*) a general term of abuse. [COCK n.² (1) + SE *face*]

cock hall n. [late 18C+] the vagina (cf. BAG n.¹). [COCK n.² (1) + SE *hall*]

cock hammer n. [1960s] (*US campus*) the penis (cf. ARSE-OPENER n.). [COCK n.⁶ (1) + SE *hammer*]

cockhead n. [1970s] (*Aus./US*) a general term of abuse, also used affectionately/intimately. [COCK n.² (1) + -HEAD sfx (1)]

cock-holder n. [late 19C–1940s] the vagina (cf. BAG n.¹). [COCK n.² (1) + SE *holder*]

cock-horse adj. [mid-18C–mid-19C] excited, elated. [the pleasure of a child riding 'a-cockhorse'; but note Nares: 'to ride a-cock-horse is a phrase of considerable antiquity, to signify being over proud and imperious […] the term *cock-horse* was commonly used in the sense of upstart']

cock-hound n. [1940s+] (*US*) a man devoted to sex before all things. [COCK n.⁶ (1) + HOUND sfx]

cockie *see under* COCKY.

cockies' clip n. [20C+] (*Aus.*) **1** a pickpocket. **2** a swim. [rhy. sl.; (1) = DIP n.⁴ (1); (2) = SE *dip*]

cocking adj. [late 17C–early 19C] impudent, cheeky. [COCK n.² (1)]

cock inn n. [late 19C+] the vagina (cf. BAG n.¹). [COCK n.² (1) + SE *inn*, a pun on the fictitious public house]

cockish adj. [17C–1930s] wanton, sexually forward, esp. of a woman. [SE *cock*, a cockerel + sfx *-ish*]

cock it v. [18C–19C; 1960s+] to have sexual intercourse (cf. BAGAGA v.). [COCK v.¹]

cock it! excl. [1920s] a mild excl. of annoyance, that's it! that's all over! [COCK v.¹; euph. for the 'harder' FUCK IT! excl.]

cock it over v. [mid-19C–1920s] to dominate, to lord it over. [SE *cock*, to behave boastfully or defiantly, to swagger]

cock it up v. [1960s+] (*Aus.*) for a woman to offer herself sexually in an obvious manner. [COCK n.⁶ (1)]

cock juice n. [1950s+] semen (cf. BABY FLUID n.). [COCK n.² (1) + JUICE n.² (1)]

cock-knob n. *see* KNOB n.¹ (2).

cock-knocker n. **1** [1950s+] (*US*) (*also* **cacknacker**) an unpleasant, worthless person. **2** [1990s+] a male homosexual (cf. BONE-EATER n.). [COCK n.² (1)/CACK n.² (1) + SE *knocker*; lit. 'penis-hitter' or 'shit-hitter']

cock-knocking adj. [1980s+] (*US*) a synon. for DAMNED adj. [COCK-KNOCKER n. (1)]

cock lane n. [late 18C+] the vagina (cf. ALLEY n.¹; BAG n.¹). [COCK n.² (1) + SE *lane*. The term was reinforced by the real-life *Cock Lane* (in the City of London), which in the 14C was the only street on which London's prostitutes were licensed to ply their trade in public. The Great Fire was supposed to have stopped at its junction with Giltspur Street, while in February 1762 thousands of the curious (including Dr Johnson, the Duke of York and other grandees) flocked to number 33 Cock Lane to hear the scratchings and knockings of the alleged 'Cock Lane Ghost']

cockle (and hen) n. *see* COCK AND HEN n.

cockles n. [19C] the labia minora.

cock linnet n.¹ [late 19C] a small but dapper East End youth.

cock linnet n.² [late 19C+] a minute. [rhy. sl.]

cockloche n. (*also* **cockloach**) [mid-17C] a term of reproach or contempt. [? Fr. *coqueluche*]

cock-locker n. [1980s] (*US*) the vagina (cf. BAG n.¹). [COCK n.² (1) + SE *locker*]

cockloft n. **1** [mid-17C–18C] the head. **2** [mid-18C–19C] the vagina (cf. BAG n.¹). [SE *cockloft*, the room over the garret; (2) COCK n.² (1)]

cock lorel n. [mid-16C–mid-17C] (*UK Und.*) the chief rogue or rascal. [COCK adj.¹ + *losel*, a worthless rogue, a profligate. Usu. as the proper name Cock Lorel, who may poss. have been a genuine person and who features largely in the literature of Elizabethan villainy, orig. as the eponymous anti-hero of *Cock Lorel's Bote* (*c*.1515), a ship-master (Rowlands claims 'a tinker'), whose 'crew' is a group of rogues drawn from the workshops and gutters of London. Together they 'sail' the country, engaging in a variety of villainies. He appears in a number of works, as well as in the glossaries compiled by Awdeley (whose *Fraternitie of Vagabondes* (*c*.1561) was 'confirmed by Cock Lorel') and Rowlands (in *Martin-Mark-all*, 1610). In all he remains at the head of his marauding beggars, sometimes plotting against the State, on one occasion even entertaining the Devil to dinner. According to Rowlands's generally fictitious 'history' of the canting crew, Cock Lorel's rule supposedly lasted *c*.1511–33]

cock manger n. [2000s] (*Irish*) a urinal. [COCK n.² (1) + SE *manger*, i.e. the supposed similarity of a urinal to the *manger* from which horses eat]

cock movie n. [1960s+] a pornographic film. [COCK adj.² + SAmE *movie*]

cockmunch n. [1990s+] a general term of abuse, a very

unpleasant person (cf. COCKSUCK n.; COCKSUCKER n.; CUNT-LAPPER n.; CUNT-LICKER n.; DICKLICK n.; DICKLICKER n.; DICKSUCKER n.; PUSSY-KISSER n.; PUSSYLICKER n.; SCUMSUCKER n.; SPUNK-GULLET n.). [COCK n.² (1) + MUNCH v.¹ (2)]

cock-my-cap n. [early–mid-18C] gin.

Cockney breakfast n. [mid-19C] (*UK Und.*) gin or brandy and soda water (cf. BARBER'S BREAKFAST n.). [SE *Cockney* + SE *breakfast*]

Cockney-shire n. (*also* **Cockneyland**) [19C–1940s] London. [SE *Cockney* + sfx *-shire*]

Cockney's luxury n. [late 19C–1950s] breakfast in bed and using the pot for defecation, rather than leaving the warm house for a trip to the outdoor privy. [SE *Cockney* + SE *luxury*]

cocko n. (*also* **cock-oh**) [1920s–50s] a general term of address. [COCK n.³ (1) + -O sfx (1)]

cock of a different hackle n. [mid-19C] an opponent of a different character. [COCK n.⁴ (1) or SE *cock, the bird* + *hackle, plumage*]

cock off v. *see* COCK UP v.

cock off oneself v. [20C+] (*W.I.*) to sit around looking important, esp. with one's feet up. [SE *cock*, to boast, to swagger]

cock of the game n. **1** [mid-16C–mid-19C] a promiscuous man. **2** [19C] (*UK Und.*) a leading villain. [SE *cock of the game*, a champion; (1) the 'game' in this case is not a sport, but that 'of love']

cock of the walk n. [late 18C+] an important man, occas. any creature. [SE *cock* + *walk*, a place or enclosure where poultry can exercise]

cock-oh n. *see* COCKO n.

cockoholic n. [1990s+] a sexually voracious woman. [COCK n.² (1) + -AHOLIC sfx]

cock-on adj. [1990s+] (*UK juv.*) first-rate, excellent.

cock on! excl. [1990s+] (*UK juv.*) fine! excellent! agreed!

cock one's beaver v. [17C] to assume an affected, swaggering air. [SE *cock*, to turn up + BEAVER n.¹]

cock one's eye v. **1** [mid–late 18C] to wink. **2** [1910s] (*Aus.*) to take a look at. [(1) thereafter SE, but note *have a cocky eye*, to glance sideways]

cock-on-hoop adj. *see* COCK-A-HOOP adj.

cock-opener n. [1920s–40s] (*US Black*) the penis (cf. ARSE-OPENER n.). [COCK n.⁶ (1) + SE *opener*]

cockowax n. *see* COCK-A-WAX n.

cock-pimp n. [late 17C–18C] a pimp who poses as his prostitute's husband (cf. ABBOT ON THE CROSS n.). [SE *cock, the male bird* + *pimp*]

cock pit n. **1** [late 18C+] the vagina (cf. BAG n.¹; BLACK HOLE n.¹). **2** [mid-18C+] the penis. **3** [1980s] (*US*) the clitoris (cf. BABY IN THE BOAT n.). [(1) and (2) COCK n.² (1); (3) COCK n.⁶ (1) + SE *pit* + a pun on SE *cockpit*]

cockpit n.¹ [late 18C] a Dissenters' meeting-house. [i.e. they are 'fighting' established religion]

cockpit n.² [1930s] (*UK Und.*) a prison's punishment cells.

cock pluck v. [1970s+] (*US Black*) to stimulate a woman's genitals manually. [COCK n.⁶ (1) + SE *pluck*]

cock puke n. [1990s+] semen (cf. BOLLOCK SNOT n.). [COCK n.² (1) + SE *puke*, vomit]

cockquean n. [mid-19C] an effeminate man, who is seen as dealing too keenly with domestic duties that are properly those of his wife. [var. on COTQUEAN n.]

cockrag n. [1960s+] (*Aus.*) a loincloth, as worn by Aborigines. [COCK n.² (1) + SE *rag*]

cockroach n.¹ [mid-19C+] (*US*) a despicable person. [the cockroach is especially loathed in New York's steam-heated apartments, where it thrives]

cockroach n.² [1940s+] a motor (rather than railway) coach. [rhy. sl.]

cockroach adj. [20C+] (*US*) used to describing something small, mean, insignificant and/or filthy. [the implication is of the insignificant size of the insect rather than the dirt that attracts it]

Cockroach Inn n. [1930s] (*US*) a shabby, run-down apartment.

cockroach killers n. [20C+] (*US*) pointed boots or shoes.

cock robin n.¹ [late 17C–18C] a complaisant, weak person. [nursery rhyme, in which the hapless *Cock Robin* is killed. The original rhyme, first noted *c.*1744, may have concerned the fall in 1742 of Prime Minister Robert Walpole's ministry. It may, on the other hand, have its roots in much earlier events, notably the mythical death of the Norse hero Balder]

cock robin n.² [1970s] the penis (cf. ANTEATER n.). [pun on SE/COCK n.² (1)]

cock rock n. [1970s+] heavy metal music with even more than the usual macho strutting and posturing; also attrib. [COCK n.² (1) + SE *rock('n'roll)*]

cock-rocker n. [1990s+] a male rock musician, or rock band, whose primary appeal lies in overt sexuality and macho posturing; also attrib. [COCK ROCK n.]

cock-rot n. [1980s+] (*US*) a venereal disease. [COCK n.² (1) + SE *rot*]

cocks n. [1930s] (*W.I.*) a sleight of hand used by a dice cheat to defraud their fellow players. [COG v. (2)]

cock sauce n. [2000s] (*US*) semen (cf. BABY GRAVY n.). [COCK n.² (1) + SE *sauce*/SAUCE n.² (7)]

cock-scratchers n. [1970s] hands. [COCK n.² (1) + SE *scratch*]

cock's eye n. [1900s] (*Aus.*) in dice games, the number 1.

cock's hair n. [1960s] (*US*) an infinitely tiny measure. [COCK n.² (1)]

cockshire n. [late 18C–1900s] the vagina (cf. ANTIPODES n.; BAG n.¹). [COCK n.² (1) + sfx *-shire*]

cock-show n. [1950s] burlesque; striptease. [COCK n.² (1)]

cockshy n. [19C] the vagina. [COCK n.² (1) + SE *shy*; a pun on SE *cockshy*, a fairground game that involved throwing broomsticks at a cock. If the thrower could knock over the cock and grab it before it regained its feet, he would win the bird]

cock-shy adj. [1990s+] of a woman, uninterested in or frightened of sex. [COCK n.² (1) + SE *shy*]

cocksman n. **1** [late 19C+] an exceptionally virile man; thus *cocksmanship*, a display of such virility. **2** [1960s] (*US Black*) a male prostitute (cf. COCKATRICE n.). [COCK n.² (1) + SE *man*]

cocksmith n. [1950s–60s] (*US*) a womanizer, a philanderer. [COCK n.⁶ (1) + sfx *-smith*]

cock-smitten adj. [19C] of a woman, keen on sex. [COCK n.² (1) + SE *smitten*]

cocksmoker n. [1990s+] (*Can.*) **1** a fellator; a semi-euph. for COCKSUCKER n. **2** any male person. **3** a general term of abuse. [COCK n.² (1) + SMOKER n.⁸]

cock snot n. [1990s+] semen (cf. BOLLOCK SNOT n.). [COCK n.² (1) + SNOT n.¹ (4)]

cock socket n. [2000s] (*gay*) the anus (cf. BUTT-PLUNGER n.). [COCK n.² (1) + SE *socket*]

cock someone's pistol v. [20C+] (*US*) to surprise, to astonish, esp. in phr. *that cocks my/his pistol*.

cock sparrow n. **1** [late 19C+] an arrow. **2** [1920s+] a street trader's barrow. **3** [1960s] a wheelbarrow. [rhy. sl.]

cock-sparrow adj. [1960s+] (*Aus.*) mad, insane (cf. APEY adj.; KING BILLY adj.; LAKES (OF KILLARNEY) adj.; MARBLES AND CONKERS adj.; MUM AND DAD adj.¹; RADIO (RENTAL) adj.; SALVATION ARMY adj.). [rhy. sl. *cock-sparrow* (pron. 'sparra') = YARRA adj.]

cockstand n. [mid-19C+] an erection; thus *this will give you the cockstand*; *cockstanding*, sexually arousing. [COCK n.² (1) + SE *stand*]

cockstrong adj. [1990s+] (*US Black/campus*) strong, muscular (cf. COCK-DIESEL n.). [COCK n.² (1) + SE *strong*]

cock-struck adj. [late 19C] of a woman, obsessed with sex, or with a particular man. [COCK n.² (1)+ SE *struck*]

cocksuck n. (*orig. US*) **1** [1940s+] the act of fellatio (cf. COCKSUCK v.; DEEP THROAT n.; DEEP THROAT v.; DICKLICK n.; DICKSUCKING n.;

GOB JOB n.; GOB THE KNOB v.; GUMJOB n.; GUMMER n.[1]; KISS v.[1]; KISS THE WORM v.; LAY THE LIP v.; LICK v.[2]; LICK LOG v.; LIP-LOCK n.; LIP SERVICE n.; MOUTH FUCK n.; MOUTH FUCK v.; MOUTH JOB n.; PRICK-LICK v.; PUT SOME SLOBBER ON THE KNOBBER v.; SUCK n.[6]; SUCK v.[1]; SUCKING n.; SUCK JOB n.; SUCK SOMEONE OFF v.; SUCK THE SUGAR-STICK v.; TONGUE v.[2]; TONGUE JOB n.; TONGUE LASH v.; WHITE MOUTH v.). **2** [1960s+] a general term of abuse (cf. COCKMUNCH n.). [backform. f. COCKSUCKER n.]

cocksuck adj. see COCKSUCKING adj.

cocksuck v. [1970s+] (orig. US) to fellate (cf. COCKSUCK n.). [backform. f. COCKSUCKER n.]

cocksucker n. **1** [late 19C] (orig. US) a sycophant, a toady. **2** [late 19C+] a fellator or fellatrix. **3** [1910s] (Aus.) a US soldier. **4** [1910s+] an abusive term, generally considered to be one of the worst? (cf. COCKMUNCH n.). **5** [1940s+] a male homosexual; thus his mouth (cf. BONE-EATER n.). **6** [1940s+] (US Black/Southern) one who performs cunnilingus. **7** [1970s+] an object, with no pej. implications. **8** [1980s+] (US) the mouth. [COCK n.[2] (1) + SE sucker/SUCKER n.[6] (1); (3) would suggest the fooling of Australians by US GIs]

cocksuckers n. [2000s] (US Black) the lips. [COCK n.[2] (1) + SUCK v.[1] (1)]

cocksucking n. [late 19C+] (orig. US) (performing) fellatio. [COCKSUCKER n. (2)]

cocksucking adj. (also **cocksuck**) [1910s+] (orig. US) vile, repellent, disgusting; one of the most taboo adj. of abuse. [COCKSUCKER n. (2)]

cocksy fuss n. (also **coxy fuss**) [early–mid-19C] amatory play, 'billing and cooing'. [COCK n.[2] (1)]

cock-tail n.[1] **1** [19C–1940s] a prostitute (cf. COCKATRICE n.). **2** [1970s+] (US gay) a male prostitute. [COCK n.[2] (1) + TAIL n.[2] (4)]

cock-tail n.[2] [mid–late 19C] an efficient, energetic, but not quite socially acceptable, person. [racing use, a horse that tries but is still no thoroughbred]

cock-tail n.[3] [mid–late 19C] a coward. [SE cock, to life up + tail]

cocktail n. **1** [1950s+] (US drugs) the very last portion of a cannabis cigarette placed on the end of a cigarette. **2** [1980s+] (drugs) a cigarette laced with cocaine or crack.

cocktail v. **1** [1960s+] (US drugs) to place the last unsmoked portion of a cannabis cigarette into the end of a regular cigarette so as to make it more easily smokeable. A folded matchbook can be used for the same effect. **2** [1980s+] (drugs) to lace a tobacco cigarette with cocaine. [COCKTAIL n.]

cocktail party n. [1970s+] (US gang) using a Molotov cocktail.

cocktails n. [1920s+] (Aus.) diarrhoea.

cock-tax n. [1950s] (Aus.) alimony. [COCK n.[2] (1) + SE tax]

cocktease v. (also **tease someone's cock**) [1920s+] to lead on in a sexual manner but never to permit actual intercourse. [backform. f. COCKTEASER n.]

cockteaser n. (also **cocktease, c.t.**) **1** [late 19C+] a woman (or man, if gay) who permits or encourages a good deal of sexual intimacy but not intercourse (cf. COCKCHAFER n.; CUNT-TEASER n.). **2** [1960s+] in fig. use. [COCK n.[2] (1) + SE tease]

cock ten v. (also **chop ten, cut ten**) [20C+] (W.I.) to sit around while others are working. [SE cock/chop/cut + ten (minutes); i.e. to take 10 minutes off the working day]

cock-trap n. [mid–late 19C] the vagina (cf. BITE n.[2]). [COCK n.[2] (1) + SE trap]

cock-trick n. see COCKATRICE n. (1).

Cock Tuesday n. [1930s] (Irish) the eve of Lent. [coarse allusion to COCK n.[2] (1)]

cock-up n. [1920s+] (orig. milit.) an error, a blunder. [SE cock, to bend at an angle, but with undertones of COCK n.[2] (1), on the pattern of FUCKUP n. (1), BALLS-UP n.]

cock up v. (also **cock off**) [1920s+] (orig. milit.) to blunder, to make a mess of. [COCK-UP n.]

cock up (one's foot) v. (also **cock up one's feet**) [20C+] (W.I.) **1** to sit around looking important while others work. **2** of a woman, to sit with one's legs sprawled in what is considered an indecent manner. [SE cock, to bend at an angle, ext. of SE use; (1) synon with SE put one's feet up]

cock (up) one's toes v. [mid-19C+] to die.

cock wagon n. [1970s] (US) a car, usu. flashy, new and expensive, that is owned spec. to attract easily impressed young women. [COCK n.[6] (1) + SE wagon]

cocky n.[1] (also **cockie**) [late 17C+] a general term of address to a man. [COCK n.[3] + sfx -y/-ie]

cocky n.[2] (also **cockie**) (Aus.) **1** [mid-19C+] a small farmer; often modified by the crop in which they specialize, e.g. spud cocky, a potato farmer. **2** [1940s+] the rural interest, whether small farmers or large landowners, with the main crop often indicated; thus cane cocky, wheat cocky etc. **3** [1950s] a lookout at a game of two-up. [COCKATOO n.[3]]

cocky adj. [mid-18C+] bumptious, self-satisfied, arrogant. [SE cock, the characteristics of the bird; the assumption is that such posturing is unjustified]

cocky v. [late 19C+] (Aus.) to work as a small farmer. [COCKY n.[2] (1)]

cockydom n. [20C+] (Aus.) the world of small farmers. [COCKY n.[2] (1) + sfx -dom]

cocky's clip n. [1920s+] (Aus.) sheep dip. [rhy. sl. but note COCKY n.[2] (1); Baker, The Australian Language (1945): 'in rural slang a cocky's clip is given to a sheep when practically every vestige of wool is removed by a shearer']

cocky's coal n. [1900s–40s] (Aus.) dry corncobs used as fuel. [COCKY n.[2] (1) + SE coal]

cocky's crow n. [20C+] (Aus.) dawn. [COCKY n.[2] (1) + pun on SE cock's crow]

cocky's delight n. (also **cocky's joy**) [20C+] (Aus.) molasses, treacle or golden syrup (cf. BULLOCKY'S DELIGHT n.). [COCKY n.[2] (1) + SE delight/joy]

cocky's friend n. [1930s] (Aus.) fencing wire. [COCKY n.[2] (1) + SE friend]

cocky's string n. [20C+] (Aus.) fencing wire, which has a variety of everyday uses in addition to marking boundaries. [COCKY n.[2] (1) + play on SE string]

coco n. **1** [mid-19C] (also **cocoa**) a hat. **2** [mid-19C+] (orig. US) (also **cocoa, cocoa-box, koko**) the head. **3** [20C+] (W.I.) a bump on the head. [abbr. SE coconut]

cocoa n.[1] [20C+] (US) a derog. term for a Black person, esp. light-skinned (cf. BLACKBELLY n.). [the colour]

cocoa n.[2] [1970s+] semen (cf. BABY GRAVY n.). [backform. f. COME ONE'S COCOA v. (1)]

cocoa n.[3] see COCO n.

cocoa adj. (also **cocoa-brown**) [1920s] **1** (US) a derog. term describing a Black person, esp. light-skinned. **2** (US Black) of a person, Black with no derog. overtones.

cocoa v. [1930s+] to speak. [rhy. sl. = SE say so]

cocoa-box n. see COCO n. (2).

cocoa-brown adj. see COCOA adj.

cocoanut n. see COCONUT n.[1].

cocoa payol n. (also **cocoa pagnol**) [20C+] (W.I., Trin.) a mixed-race person who retains traces of Spanish ancestry and culture. [SE cocoa + PAYOL n.; the payol was mainly employed on cocoa and coffee plantations]

cocoa press n. [1900s–30s] newspapers, e.g. The Daily News, owned by the chocolate-making Cadbury family.

cocoa puff n. [1980s+] (drugs) to smoke cocaine mixed with marijuana. [COCOA PUFF v.]

cocoa puff v. [1980s+] (drugs) to smoke cocaine mixed with marijuana. [abbr./redup. cocaine + PUFF v.[3] (2) + play on Cocoa Puffs, the popular breakfast cereal]

cocoa-shunter n. [1990s+] a male homosexual (cf. BROWN ARTIST n.). [the link of anything 'chocolate'/CHOCOLATE adj. (2) to sodomy/the anus]

cocobay *adj.* [20C+] (*W.I.*) having a skin covered in repulsive sores; thus *have cocobay on top of yaws*, to add new troubles to a situation that seemed bad enough already. [Twi *kokobé*, leprosy]

cocobola *n.* [1990s+] (*US*) a police nightstick. [Arawak *kakabali*, thence Sp. *cocobolo/cocobola*, the timber from any one of several species of tree of the Central American genus *Dalbergia*, or the tree itself. Nightsticks are made from this timber]

cocola *n.* [1990s+] (*US prison*) a Black person. [? var. on COCABOLA n. or Southern US pron. *co-cola* = the brand of soft drink, *Coca-Cola*, which is dark]

coconut *n.*[1] (*also* **cocoanut, coker-nut**) [mid-19C+] the head. [resemblance]

coconut *n.*[2] [1920s–40s] (*US*) $1; thus *coconuts*, money (cf. BANANAS n.[3]). [? barter imagery]

coconut *n.*[3] (*also* **coconuts**) [1940s–70s] (*US drugs*) cocaine (cf. BLANCA n.). [play on COKE n.[1] (1) and the colour]

coconut *n.*[4] [1970s+] **1** (*W.I./UK/Aus. Black teen*) a Black person who has 'sold out' to White values (cf. APPLE n.[7]). **2** (*US*) a Hispanic person trying to become White. [a SE *coconut* is brown on the outside but white within]

coconut *n.*[5] [1980s] (*Aus./N.Z.*) a South Sea islander. [the colour and the hair texture]

coconut-dodger *n.* [1920s] (*US Black*) a South American or African Black person. [the image of coconut palms shedding their fruit]

coconut head *n.*[1] [20C+] (*US*) **1** a derog. term for a Black person; thus *adj., coconut-headed* (cf. AFRICAN APE n.; BRILLOHEAD n.). **2** a derog. term for a Samoan-American. [SE *coconut* + -HEAD sfx (2); the jungle associations]

coconut head *n.*[2] [1960s] (*US*) a fool (cf. APPLEHEAD n.). [the hardness of the coconut + -HEAD sfx (1)]

coconuts *n.*[1] **1** [late 19C–1900s] large female breasts (cf. APPLES n.[1]). **2** [1990s+] the testicles (cf. ACORNS n.). [supposed resemblance]

coconuts *n.*[2] *see* COCONUT n.[3].

cocooning *n.* [1970s+] (*US*) staying at home with one's family.

cocum *n.* [mid–late 19C] **1** advantage, luck, resource; thus PLAY COCUM v. **2** knowledge. **3** (*UK Und.*) sense. [Heb. and thence Yid. *kochum*, wisdom]

cocum *adj.* (*also* **cokum**) [mid-19C–1900s] **1** resourceful, cunning. **2** sensible. **3** sorted out; arranged satisfactorily. [COCUM n.]

c.o.d. *n.* [1950s+] a male prostitute. [abbr. *cock on delivery* + a pun on SE *c.o.d.*, cash on delivery]

co-d *n.* [1990s+] a *co-d*efendant (cf. CO n.[2]). [abbr.]

cod *n.*[1] (*also* **coads, cods**) [late 16C–mid-19C] a euph. for *God*; used in oaths, e.g. *cods foot, cods my life, cods sooks, cods woons* (cf. BOB n.[2]).

cod *n.*[2] **1** [mid–late 17C] a friend; thus *honest cod*, a good friend. **2** [late 17C–18C] a fellow. **3** [late 17C+] a fool. [(2) in this context *cod* has been linked to SE *codger*, and it is found as an abbr., but *cod* is a much earlier word; (3) ? COD'S HEAD n.]

cod *n.*[3] (*also* **codshead**) [mid-17C+] the penis. [SE *cod*, a bag; thus early 16C SE *cod*, the scrotum; note sl. only in pl., i.e. CODS n.[1] (1), testicles]

cod *n.*[4] **1** [late 17C–19C] a purse. **2** [late 17C–early 19C] money; thus LUSTY COD n. **3** [1980s+] (*drugs*) a large amount of money. [SE *cod*, a bag]

cod *n.*[5] [late 19C+] a drunkard. [? COD n.[2] (3) or ? like the fish he 'swims' in alcohol]

cod *n.*[6] [20C+] (*orig. Irish*) **1** a joke, a hoax, a leg-pull, a parody. **2** deception, deceit, a lie; thus *cod-acting*, foolish behaviour. [COD v. (2)]

cod *adj.*[1] [1950s+] fake, parodic; usu. in combs., e.g. *cod-Russian, cod-typewriter* etc. [COD v. (2) + ? play on FISHY adj.[3] (1); note

theatrical jargon *cod version*, a burlesque of a well-known play]

cod *adj.*[2] (*also* **codalina, codettareenarone, codette**) [1960s–70s] a general pej. adj. [Polari]

cod *v.* **1** [18C] to cheat, to defraud. **2** [mid-19C+] (*also* **codd**) to tease, to hoax. [COD n.[2] (3)]

coddam *n.* (*also* **coddem, coddom**) [mid–late 19C] a public house game played with a button or coin. [COD v. (2); lit. *cod 'em*, hoax them, fool them. 'The game is "simplicity itself" but requires a great amount of low cunning' (Hotten, 1864)]

codder *n.* [mid-19C–1900s] a teaser, a hoaxer. [COD v. (2)]

codding *n.* [mid-19C+] teasing, chaffing, hoaxing. [COD v. (2)]

coddle *n.* [mid-19C] one who is pampered. [SE *coddle*, to nurse excessively]

coddle *v. see* MOLLYCODDLE V.

coddom *n. see* CODDAM n.

codesa-desa *v.* [1990s+] (*S.Afr.*) to negotiate (something). [CODESA, the Convention for a Democratic South Africa, held 1991–3 to prepare guidelines for a new constitution and for multi-party democracy]

codettareenarone/codette *adj. see* COD adj.[2].

code 21 *n.* [2000s] (*US prison*) masturbation. [? spec. prison rule]

codfish *n.* (*US*) **1** [late 18C–mid-19C] a fool (cf. AIREDALE n.). **2** [early 19C–1910s] one who thinks themself superior to their peers. [COD n.[2] (3). Note *codfish aristocracy*, a mocking New England term for those 19C *nouveaux riches* whose fortunes sprang from the Massachusetts cod industry]

codfish flats *n.* [1960s] (*US*) the poor area of town.

codge *n.* [late 19C–1900s] a vagrant, a tramp. [Yorks. dial. *cadger*, a beggar, a petty thief]

codge *v. see* CODGE (UP) v.

codger *n.* **1** [mid-18C+] a fellow, a man; usu. in *old codger*, with the implication of crotchety old age. **2** [mid-19C+] an affectionate term of address. **3** [late 19C] a 'roystering, ageing boon companion' (Ware). **4** [late 19C] (*Aus. prison*) a lazy person, an idler. [? 15C SE *cadger*, although its derog. use, as a whining beggar rather than the earlier, unqualified, itinerant hawker, is 19C and *codger*, by definition derog., predates this]

codger *v.* [late 19C] (*Aus. prison*) to act lazily. [CODGER n. (4)]

codge (up) *v.* [19C] to repair, usu. badly or clumsily; thus (*US*) *codge-job*, a second-rate piece of work. [Yorks. dial. *codge*, to patch up, to mend badly; ? link to SE *bodge*, to patch or mend clumsily, ult. f. *botch*]

codie *n.* [1980s] a child molester. [ety. unknown]

codology *n.* [1910s+] (*orig. Anglo-Irish*) the practice of disinformation, thus nonsense. [COD v. (2)]

cod-on *n.* [20C+] (*Irish*) a practical joke. [COD v. (2)]

cod-piece *n.* [17C] a euph. for the penis. [SE *codpiece*, the flap on breeches which covered the male genitals worn until *c.*1600]

cods *n.*[1] **1** [late 18C+] (*also* **cogs**) the testicles. **2** [late 18C–19C] a nickname for a curate. [(1) SE *cod*, a bag, thus the scrotum. (1) was SE until late 18C, when prudery rendered it taboo. (2) teases the curate for his sermonizing (with a ? ref. to his hopes of a good marriage), i.e. he is talking BALLS n.[2]; (3) fig. equation of the testicles with manliness. Note use – in sing. – as a term of affection in Urquhart, *The Complete Works of Rabelais* (1653): 'Come, my cod, let me coll [i.e. hug] thee till I kill thee']

cods *n.*[2] [1960s+] **1** a mess. **2** rubbish, nonsense. [*OED* suggests abbr. CODSWALLOP n. but ? f. CODS n.[1] (1), i.e. synon. with BALLS n.[2]]

cods *n.*[3] *see* COD n.[1].

codshead *n. see* COD n.[3].

cod's head *n.* [mid-16C–mid-19C] a dupe, a fool; thus the fool's head; also found in 19C as *cod's head and shoulders* (cf. AIREDALE n.). [dial. ? the 'thickness' of the cod's head, note slightly later COD n.[2] (3)]

cod's roe *n.* [20C+] money (cf. BEES (AND HONEY) n.). [rhy. sl. = DOUGH n.[1] (1)]

codswallop *n.* [1960s+] nonsense, rubbish, drivel. [ety. unknown; there is an implication of CODS n.[1] (1), but no proven link. Linguistically COD n.[2] (3) + dial. *wallop*, to chatter, to scold is feasible, but the chronology may militate against it]

cod trench *n.* [1990s+] the vagina (cf. AGREEABLE RUTS OF LIFE n.; BAG n.[1]). [COD n.[3] + SE *trench*]

coe *n.* [mid-16C+] (*UK Und.*) a man (cf. CO n.[1]). [abbr. COVE n. (1)]

cofe *n.* [17C] a man. [contemporary Scot. *cofe*, a chapman or peddler, or, like a number of 17C cant terms, f. Rom. *cova* or *covo*, man]

coffee *n.* **1** [1940s] (*US*) tobacco. **2** [1960s+] (*US drugs*) LSD (cf. A n.[3]).

coffee-and *n.* (*also* **coffee-an'**) [20C+] coffee and cakes or coffee and doughnuts, i.e. the cheapest meal available in a café or diner; thus in reverse, *sinkers and*, doughnuts and… (cf. SINKER n.[3]).

coffee-and *adj.* [1930s+] **1** of money, just enough to buy coffee and doughnuts. **2** in fig. use, referring to anything seen as cheap, minimal, second-rate, e.g. (*theatre*) coffee-and role, a small part that will pay for little more than snacks. [COFFEE-AND n.]

coffee-and-B *n.* [late 19C–1900s] a coffee and brandy.

coffee and cakes *n.* (*also* **two drinks and a sandwich**) [20C+] (*US*) a very small salary. [it provides just about enough to buy coffee and cakes/2 drinks and a sandwich; note late 19C local New Orleans synon. *ice-cream and cakes*]

coffee and cocoa *phr.* [1930s+] say so; usu. in I SHOULD COCOA! excl. [rhy. sl.; esp. used in *The Billy Cotton Band Show* on BBC Radio in the 1950s]

coffee-and-doughnut gun *n.* **1** [20C+] (*UK Und.*) a small, relatively powerless gun. **2** [1920s] (*US Und.*) a second-rate, unthreatening gangster. [COFFEE-AND adj. (2)]

coffee-and habit *n.* [1930s–50s] (*US drugs*) a small-time heroin habit, adopted either through grim self-control or simple poverty. [COFFEE-AND adj. (2) + HABIT n. (1)]

coffee-and pimp *n.* (*also* **coffee-and mac**) [1930s–70s] a small-time pimp, whose women barely make him a living, let alone provide the high style to which he would aspire (cf. CHILE CHUMP n.). [COFFEE-AND adj. (2) + SE *pimp*/MACK n.[1] (1)]

coffee and tea *n.* [2000s] the sea. [rhy. sl.]

coffee-bag *n.* [1910s–40s] (*US Black/tramp*) a coat pocket.

coffee-break parole *n.* [1960s+] (*US prison*) a nickname for a Special Circumstances release. [so called because it is granted very quickly]

coffee cooler *n.* **1** [late 19C+] an idler, a shirker. **2** [1910s] (*US*) a prospector. [milit. jargon *coffee cooler*, 'one who blows his coffee while the brigade is going by', i.e. a soldier who is constantly searching for a soft job]

coffee coolers *n.* [1950s–70s] (*US Black*) the lips, esp. when large and protuberant. [used to blow on hot coffee]

coffee-grinder *n.*[1] (*US*) **1** [late 19C] the vagina. **2** [1960s] a striptease artist. **3** [1960s] a prostitute.

coffee-grinder *n.*[2] **1** [1910s+] (*orig. US*) any old and unstable machine, typically a veteran propeller-driven aeroplane. **2** [1940s] (*US Und.*) a machinegun. [its noise, which resembles that of the SE *coffee grinder*; (2) orig. milit. use for a Gatling machine gun]

coffee-house *n.* [late 18C–mid-19C] a privy (cf. BACKHOUSE n.). [the colour of coffee and of urine and faeces]

coffee-house *v.* **1** [late 19C; 1970s] (*US*) to chatter, to gossip. **2** [20C+] (*gambling*) to bluff a rival verbally rather than by betting. [orig. fox-hunting use, the image is of habitués of an 18C coffee-house]

coffee-mill *n.* **1** [early–mid-19C] the mouth. **2** [mid-19C] (*UK Und.*) a watchman's rattle. **3** [mid-19C] an early form of machine gun, used in the US Civil War (1861–5). [fig. uses of SE *coffee-mill*, a coffee grinder that was worked by turning a handle]

coffee-milling *n.* [mid-19C] working very hard. [one 'grinds it out']

coffee-pot *n.* [1920s+] (*US*) a small lunch-room. [the coffee that is the mainstay of the menu, but note US regional *coffee-pot*, a small-scale operation, esp. a small lumber mill]

coffee-pot canyon *n.* [1920s–50s] (*US*) Broadway, New York City. [coined by columnist Walter Winchell (1897–1972); a real Coffee Pot Canyon exists in the San Mateo Mts, NM]

coffee-royal *n.* [1920s] (*US tramp*) coffee with a shot of pure alcohol.

coffee-shop *n.*[1] [late 18C–mid-19C] a privy (cf. BACKHOUSE n.). [the colour of its contents]

coffee-shop *n.*[2] [late 19C] the vagina. [? use of SE *coffee* to mean semen or vaginal secretions]

coffee-spout *n.* [1930s+] (*US*) the vagina. [? use of SE *coffee* to mean semen or vaginal secretions]

coffee stalls *n.* [1940s–60s] the testicles (cf. CHEESE AND CRACKERS n.). [rhy. sl. = BALLS n.[1] (1)]

coffee-strainer *n.* [1970s] (*US*) a bushy moustache.

coffee up *v.* [1960s+] (*US*) to drink a large quantity of coffee.

coffin *n.*[1] [late 17C] a man, a fellow. [var. on CUFFIN n. (1)]

coffin *n.*[2] **1** [mid–late 19C] (*US*) a clumsy, heavy boot or shoe. **2** [1920s–60s] (*US Und.*) a safe. **3** [1930s–40s] (*US Und.*) a prison cell.

coffin-dodger *n.* **1** [1900s–10s] (*US campus*) a heavy smoker. **2** [1980s+] an old person, prob. ill. [the image is of being 'one step ahead' of death or, in the case of smokers, mocking death]

coffin meat *n.* [mid-19C] (*US*) a corpse.

coffin nail *n.*[1] [19C+] a drink; thus the invitation to drink, *let's put/drive another nail in our coffins*. [the assumption that drink, esp. in the outposts of the Empire, was a killer. Folk etymology erroneously links this nail with PEG n.[5]]

coffin nail *n.*[2] (*also* **coffin screw, coffin tack**) **1** [late 19C+] a cigarette. **2** [1910s] (*US campus*) one who smokes to excess. [? no more than the resemblance of the cigarette to the nail; nicotine's cancerous potential is very much a phenomenon of 1960s+]

coffin varnish *n.* [mid-19C+] (*US*) liquor, esp. that which was sold during the Prohibition era (1920–33). [joc. use of SE + ref. to its dubious, even fatal, quality]

coff's harbour *n. see* SYDNEY HARBOUR n.

cog *n.*[1] (*UK Und.*) **1** [mid-16C–mid-19C] a lure, esp. in the form of money, designed to entice a gambler into a game, before cheating him of his own funds; thus *drop a cog*, to drop a coin and thus lure the person who picks it up into a confidence trick. **2** [17C] money. [COG v. (2)]

cog *n.*[2] [early 19C] a tooth.

cog *n.*[3] [late 19C+] (*US*) a name. [abbr. SE *cognomen*]

cog *v.* (*UK Und.*) **1** [mid-16C–mid-18C] to palm off fraudulently, to put out or utter falsely. **2** [mid-16C–19C] (*also* **cog a dice, cog a die, cog the dice**) to use any form of illicit sleight of hand, spec. to make a surreptitious change of a crooked dice for a legitimate one (or vice versa) during a game. **3** [late 16C–early 19C] to deceive, to cheat out of; thus *cog a dinner*, to cheat someone out of a dinner. **4** [17C] to have sexual intercourse. **5** [17C–early 18C] to flatter, to wheedle, to wheedle someone out of (something). **6** [17C+] to cheat at cards, or in any other manner, to crib. [ety. unknown; note that while acknowledging it as a 'ruffian's term', the *OED* categorizes the word as SE]

coge it *v.* [mid-18C–mid-19C] (*US*) to drink heavily. [Scot. *cogue*, a small drinking vessel]

cog-foist *n.* [early 17C] (*UK Und.*) a cheat. [COG v. (3) + FOIST n.[2] (2)]

cog forth *v.* [early–mid-17C] to control the fall of dice by sleight of hand. [COG v. (2)]

cogger *n.* **1** [mid-16C–early 17C] a card-sharp. **2** [late 18C+] any form of cheat or schemer. [COG v. (2)/COG v. (3)]

cogie *n.* [19C] the vagina. [Scot. *cogue*, (16C) a small pail used for milking cows, or (17C) a drinking vessel]

cogniac *n. see* CONEY *n.*

cognoscenti *n.* [1940s+] (*gay*) the world of homosexuals, its style, language, ethos etc. [Ital. *cognescenti*, the knowing ones, i.e. the cultured élite]

cogs *n.*[1] [1940s] (*US Black/Harlem*) sunglasses. [such glasses can be seen as 'fooling' other people; ? link to COG *v.* (3)]

cogs *n.*[2] *see* CODS *n.*[1] (1).

cog-shoulder *n.* [early 17C] an arrest. [SE *cog*, to place an impediment in front of + *shoulder*]

cog the dice *v. see* COG *v.* (2).

coguey *adj.* [19C] drunk (cf. ALED UP *adj.*). [Scot. *cogue*, to drink drams; *cogue*, a small drinking vessel]

Cohen *n.* (*also* **Kohen**) [1900s–10s] (*Aus.*) a generic term for a Jew, esp. when carrying out a stereotyped job, e.g. banker or bookmaker (cf. ABE *n.*[1]).

Cohentingent *n.* [1900s] (*Aus.*) an anti-Semitic slur, aimed at the alleged propensity of Jews to avoid enlisting in the Boer war, while encouraging others to join up; thus *cohentingenter.* [COHEN *n.* + SE *contingent*]

cohones *n. see* COJONES *n.*

coil *n.* [1950s+] (*W.I. Rasta*) money. [? the circular shape of coins, a roll of banknotes; or ? fig. ref. to the *mortal coil*, i.e. life and thus money as a basic necessity for life]

coiler *n.* [20C+] (*Aus.*) a vagrant who sleeps in the open air. [he simply 'coils up' and falls asleep]

coil one's ropes *v.* (*also* **coil one's cables**) [1910s+] to die. [naut. imagery, a good sailor always coiled his ropes properly at the end of his work]

coil someone's coat *v.* [mid-16C] to thrash, to beat severely. [? Fr. *cul*, the buttocks]

coin *n.* (*also* **coyne**) [mid-16C+] money.

coin collector *n.* [1970s] a male homosexual prostitute (cf. ASS PEDDLER *n.*). [play on SE]

coin (it) *v.* [mid-19C+] to make a great deal of money. [COIN *n.*]

coinkidink *n.* [1980s+] (*US campus*) coincidence. [deliberately 'jokey' mispron.]

coins *n.* [1900s–50s] (*US Black*) money, whether actual coins or notes. [COIN *n.*]

coiny *adj.* [late 19C–1910s] rich. [COIN *n.*]

coiny cove *n.* [1920s+] (*Aus.*) a rich man. [COINY *adj.* + COVE *n.* (1)]

cojones *n.* (*also* **cohones, cajun**) [1930s+] testicles, used both to mean the physical organ and metaphorical courage (cf. CULLIONS *n.*). [synon. Sp.; popularized first by the works of Ernest Hemingway (1899–1961) and latterly by Puerto Rican immigrants to US]

coke *n.*[1] (*drugs*) **1** [20C+] cocaine; thus COKED (UP) *adj.* **2** [1910s–30s] a cocaine user. **3** [1920s] any injectable opiate drug, usu. morphine or heroin. **4** [1990s+] crack cocaine (cf. BASE *n.*).

coke *n.*[2] **1** [1920s] (*US*) the head. **2** [1930s] an eccentric, a fool. [abbr. COCONUT *n.*[1]]

cokeball *n.* [1980s] (*drugs*) golfball-sized spheres of compressed cocaine. [COKE *n.*[1] (1) + SE *ball*]

coke blower *n. see* BLOW COKE *v.*

coke-blunt *n.* [1980s+] a mixture of hashish/marijuana and cocaine, made into a cigarette when rolled in a tobacco leaf taken from the wrapper of a Phillies Blunt cigar. [COKE *n.*[1] (1) + BLUNT *n.*[3] (1)]

coke bottle eyes *n.* [1980s+] (*US campus*) a state achieved by the drunkard to whom all members of the opposite sex seem far more attractive than they might be when viewed in sobriety. [similar to the effect of one's COKE BOTTLE GLASSES *n.*]

coke bottle glasses *n.* (*also* **milk-bottle bottoms**) [1950s+] (*orig. US*) spectacles with very thick lenses, used by those with seriously short sight. [such glasses supposedly resemble the glass in a trad. *Coca-Cola* bottle]

coke-date *n. see* JELLY-DATE *n.*

coked (up) *adj.* **1** [1920s+] (*drugs*) (*also* **coked out, cooked up**) under the influence of cocaine. **2** [1940s] (*US*) drunk. [COKE *n.*[1] (1)]

coke fiend *n.* [20C+] (*drugs*) a cocaine user. [COKE *n.*[1] (1) + FIEND *n.*[2] (1); later use tends to be ironic]

coke frame *n.* [1930s–40s] (*US Black*) a curvaceous figure; thus *banter play built on a coke frame*, an attractive woman with a good figure. [abbr. *Coke* for the soft drink brand *Coca-Cola* + FRAME *n.* (1), i.e. a body curved like the trad. Coca-Cola bottle; *banter* = BANTAM *n.* (2)]

coke-freak *n.* [1980s+] (*drugs*) a regular user of cocaine. [COKE *n.*[1] (1) + FREAK sfx]

cokehead *n.* [1920s+] (*drugs*) a regular cocaine user. [COKE *n.*[1] (1) + -HEAD sfx (3)]

coke horrors *n.* [1950s] (*drugs*) paranoid hallucinogenic delusions occasioned by an excessive/long-term use of cocaine. [COKE *n.*[1] (1) + HORRORS, THE *n.* (5)]

cokehound *n.* [1930s] (*drugs*) a cocaine user. [COKE *n.*[1] (1) + HOUND sfx]

coke oven *n.* [1940s–70s] (*US drugs*) a place where one buys cocaine. [COKE *n.*[1] (1) + SE *oven*]

cokeover *n.* [1980s+] (*drugs*) the after-effects of a cocaine binge. [COKE *n.*[1] (1) + SE *hangover*]

coke party *n.* [1920s–30s] (*drugs*) a party at which the principal aim is to consume cocaine. [COKE *n.*[1] (1) + SE *party*]

coker *n.*[1] [mid-17C–mid-19C] a lie. [CAULKER *n.* (3), but chronology suggests this (or at least this sp.) may have been the orig. term]

coker *n.*[2] [1980s] (*US*) a cocaine user. [COKE *n.*[1] (1) + sfx *-er*]

coker-nut *n. see* COCONUT *n.*[1].

cokes *n.* [mid-16C–17C] a fool. [? SE *Cockney*; Grose (1785) suggests *cokes* as the root of SE *coxcomb*]

cokeslut *n.* [1990s+] a regular cocaine user. [COKE *n.*[1] (1) + SLUT *n.* (3)]

coke stare *n.* [1970s+] (*US Black*) the 'evil eye', a deliberately aggressive and unpleasant look. [COKE *n.*[1] (1) + SE *stare*; the rigid gaze that may overtake the more paranoid cocaine user]

coke up *v.* **1** [1930s+] (*drugs*) to take cocaine. **2** [1970s] to consume any drug. [COKE *n.*[1] (1)]

coke-upon-littleton *n.* [mid-18C] a form of mixed drink, brandy and tent (*vino tinto*). [a famous legal textbook, the commentary upon *Littleton* by Sir Edward *Coke* (1628)]

coke-water *n.* [1930s] (*US prison*) cocaine dissolved in water. [COKE *n.*[1] (1) + SE *water*]

cokey *n.*[1] *see* COKIE *n.*

cokey *n.*[2] *see* KOKI *n.*

cokey *adj.*[1] (*US*) **1** [1930s–40s] foolish, silly. **2** [1940s+] pertaining to cocaine. [COKE *n.*[1] (1); although cocaine tends to excite rather than dull the senses]

cokey *adj.*[2] [1950s] (*US drugs*) addicted to heroin. [COKE *n.*[1] (3)]

cokey-eye *n.* [20C+] (*W.I.*) a squint; thus as a nickname *cokey*, a squinter. [COCK-EYE *n.*]

cokie *n.* (*also* **coakie, cokey**) **1** [1910s+] (*drugs*) a habitual user of heroin or opium. **2** [1920s+] (*drugs*) a habitual user of cocaine; thus [1930s–50s] *Cokie Joe*, a personification of a regular cocaine user. **3** [1920s–60s] (*US Und.*) any form of drug addict. **4** [1940s] (*US gang*) a boy, usu. pej., esp. when referring to a member of another gang. [COKE *n.*[1], on pattern of JUNKIE *n.*]

cokir *n.* [mid-17C–early 18C] a liar. [COKER *n.*[1]]

cokk *n.* [14C–mid-15C] a euph. for *God* and as such used in mild (but then blasphemous) oaths (cf. BOB *n.*[2]).

cokum *adj. see* COCUM *adj.*

cokum *v. see* PLAY COCUM *v.*

cola *n.* [1980s+] (*US drugs*) cocaine. [abbr. *coca-cola*, thus play on SE *coke*/COKE *n.*[1] (1)]

colcher *n.* (*also* **colsher**) [late 19C] a heavy fall; esp. in phr. *come a colcher*, to fall heavily. [dial. *colch*, a heavy fall, the sound of a blow]

cold *n.* [1980s+] (*US Black*) a cigarette end. [? it is no longer alight]

cold *adj.*[1] **1** [late 17C+] emotionless, unfeeling, callous, uncaring. **2** [mid-19C+] simple, unadorned. **3** [late 19C–1930s] (*US campus*) perfect, complete. **4** [late 19C+] sexually unresponsive. **5** [20C+] (*gambling*) unlucky, unfavourable. **6** [1920s+] (*US Black/teen*) unpleasant, difficult, unnecessary. **7** [1960s+] (*orig. US*) (*also* **cold-ass**) heartless, ruthless, cruel. **8** [1970s+] (*US Black/teen*) on bad = good model, excellent, first-rate, superb. **9** [1980s] (*US Black*) confrontational, provocative, conducive to violence. [all uses, positive or negative, stem from the unadorned 'iciness' of SE *cold*]

cold *adj.*[2] **1** [mid-19C+] unconscious. **2** [20C+] dead. **3** [1950s+] free of suspicion, innocent. [the chilliness of a corpse]

cold *adj.*[3] [20C+] (*US*) of money, the actual sum; i.e. abbr. *cold cash*. [COLD *adj.*[1] (2)]

cold *adj.*[4] **1** [1920s+] (*US*) of a cheque, fraudulent, worthless. **2** [1930s–60s] (*US Und.*) of a safe, wallet or other target of a crime, empty, worthless, unrewarding; thus COLD ONE *n.*[3]; COLD POKE *n.* [fig. use of SE; i.e. it has lost its 'life']

cold *adv.*[1] **1** [late 19C+] (*US*) absolutely, completely, utterly. **2** [1980s+] (*orig. US Black*) definitely, indeed, just.

cold *adv.*[2] **1** [1910s+] unprepared, unannounced. **2** [1960s] (*drugs*) in the context of giving up an addiction, without the aid of any medication.

cold as a mother-in-law's breath *phr.* (*also* **cold as a mother-in-law's kiss, ...a stepmother's breath**) [1950s+] (*Aus.*) of the climate or a person's emotions, very cold.

cold as a nun's nasty *phr.* (*also* **colder than a nun's ass, ...snatch**) [1950s+] (*US/Aus.*) of temperature, extremely cold.

cold as a polar bear's backside *phr.* (*also* **cold as a cocksucker's knees, ...a gravedigger's ass, ...an axe-head, ...a polar bear's behind/bum, ...a snowball's ass, ...a well-digger's arse, ...polar bear shit, colder than a well-digger's ass/butt**) [1920s+] (*Aus./US*) of temperature, extremely cold.

cold as a witch's tit *phr.* (*also* **cold as a witch's behind, ...teat, ...titty, colder than a witch's tit/titty**) **1** [1950s] completely without emotions. **2** [1950s+] of weather, extremely cold. **3** [1960s] sexually frigid.

cold-ass *adj. see* COLD *adj.*[1] (2).

cold biscuit *n. see* BISCUIT *n.*[1].

cold-bite *n.* [1920s+] (*Aus./N.Z.*) one who will lend money, a 'soft touch'. [COLD-BITE v.]

cold-bite *v.* [1920s+] (*Aus./N.Z.*) to ask a stranger for money. [COLD *adv.*[2] (1) + BITE v. (6); note commercial jargon *cold-call*, for a salesman to approach a potential client without making a prior appointment]

cold blood *n.* [mid-19C] a liquor store or 'off licence' that can sell beer but cannot allow it to be drunk on the premises.

cold-blooded *adj.* [1960s+] (*US*) **1** honest, open, candid. **2** harshly critical, extremely judgemental, used of actions that are done or people who act without heart. [COLD *adj.*[1] (1)]

cold botting *n. see* BOT v. (2).

cold busted *adj.* [1980s+] (*US campus*) caught in the act. [COLD *adv.*[2] (1) + BUSTED *adj.*[2] (3)]

cold case *n.* [1980s+] (*US Black, Los Angeles*) a very bad situation; a serious scolding. [COLD *adj.*[1] (6) + CASE *n.*[1]]

cold-caulk *v. see* COLD-COCK v.

cold chill *v.* [1980s+] (*US*) to relax. [COLD *adv.*[1] (2) + CHILL (OUT) v. (1)]

cold-choke *n.* [mid-19C+] (*W.I.*) cold food, which is hard to swallow. [SE *cold* + *choke*; but note CHOKE *n.*[1] (1)]

cold cock *n.* [1940s+] (*orig. US*) a knockout blow, a blow that renders someone unconscious. [COLD-COCK v.]

cold-cock *v.* (*also* **cold-caulk**) [1910s+] to knock unconscious.

[SE (*out*) *cold*, unconscious/KNOCK COLD (AS A MONKEY WRENCH) v. (1)]

cold-cock *adv.* [1980s+] (*US*) completely, utterly. [COLD-COCK v.]

cold coffee *n.*[1] [mid-19C] **1** bad luck. **2** a snub. [SE *cold coffee*, which, other than in hot weather, is usu. considered an unappetizing drink]

cold coffee *n.*[2] [late 19C–1910s] beer. [the colour + ? euph.]

cold-conk *v.* [1960s+] (*US*) to knock unconscious. [SE (*out*) *cold*, unconscious/KNOCK COLD (AS A MONKEY WRENCH) v. (1) + CONK v.[1] (1)]

cold cook *n.* [early 18C–19C] an undertaker; thus *cold cook shop*, an undertaker's shop. [pun]

Cold Country *n.* [1900s–30s] (*Aus.*) Great Britain.

cold cream *n.* [mid–late 19C] gin. [play on SE]

cold-creams *n.* [late 19C–1900s] the Coldstream Guards. [pun on the SE, but also ref. to the noted dandyism of the regiment]

cold-crushing *adj.* [1980s+] (*US Black*) a general term of approval. [COLD *adv.*[1] (2) + fig. use SE *crush*]

cold-cunt *v.* [1970s+] (*lesbian*) to ignore, to brush off. [pun on COLD-SHOULDER v.; COLD *adj.*[1] (1) + CUNT *n.*[1] (1)]

cold cut *n.* [1940s–50s] (*US*) an unfriendly, reserved person. [COLD *adj.*[1] (1) + pun on SE *cold cuts* of meat]

cold day *n.* [late 19C+] (*US*) bad luck, an unfortunate situation. [SE *cold*]

cold deck *n.* [mid-19C+] (*US Und.*) a stacked deck of cards, used by cheats; lit. and fig.

cold-deck *v.*[1] [late 19C] (*US Und.*) to cheat, to deceive. [COLD DECK n.; gambling jargon *cold deck*, for a card-sharp to introduce a prepared deck of cards into the game; thus guaranteeing his success]

cold-deck *v.*[2] [1940s+] to knock unconscious. [SE (*out cold*), unconscious/KNOCK COLD (AS A MONKEY WRENCH) v. (1) + DECK v.[3] (1)]

cold-decker *n.* [1920s+] (*US Und.*) a thug, a hoodlum, a cheat. [COLD-DECK v.[1]/COLD-DECK v.[2]]

cold enough to freeze the balls off a brass monkey *phr.* (*also* **cold enough to blow the balls off a brass monkey, ...freeze the tail/ears off a brass monkey, ...tin possum**) [mid-19C+] (*orig. US*) extremely cold in temperature. [note army var. 'cold enough to make a Jew drop his bundle']

colder than... *see also under* COLD AS...

colder than Kelsey's nuts *phr.* (*also* **colder than Kelsey's ass**) [1960s+] extremely cold. [for ety. *see* KELSEY'S NUTS n.]

cold-eye *n.* (*also* **icy eye**) [late 19C–1900s] a disdainful stare.

cold-eye *v.* [1970s] (*US*) to ignore, reject, disdain. [COLD-EYE n.]

cold-fang *v.* [1960s+] (*Aus.*) to ask a stranger for money. [COLD *adv.*[2] (1) + FANG v.[1] (1)]

cold-finger man *n.* [1940s] a pickpocket, esp. one who steals from coatrooms and cloakrooms.

cold fish *n.* [1930s+] an unemotional person. [SE *fish*/FISH *n.*[3]]

cold fish *v.* [1970s+] to be sexually unresponsive. [COLD FISH n.]

cold-footer *n.* (*also* **cold-foot**) [1910s–20s] (*orig. Aus.*) a timid, nervous person; thus *cold-footed*, timid, cowardly. [GET COLD FEET v.]

cold four *n.* [late 19C–1900s] the cheapest variety of beer. [SE *four-ale*, beer sold at 4 pence a quart]

cold gold *n.* [1980s+] (*Aus.*) a can of beer. [advertising slogan for Toohey's KB lager: 'Shake hands with a cold gold']

cold gruel *n.* [mid-19C] **1** bad luck. **2** a snub.

coldie *n.* [1950s+] (*Aus.*) a can or bottle of cold beer. [abbr. COLD ONE *n.*[2] (1)]

cold in hand *adj.* (*also* **cold hand**) [1930s–60s] (*US Black*) without money, penniless. [in gambling jargon, to be *cold* is to have poor cards, unlucky dice etc; however, in poker jargon a *cold deck* for an honest player is a good hand, requiring no change of cards, while for a sharp it is one that has been stacked, guaranteeing a win for the cheat]

cold Irish *n. see* FENIAN n.[1].

cold iron *n.* [late 17C–early 19C] a sword.

cold lamping *n.* [1990s+] (*US Black*) explaining hitherto complex, impenetrable matters. [COLD adv.[1] (2) + LAMP v.[2] (2)]

cold lead *n.* [19C–1920s] a bullet. [LEAD n.[1] (1)]

cold meat *n.*[1] **1** [late 18C+] (*also* **cold mutton**) a corpse; thus COLD MEAT BOX n.; COLD MEAT PARTY n.; *cold meat train*, a funeral procession or a train that serves a cemetery; *cold meat job* (police jargon), any case that involves a corpse. **2** [1910s] one who has been knocked unconscious. [the first use of the term appears to be that of Grose himself, used as its definition: 'A dead wife is the best *cold meat* in a man's house' (1796); note WW1 milit. *cold meat ticket*, an identity disc]

cold meat *n.*[2] *see* COLD PIE n.[1].

cold meat box *n.* [mid-19C+] a coffin. [COLD MEAT n.[1] (1) + SE *box*]

cold meat cart *n.* [early 19C+] (*US*) a hearse. [COLD MEAT n.[1] (1) + SE *cart*]

cold meat party *n.* [20C+] (*US Black*) a funeral, a wake. [COLD MEAT n.[1] (1) + SE *party*]

cold meat wagon *n.* [1940s] a hearse. [COLD MEAT n.[1] (1) + SE *wagon*]

cold mitt *n.* [1920s] (*US*) a snub, a rejection. [SE *cold*/COLD adj.[1] (1) + MITT n. (3); var. on FROZEN MITT n.]

cold muffin *n.* [late 19C–1900s] anything mediocre, second-rate.

cold mutton *n. see* COLD MEAT n.[1] (1).

cold nantz *n. see* NANTZ n.

cold on a blue *phr.* (*also* **cold on the blue**) [1990s+] (*Aus. Und.*) wrongly imprisoned or arrested. [COLD adj.[2] (3) + ? BLUE n.[3]]

cold one *n.*[1] [1900s] (*US*) $1. [COLD adj.[3]/SE *cold cash*]

cold one *n.*[2] [1920s+] (*orig. US*) **1** a bottle (latterly can) of beer. **2** a cold drink. [orig. a conscious euph. for a cold beer, used during Prohibition (1920–33) when it was better not to mention alcohol in any form]

cold one *n.*[3] [1930s–60s] (*US Und.*) an empty container for money, e.g. a safe, a wallet. [COLD adj.[4] (2)]

cold on the blue *phr. see* COLD ON A BLUE phr.

cold pie *n.*[1] (*also* **cold meat**) [1900s] (*Aus.*) an easy victim. [COLD MEAT n.[1] (1)]

cold pie *n.*[2] *see* CHOKING PIE n.

cold pig *n.* [mid-19C] a punishment or joke in which the bedclothes are stripped off a sleeper and cold water poured over them; usu. in phr. *give cold pig*. [cf. naut. jargon *cold norwester*, a bucket of seawater poured over a new recruit as an initiation ceremony]

cold-pigging *n.* [20C+] (*Aus./N.Z.*) hawking goods from door to door.

cold poke *n.* [1940s] (*US Und.*) a wallet without any money in it; thus a confidence game based on such an empty wallet. [COLD adj.[4] (2) + POKE n.[2] (2)]

cold potato *n.*[1] [late 19C–1940s] (*US*) someone or something judged to be worthless, insignificant or boring.

cold potato *n.*[2] [1950s+] a waiter. [rhy. sl.; note Cockney pron. 'pertater']

cold pudding *n.* [late 18C–19C] anything considered worthless, second-rate.

cold quack *n. see* COLD TURKEY adv. (1).

coldrifed *adj.* [1940s+] nervous, hesitant, unwilling to take a risk. [dial. *coldrife*, indifferent, spiritless; ult. SE *cold*]

cold scran *n.* [late 19C] something unappealling, distasteful, lit. 'cold food'. [SE *cold* + SCRAN n. (2)]

cold shake *n.* [1990s+] (*US drugs*) to prepare a drug for injection by shaking a capsule in cold water so as to dissolve the pill and mix together (the usual method is to heat the drug/water solution).

cold shot *n.* [1960s+] (*US Black*) **1** unnecessary and aggressive

behaviour. **2** cruel, emotionless behaviour. **3** an unpleasant surprise. [COLD adj.[1] + SHOT n.[5] (3)]

cold shoulder *n.* [early 19C+] rejection, dismissal; usu. in phrs. *get/give the cold shoulder*. [Ware roots it in 'the Italian of Dante's time', but the earliest use appears to have been in Scotland, and is found as such in Sir Walter Scott's *Antiquary* (1816) where it is explained in the book's Glossary. 19C use occas. added 'of mutton'; note COLD adj.[1] (1)]

cold-shoulder *v.* [early 19C+] to act in a reserved manner; to ignore, to snub deliberately. [COLD SHOULDER n.]

cold slaw *n.* [late 19C] (*US*) small off-cuts of material, taken from the job in hand and sold off as perks by tailors. [play on SE *coleslaw*/CABBAGE n.[1] (1)]

cold slough *n. see* SLOUGH n.[1] (1).

cold steel *n.* [1980s+] (*Aus. drugs/prison*) a hypodermic syringe.

cold storage *n.*[1] [20C+] **1** death, thus also a grave or cemetery. **2** a prison.

cold storage *n.*[2] [1910s] (*Aus.*) cheek, impudence. [play on COOL adj.[1] (1)]

cold tea *n.*[1] **1** [late 17C–18C] brandy. **2** [1900s] (*US*) beer. [TEA n.[1] (1)/the colour]

cold tea *n.*[2] *see* COLD WATER n.

cold turkey *n.* [1920s+] (*orig. US drugs*) **1** sudden and total withdrawal from heroin addiction without tapering off or using any assistance from medication; also ext. to other drugs. **2** the fundamental level, the basic situation. **3** an easy target, a vulnerable person. [COLD TURKEY adv. (1), boosted by the image of the pallid flesh of a cold, dead, plucked turkey, and a withdrawing addict; *cold turkey* is the 'word of 1922' in David K. Barnhart and Allan A. Metcalf, *America in So Many Words* (1999)]

cold turkey *adj.* [1930s–60s] (*US*) **1** dead. **2** emotionless. **3** honest, candid. [COLD TURKEY adv. (1)]

cold turkey *v.* [1920s+] to subject oneself or another addict (usu. a heroin user) to COLD TURKEY n. (1).

cold turkey *adv.* **1** [1910s+] (*US*) (*also* **cold quack**) directly, openly, candidly, without any warning. **2** [1920s–50s] (*US*) absolutely guilty, without any excuse. **3** [1950s+] (*US*) with total conviction. **4** [1950s+] (*drugs*) of withdrawal, without any form of medication to modify the pains. **5** [1960s+] without any narcotics, although not intending withdrawal. **6** [1990s+] in fig. use, lacking something, going without something. [ety. unknown]

cold water *n.* (*also* **cold tea**) **1** [late 19C–1900s] teetotalism, abstinence, thus *cold water army*, the teetotal movement. **2** [1910s] (*Aus.*) a generic term for temperance campaigners. [their favourite drink + ? ref. to Salvation Army]

coldwater walk-up *n. see* WALK-UP n. (1).

cold wire *n.* [1940s] (*US*) an unsuccessful person. [opposite of LIVE WIRE n.]

cold without *n.* [early–mid-19C] spirits and water mixed, no sugar is added. [abbr. SE *a cold drink without sugar*]

cole *n.* (*also* **coal**) **1** [late 16C–19C] (*UK Und.*) money; thus [mid–late 19C] *post the cole*, pay down money; TIP THE COLE v. (cf. ACTUAL, THE n.). **2** [1930s] a penny. [SE *coal*, the staple, as a heat-provider, of everyday life, as is money. *Cole* had faded by 19C but *post the cole* lasted, increasingly in metaphorical use, until late 19C. Also ? link to SE *cole*, brassica, an earlier play on CABBAGE n.[8]]

colfabias *n.* [mid-19C] a privy. [cod Lat.; coined at Trinity College, Dublin]

coli *n.* [1980s+] (*drugs*) marijuana. [abbr. COLIFLOR TOSTAO n. or BROCCOLI n. (1)]

coliander (seed) *n.* [late 17C–mid-19C] (*UK Und.*) money (cf. ALFALFA n.; CORIANDER (SEED) n.). [SE *coliander*, the earliest sp. (*c.*1000) of coriander, which is found as a seed. Seeds provide a form of growth, necessary for life; thus fig. synon. with money]

'colic *n.* [1970s–80s] (*UK Black*) an alcoholic, a drunkard. [abbr.]

coliflor tostao *n.* [1970s+] (*drugs*) marijuana. [Sp. sl.]

colinderies *n.* [late 19C] (*UK society*) the *Col*onial and *Ind*ian Exhibition, South Kensington, London, held in 1886 and visited by more than 2 million people. [abbr.]

coll *n.*[1] [mid-17C–mid-18C] **1** a dupe, a silly fellow. **2** a man, a fellow, a chap. [CULL *n.*[1] (2)]

coll *n.*[2] [late 18C+] a *coll*ege, esp. used of schools with *College* in their name. [abbr.]

collar *n.*[1] [mid-17C] the hangman's noose. [play on SE]

collar *n.*[2] (*US*) **1** [late 19C] in fig. use of (2), any kind of restraint, e.g. marriage. **2** [late 19C+] an arrest; in phr. *give someone the collar*. **3** [late 19C+] a policeman (cf. BEAT-POUNDER *n.*). **4** [1970s+] the person who has been arrested. [COLLAR *v.* (1)]

collar *n.*[3] [late 19C–1900s; 1960s+] legitimate work. [orig. northern UK dial.; i.e. that in which one wears a SE *collar*]

collar *n.*[4] **1** [20C+] the foam on a glass of beer. **2** [1950s+] (*drugs*) in a makeshift syringe, the strip of paper wrapped around a dropper to ensure a tight fit with the needle.

collar *v.* **1** [mid-17C+] to arrest. **2** [early 18C+] to grab, to appropriate. **3** [mid–late 19C] (*orig. UK Und.*) to catch out. **4** [mid-19C+] (*orig. UK Und.*) to understand, to work out. **5** [late 19C] in fig. use, to delight, to overwhelm. **6** [late 19C–1900s] to receive in punishment. **7** [1900s–40s] (*orig. US Black*) to get hold of, to obtain. **8** [1910s] (*US*) to master, to deal with. [SE *collar*, to get hold of]

collar a broom *v.* (*also* **cop a broom**) [1930s–40s] (*US Black*) to leave quickly, to rush away. [COLLAR *v.* (2)/COP *v.* (10) + SE *broom*, the image of a witch flying off on her broomstick]

collar a duster up the ladder *v.* [1940s] (*US Black*) to climb the stairs. [COLLAR *v.* (2) + DUSTER *n.*[3] + SE *ladder*]

collar (and cuff) *n.* [1930s+] a homosexual. [rhy. sl. = PUFF *n.*[3] (1)]

collar and elbow *adj.* (*also* **collar and shoulder**) [1920s–30s] (*US*) family style, informal, esp. of a restaurant or café. [orig. hobo jargon *collar and shoulder style*, a meal where the food is placed on the table and everyone, sitting shoulder to shoulder, grabs what he or she can from the platters. The idea of struggling for one's share may link the phr. to *collar and elbow*, a style of wrestling practised in Devon and Cornwall]

collar and tie *n.*[1] [1940s+] a masculine lesbian. [her adoption of men's clothing]

collar and tie *n.*[2] [1950s+] a lie. [rhy. sl.]

collar a nod *v.* [1940s] (*US Black*) to sleep, to take a nap. [COLLAR *v.* (2) + NOD *n.*[1] (1)]

collar-band pint *n.* [20C+] a short-measure pint of beer. [SE *collar-band*, the band to which the collar is attached (slightly lower than the collar itself). Note synon. RAF jargon *cap-tally drink*]

collar day *n.* [late 18C–early 19C] the day of execution. [COLLAR *n.*[1]]

collard greens *n. see* GREENS *n.*[4].

collared on *adj.* [mid-19C–1910s] (*Aus.*) obsessively in love with. [COLLAR *v.* (2)]

collared up *adj.* [mid-19C] kept hard at work, closely involved with one's business. [one is unable to remove one's collar, a sign of relaxation]

collar the jive *v.* [1930s+] (*US Black*) to understand every aspect of a situation. [COLLAR *v.* (4) + JIVE *n.*[1] (4)]

collar-work *n.* [late 19C] hard, strenuous work. [the image of a horse pulling against its collar]

collect *v.* (*Aus.*) **1** [1910s+] to receive one's due deserts. **2** [1960s+] to be hit by, to collide with, usu. of a car. **3** [1990s+] to be killed.

collector (of the highways) *n.* [late 18C–19C] a highwayman, esp. one who prefers cash to jewels etc (cf. RENT COLLECTOR *n.*). [he collects RENT *n.*[1] (1)]

collect rent *v. see* RENT COLLECTOR *n.*

colleen bawn *n.* [mid-19C+] an erection. [rhy. sl. = HORN *n.*[2]

(3); *Colleen Bawn* is the heroine of the opera *The Lily of Killarney* (Benedict/Oxenford & Dion Boucicault), first produced February 1862 at the Royal English Opera, Covent Garden, London; ult. the anglicized version of Irish *cailín bán*, the white or fair woman]

college *n.* **1** [early 17C] a brothel (cf. ACADEMY *n.*). **2** [late 17C–early 19C] (*UK Und.*) Newgate prison. **3** [18C+] (*UK Und.*) any prison; thus [early 18C–mid-19C] *go to college*, to go to prison (cf. CITY COLLEGE *n.*). **4** [late 18C–mid-19C] (*UK Und.*) King's (or Queen's) Bench or Fleet prison. **5** [mid-19C+] (*US Und.*) a state prison, a penitentiary. **6** [late 19C–1900s] (*UK Und.*) the workhouse. [ironic uses of SE, the overall ref. being to prison as a 'university of crime'; note mid-17C Oxbridge use *college*, a public house or tavern with a sign of a green garland or painted hoop; WW1 Aus. milit. *college*, 39 General Hospital and No. 2 Stationery Hospital, primarily treating VD]

college-called *adj.* [1950s–60s] (*US Black*) experiencing the desire to attend a college. [college attendance was still a relative rarity for young Blacks at this time]

college chum *n.* [19C] a prisoner. [COLLEGE *n.* (3) + CHUM *n.*[1] (1)]

college cove *n.* [early 19C] (*UK Und.*) the turnkey of Newgate prison. [COLLEGE *n.* (2) + COVE *n.* (1)]

college fuck *n. see* PRINCETON RUB *n.*

college hill *n.* [1960s] (*US*) that part of a town or city where the rich live. [the habit of building colleges or universities in the better-off areas of a town]

colleger *n.* [late 19C–1950s] a mortar-board.

College Street solicitor *n.* [1940s–60s] (*Aus.*) a male prostitute. [College Street, Sydney, a gay centre since the mid-19C. The street runs into Queen's Square, itself frequented by lawyers visiting the nearby law courts; thus giving puns on QUEEN *n.*[2] (1) and SE *solicitor*]

college style *adv. see* PRINCETON RUB *n.*

college try *n.* [1910s+] (*US*) a plucky effort, esp. against heavy odds; usu. in phr. (*let's*) *give it the old college try*. [the myth of 'college spirit']

college widow *n.* [late 19C–1940s] (*US*) an unmarried woman, in some way associated with a given college, whose advancing age does not deter her from associating with successive generations of students.

collegian *n.* [mid-17C+] a prisoner. [COLLEGE *n.* (3)]

collegiate *n.* **1** [mid-17C–early 19C] a prisoner. **2** [late 18C–early 19C] a shopkeeper at the Royal Exchange or Newgate prisons. [COLLEGE *n.* (3); ironic use of SE]

collegiate fucking *n.* [20C+] (*gay*) body-to-body rubbing. [SE *collegiate* + FUCKING *n.*[1]; for ety. see PRINCETON RUB *n.*]

colley thumper *n.* [late 19C] a very good hand at cards. [Gen. Sir George Pomeroy *Colley* (1835–81), defeated and killed by the Boers at the Battle of Majuba Hill, 27 February 1881; but ? note CALLITHUMPIAN *n.*]

collie *n.*[1] (*also* **callie, colly, collyweed**) [1950s+] (*W.I., Jam.*) marijuana; thus *collie-man*, a marijuana seller (cf. AFRICAN BUSH *n.*). [? joc. abbr. SE *broccoli*]

collie *n.*[2] *see* CAULI *n.*

collie knox *n.* [1960s+] venereal disease. [rhy. sl. = POX *n.*[1] (2)]

collies *n.* [1990s+] (*drugs*) drugs, esp. heroin. [abbr. COLLYWOBBLES *n.* (1); i.e. the effects of the drug on one's stomach, or those that accompany withdrawal sickness]

colli-mollie *n. see* COLLY-MOLLY *n.*

collins *n.* [1900s–20s] a thank-you letter. [fictional character William *Collins*, a foolish sycophant in Jane Austen's *Pride & Prejudice* (1813)]

Collins Street farmer *n.* (*also* **Collins Street grazier**) [1970s+] (*Aus.*) a businessman who owns or shares a farm from which he takes annual profits but rarely visits. [*Collins Street*, the financial and social centre of Melbourne]

Collins Street squatter *n.* [1960s] (*Aus.*) a man, usu. a youth, who frequents bars, cafés etc for no other reason than meeting his friends, gossiping and wasting time. [*Collins Street*, the centre of Melbourne + SAusE *squatter*, a grazier]

collogue *n.* [early–mid-19C] a private talk, a secret plan or scheme. [COLLOGUE v. (2)]

collogue *v.* **1** [late 16C–18C] to wheedle, to coax. **2** [late 18C+] (*also* **cologue**) to confer privately and confidentially, to scheme or plot. [Fr. *colloque*, conference, communication, consultation]

colloquials *n.* [late 19C–1900s] (*UK society*) informal conversation. [play on SE *colloquial*]

colly *n. see* COLLIE n.[1].

colly *v.* [1920s–40s] (*US Black*) to understand, to comprehend. [? COLLAR v. (4) or Fr. *comprendre*, to understand]

colly-molly *n.* (*also* **colli-mollie**) [17C] melancholy. [play on SE]

collyweed *n. see* COLLIE n.[1].

collywobbles *n.* **1** [early 19C+] feelings of tension, fear or sickness, usu. seen as stemming from the stomach. **2** [mid-19C] the stomach. **3** [1980s] diarrhoea. [SE *colic* + *wobble*]

colney (hatch) *n.* [1930s–70s] a match. [rhy. sl.; ult. *Colney Hatch* psychiatric hospital]

cologue *v. see* COLLOGUE v. (2).

colom *n.* [1990s+] (*drugs*) marijuana from *Colombia*. [abbr.]

Colombian *n.* (*also* **Columbian, Colombo**) [1970s+] (*drugs*) marijuana from Colombia; also ext. as Colombian *gold/green/red* etc (cf. ACAPULCO (GOLD) n.). [the mis-sp. is almost as common as the correct one]

Colombian necktie *n.* (*also* **necktie, Sicilian necktie**) [1980s+] a method of killing whereby the throat is cut and the tongue pulled through the resulting wound; such embellishment is usu. meted out to one who has betrayed the killer or his boss. [orig. in the drug wars of Colombia]

colon choker *n.* (*also* **colon commando, …cowboy, …crusader**) [1990s+] a male homosexual. [SE *colon*, the large intestine, which ends in the rectum]

Colonel Custer *n.* [1980s] (*Aus.*) **1** a muster. **2** a duster. [rhy. sl.; ult. US soldier George A *Custer* (1839–76)]

colonel of a regiment *n.* (*also* **colonel of horse**) [mid-17C–early 18C] one who 'drinks in his boots and gingling spurs'. [not necessarily a soldier]

Colonel Prescott *n. see* CHARLIE PRESCOTT n.

Colonel Sanders *n.* [1970s+] (*US gay*) an older male homosexual with a preference for young boys. [the name, quite poss. libellous, puns on the Colonel's internationally franchised product]

colonel's cure *n.* [late 19C–1900s] any form of medicine swallowed at a single gulp. [the image is of a colonel making a toast after a regimental dinner]

colonial adjective *n.* [1900s] (*N.Z.*) a euph. for BLOODY adj.[1] (1). [i.e. the 'great Australian adjective']

colonial duck *n.* (*also* **colonial goose**) [late 19C+] (*Aus.*) a boned roast shoulder (*duck*) or leg (*goose*) of mutton stuffed with sage and onions. [fig. use of *colonial* to mean second-rate, substitute]

colonial livery *n.* [19C] (*Aus.*) a bloody nose and a black eye. [the image of Aus. as a violent country]

colonial puck *n.* [1940s] (*US*) sexual intercourse. [rhy. sl. = FUCK n.[1] (1)]

colonial Robert *n.* [late 19C–1910s] (*Aus./N.Z.*) a shilling (5p). [SE *colonial* + BOB n.[4] (1)]

colonist *n.* [early–mid-19C] a louse. [it 'colonizes' one's body]

coloquaron *n. see* COLQUARRON n.

color *v.* [1960s+] (*US*) to see as, to present as. [imagery of a children's colouring book]

colora *n.* [1960s+] (*S.Afr. gay*) a mixed-race homosexual man. [SE *coloured* + fem. sfx *-a*]

Colorado Kool-Aid *n.* [1970s+] (*US*) Coors beer. [*Coors* is brewed in Colorado + the soft-drink mix *Kool-Aid*]

Colorado mockingbird *n.* [20C+] (*US*) a donkey (cf. ARIZONA CANARY n.). [the noise of its braying, the antithesis of that of a mellifluous bird]

color-blind *adj.* [1940s–60s] (*US*) larcenous. [the inability to distinguish between colours is substituted by the inability to tell the difference between one's own possessions and those of another]

colored people's time *n.* (*also* **colored folks' time**) [1920s+] (*US Black*) unpunctuality (cf. AFRICAN (PEOPLE'S) TIME n.). [racist stereotyping]

color guard *n.* [1970s+] (*US Black*) a gaudy, unfashionable dresser.

color me gone *phr.* [1980s+] (*US campus*) a phr. indicating one does not wish to be involved or present. [COLOR v.]

colors *n. see* COLOURS n.

color-struck *adj.* [1940s+] (*US Black*) **1** conceited on the grounds of one's light skin colour. **2** of a Black person, preferring light-skinned to dark-skinned Black people.

colossal *adj.* [late 19C+] immense, tremendous, magnificent, stupendous.

colouring *n.* [20C+] (*Irish*) milk as poured into tea.

colours *n.* (*also* **colors**) **1** [1960s+] of 'outlaw' motorcyclists, one's club emblem. Orig. used for the first such outlaws, the Hell's Angels, consisting of an embroidered patch of a winged skull wearing a motorcycle helmet, the name 'Hell's Angels', the name of the chapter (town etc) and the letters 'MC' (motorcycle club); thus (*N.Z.*) *run for one's colours*, to serve as a probationary member of the club. **2** [1970s+] (*US*) the insignia, e.g. a coloured bandana/headscarf/beads, sported by members of the street gangs of Los Angeles, New York etc. **3** [1990s+] (*US prison*) a prison gang tatoo.

colour the meerschaum *v.* [late 19C] to get a red nose through excessive drinking. [the gradual darkening of the white-clay bowl of a *meerschaum* pipe over years of use]

colquarron *n.* (*also* **coloquaron**) [late 17C–mid-19C] (*UK Und.*) the neck. [? Fr. *col*, neck + QUARROM n.]

colsher *n. see* COLCHER n.

colt *n.*[1] [17C–mid-19C] (*UK Und.*) anyone, usu. an inn-keeper, who provides stables and horses for a highwayman.

colt *n.*[2] **1** [17C–mid-19C] a young man who has just been initiated into crime. **2** [late 17C+] a new apprentice, modern use is usu. in a sporting context. **3** [late 18C–mid-19C] one who serves on a jury for the first time. **4** [1900s–40s] (*US Black*) a young man.

colt *n.*[3] [mid-19C] a piece of rope with something heavy fastened to the end, used as a weapon or instrument of punishment. [naut. jargon *colt*, a piece of knotted rope, used as a weapon]

colt *v.*[1] [mid-19C] to 'fine' a first-time server on a jury a sum which is spent on drink for his colleagues. [COLT n.[2] (3)]

colt *v.*[2] [mid–late 19C] to beat with a rope's end. [COLT n.[3]]

colting *n.* [mid–late 19C] a thrashing. [COLT n.[3]]

colt (over the fence) *n.* [1960s] (*US*) an illegitimate child. [abbr. BRUSH COLT n.]

colt party *n.* [late 19C] (*US society*) a party for young people only. [COLT n.[2]]

colt veal *n.* [late 17C–mid-19C] very red, coarse-grained veal. ['more like the flesh of a colt than that of a calf' (Grose, 1785)]

columbered *adj.* [early 17C] drunk. [ety. unknown; the *OED* has only this cit. and states 'derivation and meaning uncertain']

Columbian *n. see* COLOMBIAN n.

Columbia River turkey *n.* [20C+] (*US*) a salmon. [the Chinook salmon is abundant in the Columbia River]

Columbine *n.* [late 19C] a prostitute (cf. BABY JANE n.). [literary euph. *Columbine*, a character in Italian commedia dell'arte, thence trad. pantomime, the mistress of Harlequin; the original *columbine*, a flower with 'hollow horns' is cited by Williams as used for a 16C image of cuckoldry]

Columbus black n. [1980s+] (drugs) marijuana (cf. ACAPULCO (GOLD) n.). [marijuana supposedly grown in Columbus, Ohio]

columns of Venus n. [18C] the labia. [literary euph.; the image is of a temple portico, flanked by a pair of pillars]

com n.[1] **1** [mid-19C+] a commission (in a non-pecuniary sense). **2** [late 19C–1900s] a commercial traveller. **3** [late 19C+] a commission (in a pecuniary sense). **4** [1920s+] (orig. Aus.) a communist. **5** [1920s+] (US Und.) (also **comb**) the combination of a safe. **6** [1990s+] (US campus) communication(s). [abbr.]

com n.[2] see COMBIE n.

coma'd adj. [1990s+] passed out from an excess of alcohol.

comanche n. [1960s–70s] (gay) a man who uses cosmetics. [proper name Comanche; thus Native American use of warpaint]

comatose adj. [1980s+] (US campus) drunk (cf. ADDLED adj.).

comb n.[1] **1** [late 16C] (UK Und.) a hooked pole used to extract goods from shop windows. **2** [1930s–50s] (UK prison) a carpenter's file.

comb n.[2] see COM n.[1] (5).

comb v. [1940s–50s] to interrogate. [SE run a fine tooth comb over]

comb and brush n. [late 19C] a drink. [rhy. sl. = LUSH n.[1] (1)]

comb and brush v. [late 19C] to treat to a drink. [COMB AND BRUSH n.]

combat zone n. [1970s+] (US) that part of the inner city where racial, social, economic and other tensions are at their height; orig. use in Boston, Mass.

comb-brush n. [early–mid-18C] a lady's maid. [her primary task was brushing her mistress's hair]

comb-cut adj. [mid-19C–1900s] disgraced, socially or professionally embarrassed. [COMB-CUT v.]

comb-cut v. (also **cut someone's comb**) [late 16C–19C] to humiliate; to disgrace, to 'bring down a peg'. [cockfighting imagery]

comb down v. [late 19C+] (Aus.) to thrash, to beat.

comber n. [late 16C] (UK Und.) a thief who operates a hooked pole to extract goods from shop windows. [COMB n.[1] (1)]

combie n. (also **com**) [late 19C+] the all-in-one underwear known as combinations. [abbr.]

combination n. [1930s–50s] (US tramp) a vegetable stew.

combing law n. [late 16C] (UK Und.) the stealing of goods from shops by using a hooked pole to drag them from windows. [COMB n.[1] (1) + LAW n.[1]]

combo n.[1] **1** [1920s+] a partnership, esp. a group of musicians. **2** [1920s+] (UK/US Und.) combination lock (on a safe). **3** [1920s+] (US) any form of combination, whether of people, things, sandwich ingredients, wagers etc. **4** [1950s] a relationship. **5** [1980s+] (US campus) a bisexual person. [abbr. SE combination + -o sfx (6)]

combo n.[2] (also **kombo**) (Aus.) **1** [late 19C+] a White man who cohabits with or marries an Aborigine woman; thus go combo, to live with an Aborigine woman; thus combo-land, used both for the Northern Territory and for any area where such cohabitation is common. **2** [1910s] a term of address to an Aborigine. [abbr. SE combination + -o sfx (4)]

combobbolate v. see CONBOBBOLATE v.

combolo n. [1940s+] (W.I.) **1** an old, trusted machete. **2** a sexual partner. [dial. combolo, a companion, ult. Sp. compañera, friend or ? combolo, an African song-dance]

comboman n. [1920s–30s] (Aus.) a White man who cohabits with or marries an Aborigine woman. [COMBO n.[2] (1) + sfx -man]

comboozelated adj. [1970s+] (US campus) drunk (cf. ADDLED adj.). [DISCOMBOBULATE v. + BOOZE n. (1) + sfx -ated]

comb-out n. [1940s] a sorting-out. [COMB OUT v.]

comb out v. [late 19C+] to sort out, to put in order.

combs n. [late 19C+] combinations, i.e. a woman's or child's garment consisting of combined chemise or undershirt and drawers. [abbr.]

comb someone's hair v. (also **comb someone's head/noddle**) **1** [late 16C–19C] to thrash, to beat severely; sometimes ext. by ...with a joint/three-legged stool. **2** [late 18C–1920s] to tell off, to scold, to reprimand. **3** [1930s–40s] (US) (also **comb someone's wool**) to pistol-whip.

comb the kinks out of v. [1910s] (US) to correct errors in another's views or actions, to 'set straight'. [KINK n.[1] (1)]

come n. **1** [mid-17C+] an orgasm. **2** [1920s+] semen; also attrib.; thus comey, covered in semen. **3** [1940s+] vaginal secretions (cf. BINDERJUICE n.). **4** [1980s+] energy, spirit; esp. in phr. young, dumb and full of come. [COME v.[1]]

come v.[1] [late 16C+] of a man or woman, to achieve orgasm (cf. COME A BUCKET v.; COME A RIVER v.; COME OFF v.[1]; COME ONE'S COCOA v.; COME ONE'S FAT v.; COME ONE'S LOT v.; CUM v.). [abbr. SE come to a climax; Williams suggests link to SE come, of butter, to form in the churn, and thus a pun on BUTTER n.[1] (1) but this seems to predate it]

come v.[2] [late 17C–1900s] (UK Und.) to lend (money). [one 'comes' forth with the loan]

come v.[3] see COME (THE) — v.

come prep. [1990s+] in (a certain amount of time).

come about v. [late 19C] said by men of women, to have sexual intercourse.

come a bucket v. [1970s] of a man, to ejaculate copiously. [COME v.[1]]

come a clover v. [1910s–20s] to fall over, to trip over. [rhy. sl.]

come a crash v. [1910s] (Aus.) to encounter difficulties.

come a cropper v. (also **get a cropper, go a cropper**) **1** [mid-19C+] to suffer an accident, usu. a fall; also in fig. use. **2** [1900s–20s] to be killed. [CROPPER n.]

come across v. **1** [late 19C+] (also **come up**) to hand something over; to pay up money, esp. reluctantly. **2** [20C+] to acquiesce, to do what is required. **3** [1910s+] to deliver. **4** [1920s+] to surrender sexually. **5** [1920s+] to confess (to a crime).

come after with salt and spoons v. [late 17C–early 18C] to be slow, to waste time. [image of a person who is eating with their hands being pursued by a servant carrying utensils and salt]

come again v. [20C+] to repeat oneself; to redo in an improved manner.

come again? phr. **1** [20C+] a general phr. indicating either that one has failed to hear a speaker or finds it hard to believe the statement, 'please repeat yourself', 'could you say that again?', 'you must be joking'. **2** [1980s+] (W.I./UK Black teen) a call to the disc jockey to replay a piece of music.

come a Kerensky v. [1910s] (Aus.) to suffer a humiliation. [A.F. Kerensky (1881–1970), prime minister of the second Russian provisional government, deposed in the Bolshevik Revolution of October 1917]

come alive v. see LOOK ALIVE v.

come all over v. [20C+] (Aus.) **1** to thrash, to defeat completely. **2** to experience certain emotions, usu. with various modifiers, e.g. come all over queer, suddenly to feel physically unwell.

come aloft v. [late 16C–mid-17C] to have an erection.

come aloft! excl. [17C] let's have fun! let's enjoy ourselves!

come-along n. (also **pullers**) [1920s] (US Und.) a tool used to pull the lock out of a safe.

come-alongs n. [late 19C+] handcuffs; thus pull the come-along, to be arrested.

come and get it! excl. [20C+] a general cry indicating that a meal is forthcoming. [orig. milit. mess-hall use]

come and have one! excl. [late 19C–1900s] an invitation to join the speaker for a drink.

come and see your pa! excl. [mid-19C–1900s] an invitation to join the speaker for a drink. [note naut. use, come and wash your neck]

come apart v. see FALL APART v.

come apart at the seams v. (also **fall apart at the seams**)

[1940s+] **1** of people, to lose emotional control. **2** of objects, ideas, plans, to collapse.

come a purler v. (also **come a pearler**) [mid-19C+] to fall down, to trip over an obstacle, usu. sustaining some form of injury; often in fig. use. [SE come + PURLER n. (1)]

come a river v. [1970s] (US) of a woman, to have a very intense orgasm. [COME v.¹]

come-around n.¹ [1960s] (US) menstruation. [COME AROUND v.]

come-around n.² [1990s+] (W.I.) a person who is tolerated but not welcome.

come around v. [1910s–60s] (US) to menstruate. [euph.; the cyclical occurrence of menstruation]

come a stumer v. [1910s] (Aus.) to be financially ruined. [STUMER n.¹ (2)]

come at v. [20C+] (Aus./N.Z.) to undertake, to take on, to get up to, to 'try on'.

comeback n.¹ [late 19C+] (orig. US) **1** a verbal or other rejoinder. **2** repercussions, results; retaliation. [COME BACK v.]

comeback n.² [1980s+] (drugs) benzocaine and mannitol, chemicals used in the manufacture of crack cocaine.

come back v. [late 19C+] (orig. US) to give a verbal rejoinder.

come back to the field v. [1910s+] (Aus.) to come down to earth, to abandon one's fantasies and dreams.

come-bucket n. (also **cum-bucket**) [1970s+] (US) a repellent person. [COME n. (2)/CUM n.¹ (1) + SE bucket; lit. 'a bucket of ejaculate'; note RMC Duntroon (Aus.) come-/cum-bucket, come-/cum-bag, come-/cum-catcher, derog. terms for a woman, seen purely as a sex-object]

come-by-chance (child) n. [mid-18C+] an illegitimate child (cf. CHANCE CHILD n.).

come case v. see GO CASE v.

come clean v. **1** [1910s+] (orig. US) to confess, to make an admission. **2** [1920s] to get away with something, usu. a crime. **3** [1920s+] to speak the truth. **4** [1930s] (US) to pay one's debts in full.

come correct v. [1990s+] (US Black) to do something the way it should be done.

come countryman over v. [early 19C] to wheedle, to cajole, to trick. [the gullibility of the country-dweller]

come crook v. [1950s] (Aus.) to menstruate. [SE come + CROOK adj. (3)]

come-down n. **1** [mid-late 19C] a fall from grace, a humiliating decline in one's material circumstances. **2** [1950s–70s] (US Black) a bad situation, esp. an embarrassing one. **3** [1960s+] (drugs) the after-effects of drug use, or any highly emotional or stressful situation. **4** [1960s+] (drugs) the withdrawal from drug use. [(1) SE in 20C+; (3) and (4) f. COME DOWN v.³; (3) is not necessarily unpleasant and not specifically applied to addictive drugs; (4) is unpleasant and refers to addiction]

come down v.¹ [early 18C–1910s] to give or lend money; thus COME DOWN WITH v.

come down v.² **1** [1930s+] to become permanent or established. **2** [1960s] (US prison) to go to prison. **3** [1960s+] (orig. US Black) to occur, to turn out, to develop, to transpire, to happen.

come down v.³ [1940s+] **1** (drugs) to experience the ending of a drug's effects (such an experience is often emotionally distressing, although the intoxication may have been pleasurable). **2** in non-drug use, to calm down; to experience the end of an emotional 'high'. **3** (drugs) to withdraw from habitual narcotic use. [one has been HIGH adj.¹ (2)/HIGH adj.¹ (4)]

come down v.⁴ [1960s+] (US) to talk or behave; usu. in comb., e.g. she comes down all crazy. [ext. of COME DOWN v.² (3)]

come down v.⁵ see GO DOWN v.⁷ (2).

come down curtain-rods v. see COME DOWN STAIR-RODS v.

come down fonky v. [1970s+] to belittle, to insult, to talk to severely, to criticize harshly. [COME DOWN v.⁴ + FONKY adj.²]

come down front v. [1950s–60s] (US Black) to confess, to tell the

truth, to speak openly; usu. as imper. come down front! [image of a congregant approaching the front of the church to confess their sins]

come down hard v. [1930s+] (orig. US Black) to attack, whether physically or verbally. [COME DOWN v.⁴]

come down on v. **1** [late 19C+] (orig. US Black) to belittle, to insult, to talk to severely, to criticize harshly. **2** [late 19C+] to put under pressure. **3** [1940s+] (orig. US Black) to assault; to harass. **4** [1960s+] (drugs) for the pains of withdrawal symptoms, and thus the demands of drug-need, to intensify. **5** [1970s] to move one emotionally in a positive manner. **6** [1990s+] to pressurize emotionally, to depress. [fig. use of SE]

come down on someone like a ton of bricks v. (also **come down on someone like a thousand of brick**) [20C+] to unleash the full force of one's anger or aggression on someone. [COME DOWN ON v. (1) + LIKE A THOUSAND OF BRICK adv.]

come down stair-rods v. (also **come down curtain-rods, rain curtain-rods/stair-rods**) [20C+] to rain very heavily.

come down the pike v. (also **come over the pike**) [late 19C+] (US) **1** to appear, to arrive, to happen. **2** in fig. use, to imply the passing of time, progression of events. [PIKE n.² (3)]

come down to (brass) tacks v. see GET DOWN TO (BRASS) TACKS v.

come down to cases v. see GET DOWN TO CASES v.

come down to tin tacks v. see GET DOWN TO TIN TACKS v.

come down with v. [early 18C–1900s] to hand over money; usu. ext. as come down with the needful/dust/pelf etc. [ext. of COME DOWN v.¹]

come-drum n. see CUM DRUM n.

come dump n. [1960s] (US) a promiscuous female. [COME n. (2) + SE dump]

comedy n. [1910s–30s] (US) irrelevant, impertinent, cheeky talk.

come flat out with v. [late 19C+] (orig. US) to state unequivocally, to make one's point without hesitation.

come for horse and harness v. [15C–16C] to do something for one's interests. [the contemporary importance of such items]

come-freak n. **1** [1950s+] (also **fuck-freak**) anyone who is obsessed with physical sex and the delights thereof. **2** [1960s] (US gay) a fellator. [(1) COME n. (1)/FUCK n.¹ (2); (2) COME n. (2) + FREAK n.¹ (6)]

come from Liquorpond Street v. [early 19C–1900s] to be drunk.

come from Tripoli v. [mid–late 19C] to be a lively, energetic performer, esp. acrobatically. [? the troupes of North African dancers who were then popular in London or f. a play on SE trip, to tumble]

come-fuck-me's n. [1960s+] (US gay) very tight trousers (cf. FUCK-ME adj.).

come good v. [1950s+] (orig. Aus./N.Z.) **1** of things, to turn out well. **2** of people, to prove themselves (esp. after an unpromising start), to 'come up trumps'.

come grass v. [1920s+] to turn informer. [SE come + GRASS n.⁴]

come half larks with v. [1910s–20s] to deceive, to fool. [SE come + LARK n.¹ (2)]

come handsomely over v. [late 18C–early 19C] to persuade, to win over.

come home by rail v. [1930s+] (Aus.) to be so drunk that one can only proceed by hanging onto things.

come home by Spillsbury v. [late 17C–early 18C] to tumble, to fall over, to have a 'spill'; to fail.

come home by the villages v. [18C] to be reeling drunk.

come home with the milk v. [late 19C+] to come home in the very early morning. [one supposedly meets the milkman on his morning rounds]

come home with your knickers torn and say you found the money phr. [20C+] a phr. used to indicate the speaker's inability to believe an extremely unlikely story.

come-home Yankee *n.* [1930s] (*Irish*) a returned immigrant.

come-in *n. see* COME-ON *n.* (5).

come in Berlin *phr.* [1970s] (*US campus*) an exhortation to pay attention, a greeting. [? a radio call-sign]

come in like Flynn *v.* [1990s+] (*Aus.*) to 'fall for', to 'swallow' a story.

come in on a sparrow's ticket *v.* [20C+] (*Aus.*) to gain admission to a sporting event or other entertainment without paying. [one has 'flown over the wall']

come in one's pants *v.* (*also* **come in one's drawers**) [1960s+] to behave in an exaggerated, over-excited manner; the image is of extremely premature ejaculation. [fig. use of COME *v.*[1]]

come into one's own *v.* [1980s+] to masturbate. [pun on COME *v.*[1]]

come it *v.*[1] [late 17C–early 19C] to lend money to someone. [ext. of COME *v.*[2]]

come it *v.*[2] **1** [late 18C+] to act, to perform, to behave in a certain manner, usu. constructed with an adj. used adverbially, e.g. COME IT STRONG *v.* (cf. COME ON *v.*[1]; COME OVER *v.*[2]; COME (THE) — *v.*). **2** [early–mid-19C] to show off, to boast. **3** [early 19C+] to act aggressively, often with no grounds for so doing. **4** [mid-19C] to impress as a lover. **5** [mid-19C–1910s] to deceive another for one's own benefit, esp. to avoid an unpleasant task. **6** [1900s–20s] to be cheeky.

come it *v.*[3] **1** [early 19C+] to divulge a secret, to confess. **2** [early 19C+] (*Aus./UK Und.*) to betray, to inform against.

come it *v.*[4] [mid-19C] to attain, to reach, to achieve.

come it as strong as a horse *v.* [early–mid-19C] (*UK Und.*) to turn King's/Queen's evidence. [ext. of COME IT *v.*[3] (2)]

come it on *v.* (*US*) **1** [mid-19C] to treat roughly, to manhandle. **2** [1900s] to trick, to deceive. [abbr. COME IT STRONG *v.* (1)]

come it over *v.* [mid-19C+] **1** to compel, to intimidate. **2** (*US*) to trick, to deceive. [abbr. COME IT STRONG *v.*]

come-it-over man *n.* [20C+] a domineering, intimidating person. [COME IT OVER *v.* (1)]

come it strong *v.* **1** [early 19C+] (*also* **go it strong**) to act in a challenging, aggressive manner; sometimes intensified by …*as mustard*. **2** [mid-19C] to act, to practise, to perform one's part. **3** [mid-19C] to tell lies. [COME IT *v.*[2] (1)]

come it with *v.* [late 19C+] to act in a certain way in order to take advantage (of someone). [var. on COME IT OVER *v.*]

come-juice *n.* [1990s+] **1** semen (cf. BABY FLUID *n.*). **2** vaginal juices when orgasming (cf. BINDERJUICE *n.*). [COME *n.* (1) + JUICE *n.*[2] (1)]

come lickety-split *v. see* GO LICKETY-SPLIT *v.*

come-licking *adj.* [1970s] (*orig. US*) vile, disgusting. [COME *n.* (2) + SE *licking*, i.e. var. on COCKSUCKING *adj.*]

come like a parolee at the ho shack *v.* [1970s] (*US Black*) to move very fast. [pun on SE *come*/COME *v.*[1]; the image is of a long-term prisoner having the first sex of his freedom]

come-love tea *n.* [1930s+] (*Aus.*) weak tea. [the phr. *come, love* seen as a mild suggestion]

come-loving *adj.* [1950s–70s] (*US Black*) obsessed with sex. [COME *n.* (2)]

come-off *n.* [mid-19C+] (*US*) a result. [earlier use is SE]

come off *v.*[1] [17C; mid-20C+] to experience orgasm. [ext. of COME *v.*[1]]

come off *v.*[2] (*US*) **1** [late 19C–1940s] to stop, to refrain from a course of action. **2** [1960s] to hand over reluctantly.

come off *v.*[3] [1930s+] (*drugs*) to stop using a given (addictive) drug. [one has been 'on' heroin, 'on' cocaine etc]

come off! *excl.* [late 19C–1930s] (*US*) stop it! don't keep trying that line! [COME OFF *v.*[2] (1); later use is COME OFF IT! excl.]

come off bluely *v.* [mid-17C–18C] to have bad luck, to fail. [fig use of SE *blue*, considered the colour of nervousness, sorrow etc]

come off crabs *v.* (*also* **turn up crabs**) [mid-18C–mid-19C]

to turn out a failure or disappointment. [gambling jargon *crabs*, 2 aces, the lowest throw at hazard]

come off it! *excl.* (*also* **come out of it!**) [1920s+] stop it! don't keep trying that line! [later ext. of COME OFF! excl.]

come off one's game *v.* [1970s] (*US Black*) to abandon a pose, to act in a spontaneous, genuine manner. [GAME *n.*[2] (4)]

come off the bird-lime! *excl.* [1910s–20s] a general excl. of disbelief, you must be joking! you don't fool me! [COME OFF *v.*[2] (1) + the use of SE *bird-lime* as a snare or trap]

come off the grass! *excl.* [late 19C] (*orig. US*) stop telling lies! stop exaggerating! [COME OFF *v.*[2] (1)]

come off the roof! *excl.* [late 19C] an excl. used to an equal who is considered to be 'getting above themself', i.e. stop acting so superior!

come-on *n.* **1** [late 19C–1950s] (*US Und.*) a dupe, a victim of a confidence trickster; a prospective victim; a 'steered' prospect. **2** [20C+] (*US Und.*) a con-man, a swindler. **3** [20C+] (*US*) a snare, an inducement, a lure. **4** [20C+] (*US*) patter, sales or seduction talk, a line. **5** [1930s+] (*also* **come-in**) a sexual invitation, either through a look or through words. **6** [1950s] a dare. **7** [2000s] as the personification of (5), a sexually alluring woman. [SE excl. *come on!*]

come-on *adj.* [1920s+] (*orig. US*) alluring, seductive. [COME-ON *n.* (3)/COME-ON *n.* (5)]

come on *v.*[1] [late 19C+] (*orig. US*) to seem, to appear, to behave, always modified by an adj. used adverbially, e.g. *come on tough, come on nasty* etc (cf. COME IT *v.*[2]).

come on *v.*[2] **1** [1930s+] (*drugs*) for withdrawal symptoms to start affecting a narcotics addict. **2** [1940s+] (*drugs*) for a drug to begin affecting its user, esp. of a hallucinogen (which takes a period of time to enter the bloodstream and hit the brain). **3** [1980s+] for a woman, to start menstruation. [SE *come on*, to begin]

come on *v.*[3] **1** [1930s+] to approach sexually. **2** [1940s+] (*US*) to speak aggressively, forcefully. **3** [1950s] (*US*) to joke. **4** [1990s+] to harass.

come on! *excl.* [20C+] a general excl. of disbelief, disapproval, irritation.

come on bad *v.* [1960s–70s] (*US Black*) to act aggressively, to threaten; to defeat someone in a contest of words. [COME ON *v.*[1] + BAD *adj.* (2)]

come-on boy *n.* [1940s+] a male prostitute who entices a client and then, instead of sex, has him beaten and robbed by a confederate. [COME-ON *n.* (3) + SE *boy*]

come one's cocoa *v.* [1960s+] **1** to ejaculate. **2** (*UK police/Und.*) in fig. use, to inform or to confess one's crimes. [COME *v.*[1] + play on SE]

come one's fat *v.* [1970s+] **1** to ejaculate. **2** in fig. use, of a suspect, to confess. [COME *v.*[1] + SE *fat*]

come one's guts *v.* (*also* **give one's guts**) [1920s–70s] to give information (cf. THROW ONE'S GUTS *v.*). [fig. use of COME *v.*[1] + GUTS *n.*[1] (2)]

come one's lot *v.* [1970s+] **1** to ejaculate. **2** in fig. use, of a suspect, to confess. [COME *v.*[1] + SE *lot*]

come one's mutton *v.* [1960s+] to masturbate (cf. BEAT ONE'S MEAT *v.*). [COME *v.*[1] + MUTTON *n.*[3]]

come one's turkey *v.* [1960s+] to masturbate (cf. BEAT ONE'S HOG *v.*). [COME *v.*[1] + TURKEY NECK *n.*]

come-on girl *n.* [20C+] (*US*) a promiscuous woman; a prostitute (cf. AWAYDAY GIRL *n.*). [COME-ON *n.* (2) + SE *girl*]

come-on guy *n.* [1920s–50s] (*US*) (*also* **come-on ghee**, …**man**) the member of a confidence trickster team who lures the victim into the circle. **2** (*US tramp*) a hard worker, who encourages others. [COME-ON *n.* (3)/SE *come on!* + SE *guy*/man]

come on like a test pilot *v.* [1940s] (*US Black/Harlem*) to act in a speedy, efficient manner. [COME ON *v.*[1]; the test pilot, as a figure of technologically sophisticated derring-do, had a higher profile then than now]

come on one's guava v. (also **slip on one's guava**) [1970s] (S.Afr.) to make a fool of oneself. [Afk. *koejawel*, backside]

come on strong v. (also **come strong**) **1** [20C+] to speak aggressively, forcefully; to make one's presence and opinions felt; used both positively and negatively, the latter often as *come on too strong*. **2** [1950s+] to be seductive. [COME ON v.¹ + SE *strong*]

come (on) the bounce v. (also **come the bouncer**) [1910s–30s] (Aus.) to threaten, to intimidate, to suggest blackmail; thus *common bounce(r)*, a man who uses a boy to claim that he has been abused so as to threaten a homosexual with a charge of 'unnatural intercourse'. [COME (THE) — v. + BOUNCE n.¹ (3)]

come on the piper's invitation v. [19C+] (Irish) to come uninvited. [a piper always receives a welcome]

come on to v. [1950s+] (orig. US) **1** to approach reasonably aggressively, to solicit. **2** to make sexual advances towards. [ext. of COME ON v.³]

come on top v. [1970s+] to be discovered, to become unmasked.

come out v.¹ **1** [mid-19C] (US) to give up a specific religious denomination, in favour of free opinion on religious matters. **2** [mid-late 19C] (US Black) to declare one's faith in religion, to join the church.

come out v.² [20C+] (W.I.) to be born in poverty or in some unknown place, esp. in the question 'where you come out?' [i.e. 'come out from']

come out v.³ **1** [1920s+] to declare any form of self-revelation. **2** [1940s+] (gay) to declare oneself openly as a homosexual. [COME OUT v.¹ (2); (2) strengthened by abbr. COME OUT OF THE CLOSET v.]

come out v.⁴ [1970s+] (US Black) to abandon the respectable working world for a more sophisticated lifestyle. [abbr. COME OUT OF THE HOUSE v.]

come-out adj. [early-mid-19C] disgusting, appalling.

come out moldy v. (also **come up moldy**) [1980s+] (US campus) to be humiliated.

come out of a bag v. **1** [1930s] (US Black) to act in an obnoxious manner. **2** [1990s+] to act contrary to expectations, to behave illogically in a given situation. [SE *come out* +BAG n.¹⁴]

come out of it! excl. see COME OFF IT! excl.

come out of the closet v. [1960s+] (orig. US) to reveal one's gay sexuality in public; thus *out of the closet*, acknowledging one's homosexuality. [SE *come out* + CLOSET n.²]

come out of the cupboard v. [late 19C–1900s] to start work on one's first ever job.

come out of the house v. [1950s+] (US) to grow up, lit. to leave one's home life for that of the streets and the larger world.

come out of the woods v. [1960s] (US Black) of a Southerner who has moved to a Northern city, to abandon one's rural lifestyle for that of the city.

come out of the woodwork v. (also **crawl out of the woodwork**) [1970s+] to emerge, to appear, always of someone/something unpleasant. [the normal woodwork dweller being a beetle, cockroach etc]

come out strong v. **1** [mid-19C+] to speak emphatically and frankly. **2** [late 19C] to act generously.

come out the side of one's neck v. see TALK OUT OF THE SIDE OF ONE'S NECK v. (3).

come out with v. (also **come right out with**) [20C+] (orig. US) to speak openly, candidly, tactlessly.

come over v.¹ [17C+] to trick, to cheat; to get the better of. [ext. use of SE *come over*, to prevail]

come over v.² (also **come — over, come the — over**) [mid-19C+] to act in a given manner, usu. defined by the missing n. (cf. COME IT v.²). [var. on COME ON v.¹/COME (THE) — v.]

come over all unnecessary v. (also **go all unnecessary**) [1930s+] to become sexually excited. [COME OVER v.² + euph.]

come over on a whelk-stall v. [late 19C–1900s] (costermonger) to be very flashily dressed. [? the flashy dress preferred by whelk-sellers]

come over the pike v. see COME DOWN THE PIKE v.

come Paddy (over) v. see COME (THE) PADDY (OVER) v.

come-pot n. [1940s] a general term of abuse. [COME n. (2) + -POT sfx]

come Quaker on v. [1900s] (US) to defame. [COME (THE) — v.]

comer n. [late 19C+] **1** (orig. US) an ambitious, go-ahead person, 'the coming man'. **2** (US) a business, club or project promising success. [SE *come (on)*, to advance (in one's aims, development etc)]

come right out with v. see COME OUT WITH v.

come round v. [mid-19C] to get the better of by cunning or artifice; to persuade, to influence strongly, to make a serious impression.

come short home v. [17C] to be imprisoned.

come sick v. [1940s+] (US) to menstruate. [euph.]

come stain n. (also **cum stain**) [1990s+] (US) a general derog. term. [COME n. (2)/CUM n.¹ (1) + SE *stain*, lit. 'a semen stain']

comet n. [late 19C–1940s] (US tramp) the aristocrat of tramps, travelling only on express trains and only for lengthy journeys.

come (the) — v. (also **come the old —**) [late 18C+] to practise some form of dodge, to pose or act in a certain way; used in a variety of combs. always constrained by a n., e.g. *come the artful*, *come the paddy* etc. Often intensified by 'old', e.g. COME THE (OLD) ACID v. (cf. COME IT v.²). [abbr. SE *come over*, to become]

come the acid (drop) v. see COME THE (OLD) ACID v.

come the after game phr. [1920s+] (Aus.) a synon. for 'I told you so'. [COME (THE) — v. + image of those who analyse a sporting fixture *after the game*, when they naturally know better than those who actually had to play it]

come the artful v. [19C+] to hoax, to deceive. [COME (THE) — v. + SE *artful*]

come the bag v. see COME THE (OLD) BAG v.

come the big figure v. (also **go the big figure, go the whole figure**) [mid-19C–1910s] (US) to risk or do everything possible, to do or provide what is required. [COME (THE) — v. + BIG FIGURE n.]

come the big note v. [1940s+] (Aus.) to boast, to set oneself up as a richer or more important person than is true. [COME (THE) — v. + BIG-NOTE v.]

come the blarney (over) v. [early 19C+] to flatter. [COME (THE) — v./COME OVER v.² + BLARNEY n.]

come the bludge on v. [20C+] (Aus.) to sponge on. [COME (THE) — v. + BLUDGER n.² (2)]

come the carney v. see COME THE (OLD) CARNEY v.

come (the) copper v. [1930s+] to become an informer. [COME (THE) — v. + COPPER n.³ (2)]

come the cunt v. see COME THE (OLD) CUNT v.

come the don v. [mid-19C–1910s] to put on airs. [COME (THE) — v. + SE *don*, a university teacher]

come the double v. **1** [mid-19C] (US) to double-cross. **2** [1910s] (Aus.) to take more than one's fair share. [COME (THE) — v. + DOUBLE v.² (1)/SE *double*]

come the drops v. [mid-late 19C] (Aus.) to make a fuss, to burst into tears. [COME (THE) — v. + SE *teardrops*]

come the duke v. see COME THE NOB v.

come the fob on v. [mid-19C] (US) to cheat, to trick. [COME (THE) — v. + FOB n.]

come the gammon v. [19C] to wheedle. [COME (THE) — v. + GAMMON n.² (2)]

come the grope v. (also **go the grope**) [1960s+] (Aus.) to fondle someone sexually. [COME (THE) — v. + SE *grope*]

come the gum (game) over v. [mid-late 19C] (US) to hoodwink, to trick. [COME OVER v.² + GUM n.¹ (2)/GUM GAME n.]

come the heavy v. **1** [mid-late 19C] to pose as a member of a superior class to that to which one actually belongs. **2** [1970s] to act in an aggressive or moralistic manner. [COME (THE) — v. + HEAVY n.[1]]

come the heavy father v. [mid-19C+] to moralize to one's errant child. [COME (THE) — v. + HEAVY adj.[1] (4) + SE *father*, an overbearing 'Victorian' father]

come the hound v. [1970s] (*Irish*) to deceive, to trick. [COME (THE) — v. + HOUND n.[1]]

come the lardy-dardy v. [mid–late 19C] to dress in a showy manner. [COME (THE) — v. + LARDY-DARDY adj.]

come the nob v. (*also* **come the duke, come the nabob**) [early 19C+] to give oneself airs. [COME (THE) — v. + NOB n.[2] (1)/SE *duke*/NABOB n.]

come the (old) acid v. (*also* **come the acid drop**) [1910s+] to act contrarily, aggressively, to argue; to be unpleasant or offensive, to speak in a caustic or sarcastic manner, sometimes with affection. [COME (THE) — v. + ACID n.[2]]

come the (old) bag v. [1920s] (*orig. milit.*) to bluff, to 'try it on'. [COME (THE) — v. + SE *bag*]

come the (old) carney v. [early 19C–1920s] to flatter. [COME (THE) — v. + CARNEY n.[1] (1)]

come the (old) cunt v. [20C+] to act in an obnoxious or obstreperous manner; esp. in phr. *don't come the old cunt with me.* [COME (THE) — v. + CUNT n.[2] (1)]

come the old man v. [late 19C] to act in a lazy manner, to shirk one's duties. [COME (THE) — v. + SE, i.e. to pretend to infirm old age; or ? naut. use of *old man*, the captain]

come the old soldier v. (*also* **come the tin soldier, put the old soldier on**) [18C+] to deceive another for one's own benefit, esp. to avoid an unpleasant task. [COME (THE) — v. + SE *old soldier*; the skills of a veteran who, supposedly, knows every trick when it comes to avoiding onerous duties. Ware also cites the rash of beggars who proliferated in London after Waterloo (1815), all claiming to have taken part in the battle. Note naut. jargon *soldier*, a poor or lazy seaman, a shirker]

come (the) Paddy (over) v. [mid-19C] to bamboozle, to confuse, to 'blarney'. [COME (THE) — v./COME OVER v.[2] + PADDY n. (1); thus negative racial stereotyping]

come the possum over v. [mid-19C+] **1** to pretend to be ill or even dead. **2** to dissemble. [COME OVER v.[2] + SE *possum*, an animal perceived to be cowardly and dissembling]

come the raw prawn v. [1940s+] (*Aus.*) to act resentfully or unpleasantly, to be rude. [COME (THE) — v. + RAW PRAWN n. (1)]

come the roots over v. [mid-19C–1910s] (*US campus*) to defeat by trickery. [COME OVER v.[2], ? i.e. to 'trip up']

come the Rothschild v. [late 19C–1910s] to pretend to great wealth. [COME (THE) — v. + the proper name *Rothschild*, the epitome of the fabulously wealthy banker, esp. during the reign of the magnate-loving Edward VII]

come the sergeant v. [mid–late 19C] to act in an unpleasantly authoritarian manner. [COME (THE) — v. + SE *sergeant*]

come the smart-arse v. [1960s+] to pose as being cleverer than one actually is. [COME (THE) — v. + SMART-ARSE n. (1)]

come the spoon v. [mid–late 19C] to court, to make love. [COME (THE) — v. + SPOON n.[1] (2)]

come the tin man v. [20C+] **1** to deceive, to bluff. **2** to make oneself a nuisance. [COME (THE) — v. + SE *tin*, petty, worthless, counterfeit (as opposed to precious metal) + *man*]

come the tin soldier v. *see* COME THE OLD SOLDIER v.

come the touch on v. [1910s+] (*Aus.*) to adopt a manner or attitude. [COME (THE) — v. + TOUCH n.[2]]

come the Traviata v. [mid–late 19C] for a prostitute, to pretend to be suffering from phthisis or pulmonary consumption. [COME (THE) — v. + the Verdi opera *La Traviata* (1853), which was based on Dumas *fils*'s *La Dame aux Camélias*, in which the heroine dies of that disease]

come the ugly with v. (*also* **come the ugly over**) [mid–late

19C] to make threats, to menace. [COME (THE) — v./COME OVER v.[2] + SE *ugly*, unpleasant]

come through v. **1** [20C+] of an object, to deliver, to give up. **2** [20C+] to take over in an emergency, to carry out requirements. **3** [1900s] (*US*) to pay one's debts. **4** [1900s–50s] (*US*) of information, to confess. **5** [1910s+] to act as desired, to do what is wanted. **6** [1920s] to survive, to overcome problems. [fig. uses of SE; note late 19C US religious jargon *come through*, to accept conversion]

come through a side door v. [mid–late 19C] to be born out of wedlock.

come to a sticky end v. [1910s+] to meet great misfortune, esp. a violent death or a prison sentence, usu. said of a person already condemned as 'a bad lot'.

come to bat v. *see* GO TO BAT v.[1].

come-to-bed eyes n. [1920s+] eyes (of either sex) that convey infinite, if not always delivered, sexual promise.

come together v. [1970s] (*US Black*) to dress in high fashion.

come to grass v. *see* GO TO GRASS v. (1).

come to grief v. [mid-19C+] of a person, to fall into difficulties, to fail; of an object, to break (down). [GRIEF n.[1] (1); orig. a sporting phr. meaning to fall from one's horse]

come-to-heaven collar n. [20C+] (*US*) a wing collar. [the wings of the collar presumably resemble those of an angel]

come-to-Jesus adj. [1920s–30s] (*US tramp*) insincerely pious.

come-to-Jesus coat n. [1930s–40s] (*US*) a frock coat. [as worn by, *inter alia*, ministers and preachers]

come-to-Jesus collar n. [20C+] (*Can./US*) a stiff dress collar. [the preference for such collars among revivalist preachers]

come to light (with) v. [1910s+] (*Aus.*) to produce, to deliver, esp. money.

come to one's milk v. *see* BRING SOMEONE TO THEIR MILK v.

come-too-soon n. [1940s–70s] (*US*) an illegitimate child. [? *too soon* for the parents to get married]

come to stay v. [mid-19C–1910s] to become permanent or established.

come to the heath v. [early 19C] to pay out or give money. [? pun on TIP n.[2] (2)/Tiptree *Heath*, in Essex]

come to the mark v. [early 19C] (*UK Und.*) to fulfil a contract, to keep a promise. [thus SE *come up to the mark*]

come to the wrong shop v. [mid-19C+] to make a mistake, esp. in the context of asking the wrong person or going to the wrong place to get one's requirements.

come undone v. (*also* **come unstitched, come unstuck**) [late 19C+] of a person, to find oneself in difficulties; of a situation, to collapse.

come unglued v. [1940s+] to become mentally and emotionally unstable.

come unscrewed v. [1930s+] to go mad.

come unstitched/unstuck v. *see* COME UNDONE v.

come up v.[1] **1** [late 19C] (*Aus.*) to exist, to live. **2** [1930s+] (*US Black*) to turn out, to happen. **3** [1940s+] to appear, to pose. **4** [1960s+] (*US Black*) to grow up. **5** [1990s+] (*US Black*) to do well, to prosper. **6** [1990s+] (*drugs*) of a person, for a drug to start taking effect on them.

come up v.[2] *see* COME ACROSS v. (1).

come up lovely v. [20C+] to turn out well (esp. when it appeared that no such positive outcome was feasible). [ext. of COME UP v.[1] (2)]

come up moldy v. *see* COME OUT MOLDY v.

come up on v. [1950s+] to succeed at or with.

come up on the down train v. [2000s] to be stupid.

come up on the last load v. (*also* **come up the river on a bike**) [1990s+] (*Irish*) to be naïve, gullible; usu. in phrs. *do you think I came up…/I didn't come up…*

come upon the rake v. *see* RAKE v.[1] (2).

come up smelling of violets v. (*also* **come up/out smelling of roses**) [20C+] to survive an unpleasant experience not only unscathed, but actually better placed; thus *so lucky that if he fell in shit he'd come up…*

come up smiling *v.* [mid-19C+] (*orig. boxing*) to face a difficult circumstance without showing fear or complaining. [i.e. when knocked to the canvas one comes up with a (false but brave) smile]

come up tails *v.* [1970s] (*US*) to find oneself in an unpleasant or problematic situation. [the tossing of coins]

come up the Foyle in a bubble *v.* [20C+] (*Ulster*) to be naïve, gullible; usu. in phr. *do you think I came up…/I didn't come up…*. [Northern Ireland's River *Foyle*]

come up the river on a bike *v. see* COME UP ON THE LAST LOAD *v.*

come up to (the chalk) *v.* [mid-19C] (*US*) to perform as expected, to meet expectations. [the chalk mark that indicates the start of a race]

come up to the rack (or jump the fence) *v.* (*also* **stand up to the rack**) [mid-19C–1900s] (*US*) to make a decision to do one thing or another, to stop dithering, to do what one has to do, to accept one's duty. [SE *rack*, racket, i.e. the noise and bustle of a city; thus the image is of entering the urban hustle-bustle, or jumping the fence and heading off for the quiet open spaces of the country]

come up trumps *v.* [mid-19C+] to turn out satisfactorily, esp. when a bad result seems more likely. [card-playing imagery]

come up weak *v.* [1960s] (*US Black*) to disappoint, to fail to reach expectations (whether one's own or those of others). [COME UP v.[1] (2) + SE *weak*]

come up with *v.* [late 19C+] (*orig. US*) to produce, to provide, to present.

come up with the rations *v.* [1910s+] (*orig. milit.*) to be worthless, to be gained without effort. [the image of supplies being sent 'up the line' to the front-line trenches; the orig. WW1 use was to disparage a variety of medals and decorations, handed out for no real achievement]

come Vicksburgh (over) *v.* [mid-19C] (*US*) to break up someone's living quarters. [G. A. Thompson (personal correspondence): '5 gamblers had been lynched in Vicksburg, Miss. in 1835; reported in *Niles' Weekly Register*, July 25, August 1, August 8']

come with it *v.* [1990s+] (*US Black/prison*) to dare someone to do something.

comey *adj. see* COME n. (2).

come yankee over *v. see* YANKEE *v.*

come Yorkshire over *v.* (*also* **put (the) Yorkshire on**) [18C–mid-19C] to cheat. [COME OVER v.[2]; local stereotyping]

comflogsticate *v.* [19C] to astound, to puzzle. [ety. unknown, a nonsense word orig. used in the RN]

comfoozled *adj.* [mid–late 19C] exhausted, overcome (cf. BAMBOOZLE v.). [used and prob. coined by Charles Dickens (1812–70)]

comfort *n.* [early–mid-18C] gin. [its soothing effects; E.P. also notes the US liquor, *Southern Comfort*]

comfortable *adj.* [mid-19C–1950s] (*US*) a euph. for drunk (cf. ABOUT RIGHT phr.[1]).

comfortable importance *n.* **1** [late 17C] a mistress. **2** [late 17C–early 19C] one's wife. [play on SE]

comfortable impudence *n.* [18C–19C] a mistress, esp. when posing as one's wife. [play on SE and parody of COMFORTABLE IMPORTANCE n.]

comical *n.* [late 19C–1910s] a table-napkin. [? users of such items seemed amusing to those who did not usu. bother]

comical chris *n.* [1970s–80s] an act of urination (cf. ANGEL'S KISS n.). [rhy. sl. = PISS n. (2)]

comical farce *n.* [late 19C–1910s] a glass. [rhy. sl.]

comic cuts *n.* (*also* **comics**) [1940s+] (*Aus.*) **1** the stomach. **2** in the game of two-up, the 'guts', i.e. the centre of the betting circle

into which betted money is tossed. **3** the truth. [rhy. sl.; (1) and (2) = GUTS n.[1] (1); (3) fig. use of GUTS n.[1] (2)]

comic singer *n.* [20C+] a singer. [rhy. sl.]

coming *adj.* **1** [17C–18C] pregnant. **2** [late 17C–early 19C] of a woman, wanton, promiscuous. [she is fig. 'coming forward']

coming *phr.* [late 18C+] a phr. called out to say that one is on one's way, 'I'll be with you at once', 'I won't be long'; thus derisive phr., aimed at a slow person, *coming? so is Christmas*.

coming down the hill *phr.* [1940s–50s] (*US prison*) approaching the end of one's sentence.

coming-out pants *n.* [196Cs] (*US*) torn trousers, revealing one's flesh. [pun on SE *come out*, to make one's social debut]

comings *n.* [mid-19C+] semen. [COME n. (2)]

comission *n. see* COMMISSION n.

commanche *n. see* APACHE n.[1] (2).

comm-bat *n.* [2000s] (*US Black*) an aluminium baseball bat converted into a stabbing, cutting weapon. [play on SE *combat/bat*]

commercial *n.*[1] (*Aus./N.Z.*) **1** [late 19C–1910s] an itinerant worker, who travels with his pack on his back while looking for employment. **2** [late 19C+] a commercial traveller. [abbr./an ironic use of SE *commercial traveller*. Note UK Und. *commercial*, a thief who travels to pursue his profession]

commercial *n.*[2] **1** [1940s+] (*Aus./US gay*) a male prostitute, both homo- and heterosexual (cf. ASS PEDDLER n.). **2** [1970s+] (*US gay*) the 'selling point' of a homosexual man or prostitute. [SE *commercial*]

commercial *n.*[3] [1960s+] (*orig. US*) any form of praise, a good reference. [SE *commercial*, a paid advertisement, on radio or TV]

commercial *n.*[4] [1980s+] (*US drugs*) marijuana buds that come in a brick; esp. used of Colombian marijuana (which is packaged in this manner).

commercial queer *n.* (*also* **commercial trade**) [1960s+] (*gay*) a homosexual male prostitute (cf. ASS PEDDLER n.). [SE *commercial* + QUEER n. (4)/TRADE n. (3)]

commersh *n.* [1990s+] (*drugs*) average, unexceptional-quality cannabis. [SE *commercial* (*grade*); note COMMERCIAL n.[4]]

commesse *n.* [1990s+] (*W.I.*) scandal, conflict, illegal behaviour. [Fr. *commerce*, 'business', with implications of illegality, bad behaviour]

commie *n.* (*also* **commy**) [1930s+] a *commu*nist (cf. COMMO n.). [abbr.]

commie *adj.* [1940s+] communist, far-left wing. [COMMIE n.]

commish *n.* **1** [mid-19C+] a *commiss*ion (on a financial or other transaction). **2** [1910s+] a *commiss*ioner (usu. in police situations). [abbr.]

commish *v.* [1900s] to work as a commission merchant. [COMMISH n. (1)]

commissary department *n.* (*also* **commissariat region**) [late 19C–1900s] (*US*) the stomach. [SE *commissary department*, in milit. use that department that deals with the buying, preparing and distribution of food]

commission *n.* (*also* **comission**) [mid-16C–mid-19C] (*UK Und.*) a shirt. [Ital. *camisa*, shirt]

commissioner of Newmarket Heath *n.* [late 16C] a highway robber. [the site of many highway robberies]

commister *n.* [mid-19C] (*orig. UK Und.*) a clergyman. [his *chemise* or surplice]

commit oneself *v.* [20C+] (*Ulster*) usu. of children, to dirty oneself with excrement. [euph. use of SE]

commo *n.* [1940s+] (*Aus./US*) a *commu*nist, or one whose views, from hard left to mildly liberal, are seen as deviant from the speaker's (right-wing/conservative) perspective (cf. COMMIE n.). [abbr. + -O sfx (4); note Aus. *commie* does not have the same political use as UK/US, but refers to those who live in rural communes]

commode-hugging drunk *adj.* [1970s+] (*US campus*)

extremely drunk, to the point of hugging the lavatory bowl to vomit.

commodity *n.* **1** [late 16C–18C] a prostitute (cf. ASS PED-DLER n.). **2** [late 16C–19C] the female genitals. [SE *commodity*, something available for sale or trade; in both senses the woman and/or her body are seen as no more than pieces of merchandise; thus Ned Ward, *The London Spy* (1698): '*Strumpets* in the Streets were grown a scarce Commodity']

common *n.* [20C+] **1** common sense; esp. in adjuration *have/use a bit of common*, use your common sense. **2** common decency. [abbr. SE; note RN jargon *common dog*, common sense]

commoner *n.* [1970s] (*US gay*) a heterosexual.

Common Garden *n.* [early–mid-19C] Covent Garden, London WC2.

common garden gout *n. see* COVENT GARDEN GOUT n.

common law *n.* [late 18C] sexual intercourse.

commons *n.* [17C] a privy, a lavatory. [abbr. SE *common house*]

commonsensible *adj.* [late 19C] (*UK society*) being possessed of common sense.

common sewer *n.* **1** [17C–mid-18C] (*also* **common shore**) a prostitute (cf. BAG n.[4]). **2** [19C] the throat. **3** [19C] a drunkard. **4** [mid-19C] a drink. [all plays on SE *common sewer*, into which everything is poured; (1) the *common shore* was that portion of the Thames riverbank where filth could be left and then washed away by the tide]

communists *n.* [1930s] (*US*) menstruation. [pun on SE *red/*RED n.[3]]

commy *n. see* COMMIE n.

comp *n.* **1** [mid-19C+] a *comp*ositor. **2** [mid-19C+] (*US*) a *comp*liment. **3** [late 19C+] a *comp*limentary pass or ticket. **4** [20C+] (*US campus*) a course in English *comp*osition. **5** [1930s+] (*US*) a *comp*limentary gift, e.g. as given to 'high-rolling' gamblers by a resort hotel, thus also one who receives such hospitality. **6** [1950s+] *comp*etition. **7** [1950s+] *comp*ensation. **8** [1960s] (*US*) a musical *comp*osition. **9** [1980s+] a *comp*rehensive school. **10** [2000s] *comp*ilation. **11** [2000s] a *comp*arison. [abbr.]

comp *v.* [1960s+] to give free tickets, free board and lodging etc, usu. in the context of show business or casino hotels. [COMP n. (3)]

compa *n.* [1960s+] (*US*) a friend, a fellow gang member. [abbr. Sp. *compadre*, a companion]

compadre *n.* (*also* **companero**) [mid-19C+] (*US*) a close male friend. [Sp.]

Company, the *n.* [1960s+] (*US*) the Central Intelligence Agency (CIA). [Sp. *Cia*, abbr. for Company (equivalent of SE *Co.*)]

company man *n.* (*also* **company stiff**) [1940s–50s] (*US*) a worker who is seen by his peers as loyal to the employers rather than the union. [SE *company* + *man*/STIFF n.[2] (7)]

compellance weed *n.* [1940s+] (*W.I.*) marijuana (cf. AFRICAN BUSH n.). [under its influence one is supposedly 'compelled' to do something. This hardly fits, however, with the normal image of the marijuana user as a rather comatose figure. Note *compelling oil/powder*, a sweet-smelling oil or powder prepared by an obeah-man and used in the hope of winning over or controlling a lover or defeating an evil spirit]

compo *n.* [1930s+] (*Aus./N.Z.*) **1** workers' *comp*ensation, payment for time lost after an injury at work. **2** any form of *comp*ensation. [abbr. + -o sfx (4); note WW1 milit. *compo*, pay; money]

compo artist *n.* (*also* **compo king**) [1940s+] (*Aus./N.Z.*) one who is a specialist in the extraction of monetary compensation by faking or exaggerating their supposedly work-related injuries. [COMPO n. (1) + ARTIST sfx/KING n.[1] (1)]

compo-itis *n.* [1940s+] (*Aus./N.Z.*) the counterfeiting or extension of one's disability in the hope of gaining more compensation payments. [COMPO n. (1) + sfx -*itis*]

compoodle *n.* [1900s–10s] (*US*) a large, mixed-up collection of objects or people. [var. on CABOODLE n.]

compos *adj.* **1** [19C+] sane. **2** [1970s] sober. [opposite of NON COMPOS adj.]

compositum *n.* [early 18C] (*UK Und.*) a counterfeit coin made from a mixed metal.

comprador *n.* **1** [early 17C–early 19C] (*Anglo-Ind.*) a house steward. **2** [mid-19C] (*Anglo-Chinese*) a butler. [Port. *comprador*, a purchaser, in this case of household supplies]

comprende? *phr.* [1970s+] (*orig. US*) you understand? [Sp.; note WW1/WW2 *compree*, understand, f. Fr. *compris*]

compress *v.* [17C–early 18C] of a man, to have sexual intercourse. [the effect of his weight when adopting the SE *missionary position*]

compute *v.* [1960s+] (*orig. US*) to work out; usu. in negative phr. *that doesn't compute*. [lit. 'add up'. Popularized in 1964 CBS TV series *My Living Doll*. Note mid-17C–18C SE *compute*, to estimate, to reckon, to take account of, to take into consideration]

compy *v.* [1940s] (*US Black*) to understand; often as interrog. *compy?* you understand? [SE *comprehend* or f. Fr. *comprenez?*, 'do you understand?', imported by GIs returning from WW2; note WW1 equivalent *compree* (f. Fr. *compris*)]

con *n.*[1] **1** [early 17C] *con*fidant. **2** [mid-19C–1910s] *con*undrum. **3** [late 19C] *con*tract. **4** [late 19C–1910s] *con*formist. **5** [late 19C+] a railroad *con*ductor. **6** [late 19C+] a *con*fidence man. **7** [late 19C+] a *con*fidence game or trick. **8** [late 19C+] a *con*vict; thus EX-CON n. **9** [1900s–50s] a deceptive speech. **10** [1930s+] a *con*viction. **11** [1940s] *con*fidence. [abbr.; (9) *con*fidence trick]

con *n.*[2] [20C+] (*US*) **1** tuberculosis. **2** a sufferer from tuberculosis. [abbr. SE *con*sumption]

con *adj.* [late 19C+] pertaining to confidence trickery or confidence tricksters; in weakened sense, deceitful. [CON n.[1] (6)]

con *v.* (*orig. US*) **1** [late 19C+] (*also* **con along**) to fool a victim in any form of confidence trick. **2** [late 19C+] to persuade, to coax (without criminal intent), usu. as *con someone into/out of*, to trick someone into doing something or giving up something they would prefer to hold on to. **3** [1960s+] to tell stories, to fantasize. [abbr. SE *con*fidence trick]

con and coal *n.* [20C+] unemployment benefit (cf. BLESS MY SOUL n.). [rhy. sl. = SE *dole*]

Conan Doyle *n.* (*also* **Jack Doyle**) [1930s+] a boil (on the neck). [rhy. sl.; ult. Sir Arthur *Conan Doyle* (1859–1930), novelist and creator of Sherlock Holmes]

Conan Doyle *v.* [late 19C+] to boil (a kettle). [rhy. sl.; for ety. *see* CONAN DOYLE n.]

con-artist *n.* [1930s+] a confidence trickster, a fraud. [CON v. (1) + ARTIST sfx]

conbobberated *adj.* [mid-19C+] (*US*) upset, disconcerted, disturbed. [CONBOBBERATION n.]

conbobberation *n.* [mid-19C] (*US*) a disturbance, an argument. [SE sfx *con*-, together + BOBBERY n. (1)]

conbobbolate *v.* (*also* **combobbolate**) [mid-19C] (*US*) to think, to ponder, to 'calculate'. [CONBOBBERATED adj. + SE *calculate*]

con boss *n.* (*also* **boss con**) [1910s+] (*US prison*) an influential convict who runs a gang within a prison. [CON n.[1] (8) + BOSS n.[2] (1)]

concaves and convexes *n.* [early–mid-19C] 'a pack of cards contrived for cheating, by cutting all the cards from the two to the seven concave, and all from the eight to the king convex. Then by cutting the pack breadthwise a convex card is cut, and by cutting it lengthwise a concave is secured' (Hotten, 1864). [the shapes of the doctored cards]

concern *n.* [19C] **1** the penis (cf. AFFAIR n.[1]). **2** the vagina. [SE *concern*, a thing, an appurtenance]

concerned *adj.*[1] [late 17C–mid-19C] a euph. for drunk; thus *concerned with drink*, *concerned in drink*.

concerned *adj.*[2] *see* CONSARNED adj.

concertina *n.*[1] [late 19C] (*UK Und.*) a squashed top hat. [its shape]

concertina *n.*[2] [late 19C+] (*Aus.*) **1** a wrinkly sheep. **2** a side of lamb or mutton. **3** a style of leggings with wrinkles in them. [resemblance]

conch *n.*[1] **1** [mid-19C+] **1** (*W.I.*) a native of the Bahamas. **2** (*US*) a poor White native of the Florida Keys. **3** a native of North Carolina. [SE *conch*, a variety of shellfish for which such people fish]

conch *n.*[2] (*also* **conchie, conshy**) [1960s+] (*US campus/Aus.*) a devotedly hard worker. [abbr. SE *conscientious*]

conchie *n.* (*also* **concho, conchy, conscie, conshi, conshie**) [1910s+] a *conscientious* objector. [abbr.; Brophy & Partridge, *Songs and Slang of the British Soldier* (1930), note 'properly *Conscie*']

conchie *adj.* [1980s] (*Aus.*) *conscientious*. [abbr.]

Conchy *n.* [1910s–20s] (*US tramp*) Connecticut.

conchy *n. see* CONCHIE *n.*

conchy Joe *n.* [20C+] (*W.I., Baham.*) **1** a creole White or Caribbean person who has, to all appearances, no Black ancestry (although there will be a distant relation). **2** a poor White. **3** a mixed-race Bahamian, who sees themself as socially superior to Blacks. [CONCH *n.*[1] (1) + generic *Joe*]

concoct a snoot *v. see* COCK A SNOOT (AT) *v.*

con-con *n.* [1980s+] (*drugs*) a dark, oily substance that remains in a pipe after crack or FREEBASE *n.* cocaine has been smoked.

concorde *n.* [1990s+] (*W.I., Jam.*) a $100 bill. [it 'flies away' very quickly]

concrete *n.*[1] [1940s+] (*W.I.*) any starchy, indigestible foods, e.g. dumplings, fufu, usu. with peas (legumes) or beans mixed in.

concrete *n.*[2] [2000s] a city.

concrete overcoat *n.* (*also* **concrete clogs, ...drawers, ...footmuff, ...overshoes, ...slippers, ...socks**) [1970s+] a supposed gangland method of murder; the victim's feet are dunked in quick-drying concrete and they are then dumped into a river or overboard from a boat, the irremovable weight ensuring that they drown.

condemned *adj.* (*also* **condarned, condigned**) [mid-19C–1920s] a euph. synon. for DAMNED *adj.*; thus *condemnation*, DAMNATION *n.*

condo *n.* [1960s+] (*US*) a *condo*minium, i.e. an apartment house in which the units are owned individually, not by a company or cooperative. [abbr.]

condog *v.* [late 16C–17C] to concur, to agree. [*condog* is the source of a long-lived lexicographical 'chestnut'. While assembling his dictionary, the lexicographer Adam Littleton (1627–94) gave the Lat. word *concurro* (to meet, to assemble) to his assistant. The assistant, assuming, from the similarity of sounds, that the English followed the Lat., asked Littleton: 'Concur, I suppose, Sir?' Littleton replied tetchily, 'Concur! condog!' Fearing to argue, the assistant listed 'condog' in the manuscript as one of the meanings of *concurro*. It duly appeared in the first edn. Unfortunately, the story is marred by chronology, for the *OED*'s first cit. predates Littleton's work by 86 years]

conductor *n.* [1970s] (*drugs*) one who guides a person who is taking LSD. [plays on the LSD TRIP *n.*[4] (1) + SE *bus conductor*]

condy *n.* [1920s+] *Condy's* fluid, a strong solution of sodium manganate or permanganate, used as a disinfectant. [abbr.; proper name of Henry Bollmann *Condy*, 19C English manufacturer of chemicals]

condy boy *n.* [1940s–50s] (*Aus.*) a jack of all trades employed by a brothel. [the use of diluted *Condy's fluid* as a post-intercourse disinfectant]

condy's, the *n.* [1940s] (*Aus.*) advice; usu. in phr. *maleesh/ mahlish the condy's*, lit. never mind the condy's, i.e. forget the preliminaries, let's get on with it. [*Condy's fluid*, which, as a disinfectant, presumably 'deals with any problem' (+ MALEESH phr.); note Aus. milit. *Abdullah with the Condies*, an Egyptian menial]

cone *n.*[1] [late 19C] (*US*) the head. [resemblance]

cone *n.*[2] [1980s+] **1** (*Aus. drugs*) a metal cone with a hole in the centre, usu. made of aluminium or brass and used for smoking cannabis. **2** (*US drugs*) a conical cannabis cigarette, which is tapered by rolling with 2 or more papers glued at an angle (cf. BONE *n.*[11]).

conehead *n.* [1980s+] (*orig. US*) a strange and foolish person. [the *Coneheads*, a bizarre space-dwelling 'family', were created for the US TV show *Saturday Night Live* in 1976]

coner *n.* [1950s+] a pickpocket who makes contact with a prospective victim by dropping an ice-cream cone at his or her feet.

coneroo *n.* (*also* **conneroo**) [1940s] (*US*) a confidence trickster. [CON *n.*[1] (6) + -EROO sfx]

coney *see also under* CONY *and its combs.*

coney *n.* (*also* **cogniac, coniack, koniack**) [19C] (*US Und.*) counterfeit banknotes; thus *coney man*, one who passes counterfeit notes; *coney traffic*, counterfeit money trafficking.

coneyacker *n. see* KONIACKER *n.*

coney court *n. see* CUNNY ALLEY *n.*

Coney Island *n.*[1] **1** [late 19C–1960s] a glass of beer. **2** [late 19C+] a snack consisting of fried clams. **3** [1950s] a long bun filled with meat, cheese and various relishes. **4** [1950s+] a hot dog, esp. when served in a bun with fried onions, chili sauce and mustard. **5** [1950s+] a hot dog stand. [the *Coney Island* resort in Brooklyn, New York, where such foodstuffs were the staple of visitors. (2) popular 1870–80 gave way to (3) and (4)]

Coney Island *n.*[2] [1930s–40s] (*US prison/Und.*) the room used by police for interrogation. [ironic use of the place, where one normally goes for pleasure]

Coney Island chicken *n.* [20C+] a spiced, heated sausage or frankfurter, esp. when served in a bun with fried onions, chili sauce and mustard. [SE *Coney Island* + SE *chicken*]

Coney Island head *n.* [late 19C–1960s] (*US*) a beer that has more frothy head than actual beer. [the way visitors were defrauded by the bartenders of Coney Island, New York's leisure centre]

Coney Island red hot *n.* [20C+] (*US*) a spiced, heated sausage or frankfurter, esp. when served in a bun with fried onion, chili sauce and mustard. [SE *Coney Island* + RED HOT *n.*[1] (1)]

Coney Island whitefish *n.* (*also* **Canarsie whitefish**) [1930s+] (*US*) a used contraceptive floating at the edge of the beach. [the popularity with lovers of the beaches of New York's Coney Island or Canarsie]

coney warren *n. see* CUNNY WARREN *n.*

confab *n.* [18C+] a conversation, an argument. [SE *confabulation*, a chat, a conversation]

confab *v.* [1930s–40s] (*US*) to have a conversation, to argue. [CONFAB *n.*]

confeck *adj.* (*also* **confect**) [17C–early 19C] (*UK Und.*) counterfeit, fake. [SE *confect*, to prepare or mix up ingredients]

confectionary *n.* (*also* **confectionery**) **1** [mid–late 19C] a bar or liquor shop. **2** [1920s–30s] an illegal drinking establishment. [euph.]

confectionery *n. see* SWEET *n.* (1).

confessional *n.* [late 19C] the vagina. [where a FATHER CONFESSOR *n.* appears]

confess the corn *v.* (*also* **confess the cob**) [early 19C–1940s] (*orig. US*) to admit an error; thus *confession*, a tutorial. [for ety. *see* ACKNOWLEDGE THE CORN *v.*]

confidence *v.* [late 17C; late 19C–1940s] (*US*) to defraud, to swindle. [abbr. SE *confidence trick*]

confidence buck *n.* [late 19C] a confidence trick. [SE *confidence* + BUCK *v.*[2] (4)]

confidence-queen *n.* **1** [late 19C] (*US*) a female detective. **2** [1990s+] (*US campus*) a female confidence trickster. [SE *confidence* + QUEEN sfx (1); (1) ? in plain-clothes she 'cons' her victims, i.e. the criminals]

conflab *n.* [mid-19C–1940s] (*US*) a conversation, an argument. [var. on CONFAB n.]

conflab *v.* [2000s] to chat with, to argue. [CONFLAB n.]

conflabberated *adj.* [mid-19C–1910s] upset, perturbed, unnerved. [ety. unknown, a nonsense word]

conflabberation *n.* [mid-19C–1920s] a confused wrangle. [CONFLABBERATED adj.]

confloption *n.* [late 19C] an unshapely, grotesquely twisted thing. [nonsense word, ? formed f. SE pfx *con-*, together + *flop* v., collapse]

conflummox *v.* [mid-19C+] to fool, to confuse, to overcome by trickery. [ext. of FLUMMOX v.[1] (4)]

conflustercate *v. see* CONFUSTICATE v.

confo *n.* [1930s–50s] (*Aus.*) a *conf*erence. [abbr. + -o sfx (4)]

confound! *excl.* [17C+] an all-purpose euph., used as a mild oath, esp. as adj. *confounded*, and excl. *confound it!* (orig. *God confound it!* or *Mahound confound it!*). [a special use of SE *confound* to mean 'bring to perdition']

confusion *n.* **1** [late 19C+] an argument leading to a fight. **2** [1970s] a street fight, a riot.

confusticate *v.* (*also* **conflustercate**) [mid-19C–1930s] (*US*) to confuse. [SE *confound* or *confuse* and/or synon. dial. *confuscate* (+ SE *fluster*)]

con-game *n.* [late 19C+] (*orig. US*) a piece of confidence trickery. [CON v. (1) + GAME n.[2] (3)]

conger *n.* [late 17C–18C] a group of booksellers, working together in business. [? SE *conger*, a large species of saltwater eel, or f. Fr. *congrès*, a congress or SE *congeries*, a pile, a heap, a mass. B.E.'s 'knot' became known as the 'Old Conger' and was succeeded *c.*1700 by their rivals, the 'New Conger', publishers, *inter alia*, of Bailey's and Cocker's Dictionaries]

conger (eel) *v.* [1990s+] (*UK Und.*) to inform, to betray. [rhy. sl. = SQUEAL (ON) v. (1)]

Congo *n. see* CONGO (BUSH) n.

congo *n.*[1] (*also* **congou, kongo**) [late 18C–mid-19C] tea. [Chinese *kung-fu*, work, and workman; thus *kung-fu-ch'a*, tea on which work or labour is expended; *congou, congo* or *kongo* was a type of black tea, imported to England during 18C]

congo *n.*[2] [mid-19C+] a derog. term for a Black person, esp. one with a notably dark complexion (cf. AFRICAN APE n.). [US slave trade jargon *Congo*, a slave brought from the Congo nation. The term is also used in the W.I. with an additional element of poverty and a rough appearance]

congo *n.*[3] [1920s+] (*Aus./US*) a *Cong*regationalist. [abbr. + -o sfx (4)]

Congo (bush) *n.* [1960s+] (*drugs*) marijuana from the Congo area of Africa (cf. ACAPULCO (GOLD) n.; AFRICAN BUSH n.). [SE *Congo* + BUSH n.[5] (1)]

Congo croquet *n.* [20C+] (*US*) the game of craps dice (cf. ABYSSINIAN POLO n.). [CONGO n.[2]]

congo patois *n.* [late 19C] (*US*) slang, usu. Black slang. [CONGO n.[2] + SE *patois*, a local dialect]

congo-saw *n.* [early 19C] (*W.I.*) flattery. [CONGO n.[2] + SE *saw*, speech, discourse]

congou *n. see* CONGO n.[1]

congrats! *excl.* [late 19C+] *congrat*ulations; thus synon. [1930s] *congraggers*; [20C+] *congratters*. [abbr. (+ -ER sfx)]

coniack *n. see* CONEY n.

coniacker *n. see* KONIACKER n.

conish *adj.* [early–mid-19C] fashionable, smart, genteel; thus (*Scot.*) *conish cove*, a fashionable gentleman. [? CONY n.[2] on the theory that such a figure may well fall prey to a clever con-man; E.P. suggests perversion of *tonish*, fashionable]

coniwobble *n.* [early 18C] a dupe, a fool. [ext. of CONY n.[2]]

con job *n.* [1920s+] (*US*) a confidence trick. [CON n.[1] (7) + JOB n.[3] (2)]

conjobble *v.* **1** [late 17C–mid-18C] to settle, to discuss. **2** [early

18C] to have sexual intercourse. [SE pfx *con-*, together + JOB n.[4], but note *jabber*; + 17C *job*, sexual intercourse]

conjugals *n.* [20C+] sexual intercourse, esp. in a marital context.

conjuror *n.* **1** [early 17C] a pickpocket. **2** [late 17C–early 19C] (*UK Und.*) a trial judge; thus *go before the conjuror*, to be tried at the assize. [(1) their mutual dependence on sleight of hand; (2) what he 'pulls out of his hat' is a sentence]

conk *n.*[1] (*also* **konk**) **1** [early–mid-19C] (*UK Und.*) an informer, a thief who betrays his accomplices. **2** [early 19C–1900s] a policeman. **3** [early 19C+] the nose; thus a nickname for one who has a large nose. **4** [mid-19C+] the head. **5** [late 19C+] a punch, usu. on the nose. **6** [1940s] intelligence; thinking. [? Lat. *concha*, a shell, and Gk *kogcha*, anything hollow; (1) and (2) f. (3), i.e. they 'sniff things out']

conk *n.*[2] [1940s+] (*US Black*) **1** (*also* **conk job**) hair that has been straightened through the application of a special mixture. **2** pomade; hair grease. [*Congolene*, a fiery liquid, combining lye, eggs, potatoes and other ingredients, used in the artificial straightening of naturally kinky Black (Negro) hair]

conk *v.*[1] **1** [early 19C; 1920s+] (*also* **konk**) to hit, esp. on the nose or head. **2** [1910s–40s] (*US*) to kill. **3** [1930s+] (*also* **conk someone out**) to knock unconscious. **4** [1940s] in fig. use, to burden with, to assail. [CONK n.[1] (3)/CONK n.[1] (5) + echoic]

conk *v.*[2] (*also* **konk**) [1940s+] (*US Black*) to straighten hair with a mixture based on Congolene; thus *conked*, having such hair (cf. FRY (ONE'S HAIR) v.; GAS v.[2]; MAKE v.[8]; PRESS ONE'S HAIR v.; PROCESS v.; VISIT ONE'S INDIAN COUSIN v.). [CONK n.[2] (1)]

conk *v.*[3] *see* CONK (OUT) v.

conk-buster *n.* (*also* **konk-buster**) [1930s–50s] (*US Black*) **1** an intellectual. **2** a difficult problem. **3** cheap liquor. [CONK n.[1] (4) + BUST v.[1] (4); all defs. imply the straining of one's brain]

conked *adj.*[1] (*also* **conk-haired, conk-headed, konked**) [1940s+] (*US Black*) having hair that has been straightened; thus *unconked*, hair that is in its natural state. [CONK n.[2] (1)]

conked *adj.*[2] [1950s] (*US*) drunk (cf. ANNIHILATED adj.). [fig. use of CONK v.[1] (1)]

conked (out) *adj.* (*also* **conking, konked (out)**) [1910s+] **1** of a machine or engine, broken, malfunctioning, no longer working. **2** of a person, collapsed, asleep, having given up; of a situation or object, collapsed, failed. **3** of a person, dead. [CONK (OUT) v. (1)]

conked up *adj.* [1940s–70s] (*US*) injured, hurt. [CONK v.[1] (1)]

conker *n.* (*also* **konker**) [early–mid-19C] a very hard blow. [CONK v.[1] (1)]

conkers *n.* [1990s+] the testicles (cf. ACORNS n.). [resemblance to SE *conker*, a horse chestnut]

conkers deep *phr.* [1990s+] having the penis fully within the vagina. [the CONKERS n. are 'inside']

conk-haired/-headed *adj. see* CONKED adj.[1]

conkhouse *n.* [20C+] (*US Black*) the head. [CONK n.[1] (4)]

conking *adj. see* CONKED (OUT) adj.

conk job *n. see* CONK n.[2] (1).

conk off *v.* (*orig. US*) **1** [1940s] to malfunction, to fail. **2** [1940s+] to fall asleep, to sleep. **3** [1950s–60s] to stop work, to skive. **4** [1950s+] to die. [var. on CONK (OUT) v.]

conk (out) *v.* **1** [1910s+] usu. of machinery, to collapse, to break down, to malfunction. **2** [1930s+] to lose consciousness, to faint, to collapse. **3** [1940s+] to give up. **4** [1940s+] to die. **5** [1940s+] to fall asleep. [CONK v.[1]]

conkpiece *n.* [1940s] (*US Black*) the head. [CONK n.[1] (4)]

conk someone off *v.* [1940s] (*US*) to kill. [ext. of CONK v.[1] (2)]

conk someone out *v. see* CONK v.[1] (3).

conk the cardinal *v.* [late 19C+] to masturbate. [CONK v.[1] (1); var. on BANG THE BISHOP v.]

conky *n.* (*also* **konky**) [mid-19C+] a nickname given to anyone with an especially prominent nose. [CONK n.[1] (3); the best known such figure was the Duke of Wellington, widely known as 'Old Conky']

conky *adj.* [late 19C+] sub-standard, second-rate. [CONK v.¹ (1), i.e. 'knock about', strengthened by CONK (OUT) v. (1)]

con-man *n.* **1** [late 19C] (*US*) a flatterer. **2** [late 19C–1920s] (*orig. US*) (*also* **con-player**) a confidence trickster; thus *con-woman*. **3** [1930s] (*US*) a former convict. [CON v. (1); (2) later use is SE]

con merchant *n.* [1930s+] (*US*) a confidence trickster. [CON v. (1) + MERCHANT n.]

con mob *n.* [1930s–40s] (*US Und.*) a team of confidence tricksters.

connaught (ranger) *n.* [1970s] a stranger. [rhy. sl.; ult. *see* CONNAUGHT RANGERS n.]

connaught rangers *n.* [1940s–50s] (*bingo*) the number 8 (cf. ALDERSHOT LADIES n.). [the *Connaught Rangers* (disbanded 1922) were also the 88th Regiment of Foot; their army nickname was The Devil's Own]

connect *n. see* CONNECTION n.

connect *v.* **1** [mid-19C+] (*US*) to meet; usu. as *connect with*. **2** [1900s–30s] (*US*) to succeed in obtaining something, e.g. the spoils of a burglary. **3** [1920s+] (*drugs*) to obtain drugs, usu. by keeping a spec. appointment with the dealer. **4** [1930s] to achieve sexual fulfilment. [fig. uses of SE]

connected *adj.* **1** [1920s+] (*orig. US*) having links to someone influential, whether legitimate or otherwise. **2** [1970s+] (*US*) being a member of an organized crime syndicate.

Connecticut River pork *n.* [19C] (*US*) shad. [the plentiful supplies of shad in the Connecticut River]

connection *n.* (*also* **connect, connexion**) [1920s+] **1** (*orig. US*) a supplier of contraband liquor. **2** (*orig. US*) a supplier of drugs. **3** (*orig. US*) the act of contacting a drug dealer; thus *connection dough*, money for drugs. **4** (*orig. US*) the person with whom one achieves sexual fulfilment; thus the act itself. **5** (*orig. US*) any form of connection or go-between, e.g. one who helps with a crime. **6** (*US prison*) a corrupt guard who helps inmates smuggle contraband into prison; an amenable, friendly guard. [CON-NECT v.]

connector *n.* [1920s] (*US Und.*) a beggar. [CONNECT v. (2)]

connect with *v. see* CONNECT v. (1).

conned *adj.* [late 19C+] tricked, hoaxed, fooled. [CON v. (1)]

conneroo *n. see* CONEROO n.

connexion *n. see* CONNECTION n.

conney-berry/-burrow *n. see* CONY-BURROW n.

Connie *n.* **1** [1950s] a *Constellation* airliner. **2** [1970s] a Lincoln *Continental*. [abbr. + sfx -*ie*]

connie *n.* (*also* **conny**) **1** [1900s] (*US Und.*) a person with tuberculosis. **2** [1900s–70s] (*Aus./US*) a tram or bus *conductor*. [abbr.]

connie-burrow *n. see* CONY-BURROW n. (2).

conniver about *v.* [1930s+] (*Aus.*) to wander aimlessly. [dial. *conniver*, to stare or gape]

conny *see also under* CONY *and its combs.*

conny *n. see* CONNIE n.

conny wobble *n.* (*also* **conny wabble**) [late 18C–early 19C] a drink made of eggs and brandy beaten up together. [? CONY n.² + SE *wobble* or ? COLLYWOBBLES n.]

coño *n.* [1940s+] (*US*) **1** the vagina; thus, women in the context of potential seduction. **2** a general term of abuse. [Sp. sl. *coño*, CUNT n.¹ (1)/CUNT n.² (1)]

coño! *excl.* [1920s+] (*US/P.R.*) a general excl. of fury, shock etc. [Sp. *coño*, CUNT! excl.]

conoblin rig *n.* [late 18C–mid-19C] (*UK Und.*) cutting the strings that attached large pieces of coal to the doorways of coal sheds, i.e. stealing coal. [? + RIG n.² (2)]

conoodle *v. see* CANOODLE v.

con-player *n. see* CON-MAN n. (2).

Cons *n.* [1960s+] *Converse* All-Star basketball boots. [abbr. of brandname]

con safos *phr.* [1960s+] (*US*) **1** 'nobody can mess with this', a

slogan used by the Mexican gangs of Los Angeles, often abbr. as *c/s* and written, as a graffito, after the gang's name. **2** a general term of approval (and latterly used as a magazine title). [Sp.]

consarn *v.* [mid–late 19C] (*US*) a euph. for DAMN v., used in mild oaths, e.g. *consarn it!* [SE *concern*]

consarned *adj.* (*also* **concerned**) [mid-19C–1900s] (*US*) a euph. for DAMNED adj.; often ext. as *I'll be consarned, I'm consarned*. [CONSARN v.]

conscie *n. see* CONCHIE n.

conscience-keeper *n.* [late 18C–early 19C] 'a superior, who by his influence makes his dependants act as he pleases' (Grose, 1788).

consent job *n.* (*also* **owner's job**) [1950s–60s] (*US Und.*) any form of crime committed with the connivance of the victim; they will be able to collect the insurance. [SE + JOB n.³ (1)]

conshi/conshie *n. see* CONCHIE n.

conshun's price *n.* [mid-19C] (*Anglo-Chinese*) a fair price. [mispron. of *conscience's price*]

conshy *n. see* CONCH n.².

considerable *adv.* [mid-19C–1920s] (*US*) to a great extent.

considering *adv.* [mid-18C+] considering the circumstances, taking everything into account, usu. at the end of sentences.

consignment *n.* [1990s+] (*W.I.*) a term meaning adultery, usu. shouted out at a passing couple, one of whom is known to be going out with somebody else. [on *consignment* from somewhere else]

consolation *n.* [mid-19C] (*US*) alcohol, usu. whisky.

con someone into/out of *v. see* CON v. (2).

consonant-choker *n.* [late 19C–1900s] someone who slurs their 'r's and drops their 'g's.

constab *n.* [20C+] (*W.I.*) a policeman, a constable. [abbr.; note dial. *constab tick*, a cattle tick – its stripes resemble those on the constable's trousers; also *constab-macka*, a large prickle]

constant *n.* [1990s+] (*US Black*) a regular member of a given social scene. [SE *constant*]

constant screamer *n.* [late 19C–1910s; 2000s] a concertina. [joc. mispron.]

constipated *adj.* [1920s–30s] reluctant to part with money.

constitutional *n.* **1** [early 19C+] a walk taken for health's sake. **2** [1930s+] (*Aus.*) gin and bitters. **3** [1950s] (*US drugs*) the first injection of the day. [SE *constitution*, one's physical and mental state]

consult Dr Jerkoff *v.* [20C+] (*US*) to masturbate. [SE *consult* + JERK OFF v.¹ (1)]

consumah *n.* (*also* **consumer**) [17C–19C] (*Anglo-Ind.*) a butler. [Persian *khansamah*, house-steward]

consume *v.*¹ [mid-18C] a euph. for DAMN v. used in mild oaths.

consume *v.*² [1980s] (*US campus*) to drink alcohol. [euph.]

consumedly *adv.* [early 18C] extremely, very much so. [coined as sl., the term was taken up by 18C dramatists and absorbed into literary SE]

consumer *n. see* CONSUMAH n.

consumption stick *n.* [1910s] (*Aus.*) a cigarette. [SE *consumption*, tuberculosis, a disease of the lungs]

contact habit *n.* [1950s–60s] (*drugs*) the drug-like sensations a non-user, usu. a dealer, gains from constant association with users. [SE *contact* + HABIT n. (1)]

contact high *n.* (*also* **contact**) [1960s+] (*drugs*) the marijuana world's equivalent of passive smoking; the sensations that a non-smoker can achieve through the simple act of being in the same room as those who smoke; thus inhaling the drug willy-nilly, as well as picking up on the particular atmosphere generated by a roomful of smokers; similarly ext. to LSD, MDMA etc. [SE *contact* + HIGH n.¹ (1)]

contact lens *n.* [1980s+] (*drugs*) LSD (cf. A n.³). [its hallucinatory effects + ? ref. to 'making contact' with one's inner self]

con talk *n.* [late 19C–1900s] (*US*) insincerity, lies. [CON n.[1] (7) or CON v. (1) + SE *talk*]

content *adj.* [18C–early 19C] (*UK Und.*) dead. [ironic use of the SE; a euph. that compares with such as 'gone to his heavenly rest' etc]

continent *n.* [late 19C] (*US*) a euph. for *hell*, e.g. *what the continent do you mean by that?* [? link to CONTINENTAL n.]

continental *n.* [19C+] (*orig. US*) something worthless; thus phr. *not worth a continental*; also used as an adj. in combs., e.g. *a continental cuss, a continental copper, a continental damn.* [SE *continental*, a coin issued by the Continental Congress during the American War of Independence (1775–83); the coins lost all value with the ending of the war; but note Seal, *The Lingo* (1999): 'this almost obsolete phrase is much more likely to be a polite form of don't give a fuck deriving from the reputation of the Continent for liberated, even excessive sexual behaviour']

continuations *n.* [mid-19C] **1** trousers. **2** tights. [trousers 'continue' the waistcoat; orig. gaiters]

contract *n.* [late 19C+] a paid assignment usu. to murder someone but also to get them into some less severe form of difficulty; thus phr. *put/take out a contract on*, to arrange to have someone killed; *contract killer*, a killer for hire.

contract *v.* [1990s+] (*orig. US Und.*) to hire someone to kill a specific individual. [CONTRACT n.]

contrapunctum *n.* [mid-17C] the vagina. [Lat. *contrapunctum*, lit. 'counter-point'. The penis is the 'point' in this context]

contraries *n.* [mid-16C–early 19C] any form of false or legitimate dice, to be brought into and withdrawn from a game as the cheater desires. [such dice are 'contrary' to those currently in play]

contrary *adj.* [mid-19C+] antagonistic, perverse, obstinately self-willed.

control *v.* [1970s+] (*W.I. Rasta/UK Black*) **1** to be in charge of, to be responsible for, to own, to take. **2** to procure, to find, to arrange.

control freak *n.* [1970s+] (*orig. US*) a person who is never satisfied unless they are in absolute control of a situation. [SE *control* + FREAK sfx]

contwisted *adj.* [mid-19C] (*US*) a euph. for DAMNED adj. [SE pfx *con-*, together + *twisted*]

conundrum *n.* [mid-17C–19C] the vagina (cf. ARTICLE n.). [SE *conundrum*, 'a whim, crotchet, maggot, conceit'; ? intensified by 19C 'a thing that one is puzzled to name, a "what-d'ye-call-it"' (*OED*)]

convenience *n.* (*also* **place of convenience/resort**) [19C] a euph. for a privy, a chamberpot.

convenient *n.* (*also* **convenience, conveniency**) **1** [late 17C] a wife. **2** [late 17C–early 18C] a prostitute (cf. PUBLIC CONVENIENCE n.). **3** [late 17C–early 18C] the vagina, and by metonymy its possessor. **4** [late 17C–mid-19C] a mistress. **5** [late 17C–mid-19C] (*also* **convenient house**) a brothel.

convent *n.* [mid-17C–mid-18C] a brothel (cf. ABBESS n.). [ironic use of SE]

conversate *v.* [1980s+] (*US Black*) to talk, usu. in a lively, demonstrative manner. [abbr. SE *conversation*]

conversation *n.* [1990s+] (*US Black*) a romantic 'line', used for the purposes of seduction. [CONVERSATE v.; note Shakespearian *conversation*, sexual intimacy]

conversation fluid *n.* [20C+] (*US*) illicitly distilled whisky. [it 'lubricates' conversation]

conversation water *n.* (*US*) **1** [late 19C] beer. **2** [1900s–20s] champagne. [it 'lubricates' conversation]

converse with harry palm *v.* [1990s+] to masturbate (cf. FOUR SISTERS ON THUMB STREET n.; FUCK MRS PALMER v.; FUCK PALMELA v.; GO ON A DATE WITH HANDREA AND PALMELA v.; GO STEADY WITH ONE'S RIGHT HAND v.; HAVE A DATE WITH FISTY PALMER v.; MAKE A RENDEZVOUS WITH MRS HAND v.; MARY FIST n.; MEET MARY PALM AND HER FIVE SISTERS v.; MEET ROSIE HANCOCK v.; MEET WITH MOTHER THUMB AND HER FOUR DAUGHTERS v.; MR PALMER AND HIS FIVE SONS n.; MOTHER FIST AND HER FIVE DAUGHTERS n.; MRS PALM AND HER FIVE DAUGHTERS n.; ROSY PALM (AND HER FIVE SISTERS) n.; PAM AND HER FIVE SISTERS n.; PATSY PALMER AND HER FIVE DAUGHTERS n.; TAKE AN OUTING WITH TOM THUMB AND HIS FOUR BROTHERS v.). [ult. SE *palm*; *Harry* = ? pun. on the 'hairs that will grow on a masturbator's palm'; ? ref. to Len Deighton's anonymous intelligence agent anti-hero, named Harry Palmer for the 1960s films starring Michael Caine]

conversion job *n.* [1940s+] a severe beating, with or without some form of weapon. [a healthy body is 'converted' into a seriously injured, even dead one]

convertible *adj.* [1970s+] (*US gay*) bisexual.

convey *v.* [mid-15C+] to steal.

conveyancer *n.* (*also* **conveyance, conveyer**) **1** [late 16C–mid-19C] a thief. **2** [mid-19C–1930s] a pickpocket. [CONVEY v. + pun on SE; i.e. he 'conveys' one's money etc to his own pocket]

conveyancing *n.* [late 16C–19C] theft, stealing. [CONVEY v.; intensified by the pun on SE *conveyancer*, a lawyer who investigates titles to property]

convictitis *n.* [1940s–50s] (*UK prison*) the illusion, fostered by too long a career in the prison service, that every prisoner is about to attack one for no other reason than that one is a warder. [SE *convict* + sfx *-itis*, usu. used of a disease]

convincer *n.* **1** [1900s–50s] a persuasive action or speech. **2** [1930s–50s] a weapon. **3** [1940s] (*US Und.*) the large initial profit that lures a victim into a confidence trick. [SE *convincer*, that which convinces]

convincing ground *n.* [1940s] (*Aus.*) a place at which prize or grudge fights are held. [the fighters attempt to 'convince' each other of the error of their ways]

convo *n.* [1990s+] (*Aus.*) a conversation. [abbr. + -o sfx (4)]

convoy *n.* [1930s] (*Irish*) a party or gathering to say goodbye to a departing emigrant.

conwise *adj.* [1930s+] (*US prison*) **1** well-adjusted to prison life, capable of sustaining one's existence in prison. **2** manipulative of the system. [CON n.[1] (8) + -WISE sfx (1)]

con-woman *n. see* CON-MAN n. (2).

con work *n.* [1920s] (*US*) insincerity, lies. [CON v. (1) + SE *work*]

cony *n.*[1] (*also* **coney, conny, cunnie, cunny**) **1** [mid-16C–mid-17C] a general term of endearment for a woman. **2** [late 16C+] the vagina (cf. BIRD n.[8]). **3** [17C] a prostitute (cf. ALLEY CAT n.). **4** [1920s] (*US*) a sexually available woman. [SE *cony*, rabbit + play on CUNT n.[1] (1); the stereotyped sexuality of rabbits + the pubic hair is supposedly reminiscent of the rabbit's tail]

cony *n.*[2] (*also* **coney, conny, cunny**) [late 16C–mid-19C] a dupe, the victim of a confidence trick, of card-sharping etc. [SE *cony*, a rabbit]

cony-burrow *n.* (*also* **coney…, conney…, conny…, …berry**) **1** [late 16C–17C] (*also* **berry, burrow**) a brothel (cf. BIRDCAGE n.[1]; CUNNY WARREN n.). **2** [17C–19C] (*also* **connie-burrow, cony-borough, cunny-barrow, Cunnyborough**) the vagina (cf. AGREEABLE RUTS OF LIFE n.). [CONY n.[1] (3)/CONY n.[1] (2) + SE *burrow/borough*]

cony-burrow ferret *n.* (*also* **Cunnyborough ferret**) [early 17C–19C] the penis. [CONY-BURROW n. (2) + FERRET n.[2] (1)]

conycatch *v.*[1] (*also* **coneycatch**) [late 16C–17C] to go out whoring or womanizing. [CONY n.[1] (2)]

conycatch *v.*[2] (*also* **cunnycatch**) [late 16C–17C] to ensnare in a confidence trick. [CONY n.[2]]

cony-catcher *n.*[1] (*also* **coney-catcher, conny-catcher, cunny-catcher**) **1** [late 16C–early 17C] a prostitute; thus *cony-catching*, prostitution (cf. COCKATRICE n.). **2** [17C] the penis. **3** [17C–18C] a prostitute's customer. [CONY n.[1] (2); play on CONY-CATCHER n.[2]]

cony-catcher *n.*[2] (*also* **conny-catcher, cunny-catcher**) **1** [late 16C–mid-17C] a confidence trickster. **2** [late 18C] in a non-criminal context, a plausible, smooth-tongued speaker. [CONYCATCH v.²]

cony-catching n. [late 16C–17C] any form of confidence tricking, spec. card-sharping. [CONYCATCH v.²]

cony-catching adj. **1** [late 16C–mid-17C] pertaining to confidence trickery. **2** [mid-17C] in a non-criminal sense, deceitful, mendacious. [CONYCATCH v.²]

cony-dog n. [late 17C] one who assists a confidence trickster in CONY-CATCHING n. [CONY n.² + SE dog; lit. a dog that catches rabbits]

cony-fumble n. [late 17C–early 18C] a constable. [mispron.]

cony-hall n. see CUNNY ALLEY n.

cony-skin n. (also **coney-skin**, **cunny-skin**) [early 17C–19C] female pubic hair. [CONY n.¹ (2) + SE skin]

coo n. (also **cou**, **cu**) [late 19C+] **1** the vagina. **2** a woman regarded as a sex object. **3** a term of abuse. [abbr./euph. for CUNT n.¹ (1)/CUNT n.² (1)]

coo adj. [2000s] (US teen) abbr. COOL adj.¹ (2); also as excl.

coo! excl. (also **coo-er!**) [late 19C+] an excl. expressing surprise or incredulity.

cooch n.¹ **1** [1910s+] (US) a 'hootchy-kootchy' dance, i.e. belly-dancing; thus cooch dancer, coocher, a belly dancer. **2** [1960s+] (US) the vagina; thus metonymic for a woman. **3** [1970s+] (US gay) an effeminate homosexual male. [abbr./euph. for CUNT n.¹ (1); note Online Dict. Playground Slang (2001): 'This word raises all sorts of interesting possibilities since the old Welsh word "cwtch" (which has a similar pronunciation) is often used to mean a "place of comfort". It makes me wonder if the word was carried to the states by Welsh immigrants then mutated and adopted by peoples who would have no idea of its origins']

cooch n.² [1960s] (US) liquor. [? var. on HOOCH n.¹ (1)]

coochie n. [1930s+] (US) the female genitalia; thus get some coochie, to have sexual intercourse. [CUNT n.¹ (1) reinforced by SAmE cookie/COOKIE n.¹ (1) as something 'good enough to eat']

coo-coo see also under CUCKOO.

coo-coo adj. [1960s] (US) sophisticated, aware, 'hip'. [abbr./redup. COOL adj.¹ (3)]

cooda n. see COUTER n.².

coodle n. [2000s] (Irish) excrement. [ety. unknown]

coo-er! excl. see COO! excl.

cook n.¹ (orig. US drugs) **1** [late 19C–1950s] (also **cookie**, **cooky**) an expert who prepares an opium pipe. **2** [1950s] a manufacturer of illicit drugs. **3** [1990s+] a single session of manufacturing heroin. [COOK v.³]

cook n.² [20C+] (Aus.) a look, a glance; thus HAVE A COOK v. [rhy. sl.; but note Yid. guck, a look, a glance, usu. in phr. 'geb a guck', have a look]

cook n.³ see KOOK n.

cook v.¹ **1** [mid-17C+] to tamper with, to falsify; thus cook the books, cook the accounts. **2** [mid-19C–1940s] to ruin, to spoil. **3** [late 19C] to give someone their due deserts. **4** [late 19C–1950s] to overcome; thus wouldn't that cook you? wouldn't that shock/annoy you? **5** [late 19C+] to bribe, to arrange illicitly. **6** [late 19C+] (US) to kill, to murder; lit. and fig. **7** [1910s] (US) to concoct a mendacious story. **8** [1940s+] (US Black) to do something exceptionally well. **9** [1960s+] (Aus.) to scold; to criticize harshly.

cook v.² **1** [mid-19C+] to suffer from the heat. **2** [late 19C] (Aus.) to die of hanging. **3** [1930s+] (US) to die in the electric chair. **4** [1930s+] (US) to be electrocuted. **5** [1980s+] to be burned to death.

cook v.³ (drugs) **1** [late 19C] to manufacture smokeable opium from the crude product. **2** [late 19C–1950s] to heat opium before smoking it. **3** [1920s+] to prepare a narcotic (esp. heroin) for injection by heating a solution of powder and water for use in a syringe. **4** [1930s+] to distill (bootleg) alcohol. **5** [1980s] to prepare a non-narcotic drug, e.g. an amphetamine pill, for injection.

6 [1980s] to manufacture illicit drugs, e.g. heroin or crack cocaine. **7** [1980s+] to heat cocaine until it hardens.

cook v.⁴ **1** [20C+] to happen, to perform, to concoct, used to cover any activity. **2** [1940s+] (orig. US Black) of a musician or group of musicians, to be playing in harmony and particularly creatively. **3** [1970s+] to rev up a car.

cook dough v. [1940s] (UK Und.) to manufacture counterfeit money. [SE cook + DOUGH n.¹ (1)]

cook-down n. [1970s+] (drugs) the process whereby users liquefy heroin in order to inhale it. [COOK DOWN v.]

cook down v. see COOK UP v.² (3).

cooked adj. **1** [early 19C+] exhausted, finished, destroyed, in serious trouble. **2** [1920s+] (US) drunk. **3** [1970s+] (US) intoxicated by a drug. [fig. uses of SE + COOK SOMEONE'S GOOSE v.]

cooked up adj. see COKED (UP) adj. (1).

cookee n.¹ (also **cookie**, **cooky**) [19C+] (mainly US) the head cook. **2** [1910s+] (US) a cook's assistant.

cookee n.² see COOKIE n.³ (2).

cooker n.¹ **1** [mid-19C] that which settles a situation, a clincher, a finisher. **2** [1940s+] anything exciting, e.g. a sexy or sophisticated person, an emotive piece of music.

cooker n.² **1** [1910s+] (US drugs) an opium addict (who prepares his own pipes). **2** [1920s–30s] one who manufactures bootleg alcohol. **3** [1930s+] (drugs) a container, usu. a bottle cap, in which the mixture of heroin and water can be heated before drawing it into a syringe and thence injecting it into one's arm. **4** [1940s+] a container used in the illicit manufacture of spirits. **5** [1990s+] one who cooks cocaine-freebase. **6** [2000s] one who manufactures amphetamine. [COOK v.³]

cooker n.³ see CAPTAIN COOK n.¹.

cookhouse n. [1980s] (US) a very high temperature, a very hot day.

cookie n.¹ **1** [late 19C; 1950s+] the vagina. **2** [1920s+] (also **shop cookie**) an attractive woman. **3** [1920s+] (Glasgow) a prostitute (cf. BANGTAIL n.¹). **4** [1970s] a lesbian who plays the passive 'feminine' role in sex. **5** [1970s+] (US gay) an effeminate male homosexual. [SE cookie, biscuit, a common example of the equation of sex and food in sl.]

cookie n.² (also **cooky**) [1920s+] (orig. US) a man (or woman), often with a qualifying adj., e.g. SMART COOKIE n., TOUGH COOKIE n.

cookie n.³ **1** [1930s] (US prison) cocaine. **2** [1930s–70s] (US drugs) (also **cookee**) an opium addict. **3** [1950s] (US) $1 (cf. BATTER n.⁴). **4** [1960s] a good example of something, a good one. **5** [1970s] (US) a cigarette. **6** [1990s+] (drugs) crack cocaine in its solid, rock form (cf. BASE n.).

cookie n.⁴ [1950s+] (US Black) a derog. term for a Black person who is seen as espousing White values to the detriment of their own background (cf. APPLE n.⁷). [predecessor of OREO (COOKIE) n. (1)]

cookie n.⁵ [1960s] (US gay) the penis.

cookie n.⁶ [1990s+] (US) a lump of expectorated phlegm.

cookie n.⁷ see COOK n.¹ (1).

cookie n.⁸ see COOKEE n.¹.

cookie crashing n. [2000s] (US Black) slapping a woman's breasts while engaged in sexual intercourse with her. [COOKIE n.¹ (2) + SE crash]

cookie crumbs n. [1970s+] (US gay) semen stains on the trousers. [? resemblance or ? the idea of something edible]

cookie-cutter n. [1920s–60s] (orig. US Black) a policeman's badge. [resemblance]

cookie-duster n. [1930s+] (US) a moustache.

cookie-pusher n. (also **cookie-dipper**) (US) **1** [1920s+] an ambitious, but lazy, man, esp. a government career man, a sycophant. **2** [1920s+] a young man who errs on the 'feminine side of life' – tea parties, conversation, the niceties of dress and of gossip, art, rather than sport etc. **3** [1930s–50s] a waitress. [SE *cookie* + *pusher*; the cakes that such men are continually passing around such tea parties or that waitresses serve in cafés]

cookies *n.*[1] [1920s+] the contents of one's stomach, lit. things that have been cooked; usu. in phr. meaning to vomit, e.g. *chuck one's cookies*, FLIP ONE'S COOKIES v., *heave one's cookies*, THROW ONE'S COOKIES v., TOSS ONE'S COOKIES v., *woof one's cookies*.

cookies *n.*[2] [1960s+] (*US Black*) **1** any form of desired object, esp. sex or money. **2** emotions, feelings. **3** the male or female genitalia (cf. COOKIE n.[1]).

cookies and cream *n.* [2000s] (*US Black*) a mixed-race person of Black and White parentage.

cookie-shine *n.* [mid–19C–1930s] a tea-party.

cookie-truck *n.* [1970s+] (*US*) the van that transports patients to a psychiatric institution. [KOOK n. (1) + SE *truck*]

cookie-wagon *n.* [1920s+] (*US*) a police van, a 'black maria'. [? KOOK n. (1)]

cooking *n.* [1990s+] (*drugs*) manufacturing illicit drugs, e.g. heroin or crack cocaine. [COOK v.[3] (6)]

cooking *adj.*[1] [1940s+] (*orig. US Black*) excellent, doing very well, esp. of a performance. [COOK v.[4] (2)]

cooking *adj.*[2] [1960s+] **1** (*US drugs*) very intoxicated; feeling the effects. **2** (*US*) in fig. use, dramatic, aggressive. [COOK v.[4] (1)]

cook off *v.*[1] [1910s] (*US Und.*) to satisfy one's addiction by smoking opium. [COOK v.[3] (2)]

cook off *v.*[2] [1960s] in bootlegging, to heat the mix of alcohol and other ingredients preparatory to distilling spirits.

cook on all four *v.* [1940s+] (*Can./US*) to be very busy, to be working very well. [the 4 burners of a typical stove]

cook on the front burner *v.* [1940s+] (*US*) **1** to do something very well, to act or think correctly. **2** to be currently pertinent.

cookoo *adj. see* CUCKOO adj.

cook-ruffian *n.* [late 17C–early 19C] (*UK Und.*) a bad or bad-tempered cook.

cook someone's bacon *v.* (*also* **fry someone's bacon**) [mid–19C–1900s] (*US*) to ruin, to cause difficulties or unhappiness for someone else. [var. on COOK SOMEONE'S GOOSE v.]

cook someone's goose *v.* [mid–19C+] **1** to kill; thus *one's goose is cooked*, to be dying. **2** to spoil someone's chances. **3** to give someone their due deserts.

cook someone's gruel/hash *v. see* SETTLE SOMEONE'S HASH v.

cook's own, the *n.* [mid–late 19C] the police force. [a play on regimental nicknames + the force's supposed affection for the cooks working in the great London mansions]

cook the pill *v. see* COOK UP A PILL v.

cook up *v.*[1] **1** [mid-18C] to tamper with, to falsify. **2** [mid-18C+] to invent, to fabricate. **3** [late 18C+] to happen, to develop. **4** [1900s] to make. [ext. of COOK v.[1] (1)]

cook up *v.*[2] [late 19C–1960s] (*drugs*) **1** to prepare opium for smoking. **2** [1920s–40s] (*US Und.*) to boil nitroglycerine out of dynamite. **3** [1920s+] (*drugs*) (*also* **cook down**) to prepare an injection of a narcotic drug, usu. heroin, by heating a measure of the powdered drug plus some water in a teaspoon or bottle cap. **4** [1980s] (*drugs*) to manufacture methamphetamine. **5** [1980s+] (*drugs*) to prepare cocaine in order to FREEBASE v. **6** [1980s+] (*drugs*) to make crack cocaine from cocaine hydrochloride base. [COOK v.[3]]

cook up *v.*[3] [1930s–50s] (*US Black*) to enjoy oneself, to have a good time. [COOK v.[4] (1)]

cook up a pill *v.* (*also* **cook the pill**) [late 19C–1940s] (*drugs*) to prepare a pipe of opium. [COOK UP v.[2] (1)/COOK v.[3] (2) + PILL n.[4] (1)]

cook up brown *v.* [1950s] (*US*) to defeat comprehensively. [var. on DO UP BROWN v. (1)]

cook up with *v.* [1980s+] (*US campus*) to 'neck' with, to pet. [? GET HOT ON v./HOT adj.[1] (1)]

cook with gas *v.* (*also* **cook with electricity, cook with radar**) [1940s+] (*orig. US Black*) to succeed, to do very well, to

tackle a project in the right way, esp. after misdirected efforts have failed, and thus usu. in phr. *now we're cooking with gas*.

cooky *n.*[1] *see* COOK n.[1] (1).

cooky *n.*[2] *see* COOKEE n.[1].

cooky *n.*[3] *see* COOKIE n.[2].

cool *n.*[1] [late 16C] (*UK Und.*) a cut-purse. [ety. unknown; ? his 'coolness' when thieving]

cool *n.*[2] **1** [late 19C+] temper, poise, composure, attitude to life and ability to deal with it; thus KEEP ONE'S COOL v./LOSE ONE'S COOL v. **2** [1950s–60s] (*US teen*) a temporary armistice between opposing street gangs. [COOL adj.[1] (2)]

cool *n.*[3] **1** [1960s+] (*orig. US Black*) sophistication, the prevailing fashion. **2** [1970s] (*US campus*) a fashionable, drug-taking (or whatever is deemed relevant) young person, as opposed to a straight, conventional person. [COOL adj.[1] (3)]

cool *adj.*[1] **1** [17C+] emotionless, cold-blooded. **2** [19C+] relaxed, calm, self-contained. **3** [early 19C+] sophisticated, aware. **4** [mid-19C+] insolent, arrogant, impudent. **5** [late 19C; 1950s+] of situations, acceptable, satisfactory; esp. in THAT'S COOL phr. **6** [1930s+] (*orig. US Black*) good, fine, pleasing. **7** [1940s+] (*orig. US*) fashionable, chic, 'with it'. **8** [1960s+] of people, comfortable with, happy, on good terms. **9** [1970s+] trustworthy. [all fig. uses of SE *cool*; (4) note Eton College jargon *cool fish*, a cocky, self-possessed schoolboy; given that (1) is a negative use, the subseq. positive uses give it some claim to be the first example of the bad = good model of sl. terms]

cool *adj.*[2] [early 18C+] used to describe a large sum of money, e.g. *a cool thousand*, *a cool hundred*; occas. in other contexts. [? the image of a calm and deliberate counting of that money, esp. since the usu. context is of gambling in some form]

cool *adj.*[3] [1940s+] **1** (*drugs*) not carrying or owning drugs, or believing that one has hidden them well enough to defy any search of one's body or premises. **2** (*US Und.*) not suspicious, either of people or objects. **3** (*US gang*) not carrying weapons or acting aggressively.

cool *v.*[1] [mid–19C+] to look at; esp. as *cool esclop!* look, the police! [backsl.; thus *cool him*, look at him, 'a phrase frequently used when one costermonger warns another of the approach of a policeman' (Hotten, 1867)]

cool *v.*[2] **1** [1900s; 1950s+] (*orig. US*) to calm down, to deal with a problem in a controlled manner. **2** [1950s+] to calm someone or some situation down. **3** [1950s+] to knock out. **4** [1960s] (*US*) to postpone, to put off, to stop. **5** [1960s] (*US campus*) to turn down a request for a date. **6** [1960s] (*US Und.*) of stolen goods, to remain hidden until police activity quietens. **7** [1960s+] (*US*) of a criminal charge or disciplinary problem, to quash. **8** [1980s+] (*US Black/teen*) to lounge around, to 'hang out'. **9** [1980s+] to saunter. [COOL adj.[1]]

cool *v.*[3] (*US*) **1** [1920s+] to beat up. **2** [1920s+] (*also* **put the cool on**) to kill, to murder, to assassinate. **3** [1950s+] to die. [the chilliness of the corpse]

cool *v.*[4] [1970s] (*drugs*) to sell heroin; to inject (someone) with heroin. [the calming effects of the drug, either as ending withdrawal symptoms or simply removing oneself from 'reality']

cool *adv.* **1** [early 19C+] calmly, in an unruffled manner. **2** [late 19C] askance, suspiciously. [COOL adj.[1]]

cool! *excl.* [1950s–60s] (*orig. US*) relax! calm down!; thus *you cool!* goodbye! [COOL v.[2] (1)]

coolarific *adj.* [1990s+] (*US campus*) fantastic, great (cf. BONERIFIC adj.). [COOL adj.[1] (6) + SE *terrific*]

cool as a moose (and twice as hairy) *phr.* (*also* **cool as a creek stone**) [1960s+] (*US campus*) **1** very fashionable, of both persons and things. **2** handsome. [COOL adj.[1] (7)]

cool as shit *phr.* (*also* **cool as toast**) [1970s+] (*US campus*) an expression of approval. [COOL adj.[1] (6) + SHIT n.[3] (3)]

cool beans! *excl.* [1980s+] (*US teen*) excellent! wonderful! [COOL adj.[1] (6)]

cool breeze n. (*US Black/campus*) **1** [1980s] an admirable and popular person. **2** [1990s+] a person who thinks themself to be sophisticated but is not. [COOL-BREEZE adj.]

cool-breeze adj. [1960s+] (*orig. US*) **1** self-assured, sophisticated. **2** first-rate, wonderful. [COOL adj.¹ (3)/COOL adj.¹ (6) + fig. use of SE]

cool breeze! excl. [1960s+] excellent, wonderful, first-rate. [COOL-BREEZE adj. (2)]

cool cat n. [1940s+] (*mainly US Black*) a sophisticated, competent, unruffled, able person. [COOL adj.¹ (3) + CAT n.¹¹ (4)]

cool-cock v. [1930s–50s] (*US*) to knock unconscious. [var. on COLD-COCK v.]

cool-crack v. [1940s] (*US Black*) to knock unconscious. [var. on COLD-COCK v.]

cool crape n. [late 18C] a shroud; thus *be put into one's cool crape*, to die. ['*Cool-crape*, a slight Chequer'd Stuff made in imitation of Scotch Plad' (B.E.)]

cool deal! excl. [1990s+] (*US campus*) an excl. of approval, admiration. [COOL adj.¹ (6) + DEAL n.¹ (4)]

cooled out adj. [1970s+] (*orig. US Black*) **1** calm, unperturbed, in control. **2** under the influence of drugs, usu. narcotics. [COOL v.² (1)]

cooler n.¹ **1** [early 17C–early 19C] a woman, esp. a wife (who 'cools one's passions'), as opposed to a mistress or lover (who 'heats them up'). **2** [19C] a 'finisher', a 'clincher', e.g. a knockout punch, a crushing statement. **3** [19C–1900s] a glass of beer or porter taken after drinking spirits and water. **4** [early 19C] the (female) buttocks; thus phr. *kiss my cooler*. **5** [late 19C+] (*orig. US*) a prison, a police cell. **6** [20C+] (*orig. US*) a punishment or solitary confinement cell. **7** [20C+] (*Aus.*) a chilly glance, a snub, rejection. **8** [1900s] (*US campus*) an attractive young woman. **9** [1930s–60s] (*US tramp*) a silencer. **10** [1930s+] (*US Black*) a funeral home. **11** [1970s+] (*US gay*) as homosexual reverse of (1), a lover. [fig. use of SE *cool* (*down*)]

cooler n.² [late 19C–1900s] (*US campus*) an expert, an outstanding individual. [COOL adj.¹ (2)]

cool hand n. [mid-19C+] (*US*) a cool, calm, controlled and competent individual. [COOL adj.¹ + HAND n.¹; note *locus classicus*, the book title *Cool Hand Luke* (1965) by Donn Pearce]

cool-head n. **1** [mid-19C+] a calm, unflappable person. **2** [1960s] a pleasant person. [COOL adj.¹ (3)/COOL adj.¹ (6) + SE *head*]

coolie n.¹ (*also* **koelie**) **1** [mid–late 19C] (*US*) an immigrant Chinese labourer. **2** [mid-19C–1900s] (*US*) an East Asian. **3** [mid-19C+] (*S.Afr.*) a derog. term for an Indian; thus *coolie Christmas*, the Islamic festival of Moharram or the Hindu festival of Diwali; *coolie creeper*, in cricket, a ball that stays low without bouncing; *coolie pink*, shocking pink, seen as vulgar and 'typically Indian'; *coolie shop/store*, a shop owned or managed by an Indian. **4** [mid-19C+] (*Aus./S.Afr.*) a derog. term for a Black (occas. Indian) person, esp. as *coolie-boy, coolie-girl* (cf. AFRICAN APE n.; BROWNIE n.²). **5** [20C+] (*W.I.*) the trad. Jamaican epithet for East Indians, usu. in the form *coolie-man* or *coolie-oman*. [in a variety of Indian languages, the term means lit. a man for hire and thus a (menial) labourer; note Zulu *amakula*, a person of Indian origin]

coolie n.² [mid-19C] a private soldier. [fig. use of COOLIE n.¹ (3)]

coolie n.³ [1950s–60s] (*US teen*) any youth unaffiliated to a street gang. [COOL adj.¹; i.e. he remains *cool* towards their approaches]

coolie n.⁴ [1970s+] (*US*) the anus. [Sp. sl. *culo*, the anus]

coolie n.⁵ [1970s+] (*US gay*) a blunder, an error; thus *pull a coolie*, to err, to blunder.

coolie mud n. [1940s–50s] (*US drugs*) inferior opium (cf. APOSTLE n.). [COOLIE n.¹ + MUD n.³ (2)]

cool in v. [1960s] (*US teen*) to inform. [i.e. render someone COOL adj.¹ (3)]

cooling n. [1980s+] (*US*) relaxing. [COOL v.² (8)]

cooling card n. [mid-16C–17C] something that defuses one's enthusiasm or deflates one's passion. [card-playing jargon; in a now lost card-game the *cooling card* was apparently played to quash an opponent's hitherto winning card]

cool it v.¹ [1940s] (*US Black*) to strike a pose reflecting one's image as a HIPSTER n. and to show off the line of one's ZOOT SUIT n. [COOL adj.¹ (7)]

cool it v.² **1** [1950s] (*orig. US*) to leave. **2** [1950s] (*US*) to arrange to protect from the authorities. **3** [1950s+] (*orig. US Black*) to calm down, to relax, often as imper. *cool it!* **4** [1950s+] (*orig. US Black*) to stop, to cease from an action. **5** [1960s] to draw back from someone, to cease relating to someone. [COOL v.²]

cool it v.³ [1960s] (*US*) to die. [COOL v.³ (3)]

cool jerk n. [1960s–80s] (*US Black*) one who deludes himself into a belief that he is a sophisticated individual when he is not; thus *do the cool jerk*, to move in an ostentatious manner. [a JERK n.¹ (2) thinking they are COOL adj.¹ (3)]

cool lady n. [late 17C–early 19C] a female camp follower, specializing in selling brandy to the troops. [COOL NANTZ n. + SE *lady*]

cool nantz n. (*also* **cool nants**) [late 17C–early 19C] cognac.

coolness n. [1960s+] sophistication, a state of epitomizing the current fashionable stance. [COOL adj.¹ (3)/COOL adj.¹ (7)]

cool-off n. [1950s] calmness, relaxation; an escape from controversy. [COOL OFF v.² (1)]

cool off v.¹ **1** [mid-19C; 1930s–60s] to kill, to murder. **2** [1930s–60s] to knock out, to subdue with physical force. [COOL v.³]

cool off v.² **1** [mid-19C+] (*orig. US*) to calm down. **2** [20C+] (*orig. US*) to calm someone down. **3** [1920s+] (*orig. US*) to lose interest in. **4** [1930s+] (*orig. US*) of a criminal, or persons involved in conflict, to lie low until the hue and cry has passed. **5** [late 19C–1900s] (*US*) to be imprisoned. **6** [1950s] (*US*) to become bored. **7** [1990s+] (*US*) of a gambler, to run out of luck. **8** [1990s+] (*US*) of a stolen object, to be less HOT adj.² (3). [earlier var. on COOL v.²; ult. COOL adj.¹ (2)]

cool-off man n. [1930s] (*US Und.*) in a confidence trick, the gang member who calms worried members of the public. [COOL OFF v.² (2)]

cool one n. [1950s+] (*orig. US*) a bottle of beer.

cool one's copper(s) v. [mid–late 19C] to take a drink to ease the parched throat caused by excessive drinking. [SE *cool* + HOT COPPERS n.]

cool one's jets v. [1970s+] (*orig. US*) to calm down, to relax. [COOL v.² (1) + fig. use of SE]

cool one's toes v. (*also* **cool one's heels**) [17C+] to be kept waiting; to wait.

cool-out n. [1990s+] relaxation, a rest. [COOL OUT v.² (3)]

cool out v.¹ [mid-19C; 1960s+] (*orig. US*) to subdue physically, to kill. [var. on COOL OFF v.¹]

cool out v.² **1** [1910s+] (*orig. US Und.*) to calm down or calm someone down; often as imper. *cool out!* **2** [1950s+] (*W.I.*) to take a rest from work by lying in the shade of a tree. **3** [1950s+] to relax. **4** [1960s] (*US Und.*) for a confidence man, to avoid the victim from whom the money has been extracted. **5** [1960s–70s] to make manageable. **6** [1990s+] (*US drugs*) to abstain from drug use. [COOL v.²]

cool out on v. [1960s] (*US*) to fail to pay a debt to someone.

cool papa n. [1940s] (*US Black*) a self-possessed, sophisticated and, as such, alluring male. [COOL adj.¹ (3) + SE *papa*]

cool runnings n. [1980s+] (*W.I./UK Black teen*) everything is fine, all is going smoothly. [COOL adj.¹ (6) + ext. use of SE *run*]

cool smoke n. [1980s+] (*drugs*) a smoke of methamphetamine (cf. BOMBITA n.). [play on ICE n.⁶ (2)]

cool tankard n. [late 17C–early 19C] a cool drink, made of wine and water with lemon, sugar and nutmeg.

cool the beef v. [1950s+] to deal with a problem or a complaint. [COOL v.² (1) + BEEF n.² (2)]

cool whip n. [1980s+] (*US campus*) something very new and appealing. [COOL adj.¹ (6) + pun on brandname of the US sweet]

cooly n. see KALI n.

coon n. **1** [mid-19C] (US) a Native American. **2** [mid-19C] (US) a Whig. **3** [mid-19C–1900s] (US) a sly person, a cunning fellow. **4** [mid-19C+] (US) (also **koon**) a person, esp. a rustic, a peasant. **5** [mid-19C+] (orig. US) a highly derog. term for a Black person (cf. ALLIGATOR BAIT n.²). **6** [late 19C–1930s] (US) a petty thief. **7** [1910s–30s] (US Black) used non-pej. of a fellow Black person. **8** [1920s+] a clown, a fool, the image is of a 'chocolate coloured coon'. [fig. uses of SE raccoon, typified as a cunning creature. Used orig. in non-racial senses (emphasizing only cunning), by mid-19C the meaning was unequivocally racist and, as such, used in Aus. too, where it described not Blacks but Aborigines. Note *American Dialect Society-List* (Internet, 17 December 2001): 'The daughter of William Lloyd Garrison (the great American abolitionist), while tending to the needs of emancipated slaves on the Gullah Islands, anthologized Negro spirituals. She also made notes on the Gullah dialect. "Coon" was the name that the ex-slaves called each other, and she indicates that it is the word "cousin" as expressed through the dialect. [...] As with many terms that members of ethnic communities call each other, they descend into the pejorative']

coon adj.¹ (also **cooney, coonful, coony**) [mid-19C–1940s] (US) sly, cunning; thus **coonfully**, cunningly. [COON n. (3)]

coon adj.² (also **coony**) [mid-19C+] a derog. term describing a Black individual or Black culture. [COON n. (5)]

coon v. (US) **1** [mid-19C–1950s] to crawl stealthily (like a racoon). **2** [late 19C+] to pilfer, esp. fruit or other objects of little value. [COON n. (3)]

coon-ass n. (also **coonie**) [1940s+] a Cajun (a person of French descent in Louisiana). [Fr. *conasse*, the female genitals; thus *conassière*, sl. for Fr. *femelots*, the gudgeon. The Cajuns known as *coon-asses* were fishers of gudgeon]

coon-assed adj. (also **coon-bossed**) [1900s–50s] (US) a general term of abuse. [COON n. (4) + ASS n. (2); but note COON-ASS n.]

coon bottom n. (also **coon hollow**) [mid-19C–1930s] within a larger urban area, that part recognized as reserved for the Black community (cf. COON TOWN n.). [COON n. (5) + BOTTOM n.³/HOLLOW n.²]

coon chaser n. [late 19C] (US) a White man who pursues/has sex with Black women. [COON n. (5) + SE *chaser*]

coon dick n. [1920s–30s] (US) an illicitly distilled spirit compounded of 'grapefruit juice, cornmeal mash, beef bones and a few mo' things' (Zora Neale Hurston, *Mules & Men*, 1935). [COON n. (5) + DICK n.⁴ (1), i.e. racist stereotyping]

coondie n. see COONIE n.¹.

cooney/coonful adj. see COON adj.¹.

coon hollow n. see COON BOTTOM n.

coonie n.¹ (also **coondie, cundy**) [1940s+] (Aus.) a small stone suitable for a missile. [Aboriginal]

coonie n.² see COON-ASS n.

coonish adj. [mid-19C; 1990s+] (UK juv.) stupid. [? COON n. (5)]

coon jigger n. [mid-19C–1960s] (US) a derog. term for a Black child (cf. ALLIGATOR BAIT n.²). [COON n. (5) + JIGGER n.¹¹]

coonjine n. [19C+] (US) **1** the rhythmic swaying gait used when loading and unloading freight. **2** a song used by the Black dockhands to set the rhythm for loading and unloading freight. **3** sexual intercourse. [COONJINE v.]

coonjine v. [19C+] (US) **1** to move with a special rhythmic swaying gait, adapted from the shuffling step used by Black dockhands as they walked up and down the gangplanks of Mississippi steamers carrying heavy bundles and packages. **2** to sing a song to set the rhythm for loading and unloading freight by the Black dockhands. **3** to have sexual intercourse. [? SE *raccoon*, it has a notably waddling step or COON n. (5) + SE *engine*]

coon juice n. [mid-19C; 1960s+] (US) illicitly distilled whisky. [COON n. (5) + SE *juice*]

coon-lover n. [mid-19C+] (orig. US) a derog. term, as used by racists, for those who are seen as insufficiently hostile to Blacks. [COON n. (5) + SE *lover*]

coon out v. [1960s] (US) to leave surreptitiously. [COON v. (1)]

coon's age n. [mid-19C+] (US) a very long time. [the life-span of a SE raccoon although the phr. is inevitably seen as linked to COON n. (5)]

coonshine n. [late 19C] (US) an all-night party. [COON n. (5), i.e. racial stereotyping + MOONSHINE n. (2)/SE *moonshine*]

coonskin n. [mid-19C] (US) a $1 bill (cf. BAT HIDE n.). [? as used in the fur trade, when furs were the barterers' equivalent of cash]

coon squall n. [late 19C] (US) empty chatter. [COON n. (5), i.e. racial stereotyping + SE *squall*]

coon town n. [late 19C+] a derog. term for the Black section of a town or city (cf. COON BOTTOM n.). [COON n. (5) + SE *town*]

coony see under COON.

coop n.¹ **1** [late 18C+] (also **coup**) a prison; a police station. **2** [late 19C+] (US Und.) a hideout. **3** [20C+] (US police) a place for a patrolling policeman to take an unauthorized break. **4** [1900s] one's home. **5** [1910s–40s] any form of place, e.g. a nightclub, a bar. **6** [1920s–30s] a particular cell in a prison. **7** [1940s–50s] (US Und.) a solitary confinement cell.

coop n.² [1900s–20s] (US) the head, the mind. [? SE *pigeon coop*, on top of a house; note synon. Ger./Yid. *kopf*]

coop v. **1** [late 19C–1900s] (US) to stay, to hide. **2** [20C+] (US police, New York) to sleep or rest while on duty – in a motel room or similar hideaway. [COOP n.¹ (2)/COOP n.¹ (3)]

cooped up adj. [late 17C–early 18C] (UK Und.) imprisoned. [SE *coop*, an enclosure]

cooper n. see COOPER (OF CRUSTY) n.

cooper v.¹ **1** [early–mid-19C] to make presentable, to 'rig up'. **2** [mid-19C] (UK Und.) to forge, to counterfeit; thus **cooper**, a forger. **3** [mid–late 19C] to spoil, to ruin. **4** [late 19C] to consume. [fig. uses of SE *cooper*, to make casks or barrels; the journeymen coopers or barrel-makers employed on Thames vessels were meant to mend cargo containers; in fact, they often pillaged them and deliberately broke open hogsheads and barrels]

cooper v.² [late 19C] (US) to understand. [? SE *comprehend*]

coopered adj. **1** [mid-19C] spoilt, adulterated, tampered with, worn-out. **2** [late 19C] drunk. [COOPER v.¹ (3)]

cooper (of crusty) n. (also **cooper of crusty**) [19C] a mixture composed of equal parts of stout and porter. [the allowance of as much stout and porter as they liked, which was permitted to coopers (barrel-makers) at London breweries]

coose n. see COOZE n.

coosh adj. [1910s+] (Aus.) comfortable. [CUSHY adj. (1)]

coosie n. see COOZE n.

coot n.¹ **1** [mid-18C+] a fool, a simpleton; usu. as OLD COOT n., *silly old coot* etc. **2** [20C+] (Aus./US) a general derog. description. [pvb phr. 'stupid as a coot'; + ? play on Lat. *Fulica*, the species/SE *foolish*; the coot, synon. with the *Foolish Guillemot*, is seen in pvbs. as a foolish bird. The popular link with the undoubtedly eccentric Sir Eyre *Coote* (1762–1823) is specious]

coot n.² [1910s] a body louse. [abbr. COOTIE n.¹ (1)]

coot n.³ [1970s] (US campus) **1** the vagina. **2** a woman considered solely as a sexual object. [abbr. COOTER n.¹]

coot-drunk adj. see DRUNK AS A COOTIE phr.

cooter n.¹ [1970s+] (US campus) **1** a woman. **2** the vagina (cf. BEARDED CLAM n.). [US dial. *cooter*, a freshwater turtle]

cooter n.² see COUTER n.¹.

cootie n.¹ (also **cutey, cutie, koota, kooti, kootie, kuti**) **1** [1910s+] (US) a body louse, a bedbug. **2** [1920s] (US) a small car. **3** [1930s–60s] (US) a term of abuse. **4** [1950s+] (US juv.) an imaginary germ or 'bug'. **5** [1970s] (US juv.) a piece of nasal mucus. **6** [1970s+] (US) a fig. repellent quality that can be picked up from someone one dislikes. [? Malayan *kutu*, a dog tick; HDAS rejects this for lack of any real link]

cootie n.² (also **cutey, cutie**) [1980s] (US Black) an inexperienced, naïve young person, keen to improve his or her status. [fig. use of COOTIE n.[1] (1)]

cootie drapes *n.* [1940s] (*US Black*) a style of trousers, wide and draped and thus a possible home for lice. [COOTIE n.[1] (1) + DRAPES n.]

cootie garage *n.* [1920s] (*US*) the hair, esp. when styled elaborately. [COOTIE n.[1] (1) + SE *garage*, such a hairstyle may, supposedly, provide a welcome to insect infestation]

cootie-heart *n.* [1920s] (*US*) a contemptuous person; thus *cootie-hearted*, despicable. [COOTIE n.[1] (1) + SE *heart*]

cooty *adj.* [1920s+] suffering an infestation of body lice or similar vermin. [COOTIE n.[1] (1)]

cooze *n.* (*also* **coose, coosie, cooz, coozey, coozie, coozy**) (*mainly US*) **1** [1920s+] the vagina. **2** [1920s+] (*also* **couse**) a woman (usu. promiscuous or unattractive); by ext. a prostitute (cf. BANGTAIL n.[1]). **3** [1940s+] a term of abuse aimed at a woman, i.e. a CUNT n.[1] (2) (cf. BAMBA n.[1]). **4** [1950s] a passive/effeminate homosexual. **5** [1960s] a lesbian. **6** [1980s] a term of address to a sexually exciting woman. **7** [1980s+] vaginal secretions (cf. BINDERJUICE n.). **8** [1990s+] sexual intercourse with a woman. [var. on CUNT n.[1] (1)/COO n. (1)]

cop *n.*[1] **1** [mid-19C+] (*orig. US*) a policeman. **2** [late 19C+] (*orig. US*) an arrest; thus FAIR COP n. **3** [1930s] a sentence. **4** [1970s+] (*US prison*) a warder, a guard. [note Cumbrian dial. *cop*, a prison]

cop *n.*[2] **1** [late 19C+] a successful bet; thus ext. as any form of 'sure thing' or certainty. **2** [20C+] (*Aus./N.Z.*) a good job obtained by shrewdness or luck, an agreeable proposition, a bit of luck or a trick that leads to large profits; often as SOFT COP n.[1]; SWEET COP n. **3** [1910s] (*Aus.*) an experience. **4** [1930s] (*US tramp*) a theft. **5** [1940s] (*US Und.*) the money that confidence men allow a victim to win. **6** [1950s+] (*US*) an acquisition. [COP v. (4)]

cop *adj.* [1950s+] pertaining to the police or police culture. [COP n.[1] (1)]

cop *v.* **1** [early 19C+] (*also* **cob**) of people, to capture, to catch, to catch out. **2** [mid-19C] (*UK Und.*) (*also* **cob**) to imprison. **3** [mid-19C+] in fig. sense of (1), to 'catch' someone with a blow, to hit. **4** [mid-19C+] (*US*) of objects, to obtain, to purchase, to acquire; [1950s+] spec. to buy drugs. **5** [mid-19C+] (*US*) to grab for oneself, esp. unfairly. **6** [mid-19C+] to experience, to undergo, to receive, e.g. *cop a beating*. **7** [mid-19C+] (*orig. Aus.*) to notice, to look at; esp. in phr. used by one young man to another, indicating an attractive woman, *cop a load of that...* or *cop that lot!*, look at them. **8** [late 19C–1920s] to take in, to persuade. **9** [late 19C+] to steal; thus *on the cop*, engaged in theft. **10** [late 19C+] to take in an abstract sense, usu. in combs. **11** [20C+] to win, e.g. a bet, a fight. **12** [20C+] (*US*) to kill, to shoot dead. **13** [1910s] (*also* **cop out**) to win someone over. **14** [1920s+] (*orig. US*) other than of a pimp, to seduce; thus, of a man, to have sexual intercourse; thus *cop an ass*, to sodomize. **15** [1930s+] usu. of a prostitute, to fellate; thus COP A BIRD v. **16** [1940s] (*US Und.*) for a confidence man to win money from a victim. **17** [1940s–60s] (*US Black*) to understand, to 'get'. **18** [1940s+] (*US Black*) to affect a manner, to pose; esp. in phr. COP A 'TUDE v. **19** [1970s+] (*UK Und.*) to receive bribes, esp. of a policeman. **20** [1970s+] (*US Black*) of a pimp, to seduce a girl, spec. with the intention of making her into a prostitute. **21** [1990s+] (*Aus.*) to tolerate. [OF *caper*, to seize]

cop! *excl.* [mid-19C] (*Anglo-Ind.*) beware! look out! [Port. *coprador*]

copa *adj. see* COPACETIC adj.

cop a bake *v.* (*also* **cop a baking**) [1980s+] (*Aus. prison*) to receive a reprimand, a severe criticism. [COP v. (6) + BAKE v.[3]]

cop a bird *v.* [1930s–40s] (*US*) usu. of a prostitute, to fellate. [COP v. (15) + BIRD n.[8] (1)]

cop a breeze *v. see* BREEZE v.[1] (4).

cop a broom *v. see* COLLAR A BROOM v.

cop a bundle *v.* **1** [late 19C+] to earn a good deal of money, to prosper. **2** [1940s] (*Aus.*) in fig. use, to die. [COP v. (4) + lit./fig. uses of BUNDLE n.[1] (2)]

cop a buzz *v.* [1970s+] (*US*) to get drunk, to get 'high' on a drug. [COP v. (10) + BUZZ n.[3]]

copacetic *adj.* (*also* **copa, copasetic, copasetty, copesette, copus, kopasetic, kopasette**) (*US*) **1** [1910s+] excellent, first-rate; ok, satisfactory. **2** [1950s+] confidential, secret. [? Chinook jargon *copasenee*, everything is satisfactory, esp. as orig. used on the waterways of Washington state. Other etys. include (i) the painfully contrived phr. *the cop is on the settee*, i.e. the cop is not paying attention, which elided into *copacetic* and was supposedly used as such by US hoodlums; (ii) a word presumed to be Ital. but otherwise unknown; (iii) Fr. *coupersetique*, f. *couper*, to strike, thus striking or worth a strike; (iv) the Yid. phr. *hakol b'seder*, all is in order or, earlier, *kol b'tzedek*, all with justice. Note that HDAS dismisses all these and states 'ety. unknown']

cop a cherry *v.* [1920s+] to take a woman's, occas. a man's, virginity. [COP v. (10) + CHERRY n.[1] (4)]

cop a cock *v.* [1970s+] (*US gay*) to fellate. [COP v. (15) + COCK n.[2] (1)]

cop a deaf 'un *v.* (*also* **sling a deaf 'un**) [1920s+] to pretend to be deaf or at least not to hear the last statement; thus ext. to deliberately ignoring any form of wrong-doing. [COP v. (10)/SE *sling* + *deaf one*, i.e. a deaf ear]

cop a deuceways *v.* [1940s–50s] (*US Black*) to obtain $2-worth of something. [COP v. (4) + DEUCEWAYS n.]

cop a doodle *v. see* COP A JOINT v.

cop a dose *v.* [1940s+] to catch venereal disease. [COP v. (6) + DOSE n.[4]]

cop a drear *v.* [1940s–60s] (*orig. US Black*) to die. [COP v. (10) + SE *drear*]

cop a drill *v.* [1940s] (*US Black*) **1** to move off at a steady, regular pace. **2** in fig. use, to die. [COP v. (10) + SE *drill*; the orderly pace of military drill]

cop a drop *v.* [1910s+] (*UK Und.*) of police, to accept a bribe. [COP v. (10) + DROP n.[6] (1)]

cop a feel *v.* [20C+] (*US*) to indulge in some form of petting, but not intercourse. [COP v. (5) + FEEL n.]

cop a final *v.* [1940s] (*US Black/Harlem*) **1** to leave. **2** to get rid of someone who has been used temporarily to help work a confidence trick on a victim. [COP v. (10) + SE *final*]

cop a flower-pot *v.* [1930s–50s] to be severely reprimanded, punished or beaten. [rhy. sl. = COP IT HOT v. (1)]

cop a heel *v.* (*also* **cop and heel**) **1** [1920s+] (*US Und.*) to run off, to escape. **2** [1930s+] (*US prison*) to attack from behind. [COP v. (10) + HEEL v.[1] (1)]

cop a joint *v.* (*also* **cop a doodle, cop one's joint, cop one's thing**) **1** [1930s+] (*US*) to perform fellatio. **2** [1970s] (*US prison*) to smoke a cigarette. [COP v. (15) + JOINT n.[1]/DOODLE n.[2] (1)/THING n.[2] (3); (2) COP v. (10) + JOINT n.[5] (3)]

cop a moke *v.* [20C+] (*US prison*) to escape. [COP v. (10) + MOKE n.[1] (1), lit. 'take a donkey']

cop a mope *v.* (*also* **take a mope**) **1** [1930s–50s] (*US*) to leave. **2** [1930s+] (*US prison*) to escape. **3** [1940s] (*US*) to hold back, to refrain from talking. [COP v. (10) + MOPE n.[2]/MOPE n.[1] (1)]

cop a mouse *v.* [late 19C] to get a black eye. [COP v. (6) + MOUSE n.[3]]

cop a mug *v.* [late 19C] of a confidence trickster, to ensnare a victim. [COP v. (1) + MUG n.[2] (1)]

cop an ass *v. see* COP v. (14).

cop an attitude *v.* (*also* **take an attitude**) [1960s+] (*orig. US Black*) to take a negative stance on a given topic, to make one's own position adamant despite prevailing opinions and pressures (cf. COP A 'TUDE v.). [COP v. (18) + ATTITUDE n.]

cop and blow *v.* **1** [1910s–40s] (*US Und.*) for a confidence trickster to lure a victim into a dice- or card-game by playing fair, i.e. by winning and losing as dictated by the law of averages. **2** [1930s+] (*US*) to do something quickly and then leave, e.g. a theft, a quick purchase (of fast food, drugs, prostitutes etc).

3 [1940s–50s] (*US Black teen*) to run off. **4** [1940s+] (*US Und.*) to perform any kind of quick swindle. **5** [1950s–60s] (*US Black pimp*) to exploit an unsatisfactory prostitute for as much money as possible. [COP v. (1)/COP v. (4) + BLOW v.[6] (3)]

cop and heel v. *see* COP A HEEL v.

cop and pass n. [1950s] (*UK prison*) **1** the act of transferring contraband from one prisoner to another. **2** tobacco. [COP v. (4) + SE *pass* (*along*)]

cop a nod v. (*also* **cop a snooze**) [1930s–70s] (*US*) to have a nap, to go to sleep. [COP v. (10) + NOD n.[1] (1)/SNOOZE n. (1)]

cop a packet v. (*also* **get a packet, have a packet, stop a packet**) [1910s+] **1** to be killed or wounded. **2** to get into trouble. **3** to suffer a dose of venereal disease. **4** to gain a great deal, poss. more than one bargained for; this can either be good (more money than expected) or bad (a longer prison sentence than feared). [COP v. (6) + PACKET n.[2]]

cop a plea n. [1930s+] (*US Und.*) a lawyer. [COP A PLEA v.]

cop-a-plea adj. [1930s] of a lawyer, second-rate. [COP A PLEA v. (2)]

cop a plea v. (*also* **plea-cop**) **1** [20C+] to make an excuse. **2** [1920s+] (*orig. US*) to plead guilty to a lesser charge in return for the dropping of a greater one, to make a bargain. **3** [1940s–60s] (*US*) to beg, to plead, to implore. **4** [1940s–60s] to give in, to surrender, to compromise. **5** [1950s] (*US Und.*) to plead guilty as charged, and hope by so doing to get a lesser sentence. **6** [1950s] to plead guilty to a criminal charge. [COP v. (10) + SE *plea*]

cop a reeler v. [1930s] to get drunk. [COP v. (10) + SE *reel*/REELER n.[2]]

copasetic/copasetty adj. *see* COPACETIC adj.

cop a slave v. [20C+] (*US Black*) to work, to go out and find work. [COP v. (10) + SLAVE n. (2)]

cop a slew v. [1940s] (*Aus*) to take a look. [COP v. (10) + ? SLEW v.]

cop a sneak v. (*US Und./prison*) **1** [20C+] to run away or escape surreptitiously. **2** [1920s–50s] to absent oneself from work or from duty. **3** [1930s–40s] to break into and rob, esp. spontaneously. **4** [1930s–70s] to attack from behind; to ambush. **5** [1930s+] to behave surreptitiously. [COP v. (10) + SNEAK n.[1]/SE *sneak*]

cop a snooze n. *see* COP A NOD v.

cop a squat v. **1** [1940s] (*US Black*) to sit down; also as imper. *cop a squat, take a seat, make yourself at home.* **2** [1950s] (*US gay*) for a man to sit down when urinating. [COP v. (10) + SE *squat*]

cop a steal v. [1960s] (*US*) to steal. [COP v. (10) + SE *steal*]

cop (a strop) v. [2000s] to lose one's temper. [COP v. (10) + STROP n. (2)]

cop a Sunday v. [1930s+] (*US prison*) to attack suddenly, by surprise, to hit very hard. [COP v. (10) + SUNDAY PUNCH n.]

cop a tapper v. [1940s] (*US Black/Harlem*) to take a walk. [COP v. (10) + SE *tap one's feet*]

cop a 'tude v. (*also* **catch an attitude**) [1970s+] (*US campus*) to act in an uncooperative or angry manner (cf. COP AN ATTITUDE v.). [COP v. (18) + abbr. ATTITUDE n.]

cop a walk v. [1940s–70s] (*US*) to leave; usu. as imper. *cop a walk, go away*. [COP v. (10) + SE *walk*]

cop bung! excl. [mid–late 19C] (*UK Und.*) look out! the police are coming! [COP n.[1] (1) + fig. use of BUNG n. (4)]

copbusy v. [mid-19C–1930s] to hand whatever one has just stolen to a confederate or a girlfriend. [COP n.[1] (1) + SE *busy*, to busy oneself; i.e. to act fast to elude possible police interference]

cop deuces v. [20C+] (*US prison*) to make excuses. [rhy. sl. + COP v. (10) + DEUCE n.[1] (1); ? ref. to the losing roll of 2 in craps dice]

cope n. [mid-19C] a deal, a bargain. [16C SE]

cope v. [20C+] (*Ulster*) to defecate. [dial. *cope*, a pile]

Copenhagen capon n. [1960s+] (*US gay*) a transsexual (cf. DANISH PASTRY n.; GO TO COPENHAGEN v.; SOMETHING'S ROTTEN IN DENMARK phr.). [the ref. is to the pioneering operation undergone in Denmark in 1952 by Christine (formerly George) Jorgensen; a *capon* is a gelded cockerel]

copesette adj. *see* COPACETIC adj.

copess n. [1940s+] a policewoman (cf. MAMA BEAR n.; OFFICERETTE n.; ZOMBIE n.[1]). [COP n.[1] (1) + fem. sfx *-ess*]

cop for v.[1] [1950s+] **1** to have a relationship with. **2** (*US*) of a pimp, to entice a prostitute to join the group of women under his protection. **3** to make a successful seduction. [fig. use of COP v. (4)]

cop for v.[2] [1960s+] (*also* **cop to**) **1** to confess, to own up to, to admit. **2** to claim. **3** to obtain. [COP v. (4)]

cop for the blower v. [1960s] to make a phonecall. [COP v. (1) + BLOWER n.[5]]

cop hell v. *see* CATCH HELL v.

cop house n. [1920s+] (*US*) a police station. [COP n.[1] (1) + SE *house*]

co-pilot n. (*drugs*) **1** [1960s+] an amphetamine, usu. in pl. (cf. A n.[2]). **2** [1980s+] 2 or more people taking LSD together; more usu. the second person is not taking LSD and is there to look after people. [it helps you 'fly'; (1) also poss. the fact that truck drivers use it to stay awake]

cop it v. **1** [late 19C+] to get into trouble, to receive a severe reprimand. **2** [20C+] to be hit, to suffer in a given way, to die. **3** [1980s+] (*Aus. prison*) to be the passive member of a homosexual couple. [COP v. (6) + SE *it*; 'it' being trouble]

cop it hot v. **1** [late 19C+] to get into trouble, to receive a severe reprimand (cf. GET IT HOT (AND STRONG) v.). **2** [1910s+] to be hit, to suffer, to die. [COP IT v. + HOT adv. (1)]

cop it sweet v. [1960s+] (*Aus.*) **1** to accept problems without complaining, to get one's due deserts. **2** to have a stroke of luck. **3** to relax. [COP v. (6) + SWEET adv.[2]]

cop-killer n. [1980s+] (*US*) a Teflon-coated bullet capable of penetrating the body armour worn by policemen; such bullets are outlawed. [COP n.[1] (1) + SE *killer*]

cop, lock and block v. [1970s] (*US Black pimp*) to obtain a prostitute, to secure her to one's STABLE n. (2) and to ensure that no other pimp is able to lure her away. [COP v. (1) + SE *lock* + BLOCK v.[2] (4)]

cop magnet n. (*also* **copper magnet**) [1990s+] anything or anyone that attracts the unwelcome interest of the police. [COP n.[1] (1)/COPPER n.[3] (1) + MAGNET sfx]

copman n.[1] (*also* **copperman**) [late 19C–1950s] (*Aus.*) a policeman. [COP n.[1] (1)/COPPER n.[3] (1) + SE *man*]

copman n.[2] [1960s–80s] (*US drugs*) a drug dealer. [COP v. (4) + SE *man*]

cop money n. [1970s+] (*drugs*) money set aside for the purchase of drugs. [COP v. (4) + SE *money*]

cop off v.[1] (*US*) **1** [late 19C] to die. **2** [1920s] to meet someone later. **3** [1940s+] to make an excuse. **4** [1940s+] to inform someone of something. [var. on COP OUT v.[1] (1)/COP OUT v.[3] (3)]

cop off v.[2] [1900s–30s] to steal from. [COP v. (9) + SE *off*]

cop off v.[3] [1920s] (*US*) to arrest. [COP v. (1)]

cop off v.[4] **1** [1920s+] to seduce. **2** [1980s+] to embrace sexually, to indulge in petting; usu. *cop off with*. [orig. northern dial. *cop*, to act saucily or to catch (hold of) but note COP v. (14)]

cop-on n. [1990s+] (*Irish*) common sense, awareness. [COP v. (17)]

cop on v. **1** [late 19C+] to seduce, to pick up and, poss., to go to bed with. **2** [1930s+] to grab hold of. **3** [1940s+] to get a grip on oneself. [COP v.]

cop one v. [late 19C–1930s] to be hit. [COP v. (6) + ONE n.[1] (1)]

cop one's joint/thing v. *see* COP A JOINT v.

cop on the cross v. [late 19C] (*UK Und.*) to discover that someone is cheating, usu. by using cunning or deception oneself. [COP v. (1) + ON THE CROSS phr.]

cop-out n.[1] [1900s] (*US*) a chance or spontaneous meeting, esp. a pick-up by a street prostitute. [COP v. (1)]

cop-out n.[2] [1960s+] **1** a flight, an escape, a cowardly compromise or evasion, a retreat from reality. **2** a person who drops out of society. **3** a coward, someone who runs away from problems, a weakling. [COP OUT v.³ (2)]

cop-out *adj.* **1** [1950s+] compromised, defeated. **2** [1960s+] evasive. [COP OUT v.³ (2)]

cop out *v.*¹ **1** [mid–late 19C] to get into trouble. **2** [1960s] (*US campus*) to fail a test or examination. [COP v. (6)]

cop out *v.*² **1** [late 19C–1900s] (*US*) to obtain or to take for oneself. **2** [mid-19C–1940s] (*orig. UK Und.*) to arrest. **3** [1900s] (*US*) to steal. [COP v. (4)/COP v. (1)/COP v. (9)]

cop out *v.*³ **1** [1930s+] (*US Und.*) to use legal plea-bargaining to plead guilty to a lesser charge in return for having one dropped. **2** [1940s+] to avoid a problem or a difficult situation, to run away, to give up trying. **3** [1940s+] (*US Und.*) to confess, to inform. **4** [1950s] (*US Black/jazz*) to go to sleep. [COP A PLEA v.]

cop out *v.*⁴ *see* COP v. (13).

cop out on *v.*¹ [1900s] (*Aus.*) to take, to appropriate. [COP v. (5)]

cop out on *v.*² [1950s–60s] **1** to inform against. **2** to let down, to betray. [ext. of COP OUT v.³ (3)]

cop (out) to *v.* [1950s+] (*US*) to admit, to confess, to take responsibility for. [COP OUT v.³ (3)]

copped *adj.* [mid-19C+] arrested. [COP v. (1)]

copped up *adj.* [1960s] broken, old, run-down. [? euph. for FUCKED UP adj. (1)]

copper *n.*¹ (*also* **copperhide, copperskin**) [late 18C–19C] (*US*) a Native American. [the skin colour]

copper *n.*² **1** [late 18C+] a halfpenny; thus *coppers*, mixed pennies and halfpennies. **2** [late 18C+] (*US*) a cent. **3** [1930s] wages. [the colour]

copper *n.*³ **1** [mid-19C+] a policeman. **2** [late 19C+] an informer, whether in or out of prison. **3** [1910s+] (*US prison*) good conduct marks. **4** [1910s+] a prisoner who gains such marks (and who is thus considered to resemble a policeman). **5** [1940s] (*US Und./police*) parole. [the SE *copper* badges carried by New York City's first police sergeants; patrolmen had brass badges, lieutenants and captains silver ones; strengthened by COP v. (1)]

copper *v.*¹ (*US*) **1** [mid–late 19C] to steal, to embezzle. **2** [late 19C] to kill. **3** [late 19C–1920s] to outwit, to spoil. **4** [late 19C–1950s] to obtain, to make sure of getting. [COP v.; + ? Faro jargon, *copper a bet*, to bet that given card will lose]

copper *v.*² **1** [mid-19C–1920s] to arrest. **2** [1900s] (*US*) to discover. **3** [1920s] to inform. **4** [1920s+] to work as a policeman or detective. [COPPER n.³ (1)]

copper-bottomed *adj.* [late 19C+] admirable, excellent, impressive. [the positive connotations of SE *copper-bottomed*]

copper captain *n.* [mid–late 19C] a fraudulent, 'self-promoted' officer. [his BRASS n.² in posing in this way]

copper-clawing *n.* [late 19C] a fight between 2 women. [? *cap-a-clawing*, the clawing off of each other's cap]

copperhead *n.* (*US*) **1** [early–mid-19C] an unpleasant person. **2** [mid-19C] a Native American. **3** [mid-19C] a Northerner who backed the Confederacy; sometimes abbreviated to *Cop*. [SE *copperhead*, a venomous snake (*Agkistrodon contortrix*) common in the US]

copper-hearted *adj.* (*US Und.*) **1** [1930s] mean, vicious, adhering to the negative stereotypes of a policeman. **2** [1930s–60s] being an informer by nature; thus *turn copper-hearted*, to betray one's associates. [COPPER n.³ + SE *hearted*]

copperhide *n. see* COPPER n.¹.

copper house *n.* [1930s] a police station. [COPPER n.³ (1) + SE *house*]

copper jitters *n.* [1950s] (*US drugs/Und.*) excessive fear of the police, verging on obsession. [COPPER n.³ (1) + SE *jitters*]

copper john *n.* (*US Und.*) **1** [1910s] a prison warden. **2** [1930s] a prison. **3** [1940s] an informer. [COPPER n.³ (1) + JOHN n.¹ (1)]

copper nickel *n. see* WOODEN NICKEL n.

copper-nob *n.* (*also* **copper-knob**) [late 19C+] a red-headed person. [SE *copper* + NOB n.¹ (1)/KNOB n.¹ (1)]

coppernob *n.* [1910s; 1950s] (*UK juv.*) a policeman. [ext. of COPPER n.³]

copper-nose *n.* [mid-19C–1940s] (*US Black*) a drunkard. [COPPER-NOSED adj.]

copper-nosed *adj.* [late 17C–early 19C; 1940s] red-nosed (from drinking). [the broken red veins on the drunkard's nose; faded in mainstream use by 19C but was revived *c.*1940 by US Black users, albeit their pigmentation cannot turn lit. red]

copper-plated *adj.* [late 19C–1920s] (*US*) absolute, certain, definite. [var. on SE *gold-plated*]

copper shop *n.* [1910s+] a police station. [COPPER n.³ (1) + SHOP n.¹ (1)]

copper show *n.* [1900s–10s] (*Aus.*) a copper mine.

coppershy *adj.* [20C+] (*US Und.*) used of one who is terrified of the police. [COPPER n.³ (1) + SE *shy*]

copperskin *n. see* COPPER n.¹.

copper-slosher *n.* [late 19C] one who picks fights with the police. [COPPER n.³ (1) + SLOSH v.¹]

copper's nark *n.* [late 19C+] a police informer. [COPPER n.³ (1) + NARK n.¹ (1); note also COPPER n.³ (2)]

copper's shanty *n.* [late 19C] a police station. [COPPER n.³ (1) + SE *shanty*]

copper-stick *n.* [19C] **1** a policeman's truncheon. **2** the penis (cf. BAT n.⁷). [COPPER n.³ (1) + SE *stick*; (2) is fig. use of (1)/STICK n.¹ (1)]

coppertail *n.* (*also* **coppertop**) [late 19C–1950s] (*Aus.*) an unimportant person, a person of little social standing; thus a democrat rather than an aristocrat. [the inferiority of *copper* compared with silver]

copper time *n.* [1940s+] (*US Und.*) time off for good behaviour in prison. [COPPER n.³ (3) + TIME n.¹]

coppertop *n.*¹ [1910s–50s] a red-headed person.

coppertop *n.*² *see* COPPERTAIL n.

copping *n.* [1970s+] (*UK Und.*) the practice by corrupt policemen of taking bribes from criminals, to turn a blind eye when necessary, to drop charges, to lose evidence etc. [COP v. (19)]

copping clothes *n.* [1970s+] (*US*) of a pimp, a particularly smart, legitimate suit of clothes, worn specifically to entice and seduce potential prostitutes. [COP v. (20) + SE *clothes*]

copping corner *n.* (*also* **copping zone**) [1980s+] (*US drugs*) a street corner on which drug dealers collect to sell their wares. [COP v. (4) + SE *corner*]

copping fuck *n.* [1970s] (*US Und.*) the initiatory act of sexual intercourse between a newly recruited prostitute and her pimp. [COP v. (20) + FUCK n.¹ (1)]

copping zone *n.* [1980s+] (*drugs*) that area of a town or city where users will find the main drug market. [COP v. (4) + SE *zone*]

coppy *n.* [1950s–60s] a policeman. [COP n.¹ (1) + sfx *-y*]

cop shit *v.* [1980s] to suffer verbal abuse. [COP v. (6) + SHIT n.³ (8)]

cop shop *n.* [1940s+] (*orig. Aus.*) a police station. [COP n.¹ (1) + SHOP n.¹ (1)]

cop someone's drawers *v.* [1960s+] (*US*) of a man, to seduce a woman. [COP v. (10) + SE *drawers*]

cop (some) z's *v.* (*also* **count z's**) [1960s+] (*US*) to sleep, to have a nap. [COP v. (10)/SE *count* + z n.¹]

cop the brewery *v.* [mid-19C–1900s] to get drunk. [COP v. (4) + SE *brewery*]

cop the bullet *v.* [mid-19C+] to be dismissed from a job. [COP v. (6) + BULLET n.² (1)]

cop the cake/curranty *v. see* TAKE THE CAKE v.

cop the flick *v.* [1990s+] (*Aus.*) to be dismissed from one's employment. [COP v. (6) + a dismissive *flick* of the fingers]

cop the lot *v.* [late 19C+] to gain everything. [COP v. (6) + SE *lot*]

cop the needle *v.* [mid-19C+] to be extremely annoyed. [COP v. (6) + NEEDLE n.³]

cop the tale *v.* [20C+] to be fooled by a confidence trickster. [COP v. (6) + TALE n.¹ (1)]

cop to v. see COP FOR v.² (1).

cop up v. [1960s+] (drugs) to buy drugs. [COP v. (4)]

copus adj. see COPACETIC adj.

copy n. [late 19C] (US) a go, each, per item.

copycat n. **1** [late 19C+] one who mimics another, whether in their work, mannerisms, speech or other faculty. **2** [1950s+] a cheat at school. [SE copy + cat, an unpleasant person]

copyhold n. **1** [mid-17C–18C] the vagina. **2** [late 18C] a wife. [heavily joc. use of the legal terminology copyhold, 'the tenure of lands being parcel of a manor, at the will of the lord according to the custom of the manor' in law of King Richard III, 1483]

copyholder n. [mid-late 17C] a drinker who argues about the bill with the landlord. [for ety. see COPYHOLD n.]

cor! excl. (also **gor!**) [1930s+] a general excl. of amazement, surprise etc, a mild oath; occas. ext. as cor! chase me round the gasworks!/cor! chase my aunt Fanny up a gum tree/round a mulberry bush. [euph. for God]

coral n.¹ [mid-19C] money. [? its one-time role in bartering]

coral n.² [1970s+] (drugs) chloral hydrate. [mispron.]

coral branch n. (also **coral head**) [mid-17C–18C] the penis. [literary euph.]

coral stomper n. [1980s] (N.Z.) a derog. term for a Pacific islander.

corbie n. [1960s] a miser, a mean person. [OF corb, a crow]

cor blimey! excl. see GORBLIMEY! excl.

cord n. (also **corde**) [mid-19C–1900s] (US) a great deal, a large amount. [SE cord, a measure of cut wood, usu. 8ft long, 4ft broad and 4ft high (4 x 2 x 2m)]

corduroy n. [mid-19C] (US) hash, stew. [? the brown colour]

corduroy voice n. [1950s+] (US) a voice that continually fluctuates between high and low. [the up-and-down ridges in corduroy]

cordwood n.¹ [20C+] (US) a rustic, a farmer. [SE cordwood, lengths of wood cut and stacked for fuel]

cordwood n.² (US) **1** [1940s–60s] a kitchen match. **2** [1960s] a toothpick. [a joking comment on the respective sizes of 'timber' involved]

co-re n. [1910s–40s] a co-respondent in a divorce case (cf. CO n.²). [abbr.]

core v. [early–mid-19C] to steal small articles from shops (cf. CHORE v.). [Rom. cor, to steal]

-core sfx [1970s+] an all-purpose rock music sfx implying a particular heaviness (cf. HARDCORE n.³).

coriander (seed) n. [mid-18C–mid-19C] money (cf. ALFALFA n.; COLIANDER (SEED) n.].

corie n. (also **corey**) [20C+] the penis. [Rom. kori, a thorn]

coring n. [1930s] boxing. [Rom. koor, to fight]

coring mush n. [1930s] a boxer. [CORING n. + MUSH n.⁵ (2)]

corinne n. (also **corrine**) [1950s+] (drugs) cocaine (cf. AUNT NORA n.). [initial letters + play on female name; note cocaine is a 'feminine' drug, see GIRL n.²]

corinth n. [early 17C–mid-19C] a brothel. [the Greek city of Corinth, home to the temple of Aphrodite, goddess of love, was renowned for its depraved and licentious lifestyle. The term died out in the UK by the 19C but was perpetuated until the mid-century in the US]

corinthian n. **1** [late 16C–mid-19C] a dandy, a rake, one who is 'given to elegant dissipation' (OED). **2** [late 18C–early 19C] a regular frequenter of a brothel. [SE Corinth/CORINTH n.; note ancient Gk sl. corinthianize, to associate with courtesans. As 19C SE the term came to mean an idealized form of sportsman, this time in the field rather than the bedroom. It was widely popularized with the publication in 1821 of Pierce Egan's Life in London: The Day and Night Scenes of Jerry Hawthorne and his Elegant Friend, Corinthian Tom, the orig. Tom and Jerry and thus fathers to the eponymous Warner Bros. cartoon and the male leads of the 1970s BBC TV series The Good Life]

corinthian adj. [late 16C–early 19C] possessing the qualities of a dandy or rake. [CORINTHIAN n. (1)]

cork n.¹ [mid-late 19C] a bankrupt. [he bobs up and down like a cork, for lack of pecuniary 'ballast']

cork n.² [mid-19C–1900s] (US campus) the absolute inability to answer a question in class or to recite a passage from memory. [one's mouth is stopped with a cork]

cork n.³ [mid-19C+] (US) the penis (cf. BUTT-PLUNGER n.). [ext. of SE use; i.e. as a 'stopper']

cork n.⁴ [1950s–60s] (US) an Irish person; thus corktown, cork hill, the Irish part of a town or city. [proper name Cork, a city from whence many immigrants arrived in the US]

cork adj. see CORKED adj. (4).

cork v.¹ **1** [late 19C–1900s] (US campus) to baffle, to stun into silence. **2** [late 19C–1900s] to hit hard. **3** [late 19C+] to get the better of; thus wouldn't that cork you?, doesn't that infuriate or amaze you? **4** [late 19C+] (also **cork it (in)**) to be quiet, to stop talking. [fig. uses of SE cork; (2) pun on SE cork, a 'stopper']

cork v.² **1** [1970s+] of a man, to have sexual intercourse. **2** [1980s] to idle, to waste time. [CAULK v. + CORK n.³]

cork-brained adj. (also **corky-brained**) [mid-17C–early 19C] foolish, stupid (cf. AMOEBA-BRAINED adj.; CORKHEAD n.). [SE cork, which is notably light; thus lit. 'light-headed']

corked adj. **1** [late 19C+] drunk (cf. ALED UP adj.). **2** [20C+] constipated. **3** [1930s–40s] exhausted. **4** [1970s–80s] (UK Black) (also **cork**) absolutely full. [fig. uses of SE cork; (4) note CORK UP v. (3)]

corker n.¹ **1** [mid-19C] a stiff drink. **2** [20C+] (W.I.) alcohol, typically strong rum punch. [SE caulk, to fill up cracks; as a fig. sealant, rum can keep out the cold]

corker n.² **1** [mid-late 19C] the last word in an argument. **2** [mid-19C–1960s] a knockout punch; similarly in fig. use. **3** [mid-19C+] anything or anyone excellent, superlative, first-rate; sometimes used ironically; thus feminized as corkerina (cf. CAULKER n.). **4** [late 19C–1910s] something very difficult. **5** [late 19C+] an attractive young woman. [SE cork, a stopper; the cork fits the top of the bottle and thus 'tops' or 'corks up' all else]

corker adj. see CORKING adj.

corkhead n. [1940s] (US) a fool (cf. AIRBALL n.; CORK-BRAINED adj.). [SE cork + -HEAD sfx (1)]

cork-headed adj. [1910s] (US campus) arrogant, conceited. [? the idea of being SWELL-HEADED adj.]

corking adj. (also **corker**) [late 19C] excellent, wonderful. [CORKER n.² (3)]

cork it v. [1980s] to die.

cork it (in) v. see CORK v.¹ (4).

cork off v. (US) **1** [1910s–70s] to fall asleep. **2** [1940s] to go mad. **3** [1960s] to produce quickly, easily, to 'knock off'. [SE cork off, to stop up with a cork]

cork one's ass v. [1960s] (US Black) to astound, to stop and make one think.

cork out v. (US) **1** [1950s] to collapse exhausted. **2** [1960s] to fall asleep. [var. on CORK OFF v. (1)]

corks n.¹ [mid-19C] (orig. milit.) money (cf. ACTUAL, THE n.). [a cork is something that 'keeps one afloat']

corks n.² [mid-19C] a butler. [among his jobs is drawing the corks from bottles]

corksacking adj. [1970s+] a euph. for COCKSUCKING adj. [coined by Anthony Burgess in New York Times, 1972]

corkscrewed adj. [1910s] drunk (cf. ALED UP adj.). [fig. use of SE]

corkscrews n. [mid-late 19C] corkscrew curls or ringlets.

cork the air v. [1950s] (drugs) to inhale cocaine.

cork up adj. [1950s+] (W.I. Rasta/UK Black) jammed, filled, crowded. [CORK UP v. (3)]

cork up v. **1** [mid-19C–1950s] (US) to be quiet, to stop talking. **2** [late 19C] to make someone be quiet. **3** [1930s; 1970s–80s]

(*UK/UK Black*) to fill up. **4** [1960s] to get drunk. [fig. uses of SE *cork* + CORK v.[1] (1)]

corky *adj.* **1** [17C–20C] drunk, tipsy (cf. ALED UP adj.). **2** [mid-18C–19C] skittish, restless, frivolous, lively. **3** [2000s] (*US Black*) stupid, foolish. [CORKED adj.]

corky-brained *adj. see* CORK-BRAINED adj.

cor lumme! *excl.* [1930s+] a mild euph. oath, lit. 'God love me!' [COR! excl. + pron. SE *love me*]

corn *n.*[1] (*also* **seed corn**) [mid-18C+] money; thus *earn one's corn, worth one's corn,* to deserve one's wages (cf. ACTUAL, THE n.). [the roles of corn and money as staples of existence]

corn *n.*[2] **1** [19C+] (*US*) corn whisky. **2** [mid-19C+] (*US*) a drunkard. **3** [20C+] (*W.I.*) rum. [SE *corn,* its main constituent]

corn *n.*[3] [late 19C–1960s] (*US Black*) insincere chatter, flattery, deceit. [CON n.[1] (7)]

corn *n.*[4] [1930s+] (*orig. US*) anything unsophisticated, irritatingly or foolishly old-fashioned or sentimental, hackneyed, trite, inferior. [such things supposedly appeal to country people, i.e. growers of *corn*]

corn *n.*[5] [1950s+] (*W.I. Rasta*) marijuana (cf. AFRICAN BUSH n.). [euph.]

corn *n.*[6] [1950s+] (*W.I. Rasta*) a bullet. [? it resembles a small ear of corn]

cornball *n.* [1950s+] a naïve, unsophisticated person (cf. BUCKWHEAT n.). [SE *corn* + -BALL sfx]

cornball *adj.* [1940s+] (*US*) naïve, unsophisticated. [CORNY adj.]

cornbread *n.* [1950s+] **1** (*US Black*) a naïve, unsophisticated Southern person. **2** (*US*) anything old-fashioned, sentimental, hackneyed. [SE *cornbread,* a rural staple in southern US]

cornbread *adj.* [1950s+] **1** (*US*) plain, simple, down-to-earth. **2** (*US Black*) conventional, 'square'. [CORNBREAD n. (1)]

corncake *n.* [1960s] (*US*) $1 (cf. BATTER n.[4].). [SAmE *corncake,* a cake made of Indian cornmeal, but why?]

corncob *n.* [late 19C–1910s] (*Aus.*) a countryman, a peasant (cf. BUCKWHEAT n.). [his growing and eating of *corncobs*]

corncobber *n.* [1970s] (*US*) a countryman, a rustic (cf. BUCKWHEAT n.). [his growing and eating of *corncobs*]

corncob (oil) *n.* [mid-19C] (*US*) corn whisky.

corn coffee *n.* [1940s] (*US*) alcohol. [ext. of CORN n.[2] (1)]

corncracker *n.* [mid-19C+] (*US*) **1** a poor White farmer, a rustic (cf. ACORN-CRACKER n.; BUCKWHEAT n.). **2** a native of Florida, Georgia, Kentucky, Tennessee or Virginia. [? their subsisting on *corn* or maize]

corn-crackers *n. see* CORN-GRINDERS n.

corndog *n.* [1980s+] (*US campus*) someone who is socially inept or acts bizarrely. [fig. use of CORNDOG v., i.e. one who has suffered or who enjoys this; thus essentially a homophobic term]

corndog *v.* [1980s+] (*US*) to sodomize. [var. on CORNHOLE v.]

corned *adj.* [late 18C–19C] drunk (cf. ALED UP adj.). [the use of SE *corn* in the distillation of spirits; note ext. use in *Bulletin* (Sydney), 31 January 1885, 11/2: '[T]he vehicle was boarded by one of Cobb's boss employés, who, to put in mildly, had evidently anticipated Christmas, and had been where the golden corn was waving']

corned beef *n.* **1** [20C+] a thief. **2** [1950s+] (*UK prison*) a chief officer. [rhy. sl.]

corned willie *n.* [1910s–20s] (*US*) corned beef.

cornelian tub *n.* [late 18C] a sweating tub, used in the cure of venereal diseases. [? a pun on Lat. *cornu,* a horn; one's current incapacity is the result of one's HORN n.[2] (3); *see also* ety. at MOTHER CORNELIUS' TUB n.]

cornel wilder *n.* [1950s] (*Aus.*) a hairstyle once popular among Aus. youth. [the film star *Cornel Wilde* (1915–89)]

corner *n.*[1] [late 19C+] (*orig. US Und.*) a share, usu. in the spoils of a robbery; a commission on a deal.

corner *n.*[2] **1** [1950s+] (*UK Und.*) confidence trickery; thus *at the corner,* working as a confidence trickster. **2** [1970s] a confidence trick whereby shoddy goods are sold by pretending they are high-grade stolen property and playing on the 'thrill' some people derive from such a purchase. **3** [1970s] arranging to sell stolen goods and then having fake 'policemen' break in, confiscate the goods and threaten the victim with charges of receiving; the charges can, naturally, be dropped in return for a bribe, which is arranged by a fake 'solicitor', who makes sure there is no real police involvement by telling the victim that he has no rights in law and that paying and shutting up is the best thing to do. [the image of standing on the corner, waiting for a victim to appear + SE *corner,* to 'put into a tight place']

corner *n.*[3] [1960s] (*US prison*) the solitary confinement area.

corner *n.*[4] [2000s] (*US prison*) one's associates, the group with whom one spends time.

corner, the *n.* **1** [mid-19C] Tattersall's horse repository and betting rooms, sited at Hyde Park *Corner,* London W1. **2** [late 19C+] (*Aus.*) the junction of the states of Queensland, South Australia and New South Wales.

corner *v.* [early 19C+] (*orig. US*) to put into a position of difficulty or embarrassment. [ext. of SE]

corner boy *n.* (*also* **corner chap**) [mid-19C+] (*orig. US*) an idler who whiles away the time hanging around on street corners.

corner cove *n.* [mid-19C] (*orig. US*) an idler who hangs around on street corners. [SE *corner* + COVE n. (1)]

corner cowboy *n.* (*also* **corner wolf**) [1950s] (*orig. US*) a man, usu. young, given to standing around on street corners with his peers, gossiping, fooling around and ogling passing women. [SE (*street*) *corner* + COWBOY n.[1] (3)/WOLF n.[1] (1)]

corner cupboard *n.* [19C] the vagina (cf. BAG n.[1]). [the 'corner' being the fork of the legs]

cornerer *n.* [late 19C] a difficult question. [SE *corner,* to drive into a (fig.) corner]

corner man *n.* **1** [late 19C–1900s] an idler who hangs around on street corners. **2** [1940s] (*UK Und.*) a lookout.

corner wolf *n. see* CORNER COWBOY n.

cornet-player *n.* [1970s] (*drugs*) one who sniffs cocaine. [play on SE *blow*/BLOW v.[4] (3)]

corney-faced *adj. see* CORNY-FACED adj.

cornfed *n.*[1] [mid-19C] (*US*) **1** a Confederate soldier. **2** money issued by the Confederacy. [pun on SE *Confed(erate)*]

cornfed *n.*[2] [1910s–40s] (*US*) a country person (cf. BUCKWHEAT n.). [their supposed diet]

cornfed *adj.* **1** [late 18C+] plump, chunkily built. **2** [1910s+] (*orig. US*) banal, provincial, naïve. [SE *cornfed*/CORNFED n.[2]]

cornflake *n.* [1970s+] **1** an eccentric; one who stands outside the group norms. **2** a young male homosexual. [CORNY adj. + FLAKE n.[2] (2)]

cornflakes in a can *phr.* [1990s+] (*US campus*) beer. [use of corn in brewing]

corn-grinders *n.* (*also* **corn-crackers**) [mid-19C] (*US*) the teeth.

cornhole *n.* **1** [1910s+] (*orig. US*) the anus, the rectum (cf. A-HOLE n.). **2** [1970s] (*US*) an aggressor, a victimizer. **3** [1970s+] (*orig. US*) anal intercourse; thus *cornhole artist/cowboy,* one who enjoys anal intercourse. [a 'receptacle' for corn on the cob/COB n.[4]]

cornhole *v.* (*also* **corn-haul**) [1930s+] (*US*) to have anal intercourse, to sodomize; also fig. use (cf. ASK FOR THE RING v.). [CORNHOLE n. (1)]

cornholer *n.* [1950s+] (*US*) a sodomite of men or women. [CORNHOLE v.]

cornhusker *n.* [20C+] (*US*) **1** a farmer, a peasant (cf. ACORN-CRACKER n.). **2** a native of Nebraska. [SE *cornhusker,* one who strips the husks from the ears of Indian corn]

cornichon *n.* [late 19C] (*UK society*) a poor shot. [Fr. *cornichon,* lit. a gherkin, and used in Fr. argot to mean a novice or greenhorn]

corniferous *adj.* [late 17C–early 18C] cuckolded. [lit. 'horn-bearing', thus HORN n.[1] (1)]

corniferously *adv.* [late 17C–early 18C] in the state of being cuckolded. [CORNIFEROUS adj.]

corn in Egypt *n.* [19C] money (cf. ACTUAL, THE *n.*). [phr. *corn in Egypt*, a plentiful supply, f. Gen. 42:2]

Cornish duck *n.* [late 19C] a pilchard. [the fishing trade in Cornwall]

corn juice *n.* (*also* **corn-moon**) [mid-19C–1930s] (*US*) whisky, whether legally or illicitly distilled. [SE *corn* + *juice*/CORN *n.*² (1) + JUICE *n.*³/MOONSHINE *n.* (2)]

corn mission *n.* [1980s] (*UK Black*) an illegal money-making scheme, e.g. a robbery. [CORN *n.*¹ + SE *mission*]

corn mule *n.* [1920s–60s] (*US*) illicitly distilled corn whisky. [SE *corn*/CORN *n.*² (1) + MULE *n.*³ (1)]

corn off the cob *n.* [1940s+] (*Aus./US*) banality. [play on CORNY *adj.*]

corn on the cob *n.* [1970s+] (*US Black*) sexual intercourse in which the partners are partially clad. [the phallic SE *cob*/COB *n.*⁴ + ? partial clothing resembles a partially eaten corn on the cob]

cornpone *n.* [19C+] (*US Black*) a rustic, a peasant, esp. a person obviously from the southern US (cf. BUCKWHEAT *n.*). [SE *cornpone*, a cornmeal cake or bread made of maize, milk and eggs, formed into ovals and baked or fried]

cornpopper *n.* (*US*) **1** [1940s] a large truck. **2** [1970s] a cheap car. [? the noise of the exhaust]

corns and bunions *n.* [1910s+] onions. [rhy. sl.]

cornshucking *adj.* [mid–late 19C] (*US, Southern*) a euph. for DAMNED *adj.*

corn squeezings *n.* [1940s+] (*US*) illicitly distilled whisky. [its main ingredient]

cornstalk *n.* **1** [early–mid-19C] (*US*) a tall, thin person. **2** [early 19C–1940s] (*Aus.*) (*also* **cornstalker**) a European native of New South Wales; thus *John Cornstalk, Jack Cornstalk*, a generic for such people; *Cornstalkopolis*, Sydney. **3** [mid-19C+] (*N.Z.*) an Australian; also attrib. [their characteristic tall slimness or, like corn, they 'shoot up']

cornstealer *n.* [mid–late 19C] the human hand.

cornswoggled *adj. see* HORNSWOGGLED *adj.*

cornthrasher *n.* (*also* **cornthresher**) [mid-19C] (*orig. US*) a farmer, a rustic (cf. ACORN-CRACKER *n.*).

cornucopia *n.* **1** [19C] the vagina (cf. ADAM'S OWN (ALTAR) *n.*). **2** [late 19C; 1990s+] (*US*) a rich person. [Lat. *cornucopia*, the horn of plenty]

corn up *v.* [late 19C] (*US*) to get drunk. [CORN *n.*² (1)]

cornute *n.* (*also* **cornuto, cornutus**) [17C–18C] one who is cuckolded. [CORNUTE *v.*]

cornute *v.* [late 16C–mid-19C] to cuckold. [lit. 'to make horned', thus HORN *n.*¹ (1)]

cornuted *adj.* [late 17C–early 18C] cuckolded. [CORNUTE *v.*]

cornuto/cornutus *n. see* CORNUTE *n.*

corny *adj.* [1930s+] **1** sentimental, naïve, unsophisticated. **2** simple, obvious. **3** rural, socially backward. **4** banal. [such characteristics are attributed to country folk, surrounded by *corn*fields]

corny-faced *adj.* (*also* **corney-faced**) [late 17C–early 19C] acned, heavily pimpled; seen as the badge of a drunkard. [SE *corn*, a horny lump that appears on the feet]

coroner *n.* [mid–late 19C] a heavy fall. [i.e. one that may prove fatal and lead to the coroner's court]

corp *n.*¹ (*also* **corpy**) [20C+] (*orig. milit.*) *corp*oral. [abbr.]

corp *n.*² [20C+] (*Ulster*) a useless person. [SE *corpse*]

corpie *n.*¹ [1940s+] (*W.I.*) a policeman. [SE *corporal*]

corpie *n.*² [2000s] the *corp*oration (local government, not business). [abbr.]

corporal (love) *n.* [20C+] (*US*) the penis. [pun on SE; it 'stands to attention']

corporate *adj.* [1980s+] (*US campus*) appearing sophisticated, business-like. [ext. of SE use]

corporation *n.* [late 18C–1940s] the body or stomach, esp. when fat. [play on ALDERMAN *n.*¹ (4)]

corporation cocktail *n.* [1970s] coal gas bubbled through milk, a down-and-out alcoholic's tipple. [although in an age of natural gas this drink is redundant]

corporation hair oil *n.* [1950s+] (*Irish*) water, as used in smoothing down the hair.

corporosity *n.* (*also* **corporacity**) [mid-19C–1900s] (*US*) one's self, one's being, one's body; esp. in phr. *how does your corporosity sagaciate?* how do you feel? [Lat. *corpus*, the body]

corpse *n.* [1990s+] (*US campus*) a boring person.

corpse *v.* **1** [mid-19C–1930s] to kill, to murder; also in fig. use. **2** [late 19C; 2000s] (*also* **corpse it**) to die. [abbr. SE *to make a corpse of*; note theatre use *corpse*, to cause (intentionally or not) a fellow performer to forget their lines and/or laugh on stage; thus to make him or her 'die']

corpse-provider *n.* [mid-19C–1920s] a doctor. [cynical assessment of their role]

corpse-reviver *n.* [mid-19C–1930s] (*orig. US*) a kind of mixed drink, now esp. a pick-me-up for a hangover. [note lit. use in 1910 *Bulletin* (Sydney) 22 Dec. 14/4: 'On a later occasion an old native found a bottle (quart) of medicine known locally as "corpse reviver," used in cases of divers' paralysis. Mistaking it for rum, the old nigger took a long, long drink – "enough to kill four Malay seamen," said the doctor']

corpy *n. see* CORP *n.*¹.

corral *n.* [1960s–70s] a group of prostitutes working for a single pimp (cf. BROTHER-IN-LAW *n.*). [ext. of SE use; var. on STABLE *n.* (2)]

corral *v.* [mid-19C+] (*orig. US*) to secure, to lay hold of, to seize, to capture, to 'collar'. [orig. Sp. *corral*, an enclosed place, yard, courtyard, pen, poultry-yard etc]

correct card *n.* [mid–late 19C] the 'done thing', the fashionable object or style. [racing use]

correct tittup, the *phr.* [late 19C–1900s] the right thing. [SE *correct* + *tittup*, 'get-up', style of dress, ult. dial. *tittup*, an impudent or forward woman, a hussy]

corredores *n.* [1990s+] (*US drugs*) the people who work for a cocaine dealer, as guards etc. [Sp. *corredor*, broker]

corridor creepers *n. see* BROTHEL CREEPERS *n.*

corrine *n. see* CORINNE *n.*

corroboree *n.* [mid-19C+] (*Aus.*) a social gathering, a noisy party, a disturbance. [a word in the extinct language of Port Jackson, New South Wales; *corroboree*, an Aborigine dance held at night by moonlight or a bush fire, either of a festive or warlike character]

corroboree water *n.* [1920s+] (*Aus.*) cheap wine. [CORROBOREE *n.* + SE *water*]

corrode *v.* [1970s] (*US campus*) to be overcome with disgust or repulsion. [SE *corrode*, to eat away at, to wear away, esp. through the action of chemicals on metal]

corroded *adj.* [1980s] **1** (*US Black*) unappealing, unattractive. **2** (*US*) very drunk.

corybungus *n.* [early 19C] (*orig. boxing*) the posterior, the buttocks. [ety. unknown; ? link to SE *bung*, a stopper]

'cos *prep.* (*also* **'cause, 'coz, 'cuz**) [early 19C+] because. [abbr.]

cosa *n.* [1980s+] (*drugs*) marijuana. [? Sp. *cosa*, a thing; thus euph.]

cosan *n. see* CASSAN *n.*

cosey *n.* [late 19C–1900s] **1** a love affair. **2** 'a small, hilarious public-house, where singing, dancing, drinking etc goes on at all hours' (Ware). [SE *cosy*]

cosh *n.* (*also* **kosh**) **1** [mid-19C+] a stout stick, bludgeon or truncheon, a 'life-preserver'; thus *cosh-bandit, cosh-boy, cosh-man, the cosh, cosher*, one who uses a cosh. **2** [late 19C] the action of knocking out or down with a cosh. [echoic; note dial. *cosh*, stick (of any kind), but it may not predate sl.]

cosh *v.* (*also* **kosh**) [mid-19C+] to hit (with a bludgeon or 'life-preserver'). [COSH *n.*]

cosh! *excl.* [19C] an extra-mild euph. for *God!* [var. on GOSH! excl.]

cosh-carrier *n.* [late 19C] one who works with and acts as bodyguard for a prostitute. [COSH n. (1) + SE *carrier*]

cosh-poke *n.* [1950s] (*UK prison*) a club, a bludgeon. [COSH n. (1) + SE *poke*]

cosign *n.* [1970s] (*US Black/prison*) an agreement, an act of support. [CO-SIGN v.]

co-sign *v.* [1970s+] (*US Black/prison*) to agree; to underwrite or verify.

cosmic *adj.* [1970s+] excellent, first-rate, perfect. [SE *cosmic*, i.e. the contemporary interest in psychedelic drugs]

cosmo *adj.* [1980s+] (*US campus*) fashionable, trendy. [fig. use of abbr. SE *cosmopolitan*]

cosmoline *n.* [1940s] (*US milit.*) butter. [SAmE *cosmoline*, a form of purified solid paraffin]

cosmopolitan *n.* [late 19C] (*US short order*) Neapolitan ice-cream.

cosmos *n.* (*also* **cozmos**) [1970s+] (*drugs*) phencyclidine (cf. ACE n.⁴). [play on SE *cosmos*, i.e. it gets one HIGH adj.¹ (2)]

cossack *n.* [mid-19C–1930s] a policeman, esp. one used to break a strike. [proper name *Cossack*, the Turkish tribe living to the north of the Black Sea, who were organized into cavalry and fought for the Polish, then the Russian army; ult. Turki *quzzaq*, adventurer, guerrilla]

cosser *n. see* COZZER n.

cossie *n.* (*also* **cossy, cozzie**) **1** [1920s+] (*orig. Aus./S.Afr.*) a swimming costume. **2** [1970s+] (*Aus.*) any form of costume, i.e. fancy dress. [abbr.]

cost *v.* [1910s+] to prove expensive, to cost a great deal.

cost a bomb *v.* [1950s+] to cost a great deal. [COST v. + BOMB n.¹ (3)]

costa del crime *n.* [1980s+] that part of southeastern Spain where a large number of British criminals have chosen to make their homes. [coined by tabloid press on model of tourist brochure SE *Costa del Sol*]

cost a packet *v.* [1930s+] to cost a great deal. [COST v. + PACKET n.³ (1)]

costard *n.* [16C–early 19C] the human head. [SE *costard*, a large apple]

coster *n.* [mid-19C+] a costermonger. [abbr.; orig. *costard-monger*, apple seller, a street seller of fruit or vegetables, poultry or fish. 'A great being in low life, generally a sort of prince [...]. To be really royal he must make money, but save nothing, dress beautifully [...], be handsome in a rough way, be always flush of cash and liberal with it, possess a handsome girl or wife [...] and above all, fight well, and be always ready to fight. Reign generally extends five years (nineteen to twenty-four), when he either takes a shop and does well, takes to drink and does worse, or growing ancient, grizzly, or broken with disease, loses a fight, abdicates and sinks into the ranks' (Ware). Hotten (1860) prefigures this picture, noting their use of '*a Cant* or so-called *back Slang* language']

coster *v.* [mid–late 19C] to work as a costermonger or to act in a way expected of a coster. [COSTER n.]

cost ya! *excl.* (*also* **it'll cost ya!**) [1960s+] it will *cost you* something, i.e. don't ask for favours, but most things can be done – for a price. [abbr.]

cosy *adj.* [early–mid-19C] a euph. for drunk (cf. ABOUT RIGHT phr.¹).

cosy *v.* [1930s+] (*orig. US*) to comfort, to reassure, to delude. [ext. of SE use]

cosy up to *v.* [1930s+] (*orig. US*) to become intimate with, to ingratiate oneself with.

cot *n.* (*also* **quot**) [late 17C–18C] a man who meddles in 'women's work' around the house. [abbr. COTQUEAN n.]

cotbetty *n.* [mid-19C+] a man who meddles in 'women's work' around the house. [COT n. + proper name *Betty*; orig. Lincolnshire dial., the term survived up to mid-20C in areas of the US]

cot-case *n.* (*Aus./N.Z.*) **1** [1940s+] an invalid. **2** [1950s] one who is suffering from a hangover. **3** [1980s] a drunkard. [(1) and (2) one who is confined to their bed. (3) fig. use of (2)]

cotch *n.* [1970s+] (*S.Afr.*) sickness, vomit. [COTCH v.¹]

cotch *adj.* [1970s+] (*S.Afr.*) unpleasant, disgusting. [COTCH v.¹]

cotch *v.*¹ (*also* **kotch**) [1970s+] (*S.Afr.*) to vomit. [Afk. *kots*, to vomit]

cotch *v.*² [1990s+] (*W.I./UK teen*) to shirk work, to behave lazily; to relax. [SE *cotch*, to lean on, ult. f. SE *scotch*, to wedge or block]

cotch (up) *v.* [1950s+] (*W.I. Rasta*) to support something else, as with a forked stick, to balance something or place it temporarily; thus *beg someone a cotch*, to find a place on a crowded bus seat or bench; *cotch a while*, to stay somewhere temporarily. [UK dial. *scotch*, to squeeze or wedge in]

cote-si-cote-la *n.* (*also* **kote-si-kote-la**) [20C+] (*W.I.*) amusing (rather than pointedly malicious) gossip. [Fr. 'on this side and on the other']

cot house *n. see* RAG HOUSE n.

'cotics *n.* [1930s+] (*drugs*) narcotics. [abbr.]

cotquean *n.* (*also* **quotquean**) [late 16C–early 19C] an effeminate man, who is seen as dealing too keenly with domestic duties that are properly those of his wife. [SE *cotquean*, a peasant housewife]

cotso! *excl.* (*also* **cot's flesh! cots-plut!**) [late 17C–early 19C] a general excl. of annoyance, surprise etc; a euph. for 'God's oath!' [*cots*, God; ? reinforced by CATSO n.]

Cotswold lion *n.* [16C–18C] a sheep.

cott *v. see* ENDACOTT v.

cottage *n.* **1** [mid-19C] an illegal gambling establishment. **2** [late 19C+] a public convenience; thus anywhere male homosexuals gather for sex, often a public lavatory; thus *cottage-crawling*, moving from one public convenience to another in search of sex (cf. BACKHOUSE n.). [categorized by Ware as a usage of 'fast youths' and attributed to 'the published particulars of an eccentrically worded will in which the testator left a large fortune to be laid out in building "cottages of convenience"']

cottage *adj.* [1970s+] (*US campus*) bad, second-rate; eccentric. [? the perceived inadequacy of such a rural dwelling]

cottage *v.* (*also* **cottage crawl**) [1960s+] (*gay*) to frequent public lavatories, parks etc for sex; thus *cottaging*, *cottager*. [COTTAGE n. (2) + SE *crawl* (on pattern of PUB-CRAWL v.)]

cottage queen *n.* (*also* **cottage cruiser**) [1960s+] a male homosexual who solicits in public conveniences. [COTTAGE n. + QUEEN n.² (1)/QUEEN sfx (2)/CRUISER n.¹ (5)]

cotterell's salad *n.* (*also* **Sir James Cotterell's salad**) [late 18C] hemp. [a pun on proper name Sir James *Cotterell*, an Anglo-Irish nobleman, hanged for rape, itself both a crime and a plant, *Brassica napus*]

cotton *n.*¹ **1** [1930s+] (*drugs*) (*also* **charlie cotton**) a small piece of material through which heroin has been sucked up into a syringe and which can be boiled, when no better supplies exist, to extract a final measure of heroin; thus *ask for the cotton*, to ask for another addict's used cotton in the hope of using such narcotic residue as may be extracted; *down at the cotton*, reduced to boiling one's saved-up cottons to extract a last residue of heroin/morphine. **2** [1950s–70s] (*US prison/drugs*) the Benzedrine-soaked cotton wadding of a nasal inhaler.

cotton *n.*² [1930s+] money. [its role as a commodity; it 'sews' life together]

cotton *n.*³ [1960s+] (*US Black*) female pubic hair. [resemblance]

cotton *v. see* COTTON (TO) v.

cotton brothers *n.* [1930s+] (*drugs*) cocaine, heroin and morphine, esp. as saturating the cotton filter used in the injecting process. [all of which are filtered through a COTTON n.¹ (1) before injection]

cotton-chopper *n.* [1970s] (*US*) a derog. term for a Southerner.

[play on SE; the one-time importance of cotton in the economy of the Southern states]

cotton curtain *n.* [1950s] (*US Black*) the Southern states, esp. as seen by those Blacks who had moved north during the previous decade. [for ety. *see* COTTON-CHOPPER n. + a play on SE phr. the *iron curtain*]

cotton fever *n.* [1970s+] (*drugs*) a very high temperature that can result from accidentally introducing cotton fibres, impregnated with narcotics, into the bloodstream. [COTTON n.[1] (1)]

cotton freak *n.* [1960s] (*US drugs*) one who breaks open Benzedrine inhalers and eats the drug-soaked cotton they contain. [COTTON n.[1] (2) + FREAK sfx]

cotton habit *n.* [1930s–60s] (*US drugs*) a poor user's addiction, sustained by boiling cotton filters. [COTTON n.[1] (1) + HABIT n. (1)]

cottonhead *n.* (*US*) **1** [mid-19C+] a fool (cf. AIRBALL n.). **2** [2000s] a state of forgetfulness. [SE *cotton* + -HEAD sfx (1)]

cotton-headed *adj.* [1930s] (*US*) foolish, stupid (cf. AIRHEADED adj.). [COTTONHEAD n.]

cotton is low *phr.* (*also* **cotton is going down, cotton is hanging (below the market), cotton is pretty**) [1960s–70s] (*US, mainly Southern*) a warning to a woman that her slip is showing (cf. CHARLIE'S DEAD phr.).

cotton lord *n.* [mid–late 19C] a wealthy Manchester cotton manufacturer.

cottonmouth *n.* **1** [20C+] (*also* **desert mouth**) the dry mouth that comes with a hangover. **2** [1940s+] (*US Und.*) a dry mouth caused by fear; thus *cotton-mouthed*. **3** [1960s+] (*drugs*) a mouth that has become dry through smoking marijuana.

cottonocracy *n.* [mid-19C] cotton magnates viewed as a group. [SE *cotton* + (arist)*ocracy*]

cotton on (to) *v.* [19C+] **1** to become attached to; to form a liking for. **2** to realize, to understand. **3** to recognize. [ext. of COTTON (TO) v.]

Cottonopolis *n.* [late 19C] Manchester. [its world-dominating 19C cotton industry]

cotton-picker *n.* (*US*) **1** [1910s+] an unpleasant, unpopular person. **2** [1930s+] a derog. term for a Black person (cf. AFRICAN APE n.). [COTTON-PICKING adj. (1)/lit. ref. to slavery]

cotton-pickers *n.* [1960s+] (*US*) the hands. [their function]

cotton-picking *adj.* [20C+] (*US*) **1** a general term of abuse, second-rate, vulgar, insignificant (cf. PEAPICKING adj.). **2** a euph. for DAMNED adj. [the role of the slaves who picked cotton in the American South and as such an implicitly racist term]

cotton pony *n.* [1990s+] a tampon. [the string for removal resembles a tail]

cotton shooter *n.* [1930s+] (*US drugs*) one who is reduced to begging more prosperous addicts for their used COTTON n.[1] (1) in the hope of extracting some narcotic residue from them. [COTTON n.[1] (1) + SHOOTER n.[2] (1)]

cottontail *n.* [1970s] (*US*) an attractive young woman. [the common rabbit of the United States (*Lepus sylvaticus*), which has a white fluffy tail + the trad. sexuality of rabbits]

cotton (to) *v.* **1** [mid-16C+] to agree, to get on with, whether of people or objects; often as *cotton together*, for 2 people to get on well (cf. COTTON ON (TO) v.). **2** [late 17C+] to understand, to get to know about. **3** [mid-19C–1910s] (*US*) to toady. **4** [late 19C–1910s] to favour. [SE *cotton*, to succeed, to prosper. Hotten (1859) suggests to adhere to, like cotton threads sticking to a rough or napped material]

cottontop *n.*[1] [mid–late 19C] a 'loose' woman who keeps up quasi-respectable appearances. [a style of stockings of which the lower, visible portion was silk and the remainder cotton]

cottontop *n.*[2] [20C+] (*US*) **1** a person with light-coloured hair, a white blond. **2** a Swede. [equation of white cotton buds with hair; (2) stereotypically blond Swedes]

cotton up (to) *v.* [mid–19C+] **1** to make friendly overtures towards. **2** in fig. use, to get on well with, to suit, to agree.

cotton wool *v.* **1** [1980s+] (*Aus. prison*) to masturbate (cf. DRAIN CHARLES DICKENS v.; HAM SHANK v.; POLISH AND GLOSS v.; PULL RANK v.[2]; SHABBA v.; SHANK v.[3]; STRIPEY FAT v.; TAXI-RANK v.; THREE BAGS v.; WHIP AND TOP v.; YANK THE PLANK v.). **2** [1990s+] to seduce. [rhy. sl.; (1) = PULL v.[7]; (2)= PULL v.[2] (5)]

cou *n. see* COO n.

couch *v.* **1** [late 16C–mid-18C] to lie (down). **2** [1980s+] (*US*) to lounge around on the couch (watching television). [SE *couch*/COUCH POTATO n.]

couch a hogshead *v.* (*also* **couch a cod's head**) [mid-16C–early 19C] (*UK Und.*) to lie down and sleep. [SE *couch*, to lie down + SE *hogshead*, comparing the sleeper to a recumbent pig/COD'S HEAD n.; Ribton-Turner, *A History of Vagrants* (1887), suggests Welsh *hepiad*, *hephun*, a slumber or doze]

couch a porker *v.* [early 18C] to lie down and sleep. [play on COUCH A HOGSHEAD v.]

couch case *n.* [1960s+] an eccentric, a mad person, one in need of psychiatric help. [the trad. analyst's *couch* + fig. use of SE *case*]

couch checkers *n.* [1960s] (*US*) love-making on a couch. [SE *couch* + *checkers* (UK draughts)]

couch commander *n.* [1980s+] (*US campus/teen*) **1** a TV remote control unit. **2** (*also* **couch commando**) the person operating the remote control.

couch cootie *n.* [1910s–20s] (*US*) a poor or miserly man who prefers to court a woman in her own house than take her out on the town. [SE *couch* + COOTIE n.[1] (1)]

couch hockey *n.* [1990s+] sexual intercourse (on a couch). [the penis is presumably the 'stick', the vagina the 'goal']

couch hockey (for one) *n.* [1990s+] masturbation. [COUCH HOCKEY n.]

couch lock *n.* [2000s] (*US*) a state of inertia induced by excessive drug consumption.

couch potato *n.* [1970s+] (*orig. US*) one who is addicted to watching TV and who does this while sitting or lying on the couch, as inert and brain-dead as a potato. [coined 1976, allegedly a play on the earlier *boob tuber*]

cougar juice *n.* (*also* **cougar milk**) [1920s–30s] (*US*) rough, illicit whisky, esp. that sold during the Prohibition era. [modern skiers enjoy 'Cougar Milk': Put a good teaspoon of Eagle Brand Condensed Milk in a glass with an ounce of rum and a pinch of nutmeg. Fill with boiling water, stir gently and you have a smooth drink for a cold day]

couge *n.* [early 19C] (*US*) the drink, punch.

cough *n.* [1920s+] a confession (esp. one that is presumed to be sincere and factual). [COUGH v. (1)]

cough *v.* [late 19C+] (*orig. US*) **1** (*also* **cough on, cough to**) to confess, to inform. **2** (*also* **cough on**) to talk about. **3** to vomit (cf. BARF v.). **4** to hand over, to give, esp. money.

cough and choke *v.* [1990s+] to smoke. [rhy. sl.]

cough and sneeze *n.* [1910s+] cheese. [rhy. sl.]

cough and stutter *n.* [20C+] butter. [rhy. sl.]

cough drop *n.* **1** [late 19C+] poison, or anything disagreeable. **2** [late 19C+] a disagreeable person. **3** [late 19C+] a 'character', a 'card'. **4** [1940s+] (*S.Afr.*) a pretty woman. [fig. uses of SE; (1) the slogan of a popular cough lozenge, 'cough no more']

cough it (out) *v. see* COUGH UP v. (1).

cough it up *v. see* COUGH UP v.

cough medicine *n.* (*also* **cough syrup**) **1** [1910s] (*US*) whisky. **2** [1920s] (*US Und.*) bribe money. [SE/COUGH v. (1)]

cough on *v. see* COUGH v.

cough one's yoghurt *v.* [1990s+] to ejaculate.

cough syrup *n. see* COUGH MEDICINE n.

cough to *v. see* COUGH v. (1).

cough up *v.* (*also* **cough it up**) **1** [late 19C+] (*also* **cough it (out)**) to confess, to reveal (information). **2** [late 19C+] to hand over, to give, esp. money. **3** [20C+] to vomit; ext. as *cough up one's guts* (cf. BARF v.). **4** [1920s+] (*Aus.*) to speak. [ext. of COUGH v.]

could fuck up a wet dream *phr.* (*also* would fuck up a wet dream) [1960s+] referring to one who is exceptionally incompetent, stupid or clumsy (cf. CAN'T SEE THROUGH A LADDER *phr.*).

could it be Satan? *phr.* [1980s+] (*US campus*) a reaction to something seen as naughty. [the catchphrase of the Church Lady (played by Dana Carvey), in the US TV show *Saturday Night Live*]

couldn't beat a carpet *phr.* [late 19C+] a phr. used to indicate weakness.

couldn't blow the froth off a glass of beer *phr.* (*also* couldn't find a grand piano in a one-roomed house, …knock the dags off a sick canary, …knock the skin off a rice-pudding, …pick a seat at the pictures, …pull the skin off a bread and butter custard, …tell the time if the town-hall clock fell on top of them, …train a choko vine over a country dunny) [1930s+] (*Aus.*) a phr. used in contemptuous dismissal of a weakling, an incompetent or other inadequate.

couldn't brush a bee from a bucket *phr.* [1900s] (*Aus.*) said of one who is physically weak.

couldn't fight one's way out of a paper bag *phr.* [1910s+] a phr. used to imply physical weakness on the part of the subject.

couldn't fuck a frog trotting *phr.* [1980s] (*N.Z.*) a phr. used of an incompetent.

couldn't get a job on a shithouse cart *phr.* [1990s+] (*Aus.*) a phr. used of a complete inadequate/incompetent.

couldn't get pussy in a cathouse *phr.* [1970s] (*US Black*) a phr. used of someone who is utterly incompetent. [play on PUSSY n. (2) + CAT-HOUSE n.]

couldn't hit them in the behind with a red apple *phr.* [1990s+] (*US Black*) a phr. used of a conceited or arrogant person, a headstrong person or one who believes themself intellectually superior.

couldn't hit someone with a buggy whip *phr.* [1910s] (*US*) of a boxer, to be completely incompetent.

couldn't knock a chop off a gridiron *phr.* [1900s] (*Aus.*) to be feeling physically weak and/or ill.

couldn't knock a sick moll off a pisspot *phr.* (*also* couldn't pull…) [1950s+] (*Aus.*) a phr. used of a weakling or coward. [play on sl.]

couldn't organize a fuck in a brothel *phr.* [1940s+] a phr. used to indicate that the subject is utterly incompetent.

couldn't organize a piss-up in a brewery *phr.* (*also* couldn't run…) [1930s+] a phr. used of an individual with such minimal competence that, even provided with everything necessary to achieve a given aim, that aim remains beyond him or her.

couldn't push an egg off a fence *phr.* [1910s] (*Aus.*) a phr. implying weakness and/or incompetence.

couldn't raffle a chook in a pub *phr.* [2000s] (*Aus.*) a phr. used to indicate the the subject is very disorganized and incompetent.

couldn't see the road to the dunny if it had red flags on it *phr.* [1980s] (*N.Z.*) stupid; drunk (cf. CAN'T SEE THROUGH A LADDER *phr.*).

couldn't sell a statue to a pigeon *phr.* [1980s] (*N.Z.*) ineffectual.

council gritter *n.* [1990s+] the anus; usu. in phr. *go up the council*, to have anal intercourse, not necessarily homosexual (cf. BOTTLE AND GLASS n.). [rhy. sl. = SHITTER n.[1] (1)]

council houses *n.* [1930s+] trousers. [rhy. sl.]

councillor of the piepowder court *n.* [mid-18C–mid-19C] a pettifogging lawyer. [SE *Court of Piepowders*, the court of wayfarers or travelling traders; ult. Fr. *pieds poudreux*, dusty feet]

council-of-ten *n.* [mid-19C] the toes of a man whose feet turn inwards when he walks. [proper name *Council of Ten*, a secret tribunal of the Venetian Republic (1310–1797)]

counselling *n.* [1980s+] (*Aus. prison*) a beating by a prisoner officer. [ironic]

count *n.*[1] [mid-19C] a dandy, a swell. [play on SE]

count *n.*[2] [1970s] (*US drugs*) the quantity of a given drug for sale.

count *v.* [mid-19C+] to reckon, to consider, to believe. [SE *count, account regard, hold that*]

counter-caterpillar *n.* [early 18C] a constable. [SE *counter*, a prison attached to a city court or a mayor's office + CATERPILLAR n.[1] (1)]

counterfeit crank *n.* (*also* counterfeit cranker) [mid-16C–early 19C] (*UK Und.*) a mendicant villain who specializes in faking sickness, esp. epilepsy ('the falling sickness'); he would often display convincingly horrific sores and wounds, created by the application of various herbs. [SE *counterfeit* + Du. or Ger. *krenk*, sickness]

counter-hopper *n.* (*also* counter-spank) [mid-19C–1960s] a store clerk, a male shop assistant, also used as a general pej. term. [var. on COUNTER-JUMPER n.]

counter-jumper *n.* (*also* counter-jump, counter-leaper, counter-skipper) **1** [early 19C–1950s] a store clerk, a male shop assistant; also attrib.; thus *counter-jump*, to work in such a job. **2** [mid-19C+] one who has 'ideas above his or her station' and who wishes, as it were, to 'jump the counter' to the customers' side. [play on SE]

counter-rat *n.* **1** [17C–early 18C] an inferior officer of a debtor's prison. **2** [early 18C] a criminal inmate of a debtor's prison. [SE *counter*, a (debtor's) prison + SE *rat*]

countess of puddle-dock *n.* (*also* duchess of puddle-dock) [mid-17C–mid-18C] a self-appointed but spurious aristocrat. [*Puddle Dock* in London, now the site of the Mermaid Theatre, but orig. a large stagnant pool off the River Thames]

count in *v.* [mid-19C+] (*orig. US*) to include in a reckoning; esp. in phr. *count me in*, include me, don't forget me; thus the reverse, *count out, count me out*.

counting-house *n.* [late 19C] the human face. [mispron. SE *countenance*]

count lasher *n.* [1950s] (*W.I.*) a womanizer. [SE *count* + LASHER n.[2]]

count me in/out *phr. see* COUNT IN v.

count out *v. see* COUNT IN v.

country *adj.* [early 18C+] an all-purpose adj. describing a lack of sophistication, a naïveté and similar rustic stereotypes, also a direct term of address; usu. in combs., e.g. *country boob, country gook, country hink, country jig, country joker, country peck, country punk, country pumpkin, country rube, country slicker, country squash* and all combs. below.

country bookie *n.* (*also* country boo-boo, country buck) [20C+] (*W.I.*) an unsophisticated country person (cf. BOONIE n.[1]). [COUNTRY adj. + ? BUCK n.[1] (4)]

country bull *n.* [1910s] (*US*) a local, small-town policeman. [COUNTRY adj. + BULL n.[10] (1)]

country-captain *n.* [late 18C–mid-19C] (*orig. Anglo-Ind.*) a very dry curry, usu. with a spatchcocked chicken. [the dish was esp. popular among *country captains*, masters of *country ships*, vessels that traded between the ports of the East Indies]

country chub *n.* [early 18C] a fool, a dupe. [COUNTRY adj. + CHUB n.[1]]

country club *n.* [1940s+] (*US prison*) a minimum security prison, usu. housing white-collar criminals. [the supposed luxury of its facilities by prison standards]

country cokes *n.* [early 18C] a country fool, a rustic simpleton (cf. BOONIE n.[1]). [COUNTRY adj. + COKES n.]

country cousin *n.*[1] (*also* kissing cousin) [20C+] the number 12, a dozen. [rhy. sl.]

country cousin *n.*[2] [1900s] (*US*) a euph. for menstruation. [such relations make regular, if unwanted, visits]

country cracker *n.* (*also* country gawk) [19C] (*US*) an unsophisticated, backward country-dweller (cf. BOONIE n.[1]). [COUNTRY adj. + CRACKER n.[3] (1)/GAWK n.]

country harry n. [18C–early 19C] a waggoner. [COUNTRY adj. + proper name *Harry* as generic]

country hick n. [late 18C–early 19C] (*orig. UK Und.*) a country person, a rustic (cf. BOONIE n.[1]). [COUNTRY adj. + HICK n.[1] (1)]

country ike n. see IKE n. (1).

country jack n. see JACK n.[15].

country jake n. see JAKE n.[1] (1).

country jerk n. [1930s+] (*US*) a country person, a rustic (cf. BOONIE n.[1]). [COUNTRY adj. + JERK n.[1] (2)]

country johnny n. [19C] an unsophisticated country person (cf. BOONIE n.[1]). [COUNTRY adj. + JOHNNIE n.[2] (1)]

country put n. [late 17C–18C] a country person, a rustic (cf. BOONIE n.[1]). [COUNTRY adj. + PUT n.[1] (1)]

country work n. [early 19C] work that progresses very slowly. [supposed tardiness of rural workers]

count the railings v. [mid-19C–1910s] to be hungry. [SE *count* + RAILINGS n. (1)]

count (the) worms v. [20C+] to be dead.

county beef n. [1960s] (*US*) deer that has been illegally shot by poachers. [note synon. US regional (Maine) *orchard beef*]

county blues n. [1990s+] (*US prison*) a blue prison uniform, worn in a county jail. [BLUES n.[3] (4)]

county crop n. [mid-19C] a rough haircut, shorn to equal length all round the scalp. [SE *county (prison)* + *crop*; i.e. the sort of crop given to inmates of such institutions]

county down n. [19C] female pubic hair. [pun on SE *county*/CUNT n.[1] (1) + SE *down*, any substance of a feathery or fluffy nature]

county mountie n. 1 [1970s+] (*US*) a local (rather than state) policeman. 2 [1990s+] any policeman. [SE *county* + *Mountie*, a member of the Royal Canadian Mounted Police]

count z's v. see COP (SOME) z's v.

coup n.[1] see COOP n.[1] (1).

coup n.[2] see COUPE n.

Coupar justice n. see CUPAR JUSTICE n.

coupe n. (*also* coup) [1970s+] (*US Black*) a Cadillac *Coupe* de Ville.

Couper justice n. see CUPAR JUSTICE n.

couple, a n. [late 19C+] several drinks; at least, but not restricted to, 2.

couple-beggar n. [mid-18C–19C] a complaisant clergyman who specializes in solemnizing marriages among the inmates of London's Fleet prison, and in Ireland.

couple of bottles short of a six-pack, a phr. [1990s+] unstable, not very intelligent.

couple of cents n. [1960s] (*US Black*) $2. [CENT n. (1)]

couple of chips short of a fish dinner, a phr. (*also* few chips short of a cookie/computer) [1990s+] not very intelligent. [var. on NOT ALL THERE phr.]

couple of ducks n. [1950s+] (*bingo*) the number 22 (cf. ALDERSHOT LADIES n.).

couple of shakes, a n. see TWO SHAKES phr.

couple of ticks, a n. see TWO TICKS n.

couple of tinnies short of a slab, a phr. [1990s+] (*Aus.*) eccentric, foolish, simple-minded. [TINNIE n.[1] (1) + SLAB n.[1] (7); var. on NOT ALL THERE phr.]

coupler n. [19C] 1 the vagina. 2 a woman when viewed as nothing more than a sex object. [SE *coupling*, sexual intercourse]

coupling bat n. [20C+] the penis. [railway imagery]

coupling house n. [18C–19C] a brothel (cf. ACCOMMODATION HOUSE n.). [SE *coupling* + HOUSE n.[1] (1)]

coupling pin n. [1910s] (*US*) the penis. [pun on SE]

coupon n. [1980s+] (*Scot.*) the face; thus *fill in someone's coupon*, to hit in the face, esp. with a weapon.

courage n. see DUTCH COURAGE n.

courage bump n. [1960s] (*US*) acne. [dial. *courage*, sexual desire;

the assumption is that the emergent sexuality of the adolescent male manifests itself in infected pimples]

courage pills n. (*drugs*) 1 [1930s+] heroin in tablet form. 2 [1960s–70s] any form of anti-depressant. [heroin, which is based on the Gk root meaning *hero*, works to counteract one's fears]

course phr. [late 19C+] of course. [abbr.]

courses n. [late 19C–1950s] menstruation. [16C–17C SE; note Todd, *Cyclopedia of Anatomy* (1839): 'The [...] expressions of "the illness" or "the courses" are those in most common use among the vulgar']

court card n. 1 [late 17C–18C] a dandy, a 'gay, fluttering coxcomb' (Grose, 1785). 2 [early 19C] a helpful person. [note Lincolnshire dial. 'one who has risen very much in social position']

court cream n. [mid-17C–18C] empty speeches, filled only with fake sincerity. [the mannered speech of a royal court]

court element n. (*also* court holy bread, court holy water, court promises, court water) [late 16C–18C] empty speeches, filled only with fake sincerity. [the mannered speech of a royal court]

courtesy-man n. [mid-16C; 1920s] (*UK Und.*) a confidence trickster, well-dressed and spoken, and without any visible weapon, who poses as a gentleman down on his luck and tells his 'tale' to the passing victim whom he picks up in the street. They also stay in hostels from which they leave early, paying no bill but taking the bed linen with them. [SE *courtesy*]

court in v. [1980s+] (*US gang*) to subject to a ritual initiation, usu. involving a mild beating from fellow gang members, followed by some form of blooding, typically an armed attack on members of a rival gang. [the other members fig. 'hold court']

court noll n. [mid-16C–mid-17C] a courtier. [SE *court* + *noll*, a dull, drunken person]

court of assistants n. [late 18C–early 19C] the young men with whom young wives, unhappy in their marriages to older men, are likely to seek solace. [pun on SE *court of assistants*, senior members of city companies, responsible for managing their affairs]

court promises/water n. see COURT ELEMENT n.

cous-cous n. [1950s+] (*W.I.*) old, ragged work clothes. [SE *cous-cous*, granulated flour; this can be seen fig. as grains of dirt or specks of dust, and thus stretched further to encompass the sl. meaning]

couse n. see COOZE n. (2).

cousin n.[1] [mid-16C] (*UK Und.*) the victim, usu. a rural visitor to London, of a dice-player or a confidence trickster who uses counterfeit gold. [SE. The implication is of 'country cousin'; + ? pun on SE *cozen*, to cheat, to defraud]

cousin n.[2] 1 [17C] a prostitute. 2 [late 19C+] (*US*) a friend, usu. a term of address. 3 [1940s+] (*gay*) an older man's younger lover. [(1) and (3) the euph. is used when introducing the young man or woman to an acquaintance who might otherwise frown on the relationship]

cousin betty n. 1 [late 18C–early 19C] a travelling prostitute (cf. BABY JANE n.). 2 [mid-19C] a foolish woman.

cousin charlie n. [1990s+] (*drugs*) cocaine (cf. AUNT NORA n.). [ext. of CHARLIE n.[9] (1)]

Cousin Ella n. see AUNTIE ELLA n.

Cousin Jack n. (*also* Cousin Jacky, K.G.) [mid-19C+] (*Aus./US*) a Cornishman. [note dial. *cousin jack/jacky*, a fool, a coward; *K.G.* is a mis-abbr.]

cousin john n. see CUZ JOHN n.

cousin sally ann n. (*also* cousin sal, cousin sally) [mid–late 19C] (*US*) the Confederacy. [Confederate States of America]

cousin sis n. [20C+] 1 urination (cf. ANGEL'S KISS n.). 2 a drinking spree. [rhy. sl.; (1) = PISS n. (1); (2) = ON THE PISS phr.]

cousin tom *n.* [mid-19C] a madman, esp. a beggar, tramp or similar person. [SE *cousin* + TOM OF BEDLAM n.]

couter *n.*[1] (*also* **couta, cooter**) [mid–late 19C] a sovereign; thus HALF-COUTER n. [Rom. *kotor*, guinea, or Danubian-Gipsy *cuta*, gold coin]

couter *n.*[2] (*also* **cooda**) [1980s+] (*Aus. prison*) the best. [? play on *coup de grace*]

couthed up *adj.* [1960s+] (*US campus*) neat, tidy, well-behaved. [backform. f. SE *uncouth*]

cove *n.* **1** [mid-16C+] (*orig. UK Und.*) a man. **2** [late 18C–mid-19C] (*UK Und.*) a receiver. **3** [early 19C] the owner or manager of an establishment, esp. (*Aus.*) of a sheep station. **4** [early 19C] a sheriff's officer, a policeman. **5** [mid-19C] an assistant, a shop-boy. [either 16C Scot. *cofe*, a chapman or peddler or, like a number of 16C cant terms, Rom., in this case *cova* or *covo*, man]

covee *n.* [early 19C] a landlord. [COVE n. (3)]

cove-juice *n.* [1950s–60s] (*US*) illicitly distilled whisky. [dial. *cove*, a valley enclosed by mountains + SE *juice*; such valleys provide suitable hideouts for clandestine distilling]

Covent Garden *n.* [mid-19C] a farthing. [rhy. sl.; pron. of *farthing* as 'farden']

Covent Garden *adj.* [mid-17C–early 19C] allusive of sexual excess; also in combs. below. [SE *Covent Garden*, centre of 17C–18C prostitution in London]

Covent Garden abbess *n.* [late 18C–early 19C] a procuress. [COVENT GARDEN adj. + ABBESS n.]

Covent Garden ague *n.* [late 17C–early 19C] venereal disease, esp. gonorrhoea. [COVENT GARDEN adj. + SE *ague*]

Covent Garden gout *n.* (*also* **common garden gout**) [late 17C–mid-18C] venereal disease. [COVENT GARDEN adj./COMMON GARDEN n.; Williams notes 17C use of unqualified *gout* to mean venereal disease, 'partly through confusion of symptoms, partly as euphemism']

Covent Garden nun *n.* (*also* **Covent Garden lady**) [mid-17C–early 19C] a prostitute. [COVENT GARDEN adj. + NUN n. (1)/SE *lady*]

Covent Garden nunnery *n.* [18C] a brothel (cf. ABBESS n.). [COVENT GARDEN adj. + NUNNERY n.]

coventry *n.* [mid-19C] a 3-cornered puff with jam inside. [? its being first manufactured in the Warwickshire town]

cove of the dossing-ken *n.* [mid-19C] the landlord of a lodging house. [COVE n. (3) + DOSS-KEN n.]

cove of the ken *n.* (*also* **ken cove**) [early 17C–mid-19C] the master of the house, a landlord; thus *covess of the ken*, a landlady or brothel-keeper. [COVE n. (1) + KEN n.[1] (1)]

cover *n.*[1] **1** [early 19C–1950s] (*UK Und.*) (*also* **coverer, cover-up man**) a confederate who screens the operations of a thief or pickpocket. **2** [1950s–60s] (*US Black/Und.*) 'protection' as supplied by police to criminals.

cover *n.*[2] [late 19C–1920s] (*US Und.*) an overcoat.

cover all the bases *v.* [1990s+] to attend to every detail of a situation; to deal with all the relevant people. [baseball imagery]

cover-down *n.* [mid-19C] a coin that has a false cover, which can be used or removed as required, and is used by cheats in games of coin-tossing.

covered *adj.* [1900s] (*US Und.*) 'protected' from prosecution or arrest.

covered way *n.* [mid-18C–19C] the vagina (cf. ALLEY n.[1]).

coverer *n. see* COVER n.[1] (1).

cover for *v.* **1** [mid-19C; 1940s+] to protect a confederate. **2** [1940s+] to conceal wrong-doing. **3** [1940s+] to substitute for, to take over someone else's duties. **4** [1940s+] to provide 'protection'.

cover-me-decent *n.* (*also* **cover-me-decently**) [early–mid-19C] a greatcoat, an overcoat.

cover-me-properly *n.* [mid-19C] fashionable, smart clothing.

cover-me-queerly *n.* [mid-19C] ragged clothing.

cover one's ass *v.* (*also* **cover one's arse, …back**) [1950s+] to look after oneself or someone else. [SE *cover* + ASS n. (5)/ARSE n.[1] (4)/SE *back*]

cover-slut *n.* [17C] an apron. [SE *cover* v. + *slut*, a kitchen-maid]

cover the waterfront *v.* [1980s] (*US*) **1** to menstruate. **2** to change a baby's nappy or diaper. [euph. pun on SE phr., itself a journ. cliché]

cover-up *n.* **1** [1920s+] an alibi, concealment, usu. illegal or at least unethical. **2** [1940s] (*US Und.*) a criminal's associate, a confederate.

cover up *v.* [1930s–60s] (*US*) to provide someone with an alibi.

cover-up man *n. see* COVER n.[1] (1).

covess *n.* [late 18C–mid-19C] a woman. [COVE n. (1) + fem. sfx *-ess*]

covess dinge *n.* [mid-19C] (*US*) a Black woman. [COVESS n. + DINGE n. (2)]

covey *n.* (*also* **covie**) **1** [late 17C–1960s] a fellow, a man. **2** [early 19C] a landlord. **3** [1920s] a child. [COVE n.]

covey (of partridge) *n.* **1** [late 16C–early 19C] a group or collection of prostitutes, usu. as found in a brothel. **2** [mid-19C] a group of attractive young women. [joc. use of SE collective phr.]

cow *n.*[1] **1** [mid-16C+] a woman, esp. an obese or unattractive one. **2** [17C+; mid-19C+] a prostitute (cf. ALLEY CAT n.). **3** [1920s] a tramp or criminal's female companion. **4** [1950s] (*US gay*) an effeminate male homosexual. **5** [1960s+] (*Aus. teen*) a promiscuous girl. [on model of BITCH n.[1] (1)/SOW n.[1] (1)]

cow *n.*[2] **1** [late 18C; late 19C+] (*Aus./N.Z.*) an objectionable person or thing, a distasteful situation. **2** [1910s] a joc. term of adress. [ext. of COW n.[1] (1); note 1901 *Bulletin* (Sydney) 7 Dec. 30/2: 'All the cussedness of the bovine race is centred in the cow. In Australia, the most opprobrious epithet one can apply to a man or other object is "cow". In the whole range of a bullock-driver's vocabulary there is no word that expresses his blistering scorn so well as "cow". To a species of feminine perversity a cow adds a fiendish ingenuity in making trouble']

cow *n.*[3] [mid-19C] £1000 sterling (cf. FOAL n.). [ety. unknown; ? related to MONKEY n.[8]]

cow *n.*[4] **1** [late 19C–1960s] (*US campus*) an awkward or stupid person. **2** [1960s] any animal.

cow *n.*[5] (*US*) **1** [late 19C+] milk, cream (cf. COW JUICE n.). **2** [1910s–60s] beef.

cow *n.*[6] [1940s] (*W.I.*) a man who is seduced by a woman and abandoned when the money runs out. [SE *milch-cow*, one who can be easily and continually used as a source of money]

cow *n.*[7] [1960s+] (*US*) a fit, an emotional episode; usu. as *have a cow*.

cow *n.*[8] [1970s–80s] (*UK Black*) a double-sized audio speaker box, as used by sound systems. [? joc. resemblance]

cow *adj.* [1900s] (*Aus.*) unpleasant, objectionable. [COW n.[2] (1)]

cow *v.*[1] (*also* **cow-hide**) [early–mid-19C; 1930s] to whip, to beat; also in fig. use.

cow *v.*[2] *see* COW (IT) v.

cow! *excl.* **1** [mid-19C–1930s] (*US*) a mild excl., a euph. for *God!* **2** [1940s+] (*UK, mainly northern*) a euph. for FUCK v.[3]

cowabunga! *excl.* (*also* **kowabunga!**) [1950s+] (*orig. surfing*) an excl. of pleasure, victory (over the waves) etc; latterly an excl. of surprise. [the term gained a whole new currency, esp. among the pre-teens, with the popularity (*c*.1990) of the TV programme *The Teenage Mutant Ninja Turtles*, where it featured heavily. Its ultimate origin seems to have been in *Howdy Doody*, a US children's TV programme of the 1950s, in which *Cowabunga!* was the greeting exchanged by Buffalo Bob and Chief Thunderthud]

cowan *n.* [mid-19C] a sneak, an eavesdropper. [ety. unknown; Hotten (1860) offers Gk *kuon*, a dog (as general pej.) or Scot. *cowan* or *kirwan*, a man who builds dry-stone walls without mortar, and thus one who builds but is not a fully qualified mason. Note freemasons' jargon *cowan*, one who has not been initiated into the craft]

cow and calf *n.* [20C+] **1** half a pound, orig. 10 shillings, latterly 50p (cf. BEES (AND HONEY) n.). **2** (*orig. sporting*) a half-pint (of beer). **3** a laugh. [rhy. sl.]

cow and calf *v.* [mid-19C; 1930s–60s] to laugh. [rhy. sl.]

Cow and Gate *adj.* [1990s+] late, esp. in the context of a woman missing her period. [rhy. sl.; ult. brandname of baby food products *Cow and Gate*]

cow-and-kisses *n.* [mid-19C+] one's wife, a woman. [rhy. sl. = MISSIS n.]

coward's castle *n.* (*also* coward's corner) [19C–1910s] **1** a pulpit. **2** a fig. refuge for a moral coward, e.g. a religous hypocrite. [the occupier is 'above' argument]

cow-baby *n.* [late 16C–18C] a coward.

cow-banger *n.* (*also* cattle-banger) [20C+] (*Aus./N.Z.*) **1** a dairy farmer or any employee of a dairy farm; thus *cowbang*, to run a dairy farm. **2** a bullock driver. [SE *cow* + SE *bang* or BANG v.[1] (1)]

cow barn is open, the *phr.* [1960s+] (*US*) a warning to a man that his trouser-fly is undone (cf. BARN DOOR IS OPEN, THE phr.).

cowbay *n.* [mid–late 19C] a cheap brothel, a prostitute's room (cf. BIRDCAGE n.[1]). [COW n.[1] (2); New York City's red-light area was known as *Cow Bay*]

cowboy *n.*[1] **1** [20C+] (*orig. US*) a reckless man. **2** [1920s] (*US*) a man who appears to lack interest in women. **3** [1920s–30s] (*US*) a man, usu. a youth, who frequents drugstores for no other reason than to meet his friends, to gossip and to waste time. **4** [1920s+] (*orig. US*) a reckless driver. **5** [1920s+] (*US*) a ruthless, unrestrained criminal. **6** [1950s+] (*US*) in poker, a king. **7** [1950s+] a policeman. **8** [1960s+] a man; the inference is derog. **9** [1970s+] an average, run-of-the-mill criminal. **10** [1970s+] a term of address to a man. **11** [1980s+] (*US Black*) an aggressive, tough Black man; a thug. **12** [1980s+] a tradesman (esp. of the building and allied trades), who ignores the basic ethics and business standards of his peers and aims only for money; thus *cowboy builder, cowboy plumber* etc. **13** [1990s+] (*US prison*) an inmate who has no affiliation with any prison gang or group. **14** [2000s] (*US prison*) a novice officer. [fig. uses of SE; note the earliest *cowboy* (18C–early 19C) was always a Black man; his White peers were *cattlemen*]

cowboy *n.*[2] [1940s] (*US*) a western sandwich.

cowboy *n.*[3] [1970s] (*US*) a Marlboro cigarette. [the cigarette's advertising features 'the Marlboro *cowboy*']

cowboy *v.* [1940s+] (*US*) **1** to rob in a reckless manner. **2** to murder, to gun down. **3** to act in a reckless manner. [COWBOY n.[1] (1); the style (or certainly as enshrined by Hollywood) of a classic Wild West hold-up or gunfight]

cowboy Bible *n.* [1970s+] (*US, Western*) a pack of cigarette papers.

cowboy cadillac *n.* [1970s+] (*US, Southwest*) any form of open-topped vehicle, e.g. a pick-up truck.

cowboy cocktail *n.* [20C+] (*US*) straight whisky. [the modern 'cowboy cocktail' blends whisky and cream]

cowboy coffee *n.* [20C+] (*US*) black coffee.

cowboy question *n.* [1980s+] (*US campus*) a dare. [the stereotypical devil-may-care *cowboy*]

cowboys *n.* [1950s+] the police.

cowboy's breakfast *n.* [1950s] (*mainly UK juv.*) baked beans (cf. BARBER'S BREAKFAST n.).

cowboy up *v.* [1990s+] (*US*) to control one's emotions, to put on a brave, tough face. [the supposed stoicism of cowboys]

cowcatcher *n.* (*US*) **1** [mid-19C] a full moustache. **2** [1940s–60s] a large bosom. **3** [1950s] a prominent nose. [SE *cowcatcher*, an apparatus fixed in front of a locomotive engine, to remove straying cattle or other obstructions from the rails in front of a train]

cowclap *n.* [1940s–50s] (*Irish*) cow dung. [? rhy. sl. = CRAP n.[3] (1)]

cow-cocky *n.* [20C+] (*Aus./N.Z.*) a dairy farmer or any employee of a dairy farm. [SE *cow* + COCKY n.[2] (1)]

cow college *n.* [1910s+] (*US*) an agricultural college.

cow conductor *n.* [20C+] (*Aus.*) a bullock-driver.

cow confetti *n.* [1930s+] nonsense, rubbish (cf. COWYARD CONFETTI n.). [euph. for BULLSHIT n. (1)]

cow-cow *v.* [mid-19C] (*Anglo-Chinese*) to scold, to reprimand severely. [? pidgin]

cow-crazy *adj.* [1920s] (*US*) foolishly obsessed with a woman or with women in general. [COW n.[1] (1) + -CRAZY sfx]

cow-cunted *adj.* [mid-19C+] having a large vagina. [SE *cow* + CUNT n.[1] (1)]

cow-daisy *n.* [mid-19C] cow dung.

cow express *n.* [1940s] (*US Black*) shoe leather. [the *cowhide* provides leather]

cowface *n.* [1900s] a term of abuse, aimed at a woman. [COW n.[1] (1)]

cow grease *n.* (*also* cow paste, cow salve) [1940s–60s] (*US*) butter (cf. COW'S GREASE n.).

cow gun *n.* [1940s] (*US*) a revolver. [? SE *cowboy*]

cowgut *n.* [1940s] (*W.I.*) a tin lamp. [? some resemblance]

cow-handed *adj.* [late 18C–early 19C] clumsy, awkward.

cow-hearted *adj.* [mid-17C–early 19C] cowardly.

cowhide *adj.* [1950s–60s] (*Irish*) aware, knowledgeable. [rhy. sl. = WIDE adj. (1)]

cow-hide *v. see* COW v.[1].

cowing *adj.* [1950s+] (*orig. UK milit.*) a euph. for FUCKING adj. (1).

cow (it) *v.* [1970s–80s] to work as a prostitute. [COW n.[1] (2)]

cow-jerker *n.* [20C+] (*N.Z.*) a cow hand, a milker. [SE *cow* + JERKER n.[1] (1) (but note JERKER n.[2] (2))]

cow jockey *n.* [20C+] (*US*) a farmer, a rustic (cf. ACORN-CRACKER n.). [SE *cow* + JOCKEY n.[3] (2)]

cow juice *n.* [late 18C+] milk (cf. COW n.[5]).

cow-killer *n.* [late 19C] (*US*) a quack, a poor doctor. [he is barely safe with animals, let alone humans]

cowlick *n.* [mid-19C+] a hairstyle, smoothed down over the forehead, which looks as if a cow had licked it into place.

cow-neck *n.* [1940s+] (*W.I.*) newly distilled white proof rum. [ety. unknown; ? play on the *horse's neck*, a mixed drink]

cow paste *n. see* COW GREASE n.

cow-persuader *n.* (*also* oxen-persuader) [1900s] (*Aus.*) a cowboy; a herdsman.

cow pie *n.* [1970s+] (*US*) a piece of cow dung.

cowpoke *n.* [late 19C+] (*US*) a cowboy. [SE *cow* + *poke*; orig. referred spec. to those men who used long sticks to push cows aboard cattle-trains, bound for the slaughterhouses]

cow-prod *n.* (*also* cow-prodder) **1** [1900s] (*Aus.*) a dairyman. **2** [1930s] (*US*) a cowboy.

cow-puncher *n.* (*also* cattle puncher, cowpunch, puncher) [late 19C+] a cowboy; thus *cowpunch*, to work as a cowboy.

cow salve *n. see* COW GREASE n.

cow's baby *n.* **1** [late 17C–mid-19C] a calf. **2** [mid-19C] an awkward, loutish person. [lit./fig. ext. of SE]

cow's breakfast *n.* [1900s] (*Can.*) a large straw hat (cf. DONKEY'S BREAKFAST n.; MULE BREAKFAST n.).

cow's (calf) *n.* **1** [1940s–60s] 10 shillings (50p) (cf. BEES (AND HONEY) n.). **2** [1980s] £150. [rhy. sl. = half (a pound); (2) = one and a half]

cowscape *n.* [late 19C–1930s] a painting of a country scene that includes cows. [SE *cow* + *landscape*]

cow's courant *n.* [late 18C–early 19C] diarrhoea (cf. APPLE-BLOSSOM TWO-STEP n.). [SE *cow* + SE *courant, coranto*, a dance characterized by a running or gliding step; thus pun on SE *trot*/TROTS, THE n.[2]]

cow's grease *n.* [mid-19C] butter (cf. COW GREASE n.).

cowsh *n.* [1980s+] (*Aus./N.Z.*) nonsense, rubbish. [abbr. COWSHIT n. (2)]

cowshaker *n.* [1900s] (*Aus.*) a drover; thus used fig. to describe anyone who motivates or drives another.

cowshit *n.* (*US, Western*) **1** [1960s] an unpopular person. **2** [1960s+] nonsense, rubbish. [(2) var. on BULLSHIT n. (1)]

cow-simple *adj.* [1920s–70s] (*US*) foolishly obsessed with a woman or with women in general; in a homosexual context, heterosexual. [COW n.¹ (1) + SE *simple*]

cowskin *n.* [mid-19C] (*US*) a whip. [COWSKIN v.]

cowskin *v.* [late 18C–1940s] to whip. [the material]

cowskin hero *n.* [late 18C] (*W.I.*) a plantation overseer. [COW-SKIN v.]

cow's lick *n.* [1960s+] prison (cf. BUCKET n.²). [rhy. sl. = NICK n.⁶ (1)]

cow's licker *n.* (*also* **cow's lick**) [1930s+] £1 (cf. CHERRY-PICKER n.⁵). [rhy. sl. = NICKER n.² (1)]

cowson *n.* [1930s–50s] a general pej. description of a person. [on pattern of SE *whoreson*]

cowson *adj.* [1930s–60s] a general pej. [COWSON n.]

cow-spanker *n.* (*also* **cow-squeezer**) **1** [late 19C+] (*Aus./N.Z.*) a dairy farmer or any employee of a dairy farm; thus *cow-spanking*, *dairy-farming*. **2** [20C+] a bullock driver.

cow's spouse *n.* [late 18C] a bull. [facetious use of SE]

cow to cover *n.* [1940s] (*US*) a portion of butter.

cow town *n.* (*US*) **1** [20C+] any town with associated with cattle trading; thus anywhere provincial as opposed to a big city; also attrib. **2** [1960s+] Fort Worth, Texas. [its former principal industry]

cow-turd *n.* [mid-late 18C] a cheap cigar. [SE *cow* + TURD n. (1); i.e. a derog. comparison]

cow-waddie *n.* [1920s] (*US*) a cowboy, esp. a temporary cowhand. [SE *cow* + WADDIE n. (2)]

cow-week *n. see* CALF-WEEK n.

cow with the iron tail *n.* [mid-19C] a water pump. [the ref. is to the milkmen's habit, before legislation passed in 1865, of watering the milk]

cowyard *n.* [late 19C–1910s] (*US*) a cheap brothel (cf. BIRDCAGE n.¹). [COW n.¹ (2) + pun on SE]

cowyard cake *n.* [1920s–50s] (*Aus.*) a type of cake or bun that contains sultanas. [it is supposedly reminiscent of a cowpat + attendant flies]

cowyard confetti *n.* [1940s+] (*Aus.*) nonsense, rubbish (cf. COW CONFETTI n.; FLEMINGTON CONFETTI n.). [euph. for BULL-SHIT n. (1)]

cox *n.* [late 16C] a fool. [play on COCK n.² (1), i.e. one who is 'easily taken in']

coxcomb *n.* [late 16C–mid-18C] the head. [SE *coxcomb*, a cock's head; Nares notes: 'The cap of the licensed fool was often terminated at the top with a *cock's* head and *comb*, and some of the feathers']

coxy *n.* [1930s] (*US Und.*) an inexperienced salesman used by a high-pressure salesman for small deals. [ety. unknown]

coxy fuss *n. see* COCKSY FUSS n.

coyne *n. see* COIN n.

coynte *n.* [19C] the vagina. [euph. for CUNT n.¹ (1)]

coyote *n.* **1** [late 19C] (*US*) the vagina. **2** [late 19C–1940s] (*US*) a half-breed. **3** [late 19C–1970s] (*US*) a very unpleasant person. **4** [1920s; 1970s+] (*US*) a smuggler of illegal immigrants from Mexico into the US. **5** [1980s+] (*US campus*) (*also* **coyote date**) an ugly woman. [all fig. uses of SE *coyote*, a prairie dog, generally considered in pej. terms]

coyote *v.* (*US, Western*) **1** [mid-19C+] to run off, esp. in a clandestine manner. **2** [late 19C] to hoax, to deceive. **3** [1920s+] to wander about. [the perceived characteristics of the SE *coyote*]

coyote sandwich *n.* [1990s+] (*US*) a tampon. [? COYOTE n. (1)]

coyote ugly *adj.* [1980s+] (*US campus*) extremely ugly. [COYOTE n. (5)]

coz *n. see* CUZ n.

'coz *prep. see* 'COS prep.

cozies *n.* [1980s] (*US*) testicles. [? mispron./abbr. COJONES n.]

cozmos *n. see* COSMOS n.

cozo *n. see* COZZER n.

cozy *adj.* [1920s+] (*US*) sly, cunning; thus *play it cozy*, to act in a cautious or secretive manner.

cozza *n.* [mid-late 19C] pork. [Yid./Heb. *chazer*, a pig]

cozzer *n.* (*also* **cosser**, **cozo**) [1930s+] a policeman. [Yid./Heb. *chazer*, a pig]

cozzie *n. see* COSSIE n.

cozzy *n.* [1930s] (*UK Und.*) a gentlemen's public convenience. [abbr. COTTAGE n. (2)]

c.p. *n.* [mid-19C] **1** a kept man. **2** a pimp (cf. ABBOT ON THE CROSS n.). [abbr. CUNT-PENSIONER n.]

c.p.t. *n.* (*also* **c.p. time**) [1920s+] unpunctuality, usu. an hour or so later than the prescribed time, sooner or later (cf. AFRICAN (PEOPLE'S) TIME n.). [abbr. COLORED PEOPLE'S TIME n.; the stereotype is that Blacks have a less immediate sense of time than their White peers]

cpunk *n. see* CYBERPUNK n. (2).

crab *n.¹* **1** [late 16C–early 17C; late 19C+] a sour, ill-tempered person. **2** [late 19C+] an ill-tempered, thus unpopular, child; esp. as *old crab*. **3** [1900s] (*Aus.*) a policeman (cf. ANIMAL n.¹). **4** [1930s] (*US police*) a policeman who is too conscientious and thus unpopular with local politicians and his colleagues. **5** [1940s] (*US Black campus*) a freshman. **6** [1980s+] (*Aus. prison*) a prisoner whose behaviour invokes collective punishment. **7** [2000s] (*US Black*) an impoverished person. [SE *crab-apple*; (1) later use is US]

crab *n.²* [mid-17C+] usu. in pl., a pubic louse. [supposed resemblance]

crab *n.³* **1** [mid-19C] (*UK Und.*) a problem that emerges during an act of theft. **2** [mid-19C] any form of problem; that which places one at a disadvantage. **3** [late 19C–1920s] the act of complaining, of finding fault. [CRAB v.¹]

crab *n.⁴* [mid-19C–1950s] (*US*) a horse, usu. a second-rate one.

crab *n.⁵* [1990s+] (*US Black gang*) a derog. term for a member of the Crips, as used by a rival Blood.

crab *adj.¹* [1990s+] (*UK juv.*) useless, inadequate. [CRAP adj.]

crab *adj.² see* CRABBY adj.¹.

crab *v.¹* **1** [late 17C; mid-19C+] (*also* **crab on**) to tear at, to find fault, to criticize heavily, to complain; thus [early–mid-19C] *throw a crab*, to criticize harshly. **2** [early 19C–1920s] to use offensive language so as deliberately to annoy someone. **3** [mid-19C] to back down, to surrender in a humiliating manner, to run away; esp. as *crab off*. **4** [mid-19C] to inform on. **5** [mid-late 19C] to cheat, to deceive. **6** [mid-19C–1960s] (*mainly US*) to steal. **7** [mid-19C+] (*also* **put the crab on**, **crab up**) to spoil, to upset, to ruin; thus Aus. phr. *he'd crab on a marble shit house.* [all uses of SE with emphasis on the crab's snapping pincers]

crab *v.²* [1950s+] (*W.I. Rasta*) to scratch or claw. [the crustacean's movement]

crab-apple *n.* [mid-19C–1920s] (*US*) a sour, ill-tempered person. [CRAB n.¹ (1)/SE *crab-apple*, a very sour fruit]

crab-apple two-step *n.* [1960s] (*US*) diarrhoea (cf. APPLE-BLOSSOM TWO-STEP n.). [the result of eating sour fruit + pun on SE *trot*/TROTS, THE n.²]

crab-ass *n.* [1930s–60s] (*US*) an unpleasant person; also as adj. [CRAB n.¹ (1) + -ASS sfx]

crabbed *adj.* [mid-16C+] sour, ill-tempered, difficult. [CRAB n.¹ (1)]

crabber *n.* **1** [late 19C] (*US*) a small-time gambler. **2** [1930s] a fault-finder, a nag. [(1) ? one who keeps their 'claws' on their cash; (2) CRAB v.¹ (1)]

crabbit *adj.* **1** [1950s+] of a person, coarse. **2** [1980s] unpleasant, rough. [CRABBED adj.]

crabby *adj.¹* (*also* **crab**) [mid-19C+] nagging, cantankerous. [CRAB n.¹ (1)/CRAB v.¹ (1)]

crabby *adj.²* [late 19C+] infected with pubic lice. [CRAB n.²]

crabby with *adj. see* LOUSY WITH *adj.*

crabfish *n.* [17C] a cheap prostitute, likely to be infested with crab-lice. [play on SE *crabfish*, a crab/*crab-louse*]

crab lanthorn *n.* [late 18C] a peevish, surly person. [CRAB n.[1] (1) + SE *lanthorn*; *crab* in SE can mean a small machine or a trivet, which would make the fig. use more logical, but there is no record of a *crab lanthorn*]

crab off *v. see* CRAB v.[1] (3).

crab on *v. see* CRAB v.[1] (1).

crab on the rocks *n.* **1** [late 19C] itching testicles. **2** [1940s] venereal disease. [(1) pun on SE *crab*/CRAB n.[2] + SE *rocks*/ROCKS n.[4] (1); (2) rhy. sl. = POX n.[1] (2)]

crabs *n.*[1] **1** [mid-18C–19C] in the game of hazard, the lowest throw, a pair of aces; thus fig. in such phrs. as *come off crabs*, *turn out crabs*, to prove disappointing. **2** [1950s] (*US Und.*) in the context of a robbery, loot that proves valueless, and thus irritatingly so. [? the precursor of SE *craps* dice]

crabs *n.*[2] **1** [late 18C–1930s] boots, shoes. **2** [mid-19C] the feet; thus *move one's crabs*, to run off. [abbr. CRAB-SHELLS n.]

crab-shells *n.* [late 18C–mid-19C] a pair of shoes; usu. in poor condition. [a play on Norfolk dial. *cart*, the carapace or shell of a crab]

crab someone's act *v.* (*also* **crab someone's game, crab the act**) [1900s–40s] (*US*) to spoil someone's plans, to interfere. [CRAB v.[1] (7)]

crab up *v. see* CRAB v.[1] (7).

crabwalk *n.* [1970s] (*US*) the perineum. [CRAB n.[2] + SE *walk*]

crack *n.*[1] [16C–18C] a lie; a boast, an act of bragging, exaggeration.

crack *n.*[2] (*also* **bum-crack, cracker**) [late 16C+] breaking wind. [late 14C–16C SE *crack*, the breaking of wind]

crack *n.*[3] [17C–18C; 1990s+] a fool. [abbr. CRACKBRAIN n.]

crack *n.*[4] **1** [mid-17C+] any person, animal or thing that approaches perfection. **2** [late 17C] a fop, a dandy. **3** [late 18C+] the current fashion; the fashionable world, the social and sporting élite. [late 16C SE *crack*, a 'lively lad', a wag]

crack *n.*[5] **1** [late 17C+] a heavy blow, e.g. *a crack over the head*; thus *take a crack at*, to attack. **2** [mid-19C] a pistol. **3** [late 19C–1930s] a shot from a weapon; thus *take a crack at*, to shoot.

crack *n.*[6] **1** [late 17C+] (*also* **love crack**) the vagina (cf. AGREEABLE RUTS OF LIFE n.). **2** [late 17C+] a prostitute, a 'fallen woman'; latterly any woman, usu. in a derog. sense (cf. BANGTAIL n.[1]). **3** [late 19C] (*UK, London*) a narrow street or passage with houses. **4** [1940s+] (*also* **bum-crack**) the divide between the buttocks. **5** [1970s+] (*gay*) the anus.

crack *n.*[7] [18C; 1990s+] a jolly, high-spirited party (cf. CRACK, THE n.). [the *cracking* or opening of bottles]

crack *n.*[8] **1** [mid-18C–mid-19C] a burglar. **2** [late 18C–19C] a burglary; thus *on the crack*, out burgling; *do a crack*, to commit a burglary. [abbr. CRACKSMAN n.[1] (1)]

crack *n.*[9] [mid-19C] dry wood. [the noise it makes when snapped or burned]

crack *n.*[10] [mid-19C+] **1** an opportunity, a try, a chance; thus HAVE A CRACK AT v. **2** (*US*) a go, a time. [SE *crack*, the act of snapping]

crack *n.*[11] **1** [late 19C+] (*orig. US*) a telling, sharp remark. **2** [20C+] (*orig. US*) a joke. **3** [20C+] (*orig. Irish*) a conversation. **4** [1970s+] (*US campus*) a funny or witty person. **5** [1990s+] boastful talk. [ext. of CRACK n.[1], latterly strengthened by abbr. WISECRACK n.]

crack *n.*[12] [20C+] a crown. [? perversion of SE *crown*]

crack *n.*[13] [1980s+] (*drugs*) a purified and potent form of cocaine; a mixture of cocaine, baking powder and water, which is smoked rather than snorted; crack is heated and the resultant pellets are smoked through a small glass pipe (cf. BASE n.). [SE by late 1990s. Its strength, alleged addictiveness and destructive popularity have made it a source of social disruption. Unlike its powdered form, known as 'the rich man's drug', *crack*, for all that it has many middle-class devotees, is very much a drug of the ghetto and the housing estate, bringing the effects of cocaine to an underclass market]

crack, the *n.* (*also* **craic**) [20C+] (*orig. Irish*) **1** conversation, chatter, gossip. **2** fun, amusement, informal entertainment; thus *cracksome*, jolly, amusing; also of people, amusing, enjoyable (cf. CRACK n.[7]). [Irish *craic*; ult. OE *cracian*, a crack]

crack *adj.* **1** [late 18C+] (*also* **crack-up**) excellent, first-class. **2** [early 19C–1900s] best. [CRACK n.[4] (3)]

crack *v.*[1] **1** [mid-15C+] to boast or brag; thus *cracking*, boasting. **2** [mid-19C+] to talk; thus CRACK ON v.[2]. **3** [late 19C–1920s] to praise, to promote; thus CRACK INTO FAME v. **4** [late 19C+] to make a remark (to someone). **5** [1900s–10s] to chatter. **6** [1930s+] (*orig. US Black*) to tease, to insult. **7** [1980s] (*US campus*) to be very funny, to make people laugh. [SE *crack*, to make a loud or sudden noise; Nares notes: 'crake. To boast [...] To crack, in the same sense, is of rather more recent usage, and is probably only a corruption of this']

crack *v.*[2] **1** [late 16C–18C] to fall into disrepair. **2** [1920s+] to collapse, to break down (emotionally). **3** [1920s+] to change money, to break a note into change.

crack *v.*[3] **1** [late 16C–1930s] to deflower; thus CRACKED adj.[1]. **2** [late 16C+] to open, orig. of a bottle etc, meaning to have a drink (cf. CRACK A BOTTLE v.), latterly to open anything, e.g. a door etc. **3** [late 17C–mid-19C] (*also* **krack**) to break open, to break into; thus CRACKING n.; CRACK A CRIB v. and other combs. **4** [late 18C+] to escape from prison. **5** [mid-19C+] (*US*) to shoot dead. **6** [1920s+] to break someone down, e.g. during an interrogation. [later use of (2) is US]

crack *v.*[4] **1** [17C–18C; 1990s+] to break wind. **2** [18C+] to hit (with a loud noise), to slap; esp. in threat *I'll crack you one*. **3** [mid-18C+] to let off a firearm. **4** [1990s+] to break a record, to surpass. [fig. uses of SE *crack*, a sharp noise; (1) note CRACK n.[2]]

crack *v.*[5] [mid-19C+] to work something out, to find a solution. [abbr. of fig. colloq. phr. *crack a nut*]

crack *v.*[6] (*Und.*) **1** [late 19C+] to ask for, to demand; ext. as *crack on*. **2** [1940s+] to arrest. [SE *crack open*]

crack *v.*[7] **1** [20C+] (*orig. Aus.*) to act in a given manner, defined by some form of comb., e.g. CRACK HARDY v. **2** [1900s–10s] (*Aus.*) to pretend, to sham; thus *crack a deaf 'un*, to pretend to be deaf or to not hear. **3** [2000s] (*US Black*) to happen.

crack *v.*[8] [20C+] (*US*) to pass on a secret, to give information. [SE *crack open* or *crack under pressure*]

crack *v.*[9] *see* CRACK ON v.[1] (2).

crack *adv.* [mid-19C] in a first-rate manner.

crack a bell *v.* [late 19C] to tell a secret, to betray a confidence. [the belief that it is necessary to remain silent while casting a bell; the slightest sound may produce a flaw]

crack a boo *v.* [1900s–10s] (*Aus.*) to betray a secret, to display one's emotions. [? CRACK A BELL v.]

crack a book *v. see* CRACK THE BOOKS v.

crack a bottle *v.* (*also* **crack a pot/quart**) [late 16C+] to have a drink. [CRACK v.[3] (2)]

crack a brew *v.* [1990s+] to open a beer. [CRACK v.[3] (2) + BREW n.[1] (3)]

crack a case *v.* [mid–late 19C] (*UK Und.*) to break into a house. [CRACK v.[3] (3) + CASE n.[3] (1)]

crack a cherry *v.* [1960s+] **1** (*also* **pick a cherry**) to take a woman's virginity. **2** in fig. use, to become initiated in a given calling. [SE *crack*/CRACK v.[3] (1) + CHERRY n.[1] (4)]

crack a crib *v.* [19C+] (*UK Und.*) to break into a house or shop. [CRACK v.[3] (3) + CRIB n.[1] (1)]

crack a crust *v.* [mid-19C] to earn a living; ext. as *crack a tidy crust*, to make a very good living.

crack a deaf 'un *v. see* CRACK v.[7] (2).

crack a fart *v.* [late 17C; 1980s+] (*US campus*) to break wind. [SE *crack*/CRACK v.[4] (1) + FART n. (1)]

crack a fat v. [1940s+] (*Aus.*) to achieve an erection. [SE *crack*/CRACK v.[7] (1) + FAT n.[4]]

crack a grin v. *see* CRACK ONE'S FACE v.

crackajack adj. *see* CRACKERJACK adj.[1].

crack a joint v. *see* JOINT n.[5] (1).

crack a judy v. (*also* **crack a judy's tea-cup**) [early 19C+] to deflower a woman. [SE *crack*/CRACK v.[3] (1) + JUDY n.[1] (1)]

crack a ken v. (*also* **crack a swag**) [18C–early 19C] to break into and rob a house. [CRACK v.[3] (3) + KEN n.[1] (1)]

crack a kirk v. [mid-19C] (*UK Und.*) **1** to break into a church. **2** to break into a house while its owners are at church. [CRACK v.[3] (3) + Scot. *kirk*, a church]

crack a lay v. [mid-19C; 1940s+] **1** (*orig. UK Und.*) to betray, to gossip about, to 'spill the beans'. **2** to speak, to 'say the word'. [CRACK ON v.[2] (1)/CRACK v.[1] (2) + ? LAY n.[4] (1)/LAY n.[4] (3); 1940s+ use is Aus.]

crack along v. *see* CRACK ON v.[1] (2).

crack an egg v. [1980s] (*Aus.*) to have an abortion.

crack a pipkin v. (*also* **crack a pitcher, crack one's pipkin/pitcher**) [mid-17C–early 18C] **1** to take a woman's virginity. **2** to lose one's virginity. [SE *crack*/CRACK v.[3] (1) + SE *pipkin*, a small earthenware cookpot or pan/*pitcher*]

crack a pot/quart v. *see* CRACK A BOTTLE v.

crack a short v. [1960s] (*US Und.*) to break into a car; usu. in pl. *crack shorts*. [CRACK v.[3] (3) + SHORT n.[2] (2)]

crack a smile v. *see* CRACK ONE'S FACE v.

crack a stiffie v. [1960s+] to get an erection. [SE *crack*/CRACK v.[7] (1) + STIFFIE n.[1]]

crack a swag v. *see* CRACK A KEN v.

crack attack n. [1980s+] (*drugs*) a sudden craving for crack cocaine. [CRACK n.[13] + SE *attack*; play on McDonald's coinage *Mac attack*, a sudden craving for a hamburger; note WW1 Aus. milit. *Bass attack*, a drinking bout, a play on Bass ale]

crack a tube v. [1960s+] (*Aus.*) to open a can of beer. [CRACK v.[3] (2) + TUBE n.[1] (8)]

crack a whid v. [19C] to speak; thus *crack some queer whids*, to speak badly, to use coarse expressions. [CRACK v.[1] (2) + WHID n. (1)]

crack babe n. [1990s+] (*US*) a girl or woman who swaps sex for crack cocaine. [CRACK n.[13] + BABE n. (1)]

crack baby n. **1** [1980s+] the child of a crack cocaine addict. **2** [1990s+] a general pej. term. [CRACK n.[13] + SE *baby*]

crack bitch n. [1990s+] (*Black*) a female crack cocaine addict. [CRACK n.[13] + BITCH n.[1] (1)]

crack book(s) v. *see* CRACK THE BOOKS v.

crackbrain n. [16C; 19C+] a fool (cf. BAKEBRAIN n.). [SE *crack* + sfx *-brain*]

crackbrained adj. [late 17C+] stupid; eccentric (cf. AMOEBA-BRAINED adj.). [CRACKBRAIN n.]

crack diet n. [1990s+] (*drugs*) a few sweets and a soft drink. [CRACK n.[13] + SE *diet*; a minimal diet, high on sugar, that is preferred by regular crack users]

crackdown n. [1930s+] the taking of harsh measures against something, esp. used of a campaign against vice or crime.

crack down v. **1** [1930s–40s] to let off a firearm. **2** [1930s–60s] (*US*) to work hard. **3** [1940s+] to repress, to take harsh measures against, esp. used of a campaign against vice or crime.

crack down on v. [20C+] (*Aus.*) to grab and make off with something.

cracked adj.[1] [late 16C–early 18C] deflowered. [CRACK v.[3] (1)]

cracked adj.[2] **1** [17C+] insane, crazy, eccentric; thus *cracked about/on*, obsessed with, infatuated with (cf. CRACKED IN THE FILBERT phr.; CRACKERBARREL adj.; CRACKS adj.; CRACKO adj.; CRACKY adj.). **2** [early 18C] bankrupt, financially ruined. **3** [mid-19C; 1970s] at the end of one's tether; emotionally drained (rather than clinically insane). [fig. uses of SE *cracked*, broken]

cracked adj.[3] [1980s+] (*drugs*) under the influence of crack cocaine. [CRACK n.[13]]

cracked groat n. (*also* **slit groat**) [17C] something absolutely worthless. [SE *cracked*/*slit* + *groat*, a coin worth 4 pence; thus of very low value]

cracked ice n. [late 19C–1960s] (*US*) diamonds. [SE *cracked* + ICE n.[3] + joc. use of SE phr.]

cracked in the filbert phr. [late 19C] eccentric, slightly crazy. [SE *cracked*/CRACKED adj.[2] (1) + FILBERT n.[1]]

cracked in the ring adj. [late 16C–19C] deflowered. [CRACKED adj.[1] + RING n.[1] (1); note Williams: 'Gold coins were very thin, so liable to fracture [...] The inscription around the coin's circumference was enclosed within two rings. When a crack extended past the inner ring, the coin lost currency']

cracked-out adj. [1980s+] (*drugs*) wholly addicted to crack cocaine. [CRACK n.[13]]

cracked pitcher n. [mid-18C–mid-19C] **1** a woman living between respectability and prostitution. **2** a recently lost virginity. [CRACK A PIPKIN v./CRACKED adj.[1]; note *double entendre* in D'Urfey, *Pills to Purge Melancholy* (1719–20): 'Where Wenches sell Glasses and crackt Earthen-ware; / To shew that the World and the Pleasures it brings, / Are made up of Brittle and Slippery things']

cracked up adj.[1] [mid-19C–1900s] impoverished, destitute. [fig. use of SE]

cracked up adj.[2] [1980s+] (*drugs*) under the influence of crack cocaine. [CRACK n.[13]]

cracker n.[1] **1** [late 17C–18C] (*UK Und.*) the backside. **2** [early 19C] (*S.Afr.*) sheep-skin trousers. [SE *crack*, the divide between the buttocks (predates CRACK n.[6] (4))]

cracker n.[2] **1** [mid-18C] a pistol. **2** [19C] the penis. **3** [1910s+] (*N.Z.*) a cartridge. [SE *crack*, to make a sharp noise; they all 'go off']

cracker n.[3] **1** [mid-18C+] (*US*) a poor Southern US White farmer. **2** [1920s+] (*orig. US Black*) (*also* **cracker-man**) a White person, usu. a racist. [CRACK v.[1] (1); 'I should explain to your Lordship what is meant by crackers, a name they have got from being great boasters, they are a lawless set of rascalls on the frontiers of Virginia, Maryland, the Carolinas and Georgia, who often change their places of abode' (G. Cochrane, letter, 27 June 1766). Note Toschos, *Where Dead Voices Gather* (2001): 'The Georgia jurist, educator, and author A.B. Longstreet (1790–1870) wrote endearingly of the poor rural whites known as crackers in Georgia Scenes, an 1835 collection of humorous sketches whose purpose, he said, "was to supply a chasm in history which has always been overlooked—the manners, customs, amusements, wit, dialect, as they appear in all grades of society to an eye and ear witness of them." The term came to be embraced colloquially by Georgians as a source of humor and self-effacing pride; and by the mid-nineteenth century and well into the twentieth, Georgia was known as the Cracker State. In the early 1930's, Erskine Caldwell, another Georgia author, would show a darker and more sordid side of cracker life in his popular novels *Tobacco Road* and *God's Little Acre*; but only later did cracker become the pejorative epithet that it is today, a class slur leveled by other whites or a racial slur cast by blacks']

cracker n.[4] [early 19C] (*UK prison*) a small loaf served to prisoners as their daily rations. [SE *cracker*, a biscuit]

cracker n.[5] **1** [mid-19C] an aphorism. **2** [late 19C–1900s] a lie. [CRACK n.[1]/CRACK n.[11] (1)]

cracker n.[6] [mid-19C+] **1** a heavy blow. **2** a fall. [CRACK n.[5] (1)]

cracker n.[7] [mid-19C+] someone or something notable, e.g. a fast pace, a dandy, a large sum of money, an exceptional individual. [CRACK adj. (1)]

cracker n.[8] [1920s] (*US Und.*) a safe. [? CRACK v.[3] (3)]

cracker n.[9] [1920s+] (*US Black*) a very light-skinned Black person. [? SE *cracker*, a biscuit; thus biscuit-coloured, or ref. to their similarity to a CRACKER n.[3] (1)]

cracker n.[10] [1930s+] **1** (US) $1 (cf. BATTER n.[4]). **2** (Aus./N.Z.) the smallest feasible amount of money. **3** (Aus./N.Z.) anything worthless, valueless; thus *not have a cracker*, to be penniless. [SE *cracker*, a biscuit; Baker, *The Australian Language* (1945), adds *cracker*, a £1 note, and this has been taken up by the *OED*, and in Nina Pulliam, *I Travelled A Lonely Land* (1955), but Wilkes, *Dict. of Australian Colloquialisms* (1985), rejects it: 'No evidence has been found']

cracker n.[11] [1940s+] a worn-out sheep, horse or bullock. [CRACKED UP adj.[1]]

cracker n.[12] **1** [1950s+] an attractive young woman; usu. as *a little cracker*; occas a man. **2** [1960s+] (Aus.) a prostitute. **3** [1960s+] (Aus.) (also **cracker joint**) a brothel. [CRACK adj. (1), but note CRACK n.[6] (1)]

cracker n.[13] [1990s+] a regular user of crack cocaine. [CRACK n.[13]]

cracker n.[14] [2000s] a credit card computer fraudster. [ext. of CRACK v.[3] (3), the fraudster *cracks* a computer code]

cracker n.[15] see CRACK n.[2].

cracker adj.[1] (orig. US Black) **1** [mid-19C+] pertaining to the US rural South; ext. to any White person. **2** [1950s+] racist. [CRACKER n.[3]]

cracker adj.[2] [1980s+] excellent, first-rate. [CRACKER n.[7]]

cracker-ass n.[1] [1960s–70s] (US) a skinny person. [SE *cracker*, a thin biscuit + -ASS sfx]

cracker-ass n.[2] [1960s+] (US Black) a White person. [CRACKER n.[3] + -ASS sfx]

crackerbarrel adj. [1980s+] crazy, eccentric (cf. CRACKED adj.[2]). [CRACKERS adj. + SAmE *crackerbarrel*, of a philosophy, plain or unsophisticated]

cracker box n.[1] **1** [1930s–40s] (US Und.) a safe that can be broken into easily. **2** [1950s+] a small room, e.g. a nightclub, a small house. [play on (1) fragility and (2) shape of SAmE *crackerbox*]

cracker box n.[2] [1980s+] (US) **1** an eccentric, a madman. **2** a psychiatric institution. [CRACKERS adj. + SE *box*; pun on SE]

cracker box n.[3] [2000s] (US Black) a predominantly White neighbourhood. [CRACKER n.[3] (2) + SE *box*]

cracker-box adj. [1940s] (US Und.) insecure; vulnerable to theft. [CRACKER BOX n.[1] (1)]

cracker factory n. [1980s+] (US) a psychiatric institution. [CRACKERS adj. + SE *factory*; pun on SE]

crackerjack n.[1] **1** [late 19C+] (orig. US) someone or something exceptional. **2** [1910s] (US) an arrogant, 'cocky' person. **3** [1970s] (US campus) a fool, an oaf. [ext. of CRACKER n.[7]]

crackerjack n.[2] [1980s+] (drugs) a smoker of crack cocaine. [play on CRACKERJACK n.[1] (3) + ref. to CRACK n.[13] + ? JACK n.[2]]

crackerjack adj.[1] (also **crackajack**) [late 19C+] excellent, first-class, superlative. [CRACKERJACK n.[1] (1)]

crackerjack adj.[2] [1970s+] fake, make-believe. [? US sweet *Crackerjack*, which contained toy police badges]

cracker joint n. see CRACKER n.[12] (3).

cracker-man n. see CRACKER n.[3] (2).

crackers n.[1] [1900s–10s] (US) beans. [CRACK v.[4] (1)]

crackers n.[2] [1960s] (orig. US) a euph. for *Christ*, usu. as used in mild oaths.

crackers n.[3] [1960s] (drugs) LSD (cf. A n.[3]). [the distribution of LSD by placing a drop on a biscuit]

crackers n.[4] [1970s] the teeth. [SE *crack*]

crackers n.[5] [1970s] (drugs) amyl nitrite (cf. AIMIES n.). [SE *crack*, to break open, i.e. one snaps open the vial that contains the drug]

crackers n.[6] [1990s+] (Aus.) the testicles (cf. BANGERS n.). [they supposedly make a *crack* knocking together]

crackers adj. [1920s+] mad, crazy, thus *crackers about*, obsessed with. [CRACKED adj.[2] (1)]

cracker state n. [early 19C+] (US) Georgia. [CRACKER n.[3] (1) + SE *state*]

crackfart n. [late 17C–early 18C] a general term of abuse, a blusterer. [CRACK v.[4] (1) + FART n. (1)]

crack-fencer n. [mid-19C] a street-seller of nuts. [SE *crack* (of a nut) + -FENCER sfx]

crack funny v. [1980s+] (US) **1** to be cheeky, insolent. **2** to make jokes; to amuse. [CRACK v.[1] (6)]

crack gallery n. [1980s+] (drugs) a place where users of crack cocaine congregate to buy and smoke the drug. [CRACK n.[13] + SHOOTING GALLERY n. (2)]

crack halter n. (also **crack hemp**) [16C–17C] a rogue, a villain. [the *halter* is the hangman's noose; *hemp* refers to the hempen noose]

crack hand n. [mid-19C] an able, competent person. [CRACK adj. (1) + HAND n.[1]]

crack-hardy adj. [1920s] (Aus.) of a person, tough, surviving. [CRACK HARDY v. (1)]

crack hardy v. [20C+] (Aus.) **1** to put up with discomfort, to 'grin and bear it'. **2** to keep a secret. [CRACK v.[7] (1) + SE *hardy*]

crack-haunter n. see CRACK-HUNTER n.

crackhead n. **1** [1980s+] (drugs) a smoker of crack cocaine. **2** [1990s+] an idiot. [CRACK n.[13] + -HEAD sfx (3)/-HEAD sfx (1)]

crack hemp n. see CRACK HALTER n.

crack ho n. [1990s+] (US Black) a woman who will offer sex in return for crack cocaine. [CRACK n.[13] + HO n.[1] (1)]

crack house n. [1980s+] **1** a room or whole house in which users gather to take crack cocaine. **2** a place where crack cocaine is processed from base cocaine. [CRACK n.[13] + SE *house*]

crack-hunter n. (also **crack-haunter**) [late 19C] the penis (cf. ARSE-OPENER n.). [CRACK n.[6] (1) + SE *hunter/haunter*]

crackie n. [2000s] (US Black) one who is very heavily addicted to crack cocaine. [CRACK n.[13] + sfx -*ie*]

crackiness n. [mid–late 19C] eccentricity. [CRACKED adj.[2] (1)]

cracking n. [mid-19C–1920s] (UK Und.) house-breaking. [CRACK v.[3] (3)]

cracking adj. **1** [early 19C+] vigorous. **2** [mid-19C+] excellent, first-rate. **3** [1950s] as an intensifier, i.e. utter, absolute. [CRACK adj. (1)]

cracking but facking phr. [1930s–40s] (US Black) conveying hard factual information in the guise of jokes and humour. [CRACK v.[1] (6) + SE *fact*]

cracking it n. [1960s+] (Aus.) prostitution. [CRACK IT FOR A QUID v.]

crack into fame v. (also **crack into reputation/repute**) [late 19C–1920s] to make famous by constant praise. [CRACK v.[1] (3) + SE *fame*]

crackish adj. [late 17C–19C] of a woman, wanton, promiscuous. [CRACK n.[6] (2)]

crack it v.[1] [1930s+] (orig. Aus./N.Z.) **1** to succeed, to overcome obstacles, esp. to achieve a successful (from the male point of view) seduction. **2** to obtain, to get hold of, poss. by criminal means. **3** to do, to perform; usu. as *crack it for a...* [fig. use of CRACK v.[3] (3)]

crack it v.[2] see CRACK THE BOOKS v.

crack it for a quid v. [1960s+] (Aus.) to work as a prostitute. [CRACK v.[3] (2), i.e. to open her legs]

crack lay n. [late 18C–19C] (UK Und.) house-breaking. [CRACK n.[8] (2) + LAY n.[4] (1)]

crackle n. [1940s–50s] (UK Und.) banknotes, usu. £5 notes and above (cf. BANK-RAG n.; CHING n.[2]). [the noise of the paper]

crackling n. [late 19C+] attractive women, used as a generic term. [SE *crackling*, tasty roast pork fat]

crack loose v. [1900s] (US) to threaten, verbally or physically. [CRACK v.[1] (6) + SE *loose*]

crack mama n. [1990s+] (US campus) a Black woman addicted to crack cocaine; thus a derog. term for any Black woman. [CRACK n.[13] + MAMA n. (1)]

crackmans n. (also **cragmans**) [16C–18C] (UK Und.) a hedge. [SE *crack*, dry firewood + -MANS sfx]

crack monster n. [1980s+] (US drugs) a habitual user of crack cocaine. [CRACK n.[13] + MONSTER sfx]

crack mugs v. [1910s+] (*Aus.*) to sell racing tips. [CRACK v.¹ (6) + MUG n.² (1); the implication is of their worthlessness and the gullibility of the purchasers]

cracko n. [1980s+] a madman, a lunatic. [CRACKED adj.² (1) + -O sfx (2)]

cracko adj. [1980s+] eccentric, insane (cf. CRACKED adj.²). [CRACKO n.]

crack off v. [1980s+] (*US*) to make jokes, to make 'smart' comments. [CRACK v.¹ (6)]

crack of the whip phr. see WHIP n.³.

crackola n. [1990s+] (*US Black/drugs*) crack cocaine (cf. BASE n.). [CRACK n.¹³+ -OLA sfx]

crack on v.¹ **1** [mid-19C] to load up, to 'clap on'. **2** [mid-19C+] (*also* **crack, crack along**) to move along at speed, to bustle about. **3** [1940s+] to get on with one's work.

crack on v.² **1** [mid-19C–1900s; 1960s] to inform (against). **2** [mid-19C+] to talk at length. **3** [late 19C+] to tell tales, to boast. **4** [late 19C+] to pretend. **5** [1970s+] (*US Black*) to disparage, to attack verbally. [ext. CRACK v.¹]

crack on v.³ [1960s+] (*US campus*) of a man, to strike up a friendship with a woman in the hope of moving onto a deeper relationship; the alluring factor is not her status or possessions but her personality. [ext. of CRACK v.¹ (2)]

crack on v.⁴ see CRACK v.¹ (2).

crack on v.⁵ see CRACK v.⁶ (1).

crack one's face v. (*also* **crack a grin, crack a smile**) [1940s+] to laugh, to smile (cf. CRACK SOMEONE'S FACE v.).

crack one's fist v. [1940s] to masturbate. [CRACK v.⁴ (2)]

crack one's jaw v. (*also* **crack one's jib**) [1930s–50s] (*US Black*) **1** to boast, to brag. **2** to speak. [CRACK v.¹ + SE *jaw*]

crack one's marbles v. [1930s] (*US*) **1** of a man, to achieve orgasm or to induce it in a woman. **2** to delight, to please. [SE *crack* + MARBLES n.³ + pun]

crack one's nuts v. [1940s+] (*US*) of a man, to achieve orgasm. [SE *crack* + NUTS n.² (1) + pun]

crack one's pipkin/pitcher v. see CRACK A PIPKIN v.

crack one's ribs v. (*also* **crack one's guts**) [mid-19C+] to laugh uproariously, until one feels actual pain.

crack one's side v. [1930s–50s] (*US Black*) to laugh uproariously, until one feels actual pain.

crack one's whip v. [1950s–80s] (*N.Z.*) to take one's share or turn, esp. in buying a round of drinks.

crackpot n. [late 19C+] an eccentric, a madman. [SE *crack* + *pot* (*of the head*), the skull, the cranium/-POT sfx]

crackpot adj. [late 19C+] usu. of ideas, absurd, bizarre, unworkable. [CRACKPOT n.]

crack-rope n. [mid-16C–early19C] a rogue, a villain. [SE *crack* + *rope*; thus one who might stretch the hangman's rope]

crack salesman n. **1** [1940s] a pimp. **2** [1970s+] a gay male prostitute (cf. ASS PEDDLER n.). [CRACK n.⁶ (1)/CRACK n.⁶ (5)]

crack shorts v. see CRACK A SHORT v.

crackskull n. [mid-19C+] (*US*) whisky. [a melodramatic version of its effects]

cracksman n.¹ **1** [mid-18C+] a burglar; thus *swell cracksman*, a superior burglar. **2** [1920s] a safe-breaker. [CRACK v.³ (3) + sfx *-man*; the *locus classicus* is in the title of E.W. Hornung's *The Amateur Cracksman* (1899), featuring the exploits of the gentleman-thief A.J. Raffles]

cracksman n.² [19C] the penis. [CRACK n.⁶ (1) + sfx *-man*]

crack snaker n. [1990s+] (*US*) a derog. term for a lesbian (cf. BEAN FLICKER n.). [CRACK n.⁶ (1)]

crack someone's face v. [1980s] (*US campus*) to humiliate, to insult (cf. CRACK ONE'S FACE v.). [CRACK v.¹ (6)]

crack someone's lice v. [mid-19C] (*US*) to hit someone on the head.

crack someone up v. [1960s+] (*orig. US*) to make someone laugh, to reduce someone to fits of laughter. [CRACK UP v.⁴]

crack some suds v. [1940s–70s] (*orig. US Black*) to open and drink a can of beer. [CRACK v.³ (2) + SUDS n.¹ (1)]

crack spot n. [1980s+] (*drugs*) an area where people can purchase crack cocaine, but do not smoke it. [CRACK n.¹³ + SE *spot*, a place]

crack the bell v. [late 19C–1900s] to muddle, to ruin, to blunder. [a *cracked* bell is useless as it cannot ring]

crack the books v. (*also* **crack a book, crack book(s), crack it**) [1920s+] (*orig. US*) to open books; thus to read, to study. [CRACK v.³ (2)]

crack the pipe v. see HIT THE PIPE v.¹ (2).

crack-up n.¹ [1930s+] (*orig. US*) **1** a nervous breakdown, a mental collapse. **2** a motorcar or motorcycle crash. [CRACK UP v.²]

crack-up n.² [1960s+] anything considered hilariously funny. [CRACK UP v.⁴]

crack-up adj. see CRACK adj. (1).

crack up v.¹ [early 19C+] to boast or praise; esp. in NOT ALL IT'S CRACKED UP TO BE phr.[the *crack* sound of applauding hands]

crack up v.² (*orig. US*) **1** [late 19C+] to fall ill, to collapse. **2** [1910s–40s] to render ill, either mentally or physically. **3** [1930s+] to have a nervous breakdown. [SE *crack*, to break]

crack up v.³ [1920s+] to crash some form of vehicle or conveyance, e.g. a car, an aeroplane. [SE *crack*]

crack up v.⁴ [1940s+] to laugh uproariously (cf. CRACK SOMEONE UP v.). [SE *crack*, to break]

crack up v.⁵ [1990s+] (*drugs*) to smoke crack cocaine. [CRACK n.¹³]

crack whore n. [2000s] (*US campus*) a general pej., there is no need for drug use to be involved. [CRACK n.¹³ + SE *whore*, i.e. a woman who prostitutes herself to sustain a crack cocaine addiction]

crackwise n. [1940s–60s] (*US Black*) one who pretends to a greater sophistication and knowledge of 'the scene' than he or she actually possesses, a poseur. [CRACK WISE v.]

crack wise v. [1920s+] (*orig. US Black*) to make a 'clever' comment that impresses no one, to pose as more sophisticated than one actually is. [CRACK v.¹ (2) + WISE adv.]

cracky n. [1900s–40s] a mentally unstable person. [CRACKED adj.² (1)]

cracky adj. [1920s+] (*orig. Aus.*) eccentric, mentally unstable (cf. CRACKED adj.²). [CRACKERS adj.]

cracky! excl. [mid-19C+] a euph. for CHRIST! excl., usu. in mild oaths.

cradle n. [late 18C–19C] the vagina (cf. BAG n.¹).

cradle-robber n. **1** [1920s+] (*orig. US*) one who pursues lovers who are younger than they are (cf. CRADLE-SNATCHER n.). **2** [1940s] (*US*) a child molester. [ROB THE CRADLE v.]

cradle-snatcher n. [20C+] (*orig. US*) an older person, in modern use usu. a woman, who prefers affairs with people substantially younger than they are (cf. CRADLE-ROBBER n.).

craft n.¹ [mid-19C+] a woman. [20C+ use is UK Black/W.I.]

craft n.² [late 19C–1900s] a bicycle. [SE *craft*, a ship]

craft and daft n. [1990s+] (*Scot. juv.*) a course in craft and design.

craft rig n. [late 18C] (*UK Und.*) a form of river robbery. [SE *craft* + RIG n.² (2)]

craftsby n. [late 17C] a cheat, a confidence trickster.

crafty butcher n. [1990s+] a male homosexual.

crag n.¹ [mid-17C–early 19C] the neck, the head.

crag n.² [1970s+] (*US campus*) an irritable, nagging woman. [CRAB n.¹ (1) + SE *nag*]

cragmans n. see CRACKMANS n.

craik v. (*also* **crake**) [20C+] (*Ulster*) to nag, to grumble, to talk without stopping. [dial. *crake*, an ill-natured gossip; ult. SE *crake*, the cry of the corncrake]

Crail capon n. [early 19C] a salt herring. [the local fishery trade of Crail, Fife]

cram n.¹ (*UK/US campus*) **1** [mid-19C] a paper on which material necessary to be learned for a given examination or test is written down. **2** [mid–late 19C] (*also* **cram-coach**) a tutor. **3** [mid-19C+]

last-minute work for a specific test or examination; thus *cram man*, one who is working in this way; *cram-book*, a book used for intensive learning; *cram-paper*, a prepared list of examination answers, to be learned parrot-fashion; *cram-shop*, a school for this purpose; *crammable*, work that can be learned by rote; *crammed*, tutored for examinations rather than actual knowledge; (*US*) *cram session*, a burst of study immediately before an examination. [CRAM v.² (1)]

cram *n.*² [mid-19C–1900s] a lie. [CRAM v.¹]

cram *v.*¹ [late 18C–mid-19C] to lie, to deceive, to make a person believe false or exaggerated statements. [SE *cram*, to fill up, the liar's victim is 'filled up' with untruths]

cram *v.*² **1** [19C+] to study hard, esp. at the last minute. **2** [mid-19C] to train up a student for an examination. **3** [late 19C–1920s] to study for a given subject or insitution after one has been expelled from a regular school. [SE *cram*, to fill up]

cram *v.*³ **1** [mid-19C] to urge a horse on by force. **2** [mid-19C+] of a man, to have sexual intercourse.

cram it! *excl.* [1960s+] (*US*) a general excl. of dismissal, rejection, *the hell with it! shove it!* etc. [? CRAM v.³ (2)]

crammer *n.*¹ **1** [19C+] a tutor; thus [late 19C–1920s] *crammer's pup*, a pupil of such a high-pressure tutor. **2** [1910s–60s] a swot. [CRAM v.² (1)]

crammer *n.*² [mid-19C; 1960s] the stomach. [SE *cram*]

crammer *n.*³ **1** [mid–late 19C] one who lies. **2** [mid–19C–1920s] a lie. [CRAM v.¹]

cramming *n.* [early 19C+] intensive learning aimed purely at passing necessary examinations. [CRAM v.² (1)]

cram-o-matic *v.* [1980s+] (*US campus*) to study hard at the last minute. [CRAM v.² (1) + -O-MATIC sfx]

cramp *n.* [1990s+] (*US Black*) an unpleasant, unpopular woman. [? image of one suffering badly from menstrual cramps]

cramp *v.* (*US*) **1** [mid-19C] to execute by hanging, to kill. **2** [late 19C; 1960s] to annoy. [fig. uses of SE *cramp*, to compress, to restrict, to limit]

cramp! *excl.* [1950s–70s] a euph. for CHRIST! excl., usu. in mild oaths.

cramped *adj.* [mid-19C] **1** hanged. **2** killed. [CRAMP v. (1)/SE *cramp*, to torture by compressing or 'cramping' the body]

cramping-cull *n.* [mid-19C] the hangman. [CRAMP v. (1) + CULL n.¹ (4)]

cramp in the hand *n.* [late 19C] meanness.

cramp-rings *n.* (*also* **cramping-rings, queer cramp-ring**) [mid-16C–mid-19C] (*UK Und.*) shackles or fetters. [SE *cramp*: a small iron bar with its ends bent into hooks + ? pun on the orig. 15C SE *cramp-ring*, a ring worn on the finger to ward off cramp, epilepsy etc (+ QUEER adj.¹ (1))]

cramp someone's style *v.* [1910s+] to handicap, to hinder, to hold back, to get in someone's way, both fig. and lit.

cramp words *n.* [18C–mid-19C] (*UK Und.*) a sentence of death. [CRAMP v. (1) + SE *words*; note SE *cramp word*, a long, difficult or unusual word]

cranberry eye *n.* [late 19C] (*US*) a bloodshot eye (from excessive drinking). [the colour]

cranberry sauce *n.* [1930s] (*US Und.*) blood (cf. BADMINTON n.).

crane *v.* [mid–late 19C] to hesitate or balk before an obstacle. [SE *crane one's neck*, to stretch the neck to look around + hunting jargon *crane*, to pull up at a hedge or other obstacle and look over before leaping]

crank *n.*¹ **1** [mid-16C–early 19C] the 'falling sickness', epilepsy. **2** [17C–mid-18C] a mendicant villain who specializes in faking sickness, esp. epilepsy, and who often displays convincingly horrific sores and wounds, created by the application of various herbs. [Ger. *krenk*, sick]

crank *n.*² [late 18C–mid-19C] gin and water. [SE *crank*, lively]

crank *n.*³ **1** [early 19C+] an eccentric. **2** [late 19C] a crazy idea. **3** [late 19C–1910s] (*US*) a baseball fan. **4** [late 19C–1920s] (*US*) a craze, a fad, an obsession. **5** [late 19C+] an obsessive, a monomaniac; often with a defining n. **6** [1920s+] a bad-tempered person, a 'grouch'. **7** [1950s+] (*US prison*) a veteran warder or inmate who finds it amusing to persecute younger and/or newer prisoners. [CRANK adj.¹ (1); note SE *cranky*, of capricious or wayward temper, difficult to please or *crank*, an eccentric notion or action, fig. a mental twist]

crank *n.*⁴ [1960s+] (*drugs*) any form of amphetamine drug (cf. A n.²). **2** [1970s+] a thrill of excitement, esp. when drug-generated. **3** [1980s+] (*drugs*) crack cocaine (cf. BASE n.). **4** [1990s+] heroin. [SE *crank (up)*, i.e. such drugs *crank up* one's bodily 'motor']

crank *n.*⁵ **1** [1960s+] (*orig. US*) the penis. **2** [1990s+] (*Aus.*) (*also* **hand crank**) an act of masturbation performed by a woman. [resemblance to SE *crank*, a handle]

crank *adj.*¹ **1** [mid-18C+] mad, eccentric. **2** [late 18C–early 19C] brisk, pert. [SE *crank*, anything fantastic in behaviour, gesture or action]

crank *adj.*² [mid-19C] (*US*) proud. [SE *crank*, exultant, 'cocky']

crank *v.*¹ **1** [1920s+] to turn up the volume of a radio etc; to talk or sing louder. **2** [1930s+] (*also* **crank up**) to start up a mechanical device, esp. a car engine (but not with an actual crank handle); also in fig. use, to start up. **3** [1960s+] (*US*) to get, to prepare (oneself). **4** [1970s] (*US prison*) to roll a cigarette. **5** [1970s+] (*US teen*) an all-purpose v. of movement, e.g. *crank oneself together*, *crank to school...* **6** [1970s+] to intensify, to do something more energetically. [SE *crank*, to wind up, to turn a handle]

crank *v.*² (*drugs*) **1** [1960s+] (*also* **crank up**) to inject narcotics with a hypodermic syringe. **2** [1980s+] to become intoxicated by amphetamine. [fig. uses of CRANK v.¹ (2)]

crank bugs *n. see* BUG n.⁶ (2).

crank cuffin *n.* [late 17C–mid-18C] (*UK Und.*) a tramp who poses as a sufferer from a sympathy-inducing illness. [CRANK n.¹ (2) + CUFFIN n. (1)]

cranked *adj.* [late 19C–1920s] (*US*) mentally unbalanced. [CRANK adj.¹ (1)]

cranked (out) *adj.* (*also* **cranked up**) [1980s+] under the influence of amphetamine or crack cocaine. [CRANK n.⁴]

cranked (up) *adj.* (*also* **cranked**) [1950s+] (*US*) excited, 'revved up'. [CRANK v.¹ (2)]

cranker *n.*¹ [1930s–40s] (*US*) a doctor. [Ger. *krank*, sick]

cranker *n.*² [1970s] (*drugs*) a heavy user of amphetamine. [CRANK n.⁴ (1)]

cranker *n.*³ [1980s+] (*Aus. prison*) a safe-breaker. [? rhy. sl.; ? CRANK v.¹ (2); ? link to TANK n.² (3)]

cranker *n.*⁴ [1980s+] (*Aus. prison*) a masturbator. [rhy. sl. = WANKER n.; + link to CRANK ONE'S SHANK v.]

crank gang *n.* [1980s] (*US prison*) a prison work gang composed of eccentric or idle prisoners. [CRANK n.³ (1)]

crankhead *n.* [1980s+] (*US drugs*) a regular user of amphetamine. [CRANK n.⁴ (1) + -HEAD sfx (3)]

cranking *adj.* [1980s+] (*US campus*) enjoyable, exciting. [? CRANKED (UP) adj.]

crank it out *v.* [1970s+] to write (usu. rubbish) more from duty than pleasure or interest, to be a hack writer. [SE *crank*, to turn a handle]

crank it up *v.* [1980s+] to intensify, esp. to make louder, to turn up the volume. [CRANK v.¹ (1)/CRANK v.¹ (6)]

crank off *v.* [1960s+] (*US*) to fire a round from a weapon. [CRANK v.¹ (2)]

crank on *v.* [1980s+] (*US campus*) to work hard and efficiently. [CRANK v.¹ (6)]

crank one's shank *v.* (*also* **crank one's shaft, crank the shank**) [1990s+] to masturbate. [SE *crank*, to wind up, to twist + *shank*, a shaft, stem or 'neck'; note RMC Duntroon (*Aus.*) *hand crank*, an act of masturbation]

crank out *v.* [1970s] (*US campus*) to produce large amounts, e.g. of work, energy, sound etc. [CRANK v.¹ (1)]

crankpot *n.* [1960s+] (*US*) a mean, ill-tempered individual. [CRANK n.³ (1) + *pot* (*of the head*), the skull, the cranium/-POT sfx; var. on CRACKPOT n.]

crankpot *adj.* [2000s] unpleasant, ill-tempered, bigoted. [CRANKPOT n.]

crank the shank *v. see* CRANK ONE'S SHANK v.

crank up *v.*¹ *see* CRANK v.¹ (2).

crank up *v.*² *see* CRANK v.² (1).

cranky hatch *n.* **1** [20C+] (*US Und.*) a psychiatric institution. **2** [1910s+] (*US prison*) the prison segregation block. [SE *cranky*, eccentric + BOOBY-HATCH n. (2)]

cranky hutch *n.* [mid-19C] (*US*) a lunatic asylum. [SE *cranky*, eccentric + SE *hutch*]

cranny *n.*¹ [mid-17C+] the vagina (cf. AGREEABLE RUTS OF LIFE n.).

cranny *n.*² [mid-19C] (*Anglo-Ind.*) a (Bengali) clerk who writes in English; thus generic for a half-caste. [Hind. *kirani*, lit. 'a doer'; the Karana caste (Sudra mother and Vaisya father) specializes in accountancy and writing]

cranny-hunter *n.* (*also* **cranny-haunter**) [late 19C] the penis (cf. ARSE-OPENER n.). [CRANNY n.¹ + SE *hunter*]

crap *n.*¹ (*also* **crop**) [late 17C–mid-19C] money (cf. CHAFF n.²). [SE *crap*, waste, chaff]

crap *n.*² [late 18C–mid-19C] the gallows; thus *knock down/up for the crap*, to sentence to be hanged; *craping cull*, a hangman. [Du. *krap*, cramp or clasp]

crap *n.*³ **1** [mid-19C+] excrement. **2** [mid-19C+] dirt, mess. **3** [1910s+] nonsense; often as TALK CRAP v. **4** [1920s+] rubbish, anything useless or unpleasant. **5** [1920s+] an act of defecation. **6** [1930s+] (*orig. US*) the guts, the stuffing; esp. in such phrs. as KNOCK THE CRAP OUT OF v. **7** [1940s] a non-specific descriptor, 'stuff', 'things'. **8** [1940s] (*US gang*) fighting. **9** [1940s+] of people, a general derog. term. [mix of Du. *krappen*, to pluck off, cut off or separate + OF *crappe*, waste or rejected matter, siftings, particularly 'the grain trodden under feet in the barn, and mingled with the straw and dust', ult. Med. Lat. *crappa*, *crapinum*, the smaller chaff]

crap *n.*⁴ [1910s+] (*US*) insolence, cheek, e.g. *don't give me that crap!* [but note CRAP n.³ (3)]

crap *n.*⁵ (*US*) **1** [1940s+] nothing at all. **2** [1950s+] trouble, problems. [fig. uses of CRAP n.³ (3)]

crap *n.*⁶ [1950s–60s] a DAMN n.; esp. in phr. *(not) give a crap*. [CRAP n.³ (1)]

crap *n.*⁷ [1960s+] (*drugs*) **1** (*also* **crop**) low-quality heroin (cf. CACA n.). **2** marijuana. [fig. use of CRAP n.³ (1) = SHIT n.⁵ (1)]

crap, the *n.* [1940s+] (*orig. US*) used in excl., e.g. *what the crap do you want?*

crap *adj.* [1930s+] a general negative description; unpleasant, disgusting, repellent, worthless etc. [CRAP n.³ (3)/CRAP n.³ (4)]

crap *v.*¹ (*also* **crop**) [mid-18C–mid-19C] to hang; occas. as excl. *crap me! crop me!* [CRAP n.²]

crap *v.*² **1** [mid-19C+] to visit the lavatory, to defecate (cf. CACA v.). **2** [1940s+] to filthy with excrement. [CRAP n.³ (1)]

crap *v.*³ **1** [1920s+] to tell deliberate lies (to). **2** [1930s+] to complain. **3** [1940s+] to chatter; thus CRAP ON (ABOUT) v. **4** [1960s+] to annoy, to irritate. [CRAP n.³ (3)]

crap! *excl.* [late 19C+] a general excl.; thus *like crap!* a general intensifier, usu. negative.

crap around *v.* [1930s+] to fool about, to waste time (cf. CRAP SOMEONE AROUND v.). [ext. of CRAP v.³]

crap artist *n.* (*also* **crap merchant**) [1930s+] (*US*) a liar, an exaggerator, a deceiver. [CRAP n.³ (3) + ARTIST sfx/MERCHANT n.]

crap a smoke *v.* [1940s] (*US*) to smoke surreptitiously in a lavatory. [CRAP v.² (1) +SE *smoke*]

crap-ass *n.* [1970s+] (*US*) a despicable, unpleasant person. [CRAP n.³ (1) + -ASS sfx]

crap-ass *adj.* [1970s+] (*US*) second-rate, inferior. [CRAP-ASS n.]

crap-bag *n.* [1960s–70s] (*Scot.*) a coward. [CRAP n.³ (4) + -BAG sfx]

crapbrain *n.* [1950s+] a general term of abuse, based on the alleged stupidity of the recipient (cf. SHIT-FOR-BRAINS n.). [CRAP n.³ (1) + sfx *-brain*]

crap-can *n.* [1930s–40s] (*US*) the lavatory. [CRAP n.³ (1) + SE *can*/CAN n.³ (2)]

crap course *n.* [1950s+] (*US campus*) an easy course. [CRAP adj. + SE *course*]

crap creek *n.* [1970s] (*US*) a troublesome, threatening situation. [CRAP n.³ (1); var. on SHIT CREEK n.]

crape-hanger *n.* (*also* **crepe-hanger**) [1910s–60s] (*US*) a pessimist, a killjoy. [the hanging of black crape to signify mourning]

craperoo *n.* (*also* **crappadooley, crapperoo**) [1940s+] (*US*) absolute rubbish, nonsense. [CRAP n.³ (3) + -EROO sfx]

crap-happy *adj.* [1960s+] (*US*) foolishly happy. [play on SLAP-HAPPY adj.]

craphead *n.* (*also* **crapface**) [1950s+] (*orig. US*) a fool, an unpleasant person. [CRAP n.³ (4) + -HEAD sfx (1)]

craphole *n.* [1930s+] a filthy, disgusting place. [CRAP n.³ (2) + SE *hole*]

craphouse *n.* **1** [1930s+] (*orig. US*) a lavatory (cf. BACKHOUSE n.). **2** [1960s+] (*orig. US*) any unpleasant, dirty place; thus (*US*) in show business, a small, unfashionable venue. [CRAP n.³ + SE *house*]

craphouse luck *n.* [1940s–60s] (*US*) unexpectedly good luck. [CRAPHOUSE n. (1) + SE *luck*]

craphouse rat *n.* [1940s+] (*US*) an image of unpleasantness; in phrs. *as cunning as a craphouse rat, as dirty as a craphouse rat*. [CRAPHOUSE n. (1) + SE *rat*]

crap it *v.* [1960s+] to be doomed, to suffer a serious mishap, to mess something up. [fig. use of CRAP v.² (2)]

crap-kicker *n. see* SHITKICKER n. (6).

crap merchant *n.*¹ [late 18C] (*UK Und.*) the hangman. [CRAP n.² + MERCHANT n.]

crap merchant *n.*² *see* CRAP ARTIST n.

crapmound *n.* [1950s] a general term of abuse, lit. a 'heap of shit'. [CRAP n.³ (1) + SE *mound*]

crapola *n.* [1940s+] (*US*) nonsense, rubbish. [CRAP n.³ (3) + -OLA sfx]

crap on *v.* **1** [1920s+] to hell with. **2** [1940s+] (*also* **crap over**) to treat contemptuously, to victimize. [fig. use of CRAP v.² (1)]

crap on (about) *v.* [1940s+] **1** to talk lengthily, if irrelevantly (about). **2** to complain (about). [CRAP v.³ (3)]

crap oneself *v. see* SHIT ONESELF v.

crap or get off the hole *phr. see* SHIT OR GET OFF THE POT phr.

crap-out *n.* [1960s+] (*US*) a defeatist, a quitter. [CRAP OUT v. (1)]

crap out *v.* (*orig. US*) **1** [late 19C+] to back down, to give up, esp. in humiliating circumstances. **2** [20C+] to fail, to go wrong, to blunder. **3** [1940s+] of people, to collapse, to become exhausted, to fall asleep. **4** [1940s+] to die. **5** [1950s+] of machinery, to break down. **6** [1960s] to kill. [SE *crap out*, to make a losing throw in the game *craps*. Note COME OFF CRABS v., taken f. the losing cards, 2 aces, in the game of hazard; in the dice game *craps* a pair of 1s, known as *snake-eyes*, is similarly a losing throw]

crap over *v. see* CRAP ON v. (2).

crappadooley *n. see* CRAPEROO n.

crappapella *adj.* [1990s+] (*US campus*) very unpleasant, useless or disgusting. [ext. of CRAP adj.]

crap paper *n.* [1920s] (*US*) lavatory paper. [CRAP n.³ (5) + SE *paper*]

crapped *adj.* (*also* **cropped**) [late 18C–19C] (*UK Und.*) hanged. [CRAP v.¹]

crapped out *adj.* **1** [1930s+] (*US*) having been defeated in any challenge. **2** [1930s+] having hit rock bottom. **3** [1940s+] asleep, collapsed, comatose. [CRAP OUT v.]

crapper *n.*¹ **1** [1900s] (*US campus*) a very unpleasant person. **2** [1930s+] a braggart; a liar. [CRAP n.³ (1)/CRAP n.³ (3)]

crapper *n.*[2] [20C+] (*Irish*) a half-glass of whisky. [? dial. *crap*, settlings of bear at the bottom of a barrel]

crapper *n.*[3] **1** [1920s] (*US Und.*) a prison. **2** [1920s+] (*orig. US*) a lavatory. **3** [1970s] (*orig. US*) the anus, the buttocks. [CRAP v.[2] (1); popular and some scholarly sources (e.g. Seal, *The Lingo*, 1999) attribute the ety. to the eponymously named Thomas Crapper, inventor of the water closet, but this is more likely no more than a fortuitous coincidence, albeit a reinforcement of the real root]

crapper dick *n.* [1950s–70s] (*US*) a plain-clothes policeman who specializes in hanging around public lavatories in the hope of entrapping homosexual men having sex; thus an extortionist who poses as a policeman to blackmail homosexuals. [CRAPPER n.[3] (2) + DICK n.[6] (2)]

crapperoo *n. see* CRAPEROO n.

crappery *n.* [2000s] any second-rate, mediocre place or venue. [CRAP adj.]

crapping *n.* [late 18C] (*UK Und.*) hanging. [CRAP v.[1]]

crapping *adj.* [mid-19C+] a general pej. description, useless, second-rate, disgusting. [CRAP v.[2] (1)]

crapping can *n.* [1930s+] (*US*) a lavatory. [CRAP v.[2] (1) + SE *can*/CAN n.[3] (2)]

crapping casa *n.* (*also* **crapping case**) [mid-19C] a privy or water-closet (cf. BACKHOUSE n.). [CRAP v.[2] (1) + CASA n.[1]/CASE n.[3] (1)]

crapping castle *n.* [mid-19C] a privy (cf. ALTAR n.; SCRAPING CASTLE n.). [var. on CRAPPING CASA n.]

crapping cull *n.* [mid-18C–mid-19C] (*UK Und.*) the hangman. [CRAP v.[1] + CULL n.[1] (4)]

crapping ken *n.* (*also* **croppen ken, croppin ken, cropping ken**) [late 17C–mid-19C] (*UK Und.*) a privy (cf. BACKHOUSE n.). [CRAP v.[2] (1) + KEN n.[1] (1) but note CROPPEN n.]

crappo *n.* (*also* **cropoh, croppo**) [19C] a Frenchman. [Fr. *crapaud*, toad]

crappo *adj.* [1970s+] disgusting, appalling. [CRAP adj. + -o sfx (3)]

crap-pushing *adj.* [1960s] a general derisory epithet. [CRAP n.[3] (1)]

crappy *adj.* **1** [mid-19C+] fouled with excrement. **2** [1920s–30s] (*UK, Glasgow*) terrified. **3** [1920s+] (*also* **krappy**) second-rate. **4** [1950s–60s] reminiscent of excrement in colour. **5** [1950s+] unpleasant, distasteful. **6** [1960s+] unwell. [CRAP n.[3] + sfx -*y*]

crappy *adv.* [1970s+] (*US campus*) badly, in a second-rate manner. [CRAPPY adj.]

craps *n.* [1920s+] dice. [the dice game SE *craps*]

craps, the *n.* [1950s] (*US*) diarrhoea. [CRAP n.[3] (1)]

crap-shoot *n.* [1970s+] any situation in which luck, not judgement, is of paramount importance. [SE *shoot craps*; thus an image of random luck]

crap-shooter *n.* (*also* **crap-slinger**) [1930s–40s] (*US*) one who talks nonsense. [CRAP n.[3] (3) + SHOOT v.[1] (4)/SE *sling*]

crap someone around *v.* [1970s+] **1** (*also* **crap someone along**) to tell deliberate lies. **2** to annoy, to irritate. [CRAP AROUND v./ext. of CRAP v.[3]]

crap up *v.* (*orig. US*) **1** [1940s+] to ruin by adding unnecessary or distasteful accessories. **2** [1950s+] to make a mess of. [fig. use of CRAP v.[2] (2)]

crapweasel *n.* [2000s] (*US campus*) an irritatingly stupid or deceitful person.

crap work *n.* [1970s+] (*orig. US*) unpleasant, exhausting, dirty, menial or repetitive work. [CRAP adj. + SE *work*]

crash *n.*[1] **1** [late 19C–1910s] (*US*) an outstanding success. **2** [1900s] (*US campus*) a complete failure in an examination. **3** [1900s–60s] (*US campus*) a crush, an infatuation. **4** [1910s–30s] (*Aus.*) a misfortune. **5** [1930s] (*US Und.*) a police raid. **6** [1960s–70s] (*US Und.*) a break-in. [SE *crash*]

crash *n.*[2] **1** [1940s+] a nap, a sleep. **2** [1960s+] (*drugs*) the return to 'normality' that follows drug-taking. [CRASH (OUT) v.]

crash *n.*[3] *see* CRASH-OUT n.

crash *n.*[4] *see* CRASH-PAD n.

crash *v.*[1] **1** [mid-17C–early 19C] to kill. **2** [late 17C–mid-18C] to eat. **3** [mid-18C] (*UK Und.*) to steal. **4** [1920s–40s] (*US Und.*) for a burglar to break a shop window prior to plundering the contents. **5** [1920s+] (*US Und.*) to break into; lit. and fig. **6** [1920s+] (*Aus./US*) to hit someone hard. **7** [1930s] (*US Und.*) to be killed. **8** [1930s] (*US Und.*) of a gun, to go off. **9** [1990s+] (*UK juv.*) to share out, to distribute. **10** [2000s] (*US Black*) to ruin, to make a mess of. [dial. *crash*, to break violently into pieces]

crash *v.*[2] (*also* **crash in**) [1920s+] (*orig. US*) to appear uninvited at a party or other function (cf. GATECRASH v.). [abbr.]

crash *v.*[3] (*also* **crash out**) [1930s+] (*US prison*) to escape.

crash *v.*[4] *see* CRASH (OUT) v.

crashed *adj.* [1940s+] impoverished, without funds.

crasher *n.*[1] [mid-19C+] usu. of people, a (very great) bore. [(1) SE *crashing bore*]

crasher *n.*[2] [1920s+] an uninvited guest at a party. [CRASH v.[2]]

crasher *n.*[3] [1960s+] someone who collapses from fatigue, or an excess of alcohol or drugs. [CRASH (OUT) v. (3)]

crash-hot *adj.* [1950s+] (*Aus.*) first-rate, excellent. [fig. use of CRASH n.[1] (1) + SE *hot*]

crash in *v. see* CRASH v.[2].

crashing *adj.* [1910s+] overwhelming, extreme; esp. in phr. *crashing bore*, an extremely boring person. [SE *crash* + sfx -*ing*]

crashing-cheats *n.* (*also* **crassing-cheats**) (*UK Und.*) **1** [mid-16C–early 17C] apples, pears or any other fruit. **2** [mid-16C–mid-19C] the teeth. [SE *crash* + CHEAT n. (1), lit. 'crushing or crunching things'; (1) things that may be crunched]

crash-out *n.* (*also* **crash**) [1940s+] an escape from prison. [CRASH v.[3]]

crash (out) *v.* **1** [1940s+] (*orig. Aus.*) to sleep, to collapse exhausted. **2** [1960s+] to stay, to lodge, to board; often ext. as *crash at/with...*, to stay over somewhere. **3** [1960s+] (*drugs*) to collapse, esp. after a bout of heavy drug use (esp. amphetamine) or alcohol use. **4** [1960s+] (*drugs*) to lose the sensation that follows the use of a given drug. **5** [1970s+] to slip into a state of semi-conscious relaxation after taking a drug. **6** [1980s] (*UK Black*) to sit down. **7** [1990s+] to break down emotionally. [orig. from RN sl. *crash the swede*, to sleep; as such it migrated first to Aus. then to US and finally back to UK]

crash out *v. see* CRASH v.[3].

crash-pad *n.* (*also* **crash**) [1960s+] a flat or house in which any passing friends or strangers can find a bed at short notice. [CRASH (OUT) v. (2) + PAD n.[2] (2)]

crash the ash *v.* [2000s] to hand round cigarettes.

crash the ether *v.* [1940s–60s] (*orig. US Black*) to make a radio broadcast.

crash the gate *v.* [1920s–60s] (*US*) to enter uninvited. [reverse of GATECRASH v.; Vernon W. Saul, 'The Vocabulary of Bums', in *American Speech* (IV: 5, 1929), defines it (? implausibly) as 'break into jail']

crash up *v.* [1970s–80s] (*N.Z. prison*) to inject oneself with narcotics.

crassing-cheats *n. see* CRASHING-CHEATS n.

crate *n.*[1] **1** [mid–late 19C] (*US*) an old or worthless horse. **2** [1910s+] an aeroplane. **3** [1920s+] an automobile. **4** [1940s–60s] a boat. **5** [1940s+] a lorry; a bus. **6** [1950s] a railroad hand car. [SE *crate*, a container; all descriptions carry a taint of inferiority and/or the possibility of a physical or mechanical breakdown]

crate *n.*[2] **1** [1930s–60s] (*US*) a coffin. **2** [1940s–60s] (*US tramp/Und.*) a prison. [ext. of SE use]

crater *n.*[1] **1** [1950s+] (*US campus/teen*) an acne scar; thus *craterface*, a term of abuse used to mock an acne sufferer. **2** [1960s+] (*US drugs*) an abscess that is caused by the long-term injection of narcotics.

crater *n.*[2] *see* CREATURE, THE n. (3).

crater nipples *n.* [2000s] (*US Black*) inverted nipples.

crathur/cratur/crature *n.* *see* CREATURE, THE *n.* (3).

cravat *n.* *see* TIGHT CRAVAT *n.*

craven *adj.* (*also* **cravicious**) [1950s+] (*W.I. Rasta*) greedy, gluttonous. [ext. of SE *crave*, to desire intensely]

craw *n.* **1** [late 16C+] the stomach, the guts; thus *crawful*, a sufficiency. **2** [late 18C–mid-19C] a cravat that falls over the chest and stomach. **3** [20C+] (*W.I.*) cheek, audacity, nerve. **4** [2000s] (*US Black*) the jowls. [SE *craw*, the crop of a bird or insect]

crawfish *n.* **1** [mid-19C+] (*orig. US*) (*also* **crayfish**) a coward, a groveller, one who backs down from a challenge, esp. a physical one. **2** [mid-19C+] (*orig. US*) a political turncoat or rebel. **3** [1960s] (*US*) a French person. **4** [1970s+] (*US campus*) a stingy, mean person. [CRAWFISH *v.*]

crawfish *v.* [mid-19C+] (*Aus./N.Z./US*) **1** (*also* **crayfish**) to back down, to renege on a previous statement, commitment (the image is of personal humiliation). **2** to move backwards, to retreat, to run away. [SE *crawfish*, the US synon. for *crayfish*, a lobster-like crustacean. The term echoes the characteristic backwards movement of the fish]

crawful *n.* *see* CRAW *n.* (1).

crawl *n.* **1** [mid-19C+] (*orig. US*) a promenade, a street used for parading and socializing by the local youth. **2** [late 19C+] visiting of a number of different places in succession, usu. as PUB-CRAWL *n.* **3** [1900s] a walk. **4** [1910s] (*US Und.*) a trick. **5** [1920s] (*US*) a dance.

crawl *v.*[1] **1** [late 18C+] (*also* **crawl to, do a crawl**) to behave sycophantically, to act the toady. **2** [late 19C] (*US campus*) to renege on a statement.

crawl *v.*[2] **1** [late 19C] (*US*) to leave quietly, stealthily. **2** [late 19C–1930s] (*US*) to mount a horse. **3** [late 19C+] to assault. **4** [late 19C+] to spend a night moving from one nightclub, bar or public house to the next. **5** [1930s+] (*US*) to have sexual intercourse.

crawler *n.*[1] **1** [late 18C+] an insect, spec. a louse. **2** [19C] a lazy or slow person, a loiterer; thus ext. as *old crawler*. **3** [mid–late 19C] a cab moving slowly along the streets in search of a fare. **4** [mid-19C+] a general insult. **5** [late 19C] (*Aus.*) a shepherd, a musterer; one who mends boundary fences. **6** [late 19C+] (*Aus.*) a slow-moving, unexcitable domestic animal, esp. a sheep. **7** [1920s+] (*US*) a legless beggar, usu. moving with the aid of a small wheeled platform.

crawler *n.*[2] [mid-19C+] (*orig. Aus.*) one who acts in a mean or servile way. [CRAWL *v.*[1] (1)]

crawling dandruff *n.* *see* GALLOPING DANDRUFF *n.*

crawling (with) *adv.* (*also* **crawl with**) **1** [early 19C+] full of a crowd of (unappealing) people, usu. defined, e.g. *crawling with coppers*. **2** [1910s+] very rich. **3** [1910s+] full of. [SE phr. *crawling with*, describing lice]

crawl-out *n.* [1900s–50s] (*US*) an excuse, an evasion.

crawl out *v.* [1900s–50s] (*US*) to make an excuse, to get out of something, to evade.

crawl out of the woodwork *v.* *see* COME OUT OF THE WOODWORK *v.*

crawl someone's collar *v.* [late 19C] (*US campus*) to reprimand, to criticize. [orig. US milit.]

crawl someone's frame *v.* [1900s–40s] (*US*) to give someone a beating or thrashing. [CRAWL *v.*[2] (3) + FRAME *n.*[1] (1)]

crawl someone's hump *v.* [late 19C+] (*US*) to attack, to assault. [CRAWL *v.*[2] (3) + SE *hump*]

crawl to *v.* *see* CRAWL *v.*[1] (1).

crawl up the wall *v.* [late 18C–early 19C] to run up credit at a public house. [the inscribing of one's debts on a slate mounted on the wall]

crawl with *v.* *see* CRAWLING (WITH) *adv.*

crawly-mawly *adj.* [late 17C–mid-19C] ill, sickly, ailing. [Norfolk dial.; cf. synon. Sussex dial: *frobly-mobly*]

crawsick *adj.* [late 18C; 1920s+] (*Irish*) suffering from a hangover. [CRAW *n.* (1) + SE *sick*]

craw-thumper *n.* **1** [late 18C+] (*also* **claw-thumper**) a Roman Catholic. **2** [mid-19C+] (*US*) a native of Maryland. **3** [20C+] (*Irish*) an overtly pious individual. [CRAW *n.* (1) + SE *thumper*, lit. breast-beater; (2) Catholics were heavily represented among the founders of the colony that became the state of Maryland]

craw-thumping *n.* [late 19C] (*Aus.*) religiosity. [CRAW-THUMPER *n.*]

craw-thumping *adj.* [late 17C; 1920s–60s] overly religious. [CRAW-THUMPER *n.* (1)/CRAW-THUMPER *n.* (3)]

cray *n.*[1] [1910s] (*Aus.*) a *crayfish*. [abbr.]

cray *n.*[2] [1980s] (*N.Z.*) a NZ$100 note. [it is coloured red, like the SE *crayfish*]

crayfish *see under* CRAWFISH.

craythur *n.* *see* CREATURE, THE *n.* (3).

crazo *n.* [1970s+] (*orig. US*) a mad person, an eccentric. [SE *crazy* + -o sfx (2)]

crazy *n.* **1** [mid-19C+] (*orig. US*) a mad person. **2** [1980s+] (*also* **the crazies**) a feeling of madness. **3** [2000s] (*drugs*) cocaine.

crazy *adj.* **1** [mid-19C+] keen on, enthusiastic; often as *crazy about*; latterly CRAZY FOR *adj.* **2** [1940s+] (*orig. US Black*) a general intensifier, wonderful, amazing, weird, bizarre, according to context. **3** [1960s+] (*US Black*) of money, a lot, great, much.

crazy *adv.* [20C+] extremely, very much.

crazy! *excl.* [1950s+] (*orig. US*) an excl. of approval, of agreement.

-crazy *sfx* [1920s+] a sfx used to imply one's enthusiasm for the accompanying *n.*; e.g. *boy-crazy*.

crazy about *adj.* *see* CRAZY *adj.* (1).

crazy alley *n.* [1910s+] (*US prison*) a special part of a prison used for insane prisoners. [CRAZY *n.* (1)/SE *crazy*]

crazy as a bedbug *phr.* (*also* **crazy as a coot**) [mid-19C+] (*orig. US*) extremely eccentric (cf. APEY *adj.*). [such bugs make one 'itch']

crazy as a fox *phr.* (*also* **crazy like a fox**) [20C+] (*US*) cunning, shrewd. [the *locus classicus* is its use as a book title by the US humorist S.J. Perelman in 1944]

crazy as a two-bob watch *phr.* *see* SILLY AS A TWO-BOB WATCH *phr.*

crazy-ass *n.* [1960s+] (*US*) a fool, one who is out of control (cf. ASSHEAD *n.*). [CRAZY-ASS *adj.*]

crazy-ass *adj.* [1960s+] (*US*) **1** insane, utterly eccentric. **2** bizarre. [SE *crazy* + -ASS sfx]

crazy-back *n.* [late 19C] a foolish young woman.

crazy brim *n.* *see* CRAZY RIM *n.*

crazy coke *n.* [1970s+] (*drugs*) phencyclidine (cf. ACE *n.*[4]). [SE *crazy* + COKE *n.*[1] (1)]

crazy farm *n.* *see* CRAZY HOUSE *n.*

crazy fence boys *n.* [2000s] (*US prison*) inmates who wish to or are planning to escape.

crazy for *adj.* [20C+] extremely enthusiastic, obsessed by. [CRAZY *adj.* (1) + SE *for*, i.e. crazy about]

crazyhead *n.* [1970s] (*US*) a mad person. [SE *crazy* + -HEAD sfx (1)]

crazyhead whisky *n.* [late 19C] (*US*) very strong whisky. [the effect it has on one's head]

crazy house *n.* (*also* **crazy farm**) (*US*) **1** [late 19C+] a psychiatric institution. **2** [1960s+] a 'madhouse', somewhere that resembles a lunatic asylum.

crazy like a fox *adj.* *see* CRAZY AS A FOX *phr.*

crazy nigger *n.* [1960s–70s] an independent Black man, who refuses to accept an inferior social role. [SE *crazy* + NIGGER *n.*[1] (1)]

crazy rim *n.* (*also* **crazy brim**) [1960s] (*US Black*) a desirable style of hat. [CRAZY *adj.* (2) + SE *rim/brim*]

crazy timbers *n.* [early 19C] ribs.

crazy water *n.* [1930s–50s] (*Can./US*) whisky. [its effects]

creaker *n.* [1940s–60s] (*US Black*) an old person. [SE *creak*; the ref. is to one's joints]

c.r.e.a.m. *n.* (*also* **cream**) [1990s+] (*orig. US Black*) money. [abbr. *cash rules everything around me*]

cream *n.*[1] **1** [mid-17C; late 19C+] semen; thus *take in cream*, of a woman, to have sexual intercourse (cf. BABY GRAVY n.). **2** [1920s+] (*Aus.*) whisky. **3** [1930s+] vaginal secretions (cf. BINDERJUICE n.).

cream *n.*[2] [1980s+] (*US Black*) a Puerto Rican (cf. BATO n.). [the paler than Black skin colour]

cream *n.*[3] [1990s+] anything simple or very easy.

cream *n.*[4] *see* C.R.E.A.M. n.

cream *v.*[1] **1** [1910s+] of a man, to ejaculate. **2** [1940s–50s] (*US*) to vomit. **3** [1940s+] of a woman, for the vagina to become wet. **4** [1950s+] in fig. use of (1)/(3), to become excited, to find something extremely exciting, to be very desirous of doing something. [CREAM n.[1]]

cream *v.*[2] **1** [1920s+] (*orig. US*) to kill, to destroy, to beat up comprehensively, to overcome easily. **2** [1930s+] (*also* **cream up**) to win a sporting competition, to pass an examination easily or decisively, thus to do anything well. **3** [1950s–60s] of a driver, to go fast. **4** [1990s+] in fig. use, to do something to excess, e.g. drinking. [the perceived superiority of cream to milk]

cream billy *n. see* CREAM FANCY n.

cream-crackered *adj.* (*also* **cream-cracked, Jacob's crackers**) [1980s+] exhausted, tired out. [rhy. sl. = KNACKERED adj.; ult. *Jacob's cream crackers*, a brand of savoury biscuits]

cream crackers *n.* [1940s–70s] the testicles (cf. CHEESE AND CRACKERS n.). [rhy. sl. = KNACKERS n.; *see* prev. for full ety.]

creamed *adj.* **1** [1940s+] utterly defeated, lit. and fig. **2** [1960s+] (*US*) very drunk (cf. ANNIHILATED adj.). [CREAM v.[2] (1)]

creamed beef *n.* [1990s+] semen (cf. BABY GRAVY n.). [backform. f. CREAM ONE'S BEEF v.]

creamer *n.* [1950s+] **1** one who lacks control of his emotions, because of excitment or fear. **2** an outstanding example of something. **3** a chronic premature ejaculator. **4** a general term of abuse. [lit./fig. ext. CREAM v.[1] (1)]

cream fancy *n.* (*also* **cream billy**) [mid-19C] a decorated handkerchief prized by London costermongers; it had a white or cream background with a variety of patterns. [SE *cream + fancy (handkerchief)*/BILLY n.[3]]

cream-ice jack *n.* [late 19C–1900s] a street-seller of ice-cream. [SE *cream ice* + JACK n.[2]]

creamie *n.* (*also* **creamy**) [20C+] (*Aus.*) a derog. term for the offspring of White and Aborigine parents. [their complexion]

creamie piece *n.* (*also* **creamy piece**) [1970s] (*Aus.*) a half-Aboriginal woman. [CREAMIE n. + PIECE n.[1] (1)]

creaming *n.* [1960s+] (*UK Und.*) stealing from one's employer, usu. on a small, but protracted scale. [fig. 'skimming the cream' from the firm's income]

cream in one's jeans *v. see* CREAM ONE'S JEANS v. (1).

cream-jug *n.* [late 19C] the vagina (cf. BAG n.[1]). [a receptacle for CREAM n.[1] (1)]

cream jugs *n.* [20C+] the female breasts (cf. BORDENS n.).

cream money *n. see* EGG MONEY n.

cream of the valley *n.* [19C] gin.

cream one's beef *v.* [1990s+] to masturbate.

cream one's jeans *v.* [1950s+] **1** (*also* **cream in one's jeans**) to ejaculate or become wet while still fully dressed. **2** (*also* **cream one's pants**) in fig use, to become very excited. [CREAM v.[1] + SE *jeans/pants*]

cream-pot love *n.* [late 18C] false protestations of love, esp. as offered to dairymaids by amorous young men.

cream puff *n.*[1] [1910s+] **1** (*US*) an excellent person or object. **2** (*orig. US*) a weakling. **3** a male homosexual. [fig. uses of SE; (3) pun on PUFF n.[3] (1)]

cream puff *n.*[2] [1990s+] a bad temper, a rage. [rhy. sl. = SE *huff*]

cream-puff *adj.* [1910s+] (*US*) easy, undemanding of physical strength. [CREAM PUFF n.[1] (2)]

cream puff freak *n.* [1970s] (*US*) a prostitute's client who achieves sexual arousal by throwing gooey cakes at the woman. [SE *cream puff* + FREAK n.[1] (6)]

creamstick *n.* [late 19C+] the penis; thus *have a go at the creamstick, have/do a bit of creamstick*, of a woman, to have sexual intercourse (cf. BAT n.[7]). [CREAM n.[1] (1) + SE *stick*/STICK n.[1] (1); 20C+ use mainly US Black]

cream the cheese *v.* [1990s+] to masturbate; to bring to orgasm (cf. BEAT ONE'S MEAT v.). [CREAM v.[1] (1) + COCK CHEESE n. (1)]

cream up *v. see* CREAM v.[2] (2).

creamy *n.*[1] [1990s+] (*US Black/drugs*) premium-grade crack cocaine (cf. BASE n.). [CREAMY adj. (1)]

creamy *n.*[2] *see* CREAMIE n.

creamy *adj.* **1** [mid-19C+] excellent, first-rate. **2** [1990s+] of a woman, very attractive. [the superiority of cream to milk]

creamy do *n.* [1950s+] a piece of exceptionally fortunate luck. [CREAMY adj. (1) + DO n.[1]]

creamy piece *n. see* CREAMIE PIECE n.

crease *v.* **1** [late 19C+] to wound. **2** [20C+] to kill. **3** [1950s+] to beat severely. **4** [1970s+] to harm, to spoil; also in fig. use. [orig. hunting *crease*, to stun an animal by firing a shot through the cartilage at the back of the neck]

creased *adj.* **1** [1920s+] exhausted, tired out. **2** [1940s+] collapsing in laughter. [fig. use of CREASE v.; underpinned by the image of one's body bent double with laughter or tiredness; thus 'creasing' at the waist]

crease (up) *v.* [1940s+] **1** to collapse with laughter. **2** to cause someone to collapse with laughter. [CREASED adj.]

create *v.* [1910s+] to make a fuss, to 'go on about'. [abbr. SE *create a fuss*]

create fuck *v.* [1920s+] to display anger or annoyance. [SE *create* + FUCK n.[4]]

creater *n. see* CREATURE, THE n. (3).

creation *n.* [mid-19C+] a euph. for *Christ*, usu. as used in mild oaths.

creature *n.* **1** [20C+] (*W.I.*) an ugly person. **2** [1980s+] (*Aus. prison*) a police or prison officer. [? the 'creatures' that populate horror films]

creature, the *n.* **1** [mid-16C–mid-9C] wine. **2** [late 16C; early 19C] porter. **3** [late 17C+] (*also* **crater, crathur, cratur, craythur, creater, cretur**) whisky, esp. Irish whisky. **4** [early–mid-19C] brandy. **5** [early–mid-19C] gin.

crebs *adj.* [1990s+] (*W.I.*) low-life, despicable.

cred *n.* [1970s+] lit. *cred*ibility. The term, as used mainly in the 1970s–80s by young people (and those who purvey their material wants), indicates that something has a populist, anti-establishment, 'street' level of acceptability. [abbr.]

cred *adj.* [1970s+] lit. *cred*ible. The term, as used mainly in the 1970s–80s by young people (and those who purvey their material wants), means acceptable on a populist, anti-establishment, 'street' level, unaffected by puffery, artistic pretentiousness or similar negative trappings. [abbr.]

credentials *n.* [late 19C+] the male genitals.

creechy *adj.* [1990s+] (*US campus*) weird, strange. [? SE *screech*]

creeme *v.* [late 17C–mid-19C] (*UK Und.*) to slip something unobtrusively into another person's hand. [? slippery smoothness of SE *cream*]

creep *n.* **1** [1910s+] a stealthy robber, a sneak-thief, esp. one who works in a brothel. **2** [1910s+] the profession of sneak-thieving, esp. when pursued in a brothel; the individual who pursues it. **3** [1920s+] an unpleasant person, with poss. implication of some physical peculiarity or of criminality. **4** [1930s+] departure, esp. surreptitious. **5** [1960s] (*US Black*) a clandestine meeting. **6** [1970s] (*US*) a spree. [fig. uses of SE; (3) orig. dial.]

creep *adj.* [1940s+] unpleasant, distasteful. [CREEP n. (3)]

creep *v.* **1** [mid-19C+] to forgo one's pride and beg unashamedly, to curry favour, to 'suck up to'. **2** [1910s+] to rob stealthily, to work as a sneak-thief. **3** [1910s+] (*US*) for a prostitute to distract her customer while an accomplice slips into the room and rifles his wallet; since he always has to pay in advance, he won't check his money till they have parted. **4** [1920s+] (*US Black*) to flirt, to make sexual advances, to have a clandestine meeting, usu. that between 2 adulterous or cheating lovers. **5** [1920s+] (*US Black*) to sneak up on, to stalk someone with malicious intent. **6** [1930s] to 'walk', to escape punishment; to be let off. **7** [1940s+] to inform. **8** [1960s+] (*US prison*) to escape. **9** [1980s+] (*US Black teen*) to go about one's business surreptitiously and quietly. **10** [1980s+] (*US campus*) to go out on the town. **11** [1990s+] (*US Black*) to ride slowly in a car. **12** [1990s+] (*US drugs*) to sell marijuana.

creep away and die! *excl.* [1920s] a cruel dismissal.

creepazoid *n.* (*also* **creepaloid**) [1970s+] (*US*) an unpleasant person. [CREEP n. (3) + -ZOID sfx/-OID sfx]

creeped up *adj.* [1940s–60s] (*orig. US Black*) apprehensive, worried. [CREEPS, THE n.]

creeper *n.*[1] [17C+] a toady, a sycophant. [SE *creep*, to act in a servile manner]

creeper *n.*[2] **1** [17C+] a louse. **2** [early 19C] a penny-a-line hack journalist. **3** [20C+] (*US Und./police*) a sneak-thief, esp. when also a prostitute or her accomplice. **4** [1910s+] (*orig. US Black*) an adulterous or cheating lover. **5** [1940s–50s] (*US Black*) a policeman. **6** [1990s+] a burglary committed when the owners are at home. [fig. uses of SE, they all *creep around*]

creeper *n.*[3] *see* CREEP JOINT n. (2).

creeper joint *n.* [1930s] (*US*) an opium den where the semi-conscious sleepers are robbed of their possessions (cf. CREEP JOINT n.). [CREEPER n.[2] (3) + JOINT n.[4] (1)]

creepers *n.*[1] **1** [late 19C–1960s] the feet; the legs; occas. in sing. **2** [1900s–80s] (*US*) soft shoes worn by burglars, sneak-thieves and prison guards.

creepers *n.*[2] *see* BROTHEL CREEPERS n.

creep house *n.* [1910s–70s] (*US*) a brothel or unwholesome apartment house, esp. one where patrons are robbed (cf. ACCOMMODATION HOUSE n.). [CREEP v. (3) + HOUSE n.[1] (1)/SE *house*]

creepie-crawlies *n.* [late 19C+] a feeling of dread, of foreboding. [ext. of CREEPS, THE n.]

creepies, the *n. see* CREEPS, THE n.

creeping *n.* [late 16C–early 17C] (*UK Und.*) men and women robbing together. [cant use of SE *creep* (CREEP v. (2), while logical, is too late)]

creeping and tilling *n.* [1910s+] (*US Black*) diverting a store cashier's attention while a confederate opens and robs the till. [CREEP v. (2) + SE *till*]

creeping Jesus *n.* (*also* **creeping Jenny, …Judas**) **1** [early 19C+] a whining, sneaking person. **2** [1980s] a cautious, conservative person, a near-sighted person. [CREEP v. (1) + SE *Jesus* as a timid, weak person]

creeping law *n.* [late 16C–early 17C] (*UK Und.*) robbery carried out by minor thieves, concentrating on 'suburban' homes (i.e. those outside the city walls). [SE *creep*/CREEPING n. + LAW n.[1]]

creep joint *n.* **1** [1920s+] a brothel or unwholesome apartment house, esp. one where patrons are robbed (cf. BADGER-CRIB n.; CREEPER JOINT n.). **2** [1930s] (*also* **creeper**) a 'floating' gambling game, operating in a different location each night. **3** [1950s] anywhere run by unpleasant or unpopular people. [(1) and (2) CREEP v. (3); (3) CREEP n. (3) + JOINT n.[4] (3)]

creepo *n.* [1940s+] an unpleasant person. [CREEP n. (3) + -o sfx (1)]

creepola *n.* [1980s] (*US*) anything or anyone unpleasant. [CREEP n. (3) + -OLA sfx]

creep on *v.* (*US Black*) **1** [1920s–40s] to cheat, esp. sexually. **2** [1970s+] to sneak up on someone, with the intention of attacking them physically or robbing them. **3** [1990s+] to follow. [(1) CREEP v. (4); (2) and (3) CREEP v. (5)]

creep out like the Shadow *v.* [1930s–40s] (*US Black*) to make advances, in a sophisticated worldy manner. [the contemporary US radio 'crime-buster' *The Shadow*, created in late 1920s by 'Maxwell Grant' (Walter B. Gibson) for Mutual Broadcasting]

creep pad *n.* [1940s] (*US*) a brothel or unwholesome apartment house, esp. where patrons are robbed (cf. BADGER-CRIB n.). [CREEP v. (3) + PAD n.[2] (2)]

creeps *n.* [20C+] (*US Black*) the feet.

creeps, the *n.* (*also* **creepies, the**) [mid-19C+] a feeling of dread, of foreboding; usu. in phr. *give someone the creeps*, to worry, to perturb, to disgust. [the image of something creeping on one's body]

creepshow *adj.* [1980s+] awful, disgusting. [the horror film *Creepshow* (1982)]

creep someone out *v.* (*also* **creep someone up**) [1950s+] (*US*) to terrify, to unnerve. [CREEPS, THE n.]

creepsville *n.* (*also* **creepville**) [1960s+] any unappealing place. [CREEP n. (3) + -VILLE sfx[1]]

creep up someone's arse *v. see* ARSE-CREEP v.

creepy *adj.* (*also* **creepy-ass**) [late 19C+] unpleasant, sinister. [CREEP n. (3)]

creepy-crawly *n.* (*also* **creeper-crawler**) [19C+] (*mainly UK juv.*) an insect; also in fig. use of people, disgusting. [its movements]

creepy-crawly *adj.* [1960s] a general term of derision. [CREEPY-CRAWLY n.]

creepy-drawers *n.* [1970s] (*US*) a male homosexual. [CREEPY adj. + SE *drawers*]

creepy pete *n.* [1950s] (*US*) cheap, rotgut wine. [SE *creepy* + SNEAKY PETE n. (1); i.e. its effects 'creep up' on the drinker]

cremmie *n.* [1960s+] (*Aus.*) a crematorium. [abbr.]

cremorne *n.* [19C] the penis. [pun on CREAM n.[1] (1) + HORN n.[2] (1), but note *Cremorne* Gardens, Chelsea, the increasingly notorious 'pleasure gardens' (*fl.*1832–77)]

creped up *adj.* [1930s] (*US teen*) dressed up. [? wearing shoes with *crepe* soles]

crepe-hanger *n. see* CRAPE-HANGER n.

crepe sole *n.* [1940s] (*W.I.*) a large, solid cake. [resemblance, texture]

creps *n.* [2000s] (*UK teen*) trainers. [? orig. trainers had *crepe* soles]

crest *v.* [1990s+] (*US Black*) to smile. [brandname of *Crest* toothpaste]

cretin *n.* (*also* **creton**) [1940s] an obnoxious person; a stupid person.

cretur *n. see* CREATURE, THE n. (3).

crevice *n.* [19C] the vagina (cf. AGREEABLE RUTS OF LIFE n.).

crew *n.* **1** [mid-16C+] any form of gang or group. **2** [1960s+] a gang, usu. football supporters, who engage in fights with rivals. **3** [1980s+] (*orig. US Black*) a gang; orig. and spec. used in US by young Blacks to denote a teen gang, spec. of rap singers, break dancers or graffiti artists, now both Black and White UK use with the general meaning. **4** [1980s+] (*orig. US drugs*) a team of drug sellers.

Cri, the *n.* [late 19C+] the *Criterion* (bar, restaurant and theatre) at Piccadilly Circus, London W1, which was ultra-fashionable in the late 19C and revamped in the 1990s. [abbr.]

crib *n.*[1] **1** [late 16C+] (*UK Und./US Black*) a dwelling house, a shop, a public house, an apartment. **2** [early 19C+] a small, cheap brothel or 'low' saloon; thus *crib-girl*, a prostitute (cf. BADGER-CRIB n.). **3** [mid-19C] (*UK Und.*) a thieves' hideout. **4** [mid-19C] a cheap theatre. **5** [mid-19C–1900s] a berth, a situation, a job, e.g. a *snug crib*, a safe place. **6** [mid-19C–1960s] (*UK/US Und.*) a casino. **7** [mid-19C+] a bed. **8** [mid-19C+] (*US*) a prison cell. **9** [late 19C–1950s] the room in a brothel where a prostitute services her clients. **10** [1910s–60s] (*Aus./US*) a cheap café or restaurant. **11** [1920s–80s] (*orig. US Black*) a safe. **12** [1930s+] (*US Und.*) a room kept by a street-walker to which she could take her clients for sex. **13** [1970s+] (*US gay*) a private cubicle rented out at a gay bath-house. [16C SE *crib*, a small house or narrow room; (1) post-WW2 use is US Black]

crib *n.*[2] **1** [mid-17C] the stomach. **2** [18C+] provisions. **3** [late 19C+] (*Aus.*) a snack, a light meal, a piece of bread, cake etc. [SE *crib*, a container for animal fodder]

crib *n.*[3] **1** [mid-19C+] a translation of a text, classical or otherwise, for the illegitimate use of students (cf. ANIMAL *n.*[3]). **2** [1980s] (*US campus*) an easy course. [CRIB *v.*[2]; (2) abbr. CRIB COURSE *n.*]

crib *n.*[4] [mid-19C+] *cribbage.* [abbr.]

crib *n.*[5] [1940s] a grumble, a complaint. [CRIB *v.*[5]]

crib *n.*[6] *see* FENCING CRIB *n.*

crib *v.*[1] **1** [mid-18C–1910s] to indulge in petty theft; to take surreptitiously. **2** [mid-19C] 'to withhold, keep back, pinch, or thieve a part out of money given to lay out for necessaries' (Dyche, *A New General English Dict.*, 1748). [? SE *crib*, a small wickerwork container, poss. used by a poacher]

crib *v.*[2] [late 18C+] (*orig. campus*) to cheat, to take or copy (a passage, a piece of translation etc) without acknowledgement, to plagiarize (cf. HORSE *v.*[7]; JACK *v.*[2]; PONY *v.*[1]; RIDE *v.*[2]). [ext. of CRIB *v.*[1] (1)]

crib *v.*[3] [early–mid-19C] to fight, using the fists and in an honourable manner. [the prize-fighter Tom *Cribb* (1781–1848)]

crib *v.*[4] **1** [mid–late 19C] to confine. **2** [1930s+] (*also* **crib out**) to stay in a place. **3** [1960s] to live at home. **4** [1960s+] (*US Black*) to live one's uneventful, daily life. **5** [1990s+] to sleep. **6** [2000s] to offer a bed or home to. [CRIB *n.*[1]]

crib *v.*[5] [1910s+] to complain, to grumble (about). [SE *crib-biting*, of a horse, to bite the crib or fodder container]

crib *v.*[6] [1920s] (*Aus.*) to eat. [CRIB *n.*[2] (3)]

crib *phr.* [2000s] (*US campus*) one's acknowledgement of shared knowledge or of a shared experience. [? CRIB *v.*[2] or ? CRIB *n.*[1] (1)]

cribbage-faced *adj.* [late 18C–mid-19C] a face marked with smallpox scars (cf. CRUMPET-FACE *n.*; FROSTY FACE *n.*; MILDEWED *adj.*; MOCKERED *adj.*; STUB-FACED *adj.*). [the supposed resemblance of such scars to the small holes found in a cribbage board]

cribbage-peg *n.* [late 19C–1920s] a leg. [rhy. sl.]

cribber *n.*[1] [late 19C] one who uses some form of illicit aid when taking examinations or similar tests. [CRIB *v.*[2]]

cribber *n.*[2] [late 19C+] a horse that bites parts of its stall, sucking air into its lungs. [SE *crib-biter*, a horse that bites the metal crib in which its fodder is placed]

Cribbeys *n.* (*also* **Cribbey Islands**) [late 18C–early 19C] back alleys, narrow courts and by-ways. [derived f. older nicknames BERMUDAS *n.* and thence CARIBEE ISLANDS *n.*, both of which had been applied to the alleyways of 16C–18C Covent Garden, then a centre of vice and criminality. Grose (1785) offers an alternative ety.: 'perhaps from the houses built there being cribbed (stolen) out of the common way or passage']

cribbing *n.* [mid-17C] (*UK Und.*) provisions. [CRIB *n.*[2]]

cribbing cove *n.* [early 19C] a thief. [CRIB *v.*[1] (1) + COVE *n.* (1)]

crib-biter *n.* [mid-19C] a grumbler. [SE *crib-biter*, a horse that bites the metal crib in which its fodder is placed]

crib course *n.* [1960s+] (*US campus*) a very easy course. [CRIB *v.*[2]]

crib-cracker *n.* [mid-19C–1900s] a house-breaker. [CRIB-CRACKING *n.*]

crib-cracking *n.* [mid-19C–1940s] (*orig. UK Und.*) house-breaking. [CRIB *n.*[1] (1) + CRACK *v.*[3] (3)]

crib-crust Monday *n.* [mid-19C] (*UK juv.*) the Monday before Advent. [? CRIB *v.*[1] (1) + SE *crust*; one has no money for food and must scrounge crusts]

crib-girl *n.* *see* CRIB *n.*[1] (2).

crib house *n.* [1910s–40s] a brothel, esp. a small and dirty one (cf. ACCOMMODATION HOUSE *n.*). [CRIB *n.*[1] (2) + HOUSE *n.*[1] (1)]

crib joint *n.* [1920s–40s] a brothel, esp. a small and dirty one (cf. BADGER-CRIB *n.*). [CRIB *n.*[1] (2) + JOINT *n.*[4] (3)]

crib man *n.* [late 19C–1940s] (*US Und.*) **1** one who specializes

in breaking into houses and apartments. **2** a safe-breaker. [CRIB *n.*[1] (1) + sfx *-man*]

crib out *v.* *see* CRIB *v.*[4] (2).

cribsheet *n.* [1950s+] **1** a translation of a text, classical or otherwise, for the illegitimate use of students (cf. ANIMAL *n.*[3]). **2** (*US*) a police record. [CRIB *n.*[3] (1) + SE *sheet*]

cricket bats *n.* [1910s+] (*Aus.*) the teeth. [rhy. sl. = TATS *n.* (2)]

cricket match *n.* [1910s–20s] (*Aus.*) a small moustache. [it has only *11* hairs a 'side']

cricket score *n.* [1980s+] (*Aus. prison*) a very long sentence.

cricket set *n.* [1990s+] the male genitals. [i.e. a BAT *n.*[7] and 2 BALLS *n.*[1] (1)]

cries and screeches *n.* [20C+] (*Aus.*) leeches. [rhy. sl.]

crig *n.* [1940s+] (*Irish*) a testicle (cf. AGATES *n.*). [? Irish *creag/creig*, a rock, thus pun on ROCKS *n.*[4] (1)]

crikey! *excl.* [mid-19C+] a euph. for CHRIST! excl.

crim *n.* [1950s+] (*orig. US/Aus./N.Z.*) a criminal. [abbr.; 1 of the 3 classes in Aus. prison: *screws* (warders and other prison employees), *gigs* (visitors and casual workers) and *crims* (used primarily to denote those with extra-long sentences); note RMC Duntroon (Aus.) *crims*, the body of Duntoon cadets]

crimast! *excl.* (*also* **by crimus!**) [late 19C+] (*orig. US*) a euph. for CHRIST! excl., usu. in mild oaths.

crimbo *n.* (*also* **chrimbo**) [1980s+] Christmas.

crim. con. *n.* [late 18C–1900s] adultery; thus *crim. con. money*, the damages that a jury directed to be paid by a convicted adulterer as compensation to the husband whose wife had allegedly been seduced. [abbr. legal jargon *criminal conversation*, 'the trespass against the husband at common law' (the concept was abandoned in 1857). *Conversation* in this context means sexual intercourse]

crime *v.* **1** [1940s] to accuse of a crime. **2** [1980s+] to commit crimes.

crimea *n.*[1] [mid-19C] a full beard. [the troops serving in the Crimean War (1854–6) grew their beards long in a small attempt to alleviate the cold]

crimea *n.*[2] [20C+] beer. [rhy. sl.]

crime-buster *n.* [1950s+] a detective, a policeman, a melodramatic image esp. popular in tabloid press (cf. BEAT-POUNDER *n.*). [SE *crime* + BUST *v.*[1] (4)]

crimes! *excl.* (*also* **crimey!**) [mid-19C+] a euph. for CHRIST! excl., usu. in mild oaths.

crimey *n.* [1970s+] (*US Und.*) a partner in crime, an accomplice, a friend. [note the association is usu. but need not invariably be criminal]

criminy! *excl.* (*also* **crimmini!**) [late 17C+] (*orig. US*) a euph. for CHRIST! excl., usu. in mild oaths. [the euph. interpretation is the most likely, but the *OED* also suggests Ital. *crimine*, a crime, used as a 17C ejaculation]

crimmo *n.* [1950s+] (*Aus./N.Z.*) a *crim*inal. [abbr. + -O sfx (4)]

crimp *n.* **1** [late 18C–1930s] a swindler, a cheat. **2** [1940s–50s] (*US prison*) an informer. [PLAY CRIMP *v.*]

crimp *v.*[1] *see* PLAY CRIMP *v.*

crimp *v.*[2] *see* PUT A CRIMP INTO *v.*

crimper *n.* [1960s+] a hairdresser. [SE *crimp*, to curl]

crimping fellow *n.* [late 17C–early 18C] a blackguard, an untrustworthy villain. [SE *crimp*, one who 'presses' men into the RN against their will]

crimps! *excl.* [20C+] (*orig. US*) a euph. for CHRIST! excl., usu. in mild oaths.

crimp up *v.* [1950s+] (*US*) to toughen someone up by inflicting verbal and/or physical pain. [SE *crimp*, to pinch]

crimpy *adj.* [late 19C–1930s] (*US*) of weather, unpleasant; of a place, cold. [Irwin, *American Tramp and Und. Slang* (1931), suggests that such temperatures encourage *the crimps*, rheumatism]

crimson *adj.* [late 19C–1910s] (*Aus.*) a euph. for BLOODY *adj.*[1].

crimson chitterling *n.* [mid-17C–19C] the penis (cf. BACON *n.*[1]).

crimson dawn *n.* [1930s] (*Glasgow*) cheap red wine.

crimson rambler *n.* [1900s–60s] (*US*) a bedbug. [SE *crimson rambler*, a variety of climbing rose]

crinched *adj.* [1970s+] (*US campus*) bent, dented. [SE *crimped*, pinched]

cringe *n.* [1980s] (*US drugs*) methamphetamine (cf. BOMBITA n.). [ety. unknown]

crink *n.* [1970s+] (*drugs*) methamphetamine (cf. BOMBITA n.). [? CRANK n.⁴ (1)]

crinkle *n.* [1950s] paper money (cf. BANK-RAG n.).

crinklepouch *n.* [late 16C] a sixpence. [it makes barely any impact on the shape of one's purse]

crinkler *n.* [1950s+] (*Irish*) a currency note (cf. BANK-RAG n.). [ext. CRINKLE n.]

crinkle top *n.* [1970s] (*US Black*) a woman with hair that remains in an unstraightened or otherwise 'Whitened' style.

crinkly *adj.* [1980s+] (*drugs*) used to describe the user's mind after substantial and continuous use of nitrous oxide.

crinkum *n.* (*also* **crinkums, grincam, grincom, grincombe, grincome, grincum, grinkcome, grinkum**) [early 17C–early 19C] venereal disease. [for ety. *see* CRINKUM-CRANKUM n.; i.e. the sense of twisting pain that accompanies the disease]

crinkum-crankum *n.* [late 17C–19C] the vagina (cf. AGREEABLE RUTS OF LIFE n.). [SE *crinkum-crankum*, a narrow, twisting passage]

crinoline *n.* [mid–late 19C] a woman. [metonymy]

crip *n.*¹ (*also* **crippo**) **1** [1910s+] (*US tramp*) a disabled person; thus *straight crip*, a genuinely disabled person; *phoney crip*, one who poses as disabled for begging purposes. **2** [1960s] a wounded animal. **3** [1960s+] (*UK juv.*) a general insult; physical deformity is irrelevant. [abbr. SE *cripple*]

crip *n.*² [1920s+] (*orig. US campus*) anything easy, esp. of a given college course. [fig. use of CRIP n.¹ (1) or CRIB n.³ (2)]

crip course *n.* [1920s+] (*US campus*) an easy course. [CRIP n.² + SE *course*; var. on CRIB COURSE n.]

cripes! *excl.* (*also* **by cripes! for cripes sake!**) [19C+] a euph. for CHRIST! excl. (or FOR CHRIST'S SAKE! excl.).

cripple *n.*¹ [late 18C–19C] a sixpence. [play on BENDER n.¹ (1); its thin metal was susceptible to bending or distortion]

cripple *n.*² [1950s+] (*drugs*) a marijuana cigarette (cf. BOMB n.⁴). [its effect on one's mind]

cripple-cock *n.* [1960s+] a general pej. [SE *cripple* v. + COCK n.² (1). Note Dorset use *cripple-cock*, cider]

crippo *n. see* CRIP n.¹.

crippy *n.* [1930s] (*US Und.*) a paralysed beggar, or one who poses as such. [SE *cripple*]

cris *n. see* CHRISTINA n.

cris' *adj.* (*also* **criss, kris'**) [1980s+] (*W.I./UK Black teen*) used of anything rated as new, fashionable, attractive etc; thus adv. *crissly*. [CRISP adj.¹ (2)]

Crisco *v.* [1970s+] (*gay*) to lubricate. [brandname *Crisco*, a cooking oil]

crisco frisco *n.* [1950s–60s] (*US gay*) the homosexual community in San Francisco. [proper name *Crisco*, a cooking oil + 'FRISCO n.]

crisp *n.* (*also* **crispy**) [mid-19C–1950s] paper money (cf. BANK-RAG n.).

crisp *adj.*¹ **1** [1920s–30s] new, interesting. **2** [1980s+] excellent, first-rate, attractive. [the crispness of new money]

crisp *adj.*² (*also* **crispy**) [1970s+] very drunk or intoxicated by marijuana or other drug; also ext. as suffering from an excess of drugs, drink, fast living, stress etc. [play on BURNED OUT adj.¹ (3)]

crisp biscuit *n. see* CRISS BISCUIT n.

crispin *n.* [mid-17C–mid-19C] a shoemaker; thus *St Crispin's lance*, an awl; *St Crispin's holiday*, each successive Monday, and esp. 25 October (St Crispin's Day) 'whereon the whole Fraternity fail not to lay their Hearts in Soak' (B.E.). [proper name *St Crispin*, whose non-theological profession this was]

crisp one *n.* [late 19C; 1990s+] a currency note; usu. £1 (cf. BANK-RAG n.). [the crisp texture of new notes]

crispy *see also under* CRISP.

crispy (critter) *n.* (*also* **crispy batter, krispy kracker**) **1** [1960s+] (*US, orig. milit./medical*) anyone who has suffered burns or actually been burned to death. **2** [1970s] (*US drugs*) one who is under the influence of marijuana. [lit. 'crispy creature' + play on popular breakfast cereal]

criss *adj. see* CRIS' adj.

crissars *adj.* [1950s+] (*W.I. Rasta*) crisp, brand-new, slick-looking. [fig. use of SE *crisp*]

criss biscuit *n.* (*also* **crisp biscuit**) [1990s+] (*W.I./UK Black*) of people or objects, attractive, fashionable, smart. [CRIS' adj./CRISP adj.¹ (2)]

criss cross *v.* [1920s+] (*US Black*) to deceive, to cheat. [SE *double-cross*]

crisscross! *excl.* [late 19C] a euph. for *Christ's Cross*, e.g. *so help me crisscross!*

criss-miss *n.* [1950s+] (*W.I.*) a pretentious woman who over-estimates her abilities, charms and allure. [dial. *kris*, proud, aware (rightly or not) of one's beauty (ult. SE *crisp*) + SE *miss*]

cristina *n. see* CHRISTINA n.

critical *adj.* [1990s+] (*US campus*) excellent, worthy of admiration.

critter *n.*¹ [19C+] **1** a bull, thence any farm animal, including a horse. **2** (*also* **crittur**) a person. **3** a thing, an object. **4** of a person, a general derog. description. **5** any animal. [SE *creature*. The use for bull is in fact a euph. 19C US rural speech is full of such often ludicrous euphs. for *bull*, e.g. *brute, cow critter, gentleman cow, male-cow*]

critter *n.*² [mid-19C–1920s] (*US*) whisky. [regional US pron. of CREATURE, THE n. (3)]

crivens! *excl.* (*also* **crivvens!**) [1910s+] an excl. of astonishment or horror. [? *Christ + heavens*]

cro *n.*¹ (*also* **cros**) [early–mid-19C] a professional gambler. [Fr. *escroc*, a card-sharp. The 's' in *cros* is silent]

cro *n.*² [1950s+] (*Aus.*) **1** a prostitute. **2** a woman. [abbr. CHROMO n. (1)/CROW n.⁹]

croacus *n. see* CROCUS (METALLORUM) n.

croak *n.* **1** [mid–late 19C] a dying speech. **2** [mid–late 19C] a final speech from the gallows and murderers' confessions, as written down and peddled by street-sellers. **3** [late 19C–1940s] death; thus *do/pull a croak*, to die; *on the croak*, dying. **4** [1910s] (*US*) a boring complainer, a whinger. [CROAK v.² (1)]

croak *v.*¹ [late 18C–1900s] (*UK Und.*) to talk, to converse.

croak *v.*² **1** [early 19C+] to die; also in fig. use. **2** [early 19C+] to kill, to murder; thus *croaking*, a murder; *croak artist*, a murderer (cf. CROAK ONESELF v.). **3** [1900s] (*US campus*) to fail an examination or a course. [(1) the death-rattle; (3) is fig. use of (1)]

croak *v.*³ [mid-19C] (*UK society*) to act in a hypocritical manner.

croak *v.*⁴ [1920s] (*US*) to vomit (cf. BARF v.). [the noise of vomiting]

croak artist *n. see* CROAK v.² (2).

croaked *adj.* **1** [19C+] killed, dead. **2** [late 19C+] very drunk (cf. ANNIHILATED adj.). [CROAK v.²]

croaker *n.*¹ **1** [mid-17C–1930s] a congenital pessimist. **2** [mid–late 19C] a beggar. **3** [mid-19C+] a whiner or whinger. **4** [20C+] (*US*) one who backs out of undertakings they have promised to perform. **5** [1910s–40s] (*US*) one who talks too lengthily and too loudly. **6** [1940s+] an informer. [? the harsh, miserable croaking of ravens, supposedly ominous birds; (3), (5) and (6) CROAK v.¹]

croaker *n.*² [19C] a silver sixpence. [? play on CRIPPLE n.¹]

croaker *n.*³ (*also* **croker**) **1** [mid-19C] one who has collapsed, i.e. is metaphorically 'dead'. **2** [mid–late 19C] a dying person, beyond hope of recovery, a corpse. [CROAK v.² (1)]

croaker *n.*⁴ [mid-19C–1940s] (*Aus.*) a newspaper. [? CROAKER n.², i.e. the price; or CROAKER n.¹ (3)]

croaker *n.*⁵ **1** [mid-19C+] (*US*) a doctor, esp. in drug use; thus *croaker joint*, a hospital or a surgery; *nut croaker*, a psychiatrist.

2 [mid-19C+] (*orig. US Black*) (*also* **croaksman**) a murderer. **3** [1920s+] (*US prison*) the prison doctor. [CROCUS (METALLORUM) n. (1)/CROAK v.² (2), i.e. a pessimistic view of the profession]

croaker n.⁶ [1920s] (*Anglo-Irish*) a potato; usu. in pl.

croaker joint n. *see* CROAKER n.⁵ (1).

croaker sacks n. [1970s+] (*US*) shoes, orig. made of burlap sacks. [CROAKER n.⁶ + SE *sacks*]

croaker's chovey n. [mid–late 19C] a pharmacy. [CROAKER n.⁵ (1) + CHOVEY n.]

croaking n. *see* CROAK v.² (2).

croak oneself v. [20C+] to commit suicide; thus *do a gun croak*, to shoot oneself dead. [CROAK v.² (2)]

croak sheet n. [1940s–60s] (*orig. US Black*) an insurance policy. [CROAK v.² (1)]

croaksman n. *see* CROAKER n.⁵ (2).

croakumshire n. [late 18C–early 19C] Northumberland. [the guttural, rolled 'r' that typifies Northumberland speech, i.e. SE *croak* + sfx *-shire*]

croakus n. [mid-19C–1920s] a doctor, a quack. [CROCUS (METALLORUM) n. (1)/CROAKER n.⁵ (1)]

croc n. (*also* **crock**) **1** [20C+] a crocodile. **2** [20C+] a line of schoolchildren, walking in pairs. [abbr.; (2) resemblance to the long tail]

crock n.¹ (*also* **crocky**) [mid-19C+] a fool.

crock n.² **1** [late 19C–1900s] an old or broken-down horse. **2** [late 19C–1920s] a bicycle. **3** [late 19C+] a broken-down or physically debilitated person or thing. **4** [1900s] an invalid, a hypochondriac. **5** [1910s+] a broken-down or mechanically unreliable car, aeroplane or any other vehicle. [SE *crack*, to break (down); all often with pfx *old*; note medical jargon *crock*, a patient whose complaints far outweigh the seriousness of their illness]

crock n.³ [1920s–30s] (*US*) an injury, a blow. [CROCK (UP) v. (2)]

crock n.⁴ **1** [1920s+] (*US*) the head; esp. in phr. *off one's crock*, out of one's mind, crazy. **2** [1930s–50s] (*US drugs*) an opium pipe. **3** [1930s–60s] (*US*) a bottle of (illicitly distilled) whisky. [fig. and lit. uses of SE *crock*, a pot]

crock n.⁵ [1940s–50s] a drunkard. [SE *crock*, a jug]

crock n.⁶ [1940s+] (*orig. US*) a useless, unpleasant event or experience. [abbr. CROCK OF SHIT n.]

crock n.⁷ *see* CROC n.

crock v. *see* CROCK (UP) v.

crocked adj. [1910s+] **1** drunk (cf. ANNIHILATED adj.). **2** (*also* **crucked**) hurt, damaged, disabled, esp. through a sporting accident. **3** malfunctioning, going wrong. [lit. and fig. uses of CROCK (UP) v.]

crocker n.¹ [late 18C–early 19C] a shop tout. [ext. of SE *croak*]

crocker n.² *see* KIDDER n.¹ (1).

crockery n. **1** [1910s–40s] (*US*) teeth. **2** [1940s–60s] (*Aus.*) false teeth.

crockful n. [1980s+] (*US*) anything unpleasant, disgusting, repellent. [CROCK OF SHIT n.]

crocko adj. [1920s+] drunk. [CROCKED adj. (1) + -o sfx (5)]

crock of shit n. (*also* **bucket of shit, crock of bullshit, load of shit**) [1940s+] complete nonsense, a lying statement, anything useless or unpleasant. [SE *crock*, a pot + SHIT n.³ (4)]

crocks n. **1** [mid-19C] crockery and glass sellers, their wares, their trade. **2** [20C+] crockery, esp. in the context of washing it up. [abbr.]

crock (up) v. **1** [late 19C+] of a person or animal, to break down, to become disabled, to collapse, to fall ill. **2** [1910s+] (*US*) to hit on the head, to injure. [CROCK n.² (3)]

crockus n. *see* CROCUS (METALLORUM) n.

crocky n.¹ [20C+] (*Aus.*) a crocodile. [abbr.]

crocky n.² *see* CROCK n.¹.

crocky adj. [1920s+] (*Aus.*) unwell, shaky, 'under the weather'. [CROCKED adj. (2)]

crocodile n. (*Aus.*) **1** [late 19C+] a horse, esp. a broken-down,

old horse. **2** [1900s] a roustabout. [play on CROCK n.² (1); (2) is fig. use of (1)]

Crocodile Dundee n. [1990s+] a flea. [rhy. sl.; ult. the film *Crocodile Dundee* (1986)]

crocodile's adenoids n. *see* CAT'S WHISKERS n.

crocodile scam n. [1980s] (*US*) the ensnaring of a client by a woman, often a prostitute, and his subseq. robbery, either by the woman herself or, more often, by her pimp, posing as an 'outraged boyfriend', who emerges, while the pair are *in flagrante*, from a hidden door or panel in the bedroom wall. [SE *crocodile* + SCAM n.¹ (4); the amphibian opens its jaws to embrace its victims]

crocs n. [1980s+] shoes made of *crocodile* skin. [abbr.]

crocus-chovey n. **1** [late 18C–mid-19C] a chemist's shop. **2** [mid-19C–1920s] a doctor's consulting room, a surgery. [CROCUS (METALLORUM) n. (1) + CHOVEY n.]

crocus (metallorum) n. (*also* **croacus, crockus, crokus**) **1** [late 18C] (*orig. milit.*) a doctor, a surgeon, esp. a quack. **2** [mid–late 19C] a beggar who poses as a doctor. [? pun on *croak us* (though CROAK v.², to die or kill is first recorded slightly later), but *OED* suggests 'the Latinized surname of Dr Helkiah Crooke, author of a *Description of the Body of Man*, 1615, *Instruments of Chirurgery*, 1631, etc …'. The quack implication suggests a further pun on *hocus-pocus*. Note fairground use, *crocus*, a doctor, a herbalist, a miracle-worker; market use, a fair-weather trader who works only during the spring or summer (f. the flower). *Metallorum*, lit. 'of metals', plays on *crocus metallorum* or *crocus antimonii*, which are more or less impure oxysulphides of antimony, obtained by calcination]

crocus-pitcher n. [late 19C+] (*UK Und.*) an itinerant quack doctor. [CROCUS (METALLORUM) n. (1) + PITCHER n.³ (3)]

crocussing n. [mid-19C] working as a travelling quack doctor or surgeon. [abbr. CROCUSSING RIG n.]

crocussing rig n. [late 18C] (*UK Und.*) the profession of working as a wandering quack doctor. [CROCUS (METALLORUM) n. (2) + RIG n.² (2)]

crocus-worker n. [late 19C+] a seller of patent medicines. [CROCUS (METALLORUM) n. (2) + SE *worker*/WORKER n.¹ (1)]

croker n.¹ **1** [late 17C–early 19C] a groat, 4 pence. **2** [1930s–40s] a potato. [(1) CROAKER n.²; (2) CROAKER n.⁶]

croker n.² *see* CROAKER n.³.

crokus n. *see* CROCUS (METALLORUM) n.

crombie n. [1960s+] an overcoat. [the tradename of a particular coat, particularly beloved by the SKINHEAD n. in the late 1960s]

cromo n. *see* CHROMO n. (1).

croniker n. *see* CHRONICKER n.

cronk n. **1** [late 19C–1910s] (*Aus.*) (*also* **cronck, kronk**) a criminal. **2** [1930s] (*US Und.*) a bad cheque. **3** [1990s+] (*US campus*) something of poor quality. **4** [1990s+] an unattractive woman. [CRONK adj.]

cronk adj. **1** [mid-19C] (*US*) drunk (cf. AFFLICTED adj.). **2** [late 19C+] (*Aus.*) dishonest, illegal, untrustworthy. **3** [late 19C+] (*Aus.*) sick, ill. **4** [1900s] (*Aus.*) of fruit, vegetables etc, rotten. **5** [1900s] problematical, 'wrong'. [? dial. *cronk*, weak, infirm]

cronkite n. [1990s+] news, information. [the US newsreader Walter *Cronkite* (b.1916)]

cronky adj. [1920s+] **1** unsound, second-rate. **2** (*Aus./US Und.*) corrupt, dishonest, lying. [CRONK adj. + sfx *-y*; orig. racing use]

crony n.¹ [mid-17C–mid-19C] an intimate friend or associate; also as v., to be companiable. [ety. unknown; the earliest cit. has sp. *chrony*, which might suggest a root in SE *chronology*/ *chronological*, i.e. a friend of long standing. 20C+ SE use replaced 'straight' friendship with implications of (political) corruption]

crony n.² **1** [late 17C–early 18C] a tough old hen, a boiling chicken. **2** [mid-19C] an ill-tempered or malicious old woman. [SE *crone*, a gnarled old woman + sfx *-y*]

cronz n. [1990s+] (*US Black*) a gun. [ety. unknown]

crook *n.*[1] [late 18C–early 19C] a silver sixpence. [abbr. CROOK-BACK n.]

crook *n.*[2] (*orig. UK Und.*) **1** [mid-19C] the occupation of professional criminality, esp. pickpocketing; thus *on the crook.* **2** [mid–late 19C] a professional criminal. [SE *crooked*; (2) SE 20C+]

crook *n.*[3] [1940s] (*US Black/Harlem*) an elbow.

crook *adj.* [20C+] (*Aus./N.Z.*) **1** dishonest, illegal. **2** of people and objects, defective, useless, unpleasant; of food, rotten. **3** ill, out of sorts. **4** unfair, unacceptable, 'wicked'; thus *in crook (with),* in trouble with. **5** suspicious. [SE *crooked*]

crook *v.*[1] (*US*) **1** [mid-19C; 1920s–60s] to cheat. **2** [late 19C+] to steal. **3** [1940s] to truant from school. [CROOK n.[2] (2)]

crook *v.*[2] [1900s] (*Aus.*) to ruin, to render useless. [CROOK adj. (2)]

crook as Rookwood *phr.* [1980s] (*Aus.*) on the verge of death. [CROOK adj. (3) + *Rookwood* cemetery, Sydney]

crookback *n.* [late 18C–early 19C] a sixpence. [the thin silver sixpence was easily bent or distorted]

crooked *adj.*[1] **1** [mid-18C+] drunk (cf. AFFLICTED adj.). **2** [mid-19C+] wrong, out of order. **3** [20C+] ill, sick, 'under the weather'. **4** [1940s+] (*Aus.*) annoyed; thus CROOKED ON adj. [SE *crooked, bent*]

crooked *adj.*[2] [mid-19C+] used to describe anything that has been obtained dishonestly or done in a dishonest manner, e.g. *crooked whisky,* illicitly distilled whisky. [SE *crooked*; orig. sporting jargon]

crooked as a dog's hind leg *phr.* (*also* **crooked as a cow's…, a goat's…, a pigstail**) [mid-19C+] very dishonest, devious, deceptive. [CROOKED adj.[2]]

crooked as a fish-hook *phr.* (*also* **crooked as a corkscrew, …a rail fence**) [1900s–30s] very corrupt or dishonest. [CROOKED adj.[2]]

crooked as the letter zed *phr.* [late 18C–mid-19C] physically deformed. [SE *crooked*]

crooked on *adj.* [1940s+] (*Aus./N.Z.*) **1** averse to, hostile to. **2** (*also* **crook on**) angry with. [CROOKED adj.[1] (4)/CROOK adj. (3)]

crooked rib *n.* [late 18C–early 19C] an ill-tempered wife. [SE *crooked* + (*Adam's*) *rib,* a wife]

crooked stick *n.* [mid-19C+] (*US*) a dishonest person, an untrustworthy person. [SE/STICK n.[2]]

crooked tree *n. see* TREE OF THE TRIPLE CROOK n.

crooked way *n.* [late 19C] the vagina (cf. ALLEY n.[1]).

crookie *n.* **1** [20C+] a fool, an idiot. **2** [1960s–70s] something unpleasant; of food, 'off', stale.

Crooklyn *n.* [1990s+] (*US Black*) Brooklyn, New York. [SE *Brooklyn* + CROOK n.[2] (2); the borough's associations with (organized) crime]

crook on *adj. see* CROOKED ON adj. (2).

crookshanks *n.* [17C–early 19C] a bandy-legged person. [SE *crooked* + *shanks,* legs]

crook the elbow *v.* [late 18C–1940s] to drink; thus *elbow-crooking,* drinking (cf. BEND ONE'S ELBOW v.).

crook the little finger *v.* [mid-19C] (*US*) to drink. [the 'elegant' manner of drinking, usu. tea from a teacup]

crook up *v.* [1910s+] (*Aus.*) to fall ill. [CROOK adj. (3)]

crooky *v.* [mid-19C] **1** to walk arm in arm. **2** to court a woman. [the bending of the couple's arms]

croonette *n.* [1940s–60s] (*orig. US Black*) a female singer. [SE *crooner* + SE fem. sfx *-ette*]

croop *n.* [mid-19C–1910s] the stomach. [SE *crop*]

crooper *n. see* CRUPPER n.

crop *see also under* CRAP and its combs.

crop *n.*[1] **1** [late 17C–early 18C] a person with very short hair. **2** [late 18C–early 19C] a Presbyterian. [(2) the severely cropped haircut favoured by the sect]

crop *n.*[2] [1970s] (*US campus*) a fifth of a gallon of wine. [? SE *crop,* the throat or *grape crop*]

crop *v.* [mid-19C] to annoy, to irritate. [? dial. *crop,* the stomach; thus image of anger causing a pain in the stomach]

crople on *v.* [1920s+] (*Aus.*) to grab, to seize. [? dial. *criple,* to cripple or SE *grapple*]

croppen *n.* (*also* **croppin**) [18C–early 19C] the tail of either an animal or a vehicle. [dial. *croppen, croppin(g),* the tail; ult. f. SE *crop,* to cut off the extremity of the ears, tail etc]

cropper *n.* [mid-19C+] a fall; thus COME A CROPPER v. [orig. hunting jargon; one falls over the horse's crop; or ? phr. *neck and crop*]

croppie *n.* (*also* **croppy**) **1** [mid-19C] anyone who has suffered a prison haircut. **2** [late 19C] a Puritan or Roundhead (both of whom might have their nose and/or ears cropped in a judicial punishment). **3** [20C+] (*Ulster*) a derog. term for a Catholic. **4** [1930s] (*US Und.*) a prison barber. [note the *croppies* or *croppy-boys,* the Irish rebels of 1798, who wore their hair cut very short as a sign of sympathy with the French Revolution]

croppin *n. see* CROPPEN n.

croppy *n.*[1] [1920s] (*US*) **1** a corpse. **2** a dead fish. [CROPPY v.]

croppy *n.*[2] *see* CROPPIE n.

croppy *v.* [1910s] (*US*) to kill. [SE *crop,* to cut off, to harvest]

cropsick *adj.* **1** [late 17C–18C] drunk (cf. AFFLICTED adj.). **2** [late 17C–early 19C] feeling sick after a drinking bout. [SE *crop,* the throat + *sick*]

crop someone's duke *v. see* DUKE n.[3] (3).

crop the conjuror *n.* [late 18C] a nickname for one who has noticeably short hair. [it is *cropped*]

cros *n. see* CRO n.[1].

crosbite *n. see* CROSSBITE n.

crosbiter *n. see* CROSSBITER n.

croshabell *n.* [late 16C–early 17C] a prostitute. [north. dial. *crouse,* forward, wanton, vivacious + SE *belle,* beautiful; coined by and found only in the works of George Peele]

Cross, the *n.* **1** [1940s+] (*Aus.*) King's *Cross,* Sydney, the 'bohemian' area of the city; thus *crossite,* one who lives there. **2** [2000s] King's *Cross,* London WC1, the area around the mainline railway station. [abbr.]

cross *n.*[1] **1** [19C+] a trick, a deception. **2** [mid-19C] (*sporting, esp. boxing*) the deliberate losing of a fight, a race etc on payment of a bribe. **3** [mid-19C] (*UK Und.*) the underworld. **4** [1910s] an informer. [abbr. SE *double-cross*]

cross *n.*[2] [1980s+] (*Aus. prison*) any spring-loaded device, e.g. a safety-pin, held tight by a rubber band and swallowed; the gastric juices dissolve the rubber, and the resultant injury allows the prisoner to get into the hospital ward, as a means either of escaping harassment or of obtaining pain-killing drugs. [ety. unknown]

cross, the *n.* **1** [19C] (*also* **crosso**) anything deceitful or dishonest. **2** [1950s+] a double-cross. [the opposite of SQUARE adj. (1)]

cross *adj.* **1** [mid-17C+] ill-tempered, peevish. **2** [19C–1910s] dishonest, dishonestly come by. **3** [mid–late 19C] annoying, unkind. [fig. uses of SE *cross,* contrary, opposed]

cross *v.*[1] **1** [18C+] to let down. **2** [19C+] to deceive or mislead; to cheat. **3** [mid-19C+] to betray; thus *crosser,* an informer. **4** [1940s+] to oppose. [abbr. SE *double-cross*]

cross *v.*[2] **1** [mid-18C–mid-19C] to sit astride a horse. **2** [mid-19C] to have sexual intercourse. [(2) is fig. use of (1)]

cross *adv.* **1** [mid-17C–19C] unfavourably, in an unsatisfactory manner. **2** [19C] in a criminal manner. [CROSS adj.]

cross as two sticks *phr.* [late 19C+] very angry. [punning on SE *cross,* irritable, peevish/lying across each other]

cross-back *n.* [1960s+] (*US*) a Roman Catholic. [the Catholic habit of crossing oneself]

cross-bar hotel *n.* (*also* **cross-bar Hilton**) [1940s+] (*US Und.*) a prison (cf. BOARDING HOUSE n.). [17C SE *cross-bar,* a horizontal bar, as of a window or cell + HOTEL n. (2)]

crossbite *n.* (*also* **crosbite**) [late 16C–early 19C] (*UK Und.*) **1** a swindler. **2** an act of trickery. [CROSSBITE v.]

crossbite *v.* [late 16C–mid-19C] (*UK Und.*) **1** to cheat, usu. in cards or dice, esp. when the victim is another cheat. **2** to practise the CROSSBITING LAW n. (the modern BADGER GAME n. or MURPHY GAME n.[1]), i.e. to beat up an unfortunate victim, previously ensnared by the prostitute with whom the trickster works. [SE *cross*, to oppose + BITE v. (1). The image is of fleecing someone who had hoped in their turn to get 'something for nothing', although in the case of the crossbiting law, the client had merely hoped for some illicit, commercial sex]

crossbiter *n.* (*also* **crosbiter**) (*UK Und.*) **1** [late 16C] a dice cheat or card-sharp. **2** [late 16C–17C] a man who works with a prostitute to trap and then rob an unfortunate victim; his role was to rob the man and then beat him up – allegedly for his gall in attempting to seduce an innocent 'sister' or 'wife'. [CROSSBITE v.]

crossbiting *n.* [early 17C] (*UK Und.*) the ensnaring of a client by a woman, often a prostitute, and his subseq. robbery, either by the woman herself or more often by her pimp, posing as an 'outraged boyfriend' or 'husband'. [CROSSBITE v. (2)]

crossbiting cully *n.* [late 17C–19C] a swindler, a cheat. [CROSSBITE v. + CULLY n. (3)]

crossbiting law *n.* [late 16C] (*UK Und.*) the robbery of a prostitute's client by her pimp or other male accomplice, usu. posing as an aggrieved 'husband' or 'lover'. [CROSSBITING n. + LAW n.[1]]

cross-bones *n.* [1930s] (*US*) a doctor (cf. BONE-BENDER n.[1]).

cross-boy *n.* [mid–late 19C] (*Aus./US*) a criminal. [CROSS v.[1] (2) + SE *boy*]

cross-built *adj.* [mid-19C] used of a person who moves or stands in an awkward manner. [SE *cross*, contrary, opposed + *built*]

cross-buttock *n.* [mid-19C–1900s] an unexpected rebuff. [wrestling jargon *cross-buttock*, a throw over the hip]

cross-chap *n.* **1** [early 19C] (*US*) a disreputable person. **2** [mid-19C–1900s] (*UK Und./costermonger*) a thief. [CROSS adj. + CHAP n. (1)]

cross-country ballet *n.* [1990s+] (*Aus.*) a derog. term for Australian Rules football.

cross-cove *n.* [19C] a robber, anyone who lives by dishonesty or crime. [CROSS adj. (2) + COVE n. (1)]

cross-cove and mollisher *n.* [mid-19C] a man and woman who work in tandem as thieves. [CROSS-COVE n. + MOLLISHER n. (3)]

cross-crib *n.* [mid-19C] a public house frequented by thieves. [CROSS adj. (2) + CRIB n.[1] (1)]

cross dishonest *n.* [early 19C] (*UK Und.*) a villain. [CROSS adj. (2) + SE *dishonest*]

cross-drum *n.* [mid-19C] (*UK/US Und.*) a thieves' tavern. [CROSS adj. (2) + DRUM n.[3] (7)]

crosser *n. see* CROSS v.[1] (3).

crosses *n.[1]* [1930s] (*US*) the roads.

crosses *n.[2]* [1950s+] (*W.I. Rasta*) problems, vexations, trials, bad luck, misfortunes. [SE phr. *a cross to bear*]

cross-eye *v.* [1920s–50s] (*US*) **1** to look suspiciously, to look askance at. **2** to glance at, to look at furtively, to act in any way suspicious.

cross-eyed *adj.* [20C+] drunk (cf. ARSEHOLED adj.).

cross-fam *v.* (*also* **cross-fan**) [19C] (*UK Und.*) to pick a pocket by crossing one's arms in a particular position. [SE *cross*, opposed, contrary + FAM n.[1] (1)]

cross-girl *n.* [mid-19C] a prostitute who specializes in propositioning sailors, taking their money and then vanishing (cf. AWAYDAY GIRL n.). [CROSS adj. (2)+ SE *girl*]

cross-kid *n.* [late 19C–1910s] irony, teasing, deception. [CROSS-KID v.]

cross-kid *v.* (*also* **cross-kiddle**) [late 19C] to interrogate, to cross-examine. [SE *cross* adj. + KID (AROUND) v.]

cross-lad *n.* (*also* **cross-squire**) [mid-19C] (*costermonger*) a thief. [CROSS adj. (2) + SE *lad*]

cross-legged *adj.* [19C] knock-kneed.

cross-legs *n.* [19C–1900s] a tailor. [the trad. tailoring posture]

cross-life man *n.* [late 19C] (*UK Und.*) a professional thief. [CROSS adj. (2)]

cross lots *phr. see* ACROSS LOTS phr.

crossman *n.* **1** [mid-19C] a confidence trickster; a thief. **2** [1950s+] (*US Black*) anyone who manipulates others for his own advantage. [SE (*double-*)*cross* + *man*]

cross-mollisher *n.* [early 19C] a woman who works as a thief or lives in any way dishonestly. [CROSS adj. (2) + MOLLISHER n. (1)]

crosso *n. see* CROSS, THE n. (1).

cross out *v.* [1980s+] **1** (*US Black*) to perform a low-level form of gang warfare, the crossing out of a rival gang's graffiti. **2** (*US prison*) to punish.

cross over *v.* [19C+] to die, usu. in combs., e.g. *cross over the range*, *cross over Jordan*, *cross over the river*, *cross the veil*.

cross-patch *n.* [late 17C+] a grumpy person, usu. a child, or someone acting in a childish manner. [SE *cross*, quarrelsome + *patch*, a fool or clown. The original Patch was, according to mid-16C refs., Cardinal Wolsey's personal jester, so called either from his hatched, parti-coloured fool's costume or f. Ital. *pazzo*, a fool. His real name was Sexton]

crossroader *n.* [1960s+] an itinerant card-sharp who travels in search of new victims for his cheating skills. [he stands at the crossroads or crosses roads in search of victims]

crossroads *n.* [1960s+] (*drugs*) amphetamines (cf. A n.[2]). [? the cross marked on some amphetamines]

cross-road trick *n.* [late 19C] (*Aus. prison*) suicide. [the trad. burying of suicides at a crossroads]

cross-squire *n. see* CROSS-LAD n.

cross-stiff *n. see* STIFF n.[3] (1).

cross-talk *v.* [20C+] (*US Black*) to interrupt another speaker. [SE *talk across*]

cross the border *v.* (*also* **cross the river**) [late 19C–1900s] (*Aus./US Black*) to die.

cross the line *v.* (*US*) **1** [1900s] for a light-skinned Black person to attempt to pass for White. **2** [1960s] for a homosexual man to abandon his friends and marry a woman.

cross tops *n.* [1970s] (*drugs*) amphetamines (cf. A n.[2]). [the cross cut into the pill]

cross up *v.* [20C+] **1** to betray, to double-cross, to inform against. **2** in fig. use, to let down, to place someone in a negative situation. **3** to go back on one's word, to reverse one's position. [SE *double-cross*/CROSS v.[1]]

crossways *adv.* (*also* **crosswise**) [20C+] (*US*) **1** in a bad humour. **2** disagreeing with. **3** lying. [CROSS adj. + play on SE]

crotch *n.* [1970s+] a woman, seen purely as an extension of her physical sexuality. [SE *crotch*, the fork or bifurcation of the legs; thus the genital area of either sex]

crotch *adj.* [1960s+] erotic, pornographic; thus *crotch novel*, a pornographic book.

crotch cheese *n.* [1960s+] unwashed vaginal secretions (cf. BINDERJUICE n.). [var. on CHEESE n.[2] (1)]

crotch cricket *n.* (*also* **crotch monkey, ...pheasant**) [1910s; 1960s+] (*US*) a crab, a pubic louse.

crotchface *n.* [1960s] (*US campus*) a bearded person. [play on SE *beard*/BEARD n.[1] (1)]

crotch oil *n.* [1980s+] (*US*) vaginal secretions that result from sexual foreplay (cf. BINDERJUICE n.).

crotch pheasant *n. see* CROTCH CRICKET n.

crotch rocket *n.* [1970s+] a motorcycle, esp. a dirt bike.

crotch rot *n.* [1960s+] (*Can./US*) a fungal infection of the groin.

Croton (cocktail) *n.* [mid-19C–1910s] (*US, New York*) water. [the *Croton Reservoir* (now the site of the NY Public Library at 5th

Ave + 42nd St) + SE *cocktail*; the reservoir supplied the bulk of the city's drinking water]

crovey *adj.* [2000s] (*UK teen*) good, excellent. [? GROOVY adj.² (1)]

crow *n.*¹ [late 17C–mid-19C] (*UK Und.*) a *crowbar*. [abbr.]

crow *n.*² **1** [late 18C–1900s] a clergyman. **2** [mid–late 19C] a doctor. [his black clothes + (2) ? SE *carrion/crow*, reflecting on his inadequacy as a healer]

crow *n.*³ [early 19C+] a derog. term for a Black person (cf. ALLIGATOR BAIT n.²). [the blackness of the bird + JIM CROW n. (1)]

crow *n.*⁴ **1** [early 19C+] that member of a crooked dice or card-game who poses as a stranger but affirms the supposed honesty of those who run the game. **2** [mid-19C+] a thief's lookout. **3** [1930s] (*UK tramp*) a man employed by a gang of street singers to protect their territory. **4** [1970s+] a lookout in a 3-card trick game. [? the image of crows perched on a fence]

crow *n.*⁵ [mid-19C–1920s] an unexpected or flukey piece of luck; usu. in phr. REGULAR CROW n. [? one *crows* or exults over it]

crow *n.*⁶ **1** [mid-19C–1950s] (*US*) a young woman, esp. a sweetheart. **2** [1920s–50s] (*US*) an unpleasant old man. **3** [1920s+] an unattractive (old) woman; note earlier OLD CROW n. (1). **4** [1920s+] (*US*) an attractive woman. **5** [1940s–70s] (*N.Z. teen*) a derog. male description of a young girl, from her black/navy school uniform.

crow *n.*⁷ [late 19C–1910s] a bar counter. [play on/abbr. SE *crowbar*]

crow *n.*⁸ [1940s] (*US milit.*) chicken (as a meal).

crow *n.*⁹ [1940s+] (*Aus.*) a prostitute; thus *charity crow*, a prostitute who does not charge, esp. to impecunious soldiers during WW2; *society crow*, an upmarket prostitute, a courtesan (cf. ALLEY CAT n.). [CHROMO n. (1); note Ital. *cornaccia*, a crow, a loose woman]

crow *adj.* [1910s–40s] (*US Und.*) inferior, worthless, second-rate. [? negative stereotype of JIM CROW n. (1)]

crow *v.* [late 19C] (*UK Und.*) to keep a lookout. [CROW n.⁴ (2)]

crow-bait *n.* **1** [mid–late 19C] (*Aus.*) a derog. term for an Aborigine. **2** [mid-19C+] (*US*) a corpse that has been exposed to the elements. **3** [late 19C–1950s] (*US*) an unpleasant, despised person. **4** [late 19C+] (*orig. US*) an emaciated horse. **5** [1930s] (*US Und.*) an old person.

crowbar *n.* [1920s] (*US*) the penis (cf. ARSE-OPENER n.). [it 'prises open' the vagina]

crowbar brigade *n.* [mid–late 19C] (*Irish*) the police; thus *crowbar landlord*, a landlord who enforces his powers through heavy-handed policemen. [SE *crowbar* + BRIGADE n.; their breaking into houses with the help of a crowbar; the break-in was followed by the eviction of the tenants]

crowbar hotel *n.* [1940s+] a prison (cf. BOARDING HOUSE n.). [var. on CROSS-BAR HOTEL n. + ? ref. to the need of a SE *crowbar* to escape]

crowd *v.*¹ (*US*) **1** [mid-19C+] to pressurize. **2** [20C+] to assault in a group.

crowd *v.*² [1940s+] (*US*) to be getting close to a stated age, e.g. *crowding fifty*.

crowded space *n.* [20C+] a suitcase. [rhy. sl.]

crowder *n.* [18C–19C] **1** a string. **2** (*UK Und.*) a fiddler. [Shelta *crowd*, a form of fiddle]

crowd pleaser *n.* [1960s+] (*US police*) the officer's gun. [ironic use]

crowd surf *v.* [1990s+] to leap from the stage at a rock concert, be caught and passed along by the crowd.

crowd the mourners *v.* [mid-19C–1920s] (*US*) **1** to intensify someone's embarrassment; to add to someone's problems. **2** to act hastily, to act precipitately.

crowdy-headed jock *n.* [late 18C–early 19C] a North Country seaman, esp. a crewman of a collier. [Scot./northern dial. *crowdy*, a gruel made from milk and meal; thus a porridge + JOCK n.]

crow-eater *n.* [late 19C+] **1** (*Aus.*) a White inhabitant of South Australia; thus *crowland*, South Australia. **2** (*Aus./S.Afr.*) a lazy person who will scrounge and otherwise live on his wits rather than do actual work. [(1) the canard that the original settlers of the state ate crow when nothing else was available]

crow fair *n.* [late 18C] a gathering of clergymen. [CROW n.² (1) + SE *fair*; their black garments]

crow jane *n.* [1900s–20s] (*US Black*) a very dark-skinned woman. [CROW n.³ + generic proper name *Jane*]

crow jim *n.* [1950s+] (*US*) anti-White discrimination by Blacks; thus *crow jimism*, guilt-induced affection for and fascination with Blacks by White liberals. [the reverse of anti-Black discriminatory JIM CROW n. (3) laws]

crow mcgee *adj.* (*also* **crow macgee**) [1930s+] (*US prison*) no good, unreal, false. [ety. unknown; ? joc. reversal of REAL McCOY, THE n. (1)]

crown *n.*¹ **1** [late 19C] the female genital area. **2** [1970s+] (*US gay*) the glans penis.

crown *n.*² [1960s] (*US Black*) a hat.

crown *n.*³ [1980s+] (*Aus. prison*) the Principal Officer. ['a crown was worn on an insignia of rank on the lapel. This practice is now obsolete but the term still used to denote a prison officer in authority' (Tupper & Wortley, *Australian Prison Slang Glossary*, 1990)]

crown *adj.* [1920s+] (*Aus.*) very large. [? SE phr. *crowning glory*]

crown *v.* **1** [mid-19C+] to hit over the head. **2** [20C+] (*Aus. campus*) to empty a chamberpot over a victim's head. **3** [1910s+] to hit, of a ball. [orig. dial.]

crown and feathers *n.* [mid–late 19C] pubic hair. [CROWN n.¹ (1) + predate of FEATHERS n.³; playing on a typical name for a public house]

crown crap *n.* [1980s+] (*drugs*) heroin (cf. CACA n.). [? CROWN adj. + CRAP n.⁷ (1)]

crowner *n.* [mid–late 19C] a fall (from horseback) onto the top of one's head. [SE *crown*, the top of one's head]

crown jewels *n.* [1960s+] the male genitals (cf. AGATES n.). [their importance to the possessor]

crown office *n.* [late 18C–early 19C] the head. [a pun on legal SE]

crown of sense *n.* [late 17C–19C] the vagina (cf. ADAM'S OWN (ALTAR) n.; BEST IN CHRISTENDOM n.).

crowns *n. see* BURNESE n.

crown sheet *n.* [1930s–50s] (*US tramp*) the seat of one's trousers. [rhy. sl.]

crown the king *v.* [1990s+] to masturbate.

crow's foot *n.* [mid–late 19C] (*UK prison*) the 'Broad Arrow' that marked all prison property.

crow's nest *n.* **1** [late 19C–1900s] (*UK society*) a small bedroom on the higher floors of country houses, reserved for the use of bachelor guests. **2** [20C+] (*US*) a woman's hair when it has been pinned up in a bun. **3** [1960s–70s] (*US*) the upper balcony or 'gods' in a theatre. **4** [1970s+] (*US gay*) a club frequented by older homosexual men. [naut. use *crow's nest*, the platform secured high on a mast that houses a lookout]

crow tracks *n.* [late 19C+] (*US*) illegible handwriting.

croziered abbot *n.* [late 19C] a man who runs a brothel designed less for providing sex, and more for robbing or blackmailing the clients (cf. ABBESS n.; ABBOT ON THE CROSS n.). [pun SE *croziered*, bearing a crook + ABBOT n.]

c.r.s. *adj.* [1980s+] (*US campus*) forgetful. [abbr. *can't remember shit* (SHIT n.³ (3))]

crub *n.* [1970s–80s] (*UK Black*) the rubbing of one's body, esp. the genital area, against one's partner while dancing. [CRUB v.]

crub *v.* [1970s–80s] (*UK Black*) to rub one's body against one's partner when dancing. [? SE *rub*]

crubber *n.* [1920s] (*US*) one who does not buy their own cigarettes. [? var. GRUBBER n.¹ (1)]

crucial *adj.* [1980s+] a general term of praise or admiration; serious, important, excellent; thus adv. *crucially*.

crucked *adj. see* CROCKED adj. (2).

crud *n.*[1] (*also* **krud, crut**) **1** [early 16C+] any filthy and disgusting matter. **2** [19C] curds. **3** [1930s+] (*orig. US milit.*) any unidentified disease; often as *crawling crud, creeping crud.* **4** [1940s+] (*orig. US milit.*) diarrhoea. **5** [1950s+] dried semen, whether on the body, clothes or bed linen (cf. MESS n.[5]; MUCK n.[4]; SCUM n.; STUFF n.[2]). **6** [1950s+] dirt, in general. **7** [1950s+] (*US*) any venereal disease. **8** [1950s+] daylights, guts, stuffing, e.g. *kick the crud out of.* [Scot. *crud,* thickened or coagulated milk; note US regional *crud,* curdled milk]

crud *n.*[2] **1** [1930s+] anything or anyone worthless, repulsive. **2** [1940s+] (*orig. US milit.*) a slovenly, habitually dirty person. **3** [1940s+] (*US*) nonsense, rubbish. [fig. uses of CRUD n.[1]; note *HDAS* suggests all US uses are backform. f. CRUDDY adj.]

crud *adj. see* CRUDDY adj. (1).

crudball *n.* [1960s+] (*US*) a filthy or disgusting person. [CRUD n.[2] (1) + -BALL sfx]

crudball *adj.* [1960s+] (*US*) filthy, disgusting. [CRUDBALL n.]

cruddy *adj.* **1** [1930s+] (*also* **crud**) useless, no good, second-rate. **2** [1940s+] dirty, unpleasant, unsavoury. [CRUD n.[1] (1)/CRUD n.[2] (1) + sfx -*y*]

crude *adj.* [1950s+] (*US Black*) worthless, excessive and as such useless.

crud-eating *adj. see* CRUD-SUCKING adj.

crudget *n.* [1920s+] (*Aus.*) the human head. [ety. unknown]

crudhead *n.* [1980s+] a fool, an unpleasant person. [CRUD n.[2] (1) + -HEAD sfx (1)]

crud man *n.* [1970s] a term of abuse. [CRUD n.[2] (1) + sfx -*man*]

crud-sucking *adj.* (*also* **crud-eating**) [1950s+] (*US*) a general term of abuse, revolting, disgusting etc. [CRUD n.[1] (1) + SE *sucking*]

crud up *v.* [1960s+] (*orig. US*) to render disgusting, filthy; thus to spoil. [CRUD n.[1] (1)]

crud work *n.* [1950s] (*US*) any menial, unpleasant or tedious work. [CRUD n.[1] (1) + SE *work*]

crudzoid *n.* [1980s] (*US*) a repellent, disgusting person. [CRUD n.[2] (1) + -ZOID sfx]

cruel *adj.* **1** [19C–1940s] of conditions or circumstances, severe, hard. **2** [1920s+] impressive, good. [ext. of SE use]

cruel *adv.* [mid-17C+] exceedingly, very. [ext. of SE use]

cruel (the pitch) *v.* [late 19C+] (*Aus.*) to spoil, to ruin any chance of success with. [ostensibly rooted in cricket imagery, the phr. does not appear in John Eddowes's *Language of Cricket* (1996)]

cruelty man *n.* [1950s+] an officer of the NSPCC or the RSPCA. [both organizations deal with *cruelty,* to, respectively, children or animals]

cruelty-van *n.* [mid–late 19C] a 4-wheeled chaise. [? its discomfort]

cruet *n.* [1940s+] (*Aus.*) the human head; thus *do one's cruet,* to lose emotional control.

cruff *n.* [1960s+] (*W.I.*) **1** crude, coarse, uncouth manners. **2** (*also* **cruffbag**) a crude, uncouth person. [? SE *scruffy*]

cruff *adj.* [1960s+] (*W.I.*) scruffy, uncouth. [CRUFF n.]

crufty *adj.* [1980s] (*W.I., Jam.*) coarse-looking. [? SE *scruffy*; note computer jargon *crufty,* of a machine or program, poorly constructed, poss. over-complex]

crug *n.* [mid-19C] food. [? SE *crust*; orig. used by boys at Christ's Hospital school to mean bread]

cruise *n.* **1** [1950s] (*US Und.*) a male homosexual who picks up partners on the street. **2** [1960s+] (*gay*) a quick glance that assesses a passing individual in sexual terms. [CRUISE v.[1] (1)]

cruise *adj.* [1980s+] (*US teen*) easy, simple, useful. [CRUISE v.[2] (1)]

cruise *v.*[1] **1** [late 17C+] to approach someone obviously with sexual intent, both for commercial or non-commercial purposes. **2** [mid-18C] (*UK Und.*) to beg. **3** [19C] to wander through/along. **4** [20C+] (*also* **cruise around**) to drive around, often along a town's main street, surveying the situation, looking for friends or sexual encounters. **5** [1910s+] to search for sexual contacts by

walking specific streets, areas etc. **6** [1940s] (*US Black*) to walk someone along/around/through. **7** [1940s+] (*US Black*) to walk in a strutting manner. **8** [1950s–60s] (*US*) of a mugger or thief, to search out a potential victim. **9** [1950s+] to walk or drive somewhere. **10** [1970s+] to set off, to leave. **11** [1990s+] to drive someone around. **12** [1990s+] to pass, to hand over, to give. **13** [1990s+] of the police, to drive around checking on suspicious activities/individuals. [fig. uses of SE *cruise,* to sail to and fro with no particular destination; note Ned Ward, *Hudibras Redivivus* (1705–7): 'Now gently cruzing up and down, / T'observe the Follies of the Town']

cruise *v.*[2] **1** [1960s+] to do something easily, effortlessly. **2** [1980s] (*US campus*) to sleep soundly.

cruisemobile *n.* [1980s+] (*US teen*) any favoured car. [CRUISE v.[1] (4) + -MOBILE sfx]

cruiser *n.*[1] **1** [late 17C–early 19C] (*UK Und.*) a beggar, esp. one who passes on information of potential robberies to professional thieves. **2** [mid-19C] (*UK/US Und.*) 'a man who "cruises around" in search of victims and plunder' (R.H. Thornton, *An American Glossary,* 1912). **3** [mid-19C; 20C+] a prostitute. **4** [1900s] (*Aus.*) a tramp, a vagrant. **5** [1940s+] one who wanders the streets searching for a casual sexual encounter (usu. assumed to be a male homosexual but of either gender in 1980s+ use). [CRUISE v.[1]]

cruiser *n.*[2] [1920s+] (*US*) a police patrol car.

cruise the chocolate freeway *v.* [1990s+] (*orig. US*) of hetero- or homosexual anal intercourse, to sodomize (cf. ASK FOR THE RING v.). [SE *cruise/ride* + CHOCOLATE HIGHWAY n.]

cruising *n.* [1920s+] walking or driving about the streets in search of a casual sexual partner; usu. but not invariably of a male homosexual, also in a bar, club etc. [CRUISE v.[1] (4)/CRUISE v.[1] (5)]

cruising for a bruising *phr.* [1940s+] (*orig. US*) **1** looking deliberately to cause trouble. **2** acting in such a manner that will get one into trouble, usu. of a physically harmful nature. [ext. use of CRUISE v.[1] (5) + SE *bruising*]

cruising with one's lights on (dim) *phr.* [20C+] acting in a stupid manner (cf. CAN'T SEE THROUGH A LADDER phr.).

cruisy *adj.* [1940s+] (*gay*) used of the sort of place in which one is likely to make a successful pick-up. [CRUISE v.[1] (5)]

Crum, the *n.* [1970s+] (*Ulster*) the *Crum*lin Road prison in Belfast (cf. ABBOTT'S PRIORY n.). [abbr.]

crum *n.* (*also* **crumb**) **1** [mid-19C–1920s] a body louse, usu. in pl. **2** [1910s+] a filthy person, an objectionable, worthless or insignificant individual. **3** [1970s+] a cruel, vicious person. [the tiny size of the insects, the infestation of the human being]

crum *adj.* (*also* **crumb**) [20C+] (*US*) filthy, dirty, disgusting. [abbr. CRUMMY adj.[2] (2)]

crumb *see also under* CRUM *and its combs.*

crumb *n.*[1] [19C] **1** a pretty, plumpish woman. **2** plumpness. [SE *crumb,* the soft heart of a risen loaf]

crumb *n.*[2] **1** [early–mid-19C] (*US*) the head. **2** [1920s] the penis. [? the shape]

crumb *n.*[3] (*also* **crummy**) [1910s–50s] (*US tramp*) a tramp's bedding. [CRUM n. (1)]

crumb *v.* **1** [1940s–50s] (*US Black/teen*) to ruin, to undermine; usu. as *crumb a/the deal.* **2** [1960s] (*US*) to malign someone. **3** [1980s+] (*US campus*) to feel sad or depressed. [i.e. to render CRUMMY adj.[2] (3)]

crumb! *excl.* [1950s–70s] (*US*) a mild excl. of annoyance. [CRUMMY adj.[2] (3)]

crumb and crust man *n.* [mid-19C] a baker.

crumb boss *n.* (*also* **crum boss**) [1920s–30s] (*US tramp/Western*) a janitor in a construction camp or mission. [CRUM n. (1) + BOSS n.[2] (1); among his duties was delousing the beds]

crumb-catcher *n.*[1] [1940s] (*US*) a comb. [CRUM n. (1) + SE *catcher*]

crumb-catcher *n.*[2] [1940s–50s] (*US*) a hanger-on, one who acts as a parasite on the powerful or influential. [the taking of 'crumbs from the rich man's table']

crumb-catcher n.[3] (*also* **crumb-snatcher**) [1950s+] (*orig. US Black*) a baby, usu. one who is just beginning to eat solids.

crumb-cruncher n. (*orig. US Black*) **1** [1940s+] a tooth. **2** [1950s+] a baby who is just learning to eat solids.

crumb-crush v. [1940s] (*US Black*) to enjoy profoundly, to 'eat up'.

crumb-crusher n. **1** [1940s–70s] (*US Black*) a tooth. **2** [1950s+] (*orig. US Black*) a baby who is just learning to eat solids. **3** [1970s] (*US Black*) in pl., the lips.

crumb-gobbler n. [1920s] (*US*) a young man who frequents tea-parties.

crumb-grabber n. [1930s–60s] (*orig. US Black*) a baby who is just beginning to eat solids.

crumb-hall n. [1930s–40s] (*US Black*) a dining-room, esp. in an institution.

crumb in v. [1960s] (*US*) to interfere, to butt in, esp. to interfere in (and poss. ruin) another confidence man's scheme. [CRUMB v. (1)]

crumb joint n. [1930s–50s] (*US*) a filthy lodging house or hostel. [CRUM adj. + JOINT n.[4] (3)]

crumbly n. (*also* **crumblie**) [1970s+] (*UK society*) an older person, aged 50–70 years. [such people are fig. 'crumbling away']

crumbo n. [1930s+] (*orig. US*) a filthy, disgusting, despised person. [CRUM n. (2) + -O sfx (1)]

crumbs n. **1** [1920s–50s] (*US*) very small sums of money (cf. BATTER n.[4]). **2** [1980s+] (*drugs*) tiny pieces of crack cocaine. [the small sizes]

crumbs! excl. [late 19C+] (*mainly UK juv.*) a euph. for CHRIST! excl.; prob. the mildest of such euph.

crumb-snatcher n.[1] [1970s] the hand.

crumb-snatcher n.[2] *see* CRUMB-CATCHER n.[3].

crumb-stash n. [1930s–40s] (*US Black/Harlem*) a kitchen; a dining room.

crumbum n. (*also* **crumb-bum**) [1930s+] (*orig. US*) a filthy, disgusting, worthless person. [CRUM n. (2) + BUM n.[3] (2)]

crumbum adj. [1930s+] (*orig. US*) useless, awful, second-rate, inferior. [CRUMBUM n.]

crumb up v. [1910s+] (*US*) to make filthy, disgusting. [CRUM adj.]

Crum Hill n. [1920s–30s] (*US tramp*) Jefferson Park, Chicago. [CRUM n. (1)]

crum-joint n. [1920s–60s] (*US*) a second-rate, dirty dwelling-house, bar or club. [CRUM adj. + JOINT n.[4] (3)]

crummey adj. *see* CRUMMY adj.[2].

crummy n.[1] **1** [early 19C] fat, flab. **2** [mid-19C] (*US*) a louse. [(1) CRUMB n.[1] (2); (2) CRUM n. (1) + sfx -y]

crummy n.[2] **1** [1920s–50s] (*US tramp*) the caboose of a train, i.e. that coach used by railroad workmen or train guards. **2** [1950s] (*US Und.*) a local jail, police station or workhouse. [CRUMMY adj.[2] (1); such coaches or small lock-ups were trad. infested with lice; note logging jargon *crummy*, a pick-up truck that ferries loggers to and from their camps]

crummy adj.[1] (*also* **crumby**) **1** [17C] rich. **2** [mid-18C–19C] fat, fleshy; plump; attractive. [SE *crumb*, the soft inner part of a loaf, the antithesis of *crust*]

crummy adj.[2] (*also* **crumby, crumbed up**) **1** [mid-19C+] infested with lice; thus fig. 'lousy with'. **2** [mid-19C+] generally filthy. **3** [mid-19C+] (*also* **crummy-ass, crummey**) second-rate, inferior, unpleasant. **4** [1940s+] a general negative intensifier, synon. with LOUSY adj. **5** [1950s+] out of sorts, 'off colour'. [CRUM n. (1) + sfx -y]

crummy! excl. [20C+] a mild euph. for CHRIST! excl.

crummy-doss n. [mid-19C] a lousy or filthy bed. [CRUMMY adj.[2] (1) + DOSS n.[1] (1)]

crump n.[1] [late 17C–early 19C] a solicitor's assistant, who arranges for false witnesses to perjure themselves as required by a given case. [backform of phr. *I wish you had, Mrs Crump*: 'a Gloucestershire saying, in answer to a wish for any thing. It is said to have originated from the following incident: One Mrs. Crump, the wife of a substantial farmer, dining with the old Lady Coventry, who was extremely deaf, said to one of the footmen, waiting at table, "I wish I had a draught of small beer," her modesty not permitting her to desire so fine a gentleman to bring it: the fellow, conscious that his mistress could not hear either the request or answer, replied, without moving, "I wish you had, Mrs. Crump." These wishes being again repeated by both parties, Mrs. Crump got up from the table to fetch it herself; and being asked by my lady where she was going, related what had passed. The story being told abroad, the expression became proverbial' (Grose, 1785)]

crump n.[2] [early 18C–early 19C] a hunchback.

crump adj. [1990s+] (*US campus*) good, excellent. [ety. unknown]

crump v. **1** [1950s+] (*US campus*) to pass out through exhaustion, boredom or alcohol; thus *crumped (out)*, passed out drunk. **2** [1950s+] (*US*) of machinery, to break down. **3** [1950s+] (*US*) to die. **4** [1960s] (*US*) to kill. **5** [1980s] (*US*) to destroy. [SE *crump*, the noise of an object hitting the ground]

crump-backed adj. [late 17C–early 19C] hump-backed. [SE *crump*, crooked + *backed*]

crumper n. [mid–late 19C] a hard hit, a blow. [dial. *crump*, a blow]

crumpet n.[1] [late 19C+] the head; thus *barmy/balmy in/on the crumpet* or *off one's crumpet*, mad, eccentric. [the supposedly similar shapes]

crumpet n.[2] **1** [1900s] (*Aus.*) the buttocks (cf. BAKERY GOODS n.). **2** [1930s+] a generic term for women, esp. when viewed as no more than sources of sexual pleasure; thus *get a crumpet*, of a man, to have sexual intercourse. **3** [1940s+] sexual intercourse. **4** [1960s] (*US gay*) an anal virgin. **5** [1960s+] (*W.I.*) the vagina (cf. APPLE n.[6]). **6** [1990s+] men viewed as no more than sources of sexual pleasure.

crumpet n.[3] [1900s–60s] a term of endearment, often as *old crumpet*. [note the P.G. Wodehouse title, combining 3 such terms, *Eggs, Beans and Crumpets* (1940)]

crumpet n.[4] [1920s+] (*Aus.*) a weakling, a fool (cf. APPLEHEAD n.). [the softness of the comestible]

crumpet-face n. [mid–late 19C] a face that is covered with smallpox marks (cf. CRIBBAGE-FACED adj.). [similarity to the pocked surface of a crumpet]

crumpet man n. [1960s+] a womanizer. [CRUMPET n.[2] (2) + SE *man*]

crumpet-scramble n. [mid–late 19C] a tea party.

crum roll n. [1930s] (*US tramp*) a bedroll. [CRUM n. (1), i.e. the assumption/slur being that it is infested with lice]

crums n. *see* CRUM n. (1).

crum up v. (*also* **crumb up**) [1920s–50s] (*US*) to boil one's clothes to get rid of the lice. [CRUM n. (1)]

crunch n. [1970s] (*US campus*) **1** a generic term for women. **2** an infatuation. [? 'good enough to eat']

crunch adj. [1970s+] (*orig. Aus.*) critical, decisive, crucial, e.g. *a crunch situation*. [SE (*the*) *crunch*]

crunch v. **1** [mid-19C+] to beat up. **2** [1950s–60s] of a man, to have sexual intercourse (cf. BANG v.[1]).

cruncher n.[1] (*also* **crunching straight**) [1940s] (*US*) the street, the pavement. [the sound of one's feet]

cruncher n.[2] [1980s+] the ultimate aspect of a given situation. [SE (*the*) *crunch*]

crunchers n. **1** [1920s] (*US tramp*) the teeth. **2** [1940s] (*US*) the feet. [echoic, sound of biting/feet hitting the ground]

crunchie n. [1970s+] (*S.Afr.*) a derog. term for an Afrikaner. [? *mealie cruncher* or f. *krantzie*, abbr. of *krantz-athlete*, milit. sl. for an Afrikaner; the term also reflects their overall image of violence]

crunching straight n. *see* CRUNCHER n.[1].

crunch time *n.* [1980s+] the ultimate aspect of a given situation. [SE (*the*) *crunch*]

crunchy *adj.*[1] [1990s+] (*US campus*) **1** embarrassed. **2** exhausted. [? the 'crunching up' of one's face/body in embarrassment]

crunchy *adj.*[2] [1990s+] (*US campus*) vegetarian, HIPPIE adj. [CRUNCHY (GRANOLA) n.]

crunchy (granola) *n.* [1980s+] (*US campus*) **1** a vegetarian (cf. GRANOLA(-GROID) n.). **2** a devotee of New Age philosophies. **3** (*also* **earthy crunchy, hairy crunchy**) someone who identifies with the styles and concerns of the 1960s, a HIPPIE n.[2] (3). [the popular and supposedly healthy US cereal, *Crunchy Granola*; 'A hiking-boot-wearing, granola-eating, Grateful Dead/Blues Traveler-listening type of person' (Shenk & Silberman, *Skeleton Key*, 1994)]

crunk *n.* [1990s+] (*US Black*) a state of excitement; a good time. [CRUNK adj.]

crunk *adj.* [1990s+] (*US campus/teen*) **1** excellent, wonderful. **2** (*also* **crunked**) excited, exciting. **3** (*also* **crunked up**) intoxicated with drink or drugs. **4** crazy, obnoxious. [orig rap use; SE *crazy* + *drunk*]

crunk! *excl.* [1960s] (*US campus*) a mild excl. [? nothing more than the sound]

crunt *n.* [1950s–60s] (*US Black*) any form of dirt, esp. the (dried) residue of bodily fluids, e.g. blood, semen. [CRUD n.[1] (1)]

crupper *n.* (*also* **crooper**) **1** [late 16C–mid-19C] the posterior, the buttocks; thus *crupper, ride below the crupper*, to have sexual intercourse. **2** the penis. [SE *crupper*, the hind-quarters of a horse]

crusader *n.* [1990s+] (*US campus*) an evangelistic, fundamentalist Christian.

crush *n.*[1] **1** [mid-19C] a crowded social occasion. **2** [1900s–70s] a crowd, a gang. [note WW1 Aus. milit. *crush*, a unit]

crush *n.*[2] **1** [late 19C+] a romantic or sexual interest in someone, occas. the person. **2** [1980s] (*lesbian*) the vagina. [(1) one's emotions 'crush' their object]

crush *n.*[3] (*also* **crusher**) [1910s–40s] (*US*) a hat, esp. a soft, felt one. [note mid-19C UK SE *crush hat*, a soft hat that can be crushed flat, esp. a hat constructed with a spring so that it collapses and becomes flat]

crush *v.*[1] **1** [mid-19C–1940s] (*UK/US Und.*) to run away, to escape; thus *big crush*, a mass escape. **2** [1900s–20s] (*US Und.*) to break into. [? SE *crash*]

crush *v.*[2] **1** [late 19C; 1980s] (*US campus*) to amaze; to do very well. **2** [20C+] (*US campus*) (*also* **crush on**) to be fond of someone. [(1) SE; (2) CRUSH n.[2] (1)]

crush a bottle *v.* (*also* **crush a cup (of wine), crush a pot (of ale)**) [late 16C] to drink.

crushed fruit *n. see* FRUIT n.[2] (2).

crushed on *adv.* [late 19C–1920s] (*orig. UK society*) infatuated with. [CRUSH n.[2] (1)]

crusher *n.*[1] [mid–late 19C] something that overwhelms or overpowers; thus *go a crusher*, to indulge oneself. [SE *crusher*, someone or something that crushes]

crusher *n.*[2] [mid-19C+] a policeman (cf. BEAT-POUNDER n.). [the stereotype of the policeman's large, booted feet. Note naut. use *crusher*, a ship's corporal; ? link to Irish *cuir siar ar*, to force upon; an enforcer]

crusher *n.*[3] **1** [20C+] (*US*) a boor, an intruder. **2** [1930s–70s] (*Can.*) a thug. [CRUSHER n.[1]/CRUSH v.[1] (2)]

crusher *n.*[4] [20C+] (*US*) one who persists in making unwanted advances to women. [SE *crush*/CRUSH n.[2] (1) + ? MASHER n.[1] (3)]

crusher *n.*[5] *see* CRUSH n.[3]

crush in *v.* [1900s] (*US*) to attend an event when uninvited. [var. on CRASH v.[2]]

crushing *adj.* [mid-19C] excellent, first-rate. [SE *crushing*, bruising, overwhelming]

crush me! *excl.* [mid-18C] an excl. of asseveration.

crush out *n.* [1920s–50s] (*US prison*) an escape. [CRUSH OUT v. (1)]

crush out *v.* [1920s+] (*US Und.*) **1** to escape from prison. **2** to obliterate the body and the evidence of a murder by putting the corpse into a car and the car through a junkyard crushing machine. **3** to push through a crowd. [note Milburn differentiates this from simple CRUSH v.[1] (1), which does not involve violence]

crush the can *v.* [1940s] (*US prison*) to escape from jail. [CRUSH v.[1] (1) + CAN n.[3] (3)]

crush the stir *v.* [late 19C] (*UK Und.*) to break out of prison. [CRUSH v.[1] (1) + STIR n.[1]]

crust *n.*[1] **1** [19C+] a living; thus *earn/pick up a crust*, work for a living. **2** [1910s–70s] a vagrancy charge, a vagrant. [both f. SE *crust of bread*. (2) implies that a vagrant has insufficient money to buy one]

crust *n.*[2] [late 19C+] the head. [it sits on top of the body]

crust *n.*[3] [20C+] cheek, audacity, nerve (cf. RIND n.[1]). [SE *crust*, an outer covering or shell that is difficult to penetrate]

crust *v.* [1910s–70s] (*orig. Aus./N.Z.*) to charge with vagrancy; thus *do the crust*, serve a sentence for vagrancy. [CRUST n.[1] (2)]

crustafarian *n.* [1990s+] a White person who deliberately adopts the lifestyle and image of a Rastafarian. [CRUSTY n. + SE *Rastafarian*]

crust-buster *n.* [1950s+] (*US Black*) a baby who is just learning to eat solids.

crust of bread *n.* [1930s+] the head. [rhy. sl.]

crusty *n.* [1980s+] a member of the underclass of the 'punk' scene, who adopts deliberately filthy clothing (hence their 'crustiness'), lives communally (often in squats) or on the streets, enjoys an excess of drink and drugs and generally sets out to appal their less extreme peers. [note 1950s W.I. *crusty*, illiterate, backward, foolish]

crusty *adj.*[1] [mid-19C; 1930s+] unpleasant, nasty. [SE *crusty*, encrusted (with something unpleasant) + SE *crusty*, of a person, short-tempered, rebarbative]

crusty *adj.*[2] [1970s–80s] (*UK Black*) **1** of people, well-built, muscled. **2** of objects, large, heavy. [one is 'encrusted' with muscles]

crusty-beau *n.* [late 17C–early 19C] a dandy who takes especial care of his (ageing) complexion, often with cosmetics. [SE *crusty*, encrusted + *beau*]

crusty gripes *n.* [late 19C] a grumbler. [SE *crusty*, short-tempered/CRUSTY adj.[1] + SE *gripe*, a complaint]

crut *n. see* CRUD n.[1].

crutch *n.*[1] [late 19C] a crutch-handled walking-stick, the badge of the late 19C man about town.

crutch *n.*[2] [20C+] (*bingo*) the number 7; usu. as *one little crutch*; thus *all the crutches*, 77 (cf. ALDERSHOT LADIES n.). [resemblance]

crutch *n.*[3] [1930s–70s] (*US Black*) a car; thus FLY CRUTCH n.; *P-crutch*, a police car.

crutch *n.*[4] [1930s+] (*drugs*) a device (a thin piece of cardboard, usu. a matchbook cover, rolled into a cylindrical shape) used to hold the last portion of a cannabis cigarette that has become too hot to hold in the fingers.

crutch *n.*[5] [1960s] (*US*) any form of (commercially produced) cheating aid used in a test or examination. [it offers 'support']

crutch and toothpick brigade *n.* [late 19C] a broad group of men about town whose sartorial badges were a crutch-handled walking-stick and a toothpick (of the dental variety). [CRUTCH n.[1] + SE *toothpick* + BRIGADE n.; thus the music-hall rhymester's mock solicitous enquiry: 'What about that toothpick, and don't you like that crutch?/And are those trousers very tight, and do they hurt you much?']

crutch and toothpick parade *n.* [late 19C–1900s] a generic term for old and decrepit men. [punning on CRUTCH AND TOOTHPICK BRIGADE n.]

cruz *n.* [1980s+] (*drugs*) opium from Veracruz, Mexico (cf. APOSTLE n.). [abbr.]

cry *n.*[1] [17C] a group of people. [the comparison is with a 'cry' or pack of hounds]

cry *n.*[2] [mid-19C+] (*orig. Aus.*) one's turn to order a round of drinks. [var. on SHOUT n.[1] (2)]

cry *n.*[3] [mid-19C+] a fit of weeping; usu. in phr. *have a good cry.*

cry *v.* [1910s+] (*US*) to complain, to make a fuss.

cry (a) crack *v.* [16C; late 19C–1930s] to give in, to surrender, to cry 'quits'. [SE *cry* + fig. use *crack*; 20C use is Aus./Irish]

cry a go *v.* [late 19C] to give up, to surrender. [cribbage jargon *cry a go,* to pass]

cry and laugh *n.* [20C+] (*Aus.*) a scarf. [rhy. sl.]

cry a rope *v.* [late 16C] to shout a warning. [the hangman's rope that awaits those who pay no heed]

crybaby *v.* [20C+] to collapse in the face of pressure and act like a weeping, pleading child; also in fig. use. [SE *crybaby,* n.]

cry beef *v. see* CRY (HOT) BEEF v.

cry bucket-a-drop *v.* [20C+] (*W.I.*) to make a good deal of fuss (and even cry) about an unimportant matter, to shed 'crocodile tears'. [the image of filling a bucket with tears]

cry carrots (and turnips) *v.* [18C] (*UK Und.*) to be whipped at the cart's tail. [? onomat. + ironic ref. to the carter's normal cries]

cry champagne *v.* [1990s+] (*W.I.*) to express one's emotions dramatically.

cry cockles *v.* [late 18C–early 19C] to be hanged. [echoic; *cockles,* the sound made as one chokes]

cry copper *v.* [late 19C+] to raise the alarm. [SE *cry* + COPPER n.[3] (1)]

cry crack *v. see* CRY (A) CRACK v.

cry-cry *adj.* [20C+] (*W.I.*) of a child, continually or easily tearful, crybabyish.

cry halves *v. see* GO HALVES v.

cry (hot) beef *v.* (*also* **give (hot) beef, squeak beef**) [late 17C–19C] to give the alarm, to call a hue and cry. [SE *cry* + HOT BEEF! excl.]

cry Hughie *v.* (*also* **cry Ralph, cry Ruth**) [1960s+] to vomit (cf. CALL CHARLES v.). [echoic of the noise of vomiting]

crying buddy *n.* [1960s] (*US Black*) one's best friend. [? one on whose shoulder one may cry]

crying towel *n.* [1920s+] (*US*) a fig. *towel* used to mop the tears of self-pitying people.

crying weed *n.* [1950s] (*drugs*) marijuana (cf. AFRICAN BUSH n.; BOMB n.[4]). [SE *crying* + WEED n.[1] (4); ? its effects, although the tears are more likely to result from laughter than sorrow]

cry mapsticks! *excl.* [early–mid-18C] I beg for mercy! [SE *cry* + play on *mopstick,* mop handle]

cry off *v.* [1940s–50s] (*US Und.*) **1** to confess. **2** to inform.

cry pork *v.* [late 18C–early 19C] to act as an undertaker's tout. ['a metaphor borrowed from the raven, whose note sounds like the word *pork.* Ravens are said to smell carrion at a distance' (Grose, 1796)]

cry Ralph *v. see* CRY HUGHIE v.

cry roast meat *v.* [late 17C–early 19C] to boast about one's good fortune. [the assumed prosperity of those who eat roast meat. The *OED* suggests that such boasting is foolish]

cry Ruth *v. see* CRY HUGHIE v.

Crys *n.* [2000s] (*US Black*) Louis Roederer *Cri*stal Champagne, the favoured brand of many gangsters, drug dealers and hip-hop stars. [abbr.]

crystal *n.* (*drugs*) **1** [1920s+] (*also* **crystal blow**) uncut cocaine. **2** [1960s+] (*also* **crystals**) a term covering a variety of drugs of the amphetamine type, e.g. amphetamine sulphate, powdered Methedrine, desoxyn (cf. A n.[2]). **3** [1970s+] (*also* **crystal flake**) phencyclidine (cf. ACE n.[4]). [resemblance]

crystal bud *n.* [1980s+] (*US drugs*) a potent variety of marijuana in which the flowers are covered with tiny crystals (cf. AFRICAN BUSH n.). [SE *crystal* + BUD n.[4]]

crystal-gazer *n.* [20C+] a person who manages to make successful predictions; thus an intelligent person.

crystal joint *n.* [1970s] (*drugs*) phencyclidine (cf. ACE n.[4]). [CRYSTAL n. (3) + JOINT n.[5] (3)]

crystal lady *n.* [1970s+] (*US gay*) an amphetamine-using homosexual. [CRYSTAL n. (2) + SE *lady*]

crystal meth *n.* [1960s+] (*drugs*) crystal Methedrine. [it comes in a crystalline powder]

crystals *n. see* CRYSTAL n. (2).

cry the blues *v.* [1930s] (*US*) to complain, to whinge, to bemoan one's lot. [CRY v. + BLUES n.[1]]

cry uncle *v.* (*also* **holler uncle, say uncle**) [1910s+] (*US*) to beg someone to stop an action, to surrender. ['"uncle" in this expression is surely a folk etymology, and the Irish original of the word is *anacol* (*anacal, anacul*) "act of protecting; deliverance; mercy, quarter, safety", a verbal noun from the Old Irish verb *aingid* "protects"' (*American Speech* LI, 1976)]

cry whore *v.* [mid-17C–18C] to put the blame on. [lit. to accuse someone of being a prostitute]

c.s. *n.*[1] [1940s+] (*orig. US*) a coward; a contemptible, disgusting person. [abbr. CHICKENSHIT n.]

c.s. *n.*[2] [1970s–80s] (*US gay*) fellatio. [abbr. COCKSUCKING n.]

c/s *phr. see* CON SAFOS phr. (1).

c.s.p. *n.* [1980s+] (*US campus*) a casual sex partner. [abbr.]

c.t. *n. see* COCKTEASER n.

cu *n.*[1] (*also* **cue, cuke**) [1930s+] a *cu*cumber. [abbr.]

cu *n.*[2] *see* COO n.

cub *n.*[1] [17C–early 19C] a novice gambler, who is likely to be cheated of his cash. [*cub* meaning a child, a young person, a novice or a beginner was briefly sl. in early 17C but soon SE]

cub *n.*[2] *see* CUBBY n. (2).

Cuban candle *n.* [1940s–60s] (*orig. US Black*) a cigar. [the origin and shape]

Cubans *n.* (*also* **Cuban pumps**) [1970s+] (*gay*) heavy work-boots.

cubba *n.* (*also* **Miss Cubba**) [1940s+] (*W.I.*) **1** a promiscuous woman. **2** an effeminate man. [in W. African cultures *Cuba,* the day-name of a woman born on a Wednesday]

cubbitch *adj.* [1950s+] (*W.I. Rasta*) covetous, thus both mean and greedy. [SE *covetous*]

cubby *n.* (*also* **cobby**) **1** [mid-19C–1960s] (*US Black*) a small room. **2** [late 19C+] (*Aus.*) (*also* **cub**) a child's playhouse, sited in the back garden. [abbr. SE *cubby-hole*]

cube *n.*[1] (*also* **cubes**) [1910s+] (*drugs*) morphine, esp. 1oz (28g) (or what is sold as 1oz) of morphine (cf. AUNTIE EMMA n.). [the shape of bulk supplies]

cube *n.*[2] [1950s–60s] an extreme conservative, an ultra-respectable person. [an intensified version or 'superlative' of SQUARE n.[1] (3)]

cube *n.*[3] (*also* **cubes**) [1960s+] (*drugs*) LSD (cf. A n.[3]). [early LSD doses were often dripped onto sugar cubes for easy ingestion]

cube *n.*[4] [1980s+] (*US*) a derog. term for a *Cub*an. [abbr.]

cubehead *n.* (*also* **cubie**) [1960s–70s] (*drugs*) an LSD user, esp. when ingesting LSD dropped onto a sugar cube. [CUBE n.[3] + -HEAD sfx (3)]

cubes *n.*[1] [1920s] (*US tramp*) dice.

cubes *n.*[2] [1960s] (*US campus*) the testicles (cf. BALLS n.[1]).

cubes *n.*[3] *see* CUBE n.[1].

cubes *n.*[4] *see* CUBE n.[3].

cubesville *n.* [1950s–60s] the world of ultra-conservative, highly respectable people. [CUBE n.[2] + -VILLE sfx[1]]

cubie *n. see* CUBEHEAD n.

cubistic *adj.* [1960s] (*US*) extremely conventional. [CUBE n.[2] + sfx *-istic*]

cubit, the *n.* [early 19C] the treadmill, as employed in prisons; thus *punishment by the cubit,* a spell on the treadmill. [William *Cubitt* (1785–1861) who invented the treadmill (albeit for grinding corn), which, from 1818, was introduced into British prisons as a form of punishment]

cubitopolis *n.* (*also* **cubittopolis**) [mid-19C] that area of London around Warwick and Eccleston Squares; thus Pimlico. [Thomas *Cubitt* (1788–1855), the greatest London builder of the early 19C, whose major creation, backed by his patron the Duke of Westminster, is Belgravia; + ? pun on the building measure, a *cubit*]

cubs *n.* [late 19C–1920s] (*US Black*) cards that have been fixed for use in crooked games.

cuck *n.* [mid-16C–early 18C] a cuckold; thus *cuckquean*, a female cuckold. [abbr.]

cuckaboo *n. see* KOOKABOO *n.*

cuckoldshire *n.* (*also* **cuckold's crew**) [mid-16C–17C] the fig. 'world' of cuckoldry. [SE *cuckold* + sfx *-shire*]

cuckold the parson *v.* [late 18C–early 19C] to sleep with one's wife before one is married.

cuckoo *n.*[1] 1 [late 16C–early 18C] a cuckold. 2 [late 16C+] (*also* **coo-coo**) a fool, an eccentric, a silly person (cf. AIREDALE *n.*). [SE phr. *cuckoo in the nest*, denoting the oddness of such an individual; (1) the cuckoo lays its eggs in another bird's nest]

cuckoo *n.*[2] [late 19C] the penis (cf. ANTEATER *n.*). [? COCK *n.*[2] (1)]

cuckoo *n.*[3] [late 19C] (*US*) a prostitute (cf. ALLEY CAT *n.*).

cuckoo *adj.* (*also* **coo-coo, cookoo, cuckoo's nest, koo-koo**) [20C+] crazy, eccentric, insane (cf. APEY *adj.*). [CUCKOO *n.*[1] (2)]

cuckoo *v.* [1930s] (*US*) to act foolishly, to mess up. [CUCKOO *n.*[1] (2)]

cuckoo academy *n.* [1960s+] (*US*) a psychiatric institution. [CUCKOO *n.*[1] (2) + SE *academy*]

cuckoo bird *n.* [1940s+] (*US*) an eccentric, a mad person. [CUCKOO *n.*[1] (2) + BIRD *n.*[2] (1)]

cuckoo farm *n.* [1960s+] (*US*) a psychiatric institution. [CUCKOO *n.*[1] (2) + FARM *n.*[3]]

cuckoo house *n.* [1930s+] (*US*) a psychiatric institution. [CUCKOO *n.*[1] (2) + SE *house*]

cuckoo juice *n.* [1960s–70s] (*US*) strong liquor. [CUCKOO *n.*[1] (2) + JUICE *n.*[3] (3); its potency sends one crazy]

cuckoos *n.* [17C] money. [ety. unknown; link to dial. *cuckoo-penny*, a penny that, if turned in the pocket on hearing the first cuckoo, will guarantee cash for the next year]

cuckoo's nest *n.*[1] [late 18C–1960s] the female genitals. [play on SE]

cuckoo's nest *n.*[2] [1960s+] (*US*) a psychiatric institution. [CUCKOO *n.*[1] (2) + SE *nest*]

cuckoo's nest *adj. see* CUCKOO *adj.*

cuckquean *n. see* CUCK *n.*

cucumber *n.*[1] [late 17C–mid-19C] a tailor; thus *cucumber season*, *cucumber time*, the summer time; thus a slack period in a job. [in summer time, when cucumbers ripen, one's best customers, the gentry, were out of London, living on their country estates; tailors trad. took their holidays at this time]

cucumber *n.*[2] [late 19C+] the penis (cf. BANANA *n.*[2]). [resemblance]

cucumber *n.*[3] [20C+] (*Aus.*) a number. [rhy. sl.]

cud *n. see* UD *n.*

cud-chewer *n. see* CHEW THE CUD *v.* (2).

cuddie *n.* [1920s+] (*US Black*) a friend; a lover. [? Devon dial. *cuddy*, a fellow workman; a little girl]

cuddle and kiss *n.* 1 [1930s+] a woman. 2 [1960s+] an act of urination (cf. ANGEL'S KISS *n.*). [rhy. sl. = SE *miss/piss n.* (2)]

cuddle and kissed *adj.* [1960s+] drunk (cf. ADRIAN (QUIST) *adj.*). [rhy. sl. = PISSED *adj.*[1]]

cuddle-bunny *n.* [1940s–50s] (*US*) an affectionate, passionate or sexually alluring young woman. [SE *cuddle* + BUNNY *n.*[1] (2)]

cuddle-cook *n.* [1900s–10s] a policeman (cf. BEAT-POUNDER *n.*). [the popular reputation of contemporary policemen as pursuers of cooks]

cuddy *n.*[1] 1 [early 18C–mid-19C] a donkey. 2 [mid–late 19C] a fool. 3 [20C+] (*Aus./Irish*) a (small) horse. 4 [1960s] (*Irish*) a young girl. [? dial. *cuddy*, a sucking lamb or kid]

cuddy *n.*[2] [mid-19C] one's home, a room. [UK navy *cuddy*, the captain's cabin]

cuddy-wifter *n.* [1950s+] a left-hander. [? link to dial. *cuddy-finger*, a little finger]

cuds *n.* [late 16C–mid-18C] used in oaths as a euph. for *God's*, e.g. *cud's bobs!* God's body!

cudsucker *n.* [1950s] (*US*) a general term of abuse. [euph. for COCKSUCKER *n.* (4)]

cue *n.*[1] [1940s–50s] (*US Black*) a tip. [? mid-15C *cue* or *q* (Lat. *quadrans*), half a farthing]

cue *n.*[2] *see* CU *n.*[1].

cue *v.* [mid–late 19C] (*UK Und.*) to swindle by abusing one's credit. [for ety. *see* GO ON THE LETTER Q *v.*]

cue-ball *n.* [1940s] (*US*) a bald-headed person, or one with a crew cut. [resemblance to a billiard/snooker ball]

cuete *n.* [1960s+] (*US*) a gun. [Sp. *cuete*, a firecracker]

cuff *n.*[1] 1 [early 17C–early 19C] a mean, surly old fellow; often as *old cuff*. 2 [mid–late 17C] a jovial old man. [CUFFIN *n.* (1)]

cuff *n.*[2] [late 19C+] (*US*) credit, both lit. and fig.; thus ON THE CUFF phr.[1]. [the practice of pencilling debts in shops or bars on a celluloid *cuff*]

cuff *n.*[3] *see* CUFFY *n.*

cuff *v.*[1] 1 [late 19C+] (*US Black*) to hit, to fight. 2 [2000s] to defeat (in a competition). [SE *cuff*, to strike with the fist; note Rötwelsch (Ger. rogues' cant) *kuffen*, to thrash]

cuff *v.*[2] [late 19C+] to handcuff. [*OED* (2 edn) offers 2 cits. for *cuff*, to handcuff (1693, 1851), but neither is listed as sl. and the term is 'rare']

cuff *v.*[3] [1930s+] (*US*) 1 to place on credit. 2 to swindle. [CUFF *n.*[2]]

cuff *v.*[4] 1 [1960s+] to hide a (marijuana) cigarette inside the cupped fingers. 2 [1990s+] to hide anything. [one's cuffs help to obscure the cigarette]

cuffa *n. see* CUFFER *n.*

cuff a carrot *v. see* CUFF THE CARROT *v.* (1).

cuff and collar *adj. see* CUFFS AND COLLARS *adj.*

cuff and collar brigade *n. see* CUFFS AND COLLARS *n.*[1].

cuff Anthony *v.* (*also* **cuff Jonas, knock anthony**) [late 18C–early 19C] 1 for one's knees to knock together. 2 to strike the hands under the armpits to warm them. [SE *cuff*, to strike + generic use of *Anthony/Jonas*, a person, oneself]

cuffee *n. see* CUFFY *n.*

cuffer *n.* (*also* **cuffa**) [late 19C–1920s] (*Aus.*) a tale or story. [dial. *cuff*, tell a tale]

cufferoo *adj.* [1940s] (*US*) free. [ON THE CUFF phr.[1] (2) + -EROO sfx]

cuffin *n.* 1 [mid-16C–mid-19C] a man, a fellow. 2 [early 18C] (*UK Und.*) a judge. 3 [mid-19C] (*UK Und.*) a prison warder. [either CUFF *n.*[1] (1); or a simple corruption of COVE *n.* (1)]

cuffin-quire *n.* (*also* **cuffin quier**) [17C–mid-18C] a magistrate. [var. on QUEER CUFFIN *n.* (1)]

cuff Jonas *v. see* CUFF ANTHONY *v.*

cuff-link *n.* [20C+] (*Aus.*) a drink. [rhy. sl.]

cuff-link queen *n.* (*also* **cuff-link faggot, finger-bowl faggot**) [1960s] (*US gay*) a wealthy (older) male homosexual. [SE *cuff-link/finger-bowl* + QUEEN *n.*[2] (1)/FAGGOT *n.*[2] (3)]

cuffo *n.* [1970s] (*US*) credit. [CUFF *n.*[2] + -O sfx (7)]

cuffo *adj.* [1970s] (*US*) free. [CUFFO *n.*]

cuffs *n.* [mid-19C+] (*orig. UK police/Und.*) handcuffs. [abbr.]

cuffs and collars *n.*[1] (*also* **cuff and collar brigade**) [1900s] (*Aus.*) office workers.

cuffs and collars *n.*[2] [1960s+] pubic hair that matches the colour of the visible hair; thus ostensibly proving that a woman is not dyeing her hair.

cuffs and collars *adj.* (*also* **cuff and collar**) [late 19C+] (*Aus.*) middle-class, prissy, pernickety. [smart rather than more casual attire]

cuff-shooter *n.* [late 19C–1900s] a clerk. [his continual 'shooting' of his cuffs]

cuff the carrot *v.* 1 [1970s+] (*US gay/prison*) (*also* **cuff a carrot**) to fellate. 2 [1990s+] to masturbate (cf. BANG THE BISHOP v.; BEAT ONE'S MEAT v.). [SE *cuff* + CARROT n.[1]]

cuff the dummy *v.* [1990s+] (*US*) to masturbate (cf. BANG THE BISHOP v.). [SE *cuff* + DUMMY n.[3]]

cuffy *n.* (*also* **cuff, cuffee**) 1 [early 18C+] (*US*) a Black person, usu. in patronizing/derog. use; thus *cuffyism*, Black society; *proud as cuffy*, conceited, lit. proud as a Black man dressed up in his best clothes (cf. ALLIGATOR BAIT n.[2]). 2 [19C] a bear. 3 [mid–late 19C] a young boy. 4 [1940s+] (*W.I.*) a fool, a gullible person. [Twi *kofi*, a boy born on a Friday. Like other terms based on name-days, the underlying implication is always that of rural simplicity, even stupidity and backwardness]

cufuffle *n. see* KERFUFFLE n.

cuh *n. see* CUZ n.

cuirass *n. see* CURE-ARSE n.

cujo *n.* [1980s+] (*US campus*) a daredevil, one whose personal love for risk-taking tends to put others in danger. [title of *Cujo* (1983), a novel by horror writer Stephen King]

cuke *n. see* CU n.[1].

culch *n.* 1 [mid-19C] second-rate (odds and ends of) meat. 2 [late 19C] (*US*) a derog. description of a person. [southern UK dial. *culch*, rubbish, refuse]

culchie *n.* (*also* **culchy, culshie**) [1940s+] (*Irish*) a derog. term for a country-dweller, as used by a townsperson (cf. BOONIE n.[1]). [coined at University College, Galway, to describe agricultural students; ? Irish *Coillte mach* (Kiltimagh), Co. Mayo; ? Irish *coillte*, woods; ? Irish *cúl a' tí*, the backdoor of the great house, to which peasants would be directed; note Brendan Behan, *Confessions of an Irish Rebel* (1965): 'One night, Culchiemachs, as we call the Irish-speaking people, wished to play a game of pitch and toss']

cule *n.* [mid-19C] (*UK Und.*) a small bag, carried on a woman's arm. [abbr. synon. SE *reticule*]

culican *n.* [1980s+] (*drugs*) high-potency marijuana from Mexico. [proper name *Culican*, the area in which it grows]

culing *n.* (*also* **culling**) [mid-19C] (*UK Und.*) stealing (bags and purses) from carriages, esp. those parked at racecourses. [CULE n. + sfx *-ing*]

cull *n.*[1] 1 [mid-17C–mid-19C] a prostitute's customer. 2 [mid-17C–1930s] a dupe, a silly fellow, a simpleton, a fool. 3 [18C] a constable. 4 [18C–1930s] a man, a fellow, a chap. 5 [mid–late 19C] a friend. [? CULLY n.; ? CULLION n.; ? fig. use of CULLS n.; (1) Bee suggests that the cull was orig. 'a prostitute's favourite' before losing status to become merely 'a customer of any sort who pays for "favors secret, sweet, and precious"']

cull *n.*[2] [1970s] 1 (*US campus*) a socially unacceptable person. 2 (*US campus*) anyone rejected for membership in a fraternity or sorority. 3 (*US prison*) a physically weak convict. [SE *cull*, to select weak animals for killing]

cullability *n. see* CULLIBILITY n.

cull bird *n.* [1980s+] (*US campus*) any woman considered socially or physically unacceptable. [CULL n.[2] (1) + SE *bird*, play on SE]

culley *n. see* CULLY n.

cullibility *n.* (*also* **cullability**) [mid-18C–mid-19C] a willingness to be fooled. [CULL n.[1] (2) + SE *gullibility*]

culling *n. see* CULING n.

cullion *n.* (*also* **cullon**) [mid-16C–17C] a general term of contempt, a base, despicable person, a rascal; thus *cullionly*, despicable, rascally. [Fr. *coïon, coyon*, a poltroon]

cullions *n.* [17C] the testicles (cf. COJONES n.). [Fr. *couillons*, testicles]

cull of the bing *n.* [mid-19C] (*US*) a tavern-keeper. [CULL n.[1] (4) + BINGO n.[1]]

cull of the ken *n.* [18C] (*UK Und.*) the master of the house. [CULL n.[1] (4) + KEN n.[1] (1)]

cullon *n. see* CULLION n.

cullot *n.* [mid-19C] (*US Und.*) a loafer. [ety. unknown]

culls *n.* [17C] the testicles. [abbr. CULLIONS n.]

cully *n.* (*also* **culley**) 1 [mid-17C–19C] a simpleton, a victim. 2 [mid-17C–early 19C] a prostitute's customer. 3 [mid-17C–1910s] a man, a fellow, a companion; often as a term of address. 4 [late 17C–19C] a fop, a dandy. [? as fool there may be links to Ital. *coglione*, a dolt, but as a plain man it may well come from the Sp. Gypsy *chulai* or Turkish Gypsy *khulai*, both meaning man, or poss. fig. use of French *couillon*, testicles (cf. CULLIONS n.)]

cully *v.* [mid-17C–18C] to swindle, to cheat. [i.e. to render a CULLY n. (1)]

cully-rumper *n. see* RUMPER n. (1).

cully-shangy *n.* [19C] sexual intercourse. [Scot. *collie-shangie*, a disturbance, a noisy argument; ? ult. f. the sound of *collie* dogs fighting or f. Gaelic *callaidh*, wrangling, outcry]

culo *n.* [1960s+] (*US*) the buttocks, behind. [Sp. sl. *culo*, the anus]

culp *n.* [late 17C–mid-19C] a blow, a buffet. [Fr. *coup*, a blow; ult. Lat. *colaphus*, a box on the ear, although note SE *culp*, fault, blame]

culshie *n. see* CULCHIE n.

cultural fruit *n.* (*also* **culture fruit**) [1960s+] (*US*) a watermelon. [neg. racial stereotyping; i.e. *Black* cultural fruit]

culture *n.* [1950s+] (*W.I. Rasta*) reflecting or pertaining to the values and traditions respected by Rastafarians.

culture-hound *n.* [1930s] an intellectual, esp. one who is seen as too 'clever' for their own good. [SE *culture* + HOUND sfx]

culture-vulture *n.* 1 [1940s+] (*orig. US*) anyone who battens onto the prevailing cultural trends in order to debase and exploit them for economic gain, irrespective of the aesthetic loss involved. 2 [1940s+] (*US campus*) an over-zealous student. 3 [1980s] (*W.I. Rasta/US Black*) a Rastafarian term for White people. [derog. SE *culture-vulture*, one who is (affectedly) voracious for culture; thus an intellectual; (3) CULTURE n.]

culty-gun *n.* [late 19C] the penis (cf. AX n.[2]). [Lat. *cultellus*, a knife + SE *gun*]

culver-headed *adj.* [mid–late 19C] foolish, weak-minded; thus *culver-head*, a fool, a simpleton (cf. AIRHEADED adj.). [SE *culver*, a dove or young pigeon]

cum *n.*[1] [1960s+] 1 semen. 2 an ejaculation. 3 an orgasm (for either sex). [often found, e.g. in written pornography, as an alternative to COME n.; the sp. enhances the sexual aspect of the otherwise common word]

cum *n.*[2] *see* CUME n.

cum *v.* [1960s+] to achieve orgasm. [CUM n.[1] (3)]

cum-bucket *n. see* COME-BUCKET n.

cum catcher *n. see* CUM DUMPSTER n.

cumchugger *n.* [1990s+] an enthusiastic fellatrix. [CUM n.[1] (1) + CHUG v.[1] (1)]

cum drum *n.* (*also* **come-drum, cundrum**) [1930s+] a condom with a reservoir for semen. [CUM n.[1] (1) + SE *drum* + mispron. of SE *cundum* or *condom*, a contraceptive sheath]

cum dumpster *n.* (*also* **cum catcher**) [1990s+] (*US teen*) a promiscuous girl. [CUM n.[1] (1) + SAmE *dumpster* = UK *skip*]

cume *n.* (*also* **cum**) [1960s+] (*US campus*) one's *cum*ulative grade-point average. [abbr.]

cum-freak *n.* [1960s+] a promiscuous man or woman, obsessed with sexual gratification. [CUM n.[1] (3) + FREAK n.[1] (6)]

cummifo *adj.* [late 19C–1900s] as things should be, satisfactory. [mispron. of Fr. *comme il faut*]

cumshaw *n.* [19C–1950s] a bribe, a tip, a present. [Chinese *kam-sia*, the Amoy pron. of the Chinese words *kan*, to be grateful + *hsieh*, thanks; thus 'grateful thanks']

cum-shot *n.* [1970s+] (*orig. US*) in pornographic film-making, the moment of ejaculation, invariably performed (for the camera) outside the partner's body. [CUM n.[1] (2) + SE *shot*]

cum stain *n. see* COME STAIN n.

cum-sucking adj. [1990s+] (US) a general insult. [CUM n.[1] (1)]

cundrum n. see CUM DRUM n.

cundum n. [late 18C–early 19C] a false scabbard used to hide a sword. [SE cundum or condom, a contraceptive sheath]

cundy n. see COONIE n.[1].

cung n. [1980s+] (drugs) cannabis. [ety. unknown]

cuniculary warehouse n. [early 18C] a brothel (cf. ACCOMMODATION HOUSE n.). [joc. elaboration of CONY n.[1] (3)]

cunker n. (also **kunker**) [1970s+] (US gay) the vagina. [CUNT n.[1] (1)]

cunnel n. [18C–19C] (tinker) a potato. [Shelta]

cunnikin n. (also **cuntkin, cuntlet**) [18C] the vagina. [dimin. of CONY n.[1] (3); ult. CUNT n.[1] (1)]

cunning as a Maori dog phr. (also **cunning as a Maori hen**) [1920s+] (N.Z.) very cunning. [racially derog. comparison]

cunning as a shithouse rat phr. (also **cunning as a sewer rat, shifty as a shithouse rat**) [1940s+] (orig. Aus.) very cunning.

cunning as a (whole) wagon-load of monkeys phr. (also **artful as a (whole) wagon-load of monkeys, cunning as a cartload of monkeys**) [late 19C+] very cunning.

cunningberry n. (also **cunningbury**) [early–mid-19C] a fool, a gullible person. [ironic pun on SE cunning + SE -berry/-bury, a sfx. meaning 'place']

cunningham n. (also **Mr Cunningham**) [late 18C–early 19C] a fool, a gullible person. [ironic pun on SE cunning + SE -ham, a sfx. meaning 'place']

cunning man n. **1** [17C–early 19C] a confidence trickster who used a (spurious) knowledge of astrology to help convince his or (more often) her victims; the preferred swindle was the 'miraculous' recovery of stolen goods. **2** [late 18C–early 19C] a trial judge. [SE; note dial. cunning woman, a witch]

cunning shaver n. [late 18C] a clever cheat. [a pun on SE cunning + SHAVER n.[1] (1), but also one who 'shaves his victims close']

cunny see also under CONY and its combs.

cunny n. [2000s] (UK Black) cunnilingus. [abbr.]

cunny alley n. (also **coney court, cony-hall, cunny court, cunny hall**) [mid-17C–mid-18C] the vagina (cf. ALLEY n.[1]). [CONY n.[1] (2)]

cunny-fingered adj. [1930s] butter-fingered. [CONY n.[1] (2) + SE finger]

cunny-haunted adj. [late 19C] of a male, obsessed with sex. [CONY n.[1] (2) + SE haunted]

cunny-thumbed adj. [late 18C–early 19C; 1920s] 'to double one's fist, with the thumb inwards, like a woman' (Grose, 1785). [CONY n.[1] (2) + SE thumbed]

cunny-thumper n. [1970s] (US) a villain, a rascal. [CONY n.[1] (2); lit. 'vagina-hitter']

cunny warren n. (also **coney warren**) **1** [18C] a brothel (cf. BIRDCAGE n.[1]; CONY-BURROW n.). **2** [18C] a girl's boarding school. **3** [19C] the vagina (cf. AGREEABLE RUTS OF LIFE n.; BIRD n.[8]). [CONY n.[1] (2) + SE warren; the phr. puns on bunny, rabbit]

cunt n.[1] **1** [15C+] (also **cuntie, C**) the vagina. **2** [early 18C; 1930s+] a derog. term for a woman; occas. in male homosexual context. **3** [late 19C+] a woman considered purely as a sex object. **4** [20C+] copulation with a woman. **5** [1940s] (US gay) a joc. 'bitchy' term of address. **6** [1960s+] (US gay) the mouth or rectum as a sexual receptacle. **7** [1960s+] (US gay) the buttocks. **8** [1960s+] commercial sex; prostitution. **9** [1970s+] a sexually attractive woman. **10** [1970s+] any thing, object or place. [orig. ME but taboo since 15C. Cunt itself, 'a nasty word for a nasty thing', as Grose (1788) dismisses it, appears as 'C--t', although he offers roots in the Gk konnos and the Lat. cunnus, and lists the Fr. synon. con. This reticence was by no means limited to Grose (who, a single entry earlier, was perfectly happy to list CUNNY-THUMBED adj.). Not until its supplement of 1972 did the OED (albeit unphased by PRICK n. (2) since the late 19C) list the term, and

other, lesser dictionaries, on both sides of the Atlantic, showed themselves equally coy. Many otherwise authoritative American tomes, hamstrung by either the religious right or the politically correct left, have yet to break the taboo. Yet as E.P., writing in 1931 (6 years before the term was included in his DSUE), put it: 'To ignore a very frequently used word – one indeed used by a large proportion, though not the majority, of the white population of the British Empire – is to ignore a basic part of the English language.' The first use the OED can find for the term appears c.1230, when Gropecuntelane is listed among the streets that made up the 'stews' (brothel area) of Cheapside. Given the environment, it must be assumed that the term was already in general use. It would also appear from subseq. early cits. that the term, while vulgar, was descriptive rather than obscene. Lanfranc, for instance, used it while writing on surgery around 1400. But by the end of the 15C cunt was unacceptable and 2 centuries later it was deemed legally obscene, and to print the word in full rendered one liable to prosecution. Its most notorious appearance in the dock came in 1960 in the trial of Lady Chatterley's Lover. It has yet, if ever, to return to grace. As Grose suggested, the word can be traced back to the Gk, although Partridge disputes whether konnus – a trinket, a beard, or the wearing of the hair in a tuft – is actually linked to the Lat. cunnus, which meant both vagina and, like such English terms as CRACK n.[6] (1), SLIT n.[1] (1) and PUSSY n. (2), the woman who possesses it (esp. if seen as promiscuous). More likely Gk roots are kusos and kusthos, which are both related to the earlier Skrt cushi, meaning ditch. Cunnus itself, setting a pattern for its descendant, was already outlawed as obscene in Rome. Horace used it, Cicero did not. While the French, more heavily influenced by Lat., have con (and the Spanish coño), with its obvious links to cunnus, the English 'cunt' or cunte, as found in ME, takes its inspiration from a variety of Ger. (Kunte) and Scandinavian (kunta, kunte) terms. It would appear, in this form, to be a comb. of the ultimate root cu (which also lies at the basis of cow), which appears to imply quintessential femininity, and the nt of the European synons. Note val cava, 'used by Boccaccio for a woman's private parts, a hollow cavity or valley' (Florio, Worlde of Wordes, 1598)]

cunt n.[2] **1** [20C+] a fool, a dolt, an unpleasant person of either sex; a general term of abuse (cf. BAMBA n.[1]). **2** [1930s+] an infuriating object, often mechanical. **3** [1970s+] a person, usu. male, with no negative implications. **4** [1980s+] something very difficult or unpleasant to do or achieve. [fig. uses of CUNT n.[1] (1); (3) note that in some circumstances cunt, like the US Black use of MOTHERFUCKER n., is so frequent and so repetitive as to virtually lose its shock or taboo value and become a neutral synon. for 'person']

cunt n.[3] [1970s] (drugs) the area of a vein into which one injects narcotics; the crease inside the elbow. [fig. use of CUNT n.[1] (1); it, too, is a hole]

cunt n.[4] [1970s+] a synon. for FUCK n.[2] or DAMN n.; usu. in phrs., e.g. BEAT THE CUNT OUT OF v. [CUNT n.[1] (1)]

cunt adj. [1950s+] a general term of abuse, stupid, unpleasant, incompetent etc. [CUNT n.[2] (1)]

cunt v. [1990s+] to destroy, to defeat, whether physically or otherwise. [fig. use of CUNT n.[1] (1)]

cunt! excl. [1930s+] a general excl. of annoyance. [CUNT n.[1] (1)]

cunt book n. [1970s] (US prison) pornography. [CUNT n.[1] (1) + SE book]

cunt-buster n. [2000s] (US) penis (cf. ARSE-OPENER n.). [CUNT n.[1] (1)]

cunt-chaser n. [1930s] a womanizer. [CUNT n.[1] (1) + SE chaser]

cunt-collar n. [1960s] (US) the supposed entrapment of a man by a woman's sexuality. [CUNT n.[1] (1) + fig. use of COLLAR n.[2] (2); one has been 'arrested' by one's desire]

cunt-curtain n. [late 19C] female pubic hair. [CUNT n.[1] (1) + SE curtain]

cunted *adj.*[1] [late 19C] of a man, having one's penis in a woman's vagina. [CUNT n.[1] (1)]

cunted *adj.*[2] [1990s+] extremely drunk (cf. ARSEHOLED adj.). [fig. use of CUNT n.[1] (1); ? one acts like a CUNT n.[2] (1)]

cunt-eyed *adj.* [1910s+] (*US*) used of a person with narrow, squinting eyes. [fig. use of CUNT n.[1] (1) as a 'slit' + sfx *-eyed*]

cuntface *n.* [late 19C+] a term of address to an unattractive person?. [CUNT n.[1] (1) + SE *face*]

cuntfaced *adj.* (*also* **cuntface**) [1940s+] unattractive. [CUNT-FACE n.]

cunt-fringe *n.* [late 19C] female pubic hair. [CUNT n.[1] (1) + SE *fringe*]

cunt hair *n.* (*also* **pussy hair**) [1950s+] (*US*) an infinitesimally small amount. [CUNT n.[1] (1) + SE *hair*]

cunt-hat *n.* [1920s] a trilby or felt hat. [CUNT n.[1] (1) + SE *hat*; pun on 'felt', i.e. 'felt up'; ? also shape of the trilby (see also DR JIM n.)]

cunthead *n.* [1970s+] (*orig. US*) a fool. [CUNT n.[1] (1) + -HEAD sfx (1)]

cunt-hook *n.* [1990s+] (*UK juv.*) 1 the penis. 2 an insulting term of address. [CUNT n.[1] (1)]

cunt-hooks *n.* (*also* **twat-hooks**) 1 [early 19C; 1950s+] fingers. 2 [1990s+] a term of endearment; occas. used as a casual greeting. [CUNT n.[1] (1) + SE *hooks*]

cunt-hound *n.* [1950s+] a man who is obsessed with sex and seduction. [CUNT n.[1] (1) + HOUND sfx]

cuntie *n. see* CUNT n.[1] (1).

cunting *adj.* [20C+] an intensive term of derision, dismissal etc. [CUNT n.[1] (1) + sfx *-ing*]

cuntish *adj.* [1970s+] 1 stupid, unpleasant. 2 effeminate. [CUNT n.[2] (1)/CUNT n.[1] (2) + sfx *-ish*]

cunt-itch *n.* [18C–19C] sexual enthusiasm in a woman. [CUNT n.[1] (1) + SE *itch*]

cuntkin *n. see* CUNNIKIN n.

cunt-lapper *n.* 1 [1910s+] a cunnilinguist (cf. CUNT-SUCKER n.). 2 [1970s+] (*also* **cuntlap**) a general term of abuse (cf. COCKMUNCH n.). [CUNT n.[1] (1) + SE *lapper*]

cunt-lapping *n.* [1910s+] (*orig. US*) cunnilingus. [CUNT-LAPPER n. (1)]

cunt-lapping *adj.* (*also* **cunt-licking**) [1920s+] (*US*) of a person, despicable, repellent, disgusting. [CUNT-LAPPER n.]

cuntlet *n. see* CUNNIKIN n.

cunt-lick *v.* (*also* **give cunt licks**) [late 19C+] to perform cunnilingus (cf. KISS v.[1]; LAP (UP) n.; LICK v.[2]; LICK A BOX v.; LICK OUT v.[1]; LICK THE HOLY GROUND v.; SUCK v.[1]; TONGUE v.[2]; TONGUE JOB n.; TONGUE PIE n.). [CUNT n.[1] (1) + SE *lick*]

cunt-licker *n.* [1940s+] (*orig. US*) 1 a cunnilinguist. 2 a general term of abuse (cf. COCKMUNCH n.). [CUNT n.[1] (1) + SE *licker*]

cunt-licking *adj. see* CUNT-LAPPING adj.

cunt-lips *n.* [late 19C] the labia (cf. DOUBLE-SUCKER n.; JAWS n.; LOVELIPS n.; POUTER n.). [CUNT n.[1] (1) + SE *lips*]

cunt man *n.* (*also* **C man**) [1960s+] (*US campus*) a sexual athlete. [CUNT n.[1] (1)]

cuntocks *n.* [1990s+] the labia. [CUNT n.[1] (1) + COCK n.[2] (1)]

cunt-pensioner *n.* [19C] a kept man, a pimp (cf. ABBOT ON THE CROSS n.). [CUNT n.[1] (1) + Fr. *pensionaire*, a lodger]

cunt plugger *n.* [late 19C] the penis; thus *cunt plugging*, sexual intecourse (cf. BUTT-PLUNGER n.). [CUNT n.[1] (1)]

cunt positive *adj.* [1970s+] usu. in radical lesbian use, appreciating one's vagina, despite its secondary image in a phallocentric world. [CUNT n.[1] (1)]

cuntprick *n.* [1990s+] a general term of abuse. [CUNT n.[2] (1) + PRICK n. (3)]

cunt-rag *n.* [1940s–70s] a sanitary towel. [CUNT n.[1] (1) + SE *rag*]

cunt-rammer *n. see* RAMMER n. (1).

cunt rug *n.* [1990s+] female pubic hair. [CUNT n.[1] (1) + RUG n.[1] (2)]

cunt scratchers *n.* [1990s+] the hands. [CUNT n.[1] (1) + SE *scratch*]

cuntsmith *n.* [1960s] (*US*) a gynaecologist. [CUNT n.[1] (1) + sfx *-smith* on model of SE *blacksmith*]

cunt-stand *n.* [19C+] sexual enthusiasm in a woman. [CUNT n.[1] (1) + STAND n.[2] (1)]

cunt-starver *n.* [1950s+] (*Aus.*) a man who defaults on his maintenance payments. [CUNT n.[1] (1)+ SE *starver*; + the Deserted Wives & Children's Act, known as the *Cunt Act*]

cunt-stopper *n.* [late 19C] the penis (cf. BUTT-PLUNGER n.). [CUNT n.[1] (1)]

cunt stretcher *n.* [late 19C] the penis. [CUNT n.[1] (1)]

cunt-struck *adj.* [mid-19C+] (of a man) obsessed with sex, or with a particular woman. [CUNT n.[1] (1) + SE *struck*]

cunt-sucker *n.* 1 [1940s+] a cunnilinguist (cf. CUNT-LAPPER n.). 2 [1960s+] (*orig. US*) a repellent, loathed, unpleasant person. 3 [1990s+] (*US*) a derog. term for a lesbian (cf. CARPET-BITER n.). [CUNT n.[1] (1) + SE *sucker*]

cunt swab *n.* [late 19C] female underwear. [CUNT n.[1] (1) + SE *swab*]

cunt-teaser *n.* [20C+] a man who excites a woman sexually but refuses to have intercourse (cf. COCKTEASER n.). [CUNT n.[1] (1) + SE *teaser*]

cunt-tickler *n.* [1960s+] (*US*) a moustache. [CUNT n.[1] (1) + SE *tickler*]

cunt tug *n.* [1990s+] a pubic wig. [CUNT n.[1] (1) + SE *tug* (and it comes off)]

cunt up *adj.* [2000s] wrong, failed. [CUNT n.[1] (1); var. on BELLY UP adj.[2] (1)]

cunt wagon *n.* [1970s+] (*US*) a flashy car seen as an adjunct to the seduction of foolishly impressionable young women. [CUNT n.[1] (1) + SE *wagon*]

cunt-wig *n.* [late 19C] female pubic hair. [CUNT n.[1] (1)]

cunty *n.* [1950s+] a general term of abuse, as a term of address. [CUNTY adj.[1]]

cunty *adj.*[1] [1950s+] despicable, worthless, a general abusive adj. [CUNT n.[2] (1)]

cunty *adj.*[2] [1970s] 1 (*US*) sexy, attractive. 2 (*US gay*) of a man, possessing female qualities; of a place, feminine. [CUNT n.[1] (1)]

cuntyballs *n.* [1990s+] a general term of abuse. [CUNTY adj.[1] + BALLS n.[1] (1)]

cunty booby *adj.* [1990s+] to be completely confused. [CUNTY adj.[1] + BOOBY n.[1]]

cunty Italian *n.* [1970s] a generic name for a type of working-class Italian-American woman. [CUNTY adj.[2] (1) + SE *Italian*]

cup *v.* [early 19C] 1 to toast (a person). 2 to imprison.

cup and can *n.* [mid-16C–mid-19C] of 2 people, great friends. [a cup is filled from a can; thus one friend nourishes the other]

Cupar justice *n.* (*also* **Coupar justice, Couper justice**) [18C] execution without trial, i.e. hanging first and asking questions afterwards. [the alleged system in the Scottish town of *Cupar*]

cupboard *n.* [mid-19C] (*US*) the stomach.

cupboard love *n.* [18C] insincere love, however earnestly protested. [the orig. cupboard was open; thus such love is displayed rather than felt; SE f. early 19C]

cupboardy *adj.* [late 19C] close, stuffy. [the claustrophobia of a closed cupboard]

cupcake *n.* 1 [1930s+] (*US*) an attractive young woman; also as an affectionate term of address. 2 [1970s] (*US gay*) a young homosexual man. [fig. uses of SE *cupcake*, a cake baked from ingredients measured by the cupful, or baked in a small cup]

cupcakes *n.*[1] 1 [1960s+] (*US*) the female breasts (cf. APPLES n.[1]). 2 [1970s+] (*US gay*) buttocks, esp. when tight, firm and small (cf. BAKERY GOODS n.). 3 [1990s+] (*US prison*) a male homosexual. [SE *cupcake*/CUPCAKE n.]

cupcakes *n.*[2] [1980s+] (*US drugs*) LSD (cf. A n.[3]).

cupid *n.*[1] [mid-18C–early 19C] a nickname for an ugly blind man. [*Cupid*, as the god of love, is trad. blind]

cupid n.[2] [late 19C] a pimp who lives with his prostitute. [ironic use; the relationship is rarely so affectionate]

cupid's alley n. (also cupid's anvil, ...arbour, ...arms, ...cave, ...cloister, ...cupboard, ...feast, ...furrow, ...hotel, ...warehouse) [late 17C–19C] the vagina (cf. ADAM'S OWN (ALTAR) n.; AGREEABLE RUTS OF LIFE n.; ALLEY n.[1]). [literary euph.]

cupid's itch n. [1920s+] (US) gonorrhoea. [SE Cupid, the god of love + SE itch]

cupid's kettledrums n. (also kettledrums) [late 18C–early 19C] the female breasts (cf. BAGS n.[1]). [SE Cupid, the god of love + SE kettledrums]

cupid's measles n. [1940s+] (US) secondary syphilis. [SE Cupid, the god of love + SE measles; i.e. the pustules that are a sign of the disease]

cupid's torch n. (also cupid's lance, torch of love) [19C] the penis. [SE Cupid, the god of love + SE torch]

cupid's warehouse n. see CUPID'S ALLEY n.

cupman n. [mid–late 19C] a drunkard.

cup of tea n. 1 [late 19C+] a person, esp. in a teasing context, e.g. you're a nice cup of tea, aren't you? 2 [20C+] a comfort, a consolation, usu. of a person. 3 [1930s+] (also bowl of soup, cuppa, dish of tea, mug of gin, plate of meat) one's preference or taste, that which one chooses; often as not my cup of tea. [SE cup of tea as a restorative or a dependable pleasure]

cupola n. [late 19C–1950s] (US) the head. [SE cupola, a rounded vault or dome forming the roof of a building or part of a building]

cuppa n.[1] (also cupper) [1930s+] (orig. Aus.) a cup of tea.

cuppa n.[2] see CUP OF TEA n. (3).

cups n. [1930s–50s] (US Black) sleep. [the implication being that the sleep is a drunken one]

cup-shaken adj. [early–mid-17C] drunk (cf. ALED UP adj.).

cupshot adj. [mid-16C–mid-19C] drunk (cf. ALED UP adj.). [fig. shot by one's consumption of cups]

cup-sprung adj. see SPRUNG adj.

cup too low n. [late 17C–early 18C] one who remains silent in company. [they need another cup to become more loquacious]

cup-tosser n. 1 [mid-19C] a juggler. 2 [mid–late 19C] a fortune-teller who uses tea leaves (occas. coffee grounds) as a medium of prediction.

cura n. [1960s–70s] (US drugs) heroin, esp. when it is injected or smoked when one is suffering from withdrawal symptoms. [Sp. cura, a cure]

curate n. 1 [late 19C] a small poker, with an iron tip; such a poker is actually used, as opposed to the elaborate brass fire-irons that are only for show. 2 [late 19C] a handkerchief that is actually used rather than one that is worn for fashionable display. 3 [late 19C] the top half of a sliced teacake, which receives less butter. 4 [late 19C–1900s] (Anglo-Irish) a grocer's assistant. 5 [late 19C–1940s] (Irish) an assistant barman. [all play on the junior, and thus inferior, position of a curate in the local church hierarchy]

curate's delight n. [late 19C–1930s] a layered cakestand. [note CURATE n. (3)]

curb n. (also kerb) [late 16C–early 17C] (UK Und.) a pole with a hook on one end that is used to steal items from stall or shop windows. [SE curb, to bend]

curb v. (also kerb) [late 16C] (UK Und.) to use a hook on a pole to steal from stalls, windows or open shop fronts. [CURB n.]

curber n. (also curb) [late 16C–mid-17C] (UK Und.) a villain who steals by extracting goods from an open window. [CURB n.]

curbie n. [1990s+] (US juv.) lit. a student who smokes between classes on the curb outside the school; thus any rebellious schoolchild. [SE curb + sfx -ie]

curbing law n. [late 16C–early 19C] (UK Und.) theft accomplished by 'fishing' for objects through open windows, using some form of hooked pole. [CURB n. or SE curb, the roadside, from which vantage point the criminal operates + LAW n.[1]]

curb-preach v. [1990s+] (US Black) to lecture, to give advice.

curb sailor n. see CURBSTONE SAILOR n.

curbstone see also under KERBSTONE and its combs.

curbstone n. (also kerbstone) [1920s–30s] (US tramp) a cigarette made from the remains of extinguished cigarettes dropped in the gutter. [SE curbstone/kerbstone]

curbstone adj. (also kerbstone) [mid-19C+] a general term for informal, casual, often quasi-legal. [SE curbstone/kerbstone, i.e. that which is delivered in the street]

curbstone broker n. (also curbstoner, kerbstone broker) 1 [mid-19C] anyone who operates an informal and poss. illicit business. 2 [mid-19C–1900s] a street urchin. [CURBSTONE adj. + SE broker; (1) orig. used of the brokers of the New York Stock Exchange who were excluded from the reorganization of the institution in 1848 when it left the street, where it had operated, and moved indoors]

curbstone canary n. (also kerbstone canary) [1930s] (US tramp) a whingeing beggar. [SE curbstone + ironic use of CANARY n.[6]]

curbstone chapel n. [late 19C] (US Und.) preaching or using religiosity to obtain money.

curbstone justice n. (also kerbstone justice) [mid-19C] (US) rough justice, delivered impromptu and without benefit of official warning of criminal proceedings, typically the policeman's 'clip around the ear' delivered to errant youngsters. [CURBSTONE adj. + SE justice]

curbstone mixture n. (also kerbstone mixture, ...plug, ...twist) [1930s–50s] tobacco that is extracted from discarded 'fag-ends' and recycled in a pipe or 'roll-up'. [SE curbstone/kerbstone + mixture]

curbstone philosopher n. (also curbstone orator, kerbstone philosopher) [1920s] anyone who appoints themselves a purveyor of knowledge and delivers that knowledge from a position on a street corner or outside a store. [CURBSTONE adj. + SE philosopher]

curbstoner n. see CURBSTONE BROKER n.

curbstone sailor n. (also curb sailor, kerbstone sailor) [mid-19C+] a prostitute (cf. NIGHT WALKER n.). [CURBSTONE adj. + SE sailor; i.e. she 'sails' the streets]

curbstone setter n. (also kerbstone setter) [1930s+] (US) a mongrel. [CURBSTONE adj. + SE setter, a breed of dog]

curby n. [1930s] (US) a waiter or waitress who serves customers in their parked car. [SE curb + sfx -y]

curby hocks n. [mid-19C–1900s] round or clumsy feet. [SE curby hocks, the hock or other part of a horse's leg which is afflicted by a hard swelling]

curdle v. (also sour) [1930s–40s] 1 (US Und.) of a scheme or plan, to go wrong, to misfire. 2 (US) to irritate, to cause annoyance.

curdler n. [mid–late 19C] a blood-curdling story; a nightmare, a fright.

cure n. [mid–19C–1930s] an eccentric person. [abbr. SE curiosity or curious person]

cure v. (US drugs) 1 [1960s+] to improve the quality of a batch of marijuana; methods include steeping it in rum or some other spirit, placing it in the deep freeze, mixing it with another variety of marijuana or some other drug and so on. 2 [1960s+] to mix 2 drugs together to create a greater level of enjoyment. 3 [1980s+] to heat hashish so that it is easier to crumble and thus use in a cigarette or pipe. [SE cure, to improve, applied to a variety of substances including leather, rubber and plastic]

cure-arse n. (also cuirass) [late 18C–early 19C] an absorbent plaster applied to buttocks and thighs that have been chafed by too much riding. [SE cure + ARSE n.[1] (1)]

cured of a tympany with two heels, be v. [mid-17C] to give birth. [SE cured + TYMPANY WITH TWO HEELS n.]

curfuffle *n. see* KERFUFFLE n.

curious *adj.* [early–mid-19C] (*US*) excellent, first-rate. [obs. SE *curious*, of objects, carefully, delicately or beautifully made; of people, exact, punctilious, expert]

curl *n.*[1] [1960s] (*Aus.*) a term of address. [SE *curly*, one who has curly hair]

curl *n.*[2] (*also* **curler**) [1990s+] a piece of excrement. [resemblance]

curl *n.*[3] *see* CURLE n.

curl, the *n.* [1970s+] (*US Black*) a Jheri curl. [*Jheri* Redding, who in the 1970s invented this Black hairstyle, in which the normal tight curls of Black hair are replaced by straighter, softer curls, with a shiny wet look]

curl *v.* [mid-19C–1910s] (*US campus*) to do well in class, esp. to recite faultlessly; thus *curler*, a first-rate student. [? the curlicues and flourishes that adorn the handwriting of a good calligrapher. Good students would be assumed to write well as part of their overall excellence]

curl-case *n.* [1910s] a hat.

curle *n.* (*also* **curl**) [late 17C–18C] clippings from money. [the slivers of metal curled as they were clipped]

curled darlings *n.* [late 19C–1900s] (*UK society*) army officers, esp. those who had returned from fighting in the Crimean War (1854–6); by ext. one who is spoiled. [the long beards and curled moustaches such officers sported]

curler *n.*[1] [early–mid-19C] (*UK Und.*) one who 'sweats' gold coins by rubbing them together to procure gold dust. [CURLE n.]

curler *n.*[2] *see* CURL n.[2].

curler *n.*[3] *see* CURL v.

curlicue *n. see* CARLEYCUE n.

curlies *n. see* SHORT AND CURLIES n.

curl one off *v.* (*also* **curl one out**) [1990s+] to defecate (cf. BACK ONE OUT v.). [CURL n.[2]]

curl paper *n.* [late 19C] lavatory paper. [SE *curl*, i.e. its shape (the link to CURL n.[2] is coincidental) + SE *paper*]

curls *n.* [early 19C] human teeth, esp. as extracted by body-snatchers.

curl someone's hair *v.* [20C+] (*orig. US*) to scold severely. [note PUT SOMEONE'S HAIR IN(TO) A CURL v. (2)]

curl someone up *v.* [late 19C] (*US*) to kill someone.

curl-the-mo *adj.* (*also* **kurl-the-mo**) [1940s+] (*Aus.*) excellent, first-rate, a good deal, e.g. *curl-the-mo mazuma*, a great deal of money. [CURL THE MO v.]

curl the mo *v.* (*also* **kurl the mo**) [1920s+] (*Aus.*) to succeed brilliantly, to win. [SE *curl* + MO n.[1] (1); the image of a man curling the tips of his moustache in a self-satisfied manner]

curly *n.* [1910s+] a nickname for a bald person. [heavy-handed irony]

curly *adj.* [1930s+] (*N.Z.*) of a person, attractive; of an object or event, first-rate. [SE *curly* hair being seen as attractive]

curly fellas/hairs *n. see* SHORT AND CURLIES n.

curlyhead *n.* [early 19C] (*US*) a derog. term for a Black person (cf. BRILLOHEAD n.).

curly locks *n.* [20C+] (*Aus.*) socks. [rhy. sl.]

curly one *n.* [1950s+] (*mainly Aus./N.Z.*) a tricky problem, a challenge. [it is not 'straight']

curly teapot *n.* [1920s] the penis. [? the pot's spout]

curly water *n.* [20C+] (*Ulster*) a mix of sugar and water that will, allegedly, help one's hair curl.

curly wolf *n.* [1910s+] a tough, tricky individual. [qualities of the animal, but note CURLY ONE n.]

curly-wurly *n.* [2000s] a Hasidic, i.e. ultra-orthodox, Jew (cf. BIGNOSE n.). [the curled sidelocks or *payess* that are worn by Hasidic Jews]

curp *n.* (*also* **kcirp**, **kerp**) [1970s+] the penis. [backsl. = PRICK n. (2)]

currant bread *adj.* [1990s+] dead. [rhy. sl.]

currant bun *n.* **1** [1930s+] the sun. **2** [1940s+] the number 1.

3 [1960s] (*Aus.*) a German, i.e 'Hun'. **4** [1960s+] one's son. **5** [1980s] (*Aus.*) a nun. **6** [1980s] (*Aus.*) a gun. **7** [1980s+] *The Sun* newspaper. [rhy. sl.]

currant cake *adj.* [1960s–80s] (*Aus.*) awake. [rhy. sl.]

currant-cakey *adj.* [1920s+] shaky. [rhy. sl.]

currants and plums *n.* [mid-19C] 3 pence. [rhy. sl. = THRUMS n. (1)]

currency *n.* [19C] (*Aus.*) a person born in Australia; thus *currency lad/lass*, an young Australian-born man or woman.

curry *n. see* CURRY-MUNCHER n.

curry and rice *n.* [1950s+] (*Aus.*) the price. [rhy. sl.]

curry bunny *n.* [1950s+] (*S.Afr.*) vegetarian curry sold as a take-away in a hollowed-out half loaf of bread. [for ety. *see* BUNNY CHOW n.]

curry-muncher *n.* (*also* **curry**, **curry-eater**) [20C+] (*Aus./N.Z.*) a derog. term for an Indian (cf. CURRY-NIGGER n.; DOTHEAD n.). [culinary stereotyping]

curry-nigger *n.* [2000s] (*US Black*) an Indian, a Hindu (cf. CURRY-MUNCHER n.). [SE *curry* + NIGGER n.[1] (5)]

curry queen *n.* [1990s+] (*US*) a gay man who is attracted to Indian homosexuals. [SE *curry* as a staple Indian food + QUEEN n.[2] (1)/QUEEN sfx (2)]

curse *n.*[1] *see* CURSE OF GOD n.[2].

curse *n.*[2] *see* CUSS n.[1] (1).

curse, the *n.* [20C+] a euph. for a menstrual period. [abbr. SE *the curse of Eve*]

curse a blue streak *v. see* TALK A BLUE STREAK v.

cursed-cull *n.* [late 17C–18C] a person who is very ill-natured, esp. towards women. [SE *cursed* + CULL n.[1] (2)]

curse of God *n.*[1] [early 19C] a cockade. [the cockades worn by the atheistic French revolutionaries]

curse of God *n.*[2] (*also* **curse**, **curse of Cain**) [1920s–50s] (*Aus.*) the bundle or pack carried by an itinerant worker or tramp.

curse of Scotland *n.* **1** [late 18C–early 19C] the 9 of diamonds. **2** [20C+] whisky. [diamonds imply royalty and, according to legend, every 9th king of Scotland was 'a tyrant and a curse to that country' (Grose, 1785). A further suggestion is that the 9 of diamonds resembles the arms of the Duke of Argyll, who was one of the leading proponents of union with England, a move that was not wholly welcomed by his compatriots. Hotten (1860) suggests that this card was that on which 'Butcher' Cumberland wrote the orders for the mopping up of rebels after Culloden (1746); that 9 lozenges are the arms of John Dalrymple, Earl of Stair, 'detested for his share in the Massacre of Glencoe'; and that the arrangement of diamonds resembles the St Andrew's Cross; but he concludes that 'the most probable explanation is that in the game of Pope Joan the 9 of diamonds is the Pope, of whom the Scots have an especial horror']

Curse of the Pharaohs *n.* [1990s+] food poisoning, epitomized by diarrhoea suffered by tourists in Egypt (cf. AZTEC HOP n.).

curse out *v.* [1950s+] to become abusive, to swear at.

cursetor *n.*[1] (*also* **cursitor**) [mid-16C–early 18C] a tramp, spec. one of the Forty-second Order of Vagabonds. [ext. of SE *cursitor*, a courier; ult. Lat. *currere*, to run]

cursetor *n.*[2] (*also* **cursitor**) [late 18C] one of the 'broken, petti-fogging attornies or Newgate solicitors' (Grose, 1785). [SE *cursitor*, 'one of twenty-four officers or clerks of the Court of Chancery, whose office it was to make out all original writs *de cursu*, i.e. of common official course or routine, each for the particular shire or shires for which he was appointed' (*OED*); ult. Lat. *currere*, to run]

curtail *n. see* CURTAL n.

curtain climber *n.* (*also* **curtain puller**) [1960s–70s] (*US*) a small child. [its habits]

curtain lecture *n.* (*also* **curtain sermon**) **1** [mid-17C–1900s] a telling-off from a wife to her husband (occas. vice versa), after they have gone to bed. **2** [1960s] a telling-off on the quiet. [the curtains in question are those of a 4-poster bed]

curtains n.[1] [20C+] the end, finality; usu. in phr. *It'll be curtains for you*. [theatrical imagery, i.e. the curtains that come down to signal the end of a play]

curtains n.[2] [1970s+] **1** (*US gay*) the foreskin; thus *draw the curtains*, to fellate an uncircumcised penis. **2** the labia (cf. BEEF CURTAINS n.).

curtain sermon n. *see* CURTAIN LECTURE n.

curtal n. (*also* **curtail, curtall**) **1** [mid-16C–18C] a mendicant villain, one of the CANTING CREW n., distinguished by his short cloak, similar to that of the Grey Friars. **2** [late 16C–early 17C] a general insult. **3** [early 17C] a penis. **4** [early 17C–early 18C] a prostitute. **5** [18C] a cut-purse. **6** [18C–early 19C] a thief who cuts off pieces of silk, cloth, linen etc hanging from shop windows. [SE *curtal*, anything docked or cut short (orig. a horse's tail)]

curve n. **1** [late 19C–1920s] (*US*) a personal peculiarity. **2** [20C+] an occasion of unfair or surprising treatment; usu. in phr. THROW A CURVE v.; thus *get onto the curves*, to understand. **3** [1920s+] an attractive young woman. [baseball imagery]

curveball n. [1940s+] (*US*) a tricky or unexpected question or action. [baseball imagery]

curve-buster n. (*also* **curve-killer**) [1960s] (*US campus*) a student whose grades exceed the average. [such grades are above the average curve plotted on a graph]

cus n. *see* CUZ n.

cush n.[1] **1** [late 19C+] (*US*) (*also* **koosh, kush**) money. **2** [1900s] (*US Und.*) a bank teller; a cashier. **3** [1920s] (*US*) a tip.

cush n.[2] [1940s] something easy. [CUSH adj.[2]]

cush n.[3] (*also* **kush**) [1940s–60s] **1** the vagina; thus a woman seen strictly as a sex object. **2** sexual intercourse with a woman. [Arabic *cush*, the vagina]

cush adj.[1] [late 19C+] (*Aus.*) fair, honourable. [? CUSHY adj. (1)]

cush adj.[2] [1900s–10s] easy, comfortable, undemanding. [CUSHY adj. (1)]

cushat n. [19C] the vagina. [SE *cushat*, a wood pigeon or ring dove]

cushdi adj. *see* CUSHTY adj.

cushiness n. [1930s+] soft, comfortable circumstances. [CUSHY adj. (1)]

cushion n. [1950s+] (*drugs*) a vein into which a drug is injected. [it is 'plumped up' for the injection]

cushion-cuffer n. [late 17C–mid-18C] a parson.

cushion-duster n. [early 18C–early 19C] a parson. ['many of whom, in the fury of their eloquence, heartily belabour their cushions' (Grose, 1796)]

cushions n.[1] [1910s–40s] (*US Und.*) a passenger train; thus a day coach on such a train.

cushions n.[2] [1960s+] (*US gay*) the buttocks.

cushion-smiter n. [mid–late 19C] a parson.

cushion-thumper n. (*also* **thump-(the)-cushion**) [mid-17C–1930s] a parson.

cushty adj. (*also* **cushdi, cushti, custy**) **1** [1930s+] first-rate, excellent, enjoyable; also as excl. **2** [2000s] on good terms, involved with sexually. **3** [2000s] physically comfortable. [Rom. *kushto, kushti*, good; (1) widely popularized by the 1980s BBC TV series *Only Fools and Horses*]

cushty adv. [1930s+] easily. [CUSHY adj. (1)]

cushty phr. [1910s+] (*orig. costermonger*) good luck. [Rom. *kushto, kushti*, good]

cushy adj. **1** [late 19C+] soft, comfortable, easy. **2** [1970s] (*US*) of a person, soft-bodied. [? Rom. *kushto*, good or Hind. *khush*, pleasure]

cushy adv. [1970s] comfortably. [CUSHY adj. (1)]

cushy number n. *see* NUMBER n.[3] (3).

cuss n.[1] **1** [late 17C+] (*also* **curse, cuss-o'thunder**) a man, a fellow, a person; often as *old cuss*. **2** [mid–late 19C] an animal. **3** [1900s] an object, a thing. [? abbr. SE *customer*]

cuss n.[2] **1** [mid-19C+] a curse. **2** [20C+] obscenities, taboo language. [SE *curse*]

cuss v. **1** [mid-19C+] (*also* **cuss down, cuss off, cuss out**) to abuse verbally, to insult. **2** [2000s] (*UK teen*) to abuse a person's parents with the direct intent of forcing them to lose their temper; a UK version of the DOZENS n. [SE *curse*/CUSS n.[2]]

cuss a blue streak v. *see* TALK A BLUE STREAK v.

cuss-cuss n. [1940s+] (*W.I./UK Black*) a quarrel or fracas, with lots of cursing. [CUSS v. (1)+ redup.]

cuss down v. *see* CUSS v. (1).

cussed adj. [mid-19C+] cursed, damned. [SE *curse*]

cussedness n. [mid-19C–1930s] (*US*) malignity, perversity, cantankerousness, contrariness. [SE *cursed*]

cuss off v. *see* CUSS v. (1).

cuss-o'thunder n. *see* CUSS n.[1] (1).

cuss out v. *see* CUSS v. (1).

cuss-word n. [late 19C+] (*US*) an obscenity, an oath. [CUSS n.[2] (1) + SE *word*]

custard n. [1950s+] (*Aus.*) semen (cf. BABY GRAVY n.). [resemblance]

custard and jelly n. [1960s+] television. [rhy. sl. = TELLY n.]

custard arse n. [1980s+] (*Aus. prison*) one who has large buttocks, esp. used of prison officers.

custard pie n. [1990s+] (*US teen*) the female genitals.

custards n. [1920s+] (*Aus.*) pimples, acne. [the yellow pus such eructations contain]

customer n. **1** [early 19C+] a person; usu. in combs, e.g. *tough customer*; UGLY CUSTOMER n. **2** [mid-19C] an animal. [the image of humans as consumers]

custom house n. [late 17C–19C] the vagina (cf. BANK n.[1]). [in which punning institution 'Adam made the first entry']

custom house goods n. [late 18C–19C] the vagina (cf. BANK n.[1]). ['the stock in trade of a prostitute, because fairly entered' (Grose, 1796)]

custom house officer n. [mid-19C] a laxative pill. [pun on permitting goods to 'pass through']

customs officer n. [late 18C] the penis. [he 'works' in the CUSTOM HOUSE n.]

custy adj. *see* CUSHTY adj.

cut n.[1] [17C; late 19C+] a share, of profits, of loot, of the proceeds of a robbery etc.

cut n.[2] **1** [late 18C+] an act of ignoring a friend or acquaintance both deliberately and pointedly. **2** [mid–late 19C] one who deliberately avoids another person. **3** [1980s+] (*US*) an insult. [CUT v.[3] (1)]

cut n.[3] [mid-19C+] (*US campus*) **1** absenting oneself from a class. **2** the failure of a class to meet. [CUT v.[2] (3)]

cut n.[4] **1** [late 19C+] a go, an attempt. **2** [20C+] (*Aus./US/UK*) a swing with the fist; thus *take a cut at*, to menace or hit with the fist. [SE *cut*, a blow]

cut n.[5] **1** [1930s] the dilution of alcohol. **2** [1950s+] (*drugs*) an act of diluting a pure drug, usu. heroin or cocaine; thus *two-cut*, dilution with the same amount of an adulterant. **3** [1980s+] an adulterant. **4** [1990s+] a drug that has been thus diluted.

cut n.[6] [1940s+] (*US*) a vinyl record.

cut n.[7] **1** [1950s–60s] (*US Black*) a place or area where young people meet, e.g. a street corner, a drugstore, a house. **2** [2000s] (*US prison*) the area immediately surrounding an inmate's bunk. [the area is 'cut out' from its surroundings]

cut n.[8] [1950s+] (*orig. US sporting*) a pre-arranged point at which a group of competitors or recruits to a team are reduced by those who fail to achieve a given standard; thus *make the cut*, to continue on the team, in the competition etc; also in fig. non-sporting use.

cut n.[9] [1990s+] a recently received hair*cut*. [abbr.]

cut n.[10] *see* CENTRAL CUT n.

cut, the n. [1990s+] (*US Black*) the ghetto, the poor side of town.

[SE *cut*, a passage; thus note *The Cut*, London SE1, one of 19C London's best-known street markets; also f. the knives wielded in such a place (Major, *Juba to Jive: A Dict. of Afro-American Slang*, 1994)]

cut *adj.*[1] [mid-17C+] drunk. [abbr. CUT IN THE BACK adj. (1)]

cut *adj.*[2] [mid-19C+] angry, upset, hurt. [abbr. CUT UP adj.[1] (2)]

cut *adj.*[3] [1920s+] (*drugs*) adulterated, diluted, weakened; also of drink. [CUT v.[10]]

cut *adj.*[4] [1970s+] (*US gay*) circumcised.

cut *adj.*[5] (*also* **cut up**) [1980s+] (*US*) of a person, with well-defined or well-developed muscles. [the muscles are 'cut out' and thus defined from the rest of the body]

cut *v.*[1] **1** [16C–mid-19C] (*UK Und.*) to speak, to talk. **2** [20C+] (*W.I.*) to speak a language; esp. as *cut — good*. [E.P. suggests abbr. of the participle of Lat. *loquor, locutus*, spoken]

cut *v.*[2] **1** [mid-16C–19C] to walk, to go; usu. with a prep., e.g. *along, down, over, through*. **2** [mid-17C+] to leave, to desert, to run off, to escape. **3** [mid-19C+] to absent oneself without good reason. **4** [1980s+] to turn; thus *cut a left, cut a right*. [(1) 20C+ use is SE]

cut *v.*[3] **1** [mid-17C+] to ignore deliberately; often ext. as *cut dead*. **2** [late 18C+] to ignore a task, rule or obligation, e.g. homework or a college curfew. **3** [1960s+] (*US Black*) to put someone in their place by a verbal attack, to reprimand, to scold.

cut *v.*[4] [late 17C+] to pose as, to act in the manner of. [abbr. SE *cut a figure*]

cut *v.*[5] **1** [mid-19C] to stop doing something; thus *cut that*, be quiet, stop that. **2** [mid-19C+] to resign from, to leave a job. **3** [1930s+] to switch off. **4** [1960s] to switch (on).

cut *v.*[6] **1** [mid-19C] to compete in business. **2** [late 19C+] to manage, to achieve; usu. as CUT IT v.[2]. **3** [1930s+] (*US Black*) to surpass, to outdo. **4** [1960s] (*US campus*) to understand. **5** [1970s] to be convincing, to be as one wishes.

cut *v.*[7] [mid-19C+] of a man, to have sexual intercourse (cf. BANG v.[1]). [the image of the penis as a knife]

cut *v.*[8] [late 19C+] (*orig. US*) to stab.

cut *v.*[9] **1** [late 19C+] to divide, to receive or take a share, e.g. of a manager who takes a percentage of an artist's or sportsman's earnings or of criminals dividing up loot. **2** [1970s+] to give.

cut *v.*[10] **1** [1920s+] to adulterate alcohol, typically of bootleggers making illicit liquor. **2** [1930s+] (*drugs*) to dilute a drug with some adulterant; thus CUTTING n.[2]. **3** [1980s+] (*orig. US*) to adulterate one's position, to sacrifice one's standards, to equivocate.

cut *v.*[11] [1940s–80s] (*Aus./N.Z.*) to finish, e.g. a drink. [SE *cut off*]

cut *v.*[12] *see* CUT (A DEAL) v.

cut! *excl.* [mid-19C+] **1** be quiet! **2** go away! [CUT v.[5] (1)]

cut a block with a razor *v.* (*also* **cut blocks with a razor**) [mid-18C–19C] to make a futile and absurd attempt at something.

cut a bosh *v.* [mid-18C–mid-19C] (*UK Und.*) to cut a figure. [ety. unknown; ? Fr. *ébauche*, outline, a rough-hewn figure]

cut above *n.* [early 19C+] a degree or stage above, esp. socially.

cut a buck *v. see* BUCK n.[1] (3).

cut a bum card *v.* [17C] (*UK Und.*) to cheat at cards by using one that has a slightly raised surface. [? 14C colloq. *bum*, the buttocks, which are 'raised' from the plane of the back; although the meaning is alluring, the use of BUM adj. (1)is mid-19C+]

cut a cake *v. see* FROST A CAKE v.

cut a caper upon nothing *v.* [late 17C] to be hanged.

cut (a deal) *v.* [1970s+] (*orig. US*) to compromise, to make an arrangement, to make a deal?.

cut a dido *v. see* CUT UP A DIDO v.

cut a finger *v.* [late 19C–1900s] to break wind. [euph.]

cut a flash *v.* [late 18C–mid-19C] to act in a vulgar manner, to show off (cf. CUT THE FLASH v.). [CUT v.[4] + FLASH adj.[1] (1), i.e. 'pose']

cut a gut *v.* [1920s+] (*US*) to make a mistake, esp. an embarrassing one. [the butchering of an animal, when a slip of the knife, typically into the gall-bladder, can ruin the meat]

cut a hog *v.* [20C+] (*US*) **1** to make a mistake. **2** to fail in a task, esp. when it is beyond one's abilities.

cut a joke *v.* [late 18C–mid-19C] to talk, to tell a joke. [CUT v.[1] (1)]

cut a knot *v.* [2000s] (*US prison*) to assault a fellow inmate.

cut a lock *v. see* LOCK n.[2] (3).

cut a melon *v.* [20C+] (*US*) to divide up, esp. the spoils of a large coup or a crime. [fig. use of SE + CUT v.[9] (1)]

cut a mug *v.* [early–mid-19C] to make faces,e.g. of a clown or comedian. [CUT v.[4] + MUG n.[1] (3)]

cut and carried *adj.* [1930s+] married. [rhy. sl.]

cut and come again *n.* **1** [late 17C–19C] plenty, abundance. **2** [19C] the vagina. [fig. and punning use of 'Meat that cries come Eat me' (B.E.)]

cut-and-come-again *adj.* [1900s] (*Aus.*) persistent, indomitable. [CUT AND COME AGAIN n. (1)]

cut and run *v.* [19C+] to run off, to escape. [naut. jargon *cut and run*, cut one's cable and run before the wind; note CUT v.[2] (2)]

cut and tuck *n.* [1980s+] (*Aus. prison*) a male-to-female sex-change operation. [shorthand for the surgery involved]

cut a rug *v. see* CUT THE RUG v.

cut a rusty *v.* (*also* **cut some rusty**) [mid-19C+] (*US*) to show off, to behave in a silly, unsophisticated manner; to have a tantrum. [CUT v.[4] + SE *rustic*, a peasant]

cut a sham *v.* [late 17C–early 18C] to hoax, to trick. [CUT v.[4] + SHAM n.[1] (1)]

cut a shine *v.*[1] [19C] to play (practical) jokes. [CUT v.[4] + ? SE *shine*]

cut a shine *v.*[2] *see* CUT A SPLASH v.

cut a shuck *v.* [1970s] (*US*) to leave.

cut a side (of beef) *v.* [1980s+] (*US Black*) to have sexual intercourse. [CUT v.[7] + SIDE n.[4] + BEEF n.[1] (6); play on SE/music use *cut a side*, to make a record]

cut a slice (off the joint) *v.* (*also* **knock…**, **take…**) [late 18C+] of a man, to have sexual intercourse. [SE *cut*/CUT v.[7]; esp. with a married woman, since pvb 'a slice of a cut loaf is never missed']

cut a splash *v.* (*also* **cut a shine**, **…spludge**, **…splurge**, **make a shine**, **…splash**) [late 18C+] (*orig. US*) to be very well known or successful, to cut a 'fine figure'. [CUT v.[4] + SPLASH n.[1]/SE *shine/spludge/splurge*]

cut ass *v.* [1950s–60s] (*US*) to leave, to run off. [CUT v.[2] (2) + ASS n. (5)]

cut a swat *v.* [late 19C] (*US campus*) to make an impression. [SE *cut a swathe*]

cut a swell *v. see* SWELL n. (1).

cut a tooth *v.* (*also* **cut one's eye-teeth**, **…gums**, **…teeth**) [19C+] to become aware, knowing. [fig. use of SE; cutting teeth is a sign of growing older]

cut a U *v.* [1980s] (*US*) to make a U-turn. [CUT v.[2] (4) + abbr.]

cut away *v.*[1] (*also* **cut off**) [late 17C+] to leave, to run off. [CUT v.[2] (2)]

cut away *v.*[2] [early 19C] to strike a blow.

cut a wheedle *v.* [late 18C–early 19C] (*UK Und.*) to deceive by flattery. [CUT v.[4] + WHEEDLE n.]

cut behind *v.* [late 19C] (*US*) to steal a ride on a vehicle.

cut benely *v.* [mid-16C–17C] (*UK Und.*) to speak gently or kindly. [CUT v.[1] (1) + BENE adj.]

cut bene whids *v.* (*also* **cut bien whids**) (*UK Und.*) **1** [mid-16C–1900s] to speak kindly. **2** [early 17C] to tell the truth. [CUT v.[1] (1) + BENE adj. + WHID n. (1)]

cut blocks with a razor *v. see* CUT A BLOCK WITH A RAZOR V.

cut-buddy *n.* **1** [1960s] (*US Black*) a close friend. **2** [1990s+] (*US drugs*) 2 or more drug dealers who combine to adulterate a supply of drugs prior to retailing it. [CUT v.[10] + BUDDY n. (1)]

cut caper-sauce *v.* [late 18C–mid-19C] to be hanged.

cutcha *adj.* (*also* **kutcha**) [18C–19C] (*Anglo-Ind.*) makeshift, second-rate, fake, bad. [Hind. *kachcha*, raw]

cut cheese v. [late 19C–1920s] (*US campus*) to impress, to influence, to make a difference. [fig. use of SE]

cutchery n. [early 17C–19C] (*Anglo-Ind.*) a courthouse, a place of business. [Hind. *kacheri*, a hall or audience]

cutchie n. (*also* **kouchie**) [1950s+] (*W.I., Jam.*) a pipe used for smoking hashish or marijuana.

cut corners v. see CUT (THE) CORNERS v.

cut-deck n. [1950s+] (*drugs*) heroin or morphine mixed with powdered milk. [CUT v.[10] (2) + DECK n.[4] (1)]

cut dicks v. [1950s+] (*W.I.*) to affect an English accent in the hope of impressing people. [? CUT v.[4] + SE *dignity*]

cut didoes v. see CUT UP A DIDO v.

cut dirt v. [19C] (*US*) to run away, to depart at speed. [the way a horse's hooves cut into the ground as it gallops at speed; note CUT v.[2] (2)]

cut-down adj.[1] [mid-19C+] (*US Black*) dejected, miserable.

cut-down adj.[2] [1960s] of a confrontation or conflict, important, decisive. [the loser is 'cut down to size']

cut down v. [1960s+] (*US campus*) to insult. [CUT v.[1] (1)]

cute n.[1] [early 18C] (*UK Und.*) a warrant. [prosecution]

cute n.[2] see CUTER n.[2].

cute adj. 1 [mid-18C+] acute, clever, keen-witted, sharp, often ironically and esp. in phr. [20C+] *don't get cute with me.* 2 [mid-19C+] attractive, charming. [SE *acute*; early 19C adoption in US developed and spread (1)]

cute adv. [mid-19C+] cleverly, smartly, esp. with implication of 'too smart for one's own good'.

cute as a shithouse rat phr. (*also* **cute as a barrow-load of monkeys, …a bug's ear, …a cut cat**) [1920s+] extremely devious, very cunning. [CUTE adj. (1)]

cuter n.[1] [1910s] (*US Und.*) 1 a surprise. 2 a fool, a victim.

cuter n.[2] (*also* **cute, cutor, kuter, kyuter, quter**) [1910s–60s] (*US*) 25 cents, a quarter. [? pron. SE *quarter*; note hotel jargon *cuter*, one who only tips a quarter]

cuter n.[3] [1920s–40s] (*US Und.*) a prosec*utor.*

cutes n. [20C+] (*orig. US*) a pretty young woman, often as a term of address, e.g. *Hey cutes…* [CUTE adj. (2)]

cutes, the n. [1940s–50s] (*US*) coy mannerisms. [CUTE adj. (2)]

cutesie adj. (*also* **cutesie-ass, cutesy**) [1910s–20s] (*orig. US*) excessively sweet, cloying, esp. in one's behaviour. [CUTE adj. (2) + sfx -*sie*; later use is SE]

cutesie-pie n. (*also* **cutey-pie, cutie-pie**) [1920s+] 1 an attractive woman, usu. young, poss. a man's girlfriend. 2 a man, as a term of affection or ridicule. 3 a small, admirable object, esp. used ironically. 4 a child. 5 (*gay*) an attractive, feminine man. [CUTESIE-PIE adj.]

cutesie-pie adj. (*also* **cutie-pie**) [1910s+] (*orig. US*) 1 (*also* **cutesy-poo**) excessively sweet, cloying, esp. in one's behaviour. 2 usu. of a woman, very pretty. [CUTE adj. (2) + SE *pie*]

cute suit with the loop droop n. [1940s] (*US Black/Harlem*) an ostentatious drape suit, popular at the time. [CUTE adj. (2)]

cutey n.[1] see COOTIE n.[1].

cutey n.[2] see COOTIE n.[2].

cutey n.[3] see CUTIE n.

cut-eye adj. [1940s] (*US Black*) dismissive, hostile. [CUT EYE v.]

cut eye v. [19C+] (*W.I., Jam.*) to catch a person's eye then, with the intention of offering a deliberate insult, to turn away. [W.I. *cut*, to dance + *eye*]

cutey-pie n. see CUTESIE-PIE n.

cut for it v. [late 19C–1920s] to run off, to make an escape. [CUT v.[2]]

cut for the simples adj. [late 17C–19C] a phr. meaning 'cured of one's foolishness'; esp. in phr. *go to Battersea to be cut for the simples* (cf. BORED FOR THE SIMPLES adj.). [17C Battersea was best known for its market gardens and the medicinal herbs they grew, known as *simples*, basic herbs without any adulterants. The use of

simples as a cure for physical ailments evolved into one for supposed mental problems once it was absorbed in sl.]

cut gravel v. (*also* **cut grit**) [mid-19C] (*US*) to move very fast. [the image of a coach's wheels spinning up gravel]

cut Grecian v. [1940s] (*W.I.*) for a woman to walk in a self-consciously 'stylish' manner, either arrogantly or proudly. [CUT v.[4] + SE *Grecian*]

cuthbert n. [1910s–30s] 1 one who deliberately avoids military services, esp. by securing a post in a government office or the civil service. 2 a conscientious objector. [stereotype of *Cuthbert* as a slightly 'weak' or foolish name]

cut ice (with) v. 1 [late 19C+] (*orig. US*) to impress, to influence, to make a difference; usu. in negative phr. *cut no ice (with)*, to make no impression, to leave unmoved. 2 [1900s] to chat, to converse.

cutie see also under COOTIE.

cutie n. (*also* **cutey**) 1 [late 18C+] a superficially clever person. 2 [1900s] (*US*) an attractive object. 3 [1910s+] (*orig. US*) (*also* **cuttie**) a pretty young woman (occas. of a man). 4 [1910s+] (*US*) someone who is extremely shrewd or adept. 5 [1910s+] a general term of address to a (pretty) woman; also, cynically, to a handsome man. 6 [1940s+] (*US*) a smart, 'clever' move; a cunning scheme. [CUTE adj. + sfx -*y*]

cutie-pie see under CUTESIE-PIE.

cut-in n. [late 19C–1910s] 1 a share, of profits, of loot, of the proceeds of a robbery etc. 2 an interruption. [CUT IN v. (3)]

cut in v. 1 [19C+] to make a pass at another person's partner. 2 [mid-19C] (*also* **have a cut-in**) to become involved. 3 [late 19C+] to receive a share, to be included in a proposition or plan. 4 [20C+] to give a share. 5 [20C+] (*US Und.*) to introduce oneself to a potential victim. 6 [1970s] to approach.

cut in the back adj. (*also* **cut in the eye, …leg**) 1 [mid-17C–mid-19C] very drunk. 2 [19C] pregnant. [fig. use of SE]

cut into v. 1 [20C+] (*US*) to make oneself known to, to interrupt. 2 [1900s] (*US*) take a share of. 3 [1930s+] (*US*) to meet, to encounter. 4 [1960s–70s] (*US*) to introduce. 5 [1990s+] (*Aus.*) to attack verbally.

cut it v.[1] (*also* **cut it out**) [19C+] to stop doing something; often as imper. [CUT OUT v.[6] (1)]

cut it v.[2] [late 19C+] (*orig. US*) to manage, to deal with (difficult) situations; to suffice, to satisfy. [ext. CUT v.[6] (2)]

cut it (down) v. [mid-19C; 1940s+] (*US*) to dance energetically.

cut it fat v. see CUT IT (TOO) FAT v.

cut it grand v. [mid-19C] to act in a threatening, domineering manner. [CUT v.[4] + SE *grand*]

cut it out v.[1] see CUT IT v.[1].

cut it out v.[2] see CUT OUT A CHEQUE v.

cut it out! excl. (*also* **cut that out!**) [mid-19C+] just stop that! [CUT OUT v.[6] (1)]

cut it spicy v. [late 19C] to have a good, if vulgar time. [CUT v.[4] + SPICY adj. (1)]

cut it (to) v. [mid-late 19C] to run off (to). [CUT v.[2] (2)]

cut it (too) fat v. [mid-late 19C] to show off, to make a vulgar display. [SE *cut (it) fat*, to leave too much fat on a slice of meat when carving/CUT v.[4] + FAT adv.]

cut it up v.[1] [20C+] to have an uproarious good time. [CUT THE RUG v.]

cut it up v.[2] [1960s+] (*US*) to reminisce, to talk over. [abbr. CUT UP (OLD) TOUCHES v. (1)]

cutlass n. [19C] the penis (cf. AX n.[2].)

cut lemons v. [late 19C] (*US*) to impress, to appear important. [CUT v.[4]/SE; ? lemons are 'sharp']

cutlery n. [mid-19C–1910s] (*US*) any form of edged weapon, usu. a knife.

cut loose v. 1 [19C+] to abandon restraints, either in one's action or, in an argument, in one's language and abuse. 2 [mid-19C+] to leave, to walk away. 3 [20C+] to give out, to release (something). **4** [20C+] to attack; to fire a weapon. **5** [1920s+] (*US*) to escape. **6** [1930s+] (*US Black*) to give up something. **7** [1940s+] (*US Black*) to jilt; to terminate a relationship. **8** [1950s+] (*US prison*) to release, to be released. **9** [1950s+] to terminate, to let go, to get rid of. **10** [1970s] to launch someone into a situation. [fig. uses of SE; (2) CUT v.² (2)]

cut loose one's dog *v.* see CUT ONE'S DOG LOOSE v.

cut lunch *n.* [1980s+] (*Aus.*) a meal of sandwiches; thus *cut lunch commando* a regular employee, i.e. one who takes sandwiches to work. [they are cut from a loaf]

cut mud *v.* [1930s–50s] (*US*) to move very fast. [image of car wheels moving through mud]

cut mutton with *v.* [mid-19C–1900s] to share in someone's hospitality; thus *cut mutton*, to dine. [SE *cut*]

cut off *v.* see CUT AWAY v.¹.

cut off at the pass *v.* (*also* **head off at the pass**) [20C+] to intercept, to ambush, metaphorically as well as physically. [the cliché line of many Westerns]

cut off the joint *n.* [20C+] sexual intercourse. [CUT A SLICE (OFF THE JOINT) v.]

cut of one's jib *n.* [early 19C+] the way one behaves, one's character. [SE *cut*, style + *jib*, one of a variety of sails hoisted at the very front of the vessel]

cut (old) style *v.* [20C+] (*W.I.*) to behave in an exhibitionist manner to attract attention. [CUT v.⁴ + SE *style*]

cut on *v.* [1970s] (*Can. prison*) to sport a prison-made tattoo.

cut one another's throats *v.* see CUT ONE'S OWN THROAT v.

cut one's cable *v.* **1** [early 19C] to die. **2** [mid-19C] to run away. [naut. imagery]

cut one's dog loose *v.* (*also* **cut loose one's dog**) [19C+] (*US*) to act spontaneously, without restraint.

cut one's eyes *v.* (*also* **cut yai**) [mid-19C+] to glance, to look at furtively or suspiciously; to look askance at. [dial. *cut-eye*, a scornful gesture made with the eyes]

cut one's eye-teeth *v.* see CUT A TOOTH v.

cut one's foot *v.* [mid-19C+] (*US*) **1** to step in excrement. **2** to make a stupid blunder. [euph.]

cut one's gums *v.* see CUT A TOOTH v.

cut one's horns *v.* see SCRAPE ONE'S HORNS v.

cut one's last fling *v.* [18C] to be hanged. [SE *cut a fling*, to dance, implying DANCE v.²]

cut one's leg *v.* [late 17C–18C] **1** to become pregnant. **2** to get drunk. [euph; SE/CUT adj.¹]

cut one's lucky *v.* (*also* **make one's lucky**) [early 19C+] to run off. [? SE *lucky escape*]

cut one's own grass *v.* [mid–late 19C] to earn one's own living.

cut one's own throat *v.* (*also* **cut one another's throats**) [mid-19C+] to ruin oneself or oneself and another through pure bloody-mindedness rather than any rational or commercial calculation.

cut (one's) stick(s) *v.* **1** [19C–1900s] to leave quickly, to run off. **2** [mid-19C] (*US*) to die. **3** [late 19C–1900s] to travel around looking for work. [(1) Hotten (1859) suggests the rural practice of cutting a notch or tally in a stick to reckon up sheaves of corn; 'Cut your stick, then, means to make your mark and pass on'; (3) f. cutting a stick to help one as one walks along]

cut one's string *v.* [19C+] (*US*) to abandon restraint, to let oneself go. [CUT LOOSE v. (1)]

cut one's teeth *v.* see CUT A TOOTH v.

cut one's wheels *v.* [1950s] (*US*) to leave, to depart.

cut one's wolf loose *v.* [19C+] to act spontaneously, to 'let off steam'. [var. on CUT ONE'S DOG LOOSE v.]

cutor *n.* see CUTER n.².

'cutor *n.* (*also* **cutter**) [1920s–40s] (*US*) a prosecuting attorney. [abbr. SE *prosecutor*]

cut-out *n.*¹ [1910s] (*Aus.*) the end of a job. [CUT OUT v.⁴]

cut-out *n.*² [1960s+] a middleman, esp. in espionage.

cut out *v.*¹ [late 17C; mid-19C] to find (work for someone).

cut out *v.*² [late 17C; mid-19C+] (*US*) to do better than, to surpass. [ext. of SE use]

cut out *v.*³ [late 18C–1960s] (*US*) to take over as someone's preferred love-object or dance partner. [ext. CUT OUT v.²]

cut out *v.*⁴ [mid-19C] to rush away, to leave fast, to escape. [ext. CUT v.² (2)]

cut out *v.*⁵ [late 19C] (*US*) to recognize, to identify. [SE phr. *cut out from a crowd*]

cut out *v.*⁶ **1** [mid-19C+] to stop; thus CUT THAT OUT! excl. (cf. CUT IT v.¹). **2** [late 19C+] (*Aus.*) orig. shearing, to finish, to complete a job. **3** [1960s+] in fig use, to die. [ext. of CUT OUT v.⁴]

cut out *v.*⁷ **1** [1970s–80s] (*N.Z. prison*) to serve a sentence; usu. modified by the pertinent number of years. **2** [1980s+] (*Aus. prison*) to pay off fines by serving time in jail according to an established tariff.

cut out a cheque *v.* (*also* **cut it out**) [20C+] (*Aus./N.Z.*) to spend all one's earnings in one go.

cut out of *v.* **1** [late 17C+] to deprive of an opportunity. **2** [18C–19C] to cheat.

cut over the head *adj.* [late 18C–early 19C] tipsy, slightly drunk (cf. ARSEHOLED adj.). [SE/CUT adj.¹]

cutpurse *n.* [mid-16C–19C] a pickpocket. [the original *cut-purse* did just that: cut loose the bag or purse in which a person kept their money and which was attached to their belt]

cut puss *n.* [1950s] (*W.I.*) an effeminate, fat man. [SE *cut*, castrated + SE *puss*/PUSSY n. (10)]

cut queer whids *v.* (*also* **cut quire whidds**) [16C–mid-19C] (*UK Und.*) **1** to speak unpleasantly or obscenely; thus [early 18C–mid-19C] *queer whidding*, telling off, reprimanding. **2** to tell lies. [CUT v.¹ (1) + QUEER adj.¹ (1) +WHID n. (1)]

cut quick sticks *v.* [mid-19C] to be in a hurry. [var. on CUT (ONE'S) STICK(S) v. (1)]

cut-rate *n.* [1930s+] a person considered second-rate.

cut-rate *adj.* [1940s+] second-rate, inferior, unpleasant. [fig. use of SE *cut-rate*, economic, inexpensive]

cut-rate *v.* [1940s] (*US Black*) to belittle. [CUT-RATE n.]

cut-rate *adv.* [1940s+] in a cheap, unsatisfactory, limited manner. [CUT-RATE adj.]

cut round *v.* [mid–late 19C] (*US*) to show off, to make a display. [CUT v.⁴ + SE *(a)round*]

cuts *n.*¹ [mid-17C–early 18C] in oaths, a euph. for God's, e.g. *Cuts plutteranails! Cuts bobs!*

cuts *n.*² [1910s+] (*Aus./N.Z.*) corporal punishment, esp. of schoolchildren. [SE *cut*, a blow with a cane or stick]

cuts *n.*³ [1970s+] (*US gay*) the streets. [? CUT n.⁷ (1)]

cuts *n.*⁴ [1970s+] (*US campus*) muscles. [SE *cut*]

cuts and scratches *n.* (*also* **bites and scratches**) [late 19C] matches. [rhy. sl.; f. cheap imported matches which cut and scratched the box failing to ignite]

cut shit *v.* **1** [1970s+] (*orig. US*) to impress, to influence, to make a difference. **2** [2000s] (*US campus*) to act eccentrically. [CUT v.⁶ (2) + SHIT n.⁶]

cut someone a break *v.* see GIVE SOMEONE A BREAK v.

cut someone a new ass(hole) *v.* see TEAR SOMEONE A NEW ASS(HOLE) v.

cut someone down *v.* [1940s+] (*orig. US Black*) to challenge, with the intention of proving one's superiority, usu. in the context of verbal, dancing or musical competitions.

cut someone every which way but loose *v.* (*also* **turn every which way but loose**) [1920s+] (*US*) to assault comprehensively.

cut someone into *v.* (*US*) **1** [1910s+] to introduce someone to a scheme, supposedly advantageous. **2** [1930s+] to meet someone. **3** [1950s+] to introduce one person to another.

cut someone out of *v.* [mid-19C+] (*US*) to let go, to get away from someone, to release someone.

cut someone's arse v. 1 [20C+] (*W.I., Guyn.*) to thrash severely, to flog. 2 [1970s] (*US*) (*also* **cut someone's ass**) to surpass. [SE *cut*/CUT v.[6] (3) + ARSE n.[1] (1)/ASS n. (2)]

cut someone's ass(hole) v. *see* TEAR SOMEONE'S ASS(HOLE) v.

cut someone's cart v. [mid-19C–1920s] to expose someone's tricks.

cut someone's comb v. *see* COMB-CUT v.

cut some rusty v. *see* CUT A RUSTY v.

cut some slack v. (*also* **take up slack**) (*orig. US Black*) 1 [1960s+] to ease the pressure upon, to permit the subject to relax. 2 [1970s] to hand over money. [SE *cut* + SLACK n.[1] (6)]

cut some z's v. *see* BUST SOME Z's v.

cut sticks v. *see* CUT (ONE'S) STICK(S) v.

cut tail v. [1950s–60s] (*US*) to run away. [CUT v.[2] (2) + TAIL n.[2] (1)]

cut ten v. *see* COCK TEN v.

cutter n.[1] 1 [mid-16C] a braggart, a boaster, a thug. 2 [1910s–60s] (*US*) an admirable or remarkable person. 3 [1920s] (*US Black*) a pimp (cf. CANDYMAN n.). 4 [1960s–70s] (*US*) a remarkable occurrence or event. [someone or something who/that fig. 'cuts']

cutter n.[2] 1 [mid-16C; mid-19C] a pickpocket, a cut-purse. 2 [late 16C+] a thug who uses a knife or razor in fights. 3 [1920s] (*US prison*) a needle file. 4 [1930s] a robber who enters properties by cutting window bars. 5 [1940s] an oxy-acetylene blowpipe. 6 [1940s] (*US*) one who derives sexual pleasure from stabbing or cutting a woman. 7 [1970s] (*US*) a knife.

cutter n.[3] [20C+] (*US*) a revolver, esp. a Colt. [it 'cuts down' its targets]

cutter n.[4] [2000s] money. [? COUTER n.[1]]

cutter n.[5] *see* 'CUTOR n.

cut that out! *see* CUT IT OUT! excl.

cut the asparagus v. *see* CUT THE MUSTARD v. (1).

cut the buck v. [1920s–70s] (*US*) to work hard. [dial. *cut the buck*, to dance vigorously; ult. f. *buck and wing*]

cut the cackle (and come to the horses) v. [late 19C+] to come to the point, usu. as imper. [CUT v.[5] (1) + CACKLE n.[1]]

cut the cake v. [20C+] (*US Black*) 1 to get married. 2 to deflower a virgin. [fig. uses of SE]

cut the cheese v. [1970s+] to break wind; esp. in phr. *who cut the cheese?* [the smelliness of certain cheeses]

cut the comedy v. [1910s+] to stop doing something considered irritating or foolish; esp. as imper. [CUT v.[5] (1) + COMEDY n.]

cut (the) corners v. 1 [1900s] (*US*) to economize. 2 [1950s+] to perform a job of work or a duty in a way that minimizes the effort but still capitalizes on the promised rewards.

cut the crap v. (*also* **cut the shit**) [1930s+] (*US*) to stop wasting time, to stop talking or doing something irrelevant; thus *cut-the-crap*, sensible, free from nonsense. [CUT v.[5] (1) + CRAP n.[3] (3)/SHIT n.[3] (4)]

cut the crap! excl. (*also* **cut the shit!**) [1930s+] don't try to fool me! stop talking rubbish! etc. [CUT THE CRAP v.]

cut the flash v. [20C+] (*Aus.*) to show off, to be very well known or successful, to cut a 'fine figure' (cf. CUT A FLASH v.). [CUT v.[4] + FLASH n.[1] (1)/FLASH adj.[1] (1)]

cut the fool v. [1930s–60s] (*US Black*) to act the fool, esp. when dealing with White people, to play tricks. [CUT v.[4] + SE *fool*]

cut the grass v. *see* GRASS n.[1] (2).

cut the grass from under someone's feet v. [late 16C] to foil, to thwart, to trip up.

cut the gutter n. [20C+] (*Ulster*) an errand boy.

cut the knot v. [20C+] to obtain a divorce.

cut the line v. [early 19C] to cut a long story short.

cut the mustard v. 1 [late 19C+] (*also* **cut the asparagus**) (*orig. US*) to come up to a given standard, to prove satisfactory. 2 [20C+] (*W.I.*) for a man to satisfy a woman sexually. 3 [20C+] to have sexual intercourse. 4 [1950s] (*US*) to show off. 5 [1980s+] (*US*) to impress, to influence. [the image of the condiment's

piquancy. (3) is included by E.P. but his cit. suggests a journ. euph. rather than an established sl. phr.]

cut the painter v. 1 [mid-17C–mid-19C] to dismiss or send a person away. 2 [mid-19C+] to slip away clandestinely. 3 [mid-19C+] to die. 4 [1900s–10s] to bring something to an irrevocable conclusion. [in naut. use the *painter* is the rope that secures a small boat to a larger ship]

cut the rug v. (*also* **cut a rug, rug cut**) [1920s+] to dance; thus *rug-cutting*, dancing.

cut the scene v. [1940s–60s] (*orig. US Black*) to leave. [CUT v.[2] (2)]

cut the shit *see under* CUT THE CRAP.

cut-throat n.[1] 1 [late 18C–mid-19C] a dark lantern. 2 [mid-19C] a butcher. 3 [late 19C+] an open-bladed, non-safety razor.

cut-throat n.[2] [1970s+] (*US Black*) a tough, aggressive or frightening Black man. [his (potential) violence and aggressiveness]

cuttie n.[1] [1950s+] (*W.I.*) 1 a 10oz beer bottle, known as a 'reputed half pint'. 2 a very short man. [SE *cut down*]

cuttie n.[2] *see* CUTIE n. (3).

cutting n.[1] [mid-19C; 1930s+] a stabbing, a knifing. [CUT v.[8]]

cutting n.[2] [1930s+] (*drugs*) the adulteration of drugs to increase the quantity prior to retail sale. [CUT v.[10]]

cutting contest n. (*also* **carving contest**) [1940s–50s] (*US Black*) a form of musical competition; a musical version of the DOZENS n. [CUT v.[6] (3)]

cutting Dick n. [late 16C–early 17C; mid-19C] a ruffian, a braggart.

cutting-gloak n. [early–mid-19C] one who is known for using a knife to settle quarrels. [SE *cut* + GLOAK n.]

cutting ice n. [1960s–70s] (*US Black*) succeeding in a spectacular manner. [CUT ICE (WITH) v.]

cutting man n.[1] [1950s–60s] (*US Black*) one's best friend. [jazz jargon *cutting*, competing musically]

cutting man n.[2] *see* CUTTY n.

cutting-shop n. [mid–late 19C] a shop selling cheap, badly made goods. [SE *undercut*]

cutting up n. [2000s] (*US prison*) committing suicide. [the frequent use of blades to assist the suicide]

cuttle n. [late 16C–mid-17C] a knife. [obs. OF *coutel* (mod. Fr. *couteau*); ult. Lat. *cultellum*, a knife]

cuttle-bung n. [late 16C–early 17C] (*UK Und.*) a knife used for cutting purses. [CUTTLE n. + BUNG n.[1] (1)]

cutty n. (*also* **cutting man**) [1970s+] (*US Black*) a friend, a close intimate. [? dial. *cutty*, small or diminutive; thus used as an affectionate term of address]

cutty-eye v. [late 18C–early 19C] to gaze at in a suspicious manner, to look askance. [SE *cutty*, sharp + *eye*]

cutty-eyed adj. [19C] 1 suspicious (of someone). 2 suspicious-looking. [CUTTY-EYE v.]

cutty gun n. [19C] the penis (cf. AX n.[2]). [image of the penis as a weapon]

cut under v. 1 [mid-19C] to undersell. 2 [late 19C–1930s] (*US Black*) to insult.

cut-up n.[1] [mid-19C] (*US*) a slanderous attack. [CUT UP v.[1] (1)]

cut-up n.[2] 1 [late 19C+] an amusing person, a joker; also ironic use. 2 [1910s] (*US*) a smartly dressed person, a smart thing. [CUT UP v.[1] (3)]

cut-up n.[3] [1920s; 1970s] (*US Black/prison*) a knife-fight.

cut-up n.[4] [1930s–40s] a share of money, profit, loot. [CUT UP v.[2] (2)]

cut-up n.[5] [2000s] (*US Black*) sexual intercourse.

cut up adj.[1] 1 [early–mid-19C] fallen on hard times. 2 [early 19C+] unhappy, depressed, upset. [CUT UP v.[4]]

cut up adj.[2] *see* CUT adj.[5].

cut up v.[1] 1 [mid-18C+] to slander, to criticize, esp. behind the victim's back. 2 [19C+] to behave, to act, usu. with a defining adj., e.g. CUT UP ROUGH v. 3 [mid-19C+] to show off, to play the clown, to make people laugh; to act eccentrically. **4** [mid-19C+] (*US*) (*also* **cut up dickens**) to complain, to make a lot of noise; lit. and fig. **5** [20C+] to dance, to have a good time. **6** [1920s+] (*US*) to talk about. **7** [1920s+] (*US*) to cause trouble for. **8** [1990s+] (*US Black*) to fight. [fig. uses of SE]

cut up *v.*[2] **1** [late 18C] to defraud, to deprive. **2** [late 18C+] to divide, esp. money, loot. **3** [late 18C+] to leave a fortune; esp. in phr. *cut up big/large*, to leave a good deal.

cut up *v.*[3] **1** [19C] to become, to appear, to show up. **2** [mid-19C] to impress.

cut up *v.*[4] **1** [19C+] to be in a difficult situation, esp. as regards money. **2** [mid-19C+] to depress or perturb someone.

cut up *v.*[5] [early 19C; 1930s+] to overtake another vehicle by driving recklessly in front of it (and forcing it to take some form of evasive action).

cut up a curlicue *v.* [mid-19C] (*US*) to act in a deceitful manner, to play a trick. [CUT UP *v.*[1] (2) + SE *curlicue*, a twist or curl; note SE *cut up curlicues*, to cut capers]

cut up a dido *v.* (*also* **cut a dido, cut didoes, cut up didoes**) **1** [19C–1930s] (*orig. US*) to play pranks, to act the fool. **2** [mid-19C+] (*also* **kick up a dido**) to behave outrageously, to cause a fuss or indulge in a row. [CUT UP *v.*[1] (2) + DIDO *n.* (2)]

cut up dickens *v. see* CUT UP *v.*[1] (2).

cut up didoes *v. see* CUT UP A DIDO *v.*

cut up extras *v.* [mid-19C] (*US*) to behave badly. [ext. of CUT UP *v.*[1] (2)]

cut up fat *v.* [18C–19C] to leave a fortune after one's death. [CUT UP *v.*[2] (3) + SE *fat/*FAT *adv.* (1); note butchers' jargon *cut up fat*, for an animal to be divided into profitably saleable pieces]

cut up jack *v.* (*also* **kick up (high) jack, raise jack, tear up jack, turn up jack**) [mid-19C–1950s] (*US*) to cause a commotion. [ext. of CUT UP *v.*[1] (2)]

cut up nasty *v. see* CUT UP ROUGH *v.*

cut up old scores *v.* [1930s+] (*orig. US Und.*) to reminisce over old successes, major villainies etc (cf. CUT UP THE SCORE *v.*). [fig. use of CUT UP *v.*[2] (2) + SCORE *n.*[3] (4); note synon. carnival use *cut up jackpots*]

cut up (old) touches *v.* [1920s+] (*US Und.*) **1** to reminisce over old successes, villainies etc. **2** to share out the spoils of criminal acts. [CUT UP *v.*[2] (2) + TOUCH *n.*[1] (7)]

cut up rough *v.* (*also* **cut rough, cut up bad, cut up nasty**) **1** [mid-19C+] to react unpleasantly, to become annoyed, to make a fuss. **2** [1900s] to treat harshly. [CUT UP *v.*[1] (2) + SE *rough*]

cut up rusty *v.* [early 19C+] to become annoyed. [CUT UP *v.*[1] (2) + RUSTY *adj.*[2] (1)]

cut up savage *v.* [mid-19C] to become annoyed. [CUT UP *v.*[1] (2) + SE *savage*]

cut up shapes *v.* (*also* **cut up shines**) [mid-19C–1900s] to play pranks, to act in a flighty manner. [CUT UP *v.*[1] (2) + SHOW SHAPES *v.* (1)/SE *shine*]

cut up stiff *v.* [19C] to leave a large estate. [CUT UP *v.*[2] (3) + STIFF *adv.*]

cut up the score *v.* [1930s–40s] (*US Und.*) to share out illicit profits (cf. CUT UP OLD SCORES *v.*). [CUT UP *v.*[2] (2) + SCORE *n.*[3] (1)]

cut up timber *v.* [1960s] to snore. [the noise]

cut up ugly *v.* [mid-19C+] to become annoyed. [CUT UP *v.*[1] (2) + SE *ugly*]

cut up well *v.*[1] (*also* **cut up warm**) [late 18C–early 19C] to leave a fortune after one's death. [CUT UP *v.*[2] (3)]

cut up well *v.*[2] [mid–late 19C] to display a well-shaped naked body. [CUT UP *v.*[1] (2) + SE *well*]

cut-water *n.* [mid-19C–1900s] the nose. [SE *cut-water*, the prow of a ship]

cut yai *v. see* CUT ONE'S EYES *v.*

cut z's *v. see* BUST SOME Z'S *v.*

cuz *n.* (*also* **coz, cuh, cus**) [1960s+] **1** (*orig. US Black*) a form of address, usu. between men. **2** (*orig. US Black*) a friend. **3** (*US Black*) a member of the Crips gang. [abbr. SE *cousin*, a development of mid-16C–mid-19C *coz*]

'cuz *prep. see* 'COS *prep.*

cuz john *n.* (*also* **cousin john**) [mid-18C–mid-19C] (*US campus*) a privy.

cuzzy *n.* [1930s+] (*US*) the vagina. [COOZE *n.* (1)]

cuzzy-bro *n.* [1990s+] (*N.Z.*) a friend, a member of one's extended family. [SE *cousin* + *brother*; ? coined by Maori comedian Billy T. James (d.1992)]

C walk *n.* [1990s+] (*US gang*) a form of walking — a deliberately exaggerated lope — associated with the Crip gang of Los Angeles. [note William Shaw, *Westsiders* (2000): 'Many have speculated that the gang were called Crips as a short version of the word "cripples", because the new gang members copied [its founder Raymond] Washington's habit of walking as if he had a limp and carrying a cane']

c.y.a. *phr.* [1950s+] (*orig. US milit.*) a phr. meaning look after yourself before worrying about anyone else, be it colleagues, customers, the larger world, whatever; the basic admonition to anyone, at any level, working in government or a large corporation. [abbr. *cover your ass*]

cyberpunk *n.* [1990s+] (*orig. US teen*) **1** a socially acceptable, respected computer obsessive. **2** (*also* **cpunk**) the world of the computers and the Internet, with all its science fiction, futuristic, anarchic possibilities. [popular def. of SE *cyber*, computer-related + PUNK *n.*[1] (6)]

cyclone *n.* (*also* **cycline, cyclones**) [1970s+] (*drugs*) phen-cyclidine. [abbr.]

cyclops *n.* [1960s–70s] (*US Black*) a television. [proper name *Cyclops*, a 1-eyed giant who, in Greek mythology, forged thunderbolts for Zeus. A television, too, has '1 eye' or makes one myopic]

cymbal *n.* [mid-19C] a watch. [its ticking]

cynthia *n.* [1950s–60s] (*camp gay*) a 'synthetic', insincere person. [play on proper name + SE *synthetic/insincere*]

cypher *see under* CIPHER.

cypress hill *n.* [1990s+] (*US Black*) gang-rape. [? the rap band of this name]

Cyprian *n.* (*also* **Cytherean**) [late 16C–19C] a prostitute. [*Cyprian*, lit. an inhabitant of Cyprus, an island that had once been celebrated for the worship of Aphrodite or Venus; *Cytherian*, f. Gk *kuthereia*, Aphrodite]

Cyprian *adj.* [late 16C–19C] lewd, licentious; latterly used spec. of prostitutes. [CYPRIAN *n.*]

Cyprian arbour *n.* [19C] **1** (*also* **Cyprian bower**) the vagina (cf. ADAM'S OWN (ALTAR) *n.*; AGREEABLE RUTS OF LIFE *n.*). **2** a brothel. [CYPRIAN *n.*]

Cyprian cave *n.* (*also* **Cyprian strait**) [early 17C] the vagina (cf. ADAM'S OWN (ALTAR) *n.*; AGREEABLE RUTS OF LIFE *n.*). [CYPRIAN *n.*]

Cyprian sceptre *n.* [mid-17C] the penis. [CYPRIAN *n.* + SCEPTRE *n.*]

Cyril (Sneer) *n.* [1920s; 2000s] (*US*) a derog. nickname for an effeminate or homosexual man (cf. ABIGAIL *n.*). [rhy. sl. = QUEER *n.* (4); ult. cartoon character *Cyril Sneer* in the TV series *The Raccoons*]

Cytherean *n. see* CYPRIAN *n.*

czaro *n.* [1940s+] (*US Black*) a general term of address; the implication is that the addressee is superior to oneself. [SE *czar*]

D

D *n.*[1] [1970s+] (*US*) Detroit. [abbr.]

D *n.*[2] *see* D *n.*[3].

d *n.*[1] [mid-19C–1930s] an abbr. of DAMN *n.*

d *n.*[2] (*also* **dee**) **1** [mid-19C+] a pre-decimal penny. **2** [1990s+] (*US campus*) a dollar. [(1) SE £.*s.d.*; (2) abbr.]

d *n.*[3] (*also* **D**, **dee**) [mid-19C+] (*orig. Aus./N.Z.*) a *d*etective; thus (*N.Z.*) *the Dees*, the police as an organization. [abbr.]

d *n.*[4] (*drugs*) **1** [1950s+] *d*ilaudid (cf. BIG D *n.*). **2** [1960s+] LSD. [abbr.]

d *n.*[5] [1960s+] (*drugs*) heroin. [abbr. DUJI *n.*]

d *n.*[6] [1970s+] (*drugs*) phencyclidine (cf. ACE *n.*[4]). [abbr. ANGEL DUST *n.* (4)]

d *n.*[7] [1990s+] (*drugs*) cannabis. [abbr. DOPE *n.*[1] (6)]

d *n.*[8] [1990s+] (*US Black*) the penis. [abbr. DICK *n.*[4] (1)]

d *n.*[9] [1990s+] (*US Black*) looking after oneself, adopting a defensive posture to potential threats. [basketball use, *d*, defence]

d *adj.* [early 19C+] excellent, wonderful, first-rate. [? abbr. DANDY *adj.*]

d.a. *n.* **1** [1930s–50s] (*US*) a drug *a*ddict. **2** [1950s+] (*orig. US*) a style of haircut popular in the 1950s but still found. **3** [1970s] (*US campus*) a fool, an idiot. [abbr.; (1) SE *drug*/DOPE *n.*[1] (6); (2) DUCK'S ARSE *n.* (1); (3) DUMB-ASS *n.*]

da *n.* [mid-19C+] one's father. [abbr. SE *daddy*]

dab *n.*[1] [17C+] a skilful person, an expert. [gaming jargon *dab*, a top-flight gamester; ? orig. schoolboy sl., the obvious ety. is rooted in SE *adept* or *dapper*, but there is no positive proof of either]

dab *n.*[2] **1** [19C] a flat fish of any kind. **2** [late 19C] (*UK Und.*) the corpse of an impoverished, outcast woman. [SE *dab*, a small flat fish (*Pleuronectes limanda*), usu. the flounder]

dab *n.*[3] [early–mid-19C] a bed. [? backsl.; note SE *dab*, a flattish mass of a soft substance, typically butter]

dab *n.*[4] [1980s+] (*UK drugs*) a small portion of cocaine or other powdered drug, taken by dabbing one's finger into a pile or packet.

dab *adj.*[1] [18C–1910s] skilled, expert. [DAB *n.*[1]]

dab *adj.*[2] [mid–late 19C] bad. [backsl.]

dab *v.*[1] [1940s] (*UK Und./police*) to take a suspect's fingerprints. [DABS *n.*[2]]

dab *v.*[2] *see* DUB *v.*[1] (2).

dabble *n.* [late 19C+] (*UK Und.*) stolen property. [ironic use of SE]

dabble *v.* [1910s+] (*drugs*) to use drugs, esp. narcotics, in moderation.

dabbler *n.* [mid-19C] (*US Und.*) one who associates with thieves. [SE *dabble*]

dab down *v.* [19C] to hand over, to pay out. [SE *dab*, to put down with a sharp, abrupt motion]

dab hand *n.* [early 19C+] an expert at an occupation; usu. as *dab hand at.* [DAB *n.*[1] + HAND *n.*[1]]

dabheno *n.* (*also* **daheeno**) [mid-19C] (*costermonger*) something bad, usu. a poor market. [DABHENO *adj.*]

dabheno *adj.* [mid-19C] (*costermonger*) bad. [backsl.; lit. 'one bad'; DAB *adj.*[2]]

dab in the dook *n.* [1910s–20s] a tip. [SE *dab*, a pat + DUKE *n.*[3] (1)]

dab it up *v.* [early–mid-19C] to run up credit at a public house. [SE *dab*, the writing down of what is owed]

dab it up (with) *v.* [early 19C] of a man and woman, to cohabit. [DAB *n.*[3]]

dab of the brush *n.* *see* BRUSH *n.*[3] (2).

da bomb *n.* *see* BOMB, THE *n.*

dab out *v.* [mid-19C] to do the laundry. [SE *dab*, to strike or cause to strike (usu. with something soft and of broadish surface); thus the slapping of clothes on a washboard etc]

dabs *n.*[1] [late 19C] an expert. [abbr. DABSTER *n.* (1)]

dabs *n.*[2] [1920s+] fingerprints. [SE *dab*, to pat]

dabster *n.* **1** [late 19C+] an expert. **2** [1900s–10s] something excellent; also attrib. [DAB *n.*[1] + -STER *sfx*]

dab the paint *v.* [mid-19C] in boxing, to jab with the fist. [SE *dab*, to pat]

dabtros *n.* [mid-19C–1900s] a bad sort, an unpleasant person. [backsl.; DAB *adj.*[2]]

dacca *n.* (*also* **dakker**) [1970s+] (*Aus.*) marijuana. [var. on DAGGA *n.*]

dace *n.* **1** [late 17C–mid-19C] 2 pence. **2** [mid-19C; 1960s] (*US*) 2 cents. [SE *deuce*, 2]

dacehead *n.* [early 19C] a fool. [SE *dace*, a variety of freshwater fish + -HEAD *sfx* (1)]

dacha *n.* (*also* **deger**) [mid-19C] (*Ling. Fr./Polari*) the number 10. [Ital. *dieci*, 10]

dacha-one *n.* [mid-19C] (*Ling. Fr./Polari*) 11 pence. [DACHA *n.* + SE *one*]

dack up *v.* [1990s+] (*N.Z.*) to smoke marijuana. [DACCA *n.*]

dad *n.*[1] [17C+] a euph. for *God*; used in a variety of mild verbal oaths (*see* DAD-BURN *v.*) and adj. combs., mainly (*US*), e.g. *dad-binged, dad-blamed, dad-blasted, dad-blistered, dad-bloomed, dad-bob, dad-burn, dad-burned, dad-dim, dad-fetched, dad-gasted, dad-ratted, dad-rotted, dad-shaved, dad-shimmed, dad-snatched, dad-swamped* (cf. BOB *n.*[2]; DAD-GUM *adj.*). [the term flourished, like many similar euph. oaths, in the UK in the late 17C but re-emerged in the 19C in the US, where it remains in many combs., a resurgence poss. helped by the similarity to another taboo word, DAMNED *adj.*]

dad *n.*[2] [20C+] (*orig. US Black*) a term of address by one man to another, esp. when slightly older. [mainly in Black/beatnik use; thus UK jazz-orientated film *It's Trad, Dad* (1962)]

dada *n.* [20C+] (*W.I. Rasta*) one's father.

dada-mama *n.* [1970s] (*US Black*) a drum roll. [echoic]

dad and dave *n.* [1930s+] (*Aus.*) a peasant, an unsophisticated person. [for ety. *see* DAD AND DAVE *v.*]

dad and dave *v.* [1930s+] (*Aus.*) to shave; also as n. [rhy. sl.; ult. the popular 1930s radio serial *Dad and Dave* concerning various aspects of rural Aus. life. The show was based 'somewhat remotely' (Wilkes, *Dict. of Australian Colloquialisms*, 1985) on characters in the novel *Our Selection* by Steele Rudd (Arthur Hoey Davis, 1868–1935), itself taken from his columns in the *Bulletin*, starting in 1895]

dad and mum *n*. [20C+] (*Aus.*) rum or the cordial Bonox and rum. [rhy. sl.]

dad at the door *n*. [1960s+] (*bingo*) the number 24 (cf. ALDERSHOT LADIES n.). [rhy. sl.]

dad-burn *v*. (*also* **dad-blame, dad-bust, dad-fetch, dad-gone, dad-gum**) [mid-19C+] (*US*) a mild oath, GOD-DAMN v. [DAD n.[1]]

dad-burned *adv*. [20C+] (*US*) extremely, completely. [DAD-BURN v.]

daddio *n. see* DADDY-O n.

daddle *n*. [late 18C–19C] (*UK Und.*) the hand; in pl. the fists; thus TIP A DADDLE v. [dial.]

daddle *v*. [19C] to enjoy lesbian sex; the implication is of mutual masturbation. [DADDLE n.]

daddler *n*.[1] [late 19C] the hand. [DADDLE n.]

daddler *n*.[2] (*also* **dadla, dadler**) [1900s–30s] a farthing. [? SE *tiddler*, something very small]

daddy *n*. **1** [late 18C+] (*US*) a general term of address. **2** [mid-19C] (*UK Und.*) 'At mock raffles, lotteries, &c., the Daddy is an accomplice, most commonly the getter up of the swindle, and in all cases the person that has been previously arranged to win the prize' (Hotten, 1864). **3** [mid-19C] the old man, generally an aged pauper, in charge at a tramp's lodging house or casual ward. **4** [mid-19C] the man who gives away the bride at a wedding, trad., but not invariably, her father. **5** [mid-19C+] an influential, powerful person, e.g. a civic leader. **6** [mid-19C+] the supreme example, the most important, powerful, best known etc, often as *the daddy of them/us all*. **7** [1910s+] a boyfriend, a lover. **8** [1920s+] (*orig. US*) an older man who is willing to provide the various material desires of his younger mistress or, if homosexual, male lover. **9** [1920s+] (*US Black*) a form of address to a Black man, esp. by a woman to her lover. **10** [1930s] (*US tramp*) a Cadillac. **11** [1930s+] (*US*) a pimp, a prostitute's boyfriend (cf. BIG DADDY n.). **12** [1940s+] a masculine lesbian. **13** [1940s+] (*UK prison*) a leader (through intimidation and other influence) of the inmates in a borstal or prison. **14** [1950s+] an older male homosexual, a masculine homosexual (cf. AUNTIE n.[2]). **15** [1960s–70s] (*US prison*) the active, 'masculine' partner of a prison homosexual couple. **16** [1970s] (*US*) a customer, a client. **17** [1990s+] an unspecified object, a thing.

daddy *adj*. [1980s+] (*US campus*) ultimate, wonderful. [DADDY n. (6)]

daddy! *excl*. [20C+] (*W.I.*) a general expression of surprise and approval.

daddy-bag *n*. [1990s+] (*US Black*) the testes and the scrotum (cf. BALL-BAG n.). [their function in procreation]

daddy-o *n*. (*also* **daddio, dadio**) **1** [1930s+] (*orig. US Black*) a term of address between men. **2** [1940s+] (*orig. US*) a boyfriend, a male lover, a husband. **3** [1960s] (*US Black*) a thing, an object. **4** [1960s] (*US*) one's father. **5** [1960s] (*US Black*) the exemplar. **6** [1970s] a macho, 'masculine' male homosexual (cf. AUNTIE n.[2]). **7** [2000s] any male. [ext. of DADDY n.; the jazz-based Black use transferred, as did many such terms, to White beatniks in the 1950s and thence HIPPIE n.[2] (3) use; modern use usu. ironic]

daddy one *n*. [1960s+] (*US Black*) a lover or any man who provides for a woman. [DADDY n. (7) + SE (*number*) one]

daddy tank *n*. [1970s+] (*US prison*) an area set aside to provide protective custody for effeminate homosexuals. [DADDY n. (14) + TANK n.[2] (1)]

dad-fetch/-gone *v. see* DAD-BURN v.

dad-gum *adj*. (*also* **dad-gummed**) [1930s+] (*US*) a synon.

for DAMNED adj.; thus *dadgumit!* an excl. of disappointment. [DAD-GUM v.]

dad-gum *v. see* DAD-BURN v.

dadgumit! *excl. see* DAD-GUM adj.

dad-gummed *adj. see* DAD-GUM adj.

dadio *n. see* DADDY-O n.

dadla/dadler *n. see* DADDLER n.[2].

dads *n*. **1** [18C] an old man. **2** [20C+] one's father. **3** [1950s+] a term of address to anyone somewhat older than oneself. **4** [1990s+] (*W.I.*) a community leader.

da-erb *n*. [mid-19C] bread. [backsl.]

daff *n*.[1] (*also* **daffy**) [20C+] a *daffodil*; usu. in pl. [abbr.]

daff *n*.[2] [1950s+] (*Irish*) excrement. [ety. unknown]

daffadown dilly *adj*. (*also* **daffy-down dilly**) [1950s+] foolish, simple. [rhy. sl. = silly]

daffey *adj. see* DAFFY adj.

daffier *n*. [early 19C] a gin-drinker. [DAFFY n.[1] (1)]

daffies *n. see* DAFFY n.[1] (2).

daffodil *n*. **1** [1920s–80s] (*gay*) an effeminate young man. **2** [1950s–70s] a young male prostitute. [the stereotyped linking of flowers to effeminacy]

daffy *n*.[1] **1** [19C] gin. **2** [mid-19C] (*also* **daffies**) a small measure, usu. of spirits. [proper name *Daffy's Elixir*, a proprietary remedy known as 'the soothing syrup'; gin was commonly added and hence it became sl. for gin itself]

daffy *n*.[2] [late 19C] (*US*) a promiscuous woman. [abbr. dial. *daffodil*, a silly, showy woman]

daffy *n*.[3] [20C+] (*US*) an eccentric, a mad person; thus DAFFY HOUSE n. [DAFFY adj.]

daffy *n*.[4] [1910s] (*UK Und.*) a bunch; a large number. [orig. Kent dial.]

daffy *n*.[5] *see* DAFF n.[1].

daffy *adj*. (*also* **daffey**) [late 19C+] eccentric, foolish; esp. as *daffy about/on*, madly in love with. [SE *daft*]

daffy-down-dilly *n*. (*also* **daffydill**) [mid–late 19C] a dandy. [SE *daffydowndilly*, a daffodil]

daffy-down-dilly *adj. see* DAFFADOWN DILLY adj.

daffy-headed *adj*. [1980s+] foolish (cf. AIRHEADED adj.). [DAFFY adj. + SE *-headed*]

daffy house *n*. (*also* **daffy joint**) [1900s] (*US*) a psychiatric institution. [DAFFY n.[3] + SE *house/*JOINT n.[4] (3)]

daffy (it) *v*. [early–mid-19C] to drink gin. [DAFFY n.[1] (1)]

daft and barmy *n*. [1960s+] the army. [rhy. sl.]

daft ha'porth *n. see* SOFT HA'PORTH n.

daftie *n*. [late 19C+] a simpleton, a fool. [dial.; ult. SE *daft*]

dag *n*.[1] [late 19C–1900s] (*Aus.*) a feat of skill; thus [late 19C+] *be a dag at*, to be an expert at. [dial. *dag*, a feat of daring]

dag *n*.[2] [late 19C+] a euph. for *God*, usu. in adj. combs., e.g. *dag blasted, dag gone, dag-gum, dag nab, dag on* (cf. BOB n.[2]).

dag *n*.[3] (*Aus./N.Z.*) **1** [late 19C+] in affectionate use, an appealingly eccentric person, a 'character'; often ext. as *real dag, bit of a dag*. **2** [1950s+] an unenterprising person, a coward. **3** [1990s+] an unfashionable dresser. **4** [2000s] a gauche, socially awkward adolescent. [dial. *dag*, a piece of matted wool and excrement clinging to a sheep's tail; ? ult. SE *dangle*]

dag *adj*. [20C+] (*Aus.*) first-rate, excellent. [DAG n.[1]]

dag! *excl*. (*also* **dag bust it!**) [20C+] (*US/N.Z.*) a general excl. [DAG n.[2], underpinned by DAMN! excl.]

dagan *n. see* DEGEN n. (1).

dagga *n*. [20C+] (*S.Afr. drugs*) marijuana; thus *dagga-rooker*, a marijuana smoker. [Khoi, *daxab*, genus *Leonotis*; E.P. translates *dagga rooker* as 'a scoundrel, a wastrel', which may be his own moral viewpoint]

dagged *adj*. [late 17C–mid-18C] drunk. [Yorks. dial. *dagged*, damp]

dagger *n*.[1] [mid-19C+] the penis (cf. AX n.[2]).

dagger *n*.[2] [1980s] (*Aus.*) a hanger-on. [DAG n.[3]]

dagger *n*.[3] *see* BULL-DAGGER n.

dagger-ale n. [late 16C–mid-17C] very cheap ale. [the *Dagger*, a low tavern sited in Holborn; thus such food as *Dagger-pie*, *Dagger-frumety*, sold at the tavern]

dagger-cheap adj. [late 16C–mid-17C] very cheap. [for ety. *see* DAGGER-ALE n.]

dagger-pointed goldies n. [1940s–70s] (*US Black*) yellow shoes with sharply pointed toes.

daggle-tail n. [late 18C–early 19C] a prostitute. [ext. of dial. *daggle-tail*, a woman whose skirts drag in the dirt; a slattern]

daggone *see under* DOGGONE.

daggy adj. [1960s+] (*Aus.*) **1** messy, unkempt. **2** unfashionable, lacking grace. [DAG n.[3]]

dago n. **1** [early 19C+] (*orig. US*) an Italian, a Spaniard, a South American; also (*Aus.*) a Greek (cf. DING n.[2]; DINGBAT n.[9]); DINO n.[1]; EYETIE n.; EYETO n.; GANDY DANCER n.; GARLIC-EATER n.; GARLIC-SNAPPER n.; GIBRONEY n.; GINZO n.; GOOMBAH n.; GRAPE-STOMPER n.; GREASEBALL n.; GROCER'S SHOP n.; GUIDO n.; GUINEA n.; HIKE n.[2]; ICE-CREAMER n.; JIBONE n.; LUKSHEN n.; MACARONI n.[1]; MEATBALL n.[2]; MOUNTAIN WOP n.; MOUSTACHE PETE n.; ORGAN GRINDER n.[1]; PASTA-BREATH n.; RADDIE n.; REDDY n.[1]; REFFO n.; RICE AND SAGO n.; ROMAN CANDLE n.[1]; SKY n.[1]; SPAG n.[2]; SPAGHETTI n.; SPAGHETTI BENDER n.; SPAGHETTI HEAD n.; SPIC n.; SPIGGOTY n.; SPOOK n.[1]; SWAMP GUINEA n.; WALYO n.; WHITE NIGGER n.; WOG n.[1]; WOP). **2** [late 19C+] the Spanish or Italian language. **3** [20C+] (*orig. US*) a Mexican or Puerto Rican (cf. BATO n.). **4** [1900s–50s] (*N.Z.*) a Maori. **5** [1910s+] any form of foreigner. **6** [1920s] any man, esp. a sexually attractive man. **7** [1940s–50s] (*US*) San Diego, California. [Sp. proper name *Diego*, James; all uses are derog.; note Nares: '†DIEGO, DON. A popular name for a Spaniard'; John Taylor, 'The Water Poet', *Works* (1630): 'Don Coriat, chiefe Diego of our daies'; note Texas A & M college sl. *dago*, macaroni]

dago adj.[1] [mid-19C+] (*orig. US*) pertaining to a Latin, usu. an Italian, a Mexican or a Spaniard; any dark-skinned native; also (*Aus.*) Greek. [DAGO n. (1)]

dago adj.[2] [1940s+] (*W.I.*) bad. [non-specific use of DAGO n. (1) as a derog. term]

dago bomb n. [1930s+] (*US*) a large firecracker. [DAGO adj.[1] + SE *bomb*; the popularity of fireworks in the US Italian community]

dago center n. *see* DAGO TOWN n.

dagoland n. [1970s+] (*US*) a derog. name for southern Europe, esp. Italy. [DAGO adj.[1] + SE *land*]

dago red n. [20C+] **1** Italian red wine, usu. Chianti; thus the cheap, home-produced red wine made by Italian families and merchandised, during Prohibition, by Italian gangsters. **2** any cheap red wine, usu. drunk by alcoholics. [DAGO adj.[1] + SE *red wine*]

dago's piano n. [20C+] (*US*) an accordion. [DAGO n. (1) + SE *piano*; the popularity of the instrument among Italian immigrants]

dago town n. (*also* **dago center**) [1920s+] (*US*) the Italian, Mexican or Puerto Rican area of a town or city. [DAGO adj.[1] + SE *town*]

dags n.[1] [mid-19C–1920s] a feat, an achievement, a performance; thus *do/set dags*, to do something that the other person cannot do, to show off. [? OE *daeg*, a task or ? Scot. *darg*, a job, lit. 'a day's work']

dags n.[2] [late 19C+] (*Aus.*) pieces of excrement adhering to the anus; thus adj. *daggy* (cf. CLAGNUT n.). [dial. *dag*, *daglock*, a lock of wool matted with excrement on the tail parts of a sheep; ult. SE *dangle*]

dagwood n. [1940s+] (*Aus./US*) an extra-large sandwich. [the favoured food of the character *Dagwood Bumstead* in Chic Young's syndicated cartoon strip *Blondie*, launched in the US in 1930]

daheeno n. *see* DABHENO n.

daily n.[1] **1** [mid-19C+] a *daily* newspaper. **2** [1930s+] a *daily* help, a charwoman. [abbr.]

daily n.[2] [1900s–20s] one's wages. [SE *daily bread*]

daily n.[3] *see* DAILY (MAIL) n.

daily bread n. (*also* **daily breader**, **daily breadite**) [late 19C–1940s] the head of the family. [rhy. sl. + ref. to the Lord's Prayer, 'Give us this day our daily bread…']

daily dozen n. **1** [1910s+] regular physical exercises. **2** [1930s] one's work, occupation. [performed in sets of 12]

Daily Getsmuchworse n. [1970s+] the *Daily Express*.

Daily Levy n. [mid–late 19C] the *Daily Telegraph*. [its former owner, Joseph Moses *Levy* (1812–88) who took over the newly founded paper from its creator Colonel Sleigh in 1856; it was the first London paper to appear at 1d (½p) a copy]

daily (mail) n. [1920s–70s] **1** the buttocks; usu in phr. *on/up someone's daily*, following someone (cf. ALA n.). **2** a tale; thus a lie. **3** ale. **4** bail. **5** sexual enthusiasm. [rhy. sl.; (1) = TAIL n.[2] (1); (6) = TAIL n.[2] (5); ult. UK national newspaper *Daily Mail*]

Daily Wail n. (*also* **Daily Whale**) [20C+] the *Daily Mail*.

dairy n.[1] (*also* **dairies**) [18C+] the female breasts (cf. BORDENS n.). [ref. to lactation; 20C+ use is US Black]

dairy n.[2] **1** [1910s+] (*UK prison*) drawing attention to oneself so as to allow a confederate to break prison rules unnoticed. **2** [1910s+] exposure, publicity. **3** [1940s–50s] (*UK prison*) tobacco.

dairy arrangements n. [1910s–20s] the female breasts (cf. BORDENS n.). [DAIRY n.[1]]

dairy porn n. [1990s+] (*N.Z.*) pornographic magazines sold at local dairies. [SE + ? pun on DAIRY n.[1]]

dairy queen n. [1960s+] (*US gay*) **1** a homosexual milkman. **2** a homosexual farmer. **3** a sexual encounter that takes place in the early morning. [SE *dairy* + QUEEN n.[2] (1) + pun on *Dairy Queen* chain of restaurants]

daisy n.[1] (*also* **dasy**) [mid-18C] (*UK Und.*) a diamond.

daisy n.[2] **1** [mid-18C+] anything or anyone particularly appealing, excellent. **2** [late 19C] a term of affection. **3** [late 19C–1900s] (*US campus*) one who is credulous, gullible. **4** [late 19C+] (*US*) a notably attractive young woman. **5** [1900s] a person. **6** [1900s] (*Aus.*) a perfect blow. **7** [1900s] a drunkard. **8** [1940s+] a male homosexual (cf. ABIGAIL n.). **9** [1970s+] (*US Black*) a housewife. [(1) moved to the US in the 19C, then returned to the UK at end of the century]

daisy n.[3] [19C] the vagina (cf. BEAUTY SPOT n.).

daisy n.[4] [mid–late 19C] (*US*) a mule. [? popular pet name given to mules, although in the UK this name is more often given to cows]

daisy n.[5] *see* DAISY CHAIN n. (1).

daisy adj. [late 19C–1900s] (*US*) pleasant. [DAISY n.[2] (1)]

daisy adv. [late 19C] (*US*) **1** admirably, excellently, in a fine manner. **2** very. [DAISY adj.]

daisy beat v. [20C+] to cheat; also as n. [rhy. sl.]

daisy-beaters n. **1** [late 19C] feet. **2** [1940s+] (*US Black*) shoes.

daisy chain n. **1** [1930s+] (*also* **daisy**) a spintry, i.e. a circle of 3 or more people, hetero- or homosexual, all linked physically in mutual sex acts; thus *daisy-chainer*, one who participates in such activities. **2** [1960s] the group of men engaged in a gang-rape or an orgy with a single woman. **3** [1970s–80s] in business use, a situation where a group of 3 or more companies conspire together at the public's expense. **4** [1990s+] (*US campus*) the connection between people who have had sex with the same person at different times.

daisy-cutter n.[1] [late 18C–1940s] a horse that refuses to raise its feet properly when moving.

daisy-cutter n.[2] [late 19C] an attractive woman. [? ext. of DAISY n.[2] (4)]

daisy dukes n. (*also* **dazzey duks**) [1990s+] (*US Black teen*) very short shorts, 'hot pants'. [the minimal shorts worn by the character *Daisy Duke* in the 1970s US TV series *The Dukes of Hazzard*]

daisy dumpling n. [1950s–70s] (*camp gay*) a middle-class, heterosexual housewife. [her 'common' name and her shape]

daisy-kicker n. [late 18C–mid-19C] **1** a horse. **2** an ostler, working at a coaching inn.

daisyland *n.* [1950s] (*US*) the world outside the big cities.

daisy-picker *n.* [late 19C–1910s] (*Anglo-Irish*) one who accompanies an engaged couple on their walks, a chaperon(e); such an individual is invited and even paid. [ext. of SE use, i.e. she picks daisies while the couple attend to more pressing matters]

daisy (roots) *n.* (*also* **king canutes, recroots, recruits**) [mid-19C+] boots. [rhy. sl.]

daisyville *n. see* DEUSEAVILE n.

daiture *n.* [mid-19C+] (*orig. Ling. Fr./Polari*) the number 10. [Ital. *dieci*, 10]

dak *n.* [1980s+] (*N.Z. drugs*) marijuana. [DAGGA n.]

da kine *n.* [1960s] (*US*) **1** anything good, e.g. food, drugs, liquor. **2** marijuana. [Hawaiian surfing sl. *da kine*, anything of which one forgets the precise name]

dakker *n. see* DACCA n.

daks *n.* [1940s+] (*orig. Aus.*) trousers. [the proprietary name for a brand of clothes, esp. men's trousers with a self-supporting waistband, patented by the London clothiers Simpson's in 1933; supposedly an elision of *dad's slacks*]

dal *n. see* DELL n.

da land *n.* [1990s+] (*US Black/drugs*) getting intoxicated on a drug while sitting in a car with the windows rolled up, thus intensifying the effects of the ambient smoke. [? *da* (i.e. the) *land* of NOD n.¹ (1)]

'dale *n.* [1990s+] (*US Black teen*) Sunny*dale*, public housing in the southern part of San Francisco. [abbr.]

Dally *n.* (*also* **Dallie**) [1940s+] (*N.Z.*) a *Dal*matian (i.e. Balkan) immigrant; also attrib. [abbr.]

dally *v.* [1970s–80s] (*UK Black*) to leave, to go.

dally plonk *n.* [1950s+] (*N.Z.*) cheap wine manufactured by Dalmatian settlers. [DALLY n. + PLONK n.¹]

Dam, the *n.* [1990s+] Amster*dam*. [abbr.]

dam *adj. see* DAMN adj.

dama blanca *n.* [1980s+] (*drugs*) cocaine (cf. BLANCA n.). [Sp. *dama blanca*, white lady, i.e. WHITE LADY n.² (1); note cocaine is a 'feminine' drug, see GIRL n.²]

damage *n.* [late 17C+] the cost; usu. in phr. *what's the damage? how much is the bill?*

damaged *adj.* [late 18C+] (*orig. US*) drunk; occas. hungover (cf. ANNIHILATED adj.).

damaged goods *n.* **1** [1940s+] one who is no longer a virgin, but may pose as one. **2** [1990s+] an emotionally unstable person.

damager *n.* [20C+] a joc. corruption of SE *manager*, implying the alleged effect on those whose livelihoods are in his/her hands.

damask *v.* [late 17C–18C] to warm wine. [SE *damask*, to weave with richly figured designs]

damber *n.* [mid-17C–early 19C] a rogue, a rascal. [? DAMMEBOY n.]

damber-bush *n.* [late 19C] pubic hair. [? SE *dame* + BUSH n.² (1)]

damblack *adj.* [1930s–40s] (*US Black*) extremely dark-skinned. [DAMN adj. + SE *black*]

dame *n.* [mid-17C+] (*mainly US*) a woman, often with the implication of promiscuity or unattractiveness.

dame-buzzer *n. see* MOLL-BUZZER n.

Dame Nature's privy seal *n. see* NATURE'S PRIVY SEAL n.

damfino! *excl.* (*also* **damfi!**) [late 19C–1910s] (*orig. US*) damned if I know! [pron.]

damfool *adj.* (*also* **damnfool, dangfool, darnfool**) [late 19C+] stupid and irritating. [DAMN adj. + SE *fool*]

damme! *excl.* (*also* **dammy!**) [17C+] a euph. for DAMN! excl.

damme-boy *n.* (*also* **damme, God-dam-me**) [17C–early 19C] a blustering, profane, aggressive thug. [DAMME! excl. + SE *boy*]

dammed *adj. see* DAMNED adj.

dammit! *excl.* (*also* **damnit! damn it all!**) [late 17C+] a mild excl., i.e. *damn it!* (cf. DAMN! excl.). [DAMN v.]

dammy! *excl. see* DAMME! excl.

damn *n.* (*also* **tuppeny damn, twopenny damn**) [late 18C+] a miniscule or virtually non-existent amount; often in NOT GIVE A DAMN v. [the orig. ety. is based on the *dam*, a low value Indian coin, but the widely assumed link is to the oath DAMN! excl.; the inclusion of 'twopenny' was apparently popularized by the Duke of Wellington (1769–1852)]

damn *adj.* (*also* **dam**) **1** [mid-18C+] a strong expression of reprehension or dislike. **2** [late 19C+] a general intensifier, complete, utter. **3** [1940s+] as an infix, e.g. *anydamnbody*. [DAMNED adj.]

damn *v.* [late 16C+] an all-purpose v. of profanity, used in a wide variety of oaths and excls., lit. 'send to hell'; often as *damn me! damn you!* (cf. DAMMIT! excl.).

damn *adv.* [mid-19C+] a general intensifier, very, very much, exactly, completely. [DAMNED adv.]

damn! *excl.* [mid-18C+] an all-purpose profanity, used in a wide variety of contexts (cf. DAMMIT! excl.). [DAMN v.; the term is not sl. *per se*, but as cited by the *OED* is 'used profanely' and (in late 19C and beyond, still often found as *d--n* or even *d---*), thus it qualifies]

damnable *adj.* [19C+] a general abusive epithet, a term of dismissal and dislike. [prior use f. 16C is SE]

damnably *adv.* [19C+] a general intensifier. [prior use f. 16C is SE]

damn a horse if I do! *excl. see* DAMN (ME FOR) A HORSE IF I DO! excl.

damn-all *n.* [1910s+] nothing; also as general expletive, lit. 'nothing!' [DAMN adj./DAMN n.]

damn all *adj.* [1910s+] none, no. [DAMN-ALL n.]

damnation *n.* [17C+] a synon. for SE *hell*.

damnation! *excl.* [17C+] an oath of annoyance. [SE *damnation*, condemnation to eternal punishment]

damnation bow-wows *n.* (*also* **demnition bow-wows**) [mid-19C+] a euph. synon. for SE *hell*; apparently coined by Charles Dickens in *Nicholas Nickleby* (1838–9). [ext. DAMNATION n.]

damnation bow-wows! *excl.* [20C+] a general curse, an ext. of DAMNATION! excl.

damnation take it! *excl.* [19C+] a general curse, an ext. of DAMNATION! excl.

damn-but! *excl.* [1930s+] (*Irish*) an excl. of affirmation. [DAMN! excl.]

damned *adj.* (*also* **dammed, dom'd**) **1** [late 16C+] a strong expression of reprehension or dislike. **2** [mid-19C+] a general intensifier, complete, utter.

damned *adv.* (*also* **bedamned**) [late 16C+] a general intensifier, very, very much, exactly, completely. [DAMNED adj.]

damned! *excl. see* I'LL BE DAMNED! excl.

damned good swine up *n.* [late 19C] a loud quarrel, a fierce argument, prob. leading to blows. [DAMNED adv. + SE *good* + *swine*, i.e. the image of pigs fighting at the trough]

damned soul *n.* [late 18C–early 19C] a customs house clerk. [who, according to Grose (1796), 'guards against the crime of perjury, by taking a previous oath, never to swear truly on these occasions']

damnfool *adj. see* DAMFOOL adj.

damnit!/damn it all! *excl. see* DAMMIT! excl.

damn-it-skin! *excl.* [20C+] (*Ulster*) a mild excl. [ext. of DAMMIT! excl.]

damn (me for) a horse if I do! *excl.* [early 19C] an excl. implying one's absolute refusal to do something. [DAMN v.]

damn my eyes! *excl.* (*also* **blast my/your eyes! damn your eyes!**) [mid-18C+] an excl. of irritation, impatience, annoyance etc. [DAMN v./BLAST v.¹ (1)/DARN v.]

damn straight! *excl.* [1970s+] (*orig. US Black*) a general excl. of enthusiastic affirmation, absolutely! undoubtedly! [DAMN adj. + STRAIGHT adj.¹ (9)/? SE *skipping*]

damn tootin' *adv.* [1910s+] (*US*) absolutely, completely accurate, no doubt at all; also as excl. of affirmation. [DAMN adj. + SE *toot*, to blow a wind instrument]

damn well *adv.* [late 19C+] certainly, definitely, very much. [DAMN adv.]

damn your eyes! *excl. see* DAMN MY EYES! excl.

damn-your-eyes *adj.* [mid-19C–1930s] provocative. [DAMN MY EYES! excl.]

Damon (Hill) *n.* [1990s+] (*drugs*) a pill; esp. an amphetamine (cf. PILL n.⁴). [rhy. sl.; ult. racing driver *Damon Hill* (b.1960)]

damp *n.* **1** [mid-19C–1900s] a drink; thus *damp bazaar*, a bar. **2** [1950s+] the vagina, one of a number of terms that equate the organ with wetness, whether that of urine, vaginal secretions or fish-related imagery; thus *a slice of damp* (cf. BEARDED CLAM n.; DUCKPOND n.; FOUNTAIN OF LOVE n.; LIVING FOUNTAIN n.; PUMP DALE n.; SHADY SPRING n.; SLUICE n.; WATERBOX n.; WATERMILL n.). **3** [1970s] (*US*) sexual intercourse with a woman. [the wetness of the drink and of the stimulated vagina]

damp *adj.* **1** [early 19C] (*US*) tipsy, mildly drunk (cf. DRENCHED adj.; EMBALMED adj.; GET ONE'S SOUL IN SOAK v.; HALF-RINSED adj.; IN SOAK phr.²; LIQUEFIED adj.; LITTLE IN THE SUDS, A phr.; LUBRICATED adj.; MELTED adj.¹; OILED (UP) adj.; PICKLED adj.²; SATURATED adj.; SOAKED adj.; SODDEN adj.; SOGGY adj.; SOPPY adj.; SOUSED (UP) adj.; SOZZLED adj.; STEWED adj.¹; STEWED AS A PRUNE phr.; STEWED TO THE GILLS phr.; WATERLOGGED adj.; WELL-OILED adj.; WET adj.¹). **2** [late 19C–1910s] foolish, stupid.

damp *v.*¹ [mid-19C–1900s] to have a drink. [DAMP n. (1)]

damp *v.*² [1900s] (*US Und.*) to steal, by secreting a small object, a diamond, in the mouth.

damp bourbon poultice *n.* [late 19C] (*US*) a shot of bourbon. [the image is of the restorative powers of the alcohol]

dampen the dust *v.* [mid–late 19C] (*US*) to take a drink.

damper *n.*¹ **1** [late 18C–early 19C] a snack, eaten between meals. **2** [19C–1920] a glass of porter, used as a balance to a glass of spirits; any drink. **3** [late 19C] (*UK society*) the bill in a restaurant. [SE *damper*, that which damps down (the appetite) or depresses (the spirits)]

damper *n.*² **1** [mid-19C–1950s] a till, a cash drawer; thus *draw a damper, turn down the damper*, to rob a till; *damper getter*, a till robber. **2** [1930s–60s] (*US Und.*) a bank; thus *damper pad*, a bank book. **3** [1940s–50s] (*US*) a small safe, a cashbox. **4** [1950s] (*US*) in fig. use of (1), somewhere money goes. **5** [1950s+] (*US/Can. prison*) solitary confinement, punishment cells. [SE *damper*, that which calms or suppresses; (1), (2) and (3) it dampens the villain's hopes of an easy robbery, underpinned in (5) by a lit. interpretation]

damper *n.*³ [1990s+] (*UK tramp*) a bed-wetter.

damper *v.* [1970s] (*US Black*) to stop, to bring to an end. [SE *damp down*]

damp one's mug *v.* [mid-19C] to take a drink. [SE *damp* + MUG n.¹ (4)]

damson-pie *n.* (*also* **damson-tart**) [late 19C] obscene language. [pun on DAMN! excl.]

damwit *n.* [1940s] (*US*) a fool (cf. DIMWIT n.; DUMBWIT n.; FUCKWIT n.; LIGHTWIT n.; NITWIT n.; NUMBWIT n.; PANWIT n.; SPAZ-WIT n.). [DAMN-ALL n. + SE *wit*]

dan *n.*¹ [1900s–40s] dynamite. [semi-abbr.]

dan *n.*² [2000s] (*US Black*) a fool (cf. BEN n.¹). [acronym *dumb-ass nigger*]

dance *n.*¹ [mid-19C] a flight of stairs. [abbr. DANCERS n. (1)]

dance *n.*² [20C+] (*US prison*) a hanging.

dance *v.*¹ [16C+] to have sexual intercourse; also used in a variety of [17C–19C] phrs., e.g. *dance Adam's jig, dance Barnaby, dance on the mattress, dance the blanket hornpipe, …the buttock jig, …the cushion dance, …the goat's jig, …the Irish jig, …the married man's cotillion, …the matrimonial polka, …the mattress jig, …the miller's reel, dance with your arse to the ceiling, do a bit of (bum) dancing* (see *also* combs. below). [also found as a n. with a *double entendre*, e.g. in D'Urfey, *Pills to Purge Melancholy* (1719–20): 'Sukey' that Danc'd with the *Cushion*, / An Hour from the Room had been gone; And

Barnaby knew by her blushing, / That some other Dance had been done']

dance *v.*² [mid-17C+] a synon. for being hanged, used in a variety of combs. (cf. DANCE AT BEILBY'S BALL v.; DANCE AT THE SHERIFF'S BALL v.; DANCE ON AIR v.; DANCE ON NOTHING v.; DANCE THE NEWGATE HORNPIPE v.; DANCE THE PADDINGTON FRISK v.; DANCE THE TYBURN HORNPIPE ON NOTHING v.; DANCE THE TYBURN JIG v.; DO THE DANCE v.).

dance *v.*³ (*also* **dance the stairs**) [mid-19C+] to steal from first or higher floors, usu. in daytime when residents are downstairs and not in bed. [the light-footedness of the thief]

dance a haka *v.* [1940s–50s] (*N.Z.*) to express one's pleasure. [SE *dance* + Maori *haka*, a posture dance, accompanied by chants; a war-dance]

dance at Beilby's ball *v.* [mid-18C–early 19C] to be hanged; also ext. by *…where the sheriff plays the music* or *…where the sheriff pays the fiddlers*. [DANCE v.²; the ety. of Beilby is unknown; as Grose put it in 1785, 'who Mr Beilby was, or why that ceremony was so called, remains with the quadrature of the circle, the discovery of the philosopher's stone and divers other desiderata as yet undiscovered', but there exist a number of suggestions. The most obvious is that *Beilby* was a well-known sheriff; a second is that *Beilby* is a mispron. of *Old Bailey*, the court in which so many villains were sentenced to death. The third, and that espoused by E.P., is that *Beilby* refers to the *bilbo*, a long iron bar, furnished with sliding shackles to confine the ankles of prisoners and a lock by which to fix one end of the bar to the floor or ground. *Bilbo* comes from the Spanish town of Bilbao, where these fetters were invented]

dance at the sheriff's ball *v.* [late 18C–early 19C] to be hanged; ext. by *…and loll one's tongue out at the company*. [DANCE v.² + ironic use of SE]

dance at tuck 'em fair *v. see* TUCK 'EM FAIR n.

dance barefoot *v.* [late 16C–18C] for an older sister to remain single while a younger sister is married (cf. DANCE IN THE HOG TROUGH v.).

dance bobbin jo *v.* (*also* **dance bobb in-jo**) [17C] to have sexual intercourse. [DANCE v.¹ + the old dance *Bobbing Joan* although Williams suggests that Bobbing Joan might also have been a generic term for a prostitute and cites a similar use of Bobbing Bess in 1654]

dancehall *n.* (*also* **dancehouse**) [1920s+] (*US prison*) **1** the execution chamber. **2** the cell in which a prisoner is placed before being executed. [execution suggests DANCE v.² but the term is not limited to hanging; Goldin et al., *Dict. of American Und. Lingo* (1950), suggests (1) is 'erroneously used']

dance in a rope *v.* (*also* **dance on a rope**) [mid-17C; 1940s] to be hanged. [DANCE v.²]

dance in the hog trough *v.* (*also* **dance in the pig trough**) [mid-19C] (*US*) **1** for an older sibling to be left unmarried when a younger sibling has found a husband. **2** to be the last child in a family to be married. [? to have no suitors and have, therefore, to dance with the swine; later var. on DANCE BAREFOOT v.]

dance in the sandbox *v.* [1960s] (*US Black*) to scheme, to deceive. [var. on SE *throw sand in one's eyes*]

dance off *v.* [1930s] (*US*) to die by hanging. [DANCE v.²]

dance on a dime *v.* [1940s+] (*US*) to dance very close together.

dance on air *v.* [late 18C–1940s] to be hanged. [DANCE v.²]

dance on a rope *v. see* DANCE IN A ROPE v.

dance on nothing *v.* (*also* **dance upon nothing**) [late 18C–1930s] to be hanged; often ext. by *…at the sheriff's door, …in a hempen cravat, …at the tolling of a bell* etc. [DANCE v.² (+ HEMPEN CRAVAT n.); the sheriff has jurisdiction over the hanging, thus the *sheriff's door* is that of a prison, outside which the hanging took place]

dance on someone's lips *v.* (*also* **dance on someone's face**) [1980s+] (*US Black*) **1** to hit in the face. **2** to kick in the face.

dance on the carpet *v. see* ON THE CARPET phr.[2].

dancer *n.* [mid-19C+] a cat burglar who 'dances' along the roof and in through a convenient window, or a thief entering a house to rob the upstairs, when the residents are not in bed, or out; thus usu. a daylight robbery. The 20C+ use also refers to those who steal from empty offices. [DANCE v.[3]]

dancers *n.* **1** [mid-17C+] (*orig. UK Und.*) a flight of stairs. **2** [1950s+] the feet. [one *dances* down the stairs or on one's feet]

dancery *n.* [1950s] (*US*) a dance hall.

dance Sallinger's round *v.* (*also* **dance Sallenger's dance,** **...Sallenger's round, ...Sellinger's round**) [mid-17C–early 18C] to have sexual intercourse. [DANCE v.[1] + *Sallenger*, St Leger. 'St Leger's Round' was a popular ballad *c*.1600, according to Nares 'of an indelicate character']

dance someone around *v.* [1980s] (*US*) to harass, to pressurize someone.

dance the kipples *v.* [late 18C–19C] to have sexual intercourse. [DANCE v.[1] + Scot. *kipple*, couple]

dance the mill *v.* [mid-19C] (*W.I.*) to walk on the prison treadmill.

dance the Newgate hornpipe *v.* [late 18C–mid-19C] to be hanged. [DANCE v.[2] + *Newgate*, the site of London's major prison and public executions]

dance the Paddington frisk *v.* [mid-18C–early 19C] to be hanged. [DANCE v.[2] + *Tyburn*, the site of London's main 18C gallows, was in the then village of *Paddington*, near the modern Marble Arch]

dance the reels o'bogie *v.* (*also* **dance the reel...**) [late 18C–19C] (*Scot.*) to have sexual intercourse. [DANCE v.[1]]

dance the reels of stumpie *v.* [late 18C–19C] (*Scot.*) to have sexual intercourse. [DANCE v.[1] + dial. *stumpy*, something stump-like, i.e. the penis]

dance the stairs *v. see* DANCE v.[3].

dance the Tyburn hornpipe on nothing *v.* [late 18C–mid-19C] to be hanged. [DANCE v.[2] + the role of *Tyburn* as an execution ground]

dance the Tyburn jig *v.* [late 17C–early 19C] to be hanged. [DANCE v.[2] + *Tyburn*, the site of London's main 18C gallows, was in the then village of Paddington, near the modern Marble Arch]

dance to the tune of shaking the sheets (without music) *v.* (*also* **dance to the time of...**) [late 16C–19C] to have sexual intercourse. [DANCE v.[1] + 'an old country dance, often alluded to, but seldom without an indecent intimation' (Nares)]

dance upon nothing *v. see* DANCE ON NOTHING v.

dance with johnnie one-eye *v.* [1980s+] to masturbate (cf. DO A DRY WALTZ WITH ONESELF v.; HAND JIG v.; HAND JIVE v.; TAPDANCE v.).

dancing academy *n.* (*also* **dancing school**) [mid-17C–early 18C] a brothel (cf. ACADEMY n.). [DANCE v.[1] + ACADEMY n. (1)/SE *school*]

dancing dog *n.* [late 19C–1900s] a man who enjoys dancing. [SE *dancing* + SE *dog*/DOG n.[3] (2); the term was used in a period when dancing was no longer seen as fashionable]

dancing master *n.* **1** [17C] the hangman. **2** [mid-17C–early 18C] an upper-class rowdy who found his amusement in making his victims 'dance' by stabbing at their legs with his sword. **3** [mid-19C] a cat burglar. [(1) DANCE v.[2]; (2) and (3) SE *dance* but note DANCE v.[3]]

dancing school *n. see* DANCING ACADEMY n.

dand *n.* [late 19C] a *dandy*. [abbr.]

Dan Dares *n.* [1990s+] flared trousers, flares. [rhy. sl.]

d and d *n.* [late 19C+] the criminal charge of *drunk and disorderly*.

d & d *adj.* **1** [20C+] drunk *and* disorderly. **2** [1930s+] deaf *and* dumb. [abbr.]

dander *n.* [mid-19C+] (*orig. US*) temper; thus GET ONE'S DANDER UP v.; GET SOMEONE'S DANDER UP v. [? Rom. *dander*, to bite or

? SE *dander*, dandruff or ? fig. use of W.I. *dander*, the ferment created when working molasses into rum; but note various dial. uses as a commotion, a shivering fit]

dander *v.* [1910s] (*UK Und.*) to walk in a lively, brisk manner. [northern dial. *dander*, to wander, to saunter]

dandered *adj.* (*also* **dander**) [mid–late 19C] angry. [GET ONE'S DANDER UP v. (1)]

dandery *adj.* [mid-19C] (*US*) irritated, angry, alarmed. [DANDER n.]

d and i *n.* [1970s+] the criminal charge of *drunk and* incapable.

dandiprat *n.* (*also* **dandyprat**) [mid-16C–19C] an insignificant, contemptible person. [16C–17C SE *dandiprat*, a small coin worth 1½ old pence. F&H says 'half a farthing' in late 15C; Cotgrave, *Dict. French and English Tongues* (1611), defines it as 'a slender little fellow or dwarf']

dandisette/dandizette *n. see* DANDYSETTE n.

d & m *n.* [1990s+] (*orig. US teen*) a deep *and* meaningful conversation. [abbr.]

dando *n.* [mid-19C–1910s] a glutton, a great eater, esp. one who runs up a large bill at a restaurant or hotel and then leaves without paying. [a proper name of such a man, according to Hotten (1864), although no specifics have been offered]

dandruff *n.* [1950s–80s] a headbutt.

dandy *n.*[1] [late 18C+] **1** a first-rate, admirable thing. **2** an admirable person, a skilful person. [SE *dandy*]

dandy *n.*[2] [mid-19C+] (*orig. Irish*) **1** a small drink, usu. of whisky. **2** the glass in which it is served. [? fig. use of DANDY adj.]

dandy *n.*[3] [late 19C] (*UK Und.*) an imitation gold coin, a fake sovereign; thus *dandy-master*, a forger of gold coins.

dandy *adj.* [late 18C+] attractive, first-rate, excellent, a general term of approbation; thus [late 18C–mid-19C] *the dandy*, the correct thing, 'the ticket'. [SE *dandy*; i.e. something of which the fashionable dandy would approve]

dandy *adv.* [20C+] (*orig. US*) excellently, wonderfully. [DANDY adj.]

dandy-boy *n.* [1940s+] (*W.I.*) a well-dressed young man. [SE *dandy* + *boy*]

dandy-dude *n.* [1940s] (*W.I.*) a dandy. [SE *dandy* + DUDE n. (2)]

dandyfunk *n.* (*also* **dundefunk, dunderfunk**) [mid-19C–1900s] (*US*) a mixture of powdered biscuit, molasses and fat. [? SE *dandy*, a sloop, a cutter + *funk*, a smell]

dandy grey russet *adj.* [late 18C–early 19C] dirty brown in colour. [dial. *dandy-go-russet*, worn out or rust-coloured clothing]

dandy horse *n.* [early–mid-19C] a velocipede, a cross between a child's hobby-horse and the most primitive of bicycles.

dandyprat *n. see* DANDIPRAT n.

dandysette *n.* (*also* **dandisette, dandizette**) **1** [early–mid-19C] a female dandy. **2** [1960s+] (*US*) a lesbian. [SE *dandy* + SE fem. sfx *-(s)ette*]

dandy-trap *n.* [mid-19C] (*US*) a loose paving stone, on which a dandy may trip.

dang *n.*[1] [20C+] (*US*) a euph. for DAMN n. [DANG v.]

dang *n.*[2] *see* DANGLE n.

dang *adj.* [late 19C+] a euph. for DAMN adj. [DANG v.; 20C+ use mainly US]

dang *v.* **1** [late 18C+] a euph. for DAMN v. and used in similar oaths, e.g. *by dang! dang it! dang my buttons!* **2** [mid-19C] to curse, to abuse. [euph. + HANG v.[1]; orig. UK dial.; 20C+ use mainly US]

dang! *excl.* [late 18C+] a euph. for DAMN! excl. [DANG v.]

dangbatted *adj.* [1960s] (*US*) crazy. [DANG adj. + DINGBAT n.[9] (1)]

dange *n. see* DANGLE n.

danged *adj.* [mid-19C+] (*US*) a euph. for DAMNED adj. [DANG v.]

danger *n.* [1990s+] a chance, a possibility, a likelihood; e.g. *there's no danger of that*.

dangermuff *n.* [1990s+] an extremely attractive, sexy woman. [SE *danger* + MUFF n.[1] (4)]

dangerous *adj.* [19C+] (*US*) serious, even terminally ill.

danger signal *n.* [late 19C] (*UK Und.*) a policeman.

danger signal is up *phr. see* FLAG IS UP phr.

dangfool *adj. see* DAMFOOL adj.

dangle *n.* (*also* **dang, dange**) [1910s+] the penis; thus *on the dangle*, of a penis, flaccid or of a person, sexually unexcited. [metonymy]

dangle *v.* **1** [late 17C–18C] to hang. **2** [18C+] to follow a woman, without actually addressing her. **3** [early–mid-18C] to pursue. **4** [1920s–60s] to go, to travel, to move. **5** [1930s] (*US*) to go away; esp. in imper. *dangle!* go away! **6** [1960s+] to keep waiting, lit. or fig.

dangleberries *n.* [1990s+] pieces of excreta clinging to the hairs around an inadequately cleansed anus. [var. DINGLEBERRIES n. (1)]

dangle from *v.* [1910s+] of a man, to have sexual intercourse. [though the physical logic would presume a female point of view]

dangle in a Tyburn string *v.* [late 18C] to be hanged. [SE *dangle + Tyburn*, the site of the gallows]

dangle in the sheriff's picture-frame *v.* [late 18C–early 19C] to be hanged. [SE *dangle*]

dangle one's donger *v.* [1970s] to urinate. [SE *dangle +* DONGER n.[1] (1)]

danglepork *n.* [2000s] the penis (cf. BACON n.[1]). [SE *dangle/* DANGLE n. + PORK n.[2] (1)]

dangle queen *n.* [1980s+] (*US gay*) one who wears clothes that deliberately emphasize the penis, or who exposes the genitals. [DANGLE n. + QUEEN n.[2] (1)/QUEEN sfx (2)]

dangler *n.*[1] **1** [18C–mid-19C] one who follows women in the street but does not actually speak to them, a roué, a womanizer. **2** [18C+] a hanger-on, a suitor. **3** [1920s+] (*Aus./US*) an exhibitionist. [(1) and (2) DANGLE v. (2); (3) SE *dangle/*DANGLE n.]

dangler *n.*[2] **1** [mid-19C+] (*UK Und.*) any form of pendant jewellery, e.g. a watch fob, an earring. **2** [1970s+] (*US gay*) a large penis.

dangler *n.*[3] [1910s–30s] (*US tramp*) **1** a tramp who travels by hanging onto the rails and similar handgrips beneath a passenger coach. **2** a freight train.

dangler *n.*[4] **1** [1920s+] (*US*) a thief. **2** [1990s+] (*US Black*) a businessman. [? he keeps one *dangling* in expectation of money]

dangle roll *n.* [1990s+] (*US Black*) a losing throw of the dice in craps (cf. ADA FROM DECATUR n.). [it takes one's money and one must quit the game, i.e. DANGLE v. (4)]

danglers *n.* **1** [mid-19C] a bunch of seals (hanging from a watch chain). **2** [mid-19C+] the testicles (cf. BANGERS n.).

dangling modifier *n.* [1980s+] (*US campus*) a single, long, flashy earring. [pun on the grammatical term]

dangly-bits *n.* (*also* **jiggly bits**) [1990s+] the testicles (cf. BANGERS n.). [DANGLERS n. (2)]

dangnation! *excl.* [mid-19C] a euph. for DAMNATION! excl.

daniel *n.*[1] [1930s–40s] (*US Black*) the buttocks. [? corruption of SE *dangle*]

daniel *n.*[2] [1990s+] (*Aus. teen*) a rowdy person. [ety. unknown]

Danish *n.* [1980s] (*US*) conventional penetrative male–female sexual intercourse.

Danish pastry *n.* [1950s–60s] (*gay*) a transsexual. [for ety. *see* COPENHAGEN CAPON n.]

dank *n.* [1980s+] (*US Black/drugs*) extremely strong marijuana. [DANK adj. (2)]

dank *adj.* [1980s+] (*orig. US campus*) **1** bad, unpleasant. **2** excellent, first-rate. [(1) SE, which is always negative, usu. referring to swamps and marshes; (2) presumably on the bad = good model]

dank nugs *n.* (*also* **dark nuggets**) [1990s+] (*US drugs*) the very best marijuana. [DANK adj. (2) + SE *nuggets*]

danna *n.* [late 18C–mid-19C] human or other excrement; thus *danna drag*, a nightman's or dustman's cart. [DUNNAKEN n.]

dannie *n.* [20C+] a drink of liquor. [ext. of DANDY n.[2] (1)]

danny boy *n.* [2000s] (*Irish*) £20 (cf. JOYCE n.). [the picture on the pre-Euro note was of Irish politician *Daniel O'Connell* (1775–1847)]

Danny La Rue *n.* **1** [1980s] (*Aus.*) an act of defecation (cf. ANDY CAPP n.). **2** [2000s] an idea, a suspicion. **3** [2000s] (*bingo*) the number 52 (cf. ALDERSHOT LADIES n.). [rhy. sl.; (1) = POO n.[1] (2); (2) = CLUE n.[2]; ult. *Danny La Rue*, stage name of British entertainer and female impersonator *Daniel Patrick Carroll* (b.1927)]

dant *n.* [early–mid-16C] a promiscuous woman. [synon. Du. *dante*]

dan tucker *n.* (*also* **danny rucker**) [mid–late 19C; 1930s+] **1** butter. **2** breakfast. [(1) rhy. sl.; (2) ext. use; ult. ? anecdotal]

dap *n.*[1] [1970s+] (*US Black*) a ritualistic handshake, differing from area to area, involving much slapping of palms, snapping of fingers etc. [SE *dab*, to strike]

dap *n.*[2] [1970s+] (*US Black*) credit, acknowledgement, respect, self-awareness. [abbr. *dignity and pride*]

dap *adj.* [1950s+] (*US Black/P.R.*) **1** alert, aware, knowledgeable, sophisticated. **2** well-dressed. **3** of a person, pleasant, generous. [SE *dapper*, spruce, neat]

dap *v.* [20C+] to pick up, to steal, esp. luggage. [? SE *dab*, to touch lightly]

dap daddy *n.* (*also* **doogie daddy**) [1950s+] (*US Black*) a well-dressed man. [DAP adj. (2)/*doogie* = do good + DADDY n. (7)]

daphne *n.* [1980s] (*Aus.*) a foolish woman.

dapped down *adj.* [1950s+] (*US Black*) very well-dressed. [DAP adj. (2)]

dapped to a T *adj.* (*also* **dap to a T/tee**) [1950s+] (*US Black*) very well-dressed. [DAP adj. (2) + SE *to a T*]

dapper *n.* [1990s+] (*UK Black*) a general term of congratulation, an admirable person. [SE *dapper* + DAP adj. (1)]

dapper *adj.* [1960s+] (*US Black*) admirable, excellent. [ext. of SE + DAP adj. (1)]

dappy *adj. see* DIPPY adj. (1).

daps *n.* **1** [1920s–30s] slippers. **2** [1940s+] gym shoes, tennis shoes. [? dial. *dap*, the bounce of ball, a hop; the image is of bouncing along in one's rubber-soled shoes]

dapt *adj.* [1970s] (*US Black*) physically appealing, attractive, well-dressed. [DAP adj.]

dapto *n.* [1970s] (*Aus. teen*) a general insult. [the *Dapto* Dog Races, held in NSW; thus a DOG n.[3] (2)]

Dapto dog *n.* [1970s] (*Aus.*) a derog. term for a Black or Asian person (cf. FEARGAL SHARKEY n.; GOW n.[4]; GREVILLE STARKEY n.; HARVEST MOON n.; HEDGEHOG n.[2]; MECHANICAL DIGGER n.; SILVERY MOON n.; SQUARE RIGGER n.[2]). [rhy. sl. = WOG n.[1] (1); ult. *see* DAPTO n.]

d.a.r. *n.* [1930s–40s] (*US campus*) an academically successful student. [play on abbr. of *damned average raiser* and *Daughters of the American Revolution*]

darb *n.*[1] **1** [20C+] anything or anyone seen as first-rate; as *the darb*, 'the thing'. **2** [1910s–40s] (*US tramp*) an attractive woman. [? DAB n.[1] or fig. ext. of DARB n.[2]]

darb *n.*[2] [1900s–40s] (*US Und.*) money, usu. stolen. [? DARBY n.[1] (1)]

darb *adj.* [1930s–60s] (*US Und.*) highly competent. [DARB n.[1] (1)]

darberoo *n.* [1930s] a good thing. [DARB n.[1] (1) + -EROO sfx]

darbies *n.* [late 17C+] **1** shackles, fetters, handcuffs; thus *darby-ringer*, a villain; *darby ken/crib*, a blacksmith's. **2** in fig. use, anything that shackles one. [16C SE *Father Darby's bands*, a moneylender's bond of particular severity, which effectively bound the borrower to the lender while the debt remained outstanding]

darble *n.* [mid-19C] the Devil. [mangled pron. of Fr. *diable*]

darbs *n.* [late 19C–1930s] playing cards. [? backsl., i.e. the pips on a card resemble the *brads* or shoemakers' rivets in the sole of a boot]

darby *n.*[1] (*also* **derby**) **1** [late 17C–1920s] (*UK Und.*) money; thus *come down with the derbies*, to pay a bill or debt. **2** [mid-19C+]

(*UK Und.*) a haul of stolen goods. **3** [1920s] (*US*) a person with money, someone who can be relied on to pay the bill. [for ety. *see* DARBIES n.; (1) + COME DOWN WITH v.]

darby *n.*[2] [19C] (*Irish*) a glass of whisky; usu. as a *small darby*. [ety. unknown; ? anecdotal]

darby *adj.* [1910s–30s] (*US*) wonderful, excellent, first-rate. [DARB n.[1] (1)]

darby *v.* [late 19C] (*Aus. prison*) to handcuff, to shackle. [DARBIES n. (1)]

darby and joan *n.*[1] **1** [1920s+] the telephone. **2** [1940s+] (*Aus.*) a loan. [rhy. sl.; the phr. *Darby and Joan*, a synon. for an elderly, poss. impoverished but long-married couple, first appeared in the *Gentleman's Magazine* (vol. V, 1735) in a verse titled 'The joys of love never forgot, a song'. The third verse runs: 'Old Darby, with Joan by his side, / You've often regarded with wonder, / He's dropsical, she is sore-eyed, / Yet they're never happy asunder.' Whether the names refer to real-life characters (*Darby* is not a common UK name) or are taken from some earlier fiction remains unknown]

darby and joan *n.*[2] *see* JOAN n.[2].

darby and joan *adj.* [1940s–70s] alone; thus *on one's darby*, by oneself. [rhy. sl.; for ety. *see* DARBY AND JOAN n.[1]]

darby kelly *n.* (*also* **darby kel, derby kelly**) [20C+] the stomach. [rhy. sl. = belly]

darby-roll *n.* [early 19C] a style of walking that betrays an individual's experience of fetters and thus time spent in prison. [DARBIES n. (1) + SE *roll*, a swinging gait]

darby's fair *n.* [mid-19C] the day on which a prisoner is moved from one prison to another and must thus be fettered. [DARBIES n. (1) + ironic use of SE *fair*]

dard *n.* [17C–18C] the penis. [Fr. *dard*, a dart; note synon. Fr. sl. *dard* + *darder*, 'to fuck']

dargie *n. see* DOGGY n.[1] (1).

dark *n.*[1] **1** [mid-late 19C] (*Aus.*) Australian-distilled, dark, very strong brandy. **2** [1950s+] (*Aus.*) cheap red wine; usu. as FOURPENNY DARK n. **3** [1980s+] (*Aus. prison*) tobacco. [the dark red colour]

dark *n.*[2] **1** [mid-19C–1910s] (*US*) a derog. term for a Black person (cf. BLACKBELLY n.). **2** [1910s] (*Aus.*) a nickname for those with dark hair or complexion. [abbr. DARKIE n.[1]/SE *dark*]

dark *n.*[3] [1900s] (*Aus. prison*) solitary confinement in a dark cell.

dark *n.*[4] [1960s] (*US campus*) a fool, a dullard. [DARK adj.[1] (1)]

dark *adj.*[1] **1** [mid-17C–early 18C; 1940s+] stupid, ignorant. **2** [mid-19C+] weak-sighted, nearly or actually blind. [SE *dark*, unenlightened, uninformed, as in *dark ages*; (1) 1940s+ use W.I.; (2) 20C+ use Irish/W.I.]

dark *adj.*[2] [1980s+] **1** (*UK teen*) aggressive, very serious. **2** (*UK teen*) a general negative, bad, unpleasant, second-rate etc. **3** (*Aus. prison*) angry (with). [note RMC Duntroon (Aus.) *dark*, furious]

dark and dim *n.* [20C+] (*Aus.*) a swim. [rhy. sl.]

dark and dim *v.* [1900s] (*Aus.*) to swim. [rhy. sl.]

dark as an abo's arsehole *phr.* [1960s] (*Aus.*) very dark. [SE + ABO n.[1]]

dark as a nigger's pocket *phr.* [mid-19C–1910s] (*Aus.*) very dark. [SE + NIGGER n.[1] (1)]

dark as Newgate *phr. see* BLACK AS NEWGATE phr.

dark as Newgate knocker *phr. see* BLACK AS NEWGATE KNOCKER phr.

dark as the inside of a cow *phr.* [late 19C+] (*Can./US*) very dark. [UK use is naut. only]

dark brown shit *n.* [1950s–60s] (*US Black*) second-rate, inferior heroin (cf. BLACK n.[3]; CACA n.). [SE *dark brown* + SHIT n.[5] (1); pure heroin is white, although the influx of equally pure heroin from Mexico and the Far and Middle East during the 1970s, all of which was brown, meant that the equation no longer held]

dark cell *n.* [20C+] (*US Und.*) a prison punishment cell. [its lack of amenities]

Dark City *n.* [1950s–60s] (*S.Afr.*) the township of Alexandra, near Johannesburg. [SE *dark*/DARK n.[2] (1) + SE *city*]

dark cloud *n.* [1900s–50s] (*mainly Aus./US*) a derog. term for a Black person, a Native Australian (cf. BLACKBELLY n.).

dark cully *n.* [18C–mid-19C] (*UK Und.*) one who keeps a mistress and only dares visit her surreptitiously at night. [SE *dark* + CULLY n. (2)]

darkee *n. see* DARKEY n.

dark engineer *n.* [late 17C] a villain. [SE *dark* + *engineer*, to manipulate, to perform]

darken someone's daylights *v.* [mid-18C–1900s] to give someone a black eye. [SE *darken* + DAYLIGHTS n. (1)]

darkers *n.* [1950s+] (*W.I. Rasta*) sunglasses. [SE *dark* (*glasses*)]

darkey *see also under* DARKIE.

darkey *n.* (*also* **darkee, darky**) **1** [mid-18C–19C] night-time. **2** [19C] a 'dark', i.e. shuttered, lantern. **3** [early 19C] (*US Und.*) a cloudy sky. **4** [mid-19C] twilight. **5** [late 19C] a night watchman. [DARKMANS n.]

dark felt *n.* [20C+] (*Aus.*) a belt. [rhy. sl.]

dark hole *n.* [late 19C] the vagina (cf. BLACK HOLE n.[1]).

dark horse *n.* [mid-19C+] one of whom little is known, esp. one's opponent in a competition. [racing jargon *dark horse*, a horse about whose form little is known. The term appears to have been coined by Benjamin Disraeli in *The Young Duke* (1831), although his use appears to be purely descriptive]

dark house *n.* **1** [early 17C–mid-19C] a room used to confine the insane. **2** [late 17C] a tavern offering bedrooms for the night.

darkie *n.*[1] (*also* **darkey, darky**) **1** [late 18C+] a derog. term for a Black person; also used ironically by Blacks as a self-description (cf. BLACKBELLY n.). **2** [1930s] a person with dark hair (cf. BLONDIE n.). [(1) coined in the UK, the term has spread to all English-language sl., denoting Afro-Americans, Aborigines, Maoris and others]

darkie *n.*[2] [mid-19C] (*UK Und.*) a beggar who feigns blindness.

darkie *adj.* (*also* **darkey, darky**) [mid-19C+] (*US*) a derog. adj. meaning pertaining to Black people or culture.

darkies *n.* [mid-late 19C] a variety of late-night music-halls and bars on or near the Strand, London, usu. situated below ground level, e.g. the Shades, the Cider Cellars and the Coal Hole.

dark it *v.* [late 19C] to say nothing; esp. as imper. *dark it!* be quiet! keep quiet!

dark lantern *n.* [mid-19C] a thief's candle or light, made so it is possible to shut out the light when not needed.

dark lanthorn *n.* [late 17C–mid-19C] a servant or agent who takes and transmits a bribe offered to his master. [he metaphorically diverts the light of his lantern from the robbery]

darkman *n.*[1] [early–mid-18C] a nightwatchman.

darkman *n.*[2] [1970s] (*Aus.*) a derog. term for an Aborigine.

darkmans *n.* (*also* **darkman, darkum**) [mid-16C–19C] (*UK Und.*) the night. [SE *dark* + -MANS sfx]

darkmans budge *n.* [late 17C–early 19C] (*UK Und.*) a thief's accomplice, who climbs into a house through a window and opens a door to admit the rest of the gang. [DARKMANS n. + BUDGE n.[1] (1)]

dark meat *n.* **1** [late 19C; 1930s+] (*also* **dark shanks**) Black people, esp. as sex objects. **2** [1940s] the 'black sheep'. **3** [1940s+] (*US*) the Black penis or vagina (cf. BACON n.[1]; BACON SANDWICH n.).

darkness at noon *n.* [1970s+] (*US campus*) the slide shows that form the basis of lectures in Art History. [pun on the novel *Darkness at Noon* (1940) by Arthur Koestler]

darks, the *n.* **1** [late 18C] the night. **2** [2000s] depression.

dark-sambo *n.* [1950s+] (*W.I.*) a person of mixed race, with one-quarter White to three-quarters Black. [SE *dark* + SAMBO n.[1] (2)]

dark shanks *n. see* DARK MEAT n. (1).

dark stuff *n.* [1960s] (*US*) a Black person, usu. a woman, in a sexual context.

darktown n. (also **darkytown**) [late 19C+] (US) the Black area of a town or city. [SE dark/DARK n.[2] (1)/DARKIE adj.+ SE town]

darkum n. see DARKMANS n.

dark-'un n. (also **darkun**) [1930s+] (Aus.) a 24-hour shift, worked by a wharf labourer. [it involves working through the dark]

darky see also under DARKIE.

darky n. see DARKEY n.

darkytown n. see DARKTOWN n.

darl n. (also **darls**) [1930s+] (mainly Aus.) a general term of endearment. [abbr. SE darling]

darling it hurts n. [20C+] (Aus.) Darlinghurst, a rough inner-city area of Sydney. [joc. mispron.]

Darling whaler n. see MURRUMBIDGEE WHALER n.

Darlo n. [1930s+] (Aus.) Darlinghurst. [abbr. + -o sfx (4)]

darls n. see DARL n.

darn n. (also **dern, durn**) [mid-19C+] a euph. for DAMN n.; usu. found in phrs., e.g. not care a darn, to not care at all.

darn adj. (also **dern, durn**) [mid-19C+] a euph. for DAMN adj. [euph./abbr. DARNATION adj.]

darn v. [mid-19C+] a euph for DAMN v., used in mild excls.

darn adv. (also **durn**) [mid-19C+] a euph. for DAMN adv. [DARN adj.]

darn! excl. (also **dern!**) [late 19C+] (US) a euph. for DAMN! excl. [euph./abbr. DARNATION! excl.]

darnation adj. [late 18C+] (US) a euph. for DAMNED adj. [DARNATION! excl.]

darnation adv. [early 19C+] a euph. for DAMN adv. [DARNATION adj.]

darnation! excl. (also **durnation!**) [late 18C+] a euph. for DAMN! excl.

darned adj. (also **derned, durned**) [early 19C+] a euph. for DAMNED adj.; thus superlative darnedest; thus fig. do one's darnedest, to do one's very best.

darned adv. [mid-19C+] a euph. for DAMNED adv. [DARNED adj.]

darnfool adj. see DAMFOOL adj.

darn my buttons! excl. see DASH MY BUTTONS! excl.

darrel lea n. [1980s+] (Aus. prison) tea. [a well-known brand of chocolate]

Darren Gough n. [1990s+] a cough. [rhy. sl.; ult. England cricketer Darren Gough (b.1970)]

darry n. [1940s–50s] (UK prison) a look. [? DERRY n.]

darryl n. [1990s+] a general term of abuse. [? negative stereotyping of the proper name]

dart n. (Aus.) 1 [late 19C] one's fancy or favourite. 2 [late 19C] an illicit activity, a 'racket'. 3 [late 19C–1910s] a plan, an aim, a scheme. 4 [late 19C+] a try, a 'go'. 5 [20C+] a good idea. [SE dart used fig. to describe the target as much as the missile]

dart accent n. (also **dortspeak, Roadwatch accent**) [1990s+] (Irish) an affectedly quasi-British accent, adopted by the middle class in and around Dublin. [DART, Dublin Area Rapid Transit, i.e. those areas served by the system. The accent was orig. identified among radio/TV presenters (thus the ref. to the programme Roadwatch) and is typified by the use of the phoneme 'ou' in such words as 'cow']

daru n. [20C+] (W.I.) rum. [Bhojpuri daaruu, liquor]

Darwin blonde n. [1940s] (Aus.) a half-caste woman. [proper name Darwin + SE blonde; the ref. is to the Aborigine population of Northern Territory, of which Darwin is the capital]

Darwin stubby n. [1970s+] (Aus.) an extra-large beer bottle, introduced in 1958 at 80fl oz; increased in 1973 to 2.25 litres and in 1982 to 2 litres. [proper name Darwin + STUBBIE n. (1)]

d.a.'s n. [mid-19C–1920s] the menstrual flow. [domestic afflictions]

dash n.[1] [late 17C–19C] a tavern waiter. [SE dash, to rush about or dash, style, flair]

dash n.[2] [late 18C+] a tip, bribery, the money paid as a bribe. [SE dashee, a gift, present, gratuity; a 'Negrish word' used on the Guinea Coast]

dash n.[3] [19C] a drink; usu. as a dash of... [SE dash, a small quantity]

dash n.[4] [early 19C] (US) an attractive young woman. [SE dash, style]

dash n.[5] 1 [early 19C+] an attempt; usu. in phr. HAVE A DASH v. 2 [1970s+] (US gay) a latent homosexual.

dash n.[6] [1980s+] (Aus. prison) bravery. [SE dash, style]

dash adj. see DASHED adj.

dash v. [early 19C+] a general euph. for DAMN v., used in mild excls. [from the dash that replaces the 'am' in damn; thus d–n and subseq. in other 'obscenities'; note Captain Alexander Smith, History of the Lives of the Most Noted Highwaymen (5th edn, 1719): 'If we have here and there brought in some of these wicked offenders venting a profane oath or curse, which is dashed, it is to paint them in their proper colours']

dash! excl. (also **by dash!**) [mid-19C+] a general euph. for DAMN! excl. [DASH v.]

dash away belly v. see THROW AWAY BELLY v.

dashboards n. [1910s] (US) feet.

dashed adj. (also **dash**) [mid-19C+] a general adj. of annoyance or irritation; a euph. for DAMNED adj./DAMN adj. [DASH v.]

dasher n. 1 [mid-18C–19C] a flashy prostitute. 2 [19C+] a 'fast' young woman. 3 [early 19C–1950s] a smart young person, keen on parties and socializing. 4 [late 19C] a dashing attempt. 5 [late 19C+] (W.I.) a dandy. 6 [late 19C+] (W.I.) a womanizer. [ext. use of SE cut a dash]

dashing adj. [19C] showy, given to excess, esp. in dress. [SE cut a dash; SE in 20C+]

dash in the bloomers n. [1960s+] sexual intercourse, usu. quick and adulterous. [SE dash, a rush + bloomers]

dash it (all)! excl. [mid-19C+] a general euph. excl. [DASH v.]

dash my buttons! excl. (also **darn my buttons! dash my rags! dash my skin! dash my timbers! doggone my buttons!**) [19C–1910s] a mild oath. [ext. of DASH v./DARN v./DOGGONE! excl.]

dash my wig(s)! excl. [late 18C–19C] a mild oath. [ext. of DASH v.]

dashy adj. [early–mid-19C] showy, ostentatiously fashionable, stylish. [SE cut a dash]

dast v. [late 19C] (US) a euph. for DAMN v., used in mild excls. [DAMN v. + BLAST v.[1] (1)]

dasted adj. [late 19C] (US) a euph. mix of DAMNED adj. and BLASTED adj.[1] (1). [DAST v.]

dasy n. see DAISY n.[1].

date n.[1] (orig. US) 1 [late 19C+] a person with whom one makes or has made an appointment or engagement, usu. for social/sexual purposes. 2 [late 19C+] the appointment that has been made. 3 [1930s+] a prostitute's client. 4 [1950s+] a paid encounter with a prostitute.

date n.[2] [1900s–50s] a foolish or comic person; thus (UK juv.) soppy date, an affectionate term of abuse. [the common use of fruit to indicate stupidity]

date n.[3] 1 [1910s] (Aus.) a term of abuse (cf. ARSE n.[1]). 2 [1910s+] (Aus./N.Z./UK) the anus, the backside as a whole (cf. ALA n.; BOTTLE AND GLASS n.). [rhy. sl.; date and plum = BUM n.[1] (1); note 17C dog-date, dog excrement, from supposed resemblance]

date v.[1] (also **date up**) 1 [20C+] (orig. US) to have an affair with someone, to be going out together on a number of pre-arranged days; thus double date, for 2 couples to join each other on the same engagement; dated, 'booked' for an engagement or meeting; dating, making dates. 2 [1990s+] to have sexual intercourse. [DATE n.[1]]

date v.[2] [1910s+] (Aus./N.Z.) to caress the buttocks; to 'goose', i.e. to stick a thumb or finger into someone's anus. [DATE n.[3] (2)]

date bait n. 1 [1940s–50s] (US Black) a boy- or girlfriend. 2 [1940s+] (US campus) someone with whom one would like to form a relationship. 3 [1980s+] something that will persuade a member of the opposite sex to accept the offer of a date. [DATE n.[1] + SE *bait*]

date puncher n. (*also* **date packer**) [1980s+] (*Aus.*) a male homosexual (cf. ANAL ASTRONAUT n.). [DATE n.[3] (2) + SE *puncher/packer*]

date up v. see DATE v.[1].

datty adj. [2000s] (*UK teen*) mad. [? DOTTY adj. (2) + BATTY adj.[1]]

daub n.[1] (*also* **dawb**) [18C] a bribe. [DAUB v.]

daub n.[2] [mid-19C–1900s] an artist. [SE *daub*, a second-rate painting]

daub v. (*also* **dawb**) [late 17C–early 19C] to bribe. [? SE *daub*, to lay on thick; cf. SE phr. *grease one's palm*, dial. *daub*, to flatter, to 'butter up']

dauber n. (*also* **dobber**) [1910s+] (*US*) spirit, morale. [? link to dial. *dobber*, a 'wonder']

daub of the brush n. see BRUSH n.[3] (2).

daughter n. **1** [1940s–70s] a male homosexual brought into the gay world by a homosexual friend (cf. AUNTIE n.[2]). **2** [1990s+] (*UK Black/W.I.*) any young woman, irrespective of relationship.

daughters of the game n. see GAME n.[1] (2).

dave adj. [1990s+] friendly, agreeable; admirable.

Davey's locker n. see DAVY JONES'S LOCKER n.

David Gower n. [1990s+] a shower (of rain). [rhy. sl., ult. English cricketer *David Gower* (b.1957)]

David Jones n. [1980s] (*Aus.*) bones. [rhy. sl.; ult. chain of department stores in Aus.]

David Joneses n. see DAVY JONES'S LOCKER n.

davy n. [late 18C–1950s] an oath; thus *on my davy*, on my oath, on my honour. [abbr. SE *affidavit*]

Davy Crockett n.[1] [1940s] (*US Black/Harlem*) a draft board official during WW2. [proper name *Davy Crockett* (1786–1836), frontiersman, trapper, US Congressman and one of those who died defending the Alamo; in this context he was seen as 'trapping' men for the services]

Davy Crockett n.[2] [1950s+] a pocket. [rhy. sl.; for ety. see DAVY CROCKETT n.[1]]

Davy Jones's locker n. (*also* **David Joneses, Davy Jones, Davy Jones' chest-lid/dock-yard, Davey's locker, Davy's locker, Jones's locker, old Davey**) [mid-18C+] a watery grave; thus death in general; thus *go to Davy Jones's locker*, to die. [at best *Davy Jones* represents the spirit of the sea, at worst he is the ocean's own devil (thus Dickens, *Bleak House* (1853): 'If you only have to swab a plank, you should swab it as if Davy Jones were after you'); either way it is in his 'locker' that drowned seamen are stowed. The identification was first printed by Tobias Smollett in *Peregrine Pickle* (1751). The ety. remains obscure, but E.P. suggests that *Jones* refers to Jonah whose own 'locker' was the belly of the whale. *Davy*, it is proposed, may have been added by Welsh sailors]

davy large n. [late 19C] a barge. [rhy. sl.]

Davy's dust n. [mid-19C] (*UK Und.*) gunpowder. [ety. unknown]

Davy's locker n. see DAVY JONES'S LOCKER n.

daw n. see GOBDAW n.

dawamesk n. [1960s+] (*drugs*) marijuana; orig. a mixture of hashish and a variety of spices and other ingredients. [Arabic *dawamesc*, a form of 'cannabis jam', mixing hashish with oil, vanilla, pistachio, almonds and musk; plus sometimes Cantharides]

dawb see under DAUB.

dawg n. see DOG n.[2].

dawg! excl. [1980s+] (*US campus/teen*) an expression of approval or surprise and disbelief. [joc. pron. of SE *dog*; thus cf. HOT DOG! excl.]

dawner n. [1980s] (*US*) a meeting that lasts all night; lit. until dawn.

Dawn Frazer n. (*also* **Malcolm Fraser**) [1960s+] (*Aus.*) a razor. [rhy. sl.; ult. the 1960s Aus. swimming star *Dawn Frazer*

(b.1937) or Aus. Prime Minister 1975–83 *Malcolm Fraser* (b.1930)]

day and martin n. [19C–1900s] a derog. term for a Black person (cf. BLACKBELLY n.). [*Day and Martin's* shoe blacking]

day and night n. [1950s+] light ale. [rhy. sl.]

day-day phr. [1900s–30s] (*US*) goodbye, farewell. [the daytime equivalent of *night-night*, goodnight, and similarly used to children or in a consciously joc. manner]

day for the king n. (*also* **day for a king, day on the king/queen**) [1940s+] (*N.Z.*) a day off, orig. when outdoor work was impossible, but used generally to cover any unofficial day off, e.g. one that follows a night of over-enthusiastic enjoyment. [SE phr. *a day (fit for) a king*, a very pleasant day + the idea of the king/queen, as ruler, paying for the day]

daylight n. [late 18C–mid-19C] the space left in a glass between the top of the liquor and the rim; such a space is not allowed when drinking bumpers, thus the drinking toast *no daylight!*

daylight v. [1970s] (*US Black*) to enlighten, to explain. [SE *let in some daylight*]

daylights n. **1** [mid-18C+] the eyes. **2** [mid-19C+] the insides, the essence; in phrs. BEAT THE (LIVING) DAYLIGHTS OUT OF v.

day one n. [1970s+] (*orig. US*) the beginning, long ago. [lit. the first-ever day]

day on the king/queen n. see DAY FOR THE KING n.

day-opener n. [mid–late 19C] (*orig. boxing*) an eye.

days! excl. see FOR DAYS! excl. (2).

day's dawning n. (*also* **day's a-dawning**) [20C+] morning. [rhy. sl.]

daze v. [1970s+] (*US campus*) to daydream. [SE *daze*]

dazzey duks n. see DAISY DUKES n.

dazzler n. **1** [late 19C] a dazzling blow. **2** [late 19C+] one who dazzles, esp. an ostentatious woman.

d.b. n. see DOUCHEBAG n.

d-boy n. [1990s+] (*US Black teen*) a drug dealer. [abbr. SE *drugs* + SE *boy*]

D.C. n. [1980s+] (*US*) Washington, D.C. [abbr.]

d.c. n. **1** [1900s] (*Aus.*) the *d*ress *c*ircle in the theatre. **2** [1930s] (*US Und.*) a *d*angerous *c*haracter. **3** [1980s] (*UK Und.*) a *d*etention *c*entre. **4** [1990s+] (*US prison*) the *d*eath *c*ell. [abbr.]

d'd adj. [mid-19C–1930s] a euph. abbr. of DAMNED adj.

d.d.f.m.g. n. [1990s+] (*US campus*) an exceptionally attractive member of the opposite sex. [*d*rop *d*ead *f*uck *m*e *g*orgeous]

d.d.t.! excl. [1940s–50s] (*US campus*) a general phr. of dismissal, contempt. [abbr. *d*rop *d*ead *t*wice]

de n. [1970s] (*US Und.*) **1** the *de*ceased. **2** a *de*fendant. [abbr.]

deacon n. see JOEY n.[12].

deacon v. (*US*) **1** [mid-19C–1920s] to pack (fruit etc) with the finest specimens on the top. **2** [late 19C] to adulterate, to doctor, to get something for nothing, e.g. *deacon land*, to increase one's land by gradually extending one's fences or boundary lines into unclaimed or common property. **3** [1900s] to deceive, esp. to make things appear better than they actually are. [an old story: a farmer sold a barrel of apples to a minister, and when it was opened many of the apples that lay beneath the top layer were found to be bad. When the minister questioned the farmer he was informed: 'You must have opened them at the wrong end.' Henceforth the farmer took care to 'deacon' both ends of his apples]

deacon (off) v. [mid-19C] (*US*) 'to read aloud (a hymn) one or two lines at a time, the congregation singing the lines as soon as read, according to the early practice of the Congregational Churches of New England' (*OED*); thus in non-religious contexts. [as practised by church deacons]

deacon's nose n. see PARSON'S NOSE n.

dead n.[1] [mid-19C] (*US campus*) a class recitation that is judged to be a total failure; thus *to take a dead*, to fail one's recitation.

dead n.[2] [20C+] (*W.I., Bdos*) problems, trouble.

dead *adj.*[1] **1** [mid-18C+] of a bottle, finished, empty. **2** [mid-19C+] (*US Black*) of people, forgotten; of things, ideas, unfashionable, out of style. **3** [late 19C–1920s] of a house or place, uninhabited, empty, deserted. **4** [late 19C–1940s] (*US tramp*) reformed. **5** [1900s–30s] having no knowledge. **6** [1930s+] of a place, esp. a club, a party, boring, unexciting. **7** [1960s+] finished, lost, spec. arrested, captured; thus *have someone/something dead*, to have at one's mercy, to dominate completely.

dead *adj.*[2] [19C] very drunk. [abbr. DEAD *adv. drunk*]

dead *v.* **1** [mid-19C] (*US campus*) of a student, to fail completely in one's recitation. **2** [mid–late 19C] (*US campus*) of a teacher, to make a student fail a recitation. **3** [20C+] (*US*) to loaf around, to idle. **4** [2000s] (*US prison*) to remove, to steal. **5** [2000s] (*UK Black*) to die.

dead *adv.* [early 17C+] a general intensifier, very, extremely, absolutely, completely; also used as an adj. meaning complete, utter, e.g. in DEAD CERT *n.*

dead-alive *adj.* (*also* **dead and alive**) **1** [mid-19C] stupid, dull. **2** [mid-19C+] miserable, down-in-the-mouth.

deadas *n.* [1990s+] (*W.I.*) meat.

dead as… *phr.* [20C+] used in a variety of phrs. all meaning absolutely dead; *see also* combs. below.

dead as billy-be-damned *phr. see* BILLY-BE-DAMNED *n.* (1).

dead as dogshit *phr.* [1980s+] absolutely dead. [DEAD AS… phr.]

dead as Kelsey's nuts *phr.* (*also* **deader than Kelsey's nuts**) [1930s+] (*US*) very, definitely dead, out of favour. [DEAD AS… phr. in lit. or fig. use; for ety. *see* KELSEY'S NUTS *n.*]

dead ass *n.* (*also* **dead-butt**) [1950s+] (*US*) **1** the seated rump, usu. as symbolic of laziness. **2** an idler, a lazy person. **3** one who is effectively dead. **4** a listless, de-energized person. **5** an utterly boring, useless person. [SE *dead* + -ASS *sfx*/BUTT *n.*[1] (4)]

dead-ass *adj.* (*also* **dead-butt**) [1950s+] **1** (*US*) lacking energy, listless, lifeless. **2** (*US*) of a place, inactive, boring. **3** (*W.I.*) as a negative intensifier. [DEAD ASS *n.*]

dead-ass *adv.*[1] [1970s+] (*US*) lifelessly, listlessly. [DEAD-ASS adj. (1)]

dead-ass *adv.*[2] [1970s+] (*US*) completely, wholly, utterly. [DEAD adv. + -ASS *sfx*]

dead baby *n.* [1950s] (*mainly UK juv.*) suet pudding with a sauce.

dead-bang *adj.*[1] [1930s] certain, total, complete, utter. [DEAD-BANG adv.]

dead-bang *adj.*[2] [1930s+] (*US*) of a criminal prosecution, lacking any possibility of defence or argument because the case is watertight. [DEAD adv. + BANG TO RIGHTS adj.]

dead-bang *adv.* [1910s+] completely, utterly, totally, absolutely. [DEAD adv. + BANG adv. (1)]

deadbeat *n.* (*orig. US*) **1** [mid-19C] of things, a failure, a deception. **2** [mid-19C+] of people, a failure, a down-and-out. **3** [mid-19C+] a malingerer, an idler, a wastrel. **4** [mid-19C+] a cadger, a sponge. **5** [1910s+] one who reneges on their debts. [backform. f. DEADBEAT adj.]

deadbeat *adj.* **1** [early–mid-19C] absolutely defeated. **2** [early 19C+] worn-out, exhausted. **3** [mid-19C] lazy, idle. **4** [late 19C+] useless, ne'er-do-well, impoverished. [DEAD adv. + SE *beaten*; (2) note Egan, *Life in London* (1821): '"Dead beat!" or "beat to a stand still!" Common phrases in the Sporting World, when a man or horse is so completely exhausted from over-exertion, or the constitution breaking down, as to give up the object in view, not being able to pursue it any further']

deadbeat *v.* [late 19C+] (*US*) **1** to waste time, to idle around. **2** to sponge on someone. **3** to cheat. [DEADBEAT *n.*]

deadbeatism *n.* [mid–late 19C] worthlessness. [DEADBEAT *n.* + sfx -*ism*]

deadbell *n.* [20C+] (*Ulster*) a ringing in the ears.

dead bird *n.* **1** [late 19C+] (*Aus.*) a certain bet, a sure thing. **2** [1900s–10s] (*US*) a hopeless case, situation or person. [like the bird, it cannot 'move']

dead book *v.* [early 19C] (*UK Und.*) to kill, to hang. [lit. to inscribe in the 'book of the dead']

dead broke *adj.* [mid-19C+] (*orig. US*) completely without funds; thus *v. dead-broke*, to impoverish. [DEAD adv. + BROKE adj.[1]]

dead-broker *n.* [late 19C+] (*Aus.*) a down-and-out. [DEAD BROKE adj.]

dead butt *n. see* DEAD ASS *n.*

dead-butt *adj. see* DEAD-ASS adj.

dead card *n.* [late 19C–1900s] (*US*) something that is unlucky, unfashionable or unpopular. [SE *dead card*, a card that has been discarded in a game and is no longer to be used by the players]

dead cargo *n.* [late 17C–19C] (*UK Und.*) the proceeds of a robbery that have turned out to be less valuable than hoped.

dead cat up the branch *phr.* [20C+] a phr. used to suggest that something is suspicious, something is not as it should be, someone is attempting to deceive the speaker. [SE *branch*, either that of a tree or a *branch line*, thus *see* DEAD CAT UP THE LINE phr.]

dead cat up the line *phr.* (*also* **dead cat on the line**) [20C+] (*US Black*) a phr. used when something seems suspicious. [a variety of suggested etys. include (i) a dead catfish left too long on a fishing line, implying that something must have happened to the angler; (ii) a woman who is obviously having an affair since she is utterly passive (i.e. SE *dead*) during sexual intercourse; (iii) an actual dead cat that had climbed a telegraph pole and is now interrupting the telephone line]

dead cert *n.* [late 19C+] (*orig. racing*) an absolute certainty, esp. in race-course betting. [DEAD adv. + CERT *n.*]

dead chicken *n.* [1960s+] (*US*) a doomed person, a lost soul.

dead chocker *adj.* (*also* **dead chokka**) [1950s] (*orig. milit.*) very bored. [DEAD adv. + CHOCKER adj.[1]]

dead chuffed *adj. see* CHUFFED adj.

dead-copper *n.* [1920s+] (*Aus.*) a police informer. [DEAD adv. + COPPER *n.*[3] (1)]

dead cunt *n.* [1990s+] (*Aus.*) a strong term of abuse. [DEAD adv. + CUNT *n.*[2] (1)]

dead duck *n.* (*orig. US*) **1** [mid-19C+] a complete, irredeemable failure. **2** [1910s+] a hopeless person, one who has absolutely no chance. [fig. use of SE + pvb 'never waste powder on a dead duck']

dead-end street *n.* [19C; 1990s+] the vagina (cf. ALLEY *n.*[1]). [synon. for cul-de-sac; there is in *dead* an extra implication of passivity on the woman's part]

deadener *n.*[1] [mid–late 19C] (*US*) a very attractive woman. [SE *deaden*]

deadener *n.*[2] [1930s+] (*Aus.*) a bully, one who prefers to settle arguments through violence. [SE *deaden*]

deader *n.* (*orig. US*) **1** [late 19C] an exhausted person. **2** [20C+] a dead person, a corpse; thus *be a deader*, to be recently dead.

deaders *n.* [1980s+] (*W.I./UK Black teen*) animal flesh, meat by-products eaten as food. [SE *dead*; the implication is that such foods are unpalatable]

deader than Kelsey's nuts *phr. see* DEAD AS KELSEY'S NUTS phr.

deadeye *n.*[1] **1** [mid-19C] a term of abuse. **2** [1970s+] the anus. [(2) SE *dead* + EYE *sfx*]

deadeye *n.*[2] *see* DEADY *n.*

deadeye *v.* [1960s+] (*US*) to stare at in a chilly manner; thus as adv.

dead-eye dick *n.* [1930s+] (*gay*) one who performs anal intercourse. [nickname for a superlative marksman + pun on DICK *n.*[4] (1)]

deadfall *n.* **1** [mid–late 19C] a cheap, poss. corrupt, casino. **2** [mid-19C–1950s] (*US*) a rough saloon. [the drunks 'fall down dead' + ? pun on SE *deadfall*, a trap for large game]

dead finish *n.* [late 19C–1900s] (*Aus.*) the absolute, the complete. [DEAD adv. + SE *finish*]

dead fink *n.* [20C+] (*Irish*) an attractive girl. [ety. unknown]

dead-fly cake *n. see* SQUASHED FLIES *n.*

dead for *phr.* [late 19C–1920s] (*Aus./US*) desperate for, in great need of. [var. on SE *dying for*]

dead from the neck up *phr.* [1910s+] particularly stupid.

dead-game *adj.* [late 19C–1950s] (*US campus*) dissolute, ostentatious.

dead giveaway *n.* [late 19C+] (*orig. US*) **1** a complete betrayal. **2** a swindle, a deception. [DEAD adv. + SE *giveaway*]

dead hand *n.* [19C+] an expert. [DEAD adv. + HAND n.¹ + pun on SE; 20C+ use is Aus.]

deadhead *n.*¹ **1** [mid-19C+] one who receives goods or services without paying. **2** [mid-19C+] a non-participant, one who does not contribute. **3** [late 19C–1950s] (*US tramp*) an empty freight car or freight train; thus one who rides it. **4** [late 19C+] a lazy, worthless person. **5** [1930s+] a drunk. **6** [1940s+] a fool. **7** [2000s] a state of non-communication. [orig. theatre jargon *deadhead*, one who does not pay for their ticket]

deadhead *n.*² **1** [1970s+] a fan and follower of the Grateful Dead, one of the earliest psychedelic bands, and still one of the most popular in the US and the world. **2** [1980s] a HIPPIE n.² (3), esp. a devotee of a 'back to nature' lifestyle. [proper name *Grateful Dead* + -HEAD sfx (4); a development of the earlier synon. *Dead Freak*]

deadhead *adj.*¹ (*also* **deadheaded**) [mid-19C+] useless, spec. non-participant. [DEADHEAD n.¹ (2)/DEADHEAD n.¹ (4)]

deadhead *adj.*² [late 19C+] (*US*) free of charge. [DEADHEAD n.¹ (1)]

deadhead *v.*¹ (*orig. US*) **1** [mid-19C+] to obtain services or things without paying. **2** [mid-19C+] to ride for free; to allow someone to ride for free; also in fig. use. **3** [1920s+] to drive a cab, aeroplane etc without its usual load or passengers. [DEADHEAD n.¹ (1)]

deadhead *v.*² [2000s] to ignore.

deadhead *adv.* **1** [mid-19C+] for free. **2** [1920s+] of a cab, aeroplane etc, being driven without its usual load or passengers. [DEADHEAD v.¹]

deadheaded *adj. see* DEADHEAD adj.¹.

dead heart *n.* [20C+] (*Aus.*) the uninhabited centre of Australia.

dead heat *n.* [1980s] (*Aus.*) a necktie. [pun on SE (neck)*tie/tie* (dead heat or draw)]

dead horse *n.*¹ **1** [mid-17C+] work that has been already paid for but is yet to be done; thus *play a dead horse, pull a dead horse, work for a dead horse,* to perform such work. **2** [19C+] (*US/Aus./N.Z.*) a debt that has been incurred by accepting an advance on one's wages and must now be worked off; thus *ride the dead horse, work off the dead horse, bury the dead horse.* **3** [19C+] any form of debt. **4** [mid-19C] any form of useless job that does not bring in any profits but must be done; thus *draw the dead horse,* to work at such a job.

dead horse *n.*² [20C+] (*Aus.*) stew. [the disparaging comparison]

dead horse *n.*³ [1940s+] (*Aus.*) tomato sauce. [rhy. sl.]

dead house *n.* **1** [mid-19C–1940s] (*Aus.*) a room in an outback public house set aside for those who are incapably drunk. **2** [late 19C–1920s] (*US*) a particularly unappealing bar or saloon. [DEAD adj.²/SE *dead* + SE *house*]

deadie *n.* [1970s] a dead person. [SE *dead* + sfx -*ie*]

dead Indian *n.* [1960s] (*US*) an empty bottle. [the negative stereotype of allegedly alcoholic Native Americans]

dead knowledge *n.* [1900s] (*Aus.*) deceit, cunning, thus *dead-knowledge man,* a cunning or deceitful man.

deadleg *n.* [1960s–70s] a down-and-out, a failure.

dead-level best *n. see* LEVEL (BEST) n.

deadlights *n.* [19C] the eyes. [var. on DAYLIGHTS n. (1)]

dead line *n.* [late 19C–1920s] (*US*) the red-light area of a town or city. [fig. use of US milit. jargon *dead line,* a line drawn around a military prison, beyond which a prisoner is liable to be shot down]

dead loads *n.* [mid-19C+] (*US*) many, a great quantity. [DEAD adv. + LOADS OF n.]

deadlock *n.*¹ [late 19C] a lock hospital, i.e. a hospital for venereal disease.

deadlock *n.*² [1930s+] (*US prison*) solitary confinement, forfeiture of privileges; also as v.

deadlocker *n.* [1940s] (*US prison*) one who is in solitary confinement or deprived of privileges. [DEADLOCK n.²]

dead loss *n.* [1920s+] (*orig. RAF*) an absolutely useless person, idea or undertaking, a useless, unworkable object; also as adj. [SE *dead loss,* of a charge or expense, totally unproductive, unprofitable]

dead lurk *n.* **1** [mid-19C] (*UK Und.*) breaking into houses while the occupiers are at church. **2** [mid–late 19C] empty premises. [SE *dead,* abandoned, unused + LURK n. (3)]

dead-lurk *v.* [late 19C] (*UK Und.*) to break into a house when the occupants are away, esp. when they are at church on a Sunday. [DEAD LURK n. (1)]

dead lurker *n.* [mid-19C] (*UK Und.*) a thief specializing in theft from quiet or semi-dark places. [DEAD LURK n. (1)]

deadly *adj.*¹ [mid-17C+] very bad, utterly unpleasant.

deadly *adj.*² [1940s+] (*orig. US Black/campus*) excellent, first-rate. [on bad = good model]

deadly *adv.* [late 16C+] excessively, extremely.

deadly-lively *adj.* [19C] offering false joviality.

deadly nevergreen *n.* [late 18C–early 19C] the gallows. [pun on SE *evergreen*]

deadly nightshade *n.* [mid-19C–1920s] the lowest grade of prostitute (cf. MASTERPIECE OF NIGHT WORK n.; MIDNIGHT COWBOY n.; MIDNIGHT REVUE n.; MOONLIGHTER n.; NIGHTBIRD n.; NIGHTCAP n.¹; NIGHTGOWN LADY n.; NIGHTHAWK n.; NIGHTINGALE n.; NIGHT POACHER n.; NIGHT SHADE n.; NIGHT TRADER n.; NIGHT WALKER n.; NOCTURNE n.; NYMPH OF DARKNESS n.). [pun on the SE plant and night-time occupation]

dead man *n.*¹ **1** [late 17C+] (*orig. milit.*) an empty bottle. **2** [1980s] (*N.Z.*) any large object (a baulk of timber, a steel stanchion, a lump of concrete etc) used as an anchor for hawsers, guy-ropes etc.

dead man *n.*² [late 18C–19C] a baker; 'properly speaking, it is an extra loaf smuggled into the basket by the man who carries it out, to the loss of the master. Sometimes the dead man is charged to a customer, though never delivered' (Hotten, 1864). [? the role of a dead man as supernumerary to requirements]

dead man *n.*³ [late 19C] a scarecrow, esp. when made in the trad. manner of old clothes stuffed with straw. [dial.]

dead man *n.*⁴ [1930s] (*Irish*) a weekly insurance collector. [the insurance is paid off when one is dead]

dead man *n.*⁵ *see* DEAD PRESIDENT n.

dead man choppers *n.* (*also* **dead man teeth**) [1960s–70s] (*US Black*) false teeth. [SE *dead man* + CHOPPERS n. (2)/SE *teeth*]

dead man's arm *n.* [1980s+] (*N.Z.*) steamed (currant) roll pudding (cf. DEAD MAN'S EARS n.; DEAD MAN'S HEAD n.; DEAD MAN'S LEG n.). [joc. resemblance]

dead man's ears *n.* [1980s+] (*N.Z.*) stewed dried apricots (cf. DEAD MAN'S ARM n.).

dead man's hand *n.* **1** [mid-19C+] a poker hand of mixed aces and 8s or jacks and (red) 7s or 8s. **2** [1960s] bad luck. [the lawman Wild Bill Hickock (1837–76) was allegedly holding a hand of aces and 8s when he was gunned down]

dead man's head *n.* [1980s+] (*N.Z.*) a round, steamed plum pudding, eaten hot or cold (cf. DEAD MAN'S ARM n.). [resemblance]

dead man's leg *n.* [1980s] (*Aus.*) meat-loaf (cf. DEAD MAN'S ARM n.). [resemblance]

dead man's shoes *n.* [20C+] (*US Black*) anything that one would rather not have to experience but that cannot really be avoided. [note mid 16C+ SE phr. *wait for dead man's shoes,* to wait for the death of a person with the expectancy of succeeding to his possessions or office]

dead man teeth *n. see* DEAD MAN CHOPPERS n.

dead marine *n.* (*also* **marine, marine officer, marine recruit**) [late 18C+] an empty bottle. [orig. naut. jargon, now mainly Aus. use; note Fraser & Gibbons, *Soldier & Sailor Words & Phrases* (1925): 'William IV., when Duke of Clarence and Lord High Admiral, at an official dinner, is related to have said to a waiter, pointing to some empty bottles, "Take away those marines!" An elderly major of Marines present rose and said: "May I respectfully ask why your Royal Highness applies the name of the corps to which I have the honour to belong to an empty bottle?" The Duke, with the unfailing tact of his family, saved the situation. "I call them marines because they are good fellows who have done their duty and are ready to do it again!"']

dead meat *n.* **1** [mid-19C+] someone who is facing certain death; also fig. **2** [late 19C+] a corpse. **3** [late 19C+] a prostitute, esp. an older woman (cf. BANGTAIL n.¹). **4** [20C+] a horse that has no chance of winning a race. **5** [1960s] the flaccid penis (cf. BACON n.¹). **6** [1980s+] a stupid, dull person. [lit. or fig. uses of SE]

dead-meat ticket *n.* (*also* **meat ticket**) [1910s+] (*Aus./N.Z.*) an identity tag. [DEAD MEAT n. (2) + SE *ticket*; orig. milit. use, such tags identified the corpses of otherwise anonymous soldiers]

dead nail *n. see* NAIL n.¹.

dead nap *n.* [late 19C] an absolute villain. [DEAD adv. + NAPPER n.¹ (1)]

dead nark *n.* [20C+] (*Aus.*) **1** a spoilsport. **2** a very bad temper. [DEAD adv.+ NARK n.¹ (2)/NARK n.¹ (4)]

deadneck *n.* [1910s–60s] a very stupid person. [i.e. one who is DEAD FROM THE NECK UP phr.]

dead nip *n.* [late 19C] an unimportant project that turns out to be a failure. [DEAD adv. + ? SE *nip*, a fragment, a small portion]

dead number *n.* [late 19C] the last house in a row or street; the end of a street. [? link SE *dead end*]

dead nuts, the *n.* [1970s] the truth, a certainty. [DEAD-NUTS adv.]

dead-nuts *adv.* [late 19C+] (*US*) completely, absolutely, keenly for or against something. [DEAD adv. + NUTS adj. (1)]

deado *n.* [1910s+] a corpse. [SE *dead* + -o sfx (2)]

deado *adj.* (*also* **deadoh**) **1** [mid-19C+] very drunk (cf. ANNIHI-LATED adj.). **2** [late 19C–1910s] dead. **3** [1900s] as if dead. [SE *dead*/DEAD adv. *drunk* + -o sfx (2)]

dead on *adj.*¹ [mid-19C+] very fond of; determined (to do something). [DEAD adv. + SE *on*]

dead on *adj.*² [late 19C+] (*orig. US*) **1** dealing very strictly and severely with a situation or person. **2** very good at dealing with. [fig. use of DEAD adv. + SE *on*]

dead on *adj.*³ [late 19C+] (*orig. US*) absolutely right, utterly correct, exactly. [DEAD adv. + abbr. SE *dead on target*]

dead one *n.*¹ **1** [mid-19C+] (*also* **dead 'un**) a horse that seems not to have been raced to its full capacity; also in fig. use; thus *play a dead one*, to waste one's time, to act mistakenly. **2** [late 19C–1900s] (*US*) a fool. **3** [late 19C+] (*US*) a useless, unsociable, impoverished or mean person. **4** [1900s–50s] (*US*) someone or something that is doomed, on the verge of death or actually dead. **5** [1900s–60s] (*US Und.*) a reformed or retired tramp or criminal. **6** [1930s] (*US tramp*) a drunk.

dead one *n.*² *see* DEAD PRESIDENT n.

dead oodles *n.* [mid-19C+] (*orig. US*) a large quantity, many. [DEAD adv. + OODLES n.]

deadpan *n.* [1930s+] (*orig. US*) an expressionless stare. [DEADPAN adj.; *see also* ety. at DEADPAN v.]

deadpan *adj.* [1920s+] (*US*) expressionlesss. [SE *dead* + PAN n.¹ (3); *see also* ety. at DEADPAN v.]

deadpan *v.* [1930s+] (*orig. US*) to speak without expression, esp. in a situation that would normally demand some emotion. [DEADPAN adj.; *deadpan* (as n., adj., adv.) is cited as SE in *OED*, although *pan* is acknowledged to be 'orig. US slang'; it would thus seem likely to have been sl. at its coinage]

deadpan *adv.* [1930s+] (*US*) in an expressionless, emotionless manner. [DEADPAN adj.; *see also* ety. at DEADPAN v.]

deadpicker *n.* [1930s–40s] **1** (*US tramp*) one who robs passed-out drunks. **2** (*US*) a general term of abuse.

dead pickles *n. see* PICKLES n.¹.

dead pigeon *n.* [1910s–50s] **1** (*US*) a guaranteed and absolute failure, often in context of a forthcoming election. **2** (*US prison*) one who has been caught breaking a rule/committing a crime.

dead pork *n. see* PORK n.¹ (2).

dead president *n.* (*also* **dead man, dead one, president**) [1940s+] (*US*) a $1 bill; thus in pl. money (cf. ABE n.²). [the pictures of US presidents that are printed on the various denominations]

dead pudding *n.* [late 19C] (*US campus*) something easy.

dead rabbit *n.*¹ [mid–late 19C] (*US*) a street thug, a hoodlum; orig. the name of a New York City street gang. [the New York street gang, known as the Dead Rabbits, who would parade brandishing such a corpse, the symbol of their defeated rivals, as their standard; ? link to Irish *ráibéad*, a big, hulking person, a rowdy]

dead rabbit *n.*² **1** [1900s–40s] a hopeless person, one who has absolutely no chance. **2** [1960s–70s] an impotent penis, incapable of erection (cf. ANTEATER n.).

dead rag *n.* [1980s+] (*US Black gang*) a dead gang member. [the DO-RAG n. (2) or bandanna handkerchief, worn by gang members to indicate their affiliation]

dead recruit *n.* [20C+] an empty bottle. [var. on DEAD SOLDIER n.]

dead-right *adj.* [20C+] (*US*) unassailable. [DEAD adv. + RIGHT adj.¹ (2)]

dead ringer *n.* [late 19C+] (*orig. US*) usu. of people, an absolute replica (of). [DEAD adv. + RINGER n.¹ (2)]

dead ring of *n.* [1910s+] (*Aus./N.Z.*) the absolute image of. [var. on DEAD RINGER n.]

dead set *n.* **1** [18C–early 19C; 1910s] (*UK Und.*) a scheme aimed at defrauding a victim through crooked gambling. **2** [late 18C–1940s] a pointed attack on or approach to another person, often in the context of wooing. **3** [19C] (*US campus*) a complete failure to learn and recite the lesson. [DEAD adv. + SE *set*, the act of a dog in setting game; orig. used by thief-catchers referring to their imminent arrest of a villain]

dead-set *adj.* **1** [mid-19C+] fully committed. **2** [1940s+] (*Aus./US*) superlative, in both positive and negative uses. [DEAD adv. + SE *set*, positioned]

dead-set *adv.* [1970s] (*Aus*) definitely, certainly; also as excl. [DEAD-SET adj.]

dead set *phr.* [1970s] (*Aus.*) **1** a phr. denoting acquiescence, 'that's fine'. **2** an all-purpose negative phr. [DEAD-SET adj.]

dead set against *adj.* [early 19C+] totally hostile towards. [DEAD SET n. (2)]

dead set on *adj.* [late 19C+] fascinated by, obsessed with, in love with, determined. [DEAD SET n. (2)]

deadshit *n.* [1980s+] (*Aus.*) a general term of abuse. [DEAD adv. + SHIT n.² (1)]

dead shot *n.*¹ [mid-19C] (*US*) very poor-quality or adulterated whisky. [it 'kills' the drinker]

dead shot *n.*² [1970s+] (*US Black*) sexual intercourse, whether vaginal or anal. [SE *dead shot*, an expert marksman]

dead snooks on, be *v.* [1900s–30s] (*Aus.*) to be in love with. [DEAD adv. + affectionate nickname *Snooks/Snookums*]

dead soldier *n.* [late 19C+] an empty bottle.

dead spit *n.* [late 19C+] of another person (often a relative), the exact image. [DEAD adv. + SE *spit(ting image)*]

dead spotted ling of *phr.* [1930s+] (*Aus.*) the absolute image of. [rhy. sl. = DEAD RING OF n.]

dead stock *n.* [1990s+] (*W.I.*) a non-event.

dead thick *adj.* [late 19C+] (*Glasgow*) very clever. [ironic reversal of DEAD adv. + THICK adj.¹]

dead time *n.* [1970s+] (*US prison*) **1** any time spent in prison that does not actually diminish one's sentence. **2** any period of one's prison sentence when one is prohibited from associating with other prisoners. [SE *dead* + TIME n.[1]]

dead to rights *adv.* [mid-19C+] **1** caught in the act. **2** certain, sure. [DEAD adv. + TO RIGHTS adj.]

dead to the curb *adv.* [1950s] (*US Black*) completely, utterly, comprehensively.

dead to the (wide) world *phr.* (*also* **blind to the wide, out to the wide**) [20C+] (*orig. US*) **1** completely drunk (cf. ANNIHILATED adj.). **2** utterly and completely exhausted, very deeply asleep or unconscious. **3** unconscious of one's surroundings, lost in a dream.

dead tumble *n.* [1930s–50s] (*US Und.*) a discovery or arrest of someone found in the act of committing a crime. [DEAD adv. + TUMBLE n.[1]]

dead turkey *n.* [1940s+] a hopeless person, a person or thing that has absolutely no chance. [ext. of TURKEY n.[3] (5)]

dead 'un *n.*[1] [late 19C] a half-quartern loaf. [? DEAD MAN n.[2]]

dead 'un *n.*[2] **1** [late 19C] a bankrupt company. **2** [late 19C] (*UK Und.*) an uninhabited house. **3** [20C+] an empty bottle. [lit. a 'dead one']

dead 'un *n.*[3] *see* DEAD ONE n.[1] (1).

dead whiteboy *n.* [1990s+] (*US Black*) a dollar bill of any denomination (cf. ABE n.[2]). [play on DEAD PRESIDENT n.; there has as yet to be a Black president of the USA]

deadwood *n.* **1** [mid-19C] (*US*) a coffin. **2** [late 19C+] (*US Und.*) an advantage or control over someone, the thing a member of the underworld fears most, usu. arrest or being caught in the act. [(1) pun; (2) in ext. use]

deadwood *adj.* [mid-19C] (*US*) absolute, complete, unequivocal, e.g. *deadwood agreement.* [i.e. there is no possibility of further 'growth']

dead wowsers *n.* [20C+] (*Aus.*) trousers. [rhy. sl.]

deady *n.* (*also* **deadeye**) [early–mid-19C] gin or a particular quality of gin. [name of the distiller D. *Deady*, listed in the London Directory (1812) as 'Distiller and Brandy-merchant, Sol's Row, Tottenham Court Rd']

deaf and dumb *n.*[1] [1910s+] (*Aus.*) inside information, e.g. *I'll give you the deaf and dumb.* [rhy. sl. = DRUM n.[7]]

deaf and dumb *n.*[2] [1980s] (*Aus.*) the buttocks; the anus (cf. ALA n.; BOTTLE AND GLASS n.). [rhy. sl. = BUM n.[1] (1)]

deafy *n.* (*also* **deafey**) [1930s] (*US Und.*) a deaf beggar (or one who poses as such).

deak *n. see* DEKE n.

deal *n.*[1] **1** [mid-late 19C] any form of financial or commercial transaction. **2** [late 19C+] (*orig. US*) an idea, plan, scheme, arrangement, current situation, esp. with the implication of illegality or subterfuge. **3** [late 19C+] the treatment one has received, whether good or bad; thus *square deal,* fair treatment. **4** [late 19C+] (*orig. US*) the situation, the state of affairs, e.g. *that's the deal.* **5** [1910s+] (*drugs*) a purchase or sale of drugs, esp. cannabis; thus *quid deal,* one pound's worth etc. **6** [1920s+] (*US*) a turn of events, a development. **7** [1940s+] (*orig. US*) (*also* **dealie**) an individual or thing. **8** [1950s] one's concern or business, e.g. *that's my deal,* that's my business. **9** [1990s+] (*US campus*) a problem, a conflict. [ult. SE *deal,* the act or system of dividing into parts for distribution; (1) 20C+ use is SE]

deal *n.*[2] [1960s–70s] (*US Black*) a woman. [despite commercial overtones, not a prostitute]

deal *n.*[3] [1970s] (*US Black*) a sports star.

deal *n.*[4] *see* DEALER n. (2).

deal, a *n.* [late 16C+] an undefined but considerable amount or extent. [SE *deal,* a portion, an amount]

deal, the *n.* [1980s] (*US campus*) the best.

deal *v.* **1** [20C+] (*US*) to make a bargain, to conduct business. **2** [1920s] (*US*) to give, to hand over. **3** [1920s+] (*US Black*) to cause trouble for, to treat harshly. **4** [1950s+] to sell drugs, esp. marijuana. **5** [1960s+] (*US Black*) to manage a situation or circumstance. **6** [1970s–80s] (*UK Black*) to have sexual intercourse with. **7** [1980s] (*US prison*) to play the active role in a homosexual couple. **8** [1980s] (*US campus*) to make dates frequently. [DEAL n.[1]]

deal! *excl.* [1980s+] an excl. of agreement. [lit. 'it's a DEAL n.[1] (1)']

deal around me *phr.* [1940s–60s] (*orig. US Black*) leave me out, I'm not interested. [card-playing imagery]

deal dirt *v.* (*also* **deal in dirt**) [1970s+] (*US Black*) to gossip, to malign (cf. DO DIRT v.).

dealer *n.* **1** [early 19C–1920s] (*US Und.*) a wholesaler of counterfeit money. **2** [1920s+] (*drugs*) (*also* **deal**) a drug seller; often in his wholesale role, as opposed to the less important PUSHER n.[3] (1). [a specific use of an 11C SE word meaning trafficker, in whatever he or she happened to deal; note Maurer, 'Lang. of the Underworld Narcotic Addict' Pt.1 (1936): 'Often restricted to a druggist who is amenable to persuasion'; *Current Slang* III:2 (1968) suggests 'a dealer, unlike a pusher, sells marijuana to his friends as a favor and not for a profit']

dealie *n. see* DEAL n.[1] (7).

deal in coal *v.* [1930s–40s] **1** (*US Black*) to prefer dark-skinned women. **2** (*US*) for a White man to have sex with a Black woman. [DEAL v. (1) + COAL n.[1] (1)]

deal in dirt *v. see* DEAL DIRT v.

deal in zeroes *v.* [1960s] (*US Black*) to achieve nothing, to fail completely, to draw a blank. [DEAL v. (1) + SE *zero*]

deal (it) out *v.* [20C+] (*Aus.*) to attack, esp. verbally, to punish.

deal me out! *excl.* [1950s] (*US*) a general excl. of rejection, I'm not interested!, leave me out! [poker imagery]

deal on *v.* **1** [1970s] (*US Black*) to trick, to deceive, to take advantage. **2** [1980s] (*US campus*) to manage something well. [DEAL v. (3)]

deal one off the top *v.* [1960s] (*US*) to give someone a piece of good luck. [card-playing imagery]

deal out *v. see* DEAL (IT) OUT v.

deals *n.* [2000s] (*US Black*) a successful seduction. [DEAL v. (6)]

deal someone in *v.* (*also* **deal someone out**) [1940s+] (*orig. US*) to include (or exclude) in an undertaking, often a criminal one, to (not) give someone a share. [card-playing imagery]

deal someone one *v.* [1980s] (*N.Z.*) **1** to attack someone, to give someone a blow or a beating. **2** to pay someone back (for an injury or slight). [ext. SE *deal*]

deal suit *n.* [mid–late 19C] a cheap coffin, as supplied by the parish (rather than purchased through an undertaker). [SE *deal,* a form of pine wood from which cheap coffins are constructed]

deal them off the arm *v.* [1930s–40s] (*US*) to wait at tables. [the waiter's ability to carry a line of plates up the arm + ? ref. to gambling jargon *deal off the arm,* to cheat by sleight of hand; the implication is that the customer is being cheated on food quality]

deal to *v.* [1980s+] (*N.Z.*) **1** to beat up. **2** to treat roughly. [SE *deal,* to hand out]

dean *n.* [2000s] (*US Black*) a police officer. [play on academic title, the *dean* is responsible for campus discipline]

deaner *n.* (*also* **dena, denar, dener**) **1** [mid-19C–1960s] (*orig. Ling. Fr./Polari*) a shilling (5p) (cf. DEENER n.; DIENNER n.; DINARLY n.). **2** [1950s+] (*US*) 10 cents, a dime. [Ital. *dinero,* ult. f. Lat. *denarius.* 20C use is Aus. before decimalization]

dean maitland *n.* [1940s–60s] (*Aus.*) a silent person, one who does not talk. [*The Silence of Dean Maitland,* a film (1934) based on the novel (1914) by Maxwell Grey]

Dear, the *n.* [1940s] (*Aus.*) God. [abbr. *Dear Lord,* as used in prayers]

dearest bodily part *n.* [late 16C–early 17C] the vagina.

dearest member *n.* [mid-18C–19C] the penis (cf. DROPPING MEMBER n.; HOT MEMBER n.; JOLLY MEMBER n.; MASTER MEMBER n.;

MEMBER FOR COCKSHIRE n.; UNRULY MEMBER n.). [SE *dearest* + *member*, any organ of the body/MEMBER n.[1]]

Dear Jane *n.* [1980s+] a letter concluding a relationship. [feminized version of DEAR JOHN n.]

Dear John *n.* [1940s+] a letter concluding a relationship, usu. sent by the woman and received by the man, often in prison or serving in the forces. [its fig. salutation, *Dear John...*]

dear joy *n.* [late 17C–early 19C] an Irishman (cf. BOG ARAB n.). [SE *dear joy!*, a supposedly favourite Irish expression]

dear me! *excl.* (*also* **dear me suz!**) [late 18C+] a mild excl. [? Ital. *dio mio*, my God and poss. introduced to UK by Maria Beatrice of Modena (1658–1718), second wife of James II (r.1685–88)]

dear-stalker *n.* [1910s–30s] a wealthy idler who likes to follow and/or ogle attractive shopgirls or secretaries. [pun on SE *deer-stalker*, i.e. one who stalks deer, and on the 'little dears']

deasyville *n. see* DEUSEAVILE n.

death *n.* **1** [1960s] (*US campus*) an unattractive woman. **2** [1960s] (*US Black*) something excellent, something outstanding. **3** [1980s] (*US campus*) a terrible situation or event.

death! *excl.* **1** [mid-17C+] (*also* **death and furies!**) a general excl. **2** [1980s+] (*US campus*) an excl. of approval or admiration. [(2) on bad = good model]

death drop *n.* [20C+] (*drugs*) butyl chloride. [SE *death* + *drop*, a medicinal preparation]

death for *phr. see* DEATH ON phr. (1).

death-head *n.* [1990s+] a fan of GOTH n. (2) music. [SE *death* + -HEAD sfx (4)]

death house *n.* [20C+] (*US*) the execution chamber in a prison.

death-hunter *n.* **1** [mid-18C–mid-19C] one who sells stories of interesting deaths to the press. **2** [late 18C–early 19C] an undertaker. **3** [early 19C] one who visits battlefields in order to scavenge for clothes and other saleable items. **4** [mid–late 19C] a seller of the printed versions of dying speeches, usu. of those made on the gallows. [note Grose (1785): 'DEATH HUNTER, an undertaker, one who furnishes the necessary articles for funerals']

death o' day *n.* [1900s] (*Aus.*) anywhere considered by the speaker very far away or inaccessible whether lit. or fig. [BACK OF BEYOND n.]

death on *phr.* **1** [mid-19C+] (*also* **death for**) very fond of. **2** [mid-19C+] (*orig. US*) (*also* **murder on**) dealing very strictly and severely with a situation or person; very good at dealing with. **3** [20C+] (*US*) finding abhorrent or being opposed to. [fig. use of DEAD adv. + SE *on*]

death rain *n.* [1940s] (*US Black*) an extremely heavy downpour.

death row *n.* (*also* **Death Row**) [mid-19C+] (*US prison*) the condemned cells (cf. ROW, THE n.).

death seat *n.* [1960s+] the passenger seat in a motorcar, shown statistically to be the seat most likely to bring death to its occupier when the car crashes. [trotting jargon *death seat*, the position outside the leader, from which it is difficult to win]

death's head (upon a mopstick) *n.* [late 18C–19C] a miserable, impoverished, emaciated person. [image of a skull mounted on a pole]

death trip *n.*[1] [1960s+] any situation considered potentially fatal or extremely life-threatening. [SE *death* + TRIP n.[5] (2)]

death trip *n.*[2] [1960s+] a fantasy about death, often stimulated by (hallucinogenic) drugs. [SE *death* + TRIP n.[4] (1)]

death wish *n.* [1970s–80s] (*drugs*) phencyclidine (cf. ACE n.[4]). [its potentially dangerous effects]

deathy *n.* [late 19C+] (*Aus.*) a death adder, a type of venomous snake.

deausavilla-stampers *n. see* DEUSEAVILE-STAMPERS n.

deausaville *n. see* DEUSEAVILE n.

deb *n.*[1] [mid-19C] a bed. [backsl.]

deb *n.*[2] (*also* **girl-deb**) [1940s+] (*US teen*) a female member of a street gang. [SE *debutante*, itself commonly abbr. as *deb*]

de-bag *v.* **1** [late 19C+] to remove someone's trousers, either as a joke or as a form of punishment. **2** [1990s+] in fig. use, to reveal the sexual underside. [pfx *de-* + BAGS n.[2]; now obs. except in some (public) school use]

de-ball *v.* [1950s+] to castrate, lit. and fig. [SE pfx *de-* + BALLS n.[1] (1)]

debbie *n.* [1920s+] a *debutante*. [abbr.]

debblish *n.* [late 19C] (*S.Afr.*) a penny. [ety. unknown]

de-bollock *v.* [1960s+] to castrate, usu. in fig. sense of hurting or punishing severely. [SE pfx *de-* + BALLOCK n. (1)]

debs *n.* (*US drugs*) **1** [1970s] depressants, tranquillizers, barbiturates (cf. BARBIT n.). **2** [2000s] MDMA tablets (cf. ECSTASY n.). **3** [2000s] amphetamines (cf. A n.[2]). [ety. unknown]

deb's delight *n.* (*also* **debbie's delight**) [1930s+] an eligible or attractive young man who frequents the season in which upperclass or rich young women 'come out' into society. [SE *debutante*/DEBBIE n. + SE *delight*]

debug *v.* [1940s+] to remove faults from a machine, a system or, now most commonly, a computer or its software. [SE pfx *de-* + BUG n.[8] (1)]

debuggerable *adj.* [1930s] disreputable, unpleasant. [play on SE *disreputable* + BUGGER n.[1] (3)]

debut *n.* [1950s+] a first homosexual experience. [play on SE *debut*, pun on COME OUT v.[3] (2)/SE *come out*, i.e. of a debutante]

debutante *n.* **1** [1930s] (*US Und.*) a woman serving her first jail sentence. **2** [1950s+] someone new to the homosexual life. [pun on SE *debutante*]

Decatur *n. see* ADA FROM DECATUR n.

decco *n. see* DEKKO n.

dece *adj.* (*also* **dees**) [1970s+] (*US*) pleasant, amenable. [abbr. SE *decent*]

decent *adj.*[1] **1** [18C] tolerable, fairly good, acceptable. **2** [late 18C+] kind, accommodating, likeable. **3** [1940s] a general intensifier, both positive and negative. **4** [1960s+] (*US campus*) very good, excellent. [(1) SE by 1800s; (2) always mainly schoolboy use, e.g. *jolly decent chaps*, now only as a satirical/deeply ironic form]

decent *adj.*[2] [1940s+] (*orig. theatre*) fully dressed; usu. in phrs., e.g. *Are you decent?* or *Wait a minute, I'm not decent.* [SE *decent*, in accordance with or satisfying the general standard of propriety or good taste]

decent shake *n. see* FAIR SHAKE n.

deck *n.*[1] **1** [mid-19C–1950s] the roof of a train or stage-coach. **2** [mid-19C; 20C+] (*orig. US*) the floor, the ground. **3** [20C+] the roof of a building or its highest floor at a stage of building. **4** [1950s] (*US Black*) the street. [naut. use]

deck *n.*[2] (*also* **dekk**) [mid-19C+] a look, a glance. [Hind. *dekha*, sight]

deck *n.*[3] [late 19C] Seven Dials, London WC2; thus *decker*, an inhabitant of Seven Dials; *on the deck*, living in Seven Dials. [? DECK n.[2], i.e. the convergence of 7 roads means one can look in many directions; Seven Dials, near Covent Garden, was a criminal ROOKERY n. (2) of 19C London]

deck *n.*[4] **1** [1910s+] (*US drugs*) a packet of heroin, cocaine or similar narcotic. **2** [1920s+] (*US prison*) a pack of cigarettes. [SAmE *deck*, a pack of cards; ult. 16C SE, then dial.]

deck *v.*[1] **1** [late 19C–1930s] (*US tramp*) to ride on the roof of a freight car. **2** [1920s] (*US Und.*) to drill through the top of a safe. **3** [1990s+] (*orig. US teen*) to ride a skateboard. [DECK n.[1] (1)]

deck *v.*[2] (*also* **dekk**) [20C+] to see, to look at. [DECK n.[2]]

deck *v.*[3] **1** [1940s+] to knock down. **2** [1960s] to press down the accelerator pedal of a car; thus to go fast. **3** [1960s] of a man, to have sexual intercourse (cf. BANG v.[1]). [DECK n.[1] (1)]

decked *adj.* [1960s+] (*US Black*) well-dressed. [SE *decked out*]

decked (out) *adj.* [1960s–70s] (*US*) intoxicated by drink or drugs. [fig. use of DECK v.[3] (1)]

decked-out chick *n.* [2000s] (*US Black*) a woman or girl who uses an excess of cosmetics. [18C *deck out*, to decorate + CHICK n.⁴ (2)]

decked to death *phr.* [1980s] (*US Black*) exceptionally well-dressed. [DECKED adj. + SE *to death*]

decker *n.*¹ **1** [early–mid-19C] a deckhand. **2** [mid-19C+] a deck passenger. **3** [1930s+] (*Aus.*) the top deck of a double-decker bus. [SE *deck*]

decker *n.*² [20C+] (*Aus.*) a (peaked) cap or hat. [DECK n.¹ (1)]

decker *n.*³ **1** [20C+] (*US Und.*) in a pickpocketing gang, the member who surveys the street for approaching policemen; any form of lookout. **2** [1940s+] (*Aus.*) a glance. [DECK v.²]

deckhand *n.* [1900s–40s] (*US*) a menial labourer, a domestic servant.

deckie *n.* [1960s+] (*Aus.*) a *deck*hand. [abbr. + sfx *-ie*]

decko *see under* DEKKO.

decks-awash *adj.* [1930s–60s] drunk.

deck up *v.* [1960s] (*drugs*) to portion out large measures of heroin into small portions. [DECK n.⁴ (1)]

declare off *v.* [mid-18C–19C] to withdraw from an undertaking, e.g. an engagement to be married. [horseracing use]

decline, the *n.* [1900s] (*Irish*) tuberculosis.

decoct *adj.* [mid-16C] bankrupt. [SE *decoct*, well-cooked, i.e. 'done to a turn']

Decomposition Row *n.* [mid-19C] Rotten Row, the track in Hyde Park frequented by fashionable horseriders. [a pun on *Rotten Row*, itself ult. *route du roi*, the royal road, from Kensington Palace and St James's]

decorate *v.* [1910s–50s] (*US*) to injure, esp. to give a black eye.

decorate (the mahogany) *v.* **1** [1900s–50s] (*US*) to lay down money, whether for gambling or in payment of a bill. **2** [1930s+] of a man, to hand over the housekeeping money to one's wife. [SE *decorate* + MAHOGANY n.²]

decorate the parlor *v.* [1940s] (*US Und.*) to tip.

decunt *v. see* UNCUNT v.

decus *n.* [late 17C–early 19C] a crown piece, 5 shillings (25p). [the Lat. motto *decus et tutamen*, 'an ornament and a safeguard', from Virgil, *Aeneid*, Bk V, and orig. describing a breast-plate. It was subseq. engraved on coins (where it referred both to the inscription and to its helping prevent their being clipped) and has reappeared on the English version of the modern £1 coin]

deduction *n.* [1960s] (*US*) a small child. [the status in the tax laws]

dee *n.*¹ (*also* **die**) [mid-19C] a purse, a pocketbook. [orig. Rom.]

dee *n.*² *see* D n.².

dee *n.*³ *see* D n.³.

deeache *n.* [mid-19C+] the head. [backsl.]

dee-bo *v.* [2000s] (*orig. US Black*) **1** to steal. **2** to beat up, to knock down.

dee-bo! *excl.* [2000s] (*orig. US Black*) an excl. that acknowledges someone else's wit or rudeness, i.e. touché! [DEE-BO v. (2)]

dee-boed *adj.* [2000s] (*US Black*) muscular. [DEE-BO v. (2)]

deece *n.* [1940s] (*US Black/Harlem*) a dime, 10 cents. [Fr. *dix*, 10]

deeda *n.* [1960s–70s] (*US Black/Harlem/drugs*) LSD (cf. A n.³). [? redup. of the D in LSD]

deedee *n.* **1** [1920s–40s] (*US tramp*) one who poses as a deaf mute or deaf and dumb. **2** [1990s+] (*UK drugs*) a drug dealer. [abbr.]

dee-dee *adj.* [1920s] (*US tramp*) deaf and dumb. [DEEDEE n. (1)]

dee-donk *n.* [mid-19C] a Frenchman. [Fr. *dis donc*, so tell me. Note antecedents in the synon. *didones* (used in Spain after the Peninsular War (1808–14), a century earlier, *dido* (as used in Ling. Fr.) as well as, somewhat later, the Javanese *orang deedonc*, 'the dis donc people']

dee horn *n.* [1920s] (*US tramp*) denatured alcohol. [play on SE *de-horn*]

Dee-Jay *n.* [1940s] (*US Und*) an agent of the Federal Bureau of Investigation. [abbr. *Department of Justice* + pun on DJ n.]

deejay *see under* DJ.

deek *n.*¹ [1930s+] (*US*) a detective. [pron. DICK n.⁶ (1)]

deek *n.*² (*also* **deeks**) [1990s+] a look, a glance. [DEKKO n.]

deek *v.* [1990s+] to look at. [DEKKO v.]

deeker *n.* [early 19C; 1930s] (*Scot Und.*) a thief who also acts as a police informer. [? DEKKO v. although this predates it]

deeks *n. see* DEEK n.².

deelish *adj. see* DELISH adj.

deelo *adj.* (*also* **delo**, **dillo**) [mid-19C+] old. [backsl.]

deelo diam *n. see* DELO DIAM n.

deelo namo *n.* (*also* **delonammon**, **delo nammow**, **dillo namo**) [mid-19C+] an old woman; thus one's wife. [backsl.; DEELO adj. + NAMMO n.]

deemer *n.* (*US*) **1** [1920s–60s] (*also* **deem**, **demier**, **dimer**) a dime. **2** [1930s] the number 10. **3** [1930s–60s] one who tips a dime; a small tip.

deener *n.* (*also* **deena**, **deenir**) [mid-19C+] (*Aus./N.Z./UK*) a shilling, money in general. [DEANER n. (1)]

deep *adj.* [late 17C+] sly, artful. [ext. use of SE]

deep *adv.* **1** [1970s+] (*US Black*) (*also* **deep-down**) a general intensifier. **2** [1990s+] (*US Black gang*) well-supplied with members.

deep file *n.* [19C] an artful, cunning or shrewd person. [DEEP adj. + FILE n. (5)]

deep freeze *n.* (*US*) **1** [1950s] a place of imprisonment, a prison. **2** [1960s+] ostracism.

deep grief *n.* [late 19C] a pair of blackened eyes. [the blackness of not 1 but 2 eyes]

deep hole *n.* [1970s+] a serious situation, a difficult problem. [SE *deep* + HOLE n.³]

deep noser *n.* [1940s–50s] (*Aus.*) a deep glass of beer. [one has to push one's nose deep into the glass]

deep pockets *n.* [1950s+] (*US*) a person who can always be counted on to provide cash.

deep sea *phr. see* ALL AT SEA phr. (1).

deep-sea chef *n.* [1920s] (*US*) a dishwasher.

deep sea dive *n.* [1980s] (*Aus.*) the number 5.

deep-sea diver *n.*¹ [1920s] (*US Black*) a cunnilinguist. [DIVE v.²]

deep-sea diver *n.*² [1940s+] a £5 note (cf. BEEHIVE n.²). [rhy. sl. = FIVER n. (1)]

deep-sea fisherman *n.* (*also* **deep sea gambler**) [1940s–70s] a confidence trickster working the transatlantic liners.

deep-sea turkey *n.* [20C+] (*US*) **1** salt cod. **2** a codfish (dinner). **3** (*also* **submarine turkey**) salmon.

deep shit *n.* [1970s+] a serious situation, a difficult problem; usu. as phr. *in deep shit*. [SE *deep* + SHIT n.³ (1)]

deep sinker *n.* [late 19C–1950s] (*Aus.*) **1** a drinking-glass of the largest size. **2** the drink served in such a glass. [supposed resemblance to a deep mine-shaft]

deep six *n.* **1** [1920s–40s] a grave. **2** [1930s+] suicide. **3** [1950s+] death; thus *hit/take the deep six*, to die, occas. fig. **4** [1960s] a dismissal from work. [it is 6 feet under]

deep six *v.* **1** [1940s+] (*orig. US*) to get rid of, to abandon. **2** [1950s+] (*orig. US*) to ruin, to destroy. **3** [1950s+] (*US*) to kill, to die. **4** [1960s+] (*US campus*) to expel from a college. **5** [1980s+] (*US campus*) to finish a 6-pack of beer. [naut. use *deep six*, to throw overboard; ult. phr *6 feet under*, dead]

deep sugar *n.* [1940s] (*US Black*) sweet talk. [its 'sweetness']

deep throat *n.* [1970s+] deep fellatio, in which the penis is taken not simply into the mouth, but down the throat (cf. COCKSUCK n.). [the term was popularized by the 'art porn' film *Deep Throat* (1973) starring Linda Lovelace; it was also used as the nickname of the otherwise anonymous source who helped journalists investigate the Watergate Affair (1972–4)]

deep throat *v.* [1970s+] **1** to take the entire length of the penis into one's mouth, and thus down one's throat, during fellatio (cf. COCKSUCK n.). **2** in a non-sexual or semi-sexual sense. [DEEP THROAT n.]

deep yellow *n. see* HIGH YELLOW *n.*

deer *n.* **1** [17C; mid-19C–1960s] a (promiscuous) young woman. **2** [late 17C] a dupe. [abbr. WHETSTONE PARK DEER *n.*; note Shakespearian use of *deer*, a man or woman in the context of sexual activity]

deer-stalking *n.* [1920s] chasing after women. [pun on SE *deer/little dear/*DEER *n.* (1) + stalker]

Dees, the *n. see* D *n.*[3].

dees *adj. see* DECE *adj.*

deevie *adj.* (*also* **deevy**) [1900s–40s] (*UK society*) wonderful, sweet, cute. [abbr. SE *divine*]

deez (nuts) *n.* [1990s+] (*US Black*) the testicles; the male genitals. [SE *these* + NUTS *n.*[2] (1)]

def *adj.* [1970s+] (*orig. US Black*) perfect, excellent, first-rate. [? Black pron. of SE *death* or abbr. SE *definitive*. Note 1907 cit. in Cassidy & LePage, *Dict. of Jamaican English* (1967, 1992): 'I never do him one def ting', where *def* means 'single']

def *adv.* [1940s+] definitely. [abbr.]

de facto *n.* [1990s+] (*Aus.*) one of the partners in an unmarried but steady relationship. [Lat. *de facto*, in fact, as opposed to *de jure*, in law]

defense plant on a square's dim *n.* [1940s] (*US Black/Harlem*) amateur night at the Apollo Theatre, Harlem. [many performers were working in defence plants as a 'day' job]

deffo *adv.* (*also* **defo**) [1960s+] (*orig. Irish*) definitely. [DEF *adv.* + -O sfx (3)]

defi *n.* [late 19C–1960s] (*orig. Aus.*) a challenge. [abbr. SE act of *defiance*]

definitely! *excl.* [1920s+] yes!

def jam *n.* [1980s+] an outstanding record or track. [DEF *adj.* + JAM *n.*[1] (4)]

defo *adv. see* DEFFO *adv.*

def O.J. *n.* [1990s+] an extremely smart, fashionable automobile. ['In "Rapper's Delight" the term "Death OJ" is used. In current slang "death" means something good, while "OJ" is a ref. to a big car. Erstwhile football star and all-around adman O.J. Simpson does Hertz commercials featuring Ford and Lincoln Mercury cars. If we add "death" to Ford and Lincoln Mercury cars [...] we come up with the "Rapper's Delight" character driving off in a Lincoln Continental' (Nelson George, *Buppies, B-Boys, Baps and Bohos*, 1992)]

dege *adj.* (*also* **dege-dege**) [1950s+] (*W.I. Rasta*) little, skimpy, small; used both in the context of size and number. [Ewe *deká*, single, solitary]

degen *n.* **1** [late 17C–mid-19C] (*also* **dagan**) a sword. **2** [19C] an artful person. [Ger. *Degen*, a sword; (2) suggests play on *knowing blade*]

deger *n. see* DACHA *n.*

dehorn *n.* [1920s–50s] (*US*) **1** denatured or adulterated alcohol, as drunk by alcoholics, tramps etc. **2** a person who becomes ill through drinking such liquor.

dehorned *adj.* [20C+] (*US*) demoted, deprived of a position of power or authority. [SE *dehorn*, to deprive an animal of its horns]

deiner *n. see* DIENNER *n.*

deke *n.* (*also* **deak**) [late 19C+] (*US campus*) a member of the *De*lta *K*appa *E*psilon fraternity. [abbr.]

deke *v.* [1990s+] (*Can. teen*) to dodge, to avoid.

dekk *see under* DECK.

dekko *n.* (*also* **decco, decko, dekker**) [late 19C+] a look, a view; thus *keep dekko*, keep a lookout. [DEKKO *v.*]

dekko *v.* (*also* **decko**) [late 19C+] to look. [Rom. *dik*, to look; ult. Hind. *dekh-nā*, to look]

del *n. see* DELL *n.*

delec *adj.* [1960s] (*N.Z.*) delectable. [abbr.]

delf *n.* [1990s+] oneself; thus *go for delf*, release your delf. [SE *dead self*]

Delhi belly *n.* (*also* **New Delhi belly**) [1940s+] food poisoning, epitomized by diarrhoea, suffered by tourists in India (cf. AZTEC HOP *n.*). [*Delhi*, capital of India + SE *belly*]

deli *n.* [1960s+] (*orig. US*) a *deli*catessen. [abbr.]

delicate *n.* **1** [mid-19C] a fake subscription list carried by one who poses as an alms collector. **2** [late 19C] a begging-letter. [? the need for *delicacy* in pursuing these tricks]

delicatessen *n.* [1920s–30s] (*US*) a euph. for an illicit saloon.

delinko *n.* (*also* **delink**) [1950s+] (*Aus./US*) a juvenile *delink*uent. [abbr.]

delish *adj.* (*also* **deelish**) [1920s–60s] *deli*cious. [abbr./pron.]

deliver a baby *v.* [1970s] (*US gay*) to remove one's trousers in order to expose one's erect penis.

deliver (the goods) *v.* [late 19C+] to meet expectations, to fulfil one's promises.

dell *n.* (*also* **dal, del**) **1** [17C–early 19C] a young woman on the tramp, spec. a young or virgin prostitute; thus *wild dell*, such a young woman conceived or born under a hedge (cf. CANTING CREW *n.*). **2** [late 18C] a prostitute. [? SE name *Doll*; or, in the way that CUNT *n.*[1] is linked to Welsh *cwm*, a valley, ? a pun on SE *dell*, also meaning valley; Ribton-Turner, *A History of Vagrants* (1887), notes Welsh *del*, pert, smart; Lowland Scot. *dilp*, a trollop]

dell *v.* [20C+] to beat, to hit with the fists. [? SE *deal a blow*]

delo *adj. see* DEELO *adj.*

delo diam *n.* (*also* **deelo diam**) [late 19C+] an old maid. [backsl.; DEELO *adj.*]

delog *n.* (*also* **dilog, dlog**) [mid-19C] gold (cf. CANARY *n.*[5]). [backsl.]

delonammon/delo nammow *n. see* DEELO NAMO *n.*

delosis *n.* [1950s] (*US Black*) a pretty young girl. [? SE *delicious*]

Delphi *n.* [mid–late 19C] the A*delphi* Theatre, the Strand, London WC2. [abbr.]

del. trem. *n.* [mid–late 19C] *del*irium *trem*ens. [abbr.]

deluxe *adj.* [1970s+] wonderful, perfect, extreme. [ext. of SE use]

deluxe *adv.* [1970s+] to a remarkable extent. [DELUXE *adj.*]

dem *n. see* DEMO *n.*[1] (2).

dem *v. see* DEMN *v.*

demander for glimmer *n.* [mid-16C–early 17C] (*UK Und.*) a female beggar who poses as the victim of a fire (complete with fake documents to prove it) and begs alms on that basis (cf. CANTING CREW *n.*). [SE *demand* + GLIMMER *n.* (1)]

demento *n.* [1970s+] (*US*) a crazy, eccentric person. [SE *demented* + ? the 1970s US radio show *Dr Demento*]

demi-bar *n. see* DEMY *n.*

demi-beau *n.* [late 17C–early 18C] a would-be dandy. [SE *demi*, half + *beau*, a dandy]

demi-doss *n.* [late 19C–1910s] (*UK tramp*) a penny bed. [SE *demi*, half + DOSS *n.*[1] (1); ? one gets only half a bed or the comfort is substandard]

demier *n. see* DEEMER *n.* (1).

demi-rep *n.* (*also* **demi-rip, demy-rep**) [mid-18C+] a woman of doubtful reputation; ext. as a relatively classy prostitute, a figure defined by Henry Fielding in *Tom Jones* (1749) as one 'whom everybody knows to be what nobody calls her'. [SE *demi*, half + abbr. *reputation* or *reprobate*. Note synon. SE *demi-mondaine*]

demis *n.* [1970s–80s] (*US drugs*) tablets/capsules of demerol. [abbr.]

demn *v.* (*also* **dem**) [late 17C–mid-19C] a var. on DAMN *v.*, used in mild excls.; often as *demme!*

demned *adj.* [mid–late 19C] a var. on DAMNED *adj.*

demnition *adj.* [mid-19C–1920s] a var. on DAMNED *adj.* [pron. of SE *damnation* used as an adj.]

demo *n.*[1] **1** [1900s; 1930s+] (*orig. Aus.*) a *demo*nstration (of a political or pressure-group nature). **2** [1940s+] (*also* **dem**) a *demo*nstration, e.g. of a specific skill or action. **3** [1960s+] a *demo*nstration record or tape, used to promote a band's or individual musician's work. [abbr.]

demo *n.*[2] [1920s+] (*US*) a dime. [pron.]

demo *n.*[3] [1940s+] *demo*lition. [abbr.]

demob *n.* [1940s+] *demob*ilization from the armed forces; thus *demob suit*, the suit issued to discharged men on their quitting the services. [abbr.]

demob *v.* [1920s+] of a soldier, to be *demob*ilized. [abbr.]

demob-happy *adj.* [1940s+] excited at the prospect of being released from a long-term, usu. tedious job. [DEMOB n. + -HAPPY sfx; orig. milit. use, the sense of the nervous happiness that overtakes men nearing demobilization or the end of their military service. Note prison use *gate-happy*, the sense of nervous excitement that takes over those whose sentence is almost up]

demolition party *n.* [1980s+] (*N.Z.*) a party held by tenants who are leaving a house or flat, in which the fixtures and fittings are deliberately destroyed.

demon *n.*[1] (*Aus.*) **1** [early–mid-19C] a convict. **2** [late 19C] a veteran bushranger. [proper name *Van Diemen's Land*, modern Tasmania where bushranging was supposed to have been inaugurated]

demon *n.*[2] [late 19C+] (*Aus.*) a detective or policeman; often in pl. [SE *demon*/D n.[3] + *men*]

demon *n.*[3] [late 19C+] an extremely skilful person. [DEMON adj.]

demon *n.*[4] [1940s] (*US Black/Harlem*) a dime. [pron.]

demon *adj.* [late 19C+] extremely skilful; also as n. [the *locus classicus* is the late 19C Aus. cricketer F.J. Spofforth, popularly known as 'the demon bowler']

dempstered *adj.* [mid–late 17C] hanged. [Scot. *dempster*, the official who, until 1773, had the duty of repeating the judge's sentence in open court]

demure as a whore at a christening *phr.* (*also* **demure as an old whore/a harlot...**) [early 18C+] extremely demure and well-behaved.

demy *n.* (*also* **demi-bar**) [mid-16C–early 19C] a type of crooked dice. [lit. 'half a BARRED adj. dice'; post-17C use is historical]

demy-rep *n. see* DEMI-REP n.

Den, the *n.* **1** [late 18C–19C] a public house frequented by a regular group of cronies and thus named by them. **2** [early–mid-19C] the Stock Exchange. **3** [20C+] New Cross, south London, thence *The Den*, the nickname for the Millwall Football Club ground.

den *n.* **1** [late 18C] a small room, usu. occupied by a single male. **2** [late 19C+] (*US Und.*) one's home, an establishment. **3** [1920s–50s] (*US Und.*) a single prison cell. [(1) SE f. 1900]

dena/denar/dener *n. see* DEANER n.

denare/denari *n. see* DINARLY n.

dennis *n.* [early 19C] a small walking stick. [? its manufacturer]

Dennis the Menace *n.* [1990s+] MDMA. [letters M*DMA*]

dennyaiser *n. see* DINNYHAZER n.

denso *n.* [1980s+] (*US*) a very unintelligent person. [SE *dense* +-O sfx (2)]

dentals *n.* (*also* **dent**) [1960s] (*US*) teeth, false teeth.

de-nut *v.* [1950s+] to castrate. [SE pfx *de*- + NUTS n.[2] (1)]

dep *n.* **1** [mid-19C] a porter at a cheap lodging house. **2** [late 19C+] a *deputy*, e.g. a prison's deputy governor. [abbr. SE *deputy*]

dep *v.* [late 19C+] to act as deputy. [DEP n. (2)]

departer *n.* [late 19C] a last drink prior to leaving on a journey.

depresh *n.* [1930s–40s] (*orig. US*) the *Depres*sion, the financial and industrial slump of 1929 and subseq. years. [abbr./pron.]

depressed area *n.* [1940s] the stomach. [? esp. when hungry]

depresso *n.* [1960s+] (*US*) a deeply depressed individual. [SE *depressed* + -O sfx (2)]

depresso *adj.* [1960s–70s] (*US teen*) depressing; depressed. [DEPRESSO n.]

depth charge *n.* **1** [1940s–50s] (*orig. US milit./prison*) any form of stodgy food. **2** [1960s] (*US*) an ejaculation.

deputy do-right *n.* (*also* **do-right**) [1970s+] (*US Black*) the police.

derail *n.* **1** [1920s–30s] a person who becomes ill through drinking adulterated liquor. **2** [1920s–30s] (*US campus*) an unpopular student. **3** [1920s–50s] (*US/N.Z.*) denatured or adulterated alcohol, as drunk by alcoholics, tramps etc. [(1) f. (3); (2) *HDAS*, citing Weseen, *Dict. of American Slang* (1934), suggests it may be a misreading, but it may equally be be a separate or fig./ext. def. of (3)]

derailed *adj.* [2000s] (*US campus*) drunk (cf. ANNIHILATED adj.). [DERAIL n. (3)]

derb queen *n.* [2000s] (*US Black*) an enthusiastic fellatrix. [DERBY n.[1] (2) + QUEEN sfx (1)]

derby *n.*[1] **1** [1930s+] the head. **2** [1960s–70s] (*US Black*) an act of oral sex. [? the *Derby hat*, which sits on the SE *head*/HEAD n.[10]]

derby *n.*[2] *see* DARBY n.[1].

derby *v.* [late 19C] (*orig. sporting*) to pawn. [the popular excuse that a pawned watch or similar possession has been 'lost at the Derby']

derby kelly *n. see* DARBY KELLY n.

derby winner *n.* [20C+] (*Aus.*) a dinner. [rhy. sl.]

derelict *n.* [1970s] (*US campus*) a boring person.

deri *n.* (*also* **derry**) [1960s+] a *deri*lict house or other dwelling. [abbr.]

derm *n.* [1970s+] (*S.Afr.*) courage, bravery, staying power. [fig. use of Afk. *derm*, intestines]

dern *see under* DARN.

dero *n.* (*also* **derro**) [1970s+] (*Aus./N.Z.*) a *de*relict person, a down-and-out; also as a general term of abuse. [abbr. + -O sfx (4)]

derrey *n.* [mid–late 19C] (*UK Und.*) an eyeglass. [? play on SE *derry down*, one 'looks down']

derrick *n.* **1** [17C] the gallows, the hangman, the hanging. **2** [19C] the penis. **3** [1910s–40s] (*US*) a shoplifter, esp. a proficient one; also attrib.; thus *clout/root on the derrick*, to support a drug addiction by thieving. **4** [1960s] (*US gay*) a lesbian. [*Derrick*, a well-known hangman at Tyburn, *c.*1600; he appears, *inter alia*, in Thomas Dekker's *The Bellman of London* (1608); see Grose (1785): 'DERRICK, the name of the finisher of the law, or hangman, about the year 1608']

derrick *v.* **1** [mid-18C] to leave. **2** [mid-19C] (*UK Und.*) to embark on an adventure. **3** [20C+] (*US*) to execute someone or to kill oneself. **4** [1930s] (*US*) to shoplift. **5** [1970s] (*US*) to take, to remove. [DERRICK n.]

derro *n. see* DERO n.

derry *n.*[1] [mid-19C+] (*Aus./N.Z.*) **1** an aversion towards. **2** a feud. [dial. *deray*, an uproar; ult. Fr. *derroi*, confusion]

derry *n.*[2] *see* DERI n.

derwenter *n.* [late 19C] (*Aus.*) a released convict. [a veteran of the prison at the *River Derwent*, Tasmania]

des *n.* [1990s+] (*W.I.*) desperation.

desert *n.* [late 19C] (*UK society*) a ladies-only club. [i.e. the relative absence of members]

desert canary *n.* [20C+] (*US*) a mule, a donkey (cf. ARIZONA CANARY n.). [CANARY n.[10]]

desert mouth *n. see* COTTONMOUTH n. (1).

desert rat *n.* (*also* **desert-head**) [20C+] (*US*) **1** one who lives or works in the desert, esp. a prospector. **2** a native of the southwestern states. [SE *desert rat*, the jerboa]

desert wellies *n.* [1990s+] (*UK juv.*) sandals.

designer drugs *n.* [1980s+] (*drugs*) a variety of drugs, most obviously ECSTASY n., which are prepared from chemical formulae and have pre-ordained effects that can be used to influence the user's mood in a (relatively) predictable way. [play on 1980s vogue use of SE *designer*]

designer reality *n.* [1990s+] (*orig. US*) a conscious life that is determined by the planned ingestion of a variety of drugs. [ext. of SE use/DESIGNER DRUGS n.]

deskie *n.* (*also* **deskateer**) [1980s] (*US*) a desk clerk. [SE *desk* + sfx *-ie/-ateer*, the latter hinting at the spurious romance of *musketeer*]

desk jockey *n.* [1950s+] (*US*) a clerk. [SE *desk* + JOCKEY n.[3] (2)]

desk piano *n.* [1940s] (*US Black/Harlem*) a typewriter.

Desmond (Tutu) *n.* [1990s+] a lower second university degree (cf. DOUGLAS HURD n.; GEOFF HURST n.; GEORGE THE THIRD n.; PATTY HEARST n.; RICHARD (THE THIRD) n.). [rhy. sl. = '2:2'; ult. *Desmond Tutu*, South African clergyman and political activist (b.1931)]

despatcher(s)/despatches *n. see* DISPATCHER n.

despatches *n. see* DISPATCHES n.

despatch one's cargo *v.* [1910s–20s] to defecate (cf. DO ONE'S BUSINESS v.; DO ONE'S DIRTY v.; DO ONE'S DUTY v.; DO ONE'S NO-MANNERS v.; DROP ONE v.; DROP ONE'S BUNDLE v.; DROP ONE'S LOAD v.[3]; DUMP ONE'S LOAD v.; SQUEEZE (ONE'S HEAD) v.; WALK ONE'S DOG v.).

desperado *n.* [1950s+] a gambler who bets heavily but cannot pay off when he loses. [SE *desperado*, a despairing, reckless man]

desperate *adj.* [20C+] (*Irish*) **1** very bad. **2** very good, or as a general intensifier. [ext. of SE use]

desperate *adv.* [mid-17C–1900s] desperately, extremely, very much. [ext. of SE use]

de-stat *v.* [1950s–60s] for a landlord or owner to evict sitting tenants so as to gain possession of a valuable property, which can then be sold for a high profit. [SE pfx *de-* + *stat(utory tenant)*]

destroyed *adv.* [1950s+] **1** exhausted. **2** (*drugs*) under the influence of either drugs or drink.

destroyer *n.* [1950s] (*W.I.*) a deceitful man.

d.e.t. *n.* [1960s+] (*drugs*) *d*imethyl*t*ryptamine. [abbr.]

det *adj.* (*also* **dett**) [1990s+] first-rate, excellent, wonderful. [var. on DEF adj.]

detec *n.* [late 19C] a *detec*tive. [abbr.]

dethroned *adj.* [1940s–70s] (*gay*) for a gay man to be ejected from the public lavatory where he is looking for sex. [punning use of SE/QUEEN n.[2] (1) + THRONE n.]

detox *n.* [1970s+] *detox*ification after a period of drink or drug addiction; thus *Detox*, any hospital or similar establishment that specializes in detoxification of drink or drug addicts. [abbr.]

detox *v.* [1970s+] to enter a period of voluntary withdrawal from narcotic or alcohol addiction. [DETOX n.]

detrimental *n.* **1** [mid-19C] (*UK society*) a younger brother of the heir of an estate. **2** [mid-19C] a male flirt. **3** [mid–late 19C] (*UK society*) an ineligible suitor. **4** [20C+] a male homosexual. [(1) note primogeniture rendered such younger sons ineligible to inherit]

Detroit disaster *n.* (*also* **Detroit junk**) [1910s–60s] (*orig. US Black*) a car. [presumably in bad condition]

Detroit pink *n.* [1980s+] (*drugs*) phencyclidine (cf. ACE n.[4]).

dett *adj. see* DET adj.

detweed *v.* [1980s] (*Aus.*) to take off one's clothes. [SE *de-* + TWEEDS n.]

Deuce, the *n.* **1** [1960s+] the main street of downtown (less fashionable) Las Vegas. **2** [1980s+] New York's 42nd Street, between Seventh and Eighth Avenues. [(2) until the shutting down of many cinemas and bookstores specializing in pornography in the early 1990s, this was the centre of midtown vice]

deuce *n.*[1] (*also* **deucie, duce**) [16C+] **1** 2, a pair of objects and occas. individuals). **2** [late 17C–1960s] 2 pence; thus *duce hog*, 2 shillings (10p). **3** [late 19C–1960s] a useless gambler, a worthless individual. **4** [1910s+] (*US*) $2. **5** [1920s+] (*US prison*) (*also* **deuce-burger**) a 2-year sentence. **6** [1930s] (*drugs*) 2 marijuana cigarettes, sold together. **7** [1940s] (*Aus.*) 2 shillings (10p). **8** [1950s] £2. **9** [1960s–70s] (*US drugs*) a $2 package of heroin. **10** [1970s] (*US drugs*) 2 pills. [SE *deuce*, the 2 in dice or cards; (3) note the deuce is the lowest card in the deck]

deuce *n.*[2] **1** [mid–late 17C] a synon. for syphilis or the plague, used in oaths, e.g. *deuce on him, the deuce on it*. **2** [late 17C+] (*also* **dooce, duce**) a euph. for 'the devil', used in phrs., e.g. *the deuce! what the deuce! so/who/how/where/when the deuce?* (*the*) *deuce*

take it! the deuce is in it! the deuce and all/much, the deuce to pay, a deuce of a mess; thus *to play the deuce* (*with*), to cause trouble for; also lit. the Devil. **3** [1900s–10s] an inferior person, a 'devil'. [? SE *deuce*, the lowest, and thus the least lucky throw in dice]

deuce *n.*[3] (*also* **deucer**) **1** [20C+] (*Aus.*) a champion shearer capable of shearing 200 sheep in a day. **2** [1970s] a 2-hour watch. [DEUCE n.[1] (1)]

deuce *adj.* [1920s+] second in sequence, order or rank. [DEUCE n.[1] (1)]

deuce *v.* **1** [20C+] (*Aus.*) to shear approx. 200 sheep in a day. **2** [1940s] (*US drugs*) to sell 2 marijuana cigarettes. [DEUCE n.[1] (1)/DEUCE n.[1] (6)]

deuce 25 *n.* (*also* **deuce and a quarter**) [1960s+] (*US Black/teen*) **1** a Buick Electra 225. **2** any car with a 225hp engine. [DEUCE n.[1] (1)]

deuce a, the *phr. see* DEVIL A, THE phr.

deuce and ace *n.* [1910s+] the face. [rhy. sl.]

deuce and a quarter *n.*[1] [1990s+] (*US prison*) a sentence of 2 to 25 years. [DEUCE n.[1] (5)]

deuce and a quarter *n.*[2] *see* DEUCE 25 n.

deuce-burger *n. see* DEUCE n.[1] (5).

deuced *adv.* (*also* **doosid**) [late 18C–19C] a euph. for DAMNED adv.; thus [mid-19C] *deuced infernal*, very unpleasant. [DEUCE n.[2] (2)]

deuce-deuce *n.* **1** [1980s+] a .22 revolver or pistol. **2** [1990s+] a 22oz beer. [DEUCE n.[1] (1)]

deucedly *adv.* [early 19C+] a synon./euph. for *devilishly, damnably*. [DEUCED adv.]

deuce-five *n.* [1980s+] a .25 pistol. [DEUCE n.[1] (1) + SE *five*]

deuce of a — *phr. see* DEVIL OF A — phr.

deuce of a hat *n. see* HAT n.[2].

deuce of benders *n.* [1940s–60s] (*US Black/Harlem*) the knees. [DEUCE n.[1] (1) + BENDER n.[3] (4)]

deuce of boxcars *n.* [1940s] (*US Black*) 1 day, i.e. 24 hours. [DEUCE n.[1] (1) + BOXCARS n. (1)]

deuce of clubs *n.* [1940s] (*US*) the fists, used for violent assaults; thus *play the deuce of clubs*, to beat someone up. [DEUCE n.[1] (1); pun on cards/weapons]

deuce of grabbers *n.* [1940s] (*US Black*) the hands. [DEUCE n.[1] (1) + GRABBER n. (3)]

deuce of haircuts *n.* [1940s] (*US Black/Harlem*) 2 weeks. [DEUCE n.[1] (1); a fortnightly haircut]

deuce of nods on the backbeat *phr.* [1940s] (*US Black/Harlem*) 2 days ago. [DEUCE n.[1] (1) + NOD n.[1] (1) + SE *backbeat*]

deuce of peekers *n.* [1940s] (*US Black/Harlem*) a pair of eyes. [DEUCE n.[1] (1) + PEEKERS n.]

deuce of ruffs *n.* [1940s] (*US Black/Harlem*) 20 cents. [DEUCE n.[1] (1) + RUFF n.]

deuce of ticks *n.* [1940s] (*US Black/Harlem*) 2 minutes. [DEUCE n.[1] (1) + TICK n.[4] (3)]

deuce (out) *v.* [1940s+] (*US*) to back down, to act the coward. [DEUCE n.[1] (1); the weakness of the *deuce* in a pack of cards]

deucer *n.*[1] (*also* **deuce-spot**) [1920s–30s] (*US*) a $2 bill. [DEUCE n.[1] (4) + sfx *-er/-SPOT* sfx]

deucer *n.*[2] *see* DEUCE n.[3].

deuce-spot *n. see* DEUCER n.[1].

deuceways *n.* [1940s–50s] **1** (*US Black*) a pair. **2** (*US drugs*) $2 worth of narcotics. [DEUCE n.[1] (1)]

deuce wins *n.* (*also* **deux wins, dews wins**) [late 17C–mid-19C] (*UK Und.*) 2 pence. [DEUCE n.[1] (1) + WIN n.]

deucie *n. see* DEUCE n.[1].

deuseavile *n.* (*also* **daisyville, deasyville, deausaville, dewse-a-vill**) [mid-16C–19C] (*UK Und.*) the countryside. [E.P. suggests SE *daisy* + *-VILE* sfx; but *dewse* = DEUCE n.[2] (2) = the Devil and thus a generic negative. If London, the big city is RUMVILE n., the countryside from an urban perspective could be the opposite]

deuseavile-stampers n. (also **deausavilla-stampers, stampers**) [late 17C–18C] (UK Und.) members of a criminal gang who wander the country roads and frequent country inns in the hope of picking up information about possible robberies. [DEUSEAVILE n. + SE stamp]

deux wins n. see DEUCE WINS n.

devastating adj. [1920s–30s] (UK society) shocking, disturbing, distasteful etc, e.g. too, too utterly devastating.

devil n.[1] **1** [late 18C–19C] a grilled chop or steak; Grose (1796) cites a broiled, seasoned turkey-gizzard. **2** [early–mid-19C] gin seasoned with chillies. [it is hot in one's mouth; (1) subseq. use is SE]

devil n.[2] [late 18C–19C] spirit, temper, energy.

devil n.[3] [late 19C] one who performs odd tasks for others, esp. in the literary/dramatic world. [legal jargon devil, a junior counsel who works without fee to learn the profession; ult. the printer's devil, the errand boy in a printshop]

devil n.[4] [1960s+] (US Black, esp. Black Muslim) a White person. [the role of the White race in Black Muslim iconography]

devil n.[5] see LITTLE DEVIL n.

devil, the n. [1980s+] (drugs) crack cocaine (cf. BASE n.). [its effects on the individual and the community]

devil v.[1] [19C+] (US) to tease, to harass.

devil v.[2] [late 19C+] to perform odd jobs for others. [DEVIL n.[3]]

devil a, the phr. (also **deuce a, the**) [mid-16C+] a negative intensifier, e.g. the devil a thing there was...

devil among the tailors n. [mid-19C] an argument, a row. [according to F&H (and backed by OED) 'Originating in a riot at the Haymarket when Dowton announced the performance for his benefit, of a burlesque entitled "The Tailors: a Tragedy for Warm Weather." Many thousands of journeymen tailors congregated, and interrupted the performances. Thirty-three were brought up at Bow Street next day']

devil and all phr. [late 18C+] (Irish) a general intensifier, usu. positive.

devil and tommy n. see HELL AND TOMMY n.

devil beating tanbark phr. see HELL BEATING TANBARK phr.

devil-catcher n. [late 18C] a parson. [his continuing campaign against sin]

devil-chaser n. [20C+] (US) a volunteer preacher, without proper qualifications but capable of earnestly quoting what he/she has read in the Bible.

devil-dodger n. **1** [late 18C+] a clergyman, a preacher. **2** [mid-19C] one who sometimes attends an Anglican church and sometimes a Quaker meeting.

devil dogs n. [1910s+] the US Marines.

devil doubt you phr. [late 19C] a phr. meaning I agree completely; usu. as the devil doubt you – I don't.

devil-driver n. [late 18C–early 19C] a parson. [var. on DEVIL-CATCHER n.]

devil may dance in his pocket, the phr. [late 18C–early 19C] said of one who has no money. ['The cross on our ancient coins being jocularly supposed to prevent him from visiting that place' (Grose, 1785)]

devil me arse! excl. [20C+] (Anglo-Irish)a general excl.

devil of a — phr. (also **deuce of a** —) [17C+] a general intensifier, e.g. a/the devil of a row.

devil-on-the-coals n. [mid-19C–1900s] (Aus.) a small unleavened loaf hastily baked in hot ashes.

devil-pitcher n. [late 18C–19C] a clergyman. [SE devil + pitch, to throw]

devil's adj. [early 17C+] used in a variety of combs. to denote bad luck, evil intent, sinfulness and other negative qualities.

devil's bedpost n. (also **devil's bedposts**) [mid-late 19C] the 4 of clubs, considered to be an unlucky card. [note whist jargon devil's bedstead, the 13th card of whichever suit has been led]

devil's bones n. (also **devil's ribs**) [mid-17C–mid-18C] dice. [the pious identification of gaming with sin]

devil's books n. (also **devil's bible, ...picture books, ...prayer books**) [early 18C+] a pack or deck of playing cards. [the pious identification of gaming with sin]

devil's box n. [20C+] (US) a violin. [the sinfulness of music]

devil's brew n. [1940s+] (US) whisky. [the sinfulness of alcohol]

devil's claws n. [late 19C] (UK prison) the 'broad arrow' marking on convict clothes.

devil-scolder n. [mid-19C] a clergyman.

devil's colours n. (also **devil's livery**) [mid-19C] black and yellow. [the use of black to denote mourning and yellow for quarantineurs]

devil's cure! excl. [1920s–50s] (Irish) a mild excl.

devil's dandruff n. [1980s+] (drugs) crack cocaine (cf. BASE n.). [the innate evil of CRACK n.[13]; a late 20C version of the older characterization of drinking and gambling]

devil's delight n. [mid-19C+] a row, a fuss; thus kick up the devil's delight, to have a rowdy argument or make a disturbance.

devil's dick n. [1980s+] (US Black) a pipe for smoking crack cocaine. [SE devil + DICK n.[4] (1)]

devil's dinner-hour n. [late 19C] midnight.

devil's dozen n. [early 17C–19C] the number 13. [a supposedly unlucky number; the number of witches supposed to attend a sabbath]

devil's dung n. [17C–mid-19C] asafoetida (Ferula assa-foetida). [i.e. Pers. aza, mastic + Lat. foetida, stinking; the substance is used both in medicine and in cooking]

devil's dust n.[1] [mid-19C–1900s] shoddy, i.e. yarn made from reprocessed woollen rags. [SE devil, the machine that shreds the old rags + dust, refuse]

devil's dust n.[2] [1980s+] (drugs) phencyclidine (cf. ACE n.[4]). [SE devil + ANGEL DUST n. (4)]

devil's dye n. [mid-19C] (US) whisky. [the sinfulness of alcohol]

devil's eyewater n. see EYEWATER n. (1).

devil's four-poster n. [mid-19C] the 4 of clubs. [clubs, being black, are characterized as 'devilish']

devil's front porch n. see HELL'S FRONT PORCH n.

devil's guts n. [mid-17C–early 19C] a surveyor's chain. ['so called by farmers, who do not like their land should be measured by their landlords' (Grose, 1785)]

devil's half-acre n. [1950s+] (US) **1** a rough or unworkable piece of land. **2** the rough area of a town.

devil's livery n. see DEVIL'S COLOURS n.

devil's luck (and my own) n. [late 19C+] **1** extremely poor luck. **2** very good luck.

devil's necklace n. [1900s] (Aus.) a snake.

devil's nobbler n. [late 19C] (Aus.) a variety of alcoholic drink. [NOBBLER n.[3]]

devil's own —, the phr. (also **the Satan's own —**) [late 18C+] a phr. implying difficulty or problems, e.g. I've had the devil's own business finding my way.

devil's own luck n. [19C+] incredible luck, usu. very good, but occas. bad.

devil's picture books n. see DEVIL'S BOOKS n.

devil's picture gallery n. [1920s] a pack of playing cards. [the puritan's fear of gambling]

devil's pictures n. [1910s] a pack of playing cards. [the puritan's fear of gambling]

devil's playthings n. [19C] a pack of playing cards. [the puritan's fear of gambling]

devil's prayer books n. see DEVIL'S BOOKS n.

devil's rattle-bag n. [early 18C–mid-19C] a bishop's summons. [insultingly joc. ref. to the clergy]

devil's regiment (of the line) n. [mid-19C] prisoners. [coined by Thomas Carlyle (1795–1881)]

devil's ribs n. see DEVIL'S BONES n.

devil's smiles n. [19C] spring weather, esp. the alternating sun and showers of a 'typical' April.

devil's tattoo n. (*also* **tattoo**) [late 18C–1930s] the tapping of one's fingers or feet, often through boredom or irritation. [SE *tattoo*, milit. drumming; ult. ? pvb 'the devil finds work for idle hands']

devil's teeth n. [mid-19C] dice. [the puritan's fear of gambling]

devil take —, the phr. [mid-16C+] a phr. used with a suitable object to imply one's irritation with that object.

devil-teaser n. [1910s] (*US*) a clergyman.

devil thank you! excl. [1940s] (*Irish*) a mild excl.

devil to pay phr. (*also* **dickens to pay, Old Nick to pay**) [18C+] the promise of unspecified but definite problems in the future, which have been caused by an action in the present. [supposed Faustian bargains made between mortals and the Devil, the 'live now and pay later' of the 18C]

devil to pay and no pitch hot phr. **1** [18C+] a mess, a chaotic situation. **2** [early 18C–mid-19C] trouble in prospect or coming as a consequence of a particular action. [naut. jargon *pay*, to caulk + *devil*, a seam near the ship's keel]

devious adj. [1990s+] (*US teen*) extreme. [ext. of SE use]

devirginize v. [1980s+] to relieve someone of their virginity, usu. in a sexual context, but equally applicable to any first experience or rite of teenage passage, e.g. smoking marijuana, taking LSD. [a nonce-word that is grammatically correct – *de* + *virgin* + *ize* – but linguistically atrocious]

devotional habits n. [mid-19C] used of a horse that persists in falling to its knees. [pun on SE]

dew n.[1] **1** [mid-19C+] (*Anglo-Irish/US*) (*also* **dew-bowl**) whisky, usu. illicitly distilled. **2** [1970s+] (*US drugs*) marijuana. [(2) depends on illegality rather than on any image of wetness]

dew n.[2] [1970s+] (*US gay*) oily sweat exuded by the anus.

dewbaby n. [1970s] (*US Black*) a very dark-skinned man.

dew-beaters n. **1** [17C–early 19C] people who get up early, i.e. before the dew has evaporated. **2** [mid-18C–19C] (*UK Und.*) the feet. [note Norfolk dial. *dew-beaters*, heavy, waterproof shoes]

dew-bowl n. see DEW n.[1] (1).

dew-drink n. [mid-19C] a drink served to farm labourers before they start work.

dewdrop n.[1] **1** [late 18C+] a drop of mucus lodged at the opening of a nostril and hanging there before removal. **2** [1900s–10s] the lock on a gas-meter.

dewdrop n.[2] [late 19C] (*US campus*) a grudging compliment.

dewdrop v. [1900s–30s] (*US tramp*) to throw a rock or stone.

dew-dusters n. [19C] the feet.

dewey n. [mid-19C+] (*Polari*) the number 2. [Ital. *due*, 2]

dew-flaps n. [1990s+] the labia (cf. BEEF CURTAINS n.; FANNY-FLAP n.; FLAPPERS n.[1]; FLAPS n.; FUCK FLAPS n.; MUTTONFLAPS n.; PASSION FLAPS n.; PISS FLAPS n.). [var. on PISS FLAPS n.]

dewitted n. [late 17C–18C] murdered by a mob, lynched. [proper name of the brothers Jan and Cornelius *De Witt*, Dutch statesmen, who were cut to pieces by a mob in 1672]

dew o' Ben Nevis n. [late 19C–1900s] whisky. [DEW n.[1] (1) + its Scot. origin; ult. *Ben Nevis*, the highest mountain in Britain, situated in Scotland]

dew rag n. see DO-RAG n.

dews n. **1** [mid-19C] (*UK Und.*) a crown piece. **2** [1970s+] (*drugs*) $10 worth of drugs. [(2) DEUCE n.[1] (1); i.e. 2 $5 bags]

dewse-a-vill n. see DEUSEAVILLE n.

dewskitch n. [mid-19C] a severe beating, a good thrashing. [? 'catch one's due']

dews wins n. see DEUCE WINS n.

dew-treaders n. [19C] the feet. [var. on DEW-BEATERS n. (2)]

dex n. (*US drugs*) **1** [1950s+] Dexedrine, a form of amphetamine (cf. A n.[2]). **2** [2000s] MDMA (cf. ECSTASY n.). [abbr.; (2) methylenedioxymethamphetamine]

dex v. [1950s+] (*US drugs*) to take Dexedrine. [DEX n. (1)]

dexed adj. [1970s+] (*US drugs*) intoxicated on Dexedrine. [DEX n. (1)]

dexies n. see DEXY n.

dexo n. [1940s+] (*Aus. drugs*) Dexedrine. [abbr. + -O sfx (4)]

dexter n. [early 19C+] the right hand. [Lat. *dexter*, right]

dexy n. [1950s+] (*drugs*) a capsule of Dexedrine; often in pl. *dexies*, Dexedrine. [abbr.]

d.f. n. [1910s–30s] (*US*) a damned fool. [abbr.]

d.f. and l. phr. [1930s] (*US drugs*) dirty, filthy *and* lousy.

d.f.f.l. phr. [1950s+] dope forever, forever loaded, a popular patch worn by Hell's Angels, HIPPIE n.[2] (3) and other 'outlaws'. [abbr.]

DFs n. [1970s+] (*drugs*) DF 118s, painkillers mainly made of synthetic codeine.

d.h.c. n. [1980s+] (*US campus*) a very intense conversation. [*deep heavy conversation*]

dhobe n. see DOBE n.

dhobi n. (*also* **dhoby, dobee**) **1** [mid-19C+] (*orig. Anglo-Ind.*) a washerwoman. **2** [1910s+] the laundry. **3** [1980s] (*Aus.*) a bathe. [Hind. *dhob*, washing]

diabolical adj. [1950s+] outrageous, disgraceful, disgracefully bad; esp. in phr. *diabolical liberty*. [the word remains essentially SE, but for whatever reason was plucked out for this definitely sl. usage]

Diagonal Street n. [1980s+] (*S.Afr.*) the Johannesburg Stock Exchange. [its address]

dial n. [early 19C+] the human face. [SE *dial*, a clockface]

dialogue n. [1980s+] (*US teen*) a conversation, esp. one person's monologue; thus as v., to chat to.

dial out on v. [1940s] to cut off, to ignore.

dial-plate n. (*also* **dial-piece**) [19C] the human face. [SE *dial-plate*, the face plate of a clock]

Dials, the n. [early 19C+] Seven Dials, London WC2; thus *Dialler, Dialonian*, a (criminal) frequenter of Seven Dials. [in its 18C–19C prime one of London's best-known criminal enclaves]

dialtone n. [1980s+] (*US*) a fool. [? play on DINGALING n.[2] (2)]

diambista n. [1950s+] (*drugs*) marijuana. [Sp.]

diamond n. [late 19C] (*US short order*) a meat pie.

diamond adj. [1920s+] of people or objects, first-rate, excellent. [the value of the precious stone]

diamond-cracking n. [late 19C–1910s] (*Aus.*) breaking rocks as part of one's prison sentence; thus *diamond-cracker*, one who is working off such a sentence.

diamond cutter n. [1970s+] the erect penis.

diamonds n. [1960s] (*US gay*) the testicles (cf. AGATES n.). [play on CROWN JEWELS n.]

diamond squad n. [mid-19C] (*UK Und.*) rich, powerful individuals. [their jewellery]

Diana Dors n. **1** [1960s+] (*bingo*) the number 44, 'all the fours' (cf. ALDERSHOT LADIES n.). **2** [1990s+] drawers, (female) underwear. [rhy. sl.; ult. UK actress and personality *Diana Dors* (1931–84)]

diaper n. [1980s] (*US Black*) a sanitary towel.

diaper v. **1** [1930s–40s] clothes; thus *pin one's diapers on*, to get dressed. **2** [1970s+] (*US Black*) to put on a sanitary towel; usu. in phr. *diaper the baby*. [16C SE, but now SAmE *diaper*, a nappy]

diarrhoea bags n. [1980s] (*N.Z.*) knickerbockers.

diarrhoea-mouth n. [1960s+] (*US*) a very talkative individual.

diarrhoea of the mouth phr. (*also* **diarrhoea of the jaw-bone/jib**) [1940s+] (*US*) excessive loquacity. [SE/JIB n.[1] (4)]

diasticutis n. (*also* **diasticurious**) [1930s–60s] (*US Black*) the buttocks, the posterior. [cod Lat. formation based on ASS n. (2)]

diazzy n. [1990s+] (*UK drugs*) Diazepam. [abbr. + sfx -*y*]

dib n. [early 19C+] a share. [a corruption of SE *division* or *divide*]

dibb n. see DIBBLE n.[3]

dibber-dobber n. [1980s+] (*Aus.*) a tell-tale, a 'whistleblower'. [DOB (IN) v. (2)]

dibbi dibbi n. [1980s+] (*W.I./UK Black teen*) a small and insignificant thing or person. [DIBBI DIBBI adj.]

dibbi dibbi *adj.* [1980s+] (*W.I./UK Black teen*) stupid, useless, not resourceful, worthless. [? pron. of SE *little*]

dibble *n.*[1] [early 17C] a moustache. [ety. unknown]

dibble *n.*[2] **1** [late 19C–1920s] the penis. **2** [1960s] (*US campus*) a fool, a social inadequate (cf. CHOAD n.). [SE *dibbler*, a gardening implement with which one drills holes for planting]

dibble *n.*[3] (*also* **dibb**) [1980s+] a policeman. [proper name of *Officer Dibble*, a character in the TV cartoon series *Top Cat*]

dibbs *n.* (*also* **dibs**) **1** [early 19C+] money. **2** [1930s–50s] $1. [*dibs* or *dibstones*, a children's game played with the knuckle-bones of sheep]

dib-dabs *n.* [1940s] delirium tremens. [echoic of the babbling of the sufferer]

dibs *n. see* DIBBS n.

dibs and dabs *n.* [1960s+] (*Aus.*) body lice. [rhy. sl. = CRAB n.[2]]

dibs (on)! *excl.* [1930s+] (*orig. US*) that's mine! I want to do that! I want a share! A child's term used to claim the whole or an equal part of an object; the negative response to the cry is *fen dibs*. [DIB n.]

dic *n.* (*also* **dick, dicky**) [mid-19C+] **1** a *dictionary*. **2** 'jaw-breaking', pretentious language. [abbr.; (2) is fig. use of (1)]

dice *n.*[1] [1950s] (*US*) luck. [craps imagery]

dice *n.*[2] (*US drugs*) **1** [1970s] Desoxyn. **2** [2000s] crack cocaine (cf. BASE n.). [ety. unknown]

dice *v.* [1940s–50s] (*Aus.*) **1** to reject, to throw away, to leave alone. **2** of a lover, to abandon. [an image of tossing a die and losing]

dice mechanic *n. see* MECHANIC n. (3).

dicer *n.*[1] [late 19C–1960s] a hat. [its resemblance to a dice-box]

dicer *n.*[2] [1920s–30s] (*US tramp*) a fast freight train. [vagrant travellers in the boxcars feel like dice being shaken in a cup]

dicey *adj.* [1950s+] (*orig. RAF jargon*) risky, dangerous, dubious. [gambling imagery]

dichty *see under* DICTY.

dick *n.*[1] **1** [mid-16C+] a man, a fellow. **2** [mid-17C] a victim; a simpleton; note DICK n.[4] (6). **3** [mid-17C–early 18C] a man as a sexual partner. **4** [early 18C] a countryman. [generic use of proper name]

dick *n.*[2] [mid–late 19C] a riding whip. [? link to a celebrated contemporary coachman Walter Dickson, nicknamed 'Dickie the Driver']

dick *n.*[3] [mid–late 19C] an oath, a statement, an affidavit; thus *take one's dick*, to take one's declaration, to make an oath. [abbr. SE *declaration*]

dick *n.*[4] **1** [mid-19C+] the penis. **2** [1930s–40s; 1980s+] (*US Black*) a term of address between men. **3** [1950s+] sexual intercourse. **4** [1960s+] (*US teen*) an unattractive male, esp. one who has an overly high self-image. **5** [1960s+] (*US*) a mean or offensive person. **6** [1960s+] a fool (cf. CHOAD n.; DICKBRAIN n.; DICK-FUCK n.; DICKHEAD n.; DICKLICK n.; DICKSUCKER n.; DICKWAD n.; DICKWEED n.; DICKWIPE n.; DICKY-DIDO n.; DONKEY DICK n.[1]; THICK DICK n.). **7** [1990s+] in fig. use, courage, 'guts', virility, ambition. [all fig. uses of (1), itself based on DICK n.[1] (1); (1) see Williams I:382 for discussion of possible 16C uses]

dick *n.*[5] [1910s] a perambulator. [? Sheffield dial. a leather apron worn by children + link to Du. *dek*, a cover]

dick *n.*[6] [1910s+] (*US*) **1** a detective; thus *house dick*, the security officer in a hotel, office, etc (cf. DICK TRACY n.; JACK n.[19]; JOHNNY HAM n.; RICHARD n.[2]; SHERLOCK n.[1]). **2** a policeman (cf. BILLY n.[6]). [? gypsy use *dicked*, being watched (cf. DEKKO n.), DICK v.[1] or abbr. SE *detective*; the link to the fictional *Dick Tracy* (created 1931) is chronologically impossible]

dick *n.*[7] [1910s+] nothing, e.g. *we ain't got dick, not worth dick*. [use of DICK n.[4] (1) in synon. manner as FUCK n.[4] (1)/SHIT n.[3] (3)]

dick *n.*[8] [1960s] (*US*) the clitoris (cf. BABY IN THE BOAT n.). [play on COCK n.[6] (1); the clitoris, being phallic, is linked to US Black use of *dick* for penis, *cock* being used for vagina]

dick *n.*[9] *see* DIC n.

dick *v.*[1] [mid-19C] (*UK Und.*) to look at. [Rom. *dik*, to look; ult. Hind. *dekh-nā*, to look]

dick *v.*[2] **1** [1940s+] (*mainly US Black*) of a man, to have sexual intercourse (cf. BAGAGA v.). **2** [1950s+] (*US*) (*also* **dick up**) to ruin, to botch, to make a mess of; thus *dicked-up*, messed up. **3** [1960s+] (*Aus./US*) a synon. with FUCK v.[2] (1), to trick or deceive, to be unfair to, to treat meanly, to victimize. **4** [1970s+] (*US gay*) to sodomize. [DICK n.[4] (1); (2) and (3) fig. uses]

dick about with *v. see* DICK WITH v.

dick (around) *v.* **1** [1920s+] to waste time, to dither (cf. DICK SOMEONE AROUND v.). **2** [1960s+] to be sexually promiscuous, a womanizer. [(1) DICKER (AROUND) v., but with overtones of acting like a DICK n.[4] (6); (2) DICK v.[2] (1)]

dick around with *v. see* DICK WITH v.

dick-bitch *n.* [2000s] (*US Black*) an over-emotional man, esp. as regards women. [DICK n.[4] (6) + BITCH n.[1] (1)]

dickbow *n. see* DICKY BOW n.

dickbrain *n.* [1970s+] (*US*) a fool; thus a general derog. term (cf. BAKEBRAIN n.). [DICK n.[4] (1) + sfx -*brain*]

dick breath *n.* **1** [1970s+] (*US*) (*also* **cock-breath**) an unpleasant person. **2** [1990s+] anyone, esp. a superior, who has foul breath. [DICK n.[4] (1) + SE *breath*]

dick cheese *n. see* COCK CHEESE n.

dick-chewer *n.* [1970s] (*US*) a fellator. [DICK n.[4] (1) + CHEW v.[1] (4)]

dickchode *n. see* CHOAD n. (3).

dick curd *n.* [2000s] (*US Black*) one who enjoys storing up rivalry between others. [DICK WITH v.]

dick drink *n.* [1980s+] (*US gay*) semen. [DICK n.[4] (1) + SE *drink*]

Dick Dunn *n.* [late 19C+] the sun. [rhy. sl.; ult. Richard 'Dick' Dunn (d.1905), a well-known 'ready-money' bookmaker; there may have been an additional nod to the shine of the diamonds with which this 'Leviathan' of the turf adorned himself]

dick-eating *adj.* [1990s+] (*US*) a general insult, lit. 'fellating'. [DICK n.[4] (1) + EAT v.[3] (1)]

dicked *adj.*[1] [1960s+] **1** defeated, destroyed, out of luck; thus I'LL BE DICKED! excl. **2** in a mess. [DICK v.[2] (2)/DICK v.[2] (3)]

dicked *adj.*[2] [1970s+] (*US*) assured of success; completely in control (of). [fig. use of DICK v.[2] (1); thus image of potency]

dicked in the nob *phr.* [early 19C] insane. [ety. unknown; the sexual use of DICK v.[2] (1), which would work in fig. use, is too late + NOB n.[1] (1)]

dicken *v.* [1900s] (*Aus.*) to pretend. [DICKEN! excl.]

dicken! *excl.* (*also* **dickens! dickin! dickon!**) [late 19C+] (*Aus./N.Z.*) a mild oath; esp. as *dicken on/to that!*, enough of that! the hell with that! stop it! [DICKENS n. (1)]

dickens *n.* (*also* **dickings, dickins, dickons**) **1** [late 16C+] a euph. for the devil; most commonly in phr. WHAT THE DICKENS! excl. **2** [1990s+] a euph. for sexual intercourse or other sexual activity. [all euph. for SE *Devil*]

dicker *n.*[1] [late 19C–1930s] (*US*) a bargain, a deal; also *dickering*, bargaining. [SE *dicker*, to bargain]

dicker *n.*[2] (*also* **dikker**) [1920s] a *dictionary*. [abbr. + -ER sfx]

dicker *n.*[3] [1960s] (*US Black*) a sexually powerful man. [DICK v.[2] (1)]

dicker (around) *v.* [mid-19C+] (*US*) to waste time, to dither. [SE *dicker*, to bargain; ult. 13C *dicker* (Lat. *decuria*, a unit of 10 hides used in bartering)]

dickery *n.* [late 19C+] **1** a clock. **2** the penis (cf. ALMOND n.). [rhy. sl.; *dickory dock* = (2) COCK n.[2] (1)]

dickory dock *n. see* DICKORY DOCK n. (1).

dickey *see also under* DICKY and its combs.

dickey dazzler *n. see* BOBBY-DAZZLER n.

dickey-eye *n.* [1950s] (*UK juv.*) a lookout. [dial. *keep dick*, keep watch]

dickey suit *n.* [1950s] the naked body. [? DICK v.[1], i.e. something one looks at]

dickface *n.* [1970s+] (*orig. US campus*) a general term of derision. [DICK n.⁴ (1) + SE *face*]

dick-fingered *adj.* [1980s+] (*US*) maladroit. [DICK n.⁴ (1) + sfx *-fingered*]

dick-for-brains *n. see* SHIT-FOR-BRAINS n.

dick-fuck *n.* [1990s+] (*Aus.*) a general term of abuse. [DICK n.⁴ (6) + FUCK n.⁶]

dickhead *n.* [1960s+] **1** a fool, an incompetent. **2** a general term of abuse. [DICK n.⁴ (1) + -HEAD sfx (1)]

dickhead *adj.* (*also* **dickheaded**) [1990s+] stupid, foolish. [DICKHEAD n.]

dickhound *n.* **1** [1980s+] (*US Black*) a promiscuous woman. **2** [2000s] (*US gay*) a promiscuous male homosexual (cf. BONE-EATER n.). [DICK n.⁴ (1) + HOUND sfx]

dickie *see also under* DICKY *and its combs.*

dickies *n.* [1950s+] (*US*) baggy trousers, favoured by teenage gang members. [? brandname]

dickin! *excl. see* DICKEN! excl.

dickings/dickins *n. see* DICKENS n.

dick in the green *adj. see* DICKY adj.¹ (2).

dick-knob *n. see* DICKWIT n.

dickless *adj.* [1980s+] (*orig. US*) a general term of abuse implying cowardice or impotency; lit. without a penis. [DICK n.⁴ (1) + sfx *-less*; note DICK n.⁴ (7)]

dickless tracy *n.* [1960s+] (*mainly US Und.*) a woman police officer; occas. security guard. [puns on DICK n.⁴ (1) + cartoon strip *Dick Tracy* + common female name *Tracey*]

dicklick *n.* [1980s+] **1** (*US*) a fool, an idiot, an unpleasant person (cf. COCKMUNCH n.; DICK n.⁴). **2** (*US gay*) fellatio (cf. COCKSUCK n.). [backform. f. DICKLICKER n.]

dicklicker *n.* [1960s+] (*US*) a fellator or fellatrix; thus an unpleasant person (cf. COCKMUNCH n.). [DICK n.⁴ (1) + SE *licker*]

dicklicking *adj.* [1970s+] (*US*) unpleasant, disgusting, a general term of abuse. [DICKLICKER n.]

dick mac *n.* [1970s–80s] (*UK Black*) a condom. [DICK n.⁴ (1) + SE *mac(intosh)*]

dick-nailer *n.* [19C+] (*US*) something outstanding, exceptional of its type. [NAIL v. (1)]

dicknose *n.* [1970s+] (*orig. US*) a general term of derision. [DICK n.⁴ (1) + SE *nose*]

dick off *v.* [1940s–60s] (*US*) to waste time, to shirk, to avoid work. [DICK AROUND v. (1) + SE *off*]

dickon! *excl. see* DICKEN! excl.

dickon pitch *n.* [late 19C–1930s] (*Aus.*) a lie. [DICKEN! excl.]

dickons *n. see* DICKENS n.

dickory dock *n.* **1** [late 19C+] (*also* **dickery dock, dicky**) a clock. **2** [20C+] the penis (cf. ALMOND n.). **3** [1960s] a sock. [rhy. sl.; (2) = COCK n.² (1). The nursery rhyme from which this comes is itself a Rom. creation. According to Gerald Denley: 'Hickory is derived from the Romany "Ek Ore" meaning one o'clock. The word for one in Romany varies according to the tribe, so it is either "ek", "yek" or "ik". The stress is on the first vowel, so that "ek ore" is pronounced as one word. Dickory Dock is often described as London rhyming slang. But it could mean the *dock* where the *dick* puts you when you are caught *choring* or stealing']

dick out *v.* [1970s+] (*US*) to persevere, to endure. [fig. use of DICK n.⁴ (1)]

dick peddler *n.* (*also* **prick peddler**) [1940s+] a male prostitute who takes only active roles with his clients (cf. ASS PEDDLER n.). [DICK n.⁴ (1)/PRICK n. (2) + SE *peddler*]

dick sack *n.* [2000s] (*US*) **1** a contraceptive sheath. **2** the scrotum. [DICK n.⁴ (1) + SE *sack*]

dickshaft *n.* [1990s+] a general derog. description. [DICK n.⁴ (1)]

Dick's hatband *n.* [18C+] (*US*) anything makeshift; also in phrs. QUEER AS DICK'S HATBAND phr.; TIGHT AS DICK'S HATBAND phr. [the orig. *hatband* was a narrow strip of material wrapped around the hat, esp. as a badge of mourning. The identity of Dick is not known – 'some local character or half-wit' (*OED*) – but his hatband was presumably an improvised and absurd object; however, Brewer, *Dict. of Phrase and Fable* (1894) suggests *Dick* = Richard Cromwell (1626–1712) and *hatband* = a crown, which as a republican he could not wear]

dick shit *n.* [1980s+] (*orig. US*) absolutely nothing; always used with a qualifying negative v., e.g. *you don't know dick shit about…* [DICK n.⁷ + SHIT n.³ (3)]

dick-shriveler *n.* [1980s+] (*US*) an unpleasant person. [fig. us of DICK n.⁴ (1) + SE *shriveller*]

dick smith *n.* [19C+] (*US*) **1** a solitary drinker or drug-taker. **2** by ext., a mean, sponging or reclusive person. [logger jargon; ? *Richard Penn Smith* (1790–1854), a US playwright celebrated for his unsociability – and his plagiarism of others]

dick someone around *v.* [1980s+] (*US*) to harass, to impose on, to irritate, to 'mess one about' (cf. DICK AROUND v.). [DICK v.² (3) + SE *around*]

dicksplash *n.* [1990s+] a semen stain; thus an incompetent, unpleasant, unpopular person. [DICK n.⁴ (1) + SE *splash*]

dickstring *n.* **1** [1960s+] (*US Black*) the notional governor of a man's ability to attain an erection. **2** [2000s] (*US*) a general term of abuse. [DICK n.⁴ (1) + SE *string*; lit. the frenum]

dicksucker *n.* [1970s+] (*US*) **1** a fellator. **2** a general derog. term (cf. COCKMUNCH n.). [DICK n.⁴ (1) + SE *sucker*]

dicksucking *n.* [1970s+] (*US*) fellatio (cf. COCKSUCK n.). [DICKSUCKER n. (1)]

dicksucking *adj.* [1970s+] (*US*) unpleasant, disgusting, a general term of abuse. [DICKSUCKER n. (2)]

dicktease *n. see* DICKTEASER n.

dicktease *v.* [1960s+] (*orig. US*) usu. of a woman, to appear to be offering unrestrained sexual favours but stopping short of intercourse, leaving the man frustrated. [DICK n.⁴ (1) + SE *tease*]

dickteaser *n.* (*also* **dicktease**) [1960s+] **1** one who provokes their partner sexually but stops short of intercourse. **2** in fig. use, any person or thing that is frustrating, teasing, unfulfilling. [DICKTEASE v.]

dick thang *n.* (*also* **dick thing**) [1990s+] (*US campus*) something characteristically associated with males. [DICK n.⁴ (1) + joc. pron. of SE *thing*; lit. 'a penis thing']

Dick Tracy *n.* [1930s+] a policeman, esp. a detective. [the cartoon strip created by Chester Gould in 1931 for the Chicago *Tribune*/*New York News* syndicate; ult. DICK n.⁶ (1) + SE *trace*]

dickty *see under* DICTY.

dick up *v. see* DICK v.² (2).

dickup! *excl.* [1990s+] (*UK juv.*) a cry of alarm/warning, put out your cigarette — a teacher is coming!

Dick Van Dyke *n.* [2000s] (*Irish*) a bike. [rhy. sl.; ult. US actor *Dick Van Dyke* (b.1925)]

dickwad *n.* [1980s+] (*orig. US campus*) a fool, an idiot, an unpleasant person; also attrib. [DICK n.⁴ (1) + -WAD sfx/WAD n.⁶; lit. 'an ejaculation']

dickweed *n.* (*US*) **1** [1980s+] a fool. **2** [1990s+] pubic hair. [DICK n.⁴ (1) + SE *weed*]

dick-whupped *adj.* (*also* **d-whupped**) [1990s+] (*US Black*) used of a woman so besotted with her lover that she allows herself to be exploited and generally treated badly. [DICK n.⁴ (1) + SE *whipped*]

dickwipe *n.* [1990s+] (*US*) a general term of abuse. [DICK n.⁴ (1)]

dickwit *n.* (*also* **dick-knob**) [1990s+] (*Aus. teen*) a general insult. [DICK n.⁴ (1)]

dick with *v.* (*also* **dick about with, dick around with**) [1970s+] (*US*) to mess someone around, to fool around with. [DICK v.² (3)]

dicky *n.*¹ (*also* **dickey, dickie**) **1** [mid-18C–19C] a woman's under-petticoat. **2** [late 18C–mid-19C] a worn-out shirt. **3** [early 19C+] a detachable shirt-front. **4** [mid-19C–1910s] a shirt-collar.

5 [late 19C] a detachable nameplate, used on a tradesman's van. [? link to dial. *dick*, a leather apron]

dicky *n.*[2] (*also* **dickey**) [late 18C–19C] a dandy, a 'swell'. [DICKY adj.[2]; note naut. jargon *dickey*, an officer acting in commission]

dicky *n.*[3] (*also* **dickey**) **1** [19C] (*also* **dicky-box**) the seat in a carriage on which the driver sits. **2** [19C] (*also* **dickey-box**) a seat at the back of a carriage for servants etc, or of a mail-coach for the guard. **3** [1910s–30s] (*also* **dickie**) an extra seat at the back of a 2-seater motorcar, which can be closed down when not in use; also of a boat. [? *Dicky*, used as a generic name for a coachman]

dicky *n.*[4] (*also* **dickey**) [19C] a donkey. [East Anglian dial.; the habit of using proper names as sl. terms for donkeys]

dicky *n.*[5] (*also* **dickey, dickie**) [19C+] the penis. [ext. of DICK n.[4] (1)]

dicky *n.*[6] [mid-19C–1920s] an affidavit. [SE *declaration*]

dicky *n.*[7] (*also* **dickey, dickie**) [late 19C+] a word. [abbr. DICKY-BIRD n.[2]]

dicky *n.*[8] *see* DIC n.

dicky *n.*[9] *see* DICKORY DOCK n. (1).

dicky *adj.*[1] (*also* **dickey**) **1** [late 18C+] of people or animals, sickly, unhealthy. **2** [19C+] (*also* **dick in the green**) of things and people, second-rate, of poor quality, weak, sub-standard, not working as they should. **3** [late 19C] (*UK Und.*) suspicious, odd. **4** [1940s+] (*Aus./N.Z.*) stupid. **5** [1960s+] of plans, risky, ill-advised, overly complex. [dial.]

dicky *adj.*[2] (*also* **dickey**) [mid-19C–1900s] smart, fashionable. [? a DICKY n.[1] (3) shirt-front]

dicky-bird *n.*[1] (*also* **dickey-bird, dickie-bird, dicky**) **1** [mid-19C] a prostitute, esp. as NAUGHTY DICKY-BIRD n. (cf. ALLEY CAT n.). **2** [mid-19C; 1990s+] a louse. **3** [mid-19C+] a small bird. **4** [late 19C] a professional singer. **5** [1900s–40s] (*US*) an informer, a betrayer. **6** [1950s] the penis. (cf. ANTEATER n.). [(6) BIRD n.[8] (1)]

dicky-bird *n.*[2] (*also* **dickey-bird, dickie-bird**) [1930s+] a word; thus *not a dicky-bird*, lit. 'not a word', i.e. nothing at all. [rhy. sl.]

dicky-bird *n.*[3] *see* BIRD n.[7] (3).

dicky bow *n.* (*also* **dickbow, dickey bow, dickie bow**) [1970s+] a detachable bow tie. [? DICKY n.[1]]

dicky-check *n.* (*also* **dickie-check**) [1980s+] (*US Black*) the inspection by police of one's genitals as a possible hiding-place for drugs. [DICKY n.[5] + SE *check*]

dicky diaper *n.* [early 19C] a linen-draper.

dicky diddle *n.* [1950s+] an act of urination. [DICKY DIDDLE v.]

dicky diddle *v.* [20C+] to urinate (cf. APPLE AND PIP v.). [rhy. sl. = PIDDLE v. (1)]

dicky-dido *n.* (*also* **dickey-dido**) **1** [mid–late 19C] (*also* **dicky-dout**) a fool (cf. DICK n.[4]). **2** [20C+] the vagina. [ety. unknown]

dicky (dirt) *n.* (*also* **bucket of dirt, dickey**) [late 19C+] a shirt. [rhy. sl.; despite obvious links to DICKY n.[1] (3), this appears to be a discreet coinage]

dicky-doodle *n.* [1990s+] the penis (cf. BAUBLE n.). [DICKY n.[5] + DOODLE n.[2] (1)]

dicky-dout *n. see* DICKY-DIDO n. (1).

dicky fit *n.* [1990s+] (*UK juv.*) a temper tantrum. [ety. unknown; ? var. on HISSY (FIT) n.]

dicky-lagger *n.* (*also* **dickey-lagger**) [late 19C] a bird-catcher. [DICKY-BIRD n.[1] (3) + LAG v.[2] (2)]

dicky lee *n.* [20C+] (*Aus.*) tea. [rhy. sl.]

dicky-licker *n.* [1930s+] (*orig. US*) **1** a homosexual, esp. a fellator (cf. BONE-EATER n.). **2** a fellatrix. [DICKY n.[5]; var. on DICKLICKER n.]

dicky-man *n.* [late 19C] (*UK Und.*) a husband or common-law partner.

dicky sam *n.* [mid-19C] a native of Liverpool. [Lancashire dial.]

dicky ticker *n.* [1930s+] a weak heart; a person suffering from a bad heart. [DICKY adj.[1] (2) + TICKER n.[1] (3)]

dicky-waver *n.* (*also* **dickie-waver**) [1970s+] (*US*) an exhibitionist. [DICKY n.[5] + SE *waver*]

dictee *see under* DICTY.

dictionary *n.* [2000s] (*US prison*) a hacksaw blade. [ety. unknown]

dictionary *adv.* [mid-19C] (*US*) of speech, elaborately, in a complex, long-winded manner.

dicty *n.* (*also* **dichty, dickty, dictee**) [1920s+] (*orig. US Black*) a stuck-up, conceited, snobbish person. [? SE *decked*, dressed (lit. covered)]

dicty *adj.* (*also* **dichty, dickty, dictee**) [1920s+] (*US Black*) **1** arrogant, haughty, snobbish, conceited. **2** elegant, high-class, sophisticated. **3** of clothes, elegant, chic, smart. [? SE *decked*, dressed; lit. 'covered']

di-da, di-da, di-da *phr.* [1940s+] a phr. used to imply that the previous speaker's words have been overly tedious, drawn-out etc. [echoic]

diddicoi *n.* (*also* **diddikai, diddiki, didekei, dideki, didicai**) [mid-19C+] a gypsy, esp. a half-breed gypsy. [Rom.]

diddies *n.* (*also* **diddeys, diddys**) [late 18C+] the female breasts, the chest; occas. in sing. as *diddy* or *diddly*. [dial. *diddy*, the female breast, usu. when feeding a baby; also used of animals. Note mispron. of TITTY n.[1] (1)]

diddle *n.*[1] **1** [18C–19C] gin or genever; thus *diddle-cove*, a keeper of a gin or liquor tavern. **2** [19C] liquor in general. [SE *diddle*, to walk unsteadily, i.e. the effects of the liquor]

diddle *n.*[2] [early 19C] the sound of a fiddle.

diddle *n.*[3] **1** [mid-19C+] the penis. **2** [mid-19C+] the vagina. **3** [1930s+] (*also* **diddling**) sexual intercourse. **4** [1930s+] masturbation. [DIDDLE v.[1] (1)]

diddle *n.*[4] [late 19C+] a swindle. [DIDDLE v.[2] (2)]

diddle *v.*[1] **1** [mid-17C+] to have sexual intercourse. **2** [1930s+] (*also* **didle**) to molest sexually. **3** [1930s+] (*orig. US*) (*also* **diddle-fuck**) to masturbate oneself or another (cf. BOFF v.). [SE *diddle*, to jerk from side to side + *didder*, to shake, to quiver]

diddle *v.*[2] **1** [early 19C; 20C+] (*also* **diddle away**) to waste time. **2** [early 19C+] to cheat or swindle, to victimize; ext. to *diddle out of*. **3** [mid-19C] to fail. **4** [20C+] to do for, to ruin, to kill. [(1) fig. use of SE *diddle*, to jerk from side to side, to quiver; (2) ? DIDDLER n.[2]; ult. f. DIDDLE v.[1] (1); or OE *didrian, dydrian*, to deceive, delude]

diddle! *excl.* [1960s] nonsense! rubbish! [FIDDLEDEEDEE! excl.]

diddle-cove *n. see* DIDDLE n.[1] (1).

diddle-daddle *n.* [late 18C–19C] nonsense. [FIDDLEDEEDEE! excl.]

diddle daddle *v.* [1970s] to dawdle, to waste time. [SE *diddle*, to dawdle]

diddle-diddle *n.* [early 18C] violin music. [DIDDLE n.[2]+ redup.]

diddle-dumb *adj.* [1970s] (*US*) stupid. [? DIDDLE! excl.]

diddle-fuck *v. see* DIDDLE v.[1] (3).

diddlehead *n.* [1970s] (*US campus*) a fool. [DIDDLE n.[3] (1) + -HEAD sfx (1)]

diddler *n.*[1] **1** [19C] a small boy's penis. **2** [1930s–50s] a masturbator. **3** [1930s+] (*US/Can. Und.*) a child molester. [DIDDLE n.[3] (1)/DIDDLE v.[1] (3)/DIDDLE v.[1] (2)]

diddler *n.*[2] (*also* **jeremy diddler**) [early 19C] a cheat, a confidence trickster. [the character Jeremy Diddler in James Kenney's farce *Raising the Wind* (1803)]

diddler (machine) *n.* [1930s–40s] (*UK Und.*) a gambling fruit machine. [DIDDLER n.[2]]

diddle-shop *n.* [early 18C] a gin-shop. [DIDDLE n.[1] (1) + SE *shop*]

diddleums *n.* [mid-19C+] (*Aus.*) delirium tremens. [mispron.; note Baker, *The Australian Language* (1945) attributes Henry Kingsley with the coinage]

diddley *n.* (*also* **diddly**) **1** [1920s+] (*Irish*) a small monetary payment; thus the *diddley club*, a savings club, used by the poor, to which one could contribute as little as 1 halfpenny a week. **2** [1960s+] nothing whatsoever. **3** [1960s+] (*orig. US Black*) anything unimportant or insignificant; usu. in phr. *not give a diddley*, to not care at all.

diddley *adj.* (*also* **diddly**) [1960s+] (*US*) **1** crazy, eccentric. **2** insignificant, unimportant, worthless. [DIDDLEY n. (2)]

diddley-bop *see under* DIDDY-BOP.

diddley club *n. see* DIDDLEY n. (1).

diddley-damn *n.* (*also* diddly-damn) [1960s+] (*US*) anything insignificant or worthless; usu. as *not give a diddly-damn*, to not care at all. [DIDDLEY n. (3) + DAMN n.]

diddley-damn *adj.* (*also* diddly-damn) [1960s+] (*US*) insignificant, irritating. [DIDDLEY-DAMN n.]

diddley-dick *n.* (*also* diddly-dick) [1970s] (*US*) something of no value. [var. on DIDDLEY-SHIT n. + DICK n.[7]]

diddley-poo *n.* (*also* diddly-poop) [1950s+] **1** (*mainly US juv.*) excreta. **2** anything insignificant. [DIDDLEY n. (3) + POO n.[1]/ POOP n.[2]]

diddley-pout *n.* [late 19C] the vagina. [? DIDDLE n.[3] (1) for which, when stimulated, it 'pouts']

diddley-shit *n.* (*also* diddly-shit) [1960s+] (*US*) anything or anyone insignificant, unimportant. [DIDDLEY n. (3) + SHIT n.[3] (3)]

diddley-shit *adj.* (*also* diddly-shit) [1960s+] (*US*) worthless; insignificant. [DIDDLEY-SHIT n.]

diddling *n.*[1] [early 19C+] petty criminality, cheating, constant borrowing. [DIDDLE v.[2] (2)]

diddling *n.*[2] *see* DIDDLE n.[3] (3).

diddlum *adj.* [1930s] illicit, crooked, swindling. [pron. of DIDDLE v.[2] (2) + SE *them*]

diddly *see also under* DIDDLEY and its combs.

diddly *n. see* DIDDIES n.

diddly-bop *see under* DIDDY-BOP.

diddly-donce *n.* [1940s] a pimp, a ponce (cf. ALPHONSE n.[2]). [rhy. sl.]

diddly-squat *n.*[1] (*also* diddly doo, squat) [1960s+] (*orig. US*) nothing, zero; thus *it don't mean diddly-squat*, it is totally irrelevant, unimportant. [var. on DOODLEY-SQUAT n.; ult. DIDDLEY n. (2)]

diddly-squat *n.*[2] [1990s+] (*US juv.*) faeces or urine. [pun on DIDDLY-SQUAT n.[1] + SE *squat*]

diddlywhacker *n.* [1960s] (*US*) the penis (cf. BAUBLE n.). [DIDDLE n.[3] (1) + SE *whacker*]

diddums *n.* (*also* didums) [late 19C+] a term of soothing affection used by a parent to a small child; when used to older children or adults it is invariably mocking. [pron. of SE *did you/he?*]

diddy *n.*[1] [late 19C+] a gypsy. [dimin. of DIDDICOI n.]

diddy *n.*[2] (*also* didee) [1950s+] (*Aus. juv.*) a lavatory. [? DUNNY n. (2) but *see* DIDDY adj., i.e. the 'little room']

diddy *n.*[3] [1980s+] (*Irish/UK juv.*) a penis. [? DIDDLE n.[3] (1)]

diddy *n.*[4] *see* DIDDIES n.

diddy *adj.* [1930s+] small, diminutive. [nursery pron. of SE *little* + the popularity of the Diddy Men created by the UK comedian Ken Dodd (b.1927)]

diddy-bop *n.* (*also* diddley-bop, diddly-bop, ditty-bop) [1940s+] (*US Black*) **1** a pretentious Black person, pretending or trying to identify with Whites; thus a worthless person. **2** a juvenile delinquent, a street gang member. **3** a style of walking typified by an exaggerated rolling gait and swinging arms, hips and shoulders, plus the locking of one knee. [DIDDY-BOP v.]

diddy-bop *adj.* (*also* diddley-bop, diddly-bop) [1960s+] **1** (*US Black*) immature, unpleasant, stupid, bland. **2** (*US campus*) unattractive. [DIDDY-BOP n. (1)]

diddy-bop *v.* (*also* diddley-bop, diddly-bop, dirty-bop, ditty-bop) [1950s+] (*orig. US Black*) **1** to swagger, to saunter. **2** to be a street hoodlum. [? the *didd(l)y-bop, didd(l)y-bop* rhythm used in bebop jazz; note RMC Duntroon (Aus.) *diddly-bop*, to walk, esp. when on exercise]

diddy-bopper *n.*[1] (*also* diddley-bopper, diddly-bopper, dittybopper) **1** [1940s+] (*orig. US Black*) a young street thug, a gang fighter. **2** [1960s] (*US campus*) one who still acts as if at high school. [DIDDY-BOP v.]

diddy-bopper *n.*[2] [1980s+] (*US Black*) **1** an inexperienced, naïve and, on those grounds, unpopular person. **2** an upwardly mobile, pretentious or snobbish Black person. [DIDDY-BOP adj.; var. BEBOPPER n. (4)]

diddy-bopping *n.* (*also* diddly-bopping) [1960s+] (*US, orig. milit./Black*) **1** walking carelessly. **2** walking in a swaggering or strutting manner. **3** living as a teen hoodlum. [DIDDY-BOP v.]

diddy ride *v.* [1990s+] to masturbate oneself between a woman's breasts. [DIDDIES n. + RIDE v.[1] (1)]

diddys *n. see* DIDDIES n.

diddywaddle *adj.* [1970s] (*US*) insignificant, unimportant. [ety. unknown; ? DIDDY-BOP adj. (1)]

diddy-wah-diddy *n. see* DOO-WAH-DIDDY n.

didee *n. see* DIDDY n.[2].

didekei/dideki *n. see* DIDDICOI n.

didge *n.* [1990s+] a *didge*ridoo. [abbr.]

didgy *adj.* [2000s] crazy, insane. [? var. on DODGY adj.]

did I buggery! *excl.* (*also* did I fuck! ...heck! ...hell! ...shit!) [20C+] a general excl. of negation, e.g. *Did I steal that car, did I fuck!* (cf. DO I FUCK! excl.).

didicai *n. see* DIDDICOI n.

didies *n.* [1980s] underpants. [? DIDDY adj., i.e. a play on 'smalls']

did I ever! *excl.* [early 19C+] a general excl. of intensification, i.e. I certainly did! usu. in answer to a question, also with other personal pronouns or 'anyone'.

did I fuck!/heck!/hell!/shit! *excl. see* DID I BUGGERY! excl.

didle *v. see* DIDDLE v.[1] (2).

didn't ought *n.* [late 19C–1940s] port (wine). [rhy. sl.]

didn't oughter *n.* **1** [1940s+] water. **2** [1970s+] a daughter. [rhy. sl.]

dido *n.* **1** [19C+] (*US*) something fancy or frivolous. **2** [mid-19C+] a caper, a prank, a trick, an antic; often in pl.; thus CUT UP A DIDO v. **3** [1910s+] (*Irish*) an overdressed woman. [ety. unknown; E.P. suggests the Greek *Dido*, 'the tragic queen', perhaps weeping for her distant lover, Aeneas]

dido *v.* [20C+] (*Aus.*) to steal from carts in the street. [? DIDO n. (2)]

did they forget to feed the dingoes? *phr.* [1960s] (*Aus.*) a joc. phr. used to greet an unexpected arrival.

didums *n. see* DIDDUMS n.

did your mama have any sons that lived? *phr.* [1970s] (*US Black*) a phr. used by a woman to rebuff sexual cat-calling by men as she passes them.

die *n.*[1] [mid-19C] **1** a last dying speech, usu. that delivered on the gallows, or the account of an especially gruesome trial. **2** a capital trial for which the condemned man may be executed.

die *n.*[2] *see* DEE n.[1].

die *v.* **1** [early 19C; 1910s+] to fail utterly, to have a difficult time. **2** [1960s+] to collapse with laughter.

die blou *n. see* BLOU n.

die dog (or shite the licence) *v.* (*also* die dog or eat the meat-axe/hatchet, die dog for them that pats me) [mid-19C+] (*Aus./Irish*) to commit oneself unreservedly.

die dunghill *v.* [mid-18C–early 19C] to die in a cowardly manner, repenting or showing any act of contrition on the gallows, where a plucky villain was supposed to display bravado. [SE *die* + DUNGHILL n.]

die in a horse's nightcap *v.* (*also* go to rest in a horse's nightcap) [late 18C–mid-19C] to be hanged. [a *horse's nightcap* is a halter, thus a noose]

die in one's boots *v.* (*also* die with one's boots on) **1** [late 17C–early 19C] to be hanged. **2** [mid-19C–1910s] (*US*) to die by violence, esp. in a gunfight.

die in one's shoes *v.* [mid-17C–mid-19C] to be hanged.

die in the arse *v.* [1970s+] (*Aus.*) to be struck rigid, motionless, usu. through terror. [ARSE n.[1] (1)]

die in the furrow *v.* (*also* fail in the furrow) [19C] of a man, to lose one's erection during intercourse. [SE *die* + FURROW n.]

die like a dog (in a string) *v.* [late 17C–early 18C] to be hanged.

die like a hen *v.* (*also* **die like Jenkins' hen**) [18C–19C] (*Scot.*) to die unmarried. [a long-lost anecdote]

die like a rat *v.* [late 17C–18C] to be killed with poison.

diener *n.* (*also* **diender**) [1940s+] (*S.Afr.*) a policeman. [Afk. *dienaaren*, lit. one who serves; note Afk. sl. *dienaars*, prison warders known for their brutality]

dienner *n.* (*also* **deiner, diener**) [1930s–50s] a shilling (5p). [DEANER n. (1)]

die of a hempen fever *v.* [18C–early 19C] to be hanged. [SE *die* + HEMPEN QUINSY n.]

die on a fish day *v.* [late 17C–early 18C] to be hanged. [? hangings taking place on Catholic 'fish-days', i.e. Wednesdays and Fridays]

die on it *v.* [1910s+] (*Aus.*) to break one's promise, to fail to finish something one has undertaken to do.

diesel *n.*[1] [1970s+] (*UK prison*) prison tea. [its taste, supposedly reminiscent of diesel fuel]

diesel *n.*[2] [1990s+] (*US Black*) one who has a muscular, well-developed physique. [SE *diesel*, a locomotive driven by a diesel engine]

diesel *adj.* [1990s+] strong, tough, muscular. [DIESEL n.[2]]

diesel-dyke *n.* (*also* **diesel, dieseler**) [1950s+] (*orig. US*) a conspicuously masculine lesbian. [SE *diesel* + DYKE n., i.e. f. the motorcycle she is presumed to ride]

diesel therapy *n.* (*also* **circuit**) [2000s] (*US prison*) the constant movement of an inmate between prisons. [the diesel engine of the bus that transports the prisoners or the circuit of prisons around which they are taken]

die the death of a trooper's horse *v.* [late 18C–early 19C] to be hanged. [like the horse, the villain dies 'with his shoes on']

diet pills *n.* [1970s+] (*drugs*) amphetamines (cf. A n.[2]). [their appetite-reducing effects]

die with a hard-on *v.* [1960s+] (*US*) to die violently, esp. by hanging. [HARD-ON n. (1); the victim's penis becomes erect during a hanging]

die with cotton in one's ears *v.* [early 19C] to be hanged. [proper name *Cotton*, a 19C Newgate chaplain who would preach a last sermon to the condemned man]

die with one's boots on *v. see* DIE IN ONE'S BOOTS v.

dif *n.* (*also* **diff**) [late 19C+] difference, e.g. *that's the dif; what's the dif?* [? orig. Stock Exchange use]

diff *n.*[1] [late 19C] (*US*) a blow. [? Scot. *dowf*, a dull blow]

diff *n.*[2] [1940s+] (*Aus.*) the *differential* gear on a motorcar. [abbr.]

diff *n.*[3] *see* DIF n.

differ *n.* [20C+] (*Aus./Irish/N.Z.*) *difference*. [abbr.]

difference, the *n.* [20C+] (*US*) a telling advantage, e.g. a hidden weapon.

differs *n.* [1950s] (*Anglo-Irish*) *difference*. [abbr.]

diffs *n.* [late 19C] *difficulties*, usu. financial ones. [abbr.]

diffy *adj.* [1940s–50s] (*UK society*) *difficult*. [abbr. + sfx *-y*]

dig *n.*[1] **1** [early 19C+] a punch. **2** [late 19C–1910s] in fig. use, a verbal attack. [SE *dig*, a thrust, a sharp poke, as with the elbow, fist or other part of the body]

dig *n.*[2] [mid-19C–1900s] (*US campus*) a diligent or over-dedicated student, one who studies hard. [DIG v.[1]; the term also flourished briefly in UK schools in the late 19C]

dig *n.*[3] [late 19C–1910s] dignity; also as phr. *otium dig*, the dignity of leisure. [Lat. *otium cum dignitate*, the dignity of leisure, popularized in Cicero, *Ad Familiares*, I.xi.21]

dig *n.*[4] [1920s–30s] (*US tramp*) a hiding place for stolen goods. [? one *digs* a hole for the cache]

dig *n.*[5] [1930s–70s] (*US*) a sex show. [? DIG v.[5], i.e. something one enjoys or pays close attention to]

dig *n.*[6] [1940s+] (*Aus./N.Z.*) **1** an Australian or New Zealander. **2** a friend. **3** a general term of address. [abbr. DIGGER n.[3]]

dig *n.*[7] [1990s+] (*drugs*) an injection of a narcotic. [the needle 'digs into' the vein]

dig *n.*[8] *see* DIGGER n.[6].

dig *v.*[1] [early 19C–1900s] (*US campus*) to work extremely hard. [SE *dig*, i.e. to *dig* for knowledge]

dig *v.*[2] [1900s] (*US*) to leave quickly, to run off. [one *digs* oneself out of the current situation or one *digs* one's heels into the ground as one runs]

dig *v.*[3] (*also* **dig up**) (*US*) **1** [1900s–50s] to search in one's pockets for money. **2** [1920s] in fig. use, to pay for.

dig *v.*[4] [1910s+] to share lodgings with. [DIGS n.[1]]

dig *v.*[5] **1** [1930s–60s] (*orig. US Black*) to get together, to meet. **2** [1930s–60s] (*US Black*) to visit. **3** [1930s+] (*orig. US Black*) to appreciate, to enjoy, to love. **4** [1930s+] (*orig. US Black*) (*also* **dig it**) to understand. **5** [1930s+] (*orig. US Black*) (*also* **dig it**) to pay close attention to. **6** [1940s] (*US Black*) (*also* **dig the cat**) to discuss, to converse. **7** [1940s+] (*orig. US Black*) to find out, to discover; to interrogate. **8** [1950s+] to believe. **9** [1950s+] to see, to recognize. **10** [1960s] (*orig. US Black*) to imagine. **11** [1970s] (*US Black*) to borrow. [all orig. jazz musician use, thence adopted by the fans; ult. ? Smitherman, *Black Talk* (1994) suggests Wolof *dega*, to understand (although *DARE* remarks 'questionable' and *HDAS* 'not been substantiated'); ? SE *dig*, to excavate; ? TWIG v.[2]]

dig? *phr.* [1950s+] (*orig. US Black*) understand? know what I mean? [DIG v.[5] (4)]

dig a day under the skin *v.* [late 19C] to shave on alternate days.

dig a ditch *v.* [1970s+] (*US gay*) to have anal intercourse (cf. ASK FOR THE RING v.).

dig a grave *v.* [20C+] (*Aus.*) to have a shave. [rhy. sl.]

dig and dirt *n.* [1920s] (*US*) a shirt. [rhy. sl.]

Digby chicken *n.* [late 19C] a herring; when smoked it is known as a *Digby duck*. [the fishing trade of Digby, Nova Scotia]

dig dirt! *excl.* [1950s] an order to get moving fast.

dig down *v.* [1940s–50s] (*US*) to pay out of one's own pocket. [DIG v.[3]]

digest *v.* [1990s+] (*US campus*) to tolerate.

digester *n.* (*also* **jesta**) [1940s+] (*W.I.*) a large cast-iron pot, with a cover, used for cooking soup. [SE *digester*, 'an apparatus in which the carcases of beasts unfit for food are by the action of heat dissolved into their proximate elements, tallow, gelatine, earthy phosphates etc' (*OED*)]

dig foot *v.* [1930s+] (*W.I.*) to run away fast. [DIG v.[2]]

dig for gold *v.*[1] [1930s–60s] to sleep with or marry a man for his money.

dig for gold *v.*[2] [2000s] (*US campus*) to pick one's nose.

digger *n.*[1] **1** [mid-18C–19C] a spur; usu. in pl. **2** [mid-late 19C] a fingernail. **3** [mid-19C+] a card of the spade suit; thus *big digger*, the ace of spades. [resemblance to a spade or shovel]

digger *n.*[2] [early 19C–1900s] (*US campus*) a diligent student. [DIG v.[1]]

digger *n.*[3] **1** [mid-19C+] any Australian or New Zealander, although orig. a soldier. **2** [1910s+] a term of (affectionate) address. [a form of address used by miners in the 19C Aus./N.Z. goldfields; it spread after Aus./N.Z. participation in WW1; note Fraser & Gibbons, *Soldier & Sailor Words & Phrases* (1925): 'Australians specially claimed it [...] for their trench work at Gallipoli, and New Zealanders for the work of the N.Z. Tunnelling Company on the Western front']

digger *n.*[4] (*Can./N.Z./US Und.*) **1** [1920s] a county or city prison. **2** [1980s+] a solitary confinement cell. [orig. late 19C UK army use *digger*, a guardroom, in which defaulters were 'buried']

digger *n.*[5] [1920s+] (*US*) a young woman, orig. typically from the chorus line, who swaps sexual favours for the monetary and material gifts of a (usu.) older lover. [abbr. GOLD-DIGGER n. (2)]

digger n.[6] (*also* **dig**) [1930s+] (*US Und.*) a pickpocket. [Goldin et al., *Dict. of American Und. Lingo* (1950), suggests an 'unskilled' or 'crude' pickpocket only]

digger n.[7] [1960s] (*US campus*) the grade of D (cf. ACE n.[6]).

digger, the n. [1960s] (*US*) a superior figure; the government.

digger adj. [mid–late 19C] (*Aus.*) used as a qualifier to indicate the ostentation of the newly rich *diggers*, i.e. gold miners.

Diggerland n. [1910s] (*N.Z.*) New Zealand. [DIGGER n.[3] + SE *land*]

diggermania n. (*also* **diggerphobia**) [mid–late 19C] (*Aus./N.Z.*) an obsession with digging in the Antipodean goldfields, usu. fostered by one's failure to find anything. [SE *digger* + *-mania/-phobia*]

digger's delight n. [late 19C] (*N.Z.*) a wide-brimmed felt hat. [DIGGER n.[3] + SE *delight*]

diggings n. (*also* **diggins**) [mid-19C+] lodgings, temporary accommodation. [one *digs* oneself in]

diggities n. [2000s] (*US Black*) the best-quality marijuana. [? HOT DIGGETY (DOG)! excl.]

diggums n. [late 19C] cards in the spade suit. [var. on DIGGER n.[1] (3); resemblance to a spade or shovel]

diggy adj. [1990s+] (*US Black*) admirable, aware, 'hip'. [DIG v.[5] (3); lit. one who 'digs']

dig horrors v.[1] (*also* **get horrors**) [1950s+] (*W.I.*) to be emotionally troubled. [DIG v.[5] (7)/SE *get* + HORRORS, THE n. (1)]

dig horrors v.[2] (*also* **get horrors**) [1950s+] (*W.I.*) to live in material squalor. [DIG v.[4] + HORRORS, THE n. (1)]

dig in v. **1** [late 19C+] to set to work energetically. **2** [20C+] to eat heartily; often as exhortation *dig in!* **3** [1930s] to emphasize, often with malicious pleasure. **4** [1990s+] to have sexual intercourse.

dig in one's feet v. (*also* **dig in one's heels/toes**) [1930s+] to maintain one's position stubbornly.

dig in the grave n. [1910s+] (*orig. Aus.*) a shave. [rhy. sl.]

dig in the grave v. [1980s+] (*Aus. prison*) to divide up spoils.

dig in the whiskers n. [1990s+] (*Aus.*) an act of sexual intercourse.

dig into v. [1920s] (*US Und.*) to rob (a bank), to break into a safe.

dig it v. *see* DIG v.[5].

digital adj. [1990s+] (*US Black*) new, sophisticated, excellent. [as opposed to *analogue*]

digithead n. [1980s+] (*orig. US*) an obsessive computer user. [SE *digits*, numbers + -HEAD sfx (4)]

digits n. **1** [1930s+] (*US Und.*) the numbers racket. **2** [1990s+] (*US Black*) a telephone number (and address). **3** [1990s+] (*US Black*) the amount written on a cheque, usu. a pay cheque. **4** [1990s+] (*US Black*) welfare benefits.

digits baron n. [1930s] (*US Und.*) the head of a numbers betting syndicate. [DIGITS n. (1) + BARON n. (1)]

digits dealer n. [1950s+] (*US Und.*) a numbers racketeer. [DIGITS n. (1)]

dignity n. [mid–late 19C] (*W.I.*) used by Europeans to describe a dance or ball given by the native West Indians. [the implication is of the Whites' mockery of the affected mannerliness of such gatherings]

dig on v. [1980s+] (*orig. US Black*) **1** to observe, to pay attention to, to watch. **2** to find (sexually) attractive. **3** to like, to appreciate. [ext. of DIG v.[5]]

dig-out n. **1** [1900s+] (*N.Z. Und.*) a pit into which recalcitrant prisoners are placed for punishment; a solitary confinement cell. **2** [1990s+] (*Irish*) a loan.

dig out v. **1** [mid-19C–1940s] (*US*) to leave, to depart. **2** [1980s] (*Irish*) to separate from. [DIG v.[2]]

dig out after v. [1910s+] to attempt to get something one desires.

dig out someone's eye v. [1950s+] (*W.I.*) to cheat in a business deal.

digs n.[1] [mid-19C+] (*orig. Aus.*) temporary rented accommodation. [SE *diggings*, the mining districts of Aus. and California, first adopted in lodgings sense by UK actors/DIGGINGS n.]

digs n.[2] (*US Black*) **1** [1960s–70s] food. **2** [2000s] new clothes or footwear. [(1) DIG IN v. (2); (2) DIG v.[5] (3)]

digs n.[3] [1970s+] (*US*) the facts, information. [DIG v.[5] (7)]

dig someone out v. [mid-19C+] (*UK society*) to call for, to encourage one to take part in life outside one's home.

dig the cat v. *see* DIG v.[5] (6).

dig the dip on the four and two v. [1940s] (*US Black/Harlem*) to take a bath every Saturday night. [DIG v.[5] (3) +SE *dip* + SE *four and two* = 6, i.e. the 6th day]

dig up v.[1] **1** [mid-19C+] to discover, to unearth, to find. **2** [late 19C+] to obtain, to provide. **3** [1930s] to disturb, to awaken. **4** [1930s–50s] to look for.

dig up v.[2] [1920s+] to leave. [DIG v.[2]]

dig up v.[3] *see* DIG v.[3].

dig with both feet v. [20C+] (*Ulster*) to be duplicitous, cunning; in a positive sense, to be very clever. [play on DIG WITH THE... FOOT v., i.e. being both a Catholic and a Protestant]

dig with the...foot v. [20C+] (*Ulster*) a v. used in various senses to denote one's religious persuasion; e.g. *dig with the right foot*, to be a Roman Catholic; *dig with the left foot*, to be a Protestant; *dig with the other/wrong foot*, to be of another religion; *dig with the same foot*, to share a religion (cf. KICK WITH THE LEFT FOOT v.). [in the Republic of Ireland (Catholic), people usu. press on the spade with the right foot; in Northern Ireland (largely Protestant), it is the reverse]

dig you later phr. [1940s+] see you later, goodbye. [DIG v.[5] (1)]

dik n. [1970s+] (*S.Afr.*) a fool. [fig. use of Afk. *dik*, dense, thick]

dik adj.[1] [1970s+] (*S.Afr.*) **1** stupid. **2** sated, full. **3** fat. [fig. use of Afk. *dik*, dense, thick]

dik adj.[2] [2000s] (*US Black*) agreeing with. [ety. unknown]

dikbek n. (*also* **diklip**) [1970s+] (*S.Afr.*) a sour-faced or sulky person. [Afk. *dik*, thick + *bek*, mouth/SE *lip*]

dikbek adj. (*also* **diklip**) [1970s+] (*S.Afr.*) sulky, pouting. [DIKBEK n.]

dik dik phr. [2000s] (*US Black*) a statement implying one is in absolute agreement. [DIK adj.[2] + redup.]

dike *see also under* DYKE and its combs.

dike n.[1] (*also* **dyke**) [mid-19C; 1920s+] (*Aus.*) a lavatory, esp. a communal urinal used by schoolboys, soldiers etc. [SE *dike*, a pit]

dike n.[2] [mid-19C+] (*US*) someone who is dressed up; thus *out on a dike*, dressed up specially for a particular event or appointment. [DIKE UP v.]

dike n.[3] [1980s+] (*drugs*) Diconal. [abbr./pron.]

dike down v. *see* DIKE UP v.

diked up adj.[1] (*also* **diked down, diked out, dyked down, dyked up**) [mid-19C+] (*US*) well-dressed. [DIKE UP v.]

diked up adj.[2] (*also* **dyked up**) [1900s] drunk. [? SE *dike/dyke*, a water-course or channel, in this case for alcohol]

dike jumper n. (*also* **dyke jumper**) [1960s] (*US*) a person of Dutch origin. [the Netherlands is stereotypically identified with its system of dikes]

dike up v. (*also* **dike down, dike out, dyke down**) [19C+] (*US*) to dress smartly; thus DIKED UP adj.[1]. [SE *decked out* + ? 13C SE *dight*, to put or place in order, to array, to arrange]

dikk(-dari) n. [late 19C] (*Anglo-Ind.*) a state of worry. [Hind. *dik*, vexed]

dikk(-dari) adj. [late 19C] (*Anglo-Ind.*) worried. [Hind. *dik*, vexed]

dikker n. *see* DICKER n.[2].

diklip *see under* DIKBEK.

dilberry n. **1** [early 19C+] a small piece of excrement or semen clinging to the hairs around the anus or the pubic hair, usu. in pl. (cf. CLAGNUT n.). **2** [20C+] a stupid, dull or obnoxious person. **3** [1910s] a piece of nasal mucus dripping from the bottom of the nostril.

dilberry bush *n.* [mid–late 19C] pubic hair. [DILBERRY n. (1) + BUSH n.[2] (1)/SE *bush*]

dilberry creek *n.* [mid–late 19C] the anus. [DILBERRY n. (1) + SE *creek*]

dilberry-maker *n.* [early 19C] the anus. [DILBERRY n. (1) + SE *maker*]

Dilbert Dildo *n.* [1960s] (*camp gay*) a fool, a gullible person. [*Dilbert*, a comic name + DILDO n. (1)/SE *dildo*]

Dil-Dil *n.* [1990s+] (*US drugs*) Dilaudid. [abbr. + redup.]

dildo *n.* 1 [1960s+] a general term of abuse, a fool, an incompetent (cf. BOBO n.[1]). 2 [1990s+] (*Irish*) a promiscuous woman. [SE *dildo*, an artificial penis; itself ? Ital. *diletto*, a (lady's) delight; thus fig. the lack of autonomous competence of the sexual aid so named; thus Grose (1785): 'DILDO, an implement resembling the virile member, for which it is said to be substituted, by nuns, boarding school misses, and others obliged to celibacy, or fearful of pregnancy']

dildo *v.* 1 [mid-17C–mid-19C] to caress a woman sexually. 2 [late 19C] to stimulate with a dildo. [SE *dildo*]

dildock *n.* [1910s+] (*US*) a fool. [derog. implications of SE *dildo*]

dildohead *n.* (*also* **dildobrain**) [1970s+] (*US*) a general term of abuse. [DILDO n. (1) + -HEAD sfx (1)/SE *-brain*]

dill *n.* [1940s+] (*Aus./N.Z./US*) a fool. [? DILLYPOT n. (2)/backform. f. DILLY adj.[1]; the late 20C UK use may also be attributed to an abbr. of the comic name *Dilbert* (slightly transformed by the comedian Lenny Henry into his bumptious character Delbert Wilkins); also note DILDO n. (1)]

dillbrain *n.* [1950s+] (*Aus./N.Z.*) a fool (cf. BAKEBRAIN n.). [ext. of DILL n.]

diller *n.* [1960s] (*US*) the penis (cf. BAUBLE n.). [var. on DIDDLY-WHACKER n./DILLYWHACKER n.]

dill-hole *n.* [1990s+] (*US teen*) the urethra, thus used as an insult. [? SE *dildo*]

dillies *n.* [1960s+] (*US drugs*) dilaudid. [abbr.]

dillinger front *n.* [1970s+] (*US Black*) a double-breasted suit. [proper name of gangster John *Dillinger* (1903–34) + FRONT n.[2] (2)]

dillio *adj.* [1990s+] (*US teen*) ugly, esp. of a young woman. [ety. unknown]

dillo *adj. see* DEELO adj.

dillo namo *n. see* DEELO NAMO n.

dill pickle *n.* [1900s] (*US*) a fool (cf. APPLEHEAD n.). [despite appearances, the ref. is to the apparent absurdity of a gherkin (? its phallic resemblance) thus cf. WALLY n.[1]/WALLY n.[2], and not to the later DILL n.]

dillweed *n.* [1990s+] (*US campus*) a fool. [ext. of DILDO n. (1)]

Dilly, the *n.* 1 [mid-19C] the Picca*dilly* Saloon. 2 [1920s+] (*UK Und./police*) Picca*dilly*, esp. as a favoured area for prostitutes. [abbr.]

dilly *n.*[1] [late 18C–early 19C] 1 a coach. 2 a night-soil cart. [SE *diligence*, a public stage-coach]

dilly *n.*[2] [20C+] (*Aus./US*) a fool, a lunatic. [DILLY adj.[1]]

dilly *n.*[3] [20C+] (*US*) anything or anyone outstanding or remarkable, often used ironically. [? SE *delightful* and/or *delicious*]

dilly *n.*[4] [1940s–60s] (*US*) the penis (cf. BAUBLE n.). [abbr. DILLY-WHACKER n.]

dilly *adj.*[1] [20C+] (*orig. Aus.*) 1 foolish. 2 mad. [orig. dial.; ult. ? SE *silly*]

dilly *adj.*[2] [1900s–20s] *deli*ghtful. [abbr./pron. + sfx *-y*]

dilly-bag *n.* [late 19C+] (*orig. Aus.*) a small sack or similar container in which articles are carried. [synon. SE *ditty-bag*]

Dilly boy *n.* [1950s+] (*UK gay*) a teenage male prostitute. [DILLY, THE n. (2), a long-time centre for gay prostitution + SE *boy*]

dilly-dad *n.* [1960s] (*US drugs*) Dilaudid, synthetic morphine. [joc. pron.]

dilly-dally *v.* [18C] to trifle, to waste time. [SE f. 1800]

dilly dude *n.* [1960s] (*US Black*) an eccentric, an outsider. [orig. Ohio use, f. Gloucestershire dial. *dilly*, cranky, odd + DUDE n. (7)]

dillypot *n.* [1940s–60s] (*Aus.*) 1 the vagina (cf. ALL QUIET n.). 2 a fool (cf. BAMBA n.[1]; BEECHAM'S PILL n.). [rhy. sl. = TWAT n.]

dillywhacker *n.* [1920s+] (*US*) the penis (cf. BAUBLE n.). [TALLYWHACKER n.]

dilog *n. see* DELOG n.

dilsnick *n.* [1990s+] (*US Black*) a (large) penis. [ext. of DICK n.[4] (1)]

dilsy *n.* [20C+] (*Ulster*) 1 a foolish, usu. female, person. 2 an overdressed, showy woman. 3 a social climber. [ety. unknown]

dim *n.* [1940s–50s] (*US Black*) the evening, the night. [note 15C SE *dim*, the dusk]

dim *adj.* 1 [late 19C+] unintelligent, undistinguished. 2 [1920s+] unsatisfactory, disappointing, dull. 3 [1940s+] disapproving. [orig. Oxford Univ. use, with an implication of the 'subfusc' (i.e. black suit, white shirt and bow tie) formal university wear]

dimba *n.* [1980s+] (*drugs*) marijuana from West Africa. [used synon. in various west African languages]

dimber *adj.* 1 [mid-17C–1930s] (*UK Und.*) pretty; thus *dimber cove*, a handsome man; *dimber mott*, a pretty woman. 2 [mid-19C] smart, active, adroit.

dimber-damber *n.* [17C–19C] (*UK Und.*) a gang leader. [DIMBER adj. (1) + DAMBER n., lit. a 'handsome rascal']

dimber-damber *adj.* [17C–19C] smart, neat. [adj. use of the lit. meaning of DIMBER-DAMBER n.]

dimbo *n.* [1980s+] a fool of either sex (cf. BOBO n.[1]). [DIM adj. (1) + model of BIMBO n. (5)]

dimbox *n.* [1920s] (*US*) a taxi. [? its 'for hire' light]

dim bulb *n.* [1920s+] (*US/Can.*) a fool, a dullard.

dime *n.*[1] 1 [20C+] (*US*) the number 10, often as $10 (cf. CENT n.). 2 [1930s+] (*US prison*) a 10-year prison sentence; a period of 10 years. 3 [1950s+] (*US gambling*) $1000, $10,000. [SAmE *dime*, 10 cents]

dime *n.*[2] (*US drugs*) 1 [20C+] $10 worth of a given drug. 2 [1980s+] crack cocaine (cf. BASE n.). [ext. use of DIME n.[1] (1)]

dime *n.*[3] *see* DIME (PIECE) n.

dime *v.* [2000s] (*US drugs*) to divide bulk drugs into measures worth $10 each. [DIME n.[2] (1)]

dime-a-dozen *adj.* (*also* **dozen-a-dime**) [1910s+] (*orig. US*) common, undistinguished. [ext. of SE use, i.e. the cheapness of such items]

dime a pop *n.* [1930s–40s] (*US Und.*) a policeman. [rhy. sl. = COP n.[1] (1)]

dime bag *n.* [1960s+] (*US drugs*) $10 worth of a drug (cf. NICKEL BAG n.). [DIME n.[2] (1) + BAG n.[11] (1)]

dime dropper *n.* [1960s+] (*US*) an informer. [DROP A DIME (ON) v. (2)]

dime-grind palace *n.* [1930s] (*US jazz*) a cheap dancehall. [SAmE *dime* + GRIND n.[3] (3)]

dime note *n.* [1930s–60s] (*US Black*) a $10 bill (cf. CENT n.). [DIME n.[1] (1) + SE *note*]

dime (piece) *n.* [1990s+] (*US Black/campus*) an attractive woman. [fig. use of DIME n.[1] (1) + PIECE n.[1] (1)]

dimer *n. see* DEEMER n. (1).

dimes, the *n.* [mid-19C] (*US*) money (cf. CENT n.). [generic use of SAmE *dime*]

dime store *n.* [1930s] (*US Und.*) a 5- to 10-year sentence. [ext. DIME n.[1] (2)]

dime-store *adj.* [1940s+] (*US*) cheap, second-rate. [ext. of SE use, i.e. the poor quality of the goods sold in such stores]

dime-store hood *n.* [2000s] (*US Black*) a criminal who is not trusted by his/her peers. [DIME-STORE adj. + HOOD n.[1] (1)]

Dimetown, USA *n.* [1990s+] the world of street drug addicts. [DIME n.[2]/DIME BAG n.; there is an added implication of the poverty of this fig. world]

dimey *n.* [1960s+] (*US*) a glass of beer costing 10 cents. [SAmE *dime*]

dimmer *n.*[1] [1920s–30s] (*US*) a dime. [SAmE *dime* + sfx *-er*]

dimmer *n.*[2] [1930s–50s] (*US prison*) an electric light.

dimmick *n.* [mid–late 19C] counterfeit coins. [var. on DIMMOCK n.[1]]

Dimmie *n.* [1900s] a Democrat. [abbr.]

dimmo *n.*[1] (*also* **dimo**) [20C+] a Greek. [generic Greek name *Demosthenes*; mainly Cockney use]

dimmo *n.*[2] (*also* **dimo**) [20C+] (*US*) a dime, 10 cents. [SAmE *dime* + -o sfx (1)]

dimmo *n.*[3] (*also* **dimo**) [1970s+] a fool (cf. BOBO n.[1]). [DIM adj. (1) + -o sfx (2)]

dimmock *n.*[1] [early–mid-19C] money. [dial.; but note 14C *dime*, a tithe or tenth + US *dime*, 10 cents]

dimmock *n.*[2] [1990s+] an unpleasant person. [SE *dim*; ? on pattern of DILDOCK n.; *OnLine Dict.* Playground Slang (2001) suggests def. 'a person whose behaviour suggested some sort of mental imbalance']

dimmocking bag *n.* [mid–late 19C] a bag used to collect subscriptions, hold one's savings, set aside 'Christmas money' and similar tasks. [? DIMMOCK n.[1]]

dimmy *n.* [mid-19C] (*US*) money (cf. CENT n.). [DIMMOCK n.[1]/ SAmE *dime*]

dimo *see under* DIMMO.

dimp *n.* [1930s+] (*orig. milit.*) a cigarette end, esp. one that is large enough to be relit. [SE *dimple*, the indentation that is put in the cigarette when one pinches it out for further use]

dimp *v.* [1930s+] to stub out a cigarette, to extinguish a cigarette leaving a still-smokeable stub. [DIMP n.]

dimper mot *n.* [mid-19C] a delightful young woman. [var. or mis-sp. DIMBER adj. (1) + MOT n. (2)]

dimple *n.* [late 17C–19C] the vagina (cf. AGREEABLE RUTS OF LIFE n.). [SE *dimple*, a depression in the flesh]

dims and brights *n.* [1940s] (*US Black*) nights and days. [DIM n. + BRIGHT n.]

dim sim *n.*[1] [1950s+] (*Aus.*) the victim of a confidence trickster. [DIM adj. (1) + abbr. SE *simple*, but ? pun on Chinese *dim sum*, a lunchtime snack, i.e. 'I could eat him for lunch']

dim sim *n.*[2] [1980s+] (*Aus. prison*) a criminal. [rhy. sl. = CRIM n.]

dimwit *n.* [1920s+] a fool (cf. DAMWIT n.).

dim-witted *adj.* (*also* **dimwit**) [1940s+] stupid (cf. BEEF-WITTED adj.). [DIMWIT n.]

dinah *n.*[1] [late 19C–1900s] one's favourite female companion. [? var. on DONAH n.]

dinah *n.*[2] (*also* **dina, dine**) [1920s+] nitroglycerine, *dynamite* (cf. DINNY n.; DINO n.[2]). [abbr.]

dinah *n.*[3] *see* DINO n.[1] (1).

dinarly *n.* (*also* **denare, denari, dinali, dinaly, dinarla**) [mid–late 19C] (*Polari*) a shilling (5p) (cf. DEANER n.). [Lat. *denarius*. The word is part of Ling. Fr. and cognate with Sp. *dinero*]

dinch *n.* (*also* **dincher, dintch**) [1920s–30s] (*US Und.*) a cigar or cigarette end. [DIMP n. + SE *pinch*]

dinch *v.* [1920s–30s] (*US*) to pinch out a cigarette for later use. [DINCH n.]

din-din *n.* (*also* **din-dins**) [20C+] (*mainly UK juv.*) dinner. [the pl. use is 1960s+]

dine *n.*[1] [17C–18C] spite. [ety. unknown]

dine *n.*[2] *see* DINAH n.[2].

dine *n.*[3] *see* DINO n.[2].

dine at the downstairs restaurant *v.* [2000s] to have homosexual oral intercourse. [play on EAT v.[3] (1)]

dine at the Y *v.* [1940s+] (*orig. US*) to perform cunnilingus (cf. BOX LUNCH n.). [play on EAT v.[3] (1); Y = the conjunction of the thighs, plus a pun on the YMCA/YWCA]

dine out *v.* **1** [mid–late 19C] to go without a meal. **2** [1970s+] (*US gay*) (*also* **dine in**) to invite someone home for sex (as opposed to picking up a partner for alfresco coupling).

dinero *n.* [19C+] (*orig. US*) money. [Sp.]

dine with Duke Humphrey *v.* (*also* **drink a health to Duke Humphrey**) [late 16C–mid-19C] to go without a meal. [Duke Humphrey's Walk at Old St Paul's Cathedral. The real Duke Humphrey of Gloucester was actually buried in St Albans, but a statue of Sir John Beauchamp, which stood in one of the cathedral aisles, was popularly supposed to be the duke; thus to *dine with Duke Humphrey* meant to frequent this aisle, in the hope, often vain, of being invited to dinner. The Scottish equivalent was to DINE WITH ST GILES AND THE EARL OF MURRAY v.; the earl was buried in St Giles' Church]

dine with Sir Thomas Gresham *v.* (*also* **sup with Sir Thomas Gresham**) [early–mid-17C] to go without one's dinner. [*Sir Thomas Gresham* (1519–79), founder of the Royal Society and a well-known philanthropist; the image is of a poor person forced to appeal to Gresham for charity]

dine with St Giles and the Earl of Murray *v.* [18C] to go without one's dinner. [for ety. *see* DINE WITH DUKE HUMPHREY v.]

ding *n.*[1] [late 18C] (*UK Und.*) the passing of stolen goods to a confederate. [DING v.[1] (3)]

ding *n.*[2] **1** [late 19C; 1920s–40s] a beggar, a tramp, a worthless person. **2** [1940s+] (*Aus.*) a derog. term for a foreigner, esp. an Italian or Greek (cf. DAGO n.). **3** [1950s+] (*US*) a fool, a mentally unstable person. **4** [1960s] (*US prison*) an outsider. [DINGBAT n.[9]/DING v.[3] (2)]

ding *n.*[3] [1920s–70s] the penis (cf. BAUBLE n.). [abbr. DINGUS n. (2)]

ding *n.*[4] **1** [1940s] (*US Und.*) a doorbell. **2** [1990s+] (*W.I.*) a telephone call.

ding *n.*[5] **1** [1940s+] (*Aus.*) the anus. **2** [1950s+] (*Aus.*) a hole in the bottom of anything. **3** [1960s+] of an object, a small knock or dent. **4** [1960s+] (*orig. US*) of a person, a minor injury, a bruise. [DING v.[1] (1)/DING v.[1] (8)]

ding *n.*[6] [1950s] (*US drugs*) marijuana. [ety. unknown; ? the *ding* of pleasure it creates]

ding *n.*[7] **1** [1950s+] (*Aus.*) a party. **2** [1960s] (*US*) a drinking spree. **3** [1980s] a sudden feeling of pleasure, a thrill. [WINGDING n.]

ding *v.*[1] **1** [17C+] to knock down; thus fig. *ding it in someone's ears*, to criticize, to pass on information that the hearer does not wish to know. **2** [late 17C–early 18C] to act in an arrogant manner. **3** [late 18C–1930s] to throw away, esp. to get rid of contraband when threatened by arrest. **4** [early 19C] to steal by snatching, e.g. a hat. **5** [early 19C] (*UK Und.*) to pass to a confederate. **6** [early 19C+] to break off relations with, to abandon a person. **7** [1930s+] (*US campus*) to turn (someone) down, to blackball. **8** [1930s+] to dent, to scratch; thus *dinged*, scratched, dented. **9** [1960s] (*US campus*) to reject a request for a date; to blackball a candidate for a fraternity or club. **10** [1970s] in fig. use of (1), to astonish, to amaze. **11** [1970s+] to kill, to shoot. **12** [1990s+] to smash into. [fig. uses of 14C SE *ding*, to beat heavily]

ding *v.*[2] [mid-19C+] a euph. for DAMN v., used in mild excls.; thus *dingnation*, DAMNATION n.; *dingblasted*, DAMNED adj.

ding *v.*[3] **1** [1910s+] (*US*) to nag, to harass. **2** [1920s–60s] (*US tramp*) to beg money; also as *hit the ding*, *put the ding on*. **3** [1940s+] (*US*) in business, to come to a negative assessment. [SE *ding*, to nag, to bore with repetitious speech]

ding *v.*[4] [1970s+] to telephone.

dingable *adj.* [early 19C] of persons or objects, worthless, to be discarded. [DING v.[1] (3)]

dingaling *n.*[1] (*also* **ding-a-ling**) [20C+] (*Aus.*) the king. [rhy. sl.]

dingaling *n.*[2] (*also* **ding-a-ling**) **1** [1930s+] (*UK/US prison*) a prisoner whose confinement has driven him mad. **2** [1930s+] (*US*) a fool, an eccentric, a mad person. **3** [1960s+] (*US*) an effeminate man. [the ringing in the sufferer's head; (3) is seen as SE *queer*, i.e. eccentric]

dingaling n.[3] (*also* ding-a-ling, ding-a-thing, thing-a-ling) [1930s+] (*orig. US Black*) the penis. [SE *dangle* + image of the testicles as bells]

dingaling adj. [1910s+] crazy, insane, eccentric (cf. DINGBATS adj.; DING-BATTY adj.; DING-DONG adj.[4]; DINGED OUT adj.; DINGO adj.; DINGY adj.[2]).

dingbat n.[1] [mid-19C] (*US*) a strong drink. [? a specific bartender's name]

dingbat n.[2] [mid–late 19C] **1** a ball of dung on the buttocks of sheep or cattle. **2** (*US*) a cannon-ball, a bullet, a flying missile.

dingbat n.[3] [mid-19C–1900s] (*US*) a coin, a banknote; thus in pl. money. [DING v.[1] (1), i.e. the idea of smacking it down on a counter or table]

dingbat n.[4] [late 19C] a blow or slap on the buttocks. [DING v.[1] (1)]

dingbat n.[5] [late 19C] (*US*) **1** verbal squabbling, physical pushing. **2** an affectionate embrace, esp. mothers hugging and kissing their children. [DING v.[1] (1)]

dingbat n.[6] [late 19C] (*US campus*) various kinds of muffins or biscuit.

dingbat n.[7] [late 19C+] a term of admiration.

dingbat n.[8] [late 19C+] anything for which one cannot specify the proper name.

dingbat n.[9] **1** [20C+] (*orig. US*) a fool, an idiot (cf. AIREDALE n.; WOMBAT n.[1]). **2** [1910s] (*Aus. milit.*) a batman, an officer's servant. **3** [1910s–40s] (*US*) a tramp, a vagrant. **4** [1940s–60s] (*US*) a derog. term for an Italian (cf. DAGO n.). **5** [1960s] (*US*) a derog. term for a Chinese person (cf. AH CABBAGE n.). [popularized by George Herriman's carton *The Dingbat Family*, created in 1909 and revived *c.*1971 in the TV sitcom *All in the Family*]

dingbat n.[10] [1910s–40s] the penis. [DING v.[1] (1); one of the many terms equating the penis with a weapon (cf. AX n.[2])]

dingbat adj. [1930s+] foolish, stupid, idiotic. [DINGBAT n.[9] (1)]

dingbatisis n. **1** [1920s] (*N.Z.*) drunkenness, very heavy drinking. **2** [1990s] (*US*) nervousness; neurosis. [DINGBATS n.]

dingbats n. [1910s+] (*Aus./N.Z.*) **1** madness; thus *get/have the dingbats*, to be mad; *give someone the dingbats*, to drive mad, to make nervous. **2** delirium tremens; thus *be in/have the dingbats*, to be insane or suffering from delirium tremens. **3** an eccentric, a mad person. [DINGBAT n.[9] (1)]

dingbats adj. [1910s+] (*Aus.*) eccentric, crazy (cf. APEY adj.; DINGALING adj.). [DINGBATS n.]

ding-batty adj. [1910s–30s] mad, crazy (cf. APEY adj.; DINGALING adj.). [DINGBATS adj. + BATTY adj.[1]]

ding-boy n. [late 17C–mid-19C] (*UK Und.*) a thug, esp. when he acts as a bodyguard or accomplice, providing the 'muscle' for a more skilful villain. [DING v.[1] (1) + SE *boy*]

dingbust v. (*also* dingblast) [late 19C+] (*US*) a euph. for DAMN v. used in oaths or excls.; thus *dingbustit!/dingblastit!*, an excl. of annoyance. [ext. of DING v.[2] (+ BLAST v.[1] (1))]

dingbusted adj. [late 19C+] (*US*) a euph. for DAMNED adj. [DINGBUST v.]

ding-ding n. [1970s–80s] (*US prison*) a mad person. [DING n.[2] (3) + redup.]

ding-dong n.[1] **1** [mid-19C] an alcoholic drink. **2** [1920s] (*US*) the head.

ding-dong n.[2] **1** [mid-19C+] a song; a (domestic) sing-song. **2** [1920s+] (*US*) a bell, a gong. **3** [1920s+] a serious argument, a fight, esp. in phr. *a right old ding-dong*. **4** [1920s+] a noisy party or other gathering. [rhy. sl.; (3) and (4) may be more echoic]

ding-dong n.[3] [1920s; 1970s+] (*US*) a stupid, dull person. [? DING-DONG adj.[4]]

ding-dong n.[4] [1940s+] (*US*) the penis (cf. BAUBLE n.).

ding-dong n.[5] *see* DINGDONGER n. (1).

ding-dong adj.[1] [late 19C–1920s] (*US*) exciting, smart. [the ringing of bells in celebration]

ding-dong adj.[2] [late 19C+] (*Aus.*) energetic.

ding-dong adj.[3] [20C+] (*US*) a euph. for DAMNED adj., e.g. *I feel like a ding-dong fool*.

ding-dong adj.[4] [1960s+] eccentric, insane (cf. DINGALING adj.). [the supposed ringing bells heard by the sufferer]

ding-dong v.[1] **1** [mid-19C] to pressurize. **2** [20C+] (*US*) to annoy, to irritate. [SE *ding-dong*, the sound of a bell; thus its repetitiousness]

ding-dong v.[2] [1920s–50s] (*US tramp*) to beg door to door. [? the ringing of house bells prior to asking for money]

ding-dong adv. [late 18C+] in an energetic, if chaotic manner.

ding-dong bell n. [1940s+] a euph. for HELL, THE phr.[1]. [rhy. sl.]

dingdonger n. **1** [1940s] (*US Und.*) (*also* ding-dong) a house-to-house beggar. **2** [1990s+] (*US*) one who enjoys hedonistic pleasures to excess. [(1) DING-DONG v.[2]; (2) DING-DONG n.[2] (4)]

ding-dong pants n. (*also* ding-dongs) [1920s–70s] (*US*) bell-bottomed trousers. [pun]

ding-dongs n.[1] [late 19C] (*US campus*) side whiskers.

ding-dongs n.[2] [1950s+] (*US*) the testicles (cf. BANGERS n.). [DING-DONG n.[2] (2), i.e. they supposedly knock together, 'like bells']

ding-dust n. [20C+] (*Ulster*) a noise. [ON *denja*, to thrash]

ding-dust adv. [20C+] (*Ulster*) very fast. [ext. of DING v.[1] (1)]

dinge n. **1** [early 19C] (*US Und.*) a moonless night. **2** [mid-19C+] (*also* dinghe, dingy) a Black person. [SE *dingy*, grimy, shabby; ? Mandingo *den-ke*, black; now seen as pej.]

dinge adj. [mid-19C+] (*US*) racially Black. [DINGE n. (2)]

dinge blowen n. [mid-19C+] (*US*) a Black woman. [DINGE adj. + BLOWEN n. (1)]

dinged adj. [mid-19C–1910s] (*US*) a euph. for DAMNED adj. [DING v.[2]]

dinged out adj. (*US*) **1** [1960s] drunk. **2** [1970s+] insane, mentally unbalanced (cf. DINGALING adj.). [fig. use of DING v.[1] (1)]

dinge joint n. (*also* dinge palace) [1940s+] (*US*) a nightclub or similar place patronized by Black people only. [DINGE adj. + JOINT n.[4] (3)/SE *palace*]

dinge kinch n. [mid-19C] (*US*) a Black child. [DINGE adj. + KINCHIN n. (1)]

dingelberry n. *see* DINGLEBERRY n. (2).

dinge palace n. *see* DINGE JOINT n.

dinge queen n. [1960s+] (*US gay*) a male homosexual who prefers Black partners; used of both Whites and Blacks. [DINGE adj. + QUEEN n.[2] (1)/QUEEN sfx (2)]

dinger n.[1] [late 18C–19C] a thief who throws away anything he possesses that might be incriminating, e.g. a pistol, a coat. [DING v.[1] (3)]

dinger n.[2] [mid-19C+] (*Aus.*) a dingo. [abbr.]

dinger n.[3] [late 19C+] (*Aus./Irish/US*) something exceptional, something striking; also as adj., *dingery*. [fig. use of DING v.[1] (1)]

dinger n.[4] **1** [1910s] (*US Und.*) a till. **2** [1930s] (*US*) an alarm bell. **3** [1930s+] a telephone. [echoic]

dinger n.[5] (*US*) **1** [1930s] a fit. **2** [1930s+] a beggar or tramp, esp. one who pretends to have some sort of injury or throws fake 'fits'. [DING n.[2] (1)]

dinger n.[6] [1940s+] (*Aus.*) the anus, the buttocks. [DING n.[5] (1)]

dinger n.[7] [1950s] (*US*) the penis (cf. BAUBLE n.). [DINGUS n. (2)]

dingey Christian n. (*also* dingy Christian) [late 18C] a mulatto or anyone with a degree of mixed blood. ['anyone who has, as the West Indian term is, a lick of the tar-brush' (Grose, 1785); the presumption that a 'real' Christian is White]

ding farm n. [2000s] (*US*) a psychiatric institution. [DING n.[2] (3)]

dinghe n. *see* DINGE n. (2).

dinghizen n. [1930s–50s] (*US drugs*) a hypodermic syringe, or an improvised syringe based on a medicine dropper attached to a hollow needle. [ety. unknown; ? Chinese]

dingle n.[1] [1910s+] (*US*) the penis (cf. BAUBLE n.). [? DINGUS n. (2) or ? SE *dangle*]

dingle *n.*[2] [1930s] (*US campus*) the regard of one's seniors; thus *get/have a dingle with*, to be in favour; *pluck a dingle*, to toady to. [? fig. use of SE *dingle*, to ring a bell]

dingle *adj.* [late 18C] banal, clichéd, used up. [ety. unknown]

dingleberries *n.* **1** [1940s+] pieces of excreta clinging to the hairs around an inadequately cleansed anus. **2** [1970s+] the female breasts (cf. APPLES n.[1]). [SE *dangle*]

dingleberry *n.* **1** [1910s+] a testicle (cf. ACORNS n.). **2** [1920s+] (*US*) (*also* **dingelberry, dingledork**) someone stupid, dull, obnoxious. **3** [1970s] the vagina, the clitoris (cf. BABY IN THE BOAT n.).

dingleberry *adj.* [1970s] (*US*) stupid, dull, obnoxious. [DINGLE-BERRY n. (2)]

dinglebody *n.* [1950s] (*US*) a stupid, obnoxious person. [var. DINGLEBERRY n. (2)]

dingle-dangle *n.* [late 19C+] the penis. [SE *dingle-dangle*, a dangling appendage]

dingledork *n. see* DINGLEBERRY n. (2).

dingnation *n. see* DING v.[2].

dingo *n.* **1** [late 19C+] (*Aus.*) a cheat, a scoundrel, a traitor, a coward. **2** [1920s–30s] (*US*) a tramp who refuses to work, a minor confidence trickster. **3** [1950s+] (*US*) an eccentric. **4** [1980s+] (*Aus. prison*) a boy who has escaped from a children's home. [SE *dingo*, Lat. *Canis dingo*, the wild, or semi-domesticated dog of Australia]

dingo *adj.* [late 19C–1950s] (*US*) crazy, eccentric (cf. DINGALING adj.). [? Aus. *dingo dog*; or ? DINGALING adj./DINGBATS adj. + -O sfx (5) although chronology would suggest otherwise; note Brophy & Partridge, *Songs and Slang of the British Soldier* (1930), suggest Fr. sl. *dingot*, mad]

dingo *v.* [1910s+] (*Aus.*) to act in a particularly cowardly and treacherous manner, to exhibit the mannerisms of the dingo, the native Aus. dog, a despised creature. [DINGO n. (1)]

dingo's breakfast *n.* [1960s+] (*Aus.*) 'a piss and a look around' (cf. BARBER'S BREAKFAST n.).

dingswizzled *adj.* [late 19C] (*US*) a general excl., e.g. *I'll be dingswizzled!*

ding the tot! *excl.* [late 19C] run off with the lot! [rhy. sl.]

dingus *n.* **1** [late 19C+] anything for which one cannot recall the proper name. **2** [late 19C+] a euph. for the penis (cf. BAUBLE n.). **3** [1930s–50s] (*US drugs*) an improvised hypodermic syringe, made from an eye-dropper and a pin. **4** [1950s–70s] a dildo. [Du. *ding*, a thing; in S.Afr. (1) is extended to people as well as inanimate objects and usu. spelt *dinges*]

dingwallace *n.* [1920s] (*US*) the penis (cf. BAUBLE n.). [ety. unknown; ext. of DINGUS n. (2) but ? *wallace*]

dingy *n.*[1] [1950s] (*US*) one who has been beaten up. [DING v.[1] (1); note *HDAS*, using same cit., has alternative def. 'a beggar', based on ety. DING n.[2] (1)]

dingy *n.*[2] *see* DINGE n. (2).

dingy *adj.*[1] [19C+] (*US*) pertaining to the Black community. [SE *dingy*/DINGE n. (2)]

dingy *adj.*[2] [1910s+] (*US*) silly, foolish, crazy (cf. DINGALING adj.). [DING n.[2] (3)]

dingy *adj.*[3] [1960s] (*US Black*) mean; impoverished, penniless. [DING v.[3] (2)]

dingy Christian *n. see* DINGEY CHRISTIAN n.

dining room *n.* [early 19C] the mouth.

dining room chairs *n.* [early 19C] the teeth.

dining room furniture *n.* [1930s] the teeth.

dining room jump *n.* [late 18C–early 19C] (*UK Und.*) a species of robbery whereby one man poses as a lamplighter, leaning his ladder against the house that is to be robbed. The thief mounts it and makes an entry at a first-floor window. If the police appear and the 'lamplighter' runs, his partner has no means of leaving the house other than to jump.

dining room post *n.* [late 18C–early 19C] (*UK Und.*) a method of robbery in which the villain poses as a postman, sends up a sham letter to a resident of a lodging house and, while waiting for the postage to be brought down, robs the first open and empty room they encounter.

dink *n.*[1] (*also* **dinky**) [late 19C–1940s] (*US*) a Black person. [? DINGE n. (2)]

dink *n.*[2] (*also* **dinkle**) **1** [late 19C+] (*US*) the penis, esp. of a small boy or, if small, of an adult. **2** [1900s] (*US*) a flashy dresser. **3** [1920s+] any small person. **4** [1930s+] (*also* **rinky-dink**) a derog. term for an Oriental, esp. a Vietnamese person (cf. BROWNIE n.[2]). **5** [1960s+] a fool, a laughable or obnoxious figure (cf. CHOAD n.). [? SE *dinky*, small]

dink *n.*[3] [1900s] (*US campus*) failure to pass an examination. [ety. unknown]

dink *n.*[4] [1910s] (*US campus*) a small skullcap worn by freshmen. [? DINKY adj.[1]]

dink *n.*[5] [1930s+] (*Aus. juv.*) a lift on the crossbar of a bicycle (cf. BUNK v.[5]). [ety. unknown]

dink *n.*[6] (*also* **dinky**) [1980s+] *dual income no kids (yet)*, a social acronym created to describe the ideal couple of the booming 1980s.

dink *n.*[7] *see* DINKUM n. (3).

dink *adj.*[1] [1900s–30s] (*Aus.*) honest, genuine, trustworthy. [abbr. DINKUM adj.]

dink *adj.*[2] [1970s] (*US*) pertaining to an Oriental/Asian person. [DINK n.[2] (4)]

dink *adj.*[3] *see* DINKY adj.[1] (1).

dink *v.* (*also* **double-dink**) [1940s+] (*Aus. juv.*) to give someone a lift on the crossbar of one's bicycle (cf. BUNK v.[5]). [DINK n.[5]]

dinker *n.* [2000s] (*US*) something small, esp. when neat, trim or dainty. [DINKY adj.[1]]

dinker *adj.* [1920s+] (*Aus.*) honest, genuine, trustworthy. [DINKUM adj.]

dinker *v.* [late 19C] (*US*) to cheat, to swindle. [? SE *dicker*]

dinkie *adj. see* DINKY adj.[2].

dinkie dow *n.* [1960s+] (*drugs*) marijuana. [play on US milit. pidgin *dinky dau*, crazy (orig. Viet. *dien cai dau*, he is mad); imported by US troops in Vietnam (1964–75)]

dinkle *n. see* DINK n.[2].

dinkum *n.* **1** [late 19C+] (*Aus.*) work, esp. hard work, a due share of work. **2** [1910s] an Australian, spec. an Aus. soldier in WW1. **3** [1910s+] (*also* **dink**) the truth. [dial. *dinkum*, a fair share of work]

dinkum *adj.* [20C+] (*Aus.*) honest, genuine; esp. as FAIR DINKUM adj.; thus *dinkumest*. [DINKUM n.]

dinkum *adv.* [1910s+] (*Aus.*) honestly, genuinely; thus *dinkum? really?* is that so? [DINKUM adj.]

dinkum! *excl. see* FAIR DINKUM! excl.

dinkum oil *n.* [1910s+] (*Aus.*) the honest truth, the true facts. [DINKUM adj. + OIL n.[2] (3)]

dinkus *n.*[1] [1920s] (*US*) a small child. [DINGUS n. (1)]

dinkus *n.*[2] *see* DOODINKUS n.

dinky *n.*[1] [1920s] **1** (*US Black*) a second-rate, inferior person; used as an insult. **2** (*US*) a Black person, usu. derog. (cf. ALLIGATOR BAIT n.[2]).

dinky *n.*[2] [1940s] (*Aus.*) the truth. [abbr. DINKUM n. (3)]

dinky *n.*[3] [1970s+] the penis. [DINK n.[2] (1)/DINGUS n. (2)]

dinky *n.*[4] [1980s] (*UK society*) a large car. [DINKY adj.[1], i.e. deliberate understatement + ref. to *Dinky Toys*, brand of toy cars]

dinky *n.*[5] *see* DINK n.[1].

dinky *n.*[6] *see* DINK n.[6].

dinky *adj.*[1] [late 19C+] **1** (*also* **dink**) neat, trim, dainty. **2** tiny, trifling. [Scot. *dink*, smartly dressed, neat and trim; note 1920s US journ. jargon *dinky*, a 300-word, i.e. small, piece]

dinky *adj.*[2] (*also* **dinkie**) [1910s+] (*US*) second-rate, poor-quality. [RINKY-DINK adj.[2] (1)]

dinky-di *adj.* (*also* **dinky-die**) [20C+] (*Aus./N.Z.*) excellent, first-rate, the best of its type; also ext. to *dinky-di-do*. [DINKY adj.[1] (1) + SE *di(amond)*]

dinky-di *adv.* (*also* **dinky-die**) [1910s+] (*Aus./N.Z.*) truly, certainly. [DINKY-DI adj.]

dinky dirt *n.* [1930s+] (*Aus./US*) a shirt. [rhy. sl.; var. on DICKY (DIRT) n.]

dinky-doo *n.* [1910s+] (*bingo*) the number 22 (cf. ALDERSHOT LADIES n.).

dinky dyke *n.* [1980s+] (*US gay*) a feminine or boyish lesbian. [DINKY adj.[1] (1) + DYKE n.]

dinky one's slinky *v.* [1960s+] to masturbate. [assonance, but note DINK n.[2] (1)]

dinner *n.* [1940s–60s] (*US Black*) an attractive young woman. [abbr. CHICKEN DINNER n. (1)]

dinner buckets *n. see* DINNERS n.

dinner for tea, be *v.* [late 19C+] to be very easy and pleasant.

dinner masher *n.* [1980s+] a male homosexual (cf. BONE-EATER n.). [SE *dinner*, i.e. something to eat + MASHER n.[1] (3)]

dinner pailer *n.* [1940s–50s] (*US*) a regular working man or woman. [SE *dinner pail*; lit. one who carries a dinner pail]

dinners *n.* (*also* **dinner buckets**) [20C+] (*US*) the female breasts (cf. BORDENS n.). [their role as milk carriers]

dinner-set *n.* [late 19C] the teeth.

dinny *n.* [1900s] (*US Und.*) *dynamite* (cf. DINAH n.[2]). [abbr.]

dinnyhazer *n.* (*also* **dennyaiser**) [20C+] (*Aus.*) **1** a knockout blow. **2** a strenuous attempt. **3** something large, outstanding, exceptional (depending on context). [E.P. suggests the Aus. boxer *Dinny Hayes*, but note that AND and DNZE claim 'of unknown origin']

dino *n.*[1] (*US*) **1** [1910s] (*also* **dinah, dyno**) a tramp, a layabout, esp. an old one. **2** [1910s–40s] an Italian or Hispanic labourer (cf. DAGO n.). [(1) DINGBAT n.[9] (3); (2) the 'typical' Mediterranean name, *Dino*]

dino *n.*[2] (*also* **dine, dyno**) [1920s–30s] (*US*) a worker who handles dynamite (cf. DINAH n.[2]). [abbr. SE *dynamite*]

dino *n.*[3] [1930s+] (*orig. US*) a *dinosaur*. [abbr.]

dinosaur *n.*[1] **1** [1960s+] anyone who refuses to move with the times, a conservative. **2** [1980s] a large, outmoded piece of equipment. **3** [1980s+] an ageing rock star, usu. of the 1960s or early 1970s vintage. Such stars, and their bands, won't lie down and subsist gracefully on their royalties; instead they continue to stage concerts, make albums, tour the world and generally refuse to act their age. **4** [2000s] (*drugs*) a heroin user aged over 40.

dinosaur *n.*[2] [1980s+] (*US Black*) the penis (cf. ANTEATER n.). [male bravado + supposed resemblance to a dinosaur's neck]

dintch *n. see* DINCH n.

d.i.o. *phr.* [late 18C–mid-19C] damn! *I'm off*. [abbr.; the phr. satirizes the various forms of polite initials left on visiting cards]

Dip, the *n.* **1** [late 18C–early 19C] a cookshop under Furnival's Inn, London, popular among legal clerks. **2** [20C+] (*UK gay*) a stretch of Piccadilly adjoining St James's Park where gay prostitutes solicit for wealthy clients.

dip *n.*[1] [late 18C–mid-19C] a tallow-chandler. [abbr. SE *dip-candle*]

dip *n.*[2] **1** [19C+] (*US*) a blow, a hit. **2** [1940s+] a bout of quick sexual intercourse. **3** [1970s] (*US prison*) one who participates in anal intercourse. [ext. use of SE *dip*, to plunge in]

dip *n.*[3] **1** [mid-19C] (*Aus.*) a boiled flour dumpling. **2** [20C+] (*Ulster*) fried bread. **3** [20C+] (*Ulster*) hot gravy or an egg to dip in.

dip *n.*[4] [mid-19C+] **1** a pickpocket. **2** an act of pickpocketing. [DIP v.[2] (1)]

dip *n.*[5] [late 19C] a wager. [? the sideshow game, *lucky dip*]

dip *n.*[6] **1** [late 19C] (*US campus*) a diploma. **2** [1930s] (*Aus./UK/US*) *diptheria*. **3** [1940s+] a member of the *Diplomatic Service*. [abbr.]

dip *n.*[7] **1** [late 19C+] (*orig. Aus.*) a fool. **2** [1960s+] (*US campus*) (*also* **dippo**) a bore, a dullard; something tedious. [play on SE *dip*, a makeshift 'candle' made by putting some form of rudimentary 'wick' into oil or tallow and lighting it; thus a play on 'lesser light' or on one who does not 'burn very bright']

dip *n.*[8] [1900s–40s] (*US*) a hat. [one 'dips one's hat']

dip *n.*[9] [1910s–60s] (*US*) a drunkard. [SE *dip*(*somaniac*)]

dip *n.*[10] (*drugs*) **1** [1940s+] a drug addict; a drug user. **2** [1950s] a dose or portion of a drug. **3** [1980s+] crack cocaine (cf. BASE n.). **4** [2000s] a cigarette dipped into SHERM n., i.e. formaldehyde. [SE *dip*, a pinch of snuff]

dip *n.*[11] [1960s] (*US Black*) a party, a get-together, esp. of those in their teens or twenties. [the *Beale Street Dip*, a popular jazz dance of early 20C]

dip *v.*[1] [late 17C–19C] to pawn, to mortgage; thus *dipped*, in debt, mortgaged; *dip one's rigging*, to pawn one's clothes. [SE *dip*, to mortgage]

dip *v.*[2] **1** [early 19C+] (*also* **dip on**) to pick a pocket. **2** [late 19C+] to rob a till. **3** [1940s+] to steal, to take away, e.g. a prostitute's clients.

dip *v.*[3] [20C+] (*Irish*) to work.

dip *v.*[4] **1** [1900s; 1990s+] (*US Black teen*) (*also* **dip out**) to leave. **2** [1950s] (*Aus.*) to go.

dip *v.*[5] [1940s–70s] (*Aus. Und.*) to fail in an endeavour, e.g. an act of shoplifting.

dip *v.*[6] [1970s+] to eavesdrop, to butt into another's conversation, to pay more attention to other people's business than to one's own. [SE *dip in* or DIP ONE'S MOUTH IN SOMEONE'S BUSINESS v.]

dip *v.*[7] [1980s] (*US drugs*) to mix together cocaine and heroin.

dip and chuck it *n.* (*also* **dip and duck it**) [20C+] (*Aus.*) a bucket. [rhy. sl.]

dip-around *n.* [1960s–70s] (*Aus.*) an act of urination.

dipe-ducat *n.* [1920s] (*US*) a subway ticket. [? + DUCAT n. (3)]

diphead *n.* [1970s+] a fool, an unpleasant person. [DIP n.[7] (1) + -HEAD sfx (1)]

dip in the fudge pot *v.* [1980s+] (*US gay*) to have anal intercourse (cf. ASK FOR THE RING v.). [FUDGEPOT n.]

dip into *v.* **1** [early 19C] to pick a pocket. **2** [mid-19C] (*US*) to attack physically. **3** [1950s–70s] to have sexual intercourse.

dip it *v.* [1940s+] to have sexual intercourse. [abbr. DIP ONE'S WICK v.]

dip on *v. see* DIP v.[2] (1).

dip one's beak *v.* (*also* **dip one's nose**) [early 19C+] to have a drink.

dip one's bill *v.* (*also* **dip the bill**) **1** [late 17C–mid-18C] to be mildly tipsy, to be nearly drunk. **2** [1930s–60s] to take a drink.

dip one's lid *v.* (*also* **tip one's lid**) [20C+] (*orig. Aus.*) to tip one's hat, esp. in fig. use, i.e. to acknowledge, to pay respect. [SE *dip* + LID n.[1] (1)]

dip one's mouth in someone's business *v.* (*also* **dip one's nose in someone's business**) [20C+] (*W.I.*) to interfere where one's interest is not required. [var. on SE *poke one's nose in*]

dip one's nose *v. see* DIP ONE'S BEAK v.

dip one's wick *v.* (*also* **dip the wick**) [mid-19C; 1940s+] of a man, to have sexual intercourse (cf. BURY IT v.). [SE *dip* + WICK n.[1]; reinforced by HAMPTON (WICK) n. (1)]

dip out *v. see* DIP v.[4] (1).

dip out on *v.* [1950s+] (*Aus.*) **1** to fail, to miss an opportunity. **2** to refuse to join in.

dipped *adj.*[1] **1** [late 19C–1910s] (*Aus.*) mad. **2** [1950s–70s] (*US drugs*) addicted to narcotics. [? DIPPY adj.]

dipped *adj.*[2] [2000s] (*US Black*) smart, well-dressed.

dipped in the Shannon *phr.* [late 18C–early 19C] shameless, devoid of shyness. [those who are dipped in the Irish River Shannon are supposedly rendered free of any self-effacement]

dipper *n.*[1] [mid-17C+] a Baptist; an Anabaptist; thus *dipping denomination*, the Baptist Church. [SE *dip*, to plunge into water, thus the practice of baptism by total immersion; note Nares: 'A DOPER or DOPPER. An anabaptist; that is, a dipper']

dipper *n.*[2] [late 19C+] a pickpocket. [DIP v.[2] (1)]

dipper *n.*[3] [1940s] (*US Black*) a barman.

dipper *n.*[4] [1940s–50s] (*US drugs*) an opium pipe. [? the dipping of the YEN HOCK n. into the bowl of the pipe prior to lighting the opium]

dippiness n. [1960s] eccentricity, craziness. [DIPPY adj. (1)]

dipping n. [mid-19C+] the world and practice of pickpocketing; thus *dipping-bloke*, a pickpocket; *dipping gag*, pickpocketing. [DIP v.² (1)]

dipping denomination n. *see* DIPPER n.¹.

dipping (in business) n. [1970s+] (*US Black*) interfering in affairs that are none of one's concern.

dipping in the bush n. [1970s+] cunnilingus (cf. BEARD RIDE n.). [SE *dip* + BUSH n.² (1)]

dipping out n. [1980s+] (*US drugs*) of drug runners, the stealing of a portion of crack cocaine from the vials in which it is contained. [SE *dip into*]

dippit adj. *see* DIPPY adj. (1).

dippo n. *see* DIP n.⁷ (2).

dippy n. [1990s+] (*W.I.*) a deportee from the UK. [DIP v.⁴ (1)]

dippy adj. **1** [late 19C+] (*also* **dappy, dippit**) crazy, eccentric, mildly insane; thus *dippy about/over*, obsessed with, usu. a person with whom one is in love; *dippy department*, the psychiatric ward. **2** (*US campus*) unexciting. [? the image of a head that is 'not screwed on' and thus moves up and down like a bird dipping its beak]

dips n. [19C] a grocer. [a period when the grocer dipped into various sacks or boxes of goods to measure out a customer's wants]

dipshit n. **1** [1960s+] (*orig. US*) a fool (cf. DUMBSHIT n.; GOBSHITE n.¹; SHITSTAIN n.). **2** [1960s+] (*orig. US*) a derog. term of address. **3** [1990s+] (*Aus.*) a male homosexual. [(1) and (2) DIP n.⁷ (1) + SHIT n.² (1); (3) SE *dip* + SHIT n.¹ (1)]

dipshit adj. [1960s+] (*orig. US*) **1** stupid. **2** second-rate, inferior; thus *dipshitting*, horrible, vile. [DIPSHIT n. (1)]

dipso n. [late 19C+] an alcoholic; also adj. [abbr. SE *dipsomaniac*]

dip south v. [1940s+] (*Aus./N.Z.*) to put one's hand in one's pocket, esp. when one's funds are running low. [SE *dip* + SOUTH adj. (1)]

dipstick n. [1960s+] **1** the penis (cf. BAT n.⁷). **2** (*orig. US*) a fool, an incompetent (cf. CHIPSTICK n.; MOPSTICK n.). [play on SE; widely popularized by the BBC TV series *Only Fools and Horses* (from 1981), whose star, David Jason, refused to use obscenities, but *dipstick* fits neatly in the range of words that mean both penis and fool, (cf. CHOAD n.); also popularized by the character 'Boss Hogg' in US TV show *Dukes of Hazzard*]

dipstick adj. [1980s+] (*US*) stupid. [DIPSTICK n. (2)]

dipsy n.¹ [1920s–50s] (*US tramp*) a sentence of time in the workhouse.

dipsy n.² [1990s+] (*US*) a mentally retarded person. [? DIPSO n./DIPSTICK n. (2)]

dipsy adj.¹ [1970s] (*US*) drunk. [SE *dipsomaniac*]

dipsy adj.² [1980s] (*US*) eccentric. [DIPPY adj. (1)/DIPSY n.²]

dipsy-doo n. [1980s] (*US*) the anus. [? euph.]

dipsy-doodle n. (*also* **dispsy-do**) [1940s] (*US*) trickery, scheming. [baseball jargon *dipsy-do*, a deceptive sinking curveball, ult. SE *dip*]

dipsy-doodle v. (*US*) **1** [1940s–50s] to trick, to plot. **2** [1970s–80s] to wander along. [DIPSY-DOODLE n.]

dip the bill v. *see* DIP ONE'S BILL v.

dip the dagger v. (*also* **dip the candle**) [1960s–70s] of a man, to have sexual intercourse (cf. BURY IT v.). [DAGGER n.¹/SE *candle*]

dip the fly v. [1980s+] (*US Black*) of a man, to have sexual intercourse. [the dipping or lowering of the trouser fly before intercourse]

dip the schnitzel v. [1950s+] (*US*) of a man, to have sexual intercourse (cf. BURY IT v.). [SE *dip* + SCHNITZEL n. (1)]

dip the wick v. *see* DIP ONE'S WICK v.

dipwad n. [1970s+] (*US*) a general term of abuse. [DIPSHIT adj. + -WAD sfx]

dip your eye! *excl.* [1950s] (*Aus.*) a dismissive retort.

directly minute adv. [late 19C] immediately, at once.

dirk n.¹ [late 18C+] the penis.

dirk n.² [1950s+] a fool, an idiot, a failure. [var. on JERK n.¹ (2)]

dirt n.¹ [mid-17C; 19C+] money (cf. CHAFF n.²). [the guilty image of money as filth]

dirt n.² **1** [late 19C+] (*Aus./N.Z.*) a mean action or a malicious remark. **2** [late 19C+] (*orig. US*) information, not necessarily, but often scurrilous; often as [1930s+] *what's the dirt (on)...?* **3** [20C+] (*orig. US*) an unpleasant individual. **4** [1920s–60s] (*US*) a male or female prostitute who steals from clients. **5** [1920s+] (*orig. US*) gossip, malicious chatter; thus *blow some dirt*, to gossip maliciously.

dirt n.³ [1930s–40s] (*US prison*) sugar.

dirt n.⁴ [1970s+] (*US drugs*) **1** (*also* **dirt grass**) very poor-quality marijuana. **2** heroin (cf. CACA n.).

dirt n.⁵ [1970s+] (*US gay*) a homophobic thug.

dirt n.⁶ [1990s+] (*US*) one who enjoys GOTH n. (2) music and the surrounding lifestyle.

dirtbag n. **1** [1940s+] (*orig. US*) (*also* **dirthead**) a general term of abuse, irrespective of sex. **2** [1990s+] a promiscuous woman. [SE *dirt* + -BAG sfx/-HEAD sfx (1); note RMC Duntroon (Aus.) *dirtbag*, a civilian]

dirtbag adj. [1980s+] repellent, disgusting, despicable. [DIRTBAG n. (1)]

dirtball n. [1970s+] (*US*) a dirty or generally unpleasant person. [SE *dirt* + -BALL sfx]

dirtball adj. [1990s+] (*US*) unpleasant, disgusting. [DIRTBALL n.]

dirt bird n. [1940s+] (*Irish*) a general term of abuse. [? dial. *dirt bird*, the skua but prob. SE *dirt* + BIRD n.² (1)]

dirt box n. [1960s+] the anus (cf. BOURNEVILLE BOULEVARD n.; DIRT-CHUTE n.; DIRT ROAD n.²; DIRT TRACK n.; MUCKHOLE n.; POOH CHUTE n.; POO-HOLE n.; POOP-CHUTE n.; POOPER n.; POO-POO n.²; SHIT-BOX n.; SHIT-CHUTE n.; SHITHOLE n.; SHITTER n.¹). [SE *dirt* + BOX n.¹ (4)]

dirt-cheap adj. *see* CHEAP AS DIRT adj.

dirt-chute n. (*US*) **1** [1940s+] the anus (cf. ALLEY WAY n.; BOURNE-VILLE BOULEVARD n.; DIRT BOX n.). **2** [2000s] a general term of abuse.

dirt-devil n. [1980s+] (*US drugs*) an individual who has low-quality marijuana. [DIRT n.⁴ (1) + SE *devil*]

dirt-dobber n. (*also* **dirt-scratcher**) [1940s–60s] **1** (*US Southern/Western*) a poor farmer. **2** (*US*) a worthless person. **3** (*US campus*) a sandal. [SE *dirt* + *dob*, to dab, to pat/SAmE *scratcher*, a kind of wasp]

dirt-eater n. [mid-19C–1950s] (*US*) a poor White. [for ety. *see* CLAY-EATER n.]

dirt farm n. [1970s+] (*US Black*) any centre for (malicious) gossip. [DIRT n.² (5) + SE *farm* + pun on SE]

dirt grass n. *see* DIRT n.⁴ (1).

dirt, grime and dust n. [20C+] (*Aus.*) a crust (on a pie). [rhy. sl.]

dirthead n. *see* DIRTBAG n. (1).

dirties n. [1960s] (*US*) diarrhoea, sometimes modified as to source, e.g. *green-apple dirties*. [the possible effect on one's underwear]

dirt nap n. [1980s+] (*US Black*) death; esp. in phr. *take a dirt nap*, to die. [SE *nap*, a sleep, i.e. in the ground]

dirt-nap v. [1990s+] (*US Black*) to be dead. [DIRT NAP n.]

dirt road n.¹ [late 19C+] (*US*) the road, the highway (as opposed to the railroad).

dirt road n.² (*also* **dirt run, old dirt road**) [1910s+] the anus; thus GO UP THE OLD DIRT ROAD v./TAKE IT UP THE DIRT ROAD v. (cf. ALLEY WAY n.; BOURNEVILLE BOULEVARD n.; DIRT BOX n.). [fig. use of DIRT ROAD n.¹; note synon. RMC Duntroon (Aus.) *clay road*]

dirts, the n. [1920s–30s] a mean trick. [DIRT n.² (1)]

dirt-scratcher n. *see* DIRT-DOBBER n.

dirt-surfer n. [1980s+] (*US*) one who has abandoned most if not all the normal standards of hygiene and cleanliness. [SE *dirt* + *surfer* used as explorer, e.g. *net surfer*]

dirt-tamper *n.* [1940s–70s] a male homosexual, a sodomite (cf. BROWN ARTIST n.). [SE *dirt* + *tamp*, to ram down hard]

dirt track *n.* [1960s+] the anus; thus *dirt track rider/specialist*, a sodomite (cf. ALLEY WAY n.; BOURNEVILLE BOULEVARD n.; DIRT BOX n.). [note RMC Duntroon (Aus.) *dirt tracking*, hetero- or homosexual anal intercourse]

dirty *adj.*[1] **1** [17C+] bad, terrible, objectionable or a similar negative according to context. **2** [early 19C+] corrupt, morally unsound. **3** [late 19C–1960s] having money, funds. **4** [20C+] (*mainly US Black*) good, wonderful, excellent (on bad = good model). **5** [20C+] (*UK/US Und.*) dubious, unsafe, to be avoided; thus *give the dirty sign*, to warn. **6** [1900s–20s] (*US*) in possession of a large quantity. **7** [1910s+] of money, acquired through crime. **8** [1920s+] holding incriminating evidence. **9** [1960s+] (*drugs*) currently addicted to drugs. **10** [1960s+] (*drugs*) in possession of drugs. **11** [1970s+] (*US Und.*) in possession of or carrying a weapon. **12** [1970s+] (*N.Z. prison*) angry, embittered. **13** [1990s+] (*US campus*) unattractive. **14** [1990s+] (*US prison*) showing evidence of recent drug use in a urine test.

dirty *adj.*[2] [1960s+] (*Aus.*) resentful (of).

dirty *adv.*[1] [mid-19C+] a general intensifier, extremely, very, exceedingly; esp. in *dirty big*, *dirty great*.

dirty *adv.*[2] [1980s+] (*US*) illegally, in a criminal manner.

dirty acres *n.* [late 17C–mid-19C] a landed estate.

dirty a plate (with) *v.* [late 18C; 1930s–60s] to eat (with), to have a meal (with).

dirty-arsed *adj.* [1990s+] a general pej. [SE *dirty* + -ASSED sfx]

dirty barrel *n.* [1960s–70s] (*US*) the male or female genitals when suffering from a venereal disease.

dirty beau *n.* [late 17C–early 18C] a slovenly man who poses as a dandy despite his outward appearance.

dirty bird *n.*[1] [1940s–50s] (*US Black*) Old Crow whisky. [the black bird on its label]

dirty bird *n.*[2] [1950s–70s] an unappealing individual, esp. in rhetorical phr. *I'll be a dirty bird!* [coined by comedian George Gobel on his 1954 TV show]

dirty-bop *v.* see DIDDY-BOP v.

dirty bundle *n.* (*also* **old bundle**) [1940s+] (*W.I.*) an untidy person.

dirty daughter *n.* [20C+] water. [rhy. sl.; note lyrics of the once-popular song 'Wash me in the water / In which you wash your dirty daughter']

dirty dish *n.* [20C+] (*Aus.*) fish. [rhy. sl.]

dirty dishes *n.* [late 19C] poor relations. [they eat one's food]

dirty dog *n.* **1** [mid-19C+] a generally unpleasant person, often with overtones of womanizing. **2** [1940s–50s] (*US Black*) a man who habitually mistreats women. [SE *dirty* + DOG n.[3] (2)/DOG n.[3] (13)]

dirty dowager *n.* [1940s–70s] (*gay*) an unkempt, ill-preserved, older, homosexual man. [SE *dirty* + SE *dowager*, orig. the widow of a dead king, i.e. a QUEEN n.[2] (1)]

dirty dozens *n.* see DOZENS n.

dirty end of the stick *n.* see SHORT END (OF THE STICK) n.

dirty face *n.* [1990s+] a shoelace. [rhy. sl.]

dirtyfoot *n.* [2000s] (*US Black*) a fellatrix. [? ext. of DIRTY LEG n.]

dirty gertie *n.* **1** [1920s–40s] (*US*) a promiscuous or sexually enthusiastic woman. **2** [1920s+] (*bingo*) the number 30 (cf. ALDERSHOT LADIES n.). [SE *dirty* + redup. Note that *Gertie* is a 'typically' vulgar name]

dirty half-mile, the *n.* (*Aus.*) **1** [1920s+] King's Cross Road, Sydney. **2** [1930s+] William Street, Sydney. [both areas are/were known for roughness, decadence and excess]

dirty hearts *n.* [1960s+] (*US Black*) the card-game Hearts.

dirty laundry *n.* (*also* **dirty linen, dirty washing**) [20C+] unpleasant, embarrassing or revelatory information; thus *air one's dirty laundry in public*.

dirty left *n.* (*also* **dirty right**) [1900s–10s] (*Aus.*) a powerful fist, of the left or right hand.

dirty leg *n.* [1960s+] (*US*) **1** a promiscuous woman. **2** sexual intercourse. [SE *dirty* + LEG n.[7]]

dirty linen *n.* see DIRTY LAUNDRY n.

dirty-livered *v.* [1950s] (*Aus.*) a general term of abuse, grumpy, objectionable.

dirty mac brigade *n.* (*also* **dirty macintosh brigade**) [1970s+] a collective term for those (usu. middle-aged) men who frequent sex shops and have a taste for pornography. [SE *dirty* + *mac* + BRIGADE n.; such pilloried figures are invariably portrayed as skulking in a dirty raincoat]

dirty money *n.* [1910s+] money that is considered not to have been earned honourably or respectably, e.g. from crime/drug dealing. [DIRTY adj.[1] (7)]

dirty-name *v.* [1920s] (*US*) to abuse, to slander.

dirty neck *n.* [1910s–60s] (*US*) a promiscuous woman. [coined by US troops in WW1 to describe French women]

dirty night at sea *n.* [1940s–50s] (*Aus.*) an all-night drinking session.

dirty old Jew *n.* [1910s+] (*bingo*) the number 2 (cf. ALDERSHOT LADIES n.). [rhy. sl.]

dirty old man *n.* [1930s+] an older man whose sexual tastes (whether or not fulfilled) err towards much younger lovers, esp. when under the legal age of consent.

dirty 'ore *n.* see DIRTY WHORE n.

dirty pool *n.* [1940s+] (*orig. US*) unfair, duplicitous activity; thus *play dirty pool*, to behave in an underhand manner.

dirty puzzle *n.* [late 17C–early 19C] a slatternly woman. [SE *dirty* + dial. *puzzle*, a slut; ult. Fr. *pucelle*, a virgin]

dirty right *n.* see DIRTY LEFT n.

dirty sanchez *n.* [1980s+] (*US Black*) a 'moustache' of excrement, usu. obtained by finger from one's own anus by someone else. [SE *dirty* + generic Hispanic name *Sanchez*, i.e. a pun on the stereotypically moustachioed Latino]

dirty shirt *n.*[1] [1940s+] (*W.I.*) a bulla cake. [a *bulla cake* is a flat cake, sometimes with a central hole, made of flour and brown sugar and cooked by country people and the urban poor (wearers of SE *dirty shirts*)]

dirty shirt *n.*[2] [1960s] (*US Und.*) an incompetent lawyer who is given clients by court or jail officials; he has no substantial legal knowledge, charges minimal fees and usu. loses.

dirty shirt club *n.* [mid-19C] the Parthenon, a public house in Regent Street, London W1. [the 'great unwashed' who made up its clientele]

dirty shirt march *n.* [mid-late 19C] pre-Sunday lunch promenading by London slum-dwellers, before putting on clean clothes for the meal.

dirty spoon *n.* see GREASY SPOON n.[1].

dirty towel *n.* [1960s] (*US prison*) the prison barber shop.

dirty tricks *n.* [1960s+] corruption, esp. pressure to keep someone quiet.

dirty washing *n.* see DIRTY LAUNDRY n.

dirty whore *n.* (*also* **dirty 'ore**) [1910s+] (*bingo*) the number 34 (cf. ALDERSHOT LADIES n.). [rhy. sl.]

dirty work at the crossroads *n.* **1** [1910s+] underhand, dishonourable actions. **2** [1980s] sexual intercourse. [the image is of a highwayman or other robber lurking at a country crossroads]

dis *n.* (*also* **diss**) **1** [1920s; 1980s+] an act of *dis*paragement or *dis*respect. **2** [1980s] a *dis*appointment. [abbr.; (1) the earlier UK use seems to have faded before its resurrection by US Blacks in 1980s]

dis *adj.* [1920+] eccentric, mentally unstable. [orig. naut. use; ult. telegraphist's jargon *dis*, disconnected]

dis *v.* (*also* **diss**) [1980s+] (*orig. US Black/campus*) **1** to disrespect. **2** to disparage, to attack verbally. **3** to denigrate someone in public to the extent that it makes that person feel bad.

4 deliberately to break an appointment or date without consulting the second party. **5** to inform on. [abbr.]

disabilly *n. see* DISHABILLY *n.*

disc *n.* [1910s+] (*US*) a $1 coin. [the shape]

disco *n.* [1960s+] (*orig. US*) **1** a *disco*theque. **2** the type of music popular in discotheques. [abbr.; ult. Fr. *discothèque*, orig. a record library (on the model of *bibliothèque*, a (book) library) and by mid-1950s a nightclub where a selection of records replaced the trad. live band]

disco *adj.* [1980s] (*US*) applied to activities or people who are playing at being serious about something. [the innate superficiality of a DISCO *n.* (1)/SE *disco* music]

disco biscuit *n.* (*also* **disco burger**) [1990s+] (*drugs*) MDMA (cf. ECSTASY *n.*). [DISCO *n.* (1) + SE *biscuit*; its shape and the environment in which it is often consumed]

disco dancer *n.* [1980s] (*Aus.*) cancer. [rhy. sl.]

disco danny *n.* [1980s] (*US*) a male fan and frequenter of discotheques. [DISCO *n.* (1)]

discombobberate *v.* [mid-19C+] (*US*) to discomfit, to perplex, to confuse.

discombobulate *v.* (*also* **discombobligate, discomboobie, discumfuddle**) [mid-19C+] to discomfit. [a nonsense word, playing on SE *discomfit* and/or *discompose* + ? BOBBERY *n.*]

discombobulated *adj.* [1950s+] unsettled, out of sorts. [DISCOMBOBULATE *v.*]

discombobulation *n.* [mid-19C+] discomfiture, a state of nervousness or emotion. [DISCOMBOBULATE *v.*]

discomboobelate *v.* [1940s–60s] (*US*) to discomfit. [var. on DISCOMBOBULATE *v.*]

discombooberate *v. see* DISCONBOOBERATE *v.*

discomboobie *v. see* DISCOMBOBULATE *v.*

discomfolidate *v. see* DISCONBOOBERATE *v.*

discomfoozled *adj. see* FOOZLED *adj.* (3).

disconbooberate *v.* (*also* **discombooberate, discomfolidate**) [mid-19C+] to discomfit. [var. on DISCOMBOBULATE *v.*]

disco powder *n.* [2000s] amphetamine sulphate (cf. A *n.*[2]). [DISCO *n.* (1) + POWDER *n.*[2]]

discount *v.* [late 19C–1940s] (*US Black*) to disparage, to hold in very low regard. [lit. 'not count', i.e. *dis-* + *count*; ult. SE *discount*, to make a deduction in estimating the worth of]

discouraged *adj.* [mid-19C] (*US*) a euph. for drunk.

discover one's gender *v.* [1940s+] (*gay*) to accept or acknowledge one's homosexuality.

discumfuddle *v. see* DISCOMBOBULATE *v.*

discuss *v.* [early 19C–1900s] to sample or enjoy one's food and drink; thus [mid-19C] *discussion*, the sampling of a commodity's quality.

dis di program *v.* [1980s+] (*W.I./UK Black teen*) to put a planned thing on hold, to delay something, to disrupt a schedule. [DIS *v./abbr.* SE *disrupt* + SAmE *program* (UK sp. would be *programme*)]

dise *n.* [1910s–20s] (*US*) goods, commodities. [abbr. SE *merchandise*]

disease of France *n. see* FRENCH DISEASE *n.*

disguise *v.* [mid-16C–early 19C] to intoxicate, to make drunk. [SE *disguise*]

disguised *adj.* [early 17C–1900s] drunk. [DISGUISE *v.*]

dish *n.*[1] **1** [17C] the female genitals. **2** [20C+] something one likes, something suited to one's taste. **3** [1930s+] (*orig. US*) an attractive woman. **4** [1930s+] an attractive person of either sex. **5** [1950s+] (*gay*) the buttocks. [SE *dish*, an item of food; *dish* was used in 16C–17C to mean a sexually attractive person, e.g. Shakespeare, *Antony and Cleopatra* (1606): 'A woman is a dish for the gods, if the devil dress her not']

dish *n.*[2] **1** [late 19C] the act of abusing, cheating. **2** [1960s+] an embarrassing story about a subject's life; thus KNOW THE DISH *v.* [DISH *v.* (1)/DISH *v.* (3)]

dish *v.* **1** [late 18C+] to hurt, to stop another's plans, to frustrate, to cheat; thus *dish one's gravy*, to cause trouble for oneself.

2 [mid-19C–1950s] to stop, to suppress, to do away with. **3** [20C+] (*orig. US gay*) to gossip maliciously, to tell tales. **4** [1940s+] to speak, to say. **5** [1960s+] (*US gay*) to hurt verbally. [the image of food, which having been 'done' is 'dished up']

dishabells *n.* (*also* **dizybells**) [20C+] (*Irish*) a state of undress. [Fr. *déshabillé*, undressed]

dishabilly *n.* (*also* **disabilly, dishybilly**) [18C+] a state of undress. [Fr. *déshabillé*, undressed]

dishclout *n.* [early 16C–early 19C] a dirty, greasy woman. [metonymy; SE *dishclout*, a kitchen rag]

dish-down *n.* [1920s] a disappointment.

dished *adj.* (*also* **dished up**) [late 18C+] ruined, beaten, silenced; thus *I'll be dished!*, a euph. for I'LL BE DAMNED! excl. [DISH *v.* (1); 'a correspondent suggests that meat is usually *done brown* (see DO BROWN *v.* (1)) before being *dished* and conceives that the latter term may have arisen as the natural sequence of the former' (Hotten, 1867)]

dished out *adj.* [late 16C–mid-17C] dressed up (flashily). [food imagery]

dished up *adj.*[1] [1930s+] (*Aus.*) exhausted, tired out. [ext. of DISHED *adj.*]

dished up *adj.*[2] *see* DISHED *adj.*

dish it *v.* [1920s–30s] (*US*) to vomit (cf. BLOW *v.*[3]).

dish it out *v.* [20C+] (*orig. US*) to hand out, usu. punishment, blows, abuse etc.

dishlicker *n.* [1990s+] (*Aus.*) a dog.

dish of chat *n.* [mid-19C] (*US*) a talk, a conversation.

dish of rails *n.* [late 18C–early 19C] a scolding from a wife to her husband. [SE *rail*, an act of railing or reviling]

dish of red rag *n.* [early 19C–1910s] verbal abuse. [pun on SE *dish* + RED RAG *n.*[1], but note DISH *v.*]

dish of tea *n. see* CUP OF TEA *n.* (3).

dishonourable discharge *n.* [1960s+] masturbation; thus (*US gay*) *have a dishonourable discharge*, to masturbate after failing to make a sexual connection. [pun]

dish out *v.* (*also* **dish up**) [early 18C; mid-19C+] to give out, to apportion.

dish out the gravy *v.* (*also* **dish out the porridge**) [1940s–50s] for a judge to hand out a heavy sentence.

dish queen *n.* [1950s+] a homosexual who enjoys slandering his peers. [DISH *v.* (3) + QUEEN *n.*[2] (1)/QUEEN sfx (2)]

dishrag *n.* [1940s+] a person who is exploited or treated poorly.

dish ran away with the spoon *n.* [1970s+] (*Aus.*) a pimp (cf. ALPHONSE *n.*[2]). [rhy. sl. = HOON *n.* (1)]

dish the dirt *v.* (*also* **dish the dope**) [1920s+] to gossip maliciously, to slander; thus *dirt disher*, a gossip. [DISH *v.* (3) + DIRT *n.*[2] (2)/DOPE *n.*[3] (1)]

dish up *v.*[1] [late 18C+] to beat, to defeat.

dish up *v.*[2] *see* DISH OUT *v.*

dish-walloper *n.* [late 19C–1900s] (*Aus.*) a dishwasher in a restaurant.

dish-walloping *n.* [late 19C–1900s] (*Aus.*) dish-washing.

dishwater diarrhoea *n.* [1960s+] (*US*) an imaginary disease, esp. one that appears when the 'sufferer' would otherwise face an unpleasant or tedious task.

dish-wrestler *n.* [1920s–30s] a restaurant dish-washer.

dishy *adj.*[1] [1960s+] attractive, pretty. [DISH *n.*[1] (4), i.e. 'good enough to eat']

dishy *adj.*[2] [1970s+] (*US gay*) verbally cruel, negative. [DISH *v.* (3)]

dishybilly *n. see* DISHABILLY *n.*

dismal ditty *n.* [late 17C–early 19C] a psalm recited on the gallows by a criminal who is about to die. [SE *dismal*, dreary, cheerless + *ditty*]

dismal jimmy *n.* (*also* **dismal jemmy**) [mid-19C–1940s] a miserable, gloomy person.

dismals *n.* [mid-18C–mid-19C] **1** low spirits, depression. **2** mourning wear. [later use is SE]

dismiss v. **1** [mid-19C] (*US*) to leave. **2** [1980s+] (*US campus*) to end a relationship.

Disneyfied adj. [1970s] (*US Black*) sickeningly, sentimentally happy. [the 'family values' trad. associated with and propagated by the Disney Company]

Disneyland n. [20C+] (*US Und.*) a prison known for its liberal regime. [note 1960s+ US milit. use *Disneyland East*, the Pentagon, the US Air Force Academy and similar headquarters]

disobey the pope v. (*also* **punish the pope**) [1980s+] to masturbate (cf. BANG THE BISHOP v.; PLEASE THE POPE v.). [the Catholic prohibition on 'self-abuse']

dispatcher n. (*also* **despatcher(s), despatches, dispatchers, dispatches**) [late 18C–19C] a form of false dice, on which the pips are arranged in wrong numbers; a *high dispatcher* cannot throw less than 2, while a *low dispatcher* cannot throw higher than 3.

dispatches n. (*also* **despatches**) [late 18C–early 19C] a justice of the peace's warrant for the commitment of a criminal.

disremember v. [early 19C+] (*Anglo-Irish*) to forget. [pun on SE *misremember*]

diss *see under* DIS.

dissolver n. [1910s] (*Aus.*) a revolver. [rhy. sl. + effects]

distiller n. [late 19C] (*Aus.*) one who cannot take a joke. [abbr. WALKING DISTILLER n.]

distress v. [1980s] (*UK Black*) of a gang, to carry out a robbery of a collection of people, as on the underground.

District, the n. [1940s–50s] (*US Black/jazz*) the Storyville area of New Orleans, centre of the city's jazz community.

disturbance n. [late 19C] (*US*) alcohol. [its effects]

Ditch, the n.[1] [late 19C] Calcutta; thus *ditcher*, an inhabitant of Calcutta. [the *Mahratta Ditch*, built by the East India Company in 1742 to protect Calcutta from the Mahratta tribesmen; it ran for 8km (3 miles) but the work was never finished]

Ditch, the n.[2] [late 19C–1920s] **1** Shore*ditch*, east London; thus *Ditch and Chapel*, Shoreditch and Whitechapel. **2** Hounds*ditch*, London EC3. [abbr.]

ditch n.[1] **1** [17C+] the vagina; thus a term of abuse for a woman (cf. AGREEABLE RUTS OF LIFE n.; BAMBA n.[1]). **2** [1970s+] (*US gay*) the anus.

ditch n.[2] **1** [mid-19C–1910s] the Atlantic Ocean (cf. BIG DITCH n.). **2** [late 19C+] (*US*) a canal, e.g. Panama, Suez, Erie. **3** [1910s+] the sea, esp. the English Channel or North Sea.

ditch n.[3] [1960s–70s] (*drugs*) the inside of the elbow, used for injections of narcotics.

ditch v.[1] **1** [late 19C–1920s] to ruin, to stand in the way of a plan. **2** [late 19C–1930s] (*US tramp*) to throw off a moving train. **3** [late 19C+] (*also* **give the ditch**) of people and objects, to throw away, to dispense with, to abandon. **4** [1920s–30s] (*US Und.*) to be sent to prison. **5** [1920s–30s] (*US tramp*) to hide (something). **6** [1920s+] (*US*) to leave in a hurry. **7** [1980s+] (*US teen/campus*) to play truant from school.

ditch v.[2] [1940s+] (*orig. RAF*) to land one's aircraft in the sea. [DITCH n.[2] (3)]

ditched adj.[1] [late 19C+] nonplussed, at a loss. [fig. DITCH v.[1] (3)]

ditched adj.[2] [late 19C+] (*US*) in difficulties, trouble. [? DITCH v.[1] (2), i.e. a hobo being tossed from a moving train]

ditch out v. [1920s+] (*US*) to leave quickly or clandestinely. [ext. of DITCH v.[1] (6)]

ditch pig n. [1990s+] a derog. term for an unattractive, fat woman.

ditchweed n. [1980s+] (*US drugs*) **1** wild marijuana, which is usu. less powerful than cultivated varieties (cf. AFRICAN BUSH n.). **2** any inferior-quality marijuana, often from Mexico. [such plants grow lit. or fig. in the ditch]

dithered adj. [1920s+] (*Aus.*) mildly drunk, tipsy (cf. ADDLED adj.).

dits n. *see* DITZ n.[2]

ditso adj. [1970s+] (*US*) useless, second-rate, no good. [DITZ n.[2]]

ditsoon n. (*also* **titsun**) [2000s] (*US*) a Black person. [? Sicilian dial.]

ditsy *see under* DITZY.

ditsy n. *see* DITZ n.[2].

ditties n. [1990s+] female breasts. [DIDDIES n.]

ditto n. (*also* **dittoes**) [late 18C–19C] a suit of clothes (jacket, waistcoat, breeches) all the same colour. [SE *ditto*, the same. The style is common today, but less so when the sl. was coined]

ditty n.[1] **1** [late 19C+] (*Aus./N.Z.*) a lie; a 'shaggy-dog story'. **2** [1950s] (*US Black*) an anecdote, an experience.

ditty n.[2] [1990s+] (*US campus*) a small object; a penis (cf. BAUBLE n.).

ditty-bop *see under* DIDDY-BOP.

ditz n.[1] [1920s–70s] (*US*) something excellent. [ety. unknown]

ditz n.[2] (*also* **dits, ditsy**) [1970s+] (*US*) a scatterbrained person, usu. a woman, a fool, an idiot. [SE *dizzy*]

ditz v. [1970s+] (*US*) to treat like a fool, to be a fool. [DITZ n.[2]]

ditzo n. [1980s+] (*US*) a scatterbrained person; also as term of address. [DITZ n.[2] + -O sfx (1)]

ditzy adj.[1] (*also* **ditsy**) (*US*) **1** [1970s+] eccentric. **2** [1980s] fussy, intricate. **3** [1980s+] nervous, edgy. **4** [1980s+] scatterbrained, silly, esp. of women. [DITZ n.[2]]

ditzy adj.[2] (*also* **ditsy**) [1970s+] (*US*) first-rate, excellent, exceptional. [DITZ n.[1]]

div n.[1] [1900s] (*Aus.*) a sum of money, esp. money won from a bookmaker. [SE *dividend*]

div n.[2] [1970s+] a weakling, a fool. [ety. unknown; ? link to echoic *duh*!]

diva n. [1990s+] **1** (*US Black*) a stately woman, not invariably beautiful, but always of a certain grandeur. **2** any accomplished woman in any occupation. **3** (*US Black/gay*) an arrogant Black male, who indicates his feelings by elaborate finger-snaps. [SE *diva*, a distinguished female singer; ult. Ital. *diva*, goddess]

diva adj. [1990s+] (*US campus*) excellent, worthy of admiration. [DIVA n.]

dive n.[1] (*UK Und.*) **1** [early 17C–19C] a pickpocket; an act of pickpocketing. **2** [late 18C–early 19C] a thief who stands outside a house or shop, inside which is a small boy who throws out goods that have been stolen. [(1) DIVE v.[1]; (2) ? he dives to catch the falling goods/the goods 'dive' from the window]

dive n.[2] **1** [mid-19C+] (*orig. US*) an illicit drinking establishment or any similarly down-market place of entertainment, a brothel. **2** [1910s] (*drugs*) an opium den. **3** [1920s+] any unappealing place; a slum, any form of run-down housing. [SE *dive*. The implication is of both physical and social 'lowness'; such places were usu. situated in a basement, cellar or other slightly clandestine place into which patrons could 'dive' without being noticed. *Dive* reached its heyday with US Prohibition (1920–33) but the phr. *dive bar* has persisted, lending an air of spurious romance to otherwise unexceptional drinking places; (1) note 1980s use at RMC Duntroon (Aus.) *dive*, the RMC]

dive n.[3] (*also* **diveroo**) [1910s+] (*orig. US*) the voluntary losing of a fight by a boxer, presumably at the behest of a criminal bettor. [he 'dives' to the canvas (+ -EROO sfx)]

dive v.[1] [early 17C–19C] to pick a pocket; thus *diving hooks*, the hands in the context of pickpocketing. [the plunging of one's hand into another's pocket or purse; thus the name of the celebrated pickpocket *Jenny Diver*]

dive v.[2] (*also* **dive into it**) [1930s+] (*orig. US*) to perform cunnilingus (cf. CLAMDIVING n.).

dive a muff v. [1940s+] (*orig. US*) to perform cunnilingus (cf. CLAMDIVING n.). [SE *dive*/DIVE v.[2] + MUFF n.[1] (1)]

dive-bomber n. [1940s–60s] a tramp who picks up cigarette ends.

divebombing n. [1970s+] picking up cigarette ends from the pavement. [DIVE-BOMBER n.]

dive for a meal v. (also **dive for a dinner**) [late 18C–early 19C] to eat in a cellar.

dive for black pearls v. [1970s] (US) to perform cunnilingus on a Black woman (cf. CLAMDIVING n.). [DIVE v.²]

dive for pearls v. [1920s–40s] (US) to work as a dishwasher.

dive in the bushes v. [1920s+] (US) to perform cunnilingus (cf. BEARD RIDE n.; CLAMDIVING n.). [DIVE v.² + BUSH n.² (1)]

dive in the canyon v. [1960s+] to perform cunnilingus (cf. CLAMDIVING n.). [DIVE v.² + CANYON n. (1)]

dive into it v. see DIVE v.².

dive into one's sky v. [late 19C] to put one's hand in one's pocket, esp. to remove money. [SE dive + SKY (ROCKET) n.]

dive into the sack v. [late 17C–early 19C] to pick a pocket. [DIVE v.¹ + SACK n.¹ (2)]

dive into the sky v. [1970s+] to penetrate an anus with one's penis.

diver n. **1** [16C–early 17C] a small boy who, like Oliver Twist in Charles Dickens's novel (1837–9), is put in through an otherwise impassably small window; once inside the house, he either lets in the gang or passes booty out to them. **2** [17C–1940s] a pickpocket. **3** [early 17C] a man in the context of having sexual intercourse. **4** [late 18C–early 19C] one who lives in a cellar. **5** [1940s+] (US) a beggar who forages in garbage cans for food. [DIVE v.¹/SE dive]

diveroo n. see DIVE n.³.

divers n. [mid–late 19C] the fingers.

divi n. see DIVVY n.¹ (1).

dividends n. [1990s+] (US campus) money.

divide the house with one's wife v. [late 18C] to throw one's wife onto the streets. ['to give her the outside, and to keep all the inside to one's self' (Grose, 1785)]

Divine Brown n. [1990s+] fellatio (cf. BLOOD RED n.). [rhy. sl. = GO DOWN v.⁶; ult. Divine Brown, the prostitute that UK actor Hugh Grant was caught soliciting on Hollywood Boulevard in 1995]

divine line, the n. see HAPPY TRAIL n.

divine rights n. (also **divine right**) [1980s] (US Black) the police. [SE Divine Right of Kings, the concept that monarchs are answerable only to God for their actions]

diving-bell n. [late 19C] (orig. US) a basement or cellar tavern; 'a rum-shop in a basement' (Matsell). [? general use of the proper name of a well-known rough tavern in mid-19C New York's gang-infested Fourth Ward]

diving-suit n. [1940s+] (Aus.) a condom.

divoon adj. [1940s–50s] (US) divine, wonderful. [joc. mispron. of SE divine]

divorce mill n. [late 19C+] (US) a divorce court that specializes in 'quickie' separations. [SE divorce + MILL n.⁴ (4)]

divot n.¹ **1** [1930s] a toupee. **2** [1990s+] the female genitals, when heavily covered in pubic hair. [perceived resemblance to a SE divot, a piece of turf]

divot n.² [1990s+] (UK juv.) a fool. [play on SE divot, a clod of earth/CLOD n.¹]

divot-digger n. (also **divoteer**) [1920s–40s] (Aus.) a golfer, esp. an inexperienced one. [SE divot, a piece of turf/clod of earth]

divvie n. [1970s+] one who can sense the right answer even when they have no facts or expertise on which to base their opinion. [? SE diviner]

divvies! excl. [1960s] (US juv.) that's mine! I want to do that! I want a share! a child's term used to claim the whole or an equal part of a given object. [SE divide or division]

divvy n.¹ **1** [late 19C+] (also **divi**) dividend, the annual financial share-out by a cooperative society; thus **divvy-hunter**, one who joins the society purely to benefit from the dividend. **2** [late 19C+] (a share of) profits, usu. illicit. **3** [late 19C+] a share. **4** [1900s–40s] a share-out, a division (of criminal spoils). **5** [1990s+] any free sample, free trip, esp. press tours, promotions etc. [abbr.]

divvy n.² [20C+] (Aus.) a very short time. [? SE a division (of time)]

divvy n.³ [1970s+] a fool, a socially unacceptable person. [ext. of DIV n.²]

divvy adj. [late 19C] profitable, esp. in a criminal context. [DIVVY n.¹ (2)]

divvy v. (also **divy**, **divvy up**) **1** [late 19C+] to divide up, usu. illicit profits. **2** [1930s–40s] (US) to separate. [SE divide]

divvy van n. [1990s+] (Aus.) a police divisional van; esp. in sports chant 'You're going home in the back of a divvy van!'

Dixie n. [mid–late 19C] (US) the American South, esp. those states that formed the Confederacy in the Civil War (1861–5). [20C+ use is SE. The song 'Dixie's Land' was written and first performed by the 'blackface minstrel' Daniel D. Emmett (1815–1904) on 4 April 1859. The term 'Dixie Land' had appeared 2 months earlier in another Emmett song, 'Jonny Roach'. Of the various poss. etys. the preferred choice is an abbr. of the Mason–Dixon line (which divided the North and South in 1763–7). 'Dixie's land' was also a common term in 19C children's games of tag; note Asbury, Sucker's Progress (1938): 'A few years after the Louisiana Purchase one of the New Orleans banks issued ten dollar notes, on one side of which was the French word for ten, dix. To the flatboatmen one of the notes was a dix, and collectively they were dixies, while New Orleans was known as "the town of the dixies," and, later, simply as Dixie. The word does not appear to have been used to designate the entire South until after 1859, when D.D. Emmett wrote his famous song.' In Americanisms (1872), Schele de Vere, who opts for Mason-Dixon, adds another ref. to a supposed slaveholder, one Dixey, who had allegedly treated his slaves very well, thus leading to the 'minstrel' song]

dixie n. [1940s+] (Aus.) an ice-cream carton. [milit. jargon dixie, a small iron pot used for boiling tea, rice, stew etc; ult. Hind. degchi, a small iron pot]

dixie cup n.¹ [1970s+] an attractive Southern woman. [DIXIE n. + CUPCAKE n. (1)]

dixie cup n.² [1990s+] (US) anyone seen as disposable. [the brandname of America's best known disposable cup]

dixie lid n. [1990s+] a child (cf. BILLY LID n.). [rhy. sl. = KID n.¹ (1)]

diz n. see DIZZ n.

dizankster n. [2000s] (US Black) someone or something superlative. [a nonsense-word blending DOWN adj.¹ (1) + -IZ- ifx + GANGSTA n.]

dizybells n. see DISHABELLS n.

dizz n. (also **diz**) [1960s+] (US) an eccentric. [abbr. SE dizzy]

dizzie adj. [1990s+] dyslexic. [abbr. + ? DIZZY adj.¹ (2)]

dizzy n.¹ [mid-19C–1910s] a clever man; esp. in phr. quite a dizzy. [Dizzy, the popular nickname of British prime minister Benjamin Disraeli, Lord Beaconsfield (1804–81)]

dizzy n.² [1910s] (US) a madman. [DIZZY adj.¹ (2)]

dizzy n.³ [1910s] (Aus.) an Egyptian coin. [mispron. of dirham]

dizzy n.⁴ [1910s–20s] (US) a cigarette. [its effect]

dizzy adj.¹ **1** [late 18C; 1900s] drunk; thus dizzy ward, the alcoholic ward; do the dizzy, to act in an uninhibited manner (cf. ADDLED adj.). **2** [late 19C+] eccentric, mad, stupid. **3** [1920s+] obsessed by; thus dizzy with a dame, to be obsessed with a woman.

dizzy adj.² [mid-19C–1900s] (US) startling, astonishing, vivid. [it makes one SE dizzy]

dizzy-ass adj. [1970s] foolish, stupid (cf. CLAY-ASSED adj.). [DIZZY adj.¹ (2) + -ASS sfx]

dizzy flat n. [late 19C] (US) a complete fool. [DIZZY adj.¹ (2) + FLAT n.² (1) + the image of stupidity so great that it makes witnesses giddy]

dizzy limit n. (also **lurid limit**) [1910s+] (Aus.) the absolute limit.

DJ n. (also **deejay**, **dj**, **d.j.**) [1950s+] disc jockey. [abbr.]

DJ v. (also **deejay**, **dj**, **d.j.**) [1980s+] (orig. US) to work as a disc jockey. [DJ n.]

d.j. *n.* [1950s+] *d*inner jacket. [abbr.]

djamba *n.* [1930s+] (*drugs*) marijuana. [used synon. in various west African languages, e.g. Mende]

d.l. *n.* [1990s+] (*US Black*) a state of secrecy. [abbr. DOWN LOW n.]

d.l. *adj.* [1990s+] (*US Black/teen*) secret. [abbr. DOWN LOW adj.]

d.l. *v.* [1990s+] (*US teen*) to keep secret or hidden. [D.L. adj.]

d.l. *adv.* [1990s+] (*US Black*) in a clandestine, sneaky manner. [D.L. adj.]

d.l.c. *n.* [1990s+] (*US campus*) a deep or heavy conversation. [abbr. *down low conversation* (DOWN LOW adj.)]

dlog *n. see* DELOG n.

DMs *n.* [1980s+] a heavy boot favoured first by working men, then by skinheads and latterly by fashionable teenagers (cf. DOCS n.). [abbr. brandname *Dr. Martens*]

d.m.t. *n.* [1960s+] (*drugs*) *d*imethyltryptamine. [abbr.]

do *n.*[1] [mid–late 17C; 20C+] a success; esp. in phr. *make a do (of)*. [SE *do well*]

do *n.*[2] **1** [19C+] a fraud, a swindle; a (practical) joke. **2** [1990s+] (*US*) a business, an organization. [DO v.[2] (1)]

do *n.*[3] **1** [early 19C+] a party, a celebration, a dinner etc, often reasonably formal. **2** [19C] (*US*) noise, confusion.

do *n.*[4] [late 19C+] a period of suffering, usu. physical, e.g. *I've had a rotten do today*.

do *n.*[5] [1930s+] excrement, usu. animal. [euph. phr. 'do its business' (cf. DO ONE'S BUSINESS v.)]

do *n.*[6] [1930s+] an attack, a gang fight. [note 1910s milit. jargon *do*, an offensive]

do *n.*[7] [1940s+] sexual intercourse; usu. as *do the do*. [DO v.[1] (1)]

do *n.*[8] [1960s–70s] (*drugs*) a shot of a narcotic drug. [DO v.[8] (4)]

do *n.*[9] [1960s+] **1** (*US Black/campus*) a haircut. **2** (*US Black*) straightened hair. **3** (*US Black*) an Afro hairstyle. [hair that has been 'done']

do *v.*[1] **1** [16C+] (*also* **do with**) of a man, to copulate with a woman; occas. vice versa. **2** [late 18C+] to defeat. **3** [late 18C+] to murder, to kill. **4** [mid-19C+] of people, to assault, to beat up; of things, places, to break up, to destroy. **5** [1900s] to make the butt of a joke. **6** [1900s–40s] (*US*) to betray, to inform on. **7** [1940s+] of a man, to have homosexual intercourse. **8** [1940s+] to attack in a non-physical sense. **9** [1940s+] (*US gay*) to perform fellatio. **10** [1970s+] to irritate, to mess around. **11** [1990s+] to injure. [fig. uses of SE *do*, all implying a form of 'hitting']

do *v.*[2] **1** [mid-17C+] (*also* **do for**) to cheat, to defraud, to swindle. **2** [late 18C+] to rob.

do *v.*[3] [mid-18C+] (*orig. US*) to satisfy, to suffice, e.g. *that will do fine*.

do *v.*[4] [early 19C] (*UK Und.*) to counterfeit, to forge; thus *do a queer half-quid*, to counterfeit a half-guinea coin; *do a queer screen*, to counterfeit a banknote.

do *v.*[5] **1** [early 19C+] to inspect as a tourist, to visit, e.g. *do London*. **2** [late 19C] to travel, to journey. **3** [late 19C–1910s] to report on. **4** [20C+] to attend an entertainment, e.g. *do a show*. **5** [1910s–40s] (*US*) to search, to raid.

do *v.*[6] [mid-19C+] to act or behave in a manner characteristic of (a specified person etc), to mimic.

do *v.*[7] **1** [mid-19C+] to work, to repair, to prepare, to clean, to keep in order. **2** [20C+] to happen, to take place. **3** [1900s] to place a bet. **4** [1960s+] to conduct business, usu. as a drug dealer. [all rooted in SE *do* (a job)]

do *v.*[8] **1** [mid-19C+] to eat or drink, usu. with the relevant food or drink attached, e.g. *do a couple of pints*, *do a burger*. **2** [late 19C+] to serve, to make available, e.g. of accommodation, food and/or drink. **3** [1950s] (*US*) to defecate. **4** [1960s+] (*drugs*) to consume a given drug, e.g. *do a line*. **5** [1970s] to meet for a meal, esp. in a business context e.g. *do lunch*. **6** [1970s+] of a sport or hobby, to engage in; thus ext. to any experience. **7** [1990s+] (*US drugs*) to experience hallucinations from drug use.

do *v.*[9] **1** [mid-19C+] to serve a sentence in prison; usu. in phrs. *do life*; DO TIME v. etc. **2** [1920s+] to pass a period of time, other than in prison. [DO TIME v.]

do *v.*[10] **1** [mid-19C+] to dispose of, to squander, to waste, to destroy. **2** [late 19C+] to squander one's money; thus *do the lot*, to squander all one's money. **3** [1950s] to hand over, usu. money.

do *v.*[11] **1** [late 19C+] to prosecute; usu. *do for burglary, rape* etc. **2** [20C+] to arrest, to capture. **3** [1930s+] to sue, to take to court, to charge with a crime; thus *X was done for taking and driving away*.

do *v.*[12] [1940s] (*drugs*) to affect, in terms of the experience of a given drug.

d.o.a. *n.* (*drugs*) **1** [1970s+] phencyclidine (cf. ACE n.[4]). **2** [1980s+] crack cocaine (cf. BASE n.). **3** [1980s+] a street name for a variety of heroin. [orig. police jargon *dead on arrival*]

d.o.a. *v.* [1970s+] to die before one arrives at a hospital. [orig. police jargon *dead on arrival*; i.e. its potentially fatal effects]

do a... *v.* (*also* **have a...**) [17C+] used in a variety of combs. to mean to have sexual intercourse; many listed below but others include *do/have a back scuttle, ...ballocking, ...beanfeast in bed, ...bedward bit, ...belly warmer, ...bit of rabbit-pie, ...blindfold bit, ...bout, ...brush with the cue, ...buttered bun, ...dash in the bloomers, ...dash up the channel, ...dog's marriage, ...double fight, ...drop in, ...four-legged frolic, ...fuck, ...futter, ...game in the cock loft, ...goose and duck, ...grind, ...hoist-in, ...jumble up, ...knee trembler, ...lassie's by-job, ...leap (up the ladder), ...little of one with the other, ...mow, ...poke, ...roger, ...rootle, ...St George, ...shag, ...shot at the bull's eye, ...squirt and a squeeze, ...touch off, ...wallop in, ...wipe at the place* (cf. BIT n.[3]).

do a — act *v.* [late 19C+] to perform in a given manner; usu. combined with a given n. or proper name, which defines the 'act' in question.

do a backfall *v.* [late 19C] of a woman, to have sexual intercourse.

do a beer *v.* (*also* **do a drink, ...drop, ...meal**) [late 19C–1910s] to have a drink. [ext. of DO v.[8] (1) + SE *beer/drink*/DROP (OF THE CREATURE) n./SE *meal*]

do a Bertie *v.* [1970s] (*UK Und.*) to turn Crown's evidence against one's accomplices. [proper name *Bertie Smalls*, a well-known criminal turned confessor]

do a Bette Davis *v.* [1950s–60s] (*camp gay*) to act in an ostentatious and overly effeminate manner. [the actress *Bette Davis* (1908–89), a by-word for melodramatic acting and, as such, a gay icon, esp. in the film *All About Eve* (1950)]

do a big *v.* [1990s+] (*US Black*) to commit a robbery.

do a bit *v.* [mid-19C+] to have sexual intercourse; thus *do a bit of...* in all the combs. that follow; *see also under* HAVE A BIT OF... [DO A... v. + BIT n.[3]]

do a bit of beef *v. see* HAVE A BIT OF BEEF v.

do a bit of business *v.* [mid-19C+] to have sexual intercourse; often in the context of prostitution (cf. BIT n.[3]). [euph.]

do a bit of cock-fighting *v.* [19C] to have sexual intercourse (cf. BIT n.[3]). [pun on SE *cock*/COCK n.[2] (1)]

do a bit of dancing *v. see* DANCE v.[1].

do a bit of flat *v.* [19C] to have sexual intercourse, esp. of a prostitute (cf. BIT n.[3]). [SE *flat*, i.e. she is *flat* on her back]

do a bit of front-door work *v. see* FRONT DOOR n.

do a bit of giblet pie *v.* (*also* **have a bit of giblet pie**) [19C] to have sexual intercourse (cf. BELLY BUMP v.; BIT n.[3]).

do a bit of good for oneself *v. see* DO ALL RIGHT (FOR ONESELF) v.

do a bit of (ladies') tailoring *v.* [late 19C–1920s] to have sexual intercourse (cf. BIT n.[3]). [play on NEEDLE n.[1]/SEW v. (1)]

do a bit of skirt *v.* (*also* **have a bit of skirt**) [late 19C+] to have sexual intercourse (cf. BIT n.[3]). [BIT OF SKIRT n.]

do a bit of stuff *v.* [late 19C+] to have sexual intercourse (cf. BIT n.[3]).

do a bit of tailoring *v. see* DO A BIT OF (LADIES') TAILORING v.

do a bolt v. see MAKE A BOLT (OF IT) v.

do a Botany v. see BOTANY BAY v.

do a bottom-wetter v. (also have a bottom-wetter, perform…) [19C] of a woman, to have sexual intercourse (cf. CATCH AN OYSTER v.).

do a brodie v. (also throw a brodie) 1 [late 19C+] to attempt a dangerous, foolhardy stunt, esp. a dive or leap and esp. one that ends in failure. 2 [1920s] to throw oneself out of a window. 3 [1920s] to have a metaphorical fit. [Steve Brodie, a 23-year-old New York saloon-keeper who on 23 July 1886 leaped some 45m (135ft) from the city's Brooklyn Bridge in order to win a $200 wager. He survived the fall and was scooped out of the East River by a friend in a small boat]

do a brown v. see BROWN v.³.

do a brown (act) v. [1980s] (N.Z.) to act in a shy manner; to sulk.

do a bunk v. 1 [late 19C+] (orig. US) to run off, to escape, to go into hiding. 2 [1910s] (Aus.) to move or work fast. [BUNK v.¹ (1)]

do a burg v. [1990s+] (US Black gang) to commit a robbery. [BURG n.³]

do a bust v. [1990s+] (Aus. Und.) to escape. [BUST-OUT n.² (1)]

do a carrington v. [1900s] (Aus.) to run away. [? Right Hon. Charles Robert Baron Carrington sometime Governor of New South Wales, whose departure from Australia 'was marked by expressions of regret and esteem, quite without previous parallel in Australian history' (Philip Mennell, The Dictionary of Australian Biography, 1892)]

do a Chloe v. [late 19C+] (Aus.) to appear in the nude. [a nude portrait, entitled Chloe, rejected in 1883 by the Melbourne National Gallery and bought by a well-known local hotel; its popularity entered the national stock of idioms]

do a clem v. see CLEM v.

do a coin slot v. [2000s] (Aus.) to reveal the top of one's buttocks from one's low-cut trousers. [the supposed resemblance of the crack of the buttocks and a coin slot]

do a crawl v. see CRAWL v.¹ (1).

do a cross-country v. [1920s] (US prison) to make an escape.

do a crouch v. [1920s] (US Und.) to hide.

do a dive into the dark v. [late 19C+] to have sexual intercourse.

do a drink/drop v. see DO A BEER v.

do a dry waltz with oneself v. [1940s+] to masturbate (cf. DANCE WITH JOHNNIE ONE-EYE v.).

do a duck v. see DUCK v.¹ (1).

do a Dutch v. [late 19C] (orig. US) 1 to leave without paying. 2 to remove one's possessions (and oneself) from a rented apartment or house without paying one's rent. [fig. use of DUTCH ACT n.]

doady n. [2000s] (Scot.) the penis. [ety. unknown; ? Yorks. dial. doady, a penis]

do a fade-out v. see PULL A FADE-OUT v.

do a flop v. [late 19C+] 1 to sit or fall down. 2 of a woman, to prostrate oneself for intercourse. 3 to faint.

do a foreigner v. [1970s+] for a worker contracted to one job to take time off illegally to tackle another, more lucrative one. [SE foreign, i.e. somewhere 'away from home']

do a fruit salad v. [1980s+] (US campus) for a man to expose his genitals in public. [presumed resemblance to a banana and apples]

do a ghost v. [1990s+] (US Black) to leave.

do a good turn to v. [20C+] to have sexual intercourse; usu. in the arrogant male phr. I could do that a good turn.

do a grand v. [1950s–60s] (US Black) to do very well. [GRAND adj.¹]

do a grease v. see GREASE (OFF) v. (1).

do a grouse v. [mid-late 19C] to search for sexually complaisant women. [Lancashire dial. grouse, to have sexual intercourse]

do a gun croak v. see CROAK ONESELF v.

do a guy v. 1 [mid-late 19C] to escape. 2 [mid-19C–1900s] to absent oneself from work without asking permission. 3 [mid-19C+] to leave, esp. when stealthily or secretly. 4 [late 19C] to take a false name. [the early 17C anti-Parliament plotter Guy Fawkes (1570–1606)]

do a Hank Snow v. see PULL A HANK SNOW v.

do a Harvey Smith v. [1970s+] to make the V-sign gesture. [the British show-jumper Harvey Smith (b.1938), who, on 15 August 1971, gave such a sign, outraging the staid world of show-jumping]

do a homo and blow v. [1990s+] (US Black) to leave, usu. as imper. [HOMO n.² (1) + pun on BLOW v.² (3)/BLOW v.⁶ (3)]

do a Houdini v. see PULL A HOUDINI v.

do a jar up v. (also jar up) [1940s–70s] (UK Und.) to sell a piece of fake jewellery, to trick someone into buying jewellery that they do not realize is fake. [JAR n.²]

do a job v.¹ [early 19C+] (UK Und.) to commit a crime, esp. a robbery. [JOB n.³ (1)]

do a job v.² [mid-19C+] to defecate. [JOB n.⁵]

do a job v.³ [20C+] (Aus.) to make pregnant.

do a job for oneself v. [20C+] to defecate. [ext. of DO A JOB v.²]

do a job on v. 1 [early 19C+] (also do the job on) to beat up, to murder. 2 [1950s] to make someone the victim of a confidence trick or allied hoax or deception. 3 [1950s+] to cause trouble for, to harass, to persecute. 4 [1970s] to curse, to place a spell on.

do a Johnny Walker n. [1900s] to let off, to escape scot free.

do a jottle v. (also go jottling) [late 19C–1900s] to have sexual intercourse. [Lincolnshire dial. jot, to shake roughly, to jerk about + jottle, to busy oneself with trifles]

do a jumble-giblets v. (also perform a jumble-giblets) [19C] to have sexual intercourse (cf. BELLY BUMP v.).

do a kindness v. [late 19C–1920s] to have sexual intercourse (cf. ARRIVE AT THE END OF THE SENTIMENTAL JOURNEY v.). [SE kindness, affection, love, often used in 17C as euph. for sexual intercourse]

do a knock with v. (Aus.) 1 [1920s+] to arrange a meeting with someone of the opposite sex. 2 [1930s+] to have sexual intercourse with. [KNOCK n.¹ (1)]

do a line v. (also do lines) [1970s+] (drugs) to inhale cocaine. [LINE n.⁴ (4)]

do a line (with) v. (also knock a line (with)) [1930s+] 1 (Aus.) of a man, to talk amorously and seductively. 2 (Irish) to have a sexual relationship, a courtship. [SE do/KNOCK v.³ (1) + LINE n.¹ (3)]

do a living v. [1980s] (UK Black) to commit a street robbery.

do all right (for oneself) v. (also do a bit of good for oneself, do oneself a bit of good) 1 [late 19C] to make money (through betting?). 2 [1930s+] (Aus.) of a man, to seduce, to gain a woman's sexual favours. 3 [1930s+] of a prostitute, to get a client. 4 [1950s+] to improve one's situation.

do a loony v. [1990s+] (UK juv.) to lose one's temper, to become hysterical. [LOONY n.]

do a meal v. see DO A BEER v.

do a Melba v. [1970s+] (Aus.) to announce, with great fanfare, one's imminent retirement, only to return, time and time again, for another 'farewell', a practice of Dame Nellie Melba (1861–1931) and many other 'showbiz greats'.

do a mick v. (also do a mickey, do a mike) [1910s–60s] to escape, to run away. [? MIKE v. (2) or stereotyping of MICK n.¹ (1)]

do a mischief to v. [mid-19C+] (orig. UK Und.) to harm, to beat up.

do a mook v. [1900s] (Aus.) to go to. [MOOCH n.² (2)]

do a mount v.¹ [20C+] to give evidence. [one mounts the witness box]

do a mount v.² see MOUNT v.³.

do an agricultural v. [20C+] 1 to have sex in the open air. 2 to urinate or defecate in the open (cf. BURN THE GRASS v.).

do an ally slope *v.* [1920s] to escape, to make off. [the comic character *Ally Sloper*, 'a seedy proletarian loafer', featured in *Alley Sloper's Half-Holiday*, publ. by Dalziel Bros. (1884–1923) and illustrated (at first) by W.G. Baxter, an ex-patriate American. Note WW1 milit. use *Alley Sloper's cavalry*, Army Service Corps; ? underpinned by SE *slope off* + Fr. *aller*, to go]

do and dare *n.* [1920s] (*US*) underwear. [rhy. sl.]

do a nibble *v. see* NIBBLE v.[2].

do a nick *v.* [20C+] (*Aus.*) to run off. [NICK v.[3]]

do an inside worry *v.* [mid-late 19C] to have sexual intercourse. [SE *inside* + *worry*, to gnaw, to shake]

do an Oliver *v. see* CHUCK AN OLIVER v.

do a number *v.*[1] **1** [1960s+] to make a fuss, to become emotional; thus *do a number on*, to subject someone to emotional blackmail or at least some form of moral or ethical pressure. **2** [1970s+] to have sexual intercourse. **3** [1970s+] to manipulate emotionally, esp. through sexuality. **4** [1970s+] to beat savagely. **5** [1980s] (*US*) to get married. **6** [1990s+] to break, to cause harm (other than through deliberate, person-to-person violence). [NUMBER n.[3] (2)]

do a number *v.*[2] [1960s+] (*drugs*) to make and smoke a marijuana or hashish cigarette. [NUMBER n.[5]]

do a 180 *v.* [1970s+] (*orig. US campus*) to change one's life radically.

do a oner *v.* (*also* **do one's oner**) [1910s+] (*Aus.*) to die, to be killed. [it only happens once]

do a paper dolly *v.* [1940s] (*US Black/Harlem*) to play truant.

do a perish *v.* [late 19C+] (*Aus.*) to suffer extreme privation, esp. for want of a drink. [SE *perish*/PERISH v.[2] (1)]

do a perpendicular *v.* [1940s+] to have sexual intercourse while standing upright (cf. HORIZONTAL n.).

do a piece of work *v.* [20C+] (*US*) to murder, to kill.

do a plaster of warm guts *v.* (*also* **do a plaster of hot guts**) [late 17C–early 19C] to have sexual intercourse, i.e. 'one warm Belly clapt to another' (B.E.) (cf. BELLY BUMP v.). [PLAISTER OF WARM GUTS n.]

do a powder *v. see* TAKE A POWDER v.

do a push *v.* **1** [mid-19C–1920s] (*also* **make a push**) to run away. **2** [late 19C+] of a man, to have sexual intercourse. [SE *push*/PUSH n.[1]]

do a put *v.* [19C] to have sexual intercourse. [2-handed put]

do a rasp *v.* [late 19C–1900s] to have sexual intercourse. [RASP v.]

do a rat *v. see* RAT v.[1] (2).

do a rear *v. see* REAR v.

do a ride *v.* [mid-19C+] to have sexual intercourse. [RIDE n.[1] (1)]

do a rootle *v. see* ROOTLE v.

do a runner *v.* [1970s+] (*UK Und.*) to abscond from the police or to be on the run before possible capture by the police, or simply to run away. [RUNNER n.[2] (2)]

do a rural *v.* [20C+] **1** to have sex in the open air. **2** to urinate or defecate in the open (cf. BURN THE GRASS v.). [SE *rural*]

do a rush up the straight *v. see* SHOOT UP THE STRAIGHT v.

doash *n.* (*also* **dose**) [late 17C–early 19C] (*UK Und.*) a cloak. [ety. unknown]

do a shift *v.* [mid-19C+] (*Aus.*) to run off, to decamp. [SE *shift*]

do a shot *v.* [late 19C] (*S.Afr.*) to cheat, to swindle. [? link to HAVE A SHOT AT v.[2]]

do a sip *v.* [mid-late 19C] to urinate. [backsl. = PISS n. (2)]

do a skate *v. see* SKATE v.[1] (1).

do a skipper *v. see* SKIPPER (IT) v.

do a slippery *v.* [1970s] to absent oneself, usu. for dubious purposes.

do a slither *v. see* SLITHER v.

do a smile *v.* [mid-19C+] to take a glass of whisky or any other drink. [SMILE n.[1]]

do as my shirt does! *excl.* [mid-17C–18C] a euph. but derisive excl. of abuse, rejection etc. [pun on KISS MY ARSE! excl.]

do a snatch *v.* [20C+] to have quick, adulterous or paid-for sexual intercourse. [pun on SE *snatch*, to grab quickly/SNATCH n.[1] (1)]

do a sniff *v.* [1900s] (*Aus.*) to cry, to weep.

do a solid *v.* [1950s+] (*US*) to perform a great favour. [SOLID n.[3]]

do a solo *v.* [1930s–40s] (*US prison*) to confess, to turn state's evidence.

do a solomon *v.* **1** [1900s–20s] to pretend to be wiser than one actually is. **2** [2000s] to divide something in half. [the biblical king *Solomon*, supposedly of great wisdom]

do a spread *v.* [mid-19C] of a woman, to offer oneself for sexual intercourse. [SPREAD (FOR) v. (1)]

do a stamp *v.* [late 19C] (*US*) to go for a walk.

do a star pitch *v.* [mid-late 19C] to sleep in the open air. [one 'pitches one's tent' under the stars]

do a starry *v.* [1920s–30s] (*UK Und.*) to sleep in the open air. [SE *stars*]

do a starve *v.* [1910s+] (*Aus.*) to go hungry. [SE *starve*]

do a swelter *v.* [mid-late 19C] to sweat. [SE *swelter*]

do as you like *n.* [late 19C+] a bicycle. [rhy. sl. = SE *bike*]

do a thing *v.* (*also* **do the thing**) [1970s+] **1** (*US*) to have sexual intercourse (cf. ARRIVE AT THE END OF THE SENTIMENTAL JOURNEY v.). **2** (*W.I., Jam.*) to get married. **3** (*drugs*) to inject oneself with heroin. [euph. use of SE]

do a ton *v.* [1960s+] to drive a motorcycle or car at 100mph. [TON n.[1] (3)]

do a Tower of Pisa *v.* [1940s] (*US Black*) to lean over, usu. through drunkenness. [the Italian Torre Pendente di Pisa is famous for the settling of its foundation, causing it to lean 2m (7ft) from the perpendicular]

do a tread *v.* [mid-19C+] of a man, to have sexual intercourse. [SE *tread*, of the male bird, to copulate]

do a trick *v. see* TURN A TRICK v.[2] (3).

do a tumble *v.*[1] [1900s] of a woman, to have sexual intercourse with a man (cf. CATCH AN OYSTER v.). [TUMBLE n.[2]]

do a tumble *v.*[2] [1900s] (*Aus.*) to lose one's temper.

do a turn (on one's back) *v.* [late 19C+] of a woman, to make herself available for sexual intercourse. [for the woman to *turn* over onto her back + pun on theatrical use]

do a walk *v.* [1930s–70s] (*Aus.*) to abandon a rural property when one's efforts have failed to make it pay.

do a wet bottom *v.* (*also* **get a wet bottom**) [19C] of a woman, to have sexual intercourse (cf. CATCH AN OYSTER v.). [the result of male ejaculation and vaginal secretions]

do a wet 'un *v.* [19C] of a woman, to have sexual intercourse (cf. CATCH AN OYSTER v.). [for ety. *see* DO A WET BOTTOM v.]

do a whiff *v.* [late 19C] to have a smoke.

do a wiggle *v. see* GET A WIGGLE ON v.

do a wobbler/wobbly *v. see* THROW A WOBBLY v.

DOB *n.* (*also* **DOM**) [1990s+] (*drugs*) a far stronger form of MDMA. [abbr. of its chemical name 2,5-Dimethoxy-4-*b*romoamphetamine]

dob *n.*[1] [20C+] a small portion, a dab or pat or dollop. [dial.]

dob *n.*[2] [1970s] (*US*) the penis. [SE *dob*, a dab, i.e. the blow or thrust of penetration; also note Scot. *dob*, a prick]

dob *v.*[1] [20C+] (*Ulster*) usu. of boys, to play truant. [ety. unknown]

dob *v.*[2] *see* DOB (IN) v.

do-badder *n. see* DO-GOODER n.

do balloons *v.* [1980s+] to inhale nitrous oxide or 'laughing gas'. [a balloon is filled with the gas, which is then drawn into the mouth]

do bandies *v.* [20C+] (*US juv.*) to perform feats of physical daring, esp. when one dares one's companions to follow suit. [? SE *bandy legs* or ? dial. *bandy*, to toss back and forth]

dobber *n.*[1] (*also* **dobber-in**) [1950s+] (*Aus./N.Z.*) an informer, a tale-teller. [DOB (IN) v. (2)]

dobber *n.*[2] [1970s] **1** (*US*) the penis. **2** (*Aus.*) a semi-erect penis. [DOB n.[2]]

dobber *n.*³ *see* DAUBER n.

dobber-in *n. see* DOBBER n.¹.

dobbin *n.*¹ (*also* **dobin**) [late 16C+] an ordinary farm horse, sometimes a broken-down or old one. [pet-name form of Robin/Robert]

dobbin *n.*² [late 18C–early 19C] a ribbon. [? link to weaving jargon *dobby*, an attachment to a loom for weaving small figures, although this presumably relates back to DOBBIN n.¹ (dial. *dobby* = dimin. of Robert + a hobby-*horse*) or ? dial. *dobbin-wheels*, the large rear wheels of a cart, similar to spools on which ribbon was wound]

dobbin rig *n. see* DOBIN RIG n.

dob down *v. see* DOB (IN) v. (1).

dobe *n.* (*also* **dhobe**) [1900s–30s] (*US Und.*) a dollar. [? SE *dollar* bill]

do bears shit in the woods?/beavers piss on flat rocks? *phr. see* DOES A BEAR SHIT IN THE WOODS? IS THE POPE A CATHOLIC? phr.

dobee *n. see* DHOBI n.

doberman *n.* [1960s] (*US Black*) a dishonest, cowardly or deceitful person. [? the character *Doberman*, in the US TV comedy *The Phil Silvers Show* (1955–9)]

dobe-wall *v.* [late 19C–1930s] (*US*) to put up against a wall and shoot. [SE *adobe wall*]

dobie *adj.* [19C+] (*US*) inferior, second-rate. [abbr. ADOBE adj.]

dobin *n. see* DOBBIN n.¹.

dob (in) *v.* (*Aus./N.Z.*) **1** [1930s+] (*also* **dob down**) to contribute (financially). **2** [1950s+] (*also* **dob on**) to betray, to inform against. **3** [1960s] (*also* **dob it on**) to impose a responsibility on. **4** [1980s] to cause trouble for someone. [dial. *dob*, to put down with a sharp, abrupt motion]

dobin rig *n.* (*also* **dobbin rig**) [late 18C–early 19C] (*UK Und.*) the stealing of ribbons from haberdashers, usu. performed by women. [DOBBIN n.² + RIG n.² (2)]

dob oneself in *v.* [1950s+] (*Aus.*) to let oneself in for problems. [DOB (IN) v. (2)]

dob out *v.* [1960s–70s] (*Aus.*) to miss out on, to absent oneself from, to reject an offer. [antonym of DOB (IN) v.]

do brown *v.* **1** [early 17C; 19C+] (*also* **beat brown**) to surpass, to defeat comprehensively; usu. in phr. *done brown*. **2** [mid-19C+] to take to extremes, to 'go too far'. [cooking imagery]

do business *v.* **1** [late 19C+] to have sexual intercourse with a prostitute. **2** [1990s+] to purchase drugs. [euph.]

doc *n.* [mid-19C+] **1** (*US*) an all-purpose term of address to a man whose real name is unknown. **2** (*orig. US*) an abbr. of SE *doctor*.

doc and doris *n. see* JOCK AND DORIS n.

doccy *n. see* DOXY n.

dock *n.* [17C–18C] the vagina. [SE *dock*, the hindquarters of an animal; the buttocks of a human]

dock *v.*¹ [mid-16C–19C] (*UK Und.*) to have sexual intercourse; thus *dock the dell*, to deflower a young woman (cf. BANG v.¹). [SE *dock*, to cut (esp. as in a SE *tail*/TAIL n.² (3) or Rom. *dukker*, to rape (+ DELL n. (1))]

dock *v.*² [early 18C+] to cut; usu. in *dock someone's pay*, for an employer to retain a portion of someone's wages. [SE *dock*, to cut off a dog's tail]

dock-and-doris *n. see* JOCK AND DORIS n.

dock asthma *n.* [1970s+] (*UK Und.*) an ironic ref. to the gasps of alleged 'surprise' from the accused when the police produce their evidence in court.

docker *n.*¹ [1920s+] (*Aus.*) a large sum of money; thus *go a docker*, to spend extravagantly. [Scot. *docker*, to work (hard)]

docker *n.*² [1970s] a half-smoked cigarette, put out for later re-ignition. [SE *dock*, to cut the tail off]

docker *n.*³ *see* BOONDOCKER n.

docker's hook *n.* [20C+] (*Aus.*) a book, e.g. *make a docker's hook*, to lay the odds or make a book. [rhy. sl.]

dockie *n.* [late 19C+] a dock labourer. [post-1930s use is mainly Aus.]

dockin doris *n. see* JOCK AND DORIS n.

docking *n.*¹ **1** [early 18C–mid-19C] 'A punishment inflicted by sailors on the prostitutes who have infected them with the venereal disease, it consists in cutting off all their clothes, petti-coat, shift and all, close to their stays, and then turning them out into the street' (Grose, 1785). **2** [early 19C] bettering the condition of the run-down horse in order to improve the chances of selling it.

docking *n.*² [1980s+] (*US gay*) a form of mutual masturbation, involving one partner with an exceptionally long foreskin, which is drawn over the glans of the other partner before commencing masturbation. [the image of docking spacecraft]

dock rat *n.* [mid-19C–1930s] (*US/Aus.*) a vagrant that hangs around the docks.

dock-shanker *n.* [early 19C] a fellow sufferer in a venereal ward. [SE *dock*, a port, in this case a hospital + *shanker*, mis-sp. of SE *chancre*, a venereal ulcer]

dock the dell *v. see* DOCK v.¹.

dock-walloper *n.* (*US*) **1** [mid-19C–1910s] an idler who frequents the waterfront. **2** [mid-19C+] a dock-worker, a longshoreman.

Doc Martens *n. see* DOCS n.

doco *n.* [1960s+] (*Aus.*) a *doc*umentary. [abbr. + -O sfx (4)]

do cold with *v.* [20C+] (*W.I.*) not to be on speaking terms with.

do corners *v.* [2000s] (*UK Black*) to spend time socializing.

docs *n.* (*also* **Doc Martens**) [1980s+] Dr. Martens boots (cf. CHERRY REDS n.; DMs n.; EIGHTEEN-HOLER n.). [brandname *Dr. Martens*, patented in Germany in 1965 by Herbert Funck and Klaus Maertens. The original boots were for work only, but the firm diversified during the 1980s and their product, esp. in the form of a Doc Martens sole attached to one of a variety of uppers, became a leading fashion staple for both sexes]

doctor *n.*¹ [mid-17C+] anything that is considered to have restorative or healthy properties, e.g. a drink on a cold morning or the [mid-18C+] 'Doctor Wind' of the West Indies, South Africa and Western Australia, a cool sea-breeze, which usu. prevails during part of the day in summer.

doctor *n.*² **1** [late 18C–early 19C] milk and water with rum and nutmeg. **2** [late 18C–early 19C] an adulterant, e.g. alum, used in food or drink. **3** [19C+] brown sherry. **4** [1980s+] (*US campus*) any form of alcoholic drink. [SE *doctor*, to mix, to adulterate; brown sherry is a mix of sherry and wine, which gives it the darker 'brown' tint]

doctor *n.*³ [early 19C] the last throw in a game, e.g. of dice or ninepins. [? the doctor at one's end/death]

doctor *n.*⁴ [mid-19C+] (*Aus.*) the cook on a sheep station. [naut. use *doctor*, a shipboard cook or 19C N.Z. whalers' *doctor*, a Maori slave used as a cook]

doctor *n.*⁵ [late 19C+] one who mends or repairs, usu. with a qualifying n., e.g. a *play doctor*, one who fine-tunes dramatic scripts.

doctor *n.*⁶ (*also* **doctor's favourite, ...shop, ...orders**) [1910s+] (*bingo*) the number 9 (cf. ALDERSHOT LADIES n.). [milit. jargon *doctor*, pill number 9, the most frequently prescribed medicine in the Field Medical Chest + ref. to the 9 months of pregnancy, after which one 'calls for the doctor']

doctor *n.*⁷ [1940s–70s] (*US gay*) a man with a large penis. [? he gives you an 'injection']

doctor *n.*⁸ [1960s+] (*S.Afr. Und.*) a title given to a member of a prison gang, who, while prob. not qualified, is responsible for checking fellow inmates when they are sick.

doctor, the *n. see* DOCTORS n. (1).

doctor and nurse *n.* [1990s+] a purse. [rhy. sl.]

doctorate in applied chemistry *n. see* BIG JAB n.

Dr Bates *n.* [1920s] (*US Und.*) a dangerous ex-convict. [development of BEEN TO SEE CAPTAIN BATES? phr.]

Dr Brighton *n.* [late 19C] (*UK society*) Brighton. [the supposedly restorative properties of the seaside resort; according to Ware, coined by King George IV and 'one of his few small witticisms']

Dr Cotton *adj.* [1930s–60s] rotten. [rhy. sl.]

Dr Crippen *n.* [1910s+] dripping, rendered fat, occas. bread and dripping. [rhy. sl.; ult. Dr Hawley Harvey *Crippen* (1862–1910), a celebrated murderer]

Dr Death *n.* [1980s+] (*Aus. prison*) a prison doctor. [the negative image of prison doctors]

Dr Draw-fart *n.* [19C] an itinerant quack doctor.

Dr Feelgood *n.* [1960s+] **1** a doctor who obliges patients, often showbusiness or entertainment celebrities, with amphetamines or narcotics, which, although the user has no real medical need for them, guarantee 'good feelings'. **2** heroin. [the phr. was coined by the blues pianist Piano Red (William Perryman) in his record 'Dr Feelgood and the Interns' (1962); the drug ref. is a slightly later addition]

Dr Green *n.*[1] [late 18C–19C] grass; thus *send to Dr Green*, to put a horse out to grass. ['a physician, or rather medicine, found very successful in curing most disorders to which horses are liable' (Grose, 1788)]

Dr Green *n.*[2] [mid-19C] (*US*) a naïve, gullible young person. [SE *green*, innocent; note 20C+ medical jargon *Dr Green*, a hospital tannoy announcement that will not alarm patients and visitors but that signifies the 'all clear' to staff after an emergency]

Dr Hall *n. see* JOHN HALL *n.*

Dr Jim *n.* (*also* **jimkwim, jimmunt**) [late 19C] a soft felt hat, with a wide brim. [Dr *Jameson*, whose Jameson Raid (1895) brought him much notoriety, sported one; the alternative uses *jimkwim/jimmunt* mix (*Dr*) *Jim* + QUIM *n.*/CUNT *n.*[1] (1) and are thus origins of CUNT-HAT *n.*]

Dr Johnson *n.* [late 19C] the penis (cf. ABRAHAM *n.*[1]). [ext. of JOHNSON *n.*[1] (1); E.P.'s suggestion that 'there was no one Dr Johnson was not prepared to stand up to' is unlikely]

Dr Legg *n.* [1990s+] an egg. [rhy. sl.; ult. fictional doctor *Dr Legg* on the UK BBC TV soap opera *EastEnders*]

doctors *n.* [mid-16C–19C] **1** (*also* **the doctor**) false or loaded dice; thus *put the doctor(s) on someone*, to cheat someone; *load the doctors*, to prepare loaded dice. **2** counterfeit coins. [SE *doctor*, to adulterate]

doctor's curse *n.* [early 19C] a dose of calomel.

doctor's favourite *n. see* DOCTOR *n.*[6].

Dr Shop Knife *n.* [late 19C+] (*W.I.*) a deceitful, hypocritical person. [Carib.E. *doctor shop*, a chemist + SE *knife*; for semantics of ety. *see* CHEMIST BILL *n.*]

doctor's orders/shop *n. see* DOCTOR *n.*[6].

doctor('s) stuff *n.* [late 18C–mid-19C] medicine. [medicine that has been prescribed by a doctor, as opposed to folk medicines that are prepared in the home]

Dr Thomas *n. see* UNCLE TOM *n.* (1).

Dr White *n.* [1930s–50s] (*US drugs*) narcotics; narcotic addiction (cf. BLANCA *n.*). [the colour]

docxy *n. see* DOXY *n.*

DOD *n.* **1** [1920s] (*US Und.*) very strong liquor. **2** [2000s] (*US Black*) a very large penis. [? pun on phr. *death on delivery/dick of death*]

dod *n.*[1] (*also* **dodd**) [late 17C–1910s] a euph. for *God*; usu. in adj. combs., e.g. *dod-busted*, *dod-derned* or verbal oaths, e.g. DODGAST! excl., DOD ROT! excl. (cf. BOB *n.*[2]).

dod *n.*[2] [1940s] (*US*) an old, poss. infirm person. [abbr. SE *dodderer*]

do-dad *n. see* DOODAD *n.*

dodaddle *n.* [1920s] (*US*) something trivial. [ext. of DOODAD *n.* (1)]

dodd *n. see* DOD *n.*[1].

dodder *n.* [mid-late 19C] burnt tobacco that is taken from a dead pipe and placed on a fresh plug in order to strengthen the flavour. [SE *dottle*, the residue of ash remaining in the bottom of a pipe after smoking]

dodderil *n. see* DOTTEREL *n.*

doddies *n.* [late 19C] a selfish person. [the proletarian version of society's DO-UT-DES *n.*]

doddipool *n. see* DODDYPOLL *n.*

doddle *n.* [1920s+] (*orig. racing*) anything absolutely simple or easy to achieve. [? Scot. *doddle*, a small lump of homemade toffee, hence something attractive and easily obtained, or SE *dawdle/toddle*]

doddle *v.* [1930s+] to accomplish something easily, e.g. win a race. [DODDLE *n.*]

dod drot! *excl. see* DOD ROT! excl.

doddypoll *n.* (*also* **doddipool, doddy, doddypate, dodipol**) [early 16C–mid-18C] a fool. [SE *dote*, to be foolish or silly + SE *poll*, a head]

dode *n.* [1980s+] (*orig. US teen*) **1** the penis. **2** an unappealing person, a fool (cf. CHOAD *n.*). [? DORK *n.* + DUDE *n.* (7) or ? SE *dodo*, a simpleton, a silly old man; note Scot. dial. *dode*, a slow person]

dodelheimer *n.* (*also* **dodenheimer**) [1910s+] any nameless small object, typically some form of gadget. [? DOODAD *n.* + 'German' sfx *-enheimer*]

doderil *n. see* DOTTEREL *n.*

dod gast *adj.* (*also* **dodgasted**) [late 19C–1920s] a euph. for GOD-DAMN *adj.* (1). [DODGAST! excl.]

dodgast! *excl.* [early 19C–1910s] (*US*) a general imprecation, a curse. [DOD *n.*[1] + SE *gast*, to terrify]

dodge *n.* [mid-19C+] **1** a trick, a gimmick, a means of avoiding problems, esp. those encountered in work; thus *do the — dodge (over)*, to take on a pose – e.g. a clergyman, an ex-soldier – for the purposes of fraud. **2** a job, an occupation, a profession. [other than in date, it is hard to differ between the orig. 16C SE *dodge*, 'a shifty trick, an artifice to elude or cheat' (*OED*) and this sl. 'a clever or adroit expedient or contrivance' (*OED*)]

dodge *v.*[1] [mid-late 19C] to follow someone surreptitiously.

dodge *v.*[2] [1910s+] (*Aus.*) to steal, usu. cattle. [SE *dodge*, to act in a dubious, untrustworthy manner]

dodge and shirk *n.* [20C+] (*Aus.*) work. [rhy. sl.]

dodge pompey *v.* [1930s] (*Aus.*) to steal grass, rather than to grow and harvest one's own crop. [naut. jargon *dodge pompey*, to skulk around, to avoid work by the use of any semi-legitimate excuse]

dodger *n.*[1] [mid-19C] a dram of spirits or the glass that holds it. [note Kent dial. *dodger*, a nightcap, the last drink of the day]

dodger *n.*[2] [mid-19C; 1910s+] (*Aus.*) bread, a sandwich, food in general; thus *hunk of dodger*, a slice of bread. [? Northumberland dial. *dodge*, a lump, a chunk]

dodger *n.*[3] [mid-late 19C] a clergyman. [abbr. DEVIL-DODGER *n.* (1)]

dodger *n.*[4] **1** [late 19C+] (*Aus./US*) an advertising leaflet, a flyer. **2** [1930s–40s] (*US Und.*) a 'wanted' flyer distributed to law enforcement agencies, post offices etc. [SE *dodger*, a handbill]

dodger *n.*[5] [1920s] a threepenny bit coin.

dodger *n.*[6] [1990s+] (*US Black*) a cockroach. [? the cockroach, like the clergyman, has a black 'coat' or the insect's dodging of its human enemies]

dodger *adj.* [1940s–50s] (*Aus.*) excellent, first-rate. [? DODGER *n.*[2], i.e. the innate goodness of bread]

dodgie *n.* [2000s] a dubious person. [DODGY *adj.* (1)]

dodgy *adj.* **1** [mid-19C+] dubious, unreliable. **2** [late 19C+] unpredictable, tricky. **3** [1950s] suspicious. **4** [1950s+] stolen, esp. in phr. *dodgy gear*. **5** [1950s+] in poor condition, out of sorts. **6** [2000s] corrupt. [(1) temporarily popularized as the catchphrase (cf. SWINGING! excl.) of comedian Norman Vaughan, compere of UK TV's *Sunday Night at the London Palladium* during the 1960s]

dodinkus *n. see* DOODINKUS *n.*

dodipol *n. see* DODDYPOLL *n.*

do dirt v. (*also* do dirt by someone, do someone dirt) **1** [late 19C+] to harm, to injure deliberately, often verbally. **2** [late 19C+] to act in a deliberately immoral or unethical manner. **3** [1970s+] (*US gay*) to pass on gossip (cf. DEAL DIRT v.). [DIRT n.[2]]

do dixie v. [20C+] (*W.I.*) to make an exciting, successful show (of what is being done); to make events work out as one wishes. [*Dixieland* jazz and the energetic dancing it inspired]

do-do n.[1] (*also* doo-doo) [1930s+] **1** excrement, usu. animal. **2** trouble, difficulties; esp. as *deep doo-doo*, serious trouble. **3** (*US Black*) something utterly insignificant; usu. in phr. *don't mean do-do (to me)*. **4** (*US Black*) rubbish. [DO n.[5] + redup.]

do-do n.[2] [2000s] (*US Black/drugs*) cannabis, usu. marijuana. [redup. abbr. of DOPE n.[1] (6), but note DO-DO n.[1] (1), i.e. a play on SHIT n.[5] (2)]

do-do v. [1930s+] to defecate. [DO-DO n.[1] (1)]

do down v. [20C+] to cause trouble for or take advantage of someone, esp. financially or by talking behind their back in a pej. way. [DO v.[2] (1)]

dod rabbit it! excl. [mid–late 19C] (*US*) a mild oath. [DOD n.[1] + RABBIT v.[1]; lit. euph. of 16C *God rabbit it!*]

dod rot! excl. (*also* dod drot!) [mid-19C–1900s] a mild oath of exasperation; usu. as *dod rot it!* [DOD n.[1]; lit. 'God rot it!']

dodsey n. [18C–mid-19C] (*UK Und.*) a woman. [? DOXY n.]

dodunk n. [19C+] (*US*) a fool, a simpleton. [? BOHUNK n. (2)]

doe n.[1] **1** [late 16C–early 17C] a girl or young woman. **2** [late 17C–early 18C] a prostitute (cf. ALLEY CAT n.). **3** [1900s] (*US Und.*) a baby. **4** [1900s–70s] a woman. **5** [1950s–60s] (*US Black*) a fool, a potential victim. **6** [1960s] (*US*) an unaccompanied young woman. [SE *doe*, a female deer]

doe n.[2] see DOUGH n.[1].

doe-boy n. see DOUGHBOY n.[1].

doedie n. [1950s+] (*S.Afr.*) an attractive and sexually available woman. [Afk. sl. *doedie*, 'chick']

doee n. see DOOE n.

doer n.[1] [early 17C] a womanizer. [DO v.[1] (1)]

doer n.[2] **1** [mid-19C] a cheat, one who defrauds another. **2** [20C+] (*Aus.*) a character, an eccentric, one who never gives up despite any circumstances; often intensified as HARD DOER n. **3** [1990s+] (*US*) a criminal. [DO v.[2] (1)/SE *do*]

doer and gone phr. [1970s+] (*S.Afr.*) very far away, out of one's reach. [Afk. *doer*, far away]

does a bear shit in the woods? is the pope a Catholic? phr. (*also* do bears shit in the woods? do beavers piss on flat rocks? does a duck like water? do fish swim? is the pope a guinea?) [1910s+] (*orig. US*) a rhetorical question meaning 'Don't ask me stupid questions' or 'obviously.' The phr. is also found reversed, *Does the pope shit in the woods...?* [see *Maledicta* I:1 (Summer 1977) pp. 77–82 for a discussion of these 'sarcastic interrogative affirmatives and negatives']

does a chicken have lips? phr. [1970s+] (*US*) a rhetorical question meaning 'obviously not'.

doeskin n. [1960s] (*US*) money (cf. BAT HIDE n.). [var. on FROG-SKIN n.[2]]

does she? phr. [late 19C+] a comment made by men about a woman, the implication being *does she fuck?*

does your bunny like carrots? phr. [1900s–20s] a coarse comment made by a man to a passing woman. [BUNNY n.[1] (1) + CARROT n.[1]]

does your mother know you're out? phr. [mid-19C+] a sarcastic comment to a person whom the speaker feels should be elsewhere, due to immaturity, foolishness, inexperience etc.

dof adj. [1970s+] (*S.Afr.*) stupid, simple, dim; thus *doffie*, a fool, a simpleton. [Afk. *dof*, stupid]

doff v. see DUFF v.[1] (3).

do fish swim? phr. see DOES A BEAR SHIT IN THE WOODS? IS THE POPE A CATHOLIC? phr.

doflickety n. see DOOFLICKER n.

do for v.[1] [mid-18C+] **1** to beat up, to injure, to murder. **2** to ruin, to destroy, to harm. **3** to wear out completely. [DO v.[1]/abbr. SE phr. *do a bad turn for*]

do for v.[2] [mid-19C+] to take care of, to perform household chores for, esp. of a cleaning woman or char. [DO v.[7] (1) + abbr. SE *do work for*]

do for v.[3] see DO v.[2] (1).

do for v.[4] see DO v.[11] (1).

do for trade v. [1940s+] (*gay*) to perform fellatio without reciprocation (cf. GAY TRADE n.). [SE + TRADE n. (3)]

do fries go with that shake? phr. [1970s+] (*US Black*) a phr. called out by a man to a passing attractive woman (whose buttocks move as she walks). [burger bar imagery]

dofunny n. see DOOFUNNY n.

dog n.[1] [16C; late 19C+] a euph. for *God*, used in a variety of mild, semi-blasphemous oaths (cf. BOB n.[2]). [var. on DAD n.[1]/DAG n.[2]/DOD n.[1]; despite possibility, coinage is too early for backsl.; 20C use mainly US]

dog n.[2] **1** [late 16C+] a clever, cheery, hearty person; esp. in affectionate phr. *you old dog*. **2** [late 16C+] a person, irrespective of moral/social status. **3** [1980s+] (*also* dawg, dogg) a close friend. **4** [1990s+] (*also* dawg, dogg) a general term of address, usu. between men.

dog n.[3] **1** [late 16C+] an untrustworthy, treacherous, completely venal man. **2** [17C+] an unpleasant woman or man. **3** [mid-18C; 1950s+] a general negative description, something useless, worthless, broken down etc; a second rate product or one that is hard to sell, a mediocre performance. **4** [mid-19C] (*UK Und.*) a policeman (cf. ANIMAL n.[1]). **5** [mid-19C; 1960s+] unpleasantness, bad characteristics, meanness. **6** [mid-19C+] a horse that is slow, difficult to handle etc; also attrib. **7** [mid-19C+] (*Aus./US*) an informer, a 'stool pigeon', a traitor; esp. one who betrays fellow criminals; thus *dog squad*, undercover detectives; *on the dog*, branded as an informer and ostracized. **8** [late 19C+] (*orig. US*) a promiscuous man or woman. **9** [1910s+] (*US*) a disappointment, a failure, esp. in sports. **10** [1920s+] an unattractive woman or man. **11** [1920s+] (*Aus.*) a plain-clothes detective working on the railways (cf. BEAGLE n.[3]). **12** [1930s–40s] (*US Black campus*) a freshman. **13** [1930s+] (*US Black*) (*also* doggie) an offensive or abusive man. **14** [1930s+] (*US Black*) a prostitute, esp. when ageing and/or broken down (cf. ALLEY CAT n.). **15** [1950s–60s] (*US Black*) a notably brutal policeman or prison officer. **16** [1950s+] weakness, cowardice, e.g. in a boxer. **17** [1970s] (*US prison*) an older or tougher prisoner who exploits younger, weaker men as homosexual partners. **18** [1970s] (*US prison*) a guard. [negative uses of SE *dog*]

dog n.[4] **1** [17C; 20C+] (*US*) (*also* doggy) the penis. **2** [late 17C] the vagina (cf. BIRD n.[8]). **3** [1960s+] (*US Black*) lust, sexual desire. [(2) early 17C nonce-use *a dog with a hole in its head*]

dog n.[5] **1** [early 18C; mid-19C+] ostentation, showiness, style, esp. if affected or pretentious. **2** [1920s+] (*US Black*) something or someone unusual or surprising. [congratulatory phr. *you old dog* (see DOG n.[2] (1)), which has implications of the subject's swaggering around]

dog n.[6] (*also* doggie) [late 18C] (*W.I.*) a small copper or silver coin. [ety. unknown]

dog n.[7] [early 19C+] (*US*) nothing; usu. in phr. *never say dog*, to stay silent. [? the animal's inability to speak]

dog n.[8] [mid-19C] (*US*) a pistol. [pun on BARKER n.[1] (3)]

dog n.[9] (*also* doggie, dog's cock) [late 19C+] a sausage; thus *dog roll*, a hot dog. [the belief that dog-meat was used to fill cheap sausages]

dog n.[10] **1** [20C+] (*Aus.*) food. **2** [20C+] (*Aus.*) a drinking debt. **3** [1920s] (*US*) a state of drunkenness. [ety. unknown]

dog n.[11] [20C+] (*US*) a pint bottle (470ml) of liquor; thus FORTY-DOG n.; SHORT DOG n. [? Yorks. dial. *dog*, a small pitcher]

dog n.[12] **1** [20C+] a beggar who searches for cigarette ends. **2** [1930s–60s] (*drugs*) the residue of poor-quality opium or heroin.

dog n.[13] [1910s] (*Aus.*) a tout. [abbr. SALESMAN'S DOG n.]

dog n.[14] [1950s–60s] (*US*) the hardest part of the job. [once done all that is left is the 'tail']

dog n.[15] [1960s+] (*US campus*) the grade D (cf. ACE n.[6]).

dog n.[16] *see* DOG (AND BONE) n.

dog n.[17] *see* DOG (JOINT) n.

dog n.[18] *see* DOGS n.[1] (1).

dog n.[19] *see* DOG'S DISEASE n.

dog n.[20] *see* FORTY-DOG n.

dog, the n.[1] [1970s+] (*US*) a Greyhound bus. [play on its name]

dog, the n.[2] *see* OLD DOG, THE n.

dog v.[1] **1** [late 16C+] to pursue, to hunt down (often with sexual intent). **2** [18C+] to have sexual intercourse with. **3** [late 19C+] (*also* **doggy, do the dog**) to engage in sexual intercourse with the male using a rear entry position (cf. DOGFUCK n.[2]; DOGFUCK v.; DOGGIES n.; DOGGY FASHION adv.; DOGGY STYLE adv.; DOG IT v.[2]; DOG'S MARRIAGE n.; DOGWAYS adv.). **4** [1980s+] (*US*) to rape.

dog v.[2] **1** [mid-19C+] (*US Und.*) to follow. **2** [late 19C+] (*US*) to nag, to criticize, to harass, to mistreat. **3** [late 19C+] (*US*) to stare at, to glance unpleasantly at. **4** [late 19C+] (*US Black*) to abuse, to curse, to despise. **5** [20C+] to pester. **6** [20C+] (*US Und.*) to betray, to inform against. **7** [20C+] (*US*) to cheat. **8** [20C+] (*US*) to lie, to deceive. **9** [1970s+] (*US/W.I.*) to taunt, to tease, to mock, to be rude. **10** [1990s+] (*US Black teen*) to insult someone in front of their friends. [negative images of the animal]

dog v.[3] [late 19C+] (*US*) a euph. for DAMN v., used in mild excls.; often *dog it!*

dog v.[4] **1** [20C+] to act in a menial capacity. **2** [1910s–50s] to idle, to shirk work. **3** [1980s+] (*UK juv.*) to absent oneself from school. **4** [1980s+] to break an appointment, to stand someone up. **5** [1990s+] (*US Black*) to end a relationship. **6** [2000s] (*Aus.*) to abandon one friend for a new one. [one acts like a DOG n.[3] (1)]

dog v.[5] [1980s] to put out a cigarette. [DOG (END) n. (1)]

dog v.[6] [1980s+] (*US*) to filch, to steal. [abbr. BIRD DOG v.[1]]

dog v.[7] [1980s+] (*US campus*) to get a grade D in an examination. [DOG n.[15]]

dog v.[8] [1980s+] (*US campus*) to do something fast, hard or well. [? ext. DOG v.[2] (5)]

dog v.[9] [1990s+] (*US Black teen*) **1** to tear something up in the manner of a dog, to worry. **2** to defeat.

dog v.[10] *see* DOG IT v.[1].

dog adv. [late 16C+] (*US*) utterly, completely; thus DOG CHEAP adj.

dog act n. *see* BLACKFELLOWS' ACT n.

dog along v. [20C+] (*Can.*) to manage, to subsist. [? SE dogged]

dogan n. (*also* **dogun**) [mid-19C–1930s] an Irish Roman Catholic. [? Irish surname *Duggan* or ? pron. TAIG n.]

dog (and bone) n. [1940s+] telephone. [rhy. sl.]

dog and cat n. [1950s+] a mat. [rhy. sl.]

dog and goanna rules n. [1960s+] (*Aus.*) no rules at all. [the image of a fight between a dog and a goanna lizard]

dog and pony show n. (*also* **horse and dog show**) [1950s+] (*US*) any elaborately formal occasion, used for official briefings, public relations etc. [the orig. dog and pony shows were small circuses, where they were the sole animal performers; thus the image is of an event which boasts much presentation but little substance]

dog around v.[1] [20C+] to live a promiscuous life. [DOG v.[1] (1)]

dog around v.[2] [1910s+] (*US campus*) to neglect one's academic work. [DOG v.[4] (2)]

dog around v.[3] [1920s–30s] (*US Black*) to nag, to abuse verbally. [DOG v.[2] (2)]

dog around v.[4] [1920s–40s] (*orig US*) to follow. [ext. DOG v.[1] (1)]

dog-ass n. (*also* **dog-arse**) [1950s+] (*orig. US*) an objectionable, unpleasant person. [DOG-ASS adj.]

dog-ass adj. (*also* **dog-arse, dog-arsed, dog-assed**) [1950s+] (*orig. US*) inferior, second-rate, unpleasant. [SE dog + -ASS sfx/ARSE n.[1] (1)]

dog away one's time v. [late 19C] to waste time, to idle about. [DOG v.[4] (2)]

dog back v. [20C+] (*W.I.*) to swallow one's pride in the hope of regaining a formerly positive relationship. [DOG v.[4] (1)]

dog behind v. [20C+] (*W.I.*) to act in a servile manner, to toady to. [DOG v.[4] (1)]

dog bite 'em! n. (*also* **dog bite me! dog bite my ear!**) [mid-19C+] a mild, semi-blasphemous oath. [DOG n.[1]]

dog-bolt n. [mid-15C–17C] a term of contempt or reproach, a wretch, a contemptible fellow. [SE dog-bolt, a blunt-headed arrow or form of bolt, of no use other than to be aimed at a dog]

dog booby n. [late 18C] a country lout, a male peasant. [SE dog, male + BOOBY n.[1]]

dogbox n. **1** [20C+] (*Aus.*) a railway compartment with no access to other compartments, usu. on a rural railway line. **2** [20C+] (*Aus.*) a substandard railway carriage. **3** [20C+] (*Aus./N.Z.*) any small, cramped room or house. **4** [1980s] (*Aus. prison*) a cubicle.

dog-breath n. [1940s+] (*orig. US*) **1** bad breath. **2** one who has bad breath; thus an offensive person.

dog buffer n. [late 18C–early 19C] a dog stealer. [SE dog + BUFFER n.[2] (1)]

dogcart n. [1920s+] (*Aus.*) a police car.

dog cheap adj. [late 16C+] extremely cheap. [DOG adv. + SE cheap]

dog chocolate n. [1990s+] (*UK juv.*) dog excrement (cf. ADMIRAL BROWNING n.).

dog-collar n. **1** [mid-19C+] the reversed collar worn by clergymen. **2** [late 19C+] a choker necklace.

dog-dancing n. [1960s+] (*Can.*) useless activity. [a dog leaping with glee at the return of its master]

dog-days n. [1910s+] a menstrual period. [SE dog-day, an evil time, a period in which malignant influences prevail; lit. the rising of the Dog Star]

dog doctor n. [1950s–70s] (*US*) a second-rate or incompetent doctor. [ext. use of SE, i.e. one who is fit only to work with animals]

dog-drawn adj. [19C] of a woman, whose partner, in the act of intercourse, has been forcibly dragged away. [the image of 2 copulating dogs being drawn apart by their owners]

dog-driver n. [1910s+] (*W.I.*) a policeman (cf. ANIMAL n.[1]). [the term sneers at the policeman, giving him the lowly task of driving off stray dogs]

dog-drunk adj. [early 17C; mid-19C+] very drunk. [SE dog, i.e. as a dog, symbolic of excess; i.e. thoroughly, utterly, extremely]

dog-durned adj. [late 19C] (*US*) a euph. for GOD-DAMN adj. (1). [DOG n.[1]]

dog-eat-dog n. [1970s] (*Aus.*) an abusive term for a young woman. [DOG n.[3] (10)]

dog (end) n. [1930s+] **1** the last fraction of a cigarette; thus phr. *dog-ends on*, please give me the last fraction of your cigarette. **2** in fig. use, anything small or insignificant. [? SE docked end]

dog-eye n. **1** [1910s+] (*US, mainly prison*) a sidelong glance, usu. aggressive or unfriendly. **2** [1950s+] (*UK juv./Und.*) a lookout, esp. for a team of 3-card trick players. [DOG v.[1] (1) + SE eye]

dog-eye v. **1** [1910s+] (*US, mainly prison*) to cast a sidelong glance at someone. **2** [1960s] (*US prison*) to inspect, to scrutinize. [DOG-EYE n.]

dogface n. [1930s+] (*US*) **1** an unpleasant person, a term of abuse. **2** a soldier, an infantryman; thus adj. *dogfaced*. [(1) prior use from mid-19C in nicknames for specific individuals (see HDAS); (2) coined as an insult by members of the US Marine Corps, who look down on infantrymen; ult. the Cavalry took it from the old Cheyenne War Society in the Plains Wars, who called themselves Dog Soldiers]

dog fashion adv. see DOGGY FASHION adv.

dog fever n. [1910s+] (Aus.) influenza. [var. on DOG'S DISEASE n.]

dogfight n. (US) **1** [late 19C] a fistfight, a brawl. **2** [1970s] any event considered coarse or vulgar.

dog finger n. [1920s+] (US Black) the middle or index finger, depending on rival users; considered unlucky or taboo. [fig. use of DOG n.³, as a generic for bad luck; if that finger is pointed at a person, they will have bad luck]

dog food n.¹ [1940s–60s] (US) any form of canned meat.

dog food n.² [1960s] (US Black) a bribe paid to a corrupt police-man. [DOG n.³ (15) + ironic use of SE food]

dog food n.³ [1970s+] (US gay) a soldier, viewed as a potential sexual partner. [DOGFACE n. (2) + SE food, i.e. something one can EAT v.³ (1)]

dog food n.⁴ [1980s+] (drugs) heroin (cf. BLACK n.³). [ext. of SE use; ? its colour (brown) or the low status of its users]

dog-foolish adj. [mid-19C] very stupid. [backsl. dog = good + SE foolish, i.e. 'good and foolish']

dogfuck n.¹ [1970s] (US) trouble; usu. in phr. in the dogfuck. [fig. use of DOGFUCK n.²]

dogfuck n.² [1970s+] sexual intercourse in which entry is made from the rear (cf. DOG v.¹). [DOGFUCK v.]

dogfuck v. (also **doggy-fuck**) [1970s+] to have rear-entry or anal intercourse (cf. ASK FOR THE RING v.; DOG v.¹). [SE dog + FUCK v.¹]

dogfucker n. [1990s+] (US) a general term of abuse, lit. one who has sex with dogs. [SE dog + FUCKER n. (1)]

dogfucking adj. [1990s+] (US Black) a term of extreme contempt. [DOGFUCKER n.]

dogg n. see DOG n.².

dogged adj. **1** [17C; mid-19C+] a euph. for DAMNED adj. **2** [mid-19C] amazed. [abbr. DOGGONE adj.]

dogged out adj. (also **dogged up**) [1910s+] (orig. US) dressed up. [PUT ON DOG v. (1)]

dogger n.¹ (Aus.) **1** [late 19C+] a hunter of dingoes; thus dogging, dingo-hunting. **2** [20C+] one who slaughters horses for the pet-food market.

dogger n.² [1940s+] one who collects cigarette ends, cleans out the tobacco and resells it. [DOG (END) n. (1)]

dogger n.³ [1990s+] a peeping Tom who spies on couples in 'lovers' lanes' and similar places. [the excuse, 'I'm just walking my dog' used by the voyeur]

dogger out n. [1930s] (UK Und.) a lookout man. [DOG v.² (3)]

doggers n. see DOGS n.¹.

doggery n.¹ [early 19C+] (US) a low drinking house. [negative image of SE dog]

doggery n.² **1** [mid-19C] cheating. **2** [late 19C] nonsense. [SE doggery, dog-like behaviour or practice; mean and contemptible action]

doggess n. (also **dog's lady, dog's wife**) [late 18C–early 19C] a euph. for BITCH n.¹ (1).

doggie n.¹ [late 19C] an all-round stand-up collar. [SE dog-collar]

doggie n.² [1930s+] (US) a soldier, an infantryman. [abbr. DOGFACE n. (2)]

doggie n.³ see DOG n.³ (13).

doggie n.⁴ see DOG n.⁶.

doggie n.⁵ see DOG n.⁹.

doggie-bag n. see DOGGY BAG n.

doggies n. [1990s+] sexual intercourse from the rear (cf. DOG v.¹). [DOGGY FASHION adv.]

doggies, the n. see DOGS, THE n.

doggin n. (also **doggins**) [1930s+] (N.Z.) a cigarette end. [DOG (END) n. (1)]

dogging n. [1980s+] **1** spying on others having sex in parked cars. **2** (US) offering sex in return for drugs. **3** (US campus) obtaining maximum sexual pleasure from a member of the opposite sex. **4** (US) philandering. [DOG v.¹ (2)]

doggish adj. [1960s+] (US Black) obsessed with sex, lecherous; thus adv. **doggishly**. [DOG n.³ (8)]

doggo n. [1920s] (US) a fellow, a man. [DOG n.² (1)]

doggone adj. (also **doggoned, dog-goned, dog-hanged, dog on, doll-goned**) [mid-19C+] (US) a euph. for GOD-DAMN adj. (1). [DOG n.¹]

doggone adv. (also **daggone**) [mid-19C+] extremely, very, a euph. for DAMNED adv. [DOGGONE adj.]

doggone! excl. [mid-19C+] (orig. US) a general excl.; a euph. for GOD-DAMN! excl. [DOG n.¹]

doggoned/dog-goned adj. see DOGGONE adj.

doggone my buttons! excl. see DASH MY BUTTONS! excl.

doggy n.¹ **1** [1940s+] (Aus.) (also **dargie**) a hot dog. **2** [1980s+] (Aus. prison) one who is accused of bestiality. [abbr. + sfx -y]

doggy n.² see DOG n.⁴ (1).

doggy adj.¹ [late 19C+] fashionable, esp. when showy, over-ornate. [PUT ON DOG v. (1)]

doggy adj.² **1** [20C+] (US Black) hard, mean, thoughtless. **2** [20C+] obsessed with sex, lecherous. **3** [1930s] somewhat overly enthu-siastic. [DOG n.³; negative images of the animal]

doggy v. see DOG v.¹ (3).

doggy bag n. (also **doggie-bag**) **1** [1960s+] (orig. US) a bag pro-vided by some restaurants for customers to take home left-overs, ostensibly for later consumption by a pet dog. **2** [1990s+] a colostomy bag.

doggy-bag v. [1960s+] (US) to take home left-over food from one's restaurant meal, ostensibly for one's pet. [DOGGY BAG n. (1)]

doggy-do n. [1960s+] **1** a euph. for canine excrement. **2** in ext. use, anything disgusting, e.g. food. [SE doggy + DO n.⁵]

doggy-dog adj. [1990s+] (US Black) competitive, ruthless, lacking in compassion. [SE dog-eat-dog]

doggy fashion adv. (also **dog fashion**) [late 19C+] used to describe having sexual intercourse in the rear entry position (cf. DOG v.¹).

doggy-fuck v. see DOGFUCK v.

doggy paddle n. see DOG PADDLE n.

doggy style adv. (also **dog-fashion, doggy, dog style**) [1940s+] used to describe having sexual intercourse in the rear entry position (cf. DOG v.¹).

dog-hanged adj. see DOGGONE adj.

dogheart n. [20C+] (W.I. Rasta) a person who is especially cold and cruel. [negative image of SE dog + heart]

dog hours n. [1920s–30s] (US) a late-night and early morning shift.

doghouse n. **1** [late 19C–1930s] (US Und.) prison; a solitary confinement cell. **2** [late 19C+] any small structure that seems to resemble a dog kennel. **3** [1920s–50s] (orig. US) a double-bass. **4** [1930s] (US prison) a watchtower. **5** [1930s+] in fig. use of (2), a place of disgrace or punishment; sometimes spec. of mar-riage. **6** [1940s+] (US Und.) a county prison (cf. BANDHOUSE n.). **7** [1940s+] (US prison) the protective custody unit in a prison.

dogi n. [1940s+] (W.I.) a short, stocky person. [Bambara dogo, small, short]

dogie n. see DUJI n.

dog in v. [early 17C] to betray, to inform against. [DOG n.³ (1)]

dog in a blanket n. [mid–late 19C] a rolled currant dumpling ('roly-poly pudding') or jam pudding. [orig. naut. use]

dog in a doublet n. [late 17C–early 19C] a daring, bold person; thus proud as a dog in a doublet, very proud; a mere dog in a doublet, a pitiful figure, one who shows off to no avail. [the custom in Germany and Flanders to dress the dogs used to hunt wild boar in a form of buff doublet]

dog it v.¹ (also **dog**) [20C+] (orig. gambling) to act weakly, to be a loser, to lack winning spirit. [DOG n.³ (1)/SE underdog]

dog it v.² **1** [1920s] (US Black) to dance in a provocative manner. **2** [1940s+] to have sexual intercourse from the rear (cf. DOG v.¹).

3 [1980s+] (*US campus*) for a woman to make herself sexually available. [DOG v.[1] (3)/DOG n.[1] (2)]

dog it v.[3] (*US*) **1** [1920s+] to shirk, to waste time, to hang back. **2** [1920s+] to dawdle, to go slowly. **3** [1920s+] to malinger, to act lazily. **4** [1930s+] to run off. [DOG v.[4] (2)]

dog it v.[4] [1930s+] **1** to dress up, to show off. **2** (*N.Z.*) to lord it over someone. [PUT ON DOG v. (1)]

dog it v.[5] [1970s+] (*US gay*) to work as a part-time male homosexual prostitute. [DOGS n.[1] (1), i.e. walking the streets]

dog it v.[6] [1990s+] **1** (*US prison*) to betray, to inform against. **2** (*US drugs*) to spoil, to make somewhere unsafe or unsuitable for one's purposes. [DOG v.[2] (6)]

dog it! *excl. see* DOG v.[3].

dog (joint) n. [1920s] (*US*) a cheap restaurant, a hot dog stand. [SE *hot dog* + JOINT n.[4] (3)]

dog juice n. [1970s+] (*US Black*) cheap liquor or wine. [only good enough for an animal or common *dog*]

dog kennels n. [1920s] (*US*) shoes. [play on SE *dogs*/DOGS n.[1] (1)]

dog-kickers n. [mid-19C] (*US*) the feet.

dog-killer n. [20C+] (*US*) cheap or adulterated liquor. [its strength]

dog-knotted adj. [1950s+] for 2 lovers to be locked together during intercourse because of a vaginal muscle spasm brought on by a sudden shock.

dog-leech n. (*also* **dog-leach**) [17C] a quack doctor. [SE *dog leech*, a veterinary surgeon]

dog leg n. [mid–late 19C] (*US*) second-rate tobacco. [the twists in which the tobacco was sold, which resembled a dog's leg]

dog licence n. [1940s+] (*Aus.*) a certificate of exemption from the prohibition of alcohol to Native Australians (under the Aborigines Protection Act 1909–43) that permits them to buy a drink in a hotel.

dogmeat n. [20C+] (*US*) a worthless, despicable person.

dog-music n. [1900s] (*Aus.*) the howling (of a wounded person).

dog my cats! *excl.* [mid-19C+] (*US*) a general excl. of amazement, annoyance, surprise. [DOG v.[3]]

dognap v. [1940s+] (*orig. US*) to steal or kidnap a dog; thus *dognapper*, one who steals dogs. [play on SE *kidnapper*]

dog nigger n. [1970s] (*US Black*) **1** a Black person who rejects the second-class role offered by the dominant White society. **2** an unpleasant, aggressive person. [DOG n.[3] (13) + NIGGER n.[1] (1)]

dog-nose n. [late 19C–1900s] beer warmed nearly to boiling, mixed with gin or wormwood (the basis of absinthe), sugar and ginger; a later version substituted gin for the wormwood.

dog nuts n. **1** [1960s+] a term of contempt. **2** [1990s+] a friend, a general term of address. [NUTS n.[2] (1)]

dog on adj. *see* DOGGONE adj.

dog on v. [1980s+] (*US campus*) to criticize, usu. in the victim's absence. [DOG v.[2] (2)]

dog on it! *excl.* [mid–late 19C] a mild expletive. [DOG v.[3]/DOGGONE! excl.]

do good v. [1970s] (*US Und.*) to make substantial amounts of money through crime.

do-gooder n. [1920s+] a theoretically well-intentioned but often interfering and domineering figure, concerned with others' problems but lacking any real knowledge of how to alleviate them; thus the antonym *do-badder*.

do gooseberry v. [mid–late 19C] (*UK teen*) to hang around a couple who would prefer to be left alone. [GOOSEBERRY n.[3]]

do gospel v. [mid-19C] to attend church.

dog out v. **1** [1940s+] to keep a lookout. **2** [1980s+] (*US campus*) to betray, to neglect, to treat with disrespect. **3** [1980s+] (*US Black*) to approach sexually. **4** [1990s+] (*US Black/prison*) to intimidate; to abuse, to criticize. [DOG v.[2]]

dog paddle n. (*also* **doggy paddle**) [20C+] a swimming stroke that resembles the way a dog swims, usu. the style of those who cannot perform a recognized stroke; also as v.

dogpatch n. [1970s+] (*US*) a small town or hamlet. [*Dogpatch*, the hillbilly settlement in which the syndicated cartoon strip by Al Capp, *L'il Abner* (1934–77), takes place]

dogpile v. [1940s+] (*US*) for a group of people to leap on a single individual.

dog-poor adj. [late 19C–1900s] (*Aus./US*) extremely poor, whether financially or in condition. [DOG adv.]

do greasy v. [2000s] (*US prison*) to treat someone badly.

dog-robber n. **1** [mid-19C+] (*orig. milit.*) a subservient person, a menial. **2** [20C+] the tweed suit customarily worn by off-duty British officers. [milit. jargon *dog-robber*, an officer's servant, who gained his unflattering nickname from his post-mealtime habit of grabbing any edible left-overs from the mess tables before they could be tossed out to the dogs]

dog roll n. *see* DOG n.[9].

dogs n.[1] (*also* **doggers**) **1** [1910s+] (*US*) the feet, occas. sing. **2** [1910s+] (*US*) shoes. **3** [1990s+] (*US Black*) gym shoes, trainers. [coined by US sportswriter T.A. 'Tad' Dorgan (1877–1929) in the New York *Evening Journal*]

dogs n.[2] [1940s] (*US Und.*) the tumblers of a safe's combination lock. [? SE *cogs*]

dogs, the n. (*also* **the doggies**) [1920s+] the greyhound races, greyhound racing.

dog's abuse n. [1920s+] (*Irish*) harsh verbal criticism.

dog's age n. [mid-19C+] (*US*) a very long time.

dog-salmon aristocracy n. [late 19C] (*US*) one who thinks themself superior to their peers.

dogs are barking, the phr. [1980s] (*Aus.*) a phr. used to imply that one has a 'hot tip' on a racehorse.

dog's ballocks n. **1** [1920s+] anything obvious. **2** [1980s+] (*also* **ballocks, bollocks, dog's bollocks**) anything excellent, admirable, first-rate. **3** [1990s+] a derisive retort. [orig. in phr. *sticks out like a dog's ballocks*]

dogsbody n.[1] [19C–1930s] a stew, esp. pease pudding; also bully-beef.

dogsbody n.[2] [1920s+] any member of an organization who takes on all the menial and tedious tasks, often working for any senior person who gives out instructions. [naut. jargon *dogsbody*, a term for a midshipman or any junior officer; ult. ? f. 19C naut. jargon *dogsbody*, sea-biscuits soaked into a pulp with water and sugar]

dogsbody v. [1990s+] to work at menial tasks. [DOGSBODY n.[2]]

dog's bollocks n. *see* DOG'S BALLOCKS n. (2).

dog's bottom n. [1930s+] a joc. form of address.

dog's breakfast n. *see* DOG'S DINNER n.

dog's chance n. [mid-19C+] the smallest possible chance; use in negative uses.

dog's cock n. *see* DOG n.[9].

dog's dinner n. (*also* **dog's breakfast, pig's breakfast**) **1** [1930s+] a distasteful mess; usu. as *make a dog's dinner out of* but note DRESSED UP LIKE A DOG'S DINNER phr. **2** [1950s] an unpleasant person. **3** [1960s] (*US gay*) fellatio, the implication being that the fellator is a BITCH n.[1] (17) (cf. BASKET LUNCH n.).

dog's disease n. (*also* **dog**) [late 19C+] (*Aus.*) one of a variety of illnesses, e.g. influenza, malaria, a hangover.

dog's dram n. [mid-18C–early 19C] the act of spitting in someone's mouth and hitting them on the back. [SE *dog*, an unpleasant person + *dram*, a measure of spirits]

dog's eye n. [1960s] (*Aus.*) a meat pie. [rhy. sl.]

dog's foot!, the *excl.* [20C+] (*US*) a mild excl.

dogs have not dined, the phr. [late 18C–early 19C] a phr. used to alert someone whose shirt is hanging out.

dog's head n. [late 19C–1900s] (*US*) a variety of beer.

dogshit n.[1] [1950s+] (*orig. US*) the essence, the spirit; as in phrs. *kick/knock the dogshit out of*.

dogshit n.[2] [1960s+] **1** anything or anyone considered objectionable, unpleasant, disgusting. **2** nonsense.

dogshit *adj.* (*US*) **1** [1960s+] insignificant, second-rate. **2** [1980s] crazy (cf. APEY adj.). [DOGSHIT n.[2] (1)]

dogs in the grass *n.* [1930s] (*US*) frankfurters and sauerkraut.

dog's lady *n. see* DOGGESS n.

dog's licence *n.* [1930s–70s] the sum of 7 shillings and 6 pence. [a dog's licence cost 7s 6d (37½p)]

dog's marriage *n.* [1990s+] sexual intercourse in the rear-entry position (cf. DOG v.[1]).

dog's match *n.* [19C+] sexual intercourse in the open air, spec. by the wayside; thus to *make a dog's match of it*, to have sex in the open air, to have spontaneous sex. [the brevity of the intercourse and the lack of privacy of mating dogs]

dog's meat *n.[1]* [late 16C–19C] anything considered worthless, e.g. a badly written book, a poorly executed painting etc.

dog's meat *n.[2]* [1960s+] (*S.Afr.*) cheap cuts of meat which are cooked for the servants' meals. [otherwise good enough only for the dogs]

dog's mouth *n.* [1960s] (*US*) a tight vagina.

dog's nose *n.[1]* (*also* **dogsnose**) **1** [19C] a mixture of gin or brandy and beer. **2** [mid–late 19C] an alcoholic whose preferred tipple is whisky. [like the animal's nose, alcohol is cold and wet]

dog's nose *n.[2]* [1960s] (*US Und.*) a paid informer. [DOG n.[3] (7) + NOSE n.[1] (1)]

dog's paste *n.* [mid–late 19C] sausagemeat or mincemeat.

dog's paw *n.* [2000s] (*US gang*) a tattoo comprising a triangle of 3 dots, indicating gang membership. [resemblance]

dog's portion *n.* [late 18C–19C] virtually nothing; esp. of a man who pursues a woman and gets only very little for his pains. [lit. 'a lick and a smell' (Grose, 1785)]

dog squad *n. see* DOG n.[3] (7).

dog's rig *n.* [late 18C–early 19C] sexual intercourse taken to exhaustion, followed by mutual disinterest. [SE *dog* + *rig*, a romp, i.e. the style of dogs' mating]

dog's shelf *n.* [1950s] the floor.

dog's show *n.* [late 19C–1900s] (*Aus.*) a DOG'S CHANCE n., i.e. no chance at all.

dog's soup *n.* **1** [late 18C+] rainwater. **2** [mid-19C–1930s] water (for drinking). [post-19C use is US]

dog-stiffener *n.* (*also* **stiffener**) [20C+] (*Aus.*) a professional dingo-killer. [SE *dog* + STIFFEN v.[1] (3)]

dog-stiffeners *n.* [1940s+] (*Aus.*) leather leggings. [? DOGS n.[1] (1)]

dog style *adv. see* DOGGY STYLE adv.

dogsucker *n.* [1990s+] (*US Black*) a general term of abuse.

dog's wife *n. see* DOGGESS n.

dogtag *n.* **1** [1910s+] (*orig. US*) an identification disk. **2** [1950s+] (*US drugs*) a legitimate prescription for otherwise illegal narcotics. [for a dog to be 'legal' (not a stray) in the US it must have a labelled collar]

dogtown *n.[1]* [late 19C+] (*US*) an out-of-the-way or small place; thus *dogtowner*, a native of such a town. [orig. theatrical jargon *dogtown*, an out-of-town (i.e. out of New York City) theatre used to try out a new show before 'bringing it in']

dogtown *n.[2]* [1910s] (*N.Z.*) a derog. nickname for Port Chalmers. [? its fig. population of 'one man and a dog']

dog-trick *n.* [mid-16C–early 18C] a treacherous or spiteful act, an ill-turn, a mean, cruel trick. [SE *dog*/DOG n.[3] (1) + SE *trick*]

dog-tucker *n.* [late 19C+] an old or unsaleable sheep killed for dog food. [SE *dog* + TUCKER n.]

dog-tucker *adj.* [1990s+] (*N.Z.*) **1** of a person or animal, useless, second-rate. **2** in serious difficulties. [DOG-TUCKER n.]

dog turd *n.* [20C+] (*US*) a large cigar. [resemblance]

dogturd *adj.* [1980s] (*US*) obnoxious.

dogun *n. see* DOGAN n.

dog wagon *n.[1]* [20C+] (*US*) a small café or restaurant sited in a converted vehicle, a diner. [the quality of the food is generally poor]

dog wagon *n.[2]* [1960s–70s] (*US*) a prison van for conveying prisoners. [play on SE *dog wagon*, used by the dog-catcher]

dog-wallop *v.* [1900s] (*Aus.*) to beat comprehensively. [DOG adv. + WALLOP v. (2)]

dog water *n.* [1960s+] (*US*) **1** semen (cf. BABY FLUID n.). **2** urine.

dogways *adv.* [late 19C] having sexual intercourse in the rear-entry position (cf. DOG v.[1]).

dogwork *n.* [1980s+] (*US*) tedious, menial tasks.

do her job for her *v.* [mid-19C+] of a man, to have sexual intercourse and give a woman an orgasm (cf. GIVE HER A TAIL v.; GIVE HER ONE v.; GIVE HER THE JAMPOT v.; GIVE HER THE TIME v.; GO UP HER PETTICOATS v.; INTRODUCE HER TO Fagan v.; MAKE HER GRUNT v.; SINK HER v.; SLIP A LENGTH INTO v.; SLIP HER A (QUICK) CRIPPLER v.; TAKE A TURN AMONG HER FRILLS v.). [JOB v.[1] (1)]

dohickey *n.[1]* (*also* **do'hickey, do-hinky, doohickey**) [1910s+] (*orig. US*) **1** any nameless small object, typically some form of gadget. **2** something small, used for decoration. [? DOODAD n. + ? HICKEY n.[1]]

dohickey *n.[2]* [1960s+] a love-bite or a pimple. [abbr. HICKEY n.[2]]

do hooky *v.* [mid–late 19C] to make the coarse gesture of applying the thumb and fingers to one's nose. [? a *hook* nose or ? HOOKEY WALKER! excl. (1)]

do how? *excl.* [20C+] (*US*) what did you say? please repeat the question.

do I ducks! *excl.* [20C+] an excl. of absolute rebuttal, i.e. the hell I will! no I certainly won't/don't! [euph. for DO I FUCK! excl.]

do I fuck! *excl.* (*also* **do I hell! will I fuck/shit!**) [20C+] an excl. of absolute rebuttal, i.e. the hell I will! no I certainly won't/don't!; also used with 'you', 'we' etc (cf. DID I BUGGERY! excl.).

do ill to *v.* [19C–1900s] of a man, to have sexual intercourse.

do in *v.* **1** [late 19C–1910s] to steal; to rob. **2** [late 19C+] (*orig. Aus./N.Z.*) to spend one's entire funds. **3** [20C+] to kill, to murder; thus *do oneself in*, to commit suicide. **4** [20C+] (*Aus.*) to defeat. **5** [20C+] in fig. use, to kill off, of food, to finish. **6** [20C+] to wear out, to exhaust; thus DONE IN adj. **7** [1900s] to break off, to abandon. **8** [1900s–50s] to make an error, to fail in some way. **9** [1920s+] to beat up. **10** [1930s+] of machinery or objects, to break or damage. **11** [1950s+] (*drugs*) to inject a narcotic drug. **12** [1960s] (*drugs*) to consume. **13** [1990s+] (*US Black/teen*) to gang-rape. [all ext. uses of DO v.[1]]

doing *n.* **1** [mid–late 17C+] sexual intercourse. **2** [early 19C] (*UK Und.*) a crime, such as a robbery. **3** [late 19C+] (*also* **doing down**) a thrashing, a beating; lit. or fig. [DO v.[1]]

doing a hurting dance *v. see* HURTING DANCE n.

doing dab *adj.* [mid-19C] doing badly (in business). [backsl.; DAB adj.[2]]

doing down *n. see* DOING n. (3).

doings *n.[1]* **1** [late 17C+] the circumstances, the event. **2** [late 18C; 1910s+] (*orig. milit.*) anything for which the precise name cannot be recalled at the moment of speaking. **3** [mid-19C–1910s] (*US*) the trimmings or ornaments that enhance a dress. **4** [mid-19C–1930s] the components, e.g. of a meal, of a piece of engineering. **5** [late 19C–1940s] the testicles. **6** [1990s+] a condom. [ext. of SE *doing*, an act, a piece of business, a transaction]

doings *n.[2]* [1950s+] (*Aus.*) excrement, esp. animal. [ext. of DO n.[5]]

doing the bag *n. see* BAGGING n.[3].

doink *n.* [1960s+] (*US campus*) **1** a clumsy, inept person. **2** an overly hard worker, a 'grind'. [echoic of their solidity/dullness]

do in one's block *v. see* DO ONE'S BLOCK v.

do in the eye *v.* **1** [20C+] (*also* **do in the eyeball**) to cheat. **2** [1910s] to beat squarely. [DO v.[1] (4) + SE *eye*]

do it *v.[1]* **1** [mid-16C+] to have sexual intercourse (cf. ARRIVE AT THE END OF THE SENTIMENTAL JOURNEY v.). **2** [late 19C+] of a man, to ejaculate; of a woman, to reach orgasm. [euph.]

do it *v.[2]* [1910s+] to defecate or urinate.

do it *v.[3]* [1970s+] to leave, to start going; esp. in phr. *let's do it*.

do it all v. (also **get it all**) [1910s+] (*US prison*) to serve a life sentence; to serve the whole of a sentence, with no time off for good behaviour. [DO v.⁹ (1)/SE *get*]

do it brown v. [mid-19C+] to take to the limit, esp. as in prolonging one's enjoyment to the point of excess. [cooking imagery]

do-it-easies n. [1970s–80s] (*N.Z. prison*) tranquillizers. [they help one do a sentence easily]

do it fat v. [1910s–20s] to pose as a gentleman. [SE *do*, perform + FAT adv.]

do-it fluid n. [1970s+] (*US Black*) liquor, usu. gin, usu. as an enhancer of sexual potency. [DO IT v.¹ (1) + SE *fluid*]

do it like mommy v. [1980s+] to act in a domesticated manner, doing the housework, shopping etc.

do it on one leg v. see DO IT WITH ONE HAND TIED BEHIND ONE'S BACK v.

do it on someone v. **1** [late 19C–1900s] to swindle, to defraud. **2** [20C+] to get the better of, to surpass. [DO v.² (1)]

do it to death v. [late 19C+] (*orig. US*) to do anything to the extreme, e.g. perform a song.

do it up v. [early–mid-19C; 2000s] to accomplish one's object, to have success; thus *do it up in good twig*, to live a constantly enjoyable (and ever-improving) life. [SE (+ IN FINE TWIG phr.)]

do it up brown v. (also **go in the brown, hit the round brown**) [1930s+] (*US Und./gay*) to have anal intercourse (cf. ASK FOR THE RING v.). [pun. on DO UP BROWN v./DO IT v.¹ (1) + BROWN n.³ (1)]

do it up right v. [20C+] to carry out fully and correctly, to achieve a set objective. [ext. of DO IT UP v.]

do it well v. see DO ONESELF WELL v.

do it with one hand tied behind one's back v. (also **do it on one leg, ...with one's shoes on**) [20C+] (*orig. US*) to do very easily, with minimal effort.

do-it-yourself n. (also **do it yourself kit**) [1950s+] masturbation.

dojigger n. (also **dojiggie, dojiggum, dojiggus, dojiggy, dojimmie, dojinnie, dojisser, dojohn, dojohnnie, doo-jigger**) **1** [20C+] an indefinite expression used to describe a nameless object. **2** [1960s+] (also **modigger**) a euph. for the penis (cf. BAUBLE n.). [ety. unknown; ? link to SE *jiggle*]

do justice v. [late 17C–early 18C] to toast a person, to drink to a person.

do justice child v. [late 17C–mid-18C] (*UK Und.*) to act as an informer. [Sir Francis *Child* (1642–1715), banker and Lord Mayor of London]

dokus n. see TOCHES n.

dol n. (also **doll**) [mid-19C–1900s] a *dollar*. [abbr.]

do-lally adj. see DOOLALLY adj.

dolan's ass n. [20C+] (*Irish*) a time-server. [proper name Dolan + SE *ass*; it goes 'a bit of the way with everyone'; ? anecdotal origins]

doldrum n. [early 19C] a dullard, a sluggish person. [? SE *dold*, inert, stupid]

dole-bludger n. [1930s; 1970s+] (*Aus.*) (also **dole bug**) one who claims unemployment benefit either when work is available or while actually employed in the Black Economy, the Aus. equivalent of a UK 'dole-scrounger'; thus *dole-bludgery, dole-bludging*. [SE *dole* + BLUDGER n.² (2)]

dolefuls n. [mid-19C–1920s] a miserable, depressed state of mind.

do-less adj. [mid-19C+] (*US*) lazy, lethargic, shiftless. [SE *do less* + ? Scot. *dowless*, feeble, weak]

dolhja n. [2000s] (*US Black/drugs*) high-quality marijuana.

do like a kipper v. see DO (UP) LIKE A KIPPER v.

do lines v. see DO A LINE v.

do-little n. [20C+] (*Aus./US*) an idler, a lazy person.

doll n.¹ **1** [mid-16C–mid-18C; 1930s] (also **doll common**) a prostitute. **2** [mid-17C+] a woman. **3** [mid-19C+] (*US*) anything or anyone excellent, first-rate. **4** [mid-19C+] (*US*) a conceited or self-satisfied person. **5** [20C+] a conventionally attractive young woman; occas. used of (homosexual) young men. **6** [1950s+] a general term of affection. **7** [1960s] (*US*) a person, a man.

doll n.² [1960s–70s] (*drugs*) any drug in pill form, e.g. amphetamines, barbiturates (cf. PILL n.⁴). [popularized and apparently coined by the book/film *Valley of the Dolls* (1968) by Jacqueline Susann]

doll n.³ see DOL n.

doll n.⁴ see DOLLY n.³.

dollar n.¹ **1** [early 19C+] 5 shillings (25p); obs. outside films, books etc in the metric era; thus *half a dollar*, 2s 6d. **2** [1960s+] (*US Black/Und.*) $100; $100 worth of drugs. **3** [1980s+] (also **dollars**) money in general. [(1) a time when the exchange rate was US$4 to £1 sterling (20 shillings)]

dollar n.² [1990s+] (*drugs*) MDMA (cf. ECSTASY n.). [? $ sign on the pill]

dollar-an-inch man n. [1960s+] (*US gay*) a male prostitute who claims that his penis is so large that even by charging fellators by the inch he could still get rich. [? play on SAmE *dollar-a-year man*, one who works for the government at a nominal salary]

dollar house n. [20C+] (*US*) an outside lavatory (cf. BACK-HOUSE n.). [the timber required to build it costs no more than $1]

dollars n. see DOLLAR n.¹ (3).

dollars to buttons phr. (also **dollars to cobwebs**) [late 19C] (*orig. US*) a sure thing (cf. ALL THE WORLD TO A CHINA ORANGE phr.). [the disparity of the wagers underlines the certainty of the bet]

dollars to doughnuts phr. (also **dollars to dumplings/pretzels**) [late 19C+] an absolute certainty (cf. ALL THE WORLD TO A CHINA ORANGE phr.). [for ety. see prev.]

dollar store n. [late 19C] (*US Und.*) 'The dollar store displayed valuable articles priced at one dollar in order to bring in marks, who were played for with short-con games' (Maurer, *The Big Con*, 1940).

dollar-woman n. [1930s–40s] (*US*) a cheap prostitute (cf. DOLLAR-WOMAN n.; FANCY WOMAN n.; FOURPENNY n.; INGOGO n.; PENNYLINE n.; SIXPENNY SUBURB-SINNET n.; THREEPENNY UPRIGHT n.; TWO-BIT ANNIE n.; TWO-BIT HUSTLER n.; TWOFER n.; TWO PENCE WET AND TWO PENCE DRY n.). [her price]

doll baby n. [mid-19C+] (*US*) an attractive young woman; also as adj. [DOLL n.¹ (3)/DOLL n.¹ (5) + BABY n.³ (1)]

doll city n. [1980s+] (*US teen*) a conventionally pretty woman. [DOLL n.¹ (5) + CITY sfx]

doll common n. see DOLL n.¹ (1).

dolled out adj. [1920s+] (*US campus*) dressed up, esp. for a night out. [var. on DOLLED UP adj.]

dolled up adj. (also **dollied up**) [20C+] (*orig. US*) dressed up, esp. for a night out; thus ext. as *(all) dolled up like a barber's cat*. [DOLL n.¹ (5); why the barber's cat should be especially decorated is unknown]

dolled up like a sore finger/thumb/toe phr. see DRESSED UP LIKE A SORE FINGER phr.

dollface n. [20C+] an attractive woman or boy; often used as form of address *Hey, dollface!* [DOLL n.¹ (5) + SE *face*]

doll-faced adj. [late 19C] of a young woman, attractive. [? DOLLFACE n. or SE]

doll-goned adj. see DOGGONE adj.

doll house n.¹ [20C+] an outside lavatory (cf. BACKHOUSE n.). [abbr. of DOLLAR HOUSE n.]

doll house n.² [1920s–50s] (*US*) a brothel; thus *doll woman*, a prostitute (cf. ACCOMMODATION HOUSE n.). [DOLL n.¹ (1) + HOUSE n.¹ (1)]

dollied up adj. see DOLLED UP adj.

dollies n.¹ (also **dolly**) [1950s+] (*drugs*) synthetic morphine. [brandname *Dolophine*, a type of synthetic opiate slightly stronger than morphine]

dollies n.² [1960s+] (*Irish*) the female breasts. [one cuddles them]

doll of a *phr.* [1950s–60s] a phr. used of anything or anyone considered notably attractive. [DOLL n.[1] (5)]

dollop *n.* **1** [early 19C+] a lump; thus the *whole dollop*, the whole lot; *dollops of*, lots of. **2** [mid-19C] a 3-month sentence, i.e. a small 'lump' of time. [note East Anglian dial. *dollop*, an untidy woman, slattern, trollop]

dollop *v.* **1** [mid-19C] to give up a share, lit. 'dole up'. **2** [20C+] (*Irish*) to adulterate.

doll-rags *n.* [1900s] (*US*) small pieces. [SE *doll* + *rags*, clothes; thus pieces small enough to make a doll's wardrobe]

doll shop *n.* [1990s+] (*US*) a brothel (cf. BANGING-SHOP n.). [DOLL n.[1] (1) + SE *shop*/SHOP n.[1] (1)]

Doll Tearsheet *n.* [mid-19C–1930s] a prostitute (cf. BABY JANE n.). [use of Shakespeare's proper name as a generic]

doll up *v.* [20C+] to dress up a person or an object; esp. as *doll oneself up*, to smarten oneself up, put on one's best clothes; the implication is often of excess or flashiness. [DOLL n.[1] (5)]

doll woman *n. see* DOLL HOUSE n.[2].

dolly *n.*[1] **1** [17C] a female pet or favourite. **2** [mid-17C–mid-19C] a mistress, a prostitute (cf. BABY JANE n.). **3** [mid-19C] a slattern, a dull, unattractive woman. **4** [late 19C] a servant girl. **5** [20C+] any girl or woman, esp. when attractive; also as a term of affection. **6** [1960s+] a teenage girl or young woman, usu. associated with the 1960s and 'swinging London', usu. a young secretary or similar, dressed in the latest fashions, obsessed by the current 'in' rock group and other accoutrements of popular culture; post-1960s use usu. historic/ironic. **7** [2000s] (*N.Z. prison*) the younger lover of a 'butch' lesbian. [DOLL n.[1] + sfx -*y*, but note Hancock, 'Shelta and Polari' (1984), who suggests Ital. *dolce*, sweet and thus claims the word for Polari]

dolly *n.*[2] [mid-19C] anyone who has committed a *faux pas* or social solecism. [? they have as much sense as a child's doll]

dolly *n.*[3] (*also* doll) [late 19C+] the penis. [from a variety of jokes in which a supposedly innocent girl plays with a man's 'dolly', which then spits at her, vomits etc]

dolly *n.*[4] [20C+] (*UK tramp*) a candle. [ety. unknown; ? link to SE *tallow*, of which candles were made; or ? school sl. *tolly*, a candle]

dolly *n.*[5] *see* DOLLIES n.[1].

dolly *n.*[6] *see* DOLLYSHOP n.

dolly *adj.* (*orig.* Polari) **1** [mid-19C–1900s] silly, foolish. **2** [1960s+] nice or pleasant; attractive, fashionable. [note Dickens, *Bleak House* (1853): 'A dolly sort of beauty, perhaps [...] but in its way, perfect; such bloom I never saw']

dolly *v.* [1930s+] (*Aus.*) **1** to treat harshly. **2** to interrogate. [fig. use of the v. form of gold-mining *dolly*, an implement for crushing quartz; ult. UK dial. *dolly*, a wooden implement for beating clothes in the wash]

dollybird *n.* [1960s] an attractive young woman, typically a secretary or shopgirl in her late teens or early twenties and found in such centres of 'swinging London' as Carnaby Street or the King's Road. [DOLLY n.[1] (6) + BIRD n.[1] (2); post-1960s use is historical]

dolly boy *n.* [1970s+] (*orig. gay*) a young male prostitute (cf. BABY JANE n.). [male var. of DOLLYBIRD n.]

dolly cotton *adj. see* JOHNNY COTTON adj.

dolly gray *n.* [1900s] (*US*) a woman, a housewife. [? Boer War song 'Goodbye, *Dolly Gray*']

dolly-man *n.* (*also* pitchy-man) **1** [mid-19C] the keeper of an unlicensed pawnbroker's. **2** [late 19C] a Jew. [? DOLLYSHOP n., SE *trader's pitch*]

dolly mixtures *n.* [1980s+] the cinema. [rhy. sl. = SE *pictures*]

dollymop *n.* [mid-19C–1900s] **1** a part-time prostitute, often a shopgirl, esp. a milliner, who occas. sold her body to supplement her otherwise meagre income. **2** (*US*) a prostitute specializing in sailors. **3** a slovenly, ill-kempt servant girl. [DOLLY n.[1] + the equation of women and fish, in this case the SE *mop*, a young whiting

or gurnard, thus a young woman. Note obs. Ger. sl. *Backfisch*, a teenage girl, lit. a 'fish for baking']

dollymopper *n.* [mid–late 19C] a womanizer, esp. a soldier. [DOLLYMOP n.]

dollypot *n.* [1920s+] (*Aus.*) a fool (cf. BEECHAM'S PILL n.). [rhy. sl. = TWAT n. (3)]

dollyshop *n.* (*also* dolly) [mid-19C–1930s] a low or illegal pawnshop, whose owner may also act as a receiver. [orig. a marine store, signified by the black doll hanging outside as a sign]

dolly sisters *n.* [1950s–70s] (*US*) a pair of patrolmen. [the singers Janszieka (1893–1941) and Roszika (1893–1970) Deutsch, better known as Jenny and Rosie *Dolly*]

dolly sweetness *n.* [1940s] (*US Black campus*) a hitherto unknown young woman.

dolly up *v.* [20C+] (*UK tramp*) to heat water or tea with a candle. [DOLLY n.[4]]

dolly varden *n.* [late 19C+] the garden. [rhy. sl.; ult. *Dolly Varden* from Charles Dickens's *Barnaby Rudge* (1841)]

dolly-worship *n.* [late 19C–1900s] a derog. term for Catholicism. [the use of statues and religious images in Catholic churches]

dolo *adv.* [1990s+] (*US Black*) on one's own, solo. [ety. unknown]

dolomite *n.* [1980s+] (*US campus*) cocaine. [SE *dolomite*, a form of rock, composed of lime and magnesia; thus a pun on ROCK n.[3] (3); + ? ref. to 1970s+ Black comedian *Dolemite* (Rudy Ray Moore b.1937)]

d.o.m. *n.* [1950s+] a *d*irty *o*ld *m*an; poss. an actual or alleged child molester but usu. any older man who makes obvious his preference for women younger than he might be expected to pursue. [abbr.]

DOM *n. see* DOB n.

dom *n.*[1] **1** [20C+] (*Aus.*) a Dominican. **2** [1990s+] a domino; usu. in pl. [abbr.]

dom *n.*[2] [1960s+] a dominatrix or a male dominator. [abbr.]

dom *n.*[3] [1980s+] *Dom* Perignon champgane, a premier brand. [abbr.]

dom *adj.* [1980s+] in sado-masochistic sex, dominant. [DOM n.[2]]

-dom *sfx* [20C+] (*US campus*) a sfx implying 'the domain of'.

domain cocktail *n.* [late 19C–1930s] (*Aus.*) 'a lethal concoction of petrol and pepper which reputedly once had a vogue among deadbeat drinkers in the Sydney Domain' (Baker, *Australian Slang*, 1941); thus *domain dosser*, a loafer or down-and-out who frequents the Sydney Domain. [proper name of the *Domain*, a park in Sydney, Australia, popular for speech-making and frequented by the unemployed and the alcoholic]

dom'd *adj. see* DAMNED adj.

dome *n.* **1** [mid-18C+] (*orig. US*) the head; thus [1950s] *dome-doctor*, a psychoanalyst, a psychotherapist. **2** [1900s] (*US*) a hat.

do me a favour *n.* [1990s+] a neighbour. [rhy. sl.]

do me a favour *phr.* (*also* do us a favour) [1950s+] **1** a phr. meaning 'you must be joking' or 'who do you think you're fooling?' **2** a phr. meaning 'stop harassing me', 'go away'. [ironic uses of SE]

do-me-dags *n.* (*also* do my dags) [late 19C+] cigarettes. [rhy. sl. = FAG n.[4] (3); *do my dags* was orig. a children's game synon. with 'follow my leader'; the image is children encouraging each other to smoke]

do me good *n.* **1** [late 19C+] a Woodbine cigarette. **2** [20C+] wood; (*Aus.*) firewood. **3** [1910s] (*UK*) food. [rhy. sl.]

domelights *n.* [1990s+] (*US*) the eyes. [DOME n. (1)]

doment *n.* [mid-19C] a performance, a show. [orig. dial; DO n.[3] (1) + sfx -*ment*]

dome piece *n.* **1** [1970s+] (*US*) the head. **2** [1990s+] (*US Black*) a hat. [ext. DOME n.]

domes *n.* [1970s+] (*drugs*) LSD (cf. A n.[3]). [? the shape of a capsule or the effect on one's DOME n. (1)]

dome-shot *v.* [2000s] (*US Black*) to request or receive fellatio (cf. BRAIN n.[2]). [play on DOME n. (1)/SE *head*/HEAD n.[10]]

domestic *n.*[1] **1** [mid-19C–1900s] (*US*) a brand of cigar manufactured in the US (as opposed to a Cuban-made Havana). **2** [1960s+] (*drugs*) locally grown marijuana.

domestic *n.*[2] [1970s+] **1** any problems accruing to one's home (rather than criminal/professional) life. **2** an argument or fight between a married couple.

domestic afflictions *n.* [mid-late 19C] the menstrual period. [euph.]

domie *n.* (*also* **domi, dommie, dommy**) [1930s] (*US Black*) one's house, one's home. [abbr. SE *domicile*; ult. Lat. *domus*, home]

domine do-little *n.* (*also* **domini do-little, dominie, dominie do-little**) [late 18C–early 19C] an impotent old man. [SE *dominie*, a schoolmaster + *do-little*]

dominicker *n.* (*also* **dommernecker**) [20C+] (*W.I.*) **1** a coward. **2** a person of mixed race, esp. of Black, Indian and White ancestry. [SE *dominicker*, the Dominique fowl or any other chicken with mottled or barred plumage; (1) the dominicker rooster was believed always to back down when challenged by another rooster]

domino *n.*[1] **1** [early 19C–1910s] a tooth, usu. in pl., esp. when yellow and rotten. **2** [late 19C] a piano key, usu. in pl. **3** [1920s] (*US*) a die, usu. in pl.; thus *jumping dominoes*, crooked dice. **4** [1960s+] (*drugs*) a capsule containing a combination of an amphetamine and a sedative.

domino *n.*[2] [1990s+] (*UK Black*) a woman seen as a sex object. [one slams/SLAM *v.*[1] (4) it down]

domino *v.* **1** [1910s] (*Aus.*) to kill. **2** [1950s] (*US Black*) to stop. [the knocking down of a row of SE *dominoes*]

domino! *excl.* [mid-late 19C] a general excl. to signify the end of or last of a situation, that's it, that's done, all over etc; esp. among soldiers and sailors, to signify the last blow of a thrashing; thus [20C+] *it is domino with…*, it is finished, it is all over, it is hopeless. [the card-game *domino*, in which the winner is the player who gets rid of all their cards first]

domino-box *n.* [early-mid-19C] the mouth. [DOMINO *n.*[1] (1)]

dominoes *n. see* DOMINO *n.*[1].

domino-thumper *n.* [late 19C–1920s] a pianist. [DOMINO *n.*[1] (2) + SE *thumper*]

domkop *n.* [20C+] (*S.Afr.*) a fool, also as derog. form of address. [Afk. *dom*, stupid + *kop*, head; note Ger. *Dummkopf*]

dommerer *n.* (*also* **dommerar, drommerar**) [mid-16C–early 19C] (*UK Und.*) a mendicant villain who feigned dumbness, often claiming to have suffered at the hands of the infidel Turk who, on capturing him during a sea voyage, had torn out his tongue for denying Muhammad (cf. CANTING CREW *n.*). [SE *dumb*]

dommernecker *n. see* DOMINICKER *n.*

dommie *n. see* DOMIE *n.*

dommy *n.*[1] [2000s] (*US Black*) a condom. [abbr. + sfx *-y*]

dommy *n.*[2] *see* DOMIE *n.*

dommy *v.* [1940s] (*US*) to live, to stay. [DOMIE *n.*]

dommy-knocker *n. see* DONGER-KNOCKER *n.*

dompas *n.* (*also* **dompass**) [1950s+] (*S.Afr. Black*) a pass book, i.e. the mandatory identity document formerly carried by all Blacks. [Afk. *dom*, stupid + *pas*, pass]

do my dags *n. see* DO-ME-DAGS *n.*

don *n.*[1] [17C–mid-19C; 1910s–20s] a Spaniard. [the common Sp. honorific *Don*]

don *n.*[2] [17C+] a clever or outstanding person, a distinguished individual, a leader. [this original use comes from the Sp. honorific *Don*, however, the term has been re-invented, with much the same meaning, in the late 20C+ (*see* DON *n.*[3]), mainly by teen gangs, with a ref. to the Italian Mafia's use of *Don* to refer to a senior Mafioso, a use that spread with the popularity of the film *The Godfather* (1972), the story of the fictitious Don Corleone]

don *n.*[3] (*also* **donette, don man, donna**) [1970s+] (*W.I./UK Black teen*) a respected boss or leader, the master or mistress of a situation. [for ety. *see* DON *n.*[2]]

don *adj.* [mid-19C; 1990s+] ultimate, best; also adv. exceedingly. [DON *n.*[2]/DON *n.*[3]]

dona *n.* (*also* **done, doner, doney, donie, donna, donner, donny, dony**) **1** [mid-19C+] (*Ling. Fr./Polari*) a woman (cf. DONAH *n.*). **2** [1920s] a landlady. **3** [1990s+] (*W.I.*) an attractive woman. [Ital. *donna*, woman]

donagher *n.* [early 19C–1920s] a privy. [DANNA *n.*; 20C use mainly US]

donah *n.* **1** [late 19C–1910s] a wife or girlfriend (cf. DONA *n.*). **2** [late 19C+] a woman, esp. when attractive. **3** [1970s] (*UK Und.*) the 'lady', the queen in a game of the 3-card trick. [Polari *donah*; ult. Ital. *donna*, a woman]

dona highland-flinger *n.* [late 19C–1900s] a music hall singer. [rhy. sl.]

dona jack *n.* [late 19C–1900s] a pimp (cf. ABBOT ON THE CROSS *n.*). [DONA *n.* (1) + JACK *n.*[2]]

dona juanita *n.* [1930s+] (*drugs*) marijuana (cf. AUNT MARY *n.*[2]). [lit. *lady Jane*; play on Mex. *marijuana*, i.e. Mary Jane]

donaker *n. see* DUNAKER *n.*

donald *n.* [mid-late 19C] (*Scot.*) a glass of spirits, usu. whisky. [? the name of a popular brand]

Donald (Duck) *n.* **1** [1960s+] (*orig. Aus.*) sexual intercourse; often fig. in phr. *not give a Donald (Duck)*. **2** [1960s+] (*Aus.*) a truck. **3** [1970s+] luck. [rhy. sl.; (1) FUCK *n.*[1] (1)]

Donald Trump *n.* [2000s] an act of defecation. [rhy. sl. = DUMP *n.*[4] (1); ult. US millionaire property developer *Donald Trump* (b.1946)]

Don Caesar spouting *n.* [late 19C] (*UK society*) haughty after-dinner speechifying. [the gravity of Spanish Dons]

Doncaster-cut *n.* [16C] a horse. [the association of *Doncaster* with horses + SE *cut*, castrated]

Don Cheech *n.* (*also* **Don Cheechero**) [1930s+] (*US Und.*) a senior member of the US Mafia. [a generic 'Italian' name]

Don Cypriano *n.* [17C] the penis (cf. ABRAHAM *n.*[1]). [play on Sp. honorific *Don* + CYPRIAN *adj.*; coined by Sir Thomas Urquhart for his translation of *Rabelais* (1653)]

don dada *n.* [1980s+] (*W.I./UK Black teen*) the highest ranking leader, Don of Dons. [DON *n.*[3] + SE *dada*; lit. 'don father']

donder *v.* [mid-19C+] (*S.Afr.*) to beat up, to thrash. [synon. Afk.]

done *n.*[1] [mid-late 19C] (*US Und.*) a prostitute. [DONA *n.* (1); Asbury, *The Gangs of Chicago* (1940), cites 'Belle Jones's den in Clark Street which in 1871 could boast of harboring "the oldest dones in the world" — Nellie Welch and Mollie Moore']

done *n.*[2] *see* DONA *n.*

done *n.*[3] *see* DUN *n.*

done *adj.*[1] (*also* **done for**) **1** [late 16C+] exhausted; impoverished, worn-out, dead. **2** [mid-18C+] cheated, swindled. **3** [mid-19C] of an object, finished. **4** [mid-19C+] defeated. **5** [mid-19C+] killed; lit. or fig. **6** [1930s+] beaten up, assaulted. **7** [1980s+] (*UK juv.*) reprimanded, told off. [DO *v.*[2] (1)/DO *v.*[1]]

done *adj.*[2] (*also* **done for**) [early 19C+] arrested, arrested on a charge of; punished. [DO *v.*[11]]

done *v. see* DUN *v.*

done brown *phr. see* DO BROWN *v.* (1).

done deal *n.* [20C+] anything that has been brought to a satisfactory conclusion.

done fairly *phr.* [late 19C] cheated, defrauded. [DO *v.*[2] (1)]

done for *adj.*[1] *see* DONE *adj.*[1].

done for *adj.*[2] *see* DONE *adj.*[2].

done for a ramp *phr.* [early-mid-19C] arrested for stealing. [DONE *adj.*[2] + RAMP *n.*[2] (1)]

donegan *n. see* DONIGAN *n.*

done in *adj.* **1** [20C+] (*also* **done out**) very tired, exhausted. **2** [1910s+] beyond further effort. **3** [1960s] (*US*) raped. [DO IN *v.* (6)/DO IN *v.* (13); ext. of DONE *adj.*[1]]

done in a tick-tack *phr.* [late 19C] done very quickly. [SE *do* + TICK *n.*[4] (2)]

done like a dinner *phr.* [mid-19C+] (*Aus.*) 'done to a turn', i.e. utterly defeated. [DONE adj.[1] (4) + cooking imagery]

done like a dog's dinner *phr.* [1930s+] (*N.Z.*) trounced, utterly defeated. [var. on DONE LIKE A DINNER *phr.*]

done out *adj. see* DONE IN adj. (1).

done over *adj.*[1] [18C–19C] of a woman, to have been used for sexual purposes. [DO v.[1] (1)]

done over *adj.*[2] **1** [late 18C+] beaten up. **2** [19C+] drunk (cf. ANNIHILATED adj.). **3** [mid-19C] worsted, put at a disadvantage, forced to lose out in a disagreement or struggle. [DO OVER v.]

done promote *n.* [1940s+] (*W.I.*) sandals or shoes made from old automobile tyres. [? joc. allusion, *I see you done promote* (have been promoted, i.e. from bare feet)]

doner *n.*[1] [mid-19C–1930s] one who is ruined, on the verge of death or collapse. [DONE adj.[1] (5) + ? pun on GONER n.[1] (3)]

doner *n.*[2] *see* DONA n.

done thing *n.* [1920s+] whatever is currently accepted by a specific group of people, professional, social, economic etc.

done to a burn *phr. see* DONE TO A TURN *phr.* (1).

done to a frazzle *phr.* [late 19C+] (*orig. US*) **1** cooked perfectly. **2** in fig. use, completely, to the limit. [? a var. of dial. *frizzle*, to fry (with a sizzle)]

done to a turn *phr.* **1** [early 19C+] (*also* **done to a burn, done to a tee**) perfect. **2** [20C+] worsted, beaten, at a disadvantage; the image of being spit-roasted and defenceless. [positive and negative cookery images]

done to the wide *phr.* (*also* **done to the world**) [1900s–30s] defeated, beaten utterly vanquished. [DONE adj.[1] (4) + TO THE WIDE adv./SE *world*]

donette *n. see* DON n.[3].

done up *adj.*[1] **1** [late 18C–1910s] (*US*) ruined (by gambling or other forms of speculation). **2** [early 19C] (*orig. US*) beaten up. **3** [early 19C+] exhausted, worn-out, fed up. **4** [mid-19C] very drunk (cf. ANNIHILATED adj.). **5** [mid-19C+] worsted, put at a disadvantage, forced to lose out in a disagreement or struggle. **6** [20C+] ill, whether mildly or extremely. **7** [1910s] out of order, not working. [DONE adj.[1]; Grose (1785) labels it a 'modern term']

done up *adj.*[2] [late 19C+] dressed up; esp. as *done up to the nines*. [DO UP v.[4]]

done up like a dog's dinner *phr. see* DRESSED UP LIKE A DOG'S DINNER *phr.*

done up like a kipper *phr.* [1980s+] **1** beaten up. **2** caught red-handed by the police, ambushed during a crime. **3** utterly defeated. [DONE UP adj.[1]/DO (UP) LIKE A KIPPER v.]

done up like a pox doctor's clerk *phr.* (*also* **dressed up like a pox doctor's clerk, got up…, mockered up…**) [1930s+] (*UK/Aus.*) flashily dressed, overdressed. [DONE UP adj.[2]/SE *dressed up*/GOT UP adj. (1)/MOCKERED UP adj. + stereotyping of this occupation as vulgarly dressed]

done up like a sore finger/thumb/toe *phr. see* DRESSED UP LIKE A SORE FINGER *phr.*

doney *n. see* DONA n.

dong *n.*[1] (*orig. US*) **1** [late 19C+] the penis; thus (*US gay*) *dong and gongs*, the penis and testicles (cf. GONGS n.). **2** [1950s+] a general derog. term, a fool (cf. CHOAD n.). [abbr. DING-DONG n.[4] which predates general sl. use in regional cits.]

dong *n.*[2] (*also* **donger**) [20C+] a blow, esp. with the fist. [post-1930s use is mainly Aus.]

dong *v.* [20C+] to hit. [DONG n.[2]]

donger *n.*[1] [1960s+] (*orig. Aus.*) **1** the penis. **2** a general term of abuse (cf. BELL END n.). [ext. of DONG n.[1] (1), but note *donger*, a fisherman's club]

donger *n.*[2] *see* DONG n.[2].

donger-knocker *n.* (*also* **bommy-knocker, dommy-knocker, dongy-knocker**) [1930s+] (*N.Z., mainly juv.*) a club, a bludgeon. [DONG v./SE *bomb* + *knocker*]

don gorgon *n.* [1980s+] (*W.I./Rasta*) **1** outstanding dreadlocks; thus a person who is respected. **2** an enforcer. [DON n.[3] + the mythical *Gorgon*, whose 'hair' was actually writhing snakes]

dongs and gongs *n. see* DONG n.[1].

dongy-knocker *n. see* DONGER-KNOCKER n.

donicker *n.* (*also* **doniker, donneker, donnicker**) [20C+] a privy. [DUNNAKEN n.]

donie *n. see* DONA n.

donigan *n.* (*also* **donegan**) [1910s–40s] a privy. [DUNNAKEN n.]

doniker *n. see* DONICKER n.

don jem *n.* [1950s+] (*drugs*) marijuana (cf. AUNT MARY n.[2]). [var. on DJAMBA n.]

donk *n.*[1] **1** [1910s+] a donkey. **2** [1910s+] (*Aus.*) a car or boat engine, a motorcycle. **3** [1940s+] (*Aus.*) a lift on the crossbar of a bicycle (cf. BUNK v.[5]). **4** [1950s] (*N.Z.*) a racing horse; thus *on the donks*, the horses. **5** [2000s] (*US campus*) large, protruding buttocks. [(1) abbr. SE; subseq. defs. fig. use of (1)]

donk *n.*[2] **1** [1920s] illicit 'moonshine' whisky. **2** [2000s] (*US drugs*) marijuana and phencyclidine. [? both have 'a kick like a mule']

donkey *n.*[1] **1** [mid-19C] (*US campus*) a notably religious student. **2** [mid-19C+] a fool, a simpleton (cf. AIREDALE n.). **3** [1920s+] (*US*) a working-class Irish person; also attrib. (cf. BOG ARAB n.). **4** [1940s] a manual labourer.

donkey *n.*[2] (*also* **donkey's**) [1960s+] a (large) penis; thus FLOG ONE'S DONKEY v.; *pull one's donkey*, to masturbate (cf. ANTEATER n.). [the supposedly large appendage of the animal]

donkey *v.* [1990s+] (*US teen*) to do something really stupid, esp. in a social situation. [DONKEY n.[1] (2)]

donkey-cock *n. see* DONKEY DICK n.[2] (1).

donkey-deep in *phr.* [1910s–20s] (*N.Z.*) immersed in, up to one's neck. [lit. or fig.]

donkey dick *n.*[1] **1** [late 18C–early 19C] an ass. **2** [1980s+] (*US*) a fool, a simpleton (cf. DICK n.[4]). [SE *donkey* + DICK n.[4]]

donkey dick *n.*[2] (*also* **donkey-cock**) [1960s+] **1** (*orig. US*) a notably large penis or a nickname for a man with such an appendage; also adj. *donkey-dicked*, having a large penis (cf. ANTEATER n.). **2** (*US prison*) a hot dog. **3** (*US milit./prison*) sliced cold cuts. **4** (*US*) in fig. use, a problematic situation. [SE *donkey* + DICK n.[4] (1); (1) US successor to DONKEY PRICK n.; note RMC Duntroon (Aus.) *donk*, the penis (size is irrelevant)]

donkey dust *n.* [1950s+] a euph. for BULLSHIT n. (1). [SE *donkey* + *dust*, rubbish]

donkey-hung *adj.* [late 19C] possessing a very large penis.

donkey kong *n.* [1990s+] (*US Black*) an act of anal sex in which the man punches the woman in the back of the head as he climaxes. [the computer game *Donkey Kong*]

donkey lick *n.* [1940s–50s] (*Aus.*) treacle or golden syrup. [? its appeal to the animal]

donkey lick *v.* [late 19C–1940s] (*Aus./N.Z.*) to defeat easily. [SE *donkey* + LICK v.[1] (1)]

donkey price *n.* [1950s+] (*W.I.*) an inflated price, one only a fool would pay. [DONKEY n.[1] (2) + SE *price*]

donkey prick *n.* [late 19C] a notably large penis. [SE *donkey* + PRICK n. (2)]

donkey-rigged *adj.* [late 19C+] in possession of a notably large penis.

donkey roast *n.* [1960s] (*US*) a formal banquet. [? link to the US Democratic Party's mascot, the donkey]

donkey's *n.*[1] *see* DONKEY n.[2].

donkey's *n.*[2] *see* DONKEY'S (YEARS) n.

donkey's age, a *n.* (*also* **donkey's ages, a tinker's age**) [1930s–60s] a very long time.

donkey's breakfast *n.* **1** [late 19C–1960s] a straw hat (cf. COW'S BREAKFAST n.). **2** [1910s+] (*Aus./US*) a straw palliasse.

donkey's ears *n.* [mid-19C] a false collar; a detachable shirt-collar with long points.

donkey shit *n. see* SHIT n.[3] (3).

donkey show *n.* [1990s+] (*US Black*) a complete mess, a farcical situation. [? a sex show involving a donkey and a woman]

donkey's knob *n.* [1990s+] **1** anything obvious. **2** anything excellent, admirable, first-rate. [SE *donkey* + KNOB n.¹ (3), i.e. the size of the animal's penis; var. on DOG'S BALLOCKS n.]

donkey's yawn *n.* [1990s+] a large vagina.

donkey's (years) *n.* [late 19C+] a very long time. [the length of a donkey's ears + an extra *y*. Occas. as *donkey's ears*, a ref. to the beast's well-known feature + a pun on *years*]

donkey wallop *v.* [1980s] (*Aus.*) to defeat easily. [var. on DONKEY LICK v.]

donkey work *n.* [1920s+] tedious, laborious, usu. heavy tasks.

donko *n.* [1970s+] (*N.Z.*) a room set aside in the workplace for smoking, relaxation etc. [? synon. N.Z.E. *donkey room*, orig. (1920s) the enclosure on the Wellington docks where a donkey engine was kept and at the time was the only warm shelter available]

donks *n.* [1990s+] a very long time. [DONKEY'S (YEARS) n.]

don man *n. see* DON n.³

donna *n.¹ see* DON n.³

donna *n.² see* DONA n.

donna and feeles *n.* [mid-19C] a woman and children. [Ital. or Ling. Fr. *donna e figlie*, a woman and children]

donneker *n. see* DONICKER n.

donnelly *n.* [mid-19C] (*US*) a heavy blow or punch. [the prize-fighter Daniel *Donnelly* (1788–1820)]

donner *n. see* DONA n.

donner *v.* (*S.Afr.*) **1** [mid-19C+] to beat up, to thrash. **2** [1960s+] to defeat, to overcome. [Afk. *donder*, to thrash]

donnicker *n. see* DONICKER n.

donnie *n.* (*also* **donny**) [1950s–60s] (*N.Z.*) a fight, a disturbance. [abbr. DONNYBROOK n. (1)]

donny *n. see* DONA n.

donnybrook *n.* **1** [19C+] a fight, a riot, a noisy brawl. **2** [1950s] of people, a difficult, rebellious type. [the notorious *Donnybrook* Fair in Eire, at which such events were a regular feature]

donnybrook *v.* [1960s–70s] to strike, to hit. [DONNYBROOK n. (1)]

donor *n.* [1980s+] (*US campus*) a person who makes themselves available for sexual intercourse.

do-nothing stool *n.* [late 19C; 1980s] (*US Black*) the buttocks, the posterior. [used when one is sitting down idly]

donovan *n.¹* **1** [mid-19C] a nickname for an Irishman (cf. BOG ARAB n.; MICK n.¹; MICKEY n.¹; MICKSER n.; MIKE n.²; MULLIGAN n.¹; MURPHY n.²; PAD n.; PADDY n.; PADDYWHACK n.¹; PAT n.; PATLANDER n.; PATRICK n.; SEAMUS n.; TAIG n.; TEAGUELANDER n.). **2** [mid-19C+] a potato. [the commonness of the Irish surname and the stereotyping of the Irish appetite for potatoes]

donovan *n.²* [1990s+] (*W.I.*) an aspirant DON n.³ [a pej. based on the HIPPIE n.² (3) singer *Donovan* (b.1946)]

Don Pego *n. see* PEGO n.

Don Revie *n.* [1990s+] alcohol, a drink. [rhy. sl. = BEVVY n.; ult. UK football manager *Don Revie* (1928–89)]

don't be auntie *phr.* [1920s+] (*Aus.*) don't be foolish. [the stereotyping of foolish (? maiden) aunts]

don't be funny *n.* [20C+] (*Aus.*) a lavatory (cf. ANGUS ARMANASCO n.). [rhy. sl. = DUNNY n.]

don't bullshit a bullshitter *phr. see* CAN'T SHIT A SHITTER phr.

don't-care-damn *adj.* [20C+] (*W.I.*) absolutely indifferent, totally irresponsible. [NOT GIVE A DAMN v.]

don't-care-ish *adj.* (*also* **don't-care-ishified**) [1930s] (*US Black*) indifferent, uninterested.

don't do anything I wouldn't do *phr.* [20C+] an exhortation to anyone who is leaving, esp. on holiday or in search of similar supposed pleasures; the implication is usu. sexual, and the point is to wish them as excessive a time as possible.

don't do anything you couldn't eat *phr.* [1930s+] (*Aus.*) an exhortation to anyone who is leaving, in search of supposed pleasures.

don't (even) go there *phr.* [1990s+] (*orig. US Black*) advice to avoid a course of action, a form of argument etc; the emphasis is on the abstract rather than an actual place (cf. YOU DON'T WANT TO GO THERE phr.).

don't even try it *phr.* [1980s+] (*US campus*) a warning or a response to deter someone.

don't fancy yours *phr.* [20C+] a joking reflex comment when 2 young men see 2 women, irrespective of their real charms.

don't forget her *n.* [1900s] (*Aus.*) a letter. [rhy. sl.]

don't get your bowels in an uproar *phr.* [20C+] do not make so much (unnecessary) fuss.

don't get your breeches torn *phr.* [1960s] (*US*) don't get yourself over-excited.

don't get your shit hot *phr.* [20C+] don't get over-excited.

don't-give-a-damn *adj.* (*also* **don't-give-a-shit**) [1960s+] (*US*) careless, carefree. [NOT GIVE A SHIT v.]

don't-go money *n.* [1950s] (*US*) money that one cannot afford to lose.

don't go there *phr. see* DON'T (EVEN) GO THERE phr.

don't hang dirty washing in my backyard *phr.* [1940s] (*US Black*) don't lie to me; don't tell me stories.

don the beard *v. see* WEAR THE BEARD v.

don't hold no air *phr.* [1980s+] (*US Black*) a phr. meaning that something has little impact or effect on either people or events.

don't-know-what-to-call-'ems *n.* [mid-19C] (*US*) trousers (cf. DON'T-NAME-'EMS n.; DON'T-SPEAK-OF-'EMS n.; INDESCRIBABLES n.; INDISPENSABLES n.; INEFFABLES n.; INEXPRESSIBLES n.; MUSTN'T-MENTION-'EMS n.; THINGUMABOBS n.; THINGUMMIES n.; UNMENTION-ABLES n.). [euph; the image of trousers, so close to the genitals and legs, as 'obscene' or taboo]

don't let the alligator beat you to the pond *phr.* [1930s] (*US Black*) don't be slow(witted) or you will be outdone.

don't let your (alligator) mouth overload your ass *phr.* [1960s+] (*US*) keep quiet, esp. in a difficult situation where words might complicate matters.

don't let your meat loaf *phr.* [1960s+] (*US*) a general phr. of encouragement, the implication being 'don't procrastinate'. [pun on SE *meat loaf*, the food/LOAF v.¹ (2)]

don't let your mouth buy what your ass can't pay *phr.* [1970s+] (*US*) keep quiet, esp. when speaking might make matters worse.

don't let your mouth write a check your ass can't cash *phr.* [1960s+] (*orig. US Black*) keep quiet, esp. when speaking might make matters worse.

don't lose your hair *phr.* [late 19C] calm down, keep cool.

don't make a fuss *n.* [1960s] a bus. [rhy. sl.]

don't make a Judy (Fitzsimmons) of yourself *phr.* [1920s+] (*Anglo-Irish*) don't be a fool. [? a long-lost anecdote]

don't make a production out of it *phr.* [1960s+] 'don't make a mountain out of a molehill'.

don't make me laugh *phr.* [20C+] don't be stupid, ridiculous; thus [1920s–40s] ext. by *...I've got a cracked/sore/split lip*.

don't-name-'ems *n.* [mid-19C–1910s] trousers (cf. DON'T-KNOW-WHAT-TO-CALL-'EMS n.).

don't pay no rabbit foot *phr.* [1900s–40s] (*US Black*) an exhortation to ignore a person or situation. [Mezzrow & Wolfe, *Really the Blues* (1946): 'When you don't pay a man no rabbit, you're not paying him any more attention than would a rabbit's butt as it disappears hurriedly over the fence']

don't sell me a dog *phr.* [mid-19C] (*UK society*) don't try to fool me. [the perceived lack of ethics in such a transaction]

don't shit a shitter *phr. see* CAN'T SHIT A SHITTER phr.

don't sing it *phr.* [late 19C–1900s] don't exaggerate. [one 'sings' an exaggerated tale]

don't-speak-of-'ems *n.* [mid-19C] (*US*) trousers (cf. DON'T-KNOW-WHAT-TO-CALL-'EMS n.).

don't start *phr. see* DON'T (YOU) START phr.

don't sweat it *phr.* [1950s+] (*orig. US Black*) don't worry.

don't take any wooden nickels *phr.* (*also* **don't take any rubber nickels, ...wooden money**) [1920s+] (*orig. US*) beware of being defrauded or hoaxed.

don't take me there *phr.* [1990s+] (*US teen*) I am not interested, I don't want to hear it.

don't take rubber dimes *phr.* [1920s] (*US*) be careful, watch your step.

don't talk with your mouth full *phr.* [1990s+] a rejoinder to a stupid comment. [the familiar expression usu. said by parents to children at the table]

don't turn that side to London *phr.* [late 19C] a phr. used to condemn whatever object is under discussion. [the idea that only the best is good enough for display in the metropolis]

don't wake it up *phr.* [1920s+] (*Aus.*) don't talk about it. [cf. SE *let sleeping dogs lie*]

don't (you) start *phr.* [late 19C+] a phr. used to indicate that one is already sufficiently displeased or annoyed by statements that have been made and that one does not need the irritation that their repetition would cause; or, usu. to a child, meaning, 'I'm annoyed already, don't start behaving badly and make things worse'.

donut *see also under* DOUGHNUT and its combs.

donut-bumper *n.* [1990s+] (*US*) a lesbian (cf. BEAN FLICKER n.). [SAmE *donut* (UK *doughnut*) + BUMPER n.[5]]

donut hole *n.* [1990s+] (*US campus*) someone with no social skills. [the emptiness of the hole in a SAmE *donut*. Note US milit. use *donut hole*, a female volunteer worker with the US Red Cross, although the ref. is to sexuality, i.e. the HOLE n.[1] (2), rather than stupidity]

dony *n. see* DONA n.

doob *n.*[1] [1950s+] (*Aus.*) the penis. [ety. unknown]

doob *n.*[2] [1960s+] (*drugs*) amphetamine (cf. A n.[2]). [? DOOBIE n.[1]; originated with the UK Mods of the early 1960s and then spread among other users]

doob *n.*[3] *see* DOOBIE n.[1].

doobage *n.* [1980s+] (*US campus*) marijuana. [DOOB n.[2] + -AGE sfx]

doober *n.* [1970s+] (*US*) **1** a piece of excrement. **2** a foolish or unpleasant person. [ety. unknown; ? link to SE *daub*]

dooberry *n. see* DOOBRIE n.

doobie *n.*[1] (*also* **doob, doober, dube, dubee, duby**) **1** [1960s+] (*drugs*) cannabis; thus adj., *doobious*, intoxicated from cannabis. **2** [1960s+] (*drugs*) a cannabis cigarette. **3** [1970s] (*US prison*) a cigarette. [ety. unknown; ? euph.; ? same ety. as next]

doobie *n.*[2] [1980s+] (*US*) an unimportant, worthless or stupid person. [Scot. *dobie*, a dull, stupid fellow; ult. f. *Dobie*, Robert]

doobob *n.* (*also* **doobobbis, doobobbus**) [1910s+] (*orig. US*) any nameless small object, typically some form of gadget. [ety. unknown]

doobrie *n.* (*also* **dooberry, doobry, dubry**) [1950s+] (*orig. milit.*) anything for which one cannot recall the name. [orig. in the army, the term gained a new lease of life thanks to the DJ and TV performer Kenny Everett, who used it frequently in 1970s–80s]

doobs *adj.* [1990s+] unpopular, socially unacceptable. [SE *dubious*]

dooby *adj.* [1950s+] (*Aus.*) old-fashioned. [SE *dowdy* + ? BOOBY n.[1]]

dooce *n. see* DEUCE n.[2] (2).

dood *n.* **1** [1910s+] (*Aus.*) a pipe. **2** [1920s–50s] (*US*) the penis. [Irish *dudeen*, a short clay pipe]

doo-da *n. see* DOODAH n.[1].

doodackie *n.* [1940s+] (*N.Z.*) any nameless small object, typically some form of gadget; the *doodackied up*, dressed up. [ety. unknown]

doodad *n.* (*also* **do-dad, doodab, doodabbus, doogood, dudaddle, dudedad**) (*orig. US*) **1** [late 19C+] any nameless small object, typically some form of gadget. **2** [1920s+] something small, used as a decoration. **3** [1920s+] nonsense, foolish chatter. [ety. unknown; the many synon. terms for the word may represent the stammering efforts of one who is struggling to recall the correct name]

doodads *n.* [late 19C+] (*orig. US*) morsels, pieces, odds and ends. [DOODAD n. (1)]

doodah *n.*[1] (*also* **doo-da**) [1910s+] an emotional crisis, a nervous, tense state. [the refrain *doo-da(h)* of the plantation song 'Camptown Races' (1850)]

doodah *n.*[2] [1920s+] anything for which one cannot remember the name; also used of people. [DOODAD n. (1)]

doodey-squat *n. see* DOODY-SQUAT n.

doodgooi *n.* [1910s+] (*S.Afr.*) a lethal weapon. [Afk. *doodgooier*, a dumpling, lit. a 'dead-thrower', i.e. dough that has not risen]

doodibbie *n.* [1910s+] any nameless small object, typically some form of gadget. [var. on DOODAD n. (1)]

doodinkus *n.* (*also* **dinkus, dodinkus, dudinkus**) [1910s+] any nameless small object, typically some form of gadget. [var. on DOODAD n. (1)]

doodlally *adj. see* DOODLE-ALLY adj.

doodle *n.*[1] [early 17C–mid-19C] a fool, a dull person. [var. on SE *noodle*, a fool; ? link to Low Ger. *Dudeltopf*, a simpleton, lit. a 'nightcap']

doodle *n.*[2] **1** [late 18C+] the penis, esp. a child's penis; thus *whack one's doodle*, to masturbate (cf. BAUBLE n.). **2** [late 19C+] the vagina. [20C+ use of both is US]

doodle *n.*[3] (*US*) **1** [1910s] something or someone attractive. **2** [1920s+] anything completely simple or easy to achieve. [? var. on DODDLE n.]

doodle *n.*[4] [1910s] any nameless small object, typically some form of gadget. [var. on DOODAD n. (1)]

doodle *adj.* [18C] foolish. [DOODLE n.[1]]

doodle *v.*[1] [19C] to make a fool of, to cheat. [DOODLE n.[1]]

doodle *v.*[2] [late 19C–1950s] (*US*) of a man, to have sexual intercourse (cf. BAGAGA v.). [DOODLE n.[2] (1)]

doodle-ally *adj.* (*also* **doodlally**) [1940s–50s] **1** mad, eccentric. **2** very drunk (cf. ADDLED adj.). [DOODLE n.[1] + DOOLALLY adj.]

doodle (around) *v.* [1960s+] (*US*) to act idly, to laze around. [SE *doodle*, to draw idle patterns]

doodle-brain *n. see* DOODLE-HEAD n.

doodle-bug *n.* **1** [1930s+] a small cheap car or any small vehicle or machine. **2** [1940s+] a German V-1 flying bomb. [? southeastern dial. *doodle-bug*, a booming cockchafer; post-WW2 use of (2) is historical]

doodlebum *n.* [1910s] any nameless small object, typically some form of gadget. [ext. of DOODLE n.[4]]

doodle-case *n.* [late 19C] the vagina (cf. BAG n.[1]). [DOODLE n.[2] (1) + SE *case*]

doodle-dandler *n.* [19C] a masturbator; thus *do a doodle-dandler*, to masturbate. [DOODLE n.[2] (1) + SE *dandle*, to fondle, to stroke]

doodle-dasher *n.* [late 19C] a masturbator. [DOODLE n.[2] (1) + SE *dash*, to strike, to hit]

doodle-do *n.* (*also* **doodle-doo, doodly-do**) [1960s+] (*US*) **1** nothing at all, e.g. *I can't do doodle-do about it.* **2** the vagina or penis (cf. ARTICLE n.; BAUBLE n.). [(1) the trad. phonetic version of the cock's crowing, *cock-a-doodle-do*; (2) DOODLE n.[2] (1)]

doodle-doo man *n.* [early 19C] one who breeds or fights cocks. [SE *cock-a-doodle-doo*]

doodle-em-buck *n.* [late 19C] (*Aus.*) confidence trickery. [DOODLE v.[1]]

doodlefagit *n.* [1910s] any nameless small object, typically some form of gadget. [ext. of DOODLE n.[4]]

doodleflap *n.*[1] [late 19C] the flaccid penis. [DOODLE n.[2] (1) + SE *flap*, to wave up and down]

doodleflap *n.*[2] *see* FLAPDOODLE n.[2].

doodleflicker *n.* (*also* **doodleflickus, doodlegadget**) [1910s] any nameless small object, typically some form of gadget. [ext. of DOODLE n.[4]]

doodle-head *n.* (*also* **doodle-brain**) [1990s+] (*Aus. teen*) a general insult. [DOODLE n.[1]/DOODLE n.[2] (1) + -HEAD sfx (1)/SE *brain*]

doodler *n.* [20C+] a lazy person, an idler. [SE *doodle*, to draw idle patterns]

doodle-sack *n.*[1] **1** [late 18C–early 19C] a pocket. **2** [late 18C–19C] the vagina (cf. BAG n.[1]). [(2) DOODLE n.[2] (1) + SE *sack*]

doodle-sack *n.*[2] [late 18C–early 19C] (*Scot.*) a bagpipe. [Ger. *Dudelsack* bagpipes; ? ult. SE *tootle*]

doodley *n.* (*also* **doodly**) [1930s+] (*US*) an insignificant amount, nothing whatsoever, the inference is that the subject is worthless. [abbr. DOODLEY-SQUAT n.]

doodley-shit *n.* (*also* **doodly-shit**) [1950s+] (*orig. US*) anything worthless or insignificant, rubbish. [var. on DOODLEY-SQUAT n.]

doodley-squat *n.* (*also* **doodly-squat**) [1930s+] nothing, zero. [nonsense word]

doodley-squat *adv.* (*also* **doodly-squat**) [1930s+] (*US*) in no way at all. [DOODLEY-SQUAT n.]

doodly *see also under* DOODLEY and its combs.

doodly-do *n. see* DOODLE-DO n.

doo-doo *n. see* DO-DO n.[1].

doo-doo *adj.* [2000s] (*US Black*) excellent, first-rate. [DO-DO n.[1] (1), i.e. SHIT adj. (3)]

doody-squat *n.* (*also* **doodey-squat**) [1950s+] nothing. [var. on DOODLEY-SQUAT n.]

dooe *n.* (*also* **doee, dooee, due, duey**) [mid-19C+] (*Ling. Fr./Polari*) the number 2. [Ital. *due*, 2]

doof *n.* [1970s+] (*US*) a fool, a simpleton. [abbr. DOOFLUS n., but note Scot. *doof*, a dull, stupid person; ? ult. Ger. *doof*, dense, stupid, dull-witted]

doofer *n.* **1** [20C+] a partially smoked cigarette. **2** [1970s+] (*Irish*) any otherwise unnamed object. [SE *do for*]

doofless *adj.* [1970s+] (*US*) idiotic, stupid, dull. [DOOFLUS n.]

dooflicker *n.* (*also* **doflickety, dooflinkus, duflickerty**) [1900s–40s] (*orig. Can. milit.*) any nameless small object, typically some form of gadget. [? var. on DOODAD n. (1) or ? DOODLEFLICKER n.; note West Point *duflicket*, derog. term for a plebe or first-year cadet]

dooflop *n.* [1950s+] any nameless small object, typically some form of gadget. [var. on DOODAD n. (1)]

dooflus *n.* (*also* **duflus**) [1930s+] (*US Black/teen*) a bizarre, eccentric individual. [? Ger. *doof*, stupid]

doofunny *n.* (*also* **dofunny, doojumfunny, dufunny**) [1900s–40s] any nameless small object, typically some form of gadget. [? var. on DOODAD n. (1) + SE *funny*]

doofus *n.* (*also* **doofas, doufus**) [1950s+] (*orig. US Black*) an odd person, an eccentric; a fool (cf. DORKUS (PRETENTIOUS) n.; DOSCUS n.; GAZOOKUS n.[1]; GOMUS n.; GONUS n.; GOOFUS n.; OOFUS n.). [for ety. *see* DOOF n.; note also the character *Dufus*, in the cartoon strip Popeye, a foolish, bumbling individual]

doofus *adj.* [1960s+] odd, strange, eccentric. [DOOFUS n.]

doofy *adj.* [1980s] (*US, mainly juv.*) foolish, silly, eccentric. [DOOF n. + sfx -*y*]

doog *adj.* [mid-19C+] good. [backsl.]

doog eno *n.* (*also* **doogheno**) [mid-19C+] good one. [backsl.; DOOG adj. + ENO n.]

doog gels *n.* [mid-19C+] of a passing woman, good legs. [backsl.; DOOG adj.]

doogheno hit *n.* [mid-19C] a good or profitable market. [DOOG ENO n. + SE *hit*]

doogie *n. see* DUJI n.

doogie daddy *n. see* DAP DADDY n.

doogood *n. see* DOODAD n.

doogy *n. see* DUJI n.

doohickey *n. see* DOHICKEY n.[1].

dooie *n.* [1980s+] (*US campus*) an echoic equivalent of the sound of a punch or slap; thus *dooie*, to hit.

doojee *n. see* DUJI n.

doojigger *n. see* DOJIGGER n.

doojumfunny *n. see* DOOFUNNY n.

dook *see also under* DUKE and its combs.

dook *n.*[1] **1** [mid-late 19C] a notably large nose. **2** [mid-19C+] a hand; thus *put up the dooks*, to thieve, esp. to pickpocket (cf. DOOKS n.). [(1) mispron. of *duke* = Duke of Wellington (1769–1852), known for his large nose and thus nicknamed *Conky*; (2) var. on DUKE n.[3] (1)]

dook *n.*[2] [1980s+] (*US campus*) something unpleasant or worthless. [DUKIE n.[2]]

dook *v.* [1990s+] to defecate. [DUKIE n.[2] (2)]

dookering *n.* (*also* **dookin', duckering**) [mid-19C+] (*gypsy/tramp*) fortune-telling. [Rom. *dukker*, to tell fortunes]

dookey *n.* (*also* **dookie, dooky**) **1** [1960s+] rubbish, nonsense. **2** [1980s] the stuffing, the 'daylights'; thus *knock the dookey out of*. [DUKIE n.[2] (1)]

dookie *n. see* DUKIE n.[2].

dookie *adj.* (*also* **dooky**) **1** [1920s+] dirty. **2** [1990s+] (*US campus*) unpleasant, distasteful, disgusting. [DUKIE n.[2] (1)]

dookie love *n.* [2000s] (*US Black*) anal intercourse. [DUKIE n.[2] (1) + SE *love*]

dookin' *n. see* DOOKERING n.

dookin-cove *n.* [mid-late 19C] a fortune-teller. [DOOKIN' n. + COVE n. (1)]

dooks *n.* [mid-19C+] the fists; thus *put up the dooks*, to prepare to fight. [DOOK n.[1] (2)/DUKES n. (1)]

dooky *n. see* DOOKEY n.

dooky *adj. see* DOOKIE adj.

doola *n.* [1990s+] (*US Black*) a son. [ety. unknown]

doolally *adj.* (*also* **do-lally**) [late 19C+] (*orig. milit.*) **1** mad, eccentric. **2** very drunk (cf. ADDLED adj.). **3** malfunctioning, out of order. [the Deolalie military sanatorium in Bombay, to which mentally ill troops were sent. However, according to the veteran Frank Richards, writing in his memoir *Old Soldier Sahib* (1936), the illness came not before one arrived at Deolalie but during one's stay there. Time-expired troops were sent to the sanatorium to await the next troop-ship home. It was during the long hot days of tedium that men, formerly first-class soldiers, might gradually go to pieces]

doolally tap *n.* [late 19C+] madness, eccentricity, orig. a form of madness that afflicted soldiers stationed in India, and spec. at Deolalie. [DOOLALLY adj. (1) + SE *tap*, malarial fever; ult. Skrt *tapa*, heat, pain, torment]

doolally-trapped *adj.* [1910s–20s] knocked senseless. [pun on DOOLALLY TAP n.]

doolan *n.* **1** [1930s+] (*N.Z.*) (*also* **doolie, doolin**) a Catholic, usu. an Irish Catholic; also attrib. **2** [1950s] (*Aus.*) a policeman. [the common Irish surname; (2) is stereotyped link between Irish and the police]

dooley *n.* [1980s+] (*drugs*) heroin. [? DUJI n.]

doolie *n.*[1] (*also* **dooly**) [18C+] (*Anglo-Ind.*) an ambulance. [Hind. *doli*, a litter, a sedan for (working-class) women; thus a rudimentary army ambulance]

doolie *n.*[2] *see* DOOLAN n. (1).

doolin *n. see* DOOLAN n. (1).

doolittle *n.* [mid-18C] a euph. for the penis. [SE *do little*, the implication is of impotence]

doololly *n.* [1930s] any nameless small object, typically some form of gadget. [var. on DOHICKEY n.[1]/DOJIGGER n. (1)]

dooly *n. see* DOOLIE n.[1].

doom *adj.* [1960s+] (*US drugs*) of drugs, very strong or powerful.

doom *v. see* DOOM (OUT) v.

doomdust *n.* [1970s] (*US drugs*) heroin. [DOOM adj. + DUST n.⁵ (1)]

doomie *n.* [1950s] (*Aus.*) a criminally inclined teenage rebel. [? they are 'doomed']

doom (out) *v.* [1970s+] (*US*) to kill, to murder.

doondoos *n. see* DUNDUS n.

do one *v.* [1950s+] to leave, to run away.

do one! *excl.* [1990s+] a general excl. of dismissal. [DO ONE v.]

do one a treat *v.* [late 19C+] to suit one absolutely. [SE + TREAT, A adv.]

do one for me *phr.* [20C+] a phr. addressed by one male to another who is on his way to the lavatory and who may reply, 'Which side do you shake it?'

do one's arse *v.* [1990s+] (*Aus.*) to bet heavily and unsuccessfully; to lose all one's money. [DO IN v. (2) + ARSE n.¹ (4)]

do one's balls on *v.* [late 19C+] of a man, to fall obsessively in love with. [SE *do* + BALLS n.¹ (1)]

do one's bit *v.* [late 19C+] to make a contribution to the common good, esp. in joining the forces in a time of war.

do one's block *v.* (*also* do in one's block, lose one's block) [20C+] (*Aus.*) **1** to lose emotional control, to lose one's temper; thus antonym *keep the block*, to remain calm. **2** to fall in love. [BLOCK n.¹ (2)]

do one's bollocks *v.* [1990s+] to make the utmost effort. [BALLOCKS n.¹ (1)]

do one's bun *v.* [1940s+] (*orig. N.Z. milit.*) to lose emotional control. [var. on DO ONE'S SCONE v.]

do one's business *v.* (*also* do one's things) [mid-19C+] a euph. meaning to go to the lavatory, esp. used when addressing children (cf. AUNTIE n.¹; DESPATCH ONE'S CARGO v.; EXCUSED, BE v.; GO PLACES v.; GO ROUND THE CORNER v.; NATURE CALLS phr.; PAY A CALL v.; PLUCK A ROSE v.; SEE A MAN ABOUT A DOG v.). [SE *do* + BUSINESS n.³]

do one's cash *v.* [20C+] (*Aus.*) to spend all one's available funds. [DO IN v. (2) + SE *cash*]

do one's cobblers *v.* [1980s] to lose one's money. [DO IN v. (2) + fig. use of COBBLERS n. (2)]

do one's cruet *v. see* CRUET n.

do one's dash *v.*¹ [1910s] (*Aus.*) to become infatuated, to fall in love. [fig. use of DASH n.⁵ (1)]

do one's dash *v.*² (*also* lose one's dash, lose one's punch) [1910s+] (*Aus.*) to reach one's limit, to exhaust one's energies, to lose one's opportunity – and suffer accordingly. [DO IN v. (5) + SE *dash*]

do one's dirty *v.* [1970s] (*US*) to defecate (cf. DESPATCH ONE'S CARGO v.).

do one's do *v.* [20C+] (*US*) to do what is necessary, to do what one must do.

do one's dough *v.* [1910s+] (*orig. Aus.*) to lose one's money, to spend up. [DO IN v. (2) + DOUGH n.¹ (1)]

do one's duty *v.* [20C+] a euph. meaning to urinate, to defecate (cf. DESPATCH ONE'S CARGO v.). [euph.]

do oneself *v.* [1980s+] (*US*) to make a fool of oneself, to embarrass oneself. [DO v.¹ (2)]

do oneself a bit of good *n. see* DO ALL RIGHT (FOR ONESELF) v.

do oneself in *v.* **1** [20C+] to commit suicide. **2** [1930s] to put oneself in a deliberately unpleasant situation or position. [DO IN v. (3)]

do oneself (off) *v.* [1960s+] to masturbate (cf. BALL OFF v.²). [DO v.¹ (1)]

do oneself proud *v.* (*also* do someone proud) [mid-19C+] to entertain, to provide food or other material comforts to one's own (or someone else's) satisfaction.

do oneself well *v.* (*also* do it well) [late 19C+] to entertain, to provide food or other material comforts to one's own satisfaction.

do one's face *v.* [1920s+] usu. of a woman, to apply make-up.

do one's fruit *v.* [1970s] to lose one's temper, to go crazy. [joc. var. on GO BANANAS v. (1)]

do one's job (over) *v.* [1970s] (*Aus.*) to become obsessed (with).

do one's level *v.* [late 19C+] to do one's very best. [abbr. SE *do one's level best*]

do one's lolly *v. see* DO THE LOLLY v.

do one's luck *v.* [1910s+] (*Aus.*) to use up or run out of luck. [DO IN v. (2)]

do one's nana *v.* [1940s+] to lose one's temper. [NANA n. (2)]

do one's no-manners *v.* [1980s] **1** to defecate (cf. DESPATCH ONE'S CARGO v.). **2** to break wind.

do one's nut *v.* [1910s+] to lose one's temper, to lose emotional control, to get worked up. [NUT n.¹ (2)]

do one's oner *v. see* DO A ONER v.

do one's (own) thing *v.* [1960s+] **1** (*orig. US Black*) to behave as dictated by one's personal beliefs, wishes, idiosyncrasies etc. **2** (*orig. US Black*) to put on an act. **3** (*W.I./US Black*) to dance in an uninhibited manner, to enjoy oneself to the full. **4** (*US*) to perform an action. [ONE'S THING n.; ult. ? Mandingo *ka a fen ke*, to do one's thing. The term reached its peak in the 1960s, as a HIPPIE n.² (3) credo]

do one's own time *v.* [20C+] (*US prison/Und.*) to serve a prison sentence without becoming involved in any of the prison gangs, illicit business etc; thus imper. *do your own time!* mind your own business! [DO v.⁹ (1) + TIME n.¹]

do one's pegs *v.* [1940s] (*Aus.*) to become angry, excited or anxious.

do one's scone *v.* [1940s+] (*Aus./N.Z.*) to lose one's temper (with someone). [SCONE n.²]

do one's stuff *v.* **1** [mid-17C+] to perform as one is expected. **2** [1920s+] to show off a speciality.

do one's things *v. see* DO ONE'S BUSINESS v.

do on one's dick *v.* (*also* do on one's prick) [1960s+] to do with ease, esp. to endure any challenging situation, e.g. a prison sentence, with no difficulty. [SE *do* + DICK n.⁴ (1), i.e. var. on DO (STANDING) ON ONE'S HEAD v. (STAND v.¹)]

do on one's ear *v.* [1920s+] (*Aus.*) to accomplish something easily. [var. on DO (STANDING) ON ONE'S HEAD v.]

do on one's head *v. see* DO (STANDING) ON ONE'S HEAD v.

do on one's napper *v.* (*also* do on one's nob) [late 19C] to achieve something easily. [SE *do* + NAPPER n.² (2)/NOB n.¹ (1); var. on DO (STANDING) ON ONE'S HEAD v.]

do on one's prick *v. see* DO ON ONE'S DICK v.

do on the lift *v. see* LIFT v.¹ (2).

doonup *n.* (*also* dunop) [mid-19C] £1 sterling. [backsl.]

door *n.*¹ [1920s+] (*Aus.*) a brothel. [euph.; note similar imagery in 17C *door*, the vulva]

door *n.*² [2000s] (*US prison*) the end of one's sentence.

doo rag *n. see* DO-RAG n.

door and hinge *n.* [late 19C] the neck and breast of mutton. [the way in which the joint bends]

door-basher *n.* [1950s] a private detective (cf. BEAT-POUNDER n.).

doorknob *n.*¹ **1** [late 19C–1970s] a shilling (5p). **2** [20C+] a job. [rhy. sl.; (1) = BOB n.⁴ (1)]

doorknob *n.*² [1930s+] a fool. [SE, strengthened by later KNOB n.¹ (7)]

doorknob *n.*³ [1960s] (*US*) **1** a doughnut. **2** the head. **3** a female breast; usu. in pl. [resemblance]

door-knock *n.* [1950s+] (*Aus.*) a door-to-door appeal for charity or similar collection.

door-knocker *n.* **1** [mid–late 19C] a beard that runs along and just beneath the jaw line; when linking up with a moustache it was seen as resembling a door-knocker. **2** [late 19C–1900s] a female hairstyle consisting of 2 plaits bunched on top of the head. [supposed similarities]

doormat *n.* (*also* mat) [mid–late 19C] **1** a short cropped beard. **2** a moustache. [the heavy beards that veterans of the Crimean

War (1854–6) wore against the Russian cold. These were cropped short when the soldiers returned to the UK]

doormat thief *n.* (*also* **doormat grafter, doormatter**) [1900s–50s] a petty or incompetent thief.

door posts *n.* [early–mid-19C] the gallows. [the 'posts' were both those of the gallows and of the next world]

door shaker *n.* [1940s–70s] (*US*) **1** a policeman (cf. BEAT-POUNDER n.). **2** a security guard. [patrolling police or security guards shake doors to check that they are locked]

doorstep *n.* (*also* **flight of steps, step**) [late 19C+] a thickly cut slice of bread, sometimes ext. to a *couple of doorsteps* (cf. HEARTH-STONE n.). [note WW1 milit. *couple o' doorsteps*, a sandwich]

doorstep child *n.* [20C+] an illegitimate child. [such a child is trad. abandoned on a doorstep]

door-to-door *n.* [20C+] (*bingo*) the number 4 or, if the context makes this obvious, any combination ending in 4 (cf. ALDERSHOT LADIES n.).

doos *n.* [20C+] (*S.Afr.*) **1** the vagina. **2** a general term of strong abuse (cf. BAMBA n.[1]). [Afk. *doos*, box; thus used in sl. as CUNT n.[1] (1)]

doosid *adv.* *see* DEUCED adv.

doosie *n.* *see* DOOZIE n.

doosy *adj.* *see* DOOZIE adj.

dooteroomus *n.* (*also* **doot**) [mid–late 19C] (*US*) money. [? SE *duty* + *Deuteronomy*, the book of the Pentateuch that dictates the rules of society]

dooty *n.* [1960s+] (*US juv.*) excrement. [? DUKIE n.[2] (1) or ? SE *dirty*]

do out *v.* [1950s+] (*US prison*) to behave; usu. in phr. *don't do out like that*, don't behave in a way likely to debase oneself in the eyes of one's fellow convicts.

do out of *v.* [late 18C+] to deprive, to cheat someone out of.

doovah *n.* (*also* **doovah-dah**) [1930s] a cigarette end, preserved for later use. [var. on DOOVER n. (2)]

doover *n.* **1** [1930s+] (*Aus.*) (*also* **dooverlackey**) any nameless object or gadget or task. **2** [1930s+] (*Aus.*) a cigarette end, preserved for later use. **3** [1940s] (*Aus.*) a hospital urine bottle; thus *doover-joey*, a hospital orderly (among whose jobs is the emptying of such bottles). **4** [1940s] (*Aus. milit.*) a dugout. **5** [1960s] (*Aus.*) the penis (cf. BAUBLE n.). [? Heb. *davar*, a word or thing, but orig. use was as a shelter or rough dugout]

do over *v.* **1** [late 18C] in fig. use, to cause harm. **2** [late 18C–1900s] to disable, to wear out, to tire out. **3** [late 18C+] to cheat, to defraud. **4** [late 18C+] to beat up. **5** [late 18C+] of a man, to seduce, to have sexual intercourse with. **6** [mid-19C] to rob. **7** [1950s] to search thoroughly. **8** [1950s+] to ransack (a building). [DO v.[1]/DO v.[2] (1) + SE *over*]

doo-wah-diddy *n.* (*also* **diddy-wah-diddy**) [1920s–60s] (*US*) **1** an all-purpose substitute for a word or phr. one does not wish to use properly. **2** an imaginary place, a very distant place, a place one dislikes. [nonsense word derived f. musical rhythms]

doowhacker *n.* [1930s+] any nameless small object, typically some form of gadget. [var. on DOHICKEY n.[1] (1)]

doowhanger *n.* [1920s] (*US*) any nameless small object, typically some form of gadget. [var. on DOOWHACKER n.]

doowop *n.* [1970s] (*US*) a foolish, unimportant person. [SE *doowop*, a musical style esp. popular in the 1950s, featuring vocals sung against a 'backing track' of rhythmically chanted nonsense syllables]

doozer *n.* [1950s+] (*Can.*) anything notably large or outstanding. [var. on DOOZIE n. (1)]

doozie *n.* (*also* **doosie, dooze, doozy, duzey**) **1** [1910s+] (*US*) a thing or person deemed to be extraordinary, remarkable or otherwise noteworthy. **2** [1960s] (*US campus*) a hard examination. [DOOZIE adj.]

doozie *adj.* (*also* **doosy, doozy**) [1900s–20s] (*US*) splendid, wonderful. [? DAISY n.[2] (1) + ? actress Eleanora *Duse* (1859–1924)]

dop *n.[1]* (*S.Afr.*) **1** [late 19C+] brandy; thus *dop and dam*, brandy and water. **2** [1950s+] a drink, a tot; thus *doppie*, 'a little drink', 'just a small one'. [Afk. *dop*, brandy]

dop *n.[2]* [1970s] (*S.Afr.*) **1** one's head or brain. **2** a motorcycle crash helmet. [Du. *dop*, a husk, a shell, used generally for any bowl-shaped or spherical object]

dop *v.* [1950s+] (*S.Afr.*) to fail (an examination). [Afk. *dop*, to fail]

dopalicious *adj.* [2000s] (*US Black*) wonderful. [DOPE adj.[2] (2) + -LICIOUS sfx]

dop down (one's noddle) *v.* [early 18C] to duck (one's head). [SE *dop*, to duck down suddenly (+ NODDLE n. (1))]

dope *n.[1]* **1** [19C+] (*US*) (*also* **doup**) sauce, gravy. **2** [mid-19C+] any preparation, mixture or drug that is not spec. named; thus [1920s] *dope finish*, make-up. **3** [late 19C] (*US*) butter. **4** [late 19C] (*US*) coffee. **5** [late 19C+] (*US*) any form of grease, lubricant, coolant etc. **6** [late 19C+] (*orig. US drugs*) any form of illicit drug; orig. opium but taking in all popular 'recreational' drugs, esp. cannabis. **7** [20C+] (*orig. US*) any form of medicine or medicinal preparation. **8** [1900s–20s] (*Aus./US*) flattery, foolishness, nonsense. **9** [1900s–30s] alcohol, esp. whisky. **10** [1900s–40s] unspecified and wide-ranging 'stuff', varying as to context. **11** [1900s–50s] (*US*) a drug addict. **12** [1910s–20s] (*Aus./US*) an otherwise unspecified poison or adulterant. **13** [1910s–20s] (*US drugs*) a state of drugged intoxication. **14** [1910s–30s] (*US*) (*also* **doup**) a cigarette, a cigarette end. **15** [1910s+] (*US*) Coca-Cola or any other carbonated drink. **16** [1910s+] (*US*) molasses, treacle, syrup. [? SE *daub*, the axle grease used on wagons or Du. *doop*, sauce]

dope *n.[2]* **1** [mid-19C+] an ignoramus, a fool, a simpleton. **2** [1940s+] a pej. term of address. [orig. Cumberland dial.]

dope *n.[3]* [late 19C+] **1** (*orig. US*) any information; thus *get the dope on*, to find out about someone or something. **2** fraudulent information. **3** (*US*) horseracing tips. **4** (*US*) nonsense. **5** (*Aus.*) behaviour. **6** (*US*) a plan, a scheme, an idea. **7** (*US*) the right thing.

dope, the *n.* [1900s] (*US*) the suitable or ideal thing. [fig. use of DOPE n.[1] (2), i.e. a tonic]

dope *adj.[1]* [1930s+] (*US*) foolish, stupid. [DOPE n.[2]]

dope *adj.[2]* **1** [1930s+] pertaining to drugs. **2** [1980s+] (*US Black*) very good, excellent. [lit. and fig. uses of DOPE n.[1] (6); (2) note DOPE, THE n.]

dope *v.[1]* **1** [mid-19C–1930s] (*US*) to apply a lubricant or salve. **2** [mid-19C+] (*orig. US*) to poison, to put drugs into food or drink. **3** [late 19C–1930s] (*US*) to adulterate. **4** [late 19C+] (*orig. US*) to administer drugs (occas. drink) to a person, either to excite them or, usu., to knock them out. **5** [20C+] (*US*) to use 'recreational' drugs. **6** [20C+] (*orig. US*) to stimulate or undermine the performance of a racehorse, or racing. **7** [1900s–20s] (*US*) to give or take medicine. **8** [1910s] (*orig. US*) in fig. use of (6), e.g. to undermine morale. **9** [1910s] (*US*) to drink to excess. **10** [1920s+] (*US Und.*) to tamper with a gambling machine to ensure the house wins. [DOPE n.[1]]

dope *v.[2]* (*also* **dope it, dope out**) **1** [20C+] (*orig. US*) to work (something) out, to assess, esp. in working out possible winners in a horserace. **2** [1910s] (*US*) to train, to study. **3** [1920s] (*US*) to explain. **4** [1930s+] to feed biased or inaccurate information to someone. [DOPE n.[3]]

dope *v.[3]* [20C+] to idle, to loaf about. [DOPE n.[2] (1)]

dope addict *n.* [1930s+] (*orig. US*) a drug addict, orig. an opium addict. [DOPE n.[1] (6) + SE *addict*]

dope book *n.* (*also* **dope sheet**) [late 19C+] (*orig. US*) a book of information on any subject, although usu. horseracing. [DOPE n.[3] (1) + SE *book/sheet*]

dope booster *n.* [1940s–50s] (*US drugs*) a drug seller, esp. when proselytizing new customers/users. [DOPE n.[1] (6) + alternative use of BOOSTER n.[2] (1)]

dope-boy *n.* [1990s+] a drug dealer. [DOPE n.[1] (6) + SE *boy*]

dope city *n.* [1950s+] (*drugs*) any area of a town known for its high level of drugs sales/consumption. [DOPE n.[1] (6) + CITY sfx]

dope crew *n.* [1980s+] (*drugs*) a group of drug dealers who divide up, package and then retail the bulk purchases of the drug (usu. crack cocaine). [DOPE n.[1] (6) + CREW n. (3)]

doped *adj.* **1** [20C+] (*US*) drunk. **2** [20C+] (*orig. US*) under the influence of a drug; also in fig. use. **3** [1910s] addicted to a drug. **4** [1910s+] adulterated with a drug. [DOPE v.[1] (4)/DOPE v.[1] (5)]

dope daddy *n.* [1930s–50s] (*US drugs*) a drug dealer. [DOPE n.[1] (6) + SE *daddy*]

dope doctor *n.* **1** [1940s] (*US*) a general practitioner known for their (over-)prescribing of narcotics. **2** [2000s] a doctor who administers painkillers. [DOPE n.[1] (6)+ SE *doctor*]

doped out *adj.* [1990s+] (*drugs*) passed out through an excess of drugs. [DOPED adj. (2)/DOPE OUT v.[1]]

doped up *adj.* [1930s+] (*drugs*) under the influence of a drug. [DOPE UP v.[1] (1)/ext. DOPED adj. (2)]

dope fiend *n.* **1** [late 19C+] (*drugs*) a user of drugs, in modern use invariably used ironically; also attrib. **2** [1990s+] (*US Black*) *dope fiend move*, a wild, bizarre move, an extreme action taken out of desperation. [DOPE n.[1] (6) + FIEND n.[2] (1)/SE *fiend*; the original use, popularized in the US tabloid press of late 19C, referred to opium; the current incarnation refers to crack cocaine]

dope gun *n.* [1940s] (*US drugs*) a hypodermic syringe. [DOPE n.[1] (6) + GUN n.[1] (3)]

dopehead *n.[1]* [1920s+] (*drugs*) a drug user. [DOPE n.[1] (6) + -HEAD sfx (3)]

dopehead *n.[2]* [1940s–60s] (*US*) a fool. [DOPE n.[2] (1) + -HEAD sfx (1)]

dope hop *n.* **1** [1930s–70s] (*US drugs/prison*) a drug addict. **2** [1950s] (*US drugs*) the euphoric effect of a drug. [DOPE n.[1] (6) + SE *hop*]

dope house *n.* (*also* **dope shop**) [1910s+] (*drugs*) any room or apartment in which drugs are on sale. [DOPE adj.[2] (1) + SE *house/shop*]

dope in *v.* [1960s] (*US*) to explain, to inform, to recount. [DOPE v.[2] (3)]

dope it *v. see* DOPE v.[2].

dopeless *adj.* [1920s] (*US*) a general negative, useless, foolish, socially inadequate. [DOPEY adj.[2] + SE *hopeless*]

dopeman *n.* [1960s+] a drug dealer. [DOPE n.[1] (6) + SE *man*, but note MAN, THE n. (3)]

dope off *v.* **1** [1910s+] (*US*) to fall asleep, to doze off; thus *doped off*, asleep. **2** [1920s+] (*US, mainly milit.*) to be inattentive, to malinger. [DOPE v.[1] (7)]

dope out *v.[1]* [1970s] (*US*) to take drugs; to render oneself intoxicated. [DOPE n.[1] (6)]

dope out *v.[2] see* DOPE v.[2].

dope pad *n.* [1960s+] (*US drugs*) anywhere, e.g. a house, room or apartment, where drug addicts congregate to use drugs. [DOPE adj.[2] (1) + PAD n.[2] (2)]

dope peddler *n. see* PEDDLER n. (3).

doper *n.[1]* [early 17C] a female beggar, often a prostitute. [var. DOPEY n.[1]]

doper *n.[2]* [1910s+] a drug user. [DOPE v.[1] (5)]

doper *adj.* [1970s+] pertaining to drug use/users. [DOPER n.[2]]

dope rope *n.* [1980s+] (*US*) the gold chains sported by well-off drug dealers. [DOPE n.[1] (6) + SE *rope*]

dope sheet *n. see* DOPE BOOK n.

dope shop *n. see* DOPE HOUSE n.

dopeslinger *n.* [1990s+] (*US*) a drug seller. [DOPE n.[1] (6) + SLINGER n.[2]]

dopester *n.[1]* [1910s+] a poisoner. [DOPE v.[1] (2) + -STER sfx]

dopester *n.[2]* [1920s+] a drug user or seller. [DOPE n.[1] (6) + -STER sfx]

dopester *n.[3]* [20C+] (*orig. US*) one who collects information on, and forecasts the result of, sporting events, elections etc. [DOPE v.[2] + -STER sfx]

dope stick *n.* [20C+] **1** a cigarette. **2** a marijuana cigarette (cf. BAT n.[8]). [DOPE n.[1] (6)/DOPE n.[1] (14) + STICK n.[9] (3)]

dope trap *n.* [1960s] (*drugs*) any room or apartment in which drugs are on sale. [DOPE n.[1] (6) + TRAP n.[5] (3)]

dope up *v.[1]* **1** [1910s+] (*orig. US*) to administer drugs (occas. drink) to a person, either to excite them or, usu., to knock them out. **2** [1950s] (*US drugs*) to obtain one's supply of drugs. [DOPE v.[1] (7)/DOPE n.[1] (6)]

dope up *v.[2]* [1920s] (*US Und.*) to tie mustard-oil-soaked rags to one's shoes in order to put dogs off one's scent. [DOPE n.[1] (5)]

dopey *n.[1]* [17C–early 19C] a female beggar, often a prostitute. [poss., as suggested by E.P., Judges and Williams, a misprint for DOXY n. (1) and used interchangably by Dekker; however, note Henke, *Gutter Life and Language* (1988), who sees a link to SE *didapper/dydapper*, often abbr. as *doppe/dopper*, a small diving waterfowl which exhibits its hindquarters when it dives for food]

dopey *n.[2]* [late 18C] the buttocks, the rump. [ety. unknown]

dopey *n.[3]* (*also* **mopey**) [1920s+] a fool, usu. as a term of derog. address. [DOPE n.[2]]

dopey *n.[4] see* DOPIE n.

dopey *adj.[1]* [late 19C+] **1** mildly ill; comatose. **2** drunk (cf. ADDLED adj.). **3** drugged, sedated; used as a nickname for a habitual drug user. **4** sleepy. [DOPE n.[1] + sfx -*y*]

dopey *adj.[2]* (*also* **dopy**) [late 19C+] dull, stupid, vapid. [DOPE n.[2] (1) + sfx -*y*]

dopie *n.* (*also* **dopey**) [1920s–30s] a drug user. [DOPE n.[1] (6) + sfx -*ie/y*]

dopish *adj.* [1930s] (*US*) foolish. [DOPE n.[2] (1)]

dopium *n.* [1950s+] (*drugs*) opium (cf. APOSTLE n.). [DOPE n.[1] (6) + SE *opium*]

dopo *n.* [1940s–70s] a sycophant, a toady. [? DOPE n.[2] (1)]

do-pop *n.* [1970s] (*US prison*) a semi-TRUSTY n.[2]. [ety. unknown]

Dopper *n.* (*also* **Dorper**) [mid-19C+] (*S.Afr.*) a member of the strictly Calvinist Dutch Reformed Church (Gereformeerde Kerk in Suid-Afrika). [? Du. *domper*, an extinguisher, implying the Church's desire to extinguish any form of what it saw as 'progressive' or 'liberal' thinking, theological or otherwise; or ? *dorp*, a village, implying the rural backgrounds of most of its members; or ? *dop*, a shell, referring to the sect's haircuts, which resembled an inverted calabash]

dopper *n.* [1990s+] (*S.Afr.*) a drinker. [DOP n.[1] (2)]

doppess *n.* [20C+] (*US*) **1** a fool; a layabout. **2** an ineffectual observer who in a crisis offers no practical help, merely sympathetic banalities. [? Yiddish *tipesh*, a fool; ult. f. Ger. *Täppisch*, fool. The term ult. is not European Yiddish but an American word that merely seems Yiddish]

doppie *n.* [1940s+] (*S.Afr. Und.*) a measure of tobacco, about 1/40 of an ounce. [Du. *dop*, a shell, thus a container]

doption *n.* [late 19C] an adopted child. [abbr. SE *adoption*]

dopy *adj. see* DOPEY adj.[2].

doradilla *n.* [1970s+] (*drugs*) marijuana (cf. AFRICAN BUSH n.). [Sp. term for a kind of fern, ? resembling marijuana]

do-rag *n.* (*also* **dew rag, doo-rag, rag**) [1960s+] (*US Black*) **1** the scarf or similar cloth that is used to bind up one's newly straightened hair. **2** a bandanna used as part of one's gang insignia. [DO n.[9] + SE *rag*/RAG n.[2] (9)]

dora (gray) *n.* [20C+] (*Aus.*) a threepenny bit. [rhy. sl. = TRAY n. (1)]

do-ray-me *n. see* DO-RE-MI n.

dorc *n. see* DORK n. (2).

dorcas *n.* [late 19C] a seamstress, esp. one who works for a charity. [the sewing woman mentioned in the Bible, Acts 9:36; cf. Lincolnshire dial. *dorcas*, an overdressed woman]

do reason *v.* (*also* **do right**) [17C] to honour a toast, to keep up with a drinking companion.

do-re-mi n. (also **do-ray-me, dough-re-mi**) [20C+] money. [a pun on DOUGH n.[1] (1)/SE do-re-mi, the first 3 notes of a musical scale]

dorf n. (also **dorfy**) [1960s+] (US campus) a fool, an eccentric. [var. on DORK n. (2), but note UK dial. dorfer, an impudent fellow]

dorian love n. [20C+] (gay) homosexuality. [Oscar Wilde's novella The Picture of Dorian Gray (1891)]

do-right n.[1] 1 [1960s] 'first-time patients at Lexington who are considered good prospects for a cure' (Lingeman, Drugs from A to Z, 1969). 2 [1980s+] (US campus) a helpful deed. [DO-RIGHT adj.]

do-right n.[2] see DEPUTY DO-RIGHT n.

do-right adj. [1910s+] (US) law-abiding, honest, socially concerned.

do right v. see DO REASON v.

do-right boys n. [1970s+] (US) the police, esp. the Highway Patrol.

do-right daddies n. see DO-RIGHT PEOPLE n. (2).

do righteous v. [1950s+] (US) to do good (to).

do-righter n. (also **do-rightie**) [1950s] (US) a law-maker, one who lays down the law for others. [i.e. others must do what is 'right']

do-right johns n. see DO-RIGHT PEOPLE n. (1).

do-right man n. [1930s+] (US) a conformist, esp. one who follows rules within an institution. [DO-RIGHT adj. + SE man]

do-right people n. 1 [1930s–40s] (US drugs) (also **do-right johns**) people who are not addicted to narcotics. 2 [1930s+] (US) (also **do-right daddies**) honest citizens. [DO-RIGHT adj.]

Doris n. [1990s+] an older woman.

dork n. [1960s+] (orig. US) 1 the penis. 2 (also **dorc, dorko**) a fool; thus **dork out**, to behave foolishly (cf. CHOAD n.).

dork adj. [1990s+] stupid. [DORK n. (2)]

dork v. [1970s+] (orig. US) of a man, to have sexual intercourse (cf. BAGAGA v.). [DORK n. (1)]

dork around v. [1980s+] (orig. US) 1 to play around, to mess about. 2 to waste time, to act pointlessly. [DORK n. (2)]

dorkbinder n. [2000s] (US Black) a sexual athlete, one of indiscriminate appetites. [DORK n. (1)]

dorkbrain n. [1970s+] (orig. US) a fool (cf. BAKEBRAIN n.). [DORK n. (2) + sfx -brain]

dorkbreath n. [1970s+] an unpleasant person. [DORK n. (2) + sfx -breath]

dorkface n. [1970s+] (US campus/teen) an unpleasant person; thus an insulting term of address. [DORK n. (2) + sfx -face]

dorkhead n. [1980s+] (orig. US teen/campus) a fool. [DORK n. (2) + -HEAD sfx (1)]

dorkmunder n. [1980s+] (US campus) a fool, an idiot. [DORK n. (2) + ? link to Dortmünder Union Pils, a beer, i.e. those who get drunk also get foolish]

dorko n. see DORK n. (2).

dork off v. [1980s+] (US campus) 1 to fool around, to mess about. 2 to disobey orders. [DORK n. (2)]

dork out v. see DORK n. (2).

dorkus (pretentious) n. [1990s+] (US campus) a pretentious fool (cf. DOOFUS n.). [a 'Latinate' var. on DORK n. (2)]

dorky adj. [1970s+] (orig. US campus) odd, weird, bizarre, stupid. [DORK n. (2) + sfx -y]

dorm n. [20C+] (orig. school) a dormitory. [abbr.]

dormie n. (also **dorm frog, dorm rat**) [1960s+] (US campus) a student living in (and rarely leaving) a college dormitory. [DORM n. + sfx -ie]

dormouse n. [19C] the female genitals. [? resemblance]

dornick n. 1 [mid-19C] (US) a coin. 2 [1930s] a (half) brick, as thrown during riots. [Irish dornog, a pebble, a stone]

do-room n. [1970s] (US Black/drugs) a room in which drug addicts gather to inject themselves. [DO v.[8] (4)]

dorothy n. [late 19C] simple, naïve love-making. [an opera, Dorothy (1886), by Alfred Cellier, which featured such activity]

Dorothy Dix n. [1970s+] (Aus. sporting) a 6 in cricket. [proper name Dorothy Dix (pseudonym E.M. Gilmer; 1870–1951), a US journalist, who wrote a popular question-and-answer column]

Dorothy's friend n. (also **friend of Dorothy('s)**) [1960s+] a homosexual (cf. ABIGAIL n.). [Dorothy, the character played by Judy Garland (1922–69), still a deity to large parts of the gay world, in The Wizard of Oz (1939)]

Dorper n. see DOPPER n.

dors and 4s n. (also **dors 'n' fours**) (US drugs) 1 [1980s+] a combination of Doriden and Tylenol. 2 [1990s+] a mixture of codeine and Doriden. [abbr. Doriden + Tylenol 4/Codeine 4]

dorse n. [late 18C–mid-19C] 1 a bed, a lodging (cf. DOSS n.[1]). 2 sleep. [Lat. dorsus, the back, on which the sleeper lies]

dorse v. [late 18C–19C] to sleep. [var. on DOSS v. (1)]

dorse upon the queer roost v. see SLEEP UPON THE QUEER ROOST v.

dors 'n' fours n. see DORS AND 4s n. (1).

dortspeak n. see DART ACCENT n.

dos n. see DOSS n.[1].

dos a reno n. [mid-19C] a sod. [backsl.]

doscus n. (also **dosc**) [1970s+] (US campus) a fool, an idiot (cf. DOOFUS n.). [ety. unknown; ? link to DOSS v. (1), to sleep, thus one who is sleepy]

dose n.[1] [late 17C–18C; 1920s] an act of copulation; the ejaculation of semen.

dose n.[2] [late 17C–mid-19C] (UK Und.) burglary. [DOASH n.]

dose n.[3] 1 [mid-18C+] as much alcohol as one can hold (and prob. more); thus take a grown man's dose, to drink very heavily. 2 [mid-19C] (UK Und.) in fig. use of (1), as much money as is offered.

dose n.[4] [late 18C+] venereal disease. [abbr. dose of the clap]

dose n.[5] [mid-19C] 1 a 3-month sentence. 2 a short sentence. 3 any length of sentence. [SE dose, a definite quantity, on the analogy of a medical prescription]

dose n.[6] 1 [late 19C+] a bad attack of an illness. 2 [20C+] 'a sight'. 3 [1930s] (US Und.) a bullet, a gun shot. 4 [1980s] (Aus.) a distasteful feeling. [SE dose, an unpleasant experience]

dose n.[7] [20C+] (Ulster) a crowd of people. [SE dose, a quantity]

dose n.[8] [1960s+] (UK juv.) a fool.

dose n.[9] see DOASH n.

dose v.[1] [late 19C+] to infect with venereal disease; thus DOSED (UP) adj. [DOSE n.[4]]

dose v.[2] [2000s] (US teen) to give someone a dose of LSD.

dose v.[3] see GIVE SOMEONE A DOSE v. (1).

dosed adj. [20C+] (Irish) impressed. [? one is responding as if energized by a SE dose of salts]

dosed (up) adj. [late 19C+] suffering from venereal disease. [DOSE v.[1]]

dose of locust n. [late 19C] (US, New York City) a thrashing with the fists. [the locust or locust-wood club carried by New York policemen; however, this would seem to negate the use of fists]

doser n. [mid-19C] in boxing, a violent or knockout blow.

dosh n. (also **dush**) [mid-19C; 1950s+] (orig. US) money. [? DOSS n.[1] (1), a place to sleep (note in UK dial. dosh is synon. for doss), thus, by ext., the money needed for accommodation; the term appeared in the US c.1850, then vanished, to re-emerge in the UK in the 1950s]

dosh v. [1980s+] to pay. [DOSH n.]

dosh-burned adj. [late 19C–1900s] (US) a euph. for GOD-DAMN adj. (1).

do social work v. [1970s+] (US gay) to go out of one's way to have an inter-racial sexual partner; thus exhibiting one's liberal credentials. [cynical use of SE]

do someone a nasty v. [1980s+] to do something unpleasant to someone, to cause someone trouble or problems.

do someone a prop v. [1990s+] (US teen) to do someone a favour. [SE prop, support]

do someone a thick 'un v. [1920s+] to play a 'dirty trick' on someone. [SE *do* + *thick 'un*, something heavy, solid]

do someone blind v. [late 19C+] to cheat, to deceive. [DO v.² (1) + BLIND adv.¹]

do someone dirt v. see DO DIRT v.

do someone proud v. see DO ONESELF PROUD v.

do someone's job for them v. **1** [late 19C] to beat, to kill. **2** [late 19C–1920s] to ruin. [var. on DO A JOB ON v.]

do someone the dirty v. (*also* **do the dirty on**) [1910s+] to cheat, to betray, to inform against, to treat harshly.

doss n.¹ (*also* **dos**) **1** [mid-19C+] a place to sleep, a bed, a lodging; thus *do a doss*, to sleep or take to bed. **2** [mid-19C+] a sleep. **3** [late 19C; 1940s–50s] (*orig. UK Und.*) 1 month, as part of a jail sentence. **4** [1920s] (*US*) a rest. [DORSE n.; ult. Lat. *dorsus*, the back, on which the sleeper lies]

doss n.² [1960s] (*US Black*) an attractive woman. [ety. unknown]

doss n.³ [1980s+] something easy to accomplish. [ext. of DOSS n.¹ (2); lit. something one can do 'with one's eyes closed']

doss n.⁴ [1990s+] (*UK juv.*) the last few puffs of a cigarette. [? link to Scot. *doss*, a tobacco-pouch]

doss adj. [1980s+] easy, simple, undemanding; thus a general pej. [DOSS n.³]

doss v. **1** [mid-18C+] to sleep. **2** [late 19C–1900s] (*US*) to lean against. **3** [1960s+] to do nothing, to relax. **4** [1990s+] (*Irish*) to play truant. [DOSS n.¹ (1)]

doss-bag n. [1990s+] (*UK juv.*) an extremely idle person. [DOSS n.¹ (2) + -BAG sfx]

doss down n. [late 19C+] **1** a cheap lodging-house. **2** a sleep. [DOSS DOWN v. (1)]

doss down v. **1** [late 19C+] to fall asleep, usu. on the floor or at some temporary accommodation. **2** [1930s+] (*drugs*) to fall asleep after injecting heroin. [DOSS v. (1)]

dosser n. **1** [mid-19C+] (*also* **dosser-out**) a tramp, a vagrant, a homeless person. **2** [late 19C] the head of a household. **3** [20C+] someone who exists without working. [DOSS v. (1); (2) is the person who pays for/provides the place to sleep]

dossers' hotel n. [20C+] a workhouse or any form of lodging for homeless people. [DOSSER n. (1) + SE *hotel*]

dosshead n. [20C+] a fool, an idiot, a simpleton. [DOSS n.¹ (2) + -HEAD sfx (1); lit. 'sleep head']

dosshouse n. (*also* **doss, kip-house, kip-shop**) [late 19C+] a lodging house, night shelter or similar refuge for homeless people. [DOSS v. (1) + SE *house*]

dossie n. (*also* **dossy**) [late 19C–1920s] a tramp's female companion. [DOXY n. (1) + DOSS v. (1)]

dossing crib n. [mid-19C] a brothel (cf. BADGER-CRIB n.). [DOSS v. (1) + CRIB n.¹ (2)]

doss in the pure v. [late 19C] (*UK tramp*) to sleep in the open air. [DOSS v. (1) + SE *pure*, i.e. unpolluted air]

doss-ken n. (*also* **dossing crib, …drum, …ken**) [mid-19C] a lodging house. [DOSS v. (1) + KEN n.¹ (1)/CRIB n.¹ (1)/DRUM n.³ (6)]

doss-man n. [19C] the keeper of a lodging house. [DOSS n.¹ (1) + SE *man*]

doss-money n. [late 19C] the price of a night's lodging. [DOSS n.¹ (1) + SE *money*]

doss out v. [1910s–20s] to sleep in the open air. [DOSS v. (1)]

doss (out) v. [1990s+] (*Black*) to leave, to run off. [SE *dash*]

doss-ticket n. [late 19C] (*UK tramp*) a ticket giving one the right to a night's lodging. [DOSS n.¹ (1) + SE *ticket*]

dossy n. see DOSSIE n.

dossy adj.¹ [mid-19C–1900s] excellent, first-rate; smart, stylish. [the proletarian pron. of the *Count D'Orsay* (1805–52), a well-known dandy]

dossy adj.² [1940s–50s] ineffectual, weak, 'soft'. [? one who would DOSS v. (1) rather than act]

dossy adj.² [1980s+] easy, effortless. [DOSS n.³ + sfx -y]

do (standing) on one's head v. [late 19C+] to accomplish

something with the minimum of effort, to endure any challenging situation, often used of serving a jail sentence.

dot n.¹ [early 19C] a ribbon; thus *dot-drag*, a watch ribbon. [? Du. *dot*, a twirled knot of silk or thread]

dot n.² **1** [mid-19C] (*US Und.*) a useless person. **2** [late 19C] (*Aus.*) the face. **3** [late 19C] (*US*) an attractive young woman. **4** [1950s+] (*Aus.*) the anus. **5** [1960s+] (*lesbian*) the clitoris (cf. BABY IN THE BOAT n.). [lit. or fig. resemblance]

dot v. [late 19C+] to punch someone, esp. in the eye; thus *dot someone one*, to hit someone a blow. [SE *dot*, a mark, a spot]

dot and carried adj. [20C+] married. [rhy. sl.]

dot and carry one n. (*also* **dot and go one**) [late 18C+] a person with a wooden leg or a club foot. [the dot is the impression made by the bottom of the wooden leg, in an era before properly moulded 'feet' were available, while the good leg is 'carried']

dot and dash n. **1** [1920s–40s] (*US*) a moustache. **2** [1950s+] money (cf. BEES (AND HONEY) n.). [rhy. sl.; (2) = SE *cash*]

dot and go one v. [late 18C+] to waddle or hobble, esp. of those who have lost a leg. [DOT AND CARRY ONE n.]

dot and go one! excl. [early 19C] a general excl. of dismissal. [DOT AND GO ONE v.]

do tell! excl. [mid-19C+] **1** an exhortation to someone to impart a piece of juicy gossip. **2** a sarcastic or ironic rejoinder to a piece of information in which one has no interest.

dotey adj.¹ (*also* **doty**) [1920s+] (*Irish*) cute, charming; thus *dote*, a cute person or thing. [dial. *doty*, a general term of affection, usu. of a child; ult. SE *dote* (*upon*)]

dotey adj.² see DOTEY adj.¹.

do the — v. see DO THE — (THING) v.

do the — act v. (*also* **play the…, pull the…**) [late 19C+] (*US*) to pretend to a particular (by context) style of behaviour, to assume (often deceitfully) specific characteristics.

dothead n. [1980s+] (*US*) a derog. term for an Indian (cf. CURRY-MUNCHER n.). [the Hindu *bindi* or caste mark worn by married women]

do the aqua v. [mid-19C–1900s] to add water to a drink. [Ital. *acqua*, water]

do the bear v. [late 19C] (*Mex./US*) a form of courtship that involves hugging. [Sp. *hacer el oso*, do the bear; such 'hands-on' courtship was sanctioned in Mexico]

do the beat v. see BASH THE BEAT v.

do the big phr. [late 19C] (*Irish*) to self-aggrandize.

do the (big) nasty v. [1960s+] **1** (*orig. US*) to have sexual intercourse. **2** (*US Black*) to perform cunnilingus. [NASTY n.¹ (2)]

do the biz v. see DO THE BUSINESS v.

do the block v. [mid-19C–1930s] (*Aus.*) **1** (*also* **run the block**) to promenade along a variety of fashionable blocks or stretches of city street; thus *the Block*, Collins Street; *Blockite*, a fashionable individual, given to such a promenade. **2** in fig. use, to show off, to gain acclaim. [the major blocks are Collins Street between Swanston and Elizabeth Streets in Melbourne, and George Street in Sydney]

do the bolt v. see BOLT v. (6).

do the book v. [1920s+] (*US Und.*) to serve a life sentence. [DO v.⁹ (1) + THROW THE BOOK AT v.]

do the book and cover v. [1920s+] (*US Und.*) to be imprisoned for the rest of one's natural life. [ext. DO THE BOOK v.]

do the bowling hold v. see TENPIN v.

do the briny v. [mid-19C] to burst into tears; to weep.

do the brown eye express v. see BROWN EYE n. (2).

do the business v. (*also* **do the biz**) **1** [17C+] to act in the manner required. **2** [mid-18C+] to murder, to kill. **3** [mid-19C+] to settle a matter conclusively. **4** [1980s+] to succeed. [SE *business*/ BUSINESS n.¹]

do the — business v. [late 19C–1900s] to act in a given manner, as defined by the n. [DO THE BUSINESS v. (1)]

do the chewy v. [1980s] (*Aus.*) to become angry. [? one gnashes ones teeth/chews one's lips]

do the civil v. [mid-19C–1950s] to act in a civil manner, to do 'the right thing'.

do the clam v. *see* CLAM (UP) v. (2).

do the dance v. [1920s] (*US*) to be hanged. [the twitching of the victim's feet; DANCE v.²]

do the — dance v. [late 19C] to act in a given manner, presumably active, defined by the n.

do the deadly deed v. [1980s+] (*US campus*) to have sexual intercourse without using a contraceptive. [ext. of DO THE DEED (OF DARKNESS) v.]

do the deed (of darkness) v. [late 16C–17C; late 19C+] to have sexual intercourse.

do the dirty v. **1** [1990s+] (*US*) to commit a crime; to murder. **2** [2000s] to vomit.

do the dirty (deed) v. (*also* **do the dirties**) [1960s+] (*orig. US teen/campus*) to have sexual intercourse. [note RMC Duntroon (Aus.) *dirtie, dirty,* a weekend of sex with one's girlfriend, i.e. a 'dirty weekend'; *Current Slang* IV (1970) suggests 'applies only to girls']

do the dirty on v. *see* DO SOMEONE THE DIRTY v.

do the do v.¹ [1990s+] (*US Black*) to pass time.

do the do v.² *see* DO n.⁷.

do the — dodge (over) v. *see* DODGE n. (1).

do the dog v.¹ [1980s] (*US*) to show off, to strut about. [var. PUT ON DOG v. (1)]

do the dog v.² *see* DOG v.¹ (3).

do the double act v. [1910s–20s] to get married.

do the double (on) v. [mid-19C–1920s] (*Aus.*) to double-cross.

do the downy v. *see* DOWNY n.².

do the fish v. [1970s+] to suffer blackouts, seizures or convulsions following the inhalation of nitrous oxide. [the image of a fish out of water, struggling for air]

do the (five-)knuckle shuffle (on the old piss pump) v. [1970s+] to masturbate (cf. AUDITION THE FINGER PUPPETS v.).

do the full sesh v. (*also* **go full sesh**) [1980s] (*US teen*) to indulge completely, to take to the limit. [abbr. SE *session*]

do the generous v. [1900s] (*Aus.*) to act magnanimously.

do the gentleman v. [1920s] to urinate.

do the graceful v. [late 19C] to fascinate, to charm.

do the grand v. [mid-19C–1920s] to make a great display, to put on airs. [GRAND adj.¹]

do the handsome (thing) v. *see* HANDSOME adj. (2).

do the heavy v. [late 19C+] to swagger, to show off. [HEAVY adj.¹ (3)]

do the honours v. [mid-19C+] to take on the role of host in pouring out alcoholic drinks, or any drink; also in fig. use, to engage in sexual intercourse.

do the hook v. [1930s] (*US Und.*) to serve a life sentence. [? misprint for DO THE BOOK v.]

do the humpty-hump v. *see* HUMPTY n.¹.

do the job v. [mid-17C–1970s] to have sexual intercourse. [ext. of JOB v.¹ (1)]

do the job on v. *see* DO A JOB ON v. (1).

do the knuckle shuffle (on the old piss pump) v. *see* DO THE (FIVE-)KNUCKLE SHUFFLE (ON THE OLD PISS PUMP) v.

do the lardy v. *see* LARDY-DARDY adj.

do the lolly v. (*also* **do one's lolly**) [1940s+] (*Aus.*) to lose one's temper, to lose control of one's emotions or senses. [LOLLY n.¹]

do the long trot v. [mid-late 19C] to go home.

do the lot v. *see* DO v.¹⁰ (2).

do the math phr. [2000s] (*US Black*) a phr. ordering someone to work it out, to do the calculations; the implication is that what the speaker has just said 'adds up'.

do the mean v. [mid-19C] to act in an unpleasant manner. [SE *mean,* unpleasant]

do the milk route v. [1970s+] of one who is searching for or selling sex, to tour bus stations or other such places very late at night or very early in the morning looking for trade. [the image of a milk roundsman]

do the mollycoddle v. *see* MOLLYCODDLE n.

do the naked pretzel v. [1990s+] (*US campus*) to have sexual intercourse. [supposed resemblance to a SE *pretzel,* a crisp biscuit, baked in the form of a knot]

do the nasty v. *see* DO THE (BIG) NASTY v.

do the natural thing v. (*also* **get down to the natural thing**) [1970s–80s] (*US Black*) to have sexual intercourse. ['just as nature intended']

do the needful v. *see* NEEDFUL n. (1).

do the Newgate frisk v. [19C] to be hanged. [*Newgate* prison, outside which public hangings were held + *frisk,* to twitch (in one's death agonies)]

do the overdo v. [20C+] (*W.I., Guyn.*) to take things too far. [SE *do,* anything done]

do the polite v. [mid-19C–1930s] to act courteously.

do the pork sword jiggle v. *see* PORK SWORD n.

do the push v. *see* STAND THE PUSH v.

do the rosy v. [mid-late 19C] to enjoy oneself, to have a good time. [? ROSY, THE n.² or SE *rosy,* pleasant, enjoyable, positive]

do the seven v. *see* THROW A SEVEN v. (1).

do the shallow v. [mid-late 19C] to dress in rags to enhance one's appeal as a beggar. [SHALLOW DODGE n.]

do the slide v. *see* SLIDE v.¹.

do the slums v. *see* SLUM v.³ (1).

do the soft (on) v. **1** [late 19C] to make love. **2** [1910s–20s] to flatter. [SOFT SOAP n.]

do the spin v. [late 19C+] (*Aus.*) to toss the coins in a game of two-up.

do the story with v. [18C] of a prostitute, to have sex with. [SE *the old, old story;* the basic falsehood underlying the exchange of counterfeit affection for money]

do the — (thing) v. [mid-19C+] to perform a particular action, as defined by the missing adj. (or n.) and sometimes the word *thing;* thus *do the amiable* (*thing*), *do the charming* (*thing*), *do the civil* (*thing*), *do the study thing.* [all such terms have a slight air of insincerity or at least of calculated performance, although they may equally well be quite genuine]

do the thing v.¹ [1970s+] (*US gay*) to pursue a homosexual lifestyle. [THING n.⁵ (1)/SE *thing* but note THING n.⁴ (1) and THING n.²]

do the thing v.² *see* DO A THING v.

do the tight(e)ner v. [mid-19C] (*costermonger*) to have dinner. [TIGHTENER n., i.e. it *tightens* one's belly]

do the trick v. **1** [late 17C; mid-19C+] of a man, to have sexual intercourse. **2** [early 19C] (*UK Und.*) to blunder. **3** [early–mid-19C] (*orig. UK Und.*) to get what one wants, to succeed. **4** [late 19C] of a woman, to lose one's virginity, to be deflowered. **5** [late 19C] to impregnate a woman. **6** [1910s] (*Aus.*) to get married. [(3) is SE from mid-19C]

do the trick of the loop v. [1920s] to have sexual intercourse. [Gifford, *Ulysses Annotated* (1988): '"the trick of the loop", a carnival game in which the contestants try to win prizes by pitching small wooden hoops at a group of upright stakes']

do the two-fingered shuffle v. (*also* **do the two-fingered tango**) [1990s+] of a woman, to masturbate (cf. APPLY LIP GLOSS v.; AUDITION THE FINGER PUPPETS v.).

do the vonce v. [1950s] (*US Black/jazz*) to have sexual intercourse. [ety. unknown]

do the wacky v. [1990s+] to lose emotional control. [coined in late 1990s US TV show *Buffy the Vampire Slayer*]

do the wild thing v. [1980s+] (*US Black/campus*) to have sexual intercourse.

do things to v. (*also* **do things for**) [1930s+] to excite someone, usu. sexually.

do time v. 1 [mid-19C+] to serve a prison sentence. 2 [1910s+] in ext. use, irrespective of the institution. [DO v.⁹ (1) + TIME n.¹]

dot on the card n. 1 [1950s–60s] (UK Und.) a well-known individual or criminal, often too well-known. 2 [1960s] a certainty. [image of making a form of notation, e.g. on a register]

do to rights v. [late 19C] to perform satisfactorily, to do properly. [TO RIGHTS adv.]

do to wainrights v. [late 19C] to perform satisfactorily; an intensification of DO TO RIGHTS v. [pun on rights + ref. to Thomas Wainewright (1794–1852), an alleged murderer who was transported to Tasmania in 1826, but for forgery, not homicide]

dots n.¹ 1 [mid-19C+] money. 2 [1910s–30s] (UK Und.) piano keys. [? shape of coins]

dots n.² [1970s+] (drugs) LSD (cf. A n.³). [abbr. MICRODOT n.]

dot someone one v. see DOT v.

dotted adj. [late 19C] having a black eye. [DOT v.]

dotterel n. (also **dodderil, doderill**) [late 16C–19C] a dupe, a victim of a confidence trickster or fraudster; a fool. [SE dotterel, a species of plover (Eudromias morinellus); the name comes f. SE dote, to be silly or foolish or to act foolishly, the dotterel, whether bird or human allows itself to be 'taken' easily]

dot the 'i' v. [1970s+] (US gay) to have anal intercourse (cf. ASK FOR THE RING v.). [to put the DOT n.² (4) on the 'i' (i.e. add the anus to a straight line/penis); note the usual use of EYE n.¹ (2) or EYE sfx to mean anus]

dotties man n. [late 19C] a greedy, grasping person. [DOTS n.¹ (1)]

dotty adj. [late 19C+] 1 unstable, unsteady on one's feet. 2 (also **dotty in the dome**) eccentric, odd; thus dottiness, eccentricity. 3 in love with, desirous of. [orig. dial; phr. dotty on one's pins, unsteady on one's legs and thence in one's brain + ? link to DOT AND GO ONE v.]

do twelve-ounce curls v. [1980s+] (US campus) to drink beer. [a play on weight-lifting jargon; the 'curling' of the arm as when lifting a 12oz beer can to the lips]

doty adj.¹ (also **dotey**) [20C+] (US) senile, weak-minded (through old age). [dial. doty, old wood that is crumbling away or abbr. SE dotage, feeble-minded old age; both terms have the same source, MDu. doten, to be crazy]

doty adj.² see DOTEY adj.¹.

doub n. see DOUBLER n.² (3).

double n.¹ [late 18C–19C] a trick; thus tip the double, to cheat, to hoax; give the double, to escape (from one's creditors); put the double on, to bypass, to circumvent (trouble). [abbr. SE doublecross]

double n.² [20C+] (US) a $20 bill. [abbr. DOUBLE SAWBUCK n. (1)]

double n.³ [1920s+] 1 a pornographic picture that offers both the male and female genitals. 2 a sex show involving 2 women. [Williams has 17C double, 'allusive of copulation']

double v.¹ [early 19C] 1 to run off, to escape. 2 to avoid, to elude, to give the slip to. [SE double, to turn sharply and suddenly in running, to turn back on one's course]

double v.² 1 [mid–late 19C] to double-cross. 2 [1900s] (US campus) to go out on a date. 3 [1930s] (US tramp) to sleep with someone, to have sexual intercourse. 4 [1930s+] (US) to double-date, i.e. for 2 couples to go out together. 5 [1960s+] to act as a double-agent. 6 [1990s+] to double-park. [abbr./fig. use of SE double]

double adv. [mid-19C+] a general intensifier, e.g. double-choked, double-good, DOUBLE-QUICK adj.

double-arsed adj. [19C+] having very large buttocks. [SE double + -ARSED sfx¹]

double bag and stumper n. [1990s+] a very unattractive young woman. [ext. DOUBLE-BAGGER n.; she is so ugly that one would have to place paper bags over both participants' heads in order to face up to intercourse, and one would, in any case, rather cut off all one's limbs than have sex with her]

double-bagger n. (also **two-bagger**) [1980s+] (US) an intensely unappealing person, usu. used of an unattractive woman. [either

based on the need to place not just 1 but 2 bags over her before having sex or the need for each participant to be covered with a bag; note synon. RMC Duntroon (Aus.) bag job, two bag job]

double-banger n. [1980s+] (N.Z.) a multi-orgasmic woman. [SE double + bang, i.e. the 'explosion' of the orgasm]

double-bank v. 1 [late 19C–1940s] (US) to trick, to double-cross. 2 [late 19C+] (US) to attack as a gang. 3 [late 19C+] (Aus./N.Z.) to carry 2 people on a single horse. 4 [1930s] to have 2 drinks standing in front of one. 5 [1930s+] (Aus./N.Z.) to give someone a lift on the crossbar of a bicycle; thus doubling, the act of doing this (cf. BUNK v.⁵). [SAusE double-bank, to yoke together 2 oxen]

double-barrel n.¹ [late 19C] a pair of field-glasses or opera-glasses. [SE double-barrel, a double-barrelled gun]

double-barrel n.² [1990s+] of a man, more than 1 orgasm in a single session of sex. [note Cleland, Memoirs of a Woman of Pleasure (1748–9): 'My hot-mettled spark [...] loaded for a double-fire, recontinu'd the sweet battery with undying vigour']

double-barrelled adj. 1 [mid-19C–1960s] (US) extreme, utter, complete. 2 [late 19C] used of a woman enjoying simultaneous vaginal and anal intercourse. 3 [late 19C+] used of a lesbian, e.g. double-barrelled broad. 4 [1970s+] (US gay) of a woman, heterosexual, e.g. double-barrelled broad.

double-barrelled ghee n. [1970s] (gay) a male homosexual. [DOUBLE-BARRELLED adj. (4) + GHEE n.¹; i.e. his mouth and anus]

double-barrels n. [20C+] (US) men's long underwear.

double bassing n. [1990s+] performing rear-entry intercourse, with the man's hands respectively on a breast and the clitoris.

double black dog dare v. see DOUBLE DOG v.

double blue n. see BLUE n.⁹ (3).

double-bottomed adj. [late 19C–1900s] insincere, hypocritical. [? one 'bottom' is false]

double-breasted adj. [mid-19C–1930s] excellent, admirable, impressive; a general intensifier.

double-breasted feet n. see DOUBLE-BREASTERS n.

double-breasted water-butt smasher n. [late 19C] a strong, athletically built man.

double-breasters n. (also **double-breasted feet**) [late 19C] the feet, esp. when one or both is a club foot.

double bubble n. [1980s+] a double portion, an extra helping.

double bubblegum n. [1990s+] (drugs) a variety of potent marijuana. [ety. unknown]

double-bunk v. [1990s+] (US prison) of 2 inmates, to share a cell.

double burger (with cheese) n. see BURGER (WITH CHEESE) n.

double Cape Horn v. [late 18C–early 19C] to be made a cuckold. [pun on the cuckold's HORNS n. + the naut. ref.]

double carpet n. [20C+] (UK prison) a 6-month sentence. [SE double + CARPET n.² (1)]

double-click one's mouse v. [1990s+] (Aus. teen) of a woman, to masturbate.

double-clutch v. 1 [1960s] (US) to have sexual intercourse. 2 [1980s+] (US drugs) to take more than one's share of a communally smoked marijuana cigarette; US smokers ritually take only 1 puff before passing on their cigarette. [trucker jargon double-clutch, to change gears by changing first to neutral, then selecting the desired, usu. lower gear. The clutch is disengaged at each stage. The link to the drug use is the idea of doing something twice]

double-clutcher n. [1960s+] (US) a euph. for MOTHERFUCKER n. (1).

double-clutching adj. [1960s+] (US) a euph. for MOTHERFUCKING adj. (1).

doublecross n. [1970s+] (drugs) amphetamine (cf. A n.²). [the crosses stamped into the pill]

double-cunted adj. [mid-19C+] possessed of a large vagina. [SE double + CUNT n.¹ (1)]

double darse dare v. see DOUBLE DOG v.

double dash v. (also **double damn**) [mid-19C; 1970s] a more emphatic version of DASH v. [DOUBLE adv. + DASH v./DAMN v.]

double-decker n. **1** [early 19C] a form of shackles. **2** [late 19C] (US) a double-strength cocktail, used as a pick-me-up.

double deuce n. [1990s+] (US Black) a .22 calibre handgun. [SE double + DEUCE n.¹ (1)]

double-diddied adj. [19C+] having large breasts. [SE double + DIDDIES n.]

double dime n. [1960s–70s] (US) **1** $20 (cf. CENT n.). **2** 20 years. [SE double + DIME n.¹ (1)]

double-dink v. see DINK v.

double-distilled adj. **1** [19C+] worst. **2** [late 19C+] (Aus.) excellent, very best.

double dog v. (also **double black dog dare, double darse…, double nigger…, double niggle…**) [20C+] (US) to challenge defiantly.

double dome n. (also **big dome**) [1930s+] an intellectual, a scholar, esp. one who seems to hold eccentric or impractical opinions. [SE double + DOME n. (1)]

doubledonger n. [1990s+] (US) a dildo with 2 penis-shaped ends which can be used simultaneously by 2 people, usu. women. [SE double + DONG n.¹ (1)]

double dreads n. [1980s+] (drugs) a mixture of amphetamine and LSD.

double-dugged adj. [19C+] having large breasts. [SE double + DUGS n.]

double Dutch n. [mid-19C+] unintelligible gibberish. [later var. on HIGH DUTCH n.]

double-ender n. [mid–late 19C] (UK Und.) **1** a type of purse. **2** a skeleton key. **3** a fist.

double event n. **1** [late 19C] of a man, a simultaneous bout of syphilis and gonorrhoea. **2** [late 19C] of a woman, an act of intercourse that both deflowers the woman and leaves her pregnant. **3** [20C+] (mainly Glasgow) an order of a shot of whisky alongside a pint of beer.

double fair! excl. [1950s+] the intensified version of FAIR ENOUGH phr. – extremely satisfactory. [DOUBLE adv. + SE fair]

double fin n. (also **double finn, …finnif, …finnup**) **1** [mid–late 19C] a £10 note. **2** [1940s] (US Und.) a 10-year jail sentence. **3** [1940s+] (US) a $10 bill. [SE double + FIN n.²]

double-fisted adj. [mid-19C+] (US) tough, strong, over-sized.

double-fuck! excl. [1960s+] (US) an intensified form of FUCK! excl. (1). [DOUBLE adv.]

double-fucking adj. [1910s+] an intensified form of FUCKING adj. (1). [DOUBLE adv.]

double-gaited adj. [1920s+] (US) bisexual. [SE gait, a manner of walking]

double-glazing n. [1990s+] (UK juv.) an insult aimed at a spectacles-wearer.

double guts n. **1** [early 19C+] a very fat person. **2** [20C+] (US) a large stomach, a pot belly. [SE double + GUTS n.¹ (1)/-GUTS sfx]

double-gutted adj. [early–late 19C] very fat. [DOUBLE GUTS n. (1)]

double harness n. [mid-19C+] (US) marriage; usu. as jump in a double harness, take on a double harness, to get married; run in double harness, to dance with a partner. [coaching imagery]

double-headed adj. [20C+] (US Black) very clever, exceptionally intelligent. [the idea of having 2 brains; the orig. use comes f. hoodoo, a variant form of voodoo]

double-header n. **1** [late 19C–1940s] (Aus.) a double measure of a drink. **2** [1920s+] (US) a second act of intercourse with a prostitute in a single session. **3** [1970s] mutual oral-genital stimulation.

double-hocked adj. [mid–late 19C] having very thick ankles.

double in brass v. [1910s+] (orig. US) to have a wide range of abilities; to perform more than one's primary job. [circus/ vaudeville jargon double in brass, to perform one's own speciality as well as play in the orchestra]

double jugg n. (also **double juggs**) [late 17C–19C] the buttocks.

double-life man n. [1940s–60s] a bisexual man.

double master-blaster n. [1980s] (drugs) an orgasm reached through fellatio at the same time as one is smoking a pipe of crack cocaine.

double maw n. [1920s–60s] (US Black) a grandmother. [SE double + dial. pron. maw, ma, i.e. mother]

double-mouthed adj. [19C] having a notably large mouth.

double-narky n. [1950s] (US drugs) a double dose of one's preferred drug.

double nickel n. **1** [1970s+] (US) the 55mph (88.5kph) speed limit, introduced nationally in 1974; thus the road itself. **2** [1990s+] (US prison) a 10-year sentence. [SE double + NICKEL n.¹ (5)/NICKEL n.¹ (3)]

double nigger/niggle dare v. see DOUBLE DOG v.

double-O n.¹ [1910s–60s] a hard look, a serious, studious look. [the resemblance to a pair of eyes or glasses]

double-O n.² [1920s–30s] (US Und.) an act of betrayal.

double-O n.³ [1940s] (US) nothing, zero.

double-O n.⁴ [1990s+] (US prison) prison-issue bread.

double-O v. **1** [1910s–50s] (US) to stare at, to survey. **2** [1920s] to double-cross. [DOUBLE-O n.¹]

double one's milt v. [19C] to ejaculate twice without withdrawing. [MILT n.]

double-Os n. [1970s+] (US prison) Kool brand cigarettes. [the 'double-o' of the sp.]

double pay n. [1980s+] (Aus.) the upmarket Sydney suburb of Double Bay. [the area's inflated prices and the incomes of those who live there]

double peachy adj. see PEACHY adj.

double-plated blowhard n. [late 19C] (US) a consummate braggart. [SE double-plated + BLOWHARD n.¹]

double plus ungood adj. see UNGOOD adj.

double punch v. [1980s] (US Black) to assault in a group.

double-quick adj. [1920s+] extremely fast. [DOUBLE adv. + SE quick]

doubler n.¹ [early 19C] an extremely severe blow. [it causes the recipient to SE double up; note DOUBLE UP v.¹ (1)]

doubler n.² **1** [mid-19C] (N.Z.) a double portion of drink, 2 shots of a spirit in the same glass. **2** [late 19C+] (UK Und.) a corrupt policeman who not only takes the offered bribe but still arrests one for the crime. **3** [1950s+] (Aus.) (also **doub, dub, dubb**) a lift on a bicycle crossbar (cf. BUNK v.⁵).

double-ribbed adj. [17C–19C] pregnant. [i.e. the mother's ribs plus those of her unborn child]

double rough n. [1970s] (US prison) a 50-year sentence.

double-rough adj. [1970s] (US prison) serious, hard. [DOUBLE ROUGH n.]

double sawbuck n. (also **double saw, double sawski**) **1** [mid-19C+] (US) $20. **2** [1930s+] (US/Can. prison) a 20-year prison sentence. **3** [1970s] (US prison) a 25-year prison sentence. [SE double + SAWBUCK n.]

double shot n. [1970s+] 2 ejaculations of semen during a single bout of intercourse. [SHOT n.²]

double-shotted adj. [mid–late 19C] of a mixed drink, containing a double measure of alcohol. [milit. use double-shotted, loaded with 2 cannon balls]

double shuffle n. **1** [mid-19C–1960s] a double-cross; thus come the double shuffle, to double-cross. **2** [late 19C] (UK Und.) the act of repeatedly walking up and down one's prison cell. **3** [1930s] a quick getaway. [farming jargon double shuffle, a sudden shift of bucking style by a bronco, intended to throw an unwanted rider. Note also UK double shuffle, a shuffling, noisy dance, once popular among costermongers]

double-six n. [1940s] (US Black) a year, i.e. 12 months.

double slagging *n.* [1980s+] (*Aus. prison*) a 20-year jail sentence.

double slangs *n.* [early 19C] double irons. [SE *double* + SLANG n.² (1)]

double-sucker *n.* [late 19C] the labia minora, esp. when prominent (cf. CUNT-LIPS n.).

double-take *n.* [1940s+] (*orig. US*) a second glance, esp. when one 'cannot believe one's eyes' after the first one; thus intensified as *triple-take*. [film jargon]

double-take *v.* [1940s+] to look at twice (to confirm one's initial disbelief). [DOUBLE-TAKE n.]

double-team *v.* [mid-19C+] (*US*) **1** to gang up on, to use extra force against. **2** to work as a pair. [farming jargon *double-team*, to employ 2 teams of animals to haul heavy weights through difficult terrain; subseq. adopted in football use]

double-thumper *n.* [mid–late 19C] an especially audacious lie. [SE *double* + THUMPER n.² (2)]

double-time *n.* [1950s] an act of betrayal, esp. adultery. [TWO-TIME v.]

double-tongued squib *n.* [mid-19C] a double-barrelled shotgun. [SE *double-tongued* + SQUIB n.²]

double tripe *n.*¹ (*also* **Mr Double Tripes**) [late 17C–early 19C] an exceptionally fat man. [TRIPE n.¹]

double tripe *n.*² [early 19C] (*UK Und.*) lead, as used on roofs etc. [? its resemblance to thick sheets of tripe]

double trouble *n.* [1960s+] (*drugs*) Tuinal. [Tuinal is a mixture of Seconal and Amytal]

double-U *n.* [late 19C–1910s] a euph. for the lavatory. [pron. of W.C.]

double up *v.*¹ [19C] (*orig. boxing*) **1** to cause someone to collapse. **2** to die. **3** to defeat, to stop someone in their tracks. [SE *double up*, to bend double, to collapse]

double up *v.*² **1** [19C+] (*US*) to get married, to become engaged, to live together. **2** [mid-19C+] to share quarters. **3** [1920s] (*US Und.*) to work as a team. **4** [1980s+] for a man to have sexual intercourse with 2 women.

double up *v.*³ (*also* **dub**) [1980s+] (*US drugs*) for a crack dealer to offer '2 for the price of 1'.

double-ups *n.* [1990s+] (*drugs*) a $20 piece of crack cocaine that can be broken into 2 pieces, each of which is then sold for $20.

double whammy *n.* [1950s+] a double blow, an extreme problem; an intensifier of WHAMMY n. (2). [best known as the title of US thriller-writer Carl Hiaasen's 1988 novel; the term was central to the rival Conservative Party's advertising campaign in the general election of 1992 (attempting to point up the UK Labour Party threats to the UK economy)]

double-X *n.*¹ **1** [early 19C] (*US*) something superlative, outstanding. **2** [mid-19C] (*UK*) strong beer. [racetrack jargon *double-X*, the horse most likely to win; thus the optimum bet]

double-X *n.*² (*also* **XX**) (*US*) **1** [mid-19C–1910s] $20, a $20 bill. **2** [1930s+] an act of doublecrossing; also as *v.* [*X* as (1) Roman numeral 10, (2) the mark of a cross]

double-yolker *n. see* EGG n.¹ (2).

double zero *n.*¹ [1990s+] (*drugs*) prime grade hashish (cf. AFGHAN n.).

double zero *n.*² *see* ZERO n. (1).

doubling *n. see* DOUBLE-BANK v. (5).

doubloon *n.* [late 19C+] money. [SE *doubloon*, a Spanish coin orig. worth a half-pistole, i.e. 33–36 shillings]

doucer *n.* [mid-19C–1920s] (*UK Und.*) a bribe, a 'sweetener'. [orig. Fr.; SE *douceur*, 'A conciliatory present or gift; a gratuity or "tip"; a bribe' (*OED*)]

douchebag *n.* (*also* **d.b.**, **douch**, **doucher**) **1** [1950s+] (*US*) a term of general abuse, directed esp. at women; thus *have a face like a douchebag*, to be very ugly. **2** [1900s] a lesbian. [SE *douchebag*; note RMC Duntroon (Aus.) *douchebag*, an ill-kempt, unintelligent cadet (cf. -BAG sfx)]

douche can alley *n.* [1910s–50s] (*Aus.*) Palmer Street, Sydney – the city's red-light area. [the use of douches by the street's prostitutes + pun on music's *Tin Pan Alley*]

doudon *n.* [late 17C; 1910s–20s] a short, fat woman. [? SE *dowdy*]

doufas/doufus *n. see* DOOFUS n.

dough *n.*¹ (*also* **doe**) **1** [mid-19C+] (*orig. US*) money; thus *dough up*, to pay; IN THE DOUGH *phr.* (cf. BATTER n.⁴). **2** [1940s] (*UK Und.*) counterfeit coins. [the idea of bread as an essential constituent of life]

dough *n.*² *see* DOUGHBOY n.¹.

dough *adj.* [20C+] (*US campus*) excellent, first-rate. [DOUGH n.¹ (1)]

dough-baked *adj.* (*also* **dow-baked**) [late 16C] stupid, dull.

doughbanger *n.* [late 19C+] (*Aus.*) a cook; thus *dough-banging*, cooking.

doughbelly *n.* (*also* **dough-ring**) [1940s+] (*US*) a large stomach; thus a very fat person; thus *doughbellied*, fat.

dough boxer *n. see* DOUGH ROLLER n.

doughboy *n.*¹ (*also* **doe-boy**, **dough**, **doughfoot**) [mid-19C+] (*orig. US milit.*) a US soldier, orig. those serving in the Mexican War *c.*1847. [? the large round buttons worn by Civil War soldiers, reminiscent of the doughnuts or the boiled dumplings, based on flour and rice and known as *doughboys*, that were a military staple; or f. the *dough* or pipeclay used to clean US soldiers' belts in mid-19C; note Mencken, *The American Language* (3rd edn, 1936): 'Doughboy is an old English navy term for dumpling. It was formerly applied to the infantry only, and its use is said to have originated in the fact that the infantrymen once pipe-clayed parts of their uniforms, with the result that they became covered with a doughy mass when it rained']

doughboy *n.*² [1910s+] a punch in the face; usu. in *phr. give someone a doughboy*, to punch someone in the face.

dough-brain *n.* [1980s+] (*US campus*) someone who acts foolishly or as if they have not been thinking.

doughface *n.* (*US*) **1** [mid-19C] a malleable person, esp. a Northern politician who accepts slavery. **2** [20C+] a woman who wears an excess of cosmetics. [SE *doughface*, a whiteface mask made orig. of flour and water and used for fancy dress; a *doughface* and a white sheet rendered the wearer a 'ghost'; coined by John Randolph of Roanoke]

doughfoot *n. see* DOUGHBOY n.¹.

dough-god(s) *n. see* DOUGH-JEHOVAHS n.

doughguts *n.* [mid-19C] (*US*) an extremely fat person. [SE *dough* + -GUTS sfx, i.e. resemblance]

dough-head *n.* **1** [19C+] (*US*) a very silly or stupid person. **2** [1920s–60s] (*US tramp*) a baker. [SE *dough* + -HEAD sfx (1)]

dough-Jehovahs *n.* (*also* **dough-god(s)**) [late 19C–1910s] a form of meat stew or pastry. [ety. unknown]

doughnut *n.*¹ [late 19C] (*US*) a baker. [one of his popular products]

doughnut *n.*² **1** [1920s+] a rubber tyre. **2** [1930s] (*US Black*) the vagina (cf. APPLE n.⁶). **3** [1980s] of a woman, a state of sexual excitement, supposedly the vaginal equivalent of the penile erection. **4** [1980s] (*Aus.*) the anus (cf. BAKERY GOODS n.). [resemblance]

doughnut *n.*³ **1** [1920s] a rich fool (cf. APPLEHEAD n.). **2** [2000s] a person. [(1) they are surrounded by money; (2) ? the emptiness at the doughnut's centre]

doughnut *v.* (*also* **donut**) [1970s+] (*Aus./US teen*) to make an automobile spin by pulling on the hand-brake. The vehicle in question is usu. stolen. [the circularity of the doughnut and the spin]

doughnut dolly *n.* [1960s–70s] (*US milit.*) a Red Cross recreation girl. [among other things she offered coffee and doughnuts to the troops]

doughnut foundry *n.* (*also* **doughnut factory**) [1920s–60s] (*US*) a very cheap restaurant or café.

doughnut-head *n.* [1970s+] (*US*) a fool (cf. APPLEHEAD n.). [SE *doughnut* + -HEAD sfx (1)]

doughnut maker *n.* [1980s] (*Aus.*) a male homosexual (cf. ANAL ASTRONAUT n.). [DOUGHNUT n.² (4)]

doughnut poker *n.* [1980s] (*US*) a male homosexual (cf. ANAL ASTRONAUT n.). [DOUGHNUT n.² (4)]

doughnut-puncher *n.* (*also* donut-puncher) [1980s+] (*Aus./US*) a male homosexual (cf. ANAL ASTRONAUT n.). [DOUGHNUT n.² (4)]

dough-pop *v.* [1970s] **1** to hit hard. **2** to defeat completely. [SE *dough* + POP v.¹ (3); ? link to DOUGHBOY n.¹]

dough pounder/puncher *n. see* DOUGH ROLLER n.

dough-re-mi *n. see* DO-RE-MI n.

dough-ring *n. see* DOUGHBELLY n.

dough roller *n.* (*also* dough boxer, ...pounder, ...puncher) [20C+] (*US*) a cook, often spec. a baker. [navy jargon *dough roller*, the ship's cook]

dough stacks *n.* [2000s] (*US Black*) large quantities of money. [DOUGH n.¹ (1) + STACKS n.¹]

doughy *n.*¹ **1** [19C] a baker. **2** [1950s] (*Aus.*) a cook.

doughy *n.*² (*Aus.*) **1** [1950s] the buttocks (cf. BAKERY GOODS n.). **2** [1960s] a cigarette end. [(1) resemblance of plump, pale buttocks to dough; (2) ext. of (1) with its 'end' imagery]

doughy *adj.*¹ [20C+] (*Aus.*) stupid; thus *doughy over*, in love with, 'mooning over'. [the 'thickness' of dough]

doughy *adj.*² *see* IN THE DOUGH phr.

Douglas *n.* [20C+] (*Aus.*) an axe; thus *swing Douglas*, to swing an axe. [brandname of the *Douglas* Axe Manufacturing Co., East Douglas, Massachusetts]

Douglas Hurd *n.* [1990s+] **1** a piece of excrement (cf. ALI OOP n.). **2** a third-class university degree (cf. DESMOND (TUTU) n.). [rhy. sl.; (1) = TURD n. (1); ult. British Conservative MP under Margaret Thatcher, Lord *Douglas Hurd* (b.1930)]

doul *n.* [1960s–70s] (*US gay*) a very young homosexual male.

do under *v.* [1960s+] (*US Black/P.R.*) to defeat, to ruin, to kill. [play on DO OVER v. (4)]

doup *n. see* DOPE n.¹.

do up *v.*¹ [late 18C+] to rob, to cheat. [DO v.² (1)]

do up *v.*² **1** [late 18C+] to exhaust, to tire out. **2** [19C+] of people, to beat up; of objects, to smash. **3** [mid-19C+] to deal with. **4** [late 19C] to unnerve. **5** [20C+] to kill. **6** [20C+] to cause trouble for. **7** [1950s+] (*US Black*) to have sexual intercourse. [DO v.¹]

do up *v.*³ [late 19C+] (*Aus.*) to squander all one's money. [DO v.¹⁰ (2)]

do up *v.*⁴ [late 19C+] to decorate, to renovate a building or room. [DO v.⁷ (1)]

do up *v.*⁵ [1940s–70s] (*US Black*) to make something happen, to make things change. [SE *do*, to act, to perform]

do up *v.*⁶ (*drugs*) **1** [1950s+] to inject a narcotic. **2** [1950s+] to consume in non-drug context. **3** [1960s+] to take a non-narcotic drug. **4** [1980s] to give someone else an injection.

do up a joint *v.* [1960s] (*US drugs*) to smoke marijuana. [DO UP v.⁶ (3) + JOINT n.⁵ (3)]

do up brown *v.* **1** [19C+] to beat up thoroughly; also in fig. use. **2** [mid-19C+] (*also* do up blue) to do thoroughly, to perform very successfully. **3** [1950s] to deceive, to take in, to surprise. [positive and negative images DO UP v.² in overall sense of action + cooking imagery]

do (up) like a kipper *v.* [1980s+] **1** to beat up severely; thus DONE UP LIKE A KIPPER phr. **2** to take advantage of, to manipulate for one's own ends. [DO UP v.² (2)/DO UP v.¹]

do up right *v.* [1970s] to look after.

do us a favour *phr. see* DO ME A FAVOUR phr.

douse *v.* **1** [late 18C] (*Irish*) to pawn. **2** [late 18C+] to take off; thus *douse the dog vane*, take the cockade out of one's hat. [SE *douse*, to turn off, to put out]

douser *n.* (*also* douse, dowse, dowser) [18C–mid 19C] a heavy blow; esp. in phr. *douse/dowse on the chops*, a blow to the face. [SE *douse*, to strike, to punch; ult. Du. *doesen*, to beat with force and noise]

douse the glim *v.* **1** [mid-18C–1940s] to turn off the light, usu. as imper. **2** [mid-19C–1920s] (*US Und.*) to give someone a black eye. **3** [late 19C–1900s] to kill someone. [SE *douse* + GLIM n.¹]

do-ut-des *n.* [late 19C] (*UK society*) a selfish person. [Lat. *do ut des*, I give in order that you may give back]

dove *n.* [1990s+] (*drugs*) **1** a variety of MDMA (cf. ECSTASY n.). **2** a $35 piece of crack cocaine (cf. BASE n.). [(1) the picture on certain pills]

dovecotery *n. see* SOILED DOVE n.

dove of the roost *n. see* SOILED DOVE n.

dover *n.* [late 19C–1910s] (*Aus.*) a clasp-knife; thus *flash your dover*, to use one's claspknife to cut up one's food. [proprietary name]

Dover boat *n.* [1970s+] a coat. [rhy. sl.]

Dover Castle boarder *n.* [19C] a debtor. [a legally specified area around the Queen's Bench Prison in Southwark Bridge Road within which debtors, while not actually confined in the prison, were ordered to live during the period of their sentence. The nickname came from the prominent local landmark, the *Dover Castle* tavern]

Dover harbour *n. see* SYDNEY HARBOUR n.

dover's powder *n.* (*also* dover's deck) [20C+] (*drugs*) opium (cf. APOSTLE n.). [proper name Thomas *Dover* (1660–1742), an English physician whose patented preparation of opium and ipecacuanha (*Pulvis doveri*) was used as a pain-killing medicine]

dove-tart *n.* [mid-19C] a pigeon pie.

dovey *adj.* (*also* dovy) [late 19C–1910s] of people or objects, delightful, attractive, sweet. [abbr. LOVEY-DOVEY adj. (1)]

dowager *n.* [1940s+] (*gay*) an elegant, older, homosexual man. [SE *dowager*, orig. the widow of a dead king, i.e. a QUEEN n.² (1)]

dow-baked *adj. see* DOUGH-BAKED adj.

dowdy *v.* [late 18C] to play a practical joke based on one's pretending to be mad, esp. to have just escaped from one's keeper or from a psychiatric institution. [the sound *dow de dow*, the basic lyric of a song chanted by one Pearce who, according to Grose (1785), was the first to play this 'joke']

do well *v.*¹ [late 19C+] to treat, to entertain; thus *do oneself well*, to indulge oneself. [DO v.⁸ (2)]

do well *v.*² [20C+] (*W.I.*) to be inconsiderate of others or thoughtless of oneself; usu. in ironic phr. *you do well*.

do what? *phr.* [1960s+] (*US*) what did you say? please repeat the question.

do which? *phr.* [20C+] what did you say?

do with *v. see* DO v.¹ (1).

dowlas *n.* [late 18C–mid-19C] a linen-draper. [*Doulas*, near Brest, in Brittany, the eponymous name of a coarse kind of linen, much used in the 16C and 17C, and later a strong calico made in imitation of this; the sl. is more immediately linked to the character Daniel *Dowlas*, in George Colman's play *The Heir at Law* (1797)]

down *n.*¹ **1** [mid-18C+] something depressing. **2** [1940s+] a fit of misery; often as *the downs*. [DOWN adj.² (1)]

down *n.*² **1** [early–mid 19C] (*UK Und.*) a suspicion, a degree of illegality; thus *take down off*, to render a (stolen) object less suspicious; *there is no down*, there is no risk. **2** [mid-19C+] (*orig. Aus.*) a prejudice against, a suspicion of, a tendency to be unkind towards; usu. as *have a down on*. [DOWN adj.¹ (2)]

down *n.*³ [late 19C+] (*US*) a diluted or even alcohol-free drink, as consumed by a 'hostess' who is persuading her client to buy hugely overpriced 'champagne' etc. [SE *down*, under weight]

down *n.*⁴ [1940s] (*US*) a *down*-payment. [abbr.]

down *n.*⁵ (*US drugs*) **1** [1960s+] a barbiturate (cf. BARBIT n.). **2** [1980s+] codeine-based cough syrup. **3** [1990s+] heroin. [the calming, slowing down effect of the drugs]

down adj.[1] **1** [17C; 19C+] aware, conscious of, knowledgeable; thus *be down upon*, to be aware, to be knowledgeable; spec. [1940s+] to be part of the current (youth) fads and fashions; ext. as *down on the case*, to be fully aware. **2** [mid-18C] suspicious. **3** [mid-19C+] first-rate, excellent. **4** [1940s+] (*US Black*) alert, keen to get on, tough, challenging in a fight. **5** [1950s] (*US Black*) loyal, trustworthy. **6** [1960s] (*US Black*) interesting, current. **7** [1960s+] willing (to do something), enthusiastic. **8** [1960s+] (*US Black*) fashionably dressed, chic. **9** [1990s+] worked out, in a satisfactory manner. **10** [2000s] (*US Black*) feeling well, happy, at one with the world. [orig. Und. *down cove*, a potential victim of a robbery who is aware of being targeted. Originating among late 18C London criminals, the term survives mainly in US Black usage]

down adj.[2] **1** [mid-17C+] (*also* **down on it**) depressed. **2** [1950s+] depressing. **3** [1960s] in a state unassisted by any drug. [the lowering of one's spirits]

down adj.[3] [mid-19C; 1930s] (*US Und.*) serving time in prison. [abbr. DOWN THE RIVER phr.[1]]

down adj.[4] (*US*) **1** [20C+] collapsed, seriously ill. **2** [1950s+] dead. [lit. *fallen down*]

down adj.[5] [1920s+] (*US Black*) owing, deficient in. [SE *down*, under weight]

down adj.[6] [1960s+] (*US*) happening, going on.

down v.[1] (*US*) **1** [mid-19C+] to beat up, to assault. **2** [late 19C+] to defeat. **3** [1930s] to shoot dead. [abbr. SE *knock down*]

down v.[2] (*also* **down on**) [late 19C+] to denigrate. [abbr. PUT DOWN v.[3] (1)]

down v.[3] [1960s] **1** to dispose of, to sell, to get rid of. **2** of a pimp, to situate a prostitute on the street.

down adv. **1** [late 19C–1940s] very much so, exceedingly. **2** [1920s+] (*orig. US Black*) to the limit. [DOWN adj.[1] (3)]

down a cuff/lash in someone v. *see* DOWN BLOWS IN SOMEONE v.

down among the dead men phr. [mid-19C] very drunk. [SE phr. + pun on DEAD MAN n.[1] (1)]

down-and-out n. [late 19C+] (*orig. US*) a homeless or destitute person, a tramp. [*down* in the gutter and *out* of luck]

down-and-out adj. [20C+] homeless or destitute; living as a tramp. [DOWN-AND-OUT n.]

down-and-outer n. [1910s+] (*US*) a vagrant, a tramp. [ext. DOWN-AND-OUT n.]

down and up n. [20C+] (*Aus.*) a cup. [rhy. sl.]

down as a dab phr. [late 19C] very ill. [? a dead *dab* lying flat on a fishmonger's slab]

down as a hammer phr. (*also* **down as a nail/trippet**) [early–mid-19C] very aware. [DOWN adj.[1] (1) + SE *hammer/nail/ trippet*, a trivet; such a person 'hits the nail on the head']

down-ass adj. [1980s+] (*US Black*) a general term of approval. [DOWN adj.[1] (3) + -ASS sfx]

down below n.[1] [mid-19C+] a coy ref. to the vagina (cf. ARTICLE n.). [euph.]

down below n.[2] [1910s+] (*Aus.*) Sydney; any southern city, which is 'down below' the outback.

downblow n. [1940s] (*Irish*) a disaster.

down blows in someone v. (*also* **down a cuff in someone, down a lash in someone**) [20C+] (*W.I., Guyn.*) to beat up severely.

down buttock and sham file n. (*also* **downright buttock and sham file**) [19C] a prostitute who does not resort to thieving. [SE *down(right)* + BUTTOCK AND FILE n., modified by SE *sham*, fake]

down by law phr. [1980s+] (*orig. US Black*) **1** expert, professional (within one's occupation). **2** of a person, high in status; of an object or idea, wholly admirable. [DOWN adj.[1] (3)]

Down-easter n. [mid-19C+] (*US*) **1** a 'Yankee', i.e. an inhabitant or native of the northeastern states. **2** an inhabitant or native of Maine.

downer n.[1] **1** [mid-19C] (*US*) a nickel, 5 cents. **2** [mid–late 19C] a sixpence (2½p). [Rom. *tawno*, a little one]

downer n.[2] **1** [mid-19C; 1960s+] a depressing, worrying situation. **2** [1970s+] a depressing person. **3** [1970s+] a state of depression; often as *on a downer*. [DOWN adj.[2] (1)]

downer n.[3] [20C+] a grudge; esp. in phr. *have a downer on*. [DOWN n.[2] (2)]

downer n.[4] [1920s–30s] (*UK tramp*) a bed. [on which one lies down]

downer n.[5] **1** [1960s+] a barbiturate, a tranquillizer (cf. BARBIT n.). **2** [1990s+] any drug used to reduce the unpleasant experiences that can accompany the end of using any given stimulant or 'up' drug, e.g. crack cocaine. **3** [1990s+] heroin, as opposed to cocaine. [DOWN n.[5] (1)]

downey n. *see* DOWNY n.[2].

downface v. [1900s–40s] to assert something in order to make someone look foolish.

down for adv. [1960s+] (*US Black*) loyal to, committed to, in favour of. [DOWN adj.[1] (7)]

down for mine phr. [1950s+] (*orig. US Black*) able to look after oneself. [DOWN FOR adv.]

down for the count phr. [1920s–30s] (*orig. US*) as good as defeated, virtually hopeless. [boxing imagery]

down for the last count phr. (*also* **down for the long count**) [20C+] dead; also in fig. use. [boxing imagery]

down-freak n. (*also* **downs freak**) [1970s+] (*drugs*) a regular user of depressant drugs (cf. DOWN-HEAD n.). [DOWN n.[5] (1) + FREAK sfx]

down from one's high horse phr. *see* OFF ONE'S HIGH HORSE phr.

down front adj. [1950s+] (*US Black*) open, honest, candid. [var. on UP FRONT adj. (1)]

down hand on someone v. [20C+] (*W.I.*) to seize firmly.

down-head n. [1960s+] (*drugs*) a regular user of depressant drugs (cf. DOWN-FREAK n.). [DOWN n.[5] (1) + -HEAD sfx (3)]

down-hills n. [late 17C–early 19C] doctored dice that will always show low numbers.

down-home n. [1920s+] (*mainly US Black*) one's home, esp. among Black speakers, the South.

down-home adj. [1920s+] (*mainly US Black*) reminiscent or characteristic of one's home, esp. among Black speakers, of the South; thus *talk down-home*, to speak Black English. [however note (early 19C) *go down-home*, to visit one's home]

downie n. [1960s+] (*drugs*) a depressant. [DOWN adj.[2] (1)]

down in adv. [mid–late 19C] lacking in, short of. [SE *down*, under weight]

Downing Street n. [20C+] (*bingo*) the number 10 (cf. ALDERSHOT LADIES n.). [the residence of UK prime ministers at 10 Downing Street, London SW1]

down in the chops phr. (*also* **down in the gills**) [mid-19C] depressed. [DOWN adj.[2] (1) + CHOPS n.[1] (1)/GILLS n. (3) + image of the mouth being turned down in a frown]

down in the dumps phr. [late 17C+] miserable, unhappy, gloomy. [DOWN adj.[2] (1)]

down in the face the length of a fiddle phr. [1950s] looking very depressed. [DOWN adj.[2] (1)]

down in the gills phr. *see* DOWN IN THE CHOPS phr.

down in the kinks phr. [20C+] (*US*) miserable, unhappy, gloomy. [DOWN adj.[2] (1) + SE *kink*, a state of madness]

down in the mouth phr. (*also* **down in the mug, down on one's mouth**) [17C+] depressed, miserable. [DOWN adj.[2] (1)/lit. *down*, i.e. the mouth is turned down in a frown]

download one's floppy v. (*also* **download from one's own website**) [1990s+] to masturbate. [punning on computer jargon]

down low n. [1990s+] (*US Black*) a state of secrecy. [DOWN LOW adj.]

down low *adj.* [1990s+] (*US Black*) covert, secret. [i.e. keeping a *low* profile]

downmouth *v.* [1980s] (*US*) to attack verbally, to slander. [DOWN adj.[1] (2)/DOWN n.[2] (2) + SE *mouth*]

down on *phr.* **1** [19C] attacking physically. **2** [mid-19C+] annoyed with, disappointed in, holding a negative opinion of. [DOWN n.[2] (2)/DOWN adj.[1] (2)]

down on *v. see* DOWN v.[2].

down on it *adj. see* DOWN adj.[2] (1).

down on one's mouth *phr. see* DOWN IN THE MOUTH phr.

down on the knuckle(bone) *phr.* [mid-19C–1930s] virtually penniless.

down pin *adj.* [late 19C–1900s] depressed, indisposed. [skittles imagery + DOWN adj.[2] (1)]

downpressor *n.* [1950s+] (*W.I. Rasta*) a preferred term for SE *oppressor*.

downright *n.* [late 19C–1930s] (*UK tramp*) begging, tramping; esp. in phr. *on the downright*, wandering the country as a beggar.

downright buttock and sham file *n. see* DOWN BUTTOCK AND SHAM FILE n.

downrighter *n.* [1930s] a beggar, a tramp. [DOWNRIGHT n.]

Downs, the *n.* [mid-19C] (*UK Und.*) Tothill Fields prison (cf. ABBOTT'S PRIORY n.). [the site of the prison in the fields that surrounded and were geographically lower than Tothill]

downs *n.* [2000s] (*US Black*) money. [one puts it *down* as a payment]

downs, the *n. see* DOWN n.[1] (2).

downshire *n.* [19C] female pubic hair. [pun on SE *down* (i.e. below/hair) + sfx *-shire*]

down south *phr.* [1910s; 1960s] (*Aus.*) hidden, buried; in one's pocket.

downstairs *n.* **1** [19C] hell. **2** [late 19C] the urino-genital area. **3** [1910s+] the guts, the belly.

down the chute *phr.* [1920s+] (*Aus.*) in prison. [SE *chute*, a narrow passage through which animals are driven for branding, shearing etc]

down the crapper *phr. see* DOWN THE PAN phr.

down the drain *phr.* (*also* **down the plug, ...plughole, ...tube**) [1930s+] lost, wasted, useless.

down the drains *n.* [1960s+] the human brains. [rhy. sl.]

down the gurgler *phr.* [1930s+] (*Aus.*) wasted, used of something that has not worked out.

down the hatch *excl.* [1920s+] (*orig. naut.*) a popular toast before taking a drink. [HATCH n.[2]]

down the line *phr. see* LINE n.[2] (1).

down the pan *phr.* (*also* **down the crapper/shitter**) [1930s+] wasted, lost, abandoned. [i.e. the lavatory *pan*/CRAPPER n.[3] (2)/SHITTER n.[1] (4)]

down there *n.* [20C+] a coy ref. to the vagina; occas. the penis (cf. ARTICLE n.). [euph.]

down the river *phr.[1]* [late 19C+] serving time in prison. [var. on UP THE RIVER phr.; *see also* GO DOWN THE RIVER v.]

down the river *phr.[2]* (*also* **down the Swanny**) **1** [late 19C+] finished, over and done, used up. **2** [1920s] in debt. [a boat that has gone *down the river* has vanished from sight]

down the road *phr.* [mid–late 19C] **1** stylish, fashionable. **2** vulgar, showy. [Mile End *Road*, London, a favoured costermongers' market]

down the shitter *phr. see* DOWN THE PAN phr.

down the spout *phr.* [mid-19C] out of pawn. [antonym of UP THE SPOUT phr. (2)]

down the steps *phr. see* UP THE STAIRS phr.

down the Swanny *phr. see* DOWN THE RIVER phr.[2].

down the track *phr.* [1980s+] **1** experienced. **2** referring to the passage of time.

down the tube *phr. see* DOWN THE DRAIN phr.

down to *phr.[1]* (*also* **down upon**) [19C+] alert to, aware of, 'fly'. [DOWN adj.[1] (1)]

down to *phr.[2]* **1** [late 19C] to the account of. **2** [1970s+] the responsibility of. [fig. use of abbr. of SE *written down to*]

down to *phr.[3]* [1950s+] for the sake of.

down to cases *phr.* **1** [late 19C+] (*US*) down to the hard facts. **2** [1940s] (*US Und.*) down to one's last pennies.

down to larking *phr. see* LARKING n.[2] (1).

down to one's seams *phr.* [late 19C] (*US*) absolutely impoverished. [the seams of one's empty pockets]

down to the ground *adv.* (*also* **down to the bricks/muck**) [mid-19C+] (*US*) perfectly, thoroughly, completely.

down to the short strokes *phr.* [1990s+] approaching the end, very near a conclusion. [SE *short strokes*, i.e. the final thrusts of intercourse]

down to the wire *phr.* [20C+] approaching the crux, the climax; to the very limit. [horseracing imagery]

downtown *n.[1]* [1920s+] (*US Black*) the female genital area, in the context of cunnilingus (cf. AUSSIE KISS n.).

downtown *n.[2]* **1** [1930s+] (*US police/Und.*) police headquarters. **2** [1980s+] (*US*) a generic term for the city government, the police department and similar authorities. [usu. sited in the *downtown* or business area of a city]

downtown *adj.* [20C+] (*US*) sophisticated, smart, well-dressed.

downtown *v.* [1920s+] (*US Black*) to improve one's lot in society, to go 'up in the world'. [newly prosperous Harlemites signified their new status by leaving the ghetto and moving *downtown*, i.e. to more prosperous parts of New York]

down trip *n.* [1960s+] (*drugs*) **1** an unpleasant experience induced after taking LSD. **2** in fig. use., anything unpleasant, tedious, depressing. [DOWN adj.[2] (2) + TRIP n.[4] (1)]

down trou *v. see* DROP TROU v. (1).

down under *n.* [late 19C+] **1** Australia; supposedly sited 'underneath' the UK on the globe. **2** (*Aus.*) the United Kingdom. **3** New Zealand.

down upon *phr. see* DOWN TO phr.[1].

down with *adj.* **1** [1930s–40s] (*orig. US Black*) through with. **2** [1940s+] (*orig. US Black*) involved with. **3** [1940s+] (*orig. US Black*) empathetic, emotionally responsive; enjoying, appreciating. **4** [1990s+] (*US*) friendly with. [DOWN adj.[1]]

down with his apple-cart! *excl.* [mid-19C] knock him down! [northern dial.; phr. *down with* + apple-cart]

Downy *n.* [2000s] one who has Down's Syndrome. [abbr. + sfx -*y*]

downy *n.[1]* [19C] a knowledgeable, artful, aware person. [DOWN adj.[1] (1) + sfx -*y*]

downy *n.[2]* (*also* **downey**) [mid-19C–1900s] a bed; thus *do the downy*, to lie in bed. [SE *down* mattress/*lie down*]

downy *adj.[1]* **1** [19C] aware, knowledgeable. **2** [mid-19C] in fig. use, fashionable. **3** [late 19C] as (1) with overtones of criminality. [DOWN adj.[1] (1) + sfx -*y*]

downy *adj.[2]* [1950s–60s] (*drugs*) in a state that follows the climactic euphoria of a drug experience. [DOWN adj.[2] (1)]

downy bird *n.* [19C] a knowledgeable, artful, aware person. [DOWNY adj.[1] (1) + BIRD n.[2] (1)]

downy bit *n.* **1** [mid-19C] a young prostitute (cf. BANGTAIL n.[1]). **2** [late 19C] a young woman, esp. when attractive. **3** [late 19C] the vagina. [SE *down*, the first feathering of young birds + BIT n.[2] (1)]

downy cove *n.* [early–mid-19C] a knowledgeable, artful, aware person. [DOWNY adj.[1] (1)+ COVE n. (1)]

downy earwig *n.* [1920s–30s] (*UK tramp*) a sympathetic listener. [DOWNY adj.[1] (1) + EARWIG n. (3)]

downy flea-pasture *n.* [mid-19C] a bed. [SE *downy*/DOWNY n.[2]]

dowry *n.* [mid-19C] (*Ling. Fr./Polari*) a great deal, very much, plenty of. [SE *dowry*, money given with a bride; ult. Ital. *dare*, to give]

dowse/dowser *n. see* DOUSER n.

doxey/doxie *n. see* DOXY n.

doxology dumper *n.* [late 19C] (*Aus.*) a preacher, a clergyman. [SE *doxology*, the praising of God]

doxology works *n.* [late 19C] a place of Christian worship. [SE *doxology*, the praising of God]

doxy *n.* (*also* **doccy, docxy, doxey, doxie, doxsy**) (*UK Und.*) 1 [early 16C–mid-19C] the female companion of a variety of mendicant villains (cf. CANTING CREW n.). 2 [early 16C+] a general term, usu. derog., for a woman or girl, esp. a mistress. 3 [late 17C+] a prostitute. [? Du. *docke*, a doll or SE *dock*, an animal's tail; Ribton-Turner, *A History of Vagrants* (1887), suggests Lowland Scot. *doxie*, lazy]

doxy *adj.* [early 17C–mid-18C] of a woman, corrupt, amoral, whorish. [DOXY n. (1)]

doxy-dell *n.* [mid-17C] a prostitute. [DOXY adj. + DELL n. (1)]

D'Oyly Carte *n.* [1970s+] a fart. [rhy. sl.; ult. proper name Sir Richard *D'Oyly Carte* (1844–1901), late 19C producer of many Gilbert and Sullivan operas]

do you drink? *phr. see* DRINK v.

do you hold it? *phr.* [late 19C] (*Aus.*) a phr. indicating that it is your turn to buy the drinks.

do you like hospital food? *phr.* [1980s+] a threatening phr. used immediately before administering a beating. [the potential assailant asks this of a victim, who prob. replies 'No' and is told 'Well you'd better get used to it']

do you need a boy? *phr.* [1960s+] (*drugs*) a surreptitious request for heroin. [BOY n.[7] (1)]

do you savvy? *phr. see* SAVVY v. (2).

do you see any green in my eye? *phr.* (*also* **do you see any green in my eyeball, do you see anything green?**) [early 19C+] a phr. meaning do you think I'm a fool? do I look stupid? [SE *green*, innocent, naïve]

do you see skid marks on my forehead? *phr.* [1980s] (*US campus*) do you think I'm a fool? [SKID MARKS n.; thus synon. with 'do you think I'm talking out of my ass']

do you spit much with that cough? *phr.* [1910s–20s] (*Can.*) a phr. used to acknowledge that one has heard a companion break wind.

do you think you'll know me again? *phr.* (*also* **you'll know me again, won't you?**) [20C+] a phr. used to embarrass someone the speaker feels is staring too hard.

do you want jam on it? *phr.* (*also* **what do you want, jam on it?**) [1910s+] a phr. used to deride someone seen as wanting everything to come without even the slightest problem.

dozed *adj.* [mid-18C; 20C+] (*Ulster*) very drunk. [fig. use of dial. *dozed*, of wood, rotten]

dozen-a-dime *adj. see* DIME-A-DOZEN adj.

dozens *n.* (*also* **dirty dozens, dozen, snagging**) [1910s+] (*US Black*) a ritual game of testing a rival's emotional strength by insulting his various relatives, esp. his mother, in 12 'rounds' of attack and taking similar insults in return; the insults are usu. sexual and/or scatological, hence the common addition of the adj. *dirty*; usu. as PLAY THE DOZENS v. [the throw of 12 in craps, the worst possible throw, or f. its folk origins as a set of ritualized verses, usu. in rhymed couplets, which ran through 12 specific sexual acts, each rhyming with the numbers 1 to 12; dozens can be 'dirty' or 'clean', depending on the level of obscenity involved; otherwise unsupported, Legman (1968) suggests 'possibly from the Saxon word "doze", to stun or overwhelm, as in bulldozer'; for a discussion of ety. see *American Speech* XXV:3 (1950) pp.230–33]

dozer *n.* [1970s+] (*Irish*) a slow-witted person; usu. in negative phr. *no dozer*, not a fool. [SE *doze*]

dozey-arsed *adj.* [1990s+] stupid, 'slow' (cf. CLAY-ASSED adj.). [DOZY adj. + -ASSED sfx]

dozing-crib *n.* [mid–late 19C] a bedroom. [SE *doze* + CRIB n.[1] (1)]

dozo *n.* [1980s] (*N.Z.*) a fool (cf. BOBO n.[1]). [DOZY adj.]

dozy *adj.* [20C+] (*orig. milit.*) mentally sluggish, stupid, lazy; thus as a term of pej. address. [SE *doze*]

dozz *n.* [1990s+] (*US Black*) a sleep, a nap. [var. on DOSS n.[1] (2)]

D.P. *n. see* DURBAN POISON n.

d.ph. *n.* [1910s+] (*US*) a damned fool. [abbr./pron. + pun on the degree of Ph.D.]

Dr all combs. of Dr are alphabetized under DOCTOR.

drab *n.*[1] 1 [early 16C–19C] a slattern, a dirty, untidy woman. 2 [mid-16C+] a prostitute; thus *drabbery*, prostitutes as a group. [Irish *drabog*, Gael. *drabag*, a dirty female, a slattern; presumably an early cant term]

drab *n.*[2] [mid-19C] poison. [Rom. *drab*, poison; thus *drabengro*, doctor, lit. 'poison-man']

drab *v.* (*also* **go drabbing**) [17C–19C] to associate with prostitutes; thus to have sexual intercourse. [DRAB n.[1] (2)]

drabbit! *excl.* [16C–19C] a mild excl., i.e. (*Go*)*d rabbit!*, (*Go*)*d rat it!*

drabble-tail *n.* [mid-19C–1920s] a term of abuse; thus adj., *drabbled*. [? DRAGGLE-TAIL n. (1)]

drab-driver *n.* [early 17C] a pimp (cf. ABBOT ON THE CROSS n.). [DRAB n.[1] (2) + SE *driver*]

drack *n.*[1] (*also* **drac**) [1930s+] (*Aus.*) rubbishy, worthless goods. [? Yiddish *dreck*, rubbish, dirt]

drack *n.*[2] (*also* **drac**) [1960s+] (*Aus.*) 1 an unattractive woman. 2 a policeman. [proper name *Dracula* but note DRACK n.[1]]

drack *adj.* (*also* **drac**) [1930s+] (*Aus.*) second-rate, inferior, unattractive. [DRACK n.[1]]

drack sort *n.* [1930s+] (*Aus.*) an unattractive person of either sex. [DRACK adj. + SE *sort*]

dracs *n.* (*also* **duracs**) [1930s–40s] playing cards. [backsl.]

Dracula *n.* 1 [1950s+] (*Aus.*) an unattractive woman. 2 [1970s] (*US teen*) an unpleasant, severe father or person. [a cruel comparison to the well-known vampire]

draft *n.* [1940s–50s] (*US Und.*) the transportation of a convict from one prison to another. [SAmE *draft*, the selecting of a smaller group from a larger body, usu. in milit. context]

draftnik *n.* [1970s] (*US campus*) one who has avoided the military service conscription. [SAmE *draft* + -NIK sfx]

draft on the pump at Aldgate *n. see* BILL ON THE PUMP AT ALDGATE n.

draftpak *n.* [1990s+] (*Scot.*) a lowlife, an eccentric; a habitual drunkard. [Scot. *draftpak*, take-away packs of draft beer available over the bar in Scottish public houses]

draft up *n.* (*also* **draft vertical, wind vertical**) [1910s] (*Aus.*) a state of nervousness. [play on GET THE WIND UP v. (1)]

drafty *adj. see* FEEL A DRAUGHT v. (3).

drag *n.*[1] 1 [18C] (*UK Und.*) a form of 'rod', whereby robbers 'fish' items from a shop window. 2 [late 18C+] (*UK Und.*) the robbery of vehicles, initially horse-drawn, subseq. motorized; thus *go on the drag*, to pursue this as a profession. 3 [19C] (*US Und.*) a theft. 4 [1900s–20s] (*US Und.*) a burglar's tool, spec. for breaking the lock of a safe.

drag *n.*[2] 1 [mid-18C] a ferryboat. 2 [late 18C–1910s] a 1- or 2-horse wagon or cart. 3 [19C] a type of stage-coach, drawn by 4 horses, with seats on top. 4 [1900s] a prison van, a Black Maria. 5 [1910s+] a motorcar, thus vehicles in general. 6 [1920s–30s] (*US tramp*) a (slow) freight train. 7 [1930s+] a van.

drag *n.*[3] [early 19C] (*Scot. Und.*) a watch chain.

drag *n.*[4] [mid-19C+] a period of imprisonment lasting 3 months. [? DRAG n.[1]; i.e. the common sentence for such a crime; 20C+ use mainly Aus.]

drag *n.*[5] 1 [mid-19C+] a street; thus MAIN DRAG, THE n.; *back drag*, back street; *do the drag*, to wander or loiter around town; *work the drag*, to beg on the street. 2 [1920s+] a long distance, which will make for tedious travelling. 3 [1930s] (*US tramp*) a railroad line. [its use by DRAG n.[2] (3); note Allen, *The City in Slang* (1993): 'Godfrey Irwin in *American Tramp and Underworld Slang* wrote in

1931 that a "street or railroad line [is called a drag] since a tramp drags his weary way over these means of communication," and that is as good a thought as any']

drag n.[6] 1 [mid-19C+] a disappointment, a pity, a nuisance, a task that one has no desire to perform; a bore. 2 [20C+] of a person, a disappointment, a hanger-on, a pest. 3 [1940s] (US Black campus) an old-fashioned person. 4 [1950s–60s] a depressing atmosphere. 5 [1980s] second-rate drugs. [ext. use of SE drag, a bore; lit. an obstruction to progress]

drag n.[7] [late 19C–1960s] influence.

drag n.[8] 1 [late 19C+] female dress as worn by men, but not in a homosexual context, e.g. on stage. 2 [20C+] female dress as worn by homosexual males or female impersonators; also male dress as worn by lesbians. 3 [1910s+] (also **drag ball**) a party held en travesti. 4 [1920s–70s] (US/Aus.) a party (with no specific gay overtones). 5 [1920s+] (US gay) a homosexual man dressed in female clothing, a DRAG QUEEN n. 6 [1930s–40s] (US) a bar that caters primarily to a gay clientele. 7 [1950s+] clothing in general; a costume, a disguise. [orig. theatrical use, which stressed the drag of a long dress along the floor, as opposed to tight-fitting trousers; note first OED cits. (1870) imply fancy dress, gay refs. not overt until 20C]

drag n.[9] 1 [20C+] a puff of a marijuana cigarette; thus give a drag, to pass a marijuana cigarette; take a drag, to take a puff on the cigarette. 2 [1910s+] a puff of a cigarette; thus the cigarette itself; thus drag, to smoke. 3 [1980s] (UK prison) a cannabis or cannabis/tobacco cigarette. [SE drag, to draw, to pull]

drag n.[10] [20C+] (US) 1 a share of money. 2 wages. [what one can SE drag down or in]

drag n.[11] [1900s] (US campus) a joke. [ety. unknown]

drag n.[12] [1900s] (US campus) a toady, a parasite, a flatterer. [they are dragged along]

drag n.[13] [1910s+] a slow dance or the music that accompanies it.

drag n.[14] [1920s+] (US) an unkempt or immoral woman, a slattern. [16C SE draggle-tail, an unkempt, slatternly woman, whose skirts drag along the ground]

drag n.[15] (US) 1 [1920s+] a young woman who is being taken to a party. 2 [1950s] a girlfriend, a young woman. [SE drag, a heavy weight, an impediment]

drag n.[16] [1930s–60s] (US Und.) a police dragnet, i.e. the systematic searching of a large area, even a whole town or city. [abbr.]

drag n.[17] [1990s+] (US Black) a ritual game of testing a rival's emotional strength by insulting his various relatives. [note this version of the DOZENS n. is characterized by its extreme vulgarity and coarseness]

drag adj.[1] 1 [late 19C+] pertaining to female impersonation (not invariably by homosexuals), usu. in a theatrical context. 2 [1920s+] relevant to the gay lifestyle. [DRAG n.[8] (1)/DRAG n.[8] (2)]

drag adj.[2] [1960s+] (US) boring.

drag v.[1] (UK Und.) 1 [late 18C–1950s] to rob from vehicles. 2 [1970s] to steal a car. [DRAG n.[2]]

drag v.[2] [late 19C] (US) to search for contraband.

drag v.[3] [late 19C] (US campus) to escort to a dance. [SE drag]

drag v.[4] 1 [20C+] (US) to leave something unfinished. 2 [20C+] to leave quickly. 3 [1920s+] (US) (also **drag it**) to resign from a job, or participation in a betting game.

drag v.[5] [1900s] (US campus) to understand. [? SE drag, i.e. into one's brain]

drag v.[6] [1900s] (US campus) to joke, to jest. [DRAG n.[11]]

drag v.[7] [1900s] (US campus) to toady to, to curry favour with a superior. [DRAG n.[12]]

drag v.[8] 1 [1920s+] to force someone to go to a place against their will, often as drag along. 2 [1950s+] (US Black/prison) to lead someone on, to persuade, to trick.

drag v.[9] [1940s–70s] (US) to irritate, to bore, to 'bring down'. [DRAG n.[6] (2)]

drag v.[10] [1950s+] 1 to drive up and down, chatting to one's friends and displaying one's automobile. 2 (US campus) to race a car. [DRAG n.[5] (1)]

drag v.[11] [1960s+] to waste time, to idle; usu. as drag around; to move slowly.

drag a blind v. [1920s] (US) to go out with someone one has never met. [DRAG v.[3] + SE blind date]

drag-ass adj. (US) 1 [1930s+] annoying, irritating. 2 [1950s] of a person, lazy, bedraggled. 3 [1950s+] of a thing, or person, tedious. [DRAG ASS v./DRAG n.[6] (1) + -ASS sfx]

drag-ass adv. [1990s+] (US) lazily, hesitantly. [DRAG-ASS adj. (2)]

drag ass v. (also **drag tail**) [1930s+] (US) 1 to act slowly, lazily. 2 to do badly. 3 to go, to travel (the subtext is of reluctance) (cf. DRAG ONE'S ASS v.). [SE drag + ASS n. (5)/TAIL n.[2] (1); note DRAG ONE'S TAIL v.]

drag ball n. see DRAG n.[8] (3).

drag-butch n. see DRAG-KING n.

drag-cove n. [early 19C] a cart-driver. [SE drag, a cart, a wagon + COVE n. (1)]

drag down v. [1920s+] (US) to earn a salary, wages. [SE drag; note DRAG n.[10] (2)]

drag-dyke n. [1960s+] a 'masculine' lesbian who chooses to dress in male clothing. [DRAG n.[8] (2) + DYKE n.]

dragged (out) adj. 1 [mid-19C+] (orig. US) (also **dragging**) exhausted, sickly. 2 [1950s] angry. 3 [1960s] suffering adverse reactions after smoking cannabis. 4 [1990s+] drunk.

dragged up adj. [late 17C+] educated or brought up 'any how'. [DRAG UP v.[1]]

dragger n.[1] [20C+] one who robs vehicles. [DRAG v.[1] (1)]

dragger n.[2] [1990s+] (US campus) one who is so drunk that have to be dragged back to their room.

dragging n.[1] [mid-19C+] stealing from carts and vans. [DRAG v.[1] (1)]

dragging n.[2] [1980s+] (US campus) the state of feeling ill or lethargic. [abbr. dragging one's ass, feeling exhausted]

dragging adj. see DRAGGED (OUT) adj. (1).

dragging lark n. (also **dragging game**) [1920s–30s] stealing from automobiles. [DRAGGING n.[1] + LARK n.[1] (5)]

dragging time n. [mid-19C] the evening of a country fair, when everyone has been drinking and the men begin to make robust physical advances towards the women.

draggin' wagon n. [1950s] (US teen) a fast car. [SE drag racing]

draggle-tail n. 1 [mid-17C+] a prostitute; thus draggletailed, draggled, promiscuous, a general abusive term. 2 [1900s] (Aus.) a female servant. [16C SE draggle-tail, an unkempt, slatternly woman, whose skirts drag along the ground]

draggle-tailed adj. (also **draggle-skirted, draggle-tail**) [late 17C+] impoverished.

draggy adj.[1] (also **draggly**) [late 19C+] (orig. US) unwell, sickly-looking. [DRAGGED (OUT) adj. (1)]

draggy adj.[2] [1920s+] of people or events, boring. [DRAG n.[6] (1)]

drag in v. [20C+] (US) to arrive, to appear.

drag it v.[1] see DRAG v.[4] (3).

drag it v.[2] see DRAG ONE'S ASS v.

drag it through the garden v. [2000s] (US) to add salad etc to a portion of meat/fish.

drag joint n. [1930s+] (US gay) a bar or club that caters predominantly to transvestites. [DRAG n.[8] (2) + JOINT n.[4] (3)]

drag-king n. (also **drag-butch**) [1990s+] (gay) a woman who dresses as a man. [DRAG n.[8] (2) + KING n.[1] (3)/BUTCH n.[4] (3)]

drag lay n. [late 18C–early 19C] the robbery of vehicles. [DRAG n.[1] (2) + LAY n.[4] (1)]

dragon n.[1] 1 [17C–early 18C] a slattern, a promiscuous woman. 2 [1950s–60s] an old prostitute. 3 [1960s] (N.Z.) a wife. [note RMC Duntroon (Aus.) dragon, a girlfriend]

dragon n.[2] [19C] a sovereign. [the image of St George and the dragon engraved on the obverse of the coin]

dragon n.[3] [1980s+] (drugs) heroin. [backform. f. CHASE THE DRAGON v. (1)]

dragon n.[4] [1980s+] (US) the penis (cf. ANTEATER n.).

dragon n.[5] [1980s+] (US campus) a person with particularly bad breath. [DRAGON BREATH n., i.e. such a person 'breathes fire']

drag on v. [1910s+] (Aus.) 1 to marry a woman. 2 to perform a task.

dragon breath n. [1970s+] (US) bad halitosis, or any bad smell. [the image of one who 'breathes fire']

drag one's anchor v. (also drag one's drawers) [1920s+] (US) to go slowly, to idle, to dawdle.

drag one's ass v. (US) (also drag it, drag one's butt) 1 [1920s+] to leave, to go, to move (cf. DRAG ASS v.). 2 [1930s+] to be fatigued, run-down, miserable. [SE drag + ASS n. (2)/BUTT n.[1] (2)]

drag one's heels v. [1970s] (US campus) to walk, to stroll.

drag one's hook v. [1960s] (N.Z.) to leave. [SE drag + naut. hook, an anchor]

drag one's tail v. [1920s+] (US) to mope around, to look miserable. [the image of a dog with its tail down, supposedly a sign of its unhappiness]

dragon upon St George n. [late 17C–18C] a position of sexual intercourse in which the woman is on top of the man. [the female dragon is on top of a male St George]

dragoon (it) v. [late 18C–19C] to work at 2 jobs simultaneously. [SE dragoon, orig. a horse soldier, i.e. one who rode to battle on horseback but dismounted to fight like infantry]

drag-out n. [mid-19C] (US) 1 a rough party, a brawl. 2 one who indulges in a fierce fight. 3 a dance. [the loser, knocked unconscious, is dragged out of the way/room]

drag queen n. (also queen drag) 1 [1930s+] a feminine homosexual who prefers to dress as a woman; sometimes as a professional female impersonator. 2 [1990s+] in fig. use, as a general insult. [DRAG n.[8] (2) + QUEEN n.[2] (1)/QUEEN sfx (2)]

dragsman n. [19C] 1 a coachman; a cart or wagon driver. 2 a thief who robs goods or trunks from the back of vans or carts. [DRAG n.[2] (3) + SE man; (1) 20C+ use is SE]

drag-sneak n. [mid-19C] a thief who specializes in the robbery of vehicles. [DRAG n.[1] (2) + SNEAK n.[1] (2)]

dragsville n. see -VILLE sfx[1].

drag tail v. see DRAG ASS v.

drag the chain v. [1930s+] (Aus./N.Z.) to be slow, to be inferior, to be last in any work or contest, to be the slowest drinker of a group. [sheep-shearing jargon]

drag the gut v. see SHOOT THE GUT v.

drag the rag v. [20C+] (US) to hurry up. [SE drag + ? fig. use of RAGS n. (1), or simply assonance]

drag up v.[1] [late 17C+] to bring up or educate a child roughly, without controls, manners or discipline. [B.E. notes 'as the Rakes call it', i.e. upper-class society use; thus the irony is deliberate]

drag up v.[2] [1920s] (US) to leave one's job, to resign. [DRAG v.[4] (3)]

drag up v.[3] [1960s+] to get dressed (up). [DRAG n.[8] (7)/DRAG n.[8] (2)]

drag weed n. [1940s–50s] (US drugs) marijuana (cf. AFRICAN BUSH n.).

d-railed adj. [2000s] (US campus) drunk. [SE derailed, but note DERAIL n. (3)]

drain n.[1] 1 [early–mid-19C] gin. 2 [early 19C+] a drink; thus drain of pale, a glass of brandy; do a drain, to have a drink (with a friend). [SE drain a glass]

drain n.[2] 1 [late 19C] the vagina (cf. AGREEABLE RUTS OF LIFE n.). 2 [1930s] the throat.

drain n.[3] [1930s] an act of urination.

drain v. see DRAIN (OFF) v.

drain Charles Dickens v. [1990s+] to masturbate (cf. COTTON WOOL v.). [rhy. sl. = chickens, i.e. CHOKE THE CHICKEN v. (1)]

drainies n. [1970s+] very narrow 'drainpipe' trousers. [abbr. DRAINPIPES n. (2)]

drain-off n. [2000s] an act of urination. [DRAIN (OFF) v.]

drain (off) v. [19C] to urinate.

drain one's lizard v. see DRAIN THE DRAGON v.

drain one's radiator v. [1940s+] to urinate (cf. BLEED ONE'S TURKEY v.).

drainpipes n. 1 [late 19C] macaroni. 2 [1950s+] tight trousers.

drain the anaconda v. see EMPTY THE ANACONDA v.

drain the dragon v. (also drain one's/the lizard) [1960s+] to urinate (cf. BLEED ONE'S TURKEY v.). [DRAGON n.[4]/LIZARD n.[3]]

drain the lily v. [1940s] to urinate (cf. BLEED ONE'S TURKEY v.). [LILY n.[4] (1)]

drain the (main) vein v. [1940s+] (orig. Aus.) to urinate (cf. BLEED ONE'S TURKEY v.).

drain the monster v. [1980s+] to masturbate (cf. BEAT ONE'S HOG v.).

drake n. [20C+] (US) a cigar or cigarette end. [play on SE drakes + DUCK n.[8]]

drake v. [early 19C] to duck in a pond, a punishment sometimes meted out to pickpockets captured at fairs or races. [play on SE duck]

drake and duck n. [1940s] sexual intercourse. [rhy. sl. = FUCK n.[1] (1)]

drama queen n. [1960s+] (orig. gay) anyone considered to be making an excessive fuss or 'making a mountain out of a mole-hill'. [SE drama + QUEEN n.[2] (1)]

dram-a-tick n. [late 18C–early 19C] a shot of spirits obtained on credit. [SE dram + TICK n.[3] (1); a pun on SE dramatic (credit in a public house being hard to obtain)]

dranka n. [2000s] (US Black) a close friend, esp. a fellow gang member. [ety. unknown]

drap n. [late 18C] a 'nasty, sluttish whore' (Egan's Grose). [var. on DRAB n.[1] (2)]

drape n. 1 [1930s–60s] (orig. US Black) a suit, typified by its generously cut, long, draped jacket with padded shoulders and high-waisted, tapering trousers. 2 [1950s+] (orig. US Black) a person who wears such a suit. 3 [1990s+] (W.I.) 'the act of grabbing someone in the waist and hoisting him onto his toes' (Francis-Jackson, Official Dancehall Dict., 1995). [after its rejection by US Blacks, the drape suit was taken up by Teddy Boys in the UK in the 1950s]

drape v.[1] [1930s+] to place oneself closely against someone (or something) else, esp. when amorous and/or drunk.

drape v.[2] [1940s–50s] (US Black) to dress (up). [DRAPE n. (1)]

drape crib n. [1940s] (US Black) a wardrobe. [DRAPE n. (1) + CRIB n.[1] (1)]

draped adj.[1] [1940s] (orig. milit.) drunk. [? one is draped across the bar or around another's shoulders]

draped adj.[2] 1 [1970s+] (US gay) uncircumcised. 2 [1970s+] (US gay) having a large penis. 3 [1990s+] (US Black) wearing large amounts of gold jewellery. [SE draped (in), covered in]

draped down adj. [1940s] (US Black) dressed in the height of urban fashion. [DRAPE v.[2]]

draper n. see ALE-DRAPER n.

drapers n. [1990s+] (W.I.) suspenders, braces.

drapery miss n. (also bit of drapery) [late 19C–1900s] a woman who is considered sexually forward and who emphasizes her appeal by a flashy style of dress. [orig. cited by Lord Byron c.1811 as 'a pretty, a high-born, a fashionable young female, well-instructed by her friends, and furnished by her milliner with a wardrobe upon credit, to be repaid, when married, by her husband']

drapes n. [1930s+] (orig. US Black) clothes, a suit. [DRAPE n. (1)]

drapes v. [1970s–80s] (UK Black) 1 to mug, to rob with violence. 2 to beat up.

drape shape n. [1940s–50s] a style of man's suit, typified by its generously cut, long, draped jacket with padded shoulders and high-waisted, tapering trousers. [DRAPE n. (1) + SE *shape*]

drat v. (*also* **drot**) [19C–1950s] lit. *God rot it*; usu. used in mild excls. as a euph. for DAMN v.

drat! *excl.* (*also* **drats!**) [1940s+] a euph. for DAMN! excl. [DRAT v.]

dratsab n. [mid-19C+] a bastard. [backsl.]

dratted adj. (*also* **drotted**) [mid-19C+] irritating, infuriating, a euph. for DAMNED adj. [DRAT v.]

draught-board suit n. *see* PENGUIN SUIT n.

draught on the pump at Aldgate n. *see* BILL ON THE PUMP AT ALDGATE n.

draw n.[1] [19C] **1** any device (or person) used to extract information from a third party. **2** the person from whom the information may be extracted.

draw n.[2] **1** [1920s–30s] (*also* **long draw**) a pipeload of opium. **2** [1940s+] (*Aus.*) a cigarette. **3** [1980s+] (*drugs*) cannabis, a portion of cannabis; esp. as 1oz (28g) or multiples thereof, e.g. *five-draw*, *seven-draw* etc. **4** [1990s+] a cannabis cigarette. [one *draws* upon it]

draw n.[3] [1940s–50s] (*US prison*) a suspended sentence.

draw v.[1] [late 16C–19C] to pick a pocket; thus *on the draw*, working as a pickpocket. [abbr. SE *withdraw*]

draw v.[2] (*also* **draw out**) [19C–1910s] to tease, to irritate, to exasperate, to induce (through teasing) to action.

draw v.[3] [20C+] (*W.I.*) to be born with a skin-colour noticeably different from that of the rest of one's family. [SE *drawn*]

draw v.[4] [1930s; 1990s+] (*drugs*) to take a drug, e.g. cocaine or cannabis.

draw a blank v. *see* DRAW BLANKS v.

draw a cork v.[1] [19C] (*UK Und.*) to give someone a bleeding nose.

draw a cork v.[2] [late 19C] of a woman, to have sexual intercourse (cf. CATCH AN OYSTER v.). [the image is of an exhausted, post-coital male]

draw a good ticket v. [1910s] to have good luck, to be successful. [lottery imagery]

draw a long bow v. (*also* **draw the long bow, shoot with the long bow**) [mid-17C+] to tell lies, to exaggerate; thus LONG-BOW MAN n. [tales of Irish archers who could allegedly kill at 5 miles distance, etc]

drawback n. [20C+] (*W.I.*) a small bribe. [the recipient *draws back* some money for themself]

draw blanks v. (*also* **draw a blank, draw it blank**) [19C+] to fail, to be disappointed or frustrated. [SE *draw a blank*; ult. drawing a blank ticket in a lottery]

draw bungy v. [1950s+] (*W.I.*) to snore. [? the sound of a bung being withdrawn from a cask]

draw caad v. (*also* **draw card**) [1950s+] (*W.I./UK Black teen*) to trick or connive, to mislead, to 'pull a fast one' on someone. [SE *draw* + CARD v.[1]]

draw down v. [1990s+] (*W.I.*) to approach someone with sexual intentions.

draw drapes n. [1970s] (*US gay*) a foreskin.

drawers n. [mid-16C–18C] (*UK Und.*) stockings. [? their being drawn on and off; the subseq. colloq. use to mean underpants does not materialize until 17C]

draw iron v. [mid-late 19C] (*US*) to draw a pistol. [SE *draw* + SHOOTING IRON n. (1)]

draw it blank v. *see* DRAW BLANKS v.

draw it easy! *excl.* [mid-19C] (*US*) a general excl. expressing incredulity or derision.

draw it mild v. **1** [mid-19C] to amaze, to impress. **2** [mid-19C+] to restrain oneself, usu. in speech. [public house imagery; i.e. the *drawing* of pints of beer]

draw it mild! *excl.* [mid-19C+] a general excl. expressing incredulity or derision, i.e. don't exaggerate! [DRAW IT MILD v. (2)]

draw it strong v. [mid-late 19C] to exaggerate. [opposite of DRAW IT MILD v. (2)]

draw-latch n. (*also* **draw-lock**) [mid-16C–mid-19C] a thief who enters a house by lifting the latch. [SE *draw-latch*, a string hanging on the outside of a door by which a latch is drawn or raised]

draw off v.[1] [late 19C] of a woman, to calm a man's passion by consenting to sleep with him. [SE *draw off*, to divert one's attention]

draw off v.[2] [20C+] of a man, to urinate (cf. BLEED ONE'S TURKEY v.). [SE *draw off*, to drain away]

draw one phr. [late 19C–1940s] (*US short order*) pour me a cup of coffee; thus ext. as *draw one in the dark*, pour me a black coffee.

draw out v. *see* DRAW v.[2].

draw someone for v. [19C] to borrow money from someone. [SE *draw*, to extract]

draw someone's fireworks v. [late 19C] of a woman, to calm a man's passion by consenting to sleep with him.

draw straws v. (*also* **gather straws, pick straws**) [mid-18C–mid-19C] to show signs of sleep; esp. as *one's eyes draw straws*. [pvb 'one eye draws straw, t'other serves the thatcher'; Grose (1796) has a single *straw*]

draw teeth v. [mid-late 19C] (*UK Und.*) to wrench off door-knockers.

draw the blinds v. (*also* **draw the veil**) (*US gay*) **1** [1920s] to engage in homosexual activity. **2** [1970s+] to pull back the foreskin. **3** [1980s+] to fellate an uncircumcised penis (cf. MAKE THE BLIND SEE v.). [the foreskin represents the *blinds* that cover the penis]

draw the crabs v. [1930s+] (*Aus.*) to attract unwelcome attention, to draw enemy fire (actual or metaphorical).

draw the crow v. [1940s+] (*Aus.*) to come off worst, usu. in a share-out or division of spoils, labour, prizes etc. [an anecdote in which a number of game birds and 1 crow were on offer and a hapless person *drew the crow*]

draw the king's picture v. (*also* **draw the queen's picture**) [late 18C–19C] (*UK Und.*) to create counterfeit banknotes. [UK banknotes always carry the current monarch's head]

draw the long bow v. *see* DRAW A LONG BOW v.

draw the queen's picture v. *see* DRAW THE KING'S PICTURE v.

draw the twine v. [1990s+] (*Irish*) to pursue a profitable activity. [? the twine used in bricklaying]

draw the veil v. *see* DRAW THE BLINDS v.

draw water v. [20C+] to have influence. [naut. jargon, a large ship draws more water than a smaller one]

drayman bible n. [1940s+] (*W.I.*) a bulla cake. [the *bulla cake* is a food of the poor; thus a drayman would rely on it for sustenance]

dread n.[1] [1940s–60s] (*Irish*) an object of pity or distaste.

dread n.[2] [1950s+] (*W.I. Rasta/UK Black*) **1** a Rastafarian. **2** one who wears dreadlocks but follows no other Rastafarian teachings. **3** the beliefs, practice or expression of Rastafarianism. **4** a youngster, usu. a male teenager, who shows off by taking dangerous risks. **5** (*also* **dred**) dreadlocks; usu. in pl. **6** as a term of address; the person addressed need not be a Rastafarian or wear dreadlocks. [Exod. 15:16: 'Fear and dread shall fall upon them; by the greatness of thy arm they shall be as still as a stone']

dread adj. [1960s+] (*W.I./Rasta*) of a situation, serious, important, amazing, whether positively or negatively. [DREAD n.[2]]

dread! *excl.* [1950s+] (*W.I./Rasta*) **1** a form of address, e.g. *You looking good, dread!* **2** a form of emphasis, underlining what has been said, e.g. *This herb is irey, dread!* [DREAD n.[2]]

dreaded lurgi phr. *see* LURGI n.

dreadful n. [late 19C] a sensationally written 'true crime' story, sold for a penny. [abbr. PENNY DREADFUL n.]

dreadlocks n. [1960s+] (*orig. W.I.*) **1** the long, braided hair worn by Rastafarians. **2** one who wears such locks, a Rastafarian. [DREAD n.[2] (1) + SE *locks*; Rastas have worn beards from the formation of the cult in the early 1950s, but *dreadlocks* were adopted later, in conscious imitation of Somali and Masai tribesmen, whose pictures were circulated in Jamaica]

dreadnought n.[1] **1** [mid-19C] an overcoat. **2** [1900s] a male pessary or suppository. **3** [1900s–10s] a high, stiff corset. **4** [1910s] (*Aus. milit.*) a prophylactic kit. [all plays on SE; lit. 'fear nothing']

dreadnought n.[2] (*Aus.*) **1** [1910s–30s] a long, deep glass of beer. **2** [1980s+] a shearer who can shear 300 sheep in a day. [fig. uses of SE *dreadnought*, a large battleship, the first of which, HMS *Dreadnought*, was launched on 18 February 1906 and became the world's greatest armaments platform]

dreadnoughts n. [1900s–40s] tight-fitting flannel or woollen female drawers. [their role as 'passion-killers']

dreads n. see DREAD n.[2] (5).

dready n. [1950s+] (*W.I. Rasta*) a friendly term for a fellow Rastafarian. [DREAD n.[2] (1) + sfx -*y*]

dream n.[1] **1** [late 19C+] a very attractive, charming, personable individual. **2** [late 19C+] someone or something exceptional, remarkable; often in ironic use. **3** [1910s] an expert.

dream n.[2] [late 19C+] (*Aus.*) a 6-month prison sentence. [? one can do it in one's sleep]

dream n.[3] [1910s] (*US*) a hand-rolled cigarette. [? a brandname]

dream n.[4] (*drugs*) **1** [1920s+] opium, morphine; thus *dream beads*, pellets of opium (cf. APOSTLE n.; AUNTIE EMMA n.). **2** [1940s] marijuana (cf. BOMB n.[4]). **3** [1980s+] cocaine. [the effects on one's brain]

dreamboat n. [1940s+] (*orig. US*) **1** (*also* **charmboat, dream bait**) a particularly attractive man or woman, the fuel of one's fantasies. **2** something particularly attractive, esp. a car. **3** a general term of admiration or affection (also used ironically).

Dream Boulevard n. see DREAMLAND n.

dreambox n. [1910s–40s] (*US Black*) the head.

dream dust n. (*also* **dream powder**) [1950s+] (*drugs*) any narcotic in a powdered form. [DREAM n.[4] (1) + SE *dust*/POWDER n.[2]]

dreamer n. [1960s+] (*drugs*) morphine (cf. AUNTIE EMMA n.). [DREAM n.[4] (1)]

dreamers n. [1930s–40s] (*US Black*) sheets and blankets. [SE *dream*; one dreams between them]

dream girl n. (*also* **dream guy**) [1920s+; 1980s+] (*orig. US*) the ideal(ized) young woman or young man.

dream gum n. [1930s–50s] (*drugs*) opium (cf. APOSTLE n.). [DREAM n.[4] (1) + GUM n.[3]]

dreamland n. (*also* **Dream Boulevard**) [20C+] unconsciousness.

dream off v. (*US*) **1** [late 19C] to have a nocturnal emission of semen, a 'wet dream'. **2** [1930s–40s] to fall asleep on the job, to drift off.

dream powder n. see DREAM DUST n.

dream puss n. [1940s] (*US campus*) the idealized young woman. [SE *dream* + PUSS n.[3] (1)]

dreams n. [1920s–50s] (*US drugs*) opium, usu. in pellet form for eating (cf. APOSTLE n.). [DREAM n.[4] (1)]

dream stick n. (*US drugs*) **1** [1930s–50s] an opium pipe. **2** [1940s–50s] (*also* **dream stuff**) a marijuana cigarette (cf. BAT n.[8]). [DREAM n.[4] (1)/SE *dream* + STICK n.[9]]

Dream Street n. [1930s+] 47th Street, New York City, between Sixth and Seventh Avenues. [the term was coined by the short story writer and chronicler of Broadway, Damon Runyon (1880–1946); the block was the site of the stage door to B.F. Keith's Palace Theater, 1913–32, the headquarters of American vaudeville]

dream wax n. [1920s–50s] (*US drugs*) opium (cf. APOSTLE n.). [its effects and its consistency]

dreamy adj. [1940s+] (*orig. US teen*) perfect, ideal, delightful, beautiful. [DREAM n.[1]]

drear n. [1950s+] a depressing person. [abbr. SE *dreary*]

drear v. [1950s] to act in a depressed, miserable manner. [SE *dreary*]

dreck n. (*also* **drek**) **1** [1920s+] (*US*) excrement, filth. **2** [1920s+] (*US*) anything worthless, second-rate, rubbishy. **3** [1970s+] (*US*

drugs) heroin (cf. CACA n.). [Yid. *drek*, thence Ger. *dreck*, excrement, dung]

drecky adj. [1950s+] second-rate, trashy, rubbishy, dirty. [DRECK n. (2)]

dred n. see DREAD n.[2] (5).

dredgerman n. [mid-19C] a thief who poses as a dredgerman in order to get on board a boat and rob its passengers.

dreds n. see DREAD n.[2] (5).

dreg n. [1980s] (*Aus.*) a term of abuse, esp. by women towards men. [SE *dreg*]

dregged adj. [1980s+] (*Aus. drugs*) tired and lethargic after smoking cannabis. [17C SE *dreg*, to render mentally confused, perplexed]

dreggy n. [1980s+] (*Aus./US drugs*) cannabis that causes one to become tired and lethargic. [DREGGED adj.]

drek n. see DRECK n.

drenched adj. [1920s–60s] (*US*) very drunk (cf. DAMP adj.). [ME *drench*, drink]

drench one's gizzard v. [20C+] to drink heavily.

dress v. **1** [late 18C–early 19C] to beat, to thrash. **2** [early–mid-19C] to tell off, to reprimand, to criticize. **3** [mid-19C] (*UK Und.*) fig. use of (1), to subject to robbery. [ironic use of SE *dress*, to treat a person properly]

dress a hat v. [mid-19C] to carry out various methods of robbery contrived by 2 or more servants or shopmen, either exchanging their master's goods (e.g. shoes for a hat) or pooling them (the butcher's boy steals steaks, the potboy steals beer etc) and all is sold to a third party.

dress-and-breath n. [1920s–30s] (*US Black*) a very lazy woman. [the most effort she makes is to get dressed and breathe]

dress and res v. [1990s+] (*US Black*) to dress smartly, fashionably. [SE *dress* + ?]

dress down v. **1** [18C+] to tell off, to reprimand, to criticize. **2** [19C+] to beat, to thrash. [ext. of DRESS v.; but note SE *dress*, to treat leather; thus to 'tan a hide']

dressed adj. [1910s+] (*US Black*) of a car, filled with every conceivable decoration, gimmick and similar flashy adornment. [SE *dressed up*]

dressed down adj. (*also* **dressed tight**) [1970s+] (*US Black*) very well-dressed. [but note recent 'dress down Friday', a day on which office workers are allowed to dress casually]

dressed in n. [20C+] (*US prison*) a new inmate. [i.e. *dressed in* newly issued clothes]

dressed out to the nines phr. see DRESSED TO THE NINES phr.

dressed tight adj. see DRESSED DOWN adj.

dressed to death phr. [mid-19C+] (*US*) dressed in one's very best clothes.

dressed to kill phr. (*also* **got up to kill**) [early 19C+] dressed up in one's smartest clothes, esp. with the intention of using one's appearance for (sexual) advantage. [SE *dressed*/GOT UP adj. (1)]

dressed to the nines phr. (*also* **dressed out to the nines, dressed up to the nines**) [mid-19C+] dressed up to the height of fashion; occas. intensified as *dressed to the tens*. [UP TO THE NINES adv.]

dressed up like a Christmas tree phr. [1920s] (*US*) dressed in one's best clothes.

dressed up like a dog's dinner phr. (*also* **done up like a dog's dinner, got up...**) [1930s+] dressed in the height of chic and fashion. [SE *dressed up*/DONE UP adj.[2]/GOT UP adj. (1)]

dressed up like a lighthouse phr. [1920s–30s] (*US*) flashily, ostentatiously dressed.

dressed up like a pox doctor's clerk phr. see DONE UP LIKE A POX DOCTOR'S CLERK phr.

dressed up like a sore finger phr. (*also* **dressed up like a sore thumb/toe, dolled up like a sore finger/thumb/toe, done up like a sore finger/thumb/toe**) [20C+] (*Aus./N.Z./US*) overdressed, flashily dressed. [SE *dressed up*/DOLLED UP adj./DONE UP adj.[2]]

dressed up to the knocker *phr.* [19C] dressed in one's best clothes.

dressed up to the nines *phr. see* DRESSED TO THE NINES *phr.*

dresser *n.* [1990s+] (*gay*) a transvestite. [abbr. SE *cross-dresser*]

dress flash *v.* [19C] to dress in a manner adopted by the fashionable or criminal classes. [FLASH adj.[2] (1)]

dress for the part *v.* [late 19C] (*UK society*) to act hypocritically. [theatrical imagery]

dressing down *n.* [mid-19C+] a reprimand, a telling-off. [DRESS DOWN v. (1)]

dress it in mourning *v.* [1930s] (*US*) of a White man, to have sexual intercourse with a Black woman.

dress like a million dollars *v. see* LOOK LIKE A MILLION DOLLARS v.

dress-lodger *n.* (*also* **dress-lady, dress-woman**) [mid-19C] a prostitute who is dressed in finery by her landlady and repays the favour by walking the streets and turning over her profits. [Bee notes *dress house*, a dress-hire shop where smart outfits were rented by the night, but suggests no Underworld overtones]

dress-puss *n.* [1940s+] (*W.I.*) an overdressed or fashionably dressed person, a provocatively dressed woman. [SE *dress* + PUSSY n. (9)]

dress suit burglar *n.* [1910s] (*US Und.*) a lobbyist.

dress-up *n.* **1** [1930s] (*US Und.*) an outfit of one's best clothes. **2** [1970s] a prostitute's client who enjoys dressing up, usu. in her clothes and make-up, although some prefer to provide their own wardrobe.

dress up drunk *v.* [19C] (*US*) to dress in an ostentatious manner. [the lack of discrimination in dressing supposed to be shown by a drunkard]

dress-woman *n. see* DRESS-LODGER n.

dreykop *n.* [1960s–70s] a trickster, a fraudsman. [Yid. *dreykop*, lit. 'twisted head']

drib *v.* [late 17C] (*UK Und.*) to crop, to cut off. [SE *drib*, to fall drop by drop]

dribble *n.* [late 19C+] meaningless chatter.

dribble *v.* [1930s–40s] (*US Black*) to stutter.

dribble-lipped *adj.* [1980s+] (*US Black*) having a notably pendulous bottom lip.

dribble-puss *n.* [1940s+] (*US*) a person, usu. a child, with a runny nose. [SE *dribble* + PUSS n.[3] (1)]

dribbling shits *n.* (*also* **dribbles**) [20C+] incontinence, diarrhoea. [SE *dribble* + SHITS, THE n. (1)]

dribs and drabs *n.* [20C+] (*Aus.*) body lice. [rhy. sl. = CRAB n.[2]]

dried-barkers *n.* [1940s] (*US Black*) furs. [SE *dried* + *barker*, a dog, thus any furred animal]

drift *v.* (*orig. US*) **1** [mid-19C; 20C+] to leave, to depart; esp. as imper. *drift*, go away. **2** [1920s+] to arrive. [the overtone is of moving slowly and aimlessly, although the imper. dispenses with it]

drill *n.* **1** [late 17C] a gigolo. **2** [1910s–20s; 1970s] (*US*) the penis (cf. AX n.[2]).

drill, the *n.* [1940s+] the proper way of doing things, the recognized procedure, esp. in phr. *what's the drill?* how are things done (round here)?; *know the drill*, to understand the way things are done. [ext. of milit. use]

drill *v.[1]* [early 17C+] to have sexual intercourse, usu. of a man (cf. BANG v.[1]).

drill *v.[2]* **1** [late 17C–18C] to lure, to entice slowly. **2** [1960s] (*US*) to stare. [the slow progress of a *drill* as it penetrates wood]

drill *v.[3]* **1** [late 18C+] to shoot (dead). **2** [1990s+] to punch, to beat. **3** [1990s+] to finish a drink.

drill *v.[4]* [late 19C+] (*US*) to walk, esp. of a tramp who would normally ride in a boxcar. [SE *drill*, to perform military exercises on a parade ground]

drill for Marmite *v.* [1990s+] to sodomize (cf. ASK FOR THE RING v.). [*Marmite*, a spread made of yeast extract and, as such, brown]

drill for oil *v.* [1940s] (*orig. US Black*) **1** of a man, to have sexual intercourse. **2** of a woman, to masturbate (cf. APPLY LIP GLOSS v.).

drill for Vegemite *v.* [1980s+] (*Aus.*) to perform homosexual anal intercourse; thus to be a male homosexual (cf. ASK FOR THE RING v.).

drillions *n.* [1940s+] an enormous, unspecified amount.

drink *n.[1]* **1** [mid-19C+] the ocean, the sea, a lake. **2** [1930s+] the river Thames.

drink *n.[2]* [late 19C+] one who is too tall for their age. [Scot. *drink*, a lanky, overgrown person]

drink *n.[3]* [1970s+] **1** a bribe, a sum of money that would supposedly purchase 'a drink' but is usu. much larger. **2** a tip, a commission, a bonus.

drink *v.* [1970s+] (*UK Und.*) to be susceptible to bribery; thus *do you drink?* a coded invitation by a criminal to a police officer whom they are hoping to bribe. [DRINK n.[3] (1)]

drinkage *n.* [1980s+] (*US campus*) alcohol, esp. beer. [SE *drink* + -AGE sfx]

drink a health to Duke Humphrey *v. see* DINE WITH DUKE HUMPHREY v.

drink all out *v.* [mid-16C–early 17C] to empty one's glass.

drink at Freeman's Quay *v.* (*also* **lush at Freeman's Quay**) [19C] to drink at another's expense. [SE *drink*/LUSH v.[1] (2); the free drinks distributed at this quay near London Bridge to porters and carmen in 1810–80; the RN amplified it to *Harry Freemans* (and used it for anything, not merely drink, that was free), while the British Army shortened it to *Freemans*]

drink at St Patrick's well *v.* [mid-17C] to drink (Irish) whisky. [*St Patrick*, patron saint of Ireland]

drink at the fuzzy cup *v. see* SIP AT THE FUZZY CUP v.

drink by word of mouth *v.* [late 18C–early 19C] to drink straight from the bottle.

drink coffee *v. see* DRINK MUDDY WATER v.

drink den *n.* [1940s] (*US Black*) a bar, a saloon.

drinker *n.* [1970s+] **1** an after-hours or unlicensed drinking club. **2** a public house.

drinkery *n.* [mid-19C–1910s] (*orig. US*) a liquor store, a bar, anywhere where alcohol is sold.

drink from both taps *v.* [1990s+] to be bisexual.

drinkie *n. see* DRINKY-POO n.

drinkitite *n.* [late 19C] thirst; thus *on the drinkitite*, on a drunken spree. [pun on SE *appetite* + TIGHT adj.[5]]

drink like a fish *v.* (*also* **drink like a sieve/well**) [mid-17C–19C] to drink heavily. [SE 20C+]

drink link *n.* [2000s] a cashpoint machine, an ATM. [the money taken out will be spent on alcohol]

drink muddy water *v.* (*also* **drink coffee**) [1950s–60s] **1** (*US*) to be very thin. **2** (*US Black*) to suffer, to experience hard times. [one cannot see through muddy water; thus those who are so thin as to be virtually invisible have to drink muddy water to give themselves some substance]

drink of water *n.* [20C+] (*Ulster*) **1** an irritating person. **2** a weakling, a dull or boring person.

drink on the whip *v.* (*also* **lick on the whip**) [15C–16C] to receive a thrashing.

drink out of the island *v.* [late 18C–19C] to drink to the bottom of a wine bottle. [the *island* is the inverted glass 'hillock' in the base of a wine bottle]

drink out one's cheque *v. see* KNOCK DOWN ONE'S CHEQUE v.

drink soup off someone's head *v.* (*also* **drink soup over someone's head**) [20C+] (*W.I.*) to be taller than someone.

drink's talking *phr. see* IT'S THE BEER TALKING phr.

drink the cross off an ass *v.* [20C+] (*Irish*) to have a substantial capacity for alcohol.

drink to one's oysters v. [late 15C–early 16C] to take life (usu. as regards its negative aspects) as it comes. [ety. unknown; image of opening oysters – some bad, some good – and drinking anyway]

drink wagon n. [1940s] (US Black) a ship. [DRINK n.¹ (1) + SE wagon]

drink with the flies v. [20C+] (Aus.) to drink by oneself. [a situation in which there are no companions other than the flies – whose presence is, of course, unwelcome]

drinky adj. [1900s] (Aus./US) mildly drunk, tipsy (cf. ALED UP adj.).

drinky-poo n. (also **drinkie, drinky-winky**) [1950s+] a drink, rendered facetious by this arch baby-talk.

drip n.¹ **1** [1910s–40s] (US) nonsense, flattery, sentimental drivel. **2** [1940s+] complaints, grumbling. [the words drip from one's mouth; note RN dripper, an habitual whinger]

drip n.² [1930s+] a weakling, a spineless person. [SE drip, i.e. weak rather than full flow]

drip n.³ (also **drips, dripsy**) [1940s+] venereal disease, esp. gonorrhoea. [the discharge that oozes from one's penis]

drip v. [1900s–40s] (Aus.) to complain, to nag; thus **dripping**, nagging.

drip-dry lover n. [1970s] (US gay) a homosexual man with a small penis. [the joke is that he has to let it drip dry – it's too short to shake]

dripper n.¹ **1** [late 17C–early 19C] venereal disease, esp. gonorrhoea; the discharge that accompanies it. **2** [1930s+] an ageing prostitute. **3** [1970s+] a prostitute, a promiscuous woman; the implication is of her de facto carrying a venereal disease. [SE drip, a falling drop; the pus-like discharge is a primary symptom of gonorrhoea]

dripper n.² [1920s+] (drugs) an eye-dropper, used to make a makeshift syringe or to drop LSD onto sugar-cubes, blotting-paper or some other medium of delivery; thus lip the dripper, to use suction to remove all traces of air from the makeshift syringe.

dripping n. [mid-19C] a cook. [SE dripping, rendered animal fat]

dripping for it (like a butcher's daughter) phr. [1910s+] (orig. Aus.) sexually voracious; sometimes abbr. to like a butcher's daughter. [pun on dripping, fat/dripping, sexually excited; the image is of uncontrollable vaginal secretions]

dripping pan n. [mid-17C; 19C] the vagina. [DRIPPINGS n. + SE pan]

drippings n. [18C] vaginal secretions.

dripping (toast) n. [1960s+] a publican. [rhy. sl. = SE (mine) host]

dripping with adj. [1920s+] abundant with, overloaded with, usu. in context of jewels or money.

drippy adj. [1950s+] weak, ineffectual. [DRIP n.²]

drippy tummy n. [1960s] (US) diarrhoea. [the watery stools thus engendered]

drips/dripsy n. see DRIP n.³.

drive n.¹ [20C+] (US Black) a highway.

drive n.² [1920s–60s] (US drugs) a thrill, a feeling of excitement, esp. after using narcotics. [SE drive, energy, intensity]

drive v.¹ [late 17C–18C; 1920s+] (US Black) of a man, to have sexual intercourse (cf. BANG v.¹).

drive v.² [1940s+] (orig. Aus.) to infuriate. [abbr. SE drive mad, drive crazy etc]

drive a nail/peg into one's coffin v. see ADD A NAIL TO ONE'S COFFIN v.

drive at v. [mid-19C] to work hard at.

drive-by n. [1980s+] **1** a shooting that is carried out by gunmen firing from a moving car. **2** a slow drive past a given place; no violence is involved. **3** surveillance from a moving car. [the subjects 'drive by' the victim/place]

drive by v. [1990s+] (US) to shoot at or be shot at from a moving car. [DRIVE-BY n. (1)]

drive iron v. see BUMP IRON v.

drive licks in someone's skin v. (also **drive licks in someone's tail**) [20C+] (W.I.) to beat severely. [SE drive + LICKS n. (1) + SE skin/TAIL n.² (1)]

drive on v. **1** [1950s+] (orig. US Black) to hit hard and without warning. **2** [1960s+] (US) to trick, to deceive.

drive one's ducks to a poor market v. (also **drive one's ducks to a poor puddle, drive one's geese to a poor market/puddle**) [20C+] (US) to marry unwisely, esp. to marry 'beneath oneself'. [the market in question is the marriage market]

drive one's hogs (to market) v. [early 18C–19C] to snore.

drive one's hos v. [1960s+] (US Black) to keep one's group of prostitutes hard at work, observing one's rules and earning plenty of money. [SE drive + HO n.¹ (1)]

drive (one's) pigs to market v. (also **drive the pigs home**) [18C+] to snore.

drive on the other side of the road v. [1990s+] to be homosexual.

driver n. [mid-19C] a manager or foreman who forces employees to work much harder than their wages demand. [abbr. SE slave-driver]

drivers n.¹ [1970s] (US campus) legs. [they 'drive one along']

drivers n.² (US drugs) **1** [1970s+] amphetamine (cf. A n.²). **2** [2000s] MDMA (cf. ECSTASY n.).

drive someone bananas v. [1970s+] (orig. US) to drive mad, to infuriate. [SE drive, to impel, to push + BANANAS adj. (1)]

drive someone nuts v. [1930s+] to drive crazy, insane. [NUTS adj. (2)]

drive someone up the wall v. [20C+] to infuriate, to annoy intensely, fig. to the point of insanity.

drive tab v. [late 18C–early 19C] to go out for a drive with one's family.

drive the bus v. see DRIVE THE (PORCELAIN) BUS v.

drive the car v. [1990s+] (US drugs) in prison, for a prisoner to purchase the day's supply of marijuana for a small group of friends. Members of the group take it in turns to provide for their fellows. Those who are smoking the drugs but not purchasing that day are hitching a ride or hitchhiking. [SE drive + car]

drive the pigs home v. see DRIVE (ONE'S) PIGS TO MARKET v.

drive the (porcelain) bus v. [1970s+] (US campus) to vomit, spec. when hugging the circular (i.e. steering-wheel-shaped) lavatory bowl and vomiting therein (cf. KISS THE PORCELAIN GOD(DESS) v.; MAKE LOVE TO THE LAV v.; MAKE LOVE TO THE POR-CELAIN GODDESS v.; RIDE THE PORCELAIN BUS v.; TALK TO THE BIG WHITE (TELE)PHONE v.).

drive turkeys to market v. [mid–late 19C] to walk in a drunken, unsteady manner. [the turkey-driver is forced to follow the birds' meandering course along the road]

driving stealth n. [1980s+] (US) driving a car without any bumper-stickers or similar advertisements of one's political affections, use of drugs or other beliefs that might antagonize the authorities. [milit. jargon stealth, a form of technology, best seen in the stealth bomber used in the second Gulf War (1991), in which all surfaces are made as radar-resistant as possible, thus helping the aircraft to operate largely unobserved by surveillance systems; similar anti-radar systems, although termed stealth, are available for automobiles to evade speed traps etc]

driz n. [early–mid-19C] lace; thus driz fencer, one who sells lace; driz camesa/kemesa, a lace-adorned shirt. [Rom. doriez, thread, lace]

drizzle n. **1** [late 18C] tears. **2** [1920s] (US) nonsense, empty chatter. **3** [1930s–60s] (US campus) a weakling, a whinger; thus adj. drizzly.

drizzlepuss n. [1930s–50s] (US) a sour-faced person, a grumbler, a killjoy. [DRIZZLE n. (1)/DRIZZLE n. (3) + PUSS n.³ (1)]

drizzlies, the n. [1960s–70s] (US) diarrhoea.

drizzunk adj. [2000s] (US campus) drunk.

droddum n. [mid–late 19C] the buttocks, the posterior. [synon. Scot.]

drol n. [1960s+] (S.Afr.) a general term of abuse. [Afk. drol(letjies), animal droppings]

dromaky n. [19C] (mainly northern) a prostitute. [abbr. Andromache, wife of the Trojan hero Hector, referring to the poor reputation of the travelling actresses who played her in Euripedes' play (5C BC)]

drome n. (also 'drome) [1900s–40s] an aerodrome. [abbr.]

dromedary n. (also purple dromedary) [late 17C–18C] (UK Und.) a thief, esp. an incompetent or novice one. [SE dromedary, a bungling fellow (although the dromedary or Arabian single-humped camel is, according to the OED, 'a light and fleet breed')]

drommerar n. see DOMMERER n.

drone n. [early 19C; 1940s+] (US campus) a tedious, unpleasant person. [SE drone, a parasite]

droned adj. [1970s+] (US drugs) simultaneously drunk and intoxicated by drugs (cf. DRY adj.[3]). [SE drunk + STONED (OUT) adj. (2)]

drongo n. [1940s+] (orig. Aus.) a simpleton, a stupid person. [orig. used of a recruit to the RAAF. Baker, The Australian Language (1945) links the term to 'Drongo [...] the name of a horse [...] which won a certain claim to fame by consistently finishing last or near last.' The OED dismisses this as 'highly speculative', while the AND suggests that the horse's name might have 'influenced' the earlier use; thus ? f. drongo cuckoo, the cuckoo genus Surniculus; this relates to CUCKOO n.[1] (2), thus cf. BOOBY n.[1]; note Seal, The Lingo (1999): 'drongo, a very Australian insult, was the name of a racehorse of the mid-1920s. Named after an Australian bird (Chibea bracteatus), commonly known as the DRONGO, the four-legged version was totally unable to win a race. This prolonged ineptitude was so spectacular that punters began to refer to any horses that failed to win (rather a lot) as a DRONGO. The term spread very quickly from this racegoers' little lingo into the Great Australian Lingo'; see also Bruce Moore (ed. AND), in Ozwords, October 1996, who maintains the centrality of the horse]

drongo adj. [1940s+] (Aus.) silly, foolish. [DRONGO n.]

droob n. (also drube) [1930s+] (Aus.) a useless, foolish, depressing person. [? link to RUBE n.[1] (2)]

droodle v. [20C+] (US) to wander aimlessly, to laze around. [SE drift + dawdle]

droog n. (also droogie) 1 [1970s] a thug, a gangster. 2 [1990s+] (US teen) a good friend. 3 [1990s+] a dull person. 4 [1990s+] a young man, esp. working-class. [coined by Anthony Burgess in A Clockwork Orange (1962); ult. Rus. drug, friend]

drool n. (orig. US) 1 [mid-19C+] spittle. 2 [20C+] nonsense, rubbish. 3 [1930s] vaginal secretions (cf. BINDERJUICE n.). 4 [1940s+] a socially unacceptable person. [SE drivel]

drool v. 1 [1900s–20s] to talk nonsense. 2 [1920s+] (orig. Aus.) to waste time, to idle around. [DROOL n. (2)]

drooly n. [1940s–60s] (US) a stupid, unpopular person; also adj. [DROOL n. (2) + sfx -y]

drooly adj. [1990s+] (US) sexy. [one who causes admirers to SE drool]

droop n.[1] [1910s–60s] (US campus) an unpleasant, esp. boring person.

droop n.[2] (also droops) [20C+] a feeling of unhappiness, depression.

droopy adj. [1930s+] 1 unpleasant, dull, weak. 2 depressed. [DROOP n.[1]/SE]

droopy-drawers n. [1910s+] an untidy, sloppy or depressing person.

drop n.[1] 1 [late 18C+] (UK/US Und.) a confidence trick, spec. ring-dropping. 2 [mid-19C] (UK Und.) a confidence trickster.

drop n.[2] 1 [mid-19C+] an advantage; usu. in phr. GET THE DROP ON v. 2 [1960s] (Aus) a good thing.

drop n.[3] 1 [late 19C] a financial loss. 2 [late 19C] (UK Und.) a share of stolen goods or money. 3 [1910s+] a receiver of stolen goods. 4 [1910s+] a delivery, usu. of stolen goods, drugs, contraband etc. 5 [1920s+] a hiding place for stolen, smuggled or illicit goods. 6 [1930s+] (drugs) a delivery point for drugs. 7 [1930s+] a payment of money. 8 [1950s+] a place where letters, papers and similar material (usu. secret) can be left for subseq. collection by another person. 9 [1970s] one who temporarily stores stolen goods immediately after a robbery, but who does not actually buy them from the thief. 10 [2000s] (drugs) the consumption of a pill or drug, taken orally.

drop n.[4] [20C+] (US Black) an orphan, esp. one whose parents are unknown. [farming jargon drop, an animal bred by accident]

drop n.[5] [1900s] (US campus) an unexpected examination.

drop n.[6] 1 [1910s+] a bribe. 2 [1910s+] the money used for a bribe. 3 [1930s] the money paid to a street beggar. 4 [1960s] (Aus. Und.) an informer. [one drops off the money]

drop n.[7] [1950s] (Aus.) the penis. [? DROPPING MEMBER n.]

drop n.[8] [1950s+] (W.I.) a free ride in a car or cart, at the end of which one is dropped off.

drop n.[9] [1980s] (US drugs) the physical discomfort that accompanies withdrawal from crack cocaine.

drop n.[10] see DROP (OF THE CREATURE) n.

drop, the n. (also the long drop) [mid-19C+] (Aus./UK prison) execution by hanging.

drop v.[1] 1 [early 17C+] to abandon a friendship or relationship; to snub. 2 [early 19C+] of an idea or train of thought, to overlook, to ignore, to give up on. 3 [mid-19C–1950s] to quit, to turn aside, e.g. on a road. 4 [1940s+] to evade.

drop v.[2] 1 [late 17C+] to pay over money, to spend money. 2 [19C+] to lose money. 3 [mid-19C; 1920s+] (US Und.) to sell stolen property to a receiver. 4 [mid-19C; 1960s] (US Und.) to sell something inferior for more than it is worth. 5 [1920s+] (orig. US) to pass dud cheques or counterfeit money. 6 [1930s] to hand over drugs. 7 [1950s] to bribe. 8 [1960s] (US) to bet. [the money is dropped on the table]

drop v.[3] 1 [early 18C+] to shoot down, to kill. 2 [late 18C+] to die. 3 [early 19C+] to knock down; also in fig. use. 4 [20C+] (US Und.) to arrest. 5 [1920s+] (US) to be convicted of a crime. 6 [2000s] to fire a bullet. [SE drop, to fall or make another fall to the ground]

drop v.[4] 1 [late 18C–1920s] to get to know about, to become aware of; thus drop cull, one who gives information. 2 [late 19C–1900s] to understand. 3 [1900s] (US) to reveal. 4 [1940s+] (US Black) in jazz/rap music, to produce, to deliver. 5 [1960s+] (US Black) to explain, to enlighten. [one drops or drops onto the information]

drop v.[5] [20C+] to give birth. [SE drop, usu. of a sheep, to give birth]

drop v.[6] 1 [1960s+] (drugs) to consume pills or any drug that can be taken orally. 2 [1980s] to drink (beer). [one drops them down one's throat]

drop a ballock v. (also drop a bollock) [1920s+] to make a mistake, to blunder. [fig. use of BALLOCK n. (1)]

drop a banger v. see DROP A CLANGER v.

drop a beast v. [1970s+] (UK society) to break wind.

drop a bollock v. see DROP A BALLOCK v.

drop a bombshell v. (also drop a bomb, drop the bomb) [1920s+] to deliver a shocking piece of news or a surprise.

drop a brick v. 1 [1920s+] to make an error, a mistake, esp. verbally. 2 [1990s+] to be shocked.

drop a clanger v. (also drop a banger) [1940s+] to make a social error, the awfulness of which reverberates around the assembled gathering. [SE clang/bang]

drop a cog v. [late 17C] (UK Und.) to drop a gold piece with the aim of ensnaring a victim into a confidence trick. [COG n.[1] (1)]

drop a dime (on) v. (also drop the dime) (US) 1 [1930s] to leave a tip. 2 [1960s+] to inform, to inform against. 3 [1960s+] to explain, to recount, to pass on information (in a non-criminal context). [(2) and (3) the act of making a call from a public telephone, which in the 1960s cost 10 cents. Note basketball jargon *drop a dime*, to shoot a 3-point basket]

drop a frog *v.* [1970s] (*US*) to give birth.

drop a hand in *v. see* DROP HAND *v.*

drop a hype *v. see* HYPE *n.*[1] (2).

drop a line *v.* **1** [mid-18C+] (*also* **drop a scrawl, send a line**) to send a letter; to write a note. **2** [1990s+] (*US Black*) to start a conversation with someone in the hope of establishing a longer relationship. **3** [1990s+] (*US Black*) to ring on the telephone.

drop anchor *v.* [1990s+] to defecate.

drop anchor in the bum bay *v.* [1980s] to have anal intercourse (cf. ASK FOR THE RING *v.*).

drop a net on *v.* [1940s+] (*US*) to commit to a psychiatric institution.

drop a packet *v.* [1930s] to give birth.

drop a rack *v.* (*also* **drop a roll**) [1980s+] (*US drugs*) to take 3 to 5 pills, of various types of drug.

drop a scrawl *v. see* DROP A LINE *v.* (1).

drop a thumper *v.* [1960s+] to break wind loudly. [SE *drop* + THUMPER *n.*[2] (1)]

drop away *v.* [late 17C] to give, lose or part with something, usu. money.

drop blue lights *v.* [1960s] to swear, to use obscenities.

drop bottom *v.* [1990s+] (*orig. US Black*) to drive around in one's car playing loud (hip-hop) music with a heavy bass-line.

drop car *n.* [2000s] (*US Und.*) a vehicle parked at some distance from a crime scene, which the perpetrators pick up after abandoning the one in which they actually committed the crime (and which might thus be identifiable).

drop-case *n.* [1970s] (*US*) a fool.

drop-cove *n.* [early 19C+] (*UK Und.*) a confidence trickster, specializing in RING DROPPING *n.* (1). [DROP GAME *n.* (1) + COVE *n.* (1)]

drop cull *n. see* DROP *v.*[4] (1).

drop dead! *excl.* [1920s+] (*orig. US*) a general excl. of dismissal.

drop-dead money *n.* [1980s+] money, the possession of which enables one to say to the world DROP DEAD! excl., i.e. it bestows freedom on its possessor.

drop down on *v.* [late 19C] to visit.

drop down on oneself *v.* [early–mid-19C] to feel depressed, esp. at the prospect of prison or judicially sanctioned death, to sink beneath one's problems. [DOWN *adj.*[2] (1)]

drop down to *v.* [early 19C] to find out about someone's character or plans. [var. on DROP *v.*[4] (1)]

drop 'em *v.* [1940s+] of a woman, to have sexual intercourse (cf. CATCH AN OYSTER *v.*). [*'em* are her knickers]

drop foot *v.* [1950s+] (*W.I., Jam.*) to dance energetically.

drop game *n.* **1** [mid-19C+] (*UK Und.*) a confidence trick whereby the victim is persuaded to pay money for a wallet, ring or some valuable, supposedly found on the ground but actually planted by the con-man. **2** [late 19C] in gambling, a trick whereby a gambler substitutes a note of higher value than that which was apparently bet, then reveals its worth and demands to be paid the correspondingly greater winnings.

drop gamester *n.* [mid-19C] (*US Und.*) a confidence trickster who performs the DROP GAME *n.* (1).

drop hairpins *v.* [1960s+] (*gay*) to reveal one's sexual preferences by dropping broad hints; thus *keep your hairpins up*, to maintain a 'normal' mask. [SE *hairpins* are seen as a quintessentially feminine possession]

drop hand *v.* (*also* **drop a hand in**) [1950s+] (*W.I.*) to hit with the clenched fist.

drop house *n. see* DROP JOINT *n.*

drop-in *n.*[1] **1** [early 19C+] an unexpected or casual visit or visitor; also of a surprising event. **2** [1940s+] (*orig. US*) a place or function which one may visit without prior arrangement.

drop-in *n.*[2] [1930s–40s] (*US*) **1** something that is easy; easy money.

2 a victim, a sucker. [the image of a gullible victim who may sometimes *drop in* to a confidence game without having to be steered there first]

drop in one's eye *n.* [late 17C–18C] a state of mild drunkenness. [? SE *drop* of liquor, or one is on the verge of drunken tears]

drop in the bucket *v. see* BUCKET *n.*[2].

drop into *v.* [mid-late 19C] to beat, to thrash. [the whip or fist is *dropped into* the victim]

drop it *v.* [1990s+] (*W.I.*) successfully to achieve a streetwise image, in terms of clothes, speech, walk etc.

drop it! *excl.* [mid-19C+] change the subject! stop talking that way! stop what you are doing!

drop it across *v.* [1910s] to reject someone.

drop joint *n.* (*also* **drop house**) [1930s–50s] (*US Und.*) a place used for storing and hiding stolen goods. [DROP *n.*[3] (5) + JOINT *n.*[4] (3)/SE *house*]

dropkick *n.* [1980s+] (*Aus./N.Z.*) a general term of abuse. [rhy. sl. = PRICK *n.* (3)]

dropkick and punt *n.* [1980s+] (*Aus.*) the vagina; thus a general insult (cf. ALL QUIET *n.*). [rhy. sl. = CUNT *n.*[1] (1)/CUNT *n.*[2] (1)]

drop knowledge *v.* [1980s+] (*US Black*) to demonstrate wisdom or skill. [DROP *v.*[4] (4) + SE *knowledge*]

drop lullaby *n.* [1950s] (*Aus.*) execution by hanging.

drop man *n.* [1960s] (*drugs*) a wholesale drug dealer's runner, who delivers bulk supplies to less important dealers. [SE *drop off*/DROP *v.*[2] (6)]

drop off *v.*[1] [late 18C+] to die. [fig. use of SE]

drop off *v.*[2] [1990s+] (*Aus. Und.*) to reject, to abandon.

drop off a style *v.* [1990s+] (*W.I.*) to lose one's figure or attractiveness.

drop off the hook(s) *v.* [mid-19C–1930s] to die.

drop off the perch *v.* **1** [18C+] to climb down, to adopt a less arrogant or condescending manner. **2** [18C; 1990s+] to die.

drop off the twig *v.* [1960s+] to die, as if one were a bird.

drop (of the creature) *n.* [late 18C+] a drink. [SE *drop* + CREATURE, THE *n.* (3)]

drop of the old author *n. see* LEAF OF THE OLD AUTHOR *n.*

drop on *v.*[1] **1** [mid-19C–1910s] to accuse, to rebuke. **2** [late 19C] to encounter.

drop on *v.*[2] *see* DROP TO *v.*

drop one *v.* **1** [1960s+] to defecate (cf. DESPATCH ONE'S CARGO *v.*). **2** [1990s+] (*Aus.*) to break wind.

drop one's bait-can *v.* [late 19C] (*US Black*) to make a serious mistake. [the most serious mistake an angler can make is to drop his bait-can]

drop one's beads *v.* [1970s+] (*gay*) **1** to accidentally reveal one's homosexuality by a slip of the tongue or other blunder. **2** to be shocked. [the stereotypical effeminacy of beads + BEADS *n.*[2]]

drop one's bundle *v.* (*Aus./N.Z.*) **1** [20C+] to panic, to lose (emotional) control, to give up hope. **2** [1980s] to defecate (cf. DESPATCH ONE'S CARGO *v.*). **3** [1980s] to give birth.

drop one's candy *v.* (*also* **drop one's watermelon**) [1900s–30s] (*US*) to make a serious mistake.

drop one's cookies *v. see* SHOOT ONE'S COOKIES *v.*

drop one's drawers *v.* [1970s+] of a woman, to allow intercourse; to lead a promiscuous sex life.

drop one's ears *v.* [mid-19C] to give up, to be discouraged.

drop one's gear *v.* [1950s+] (*Aus./N.Z.*) to undress. [SE *drop* + GEAR *n.*[1] (1)]

drop one's guts *v.* **1** [1970s–80s] (*N.Z. prison*) to act in a cowardly manner, to back down. **2** [1990s+] to break wind. [(1) GUTS *n.*[2] (1); (2) GUTS *n.*[1] (2)]

drop one's harness *v. see* HANG UP ONE'S HARNESS *v.* (1).

drop one's leaf *v.* [19C] to die. [autumnal imagery, but note GO OFF WITH THE FALL OF THE LEAF *v.*]

drop one's load *v.*[1] **1** [late 19C] of a woman, to give birth. **2** [1930s] to have a miscarriage.

drop one's load v.[2] [1940s+] (*US Black*) to reduce tension by having sexual intercourse. [SE *drop* + LOAD n.[5] (2)]

drop one's load v.[3] [1960s+] **1** to defecate (cf. DESPATCH ONE'S CARGO v.). **2** [1970s] to experience a shock. **3** [1990s+] to act in a cowardly manner; a synon. with SHIT ONE'S LOAD v. [LOAD n.[5] (1); (2) and (3) are fig. uses of (1)]

drop one's lunch v.[1] *see* LOSE ONE'S LUNCH v.

drop one's lunch v.[2] *see* OPEN ONE'S LUNCHBOX v.

drop one's tweeds v. [1960s] to have sexual intercourse. [TWEEDS n. (1)]

drop one's watermelon v. *see* DROP ONE'S CANDY v.

drop one's wing v. [late 19C] (*US Black*) to flirt. [the way in which one bird drops a wing in order to attract the attention of another. Note UK dial. *wing down*, to court]

drop onto v. (*also* **drop upon**) [mid–late 19C] **1** to become aware of. **2** to accuse, to turn on someone suddenly. [ext. DROP v.[4]]

dropout n. [20C+] (*orig. US*) a dull, boring person. [SE *dropout*, one who abandons their education]

drop out v.[1] [20C+] to die.

drop out v.[2] [1970s+] to dismiss, to get rid of.

dropped adj.[1] [mid–late 19C] of foodstuffs, coarse, stale, decaying.

dropped adj.[2] [20C+] arrested. [DROP v.[3] (4)]

dropped adj.[3] [1970s] (*US campus*) unofficially but dedicatedly engaged to be married. [the trad. gift by the man of a pendant or *drop*, bearing his initials]

dropper n.[1] [mid-19C+] one who passes counterfeit money, whether cheques or notes. [DROP v.[2]]

dropper n.[2] **1** [late 19C] (*US*) a gun, a pistol. **2** [1920s+] (*US*) a paid killer. **3** [1930s] (*US prison*) one who carries a knife. **4** [1930s+] (*US Und.*) a violent robber. [DROP v.[3]]

dropper n.[3] (*Aus./N.Z.*) **1** [1910s+] one who delivers supplies of contraband liquor. **2** [1940s–50s] one who makes deliveries of goods to retailers. [abbr. *shop-dropper*]

dropper n.[4] [1930s+] (*drugs*) an eye-dropper used by narcotics addicts as a makeshift syringe when proper hypodermics are unavailable.

dropper n.[5] [1960s] (*US prison*) a device for heating drinks.

dropper n.[6] *see* GOLD-DROPPER n.

dropper n.[7] *see* RUM DROPPER n. (1).

dropping member n. [19C] the flaccid penis, esp. when afflicted with (temporary) impotence or with venereal disease (cf. DEAREST MEMBER n.). [MEMBER n.[1]]

drop plates (on this mother) v. [1970s] (*US Black*) to lose one's temper, to get sufficiently annoyed to resort to physical violence. [fig. use of SE + MOTHER n.[4] (1)]

drops n. [1970s] **1** money left in pre-arranged (secret) places for bribes, pay-offs, shares of a robbery etc. **2** the weekly housekeeping money for one's wife. [DROP n.[3] (8)/DROP n.[3] (7)]

drop science v. [1980s+] (*US Black*) to demonstrate wisdom or skill. [DROP v.[4] (4) + SCIENCE n. (3); note W.I. dial. *science*, obeah, or ritual magic]

dropsey n. *see* DROPSY n.[2].

drop shit on v. *see* DROP (THE) SHIT ON v.

drop someone in it v. (*also* **drop someone in the shit**) [1930s+] to put someone deliberately into difficulties. [*it* is trouble, but the implication is also of excrement]

drop someone one v. [1920s+] to hit, to knock down. [DROP v.[3] (3) + ONE n.[1] (1)]

drop sticks v. [1960s+] (*UK/W.I. Und.*) to work as a pickpocket.

dropsy n.[1] **1** [mid-19C] one who 'drops off' to sleep. **2** [1930s+] the habit of dropping things; usu. as *the dropsy*. **3** [1990s+] (*W.I.*) an illness whereby the sufferer is prone to sudden sleepiness. [pun on SE *dropsy*, the falling sickness + (2) SE *drop off*]

dropsy n.[2] (*also* **dropsey**) [1930s+] **1** a bribe. **2** a tip. **3** money. [SE *drop*/DROP v.[2] (1); the giver *drops* the money in someone's

pocket or hand; a single nonce-use 'the silver dropsie' has been cited for 1616]

drop the arm on v. [1920s+] (*US*) to arrest. [the physical action + the fig. SE *arm of the law*]

drop the ball v. [1940s+] (*orig. US*) to make a mistake at a crucial moment. [sporting imagery]

drop the bomb v. *see* DROP A BOMBSHELL v.

drop the boom (on) v. *see* LOWER THE BOOM (ON) v.

drop the bucket v. [1940s+] (*Aus.*) to 'leave in the lurch'.

drop the bucket on v. (*also* **tip the bucket on**) [1950s+] (*Aus.*) to make damaging revelations about, esp. in a political context.

drop the chuck on v. [1920s–50s] (*US Und.*) to conspire with the police against a fellow criminal. [? fig. use of CHUCK n.[2] (2)]

drop the cue v. [20C+] to die. [billiards/snooker/pool imagery]

drop the dime v. *see* DROP A DIME (ON) v.

drop the hammer v. [1970s+] (*orig. US*) to take decisive action (against).

drop the hook on v. **1** [1930s] to become involved with, to take advantage of. **2** [1950s] to make an arrest. [(2) ext. HOOK v.[3] (1)]

drop the kids off v. *see* TAKE THE KIDS TO THE POOL v.

drop the lashes on v. [20C+] (*W.I.*) **1** to beat severely. **2** to make a surprising, shock decision.

drop the lug on v. *see* PUT THE LUG ON v.

drop the pill on v. [1990s+] (*US Und.*) to execute in the gas chamber. [the gas is triggered by breaking open a pill of cyanide]

drop the rag v. [20C+] (*US*) to give a signal, to set events in motion. [RAG n.[2] (4); the dropping of a flag to signal the start]

drop (the) shit on v. [1970s] (*US*) to give someone a hard time, to persecute. [SHIT n.[3] (8)]

drop the soap v. [1950s+] to make oneself available for anal penetration (cf. PLAY DROP THE SOAP v.). [orig. gay use, but also as a semi-joc. warning from one self-proclaimedly heterosexual young man to another, *I wouldn't drop the soap while he was around*]

drop to v. (*also* **drop on**) **1** [mid-19C+] to become aware of, to work out, to recognize. **2** [1900s] (*US Und.*) to obtain, to gain. [ext. DROP v.[4]]

drop-top n. [1970s] (*US Black*) a convertible, a soft-topped automobile.

drop trou v. (*US campus*) **1** [1950s] (*also* **down trou**) to drop one's trousers (in public). **2** [1960s+] in fig. use, to be amazed, astonished. [abbr.; a classier version (supposedly) of MOON v.[2] (2)]

drop up v. [1940s–50s] to visit.

drop upon v.[1] [late 19C] to treat badly, to victimize.

drop upon v.[2] *see* DROP ONTO v.

drop words v. (*also* **drop word**, **throw words**) [20C+] (*W.I.*) to utter veiled insults, to make sarcastic comments.

dross n. [mid-18C–early 19C] (*Scot. Und.*) gold coins, money; also as adj., gold (cf. CHAFF n.[2]). [the trad. (if high-minded) equation of money and rubbish]

drot v. *see* DRAT v.

drotted adj. *see* DRATTED adj.

drought n. **1** [1960s+] (*drugs*) a period when drugs are in very short supply or even non-existent. **2** [1980s+] (*orig. US campus*) a period without sex or even dates.

drove adj. **1** [1960s+] (*US*) very angry, infuriated. **2** [1970s] exhausted. [SE *driven*]

drover's breakfast n. [1940s+] (*Aus.*) a cough and a look around (cf. BARBER'S BREAKFAST n.). [SE *drover*, a shepherd; either the lack of 'civilized' amenities in the bush or his lack of desire for anything more]

drover's dog n. [1970s+] (*Aus.*) a useless or insignificant person, a drudge. [the *drover's dog* never stops working]

drover's guide, the n. [1920s+] (*Aus.*) gossip and rumour, reified as an imaginary newspaper.

drove up adj. [1970s] **1** (*US Black*) excited. **2** (*US prison*) frightened. [DRIVE ON v.]

drowned in the mercer's book *phr.* [late 16C] deeply indebted, i.e. 'over head and ears in debt'.

drown the miller *v.* (*orig. Scot.*) **1** [mid-18C–19C] (*also* **drown the miller's thumb, put out the miller's thumb**) to put too much water in one's liquor, to over-dilute a cup of tea or add too much liquid to one's dough mixture. **2** [early 19C] to go bankrupt. [*pvb* 'too much water drowned the miller', one can have too much of a good thing]

drown the shamrock *v.* [late 19C+] (*Irish*) to get very drunk on St Patrick's day. [the *shamrock* is the national plant of Ireland]

drozel *n.* **1** [early 18C] a young woman. **2** [early 19C] (*US*) a slattern. [Yorks. dial. *drasil*, 'a dirty slut, a draggle-tailed person' (*EDD*)]

drube *n. see* DROOB *n.*

drudge *n.* [mid–late 19C] (*US*) whisky. [ety. unknown; ? link to SE *draught*]

drudge *v.* [1940s+] (*W.I.*) to wear boots regularly (rather than go barefoot); shoes would normally have been worn only on special occasions. [SE *drudge*, a menial job; the implication is that the wearer has to wear shoes in their job]

drug *adj.* (*also* **drugg**) [1940s+] (*US Black*) exhausted, disinclined, bored; thus *I'm too drug to go out tonight.* [DRAG v.9]

drug *v.* [late 19C+] to take drugs.

drugged *adj.* [1960s] (*US*) annoyed, irritated. [ext. DRUG adj.]

drugger *n.* [1980s+] a drug user.

druggist *n.* [1990s+] (*W.I.*) a general term of address.

druggy *n.* (*also* **druggie, druggo**) (*US*) **1** [20C+] a drugstore owner, a druggist. **2** [1960s+] a drug user; rarely used by anyone involved with drugs. [SE *drug*]

druggy *adj.* (*also* **druggie**) [1970s+] (*orig. US*) **1** of, pertaining to, or characteristic of recreational drugs or their users. **2** consisting of drug-takers. [DRUGGY n. (2)]

drughead *n.* [1960s–70s] (*US*) a consumer of illicit, recreational drugs. [SE *drug* + -HEAD sfx (3)]

drugola *n.* [1970s+] (*orig. US*) bribery in which the pay-off comes not in money but in drugs. [SE *drug* + -OLA sfx]

drugsman *n.* [2000s] a drug dealer.

drugstore cowboy *n.* [1920s+] (*US*) a man, usu. a youth, who frequents drugstores for no other reason than to meet his friends, gossip and waste time.

drugstore stuff *n.* [1960s+] (*US drugs*) painkillers, synthetic opiates, available from drugstores but less effective than heroin. [SAmE *drugstore* + STUFF n.3 (2)]

drukkie *n.* [20C+] (*S.Afr.*) a hug, an affectionate squeeze. [Afk. *druk*, squeeze]

drum *n.1* **1** [mid–late 17C] the penis. **2** [late 18C] (*also* **drummers**) the testicles; usu. in pl.

drum *n.2* [late 18C–19C] the road, the street. [Gk *dromos*, thence Rom. *drom*]

drum *n.3* **1** [late 18C–19C] a social gathering, a party. **2** [mid-19C] (*UK Und.*) a casino. **3** [mid–late 19C] (*UK Und.*) a travelling salesman's stall. **4** [mid-19C–1950s] (*orig. UK Und.*) a saloon, a drinking house, a speakeasy, a nightclub. **5** [mid-19C+] (*orig. UK Und.*) a brothel (cf. BADGER-CRIB n.). **6** [mid-19C+] (*orig. UK Und.*) a house, a home. **7** [20C+] a prison cell, a prison. **8** [1900s; 1980s] (*Aus./US*) a room. **9** [1930s] (*US tramp*) a safe. **10** [1960s] (*US prison*) a criminal's hideout. [ety. unknown; ? the image of the hollow drum resembling a hollow house or room or the use of DRUM n.2 as a fig. house for wandering gypsies and tinkers]

drum *n.4* [mid-19C+] (*Aus.*) a pack. [the shape of the rolled pack]

drum *n.5* [late 19C] (*US*) any hat but a silk one. [? shape]

drum *n.6* **1** [1910s+] a tin or can in which tea etc is made. **2** [1950s] (*UK prison*) a primitive and illicitly constructed cooking stove, using a small tin bowl, a basic adjustment lever and as a wick a hospital bandage, rubbed with mutton fat. [shape]

drum *n.7* [1940s+] (*Aus.*) a piece of information, esp. a racing tip; thus *the drum*, the facts, true or reliable information. [the image

of drummers beating out information for transmission through jungles etc]

drum *v.1* [1920s+] **1** to knock on a front door to ascertain whether or not the home owner is in; if they are not, the house is broken into and robbed. **2** to steal from an empty or unoccupied house. [DRUM n.3 (6)]

drum *v.2* [1940s+] (*Aus.*) to inform, to 'tip off'. [DRUM n.7]

drum *v.3* [1940s+] (*US*) to work as a commercial traveller. [DRUMMER n.2]

drum and fife *n.* [20C+] **1** (*also* **duke of Fife**) a knife. **2** a wife.

drum-arsed *adj.* [mid-17C] having large buttocks. [SE *drum* + -ARSED sfx1]

drumbelo *n.* [late 17C–mid-19C] 'a dull heavy Fellow' (B.E.). [ety. unknown]

drummed up *adj.* [late 19C+] **1** artificially inflated, made to appear more important than reality allows. **2** of people, excited. [SE *drum*, to obtain custom, draw attention, make an announcement, by beating a drum]

drummer *n.1* [mid-19C] a thug who robs drunks, often after helping them to oblivion with a knockout draught. [? the 'beating' he administers]

drummer *n.2* [mid-19C+] (*US*) a commercial traveller, a salesman. [SE *drum up trade* + DRUM n.3 (3)]

drummer *n.3* [late 19C] (*Aus./N.Z.*) an itinerant. [DRUM n.2]

drummer *n.4* [late 19C+] (*Aus./N.Z.*) the laziest and therefore the slowest shearer in a shed. [? DRUMMER n.2; i.e. a commercial traveller is not a *real* workman]

drummer *n.5* [1930s+] a thief who specializes in robbing houses while their occupants are out, usu. for a short time. [DRUM v.1]

drummer *n.6* [1990s+] (*Aus.*) a racecourse tipster. [DRUM n.7]

drummers *n. see* DRUM n.1 (2).

drumming *n.* [1920s+] (*UK Und.*) posing as a door-to-door salesman to tour houses and thus identify empty ones, ripe for robbery. [DRUM v.1]

drummond *n.* [early 19C] (*UK Und.*) a supposedly infallible scheme; any certainty. [the fabled stability of the bankers *Drummond & Co*]

drummond and roce *n.* [1940s–70s] a knife and fork. [rhy. sl.; *drummond* = drum = DRUM AND FIFE n. (1); *roce* = roast = roast pork = SE *fork*]

drum out *v.* **1** [mid-19C+] to send away, to dismiss; thus *phr. give someone the drum*. **2** [1930s] (*US Und.*) to shoot dead. [milit. *drum out*, 'to expel or dismiss publicly by beat of drum, so as to heighten the disgrace' (*OED*)]

drumstick *n.* [mid-17C; late 19C+] the penis (cf. BAT n.7).

drumstick case *n.* [1970s+] (*US Black*) rape. [DRUMSTICK n. (but note DRUMSTICKS n. (3)) + SE *case*, a legal proceeding]

drumstick cases *n.* [mid-19C] trousers. [DRUMSTICKS n. (1) + SE *cases*]

drumsticks *n.* **1** [late 18C–1940s] the legs. **2** [mid-19C] the arms. **3** [1970s+] (*US Black*) the well-rounded thighs of an attractive woman. [(2) ext. of (1) but ? reflects the shape of a chicken drumstick like (3)]

drum-up *n.* [1910s+] the preparation of a cup of tea or meal. [DRUM n.6 (1)]

drum up *v.* **1** [mid-19C+] to obtain or create anything despite a difficult situation. **2** [1910s+] to make tea in a billy-can or similar container. **3** [1930s] to prepare a meal under rough conditions (typically on a battlefield or out of doors). [SE *drum*/ DRUM n.6 (1)]

drunk *n.* [mid-19C+] (*orig. US*) a bout of drinking, usu. to excess or oblivion.

drunk as (a)... *phr.* (*also* **pissed as (a)...**) [late 16C+] the images of drunkenness are many and varied, for all that some comparisons seem somewhat far-fetched. As well as the following whole entries, all the following nouns have been allied with the *phr. drunk as a...: bastard, bat, beggar, besom, big owl, bowdow,* *brewer's fart, cook, coon, dog, fiddler, fiddler's bitch, fish, fly, fowl, forty, Gosport fiddler, hog, jaybird, king, little red wagon, log, loon, monkey, Perraner, pig, piper, poet, rolling fart, sailor, skunk in a trunk, sow, swine, tapster, tick, top, wheelbarrow* (cf. PISSED AS A... phr.). [for *drunk as a tick* note RMC Duntroon (Aus.) *maggoted, exceedingly drunk*]

drunk as a boiled owl *phr.* (*also* **drunk as a biled owl, ...a fresh-boiled owl, ...an owl, full as a boiled owl, stewed as an owl, tight as a boiled owl, ...an owl**) [late 18C+] (*orig. US*) very drunk; intensified as *drunker than a boiled owl*; thus a *boiled owl*, a drunk person.

drunk as a cootie *phr.* (*also* **coot-drunk, drunk as a coot, drunk as a cooter, tight as a coot**) [early 19C+] very drunk. [COOTIE n.¹ (1)]

drunk as a duck *phr.* [1910s+] drunk; often ext. by *and don't give a fuck/quack*.

drunk as a lord *phr.* [mid-17C+] very drunk.

drunk as an emperor *phr.* [late 18C–mid-19C] very drunk. ['ten times as drunk as a lord' (Grose, 1796)]

drunk as (a) peep *phr. see* TIGHT AS PEEP phr.

drunk as a polony *phr.* [late 19C] extremely drunk. [? Fr. phr *soul comme un Polonnais*, drunk as a Pole (supposedly mocking the Polish-French Maréchal de Saxe, a great tippler), although the phr. might simply mean drunk as a POLONY n.¹ (1) or sausage, which cannot stand upright]

drunk as a rat *phr.* (*also* **drunk as a mouse**) [mid-16C+] very drunk.

drunk as Chloe *phr.* (*also* **blind as Chloe, tight as...**) [late 18C+] very drunk. [SE *drunk*/BLIND adj.¹ (1)/TIGHT adj.⁵; 20C+ use mainly Aus; Bee noted: 'she must have been an uproarious lass.' Poss. popularized in Aus. by the picture, *Chloe*, rejected in 1883 by the Melbourne National Gallery and bought by a well-known local hotel, where it became a point of attraction for many visitors; but note ref. in George Parker's 1789 poem 'The Bunter's Christening' to one 'dust-cart Chloe' as a guest at the christening — the orig. ref. may thus be to a 'real' person in the foregoing narrative]

drunk as cooter brown *phr.* (*also* **drunk as kooter brown**) [1900s–40s; 1980s] (*orig. US Black*) very drunk. [? anecdotal; but note DRUNK AS A COOTIE phr.]

drunk as David's sow *phr.* (*also* **drunk as Davy's sow, tipsy as David's sow**) [late 17C+] very drunk. [according to Grose (1785), the phr., which dates at least to Ray's *Proverbs* (1678), refers to one David Lloyd, a publican of Hereford, who had both a 6-legged sow and an alcoholic wife. On one occasion the wife, hoping to sleep off her excesses, threw out the sow and passed out in the stye. Unfortunately, Lloyd had chosen this time to exhibit his 6-legged freak to a group of friends. He escorted them to the stye, announcing: 'There's a sow for you, did you ever see another?' The friends saw only his wife and responded that it was indeed the drunkenest sow they had ever seen. The phrase stuck]

drunk as dogshit *phr.* [1980s+] very drunk.

drunk as floey *phr.* [late 19C–1900s] very drunk. [? misuse of DRUNK AS CHLOE phr.]

drunked up *adj.* (*also* **drunked out**) [1940s+] (*US*) drunk.

drunken piece *n.* [1910s–20s] a drunkard.

drunken tinker *n.* [16C–19C] a ne'er-do-well who, accompanied by his woman, wanders the country, mixing villainy and legitimate work, pursuing neither, it appears, with particular enthusiasm (cf. CANTING CREW n.; PRIG n.¹).

drunkery *n.* [19C] a cheap saloon. [SE *drunk* + sfx -*ery*]

drunk farm *n. see* DRY-OUT FARM n.

drunkie *n.* (*also* **drunkman**) [mid-19C; 1950s+] (*orig. W.I.*) a drunkard.

drunkie *adj.* (*also* **drunky**) [mid-19C+] (*US*) drunken; esp. with a name, e.g. *drunkie John*.

drunkin *adj.* (*also* **drunking**) [1950s+] (*W.I.*) extremely drunk. [pron. of SE *drunken*]

drunkman *n. see* DRUNKIE n.

drunk-on *n.* [mid-19C–1920s] (*US*) the state of being drunk, a spree; also attrib.

drunk's lagging *n.* [1960s] (*Aus.*) a short prison sentence, as given to one convicted of being drunk and disorderly. [SE *drunk* + LAGGING n. (2)]

drunk tank *n.* [1940s+] (*Can./US*) a short-term lock-up, where the night's drunks are held before sending them to court. [SE *drunk* n. + TANK n.² (2)]

drunk to the pulp *adj.* [1970s] (*US Black*) drunk to the point of passing out.

drunk with a bad cold *n.* [1940s] (*US*) oyster stew. [play on OYSTER n.² (1)/SE *oyster*]

drunky *adj. see* DRUNKIE adj.

Druriolanus *n.* [late 19C] the Drury Lane Theatre, London WC2. [its street address + pun on Shakespeare's *Coriolanus*, coined by its celebrated manager Augustus Harris (1852–96), who (see the writings of J.B. Booth) was also called by the nickname]

Drury Lane ague *n.* [mid-18C–early 19C] venereal disease, esp. gonorrhoea. [the reputation of *Drury Lane* as a centre of prostitution]

Drury Lane vestal *n.* (*also* **Drury**) [mid-18C–early 19C] a prostitute. [for ety. *see* prev.; note 'Foreigners in England' (in Hindley, *Curiosities of Street Literature*, 1871): 'If he wants some wives for the Ottoman plains / He can have all the women in Drury Lane']

druthers *n.* (*also* **rathers, ruthers**) [late 19C+] (*orig. US*) an alternative choice, a preference; esp. in phr. *have one's druthers*, to gain one's preference. [pron. of SE *I'd rather*]

dry *n.*¹ [late 19C+] (*US*) a Prohibitionist, dedicated to the cause of eradicating alcohol; also attrib. [the term was picked up under Margaret Thatcher's rule of the UK Conservative party (1979–90) to define those who opposed policies dedicated to free-ranging, deregulated market forces and the resulting mass-unemployment, false economic booms etc]

dry *n.*² [1930s] (*US prison*) the bread and water diet given as a punishment.

dry, the *n.* [mid-19C+] (*Aus.*) the dry season.

dry *adj.*¹ **1** [18C+] abstaining from alcohol; teetotal. **2** [19C+] bereft of alcohol. **3** [20C+] without supplies. **4** [1920s+] (*US*) without money. **5** [1970s+] (*drugs*) bereft of drugs.

dry *adj.*² [mid-18C–19C] drunk. [play on SE *dry*, thirsty]

dry *adj.*³ [1990s+] (*US Black*) simultaneously drunk and intoxicated by drugs (cf. DRONED adj.). [SE *drunk* + HIGH adj.¹ (2)]

dry *v.* [1940s+] to deprive a person of everything they possess.

dry as a... *phr.* [16C+] (*Aus./N.Z.*) used in various combs. to denote the intensity of one's thirst, e.g. [late 19C] *dry as a sack of gum-dust*; [1900s] *dry as a cocky's selection* [i.e. a small farm] *after a long drought*; [1910s] *dry as the rim of a lime-burner's hat*; [1950s+] *dry as a wooden god, dry as a lime kiln*.

dry as a dead dingo's donger *phr.* [1960s+] (*Aus.*) of weather or one's throat, extremely dry.

dry as a pommie's bath-mat *phr.* (*also* **dry as a pommie's towel**) [1980s+] (*Aus.*) of the weather, extremely dry. [POMMIE n.; the ref. is to the belief that British people don't wash]

dryball *n.* [1920s] (*US campus*) a student who does nothing but study. [SE *dry* + -BALL sfx, i.e. he refuses to 'get wet', to drink and enjoy himself]

dryball *v.* [1930s] (*US campus*) to study hard. [DRYBALL n.]

dry balls *n.* [1920s–40s] (*US*) an impotent man. [SE *dry* + BALLS n.¹ (1), i.e. they have 'dried up']

dry bang *n. see* DRY RIDE n.

dry bath *n.* [1920s+] (*UK Und.*) the search of a prisoner who has been first stripped naked; or a prison cell.

dry behind the ears *phr.* (*also* **dry back of the ears**) [20C+] (*US*) experienced, sophisticated; thus in negative to mean unsophisticated, naïve. [antonym of WET BEHIND THE EARS phr.]

dry bob *n.* **1** [late 16C–early 19C] a smart response, sharp repartee. **2** [late 17C–19C] sex without ejaculation by the man. [SE *dry bob*, a blow that fails to break the skin; in (1) positive and (2) negative uses]

dry-bone *n.* (*also* **dry-bones**) [mid-17C–mid-19C] 'a contemptuous or familiar term for a thin or withered person, who has little flesh on his bones' (*OED*) (cf. BAG OF BONES n.¹).

dry boots *n.* [late 18C–early 19C] 'a sly, humorous fellow' (Grose, 1785).

dry-clean Methodist *n.* [20C+] a Methodist. [Methodists baptize by sprinkling, rather than total immersion]

dry date *n.* [1970s+] (*US gay*) a platonic date; any appointment other than a sexual one; also thus pornography. [SE *dry* + DATE n.¹ (2)]

dry Dutch courage *n.* [1940s+] narcotics, esp. as a fig. 'killer of pain'. [a modern play on the trad. wet DUTCH COURAGE n. which refers to alcohol]

dry-eye *adj.* [1990s+] (*W.I.*) daring, dauntless.

dry fuck *n.* (*orig. US*) **1** [1930s+] (*also* **dry rub**) a simulated act of sexual intercourse, without penetration and usu. without removing the clothes (cf. DRY FUCK v.; DRY HUMP v.; DRY RIDE n.; DRY ROOT n.; DRY SCREW n.; DRY SCREW v.). **2** [1930s+] an unsatisfactory act of intercourse, esp. one that does not result in ejaculation or orgasm. **3** [1940s] something tedious or disappointing. **4** [1950s+] (*gay*) anal intercourse without any form of lubricant. [SE *dry* + FUCK n.¹ (1)]

dry fuck *v.* **1** [1930s+] to simulate intercourse by rubbing one's clothed body against that of one's partner. **2** [1950s+] to have (anal) intercourse without any form of lubrication. **3** [1970s+] to have lesbian sex, rubbing the vaginas together. [DRY FUCK n.]

dryfucking *adj.* [1950s] (*orig. US*) infuriating, disappointing or any other negative relevant to the context. [fig. use of DRY FUCK n. (1)]

dry gin *n.* [1930s] (*W.I.*) marijuana. [GANJA n. + pun on SE]

dry goods *n.*¹ [mid-late 19C] (*US*) a derog. term for a woman. [retail jargon *dry goods*, items of drapery, haberdashery etc, as opposed to groceries; i.e. the forerunner of a PIECE OF SKIRT n. etc]

dry goods *n.*² **1** [mid-19C–1960s] (*US*) (outer) clothing; thus phr. *kick into dry goods*, to get dressed. **2** [1920s–40s] (*US Black*) a style of suit characterized by a long, draped jacket with padded shoulders and high-waisted, tapering trousers. [for ety. *see* prev.]

dry grog *n.* [1940s–50s] (*US drugs*) narcotics. [drugs have a similar effect to 'wet' GROG n.¹ (1), i.e. alcohol]

dry gulch *v.* [1930s+] (*US*) **1** to murder. **2** to assault. [Western outlaws often ambushed and shot their victims as they passed through the narrow confines of a SE *dry gulch*; or ? f. the rustlers' killing of stolen animals by driving them over the edge of such a gulch]

dry head *n.* [1940s+] (*W.I.*) a bald person. [DRY-HEAD adj.]

dry-head *adj.* (*also* **dry-headed**) [1930s+] (*W.I.*) bald, when used of women it is an insult.

dry horrors *n.* **1** [1900s] (*Aus.*) delirium tremens. **2** [1910s] (*Aus.*) a negative reaction to alcohol, due to one's having been without drink for a long period. **3** [1970s+] (*Aus. drugs*) a dry mouth and throat after smoking marijuana. [SE *dry* + HORRORS, THE n.]

dry house *n.* [mid-19C] (*US Und.*) a dungeon.

dry hump *v.* [1960s+] **1** (*also* **dry root**) to simulate intercourse; thus as n. (cf. DRY FUCK n.). **2** in fig. use, to do something ultimately disappointing. [SE *dry* + HUMP v.¹/ROOT v.³ (1)]

dry jag *n.* [20C+] (*US*) a sense of brief excitement similar to that produced by alcohol, but without any drinking. [SE *dry* + JAG n.¹ (1)]

dry land *n.* [1970s] (*US Black*) a situation of safety; thus *dry land!* all clear! [one has fig. reached *dry land*]

dry land? *phr.* [mid–late 19C] do you understand? [rhy. sl.]

dry-land sailor *n.* (*also* **dry-land Jack**) [mid–late 19C] a criminal beggar who claims to have suffered shipwreck or piracy and requests alms to return home; or one who claims his goods are smuggled and thus sells them at an exhorbitant rate.

dry malice *n.* [1990s+] (*W.I.*) the act of ignoring somebody, esp. by using a third person to communicate via.

dry money *n.* [1900s] (*Irish*) cash, ready money.

dry out *n.* [1960s+] (*US drugs*) a period in jail, in order to withdraw compulsorily from drug addiction. [DRY OUT v. (2)]

dry out *v.* (*orig. US*) **1** [1950s+] to stop drinking alcohol; usu. to recover from alcoholism or from a bout of excessive drinking. **2** [1960s+] to withdraw from narcotics addiction.

dry-out farm *n.* (*also* **drunk farm**) [1950s] a rehabilitation clinic. [DRY OUT v.]

dry ride *n.* (*also* **dry bang**) [1930s+] a simulated act of sexual intercourse, without penetration and usu. without removing the clothes (cf. DRY FUCK n.). [SE *dry* + RIDE n.¹ (1)]

dry room *n.* **1** [19C] a prison; the inference is that its cells are damp. **2** [1930s] an interrogation room. [irony]

dry root *n.* [1970s] (*Aus.*) a simulated act of sexual intercourse, without penetration and usu. without removing the clothes (cf. DRY FUCK n.). [SE *dry* + ROOT n.¹ (5)]

dry root *v. see* DRY HUMP v. (1).

dry rub *n. see* DRY FUCK n. (1).

dry-rub *v.* **1** [late 19C] to beat severely. **2** [1950s+] (*US gay*) to wrestle or engage in similar 'horseplay' with strong homosexual overtones.

dry run *n.* **1** [1940s+] a test, a rehearsal. **2** [1950s] an act of sexual intercourse using a contraceptive. **3** [1950s] (*US gay*) sex without ejaculation; frottage.

dry screw *n.* [1920s] an act of simulated sexual intercourse, usu. with one's clothes on (cf. DRY FUCK n.). [SE *dry* + SCREW n.¹ (2)]

dry screw *v.* [1920s] (*US*) to simulate intercourse (cf. DRY FUCK n.). [SE *dry* + SCREW v.² (1)]

dry shave *v.*¹ [17C–18C] to deceive, to defraud, to rob.

dry shave *v.*² [19C+] to carry out an act of 'effrontery' (F&H) whereby one rubs one's knuckles hard across the victim's skull or chin (cf. DUTCH RUB v.; NOOGIE v.). [orig. a milit. punishment, men who had failed to shave adequately were roughly shaved on the parade-ground without benefit of soap or water]

dry shite *n.* [2000s] (*Irish*) a boring, unpopular person. [SE *dry* + SHITE n. (4)]

dry skull *n.* [1950s] (*W.I.*) a completely bald person.

dry snap *v.* [1940s+] to fire a gun that is either empty or does not have a round ready in the barrel.

dry snitch *n.* [1990s+] (*US prison*) **1** an act of informing committed by innuendo, or even error, rather than by direct accusation. **2** an individual who passes on information in this manner. [DRY SNITCH v.]

dry snitch *v.* [1950s+] (*US prison*) to inform by innuendo, or even error, rather than by direct accusation. [SE *dry* + SNITCH v. (1)]

dry stick *n.* [20C+] an unpleasant, humourless person. [SE *dry* + STICK n.²]

dry straight *v.* [late 19C–1930s] for a situation to work out satisfactorily or in time. [woodworking imagery, of wood that dries without warping]

dry up *v.* **1** [mid-19C+] to stop talking; esp. as DRY UP! excl. **2** [1980s] (*US Und.*) to refuse to give information (to the police).

dry up! *excl.* [mid-19C+] be quiet! [DRY UP v. (1)]

dry your arse! *excl.* [2000s] (*Irish*) stop whining! stop complaining! [ARSE n.¹ (1)]

dry your eyes! *excl.* [1940s+] (*Aus.*) stop complaining! stop whingeing! [lit. 'stop crying']

D. S., the *n.* [1960s+] the Drug Squad. [abbr.]

DSL *n.* [2000s] (*US Black*) a mouth seen as well suited for the performance of fellatio. [*d*ick *s*uckin' *l*ips]

DT *n. see* DTs n.

d.t. *n.* [1920s+] (*US*) a *d*etective, in later 20C+ esp. a member of the drug squad. [abbr.]

d/t *n.* [1970s+] in sex contact advertisements, *d*irty *t*alk; *dom*inance *t*raining. [abbr.]

d.t. centre *n.* [late 19C–1900s] a small literary club. [DTs n. (1) and thus a ref. to the enthusiastic drinking that takes place]

D-town *n.* [1970s] (*US*) Dallas, Texas.

d.t.r. *phr.* [1990s+] (*US campus*) defining the relationship. [abbr.; used of a conversation, often between the partners]

DTs *n.* (*also* DT) **1** [mid-19C+] delirium *t*remens. **2** [1940s+] a general malaise, not based on alcohol. [abbr.]

Dub *n.* [1920s+] (*Irish*) **1** *Dub*lin. **2** a *Dub*liner. [abbr.]

dub *n.*[1] **1** [late 17C–mid-19C] a key, a picklock; thus *dubs*, a bunch of keys. **2** [18C] (*UK Und.*) opening a door with a skeleton key or picklock. **3** [early 18C] a picklock boy. **4** [early 19C] a toll collector. **5** [late 19C] a prison warder. [DUB v.[1]]

dub *n.*[2] **1** [mid-19C] filth; thus a piece of excrement. **2** [1940s+] (*Aus./N.Z.*) (*also* **dubs**) a lavatory. [Scot. *dub*, filth, a dirty puddle; (2) + abbr. of *double-you see*, i.e. W.C.]

dub *n.*[3] [late 19C+] (*orig. US*) **1** a failure, an incompetent, a novice, an oaf. **2** something that fails, a disaster. [? SE *dubbed*, blunted, without a point]

dub *n.*[4] **1** [1940s+] (*US Black*) a $20 bill. **2** [1950s] (*N.Z.*) a double-decker tram. **3** [2000s] the number 20. [abbr./pron.; (1) and (3) = *double* 10]

dub *n.*[5] [1960s] (*US Black*) a friend.

dub *n.*[6] **1** [1970s] (*US*) (*also* **dubber**) a cigarette. **2** [1990s+] (*US drugs*) a marijuana cigarette. [? link to DUB v.[1] (2), i.e. it 'shuts up' one's mouth; or ? northern dial. *tab*, a cigarette]

dub *n.*[7] [1970s+] (*W.I./UK Black*) music with or without vocals invariably spiced up with snatches of echo and similar special effects, created by skilful, artistic re-engineering of existing recorded tracks.

dub *n.*[8] [1990s+] a piece of graffito, painted on a wall or train. [SE *dub*, to smear, but given the lifestyle of the artists note DUB n.[7]]

dub *n.*[9] [2000s] (*US Black*) one's local neighbourhood.

dub *n.*[10] *see* DOUBLER n.[2] (3).

dub, the *n.* [1910s] the Atlantic Ocean (cf. BIG DITCH n.). [northern dial. *dub*, a deep, dark pool]

dub *v.*[1] **1** [late 17C] to open a door. **2** [mid-18C–19C] (*also* **dab**) to lock up, to shut up, esp. in prison use. [dial. *dup*, to open; ult. SE *do up*]

dub *v.*[2] [1990s+] (*W.I.*) to make sexual advances. [SE *dub*, to thrust, to poke]

dub *v.*[3] *see* DOUBLE UP v.[3].

dub along *v.* (*also* **dub around**) [late 19C–1960s] (*US*) to idle, to loaf, to fool about, to spend time with; thus *dubber*, a time waster. [DUB n.[3] (1)]

dubash *n.* [mid-19C–1900s] (*Anglo-Ind.*) **1** an agent. **2** an interpreter. **3** a commissionaire. [Hind. *dobāshī*, a 2-language man]

dubb *n. see* DOUBLER n.[2] (3).

dubbe *n.* [1990s+] (*drugs*) cannabis. [DOOBIE n.[1] (1)]

dubber *n.*[1] [late 17C–mid-19C] (*UK Und.*) a thief who specializes in picking locks. [DUB v.[1] (1)]

dubber *n.*[2] [18C–19C] the mouth; thus MUM YOUR DUBBER! excl. [DUB v.[1], i.e. something that opens and shuts]

dubber *n.*[3] *see* DUB n.[6] (1).

dubber-mumed *adj.* [late 18C] silent. [DUBBER n.[2] + MUM adj.]

dubbies *n.* [1960s+] the female breasts. [var. on BUBBIES n.]

dubbo *n.* [1970s+] (*Aus.*) a fool, a general term of abuse (cf. BOBO n.[1]). [DUBBO adj.]

dubbo *adj.* [late 19C+] (*Aus.*) stupid; senile. [DUB n.[3] (1) + -o sfx (4)]

dubbs *n. see* DUBS n.[1].

dub-cove *n.* (*also* **dub cull**) [mid-18C–mid-19C] a turnkey. [DUB n.[1] (1) + COVE n. (1)/CULL n.[1] (4)]

dube/dubee *n. see* DOOBIE n.[1].

dub in *v.* [early 19C+] to pay a share of money, to contribute. [? fig. DUB v.[1] (1), i.e. 'open' one's pocket or purse]

dub lay *n.* (*UK Und.*) **1** [18C] picking pockets. **2** [late 18C–19C] robbery of a house by picking the lock. [DUB n.[1] (2) + LAY n.[4] (1); given the ety., (1) may be a misinterpretation; the only cit. is in *The Tyburn Chronicle*, there are no refs. in any other dict.]

Dublin *n.* [20C+] (*US*) the Irish area of a town or city. [*Dublin*, the capital of the Republic of Ireland]

Dublin fair *n.* [20C+] (*Aus.*) the hair. [rhy. sl.]

Dublin jackeen *n. see* JACKEEN n.

Dublin rules *n.* [1900s] (*Aus.*) no rules at all. [stereotyping the Irish as rough-and-ready brawlers]

Dublin trick *n.* [late 19C] a brick. [rhy. sl.; the identification of Irishmen with the building trade]

Dublin University graduate *n.* [1950s+] a particularly stupid person. [an unexceptional example of the clichéd condemnation of the Irish as fools]

dub off *v.* [1910s] (*US*) to masturbate (cf. BALL OFF v.[2]). [? SE *dub*, to beat blunt]

dub one's mummer *v.* [early 19C] to be quiet, esp. as imper. [fig. use of DUB v.[1] (2) + MUMMER n. (1)]

dubry *n. see* DOOBRIE n.

dubs *n.*[1] (*also* **dubbs**) [early 19C–1910s] money. [DUB UP v.[1]]

dubs *n.*[2] [1910s+] (*Aus.*) marbles. [SE *doubles*]

dubs *n.*[3] [2000s] (*US Black/campus*) 20-inch tyre rims; thus *sit on dubs*, of a car, to have such tyre rims.

dubs *n.*[4] *see* DUB n.[1] (1).

dubs *n.*[5] *see* DUB n.[2] (2).

dubsman *n.* [mid-19C] a prison warder or turnkey. [DUB n.[1] (1) + sfx -*man*]

dub the gigger *v.* (*also* **dub the gig/jigger, dup the giger/jigger**) [mid-16C–19C] to open a door. [DUB v.[1] (1)/DUP v. + GIGGER n.[1] (1)/JIGGER n.[1] (1)]

dub up *v.*[1] [early 19C+] to pay over money, to pay on demand. [ety. unknown]

dub up *v.*[2] [early 19C+] to lock up, e.g. in a cell or in handcuffs. [DUB v.[1] (2)]

dub up *v.*[3] [mid-19C] of a man, to ejaculate. [SE *dub*, to thrust, to poke]

duby *n. see* DOOBIE n.[1].

ducat *n.* **1** [late 18C; mid-19C+] usu. in pl., money, cash. **2** [mid-19C+] (*US*) $1. **3** [mid-19C+] a ticket, for the theatre, a sporting event etc. **4** [1920s] a (business) card. **5** [1920s–30s] (*US tramp*) a counterfeited letter identifying one as some form of victim, used to facilitate begging. **6** [1920s+] (*US prison*) any form of document. [SE *ducat*, 'a gold coin of varying value, formerly in use in most European countries. That current in Holland, Russia, Austria and Sweden being equivalent to about 9s 4d. Also applied to a silver coin of Italy, value about 3s 6d' (*OED*)]

ducat *v.* [1970s+] (*US prison*) to single out, to place on a list. [DUCAT n. (6)]

duce *see under* DEUCE.

ducey *n.* [1900s–50s] (*US*) the penis. [ety. unknown; ? link to SE *juicy* or DOOZIE n. (1)]

duchess *n.*[1] **1** [late 17C–18C] a woman, esp. when good-looking, even showy. **2** [early 18C] an old woman. **3** [late 18C] a prostitute. **4** [19C+] a general term of address to a woman. **5** [late 19C–1900s] one's mother. **6** [20C+] a wife. **7** [1920s+] a woman who is making money in films. **8** [1970s] an ageing, affected male homosexual (cf. GRAND DUCHESS n.; PINEAPPLE PRINCESS n.; PRINCESS n.; QUEEN n.[2]; QUEENIE n.). [play on SE, esp. in (1) the image of a *duchess* as an imposing figure; (6) also rhy. sl. (note DUCHESS OF FIFE n.)]

duchess *n.*[2] [late 18C–early 19C] **1** a woman who has intercourse while still half-dressed. **2** a man who has intercourse without removing his boots; thus *make a duchess*, to have intercourse in this spontaneous manner. [? the diary of Sarah, *Duchess of Marlborough* (1660–1744), who, following the return of her husband, wrote: 'Today my Lord returned from the wars and pleasured me twice in his top-boots']

duchess *v.* [1950s+] (*Aus.*) to treat in a patronizing manner, in the image of a stereotyped duchess; trad. attributed to the treatment by certain Britons of visiting Australians. [note letter from Paul Kunino Lynch, 12 September 2000, where he says that *duchess* is 'widely understood here as meaning what happens when an Australian or other provincial goes to the UK, and British power figures try to sap the visitor's will & judgment by overpowering them with experiences such as weekends in the luxurious homes of the mighty, duchesses and such. Presumably this used to work once upon a time, and it was at its peak during WWI. Verb both transitive & intransitive. I was duchessed, they duchessed or tried to duchess me. Stupid bastard went to London and let them duchess him [...] So the central meaning of the word is "treated by (generic) duchesses", rather than like them']

duchess of Fife *n. see* DUCHESS n.[1] (6).

duchess of puddle-dock *n. see* COUNTESS OF PUDDLE-DOCK n.

duchill *n.* (*also* **ducle**) [20C+] (*Ulster*) a general term of abuse. [? SE *dunghill* or ? Scot. *dochle*, an easy-going man]

duck *n.*[1] **1** [late 16C+] a lover, a sweetheart; a general term of affection; thus *duckheaded*, romantic, sentimental. **2** [17C] a prostitute (cf. ALLEY CAT n.). **3** [early 19C+] a fine example of; usu. in phr. *(a) duck of a —*. **4** [early 19C+] a fellow, a person.

duck *n.*[2] [mid-19C] a faggot, a parcel of meat scraps sold cheaply to the poor. [Yorks. dial.]

duck *n.*[3] [mid-late 19C] (*Anglo-Ind.*) a nickname for a soldier of the Bombay Presidency. [the Bombay *duck*, the bummalo (*Harpodon nehereus*), a small local fish, usu. eaten dried as a relish]

duck *n.*[4] **1** [mid-19C+] (*orig. US Und.*) a gullible fool (cf. AIREDALE n.). **2** [late 19C+] (*US campus*) a misfit, an unappealing person. [? SE *lame duck*]

duck *n.*[5] [late 19C] a type of watch.

duck *n.*[6] [late 19C–1910s] (*US*) a container used to bring back beer from the saloon; usu. as *chase the duck*, to bring beer from the tavern to drink at home (cf. RUSH THE GROWLER v.). [? its spout resembles a duck's neck]

duck *n.*[7] [late 19C–1950s] an evasion; thus *do/cop a duck*, to keep out of sight, to hide, to leave.

duck *n.*[8] (*also* **ducks**) [20C+] (*US*) a cigarette or cigar end; thus *shoot ducks*, to relight a cigar or cigarette end. [i.e. one 'ducks down' to pick them off the street]

duck *n.*[9] **1** [1910s+] (*US*) in gambling, **2**. **2** [1970s] (*US prison*) a 2-year prison sentence. [DEUCE n.[1] (1)]

duck *n.*[10] [1940s–50s] (*US*) a ticket, e.g. for the theatre, a sporting event. [abbr. DUCAT n. (3)]

duck *n.*[11] [1950s–60s] a type of hairstyle in which the back turns up. [DUCK'S ARSE n.]

duck *n.*[12] [1980s+] (*US prison*) **1** a weakling; an inferior. **2** an officer who passes on information to the inmates.

duck *n.*[13] [1980s+] (*US campus*) **1** a snob, a conceited, stuck-up young woman. **2** an unpleasant or ugly person. **3** a silly person. [? SE *duchess*]

duck *v.*[1] **1** [late 19C–1920s] (*also* **do a duck**) to travel, to go. **2** [late 19C+] (*also* **duck the nut**) to avoid, to escape from. **3** [late 19C+] to hide. **4** [1910s] to avoid an activity. **5** [1950s] to get rid of. [SE *duck* (one's head)/DUCK n.[7]]

duck *v.*[2] [1930s–40s] (*US*) a euph. for FUCK v.[1]/FUCK v.[3].

duck *v.*[3] [1940s+] to bend over in preparation for anal intercourse; usu. in phr. *fuck, suck and duck*.

duck *v.*[4] *see* DUKE v.[1] (3).

duck arse *n.* [1980s+] (*Aus. prison*) a lazy prison officer. [DUCK v.[1] (4) + ARSE n.[1] (4)]

duck-arsed *adj.* [1940s–60s] **1** (*Irish*) short and squat, with large buttocks. **2** a general derog. epithet. [SE *duck* + -ARSED sfx[1]]

duck buddy *n.* [1910s] (*US*) one who, bereft of a cigarette himself, is given the last few puffs on a friend's. [DUCK n.[8] + BUDDY n. (1)]

duckbutt *n.* [1930s+] (*US*) a short person. [SE *duck* + BUTT n.[1] (4)]

duck butter *n.* [1930s+] (*US*) **1** semen (cf. BABY GRAVY n.). **2** smegma. [the smell, reminiscent of duck droppings + the colour of butter]

Ducker *n.* [1930s–50s] (*US tramp*) a Dodge automobile. [play on DUCK v.[1]]

duckering *n. see* DOOKERING n.

ducket *n.* **1** [mid-19C–1930s] a ticket, for the theatre, a sporting event etc; thus fig. in phr. *that's the ducket*, i.e. THAT'S THE TICKET! excl. **2** [late 19C] a hawker's license. **3** [1920s–30s] (*US*) a union card. **4** [1920s–30s] (*US tramp*) a cripple's begging letter. **5** [1940s] (*US Und.*) a pardon. [var. on DUCAT n.]

duckets *n.* (*also* **duckettes**) [1990s+] (*US Black/teen*) money, cash. [var. on DUCAT n. (1)]

duck fart *n.* [1940s–60s] (*N.Z. juv.*) the 'plop' of a stone falling into water.

duck fit *n.* **1** [1900s] laughter, hysterics. **2** [1900s–20s] (*US*) a temper tantrum. [the noise of a duck]

duck-fucker *n.* [1970s+] (*US*) an unpleasant, unpopular person. [SE *duck* + FUCKER n. (3); note Grose (1785): '*Duck f-ck-r*, The man who has care of the poultry on board a ship of war']

duckhead *n.* [1970s+] (*US Black*) a woman with short, nappy hair. [? resemblance]

duckhole *n.* [2000s] a hideout. [DUCK v.[1] (3) + SE *hole*]

duck-house door *n.* [20C+] (*Ulster*) a very thick slice of bread (and butter).

duckie *n. see* DUCKY n.

duckies *n.* [1970s+] (*US Black/campus*) money. [DUCAT n. (1)]

ducking and diving *n.* [1960s+] living a life on the (criminal) margins; avoiding organized jobs, society etc. [rhy. sl. = SKIVE (OFF) v.]

duck it out *v. see* DUKE IT OUT v.

duck legs *n.* [late 18C] short legs; thus *duck-legged*, short.

duck of a —, (a) *phr. see* DUCK n.[1] (3).

duck-out *n.* [2000s] a failure, something that fails a test. [DUCK OUT v. (3)]

duck out *v.* (*also* **duck out of**) **1** [20C+] to back out, to withdraw. **2** [20C+] to make off, to leave, to abscond. **3** [1970s+] to default on, to avoid. [DUCK v.[1]]

duckpond *n.* **1** [mid-17C; late 19C] the vagina (cf. DAMP n.). **2** [1920s] a joc. name for the Atlantic Ocean (cf. BIG DITCH n.).

ducks *n.*[1] (*also* **ducksey**) [mid-17C+] a term of address, generally affectionate or friendly. [DUCK n.[1] (1)/DUCKY n.]

ducks *n.*[2] *see* DUCK n.[8].

ducks! *excl.* [1930s+] (*US, mainly juv.*) a claim, esp. a claim of first rights to something.

ducks and drakes *n.* **1** [early 19C+] a mess. **2** [1960s+] (*Aus.*) delirium tremens. [(1) fig. use of SE, i.e. a crowd of poultry; (2) rhy. sl. = SHAKES, THE n. (1)]

ducks and geese *n.* [20C+] (*Aus.*) the police. [rhy. sl.]

duck's arse *n.* (*also* **duckass**, **duck's ass**, **…behind**, **…butt**) **1** [1950s+] (*orig. US*) a type of hairstyle, esp. as adopted by teddyboys and rockers, in which the back of the hair is turned upwards in a manner similar to a duck's tail (cf. DUCKTAIL n.). **2** [1990s+] (*Irish*) a soggy cigarette butt. [SE *duck* + ARSE n.[1] (1)/ASS n. (2)/BUTT n.[1] (2); (2) pun on BUTT n.[2] (1)]

duck's breakfast *n.* [1900s–10s] (*Aus.*) a drink of water and a wash (cf. BARBER'S BREAKFAST n.).

duck's butt *n.*[1] [1970s] (*US Black*) a woman with unkempt hair. [SE *duck* + BUTT n.[1] (2); ? resemblance; presumably it sticks up at the back; but note DUCK'S ARSE n. (1)]

duck's butt n.[2] *see* DUCK'S ARSE n.

duck's dinner n. [1990s+] (*Aus.*) a drink of water, but no food to accompany it.

duck's disease n. [1910s+] having short legs. [like a duck, one waddles around with one's buttocks close to the ground]

ducksey n. *see* DUCKS n.[1].

duck shoot n. [1940s+] (*orig. milit.*) a simple operation. ['like shooting ducks on a pond']

duck-shoving n. [1910s+] (*Aus./N.Z.*) fighting for status, rank, position, esp. in political terms; in gambling, manipulating, using sleight of hand; thus *duck-shover*, one who uses unfair business methods. [19C cabman's jargon *duck-shoving*, touting for passengers rather than waiting one's turn in line; ult. image is of the farmyard; note WW1 milit. *duck shoving*, evading duty]

duck's meat n. [1990s+] (*Ulster*) mucus produced in the eye.

duck's neck n. [20C+] (*Aus.*) a cheque. [rhy. sl.]

duck soup n. (*US*) 1 [late 19C+] the total destruction of; usu. as *make duck soup of*. 2 [late 19C+] anything simple, easy. 3 [1900s] a guaranteed success. 4 [1910s–50s] something that suits one perfectly. 5 [1920s–30s] of a person, easily persuaded or victimized. 6 [1940s] something strange; as in phr. *queer as duck soup*.

duck's quack n. [1920s] (*US*) the very best, of a person or thing. [var. on CAT'S WHISKERS n.]

ducktail n. 1 [1940s+] (*also* **duck's tail**) a type of hairstyle in which the back of the hair is turned upwards in a manner similar to a duck's tail (cf. DUCK'S ARSE n.). 2 [1940s] (*S.Afr.*) a teddyboy. [the preferred hairstyle of the teen sub-culture]

duck the nut v. *see* DUCK v.[1] (2).

duck the scone v. [1940s+] (*Aus.*) to plead guilty in court. [SE *duck* + SCONE n.[2], i.e. the nod that is required]

duck Uncle v. *see* UNCLE n.

ducky n. (*also* **duckie**) 1 [early 19C+] a term of address; when used between men there is an implication of effeminacy. 2 [1990s+] a person.

ducky adj. [mid-19C+] sweet, delightful, charming. [DUCK n.[1] (3); an example of the supposed charm of farmyard animals; late 20C+ use generally ironic]

ducle n. *see* DUCHILL n.

dud n.[1] (*also* **dudde**) [mid-15C+] an article of clothing, esp. a cloak made from rough, coarse cloth. [ety. unknown]

dud n.[2] 1 [early 19C; 20C+] of a person, a failure, an incompetent, a weakling, a bore. 2 [20C+] anything that lit. or fig. 'does not work', a fake. 3 [20C+] of a thing or event, a failure, a disappointment, a 'flop'. [? DUD n.[1]; thence rags and thus one who dresses in them, esp. a *dudman*, a scarecrow]

dud adj. [20C+] 1 fake, false, counterfeit. 2 second-rate, unsuccessful. 3 broken. [DUD n.[2]]

dud v.[1] [20C+] (*US*) to dress up, to dress smartly. [DUD n.[1]]

dud v.[2] [1970s+] (*Aus. Und.*) to misrepresent the origin, quality and value of goods; thus n. *dudding*. [DUD n.[2] (2)]

dudaddle n. *see* DOODAD n.

dudde n. *see* DUD n.[1].

dudder n.[1] (*also* **whispering dudder**) [18C–mid-19C] a criminal beggar who wanders the country, selling goods that have supposedly been smuggled through the customs; thus capitalizing on the greed and gullibility of their provincial customers. The clandestine style of their encounter with a customer gives the synon. *whispering dudder*. [DUD n.[1]]

dudder n.[2] [late 19C] (*UK Und.*) money. [synon. Rom.]

duddering rake n. (*also* **dundering rake**) [late 17C–early 19C] 'a thundering rake, a buck of the first head, one extremely lewd' (Grose, 1785).

duddies n. *see* DUDS n.[1].

dud-dropper n. [1940s+] (*Aus.*) 1 a seller of stolen or inferior clothes. 2 a confidence trickster specializing in selling otherwise second-rate goods to those who believe that they have 'fallen off the back of a lorry'. [DUD n.[1]/DUD n.[2] (2) + DROPPER n.[3] (2)]

dudds n. *see* DUDS n.[1].

duddy adj. [1950s] (*Aus.*) useless, incompetent. [DUD adj. (2)]

dude n. 1 [late 19C+] (*orig. US*) (*also* **dudelet**) a man, a fellow. 2 [late 19C+] (*orig. US*) an overdressed, showy person, a fop or dandy; as *dudine*, a similarly showy woman. 3 [1900s] (*US campus*) a fool. 4 [1910s] (*US*) an expert. 5 [1960s+] a form of address. 6 [1970s+] (*US*) a thing. 7 [1970s+] (*US campus*) a person, irrespective of gender. [? DUDS n.[1] (1) or ? abbr. SE *attitude*. The term gained a whole new currency, especial among the pre-teens, with the popularity *c.*1990 of the cartoon characters Teenage Mutant Ninja Turtles, where it featured heavily; note also in *Comments on Etymology* (April 1997), Gerald Cohen has posited an orig. pron. of *doo-dee* and suggested an origin in Yankee *Doodle* + SE *dandy*]

dude adj. 1 [late 19C+] showy, smart. 2 [late 19C+] a general term of approbation. 3 [1930s+] used of one who is posing as a cowboy. [DUDE n. (2)]

dude! excl. [1980s+] (*US campus*) a mild excl., synon. with SE *wow!*, GEE! excl., SHIT! excl. etc and generally implying agreement or approval.

dudedad n. *see* DOODAD n.

duded up adj. (*also* **dudied up**) [late 19C+] (*US*) dressed up, esp. for a party or night out. [DUDE UP v.]

dudelet n. *see* DUDE n. (1).

dudester n. [1980s] (*US*) a person, irrespective of gender. [DUDE n. (7) + -STER sfx]

dudette n. (*also* **dudinette**) [late 19C+] (*US*) a girl, a woman. [DUDE n. (2)/DUDE n. (7) + SE fem. sfx *-ette*]

dude up v. [late 19C+] (*US*) to dress (oneself) up. [DUDE n. (2); ult. DUDS n.[1] (1)]

dudhead n. [1960s+] (*US*) an idiot. [DUD n.[2] (1) + -HEAD sfx (1)]

dudied up adj. *see* DUDED UP adj.

dudine n. *see* DUDE n. (2).

dudinette n. *see* DUDETTE n.

dudinkus n. *see* DOODINKUS n.

dudish adj. (*also* **dudeish**) [late 19C+] smart, dandyish. [DUDE n. (2)]

duds n.[1] (*also* **duddies**, **dudds**) 1 [16C+] clothing; thus *drop the duds*, to get undressed. 2 [mid-17C+] one's possessions, one's things in general. 3 [1900s] imitation jewels. 4 [1960s+] (*Aus./UK juv.*) trousers. [DUD n.[1]; Vaux glosses (1) 'women's apparel in general']

duds n.[2] [1960s] (*N.Z.*) the female breasts. [? BUBS n.[1]]

dudsman n. [18C–mid-19C] a criminal beggar, often dressed as a sailor, who wanders the country, selling goods that they claim fraudulently to have been smuggled. [var. DUDDER n.[1]]

dudueish adj. *see* DUDISH adj.

dud up v. [1930s+] (*Aus.*) to misinform, to cheat, to swindle; thus *dudder(-upper)*, one who fraudulently misrepresents the price and/or value of the goods he is selling, e.g. selling dyed aspirins as 'purple hearts', or claiming that perfectly legitimately purchased goods are actually 'off the back of a lorry' (and thus more glamorous) (cf. DUD v.[2]). [DUD n.[2] (2)]

due n.[1] [1980s+] (*drugs*) the cocaine oil that remains in a pipe after freebasing. [abbr. SE *residue*]

due n.[2] *see* DOOE n.

due adj. 1 [1930s] (*US Und.*) marked for assassination. 2 [1950s+] (*UK Und.*) due to be arrested, as part of the everyday problems of a regular, known criminal, irrespective of whether the person in question had actually committed the crime of which he was suspected.

dues n. [19C] money.

duey n. *see* DOOE n.

duff n.[1] 1 [late 18C+] counterfeit money, smuggled goods. 2 [1920s] a fake. 3 [1950s+] (*UK prison*) contraband tobacco. [? Yorks dial. *duff*, to avoid, to dodge]

duff n.[2] 1 [mid-19C+] the buttocks; thus [1980s+] (*US gay*) *fluff* *the duff*, to have anal intercourse. **2** [late 19C] the vagina. [west Yorks. dial. *duff*, the posterior]

duff *n.*[3] [1950s] *(US)* a *duff*el bag. [abbr.]

duff, the *n.* [late 19C] *(UK Und.)* the passing off of false jewellery. [DUFF v.[1]]

duff *adj.* **1** [late 19C+] fake, spurious. **2** [1920s+] of objects, useless, broken down, inferior. **3** [1930s+] of people, inadequate, incompetent. [DUFF n.[1]]

duff *v.*[1] **1** [late 18C–19C] to sell ordinary goods that are touted as smuggled contraband. **2** [mid-19C] to make old goods look like new. **3** [mid-19C] *(also* **doff***)* to make poor-quality new goods look old, and thus of better quality. **4** [mid-19C] to cheat out of, to defraud. **5** [mid-19C+] *(Aus.)* to alter the brands on (stolen) cattle. **6** [mid-19C+] *(Aus.)* to steal (cattle or horses). **7** [late 19C+] to blunder, to make a mess of. **8** [1900s–10s] *(Aus.)* in weakened use, to use (a possession, a place) without the owner's permission; spec. to pasture cattle on someone else's land. **9** [1940s] to smuggle. [DUFF n.[1] (1)]

duff *v.*[2] **1** [1960s] *(Aus./US)* to have sexual intercourse with (cf. BANG v.[1]). **2** [1960s+] *(Aus./N.Z.)* to impregnate. [DUFF n.[2] (2) or fig. use of DUFF UP v.[2]]

duff around *v.* [20C+] to sit about, to act lazily. [DUFF n.[2] (1)]

duffer *n.*[1] **1** [mid-18C–19C] *(UK Und.)* a crooked salesman who pretends to deal in smuggled goods but whose stock is actually cheap, mass-produced items, sold at a substantial mark-up and who targets especially provincials up in London, mainly from a site at St Clement's Church in the Strand. **2** [mid-18C+] *(UK Und.)* a hawker or peddler. **3** [mid-19C] *(UK Und.)* an inferior prostitute. **4** [mid–late 19C] *(UK Und.)* a counterfeit coin or article; any spurious article. **5** [mid–late 19C] *(UK Und.)* a petty swindler. **6** [late 19C–1920s] *(US)* a liar, a trickster. [DUFF v.[1]]

duffer *n.*[2] [mid-19C+] **1** an incompetent, foolish person. **2** *(Aus.)* an unproductive mine or goldfield. **3** a failure. [DUFF v.[1]; i.e. the item is 'no good' and so is the person; or ? Scot. *duffar*, a blunt, stupid person, or *dofart*, *doofart*, *dowfart*, a dull, heavy-headed, inactive fellow. Note 1920s angling jargon *duffer's fortnight*, a fortnight of the angling season during which trout are supposed to be caught easily]

duffer *n.*[3] [mid-19C+] *(Aus./UK Und.)* a cattle-stealer. [DUFF v.[1] (6)]

duffer *n.*[4] [1900s–40s] *(UK prison)* food, esp. pudding. [SE *dough*]

duffer *n.*[5] [1980s+] *(drugs)* a girl or woman who offers sex in return for drugs. [DUFF v.[1] (1)]

duffer (out) *v.* [mid-19C+] *(Aus.)* **1** for a mine or goldfield to prove unproductive. **2** for a miner or prospector to fail in his searches. [DUFFER n.[2] (2)]

duff-flogger *n.* [1930s] *(US)* a male masturbator. [? DUFF n.[2] (1) + SE *flogger*]

duffing *n.* [mid-19C] passing off of a worthless article as valuable. [DUFF v.[1]]

duffing *adj.* **1** [mid-19C] worthless, false, esp. of goods sold as more valuable than they really are. **2** [late 19C] foolish, incompetent. [DUFF v.[1]]

duffing yard *n.* [late 19C] *(Aus.)* an isolated place where cattle-stealers can hide rustled cattle, rebrand it etc. [DUFF v.[1] (5)/DUFF v.[1] (6)]

duffis *n. see* DUFUS n. (1).

duffle-headed *adj.* [mid-19C] stupid, dull-witted (cf. AIRHEADED adj.). [? var. on BUFFLEHEADED adj.]

duffman *adj.* [1910s–20s] *(UK Und.)* inferior, bad. [DUFF adj.]

duff over *v. see* DUFF UP v.[2].

duff-trap *n.* [1900s] *(Aus.)* the mouth. [SE *duff*, a form of pudding + SE *trap*/TRAP n.[3]]

duff up *v.*[1] [1940s] to become foggy or hazy. [orig. dial.; ult. dial. *duff*, coal dust]

duff up *v.*[2] *(also* **duff over***)* [1940s+] to beat up. [orig. RAF jargon; ? Scot. *duff*, to hit, to strike]

duffus *n.* [1940s] *(US)* the posterior, the buttocks. [var. on DUFF n.[2] (1)]

duffy *n.*[1] [early 19C] a quarter-pint of gin. [? a brandname; ? var. on DAFFY n.[1] (1)]

duffy *n.*[2] [1900s] *(US)* bread. [var. on DUFFER n.[4]]

duffy *n.*[3] [1920s–30s] *(US)* a derby hat. [? its popularity among Irish wearers, i.e. the common surname *Duffy*]

duffy *n.*[4] [1950s] *(US prison)* state issue tobacco. [a 'tribute' to Clinton *Duffy*, San Quentin warden 1942–54]

duflickerty *n. see* DOOFLICKER n.

duflus *n. see* DOOFLUS n.

dufunny *n. see* DOOFUNNY n.

dufus *n.* [1970s+] **1** *(also* **duffis***)* an eccentric, foolish or gauche person. **2** a thingummyjig. [var. on DOOFUS n.]

dufus *adj.* [1970s+] *(US)* strange, unlikely. [DUFUS n. (1)]

dugie *n. see* DUJI n.

dug-in *adj.* [1910s+] safe, secure, entrenched, firmly established in a position. [imagery of 'digging in' for safety during a battle]

dugout *n.*[1] [1910s+] an old-fashioned person, either in ideas or appearance, esp. a retired officer etc, recalled for temporary milit. service. [SE *dugout*, a roofed shelter used in trench warfare; note Fraser & Gibbons, *Soldier & Sailor Words & Phrases* (1925), suggest: 'It first came in apparently during the South African War of 1899–1902 for pensioned or retired officers who came back to service in consequence of the depleting of the active establishment through casualties in the field', however, the *OED*'s first cit. is 1912]

dugout *n.*[2] **1** [1930s–50s] *(US drugs)* the lowest class of addict. **2** [1930s–70s] *(US prison)* a voracious eater.

dugs *n.* [mid-16C+] female breasts (cf. BORDENS n.). [SE *dug*, the udder or teat of a female animal]

dugu-dugu *n.* [1990s+] *(W.I.)* sexual intercourse.

duh-brain *n. see* DUR-BRAIN n.

duji *n.* *(also* **dogie, doogie, doogy, doojee, dugie, dujie***)* [1960s+] *(drugs)* heroin. [ety. unknown]

duke *n.*[1] [late 17C+] a showy, ostentatious man. [abbr. RUM DUKE n. (2); 20C+ use is US although its root may lie in the more recent DUDE n. (2)]

duke *n.*[2] [mid-19C] gin. [used by servants in upper-class houses]

duke *n.*[3] **1** [mid-19C+] *(US)* *(also* **juke***)* a hand; usu. in pl.; also in fig. use; occas. an arm; thus *dukefull*, a handful. **2** [1900s–40s] *(US Und.)* a form of confidence game. **3** [1910s–50s] a hand of cards; thus *crop someone's duke*, to read an opponent's cards by trickery. **4** [1930s–70s] in boxing, a decision. **5** [1950s] the bill, usu. in a restaurant. **6** [1970s] in fig. use, a plan, i.e a hand of cards that one deals or is dealt. [? rhy. sl. *duke of yorks* = FORKS n.; (4) the referee raises the winning boxer's hand]

duke *n.*[4] **1** [1920s] a champion, one of the best. **2** [1930s+] a tough, dominant individual, a leader or boss, esp. in the criminal world. **3** [1940s] *(US prison)* the warden. **4** [1970s+] *(US gay/prison)* a predatory prison homosexual.

duke *n.*[5] *see* DUKE (OF KENT) n.

duke *v.*[1] **1** [mid-19C–1920s] *(also* **dook (it), duke it***)* to shake hands, to welcome. **2** [1920s+] *(also* **dook (it), duke it, duke on***)* to give out, to hand over. **3** [1930s+] *(also* **duck***)* to fight with the fists. **4** [1960s+] to inform. **5** [1980s+] *(US gay)* to push one or more fingers or even the whole fist into one's partner's anus. [DUKE n.[3] (1); note WW1 Aus. milit. *dook 'im one*, to salute]

duke *v.*[2] [1980s+] to get dressed. [ety. unknown; ? link to DUDE n. (2); ? var. on DUDE UP v.]

duked out *adj.* *(also* **duked up***)* [1930s–50s] *(US)* dressed up. [? var. on DUDED UP adj.]

dukee *n. see* DUKIE n.[1] (1).

duke in *v.* *(US)* **1** [1930s+] to introduce, to bring in to a plan or group; also as n. **2** [1950s+] to fool, to trick. **3** [1960s] to give a share. [DUKE v.[1] (1); handshaking in both deceitful and sincere contexts]

duke it v. see DUKE v.[1].

duke it out v. (*also* **duck it out**) **1** [1930s+] (*US*) to fight with fists. **2** [1990s+] to argue, to dispute. [DUKE v.[1] (3)]

duke of Cork n. see EARL OF CORK n.[2].

duke of Fife n. see DRUM AND FIFE n. (1).

duke (of Kent) n. **1** [1930s+] the rent. **2** [1960s+] (*Aus.*) (*also* **dukers**) a cent. **3** [1970s+] a homosexual. **4** [1980s] (*Aus.*) a tent. [rhy. sl.; (3) = BENT n.]

duke of limbs n. [mid-18C–mid-19C] an awkward, ungainly person.

duke of Seven Dials n. [late 19C] a conceited, self-opinionated (young) man. [*Seven Dials*, a well-known criminal enclave and, as such, unlikely to boast many peers]

duke of York n. **1** [mid–late 19C] a walk. **2** [late 19C+] a fork. **3** [late 19C+] in pl., fingers, i.e. FORKS n. (1). **4** [late 19C+] talk. **5** [1930s+] chalk. **6** [1950s] a cork. **7** [1960s] pork. [rhy. sl.]

duke of York v. **1** [mid-19C+] to walk. **2** [late 19C+] to talk. [rhy. sl.]

duke on v. see DUKE v.[1] (2).

duke-out n. [1970s+] (*US*) an argument, a fight. [DUKE OUT v. (2)]

duke out v. **1** [1950s] (*US Und.*) to throw out, to get rid of. **2** [1970s+] (*US*) to knock out. [DUKE v.[1] (3)]

duke player n. [1930s] (*US Und.*) a gambler who cheats at cards. [DUKE n.[3] (3)]

duker n.[1] (*also* **dooker**) [1920s–50s] (*US Und.*) the member of a team of cheats, con-men or similar groups who pretends to be an 'innocent bystander' to lure in genuine victims. [DUKE v.[1] (1)]

duker n.[2] [1970s] (*US*) a boxer, a fist-fighter. [DUKES n. (1)/DUKE v.[1] (3)]

dukers n. see DUKE (OF KENT) n. (2).

Duke's, The n. [late 19C] the Argyll Rooms, Windmill Street, London W1. [*fl.*1860–1900 and named, presumably, for the earlier and more fashionable Argyll Rooms in Little Argyll Street, W1 (*fl.*1806–30). Liszt and Mendelssohn played there, and Byron versified upon its excesses]

dukes n. **1** [mid-19C+] the fists; thus *put up your dukes, go to dukes, get ready to fight.* **2** [1940s] (*US Black*) the knees. [DUKE n.[3] (1)]

dukey n. [mid–late 19C] a cheap theatre or music hall. [a particular theatre whose Jewish proprietor had a large nose, i.e. a DOOK n.[1] (1)]

dukey rope n. [1990s+] (*US Black/teen*) a large, heavy gold chain, worn as jewellery. [? SE *duke* or ? DUKIE n.[2] (1), i.e. a SHITLOAD n. of gold]

dukie n.[1] (*also* **dookey, dukey**) **1** [1910s–40s] (*US Und.*) (*also* **dukee**) a meal (of scraps/left-overs) given to a tramp. **2** [1920s+] (*US*) a light meal, esp. that carried to work by a labourer or factory worker. **3** [1960s] (*US prison*) a sandwich. [DUKE n.[3] (1); thus something one can carry or ? dial. *docky,* a light meal taken in the fields]

dukie n.[2] (*also* **dookey, dookie**) **1** [1960s+] excrement; thus *do dukie, drop a dookie, blast a dookie, take a dookie,* to defecate. **2** [1970s+] (*US Black*) an act of defecation; thus *dukie hole,* the anus. **3** [1990s+] (*US campus*) an unpleasant, obnoxious person. [? Scot. *dook,* the bung of a cask]

dukie v. [1990s+] to defecate (cf. CACA v.). [DUKIE n.[2] (1)]

Dulcibella n. [18C] a prostitute, a mistress. [note *The Lantern* (N.O.) (1887): 'I seed him last Saturday night with a dolcina']

dull as dogshit adj. [1960s+] utterly tedious.

dullhead n. [1970s] (*US*) a dullard. [SE *dull* + -HEAD sfx (1)]

dull-pickle n. [late 17C–18C] a fool, a dullard. [SE *dull* + PICKLE n.[1] (1)]

dullsville n. [1950s+] an imaginary town, characterized by extreme dullness or boredom; thus a state, environment or situation of extreme dullness. [SE *dull* + -VILLE sfx[1]]

dullsville adj. [1960s+] (*orig. US*) tedious. [DULLSVILLE n.]

dull swift n. [late 18C–early 19C] a stupid, sluggish person. [lit. 'a stupid messenger']

dum adj. (*also* **dumb**) [late 19C–1920s] (*US*) a general intensifier, great, complete, e.g. *dumb shame.* [DUM adv.; ult. euph. for DAMN adj.]

dum adv. (*also* **dumb**) [late 18C+] (*US*) extremely, very. [euph. for DAMN adv.]

dum-ass n. see DUMB-ASS n.

dumb see also under DUM and its combs.

dumb n. **1** [1920s+] (*orig. US*) a fool, a stupid person (cf. DUMB-ASS n.; DUMB-BELL n.; DUMB BUNNY n.; DUMBBUTT n.; DUMB CLUCK n.; DUMBELLINA n.; DUMB FUCK n.; DUMBHEAD n.; DUMB ISAAC n.; DUMBNUTS n.; DUMBO n.; DUMBSHIT n.; DUMBSKI n.; DUMBSMACK n.; DUMB SOCK n.; DUMBSQUAT n.; DUMBUM n.; DUMBWAD n.; DUMBWIT n.). **2** [1990s+] stupidity.

dumb adj. (*also* **dumm**) [early 19C+] (*orig. US*) stupid, ignorant. [Ger. *dumm,* stupid; note Sinclair Lewis, writing of the German-influenced mid-West, uses sp. *dumm*]

dumb arm n. [late 18C–early 19C] a lame or maimed arm.

dumb-arse n. see DUMB-ASS n.

dumb-arsed adj. see DUMB-ASS adj.

dumbarton n. (*also* **dumby**) [1910s] (*W.I.*) the buttocks. [joc. use of proper name, but note *dounby,* buttocks, used by Sir Thomas Urquhart (*c.*1611–60) in his translation of Rabelais]

dumb as a box of rocks phr. (*also* **dumb as a deep sea oyster, ...a doornail, ...a rock, ...whale crap**) [1910s+] (*US*) extremely stupid (cf. KNOWING AS KATE MULLET phr.; SO DUMB SHE THINKS HER BOTTOM IS JUST TO SIT ON phr.; STUPID AS ARSE-HOLES phr.; THICK AS... phr.[1]; THICK AS TWO SHORT PLANKS phr.).

dumb-ass n. (*also* **dum-ass, dumb-arse**) [1950s+] (*orig. US*) a fool (cf. ASSHEAD n.; DUMB n.). [DUMB-ASS adj.]

dumb-ass adj. (*also* **dumb-arsed, dumb-assed**) [1930s+] (*orig. US*) stupid, unintelligent (cf. CLAY-ASSED adj.). [DUMB adj. + -ASS sfx/-ASSED sfx]

dumb as whale crap phr. see DUMB AS A BOX OF ROCKS phr.

dumb-bell n. [mid-19C+] an idiot, a fool (cf. DUMB n.). [DUMB adj. + SE *bell,* i.e. lit. a bell that will not ring]

dumb-bell adj. [1920s] stupid, foolish. [DUMB-BELL n.]

dumb bunny n. (*also* **dumb rabbit**) [1920s+] (*US*) a fool (cf. AIREDALE n.; DUMB n.). [DUMB adj. + BUNNY n.[3] (1)/RABBIT n.[6] (2)]

dumbbutt n. [1950s+] (*US*) a fool (cf. DUMB n.). [DUMB adj. + BUTT n.[1] (3)]

dumb cluck n. [1930s+] (*orig. US*) a fool (cf. DUMB n.). [DUMB adj. + CLUCK n.[1] (1)]

dumb dora n. [late 19C–1920s] (*US*) **1** a pretty, but empty-headed woman, often a member of the chorus line. **2** a stupid person. [allegedly coined *c.*1890 by Anita Pines, the first woman manager of a burlesque theatre but popularized in 1920s via Chic Young's eponymous comic strip]

dumbed adj. [late 19C] (*US*) a euph. for DAMNED adj.

dumbellina n. [1950s+] (*camp gay*) a fool (cf. DUMB n.). [DUMB-BELL n. + fem. sfx *-ina* + pun on Disney character *Thumbellina*]

dumb fuck n. [1940s+] (*orig. US*) a fool, an idiot; thus *dumb-fuckery,* behaviour typical of such an individual (cf. DUMB n.; FUCKBRAIN n.). [DUMB adj. + FUCK n.[6]]

dumb-fuck adj. (*also* **dumb-fucker**) [1960s+] absurd, stupid, with undertones of unpleasantness. [DUMB FUCK n.]

dumb glutton n. [mid-18C–19C] the vagina (cf. DUMB ORACLE n.; DUMB SQUINT n.). [it 'eats' the penis]

dumbhead n. [late 19C+] (*orig. US*) a fool (cf. DUMB n.). [lit. translation of Ger. *Dummkopf,* a dumbhead]

dumbie n. [early 19C] (*Scot. Und.*) a pocketbook. [DUMMY n.[2]]

dumb isaac n. [1900s–20s] (*US*) a fool (cf. DUMB n.). [play on SMART ALEC(K) n.]

dumb it v. [mid-19C] for a beggar to pose as a mute in order to extract money.

dumbness n. [mid-19C+] (*orig. US*) stupidity. [DUMB adj.]

dumbnuts n. [1970s+] (*US*) a fool (cf. DUMB n.). [DUMB adj. + play on NUMBNUTS n.]

dumbo *n.* (*orig. US*) **1** [1930s+] a fool, a dullard; also a term of address (cf. BOBO n.¹; DUMB n.). **2** [1950s] a foolish blunder. [DUMB adj. + -O sfx (2). Note the Walt Disney cartoon *Dumbo* (1941), although the elephant in question was naïve rather than stupid]

dumbo *adj.* [1960s+] (*Aus.*) stupid, senile. [DUMBO n. (1)]

dumb oracle *n.* [18C] the vagina (cf. DUMB GLUTTON n.).

dumb ox *n.* [1940s+] a large, stupid man. [DUMB adj. + SE *ox*]

dumb rabbit *n. see* DUMB BUNNY n.

dumbshit *n.* [1960s+] (*US*) a fool; thus as a term of address (cf. DIPSHIT n.; DUMB n.). [DUMB adj. + SHIT n.² (1)]

dumbshit *adj.* [1960s+] (*US*) stupid. [DUMBSHIT n.]

dumbski *n.* [1950s+] (*US*) a fool (cf. DUMB n.). [DUMB n. (1)/DUMBO n. (1) + -SKI sfx]

dumbsmack *n.* [1950s+] (*US*) a fool (cf. DUMB n.). [ext. of DUMB n. (1); ? the smacking of the forehead in perplexity]

dumb sock *n.* [1930s+] (*US*) **1** a fool (cf. DUMB n.). **2** a Swede or any Scandinavian immigrant. [DUMB adj. + ? SOCK n.³ (1)]

dumbsquat *n.* [1960s+] (*US*) a fool (cf. DUMB n.). [DUMB adj. + ? DIDDLY-SQUAT n.¹]

dumb squint *n.* [18C] the vagina (cf. DUMB GLUTTON n.).

dumbum *n.* [1980s+] (*UK/N.Z.*) a fool (cf. DUMB n.). [DUMB adj. + BUM n.³ (2)]

dumbwad *n.* [1960s+] (*US campus*) a fool (cf. DUMB n.). [DUMB adj. + -WAD sfx]

dumb watch *n.* [late 18C–early 19C] a venereal bubo in the groin. [SE *dumb* + ? *watch*, a sentinel; such a sentinel is looking out for any further sexual misadventures]

dumbwit *n.* [1930s+] (*US*) a fool (cf. DAMWIT n.; DUMB n.). [DUMB adj. + SE *wit*, on pattern of FUCKWIT n.]

dumby *n. see* DUMBARTON n.

dum-dum *n.¹* (*also* **dumb-dumb**) (*orig. US*) **1** [1930s+] a fool, an idiot, a general term of abuse. **2** [1970s] the penis. [DUMB n. (1) + redup.]

dum-dum *n.²* (*also* **dumb-dumb**) [1940s+] (*orig. US*) a deaf mute. [SE *dumb* + redup.]

dumfoozle *v. see* BUMFUZZLE v.

dumifutchit *n.* [20C+] (*US*) any nameless small object, typically some form of gadget. [ety. unknown]

dumm *adj. see* DUMB adj.

dummacker *n.* [mid-19C–1900s] a knowing, aware person. [? devel. of DUNAKER n.]

dummee *n. see* DUMMY n.².

dummerer *n.* (*also* **dummerar**) [17C–mid-18C; 1920s] a beggar who fakes dumbness in order to gain alms. [DOMMERER n.]

dummie *see also under* DUMMY.

dummied up *adj.* [1920s+] (*US Und.*) silent, e.g. under interrogation. [DUMMY UP v.¹ (2)]

dummo *n.* [1970s] (*US*) a fool (cf. BOBO n.¹). [var. DUMBO n. (1)]

dummock *n.* [late 19C] the buttocks. [Yorks. dial. + ? Rom. *dummock*, back]

dummy *n.¹* **1** [late 16C+] a dumb (i.e. mute) person; thus [1970s] (*US prison*) *catch a dummy*, to refuse to talk. **2** [19C+] (*also* **dummy head**) a fool, an idiot. **3** [mid-19C; 1910s+] a deaf mute, or a tramp or beggar who pretends to be deaf and dumb. **4** [1920s] (*US Und.*) a detective. **5** [1930s] (*UK Und.*) one who poses as the law-abiding owner of an establishment, e.g. a nightclub, to shield the criminal who is the actual owner. **6** [1930s+] (*also* **dummie**) a retarded person. [SE *dumb*/DUMB adj.; (2) note Egan, *Life in London* (1821): 'A cant phrase for a stupid fellow; a man who has not a word to say for himself. The family of the *dummies* is very numerous']

dummy *n.²* (*also* **dummee, dummie**) [early 19C+] a pocketbook, a wallet. [SE *dumb*; Hotten (1864) suggests that money in a pocket-book or wallet makes no noise, while coins in a purse chink together]

dummy *n.³* [mid-19C+] the penis; usu. in combs. meaning to masturbate (cf. BEAT ONE'S DUMMY v.). [its silence or its use for sucking on]

dummy *n.⁴* [late 19C+] (*Can./UK/US Und.*) bread. [? the softness of the crumb]

dummy *n.⁵* [20C+] an empty bottle. [like a baby's *dummy* one can suck it, but nothing will come out]

dummy *n.⁶* **1** [1930s–60s] (*US Und.*) a roll of counterfeit money. **2** [1960s+] (*drugs*) poor-quality or fake drugs. [they are effectively SE *dummy*, or fake]

dummy *n.⁷* [1950s+] (*N.Z. Und.*) solitary confinement; the solitary confinement/punishment cell in a prison. [SE *dumb*; the isolation renders the inmate silent]

dummy *v.* [1960s] (*US Und.*) to disguise. [SE *dummy*, fake]

dummy-chucker *n.* [1910s–30s] (*US*) one who throws fake fits. [CHUCK A DUMMY v. (2)]

dummy dust *n.* [1970s+] (*drugs*) phencyclidine (cf. ACE n.⁴). [a drug that appeals to or creates a DUMMY n.¹ (2) + DUST n.⁵ (5)]

dummy head *n. see* DUMMY n.¹ (2).

dummy-hunter *n.* [late 19C–1900s] a pickpocket specializing in stealing wallets. [DUMMY n.² + SE *hunter*]

dummy out *v.* [1970s] (*drugs*) to lose awareness and coordination through drug use. [DUMMY n.¹ (6)]

dummy up *v.¹* (*orig. US*) **1** [1920s] to pose as a mute. **2** [1920s+] to stop talking, to keep quiet. **3** [1950s] to keep something secret. [DUMMY n.¹ (1)/DUMMY n.¹ (3)]

dummy up *v.²* [1950s+] (*US*) to concoct a fraud, to fake something up. [SE *dummy*, a sham]

dump *n.¹* (*Aus./US*) **1** [19C+] a small coin or small sum of money; thus *not worth a dump*, utterly worthless. **2** [mid-19C–1900s] a button, often as sold by a street-hawker; thus *not care a dump*, not care at all. **3** [1960s+] a bill or fare. [SE *dump*, a coin worth 1s 3d (6½p), formerly current in Australia, made by punching a disc out of the middle of a Spanish dollar and milling the edge]

dump *n.²* [mid–late 19C; 1960s] (*US*) a short, fat person. [? abbr. SE *dumpling*]

dump *n.³* **1** [late 19C–1960s] (*US tramp*) a lodging house or criminal rendezvous. **2** [20C+] (*orig. US*) an unpleasant, disgusting and unappealing place. **3** [20C+] (*orig. US*) a place in general. **4** [1900s–30s] (*US Und.*) a prison. **5** [1910s] (*US Und.*) a restaurant. **6** [1920s+] (*orig. US*) one's home, irrespective of its appearance. **7** [1960s] (*Aus.*) a rest, a sleep. [SE *dump*, a pile or heap of refuse or other matter 'dumped' or thrown down]

dump *n.⁴* **1** [1940s+] (*orig. US*) an act of defecation; often as TAKE A DUMP v. **2** [1950s+] (*drugs*) the vomiting that may follow an injection of heroin. **3** [1970s+] (*orig. US*) a piece of excrement. [SE *dump*, a heap]

dump *n.⁵* [1990s+] (*US prison*) a rejection of parole. [DUMP v.¹ (1)]

dump *v.¹* **1** [late 18C+] (*orig. US*) to get rid of, to dispose of. **2** [mid-19C+] (*US*) to injure or kill by gunfire. **3** [20C+] to beat up; to knock down. **4** [1940s–70s] to murder. **5** [1940s+] to jilt, to terminate a relationship. **6** [1950s+] to lose a game, esp. on purpose. **7** [1960s] (*US*) to leave. **8** [1960s] to dismiss from a job. **9** [1960s] (*US prison*) to reject a parole application. **10** [1970s] to defeat, to ruin. **11** [1980s] (*US Black*) to attack verbally. [SE *dump*, to throw down in a lump or mass]

dump *v.²* **1** [1940s] (*US*) to confess, to betray. **2** [1950s–70s] (*drugs*) to vomit through drug withdrawal sickness. **3** [1950s+] (*orig. US campus*) (*also* **dump it out**) to defecate (cf. CACA v.). **4** [1960s+] (*drugs*) to vomit after taking drugs and prior to the mental effects. [SE *dump*]

dump all over *v. see* DUMP ON v.¹.

dumper *n.¹* (*US*) **1** [1940s] a lavatory. **2** [1950s] a sexual sadist (poss. one with an obsession with excrement/defecation), usu. as encountered by prostitutes. [DUMP v.² (3)]

dumper *n.²* [1960s+] (*N.Z. Und.*) a racecourse detective. [ety. unknown]

dumper n.[3] [1970s] (US) an ageing prostitute, i.e. over 40. [one who should be thrown into a DUMPER n.[1] (1)/SE *dumpster*, a large rubbish container or (UK) *skip*]

dump-fencer n. [mid-19C] a button-seller. [DUMP n.[1] (2)/SE *dump*, a lead counter, used for playing children's games + -FENCER sfx]

dumpie n. (*also* **dumpy**) [1960s+] (*S.Afr.*) a non-returnable 340ml (12fl oz) beer bottle.

dumpish adj. [mid-16C–1900s] miserable, wretched, grumpy. [DUMPS, THE n.]

dump it out v. *see* DUMP v.[2] (3).

dumpling n. [late 19C] a native of Norfolk. [such individuals are supposed to be excessively fond of *dumplings*]

dumpling depot n. [mid-19C] the stomach. [boxing jargon]

dumplings n. [early 18C+] the female breasts; thus [20C+] (*Aus.*) *her dumplings are boiling over*, her breasts are falling out of a low-cut dress (cf. APPLES n.[1]).

dump on v.[1] (*also* **dump all over**) (*orig. US*) **1** [1940s+] to criticize, to abuse. **2** [1950s–70s] to better in an argument; thus *dumped on*, abused, out-argued. **3** [1960s–70s] to reject, e.g. a lover, an application to join a club or fraternity. **4** [1970s+] to impose oneself or one's emotions on another person. [SE *dump*]

dump on v.[2] [1970s+] (US) to defecate. [DUMP v.[2] (3)]

dump one's change v. [2000s] (*US Black/drugs*) to excrete bags of drugs after swallowing them when facing a police search. [play on SHIT DIMES AND QUARTERS v.]

dump one's load v. [1960s+] **1** to vomit. **2** (*N.Z.*) to ejaculate. **3** to defecate (cf. DESPATCH ONE'S CARGO v.). [SE *dump*/DUMP v.[2] + LOAD n.[5]]

dumps, the n. [16C+] a depression; esp. as DOWN IN THE DUMPS phr. [one's emotions have been 'dumped' in a heap; OED notes similarities in MDu. *domp*, exhalation, haze, mist; 'possibly the original notion might be a mental haze or mist, in which the mind is befogged; but connecting links are not known'; Ger. *dumpf*, mentally depressed, clouded, dazed, or dulled suits the sense, but comes 200 years later than UK use]

dumps! excl. [2000s] (*US campus*) an excl. of commiseration, 'what a shame!' [DUMPS, THE n.]

dump someone in it v. *see* LAND SOMEONE IN THE SHIT v.

dumpster-ass bitch n. [2000s] (*US Black*) a derog. term for a woman. [SAmE *dumpster*, a skip + -ASS sfx + BITCH n.[1] (1)]

dumptruck n.[1] [1970s] (*US gay*) **1** a car full of lesbians. **2** a masculine lesbian. [the innate masculinity of the SAmE *dumptruck*]

dumptruck n.[2] [1970s+] (*US Und.*) a public defender. [? one can DUMP v.[1] (1) all ones troubles on them or their incompetence *dumps* one in jail]

dumptruck v. [1960s+] (*US prison*) to fail through a lack of nerve and courage, rather than through actual physical inadequacy. [DUMP v.[2] (3); the image of losing control of one's bowels + pun]

dumptruck date n. [1980s+] (*US campus*) an overweight female. [SAmE *dumptruck* + DATE n.[1] (1)]

dumpty n. (*also* **dumpty-doo**, **dumpy**) [1960s+] (*Aus./N.Z.*) an outside privy. [? DUNNY n. (1), but note DUMP v.[2] (3)]

dumpy n.[1] [1920s] a short, squat umbrella.

dumpy n.[2] *see* DUMPIE n.

dumpy adj.[1] [mid-19C+] (US) miserable, out of sorts. [DOWN IN THE DUMPS phr. + 16C SE *dumpy*, melancholy, dejected]

dumpy adj.[2] [1960s–80s] of a place, dirty, run-down, squalid. [DUMP n.[3] (2)]

dun n. (*also* **done**, **dunn**, **dunner**) [late 16C–18C] a demanding creditor or his agent. [? Fr. *donner*, to give, or eponymous *Joe Dun*, a notorious bailiff operating in Lincoln *c*.1500; SE f. 19C]

dun v. (*also* **done**, **dunn**) [late 16C–18C] to demand one's debts; also in fig. use. [DUN n.; SE f. 1900]

dunaker n. (*also* **donaker**) [late 17C–18C] a cow-stealer. [DUNNOCK n.]

Dunbar wether n. [late 19C] a red herring. [the fishing trade of *Dunbar*, Scotland + SE *wether*, a castrated ram]

duncarring n. [late 17C–18C] the practice of male homosexuality. [? a proper name or ? corruption of DUNNAKEN n.]

dunced out adj. [1960s–70s] (US) dumbfounded, stupid. [SE *dunce*]

duncehead n. **1** [mid-19C+] (US) (*also* **dunce-cap**) a fool, a simpleton. **2** [1980s] (*US Black*) one who shows off or 'acts the fool'. [SE *dunce* + -HEAD sfx (1)]

dundee adj. [1950s] (US) exhausted. [? SE *done*]

dundefunk/dunderfunk n. *see* DANDYFUNK n.

dunderhead n. (*also* **dundernapper**, **dunderpate**, **thunderhead**) [late 17C+] a fool, an idiot, an incompetent. [? Scot. *dunner*, to fall down with a loud noise, or *dunnered*, stunned, stupefied, stupid, 'in a state of gross stupor'; both ult. Scot. *donner*, to stupefy as with a blow or a loud noise + -HEAD sfx (1)]

dunderheaded adj. (*also* **dunderhead**) [late 19C+] stupid (cf. AIRHEADED adj.). [DUNDERHEAD n.]

dundering rake n. *see* DUDDERING RAKE n.

dundernapper/dunderpate n. *see* DUNDERHEAD n.

Dundreary n. [mid-19C–1920s] one who poses as a dandy or swell; thus *Dundreary whiskers*, long side whiskers worn without a beard. [the name of Lord *Dundreary*, a character in Tom Taylor's comedy *Our American Cousin* (1858)]

dundus n. (*also* **doondoos**) [1940s+] (*W.I.*) **1** an albino. **2** a freak. [Kongo *ndundu*, an albino]

dune coon n. [1990s+] an Arab (cf. ABDUL n.). [SE (*sand-)dune* + COON n. (5)]

dunegan n. *see* DUNNAKEN n.

dung n. [late 18C–19C] a workman who accepts less than union wages; thus a strike-breaker. [mid-18C tailors' jargon *dung*, a tailor who accepts the master's terms without argument, or who works when his fellows are striking; the *dung* is 'soft' (and abhorrent), while the union man, the FLINT n.[1], is 'hard' (and admirable)]

dunga n.[1] [1980s] (*N.Z.*) the penis. [? 'combining "donger" and "punga", the tree fern with the suggestive penis shape' (McGill, *Dict. of Kiwi Slang*, 1988)]

dunga n.[2] *see* DUNGER n.

dungaree adj. [mid-19C] (*Anglo-Ind.*) low, common, vulgar. [Hind. *dungrī*, a coarse calico; also name of a disreputable Bombay suburb]

dungaree doll n. [1950s] (*US teen*) a young woman or girl wearing blue jeans.

dungeon n. **1** [1930s] (*US Black*) a gun. **2** [1990s+] (*UK prison*) an open area on the floor of a wing used for recreation, association etc.

dungeon head n. [1960s] (US) a fool. [SE *dungeon* + -HEAD sfx]

dunger n. (*also* **dunga**) [1980s+] (*Aus./N.Z.*) anything, usu. mechanical, that is worn-out or malfunctioning, e.g. an old car. [echoic of the engine noises]

dunghill n. [mid-18C–early 19C] a coward. [cock-fighting jargon *dunghill*, any cock but a fighting cock]

dungle adj. [1990s+] (*W.I.*) ordinary, worthless, of no account. [ety. unknown]

dung-puncher n. (*also* **dung-pusher**) [1960s+] (*Aus.*) a derog. term for a male homosexual (cf. BROWN ARTIST n.). [SE *dung* + fig. use of *punch/push*]

dung-stabber n. [1990s+] the penetrative partner in anal sex. [SE *dung* + fig. use of *stabber*]

dunhead n. [1950s] (*Aus.*) a general term of abuse. [? DUNDERHEAD n., but note DUNNY n., i.e. synon. with SHITHEAD n.]

dunk v. **1** [1970s+] (*US gay*) to charge, to use a credit card. **2** [1990s+] (*US Black*) to outwit, to overcome an opponent by an unorthodox move. [baseball use *dunk*, to push (the ball) down through the basket, esp. by jumping so that the hand is above the level of the ring]

dunker *n.* [1960s] a condom. [? one *dunks* the penis in the condom/vagina]

dunkie *n.* [1990s+] a condom. [var. DUNKER n.]

Dunkirk *n.* [2000s] work. [rhy. sl.]

Dunlop cheque *n.* [1980s+] (*Aus.*) a cheque that has 'bounced', i.e. been marked 'return to drawer' by the bank. [the *Dunlop* Rubber Company, i.e. a RUBBER CHEQUE n.]

Dunlop overcoat *n. see* OVERCOAT n. (3).

Dunlop tyre *n.* [1960s+] a liar.

dunn *see also under* DUN n.

dunnage *n.* **1** [mid-19C] clothes. **2** [mid-19C+] baggage, esp. carried by a tramp or a sailor. [naut. use *dunnage*, material such as brushwood or mats, used to protect valuable or easily broken cargo; ult. Low Ger. *dün*, thin and *dünne Twige*, brushwood]

dunnaken *n.* (*also* **dunegan, dunnakin, dunniken, dunnyken, dunyken**) [late 18C–mid-19C] a lavatory (cf. BACKHOUSE n.; DONIGAN n.; DUNNIGAN n.; DUNNY n.). [DANNA n. + KEN n.¹ (1)]

dunnee *n. see* DUNNY n.

dunner *n. see* DUN n.

dunney *n. see* DUNNOCK n.

dunnigan *n.* (*also* **dunnikan**) [20C+] (*Aus.*) a lavatory (cf. BACKHOUSE n.). [var. on DUNNAKEN n.; note synon. US carnival use *donniker*]

dunnigan worker *n.* (*also* **donegan worker**) [1930s] (*US Und.*) a thief who hangs around public lavatories, hoping to steal from discarded coats or take parcels etc that have been put down. [DUNNIGAN n./DONIGAN n. + WORKER n.¹ (1)]

dunnikan *n. see* DUNNIGAN n.

dunniken *n. see* DUNNAKEN n.

dunnock *n.* (*also* **dunney**) [late 17C–mid-19C] (*UK Und.*) a cow. [SE *dun*, brown, the colour of many cows]

dunny *n.* (*also* **dunnee**) [1930s+] (*Aus./N.Z.*) **1** an outside lavatory or privy. **2** any lavatory; thus *dunny cart*, a vehicle used to remove excrement; *dunny man*, a night-soil cleaner. [DUNNAKEN n.]

dunny budgie *n.* [1990s+] (*Aus.*) a fly. [DUNNY n. + facetious use of BUDGIE n.¹ (1), i.e. the size or noisiness of the flies is reminiscent of the bird]

dunnyken *n. see* DUNNAKEN n.

dunop *n. see* DOONUP n.

duns *n.* (*also* **dunsa, dunsie**) [1950s+] (*W.I. Rasta*) money. [DUN v.]

dunsy *adj.* [20C+] (*Ulster*) foolish, 'slow'. [SE *dunce*]

dunt *n.* [1980s+] (*US campus*) a person of ambivalent sexuality. [DICK n.⁴ (1) + CUNT n.¹ (1)]

dunyken *n. see* DUNNAKEN n.

d-up *v.* [1990s+] **1** (*US Black*) to protect oneself in those areas of one's life where one might be vulnerable. **2** to defecate. [(1) D n.⁹; (2) is pun on (1) and initial letter of SE *defecate*]

dup *v.* [mid-16C–mid-19C] (*UK Und.*) to open (a door). [? DUB v.¹ (1) or ? SE *do up*, although this would imply closing, unless the image is of fastening the door]

dupa *n.* [20C+] (*US*) the buttocks, the posterior, often used as an affectionate term, esp. among Polish speakers or the families of Polish immigrants. [Polish *dupa*, little ass]

dupe *n.* [late 19C+] a duplicate, e.g. key, identification card. [abbr.]

dupe *v.* [1980s+] (*US campus*) to abuse, to do wrong to.

dupey-dupe *n.* [1970s+] a foolishly naïve (young) policeman.

dup the giger/jigger *v. see* DUB THE GIGGER v.

dup the ken *v.* [late 17C–18C] to enter a house. [DUP v. + KEN n.¹ (1)]

duracs *n. see* DRACS n.

Durban poison *n.* (*also* **Durban, D.P.**) [1960s+] (*orig. S.Afr.*) an exceptionally well-regarded variety of marijuana, grown near Durban, Natal (cf. ACAPULCO (GOLD) n.). [similarity in pron. between Afk. *gif*, poison and KIF n./KIF adj.]

dur-brain *n.* (*also* **duh-brain**) [1990s+] (*UK juv.*) a fool (cf. BAKEBRAIN n.). [echoic of the stupid person's grunt *duh!* or *dur!*]

dur-brained *adj.* (*also* **durr-brained**) [2000s] stupid, idiotic (cf. AMOEBA-BRAINED adj.). [DUR-BRAIN n.]

Durbs *n.* [1970s+] (*S.Afr.*) *Durb*an. [abbr.]

durgen *n.* [late 17C–early 19C] an insignificant person. [ety. unknown]

Durham man *n.* [late 18C–early 19C] one whose knees knock or rub together. [proper name *Durham*, home of high-quality mustard, which was ground between 2 stones]

durn *see also under* DARN and its combs.

durog *n.* [1970s+] (*drugs*) marijuana. [poss. misreading of DUROS n.]

duros *n.* [1970s] (*drugs*) marijuana. [Sp. *duros*, hard, i.e. tough]

durr-brained *adj. see* DUR-BRAINED adj.

durry *n.* [1940s+] (*Aus./N.Z.*) **1** a cigarette butt. **2** a cigarette, esp. when hand-rolled. [? Ulster *durrie*, anything small; ? link to rolling tobacco Bull *Durham*]

durry *v.* [1960s+] (*N.Z., mainly teen*) to smoke illicitly. [DURRY n. (2)]

durrynacker *n.* [mid-19C] a female lace-hawker who may also tell fortunes to her customers. [Rom. *dukker*, to tell fortunes]

durrynacking *n.* (*also* **duryking, durynacking**) [mid-19C] **1** begging. **2** fortune telling, under the guise of lace-selling, usu. practised by gypsy women. [DURRYNACKER n.]

dush *n. see* DOSH n.

dusky *adj.* (*also* **dusk**) [early 19C+] used to describe a Black person.

dust *n.*¹ [mid-16C–1920s] a fight, an argument, a disturbance.

dust *n.*² [17C–19C] money; thus *down with one's dust*, to lay down one's money (cf. CHAFF n.²). [? SE *gold-dust*, but note the religious equation of money with dirt; note Egan, *Book of Sports* (1832): 'Sovereigns were golden dust, which blew about in the breath of his opinion']

dust *n.*³ [late 18C–19C] **1** excrement. **2** fig. nothing, a worthless object.

dust *n.*⁴ **1** [mid–late 19C] (*Aus.*) gunpowder. **2** [late 19C–1930s] (*Aus.*) flour; thus *dust*, to fill (a bag) with flour. **3** [1900s–80s] (*Aus./US*) tobacco. **4** [1930s+] (*US*) rolling tobacco. [the consistency of these substances]

dust *n.*⁵ (*drugs*) **1** [1910s+] heroin. **2** [1910s+] cocaine (cf. BIRDIE POWDER n.). **3** [1940s–50s] morphine (cf. AUNTIE EMMA n.). **4** [1950s] marijuana. **5** [1970s+] phencyclidine (cf. ACE n.⁴). **6** [1980s+] marijuana mixed with phencyclidine, cocaine or any other powdered drug. [all these drugs (except marijuana) come in powdered form]

dust *adj.* [1980s+] (*US campus*) ruined, utterly exhausted; in serious trouble. [SE *dust*, the condition of human decay]

dust *v.*¹ **1** [early 17C; 19C+] to thrash, to beat up, to hit hard. **2** [1960s+] (*US*) to defeat. **3** [1970s+] (*US*) to destroy. **4** [1970s+] to kill, to murder. **5** [1980s+] (*US campus*) to humiliate, to insult. [image of knocking the dust from someone's coat or jacket]

dust *v.*² (*also* **dust off, dust out**) **1** [mid-17C; mid-19C+] (*orig. US*) (*also* **dust it**) to rush off, to leave fast. **2** [late 19C+] (*US*) to overtake, to pass on the road. **3** [1930s+] (*US*) to get rid of, to jilt. [all reflect an image of the dust raised by one's speedy movement]

dust *v.*³ **1** [early 19C] (*also* **dust down**) to deceive, to mislead. **2** [1950s] (*US*) to tease, to hoax. ['throw dust in one's eyes']

dustbag *n.* [late 19C–1900s] (*US*) a wallet. [DUST n.² + SE *bag*]

dustbin *n.* [1940s] (*US Black*) a grave.

dustbin lid *n.* **1** [20C+] a child; usu. in pl. **2** [1990s+] (*UK juv.*) a handicapped person, esp. one suffering the after-effects of Thalidomide. [rhy. sl.; (1) = KID n.¹ (1); (2) = FLID n. (1)]

dust bunny *n.* [2000s] (*US drugs*) a user of phencyclidine. [DUST n.⁵ (5)]

dust-cutter *n.* [late 19C–1950s] (*US*) a drink, esp. as a 'pick-me-up' or 'reviver'.

dust down *v. see* DUST v.³ (1).

dusted *adj.*¹ **1** [1930s+] beaten, defeated, killed. **2** [1980s+] shamed, humiliated. [DUST v.¹]

dusted *adj.*[2] 1 [1950s–70s] (*drugs*) having consumed and finished off a drug. 2 [1960s] (*US campus*) drunk. [SE *dust*, to clean up]

dusted *adj.*[3] [1970s+] (*drugs*) under the influence of phencyclidine. [DUST n.[5] (5)]

duster *n.*[1] [1910s] (*Aus.*) a knuckleduster. [abbr.]

duster *n.*[2] [1930s] (*US tramp*) one who steals from freight trains or box cars. [DUST v.[2] (1)]

duster *n.*[3] [1940s] (*US Black*) the act of moving; usu. in phr. *dig a duster*, thus COLLAR A DUSTER UP THE LADDER v. [DUST v.[2] (1)]

duster *n.*[4] [1940s+] (*US Black*) the buttocks, the posterior. [RUSTY-DUSTY n.]

duster *n.*[5] [1950s] (*US Und.*) a thug. [DUST v.[1] (1) + ? late 19C New York City gang the Hudson *Dusters*]

duster *n.*[6] (*drugs*) 1 [1960s–70s] a cigarette laced with heroin. 2 [1970s+] a user of phencyclidine. [DUST n.[5] (1)/DUST n.[5] (5)]

dusters *n.* [1950s+] (*orig. milit.*) the testicles (cf. BANGERS n.). [? boastful image of testicles that hang so low as to 'dust' the floor]

dust-head *n.* [1970s+] a phencyclidine user or addict. [DUST n.[5] (5) + -HEAD sfx (3)]

dustie *n.*[1] [1950s] (*US drugs*) a narcotics user. [DUST n.[5] + sfx -*ie*]

dustie *n.*[2] *see* DUSTY n.[1].

dusting *n.*[1] [late 18C+] a beating or thrashing. [DUST v.[1] (1)]

dusting *n.*[2] [1970s+] (*drugs*) adding phencyclidine, heroin or another drug to marijuana. [DUST n.[5] (5)]

dust it *v. see* DUST v.[2] (1).

dust it away *v.* [late 18C–early 19C] 'to drink about' (Grose, 1785).

dust joint *n.* [1970s+] (*drugs*) a cigarette made with phencyclidine. [DUST n.[5] (5) + JOINT n.[5] (3)]

dustman *n.*[1] [late 18C–early 19C] a corpse. [the line in the Church of England burial service: 'ashes to ashes and dust to dust']

dustman *n.*[2] [mid–19C] (*mainly nursery*) sleep, personified; thus soothing phr. *the dustman's coming*. [he throws *sleep-dust* (or sand) into sleepy eyes]

dustman *n.*[3] [mid–late 19C] an energetic, fanatic preacher. [DUST v.[1] (1), i.e. he thumps the pulpit as he preaches]

dustman's bell *n.* [mid–late 19C] (*nursery*) bedtime. [the DUSTMAN n.[2] who brings sleep]

dust off *v.*[1] 1 [1920s+] to finish off. 2 [1930s+] (*US*) to beat up. 3 [1940s+] (*US*) (*also* **give someone the dust-off**) to reject, to snub. 4 [1980s] to kill. [DUST v.[1]]

dust off *v.*[2] *see* DUST v.[2].

dust one's broom *v.* [1930s–50s] (*US Black*) to leave. [SE/DUST v.[2] (1)]

dust one's throat *v.* [late 19C] (*US*) to take a drink.

dustoor *n.* (*also* **dustoorie**) [late 17C–19C] (*Anglo-Ind.*) a bribe, a sweetener, a commission. [Hind. *dastur*, custom, what is customary]

dust out *v. see* DUST v.[2].

dust someone's jacket *v.* (*also* **dust someone's back, …coat, …linen**) [late 17C–1910s] to thrash, to beat someone up. [DUST v.[1] (1) + JACKET n.[1]]

dust-up *n.* [late 19C+] (*orig. milit.*) 1 a fight. 2 a quarrel. 3 in weak form, a party, an exciting event. [DUST n.[1] + image of the dust generated by struggling men and horses]

dusty *n.*[1] (*also* **dustie**) [mid–late 19C] a *dustman*. [abbr. + sfx -*y*/-*ie*]

dusty *n.*[2] 1 [1970s] (*US Black*) an old record. 2 [1980s+] (*UK society*) a very old person, 70 years old and onwards. [(2) one of a set of words implying the physical disintegration of the body as one ages]

dusty *adj.*[1] 1 [mid–19C] (*US*) tough, dangerous. 2 [mid–19C+] of a person, uncouth, unattractive; of a thing, bad; esp. in phr. NOT SO DUSTY phr. 3 [1980s+] (*US campus*) tetchy, irritable, out of sorts. [17C SE *dusty*, worthless, distasteful; ult. *dust*, rubbish, garbage]

dusty *adj.*[2] [1970s] (*US Black*) unclear, unable to predict the future. [there is *dust* in one's eyes]

dusty *adj.*[3] [1990s+] (*US drugs*) pertaining to narcotic use. [DUST n.[5]]

dusty answer *n.* [mid-19C+] an unhelpful, unpleasant or intolerant response to a question; usu. as *give/get a dusty answer*. [DUSTY adj.[1] (2)]

dusty behind *n.* [1980s+] (*US Black*) the buttocks, the posterior. [RUSTY-DUSTY n. + SE *behind*]

dusty bread *n.* [1970s] (*US Black*) a conventional, conservative woman. [? the poor quality of everyday bread]

dusty butt *n.* 1 [1900s–50s] (*US Black*) a low-grade, unattractive prostitute. 2 [1960s] (*US*) a short person. [SE *dusty* + BUTT n.[1] (2)]

dusty diamonds *n. see* BLACK DIAMONDS n. (1).

dusty line *n.* [1980s+] (*US Black*) a piece of outmoded slang. [SE *dusty* + LINE n.[1] (3)]

dusty pup *n.* [1950s] (*Aus.*) an unpleasant person, a synon. for 'dirty dog'.

Dutch *n.*[1] 1 [mid-19C–1950s] the German language. 2 [mid-19C+] (*US*) a German. 3 [1900s–50s] (*US*) a nickname for a German. [Ger. *Deutsch*]

Dutch *n.*[2] [mid-19C+] nonsense, incomprehensible rubbish; often as *talk Dutch*. [abbr. DOUBLE DUTCH n.]

Dutch *n.*[3] (*US*) 1 [mid-19C+] bad temper, irascibility. 2 [1960s+] a crewcut haircut. [stereotyping; (2) confusion between Dutch and *Deutsch*, German]

Dutch *n.*[4] [1990s+] (*US*) intercourse between the breasts.

Dutch *adj.*[1] [early 17C+] German. [Eng. pron. of Ger. *Deutsch*, German, as 'Dutch'; popularized in US by the growth of German settlements, notably in Pennsylvania; *see also* some of the combs. below]

Dutch *adj.*[2] [mid-17C+] a derog. racial stereotype, meaning stolid, miserly, dour and bad tempered, and used as such in many of the combs. below. [the mid-17C when the UK fought the Dutch as a national enemy]

dutch *n.* [late 19C+] (*Cockney*) a wife. [the precise origins of this term remain debatable. Either the term is an abbr. of SE *duchess*, strengthened by RUM DUCHESS n. and the rhy. sl. DUCHESS n.[1] (6) (of Fife); or, according to the 19C music-hall star Albert Chevalier (1861–1923), whose signature song was entitled 'My Old Dutch', the term was semantically linked to another piece of sl., DIAL n., face. In Chevalier's version, the orig. term was 'my old Dutch clock', whose face, i.e. dial, resembled that of his wife. E.P., formerly a partisan of the *duchess* theory, claimed to have changed his mind in the later editions of the *DSUE*. The *OED*, however, while citing Chevalier's song in 1893, has a previous cit., dated 4 years earlier, and states unequivocally that in this context *dutch* is 'an abbr. of duchess']

dutch *v.* (*US*) 1 [1910s+] to ruin another's business, social standing, enjoyment etc with deliberate malice. 2 [1970s] to bet in such a way that the bank is broken. 3 [1970s] to speak emphatically. [all racial stereotypes of Dutch]

Dutch act *n.* (*also* **Dutch route**) [late 19C+] (*Can./US Und.*) suicide; thus *dutch (oneself out)/do the Dutch (act)/go Dutch*, to commit suicide (cf. DO A DUTCH v.). [DUTCH adj.[2]]

Dutch almanacs *n.* [late 17C] gibberish. [HIGH DUTCH n.]

Dutch auction *n.* [mid-19C+] a mock auction or sale in which the much-touted 'reductions' have no bearing in commercial fact. [DUTCH adj.[2]]

Dutch bargain *n.* [late 17C] 1 a one-sided bargain. 2 a deal concluded over drinks. [DUTCH adj.[2]]

Dutch bath *n.* [20C+] (*US*) a very cursory wash. [DUTCH adj.[2]]

Dutch boy *n.* [1990s+] (*US gay*) a man, irrespective of sexuality, who enjoys the company of lesbians. [play on the story of the 'little Dutch boy' who 'put his finger in the dyke', i.e. DYKE n.]

Dutch build *n.* [19C] a stocky, thickset individual.

Dutch-buttocked *adj.* [late 17C] fat, 'broad in the beam'. [SE *Dutch-buttocked*, of cattle, having large hind-quarters]

Dutch by injection *n.* [1920s+] any woman living with a foreigner. [note INJECTION n.]

Dutch cheese *n.* [19C] a bald person. [the Dutch Edam cheese, which is round, red and shiny]

Dutch clock *n.* **1** [late 19C] the vagina. **2** [late 19C–1910s] a woman. [(2) resemblance of a woman's face to a clockface; (1) f. (2)]

Dutch comfort *n.* [late 18C–early 19C] a style of comforting in which the speaker intones 'Thank God it is no worse'. [DUTCH adj.²]

Dutch concert *n.* (*also* **Dutch medley**) [late 18C–19C] any performance in which each musician plays a different tune; thus a general pej. for a bad performance, musical or metaphorical. [DUTCH adj.²]

Dutch consolation *n.* [mid–late 19C] a style of comforting in which the speaker intones 'Thank God it is no worse'. [DUTCH adj.²]

Dutch courage *n.* (*also* **courage**) [19C+] (temporary) bravery, fortified by generous quantities of alcohol; the implication is of innate cowardice; also from drugs. [coined as a propagandist measure during various Anglo-Dutch wars of 17C/18C]

Dutch daub *n.* (*also* **Dutch dab**) [late 19C] (*US*) a badly executed picture. [orig. the second-rate Dutch still lifes that were imported in bulk into the US during the 1880s, an influx that was slowed only by the imposition of a 35% duty on such pictures]

Dutch distemper *n.* [early–mid-19C] (*US*) jail fever. [the disproportionately large number of Dutch (or Germans) in the prison population]

Dutch doggery *n.* [mid-19C] a grog-shop. [SE *Dutch* + DOGGERY n.¹, reinforced by the stereotypical surliness of the Dutch (cf. DUTCH adj.²)]

Dutch door *n.* [1990s+] a bisexual woman. [she 'swings both ways' but note DUTCH GIRL n.]

Dutch dumplings *n.* [1950s–70s] (*gay*) the buttocks.

Dutch father *n. see* DUTCH UNCLE n.

Dutch feast *n.* [late 18C–19C] any meal where the host gets drunk before his friends. [DUTCH adj.²; the assumption is that he has monopolized the supply of alcohol]

Dutch fit *n.* [mid-19C] (*US*) a fit of temper, an explosion of rage. [DUTCH adj.¹/DUTCH adj.²]

Dutch foil *n.* (*also* **Dutch gilding, …gold, …metal**) [1970s] (*US*) an alloy of 11 parts copper and 2 parts zinc, used as a substitute for gold leaf – and presumably passed off as such to the unwary. [DUTCH adj.²]

Dutch fuck *n.* **1** [1950s+] the lighting of one cigarette from another, thus saving matches. **2** [1990s+] (*US*) intercourse between the breasts; also as v. [the implication in both is of meanness (cf. DUTCH adj.²)]

Dutch fustian *n.* [late 16C–early 17C] to talk nonsense. [SE *fustian*, lofty or turgid language, accentuated by ref. to HIGH DUTCH n.; note late 16C *fustian*, Und. or thieves' jargon]

Dutch gilding/gold *n. see* DUTCH FOIL n.

Dutch girl *n.* [1930s+] a lesbian. [pun on SE *dike* (i.e. the dikes that form the basis of Holland's coast defences)/DYKE n.]

Dutch gleek *n.* [17C] any form of drink. [derog. use of *Dutch* (implying generic drunkenness) + SE *gleek*, 'a game at cards, played by three persons; forty-four cards were used, twelve being dealt to each player, while the remaining eight formed a common "stock"' (OED)]

Dutch guts *n.* [1990s+] (*Aus.*) courage created by alcoholic intake. [SE *Dutch* + GUTS n.² (1); var. on DUTCH COURAGE n.]

Dutch it *v.* [1910s+] to share expenses, usu. in the context of a meal. [DUTCH adj.²]

Dutch kiss *n.* [20C+] (*US*) a kiss in which both participants grab the other's ears. [ety. unknown; ? a national peculiarity]

Dutch leave *n.* [late 19C] (*US*) taking time off without permission, absenting oneself illegally. [DUTCH adj.¹/DUTCH adj.²]

Dutch lunch *n. see* DUTCH TREAT n.

Dutchman *n.* **1** [17C+] (*US*) anyone of German (occas. Scandinavian) origin. **2** [1910s–30s] (*orig. US*) a foreigner, one who does not speak English well. **3** [1930s] a bar- or saloon-keeper. [Ger. *Deutsch*, German; (3) Germans were trad. linked to the brewing industry]

Dutchman, the *n.* [late 19C] Deutz and Gelderman champagne.

Dutchman's breeches *n.* [19C] 2 streaks of blue in an otherwise cloudy sky. [the trad. Dutchman is pictured in blue pantaloons]

Dutchman's cape *n.* [20C+] a cloudbank on the horizon that gives the impression of being land. [SE *cape*, a promontory; the image is of the stupid Dutch sailor who confuses clouds with land]

Dutchman's drink *n.* [19C] a drink that empties the pot or drains some form of communal drinking vessel. [DUTCH adj.²]

Dutchman's fart *n.* [20C+] a sea urchin. [derog. joke]

Dutchman's headache *n.* [19C] a state of drunkenness. [DUTCH adj.²]

dutchmasta *n.* [1990s+] (*US Black*) a cigar, esp. when its tobacco is removed and replaced by marijuana. [brandname *Dutchmaster*]

Dutch medley *n. see* DUTCH CONCERT n.

Dutch metal *n. see* DUTCH FOIL n.

Dutch milk *n.* [1900s–40s] (*orig. US Black*) beer. [DUTCH adj.¹ + SE *milk*; the stereotyping of Germans as beer-drinkers]

Dutch nickel *n.* [20C+] (*US*) a kiss. [in racial stereotyping *Dutch* = thief, therefore such a kiss has been 'stolen']

Dutch nightingale *n.* [late 18C–mid-19C] a frog (cf. CAMBRIDGE NIGHTINGALE n.). [the implied inability of the Dutch to sing]

dutch (oneself out) *v. see* DUTCH ACT n.

Dutch oven *n.* **1** [1920s] the mouth. **2** [1980s+] (*also* **Greek sauna**) the smell of a bed in which someone has just broken wind. **3** [1980s+] (*Aus. drugs*) an enclosed area or room filled with cannabis smoke. [SE *Dutch oven*, a large pot that gains heat from coals placed around and on top of it; (3) is underpinned by Holland's liberal understanding of the harmless uses of cannabis]

Dutch palate *n.* [late 17C–18C] a coarse palate, with no appreciation of the finer comestibles. [DUTCH adj.²]

Dutch parliament *n. see* DUTCH ROW n.

Dutch party *n. see* DUTCH TREAT n.

Dutch pegs *n.* [20C+] legs. [rhy. sl.]

Dutch pink *n.* (*also* **pink**) [early–mid-19C] blood (cf. BADMINTON n.). [SE *Dutch pink*, a yellow lake pigment]

Dutch (plate) *n.* [1960s+] a friend. [rhy. sl. = SE *mate*]

Dutch reckoning *n.* **1** [late 17C] a bill that, if disputed, only gets higher. **2** [late 17C–early 19C] a bill presented as a lump sum, with no details attached. **3** [19C] (*naut.*) a bad day's work. [DUTCH adj.²; the poor image of Dutch businessmen]

Dutch rod *n.* [1940s] (*US Und.*) a Luger pistol. [DUTCH adj.¹ + ROD n.¹ (2)]

Dutch route *n. see* DUTCH ACT n.

Dutch row *n.* (*also* **Dutch parliament**) [late 19C–1910s] a spurious argument, generating far more sound than any real fury. [note Fr. synon *une querelle d'Allemand*, lit. a 'German argument']

Dutch rub *v.* [1930s+] to rub one's knuckles hard across one's victim's skull (cf. DRY SHAVE v.²).

Dutch supper *n. see* DUTCH TREAT n.

Dutch town *n.* [20C+] (*US*) that area of a town predominantly populated by German immigrants or their descendants. [DUTCH adj.¹ + SE *town*]

Dutch treat *n.* (*also* **Dutch lunch, …party, …supper**) [late 19C+] an outing, a visit to a restaurant etc in which costs are shared equally, i.e. there is no 'treat' at all in the sense of one party being entertained at the other's expense; occas. as v. [DUTCH adj.[2]]

Dutch uncle n. (*also* **Dutch father, uncle**) [mid-19C+] one who talks severely and critically, who lays down the law; usu. in phr. *talk like a Dutch uncle.*

Dutch widow n. [early 17C] a prostitute.

Dutch wife n. [late 19C+] a bolster, otherwise defined as a 'masturbation machine'.

Dutchy n. **1** [late 18C+] (*US*) a German; a nickname for a German. **2** [late 19C–1920s] a Dutchman. [DUTCH adj.[1] + sfx -*y*; (2) SE *Dutch*]

Dutchy adj. (*US*) **1** [mid-19C–1900s] typically German, esp. recent immigrants who have yet to adapt to America and still retain their old-country crudities. **2** [1900s–10s] low-class, dowdy, slovenly. **3** [1940s] typically Dutch. [DUTCHY n.]

dutchy n. [20C+] (*W.I. Rasta*) **1** a Dutch cooking pot, a low, round-bottomed heavy pot. **2** a pipe or bowl used for smoking marijuana.

duty n. [late 19C] pawnbrokers' interest. [pun on SE]

duzey n. *see* DOOZIE n.

D.V. n. [1970s+] (*US Black*) Cadillac Coupe *De Ville.* [abbr.]

d.v. n. [late 19C] (*UK society*) *d*ivorce. [abbr. but also a cynical ref. to Lat. *deo volente*, God willing]

D.V.D.A. n. [1990s+] a variety of pornographic film that features *d*ouble-*v*aginal and *d*ouble-*a*nal penetration.

dwaal n. [1960s–70s] (*S.Afr.*) a daze, a confusion; esp. in phr. *in a dwaal*, in a daze. [Afk. *dwaal*, to wander, to lose one's way]

dwaas n. [20C+] (*S.Afr.*) a fool, an idiot. [Du. *dwaas*, a silly fellow]

dweasal n. *see* DWEEZLE n.

dweeb n. (*also* **dweeber, dweebie, dweeble**) [1960s+] (*orig. US teen*) an idiot, someone lacking social qualities; thus fem. *dweebette*; also attrib. [ety. unknown; ? the name of a lost SF alien]

dweezle n. (*also* **dweasal**) [1980s+] (*US campus*) a socially inept person. [ety. unknown; ? DWEEB n. + SE *weasle*]

-dweller sfx [1980s+] (*US campus*) a combining form to indicate someone who frequents a particular place.

dwelling dancer n. [1940s] (*Aus.*) a thief. [SE *dwelling* + DANCER n.]

dwell in the box v. [1930s–50s] (*UK Und.*) to pickpocket at a racecourse.

d-whupped adj. *see* DICK-WHUPPED adj.

-dya sfx [1950s+] a sfx meaning 'do you', e.g. *whaddya, whodya.*

dyestuffs n. [mid-late 19C] (*US*) money. [a pun on SE + the metal *dies* used for printing notes]

dying adj. [1940s–70s] (*US*) absolute. [DEAD adv.]

dying duck in a thunderstorm n. [late 19C+] a lazy, weak, vapid person.

dyke *see also under* DIKE and its combs.

dyke n. (*also* **dike**) [1930s+] a lesbian (cf. BOYDYKE n.; BULL-DYKE n.; DIESEL-DYKE n.; DINKY DYKE n.; DRAG-DYKE n.; DYKEFACE n.; LEATHER DYKE n.; VAN DYKE n.[2]). [ety. unknown; ? f. DIKED UP adj.[1], dressed up; certainly some lesbians have always dressed as men. Another theory suggests the gradual corruption of SE *herma-phrodite* to *morphodite* to *dike* and *dyke* and thence, with the masc. generic *bull* to BULL-DYKE n. and BULL-DAGGER n.; however, the first uses of both these appear to predate *dyke*, which may thus mean this is an abbr.]

dyke adj. (*also* **dike**) [1930s+] pertaining to lesbians or lesbianism. [DYKE n.]

dyke v. (*also* **dike**) **1** [1940s] to engage in lesbian sex. **2** [1960s] to live as a lesbian. [DYKE n.]

dykeface n. [1990s+] a general term of abuse, aimed at a woman; lit. 'lesbian-face'. [DYKE n.]

dykey adj. (*also* **dikey, dykey-ass, dykish**) [1960s+] having the appearance or characteristics of a lesbian. [DYKE n. + sfx -*y*]

dykon n. [1990s+] (*US gay*) a lesbian icon. [DYKE n. + SE *icon*]

Dyna n. [1950s] (*US*) a Buick *Dyna*flow automobile. [abbr.]

dyna n.[1] [1920s] *dyna*mite. [abbr.]

dyna n.[2] [1960s] a male homosexual. [rhy. sl.; *dynamite* = SE *catamite*]

dynamite n.[1] [late 19C] tea. [the use of 'tea' as a codeword for *dynamite* as revealed during a trial of 1888; but note SE *gunpowder*, a fine, green-leafed tea, popular in the UK from the 1770s]

dynamite n.[2] (*drugs*) **1** [late 19C+] whisky. **2** [1920s+] heroin, morphine; esp. good-quality, highly potent drugs (cf. AUNTIE EMMA n.). **3** [1930s] cocaine. **4** [1930s] (*US prison*) a form of ersatz 'snuff' used by convicts; it is made of tobacco, soda, salt and sugar. **5** [1940s+] hashish or marijuana (cf. BOMB n.[4]). **6** [1950s+] a mixture of cocaine and morphine/heroin. **7** [1960s+] any pure, undiluted drugs. [the strength and effect]

dynamite n.[3] [1940s+] (*Aus.*) baking powder. [it makes things 'blow up']

dynamite adj. **1** [20C+] very strong; intense. **2** [1920s+] (*also* **dynamo**) excellent, wonderful, first-rate; often as *dynamite!* wonderful! **3** [1930s+] very important, extremely effective; used both positively and negatively.

dynamite v. (*US*) **1** [1920s] to talk loudly, to complain, to make a fuss. **2** [1920s–50s] to talk in an aggressive manner, esp. when trying to sell something or seduce someone. **3** [1930s] to push something through, to make it happen fast. [i.e. to 'go off with a bang']

dynamiter n.[1] (*US*) **1** [1910s] a whinger, a complainer. **2** [1910s–30s] a sponger, a cadger. **3** [1920s–40s] a very aggressive sales-person. **4** [1930s–60s] a very ambitious person, a trouble-maker. [DYNAMITE v.]

dynamiter n.[2] **1** [1950s] (*US drugs*) a cocaine user. **2** [1950s–60s] (*UK Und.*) a drug pusher. [DYNAMITE n.[2] (3)]

dynamo adj. *see* DYNAMITE adj. (2).

dyno n.[1] **1** [1920s–60s] (*US prison*) a manual labourer. **2** [1940s–60s] (*drugs*) (*also* **dyno-pure**) heroin. **3** [1960s] (*US prison*) liquor. [SE *dynamite*/DYNAMITE n.[2]]

dyno n.[2] *see* DINO n.[1] (1).

dyno n.[3] *see* DINO n.[2].

dyno n.[4] *see* DYNO ROUSTER n.

dyno adj.[1] [1960s+] (*drugs*) uncut, therefore stronger than usual heroin or any other drug. [DYNAMITE n.[2] (2)]

dyno adj.[2] [1980s] (*US campus*) **1** pretty. **2** excellent, first-rate. [DYNAMITE adj. (2)]

dyno-pure n. *see* DYNO n.[1] (2).

dyno rouster n. (*also* **dyno**) [1920s–30s] (*US tramp*) one who robs drunks. [DINO n.[1] (1) + SE *roust*]

dyspepsia in a snow storm n. [late 19C] (*US short order*) an order of pie topped with powdered sugar.

d.y.w.y.k. phr. [late 19C] (*US campus*) a phr. of mocking dismissal and exclusion. [abbr. *don't you wish you knew*]

E

E *n.* [1980s+] the popular nickname of the hallucinogenic drug MDMA (methylene dioxymethamphetamine). [abbr. ECSTASY n.]

E.A. *n. see* AMATEUR n.[1].

each mother's son *n. see* EVERY MOTHER'S SON n.

eager beaver *n.* [1940s+] (*orig. US*) an excessively earnest, keen person whose efforts are sometimes more notable for their sound and fury than their actual usefulness. [the ever-industrious beaver]

eager beaver *adj.* [1940s+] earnest, usu. excessively so. [EAGER BEAVER n.]

eagers, the *n.* [1920s–60s] (*US*) anxiety, apprehension or excessive keenness. [SE *eager*]

eager up *v.* [1960s] (*US*) to excite.

eagle *n.*[1] [early 17C–early 18C] (*UK Und.*) a gambler, presumably a cheat, who wins. [? the strength of the predatory bird]

eagle *n.*[2] **1** [late 18C–1930s] a 10-dollar coin; thus *half-eagle*, a $5 coin; *double-eagle*, a $20 coin. **2** [mid–late 19C] a silver dollar. **3** [late 19C+] a dollar bill (cf. BIRD n.[6]). [the eagle that appears on the coin or note]

eagle *n.*[3] [1960s] (*US campus*) the grade of E (cf. ACE n.[6]). [the initial letter]

eagle beak *n.* [1920s–50s] (*US*) a derog. term for a Jew (cf. BIGNOSE n.). [the stereotypically large-nosed Jew]

eagle day *n.* (*also* **eagle's day**). [1940s+] (*US*) payday. [EAGLE n.[2] (3)/WHEN THE EAGLE SHITS phr.]

eagle eye *n.* [1910s–30s] (*US Und.*) a detective (cf. BEAGLE n.[3]; EYE n.[2]; PINK n.; PRIVATE EYE n.). [EYE n.[2]]

eagle eye *v.* [1960s] (*US*) to look closely, scrutinize. [EAGLE-EYED adj.]

eagle-eyed *adj.* [20C+] scrutinizing, paying close attention, watching. [the visual acuity of the bird]

eagle fly *v.* [1950s–70s] (*US Black*) to pay wages; thus *eagle flies on Friday*, Friday will be payday. [EAGLE n.[2] (3)/WHEN THE EAGLE SHITS phr.]

eagle-flying day *n.* [1940s+] (*US Black/campus*) payday. [EAGLE n.[2] (3)/WHEN THE EAGLE SHITS phr.]

eagle's day *n. see* EAGLE DAY n.

ear *n.* [mid-19C] (*US Black*) a tuning peg on a guitar or fiddle. [resemblance]

earbash *v.* (*also* **bash someone's ear**) [1940s+] (*orig. Aus./N.Z.*) **1** to talk incessantly. **2** to subject to one's opinions, grievances etc. [SE *ear* + BASH v.[1] (1); lit. to 'hit one's ear']

ear-basher *n.* [1940s+] (*orig. Aus./N.Z.*) a bore, a loudmouth who refuses to stop talking. [EARBASH v.]

earbashing *n.* **1** [1940s+] (*orig. Aus.*) nagging, non-stop chatter. **2** [1990s+] (*UK Black*) reprimands, scoldings. [EARBASH v.]

ear between the legs *n.* [19C] the labia minora. [resemblance]

ear-biter *n.*[1] [mid-19C] (*US*) a special agent of the US Post Office. ['so-called because one of the agents about 1845 chewed off the ear of an opponent in a fight' (Craigie, *Dictionary of American English*, 1944)]

ear-biter *n.*[2] [late 19C+] a cadger, one who seeks constantly to borrow money. [BITE SOMEONE'S EAR v. (2)]

ear-biting *n.* [1900s] (*Aus.*) cadging, begging. [BITE SOMEONE'S EAR v. (2)]

ear flap *n.* [mid-19C; 1930s] (*US*) an ear.

earful *n.* **1** [20C+] (*US*) a forceful expression of opinion, esp. a complaint or rebuke; usu. as *get an earful*; occas. *give an earful*. **2** [1910s–30s] information, the implication is of illicitly overheard.

earguard *n.* [1940s] (*Aus.*) short side-whiskers, sideboards or sideburns. [SE *earguard*, a small flap, attached to the cap and covering the ear]

earhole *n.* **1** [mid-19C+] the ear. **2** [1960s] an act of listening, of eavesdropping. [(2) from EARHOLE v.]

earhole *v.* [1950s+] to listen, to overhear, to eavesdrop. [put one's 'ear' to a metaphorical 'hole']

ear hustle *v.* [1990s+] (*US Black/prison*) to eavesdrop. [SE *ear* + HUSTLE v. (3)]

ear hustler *n.* [1990s+] (*US Black*) a gossip, an eavesdropper. [EAR HUSTLE v.]

ear job *n.* **1** [1960s] (*US*) the kissing and caressing of someone's ear with one's tongue. **2** [1970s] a phone call to a sexual phone service, sexually stimulating talk on the telephone. [SE *ear* + JOB n.[4]]

earl *v.* [1960s+] (*US*) to vomit; thus *go to see earl, earl's knocking at the door* (cf. BARF v.; CALL CHARLES v.). [echoic]

earl of Cork *n.*[1] [mid-19C] (*Anglo-Irish*) the ace of diamonds. ['the worst ace and the poorest card in the pack', so called from the contemporary earl, who was the poorest nobleman in Ireland]

earl of Cork *n.*[2] (*also* **duke of Cork**) [1940s] **1** a talk. **2** a walk. [rhy. sl.]

ear-lugger *n.* [20C+] (*Aus.*) a cadger, a scrounger. [SE *ear* + LUG v.[1] (2)]

early *adj.* [1980s+] (*US Black*) up-to-date.

early Battersea *n. see* EARLY HALLOWEEN n.

early beam *n.* [1930s–40s] (*US Black*) dawn, the early morning. [the first sunbeams]

early bird *n.*[1] **1** [mid-19C+] one who habitually gets up or arrives early. **2** [1930s] one who goes to bed early.

early bird *n.*[2] [20C+] a word. [rhy. sl.]

early-bird *adj.* [20C+] first of the day, e.g. *early-bird matinee*. [EARLY BIRD n.[1] (1)]

early black *n.* (*also* **early blue**) [1930s–50s] (*US Black*) dusk, nightfall. [the initial darkening of the sky]

early bright *n.* [1940s–70s] (*US Black*) the early morning.

early door *n.* [late 19C] a prostitute, a whore. [rhy. sl.]

early doors *n.* [20C+] underwear. [rhy. sl. = SE *drawers*]

early doors *adj.* [1980s+] early.

early doors *adv.* [1980s+] prematurely.

early Halloween *n.* (*also* **early Battersea**, ...eclectic,

...homosexual) [1970s+] vulgar, tasteless decor (cf. YIDDISH RENAISSANCE n.). [all considered in poor taste; on model of 'early Georgian' etc]

early hours n. see HAPPY HOURS n.

early morn n. see SUNDAY MORN n.

early parole n. [1990s+] (Aus. prison) suicide.

early purl n. [late 19C–1900s] a drink made of hot beer and gin. [SE early + PURL n.[1]]

early riser n. [1960s+] (US prison) an inmate who is granted an early parole.

ear man n. [1970s] (US Black) an individual expressing a natural ability to excel at an endeavour, a virtuoso. [he picks it up by ear]

ear music n. [1970s] (US Black) improvised music.

earn v. [1950s+] (UK Und.) 1 to work as a prostitute. 2 of a policeman, to take bribes. 3 to make a dishonest profit from a crime.

earner n. (also earn) [1960s+] 1 (orig. UK Und.) any job or plan that pays well, almost invariably criminal; often as nice little earner. 2 (UK police) a bribe, often paid as regularly as more legitimate wages. [EARN v.]

earnest n. [late 17C–mid-18C] (UK Und.) a share (of the booty); thus tip one their earnest, to hand out a share. [SE earnest, money, esp. as paid as a pledge for securing a contract]

earn one's stripes v. [1990s+] (US Black gang/teen) for a young gang member to commit a crime to advance their status. [milit. imagery]

earn one's tucker v. (also earn one's peasoup, make one's tucker) [late 19C] to earn (at least enough for) one's bed and board. [SE earn/make + TUCKER n.]

ear of corn n. [1910s–30s] (US) a country person (cf. BUCK-WHEAT n.).

ear-piece n. [1980s] (UK Black) an ear.

ears n. 1 [1920s–30s] a euph. for ARSE n.[1] (1). 2 [1970s] (orig. US) a Citizen's Band radio, its antenna or the vehicle carrying it; thus have one's ears on, to be tuned into one's CB transceiver.

ear sex n. [1980s+] (US) an instance of sexual talk on the phone.

earth n.[1] (also eerth, erth) [mid-19C+] 3; thus earth sis noms, a 3-month prison term. [backsl.]

earth n.[2] [1980s+] (drugs) a marijuana cigarette. [? its organic (rather than chemical) origins]

earth, the n. [late 19C+] everything, a large amount or quantity, e.g. cost the earth, pay the earth, want the earth.

Eartha (Kitt) n. [1950s+] 1 excrement; also in fig. use (cf. ALI OOP n.). 2 an act of defecation; also fig. in phr. not give a shit (cf. ANDY CAPP n.). 3 in pl., diarrhoea (cf. BANANA (SPLITS) n.). 4 in pl., the female breasts (cf. BRACE AND BITS n.). [rhy. sl.; (1) =SHIT n.[1] (1); (2) = SHIT n.[1] (3); (3) =SHITS, THE n. (1); (4) = TIT n.[3] (1); ult. US singer Eartha Kitt (b.1928)]

earth biscuit n. [1990s+] (US campus) someone who identifies with the styles and concerns of the 1960s. [the save the earth attitudes of the period + the 'whole-grain' image of the biscuit]

earth daddy n. [1980s+] (US campus) an older than average college male who professes the values of the 1960s. [play on a classic figure of the 1960s, the earth mother]

earth gens n. (also erth gens) [mid-19C] 3 shillings. [backsl.; EARTH n.[1] + GEN n.[1]]

earthly n. 1 [late 19C+] a chance, usu. in negative e.g. NO EARTHLY phr. 2 [1920s+] an idea. [SE earthly, emphatic epithet meaning 'on earth'; (2) f. (1)]

earth muffin n. [1980s+] (US campus) an older than average college male; used pej. to indicate one who pursues a HIPPIE n.[2] (3) lifestyle. [SE earth, i.e. one who espouses the values of the 1960s + MUFFIN n.[1] (3)]

earth pads n. (US Black/campus) 1 [1940s] feet. 2 [1960s] shoes.

earth-pu n. (also erth-pu) [mid-19C] three-up, a street gambling game based on coin-tossing. [backsl.; EARTH n.[1]]

earthquake n. [mid–late 19C] (US) an alcoholic mixed drink (cf. BOTTLED EARTHQUAKE n.). [its effects]

earth sith-noms n. [mid-19C] 3 months, usu. as a prison sentence. [backsl.; EARTH n.[1] + SITH-NOM n.]

earth to — phr. [1970s+] (US) a phr. used to call someone's attention, also to tease someone. [the image is that the person is day-dreaming, 'out in space']

earthworm n. [1990s+] the penis (cf. ANTEATER n.).

earth yannops n. (also earth yenneps, erth yannops/ yenneps) [mid-19C] 3 pence. [backsl.; EARTH n.[1] + YENNEP n.]

earthy crunchy n. see CRUNCHY (GRANOLA) n. (3).

earwag v. [1980s] (N.Z.) to gossip.

earwig n. 1 [mid-17C–19C] a malicious gossip or flatterer. 2 [mid-19C] a clergyman. 3 [mid-19C] a close, intimate friend. 4 [mid-19C] (UK Und.) information. 5 [mid-19C; 1930s+] (also wiggin's) an eavesdropper. 6 [late 19C] an inquisitive person. 7 [1940s+] a lookout, one who listens for approaching steps, then checks the owner before admitting them. [play on SE ear]

earwig v.[1] 1 [19C] to gossip, esp. maliciously, to feed another with unpleasant rumours. 2 [mid–late 19C] to lecture, to sermonize. 3 [mid-19C+] (also earwag) to eavesdrop. [EAR-WIG n.]

earwig v.[2] [1910s+] to understand. [rhy. sl. = TWIG v.[2] (2)]

earwigger n. (also wiggin's) [mid-19C; 1920s+] an eavesdropper. [EARWIG v.[1] (3)]

earwigging n. 1 [mid-19C] a private rebuke. 2 [mid-19C+] eavesdropping. [EARWIG v.[1]]

ease v.[1] [early 17C–19C] 1 to rob, to steal. 2 to have sexual intercourse, esp. to deflower. [SE ease, to deprive, to despoil]

ease v.[2] (also ease in, ...off, ...out) [1920s+] (US) 1 to leave, esp. quietly and discreetly; usu. as ease out. 2 to get rid of, to leave behind. 3 to move quietly. 4 to move, to travel.

ease it v. [1940s+] (UK prison) to relax, to let up on some form of crime or rule-breaking.

easeman n. see EASTMAN n.

ease off v. see EASE v.[2].

ease on v. [1950s] (US Black) to go, to make one's way. [EASE v.[2]]

ease out v. see EASE v.[2].

ease over v. [1930s] (orig. US) to move towards. [EASE v.[2]]

ease-up n. [20C+] (W.I.) assistance, esp. in a difficult situation; thus give someone an ease-up, to help. [orig. dial.]

ease up v. [mid-19C+] to relax, to 'lighten up'; often as imper.

easies n. [1950s+] (N.Z.) a woman's elasticated foundation garment.

easily adv. [1940s+] at least, more than, e.g. easily twenty.

easing powder n. [20C+] (drugs) opium (cf. APOSTLE n.). [SE ease, to relieve pain + powder]

east and south n. [mid–late 19C] the mouth (cf. NORTH AND SOUTH n.). [rhy. sl.]

east and west n. 1 [late 19C] the male chest. 2 [1920s+] a vest. 3 [1970s+] the female breast. [rhy. sl; note SE vest is an undergarment; SAmE vest is a waistcoat]

east and west adj. (also east, west and crooked) [20C+] (US) disorderly, confused.

east buttfuck n. see BUMFUCK, EGYPT n.

Easter bunny n.[1] [1990s+] money (cf. BEES (AND HONEY) n.). [rhy. sl.]

Easter bunny n.[2] [1990s+] (US campus) a benefactor, someone who does a favour. [the Easter bunny is a beneficent creature]

Easter egg n.[1] [20C+] (US) a woman wearing too much make-up. [the trad. painted Easter eggs created annually in some cultures]

Easter egg n.[2] [1990s+] the human leg. [rhy. sl.]

Easter queen n. [1960s+] (US gay) one who ejaculates

prematurely. [SE *easter* (*bunny*), i.e. he 'comes quick as a rabbit' + QUEEN n.² (1)]

East Hell *n. see* WEST HELL n.

East India docks *n.* [1990s+] socks. [rhy. sl.]

East Jesus(, Kansas) *n.* [1950s+] an out-of-the-way place, a small town.

Eastman *n.* (*also* easeman) [1910s–40s] (*US Black*) a kept man, one who lives on money earned by a woman; a pimp (cf. CANDYMAN n.). [Black pron. of *yeast* as *east*; thus the image of yeast as expanding and thus making a 'big man'; or *yeast* = BREAD n.¹ (2)/DOUGH n.¹ (1)]

Eastside O *n.* [1990s+] (*US Black teen*) East Oakland. [abbr.]

east, west and crooked *adj. see* EAST AND WEST adj.

easy *n.*¹ [1900s] (*US*) a gullible person. [abbr. EASY MARK n. (1)]

easy *n.*² [1970s+] (*US*) New Orleans, Louisiana. [abbr. of BIG EASY, THE n.]

easy *adj.* **1** [late 17C–early 19C; 20C+] of a woman, sexually promiscuous. **2** [late 17C+] innocent, gullible. **3** [late 19C] (*UK/ US Und.*) amenable to bribery. **4** [20C+] (*Can.*) easily imposed upon.

easy! *excl.* [mid-19C+] an exhortation to relax, not get flustered, stay cool. [TAKE IT EASY v. (1)]

easy as... *phr.* [17C+] used in a variety of combs. all of which mean very easy indeed, sometimes almost criminally so, e.g. ...ABC, ...a gum shoe, ...a pig would eat a daisy, ...apple pie/tart, ...damn it, (Aus.) ...drinking beer, ...eating a mango, ...go and be blowed, ...kiss my arm/arse/eye, kiss your hand, ...ninepence, ...peas, (orig. US) ...pie, ...pissing backwards/the bed, (Aus.) ...pulling a cork, ...shelling peas, ...shit, (Aus.) ...shitting in bed, ...stirring a foot, ...taking candy from a baby/money from a child, ...tilly, ...wink/winking (see also combs. below).

easy as cake (and ice-cream) *phr.* [1930s+] very easy. [the ease and pleasure with which one consumes such food-stuffs]

easy as falling off a log *phr.* (*also* easy as falling off a horse, ...rolling off a log, like falling off a log, simple as falling off a log) [late 19C+] very easy indeed.

easy as piss *phr.* [1990s+] extremely easy. [note local Aus. use *easy as pee-the-bed-awake*]

easy digging *n.* [1930s] (*US*) granulated sugar. [ety. unknown; ? the ease with which one can spoon it into a cup]

easy-doer *n.* [1940s] (*US prison*) one who copes well with prison life.

easy does it *phr.* [late 19C+] a phr. used as a warning, go easy, take your time, careful.

easy game *n.* [late 19C+] a sexually available woman. [SE *easy*/EASY adj. (1) + SE *game*]

easy lay *n.* [1920s+] usu. of a woman, one who can be easily seduced; also used fig. of anything that is easily obtained. [SE *easy*/EASY adj. (1) + LAY n.³ (1)]

easy lines *n. see* HARD LINES n.

easy make *n.* [1940s+] (*US*) a promiscuous or easily seducible woman; also in homosexual use. [SE *easy*/EASY adj. (1) + MAKE n.³ (2)]

easy mark *n.* **1** [late 19C+] someone or something over-come, mastered or persuaded without difficulty, anything achieved with ease. **2** [1930s] an obvious suspect. [SE *easy* + MARK n.¹ (1)]

easy meat *n.* [late 19C+] someone who is easily fooled or seduced. [SE *easy*/EASY adj. (1) + MEAT n. (5)]

easy mort *n.* [mid-17C–early 18C] a promiscuous, 'forward' woman. [SE *easy*/EASY adj. (1) + MORT n.]

easy on! *excl.* [1920s+] a general excl., go easy! stop it! be sen-sible!

easy on the eye *adj.* [1920s+] (*orig. US*) attractive, esp. of women or girls. [note 1900s synon. *easy to look at*]

easy over *phr.* [1960s] (*US*) no problems, don't worry.

easy ride *n.* [1980s+] (*US*) a sexually available woman. [SE *easy* + RIDE n.¹ (2)]

easy rider *n.*¹ [20C+] (*US Black*) **1** a male sexual athlete; a promiscuous woman (cf. BANBURY n.). **2** a pimp, a kept man (cf. CANDYMAN n.). **3** a guitar. [SE *easy* + RIDE n.¹ (2); the term crossed briefly into White vocabulary with the release of the hit film *Easy Rider* (1969)]

easy rider *n.*² [1960s] any 'outlaw' motorcyclist. [film title (1969)]

easy rider *n.*³ [1970s] a calm, unruffled person.

easy six *n.* [20C+] (*US gambling*) the point of 6 in craps dice (cf. ADA FROM DECATUR n.). [it is *easy* because of the number of combinations that equal 6]

easy street *n.* **1** [late 19C] a euph. for a town's red-light area. **2** [late 19C+] a secure, comfortable life, a situation free of problems, esp. material ones; usu. in phr. *on easy street.*

easy stuff *n.* [1950s+] (*US*) a sexually available woman. [SE *easy*/EASY adj. (1) + STUFF n.⁶ (2)]

easy time *n.* [20C+] (*US Und.*) an uneventful time in prison. [SE *easy* + TIME n.¹]

easy touch *n.* **1** [1930s+] one who can be easily solicited for money or favours. **2** [1970s+] a situation which is easily exploitable. **3** [1970s+] (*UK Und.*) a robbery that can be carried out without difficulty. [SE *easy* + TOUCH n.¹ (7)]

easy virtue *n.* [late 18C–early 19C] a prostitute. [SE *easy*, careless, unconcerned + *virtue*]

easy walkers *n.* [1920s–60s] (*US Black*) comfortable, well-fitting shoes.

eat *n. see* EATS n.

eat *v.*¹ **1** [19C+] to defeat, to destroy; thus *I'll eat him alive.* **2** [mid-19C+] (*also* eat off) to annoy, to bother; thus *what's eating you?* **3** [1970s+] to strike face-first or be hit by (e.g. a bullet).

eat *v.*² [early 19C–1920s] (*US*) to provide with food.

eat *v.*³ **1** [late 19C+] to perform cunnilingus or hetero- or homosexual fellatio (cf. BASKET LUNCH n.; BOX LUNCH n.). **2** [2000s] to perform anilingus (cf. AUSTRALIAN n.). [note RN synon. *chew*]

eat *v.*⁴ [1920s+] (*US Und.*) to take a profit from criminality.

eat *v.*⁵ *see* EAT THE HEAD OFF v.

eat *v.*⁶ *see* EAT UP v.

eat a child *v.* [late 18C–19C] to share in a treat given to the parish officers. [the price for the commutation (registering as legitimate) of a bastard child was 'ten pounds and a greasy chin' (Grose, 1785), i.e. a good meal]

eat acorns *v.* [1930s] (*US Black*) to suffer humiliation, to accept defeat. [a peasant might eat acorns when deprived of a more nutritious source of food]

eat a dick *phr.* [1990s+] (*US Black teen*) a general phr. of dislike or dismissal. [SE *eat* + DICK n.⁴ (1)]

eat a fig *v.* [mid-19C] to commit burglary, to rob a house. [rhy. sl. = CRACK A CRIB v.]

eat a furburger *v.* [1980s+] (*US*) to perform cunnilingus (cf. BEARD RIDE n.; BOX LUNCH n.). [EAT v.³ (1) + FURBURGER n.]

eat alone *v.* [1990s+] (*US Und.*) to be greedy.

eat at the Y *v.* (*also* eat box lunch at the Y) [1950s+] (*US*) to perform cunnilingus (cf. BOX LUNCH n.). [EAT v.³ (1) + Y n./SE *Y*, referring to the spread legs]

eat (boiled) crow *v.* [mid-19C+] to suffer humiliations and insults without responding in kind. [the mid-19C story of a man who bet that he was able to eat a cooked crow, and duly did so, but remarked as he chewed the bird: 'Yes, I can eat a crow, but I'll be darned if I hanker after it!']

eat bull beef *v.* [late 16C–19C] to become strong, to become fierce. [the image of *bull beef* as tough meat]

eat cauliflower *v. see* CAULIFLOWER n.¹ (1).

eat cheese *v.*¹ **1** [1940s+] (*orig. US Black*) to toady to, to ingratiate oneself with. **2** [1950s+] (*US*) to inform on, to betray. [SE *eat* + CHEESY adj.³, i.e. the quality of one's smiles]

eat cheese v.[2] [1970s] (*US Black*) to be in love.

eat concrete v. [1970s] (*US*) to drive fast, esp. a truck, down a highway.

eat crap v. [1930s+] (*orig. US*) to suffer and accept humiliation, to humble oneself, usu. in order to attain a desired goal. [SE *eat* + fig. use of CRAP n.[3] (1)]

eat crow v. *see* EAT (BOILED) CROW v.

eat dirt v.[1] [mid-19C+] **1** (*also* **eat dirt pie, eat dust**) to retract a previous statement, usu. incurring humiliation and embarrassment by so doing. **2** to act in a demeaning, humiliating manner. [pvb 'Every man must *eat a peck of dirt* (i.e. retract a number of errors) before he dies']

eat dirt v.[2] *see* EAT GRAVEL v.

eat dog v. [19C+] to suffer humiliation and insult without reciprocating.

eat dong v. [1970s] (*US*) to suffer humiliation.

eat dried apples v. (*also* **eat peaches, ...pumpkin seeds**) [1960s–70s] (*US*) to become pregnant. [the way in which dried fruit swells up when placed in water]

eat dust v.[1] (*US*) **1** [late 19C] to be killed. **2** [late 19C+] to leave, to travel.

eat dust v.[2] *see* EAT DIRT v.[1] (1).

eater n. [1990s+] a café, a restaurant.

eaters n. [1910s] (*Aus.*) false teeth.

eatery n. (*also* **eaterie**) [20C+] (*orig. US*) a restaurant.

eat face v. [1960s+] (*US campus*) to kiss passionately on the mouth and face.

eat fish v. *see* FISH v.[3].

eat fist-meat v. [mid-16C] to receive a punch in the mouth.

eat gravel v. (*also* **eat dirt, eat grass**) [20C+] (*US*) to be thrown or to fall on one's face.

eat hair pie v. (*also* **eat fur pie**) [1940s+] to perform cunnilingus (cf. BEARD RIDE n.; BOX LUNCH n.). [EAT v.[3] (1) + HAIR PIE n.]

eat hempseed v. [early 17C] to be hanged. [the rope is made from *hemp*]

eat-house n. [2000s] (*US*) a café or restaurant.

eat in Dutch street v. [1910s+] to share expenses. [GO DUTCH v.[1], i.e. stereotyping]

eating corn phr. *see* ON THE CORN phr.

eating irons n. [1940s+] utensils, knives and forks.

eating match n. [mid-19C] (*W.I.*) a feast.

eatings n. [1900s–30s] food.

eating tackle n. [20C+] teeth.

eating tobacco n. [1900s–60s] (*US*) chewing tobacco.

eating tool n. [1920s–60s] (*US*) an eating utensil.

eat it v.[1] [1910s+] to perform oral sex (cf. BASKET LUNCH n.; BOX LUNCH n.). [EAT v.[3] (1)]

eat it v.[2] **1** [1930s+] to suffer humiliation, esp. in attaining a desired goal. **2** [1960s] (*US campus*) to do poorly, to achieve low marks. **3** [1970s] (*US*) to be unpleasant. **4** [1970s+] to die.

eat it! excl. [20C+] a general term of dismissal, disdain. [*it is the penis*]

eat its head off v. *see* EAT ONE'S HEAD OFF v.

eat jam v. [1940s+] (*US gay*) to perform anilingus (cf. AUSTRALIAN n.). [SE *eat* + JAM n.[7] (1)]

eat joint n. [1920s] (*US*) a restaurant, a café. [SE *eat* + JOINT n.[4] (3)]

eat lead v. [1920s+] (*orig. US*) to be shot, usu. fatally. [SE *eat* + LEAD n.[1] (1); note 16C SE *eat iron*, to be stabbed]

eat like a beggar man and wag one's under jaw phr. [late 18C–early 19C] 'a jocular reproach to a proud man' (Grose, 1785).

eat me! excl. [1960s+] (*US*) shut up! you make me sick! the hell with you! go away! [EAT v.[3] (1)]

eat my shorts! excl. [1970s+] (*US*) a dismissive phr., drop dead! go to hell! etc. [SAmE *shorts* = SE *underpants*; the phr. moved into

the mainstream with the success of the TV cartoon family, *The Simpsons*, whose renegade son Bart took it as his personal catchphrase; note EAT ONE'S SHORTS v.]

eat off v. *see* EAT v.[1] (2).

eat one's gun v. (*also* **eat the gun**) [1970s+] (*US*) to commit suicide by shooting oneself in the mouth.

eat one's hat v. (*also* **eat one's, eat one's bonnet, ...boots, ...cap, ...pants, ...shirt**) [late 18C+] to go back on one's words, esp. to admit that a public statement was, in fact, wrong.

eat one's head v. [mid-19C+] to go back on one's words, esp. to admit that a public statement was, in fact, wrong.

eat one's head off v. (*also* **eat its head off**) [18C+] of a person or thing, to cost more than it is worth, lit. to eat too much.

eat one's heart out v. [late 19C+] to be consumed by jealousy.

eat one's nails v. [early 18C] to do something foolish. [ety. unknown]

eat one's pants/shirt v. *see* EAT ONE'S HAT v.

eat one's shorts v. [1970s+] (*US*) to die, to suffer. [note EAT MY SHORTS! excl.]

eat one's tutu v. (*also* **eat one's toot**) [mid–late 19C] (*N.Z.*) to become acclimatized, esp. to colonial life. [Maori *tutu*, a New Zealand shrub yielding shining black juicy berries which can be eaten, but also containing poisonous seeds]

eat out v.[1] [1940s] (*US*) to tell off, to reprimand. [var. on CHEW OUT v.]

eat out v.[2] [1960s+] (*US*) to perform cunnilingus, occas. anilingus (cf. AUSTRALIAN n.; BOX LUNCH n.). [EAT v.[3] (1)]

eat parrot backside v. (*also* **eat bird-seed, eat parrot bambam/bottom, eat parrot-head soup**) [20C+] (*W.I.*) to chatter on incessantly and irritatingly.

eat peaches v. *see* EAT DRIED APPLES v.

eat pie v. [1980s+] to perform cunnilingus (cf. BOX LUNCH n.). [EAT v.[3] (1) + HAIR PIE n.]

eat popcorn v. [1960s] (*US drugs*) to take some form of pill.

eat poundcake v. **1** [1940s+] (*gay*) to suck a partner's anus. **2** [1970s+] (*US Black*) to have sexual intercourse. [pun on SE + POUND v.[2] (1)]

eat pumpkin seeds v. *see* EAT DRIED APPLES v.

eat pussy v. [1930s+] to perform cunnilingus (cf. BOX LUNCH n.). [EAT v.[3] (1) + PUSSY n. (2)]

eat razor soup v. [1930s] (*US*) to say something cheeky or impertinent.

eats n. (*also* **eat**) [mid-19C+] food; a meal. [orig. UK but in 20C+ US only]

eat sausage v. [1980s+] (*N.Z.*) of a woman, to fellate (cf. BASKET LUNCH n.). [EAT v.[3] (1) + SAUSAGE n.[1] (1)]

eat shit v. **1** [1930s+] (*also* **eat shit and die**) to suffer and accept humiliation. **2** [1930s+] to humble oneself, usu. to attain a desired goal. **3** [1940s+] to be utterly contemptible. [SE *eat* + SHIT n.[1] (1)]

eat shit (and die)! excl. [1960s+] (*US*) a general, dismissive, derog. expression; it has no spec. meaning. [EAT SHIT v. (1)]

eat snowballs v. [1930s] (*US tramp*) to stay in the north during the winter (many tramps wintered in the warmer south).

eat someone for breakfast v. *see* HAVE SOMEONE FOR BREAKFAST v.[2].

eat someone's ass off v. (*also* **eat someone's ass out, eat someone's arse off**) [1940s+] (*US*) to criticize severely, to punish heavily. [fig. use SE *eat* + ASS n. (2)/ARSE n.[1] (1)]

eat someone's bird v. *see* BIRD n.[8] (1).

eat someone's cookies v. [1970s] (*US*) to defeat someone.

eat someone's lunch v. [1950s+] (*US*) to defeat, injure or outdo someone.

eat someone's meat v. [1920s+] to perform oral intercourse. [EAT v.[3] (1) + MEAT n. (2)]

eat supper before you say grace *v.* [20C+] (*US*) to conceive a child before one gets married.

eat the big one! *excl.* [1980s+] (*US*) to hell with you! [var. on EAT ME! excl.]

eat the carpet *v. see* CHEW THE CARPET v.[1].

eat the cookie *v.* [1970s] (*US*) to be defeated.

eat the face off *v. see* EAT THE HEAD OFF v.

eat the greaser *v.* [20C+] (*US*) to swallow one's words, to recant. [dial. *greaser*, a lump of salt pork used to grease the bars of a griddle]

eat the green weenie *v.* [1970s+] (*US, orig. milit.*) to get killed. [? the grass; thus cf. BITE THE DUST v.]

eat the gun *v. see* EAT ONE'S GUN v.

eat the head off *v.* (*also* **eat**, **eat the face off**) [1930s+] to verbally abuse.

eat the leek *v.* [late 19C] to be forced to address unpleasant consequences. [the 'sharpness' of the SE *leek*]

eat turkey *v.* [1960s–70s] (*US*) **1** to suffer humiliation and insult without reciprocating. **2** to take second best, to accept an inferior role. [var. EAT (BOILED) CROW v.]

eat-unda-table *n.* [1990s+] (*W.I.*) a man who performs oral sex.

eat-up *n.* [1910s] (*Aus.*) a meal.

eat up *adj.* (*also* **ate up**) **1** [1970s] (*US campus*) tired out, exhausted. **2** [1990s+] disorganized, messy, all over the place. **3** [1990s+] strange, unusual, crazy. **4** [1990s+] keen on, obsessed with. [SE *eaten up*/EAT UP v.]

eat up *v.* **1** [mid-19C–1950s] to scold, to rebuke. **2** [mid-19C+] to defeat, to destroy. **3** [late 19C+] (*also* **eat**) to believe unquestioningly. **4** [1900s–10s] to do well; to act competently; to deal with efficiently. **5** [1910s+] (*orig. theatre*) (*also* **eat**) to enjoy immensely, to acclaim. **6** [1930s+] to take control of, to 'consume'.

eat vinegar with a fork *v.* [late 19C–1900s] to have a sharp tongue.

eau-de-Cologne *n.* **1** [1960s+] (*Aus.*) the telephone. **2** [1990s+] a woman. [rhy. sl.; (2) = POLONE n. (1)]

ebb-water *n.* [late 17C–18C] (*UK Und.*) a lack of money.

ebenezer *n.* (*also* **ebeneser**) [mid-19C] (*US*) temper, passion. [Heb. *eben ha-ezer*, the stone of help, the memorial stone set up by Samuel after the victory of Mizpeh (1 Sam. 7:12); a misreading of Samuel's 'raising' of a memorial]

ebony *n.* (*also* **ebon**, **son of ebony**) **1** [mid-19C+] (*US*) a Black person. **2** [20C+] (*US Black*) the quintessence of Black sensibility.

ebony *adj.* [mid-19C+] (*US*) racially Black, e.g. *ebony chick/pidgeon*, a Black girl. [EBONY n. (1)]

ebony-kugel *n. see* KUGEL n.

E-boy *n.* [1980s+] a devotee of MDMA. [E n. + SE *boy*]

ecaf *n. see* EEK n.

eccer *n.* (*also* **eccker**, **ecker**, **ekker**) **1** [late 19C] physical exercise. **2** [1910s+] (*Aus./Irish*) homework. [SE *exercise* + -ER sfx]

eccy *n.* [1920s+] (*US campus*) economics. [abbr.]

eccy/eccky *n. see* ECKY n.

echohead *n.* [1990s+] a foolish person, usu. female. [SE *echo* + -HEAD sfx (1), i.e. thoughts 'echo' around the empty skull]

ecker *n. see* ECCER n.

eckied (up) *adj.* [1980s+] (*drugs*) under the influence of MDMA. [ECKY (UP) v.]

ecky *n.* (*also* **eccy**, **eccky**) [1980s+] (*drugs*) MDMA (cf. ECSTASY n.). [abbr. ECSTASY n.]

ecky-becky *n.* [20C+] (*W.I., Bdos*) a poor White. [? redup. of Ijo *beke*, a European or ironic use of Ijo *ekee*, God + *beke*]

ecky (up) *v.* [1980s+] (*drugs*) to take MDMA. [ECKY n.]

E class *n.* [2000s] (*US teen*) a very expensive car. [Mercedes *E class*; although the sl. term can mean any luxury brand]

ecnop *n.* [1950s–80s] a ponce. [backsl.]

eco *n.* [2000s] (*US Black*) money. [abbr. SE *economy/economics*]

ecod! *excl.* (*also* **icod!**) [18C–19C] a euph. for *God!*, also used in a variety of oaths (cf. ADAD! excl.).

ecofreak *n.* (*also* **eco-warrior**) [1970s+] an extremist in the cause of environmentalism. [SE *ecology* + FREAK sfx/SE *warrior*]

econut *n.* [1970s+] (*US*) an extremist in the cause of environmentalism. [SE *ecology* + NUT n.[4] (2)]

ecstasy *n.* [1980s+] the main 'unofficial' term for the drug known officially as methylene dioxymethamphetamine (MDMA) (cf. ACID n.[4]; ADAM n.[3]; APPLES n.[2]; B-BOMB n.; BENZ n.; BIG BROWN ONES n.; BISCUIT n.[6]; BURGERS n.; CLARITY n.; DEBS n.; DEX n.; DISCO BISCUIT n.; DOLLAR n.[2]; DOVE n.; DRIVERS n.[2]; E n.; ECKY n.; EGGS n.[2]; ENERGIZER n.; ESSENCE n.[2]; FANTASIA n.; GREENIES n.[2]; GREY BISCUIT n.; HAMBURGER n.[3]; HAMMER AND SICKLES n.; HUG DRUG n.; KINDER EGGS n.; LOVE DOVE n.; LOVE DRUG n.; LUCKY CHARMS n.; M25 n.; MELLOW DRUG OF AMERICA n.; MITSUS n.; NEW YORKERS n.; NEXUS n.; ORBIT n.; PINK CALLY n.; PINK FLAMINGOES n.; PINK STUDS n.; RHUBARB AND CUSTARDS n.; ROLL n.[6]; ROLLING n.[3]; SHAMROCK n.; SNOWBALL n.[4]; SPACE PILL n.; SPEED FOR LOVERS n.; SUPER ECSTASY n.; SWANS n.; TABLET n.; VITAMIN A n.; VITAMIN E n.; VITAMIN X n.; WEST COAST TURNAROUNDS n.; WHITE CALLIES n.; WHITE DOVE n.; WHIZZ-BOMB n.; X n.[3]; XTC n.). [*ecstasy* existed in the 1960s, as one of many synthetic hallucinogens (although it is more amphetamine than a 'real' hallucinogen) from a group known as 'Schulgin's Compounds' but only reached its apotheosis in the late 1980s. Its nickname comes from the euphoria and indiscriminate affection that its ingestion promotes, and the earlier popular name of 'love-drug'; virtually SE by mid-1990s]

EC women *n.* [late 19C] (*UK society*) the wives of City businessmen. [the London postal code EC1, the location of the City of London; a snobbish usage by those who despise 'trade']

E'd *adj. see* E-ED adj.

Eddie *n.* [1920s] (*US Black*) a White male. [abbr. MR EDDIE n.]

eddie *n.* [1980s+] (*US campus*) **1** an ugly man. **2** anything stupid. [ety. unknown; ? anecdotal or ? link to EDDIE n.]

Eddie Grundys *n.* [2000s] underwear. [rhy. sl. = UNDIES n.; ult. fictional character *Eddie Grundy* in BBC radio soap opera *The Archers*]

eddress *n.* [1990s+] (*US teen*) an electronic-mail a*ddress*. [abbr. + pun on SE *address*]

e.d.'ed *adj.* [1920s] finished, worn-out. [SE *exhausted*]

edgabac *n.* (*also* **egabac**) [mid-19C] cabbage. [backsl.]

Edgar Britt *n.* [1960s+] (*Aus.*) **1** excrement, an act of defecation (cf. ALI OOP n.; ANDY CAPP n.). **2** in pl., diarrhoea (cf. BANANA (SPLITS) n.). [rhy. sl.; (1) = SHIT n.[1] (1); (2) = SHITS, THE n. (1); ult. Aus. jockey *Edgar Britt* (b.1913)]

Edgar Wallace *v.* [1970s] to thrill. [the thriller writer *Edgar Wallace* (1875–1932)]

edge *n.*[1] **1** [late 19C–1960s] a state of mild intoxication; often as *have/get an edge on*. **2** [late 19C+] an advantage. **3** [1930s+] (*also* **edgies**) drug-created stress; or symptoms of withdrawal from a drug. **4** [1940s+] tension, usu. creative. [(1) one is on the *edge* of inebriation]

edge *n.*[2] [1960s+] (*US Black*) a knife; thus *pack an edge*, carry a knife.

edge *v.* **1** [late 19C–1960s] (*UK Und.*) to escape, to run away, to avoid or keep away; esp. as excl. called out by a lookout *edge!*, run for it!; thus *keep the edge up*, to act as a lookout. **2** [1910s–20s] (*Aus.*) to discontinue. **3** [1950s] (*Aus.*) to be unreasonable.

edge city *n.* [1960s+] the extremes of experience, whether spiritual, physical, drug induced or whatever; usu. with overtones of fear and challenge. [EDGE n.[1] (4) + CITY sfx]

edged *adj.*[1] [late 19C–1930s] (*US*) tipsy. [EDGE n.[1] (1)]

edged *adj.*[2] [1980s+] (*US*) angry. [EDGE n.[1] (4)]

edge it! *excl.* [1930s] (*Aus.*) be quiet! shut up!

edgenaro *n.* [mid-19C] an orange. [backsl.]

edge-up *adj.* [20C+] (*W.I.*) used of one who is trying excessively hard to become friends. [the image is of physically moving close]

edge work *n.* [1930s–50s] (*US Und.*) barely perceptible markings on the edges of cards; used by cheats.

edgies *n. see* EDGE n.[1] (3).

edie *n.* [1940s–50s] a prostitute (working Piccadilly, Bayswater Road and other 'cheap' streets in London]. [the image of *Edie* as a poor person's name]

edison *v.* [1920s] (*US*) to interrogate. [the inventor of the electric light, Thomas Edison; it is presumably shone on the person being interrogated]

Edison medicine *n.* [1990s+] (*US*) electro-shock therapy. [proper name Thomas Alva *Edison* (1847–1931), inventor of the electric light-bulb + SE *medicine*]

Edison special *n.* [1970s] (*US prison*) death in the electric chair. [see prev. + SE *special*]

edmundo *n.* [1960s+] the leader, the most important person. [rhy. sl.; *Edmundo Ros* = BOSS n.[2] (1); ult. *Edmundo Ros* (b.1910), a popular Latin American band leader]

Edna (May)! *excl.* [20C+] (*UK Und.*) a general excl. of dismissal, be off! go away! [rhy. sl. = on your way!; ult. early 20C music-hall artiste *Edna May* (1878–1948)]

-ed out *sfx* [1970s+] glutted with, full of; both lit. and fig. uses.

educated *adj.* **1** [20C+] (*US*) fraudulent, esp. of a card deck that has been fixed. **2** [1940s+] clever but criminal. [ironic use of SE]

educated fool *n.* (*also* **educated ignorant**) [1950s+] (*orig. US Black*) one who is academic but not very sophisticated or worldly wise.

educated pussy *n.* [1950s–60s] (*US Black*) a weakling, an inadequate. [SE *educated* + PUSSY n. (10); the image is of one who is 'not a real man']

-ed up *sfx* [1990s+] wearing a specific (designer) brand of clothing, e.g. *Guccied up*.

edward *n.* [1960s] a Teddy boy. [SE *Teddy Boy*, or 'Edwardian']

E-ed *adj.* (*also* **E'd**) [1980s+] under the influence of MDMA; usu. as *E'd up*. [E n.]

eejit *n.* (*also* **eedjit, eejut, idjeet, idjit, idjut, ijet, ijit, ijjit, ijut**) [mid-19C+] (*mainly Irish*) a fool, an idiot. [Irish pron./ mispron. of SE *idiot*]

eejity *adj.* (*also* **eejit**) [late 19C+] stupid, idiotic. [EEJIT n.]

eek *n.* (*also* **ecaf**) [1960s+] (*Ling. Fr./Polari*) the face. [backsl.]

eekcher *n.* [late 19C–1900s] cheek, audacity. [cod Lat.]

eeks *n.* [1950s+] the eyes. [Polari]

eel *n.*[1] **1** [17C; mid-19C+] the penis (cf. ANTEATER n.). **2** [1920s] a very thin person. [resemblance]

eel *n.*[2] **1** [mid-19C] (*US, Western*) a native of New England. **2** [mid-19C+] (*orig. US*) anyone who possesses the 'slippery' qualities of the fish, e.g. an accomplished escaper from prison, a spy, a confidence trickster. [SE *eel*, seen anthropomorphically as an untrustworthy creature]

eelerspee *n.* (*also* **eeler-spieler**) [1910s+] (*Aus. Und.*) a confidence trickster. [backsl. = SPIELER n. (1)]

eel juice *n.* [20C+] liquor. [? it makes one wriggle like an eel; note SE *liquor*, the green sauce that is served with eels at pie and mash shops]

eel out *v.* [1920s] (*US*) to avoid a problem, esp. in a deceitful, self-serving way. [SE *eel*, i.e. its slippery qualities]

eel pot *n.* (*also* **eel trap**) [late 18C–early 19C] the vagina (cf. BAG n.[1]). [EEL n.[1] (1)]

eel's ankle *n.* (*also* **eel's hips, trout's ankles**) [1920s] (*US*) something extraordinary or very special. [on pattern of BEE'S KNEES n.]

eel's eyebrows *n.* [1920s] something utterly repellent.

eel skin *n.*[1] [mid-19C] a banknote (cf. BAT HIDE n.). [? the green colour]

eel skin *n.*[2] [mid-19C] a New Englander. [EEL n.[2] (1)]

eel skin *n.*[3] [late 19C] a tight skirt, fashionable *c.*1881. [it fits the wearer like an eel's skin]

eel skin *n.*[4] [late 19C] a cosh, made from a canvas tube filled with sand. [resemblance]

eel-skinner *n.* [late 18C–early 19C] the vagina (cf. BITE n.[2]). [EEL n.[1] (1)]

eel skins *n.* [mid-19C] extremely tight trousers.

eel trap *n. see* EEL POT n.

eely *n.* [1980s] (*Aus.*) a confidence trick. [the 'slippery' characteristic of an eel]

eemosh *n.* [mid-19C+] home. [backsl.]

eenin *n. see* ENIN n.

eenque *n.* [late 19C] the queen. [backsl.]

eensie-teensie/eensy-beensy/eensy-weensy/eentsy-weentsy *adj. see* TEENSIE-WEENSIE adj.

eerht *n.* [mid-19C] the number 3. [backsl.]

eerquay *n.* [1930s–40s] (*US*) a male homosexual; also adj. [cod Lat. = QUEER n. (4)/QUEER adj.[1] (3)]

eerth *n. see* EARTH n.[1].

eeson *n.* [mid-19C+] nose. [backsl.]

eetswe *adj.* [late 19C] fond of. [backsl. = SWEET ON adj. (1)]

eevach a kool *v.* [late 19C] to have a look. [backsl.]

eevige *v.* [late 19C] to give. [backsl.]

efegs! *excl. see* FAGS! excl.

eff *v.* (*also* **f**) [1910s+] a euph. for FUCK v.[1]/FUCK v.[2]; thus *effing*, a euph. for FUCKING adj. (1).

eff-all *n. see* FUCK-ALL n.

eff (and blind) *v.* (*also* **F and blind, fuck and blind**) [1920s+] to swear intensely; thus *effing and blinding*, using obscenities. [EFF v. + BLIND v.[2]]

effer *n.* [1970s] (*Irish*) a term of abuse, a FUCKER n. (3). [EFF v.]

effie *n.*[1] [1930s] (*US gay*) an *eff*eminate male homosexual. [abbr.]

effie *n.*[2] *see* HEIFER n. (2).

effing *adj. see* EFF v.

effing and blinding *phr. see* EFF (AND BLIND) v.

eff off! *excl.* [1950s+] a euph. for FUCK OFF! excl. [EFF v.]

e-fink *n.* [mid-19C] a knife. [backsl.]

efter *n.* [mid-19C] a thief (who specializes in theatre audiences). [? SE *after*, he is *after the valuables*; or ? backsl. *thief*]

egabac *n. see* EDGABAC n.

egad! *excl.* [late 17C+] a euph. for *God!* (cf. ADAD! excl.). [? A God!]

egg *n.*[1] **1** [mid-19C+] a person; usu. qualified as GOOD EGG n., BAD EGG n. etc. **2** [1920s+] (*also* **double-yolker**) a fool or obnoxious person (cf. APPLEHEAD n.). **3** [1940s] (*US Und.*) the victim of a confidence trick.

egg *n.*[2] [20C+] (*US campus*) a conspicuously studious and intellectual student. [abbr. EGGHEAD n.[1] (2)]

egg *n.*[3] [20C+] (*US*) a henpecked husband. [pun on SE *egg*, thus *hen*]

egg *n.*[4] **1** [1900s–30s] the head or skull; thus *out of one's egg*, insane. **2** [1910s–40s] (*UK/US Und.*) a bomb. **3** [1970s+] (*drugs*) a capsule of a drug; usu. as EGGS n.[2] (cf. PILL n.[4]). [resemblance; (2) orig. US Civil War milit. use]

egg *n.*[5] [1910s] (*US*) $1. [? abbr. SE *nest-egg*]

egg *n.*[6] *see* GOOSE EGG n.[1].

egg *v.*[1] [late 19C+] (*US*) to move carefully, quietly. [phr. *walk on eggshells*, to tread delicately]

egg *v.*[2] [1920s+] to make fun of someone. [SE *egg on*]

egg-a-muffin! *excl.* [1980s+] (*US campus*) an enthusiastic response of agreement. [SE *egg on* + McDonald's *egg McMuffin*]

egg-and-butter/-chicken money *n. see* EGG MONEY n.

egg and spoon *n.* **1** [1960s+] a Black person. **2** [1970s+] (*Aus.*) a fool, a silly person (cf. BEECHAM'S PILL n.). **3** [1970s+] (*Aus.*) a pimp (cf. ALPHONSE n.[2]). [rhy. sl.; (1) = COON n. (5); (2) = GOON n.[1] (1); (3) = HOON n.[1] (1)]

eggbeater *n.* 1 [1930s+] (*US*) an autogiro or helicopter. 2 [1970s+] an old motorcar.

egg-boiler *n.* [1930s] (*Aus.*) a bowler hat. [in hot weather it 'boils' one's EGG n.⁴ (1)]

egg crate *n.* 1 [1920s–50s] (*US*) an old car or aeroplane. 2 [1930s] an old elevator. [resemblance]

egg flip *n.* [20C+] (*Aus.*) a piece of inside information in horseracing. [rhy. sl. = TIP n.⁵ (1)]

egg-for-fuck *n.* [1990s+] (*US campus*) a fool, a simpleton, an obnoxious person (cf. FUCKBRAIN n.). [SE *egg* + FUCK v.¹; joc. var. on SHIT-FOR-BRAINS n.]

egghead *n.*¹ [20C+] (*orig. US*) 1 an idiot (cf. APPLEHEAD n.). 2 an intellectual, anyone considered to work with the brain rather than brawn. 3 a pretentiously intellectual type.

egghead *n.*² [20C+] 1 a bald person. 2 a bald head. [resemblance]

egghead *adj.* [1950s+] (*orig US*) intellectual, or pretentiously so. [EGGHEAD n.¹ (2)]

eggheaded *adj.*¹ [1910s+] intellectual, or posing as such. [EGGHEAD n.¹ (2)]

eggheaded *adj.*² [1940s+] (*US*) bald. [EGGHEAD n.² (2)]

egg hits the fan, the *phr. see* SHIT HITS THE FAN, THE phr.

egg in your beer *phr.* [1930s+] (*US*) something for nothing, used as an ironical retort.

egg money *n.* (*also* **butter money, cream money, egg-and-butter money, egg-and-chicken money**) [late 19C+] (*US*) money earned by a farmer's wife through the sale of eggs, butter and other dairy products.

eggnog *n.* [1920s] (*US*) a foolish or unpleasant person.

eggo *n.* [1980s+] (*US campus*) a fool, a misfit, a social anachronism (cf. APPLEHEAD n.; BOBO n.¹). [? EGG n.¹ (2) + -O sfx (1)]

egg on *phr.* [1950s] (*Aus.*) hurry up.

eggplant *n.*¹ [1940s] (*US Black*) a $5 bill. [ety. unknown]

eggplant *n.*² [1970s] (*US*) a Black person. [SE *eggplant* or aubergine, the vegetable has a shiny purple-black skin; also 'translation' of MULENYAM n.]

egg roll *n.* 1 [1970s–80s] (*N.Z. prison*) a general term of abuse. 2 [1980s] (*US*) a derog. term for a Korean immigrant. 3 [1980s+] (*US gay*) a Chinese man's penis. [SE *egg roll*/Chinese *egg roll*, the quintessential US Chinese restaurant dish]

eggs *n.*¹ 1 [mid-15C+] the testicles (cf. ACORNS n.). 2 [1950s–60s] in fig. use, courage, virility.

eggs *n.*² (*drugs*) 1 [1970s+] a drug in capsule/tablet form (cf. PILL n.⁴). 2 [1980s+] temazepam, tranquillizers. 3 [1990s+] (*Aus.*) MDMA tablets (cf. ECSTASY n.). [the shape; EGG n.⁴]

eggshell blond *n.* [1950s+] (*Aus./N.Z.*) a bald person.

eggs in the basket *n.* [1940s–60s] (*US gay*) the testicles (cf. ACORNS n.). [EGGS n.¹ (1) + BASKET n.¹ (2)]

eggs in the coffee *phr.* [1920s–30s] (*US*) a general phr. of approval, satisfaction, everything is excellent, wonderful, ideal.

egg suck *v.* [1970s+] (*US*) to curry favour. [SUCK UP v. (1)/obs. SE *suck-egg*, a foolish person]

egg-sucker *n.* 1 [19C+] (*US*) a worthless and unpleasant person. 2 [1950s+] (*US gay*) an ageing or old homosexual. [dial. *egg-sucker*, a worthless animal, esp. a dog; in (2) the pun is on the *egg*, i.e. an unformed youth, who is the target of the older man's desires]

egg-sucking *adj.* [19C+] (*US*) worthless, contemptible, unpleasant. [EGG-SUCKER n. (1)]

egg-white *n.* [1910s+] semen, thus *egg-white cannon*, the penis (cf. BABY GRAVY n.).

eggy *adj.* [1920s+] (*orig. US*) angry, irritated. [EGG v.²]

eggy! *excl.* [1990s+] (*UK juv.*) excellent! wonderful!

Egon (Ronay) *n.* [1990s+] an act of defecation (cf. ANDY CAPP n.). [rhy. sl. = PONY (AND TRAP) n.; ult. food guidebook pioneer *Egon Ronay* (b.1920)]

ego-surfing *n.* [2000s] surfing the Internet in search of one's own name.

ego trip *n.* [1960s+] (*orig. US*) self-aggrandizement, boastfulness, egocentricity. [SE *ego* + TRIP n.⁵ (1)]

ego trip *v.* [1970s+] (*orig. US*) to act in an egocentric, self-aggrandizing manner. [EGO TRIP n.]

E.G.Y.P.T. *phr.* [20C+] eager to grab your pretty tits, written on envelopes of love letters (cf. B.O.L.T.O.P. phr.). [abbr.]

Egypt *n.*¹ [19C+] (*US*) an outside lavatory. [image of *Egypt* as a far distant place]

Egypt *n.*² [20C+] (*US*) the Black section of a town or city. [the dark complexion of actual Egyptians and the exotic myths that, just as they do in regard to the Middle East, abound around Black culture]

Egypt *n.*³ *see* BUMFUCK, EGYPT n.

Egyptian charger *n.* [early 19C] a donkey. [the association of the animal with the gypsies or *Egyptians*]

Egyptian flu *n.* [1980s+] (*US*) a pregnancy. [i.e. one is going to be a *mummy*]

Egyptian hall *n.* [mid-19C] a ball. [rhy. sl.; the *Egyptian Hall* was the popular name for the London Museum, established at today's 170 Piccadilly *c.*1812, holding 'upwards of Fifteen Thousand Natural and Foreign Curiosities, Antiques and Productions of the Fine Arts'. It featured an 'Egyptian' façade and among the many visitors was, in 1844, General Tom Thumb. The hall was demolished in 1905]

Egyptian queen *n.* [1960s+] (*gay*) a homosexual Black man, particularly if he is stately and proud. [QUEEN n.² (1) + the well-known picture of Queen Nefertiti]

eh? *excl.* [mid-19C+] used interrogatively, as a request for the repetition or explanation of something that has just been said, i.e. 'What did you say?'

E-head *n.* [1990s+] (*drugs*) a regular user of MDMA. [E n. + -HEAD sfx (3)]

eh-eh *n.* [1960s+] (*US gay*) the anus; thus used of anything seen as tasteless/unpleasant. [Yid. *eh-eh* = baby's word for faeces]

eh, what! *excl. see* WHAT! excl. (2).

eicespie *n.* [late 19C] money. [backsl. = *pieces* (of gold)]

Eiffel Tower *n.* 1 [20C+] (*Aus.*) a shower. 2 [1980s] a flower. [rhy. sl.]

eight *n.* [1970s–80s] (*US drugs*) 1 heroin. 2 ¹⁄₈oz (4g) of a narcotic, usu. heroin. [*H* is the eighth letter of the alphabet]

eightball *n.*¹ (*US*) 1 [1910s+] a derog. term for an Afro-American, a Black person (cf. BLACKBELLY n.). 2 [1930s+] an incompetent; a fool. 3 [1950s] a conventional, law-abiding person. [pool imagery; the eight ball is black; sinking it out of turn will lose the game]

eightball *n.*² (*drugs*) 1 [1980s+] ¹⁄₈oz (4g) of a drug. 2 [2000s] a 'cocktail' of crack cocaine and heroin.

eightball *n.*³ [1980s+] (*US Black*) Olde English 800, a popular beer in Black neighbourhoods.

eightball *n.*⁴ [1990s+] excrement, a turd. [the colour]

eightball *n.*⁵ [2000s] (*US prison*) 1 a prison gang or clique. 2 an 8-year prison sentence.

eight ball *v.* [1940s+] (*US*) to ruin or frustrate, esp. by cheating. [pool imagery]

eightball chick *n.* [1990s+] (*US*) a girl gang member. [EIGHTBALL n.⁵ (1) + CHICK n.⁴ (2)]

eight-day clock *n.* [1980s] (*Aus.*) the penis (cf. ALMOND n.). [rhy. sl. = COCK n.² (1)]

eighteen *n.* [1910s+] (*Aus.*) an 18-gallon (82-litre) keg of beer.

eighteen-carat *adj.* (*also* **fourteen-carat, nineteen-carat, seventeen-carat**) [late 19C–1910s] (*US*) 1 first-class. 2 absolute, complete; often in phr. EIGHTEEN-CARAT LIE n. [the measurement of gold, but note the best is not 18 but 22 carat]

eighteen-carat lie *n.* [late 19C] (*US*) a downright, deliberate lie. [EIGHTEEN-CARAT adj. (2)]

eighteen-holer *n.* [1990s+] (*UK teen*) the highest lacing version of Dr. Martens boots (cf. DOCS n.).

eighteen pence *n.* **1** [1910s+] sense. **2** [1950s+] (*Aus.*) a garden fence. **3** [1950s+] (*Aus./UK*) a receiver of stolen goods. [rhy. sl.; (3) = FENCE n.¹ (1)]

8–8–16 *n.* [1990s+] (*US Und.*) a prison cell. [the dimensions in inches of a single one of the concrete blocks that make up the cell walls]

eighter (from) Decatur *n. see* ADA FROM DECATUR n.

eighth *n.* [1930s+] (*drugs*) ¹/₈oz (4g) of a drug, usu. a narcotic.

808 *n.* [1990s+] in rap music the bass drum from a Roland TR-808 drum machine, which is now a popular make. [the Roland *808* drum machine]

eight-pack *n. see* SIX-PACK n.¹.

eight-pager *n.* (*also* **sixteener**) [1930s+] a small, illustrated 8-page (or 16-page) pornographic booklet in which popular cartoon characters (Popeye, Mickey Mouse, Blondie etc) are crudely pastiched in erotic scenarios far removed from their everyday antics.

eight rock *n.* [1930s–50s] (*US Black*) a very dark-skinned Black person. [EIGHTBALL n.¹ (1)]

eight-six *v. see* EIGHTY-SIX v.

eight track *n.* [1990s+] (*US Black*) ¹/₈oz (4g) of crack cocaine. [EIGHTBALL n.² (1)]

eight-wheeler *n.* [1930s–50s] (*US tramp*) one who robs trains whether en route or stationary. [the wagon has 8 wheels]

eighty days *n.* (*also* **eighty miles**) [1900s–10s] (*US*) the point of 8 in craps dice (cf. ADA FROM DECATUR n.).

eighty-eight *n.*¹ [1930s–50s] (*US Black*) a piano. [? number of keys or 8:8 time]

eighty-eight *n.*² (*also* **88**) [1950s] (*US*) an Oldsmobile 88, a.k.a. *Rocket 88*.

eighty-eighter *n.* [1940s+] (*US*) a pianist. [EIGHTY-EIGHT n.¹]

eighty-eights *n.* [1930s–70s] (*US*) love and kisses. [orig. used by telegraph operators]

85% *n.* [1990s+] (*US Black*) the great uneducated mass of (Black) people, who are destined to be taught and led by the knowledgeable 5%. [for full ety. *see* 5% NATION n.]

eighty miles *n. see* EIGHTY DAYS n.

eighty-six *adj.* (*also* **86**) [1960s–80s] (*US*) unwelcome, esp. as at a bar. [EIGHTY-SIX v. (1)]

eighty-six *v.* (*also* **eight-six, 86**) **1** [1940s+] (*US*) to throw out, to get rid of; thus as n., an unwanted item. **2** [1970s+] (*US*) to kill, to murder; to execute judicially. **3** [1980s+] (*US campus*) to be finished, to be ready to leave. [rhy. sl. = NIX v.¹ (1); orig. restaurant and bar use, indicating that the supply of an item is exhausted or that a customer is not to be served]

eighty-six! *excl.* [1960s+] **1** get out! go away! **2** (*US campus*) no! [EIGHTY-SIX v.]

eina! *excl.* [1910s+] (*S.Afr.*) an excl. of pain, i.e. ouch! [Khoi *é* + *ná*]

einstein *n.* **1** [1960s] (*US campus*) an intellectual. **2** [1980s+] (*US campus*) pubic hair. **3** [1990s+] brains. [the crinkly grey hair/genius of the scientist Albert *Einstein* (1879–1955)]

einstein *v.* [1950s] to think. [for ety. *see* EINSTEIN n.]

ekame *n.* [mid-19C] a swindle. [backsl. = MAKE n.² (1)]

eke *n.* [1970s] (*gay*) make-up, cosmetics. [EEK n., i.e. FACE n.² (12)]

Ekka, the *n.* [1970s+] (*Aus.*) the annual Exhibition held at the Brisbane Exhibition Grounds. [abbr. SE *exhibition*]

ekker *n. see* ECCER n.

ekom *n.* [mid-19C] a donkey. [backsl. = MOKE n.¹ (1)]

El *n.* (*also* **el, L, L train**) [late 19C+] (*US*) the *el*evated railway, usu. that of New York (opened in 1879), but also in other cities, e.g. Chicago, where such transport systems existed. [abbr./pron.]

El, the *n.* [1940s] (*US prison/Und.*) *El*mira prison, New York City (cf. ABBOTT'S PRIORY n.). [abbr.]

el *n.*¹ [1980s] (*US Black*) a *l*imousine. [abbr.]

el *n.*² *see* L n.³.

el *pfx* [1920s+] (*orig. US*) a cod-Sp. pfx added to the front of a n. or adj. with an '-o' sfx, used to describe a person or situation, usu. pej., e.g. EL CHEAPO adj., EL DORKO n.

elakazoo *n.* [1900s] (*US*) money. [ety. unknown]

elbow *n.*¹ **1** [late 19C–1900s] (*US*) a detective, a policeman. **2** [1940s] (*US Und.*) a general term of abuse. [pun on the 'long arm of the law'; note Casey, *The Gay-cat* (1921): "'Elbow" comes from the detective's way of elbowing through a crowd']

elbow *n.*² [1900s–30s] (*UK Und.*) a pickpocket's assistant. [he *elbow*s the victim to distract their attention from the pickpocketing]

elbow *n.*³ [1970s+] rejection, dismissal. [the image of an *elbow* pushed into someone's ribs]

elbow *v.*¹ [mid-19C–1930s] (*US Und.*) to warn an accomplice to get out of sight when police appear; usu. as excl. *elbow!* [ELBOW n.¹ (1); + ? one nudges the person with an *elbow*]

elbow *v.*² [1970s+] to reject, to dismiss. [ELBOW n.³]

elbow bender *n.* (*also* **elbow crooker**) [20C+] a heavy drinker. [BEND ONE'S ELBOW v./CROOK THE ELBOW v.]

elbow-crooking *n. see* CROOK THE ELBOW v.

elbow crooker *n. see* ELBOW BENDER n.

elbow exercise *n.* [1910s] (*US*) drinking.

elbow grease *n.* **1** [late 17C+] physical effort. **2** [mid-19C] fiddle-playing. [the movement of one's *elbow*; B.E. defines *elbow-grease* as 'a derisory term for sweat' but his extra examples, e.g. *it will cost nothing but a little elbow-grease*, imply def. (1)]

elbow jigger *n.* (*also* **elbow scraper**) [mid-19C] a fiddle-player.

elbow shaker *n.*¹ [18C–mid-19C] a dice-player. [the action of shaking the dice cup]

elbow shaker *n.*² [1950s+] (*US Black*) one who reminds others of a forgotten or overlooked fact or event by (fig.) digging them in the ribs.

elbow-titting *n.* [1960s] (*US*) a game whereby a male accosts an unknown female and rubs his elbows against her breasts before running off – or getting hit or shouted at.

el bummero *n. see* BUMMER n.⁴ (3).

el cheapo *adj.* [1960s+] (*US*) cheap. [EL pfx + SE *cheap*]

El D *n.* (*also* **eldo**) [1970s+] (*US*) a Cadillac *El D*orado. [abbr.]

elderberry *n.* [1950s–60s] (*gay*) an ageing or old homosexual. [pun on SE *elder* and FRUIT n.² (2)]

elderly jam *n.* [late 19C] an old woman. ['Elderly jam is – elderly jam, and heaven preserve it, for man turns from it' (Ware)]

elders *n.* [1960s+] (*Irish*) **1** the female breasts (cf. BORDENS n.). **2** a term of abuse, as in *dirty elders*. [SE *udders*]

el diablito *n.* (*also* **el diablo**) [2000s] (*drugs*) a mixture of marijuana, cocaine, heroin and phencyclidine. [Sp. 'the little devil']

el dingo *adj.* [1980s] (*US*) crazy. [EL pfx + DINGY adj.²]

eldo *n. see* EL D n.

el dorko *n.* [1980s+] (*US*) a fool, an incompetent (cf. BOBO n.¹). [EL pfx + DORK n. (2)]

electric *adj.* **1** [1960s–70s] containing LSD. **2** [1970s] weird and wonderful, marvellous.

electric cure *n.* [1920s+] (*US prison*) the electric chair.

electric lettuce *n.* [1990s+] (*drugs*) very potent cannabis (cf. AFRICAN BUSH n.).

electric machine *n. see* MACHINE n.¹ (2).

electric queen *n.* [1960s–70s] (*US gay*) a gay HIPPIE n.² (3). [fig. use of SE *electric*, to mean drugged + QUEEN n.² (1)]

electrified *adj.* [late 19C] drunk (cf. ABOUT RIGHT phr.¹).

elegant *n.* [1950s] (*US Und.*) an escape from prison.

elegant *adj.* [mid-18C+] excellent, first-rate.

elegantifferously *adv.* [mid-19C] (*US*) outstandingly. [SE *elegant* + SPLENDIFEROUS adj.]

element *n.* [mid-18C–mid-19C] (*US*) an alcoholic drink; thus *in one's element*, intoxicated.

elephant *n.*[1] [mid-19C+] an extraordinary sight or remarkable situation and the experience of such that leads to gaining knowledge or the loss of innocence; thus SEE THE ELEPHANT *v.* [the exoticism of the creature]

elephant *n.*[2] [late 19C+] the *Elephant* and Castle, London SE1. [abbr.]

elephant *n.*[3] **1** [20C+] (*US*) a clumsy, awkward person. **2** [1980s] (*US gay*) a fat person. [reverse anthropomorphism]

elephant *n.*[4] [1980s+] (*drugs*) **1** heroin. **2** phencyclidine (cf. ACE n.[4]). [such drugs could 'knock out an elephant']

elephant (and castle) *n.* **1** [20C+] the anus (cf. BOTTLE AND GLASS n.). **2** [1920s+] a parcel. [rhy. sl. = ARSEHOLE n. (1) (pron. 'arssle'); ult. the *Elephant and Castle*, London SE1]

elephant business *n.* [late 19C] (*US*) sightseeing. [SEE THE ELEPHANT v. (1)]

elephant ears *n.* [1920s–50s] (*US Und.*) a detective or policeman (cf. BEAGLE n.[3]).

elephant's fallen arches *n. see* CAT'S WHISKERS n.

elephant's (trunk) *adj.* (*also* **Jumbo's trunk**) [mid-19C+] drunk (cf. ADRIAN (QUIST) adj.). [rhy. sl.]

elephant teeth *n.* [1950s] (*US Black*) piano keys. [the ivory keys]

elephant tranquillizer *n.* [1970s+] (*drugs*) phencyclidine (cf. ACE n.[4]). [phencyclidine is an animal (pig) tranquillizer]

elevate *v.*[1] [late 19C–1920s] (*US*) in poker, to raise an opponent.

elevate *v.*[2] [1910s–50s] (*UK/US Und.*) **1** to rob at gunpoint. **2** to hold someone up (other than for robbery). **3** to put up one's hands in a hold up; thus used as imper. [pun on HOLD UP v.[1] (1)]

elevated *adj.* [mid-17C+] drunk, one of a number of words and phr. that equate drunkenness with 'getting high' (cf. EXALTED adj.; FLYING HIGH phr.; HALF-HIGH adj.; HAVE ONE'S SAILS HIGH v.; IN ONE'S ALTITUDES phr.; IN ORBIT phr.; KITED adj.; TALL adj.[4]). [pun on SE]

elevator *n.*[1] [late 19C] a crinolette or bustle used for distending the back of a woman's skirt. [it raises or 'elevates' the back of the skirt]

elevator *n.*[2] [1910s–20s] (*UK Und.*) a hold-up man, a robber; a shoplifter. [ELEVATE v.[2] (1)]

elevator jockey *n.* [1960s–70s] (*US*) a lift operator. [SE *elevator* + JOCKEY n.[3] (2)]

eleven forty-fiver *n.* [1940s] (*US*) a blackface minstrel. [the trad. time – 11.45 a.m. – of the pre-show parade that passed through a town where the minstrels were performing]

eleven steps *n.* [1950s] (*W.I.*) an arrest, a trial. [the 11 steps that led to the front door of a well-known court house]

eleven, twenty-nine, twenty-three *n.* [1920s] (*US Und.*) a jail sentence of 1 hour less than a whole year, thus avoiding the mandatory loss of citizenship that in some states comes with a 1-year sentence. [i.e. 11 months, 29 days and 23 hours]

eleventy-eleven *n.* (*also* **eleventeen, leventy-leven**) [late 19C+] (*US Black*) a very large or infinite number.

el foldo *n.* [1930s+] (*US*) a failure, esp. in sport or a feigned knockout in boxing. [EL pfx + FOLD v. (3)]

Eli *n.* [19C+] (*US campus*) Yale University; thus *Elis*, alumni of Yale. [*Elihu* Yale (1649–1721), founder of the original college at Saybrook before it moved to New Haven]

elick *n. see* ELLICK n.

Elijah two *n.* [late 19C] (*US*) a false prophet. [Dr John Alexander Dowie (1847–1907), a US evangelist, who was thus satirically christened in memory of the original, biblical *Elijah*; his son, in time, became *Elijah three*]

Elkie Clark *n. see* L.K. CLARK n.

ell *n.* [late 16C–18C] the vagina. [play on SE *ell*, 45 inches (a Flemish ell was 27 inches) + YARD n.[1] + Fr. *elle*, she]

Ellen *n.* [1990s+] (*US campus*) a lesbian (cf. AMY-JOHN n.). [US lesbian actress *Ellen Degeneres* (b.1958)]

Ellenborough's lodge *n.* (*also* **Ellenborough's park/spike**) [early 19C] the King's Bench prison (cf. ABBOTT'S PRIORY n.; BOARDING HOUSE n.). [Lord *Ellenborough* (1750–1818), Lord Chief Justice 1802–17]

Ellenborough's teeth *n.* [early 19C] the spiked *cheveux-de-frise* that top the walls of the King's Bench prison. [Lord *Ellenborough* (see ELLENBOROUGH'S LODGE n.) + SE *teeth*]

Ellen Terry *n.* [1920s+] a chamberpot. [rhy. sl. = JERRY n.[6] (1); ult. Shakespearian actress *Ellen Terry* (1847–1928)]

ellersby *n.* [late 19C] the London School Board. [pron. of abbr. (LSB). Note printers' use *Ellessea*, London Society of Compositors (LSC)]

ellick *n.* (*also* **elick**) [1900s–20s] (*US*) the penis. [ety. unknown; ? proper name *Alec*]

elly-bay *n.* [mid-19C+] the belly. [cod Lat.]

el magnifico *adj.* [1990s+] wonderful, excellent, magnificent. [EL pfx + SE *magnificent*]

elmer *n.* [1920s–60s] (*US*) a rural or unsophisticated man (cf. ALVIN n.). [the use of *Elmer* as a 'typical' country name]

elmer fudge *n.* [1980s] (*Aus.*) a judge. [rhy. sl.; ult. cartoon character *Elmer Fudd*]

el paso *n.* [1990s+] (*US*) an act of rejection, ignoring. [EL pfx + PASS v.[1]]

el pee *n.* [1990s+] (*US Black*) an El *P*roducto cigar. [abbr.]

el primo *adj.* [1980s+] (*US*) first-class. [Sp. *primo*, the best]

elrig *n.* [mid-19C+] girl. [backsl.]

el ropo *n.* (*also* **el ropo stinkadoro, el stinko**) [1940s+] (*US*) a cheap, strong cigar. [EL pfx + ROPE n.[1] (1)/SE *stink*; note Rudyard Kipling, *Stalky & Co.* (1899), 'pomposo stinkadoro', a large, malodorous cigar]

Elsie Tanner *n.* [2000s] a hammer. [rhy. sl.; ult. fictional character *Elsie Tanner* in UK ITV's soap opera *Coronation Street*]

elsin *n.* [late 19C+] (*Ulster*) a 'sharp' individual. [dial. *elsin*, a shoemaker's awl; ult. MDu. *elssene*, an awl]

el sleazo *n. see* SLEAZO n.

el stinko *n. see* EL ROPO n.

el stinkola *n.* [1940s] (*US*) anything or anyone considered worthless, useless. [EL pfx + STINK v. + -OLA sfx]

Elton (John) *n.* [1990s+] a confidence trick. [rhy. sl. = CON n.[1] (7); ult. UK singer/songwriter *Elton John* (b.1947)]

elvis *v.* [1990s+] (*drugs*) of a cannabis cigarette, to burn unevenly, proceding faster down one side than the other. [a play on the SAmE *sideburns* (UK *side-boards*), which adorned the cheeks of the singer *Elvis* Presley (1935–77)]

el zilch-o *n.* [1970s] (*US*) nothing. [EL pfx + ZILCH n.[1] (1)]

elzoo *n.* [1920s] (*US Und.*) a surveillance preparatory to committing a crime. [ety. unknown]

em *n. see* M n. (1).

emag *n.* [late 19C+] a game, usu. as a term of disgust or disappointment meaning 'what's your game?' etc. [backsl.]

embalmed *adj.* [1920s+] very drunk (cf. DAMP adj.). [play on SE + EMBALMING FLUID n. (1)]

embalmed horse *n. see* HORSE n.[7].

embalmer *n.* [1920s–30s] (*orig. US Black*) a bootlegger. [EMBALMING FLUID n. (1)]

embalming fluid *n.* **1** [1920s+] second-rate whisky. **2** [1920s+] (*US tramp*) coffee. **3** [1980s] (*drugs*) phencyclidine (cf. ACE n.[4]). **4** [1980] marijuana mixed with cocaine.

embarrassed *adj.* [1960s] (*W.I.*) of a woman, pregnant; of a man, castrated; thus as the major insult, *embarrassed sow*, *embarrassed hog*.

emboosticated *adj.* [1970s] (*US campus*) embarrassed.

embroidery *n. see* CHINESE NEEDLEWORK n. (2).

emcee *n. see* M.C. *n.*

em-eff *n.* (*also* **emm-eff**) [1960s+] (*orig. US*) a euph. for MOTHERFUCKER *n.* (1). [pron. of initial letters, i.e. M.F. *n.*]

em-eff *adj.* (*also* **emeffing, emm-eff**) [1950s+] (*orig. US*) a euph. for MOTHERFUCKING *adj.* (1). [pron. of initial letters; M.F. *adj.*]

emergency gun *n.* [1930s+] (*drugs*) any makeshift instrument used to inject when one does not have a syringe. [SE *emergency* + GUN *n.*[1] (3)]

emigrate *v.* [mid-19C] (*US*) to leave.

emily post *n.* [1980s+] (*Aus.*) a creditor. [rhy. sl. = GHOST *n.*[4]; ult. author of popular etiquette manual *Emily Post* (1872/3–1960)]

Emma Freuds *n.* (*also* **Clement Freuds, emmas**) [1990s+] haemorrhoids. [rhy. sl.; ult. UK TV presenter *Emma Freud*, daughter of UK food writer and broadcaster *Clement Freud* (b.1924)]

emm-eff *see under* EM-EFF.

Emmerdale (Farm) *n.* [1990s+] an arm. [rhy. sl.; ult. UK soap opera *Emmerdale Farm*, now renamed *Emmerdale*]

emok nye *phr.* [late 19C] come in. [backsl.]

empty *n.*[1] [20C+] any container or vessel that has been emptied, esp. a bottle once containing alcohol.

empty *n.*[2] [1980s] (*Aus.*) an ejaculation of semen; thus *have an empty*, to masturbate.

empty *adj.* [1940s–50s] (*US*) penniless, broke.

empty *v.*[1] [late 19C] (*UK Und.*) to trick, to swindle.

empty *v.*[2] **1** [1980s+] (*Aus. prison*) to be transferred suddenly to another prison. **2** [1990s+] (*Aus. Und.*) to dismiss from a job.

empty bottle *n.* [early–mid-19C] (*UK campus*) at Cambridge University, a fellow-commoner, i.e. a rich or aristocratic undergraduate, with special privileges and a reputation for self-indulgent laziness.

empty house is better than a bad tenant, an *phr.* [1930s+] (*N.Z.*) a phr. used after breaking wind in public.

empty one's trash *v.* [1970s] (*US Black*) to have sexual intercourse; usu. to ejaculate.

empty suit *n.* [1980s+] (*US*) a useless or insincere person.

empty the anaconda *v.* (*also* **drain the anaconda**) [1990s+] to urinate (cf. BLEED ONE'S TURKEY *v.*).

empty the bag *v.* [19C] to tell the whole story.

empty the butter-boat *v.* [mid–late 19C] to flatter lavishly (and insincerely). [BUTTER UP *v.*]

emsel *n.* [1950s–70s] (*US drugs*) morphine (cf. AUNTIE EMMA *n.*).

emu *n.* [1960s+] (*Aus.*) a racecourse idler who picks up discarded tote tickets in the hope of finding one that has not been cashed. [the image of an *emu* pecking at the ground; note *Ozwords* Oct. 1996: 'The term appears to have its origin in the early twentieth century when it was used to describe people picking up pieces of timber after clearing or burning (and bobbing up and down in emu-fashion). It was also used of people picking up litter']

emu-bobber *n.* [1920s+] (*Aus.*) a man employed to pick up the remnants after clearing or burning off in the bush. [for ety. see EMU *n.*]

enamel *n.* [1940s] (*US Black*) skin.

enchilada *n.* [1970s] (*US*) the penis (cf. BURRITO *n.*). [resemblance]

encore *n.* [20C+] sexual intercourse for the second time, usu. soon after one has just had the initial bout.

end *n.*[1] **1** [late 16C–mid-17C; 1920s+] the penis; esp. in phr. GET ONE'S END AWAY *v.* **2** [17C–18C] the vagina, the female genitals. **3** [late 18C+] the buttocks, the posterior (cf. ARSE-END *n.*).

end *n.*[2] **1** [late 19C+] a share, usu. of criminal profits or responsibility. **2** [1940s] that proportion of one's illicit gains that is used to bribe the police.

end *n.*[3] **1** [20C+] that area of a football stadium, behind the respective goals, trad. reserved for the hardcore supporters of home and away teams and the scene of most fighting. **2** [1990s+] (*UK Black/teen*) an area of a city.

end, the *n.* **1** [1910s+] the absolute limit that the speaker will tolerate, 'the last straw'. **2** [1940s+] (*orig. US Black*) perfection, absolute excellence, the best possible.

endacott *v.* (*also* **cott, endicott**) [late 19C] to arrest on false pretences, spec. those of being a prostitute. [one Constable *Endacott* who, in 1887, was tried and acquitted for the arrest on these grounds of a respectable dressmaker; the term was poss. coined by Annie Besant (1847–1933)]

endjie *n. see* ENTJIE *n.*

endo *n.* [1980s+] (*drugs*) marijuana. [var. INDO *n.* (2)]

end of the ball-game *n.* [20C+] (*US*) **1** death; one of a number of games-playing/sporting metaphors for life's termination. **2** the definitive conclusion to something.

end over appetite *phr.* [20C+] (*US*) head over heels. [END *n.*[1] (3) + SE *appetite*]

ends *n.*[1] [1960s+] (*US Black*) money; living expenses. [SE phr. *make ends meet*]

ends *n.*[2] [1960s] (*US Black*) shoes.

endsville *n.* [1950s+] (*US*) **1** the best, the ultimate. **2** the limit, the end, as far as one can go, death. **3** absolute, irretrievable failure. [END, THE *n.* + -VILLE sfx[1]]

endways *adv.* [1900s–40s] (*US Black*) backwards, back-to-front. [SE *endways*, end on, with the end facing]

enemy *n.*[1] [mid-19C–1930s] time; thus *kill the enemy*, to pass time; *how goes the enemy?, what says the enemy?*, what time is it?

enemy *n.*[2] [late 19C] **1** the penis. **2** the vagina.

energizer *n.* (*drugs*) **1** [1980s+] phencyclidine (cf. ACE *n.*[4]). **2** [1990s+] MDMA (cf. ECSTASY *n.*).

enforcer *n.* **1** [1920s+] a person, usu. a thug, used to enforce his (or another's) will through violence or threats of violence. **2** [1950s+] (*gay*) a lesbian who keeps the other women in line.

engabachado *n.* [1960s+] (*US*) a Mexican who attempts to 'pass' as White. [Mex. Sp. *engabachado*, rendered white]

engage in three to one (and bound to lose) *v.* [late 18C–19C] to have sexual intercourse. [the image is of a conflict between the penis and 2 testicles and the vagina; the 'loss' is of semen]

engagement *n. see* NAVAL ENGAGEMENT *n.*

Engelbert (Humperdinck) *n.* [1990s+] a drink. [rhy. sl.; ult. UK pop star *Englebert Humperdinck*, real name Arnold George Dorsey (b.1936)]

engine *n.* **1** [early 17C–19C] the penis (cf. FORNICATING ENGINE *n.*; GARDEN ENGINE *n.*). **2** [late 17C–mid-18C; 1910s+] the vagina. **3** [1930s–50s] (*US drugs*) the equipment used by an opium smoker.

engka *v.* [1990s+] (*W.I.*) to associate with someone in the hope of begging a loan.

English *n.*[1] [17C] ale. [the national drink]

English *n.*[2] [mid-19C+] (*orig. US*) deceptiveness, duplicity, 'spin'. [billiards jargon *English*, spin imparted to one or the other side of the ball]

English *n.*[3] [1990s+] (*US*) Olde *English* Malt Liquor. [abbr.]

English *adj.* [1960s–70s] (*US*) sado-masochistic. [the national stereotype of the English as loving beatings]

English burgundy *n.* [late 18C–mid-19C] porter (a type of dark beer brewed from malt). [the real *Burgundy* is a variety of French wine]

English cane *n.* [late 17C–early 18C] a cudgel.

English channel *n.*[1] [1950s–70s] the National Health Service. [rhy. sl. = SE *panel* (of doctors)]

English channel *n.*[2] [1970s] (*US campus*) bloodshot or drooping eyes, the effect of smoking cannabis. [ety. unknown]

English cold *n.* (*also* **English winter**) [20C+] (*US*) iced tea. [tea (hot) is seen as a quintessential English pleasure]

English culture *n.* [1960s+] sex advertisements for bondage and discipline. [ENGLISH adj. + ironic use of SE *culture*]

English disease *n.* **1** [18C–19C] melancholy, depression. **2** [mid–late 19C] rickets. **3** [1960s+] a propensity for industrial action and strikes. **4** [1960s+] erotic flagellation.

English guidance *n.* [1960s+] bondage and discipline. [the popular assumption that all Englishmen enjoy such activities]

Englishified *adj.* [20C+] (*W.I.*) **1** said of one who has returned from a stay in England with an English accent and a generally more sophisticated persona. **2** of East Indians, generally urbanized or westernized (there need have been no visit to the UK).

English manufacture *n.* (*also* **manufacture**) [late 17C–early 19C] ale, beer or cider. [SE; all these are native drinks, as opposed to wine or brandy]

English martini *n.* [1960s+] (*US gay*) tea; esp. when spiked with gin.

English method *n.* [1960s+] (*US gay*) intercrural homosexual intercourse, i.e. non-penetrative rubbing between closed thighs.

English muffins *n.* [1960s+] (*US gay*) a boy's buttocks (cf. BAKERY GOODS n.). [the sexual image of the *English* + MUFFINS n.]

English sentry *n.* [1960s+] (*US gay*) the erect penis. [it 'stands to attention' + ? reputation of Guardsmen for gay prostitution]

English shower *n. see* POLISH SHOWER n.

English sunbathing *n.* [1970s+] (*N.Z.*) sitting fully-clothed in the sun. [the foolishness of recent immigrants from the UK]

English winter *n. see* ENGLISH COLD n.

enif *adj.* [mid–late 19C] fine, attractive. [backsl.]

enin *n.* (*also* **eenin**) [mid-19C+] the number 9. [backsl.]

enin gens *n.* [mid-19C+] 9 shillings (45p). [backsl.; ENIN n. + GEN n.[1]]

enin yeneps *n.* (*also* **enine yenep, enin yannops, enin yenneps**) [mid-19C+] 9 pence. [backsl.; ENIN n. + YENNEP n.]

enlightened *adj.* [2000s] (*US Black*) intoxicated by marijuana.

eno *n.* [mid-19C+] the number 1. [backsl.]

enob *n.* **1** [late 19C+] a bone. **2** [1980s] the penis. [backsl.]

enoch *n.* [1990s+] a towel. [rhy. sl.; ult. UK right-wing, racist politician *Enoch Powell* (1912–98)]

enormous *adj.* [late 19C] (*US*) splendid.

enough to gag a maggot *phr.* [1960s] (*US*) **1** describing something utterly repulsive. **2** describing something in great or overwhelming quantity.

enough to make a Black man choke *phr.* [20C+] a phr. indicating that something (usu. food and medicines but also of abstract objects, emotions etc) is unpalatable. [negative stereotyping, on the basis that Blacks have a less refined palate]

enough to make a cat laugh *phr.* (*also* **enough to make a cat sick, ...cow satirical, ...dog/mouse/rat laugh, it would make a cat laugh**) [late 16C; mid-19C+] utterly hilarious, devastatingly funny.

enough to split the grain *phr.* [1900s] enough to render one very drunk.

ensign-bearer *n.* [mid-17C–early 19C] a red-faced drunkard. [the colours of the face resemble those of the Union Jack]

entered *adj.* [early 18C] (*US*) intoxicated.

enter for the gelding stakes *v.* [late 19C] to castrate someone; thus *entered...*, to be a eunuch. [joc. use of racing imagery]

entertain the general *v.* [20C+] (*US*) to menstruate.

enthroned *adj.* **1** [1940s] (*US*) using the lavatory. **2** [1950s–60s] (*gay*) searching for sex in public lavatories. [THRONE n.; (2) + pun on QUEEN n.[2] (1)]

enthusiastic amateur *n. see* AMATEUR n.[1].

enthuzimuzzy *n.* [late 19C] enthusiasm.

entire *adj.* [late 19C+] (*Ulster*) financially independent; retired from business. [also in Lincolnshire dial.]

entire animal *n.* (*also* **extreme animal**) [mid-19C] absolutely everything, 'the lot'. [semi-euph. for WHOLE HOG, THE n.]

entjie *n.* (*also* **endjie**) [1980s+] (*S.Afr.*) a cigarette end. [Afk. *end*, *end* + dim. sfx *-ie*]

entrance *n.* [late 17C; late 19C–1900s] the vagina (cf. BELLY ENTRANCE n.).

entry *n.* [1930s] a couple. [? entered on a marriage certificate]

enzed *n.* [1910s+] (*Aus./N.Z.*) New Zealand; thus *enzedder*, a New Zealander; also attrib.

ep *n.* [2000s] event, situation. [abbr. SE *episode*]

epar! *excl.* [1950s–70s] (*US campus*) a cry of distress used ironically. [reverse of SE *rape!* used fig.]

Eph *n.* [1910s] (*US*) a Black servant, a porter, a waiter. [? abbr. popular Black proper name *Ephraim*]

ephus *n.* **1** [1930s–50s] (*US*) the truth. **2** [1950s] a trick or gimmick. [ety. unknown]

eppes *n.* (*also* **eppis, eppus**) [20C+] **1** something, a little. **2** a somebody. **3** nothing. [Ger. *etwas*, something, thence Yid. *eppes*; like many Yiddish terms *eppes* is capable of many uses, often ironic, and all dependent on context. It entered the sl. vocabulary via the underworld, which used it to mean low-class or worthless. Subseq. meanings have developed since]

eppes *adj.* (*also* **eppis, eppus**) [20C+] debatable, worthless, unsatisfactory. [EPPES n.]

eppes *adv.* (*also* **eppis, eppus**) [20C+] quite, perhaps, maybe, for some inexplicable reason. [EPPES n.]

eppy *n.* (*also* **ep**) [1980s+] **1** an *epi*leptic. **2** an *epi*leptic fit; a temper tantrum. **3** a very stupid or unpopular person. [abbr.; (3) f. (1)]

Epsom races *n.* [mid-19C] **1** a pair of braces. **2** faces. [rhy. sl.]

equalizer *n.* [late 19C+] (*US*) **1** a gun. **2** any weapon, a cosh, a knife. [it reduces all before it to the same abject level; note McCall, *Makes Me Wanna Holler* (1994): 'For me guns were life's great equalizer']

equipment *n.* **1** [late 19C+] the male genitals. **2** [1940s+] the female breasts. [euph.]

equipped *adj.* **1** [late 17C–early 19C] rich. **2** [late 17C–early 19C; 1960s] well-turned out, well-dressed. **3** [1970s] (*US Black*) emotionally and socially poised. **4** [1990s+] carrying a weapon of one sort or another. [(2) 1960s use US Black]

-er *sfx* (*also* **-ers**) [late 19C+] used to create slangy formations of nouns by shortening the original n. and replacing the missing letters with *-er(s)*. When the word is a monosyllable, it can be ext. by *-agger(s)* or *-ugger(s)*. [the 'Oxford' *-er* sfx appeared 'early in the Queen's [i.e. Victoria] reign' (Ware) or was 'introduced from Rugby School into Oxford University slang, orig. at University College, in Michaelmas Term, 1875' (*OED*). The absence of any such terms from the seminal (and sl.-laden) Oxford novel *The Adventures of Mr Verdant Green* (1853, by 'Cuthbert Bede') makes the later date far more likely. Strictly jargon, given its use at Oxford, it has moved into wider areas, typically *fresher*, a university freshman, *footer*, football, *soccer*, football and *rugger*, rugby. The extreme uses, e.g. *pragger-wagger*, the Prince of Wales and *wagger-pagger-bagger*, a wastepaper basket remain strictly Oxford University and 1900s–20s Oxford at that. For a fuller discussion see M. Marples, *University Slang* (1950); *inter alia* he suggests the importation came not from Rugby but from Harrow]

-erama *sfx see* -ORAMA sfx.

erase *v.* [1930s+] to murder, to kill.

erb *n.* [1910s+] **1** a wag, a humourist. **2** anyone whose real name is unknown. [abbr. proper name H*erbert*, which is seen to be 'funny']

'erbert *n. see* HERBERT n.

erection section *n.* [2000s] (*Irish*) a slow song at a disco.

-ereenie *sfx see* -EROONIE sfx.

erie v. [1940s] (US Und.) to overhear. [ON THE EARIE phr. (2)]

erif n. [mid-19C] fire. [backsl.]

eriff n. [late 17C–19C] a young or novice criminal. [SE *eriff*, a 2-year-old canary; the term migrated to the US during the 19C]

-erino sfx (also **-arina, -arino, -erina, -erine**) [late 19C+] (US) an intensifier applicable to various adjs. or nouns, generally implying further excellence, appeal etc, e.g. PEACHERINO n.

erk n. [1940s+] a general term of contempt, an insignificant person. [orig. WW1 milit. use, either RN *erk*, a lower deck rating, or RAF *erk*, aircraftsman, second class]

erk v. [2000s] (US Black) to annoy, to irritate. [? JERK AROUND v. or SE *irk*]

erky adj. [1950s–60s] (Aus.) unpleasant, distasteful. [ERK n. + sfx *-y*, but note *yuck*, a grunt of distaste]

ernie marsh n. [20C+] the grass. [rhy. sl.]

-eroo sfx (also **-aroo**) [late 19C; 1930s+] (orig. US) a general intensifier, implying a greater flamboyance or exaggeration; allied to a variety of terms, usu. nouns, e.g. BOOZEROO n.; FLOPEROO n.; SMACKEROO n.; STINKEROO n.

-eroonie sfx (also **-aroon, -arooney, -aroonie, -arootie, -ereenie, -eroon, -ooney, -oroonie**) [1910s+] (US) an intensifier, usu. positive and added to various words, e.g. *smackeroonie*. [ext. of -ERINO sfx]

Eros and Cupid adj. [1990s+] stupid. [rhy. sl.]

Errol Flynn n. [1940s+] the chin. [rhy. sl.; ult. Hollywood star *Errol Flynn* (1909–59)]

-ers sfx see -ER sfx.

erth see under EARTH and its combs.

ervine n. [1960s] (US Black) a policeman. [Los Angeles use; the *E* on number plates that in LA signifies a police vehicle]

esaff n. [late 19C] the face. [backsl.]

escamado adj. [1960s+] (US) nervous, shaken up. [Sp. sl. *escamao*, 'losing it']

escape out v. [mid-19C] (US) to speak, to request. [SE *escape*, to let a word out inadvertently]

escargot n. [1980s] (US campus) a male walking arm in arm with his date. [Fr. *escargot*, a snail; the couple appear curled up as tightly as a snail in its shell; Eble prefers play on (she is) *his cargo*]

esclop n. (also **esilop, eslop**) [mid-19C+] the police. [backsl., neither the *e* nor the *c* are pron.]

ese n. (also **essay**) [1960s+] **1** (US/Hispanic) a fellow Hispanic, esp. in the context of a street gang. **2** (US Black) a congratulatory term for a Hispanic; the inference is that such a person is effectively Black; qualified as *ese bato, ese vato, ese vacho, cool ese, okay ese, righteous ese*. [Sp. *ése*]

esel n. (also **ezel**) [1910s] (S.Afr.) a fool, a simpleton. [Afk. *ezel*, a donkey, an ass]

esilop n. see ESCLOP n.

eski/eskie n. see ESKY n.[2].

Eskimo Nell n. [1990s+] a call on the telephone. [rhy. sl. = BELL n.[8]]

Eskimo pie n. [1970s] (US) the vagina of a frigid woman (cf. APPLE n.[6]).

esky n.[1] [1910s+] (US) a derog. term for an Inuit, an Eskimo person or an Eskimo dog. [abbr. SE *Eskimo*]

esky n.[2] (also **eski, eskie**) [1950s+] (Aus.) a portable drinks cooler, popularly filled with beer for cricket watching etc. [SE *eskimo* and thus chilliness]

eslop n. see ESCLOP n.

Esprit chick n. [1990s+] (US teen) a girl who wears only designer clothing and looks down on others who dress differently. [the fashion store *Esprit* + CHICK n.[4] (2)]

espysay n. [late 19C] the Society for the Prevention of Cruelty to Animals. [initials SPCA, 'secretive in its nature, being created by people about horses and cattle, many of whom go about in savage fear of this valuable society' (Ware)]

esra n. (also **esrar**) [1930s+] (drugs) marijuana. [Turkish *esrar*, cannabis]

es-roph n. (also **es-roch**) [mid-19C] a horse. [backsl.]

essay n. see ESE n.

essedartus n. [early 18C] a coachman. [Lat. *essedarius*, a fighter in a Gaulish war-chariot]

essence n.[1] [mid-19C] (US) whisky. [SE *essence*, an extract obtained by distillation or otherwise from a plant]

essence n.[2] [1980s+] (drugs) MDMA (cf. ECSTASY n.). [EC-STASY n.]

essence of hickory n. [mid-19C] (US) a whipping with a hickory switch.

essence-peddler n. [mid-19C–1970s] (US) a skunk. [the skunk's notoriety as a smelly animal]

Essex calf n. (also **calf**) [17C–19C] a native of Essex, as used by those of Suffolk, who look down on their southern neighbours.

Essex lion n. **1** [mid-17C–19C] a calf. **2** [late 19C–1900s] a pej. term for a native of Essex, as used by those of Kent. [Essex was a popular source of cattle for the London meat markets]

Essex stile n. [late 18C–mid-19C] a ditch. [Essex being a low, marshy county, there are more ditches than stiles]

Establishment, the n. [mid–late 19C] (Aus.) the Fremantle jail. [SE *establishment*, an institution]

esther (the queen) n. [1950s–60s] (camp gay) a Jewish homosexual male (cf. ABIGAIL n.). [joc. ref. to the biblical *Esther*, who was a SE *queen*, thus pun on QUEEN n.[2] (1)]

estuffa n. [1980s+] (drugs) heroin. [Sp.]

etarnal adj. see TARNAL adj.

et-caetera n. (also **etcetera**) **1** [late 16C–early 17C] the vagina (cf. ARTICLE n.). **2** [mid-19C] venereal disease. **3** [late 17C–mid-18C] sexual intercourse. [euph.]

eternity box n. [late 18C+] a coffin.

ethel n. [1920s+] a male homosexual (cf. ABIGAIL n.). [the female name]

ether n. [1920s+] a fig. use for communication through the radio or the wireless.

Ethiopian paradise n. (also **Ethiopian heaven**) [20C+] (US) the top gallery in a theatre. [poor Black theatre-goers could usu. afford only the cheapest seats]

ethno n. [1970s] (Aus.) an immigrant to Australia, of various ethnic persuasions. [SE *ethnic* + -O sfx (4)]

ethy meat n. [20C+] a Black woman. [SE *Ethiopian* + MEAT n. (1)]

-ette sfx [late 19C+] an all-purpose dimin., used by the middle-classes in a generally twee manner, e.g. *smidgeonette*, a very, very small portion, *drinkette*, a very small measure of alcohol.

euchre v. **1** [mid-19C+] (US) to swindle, to trick, to cheat. **2** [1970s+] to destroy. [for ety. see next]

euchred adj. [late 19C+] (Aus.) exhausted, destitute, faulty. [the card-game *euchre* (orig. US) in which, if a player chooses to play a round and fails to take three tricks, they are 'euchred' (OED)]

European accentuation n. [1950s+] (gay) a tapered body with jutting buttocks. [? body-building use]

evaporate v. [mid-19C+] to leave, to vanish, to escape.

evatch v. [mid–late 19C] to have. [backsl.]

eve n.[1] [early 18C–early 19C] a hen-roost. [Somerset dial.]

eve n.[2] [2000s] (drugs) MDEA, a synthetic hallucinogen similar to MDMA. [play on ADAM n.[3]]

even adv. [1980s+] (US) at all, used as a negative emphasis.

even break n. [20C+] (orig. US) a fair chance. [SE *even* + BREAK n.[1] (1)]

even-even adj. [20C+] (US) equal.

evening phr. [late 19C+] good *evening*. [abbr.]

evening sneak n. (also **night sneak**) [mid-18C–early 19C] (UK Und.) a thief who works after dark. [SE *evening/night* + SNEAK n.[1] (2)]

evening socket *n.* [1990s+] the female genitalia. [the male 'plugs in' at night]

evening star *n.* [mid–late 19C] (*US*) a prostitute.

evening wheeze *n.* [late 19C] false news, rumours. [SE *evening* + WHEEZE n.; the exciting but implausible stories used to sell evening papers]

evens *n.* [1910s+] (*US*) revenge, a person as an object of revenge.

even shake *n.* (*also* **good shake**) [1960s+] an equal chance. [the shaking of dice; ult. FAIR SHAKE n.]

even-up *n.* [1990s+] (*W.I.*) presumptuousness.

evergreen *n.* [1900s] (*US*) money (cf. ALFALFA n.). [its colour]

evergreens *n.* [late 19C] the vagina (cf. BEAUTY SPOT n.; CABBAGE n.⁷). [SE *ever* + GREENS n.²]

everlasting *adj.* [mid-19C–1940s] (*US*) a general intensifier, very, exceeding, excessive.

everlastingly *adv.* [mid–late 19C] (*US*) beyond measure; immeasurably, excessively. [EVERLASTING adj.]

everlasting shoes *n.* [mid–late 19C] the feet.

everlasting staircase *n.* [mid–late 19C] the prison treadmill. [invented by the builder William Cubitt (1785–1861) for use in prisons; it was improved by Colonel Chesterton, thus its expanded name *Colonel Chesterton's everlasting staircase*]

everlasting wound *n.* [late 17C; mid–late 19C] the vagina.

ever-loving *n.* **1** [1930s+] one's wife. **2** [1960s–70s] one's mind. [(1) apparently coined and primarily used by Damon Runyon (1884–1946)]

ever-loving *adj.* [1910s+] (*US*) a general intensifier.

ever so *phr.* [late 19C+] much, e.g. *thanks ever so*.

everton toffee *n.* [mid-19C] coffee. [rhy. sl.; like white coffee, this toffee is also made with cream or (later) evaporated milk. Note nickname for the British football club Everton, 'the Toffees']

everybody and his cousin *n.* (*also* **everybody and his aunt, ...his mother, ...their mothers-in-law**) [mid-19C+] (*US*) absolutely everybody.

every daddy's babby *n. see* EVERY MOTHER'S SON n.

every dog and devil *n.* [20C+] (*Irish*) everyone.

every jack man *n. see* EVERY MAN JACK n.

every last (one) *phr.* [late 19C+] (*orig. US*) every one or thing without exception.

every living ass *n.* [1940s+] (*US*) every single person. [play on SE + ASS n. (5)]

every man jack *n.* (*also* **every jack man, every man jag/john**) [early 19C+] every single one; thus *not a man jack*, not a single one. [JACK n.² as generic for a man]

every mother's son *n.* (*also* **each mother's son, every daddy's babby, every woman's babe/son**) [late 16C+] every single person or thing.

everyone and his brother *n.* [20C+] a large number of people. [the implication is that the numbers are more than the speaker desires]

every postman on his beat *n.* [1930s–40s] (*US Black*) kinky hair that stands up in odd strands or areas of the head.

everything but the kitchen sink *n.* [1910s+] every imaginable object, whatever is available, no matter what it is, relevant to the situation or not.

everything cook and curry *phr.* [1950s+] (*W.I. Rasta*) all is well, all is taken care of. [culinary imagery]

everything in the book *n.* [1950s] (*US*) whatever is available, whatever is known.

everything is everything *phr.* [1960s+] (*US teen/W.I.*) everything is fine.

every time! *excl.* [1920s+] (*US*) a general affirmative excl.

everywheres *adv.* [mid-19C+] (*US*) everywhere.

every woman's babe/son *n. see* EVERY MOTHER'S SON n.

Eve's custom house *n.* [late 18C–early 19C] the vagina (cf. BANK n.¹). [ext. of CUSTOM HOUSE n.]

evesdropper *n.* **1** [mid-17C] the penis. **2** [early 18C–19C] a burglar who lurks outside a house waiting for the chance to break in while the owners are absent; thus a petty thief. **3** [late 18C–mid-19C] a robber of hen-houses. [pun on SE *eaves* + *eavesdropper*]

eve with the lid on *n.* [1930s–40s] (*US*) apple pie. [the Garden of Eden story]

evif *n.* (*also* **ewif**) [mid-19C] the number 5. [backsl.]

evil *n.*¹ [18C–early 19C] a halter. [dial. *evil*, a swelling on the neck]

evil *n.*² [early–mid-19C] one's wife, 'an admirable synonyme' (Egan's Grose). [sl.'s usu. negative image of marriage]

evil *adj.* **1** [1920s–70s] excellent, wonderful, the best. **2** [1930s+] unpleasant, cruel. **3** [1930s+] in a bad mood. [ext. of SE; (1) on bad = good model]

evilling *n.* [1930s+] (*US Black*) acting in a deliberately negative manner, e.g. riotously, argumentatively, criminally. [SE *evil*/EVIL adj. (2)]

evlenet gens *n.* [mid-19C] 12 shillings. [backsl.; GEN n.¹]

evlenet sith-noms *n.* [mid-19C] 12 months, usu. as a prison sentence. [backsl.; SITH-NOM n.]

evo *n.* [1950s+] (*Aus.*) evening. [SE *ev(ening)* + -o sfx (4); var. on ARVO n.]

ewe *n.* [late 17C–18C] (*UK Und.*) a young and beautiful female member of a criminal gang.

ewe-mutton *n.* [late 19C] **1** an ageing prostitute (cf. ALLEY CAT n.; BIT OF MUTTON n.). **2** an amateur prostitute. [SE *ewe* + MUTTON n.¹ (1)]

ewif *n. see* EVIF n.

ewif gens *n.* [mid-19C] 5 shillings, a crown. [backsl.; EVIF n. + GEN n.¹]

ewif yeneps *n.* (*also* **evif yenneps, ewif yenneps**) [mid-19C] 5 pence. [backsl.; EVIF n. + YENNEP n.]

ewscray *v.* [1930s–40s] (*US*) to go away, used as a command. [cod Lat. = SCREW v.⁵]

ex *n.* **1** [early 19C+] an ex-husband, ex-wife, ex-lover, the other half of a lapsed relationship. **2** [1900s–30s] (*US prison*) an ex-convict. [SE pfx *ex-*, former, previous]

ex *adj.*¹ [20C+] superlative, first-rate. [abbr. SE *excellent*]

ex *adj.*² *see* X adj.

ex *v. see* X v.

ex! *excl.* [1920s; 1980s+] (*UK juv.*) excellent! [abbr.; used in preparatory schools]

exalted *adj.* [mid-17C–mid-18C] slightly drunk (cf. ABOUT RIGHT phr.¹; ELEVATED adj.).

excellent *adj.* [1980s+] (*US campus*) extremely good or exciting. [popularized by the film *Bill and Ted's Excellent Adventure* (1988)]

excess baggage *n.* [1940s+] (*US Und.*) a second-rate confidence man. [play on SE]

exchange spit *v.* [1970s] (*US*) **1** to kiss. **2** to have sexual intercourse.

exchequer *n.* [early–mid-16C] the vagina (cf. BANK n.¹). [into which one makes a 'deposit' or the image of the vagina as a commodity]

ex-con *n.* [20C+] (*orig. US*) a former convict. [SE *ex*, former + CON n.¹ (8)]

excremental *adj.* [1960s+] a euph. for SHITTY adj.¹ (1).

excused, be *v.* [1950s+] (*mainly school*) a euph. for to be allowed to visit the lavatory; usu. as *may I be excused?* (cf. DO ONE'S BUSINESS v.).

excuse-me *n.* [1960s+] (*S.Afr.*) a member of the educated middle class. [their good manners]

excuse me while I whip this out *phr.* (*US Black teen*) **1** [1970s] one's last words before commencing a fight. **2** [2000s] a phr. said before exposing one's penis. [(1) *this* is one's fist or poss. a weapon]

excuse my French *phr.* (*also* **excuse the French**) [late 19C+] a genteel euph. automatically offered after the speaker has sworn in public. [FRENCH n.² (2)]

exec *n.* [late 19C+] an *exec*utive (of a firm or business). [abbr.]

execution day *n.* **1** [late 18C] washing day. **2** [20C+] (*US*) Monday. [(1) the washing is 'hanged' out to dry; (2) Monday is the trad. washing day]

exercise me *phr.* [1990s+] (*W.I.*) a request to dance.

exercise the ferret *v.* (*also* **exercise one's pecker/the armadillo**) [1950s+] to copulate (cf. BURY IT v.). [SE *exercise* + CHUTNEY FERRET n. (1)]

exes *n.¹* (*also* **exies, ex's**) [mid-19C+] *ex*penses. [abbr.]

exes *n.²* *see* EXIS n.

Exeter hall *n.* [19C] the vagina (cf. ANTIPODES n.). [a teasing allusion to Exeter Hall, best known for its temperance sermons and, later, as the first London site of a YMCA]

exflunct *v.* [mid-19C–1970s] (*US*) to destroy or overwhelm; usu. as adj. *exflunctified*, overwhelmed, destroyed. [? SE *fling*]

exhaust pipe *n.* [1970s+] (*US gay*) the anus.

exhibition meal *n.* [1920s–30s] (*US tramp*) food left for a beggar outside the door.

exies *n.* *see* EXES n.¹.

exis *n.* (*also* **exes, xis**) **1** [mid-19C] a sixpence. **2** [mid-19C+] the number 6. **3** [1930s+] £6 sterling. **4** [1980s] (*UK Und.*) a 6-month prison sentence. [backsl.]

exis-evif yeneps *n.* [mid-19C] 11 pence. [backsl.; EXIS n. + EVIF n. + YENNEP n. (lit. '6 plus 5 pence')]

exis-ewif gens *n.* [mid-19C] 30 shillings, £1 10s (£1.50). [backsl.; EXIS n. + EVIF n. + GEN n.¹ (lit. '6 times 5 shillings')]

exis gens *n.* [mid-19C] 6 shillings (30p). [backsl.; EXIS n. + GEN n.¹]

exis sith-noms *n.* [mid-19C] 6 months, usu. as a prison sentence. [backsl.; EXIS n. + SITH-NOM n.]

exis yeneps *n.* (*also* **exis-yenneps**) [mid-19C] a sixpence (2½p). [backsl.; EXIS n. + YENNEP n.]

expat *n.* [1960s+] **1** an *expat*riate, any citizen of one country living abroad. **2** (*W.I.*) an immigrant, esp. a White foreigner, working in a local job. [abbr.]

expecting *adj.* [late 19C+] pregnant. [abbr. SE *expecting a baby*]

expense *n.* [1940s] (*US Black*) a baby. [the cost of bringing up a child]

explore me! *excl.* [1910s] (*US*) used to express lack of knowledge.

explorers' club *n.* [1970s+] (*drugs*) a group of LSD users. [they go on a TRIP n.⁴ (1)]

ex's *n.* *see* EXES n.¹.

exsie *adj.* [1990s+] (*Aus.*) expensive. [abbr.]

extensive *adj.* [mid-19C] showy, vulgar. [euph.]

extensive *adv.* [late 19C] to a great extent, unreservedly, ostentatiously. [EXTENSIVE adj.]

extortion *n.* [late 19C] (*US*) the cost. [hyperbole]

extra *n.* [1990s+] (*W.I.*) a show-off.

extra *adj.* **1** [1940s–60s] (*Aus./US*) extraordinarily good. **2** [1980s] (*N.Z.*) a general intensifier.

extract the michael *v.* (*also* **take the michael**) [1950s+] consciously 'genteel' version of TAKE THE MICKEY (OUT OF) v.

extract the urine *v.* [1930s+] (*orig. milit.*) a euph. for TAKE THE PISS (OUT OF) v.

extreme animal *n.* *see* ENTIRE ANIMAL n.

e ya later *phr.* [1990s+] (*US teen*) goodbye; spec. on the Internet, an electronic version of *see you later*. [var. on *see you later* + joc. ref. to the drug ECSTASY n. or E n.]

eye *n.¹* **1** [late 16C; mid-19C] the vagina. **2** [1930s–70s] (*US gay/prison*) the rectum, the anus. [(1) the eye is similarly shaped, is surrounded by hair, and can 'water'; (2) note EYE sfx]

eye *n.²* **1** [20C+] a detective, a private eye (cf. EAGLE EYE n.). **2** [20C+] (*US Und.*) (*also* **the Eye**) Pinkerton's Detective Agency.

3 [1940s] a warning. **4** [1950s] a lookout. [the logo of Pinkerton's detective agency]

eye *n.³* (*also* **eyeball**) [1950s–70s] (*US campus*) a television set. [its monocular screen]

eye *n.⁴* [1950s] (*US Black*) a hole.

eye *adj.* [1900s–40s] (*US Und.*) under the protection of the Pinkerton Detective Agency. [EYE n.² (2)]

eye *sfx* [20C+] used in combs. meaning anus (cf. BACK EYE n.; BLIND EYE n.; BROWN EYE n.; DEADEYE n.¹; HAWAIIAN EYE n.; HOG-EYE n., RED-EYE n.³; ROUNDEYE n., THIRD EYE n.); note also words like EYE DOCTOR n. [note EYE n.¹ (2)]

eye ache *n.* [1990s+] a bore, a nuisance, an irritation. [i.e. a pain in the BROWN EYE n. (1)]

eyeball *n.¹* [20C+] (*W.I.*) the most beloved child in a family. [play on SE *the apple of one's eye*]

eyeball *n.²* **1** [1960s+] a look or glance; an inspection. **2** [1990s+] a careful person. [EYEBALL v. (2)]

eyeball *n.³* *see* EYE n.³.

eyeball *adj.* [1950s+] (*US*) used of a personal inspection or eyewitness account. [EYEBALL v. (2)]

eyeball *v.* **1** [mid-19C; 20C+] (*orig. Aus.*) (*also* **highball**) to stare at, to ogle. **2** [1940s+] (*orig. US*) to inspect, to examine. **3** [1970s] (*US*) to meet or experience in person.

eyeballer *n.* [1920s+] (*US*) a know-it-all, esp. one who takes it upon themself to tell others what to do. [EYEBALL v.]

eyeballing *n.* [mid-19C; 1940s+] staring, esp. by a man at a woman. [EYEBALL v. (1)]

eyeball queen *n.* [1960s] (*US gay*) one who stares rather than talks. [EYEBALL v. (1) + QUEEN n.² (1)]

eye booger *n.* [1980s+] (*US campus*) the small pieces of 'sleep' or mucus that collect in the corners of the eyes. [SE *eye* + BOOGER n.¹ (1)]

eye-bunger *n.* [late 19C] a setback, lit. something that 'blacks one's eye'. [SE *eye* + BUNG v. (1)]

eye candy *n.* [1970s+] (*orig. US*) a person or thing (e.g. printed or televisual matter) that pleases the eye (esp. in a sexual manner) but has no intrinsic worth (cf. ARM CANDY n.).

eye cheaters *n.* *see* CHEATERS n.² (1).

eye doctor *n.* [1930s+] (*gay*) a male homosexual, i.e. one who practises anal intercourse (cf. ANAL ASTRONAUT n.). [EYE n.¹ (2) + SE *doctor* + pun on SE]

eye-eye! *excl.* [1940s+] look at that! what's all this! take a look around!

eyefuck *n.* [1990s+] (*US*) an aggressive, challenging stare. [EYEFUCK v. (3)]

eyefuck *v.* (*US*) **1** [1910s; 1970s+] to stare pointedly and lustfully at a sexually desirable person; thus *eyefucking*. **2** [1970s+] to stare, without sexual overtones. **3** [1970s+] to stare with deliberate, challenging aggression. [SE *eye* + FUCK v.¹]

eyeful *n.* **1** [late 19C+] a good look at. **2** [1930s+] an attractive woman.

eyeglass weather *n.* [late 19C] foggy weather, in which one cannot see clearly. [one requires an *eyeglass*]

eye in the sky *n.* (*orig. US*) **1** [1960s+] a 2-way mirror used for security in a casino. **2** [1970s+] a police or traffic helicopter.

eyelid movies *n.* [1970s+] (*US*) daydreams, fantasies enjoyed with the eyes closed, often as stimulated by a hallucinogenic drug; often masturbation fantasies; thus *watch eyelid movies*, to masturbate.

eye-limpet *n.* [late 19C] an artificial eye. [it sticks to one's eye socket]

eye of one's arse *n.* [20C+] (*Irish*) the anus. [EYE n.¹ (2) + ARSE n.¹ (1)]

eye-opener *n.¹* **1** [early 19C+] (*orig. US*) the first drink of the day. **2** [mid-19C+] a surprise, a shock, not necessarily unpleasant. **3** [1920s] an attractive woman. **4** [1930s+] (*drugs*) the day's first dose of a drug. **5** [1970s+] (*drugs*) amphetamine (cf. A n.²). **6** [2000s+] (*drugs*) crack cocaine (cf. BASE n.). [all 'wake you up']

eye-opener *n.*² **1** [late 19C] the penis (cf. ARSE-OPENER n.). **2** [1920s+] (*US Und.*) a tramp who has homosexual sex with a young companion.

eye-popper *n.* [1940s+] (*US*) something sensational. [one's eyes *pop out of one's head*]

eyes *n.*¹ **1** [1930s+] the nipples or female breasts (cf. BAGS n.¹). **2** [1990s+] (*US Black*) sunglasses. [resemblance]

eyes *n.*² [1990s+] (*US prison*) mirrors held through the bars of one's cell and used to survey the outer world. [the mirror extends the range of one's eyesight]

eye-shoot *v.* [2000s] (*US*) to stare at aggressively.

eyes like pissholes in the snow *phr.* (*also* **eyes like two burnt holes in a blanket**) [1920s+] (*orig. milit.*) deeply sunken eyes, often bloodshot. [poss. the result of an excess of alcohol]

eyes out *phr.* [1980s] (*N.Z.*) a phr. meaning do something as fast as possible.

eyes set at eight in the morning *phr.* [early 17C] drunk (cf. ARSEHOLED adj.). [one's eyes are staring in different directions]

eyes set in one's head *phr.* [early 17C] drunk (cf. ARSEHOLED adj.).

eye that weeps most when best pleased *n.* [19C] the vagina. [the secretions that indicate excitement]

Eyetie *n.* (*also* **Eyetalian, Eyetallyano, Eytie, Ite, Itie**) [1910s+] (*orig. US*) **1** a derog. term for an Italian (cf. DAGO n.). **2** the Italian language. [exaggerated pron. of *Italian*]

Eyetie *adj.* (*also* **Itie**) [1910s+] Italian or pertaining to Italian culture or language. [EYETIE n.]

eyeto *n.* [1940s–50s] (*Aus.*) **1** an Italian (cf. DAGO n.). **2** the Italian language. [EYETIE n. + -O sfx (4)]

eye-trouble *n.* [1980s+] (*N.Z. prison*) a propensity (real or imagined) for staring at other prisoners or at warders; usu. in challenging phr. *have you got eye-trouble?*, often the start of a fight.

eyewash *n.* **1** [late 19C+] (*orig. milit.*) rubbish, nonsense, humbug, anything done for appearance rather than effect. **2** [1910s–70s] cheap liquor. [the army use meant anything, e.g. washing the eyes, that is done for effect rather than for any practical purpose]

eyewater *n.* **1** [early 19C] (*also* **devil's eyewater**) brandy. **2** [early–late 19C] gin. **3** [1940s+] (*US*) illicitly distilled whisky.

Eytie *n. see* EYETIE n.

ezel *n. see* ESEL n.

F

F *n.*[1] [1920s+] a euph. for FUCK *n.*[1], as a swearword.

F *n.*[2] [1980s] (*US*) a $50 bill. [SE *fifty*]

f *v. see* EFF *v.*

F.A./f.a. *n. see* FANNY ADAMS *n.*[2].

faas *v.* (*also* **fass**) [20C+] (*W.I.*) to be nosy, inquisitive; thus *n.*, impudence, cheek. [SE *fuss*]

faastie *adj.* [1950s+] (*W.I., Jam.*) rude, impertinent, impudent. [? Surinam Creole *fiesti*, nasty; or ? FEISTY adj. (1)]

faastiness *n.* [1950s+] (*W.I.*) rudeness. [FAASTIE adj.]

FAB *n.* [2000s] (*US Black*) a derog. term for a woman. [FAKE-ASS adj./FAT-ASS adj. + BITCH *n.*[1] (1)]

fab *adj.* (*also* **fabbo, fabby**) [1960s+] a general term of approbation, first popularized by The Beatles *c.*1963 but still used, often with an ironic intonation (cf. GEAR adj.[1]). [abbr. SE *fabulous*, but Hancock, 'Shelta and Polari' (1984), suggests Sp. *fabulosa*, and sees it as orig. Polari]

fab! *excl.* [1960s+] a general excl. of approbation. [FAB adj.]

faboo *adj.* [1990s+] (*US gay*) fabulous. [abbr.]

fabric *n.* [1970s] (*US Black*) clothes.

fabu *adj.* [1990s+] (*US*) excellent. [abbr. SE *fabulous*]

fabuloso *adj.* [1990s+] (*orig. gay*) wonderful. [cod-Ital. version of SE *fabulous*]

fabulous drop *n.* [1940s+] (*Aus.*) an attractive young woman. [the comparison is with a good drink, 'a good drop' (of liquor)]

faburrific *adj.* [2000s] (*US*) excellent (cf. BONERIFIC adj.). [SE *fabulous* + terrific]

face *n.*[1] **1** [16C–18C] a coin. **2** [mid-18C–mid-19C] credit at a public house. [the face, usu. royal, engraved on one of a coin's sides]

face *n.*[2] **1** [late 16C–early 17C] a grimace. **2** [17C+] (*US*) (*also* **facial area**) audacity, impudence. **3** [mid-19C+] (*US*) the mouth, as the source of speech; thus *shut your face*. **4** [late 19C–1910s] (*US*) the mouth, as used for eating and drinking. **5** [late 19C–1950s] (*US*) interference, nosiness; thus *stick one's face in*. **6** [late 19C+] a general term of greeting, e.g. *Hello, face*. **7** [1920s+] (*Aus.*) one's personal appearance. **8** [1920s+] (*US*) fellatio or cunnilingus; usu. as *get/give face* (cf. BRAIN *n.*[2]; FACE ARTIST *n.*; FACE-FUCK *v.*; FACE-FUCKING *n.*; FACE JOB *n.*; FACE PUSSY *n.*; FACE THE NATION *v.*; SIT ON SOMEONE'S FACE *v.*). **9** [1930s–40s] (*US Black*) a stranger, esp. a White stranger. **10** [1930s+] (*US Und.*) a respectable image, a 'front'. **11** [1940s] (*US Black*) a White person. **12** [1940s+] (*US*) a cosmetic kit, make-up. **13** [1940s+] a person; esp. in police use, a known criminal. **14** [1960s+] a recognizable person. **15** [1960s+] a fellow member of a mod gang, esp. one who is considered particularly fashionable. **16** [1960s+] (*UK Und.*) a professional criminal, usu. an armed robber with no territorial ambitions.

face *v.* **1** [1920s+] (*Irish*) of a man, to pay court to a woman. **2** [1950s+] (*US campus*) to outperform, to correct, to show up, to humiliate, to insult. [15C SE *face*, 'to show a bold face, look big; to brag, boast, swagger' (*OED*)]

face! *excl.* [1980s] (*US campus*) an excl. delivered to a person whom one has just insulted or humiliated. [FACE *v.* (2)]

face-ache *n.* [1930s+] a joc. form of address. [despite the apparent rudeness of the phr., the *ache* presumably comes f. laughter]

face and brace *v.* [16C] to bluster, to defy, to bully verbally. [SE *face*]

face artist *n.* [1920s+] (*US Und.*) a fellator or fellatrix. [FACE *n.*[2] (8) + ARTIST sfx]

face bowl *n.* [1900s–50s] (*US Black*) a small bowl in which to wash the face.

face cream *n.* [1970s+] (*US gay*) semen, esp. as when ejaculated onto a fellator's face. [SE *face*/FACE *n.*[2] (8) + CREAM *n.*[1] (1), punning on the good effects that semen is reputed to have on the complexion]

faced *adj.*[1] **1** [1960s+] (*US teen*) extremely drunk (cf. ARSEHOLED adj.). **2** [1980s] (*drugs*) stunned by the potency of a drug, usu. cannabis. [abbr. SHITFACED adj.[2]]

faced *adj.*[2] [1980s+] (*US campus*) humiliated, embarrassed. [FACE *v.* (2)]

face fannies *n.* [1990s+] sideboards, sideburns.

face-feeding *n. see* FEED ONE'S FACE *v.* (1).

face fins *n.* [20C+] a moustache, presumably a large one that protrudes on either side of the cheeks.

face fittings *n.* [20C+] (*Aus.*) a beard and/or moustache.

face-fuck *v.* [1970s+] to place one's penis in a passive person's mouth in order to 'actively' receive fellatio (cf. BRAIN *n.*[2]; FACE *n.*[2]).

face-fucking *n.* [1970s+] fellatio where the person being fellated is the active partner and the other person is passive with an open mouth (cf. BRAIN *n.*[2]; FACE *n.*[2]). [FACE-FUCK *v.*]

face fungus *n.* [1910s+] male facial hair, i.e. a beard and/or moustache; occas. as a term of address (cf. FUNGUS *n.*).

face it out with a card of ten *v. see* BRAG IT OUT WITH A CARD OF TEN *v.*

face job *n.* [late 19C–1930s] (*US*) cunnilingus (cf. FACE *n.*[2]).

face-lace *n.* [1920s–40s] whiskers; a beard.

face like a stopped clock *phr.* [1980s] (*Aus.*) a phr. describing a very unattractive (usu. female) face; also of one who is momentarily stunned.

face like a stripper's clit *phr.* [1990s+] a derog. description of the face of an unattractive woman. [SE + CLIT *n.*]

face like yesterday *phr.* [1900s–10s] a phr. describing a very miserable-looking face.

face-making *n. see* MAKE FACES *v.*

faceman *n.* [1960s–80s] (*orig. W.I.*) an attractive man, a 'pretty boy'. [note the character *Faceman* in the 1980s US TV series *The A-Team*]

face-painting *n.* [1990s+] the ejaculation of semen over one's partner's face.

face-plaster *n.* [1940s+] (*Aus.*) an alcoholic drink. [it 'bandages up' a miserable face]

face pussy *n.* [1980s+] (*US gay*) fellatio (cf. BRAIN n.²; FACE n.²). [SE *face* + PUSSY n. (2)]

facer *n.*¹ **1** [late 17C–mid-19C] a brimming glass. **2** [mid-19C] a glass that holds a single dram of spirits. **3** [mid-19C] a glass of whisky punch. [all are poured into the face]

facer *n.*² **1** [early–mid-19C] a blow in the face. **2** [mid-19C+] an unexpected problem or obstacle, anything to which one must face up.

facer *n.*³ [mid-19C] (*US Und.*) a criminal who stalls those in pursuit of their accomplices. [SE *face off*]

face rape *v.* [1980s+] (*US campus*) to kiss passionately. [on model of SE *date rape*]

face stretcher *n.* [1920s] (*US*) an old woman who attempts to look young.

face the music *v.* [mid-19C+] **1** to deal stoically with a problem or difficult situation. **2** to take one's punishment. [MUSIC n.³ (2)]

face the nation *v.* [1970s+] (*US Black*) to perform cunnilingus (cf. FACE n.²).

facety *adj.* [1940s+] (*W.I./UK Black*) cheeky, impudent; thus *facetyness*, impudence. [SE *feisty* but ? note Surinam Creole *fiesti*, dirty, nasty and SE *fist*, a FART n. (1)]

facey *adj.* (*also* **facy**) [early 17C+] cheeky, rude, impudent. [SE *face*, effrontery; 20C+ use is W.I. only]

facial *n.* [1970s+] **1** a prostitute's client who likes the woman to sit on his face, sometimes after she has inserted a suppository or even when she is having intercourse with another man. **2** ejaculation in one's partner's face. [SE *facial*, cosmetic treatment for the face]

facial area *n. see* FACE n.² (2).

facker *n. see* FUCKER n. (3).

facking *adj. see* FUCKING adj.

fack off *v. see* FUCK OFF v.

facquing *adj. see* FUCKING adj.

factor *n. see* FATER n.

factor *sfx* [1970s+] (*US campus*) in comb. with a relevant n., a quantity of, a degree of, e.g. *dork factor*, the number of fools, *dog factor*, the number of ugly women.

factory *n.*¹ [mid-19C+] (*UK Und.*) a large, forbidding Victorian police station in the London Metropolitan area. [resemblance to the architecture of 19C factories + ? allusion to the 'manufacturing' of evidence]

factory *n.*² [1930s+] (*drugs*) **1** the kit used by a narcotics addict for injections. **2** a place where drugs are packaged, diluted or manufactured.

factotum *n.* [late 19C] the vagina. [SE *factotum*, a man of all work; a servant who has the entire management of his master's affairs]

facy *adj. see* FACEY adj.

fadangle *v.* [2000s] (*US Black*) to cheat, to do wrong. [FINAGLE v. (1)]

fad-cattle *n.* [19C] a generic term for sexually available women. [dial. *faddle*, to make much of (a child) + SE *cattle*]

faddle *n.* [19C] **1** a trifling person, a busybody. **2** an affected and/or homosexual man. [Midlands dial. *faddle*, an over-particular, fussy person]

fade *n.*¹ **1** [late 19C] (*US*) a former dandy, now fallen on hard times and thus less resplendent. **2** [1990s+] (*US campus*) a badly dressed person. [SE phr. *faded glory*]

fade *n.*² (*US Black*) **1** [20C+] a derog. term for a White person. **2** [1970s+] a Black person who becomes immersed in the White world and thus 'fades away'. [SE *faded*, pale, wan]

fade *n.*³ (*also* **fadeaway**) [1900s–60s] (*US*) a departure, an escape. [FADE v.² (1)]

fade *n.*⁴ [1980s+] (*US Black*) short-cropped Black hair, pioneered by the hip-hop culture. [? it fades into the skull]

fade *v.*¹ **1** [late 19C+] (*gambling*) in dice games, to bet against the player holding the dice, or, in poker, to match the previous bet.

2 [late 19C+] (*US*) to put at a disadvantage, to cause problems for someone; esp. in phr. *don't fade me*; thus *have someone faded*, to have someone at a disadvantage. **3** [1920s–30s] in fig. use of (1), to respond, to counter. **4** [1920s–40s] (*US Und.*) to hold up with a gun. **5** [1960s] (*US*) to put up with, to manage something. **6** [1990s+] (*US Black teen*) to fool around or tinker with something or someone.

fade *v.*² **1** [20C+] (*also* **fade away**) to leave, to vanish. **2** [1940s–70s] (*US*) to die. **3** [1940s] (*US Black/campus*) to stop talking. **4** [1960s] (*US campus*) to miss a class; to waste time rather than work. **5** [1960s] (*US Und.*) to withstand interrogation. **6** [1960s] (*US Und.*) to obtain a verdict of 'not guilty'. **7** [1980s] (*US Black*) to drop a topic of conversation, to change an unpalatable subject. **8** [1980s] (*US Black*) to remain sufficiently silent not to be noticed. **9** [1980s] (*US campus*) to become tired, to feel increasingly exhausted. **10** [1990s+] (*US*) to let down, to renege. [SE *fade*, to grow dim, faint or pale]

fade *v.*³ [1990s+] (*US Black*) to ignore, to erase, to get rid of. [SE *fader*, a slider on the mixing board used in rap music; if one pulls the fader down it gradually reduces the volume; note also FADE v.¹ (2)]

fadeaway *n. see* FADE n.³.

fade away *v. see* FADE v.² (1).

faded *adj.* [1980s+] (*US Black/campus*) **1** drunk, under the influence of drugs. **2** unfashionable. **3** used to excess. [SE *fade*, to grow pale]

faded boogie *n.* (*also* **faded bogey**) [1920s+] (*US Black*) **1** a Black informer. **2** a Black who apes Whites and loses his own ethnicity. **3** a White who imitates Blacks. [SE *faded* + BOOGIE n.² (1); note Irwin, *American Tramp and Und. Slang* (1931): 'Why the adjective "faded" is applied is hard to say, unless it is felt that the negro who turns informer has still less claim to identity than as a negro, and that he has faded from what small importance he formerly had']

fade-out *n.* (*US*) **1** [1910s–60s] a disappearance, a departure, an escape; thus *on the fade-out*, evading the police, on the run. **2** [1920s–50s] death. [film imagery + FADE v.² (1)]

fade out *v.* [1920s–50s] (*orig. US*) **1** to die. **2** to leave. [film imagery + FADE v.² (1)]

fadge *n.* [late 18C–1900s] a farthing. [pron.]

fadge *v.* [late 16C–mid-19C] to suit, to work out, to 'do'. [ety. unknown]

fadger *n.* [late 19C–1910s] a farthing. [FADGE n.]

fadoodle *n.* [mid-17C; 1920s+] a nothing, a trifle. [cited in Manchon; *OED* has one SE cit. for 1670]

fadoodling *n.* [17C] a euph. for sexual intercourse. [SE *fadoodle*, nothing, nonsense, a foolish trifle; the *OED*'s first and only use is 1670, but the term is used in Thomas Middleton's *The Roaring Girl* (1611) V.i when, midway through a scene in which the whole canting vocabulary is paraded and properly translated, the authors back away from explaining *wapping* (*see* WAP v.) and NIGGLING n., dismissing them as 'fadoodling, if it please you']

faff *n.* [2000s] a nuisance. [FAFF v.]

faff *v.* (*also* **faff about/around**) [1950s+] to play around, to mess about, a euph. for FUCK ABOUT v. (1). [orig. dial. *faff*, to fuss (about); note echoic dial. *faffle*, to stutter or stammer, to utter incoherent sounds]

fag *n.*¹ **1** [late 18C–mid-19C] a young female fish seller. **2** [early–mid-19C] (*US*) an errand boy or clerk. **3** [20C+] (*Aus.*) a lawyer's clerk. [public school jargon *fag*, a junior boy who performs (menial) tasks for a senior; ult. SE *fag*]

fag *n.*² **1** [late 18C+] a bore, a chore, an unpleasant, tedious task. **2** [mid-19C; 1960s] (*US campus*) a hard worker. [SE *fag*, to tire, to perform a wearisome task; ? ult. *flag*, to droop, to tire; (1) is based on UK public school jargon *fag*, a junior boy performing tasks for seniors; (1) usu. considered UK, Jim Thompson, *Now and On Earth* (1942), has it in a US setting in the 1920s]

fag *n.*³ (*also* **fish-fag**) [mid-19C] a pickpocket. [? SE *fag-end*, the way a pickpocket tugs at handkerchiefs, watch-chains etc, or dial. *fag*, to cut corn with a sickle]

fag *n.*⁴ [late 19C+] **1** a cigarette end. **2** a cheap cigarette, usu. as issued to troops in WW1. **3** any cigarette; thus *fag-ash*, cigarette ash; *Fag-Ash Lil*, a nickname for a woman who smokes heavily. [abbr. FAG END *n.* (4)]

fag *n.*⁵ **1** [1920s+] (*orig. US*) a male homosexual. **2** [1970s+] (*US campus/teen*) an offensive person. [abbr. FAGGOT *n.*² (3)/FAGGOT *n.*² (5) but note comment in ety. there]

fag *adj.* [1930s+] homosexual; pertaining to homosexuality. [FAG *n.*⁵ (1)]

fag *v.*¹ [late 17C–19C] (*UK Und.*) to beat; thus *fagging*, a beating; *fag the bloss*, hit the wench; *fag the fen*, drub the prostitute. [SE *feague*, to beat, to whip; ult. Ger. *fegen*, to polish]

fag *v.*² [late 18C–1910s] to work hard academically. [FAG *n.*² (1)/SE *fag*, to work]

fag *v.*³ (*also* **fag along**) [20C+] (*US*) **1** to move quickly, to leave in a hurry. **2** to move when it requires an effort. [? SE *fag*, to tire (of a situation)]

fag *v.*⁴ [1920s–50s] to supply with a cigarette, to smoke a cigarette. [FAG *n.*⁴ (3)]

fag *v.*⁵ [1960s] (*US*) a derog. term, meaning to engage in or subject another to homosexual practices. [FAG *n.*⁵ (1)]

fag along *v.* see FAG *v.*³.

fagan *n.* (*also* **fagin**) [1940s+] the penis (cf. BURY OLD FAGIN *v.*; INTRODUCE HER TO FAGAN *v.*). [the character *Fagin* from Charles Dickens's *Oliver Twist* (1837–9); despite Fagin's poss. paedophilia and the use of 'fag', no specific gay context is implied]

fag around *v.* [1960s+] (*US*) for heterosexual men to play at acting in a 'homosexual' manner. [FAG *v.*⁵]

fag-bagging *v.* [1970s] (*US*) to beat up and rob a homosexual. [FAG *n.*⁵ (1) + BAG *v.*² (2)]

fag-basher *n.* [1980s+] (*orig. US gay*) **1** an ostensibly heterosexual man who specializes in beating and terrorizing gay men. **2** any anti-gay spokesperson. [FAG *n.*⁵ (1) + BASH *v.*¹ (1)]

fag-bashing *n.* [1980s+] the homophobic beating up of male homosexuals. [*see prev.* + BASHING *n.*¹ (1)]

fag-butt *n.* [1930s+] a cigarette end. [FAG *n.*⁴ (3) + BUTT *n.*² (1)]

fag end *n.* (*also* **butt-end**) **1** [17C+] the last part or remnant of anything. **2** [early 18C+] of ropes, the end of, a part near the end of. **3** [early 19C+] a fragmentary part of a speech or conversation that one might overhear, just as it tails off. **4** [mid-19C+] the butt of a cigarette or cigar. [SE *fag*, to droop, to decline, to flag]

fag-end man *n.* [1910s–20s] a man who collects cigarette ends from the pavement. [FAG END *n.* (4)]

fagery *n.* see FEGARY *n.*

faggamuffin *n.* [1980s+] (*Black*) a homosexual Black person, usu. male. [FAG *n.*⁵ (1) + RAGAMUFFIN *n.*]

fagged (out) *adj.* **1** [mid-18C+] exhausted. **2** [1900s] shocked, mentally destroyed. [FAG *v.*²]

fagger *n.* (*also* **figger, figure**) [17C–18C] a small boy used by robbers to enter a house through a window that would be too small to allow a man to climb through it. [SE *fag*, to work (for another)]

fagging *n.* see FAG *v.*¹.

fagging *adj.* [late 19C] exhausting. [FAG *v.*²]

fagging law *n.* see FIGGING LAW *n.*

faggish *adj.* [1950s] (*US*) homosexual in style or manner. [FAG *n.*⁵ (1)]

faggot *n.*¹ [late 17C–early 19C] a man mustered for duty in the army (and thus 'bound' to service) but not yet formally enlisted. [SE *faggot*, a bundle (usu. of sticks) bound together]

faggot *n.*² **1** [early 18C+] a general term of abuse, usu. of women or children. **2** [late 18C] a prostitute. **3** [1910s+] (*orig. US*) a homosexual man; in general use the term covers any gay man; in gay use the implication is of overt effeminacy. **4** [1950s] (*US*) a

lesbian. **5** [1950s+] (*US*) a general term of abuse, irrespective of sex. **6** [1970s+] (*US teen/campus*) an unattractive young woman. **7** [1970s+] a coward, a weakling. [(3) is usu. seen as a US coinage, but *faggot* has an older, if debatable, UK ety. One, somewhat fanciful, version suggests that a *faggot* was used in the burning of heretics, and thus became transferred to the name of an embroidered patch (like the pink triangles of the Nazi concentration camps) worn by unburned heretics; homosexuals are certainly considered fig. heretics, therefore *faggot* means homosexual. More feasible is the descent from (1), the 18C use of *faggot* as a woman (thus playing on homosexual effeminacy), esp. in the derog. form of a 'baggage', which stems from the faggots that one had to haul to the fire. The abbr. FAG *n.*⁵ (1) may be linked independently to the British public school *fag*, a junior boy performing menial tasks and poss. conducting homosexual affairs with the seniors. Rodgers, *The Queen's Vernacular* (1972), acknowledges all these and adds 'fr WW I sl *fag* = cigarette, because cigarettes were considered effeminate by cigar-smoking he-men.' Finally, there is the Yid. FAYGELE *n.*, meaning little bird (thus the synon. *birdie*), and thence homosexual]

faggot *n.*³ [late 18C] the penis. [? supposed resemblance to SE *faggot*, a stick]

faggot *adj.* **1** [1940s+] (*US*) pertaining to homosexuality or homosexuals. **2** [1960s+] in fig. use, weak, ineffectual. [FAGGOT *n.*² (3)]

faggot *v.* [late 18C–early 19C] (*UK Und.*) to bind, to tie up. [SE *faggot*, to tie up bundles of wood]

faggot and stall *n.* (*also* **faggot and storm**) [early 18C] (*UK Und.*) a burglar who enters a house, ties up the residents and then robs them. [FAGGOT *v.* + SE *stall*, to confine/*storm* (one's way in)]

faggot-ass *adj.* [2000s] (*US Black*) weak, cowardly, contemptible. [FAGGOT *adj.* (2) + -ASS *sfx*]

faggoteer *n.* see FAGGOT-MASTER *n.*

faggoter *n.* [1960s+] (*US Black*) a pimp who specializes in selling the services of male homosexual prostitutes (cf. CANDYMAN *n.*). [FAGGOT *n.*² (3)]

faggot-lover *n.* [1960s+] (*Aus./US*) one who has no feelings of homophobia. [FAGGOT *n.*² (3) + sfx *-lover*]

faggot-master *n.* (*also* **faggoteer**) [19C] a pimp, a lecher (cf. ABBOT ON THE CROSS *n.*). [FAGGOT *n.*² (2) + sfx *-master*]

faggot's lunchbox *n.* [1960s] (*US gay*) an athletic supporter. [FAGGOT *n.*² (3) + SE *lunchbox* but note LUNCHBOX *n.*²]

faggoty *adj.* (*US*) **1** [1920s+] (*also* **faggot-assed**) effeminate, homosexual. **2** [1960s+] cowardly, useless, second-rate. [FAGGOT *n.*² (3)]

faggy *adj.* [1940s+] (*orig. US*) effeminate, homosexual. [FAG *n.*⁵ (1) + sfx *-y*]

fag-hag *n.*¹ [1940s–50s] (*Can.*) a woman who smokes excessively. [FAG *n.*⁴ (3) + SE *hag*]

fag-hag *n.*² [1960s+] (*orig. US*) **1** a woman, prob. heterosexual, poss. ageing, who courts and indulges the company of male homosexuals. **2** a heterosexual man, irrespective of age, who prefers the company of homosexuals to that of his heterosexual peers. [FAG *n.*⁵ (1) + SE *hag*]

fag-hag *v.* [1960s+] of a woman, to associate with and choose one's close friends from homosexual men. [FAG-HAG *n.*² (1)]

fag-hole *n.* [1940s+] the mouth. [FAG *n.*⁴ (3) + SE *hole*]

fag hots *n.* [1960s+] (*gay*) cheap pornography aimed at the male homosexual readership. [FAG *n.*⁵ (1) + ? HOT STUFF *n.*² (3) + play on FAGGOT *n.*² (3)]

fagin *n.* see FAGAN *n.*

faginy-fagade *n.* [1920s–30s] (*US Black*) a White person. [cod Lat. version of FADE *n.*² (1)]

faglish *n.* [1980s+] (*US gay*) gay slang. [FAG *n.*⁵ (1) + SE *English*]

fagola *n.* [1960s+] (*US*) a male homosexual. [FAG *n.*⁵ (1) + -OLA *sfx* but note FAYGELE *n.*]

fag-paper *n.* [1910s+] a cigarette paper. [FAG n.⁴ (3) + SE *paper*]

fags! *excl.* (*also* **efgs!**) [mid-17C–18C; 1920s+] a mild excl. [? SE *faith!*]

fag stag *n.* [1990s+] (*US*) a heterosexual male who enjoys the company of homosexual men. [FAG n.⁵ (1) + STAG n.³ (1)]

fag tag *n.* [1980s+] (*US campus*) the small loop (ostensibly for hanging the shirt when no hanger is available) on the upper back of many shirts; such a loop, supposedly, can be used to hold a victim ready for buggery (cf. FAIRY LOOP n.). [FAG n.⁵ (1) + SE *tag*]

fag-topper *n.* [1900s] a cigarette end. [FAG n.⁴ (3) + SE *top*]

fag water *n.* [1980s] (*US*) cologne. [FAG n.⁵ (1) + SE *water*]

faigelah *n. see* FAYGELE n.

faike *n.* [late 19C] (*UK Und.*) an experienced, senior criminal. [? FAKE n.¹ (1)]

fail *v.* [1980s+] (*US campus*) to fail to understand, to be unable to understand.

fail in the furrow *v. see* DIE IN THE FURROW v.

fains! *excl.* (*also* **fains I!**) [mid-19C+] (*UK juv.*) a call for a truce during a game, or a statement that one is ineligible for a given duty or command. [SE *fen*, to forbid; ? ult. *fend*, forbid]

faint *adj.* [mid-19C] (*US*) a euph. for drunk (cf. AFFLICTED adj.).

fainting fits *n.* [1940s+] the female breasts (cf. BRACE AND BITS n.). [rhy. sl. = TIT n.³ (1)]

fair *n.* (*also* **fair-skin**) [20C+] (*US Black*) a light-skinned Black person.

fair *adj.* [late 19C+] (*orig. Aus.*) absolute, complete, total; usu. in combs., e.g. FAIR COW n. (1). [FAIR adv.]

fair *adv.* [mid-19C+] very, absolutely, really, e.g. *fair old.*

fair buck *n.* [1940s+] (*N.Z.*) a fair chance; usu. as excl. *fair buck!* be fair! give me a chance! [SE *fair* + BUCK n.⁶ (1)]

fair cop *n.* [late 19C+] (*orig. UK Und.*) **1** a justifiable arrest; usu. in the tongue-in-cheek phr. *it's a fair cop guv* (slap the bracelets on). **2** any situation seen as fair and about which there is no complaint. [SE *fair* + COP n.¹ (2)]

fair cow *n.* [20C+] **1** (*Aus./N.Z.*) (*also* **fair lizard**) a general negative, applied to persons or things to which the speaker takes great exception, e.g. *fair cow of a day, he's a fair cow*; often in phr. *it's a fair cow.* **2** (*N.Z.*) a call for fair treatment. [FAIR adj./SE *fair* + COW n.² (1)]

fair crack of the whip *n.* [1920s+] (*Aus.*) an equitable opportunity, a reasonable chance.

fair crack of the whip! *excl.* [1960s+] (*Aus./N.Z.*) be fair! give someone a chance! [FAIR CRACK OF THE WHIP n.]

fair deal *n.* [1910s+] (*orig. US*) an honest transaction, a fair bargain. [SE *fair* + DEAL n.¹ (1)]

fair dinkum *adj.* (*also* **fair dink**) [20C+] (*Aus.*) honest. [FAIR DINKUM! excl.]

fair dinkum! *excl.* (*also* **dinkum!**) [late 19C+] (*mainly Aus.*) honest! really! on the level! [SE *fair* + DINKUM adj.]

fair dos! *excl.* (*also* **fair do! fair dues!**) [mid-19C+] (*Aus./N.Z.*) a general statement of agreement, acceptance; as n., decent treatment. [SE *fair* + *do*, dealing, treatment]

fair enough *phr.* [20C+] a statement of acceptance, agreement.

fair fucks to *phr.* [1980s+] (*Irish*) good luck (to).

fair gang *n.* [19C] the gypsies. [? their regular appearances at fairs; or ? f. *Faa*, the Scot. gypsy equivalent of Smith]

fair go *n.* (*also* **open go**) [20C+] (*Aus.*) **1** any situation that meets a basic requirement of impartiality to all without fear of favour or prejudice. **2** a fair fight. [a call in a game of 'two-up' that indicates all relevant rules were satisfied and that the coins could be spun]

fair go! *excl.* [20C+] **1** (*Aus.*) be reasonable! be fair! **2** (*N.Z.*) an interrog. meaning really? [FAIR GO n.]

fair-haired boy *n.* [20C+] (*US*) an especial favourite, one who can, in supportive eyes, do no wrong.

fairish *adj.* [late 19C+] considerable in amount.

fair itch *n.* [late 19C–1930s] an absolute imitation.

fair lizard *n. see* FAIR COW n. (1).

fair nark *n.* [20C+] (*Aus./N.Z.*) something or someone inexpressibly tedious or baffling. [FAIR adj. + NARK n.¹ (2)]

fair one *n.* [1950s+] (*US gang*) a (street gang) fight conducted under some sort of mutually recognized rules and poss. preceded by a verbal argument.

fair-play artist *n.* [1950s] a trustworthy, honest person. [SE *fair play* + ARTIST sfx]

fair pop *n.* [late 19C+] a good opportunity, a fair chance; thus *not a fair pop*, not a fair chance. [SE *fair* + POP n.³ (1)]

fair roebuck *n.* [early 18C] a woman at the peak of her beauty. [SE *fair roebuck*, a roebuck in its 5th year]

fair shake *n.* (*also* **decent shake, shake**) [early 19C+] **1** a fair or acceptable situation. **2** equable treatment. [abbr. FAIR SHAKE OF THE DICE! excl.]

fair shake of the dice! *excl.* [early 19C+] (*Aus.*) be fair!

fair shakes! *excl.* [mid-19C+] (*Aus.*) a general statement of agreement, acceptance. [FAIR SHAKE OF THE DICE! excl.]

fair-skin *n. see* FAIR n.

fair spin *n.* [1910s+] fair treatment, a reasonable chance. [SPIN n.³]

fair suck (of the sav) *n.* (*also* **fair suck of the pineapple,** ...**sauce bottle/stick**) [1960s+] (*Aus./N.Z.*) a fair or equal chance. [SE *sav*, a saveloy]

fair thing *n.* [1910s+] (*Aus.*) a sensible, judicious action or decision.

fair treat *n.* [late 19C+] something or someone highly enjoyable or satisfactory, also used ironically to describe something or someone quite the opposite.

fair trod on *adj.* [late 19C] abused, treated very badly. [FAIR adv. + SE]

fair-weather drink *n.* [1970s] a small celebration before initiating some project or journey. [one toasts actual and fig. *fair weather*]

fair whack *phr.* [20C+] (*N.Z.*) an appeal for equable treatment. [SE *fair* + WHACK n.² (3)]

fairy *n.*¹ **1** [mid–late 17C; mid-19C–1930s] a young woman, with the poss. implication of promiscuity. **2** [19C] a drunken old hag. **3** [20C+] (*N.Z.*) a blonde-haired woman. [(1) US mid-19C–1930s]

fairy *n.*² [late 19C] (*US drugs*) a lamp for preparing opium.

fairy *n.*³ [late 19C+] (*orig. US*) a homosexual man. [a note in vol. VII of the *American Journal of Psychology* (1895) cites: 'the peculiar societies of inverts. Coffee-clatches, where the members dress themselves with aprons etc, and knit, gossip and crotchet; balls, where men adopt the ladies' evening dress, are well known in Europe. "The Fairies" of New York are said to be a similar secret organization']

fairy *n.*⁴ (*also* **fairy-twister**) [1900s–20s] (*Aus.*) **1** a fanciful tale, a 'tall story'; thus *pitch a fairy*, to tell a 'tall story'. **2** the teller of fanciful tales. [FAIRY STORY n.]

fairy *adj.* [1920s+] effeminate, homosexual. [FAIRY n.³]

fairy bower *n.* [20C+] (*Aus.*) **1** a shower (of rain). **2** a shower (for bathing). **3** an hour. [rhy. sl.]

fairydiddle *n.* [20C+] (*US*) nonsense, rubbish. [SE *fadoodle*, nonsense]

fairy dust *n.* [1970s+] (*drugs*) phencyclidine (cf. ACE n.⁴). [play on ANGEL DUST n. (4)]

fairy hawk *n.* [1960s+] (*US gay*) one who attacks (and robs) homosexuals. [FAIRY n.³ + SE *hawk*, an aggressive person]

fairy house *n.* (*also* **fairy joint**) [late 19C–1930s] (*US gay*) a male brothel for homosexuals (cf. ACCOMMODATION HOUSE n.). [FAIRY n.³ + HOUSE n.¹ (1)/JOINT n.⁴ (3)]

fairy lady *n.* [1940s–60s] (*US*) a lesbian, esp. a 'feminine' one. [FAIRY n.³ + SE *lady*]

fairy loop *n.* [1990s+] (*US*) the small loop on the upper back of many shirts; such a loop, supposedly, can be used to hold a victim ready for buggery (cf. FAG TAG n.). [FAIRY n.³ + SE *loop*; despite the link to homosexuality implicit in *fairy*, the term is sometimes capable of more fanciful interpretation, i.e. the practice cited in *DARE* as regards a Utah high school where 'a group of girls … will run a contest. They were to pick a boy, usually in their class. The girl who gets the most of his "fairy loops" … would be the one to marry him']

fairy pipe *n. see* FAIRY STORY n.

fairy powder *n.* [1950s–70s] (*drugs*) any form of powdered narcotic. [SE *fairy* + POWDER n.²]

fairy-shaking *n.* [1990s+] (*US*) blackmailing married men who frequent gay bars and similar centres. [FAIRY n.³ + SHAKE DOWN v.¹ (1)]

fairy snuff *phr.* [20C+] a joc. mispron./corruption of FAIR ENOUGH phr.

fairy's phonebooth *n.* [1960s+] (*US gay*) a public lavatory cubicle. [FAIRY n.³ + SE *phonebooth*, but note BONE PHONE n. and TELEPHONE n.²]

fairy story *n.* (*also* **fairy tale, fairy pipe**) [late 19C+] (*orig. US*) a fanciful, mendacious tale, often in aid of obtaining money or favours.

fairy's wand *n.* [1960s+] (*US gay*) any phallic object carried by a cruising gay man, e.g. a cigarette holder, a rolled umbrella (on a dry day), a long-stemmed rose. [FAIRY n.³ + SE *wand*]

fairy-twister *n. see* FAIRY n.⁴.

fake *n.*¹ **1** [19C–1940s] a dodge, a swindle, some form of fraudulent money-making scheme. **2** [mid-19C–1910s] (*US*) an invented newspaper story or false rumour. **3** [mid-19C+] any form of action, often a trick, varying as to context. **4** [late 19C] used fig. to describe any situation (the underlying image is of trickery or deception). **5** [late 19C] (*US*) a patent medicine. **6** [late 19C] (*US*) cheap, esp. worthless, merchandise sold by street vendors. **7** [late 19C+] (*US*) an impostor or insincere person. **8** [late 19C+] (*US*) a confidence trickster. **9** [1930s+] (*US drugs*) (*also* **fake-a-loo**) any form of substitute for a hypodermic syringe. [FAKE v.¹]

fake *n.*² [20C+] (*Ulster*) cancer. [dial. *fake*, to hurt, *fakement, pain*]

fake *adj.* [1990s+] (*US campus*) bad, disappointing, negative. [SE *fake*, counterfeit]

fake *v.*¹ **1** [early 19C] to shoot, to wound, to hit or cut. **2** [early 19C+] (*Ling. Fr./Polari*) to make, to do. **3** [early 19C+] to steal, to rob. **4** [mid-19C+] to cheat, to deceive, to swindle, to counterfeit; thus *faked (up)*, counterfeit, spurious. **5** [late 19C–1900s] to dress the hair, to make up the face. **6** [late 19C+] to pretend. **7** [late 19C+] (*US*) to malinger by feigning illness. **8** [1990s+] to fail to meet someone. [prob. fig. uses of SE *feague* + Ger. *fegen*, to furbish up, clean, sweep or Ital. *faccio*, I make; note FAKER n. predates this]

fake *v.*² [early 19C] to hurt, e.g. *this shoe fakes my foot*, this shoe pinches my foot. [dial. *fake*, to hurt, *fakement, pain*]

fake! *excl.* [1980s+] (*US campus*) an expression used by the trickster to underline that someone has been tricked or duped.

fake a cly *v.* [early–mid-19C] to pick or search a pocket. [FAKE v.¹ (3) + CLY n. (2)]

fake-a-loo *n. see* FAKE n.¹ (9).

fake (and) bake *v.* [1980s+] (*US campus*) to get a tan in a tanning booth. [FAKE v.¹ (6) + SE *bake*]

fake a pin *v.* [early 19C] (*UK Und.*) to create a sore leg or to cut it, as if accidentally, in the hope of getting onto the doctor's list. [FAKE v.¹ (1) + PINS n.]

fake a poke *v.* [late 19C] (*UK Und.*) to pick a pocket. [FAKE v.¹ (3) + POKE n.² (2)]

fake a screeve *v.* [early 19C] to write a (begging) letter. [FAKE v.¹ (4) + SCREEVE n. (5)]

fake a screw *v.* [19C] to make a skeleton key. [FAKE v.¹ (4) + SCREW n.² (1)]

fake-ass *adj.* [1990s+] (*US*) fraudulent. [SE *fake* + -ASS sfx]

fake away (there's no down)! *excl.* [19C] carry on! don't stop! [FAKE v.¹ (2) + SE *away*]

fake-bake *n.* [1980s+] (*US campus*) **1** a tanning salon. **2** a fake tan. [FAKE (AND) BAKE v.]

fake bake *v. see* FAKE (AND) BAKE v.

fake bandager *n.* [1900s] (*US Und.*) a beggar who poses as a cripple to elicit sympathy.

fake boodle *n.* [late 19C] (*US*) a roll of money in which small bills (or even paper cut to the right size) are surrounded, for ostentation's sake, by a large one. [SE *fake* + BOODLE n.¹ (4)]

fake down *v.* [mid-19C] (*N.Z.*) to carry out a crime. [FAKE v.¹ (4)]

fake it *v.* [1930s+] to pretend. [FAKE v.¹ (6)]

fakeloo *n.* [1920s+] (*US*) a spurious tale, a 'fairy story'.

fake-man *n.* [1900s] (*Aus.*) a confidence trickster. [FAKE v.¹ (4)]

fakement *n.* **1** [19C] any act of robbery or swindling. **2** [19C] a forged signature. **3** [early 19C] a letter, a note. **4** [mid-19C] scraps. **5** [mid-19C] any form of printed material. **6** [mid-late 19C] a false begging petition. **7** [late 19C] activity. **8** [late 19C–1900s] a trimming, a superfluous thing. **9** [1910s] (*UK Und.*) burglar's tools. [FAKE v.¹ (4) + sfx -*ment*]

fakement charley *n.* (*also* **fakeman charley, fakement chorley**) [early–mid-19C] a private sign or mark. [FAKEMENT n. (2) + CHARLIE n.¹]

fakement dodge *n.* [mid-19C–1900s] the writing of spurious begging letters; thus *fakement dodger*, the individual who does this. [FAKEMENT n. (6) + DODGE n. (1)]

fake oneself *v.* [19C] to inflict wounds or otherwise disfigure oneself for a criminal purpose. [FAKE v.¹ (1)]

fake one's slangs *v.* [19C] to cut off one's chains or irons to make an escape from prison. [FAKE v.¹ (4) + SLANG n.² (1)]

fake on someone *v.* [1970s+] (*US Black*) **1** to ignore. **2** to humiliate, to deceive. [FAKE v.¹ (4)]

fake out *n.* [1950s+] (*US*) a bluff, a deception, an unpleasant surprise. [FAKE OUT v.¹ (1)]

fake out *v.*¹ **1** [late 19C; 1940s+] to fool, to get the better of. **2** [1950s] to sneak away. [FAKE v.¹ (4)]

fake out *v.*² [1990s+] (*US Black*) **1** to ignore. **2** to humiliate, to deceive. [var. on FAKE ON SOMEONE v.]

fake out and out *v.* [early 19C] to kill, to murder. [FAKE v.¹ (4) + SE *out and out*, complete, extreme]

fake pie *n.* [late 19C] (*UK society*) a pie made up of left-overs. [users are usu. somewhat impoverished and no longer very smart]

faker *n.* **1** [late 17C–19C] a maker. **2** [19C+] a forger. **3** [mid-19C–1910s] (*US*) a thief. **4** [mid-19C–1920s] a street salesman of cheap goods. **5** [mid-19C–1920s] a confidence trickster, a fraudster. **6** [late 19C] a pimp (cf. ABBOT ON THE CROSS n.). **7** [1910s–50s] (*US*) a person feigning illness or injury. [Fr. *faire*, to make; ult. Lat. *faceo*]

faker of loges *n.* (*also* **feager of loges**) [17C] a beggar, esp. one who backs up his fraudulent tales with especially created fake documents. [FAKER n. (1)/SE *feague* + LOGES n.]

fake the broads *v.* (*also* **work the broads**) [19C] to cheat at cards, to perform the 3-card trick. [FAKE v.¹ (4) + BROADS n. (1)]

fake the duck *v.* [mid-late 19C] to adulterate drink, to cheat, to swindle. [FAKE v.¹ (4) + SE (*decoy*) *duck*]

fake the funk *v.* [1970s+] (*US Black*) to pose as more sophisticated than one actually is. [FAKE v.¹ (6) + FUNK n.¹ (5)]

fake the rubber *v.* [mid-19C] to stand treat. [FAKE v.¹ (4) + RUBBER n.¹ (2)]

fake the sweeteners *v.* [mid-late 19C] to kiss. [FAKE v.¹ (2) + SWEETENERS n.]

faking *n.* [mid-late 19C] **1** (*UK Und.*) thieving. **2** (*UK Und.*) cheating (e.g. at a card-game). **3** (*UK prison*) counterfeiting illness. [FAKE v.¹]

faking-boy *n.* [mid-19C] (*UK Und.*) a thief. [FAKE v.¹ (3)]

fakir *n.* **1** [mid-19C–1930s] a street salesman of cheap goods, an itinerant repairman etc. **2** [late 19C] (*US*) an actor. **3** [1900s] a street card-sharp. [FAKER n. (4); note the additional exotic tinge of SE *fakir*, a Muslim or Hindu holy mendicant]

fakus *n.* [1910s] (*Aus.*) something, without a specific name, that has been 'thrown together' or 'knocked up'. [? FAKE n.[1] (6)]

fal *n.* [late 19C] a young woman. [rhy. sl. = GAL n. (1)]

falairy *adj.* [20C+] (*Ulster*) unpleasant. [SE *floury*]

falconer *n.* [17C] (*UK Und.*) a confidence trickster, spec. one who poses as a poor scholar and thus persuades his victims to put up money in order to back the printing of some spurious learned pamphlet.

fall *n.* (*UK/US Und.*) **1** [late 19C+] an arrest. **2** [1910s+] problems, difficulties, a 'fall from grace'. **3** [1920s+] the blame, the consequences, esp. the blame taken on behalf of another; usu. as TAKE THE FALL v. **4** [1930s+] a conviction and the concomitant spell of imprisonment.

fall *v.*[1] **1** [late 19C–1920s] to commit oneself. **2** [1910s] to get married. **3** [1910s+] to fall in love.

fall *v.*[2] **1** [late 19C+] to be caught in illegal activities and subseq. arrested, tried and convicted. **2** [1990s+] to lose status, to be deprived of a comfortable situation. [(1) orig. UK but mainly US since the 1930s]

fall *v.*[3] (*also* **fall for**) [late 19C+] to become pregnant (with/by). [abbr. SE *fall pregnant*]

fall *v.*[4] **1** [1920s–50s] (*US Black*) to leave. **2** [1940s+] (*Aus.*) to arrive suddenly, usu. of the police.

fall about *v.* [1940s+] (*orig. US*) to collapse in laughter.

fall all over oneself *v.* [late 19C+] to make extreme, if chaotic, efforts to achieve what one or another wants.

fall apart *v.* (*also* **come apart**) [1930s+] to collapse emotionally, to lose control of one's feelings.

fall apart at the seams *v. see* COME APART AT THE SEAMS v.

fall back *v.* [early 19C] (*US*) to run off.

fall bitch *n. see* FALL GUY n.

fall by *v.* [1950s+] (*orig. US Black*) to visit without prior warning, to drop in.

fall dough *n.* [1910s–50s] (*US Und.*) money set aside by a criminal for bribing policemen or obtaining bail if he is arrested. [FALL n. (1) + DOUGH n.[1] (1)]

fall down (on) *v.* (*US*) **1** [mid-19C+] to fail, to blunder, to 'come to grief'. **2** [1960s] to experience, to enjoy.

fall-downs *n.* [late 19C] fragments of a pie that fall from the larger piece or slice when it is being cut up; plates of such fragments were sold at a halfpenny a plate in cookshops.

fall downstairs *v.* [20C+] (*US*) to get a haircut. [Ger. *die Treppe herunterfallen*, to fall downstairs; the sl. is found in Ger. areas of the US]

fallen angel *n. see* ANGEL n.[1] (1).

fallen on *adj.* [1930s+] pregnant. [FALL v.[3]]

fall for *v.*[1] [20C+] **1** to fall in love with a person or an idea or plan etc. **2** to be fooled by (a plan, a trick).

fall for *v.*[2] *see* FALL v.[3].

fall guy *n.* (*also* **fall bitch**) [20C+] **1** one who bears the punishment for another's wrong-doing. **2** a person who is easily duped, a victim. [according to Bentley & Corbett, *Prison Slang* (1992), there was a real-life *fall guy*, Albert Bacon Fall (1861–1944), who in 1922 took upon himself the entire blame for the Teapot Dome Scandal; despite the involvement of many top government officials, Fall was the only one to serve time, a sentence of 1 year and 1 day; this, however, does not match earlier available cits.]

fall in *v.* **1** [mid-19C–1910s] (*also* **fall to**) in fig. use of (2), to become involved. **2** [mid 19C+] (*orig. US Black*) (*also* **fall on in, fall out, fall over**) to arrive, to go to, to visit. **3** [20C+] (*US*) to go to bed.

falling *n.* [2000s] (*US Black*) acting insanely.

falling den *n.* [1920s] (*US Black*) a bed. [FALL IN v. (3)]

falling sickness *n.* [17C–early 18C] sexual intercourse. [pun on SE *falling sickness*, epilepsy]

fall in the furrow *v.* [20C+] to ejaculate. [SE *fall in* + FURROW n.]

fall in (the shit) *v.* [mid-19C+] to find oneself in difficulties. [SE *fall in* + SHIT n.[3] (1)]

fall in the thick *v.* [late 19C] to become very drunk.

fall into *v.*[1] [1930s] to come upon, to obtain.

fall into *v.*[2] [1940s–60s] (*US*) **1** to stay. **2** to visit. [ext. of FALL IN v. (2)]

fall money *n.* [late 19C+] (*US Und.*) bail and legal fees, just in case one is arrested. [FALL n. (1) + SE *money*]

fall off the christmas tree *v.* [late 19C] (*US campus*) to be amazed.

fall off the perch *v.* [late 18C+] to die.

fall off the roof *v.* **1** [1950s+] to be menstruating. **2** [1970s] (*US gay*) to be in a nervous, irritable state.

fall off the twig *v.* [2000s] to die.

fall off the (water) wagon *v.* [late 19C+] **1** to drink heavily, usu. in the context of resuming drinking after a period of abstinence. **2** in ext. use, to abandon any good resolution. [ON THE WAGON phr.]

fall of the leaf *n.* [early 18C] death.

fall on in *v. see* FALL IN v. (2).

fall on one's feet *v. see* LAND ON ONE'S FEET v.

fall on the wrong side of the hedge *v.* (*also* **be on the wrong side of the hedge**) [late 19C] to be thrown from a coach. [one lands off the road and in a field]

fall-out *n.* **1** [1950s+] (*Aus.*) the threat of pieces falling from an old, unsafe automobile. **2** [1960s+] (*orig. Aus.*) of a woman's breasts, their falling out of a badly secured or overly low-cut bikini or swimsuit. **3** [1970s] (*US Black*) a fainting fit.

fall out *v.*[1] **1** [1930s+] to leave. **2** [1930s+] to enthuse, to be delighted by. **3** [1940s+] (*US Black*) to faint, to collapse, to fall asleep; often when overcome by drug consumption or excessive drinking. **4** [1940s+] to be overcome with laughter. **5** [1940s+] to lose control of a situation. **6** [1940s+] (*US Black*) to be surprised. **7** [1950s] to relax.

fall out *v.*[2] *see* FALL IN v. (2).

fall out of one's standing *v.* [1990s+] (*Irish*) **1** to collapse from exhaustion. **2** to be surprised, stunned.

fall over *v. see* FALL IN v. (2).

fall over backwards *v. see* BEND OVER BACKWARDS v.

fall over oneself *v.* [20C+] to go out of one's way to do something (usu. altruistic).

fall partner *n.* [1950s+] (*US Und.*) one of 2 or more people who are arrested or sentenced to prison at the same time for the same crime; also one of a pair of thieves working together. [FALL n. (1)]

fall scratch *n.* [1960s] (*US Und.*) money that is held ready for use as bail, e.g. by a pimp for one of his prostitutes. [FALL n. (1) + SCRATCH n.[4] (4)]

fall through one's (own) asshole *v.* [1960s–70s] (*US*) to be extremely surprised, utterly shocked.

fall to *v.* [1900s] (*US Und.*) to notice.

fall togs *n.* [1920s–40s] (*US Und.*) respectable/smart clothing worn for a court appearance. [FALL n. (1) + TOGS n. (1)]

fall to pieces *v.* [late 19C+] to go into labour, to give birth. [19C Leicester dial.; 1940s+ use is Aus.]

fall up *v.* [late 19C+] (*US Black*) to arrive, to turn up.

faloose/falouse *n. see* FELOOSE n.

false *n.* [1920s–30s] (*US Black*) a lie. [SE *falsehood*; note 16C–18C SE *false*, a lie, a deception]

false *v.* [1930s+] (*Aus.*) to lie, to deceive. [obs. SE *false*, to cheat, to betray, to defraud, to break one's word]

false! *excl.* [1980s+] (*US campus*) no! impossible! that's not true! [SE, but note *true/false* answers required in various forms of examination]

false alarm *n.*[1] [1900s–50s] **1** a braggart, a boaster. **2** something or someone that does not live up to expectations. [play on SE]

false alarm *n.*[2] [1910s+] (*orig. milit.*) the arm. [rhy. sl.]

false face *n.* [1970s+] (*US campus*) a hypocrite, an insincere person.

false gig *v.* [1940s+] (*Aus.*) to pretend to be what one is not, to act under false pretences; thus *falsing, shamming, malingering.* [SE *false* + GIG v.⁴]

false hereafter *n.* [late 19C] (*US society*) a bustle. [pun]

falsies *n.* **1** [1940s+] pads placed in a brassiere that accentuate the shape and dimensions of otherwise small female breasts. **2** [1940s+] anything fake added to the body. **3** [1950s–60s] padding inserted in the trousers to resemble large genitals. **4** [1990s+] false teeth.

fam *n.*¹ **1** [late 17C–1910s] (*also* **famm, fem, feme**) a hand. **2** [18C–mid-19C] a ring. [abbr. FAMBLE n.]

fam *n.*² [1970s+] **1** (*US Black/gay/teen*) the *family.* **2** (*US gay*) a large number. [abbr.; (2) f. (1)]

fam *v.* [mid-18C–early 19C] to feel, to handle. [FAM n.¹ (1)]

fam a dona *v.* (*also* **fam a donna**) [late 19C] to take liberties with a woman. [FAM v. + DONA n. (1)]

famble *n.* **1** [mid-16C–1900s] a hand. **2** [late 17C–mid-19C] (*UK Und.*) a ring. [? SE *fumble*]

famble-cheat *n. see* FAMBLING-CHEAT n.

fambler *n.* (*also* **famble**) [late 17C–early 18C] a dealer in fake 'gold' rings. [FAMBLE n. (2)]

famblers *n.* [17C] a pair of gloves. [FAMBLE n. (1)]

fambling-cheat *n.* (*also* **famble-cheat, fam-cheat**) [mid-16C–early 19C] (*UK Und.*) a ring; a glove. [FAMBLE n. (1)/FAM n.¹ (1) + CHEAT n. (1); lit. 'hand thing']

fam-cloth *n.* [late 17C–18C] a handkerchief. [FAM n.¹ (1) + SE *cloth*]

fam-grasp *v.* [late 17C–18C] to shake hands (and make up one's differences). [FAM n.¹ (1) + SE *grasp*]

familiars *n.* [19C] lice.

family *n.*¹ **1** [mid-18C+] the criminal fraternity; thus FAMILY MAN n. **2** [1910s+] an intimate, whether related by blood or ties of friendship; usu. in phr. *he/she's family* etc. **3** [1950s+] the American Mafia. **4** [1970s] (*US Black*) a pimp and the women who work for him (cf. BROTHER-IN-LAW n.). **5** [1970s+] (*US gay*) the world of homosexuality.

family *n.*² [1940s+] (*US*) crab lice. [note the prostitute's phr.: 'Sleep with that pig and you'll end up with a family to feed']

family disturbance *n.* [19C] (*US, Western*) whisky. [the supposedly deleterious effects of alcohol on family life]

family hotel *n.* [mid-late 19C] a prison (cf. BOARDING HOUSE n.). [FAMILY n.¹ (1) + SE *hotel*]

family jewels *n.* **1** [1910s+] (*also* **jewelry**) the male genitalia. **2** [1950s] wealth, ready money (cf. BRASS n.¹). **3** [1960s] something very valuable.

family man *n.* (*also* **family woman**) **1** [late 18C–1930s] a member of the criminal fraternity, a thief. **2** [early 19C] a receiver of stolen goods. [ext. of FAMILY n.¹ (1)]

family of love *n.* [late 17C–early 19C] prostitutes, considered as a group or occupation. [SE *family of love,* a 16C–17C religious sect, based in Holland, and very popular in England; its main tenets were that religion could best be realized through sex and that all governments, however tyrannical, must be obeyed]

family organ *n.* [1920s–50s] (*US*) the penis. [pun]

family people *n.* [late 18C–mid-19C] thieves, robbers. [FAMILY n.¹ (1) + SE *people;* Vaux glosses this as 'persons living by fraud and depredation']

family plate *n.* [19C] silver coins (cf. BRASS n.¹). [SE *family* + (*silver*) *plate,* silver coins]

family pound *n.* [late 19C] a family grave. [SE *family* + *pound,* an enclosure]

family ram *n.* [1990s+] (*W.I.*) an incestuous male; a man who sleeps with 2 or more female members of the same family. [SE *family* + *ram*/RAM n.¹ (2)]

family style *adv.* [1970s+] (*US prison*) anal intercourse in which

the passive partner's legs are thrown over the head. [it supposedly mimics the 'missionary position' of heterosexual intercourse]

family woman *n. see* FAMILY MAN n.

fam-lay *n.* [18C–19C] shoplifting; thus *fam-layer,* a shoplifter. [FAM n.¹ (1) + LAY n.⁴ (1)]

famm *n. see* FAM n.¹ (1).

fam-snatcher *n.* [early 19C] a glove. [FAM n.¹ (1) + SE *snatcher*]

fam-squeeze *n.* [early 19C] throttling. [FAM n.¹ (1) + SE *squeeze*]

famstrings *n.* [18C] (*UK Und.*) gloves. [FAM n.¹ (1)]

fan *n.*¹ [mid-late 19C] (*Aus./UK Und.*) a waistcoat. [? FANCY, THE n. (1) who sported such garments, or its fan-like expanse across the frame]

fan *n.*² [mid-19C+] the vagina. [abbr. FANNY n.¹ (1)]

fan *v.*¹ **1** [late 18C+] to beat; also in fig. use. **2** [mid-19C+] to run one's hands over a potential victim's clothes to see if they have anything in their pockets that can be stolen. **3** [1910s+] (*orig. US*) to conduct a search of a suspect's clothes, possessions or premises. **4** [1920s+] (*also* **give the fan**) to pick pockets. [all SE *fan,* to wave a fan; but note (1) underpinned by *fan,* to winnow or thresh corn; (1) is US in 20C+; (2), (3) and (4) poss. link to FAM v.]

fan *v.*² **1** [late 19C+] (*US*) to move around quickly, to run, to escape. **2** [20C+] (*US*) to flaunt oneself deliberately to gain sexual interest. **3** [1980s] (*US campus*) to play truant, to miss a class.

fan *v.*³ [1900s–50s] (*US*) to converse, to chat, usu. about sport. [SE *fan,* a supporter; ult. *fanatic*]

fan *v.*⁴ [1970s+] (*US*) to calm someone down.

fanciness *n.* [1990s+] (*W.I.*) luxury items, jewellery, expensive clothing etc.

Fancy, the *n.* **1** [19C] the sporting fraternity. **2** [mid-late 19C] (*Aus./US*) the underworld. **3** [mid-19C–1940s] (*US*) the aristocracy, the wealthy and powerful. **4** [mid-19C+] (*US*) the world of professional boxers. [orig. used of any adherents of a given amusement, thus 1735 J. Moore, *Columbarium* 40: 'These Pigeons by their Flight afford an admirable Satisfaction, to those Gentlemen of the Fancy that have time to attend them']

fancy *n.*¹ **1** [mid-17C–early 18C] the vagina. **2** [early 19C+] a girlfriend; a mistress.

fancy *n.*² *see* FANCY MAN n.².

fancy *adj.* [early 19C] pertaining to boxing or prize-fighting. [FANCY, THE n. (1)]

fancy *v.* **1** [late 17C; late 19C+] to find attractive; esp. in phr. *I could fancy that,* used of a passing attractive member of the opposite sex; thus *fancy the knickers/pants off.* **2** [1920s+] of a gambler, to select as worthy of a bet, usu. of a horse or dog. [SE *fancy,* to take a fancy to]

fancy *adv.* [1940s–50s] fancily, affectedly.

fancy! *excl.* [mid-19C+] an excl. of surprise. [abbr. of SE *fancy me!* *fancy that!*]

fancy-ass *adj.* [2000s] showy, smart. [SE *fancy* + -ASS sfx]

fancy bit *n.* [19C] the vagina; thus a young woman. [SE *fancy*/FANCY n.¹ (1) + BIT n.² (2)]

fancy bloke *n.* **1** [mid-19C] a member of the sporting world. **2** [late 19C+] a male lover, not always adulterous, but the relationship usu. refers to a married or older woman. [SE *fancy*/FANCY, THE n. (1) + BLOKE n. (1)]

fancy cove *n.* [19C] **1** a pimp, a procurer (cf. ABBOT ON THE CROSS n.). **2** a thief. [SE *fancy* + COVE n. (1)]

fancy crib *n.* [20C+] (*US Black*) a fashionable, chic, well-designed home. [SE *fancy* + CRIB n.¹ (1)]

fancy Dan *n.* [1930s+] (*orig. US*) **1** a flashily dressed man, a dandy. **2** a ladies' man. **3** a showy but ineffective sportsman or worker. **4** (*also* **fancy damn**) anything showy. [SE *fancy* + *Dan* as generic for man]

fancy girl *n.* **1** [early 19C+] a man's girlfriend. **2** [early 19C+] the woman with whom a married man is having an affair. **3** [early 19C+] (*US*) a prostitute (cf. AWAYDAY GIRL n.). **4** [1990s+] (*W.I.*) a materialistic woman. [SE *fancy* + *girl;* note US use pre-Civil War *fancy girl*, a slave girl or woman used for the sexual enjoyment of her master]

fancy house *n.* [late 19C–1930s] a whore-house, a house of ill-repute, a brothel (cf. ACCOMMODATION HOUSE n.). [FANCY n.¹ (2) + HOUSE n.¹ (1)]

fancy joseph *n.* [19C] a boy or young man who is a favourite of prostitutes (but not a customer or a pimp). [SE *fancy*/FANCY n.¹ (2) + generic use of Joseph or ? link to JOSEPH n. (2)]

fancy-lay *n.* **1** [19C] the sport of boxing, prize-fighting. **2** [1910s] (*UK Und.*) any form of swindling or robbery. [FANCY, THE n. + LAY n.⁴ (1)]

fancy man *n.*¹ [early–mid-19C] a member of the fashionable sporting world. [FANCY, THE n. (1) + SE *man*]

fancy man *n.*² [early 19C+] **1** (*also* **fancy**) a man who lives on the earnings of a prostitute. **2** (*also* **fancy**) a male lover, not always adulterous, but the relationship usu. refers to a married or older woman; occas. used of male homosexuals. **3** in weak form of (2), a (younger) man who is befriended by a (older) woman. [SE *fancy* + *man*, lit. one who is fancied]

fancy man *n.*³ [1970s+] (*US*) a male homosexual or transvestite. [SE *fancy*, over-adorned, ornamental + *man*]

fancy one's chances *v.* [20C+] to feel confident of success.

fancy oneself *v.* [late 19C+] to have a (smugly) good opinion of oneself. [SE *fancy*, take a liking to]

fancy pants *n.* **1** [1910s+] an overdressed man, erring towards the effeminate in this preoccupation. **2** [1930s+] (*orig. US*) the social élite, the aristocracy; also fig. someone who puts on airs. [SE *fancy* adj. + *pants*]

fancy pants *adj.* [1940s+] smart, pretentious. [FANCY PANTS n. (1)]

fancy pants *v.* [1940s+] **1** to act in an arrogant or supercilious manner. **2** to play around, to 'mess about'. [FANCY PANTS n.]

fancy piece *n.* **1** [early 19C] a prostitute, a mistress. **2** [1920s+] a girlfriend, a 'best girl'. [SE *fancy* adj. + PIECE n.¹ (1); (1) note def. in Egan, *Life in London* (1821): 'A sporting phrase for a "bit of *nice* game" kept in a *preserve* in the suburbs. A sort of Bird of Paradise!']

fancy sash *v.* [20C+] (*Aus.*) to hit. [rhy. sl. = BASH v.¹ (1)]

fancy smile *n. see* SMILE n.¹.

fancy stroll *n.* [1980s+] (*US Black*) the main street on which the high life happens. [SE *fancy* + STROLL n. (1)]

fancy woman *n.* [early 19C+] **1** a man's favourite girl or woman. **2** a prostitute (cf. AWAYDAY GIRL n.; BANKSIDE LADY n.; DOLLAR-WOMAN n.; FIVE-LETTER WOMAN n.; FLASHWOMAN n.; LIGHT WOMAN n.; NEEDLE WOMAN n.; PY-WOMAN n.; SWELL WOMAN n.; WOMAN ABOUT TOWN n.). **3** a mistress, a 'bit on the side'. [SE *fancy* v. + *woman*]

fancy work *n.* **1** [late 19C] prostitution; thus *take in fancy work*, to work secretly as a prostitute. **2** [late 19C] sexual intercourse. **3** [20C+] the (usu. male) genitals and pubic hair. [(1) and (2) play on SEW v. (1)/FANCY n.¹ (1)]

fandangle *n.* **1** [late 19C] nonsense, excessively ornate speech. **2** [1940s+] (*W.I.*) any form of fussy ornamentation, whether of clothes, buildings, automobiles etc. **3** [1940s+] (*W.I.*) stupidity, foolishness.

fandango girl *n.* [mid-19C] (*US*) a prostitute (cf. AWAYDAY GIRL n.). [SE *fandango*, a boisterous, energetic Spanish/Spanish-American dance, which was associated with dancehalls, which, in turn, were seen by their critics as quasi-brothels]

F and blind *v. see* EFF (AND BLIND) v.

fanfoot *n.* [20C+] (*US Black*) a promiscuous woman, one who openly seeks sex; thus *fan-foot*, to play around. [FAN v.² (2) + SE *foot*]

fanfuckingtastic *adj.* [1980s+] absolutely amazing, often ironic. [SE *fantastic* + FUCKING adj. (4)]

fang *n.* **1** [late 18C+] a tooth; also in fig. use, something that 'bites'. **2** [1950s+] the penis; thus *bury the fang*, to have sexual

intercourse. [SE *fang*, an animal tooth; the pointed tapering part of anything which is embedded in something else]

fang *v.*¹ [1910s+] (*Aus.*) **1** to demand money, to cadge, to beg for a loan; thus *put the fang on, put in the fangs*, to beg; *fanging for*, desperate for. **2** to eat. [FANG n. (1); note SE *fang*, to tear or seize with the teeth]

fang *v.*² [1960s] (*Aus.*) **1** to drive fast. **2** to do something fast, to send something quickly. [abbr. of proper name of the Argentine racing driver Juan *Fangio* (1911–95)]

fang artist *n.*¹ [1970s+] (*Aus.*) **1** one who is particularly adept at obtaining loans. **2** a glutton. [FANG v.¹ + ARTIST sfx]

fang artist *n.*² [1970s+] (*Aus.*) a lecher, a womanizer. [FANG n. (2) + ARTIST sfx]

fang-bandit *n.* (*also* **fang-carpenter**) [1950s+] (*Aus.*) a dentist (cf. FANG-FAKER n.; FANG-LIFTER n.). [FANG n. (1) + BANDIT sfx/SE *bandit/carpenter*]

fang-chovey *n.* [mid–late 19C] a dental surgery. [FANG n. (1) + CHOVEY n.]

fang factory *n.* [1970s+] a dental surgery. [FANG n. (1) + SE *factory*]

fang-faker *n.* [late 19C] a dentist (cf. FANG-BANDIT n.). [FANG n. (1) + FAKER n.; cf. 20C+ milit. jargon *fang-farrier*, a dentist]

fang job *n.* [1960s] criticism, esp. a critical article. [FANG n. (1) + JOB n.⁴]

fang-lifter *n.* [1930s] (*US Und.*) a dentist (cf. FANG-BANDIT n.). [FANG n. (1) + SE *lift*]

fangs *n.* [1950s–60s] (*US Black/jazz*) the lips; thus, in fig. use, the equivalent of CHOPS n.¹ (4). [FANG n. (1)]

fanning *n.* **1** [mid-19C] a beating, a thrashing. **2** [1900s–40s] (*US Und.*) a pickpocket's preliminary running of their hands over a victim to find a wallet or bankroll. **3** [1930s] a search of a person, usu. for weapons. [FAN v.¹]

fanny *n.*¹ **1** [mid-19C+] the vagina. **2** [1910s+] (*US*) (*also* **fannie**) the buttocks; thus *fanny-shaker*, a bellydancer. **3** [1920s+] (*US*) one's self. **4** [1990s+] women, considered simply as sex objects. [ety. unknown; E.P. suggests link to *Fanny* Hill, the heroine of John Cleland's *Memoirs of a Woman of Pleasure* (1748–9)]

fanny *n.*² **1** [1910s+] verbal effusiveness, usu. nonsensical. **2** [1920s+] any form of story (poss. mendacious) designed to elicit money, sympathy, provide excuses etc. **3** [2000s] a fit of temper.

fanny *n.*³ **1** [1950s+] (*camp gay*) a proper name, with its sl. allusions, used for a variety of camp nicknames, e.g. *Fanny Fed*, the FBI. **2** [2000s] an idiot.

fanny *v.* [1930s+] to deceive or persuade by glib talk. [FANNY n.² (2)]

fanny about *v.* (*also* **fanny around**) [1970s+] to waste time, to act aimlessly. [euph. FUCK ABOUT v. (1)]

fanny adams *n.*¹ [late 19C–1910s] (*orig. RN*) tinned mutton. [the brutal murder and dismemberment of 8-year-old *Fanny Adams*, at Alton, Hampshire, on 24 August 1867; the murderer, one Frederick Baker, was hanged at Winchester on Christmas Eve; 5000 people watched the execution]

fanny adams *n.*² (*also* **F.A., f.a.**) [1910s+] a euph. for FUCK-ALL n., i.e. nothing, anything meaningless, nonsense, rubbish etc. [initial letters; for ety. *see* prev.]

fanny around *v. see* FANNY ABOUT v.

fanny-artful *n.* (*also* **fanny-fair**) [19C] the vagina. [ext. of FANNY n.¹ (1)]

fanny batter *n.* [1990s+] vaginal secretions (cf. BINDERJUICE n.). [FANNY n.¹ (1) + SE *batter*]

fanny blair *n.* [mid-19C] the hair. [rhy. sl.]

fanny-fair *n. see* FANNY-ARTFUL n.

fanny-flap *n.* [1990s+] the labia (cf. DEW-FLAPS n.). [FANNY n.¹ (1) + FLAPS n. (2)]

fanny flask *n. see* FANNY PACK n.

fanny hat *n.* [1930s–60s] a trilby hat. [FANNY n.¹ (1) + SE *hat*; the dent in its crown, i.e. a euph. for CUNT-HAT n.]

fanny magnet *n.* [1990s+] anything that attracts women, e.g. a very attractive (young) man, an attractive motorcar. [FANNY n.¹ (4) + MAGNET sfx]

fanny merchant *n.* [1990s+] one who offers 'all talk and no action', esp. in the context of sex. [FANNY n.¹ (1) + MERCHANT n.]

fanny mob *n.* [1970s] (*UK Und.*) confidence tricksters. [FANNY n.² (2) + MOB n.² (3)]

fanny nosher *n.* [1990s+] a lesbian (cf. CARPET-BITER n.). [FANNY n.¹ (1) + NOSH v. (2)]

fanny-nudger *n.* [1990s+] a vibrator. [FANNY n.¹ (1) + SE *nudge*]

fanny pack *n.* (*also* **fanny flask**) [1950s+] (*US*) a small pouch-like bag strapped around the wearer's waist (cf. BUM BAG n.). [FANNY n.¹ (2) + SE *pack*]

fanny rag *n.* [1940s+] (*Aus.*) a sanitary towel. [FANNY n.¹ (1) + SE *rag*]

fanny rat *n.* **1** [1940s–50s] a pubic louse. **2** [1990s+] the penis (cf. ANTEATER n.). **3** [1990s+] a sexually promiscuous man. **4** [1990s+] a general term of abuse. [FANNY n.¹ (1) + SE *rat*]

fan one's ass *v.* [1960s+] (*US Black*) **1** to move one's buttocks in an exaggerated manner with the deliberate intention of attracting one's audience sexually; usu. of homosexuals. **2** to move, to walk. [FAN v.² (2) + ASS n. (2)]

fan one's pussy *v.* [1960s+] (*US Black*) of a woman, to flaunt oneself sexually. [FAN v.² (2) + PUSSY n. (2)]

fanqui *n.* [mid-19C] (*Anglo-Chinese*) a European. [lit. 'foreign devil']

fantabulosa *adj.* [1950s+] excellent, perfect. [Polari; SE *fantastic* + f*abulous*]

fantabulous *adj.* [1950s+] incredibly wonderful. [SE *fantastic* + f*abulous*]

fantadlins *n.* [mid-19C] a pastry. [SE *tantoblin*, a sweet tart]

fantail *n.*¹ [19C] a coal-heaver's or dustman's hat, resembling a sou'wester; thus *fantail gentleman*, a coal-heaver. [naut. jargon *fantail*, 'the projecting part of the stern of a yacht or other small vessel when it extends unusually far over the water abaft the stern post' (*Century Dict.*, 1889)]

fantail *n.*² [1960s+] (*US prison*) a highly promiscuous prison homosexual. [FAN ONE'S ASS v. (1) + TAIL n.² (1)]

fantail banger *n.* [late 19C] (*Aus.*) a morning coat. [naut. jargon *fantail* (*see* ety. at FANTAIL n.¹) + BANGER n.²]

fantail-boy *n.* [early 19C] a dustman. [FANTAIL n.¹, i.e. the sou'wester that was part of his 'uniform']

fantailer *n.* [early 19C] a person whose tail coat is excessively long. [SE *fantail*]

fantasia *n.* [1980s+] (*drugs*) **1** MDMA (cf. ECSTASY n.). **2** mescaline. **3** dimethyltryptamine. [the hallucinogenic effects; ult. Disney's *Fantasia* (1940)]

fantastic *adj.* [1930s+] excellent, good beyond expectation. [loose use of the SE]

fantastic plastic *n.* [1990s+] (*Aus.*) a contraceptive sheath, a condom.

fan the breeze *v.*¹ (*also* **fan the air, fan the fire**) [20C+] (*US*) to chatter, to gossip.

fan the breeze *v.*² *see* BREEZE v.¹ (1).

fan the fire *v. see* FAN THE BREEZE v.¹.

fan the hammer *v.* [late 19C] (*US*) to act in a brilliant but unscrupulous manner. [the action of fanning the hammer of a pistol or revolver in order to fire more speedily]

fanti *adj.* [1910s] crazy, insane; thus *go fanti*, to go crazy, to run amok. [SE *go fanti*, to 'go native', to adopt the habits of a native tribe; ult. W. African Fantee, a tribe in Ghana]

fantod *n.* (*also* **fantods, fant-tods**) [19C+] (*US*) **1** a feeling of uneasiness, a feeling of depression. **2** a feeling of excitement. **3** a minor or imaginary disease. **4** diarrhoea. [SE *fantod*, a crotchety way of acting; ult. ? f. *fantasy, fantastic*]

fap *adj.* [late 16C; early 19C] drunk.

far along *adj. see* FAR GONE adj. (3).

far and near *n.* [late 19C–1980s] (*US*) beer. [rhy. sl.]

far away *phr.* [late 19C] in pawn; thus *far away*, to pawn. [the hymn 'There is a happy land, / Far, far away', which was often parodied in such lines as 'Where are my Sunday clothes? / far, far away']

farblondjet *adj.* [20C+] (*US*) confused, lost, astray. [Yid. *farblondzhen*, to lose one's way, to go astray]

farchadet *adj.* [20C+] (*US*) confused, befuddled. [Yid. *fartschadat*, confused; ult. Slavic, *chad*, smoke, daze]

farcing *n.* [late 16C–early 17C] (*UK Und.*) the picking of a lock. [SE *force*]

fardel *n.* [late 19C+] (*Irish*) a farthing. [OE *féorða dæ'l*, fourth part]

farden *n.* [mid-18C+] a farthing. [pron.]

far-down *n.* **1** [mid–late 19C] (*US*) an Irish-American Catholic whose forebears come from Northern Ireland; thus *fardownianism*. **2** [late 19C] (*Aus.*) Ulster. [County *Down*, one of the 6 counties of Northern Ireland]

fare *n.* [1930s+] a male or female prostitute's client. [someone who 'pays for a ride']

Far East Two-step *n.* [1960s] (*US*) diarrhoea; dysentery (cf. APPLE-BLOSSOM TWO-STEP n.; AZTEC HOP n.). [SE *Far East* + pun on SE *trot*/TROTS, THE n.²]

farger *n.* [late 16C–early 17C] (*UK Und.*) a false die. [play on SE *forger*]

far gone *adj.* [mid-19C+] **1** exhausted, worn-out. **2** mad, eccentric, insane. **3** (*also* **far along**) drunk or otherwise intoxicated (cf. ADDLED adj.).

farkakte *adj.* [1930s+] (*US*) unpleasant, disgusting. [synon. Yid.]

Farm, the *n.* [1960s+] (*Aus.*) Monash University, Melbourne. [Monash, which opened in 1961 with 363 students, was orig. set on a rural campus where cows still grazed and wildlife was a common sight]

farm *n.*¹ [late 19C–1930s] a prison infirmary; thus *fetch the farm*, have oneself admitted to the infirmary. [SE *farm*, an institution for poor children]

farm *n.*² [20C+] (*US*) a prison; thus *junk farm*, a federal rehabilitation institution. [abbr. SE *work farm*]

farm *n.*³ [1940s+] (*US*) a psychiatric institution. [abbr. FUNNY FARM n.]

farm *v.* [1970s+] (*US campus*) to drink alcohol; thus *farmed*, drunk. [one 'harvests' the CROP n.²]

farmer *n.*¹ [mid-19C] an alderman. [SE *farm*, to lease or let the proceeds or profits of customs, taxes etc for a fixed payment]

farmer *n.*² **1** [mid-19C+] (*US*) a derog. term for a peasant, an unsophisticated country person, whether an actual farmer or not (cf. ACORN-CRACKER n.). **2** [mid-19C+] a stupid or unsophisticated person; also as adj., foolish. **3** [1940s+] (*US Black*) recently arrived Southern farm workers who persist in their country ways despite the pressing sophistication of the Northern cities.

farmer giles *n.* (*also* **farmers, johnny giles**) [1950s+] (*UK/Aus.*) haemorrhoids. [rhy. sl. = piles]

farmer's alliance *n.* [late 19C] (*US*) pumpkin pie.

farmer's beef *n.* [20C+] (*US*) illegally shot deer, butchered and eaten by its hunter.

farmer's haircut *n.* [20C+] (*US*) a short haircut that leaves a white strip of skin showing between the bottom of the hair and the tanned portion of the neck. [the farmer's outdoor life gives the tan]

farmer's time *n.* [20C+] (*US*) 30 minutes early or fast.

farmer's wine *n.* (*also* **farm liquor**) [20C+] (*US*) illicitly distilled whisky. [joc. euph.]

farmisht *adj.* [20C+] (*US*) confused, mixed up. [Yid. *farmisht*, confused]

farm liquor *n. see* FARMER'S WINE n.

farmyard confetti *n.* [1940s+] (*Aus.*) nonsense, rubbish. [euph. for BULLSHIT n. (1)]

farmyard talk *n.* [late 19C] rude, abusive talk.

faro-bank *v.* [mid-19C; 1940s] (*US Und.*) a form of cheating whereby the victim is allowed to win, but never as much as he loses.

far out *adj.*[1] **1** [1920s+] bizarre, eccentric, strange. **2** [1950s+] extreme.

far out *adj.*[2] [1950s+] (*orig. US Black*) excellent, wonderful, first-rate. [with its implication of 'other-worldliness' – and thus hallucinogenic drugs – the term became a staple of the white HIPPIE n.[2] (3) vocabulary of the 1960s and faded, other than in ironic use, by the 1970s]

far out! *excl.* [1960s+] amazing! remarkable! wonderful! [FAR OUT adj.[2]]

farputst *adj.* [20C+] (*US*) dressed up to excess. [Yid. *farpotshket*, sloppy, messy; ult. Ger. *Patsche*, a slap]

Farringdon hotel *n.* [mid-19C] the Fleet prison, in Farringdon Road, London EC4 (cf. ABBOTT'S PRIORY n.; BOARDING HOUSE n.). [ironic euph.]

farshtinkener *adj.* [1940s+] (*US*) stinking. [Yid.; ult. Ger. *verstinken*, stink up]

fart *n.* **1** [late 14C+] an act of breaking wind. **2** [mid-18C; 1930s+] a fool, an unpleasant person, often older than the speaker; thus synon. *old fart*. **3** [1930s+] as (2), but used affectionately. **4** [1940s] something worthless. **5** [1970s] something important, worthwhile. [FART v. (1)]

fart, a *n.* [17C–18C] a dismissive excl., usu. as *a fart for…*

fart *v.* **1** [late 14C+] to break wind; thus in fig. use. **2** [1970s–80s] (*UK Black*) to suffer. [cognate with various words in Teutonic and Indo-Germanic languages, e.g. Skrt *pard*, MHG *verzen*, ON *freta*, Lithuanian *pérdzu*, Rus. *perdet*]

fart about *v.* (*also* **fart around**) **1** [1910s+] to dawdle, to mess around. **2** [1980s] to irritate. [fig. use of FART v. (1)]

fart along *v.* [1990s+] (*US*) to do something very slowly, without conviction. [fig. use of FART v. (1)]

fart-arse *n.* [1940s+] a general term of contempt, a fool, an incompetent (cf. SILLY-ARSE n.). [fig. use of FART v. (1) + ARSE n.[1] (1)/ASS n. (2)/-ASS sfx]

fart-arse *v.* (*also* **fart-arse around/about**) [1940s+] to dawdle, to mess around, to waste time. [FART-ARSE n.]

fart-arsed *adj.* (*also* **fart-arseing**) [1940s+] useless, incompetent, 'half-baked'. [FART-ARSE v.]

fart box *n.* [1960s+] (*US*) the anus or rectum. [FART n. (1) + SE box/BOX n.[1] (4)]

fartbreath *n. see* FART-FACE n.

fart-catcher *n.* [late 18C–early 19C] a footman. [later var. on CATCH-FART n.]

fart-daniel *n.* [19C] the vagina. [? misprint for dial. *fare-daniel*, a sucking pig that is the youngest of a litter]

farteen *n.* [1960s] (*Irish*) anything totally insignificant. [FART n. (4) + Irish dimin. sfx *-een*]

farter *n.*[1] **1** [mid-17C; 1910s+] one who breaks wind (in a noticeable and even ostentatious manner). **2** [1920s–40s] the anus. [FART v. (1)]

farter *n.*[2] *see* FART-SACK n. (1).

fart-face *n.* (*also* **fartbreath, fart-hammer**) [1930s+] a general term of abuse. [FART n. (1) + SE]

fart-faced *adj.* [1970s+] a general term of abuse. [FART-FACE n.]

fartful *n.* [1970s] a very small or insignificant amount. [FART n. (1)]

fart-hammer *n. see* FART-FACE n.

fart-head *n.* **1** [1960s+] (*US*) a contemptible person. **2** [1990s+] a conservative, traditional old person. [FART n. (1) + -HEAD sfx (1) + play on FAT-HEAD n.]

farthing *n.* [mid–late 19C] worthlessness. [SE *farthing*; thus the minimal value of the coin]

farthing-faced *adj.* [late 19C+] mean-faced, pinched features. ['as insignificant as a farthing' (Ware)]

farthing-faced chit *n.* [1900s] a small, pinch-faced, insignificant person. [FARTHING-FACED adj. + SE *chit*, a brat]

farthing-taster *n.* [late 19C] the smallest available portion of ice-cream as sold by street vendors.

fartick *n.* (*also* **fartkin**) [late 19C] a small act of breaking wind. [FART n. (1)]

farting *adj.* [1930s+] a general pej., piffling, trivial, irrelevant. [FART v. (1)]

farting-crackers *n.* [late 17C–18C] (*UK Und.*) breeches, trousers. [FARTING adj. + CRACKER n.[1] (1)]

farting strings *n.* (*also* **puckering string**) [1910s+] a fig. part of the body, which can be damaged by some form of excess, usu. laughter, e.g. in phr. *If you don't stop that, I'll bust my farting strings!*

farting-trap *n.* [late 19C–1910s] (*Anglo-Irish*) a jaunting car, a light 2-wheeled vehicle carrying 4 people, seated 2 on each side, back to back. [FARTING adj. + SE *trap*]

fartkin *n. see* FARTICK n.

fartknocker *n.* [1950s+] (*US*) **1** an obscure person. **2** a braggart. **3** one who does not know what they are talking about, an idiot. [FART n. (1) + SE *knocker*, i.e. one who *knocks* or makes *farts*; created or at least popularized in the 1990s TV cartoon *Beavis and Butthead*]

fartleberried *adj.* [1940s] a term of disdain. [FARTLEBERRIES n.]

fartleberries *n.* [late 18C+] pieces of excrement clinging to the anal hairs (cf. CLAGNUT n.). [FART n. (1) + joc. use of SE *berries*]

fart-off *n.* [1940s+] (*US*) one who shirks responsibilities, a loafer. [fig. use of FART n. (1)]

fart off *v.* [1960s+] (*US*) to idle, to avoid responsibilities. [FART-OFF n.]

fart-sack *n.* [1940s+] **1** (*also* **farter**) a bed. **2** a term of abuse. [FART n. (1) + SE *sack*]

fart's end *n.* [early 18C] a term of abuse.

fart sparks *v.* [1990s+] (*Aus.*) to be very angry. [FART v. (1) + SE *sparks*]

fart-sucker *n.* [late 19C; 1970s] a toady, a parasite. [fig. use of FART n. (1) + SE *sucker*]

fart through silk *v.* [1920s+] (*US*) to live prosperously, to feel happy, to be important.

fas' *v.* [1950s+] (*W.I. Rasta*) to be fast with, to be rude, impertinent, to meddle with somebody's business, to be forward. [FAASTIE adj.]

fascio *n.* [2000s] (*UK Black/teen*) an antagonistic, hostile person. [? *fascist*]

fash *v.* [early 19C+] (*orig. UK Und.*) to trouble, to bother.

fashion arrest *n.* [1980s+] (*orig. US campus*) a fig. 'arrest' (most likely heavy verbal criticism) of one whose style is considered unacceptably unfashionable; usu. as *make a fashion arrest*. [SE *arrest*; note 'fashion police', journalists and other 'style makers' who determine what is and is not fashionable]

fashion criminal *n.* (*also* **fashion mutant**) [1980s+] (*US campus*) one whose style is considered outside the bounds of acceptable fashion.

fass *v. see* FAAS v.

fast *n.* [1980s+] (*drugs*) amphetamine (cf. A n.[2]).

fast *adj.*[1] [early 19C+] **1** immoral, illegal, corrupt; hedonistic. **2** of a man or woman, promiscuous. **3** of a woman, one who acts in a 'masculine' and thus socially unacceptable/unnerving manner. ['A *fast* man – a person who, by late hours, gaiety and continual rounds of pleasure, lives too fast, and wears himself out […] a *fast* young lady is one who affects mannish habits, or makes herself conspicuous by some unfeminine accomplishment, – talks Slang, drives about in London, smokes cigarettes, is knowing in dogs, horses, &c.' (Hotten, 1859); the *Saturday Review* (28 July 1860) defines a *fast* woman as 'a woman who has lost her respect for men, and for whom men have lost their respect also']

fast *adj.*[2] [mid-19C] in financial difficulties.

fast *adj.*[3] [1940s+] (*W.I.*) **1** interfering, meddlesome. **2** cheeky, rude, impertinent. [FAASTIE adj.]

fast *adj.*[4] [1960s+] (*US Black*) illegal, obtained through crime; thus *get fast*, to act in an illegal manner.

fast *v.*[1] [mid-19C] to be out of pocket. [FAST adj.[2]]

fast *v.*[2] [1950s+] (*W.I.*) to interfere, to meddle. [FAST adj.[3] (1)]

fast alec(k) *n.* [1930s] (*US Black*) anyone who moves fast. [var. on SMART ALEC(K) n.]

fast and loose *n.* [late 16C] a gambling and cheating game, often practised by thimbleriggers, in which a garter is folded and held out to the punter who bets that by pricking with a pin they can hit the place where the material is folded; almost inevitably they fail and lose their money (cf. PRICK THE BELT n.).

fast-ass *adj.* [1930s] (*US*) **1** peremptory. **2** fast, quick. [SE *fast* + -ASS sfx]

fast black *n.* [1960s+] (*UK society*) a black London taxi.

fast buck *n.* (*also* **fast quid, quick buck**) [1940s+] (*orig. US*) money that is earned quickly, and poss. illicitly. [SE *fast* + BUCK n.[3] (3)]

fast-buck *adj.* [1960s+] (*US*) greedy, 'get rich quick'. [FAST BUCK n.]

fast-buck artist *n.* (*also* **fast-buck guy**) [1970s+] (*US*) anyone keen on (and successful in) making a great deal of money. [FAST BUCK n. + ARTIST sfx/GUY n.[2] (1)]

fast dollar boy *n.* [1940s] (*US*) one who is unscrupulous as to the source of their income.

fastener *n.* [late 17C–mid-19C] (*UK Und.*) an arrest warrant.

fast-fast *adj.* [20C+] (*W.I.*) very fast. [redup.]

fast-fast mouth *n. see* FAST-MOUTH adj.

fast food sex *n.* [1980s+] (*US gay*) spontaneous, short-term sex, e.g. that enjoyed in lavatories, bath-houses and similar places of anonymous assignation.

fast fuck *n.* [20C+] **1** sexual intercourse that, through various circumstances, has to be hurried and brief. **2** of a man, one who is unable to delay his own orgasm until his partner is satisfied too; a premature ejaculator. [SE *fast* + FUCK n.[1] (1)]

fast house *n.* [mid-19C–1940s] (*US*) a brothel (cf. ACCOMMODA- TION HOUSE n.). [FAST adj.[1] + HOUSE n.[1] (1)]

fastidious cove *n.* [late 19C] a fashionable swindler who poses as a member of the class he deceives. [ironic use of SE *fastidious* + COVE n. (1)]

fast lane *n.* [1970s+] the active, competitive and ruthless world fought over by those of ambition and intent.

fast lane *v.* [1980s+] (*Aus. prison*) to indulge in a crime spree. [FAST LANE n.]

fast laner *n.* [1990s+] (*US campus*) one who takes illegal hard drugs. [? to live in the FAST LANE n.]

fast life *n.* [1960s+] (*US*) the worlds of gambling, drug-dealing, prostitution etc. [FAST adj.[1] (1)]

fast-mouth *adj.* (*also* **fast-fast mouth**) [1940s+] (*W.I.*) cheeky, impertinent. [FAST adj.[3] (2)]

fastner *n.* [late 17C–mid-19C] a warrant (of arrest).

fast one *n.* [1920s+] any scheme seen as amoral, corrupt, underhand; usu. as PULL A FAST ONE v.

fast quid *n. see* FAST BUCK n.

fast-rod *adj.* [1960s] (*US*) used of one who is quick to use a gun. [SE *fast* + ROD n.[1] (2)]

fast-sheet hotel *n.* (*also* **fast-sheet joint/set-up**) [1940s+] (*US*) a cheap hotel that rents out its rooms by the hour to prostitutes and their clients or to illicit lovers. [the pillows (and beds) are always in use]

fast stuff *n.* [1930s] cheating, swindling. [FAST adj.[1] (1)]

fast-talker *n.* [1930s+] a confidence trickster.

fast-talking charlie *n.* [1960s+] (*US Black*) a Jew, esp. a Jewish storekeeper (cf. FOX IN THE BUSH n.; GOOSE n.[4]; MR MONEY n.; MOCK n.[2]; MOCKIE n.; MOUCHEY n.; NICKELNOSE n.; NUNKY n.;

SCHNEIDER n.; SHONNICKER n.; SLICK-'EM-PLENTY n.; SMOUS n.; THREE BALLS n.). [SE *fast-talking* + CHARLEY n.[4]]

fast track *n.* (*also* **big track**) [1960s+] (*orig. US*) **1** those streets or blocks in a city where prostitutes work; esp., in US, differentiating the East Coast cities from the slower world of the West, esp. California (cf. SLOW TRACK n.). **2** the lifestyle pursued by the ambitious and successful. [TRACK n.[2] (4)]

fast with *adj.* [1950s+] (*W.I.*) cheeky, impertinent. [FAASTIE adj.]

fast worker *n.* (*also* **quick worker**) [1910s+] a successful womanizer, who achieves his seductions quickly; occas. of a woman. [modern use could extend to a sexually active woman, although the nature of male sexuality hardly calls for her to 'work' for sex]

fat *n.*[1] [mid-19C; 1960s] (*Aus.*) money; thus *get the fat off*, to relieve someone of their money, usu. by some form of trickery.

fat *n.*[2] (*also* **fatman, harry fat, Mr Fat**) [late 19C–1950s] (*Aus./N.Z.*) a generic term for the business élite, the wealthiest members of the community.

fat *n.*[3] [1940s–80s] (*mainly gay*) a fat person, esp. as used in small ads.

fat *n.*[4] [1940s+] (*Aus./N.Z.*) an erection; esp. in phr. CRACK A FAT v.

fat *adj.*[1] **1** [17C; mid-19C+] good. **2** [1960s+] a general term of approval, first-rate, excellent. **3** [1970s+] well supplied with drugs.

fat *adj.*[2] **1** [late 17C; late 18C+] substantial; wealthy, rich; thus *fat cull*, a rich man. **2** [20C+] self-obsessed, smug.

fat *adj.*[3] [1950s+] (*US Black*) pregnant.

fat *adv.* **1** [late 19C+] (*US campus*) successfully. **2** [1900s] comfortably. **3** [1960s] very, extremely.

fat ale *n.* [mid-19C] strong beer.

fat and wide *n.* [20C+] a bride. [rhy. sl.]

fat arm *n.* [1960s] (*drugs*) a serious narcotics addiction. [the image of an arm fat enough to take the many injections demanded by such an addiction]

fat around the heart *adv.* [1930s] (*US Black*) cowardly. [fat around the heart clogs the arteries and makes one's blood, fig. courage, flow more slowly]

fat-arse *n.* (*also* **fat-ass**) [1930s+] a very fat person. [FAT-ARSE adj.]

fat-arse *adj.* (*also* **fat-arsed**) [18C+] fat, large-buttocked; also of objects, large. [SE *fat* + ARSE n.[1] (1)/-ARSED sfx[1]]

fat as a buggy-whip *phr.* [19C+] (*US*) very thin.

fat as a match *phr.* [late 19C+] (*US*) very thin.

fat-ass *n. see* FAT-ARSE n.

fat-ass *adj.* (*also* **fat-assed, fat-assing**) (*US*) **1** [1950s+] fat; in fig. use, comfortably off. **2** [1970s+] large. **3** [2000s] money-grabbing, superficial, fake, a general pej. [SE *fat* + -ASS sfx/-ASSED sfx]

fat ass *v.* [1960s+] (*US*) to loaf, to idle. [FAT-ASS adj. (1)]

fat as Sir Roger *adj.* [late 19C] extremely fat. [the weighty Arthur Orton (1834–98), self-styled *Sir Roger* Tichborne, 'star' of the 1871 'Tichborne claimant' case]

fat-brain *n. see* FAT-HEAD n.

fat-brained *adj. see* FAT-HEADED adj.

fat cat *n.* [1920s+] (*orig. US*) any successful, wealthy, influential person; recent UK use has tended to impute a degree of self-serving corruption to such individuals.

fat-cat *adj.* [1950s+] (*orig. US*) prosperous; the implication is that such prosperity has been gained by corruption. [FAT CAT n.]

fatcha *n.* [20C+] (*Ling. Fr./Polari*) the human face; thus *fake the fatcha*, to shave, to put on make-up. [Ital. *faccia*, face]

fat chance *n.* [mid-19C+] no chance at all; also as excl.

fat city *n.*[1] [1960s+] success, wealth, often from criminal activities; also as adj., excellent, splendid. [SE *fat*, abundant, stimulating + CITY sfx]

fat city *n.*[2] [1970s+] (*US*) the process of gaining weight or the state of being fat. [SE *fat* + CITY sfx]

fat cock *n.*[1] [mid-19C] a fat old man. [SE *fat* + COCK n.[4] (1)]

fat cock n.² [late 19C] the labia minora, esp. when prominent. [SE *fat* + COCK n.⁶ (1)]

fater n. (*also* **factor, fayter**) [16C–early 19C] (*UK Und.*) a cheat or impostor; a fraudulent fortune-teller. [Fr. *faiteur*, maker; 'the Second (old) Rank of the Canting Crew' (B.E.)]

fat-face n. [mid-18C] a general term of opprobrium.

fat-fancier n. (*also* **fat-monger**) [19C] a man who prefers plump women.

fat farm n. [1960s+] (*orig. US*) a slimming clinic.

fat-guts n. (*also* **fatgut, gutfatty**) [late 16C+] a term of abuse, used of one who has a fat stomach. [SE *fat* + SE *gut*/GUTS n.¹ (1)/ -GUTS sfx]

fat head n. [1910s+] **1** a hangover. **2** a headache. [SE *fat* + HEAD n.⁵ (1)]

fat-head n. (*also* **fat-brain**) [late 16C; mid-19C+] a fool, an idiot, often used affectionately as well as derog. [SE *fat* + -HEAD sfx (1)]

fat-headed adj. (*also* **fat-brained**) [late 18C+] foolish, stupid (cf. AIRHEADED adj.). [FAT-HEAD n.]

father n. **1** [mid-19C] a receiver of stolen goods. **2** [mid-19C] the owner of a common lodging house. **3** [1960s] (*US drugs*) a large-scale drug dealer. [(1) play on UNCLE n.¹ (1)]

father abraham n. [19C] the penis (cf. ABRAHAM n.¹).

father (and mother) of — phr. (*also* **mama and papa of** —, **mother and father of** —) [mid-19C+] a general intensifier; usu. ...*of a thrashing*, ...*of a row*.

father confessor n. [19C] the penis. [play on SE + ? ref. to popular image of the venal priest]

father-fucker n. [1960s] (*US gay*) a synon. for MOTHERFUCKER n. (1).

father-fucking adj. [1960s] (*US gay*) a synon. of MOTHERFUCKING adj. (1).

father-grabber n. see MOTHER-GRABBER n.

father-grabbing adj. see MOTHER-GRABBING adj.

father of — phr. see FATHER (AND MOTHER) OF — phr.

father-of-all n. [19C] the penis.

Father O'Flynn n. [1960s+] the chin. [rhy. sl.]

father something on someone v. [20C+] to put the blame for something on someone else, to 'pass the buck'.

father time n. **1** [1920s] (*US campus*) an older man (but poss. still attractive). **2** [1940s] (*US prison*) the warden. [(2) play on TIME n.¹]

fat is in the fire, the phr. (*also* **all the fat is in the fire**) **1** [mid-16C–mid-19C] a phr. used to indicate that a plan has failed. **2** [late 19C+] a phr. used to indicate that the result of an action will be to provoke anger.

fat jack of the bone-house n. [mid-19C–1900s] a very fat man. [JACK n.² as a generic + obs. SE *bonehouse*, the human body]

fat knacker n. [1990s+] (*UK juv.*) an unattractive, promiscuous woman. [SE *fat* + KNACKER n. (1)]

fat knot n. [1970s+] (*US Black*) a substantial roll of dollar bills.

fat lip n. **1** [1940s–60s] unpleasant talk. **2** [1940s+] a bruise; the result of a blow.

fat lot n. [mid-19C+] not very much, if anything at all; often as phr. *a fat lot of good* (*that will do*). [an ironic reversal]

fatman n. see FAT n.².

fat meat n. [1940s–60s] (*US Black*) the truth. [phr. *fat meat is greasy*]

fat-monger n. see FAT-FANCIER n.

fatmouth n. [1920s+] (*US Black*) a braggart, a boaster; the quality of being one. [fig. use of SE or lit. trans. of Mandingo *da-ba*, big, fat mouth; thus fig. excessive talking]

fatmouth adj. (*also* **fat-mouthed**) [1960s+] (*orig. US Black*) boastful, noisy, verbose. [FATMOUTH n.]

fatmouth v. [1960s+] (*orig. US Black*) to argue, to answer back, to be cheeky, to talk excessively, to boast. [FATMOUTH n.]

fatness n. [19C] wealth. [FAT adj.² (1)]

fat one n.¹ (*also* **fat 'un**) [19C] an especially noisy breaking of wind.

fat one n.² **1** [1950s–60s] (*US*) a $100 bill. **2** [1990s+] (*US*) a large cigar. **3** [1990s+] (*drugs*) a marijuana cigarette (cf. BONE n.¹¹).

fat on top adj. [1970s+] (*US gay*) **1** intellectual. **2** drunk.

fats n. **1** [1910s–30s] (*orig. US Black*) a generic term for jazz musicians. **2** [1930s+] (*US*) a nickname for anyone seen as overweight.

fat's a-running phr. [late 19C] (*UK Und.*) a phr. used to indicate that a loaded van is passing along the street and may be robbed, to the greatest possible extent, by opportunists.

fat scraps and glorious bits n. [17C] (*UK Und.*) a sound beating.

fat show n. [1930s+] (*N.Z.*) no chance at all.

fatso n. [1930s+] (*orig. US*) a fat person, esp. as a derog. term of address.

fats or fems n. [1970s+] (*gay*) fat or effeminate male homosexuals, as described in gay advertisements.

fat-tailed adj. [1950s] (*US*) overweight. [SE *fat* + TAIL n.² (1)]

fat talk n. [1970s] (*US Black*) nonsense, rubbish.

fat tape n. (*also* **phat tape**) [1990s+] (*US Black teen*) an exceptionally good mix tape. [FAT adj.¹ (2)/PHAT adj. (2) + SE *tape*]

fatten frogs for snakes v. [1950s] to prepare a victim (including oneself) for exploitation by a criminal or trickster.

fattoon n. [1950s] (*W.I.*) a very fat person. [SE *fat* + sfx -*oon*; on model of *octaron*, *quadroon* etc]

fatty n. **1** [early 19C+] a fat person, esp. as a nickname. **2** [1960s+] (*drugs*) (*also* **fattie**) a particularly large marijuana cigarette (cf. BONE n.¹¹).

fatty bum-bum n. [1950s+] (*W.I., Gren./Trin.*) a fat person, esp. a woman with large buttocks. [SE *fatty* adj. + redup. BUM n.¹ (1)]

fatty cake n. [1940s] (*US Black campus*) a plump woman.

fat 'un n. see FAT ONE n.¹.

fatymus n. (*also* **fatyma, fattyma, fattymus**) [mid–late 19C] a fat man or woman. [cod Lat.]

faucet n. [mid-18C; 1980s] (*US*) a penis.

faulkener n. (*also* **faulkner**) (*UK Und.*) **1** [late 17C–18C] one who lures an innocent player into a crooked gambling game. **2** [late 17C–mid-19C] a juggler, a tumbler. [? SE *faulconer*, one who lures his hawks onto his hand or into a cage]

faulties n. [1990s+] (*US Black teen*) a mobile telephone that is being used illegally. [SE *faulty*]

Fauntleroy v. [early 19C] (*US*) to act as a forger. [Henry *Fauntleroy*, a British criminal, hanged for forgery in 1824]

fauny shop n. see FAWNEY SHOP n.

faust n. [1930s–50s] (*US Black*) **1** an ugly person of either sex. **2** a blind date. [? the fictional *Dr Faustus*]

faux n. [1980s+] (*US campus*) a mistake. [abbr. Fr. *faux pas*, a blunder]

faux v. [1980s+] (*US campus*) to make a mistake. [FAUX n.]

fave n. (*also* **fav**) [1930s+] (*orig. US*) a favourite. [abbr.]

fave adj. (*also* **fav**) [1930s+] (*orig. US*) favourite. [abbr.]

fave rave n. [1960s+] (*UK teen*) most favoured person, most enjoyable experience, preferred food etc. [FAVE adj. + RAVE n.¹]

favourite vice n. [late 19C–1910s] one's preferred drink; usu. in phr. *what's your favourite vice?* what would you like to drink?

fawney n. (*also* **fawny, forney, forny**) **1** [late 18C–1900s] a ring. **2** [late 18C–1930s] one who practises the fraud involving bogus jewellery; thus *go on the fawney*; *fawney-man*, a seller of bogus jewellery. [Irish *fáin(n)e*, a ring]

fawney-bouncing n. [mid-19C] selling a ring to a victim; the justification for the sale is a supposed wager, which the seller can win only by selling the ring. [FAWNEY n. (1) + SE *bounce*]

fawney-dropper n. [mid–late 19C] (*UK Und.*) one who practises the FAWNEY-RIG n. [FAWNEY n. (1) + DROP v.² (4)]

fawney-rig n. (*also* **fawney-dropping**) [late 18C–mid-19C] 'A common fraud thus practised. A fellow drops a brass ring, double gilt, which he picks up before the party meant to be cheated, and to whom he disposes of it for less than its supposed, and ten times more than its real, value' (Grose, 1796). [FAWNEY n. (1) + RIG n.² (2)]

fawney shop n. (also **fauny shop**) [1900s] (US Und.) a shop selling fake or cheap jewellery. [FAWNEY n. (1) + SE shop]

fawnied adj. (also **fawned**) [late 18C–mid-19C] wearing more than one ring on a single finger; often as fawnied famm, a ringed hand. [FAWNEY n. (1) (+ FAM n.¹ (1))]

fawny n. see FAWNEY n.

fax the pope v. see PLEASE THE POPE v.

fay n. see OFAY n.

fay adj. see OFAY adj.

fay broad n. [1910s+] (US Black) a light-skinned Black woman or a White woman. [FAY adj. + BROAD n.² (3)]

faygele n. (also **faigelah, fegala, feigele, feygele**) [20C+] (US) a male homosexual. [Yid. feygele, little bird + FAG n.⁵ (1); Yid. Feygel is also a woman's proper name]

fayter n. see FATER n.

fazzled adj. [1920s] (US) disconcerted, worried.

f.b.i. adj. [1970s] (US Black) fat, black and ignorant.

f.b.i.! excl. [1990s+] a general term of abuse, fucking bloody idiot! [abbr.]

f.d.a. v. [2000s] (US Black) to have sexual intercourse. [fuck/fuckin dat ass]

f.d.r. n. (also **roosevelt**) [1930s–60s] (US) an outdoor toilet. [abbr. Franklin Delano Roosevelt (1882–1945); one of the projects of Roosevelt's New Deal WPA programme was the building in deprived rural areas of new outdoor toilets]

f'd up adj. see FUCKED UP adj. (2).

f.e. n. [1990s+] (S.Afr.) a condom. [abbr. French envelope]

feager of loges n. see FAKER OF LOGES n.

feague v. 1 [mid-late 17C] to have sexual intercourse (cf. BANG v.¹). 2 [late 18C–early 19C] to enliven, usu. of a horse. [SE feague, to beat, to whip; ult. Ger. fegen, to polish]

feak n. [early 19C] the posterior, the buttocks. [? link to FEAGUE v.]

fear! excl. [1980s+] (US campus) a negative response to anything the speaker finds distasteful, rather than actually frightening.

fearful adj. [mid-17C; mid-19C–1920s] a general intensifier; thus fearfully.

fearful frights n. [late 19C] a kick in the posterior.

Feargal Sharkey n. [1990s+] a derog. term for a Black person (cf. DAPTO DOG n.). [rhy. sl. = DARKIE n.¹; ult. Northern Irish pop star Feargal Sharkey (b.1958)]

fearnought n. [late 19C] a drink to boost one's morale.

feather n.¹ 1 [late 17C+] pubic hair. 2 [mid-19C] (UK Und.) the hair.

feather n.² [late 19C–1920s] (UK tramp) a bed (cf. FEATHER (AND FLIP) n.). [abbr. SE feather bed]

feather v. [20C+] (US) to curry favour with, to toady to. [phr. feather one's own nest]

feather (and flip) n. [1930s+] a sleep or a bed (cf. FEATHER n.²). [rhy. sl. = KIP n.¹ (2)/KIP n.¹ (4)]

feather-bed n. [late 19C; 1950s] (US) an extremely fat person. [resemblance]

feather bed v. [1920s+] to make things (unfairly) easy for a friend, relation or confederate. [fig. use of the softness of the bed]

feather-bed and pillows n. [19C] a fat woman. [resemblance]

feather-bedding n. [20C+] the practice of making things easy for one's associates, handing out easy 'jobs for the boys'. [FEATHER BED v.]

feather-bed jig n. [late 18C–19C] sexual intercourse.

feather-bed lane n. [late 17C–18C] a notably rough road or track. ['particularly that betwixt Dunchurch and Daintrie' (B.E.)]

feather-bed soldier n. 1 [late 19C] (US) a soldier who avoids hard tasks. 2 [1910s] a womanizer, a lecher.

featherbrain n. see FEATHERHEAD n. (2).

feather-brained adj. see FEATHER-HEADED adj.

feather-driver n. [late 16C–early 17C] a clerk. [his quill pens]

feather-duster n. [1920s] (US) a style of facial whisker.

feathered oof-bird n. [late 19C–1920s] a source or supplier of a large amount of money. [ext. of OOF-BIRD n.]

featherhead n. (US) 1 [mid-19C+] a Native American. 2 [mid-19C+] (also **featherbrain**) a scatterbrain (cf. AIRBALL n.). 3 [20C+] one who takes foolish chances. [SE feather + (1) SE head; (2), (3) -HEAD sfx (1)]

feather-headed adj. (also **feather-brained**) [mid-17C; 20C+] (US) scatterbrained. [FEATHERHEAD n. (2)]

feather-legged adj. [1930s+] (US) terrified, extremely frightened. [i.e. one's legs are shaking like feathers in the wind]

feather-merchant n. [1930s+] (orig. US milit.) 1 a physical weakling. 2 a foolish, silly person. 3 a shirker. [(1) his physical size; (2) and (3) he does not 'pull his weight']

feather-plucker n. [1940s+] a general term of abuse, usu. used to refer to someone unpleasant. [euph. rhy. sl. = FUCKER n. (3)]

feathers n.¹ 1 [early 17C; mid-19C] wealth, money (cf. ACTUAL, THE n.). 2 [late 19C+] (US) fancy clothes; thus fine feathers. [SE phr. feather one's nest; ? they help you fly]

feathers n.² [mid-19C+] (US) a bed; thus a date with the feathers, bedtime; hit the feathers, to go to bed.

feathers n.³ [1940s+] facial or body hair.

feathers n.⁴ see HORSEFEATHERS n.

feather up v. [1930s–50s] (US) to prepare to fight. [the action of birds]

featherweight n. see LIGHTWEIGHT n. (1).

featherweight adj. see LIGHTWEIGHT adj.

featherwood n. [1990s+] (US prison) 1 a White prisoner's wife or girlfriend. 2 a White female inmate. [play on PECKERWOOD n.; or ? she 'flies in and out' of the jail or is clad in metaphorical feminine feathers]

feature n. [1960s–70s] (Aus.) an act of sexual intercourse. [FEATURE WITH v.]

feature v. 1 [1920s+] (US) to note, to pay attention to, to understand; often as feature this. 2 [1950s+] to like, to appreciate.

features n. [late 19C–1900s] a term of address, e.g. Hello, features.

feature with v. [1960s+] (orig. Aus.) to seduce a compliant woman. [coined by the Aus. comedian and writer Barry Humphries (b.1934) for his strip character Barry Mackenzie]

feaze v. see FEEZE v.

February adj. [1990s+] unfashionable.

feck see also under FUCK and its combs.

feck v. 1 [late 18C–mid-19C] (UK Und.) to ascertain the best method of committing a robbery. 2 [late 19C] (Irish/Scot.) to steal. [? OE feccan, to fetch; Ger. fegen, to plunder]

feckins!/fecks! excl. see FUCK! excl.

Fecky the Ninth n. [2000s] (Irish) an utter fool.

Fed n. (also **fed**) 1 [late 18C–early 19C] (US) a Federalist. 2 [mid-19C] (US) a supporter of the Northern cause in the US Civil War, fighting for federal rather than states' rights. 3 [1910s+] (US) (also **Federales**) a member of the Federal Bureau of Investigation, often in pl. 4 [1950s+] (US) the Federal governent. 5 [1960s+] (Aus.) a federal police officer. 6 [1970s+] (Aus.) a member of the Federal government. 7 [1990s+] (US campus) money, i.e. Federal dollar bills. 8 [1990s+] (UK Black/teen) a policeman. [abbr.]

Fed adj. [1950s+] (US) pertaining to the federal government. [FED n. (4)]

fed adj. see FED UP adj.

feddy n. [2000s] (US Black) money. [FED n. (7)]

federal adj. 1 [1990s+] used of something of exceptional quality or of an extreme nature. 2 [2000s] (US teen) criminal. [SE federal, pertaining to the federal, i.e. national rather than state (local) government]

federal building n. [1940s–60s] (US) an outdoor toilet (cf. ALTAR n.).

Federales *n. see* FED n. (3).

federal joint *n.* [1950s+] (*US Und.*) a federal, rather than state, prison. [SE *federal* + JOINT n.⁴ (8)]

federating *n.* [1900s–50s] (*Aus.*) having sexual intercourse. [SE *federate*, to join together]

fedex *n.* [1990s+] (*US Black teen*) an individual who pays debts quickly. [popular abbr. for the *Federal Express* courier company]

feds *n.* [1990s+] (*US prison*) a federal, rather than a state, prison.

fed up *adj.* (*also* **fed**) [20C+] irritated, annoyed, bored; ext. as *fed up to the back teeth*, *fed to the teeth* and (*orig. milit.*) *fed up*, *fucked up* and *far from home*.

fed up *v.* [1910s–30s] (*Aus./US*) to annoy. [FED UP adj.]

fed with a fire-shovel *phr.* [late 18C–19C] a phr. used of someone who has a notably wide mouth.

fedy *adj.* [1990s+] (*US Black*) aggressive. [FEDERAL adj. (1); ult. abbr. *Federal* (Bureau of Investigation)]

Feeb *n.* (*also* **Feebee, Feebie, Phoebe**) [1920s+] (*US*) the FBI, an FBI agent.

feeb *n.* [1910s+] a feeble, useless person. [FEEB adj.]

feeb *adj.* [1910s+] *feeble.* [abbr.]

Feebee/Feebie *n. see* FEEB n.

feeblo *n.* [1930s–50s] (*US prison*) **1** one who is mentally impaired. **2** a drug addict. [SE *feeble* + -O sfx (2)]

fee-chaser *n.* [20C+] (*US*) a lawyer. [their supposed primary interest]

feed *n.* **1** [early 19C+] food and drink, usu. as served in a meal, esp. a substantial one. **2** [1940s–50s] (*US drugs*) drugs.

feed *v. see* FEED (SOMEONE) A LINE v.

feedback *n.* [1970s] (*US*) cheek, insolence.

feed bag *n.* **1** [1900s] (*Aus.*) the face; the mouth. **2** [1960s+] (*drugs*) a container for narcotics or marijuana.

feed box *n.* [20C+] **1** the mouth; usu. in STRAIGHT FROM THE FEED BOX phr. **2** food, a meal. [horseracing imagery]

feeder *n.*¹ [18C–19C] (*UK Und.*) a (silver) spoon.

feeder *n.*² **1** [1900s–20s] (*US*) the mouth or throat. **2** [1950s–70s] (*US drugs*) a hypodermic syringe.

feeder-prigger *n.* [late 18C–19C] (*UK Und.*) a thief specializing in silver spoons. [FEEDER n.¹ + PRIGGER n.¹ (1)]

feed from home *v.* [late 16C–early 17C] to commit adultery.

feed (hot) lead *v.* [1940s–50s] (*US*) to shoot, usu. to shoot dead. [LEAD n.¹ (1)]

feeding *n.* [20C+] (*W.I.*) **1** sexual intercourse. **2** a woman with whom a man wishes to have sex.

feeding birk *n.* [late 19C] (*UK Und.*) a cookshop. [SE *feeding* + ? *barrack*]

feeding bottles *n.* [20C+] the female breasts (cf. BORDENS n.).

feed joint *n.* [1900s–10s] (*US*) a café or restaurant. [SE *feed* + JOINT n.¹ (3)]

feed one's face *v.* **1** [late 19C+] to eat, esp. to stuff oneself with food; thus *face-feeding*, over-eating; *feed someone's face*, to feed someone else. **2** [1980s+] to indulge in oral sex.

feed one's habit *v.* [1950s+] (*drugs*) **1** to inject oneself with a narcotic, usu. heroin. **2** habitually to consume any drug or alcohol. [HABIT n. (1)]

feed one's pussy *v.* [19C+] of a woman, to have sexual intercourse (cf. CATCH AN OYSTER v.). [SE *feed* + PUSSY n. (2); play on SE]

feed pap with a hatchet *v.* (*also* **give pap with a hatchet**) [late 16C–early 18C] to perform a kind act in an unkind manner, to be 'cruel to be kind'. [SE *pap*, baby food; thus one feeds the baby (a kindness) with a hatchet (a cruelty)]

feed (someone) a line *v.* (*also* **feed**) [1950s+] to deceive through a cunning story or excessive charm, to persuade, to talk smoothly. [SE *feed* + LINE n.¹ (3)]

feed someone chunks *v.* [late 19C] (*US campus*) to attempt verbal deception.

feed someone stuff *v.* [1970s+] (*US Black*) to deceive, to pass on false (and self-serving) information.

feed the bears *v.* [1970s+] (*orig. Citizen's Band radio*) to pay a parking fine, to get a parking ticket. [SE *feed* + BEAR n.⁷]

feed the ducks *v.* [1990s+] (*US*) to masturbate (cf. BEAT ONE'S HOG v.). [the similarity in hand motions]

feed the dumb glutton *v.* [19C] to have sexual intercourse. [SE *feed* + DUMB GLUTTON n.]

feed the dummy *v.* [19C] to have sexual intercourse. [FEED THE DUMB GLUTTON v.]

feed the fishes *v.* **1** [19C+] to die by drowning. **2** [late 19C+] (*US*) to vomit, esp. over the side of a ship.

feed the goldfish *v.* (*also* **feed the kippers**) [20C+] (*US*) to vomit, esp. over the side of a ship. [FEED THE FISHES v. (2)]

feed the monkey *v.*¹ (*also* **scratch the monkey**) [1950s+] (*drugs*) to maintain one's addiction to narcotics. [MONKEY n.¹² (1)]

feed the monkey *v.*² *see* MONKEY n.¹⁰ (1).

feed the pigeons *v.* [2000s] to masturbate (cf. BEAT ONE'S HOG v.). [the image of a hand shaking out breadcrumbs]

feed the pony *v.* [1990s+] the digital stimulation of a woman's genitals.

feed the roots of daisies *v.* [1930s] to die. [var. PUSH UP (THE) DAISIES v.]

feed the worms *v.* [mid-19C+] to die. [although the image dates to the early 17C, the sl. use is modern]

feed with a spoon *v.* [1910s–20s] to bribe.

fee-faw-fum *n.* [19C] nonsense, esp. bloodthirsty, threatening nonsense. [the favoured phr. of the Giant in the nursery tale of Jack the Giant-Killer]

feel *n.* [late 19C+] an act of sexual groping. [FEEL v. (1)]

feel *v.* **1** [mid-17C+] to caress sexually, whether or not the advance is desired. **2** [1960s+] (*US Black*) to empathize with. **3** [1990s+] to arrest.

feel a draught *v.* (*also* **feel a draft**) **1** [1920s+] to feel a general sense of hostility. **2** [1920s+] to feel insecure, esp. financially. **3** [1930s–40s] (*US Black*) to sense racial antagonism in one's conversation or dealings with Whites; thus *drafty*, unfriendly to Blacks. **4** [1930s–40s] (*US Black*) to warn one's friends that a White person has entered the room. [the phr. is generally credited to the jazz musician Lester Young (1909–59)]

feel all round my hat *v.* (*also* **feel all around my hat**) [mid-19C–1910s] to feel unwell. [? ballad 'all round my hat I wears a green willow'; thus ? ref. to the green pallor of an ill complexion]

feel as if a cat had kittened in one's mouth *v.* [late 19C+] to feel the nauseous after-effects of drinking the morning after.

feel cheap *v.* [late 19C–1930s] to feel ill, esp. hungover; often as *feel very cheap*. [SE *feel* + CHEAP adj. (1)]

feel day *n.* [1910s+] (*Can.*) heavy petting. [FEEL n. + SE *day*; a pun on SE *field day*]

feele *n.* (*also* **feelia, feelier**) [mid-19C] (*Ling. Fr./Polari*) a child; thus *donah and feeles*, a woman and (her) children; *feele omi*, a young (and poss. underage) man. [Ital. *figlie*, children]

feeler *n.*¹ [mid-19C] (*US*) a knife or other pointed weapon. [the victim *feels* the point]

feeler *n.*² **1** [mid-19C] (*US Und.*) a small boy who pilfers small items, then hands them over to his elders in a gang for sale to a junk-shop. **2** [late 19C+] a hand. **3** [1910s+] a finger, usu. in pl.

feel fine *n.* [1980s+] £9. [rhy. sl.]

feel froggy *v.* (*also* **feel froggish**) [1970s+] (*US Black*) to feel like fighting; thus the challenge *if you feel froggy/froggish, leap!* [FROGGY adj.²]

feel funny *v.* **1** [early 19C+] to feel (unpleasantly) drunk. **2** [mid-19C+] to feel very emotional. **3** [20C+] to feel ill.

feel good *v.* (*orig. US*) **1** [mid-19C+] to feel in good spirits or health. **2** [late 19C+] to feel mildly drunk (cf. ABOUT RIGHT phr.¹).

feelia/feelier *n. see* FEELE n.

feelies *n.* [1980s–90s] sexual petting (and intercourse). [FEEL n.]

feelies, the *n.* [1940s+] (*Aus.*) petting in a darkened cinema. [FEEL n.]

feeling no pain *phr.* **1** [1920s+] drunk (cf. ABOUT RIGHT phr.[1]). **2** [1950s+] unconcerned, casual; a state achieved with or without drugs. [i.e. anaesthetized (by liquor)]

feeling right royal *phr.* [late 19C+] drunk (cf. ABOUT RIGHT phr.[1]). [SE *feeling* + RIGHT adv. (2) + SE *royal*]

feel in one's pocket for one's big hairy rocket *v.* [20C+] to masturbate.

feel like *v.* [mid-19C+] (*orig. US*) to desire, to have an inclination for.

feel like a ball of string *v.* (*also* **feel like a bag of string**) [1950s] (*Aus.*) to feel exhausted. [pun on Aus. phr. a *ball of muscle*, an energetic person, but note possible pun on phr. *all wound up*, emotional, tense]

feel like a boiled rag *v.* (*also* **feel like a piece of chewed rag/string**) [20C+] to feel ill.

feel like a (fresh-)boiled owl *v.* (*also* **feel like a stewed monkey/witch**) [mid-19C–1900s] (*US*) to be extremely hungover, to be very exhausted, run-down.

feel like a million dollars *v.* (*also* **feel like a million big ones, ...bucks, ...seeds**) [1920s+] (*orig. US*) to feel excellent, very cheerful, extremely well, in the best of spirits; thus *taste like a million*, to taste very good (cf. LOOK LIKE A MILLION DOLLARS v.).

feel like death warmed up *v.* (*also* **feel like a warmed-up corpse, ...death on a bun/cracker**) [1910s+] to feel absolutely appalling, often used by those suffering from hangovers (cf. LOOK LIKE DEATH WARMED UP v.).

feel like shit *v.* (*also* **feel shit/shitty**) [1940s+] to feel very bad, whether emotionally or physically (cf. LOOK LIKE SHIT v.). [SE *feel like* + SHIT n.[1] (2)]

feel like thirty cents *v. see* LIKE THIRTY CENTS phr.

feel moldy *v.* [1980s+] (*US campus*) to feel humiliated, embarrassed. [SE *mouldy*]

feel much of an onion *v.* [1910s–20s] to feel bored. [one is 'bored to tears']

feel no way *phr.* [1950s+] (*W.I. Rasta*) don't take offence, don't be sorry, don't worry.

feel off *v.* [1970s+] to manipulate a sexual partner to orgasm. [FEEL v. (1) + *off* used to imply agency as in JERK OFF v.[1] etc]

feel oneself *v. see* ONESELF, BE v.

feel one's hell rise *v.* [1920s] (*US Black*) to become angry.

feel one's keeping *v.* [20C+] (*US*) to be in good health. [SE *keeping*, taking care, maintaining in good condition]

feel one's piss *v.* [1940s] to become infatutated with one's own importance. [fig. use of PISS n. (1) as in PISS AND VINEGAR n.]

feel one's stuff *v.* [1930s–50s] (*US Black*) to base one's actions or speech on one's most intense and sincere emotions.

feel one's way to heaven *v.* [late 19C–1910s] to caress a woman, becoming increasingly intimate. [SE *feel one's way* + HEAVEN n.]

feel shit/shitty *v. see* FEEL LIKE SHIT v.

feel someone's collar *v.* [1950s+] (*UK Und.*) to arrest, to place under suspicion. [the physical act of grabbing a villain]

feel the draught *v.* **1** [1920s] to be inconvenienced, suffering the consequences of something. **2** [1940s+] to have serious money problems.

feel the miss of *v.* [mid-19C–1900s] to long for something. [prior use was SE]

feel the steel *v.* [1980s+] (*Aus. prison*) to inject heroin. [COLD STEEL n.]

feel up *v.* [20C+] to caress (usu. a woman) sexually.

feel-up *n.* [1980s+] an intimate caress, usu. of a woman by a man. [FEEL UP v.]

feero *n.* [1930s] (*US prison*) an arsonist.

feese *see under* FEEZE.

feet-casements *n.* [mid-19C–1910s] boots, shoes. [SE *feet* + *casement*, a frame]

feet uppermost *adj.* [19C+] used to describe a woman lying supine, in the sexual 'missionary position'.

feevee *n.* [1910s] (*US*) $15. [pron. of SE]

feeze *n.* (*also* **feese, pheeze**) [mid-19C] (*US*) a state of worry or alarm. [SE *feeze*, to frighten, to put into a state of alarm]

feeze *v.* (*also* **feaze, feese, feize, pheeze**) [17C] to have sexual intercourse (cf. BANG v.[1]). [SE *feeze*, to beat, to flog; ult. OE *fesian*, to drive]

fegala *n. see* FAYGELE n.

fegary *n.* (*also* **fagery, figary, flagary**) **1** [17C; late 19C+] a prank, a freak, a whim, an eccentricity. **2** [early 18C–early 19C] in pl., trinkets, trifles, adornments of dress. [SE *vagary*]

fegary *v.* (*also* **flagary**) [early 19C] to concern oneself about trifles in dress; thus *figaried up*, dressed up. [FEGARY n. (2)]

fegs! *excl. see* FUCK! excl.

feh true *adv.* (*also* **for true**) [20C+] (*orig. W.I.*) a general intensifier, in all honesty, without a doubt.

feigele *n. see* FAYGELE n.

feint *n.* [mid-19C] (*UK Und.*) a pawnbroker.

feist *n.* [20C+] (*US*) a truculent, short-tempered person or animal. [FEISTY adj. (1)]

feisty *adj.* **1** [late 19C+] (*orig. US*) truculent, irascible, impertinent. **2** [20C+] (*orig. US*) (*also* **fisty**) of young women, flirtatious (to a greater extent than the speaker sees as proper), showing off, putting on airs, of dubious morality etc. [SE *fist*, a small dog; thus having the characteristics of such a yappy, snappy, energetic creature; the dog shares an ety. with 15C *fist*, a foul smell, the breaking of wind, but whether, as Wentworth & Flexner suggest in *Dict. American Slang* (1960, 1975), the dog was so named because one's own smells could be blamed upon it remains debatable. Equally feasible is the 19C suggestion that such dogs were not much bigger than a man's fist. Note dial. *feist*, to strut about, to flirt or show off]

feize *v. see* FEEZE v.

feke *n.* [1910s–30s] methylated spirits; thus *feke-drinker*, a drinker of 'meths'. [*feke* = *fake*, i.e. fake alcohol]

fel *n.* [mid-19C] (*US*) a fellow, a chap, as a term of address. [abbr. SE *fellow*]

felch *v.* [1970s+] (*mainly gay*) to lick out the semen from the anus of someone who has just been sodomized; the semen is then often spat into the partner's mouth (cf. AUSTRALIAN n.). [? echoic; but note suggestion by the linguist Laura Wright (in personal correspondence): '"Filch" [FILCH v.] originally meant to hook something out of something with a stick according to the OED and in the Bridewell it always involves the hooking of something with a stick covered in sticky lime, so when I heard about modern 'felch' [...] I figured that the two variants have a common source, and the usual P-DE meaning has lost the sense of hooking and kept the sense of stealing, whereas the homosexual sense has kept the sense of hooking and lost the sense of stealing']

felcher *n.* [1970s] (*gay*) a man who ejaculates into another man's rectum and then eats all of what he has deposited there. [FELCH v.]

felch queen *n.* [1970s+] a male homosexual who is stimulated by *felching*. [FELCH v. + QUEEN n.[2] (1)/QUEEN sfx (2)]

felicia *n.* [1970s+] (*US gay*) a fellator. [SE *fellatio* + ? ref. to FELIX n.[1]]

Felipe *n.* [1980s] (*US Black*) a familiar name for a Chicano or Latino (cf. BATO n.). [the common Latino name]

felix *n.[1]* [1950s] the penis. [ety. unknown; ? a nonce-word coined by Colin MacInnes in his novel *Absolute Beginners* (1959)]

felix *n.[2]* [1950s+] (*W.I.*) a very large, tough dumpling. [? the cartoon character *Felix* the Cat (1931), known for his toughness; or ? onomat., the dumpling makes a noise like 'flix' when one bites it]

fellow *n.[1]* **1** [late 19C+] one's husband or regular male partner.

2 [1960s+] (*US gay*) a lesbian. **3** [1970s+] (*US gay*) an effeminate homosexual.

fellow *n.*² [1930s–40s] (*US Black*) a White person. [deliberate reversal of dismissive White description of a 'Black fellow']

fellow, a *n.* (*also* **a chap**) [mid-19C+] oneself, e.g. *a fellow ought to get drunk once in a while.*

fellow commoner *n.* [late 18C] an empty bottle (cf. GENTLEMAN COMMONER n.). [orig. Cambridge University use; as opposed to scholars, commoners were 'not in general considered as over-full of learning' (Grose, 1785)]

fellow-feeling *n.* [late 19C–1950s] a ceiling. [rhy. sl.]

felon fodder *n.* [2000s] (*US prison*) prison inmates (seen as an indistinguishable mass).

felon swell *n.* [early–mid-19C] (*Aus.*) a gentleman convict. [SE *felon* + SWELL n. (1)]

felony shoes *n.* (*also* **felony flyers**) [1980s+] (*US*) any brand of the high-priced trainers (Nike, Adidas etc) worn by teenagers. [the term is implicitly racist, suggesting that the (orig. Black) teenagers who particularly favour such footwear are automatically up to no good]

feloose *n.* (*also* **faloose, falouse, feloos, felooze, filoose, fils**) [1910s–40s] (*N.Z.*) money. [synon. in Arabic]

felt-head *n. see* CLOTH-HEAD n.

fem *see also under* FEMME.

fem *n. see* FAM n.¹ (1).

female unit *n. see* UNIT n. (4).

fembo *n.* [1980s+] (*US campus*) a homosexual man. [SE *female* + BIMBO n. (1)/? proper name of the 1980s macho film hero *Rambo*]

feme *n. see* FAM n.¹ (1).

fem fatale *n.* [1990s+] (*US gay*) an overtly effeminate male homosexual. [adopted SE *femme fatale*]

femme *n.* (*also* **fem**) (*orig. US*) **1** [late 19C+] a young woman. **2** [1930s+] (*also* **femmie**) an effeminate homosexual man. **3** [1940s+] a feminine lesbian. **4** [1960s+] the 'female' partner of a couple whether hetero- or homosexual. [Fr. *femme*, a woman; note West Point jargon *femme*, a young woman; note synon. use for (1) in Kendall, *Flowers of Epigrammes* (1577): 'Which are three ills that mischief men […] The fem, the flud, the fire']

femme *adj.* (*also* **fem**) **1** [20C+] female. **2** [1930s+] (*gay*) used of an effeminate male homosexual. **3** [1940s+] (*gay*) used of a 'female' lesbian. [FEMME n.]

femo *n.* [2000s] (*Aus.*) a *fem*inist. [abbr. + -o sfx (4)]

fen *n.* (*UK Und.*) **1** [late 17C–early19C] a prostitute; thus *fag the fen*, beat the prostitute. **2** [18C–early 19C] a madame, a procuress. **3** [late 18C] a receiver of stolen goods. [SE *fen*, a marshy bog; the image is of the 'dirtiness' of the prostitute or the receiver]

fen *v. see* FEND v.

fen! *excl.* [mid–late 19C] a call for a truce during a game, a statement that one is ineligible for a given duty or command. [SE *fen*, to forbid, ult. ? f. *fend*, forbid]

fenagle *v. see* FINAGLE v.

fence *n.*¹ **1** [17C+] a receiver and seller of stolen property; also attrib. **2** [mid-19C–1960s] (*US Und.*) the place where stolen goods are received, kept and sold. **3** [2000s] (*Aus.*) a procurer of the sexually complaisant for customers who prefer something 'out of the ordinary'. [? as a middleman he provides a *fence* between the thief and the buyer of the goods]

fence *n.*² [1910s] (*US*) a man's detachable collar. [i.e. the collar provides a *fence* around the neck]

fence *v.* **1** [17C+] to buy and sell stolen property. **2** [late 17C–early 18C] to spend money. [FENCE n.¹ (1)]

fence con *n.* [20C+] (*US prison*) an escapee, a prisoner who is planning an escape. [SE *fence* + CON n.¹ (8)]

fence-corner *adj.* [20C+] (*US*) illegitimate; thus *fence-corner child*, an illegitimate child; *hatched on a fence post*, illegitimate.

fence-jumping *n.* [1990s+] (*N.Z.*) race mixing. [farmyard imagery, i.e. a bull *jumping* a *fence* to reach the cows]

fence master *n.* [early 17C–18C] (*UK Und.*) a receiver and seller of stolen goods. [FENCE v. (1) + SE *master*]

fence parole *n.* [1990s+] (*US prison*) the attempt to make an escape by climbing the prison fence or wall; such efforts, inevitably, lead to death.

fencer *n.* [17C–19C] a receiver and seller of stolen property. [FENCE v. (1)]

-fencer *sfx* [19C] a (street) seller of various commodities (cf. BILLY-FENCER n.; BLINK-FENCER n.; BOOZE-FENCER n.; BROAD-FENCER n.; CAKEY-PANNUM FENCER n.; CHAUNT-FENCER n.; CHIVE-FENCER n.; CRACK-FENCER n.; DUMP-FENCER n.; JEW-FENCER n.; LETTER-FENCER n.; SPUNK-FENCER n.; STIFF-FENCER n.; STRETCHER-FENCER n.; SWELL-FENCER n.; TAX-FENCER n.; TOG-FENCER n.; TOP-FENCER n.). [weak use of FENCER n.]

fence rail *n.* [20C+] (*US*) a very thin person. [dimensions of a fence rail]

fence-shop *n.* [late 18C] a shop where stolen property is on sale. [FENCE n.¹ (1)]

fencing *n.* [late 18C+] receiving or dealing in stolen goods. [FENCE v. (1)]

fencing crib *n.* (*also* **crib**) [19C–1900s] the shop, house or room from which a receiver operates. [FENCING n. + CRIB n.¹ (1)]

fencing cully *n.* [mid-17C–18C] a receiver and seller of stolen goods. [FENCING n. + CULLY n. (3)]

fencing ken *n.* (*also* **ken**) [late 17C–19C] the shop, house or room from which a receiver operates. [FENCING n. + KEN n.¹ (1)]

fend *v.* (*also* **fen**) [1920s–30s] (*US Black*) to *defend*. [abbr.]

fender-bender *n.* **1** [1960s+] (*US*) a minor automobile accident. **2** [1970s+] (*drugs*) a barbiturate capsule (cf. BARBIT n.). [SAmE *fender* (UK bumper) + *bender*; the effects of (2) are likely to cause (1)]

fenderhead *n.* [1970s] a fool.

fend off *v.* [1930s] (*N.Z.*) to take, to steal. [one *fends off* the object from its owner so that one may keep it oneself]

feng *v.* [mid-16C] (*UK Und.*) to steal. [Anglo-Saxon *feng*, a gasp, a hug]

Fenian *n.*¹ (*also* **cold Irish, three cold Irish**) [late 19C] threepennyworth of whisky and water; thus generic for any quantity of whisky. [a pun on 'three cold Irish', itself referring to the hanging of the Fenians Allen, Larkin and O'Brien for the 'Manchester Murder' of PC Brett in 1867 or for 3 men, also Fenians, hanged for the Phoenix Park murders of Lord Frederick Cavendish and Thomas Henry Burke, Under-Secretary for Ireland, on 6 May 1882]

Fenian *n.*² [1910s+] (*Ulster*) a Protestant term of abuse, used of Ulster Catholics/nationalists. [SE *Fenian*, a member of the mid–late 19C Fenian Brotherhood; ult. Irish *na Fianna*, the legendary warrior band led by Fionn Mac Cumhail]

fenky-fenky *adj.* [1940s+] (*W.I.*) **1** cowardly, effeminate, 'crybabyish'. **2** ordinary. [? SE *finicky* + redup.]

fenneh *v.* [1950s+] (*W.I. Rasta*) to feel physical distress or pain. [Twi *fene*, to vomit; Fante *fena*, to be troubled; Lumba *feno*, to faint]

fen nightingale *n.* [late 18C–19C] a frog (cf. CAMBRIDGE NIGHTINGALE n.). [the large population of frogs in England's marshy fenlands]

feral *adj.* [2000s] (*Aus.*) disgusting. [SE *feral*, savage, untamed]

ferchrissakes! *excl. see* FOR CHRIST'S SAKE! excl.

ferculate *v.* [1990s+] (*W.I.*) a mild obscenity meaning to mess about. [i.e. FUCK ABOUT v. (1)]

fergler *n. see* FURGLE v.

feria *n.* [1960s+] (*US*) money. [SE *fare* + Hispanic sfx *-ia*]

feringee *n.* [17C–19C] (*Anglo-Ind.*) a foreigner, a European. [Arabic *faranji*, a Frank, a European]

ferk *v.* [17C; 1920s+] lit. to dance about, but used as a euph. for

FUCK v.[1]. [SE *firk/ferk*, to move about briskly; to dance, to frisk about; note D'Urfey, *Pills to Purge Melancholy* (1719–20): 'Oh, how they did jerk it, / Caper and ferk it, / Under the Green-wood Tree']

ferme n. [early 17C–early 19C] (*UK Und.*) a hole; thus a prison, a cave. [Fr. *fermer*, to shut, to close]

fermedy beggars n. (*also* **fermerly beggars**) [late 17C–early 18C] (*UK Und.*) beggars in general, other than those who parade their (faked) open sores. [? Fr. *fermer*, to close; i.e. their skin is 'closed' or 'shut']

fern n.[1] [1950s+] **1** (*US*) the female genitals and pubic hair. **2** (*US campus*) the buttocks. **3** (*US campus*) a homosexual. [? ref. to SE *maidenhair fern*]

fern n.[2] [1980s+] (*US campus*) someone who clings to the styles of the 1960s; an environmentalist; thus adj. *ferny*. [image of flowers and 'love']

Fernandez talking n. *see* APPLETON TALKING phr.

ferninster n. [1940s+] (*US*) a devoted nay-sayer, one who consistently opposes. [dial. *fornenst*, opposite; ult. SE *foreign*]

fernleaf n. [1910s+] (*N.Z.*) a New Zealander, usu. a soldier. [the SE *silver fern*, adopted as a national emblem, also seen on the uniforms of some representative N.Z. sporting teams]

ferret n.[1] **1** [17C–early 18C] a tradesman who entices the young and naïve to spend money on credit, then promptly duns them for his bill. **2** [early 18C–mid-19C] a pawnbroker. **3** [late 19C] a young thief who gets into a coal barge and throws coal over the side to his confederates. [SE *ferret*, a thief; ult. Lat. *fur*, a thief + image of a SE *ferret*, a predator used in the hunting of rabbits (cf. CONY n.[2])]

ferret n.[2] **1** [17C+] the penis (cf. ANTEATER n.). **2** [1980s+] (*UK juv.*) a male homosexual, a sodomite. [SE *ferret*; like the animal, it burrows into holes]

ferret n.[3] **1** [late 19C–1920s] (*US*) a detective (cf. BEAGLE n.[3]). **2** [1940s] (*UK Und.*) an informer. [SE *ferret (out)*, to search]

ferret v. [late 17C–18C] to cheat, to defraud. [FERRET n.[1] (1)]

ferret-face n. [1990s+] (*UK juv.*) an insult aimed at a teenage boy whose facial hair is appearing early.

ferreting n.[1] [17C] (*UK Und.*) a confidence trick that involves the offering of spurious credit and the subseq. profitable dunning of the victim who has taken it. [FERRET v.]

ferreting n.[2] [19C] sexual intercourse. [FERRET n.[2] (1)]

ferricadouzer n. [mid-19C+] **1** a knockout blow. **2** in fig. use, something outstanding or overwhelming. [Ital. *fare cadere*, to knock down + *dosso*, back; or ? Lat. *ferri*, iron + intensifier *ca* + *douse*, a heavy blow. Hancock, 'Shelta and Polari' (1984), suggests an origin in Polari]

ferry n. **1** [1940s] (*US Black*) a homosexual. **2** [1960s+] (*Aus./US*) a prostitute (cf. BANBURY n.). [many men get to 'ride on her']

ferryboat n. [1900s] (*US*) **1** a large, clumsy shoe. **2** a large automobile.

ferry dust n. [1980s+] (*drugs*) heroin. [? var. on FAIRY DUST n.]

ferschlugginer adj. (*also* **furschlugginer**) [1950s+] (*US*) confounded, darned, wretched. [Yid. *farshlogn*, worried, careworn]

fescue n. [17C–mid-18C] the penis (cf. BAT n.[7]). [SE *fescue*, 'a small stick, pin, etc. used for pointing out the letters to children learning to read; a pointer' (*OED*)]

fess v. **1** [19C+] to admit, to confess; esp. in phr. *fess up (to)*. **2** [19C+] (*US campus*) to fail in one's recitation, to admit that one has not prepared the lesson's work. **3** [1980s+] (*US Black*) to back down or decline. **4** [1990s+] to complain, to whinge. **5** [1990s+] to annoy or irritate someone. [abbr. SE *confess*; defs. (4) and (5) suggest an image of insincere or excessive confession, i.e. verbal manipulation]

fessor n. [20C+] (*US Black*) **1** a *professor*, i.e. any male teacher. **2** any intelligent man. [abbr.; (2) is fig. use of (1)]

-fest sfx [late 19C+] (*orig. US*) combined with a relevant n., this indicates a gathering or get-together. [abbr. SE *festival*]

festive adj. [mid-19C–1930s] 'loud, fast, a kind of general utility word' (F&H).

fetch n.[1] (*UK Und.*) **1** [late 17C–early 19C] a trick, a fraud. **2** [early 19C] the act of eliciting secrets from a victim.

fetch n.[2] [19C] **1** a success; one who appeals. **2** a likeness; thus *the very fetch of*, the image of. [northern dial. *fetch*, an apparition, a double of a living person]

fetch n.[3] [19C] semen. [SE *fetch*, to draw forth]

fetch n.[4] [20C+] (*US Black*) an illegitimate or abandoned child.

fetch v.[1] **1** [late 16C+] to attract, to interest. **2** [mid-19C] to obtain a summons against someone. **3** [late 19C] to excite sexually. **4** [late 19C+] to gain access to, to go to (esp. prison).

fetch v.[2] **1** [18C+] to hit; esp. as *fetch someone one*. **2** [late 19C] of a man, to ejaculate, to come to orgasm. **3** [late 19C] to give one's partner an orgasm. [13C SE *fetch*, to give a blow]

fetch a howl v. [late 19C] to cry out, to weep loudly.

fetch a Tyburn stretch v. [16C] to be hanged. [TYBURN n. + SE *stretch*, the extension of the limbs]

fetch away v. [mid-late 19C] to divide, to separate, to take away (something) from.

fetched adj. [mid-19C] (*US*) a euph. for DAMNED adj.

fetch law of v. [early–mid-19C] to bring a court case or summons against.

fetch mettle v. [17C–early 19C] to masturbate. [SE *fetch*, to draw forth + METTLE n.]

fetch one's pennyworth out of v. [late 17C–early 18C] to ensure that a person works hard for their wages, to get one's moneysworth out of someone.

fetch over the coals v. [late 16C–early 18C] to reprimand. [the burning of heretics at the stake]

fetch someone a crack v. [mid-19C] to hit someone. [FETCH v.[2] (1) + CRACK n.[5] (1)]

fetch someone a stinger v. [late 19C] to hit someone a sharp blow. [FETCH v.[2] (1) + STINGER n.[1] (1)]

fetch the brewer v. [mid-19C] to become drunk. [FETCH v.[1] (1)]

fetch up v. **1** [mid-late 19C] to recuperate from an illness, to recover one's health. **2** [mid-19C+] (*orig. US naut.*) to arrive at a destination, intentionally or otherwise.

fete down v. [20C+] (*W.I.*) to go on a (lengthy) spree. [SE *fête*, a party]

fete up v. [20C+] (*W.I.*) to take out and entertain in the hope of persuading one's guest to agree with one's plans, esp. in a political or business context. [SE *fête*, a party]

fetti n. [1990s+] (*US Black teen*) money. [abbr. SE *confetti*]

fettled adj. [19C] tipsy, drunk (cf. ABOUT RIGHT phr.[1]). [SE phr. *in fine fettle* + note Cheshire dial. *fettled ale*, ale mulled with ginger and sugar]

fever (in the South) n. **1** [1950s+] (*US gambling*) the point of 5 in craps dice (cf. ADA FROM DECATUR n.). **2** [1970s] (*US prison*) a 5-year sentence. [i.e. FIVER n.]

feverish adj. [mid-19C] (*US*) a euph. for drunk (cf. AFFLICTED adj.).

fevvers n. [1910s] (*Aus.*) a Cockney woman. [Cockney pron. of SE *feathers*, which adorn her hat]

few, a n. **1** [mid-19C] someone extreme in manner. **2** [late 19C+] a number, unspecified, of drinks; usu. as HAVE A FEW v. **3** [1900s–50s] (*US prison*) a short prison sentence. **4** [2000s] a short time, i.e. a few minutes.

few, a adv. [mid-18C–1910s] a good deal, to a degree.

few!, a excl. [late 18C–1950s] a deliberately down-played rejoinder to a suggestion that an event is worth noticing. [FEW, A adv.]

few bob short of the pound, a phr. [1960s+] unintelligent, eccentric. [var. on NOT ALL THERE phr.]

few french fries short of a happy meal, a phr. *see* FEW SPRING ROLLS SHORT OF A BANQUET, A phr.

few pence short in the shilling, a phr. [20C+] unintelligent, eccentric; thus also *eighteen shillings* (short of a pound). [var. on NOT ALL THERE phr.]

fews and twos *n.* [1930s–40s] (*US Black*) a very small amount of money.

few snags short of a barbie, a *phr.* [1980s+] (*Aus.*) eccentric, crazy. [var. on NOT ALL THERE phr.]

few spring rolls short of a banquet, a *phr.* (*also* **a few french fries short of a happy meal**) [1990s+] unintelligent, eccentric, mad; used of someone considered to be NOT ALL THERE phr.

few tickers, a *n.* [1940s] (*US Black*) a few minutes. [SE *few* + TICK n.[4] (2)]

fey *n. see* OFAY n.

fey cat *n.* [1940s–70s] (*US Black*) a White man. [FEY n. + CAT n.[11] (4)]

feygele *n. see* FAYGELE n.

f.f. *n. see* FIST-FUCKING n.

f.f.f. *phr.* [1910s] (*Aus.*) utterly miserable (on account of the war). [abbr. frig[gled, fucked and far from home; or forlorn, famished and far from home]

F-40 *n.* [1980s+] (*drugs*) a capsule of Seconal (cf. F-60 n.; F-66 n.). [the pharmaceutical identification stamped on the capsule]

f.f.v. *n.* [20C+] an important person or one who poses as such, often used teasingly or derisorily. [abbr. First Family of Virginia, a member of the founding families of Virginia; thus one of the élite. 'Used quite seriously in the South of the USA and satirically in the North' (Ware)]

f.h.b. *phr.* (*also* **f.h.o.**) [1910s+] a phr. often used by a host/hostess when there is only enough food to feed the guests properly. [abbr. family hold back/family hold off]

fiasco *n.* [20C+] a fiancé; occas. a fiancée. [joc. mispron.]

fib *n.*[1] **1** [late 16C; mid-19C] a liar. **2** [early 17C+] a lie, usu. but not invariably a trivial one. [? link to dial. *fible-fable*, a story, a fable]

fib *n.*[2] [early 19C] a blow, a punch; thus *fibbery*, boxing. [FIB v.[1]]

fib *v.*[1] [mid-17C–mid-19C] to beat, to thrash; to box. [note def. in Egan (1832): 'Technical, in the P.R., to *hammer* your opponent repeatedly in close quarters; and to get no return for the compliment your are bestowing on him']

fib *v.*[2] [late 17C+] (*mainly UK juv.*) to lie. [FIB n.[1]]

fibber *n.* [early 18C+] a liar; thus [mid-19C–1920s] *fibbery*, the telling of lies. [FIB v.[2]]

Fibber McGee's closet *n.* [20C+] (*US*) a very untidy room or cupboard. [*Fibber McGee*, a character in the radio show 'Fibber McGee & Molly' (1935–50); whenever he opened his closet door, the entire contents fell out]

fibbing *n.* [early–mid-19C] prize-fighting, boxing; thus *fibbing gloak*, a boxer; *fibbing-match*, a prize-fight. [FIB v.[1]]

fibre *n.* [1940s] (*S.Afr.*) a matchbox. [SE *wood fibre*]

fice *n.* (*also* **fico, foyse**) [late 18C–early 19C] a silent breaking of wind, 'more obvious to the nose than to the ears; frequently by old ladies charged on their lapdogs' (Grose, 1796). [FOIST n.[1]; note 19C US dial. *fice*, a small dog]

ficky-fick *n.* (*also* **ficky boom-boom, ficky-ficky**) [20C+] sexual intercourse. [pidgin var. of FUCK n.[1] (1) + redup.]

fico, a *n. see* FIG, A n.

fid *n.* [late 19C–1900s] (*US*) a violin. [abbr. SE *fiddle*]

fidas *n. see* FIETAS n.

fiddle *n.*[1] **1** [16C–early 18C] the penis (cf. ACCORDION n.). **2** [17C+] the vagina. [one 'plays on it']

fiddle *n.*[2] [late 17C–18C] a writ of arrest. [the victim must 'face the music']

fiddle *n.*[3] **1** [late 18C] a swindler, a card-sharp. **2** [mid-19C+] (*orig. US*) a swindle, a fraud. [FIDDLE v.[2] (2)/SE *fiddle*, to swindle]

fiddle *n.*[4] [19C] a watchman's rattle (the precursor of the policeman's whistle). [? the noise, the watchman 'plays' his rattle]

fiddle *n.*[5] [mid-19C] a whip. [abbr. SE *fiddlestick*]

fiddle *n.*[6] [late 19C] a sixpence. [abbr. FIDDLER n.[3] (2)]

fiddle *n.*[7] [late 19C] (*UK prison*) a primitive 'machine' used in prison to 'pick' oakum.

fiddle *n.*[8] [20C+] (*Aus.*) a maize grater. [resemblance/the movement of one's arm]

fiddle *n.*[9] [1910s–20s] an unrewarding, annoying job of work. [FIDDLE v.[2] (1)]

fiddle *n.*[10] [1930s] (*N.Z.*) a dressed hindquarter of mutton. [the shape]

fiddle *v.*[1] **1** [early 17C+] to take liberties with a woman. **2** [20C+] to abuse sexually, usu. a child.

fiddle *v.*[2] **1** [mid-19C–1920s] to make one's living taking small jobs on the street, e.g. unloading a cart. **2** [mid-19C+] to cheat, to swindle. **3** [late 19C] to drug liquor. **4** [1930s] (*UK tramp*) to beg. **5** [1940s+] to cheat on one's expenses. **6** [1960s] to work as a petty thief. [ult. SE *fiddle*, the swindler can 'make people dance to his tune'; (2) 17C–early 19C use is SE]

fiddle and flute *n.* [1910s+] (*US*) a suit. [rhy. sl.]

fiddle-arse (about) *v.* (*also* **fiddle-arse around**) [20C+] (*Aus.*) to mess around, to waste time. [SE *fiddle* + ARSE ABOUT v.[1]]

fiddle-bow *n.* [19C] the penis (cf. ACCORDION n.). [it 'plays' the FIDDLE n.[1] (2)]

fiddle-britches *n.* [20C+] (*US*) anyone who is too clever for their own good.

fiddlecases *n.* [1940s] (*US Black*) shoes, esp. large ones. [resemblance]

fiddle-come-faddle *n.* [early 18C] an indecisive person.

fiddledeedee *n.* (*also* **fiddlededee**) [late 19C–1930s] nonsense. [FIDDLEDEEDEE! excl.]

fiddledeedee! *excl.* [late 18C+] a mild excl. denying the validity of the other speaker's remark. [SE *fiddle* + a nonsense sfx]

fiddle-diddle *n.* [19C] the penis. [FIDDLE n.[1] (1) + DIDDLE n.[3] (1)]

fiddle-face *n.* [mid–late 19C; 1950s] **1** one who has a wizened, drawn face. **2** one who has a miserable, 'long' face; thus *fiddle-faced*, wizened, miserable; foolish, empty-headed. [the long face resembles the shape of a violin]

fiddle-fart (around) *v.* [1910s+] to waste time, to shirk one's duties. [ext. FART ABOUT v. (1); note *fiddlefoot*, for a horse to make jumpy, skittish movements; thus *fiddlefoot*, to wander aimlessly]

fiddle-fuck (around) *v.* [1940s+] to waste time, to shirk one's duties. [SE *fiddle* + FUCK AROUND v. (1)]

fiddle-fucked *adj.* [1970s+] (*US*) damned; esp. in phr. *I'll be fiddle-fucked*. [SE *fiddle* + FUCKED adj.[2]]

fiddle-fucking *adj.* [1970s] an elaboration of FUCKING adj. (1).

fiddler *n.*[1] **1** [late 18C] a ne'er-do-well. **2** [mid-19C+] a cheat, a swindler. [FIDDLE v.[2] (2)]

fiddler *n.*[2] [early 19C] a coachman.

fiddler *n.*[3] [mid–late 19C] **1** a farthing. **2** a sixpence. [? the old custom of each couple at a dance paying the fiddler a farthing, and later sixpence]

fiddler's fare *n.* [mid-17C–early 19C] meat, drink and money. [SE *fiddler* + *fare*, the wages paid to an itinerant fiddler]

fiddler's fuck *n.* [1930s+] (*US*) anything considered utterly insignificant, a DAMN n.; usu. in *not worth a fiddler's fuck* or NOT GIVE A FIDDLER'S FUCK v. [fig. use of FUCK n.[1]]

fiddler's green *n.* [19C–1900s] (*orig. naut.*) paradise, a place of unlimited rum, women and tobacco, i.e. 'nine miles this side (or the other side) of hell'.

fiddler's money *n.* [late 18C–mid-19C] small change. [fiddlers receive only very small wages]

fiddler's pay *n.* [late 17C–early 19C] wine and thanks. [i.e. no actual money]

fiddler's wages *n.* [late 16C] no wages at all, but simply a thank you. [ironic use of SE]

fiddles and flutes *n.* [20C+] (*Aus.*) boots. [rhy. sl.]

fiddlestick *n.*[1] **1** [late 16C–early 17C] a sword. **2** [18C+] the penis (cf. BAT n.[7]). **3** [early 19C] (*Scot. Und.*) a spring saw.

[resemblance; in (2) note Jonson (1614): 'My Fiddle-stick does fiddle in and out too much']

fiddlestick *n.*[2] [late 18C–mid-19C] nonsense. [backform. f. FIDDLESTICKS! excl.]

fiddlesticks! *excl.* [17C+] a general expletive; spec. nonsense! rubbish! [the inconsequence of a *fiddlestick* or ? FIDDLESTICK *n.*[1] (2)]

fiddlestick's end *n.* [late 18C–1900s] nothing; thus as excl., a dismissive retort. [a SE *fiddlestick* ends in a point]

fiddley(-did) *n.* (*also* **fiddlie**) [1920s+] (*Aus.*) £1; often in pl. (cf. CHERRY-PICKER *n.*[5]). [rhy. sl. = QUID *n.* (2)]

fiddling *n.* **1** [mid-19C] picking up a variety of odd jobs in the streets, holding horses, carrying parcels etc. **2** [1910s] buying cheap and selling dear. **3** [1920s–30s] (*UK tramp*) to sell matches. [FIDDLE *v.*[2] (1)]

fiddling-stick *n.* [19C] the penis (cf. BAT *n.*[7]). [var. on FIDDLESTICK *n.*[1] (2)]

fiddly-fuck *n.* [1960s+] (*US*) anything considered utterly insignificant. [var. on FIDDLER'S FUCK *n.*]

fidlum-ben *n.* (*also* **fidlam-ben, fidlam-cove**) [late 18C–mid-19C] (*UK Und.*) a petty thief, one who will grab anything, irrespective of its value. [FIDDLE *v.*[2] (2) + abbr. *'em* + BENE CULL *n.*/COVE *n.* (1)]

f.i.d.o. *phr.* [1980s+] a term of emotional resignation (cf. F.I.F.I. phr.). [abbr. *fuck it, drive on*]

fido *n.* [1930s–40s] (*US prison*) a trusty. [Lat. *fidus,* faithful; as *Fido,* a dog's name]

fi-do-nie *n.* [1950s] (*drugs*) opium (cf. APOSTLE *n.*). [ety. unknown]

fie-fie *n.* [19C] a 'fallen' woman. [redup. excl. of *Fie!* on encountering such a person]

fie-fie *adj.* [19C] improper, of improper character. [FIE-FIE *n.*]

fie-fie *v.* (*also* **put on the fie-fie**) [late 19C] to make a fuss, to upbraid. [SE *fie!*]

fie for shame *n.* **1** [mid-19C] breeches. **2** [late 19C] the vagina. **3** [late 19C] tights. [all are seen as shameful things; thus (2) is the common English use for the euph. Lat. *pudendum* (lit. 'that of which one ought to be ashamed'), e.g. throughout E.P. as the def. for the many sl. terms for the female genitals]

field artillery *n. see* ARTILLERY *n.*[2].

field colt *n.* (*also* **field rabbit**) [1940s+] (*US*) an illegitimate child.

Field Lane duck *n.* [late 18C–19C] a baked sheep's head. [*Field Lane,* which once linked Holborn to Clerkenwell]

field nigger *n.* **1** [20C+] (*W.I.*) a term of abuse for a deferential Black, who curries favour with Whites. **2** [1960s+] (*US Black*) working-class, street Blacks, as opposed to Black bourgeoisie. **3** [1960s+] (*US Black*) Blacks from the rural, Southern states rather than the Northern cities. [SAmE *field negro/nigger,* a Black slave who worked in the fields; (1) is a paradox, or an erroneous def., since the usu. meaning is (2) f. the slavery era distinction between the rougher, less refined field workers and those who worked as 'house' servants]

field of wheat *n.* [late 19C+] a street. [rhy. sl.]

field rabbit *n. see* FIELD COLT *n.*

field whisky *n.* [1950s] (*US*) illicitly distilled whisky.

fiemies *n.* [20C+] (*S.Afr.*) whims, fads; thus *full of fiemies,* capricious, pernickety. [Afk. *fiemies,* whims]

fiend *n.*[1] **1** [late 19C–1910s] (*US campus*) a clever student. **2** [late 19C–1910s] (*US campus*) a fool. **3** [1960s] (*US Black*) a general term of praise for any person or thing. [on bad = good model]

fiend *n.*[2] (*orig. US drugs*) **1** [late 19C+] a drug addict, esp. of opium. **2** [late 19C+] an addict, an obsessive, other than of drugs. **3** [2000s] someone who smokes marijuana alone (since smoking is usu. a communal experience). [contemporary use is always ironic]

fiend *v.*[1] **1** [1980s+] (*US Black*) to steal, esp. in the street. **2** [1990s+]

(*US drugs*) to be addicted to narcotics. **3** [1990s+] (*US prison*) to need intensely; to be addicted to. [fig. use of FIEND *n.*[2]]

fiend *v.*[2] *see* FIEND (ON) v.

fiender *n.* [1990s+] (*US*) a drug addict. [ext. of FIEND *n.*[2] (1)]

fiendish(-back) *adj.* [1900s; 1960s+] (*US Black*) excellent, wonderful, admirable. [on bad = good model]

fiendishly *adv.* [1980s] (*US Black*) especially, very much so.

fiend (on) *v.* [1960s+] (*US Black*) **1** to show off, to outdo a rival. **2** to covet, to lust after, to become obsessed with. [FIEND *n.*[1] (3)]

fierce *adj.* [20C+] (*orig. US*) **1** very bad or unpleasant. **2** great, large, fast. **3** a general adj. of approval, excellent, wonderful, first-rate. [(2) and (3) on bad = good model]

fierce *adv.* (*also* **fiercely**) [mid-18C; late 19C+] a general intensifier, whether positive or negative.

fiery lot *n.* [late 19C] a 'fast', 'sporting' man. [var. on HOT STUFF *n.*[2] (2)]

fiery snorter *n.* [mid-19C] a drink-reddened nose. [SNORTER *n.*[1] (2)]

fietas *n.* (*also* **fidas, vietas**) [1980s] (*S.Afr.*) Vredeorp/Pageview, i.e. Soweto District Six, an area from which the occupants were forcibly removed under the Group Areas Act. [Afk. *fiela,* a backward, slovenly person + Du. *vielt,* a scoundrel and/or ? Zulu *i-vila,* a loafer]

fiezle *n. see* FIZZLE *n.*[1].

fife and drum *n.* [1930s+] the buttocks, the posterior (cf. ALA *n.*). [rhy. sl. = BUM *n.*[1] (1)]

fiff *n. see* FIFI *n.* (1).

f.i.f.i. *phr.* [1980s] (*US campus*) an expression of frustration, anger (cf. F.I.D.O. phr.). [abbr. *fuck it, fuck it*]

fifi *n.* **1** [1900s] (*also* **fiff**) an effeminate or 'aesthetic' man. **2** [1940s] (*US gay*) one who enjoys oral sex. **3** [1940s–50s] a French prostitute working in London. **4** [1980s+] (*US campus*) an attractive, sexy young woman, who dresses to match but is, in the end, considered superficial. [? *Fifi,* the clichéd name of the stereotyped sexy French maid of farce and fantasy; note Hotten (1864): 'Fi-Fi, Mr Thackeray's term for Paul de Kock's novels, and similar modern French literature']

fifi *adj.* [1900s; 1960s+] (*orig. US prison*) effeminate. [FIFI *n.* (1)]

fifi (bag) *n.* [1960s+] (*US prison*) a substitute 'vagina' for masturbation; one version uses a container stuffed with a towel soaked in warm water. [FIFI adj. + SE *bag*]

fifi water *n.* [1970s+] (*US prison*) aftershave. [FIFI adj. + SE *water;* the presumed effeminacy of those who use it]

fifteen and two *n.* (*also* **fifteen-two**) [1930s+] (*US*) a Jew (cf. BILLY THE KID *n.*). [rhy. sl.]

fifteen puzzle *n.* [late 19C] absolute chaos, utter confusion. [SE *fifteen puzzle,* a popular puzzle, *c.*1879; like a prototype Rubik's cube, it required players to arrange a set of numbered, moveable cubes in rows, each of which had to add up to 15]

fifteen-two *n. see* FIFTEEN AND TWO n.

fifth *n.* [1920s+] (*US*) **1** a fifth part of a gallon of liquor. **2** a bottle containing such a part.

Fifth Avenoodles *n. see* AVENOODLES *n.*

fifth calf *n. see* FIFTH WHEEL *n.*

fifth gear *n.* [1990s+] an ear. [rhy. sl.]

fifth point of contact *n.* [1990s+] (*US*) the anus, usu. of a woman in a sexual sense. [the other 4 points are mouth, nipples and vagina]

fifth wheel *n.* (*also* **fifth calf**) [mid-19C+] (*US*) a superfluous person, one who does not fit in. [an extra wheel on a 4-wheeled vehicle; or a cow's 4 udders whereby 4 calves can drink at a time, the fifth must wait its turn or force its way in]

fifty *n.*[1] [1970s+] (*Aus.*) a pint of beer composed of 50% old beer and 50% new.

fifty *n.*[2] [1980s] (*US drugs*) a packet of a drug worth $50.

fifty *n.*[3] [1990s+] (*US Black*) the police. [FIVE-OH *n.* (1)]

fifty-cent bag *n.* [1960s+] (*US drugs*) $50 worth of marijuana. [CENT n. (1)]

fifty cents *n.* [1990s+] (*US prison*) $50 worth of drugs. [CENT n. (1)]

fifty-cent word *n.* [1930s+] (*US*) a polysyllabic or supposedly 'difficult' word.

fifty-eleven *n.* (*also* **fifty-'leven**) [late 19C–1950s] (*US Black*) a large or infinite quantity.

fifty-fifty *n.* [1930s+] (*gay*) a sexual act in which the 2 partners alternately perform fellatio and sodomy on each other. [FIFTY-FIFTY adj.]

fifty-fifty *adj.* [1910s+] (*orig. US*) equal, of shares or of chances; thus *go fifty-fity*, to take equal shares. [SE *fifty per cent*]

fifty-'leven *n. see* FIFTY-ELEVEN n.

fifty-one *n.* [1990s+] (*drugs*) **1** crack cocaine (cf. BASE n.). **2** a cigarette made from a mix of marijuana and crack cocaine. [ety. unknown]

5150 *n.* [1990s+] (*US Black/prison*) someone in need of mental health treatment; an eccentric, a crazy person. [police code, an insane person is annoying the public]

5150 *adj.* (*also* **fifty-one/fifty**) [1990s+] (*US Black/prison*) psychotic, crazy, eccentric. [5150 n.]

52-20 Club *n.* [1960s] (*US*) a notional club that took advantage of the US government's payment to ex-GIs of $20 a week for 1 year (52 weeks) or until they could find a job.

52-26 Club *n.* [1960s] (*US*) unemployment insurance. [? 52 weeks, i.e. 1 year + 26 weeks, i.e. 6 months]

fig *n.*[1] [late 16C–17C; late 19C] the vagina (cf. APPLE n.[6]). [Ital. sl. *fica*, the vagina (lit. a fig)]

fig *n.*[2] (*also* **figthing**) [late 18C–19C] a counterfeit coin. [phr. *not worth a fig*]

fig *n.*[3] [1970s+] (*N.Z. prison*) a 1oz (28g) packet of prison-issue tobacco. [SNZE *fig*, tobacco, used as a unit of barter between settlers and Maoris in the mid-19C; note also Clarke, *For the Term of His Natural Life* (1874): 'You may flog, and welcome, master [...] if you'll give me a fig o' tibbacky'; Price Warung, *Tales of the Early Days* (1894): 'Distribute that tobacco — half a fig to a man']

fig, a *n.* (*also* **a fico**) [late 16C+] a dismissive excl.; usu. as *a fig for...* [Ital. *fico*, a fig]

fig *v.*[1] [mid-16C–early 19C] to pick pockets. [SE *feague*, to overcome by trickery, to beat]

fig *v.*[2] [late 16C] 'to put something useless into one's head. Low Cant' (Johnson, 1755). [FIG, A n.; the *OED* def. is Johnson's quote; the presumed implication is of fooling one's hearer with specious nonsense]

fig (a horse) *v.* (*also* **fig a nag**) [late 18C–19C] 'to play improper tricks with [a horse] in order to make him lively' (Hotten, 1860). [FEAGUE v. (2)]

figaro *n.* [mid-19C–1920s] a barber. [Beaumarchais' story *Le Mariage de Figaro* (1784) and Mozart's opera *Le Nozze di Figaro* (1786)]

figary *n.*[1] [mid-17C] the vagina. [lit. 'a fig garden', thus FIG n.[1]]

figary *n.*[2] *see* FEGARY n.

fig-boy *n.* [mid-16C–early 17C] (*UK Und.*) a pickpocket or cutpurse. [FIG v.[1] + SE *boy*]

figdean *v.* [early 19C] to kill. [? Fr. *figer*, to freeze]

figger *n.*[1] [mid-16C] (*UK Und.*) a pickpocket. [FIG v.[1]]

figger *n.*[2] *see* FAGGER n.

figger *v. see* FIGURE v.[1].

figging law *n.* (*also* **fagging law**) [16C–early 19C] (*UK Und.*) the art of picking pockets. [FIG v.[1] + LAW n.[1]]

figgins *n. see* FIGS n.

fight *n.* [late 19C–1950s] (*US*) a party, a brawl. [abbr. BUN-FIGHT n.]

fight at the leg *v.* [late 18C–19C] to take unfair advantage. [back-sword or single-stick rules, in which it is considered unfair to hold the opponent by the leg]

fight cocum *v. see* PLAY COCUM v.

fight cunning *v.* [mid-18C–1900] to act smartly or astutely, to 'box clever'.

fight in armour *v. see* IN ONE'S ARMOUR phr.[2]

fighting *adj.* [late 19C+] (*orig. US*) used of words or speeches to imply ferocity and aggression, e.g. *fighting talk*.

fighting drunk *adj.* (*also* **fighting tight**) [20C+] so drunk as to wish to fight, for no apparent reason, one's companions or some hapless stranger. [FIGHTING adj. + *drunk*/TIGHT adj.[5]]

fighting Irish *n.* [20C+] (*US*) a boast. [racial stereotyping]

fighting mad *adj.* [late 19C+] (*US*) so angry as to wish to hit someone. [FIGHTING adj. + SAmE *mad*, angry]

fighting tight *adj. see* FIGHTING DRUNK adj.

fightist *n.* [late 19C] a prize-fighter, a boxer. [SE *fight* + sfx *-ist*]

fight like Kilkenny cats *v.* [mid-19C+] to fight savagely and without restraint, to fight to the death. [one of a pair of cats fabled to have fought until only their tails remained. Brewer, *Dict. of Phrase and Fable* (1894) suggests that the first such fight came from Oliver Cromwell's troops in Ireland who, in the 1650s, would cruelly tie 2 cats together by their tails and hang them over a washing line; the maddened cats tore each other to pieces]

fight nob work *v.* [early 19C] (*UK Und.*) to succeed without working in the respectable world. [? to act like a NOB n.[2] (1)]

fight off *v.* (*also* **fight up with**) [20C+] (*W.I.*) to attack with unexpected aggression.

fight one's hat *v.* [20C+] (*US*) to struggle uselessly. [pvb 'if the hat fits, wear it', the image is of struggling against a metaphorical 'hat that fits']

fight the tiger *v.* (*also* **twist the tiger's tail**) [mid-19C+] (*US*) to play the game of faro. [SE *fight* + TIGER n.[3] (1)]

fight up oneself *v.* [20C+] (*W.I.*) to struggle for survival.

fight up with *v. see* FIGHT OFF v.

fight-water *n.* [late 19C–1900s] (*Can.*) spirits. [their effect]

fight with the nails on your toes *v.* (*also* **fight with your own toenails**) [1990s+] (*Irish*) to be obsessively, continually aggressive.

fig-leaf *n.* [early 18C–19C] an apron.

f.i.g.m.o. *phr.* [1960s+] *fuck it, got my orders*; sometimes bowdlerized as *finally I... or forget it...* (cf. S.N.A.F.U. n.)[abbr.]

fig (of Spain) *n.* [late 16C–19C] a coarse gesture of dismissal whereby one sticks one's thumb up between 2 forefingers; thus GIVE THE FIG v.

fig-picker *n.* [2000s] (*US Black*) a cadger.

figs *n.* (*also* **figgins**) [late 19C] a grocer. [his stock]

figthing *n. see* FIG n.[2].

fig up *v.* [early 19C] to invigorate, to cheer up, to improve morale. [fig. use of FIG (A HORSE) v.]

figure *n.*[1] [late 18C–mid-19C] an untidy, unkempt person.

figure *n.*[2] [mid–late 19C] a sum of money, esp. a bill. [SE *figure*, a number]

figure *n.*[3] *see* FAGGER n.

figure *v.*[1] (*also* **figger**) (*orig. US*) **1** [mid-19C+] to consider, to feel, to estimate. **2** [1920s+] to think of a person or object in a given way; usu. *figure him/her for...* **3** [1930s+] (*also* **figure on**) to intend, to plan. **4** [1940s+] to work out as expected; esp. as THAT FIGURES phr. **5** [1990s+] to understand. [SE *figure*, to calculate, to ascertain]

figure *v.*[2] *see* FIGURE (ON) v.

figure-dancer *n.* [late 18C–early 19C] a forger who specializes in altering the figures on banknotes, usu. adding a zero to make 10 into 100. [they make the 'figures dance' + pun on SE *figure-dancer*, one who performs in a figure-dance, i.e. a dance that offers representations of famous historical events]

figure-eight *n.* [1930s–50s] (*US drugs*) a fake fit or similar spasm, used by an addict attempting to persuade a doctor to give out drugs. [? the twisting of the body]

figure-fancier *n.* [19C] a man who prefers plump women.

figure-maker *n.* [late 19C] a womanizer. [SE *figure*, a woman's shape]

figure (on) *v.* [late 18C] to total up, e.g. a bill or account (against).

figure on *v. see* FIGURE v.¹ (3).

figure out *v.* [mid-19C+] (*orig. US*) **1** to work out, to understand. **2** to assess (a person's character). **3** to make a plan. **4** to seem, to appear.

figure-six (curls) *n.* [mid-19C] a hairstyle in which the hair is greased, twisted into spirals and then stuck to the face.

figuring *n.* [1950s] calculation, assumption, assessment. [FIGURE v.¹ (4)]

fi-heath *n.* [mid-19C] a thief. [backsl.]

Fiji uncle *n.* (*also* **uncle from/in Fiji**) [1900s–20s] (*Aus.*) a mythical figure, the human equivalent of Billy Bunter's never-materialized postal order, whose supposed wealth is ready and waiting to bail one out of any problems. [one's refs. to 'when my uncle in Fiji…']

filbert *n.*¹ [late 19C–1930s] the human head. [SE *filbert*, a hazelnut, which in France trad. ripened on or near St Philibert's day, 22 August (Old Style); thus play on NUT n.¹ (2)]

filbert *n.*² [1900s–10s] a fashionable dandy. [pun on KNUT n.; esp. in song 'Gilbert the Filbert/Colonel of the Knuts', by Arthur Wimperis (1874–1953) featured in a 1914 version of *The Passing Show*]

filbert *n.*³ [1910s–50s] (*US*) a crazy person; a clownish person. [SE *filbert*, a hazelnut, thus play on NUT n.⁴ (1)]

filberts on *adj. see* NUTS ON adj.

filch *n.* **1** [17C–mid-19C] a short pole with a hook on one end, used to steal small, portable items from windows, stalls etc. **2** [late 17C–18C] that which is stolen, the booty of a theft. **3** [1990s+] a thief. [a cant word of no certain origin; despite a 40-year gap between printed first uses, it is poss. that (1) may have been the source of FILCH v. (note also FILCHMAN n.); Ribton-Turner (1887) suggests Welsh *yspeilio*, to steal, with a 'common' change from 'p'/'sp' to 'f', + Lowland Scot. *pilk*, to pilfer]

filch *v.* **1** [mid-16C–early 18C] to beat, to strike. **2** [mid-16C+] (*orig. UK Und.*) to steal. **3** [mid-19C] (*US*) to defraud, to cheat. [*see* ety. at FILCH n.]

filcher *n.* [mid-16C–18C; 1990s+] a thief, orig. one who uses a FILCH n. [FILCH v. (2)]

filching-cove *n.* [17C–early 19C] a thief. [FILCH v. (2) + COVE n. (1)]

filching-mort *n.* [17C–early 19C] a female thief. [FILCH v. (2) + MORT n.]

filchman *n.* [mid-16C–17C] a cudgel or staff. [FILCH n. (1) + -MANS sfx; this predates FILCH n. (1) but *see* ety. there]

file *n.* (*UK Und.*) **1** [17C–early 18C] an act of pickpocketing. **2** [mid-17C–19C] a pickpocket. **3** [mid-18C] a shoplifter. **4** [early–mid-19C] an experienced fraudster or confidence trickster; thus *old file upon the town*. **5** [early 19C–1900s] an artful, cunning or shrewd person, a man, a 'fellow'; thus *old file*, an old and/or experienced person. **6** [mid-19C] a pickpocket's assistant. [ety. unknown; despite chronology *OED* suggests abbr. FOIL-CLOY n., thence FILE-CLOY n.; Weekley, *Etymological Dict. of Modern English* (1921), offers link to Fr. *filou*, a pickpocket; E.P. suggests SE *file*, a metal tool used to cut through things, and *file*, a rascal; 18C Fr. argot also has *filer doux*, to flatter, wheedle, 'play the sleeping dog', i.e. lie in wait]

file *v.*¹ (*UK Und.*) **1** [early 17C–18C] to pick a pocket. **2** [early 18C] to break into. **3** [mid-18C–early 19C] to cheat, to rob. [FILE n.]

file *v.*² [mid-19C+] to go, to leave.

file *v.*³ [1930s+] (*US campus*) to throw away into a wastepaper bin (cf. CIRCULAR FILE n.).

file *v.*⁴ [1960s] (*US Black*) to act in a brutal, cruel manner. [? 13C SE *file*, defile or ? SE *vile*]

file *v.*⁵ [1970s+] (*US campus*) to show off, to dress up. [clipping of PROFILE v.]

file a cly *v.* [mid-17C–early 19C] (*UK Und.*) to pick a pocket. [FILE v.¹ (1) + CLY n. (2)]

file-cloy *n.* (*also* **file-cly, file coy**) [18C–mid-19C] a pickpocket. [FOIL-CLOY n.]

file lay *n. see* FILING-LAY n.

file-lifter *n.* [late 17C–18C] a pickpocket. [FILE n. (2) + SE *lifter*]

file on *v.* [1960s] (*US Und.*) to arrest; to charge.

file onto *v.* [1920s–30s] (*Can.*) to grab hold of, to seize.

filer *n.* [mid-17C–mid-18C] a pickpocket. [FILE v.¹ (1)]

filet *n.* [1980s+] (*US campus*) a very attractive young woman. [Fr. *filet de boeuf*, fillet steak + ? joc. ref. to LAY n.³ (1)]

filing-lay *n.* (*also* **file lay**) [18C] (*UK Und.*) pickpocketing. [FILE v.¹ (1) + LAY n.⁴ (1)]

filiome *n.* [mid-19C+] (*Ling. Fr./Polari*) a child that is under the age of consent. [FEELE n. + OMEE n. (3), lit. 'child-man']

filipinyock *n.* [1940s] (*US*) a derog. term for a Filipino. [? *Filipino* + ? HUNYAK n.]

fill a blanket *v.* [1940s–50s] (*US Und.*) to roll a cigarette; thus *filled blanket*, a hand-rolled cigarette.

fill a bottle with a tun-dish *v.* [late 16C–early 17C] of a man, to have sexual intercourse. [fig. use of SE *bottle* as vagina + SE *tun-dish*, 'a wooden dish or shallow vessel with a tube at the bottom fitting into the bung-hole of a tun or cask, forming a kind of funnel used in brewing' (*OED*)]

fillaloo *n.* (*also* **phililoo**) [19C–1920s] a commotion, a row. [SE *hullaballo*]

fill an eye *v.* [1910s–30s] (*Aus.*) to punch in the eye.

fill a woman's pannier *v.* [17C] to impregnate a woman.

filled *adj.* [1990s+] (*US campus*) of a woman, attractive.

filled up *phr.* [1960s+] (*Ulster*) on the verge of tears. [one's eyes are filled with tears]

fillet of cod *n.* [1970s] a mild term of abuse. [rhy. sl. = SOD n.¹ (1)]

fillet of veal *n.* **1** [mid-19C] a treadmill. **2** [mid-19C] a prison, i.e. the site of (1) (cf. BUCKET n.²). **3** [1940s] (*US*) a wheel. [rhy. sl.; (1) = *wheel*; (2) = STEEL, THE n. (2)]

fillibrush *v.* [mid-19C] to flatter, to praise ironically. [? SE *filibuster*]

fill-in *n.* [1950s] information. [FILL IN (ON) v.]

fill in *v.*¹ [1900s–50s] (*US Und.*) **1** to join a criminal gang. **2** to recruit into a criminal gang.

fill in *v.*² [1920s+] (*orig. naut.*) to beat up. [the image is of 'filling' one's victim's face with a fist, to give them a black eye]

fill in *v.*³ [1950s+] (*Aus.*) to make pregnant; thus *filled in*, pregnant.

filling station *n.*¹ (*US*) **1** [1920s–40s] an urban description of a small town. **2** [1930s–40s] a place to eat or drink, esp. a nightclub. [SE *filling station*, a petrol or gas station. Apart from its filling station, such a town holds no use or appeal to a passing city-dweller]

filling station *n.*² [1970s+] (*US Black*) a liquor store. [pun]

fill in (on) *v.* [1940s+] (*orig. US*) to inform, to explain. [i.e. to fill in blank spaces]

fillmill *n.* [1940s] (*orig. US Black*) a bar, a saloon. [SE *fill + mill*, a building characterized by the task performed within it, in this case 'filling']

fill one's boots *v.* [1970s–80s] **1** to take as much of something as one can. **2** as a drinking toast.

fill one's collar *v.* [late 19C] (*US*) to perform adequately, to come up to expectations. [SE *fill + collar*, that part of a draft harness that fits the lower part of the neck; the image is of a draft horse pulling wagons as required]

fill one's pipe *v.* [early 19C] to attain a comfortable lifestyle, to amass wealth; thus ext. by *…and leave others to enjoy it.* [one can lie back and smoke; in ext. the implication is that it has taken so long that one is dead]

fill one's shirt *v.* [20C+] (*US*) to eat heartily. [a full, bulging stomach fills one's shirt]

fill someone up v. [1970s+] (*US Black*) to gratify and satisfy completely; with obvious sexual overtones, although sex need not invariably be involved.

fill the bill v. [late 19C+] (*orig. US*) **1** to suit ideally, to satisfy. **2** to work out, to be effective. [theatrical use, 'to excel in conspicuousness, as a star actor whose name is "billed" to the exclusion of the rest of the company' (F&H)]

fill the funnel v. [1960s] (*US*) to attain a target, e.g. a given monetary sum.

fillupy adj. (*also* **filluppey**) [mid-19C] satisfying. [it 'fills you up']

filly n. **1** [17C+] a girl, a young woman; occas. older. **2** [late 19C] (*UK society*) a girl or woman who dances noticeably quickly. **3** [20C+] (*US*) an illegitimate daughter. **4** [1970s+] (*US gay*) an effeminate male homosexual. **5** [1970s+] (*US gay*) a passive lesbian. [SE *filly*, a young mare, a female foal]

filly and foal n. [late 19C] a couple who have left a larger group in search of privacy.

filly-hunting n. [19C] the pursuit of women. [FILLY n. (1) + SE *hunting*]

film for your brownie n. [1970s+] toilet paper. [pun on the Brownie (camera) + BROWNIE n.⁴ (1)]

filoose/fils n. *see* FELOOSE n.

filter v. **1** [late 19C] (*US*) to catch on (to a story or joke). **2** [1980s] to desert.

f.i.l.t.h. phr. [1980s+] used of one who is attempting to resuscitate their career in the Far East, after it has stalled in London. [abbr. *failed in London, try Hong Kong*]

filth n.¹ [late 16C–early 17C] a prostitute. [guilty equation of prostitution and dirt]

filth n.² [1960s] (*UK Und.*) the police, esp. the CID (Criminal Investigation Department).

filthily adv. [1920s–30s] very, extremely. [play on SE]

filthy, the n. [19C+] money (cf. CHAFF n.²). [SE *filthy lucre*]

filthy adj.¹ [late 16C; 18C+] a general intensifier, e.g. *filthy temper*.

filthy adj.² **1** [1960s] (*US Und.*) in possession of incriminating items, esp. drugs. **2** [1990s+] (*US campus*) amazing, excellent. [(1) synon. DIRTY adj.¹ (10); (2) on bad = good model]

filthy adv. [late 19C+] extremely, very, e.g. *filthy rich*.

Filthy MacNasty n. [1930s] a nickname for an unpleasant man, esp. a peeping Tom or dirty old man.

filthy on adj. [1990s+] (*Aus. Und.*) furious with.

filthy pillows n. [1990s+] the female breasts.

filthy with adj. [20C+] full with, over-loaded with, usu. money (cf. LOUSY WITH adj.; ROTTEN WITH adj.; STINKING WITH adj.). [phr. *filthy rich*, but note FILTHY, THE n.]

fimble-famble n. [mid-19C] a lame, prevaricating excuse. [the image is of fumbling weakly for the excuse]

fimpted adj. [20C+] (*US Black*) very ugly. [ety. unknown]

fi'muth n. [1900s] (*US*) a $5 bill.

fin n.¹ [late 18C+] the hand and sometimes the arm. [SE refers only to fish; Grose (1785) defines it as 'a sea phrase']

fin n.² (*also* **finn**) **1** [mid–late 19C] £5, a £5 note. **2** [1920s+] (*US*) a $5 bill. **3** [1930s+] (*Can./US Und.*) a sentence of 5 years. **4** [2000s] (*US*) a throw of 5 in craps dice (cf. ADA FROM DECATUR n.). [abbr. FINNIF n./FINNIP n.]

fin n.³ [1980s] (*US Black*) a female hip that resembles in its opulent curve the fins of a 1950s model automobile.

finagle v. (*also* **fenagle**, **phenagle**) **1** [1920s+] (*orig. US*) to use dishonest or devious methods to bring something about; to fiddle; to 'wangle', to scheme, to get (something) by trickery. **2** [1930s–60s] to associate with (for hedonistic purposes).

finagler n. (*also* **phenogler**) **1** [1920s] (*US*) one who plays for time until a fellow-diner or drinker picks up a bill. **2** [1930s+] a trickster. [FINAGLE v. (1)]

final n. [1930s] the fourth round of a pub drinking session.

final v. [1920s–40s] (*US Black*) to move, to go, to travel.

final curtain n. [20C+] death, the end, the conclusion.

finale n. [1940s] (*US Black*) death.

finale hopper n. [1920s] (*US*) one who arrives after any possible bill has.

final gallop n. [1990s+] an orgasm. [horseracing imagery]

final trill n. [1940s] (*US Black*) death. [SE *final* + TRILL n.² (1)]

finance n. [1900s–10s] a (rich) fiancé(e). [joc. mispron.]

financial adj. [late 19C+] (*Aus./N.Z.*) in credit, solvent, 'in the black'.

financier n. *see* SPONSOR n. (4).

find v. [mid-19C–1940s] to steal; a self-serving euph.

find a clue v. *see* GET A CLUE v. (1).

find a home v. [1940s–50s] (*US prison*) of a prisoner, to be completely dependent on the prison system for stability.

find cold weather v. [late 19C] to be thrown out of a public house.

finder n. **1** [mid-19C] one who gathers the scraps from the floors of a meat-market. **2** [mid-19C–1940s] a thief. [FIND v.]

find fault with a fat goose v. [late 17C–18C] to find fault for no apparent reason. [general opinion holds that the fatter the goose the better]

find fish on one's fingers v. [late 16C] to make up an excuse. ['something smells']

find no bones v. *see* MAKE NO BONES v.

find one's sex and size v. [20C+] (*W.I.*) to mix with people of one's own age and class; thus *not be sex and size with*, not to fit in with on an age or social level. [shopping imagery]

find the lady n. [late 19C+] (*UK Und./gambling*) the 3-card trick, usu. played on the street, the 'lady' being a solitary queen alongside 2 nondescript cards; also as v. and thus fig. to catch a culprit.

find where you live! excl. (*also* **find your hole! ...place! ...yard!**) [20C+] (*W.I.*) an aggressive command, go home! go away!

fine n. [early–mid-19C] (*UK Und.*) one who has been imprisoned for any offence.

fine adj.¹ **1** [early 17C] smart, clever. **2** [early–mid-19C] (*orig. US*) drunk (cf. ABOUT RIGHT phr.¹).

fine adj.² (*also* **foine**) [1930s+] (*orig. US Black*) **1** attractive, good-looking. **2** first-rate, satisfactory.

fine adv. **1** [late 19C+] very well. **2** [1930s+] (*orig. US Black*) attractively.

fine and dandy n. [1930s+] brandy. [rhy. sl.]

fine as a cow turd stuck with primroses phr. [late 18C–early 19C] excellent, first-rate, very fine.

fine as frog hair phr. **1** [20C+] (*US*) feeling very well or very cheerful. **2** [1990s+] (*US campus*) very attractive. [pun on SE *fine*, thin/*fine*, well/FINE adj.² (1)]

fine-ass adj. [1960s+] (*US Black*) first-rate, excellent. [FINE adj.² (1) + -ASS sfx]

fine as wine phr. [1940s+] (*US Black*) **1** of an object or idea, satisfactory, pleasing; of a person, pleasant, amusing, a 'good guy'. **2** referring to any particularly attractive man or woman. [FINE adj.² + assonance]

fine banana n. [1940s] (*US Black*) an attractive, light-skinned young woman. [FINE adj.² (1) + BANANA n.² (2)]

fine brown frame n. [1930s–60s] (*US Black*) (the figure of) an attractive Black woman. [FINE adj.² (1) + FRAME n.¹ (2)]

fine dinner n. (*also* **fine fryer**) [1930s–40s] (*US Black*) a good-looking Black woman. [FINE adj.² (1); she is 'good enough to eat']

fine-fine adj. [20C+] (*W.I., Guyn.*) in infinite and thus irritating detail. [redup.]

fine-haired adj. [late 19C–1910s] (*US*) **1** arrogant, conceited. **2** over-fastidious, pernickety.

fine madam n. [late 19C] a derog. term for a woman who is seen to consider herself 'above her station'.

fine Scot n. *see* SCOT n. (1).

fine stuff *n.* [1980s+] (*drugs*) marijuana. [FINE adj.² (2) + STUFF n.³ (2)]

fine thing *n.* [1940s+] (*Irish/US Black*) an attractive woman. [FINE adj.² (1)]

fine weather *n.* [1940s] (*US Black/Southern campus*) an attractive woman.

fine wirer *n.* (*also* **fine worker**) [mid-19C–1900s] the most skilful grade of pickpocket, esp. one who steals from women. [? *wire*, a small implement, similar to a grappling hook, used to hook items from the victim's pocket; SE *fine*, high-quality goods]

finger *n.*¹ [17C] the penis.

finger *n.*² [19C+] (*orig. US*) a measure of alcohol; thus *three fingers of rye* etc.; abbr. to *three*. [the width of a finger, measured against the side of the glass]

finger *n.*³ **1** [late 19C] (*Aus.*) the manager or boss in a shearing shed. **2** [late 19C–1940s] a policeman (cf. BEAT-POUNDER n.). **3** [1910s+] a police informer. **4** [1910s+] a person. **5** [1920s] (*N.Z.*) one's father; often as *old finger*. **6** [1930s+] an unpopular person. **7** [1930s+] (*US police*) an identified suspect. **8** [1940s–50s] an identification. **9** [1970s] (*UK Und.*) a thief. [FINGER v.²; (2) note Casey (1921): 'Fingers — policemen. From the policeman's method of fingering and frisking the arrested hobo']

finger *n.*⁴ [1910s] (*Aus.*) an amusing person. [ety. unknown]

finger *n.*⁵ (*US drugs*) **1** [1930s–60s] a quantity of drugs smuggled into prison in a rubber finger. **2** [1960s] a finger-shaped piece of hashish. **3** [2000s] a marijuana cigarette (cf. BONE n.¹¹).

finger *n.*⁶ [1970s] (*Aus.*) the manual stimulation of the vagina and clitoris. [FINGER v.¹]

finger *n.*⁷ *see* FINGER AND THUMB n. (1).

finger *n.*⁸ *see* FINGER MAN n. (1).

finger, the *n.* (*orig. US*) **1** [late 19C+] contemptuous or mocking treatment; esp. as GIVE SOMEONE THE FINGER v.; *shoot someone the finger*. **2** [1940s+] an obscene gesture of contempt; usu. as GIVE SOMEONE THE FINGER v. [despite the chronology, the act of (2) is the origin of (1)]

finger *v.*¹ [late 16C+] to indulge in sexual foreplay; usu. stimulation of the female genitals.

finger *v.*² **1** [late 18C+] to steal; to rob. **2** [late 19C+] (*US Und.*) to arrest. **3** [1920s+] to identify a target or possible victim, to incriminate. **4** [1930s+] (*orig. US*) to inform on, to tip off. **5** [1940s] to put a curse on. **6** [1950s+] to point out. [the image of pointing the *finger*]

finger and thumb *n.* **1** [mid-19C–1960s] (*also* **finger**) rum. **2** [20C+] a road. **3** [1930s+] a friend. **4** [2000s] one's mother; also as *keep finger and thumb*, keep quiet. **5** [2000s] a drum. [rhy. sl.; (2) DRUM n.²; (3) CHUM n.¹ (1); (4) SE *mum*/MUM adj.]

finger artist *n.* [1940s–70s] (*US Black*) a lesbian (cf. BEAN FLICKER n.). [FINGER v.¹ + ARTIST sfx, i.e. her manipulation of her partner's clitoris]

finger-bang *v.* [1970s+] to stimulate a woman's genitals with the fingers. [SE *finger* + BANG v.¹ (2)]

finger blasting *n.* [1990s+] masturbation.

finger-bowl *n.* [1960s+] (*Can.*) an open-air cinema. [FINGER v.¹ + a pun on the various sporting 'bowls']

finger-bowl faggot *n. see* CUFF-LINK QUEEN n.

finger-egg *n.* [1940s] (*US Und.*) an informer. [FINGER n.³ (3) + EGG n.¹ (1)]

fingerer *n.* [16C] (*UK Und.*) **1** a pilferer, one who uses his fingers to remove small objects. **2** the accomplice of a team of card-sharps, the fingerer appears as an old, poor man and dresses accordingly; he then allows himself to be lured into some form of gaming by a group of young confederates, and, through his apparent inability to win, persuades the real victim to bet and, inevitably, lose heavily. [SE *finger* or Lat. *fingere*, to feign, to cheat]

finger fuck *n.* [1960s+] the manual stimulation of the female genitals or of a man's anus. [FINGER FUCK v. (1)]

finger fuck *v.* **1** [late 17C+] to stimulate the vagina or anus.

2 [1960s+] of a woman, to masturbate (cf. APPLY LIP GLOSS v.; AUDITION THE FINGER PUPPETS v.). [SE *finger* + FUCK v.¹]

finger fucking *n.* [mid-19C+] using the fingers to stimulate the clitoris or penetrate the vagina. [FINGER FUCK v. (1)]

finger man *n.* **1** [1910s+] (*orig. US*) (*also* **finger**, **finger guy**, **finger merchant**) a traitor, an informer; in criminal terms one who helps with a robbery 'from the inside'. **2** [1930s] a safe-breaker. [criminal var. on FINGER n.³ (3) + SE *man*]

finger map *n.* [1940s] (*US Und.*) a fingerprint. [SE *finger* + *map*/MAP n. (1)]

finger mob *n.* [1930s–40s] (*US Und.*) a criminal gang who have paid off the police; they may also inform on rival gangs. [FINGER n.³ (3) + MOB n.² (3)]

finger pie *n.* [1950s+] the manual stimulation of the female genitals. [note FINGER v.¹]

finger-pointing *n.* [mid-19C+] the making of (false) accusations.

finger-popping *adj.* [1950s–60s] (*US*) enjoying music intensely; thus *fingerpopping daddy*, one who affects to enjoy music but lacks any real knowledge or understanding. [the 'popping' or snapping of one's fingers in time to the beat]

finger post *n.* [late 18C] a parson. [he points the way (that one should live one's life) but does not follow his own directions; 'like the finger post he points out a way he has never been, and probably will never go, i.e. the way to heaven' (Grose, 1785)]

fingers are made of lime-twigs *phr.* [late 16C–mid-18C] a phr. used of a thief (cf. BIRDLIME n.¹). [lime-twigs are sticky]

finger-smith *n.* **1** [19C] a midwife. **2** [19C+] a pickpocket; a thief. [SE *finger* + sfx *-smith*, an adept, an expert]

finger-stink *n.* [late 19C] the manipulation of the vagina with (male) fingers. [FINGER-STINK v.]

finger-stink *v.* [late 19C] usu. of a man, to manipulate the vagina with the fingers.

finger wave *n.* [1980s] (*UK Und./police*) an anal examination for drugs.

fingy *n.* [1910s+] (*orig. US Und.*) a person lacking 1 or more fingers. [on pattern of WINGY n.]

finick *n.* [early 18C+] a faddy, 'picky' person; thus *adj.* **finickity**. [Cheshire dial. *finnick*, a mincing, over-fastidious person]

finicky *adj.* (*also* **finicking**) [late 17C; early 19C+] in the manner of an obsessive, petty person, concerned with minutiae and, as such, often irritating to others; often in phr. *finicky Dick*. [FINICK n. + sfx *-y*]

finif/finiph *n. see* FINNIF n.

Finish, the *n.* **1** [18C–19C] Carpenter's late-night coffee-shop, sited in Covent Garden opposite Russell Street and ostensibly catering to the market porters, which closed only when the last customer had gone home at dawn. **2** [19C] any late-night/early-morning café. [a place where one finishes one's night out; Bee notes that the owner, Carpenter, 'was a lecher, his handy bar-maid Mrs. Gibson, a travelled dame']

finish *n.* [1930s] (*UK tramp*) methylated spirits; thus *finish-drinker*. [? it *finishes* one off]

finish *v.* [19C+] to put an end to, to terminate, to destroy.

finisher *n.* [early 18C+] **1** something that puts an end to, discomfits or 'does for' someone; in boxing, a knockout blow. **2** something that settles a dispute. [FINISH v.]

finisher (of the law) *n.* [18C–19C] the hangman.

finishing academy *n.* (*also* **finishing school**) [18C] a brothel (cf. ACADEMY n.). [? pun on SE *finish*, to end a girl's education/to reach orgasm + ACADEMY n. (1)]

finishing school *n.* [1930s–40s] (*US Und.*) a women's prison (cf. BIG SCHOOL n.). [SE *finish*, to end a girl's education]

finish one's circle *v.* [20C+] (*US*) to die. [Western jargon, orig. used of a dead cowman, whose jobs, when alive, included riding the boundaries of the ranch]

finish out one's row *v.* [20C+] (*US*) to die. [the image is of a ploughman]

finito *adj.* [1970s+] over, finished, completed. [FINITO! excl.]

finito! *excl.* [1950s+] an excl. used to signify the end, a completion. [Ital. *finito*, finished]

fink *n.* [20C+] **1** an unpleasant or contemptible person, one who cannot be trusted. **2** a strike-breaker, a company policeman. **3** a contemptible object or thing. **4** an informer. **5** (*US Und.*) a confidence trickster's victim. **6** (*US*) (*also* **fink-out**) an act of backing down. [the claim that 'dating from the famous Homestead strike of 1892 is the odious *fink*. [It] according to one version was originally Pink, a contraction of Pinkerton, and referred to the army of strike-breakers recruited by the detective agency' (*American Mercury*, January, 1926) is prob. spurious. Note *HDAS*: 'G *Fink* student not belonging to the students association [...] hence, not "one of the guys"; [...] or G. *Schmierfink* "a low dirty hack"']

fink *v.* (*also* **fink on, fink out**) (*US*) **1** [1920s+] to inform, to inform on. **2** [1960s+] to back down. [FINK n.]

finky *adj.* (*also* **fink**) [1950s] (*US Und.*) given to acting as an informer, untrustworthy. [FINK n. (4)]

finkydiddle *v.* [late 19C–1940s] to indulge in foreplay. [var. on FIRKYTOODLE v. + DIDDLE v.[1]]

finn *n. see* FIN n.[2].

finna *v.* (*also* **funna**) [1990s+] (*US Black*) to get oneself ready, to prepare.

finnif *n.* (*also* **finif, finiph, finnuff, finuf**) **1** [mid-late 19C] (*UK Und.*) £5, a £5 note; thus *half a finnuff*, £2 10s. **2** [mid-19C+] (*US*) $5. **3** [1900s–40s] (*US Und.*) a 5-year jail sentence. [Yid. *fünf*, 5]

finnip *n.* (*also* **finnep, finnio, finnup**) [mid-19C+] a £5 note; thus *double finnip*, £10; *cross-finnep*, a forged note. [Yid. *fünf*, 5]

finny *n.*[1] [18C] (*UK Und.*) a funeral. [? abbr.]

finny *n.*[2] [mid-late 19C] a £5 note. [FIN n.[2] (1)]

finuf *n. see* FINNIF n.

fin up *n.* [1930s+] (*US Und.*) a sentence of 5 years to life. [FIN n.[2] (3) + SE *up*(*wards*)]

fip *n.*[1] **1** [19C] (*US*) a 5-penny bit, the nickname for the Spanish *half-real*, worth about 4½ cents or 6 cents in some states. **2** [19C] any very small amount of money. [elision of SE *fivepence*]

fip *n.*[2] *see* FIPPENCE n.

fipenny *n.* (*also* **fippeny**) [mid-19C] a 5-penny coin.

fi'penny *n.* [early 19C–1910s] a clasp-knife. [? its original price]

fipp *n.* [1900s] (*US*) a general derog. term. [ety. unknown]

fippence *n.* (*also* **fip**) [mid-19C–1940s] (*UK/W.I.*) a threepenny bit.

fippenny *n. see* FIPENNY n.

fir *n.* [1980s+] (*drugs*) marijuana (cf. AFRICAN BUSH n.). [? resemblance to fir leaves]

fire *n.*[1] [early 16C–19C] venereal disease; thus v., to give a partner such a disease. [the pain it causes; note Ned Ward, *The London Spy* (1699): 'The Doctor undertook to extinguish [...] all *Venereal Fires* that had unhappily taken hold of the Instruments of *Generation*']

fire *n.*[2] [late 17C; 19C] the vagina (cf. BLACK HOLE n.[1]).

fire *n.*[3] **1** [mid-19C+] (*US Und.*) danger, esp. from the police; thus *on fire*, very dangerous. **2** [1940s] (*US Black*) a cigarette. **3** [1940s] (*US Black*) a marijuana cigarette. **4** [1940s–60s] (*US*) matches or a cigarette lighter. **5** [1990s+] (*US Und.*) a firearm.

fire *n.*[4] **1** [1980s+] a mixture of crack cocaine and methamphetamine. **2** [1980s+] bad or weak crack cocaine. **3** [1990s+] (*US Black/drugs*) potent marijuana. [? it burns the throat or ? play on BURN v.[2] (10)]

fire *v.*[1] **1** [18C+] to ejaculate semen (cf. FIRE A BLANK v.; FIRE A SHOT v.; FIRE IN THE AIR v.; GET ONE'S GUN (OFF) v.; GET SOMEONE'S GUN (OFF) v.; GO OFF AT HALF-COCK v.; POP v.[1]; POP A NUT v.; POP ONE'S COOKIES v.; POP ONE'S CORK v.; POP ONE'S DRAWERS v.; POP ONE'S NUTS v.; POP ONE'S ROCKS v.; POP ONE'S WAD v.; SHOOT v.[1]; SHOOT BLANKS v.[1]; SHOOT OFF v.[2]; SHOOT ONE'S LOAD v.; SHOOT ONE'S MILT v.; SHOOT ONE'S ROCKS v.; SHOOT ONE'S ROE v.; SHOOT ONE'S WAD v.; SHOOT THE WORKS v.; SHOOT WHITE v.). **2** [20C+] in sport, to play at maximum capacity. **3** [1950s+] (*US Black*) to strike a blow. **4** [1980s] (*Aus.*) to excel. **5** [1990s+] (*UK Black*) to prosper, to do well. **6** [1990s+] (*US*) to have sexual intercourse. [(1) note Burns poem *c*.1800 in *Merry Muses of Caledonia*: 'He turned about to fire again / And give me t'other sally / And as he fired I ne'er retired / But received him in my alley']

fire *v.*[2] (*also* **fire out**) [late 19C+] **1** (*orig. US*) to dismiss from a job, to throw out or expel. **2** (*Aus./US*) to eject, in a non institutional context. [pun on SE *fire*, discharge (a weapon)]

fire *v.*[3] [20C+] (*W.I.*) used in several phr. to denote aggressive or decisive action; thus *fire a blow/box/chop/cuff/hand/kick/lash*, to hit hard; *fire yourself/your skin*, hurry up. [SE *fire*, to stimulate, to inflame with passion]

fire *v.*[4] [20C+] (*orig. W.I.*) **1** to obtain a drink, esp. of a barman, e.g. *fire me a rum*. **2** to drink strong liquor; thus *fire a booze/a drink/a few/a rum/the grog*, to take a drink.

fire *v.*[5] [1910s+] (*drugs*) to inject a drug.

fire *v.*[6] [1940s+] (*US*) to light a cigarette (drugged or otherwise). [FIRE UP v.[3]]

fire a blank *v.* (*also* **fire blanks**) [1960s+] **1** of an impotent man or one who has had a vasectomy, to have intercourse despite one's inability to impregnate one's partner. **2** of a man, to have an orgasm without ejaculation (cf. FIRE v.[1]).

fire a gun *v.* [late 18C–early 19C] to push a topic unsubtly into the conversation. [the firing of a warning gun + the suddenness of the explosion]

fi real *adv.* [1970s+] (*W.I./UK Black teen*) precisely or genuinely. [pron. of FOR REAL adv.]

fire-alarm *n.* [1920s] (*US*) a divorcée.

fire-alarms *n.* [1910s] the arms. [rhy. sl.]

fire a shot *v.* [late 19C+] of a man, to ejaculate. [FIRE v.[1] (1) + SHOT n.[2]]

fire a slug *v.* [late 18C–early 19C] to drink a dram. [pun on *slug*, bullet/SLUG n.[3] (2) of liquor]

fire blanks *v. see* FIRE A BLANK v.

firebox *n.* [late 19C] a constantly passionate man. [he is 'heated' with passion]

firebug *n.* [late 19C+] (*US*) an arsonist. [SE *fire* + BUG n.[5] (2)]

fire-burn *n.* [20C+] (*W.I.*) a rowdy, riotous person. [such a person might, when enjoying themself, start a fire]

fireburn *v.* [2000s] (*UK Black*) to attack verbally.

fire-burner *n.* [1960s] (*US Und.*) a very enthusiastic, passionate lawyer.

fire-catcher *n.* [1950s] (*W.I.*) old, ragged, workclothes. [such clothes are worth using only to light a fire]

fire down town! *excl.* [1950s] (*W.I.*) a call for speedy and generous service, esp. on arriving at a bar and calling for a quick round of drinks.

fired up *adj.* **1** [mid-19C] drunk (cf. ABOUT RIGHT phr.[1]). **2** [1950s+] (*US*) angry. **3** [1960s+] (*also* **fired**) energized; thus *unfired*, unenthusiastic.

fire-eater *n.*[1] **1** [late 18C+] a braggart, an aggressive person always spoiling for a fight. **2** [mid-late 19C] a quick worker. **3** [mid-19C+] a noticeably courageous person, with the supposed daring of the performer.

fire-eater *n.*[2] [1920s+] (*US*) a firefighter.

fire-eating *adj.* [mid-19C; 1930s+] of a person, being aggressive and spoiling for a fight. [FIRE-EATER n.[1] (1)]

fire-escape *n.* [mid-19C–1920s] a clergyman. [the *fire* is that of hell; 20C use is naut. jargon]

fire escapes *n.* [1900s] (*US*) a style of side whiskers.

firefight *n.* [1980s+] (*US Black*) a street battle involving guns. [milit. jargon *firefight*, a battle between infantrymen on the ground]

fire fluid *n.* [late 19C] (*Aus.*) strong liquor; spirits.

fire in v.[1] [1910s] to send in.

fire in v.[2] [2000s] to fight, to throw a punch. [ext. FIRE v.[1] (3)]

fire in the air v. **1** [19C] of a man, to have sexual intercourse. **2** [late 19C+] of a man, to ejaculate outside their partner's body. [FIRE v.[1] (1)]

fire into v. [20C+] to approach sexually, to pick up, to seduce. [FIRE v.[1] (1)]

firelock n. (also **fireplace, firework, tinder-box**) [late 17C–19C] the vagina (cf. BLACK HOLE n.[1]). [FIRE n.[1]]

fireman's hose n. see GARDEN HOSE n.

fire on v. [1960s+] (US Black/campus) **1** to disparage, to ridicule. **2** to hit, to assault, usu. with a weapon. [FIRE v.[1] (3)]

fire on all cylinders v. [20C+] to work properly; thus *fire on one cylinder*, to work badly. [automobile imagery]

fire one across the bows v. [1990s+] to indulge in coitus interruptus. [SE *shot across the bows* is fired to warn another vessel to stop]

fire out v. see FIRE v.[2].

fireplace n. see FIRELOCK n.

fireplug n.[1] [19C] a man who is suffering from a venereal disease. [FIRE n.[1] + pun]

fireplug n.[2] **1** [20C+] (US) a short, squat person. **2** [1930s–40s] (US drugs) a large piece of opium (cf. APOSTLE n.). [supposed resemblance]

fire power n. [1980s] (US Black) physical strength and ability.

fire prigger n. [late 18C–early 19C] one who robs those who are otherwise preoccupied with watching their, or someone else's, home burn down. [SE *fire* + PRIGGER n.[1] (1)]

fireproof adj. [mid-19C+] (orig. US) invulnerable, guaranteed against failure.

fire queen n. [1980s+] (US gay) a militant gay activist. [SE *fire* + QUEEN n.[2] (1); they wish to 'set the world on fire']

fire-rage n. [20C+] (W.I.) **1** intense anger, uncontrolled fury; thus *pick up someone's fire-rage*, to take someone's side in a quarrel as energetically as if it were one's own. **2** of a man, one who loses his temper easily, who 'flies off the handle'.

fireship n. [mid-17C–18C] a diseased prostitute. [FIRE n.[1] + pun]

fires of hell n. [19C] the vagina (cf. BITE n.[2]; BLACK HOLE n.[1]). [the image of the vagina as a threat and a source of evil]

fire-tail n. [20C+] (W.I., Guyn.) of a woman, one who loses her temper easily.

fire the acid v. see ACID n.[1].

fire the question v. [late 19C] (US) to make a proposal of marriage.

fire up v.[1] (US) **1** [mid-19C+] to begin, to get ready. **2** [1950s+] to start up a mechanical device, e.g. a car.

fire up v.[2] **1** [late 19C] to become emotional, angry. **2** [20C+] to anger, to arouse emotionally. **3** [1960s+] to excite in general. **4** [1970s] (US campus) to drink with the intention of boosting one's spirits. **5** [1970s+] (orig. US Black/campus) to excite sexually; to have sexual intercourse. **6** [1970s+] to hit; to shoot or kill. **7** [1980s] (US campus) to get excited, to dedicate oneself to; to be happy.

fire up v.[3] **1** [late 19C+] to light a pipe, cigarette or cigar. **2** [1960s+] to light a marijuana cigarette. **3** [1990s+] to heat up crack cocaine.

fire up v.[4] [1940s+] (drugs) to pump the blood and heroin mixture out of the hypodermic into the vein or muscle.

firework n. see FIRELOCK n.

fireworks n.[1] [17C; late 19C+] an emotional outburst, a state of intense excitement.

fireworks n.[2] **1** [mid-19C] (US) guns. **2** [late 19C] (US) matches. **3** [1920s+] (US Und.) gunplay, shooting.

fire your tail! excl. [20C+] (W.I.) get out! go away! [TAIL n.[2] (1)]

firing (to) phr. [1960s] (US Black) eager (to), keen (to).

firk v. [late 16C–early 18C] to have sexual intercourse; thus *firking school*, a brothel or any place of unrestrained sexual frolics (cf.

BANG v.[1]; FRIG v.). [SE *firk*, to move about briskly; to whip, to beat + euph. FUCK v.[1]]

firking adj. [1970s+] a euph. for FUCKING adj. [FIRK v.]

firkin of foul stuff n. [late 17C–early 18C] a very plain, fat, coarse woman.

firkytoodle v. [late 19C] to indulge in foreplay. [FIRK v. + SE *toodle/tootle*, to play upon]

firm n. **1** [early 19C; 20C+] a criminal gang, large or small. **2** [1910s+] any form of gang, e.g. of football hooligans.

firme adj. [1960s+] (US) a general term of high approval. [Sp.; also used as a magazine name in 1970s–80s]

firming n. [1980s] (UK Und.) an assault or beating by a gang. [FIRM n. (1)]

firmota n. [1960s+] (US) a very attractive young woman. [FIRME adj.]

first, the n. [mid-19C+] (orig. US) nothing, not a single one, usu. in negative.

first and fifteenth n. [2000s] (US Black) those days in a month on which welfare cheques are distributed.

first base n. [1920s+] (orig. US) **1** a man's initial advances on a young woman, usu. implying just kissing, but sometimes also caressing some part of the body or even the removal of some clothing; such a 'base' is always above the waist (cf. HOME RUN n.; SECOND BASE n.; THIRD BASE n.). **2** the start of something, e.g. a relationship, usu. applied in terms of failing to reach it, e.g. *he couldn't even get to first base*. [baseball jargon]

first base v. [1930s+] (US) to take one's first steps towards an objective. [FIRST BASE n. (2)]

first belly pain n. [1950s] (W.I.) one's first-born child.

first bird n. see BIRD n.[10] (1).

first cab off the rank n. (Aus.) **1** [1960s+] the speediest one to react, the first one off the mark. **2** [1980s] one's primary interest.

first cab on the rank n. [1950s+] (Aus.) a prime suspect.

first chop n. [1910s] the first opportunity.

first chop adj. [early 19C+] excellent, first-rate. [from Hind. *chhaap* meaning a print, and thus a seal, notably that which is placed on first-rate merchandise; Schele de Vere, *Americanisms* (1872), however, cites it as 'Canton-jargon of the Anglo-Chinese']

first crack out of the box phr. (also **first rattle out of the box**) [20C+] at once, immediately, at the first attempt.

first feel n. [1950s+] (W.I.) the first chance, the earliest opportunity.

first fiddle n. see SECOND FIDDLE n.

first fleeter n. [mid–late 19C] (Aus.) one of the original emigrants from Britain to New South Wales. [SE *First Fleet*, the original fleet of ships, carrying mainly transported convicts, which arrived in New South Wales in 1788]

first line n. [1970s] (drugs) morphine (cf. AUNTIE EMMA n.). [SE *first*, best + *line* (of merchandise)]

first national bank n. [20C+] (US) an outside lavatory (cf. ALTAR n.). [the resentment of the farming community towards the banks, which regularly repossessed their land when times became hard]

first-nighter n. [1970s+] (US Black) a one-time sexual encounter, unlikely to be repeated.

first of May n.[1] [mid–late 19C; 1970s] the tongue; ext. to firm speech as in 'have one's say'. [rhy. sl. = say]

first of May n.[2] [1930s–50s] (US tramp) a new recruit to the carnival or circus; in ext. use, any new, inexperienced person, esp. one who does not stay the course. [i.e. the date of the start of the summer season]

first-rate adv. [mid-19C+] excellently, very well. [adj. use is SE]

first rattle out of the box phr. see FIRST CRACK OUT OF THE BOX phr.

firsts n. **1** [20C+] (US Black) any Blacks who are the first to take on a specific job in a formerly all-White world. **2** [1950s+] the first chance, the first opportunity; often as excl. *firsts!* I want to do something first.

first thing smoking *n.* [1940s] (*US Black*) a railroad train.

first thirty *n.* [1940s] (*US Black*) January. [although January has 31 days]

first-timer *n.* [late 19C+] (*Aus. Und.*) one who is serving their first sentence in prison; thus *second-timer*.

first up *adv.* [20C+] (*Aus.*) for the first time, at the first try.

fisgig *n.* (*also* **fizgig**) [early–mid-19C] amusement gained at the expense of others. [SE *fizz*, animal spirits + *gig*, a frivolous person]

fish *n.*[1] **1** [mid-16C+] the vagina (cf. BEARDED CLAM n.). **2** [late 16C–early 17C; 1970s+] a woman. **3** [late 19C+] (*US*) a prostitute (cf. ALLEY CAT n.). **4** [1920s+] (*US gay*) a heterosexual woman, sometimes derog. **5** [1930s–40s] (*US gay*) one who masturbates while performing oral intercourse. **6** [1930s–50s] (*US gay*) an effeminate male homosexual. **7** [1960s+] (*US*) a feminine lesbian. [(1) is derog. ref. to the supposed odour; (2)–(8) are ext. uses]

fish *n.*[2] **1** [early 18C–19C] a gambling chip. **2** [late 19C+] (*US*) a dollar. **3** [1940s] a pound sterling. [(2) may exist only in the works of P.G. Wodehouse, living in the US and using its sl., but usu. in a UK context]

fish *n.*[3] [early 18C+] a man, a person; esp. as qualified in various combs., e.g. *bad fish, cool fish, loose fish, old fish, poor fish, rare fish, shy fish, strange fish, timid fish* (cf. BIG FISH n.; COLD FISH n.; FLAT FISH n.; LITTLE FISH n.; ODD FISH n.; QUEER FISH n.; YELLOW FISH n.).

fish *n.*[4] [late 18C–early 19C] a sailor; thus SCALY FISH n.

fish *n.*[5] (*also* **fisher**) [19C] a toady, a sycophant, a parasite. [FISH v.[1] (1)]

fish *n.*[6] **1** [mid-19C+] (*Can./US prison*) a new inmate; thus *fish number*, the number issued to each prisoner by the US Department of Corrections; *fish gallery*, a segregated area of the prison where new inmates are housed. **2** [late 19C–1940s] (*US campus*) a freshman. **3** [late 19C+] (*US*) any form of novice, esp. a gullible innocent. **4** [20C+] (*US*) a fool, a 'sucker' (cf. AIREDALE n.). **5** [1970s] (*US campus*) a socially inexperienced boy. **6** [1990s+] (*UK juv.*) a very unpopular person. **7** [1990s+] a virgin or someone who has not even been kissed. [abbr. SE *fresh fish*; (4) note Robert Greene, *The Blacke Bookes Messenger* (1592): 'He that drawes the fish to the bait, *the Beater*']

fish *n.*[7] [1910s+] (*US*) a heavy drinker. [SE phr. *drink like a fish*]

fish *n.*[8] [1950s+] (*W.I.*) any form of sauce that accompanies the staple, some form of starch, which need not contain fish.

fish *n.*[9] [1950s+] (*US*) a Roman Catholic. [the Catholic tradition of abstaining from meat on Fridays]

fish *n.*[10] [1970s+] (*US gay*) semen (cf. BABY GRAVY n.).

fish *n.*[11] [1970s+] (*US*) a derog. term for a Newfoundlander. [the staple industry]

fish *adj.*[1] [1930s+] (*Can./US prison*) fresh, uninitiated, new, esp. of a prisoner. [FISH n.[6] (1)]

fish *adj.*[2] *see* FISHY adj.[3] (1).

fish *v.*[1] **1** [late 18C+] (*US campus*) to toady, to ingratiate oneself. **2** [late 19C] to interrogate. [? SE *fish* for compliments or favours]

fish *v.*[2] [1940s–60s] to shoplift, to steal.

fish *v.*[3] (*also* **chew fish, eat fish**) [1970s+] (*US gay*) to perform cunnilingus (cf. BOX LUNCH n.). [FISH n.[1] (1)]

fish! *excl.* [late 19C; 1990s+] a general excl. of dismissal, a euph. for FUCK! excl. (1).

fish and shrimp *n.* [1930s+] a procurer, a pimp (cf. ALPHONSE n.[2]). [rhy. sl.]

fish and tank *n.* [1990s+] (*UK Und.*) a bank. [rhy. sl.]

fishbagger *n.* [late 19C] a suburbanite who works in the City. [they use their supposedly important briefcase to take home food, esp. cheap fish]

fishbelly *n.* [1960s] (*US Black*) a derog. term for a White person. [the colour of the stomachs of many fish]

fish bits *n.* [1980s+] (*UK juv.*) that portion of the hair that hangs down at the back of a MULLET n.[2] haircut.

fish-black *n.* [1940s] (*US Black*) Friday night. [the Catholic tradition of eating fish on Friday + the *blackness* of night]

fish bowl *n.*[1] (*also* **fish tank**) [1930s+] **1** (*US Und.*) a holding cell in a police station. **2** (*US prison*) the processing unit for new arrivals at a prison. [(1) play on SE, the visibility of the prisoners; (2) FISH n.[6] (1)]

fish bowl *n.*[2] [1960s] (*US*) steam baths frequented by homosexual men. [play on FISH n.[1] (6)/SE *fish bowl*]

fish-brained *adj.* [1910s–40s] (*UK school*) stupid (cf. AMOEBA-BRAINED adj.).

fish-broth *n.* [late 16C–early 17C] water, esp. when salted.

fishcunt *n.* [1990s+] a general term of abuse, aimed at a woman; the implication is that her vagina smells (cf. FISH-FANNY n.). [CUNT n.[1] (1)]

fish dinner *n.* [1970s+] (*US gay*) sexual intercourse with a woman; thus a woman. [FISH n.[1] (1)/FISH n.[1] (4)]

fish-eater *n.* [1930s+] **1** a Roman Catholic. **2** (*Can.*) an inhabitant of Nova Scotia.

fished *adj.* [1980s] (*US campus*) drunk.

fisher *n.*[1] [1910s–30s] a banknote. [proper name of Sir Warren *Fisher*, secretary to the Treasury *c*.1919–33]

fisher *n.*[2] *see* FISH n.[5].

Fisheries *n.* [late 19C] the *Fisheries* Exhibition, London, 1883.

fisherman's daughter *n.* [late 19C+] water (that which one drinks, rather than that making up lakes, rivers, seas etc). [rhy. sl.]

fisherman's luck *n.* [19C+] (*Aus./US*) no luck at all, bad luck. [popularly defined as 'a wet ass and a hungry gut']

fisher of fogles *n.* [early–mid-19C] a pickpocket, specializing in handkerchiefs. [SE *fisher* + FOGLE n.]

fisher's flimsies *n.* [1910s–30s] (*Aus.*) currency notes issued during the government of Prime Minister Andrew *Fisher* (1862–1928).

fishery *n.* [1930s] (*US tramp*) a mission hall. [they are 'fishing' for souls]

fishes' eyes *n. see* FISHEYES n.

fish-eye *n.* [1910s] (*US Und.*) a diamond.

fisheyes *n.* (*also* **fishes' eyes**) [20C+] (*orig. US milit./prison*) tapioca (pudding) (cf. FROG'S EGGS n.; FROGSPAWN n.; GLOUTER n.; SNAKE EYES n.[1]). [supposed resemblance]

fish-face *n.* [early 17C; 1910s+] a stupid or ugly looking person; also used as a derog. term of address.

fish-faced *adj.* [1920s+] stupid- or ugly-looking. [FISH-FACE n.]

fish-fag *n. see* FAG n.[3].

fish-fanny *n.* (*also* **fishy-fanny**) [2000s] a general insult aimed at a woman; the implication is that her vagina smells (cf. FISHCUNT n.). [FANNY n.[1] (1)]

fish fingers *n.* [1990s+] (*UK juv.*) one who having placed his finger(s) in a girl's vagina, fails to wash them; thus his fingers supposedly smell of fish. [play on SE *fish fingers*/FISH n.[1] (1)]

fish for brown trout *v. see* BROWN TROUT n.

fish for food *v.* [1940s–70s] (*US Black*) to gossip. [FOOD n. (1)]

fish-fosh *n.* [late 19C] kedgeree. [? redup.]

fish-fry *n.* [1920s+] (*US Black*) a party to which guests bring refreshment, or pay to attend; thus adj., well supplied with money (cf. HOUSE HOP n.; JUMP n.[2]; JUMP JOINT n.; PERCOLATOR n.; RENT PARTY n.; SHAKE n.[2]; SHOUT n.[2]; SKIFFLE n.; STRUT n.).

fish-head *n.*[1] **1** [20C+] (*US*) a native of the west Florida coast. **2** [20C+] anyone who lives alongside a river. **3** [20C+] a West Indian. **4** [20C+] a worker in a fish cannery. **5** [1970s+] an East Asian (cf. BROWNIE n.[2]). [all uses are derog.; their consumption of and/or occupation with fish]

fish-head *n.*[2] [1950s] (*W.I.*) a bribe, a tip. [among the poor a fish-head was considered a treat or delicacy]

fish-hook *n.* **1** [mid-19C+] a hand. **2** [1980s] (*N.Z.*) a problem.

fish-hooks *n.* [late 18C+] the fingers. [the term, derived f. 19C naut. use, was UK and then moved to US Black use by 1930s]

fish-horn *n.* [mid-19C+] (*US*) a wind instrument; [1930s+] a saxophone.

fishing expedition *n.* [1980s] a search for a wife.

fishing fleet *n.* [late 19C+] (*UK society*) those young women who visit Hong Kong, and once many more centres of the British Empire, esp. India, in the hope of catching a rich husband.

fish line *n.* (*US prison*) **1** [1960s] a bus that brings in new inmates. **2** [2000s] a line used to pull items from one cell to another. [FISH n.[6] (1)]

fish market *n.* **1** [mid-19C–1900s] the vagina (cf. BEARDED CLAM n.). **2** [mid-19C–1900s] a brothel (cf. BANGING-SHOP n.; BIRDCAGE n.[1]). **3** [1960s] (*US campus*) a women's dormitory. [FISH n.[1] (1) + SE *market* + pun]

fish mitten *n.* [1990s+] the vagina (cf. BEARDED CLAM n.). [FISH n.[1] (1) + SE *mitten*, i.e. for the penis]

fishmonger *n.* [17C] **1** a womanizer, a promiscuous man. **2** a madame, a bawd. [FISH n.[1] (1) + sfx *-monger*]

fishmonger's daughter *n.* [late 16C–early 17C] a prostitute. [play on FISH n.[1] (1)]

fish 'n' chip mob *n.* [1970s+] (*UK society*) anyone considered socially unacceptable. [Sandhurst jargon *fish 'n' chip mob*, unfashionable regiments]

fisho *n.* [1920s+] (*Aus.*) a professional fisherman; a fish-seller. [SE *fish* + -o sfx (4)]

fisho *v.* [1960s] (*Aus.*) to fish professionally. [FISHO n.]

fish or cut bait *phr.* [mid-19C+] a phr. suggesting that you either carry out what you're doing to the fullest extent or let someone else more competent get on with it while you take a secondary role.

fish out *v.* (*also* **fish up**) [late 19C+] to obtain, to produce.

fishpond *n.* [17C–18C] the vagina (cf. BEARDED CLAM n.). [euph.; ext. FISH n.[1] (1)]

fishpond, the *n.* [early 19C] (*Anglo-Irish*) the Irish Sea; thus *over the fish-pond*, England.

fish queen *n.*[1] **1** [1940s] (*US gay*) a male homosexual who openly associates with women, with the supposed aim of appearing to be bisexual. **2** [1940s+] (*US gay*) any man, homo- or heterosexual, who enjoys cunnilingus. **3** [1960s–70s] (*US gay*) a heterosexual man. [FISH n.[1] (4) + QUEEN n.[2] (1)/QUEEN sfx (2)]

fish queen *n.*[2] [1970s+] (*US prison*) a gay inmate who has newly arrived at the prison. [FISH n.[6] (1) + QUEEN n.[2] (1)]

fish-queen *v.* [1940s–50s] (*US*) to perform cunnilingus (cf. BOX LUNCH n.). [FISH QUEEN n.[1] (2)]

fish roll *n.* [1990s+] (*US prison*) the clothing and other necessities issued to a new inmate. [FISH n.[6] (1)]

fish scales *n.* [1980s+] (*drugs*) crack cocaine (cf. BASE n.). [? resemblance to the flakes of crack cocaine]

fishsticks *n.* [2000s] (*US Black*) money. [ext. FISH n.[2] (2)]

fish supper *n.* [1990s+] sexual intercourse, esp. in the context of a conjugal right. [FISH n.[1] (1) + *supper* + pun on SE]

fish tank *n.*[1] [1980s+] (*US gay*) the vagina of a heterosexual woman (cf. BEARDED CLAM n.). [FISH n.[1] (1) + SE *tank* + pun]

fish tank *n.*[2] *see* FISH BOWL n.[1].

fish up *v. see* FISH OUT v.

fish wrapper *n.* (*also* **fried fish wrapper, meat wrapper**) [late 19C+] (*orig. US*) a newspaper. [the assumption that newspapers were good only for wrapping fish]

fishy *adj.*[1] [mid-18C–mid-19C] looking ill, esp. around the eyes, after a drinking session. [one's eyes resemble those of a dead fish]

fishy *adj.*[2] [mid-19C] (*US*) of whalers and professional fishermen, dedicated, steadfast. [the qualities of the work have transferred themselves to the man]

fishy *adj.*[3] **1** [mid-19C+] (*also* **fish**) suspect, dubious, unreliable, questionable. **2** [1910s] (*US*) supercilious. [the smell of rotting fish or the slipperiness of fresh fish]

fishy about the gills *phr.* [late 19C] hangover. [ext. OF FISHY adj.[1] + GILLS n. (1)]

fishy-fanny *n. see* FISH-FANNY n.

fisk *v. see* FRISK v.[2] (1).

fisle *v. see* FIZZLE v.[1] (2).

fisno *n.* [late 19C] (*UK tramp*) a warning. [backsl. = OFFICE n.[3] (1)]

fist *n.*[1] **1** [mid-16C+] handwriting. **2** [early 19C; 20C+] a competent person. **3** [early 19C+] an attempt, a try. **4** [mid-19C] a signature.

fist *n.*[2] *see* FIST-FUCK n. (2).

fist *v. see* FIST FUCK v.

fist city *n.* (*also* **fist holler**) [1930s+] (*US*) a fist fight. [SE *fist* + CITY sfx/SE *hollow*; an imaginary place where quarrels are settled with the fists]

fist-fuck *n.* (*also* **fist**) **1** [1960s+] an act of masturbation. **2** [1970s+] (*mainly gay*) the insertion of the hand (and forearm) into the vagina or anus. [FIST FUCK v.]

fist fuck *v.* (*also* **fist**) **1** [late 19C; 1960s+] (*also* **fuck one's fist**) to masturbate. **2** [1970s+] (*mainly gay*) to insert one's hand (and forearm) into someone's anus or vagina. [SE *fist* + FUCK v.[1]; (1) note synon. RMC Duntroon (Aus.) *fuck (one's) knuckles*]

fist-fucker *n.* **1** [1960s] (*US*) a habitual masturbator. **2** [1970s] (*US*) a generally unpleasant person. **3** [1970s+] (*mainly gay*) one who practises FIST-FUCKING n. (2). [FIST FUCK v.]

fist-fucking *n.* (*also* **f.f., fisting**) **1** [1960s+] male masturbation. **2** [1970s+] (*mainly gay*) the insertion of the hand (and forearm) into the anus or vagina of one's partner for purposes of sexual stimulation. [FIST FUCK v.; (2) popular in the 1970s but latterly in decline through fears of injury and hence the possibility of spreading AIDS]

fistful *n.* [1930s] (*US Und.*) a 5-year jail sentence. [the 5 fingers]

fist holler *n. see* FIST CITY n.

fist in *v.* [1990s+] to interrupt.

fisting *n. see* FIST-FUCKING n.

fist it *v.* **1** [19C] of a woman, to caress a man's penis. **2** [mid–late 19C] (*Aus./N.Z.*) to eat with one's hands.

fist junction *n.* [1970s+] (*US Black*) that point of confrontation at which a physical fight takes over from mere words.

fist one's mister *v.* [20C+] to masturbate.

fist sandwich *n. see* KNUCKLE SANDWICH n.

fist up *v.* [1990s+] to clench one's fingers into a fist, preparatory to fighting or hitting.

fisty *adj. see* FEISTY adj. (2).

fit *n.*[1] [1950s–60s] (*US Black*) a suit of clothes, esp. a well-cut garment. [abbr. SE *outfit*]

fit *n.*[2] [1950s+] (*drugs*) the equipment (a needle, a spoon, a dropper) required for injecting narcotics; thus *have a fit (up)*, to inject heroin. [abbr. OUTFIT n.[3] (2)]

fit *adj.*[1] **1** [late 18C+] of things, likely. **2** [mid-19C+] of people, inclined, disposed.

fit *adj.*[2] **1** [late 19C] very well, healthy, usu. in response to the query 'How are you?' **2** [late 19C+] good-looking. [(2) later 20C+ use is UK Black; note agricultural use *fit*, of fruits and vegetables, ready to pick, full-grown, though not necessarily fully ripe; note Shakespearian use of *fit*, of a woman, aptitude for love-making]

fit *v.*[1] [late 19C+] to identify someone as the perpetrator of a crime.

fit *v.*[2] *see* FIT UP v.

fit! *excl.* [1950s+] (*orig. W.I.*) a general excl. of approval, excellent! first-rate! very good!

fit as a fiddler *phr.* [20C+] (*Aus.*) extremely healthy.

fit as a trout *phr.* [1960s–80s] (*Aus./N.Z.*) very healthy.

fitch *n.* [1920s] (*US Und.*) fur, as worn in a coat. [SE *fitch*, the hair of a polecat]

fit end to end *v.* (*also* **fit ends to end**) [late 19C–1900s] to have sexual intercourse.

fit house *n.* [1920s] (*US Und.*) a hospital for the criminally insane. [SE *fit*, a paroxysm]

fit in the arm *n.* [late 19C] a blow, a punch. ['In June 1897 one Tom Kelly was given into custody by a woman for striking her. His defence was that "a fit had seized him in the arm", and for months afterwards backstreet frequenters called a blow a fit' (Ware)]

fit like a ball of wax *v.* [mid–late 19C] of clothes, to fit very tightly.

fit like a tattoo *v.* [1970s] (*US*) to fit well.

fit-me-tight *n.* [1960s] (*Irish*) a journeyman tailor.

fitness *n.* [1970s+] (*UK Black*) attractiveness; an attractive (young) woman. [FIT adj.[2] (2)]

fitshaced *adj.* [1990s+] drunk. [play on SHITFACED adj.[2]; the idea being that one is too drunk to be able to say the word properly]

fitted *adj.* [1990s+] well-dressed.

fitter *n.* [1940s] (*UK Und.*) a corrupt supplier who provides criminals with disguises, weapons, transport etc.

fit to be tied *adj.* [late 19C+] furious, enraged and in need, therefore, of restraint. [the image of one so hysterically furious that they need to be tied down]

fit to bust *adv.* (*also* **fit to burst, fit to split**) [mid-19C+] to a very great extent, usu. of emotions, i.e. moved to a great degree, whether with anger of tearfulness or ecstasy etc, depending on context.

fit to kill *adv.* [mid-19C+] (*orig. US*) used of something done to excess, esp. of one's dress.

fit-up *n.*[1] [mid-19C+] any temporary structure, esp. a stage, boxing-ring etc, which can be assembled, then knocked down for assembly at another venue. [orig. theatre use]

fit-up *n.*[2] [1930s+] (*UK Und.*) a false accusation or perjured evidence used to have an innocent suspect (albeit one who has a criminal record) arrested and found guilty. [FIT UP v. (2)]

fit up *v.* (*also* **fit, fix up**) **1** [mid-19C–1910s] (*UK Und.*) to prepare. **2** [20C+] to incriminate by using false evidence, both physical and verbal. **3** [1970s] to make responsible (for).

fitz *n.*[1] [late 19C–1900s] the illegitimate child of a royal person. ['the Anglo-French word for "son"; chiefly Hist. in patronymic designations, in which it was followed by the name of a parent in the uninflected genitive. Some of these survive as surnames, e.g. Fitzherbert, Fitzwilliam etc; in later times new surnames of the kind have been given to the illegitimate children of royal princes' (*OED*)]

fitz *n.*[2] [20C+] (*Aus./S.Afr.*) a large sausage used for cutting into slices for sandwiches or to eat with salad. [? a brandname]

Fitzroy cocktail *n.* [1920s+] (*Aus., Melbourne*) a drink based on methylated spirits with some form of mixer to mediate the taste. [*Fitzroy* is a suburb of Melbourne]

Fitzroy Yank *n.* [1940s+] (*Aus.*) a relatively unsophisticated person who attempts to ape the supposedly smart style of an American. [for ety. *see* FITZROY COCKTAIL n.]

five *n.*[1] **1** [20C+] a 5-year prison sentence. **2** [1910s+] 5 minutes; usu. as TAKE FIVE v. (1). [abbr.]

five *n.*[2] **1** [1930s+] (*US*) a blow with the fist. **2** [1940s] (*US Black*) the 5 fingers, thus the hand. [BUNCH OF FIVES n.]

five-acre farm *n.* [mid-19C] an arm. [rhy. sl.]

five-acre Tory *n.* [1980s+] (*N.Z.*) a very conservative small farmer.

five against one *n.* [20C+] masturbation (cf. FIVE ON ONE n.). [5 fingers vs 1 penis or vagina]

five and dime *n.* (*also* **five and ten**) [late 19C+] (*US*) a small store where articles are all priced at 5 or 10 cents. [the original such store was that opened (1879) by F.W. Woolworth (1852–1919)]

five and dime *adj.* [1960s+] (*US Black*) **1** insignificant, paltry. **2** badly dressed, cheap, unattractive, sleazy. [FIVE AND DIME n.]

five-and-dimer *n.* [1940s] (*US*) an insignificant person. [fig. use of FIVE AND DIME n.]

five and ten *n. see* FIVE AND DIME n.

five and two *n.* (*also* **seven and a three, twenty and a ten**) [1970s] (*gay*) a male homosexual prostitute. [at 1970s rates he charges $5 for his services plus $2 for a room; ? the alternatives suggest inflation]

five-barred gate *n.* [late 19C] a policeman. [the majority of policemen were recruited from the countryside, home of such gates]

Five by Five *n.* [1940s+] (*Can./US Black*) a short fat person. [their girth presumably equals their height]

five by two *n. see* FIVE TO TWO n.

five-cent bag *n.* (*also* **five-cent balloon/paper**) [1960s] (*US drugs*) a small amount of heroin, less than 28g (1oz), sold for $5. [SE *five-cent* + BAG n.[11] (1)/BALLOON n.[4] (2)/PAPER n.[2] (2)]

fivecenter *n.* (*also* **five-cent word**) [1990s+] (*US*) a long and supposedly 'difficult' word.

five-dollar *n.* [2000s] (*US Black*) fellatio for which the woman charges $5.

five-dollar bag *n.* [1960s] (*US drugs*) a bag of heroin costing $5 or $50. [SE *five-dollar* + BAG n.[11] (1)]

five-dollar expression/words *n. see* TWO-DOLLAR WORDS n.

five-eight *n.* [1980s+] (*Aus. prison*) a friend. [rhy. sl. = SE *mate*; a position in the game of rugby]

five-finger *v.* [1910s; 2000s] (*US Black*) to steal.

five-finger discount *n.* [1960s+] (*orig. Aus./N.Z./US*) the act and proceeds of shoplifting, stealing.

five-fingered Annie/Mary *n. see* FIVE-FINGER MARY n.

five-finger(ed) exercise *n.* [1960s+] masturbation.

five-fingered salute *n.* [1940s] (*US*) a gesture of derision, placing the thumb on the tip of the nose and fanning out and wriggling the fingers.

five-fingered widow *n.* (*also* **widow five-finger**) [1970s+] masturbation.

five-fingered words *n.* [1910s] (*US*) insulting language. [the 5 fingers are those of the fist, raised as a result of the language]

five-finger Mary *n.* (*also* **five-fingered Annie/Mary**) [1940s+] the hand, as used for masturbation.

five fingers *n.* **1** [late 16C–17C; mid-19C] in card-games, the 5 of trumps. **2** [1930s] (*US Und.*) a 5-year jail sentence. [ety. unknown]

five fingers *adj.* [20C+] (*Irish*) first-rate, excellent. [*five fingers* make a fig. whole hand]

five-finger sandwich *n.* [1990s+] (*Aus.*) a punch.

five-finger shuffle *n.* (*also* **five-knuckle shuffle**) [1990s+] masturbation.

five-finger solo *n.* [1990s+] masturbation.

five hundred *n.* [1990s+] (*US Black*) a BMW automobile. [a specific model number, the series 500]

five in the south *n.* [20C+] (*US gambling*) the point of 5 in craps dice (cf. ADA FROM DECATUR n.).

five-knuckle shuffle *n. see* FIVE-FINGER SHUFFLE n.

five-letter woman *n.* [1920s+] a prostitute, i.e. a *w-h-o-r-e* or *b-i-t-c-h* (cf. FANCY WOMAN n.; FOUR-LETTER MAN n.).

five miles of bad road *n. see* TEN MILES OF BAD ROAD n.

five o'clock *n.* [late 19C] afternoon tea. [obs. in English but perpetuated in synon. Fr. *le five o'clock* and in Romania, where the English term is used]

five of clubs *n.* [1940s] (*US*) the fist.

five-oh *n.* (*also* **5-0, five-o**) [1980s+] **1** (*US Black/teen*) the police; also attrib. **2** (*US Black/teen*) a 50-litre Ford Mustang (used as a police vehicle in some areas). **3** (*US prison*) a prison officer. [1960s TV police show *Hawaii 5-0*]

502 *n.* [1990s+] (*US Black/teen*) drunk driving. [California police code for the offence]

five on it *phr.* [2000s] (*US teen*) a phr. meaning that one either has $5 worth of marijuana or $5 to contribute to the purchase of marijuana.

five on one *n.* [20C+] masturbation. [var. on FIVE AGAINST ONE n.]

five or seven *n.* [late 19C] a drunkard. [the popular sentence, a 5-shilling fine or 7 days in prison]

five over five *phr.* [late 18C] used of people who turn in their toes.

five pennyworth *n.* [late 19C] (*UK tramp*) a jail sentence of 5 years.

5% Nation *n.* [1990s+] (*US Black*) a Black radical group, an offshoot of the Nation of Islam; thus *Five Percenter*, a member of the group. [it teaches that any large group of people, and more specifically, the African American nation, can be divided into 3 groups, the 85%, basically the ignorant masses that need to be led, the 5%, the people with true knowledge of the self whose job it is to lead the masses and fight against the 10%, the people who have partial knowledge of the self and use it to gain power and wealth by exploiting the 85%, also referred to as 'blood-suckers of the poor'. The chosen percentages are those they feel are the percentages within the Black community. These numbers are neither universal (although these groups do exist within any large group) nor unchangeable]

five pot piece *n.* [mid-19C] 2 shillings and 6 pence (2s 6d; 12½p). [orig. medical student use, f. the contemporary price of a quart or *pot* of mixed mild and bitter beer]

fiver *n.* **1** [mid-19C+] a £5 note, £5. **2** [mid-19C+] (*US*) a $5 bill. **3** [late 19C–1920s] (*Aus./US*) a 5-year prison sentence; one serving such a sentence. **4** [20C+] £500. **5** [1970s] (*US drugs*) a quantity of heroin costing $5.

fives *n.*[1] **1** [17C] a foot. **2** [late 18C+] the hand, usu. when clenched in a fist; thus TIP SOMEONE THE FIVES *v.*; *man of fives*, a professional fighter. **3** [mid-19C+] a street fight. **4** [1990s+] masturbation.

fives *n.*[2] [1960s] (*drugs*) 5mg Benzedrine or amphetamine tablets (cf. A N.[2]).

five-slap *v. see* SLAP FIVE *v.*

five specker *n.* [1920s–30s] (*US Und.*) a 5-year prison sentence. [? var. on FIVE-SPOT *n.* (2)]

five-spot *n.* **1** [late 19C+] a $5 or £5 note. **2** [1900s–60s] (*US*) a 5-year prison sentence. **3** [1910s] (*US*) a $5 gold piece. **4** [1980s] (*N.Z.*) NZ$500. [SE *five* + -SPOT sfx]

5000 *phr. see* AUDI (5000) *phr.*

five-time *v. see* TWO-TIME *v.* (1).

five to six rush *n.* (*also* **five to six swill**) [1950s–70s] (*N.Z.*) the nightly rush to the public house, caused by severely restricted licensing laws. [SE *five/six o'clock* + *rush/swill*]

five to two *n.* (*also* **five by two**) [1930s+] a Jew (cf. BILLY THE KID *n.*). [rhy. sl.; ult. ref. to betting]

five to twos *n.* [1930s] shoes. [rhy. sl.; ult. ref. to betting]

five-twenty-nine *n.* [1950s] (*US Und.*) the sentence of 5 months and 29 days for 'jostling' a drunk, i.e. robbing them.

fix *n.*[1] [19C] (*orig. US*) a dilemma, a problematic situation. [lit. the state in which one is 'fixed'; SE by 1900]

fix *n.*[2] **1** [mid-19C] (*US*) an outfit. **2** [1900s] (*Aus.*) fitness, 'condition'. [FIX *v.*[1] (4)]

fix *n.*[3] [1910s+] (*orig. US Und.*) **1** any corrupt deal, a bribe, a favour; thus *put the fix in*, to ensure a plan or event favours whoever has paid the bribe, arranged the deal etc. **2** the person who makes such deals.

fix *n.*[4] **1** [1930s+] (*drugs*) an injection of narcotics; a generic for the drug itself. **2** [1960s–70s] (*drugs*) a small amount of cocaine. **3** [1960s+] an ingestion of any drug, e.g. coffee. **4** [1960s+] (*US*) a compulsive desire or thrill. **5** [1980s+] anything that satisfies a craving, e.g. for food. [it 'fixes' one's emotional and/or physical state]

fix *n.*[5] [1950s] (*US*) a meeting. [FIX *v.*[1]]

fix *v.*[1] **1** [late 17C; mid-19C+] to prepare some form of trick. **2** [late 18C+] to bribe, to suborn, esp. in the context of sports or politics. **3** [late 18C+] to take revenge upon, to get even with, to foil an antagonist's plans; thus *fix oneself*, to get oneself into

trouble. **4** [mid-19C+] (*orig. US*) to arrange, to prepare, to get ready. **5** [mid-19C+] to prepare food or a meal. **6** [mid-19C+] (*also* **fix off**) to kill, to murder. **7** [late 19C] (*US*) to look after. **8** [late 19C+] to intend. **9** [late 19C+] to attack, to beat up. **10** [late 19C+] to sort out. **11** [1900s] to pay.

fix *v.*[2] **1** [mid-19C; 1930s+] to have sexual intercourse. **2** [1960s] to make pregnant.

fix *v.*[3] **1** [1930s+] (*drugs*) to inject oneself with narcotics; thus *fixer*, one who injects. **2** [1940s+] (*drugs*) to give someone else an injection. **3** [1960s] (*US prison*) in ext. use, to eat heavily. [the over-riding image is of 'fixing' a problem, i.e. the pain of withdrawal; note William Burroughs, *Junkie* (1953): 'If you have any habit at all it takes two papers to fix you, and I mean just fix']

fixed *adj.*[1] [mid-19C+] situated materially or financially, e.g. *how are you fixed?* how much money do you have?

fixed *adj.*[2] (*also* **fixed up**) **1** [mid-19C+] sorted out, situated. **2** [late 19C+] in funds. **3** [late 19C+] (*orig. US*) corrupted, bribed, 'squared', tampered with. **4** [20C+] of a sporting contest, having had the result pre-arranged (to favour a group of gamblers). [FIX *v.*[1]]

fixed *adj.*[3] [late 19C] (*US*) armed; carrying a weapon.

fixed *adj.*[4] [1910s] (*Aus.*) 'out of sorts', unwell. [SE *in a fix*]

fixed *adj.*[5] [1960s+] (*drugs*) using or under the influence of injectable narcotics. [FIX *v.*[3] (1)]

fixed bayonet *n.* **1** [19C] an erect penis (cf. AX *n.*[2]). **2** [1910s] (*Aus. milit.*) red wine. **3** [1940s] (*N.Z. milit.*) methylated spirits.

fixed up *adj.*[1] **1** [late 19C] (*US*) (*also* **fixed out**) dressed up. **2** [1990s+] (*S.Afr.*) fine, good, worked out, happy, content.

fixed up *adj.*[2] *see* FIXED *adj.*[2].

fixer *n.*[1] [late 19C+] (*orig. US*) one who arranges or adjusts matters, a go-between, esp. in an illegal context. [SE *fix*/FIX *v.*[1] (2)]

fixer *n.*[2] [1980s+] (*US drugs*) a drug dealer. [FIX *v.*[3] (2)]

fixing *n.* [late 19C] (*Aus.*) strong drink. [it *fixes* one up]

fixings *n.*[1] [19C+] (*US*) **1** equipment. **2** food. **3** anything used to dilute or mix with alcohol, e.g. tonic water. **4** the tobacco and matches required to light a pipe. [SE *fixing*, the garnishing of food]

fixings *n.*[2] [late 19C–1910s] **1** furniture. **2** ext. in fig. use, 'extras'. [it is *fixed* in the house]

fixings *n.*[3] [1930s–60s] (*US*) sexual intercourse. [the couple are *fixed* together]

fix off *v. see* FIX *v.*[1] (6).

fix one's bones *v.* [1990s+] (*drugs*) to take some heroin in order to ward off the pains of an unsatisfied heroin addiction. [FIX *v.*[3] (1)/SE *fix, mend*; the aching bones that are part of the symptoms of heroin withdrawal]

fix one's face *v.* [1930s+] (*orig. US*) to apply one's make-up.

fix someone's clock *v.* [20C+] (*US*) to thwart another's plans, to cause trouble for an enemy, to get even with. [ironic use of SE *fix* + *clock*; the image is that the clock will indeed be 'fixed', not in the way its owner desires]

fix someone's flint *v.* [mid-19C–1910s] (*US*) to thwart another's plans, to cause trouble for an enemy, to get even with. [ironic use of SE *fix* + *flint*, the flint of a matchlock or musket]

fix someone's hash *v. see* SETTLE SOMEONE'S HASH *v.*

fix someone's little red fire engine *v.* [1960s+] (*orig. US*) to deal with, to take revenge on.

fix someone's wagon *v.* (*also* **fix someone's little red wagon**) [1930s+] to thwart someone's plans. [ironic use of SE *fix* + *wagon*]

fix the old gum tree *v.* [20C+] (*Aus.*) of a former wanderer, to settle down at last.

fix-up *n.* **1** [mid–late 19C] (*US*) an alcoholic drink. **2** [1930s] (*drugs*) an injection of a narcotic drug. [SE *fix*/FIX UP *v.*[2]]

fix up *v.*[1] **1** [mid-19C+] to set up a meeting (usu. for someone else); thus [20C+] *fixed up*, having an appointment. **2** [late 19C+]

to provide food, clothing, living quarters, accommodation, a job etc for someone. **3** [1930s+] to initiate a relationship or bring 2 people together for sex, to marry. **4** [1940s] (*US gay*) to fellate. **5** [1940s–60s] to have sexual intercourse. **6** [1950s] to pay someone.

fix up *v.*[2] **1** [20C+] (*US drugs*) to inject heroin or morphine. **2** [1950s] to give someone, usu. an alcoholic, a drink. **3** [1950s+] to give (or sell) someone some narcotics. [ext. of FIX n.[4] (1)]

fix up *v.*[3] *see* FIT UP v.

fix up! *excl.* [1990s+] a general excl. of admonition.

fixy *adj.* [1950s] (*US*) fussy, esp. as regards one's clothes and appearance. [SE *fix oneself up*, to arrange one's clothes, to get ready]

fiz *n.*[1] *see* FIZZ n.[1] (3).

fiz *n.*[2] *see* PHIZ n.[1].

fizgig *n.*[1] [16C; mid-19C] a promiscuous woman. [ext. of GIG n.[1] (1); despite logical imagery of FIZZ n.[1] (2), i.e. one who fizzes (with animal spirits), the chronology renders this impossible]

fizgig *n.*[2] (*also* **fizzgig, phizgig**) [20C+] (*Aus.*) a police informer. [ety. unknown; *AND* suggests an ext. use of FIZGIG n.[1], i.e. one who runs around and chatters indiscreetly]

fizgig *n.*[3] *see* FISGIG n.

fizz *n.*[1] **1** [mid-18C] a fuss, a commotion. **2** [mid-19C+] animal spirits, raw energy. **3** [mid-19C+] (*also* **fiz, pfiz, phiz**) champagne, occas. lemonade and ginger beer mixed; thus *fizzler*, a champagne bottle. **4** [1930s] sparkling water; soda water. **5** [1970s] sherbet.

fizz *n.*[2] [1940s+] (*Aus.*) an informer. [abbr. FIZGIG n.[2]]

fizz *v.* [1900s] (*Aus.*) to be an informer. [FIZGIG n.[2]]

fizz around *v.* [1910s] to rush around energetically. [FIZZ n.[1] (2)]

fizzer *n.*[1] [mid-19C–1920s] anything or anyone excellent or first-rate. [FIZZ n.[1] (2)]

fizzer *n.*[2] **1** [1910s+] (*US*) a firecracker that fails to go off. **2** [1940s+] (*Aus.*) a disappointing failure, a fiasco. [FIZZLE v.[2] (3)]

fizzer *n.*[3] (*also* **phizzer**) [1950s+] (*Aus.*) an informer. [FIZGIG n.[2]/FIZZ v.]

fizzgig *n. see* FIZGIG n.[2].

fizzical culturalist *n.* [1940s+] (*US Black*) a bartender. [puns on SE *fizzy/physical*]

fizzing *adj.* **1** [mid-19C+] wonderful, excellent, first-rate. **2** [1950s+] a general negative. [(2) is a euph. for FUCKING adj. (1) but the positive use is more prob. an innocent ref. to the effervescence of champagne, i.e. FIZZ n.[1] (3)]

fizzing at the bung(hole) *phr.* (*also* **fizzing at the slit**) [1990s+] of a woman, sexually excited. [SE *fizzing*, effervescing + BUNG n.[2] (4)/BUNGHOLE n.[1] (1)/SLIT n.[1] (1)]

fizzle *n.*[1] (*also* **fiezle**) [mid-17C–1900s] a breaking of wind. [FIZZLE v.[1]]

fizzle *n.*[2] [mid-19C+] **1** (*US campus*) a (partial) failure in recitation or examination. **2** (*orig. US*) a failure. **3** (*US*) a minor quarrel. [FIZZLE v.[2]]

fizzle *v.*[1] **1** [late 16C–early 18C] to defecate. **2** [mid-17C] (*also* **fisle**) to break wind. [echoic]

fizzle *v.*[2] **1** [mid-19C] (*US campus*) to fail someone in an examination. **2** [mid-19C–1920s] (*US campus*) to fail in an examination. **3** [mid-19C+] to fail, to make a mess of.

fizzle-fart *n.* [1930s] (*US teen*) a term of abuse.

fizzle (out) *v.* **1** [mid-19C] to kill. **2** [mid-19C+] (*orig. US*) to peter out, to fail gradually but surely. [the sound of escaping air + FIZZLE v.[2] (3)]

fizzog *n. see* PHIZ n.[1].

fizz out on *v.* [1940s+] (*Aus.*) to let down, to fail in a promise. [FIZZLE v.[2] (3)]

fizzy *n.* [1920s–30s] champagne. [ext. FIZZ n.[1] (3)]

fizzy *adj.* [1930s–50s] energetic, excitable. [FIZZ n.[1] (2)]

fla/flaa *n. see* FLAH n.

fla/flaa *v. see* FLAH v.

flaaitaal *n. see* FLY TAAL n.

flab *n.* [1920s+] **1** fat, fatness. **2** (*UK juv.*) a fat person. [onomat. for something hanging down; (1) now virtually SE]

flaba-flaba *adj.* [1950s] (*W.I.*) **1** worthless, good-for-nothing. **2** stocky, short and thickset. [SE *flabby* + redup.]

flabbergast *n.* (*also* **flabagast**) [20C+] (*US*) **1** an awkward, clumsy person. **2** (*also* **flabbergastment**) confusion, surprise. [FLABBERGAST v.]

flabbergast *v.* (*also* **flabagast**) [late 18C+] to astound, to astonish, to confuse. [? SE *flabby* or *flap* + *aghast*; it was first mentioned in the *Annual Register* (1772) as a new piece of fashionable sl. It is poss. of dial. origin; the *EDD* has it as a Suffolk word, while Scot. has *flabrigast*, to boast extravagantly and *flabrigastit*, worn out with exertion]

flabbergasted *adj.* (*also* **flabagasted, flambergasted**) [late 18C+] **1** astonished, exhausted, annoyed or disgusted. **2** (*US*) a euph. for DAMNED adj. [FLABBERGAST v.]

flabbergastment *n. see* FLABBERGAST n. (2).

flabby-knackers *n.* [1950s+] a term of affectionate ribaldry. [SE *flabby* + KNACKERS n.]

flab-stabbing *n.* [2000s] (*US Black*) having sexual intercourse with a fat woman. [FLAB n. (1) + STAB v.]

flach *n. see* FLATCH n.

flack *n. see* FLAK n.

flack *v.* [1960s+] (*US*) to publicize; to work as a press agent. [FLAK n. (1)]

fladge *n.* (*also* **flage**) [1950s+] *flag*ellation, only when used in a sexual context; also attrib., used of flagellants. [abbr./pron.]

fladge queen *n.* (*also* **fladge fiend/freak**) [1970s+] a homosexual who enjoys flagellation. [FLADGE n. + QUEEN n.[2] (1)/QUEEN sfx (2)/FIEND n.[2] (2)/FREAK n.[1] (6)/FREAK sfx]

flag *n.*[1] (*also* **flagg**) **1** [mid-16C–mid-19C] (*UK Und.*) a groat, 4 pence. **2** [1930s+] (*US*) a $1 bill. **3** [1940s–60s] (*Aus.*) a £1 note. [(1) ? f. MLG *vleger*, 'a coin worth somewhat more than a Bremer groat'; (2) var. on (1) or abbr. JEWISH FLAG n.]

flag *n.*[2] **1** [mid–late 19C] an apron; thus *flag-flasher*, one who wears an apron when not actually working. **2** [mid-19C+] a sanitary towel. **3** [1960s] (*US*) the desire to avoid looking at a partner's face during sexual intercourse.

flag *n.*[3] **1** [late 19C] the labia. **2** [1960s] (*US*) an erect penis; thus *grow a flag*, to have an erection.

flag *n.*[4] [1930s–60s] (*US Und.*) an assumed name, an alias. [SE *flag of convenience*]

flag *n.*[5] [1960s] a cigarette. [? one waves it]

flag *n.*[6] [1960s] (*US prison*) a warning.

flag *n.*[7] [1970s] (*US*) instinct, personal standard or belief.

flag *n.*[8] [1970s+] (*drugs*) the flow of blood from the vein into the syringe, where it blends with the narcotic/water mixture before being pumped back into the vein; thus *have the flag up*, to have the needle in a vein. [the blood 'waves' as it enters the syringe; note 19C whaling jargon *flag*, the blood spouted by a harpooned whale]

flag *n.*[9] [1980s] (*US campus*) the grade of F (fail) (cf. ACE n.[6]). [initial letter; FLAG v.[2] (3)]

flag *n.*[10] [1990s+] (*US Und.*) the bottom row of cells in a prison block. [SE *flagstone*]

flag *v.*[1] **1** [late 19C–1950s] (*gay*) to attract a stranger with the eyes or with a slight gesture of the head. **2** [late 19C+] (*US*) to signal an interest in someone in anticipation of romantic or sexual involvement or to accost; thus as n. the gesture that signifies attraction. **3** [late 19C+] (*US*) to allow someone to pass by, esp. the intended victim of a pickpocket, to avoid. **4** [late 19C+] to refuse service to someone in a bar, to stop someone drinking; often as *flagging*, refusing service. **5** [1900s] to attract someone's attention. **6** [1900s–30s] (*US tramp*) to reject, turn away. **7** [1920s] (*US tramp*) to beg. **8** [1930s] to leave.

flag *v.*[2] **1** [1920s–60s] (*US Und.*) to arrest. **2** [1920s+] (*US Und.*) to release from custody. **3** [1950s+] (*US campus*) (*also* **fly a flag**) to fail a test or examination; thus to get a grade F in an examination. **4** [1990s+] (*US campus*) to fail to attend a class. [? SE *wave the white flag*, to surrender; (3) and (4) + initial letters]

flag *v.*[3] [1990s+] (*US, esp. prison*) to label someone in a certain way, usu. with derog. undertones, e.g. *he was flagged a homosexual* (cf. FLY A FLAG v.[1]).

flag-about *n.* [mid-19C] a street-walking prostitute (cf. FLAGGER n.; FLAG-HOPPER n.). [? she waves her fig. flag to attract customers or walks on *flag*stones]

flagary *see under* FEGARY.

flag day *n.* [1960s] (*US campus*) the menstrual period. [FLAG n.[2] (2)/HAVE THE FLAGS OUT v.]

flage *n. see* FLADGE n.

flag-flapper *n.* [late 19C+] one whose noisy patriotism is surpassed only by the care with which they ensure their ineligibility for active service.

flag-flasher *n.* [mid–late 19C] any member of the services who wears their uniform despite being off duty and in civilian surroundings.

flagg *n. see* FLAG n.[1]

flagger *n.* [mid-19C] a street prostitute (cf. FLAG-ABOUT n.). [SE *flag*, a paving stone, upon which she walks; + ? her *showing the flag*]

flagging *n.*[1] [1930s] (*US*) menstruation. [HAVE THE FLAGS OUT v.]

flagging *n.*[2] [1990s+] (*US gay*) wearing a handkerchief, in a back trouser pocket, to indicate a sexual preference.

flaggings *n.* [20C+] (*orig. US tramp*) meat or any other foodstuff, usu. cold. [? the *flagging down* by the tramp of a passing citizen, in the hope of getting a hand-out]

flaggin', saggin' and braggin' *phr.* [1990s+] (*US Black gang*) a phr. describing the means of identifying oneself as a member of a gang, esp. in prison. [spec. wearing the gang colours (cf. FLAGGING n.[2]), wearing one's trousers low on the hips and boasting about one's exploits in the free world. Such activities are often spec. prohibited in prisons in the (vain) hope of minimizing inter-gang tensions]

flaggot *n.* [1990s+] (*US gay*) an overt and ostentatious effeminate gay man. [*flaming faggot*]

flag-hopper *n.* [mid-19C] a street prostitute (cf. FLAG-ABOUT n.). [she 'hops' along the *flag*stones/pavement]

flag is up *phr.* (*also* **danger signal is up**) [late 19C+] a phr. used of a woman who is menstruating.

flag of defiance is out *phr.* [late 17C–early 19C] a phr. used of someone who is drunk. [the aggressiveness that so often accompanies heavy drinking]

flag of distress *n.* [mid-19C] **1** an advertisement or similar statement of charges for board and lodging. **2** thus a generic term for poverty. **3** the end of a person's shirt protruding through a hole in their trousers. [(1) those who have to pay suffer the distress]

flagon-wagon *n.* [1960s+] (*N.Z.*) a beer truck.

flags *n.* [mid–late 19C] clothes drying in the open air.

flag spot *n.* (*also* **flag stop**) [1930s–40s] (*US Black*) a bus stop. [SE *flag down*]

flag the banner *v.* [1940s] (*UK Und./gay*) of a male prostitute, to solicit.

flag the bone *v.* (*also* **flip the bone**) [1960s+] (*US*) to make a gesture of contempt by raising the middle finger. [the SE *bones* inside the finger]

flag unfurled *n.* [mid–late 19C] a man of the world. [rhy. sl.]

flag-wagger *n.* (*also* **flag-waver**) **1** [late 19C+] an overt and excessive patriot, esp. as found during the Anglo-Boer Wars. **2** [1920s+] (*US*) a song, film or oration which arouses patriotic fervour. [note jazz use *flagwaver*, 'a spectacular piece of music or part of a musical performance intended to excite the listeners and win their applause' (Gold, *A Jazz Lexicon*, 1964)]

flag-waver *n.*[1] [20C+] (*US*) an assistant to the boss. [such an assistant is given an order, he or she then communicates it to the rest of the workforce; the image is of semaphore flags]

flag-waver *n.*[2] [1980s+] (*Aus. prison*) an exhibitionist.

flah *n.* [1990s+] (*Irish*) (*also* **fla, flaa**) a sexually attractive/active young person, usu. a woman. [FLAH v.]

flah *v.* [1990s+] (*Irish*) (*also* **fla, flaa**) to have sexual intercourse. [Irish *fleadh* (pron. flah), a party]

flahoola *n.* [late 19C–1900s] (*Irish*) a fat, noisy, extremely vulgar woman. [Irish]

flail *n.* [1970s+] (*US*) a confused, anxiety-provoking activity. [SE *flail*, to act energetically but without direction]

flail *v.* [1980s+] (*US campus*) to fail a test through being flustered or over-pressured. [SE *fluster + fail*; SE *flail*, to act energetically but without direction]

flailing *adj.* [1990s+] very intoxicated, usu. with marijuana. [SE *flail*/FLAIL v.]

flak *n.* (*also* **flack**) **1** [1930s+] (*US*) (*also* **flak artist, flak merchant**) a publicity man/woman, a press or public relations agent, i.e. one whose job it is to catch adverse 'flak'. **2** [1940s+] interference, annoyance, problems. **3** [1960s+] (*orig. US*) cheek, negative criticism, verbal attacks. **4** [1970s+] publicity material. [SE *flak*, anti-aircraft fire, ult. the initials of the elements of Ger. *fliegerabwehrkanone*, 'pilot-defence-gun'; however, (1) is apparently an eponym from Gene *Flack*, a US publicist]

flak catcher *n.* [1970s+] a civil servant or similar figure in private industry whose task is to intercept complaints, queries etc from the public, before such problems reach their superiors. [SE *flak*, anti-aircraft fire + *catcher*]

flake *n.*[1] (*drugs*) **1** [1920s+] cocaine, spec. pieces that are smaller than average (cf. BASE n.). **2** [1950s] heroin. **3** [1980s] crack cocaine.

flake *n.*[2] **1** [1950s+] (*orig. US*) (*also* **flakeout, flako**) a boring, unappealing, incompetent, undesirable person. **2** [1950s+] (*US*) an eccentric, crazy person. **3** [1960s+] (*US*) a disappointment, a failure. **4** [1990s+] anything worthless or second-rate. [FLAKY adj.]

flake *n.*[3] [1980s] (*Aus.*) shark meat, esp. as sold in fish 'n' chip shops. [SE *flake*, a thin broad piece peeled or split off from the surface of something]

flake *v.*[1] [mid-19C+] (*Aus./Irish*) to beat, to thrash.

flake *v.*[2] [1970s] (*US Und.*) of police, to plant evidence; thus as n., planted evidence. [FLAKE n.[2] (1), i.e. to act in that way]

flake *v.*[3] *see* FLAKE OFF v. (5).

flake *v.*[4] *see* FLAKE (ON) v.

flake *v.*[5] *see* FLAKE (OUT) v.

flaked *adj.* [1910s+] drunk (cf. ADDLED adj.). [abbr. FLAKED OUT adj.]

flaked out *adj.* [1940s+] (*orig. US*) exhausted, unconscious, asleep, lying down, resting. [FLAKE (OUT) v.]

flake off *v.* [1950s+] **1** (*US campus*) to depart, to go away; to leave someone in peace; also as imper. meaning 'go away!' **2** (*US campus*) to loaf, to idle. **3** (*US Black*) to break off one's line of thought. **4** (*US campus*) to irritate. **5** (*US*) (*also* **flake**) to back down in an argument or fight.

flake (on) *v.* [1980s+] (*US campus*) to fail to keep an appointment or other commitment.

flakeout *n. see* FLAKE n.[2] (1).

flake (out) *v.* **1** [1940s+] to collapse from exhaustion or an excess of drink or drugs. **2** [1940s+] (*US*) to recline or lie down, to sleep. **3** [1950s+] to go crazy. **4** [1960s+] (*US*) to die. **5** [1970s+] (*US campus*) to astound. **6** [1980s+] to fail, to let down. [? SE *flag*, to grow weak, to become exhausted, or US commercial fishing jargon *on the flakes*, dead, laid out for burial; this refers to the laying out of split fish on wooden racks or *flakes*]

flaker *n.* [1910s+] (*Aus.*) a fall; a crash.

flakers *adj.* [1950s+] (*orig. naut.*) drunk (cf. ADDLED adj.). [FLAKE (OUT) v. (1) + -ER sfx]

flakes n. [1970s+] (drugs) phencyclidine (cf. ACE n.[4]).

flakey adj. see FLAKY adj.

flak merchant n. see FLAK n. (1).

flako n. see FLAKE n.[2] (1).

flako adj. [1950s+] drunk (cf. ADDLED adj.). [FLAKED OUT adj.]

flaky adj. (also **flakey, flako**) [1960s+] (orig. US) **1** of a person, second-rate, unreliable, distasteful, eccentric, crazy. **2** of an object, eccentric, crazy, outrageous, unusual, unreliable or erratic. [orig. baseball use. 'It's an insider's word [...] It does not mean anything so crude as "crazy", but it's well beyond "screwball" and far off to the side of "eccentric"' (New York Times, 26 April 1964); ? SE fall/crumble into flakes, i.e. to come apart]

flaky ho n. [1970s+] an unstable, unreliable prostitute, whose desire for clients and money is undermined by her inability to maintain a good front and economic and social discipline. [FLAKY adj. (1) + HO n.[1] (1)]

flam n.[1] [late 17C–1910s] **1** a lie, a deception. **2** an idle tale, a piece of nonsense. [FLAM v. (1); but note FLIM-FLAM n.[1] (1) + Scot. flamfew, a trifle, a trinket]

flam n.[2] [mid-19C] a ring. [? FAMBLE n. (2)]

flam v. **1** [17C–19C; 1980s+] (also **flam off**) to hoodwink, to deceive. **2** [mid-19C] (US campus) to be attentive to a woman. **3** [1900s] (US campus) to fail. **4** [1970s] (US) to flirt with or be aggressively forceful towards someone. [SE flam, to deceive by a sham story, trick or flattery]

flambasted adj. [1990s+] (US teen) utterly intoxicated by drink and drugs taken in tandem. [FLAMING adj.[2] (1) + SE lambaste, to thrash]

flambergasted adj. see FLABBERGASTED adj.

flam-blam n. see FLIM-FLAM n.[1] (1).

flamboast v. [1990s+] (US teen) to show off or flaunt material items. [? FLAM v. (4) + SE boast]

flamdoodle see under FLAPDOODLE.

flame n.[1] [18C] venereal disease; thus flaming, diseased. [the association of VD with heat]

flame n.[2] **1** [mid-18C+] a (female) lover; a heart throb. **2** [1930s] (US) an infatuation.

flame n.[3] see FLAMER n.[1] (4).

flame v.[1] **1** [1950s+] to talk arrant and apparent nonsense about an otherwise interesting subject. **2** [1960s] (US campus) to be sexually aroused, to flirt, esp. when drunk. **3** [1960s+] to exaggerate, to bore. **4** [1960s+] to rant in an unacceptable manner, esp. to insult a specific individual, via a communications network, e.g. the Internet.

flame v.[2] (also **flame it up**) [1960s+] **1** (US gay/campus) of a man (whether actually homosexual or not), to look exaggeratedly 'feminine' in dress and style; thus flaming, acting in an obviously homosexual manner. **2** (US gay) to wear make-up. [FLAMER n.[1] (4)]

flame artist n. see FLAMER n.[1] (4).

flame cooking n. [1980s+] (drugs) smoking FREEBASE n. cocaine by placing the pipe over the gas burner of a domestic stove.

flame it up v. see FLAME v.[2].

flamer n.[1] **1** [late 17C+] an admirer, a lover, a promiscuous woman. **2** [early–mid-19C] a conspicuous, ostentatious person who 'burns brightly'. **3** [late 19C; 1960s–70s] an enthusiast; a success with the female sex, a ladies' man. **4** [1940s+] (US) (also **flame, flame artist, flame thrower**) a blatantly homosexual man. [they all 'burn brightly', although (4) is underpinned by abbr. of flaming faggot/FAGGOT n.[2] (3)]

flamer n.[2] [late 19C] a safety match burning with a notably bright flame.

flamer n.[3] (US campus) **1** [1930s+] a clumsy, embarrassing or highly unpleasant person. **2** [1960s+] anyone who commits a major social error; thus the error itself. [such blunders mean that one 'goes down in flames']

flames n. [19C] a nickname for a red-headed person.

flame thrower n. see FLAMER n.[1] (4).

flaming n. **1** [1950s+] speaking incessantly and obsessively on a particular topic of little interest to anyone but oneself. **2** [1980s+] using computer 'bulletin boards' and other communications links to circulate obscene messages, pictures etc. [FLAME v.[1]]

flaming adj.[1] **1** [mid-18C–19C; 1990s+] excessively noticeable, flagrant, monstrous. **2** [1960s+] (US gay) ostentatiously homosexual. **3** [2000s] (Irish) drunk. [SE flaming, burning brightly]

flaming adj.[2] (orig. Aus.) **1** [late 19C+] a mildly pej. negative adj. **2** [1940s+] a congratulatory epithet. **3** [1960s+] (1) used as an infix. [synon. SE hellish or euph. FUCKING adj. (1)]

flaming fury n. [1960s] (Aus.) an outside lavatory, the contents of which were periodically burned off.

flammy adj. [1990s+] (US Black teen) flamboyant. [abbr.]

flam off v. see FLAM v. (1).

flanderkin n. [late 17C–early 19C] a notably fat man or horse. [proper name Flanders + sfx -kin]

Flanders fortune n. [late 17C–18C] a relatively small fortune or inheritance. [stereotyping of the Dutch as mean]

Flanders piece n. [late 17C–18C] a painting that looks good from a distance but not so good close to. [stereotyping of the Dutch as mean, hypocritical or deceitful]

Flanders reckoning n. [early 17C] spending money in a place that has no links to that where one received it. [stereotyping of the Dutch as mean or deceitful]

flange n. **1** [1960s+] the head of the penis. **2** [1990s+] (orig. US) the vagina. [SE flange, (1) that which stands out from the surface; (2) a collar]

flangehead n. [1940s] a derog. term for an East Asian (cf. BROWNIE n.[2]). [derog. use of SE]

flank v. [mid-19C] (US, orig. milit.) **1** to dodge, to evade. **2** to trick out of. [SE flank, to go around the side]

flankard n. [16C–17C] a venereal sore. [hunting jargon flankard, a wound in a deer's flank or side]

flanker n. **1** [mid-19C–1900s] a blow or punch. **2** [mid-19C–1900s] a verbal response. **3** [1920s+] (orig. milit.) a trick, a swindle, a hoax; thus do/pull/work a flanker, to trick, to swindle. [SE flank, to go around the side; note WW1 milit. flanker, a shirker]

flankey n. [mid-19C] (UK Und.) the buttocks. [SE flank, 'the fleshy or muscular part of the side of an animal or a man between the ribs and the hip' (OED)]

flannel n.[1] [early–mid-19C] grog, punch or gin-twist, with a dash of beer. [SE flannel, a form of woollen cloth; the drink 'keeps one warm']

flannel n.[2] [20C+] rubbish, nonsense, albeit plausible rubbish. [? 19C tradesmen's jargon flannel, the ornate, scroll-ridden letterheads with which tradesmen garlanded the invoices they sent to their aristocratic clients. There is no proof, however, that this is linked to the 20C use, albeit a similar one]

flannel v. [1940s+] to flatter, to curry favour, to talk nonsense in a soothing, plausible manner, esp. for the purposes of charming a woman one wishes to seduce. [FLANNEL n.[2]]

flannel back n. see FLANNEL JACKET n.

flannel face n. see FLANNEL MOUTH n.

flannel feet n. [20C+] (US) **1** large feet. **2** a clumsy person.

flannel jacket n. (also **flannel back**) [late 19C] a navvy, who wears such a garment.

flannel mouth n. (also **flannel face**) **1** [late 19C–1960s] (US) a derog. term for an Irishman (cf. BOG ARAB n.). **2** [20C+] (Can.) a well-spoken person. **3** [1910s+] (US) a loudmouth, a braggart, one who talks too much and with too little sense. **4** [1940s] (US) a derog. term for a Pole. [FLANNEL-MOUTHED adj.]

flannel-mouthed adj. (also **flannel-tongued**) (orig. US) **1** [late 19C+] having a large mouth. **2** [late 19C+] loud-mouthed. **3** [1930s] talking thickly or with a brogue. [SAmE flannelmouth, a catfish]

flannel-shirt dyke *n.* [1990s+] (*US gay*) a casually dressed lesbian, neither particularly feminine or masculine. [SE *flannel shirt* + DYKE n.; 'so called for the habit of wearing plaid flannel shirts whenever the weather permits. They tend to be outdoors-types. There are flannel-shirt butches and femmes, but not as many of them, since the stereotype of the flannel-shirt dyke emerged during the 1970s when "The Uniform" for lesbians was jeans and a flannel shirt']

flap *n.*[1] **1** [early 17C] a cap. **2** [late 18C–1920s] any garment that has a pendant flap or flaps.

flap *n.*[2] **1** [early–mid-17C; 1910s+] a promiscuous woman; a prostitute. **2** [late 19C–1910s] the vagina. **3** [1950s+] (*US*) the mouth.

flap *n.*[3] [late 19C] (*UK Und.*) a strip of lead used on roofs. [? it *flaps* about as one removes it]

flap *n.*[4] [20C+] excrement, esp. animal. [? abbr. SE *flapjack*]

flap *n.*[5] **1** [1910s+] panic, excitement, commotion. **2** [1970s] an argument. [orig. WW1 milit. use]

flap *n.*[6] [1950s–60s] (*US*) nonsense, rubbish. [abbr. FLAPDOODLE n.[2] (1)]

flap *n.*[7] [1980s] (*Aus.*) a cheque.

flap *n.*[8] *see* FLAPS n. (1).

flap *v.*[1] (*also* **chuck a flap**) [mid-17C–mid-19C] to fall or throw oneself down suddenly. [? SE *flop*]

flap *v.*[2] [late 19C] to rob, to swindle; thus *flap the dimmock*, to pay (money).

flap *v.*[3] [late 19C] of a man, to have sexual intercourse. [FLAP n.[2]]

flap *v.*[4] **1** [1910s] to chatter. **2** [1910s+] to become over-excited, to lose control, esp. when faced by an unforeseen problem. **3** [1970s+] (*US gay*) to act in an exaggeratedly effeminate manner. [FLAP n.[5] (1)]

flap a jay *v.* [late 19C+] (*UK Und.*) to trick a simpleton, to swindle an innocent victim. [FLAP v.[2] + JAY n.[3] (2)]

flap at the jibs *v.* [1950s+] (*US Black*) to talk wildly, out of control, in a panicky, unrestrained manner. [SE *flap* + JIB n.[1] (4)]

flap-cap *n.* [early 18C] a prostitute.

flapdash *adj.* [1910s–20s] very clean, shiny. [? confusion of the 2 parts of *slapdash*, assuming the imagery to be of dusting]

flapdoodle *n.*[1] **1** [17C] the penis. **2** [19C] the vagina. **3** [19C] a sexually incompetent man, either one who is still too young to have had sex or one who is now too old to attempt it. [SE *flap*, something hanging down + DOODLE n.[2] (1)]

flapdoodle *n.*[2] (*also* **doodleflap, flamdoodle**) **1** [19C+] nonsense, rubbish; thus *flapdoodler*, a charlatan, a politician, a speaker of portentous but empty words. **2** [20C+] (*US Black*) mischief, malicious behaviour. **3** [1920s] (*US*) any thing. **4** [1950s] a fuss, an uproar. [ety. unknown; the image is of flapping lips]

flapdoodle *adj.* (*also* **flamdoodle**) [late 19C+] (*US*) absurd, nonsensical. [FLAPDOODLE n.[2] (1)]

flapdragon *n.* **1** [17C] a derog. term for a German or Dutchman. **2** [late 17C–early 19C] venereal disease. [imagery drawn on SE *flapdragon/snapdragon*, a game 'in which they catch raisins out of burning brandy and, extinguishing them by closing the mouth, eat them' (Johnson, *Dictionary*, 1755); (1) supposes an image of the German or Dutchman as all display but no substance and as races that for all their external show can be 'eaten up' by an Englishman; (2) the 'heat' affects the penis]

flap it in someone's face *v.* (*also* **fling it in someone's face**) [late 19C] of a prostitute, to expose her genitals or breasts.

flapjack *n.* [1940s+] (*Aus.*) a powder compact. [the 'flap']

flapjack invalid *n.* [late 19C] (*US*) one who is suffering from an excess of food and drink. [they are reduced to eating *flapjacks*]

flapjaw *n.* [1950s–60s] (*US*) a noisy talker, a braggart. [FLAP ONE'S JAW v.]

flap one's chops *v.* [20C+] to talk incessantly, to gossip. [SE *flap* + CHOPS n.[1] (1)]

flap one's ears *v.* [1920s+] (*US*) to listen (hard).

flap one's horns *v.* [1960s] (*US Black*) to listen.

flap one's jaw *v.* [1940s+] (*US*) to talk idly, to gossip.

flap one's mouth *v.* (*also* **flap one's lips, flap one's tongue**) [1910s+] to chatter, to say more than is sensible or proper. [now mainly W.I. use]

flapp *n. see* FLAPPER n.[3] (2).

flapper *n.*[1] **1** [17C] the (flaccid) penis. **2** [19C] an impotent old man. [FLAPDOODLE n.[1]]

flapper *n.*[2] [19C] the hand.

flapper *n.*[3] **1** [late 19C–1910s] a very young prostitute (usu. in her early teens) (cf. FLIPPER n.[3]). **2** [late 19C+] (*orig. US*) (*also* **flapp**) a flighty girl or young woman, usu. middle-class, in her late teens or very early 20s, who sported short, bobbed hair, lipstick and skimpy dresses and generally led a lifestyle as far as possible removed from that desired by her parents; thus combs. *flapper-seat*, a seat at the back of a bicycle to accommodate a young woman; *flapper vote*, a contemptuous expression for the parliamentary vote, which was granted to women aged 21 years in 1928 (the over-30s having been enfranchised in 1918); also attrib. [various etys. have been offered, each of which may have some claim to accuracy: the Northumbrian dial. *flap*, an unsteady young woman; SE *flapper*, a young wild duck or partridge (which flaps its wings as it experiments with flying); SE *flap*, to act in an emotional manner, supposedly typical of such young women. Whatever the ety. the heyday of the *flapper* (2) was the 1920s, Scott Fitzgerald's 'Jazz Age', an era of which they were as emblematic as the 'swinging dolly-bird' of the 1960s]

flapper *n.*[4] [20C+] (*US*) a large foot or the shoe that encases it.

flapper *n.*[5] [1940s+] (*US Black*) the mouth; thus in pl. the lips.

flapper *n.*[6] *see* FLAPPING TRACK n.

flapper-bracket *n.* [1920s] a motorcycle pillion. [FLAPPER n.[3] (2) + SE *bracket*]

flappers *n.*[1] [late 19C] the labia (cf. DEW-FLAPS n.).

flappers *n.*[2] **1** [late 19C] exaggeratedly long, pointed shoes. **2** [1930s] (*UK tramp*) the boards carried by a 'sandwich-man'. **3** [1930s–40s] the arms. **4** [1930s+] (*US*) the ears. [plays on SE]

flappers *n.*[3] *see* FLAPPING n.

flapper-shaker *n.* [19C] the hand; thus *flapper-shaking*, hand-shaking. [ext. of FLAPPER n.[2]]

flapper steaks *n.* [1940s] (*US Black*) pigs' ears (eaten as a 'soul food' dish). [FLAPPERS n.[2] (4)]

flapping *n.* (*also* **flappers**) [1910s+] any form of racing, e.g. horses or dogs, that is not subject to Jockey Club or National Hunt Committee regulations or, in greyhound racing, to those of the National Greyhound Racing Club.

flapping track *n.* (*also* **flapper**) [1910s+] a small, unlicensed racetrack for horses or dogs. [FLAPPING n. + SE *track*]

flaps *n.* [late 19C+] **1** (*also* **side-flaps**) the ears, usu. large ones; occas. sing. **2** the labia (cf. DEW-FLAPS n.). [note. juv. use *flap-ears*, nosy, inquisitive people]

flapsauce *n.* [20C+] nonsense, rubbish.

flap shot *n.* [1970s+] in pornographic still or moving pictures, a close-up shot of the labia and open vagina. [FLAPS n. (2) + SE *shot*, a picture]

flap snot *n.* [1990s+] vaginal secretions (cf. BINDERJUICE n.). [FLAPS n. (2) + SNOT n.[1] (4)]

flaptabs *n.* [1950s+] the ears. [SE *flaps*/FLAPS n. (1) + TAB n.[1]]

flap-trap *n.* [1940s] (*US*) the mouth. [SE *flap* + TRAP n.[3]; note FLAP n.[2] (3)]

flap with a fox-tail, a *n.* [17C] a contemptuous dismissal, a trivial rebuke. [the lightness of a SE *foxtail*]

flare *n.* [mid–late 19C] **1** a quarrel, an argument. **2** a spree, an outing. [FLARE-UP n.[1]]

flare *v.* [mid-19C] **1** to swagger. **2** to steal by sleight of hand.

flared *adj.* [1960s+] (*Can.*) slightly drunk. [? abbr. FLARING adv. (drunk)]

flare-up *n.*[1] (*also* **flare-out**) [mid-19C–1900s] **1** an argument, a fight. **2** a jovial social gathering. **3** one who seeks a good time. **4** one who is socially adept. **5** an orgy.

flare-up *n.*[2] [1900s–10s] brandy. [its flammability]

flare up *v.* [mid-19C+] to lose one's temper (suddenly), to speak forcefully.

flare up! *excl.* [mid-19C] a cry of delight, triumph or defiance. [coined at the burnings that accompanied the Reform Riots of 1832, esp. in Bristol]

flaring *adv.* [19C–1910s] very, extremely.

flash *n.*[1] **1** [late 17C–mid-19C] a nouveau riche, an ostentatious person, a showy swindler. **2** [mid-18C+] cant or criminal slang. **3** [19C] a generic term for the criminal underworld. **4** [early 19C] sporting jargon. **5** [mid-19C+] ostentation, showiness, vulgarity. **6** [1940s] a success. **7** [1970s] a general term of address. [FLASH adj.[1] (1)]

flash *n.*[2] [late 17C–18C] a periwig; thus *rum flash*, a long, full, expensive wig; *queer flash*, an old, raggedy wig. [? its being worn by a FLASH n.[1] (1), i.e. an ostentatious person]

flash *n.*[3] **1** [mid-19C+] (*UK Und.*) a large bundle of notes, esp. when used in a game of 3-card trick to entice victims; thus phr. *make a flash*, to exhibit a large bundle of notes. **2** [late 19C+] (*UK Und.*) imitation gold coins or banknotes. **3** [1920s+] (*UK/US Und.*) cheap but alluring items, e.g. cheap jewellery, used to lure players into carnival games, confidence tricks etc. **4** [1970s+] (*US gay*) cheap jewellery worn by homosexual males. [abbr. FLASH ROLL n.]

flash *n.*[4] **1** [late 19C–1950s] (*orig. US*) a quick look around. **2** [20C+] (*orig. US*) a brief glimpse. **3** [1930s+] a brief glimpse by a man of a woman inadvertently revealing her thighs, breasts or genitals; or vice versa, of a penis. **4** [1980s] a sign of flirtatious behaviour. [(3) was initially a ref. to the conscious 'flashing' by stripteasers/burlesque artists]

flash *n.*[5] **1** [late 19C–1970s] (*US*) a surprising piece of news or a rumour. **2** [1920s+] (*US*) a burst of inspiration, a sudden idea. **3** [1920s+] a flashback.

flash *n.*[6] **1** [1920s–50s] (*US Und.*) a suit of clothes. **2** [1920s+] (*Aus.*) one's personal appearance. [FLASH n.[1] (1)]

flash *n.*[7] (*drugs*) **1** [1940s+] the instantaneous effect that follows the injection of a narcotic or other drug; also in non-drug use. **2** [1970s+] LSD (cf. A n.[3]). **3** [1970s+] the effect of LSD.

flash *n.*[8] [1960s] (*US campus*) the grade of F (cf. ACE n.[6]). [initial letter]

flash *n.*[9] [1970s] a cigarette lighter.

flash *adj.*[1] **1** [mid-17C+] of a person or thing, ostentatious, showy. **2** [18C+] expert, understanding what someone else means, 'knowing the ropes', esp. of the underworld. **3** [mid-19C] fashionable, smart, chic. **4** [1950s+] cheeky; arrogant, boastful.

flash *adj.*[2] **1** [late 17C+] belonging to or connected with the underworld. **2** [late 18C–19C] amoral, promiscuous; thus FLASH GIRL n.[1]. **3** [early 19C–1910s] belonging to, connected with or resembling the world of 'sportsmen', esp. the patrons of the prize-fight 'ring'. **4** [early 19C–1950s] (*UK Und.*) counterfeit; thus FLASH NOTE n.

flash *v.*[1] [mid-18C+] to 'cut a figure', to show off, usu. one's material possessions and gross self-esteem. [FLASH adj.[1] (1)]

flash *v.*[2] **1** [mid-18C+] to display, e.g. a gun; also in non-material use, e.g. to display an idea. **2** [mid-19C+] (*orig. US*) to expose a part of the body in a quick or provocative manner. **3** [mid-19C+] to expose one's genitals, esp. in a public place. **4** [1920s–30s] (*US tramp*) to turn state's evidence. **5** [2000s] (*US teen*) to shout at, while others are watching.

flash *v.*[3] **1** [early 19C] (*UK Und.*) to buy and sell stolen property. **2** [1900s] (*US Und.*) to acquire through pickpocketing.

flash *v.*[4] **1** [1920s+] to notice. **2** [1960s+] to realize, to think, usu. suddenly or spontaneously. [FLASH n.[5] (2), compounded by drug imagery]

flash *v.*[5] [1950s+] (*UK Black*) to rush, to run away. [SE phr. *quick as a flash*]

flash *v.*[6] [1950s+] (*US campus*) to vomit; also as *flash one's cookies* (cf. BLOW v.[3]).

flash *v.*[7] [1960s] (*US campus*) to do badly in a test or examination. [FLASH n.[8]]

flash *v.*[8] [1960s+] (*US*) to experience the effects of taking a drug, esp. hallucinatory. [FLASH n.[7] (1)]

flash *adv.* [1950s+] boastfully, arrogantly, in a showing-off manner. [FLASH adj.[1] (4)]

flash a bit *v.* [mid–late 19C] of a woman, to behave immodestly. [FLASH v.[2] (2)]

flash a fawney *v.* [19C] to wear a counterfeit ring. [FLASH v.[2] (1) + FAWNEY n. (1)]

flash alf *n.* [1900s–70s] a fashionable man. [FLASH adj.[1] (3) + generic *Alf*]

flash as a rat with a gold tooth *phr.* (*also* **flash as a chinky's horse**) [20C+] (*Aus.*) extremely ostentatious. [FLASH adj.[1] (1)]

flash a tatler *v.* (*also* **flash a tattler**) [late 18C–19C] to wear a watch. [FLASH v.[2] (1) + TATLER n.]

flashback *n.* [1970s+] (*drugs*) the repetition after the event of emotions and sensations, typically a recurrence without the presence of any drug of the hallucinations provoked by LSD, first experienced while using a drug.

flash blone/blowen *n. see* FLASH COVE n.

flash boy *n.* [late 19C] (*UK Und.*) a swindler.

flash cane *n. see* FLASH KEN n. (1).

flash captain *n.* [mid-18C] a thug employed by a casino to ensure order. [FLASH adj.[2] (1) + CAPTAIN n.[1] (3)]

flash case *n.*[1] (*also* **flash crib**) [early 18C–19C] a public house frequented mainly by criminals. [FLASH adj.[2] (1) + CASE n.[3] (1)/CRIB n.[1] (2)]

flash case *n.*[2] [1930s+] (*US Black*) a satchel or bag that contains illegal drugs or any other contraband. [FLASH adj.[2] (1) + SE *case*]

flash chant *n.* (*also* **flash chaunt**) [early 19C] a song filled with criminal slang. [FLASH adj.[2] (1) + CHANT n. (2)]

flash chap *n. see* FLASHMAN n. (3).

flash cove *n.* (*also* **flash blone, …blowen, …covess**) [19C] **1** a thief. **2** a landlord or landlady, esp. of a criminal public house. **3** a receiver of stolen goods; thus as v., to sell stolen goods to a receiver. [FLASH adj.[2] (1) + COVE n. (1)/COVESS n.]

flash crib *n. see* FLASH CASE n.[1].

flash cull *n.* [early 18C] (*UK Und.*) one who enjoys the society of the underworld. [FLASH adj.[2] (1) + CULL n.[1] (4)]

flash dona *n.* [late 19C] a showy, working-class woman. [FLASH adj.[1] (1) + DONA n. (1)]

flash dough *n.* [1940s] (*US Und.*) counterfeit money, used in a confidence trick. [FLASH adj.[2] (4) + DOUGH n.[1] (1)]

flash drum *n.* [mid-19C] **1** a criminal lodging house. **2** a brothel (cf. BADGER-CRIB n.). [FLASH adj.[2] (1) + DRUM n.[3]]

flashed-up *adj.* [20C+] dressed up in one's best clothes. [FLASH adj.[1] (3)]

flasher *n.*[1] [late 19C; 1960s+] an exhibitionist, one who reveals parts of their naked body. [FLASH v.[2] (3)]

flasher *n.*[2] [20C+] (*US*) a spendthrift, one who shops ostentatiously. [FLASH v.[1]]

flashes *n.* [1910s–30s] used as an intensifier, e.g. *swearing flashes, cursing flashes*.

flash gentry *n.* [18C–19C] thieves as a group. [FLASH adj.[2] (1) + SE *gentry*]

flash girl *n.*[1] (*also* **flash madam**) [late 18C–19C] a prostitute (cf. AWAYDAY GIRL n.). [FLASH adj.[2] (2) + SE *girl*]

flash girl *n.*[2] [late 19C] a showy dresser. [FLASH adj.[1] (1) + SE *girl*]

flash harry *n.* [1910s+] an ostentatious, loudly dressed and usu. ill-mannered man. [FLASH adj.[1] (1) + generic *Harry*; best known as the nickname of the conductor Sir Malcolm Sargeant

(1895–1967) and as the SPIV n. character played by George Cole (b.1925) in the 'St Trinian's' films in the 1950s]

flash house *n.* 1 [mid-18C–19C] a public house frequented mainly by the underworld. 2 [mid-19C–1920s] a brothel (cf. ACCOMMODATION HOUSE n.). [FLASH adj.² (1)/FLASH adj.² (2) + SE *house*/HOUSE n.¹ (1)]

flashing *n.* [1960s+] indecent exposure. [FLASH v.² (3)]

flash in the pan *n.* 1 [late 17C–18C; 1980s+] sex without ejaculation. 2 [18C+] an incompetent, useless person. 3 [18C+] an abortive effort or outburst. [SE phr. *flash in the pan*, an explosion of gunpowder without any communication beyond the touch-hole, thus the gun fails to fire]

flash in the pan *v.* 1 [18C–mid-19C] to be incompetent. 2 [mid-19C] to have sex without ejaculation. [FLASH IN THE PAN n.]

flash it *v.*¹ [late 18C–mid-19C] to show off. [FLASH v.¹]

flash it *v.*² [late 19C+] to reveal one's genitals. [FLASH v.² (3) + IT n.¹ (2)]

flash it about *v.* (*also* **flash it away**) 1 [mid-19C+] to act in a showy manner. 2 [1960s+] to show off one's money or wealth in an ostentatious manner. [ext. FLASH IT v.¹; (2) + SE *flash*]

flash jack *n.* [late 19C–1960s] (*Aus.*) a dandy, a swell, esp. in the context of a sheep station; thus *flash jane*, a showy woman. [FLASH adj.¹ (1) + generic *Jack*]

flash ken *n.* 1 [late 17C–19C] (*also* **flash cane/kane**) a criminal lodging house. 2 [mid-19C–1910s] a brothel (cf. BADGER-CRIB n.). [FLASH adj.² (1) + KEN n.¹ (1)]

flash kiddy *n.* [19C] a dandified young thief. [FLASH adj.¹ (1) + KIDDY n.¹ (1)]

flash lingo *n.* [late 18C–19C] the jargon of the criminal underworld. [FLASH adj.² (1) + LINGO n. (1)]

flashly *adv.* [early–mid-19C] 1 in an ostentatious, showy manner. 2 using the language of the criminal underworld. [FLASH adj.¹ (1)/FLASH adj.² (1)]

flash madam *n. see* FLASH GIRL n.¹.

flashman *n.* 1 [late 18C] a highwayman. 2 [late 18C] a thug employed by a brothel to deal with undesirables and drunks. 3 [late 18C–mid-19C] (*also* **flash chap**) a pimp (cf. ABBOT ON THE CROSS n.). 4 [late 18C–19C] anyone conversant with the criminal world and thus its vocabulary. 5 [mid-19C] (*US*) a man about town, a loafer with no visible means of support but an endless appetite for good clothes, parties and places of entertainment; such a man lived by his wits and often off foolish women. 6 [mid-19C] an itinerant hawker. [FLASH adj.² (1) + SE *man*; (5) FLASH adj.¹ (1)]

flash mob *n.* [1940s] (*US Und.*) a gang of thieves or confidence tricksters. [FLASH adj.² (1) + MOB n.² (3)]

flash moll *n.* [mid-19C] a thief's female companion. [FLASH adj.² (2) + MOLL n.¹ (3)]

flash mollisher *n.* [early 19C] a female criminal or habitué of the underworld; a prostitute. [FLASH adj.² (2) + MOLLISHER n. (1)]

flashness *n.* [mid–late 19C] ostentation, showing-off. [FLASH adj.¹ (1)]

flash note *n.* (*also* **flash 'un**) [early 19C–1950s] a piece of paper that at first glance looks like a banknote; a forged note of any sort, e.g. a licence, certificate etc. [FLASH adj.² (4) + SE *notes*]

flash of light *n.* 1 [late 19C] a gaudily dressed woman. 2 [1970s+] a sight. [(1) 'upon the model of a rainbow' (Ware); (2) rhy. sl.]

flash of lightning *n.* [late 18C–mid-19C] a glass of gin. [SE *flash* + LIGHTNING n.¹ (1) + play on SE]

flash on *v.* 1 [1920s+] (*US*) to catch sight of. 2 [1960s+] to have a sudden inspiration, memory, moment of absolute comprehension etc. [FLASH v.⁴ (1)]

flash one's gab *v.* [early 19C] to talk, esp. to brag, to boast. [FLASH v.² (1) + GAB n. (2)]

flash one's gash *v.* [1990s+] (*Aus.*) of a woman, to expose her vagina as an incitement/invitation to intercourse. [FLASH v.² (3) + GASH n.¹ (1)]

flash one's hand *v.* [1960s] (*US*) to let down one's guard; to reveal one's secrets, plans etc. [card-playing imagery]

flash one's ivories/ivory *v. see* FLASH THE IVORIES v.

flash one's rags *v.* [mid–late 19C] to show off one's bankroll. [FLASH v.² (1) + RAG n.¹ (3)]

flash one's roll *v.* [20C+] to display one's money. [FLASH v.² (1) + ROLL n.²]

flash one's ticker *v.* [mid–late 19C] to take one's watch out frequently. [FLASH v.² (1) + TICKER n.¹ (1)]

flash panny *n.* (*also* **flash panney**) 1 [early 19C] a public house used primarily by criminals. 2 [mid-19C] a brothel. [FLASH adj.² (1)/FLASH adj.² (2) + PANNEY n.² (1)]

flash piece *n.* [19C] a prostitute. [FLASH adj.² (2) + PIECE n.¹ (1)]

flash queen *n. see* MISS FLASH n.

flash roll *n.* [mid-19C+] a sum of money that is revealed as proof that a person, esp. a narcotics dealer or other criminal, is willing to do business; the money is 'flashed' before the client (cf. CALIFORNIA BANKROLL n.). [SE *flash*/FLASH adj.² (1) + ROLL n.²]

flash song *n.* [early 19C] a song filled with criminal slang. [FLASH adj.² (1) + SE *song*]

flash-sport *n.* [1950s] (*US Black*) a notably stylish man. [FLASH adj.¹ (1) + SPORT n.² (1)]

flashtail *n.* 1 [mid-19C] a prostitute, esp. one seeking wealthy customers who will be robbed by her pimp (cf. BANGTAIL n.¹). 2 [1970s+] (*US Black*) any prostitute. [FLASH v.² (2) + TAIL n.² (3)]

flash the ash *v.* [20C+] to hand around one's pack of cigarettes. [FLASH v.² (1) + SE *ash*]

flash the dibs *v.* [mid-19C–1920s] to spend one's money. [FLASH v.² (1) + DIBBS n. (1)]

flash the dicky *v.* [mid-19C] to expose one's shirt-front. [FLASH v.² (2) + DICKY n.¹ (3)]

flash the drag *v.* [late 19C] (*UK Und.*) of a man, to wear female clothes for criminal purposes. [FLASH v.² (1) + DRAG n.⁸ (1)]

flash the gab *v.* [late 19C] to show off, to act ostentatiously. [FLASH v.² (1) + GAB n. (2)]

flash the gallery *v. see* FLASH THE RANGE v.

flash the hash *v.* [late 18C+] (*orig. UK Und.*) to vomit. [FLASH v.² (1) + SE *hash*, stew; 20C+ use is US]

flash the ivories *v.* (*also* **flash one's ivories/ivory**) [late 18C+] to smile, to grin, to laugh with a wide-open mouth. [IVORY n. (1)]

flash the muzzle *v.* [19C] to draw a pistol. [FLASH v.² (1) + SE *muzzle*]

flash the narl *v.* [early 19C] to complain aggressively, to take exception (to). [FLASH v.² (1) + SE *gnarl*, a snarl]

flash the patter *v.* [late 18C–19C] 1 to talk fast and meaninglessly. 2 to talk in cant. [FLASH v.² (1) + PATTER n.]

flash the range *v.* (*also* **flash the gallery**) [1950s+] (*US prison*) the scanning of the area outside one's cell by using a hand mirror to catch any reflections of approaching warders etc. [SE *flash* + RANGE n.]

flash the tongue *v.* [19C] to talk fast and, usu., meaninglessly. [FLASH v.² (1) + SE *tongue*]

flash the wedge *v.* [19C] (*UK Und.*) to dispose of one's 'swag' or booty. [FLASH v.² (1) + WEDGE n.¹]

flash toggery *n.* (*also* **flash togs**) [mid–late 19C] smart clothes. [FLASH adj.¹ (3) + TOGGERY n. (1)/TOGS n. (1)]

flash 'un *n. see* FLASH NOTE n.

flash up *v.* (*US*) 1 [late 19C] to produce, to hand over. 2 [1930s] of a woman, to dress showily, to use an excess of cosmetics. [FLASH v.¹]

flashwoman *n.* [19C] a prostitute (cf. FANCY WOMAN n.). [FLASH adj.² (2) + SE *woman*]

flashy *adj.* [late 18C+] pertaining to the sporting and criminal worlds. [FLASH adj.²]

flash yad *n.* [mid-19C–1900s] a pleasant day out. [FLASH adj.[1] (3) + YAD n.]

flashy blade *n.* (*also* **flashy fop, flashy spark**) [18C–19C] a dandy. [FLASH adj.[1] (1) + BLADE n.[2] (1)/SE *fop/spark*, a dandy]

flat *n.*[1] **1** [mid-16C–18C; 1930s] (*UK Und.*) a type of false die, in which one side is fractionally shorter than the others. **2** [late 19C] (*Aus.*) a third-rate painting.

flat *n.*[2] (*also* **flatt**) **1** [mid-18C+] a peasant, a rustic and as such considered a fool or innocent; antonym of SHARP n.[1]; thus (*UK Und.*) *it's a good flat that's never down*, even the most naïve of dupes must realize what's happening eventually; thus *strike a flat*, to encounter a gullible victim. **2** [mid-19C] a prostitute's customer. **3** [late 19C–1900s] (*also* **flatite**) a common person, one who not a member of an élite, i.e. a minor criminal.

flat *n.*[3] [mid-19C] (*US*) a rejection; thus *give someone the flat*, to turn down a suitor. [SE turn down *flat*/a *flat* refusal]

flat *n.*[4] [1900s–40s] (*US Black*) 5 cents, a nickel. [the thin, flat coin]

flat *n.*[5] [1940s+] a *flat* tyre. [abbr.]

flat *n.*[6] [1950s] (*US drugs*) a thin packet of heroin. [its shape]

flat *n.*[7] *see* FLATFOOT n.[1] (3).

flat *n.*[8] *see* FLATS n.[2].

flat *adj.*[1] **1** [late 16C–17C; 19C+] total, complete, unchangeable; esp. in phr. *that's flat*. **2** [early 17C; late 18C–mid-19C] naïve, unsophisticated. **3** [mid-19C+] without any money. [(3) abbr. FLAT BROKE adj.]

flat *adj.*[2] [20C+] **1** emotionally crippled. **2** exhausted, worn-out. [(2) abbr. FLAT OUT adj.[2] (1)]

flat *v.* [mid-19C] (*US*) to reject a suitor. [abbr. SE turn down *flat*]

flat *adv.* **1** [mid-19C+] completely, utterly. **2** [mid-19C+] unreservedly, candidly. **3** [1920s+] of time, exactly. **4** [1940s+] of money, a payment, exact.

flat as a tack *phr.*[1] [1960s+] (*Aus.*) very depressed. [FLAT adj.[2] (1)]

flat as a tack *phr.*[2] (*also* **flat tack**) [1950s+] (*Aus./N.Z.*) at full speed (cf. FLAT STICK adv.). [SE *flat*, i.e. with the car's accelerator pressed to the floor]

flat-back *n.* [mid-19C] a bedbug. [ext. of FLATS n.[4]]

flatback *v.* [1950s+] (*US*) **1** to work as a prostitute, the image is of working from a given place, rather than walking the streets; also *adj.*, pertaining to intercourse, esp. when for money. **2** to have sex in the missionary position.

flatbacker *n.* [1960s+] (*US Black pimp*) a prostitute, esp. one who specializes in quantity rather than quality in her clients; also an honest prostitute (i.e. who delivers the promised sex and neither tricks nor robs her client). [FLATBACK v. (1); she does no more than lie *flat on her back*]

flatbacking *n.* [1960s+] (*US Black*) working as a prostitute. [FLATBACK v. (1)]

flat bit *n.* (*also* **flat time**) [1940s+] (*US Und.*) a sentence served with no remission for good behaviour. [FLAT adj.[1] (1) + BIT n.[5]/TIME n.[1]]

flat blues *n.* [1970s+] (*drugs*) LSD (cf. A n.[3]). [packaging]

flatboat *n.* (*also* **flatboot**) [20C+] (*US*) a large, clumsy shoe. [play on SE *flatboat*, a broad flat-bottomed boat, used for transport]

flat broke *adj.* [mid-19C+] totally impoverished. [FLAT adv. (1) + BROKE adj.[1]]

flat-cap *n.* **1** [late 16C–early 18C] a citizen of London; thus a tradesman. **2** [late 17C–early 18C] a Billingsgate fishwife. [the headgear; thus Jonson, *Every Man in his Humour* (1598): 'Mock me all over From my flat-cap unto my shining shoes' or Dekker, *Honest Whore* (1630): 'Flat caps as proper are to Citty Gownes / As to armour helmets, or to kings their Crownes']

flat-car *n.* [1920s–30s] (*US tramp*) a pancake.

flat-car tourist *n.* [late 19C–1900s] (*US*) an itinerant who travels in freight cars.

flat-catcher *n.*[1] **1** [19C] anything that will serve to dupe the public. **2** [early 19C+] (*also* **catcher**) a confidence trickster, one who indulges in 'sharp practice'. [FLAT n.[2] (1) + SE *catcher*]

flat-catcher *n.*[2] [mid-19C–1920s] a horse that looks good but fails to win races. [it is always caught and passed *in the flat*]

flat-catching *n.* [early 19C–1910s] confidence trickery, fraud. [FLAT-CATCHER n.[1] (2)]

flatch *n.* (*also* **flach**) [mid-19C+] **1** a half. **2** a halfpenny. [backsl.]

flatchenorc *n.* (*also* **flatch yenork/ynork**) [mid-19C] half-a-crown, 2s 6d (12½p). [backsl.; FLATCH n. (1) + YENORK n.]

flat chicken *n.* [late 19C] stewed tripe. [? the taste, the consistency, the look]

flatch-kennurd *adj.* [mid–late 19C] tipsy, mildly drunk. [backsl.; FLATCH n. + KANURD adj.; lit. 'half-drunk']

flatch yenep *n.* (*also* **flatch yennep/yennop**) [mid-19C] a halfpenny. [backsl.; FLATCH n. + YENNEP n.]

flatch yenork/ynork *n. see* FLATCHENORC n.

flat-cock *n.* [late 18C–19C] a woman. [the anatomical difference]

flat-cocking *n.* (*also* **flat cocks**) [late 19C] of 2 women, rubbing their bodies togther for sexual stimulation. [FLAT-COCK n.]

flat dog *n.* [1960s–70s] (*US prison*) bologna sausage.

flat fish *n.* (*also* **regular flat fish**) **1** a fool, a dullard (cf. AIREDALE n.). **2** a beggar's or confidence trickster's prey. [FLAT n.[2] (1) + FISH n.[3]; but ? a simple joc. use of SE]

flatfoot *n.*[1] **1** [mid-19C] a sailor. **2** [mid-19C] a Black person. **3** [mid-19C+] (*also* **flat, flatheel**) a policeman (cf. FLATTER n.[1]; FLATTIE n.[3]; GUM HEEL n.; GUMSHOE n.; GUMSHOE ARTIST n.; RUBBER HEEL n.; SHOE n.[2]). **4** [late 19C+] an infantryman. **5** [1960s] (*US*) an Irish immigrant. [all refer to marching or to walking in menial jobs]

flatfoot *n.*[2] [late 19C] (*US*) a man who stands firmly for a particular political party, come what may. [FLAT-FOOTED adj.[1]]

flatfoot *n.*[3] [1910s–20s] a person who has flat feet.

flatfoot *v.*[1] [1930s+] (*US*) to walk like a policeman. [FLATFOOT n.[1] (3)]

flatfoot *v.*[2] [1960s] (*US*) to down a glass of liquor in a single gulp. [? after drinking one slaps the glass *flat* on the table or bar]

flat-footed *adj.*[1] [early 19C+] downright, positive, undeviating, straightforward. [the image of 'putting one's foot down']

flat-footed *adj.*[2] [mid-19C] (*US*) destitute, penniless. [FLAT adj.[1] (3) + pun on SE]

flat-footed *adj.*[3] [20C+] (*US*) **1** of food, plain, devoid of any further cooking or mixing. **2** insipid, maladroit. **3** unprepared, caught unawares; thus *catch flat-footed*, to catch unawares. [sporting imagery]

flat-footed *adj.*[4] [1920s–30s] used of a policeman. [FLATFOOT n.[1] (3)]

flat-footed *adj.*[5] *see* FROG-FOOTED adj.

flat-footed *adv.* [mid-19C+] (*US*) plainly, firmly, without adornment, undeviating; usu. in phr. *come out flat-footed*, to state an unequivocal opinion. [FLAT-FOOTED adj.[1]]

flat-footed Dutch *n.* [1960s] (*US*) a German immigrant. [FLATFOOT n.[1] (5) + DUTCH n.[1] (2)]

flat-footer *n.* [late 19C–1900s] a pedestrian, a walker.

flat fuck *n.* [1960s+] (*gay*) sexual relations between 2 women, rubbing their bodies together. [FLAT FUCK v.]

flat fuck *v.* [late 19C; 1960s+] of 2 women, to rub their bodies together for sexual stimulation. [SE *flat* + FUCK v.[1]]

flathead *n.* [late 18C+] **1** a foolish, stupid person; thus *adj. flat-headed*. **2** a Jew. **3** a Lithuanian. **4** an inhabitant of the Illinois-Ohio lowlands. **5** a German settler in Dakota or Wisconsin. [all uses are derog.]

flatheads *n.* [1980s] (*US drugs*) barbiturates as sold by a dealer (rather than a proprietary brand) (cf. BARBIT n.).

flatheel *n. see* FLATFOOT n.[1] (3).

flat-iron *n.* [mid–late 19C] any wedge-shaped house, usu. at the diagonal confluence of 2 streets, orig. a public house sited on a corner. [note the *locus classicus* is New York's Flatiron

Building, at the corner of Broadway and Fifth Avenue at 23rd Street]

flatite *n.*[1] [1940s+] (*Aus.*) a flat-dweller. [SE *flat* + sfx *-ite*, connected with or belonging to]

flatite *n.*[2] *see* FLAT *n.*[2] (3).

flat joint *n.* [20C+] (*US Und.*) a crooked gambling game or casino; orig. fair/carnival use, when a flat was a crooked or doctored 'wheel of fortune'; thus as *v.*, to operate a crooked gambling device. [SE *flat* + JOINT *n.*[4] (3); the flat surface that is vital to the playing of the sort of game (3-card monte, the shell game etc) featured at such places]

flatlander *n.* (*also* **flatter**) [1930s+] (*US*) an outsider, an incompetent person. [lit. one who comes from the flatlands, the plains and thus seen as inferior by those who live in the mountains]

flatline *v.* (*also* **catch a flatline**) [1980s+] (*US*) **1** of a person, to die. **2** of an inanimate object, to fail, to collapse. [the flattening on the electronic line on the monitor of a piece of medical equipment that indicates the patient's heart has stopped]

flat-move *n.* [early 19C] (*orig. UK Und.*) any plan – criminal or otherwise – that fails. [SE *flat*, i.e. lifeless, disappointing + MOVE *n.* (1)]

flat on one's ass *phr.* (*also* **flat on one's can**) [1940s+] (*US*) out of work, without money. [SE *flat* + ASS *n.* (2)/CAN *n.*[1] (2)]

flat out *adj.*[1] [late 19C+] straightforward, unadorned, blunt, esp. of speech.

flat out *adj.*[2] [1940s+] (*orig. Aus.*) **1** exhausted. **2** busy. **3** hard put.

flat-out *adv.* [1940s+] (*US*) **1** completely, utterly, totally. **2** openly.

flats *n.*[1] [mid-17C–18C] lesbian sexual intercourse.

flats *n.*[2] [late 18C–19C] counterfeit coinage; occas. sing. [the *flat* metal sheets from which it is stamped]

flats *n.*[3] **1** [late 18C+] playing cards. **2** [1970s+] plastic credit cards. [the shape; but note FLAT *n.*[1] (1) for overtones of possible criminal use]

flats *n.*[4] [19C] bugs or lice.

flats *n.*[5] [1920s–30s] (*US tramp*) griddlecakes or pancakes.

flats *n.*[6] [1950s+] (*US Und.*) the bottom row of cells in a prison block. [19C SE *flat*, a floor or storey in a house]

flats and sharps *n.* [late 18C–early 19C] edged weapons.

flatsey *n.* [1970s] (*Aus. teen*) a nickname, used as a term of abuse, for a girl whose breasts are small or undeveloped.

flat stick *adv.* (*also* **flat tap**) [1970s+] (*Aus./N.Z.*) at top speed, at the limit of one's abilities or resources (cf. FLAT AS A TACK *phr.*[2]).

flatt *n.* *see* FLAT *n.*[2].

flat tack *adv. see* FLAT AS A TACK *phr.*[2].

flat tap *adv. see* FLAT STICK *adv.*

flatten *v.* [late 19C+] **1** to get the better of. **2** (*also* **flatten out**) to knock down. **3** in fig. use of (2), to defeat.

flattener *n.* [late 19C] a hard blow.

flatter *n.*[1] [late 19C] a policeman. [FLATFOOT *n.*[1] (3)]

flatter *n.*[2] *see* FLATLANDER *n.*

flatters *adj.* [1950s+] absolutely penniless. [FLAT *adj.*[1] (3) + -ER sfx]

flatter-trap *n.* [mid-19C] the mouth, esp. that of a sycophant or toady. [SE *flatter* + TRAP *n.*[3]]

flattie *n.*[1] (*also* **flatty**) [mid–late 19C] a dupe, a naïve countryman. [FLAT *n.*[2] (1)]

flattie *n.*[2] (*also* **flatty**) [mid-19C+] a small, flat-bottomed sailing boat.

flattie *n.*[3] (*also* **flatty**) **1** [late 19C+] a police officer. **2** [1920s] (*US tramp*) a railroad policeman. [abbr. FLATFOOT *n.*[1] (3)]

flattie *n.*[4] (*also* **flatty**) [1980s+] (*N.Z.*) a *flat* tyre. [abbr.]

flattie *adj.* (*also* **flatty**) [mid-19C] (*UK Und.*) gullible, naïve. [FLATTIE *n.*[1]]

flatties *n.* [1940s+] low-heeled or flat shoes.

flat time *n. see* FLAT BIT *n.*

flat top *n.* **1** [1950s+] a style of haircut. **2** [1960s] a style of hat.

flatty *see also under* FLATTIE.

flatty *n.* [1950s+] (*US*) a confidence trickster; a crooked carnival game operator.

flatty-gory *n.* [early 19C] **1** a counterfeit coin. **2** the potential victim of a confidence trickster. [FLATS *n.*[2]/FLATTIE *n.*[1] + GOREE *n.*]

flatty-ken *n.* [mid-19C] a public house that is frequented by members of the underworld but where the landlord remains oblivious of their activities. [FLATTIE *n.*[1] + KEN *n.*[1]]

flat tyre *n.* [1920s–60s] **1** (*US campus*) an unattractive young woman. **2** (*US*) a woman who has been thrown over by a lover; a prostitute who has been rejected by her pimp. **3** (*orig. US Black*) a letdown, a disappointment. **4** (*US*) a failure, an inadequate. **5** (*US*) an impotent man.

flat-wheel *n.* (*US*) **1** [1920s] a dull, boring person. **2** [1930s–50s] one who walks with a limp. [railroad jargon *flat wheel*, a car wheel that has worn flat spots on its tread and thus rolls slightly askew]

flat wheeler *n.* [1920s] (*US*) one who is mean or impoverished. [FLAT-WHEEL *n.* (1)]

flat wig *v.* [2000s] (*US prison*) to knock down violently.

flat worker *n.* [1900s–70s] (*US Und.*) a burglar. [SE *flat* + WORKER *n.*[1] (1)]

flava *n.* [1990s+] (*orig. US Black*) style. [deliberate mis-sp. of FLAVOR *n.*[2] (1)]

flavor *n.*[1] **1** [1980s+] (*US drugs*) top-quality cocaine. **2** [2000s] (*US prison*) a brandname cigarette. [abbr. SE *flavor of the month*]

flavor *n.*[2] [1990s+] (*US Black*) **1** style. **2** attractiveness; thus an attractive young woman.

flavour of the month *n.* [1970s+] a derisory ref. to a contemporary and, it is presumed, short-lived fashion or fad, or a person chosen as favourite. [orig. coined in 1937 as SE for varieties of ice-cream]

flaw *v.* [late 17C–early 18C] to make drunk.

flawed *adj.* **1** [mid-17C–19C] drunk. **2** [19C] of a woman, deflowered but still unmarried.

flaxation! *excl.* [late 19C] (*US*) a euph. version of *damnation!* [ety. unknown; ? link to *flax*, humbug]

flaxie *n.* [1910–20s] (*N.Z.*) a *flax*-cutter. [abbr.]

flaxstick *n.* [1900s] (*Aus.*) a derog. term for a New Zealander.

flay a flint *v.* [mid–late 17C] to undertake the worst sort of meanness or excess to extract money from another person. [cf. SE *get blood from a stone*]

flaybottomist *n.* (*also* **flaybottom**) [late 18C–19C] a schoolmaster.

flay the fox *v.* [mid-17C–early 19C] to vomit. [lit. trans. of Fr. sl. *écorcher le renard*]

flea and louse *n.* [mid-19C; 1930s+] a house, esp. a house with a bad reputation. [rhy. sl.]

fleabag *n.* **1** [late 18C+] (*orig. milit.*) (*also* **flea-park**) a sleeping bag or bed; a bedroll. **2** [20C+] a cheap hotel or lodging house. **3** [20C+] (*US*) an ageing, ill dog. **4** [1930s+] (*US*) an old, worn-out prostitute who is forced to seek equally run-down clients, often on Skid Row, in cheap hotels etc. **5** [1940s+] a general term of abuse. **6** [1950s+] (*US Black*) a troublesome, difficult person who tends, like fleas, to follow around and keep irritating the individual who has been made subject of their woes. **7** [2000s] a smelly person, i.e. a tramp, a vagrant. [(1) note WW1 Aus. milit. *fleabag*, an officer's valise; (2) note *c*.1910 there was an actual *Fleabag* in New York City, a cheap saloon at 241 Bowery]

fleabag *adj.* [1950s+] (*US*) of a hotel or anything, cheap, run-down, second-rate. [FLEABAG *n.* (2)]

flea box *n.* [1930s–40s] a cheap hotel or lodging house.

flea-catcher *n.* [early 19C] a tailor.

flea circus *n.* [1920s+] (*Aus.*) a cheap, tawdry, run-down cinema.

fleapit *n.* **1** [20C+] (*also* **flea joint**) a cheap, tawdry, run-down hotel, motel or club, or any place; also attrib. **2** [1910s] a (run-down) flat. **3** [1930s+] (*also* **fleahouse**) a cheap, tawdry, run-down cinema.

flea powder *n.* [1950s+] (*drugs*) second-rate or poor-quality drugs.

flea-powder habit *n.* [1950s] (*drugs*) a low-level narcotics addiction or an addiction to weak heroin. [FLEA POWDER n. + HABIT n. (1)]

fleas and ants *n.* [1930s–50s] (*US*) trousers. [rhy. sl. = PANTS n.[1] (2)]

fleas and itches *n.* (*also* **flies and itchers**) [1940s+] (*Aus.*) the cinema; paintings. [rhy. sl. = SE pictures]

fleas and scratches *n.* [20C+] (*Aus.*) matches. [rhy. sl.]

flea taxi *n.* [1980s] (*N.Z.*) a sheepdog pup.

flea trap *n.* **1** [1930s+] (*US*) an ageing, ill dog. **2** [1940s+] a cheap and dirty hotel.

flee *n.* [1970s] (*drugs*) second-rate narcotics. [FLEA POWDER n.]

fleece *n.*[1] **1** [mid-19C] the hair on the head. **2** [late 19C] a generic term for women as sex objects; esp. in *fleece-hunter, fleece-monger,* a womanizer. **3** [late 19C+] the pubic hair of either sex. [Williams offers examples of synon. plays on *golden fleece*; (2) f. (3)]

fleece *n.*[2] [2000s] (*US Black*) second-rate drugs. [? FLEE n. or SE *fleece*, to cheat]

fleecer *n.* [20C+] a confidence trickster. [SE *fleece*, to plunder, to rob heartlessly, to victimize]

fleecy-claiming *n.* [late 19C] sheep-stealing.

Fleet *n.* [1990s+] (*US Black*) a *Fleet*wood Cadillac. [abbr.]

fleet *adj.* [early 19C] counterfeit. [? the *Fleet* Prison]

fleet of blows *n.* (*also* **fleet of licks**) [20C+] (*W.I., Guyn./Trin.*) a painful thrashing.

Fleet Street dove *n.* (*also* **Fleet Street houri**) [19C] a prostitute (cf. ALLEY CAT n.). [proper name *Fleet Street*, London EC4, the late 19C–1980s centre of London journalism, also celebrated for its population of prostitutes + SE *dove/houri*, a nymph of the Muslim paradise, thus a beautiful woman]

Fleet-Streeter *n.* [late 19C] 'a journalist of the baser sort, a spunging prophet; a sharking dramatic critic; a spicy paragraphist; and so on' (F&H); thus *Fleet-Streetese,* 'the so-called English, written to sell by the Fleeter-Streeter, a mixture of sesquipedelians and slang, of phrases worn threadbare and phrases sprung from the kennel; of bad grammar and worse manners; the like of which is impossible outside Fleet Street, but which in Fleet Street commands a price, and enables not a few to live' (F&H). [*Fleet-Street,* 'the estate of journalism, especially journalism of the baser sort' (F&H)]

fleggy *n.* [1970s+] (*UK juv.*) a gob of spit. [SE *phlegm*]

Flemington confetti *n.* [1920s+] (*Aus.*) rubbish, nonsense, 'tripe' (cf. COWYARD CONFETTI n.). [? *Flemington* racecourse, covered in torn-up betting slips etc at the end of a major meeting; or *Flemington* saleyards in Sydney and Melbourne]

Flemington races *n.* [1920s+] (*Aus.*) braces. [rhy. sl.]

Flemish account *n.* [late 17C–mid-19C] a badly prepared account or books that do not balance. [successor to FLANDERS RECKONING n.; the Flemish *livre* or pound was worth only 12 rather than 20 shillings; the main implication, however, is of the grasping stereotype attributed to any native of the Low Countries]

Flemo *n.* [20C+] (*Aus.*) the suburb of *Flem*ington, northwest of Melbourne. [abbr. + -o sfx (4)]

flesh! *excl.* (*also* **flesh and eels! …fire! …nouns!**) [late 17C–early 18C] a blasphemous excl. [abbr. of SE *God's flesh!*]

flesh-and-blood *n.* [mid–late 19C] a drink composed of equal measures of port and brandy. [a loose approx. of the colours of the drinks]

fleshbag *n.* [late 18C–19C] a shirt.

flesh broker *n.* [17C–mid-19C] a madame, a procuress; a match-maker.

flesh-dresser *n.* [17C] an official who punishes prostitutes with flogging. [SE *flesh-dresser,* a butcher]

flesh-fly *n.* **1** [mid-16C–mid-17C] a lecher, a womanizer. **2** [early 17C] a prostitute (cf. ALLEY CAT n.). **3** [early–mid-17C] a madame, a bawd; occas. a pander.

flesh hooks *n.* [mid-16C–early 17C] the hands.

flesh hound *n.* [1980s] (*US Black*) an obsessive womanizer. [SE *flesh* + HOUND sfx]

flesh (it) *v.* [late 16C–early 17C; 1990s+] of a man, to have sexual intercourse; modern use is by both sexes (cf. BURY IT v.). [SE *flesh,* to plunge one's weapon into flesh, to gratify one's lusts]

fleshly part *n.* [19C] the vagina. [SE *fleshly,* sexual, carnal]

flesh market *n.* **1** [mid-18C–early 19C] any street or urban area, e.g. Cheapside, the Strand, Covent Garden, that is paraded by prostitutes. **2** [mid-19C] a brothel (cf. BANGING-SHOP n.).

fleshmonger *n.* [early 16C–early 18C] a lecher, a womanizer. [SE *flesh* + sfx -*monger*; despite the lit. meaning of 'flesh seller' and the *OED* def., Williams states that 'the word seems not to be used for pander']

flesh one's will *v.* [early 17C] of a man, to have sexual intercourse (cf. BURY IT v.). [on the pattern of SE *flesh one's sword,* to thrust a sword into an adversary's flesh]

flesh peddler *n.* **1** [late 17C–18C] a match-maker, a procuress. **2** [1930s+] (*US*) a film or theatrical agent. [(2) allegedly coined by the columnist Walter Winchell]

flesh pencil *n.* (*also* **flesh pen**) [1990s+] the penis (cf. BLACK PENCIL n.).

fleshpot *n.* **1** [late 19C] the vagina (cf. BAG n.[1]). **2** [1910s+] a brothel. **3** [1930s+] (*US Black*) a woman, viewed strictly (and thus offensively) as a sex object. [note synon. RMC Duntroon (Aus.) *flesh*]

flesh-presser *n.* **1** [1920s+] (*orig. US*) a politician who attempts to curry favour with the voters by shaking as many hands, kissing as many babies and patting as many backs as possible during a campaign. **2** [2000s] (*US*) a porn star. [PRESS THE FLESH v.]

flesh-shambles *n.* [early 17C] a brothel. [SE *flesh* + *shambles,* a slaughterhouse]

flesh-tailor *n.* [mid-17C] a surgeon.

fleshy bagpipes *n.* [1990s+] the female breasts (cf. BAGS n.[1]).

flex *n.* [1990s+] **1** (*US Black*) guts, courage, integrity, energy. **2** (*W.I./UK Black teen*) a person's mannerism, idiosyncrasies etc.

flex *v.*[1] [1980s+] **1** (*US prison*) to get emotionally prepared for a (gang) fight. **2** (*US Black*) to make others aware of one's potential for violence and willingness to use it; thus *on the flex,* acting in an excessively macho manner in the hope of impressing onlookers. **3** to show off generally. **4** to hit or intimidate someone. **5** to go well, to work out. [SE *flex one's muscles*]

flex *v.*[2] [1980s+] (*US Black*) **1** to scratch records, i.e. to move the record backwards and forwards so the needle scratches across the record, thus repeating or distorting a chosen section. **2** to rap well. [the required *flexing* of the muscles in (1) the wrist and (2) the brain]

flex *adv.* [1990s+] (*UK Black*) quickly, at high speed. [FLEX v.[1] (5)/FLEX v.[2]]

flex (one's sex) *v.* [1990s+] (*US Black teen*) to have an erection. [pun on SE *flex one's muscles*]

flex with *v.* [1990s+] (*UK Black*) to associate with. [ext. of FLEX v.[1]]

flic *n. see* FLICK n.[3] (1).

flick *n.*[1] [early 17C] a thief. [this word orig. appeared as *afflicke* (albeit at F in Rowlands' A–Z listing in Rowlands, *Martin-Mark-all,* 1610) and has always been assumed, by the *OED* and others, to have been a misprint of *a flick.* That said, it has no proven ety. and may indeed be one, equally incomprehensible word]

flick *n.*[2] [mid-19C–1930s] an amusing person; esp. as *old flick.*

flick *n.*[3] **1** [1910s+] (*also* **flic**) a film; often in pl. as cinema in general. **2** [1960s+] (*US Black/prison*) a photograph. [(1) early films jerked or 'flicked' slightly as they ran through the projector, mainly used historically/ironically post-1950s; (2) f. (1) or the flash]

flick n.[4] **1** [1950s+] a knife with a spring-loaded blade. **2** [1980s] a razor blade with one side taped so that it can be held as a weapon. [abbr. SE *flick-knife*]

flick v.[1] [late 17C–mid-19C] (*UK Und.*) **1** to cut. **2** to cut off.

flick v.[2] [1970s+] (*US Black*) to fail deliberately to turn up for work or school.

flicker n.[1] [late 17C–mid-19C] (*UK Und.*) a glassful of alcohol; thus *rum flicker*, a large glass; *queer flicker*, an ordinary glass. [ety. unknown; ? one 'flicks' the contents down one's throat]

flicker n.[2] *see* FLICKERS n.

flicker v.[1] [early 17C] to kiss or caress a woman. [? the SE *flick* of the tongue or fingers]

flicker v.[2] **1** [late 17C–early 19C] to grin, to laugh in someone's face. **2** [late 19C–1960s] (*US tramp*) to faint or pretend to faint, to die; thus as *flicker/flickers*, a faked faint.

flicker v.[3] [mid-19C] to drink. [FLICKER n.[1]]

flickerbox n. [1970s] (*Aus.*) television.

flickers n. [1920s+] moving pictures, the cinema in general; occas. in sing. as a film. [ext. of FLICK n.[3] (1)]

flickertail n. [20C+] (*US*) a native of North Dakota. [dial. *flickertail*, the ground squirrel, the state's best known native animal]

flicking adj. *see* FLIPPING adj.

flick-off n. [1950s+] an act of rejection, a snub. [FLICK OFF v.[1]]

flick off v.[1] [1950s+] to snub, to reject, to ignore. [a dismissive *flick* of the fingers (cf. FLIP OFF v.[2])]

flick off v.[2] *see* FLIP OFF v.[2].

flick one's wick v. [1950s] (*N.Z.*) to hurry up. [the flicking of a cigarette lighter]

flicks n. *see* FLICK n.[3] (1).

flick the bean v. [1990s+] of a woman, to masturbate (cf. APPLY LIP GLOSS v.). [SE *flick* + BEAN n.[4] (3)]

flick the bic v. [1970s+] to stimulate the genitals with a hand, whether one's own or those of a partner. [SE *flick* + *bic*, a popular brand of pen]

flick the switch v. [1980s+] (*Aus.*) of a woman, to masturbate (cf. APPLY LIP GLOSS v.).

flick the vee(s) v. (*also* **flick the vick**) [1990s+] to make the 'V-sign' gesture.

flick up v. [2000s] (*US prison*) to take a photo. [FLICK n.[3] (2)]

flid n. [1990s+] **1** (*UK juv.*) a handicapped person, esp. one suffering the after-effects of Thalidomide, which drug, erroneously distributed to pregnant women in the 1960s as a counter to morning sickness, caused massive physical disability in the babies. **2** a general term of abuse. [elision of *Thalid*(omide) as '*flidomide*']

flier *see also under* FLYER.

flier n.[1] [1940s–50s] (*US drugs*) a drug addict. [they are always HIGH adj.[1] (2)]

flier n.[2] *see* HIGH-FLYER n.[1].

Flies n. [1970s] (*UK Und.*) the Flying Squad.

flies' skating rink n. *see* SKATING RINK n.

flight n. [1950s] an experience of a drug. [FLY v.[4] (1)]

flight deck n. [1980s] the female breasts. [? nonce-word created by Posy Simmonds for her raffish character Edmund Heap]

flight of steps n. *see* DOORSTEP n.

flim n.[1] **1** [mid-19C+] a £5 note. **2** [1940s–50s] a 5-year prison sentence. [(1) FLIMSY n. (1)]

flim n.[2] [1910s+] a swindle, a fraud, a confidence trick. [abbr. FLIM-FLAM n.[1] (2)]

flim v. [late 19C–1920s] to swindle, to defraud, to trick. [FLIM-FLAM v. (1)]

flim-flam n.[1] **1** [mid-16C+] (*also* **flam-blam**) an idle tale, a piece of nonsense. **2** [late 19C] (*orig. US*) a confidence trick, a criminal hoax, orig. a short-change swindle. **3** [1900s–30s] (*US*)

a deceptive, untrustworthy person. **4** [1990s+] (*US*) a confidence trickster. [? ON *flim*, a lampoon, *flimska*, mockery]

flim-flam n.[2] [1950s–70s] (*US*) the penis (cf. BAUBLE n.). [SE *flim-flam*, a trifle]

flim-flam adj. [mid-17C; 20C+] nonsensical. [FLIM-FLAM n.[1] (1)]

flim-flam v. **1** [late 19C+] (*US*) to perpetrate a confidence trick or hoax, orig. to practise a short-change swindle. **2** [1900s] to perform a task inadequately. **3** [1930s] (*US Und.*) to scold, to berate. [FLIM-FLAM n.[1]]

flim-flammer n. (*also* **flim-flam man**) [late 19C+] (*US*) confidence trickster. [FLIM-FLAM v. (1)]

flimmer n. [late 19C] (*US campus*) a cheat. [FLIM v.]

flimp v. **1** [mid-19C–1900s] to steal by snatching items from their owners (rather than carefully picking a pocket), often using violent means, esp. of watches. **2** [mid-19C+] to have sexual intercourse (cf. BANG v.[1]). **3** [1910s–50s] to swindle, to cheat. [western Flemish *flimpe*, to hit in the face; *flimping* is equivalent to 2-man mugging, one person pushes the victim from behind, the other robs him]

flimper n. (*also* **flimp**) [mid–late 19C] a mugger or thief, working in a team, where one man grabs the victim from behind, while the *flimper* steals the item, usu. a watch. [FLIMP v. (1)]

flimping n. [mid-19C] stealing by snatching items, usu. watches, rather than carefully and surreptitiously removing them. [FLIMP v. (1)]

flimsy n. **1** [early 19C+] a banknote, esp. a £5 note (cf. BANK-RAG n.). **2** [mid-19C] (*US*) a $100 dollar note. **3** [mid-19C] (*UK Und.*) a counterfeit banknote. **4** [mid-19C–1910s] multi-leaved copy paper used by journalists. **5** [late 19C] (*Aus.*) a cheque. **6** [1940s–70s] in pl., papers, a report. [the *flimsy* paper on which it is printed or written]

flimsy v. [late 19C] to copy out on tracing paper. [FLIMSY n. (4)]

fling v. **1** [early 18C] to snatch. **2** [mid-18C–mid-19C] to get the better of, to cheat, to deceive; esp. as *fling out of; fling for*, to be caught out. [SE *fling*, i.e. to fling money out of]

fling down n. [early 19C] (*Anglo-Irish*) a fight.

fling-dust n. (*also* **fling-stink**) [17C] a street-walking prostitute. [the dirt or dust that she stirs on her walk]

fling it in someone's face v. *see* FLAP IT IN SOMEONE'S FACE v.

fling-it-up n. [1990s+] (*W.I.*) of dancing or sex, wild abandon.

fling mud v. *see* SLING MUD v.

fling of a cow's tail, a phr. *see* TWO SHAKES OF A LAMB'S TAIL phr.

fling-stink n. *see* FLING-DUST n.

fling the hoof v. *see* SLING THE HOOF v.

fling the house out of the windows v. [early 17C] to make a great deal of noise or disturbance in one's house.

flink v. **1** [late 19C] (*US*) to act like a coward, to shirk one's duties. **2** [1960s] (*US*) to play truant from school. **3** [1970s+] (*gay*) for a male homosexual to go out with a woman in order to appear 'normal'. [? SE *flinch*, to slink off, to sneak away]

flint n.[1] [late 18C–mid-19C] a worker who refuses to accept anything but full, union-negotiated wages (cf. DUNG n.). [the hardness of SE *flint*]

flint n.[2] [1970s] (*US Black*) a cigarette lighter. [the flint that it contains]

Flip n. [1930s+] (*US*) a derog. name for a *Filipino*. [abbr.]

flip n.[1] (*also* **phlip**) [late 17C–19C] a mixture of beer and spirit sweetened with sugar and heated with a hot iron. [SE *flip*, to whip up]

flip n.[2] [late 19C+] a bribe or tip. [one 'flips' the recipient a coin]

flip n.[3] **1** [late 19C+] a triviality, an irrelevance; a tiny amount. **2** [1910s+] an impudent, flippant, 'lightweight' person. **3** [1940s–60s] (*Aus.*) an act of sexual intercourse. **4** [1940s+] (*US*) an eccentric, a madman; thus *go flip*, to go crazy, to lose control.

5 [1950s+] (*US*) a state of high excitement, delight or craziness, esp. as produced by drug use.

flip *n.*[4] [1910s+] a short trip, orig. in an aeroplane, but also in other forms of conveyance. [SE *fillip*]

flip *n.*[5] **1** [1960s] (*US Und.*) an informer. **2** [1970s+] (*US Black*) a passive male homosexual. [(1) he 'flips over' on his fellow inmates; (2) he 'flips over' for anal penetration]

flip *n.*[6] [1960s+] (*US*) a DAMN n., anything at all; thus *couldn't give a flip*. [euph. for FUCK n.[4]]

flip *adj.* (*orig. US*) **1** [late 19C+] nonchalant, unconcerned, in control. **2** [1920s+] exciting, excitable, eccentric, crazy (cf. FLIPPED-OUT adj.; FLIPPY adj.[1]). [Devon dial. *flip*, glib, flippant]

flip *v.*[1] **1** [19C] to shoot with a pistol or revolver. **2** [20C+] (*US*) to steal a ride, esp. on a freight train. **3** [1930s] (*US drugs*) to make another addict unconscious in order to steal his drugs. **4** [1940s] (*US Black*) to reject someone. [SE *flip*, to strike at sharply]

flip *v.*[2] [late 19C+] (*orig. Aus.*) to masturbate (cf. BOFF v.). [SE *flip*, to give a flip with (the finger)]

flip *v.*[3] [1930s] (*US*) to hand over, to give.

flip *v.*[4] **1** [1950s] (*US drugs*) to become unconscious through an overdose of a drug. **2** [1950s+] (*orig. US*) (*also* **flit**) to lose control, to get over-excited or very worried; often ext. in phrs. starting *flip one's...* (cf. FLIP ONE'S BANANAS v.). **3** [1950s+] to excite (sexually). **4** [1960s] to become drunk. **5** [2000s] (*US Black*) to start an argument, esp. with an intimate. [(2) abbr. FLIP ONE'S WIG v.]

flip *v.*[5] **1** [1960s] (*US*) to 'come out' as a homosexual. **2** [1970s+] (*US gay*) to reverse one's primary sexual activity, i.e. for a masculine lesbian to turn 'femme' or a sadist to play masochist; thus *flippy*, describing a homosexual who will take the active or passive role in intercourse. **3** [1990s+] (*US prison*) to convert a fellow inmate to homosexuality.

flip *v.*[6] **1** [1960s+] (*US Und.*) to inform. **2** [1980s+] to turn state's evidence. **3** [1990s+] to tell a story. [FLIP n.[5] (1) in lit. and ext. uses]

flip *v.*[7] [2000s] (*US Black*) to increase, e.g. money or stocks of drugs.

flip *v.*[8] [2000s] (*US Black*) to roll a marijuana cigarette.

flip! *excl.* [20C+] a euph. for FUCK! excl. (1).

flip a bitch *v.* [1980s+] (*US campus*) to make an illegal U-turn. [BITCH n.[1] (1); the stereotype of the poor woman driver]

flip da scrip *v. see* FLIP THE SCRIP v.

flip-flap *n.*[1] **1** [mid-17C] the penis. **2** [18C] copulation. **3** [late 19C] a broad fringe of hair falling across the forehead, esp. as used by street boys. [both (1) and (3) 'flap' around]

flip-flap *n.*[2] [18C–19C] 'a kind of somersault in which the performer throws himself over on his hands and feet alternately'; also 'a peculiar rollicking dance indulged in by costers' (Hotten, 1864).

flip-flap *n.*[3] **1** [late 19C] a type of firework. **2** [1940s] (*Aus.*) nonsense. [echoic]

flip-flop *n.*[1] **1** [20C+] (*US prison*) an individual who first gains parole and then returns to the same prison after breaking the terms of that parole or committing a new crime. **2** [1960s+] mutual oral-genital stimulation. **3** [1970s] a bisexual. **4** [1970s] a homosexual who takes either the active or passive role in sex. [SE *flip-flop*, a somersault/FLIP-FLOP v.]

flip-flop *n.*[2] [1920s] (*US*) a trick, a gimmick.

flip-flop *n.*[3] [2000s] an Albanian. [coined on Saudi construction sites, where Albanians wear non-protective footwear]

flip-flop *v.* **1** [1960s+] (*US prison*) (*also* **turn flip-flops**) to indulge in gay sex. **2** [1990s+] (*US prison*) for a male homosexual to take either the active or passive role in intercourse. **3** [1990s+] (*US prison*) to practise bisexuality. [SE *flip-flop*, to turn over; (1) for anal sex]

flip for *v.* [1950s+] (*orig. US*) to become fascinated, obsessed by. [FLIP v.[4] (2)]

flip off *v.*[1] [1930s+] to masturbate (cf. BALL OFF v.[2]). [ext. FLIP v.[2]]

flip off *v.*[2] (*also* **flick off**) [1980s+] **1** to make an obscene, dismissive gesture by raising the middle finger from the otherwise clenched fist. **2** in fig. use, to insult, to annoy. [var. on FLIP THE BIRD v.]

flip off! *excl.* [1950s+] go away! [FLIP OFF v.[2] (1); euph. FUCK OFF! excl. (1)]

flip off at the jibs *v.* [2000s] (*UK Black*) to speak in such a manner as to provoke a fight. [FLIP v.[4] (2) + JIB n.[1] (4)]

flip one's bananas *v.* [1970s] (*US*) to go suddenly insane (cf. FLIP ONE'S BEAN v.; FLIP ONE'S CORK v.; FLIP ONE'S LID v.; FLIP ONE'S TOP v.; FLIP ONE'S WIG v.). [SE *flip*/FLIP v.[4] (2) + BANANAS adj. (1)]

flip one's bean *v.* (*also* **flip one's beanie**) [1960s] (*US*) to go crazy, to lose emotional control (cf. FLIP ONE'S BANANAS v.). [SE *flip*/FLIP v.[4] (2) + BEAN n.[5]]

flip one's cookies *v.* [1950s+] to vomit (cf. BLOW CHOW v.). [SE *flip* + COOKIES n.[1]]

flip one's cork *v.* [1960s] (*US*) to lose one's temper (cf. FLIP ONE'S BANANAS v.). [FLIP v.[4] (2)]

flip oneself off *v.* [1930s+] (*Aus.*) to masturbate (cf. BALL OFF v.[2]). [FLIP OFF v.[1]]

flip one's gourd *v. see* BLOW ONE'S GOURD v.

flip one's lid *v.* [1940s+] (*orig. US*) to go crazy, to lose emotional control (cf. FLIP ONE'S BANANAS v.). [SE *flip*/FLIP v.[4] (2) + LID n.[1] (2)]

flip one's top *v.* [1940s–60s] (*US Black*) to go crazy, to lose one's temper; thus *fliptop*, adj., crazy; n., a crazy person (cf. FLIP ONE'S BANANAS v.). [SE *flip*/FLIP v.[4] (2) + fig. use of *top*]

flip one's wig *v.* [1930s+] (*orig. US*) **1** to lose one's temper (cf. FLIP ONE'S BANANAS v.). **2** to lose one's sanity; in weak use, to become emotional, e.g. through love. [SE *flip*/FLIP v.[4] (2) + WIG n.[3] (1)]

flip-out *n.* [1960s+] (*US*) **1** an eccentric, a madman. **2** a crazy, uncontrolled reaction to a drug or a situation. [FLIP OUT v.]

flip out *v.* [1960s+] **1** (*orig. US*) to lose emotional control, to go mad. **2** (*US campus*) to be intoxicated. **3** (*US*) to be overjoyed. **4** (*US*) to amaze, to delight. **5** (*US*) to cause someone emotional problems. [FLIP v.[4] (2)]

flip over *v.* [1960s+] (*gay*) to make oneself/a partner available for anal intercourse. [SE *flip* + *over*]

flipped-out *adj.* (*also* **flipped**) **1** [1940s+] crazy, over-reacting; fascinated (cf. FLIP adj.). **2** [1990s+] (*US campus*) intoxicated with drink or drugs. [FLIP OUT v./FLIP v.[4] (2)]

flipper *n.*[1] [19C+] the hand or arm. [reverse anthropomorphism]

flipper *n.*[2] [mid-19C–1900s] (*Aus./US*) a pancake. [SE *flip*; one flips it over in the pan]

flipper *n.*[3] **1** [late 19C–1910s] (*orig. US*) a very young prostitute (cf. FLAPPER n.[3]). **2** [1920s] (*US*) a male FLAPPER n.[3] (2). **3** [1950s] a general term of abuse, a euph. for FUCKER n. (3). **4** [1960s] a friend. **5** [1980s] (*Aus.*) a fool.

flipper *n.*[4] **1** [20C+] (*Irish*) a messy, untidy man. **2** [1980s] (*US campus*) an impulsive person. [? he 'flips' things around or ? SE *flippant*]

flipper *n.*[5] [1930s] (*US tramp*) a tramp who rides the railroads, rather than travels by road. [FLIP v.[1] (2)]

flippers *n.* **1** [late 18C–1910s] (*US*) the legs. **2** [1900s–40s] (*US Black*) the ears.

flipping *adj.* (*also* **flicking, flopping**) **1** [1910s+] a general intensifier, a euph. for FUCKING adj. (1); esp. in *flipping heck!* **2** [1960s+] (*US campus*) splendid.

flippy *adj.*[1] **1** [1920s] (*US*) flippant, 'lightweight'. **2** [1950s–70s] crazy, eccentric (cf. FLIP adj.). [FLIP n.[3] (2)/FLIP n.[3] (4)]

flippy *adj.*[2] *see* FLIP v.[5] (2).

flipside *n.* **1** [1960s+] the reverse, the alternative. **2** [1980s+] (*US gay*) the anus; the buttocks. [rock music use, the 'other side' of a record, the B-side; in (2) the man 'flips over' to offer his anus for sex]

flipside *adj.* [1990s+] (*US*) pertaining to the world of criminality. [i.e. the FLIPSIDE n. (1) of respectable society]

flip the bird *v.* [1960s+] to make an obscene gesture. [SE *flip* + BIRD n.[13]]

flip the bishop *v.* [1990s+] to masturbate. [FLIP v.[2]; var. on BANG THE BISHOP v.]

flip the bone *v. see* FLAG THE BONE v.

flip the scrip *v.* (*also* **flip da scrip**) [1990s+] (*US Black teen*) to change completely, to take an utterly fresh direction. [SE *flip*, turn over + *script*]

flipwreck *n.* [1910s+] (*Aus.*) **1** a person who has (supposedly) masturbated themselves into physical and mental decline. **2** a fool, an idiot. [FLIP v.[2]; pun on SE *shipwreck*]

flirt *n.* (*also* **flurt**) [late 16C–17C] a prostitute.

flirt-gill *n.* [late 16C–early 18C] a prostitute; a promiscuous female. [SE *flirt + gill*, a lass, a wench]

flirtina cop-all *n.* [mid–late 19C] a woman, esp. when considered 'too fond of men' (B&L). [play on SE *flirt* + fem. sfx *-ina* + COP v. (1) + SE *all*]

flit *n.*[1] [1920s+] (*US prison*) prison-made coffee. [brandname *Flit*, an insect repellent spray]

flit *n.*[2] [1930s+] (*US*) **1** (*also* **flitty**) a male homosexual. **2** a silly person. [SE *flit*, a flutter, a light movement; the stereotypical effeminacy of male homosexuals]

flit *n.*[3] [1940s+] (*US*) drunkenness. [SE *flit*, a sudden movement]

flit *n.*[4] *see* MOONLIGHT FLIT n.

flit *v.*[1] [mid-19C+] (*US*) to run away, to escape.

flit *v.*[2] [1980s] to be a homosexual. [FLIT n.[2] (1)]

flit *v.*[3] *see* FLIP v.[4] (2).

flitter *n.* [19C] (*US*) the vagina (cf. APPLE n.[6]). [dial. *flitter*, a pancake]

flitter *v.* [mid-19C; 1920s+] (*Irish*) to reduce to rags and tatters, both lit. and fig., thus *flitters*, bits and pieces. [dial. *flitter*, to fluster]

flitty *n. see* FLIT n.[2] (1).

flitty *adj.* [1900s–50s] effeminate. [FLIT n.[2] (1)]

flivver *n.* (*US*) **1** [1900s–60s] (*also* **fliv**) a failure, a disappointment, something cheap and inferior. **2** [1910s] something or someone that has a negative influence on others. **3** [1910s+] (*also* **fliv, fliver**) a cheap automobile, spec. a Model T Ford. [ety. unknown; note US Navy 1920s use, 'a destroyer of 750 tons or less']

flivver *v.* [1910s–20s] to fail, to falter. [FLIVVER n. (1)]

flivver tramp *n.* [1930s] (*US tramp*) a tramp who travels in an old car. [FLIVVER n. (3)]

Flo *n. see* AUNT FLO n.

float *n.* [1960s+] a small loan. [SE *float*, a sum of money in a shop used to provide change etc at the start of business]

float *v.*[1] **1** [late 19C] (*US*) to leave; thus *to do a float*, of objects, to disappear. **2** [late 19C+] (*orig. US*) to wander around. **3** [1910s] (*Aus.*) to die. **4** [1920s–30s] to eject, to send away.

float *v.*[2] [1930s+] **1** (*drugs*) to experience the 'other-worldliness' that can accompany the use of certain drugs, typically cannabis and the hallucinogens. **2** to be drunk. [play on SE *float*; one of a number of drug-related synon. that play on 'getting high']

float *v.*[3] [1960s+] (*US campus*) to pay for, to lend money. [FLOAT n.]

float an air biscuit *v.* **1** [1980s] to vomit (cf. BLOW CHOW v.). **2** [1990s+] to break wind silently, but with a pervasive odour. [SE *float* + AIR BISCUIT n.]

float around *v.* [20C+] to wander aimlessly. [ext. FLOAT v.[1] (2)]

floater *n.*[1] **1** [mid-19C–1910s] a suet dumpling. **2** [late 19C] (*orig. US*) a dead body found floating in the water. **3** [1910s+] (*Aus./N.Z.*) (*also* **pie floater**) a meat pie floating in pea soup. **4** [1980s+] a large piece of excrement that cannot be flushed away. **5** [1990s+] (*N.Z.*) a fried scone.

floater *n.*[2] **1** [mid-19C+] (*Aus./US*) a wanderer; a person of no fixed occupation, living on their wits. **2** [late 19C+] (*US*) a migratory worker. **3** [1930s+] (*UK prison*) an old magazine, book or newspaper that is smuggled irregularly from cell to cell. **4** [1940s+] (*gay*) a gay prostitute who works only in towns where he is unknown and in which he does not live. **5** [1970s] a prisoner on a short term sentence. [FLOAT v.[1]]

floater *n.*[3] [late 19C] the (flaccid) penis.

floater *n.*[4] [1910s+] an error, a faux pas. [orig. Oxbridge use; ? corruption of *faux pas* as 'foper', thence 'floater'; SE *float*, to circulate a rumour]

floater *n.*[5] [1910s+] (*US*) **1** an official order to leave a town or district. **2** a sentence suspended on condition that the offender leaves the area.

floater *n.*[6] (*also* **butterfly**) [1940s+] (*Aus.*) in the game of two-up, a coin that fails to spin.

floater *n.*[7] [1970s] (*US drugs*) a Quaalude. [the sensations it creates in the user]

floaters *n.* (*also* **flying flies**) [1950s+] spots before one's eyes.

floating academy *n.* [late 18C–mid-19C] the prison hulks. [SE *floating* + ACADEMY n. (4); run-down or part-derelict ships, no longer seaworthy, were recycled as prison ships, moored in the Thames estuary]

floating boat *n.* [1950s] (*W.I.*) cooked breadfruit. [? resemblance]

floating bullet *n.* [1940s+] (*W.I.*) a large, spherical cooked breadfruit. [? resemblance]

floating buoy *n.* [1950s] (*W.I.*) a dumpling made of flour and baking soda. [it rises to the surface when cooking]

float someone's boat *v.* [1980s+] to satisfy, to be to one's liking, e.g. *whatever floats your boat*.

float the note *v.* [1990s+] (*US teen*) to loan money to a friend to get them to participate in an activity. [SE *float*, to arrange a loan]

float-up *n.* [20C+] (*N.Z.*) a casual approach to someone. [FLOAT UP v.]

float up *v.* [20C+] (*N.Z.*) to approach casually, to stroll up. [FLOAT v.[1] (2)]

flob *n.* [1990s+] (*UK juv.*) saliva, in the context of spitting. [FLOB v. (1)]

flob *v.* [1930s+] (*mainly juv.*) **1** to spit. **2** to vomit (cf. BARF v.). [note Yorks. dial. *flob*, to puff, to cause to swell, i.e. the puffing of the cheeks that accompanies the action of spitting]

flock *n.* [1980s] (*US*) those women currently working for a pimp (cf. BROTHER-IN-LAW n.).

flock of bull *n.* [1920s] (*US*) nonsense, lies. [SE *flock*, i.e. of birds + BULL n.[11] (1)]

flock of sparrows flying out of one's backside *phr.* (*also* **flock of geese/peacocks/swallows…, nest of sparrows…**) [1950s+] (*Aus.*) a phr. used to describe the sensation of the male orgasm.

flog *v.*[1] **1** [late 17C–18C] (*UK Und.*) to whip. **2** [early 18C; 20C+] to have sexual intercourse (cf. BANG v.[1]). **3** [19C] to beat, to surpass. **4** [20C+] to masturbate; thus *flogger*, a masturbator (cf. BANG THE BISHOP v.; BOFF v.). **5** [1980s] (*Aus. prison*) to beat up. [(1) SE *flog*, to whip]

flog *v.*[2] **1** [late 18C+] (*also* **flog on**) to proceed by violent or painful effort. **2** [late 18C+] to obtain, usu. by violent effort. **3** [mid-19C] (*UK Und.*) to drink heavily. **4** [1910s] (*Aus.*) to worry. **5** [1970s+] (*US*) (*also* **flog it**) to hurry. [SE *flog*, to urge forward (a horse etc) by flogging]

flog *v.*[3] **1** [1910s+] (*also* **flog off**) to sell, currently non-specific, but orig. with criminal overtones. **2** [1980s+] (*US*) to advertise. **3** [1990s+] of an idea or a complaint, to belabour. [SE *flog*, to urge forward (a horse etc) by flogging; here it is the merchandise that is being 'urged']

flogged *adj.* **1** [1940s–50s] (*US drugs*) overcome by a drug. **2** [1960s–70s] exhausted. [fig. use FLOG v.[1] (1)]

flogged at the tumbler *phr.* [late 17C] whipped at the cart's end, a judicial punishment. [SE *flogged* + TUMBLER n.[2]]

flogger n.[1] [mid-18C–mid-19C] (*UK Und.*) a whip. [FLOG v.[1] (1)]

flogger n.[2] (*also* **flogger coat**) **1** [1900s–10s] (*Aus.*) a morning coat. **2** [1900s–40s] (*Aus./US*) an overcoat. [pun on FLOGGER n.[1], like a whip, esp. a cat-o-nine-tails, it has 'tails']

flogging *n.* [2000s] (*US Black*) acting eccentrically. [? ext. use of FLOG v.[1] (4)]

flogging *adj.* [1920s+] (*Aus.*) a euph. for FUCKING adj.

flogging-cove *n.* (*also* **flogging cull**) [late 17C–early 19C] one who gives out corporal punishment as authorized by the courts; often synon. with a beadle. [FLOG v.[1] (1) + COVE n. (1)/CULL n.[1] (4)]

flogging cully *n.* (*also* **flogging cull**) [late 17C–early 19C] one who enjoys receiving a whipping as sexual stimulation. [FLOG v.[1] (1) + CULLY n. (2)/CULL n.[1] (1)]

flog it *v. see* FLOG v.[2] (5).

flog my dolphin! *excl.* [1980s+] (*US*) a general excl. of surprise.

flog off v.[1] [1950s+] (*N.Z.*) to leave. [FLOG v.[2]]

flog off v.[2] *see* FLOG v.[3] (1).

flog on *v. see* FLOG v.[2] (1).

flog one's chops *v.* [1960s+] (*Aus.*) to work very hard. [SE *flog* + CHOPS n.[1] (3)]

flog one's doggin *v.* [1950s] to masturbate (cf. BANG THE BISHOP v.; BEAT ONE'S HOG v.). [SE *flog* + ext. DOG n.[4] (1)]

flog one's dong *v.* [1960s+] to masturbate (cf. BANG THE BISHOP v.). [SE *flog* + DING-DONG n.[4]]

flog one's donkey *v.* [1960s+] to masturbate (cf. BANG THE BISHOP v.; BEAT ONE'S HOG v.). [SE *flog* + DONKEY n.[2]]

flog one's dummy *v. see* BEAT ONE'S DUMMY v.

flog one's guts out *v.* [1970s+] to work very hard, to make an extreme effort. [SE *flog* + fig. use of GUTS n.[1] (2)]

flog one's meat *v. see* BEAT ONE'S MEAT v. (1).

flog one's mutton *v.* (*also* **thump the mutton**) [late 19C+] to masturbate (cf. BANG THE BISHOP v.; BEAT ONE'S MEAT v.). [SE *flog* + MUTTON n.[3]]

flog one's pork *v. see* POUND ONE'S PORK v.

flogster *n.* [mid-late 19C] one who enjoys flagellation for sexual purposes. [SE *flog* + -STER sfx]

flog the bishop *v. see* BANG THE BISHOP v.

flog the dog *v.* [20C+] to masturbate (cf. BANG THE BISHOP v.; BEAT ONE'S HOG v.). [SE *flog* + DOG n.[4] (1)]

flog the (finless) dolphin *v.* [1920s+] (*orig. naut.*) to masturbate (cf. BANG THE BISHOP v.; BEAT ONE'S HOG v.).

flog the hog *v.* [1960s+] to masturbate (cf. BANG THE BISHOP v.; BEAT ONE'S HOG v.). [SE *flog* + HOG n.[6]]

flog the lizard *v.* [1960s] (*Aus.*) to urinate (cf. LET ONE'S HORSE OUT OF THE STABLE v.; SHOOT A LION v.; STRANGLE THE GOOSE v.; TAKE ONE'S SNAKE FOR A GALLOP v.; WALK ONE'S DOG v.; WRING THE RATTLESNAKE v.). [SE *flog* + LIZARD n.[3]]

flog the log *v.* [1950s+] to masturbate (cf. BANG v.[1]). [SE *flog* + LOG n.[4]]

flood *v.* (*US Black*) **1** [1920s–30s] to have a menstrual period. **2** [1970s+] to have an erection, for the penis to 'flood' with blood.

flood-pants *n.* [20C+] (*orig. W.I.*) trousers that are too short and narrow. [such trousers are ideal for walking through a flood – the legs are too short to get wet]

flooey! *excl.* [20C+] (*orig. US*) an echoic excl. designed to resemble the sound of an explosion.

floor v.[1] [early 19C+] **1** to confuse, to confound, to puzzle, to defeat intellectually. **2** to amaze. **3** to knock down, to defeat utterly; to kill, lit. and fig. **4** to drink alcohol. **5** to finish properly, to do thoroughly. [boxing or wrestling imagery; SE *floor*, to knock to the ground]

floor v.[2] **1** [1950s+] (*orig. US*) to make a car go faster by pressing the relevant pedal. **2** [1970s+] (*US*) in fig. use, to hurry, to get a move on. [the pressing down on the accelerator pedal]

floorboard *v.* [1960s+] (*US*) to make a car go faster. [the pressing down on the accelerator pedal]

floorburners *n.* [1950s–70s] (*US Black*) shoes. [the idea of heat being generated by wildly dancing feet]

floored *adj.* **1** [early 19C; 1930s+] very drunk (cf. ANNIHILATED adj.). **2** [early 19C+] astounded, amazed, confused. [FLOOR v.[1]]

floorer *n.* **1** [19C] a blow that will knock its recipient down; thus anything, e.g. a piece of bad news, that renders its recipient 'floored'; also in fig. use. **2** [mid-19C] (*UK Und.*) one who knocks a person down, at which point a confederate appears and, under the pretext of 'helping', robs the victim. [FLOOR v.[1] (3)]

floor fuck *n.* [1910s+] (*orig. Aus.*) sexual intercourse on the floor. [SE *floor* + FUCK n.[1] (1)]

floor fuck *v.* [1910s+] (*orig. Aus.*) to have sexual intercourse on the floor. [FLOOR FUCK n.]

floor one's licks *v.* [mid-late 19C] to surpass, to do very well. [FLOOR v.[1] (3) + LICK n.[2] (1)]

floor polish *v.* [1940s] to defeat comprehensively. [pun]

floor the pig and bolt *v.* [early 19C] to knock down a policeman and run off. [FLOOR v.[1] (3) + PIG n.[3] (1) + BOLT v. (1)]

flooze up *v.* [1930s] (*US*) to make a mess, to bungle. [? euph. FUCK UP v. (1)]

floozie *n.* (*also* **floosie, flooze, floozy, flusie, fluzie, he-fluesy**) [20C+] (*orig. US*) a promiscuous young woman; also of homosexual men. [dial. *floosy*, flossy, thus soft; note Irish *Floozie in the Jacuzzi*, the monument in O'Connell Street, Dublin, representing the spirit of the River Liffey]

floozie *adj.* [1910s+] **1** (*US*) showy, stylish. **2** (*US*) over-dressed, over-made-up. **3** (*US*) silly or light-headed. **4** (*US Und.*) immoral, corrupt, dissipated. **5** (*US campus*) (*also* **floozy**) sexy. [FLOOZIE n.]

floozie up *v.* [1970s] (*US*) to embellish, either of one's own appearance or by adding decoration to a garment. [FLOOZIE n.]

floozled *adj.* [1990s+] drunk (cf. ADDLED adj.).

floozy *see under* FLOOZIE.

flop n.[1] [mid-19C–1910s] (*orig. US campus*) **1** any action by which someone else is deceived. **2** any form of cheating in an examination that leads to scoring high marks. [SE *flop*, i.e. one fig. lets something fall on the person one is cheating]

flop n.[2] [late 19C] **1** a male hairstyle, in which the hair is worn low over the brow. **2** a similar female hairstyle. [Ware notes the synon. *cretin* and *poodle* style]

flop n.[3] [late 19C–1920s] (*US*) a sudden political change of policy. [abbr. SE *flip-flop*]

flop n.[4] **1** [late 19C+] a failure, esp. of a film or stage play; also adj. unsuccessful, failed. **2** [1900s–30s] a fat, ungainly, slovenly person, esp. a woman. **3** [1900s–50s] (*US Und.*) an arrest. **4** [1920s+] a dull, unpleasant person, a misfit, a failure. **5** [1930s+] (*US prison*) the rejection of one's application for parole.

flop n.[5] **1** [20C+] (*US*) a cheap room or bed; thus *hit the flop*, to go to bed. **2** [1910s+] (*US*) a drunk who has passed out and as such is a potential victim for a robber. **3** [1910s+] (*US*) a sleep, esp. a prisoner's last night in prison; thus *2 weeks and a flop*, 2 weeks and 1 morning left in prison. **4** [1920s–50s] (*US Und.*) a legless beggar. **5** [1920s–60s] (*US*) an act of sexual intercourse. **6** [1930s] a blow. **7** [1940s–60s] (*US*) a seat. **8** [1960s+] (*UK Und.*) anywhere a thief or gang can leave the loot so as to avoid detection during the immediate aftermath of a crime. [SE *flop*, to fall down in a heap]

flop n.[6] [1930s+] (*US*) excrement; esp. *cow-flop*; thus as a dismissive retort. [Wiltshire dial. *flop*, thick liquid]

flop n.[7] *see* FLOPHOUSE n.

flop, the *n.* [1920s–40s] (*US Und.*) a form of confidence trick. [FLOP v. (6)]

flop v. 1 [mid-19C] (US campus) to cheat in an examination, esp. by faking sickness. 2 [mid-19C–1910s] to hit. 3 [late 19C–1910s] (US) to knock down an opponent; also in fig. use. 4 [20C+] to fall asleep, to go to bed. 5 [20C+] to lodge, i.e. in a hotel. 6 [1910s] (US Und.) to short-change. 7 [1910s] to move, to walk; often ext. as flop around, flop in etc. 8 [1910s–30s] (US) to become enamoured of someone. 9 [1910s+] (also go flop) to collapse, to fail, esp. of a stage entertainment or similar undertaking. 10 [1930s] (US) to fall to the ground for protection. 11 [1930s–40s] (US) to copulate. 12 [1940s–50s] (US prison) to deny a parole appeal; to be denied parole. 13 [1970s] (Aus.) to die. 14 [1970s+] (US) to demote.

flop about v. (also flop around, flop out) [late 19C+] to lie around. [ext. FLOP v. (4)]

flop a judy v. [late 19C] to lay a woman down preparatory to intercourse. [weak use of FLOP v. (3) + JUDY n.[1] (1)]

flop-and-slop n. [1990s+] a hostel, a cheap lodging. [FLOP n.[5] (1) + SLOP n.[1] (2)]

flop around v. see FLOP ABOUT v.

flop dough n. [1930s–40s] (US Und.) money set aside for lodging. [FLOP n.[5] (1) + DOUGH n.[1] (1)]

flop-ear n. see LOP-EAR n.

flop-eared adj. see LOP-EARED adj.

floperoo n. [1950s+] (orig. US) an extreme failure, esp. in a show business context. [FLOP n.[4] (1) + -EROO sfx]

flophouse n. (also flop) [20C+] (mainly US) 1 a lodging house or night shelter for tramps, down-and-outs, alcoholics etc. 2 a cheap restaurant or café. 3 a prison (cf. BANDHOUSE n.). [FLOP n.[5] (1) + SE house]

flop in v. [19C] of a man, to commence sexual intercourse.

flop joint n. [1930s+] (US) a tramp's lodging, a cheap hotel. [FLOP n.[5] (1) + JOINT n.[4] (3)]

flop off v. [1950s] to lose control emotionally.

flop one v. [1990s+] (US teen) to masturbate.

flop on the gills n. [mid–late 19C] a punch in the mouth. [FLOP v. (3)/Yorks. dial. flop, a blow, a slap + GILLS n. (3)]

flop out v.[1] 1 [late 19C–1910s] to jump out. 2 [1930s] to knock down, to make someone fall into a heap. [Yorks. dial. flop, to strike with a sudden blow]

flop out v.[2] see FLOP ABOUT v.

flopover v. [1980s] to assume a position with the buttocks in the air or with the body bent at 45° and the hands thus supported by the knees; both positions will permit the easy introduction of the penis into the anus or vagina.

flopped out adj. [20C+] (US) exhausted, tired out. [FLOP v. (4)]

flopper n. 1 [late 19C+] (UK Und.) a criminal who pretends to have 'slipped' on a shop floor or 'been knocked down' by a slow-moving automobile; they then claim damages, usu. offering to take a quick cash payment rather than go to an insurance company; thus flop racket, performing such frauds. 2 [1910s] (US Und.) a petty swindler. 3 [1910s–20s] a weakling, a spineless person. 4 [1910s+] (US Und.) a beggar who pretends to be crippled. [FLOP v.]

flopper-stopper n. [1950s+] (Aus./US) a brassiere.

flopping n. [1900s–20s] (US tramp) a sleeping bag or similar covering; in pl., a place where one sleeps. [FLOP n.[5] (1)]

flopping adj. see FLIPPING adj.

floppy n.[1] [20C+] (US) a fat, ungainly, slovenly person, esp. a woman. [FLOP n.[4] (2) + sfx -y]

floppy n.[2] [1970s+] (S.Afr.) a derog. term for a Black person. [orig. Rhodesian milit. use, one who 'flops down dead' when hit by bullets; the targets of such bullets were invariably Black]

flop racket n. see FLOPPER n. (1).

floptious adj. [20C+] (Irish) generous. [? the gifts flop into the receiver's hand]

flop-whop n. [late 19C] a heavy fall. [echoic]

flop worker n. [1930s] (US tramp) one who robs sleepers, usu. fellow tramps. [FLOP n.[5] (2) + WORKER n.[1] (1)]

floral arrangement n. [1960s+] (US gay) a spintry, i.e. a circle of 3 or more people, hetero- or homosexual, all linked physically in mutual sex acts. [pun on DAISY CHAIN n. (1)]

flor di cabbagio n. [1900s–10s] a cheap cigar. [CABBAGIO PERFUMO n.]

florence n. [late 17C–18C] an untidily dressed young woman. [Northamptonshire dial. florence, one who dresses untidily; whether this comes from the proper name and thus memorializes a long-forgotten woman is unknown; Williams prefers a link to the whores of Florence, Italy, and their speciality, the Florentine kiss, synon. with a French kiss]

florid adj. [late 18C–mid-19C] tipsy. [i.e. red-faced with drink]

Florida n. [20C+] (US prison) the solitary confinement/ punishment block. [the siting of such cells in the warmest areas of the prison, often underground]

Florida chicken n. [20C+] (US) a turtle. [the abundance of the turtle, Gopherus polyphemus]

floss n. [1990s+] (US) money. [ety. unknown]

floss v.[1] [1990s+] (US Black) 1 to relax. 2 to pose, to present a false image of oneself. 3 to appear stylish and attractive.

floss v.[2] [2000s] (US Black) to harass.

flossed up adj. see FLOSSY (UP) v.

flossie n. (also flossy) 1 [20C+] (Aus./N.Z./S.Afr.) a prostitute; thus flossiedom, the world of prostitution. 2 [1900s] an overdressed, over-affectionate woman. 3 [1900s] a barmaid. 4 [1910s–20s] a girlfriend, esp. one who is older than her partner. [FLOOZIE n.]

floss the cat v. [1990s+] of a woman, to masturbate (cf. APPLY LIP GLOSS v.; BEAT ONE'S HOG v.). [SE floss, to clean the teeth with dental floss + CAT n.[3] (1)]

flossy adj. 1 [late 19C+] (US) showy, slick, saucy, impertinent, ostentatious, attractive. 2 [1960s–70s] of homosexuals, flagrant, ostentatious. [SE floss, silk used for embroidery]

flossy (up) v. [1940s+] (Aus.) to dress oneself up, esp. in a showy, excessive manner; thus adj. flossed up. [? FLOOZIE n. or FLOSSIE n.]

floster n. [late 19C] a mixed drink consisting of sherry, soda water, lemon, ice etc. [ety. unknown]

flotch n. [1990s+] (UK juv.) feacal stains in one's underwear. [? SE flotsam]

flounder n.[1] [mid–late 19C] a drowned man, his corpse. [pun]

flounder n.[2] [1910s] (US) a Newfoundlander. [SE flounder, i.e. the fishing industry]

flounder (and dab) n. [mid-19C+] a taxi-cab. [rhy. sl.]

flounder mouth n. [mid-17C–mid-18C; 20C+] (US) a person with a notably large mouth. [SE flounder, a fish with a large mouth]

flourbags n. [1910s] (Aus.) a bush cook.

flour mixer n. [20C+] 1 a non-Jewish woman. 2 an inoffensive man, a clerk. [rhy. sl.; (1) = SHIKSA n. (1); (2) = ext. of image of SHIKSA n. (2)]

flous v. [1900s–10s] (S.Afr.) to cheat, to trick, to put at a disadvantage. [Ger. Flause, deceit]

floush v. (also go flouch) [early 19C] to collapse. [echoic]

flow n. [2000s] (US Black) money. [abbr. SE cash flow]

flow v. [1990s+] 1 (orig. US Black) to perform rap music very well, esp. one's creation of lyrics. 2 (US campus) to speak eloquently.

flower n. [1910s–70s] an effeminate male homosexual. [the 'feminine' image of flowers]

flower-fancier n. [late 19C–1900s] a womanizer, a lecher, presumably specializing in 'flowers', i.e. virgins.

flower of chivalry n. [19C] the vagina (cf. ADAM'S OWN (ALTAR) n.; BEAUTY SPOT n.). [pun on orig. use of SE chivalry, a body of men who ride; thus cf. RIDE v.[1] (1)]

flower patch n. [1980s] (US) the female genital area.

flowerpot n. [19C; 2000s] the vagina (cf. BAG n.[1]; BEAUTY SPOT n.).

flowers *n.* **1** [late 17C–1950s] a euph. for menstruation. **2** [1980s+] (*orig. US*) the vulva; thus *eat someone's flowers*, to perform cunnilingus. [prior use of (1) is SE since 15C]

flowers and frolics *n. see* FUN AND FROLICS n.

flowers-on-his-grave *n.* [1910s] (*Aus.*) fastidiousness.

flower tops *n.* [1960s+] (*drugs*) marijuana (cf. AFRICAN BUSH n.). [the most powerful part of the plant]

flowery (dell) *n.* [20C+] a cell. [rhy. sl.]

flowery dell *n.* [mid-19C] a room, esp. a room in an inn. [pedlars' Ling. Fr.]

flowing hope *n.* [mid–late 19C] a gambler's last, despairing bet. [for ety. *see* FORLORN HOPE n.]

flub *n.* (*also* **flubdub, flubdubbery**) [1910s–30s] nonsense. [FLUB v.]

flub *v.* [20C+] (*US*) **1** (*also* **flub up**) to botch, to bungle, to make a mess of. **2** to confuse. **3** to waste time, to fool around. [? link to FLUFF v.[1] (2)]

flubdub *v.* [20C+] (*US*) to mess around, to waste time. [FLUB v. (3) + redup. or ? DUB n.[3] (1)]

flubdubbery *n. see* FLUB n.

flub the dub *v.* [1940s+] **1** (*orig. US milit.*) to shirk, to evade one's duties. **2** (*US*) to blunder, to fail in a task. **3** (*US*) to masturbate. [FLUBDUB v.]

flub up *v. see* FLUB v. (1).

flue *n.*[1] **1** [17C+] (*US*) the vagina. **2** [early–mid-19C] a lift formerly in use in pawnbrokers' shops, up which the articles pawned were taken for storage; thus phr. *put up the flue*, to pawn. **3** [1920s+] the anus (cf. ALLEY WAY n.). [SE *flue*, a chimney, thus any form of passage for conveying heat]

flue *n.*[2] [1940s–50s] (*UK prison*) a warder. [rhy. sl. = SCREW n.[2] (3)]

flue *n.*[3] [1970s] (*US Black*) a room, as used by a prostitute for work.

flue *v.* [late 19C] to put in pawn. [FLUE n.[1] (2)]

flue-faker *n.* [19C] **1** a chimney sweep. **2** (*racing*) 'low sporting characters, who are so termed from their chiefly betting on the Great Sweeps' (sweepstakes) (Hotten, 1860). [SE *flue* + FAKER n. (1)]

fluence *n.* [late 19C+] **1** hypnotism, lit. or fig. **2** delicate, subtle influence, either in the context of business, politics etc, or in actual physical acts, e.g. the spinning of a cricket ball.

fluff *n.*[1] **1** [mid-19C] the pubic hair of either gender. **2** [20C+] a young, attractive, but empty-headed woman; esp. as BIT OF FLUFF n.; also used of men. **3** [1940s+] the passive, 'feminine' partner in a lesbian couple. **4** [1960s+] (*gay*) an effeminate male homosexual. **5** [1970s+] (*US Black*) the vagina. **6** [1970s+] (*US gay*) male sex organs, esp. the anus. [note RMC Duntroon (Aus.) *fluff*, a woman, a girlfriend (no derog. meaning)]

fluff *n.*[2] **1** [mid-19C+] (*Aus.*) rubbish, nonsense, something superficial. **2** [1900s–20s] (*US*) a foolish person.

fluff *n.*[3] [1920s+] (*Aus.*) a railway ticket. [ety. unknown; ? link to FLUFF v.[1] (1)]

fluff *n.*[4] [1940s+] lightweight writing. [FLUFF adj.]

fluff *adj.* [1930s+] of writing, lightweight, nonsensical, meaningless.

fluff *v.*[1] **1** [mid–late 19C] of railway booking clerks, to give short change. **2** [mid-19C+] (*orig. theatre*) to make a mistake, to bungle. **3** [late 19C] to disconcert or put off a public speaker. **4** [1900s–50s] to bluff, to lie. **5** [1900s–50s] to falsify (accounts etc).

fluff *v.*[2] **1** [1930s–40s] to realize, to work out. **2** [1950s] to understand.

fluff *v.*[3] [1960s+] (*N.Z. juv./US campus*) to break wind. [echoic + SE *fluff*, a puff, an explosion]

fluffbrain *n. see* FLUFFHEAD n.

fluffed *adj.* **1** [mid-19C] drunk. **2** [20C+] intoxicated by drugs.

fluffer *n.*[1] [late 19C] a drunkard. [FLUFFED adj.]

fluffer *n.*[2] **1** [1980s+] (*US*) a person employed on a film set to arouse an actor physically before filming a sexual episode. **2** [2000s] an erection. [FLUFF IT UP v.]

fluffhead *n.* (*also* **fluffbrain**) [1960s+] an insubstantial, superficial person. [SE *fluff* + -HEAD sfx (1)]

fluff in *v.* [late 19C] to deceive by smooth talk. [SE *fluff*, to puff]

fluffiness *n.* [late 19C] drunkenness. [FLUFFED adj.]

fluff in the pan *n.* [mid–late 19C] a failure. [FLUFF v.[1] (2) + play on phr. FLASH IN THE PAN n.]

fluff it! *excl.* [mid–late 19C] take it away! I don't want it!

fluff it up *v.* [1970s+] (*US gay*) to make the penis erect prior to appearing on the street in tight trousers.

fluff off *v.*[1] [1940s+] (*US*) to dismiss or reject, also as imper. [SE *fluff*, to blow, to puff]

fluff off *v.*[2] [1950s+] to avoid work, to shirk. [? euph. for FUCK OFF v. (2)]

fluff the duff *v. see* DUFF n.[2] (1).

fluff up *v.* [1990s+] to get drunk, to become intoxicated by drugs. [FLUFFED adj.]

fluffy *adj.* **1** [late 19C] drunk and incapable. **2** [1920s] gentle, unaggressive, sympathetic. **3** [1980s] (*US campus*) a general intensifier. **4** [1990s+] (*US lesbian*) sexually excited. **5** [1990s+] (*US gay*) among leather-wearing gay men, refusing to accept the dress-code. [SE *fluffy*, soft, covered in down; (1) ? link to theatre jargon *fluff*, to forget one's lines]

fluffy duck *n.* [1980s] (*Aus.*) an act of sexual intercourse. [rhy. sl. = FUCK n.[1] (1)]

flugens! *excl.* [mid-19C–1950s] a general, mild oath. [ety. unknown; ? link to Ger.]

fluke *n.*[1] [early 19C; 1930s–60s] a gullible victim. [SE *fluke*, a flat fish thus ? play on FLAT n.[2] (1)]

fluke *n.*[2] **1** [mid-19C+] an unforeseen success, a piece of unexpected good luck; thus *flukiness*, fortuitous good fortune. **2** [late 19C] (*orig. US campus*) a failure, a worthless person or thing. **3** [1990s+] (*Aus.*) a lucky person. [? billiards jargon *fluke*, to succeed in a given shot more through luck than judgement; thus a player who wins through flukes cannot be judged as capable as one who wins through skill alone; ult. ety. unknown; ? link to dial. *fluke*, a guess]

fluke *v.*[1] **1** [late 19C–1940s] to fail; thus *fluke up*, to do badly; thus *go up the fluke*, to fail in a recitation or examination. **2** [20C+] to steal. **3** [20C+] to back out, to renege on a promise. **4** [1950s] (*US*) (*also* **fluke out**) to die.

fluke *v.*[2] [late 19C+] to get a piece of good luck. [FLUKE n.[2] (1); the implication is always one of some degree of unfairness in such luck]

fluked out *adj.* [1940s–50s] intoxicated with a drug.

fluke out *v. see* FLUKE v.[1] (4).

fluker *n.* [early 19C] a lucky blow. [logically FLUKE n.[2] (1) but earlier than available cites]

flukum *n.* [1930s] (*US tramp*) cheap, nickel-plated goods sold as 'silver plate'. [? it's a FLUKE n.[2] (1) that any of it gets sold]

fluky *adj.* (*also* **flukey**) [late 19C+] **1** lucky; thus adv. *flukily*. **2** (*US*) peculiar, bizarre. [FLUKE n.[2] (1) + sfx -*y*]

flumdiddle *n.* [1910s–20s] empty flattery, humbug. [var. on FLUMMADIDDLE n. (1)]

flumdoodle *v.* [1910s+] (*Aus.*) to cheat, to trick, to hoax (someone); thus *flumdoodle*, a trick, a hoax. [FLUMDIDDLE n.]

flummadiddle *n.* [mid-19C+] (*US*) **1** nonsense, empty flattery, humbug. **2** something trivial or ridiculous. [? FLUMMERY n. + ? DIDDLE n.[4]; *flummery* was also a variety of sweet dish thus note *flummadiddle*, 'stale bread, pork-fat, molasses, cinnamon, allspice, from which a kind of mush is made, which is baked in the oven and brought to the table hot and brown' (Schele de Vere, *Americanisms*, 1872)]

flummer *v.* [mid-18C] to flatter, to 'soft soap'. [backform. f. FLUMMERY n.]

flummery *n.* [mid-18C–early 19C] empty flattery, humbug. [later use is SE; *see also* ety. at FLUMMADIDDLE n.]

flummocky *adj.* [late 19C] in poor taste. [FLUMMOX n.]

flummox *n.* (*also* **flummux**) [19C] (*US*) **1** a failure. **2** a stupid person. [FLUMMOX v.¹ (3)]

flummox *v.*¹ (*also* **flummux**) **1** [mid-19C] to move in a clumsy manner. **2** [mid-19C–1910s] to back down, to back out of a promise; to disappoint; to opt out of a round of betting. **3** [mid-19C–1910s] (*US*) to blunder, to fail; to die. **4** [mid-19C+] to fool, to confuse, to overcome (by trickery). [? dial. *flummocks*, to maul, to mangle; *flummock*, a slovenly person or *flummock*, to make untidy, to disorder, to confuse, to bewilder + onomat. element based on throwing down roughly and untidily. As such, the term is reminiscent of *flump*, a hummock, and *slommock*, a sloven]

flummox *v.*² [mid-late 19C] (*US*) to titivate one's hair. [fig. use of FLUMMOX v.¹]

flummox by the lip *v.* [late 19C] to talk down. [FLUMMOX v.¹ (4)]

flummoxed *adj.*¹ (*also* **flummuxed**) [mid-19C] (*UK Und.*) imprisoned for 1 month. [FLUMMUT n. + fig. use of FLUMMOX v.¹; in tramp jargon *flummoxed* refers to a place that is unsafe to visit, the owners or guardians are likely to have one imprisoned]

flummoxed *adj.*² [mid-19C+] **1** (*also* **flummoxed up**) confused, let down, outwitted. **2** ruined. **3** drunk (cf. ADDLED adj.). [FLUMMOX v.¹]

flummut *n.* [mid-late 19C] a 1-month prison sentence. [tramp/tinker use, *flummut*, a mark placed on a door to indicate a house that will be unfriendly; 'flummut, sure of a month in quod' (Mayhew); ult. FLUMMOX v.¹]

flummux *see under* FLUMMOX.

flump *n.* **1** [late 18C+] a sudden heavy fall. **2** [1990s+] (*US teen*) the act of sitting down in a casual manner. [dial./echoic]

flump *v.* [mid-19C+] **1** to collapse or fall heavily. **2** to move determindly. [FLUMP n. (1)]

flunk *n.*¹ **1** [mid-19C+] (*US campus*) a total failure in academic work, a grade F; thus a student who has failed (cf. ACE n.⁶). **2** [mid-19C+] (*US*) a failure. **3** [late 19C–1910s] (*US*) an idler, a loafer; thus *flunky*, ignorant, second-rate. [FLUNK v. (1)]

flunk *n.*² [1920s–50s] (*US Und.*) the strongbox within a safe. [ety. unknown]

flunk *v.* **1** [early 19C+] (*orig. US campus*) (*also* **flunk out**) to fail an examination; to give a fail mark. **2** [early 19C+] (*US*) to give in, to back down or renege in a cowardly manner. **3** [mid-19C] (*US gambling*) to 'fold' one's cards. **4** [mid-19C+] (*US campus*) to be dismissed or to dismiss on the grounds of academic failure. **5** [late 19C+] (*US*) to fail (in a non-academic context), to blunder, to make a mistake. **6** [late 19C+] to embarrass someone (by an indiscreet remark). **7** [late 19C+] (*orig. US*) to do a skimpy, inadequate job. [? US dial. *flink*, ult. SE *flinch*, to act in a cowardly way, to shrink from one's duties; + 18C Oxford jargon (later sl.) *funk*, to exhibit a state of complete fear or panic]

flunker *n.* [late 19C–1910s] (*US campus*) **1** one who regularly fails their examinations or recitations. **2** a teacher who often fails students. [FLUNK v. (1)]

flunky *n.*¹ (*also* **flunkee, flunkey**) **1** [19C+] (*US campus*) one who fails an examination. **2** [20C+] a menial, a stooge. **3** [20C+] (*US*) an assistant cook in a mining or lumber camp. **4** [1920s–50s] one who is expelled, due to failing examinations. **5** [1960s+] (*US Black*) an undistinguished person. [SE *flunkey*, servant; (1) Hall, *College Words and Customs* (1856), does not support Schele de Vere's idea, in *Americanisms* (1872), of 'backing out' of an exam; the def. is simply that of failure]

flunky *n.*² [1990s+] a condom. [? joc. use of FLUNK n.¹ (1)]

flurgle *v. see* FURGLE v.

flurry *n.* [2000s] (*Aus.*) a promiscuous woman. [McDonald's *McFlurry* ice cream]

flurry one's milk *v.* [early–mid-19C] to be worried, perturbed, annoyed. [SE *flurry*, to agitate]

flurt *n.*¹ [early 18C] an act of copulation.

flurt *n.*² *see* FLIRT n.

flush *n.*¹ [1940s+] (*W.I.*) a 6-month prison sentence. [ety. unknown]

flush *n.*² [1960s+] (*US*) the lavatory.

flush *adj.*¹ (*also* **flushed**) [18C+] drunk. [the level of the liquid that is *flush* with the rim of the glass]

flush *adj.*² *see* FLUSH (IN THE POCKET) adj.

flush *v.*¹ [mid-19C] to whip; thus *flushed on the horse*, privately whipped in prison. [some punitive whipping was still carried out in public; the *horse* is a wooden frame to which the victim is secured]

flush *v.*² [1950s+] (*US*) to reject, to cancel, to discard. [SE *flush*, to empty/refill a lavatory bowl]

flush a wild duck *v.* [19C] to single out a woman in the hope of seducing her. [sporting imagery]

flushed *adj. see* FLUSH adj.¹.

flushing *n.* [1970s+] (*UK drugs*) the act of drawing blood into the syringe when injecting a narcotic.

flush (in the pocket) *adj.* [early 17C–18C] well supplied with money. [SE *flush*, to burst with, usu. of a stream or river. The term remained sl. (the image being of a pocket running over with money) until 19C when it became SE]

flusie *n. see* FLOOZIE n.

flustered *adj.* [mid-17C–mid-19C] drunk (cf. ADDLED adj.). [17C SE *fluster*, to make half-tipsy]

flusticate *v.* [mid-late 19C] to confuse. [SE *fluster*]

flustrate *v.* [early 18C–19C] to confuse, to excite; thus *flustration*, excitement, confusion, bustle. [SE *fluster*]

flustrated *adj.* [1930s] mildly drunk. [SE *flustered/frustrated*]

flute *n.*¹ [late 17C–mid-19C] the Recorder of London. [pun on SE *recorder*, a flute-like instrument]

flute *n.*² **1** [late 17C+] the penis (cf. ACCORDION n.). **2** [late 19C] (*US drugs*) an opium pipe; thus *hit the flute*, to smoke opium. **3** [late 19C+] a policeman's whistle. **4** [1930s] a male homosexual.

flute *n.*³ [mid-19C] a pistol. [resemblance]

flute *n.*⁴ (*also* **highland flute**) [1910s+] a suit. [abbr.]

flute *v.*¹ [late 19C+] (*Aus.*) to talk incessantly; thus *on the flute*, talking continually; *hold the flute*, to monopolize the conversation; *pass the flute*, to let someone else speak; *put your flute away!* stop talking! [SE *flute* v.]

flute *v.*² [1930s] (*US gay*) to fellate (cf. BLOW v.²). [FLUTE n.² (1)]

flute! *excl.* [20C+] (*Irish*) a general excl. of surprise or annoyance. [? euph. for FUCK! excl.]

flute mute *n.* [1990s+] a condom. [FLUTE n.² (1) + SE *mute*]

flute-player *n.* [1950s+] (*US*) a fellator or fellatrix. [FLUTE n.² (1) + pun]

fluter *n.*¹ [late 19C–1950s] (*Aus.*) an incessant talker. [FLUTE v.¹]

fluter *n.*² [20C+] a fellator (thus generic for a male homosexual) or fellatrix (cf. BONE-EATER n.). [FLUTE n.² (1)]

fluthered *adj.* [1940s+] (*Irish*) very drunk (cf. ADDLED adj.). [? SE *fluttered*]

flutter *n.*¹ [mid-late 19C] **1** a spree, an adventure; thus *on the flutter*, out on a spree. **2** a small, swift trip. **3** a burst of speed.

flutter *n.*² **1** [mid-late 19C] an attempt, a try; thus *have a flutter for*, to attempt something. **2** [late 19C+] a bet, usu. presumed to be small, unless used ironically; usu. as *have a flutter*, occas. *do a flutter*, to bet. [the excitement that flutters one's heart or the punter fluttering their money at the bookmaker]

flutter *n.*³ **1** [late 19C] any form of sexual experience; thus *be on the flutter*, to be a sexual sophisticate; *do/have a flutter*, to enjoy hedonistic rather than procreative intercourse; *have had a flutter*, to have lost one's virginity. **2** [1930s–40s] (*US*) (*also* **flutterer**) a male homosexual.

flutter *v.*¹ [late 19C] to have sexual intercourse; thus *flutter a judy*, to pursue and/or seduce a woman. [FLUTTER n.³ (1)]

flutter *v.*² [late 19C–1900s] **1** to enjoy oneself. **2** to gamble, to wager. [FLUTTER n.² (2)]

flutter a skirt *v.* [late 19C–1900s] to work as a prostitute.

flutterbudget *n.* (*also* **flutter-guts**) [20C+] (*US*) a particularly fussy person. [var. on FUSSBUDGET n. (1)]

flutterer *n. see* FLUTTER n.[3] (2).

flutter someone's kidneys *v.* [late 19C] to annoy, to disturb, to irritate.

flux *v.*[1] [18C–mid-19C] to cheat, to deceive. [SE *flux*, to confuse]

flux *v.*[2] [late 18C–early 19C] to salivate. [SE *flux*, to make salivate, to purge]

flux me! *excl.* [18C] an excl. of asseveration, a synon. with I'LL BE DAMNED! excl.

fluxy *adj.* [1970s+] (*W.I.*) superficially impressive. [orig. used of under-ripe or blemished mangoes]

fluzie *n. see* FLOOZIE n.

fly *n.*[1] [18C–early 19C] (*UK Und.*) a wagon. [SE *fly*, a fast carriage, a stage-coach]

fly *n.*[2] [mid–late 19C] a trick, a dodge. [SE *fly*, i.e. one is 'flying a kite']

fly *n.*[3] [mid–late 19C; 1950s] a policeman. [pun on BLUEBOTTLE n. (2) but note FLY COP n.]

fly *n.*[4] [late 19C] a spree, a 'lark'.

fly *n.*[5] [late 19C+] (*Aus.*) **1** the act of tossing a coin, esp. in a game of two-up. **2** in fig. use, a try, a 'go'. [SE *fly*, a throw, a toss]

fly *n.*[6] *see* FLY COP n. (2).

fly *n.*[7] *see* FLY (TIPPER) n.

fly *adj.* **1** [early 18C+] aware, knowledgeable. **2** [mid-18C–early 19C; 1950s+] fashionable. **3** [mid-18C+] smart, sharp, perspicacious; thus *flyness*, perspicacity. **4** [mid-19C–1910s] dexterous, agile. **5** [late 19C] enjoying a run of good luck. **6** [late 19C+] of a woman, occas. a man, promiscuous, flirtatious. **7** [late 19C+] sophisticated. **8** [20C+] (*US*) rebellious, uninhibited in behaviour. **9** [1940s] (*orig. US*) insolent, brash. **10** [1950s+] (*US campus*) of a woman, attractive, pretty, stylish. **11** [1990s+] (*US*) terrific. [Scot. *flee*, aware; 20C+ US Black uses may be further influenced by Gullah *fly*, to be fast and ecstatic]

fly *v.*[1] **1** [mid-16C+] to go quickly, to rush; esp. in phr. *I must fly*, I must hurry away. **2** [mid–late 19C] to send quickly.

fly *v.*[2] [mid-19C] (*UK Und.*) to lift, to raise; thus *fly a window*, to open a (sash) window for the purpose of breaking into a house. [note theatre jargon *fly*, to suspend scenery or lights from above the stage]

fly *v.*[3] [late 19C+] of an idea, a plan, to work out, usu. in negative. [the same metaphorical 'flag' as found in the SE phr. *run it up the flagpole and we'll see who salutes*]

fly *v.*[4] **1** [1930s+] (*US drugs*) to take or to be intoxicated by psychotropic drugs. **2** [1970s+] to be drunk. [one gets HIGH adj.[1]]

fly *adv.* [1950s] (*US Black*) smartly, fashionably. [FLY adj. (2)]

fly a blue pigeon *v.* (*also* **fly the blue pigeon**) [late 18C–1900s] to steal the lead from a church roof; thus *pigeon-flying*, conducting such thefts. [SE *fly*/FLY v.[2] + BLUE PIGEON n. (2); the verse from a sporting song quoted in Egan, *Book of Sports* (1832): 'I'll race my *Jack*, or bait a *bull*, / Or fight my *Doodle-doo*, / I'll flash a *quid* with any *cull*, / And fly a *pigeon* blue' is presumably to be taken lit.]

fly a flag *v.*[1] [1990s+] **1** (*US, esp. prison*) to betray one's personality, esp. in a situation, e.g. prison, where such honesty may be foolish (cf. FLAG v.[3]). **2** (*US Black teen*) to wear gang colours.

fly a flag *v.*[2] *see* FLAG v.[2] (3).

fly a kite *v.*[1] **1** [19C+] (*also* **fly the kite**) to obtain credit against bills, whether or not the 'paper' is valid or fraudulent. **2** [late 19C–1910s] to raise money. **3** [1920s+] (*US prison*) to smuggle a letter out of prison; also occas. within prison. **4** [1920s+] to pass a dud cheque; ext. as *fly a dodgy kite*. **5** [1940s–70s] (*US*) to send a letter. [SE *fly* + KITE n.[2]]

fly a kite *v.*[2] **1** [late 19C] to make public, to publicize. **2** [late 19C] (*UK Und.*) to write a letter to a receiver of stolen goods, prior to a robbery, to ascertain the value of the goods to be stolen. **3** [20C+] (*US*) to show off, to make a big display. **4** [1920s+] to present a false front or a deceitful line of talk in order to persuade one's victim that one's intentions are other than they really are. **5** [1930s+] to sound out public opinion, by taking initial steps in a given project or idea. **6** [1950s] (*Aus.*) to lie.

fly a kite at *v.* [mid-19C] to court, to pursue a woman.

fly a line *v.* [mid-19C] to send a letter. [FLY v.[1] (2) + SE *line*, a short letter or note]

fly around *v.* [mid-19C] (*US*) to get busy, to rush about; thus *flyaround*, a burst of activity. [FLY v.[1] (1)]

fly around and tear one's shirt *v.* [late 19C–1900s] to get on with things. [ext. of FLY AROUND v.]

fly-ass *adj.* [1990s+] (*US Black*) sophisticated, up-to-the-minute. [FLY adj. (7) + -ASS sfx]

fly a tile *v.* [early 19C] to knock off a man's hat as a form of practical joke. [SE *fly*/FLY v.[2] + TILE n.]

fly-away *n.* **1** [late 19C] a tricycle. **2** [1910s–30s] (*US*) a deserter. **3** [1940s] (*US prison*) a fugitive.

flyball *n.* **1** [1920s–30s] (*US tramp*) a city detective. **2** [1960s–70s] (*US*) a male homosexual. [? pun on baseball jargon *flyball*, a ball that can be caught 'on the fly'; the image of (2) is of a ball that travels far and fast]

fly-blister *n.* [late 19C] (*Aus.*) a minor newspaper. [? its minimal impact]

fly-blow *n.* [mid–late 19C] an illegitimate child. [BY-BLOW n. + ? SE *fly-blown*]

fly-blow *v.* **1** [19C–1900s] (*US*) to gossip maliciously about an absent third party, to attack behind one's back. **2** [20C+] (*Aus.*) to take money from someone, often by chicanery. [SE *flyblow*, the egg of a fly, which turns into a maggot that will, in this context, fig. devour the victim's reputation or money]

fly-blown *adj.* (*also* **fly-blowed**) **1** [17C–19C] deflowered, no longer virgin, thus, of a prostitute, thought to be used by many men. **2** [19C] drunk. **3** [mid-19C–1950s] (*Aus./N.Z.*) ruined, penniless, without funds. **4** [late 19C] suspected of carrying venereal disease. **5** [late 19C] tired out, exhausted. [fig. uses of SE]

flybog *n.* [1910s+] (*Aus.*) treacle, jam. [flies that land on jam tend to get stuck]

fly-boy *n.*[1] **1** [late 19C; 1980s+] (*US Black*) (*also* **fly guy**) a sophisticated, intelligent, stylish young man. **2** [1940s+] a 'wide boy', a SPIV n. [FLY adj.]

fly-boy *n.*[2] **1** [1910s] (*Anglo-Irish*) a British citizen who escaped to Ireland to avoid conscription in WW1. **2** [1930s+] (*US*) a pilot, civil or milit., usu. with a slight implication of disdain or dislike. [joc. uses of SE *fly* + *boy*]

fly bull *n. see* FLY COP n.

fly-buzzing *n. see* BUZZING n.

fly-by-night *n.* **1** [19C+] (*also* **fly-by-nighter**) one who defrauds the landlord by leaving their lodgings in the middle of the night, having failed to pay the rent. **2** [early–mid-19C] a sedan chair on wheels. **3** [late 19C] (*US*) a small touring theatrical company. **4** [20C+] (*also* **fly-by-nighter**) anyone dubious, crooked, criminal, esp. of a businessman who takes one's money but fails to provide any or at least adequate recompense. **5** [1930s] (*UK Und.*) itinerant casinos, moving every night to avoid the detection of illegal gambling. [lit. one who 'flies by night'. Grose (1796) adds his punning joke: 'an ancient term of reproach to an old woman, signifying that she was a witch']

fly-by-night *adj.* [20C+] **1** dubious, untrustworthy, undependable. **2** crooked, criminal. [FLY-BY-NIGHT n. (4)]

fly-by-night, pitch-by-day *n.* [1950s] (*W.I.*) an idle, worthless person with no home. [FLY-BY-NIGHT n.]

fly-by-nights *n.* [1970s+] tights. [rhy. sl.]

fly by the seat of one's pants *v.* [1940s+] to fly an aircraft using natural ability and daring rather than instruments and technology; thus fig. to gamble with one's life, to take extravagant risks.

fly-cage n. (also **flycatcher, flytrap**) [late 19C] the vagina (cf. BITE n.[2]). [joc. use of SE + ? ref. to the FLY adj. (1) young gentleman it ensnares]

flycar n. [1980s+] (US Black) a desirable automobile. [FLY adj. (2) + SE car]

fly card n. [late 19C] a knowledgeable, aware, cunning person. [FLY adj. (1) + CARD n.[2] (2)]

flycatcher n.[1] [mid-17C–19C] a gawping fool. [his open mouth]

flycatcher n.[2] see FLY-CAGE n.

fly cemetery n. **1** [1930s+] (N.Z.) a pastry square filled with mincemeat. **2** [1930s+] (N.Z.) a raisin biscuit. **3** [1950s–60s] steamed pudding with currants. **4** [2000s] (Irish) a currant bun. [resemblance]

flychick n. [1940s] (US Black) a hedonistic young woman who enjoys parties and her social life. [FLY adj. (6) + CHICK n.[4] (2)]

fly cop n. (also **fly bull, fly dick**) (US) **1** [mid–late 19C] an alert or experienced police officer. **2** [mid-19C+] (also **fly**) a plain-clothes policeman. **3** [late 19C+] a detective. [FLY adj. (1) + COP n.[1] (1)]

fly coy v. [1960s–70s] (US Black) to become suddenly reticent and coy. [SE fly, to become + coy]

fly crutch n. [1970s+] (US) any fashionable automobile. [FLY adj. (2) + CRUTCH n.[3]]

fly dick n. see FLY COP n.

fly-disperser soup n. [mid-19C–1900s] oxtail soup (cf. FLY-SWISHER STEW n.). [the ox swishes its tail to get rid of clustering flies]

fly donah n. [late 19C] a cunning woman. [FLY adj. (3) + DONAH n. (2)]

fly-dusters n. [late 19C–1900s] the fists.

flyer n.[1] (also **flier**) **1** [late 17C–19C] a shoe. **2** [mid-19C] a shoe that has been soled without having been welted. [? play on 'flying away' in one's footwear]

flyer n.[2] (also **flier**) [early 19C+] (US) **1** a wager or investment; thus take a flyer, to take a gamble, a risk. **2** a lark. **3** a try, an attempt.

flyer n.[3] (also **flier**) **1** [mid–late 19C] a racehorse, a fast horse. **2** [mid-19C+] (Aus.) a fast-running kangaroo. **3** [late 19C] in ext. use of (1), an attractive young woman. **4** [late 19C] in ext. use of (1), a successful person. [SE fly, to go fast]

flyer n.[4] (also **flier**) [1940s+] (US prison) suicide by throwing oneself from an upper gallery in a cell-block; thus take a flier, to kill oneself thus.

flyer n.[5] (also **flier**) [1960s] (US campus) an idiotic or obnoxious person. [FLY A KITE v.[2] (3)]

fly-flapped adj. [late 18C] whipped at the cart's tail or in the stocks. [SE fly-flap, to beat, to whip, orig. to hit flies with a swatter]

fly-flapper n. [mid-19C–1920s] a heavy club.

fly-flat n. **1** [late 19C–1940s] (also **fly gee**) a con-man's victim who believes himself to be cleverer than he actually proves. **2** [1910s] in ext. use, anyone gullible. **3** [1940s] (US) a gun. [FLY adj. (1) + FLAT n.[2] (1)/GEE n.[3] (1)]

fly-girl n. **1** [late 19C] a prostitute (cf. AWAYDAY GIRL n.). **2** [1980s+] (US/UK Black) a smart, attractive woman. [FLY adj. (6)/FLY adj. (10) + SE girl]

fly high v. [mid-19C+] to get drunk; usu. as FLYING HIGH phr.

fly hot v. [1900s–40s] (US Black) suddenly to lose one's temper. [SE fly, to become + HOT adj.[1] (4)]

flying n. [late 18C–mid-19C] (UK Und.) a bout of hedonistic enjoyment; a brief act of intercourse. [synon. with SE fling]

flying adj. [1950s+] (drugs) under the influence of drink or drugs. [FLY v.[4]]

flying baker n. [1940s+] menstruation. [naut. jargon baker = B; in semaphore, the flag signifying the second letter of the alphabet is red, i.e. FLY THE RED FLAG v.]

flying bedstead n. [19C] a stall used by a bric-a-brac dealer. [note WW1 milit. flying bedstead, a milit. bicycle or motorcycle]

flying camps n. [late 17C–early 19C] a group of beggars who work as a team at funerals. [SE flying camp, 'a little army of horse and foot, that keeps the field, and is continually in motion' (Phillips, The New World of Words, 1671)]

flying cat n. [late 17C–early 18C] (UK Und.) an owl. [its predilection for mice and other small rodents]

flying dustman n. [early 19C] a 'pirate' dustman, who collects garbage before the contracted dustman can arrive. [pun on the Flying Dutchman]

flying flies n. see FLOATERS n.

flying fuck n. (also **flying shit**) [1950s+] an all-purpose negative epithet; usu. in comb., e.g. (not) give a flying fuck, TAKE A FLYING FUCK v.

flying giggers n. [late 18C–early 19C] turnpike gates. [GIGGER n.[1] (1)]

flying handicap n. [1950s] (Aus.) diarrhoea.

flying high phr. [mid-19C+] drunk or intoxicated by drugs; often with rather (cf. ELEVATED adj.). [fig. use of SE, but cf. FLYING adj. and HIGH adj.[1]]

flying horse n. [1950s] (W.I.) a bent pin or similar sharp object placed on a chair. [the person who sits on it 'flies']

flying jib n. [1930s–60s] a talkative person. [JIB n.[1] (4)]

flying knacker n. [mid–late 19C] a small-scale, travelling horseflesh butcher. [SE flying, moving fast + knacker]

flying lessons n. [1990s+] (UK/US prison) the throwing of a guard or fellow inmate off the balcony of a cell tier.

flying light phr. [1930s–60s] (US tramp) hungry; unencumbered by a pack or similar possessions. [Irwin (1931): 'From the railroads, where a "light engine" is one travelling over the line without a train, and so able to move swiftly and without needless delay']

flying low phr. [1960s+] (Irish) a phr. warning someone their flies are open.

flying officer Biggles n. [2000s] sexual intercourse. [rhy. sl. = SE wriggles; ult. the fictional character James Bigglesworth known as Biggles, created by Captain W.E. Johns in the 1930s]

flying pasty n. **1** [late 18C–early 19C] a packet of excrement wrapped in paper and flung over a neighbour's wall. **2** [19C] (US prison) a similar package wrapped in newspaper and tossed out of one's cell window.

flying porter n. [late 18C–early 19C] a cheat who approaches the victim of robbery, tells him that he can regain the stolen goods for him and demands a payment for fetching them. [SE fly, to run off]

flying saucer n.[1] **1** [1950s+] (orig. US) a diaphragm. **2** [1990s+] (W.I.) a motorcycle policeman. [(1) shape]

flying saucer n.[2] **1** [1960s+] (drugs) the seeds of the plant Ipomoea, popularly known as morning glory. **2** [1970s–80s] (N.Z. prison) a capsule of the strong tranquillizer, Largactil. [their shape and their effect on the user]

flying shit n. see FLYING FUCK n.

flying sixty-nine n. [1990s+] mutual oral-genital stimulation. [SE flying + SIXTY-NINE n. (1)]

flying sixty-six n. [20C+] oral sex. [rhy. sl. = FRENCH TRICKS n.]

flying stationer n. [late 18C–19C] a street seller of cheap ballads, criminal 'confessions' and similar popular material. [SE flying, moving + stationer, a bookseller]

flying trapeze n. [late 19C+] cheese. [rhy. sl.]

fly in one's head v. see FLY (UP) IN ONE'S HEAD v.

fly-in-the-milk n. [20C+] (US) a mulatto, a child of mixed Black and White parentage. [the black fly in the white milk]

fly jay n. [1970s+] (US Black) an attractive woman. [FLY adj. (10) + JAY n.[2]]

fly jerks n. [late 19C+] (Aus.) the small pieces of cork suspended from a hat to ward off flies.

fly loo n. (also **Kentucky loo**) [mid–late 19C] a form of betting, on the actions of flies, indulged in by students. [SE fly/Kentucky + loo, a card-game similar to whist. The participants stand around a table and each has a sugar lump daubed with a little honey in front of them; they then bet on which lump attracts a fly first]

fly machine *n.* [1980s] (*S.Afr. Black*) methylated spirits. [? the effect of the drink makes one 'fly']

fly-man *n.* **1** [mid-19C–1910s] a private or plain-clothes detective. **2** [late 19C–1950s] a shrewd, cunning, usu. criminal man. **3** [1920s] an expert thief. [FLY adj. (1) + SE *man*]

fly me! *excl.* [late 19C] a mild excl. [SE *flay me!*]

fly member *n.* [late 19C] a smart, even cunning man, good at picking up on and exploiting the current fashions. [FLY adj. (1) + SE *member*]

fly Mexican airlines *v.* [1960s+] (*drugs*) to smoke marijuana. [the easy access to marijuana in Mexico + flying HIGH adj.¹ (2)]

fly mobsman *n.* [1930s] (*UK Und.*) a confidence trickster who poses as a gentleman. [FLY adj. (1) + MOBSMAN n. (1)]

flymy *adj.* [mid–late 19C] sly, roguish, cunning. [FLY adj. (1) + SE *slimy*]

fly my kite *n.* [mid-19C] a light. [rhy. sl.]

fly off *v.*¹ [20C+] (*US*) to suffer from diarrhoea.

fly off *v.*² *see* FLY OFF (THE HANDLE) v.

fly off at the deep end *v.* (*also* **go off (at) the deep end**) [1910s+] **1** to lose control, to become extremely angry or depressed, to show any extreme of emotion. **2** to become emotionally involved with or obsessed by.

fly off in one's face *v.* (*also* **fly up in one's face**) [20C+] (*W.I.*) to lose control, to become extremely angry. [var. on FLY OFF (THE HANDLE) v.]

fly off (the handle) *v.* [19C+] (*orig. US*) to lose control, to become extremely angry (cf. GO OFF THE HANDLE v.). [the image of an axe-head 'flying' from its handle]

fly one's mouth *v. see* RUN ONE'S MOUTH v.

fly out *v.* [mid-19C] to lose control of one's temper.

fly out of one's skin *v.* [20C+] (*W.I.*) to become violently excited.

fly-over people *n.* [20C+] (*US*) inhabitants of those states of the US over which one passes in an aeroplane flying from coast to coast; 'middle America'.

flypaper act *n.* [1900s–30s] the Prevention of Crimes Act, 1909; thus *on the flypaper*, subject to this Act, to be a criminal known to the police. [the criminal remains on record like a fly stuck to a flypaper]

fly pies *n. see* SQUASHED FLIES n.

fly-pitch *n.* [20C+] any form of street stall or other place where goods are sold in the open air; thus *fly-pitcher*, a street-seller. [FLY v.¹ (1), i.e. they run off when a policeman approaches]

fly right *v.* [1940s+] (*orig. US Black*) to behave oneself, to mend one's ways, to see sense. [song by N. Cole & I. Mills 'Straighten Up and Fly Right', written for the film *Here Comes Elmer* (1943)]

fly rink *n. see* SKATING RINK n.

fly salty *v. see* JUMP SALTY v.

fly slicer *n.* **1** [late 18C–early 19C] a member of the Life Guards. **2** [19C] a cavalryman. ['from their sitting on horse-back, under an arch, where they are frequently observed to drive away flies with their swords' (Grose, 1785)]

fly speck (isle) *n.* [20C+] (*Aus.*) Tasmania; thus *fly-speck(er)*, an inhabitant of Tasmania, *fly-speck*, Tasmanian. [its relative size compared to Australia]

fly-swisher stew *n.* [1910s+] (*Aus.*) oxtail stew (cf. FLY-DISPERSER SOUP n.). [the ox swishes its tail to get rid of clustering flies]

fly taal *n.* (*also* **flaaitaal**) [1950s+] (*S.Afr. Black*) a form of urban sl. used by streetwise young people. [FLY adj. (1) + Afk. *taal*, language]

fly the basket *v.* [late 18C] (*UK Und.*) to steal a parcel or luggage from the basket or rear part of a stage-coach.

fly the blue pigeon *v. see* FLY A BLUE PIGEON v.

fly the coop *v.* [mid-19C+] (*US*) **1** to leave, esp. suddenly. **2** to

die. **3** to stop working. **4** to lose control, to lose one's temper. **5** to go wrong, to blunder. **6** to escape from prison.

fly the flag *v.*¹ **1** [mid-19C] of a prostitute, to walk the streets looking for trade. **2** [1940s+] to be menstruating. [(2) var. on FLY THE RED FLAG v.]

fly the flag *v.*² **1** [1970s+] (*Aus. Und.*) (*also* **raise the flag**) to appeal to a higher court. **2** [1990s+] to make a fuss for form's sake.

fly the kite *v.*¹ [mid-19C] to toss excrement from a window.

fly the kite *v.*² *see* FLY A KITE v.¹ (1).

fly the mags *v.* [early–mid-19C] (*orig. UK Und.*) to gamble by tossing halfpence, to play pitch and toss; thus MAG-FLYING n. [SE *fly*/FLY v.² + MAG n.³ (1)]

fly the red flag *v.* [1940s+] to be menstruating.

fly the track *v.* [19C+] (*US*) to abandon one's duties, to depart from an expected course of action.

flytime *adj.* [1950s] (*US Black*) fashionable, sophisticated. [ext. FLY adj. (2)/FLY adj. (7)]

fly (tipper) *n.* [1990s+] a child. [rhy. sl. = NIPPER n.³ (2)]

fly to flinders *v.* **1** [late 19C+] (*US*) (*also* **fly to pieces**) to lose one's temper. **2** [1990s+] to break into pieces. [SE *flinders*, fragments, splinters]

fly to the time of day *phr.* [early 19C] to be well aware of what is going on. [FLY adj. (1)]

flytrap *n.*¹ **1** [late 18C–1930s] the mouth. **2** [20C+] a run-down hotel or similar establishment. [SE *fly + trap*; (1) note TRAP n.³]

flytrap *n.*² *see* FLY-CAGE n.

fly up *v.*¹ [1920s–60s] (*US*) to go to bed. [the action of chickens in 'flying up to the roost']

fly up *v.*² *see* FLY UP (IN THE AIR) v.

fly up in one's face *v. see* FLY OFF IN ONE'S FACE v.

fly (up) in one's head *v.* [20C+] (*W.I.*) of alcohol, to go to one's head, to make one extremely and thus dangerously drunk.

fly up (in the air) *v.* [19C+] (*US*) to lose one's temper, to lose control.

fly-up-the-creek *n.* [late 19C+] (*US*) **1** an inhabitant of Florida. **2** a capricious person. **3** an immoral woman. [regional use *fly-up-the-creek*, a popular name of the small green heron (*Butorides virescens*), a native of Florida]

flyweight *n.* [1940s–70s] (*US*) a person, usu. criminal, of little or no importance or influence. [boxing imagery]

FM boots *n. see* FUCK-ME BOOTS n.

f.n.g. *n.* [1960s+] (*orig. US milit.*) an innocent, a novice. [*fucking new guy*]

f.o. *v. see* FUCK OFF v. (2).

f.o.! *excl.* [1940s+] (*US*) go away! leave me alone! [abbr. FUCK OFF! excl.]

f.o.a.d.! *excl.* [1980s+] *fuck off and die!* [abbr.]

foal *n.* [1990s+] £1 (cf. COW n.³; GORILLA n.³; HORSE n.³; MONKEY n.⁸; PONY n.¹; WALRUS n.). [a play on a small PONY n.¹ (2)]

foal and filly dance *n.* [late 19C] (*UK society*) a dance for young people only. [equine imagery]

foam *n.* [20C+] (*US Black*) beer.

foamin' at the gash *phr.* [1990s+] of a woman, becoming damp with sexual arousal. [SE *foam* + GASH n.¹ (1)]

foaming (at the mouth) *phr.* **1** [20C+] absolutely furious. **2** [1960s+] (*US*) of a penis, on the verge of ejaculation.

foamy *n.* [1950s] a bottle, can or glass of beer. [FOAM n.]

f.o.b. *n.* [1930s+] (*Aus./N.Z./US*) a newly arrived immigrant, usu. Black or Asian; ext. as a derog. term for any minority group. [abbr. *fresh off the boat*]

fob *n.* [late 17C–early 19C] a trick, a deceit. [the term was SE in 1622 (*OED* first cit.) but sl. by late 17C; thus SE use *fob off*, to sidetrack, to put off with a lie or deceit]

fob *v.* **1** [late 17C–mid-19C] to trick, to deceive, to steal from. **2** [mid-19C–1900s] to place in one's fob pocket. **3** [late 19C–1940s] (*US Und.*) to steal from a fob pocket.

fobber *n.* [late 19C–1940s] (*US Und.*) a pickpocket who specializes in removing small change from the victim's fob pocket. [SE *fob*; Irwin, *American Tramp and Und. Slang* (1931), suggests that such a pickpocket has lost his skills and can no longer attempt less accessible pockets]

fob-diver *n.* [late 19C–1900s] a pickpocket. [SE *fob* (pocket) + DIVER n. (2)]

fobus *n.*[1] [late 17C] a general term of dislike. [ety. unknown; ? link to dial. *fobey*, an eccentric]

fobus *n.*[2] [late 19C] the vagina. [ety. unknown; ? link to SE *fob*, a small pocket]

focus *n. see* FOGUS n.

focus *v.* [1930s–40s] (*US Black*) to look, to see.

fodder *n.*[1] [mid-19C; 1910s+] food, often metaphorical. [although it covered all forms of food in 11C–14C the SE is now only used for animal food]

fodder *n.*[2] [late 19C+] lavatory paper. [abbr. BUM-FODDER n. (1)]

fodder forker *n.* [20C+] (*US*) a derog. term for a farmer, as seen by cowboys. [his usual task]

fofi-eye *n.* [20C+] (*W.I., Bdos/Guyn.*) an eye with a discoloured, whitish eyeball. [ety. unknown; ? link to *fufu*, a plantain dough, which is white]

fog *n.* **1** [18C–mid-19C] (*UK Und.*) smoke. **2** [1940s] (*US Und.*) shooting.

fog *v.* **1** [early 17C; mid-19C–1910s] (*also* **fogify**) to perplex, to confuse, to mystify. **2** [18C–early 19C; 1920s] to smoke a pipe. **3** [1900s–30s] (*US*) to go fast, to rush around, to chase. **4** [1900s–60s] (*US*) to fire a gun rapidly. **5** [1920s–40s] (*US*) to attack, to kill. **6** [1930s] (*US*) to scold, to complain. **7** [1990s+] (*US prison*) to delouse a new prisoner.

fogare *n. see* FOGUS n.

fog-bound *adj.* **1** [1920s–30s] slightly drunk (cf. ADDLED adj.). **2** [1920s–40s] (*US*) confused, dazed. [SE *fog*/FOG v. (1)]

fog-cutter *n. see* ANTIFOGMATIC n.

fogey *n.* **1** [late 18C–early 19C] (*also* **foggy**) an invalid soldier. **2** [late 19C] an old maid. [Fr. *fourgeaux*, fierce, fiery; or Scot. dial. *foggy*, fat, bloated. Note SE *fogram/fogrum*, an old-fashioned, out-of-date person; (1) thence the SE use, usu. with pfx *old*]

fogey *adj.* (*also* **fogy**) [mid-19C+] (*orig. Scot.*) old-fashioned, 'stuck-in-the-mud'. [SE *fogey*, n.]

fogged *adj.* **1** [mid-19C+] (*also* **befogged**) drunk, tipsy (cf. ADDLED adj.). **2** [mid-19C+] confused, bewildered. **3** [1930s] exhausted. **4** [1940s] under the influence of a drug. [FOG v. (1)]

fogger *n. see* FUCKER n.

fogging *adj. see* FUCKING adj.

foggy *n. see* FOGEY n. (1).

foggy *adj.* **1** [late 16C+] drunk, tipsy (cf. ADDLED adj.). **2** [late 18C+] confused, not very intelligent. [play on SE]

Foggy Bottom *n.* (*also* **Foggy Butts**) [1940s+] (*US*) the US State Department. [derived both f. the name of an area of Washington, D.C., and from the 'foggy' obfuscations produced by its bureaucrats]

foghorn *n.* (*US*) **1** [1910s–30s] a tuba or saxophone. **2** [1940s+] the nose. **3** [1960s] one who talks too loudly. [the noise made]

fogie *n.* [2000s] (*US Black*) a 40fl oz (2-litre) bottle of malt liquor. [var. pron. of FORTY n.[2]]

fogify *v. see* FOG v. (1).

fog in *v.* [late 19C] (*UK society*) to see a place by accident; to achieve one's object by accident.

fogland *n.* [1910s] (*Aus.*) Britain; thus *Fogtown, Fogville-on-Thames*, London. [the weather and the contemporary smogs in London]

fogle *n.* [19C] (*orig. Ling. Fr./Polari*) a silk handkerchief; thus *draw a fogle*, to steal a silk handkerchief. [? Ital. *foglia*, leaf; thus handkerchief; or ? Fr. sl. *fouille*, a pocket; less likely is Ger. *vogel*, bird, and thus the 'bird's eye' pattern of some handkerchiefs]

fogle-hunter *n.* (*also* **fogle-drawer**) [early–mid-19C] a pickpocket who specializes in stealing silk handerchiefs. [FOGLE n.]

fogle-hunting *n.* (*also* **fogle-drawing**) [early–mid-19C] (*orig. Ling. Fr./Polari*) the stealing of silk handkerchiefs. [FOGLE-HUNTER n.]

fogmatic *n.* [early–mid-19C] (*US campus*) a bracing drink of alcohol. [ANTIFOGMATIC n.]

fogmatic *adj.* [mid-19C] (*US campus*) drunk (cf. ADDLED adj.). [FOGMATIC n.]

fogo *n.* [mid-19C] a stench, esp. of breaking wind. [? SE *fog* + *hogo*, f. Fr. *haut gout*, high taste, i.e. a high or putrescent flavour, an offensive taste or smell, or *foh!*, an excl. of disgust]

fog out *v.*[1] [1980s+] (*US drugs*) to fill a room or car with smoke.

fog out *v.*[2] [1990s+] (*US*) to daydream.

fogram *n.* (*also* **fogrum**) **1** [mid-18C–19C] an antiquated or old-fashioned person, a fogey. **2** [early 19C] an ageing lecher. [SE *fogram*, antiquated, out-of-date]

fogramite *n.* [late 18C–early 19C] a fogey. [FOGRAM n. (1) + sfx -*ite*]

fogue *v.* [1920s–30s] (*Aus./N.Z.*) to stink. [FOGO n.]

fogus *n.* (*also* **focus, fogare**) [mid-17C–mid-19C] tobacco. [? SE *fog*, in this case that produced by a pipe]

fogy *adj. see* FOGEY adj.

foil *n.* [1960s+] (*drugs*) a quantity of drugs, e.g. amphetamines, heroin or cannabis, wrapped in foil ready for sale.

foil *v.* [1990s+] (*UK Und.*) to wrap a copper coin in silver foil to create a silver one, which can be used in slot or gaming machines.

foil-cloy *n.* (*also* **foyl-cloy**) [mid-17C–early 18C] (*UK Und.*) a pickpocket; thus *foyl someone's cloy*, to pick someone's pocket. [FILE v.[1] (1) + CLY n. (2)]

foily *n.* [1990s+] (*Aus. drugs*) a foil-wrapped package of heroin.

foin *n.* [late 16C] (*UK Und.*) a cut-purse or pickpocket. [SE *foin*, a thrust with a pointed weapon]

foin *v.* [14C–17C] of a man, to have sexual intercourse (cf. BANG v.[1]). [SE *foin*, to make a thrust with a pointed weapon]

foine *adj. see* FINE adj.[2].

foining *n.* [late 16C] indulging in sexual intercourse. [FOIN v.]

fois *adj.* [1980s+] (*US campus*) reminiscent of European style. [? Fr. *fois*, time, i.e. the perceived antiquity of such styles]

foist *n.*[1] (*also* **foyst, fyst**) [late 16C–early 18C] a silent breaking of wind. [FOIST v.[1]]

foist *n.*[2] (*also* **foister, foyst, fyst**) (*UK Und.*) **1** [late 16C–mid-19C] a pickpocket or cut-purse. **2** [late 16C–mid-19C] a card-sharp, a cheat. **3** [17C] a trick, a hoax. [FOIST v.[2]]

foist *v.*[1] (*also* **fyst**) [16C–early 18C] to break wind silently. [15C SE *fist*, to break wind; 16C SE *foist*, to smell or grow musty]

foist *v.*[2] (*also* **foyst, fyst**) **1** [mid-16C–early 17C] to palm a false die so as to be able to introduce it into the game when required. **2** [mid-16C–early 17C] to cheat by this means; thus *foist in*, to introduce a false die surreptitiously when palmed. **3** [late 16C–19C] to steal, esp. to pick a pocket. [prob. Du. dial. *vuisten*, to take in the hand, f. *vuist*, fist; the Du. means to play at a game in which one player holds some coins in his hand, and the others guess their number]

foister *n. see* FOIST n.[2].

fold *n.*[1] [1990s+] (*US drugs*) a piece of paper folded to contain a measure of a given drug; the standard price is $25 per fold. [powdered narcotic drugs are sold in folds of paper]

fold *n.*[2] [2000s] a collapse into laughter.

fold *v.* **1** [1930s+] (*US*) to become exhausted, to tire. **2** [1930s+] (*orig. US*) to shut down completely, esp. in show business use, e.g. *it folded* or *the cops folded it*. **3** [1950s+] (*US Und./Black*) to collapse, to fail, e.g. in the context of a town becoming useless for criminal activities. **4** [1950s+] (*US*) to give up. **5** [1970s] (*US Black*) of a shop, club etc, to close at the end of the day/night. **6** [1990s+] (*US Und.*) to collapse under pressure, e.g. police interrogation. [poker imagery]

folder *n.* [1980s+] (*US campus*) one who tires easily; thus a poor companion for partying. [FOLD v. (1)]

fol-de-riddle-ido *n.* [late 19C–1920s] a trilby hat. [? SE *fol-de-rol*, a trifle]

fol-de-rol *n.* [mid-19C–1900s] a temporary, prob. self-induced depression, pique. [SE *fol-de-rol*, a trifle]

folding *n.* (*also* **folding dough, ...money, ...stuff**) [1930s+] (*orig. US*) paper money (cf. BANK-RAG n.).

folding green *n.* (*also* **green folding**) [1940s+] (*US Black*) paper money, dollar bills (cf. ALFALFA n.; BANK-RAG n.). [SE *folding/* FOLDING n. + GREEN n.[2] (1)]

fold out *v.*[1] [20C+] (*US*) to go to bed. [the unfolding of one's bedroll]

fold out *v.*[2] *see* FOLD UP v. (4).

fold someone's ears *v.* [1960s–70s] (*US Black*) to lecture or advise someone at great and serious length.

fold up *v.* **1** [1910s+] to collapse or surrender under unbearable pressure. **2** [1930s–40s] to terminate an activity. **3** [1930s–50s] (*drugs*) to withdraw from drug use. **4** [1960s] (*also* **fold out**) to leave. **5** [1970s] to shut down someone's business or other activity. [poker use, *fold (up)*, to withdraw from a round of betting]

folks *n.* **1** [late 19C] (*US Und.*) fellow criminals; also in sing. **2** [late 19C+] (*US teen*) one's group of friends. **3** [1990s+] (*US Black teen*) fellow gang members, esp. used in prison where gang membership is, where possible, hidden from the authorities. **4** [2000s] (*US Black*) the police. [SAmE *folks*, one's family]

follies *n.* (*also* **fullies**) [1940s–50s] (*UK prison*) the Quarter Sessions. [ironic use]

follow a whereas *v.* [late 18C–mid-19C] to become bankrupt. [notices of bankruptcy in the *London Gazette* invariably began with the word *Whereas...*]

follow-cat *n.* (*also* **follow-pot, follow-pup**) [1950s–60s] (*US*) one who tags along, whether invited to or not.

follower *n.* [mid-19C+] a man who courts a maidservant; thus the common admonition on hiring a cook or maid, *No followers.*

follower-upper *n.* (*also* **follyer-upper, follyinupper, folly-up**) (*Irish*) **1** [1940s–50s] a weekly cinema serial, usu. screened on Saturday mornings. **2** [1950s+] any form of sequel. [SE *follow-up*]

follow-foot monkey *n.* [20C+] (*W.I.*) someone, often a young person, who 'apes' (as far as they can) the famous.

follow-foot monkey *v.* [20C+] (*W.I.*) to 'ape' the famous. [FOLLOW-FOOT MONKEY n.]

follow like a tantony pig *v.* [mid-18C–early 19C; 1920s] to follow closely. [ANTHONY n.]

follow-me(-home)-and-fuck-me shoes *n. see* FUCK-ME SHOES n.

follow-me-lads *n.* [mid-19C–1900s] curls that hang over a woman's shoulder. [the apparent sexual invitation implicit in the hairstyle]

follow one's nose *v.* [1980s] (*US Black*) to lead a law-abiding life, whatever temptations may exist to the contrary. [SE *follow one's nose*, to go (lit.) straight]

follow-pot/-pup *n. see* FOLLOW-CAT n.

follow through *v.* **1** [20C+] to ejaculate twice without withdrawal. **2** [1990s+] to soil one's underwear by mistake.

follyer-upper/follyinupper/folly-up *n. see* FOLLOWER-UPPER n.

fondle *v.* [19C] to have sexual intercourse.

fond of meat *phr.* [19C+] used to describe a man who is fond of sex, esp. with prostitutes. [euph.; SE *fond* + MEAT n. (6)]

fond of one's drops *phr.* [late 19C] used of a heavy drinker. [euph., i.e. 'drops' of liquor]

fonfen *n.* [1960s–70s] the verbal trickery created by con-men to further a given fraud or trick. [Yid. *fonfer*, a cheat, one who deceives, fails to deliver on their promises]

fong *n.*[1] (*also* **fong-eye**) [1940s+] (*N.Z.*) **1** strong liquor. **2** methylated spirits as drunk by alcoholics. **3** a very heavy drinker, a drunkard.

fong *n.*[2] [1960s] (*Irish*) a kick. [? echoic]

fonged (up) *adj.* (*also* **half-fonged**) [1940s+] (*N.Z.*) drunk, tipsy. [FONG n.[1]]

fong-eye *n. see* FONG n.[1].

fonk *n. see* FUNK n.[1].

fonk *v.* (*also* **fonk out**) [1960s+] (*US Black*) **1** to show off; to upstage. **2** to praise. [FONKY adj.[1]]

fonked out heavy *adj.* [1960s+] (*US Black*) very well-dressed. [FUNKED OUT adj. (2) + HEAVY adv. (1)]

fonky *adj.*[1] [1960s+] (*US Black*) positive or negative intensifier depending on context; thus exceptionally good or bad, smelling sweet or vile etc. [pron. of FUNKY adj.[1]/FUNKY adj.[3] (1)]

fonky *adj.*[2] [1970s+] (*US Black*) aggressive; thus COME DOWN FONKY v. [FUNKY adj.[3] (1)]

fonky fresh *adj. see* FUNKY FRESH adj.

fonky to the bone *phr.* [1940s+] (*US Black*) **1** exceptionally well-dressed. **2** handsome. [FONKY adj.[1] + TO THE BONE phr.]

foo *n. see* FOOL n.

foo *adj.* [1910s] (*Aus.*) drunk (cf. ADDLED adj.). [? SE *foolish* or ? FOO-FOO adj. (1)]

food *n.* **1** [1940s] (*US Black*) gossip. **2** [1970s+] (*US gang/gay*) a victim, prey; a sex object. [something one (1) 'chews' over or (2) 'eats']

food boat *n.* [2000s] a group of prisoners who cook their own food.

foodie *n.* [1980s+] a gourmet, a food obsessive; one of a self-elected circle of eaters devoted to the best and newest in eating and drinking. [coined by food writer Paul Levy, 1981]

food inspector *n.* [1900s–50s] (*Aus.*) a tramp. [his 'inspection' of whatever food he can obtain]

food one's beast *v.* [2000s] to obtain sexual gratification.

fooey! *excl. see* PHOOEY! excl.

foof *n.* [1960s+] (*US campus*) a superficial person; thus *foofy*, silly. [? echoic of an insubstantial puff of wind]

foo-foo *n.*[1] **1** [mid-19C] (*orig. US*) an effeminate or weak man. **2** [mid-19C+] (*US/W.I.*) a naïve, gullible, foolish person. [SE *fool* + redup.]

foo-foo *n.*[2] [1990s+] the vagina. [ety. unknown; ? fig. use of FOO-FOO n.[1] (1)]

foo-foo *adj.* (*also* **foo-fool, fool-fool**) **1** [mid-19C+] simple-minded, stupid, oafish; thus as v., to act stupidly. **2** [1950s] credulous, gullible. [FOO-FOO n.[1] (2)]

foo-foo dust *n.* (*also* **foo-foo stuff**) [1940s+] (*drugs*) any form of powdered narcotic. [var. on FOO-FOO POWDER n.]

foo-foo powder *n.* (*also* **foo-foo dust**) [1910s+] (*US*) talcum powder, baby powder, anti-louse powder etc. [orig. naut. jargon *foo-foo*, cologne; ult. FOO-FOO n.[1] (1)]

fool *n.* **1** [late 19C] a stupid or foolish thing. **2** [late 19C–1900s] an easy thing, in comparison; usu. in phr. *a fool to it.* **3** [late 19C+] anyone excessively enthusiastic about a given activity or topic, e.g. *dancing fool, singing fool*; often found as *a fool for...* **4** [1960s+] a person, irrespective of their actual intelligence. **5** [1960s+] (*also* **foo**) a general term of address. **6** [1990s+] (*also* **foo**) a stupid person.

fool *adj.* [19C+] (*US*) stupid, ludicrous, absurd. [abbr. SE *foolish*]

fool *v.* [late 17C; mid–late 19C] (*US*) to make advances to, to curry favour with.

fool around *v.* **1** [1920s+] to conduct a promiscuous sex life; thus the invitation *let's fool around*, a suggestion by one of a couple that they should abandon speech for (sexual) action. **2** [1930s+] to enjoy sexual activity short of intercourse. **3** [1950s] to tease.

fool-ass *adj.* [1970s+] a general term of disparagement; the inference is of stupidity. [SE *fool* + -ASS sfx]

fool away *v.* [18C+] (*US*) to waste time or resources, to fritter something away.

fooleries, the *n.* [late 19C–1920s] the amusements of April Fool's Day (1 April).

fool-finder *n.* [late 18C–early 19C] a bailiff. [? because only fools are available when he comes to call]

fool-fool *adj. see* FOO-FOO adj.

fool-fool house *n.* [1970s–80s] (*UK Black*) a psychiatric institution. [FOOL-FOOL adj. + SE *house*]

foolhead *n.* [20C+] a fool; thus *foolheaded*, stupid, foolish. [SE *fool* + -HEAD sfx (1)]

foolish *adj.* [late 18C–early 19C] used by prostitutes to distinguish a casual customer from a more sophisticated client; thus the query, *Is he foolish or* FLASH adj.[1] *(2)?*

foolish house *n.* (*also* **foolish factory**) [1900s–30s] (*US*) a psychiatric institution.

foolish powder *n.* [1930s+] (*drugs*) any powdered narcotic, i.e. heroin, cocaine, morphine (cf. AUNTIE EMMA n.; BIRDIE POWDER n.). [the effects]

foolish water *n.* [1900s] (*US*) alcohol. [its effects]

fool-maker *n.* (*also* **fool-sticker**) [19C] the penis. [the *fool* in this case is presumably a cuckolded husband]

fool-monger *n.* [late 16C–early 18C] **1** one who 'trades on' the credulity of fools, a swindler. **2** a gambler. [SE *fool* + sfx *-monger*]

fool's gold *n.* [1980s] (*US Und.*) fake jewellery. [SE *fool's gold*, iron pyrites, which fool novice miners into believing they have struck the real thing]

fool's rush *n. see* BUM'S RUSH n. (3).

fool-sticker *n. see* FOOL-MAKER n.

fool's wedding *n.* [late 19C] a party of women. [? pvb]

fool-taker *n.* [late 16C–early 17C] (*UK Und.*) a dice- or card-sharp; thus *fool-taking*, the swindling of gamblers.

fool trap *n.* **1** [late 16C–early 18C] one who 'trades on' the credulity of fools, a swindler. **2** [19C] the vagina (cf. BITE n.[2]). **3** [19C] a high-class prostitute (cf. COCKATRICE n.).

fool up *v.* [1950s] (*W.I.*) to deceive, to trick.

foon *n.* (*also* **fun**) [1920s–50s] (*US drugs*) a pellet of prepared opium (cf. APOSTLE n.). [Chinese measurement]

foont *n. see* FUNT n.

foop *n.* [1900s–10s] a homosexual man. [backsl. = POOF n. (1)]

foop *v.* **1** [1920s] (*US Black*) to dance uninhibitedly. **2** [1970s] (*US campus*) to engage in homosexual acts. [FOOP n.]

fooper *n.* [1970s] (*US campus*) a homosexual. [FOOP n.]

foostie-minged *adj.* [1990s+] (*Scot.*) a general term of abuse aimed at a woman; lit. 'smelly cunted'. [Scot. *foost*, a stench + MINGE n. (1)]

foot, the *n. see* GIVE SOMEONE THE FOOT v.

foot *v.* (*also* **footer, footy**) [17C] to have sexual intercourse; a euph. for FUCK v.[1]. [Fr. *foutre*, to fuck]

footback *adv.* [late 16C; 19C+] travelling on foot. [pun on SE *horseback*]

footback it *v.* [1930s] (*Aus.*) to travel by foot, with a pack on one's back. [FOOTBACK adv.]

football *n.* [1960s+] (*drugs*) **1** a measure of one half grain of a narcotic. **2** a capsule of a psychotropic drug.

footballer *n.* [1910s–20s] **1** (*Aus. prison*) a prison warder, who disciplines through kicking the prisoners. **2** (*Aus.*) anyone who fights with their feet. [the use of the feet as an agent of violence]

footballs *n.* [1960s+] (*drugs*) amphetamine (cf. A n.[2]). [packaging]

foot-bath *n.* [late 19C–1900s] an overfilled glass.

footer *n.*[1] [mid-18C–mid-19C] a general term of contempt, a 'scurvy fellow', a 'low fellow'. [FOOT v./Fr. *foutre*, to fuck, thus cf. FUCKER n. (3)]

footer *n.*[2] **1** [mid-19C+] football, a football. **2** [1910s+] (*Aus.*) Australian Rules football. [SE *football* + -ER sfx]

footer *n.*[3] [1920s] (*US*) a footstep.

footer *v.*[1] [mid-19C] to idle around. [FOOTER n.[1]]

footer *v.*[2] *see* FOOT v.

footermans *adj.* [1960s] (*US, Western*) on foot. [a very late example of the 16C–17C -MANS sfx]

footey *n. see* FOOTIE n.

foot! (foot!) *excl.* [late 19C–1900s] go away! [Fr. *foutre*, to fuck; usu. addressed to 'the respectably dressed person who wanders into strange and doubtful bye-ways' (Ware)]

footie *n.* (*also* **footy, footey**) [1940s+] **1** (*Aus./N.Z.*) Australian Rules football. **2** football (soccer).

foot-in-mouth disease *n.* [1960s+] the continual problem of making grossly tactless or embarrassing statements. [pun on SE *foot and mouth disease* + PUT ONE'S FOOT IN ONE'S MOUTH v.; note the cod-academic synon. *dontopedology*]

foot is hot *phr.* [20C+] (*W.I., Trin.*) used of one who is restless, esp. a woman.

foot is too short *phr.* [20C+] (*W.I.*) said of one who has missed their chance or has arrived too late, esp. for a meal.

foot it *v.* **1** [16C–1900s] to dance. **2** [17C+] (*US Black*) to walk, esp. to walk a long way.

foot juice *n.* [1920s] (*US tramp*) cheap red wine.

foot-kisser *n.* [20C+] (*US*) a sycophant, a toady.

foot land-raker *n.* [late 16C–early 17C] a highway robber. [SE *foot* + LAND-RAKER n.]

footle *n.* [late 19C–1910s] nonsense, rubbish. [FOOTLE v. (2)]

footle *adj.* [late 19C] paltry, trifling, insignificant. [FOOTLE v. (2)]

footle *v.* **1** [late 18C] to titivate, to enhance. **2** [late 19C+] to act or talk foolishly. **3** [1920s–30s] to potter around. [OED has 'of obscure origin' and suggests link to FOOTER v.[1], but EDD offers Nottingham dial. *footle*, to do anything in a feeble, ineffectual manner]

footled *adj.* [1900s] rendered foolish or stupid. [FOOTLE v. (2)]

footless *adj. see* LEGLESS adj.

footling *adj.* [late 19C+] incompetent, inadequate, mediocre. [FOOTLE v. (2)]

footman's inn *n.* [early–mid-17C] very poor lodgings. [the poor status and negative image of the SE *footman*]

footman's mawnd *n.* [late 17C–early 19C] a counterfeit sore that represents a kick or bite from a horse. [SE *footman* + MAUND n.]

footmobile *n.* [1910s+] (*US*) transportation by foot.

footpad *n.* [late 17C+] a highway robber, although not a highwayman, the former operated on foot, the latter from a horse; the act of highway robbery; also attrib.; thus *horsepad*, one who robbed from a horse. [SE *foot* + PAD n.[1] (3)]

foot-rot *n.* [late 19C] cheap (4-penny) ale. [? link to dial. *foot-ale*, in mining communities a miner uses his first day's pay to 'stand his foot-ale', i.e. buy drinks for his fellows]

foot-rotting *n.* [1930s+] (*Aus.*) idling away one's time in boredom. [SAusE *footrot*, to treat a sheep's foot for rot]

footsack! *excl.* [mid-19C+] (*orig. S.Afr.*) a general excl. of dismissal, go away! be off! get out! [anglicized version of VOETSAK! excl.]

foot-scamp *n.* (*also* **scamp-foot**) [18C] (*UK Und.*) a highway robber who works on foot. [SE *foot* + SCAMP n. (2)]

foot scamper *v.* [18C] (*UK Und.*) to work as a highway robber. [FOOT-SCAMP n.]

foot scamperer *n.* [18C] (*UK Und.*) a highway robber who works on foot. [FOOT SCAMPER v.]

foot-shaker *n.* [1900s] (*US*) an infantryman.

footsie *n. see* PLAY FOOTSIE v.

footslog *v.* [late 19C+] to walk long and hard; usu. as *footslogging*. [orig. Boer War milit. sl.]

footslogger *n.* **1** [late 19C+] an infantryman. **2** [20C+] a pedestrian. **3** [1920s+] (*Aus.*) a policeman who walks his beat (cf. BEAT-POUNDER n.). **4** [1930s] a tramp.

foot soldier *n.* [1970s+] (*US gay*) a male street prostitute.

footstool *n.* [early 19C–1950s] (*US*) the earth. [Isa. 66:1, 'Thus saith the Lord, The heaven is my throne, and the earth is my footstool']

foot the bill *v.* [19C+] (*orig. US*) to pay a bill. [SE *foot the bill*, to add up and set the sum at the foot of an account or bill]

foot up *v.* [mid–late 19C] (*US*) to work out, to sum up a person. [the placing of the final result at the foot of a column of figures]

foot-wabbler *n.* (*also* **foot-wobbler, wabbler**) [late 18C–mid-19C] an infantryman, esp. as described by a cavalryman. [SE *foot + wobbler*]

foot-walk it *v.* [1940s+] (*Aus.*) to travel by foot.

footwasher *n.* [19C+] (*US*) a traditional, fundamentalist Baptist. [the religious rite whereby Primitive Baptists wash each other's feet, as commanded in John 13:14, 'If I then, your Lord and Master, have washed your feet, ye also ought to wash one another's feet']

foot-wobbler *n.* see FOOT-WABBLER *n.*

footy *n.* see FOOTIE *n.*

footy *adj.* **1** [18C+] insignificant, worthless, despicable, futile. **2** [19C+] (*US*) foolish, simple. [Fr. *foutu*, fucked or SE *futile*; (1) 19C+ use is US]

footy *v.* see FOOT *v.*

foozilow *v.* [late 19C] (*Anglo-Ind.*) to flatter. [Hind. *p'huslana*, to flatter or cajole]

foozle *n.* **1** [mid–late 19C] a conservative, one who is behind the times; a gullible fool. **2** [20C+] (*orig. sporting*) a miss, a blunder. [FOOZLE *v.* (1) but in (1) note SE *fossil*]

foozle *v.* **1** [19C+] to perform clumsily, to bungle, to make a mess of (cf. BAMBOOZLE *v.*). **2** [20C+] (*sporting*) to miss a shot. [Ger. *fuseln*, to work too fast and thus badly]

foozle about (with) *v.* **1** [mid-19C] to have sex on a casual basis. **2** [1930s+] to fool around (with). [SE *fool around*/FOOL AROUND *v.* (1)]

foozled *adj.* (*also* **foozlified, foozly**) **1** [17C–1900s] (*also* **fusled**) drunk (cf. ADDLED *adj.*). **2** [mid-19C+] (*also* **fuzzled**) blurred, spoilt. **3** [mid-19C+] (*also* **befoozeled, discomfoozled**) confused. [FOOZLE *v.* (1)]

foozler *n.* [late 19C] a bungler, one who does things clumsily. [FOOZLE *v.* (1)]

fopdoodle *n.* [17C] a fool, a simpleton. [15C SE *fop*, a fool + DOODLE *n.*[1]]

fopdoodle *v.* [17C] **1** to have sexual intercourse. **2** to deceive, to cheat.

fop fops *v.* [2000s] (*US prison*) to have a fistfight.

foplin *n.* (*also* **fopling**) [late 17C–18C] a young fop.

fopper *n.* [late 19C] a blunder, a mistake. [mispron. Fr. *faux pas*]

f.o.q.! *excl.* [1910s] (*Aus.*) leave! go away! [SE *fly off*/FUCK OFF! excl. *quickly*]

for Africa *phr.* [1970s+] (*S.Afr.*) a lot, a great many, a great deal.

forakers *n.* [mid-19C] the lavatory. [orig. Winchester School jargon; ? synon. Lat. *forica* or SE *four acres*, i.e. a field (cf. BOG *n.*[1])]

for a kicker *phr.* see FOR KICKERS *phr.*

for a motherfucker! *excl.* [1960s+] (*orig. US Black*) an intensifying expletive, e.g. *he has guns for a motherfucker*, he has a great many guns; *I'm throwing bricks for a motherfucker*, I'm throwing bricks continually and passionately etc.

for beans *adv.* [1950s+] (*orig. US*) in no way whatsoever. [BEAN *n.*[1] (4)]

forbidden fruit *n.*[1] [1930s–40s] (*Irish*) the 'Adam's apple' in the throat. [the biblical myth]

forbidden fruit *n.*[2] [1940s–60s] an underage sexual partner of either sex.

for cat's sake! *excl.* [1920s] (*US*) a euph. for FOR CHRIST'S SAKE! excl.

force-meat ball *n.* [early 19C] anything essentially unpleasant, endured whether one likes it or not.

force-ripe *adj.* [1950s+] (*W.I.*) precocious. [the image of 'forced' (i.e. grown at abnormal speed) fruit or vegetables]

force-up *adj.* [1990s+] (*W.I.*) socially ambitious. [for ety. *see* FORCE-RIPE *adj.*]

for Christ's sake! *excl.* (*also* **ferchrissakes! for Chrissake(s)! for crissake!**) [20C+] a now mildly blasphemous excl. of rage, annoyance, surprise, amazement.

for crap's sake! *excl.* [1930s+] (*orig. US*) a general excl. of annoyance, surprise etc. [euph. for FOR CHRIST'S SAKE! excl.]

for crazy *phr.* [1960s] (*US*) for fun, for pleasure.

for cripes sake! *excl. see* CRIPES! excl.

for crissake! *excl. see* FOR CHRIST'S SAKE! excl.

for crying out loud! *excl.* [1920s+] a euph. for FOR CHRIST'S SAKE! excl.

ford *n.* [2000s] (*US prison*) any generally antagonistic or unhelpful doctor. [anecdotal]

for days! *excl.* [1950s+] **1** (*gay*) an excl. implying shock or amazement. **2** (*orig. US Black*) (*also* **days!**) a general intensifier implying an extreme, e.g. for a very long time, absolutely truthfully. [the orig. implication was of having sex continually, for day after day]

Ford car salesman *n.* [1980s+] (*Aus. prison*) a prison superintendent who promises reforms but never carries them out.

for ducks *phr.* [1900s–60s] (*US*) for no special reason, 'for the hell of it'. [ety. unknown]

fore *adj.* [1970s+] (*US gay*) of a homosexual male, passive (cf. AFT *adj.*). [naut. imagery, i.e. lying on his front for anal intercourse]

fore and aft *adj.* [2000s] daft. [rhy. sl.]

fore and after *n.* [19C] a woman, usu. a prostitute, who is agreeable to group sex, involving vaginal (*fore*) and anal (*aft*) intercourse.

forebuttocks *n.* [early–mid-18C] the female breasts.

forecaster *n.* [19C] the vagina (cf. BELLY ENTRANCE *n.*).

forecastle *n.* [19C] the vagina (cf. BELLY ENTRANCE *n.*). [SE *forecastle*, the forward area of a ship]

fore coach-wheel *n.* [late 18C–19C] a half-a-crown (12.5p). [the fore or front coach-wheels were smaller than those at the rear]

fore-court *n.* [19C] the vagina (cf. BELLY ENTRANCE *n.*).

foredeck *n.* [17C] the vagina (cf. BELLY ENTRANCE *n.*). [SE *foredeck*, the forward deck of a boat]

forefoot *n.* (*also* **forepaw**) [late 16C–early 19C] the human hand.

foregather *v.* [18C] to have sexual intercourse. [SE *foregather*, to meet together, to associate with]

foregut *n.* [19C] the vagina (cf. BELLY ENTRANCE *n.*). [SE *fore*, front + *gut*]

fore-hatch *n.* [19C] the vagina (cf. BELLY ENTRANCE *n.*).

foreign *adj.* [1900s–40s] (*US Black*) referring to any form of sexual activity considered 'unnatural'; thus *foreigner*, one deemed a sexual 'pervert'. [the automatic xenophobia that attaches itself to fantasies about 'foreign' sexual practices]

foreigneering cove *n.* [mid–late 19C] a foreigner; also adj. *foreigneering*. [SE *foreign* + COVE *n.* (1)]

foreigner *n.* **1** [1930s] (*US Und.*) any convict who is not a professional thief. **2** [1970s+] (*US Black*) a homosexual; thus *speak in a foreign tongue*, to have oral sex. [(2) the 'foreign tongue' is FRENCH *n.*[2] (3)]

foreman *n.*[1] [early 17C] ? a goose. [OED marks this as '? slang ? goose'; the def. is assumed f. one use in Beaumont & Fletcher's *Philaster* (1622) referring to Michaelmas (29 Sept.); Michaelmas is a trad. goose-eating day; ? a foreman precedes an alderman in a procession as Michaelmas precedes Christmas when one eats an ALDERMAN *n.*[1] (1), i.e. turkey]

foreman *n.*[2] [late 19C] the penis. [it stands at the *fore*front of the body]

foreman of the jury *n.* [mid-17C–early 19C] one who takes over the conversation. [a specific 'tavern term' drawn from the anonymous *The English Liberal Science, or a new-found Art and Order of Drinking* (1650)]

forenoon *n.* [19C] an alcoholic drink taken before breakfast.

forepaw *n. see* FOREFOOT *n.*

fore-pokers *n.* [late 18C–early 19C] in cards, aces and kings.

fore-room *n.* [19C] the vagina (cf. BELLY ENTRANCE *n.*).

foreskin hunter *n.* [19C] a prostitute (cf. COCKATRICE *n.*).

forest *n.* [17C+] female pubic hair.

forever gentleman *n.* [late 19C] (*UK society*) one in whom good breeding is ingrained, rather than the parvenu, in whom it is affected.

forewoman *n.* [late 19C] the vagina (cf. BELLY ENTRANCE *n.*). [antonym of FOREMAN *n.*[2]]

for fair *adv.* [late 19C+] (*US*) completely, absolutely, altogether.

for-free *n.* [1940s] (*orig. US*) a prostitute who undercuts the going price, an amateur (cf. CHARITY *n.*). [she effectively 'gives it away for free']

for freezies *phr.* [1960s] (*US Black/teen*) without rules or restrictions. [SE *free* + -IZ- ifx]

for fuck's sake! *excl.* (*also* **for fuck sake! fuck's sake!**) [1920s+] a general excl. of exasperation.

forge *n.* [18C–19C] the vagina (cf. BLACK HOLE *n.*[1]). [where the male 'rod' is softened]

forgers *n.* [late 16C] crooked dice.

forget it! *excl.* [20C+] **1** an excl. implying absolute dismissal of a suggestion or concept. **2** [1940s+] an excl. implying that the previous speaker doesn't understand the gist of the conversation. **3** [1990s+] (*US Black*) a euph. for FUCK IT! excl.

forget you! *excl.* [1960s+] (*US teen*) a euph. for FUCK YOU! excl.

forgive and forget *n.* [20C+] (*Aus.*) a cigarette. [rhy. sl.]

for God's sake! *excl.* [18C+] a once-blasphemous oath of irritation. [orig. 14C SE and used as an earnest appeal or exhortation]

for gosh sake! *excl.* [20C+] (*US*) a euph. version of FOR GOD'S SAKE! excl. [GOSH *n.*]

for greens *phr.* [mid-19C–1900s] (*US*) for fun, for no special reason.

for grins *phr. see* GRIN *n.*[2].

for heaven's sake! *excl.* [mid-18C+] a euph. version of FOR GOD'S SAKE! excl.

fork *n.*[1] **1** [late 17C–18C] a spendthrift, a wastrel. **2** [late 17C–mid-19C] (*UK Und.*) a pickpocket.

fork *n.*[2] [late 19C+] the crotch, thus ext. as the penis. [SE *fork*, the division of the legs where they join the torso]

fork *n.*[3] *see* FORK AND KNIFE *n.* (1).

fork *n.*[4] *see* FORKS *n.*

fork *v.*[1] [late 17C–early 19C] to pick pockets, using the fore and middle fingers, extended like the tines of a fork, which are thrust into the pocket, then closed tight on any object within; this is then withdrawn between the 'fork'.

fork *v.*[2] **1** [mid–late 19C] (*also* **fork out**) to lay a woman down with spread legs preparatory to intercourse. **2** [late 19C+] (*US*) to mount a horse. **3** [20C+] (*Aus.*) to ride a horse. [SE *fork*, the division of the legs where they join the torso]

fork *v.*[3] [1950s] a euph. for FUCK *v.*[1].

fork *v.*[4] *see* FORK OUT *v.*[1].

fork! *excl.* [early 19C+] give! [abbr. FORK OUT *v.*[1]]

fork and knife *n.* [20C+] **1** (*also* **fork**) life. **2** a wife. [rhy. sl.]

fork and spoon *n.*[1] [1930s] (*US*) mutual oral-genital stimulation. [the shape]

fork and spoon *n.*[2] [1980s+] (*Aus. prison*) a lout, a hooligan. [rhy. sl. = HOON *n.* (2)]

for keeps *phr.* [mid-19C+] **1** for the duration, for a long time, for ever. **2** in absolute earnest.

forker *n.* [mid-19C] one of those 'who reside in seaports for the sake of stealing dockyard stores, or buying them, knowing them to be stolen' (Smyth, *Sailor's Word-book*, 1867). [? FORKS *n.*]

fork-hooks *n.* [20C+] (*US*) the fingers. [FORKS *n.* + HOOK *n.*[1] (1)]

for kickers *phr.* (*also* **for a kicker, for the kickers**) [1960s+] (*US*) for good measure. [KICKER *n.*[7]]

for kicks *phr.* [1940s+] for pleasure, for amusement. [KICK *n.*[5] (3)]

for kid *adv.* [1950s] as a joke. [KID (AROUND) *v.* (2)]

fork leather *v. see* LEATHER *n.*[3] (7).

forklifts *n.* [1960s] (*Aus.*) a pair of cushions placed on the rear window of a car to be used for in-car sex. [SE *fork* n. + pun]

fork-out *n.* [mid-19C] a price, a payment. [FORK OUT *v.*[1] (1)]

fork out *v.*[1] (*also* **fork, fork up**) [19C+] **1** to pay, to donate. **2** to hand over. [FORKS *n.*]

fork out *v.*[2] *see* FORK *v.*[2] (1).

fork over *v.* [early 19C+] to hand over, to give out. [FORKS *n.*]

forks *n.* **1** [early 19C+] (*orig. UK, later use mainly US Black*) the fingers, esp. the middle and forefingers; occas. in sing. **2** [mid-19C+] the hands; occas. in sing.

fork up *v. see* FORK OUT *v.*[1].

forlorn hope *n.* **1** [17C] the losers at a gaming table. **2** [late 18C–early 19C] a gambler's last, despairing bet. [Du. *verloren hoop*, a lost troop (of soldiers); the orig. 16C use described a band of skirmishers or assault troops who were sent ahead of the main force; this mutates into a desperate band of men and thence a desperate enterprise]

form *n.*[1] **1** [mid-19C+] character, style. **2** [late 19C+] the accepted way of doing things. **3** [1950s+] (*UK Und.*) previous convictions. [horseracing use]

form *n.*[2] **1** [late 19C+] liveliness, high spirits, conversational articulacy; esp. in phrs. *in great form* or *on form*. **2** [1960s] habit, occupation.

form *n.*[3] [late 19C+] (*S.Afr.*) a prison. [abbr. SE *reformatory*]

form *n.*[4] [1950s+] (*US*) the body as an object of sexual interest; thus *warm for someone's form*, sexually attracted to someone. [SE *form*, shape]

form, the *n.* [1930s+] the situation, the status quo, what is happening, how things are usu. done; often in query, *what's the form?* [SE *form*, the proper way of doing things]

formula *n.* [1980s] (*drugs*) fake cannabis. [? SAmE *formula*, baby food, pap]

for my money *phr.* (*also* **for my tin**) [mid-16C+] **1** what one would like, what one would choose. **2** in one's opinion, as far as one is concerned. [i.e. if one were having to pay or to wager]

forney *n. see* FAWNEY *n.*

fornicate the poodle *v.* [1910s+] (*US*) to waste time (and loaf on the job). [euph. for FUCK THE DOG (AND SELL THE PUPS) *v.* (1)]

fornicating *adj.* [20C+] a euph. for FUCKING *adj.*

fornicating engine *n.* (*also* **fornicating member/tool**) [19C] the penis. [FORNICATING *adj.* + ENGINE *n.* (1)/MEMBER *n.*[1]/TOOL *n.*[1] (1)]

fornicator *n.* [19C] the penis; thus *fornicator's hall*, the vagina.

fornicators *n.* [late 19C] trousers with a flap front rather than the modern fly. [their ease of exposure]

for nuts *adv.* [late 19C+] at all, in no way, e.g. *she can't cook for nuts.* [the relative insignificance of a *nut*]

forny *n. see* FAWNEY *n.*

for one's gills *phr.* [mid-19C] (*UK Und.*) to one's gain, to one's advantage. [GILLS *n.* (1)]

for Pete's sake! *excl.* [20C+] (*orig. US*) a euph. excl. for FOR CHRIST'S SAKE! excl., usu. used to indicate one's mild annoyance.

for real *adj.* (*also* **4-real**) [1950s+] (*US*) genuine. [FOR REAL *adv.*]

for real *adv.* (*also* **fo' rilla**) [1930s+] (*orig. US Black*) genuinely, honestly, sincerely, to be taken at face value.

for real? *phr.* (*also* **for reals**) [1930s+] (*US teen*) used as a question to ask whether someone is teasing or telling the truth. [FOR REAL *adv.*]

for real! *excl.* **1** [1970s+] an affirmative excl. absolutely! genuinely! **2** [1990s+] an excl. of alarm or threat. [FOR REAL *adv.*]

fo' rilla *adv. see* FOR REAL *adv.*

for shit *adv.* [1940s+] (*orig. US*) **1** whatsoever, at all, in any way. **2** awful, very badly. **3** pointlessly.

for skins *adv.* [20C+] (*Irish*) at all, in any way. [? SKIN n.²]

for sure *adj.* [1960s] absolute, certain. [FOR SURE adv.]

for sure *adv.* (*also* **fo' sho**) [20C+] (*US*) definitely, certainly, absolutely.

for sure! *excl.* (*also* **fo' shizzle (my nizzle)! fo' sho!**) [20C+] certainly! definitely! absolutely! [FOR SURE adv.; the excl. gained a new lease of life as part of the Valley Girl vocab. of the early 1980s+]

Forsyte Saga *n.* [1970s+] lager. [rhy. sl.; ult. John Galsworthy's early 20C literary saga of British business/social life, the first book of which was *The Forsyte Saga* (1922)]

fort *n.* (*also* **fortress**) [mid-16C–19C] the vagina; thus fig. the state of chastity or honour. [lit. euph.]

fort bushy *n.* [1960s+] **1** the vagina. **2** (*gay*) pubic hair. [FORT n. + BUSH n.² (1)]

forteyed *adj.* [1990s+] (*US Black*) drunk or intoxicated by a drug (cf. ALED UP adj.; ARSEHOLED adj.). [FORTY n.²]

Forth Bridge job *n.* [1970s+] anything that requires constant redoing, updating, amending. [the erroneous but trad. belief that the painting of Scotland's Forth Bridge is never finished – as soon as one end has been completed it is time to return to the other]

for the birds *phr.* [1940s+] (*orig. US*) trivial, worthless, appealing only to gullible people; ext. as *strictly for the birds* and coarsely as *shit for the birds.*

for the fuck of it *phr.* [20C+] for the fun of it. [FUCK n.⁴]

for the good of the loo *phr.* [late 18C–early 19C] for the good of all, for the benefit of the community. [SE *loo*, a card-game resembling whist; the ref. to the game extends to its players and thus, fig., to the whole community]

for the high jump *phr.* [1920s+] in serious trouble; often as *in for...* [? steeplechasing; or of trouble so bad that one will metaphorically have to 'jump very high' to get over it; but ? image of death by judicial hanging]

for the kickers *phr. see* FOR KICKERS phr.

for the love of Mike! *excl.* (*also* **for the love of Moses! ...Pete!**) [mid-19C+] (*orig. US*) a euph. excl. of exasperation or surprise, for goodness' sake! [*Mike*, like *Pete*, is irrelevant, other perhaps than as a euph. for *Moses*]

for the ride *phr.* [1940s+] (*orig. US*) as a non-participant, as an observer only, esp. in phr. *be/come/go along for the ride.*

for the (sheer) hell of it *phr.* [1920s+] (*orig. US*) with no other justification than a (momentary) whim or self-indulgence.

Forties *n. see* ROARING FORTIES n.

fortnighter *n.* [1950s–70s] (*US drugs*) an occasional, notionally fortnightly, use of narcotics.

Fortnum and Mason *n.*¹ [late 19C] a large and sumptuous hamper, as provided by the famous London provisioners.

Fortnum and Mason *n.*² [1990s+] **1** a basin. **2** a pudding-basin haircut, a 'short back and sides'. [rhy. sl.; ult. *see* prev.]

fortress *n. see* FORT n.

for true *adj.* [late 19C] (*US*) genuine.

for true *adv. see* FEH TRUE adv.

fortune-biter *n.* [18C] a swindler, a confidence trickster. [SE *fortune* + BITE v. (4)]

fortune cookie *n.* [1960s+] (*Can.*) a young woman, orig. typically from the chorus line, who swaps sexual favours for the monetary and material gifts of a (usu.) older lover. [SE *fortune* + COOKIE n.¹ (2) + pun]

fortune-teller *n.* [late 17C–early 19C] a trial judge. [he tells you your *fortune*, i.e. your sentence]

forty *n.*¹ **1** [19C] (*US Und.*) a gang, properly the 'Forty Thieves', based in New York's Five Points area. **2** [late 19C+] (*Aus.*) a crook, a confidence trickster. [(2) a Sydney gang of the mid-19C; poss. called the *Forty Thieves*, although that name may have been a subseq. journ. invention]

forty *n.*² (*also* **40, forty ounce, four-oh**) [1980s+] (*US Black*) a 40fl oz (1-litre) bottle of beer. [its contents, *40 ounces* of beer]

forty *adj.*¹ [17C+] many.

forty *adj.*² (*also* **thirty-eight and two, thirty-eight plus two, twice twenty**) [1930s–50s] (*US Black*) used of anything pleasing.

forty acres *n.* [20C+] (*US*) extremely large feet. [their supposed dimensions]

Forty-Deuce *n.* [1980s+] (*US*) 42nd Street from Eighth Avenue to Times Square; the centre of New York's tourism, nightlife and underworld. [ext. DEUCE, THE n. (2)]

forty-dog *n.* (*also* **dog**) [1980s+] (*US Black*) a 40fl oz (1-litre) bottle of beer. [FORTY n.² + DOG n.¹¹]

forty-eleven *adj.* (*also* **forty-leven**) [mid-19C–1960s] (*US Black/W.I.*) too many, infinite.

forty-faced *adj.* [late 19C–1950s] shameless; thus in combs. *forty-faced liar, forty-faced flirt.* [? one has 'forty faces', none of them trustworthy, but note FORTY adj.¹ + dial. *forty-legs*, a millipede, where *forty* is generic for 'many']

forty fits *n.* [late 19C+] an extreme loss of emotional control; thus *have forty fits*, to lose all control. [FORTY adj.¹ + SE *fits*]

forty-five *n.* [20C+] a .45 calibre pistol. [the popular Colt .45 revolver]

forty-five minute psychosis *n.* [1970s+] (*drugs*) dimethyltryptarine (DMT). [the short duration and intensity of the drug experience]

forty-fives *n.* [1930s] (*US tramp*) beans. [? the pistol-shot like explosion of bean-induced breaking wind]

forty-foot *n.* [mid-19C] a short person. [? ironic ref. to height]

forty-four *n.*¹ [1920s+] a .44 calibre pistol. [abbr.]

forty-four *n.*² **1** [1930s+] a prostitute, a whore (cf. BOAT AND OAR n.). **2** [1950s+] a door-to-door salesman. [rhy. sl.]

forty-four *adv.* [20C+] door-to-door. [rhy. sl.]

forty-guts *n.* [mid-19C] a fat man. [FORTY adj.¹ + SE *guts*/-GUTS sfx]

forty h.p. *adj.* [late 19C] (*Aus.*) substantial, very great. [lit. 40 horse *power*, a high speed for the period]

forty-jawed *adj.* (*also* **forty-lunged**) [1910s+] loquacious, talkative. [SE phr. *talk forty to the dozen*]

forty-leven *adj. see* FORTY-ELEVEN adj.

forty miles of bad road *n.* [1920s+] (*US*) **1** a very unattractive person, sight or situation; the number can differ. **2** one who is very exhausted.

forty-niner *n.* **1** [mid-19C] (*US*) an early immigrant to California, drawn there because of the gold rush of 1849. **2** [1950s–70s] (*US drugs*) a cocaine user. [(2) the image is of cocaine as GOLD DUST n. (1)]

forty-one *n.*¹ [1910s+] (*US*) a .41 calibre pistol.

forty-one *n.*² [1930s] (*US*) orangeade. [? a menu number; ? orig. short order]

forty ounce *n. see* FORTY n.².

forty-pounder *n.* [19C] a policeman. [the £40 cash bonus awarded to any policeman who secured a 'Tyburn ticket', i.e. captured a murderer]

forty-rod (lightning) *n.* [mid-19C–1930s] cheap, strong whisky. [its strength; such whisky was jokingly said to be powerful enough to kill at a distance of 40 rods (about 17km/11 miles). Alternatively, its strength empowered the drinker to run at top speed for a similar distance, or the drinker is guaranteed to collapse if he attempts to walk much further than this]

forty-shilling word *n.* [1960s] (*W.I.*) an obscene word, for the use of which one can be fined 40 shillings or £2.

forty ways (from the jack) *phr.* [20C+] (*US, orig. gambling*) in every way possible.

forty weeks favour *n.* [early 17C] the state of pregnancy, often in the context of an illegitimate child. [SE *forty weeks*, the approx. period of gestation + *favour*, something given as a mark of favour, e.g. a gift to a lover such as a handkerchief]

forty winks *n.* (*also* **forty-winker, winks**) [early 19C+] a brief nap, often after a meal.

forward *adj.* [late 18C] drunk.

forward *v.* [1980s] (*UK Black*) to go to.

forward (pass) *n.* [1990s+] (*Aus.*) a beer or wine glass. [rhy. sl.]

forwards *n.* [1960s+] (*drugs*) amphetamine (cf. A n.²). [it impels its users to action]

fo' shizzle (my nizzle)! *excl. see* FOR SURE! excl.

fo' sho *adv. see* FOR SURE adv.

fo' sho! *excl. see* FOR SURE! excl.

foss *n. see* PHOS n.

fossick *n.* (*also* **fossicker, night-fossick(er)**) [mid–late 19C] (*Aus.*) a thief who specializes in taking gold dust or gold quartz. [SE *night* + SAusE *fossick*, to search for/pick up gold on the surface; ult. Warwicks dial. *fossick*, a troublesome person]

fossil farming *n.* [1980s+] (*Aus. prison*) snatching purses from old women.

fossy jaw *n. see* PHOSSY JAW n.

fotie *n. see* PHOTIE n.

fotog *n. see* PHOTOG n.

fou *adj.*¹ (*also* **fu**) [late 17C–1910s] drunk (cf. BITCH-FOU adj.; GREETIN' FOU adj.; PIPER FOU adj.; PISSING FOU adj.; ROARING FOU adj.). [Scot. pron. of SE *full*/FULL adj.¹ (1)]

fou *adj.*² [20C+] (*W.I.*) crazy, mad. [Fr. *fou*, mad]

foul *adj.* [20C+] **1** a general negative, revolting, disgusting. **2** (*US Black*) of talk, deliberately belligerent. **3** of a person, aggressive.

foul *adv.* [mid-19C–1920s] (*US Und.*) in the act, red-handed; usu. in phr. *caught foul*, caught red-handed. [14C–17C SE *foul*, 'guilty of a charge or accusation; criminally implicated' (*OED*)]

foul a plate with *v.* [late 18C–early 19C] to share a meal with. [SE *foul*, to dirty]

foul ball *n.* [1920s+] (*US*) an unpleasant, poss. criminal character. [baseball jargon *foul ball*, a ball struck so that it falls outside the lines drawn from the home base through the first and third bases]

foulcher *n.* [late 19C] (*UK Und.*) a purse.

fouled up *adj.* (*US*) **1** [1940s+] in a mess, in chaos, disorganized. **2** [1950s+] useless, worthless. **3** [1960s] mistaken. [euph. for FUCKED UP adj.]

foul out *v.* [1940s+] (*US*) to go wrong, to fail. [baseball imagery]

foul-up *n.* [1940s+] (*US, orig. milit.*) **1** a state of confusion or chaos occasioned by bungling and/or ineptitude. **2** the individual who causes or is capable of causing such chaos. [FOUL UP v.]

foul up *v.* [1940s+] (*US, orig. milit.*) **1** to blunder, to make a mistake. **2** to ruin, to destroy. **3** to fall into confusion, to fail through personal inadequacy, to get into trouble. **4** to cause trouble for; to annoy. [euph. for FUCK UP v.]

foundling temper *n.* [late 19C] an extremely bad temper. ['proverbially said of the domestic servants poured upon London by the Metropolitan Foundling Hospital' (Ware)]

found on *adj.* [20C+] (*Irish*) arrested for drinking in a public house after licensing hours. [police charge sheet, *found on licensed premises...*]

foundry *n.* **1** [late 19C] a shop, esp. a pork butcher's shop because of the noise of the sausage machine. **2** [1900s] (*US*) a restaurant.

fountain of love *n.* [late 16C–19C] the vagina (cf. ADAM'S OWN (ALTAR) n.; DAMP n.).

fountain palaces *n.* (*also* **fountain temples**) [late 19C] public conveniences.

four *n.* [mid-19C–1910s] 4-pennyworth of a given drink, as sold in a public house.

four-'alf *n. see* FOUR-HALF n.

four and nine (penny) *n.* [mid-19C] a cheap hat. [the 1844 advertisement, which declared 'Whene'er to slumber you incline / Take a *short nap* at 4 and 9']

four and one *n.* [1940s] (*US Black*) the fifth day of the working week, i.e. payday, which is Friday.

four-and-twenty (steps) *n.* [1950s] (*W.I.*) an arrest, a trial.

[ety. unknown; ? the number of steps from a particular courtroom to the cells]

four-and-two *n.* [1930s] a sandwich. [? of the 4 sides of bread, only 2 are buttered]

four annas in the rupee *n.* [late 19C–1900s] a Eurasian quadroon. [16 annas = 1 rupee; thus 4 annas = 1 quarter]

four-'arf *n. see* FOUR-HALF n.

four-bit *n.* [mid-19C+] (*W.I.*) 1 shilling and 6 pence.

four bits *n.* **1** [late 19C+] (*US*) 50 cents. **2** [1970s] (*US prison*) a 50-year prison sentence. [BIT n.¹ (4); (2) f. (1)]

four bones *n.* [1910s–20s] (*Irish*) the human body.

four-by *n.* [1990s+] a 4-wheel-drive vehicle, usu. a form of Jeep, popular among drug dealers, rappers and their fans. [abbr. of SE *four-by-four*, i.e. 4x4]

four-by-three *adj.* [1920s–30s] small, unimportant. [? the relatively small dimensions]

four by two *n.* **1** [1910s+] a Jew (cf. BILLY THE KID n.). **2** [1970s] (*mainly Aus./N.Z.*) a prison warder. [rhy. sl.; (2) = SCREW n.² (3)]

four cautions, the *n.* [late 18C–early 19C] 'I. Beware of a woman before. – II. Beware of a horse behind. – III. Beware of a cart sideways. – IV. Beware of a priest every way' (Grose, 1785).

four-cornered *adj.* [20C+] (*US prison*) caught in the act. [elaboration of SE *cornered*]

four corners *n.* [19C+] (*US*) a small, out-of-the-way place. [*four-corners*, a crossroads and thus a small settlement that might grow up around it]

four-decker *n.* [1980s] group sex, involving 2 heterosexual couples.

four-eleven *n.* (*also* **four-one-one, 411**) [1980s+] (*US Black/campus*) information; thus as an excl. give me the facts, give me some details. [the US phone number for information]

four-eleven-forty-four *n.* (*also* **4-11-44**) [1960s] (*US Black*) the penis. [a 'lucky number' popularized by NUMBERS, THE n. or POLICY n. bettors from late 19C+, and known in numbers jargon as the *fancy gal roll* or the *Washerwoman's Number*; note 1872 *The Galaxy* (NY) 495: 'Sometimes a mania seizes the entire fraternity of colored players to play some particular "flat gig," which is generally 4—11—44, and the numbers being sure to be drawn only after everybody has been tired out and quit betting on them, their appearance evokes a storm that is comical in its intensity when its occasion is remembered']

four-eyed *adj.* (*also* **four-eyes**) [late 19C+] a pej. epithet aimed at those who wear spectacles. [FOUR-EYES n. (2)]

four-eye puss *n.* [1940s] (*W.I.*) one who wears glasses. [FOUR-EYED adj. + PUSS n.³ (1)]

four-eyes *n.* **1** [early 19C] spectacles. **2** [mid-19C+] one who wears spectacles; the pej. term has overtones of distrust of anyone 'intellectual'.

four-eyes *adj. see* FOUR-EYED adj.

4-F *adj.* (*also* **Four-F**) [1940s+] (*US*) useless, inferior, weak. [milit. specification for anyone unfit to serve]

4-F club *n.* [1950s+] (*US*) a metaphorical 'club' based on the slogan 'find 'em, feel 'em, fuck 'em (or euph. as fool 'em) and forget 'em', the axiom for macho US youth in its dealings with women. [FOUR-Fs n.]

four-fingered shuffle *n.* [1980s+] masturbation.

459 *n.* [1980s+] (*US Und.*) a burglary; thus as v. *459*, to steal.

four-flush *n.*¹ [1900s] an act of deception. [FOUR-FLUSH v.]

four-flush *n.*² *see* FOUR-FLUSHER n.

four-flush *adj.* (*also* **four-flushing**) [late 19C+] (*US*) cheating, lying, bragging, untrustworthy. [FOUR-FLUSH v.]

four-flush *v.* [late 19C+] (*US*) to cheat or bluff; thus n. *four-flushing*. [FOUR-FLUSHER n.]

four-flusher *n.* (*also* **four-flush, four of one suit**) (*US*) **1** [late 19C+] a cheat, a bluffer. **2** [20C+] a braggart, a boaster. **3** [1910s] something worthless. **4** [1910s+] a scrounger, one who fails to pay due debts. [poker jargon; a real flush requires 5 cards of the same suit, 4 is merely a bluff]

four-flushing *adj. see* FOUR-FLUSH *adj.*

four-foot amelia *n.* [1930s] (*W.I.*) a flimsy or roughly constructed bed.

four-four *n.* [1990s+] (*US*) a .44 calibre weapon.

four-Fs *n.* [1940s+] (*US*) a young man's guide to sexual ethics, i.e. 'find 'em, feel 'em, fuck 'em and forget 'em'; sometimes amplified to *five Fs* by adding 'feed 'em' after 'find 'em'; thus 4-F CLUB *n.* [note Mae West in *I'm No Angel* (1933) tells her maid to 'find 'em, fool 'em and forget 'em' when it comes to men; the rap group NWA used 'find 'em, fuck 'em and flee' in 1991]

four-half *n.* (*also* **four-'alf/-'arf**) [late 19C–1920s] a mix of ale and porter, sold at 4 pence a quart.

four-headed *adj.* [1930s] (*US Black*) very clever, exceptionally intelligent. [for ety. *see* DOUBLE-HEADED *adj.*]

four-kind *adj.* [1960s] a general intensifier; a euph. for FUCKING *adj.*

four-legged fortune *n.* [late 19C–1910s] (*UK society*) a winning racehorse.

four-legged frolic *n.* [mid-19C] sexual intercourse. [popular euph. for *the beast of two backs*]

four-letter man *n.* **1** [1920s+] (*UK society*) an unpleasant person; the 4 letters are perhaps *s-h-i-t* (as suggested by Manchon) or *c-u-n-t* (cf. FIVE-LETTER WOMAN *n.*). **2** [1940s+] (*US*) a male homosexual, i.e. both as an ext. of (1) and as *h-o-m-o*.

four-letter word *n.* [20C+] an obscenity, notably CUNT *n.*[1], FUCK *n.*[1], SHIT *n.*[1] etc; thus *six-letter word*, BUGGER *n.*[1]; and *ten-letter word*, COCKSUCKER *n.* etc. [euph.]

four-liner *n.* [late 19C] (*UK society*) something considered very important. [the '4-line whips' issued in Parliament]

four-minute job *n.* [2000s] (*US prison*) a shower. [SE *four minutes* + JOB *n.*[4]]

four of one suit *n. see* FOUR-FLUSHER *n.*

four-oh *n. see* FORTY *n.*[2].

four-oh-four *n.* (*also* **404**) [1990s+] (*US teen*) a fool. [computer use *404*, 'File Not Found' message on the Web]

four-one-one/411 *n. see* FOUR-ELEVEN *n.*

fourpenny *n.* **1** [mid-19C] beer costing 4 pence a pint. **2** [late 19C–1900s] an ugly, worn-out old prostitute (cf. DOLLAR-WOMAN *n.*). **3** [late 19C–1900s] (*also* **fourpenny touch**) a short, commercial act of intercourse. **4** [1950s] (*UK Und.*) a cheap lodging house. [the price of the various commodities]

fourpenny cannon *n.* [late 19C] a steak and kidney pie. [its shape and/or its consistency resembles a cannon ball + the cost]

fourpenny dark *n.* [1950s+] (*Aus.*) cheap red wine. [the cost + DARK *n.*[1] (2)]

fourpenny (one) *n.* [late 19C+] 'a clip round the ear-hole'; usu. as *get/give a…* [rhy. sl. *fourpenny bit* = hit]

fourpenny pit *n.* [late 19C] a fourpenny bit or groat, the predecessor of the threepenny bit. [rhy. sl.]

fourpenny touch *n. see* FOURPENNY *n.* (3).

4 piece *n.* [2000s] a full set of restraints, comprising 4 pieces: cuffs, leg irons, waist and security cover. [pun on SE *three-piece suit*, i.e. jacket, waistcoat and trousers]

four pound *n.* (*also* **4-pound**) [1990s+] (*US Black*) a gun.

four prices *adj.* [20C+] (*Ulster*) very expensive. [? it costs fig. '4 times as much' as a normal item]

4-real *adj. see* FOR REAL *adj.*

four sisters on thumb street *n.* [1970s+] (*US Black*) masturbation. [cf. CONVERSE WITH HARRY PALM v.].

foursome *n.* [1940s+] (*US*) 4 people involved in sex together; it can involve any combination of genders.

14 *n.* [1990s+] (*US prison*) N, the 14th letter of the alphabet; the ref. is to gangs from North California.

fourteen-carat *adj. see* EIGHTEEN-CARAT *adj.*

fourteen penn'orth *n.* [early 19C] a sentence of 14 years' transportation.

fourth *n.* [mid-19C] a lavatory. [? orig. used at Trinity College, Cambridge University; at that time the college privies were sited in the fourth court and thus an undergraduate who had temporarily gone there would write upon his door 'Gone 4'; an alternative ety. suggests that one's morning went through 4 stages, chapel, breakfast, pipe, visit to the lavatory]

four thick *n.* [late 19C] beer sold at 4 pence a quart.

four-twenty *n.* (*also* **4:20**) [1970s+] (*US Black/drugs*) marijuana. [email to *American Dialect Society-List* (Internet, 10 May 2001): '[The term] originated at San Rafael High School in San Rafael, CA, in the early 1970s as a code for smoking marijuana at 4:20 pm (70 minutes after school dismissal). The Grateful Dead were long based out of San Rafael, and the phrase was used on a flyer at Grateful Dead shows in 1990, leading to its wider use']

four-twenty *v.* (*also* **4:20**) [1990s+] (*US Black/drugs*) to smoke marijuana. [FOUR-TWENTY *n.*]

four-wheeler *n.*[1] [19C] a beefsteak. [? the cow's 4 legs]

four-wheeler *n.*[2] (*also* **four-wheel Christian**) [1960s] anyone (orig. Roman Catholic) who only visits a church for weddings, christenings, funerals and other 'social' rather than purely religious events. [they drive to church]

four-wheel (skid) *n. see* FRONT-WHEEL SKID *n.*

foutra *v.* (*also* **foutre**) [17C] to have sexual intercourse; a euph. for FUCK *v.*[1]. [Fr. *foutre*, to fuck]

foutre! *excl.* [late 16C–mid-17C; mid-19C] a general oath of dismissal; thus *a foutre*, a synon. with FUCK *n.*[4] [Fr. *foutre*, to fuck; note 19C US regional (Pennsylvania) *fouty*, trifling]

f.o.w.b. *phr.* [1940s–50s] (*US Black/teen*) used to a girl who has been taken out in a car: *fuck or walk back*.

fox *n.*[1] **1** [late 16C+] (*also* **Mr Fox**) a cunning, duplicitous person. **2** [1910s–30s] (*US Und.*) a tramp who rides on passenger trains by tricking the conductor as to their legitimacy. **3** [1930s] (*US Und.*) an escape, either from the police or from prison. **4** [1970s+] (*orig. US*) a drinker who slips out of the bar when it is his turn to pay for a round. [stereotypical negative characteristics of the animal]

fox *n.*[2] [late 17C–early 18C] a state of drunkenness; thus *catch a fox*, to be drunk. [FOXED *adj.*]

fox *n.*[3] **1** [mid-19C] an artificial sore. **2** [1900s] (*Aus.*) a lie, nonsense. [FOX *v.*[1] (1)]

fox *n.*[4] [mid-19C] (*US*) an inhabitant of Maine. [? the preponderance of foxes; ? their cunning characteristics]

fox *n.*[5] **1** [1940s+] (*orig. US Black*) a girl, a woman, esp. an attractive and sexually active one; thus *superfox*, an extreme example. **2** [1940s+] a womanizer. **3** [1960s] (*US prison*) the passive partner in a lesbian relationship. **4** [1970s+] (*US campus*) a sexually attractive person of the opposite sex. [stereotypical positive characteristics of the animal + FOXY *adj.*[2] (4)]

fox *v.*[1] **1** [early 17C+] to fool, to trick, to dissemble. **2** [mid-17C] to make drunk. **3** [late 18C] (*UK Und.*) to perform a specific trick practised by prisoners on visitors to the jail. [SE *fox*, to confuse]

fox *v.*[2] **1** [mid-19C–1900s] to observe surreptitiously. **2** [late 19C–1900s] (*Aus./N.Z.*) to be a voyeur, esp. when spying on couples in the open air.

fox *v.*[3] [mid-19C+] to feign sleep or (*Aus.*) to feign unconsciousness.

fox around *v.* [1930s] (*US*) to sneak about, to act in a surreptitious manner.

fox bait *n.* [20C+] (*US*) an old horse, ready for the knacker.

fox-drunk *adj.* [late 16C] drunk but still cunning. [SE *fox* as a symbol of cunning + *drunk*]

foxed *adj.* (*also* **foxified**) [early 17C+] drunk. [SE *fox*/FOX *v.*[1] (1)]

foxer *n.*[1] [1900s] (*Aus./N.Z.*) a voyeur, esp. one who spies on couples in the open air. [FOX *v.*[2] (2)]

foxer *n.*[2] *see* NIXER *n.*

foxhead *n.* [20C+] (*US*) illicitly distilled whisky. [SE *fox*, to confuse + *head*]

foxiness *n.* [1990s+] (*US*) flirtatiousness. [FOXY adj.[2] (4)]

foxing *n. see* FOX'S SLEEP n.

fox in the bush *n.* [1900s–20s] (*US*) a derog. term for a Jew (cf. FAST-TALKING CHARLIE n.). [the stereotype of Jewish cunning]

fox's paw *n.* [late 18C–early 19C] a mistake, a blunder. [Fr. *faux pas*]

fox's sleep *n.* (*also* **foxing**) [mid-19C] an air of indifference to what is going on. [the belief that a fox sleeps with 1 eye open]

foxy *n.* [late 19C+] (*Aus.*) a fox terrier.

foxy *adj.*[1] [mid-19C; 1950s] having red hair. [the fox's colouring]

foxy *adj.*[2] **1** [mid-19C–1900s] (*UK Und.*) avoiding trouble. **2** [mid-19C+] cunning, perspicacious. **3** [late 19C] (*US campus*) artistic, neat. **4** [late 19C+] (*orig. US*) attractive, sexy. **5** [1900s–50s] (*US Black*) splendid, good. **6** [1900s–60s] clever, intellectual. [FOX n.[1] (1) + sfx -*y*]

foxy grandpa *n.* [20C+] (*US*) a sly person, neither necessarily old nor a grandfather. [the cartoon character *Foxy Granpa*, by C.E. Schultze (1866–1939), which appeared *c.*1900 and featured an adult who, in a reverse of the usual cartoon situation, played tricks on children]

foy *n.* [late 16C–early 17C] a swindler. [abbr. FOIST n.[2]]

foy! *excl.* [late 17C] a general excl. [SE *fay*, faith]

foyl-cloy *n. see* FOIL-CLOY n.

foyse *n. see* FICE n.

foyst *see under* FOIST.

f.p. *n.* [20C+] (*UK Und.*) false pretences, thus fraud. [abbr.]

fraai *v. see* VRY v.

frabbajabba *n.* [1950s] (*US*) nonsensical chatter.

fracture *v.* **1** [1930s–70s] (*US*) to beat up, to trounce. **2** [1940s–70s] (*US*) to astonish, to disconcert. **3** [1940s+] to make one laugh, to amuse greatly, e.g. *that fractures me*, that's an amusing joke.

fractured *adj.* [1950s+] **1** very drunk (cf. ANNIHILATED adj.). **2** emotionally overcome. **3** divorced.

fracture one's wig *v. see* BLOW ONE'S WIG v. (1).

fraggle *n.* [2000s] (*UK prison*) someone who is mentally disturbed. [the 1980s TV series *Fraggle Rock*]

fraho *n.* (*also* **frajo**) **1** [1950s+] (*US drugs*) marijuana. **2** [1990s+] (*US prison*) a cigarette. [Sp.]

fraidy *adj.* (*also* **fraidy-fraidy**) [1950s] (*W.I.*) timid, fearful. [SE *afraid*]

fraidy-cat *n.* (*also* **fraid-cat, fraidy-pants**) [20C+] (*US juv.*) a coward, a timorous person; also as adj. [SE *afraid*]

frail *n.*[1] **1** [mid-19C–1930s] a prostitute, a mistress. **2** [20C+] (*orig. US*) a girl, a woman. **3** [1950s] (*US prison*) a passive partner in a lesbian relationship. [the image of women as weaklings; thus Victorian euph. *the frail sisterhood*, prostitutes as a class]

frail *n.*[2] [1940s] (*US Und.*) a stolen cheque. [? its insubstantiality]

frail eel *n.* [1930s–40s] (*US Black*) an attractive woman. [SE *frail* + SE *eel*, an elusive creature which is hard to hold on to]

frajo *n. see* FRAHO n.

fram *v.* [1930s+] (*orig. US Black*) to beat, to strike, to attack. [? Midlands dial. *fram*, to be in a temper or passion]

frame *n.*[1] **1** [17C+] the body. **2** [20C+] (*US Black*) a person. **3** [1940s] (*US Black*) a suit of clothes.

frame *n.*[2] *see* FRAME(-UP) n.

frame *v.*[1] **1** [20C+] (*US Und.*) to create the environment – a fake bookmaker's, a fake stock dealer's – in which an elaborate confidence trick can take place; to arrange a 'fixed' boxing match. **2** [1900s] (*US Und.*) to place in a Rogues' Gallery. **3** [1910s–50s] to fake. **4** [1910s+] in fig. use, to arrange, to prepare. **5** [1920s–40s] (*US*) to trick or hoodwink. [SE *frame*, to put in a frame]

frame *v.*[2] [1900s] (*US*) to dress. [SE *frame* (a picture)]

frame in *v.* [1900s] (*US Und.*) to join up with.

framer *n.* [1940s] one who accuses another person unfairly,

and/or through the provision of faked evidence. [FRAME (UP) v. (4)]

frames *n.* [1950s] (*US Black*) spectacles, glasses.

frame(-up) *n.* (*orig. US*) **1** [20C+] a plot, a plan. **2** [20C+] the concoction of criminal guilt or charges; any circumstances that combine to place an individual in a disadvantageous position, usu. leading to their arrest. **3** [1910s] a 'fixed' sporting encounter. **4** [1910s] corruption, malpractice. **5** [1930s+] the general situation, esp. that surrounding the suspects in a given crime. [FRAME (UP) v.]

frame (up) *v.* **1** [1900s] (*US*) to explain. **2** [1900s–30s] (*orig. US*) to form a plan of action, esp. in secret. **3** [1910s] to set someone up with something (non-criminal). **4** [1910s+] (*orig. US*) to trap a suspect (poss. innocent) by creating false evidence, witnesses etc against them, to devise a scheme or plot with regard to. [ext. of FRAME v.[1] (1)]

frammagemed *adj. see* FRUMMAGEMED adj.

frammis *n.* [1950s+] (*US*) **1** (*also* **frammiss**) any form of confidence trick. **2** a thingumibob. [? FRAME(-UP) n.]

France *n.* [1920s+] (*W.I.*) a euph. for FUCK n.[1] or *hell* (cf. CATCH FRANCE v.; GIVE FRANCE v.; GO TO FRANCE! excl.; PUT FRANCE ON v.; SEE FRANCE v.). [the basic use, *France!*, is as an oath, and refers to the horrors of WW1, when many West Indians fought and died in the trenches of Flanders. Other uses, all of which can be paralleled by a use of fuck and/or hell, include such phrs. as *to France with that; how/what/when/who/why/where the France*. The phrs. may also have some background in the Du. *Loop naar de Franschen*, run to the French, i.e. go to the devil]

France and Spain *n.* [late 19C+] rain. [rhy. sl.]

frances *n.* (*also* **francesca**) [1930s–60s] (*US*) the buttocks. [FANNY n.[1] (1)/proper name *Fanny*, which is an abbr. of this]

franc-fileur *n.* [late 19C–1900s] (*UK society*) at a ball, a man who will not dance and refuses to talk to any woman for more than a moment. [Fr. *franc-fileur*, free runner]

franger *n.* [1970s+] (*Aus.*) a condom. [? FRENCH LETTER n.]

Frank Bough *adj.* [1990s+] of food or drink, stale, sour. [rhy. sl. = OFF adj.[1] (4); ult. UK sportscaster and TV personality *Frank Bough* (b.1933), pron. 'Boff']

Frankie Fraser *n.* [1990s+] a razor. [rhy. sl.; ult. the London gangster 'Mad' Frankie Fraser (b.1923)]

Franklin *n. see* BEN FRANKLIN n.

franklin teeth *n.* [1920s–30s] (*Can.*) projecting or 'buck' teeth. [the protruding grille of the Franklin automobile]

frank thring *n.* [1970s+] (*Aus.*) a (wedding) ring. [rhy. sl.]

Frank Zappa *n.* [1990s+] a lavatory (cf. ANGUS ARMANASCO n.). [rhy. sl. = CRAPPER n.[3] (2); ult. US rock star and experimental musician *Frank Zappa* (1940–93)]

fransman *n.* (*also* **franse, Frenchman**) [1970s+] (*S.Afr. Und.*) an outsider, a convict who is not affiliated to a prison gang. [Afk. *fransman*, Frenchman, thus fig. a foreigner]

frantic *n.* [1950s] (*US Black*) a lively, remarkable person. [SE *frantic*/FRANTIC adj. (2)]

frantic *adj.* **1** [late 19C–1950s] a general intensifier, terrific, awful. **2** [1930s–60s] exciting, amusing, enjoyable. **3** [1940s–60s] of people or things, good-looking, fashionable.

frantically *adv.* **1** [1900s] a general intensifier, terrifically, awfully. **2** [1950s] of a party, in a lively style, frenetically. **3** [1950s–60s] excitingly, amusingly, enjoyably. [FRANTIC adj.]

franzy house *n.* [20C+] (*US*) **1** a brothel (cf. ACCOMMODATION HOUSE n.). **2** a psychiatric institution. [dial. *franzy*, SE *frenzy*, craziness, madness + HOUSE n.[1] (1)/SE *house*, as in SE *madhouse*]

frap *n.* [1990s+] a euph. for FUCK n.[1] in all senses. [note dial. *frap*, to strike, to beat]

frapping *n.* [mid-19C] a beating. [Fr. *frapper*, to beat]

frapping *adj.* [1990s+] a euph. for FUCKING adj. (1). [FRAP n.]

frat *n.* [late 19C+] (*US*) **1** a college *fraternity*. **2** (*also* **frat boy, frat head**) a member of a *fraternity*; thus also *non-frat*. [abbr.]

frat *v.* [1980s] **1** to associate with. **2** (*US campus*) to participate in fraternity parties or events, in order to pick up girls. [SE *fraternize*; (1) orig. US milit. at end of WW2; (2) also FRAT n. (2)]

fratastic *adj. see* FRATTY adj.

frat boy/brat *n. see* FRAT RAT n.

frat dick *n.* (*also* **frat fag**) [1980s] (*US campus*) a derog. description of a typical fraternity member. [FRAT n. (1) + DICK n.[4] (4)/FAG n.[5] (2)]

fratdom *n.* [1980s+] (*US campus*) the world of fraternities. [FRAT n. (1) + sfx *-dom*]

frater *n.* [mid-16C–early 18C] (*UK Und.*) a mendicant villain who poses as a friar and claims, as such, to beg alms for a hospital or charitable institution, specializing in poor, gullible women (cf. CANTING CREW n.). [Lat. *frater*, brother]

frat head *n. see* FRAT RAT n.

fratosoralingoid *n.* (*also* **fratosororalingoid**) [1990s+] (*US campus*) an obnoxious fraternity or sorority member. [SE *fraternity* + *sorority* + SF sfx *-lingoid/-*OID sfx]

frat out *v.* [1970s] (*US campus*) to dress and act like a fraternity member. [FRAT n. (2)]

frat rat *n.* (*also* **frat boy**, *…***brat**, *…***head**, *…***star**) [1960s+] (*US campus*) a member of a fraternity. [FRAT n. (1) + SE *rat/boy/*-HEAD sfx (1)/*star*]

fratting *n.* [1940s+] having sexual intercourse. [essentially abbr. of SE *fraternizing*, but used as euph. for FUCKING n.[1]]

fratty *adj.* (*also* **fratastic**, **fratstar**) [1970s+] (*US campus*) pertaining to fraternity life. [FRAT n. (1) + sfx *-y/fraternity* + -TASTIC sfx/*star*]

fratty-bagger *n.* (*also* **bag**, **bagger**) [1970s] (*US campus*) a stereotypical fraternity member. [FRATTY adj. + BAGS n.[2]]

frau *n.* [1900s–40s] (*US*) a wife. [synon. Ger. *frau*]

fraughty issue *n.* [1930s–40s] an unacceptable or unpleasant situation. [SE *fraught*]

fray *v. see* VRY v.

fray bentos *adj.* [1910s] (*Aus. milit.*) very good. [pun on pron. Fr. *tres bien*; ult. *Fray Bentos*, a brand of meat pies]

frazer nash *n.* [1970s] an act of urination (cf. ANGEL'S KISS n.). [rhy. sl. = SLASH n.[3] (1); ult. the sports car *Frazer-Nash*, manufactured before 1940]

frazzle *n.* [mid-19C+] (*orig. US*) a state of emotional and/or physical exhaustion; esp. in phr. *worn to a frazzle*, utterly exhausted; *beat to a frazzle*, comprehensively defeated. [SE *frazzle*, a frayed end, a fragment, a shred]

frazzle *v.* **1** [19C+] to fray, to become unravelled, often used of a whip's end. **2** [20C+] (*Aus.*) to rob. **3** [1900s] (*US*) to whip. **4** [1960s] (*US*) to excite, to render upset. [East Anglia dial. *frazzle*, to wear away, to unravel; ult. SE *fray*]

frazzled *adj.* (*also* **frazzle-assed**, **frazzled out**) **1** [19C+] (*orig. US*) emotionally drained, physically exhausted. **2** [19C+] (*orig. US*) drunk (cf. ADDLED adj.). **3** [1970s+] (*US drugs*) under the influence of a drug, e.g. cocaine or marijuana. [fig. use of FRAZZLE v. (1)]

frazzle-headed *adj.* [1980s] wild, crazy, unkempt.

frazzling *adj.* [1900s–40s] (*US*) a general intensifier, a euph. for FUCKING adj. (1).

freak *n.*[1] **1** [late 19C] (*US campus*) a student who is exceptionally proficient in a subject. **2** [late 19C+] (*orig. US*) (*also* **freako**) an offensively eccentric or crazy person. **3** [1900s] (*US campus*) a fool. **4** [20C+] an obsession. **5** [20C+] an obsessive. **6** [1920s+] one who enjoys non-standard sexual practices. **7** [1940s] an impotent man. **8** [1950s+] (*orig. US Black*) an effeminate man, a male homosexual. **9** [1950s+] (*US Black*) (*also* **freakette**) a woman, usu. sexually aggressive and adventurous. **10** [1960s+] (*orig. US*) a young person devoted to the 'counter-culture' or 'alternative society'; thus, a drug user. **11** [1960s+] (*US campus*) an unattractive person. **12** [1970s+] a lesbian; a prostitute who deals with lesbian clients. **13** [1980s+] (*US campus*) an extremely beautiful, good-

looking woman, usu. but not always a member of one's own peer group. [SE *freak*, a monstrosity (of nature), often as exhibited in a show; note also 16C *freke*, a man, often derog; (10), like many parallel bad = good usages, the young people in question adopted the name, synon. with 'extreme HIPPIE n.[2] (3)', after they had been branded as 'freaks' by their critics]

freak *n.*[2] [1990s+] a euph. for FUCK n.[1] in various contexts.

freak *n.*[3] *see* FREAK-OUT n.

freak *adj.*[1] [1910s; 1960s+] **1** (*orig. US*) obsessive, crazy. **2** (*US*) promiscuous. **3** (*US*) pertaining to the world of hippies. **4** (*US campus*) good. [FREAK n.[1]]

freak *adj.*[2] *see* FREAKISH adj. (2).

freak *v.*[1] **1** [1960s+] (*drugs*) to lose psychological control, whether enjoyably or otherwise, as the result of drugs, usu. hallucinogens; usu. as *freaking*. **2** [1960s+] orig. in HIPPIE n.[2] (3) use, to worry, to disturb, to cause severe anxiety (the extent of the disturbance varies totally as to context). **3** [1960s+] (*orig. US*) (*also* **freak one's mind**) to be worried, to be severely anxious. **4** [1960s+] (*orig. US*) to act in an emotional, melodramatic manner; thus *freaked*, emotionally overwhelmed. **5** [1970s+] (*US gay*) to be uninhibited, esp. at a party. [abbr. FREAK OUT v.]

freak *v.*[2] **1** [1960s+] to have adventurous sex. **2** [1980s+] (*US campus*) (*also* **freak all over**, **freak on**) to dance in a highly sexual manner, to simulate sex on the dance floor. **3** [1990s+] to have sexual intercourse, usu. forced. [FREAK n.[1] (6)/euph. for FUCK v.[1]]

freak *v.*[3] [1980s+] a euph. for FUCK v.[3].

freak *sfx* [20C+] (*orig. US campus*) a combining form that indicates an obsessive, one who is extremely interested in or overly fond of something, e.g. *health freak*, *dope freak* etc. [FREAK n.[1] (5)]

freak all over *v. see* FREAK v.[2] (2).

freak around *v.* [1970s+] (*US gay*) to waste time, to idle. [euph. FUCK ABOUT v. (1)]

freak attack *n.* [1990s+] (*US teen*) a state of extreme tension. [FREAK v.[1] (3) + SE *attack*]

freak-a-zoid *n.* [1990s+] (*US Black teen*) an eccentric, an obsessive, a freak. [FREAK n.[1] (2)/FREAK n.[1] (5) + -ZOID sfx]

freak book *n.* [1960s] (*US prison*) a pornographic book. [FREAK n.[1] (9) + SE *book*]

freak daddy *n.* [1980s+] (*US campus*) an attractive man. [FREAK n.[1] (9) + DADDY n.]

freaked *adj. see* FREAK v.[1] (4).

Freakeries, the *n.* [late 19C] Barnum's freak and acrobat shows, put on at Olympia. [SE *freak*, a monstrosity + sfx *-eries*]

freakette *n. see* FREAK n.[1] (9).

freak fuck *n.* [1960s+] **1** any variation on 'straight' heterosexual intercourse, esp. anal intercourse. **2** (*orig. US Black*) a client who demands unusual or poss. physically dangerous services from a prostitute. [FREAK n.[1] (6) + FUCK n.[1] (1)/FUCK n.[3]]

freak fuck *v.* [1970s+] (*orig. US Black*) **1** to engage in anal intercourse with a woman (cf. ASK FOR THE RING v.). **2** to engage in cunnilingus. [FREAK n.[1] (6) + FUCK v.[1]]

freaking *n. see* FREAK v.[1].

freaking *adj.*[1] **1** [1920s+] (*US*) a euph. for FUCKING adj. **2** [1980s+] (*US campus*) extraordinary, good.

freaking *adj.*[2] [1970s+] sexually perverse. [FREAK n.[1] (6)]

freakish *adj.* [1920s+] (*US Black*) **1** homosexual or lesbian. **2** (*also* **freak**) sexually deviant or lustful. [FREAK n.[1] (2)/FREAK n.[1] (6)]

freak it up *v.* [1970s] (*US gay*) to behave extravagantly, whether sexually, socially or on a dance floor. [FREAK v.[1] (5)]

freak magazine *n.* [1990s+] (*US Black*) a pornographic magazine. [FREAK n.[1] (9)]

freak mama *n.* [1980s+] (*US campus*) an attractive woman, with overtones of sluttishness. [FREAK n.[1] (9) + MAMA n. (1)]

freaknasty *adj.* [2000s] (*US*) sexually exciting and poss. perverse. [FREAK n.[1] (6) + NASTY adj. (2)]

freako *n. see* FREAK n.[1] (2).

freak-off *n.* [1960s] (*US Black*) an act of sexual intercourse. [FREAK OFF v.]

freak off *v.* **1** [1950s+] (*US Black*) to masturbate (cf. BALL OFF v.[2]). **2** [1950s+] (*US Black*) to engage in unrestrained or unorthodox sexual activity. **3** [1960s] to flirt, to attempt to pick up. **4** [1960s–70s] (*US Black*) to express one's enjoyment. **5** [1960s–80s] to decorate, esp. to create something beautiful. **6** [1970s+] (*US Black*) to have homosexual sex. [FREAK n.[1] (6)]

freak on *v. see* FREAK v.[2] (2).

freak one's mind *v. see* FREAK v.[1] (3).

freak-out *n.* (*also* **freak**) [1960s+] (*orig. US drugs*) **1** any unpleasant experience caused by drug use, esp. with LSD. **2** anxiety, ranging from twinges of fear to a full nervous breakdown, varying as to context. **3** a gathering of young people, esp. hippies, to enjoy music and take drugs together. [FREAK OUT v.]

freak out *v.* [1960s+] (*orig. US drugs*) **1** to experience an altered state of consciousness from the effects of a hallucinogenic drug; usu. an unpleasant effect. **2** to worry, to disturb, to horrify – the level of trauma depends on context. **3** to engage in unorthodox or unrestrained sexual activity. **4** to go crazy, wild or out of control from fear or instability. **5** to experience intense emotional pleasure, to have a good time, often in terms of dancing. **6** to engender or create such pleasure in someone. **7** to be upset, worried; thus to back down, retreat. [FREAK n.[1] (2); (2) FREAK n.[1] (6)]

freak party *n.* [1960s+] perverted or otherwise out of the ordinary sex. [FREAK n.[1] (6)]

freak rock *n. see* ACID ROCK n.

freak show *n.* [1960s+] a sexual display or performance, usu. of unorthodox sex. [FREAK n.[1] (6)]

freaksome *adj.* [1990s+] eccentric, bizarre. [FREAK n.[1] (2); coined in late 1990s US TV show *Buffy the Vampire Slayer*]

freak trick *n.* [1960s+] (*US prostitute*) any customer who requires out-of-the-way sex or who attacks the woman physically. [FREAK n.[1] (6) + TRICK n.[1] (3)]

freaky *adj.*[1] **1** [late 19C+] odd, bizarre, unnerving. **2** [1960s+] (*drugs*) hallucinogenic, psychedelic. **3** [1970s] (*drugs*) strong, powerful. [FREAK n.[1] (2) + sfx *-y*]

freaky *adj.*[2] [1960s+] **1** sexually aroused. **2** sexually deviant. **3** sexually exciting. [FREAK n.[1] (6)]

freaky-deaky *adj.* [1980s+] (*US*) weird, bizarre. [FREAKY adj.[1] (1) + assonance]

freaky-freak *n.* [1990s+] an eccentric; also used as term of affection. [FREAKY adj.[1] (1) + FREAK n.[1] (2)]

freaky-straight *n.* [1960s] 'either ordinary-looking people with fanatical ideas on one particular theme, [...] or people whose appearance is very weird but whose minds are channelled into one usual line of thought and on all other subjects their thinking is just as stereotyped as "Mr. Average"' (*Gandalf's Garden*, 1969). [FREAKY adj.[1] (1) + STRAIGHT n.[2] (2)]

freckle *n.* [1960s+] (*Aus.*) the anus.

freckle-nature *n.* [1950s] (*W.I.*) an albino.

freckle-puncher *n.* [1960s+] a male homosexual (cf. ANAL ASTRONAUT n.). [FRECKLE n. + SE *puncher*]

fred *n.*[1] [1970s+] (*US campus*) **1** a socially unacceptable person, a freeloader. **2** a fool. **3** (*also* **freddie**) a term of address to a friend. [the character *Fred Flintstone* in *The Flintstones* cartoon and film (1994)]

fred *n.*[2] [1970s+] (*Aus.*) the average Australian. [the commonness of the name]

fred *v.* [1980s+] (*US campus*) to vomit (cf. BARF v.; CALL CHARLES v.). [echoic]

Fred Astaire *n.* [1960s+] (*Aus.*) **1** a chair. **2** the hair. **3** a dandy. [rhy. sl.; (3) = LAIR n.; ult. film star and dancer *Fred Astaire* (1899–1987)]

Fred Astaire *adj.* [1940s] (*US campus*) stylish. [his style; for full ety. *see* prev.]

Fred Astaires *n.* [1940s] stairs. [rhy. sl.; for ety. *see* FRED ASTAIRE n.]

freddie *n. see* FRED n.[1] (3).

Fred Karno's army *n.* [1910s–50s] a group of people considered incompetent. [the popular comedian *Fred Karno* (1866–1941), who fronted a series of slapstick mini-shows, often burlesquing music-hall. Orig. milit. use in WW1 for the 'New', i.e. conscripted, army and in WW2 for any platoon or section seen as inept]

Fred McMurrays *n.* [2000s] worries. [rhy. sl.; ult. US film star *Fred MacMurray* (1908–91)]

fred nerk *n.* [1990s+] (*Aus.*) an imaginary person, esp. one on whom the blame can be placed, e.g. in phr. *I suppose it was Fred Nerk* (who did it).

Fred's out *phr.* [1970s] (*US campus*) expression used to admit to breaking wind.

free *n.* [1960s+] (*US prison*) the free world, i.e. the world outside prison.

free *v.* [mid-19C] to steal, usu. a horse; thus *free a cat*, to steal a muff. [ironic use of SE]

free-and-easy *n.* **1** [early 19C–1900s] a convivial gathering for singing, at which one may drink, smoke etc. **2** [late 18C–19C] a cheap brothel.

freebase *n.* (*drugs*) **1** [1970s+] cocaine base, purified by ether and smoked rather than sniffed or injected. **2** [1980s+] crack cocaine (cf. BASE n.). [the image of 'freeing' the SE *base* cocaine]

freebase *v.* [1980s+] (*drugs*) to intensify the effect of cocaine by heating it in combination with ether or other chemicals before inhaling. [FREEBASE n. (1)]

freebasing *n.* [1980s+] (*drugs*) intensifying the effect of cocaine by heating it in combination with ether or other chemicals before inhaling it. [FREEBASE v.]

freebie *n.* **1** [1920s+] (*orig. US*) (*also* **freeby**) any free sample, free trip, esp. press tours, promotions etc. **2** [1940s+] (*US*) one who gives their services for free, esp. a prostitute (cf. CHARITY n.). **3** [1970s+] (*drugs*) a free sample. **4** [1990s+] something, e.g. food, given away for free (in a non-promotional context).

freebie *adj.* [1940s+] (*orig. US*) used of anything or anyone free or obtaining something without paying. [FREEBIE n.]

freedom cut *n.* [1960s+] (*US Black/campus*) a hairstyle for which normally short, curly Black hair is allowed to grow out in a bush around the head. [the Afro cut was equated with a statement of Black freedom]

free-fishery *n.* [late 19C–1900s] the vagina (cf. BEARDED CLAM n.). [FISH n.[1] (1); but note SE *free fish*, a soft-bodied fish (as opposed to a crustacean)]

free-for-all *n.* [20C+] (*US*) a sexually available woman (cf. CHARITY n.).

free-fuck *v.* [late 19C+] of a woman, esp. a potential prostitute, to have sexual intercourse without charging. [SE *free* + FUCK v.[1]]

freeholder *n.* **1** [late 17C–18C] a man whose wife accompanies him to the tavern. **2** [late 19C–1900s] a prostitute's companion. [(1) a specific 'tavern term' drawn f. *The English Liberal Science, or a new-found Art and Order of Drinking*; ult. ? pun on SE *freeholder*, one who has land worth 40s (£2) a year; presumably one needed such an income to buy a wife a drink; (2) ? pun is on owning the prostitute/her income]

free hotel *n.* (*also* **free motel**) [20C+] (*US*) a prison (cf. BOARDING HOUSE n.). [i.e. one pays nothing for one's accommodation]

free kirker *n. see* KIRKER n.

freelance *n.* [19C] a habitual adulteress, although not a professional prostitute (cf. CHARITY n.).

freelance *v.* [1960s+] for a woman to work as a prostitute without informing her pimp or without a pimp at all.

freeload *v.* [1940s+] to enjoy for free the pleasures that are primarily made available to a celebrity or laid on at an important event but become equally available to anyone who cares to struggle hard enough to grab them; in general use, to define the taking of any benefits that one has not made due efforts to deserve. [backform. f. FREELOADER n.]

freeloader n. [1940s+] (orig. US) a parasite, one who eats and drinks without spending any money; more recently those who form a celebrity's entourage and enjoy the crumbs from their various tables. [SE free + load up, to fill (oneself) up]

freeloading adj. [1960s+] describing one who is enjoying pleasures for free; taking benefits that one has not earned. [FREELOAD v.]

free lunch n. [1910s+] (orig. US) something for nothing; often in phr. there's no such thing as a free lunch.

freeman n. [19C] an adulterer.

freeman of a corporation's work n. [late 18C] an unattractive, weak man. [SE corporation, the magistrates of a provincial town]

freeman of bucks n. [19C] an adulterer. [FREEMAN n. + pun on BUCK n.[1] (1)]

freeman's n. (also **harry freeman's**) [1910s+] anything obtained for free, esp. as a bribe given to a corrupt policeman. [for ety. see DRINK AT FREEMAN'S QUAY v.]

freeman's key n. [late 19C–1910s] (Aus.) any situation in which payment, esp. for alcohol, can be put off. [corruption of/var. on. DRINK AT FREEMAN'S QUAY v.]

free motel n. see FREE HOTEL n.

free object n. [19C] (Aus.) a 'civilian' settler who has not been transported. [pun on free subject (of His/Her Majesty)]

free of fumbler's hall phr. [late 17C–early 19C] referring to an impotent husband. [SE free of + FUMBLER'S HALL n. (2)]

free of the bush phr. [late 19C] sexually intimate with a woman. [SE free of + BUSH n.[2] (1)]

free ride n. **1** [20C+] an easy time. **2** [1910s] (US) an arrest. **3** [1990s+] an unpaid sexual encounter with a prostitute.

free shot n. [1970s+] the unpaid-for services of a prostitute. [SHOT n.[2]/SHOT n.[5] (1)]

free show n. [20C+] the inadvertent revelation by a woman of her body, in all or part, glimpsed by a passing man.

free side n. see FREE WORLD n. (1).

Free State coal n. [late 19C] (S.Afr.) dried cow-dung, used as fuel.

freestyle n. [1990s+] (US Black/teen) unwritten rap lyrics (occas. used of other forms of music), using whatever comes to mind at the spur of the moment.

freestyle v. [1990s+] (US Black/teen) **1** to create spontaneous rap rhymes, without prior preparation. **2** to act in a spontaneous manner, to live by one's own rules, wear one's own styles of clothes etc.

free the tadpoles v. [1990s+] to masturbate (cf. BEAT ONE'S HOG v.).

free-traders n. [late 19C–1930s] women's knickers, open at the crotch. [the freedom of access to the vagina]

freeway Freddie n. [1970s+] (US Black) a highway patrolman. [California use]

free, white and (over) twenty-one phr. [1920s+] (orig. US) a phr. describing a free agent, one who is free to make their own decisions. [21 is the age of consent in many countries and US states]

free willy v. [1990s+] to masturbate (cf. BEAT ONE'S HOG v.). [SE free + WILLIE n.[5] + pun on title of film (1993) about freeing a whale (? thus also pun on sperm/tadpoles)]

free world n. [1960s+] (US prison) **1** (also **free side**) the home of life outside prison. **2** (also **worlds**) a tailormade cigarette.

free-world adj. [1960s+] (US prison) pertaining to the non-prison environment. [FREE WORLD n. (1)]

free-world girl n. (also **free-world gal/punk**) [1960s+] (US

prison) a jail homosexual who has also been a homosexual in 'civilian' life. [FREE-WORLD adj. + SE girl/GAL n. (1)/PUNK n.[1] (2)]

freeze n.[1] [late 17C–early 19C] a thin, hard cider, used by vintners to dilute wines; thus freezing vintner, a vinter who dilutes their wine.

freeze n.[2] **1** [1930s+] (Aus.) a wife's deliberate withholding of sexual favours; often as do the freeze. **2** [1940s+] (orig. US) a snub, a rejection; thus do a freeze, to ignore. [FREEZE v.[3]]

freeze n.[3] [1970s+] (drugs) **1** cocaine. **2** the 'freezing' sensation that results from using cocaine. **3** a taste, a pinch of cocaine. [the effects as denoted by FREEZE ONE'S NOSE v.]

freeze v.[1] (also **freeze up**) **1** [mid-19C] to stay where one is, to remain. **2** [mid-19C; 20C+] to stand absolutely still, to remain motionless. **3** [1920s+] to become silent, to quieten down, to refuse to answer questions or make conversation. **4** [1920s+] to stop what one is doing. **5** [1960s+] to act calmly, to 'play it cool'.

freeze v.[2] [mid–late 19C] (US) to yearn for; thus froze for, desirous of. [FREEZE ON v. (1)]

freeze v.[3] **1** [mid–late 19C] to exclude from society, business etc, by intimidating, snubbing behaviour. **2** [20C+] (US) to intimidate. **3** [20C+] (US) to snub, to ignore. **4** [1930s] (US) to end a relationship; to obtain a divorce. **5** [1930s+] (Aus.) of a woman, to refuse sexual favours. **6** [1960s+] (drugs) to renege on an agreement, esp. on a drug deal.

freeze! excl. [1910s+] don't move! stay where you are! [FREEZE v.[1] (2)]

freeze-a n. [1910s] (Aus.) 'a catch word satirically applied to a popularity-hunter' (Downing, Digger Dialects, 1919). [abbr. of SE phr. 'for he's a jolly good fellow!']

freeze-cat n. (also **freezy-cat**) [1940s+] (US) one who has a low tolerance for cold weather. [on pattern of FRAIDY-CAT n./SCAREDY-CAT n.]

freeze off v. [1900s–30s] to kill, also in fig. use.

freeze on v. **1** [mid-19C+] (orig. US/Aus.) (also **freeze on to**) to take a tight grip of, to grasp something, e.g. to refuse to leave someone alone or to get behind someone; thus also to steal. **2** [late 19C+] (also **freeze up on**) to ignore, to snub, to reject.

freeze one's nose v. [1960s] to inhale cocaine. [the effects of the drug when inhaled or rubbed on the gums]

freeze-out n.[1] [mid-19C+] (orig. US) the act of deliberately excluding someone; sometimes the person excluded; thus freeze-out game, the act of doing this. [FREEZE OUT v.]

freeze-out n.[2] [1940s] (US) a situation that offers no opportunities, e.g. for theft.

freeze out v. [mid-19C+] (orig. US) to snub, to render socially unacceptable, to exclude from a (business) deal.

freezer n.[1] **1** [late 18C+] a rebuff, a snub. **2** [mid–late 19C] a chilly look, a dismissive remark. [play on SE]

freezer n.[2] [1920s–50s] (Aus./US) a prison.

freeze to v. [mid–late 19C] (orig. US) of people or objcts, to be very keen on, to fancy greatly.

freeze up v. see FREEZE v.[1].

freeze up on v. see FREEZE ON v. (2).

freezing weather n. [1930s–40s] (US Black) an unattractive woman.

freezy-cat n. see FREEZE-CAT n.

freight n. [1920s+] (US) payment, cost, e.g. one's rent or a subway fare; a bribe.

freight (it) v. **1** [late 19C] to travel a long distance. **2** [1910s–40s] (US tramp) to travel on a freight train.

French n.[1] [18C–19C] brandy (cf. FRENCH ARTICLE n.[1]; FRENCH CREAM n.; FRENCH ELIXIR n.; FRENCH LACE n.; FRENCHMAN, THE n.). [France as the home of brandy]

French n.[2] **1** [late 16C+] syphilis. **2** [late 19C+] taboo language; usu. in phr. EXCUSE MY FRENCH phr. **3** [1910s+] (also **French art, Frenchie, full French**) fellatio (cf. FRENCH ACTIVE n.; FRENCH BATH n.; FRENCH BY INJECTION n.; FRENCH CULTURE n.; FRENCH

DATE n.; FRENCH DRESSING n.; FRENCH GIRL n.; FRENCH HEAD JOB n.; FRENCH JOB n.; FRENCH LANGUAGE EXPERT n.; FRENCH LANGUAGE TRAINING n.; FRENCH LOVE n.; FRENCH PASSIVE n.; FRENCH POLISHING n.; FRENCH STYLE n.; FRENCH WAY n.). **4** [1970s] pornography. [racial stereotyping; Anglo-Saxons blame the French for anything remotely 'dirty']

French adj. **1** [late 16C–mid-18C] used in various combs. meaning syphilis (see relevant headwords below). **2** [17C+] a racial stereotype used in various contexts, the English (and thus US) belief in 'gay Paree' and its supposedly sex-obsessed denizens has long equated 'French' with sexy or, pej., pornographic and 'dirty'. **3** [mid-19C–1900s] (US) unfashionable, vulgar, distasteful. **4** [20C+] used in various combs. meaning fellatio/fellate (see relevant headwords below); thus by ext., denoting homosexuality. **5** [1930s] used of a prostitute, willing to give oral sex.

French v.[1] [20C+] (US) to rearrange the bedclothes for a practical joke. [for ety. see APPLE-PIE ORDER n.]

French v.[2] **1** [1920s+] (also **French it, French off**) to fellate; thus *Frenching*, giving fellatio. **2** [1950s+] to deep kiss. [(1) FRENCH n.[2] (3); (2) abbr. FRENCH KISS v.]

French active n. [1950s+] (gay) the passive (sucked) partner in fellatio (cf. FRENCH n.[2]; FRENCH PASSIVE n.). [FRENCH adj. (4)]

French art n. see FRENCH n.[2] (3).

French article n.[1] [18C] brandy. [SE French/FRENCH n.[1] + SE article]

French article n.[2] [mid-19C+] a French prostitute. [SE French/FRENCH adj. (2) + ARTICLE n. (2)]

French artist n. [1970s+] (US gay) a fellator. [FRENCH adj. (4)]

French aunt n. [20C+] (US) a flighty woman. [FRENCH adj. (2) + SE aunt]

French bath n. [1930s] (US) fellatio (cf. FRENCH n.[2]). [FRENCH adj. (4)]

French bathe n. [1950s+] (gay) the use of perfumes as a deodorant in lieu of bathing. [stereotyping of the French as physically as well as morally dirty]

French bathe v. [1950s+] (gay) to use perfumes as a deodorant in lieu of bathing. [FRENCH BATHE n.]

French blue n. [1960s+] **1** (drugs) a mix of barbiturate and amphetamine (cf. BAM n.[2]). **2** (US drugs) amphetamine. [manufacturers Smith, Kline and French + BLUES n.[2] (2)]

French bore n. see BORE n.[1] (1).

French by injection n. **1** [1950s–60s] (US gay) said of anyone considered particularly well-versed in fellatio (cf. FRENCH n.[2]). **2** [1960s] (US) any prostitute who opts for foreign customers. [SE French/FRENCH adj. (4) + SE injection, i.e. by the penis]

French cannibal n. see FRENCH MEASLES n.

French cap n. [1920s] (US) a condom. [var. SE Dutch cap]

French chillblains n. [17C] venereal disease. [FRENCH adj. (1)]

French cream n. [18C] brandy. [SE French/FRENCH n.[1]; 'so called by the old tabbies and dowagers when they drink their tea' (Grose, 1796)]

French crown n. (also **French goods/gout**) [late 17C–19C] venereal disease. [also known as Corona Veneris; stereotyping of FRENCH adj. (1) + joc. uses of SE crown, the ring of spots around the forehead/ goods/gout]

French culture n. [1960s+] fellatio, obs. except in homosexual contact advertisements (cf. FRENCH n.[2]). [FRENCH adj. (4)]

French date n. **1** [1930s] (US Und.) a prostitute's client who enjoys fellatio (cf. FRENCH n.[2]). **2** [1960s] (US) a paid-for act of fellatio. [FRENCH adj. (4)]

French deck n. [1960s+] (US) a pack of playing cards decorated with erotic pictures. [FRENCH adj. (2) + SE deck]

French dip n. [1950s+] (gay) vaginal juices (cf. BINDERJUICE n.). [FRENCH adj. (2)]

French disease n. (also **disease of France, malady of France**) [late 16C–18C] venereal disease, esp. syphilis. [FRENCH adj. (1); stereotyping]

French dressing n. [1950s+] (US gay) semen, in the context of fellatio (cf. BABY GRAVY n.; FRENCH n.[2]). [FRENCH adj. (4)]

French elixir n. [19C] brandy. [SE French/FRENCH n.[1]]

French embassy n. [1960s] (US gay) any location, esp. a gym or YMCA, where homosexual activity is extensive and unchecked. [FRENCH adj. (4) + pun on SE]

Frencher n.[1] [mid-late 19C] a Frenchman. [SE French]

Frencher n.[2] [20C+] one who enjoys oral sex, usu. a man. [FRENCH v.[2] (1)]

Frenchery n. [mid-19C+] a brothel. [FRENCH adj. (2) + sfx -ery]

French fits n. [1940s–50s] (US) delirium tremens. [? a link to insanity attendant on syphilis, i.e. the FRENCH DISEASE n.]

French-fried ice-cream n. [1960s+] (gay) semen (cf. BABY GRAVY n.). [FRENCH adj. (4) + ICE-CREAM n.[2] + pun]

French-fried ice water n. [1960s+] (US gay) lumpy semen (cf. BABY FLUID n.; BABY GRAVY n.). [FRENCH adj. (4)]

French fuck n. [1930s+] (US) the rubbing of a man's penis between a woman's breasts. [FRENCH adj. (2) + FUCK n.[1] (1)]

French girl n. [1930s] (US Und.) a prostitute who offers fellatio (cf. AWAYDAY GIRL n.; FRENCH n.[2]). [FRENCH adj. (4)]

French goods/gout n. see FRENCH CROWN n.

French handshake n. [1970s] (US teen) a form of handshake signifying sexual interest or invitation. [FRENCH adj. (2) + SE handshake]

French harp n. [late 19C–1940s] (US) a harmonica. [SE French + HARP n.[2] (1)]

French head job n. [1980s+] (gay) fellatio (cf. FRENCH n.[2]). [FRENCH adj. (4) + HEAD JOB n.]

Frenchie n.[1] (also **Frenchy**) **1** [mid-19C+] (US) a Frenchman, a person of French descent, a French-Canadian; one who is assumed to be French. **2** [late 19C] anyone seen in the street and classified as foreign. **3** [late 19C+] a term of address to a French person. **4** [20C+] (US) a Cajun. **5** [20C+] (W.I., St Kitts) a poor White, a descendant of the original French settlers on St Kitts who, as Roman Catholics, lost their status when the island was taken over by the Protestant British in 1690. **6** [1930s] something French, e.g. a play. [SE French + sfx -ie/-y]

Frenchie n.[2] see FRENCH n.[2] (3).

Frenchie adj. **1** [1910s–40s] lightheaded, frivolous. **2** [1910s+] (also **Frenchy**) French. **3** [1970s] (US campus) smartly dressed. [FRENCHIE n.[1] (1); (1) f. (2)]

frenchie n.[1] (also **frenchy**) [20C+] a contraceptive sheath. [abbr. FRENCH LETTER n. + sfx -ie]

frenchie n.[2] (also **frenchy**) **1** [20C+] (US) a foolish man. **2** [20C+] (US) a flighty woman. **3** [20C+] (Irish) a French kiss. **4** [1960s+] (US gay) a fellator. [stereotyping/FRENCH adj. (4)]

frenchie n.[3] (also **frenchy**) [1990s+] (N.Z.) a potato chip. [SE French fry]

frenchified adj. **1** [late 17C–early 19C] having venereal disease. **2** [1980s] usu. of a woman, sexually talented. [FRENCH adj. (1)/FRENCH adj. (2) + sfx -ified]

French inhale v. [1950s+] (US) to blow out cigarette smoke through the nose. [the supposed sophistication of the French]

French it v. see FRENCH v.[2] (1).

French job n. [1960s+] (US gay) fellatio (cf. FRENCH n.[2]). [FRENCH adj. (4) + JOB n.[4]]

French kiss n. [1930s+] a deep kiss, using the tongue as well as the lips. [FRENCH KISS v.]

French kiss v. [1910s+] to kiss with the tongue. [FRENCH adj. (2) + SE kiss]

French kiss filter n. [1950s+] (gay) any filter-tipped cigarette. [FRENCH KISS n.]

French lace n. [early 19C] brandy. [SE French/FRENCH n.[1]]

French lady n. (also **French woman**) [1980s] (US) a fellator. [FRENCH adj. (4)]

French language expert n. [1950s+] (gay) a fellator (cf. FRENCH n.[2]). [FRENCH adj. (4)]

French language training n. [1970s+] (*gay*) teaching another person fellatio (cf. FRENCH n.²). [FRENCH adj. (4)]

French leave n. [mid-18C+] absenting oneself from a job or duty without prior permission; thus *take French leave*, to do something without requesting permission. [negative national stereotyping]

French letter n. (*also* **letter**) [mid-19C+] a contraceptive sheath. [FRENCH adj. (2) + SE *letter*; accepted as SE since 1950s]

French loaf n. [20C+] £4. [rhy. sl. = ROUF n. (3)]

French love n. [20C+] fellatio (cf. FRENCH n.²). [FRENCH adj. (4) + SE *love*]

Frenchman n.¹ [mid-17C–early 19C] a scholar of French.

Frenchman n.² *see* FRANSMAN n.

Frenchman, the n. **1** [late 16C–19C] syphilis. **2** [late 19C–1900s] a bottle of brandy (cf. FRENCH n.¹). [the association of the disease and the drink with France]

Frenchman's parole v. [1950s] an escape from prison. [play on FRENCH LEAVE n.]

French marbles n. [late 16C] venereal disease, esp. syphilis. [FRENCH adj. (1); stereotyping]

French measles n. (*also* **French cannibal, French mole**) [early 17C–18C] venereal disease, esp. syphilis. [FRENCH adj. (1); stereotyping]

French off v. *see* FRENCH v.² (1).

French passive n. [1950s+] (*gay*) the fellator (cf. FRENCH n.²; FRENCH PASSIVE n.). [FRENCH adj. (4)]

French peasoup n. [19C+] (*US/Can.*) a French immigrant.

French photographer n. [1950s+] (*gay*) a homosexual photographer. [FRENCH adj. (4) + SE *photographer*]

French pig n. [late 19C–1900s] syphilis, esp. the syphilitic pustule or bubo. [FRENCH adj. (1) + PIG n.⁴]

French polishing n. [1980s] fellatio; thus *French polisher*, a fellatrix (cf. FRENCH n.²). [FRENCH adj. (4)]

French postcard n. **1** [1910s+] (*orig. US*) an erotic picture postcard. **2** [1950s+] (*gay*) an exciting prospective sexual partner. [FRENCH adj. (2) + SE *postcard/picture*]

French pox n. [early 16C–18C] venereal disease, esp. syphilis. [FRENCH adj. (1); stereotyping]

French prints n. **1** [mid-19C+] pornographic pictures and engravings. **2** [1950s+] (*gay*) unusual heterosexual pornography. [FRENCH adj. (2) + SE *prints*]

French razor n. [early 17C] syphilis. [FRENCH adj. (1) + the pain]

French revolution n. [1950s–60s] (*gay*) the movement for homosexual and lesbian rights. [FRENCH adj. (4) + SE *revolution*; pun on SE]

French safe n. [late 19C+] (*Can./US*) a condom. [FRENCH adj. (2) + SAFE n.¹]

French screwdriver n. [20C+] a hammer. [supposed French inability to perform simple manual tasks]

French 75 n. [1930s+] (*US*) a cocktail of champagne, cognac, lemon juice and sugar. [a tribute to the large French gun, used in WW1]

French stuff n. [1970s] (*gay*) **1** pornography. **2** any unusual sexual activity. [FRENCH adj. (2) + SE *stuff*]

French style n. [1970s] fellatio (cf. FRENCH n.²). [FRENCH adj. (4)]

French tickler n. (*also* **tickler**) [1910s+] a contraceptive sheath with extra protrusions for added stimulation. [FRENCH adj. (2) + SE *tickler*]

French tricks n. [1960s+] oral sex, of a man or a woman. [FRENCH adj. (4) + SE *tricks*; Williams cites 17C use of *French tricks* as a general euph. for degeneracy/debauchery]

French vanilla n. [1990s+] (*US Black teen*) **1** a sexy White woman. **2** a light-skinned Black woman. [play on popular variety of ice-cream]

French walk n. [late 19C] (*US*) the posture assumed by those being thrown bodily out of a saloon. [a pun on FROG n. (2) + SE

walk; unwelcome or obstreperous drinkers would be grasped by a couple of bouncers, held up with all 4 limbs spread out (like a frog) and tossed into the street]

French wank n. [1990s+] the action of being masturbated between a woman's breasts. [FRENCH adj. (2) + WANK n.¹ (1)]

French way n. [1960s+] fellatio (cf. FRENCH n.²). [FRENCH adj. (4) + SE *way*]

French welcome n. [17C] a dose of syphilis. [FRENCH adj. (1)]

French woman n.¹ [1920s+] (*W.I.*) a fortune-teller. [fig. use of *French* to mean strange, mysterious]

French woman n.² *see* FRENCH LADY n.

Frenchy/frenchy *see under* FRENCHIE/FRENCHIE.

freney n. [late 18C–early 19C] (*Irish*) a 1-eyed person. [the 18C highwayman James *Freney*, who had 1 eye]

fresh n. *see* FRESHER n.

fresh adj.¹ (*also* **freshish**) [19C] tipsy, slightly drunk (cf. ABOUT RIGHT phr.¹). [SE *fresh wind*, a light wind that is noticeable but that wouldn't blow one over; Egan, *Life in London* (1821) defines it as 'a country phrase altogether']

fresh adj.² [mid-19C+] familiar, cheeky, over-intimate. [earlier meaning of naïve, 'green'; the implication is that such a person would innocently presume a greater intimacy than is acceptable; Shakespeare uses the term similarly in *Measure for Measure* (1603): 'Your fresh whore', although the primary image is of a pun on SE *fresh*, unused]

fresh adj.³ **1** [20C+] (*W.I.*) sexually aggressive, making open advances to the opposite sex. **2** [1980s+] (*US Black/campus*) smart, 'on the ball', aware, attractive; a general term of approval, varying as to context and applying to objects and events as well as people.

fresh v. [1980s] (*US Black*) to compliment. [i.e. calling someone FRESH adj.³ (2)]

fresh adv. [1900s–30s] cheekily, familiarly. [FRESH adj.²]

fresh and fast adj. (*also* **fresh and forward**) [20C+] (*W.I.*) **1** cheeky and impertinent. **2** sexually promiscuous. **3** of meat, smelling raw (although not stale). **4** of fish, smelling stale, past it, 'off'. **5** of popular music, in the latest style.

fresh as paint adj. [1910s] (*Aus.*) naïve. [play on SE *fresh as paint*, blooming, healthy]

fresh bit n. [mid–late 19C] a sexually inexperienced woman; a new mistress. [SE *fresh* + BIT n.² (1)]

fresh bull n. *see* BULL n.¹⁰ (1).

fresh cat n. [1920s–30s] (*US tramp*) a new, inexperienced tramp. [CAT n.⁹]

fresh-cool adj. [1990s+] (*US Black*) used to describe any superlative example, according to context. [FRESH adj.³ (2) + COOL adj.¹ (6)]

fresh cow n. [1920s–30s] (*US tramp*) one who has just developed a venereal disease.

fresh cut n. [1980s+] (*US Black*) a short, neat haircut. [FRESH adj.³ (2) + SE *haircut*]

fresher n. (*also* **fresh, freshie**) [late 19C+] (*UK/US campus*) a student in their first term at a university. [one of the last survivors of the 'Oxford' -ER sfx]

fresh fish n. [late 19C+] **1** (*US prison*) a new inmate in a prison; thus *fresh fish special*, the prison crop given to a new inmate. **2** any novice, e.g. a new recruit. **3** a new young prostitute (cf. ALLEY CAT n.). [SE *fresh* + FISH n.⁶ (1)/FISH n.⁶ (3)/FISH n.¹ (3)]

fresh greens n. [mid–late 19C] a new, young prostitute. [SE *fresh* + GREENS n.²]

fresh hide n. [1980s+] (*US Black*) a new lover or sexual partner. [SE *fresh* + HIDE n.¹ (2)]

freshie n.¹ [1910s] (*US*) one who is considered sexually or verbally forward. [FRESH adj.²]

freshie n.² [1960s+] (*Aus.*) a *fresh*water crocodile. [abbr. + sfx *-ie*]

freshie n.³ *see* FRESHER n.

freshish adj. *see* FRESH adj.¹.

fresh lodger n. [20C+] (*Ulster*) a loaf of bread.

freshman *n.* [1950s] (*US drugs*) a novice drug user.

fresh meat *n.* **1** [19C+] a newly fledged prostitute (cf. BIT OF MUTTON n.). **2** [20C+] any form of novice, e.g. a new recruit. **3** [1960s+] a new sexual partner. **4** [1960s+] (*US Und.*) a new, young inmate, a potential victim of predatory prison homosexuals. [SE *fresh* + MEAT n.; pun]

fresh nugs *n. see* NUGS n.[2].

fresh off the irons *phr.* (*also* **new off the irons**) [late 17C–19C] newly graduated from university, just left school; thus inexperienced, brand-new. [SE *leg-irons*]

fresh out of *phr.* [20C+] (*US/Can.*) absolutely bereft of; usu. used of some form of commodity.

fresh union *adj.* [1980s+] (*US*) clean, healthy. [? SAmE *union suit*, a suit of 1-piece underwear]

fresh-up *adj.* [20C+] (*W.I.*) **1** precocious. **2** sexually cheeky, suggestive. [FRESH adj.[2]/FRESH adj.[3] (1)]

fresh vegetable *n.* [1990s+] (*W.I.*) a young man who is dating an older woman.

freshwater *n.* **1** [mid–late 19C] an emigrant who works their passage rather than pays a fare. **2** [20C+] (*W.I., Trin.*) a West Indian who visits America and comes back with a US accent.

Freshwater Bay *n.* [early–mid-19C] (*UK Und.*) **1** the Fleet prison (cf. ABBOTT'S PRIORY n.). **2** Fleet Street Market. [the then adjacent Fleet River; the prison closed in 1842, the market in 1826]

freshwater mariner *n.* (*also* **freshwater seaman**) [mid-16C–17C] (*UK Und.*) 'their shippes were drowned in the playne of Salisbury' (Harman), such criminal beggars claimed to have suffered shipwreck or piracy and requested alms to return home (cf. CANTING CREW n.).

freshwater soldier *n.* [early 17C] a professional beggar who trades on his spurious reminiscences of battles and campaigns of which, in fact, he has no personal experience.

freshwater trout *n.* [1940s] (*US Black*) an attractive woman, usu. in a group. [play on FISH n.[1] (4)]

fresh-whites *n.* [late 19C] a pallid complexion.

fress *v.* [20C+] (*orig. US*) **1** to eat greedily, to snack. **2** to perform oral intercourse, usu. cunnilingus (cf. BOX LUNCH n.). [Yid. *fress*, to eat/EAT v.[3] (1)]

fresser *n.* [20C+] (*US*) **1** a glutton. **2** one who performs cunnilingus or fellatio. [FRESS v.]

fret one's cream *v.* [mid-19C] to worry.

fret oneself to fiddlestrings *v.* [mid-19C–1920s] to worry to excess.

fret one's fat *v.* [late 19C+] to worry; also as phr. *God fret my fat.*

fret one's gizzard *v.* (*also* **fret one's eyelids**, **...giblets**, **...guts**, **...kidney**, **...soul**) [mid-16C–19C] to worry. [vry *see* VRY v.

frey *v. see* VRY v.

friar tuck *n.* [20C+] sexual intercourse; thus as a euph; also as excl. [rhy. sl. = FUCK n.[1] (1)]

friar tuck *v.* [20C+] to have sexual intercourse. [FRIAR TUCK n.]

friar tucked *adj.* [1990s+] a euph. for FUCKED adj.[1]. [FRIAR TUCK n.]

fribble *n.* [mid-17C–mid-19C] a sexually inadequate male; thus adj. *fribbled, fribbling*; as v., to behave in a sexually inadequate manner. [echoic + ? SE *frivol*]

frick and frack *n.* [1980s+] (*US Black*) the testicles (cf. BANGERS n.). [echoic of the sound of their knocking together; ult. *Frick and Frack*, the 1920s–30s Swiss comedy skating team, who performed in the US and Europe. They were famous for a routine where they would put the heels of their skates together, bend their knees and skate in large circles with their bodies leaning outwards]

frickinchaten *n.* [2000s] (*US Black*) talking seductively to a woman. [? FRIGGING n. (4) + SE *chatting*]

fricking *adj.* [1930s+] a euph. for FUCKING adj. (1).

Friday face *n.* [late 16C–1910s] a miserable or dour face; thus

Friday-faced, miserable, gloomy. [Friday's trad. status as a day of abstinence either from all food or from meat]

fridge *n.* **1** [1910s+] (*Aus.*) a prison. **2** [1990s+] a person, usu. a woman who is frigid.

fridge freezer *n.* [2000s] a man. [rhy. sl. = GEEZER n.[1] (1)]

fried *adj.*[1] **1** [1920s+] very drunk; thus *fried to the gills/tonsils*, extremely drunk. **2** [1960s] (*US*) dead. **3** [1960s+] (*drugs*) extremely intoxicated by a drug, usu. cannabis. **4** [1960s+] (*US campus*) angry. **5** [1970s+] (*US*) (*also* **fried out**) very tired, worn-out, hungover. **6** [1980s] (*US campus*) defunct. [fig. uses of SE]

fried *adj.*[2] [1980s] (*US campus*) sunburned.

fried bread *adj.* [1990s+] dead. [rhy. sl.]

fried carpet *n.* [late 19C] fish and chips. [? resemblance of the fried fish]

fried, dyed, laid to the side *adj.* (*also* **fried, dyed, swept to the side; fried, dyed, swooped to the side**) [1970s+] (*US Black*) straightened Black hair that is attempting to emulate the texture and even colour of a White person's hair. [FRY (ONE'S HAIR) v.; the 3 processes that are undertaken to straighten and arrange Black hair into a 'White' style]

fried eggs *n.*[1] [20C+] (*Aus.*) legs. [rhy. sl.]

fried eggs *n.*[2] [1930s+] (*orig. Aus.*) small or undeveloped female breasts (cf. APPLES n.[1]). [supposed resemblance]

fried fish wrapper *n. see* FISH WRAPPER n.

fried out *adj. see* FRIED adj.[1] (5).

fried potato *n.* (*also* **baked potato**) [1920s] (*US*) a waiter. [rhy. sl.; note Cockney pron. 'potater']

fried rice *n.* [20C+] (*Aus.*) the price. [rhy. sl.]

fried shirt *n.* [20C+] (*US*) a heavily starched shirt, a dress shirt. [var. on BOILED SHIRT n. (1)]

friend *n.*[1] [early 19C; 1950s–60s] a prostitute's boyfriend or lover, but not necessarily her pimp.

friend *n.*[2] [1940s+] (*US Black*) menstruation; thus euph. phr. *I have friends to stay*, I am menstruating.

friend-boy *n.* (*also* **friend-girl**) [1900s–70s] (*US Black/Southern*) a boyfriend or girlfriend.

friend form *n.* [1950s+] (*US prison*) official papers that must be completed to facilitate outside visits to the inmates.

friendly lead *n.* [late 19C] a subscription to help an unfortunate friend, usu. held by a 'whip-round' in a public house.

friendly pannikin *n.* [late 19C] (*Aus.*) a shared drink. [the *pannikin* or small tin container from which many Aus. 'diggers' ate and drank]

friendly road, the *n.* [1930s] (*N.Z.*) of workers, the decision to side with one's employer during an industrial dispute.

friend of Dorothy('s) *n. see* DOROTHY'S FRIEND n.

friend of Oscar *n.* [1920s+] a male homosexual (cf. ABIGAIL n.). [the gay icon, playwright Oscar Wilde (1854–1901)]

friend of Pedro *n. see* PEDRO n.[2].

frig *n.* **1** [late 18C–19C] an act of masturbation. **2** [late 19C+] sexual intercourse. **3** [1940s+] a euph. for FUCK n.[4] in various contexts. **4** [1990s+] (*US gay*) lesbian sexual intercourse, based on the partners rubbing against each other's body. [FRIG v.]

frig *v.* **1** [early 16C+] to have sexual intercourse; latterly used as a euph. for FUCK v.[1] (cf. FIRK v.; FURGLE v.; ROOT v.[3]; ROOT, HOG OR DIE n.; SCREW v.[2]; SHAG v.[1]; STUFF v.[1]). **2** [late 16C+] to masturbate (cf. BOFF v.). **3** [mid-17C+] to masturbate another person. **4** [late 17C–1950s] to cheat. **5** [late 18C+] to trifle or fool around. **6** [1920s+] a euph. for FUCK v.[1] in non-sexual senses, e.g. to waste time, to cause someone trouble, as FUCK v.[3] etc. **7** [1930s] (*US*) to cause to happen. **8** [1950s+] to perform lesbian sex, where the genitals are rubbed together. [Lat. *fricare*, to rub; note 18C SE *frication*, rubbing, in sexual context masturbating a partner]

frig about *v.* (*also* **frig around**) [1920s+] to trifle, to waste time, to fool around. [FRIG v. (6)]

frigate *n.* [mid-17C–19C] a woman. [SE *frigate*, a light, swift vessel; there may also be some punning connection to FRIG v. (1)]

frigate on fire n. [early–mid-19C] a prostitute who has venereal disease. [FRIGATE n. + FIRE n.[1]]

frigate well rigged n. [late 17C–18C] an attractive, well-dressed woman. [FRIGATE n. + SE *well-rigged*]

frig-beard n. [early 18C] a degenerate, a seducer. [FRIG v. (1) + SE *beard*; the image is of the adult, bearded male]

frigged out adj. [late 19C] exhausted by excessive masturbation and thus incapable of ejaculation. [FRIG v. (2)]

frigger n.[1] **1** [late 17C] the finger or hand with which one masturbates. **2** [late 17C] the penis. **3** [late 19C–1900s] a masturbator. [FRIG v.]

frigger n.[2] [1950s] a general derog. term. [FRIG v. (1); semi-euph. for FUCKER n. (3)]

frigging n. **1** [late 16C+] an act of masturbation. **2** [late 19C+] an act of copulation. **3** [1920s] a beating, lit. or fig. **4** [1940s–50s] attrib., pertaining to sex; thus *frigging book*, a pornographic magazine. [FRIG v.]

frigging adj. **1** [late 18C] insignificant, petty, worthless. **2** [late 19C+] a euph. for FUCKING adj. **3** [1970s+] as an infix. [FRIG v. (1)]

friggish adj. [1960s] sexy. [FRIG v. (1)]

frigg-up n. *see* FRIG-UP n.

frigg up v. *see* FRIG UP v.

fright n. [mid-18C+] a person or thing of a shocking, grotesque, unkempt or ridiculous appearance.

frighten adj. [1990s+] (*W.I.*) easily impressed.

frightener n. (*also* **frighteners**) **1** [1930s+] (*also* **frights**) threats, violence, anything that will terrify a given person into doing what is required. **2** [1960s] fear; thus *get the frighteners*, to become terrified. **3** [1960s+] a thug, esp. as used by gangsters, casino-owners etc to commit violence for them.

frighten Friday n. [20C+] (*W.I.*) a timid person. [SE *frighten*, frightened + FRAIDY adj. or *Man Friday*, the Black character in Daniel Defoe's *Robinson Crusoe* (1719)]

frighten into (forty) fits v. [late 19C+] to terrify someone.

frighten the Jew Jesus out of v. [1940s] (*Irish*) to terrify.

frighten the (living) daylights out of v. (*also* **frighten the shite out of, …lard out of**) [late 19C+] to terrify. [SE *frighten* + DAYLIGHTS n. (2)/SHITE n. (5)/LARD n. (3)]

frightful adj. [mid-18C+] a general intensifier, awful, terrible, annoying, shocking. ['A cant word among women for anything unpleasing' (Johnson, *Dictionary*, 1755)]

frightfully adv. (*also* **frightful**) [mid-19C+] extremely, very much. [now only used ironically or in mockery of 'upper-class' usage]

frights n. *see* FRIGHTENER n. (1).

frig off v. [20C+] to masturbate, oneself or another (cf. BALL OFF v.[2]). [FRIG v.]

frig off! excl. *see* FUCK OFF! excl.

frig pig n. [late 18C–19C] a fussy, trifling person. [FRIG v. (5) + SE *pig*]

frigster n. (*also* **frigstress**) [late 17C–19C] a masturbator. [FRIG v. (2) + -STER sfx/-*stress*]

frig-up n. (*also* **frigg-up**) [1940s+] (*orig. Aus.*) a disaster, a blunder, a mess. [FRIG UP v.; semi-euph. for FUCKUP n. (1)]

frig up v. (*also* **frigg up**) [1930s+] (*orig. Aus.*) to make a blunder, to make a mess of; thus *frigged up*. [FRIG v. (6); semi-euph. for FUCK UP v. (1)]

frig you! excl. [1960s+] a semi-euph. synon. for FUCK YOU! excl.

frig your buddy week phr. *see* FUCK YOUR BUDDY WEEK phr.

fri-high-day n. [1990s+] (*US Black teen*) a day devoted to drinking. [? play on FLY HIGH v./FRY ONE'S BRAINS v.; SE *Friday* being the typical day for drinking]

frijole-eater n. (*also* **frijole guzzler**) [20C+] (*US*) a derog. term for a Mexican (cf. BEAN n.[8]). [Mex. Sp. *frijol*, a bean + SE *eater*]

frikkie n. (*also* **frikky**) [1970s+] (*S.Afr.*) a condom. [? FRIG v. (1)]

frildo adv. [1990s+] (*US Black teen*) really, honestly, a phr. of agreement or assertion. [elided pron. of 'FOR REAL adv. though']

frill n.[1] [1920s–60s] a woman. [her clothing]

frill n.[2] *see* FRILLS n.

frilled lizard n. [20C+] (*Aus.*) a bearded man.

frillery n. [19C] women's underwear; thus *explore someone's frillery*, to caress a woman intimately.

frillies n. [20C+] a frilled feminine undergarment.

frills n. (*also* **frill**) [mid-19C+] affectations of dress, speech, writing, painting or manner; ornamentation for its own sake.

frilly adj. [20C+] (*Aus./US*) arrogant, pretentious, snobbish.

frimped adj. [1920s–40s] (*US Black*) ugly, unattractive; thus *frimpet*, a term of abuse, an ugly person. [? SE *frump*]

fringe v. [1940s] (*US Black campus*) to sponge.

fringer n. [1940s–50s] an outcast; one who exists on the *fringes* of a given group.

fringes n. [1940s] (*US Black campus*) eyes.

frip n. (*also* **friphead**) [1970s+] (*US campus*) a weak, ineffectual person. [? SE *frippery* or FRIPPING n.]

frip v. [1960s] to tease.

frippet n. [20C+] a frivolous or showy young woman. [? *flibbertigibbet*]

fripping n. [1910s–20s] domestic bickering between husband and wife. [? SE *fripperies* or Lancashire dial. *frip*, something worthless]

'Frisco n. [mid-19C+] (*US*) San Francisco. [abbr.]

frisco n. (*also* **frisko**) [mid-17C] a term of endearment. [a 'frisky' person]

frisco v. [1930s] (*US gang*) to act in a provocative manner. [? stereotyping of 'FRISCO n.]

'Frisco speedball n. (*also* **'Frisco special**) [1960s–70s] (*drugs*) a drug cocktail containing LSD, cocaine and heroin.

frisk n.[1] **1** [early 18C+] sexual intercourse. **2** [early–mid-19C] fun, amusement.

frisk n.[2] (*also* **frisking**) [late 18C+] (*orig. UK Und.*) a search. [FRISK v.[2] (1)]

frisk v.[1] [mid-16C–19C] to have sexual intercourse; to be adulterous; thus *frisking*, foreplay; *frisker*, one who engages in sexual intercourse, a prostitute.

frisk v.[2] **1** [early 18C+] (*orig. UK Und.*) (*also* **fisk, friz**) to search, usu. for weapons, illicit drugs, stolen goods etc; usu. of people, occas. things. **2** [late 18C+] (*orig. US*) to rob or steal, esp. from a sleeping or helpless person. **3** [early 19C] to trick, to hoax. **4** [mid-19C; 1960s] to search, e.g. one's own pockets, in a non-criminal context. [one's hands or schemes 'frisk' over the victim]

frisk and frolic n. [late 19C–1910s] carbolic (soap). [rhy. sl.]

frisker n. **1** [19C+] a pilferer, a petty thief; a pickpocket. **2** [mid-19C] (*UK Und.*) one who conducts a body search. [FRISK v.[2]]

frisk in a hempen cravat v. *see* HEMPEN CRAVAT n.

frisking n. *see* FRISK n.[2].

frisko n. *see* FRISCO n.

frisk the whiskers v. [1930s–40s] (*US Black/jazz*) to play a few bars preparatory to a session.

frisky adj. [late 19C–1900s] ill-tempered.

frisky powder n. [1950s] (*drugs*) cocaine (cf. BIRDIE POWDER n.). [its effects]

frit n. [1940s–60s] (*US*) an effeminate male homosexual. [FRIT adj.; his supposed cowardice]

frit adj. [20C+] frightened. [SE *fright*, to scare, to terrify]

frito n. [1950s–60s] (*US*) a derog. term for a Mexican or Spanish-American (cf. BEAN n.[8]). [advertisements for *Frito Bandito* corn chips, which feature a stereotypical 'Mexican bandit']

frito toes n. [1980s+] (*US campus*) very smelly feet. [brandname *Fritos*, a US snack food]

fritter around v. (*US*) **1** [1950s] to act nervously. **2** [1990s+] to waste time, to act ineffectually.

fritters! *excl.* [1900s] (*Aus.*) an excl. of dismissal or contempt.

Fritz *n.* (*also* **Fritzer, Fritzey, Fritzie**) [late 19C+] a German, esp. a German soldier. [Ger. dimin. of proper name *Friedrich*; the usage emerged *c.*1880 but came into widespread use during WW1, although it fell from favour afterwards; Brophy & Partridge, *Songs and Slang of the British Soldier* (1930), suggest it was generally replaced by JERRY *n.* after 1915]

Fritz *adj.* [1910s] German. [FRITZ *n.*]

fritz *n.* (*also* **pork fritz**) [20C+] (*Aus.*) a large, but not especially spicy sausage. [Ger. name *Fritz*, linked to a German sausage]

fritz *v.* (*US*) **1** [1910s+] (*also* **fritz out**) to go out of order, to break down, to malfunction. **2** [1940s+] to put out of order, to break. [ON THE FRITZ *phr.* (3)]

Fritzer/Fritzey/Fritzie *n. see* FRITZ *n.*

fritzy *n.* [1930s] (*US Und.*) an epileptic beggar, or one who poses as such. [ON THE FRITZ *phr.* (2)]

friz *v. see* FRISK *v.*[2] (1).

friz out *v.* [1990s+] (*US teen*) to lose one's temper, to argue. [ext. FRITZ *v.* (1)]

frizzle *n.*[1] [18C] the vagina. [abbr. OLD FRIZZLE *n.* (2)]

frizzle *n.*[2] [mid-19C] champagne. [? FIZZ *n.*[1] (3)]

frizzler *n. see* SIZZLER *n.* (2).

fro *n. see* FROE *n.*[1].

'fro *see under* AFRO.

frock *n.*[1] [1900s–10s] a man wearing a frock-coat. **2** [1920s] (*US Und.*) a suit of clothes.

frock *n.*[2] [1980s+] (*US gay*) the man who poses as a lesbian's 'husband' for the sake of 'passing' in an intolerant society. [the image of the lesbian as a trouser-wearing woman for whom a frock is automatically unnatural]

frock *n.*[3] [1980s+] (*UK juv.*) a euph. substitute for FUCK *n.*[1] in various contexts.

frock and frill *n.* [late 19C–1900s] a chill. [rhy. sl.]

frocked down *adj.* [1940s] (*US Black/Harlem*) of a woman, dressed up. [SE *frock*]

frocker *n.* [1900s–10s] (*Aus.*) a woman dressed up in a (fashionable) frock; thus **frocky**, fashionably dressed.

frock-hitcher *n.* [late 19C–1900s] a milliner.

froe *n.*[1] (*also* **fro, vroe, vrow**) [mid-17C–early 19C] a woman, esp. a prostitute; also as *adj.*, female, e.g. *fro file*, a female pickpocket. [Du. *vrouw*, a woman]

froe *n.*[2] [late 19C–1930s] (*US Black*) a trad. plantation slave pocket knife. [ety. unknown]

Frog *n.* **1** [mid-17C–18C] a Dutch person. **2** [mid-17C+] (*also* **bullfrog**) a French person. **3** [mid-19C] (*US*) a contemptible person. **4** [1910s] (*Aus.*) a French franc. **5** [1920s+] the French language. **6** [1970s+] (*Can.*) a French-Canadian. **7** [1980s] (*US*) a Cajun. [orig. 14C SE *frog*, a contemptible or offensive person; used in early 17C to refer to Jesuits, then in 1650 to the Dutch, England's national enemy; when they were replaced by the French, the def. changed accordingly]

frog *n.*[1] [mid–late 19C] (*US*) a policeman (cf. ANIMAL *n.*[1]). [his sudden 'leaping' onto criminals]

frog *n.*[2] [late 19C–1900s] a foot; thus *on the frog*, walking. [SE *frog*, an elastic, horny substance growing in the middle of the sole of a horse's hoof]

frog *n.*[3] **1** [20C+] (*US Black/campus/Und.*) (*also* **alligator skin, frogskin**) a banknote, $1 bill (cf. BAT HIDE *n.*). **2** [1920s] (*US Und.*) a counterfeit dollar bill. **3** [1930s–60s] (*Aus.*) a £1 note. [such notes are/were green; Franklyn, *Dict. of Rhyming Slang* (1960), suggests rhy. sl. *frogskin* = SE *sovereign*]

frog *n.*[4] (*US campus*) **1** [1940s–70s] a freshman. **2** [1960s+] a grade of F (cf. ACE *n.*[6]). [initial letters]

frog *n.*[5] [1950s+] (*orig. Aus.*) a condom. [pun on FROG *n.* (2), i.e. a FRENCH LETTER *n.*]

frog *n.*[6] *see* FROG (AND TOAD) *n.*

frog *adj.* [1910s+] French. [FROG *n.* (2)]

frog *v.*[1] **1** [late 19C] to write for money. **2** [1900s+] (*US campus*) to cheat. [stereotype of the French as deceitful and idle]

frog *v.*[2] [1960s] (*US Black*) to leap, to jump.

frog (and toad) *n.* [mid-19C+] the road. [rhy. sl.]

frog and toad *v.* **1** [late 19C] (*also* **frog it**) to walk. **2** [1980s+] (*Aus. prison*) to leave, esp. to escape. [FROG (AND TOAD) *n.*]

frog and toe *n.* [mid-19C] **1** London. **2** (*US Und.*) New York City. [ety. unknown; Franklyn, *Dict. of Rhyming Slang* (1960), suggests for (1) that it was a destination towards which one travels on FROG *n.*[2] i.e. foot + *toe*]

frog-eater *n.* [late 18C+] a French person; thus *adj. frog-eating*.

frog eggs *n. see* FROG'S EGGS *n.*

frog-footed *adj.* (*also* **flat-footed**) [late 19C–1900s] used of one who travels on foot.

froggie *n.* (*also* **froggee, froggy**) **1** [mid-19C+] (*orig. US*) a French person. **2** [1930s+] the French language. [FROG *n.* (2)/FROG *n.* (5)]

froggy *adj.*[1] (*also* **froggie**) [mid-19C+] French. [FROGGIE *n.* (1)]

froggy *adj.*[2] (*also* **froggish**) [1960s+] (*US Black*) aggressive, belligerent, keen to fight, keen to start 'jumping'; thus FEEL FROGGY *v.*

frog in the throat *n.* [1950s+] a boat. [rhy. sl.]

frog it *v. see* FROG AND TOAD *v.* (1).

Frogland *n.* [mid-19C+] France. [FROG *n.* (2)]

froglanders *n.* [late 17C–mid-19C] the Dutch. [FROG *n.* (1) + SE *frogland*, marshy land that is full of frogs, orig. used of the Fens and of Holland]

frogmarch *v.* (*also* **frog's-march**) [mid-19C+] to carry someone face-down, one person holding onto each limb; used on drunks or recalcitrant prisoners. [the image of a spreadeagled frog]

Frogolia *n.* [1970s+] (*N.Z.*) a derog. term for France; thus *Frogolian*, a French person. [FROG *n.* (2)]

frog's eggs *n.* (*also* **frog eggs, frog's eyes**) [1910s+] boiled sago or tapioca (pudding) (cf. FISHEYES *n.*).

frog's eyebrows *n. see* CAT'S WHISKERS *n.*

frogsh *n.* [1910s] (*Aus.*) nonsense, rubbish. [abbr. *frogshit*]

frog's hair *n.* [late 19C+] the very smallest degree; in phr. like *within a frog's hair*, *to a frog's hair*.

frogskin *n.*[1] [1920s+] (*orig. Aus./N.Z.*) a condom.

frogskin *n.*[2] *see* FROG *n.*[3] (1).

frog's-march *v. see* FROGMARCH *v.*

frog (spawn) *n.* [1990s+] an erection. [rhy. sl. = HORN *n.*[2] (3)]

frogspawn *n.* [1950s+] (*mainly school*) sago or tapioca (cf. FISHEYES *n.*).

frogsticker *n.* [mid-19C+] (*US*) a long-bladed pocket-knife.

frog-swallower *n.* [late 19C] a derog. term for a French person. [the stereotyped eating of frogs by the French]

frog's wine *n.* [mid-19C] **1** brandy. **2** gin. [(1) FROG *n.* (2); (2) FROG *n.* (1) + SE *wine*; brandy is always linked to France, gin to Holland]

frogtown *n.* [19C+] (*US*) a small or out-of-the-way place. [the swampy, frog-ridden pond that is trad. associated with such rural settlements]

frog up *v.* **1** [1920s–60s] (*US Black*) to cheat, to confuse, to trick. **2** [1920s–60s] (*US Black*) to be confused, to be tricked. **3** [1950s–70s] (*US*) to waste time, to idle on the job. [ext. FROG *v.*[1] (2)]

frolic pad *n.* [1940s] (*US Black*) a nightclub. [SE *frolic* + PAD *n.*[2] (2)]

from *prep.* [20C+] because of, as a result of; used in a variety of combs., e.g. *from hunger*, *from grief*.

fromage *adj.* [1920s+] (*US campus*) objectionable. [Fr. *fromage*, cheese, i.e. CHEESY *adj.*[2] (1)]

from a (great) height *phr.* [1970s+] intensely.

from Alice Springs to breakfast time *phr.* [1930s+] (*Aus.*) everywhere.

from arsehole to breakfast table *phr.* [1940s+] (*N.Z.*) completely, entirely. [ARSEHOLE *n.* (1)]

from arsehole to breakfast time *phr.* (*also* **from haircut to**

breakfast time) [late 19C+] **1** all the way, all the time. **2** (*Aus.*) referring to a chaotic situation. [ARSEHOLE n. (1)]

from asshole to appetite *phr.* [1950s] (*US*) thoroughly, absolutely, totally. [ASSHOLE n.¹ (1)]

from back *phr.* [1930s–50s] (*US Black*) for a long time. [abbr. SE *from way back*, from a long time ago]

from bitter creek *phr.* [late 19C–1900s] (*US, Western*) very tough. [the image of Bitter Creek, Wyoming, as an outlaw town]

from boots to breakfast *phr. see* FROM HELL TO BREAKFAST phr.

from can to can't *phr.* [1960s+] (*US*) all day long. [from dawn, when one *can* see the sun, to dusk, when one *can't* see the sun; also the image of one's waning strength as the day continues]

from Chicago *phr.* **1** [1950s] (*US Und.*) of a fellow criminal, acceptable, trustworthy. **2** [1980s+] (*US campus*) unaware of what's going on, behaving like an 'air-head'. [(1) Chicago's association with gangster Al Capone; (2) play on Chicago as the WINDY CITY n. (1)]

from Dogleg to the Day of Judgement *phr.* [1900s] (*Aus.*) anywhere; everywhere.

from ears to crupper *phr.* [1900s] (*Aus.*) to the fullest extent. [horse imagery]

from go to whoa *phr.* [1970s+] (*Aus.*) from start to finish.

from haircut to breakfast time *phr. see* FROM ARSEHOLE TO BREAKFAST TIME phr.

from head to heinie *phr. see* HEINIE n.² (1).

from hell to breakfast *phr.* (*also* **from boots to breakfast**) [late 19C+] (*US*) **1** in all directions, everywhere. **2** decisively, violently. **3** for a long time, for a long distance. **4** to a very great extent.

from hell to Hackney *phr.* [early 19C] extensively, to a great degree.

from here to hell and gone *phr. see* HELL AND GONE phr.

from horse and buggy *phr.* [2000s] unsophisticated, from the backwoods.

from in front *phr.* [1950s–60s] (*orig US Black/jazz*) from the beginning.

from Mars *phr.* [1980s+] (*US*) weird, bizarre, eccentric. [the image of 'little green men']

from now on *n.* [1930s–50s] (*US Und.*) a life sentence; indefinite confinement on the punishment block.

frompy *adj.* [1930s–40s] (*US Black*) of a woman, dowdy, ill-kempt. [pron. of SE *frumpy*]

from shit to Shinnecock *phr.* [1970s] (*US*) of any sort whatsoever, across the entire spectrum.

from soup to nuts *phr.* (*also* **from soda to hock**) [late 19C+] (*US*) from first to last, completely, comprehensively. [the image is of a meal]

from the door *phr.* [1960s] (*US*) from the very beginning.

from the drop *phr.* [20C+] from the outset. [the drop of a flag that signals the start of a race]

from the gate *phr.* [1940s+] from the outset, from the beginning. [racecourse jargon]

from the giddy-ap *phr.* (*also* **from the giddyup**) [1970s+] (*orig. US*) right from the start, the beginning; often as *right/ straight...* [the image is of starting a horse with a cry of *Giddyap!*]

from the git-go *phr.* (*also* **from the get, ...get-go, ...git**) [1960s+] (*orig. US Black*) from the very start. [SE *get ready, get set, go!*]

from the ground up *phr.* [late 19C+] **1** (*US*) of a person, sturdy. **2** (*orig. US*) from the very beginning, from first principles, in essence.

from the rip *phr.* [1990s+] (*US Black*) from the start. [? RIP AND RUN v.]

from the sublime to the gorblimey *phr.* (*also* **from the sublime to the ridiculous**) [20C+] to the absolute extreme. [SE + GORBLIMEY! excl.]

froncey *n.* [mid–late 19C] a Frenchman, the French language. [mispron. of Fr. *Français*, French]

frone *n.* [1940s] (*US Black*) an unattractive woman. [? Ger. *Frau*, woman or SE *frown* + *crone*]

Front, the *n.* **1** [1940s+] (*UK gay/Und.*) any street that is known as a centre of street prostitution, e.g. Piccadilly, Oxford Street. **2** [1950s] (*UK teen*) the main street of a gang's territory.

front *n.*¹ **1** [19C+] (*orig. UK society*) (*also* **frontage**) cheek, audacity. **2** [mid-19C+] self-respect, 'face'. **3** [mid-19C+] a respectable appearance, esp. as a mask for illegal activities; used of both people and places. **4** [late 19C+] (*UK Und.*) anything one needs, fancy clothes, a clever line of patter, a personal style, a mental attitude, for the successful promotion of one's schemes. **5** [20C+] one who maintains a respectable appearance for the pursuit of crime. **6** [1910s] (*US Und.*) an assistant, usu. for purposes of diversion, in a criminal act. **7** [1980s] (*US drugs*) a payment for drugs, i.e. not on consignment.

front *n.*² **1** [late 19C–1920s] (*US Und.*) a watch and chain; jewellery. **2** [late 19C–1970s] (*US*) a suit of clothes.

front *n.*³ [1950s] (*US Black*) a place.

front *n.*⁴ [1990s+] (*UK Und.*) prostitution. [? FRONT, THE n. (1)]

front *n.*⁵ *see* FRONT LINE n.

front *n.*⁶ *see* FRONT MONEY n.

front *adj.* [1930s+] providing a respectable image for illegal activities. [FRONT n.¹ (3)]

front *v.*¹ **1** [late 16C; mid-19C+] to confront. **2** [mid-19C–1910s] (*UK Und.*) of a pickpocket team, to distract a victim's attention while the actual theft is carried out. **3** [1960s–70s] (*also* **front up**) to approach. **4** [1960s+] (*US campus/Black*) to disrespect, to snub. [SE *confront*]

front *v.*² (*also* **front for**) **1** [late 19C+] (*US Und.*) to act as a decoy for a fellow criminal. **2** [1920s+] (*orig. US*) to be the public face or maintain a respectable image for what is in fact a criminal organization, e.g. a restaurant, a nightclub. **3** [1930s] (*US Und.*) to take the blame. **4** [1960s] to represent, e.g. as a lawyer. **5** [1960s+] (*US Black*) (*also* **front off**) to deceive, to trick, esp. with glib verbosity for monetary or sexual gain. **6** [1970s+] (*US Black*) (*also* **front off, front out**) to pose as something one is not. **7** [1970s+] (*US Black*) (*also* **front off**) to show off, to pose. **8** [1990s+] (*US campus*) to act foolishly. [FRONT n.¹]

front *v.*³ [1940s+] (*Aus.*) to appear in front of.

front *v.*⁴ [1960s+] to advance either money or any other commodity (esp. drugs) as a loan or a sample of goods on offer; when buying drugs the seller may ask for the money to be 'fronted' so he, in turn, can make a bulk purchase from his superior in the sales chain. [UP FRONT adv. (1)]

front *v.*⁵ *see* FRONT OFF v.².

fronta *n.* [20C+] (*W.I. Rasta*) a tobacco leaf used to roll a marijuana cigarette. [it provides a *front* to the marijuana within]

frontage *n.*¹ [mid-19C+] **1** the face. **2** a woman's chest, i.e. breasts.

frontage *n.*² *see* FRONT n.¹ (1).

front and rear *n.* [1990s+] a year. [rhy. sl.]

front attic *n.* [19C] the vagina (cf. BELLY ENTRANCE n.).

front bottom *n.* [1980s+] the vagina (cf. BELLY ENTRANCE n.).

front bum *n.* [1980s+] the labia majora; the vagina (cf. BELLY ENTRANCE n.). [SE *front* + BUM n.¹ (1)]

front door *n.* [late 19C+] the female genitals; thus *do a bit of front-door work*, to have sexual intercourse.

front door *adj.* [1980s+] (*Aus. prison*) honest.

front-door mat *n.* [1950s+] female pubic hair. [FRONT DOOR n. + play on SE *mat*]

front entrance *n.* [late 19C] the vagina (cf. BELLY ENTRANCE n.).

fronter *n.* **1** [1930s] (*US tramp*) one who maintains a respectable appearance as a mask for criminality. **2** [1970s+] (*US Black*) a show-off. [FRONT v.²]

front for v. *see* FRONT v.[2].

front garden n. (*also* **front gate**) [19C] the vagina (cf. BEAUTY SPOT n.; BELLY ENTRANCE n.).

front gee n. [1930s–40s] (*US Und.*) a member of a pickpocket team who diverts the victim. [FRONT adj. + GEE n.[3] (1)]

front gut n. [19C] the vagina (cf. BELLY ENTRANCE n.).

frontispiece n. **1** [18C–1910s] the face. **2** [mid-19C] the forehead.

front job n. [1930s] (*US Und.*) a bank robbery in which no money is taken from the safe; only that in the tellers' drawers. [SE *front*, i.e. of the bank (rather than the hidden strongroom) + JOB n.[3] (1)]

front line n. (*also* **front, line**) [1970s+] **1** (*W.I./UK Black teen*) the main street or area, the main area of attraction or focus of activities. **2** (*UK Black*) that area of a city where the Black community is most likely to clash with the forces of White law and order, e.g. at various times All Saints Road, Notting Hill, Railton Road, Brixton etc. [weakened/fig. use of milit. *front line*, the place where 2 opposing armies face each other]

frontload v. [1990s+] (*US campus*) to get drunk before attending an event where no alcohol will be available. [SE *frontload*, 'to concentrate a load at the front of (a vehicle)' (*OED*)]

front-man n. [1930s+] (*orig. US*) anyone who covers for illegal activities, posing as a 'legitimate' citizen. [FRONT adj. + SE *man*]

front marriage n. [1950s+] (*US gay*) an unconsummated marriage between a gay man and a gay woman to satisfy the norms of non-gay society. [FRONT adj./FRONT n.[1] (3) + SE *marriage*]

front money n. (*also* **front**) **1** [1920s+] any form of money paid over in advance. **2** [1930s+] (*US*) money to show and impress others. **3** [1960s+] (*drugs*) money advanced to a dealer for the purchase of drugs.

front name n. [late 19C–1910s] a given or Christian name.

front off v.[1] [1980s+] (*US prison*) **1** to betray, to inform on, to reveal information about. **2** to confide in. **3** to confront. **4** to put someone else in trouble. [SE *confront*]

front off v.[2] *see* FRONT v.[2].

front on v. [1960s+] (*US Black*) to pretend, to deceive; the image of putting up a front. [ext. FRONT v.[1] (4)]

front oneself off v. [1960s] (*orig. US Black*) to reveal oneself, one's motives, actions etc. [? FRONT OFF v.[1] (1), although this predates; ? FRONT v.[2] (5)]

front out v. *see* FRONT v.[2] (6).

front parlour n. [late 19C] the vagina (cf. BELLY ENTRANCE n.).

front porch n. **1** [1910s] (*US*) a protruding stomach. **2** [1970s] the penis.

front room n. **1** [early 19C] the vagina (cf. BELLY ENTRANCE n.). **2** [1930s–50s] (*US Und.*) a sedan; a limousine.

fronts n.[1] [1940s] a woman's breasts.

fronts n.[2] [1950s+] (*US Black*) clothes. [? show business jargon *front*, a large diamond tie pin or ring worn by vaudevillians to indicate prosperity/FRONT n.[2] (2)]

fronts n.[3] [2000s] (*US Black*) the teeth.

front street n. (*also* **Front Street**) [1960s+] (*US Black*) **1** the main street of a town, the street on which most of the (illegal) action takes place. **2** the state of being on public display and thus open to attack, whether verbal or physical; a situation in which one must be responsible for one's words and deeds. [note the actual Front Street, New York City, once a mercantile centre]

front tottie n. [1980s] (*Aus.*) the female genitals (cf. BACK TOTTIE n.). [SE *front* + TOTTIE n.[2] (2)]

front up v.[1] [1960s+] (*Aus./N.Z. Und.*) to appear, esp. in court. [i.e. in *front* of the judge]

front up v.[2] *see* FRONT v.[1] (3).

front-wheel skid n. (*also* **backward skid, back-wheel skid, four-wheel (skid), front-wheeler, three-wheel (skid)**) [1920s+] a derog. term for a Jew (cf. BILLY THE KID n.). [rhy. sl. = YID n.[1]]

front window n. [19C] the vagina (cf. BELLY ENTRANCE n.).

front windows n. **1** [mid-19C] the eyes. **2** [1900s–10s] spectacles.

front yard n. [20C+] (*US*) the area of a town where the well-off citizens live.

frootloop n. *see* FRUIT LOOP n.[2].

frosh n. (*also* **froshie**) [1910s+] (*US*) **1** a college freshman. **2** a member of a freshman sports team. **3** a collective term for freshmen. [SE *freshman* + ? Ger. dial. *Frosch*, frog, a grammar-school pupil]

frost n.[1] [late 19C+] **1** (*orig. theatre*) a failure. **2** coolness (between 2 people).

frost n.[2] [1960s+] (*US Black*) cocaine (cf. BLANCA n.).

frost v. [late 19C+] **1** (*US*) to treat in a distant manner. **2** (*US*) to anger; to cause coolness in relations. **3** (*US campus*) to shock; esp. in phr. *wouldn't that frost you*.

frost a cake v. (*also* **cut a cake**) [1900s; 1960s] (*US*) to make a difference.

frost bite me! *excl.* [late 19C–1920s] a general excl.

frost-bitten adj. [2000s] (*US drugs*) under the influence of cocaine. [FROST n.[2]]

frosted adj. [1960s] (*drugs*) heavily intoxicated by cocaine. [FROST n.[2]]

frosty n. (*also* **frostie**) [1950s+] (*Aus./US*) a chilled glass or can of beer.

frosty adj. **1** [late 19C+] (*US*) very unfriendly. **2** [1900s] unsuitable, inappropriate, 'bad'. **3** [1950s] (*US drugs*) under the influence of cocaine. **4** [1970s+] cool, unemotional. **5** [1980s+] stylish, fashionable. [FROST v.]

frosty face n. **1** [late 18C–19C] one whose face is pitted with smallpox scars (cf. CRIBBAGE-FACED adj.). **2** [20C+] (*Ulster*) the joker in a pack of cards. **3** [1920s+] (*also* **Miss Frosty Pants**) a severe person.

frot v. [1970s+] to rub up against (for sexual pleasure and usu. in a clandestine manner). [Fr. *frottage*, rubbing (in a sexual context); note Urquhart, *The Complete Works of Rabelais* (1653): 'These two did oftentimes do the two-backed beast together, joyfully rubbing and frotting their bacon against one another']

froth n. [early–mid-17C] beer.

froth and bubble n. [1960s+] (*Aus.*) **1** a racing double, the daily double. **2** trouble. [rhy. sl.]

frottage n. [2000s] (*US Black*) sexual desire. [FROT v. + -AGE sfx/SE *frottage*]

frotting n. [1990s+] the rubbing of bodies together for sexual pleasure. [FROT v.]

froudacious adj. [late 19C] (*Aus.*) absurd, ludicrous. [the erroneous comments made on Aus. (and N.Z.) by the historian J.A. Froude (1818–94)]

frow n. **1** [early 18C–mid-19C; 1950s] a woman. **2** [mid-18C; 1920s] a prostitute. [Du. *vrouw* or Ger. *Frau*, a woman]

frowst n. (*also* **froust**) [1900s–40s] the stuffy, close air of a room without adequate ventilation that is used by too many people. [FROWST v.]

frowst v. (*also* **froust**) [late 19C+] to lie around in a stuffy, ill-ventilated room. [dial. *frowsty*, fusty; having an unpleasant smell]

froyo n. [1980s+] (*US teen*) frozen yoghurt. [abbr.]

froze adj. [1980s] under the influence of cocaine. [FROST n.[2]]

frozen adj.[1] [late 19C–1920s] absolute, complete; usu. in phrs. *the frozen limit* or *the frozen truth*.

frozen adj.[2] [1980s] (*US Black*) extremely intoxicated by a drug. [one is rendered immobile, i.e. *frozen* to the spot]

frozen fruit n. [1970s] (*US gay*) a sexually frigid gay man. [pun on SE *frozen* + FRUIT n.[2] (2)]

frozen mitt n. (*also* **frozen face/mitten, icy mitt**) [late 19C+] (*US*) a rejection, an unfriendly reception (cf. CHILLY MITT n.; COLD MITT n.). [SE *frozen/icy* adj. + MITT n. (3)]

fruit *n.*[1] **1** [late 19C–1930s] (*US*) a dupe, an easy victim, one who is easily influenced. **2** [1900s–50s] something or someone delightful or pleasant; thus OLD FRUIT n. **3** [1930s; 1990s+] (*US teen*) an unintelligent, dull person. **4** [1960s+] an eccentric person. [? such a person is considered 'easy picking']

fruit *n.*[2] **1** [1900s–40s] a promiscuous woman. **2** [20C+] a derog. term for a male homosexual; in general use any homosexual; in gay use esp. one who pays for sex; thus *canned/crushed fruit*, a homosexual who does not reveal his sexual proclivity; *fruitette*, a school-age homosexual. [the 'softness']

fruit *adj.*[1] (*also* **fruity**) [1900s] (*US campus*) easily achieved. [it is 'soft']

fruit *adj.*[2] [1920s+] (*US*) homosexual, pertaining to homosexuality. [FRUIT n.[2] (2)]

fruit *v.* [1930s–40s] (*US*) **1** to romance, to 'sweet-talk'. **2** to waste time.

fruitball *n.* (*also* **fruitbat, fruit basket/merchant**) [1970s+] (*US*) an eccentric. [var. on FRUITCAKE n.[1] + -BALL sfx]

fruit bat *n.* [1990s+] **1** (*US gay*) a heterosexual woman who prefers the company of male homosexuals (cf. FRUIT-FLY n.). **2** (*US Und.*) a heterosexual man who specializes in robbing homosexuals whom he has fooled into believing he is looking for gay sex. [pun on SE *fruit bat* + FRUIT n.[2] (2)]

fruit boots *n.* [1950s–70s] (*orig. US gay*) **1** white tennis shoes, white suede shoes. **2** 'Beatle boots' or any Italian-style shoes with pointed toes. [FRUIT n.[2] (2) + SE *boots*; in more restrained eras, such shoes were seen as badges of effeminacy]

fruitcake *n.*[1] [1910s+] an eccentric, a peculiar person; esp. in phr. *nutty as a fruitcake*; thus *fruitcake factory*, a psychiatric institution. [they are both NUTTY adj.[2] (2)]

fruitcake *n.*[2] [1930s+] a male homosexual. [FRUIT n.[2] (2)]

fruitcake *adj.* [1940s+] (*US*) crazy, eccentric (cf. BANANAS adj.). [FRUITCAKE n.[1]]

fruiter *n.* [1910s+] (*US*) a male homosexual. [FRUIT n.[2] (2)]

fruitette *n. see* FRUIT n.[2] (2).

fruit factory *n.* [1960s] (*Aus.*) a psychiatric institution. [FRUIT n.[1] (4)]

fruit-fly *n.* **1** [1950s+] a homosexual man. **2** [1960s+] a woman who enjoys the company of homosexual rather than heterosexual men. [(1) ext. of FRUIT n.[2] (2); (2) idea of hovering around]

fruit for monkeys *n.* [1930s–70s] (*US*) a passive homosexual man. [FRUIT n.[2] (2) + SE *monkey*]

fruit for the monkeys *n.* [1950s+] (*gay*) the penis. [pun on BANANA n.[2] (1) + FRUIT n.[2] (2)]

fruit for the sideboard *n.* [1950s+] (*Aus.*) **1** 'easy money', esp. as won while gambling. **2** (*also* **fruit on the sideboard**) a person who is seen as a source of 'easy money'. [the implication is of 'extras' or luxuries; fruit would normally be placed on the table and soon eaten]

fruitful vine *n.* [19C] the vagina (cf. ADAM'S OWN (ALTAR) n.; BEAUTY SPOT n.). [it 'bears flowers' (menstruation) every month]

fruit hustler *n.* [1950s+] (*US*) one who pursues passive homosexuals for sex. [FRUIT n.[2] (2) + HUSTLER n. (3)]

fruiting *n.* [1940s+] (*US Black*) promiscuity. [FRUIT n.[2] (1)]

fruit jar *n.* [1960s] (*US*) illicitly distilled whisky; thus *fruit-jar nose*, a sore across the top of the nose, which has been irritated by the rubbing of the fruit jars from which the whisky is drunk. [SE *fruit jar*, in which the whisky is stored and from which it can be drunk]

fruit jockey *n.* [1980s] (*US prison*) a homosexual. [FRUIT n.[2] (2) + JOCKEY n.[3] (2)]

fruit juice *n.* [1970s+] (*US gay*) semen (cf. BABY FLUID n.; BABY GRAVY n.). [FRUIT n.[2] (2) + JUICE n.[2] (1) + pun on SE]

fruit loop *n.*[1] [1980s+] **1** (*US campus*) the small loop (ostensibly for hanging the shirt when no hanger is available) on the upper back of many shirts; such a loop, supposedly, can be used to hold a victim ready for buggery. **2** (*US*) a homosexual man. **3** (*US gay*) a freedom ring. **4** (*US gay*) an area frequented by homosexual men in search of partners. [pun on the US breakfast cereal *Fruit Loops*/FRUIT n.[2] (2); (3) *freedom rings* are a set of 6 metal rings in the colours of the rainbow worn to indicating that one is gay or sympathetic to gay people and causes]

fruit loop *n.*[2] (*also* **frootloop**) [1980s+] (*US*) a crazy or stupid person. [pun on the US breakfast cereal *Fruit Loops*/LOOPY adj. (1)]

fruit of the gibbet *n.* [early 18C; late 19C] a hanged man.

fruit on the sideboard *n. see* FRUIT FOR THE SIDEBOARD n. (2).

fruit picker *n.* (*US gay*) **1** [1960s] an ostensibly heterosexual man who enjoys homosexual encounters. **2** [1970s+] one who blackmails or robs homosexuals. [FRUIT n.[2] (2) + pun on SE]

fruit-plate *n.* [1930s+] (*US*) a male homosexual. [FRUIT n.[2] (2) + pun on SE]

fruit roller *n.* [1980s+] (*US*) a thug who specializes in mugging or beating up homosexuals; thus v. *fruit-roll*. [FRUIT n.[2] (2) + ROLL v.[4]]

fruit salad *n.*[1] **1** [1940s+] badges, medals. **2** [1960s+] (*US drugs/teen*) a random combination of any pills or capsules of drugs available, including psychotropic and medicinal, on which to get intoxicated. [pun on SE, suggested by the assorted colours]

fruit salad *n.*[2] **1** [1960s] (*US*) sexually attractive young women. **2** [1970s+] (*US gay*) a group of gay men. [pun on FRUIT n.[2] (1)/FRUIT n.[2] (2)/SE]

fruit salad bowl *n.* [1980s+] (*US drugs*) a pipe or bowl filled with a mix of marijuana and hashish. [pun]

fruit stand *n.* [1960s] (*US gay*) a place to find male homosexual prostitutes. [FRUIT n.[2] (2)]

fruit that made man wise *n.* [early 17C] sexual intercourse. [the eating of the apple in the Garden of Eden]

fruit tramp *n.* [20C+] (*US*) a migratory worker who follows the fruit harvest; such people are not tramps as such, but simply move as the job demands.

fruity *n.* [2000s] a *fruit* machine. [abbr.]

fruity *adj.*[1] [20C+] **1** sexually aroused. **2** full of a rich or strong quality, highly interesting, attractive or suggestive. [the fig. *fruit* is 'ripe' for enjoyment]

fruity *adj.*[2] [1910s+] (*US*) crazy (cf. BANANAS adj.). [FRUITCAKE n.[1]]

fruity *adj.*[3] [1910s+] (*US*) homosexual; effeminate. [FRUIT n.[2] (2)]

fruity *adj.*[4] [1930s] painful. [fig. use of SE *fruity*, full of flavour]

fruity *adj.*[5] *see* FRUIT adj.[1].

frum *adj.* [late 19C+] religious, orthodox. [Ger. *fromm*, pious, thence Yid. *frum*]

frummagemed *adj.* (*also* **frammagemed, frummagem**) [mid-17C–mid-19C] (*UK Und.*) choked, strangled, spoilt.

fruppencies *n.* [1970s] the female breasts. [Cockney pron. of SE *three-pences*]

fry *n.* (*also* **skull fry**) [1940s] (*US Black*) the act of having one's hair straightened; thus the straightened hair. [FRY (ONE'S HAIR) v.]

fry *v.*[1] (*US*) **1** [1910s+] to punish or be punished. **2** [1960s+] to ruin someone or to impair the mind. **3** [1960s+] to infuriate. [fig. uses of SE]

fry *v.*[2] **1** [1920s+] (*US Und.*) to electrocute or be electrocuted in the electric chair. **2** [1970s+] to be electrocuted, to get an electric shock.

fry *v.*[3] *see* FRY (ONE'S HAIR) v.

fry-ass *v.* [1960s] (*US*) to be executed in the electric chair. [ext. FRY v.[2] (1)]

fryer *n.* [1990s+] the electric chair. [FRY v.[2] (1)]

fryers *n.* [1940s+] (*US Black/W.I.*) an insignificant person; a sidekick.

frying pan *n.*[1] [mid-19C] (*UK Und.*) a large, silver pocket watch. [resemblance]

frying pan *n.*[2] [20C+] **1** an old man. **2** a hand. [rhy. sl.]

frying pan *n.*[3] [1930s] (*US prison*) the electric chair.

frying-pan *adj.* [mid-19C; 1960s] (*Aus. Und.*) small-time, petty. [shearer jargon *frying-pan brand*, a crude brand laid over the legitimate one by a cattle-thief; some rustlers lit. used a red-hot frying pan]

frying size *n.* [1900s–10s] (*US*) a young person, esp. a young woman. [SE *frying size*, a young chicken which has reached the proper size for killing and then frying]

fry-meat preacher *n.* [20C+] (*US*) an unprofessional, part-time lay preacher. [dial. *fried meat*, bacon, served to the preacher in return for his sermon]

fry one's brains *v.* [1970s+] to indulge in an excess of drugs.

fry (one's hair) *v.* [1930s+] (*US Black*) to straighten the hair (cf. CONK v.²). [the treatment with Congolene, a liquid that burns the scalp, that is part of straightening Black hair]

fry someone's ass *v.* [1960s] (*US*) to have completely at one's mercy; to punish comprehensively.

fry someone's bacon *v. see* COOK SOMEONE'S BACON v.

f.s. *n.* [1960s+] a woman who likes to sit on a man's face while he performs cunnilingus. [abbr. *face sitter*]

f sharp *n.* [mid-19C] a flea. [play on B FLAT n.]

F-60 *n.* [1980s+] (*drugs*) Histadyl (cf. F-40 n.). [the pharmaceutical identification stamped on the capsule]

F-66 *n.* [1980s+] (*drugs*) Tuinal (cf. F-40 n.). [the pharmaceutical identification stamped on the capsule]

F. S. man *n.* [late 19C] (*Aus.*) a convict who, after transportation, has worked long enough to gain their freedom. [abbr. *free by servitude* + SE *man*]

f.t.b. *phr.* [1910s] a phr. used to denote that one has had more than enough to eat. [abbr. *full to bursting*]

f.t.d. *v. see* FUCK THE DOG (AND SELL THE PUPS) v.

FTM *n.* [1990s+] (*US gay*) a female to male transsexual (cf. MTF n.; MTM n.). [abbr. *female to male*]

f.t.w.! *excl.* [1970s+] (*US, mainly bikers/campus*) fuck the world! [abbr.]

f.u.! *excl. see* FUCK YOU! excl.

fu *n.* [1960s+] (*drugs*) marijuana. [? Sp. *fumar*, to smoke]

fu *adj. see* FOU adj.¹.

fub *n.* [early 17C] a cheat.

fub *v.* [late 16C–mid-17C] to cheat, to impose upon. [earlier var. on FOB v. (1)]

f.u.b.a.r. *v.* [1940s+] (*orig. US milit.*) to blunder, make a mess, make a mistake. [F.U.B.A.R. phr. (2)]

f.u.b.a.r. *phr.* **1** [1940s+] (*orig. US milit.*) extremely unhappy. **2** [1940s+] (*orig. US milit.*) totally beyond repair and/or control (cf. S.N.A.F.U. n.). **3** [1970s+] (*US campus*) very unattractive. **4** [1990s+] (*US campus*) very drunk; completely intoxicated by a given drug. **5** [1990s+] (*US*) exhausted. [abbr. *fucked up beyond all recognition*]

f.u.b.b. *phr.* [1950s+] (*US, orig. milit.*) in a very parlous state, whether from physical injury, emotional instability, the effects of drink and/or drugs etc (cf. S.N.A.F.U. n.). [abbr. *fucked up beyond belief*]

fubbery *n.* [early 17C] cheating, deception. [FUB v.]

fubbs *n.* [early 17C–18C] an affectionate term, applied to small children and women with whom one is in love. [thus later SE *fubsy*, plump, dumpy; allegedly coined by Charles II (r.1660–85) to describe the Duchess of Portsmouth; Grose (1785) cites this as sl.]

fubby *adj.* (*also* **fubsey, fubsy**) [late 17C–1900s] pleasantly plump; thus *fubsiness*, fatness, plumpness.

f.u.b.i.s. *phr.* [1940s+] fuck you buddy, I'm shipping out (cf. S.N.A.F.U. n.). [abbr.]

fuck *n.*¹ **1** [mid-17C+] an act of copulation. **2** [late 17C–early 18C; 1930s+] copulation. **3** [1980s] (*gay*) anal intercourse. [FUCK v.¹]

fuck *n.*² **1** [late 19C; 1970s+] semen. **2** [1970s+] the essence, the spirit, 'the daylights', e.g. *kick the fuck out of*.

fuck *n.*³ [late 19C+] a person (usu. a woman but covering both sexes since the 1970s) considered purely as a sex object; thus a *good/bad fuck*, someone who is seen as a sexual adept or incompetent. [FUCK n.¹ (1)]

fuck *n.*⁴ [20C+] **1** anything at all, usu. in negative (i.e. nothing); usu. in phrs., e.g. GIVE A FUCK v.; NOT CARE A FUCK v.; NOT GIVE A FUCK v.; NOT WORTH A FUCK phr. **2** nonsense, rubbish.

fuck *n.*⁵ [1910s+] a general swear word, indicating excessive quantity or quality; often used in comparisons, e.g. *as big as fuck*, *hurts like fuck*, *bigger than fuck*; thus AS FUCK adv.; LIKE FUCK adv.; TO FUCK adv.

fuck *n.*⁶ [1920s+] a despicable person, usu. with qualifying adj., e.g. *dumb fuck, useless fuck*.

fuck *n.*⁷ [1970s+] a general negation of the previous statement, usu. a v., e.g. *do I fuck* or *is it fuck*.

fuck *n.*⁸ [1970s+] a turn of ill-fortune, a piece of bad luck, e.g. *I lost the gig, ain't that a fuck*.

fuck, the *n.* (*also* **fuck**) [1910s+] **1** var. on HELL, THE phr.², e.g. *why the fuck did you do that? who the fuck wants to know? the fuck I care*. **2** as an infix, a general intensifier, e.g. *sit the fuck down*.

fuck *adj.* [1940s+] (*orig. US*) **1** used as a description of something obscene or pornographic, e.g. *fuck movie*. **2** used as an intensifier. [FUCK v.¹]

fuck *v.*¹ [16C+] to have sexual intercourse, usu. of a man, but increasingly of either sex; also of anal intercourse. [strictly, the ety. of *fuck* remains unknown, although the word has been linked to a supposed, if unsubstantiated, ME v. *fuken*. Neither Ger. *ficken*, nor the Fr. *foutre* (f. Lat. *fotuere*), both of which mean the same, can be linked semantically. *HDAS* notes MDu. *fokken*, to thrust, to copulate with; Nor. dial. *fukka*, to copulate; Swed. dial. *focka*, to strike, to push, to copulate + *fock*, the penis. Given the plethora of euphemisms equating intercourse or penetration with striking or hitting (BANG v.¹ (2), SCREW v.² (1), POKE v. (1) etc), there may be some substance in E.P.'s suggestion of a root in the Lat. *pugnare*, to fight or strike. Considered (with CUNT n.¹ (1) and the compound MOTHERFUCKER n.) as the ultimate in taboo terms, *fuck* is in fact SE, but has been listed as taboo, and thus as sl., since *c*.1690. The first print cit. is dated 1503, in a line from the poetry of William Dunbar (?1456–?1513); the first dictionary listing is in Florio's *Worlde of Wordes* (1598): '*Fottere*, to iape, to sard, to fucke, to swive, to occupy.' By the 18C, if printed at all, the form was usu. *f—k*. The term returned to literary use with James Joyce's much-banned *Ulysses* (1922) but remained taboo in the popular media and in 'polite' speech. This position has been eroded ever since, with the term and its compounds appearing today in films, books and on television, although the press, esp. the tabloids, pretend to a continuing squeamishness. 'Officially', for all that the realities of everyday speech (irrespective of class) disprove the theory, *fuck* remains an outlaw in conversation]

fuck *v.*² **1** [mid-19C+] to harm irreparably, to cheat, to victimize, to betray, to deceive. **2** [1920s+] to stop, to abandon or give up (on). **3** [1940s+] to trifle with, to 'mess around', to interfere. **4** [1960s] to kick, to stomp on. **5** [1960s+] to blunder, to make a mess (of). **6** [1970s+] to throw. **7** [1980s] to use or exploit for one's benefit. **8** [1980s+] to dismiss, to expel. [fig. use of FUCK v.¹]

fuck *v.*³ [1920s+] used as a synon. for TO HELL WITH —! excl. in dismissive excls.

fuck! *excl.* (*also* **feck! feckins! fecks! fegs!**) **1** [17C+] an excl. of anger, surprise, dismay, disbelief, resignation, esp. in combs. **2** [1970s+] a verbal punctuation, with no real meaning.

-fuck *sfx* [1970s+] (*orig. US*) a sfx implying the destruction of the appended n., usu. of something subversive, e.g. CLUSTERFUCK n. (3), GENDER-FUCK n. (2), MINDFUCK n., RAT FUCK n.² (1). [FUCK n.¹ (1)]

fuckability *n.* [1960s+] sex appeal. [FUCK v.¹ + sfx *-ability*]

fuckable *adj.* **1** [late 19C+] sexually desirable. **2** [1970s+] (*US campus*) sexually available. [FUCK v.[1] + sfx -*able*]

fuck-about *n.* (*also* fuckaround) [1930s+] of a person, task, occupation etc, a time-waster, an act of time-wasting. [FUCK ABOUT v. (1)]

fuck about *v.* (*also* feck about, fuck around, fug around, fugh around) **1** [1910s+] to mess about, to waste time, to fool around. **2** [1920s+] to annoy, to inconvenience, to waste someone's time. **3** [1960s+] to wander about aimlessly. **4** [1960s+] to have sex outside one's primary relationship. **5** [1970s+] to astonish. [fig. use of FUCK v.[1]/FUG v.[2]/FUGH v. + SE *about/around*]

fuck-a-bush *adj.* [1950s+] (*W.I., Jam.*) promiscuous. [lit. one who 'fucks in the bushes']

fuck a duck *v.* [1930s+] to live a sexually promiscuous life. [FUCK v.[1] + assonance]

fuck a duck! *excl.* [1930s+] an excl. of surprise, disbelief, dismissal or rejection. [cited occas. as rhy. sl., but only by redup. and not a genuine e.g.]

fuckaholic *n.* [1980s+] one who is obsessed with having sexual relations. [FUCK v.[1] + -AHOLIC sfx]

fuck-all *n.* (*also* bollock-all, eff-all, feck-all, fugh-all, shag-all, shit-all) [1910s+] **1** none, nothing; often ext. to SWEET FUCK-ALL n. **2** a second-rate or worthless person. **3** a synon. for a DAMN n., e.g. *I don't give fuck-all.* **4** a synon. for HELL, THE phr.[2], e.g. *who the fuck-all does he think he is?* [fig. uses of FUCK n.[1]/BALLOCKS n.[1] (1)/EFF v./FUGH n./SHAG n.[1] (1)/SHIT n.[1] (1)]

fuck-all *adj.* [1930s+] no; as an intensifier. [FUCK-ALL n.]

fuck-all! *excl.* [1910s+] an ext. version of FUCK! excl.

fuck (all) else *n.* [1950s+] absolutely nothing, e.g. *there's fuck else to do around here.* [FUCK-ALL adj. + SE *else*]

fuck and blind *v. see* EFF (AND BLIND) v.

fuck-a-rama *n.*[1] [1960s+] (*orig. US*) a long sexual orgy. [FUCK v.[1] + -ORAMA sfx]

fuck-a-rama *n.*[2] [1990s+] an absolute disaster, utter chaos. [FUCKUP n. (1) + -ORAMA sfx]

fuck-a-rama! *excl.* [1990s+] an excl. of frustration, annoyance. [ext. of FUCK! excl. + -ORAMA sfx]

fuckaround *n.*[1] [1970s+] (*US*) bad treatment, 'messing about'; thus *play fuckaround*, to treat someone badly or contemptuously. [FUCK AROUND v.[2]]

fuckaround *n.*[2] *see* FUCK-ABOUT n.

fuck around *v.*[1] [1930s+] to lead a promiscuous sex life. [FUCK v.[1] + SE *around*]

fuck around *v.*[2] *see* FUCK ABOUT v.

fuck around! *excl.* [1990s+] (*US*) an excl. of mild annoyance.

fuckarse *n.* (*also* fuckass) [1960s+] a general term of contempt. [FUCK v.[1] + ARSE n.[1] (1)/ASS n. (2)]

fuckarse *v.* (*also* fuckass) [2000s] to play the fool, to act stupidly (cf. ACT THE ANGORA v.). [FUCKARSE n.]

fuckathon *n.* [1960s+] (*orig. US*) a long sexual encounter or orgy. [FUCK n.[1] (1) + sfx -*athon*]

fuckation *n.* [mid–late 17C] sexual intercourse. [FUCK n.[1] (1) + sfx -*ation*]

fuck away *v.* [1970s+] to waste, to squander. [FUCK v.[2] (6)/fig. use of FUCK v.[1] + SE *away*]

fuckbag *n.* [1970s+] a general term of contempt for an unpleasant, disgusting person. [FUCK n.[1] (1) + -BAG sfx; note RMC Duntroon (Aus.) *fuck bag*, a woman believed by cadets to be a good fuck and/or readily available for a fuck]

fuckball *n.* [1990s+] a general derog. term. [FUCK n.[1] (1) + -BALL sfx]

fuck-beggar *n.* [18C] 'An impotent or almost impotent man whom none but a beggar-woman will allow to "kiss" her' (Grose, 1785). [FUCK v.[1]]

fuck book *n.* [1940s+] pornography. [FUCK adj. + SE *book*]

fuckboy *n.* [1950s] **1** one who is victimized by their superiors

or associates. **2** a passive male homosexual, a catamite. [FUCK n.[1] (1) + SE *boy*]

fuckbrain *n.* [1970s+] a fool, a simpleton; thus *fuckbrained*, stupid (cf. BAKEBRAIN n.; DUMB FUCK n.; EGG-FOR-FUCK n.; FUCKFACE n.; FUCKHEAD n.; FUCK-KNUCKLE n.; FUCKNOB n.; FUCKWAD n.; FUCKWIT n.). [FUCK n.[1] (1) + sfx -*brain*]

fuck buddy *n.* [2000s] one with whom one has a sexual, but no deeper, relationship. [FUCK n.[1] (1) + BUDDY n. (1)]

fuckchop *n.* [1990s+] an imbecile, a stupid person. [FUCK n.[1] (1) + CHOPS n.[1] (1)]

fuckdog *n.* [1970s+] a promiscuous woman; one who is eager for sex. [FUCK n.[1] (1) + DOG n.[3] (8)]

fuckdust *n.* [2000s] a general term of abuse. [FUCK n.[1] (1) + SE *dust*]

fucked *adj.*[1] **1** [20C+] bothered, concerned, e.g. *I can't be fucked to do it.* **2** [1920s+] of people, exhausted, unhappy, wretched. **3** [1940s+] of things, broken, out of order, ruined, spoilt. **4** [1940s+] cheated, tricked, defeated, deceived. **5** [1950s+] in serious trouble. **6** [1960s+] intoxicated by a drug or drink. **7** [1960s+] lacking in good sense, crazy. **8** [1960s+] very bad, offensive, rotten, unfair. **9** [1970s+] psychologically maladjusted. [FUCK v.[2]/fig. uses of FUCK v.[1]]

fucked *adj.*[2] (*also* fugged) [1940s+] used as an intensified version of DAMNED adj.; often as *fucked if...* [FUCK v.[1]/FUG v.[2]]

fucked by the fickle finger of fate *phr.* [1940s+] (*orig. US*) used of a victim of adverse circumstances or bad luck. [FUCKED adj.[1] (4)]

fucked duck *n.* [1930s–60s] (*US*) one who is about to die or doomed to die. [FUCKED adj.[1] (5)]

fucked off *adj.* [1940s+] annoyed, furious. [fig use of FUCK v.[1] + SE *off*]

fucked out *adj.* **1** [mid-19C+] exhausted by an excess of sex. **2** [1940s+] (*orig. US*) exhausted. [(1) FUCK v.[1]; (2) ext. of FUCKED adj.[1] (2)]

fucked over *adj.* [1970s+] **1** suffering (not always painfully) from the use of drugs or alcohol to excess. **2** unpleasant, rotten, sick, dazed. [ext. of FUCKED adj.[1]]

fucked to a fair-thee-well *adj.* [1980s+] (*US*) ruined beyond repair. [FUCKED adj.[1] (3)]

fucked up *adj.* **1** [1930s+] of objects, intentions or plans, broken, wrecked, ruined. **2** [1940s+] (*also* f'd up) of people, distressed, unhappy, mentally unstable. **3** [1940s+] (*also* fuck-up) suffering (not always painfully) from the use of drugs or alcohol to excess. **4** [1940s+] (*orig. US milit.*) of people, badly hurt, wounded or killed. **5** [1940s+] worthless, contemptible, miserable. **6** [1940s+] an intensified var. of DAMNED adj. **7** [1950s] (*US*) confused, in a muddle. **8** [1960s+] of places, unpleasant. **9** [1970s+] unappealing, unpleasant. **10** [1980s+] exhausted, worn-out. **11** [1990s+] weird, strange, unusual. **12** [1990s+] drunk (cf. ANNIHILATED adj.). [FUCK v.[2]/fig use of FUCK v.[1] + SE *up*]

fucked up and far from home *phr.* (*also* bitched, buggered and bewildered) [late 19C+] in an utterly awful situation, miserable and lonely. [ext. of FUCKED UP adj. (2); orig. milit. in the depths of misery, both physical and mental; f. the image of a seduced and abandoned woman]

fucked with no Vaseline *phr.* [1990s+] suffering extreme physical or emotional pain. [the use of Vaseline to facilitate sexual (usu. anal) intercourse]

fuckee *n.*[1] [late 19C] the 'passive' recipient during copulation. [FUCK v.[1]; the opposite of FUCKER n. (1); lit. 'one who is fucked']

fuckee *n.*[2] [1970s] one who is treated badly; one who suffers harm or punishment. [FUCK v.[2] (1); the opposite of FUCKER n. (10); lit. 'one who is fucked']

fuck else *n. see* FUCK (ALL) ELSE n.

fuck 'em (all)! *excl.* [1940s+] a general excl. of dismissal, bravado, 'to hell with them'. [the orig. words for the bowdlerized soldiers' song 'Bless 'Em All']

fucken *adj. see* FUCKING adj.

fucker *n*. **1** [late 16C+] one who has sexual intercourse. **2** [19C] a pimp. **3** [early 19C; 1920s+] (*also* **facker, fecker, fugger, fugher**) a general term of abuse, e.g. *You stupid fucker!* **4** [1910s] (*Aus.*) an English private soldier. **5** [1920s–40s] a vagina. **6** [1920s+] (*also* **fugger, fugher**) a man, a fellow, with no particular abuse intended and even some degree of affection. **7** [1940s+] (*also* **fecker, fogger, fugger, fugher**) an unspecified object, irrespective of its qualities; an animal. **8** [1940s+] a difficult or irritating thing or task. **9** [1960s+] an extreme example, whether positive or negative. **10** [1970s+] one who harms others. [FUCK v.^{1}/FUCK v.^{2}/FUG v.^{2}/FUGH v.; (4) is either tongue-in-cheek or the result of deliberate misinformation; note COCKSUCKER n. (3)]

fuckermother *n*. [2000s] a var. on MOTHERFUCKER n. (1).

Fuckerware party *n*. [1980s+] (*US*) a party organized for the sale of erotic 'toys' and clothing. [a play on a *Tupperware* party]

fuckery *n*.^{1} [19C] a brothel. [FUCK n.^{1} (1) + sfx *-ery*; 'a place where an indicated article or service may be purchased or procured' (*OED*)]

fuckery *n*.^{2} [1970s+] **1** unfairness, ill treatment; treachery. **2** (*W.I. Rasta/UK Black*) (*also* **fuckry**) nonsense. **3** (*UK Black*) the personification of (1) + (2), i.e. a stupid mean person. [FUCK UP v. (1)]

fuckery *adj*. [1970s+] **1** wrong, unfair. **2** (*W.I. Rasta/UK Black*) stupid, nonsensical. [FUCKERY n.^{2}]

fuck eye, the *n*. [1980s+] (*US campus*) a flirtatious, sexually encouraging glance. [FUCK n.^{1} (1) + SE *eye*]

fuck eyes *n. see* FUCK-ME EYES n.

fuckface *n*. [1960s+] (*orig. US*) a fool, an idiot, a generally contemptible person (cf. FUCKBRAIN n.).

fuckfaced *adj*. [1940s+] **1** having an ugly, miserable face. **2** drunk (cf. ARSEHOLED adj.). **3** bleary-eyed, half-awake.

fuckfest *n*. [1970s] (*US*) an orgy. [FUCK n.^{1} (1) + -FEST sfx]

fuck-film *n*. [1970s+] a pornographic film. [FUCK adj. + SE *film*]

fuck-fist *n*. (*also* **fuck-finger**) [late 19C–1900s] a male or female masturbator. [FUCK v.^{1} + SE *fist/finger*]

fuck flaps *n*. [1990s+] the labia (cf. DEW-FLAPS n.). [FUCK v.^{1} + FLAPS n. (2)]

fuck flick *n*. [1990s+] (*orig. US*) a pornographic film. [FUCK adj. + FLICK n.^{3} (1)]

fuck-freak *n. see* COME-FREAK n. (1).

fuck-fuck *n. see* FUCKY-FUCKY n.

fuck handles *n. see* LOVE HANDLES n.

fuckhead *n*. [1960s+] a fool, a complete idiot; the use of fuck merely intensifies the disdain by its own taboo status; esp. as a term of address (cf. FUCKBRAIN n.). [FUCK n.^{1} (1) + -HEAD sfx (1)]

fuckheaded *adj*. (*also* **fuckhead**) [1970s+] stupid, moronic, incompetent, contemptible (cf. AIRHEADED adj.). [FUCKHEAD n.]

fuckhole *n*. **1** [late 19C+] the vagina; the female genitals (cf. BLACK HOLE n.^{1}). **2** [1950s+] an unpleasant, disgusting place. **3** [1980s+] a contemptible, unpleasant person. [lit. + fig. uses of FUCK v.^{1} + HOLE n.^{1} (2)]

fuck-in *n*. [1960s–70s] (*orig. US*) an orgy, mainly in HIPPIE n.^{2} (3) use. [FUCK v.^{1}; on the pattern of LOVE-IN n.]

fucking *n*.^{1} [mid-16C+] the act of copulation. [FUCK v.^{1}]

fucking *n*.^{2} (*also* **fuggin**) [mid-19C+] harsh and/or unfair treatment. [FUCK v.^{2} (1)/FUG v.^{2}]

fucking *adj*. (*also* **facking, facquing, fecking, fogging, fucken, fugging, fughing**) **1** [mid-19C+] a general intensifier, e.g. *fucking idiot.* **2** [mid-19C+] pertaining to sexual intercourse. **3** [20C+] implying a variety of negatives, e.g. vile, despicable, unpleasant, corrupt, dirty. **4** [1910s+] as an infix, *-fucking-*, whether within words, e.g. ABSOFUCKINGLUTELY adv.; FANFUCKING--TASTIC adj.; GUARANFUCKINGTEE v., or within phrs. e.g. *Happy fucking Christmas.* [FUCK v.^{1}/FUG v.^{2}/FUGH v.]

fucking *adv*. **1** [mid-19C+] a general intensifier, totally, completely, e.g. *fucking stupid.* **2** [1970s+] used, usu. in the negative, to imply definitely (not), certainly (not), e.g. *fucking thanks.*

fucking-A *n*. [1960s] (*orig. US*) very little, as good as nothing, e.g. *I don't know fucking-A about it.* [FUCK-ALL n. (1)]

fucking-A *adj*. (*also* **fucking A-OK, fuggin ay**) **1** [1940s+] excellent, superb, the best. **2** [1950s+] goddamned, damned. **3** [1950s+] right, correct. [FUCKING adv. (1) + A-OK adj.]

fucking-A *adv*. [1950s+] completely, totally, absolutely, very well, very much, extremely, e.g. *You're fucking-A right* or *fucking-A well.* [FUCKING-A adj. (3)]

fucking-A! *excl*. **1** [1950s+] (*also* **fucking-aye!**) an excl. generally used for emphasis, absolutely! definitely! **2** [1970s+] an excl. used to denote astonishment, dismay, acceptance, praise, recognition. [FUCKING-A adj.]

fucking Ada! *excl*. [20C+] a general excl. [the *Ada* is either a nonsense word or a euph. for the stronger alternative *fucking arseholes!* as with FUCKING HELL! excl./'KIN'ELL! excl. the *fu* may be deliberately abandoned; thus *'kin'Ada!*]

fucking A-OK *adj. see* FUCKING-A adj.

fucking-aye! *excl. see* FUCKING-A! excl. (1).

fucking hell! *excl*. (*also* **shagging hell!**) [1910s+] an excl. of surprise, annoyance, wonder etc; thus 'KIN'ELL! excl. [FUCKING adj. (1) + SE *hell*]

fuckingly *adv*. [1920s+] extremely, very much, damned. [FUCKING adj. (1)]

fucking Nora! *excl*. (*also* **bleeding Nora!**) [1990s+] an excl. used to denote astonishment, dismay, acceptance, praise, recognition. [var. on FUCKING ADA! excl.]

fucking stick *n. see* FUCKSTICK n. (2).

fucking well *adv*. [1910s+] generally used for emphasis, absolutely, very well, very much, extremely. [FUCKING adv. (1) + SE *well*]

fuck into a cocked hat *v. see* KNOCK INTO A COCKED HAT v.

fuckish *adj*. [late 19C+] sexually forward. [FUCK v.^{1}]

fuck it! *excl*. (*also* **feck it! fug it!**) [1920s+] a general dismissive excl. [fig. uses of FUCK v.^{1}/FUG v.^{2}/FUGH v.]

fuck job *n*. [1970s+] victimization, an act of victimization. [FUCK v.^{2} (1) + JOB n.^{4}]

fuck knows *phr*. [1970s+] a general intensifier, underlining one's ignorance or disinterest.

fuck-knuckle *n*. [1980s+] (*Aus./N.Z.*) a fool, an incompetent (cf. FUCKBRAIN n.). [a mix of FUCKWIT n. (1) and KNUCKLEHEAD n., the first of which implies plain stupidity, the second adds physical inadequacy]

fuck like a bunny *v*. [1940s+] to copulate enthusiastically (cf. GO LIKE A RABBIT v.).

fuck like a mink *v*. [1910s+] (*Aus./US*) of a woman, to copulate enthusiastically.

fuck like a rattlesnake *v*. (*also* **root like a rattlesnake, shag...**) [20C+] to copulate enthusiastically, often used by a man of a woman who is presumed to be a sexual enthusiast; usu. in phr. *I'll bet she...* [FUCK v.^{1}/ROOT v.^{3} (1)/SHAG v.^{1} (1)]

fuck like a stoat *v*. [late 19C+] to copulate enthusiastically.

fuckload *n*. [1960s+] a great many, a large amount.

fuck me! *excl*. [1910s+] **1** an excl. of surprise, astonishment, resignation; often in combs., e.g. *fuck me rigid! fuck me insensible! fuck me dead!* **2** (*US campus*) an excl. of annoyance, of contempt, shut up! go away! you make me sick!

fuck-me *adj*. [1980s+] outrageous, esp. when extremely sexy; thus FUCK-ME BOOTS n.; FUCK-ME EYES n.; FUCK-ME SHOES n. (cf. C.F.M. adj.). [FUCK v.^{1}]

fuck me backwards! *excl*. (*also* **fuck me sideways!**) [1940s+] a general excl.

fuck-me boots *n*. (*also* **FM boots, fuck-me booties**) [1980s+] (*US*) sexually alluring footwear, usu. as worn by a woman, thus often high-heeled boots, esp. when worn with a mini-skirt. [FUCK-ME adj.]

fuck-me eyes n. (also **fuck eyes**) [1980s+] (US) flirtatious, sexually encouraging stares or glances. [FUCK-ME adj.]

fuck me gently! excl. (also **fuck me dead! ...pink! ...rigid!**) [1910s+] a general excl. of surprise, alarm etc.

fuck me gently with a chainsaw! excl. [1980s+] a general excl. of surprise or annoyance.

fuck me hard! excl. [1980s+] (US) an expression used in response to an unwanted and undesirable action done to the speaker.

fuck-me pink! excl. see FUCK ME GENTLY! excl.

fuck-me pumps n. see FUCK-ME SHOES n.

fuck me ragged! excl. [1980s] a general excl.

fuck me rigid! excl. see FUCK ME GENTLY! excl.

fuck-me shoes n. (also **follow-me(-home)-and-fuck-me shoes, fuck-me pumps, fuck-me's, hump-me pumps**) [1970s+] ankle-strapped, wedge-heeled shoes. [FUCK-ME adj.; allegedly first worn, at least for mass delectation, by film star Joan Crawford (1906–77)]

fuck me sideways! excl. see FUCK ME BACKWARDS! excl.

fuckmobile n. [2000s] a car that improves one's attractiveness to the opposite sex. [FUCK n.[1] (1) + -MOBILE sfx]

fuck Mrs Palmer v. [1990s+] to masturbate (cf. CONVERSE WITH HARRY PALM v.). [ironic use of FUCK v.[1] + SE palm]

fuck muscle n. [1980s+] (US gay) the penis.

fuck my days! excl. [1970s–80s] (UK Black) an excl. of surprise, annoyance etc. [fig. use of FUCK v.[1] + FOR DAYS! excl. (2)]

fuck my luck! excl. [1990s+] I don't believe it!

fuck my old boots! excl. (also **blast my old boots!**) [late 18C; 20C+] an excl. denoting one's astonishment; orig. milit. use, sometimes euph. as seduce my ancient footwear!

fuck nest n. see FUCK PAD n.

fucknob n. [1990s+] a fool, an unpleasant person (cf. FUCKBRAIN n.). [FUCK n.[1] (1) + KNOB n.[1] (7)]

fuck-nut n. [1980s+] (UK juv.) a general term of abuse.

fuck-nutty adj. [1940s] obsessed with thoughts of sex. [FUCK n.[1] (1) + NUTTY adj.[2] (1)]

fucko n. [1960s+] (orig. US) **1** a general term of address, with no particular overtones whether positive or negative. **2** an unpleasant person. [FUCK n.[1] (1) + -o sfx (1)]

fuck of a, a phr. [1920s+] (orig. US) **1** large or notable in amount. **2** a general intensifier.

fuck-off n. (also **fug-off**) **1** [1940s+] a lazy or inefficient person. **2** [1950s] a despicable thing. **3** [1980s+] a gesture of contempt. **4** [1980s+] a statement of prohibition. **5** [1980s+] an irritating or frustrating situation. [FUCK OFF v./FUG v.[2]; (1) they prefer to fuck off rather than work]

fuck-off adj. [1990s+] **1** annoying. **2** arrogant, ostentatious. **3** large, showy. [FUCK OFF v.]

fuck off v. (also **fack off, feck off, feck off**) **1** [1910s+] (also **fuck out**) to leave, to go away. **2** [1940s+] (orig. US) (also **f.o.**) to waste time, to idle, to avoid one's duties; thus fucking off, wasting time, acting lazily. **3** [1940s+] a synon. for GO TO HELL! excl. **4** [1960s+] (US Black) to waste, to squander. **5** [1960s+] to disregard, to brush aside, to put off. **6** [1970s] to miss out on something through one's own or another's ineptitude. **7** [1980s] to expel, to reject. **8** [1990s+] to stop. **9** [2000s] to annoy.

fuck off! excl. (also **feck off! frig off!**) **1** [1930s+] in aggressive use, 'go away!', often compounded as fuck off out of it! **2** [1980s+] in joc. use, 'don't be silly!'

fuck-off money n. [2000s] a sum of money or an income large enough to give one the power of freedom from everyday constraints, i.e. one can tell one's employer to fuck off. [FUCK OFF v. (1); var. on FUCK-YOU MONEY n.]

fuck one n. [1970s] the very beginning. [an emphatic/coarse var. on DAY ONE n.]

fuck one's fist v. see FIST FUCK v. (1).

fuck out v.[1] [1970s+] to break down. [backform f. FUCKED OUT adj. on pattern of SE wear out]

fuck out v.[2] [1980s+] to be sexually unfaithful. [to have sex 'out' of the house, 'out' of one's relationship]

fuck out v.[3] see FUCK OFF v. (1).

fuck out of v. [mid-19C+] to cheat someone. [ext. FUCK v.[2] (1)]

fuck over v. [1960s+] **1** of people, to harm, to beat up, to hurt emotionally, to act cruelly, to interfere, to mess around with. **2** of ideas or objects, to adulterate.

fuck pad n. (also **fuck nest**) [1950s+] (orig. US) a room or apartment that a man keeps for seductions and sex. [FUCK n.[1] (1) + PAD n.[2] (2)]

fuck palmela v. [1990s+] to masturbate (cf. CONVERSE WITH HARRY PALM v.). [ironic use of FUCK v.[1] + SE palm]

fuckpig n. [1920s+] a general term of derision; the implication is of grubbiness, slovenliness.

fuck-plug n. [1980s+] **1** a contraceptive diaphragm. **2** a term of abuse. [FUCK n.[1] (1) + SE plug]

fuckpole n. [1990s+] **1** the penis (cf. BAT n.[7]). **2** a general term of dislike. [FUCK v.[1] + SE pole/POLE n.]

fuckpump n. [20C+] a married man. [the monotonous regularity of his sex life]

fuck rubber n. [1980s] (US) a contraceptive sheath. [FUCK n.[1] (1) + RUBBER n.[5]]

fuckry n. see FUCKERY n.[2] (2).

fucksauce n. [1990s+] semen (cf. BABY GRAVY n.). [FUCK n.[1] (1) + SE sauce/SAUCE n.[2] (7)]

fuck show n. [1960s+] a live sex show. [FUCK adj. + SE show]

fucksock n. [1990s+] a sock used as a repository for the ejaculation that climaxes masturbation. [FUCK n.[1] (1) + SE sock]

fucksome adj. [late 19C+] of a woman, sexually desirable. [FUCK v.[1] + sfx -some]

fuck someone's arse/ass off v. see FUCK THE ARSE OFF v.

fuck someone's brains out v. (also **ball someone's brains out**) [1950s+] to copulate very strenuously and poss. sadistically, usu. of a man to a woman.

fuck someone's head/mind (up) v. see FUCK WITH SOMEONE'S MIND v.

fuck's sake! excl. see FOR FUCK'S SAKE! excl.

fuckster n. [late 17C; late 19C] a promiscuous man; occas. a woman. [FUCK v.[1] + -STER sfx]

fuckstick n. [1950s+] a worthless, contemptible or despicable person. **2** [1960s+] (also **fucking stick**) the penis (cf. BAT n.[7]). [fig. + lit. uses of FUCK n.[1] (1) + SE stick/STICK n.[1] (1); cits. give this order, but presumably (2) actually predates (1)]

fucks to phr. [2000s] a dismissive phr., a synon with TO HELL WITH —! excl.

fuckstrated adj. [1980s+] (US campus) sexually frustrated. [FUCK n.[1] (1) + SE frustrated]

fuckstress n. [19C+] **1** a prostitute. **2** a female sexual sophisticate. **3** a nymphomaniac. [FUCK v.[1] + sfx -stress, a female agent or 'doer' (i.e. fem. -STER sfx)]

fuck-struck adj. [1960s] obsessed with sex. [FUCK n.[1] (1) + SE struck]

fuck that! excl. [20C+] a dismissive excl., often in combs., e.g., fuck that for a bowl of cherries, fuck that for a comic song, fuck that for a top hat. [fig. use of FUCK v.[1]]

fuck that for a game of soldiers! excl. (also **bugger that for a game of soldiers! fuck this...!**) [20C+] an excl. of derision, indicating something is not working; often modified. [ext. FUCK THAT! excl.]

fuck that for a lark! excl. (also **fuck this for a geg! ...this for a lark! ...this lark!, shag that for a lark!**) [20C+] **1** an excl. of derision, indicating something is not working. **2** don't expect me to get mixed up! that's a stupid idea! [fig. use of FUCK v.[1]]

fuck that for a laugh! excl. (also **fuck this for a laugh!**)

[1940s+] an excl. of derision, indicating that something is not satisfactory or rejecting an idea that is unfeasible. [ext. FUCK THAT! excl.]

fuck that noise! *excl.* [1980s+] (*US*) forget it! rubbish! what a bore! [FUCK v.² (8)]

fuck the arse off *v.* (*also* fuck someone's arse/ass off, fuck the ass off) [1940s+] to copulate enthusiastically, usu. from the male point of view; often in wishful phr. voiced by a man watching a passing woman, *I could/I'd like to fuck the arse off that* (cf. SCREW THE ARSE OFF v.). [FUCK v.¹ + ARSE n.¹ (1)/ASS n. (2); there is no implication of anal intercourse/homosexuality; the ref. is merely to the movement of the male buttocks]

fuck the begrudgers! *excl.* [1980s+] (*Irish*) a general excl. of defiance or scorn.

fuck the crap out of someone *v.* (*also* fuck the cum out of someone, fuck the shit...) [1970s+] of a man, to have sexual intercourse; usu. very energetically and repeatedly. [FUCK v.¹ + CRAP n.³ (6)/CUM n.¹ (1)/SHIT, THE n.²]

fuck the dog (and sell the pups) *v.* (*also* f.t.d., screw the dog/pooch) [1910s+] (*US*) **1** to idle, to waste time, to loaf on the job. **2** to bungle, to blunder. [FUCK v.¹/SCREW v.² (1) + SE *dog*/POOCH n.]

fuck the duck *v.* [1960s+] **1** to waste time; to relax. **2** to make a mistake. [var. on prev.]

fuck them all but six! *excl.* (*also* fuck them all but eight!) [1910s+] (*US, orig. milit.*) a general oath of annoyance and hostility; often ext. with *...and save them for pallbearers*.

fuck this...! *see under* FUCK THAT...!

fuck truck *n.* [1970s+] (*Aus.*) any vehicle, usu. a small van (poss. with a mattress in the back), in which a young man hopes to seduce women. [FUCK n.¹ (1)]

fuck udders *n.* [1990s+] the female breasts (cf. BORDENS n.). [FUCK n.¹ (1)]

fuckup *n.* (*also* fug-up) **1** [1930s+] (*orig. US*) an error, a mistake, bungling, incompetence. **2** [1940s+] (*orig. US*) a bungler, an incompetent, a hopeless failure. **3** [1990s+] (*US*) a negative attitude. [FUCK UP v./FUG n.²]

fuck-up *adj.*¹ [1960s+] (*orig. US*) incompetent, inadequate. [FUCKUP n. (2)]

fuck-up *adj.*² *see* FUCKED UP adj. (3).

fuck up *v.* (*also* fug up, fugg up) **1** [1910s+] to ruin, to destroy; to make a mess of; thus *fucker-up*, that which ruins or destroys. **2** [1940s+] to confuse, to confound. **3** [1950s+] to blunder, to make a mistake. **4** [1960s+] (*US Black*) to fool around. **5** [1960s+] (*orig. US Black*) to hurt, to injure. **6** [1960s+] to cause problems for someone. **7** [1960s+] (*orig. milit.*) to kill, to thwart. **8** [1970s+] to make drunk or drugged. **9** [1980s+] to go wrong, to malfunction, to break down. **10** [1990s+] to infect with a venereal disease. [FUCK v.²/fig. use of FUCK v.¹/FUG v.²]

fuck up! *excl.* [1980s+] (*Irish*) shut up! stop it!

fuck up someone's pussy *v.* [1960s+] (*US Black*) to interfere with a rival, a companion's efforts at seducing a woman. [FUCK UP v. (1) + PUSSY n. (2)]

fuckwad *n.* [1970s+] (*US*) a fool, a stupid or contemptible person; often in direct address (cf. FUCKBRAIN n.). [FUCK v.¹ + -WAD sfx]

fuckwank *n.* [1990s+] a general term of derision, abuse. [FUCKER n. (3) + WANKER n. (2)]

fuckwit *n.* [1980s+] **1** a fool; thus *fuckwitted*, stupid (cf. DAMWIT n.; FUCKBRAIN n.). **2** a general term of derision. [FUCK v.¹+ SE *wit*; note synon. RMC Duntroon (Aus.) *shitwit*]

fuck with *v.*¹ (*also* fug with) [1940s+] **1** to mess about with, to become involved with. **2** to interfere, often by physical or mental intimidation. **3** (*US Black*) to impress, to overwhelm, to manipulate. **4** to play around with. [ext. of FUCK v.²/FUG v.²]

fuck with *v.*² [1960s+] to copulate with (a partner is usu. cited). [ext. of FUCK v.¹]

fuck with someone's mind *v.* (*also* fuck someone's head (up), ...mind (up), fuck with someone's head) [1960s+] to disturb and harm someone emotionally, to intimidate, to astonish or confuse another or oneself. [FUCK WITH v.¹ (3) + SE *mind/head*]

fucky *adj.* [20C+] nubile, ostensibly sexually enthusiastic; usu. of a woman. [FUCK v.¹ + sfx -*y*]

fucky-fucky *n.* (*also* fuck-fuck) [20C+] sexual intercourse; esp. as used in Asia, often by prostitutes. [FUCK v.¹ + redup.]

fuck-you *n.* [1970s+] (*orig. US*) a statement of dismissal or contempt. [FUCK YOU! excl.]

fuck-you *adj.* [1930s+] dismissive, contemptuous. [FUCK YOU! excl.]

fuck you! *excl.* (*also* f.u.! fug you! fugh you!) [1930s+] a general excl. of dismissal, contempt, I don't believe you! go to hell! nonsense! (cf. GO FUCK YOURSELF! excl.). [fig. uses of FUCK v.¹/FUG v.²/FUGH v.]

fuck you, Charley! *excl.* [1930s+] a general term of dismissal; often reversed as CHUCK YOU, FARLEY! excl. [FUCK YOU! excl.]

fuck you Jack, I'm all right! [late 19C+] a general dismissive excl., don't bother me! I don't care! [orig. naut. catchphrase, denoting utter selfishness and disinterest in the plight of anyone else; general milit. use by WW1 and thence to civilians; the best known use is bowdlerized in the film title *I'm Alright, Jack* (1959), which burlesqued bloody-minded industrial relations]

fuck-you money *n.* [1950s+] a sum of money or an income large enough to give one the power of freedom from everyday constraints, i.e. one can tell one's employer, *fuck you!* (cf. FUCK-OFF MONEY n.). [FUCK YOU! excl.]

fuck your buddy week *phr.* (*also* frig your buddy week, screw...) [1950s+] (*orig. US milit.*) used in response to any moment or act of betrayal; usu. as *so it's fuck your buddy week, is it?* [FUCK v.² (1)/FRIG v. (6)/SCREW v.² (5) + BUDDY n. (1)]

fuck yourself! *excl. see* GO FUCK YOURSELF! excl.

fud *n.*¹ [late 18C–19C] pubic hair. [dial. *fud*, a rabbit's tail]

fud *n.*² *see* FUDDY-DUDDY n.

fuddle *n.* [late 17C–1940s] **1** drink, alcohol; thus *on the fuddle*, on a drunken spree. **2** intoxication, an intoxicated or generally muddled state; occas. a drunken person; thus *fuddle-headed*, *fuddlement*. [FUDDLE v.]

fuddle *v.* **1** [mid-17C–1910s] to become drunk, to make oneself drunk; thus *fuddling school*, an ale house. **2** [18C–mid-19C] to render drunk. [ety. unknown; *OED* suggests poss. links to Du. *vod*, soft, slack, loose; Ger. dial. *fuddeln*, to swindle]

fuddlecap *n.* [late 17C–mid-19C] a drunkard; thus *fuddle-caps' hall*, a tavern. [FUDDLE n.]

fuddled *adj.* [early 17C+] drunk (cf. ADDLED adj.). [FUDDLE v. (1), although cits. here predate slightly]

fuddle-headed *adj. see* FUDDLE n. (2).

fuddy-duddy *n.* (*also* fud, fuddy, fuddy-dud) [20C+] a fussy, pernickety, narrow-minded person, often with the assumption of their being old. [? Cumberland dial. *duddy fuddiel*, a ragged fellow]

fuddy-duddy *adj.* [20C+] fussy, pernickety, narrow-minded. [FUDDY-DUDDY n.]

fudge *n.*¹ **1** [mid-18C–1920s] nonsense, stupidity. **2** [early 19C] a lie. [SE *fudge!* rubbish! bosh!]

fudge *n.*² [1960s+] (*US*) excrement, usu. in association with homosexual practices; thus *pack/stir fudge*, to perform anal intercourse; *park one's fudge*, to defecate; also as adj., *fudgy* (cf. ADMIRAL BROWNING n.). [SE *fudge*, a sweetmeat (+ PACK v.⁴)]

fudge *v.*¹ **1** [late 18C+] to blunder, to err. **2** [mid-19C+] to lie, to 'tell stories'. **3** [20C+] to fabricate. **4** [20C+] to cheat in an examination. [FUDGE n.¹]

fudge *v.*² [1980s+] (*US*) to foul with excrement. [FUDGE n.²]

fudge! *excl.* [1930s+] a euph for FUCK! excl. [note SE *fudge!* rubbish!]

fudge baby *n.* [1990s+] a piece of excrement (cf. ADMIRAL BROWNING n.). [FUDGE n.² + SE *baby*]

fudge-nudger *n.* [1990s+] a derog. term for a male homosexual, a sodomite (cf. BROWN ARTIST n.). [FUDGE n.² + SE *nudger*]

fudge-packer *n.* (*also* **packer**) [1980s+] (*US*) a derog. term for a homosexual man (cf. BROWN ARTIST n.). [FUDGE n.² + PACK v.⁴]

fudgepot *n.* [1980s+] (*US gay*) the anus; thus DIP IN THE FUDGE POT v. (cf. BOURNEVILLE BOULEVARD n.). [FUDGE n.²]

fudge tunnel *n.* [1990s+] the anus (cf. ALLEY WAY n.; BOURNEVILLE BOULEVARD n.). [FUDGE n.² + SE *tunnel*]

fudgsicle *n.* [1940s–60s] (*US*) a Black person who is criticized by other Blacks as behaving in a 'White' manner. [proprietary name of the *Fudgsicle* ice-cream-bar, although the bar is, in fact, all-chocolate; the usual image in such terms (cf. APPLE n.⁷) is of something that, while coloured outside, is White within]

fuel *n.* [1980s+] **1** (*drugs*) marijuana mixed with insecticides. **2** (*drugs*) phencyclidine (cf. ACE n.⁴). **3** (*Aus. prison*) drink.

fuete *n.* [1980s+] (*drugs*) a hypodermic needle. [Cuban Sp. *fuete*, a whip]

fug *n.*¹ **1** [late 19C+] (*orig. public school*) a thick, close, stuffy atmosphere, esp. as experienced in a smoky, unventilated room; thus *fugged*, stuffy. **2** [2000s] (*US prison*) a cigarette. [? SE *fog*; note Lancashire dial. *fug*, stinking sweat, esp. accruing to the feet + Norfolk dial. *fugga*, to spend one's time indoors]

fug *n.*² [1940s+] a euph. for FUCK n.¹ in a variety of contexts. [FUG v.²]

fug *v.*¹ [late 19C+] to stay in a stuffy atmosphere. [FUG n.¹ (1)]

fug *v.*² (*also* **fog**) [1940s+] a euph. for FUCK v.¹ in all uses. [coined by Norman Mailer (b.1923) as an all-purpose replacement for the taboo word in his book *The Naked and The Dead* (1948)]

fug around *v. see* FUCK ABOUT v. and for all combs. with fug, *see under* FUCK.

fugazi *adj.* (*US*) **1** [1980s+] a euph. for FUCKED UP adj. **2** [1990s+] fake, artificial, false. [acro. Fucked Up, Got Ambushed, Zipped In]

fugel *v.* (*also* **fugle**) [early 18C–19C] to seduce; to have sexual intercourse. [? Yorks. dial. to trick, to deceive]

fugged *adj. see* FUG n.¹ (1).

fuggy *adj.* **1** [1910s] of people, preferring stuffy rooms, and thus smelly. **2** [1910s+] of a place or room, close, stuffy, lacking in ventilation. [FUG n.¹ (1) + sfx -*y*]

fugh *n.* [20C+] a euph. for FUCK n.¹, used in a variety of contexts. [FUGH v.]

fugh *v.* [20C+] a euph. for FUCK v.¹ in all uses. [used mainly by its popularizer Brendan Behan (1923–64) in his autobiographies *Borstal Boy* (1958) and *Confessions of an Irish Rebel* (1965)]

fugh-all *n. see* FUCK-ALL n. and for all combs. with fugh, *see under* FUCK.

fugitive from the chain gang *n.* [1960s+] (*US gay*) a man who has been one of a spintry. [play on DAISY CHAIN n.]

fugle *v. see* FUGEL v.

fugly *n.* [2000s] a very unattractive woman. [FUGLY adj.; note RMC Duntroon (Aus.) *fugly*, an unsightly woman; a term one might use ribbingly of the girlfriend of another]

fugly *adj.* [1980s+] (*orig. US Black*) very unattractive. [elision of FUCKING adj. (1) + *ugly*]

fugo *n.* [17C–18C] the rectum or anus. [Cornish dial. *fogo*/*fougo*, a cave or underground storage chamber]

F.U.J.I.A.M.A. *phr.* [1930s] written across the back of an envelope, *fuck you Jack, I am all right*. [abbr.; note US milit. *f.u.j.i.g.m.o.* *fuck you Jack, I got my orders*; ult. FUCK YOU JACK, I'M ALL RIGHT!]

fulhams *n.* **1** [mid-16C–mid-19C] (*UK Und.*) (*also* **fullams**, **fullums**) crooked dice that appear to be perfectly honest but have in fact been weighted with lead to ensure that they roll as the user wishes. **2** [mid-17C] in fig. use, a trick. [*Fulham*, southwest London, presumably a centre of their manufacture, although Walker, *A Manifest Detection of Dice-play* (1552), recommends the King's Bench, the Marshalsea and, above all, 'Bird, in Holborn, is the finest workman'; Nares dismisses such criminality in 'so

quiet a village', and suggests that the dice were 'full, or loaded, with some heavy metal on one side, so as to produce a bias']

Fulham tractor *n.* [2000s] a sports utility vehicle. [the popularity of SUVs among the rich inhabitants of Fulham, London SW10]

Fulham virgin *n.* [19C] a prostitute. [? the louche reputation of Cremorne Gardens, in neighbouring Chelsea]

fulke *v.* [early 19C] to have sexual intercourse. [coined by Lord Byron in *Don Juan* (1819–24)]

fulker *n.* [mid–late 16C] a pawnbroker or moneylender. [Ger. *fucker, fugger*, a usurer, a great merchant]

full *adj.*¹ **1** [mid-19C+] (*also* **full of it**) drunk (cf. FULL AS... phr.; FULL TO THE BOW-TIE phr.; FULL TO THE BUNG phr.; FULL TO THE GILLS phr.). **2** [1980s] drugged.

full *adj.*² [1960s+] **1** absolute, complete, total. **2** good, amazing.

full! *excl.* [1990s+] an affirmative excl.

full about *phr. see* FULL OF phr.

fullams *n. see* FULHAMS n. (1).

full as... *phr.* [late 19C+] used in various phrs. meaning very drunk, e.g. *a boot, a bull, a bull's bum, a Catholic school, a fairy's phone book, a fiddle, a fiddler, a fiddler's fart, a fiddler's bitch, a footie final, a goat, a goog, a googy egg, a goose, a lord, an egg, a pommie complaint box, a seaside shithouse on Boxing Day, a state school* (*hat rack*), *a tick, the family po, the moon, two/three race trains*. [FULL adj.¹; note also used lit., i.e. of food]

full as a boiled owl *phr. see* DRUNK AS A BOILED OWL phr.

full-blown stallone *n.* [1990s+] an erection. [rhy. sl. = BONE n.¹ (2); ult. US film star Sylvester *Stallone* (b.1946), known for his macho 'hard' roles]

full bob *adv.* [17C–18C] suddenly, esp. in an unexpected collision. [SE *full* + *bob*, a blow (with the fist)]

full bottle, the *n.* [1960s+] (*Aus.*) an expert.

full-bottomed *adj.* (*also* **full-breeched, full-pooped, full-rigged**) [late 19C–1970s] having large buttocks; thus *full-bottom*, one with large buttocks.

full buf *adj.* [1980s] (*US teen*) dressed up in one's finery, 'dressed to kill'. [SE *full* + BUF adj.]

full butt *adv.* [17C+] (*US*) at full speed; thus (*W.I.*) rushing forward without hesitation or thought. [the image of a charging bull, which 'butts' those in its way]

full enchilada, the *n. see* WHOLE ENCHILADA, THE n.

fuller's *n.* [1910s+] (*N.Z.*) **1** a vaudeville, 'variety' show. **2** New Zealand. [the *Fuller Bros.*, contemporary impresarios and owners of many theatres and cinemas]

fuller's earth *n.* [early–mid-19C] gin. [SE *Fuller's earth*, 'a hydrous silicate of alumina, used in cleansing cloth' (*OED*); thus gin is a scourer and 'cleaner out']

full-fledged *adj.* [19C] of a virgin, ripe for defloration. [SE *full-fledged*, of a bird, fully feathered, grown to maturity]

full French *n. see* FRENCH n.² (3).

full-growner *n.* [mid-19C] an adult.

full-guts *n.* [19C] a fat-stomached person; thus *full-gutted*, fat. [SE *full* + GUTS n.¹ (1)/-GUTS sfx]

full hand *n.* [1940s+] (*Aus.*) **1** something important, significant or powerful that is withheld or hidden away, a secret 'weapon', something that will 'win'. **2** a life sentence. [fig. uses of poker jargon *full hand*, the Aus. var. of *full house*, the winning hand of 1 pair and 3 of a kind]

full hop *adv.* [late 19C] very enthusiastically, unreservedly. [var. ON THE HOP phr.¹]

full house *n.*¹ [mid-19C+] a very busy time. [theatrical use]

full house *n.*² [1940s+] (*mainly US, orig. milit.*) **1** a simultaneous dose of both syphilis and gonorrhoea. **2** an infestation of both head and body lice. **3** a combination of any varieties of disease. [fig. uses of poker jargon *full house*, the winning hand of 1 pair and 3 of a kind]

fullie *n.* (*also* **fully**) [1990s+] (*US gang*) an automatic weapon, e.g. an Uzo, Glock or Tech Nine, as used in gang wars. [SE *fully automatic*]

fullied *adj.* [mid-19C–1930s] committed for trial. [FULLY v.]

fullies *n. see* FOLLIES n.

full in the belly *phr.* (*also* **big-bellied**) [18C–19C] pregnant.

full jerry *n.* [20C+] (*Aus./N.Z.*) the whole truth, all the information, 'the facts'. [FULL JERRY adj.]

full jerry *adj.* [late 19C+] knowledgeable, informed. [SE *full* + JERRY adj. (1)]

full monty *n. see* MONTY n.[1].

full moon *n.*[1] [1970s+] the bared buttocks, deliberately exhibited in public. [MOON v.[2] (2)]

full moon *n.*[2] *see* MOON n.[5].

full mourning *n. see* MOURNING n. (1).

full mouth *n.* [late 16C–early 17C] a talkative person. [SE *with full mouth*, loudly, aloud]

fullmouth *adj.* [20C+] (*W.I.*) bad-mannered, unrestrained. [FULL MOUTH n.; image of 'talking with one's mouth full']

full of *phr.* (*also* **full about**) [mid-19C–1910s] (*Aus.*) thoroughly displeased by, 'fed up with'.

full of bean soup *phr. see* FULL OF PRUNES phr.

full of crap *phr.* [1930s+] (*orig. US*) contemptible, stupid, nonsensical. [CRAP n.[3] (1)/CRAP n.[3] (3); var. on FULL OF SHIT phr.]

full of doo doo *phr. see* FULL OF SHIT phr.

full of 'em *phr.* [late 19C–1900s] infested with fleas.

full of gifts as a brazen horse of farts *phr.* [late 18C–early 19C] a phr. used of a notably mean person. [SE *gift*, a white spot beneath the fingernail, supposedly a sign of gifts or presents; the stingy man hoards such items for himself; a *brazen horse* is a bronze horse and as such does not FART v. (1)]

full of glue *phr.* [1920s] (*US*) worthless, contemptible. [ety. unknown]

full of hop *phr.* (*also* **full of hops**) [1900s–20s] (*US*) behaving as if one were drugged, acting without sense. [HOP n.[2]]

full of it *phr.*[1] [late 19C] pregnant. **2** [late 19C] (*US campus*) unwilling. **3** [1940s+] of a person, lying, spinning a line, telling tales. [(3) euph. for FULL OF SHIT phr. (1)]

full of it *phr.*[2] *see* FULL adj.[1] (1).

full of money as a toad is of feathers *phr.* [late 18C–19C] penniless, impoverished.

full of piss and vinegar *phr.* [1940s+] (*orig. US*) healthy in mind and body, full of energy and élan. [note late 19C local New Orleans synon. *full of prunes*]

full of prunes *phr.* (*also* **full of bean soup, …prune juice**) [late 19C–1930s] (*US campus*) mistaken, nonsensical, stupid. [the laxative powers; thus euph. for FULL OF SHIT phr.]

full of shit *phr.* (*also* **full of doo doo, …stuff**) [1930s+] **1** of a person, lying, spinning a line, telling untrue tales of an experience. **2** unpleasant, distasteful. [SE *full* + SHIT n.[1] (1)/SHIT n.[3] (3)]

full of shit and sticks *phr. see* ALL PISS AND WIND phr.

full-pooped *adj. see* FULL-BOTTOMED adj.

full quid *n.* (*also* **full pound/shilling**) [1930s+] (*Aus./N.Z.*) sensible, intelligent, aware, trustworthy, 'all there'; esp. in negative phr. NOT THE FULL QUID phr., not very intelligent, slightly eccentric, odd. [QUID n. (2)/SE *pound/shilling*; lit. the 'whole pound'; var. on NOT ALL THERE phr.]

full-rigged *adj. see* FULL-BOTTOMED adj.

full scream *n.* [20C+] **1** (*US Black*) total commitment, no holds barred. **2** (*UK Und.*) at the highest estimate.

full sheet *n.* [1950s+] (*UK prison*) a report against an officer for a serious offence against a prisoner. [the sheet of paper on which the complaint is written]

full shilling *n.*[1] [1960s] (*Irish*) the proper, complete thing.

full shilling *n.*[2] *see* FULL QUID n.

full split *adv.* [19C] (*US*) at full speed. [the person fig. 'splits' away from the place they have left]

full stop *n.* [mid-19C] (*boxing*) a hard blow.

full suit of mourning *n. see* MOURNING n.

full team *n. see* WHOLE TEAM (AND THE DOG UNDER THE WAGON) n.

full time *n.* [1940s] (*US Und./prison*) a life sentence. [TIME n.[1]]

full tit *n.* [1950s+] (*N.Z.*) the greatest possible effort. [TIT n.[3] (2), i.e. the image of pressing hard on a button or switch]

full to the bow-tie *phr.* [1950s] very drunk, or having drunk a large quantity. [FULL adj.[1] (1)]

full to the bung *phr.* (*also* **full to the brim**) [mid-late 19C] very drunk. [SE/FULL adj.[1] (1) + SE *bung*, the stopper of a barrel of beer]

full to the gills *phr.* [1910s+] (*orig. US*) very drunk (cf. ARSEHOLED adj.). [FULL adj.[1] (1) + GILLS n. (1)]

full treatment *n.* [1940s+] (*orig. US*) 'the works', the most complete way of dealing with something.

full two bob, the *phr.* [1960s+] (*Aus.*) worthwhile, as good as advertised. [lit. worth the two shillings that is charged]

fullums *n. see* FULHAMS n. (1).

full up *adj.* [20C+] (*W.I.*) of an unmarried woman, pregnant.

full up (of) *phr.* [late 19C+] (*Aus.*) disgusted with, surfeited with.

fully *n. see* FULLIE n.

fully *v.* [mid-19C–1930s] to commit for trial; as n., *fulley*, a trial. [phr. *the prisoner was fully committed for trial*, commonly found in penny-a-line journalism]

fully *adv.* [1990s+] (*US Black*) an intensifier, totally, completely.

fumble *v.* **1** [16C+] to indulge in sexual foreplay; the inference is usu. of feebleness, as exhibited by an ageing lecher. **2** [mid-17C–19C] to be impotent. [joc. uses of SE]

fumbler *n.* **1** [late 17C–18C] an impotent man, esp. a husband; thus *fumbling*, impotent. **2** [early 18C] a young lecher. [FUMBLE v.]

fumbler's hall *n.* [mid-17C–19C] **1** the vagina. **2** a metaphorical place where impotent men might be confined as punishment for their failings. [FUMBLER n. + SE *hall*]

fumigate (one's brains) *v.* (*also* **fume**) [late 19C–1960s] (*US campus*) to smoke.

fumo d'Angola *n.* [1960s+] (*drugs*) marijuana (cf. ACAPULCO (GOLD) n.). [Port., lit. 'the smoke of Angola']

f.u.m.t.u. *phr.* [20C+] *fucked up more than usual* (cf. S.N.A.F.U. n.). [abbr.; FUCKED UP adj.]

fumunda cheese *n.* [1980s+] (*US campus*) smegma. [SE *from under* (the foreskin) + CHEESE n.[2] (1)]

fun *n.*[1] [late 17C–early 19C] the buttocks, the backside. [SE *fundament*]

fun *n.*[2] [late 17C–19C] a cheat, a trick; thus phr. *put the fun upon*, to trick, to cheat.

fun *n.*[3] *see* FOON n.

fun *v.* **1** [late 17C–19C; 1960s+] to cheat, to deceive, to swindle. **2** [19C+] to joke with, to tease. [FUN n.[2]; (1) 1960s+ use is US Black]

fun and frolics *n.* (*also* **flowers and frolics**) [1940s+] the testicles (cf. CHEESE AND CRACKERS n.). [rhy. sl. = BALLOCKS n.[1] (1)]

funbags *n.* (*also* **funsacks**) [1960s+] the female breasts, esp. when large. [SE *fun* + BAGS n.[1] (2)]

fun bone *n.* [1970s] (*gay*) the penis. [SE *fun* + SE *bone*/BONE n.[1] (1)]

fun-button *n.* [1990s+] the clitoris (cf. BABY IN THE BOAT n.). [ext. BUTTON n.[1] (3)]

funch *n.* [1970s+] sexual liaisons at lunchtime. [FUCK v.[1] + SE *lunch*; the trad. genteel term is euph. SE *matinée*]

funds *n.* [late 19C+] (*US Black/campus*) money.

fungoo! *excl. see* BAH-FUNGOO! excl.

fungus *n.* **1** [late 18C+] an unpleasant person. **2** [mid-late 19C] an old man. **3** [1920s+] a moustache; a beard; thus as insult *fungus-face, fungus-features* etc (cf. FACE FUNGUS n.).

fun hatch *n.* [1990s+] the vagina.

fun joint *n.* [1940s–50s] (*US drugs*) an opium den. [Chi. *fun*, a measure of opium + JOINT n.[4] (1)]

Funk *n. see* PETER FUNK n.

funk *n.*[1] (*also* **fonk**) **1** [late 17C–18C] tobacco. **2** [late 17C–18C] tobacco smoke. **3** [early 19C; 1940s+] a stench. **4** [1930s+] (*orig. US Black*) sweat generated during sex, dancing, general body odour. **5** [1930s+] (*orig. US Black*) anything basic, elemental, earthy; the essence of being. **6** [1970s] (*US*) anything attractive or beautiful. **7** [2000s] (*US campus*) any sexually transmitted disease.

funk *n.*[2] **1** [18C+] (a state of) cowardice, terror. **2** [late 18C+] a black mood; a state of depression; thus *funking*, furious. **3** [late 19C] (*US Und.*) a cheat, a swindler. **4** [late 19C+] a coward. **5** [1900s] (*Aus./US Und.*) an informer. **6** [1920s–30s] (*US tramp*) a sneak-thief. [orig. Oxford Univ. use; ult. Flemish *fonck*, fear]

funk *v.*[1] [late 17C+] **1** to smoke a pipe. **2** to make a stench. **3** to blow smoke on someone. **4** of an object, to smoke. [FUNK n.[1]]

funk *v.*[2] **1** [early 18C+] (*also* **funk it, funk on**) to act in a cowardly manner, to flinch or shrink through fear; to worry. **2** [19C+] (*also* **funk it**) to try to back out of anything, to fight shy of, to wish or try to shirk or evade (an undertaking, duty etc.). **3** [mid-19C–1910s] (*also* **funkify**) to frighten or scare someone. **4** [late 19C–1910s] to fear, to be afraid of someone.

funked out *adj.* [1990s+] **1** in the style of the music and clothes promoted by the funk bands of the 1970s, esp. George Clinton's Parliament/Funkadelic. **2** sophisticated, blasé.

funked up *adj.*[1] [1990s+] (*US Black*) excellent, splendid, first-rate. [FUNK n.[1] (6)]

funked up *adj.*[2] [2000s] (*US*) hurt, destroyed. [euph. for FUCKED UP adj. (4)]

funker *n.*[1] **1** [19C] a petty criminal, rated as the lowest order of thieves. **2** [mid-19C+] one who is a coward, a weakling or a shirker. **3** [late 19C] a prostitute who quits the streets when the weather is bad. [FUNK v.[2] (1)]

funker *n.*[2] [early–mid-19C] **1** a pipe, a cigar. **2** a fire. [FUNK v.[1]]

funkhole *n.* [1910s+] (*orig. milit.*) anywhere one can hide. [FUNK n.[2] (1) + SE *hole*]

funkify *v. see* FUNK v.[2] (3).

funk in the trunk *n.* [1990s+] (*US Black teen*) **1** music issuing from one's car trunk or boot. **2** a general term for being FUNKY adj.[3] (1). [SE *funk music*, used as a generic; the stereo speakers are usu. sited in the car boot]

funk it *v. see* FUNK v.[2].

funk on *v. see* FUNK v.[2] (1).

funk on a dunk *v.* [1990s+] (*US Black*) to joke, to act insincerely. [FUNK v.[2] (2) + basketball jargon *dunk*; basketball star Shaquille O'Neal's dictum, 'Don't fake the funk on a nasty dunk']

funk the cobbler *v.* [late 17C–early 19C] (*UK juv.*) to 'smoke out' a schoolmate, usu. with asafoetida. [FUNK v.[1] (2); the trick was apparently first performed by blowing the foul fumes into the cracks in a cobbler's stall]

funkum *n.* [1930s] lavender, as sold in sachets. [FUNK n.[1] (3)]

funk up *v.* [1960s] (*US Black*) fig. or lit., to 'stink out', to make a smell. [FUNK v.[1] (2)/FUNK n.[1] (4)]

funky *adj.*[1] [late 17C; 20C+] lit. or fig., smelling very unpleasant. [FUNK n.[1] (3) + sfx -*y*]

funky *adj.*[2] [mid-19C+] fearful, timid, nervous, cowardly. [FUNK n.[2] (1) + sfx -*y*]

funky *adj.*[3] **1** [20C+] (*orig. US Black*) soulful, elemental. **2** [1950s+] (*orig. US Black*) pertaining to funk music. **3** [1960s+] (*orig. US Black*) fashionable, 'with it'. **4** [1980s+] (*US campus*) weird. [FUNK n.[1] (5) + sfx -*y*; but note isolated *c.*1900 cit. in (1) in Buddy Bolden lyrics]

funky *adj.*[4] **1** [20C+] a general term of disparagement, unpleasant, unappealing etc. **2** [1990s+] (*US teen*) wrong, unsatisfactory. [FUNK n.[2] (1)/FUNK n.[2] (2) + sfx -*y*]

funky-ass *adj.* [1960s+] (*US Black*) **1** a general term of derision, with overtones of bad odours. **2** on bad = good pattern,

something excellent, exciting. [FUNKY adj.[4] (1)/FUNKY adj.[3] (3) + -ASS sfx]

funky Broadway *n.* [1950s] (*US Black*) the main street of any town, where the high life is to be found. [FUNKY adj.[3] (1) + *Broadway* as a generic]

funky dude *n.* [1950s+] (*US Black*) a confidence trickster's victim, a dupe. [FUNKY adj.[3] (3) + DUDE n. (2); a reversal of the lit. meaning, i.e. *not* a smart, fashionable city slicker]

funky fresh *adj.* (*also* **fonky fresh**) [1980s+] (*US Black*) a general adj. of high praise, the most sophisticated, the smartest, the most attractive. [FONKY adj.[1]/FUNKY adj.[3] (1) + FRESH adj.[3] (2)]

funna *v. see* FINNA v.

funned-up *adj.* [1950s] (*US*) pleasure-loving. [SE *fun*]

funnel *n.* **1** [early 18C; 1900s] the throat. **2** [20C+] (*orig. US Black*) a drunkard.

funnies *n.*[1] (*orig. US*) **1** [mid-19C+] jokes, humorous conversation. **2** [1920s+] comic strips in daily/weekly newspapers. [abbr. SE *funny papers*]

funnies *n.*[2] *see* FUNNY BUSINESS n.

funniment *n.* [19C] the vagina. [FUNNY BIT n. + play on SE *fundament*]

funny *n.* [1950s+] a joke. [abbr. SE *funny story*]

funny *adj.*[1] [mid-18C–mid-19C] tipsy, slightly drunk. [SE *feeling funny*]

funny *adj.*[2] **1** [late 19C+] difficult, problematic; usu. in GET FUNNY (WITH) v. **2** [20C+] corrupt, fraudulent. **3** [20C+] weak, out of control. **4** [20C+] (*US*) sexually aroused.

funny *adj.*[3] [1930s+] of a man, homosexual, effeminate. [abbr. fig. use of SE *funny one/funny fellow*]

funny as a bit of string *phr.* (*also* **funny as a piece of string**) [1930s+] (*N.Z.*) highly amusing.

funny as a box of worms *phr.* [1900s] (*N.Z.*) very funny; often used ironically.

funny as a crutch *phr.* [1910s–60s] (*US*) **1** very funny. **2** not funny at all.

funny bin *n. see* FUNNY HOUSE n.

funny bird *n.* [late 19C] an odd, eccentric person. [SE *funny* + BIRD n.[2] (1)]

funny bit *n.* [19C] the vagina.

funny book *n.* [1960s] a comic book (cf. FUNNY PAGES n.).

funny bunny *n.* [1960s] (*US*) a victim.

funny-bunny *adj.* [1960s+] (*US*) weird, odd, eccentric (cf. APEY adj.). [SE *funny* + redup.]

funny business *n.* (*also* **funnies, funny stuff, funny work**) [late 19C+] deceitful or underhand practices.

funny cigarette *n. see* HAPPY CIGARETTE n.

funny-face *n.* **1** [late 19C+] a term of derision. **2** [1920s+] a term of affectionate address.

funny farm *n.* [1940s+] a psychiatric institution.

funny house *n.* (*also* **funny bin, funny place**) [20C+] (*US*) a psychiatric institution.

funny man *n.*[1] [mid-19C+] a joker. [later 20C+ use often sarcastic and derog.]

funny man *n.*[2] [1970s+] (*US Black*) a homosexual man. [FUNNY adj.[3] + SE *man*]

funny money *n.* **1** [1910s+] (*UK/US Und.*) (*also* **funny paper**) counterfeit money. **2** [1960s–70s] substitute money, i.e. coupons, certificates etc. **3** [1960s+] tricks, deceits. **4** [1980s] (*US Black*) a small amount of money. **5** [1980s+] any money that has been gained illegally, usu. through some form of fraud. [FUNNY adj.[2] (2) + SE *money*]

funny pages *n.* (*also* **funny papers**) [1930s+] those pages which newspapers reserve for comic strips; thus the comics themselves (cf. FUNNY BOOK n.).

funny place *n. see* FUNNY HOUSE n.

funny stuff *n.*[1] [1980s+] (*Aus. prison*) alcohol. [? a revival of 19C FUNNY adj.[1]]

funny stuff n.[2] see FUNNY BUSINESS n.

funny style n. [1980s] (US Black) **1** referring to someone seen as different from the speaker. **2** a homosexual.

funny-time adj. [1950s–70s] (US Black) strange, bizarre.

funny trap n. [1960s] a semi-joc. term of abuse. [SE funny + TRAP n.[3]]

funny work n. see FUNNY BUSINESS n.

fun of Cork, the n. [20C+] (Aus.) a very jolly time. [imported by Irish immigrants]

funsacks n. see FUNBAGS n.

funt n. (also **foont, phunt**) [mid-19C+] £1. [Ger. pfund, thence Yid.]

fur n. **1** [late 16C+] female pubic hair. **2** [18C+] the vagina. **3** [1950s–60s] (US Black) a woman's wig. **4** [1960s] (US Black) a woman.

furbelow n. [18C–mid-19C] female pubic hair; the vagina. [SE furbelow, an adornment to a dress or other garment; ult. f. falbala, trimming for women's petticoats, scarves etc + pun on FUR n. (1) + SE below; the term begins as a ref. to a petticoat typically worn by a prostitute, then by metonymy to the woman herself, thence the pubic hair and/or vagina]

furburger n. [1960s+] the vagina, esp. during the act of cunnilingus since then it is 'eaten' (cf. BACON SANDWICH n.; BEARD RIDE n.; BOX LUNCH n.). [FUR n. (1) + play on SE hamburger; note synon. RMC Duntroon (Aus.) muffburger]

furch n. [1920s] a euph. for FUCK n.[1], in various contexts.

fur doughnut n. [1970s] the vagina (cf. APPLE n.[6]). [FUR n. (1); the doughnut has a HOLE n.[1] (2)]

furgle v. (also **flurgle**) [1920s–70s] to have sexual intercourse; thus furgler/fergler, a FUCKER n. (1) (cf. FRIG v.). [euph. for FUCK v.[1]]

furioso n. [late 17C–early 18C] a boaster, a braggart; an angry person.

furk n. [1920s+] a euph. for FUCK n.[1], used in a variety of contexts.

furking adj. [1920s+] a euph. for FUCKING adj.

furman n. [late 17C–mid-19C] (UK Und.) an alderman. [SE fur + man; the fur trimmings that adorn his official robes]

furmity-faced adj. [16C–17C] light-complexioned. [SE frumenty, hulled wheat (Lat. frumentum) boiled in milk and sweetened]

furnish n. [late 19C] an embellishment (to furnishing, clothing etc). [16C–17C SE]

furniture-polish n. see SHOE-POLISH n.

furphy n. (also **furph**) [1910s+] (Aus.) a groundless rumour; thus furphy-king/-monger, a gossip. [proper name John Furphy, the proprietor of sanitary carts used by the Aus. forces in WW1; the gossip and chat around these carts developed into the general word. Furphy, a former ironfounder, made his carts of iron, and on them was inscribed 'Good, better, best, / never let it rest, / till your good is better / and your better best.' The same slogan was also inscribed in Pitman's shorthand. Note UK services, Elsan gen, a rumour, lit. news from the chemical toilet]

fur pie n. [1930s+] the female pubic hair and genitals. [FUR n. (1) + SE pie]

furpiece n. [1990s+] the vagina. [FUR n. (1)]

furrow n. [17C–19C] the vagina (cf. AGREEABLE RUTS OF LIFE n.).

furry adj. [1990s+] (US campus) of a woman, attractive. [? extrapolated f. FOX n.[5] (1)]

furry bicycle stand n. [1990s+] the vagina. [SE fur/FUR n. (1); the bicycle stand is a groove moulded into a concrete block]

furry front bottom n. [1990s+] the female genitals. [SE furry/FUR n. (1) + FRONT BOTTOM n.]

furry hole n. [1990s+] the vagina (cf. BLACK HOLE n.[1]). [SE fur/FUR n. (1) + SE hole/HOLE n.[1] (2)]

furry hoop n. [1960s+] (Aus.) the vagina. [SE fur/FUR n. (1) + SE hoop/HOOP n.[2] (1)]

furry letterbox n. [1990s+] the vagina (cf. BAG n.[1]). [SE fur/FUR n. (1) + SE letterbox, i.e. an 'opening']

furry monkey n. [2000s] the vagina. [SE fur/FUR n. (1) + SE monkey]

furschlugginer adj. see FERSCHLUGGINER adj.

further behind than Walla Walla phr. [1950s+] (Aus.) delayed, at a disadvantage. [proper name of the racehorse Walla Walla, celebrated for his ability to come from far behind and still win]

fur trade n. [mid-19C] (UK Und.) the legal profession.

fury n. [19C+] a euph. for hell.

furze-bush n. [mid-19C] female, occas. male, pubic hair. [SE furze, a spiny evergreen shrub with yellow flowers + BUSH n.[2] (1)/SE bush]

fusby n. [early 18C–mid-19C] a woman (in any negative context). [? FUBBY adj. + FUSSOCK n.]

fuse n. [1970s] (S.Afr.) a cigarette. [the image of the cigarette as a fuse attached to the 'bomb', i.e. the head]

fusebox n. [1940s–60s] (orig. US Black) the head.

fusel oil n. see FUSIL OIL n.

fushme n. [mid–late 19C] 5 shillings (25p). [ety. unknown]

fusilier n. [1900s] beer. [rhy. sl.]

fusil oil n. (also **fusel oil**) [late 19C–1900s] (US) whisky. [SE fusel oil, 'a term for a mixture of several homologous alcohols, chiefly amylic alcohol, and especially applied to this when in its crude form' (Syd. Soc. Lex. 1885)]

fusled adj. see FOOZLED adj. (1).

fuss n. [mid-17C–early 18C] a lazy, fat woman. [abbr. FUSSOCK n.]

fuss v.[1] (US) **1** [late 19C+] to quarrel, to pick a fight. **2** [1900s–20s] to court, to date. **3** [1920s–30s] to engage in sexual activity short of intercourse. [SE make a fuss (of)]

fuss v.[2] see FUSS (UP) v.

fussbox n. [1950s+] a notably fussy person.

fussbudget n. [20C+] (US) **1** a particularly fussy person. **2** (also **fuss-bug, fuss-butt, fuss-button, fuzz-button, fuzzy-dud**) a bad-tempered person. [SE fuss + budget, one who embodies certain characteristics]

fusser n. [1900s] (US) a womanizer.

fussock n. (also **fussocks, fuzzock**) [mid-17C–19C] a lazy, fat woman; thus fat fussock, a fat, strapping woman; old fussock, an ill-kempt old woman. [Yorks. dial. fussock, a stupid person, a coarse, fat woman; 'a lazy, fat-arsed bitch' (B.E.)]

fussock v. [1910s–20s] to make a fuss, to cause a commotion, to be noisy. [ext. SE fuss]

fusspot n. [1920s+] a notably fussy person. [SE fuss + -POT sfx]

fuss (up) v. [1920s] (US) to agitate, to annoy, to irritate, to disturb. [ext. of SE fuss]

fussy adj. [1920s+] **1** of clothes, over-ornamented. **2** in general, over-ornamental.

fustian n. [late 17C–19C] alcohol. [SE fustian, a kind of coarse cloth made of cotton and flax; thus note the contrast with 'smooth' SATIN n.[1] (1)]

fustilugs n. (also **fusty luggs**) [17C–mid-19C] 'a Fulsom, Beastly, Nasty Woman' (B.E.). [lit. 'dirty ears']

fut! excl. [early 17C] a general excl.; a synon. with FUCK! excl. (1). [Fr. foutre, to fuck]

futhermucker n. [1960s+] (US) a joc. reverse of MOTHER-FUCKER n. (1).

futt about v. [1930s] a euph. for FUCK ABOUT v.

futter n. [late 19C] sexual intercourse. [FUTTER v. (1)]

futter v. **1** [17C; late 19C+] to have sexual intercourse with. **2** [1990s+] to waste time, i.e. semi-euph. for FUCK ABOUT v. (1). [Fr. foutre, to fuck]

future n. **1** [1970s+] (US campus) an unattractive man. **2** [1980s] the male genitals. [ety. unknown; ? link to LATER FOR — phr.]

futy n. **1** [20C+] the vagina. **2** [1970s+] (US gay) the passive partner in homosexual intercourse. [FUTZ n. (3)]

futz n. (US) **1** [1930s–50s] (also **phutz**) a fool, an unpleasant person. **2** [1930s+] a euph. for FUCK n.[1]. **3** [1940s+] the vagina. [FUTZ v.; (3) ? link to PFOTZ n.]

futz v. (also **futz around, phutz around**) (US) **1** [1910s+] to waste time, to mess around, to trifle with. **2** [1940s+] to fiddle with. **3** [1940s+] to treat with contempt. [Ger. *furzen*, to fart or Yid. *arumfartzen zikh*, to fart around; the term is also a euph. for FUCK ABOUT v.]

futzer n. [1930s] a foolish or unpleasant person. [FUTZ v. (1)]

futzing adj. [1930s–60s] (US) a euph. for FUCKING adj. [FUTZ n. (2)]

futz off v. [1920s+] to leave, to go away. [euph. for FUCK OFF v. (1)]

futz out v. [1960s] (US) to spoil, to confound. [var. on FUTZ UP v.]

futz up v. [1940s–60s] (US) to spoil, to confound. [euph. for FUCK UP v.]

fuz-chats n. [late 19C] (UK tramp) those who sleep in the open air. [SE *furze* + CHEAT n. (1)]

fuzz n.[1] **1** [1920s+] (orig. US) a policeman; the police in general. **2** [1930s–40s] (US) a detective. [? SE *fuss*, which a policeman makes; or ? MAN WITH (THE) FUZZY BALLS n. although this pre-dates; without detailed context (1) and (2) can be indistinguishable]

fuzz n.[2] **1** [1930s+] pubic hair. **2** [1970s] (US Black) a goatee beard.

fuzz v.[1] [late 17C–early 18C] to make drunk; esp. as *fuzzed*, tipsy, drunk. [? SE *fuzz*, light, insubstantial particles; the obvious link, FUZZY adj., drunk, is a later coinage]

fuzz v.[2] **1** [mid-18C] to deal twice together with the same pack of cards, for luck's sake, at whist. **2** [mid-18C–19C] to shuffle cards very carefully, to change the pack. [? onomat. sound of riffling cards, or ? SE *fuss*]

fuzz-brain n. [1960s+] a stupid person. [SE *fuzz(y)*, blurred + sfx *-brain*]

fuzz-brained adj. [20C+] (US) stupid (cf. AMOEBA-BRAINED adj.). [FUZZ-BRAIN n.]

fuzz bumper n. [1980s+] (US campus) a lesbian (cf. BEAN FLICKER n.). [FUZZ n.[2] (1) + SE *bumper*/BUMPER n.[5]]

fuzzburger n. [1960s+] the vagina, esp. during the act of cunnilingus (cf. BACON SANDWICH n.; BEARD RIDE n.; BOX LUNCH n.). [FUZZ n.[2] (1) + play on SE *hamburger*; var. on FURBURGER n.]

fuzz-button n. see FUSSBUDGET n. (2).

fuzzface n. [20C+] (US tramp) a young tramp (whose beard has not properly grown).

fuzzhead n. [1980s] (US Black) a woman with tightly curled or 'nappy' hair. [FUZZ n.[2] (1)]

fuzzies n. [1960s] (US) pubic hair. [FUZZ n.[2] (1)]

fuzzled adj. see FOOZLED adj. (2).

fuzzmobile n. [1970s–80s] (US) a police car. [FUZZ n.[1] (1) + -MOBILE sfx]

fuzz nutted adj. [1970s–80s] stupid. [? the image of immaturity, i.e. one's pubic hair is as yet no more than *fuzz*]

fuzzock n. see FUSSOCK n.

fuzz tail n. see FUZZY TAIL n.

fuzzy n.[1] [1940s+] a policeman. [FUZZ n.[1] (1) + sfx *-y*]

fuzzy n.[2] see FUZZY-WUZZY n.[1].

fuzzy adj. [late 18C+] drunk; thus *fuzziness*, drunkenness (cf. ADDLED adj.).

fuzzy cup n. [1970s+] (US Black) the vagina (cf. BAG n.[1]). [FUZZ n.[2] (1)]

fuzzy-dud n. see FUSSBUDGET n. (2).

fuzzy end of the lollipop n. [1950s] (US) the worst treatment, a situation where everything is against one (cf. HAVE THE SWEETEST END OF THE STICK v.; HAVE THE WORSE END OF THE STAFF v.; ROUGH END OF THE PINEAPPLE n.; SHORT END (OF THE STICK) n.). [coined by Billy Wilder for Marilyn Monroe in the film *Some Like It Hot* (1958)]

fuzzy-face n. [1920s–60s] (US) a young man. [his light facial hair]

fuzzy lap flounder n. [1990s+] (orig. US) the vagina (cf. BEARDED CLAM n.). [FUZZ n.[2] (1) + SE *lap* + *flounder*, the fish]

fuzzy tail n. (also **fuzz tail**) **1** [1910s–30s] (US tramp) the lowest category of vagrant or tramp. **2** [1920s–30s] an ill-natured person. **3** [1930s] a conceited person. [? the way the fur of an angry or frightened animal bristles]

fuzzy-wuzzy n.[1] (also **fuzzy**) **1** [late 19C+] a soldier's derog. nickname for a Sudanese warrior. **2** [20C+] 'a coloured native of other countries, such as Fiji and New Guinea' (OED). [orig. the Sudanese method of dressing the hair; latterly used of anyone with tightly curled 'fuzzy' hair (and Black skin)]

fuzzy-wuzzy n.[2] [1900s] (Aus.) a derog. term for an intellectual. [? their obscurantism, i.e. they render things 'fuzzy']

fye-buck n. see SYEBUCK n.

f.y.f.i. phr. [1960s+] *for your fucking information*, acronym often appended to memos in business. [abbr.]

f.y.o. n. [1980s+] (N.Z.) an invitation to a party at which the guests are asked to supply the drink. [abbr. *fill your own*, i.e. a beer flagon]

fy out v. [late 19C] to spy, to survey. [? SE *spy*]

fyst see under FOIST.

G

G *n.*[1] **1** [1920s+] (*orig. US*) (*also* **gee**) 1000 (usu. dollars or pounds) (cf. C *n.*[1]; K *n.*[2]). **2** [1990s+] (*US Black*) money. [abbr. GRAND *n.*[1]]

G *n.*[2] [1970s–80s] (*UK Black*) a Giro cheque, thus money. [abbr.]

G *n.*[3] [1980s+] **1** (*US Black*) a gangster. **2** (*orig. US Black*) a friend, a partner; also as a term of address. **3** (*US campus*) a smart and attractive male. **4** (*US Black*) a girlfriend. [abbr.; (2) is affectionate use of (1)]

G *n.*[4] *see* G-MAN *n.*[1] (1).

G, the *n.* [1930s+] (*US Und.*) the US government (cf. G *adj.*). [abbr.]

G *adj.* [1920s+] (*US*) federal (cf. G, THE *n.*; G-GIRL *n.*; G-GUY *n.*; G-HEAT *n.*; G-MAN *n.*[1]; G-WOMAN *n.*). [i.e. government]

g *n.*[1] (*also* **gee**) **1** [1920s] (*US tramp*) a gallon of liquor. **2** [1950s+] (*US drugs*) a grain, usu. of morphine. **3** [1990s+] (*drugs*) a gram, orig. of heroin or cocaine, and latterly also of cannabis. **4** [2000s] (*US drugs*) gamma hydroxybutyrate (GHB). [abbr.]

g *n.*[2] [1940s–60s] (*US*) a cheating device. [abbr. GAFF *n.*[3] (1)]

g *n.*[3] [1970s+] (*US Black*) the female genitals, the vagina. [abbr. GOODIES *n.* (7)]

g *n.*[4] [1990s+] (*US prison*) prison-made cigarettes. [abbr. SE *generic*, no-brand]

g *n.*[5] [2000s] a G-string. [abbr.]

gaan kak! *excl.* [1970s+] (*S.Afr.*) a synon. of GO TO HELL! excl. [KAK *v.* (2); lit. 'go shit!']

gaan to bed *phr.* [1950s+] (*W.I. Rasta*) a general intensifier, following a v. of liking or loving, in any context, e.g. *I love hafu yam gaan to bed!*

gaan vrek *v. see* VREK *v.*

gab *n.* **1** [18C+] the mouth. **2** [19C+] idle chatter. **3** [mid-19C+] talk, conversation, esp. charming and persuasive. **4** [1920s] (*US*) one who talks freely, one who cannot keep a secret. [Scot. *gab*, the mouth]

gab *v.* [late 18C+] to talk. [GAB *n.* (1)]

g.a.b.a. *n.* [1980s] (*Aus.*) the outback. [abbr. the great Australian *bugger all*]

gab-artist *n.* [1940s–50s] (*US*) a talker, esp. a convincing talker. [GAB *v.* + ARTIST sfx]

gabba *n.* [1960s+] (*S.Afr.*) a friend. [Heb. *chaver*/Yid. *khaver*, a comrade]

gab-bag *n.* [1940s] (*Aus.*) a gossip. [GAB *n.* (2) + -BAG sfx]

gabber *n.*[1] [mid-19C] talk, loquacity. [GABBER *v.*]

gabber *n.*[2] **1** [1930s+] a chatterer, an indiscreet talkative person, a gossip. **2** [1940s] a lawyer. **3** [1940s–60s] (*US*) a radio commentator. **4** [1980s] a policeman (cf. BEAT-POUNDER *n.*). [GAB *v.*]

gabber *v.* [mid-17C+] to talk; thus *gabbering*, verbose. [dial. *gabber*/SE *gabble*/GABBLE *v.*]

gabberlooney *n.* (*also* **gobaloon, gobberloony**) [20C+] (*Ulster*) one who talks too much, acts the fool. [Scot. *gaberlunzie*, a strolling beggar; or ? GAB *v.* + LOONY *n.*]

gabbey *adj. see* GABBY *adj.*

gabble *n.* **1** [18C+] verbosity, chatter. **2** [19C] a chatterer, a gossip. [GABBLE *v.*]

gabble *v.* [18C+] to chatter, to talk meaninglessly. [16C–18C SE]

gabbleblooter *n.* [20C+] (*Ulster*) a loudmouth, a prattler. [SE *gabble* + BLOOTER *n.*]

gabbletrap *n.* [mid-19C] (*Aus.*) a silly chatterer. [GABBLE *n.* (1)]

gabbo *n.* (*also* **gabo**) [1930s–50s] (*US*) a chatterer. [GAB *v.* + -O sfx]

gab-box *n.* [20C+] (*US*) **1** the mouth. **2** a chatterer. [GAB *n.* (1) + SE *box*]

gabby *n.*[1] [mid-19C+] (*Aus.*) water. [? Aboriginal]

gabby *n.*[2] *see* GABY *n.*

gabby *adj.* (*also* **gabbey, gaby**) [late 19C+] talkative. [orig. Scot.; GAB *v.* + sfx -*y*]

gabby-guts *n.* [1940s] (*Irish*) an excessive talker. [GABBY *adj.* + -GUTS sfx]

gabby row *n.* [20C+] (*US*) the area of town where the poor live. [GAB *v.* + SE *row*; the closeness of the houses leads to much neighbourly conversation]

Gabe's off-ox *n.* [late 19C+] a headstrong person. [lit. 'Gabriel's off-ox'; the offside ox of a pair is presumed to be the less tractable]

gabey *n. see* GABY *n.*

gabfest *n.* (*also* **gab session, jabfest**) [late 19C+] (*orig. US*) **1** a gathering for talk; a spell of talking; a prolonged conference or conversation. **2** garrulous, unrestrained talk. [GAB *v.* + -FEST sfx; *jab* is mis-sp. of *gab*]

gable (end) *n.* [late 19C] the head.

gabo *n. see* GABBO *n.*

gaboon *n. see* GOBOON *n.*

gabriel *n.* **1** [1930s–40s] (*US Black*) a trumpet-player. **2** [1930s–40s] (*US Black*) a puritan, a killjoy, a 'bible-thumper'. **3** [1930s–50s] (*UK prison*) the chapel organist. [the archangel *Gabriel* who sounds the 'last trump']

gabs, the *n.* [1990s+] a propensity to talk too much. [GAB *v.*]

gab session *n. see* GABFEST *n.*

gabshite *n. see* GOBSHITE *n.*[1] (2).

gabslick *n.* [20C+] (*Ulster*) a talkative person. [GAB *v.* + SLICK *n.*[1] (1)]

gabster *n.* [late 19C] a chatterer, an idle talker. [GAB *v.* + -STER sfx]

gab string *n.* (*also* **gob string**) [late 18C–early 19C] a bridle. [GAB *n.* (1)/GOB *n.*[1] (1) + SE *string*]

gaby *n.* (*also* **gabby, gabey**) [late 18C–1960s] a fool. [Yorks. dial. *gabes*, a fool, one who gapes or stares vacantly]

gaby *adj. see* GABBY *adj.*

gack *n.*[1] (*also* **gak**) [1990s+] (*UK drugs*) cocaine. [? link to dial. *gack*, to chatter to talk idly, i.e. one of the drug's primary effects]

gack *n.*[2] *see* GECK *n.*

gack *adj.* [1980s] unappealing, pretentious. [? echoic of a sound of distaste]

gacked *adj.* [1990s+] overcome by drink or drugs. [echoic of the vomiting that may accompany this + ? GACK n.[1]]

gacky *adj.* [2000s] stupid, odd. [GECK n. (1)]

gad *n.*[1] [late 16C+] a euph. for *God*, used in a variety of oaths, which have gradually become milder as the decline of religiosity has robbed them of their import, e.g. *gadsbobs! gadsbud!* (body), *gadsbodikins! gadsbudlikins!* (little body), *gadslid!* (eyelid), *gadsnigs! gadsniggers!* (unknown), *gadsokers! gadsookers! gadswookers!* (hooks), *gadsprecious!* (precious (heart)), *gadsnouns! gadswoons! gadzoons! gadzounds!* (wounds); also GADS-O! excl.; GADZOOKS! excl. (cf. BOB n.[2]).

gad *n.*[2] (*also* **gadder**) [mid-17C; mid-19C] a loose woman, a slattern. [SE *gad*, to rush from place to place]

gad! *excl.* (*also* **gads!**) [late 16C+] a semi-euph. excl., i.e. *God!* [GAD n.[1]]

gadaha *n.* [20C+] (*W.I.*) a fool, an idiot. [Hind. *gadha*, a donkey; used as a general derog. term by East Indians; the female version *gadahee* is more offensive]

gadder *n. see* GAD n.[2].

gadderman *n.* [20C+] (*Ulster*) a rogue. [Irish *cadramán*, a boor]

Gadfrey *n. see* GODFREY n.

gadget *n.* (*also* **gidget**) [1940s+] (*US*) the penis; thus, in pl., the male genitals.

gadgy *n.* **1** [mid-19C+] (*also* **gadge, gadgie**) any male, including a husband. **2** [1960s+] (*gay*) a male prostitute's client. [Rom. *gorgio*, a non-Gypsy male, and thus fig. in a sexual context a STRAIGHT n.[2] (2)]

gads! *excl. see* GAD! excl.

gadso *n.* [17C–early 19C] **1** the penis. **2** a fool (cf. BOBO n.[1]; CHOAD n.). [Ital. *cazzo*, the penis]

gads-o! *excl.* [late 17C–mid-19C] a general excl., lit. 'God's oath!' [GAD n.[1], although there may be a link to GADSO n.]

gad the hoof *v.* [mid-19C] to walk without shoes. [SE *gad*, to go from one place to another, to wander + HOOF n. (1)]

gad up and down *v.* [late 17C–early 18C] to go out gossiping. [SE *gad*, to move around]

gadzooks! *excl.* [17C+] a mild excl., lit. 'God's hooks!' [GAD n.[1]; in this context *hooks* means either the nails used in the crucifixion or the hands (i.e. HOOK n.[1] (1) although it postdates)]

Gaelically utter *n.* [late 19C] (*UK society*) a Scottish accent, esp. when modified to move in snobbish English circles.

Gaelick *n.* [1980s+] (*US gay*) a gay Irishman. [puns on SE *Gaelic* + *gay lick*]

gaff *n.*[1] **1** [mid-18C–early 19C] a fair. **2** [late 18C–1950s] a cheap music hall or theatre. **3** [19C+] a show, an exhibition. **4** [late 19C+] a prison. **5** [late 19C+] a place, an area, e.g. a street. **6** [1910s] (*UK Und.*) a warehouse. **7** [1910s–60s] a job, an occupation. **8** [1920s+] a house or shop, a home. **9** [1930s] a dance hall. **10** [1930s–50s] (*US Und.*) a crooked casino or similar place designed to fleece innocent victims. **11** [1930s+] a hotel. **12** [1930s+] a bar. **13** [1930s+] a restaurant. **14** [1940s+] a club. **15** [1960s] (*UK Und.*) a prostitute's room, where she works, but usu. does not live. [Rom. *gav*, a town, esp. a market town]

gaff *n.*[2] **1** [early 19C–1910s] an outcry, a noise; thus imper. *stow your gaff!* be quiet! **2** [late 19C–1920s] (*US*) as the *gaff*, a dismissal; ridicule. **3** [late 19C–1960s] (*US*) severe treatment, criticism, punishment or hardship; thus STAND THE GAFF v.; *give the gaff/put the gaff into*, to deliver criticism. **4** [late 19C–1960s] humbug, nonsense. **5** [1910s] a legitimate job, work. **6** [1920s] talk. **7** [1920s–50s] interrogation. **8** [1940s] (*Ulster*) news, gossip. [SE *gaff*, the steel spur attached to a fighting cock; ? Fr. *gaffe*, a verbal blunder or Scot. *gaff*, to talk loudly and merrily or dial. *gaff*, loud, coarse talk; (1) ? also link to GAFF n.[1] (1), a fair, where 'outcry' would naturally be the order of the day]

gaff *n.*[3] **1** [early 19C+] a cheating device in gambling, orig. a small hook set in a ring used by a card-sharp. **2** [1930s] (*UK Und.*) a place chosen for a robbery. **3** [1930s+] (*US Und.*) a fraud, a racket.

4 [1940s] (*US Und.*) the place – a fake 'bookmaker's' or 'stockbroker's' office – in which a confidence trick is carried out. **5** [1940s–50s] (*US*) in pl., crooked dice. **6** [1960s] a gimmick, a hidden trick. [SE *gaff*, a spur for a fighting cock + GAFF n.[1] (1), a fair, where such gambling was most likely to be found]

gaff *n.*[4] [1960s+] (*US*) the penis (cf. AX n.[2]). [SE *gaff*, a barbed fishing spear]

gaff *n.*[5] *see* GAFFER n.[1].

gaff *adj.*[1] [19C+] excellent, simple. [ety. unknown; ? link to dial. *gaff*, to laugh loudly]

gaff *adj.*[2] [1930s+] (*US gambling*) rigged. [GAFF n.[3]]

gaff *v.*[1] **1** [19C] to gamble, esp. to toss coins. **2** [20C+] (*US gambling*) to cheat, to rig, to fix. **3** [1930s+] (*US gambling*) to make a game crooked or dishonest, typically to tamper with a fruit machine or roulette wheel. [dial. + GAFF n.[3]]

gaff *v.*[2] [mid–late 19C] to play or perform in a music hall. [GAFF n.[1] (2)]

gaff *v.*[3] **1** [late 19C] (*US*) to tease. **2** [late 19C+] (*orig. Scot.*) to talk; to talk loudly; to talk nonsense. **3** [1980s+] (*US campus*) to insult, to ignore. [GAFF n.[2]]

gaff *v.*[4] **1** [1920s–30s] (*US tramp*) to stay where one is for too long. **2** [1930s] (*US tramp*) to punish. **3** [1970s+] (*US campus*) to endure. [GAFF n.[2] (3)]

gaffer *n.*[1] **1** [late 16C+] (*also* **gaff**) an old man. **2** [18C] a husband. **3** [late 19C–1960s] one's father. **4** [1900s–60s] (*Anglo-Irish*) a boy, a young fellow. [abbr. of *granfer*, i.e. SE *grandfather*]

gaffer *n.*[2] **1** [18C+] a boss or master, esp. of a show or circus; also as a term of address. **2** [late 19C+] (*US*) a foreman, esp. an electrician. **3** [1980s+] (*Aus. prison*) a dominant prisoner. [GAFF n.[1]; note Lincolnshire dial. *gaffman*, the bailiff or superintendent of a farm]

gaffer *n.*[3] **1** [early 19C+] one who tosses up coins in a gambling game based on guessing heads or tails. **2** [1970s] the 'straight' front man for any form of fraud or marginal business. [GAFF v.[1]]

gaffing *n.* **1** [early–mid-19C] tossing 3 coins in a hat in order to determine who pays for drinks; he who guesses right is exempt from payment. **2** [mid-19C] coin-tossing, pitch and toss. [GAFF v.[1] (1)]

gaff joint *n.* [1920s–50s] (*US Und.*) a casino where the games are crooked. [GAFF adj.[2] + JOINT n.[4] (3)]

gaffle *n.* [1990s+] (*US Black*) defeat, failure, betrayal. [GAFFLE v.]

gaffle *v.* **1** [20C+] (*US*) to snatch, to steal, to round up. **2** [1950s+] (*US Und.*) to arrest. **3** [1960s] (*US prison*) to lock up in solitary confinement. **4** [1970s+] (*US*) to hoax, to deceive. **5** [1990s+] (*US teen*) to ruin someone's plans. **6** [2000s] (*US prison*) to place in handcuffs. [dial. *gaffle*, to encumber, to tease, to incommode]

gaffled *adj.* [1990s+] **1** in an unfortunate condition. **2** (*US Black*) dead. [GAFFLE v.]

gaffler *n.* [1990s+] (*US Black*) a businessman, a thief. [GAFFLE v. (1)]

gaffus *n.* [1960s+] (*drugs*) a hypodermic needle. [? SE *gaff*, a hook]

gafone *n. see* GAVONE n.

g.a.f.u. *n. see* S.N.A.F.U. n.

gag *n.* **1** [early 19C+] a joke, a tease; a deception, a lie; thus *gaggery*, deception; *gaggist*, a joke-teller. **2** [mid-19C–1910s] (*US*) a fool, a laughing-stock. **3** [mid-19C–1930s] the salestalk of a street-seller of broadsides; the 'patter' of a beggar. **4** [mid-19C–1950s] an ad-lib remark. **5** [mid-19C+] a plan, a scheme. **6** [late 19C] oratory, speechifying. **7** [late 19C] chatter (as in a restaurant or bar). **8** [late 19C–1920s] (*UK tramp*) an account; a begging tale. **9** [late 19C–1930s] (*US*) any form of behaviour or practice. **10** [1900s] (*US drugs*) narcotic drug addiction. **11** [1900s–10s] (*US*) a thing or aspect. [fig. uses of SE *gag*, something thrust into the mouth to procure the victim's silence; note that Share suggests ON *gaghals*, with one's neck thrown back]

gag *adj.* [1990s+] joking. [GAG n. (1)]

gag *v.* **1** [mid-18C; 20C+] (*UK tramp*) (*also* **gagg**) to beg. **2** [late

18C+] (*also* **gagger**) to deceive, take in or impose upon (a person). **3** [early 19C+] to amuse. **4** [mid-19C] to scold, to nag. **5** [mid-19C+] to ad-lib. **6** [late 19C] (*also* **gag on**) to inform against, to betray. **7** [late 19C–1920s] to persuade, to boost, to promote. **8** [late 19C+] to make a joke. **9** [1910s] to fix a horserace. **10** [1960s+] (*US campus*) to find disgusting; thus GAGGED adj. **11** [1990s+] (*US prison/drugs*) to cheat; to sell fake drugs. [SE *gag*, to choke, to mute; the image is of making someone 'swallow' a lie or imposture]

gag! *excl.* [1980s] (*US campus*) an excl. of disgust. [SE *gag*, to choke]

gaga *n.*[1] (*also* **gagagootz**) [1930s+] an eccentric or senile person. [GAGA adj. (1)]

gaga *n.*[2] (*US gay*) **1** [1940s+] an inexperienced, immature homosexual. **2** [1960s] homosexual foreplay. [? play on the *ga-ga* noises of babytalk or GAGA adj. (2)]

gaga *adj.* (*also* **gugga**) **1** [1910s+] eccentric, senile. **2** [1920s+] sentimental (about), infatuated (with); usu. as *gaga over*. **3** [1930s+] drunk (cf. ADDLED adj.). [Fr. *gaga*, a senile person]

gaga *v.* (*US*) **1** [1930s] to act sentimentally. **2** [1990s+] to persuade, to 'sweet talk'. [GAGA adj. (2); + ? the *ga-ga* noises of babytalk]

gaga *adv.* [2000s] madly, both lit. and fig. [GAGA adj. (1)]

gagagootz *n. see* GAGA n.[1].

gag-awful *adj.* [1980s] (*US campus*) terrible. [SE *gag*, to choke, to vomit]

gage *see also under* GAUGE.

gage *n.*[1] **1** [mid-15C–18C] (*UK Und.*) (*also* **gauge**) a mug holding a quart (2 pints/1 litre) of beer; occas. a pint. **2** [17C–18C] (*also* **gagg**) any mug or container. **3** [mid-17C–1940s] (*also* **gagg**) a pipe, a pipeful of tobacco. **4** [mid-19C] a small quantity; thus *a gage of tobacco, a gage of gin*. **5** [1930s–50s] (*US Und.*) cheap whisky. [SE *gage*, a measure or, alternatively, a pledge, and thus, in the drinking context, a toast]

gage *n.*[2] (*also* **gauge**) [1930s+] (*US drugs*) marijuana. [modern ext. of GAGE n.[1] (3)]

gage *adj. see* GAGED adj. (2).

gage butt *n.* (*also* **gauge butt**) [1930s–50s] (*drugs*) a marijuana cigarette. [GAGE n.[2]+ BUTT n.[2] (2)]

gaged *adj.* (*also* **gauged**) **1** [1930s–40s] (*US*) drunk (cf. ALED UP adj.). **2** [1950s] (*US drugs*) (*also* **gage**) intoxicated by marijuana. [GAGE n.[1] (5)/GAGE n.[2]]

gagers *n.* (*also* **gaggers**) [mid-19C] (*US*) the eyes. [? they *gauge* the situation]

gage up *v.* [1930s+] (*US Black*) to smoke marijuana. [GAGE n.[2]; var. on GET ONE'S GAGE UP v.]

gagg *n. see* GAGE n.[1].

gagg *v. see* GAG v. (1).

gagged *adj.* [1960s–70s] (*US campus*) disgusted. [GAG v. (10)]

gagger *n.*[1] **1** [late 18C–early 19C] a confidence trickster, a cheat, esp. when telling 'sob-stories' or posing as a deaf mute. **2** [mid-19C–1910s] a joker. **3** [1930s] a tramp, a beggar. **4** [1940s] (*US Und.*) a receiver of stolen goods. **5** [1940s] (*US tramp*) a tramp who makes a living by telling stories. [GAG v.]

gagger *n.*[2] **1** [1920s–30s] (*US tramp*) one who pimps his own wife. **2** [1980s+] (*US campus*) a disgusting person or thing, lit. a 'sickener'. [(1) JOCKUM-GAGGER n.; (2) GAG v. (10)]

gagger *v. see* GAG v. (1).

gaggers *n. see* GAGERS n.

gagging *n.* [early 19C] (*UK Und.*) a form of confidence trick, based on persuading a stranger that one is an old, if forgotten, friend. [GAGGER n.[1] (1)]

gagging for *adj.* (*also* **gagging to**) [1970s+] desperate for/to; thus *gagging for it*, desperate for sex, usu. but not invariably of a girl or woman. [SE *gag*, to choke + SE *it*//IT n.[1] (1)]

gagging lark *n.* [1930s] begging. [GAG v. (1) + LARK n.[1] (5)]

gaggler's coach *n.* [mid-19C] (*UK Und.*) a hurdle on which the condemned were dragged to the gallows. [one *gags*, i.e. chokes, on the gallows]

gaggy *adj.* [1960s+] (*US gay*) sordid, highly distasteful. [SE *gag*, to choke, to vomit]

gag me with a spoon! *excl.* [1980s+] (*US teen*) an expression of disgust. [SE *gag*, to make someone choke]

gag on *v. see* GAG v. (6).

gah damn *n. see* GOR DAMN n.

gahn! *excl. see* GO ON! excl.

Gainesburger *n.* [1970s+] (*US prison*) Salisbury steak; hamburger. [proprietary brandname Gainesbury Puppy Chow, i.e. dog food]

gaishen *n. see* GATION n.

gait *n.* **1** [mid-19C–1900s] (*US*) one's trade or occupation. **2** [1930s] one's manner or way of being; thus *get a gait on*, to hurry. [SE *gait*, manner of walking or stepping, bearing or carriage while moving]

gaiter *n. see* GATOR n.[1] (1).

gajillion *n. see* ZILLION n.

gajoungas *n. see* GAZONGAS n. (1).

gak *n.*[1] *see* GACK n.[1].

gak *n.*[2] *see* GECK n.

gal *n.* **1** [late 18C+] a girl, a woman; also attrib. **2** [mid-19C+] a general term of address to a woman. [SE *girl*]

gal *v.* [mid-19C–1930s] (*US*) to court young women; thus *go a-gallin*, go courting. [GAL n. (1)]

galah *n.* [1930s+] (*Aus.*) **1** a fool. **2** a chap, a fellow. [SE *galah*, the rose-breasted grey-backed Aus. cockatoo 'much given to chatter']

galah session *n.* [1950s+] (*Aus.*) an interval set aside regularly on the Flying Doctor radio network for anyone who wishes to exchange news and gossip rather than make emergency calls. [SAusE *galah*, the rose-breasted grey-backed Aus. cockatoo 'much given to chatter' + SE *session*]

galaney/galany *n. see* GALENY n.

gal a tek life *n.* [1990s+] (*W.I.*) a very attractive woman. [lit. 'girl (who) takes life' thus play on KILLER n.[1] (1)]

galay *v.* [20C+] (*W.I., Trin.*) to hesitate, to speak or act indecisively. [Fr. *galeux*, itching, suffering from scabies, thus the image is of one who is constantly scratching their head – in this context through perplexity. In 19C Fr. sl. the term, from the same basic meaning, also meant boss or master]

galbe *n.* [late 19C] (*UK Und.*) an aggressive and frightening profile; any physical deformity occurring above the knee. [Fr. *galbe*, 'in art, the general outline or form of any rounded object, as a head or vase; especially, in architecture, the curved form of a column, a Doric capital, or other similar feature' (*Century Dict.*, 1889)]

gal-boy *n.* (*US*) **1** [19C+] a tomboy. **2** [late 19C+] a feminine young man, thence an effeminate (young) homosexual; a prison catamite (cf. BOY-GIRL n.[1]). [GAL n. (1) + SE *boy*]

galdarned *adj. see* GOLDARNED adj.

gale *n. see* WHALE n. (4).

gale *adj.* [20C+] (*W.I.*) covered in scabs, itching, suffering from scabies, eczema or some other skin disease. [for ety. *see* GALAY v.]

galee *n.* [late 19C] (*Anglo-Ind.*) bad language. [Hind. *gali*, abuse, bad language]

galeeny *n. see* GALENY n.

galeery *adj.* [20C+] (*Ulster*) foolish. [ety. unknown; ? link to ON *gola*, to howl or GALLEY adj.]

galen *n.* [late 19C] an apothecary. [*Galenus* (AD 129–*c*.199), the Greek physician, born at Pergamum in Asia Minor]

galena *n.* [mid-19C] (*US*) salt pork. [*Galena*, Illinois, a centre of the pork rearing and packing industry]

galeny *n.* (*also* **galaney, galany, galeeny**) [late 18C–1900s] **1** a guinea-fowl. **2** any sort of fowl. [Sp. *gallina morisca*, a Moorish hen]

gal Friday *n. see* GIRL FRIDAY n.

Galilee *n.* [1920s–50s] (*US Black*) the Southern states. [? the image of '*Galilee* of the Gentiles' (Matt. 4:15), the 'gentiles' in this case being White segregationists]

Galilee stompers *n.* [1970s–80s] (*gay*) sandals, flip-flops. [*Galilee* as metonymic for Jesus Christ, trad. pictured in sandals + STOMPERS n.]

galimony *n.* [1990s+] (*US gay*) the lesbian version of palimony. [GAL n. (1) + SE *alimony*]

gall *n.* [mid-19C+] (*orig. US*) impudence, arrogance, self-possession. [SE *gall*, bitterness of spirit, asperity, rancour]

galla *v.* [1960s+] (*S.Afr.*) to crave, to desire very much, esp. of food. [Xhosa *ukurhala*, to be greedy for]

gallagher and sheehan *n.* [1910s] (*US*) a policeman. [pun on *Gallagher and Shean*, Irish/Jewish vaudeville stars, touring America 1910–11, namely Ed *Gallagher* (*c.*1872–1929) and Al *Shean*, stagename for Al Schoenberg (1868–1949), the Marx Brothers' uncle, who wrote their hit show *Home Again* in 1914. Note sp. changed from the Jewish *Shean* to the Irish *Sheehan*, as there weren't many Jews on the force]

gallersgood *n.* [18C] (*UK Und.*) anything considered so bad or useless that it is fit only for the gallows. [lit. SE *gallows good*; E.P. states that Ware's 18C dating is 'almost certainly erroneous', but offers no alternative]

gallery *n. see* SHOOTING GALLERY n.

gallery 13 *n.* [1990s+] (*US Und.*) a prison cemetery. [SE *gallery*, a floor of cells + the trad. bad luck associated with the number 13]

galley *n.* (*also* **gallery**) [20C+] (*Irish*) fun, enjoyment. [Scot. *galliard*, cheerful, lively]

galley *adj.* (*also* **gallery**) [20C+] (*Irish*) cheerful, lively. [GALLEY n.]

galley-west *adv.* (*also* **gally-west**) [19C+] (*US*) askew, crooked, scattered in all directions; usu. as *go galley-west, knock galley-west*. [Eng. dial. *colleywest(on)*, contrarily, askew; Collyweston is an actual village in Northamptonshire, although sources do not specify its particular skewedness; it is usu. found in relation to Collyweston roofing slates]

gallfired *adj.* [1900s] (*US*) a euph. for GOD-DAMN adj. (1).

gallied *adj.* **1** [early 18C–1940s] hurried. **2** [late 19C] worried. [? dial. *gally*, to frighten, to alarm]

gallies *n.* [mid–late 19C] shoes. [? SE *galligaskins*, leggings or wide hose]

galligaskins *n.* (*also* **galligastins**) [17C–19C] a joc. term for any form of breeches. [SE *galligaskins*, a form of wide hose popular in the 16C–17C; later use is joc.; Nares suggests 'GALLO-GASCOINS, being a kind of trowsers first worn by the Gallic Gascons, i.e. the inhabitants of Gascony']

gallihoot *v. see* GALLYHOOT v.

gallimaufry *n.* **1** [late 16C–17C] a mistress. **2** [19C] the vagina. [SE *gallimaufry*, a mess or jumble (usu. of food)]

gallion *n.* [1940s] (*US Black*) the slave quarters; thus the Black ghetto and fig. the Black world. [17C SE *galion*, the fore-parts of a ship; thus that part in which slaves were transported from Africa and, once landed, the slave quarters of a plantation]

gallipot *n.* [mid-18C–mid-19C] an apothecary. [SE *gallipot*, a small earthen glazed pot, esp. one used by apothecaries for ointments and medicines; *gallipot* itself means lit. a pot that has been carried/imported in a galley]

gallivant *n.* [early–mid-19C] 'a nest of whores' (Bee). [SE *gallivant*, to parade around in a showy fashion, esp. with persons of the other sex]

gallon distemper *n.* [early 19C–1900s] **1** a hangover. **2** delirium tremens. [SE *gallon*, joc. ref. to the amount one has drunk + *distemper*, mental or physical disease]

gallon head *n.* [1980s+] (*US Black*) **1** a person with a large head. **2** an intelligent person. [their skull could hold a gallon of liquid]

galloot *n. see* GALOOT n. (2).

gallop *n.* [1970s] an act of sexual intercourse.

galloper *n.* [18C–early 19C] a blood horse, a hunter.

galloping *adj.* [early 17C+] (*orig. US*) worsening or increasing.

galloping dandruff *n.* (*also* **crawling dandruff, leaping..., mechanized..., mobile..., mobilized..., travelling..., walking...**) [1910s–70s] (*Aus./US*) head or body lice.

galloping freckles *n.* [1920s] (*US*) head or body lice.

galloping goose *n.* [1910s–60s] (*US*) a train, car or plane that runs badly.

galloping horse *n.* (*also* **gallup**) [1950s+] (*drugs*) heroin. [ext. of HORSE n.[8]]

galloping snapshots *n.* [1920s–40s] (*US*) movie films.

gallop one's antelope *v.* (*also* **gallop one's maggot, ...the antelope, ...the maggot**) [20C+] to masturbate (cf. BEAT ONE'S HOG v.). [SE *antelope*/MAGGOT n.[2]]

gallop the (old) lizard *v.* (*also* **choke one's lizard**) [1960s+] to masturbate (cf. BEAT ONE'S HOG v.). [SE *gallop* + LIZARD n.[3]]

gallous *adj.* [19C+] **1** excellent, first-rate, with criminal overtones. **2** lively, spirited. [Scot. *gallows*, rascally, dissolute]

gallow-grass *n.* [mid-16C–early 17C] hemp. [it is used for making hangman's ropes]

gallows *n. see* GALLOWS-BIRD n.

gallows *adj.* (*also* **gallus**) [mid-16C; late 18C+] a general intensifier, very great, excellent, fine, absolute etc; also used ironically. [20C+ use is US; on pattern of BLOODY adj.[1] (1), i.e. fig. use of violence as synon. for extremism]

gallows *adv.* (*also* **gallus**) [late 18C–19C] extremely, very much, e.g. *gallows poor*, very poor. [GALLOWS adj.]

gallows —! *excl.* (*also* **gallus — !**) [mid-19C] an excl. of annoyance, lit. go/send to the gallows, e.g. *gallows me if...*

gallows apple *n.* [late 17C–early 19C] a candidate for the gallows.

gallows-bird *n.* (*also* **gallows, gallus**) **1** [late 16C–mid-19C] a thief or pickpocket or one who associates with them. **2** [mid-17C–1930s] (*also* **gallows-clapper**) a general insult, i.e. one who is destined for the gallows. **3** [mid-19C] the corpse of one who has been hanged. **4** [1920s–40s] one who has been sentenced to be hanged. [the image is of one destined to 'fly' to the gallows]

gallowses *n. see* GALLUSES n.

gallows-looking *adj.* (*also* **gallows-faced**) [mid-18C–mid-19C] fit for the gallows, having a hang-dog, run-down, shifty look.

gallowsness *n.* [mid-19C] mischief, perversity.

gallows-trap *n.* [early 19C] (*UK Und.*) a policeman. [SE *gallows* + TRAP n.[2]]

gallstone *n.* [1960s] (*US*) an irritating person.

gallup *n. see* GALLOPING HORSE n.

galluptious *adj. see* GOLOPSHUS adj.

gallus *see under* GALLOWS.

gallus *n. see* GALLOWS-BIRD n.

galluses *n.* (*also* **gallowses**) [mid-18C+] (*US*) braces, suspenders. [play on SE *gallows*]

gallyhoot *v.* (*also* **gallihoot**) [1940s–60s] (*US*) to go gallivanting; thus *gallihoot*, a spree. [SE *gallivant* + US regional *scallyhoot*, to be off, to 'skedaddle']

gallypot baronet *n.* [late 19C] an ennobled physician. [SE *gallipot*, a small earthen glazed pot, esp. one used by apothecaries for ointments and medicines + *baronet*; the term implies a snobbish disdain for the parvenu]

gallyslopes *n.* [late 19C] leggings, gaiters. [SE *galligaskins*, wide breeches or hose]

gally-west *adv. see* GALLEY-WEST adv.

gal officer *n.* [1940s–50s] (*US Black*) a lesbian. [GAL n. (1) + SE *officer*; ? play on TOP SERGEANT n.]

galoot *n.* **1** [19C–1910s] a soldier, a marine. **2** [19C+] (*orig. US*) (*also* **galloot, galoon, galoosh**) an awkward or uncouth person, often used affectionately. [? pfx. *ga-* = KER- pfx + Scot. *loot*, lout]

galopshus/galoptious *adj. see* GOLOPSHUS adj.

gal pal *n.* [1970s+] (*US gay*) a homosexual man's female friend. [GAL n. (1) + PAL n. (1)]

gal's at the stockyards *phr.* [20C+] (*US*) a woman is menstruating. [the blood flows at the SE *stockyards*]

gal-sneaker *n.* [late 19C] a seducer, esp. of other men's women. [GAL n. (1) + SE *sneaker*]

galtee *v.* [late 19C] (*UK tramp*) to spend. [ety. unknown]

galter *n.* [mid-19C] (*UK Und.*) a racecourse swindler; a gambler. [? GALTEE v.]

galumptious *adj.* *see* GOLOPSHUS *adj.*

galvanized *adj.* [late 19C–1910s] (*US*) in disguise. [joc. mispron.]

galvo *n.* [1970s+] (*Aus.*) galvanized iron. [SE *galv(anized)* + -o sfx (4)]

Galway *n.* [late 19C–1930s] (*US*) a Catholic priest. [the birthplace of many such priests]

galway *n.* [1920s] (*US*) a style of facial whisker. [such whiskers, popular in Co. *Galway*, Ireland, are grown on the upper part of the cheek only]

gam *n.*[1] (*also* **gamb**) **1** [late 18C+] a leg, esp. [20C+] (*US*) a female leg; thus [late 18C; 1940s] *gam-case*, a stocking (1940s use is US Black); [early 19C] *queer gams*, bandy legs. **2** [2000s] (*Aus.*) a tampon, a sanitary towel. [Fr. *jambe*, a leg or Ling. Fr. *gamba*, leg; (2) refers to the position of the vagina at the top of the legs]

gam *n.*[2] (*also* **gamb**) [late 19C–1900s] (*US*) a gambler. [abbr.]

gam *n.*[3] (*also* **gamb**) [20C+] an act of fellatio. [GAM v.[2] (1)]

gam *n.*[4] *see* GOM n.[2].

gam *v.*[1] **1** [early 19C–1900s] (*US*) to chat, to pay a social call; thus TIP THE GAM v. **2** [1920s+] (*US Black*) to boast, to show off. [GAMMON v. (4)]

gam *v.*[2] **1** [mid-19C+] to fellate. **2** [1980s] (*US campus*) (*also* **gam around**) to kiss. [abbr. GAMAHUCHE v.]

gamahuche *v.* (*also* **gama, gamahoosh, gamahouch, gamaroosh, gamaruche**) [mid-19C+] to perform oral sex, esp. fellatio. [? Gk *gamos*, wedding or Northumbrian dial. *rouched*, wrinkled, puckered]

gamb *see under* GAM.

gambetter *v.* [late 19C] to deceive, to hoax. [proper name (and negative reputation) of French politician Léon *Gambetta* (1838–82)]

Gamble and Proctor *n.* [1990s+] a doctor. [rhy. sl.; ult. pharmaceuticals manufacturer *Proctor and Gamble*]

gamble one's socks *v. see* BET ONE'S BOOTS v.

gambler *n.* **1** [mid-18C] a confidence trickster who drops a supposedly valuable object, e.g. a ring, a wallet, and rather than claim it for himself, persuades a passer-by to buy it from him. **2** [mid-18C–19C] a cheating card- or dice-player. [Johnson, *Dictionary* (1755), cites it as 'a cant word, I suppose, for [...] gamester' and defines it as 'a knave whose practice it is to invite the unwary to game and cheat them'. The cheating inference had worn off by early 19C; even so, the modern professional gambler is assumed to depend on skill, albeit honest, rather than on luck]

gambler's roll *n.* [1980s] (*US*) a roll of money with a high-value note visible on the outside, hiding only small-denomination notes (cf. CALIFORNIA BANKROLL n.). [ROLL n.[2]]

gambolier *n.* [mid-19C–1910s] (*US*) a gambler. [joc. blend of SE *gambol* + *gambler*]

gamdiddle *v.* [late 19C] to cheat. [GAMMON v. (4) + DIDDLE v.[2] (2)]

Game, the *n.* [1950s+] (*US Black*) **1** the sophisticated, streetwise person's lifestyle. **2** spec. drug-dealing. **3** prostitution and/or pimping. **4** deception, trickery. **5** courting the desired person with Black sl. talk. [(3) abbr. PUSSY GAME n.]

game *n.*[1] (*UK Und.*) **1** [late 16C–19C] (*also* **Venus's game**) sexual intercourse. **2** [late 16C–early 19C] (*also* **daughters of the game**) a group of prostitutes, esp. in a brothel. **3** [mid-17C+] (*also* **Venus's game**) the world of prostitution; esp. in phr. *on the game*. **4** [1980s] any variety of unconventional sexual 'play', e.g. sado-masochism.

game *n.*[2] **1** [mid-17C] (*UK Und.*) the proceeds of a robbery. **2** [18C–mid-19C] (*UK Und.*) the profession of robbery; thus *put the high game on*, to rob, to pick someone's pocket. **3** [18C+] (*later use US Black*) any attempt to manipulate humanity for one's own ends, usu. financial ones. **4** [19C+] any form of negative activity, e.g. deception, fooling around. **5** [mid-19C–1910s] an amusing incident, a piece of fun, a 'lark'. **6** [mid-19C–1920s] spirit, 'pluck'; thus *keep the game up*, to continue enjoying oneself. **7** [mid-19C+] (*orig. US*) a calling, business or interest; esp. in phr. *what's your game?* **8** [mid-19C+] (*US*) a situation, a state of affairs. **9** [1950s+] expert ability at a particular skill; knowledge, power or influence in a particular industry or environment. **10** [1960s] (*US*) money, possessions. **11** [2000s] (*US Und.*) benefits or gains that, while illegally obtained, are seen as worth the poor reputation such actions might engender; thus *have the game without the name*.

game *n.*[3] [late 17C–19C] a fool, a simpleton, esp. a victim. [he provides a 'game' for his tormentors]

game, the *n.* [mid-17C+] an occupation, differing as to the group concerned; thus [mid-17C+] for lovers, sexual intercourse; [late 17C–early 18C] for sportsmen, cock-fighting; [early 19C] for criminals, robbery; [mid-19C] for sailors, slave-trading; and [mid-19C+] for prostitutes, commercial sex.

game *adj.*[1] **1** [late 17C+] of women, promiscuous; thus adj. *gamey*. **2** [late 18C+] criminal or associated with the underworld; thus [late 18C–early 19C] *game woman*, a prostitute; [19C] *game cove*, an associate of thieves; [19C] *game publican*, a publican who affects not to notice the breaking of the law. **3** [early 19C] of an animal, cantankerous. **4** [early 19C–1920s] of men, cunning, villainous. **5** [1990s+] (*US campus*) attractive.

game *adj.*[2] *see* GAMMY adj.[2].

game *v.* **1** [late 17C+] to jeer, to mock, to delude. **2** [1960s+] (*US Black*) to manipulate humanity for one's own ends, usu. financial ones; to trick, to deceive.

game as a badger *phr.* [1910s] (*US*) very enthusiastic, 'raring to go'. [SE *game*, enthusiastic, keen, 'up for']

game as a meat ant *phr.* (*also* **game as an ant, ...as goats, ...as hornets**) [late 19C+] (*Aus.*) very brave. [SE *game*, enthusiastic, keen, 'up for' + *meat ant*, a large ant with a painful bite]

game as a pebble *phr.* (*also* **game as pebbles**) [mid-19C+] extremely courageous, 'raring to go'. [SE *game*, enthusiastic, keen, 'up for']

game as a pissant *phr.* [late 19C+] (*Aus.*) brave, courageous. [SE *game*, enthusiastic, keen, 'up for' + *piss ant*, a large ant with a painful bite]

game as Ned Kelly *phr.* [1930s+] (*Aus.*) plucky, courageous, willing to go up against overwhelming odds. [SE *game*, enthusiastic, keen, 'up for' + proper name *Ned Kelly* (1855–80), Australia's most celebrated bushranger, who ended his days on the gallows, remarking 'Such is life']

gameball *adj.* [1910s+] (*Irish*) excellent, first-rate. [SE *gameball*, the final round in a game of handball]

game boy *n.* [2000s] a football supporter who looks for fights with rival supporters.

gamecock *n.* [19C] a womanizer, a philanderer. [SE *gamecock*, a fighting cock]

game face *n.* [1980s+] (*US Black*) one's public face. [GAME n.[2] (3) + SE *face*; play on sporting *game face*, an aggressive look adopted for sporting encounters]

game of nap *n.* [20C+] **1** a cap. **2** excrement (cf. ALI OOP n.). [rhy. sl.; (2) = CRAP n.[3] (1)]

game on *v.* (*also* **game off**) [1960s+] (*orig. US Black*) to act deceitfully, to manipulate, to get an advantage over someone by underhand means. [GAME v. (2)]

game on! *excl.* [1980s+] **1** an excl. of excitement or anticipation, usu. about a possible sexual conquest or when a night out or drinking session is arranged. **2** an excl. of triumph at having sorted out initial arrangements. [darts jargon *game on!* the game is about to start]

game-playing *adj. see* PLAY GAMES v.

game pullet *n.* [18C] a young prostitute; a promiscuous girl. [GAME adj.¹ (1) + *pullet*, a young chicken; the 'Game Chicken', however, was the nickname for the early 19C prize-fighter Henry 'Hen' Pearce]

gamer *n.* **1** [1970s] a pimp, a confidence trickster, one who lives by their wits. **2** [1990s+] (*US campus*) one who is willing to take a challenge. [GAME n.² (3)]

game room *n.* [1960s+] in sado-masochistic sex, a torture chamber.

gamester *n.* **1** [17C–mid-19C] a prostitute; a promiscuous woman. **2** [early 17C–early 18C] a womanizer, a promiscuous man. **3** [late 17C] a mistress. **4** [early 18C] a pimp (cf. ABBOT ON THE CROSS n.). [GAME n.¹ + -STER sfx]

game-stock *n.* [1940s+] (*W.I.*) a risible figure, a laughing-stock. [SE *game*, an object of ridicule, laughing-stock]

gamfral/gamfril/gamful *n. see* GAMPH n.

gaming *n.* [late 19C+] (*US Black*) playing a confidence trick or otherwise manipulating another. [GAME v. (2)]

gam it *v.* [19C] (*UK Und.*) to walk, to run (away). [GAM n.¹ (1)]

gammat *n.* [1950s+] (*S.Afr.*) **1** a Cape Malay, a Coloured person. **2** the stereotypical Cape Malay, esp. as the subject of jokes; thus *gamtaal*, *gammat-taal*, a street-gang argot, a mix of English, Afrikaans and Xhosa. [proper name *Muhammad*]

gammer cook *n. see* HEY GAMMER COOK n.

gammo *v. see* GAMO v.

gammocks *n.* [19C] unrestrained, noisy activities. [dial. *gammocking*, rough horseplay]

gammon *n.¹* [early–late 18C] (*UK Und.*) a pickpocket's accomplice who jostles the victim while the pickpocket actually performs the theft; a shoplifter's accomplice. [GAMMON v. (1)]

gammon *n.²* **1** [mid-18C–early 19C] the language or jargon of thieves, i.e. cant. **2** [late 18C+] nonsense, lies, humbug; thus *gammoner*, *gammoning*; thus *pay out the slack of one's gammon*, to recount too many anecdotes. **3** [19C] chatter. **4** [early–mid-19C] persuasive talk. [GAMMON v.]

gammon *n.³* [1990s+] the vagina. [SE *gammon*, ham, i.e. the haunch of a pig; note Urquhart, *The Complete Works of Rabelais* (1653): 'And therefore, that we lose no time, put on, thrust out your gammons ']

gammon *v.* **1** [late 17C–early 18C] to cheat (at a game). **2** [mid-18C] (*UK Und.*) to help. **3** [late 18C] to talk criminal sl. or cant. **4** [late 18C+] to deceive, to fool, to talk humbug, to pretend. **5** [19C] to persuade. **6** [mid-19C] to tease amicably. [? GAME v. (1) or ? SE (*back*)*gammon* or ? fig. tying up of a *gammon* or ham]

gammon! *excl.* [19C] nonsense! humbug! rubbish! [GAMMON v. (4)]

gammon and patter *n.* [late 18C–19C] **1** criminal cant. **2** any form of jargon or professional sl. **3** verbose chatter. [GAMMON n.² + PATTER n.]

gammon and pickles *n.* (*also* **gammon and jalap, ...spinach**) [early 19C+] nonsense, rubbish, humbug. [pun on SE *gammon*/GAMMON n.² (2) + *pickles/jalap/spinach*; for jalap *see* ety. at JOLLOP n.¹]

gammoner *n.* **1** [early 19C] one who covers for an accomplice. **2** [early 19C–1950s] one who 'spins a yarn' or tells deceitful tales; thus *a prime gammoner*, an expert at such tale-spinning. [GAMMON v. (4)]

gammon lushy *v.* (*also* **gammon queer**) [early 19C] to pretend to be drunk. [GAMMON v. (4) + LUSHY adj.¹ (1)/QUEER adj.² (1)]

gammon rasher *n.* [1970s] anything excellent, first-rate. [rhy. sl. = SMASHER n.² (1)]

gammon the draper *v.* [early 19C] 'When a man is without a shirt, and is buttoned up close to his neck, with merely a handkerchief round it, to make an appearance of cleanliness, it is

termed, *gammoning the draper*' (Egan, *Life in London*, 1821). [GAMMON v. (4) + SE *draper*]

gammon the twelve (in prime twig) *v.* [late 18C–early 19C] (*UK Und.*) to gain an acquittal in court; the implication is that the defendant has managed to fool the jurymen. [GAMMON v. (4) + SE *twelve*, generic for the jury (+ IN PRIME TWIG phr.)]

gammy *n.¹* [late 18C] (*UK Und.*) cant or criminal language; thus *stoll the gammy*, to understand thieves' jargon. [? GAMMON AND PATTER n. (1)]

gammy *n.²* [mid-19C+] a lame person. [GAMMY adj.² (1)]

gammy *n.³* [late 19C–1900s] (*Aus.*) a fool. [GAMMY adj.²; he is mentally 'lame']

gammy *n.⁴* (*also* **gummer**) [20C+] (*US*) grandmother. [SE *gammer*, i.e. SE *grandmother*]

gammy *adj.¹* **1** [mid-19C+] (*UK Und.*) bad; usu. in combs., e.g. *gammy lour*, counterfeit coins; *gammy monicker*, a forged signature; *gammy stuff*, spurious soap or medicine; *gammy vendor*, one who sells bad goods; *gammy vial* (*ville*), a place where begging or hawking is prohibited. **2** [late 19C] idle, lazy. [according to Mayhew (1862), Welsh *gam*, crooked, queer]

gammy *adj.²* (*also* **game, gamy**) [mid-19C+] **1** lame, crippled; usu. in *gammy leg*, a lame leg. **2** in fig. use, spoilt, useless, second-rate. [GAM n.¹ (1) + sfx -*y*; but ? ext. of GAMMY adj.¹ (1); note Share suggests Shelta *geamhchaoch*, bad; note dial. *gammy*, left-handed]

gamo *v.* (*also* **gammo**) [1910s+] to perform oral sex. [abbr. GAMAHUCHE v.]

gam on *v.* [1940s+] (*Irish*) to pretend, to make out that. [GAMMON v. (4)]

gamot *n.* [1970s+] (*drugs*) morphine; heroin. [ety. unknown]

gamp *n.* **1** [mid–late 19C] an interfering busybody. **2** [mid-19C–1920s] a monthly nurse, a midwife. **3** [mid-19C–1920s] an umbrella. [the fictional Sarah *Gamp*, created by Charles Dickens in *Martin Chuzzlewit* (1843–4)]

gamph *n.* (*also* **gamfral, gamfril, gamful**) [20C+] a fool, a buffoon. [Scot. *gamf*, a fool, an idiot]

gamy *adj. see* GAMMY adj.².

gan *n.* [mid-16C–mid-19C] (*UK Und.*) the mouth, the lips; occas. the throat. [? Welsh *geneu* or Cornish *ganau*, mouth; Scot. *gane* or *ganne*, mouth (orig. of a fish); itself linked to Norw. *gan*, a fish-gill]

ganaglii *n.* [1940s+] (*W.I.*) a bully. [SE *gang*]

ganch *n.* (*also* **gaunch**) [20C+] (*Ulster*) a fool, a boor. [Irish *gaimse*, a fool]

gander *n.¹* **1** [late 18C–19C] a husband. **2** [mid–late 19C] (*US*) a man or husband who is away from home, a 'grass-widower'. [reverse anthropomorphism]

gander *n.²* [early–mid-19C] a dandy, a fop. [Fr. *gandin*, a fop]

gander *n.³* [1910s+] a look, a survey; thus *cop a gander*, to take a look; TAKE A GANDER (AT) v. [GANDER v.²]

gander *v.¹* [mid-19C–1950s] (*orig. Aus.*) to walk. [early 19C SE *ganderheel*, to wander aimlessly]

gander *v.²* [20C+] to have a look at. [the bird's long neck]

gander-faced *adj.* [late 19C] foolish-looking. [SE *gander*, the male goose]

gander-gut *n.* [mid-19C+] (*US*) one who is thin and awkward; thus *gander-gutted/-bellied*, scrawny. [SE *gander* + *gut*]

gander-legged *adj.* [19C] (*US*) thin-legged. [resembling the bird]

gander month *n.* (*also* **gander-moon**) [late 18C–19C] the period immediately following childbirth, during which time it was considered acceptable for a man temporarily to abandon his domestic fidelity; thus *gander-moooner*, a man enjoying this privilege; *gander-party*, the male equivalent of a HEN PARTY n. [GANDER n.¹ (1) + SE *month*]

ganderneck *v.* [1970s+] (*US*) to look at; thus *gandernecker*. [ext. of GANDER v.²; on pattern of RUBBERNECK v.¹]

gander-shanked *adj.* [19C+] (*US*) referring to a thin, awkward person. [SE *gander* + *shank*]

Gandhi's revenge *n.* [1980s] an upset stomach.

g. and t. *n.* [1970s+] gin *and* tonic (cf. V.A.T. n.). [abbr.]

gandy dancer *n.* (*US*) **1** [20C+] an Italian (cf. DAGO n.). **2** [1910s+] a petty crook, a tramp. **3** [1940s] a jitterbug. **4** [1990s+] a womanizer, an active socialite. [railroad jargon *gandy dancer*, one who works in a railroad maintenance crew, ult. the *Gandy* Mfg. Co., maker of railroad repair equipment. Such workers might spend their unemployed time tramping the country]

gandy stiff *n.* [1910s] (*US tramp*) **1** a street beggar. **2** a tramp who occasionally takes a short-term job. [GANDY DANCER n. (2) + STIFF n.² (4)]

ganef *n. see* GONNOF n.

gang *n.*¹ **1** [late 16C+] any social group (with no criminal overtones). **2** [19C+] (*US*) a large amount of anything.

gang *n.*² [1980s] (*US*) an act of usu. non-consensual intercourse, involving a number of men and a single woman. [GANG v. (3)]

gang *v.* (*US*) **1** [1910s+] to act or move as a group. **2** [1920s+] to attack or kill as part of a gang, to gang up on. **3** [1930s+] to engage in multiple, usu. non-consensual sexual intercourse with 1 woman as part of a gang.

ganga *n. see* GANJA n.

gangbang *n.* **1** [1940s+] the multiple rape of (usu.) a woman, or in gay use, a man. **2** [1950s] (*US drugs*) a number of individuals taking drugs together, esp. a group marijuana-smoking session. **3** [1950s+] an orgy, irrespective of sexuality, in which there is no compulsion. **4** [1960s] (*Aus.*) a woman willing to take on multiple sexual partners in a single session. **5** [1970s] (*US Black*) a fight. **6** [1970s+] (*US*) a confusing or chaotic situation. **7** [1990s+] a group (of men) conducting the mass rape of a single woman. [SE *gang* + BANG n.² (2)/SCREW n.¹ (2)]

gangbang *adj.*¹ [1970s+] of a woman, willing to indulge in multiple sex. [GANGBANG n. (4)]

gangbang *adj.*² [1990s+] (*orig. US Black*) pertaining to the lifestyle of a teen gang member. [GANGBANGER n. (1)]

gangbang *v.* **1** [1940s+] to engage in (usu. coerced) multiple sexual intercourse with a woman (or gay man) as part of a gang. **2** [1970s+] of a woman, to offer sex to a group of men. **3** [1970s+] (*US*) to belong to a gang or to engage in a gang fight; to engage in general gang activities. **4** [1970s+] (*US*) to victimize or destroy. **5** [1990s+] to target as a group, in order to influence or persuade someone. [GANGBANG n.]

gangbang, thank you ma'am *phr. see* WHAM BAM, THANK YOU MA'AM phr.

gangbanger *n.* **1** [1970s+] (*US Black*) a member of a teenage gang. **2** [1980s] (*US prison*) a member of an aggressive prison gang. [GANGBANG v. (3)]

gang-banging *n.*¹ [1960s+] (*orig. US*) gang-rape. [GANGBANG v. (1)]

gang-banging *n.*² (*US Black*) **1** [1970s] fighting, esp. in a group. **2** [1980s+] being and living the life of a member of a US youth gang, usu. in Los Angeles.

gange *n. see* GANJA n.

gang fairy *n.* [1960s] (*US prison*) a man subjected to serial anal rape. [GANG v. (3) + FAIRY n.³]

gangfuck *n.* **1** [1940s+] the multiple rape of (usu.) a woman. **2** [1970s+] (*US gay*) a male homosexual orgy. [GANG-FUCK v.]

gangfuck *v.* [1910s+] to engage in the multiple rape of (usu.) a woman. [SE *gang* + FUCK v.¹]

gangfucker *n.* [1960s] one who joins in the multiple rape of (usu.) a woman. [GANGFUCK v.]

gangie *v.* [1980s] (*Aus.*) of a woman, to make oneself available for sex with a number of men in sequence. [GANGBANG v. (2)]

gang of *adj.* [1930s] (*US Black*) excellent.

gang roll *n.* [late 19C] (*US*) a sexual orgy or gang-rape. [SE *gang* + ROLL v.¹]

gang-shag *n.* [1920s+] **1** (*orig. US*) the mass rape of a single

woman by a gang; also in gay use. **2** (*US Black*) a riotous, noisy party. [GANG SHAG v.]

gang shag *v.* [1920s+] (*orig. US*) of a gang, to engage in the mass rape of a single woman. [SE *gang* + SHAG v.¹ (1)]

gang-splash *n.* **1** [1960s+] (*Aus.*) a heterosexual orgy. **2** [1970s+] (*US gay/prison*) a homosexual rape or orgy. [SE *gang* + *splash*, i.e. of bodily fluids]

gangsta *n.* (*also* **G-ster**) [1980s+] (*US Black*) **1** a rebellious, non-conformist individual, who refuses to accept establishment (White) authority. **2** (*also* **gansta**) a gangster, a criminal, esp. a member of organized crime or an urban gang. [SE *gangster*; the sp. is deliberately geared to emphasize the anti-establishment pose. The gangsta image, as propounded through rap music, offers an alluring mix of sex (often coerced), violence, drugs and illicitly gained money, but those same characteristics have made it a threatening force for conformists, whether Black or White]

gangsta *adj.* [1980s+] (*US Black*) used to describe the hedonist, violent lifestyle as epitomized in lyrics of 'gangsta' rappers. [GANGSTA n. (1)]

gangsta-ass *adj.* [1990s+] (*US Black*) pertaining to the street culture of a Black urban GANGSTA n. (1). [GANGSTA n. (1) + -ASS sfx]

gangsta bitch *n.* [1990s+] (*US*) a woman who associates with a male gang and may participate in its activities. [GANGSTA n. (1) + BITCH n.¹ (1)]

gangsta class *n.* [1980s+] (*US Black*) the style affected by a young street thug and/or drug dealer. [GANGSTA n. (1) + SE *class*]

gangsta limp *n.* [1990s+] (*US Black*) a style of walking, characterized by a slight dip in the stride, adopted by young urban Black men. [GANGSTA n. (1) + SE *limp*]

gangsta rap *n.* (*also* **gangster rap, gansta rap**) [1990s+] (*orig. US Black*) a style of music that evolved in South Central Los Angeles. [GANGSTA n. (1) + RAP n.⁵]

gangsta roll *n.* [1980s+] (*US Black*) a large wad of paper money (cf. CALIFORNIA BANKROLL n.). [GANGSTA n. (1) + ROLL n.²]

gangster *n.*¹ (*US Black*) **1** [1960s+] marijuana. **2** [1970s] a cigarette. [? its rebel image, but note GANJA n.]

gangster *n.*² [1970s+] (*US Black*) **1** a troublemaker; an aggressive, abusive person. **2** a rebellious, non-conformist individual.

gangster *n.*³ [2000s] (*US prison*) HIV/AIDS.

gangster *adj.* [1960s+] (*US Black*) pertaining to a rebellious, non-conformist lifestyle. [GANGSTER n.² (2)]

gangster *v.* [1970s+] (*US Und.*) to take by force. [GANGSTER n.² (1)]

gangster doors *n.* [1970s+] (*US Black*) a 4-door saloon. [GANGSTER adj. + SE *doors*; the car preferred by prominent ghetto criminals]

gangster front *n.* [1980s+] (*US Black*) a double-breasted suit. [GANGSTER adj.+ FRONT n.² (2); the style of suit worn by the (movie) gangsters of the 1920s–30s and adopted by latter-day ghetto criminals]

gangster lean *n.* [1970s+] (*US Black*) the supposedly sophisticated style of driving a car, with one's elbow out of the window and the body leaning in the same direction; thus, fig., an attitude to life and a lifestyle. [GANGSTER adj. + SE *lean*]

gangster lean *v.* [1970s+] (*US Black*) to adopt the driving posture known as the GANGSTER LEAN n.

gangster pills *n.* [1960s+] (*US Black*) barbiturates (cf. BARBIT n.). [? they slow down the gangster's natural energy]

gangster rap *n. see* GANGSTA RAP n.

gangster ride *n.* [1970s+] (*US Black*) an old-fashioned, large, poss. black car. [GANGSTER adj.+ RIDE n.² (1)]

gangster stick *n.* [1950s+] (*US Black*) a marijuana cigarette (cf. BAT n.⁸). [GANGSTER adj. + STICK n.⁹ (3); but note GANGSTER n.¹ (1)]

gangster-style *adv.* [1960s+] (*US Black*) in an aggressive manner. [GANGSTER adj.]

gangster walls n. [1970s+] (US Black) white-walled tyres. [GANGSTER adj. + (white)-walls; the style of wheel preferred by successful ghetto villains]

gang up (on) v. [1920s+] (orig. US) to combine in a group, usu. against someone.

gangy n. [1980s] (Aus.) a woman who makes herself available for group sex with a number of males in sequence. [GANGIE v.]

ganja n. (also ganga, gange, ghanja, gunga, gunja) [1920s+] marijuana, spec. that grown in Jamaica. [Hind. ganja, the hemp plant]

ganja stick n. [1950s] (W.I.) a device for smoking marijuana. [GANJA n. + SE stick]

gank n. (also ganker) [1980s+] (drugs) fake crack cocaine. [GANK v.]

gank v. 1 [1980s+] (orig. US Black teen) (also jank) to trick, to tease. 2 [1990s+] (orig. US teen) (also jank) to rob, to steal. 3 [1990s+] (US Black teen) to shoot someone. [? SKANK v.]

ganky n. [2000s] (Irish) an unattractive woman. [ety. unknown]

gannet n. [1920s+] (orig. naut.) a glutton, a heavy eater; a greedy person (for items other than food). [SE gannet]

ganns n. [late 17C–18C] the lips. [GAN n.]

ganov n. see GONNOF n.

gansta n. see GANGSTA n. (2).

gansta rap n. see GANGSTA RAP n.

ganting adj. [20C+] (Scot.) desperate (for). [SE gant, yawn or gape, thus a mouth hanging open]

ganymede n. 1 [late 16C+] a young male homosexual, a catamite. 2 [17C–19C] a potboy. [Ganymede, in Greek mythology, the cup-bearer to Zeus]

gaol see also under JAIL and its combs.

gaolbird n. (also jailbird, prison-bird) [17C–18C] a prisoner, a former prison inmate; also attrib. [SE f. 1800; SE gaol/jail/prison + BIRD n.³ (2)]

gaoler's coach n. [late 17C–19C] a hurdle. [SE hurdle was a kind of frame or sledge on which traitors used to be drawn through the streets to execution; this remained part of the legal punishment for high treason till 1870]

g.a.p. n. [1960s+] (US) the Great American Public. [abbr.]

gap n.¹ 1 [17C+] the vagina (cf. AGREEABLE RUTS OF LIFE n.). 2 [20C+] the mouth.

gap n.² [1900s–40s] (US) a look, a glance. [GAP v. (1)]

gap v. 1 [late 19C–1950s] (US) to stand and stare, esp. at a crime and not take part. 2 [1930s] (US drugs) to exhibit the yawning that is a symptom of the onset of withdrawal from narcotics. [SE gape]

gape n. [1970s+] (US Black) anyone who is not part of the hip subculture and who thus 'gapes' in wonder or horror at its antics. [SE gape]

gape for gudgeons v. see GUDGEON n.

gape (over the garter) n. [mid-19C] the vagina (cf. AGREEABLE RUTS OF LIFE n.). [SE gape, an opening; note Williams refers to 17C use of gape as v. allusive of the vagina]

gaper n. 1 [1930s+] (US gambling) a small mirror or similar used for cheating in card-games. 2 [1940s] (US Black) a mirror, a looking-glass. [SE gaper, one who gapes; one who stares or gazes in wonder or curiosity]

Gaperies, the n. [1900s] Paris. [elision of the cliché gay Paris + sfx -eries; plus an image of the gaping British visitor]

gapes, the n. [early–mid-19C] 1 boredom, a fit of yawning. 2 amazement.

gapeseed n. 1 [late 16C–mid-19C] anything considered worthy of pause, an exciting event; esp. in phrs. seek/buy/sow gapeseed, to gaze in wonder when one should be getting on with work, business etc. 2 [mid-18C–mid-19C] one who stares (with open mouth). [SE gape + seed; the term is usu. derog.; such 'excitements' are presumed to appeal to the gullible or unsophisticated]

gapia-mouth n. [20C+] (W.I., USVI) one whose mouth hangs open or gapes. [SE gape + mouth; but note Du. gapen, one who yawns from hunger]

gaping n. [1950s–60s] (drugs) a desire for narcotics. [GAP v. (2); the yawning that is typical of an addict suffering from withdrawal]

gap-lapper n. [1990s+] a lesbian (cf. CARPET-BITER n.). [GAP n.¹ (1) + LAPPER n.³]

gapped adj. [mid-18C–early 19C] defeated, vanquished. [SE gapped, broken through at intervals, full of holes or breaches]

gapper n.¹ 1 [1910s–50s] (US Und.) a foolish bystander, esp. one who witnesses a crime but is not taking part. 2 [1930s+] (US prison) a mirror used as a periscope to watch a prison guard; thus the lookout who uses one. [SE gape/GAP v. (1)]

gapper n.² 1 [1930s–50s] a narcotics user in the first stages of withdrawal. 2 [1950s–70s] (US Black) a narcotic drug, usu. heroin. [GAP v. (2); the immediate effect of such a drug is to make one sleepy, thus one's mouth 'gapes' open; yawning is also a symptom of withdrawal]

gapper n.³ (US) 1 [1960s+] a view of a fully exposed vulva. 2 [1980s+] the mouth. [GAP n.¹]

gappings n. [1930s–40s] (US Black) pay, wages, salary. [? phr. 'fill the gap']

gap-stopper n. 1 [18C] a pimp or whoremaster (cf. ABBOT ON THE CROSS n.). 2 [19C] the penis (cf. BUTT-PLUNGER n.). [GAP n.¹ (1)]

gar n.¹ [late 16C–1900s] a euph. for God (cf. BOB n.²).

gar n.² [early 18C] (UK Und.) a lip. [ety. unknown]

'gar n. [1960s+] (US) a derog. term for a Black person (cf. ALLIGATOR BAIT n.²). [abbr. 'neegar', i.e. NIGGER n.¹ (1)]

garage n. [1910s] (US) a restaurant.

garage door is open phr. [1970s+] (US) a phr. used to warn a man that his fly is open.

garb n. (also garby) [1910s] (US) a sailor. [GOB n.⁴ (2)]

garbage n. 1 [late 16C–early 17C] (UK Und.) stolen goods, esp. parcels or packages. 2 [late 19C+] nonsense, often as used in criticism, e.g. of a record. 3 [20C+] bad food. 4 [1940s–50s] cabbage. 5 [1960s+] (drugs) poor-quality or heavily adulterated drugs; orig. heroin, but since expanded to cover all drugs. 6 [1970s+] trivia, anything unimportant. 7 [1980s] (drugs) drugs that have the potential of adverse effects. [fig. uses of SE; note orig. 15C–19C SE garbage, 'the offal of an animal used for food; esp. the entrails. Rarely, the entrails of a man' (OED)]

garbage can n. [1920s–70s] (US) a disgusting person, esp. an old prostitute (cf. BAG n.⁴).

garbage head n. (drugs) 1 [1960s+] (also garbage freak) a drug user who will consume anything on offer, irrespective of quality, purity etc. 2 [1980s+] a drug user who buys crack cocaine from a street dealer instead of cooking it themselves. [GARBAGE n. (5) + -HEAD sfx (3)/FREAK sfx]

garbage hound n. [1960s] (US prison) a voracious eater who enjoys even prison food. [GARBAGE n. (3) + HOUND sfx]

garbage mouth n. [1970s+] a regular, even obsessive user of obscenity or profanity; thus as v., to abuse.

garbage wagon n. [1950s+] a motorcycle that still retains its basic style and specifications, before being adapted for use by an outlaw motorcycle gang.

garbar n. [20C+] (W.I., Guyn./Trin.) nonsense, confusion; thus make garbar, to make trouble; play garbar, to play the fool. [Hind. garbar, disorder, chaos]

garbo n. [1950s+] (Aus.) a garbage man, a dustbin man. [SE garbage + -O sfx (4)]

garbonzas n. [1980s+] (US) the breasts (cf. BAZONGAS n.). [var. on GAZONGAS n. (1)]

garbonzo n. [1980s+] (US) a crazy idiot, a fool (cf. BOBO n.¹). [? GONZO n.]

garboon *n.* [1990s+] one who sniffs bicycle seats for sexual excitement. [ety. unknown]

garbroth *n.* [mid-19C+] (*US*) any poor or worthless person; often in phr. *mean as garbroth, poor as garbroth*. [lit. broth made from the *gar*, a fish generally seen as the food of the very poorest and as such not properly fit for human consumption]

garby *n. see* GARB n.

Garden, the *n.* **1** [mid-17C–1930s] Covent *Garden* market, London WC2; initially as an area frequented by prostitutes. **2** [mid-18C–19C] Covent *Garden* Theatre, London WC2. **3** [late 19C–1950s] Hatton *Garden*, London EC1. **4** [1940s+] Madison Square *Garden*, New York City. [abbr.]

garden *n.* **1** [mid-18C+] the vagina (cf. BEAUTY SPOT n.). **2** [19C+] pubic hair.

garden engine *n.* [19C] the penis. [GARDEN n. (1) + ENGINE n. (1)/play on SE *garden engine*, 'a portable force-pump used for watering gardens' (*OED*)]

gardener *n.*[1] [mid-19C] the penis. [which 'works' in the GARDEN n. (1)]

gardener *n.*[2] [mid-19C] an insult hurled at a second-rate, incompetent coachman. [the relative status of their employment, the implication being that this coachman would make a better gardener]

garden gate *n.*[1] [mid-19C+] the labia minora (cf. GATE IN THE ORCHARD n.). [GARDEN n. (1) + SE *gate*]

garden gate *n.*[2] **1** [mid-19C+] a magistrate. **2** [1940s+] (*bingo*) the number 8 (cf. ALDERSHOT LADIES n.). **3** [1960s+] £8. **4** [1960s+] a friend. [rhy. sl.; (4) = SE *mate*]

garden gates *n.* [20C+] rates, taxes. [rhy. sl.]

garden gnome *n.* [1990s+] a comb. [rhy. sl.]

Garden goddess *n.* (*also* **Garden whore**) [early 19C] a Covent Garden prostitute. [GARDEN, THE n. (1)]

garden gout *n.* [early 19C] venereal disease, whether syphilis or gonorrhoea. [abbr. Covent *Garden*, London, a centre for prostitution + SE *gout*; + ? link to GARDEN n. (1)]

garden hop *v.* [late 19C+] (*UK Und.*) to inform against, to betray. [rhy. sl. = SHOP v.[3]]

garden hose *n.* (*also* **fireman's hose**) [2000s] the nose. [rhy. sl.]

garden house *n.*[1] **1** [17C–19C] the house where one's mistress was kept, or which either sex kept for secret assignations. **2** [19C] a brothel (cf. ACCOMMODATION HOUSE n.). [? GARDEN n. (1)/GARDEN, THE n. (1) + HOUSE n.[1] (1)]

garden house *n.*[2] [20C+] (*US*) an outside lavatory, a privy (cf. BACKHOUSE n.).

garden of Eden *n.* (*also* **garden of Venus**) [16C–17C; 20C+] the vagina (cf. ADAM'S OWN (ALTAR) n.; BEAUTY SPOT n.). [SE/GARDEN n. (1); 20C+ use is US Black]

garden of pleasure *n.* (*also* **garden of delight**) [mid-17C] the vagina (cf. ADAM'S OWN (ALTAR) n.; BEAUTY SPOT n.). [SE/GARDEN n. (1)]

garden plant *n.* [20C+] an aunt. [rhy. sl.]

garden rake *n.* [late 19C] a comb.

garden tool *n.* [1990s+] (*US campus*) a sexually promiscuous woman, a 'whore'. [pun on HO n.[1] (1)/SE *hoe*]

garden violet *n. see* VIOLET n.

Garden whore *n. see* GARDEN GODDESS n.

gargle *n.* **1** [mid-19C+] a drink. **2** [20C+] strong drink in general. [orig. medical student use]

gargle *v.* [late 19C+] to have a drink. [GARGLE n. (1)]

gargled *adj.* [20C+] drunk. [GARGLE v.]

gargle factory *n.* (*also* **gargle house**) [20C+] a public house or bar. [GARGLE n. (2) + SE *factory*]

gargler *n.* [late 19C] the throat. [SE *gargle*]

gargle trap *n.* [1940s] the throat.

Garibaldi biscuit *v.* [20C+] to risk it. [rhy. sl.; ult. the *Garibaldi*

biscuit, whose name comes from the Italian nationalist Giuseppe Garibaldi (1807–82)]

garlic-eater *n.* (*also* **garlic mouth**) [mid-19C–1940s] (*US*) a derog. term for a French, Spanish, Portuguese or Italian person; thus *garlic-eating*, foreign (in a derog. context) (cf. DAGO n.).

garlic-snapper *n.* [1940s] (*US*) an Italian (cf. DAGO n.).

garm *n.* [1990s+] (*UK Black*) usu. in pl., clothes, clothing. [abbr. SE *garment*]

garment-peg *n. see* CLOTHES-PEG n.[1].

garmouth *v.* [20C+] (*US*) to boast, to brag, to make empty threats. [SE *gar*, a fish that is generally considered not worth eating other than in the direst extremity]

garm up *v.* [1990s+] (*UK Black/W.I.*) to dress oneself up. [GARM n.]

garn! *excl. see* GO ON! excl.

garnish *n.* [late 16C–mid-19C] **1** money extorted from a new prisoner, either as a gaoler's fee or as drink money for the other prisoners. **2** fetters. [SE *garnish*, to embellish, to add on; (1) the practice was abolished in 1824, after which time the term was restricted to SE; (2) although both Johnson (1755) and F&H cite this meaning, it may have stemmed from a misreading of (1)]

garnish *v.* [mid-18C–19C] to fit a prisoner with fetters. [GARNISH n. (2)]

garp *n.* [1960s–70s] (*US campus*) nonsense. [? film *The World According to Garp* (1982), based on the novel by John Irving]

garret *n.* **1** [late 18C–1930s] the head. **2** [early–mid-19C] (*UK Und.*) the fob pocket. **3** [late 19C] the mouth. **4** [late 19C+] a woman's handbag.

garreter *n.* (*also* **garreteer**) [mid–late 19C] (*UK Und.*) a thief who crawls over house-tops and breaks in through garret windows. [SE *garret*]

Garrison finish *n.* [late 19C] (*US*) orig. in horseracing, any finish, lit. or fig., in which the winner comes from behind. [the US jockey Ed 'Snapper' Garrison, known for this ability]

garrison hack *n.* [late 19C] a prostitute (cf. BANBURY n.). [ironic use of SE *garrison hack*, a regular attender at military balls; such a woman, like the horse, can be 'ridden' by anyone]

garrot *n.* [1960s+] (*W.I., UKVI*) one who is not a native of the Virgin islands, an outsider. [ety. unknown]

garrotty *adj.* [1980s+] crazy, insane. [? SE *garrotte*]

garsoon *n.* (*also* **garsun, gassan, gasur, gorsoon, gossoon**) [19C+] (*Irish*) a boy, esp. in derog. contexts. [synon. Irish *garsún*, but note Fr. *garçon*, boy]

garter *n.* [1930s+] (*US prison*) an indeterminate prison sentence. [SE *garter*, i.e. something that stretches]

Gary Ablett *n.* [1990s+] (*drugs*) a tablet. [rhy. sl.; ult. the footballer *Gary Ablett* (b.1965); the term is thus a pun on SE *pill*/PILL n.[1] (4), a ball]

Gary Glitter *n.* **1** [1980s+] (a pint of) bitter. **2** [1990s+] the anus (cf. BOTTLE AND GLASS n.). [rhy. sl.; (2) = SHITTER n.[1] (1); ult. UK pop singer *Gary Glitter*, real name Paul Gadd (b.1940)]

Gary Lineker *n.* [1990s+] vinegar. [rhy. sl.; ult. UK football star and TV personality *Gary Lineker* (b.1960), also recently famous for starring in adverts for Walker's crisps with a flavour temporarily renamed 'Salt and Lineker']

gas *n.*[1] **1** [late 18C+] idle or boastful talk, bombast, humbug. **2** [1910s+] (*US*) energy; thus *out of gas*, tired out. [SE *gas*]

gas *n.*[2] [1910s–60s] (*US tramp*) any form of very strong, if poss. poisonous drink.

gas *n.*[3] [1910s+] (*orig. Irish*) **1** a very enjoyable, pleasant situation or experience. **2** someone who is very pleasing, exciting, impressive.

gas *n.*[4] [1940s+] (*US Black*) hair that has been artificially straightened or 'processed'. [GAS v.[2]]

gas *adj.*[1] **1** [1930s+] of objects or people, enjoyable, exciting, funny. **2** [1960s+] impressive, extraordinary. [GAS n.[3]]

gas *adj.*[2] *see* GASSY *adj.*[1] (2).

gas *v.*[1] **1** [mid–late 19C; 2000s] (*US campus*) to deceive. **2** [mid-19C+] (*also* **gas off**) to chatter, to talk inconsequentially and continually, to offer only 'hot air'. **3** [late 19C–1910s] to boast. **4** [1940s] (*US Black*) to tell, to inform. [GAS *n.*[1] (1)]

gas *v.*[2] [1940s+] (*US Black*) to straighten one's hair (cf. CONK *v.*[2]). [the gas canister used as part of straightening Black hair]

gas *v.*[3] [1940s+] **1** to enjoy, to have a good time. **2** to impress or please enormously. **3** to excite or thrill. [GAS *n.*[3]]

gas *v.*[4] [1970s+] (*US drugs*) **1** to sniff gasoline fumes. **2** to commit suicide by inhaling car exhaust fumes.

gas! *excl.* [mid-19C] rubbish! nonsense! [GAS *n.*[1] (1)]

gasbag *n.* (*also* **gasman**) [mid-19C+] a talkative person.

gas buggy *n. see* BUGGY *n.*[1] (1).

gaseous *see under* GASSY.

gasface *n.* [1980s+] (*US teen*) a contorted face, either from pleasure or disgust. [? the image is of a user of laughing gas; coined by the hip-hop group *3rd Bass*]

gas-guzzler *n.* (*also* **guzzler**) [1970s+] the trad. enormous US automobile, profligate of petrol and dwarfing its European rivals; symbolic of the 1950s, out of favour in the energy-conscious 1970s, it staged a brief renaissance in the early 1990s. [SAmE *gas*, gasoline, i.e. petrol + GUZZLER *n.*[1]]

gash *n.*[1] **1** [late 18C+] the vagina (cf. AGREEABLE RUTS OF LIFE *n.*). **2** [1910s+] any girl or woman, including a prostitute; thus sexual gratification (cf. BANGTAIL *n.*[1]). **3** [1950s+] (*US*) an effeminate, passive homosexual. **4** [1950s+] (*US gay*) the anus, as used for sodomy. [as simple anatomy in the 18C, e.g. Burns c.1786 in *Merry Muses of Caledonia*: 'The lasses they hae wimble-bores [i.e. small holes] / The widows they hae gashes'; but 20C+ use is derog. thus poss. augmented by GASH *adj.*; note RMC Duntroon (Aus.) *gash*, sexual intercourse]

gash *n.*[2] [mid-19C–1960s] (*US*) the mouth.

gash *n.*[3] [1940s–50s] (*Aus.*) a second helping. [printers' jargon *gash*, waste matter]

gash *n.*[4] [1980s+] (*drugs*) marijuana.

gash *adj.* [1940s+] extra, superfluous, spare. [? dial. *gaishen*, a skeleton, something or someone ridiculous, an obstacle]

gash *v.* **1** [1940s+] (*US campus*) to have sexual intercourse (cf. BANG *v.*[1]). **2** [1990s+] to suffer from any form of sexually transmitted disease. [GASH *n.*[1]]

gas-head *n.* [1960s+] (*US Black*) **1** one who has had their hair straightened with a 'process' haircut. **2** in fig. use, a Black person who rejects their racial origins. [GAS *n.*[4] + SE *head*]

gash-eater *n.* [1940s+] one who performs cunnilingus (cf. BOX LUNCH *n.*). [GASH *n.*[1] (1) + SE *eater*; note EAT *v.*[3] (1)]

gashgrinder *n.* [1990s+] (*US*) a promiscuous woman; thus a general derog. term for a woman. [GASH *n.*[1] (1) + GRIND *v.*[1] (1)]

gash-hound *n.* (*also* **gashman**) **1** [1910s–60s] (*US*) a womanizer. **2** [1950s+] (*US prison*) an older homosexual man with a taste for young men or boys. [GASH *n.*[1] + HOUND *sfx*/SE *man*]

gashle *adv.* [late 19C+] (*S.Afr.*) gently, carefully. [Zulu/Xhosa *kahle*, sweetly, peacefully]

gash mag *n.* [1990s+] a 'men's magazine'. [GASH *n.*[1] (1) + colloq. SE *mag*, a magazine]

gashman *n. see* GASH-HOUND *n.*

gas hound *n.* [1920s–40s] (*US tramp*) a drinker of wood alcohol, ether and similar intoxicating, poss. poisonous, stimulants. [GAS *n.*[2] + HOUND *sfx*]

gas-house district *n.* [late 19C+] (*US*) a slum. [the original gas-houses that lined New York's East River between 14th Street and 22nd Street. The first gas-house appeared in 1842 and its peers followed over the next 50 years; the orig. Gas-house District covered 3rd Avenue to the river and 14th Street to 27th Street. The smell of leaking gas and the poor neighbourhood housing meant that few lived there by choice, but among those who did were the feared thugs of the Gas-house gangs]

gas-house mick *n.* [1920s–30s] (*US*) a poor or working-class Irish person (cf. BOG ARAB *n.*). [GAS-HOUSE DISTRICT *n.* + MICK *n.*[1] (1)]

gashun *n. see* GATION *n.*

gas it *v.* [1960s] (*US campus*) to do badly on an examination.

gas jockey *n.* [1950s+] (*US*) a gas/petrol station attendant. [SAmE *gas* + JOCKEY *n.*[3] (2)]

gasket *n.*[1] [1940s] (*US*) a doughnut or flapjack. [resemblance]

gasket *n.*[2] [1960s–70s] (*US drugs*) anything used to seal a hypodermic needle to a syringe.

gaskins *n.* [late 17C–early 19C] breeches. [SE *galligaskins*, a form of wide hose popular in the 16C–17C]

gaslight *v.* [1950s+] (*US*) to confuse someone, causing them to feel insane. [the 1944 film of Patrick Hamilton's play *Gaslight* (1939), in which such deliberate cruelty forms the basis of the plot]

gaslighter *n.* [early 19C] (*UK Und.*) a stunning blow. [ety. unknown]

gasman *n. see* GASBAG *n.*

gas-meter bandit *n.* [1970s] a petty thief. [the biggest 'job' he attempts is robbing the gas-meter]

gas monkey *n.* [1930s] (*US*) a gas/petrol station attendant. [SE *gas* + MONKEY *n.*[2] (3)]

gas off *v. see* GAS *v.*[1] (2).

gasoline *n.* [1900s–20s] alcohol, esp. Jack Daniel's whisky.

gasoline buggy/go-cart *n. see* BENZINE BUGGY *n.*

gasp *n.* [late 19C] a drink, a shot of liquor. [? the effect on one's throat]

gasp *v.* [late 19C] to drink a dram of spirits. [GASP *n.*]

gasp and grunt *n.* [1940s–60s] the vagina (cf. ALL QUIET *n.*). [rhy. sl. = CUNT *n.*[1] (1) + ref. to the sounds of intercourse]

gasper *n.* **1** [1910s+] a cigarette, esp. a cheap brand (orig. Virginia rather than the more exotic Turkish tobacco); also a cigar. **2** [1980s+] (*drugs*) a marijuana cigarette.

gas pipe *n.*[1] [mid-19C–1910s] (*US*) a talkative person. [GAS *n.*[1] (1) + SE *pipe*]

gas pipe *n.*[2] [1930s–40s] (*US*) a slide-trombone.

gas pipes *n.* [late 19C] tight trousers.

gas queen *n.* [1980s] (*US gay*) a man who picks up male prostitutes from his car. [SAmE *gasoline* + QUEEN *n.*[2] (1)/QUEEN *sfx* (2)]

gas round *v.* [late 19C–1910s] to ferret out information in a clandestine manner.

gassan *n. see* GARSOON *n.*

gassed *adj.*[1] [1910s+] drunk or drugged; thus *half-gassed*, tipsy. [GAS *n.*[2]]

gassed *adj.*[2] [1940s+] (*US Black*) used of hair that has been chemically straightened. [GAS *v.*[2]]

gassed *adj.*[3] [1950s–60s] (*US*) delighted. [GAS *v.*[3] (2)]

gassed-out *adj.* [1960s] (*US*) worn-out. [one has run out of GAS *n.*[1] (2)]

gasser *n.*[1] [mid-19C–1950s] a loudmouth, a chatterer. [GAS *v.*[1] (2)]

gasser *n.*[2] **1** [1940s+] anything considered very enjoyable, superlative, first-rate. **2** [1950s–60s] a man or woman highly admired, considered to be the best. **3** [1960s] a friend. [GAS *n.*[3]]

gassing *n.* [2000s] (*US prison*) throwing a liquid substance on an officer from a cell. [the image of throwing petrol, US *gas*, over a victim]

gas someone's head up *v. see* GAS UP SOMEONE'S HEAD *v.*

gassy *n.* [1930s–50s] (*US prison*) a chatterer. [GASSY *adj.*[1] (2)]

gassy *adj.*[1] **1** [mid–late 19C] (*also* **gaseous**) irascible, likely to 'flare up' without warning. **2** [mid-19C+] (*also* **gas**) talkative, verbose, boastful. [fig. uses of SE/GAS *v.*[1] (2)]

gassy *adj.*[2] (*also* **gaseous**) [1960s–70s] (*US*) superlative, fantastic. [GAS *n.*[3]]

gasumph *v. see* GAZUMP *v.*

gas up someone's head *v.* (*also* **gas someone's head up**) [1990s+] **1** (*US*) to destroy someone, usu. emotionally but occas. physically. **2** to pressurize. [fig. use of SAmE *gas up*, to fill up with petrol]

gasur *n. see* GARSOON n.

gas wagon *n.* [1910s–20s] (*US*) a car; also fig. use. [SAmE *gas* + *wagon*]

gasworks *n.* [1990s+] (*Irish*) an asthma inhaler.

gat *n.*[1] (*also* **gatt**) **1** [late 19C+] (*orig. US*) a pistol or revolver. **2** [1920s] (*US*) a gunman. **3** [2000s] (*US prison*) a prison-made knife. [*Gatling* gun; note British Army *gatt*, a rifle during 2003 Iraq War]

gat *n.*[2] [1940s+] (*S.Afr.*) the anus; also used as a general excl. [Afk. *gat*, hole, vent]

gat *v.* [1930s] to shoot; thus *gatting*, shooting, a shoot-out. [GAT n.[1] (1)]

gata *n.* [1970s+] (*S.Afr.*) **1** the police. **2** a prison warder. [Sotho sl. *legata*, a member of the police force, lit. 'catch a thief'; or ? GAT n.[1] f. their guns]

gat-creeper *n.* [1980s+] (*S.Afr.*) a sycophant, a toady. [GAT n.[2] + SE *creeper*]

Gate, the *n.* **1** [early 18C–19C] New*gate* prison, London (cf. ABBOTT'S PRIORY n.). **2** [mid-19C] Billings*gate*, London. **3** [1950s+] Notting Hill *Gate*, London W11. [abbr.]

gate *n.*[1] **1** [1910s+] (*orig. N.Z. milit.*) the mouth. **2** [1950s–70s] (*US drugs*) the vein into which one injects a narcotic. **3** [1990s+] one's appearance, looks. [note Shakespearian use of *gate*, the vulva]

gate *n.*[2] (*also* **gates**) [1930s+] (*US Black*) a person, a man, esp. as a term of address. [jazz jargon *gate*, a swing musician, ult. the 'swinging' of a gate + abbr. ALLIGATOR n.[3] (2); the term, at its peak 1935–43, was popularized by the comedian Jerry Colonna, who used it widely on Bob Hope's radio show]

gatecrash *v.* [1920s+] (*orig. US*) **1** to gain admission to a social or public event without an invitation or admission ticket (cf. CRASH v.[2]). **2** to gain admission to any group, uninvited. [backform. f. GATE-CRASHER n.]

gate-crasher *n.* [1920s+] (*orig. US*) a person who gets into a social or public event without an invitation or admission ticket.

gate fever *n.* [1920s+] (*UK prison*) the nervous feeling that overtakes many prisoners as their sentence draws to its close (cf. GATEY adj.).

gate in the orchard *n.* [19C] the labia minora (cf. GARDEN GATE n.[1]).

gate money *n.* [1930s–60s] (*US prison*) money given to a prisoner on release.

gatemouth *n.* [1920s–40s; 1990s+] (*US Black*) **1** a person, a man. **2** a gossip, a loudmouth. [allegedly coined by jazz maestro Louis Armstrong (1901–71); Columbia records ad. 1926: 'Gate Mouth [...] is the kind of mouth that stretches from ear to ear and buttons in back']

gate of horn *n.* [19C] the vagina (cf. ADAM'S OWN (ALTAR) n.; BELLY ENTRANCE n.). [pun on SE *gate* + HORN n.[2] (1)]

gate of life *n.* [late 18C] the vagina (cf. ADAM'S OWN (ALTAR) n.; BELLY ENTRANCE n.).

gater *n. see* GATOR n.[1] (1).

gates *n.*[1] [1950s+] (*W.I. Rasta/UK Black*) one's home. [i.e. one's front *gate*]

gates *n.*[2] [1970s+] (*US gay*) the buttocks (cf. ARSE-END n.).

gates *n.*[3] *see* GATE n.[2].

gates of heaven *n.* [1940s] the number 7. [rhy. sl.]

gates of Rome *n.* [20C+] home. [rhy. sl.]

gateswinger *n.* [1970s+] (*US gay*) a bisexual.

gatey *adj.* [1950s] (*UK prison*) suffering from the nervousness that precedes the end of one's sentence (cf. GATE FEVER n.). [the opening of the prison *gate*]

gather *n.* [2000s] (*UK Und.*) a detective. [GATHER v.]

gather *v.* [1970s] (*Aus. Und.*) to arrest.

gather-em-up *n.* (*also* **gather-up**) [1970s+] (*Irish*) a useless person. [Irish/Ulster *gather-up*, a rag-and-bone man]

gather straws *v. see* DRAW STRAWS v.

gather-up *n. see* GATHER-EM-UP n.

gation *n.* (*also* **gaishen, gashun**) [20C+] (*Ulster*) a very thin person. [Scot. Gael. *gaisean*, a stalk; thus a young boy]

gatkas *n.* [20C+] trousers. [synon. Yid.]

gatling *n.* [late 19C–1960s] (*US*) a gun. [abbr. *Gatling gun*, a form of machine gun, invented by Dr R.J. *Gatling* (1818–1903), and first used in the US Civil War (1861–5)]

gato *n.* [1980s+] (*drugs*) heroin. [Sp.]

gator *n.*[1] **1** [mid-19C+] (*orig. US*) (*also* **gaiter, gater**) an alligator. **2** [1950s+] (*orig. US*) an alligator skin shoe; often in pl. **3** [1980s+] (*US campus*) a typical fraternity boy. [abbr.; (3) the alligator emblem that is the trademark of Izod shirts, popular among fraternity wearers]

gator *n.*[2] [20C+] (*US*) an inhabitant of Florida. [abbr. ALLIGATOR n.[2]]

gator *n.*[3] [1930s–50s] (*orig. US Black*) **1** a jazz fan. **2** any person considered to be in the swing of things. **3** a term of address used between men. [abbr. ALLIGATOR n.[3]]

gator bait *n.* [1970s+] (*US*) a Black person. [abbr. ALLIGATOR BAIT n.[2] (1)]

gator-faced *adj.* [1940s–50s] (*US Black*) someone who has a long face and a large mouth. [GATOR n.[1] (1)]

gator-mouth *n.* [1990s+] (*US campus*) **1** a person who talks too much. **2** a fellatrix. [GATOR n.[1] (1) + SE *mouth*, the idea of alligators having big mouths]

gatt *n. see* GAT n.[1].

gatter *n.* (*also* **gatta**) **1** [19C–1900s] beer; esp. in phr. *shant of gatter*, a pot of beer. **2** [mid-19C] gin. [ety. unknown; E.P. suggests poss. Ling. Fr. or mix of *agua* + *water*]

gatter *v.* [late 19C] to drink beer. [GATTER n. (1)]

gattering *n.* [mid–late 19C] a public house; a drinking spree. [GATTER n.]

gattes *n.* [1960s+] **1** (*S.Afr. Black*) the police. **2** (*S.Afr. Jewish*) an Afrikaner. [? Sotho *gata*, to trample or Yid. *khates*, a bad person]

gat up *v.* [1920s–30s] (*US Und.*) **1** to hold someone up with a gun. **2** to arm oneself. [GAT n.[1] (1)]

gatvol *adj.* [1980s+] (*S.Afr.*) bored, disgusted, 'having a bellyful'. [GAT n.[2] + Afk. *vol*, full]

gauber-grubber *n. see* GOOBER-GRABBER n.[1].

gaubey *n.* [early 19C+] (*Irish*) a gawper, one who looks on while others are doing something. [Irish *gabhgaire*, an onlooker (at a card-game)]

gaudeamus *n.* [19C] a student feast; thus any form of party, merry-making. [first lines of students' song: *Gaudeamus igitur, / juvenes dum sumus*, 'Then let us be merry while we are young']

gaudy *adj.* [late 19C–1940s] a general intensifier, great, complete, utter; also as adv., very, extremely. [? euph. for BLOODY adj.[1] (1)]

gauge *see also under* GAGE and its combs.

gauge *n.*[1] (*also* **gage**) [1930s–50s] temper; often in phr. *get one's gauge up*.

gauge *n.*[2] (*also* **gage**) [1970s+] (*US Black*) a shotgun. [abbr. *12-gauge*, a 12 bore]

gaul darned *adj. see* GOLDARNED adj.

gaulder *n.* (*also* **gulder**) [20C+] (*Ulster*) a shout; also as v., to shout. [Scot. *gulder*, a noisy, energetic shout]

gaully! *excl. see* GOLLY! excl.

gaum *n.*[1] (*also* **gaumhead**) [late 19C–1900s] (*US*) a fool, a clumsy oaf. [dial. *gaumless*, stupid (+ -HEAD sfx (1)); note synon. dial. *gaumless-head*]

gaum *n.*[2] *see* GOM n.[2].

gaumy *adj.* [20C+] (*US*) stupid, clumsy. [GAUM n.[1]]

gaunch *n. see* GANCH n.

gauzer n. (also **gawzer**) [20C+] (Irish) a very pretty girl. [? SE gorgeous or gaze, to stare at]

gavacho n. [1960s+] (US Hisp.) a White person.

gavel and wig v. [20C+] to scratch (an itchy anus). [rhy. sl. = SE twig, i.e. the image of using a twig to do the scratching]

gavone n. (also **cafone, gafone**) [1960s+] a fool. [? JIBONE n.]

gaw n. (also **gawd**) [mid-19C+] a mispron. of or euph. for God and as such used in a variety of oaths (cf. BOB n.[2]).

gawd aggie! excl. [20C+] (Aus.) a general expletive of surprise, annoyance etc. [SE God! + proper name Aggie, i.e. Agatha]

gawdelpus n.[1] (also **God-help-us, gordelpus**) [late 19C–1900s] an impoverished labourer. ['from his ordinary excl. "Gordelpus – what's a cove to do?"' (Ware)]

gawdelpus n.[2] (also **God-help-us, gordelpus**) [20C+] **1** an irritating or helpless person; often used of a child, e.g. You 'orrible little gawdelpus. **2** a generally miserable looking person. [SE God help us; unstated is 'what shall we do about you?']

gawd-forbids n. see GOD-FORBIDS n. (1).

gawd love a duck! excl. see LORD LOVE A DUCK! excl.

gawf n. [mid-19C] a red-skinned apple, considered inferior produce but capable, with judicious polishing, of being sold as something better. [? 'go for more'; 'Gawfs are sweet and sour at once […] and fit only for mixing' (Mayhew)]

gawie n. [1960s+] (S.Afr.) a country bumpkin, an unsophisticated peasant (cf. BLOOTER n.). [Afk. gawie, lout]

gawk n. (also **gawke, gawkhead, gawky**) **1** [early 18C+] a simpleton, a fool. **2** [late 19C] a peasant, a rustic (cf. BLOOTER n.). [GAWK v.[1]]

gawk v.[1] [late 19C+] to stare; also as n., a look. [(1) Scot. gowk, cuckoo and thus fool or gawk, to stare at; the OED sees gowk as an independent word, claiming that Johnson, among others, confuses them]

gawk v.[2] [2000s] (Irish) to vomit (cf. BARF v.). [echoic/GAWKS, THE n.]

gawke n. see GAWK n.

gawker n. [1950s+] one who stares (stupidly). [GAWK v.[1]]

gawkey n. **1** [late 18C–1900s] a tall, thin, physically un-coordinated young person. **2** [mid-19C] a clumsy or ridiculous event.

gawkhead n. see GAWK n.

gawks, the n. [1990s+] (Irish) feelings of nausea; thus phr. have the gawks, to feel sick. [echoic of vomiting]

gawky n. see GAWK n.

gawky adj. [mid-18C+] foolish, simple. [GAWK n. (1)]

gawm n. see GOM n.[2].

gawney n. [18C] a fool. [Midl. dial. gawney, to stare vacantly]

Gawney (Mac)! excl. [1980s+] (Irish) a euph. for JESUS (CHRIST)! excl. (cf. JANEY (MACK)! excl.).

gawp n. **1** [early 19C+] (orig. Scot.) a fool, a simpleton. **2** [2000s] a foolish stare. [GAWP v.]

gawp v. [early 19C+] to stare. [obs. SE galp, to gape, yawn, orig. of animals]

gawsave n. [20C+] the British national anthem. [the first line, 'God save our gracious king/queen']

gawzer n. see GAUZER n.

gay n.[1] [1920s–60s] (Aus.) a dupe, a sucker, a gullible person. [? GALAH n. (1) or ? JAY n.[3] (3)]

gay n.[2] **1** [1920s+] a male homosexual. **2** [1990s+] (mainly UK juv.) a term of abuse for an unpopular individual. [GAY adj.[1] (3)]

gay n.[3] see GAY (AND FRISKY) n.

gay n.[4] see GAY (AND HEARTY) n.

gay adj.[1] **1** [late 14C; mid–19C–1920s] of a woman, leading an immoral life, working as a prostitute. **2** [17C–1930s] promiscuous, dissipated. **3** [1920s+] (orig. US) of sexual orientation, homosexual. **4** [1920s+] of a place, catering for or frequented by homosexuals. **5** [1920s+] of behaviour, mannerisms, feelings, events, social circles etc, homosexual. [(3) the use of gay as a self-description

by homosexuals originated shortly after WW1, prob. an abbr. of US tramps' sl. GAYCAT n. (4), the young homosexual companion of an older tramp; but note Rodgers, The Queen's Vernacular (1972): 'fr. 16th cent Fr gaie = homosexual man'; the wider use in the heterosexual world did not begin until c.1970, with the emergence of the Gay Liberation Front, first in the US and subseq. in the UK. With the decline of derog. terms, such as QUEER adj.[1] (3), gay is now effectively SE; thus note George Melly, Owning Up (1965): 'I'd never heard the word "gay" at that time [1945]. "Queer" was in more general use even among homosexuals']

gay adj.[2] **1** [19C–1920s] slightly drunk, tipsy (cf. ABOUT RIGHT phr.[1]). **2** [late 19C–1910s] (US) forward, impertinent, over-familiar; esp. in phr. GET GAY (WITH) v. [SE gay, cheerful]

gay adj.[3] (also **gey**) [mid-19C–1920s] (orig. US) fine, first-rate.

gay adj.[4] [1980s+] (orig. US campus) a general pej. epithet, stupid, ugly, eccentric. [a paradoxical use of the otherwise politically correct term GAY adj.[1] (3) as a derog.]

gay (and frisky) n. [1910s+] whisky. [rhy. sl.]

gay (and hearty) n. [1960s+] (Aus.) a party. [rhy. sl.]

gay-basher n. [1980s+] an ostensibly 'real man' who specializes in beating and terrorizing homosexual men. [GAY n.[2] (1) + BASH v.[1] (1)]

gay-bashing n. [1980s+] (orig. US) the homophobic beating up of homosexual men; thus gay-bash, to beat up homosexuals. [GAY n.[2] (1) + BASHING n.[1] (1)]

gay bit n. [mid–late 19C] a prostitute. [GAY adj.[1] (1) + BIT n.[2] (1)]

gaybo n. [1980s] a male homosexual?. [GAY adj.[1] (3) + SE boy]

gay boy n. [1950s+] (US) a male homosexual. [GAY adj.[1] (3) + SE boy]

gaycat n. **1** [late 19C–1950s] (US tramp) a young or inexperienced tramp. **2** [late 19C–1950s] (US tramp) a tramp who accepts occasional or seasonal work. **3** [1900s–40s] (US Und.) the junior member of a criminal gang, employed to run errands or spy out possible crimes. **4** [1910s–20s] (US tramp) (also **geycat**) a tramp's younger, homosexual companion. [ety. unknown; the best possibility is that (1) and (2) were often homosexual, and thus (4) which in turn may suggest a transitional point between SE gay, cheerful, and GAY adj.[1] (3); note 'The Kid' who appears in the eponymous The Gay-cat (1921) is not openly homosexual, although this may be contemporary self-censorship by the author]

gaycat v.[1] [late 19C–1950s] **1** (US tramp) (also **geycat**) to act as a tramp's (homosexual) companion. **2** (US Und.) to act as a spy for a criminal gang. [GAYCAT n.]

gaycat v.[2] [1920s–40s] (US Black) **1** to have a good time. **2** to loiter and chat in the street. [SE gay adj. + CAT n.[11] (2)]

gaychick n. [1980s+] (US gay) a lesbian. [GAY adj.[1] (3) + CHICK n.[4] (2)]

gaydar n. [1980s+] (mainly gay) the (alleged) sensory perception that lesbians and gays have of other gay people in their midst. [play on GAY adj.[1] (3) + radar]

gay deceivers n. **1** [1940s+] a padded brassiere that accentuates the shape and dimensions of otherwise small female breasts. **2** [1960s] (US gay) a large artificial penis worn beneath the trousers to accentuate one's apparent sexual allure. [pun on orig. use, a deceitful rake]

gay girl n. (also **gay woman**) **1** [mid-19C] a promiscuous girl or woman. **2** [1970s+] (US gay) an effeminate homosexual. [GAY adj.[1] (1)/GAY adj.[1] (3) + SE girl]

gay goddess n. [1990s+] (US gay) a heterosexual woman who prefers the company of homosexual men. [GAY adj.[1] (3)]

gay gordon n. [1990s+] (US) a traffic warden. [rhy. sl.]

gay house n. [18C–1900s] a brothel (cf. ACCOMMODATION HOUSE n.). [GAY adj.[1] (1) + HOUSE n.[1] (1)]

gaying instrument n. [18C] the penis. [GAY adj.[1] (1)/GAY adj.[1] (2) + SE instrument]

gaying it n. [19C] having sexual intercourse. [GAY adj.[1] (1)/GAY adj.[1] (2)]

gay in the arse adj. (also **gay in the groin**) [19C] of a woman, promiscuous. [GAY adj.¹ (1) + ARSE n.¹ (2)]

gay lady n. [mid–late 19C] a prostitute (cf. BANKSIDE LADY n.). [GAY adj.¹ (1) + SE lady]

gayola n. **1** [1960s+] (US Und.) pay-offs and bribes made to police or organized crime in order to allow the running of gay clubs. **2** [1980s+] (US) a homosexual man. [GAY adj.¹ (3) + -OLA sfx; on pattern of PAYOLA n.]

gay trade n. [1940s+] a homosexual man who is happy to fellate or to perform anal intercourse but will not reciprocate (although he may kiss and otherwise fondle his partner) (cf. DO FOR TRADE v.). [TRADE n. (3)]

gayumbas n. see GAZONGAS n. (1).

Gay White Way n. [1910s–30s] Broadway, New York City; thus used generically for similar entertainment centres in other cities. [the term, in which gay is used in the conventional SE manner, i.e. cheerful, jolly, was a short-lived alternative to the longer-lasting GREAT WHITE WAY n.]

gay woman n. see GAY GIRL n.

gazabo n. (also **gazab, gazabe, gazaybe, gazebo, gazebu, gazee, gazooney, gezeybo**) [late 19C+] (Irish/US) an awkward, strange or stupid person; thus fem. gazaboine, used of women. [? Sp. gazapo, a sly fellow + SE gaze, i.e. their vacant stares]

gaze at the melody v. [late 19C] to deal stoically with a problem or difficult situation; to take one's punishment. [play on FACE THE MUSIC v.]

gazebo n.¹ [1900s] (US) the mouth. [SE gazebo, a form of garden hut, or a turret on the roof of a house]

gazebo n.² see GAZABO n.

gazebos n. [1980s] (US) the testicles. [? nonce-word]

gazebu/gazee n. see GAZABO n.

gazelle n. [late 19C–1940s] (US) a young woman.

gazer n.¹ **1** [1930s–40s] (US Black) a flirtatious woman looking for a new partner. **2** [1930s–50s] (US Und.) a federal narcotics agent. [SE gaze, to stare at; (1) the assumption being that she is gazing at other men in the hope of finding a new husband]

gazer n.² [1940s] (US Black) **1** a mirror. **2** a window.

gazlon n. [20C+] (UK Und.) a small-time, poss. timid thief. [Yid. gozlin, a swindler, an unethical person]

gazob n. [1900s–40s] (Aus.) a fool, a simpleton. [var. GAZABO n.]

gazock n. see GAZOOK n. (2).

gazongas n. **1** [1960s+] (also **gajoungas, gayumbas, gazonkas, gazungas**) the female breasts, usu. large (cf. BAZONGAS n.). **2** [2000s] the male breasts.

gazoo n. (also **gazool**) **1** [1960s+] the anus. **2** [1970s] (also **gazookus**) the vagina. [var. on KAZOO n.]

gazook n. (also **gazoo, gazoop, gazoopus**) **1** [1900s–60s] (US) a lout, a boor, a fool. **2** [1930s–40s] (US tramp) (also **gazock**) a tramp's young (homosexual) companion. [GAZABO n.]

gazookus n.¹ (US) **1** [1900s–40s] a lout, a boor, a fool (cf. DOOFUS n.). **2** [1920s] (also **gazukus**) a thing; thus the real gazookus, the genuine article. [ety. unknown]

gazookus n.² see GAZOO n. (2).

gazool n. see GAZOO n.

gazooma n. [1950s] (US Und.) a thug, a stupid man.

gazoomph v. see GAZUMP v.

gazooney n.¹ [1910s+] (US tramp) a young, homosexual sidekick who accompanies a tramp. [Anglo-Irish gossoon, ult. Irish garsuin, a boy, a lad]

gazooney n.² [1990s+] (US) an amusing person.

gazooney n.³ see GAZABO n.

gazoop/gazoopus n. see GAZOOK n.

gazoopie n. (also **gazoopy, gazupie**) [1930s–70s] (US) a sex show. [? GAZOO n. (2)]

gazukus n. see GAZOOKUS n.¹ (2).

gazump n. [1920s] (US) a general pej. term. [var. GAZABO n.]

gazump v. (also **gasumph, gazoomph, gazumph, gezump,**

gezumph, gezzump) **1** [1920s+] to swindle; thus gazumper, a swindler. **2** [1970s+] (orig. estate agent) to accept a stated price for one's property and then to raise that price, using as a threat a supposed, but usu. non-existent, 'offer' from elsewhere; alternatively, the seller accepts one price and then, tempted by a genuinely greater offer, dumps the first buyer without sorrow or ceremony. [? Yid. gezumph, to cheat or to overcharge]

gazunder v. [1980s+] for the buyer to cut the agreed house price, after contracts have been exchanged, at the last minute. [antonym of GAZUMP v. (2), i.e. + SE under]

gazungas n. see GAZONGAS n. (1).

gazupie n. see GAZOOPIE n.

g.b. n.¹ [late 19C–1920s] (US) grand bounce, a forceful ejection or dismissal. [abbr. SE grand + BOUNCE, THE n.]

g.b. n.² [1950s] (W.I.) gym shoes or boots that lace at the front with buckles at the side. [ety. unknown]

g.b. n.³ [1960s+] (drugs) a barbiturate, a depressant (cf. BARBIT n.). [abbr. GOOFBALL n.¹ (2)]

g.b. n.⁴ see GREENBACK n.² (1).

g.b. phr. [1970s+] (US campus) goodbye. [abbr.]

g.b.h. n. [1950s+] (orig. UK Und.) grievous bodily harm; also in fig. use, e.g. g.b.h. of the brain, pressure or strain; g.b.h. of the ear, excessive noise. [abbr.]

G-clip n. [2000s] (US Black) a sign that indicates to a woman that one wishes to have sex. [ety. unknown; ? link to G n.¹ (2) or G n.³ (1)]

G.D. adj. (also **G.d., g.d.**) [mid-19C+] (US) God-damned; thus g.d.f., God-damned fool. [abbr.]

g.d.i. n. [1960s+] (US campus) a student who is not a fraternity or sorority member. [abbr. God-damned independent]

G'd up adj. [1990s+] (US Black/campus) dressed in the style currently favoured by Black urban GANGSTA n. (2) youth. [G n.³ (1)]

g'd up adj. see GEED-UP adj.².

ge n. [1980s+] (S.Afr.) **1** a friend, a pal. **2** a tough, a thug. [Afk. gê, trash, rubbish]

geach n. [early 19C] a thief. [? Scot. geck, an act of deception; ult. Ger. Gecken, tricks]

geach v. [early 19C] to steal. [GEACH n.]

gear n.¹ **1** [late 15C+] (also **geer, gere**) dress, equipment. **2** [mid-16C+] an object or objects; things, varying as to context. **3** [late 17C–early 18C] trash, rubbish. **4** [1950s+] stolen property. **5** [1960s] in the sex industry, photographs, magazines, films etc. **6** [1960s+] (drugs) drugs, esp. cannabis, heroin. **7** [1970s+] the equipment used in sado-masochistic sex. **8** [2000s] (US Black) one's personal space. [14C SE]

gear n.² **1** [mid-16C–early 18C; late 19C] the female genitals. **2** [mid-16C–mid-18C; 1970s+] (also **geer**) the male genitals; thus [17C] gear-itch, lecherousness. [SE gear, accoutrements]

gear n.³ [1930s–70s] (US prison) a homosexual. [fig. use of GEAR n.¹ (4), the gay man is 'stolen away' to become an object of gratification for others]

gear n.⁴ [1950s+] (US) an important or influential person. [SE 16C–18C]

gear adj.¹ (also **geer**) [1920s+] excellent, wonderful, just right; often as the gear. [abbr. that's the gear, that's the stuff; at peak popularity one of The Beatles' supposed favourite words; post-1960s use is ironic (cf. FAB adj.)]

gear adj.² [1930s+] homosexual. [GEAR n.³ + rhy. sl. = QUEER adj.¹ (3)]

gearbox n. [1940s+] the female genitals. [GEAR n.² (1) + SE box/BOX n.¹ (1)]

geared adj. [1930s+] (US Und.) sexually aberrant. [GEAR adj.²]

geared up adj. **1** [1930s+] (US) intoxicated. **2** [1960s+] (Scot./US Black) dressed up. **3** [1970s+] (US) very (sexually) excited. **4** [1990s+] prepared, ready. [GEAR n.¹]

gearhead n. **1** [1970s+] (orig. US campus) an engineering student, someone mechanically minded; thus ext. to one who is obsessed with automobiles. **2** [1990s+] (*US*) a car factory worker. [mechanical sense of SE *gear* + -HEAD sfx (4)]

gear job *n.* [1970s] (*US prison*) a homosexual. [GEAR n.³ + JOB n.⁴]

gears *n.* [1960s+] (*W.I.*) one's best clothing. [SE *gear*, apparel, attire + 1960s use of GEAR n.¹ (1)]

gear stick *n. see* JOYSTICK n.¹.

gear up *v.* [20C+] to prepare oneself mentally and physically for dealing with something, usu. the day ahead. [automobile imagery]

geck *n.* (*also* **gack, gak, geek**) **1** [early 19C; 1990s+] an odd, eccentric-looking person. **2** [20C+] (*Ulster*) a person who tells tales behind another's back, a gossip. **3** [1990s+] a person who uses LSD. [dial. *geck*, a fool]

geck *v.* [1990s+] to lose one's self-confidence. [? GECK n. (3)]

ged *n.* [late 17C–mid-18C] a euph. for *God* in a variety of oaths/ excls., e.g. *ged's curse it! 'fore ged!* (cf. BOB n.²).

gedoente *n.* [1970s+] (*S.Afr.*) a fuss, a carry-on, a 'to-do'. [Afk. *gedoente*, bustle]

gee *n.*¹ [late 19C–1930s] a horse. [abbr. GEE-GEE n.¹ (1)]

gee *n.*² **1** [late 19C+] (*Aus.*) (*also* **gee-er, gee-man**) one who 'gees up' the potential customers into a sideshow, strip-club, confidence trick etc. **2** [1920s+] idle chatter, empty talk, 'blarney'. [GEE (UP) v. (1); (2) f. (1)]

gee *n.*³ [20C+] (*US*) **1** a male, esp. a male friend. **2** the most important person in a given environment; the leader; **3** usu. as *the whole gee*. [GUY n.² (1)]

gee *n.*⁴ **1** [1910s+] a woman considered solely as a sex object. **2** [1930s; 1990s+] (*also* **gee box**) the vagina. [? Irish sl. *gowl*, the vagina, ult. Irish *gabhal*, the fork (of the body)]

gee *n.*⁵ [1930s] (*US tramp*) a glass of alcohol. [the initial letter]

gee *n.*⁶ [1930s–60s] (*US drugs*) **1** opium (cf. APOSTLE n.). **2** narcotics other than opium. [the initial letter of various sl. terms for opium, e.g. GONG n.² (2), GOW n.¹ (2), GUM n.³; ? or of SE *guy*, which is synon. with BOY n.⁷ (1), i.e. heroin; further-fetched is poss. pun on SE *gee-up!*, used of horses, thus linked to HORSE n.⁸, heroin; Maurer, 'Lang. of the Underworld Narcotic Addict' Pt.2 (1938), suggests Hindi *ghee*, refined butter; also note Chinese *yi-yin*/GEE YEN n., seconds, i.e. opium residue]

gee *n.*⁷ (*also* **boo-gee, gee rag**) [1930s+] a paper 'collar' used by a drug user to secure the needle to the eye-dropper prior to injecting the heroin/water solution; earlier use in opium smoking. [? ext. of GEE n.⁶ (1) but, despite dates, poss. abbr. GASKET n.². Note that, unlike in the UK, where registered addicts (and via them other users) were allowed to use proper medical syringes, US users were often forced to make their own WORKS n.² (1), a do-it-yourself assemblage of a hollow needle and an eye-dropper]

gee *n.*⁸ *see* G n.¹ (1).

gee *n.*⁹ *see* G n.¹.

gee *n.*¹⁰ *see* GUEE n.

gee *v.*¹ (*also* **jee**) [late 17C–1920s] to fit, to suit, to behave as required or expected; usu. in phr. *it won't gee*, it doesn't suit, it doesn't work. [? pron. of initial letter of SE *go*]

gee *v.*² [1970s+] (*US Black*) to have sexual intercourse. [? fig. use of SE *gee up*, to urge a horse forward, thus play on RIDE v.¹ (1)]

gee *v.*³ *see* GEE (UP) v.

gee! *excl.* (*also* **jee!**) [mid-19C+] (*US*) a mild oath, a euph. for JESUS! excl.

geeba *n.* [2000s] (*US campus*) marijuana. [var. on CHIBA n.² (1)]

gee bag *n.* [2000s] (*Irish*) a term of abuse. [? Irish sl. *gowl*, the vagina, ult. Irish *gabhal*, the fork (of the body) + -BAG sfx]

gee box *n. see* GEE n.⁴ (2).

geebung *n.* [mid-19C–1910s] (*Aus.*) **1** an unsophisticated, uncultured, philistine native-born Australian, who values material gain above everything else; personified as *Tommy Geebung*. **2** a place-name for any out-of-the-way place. **3** a gadget. [SE *geebung*, a shrub or tree of the genus *Persoonia*]

geech *n.* [1960s] (*US*) money. [? GEETUS n. (1)]

geechee *n.* [20C+] (*US Black*) a derog. term for anyone (typically a rural Southerner, newly migrated to the urban North) whose speech is made incomprehensible by a heavy accent. [proper name *Geechee*, an inhabitant (usu. Black) of the coastal areas of Georgia, North Carolina or northern Florida; the language such people speak is itself *Geechee*]

geechie *adj.* (*also* **geechy**) (*US Black*) **1** [20C+] unintelligible; thus unsophisticated, provincial. **2** [1980s] of a Black person, light-skinned, or having Native American forebears. [GEECHEE n.]

geed-up *adj.*¹ **1** [1900s–60s] (*US*) crippled, in disrepair. **2** [1930s] (*US drugs*) impoverished. [ety. unknown]

geed-up *adj.*² (*US*) (*also* **g'd up**) **1** [1920s–70s] drunk (cf. ABOUT RIGHT phr.¹). **2** [1920s+] excited. **3** [1930s–70s] intoxicated by drugs. **4** [1990s+] modified and thus increased in value. [? GEE (UP) v. (1); or ? (1) GEE n.⁵; (3) GEE n.⁶]

geedus *n. see* GEETUS n.

gee-er *n.*¹ *see* GEE n.² (1).

gee-er *n.*² *see* GEE (UP) v. (4).

gee-eyed *adj.* [2000s] (*Irish*) drunk (cf. ARSEHOLED adj.).

gee-fat *n.* [1930s–50s] (*US drugs*) narcotics, usu. the residue of opium. [? GEE YEN n.]

gee for *v.* [1900s] (*N.Z.*) to support enthusiastically. [GEE (UP) v. (1)]

gee-gee *n.*¹ (*also* **gee-gaw**) [mid-19C+] **1** a horse; often as *gee-gees*, horses, esp. those on racecourses; thus *play the gee-gees*, to gamble on horseraces. **2** horse-meat. [SE *gee up!*]

gee-gee *n.*² [1920s] a man, a fellow. [GEEZER n.¹ (1)/GEE n.³ + redup.]

gee-gee *n.*³ [1960s–70s] (*US*) the anus or vagina. [? play on GEE-GEE n.¹; i.e. it is 'ridden' during intercourse + note GEE n.⁴]

gee-gee *n.*⁴ [1980s] (*UK Und.*) £1000. [redup. G n.¹ (1)]

gee hair *n. see* GNAT'S EYEBROW n.

geek *n.*¹ **1** [late 19C+] (*US*) (*also* **geke, geekoid**) a clumsy, eccentric or offensive person. **2** [20C+] a carnival freak who specialized in biting the heads off live chickens or snakes. **3** [1940s] a generally unpleasant person, irrelevant of class. **4** [1950s+] (*US Black/teen*) an eccentric, an intellectual; esp. an obsessive; thus *geekize*, to render something thus appealing. **5** [1980s+] (*US teen*) a vulgar, working-class youth. **6** [1980s+] (*US campus*) one who is considered to devote too much time to their books; thus *geek out*, to work (too) hard. **7** [1980s+] (*orig. US campus*) a devotee of and expert in computers and computer-related culture; thus *geekware*, technology that appeals to such individuals. [dial. *geck*, a fool; 20C+ uses allegedly invented by one Wagner, of Charleston, West Virginia, who had a celebrated touring snake-eating act; his ballyhoo ran in part, 'Come and see Esau / Sitting on a see-saw / Eatin' 'em raw!'; thus note *Variety*, 8 Sep. 1922: 'The old and reliable snake charmer retired to make room for the snake eater, and weird creatures appeared in dens filled with small reptiles, outside of which huge banners proclaimed the fact that "Bosco" or "Esau" "eats 'em alive"']

geek *n.*² [1910s+] (*Aus.*) a glance, a look. [Cornish dial. *geek*, to peer, to look intently]

geek *n.*³ *see* GECK n.

geek *adj.* **1** [1960s+] clumsy, uncoordinated. **2** [1980s+] pertaining to the world of obsessives, esp. in the context of computing, the Internet etc. [GEEK n.¹ (1)/GEEK n.¹ (7)]

geek *v.*¹ [1910s+] (*Aus./N.Z.*) to stare at, to look at. [GEEK n.²]

geek *v.*² **1** [1950s+] (*US Black/drugs*) (*also* **geek out**) to experience severe symptoms of heroin withdrawal; also to deal obsessively with surrounding inanimate objects after a binge on strong amphetamine drugs. **2** [1980s+] (*orig computing/US campus*) (*also* **geek out**) to devote oneself to one's own (computing, obsessive) pursuits in an environment where such pursuits are disdained.

3 [1980s+] (*US campus*) to act stupidly or in a way that counters the cultural norm. [GEEK n.[1]]

geek v.[3] [1990s+] (*US*) to sell items in the street. [? GEEK n.[1] (5)]

geeked (up) adj. [1990s+] (*US*) naively excited or thrilled by something. [GEEK n.[1] (1)]

geekiness n. [1980s+] social ineptitude. [GEEK n.[1] (1)]

geekish adj. (*also* **geekified, geeking**) [1990s+] eccentric, freakish. [GEEK n.[1] (1)]

geek it v. (*also* **geek out**) [1930s–50s] (*US*) to quit or back down. [GEEK n.[1] (1)]

geekoid n. *see* GEEK n.[1] (1).

geek out v.[1] *see* GEEK n.[1] (6).

geek out v.[2] *see* GEEK v.[2].

geek out v.[3] *see* GEEK IT v.

geek up v. [1980s+] (*US*) to frighten, to make nervous. [i.e. to render one a GEEK n.[1] (1)]

geeky adj. **1** [1970s+] (*US gay*) unethical, villainous. **2** [1980s+] (*US Black*) of a man, unattractive. **3** [1990s+] (*orig. US campus*) socially inept, overly studious. [GEEK n.[1] + sfx -*y*]

gee-man n. *see* GEE n.[2] (1).

gee mo nitty! *excl.* [20C+] (*US Black*) a general excl. of annoyance or bewilderment. [ety. unknown; ? ext. of GEE! excl.; ? pron. of JIMINETTY! excl.]

geep n. (*also* **geepo**) [1940s–50s] (*US*) an obnoxious, inept or suspicious looking person. [? GEEK n.[1] (1)]

geepie n. [1950s–70s] a youthful hipster, spec. a fan of P-Funk. [pron. with hard 'g'; echoic, i.e. the squeaky tones of the youthful enthusiast]

geer *see under* GEAR.

gee rag n. *see* GEE n.[7].

geese n. [1950s] (*US gang*) a theft. [ety. unknown]

geesefeathers n. [1910s–20s] (*US*) snow. [resemblance]

geeser *see under* GEEZER.

gee stick n. [1930s–50s] (*US drugs*) an opium pipe. [GEE n.[6] (1) + SE *stick*/STICK n.[9] (2)]

geetus n. (*also* **geedus, geetas, geeters, geetis, geets, ghedis, gietus**) [1920s] (*US*) **1** money. **2** power. [ety. unknown; ? SE *get us*]

gee up n. **1** [1920s+] (*Aus.*) a spree, any form of merry-making. **2** [1940s] (*also* **jee up**) encouragement, stimulus. [GEE (UP) v. (1)]

gee (up) v. **1** [mid-19C+] to encourage, to persuade, to incite, esp. when working as a showman's or market-trader's assistant. **2** [1930s+] to act as an agent provocateur, esp. when using entrapment for sexual crimes. **3** [1930s+] to provoke trouble deliberately, to tease maliciously; to deceive; thus *geed up*, furious, very angry. **4** [1940s+] (*orig. UK prison*) to inform (against a fellow prisoner); thus *gee-er*, an informer. **5** [1990s+] to give up, to surrender. [SE *gee up*, to urge a horse forward; (5) may be SE *give up to*, hand over]

gee vet *excl.* [20C+] (*S.Afr.*) hurry up! get a move on! 'step on it!' [Afk. *gee vet*, lit. to 'give grease']

gee whillikins! *excl.* (*also* **gee whillikers! geewhittaker(s)!**) [mid-19C+] (*mainly US juv.*) a mild excl., a euph. for JESUS (CHRIST)! excl.

gee-whiz adj. [1950s+] exciting. [GEE WHIZ! excl. (1)]

gee whiz! *excl.* **1** [late 19C+] a euph. for JESUS! excl. and as such a mild excl. **2** [1930s] a term used to describe popular speech-forms.

geewillies n. [20C+] nerves, tension, fear. [GEE! excl. + WILLIES n.; ? underpinned by GEE WHILLIKINS! excl.]

gee yen n. (*also* **yi-yen**) [late 19C–1930s] (*US drugs*) the residue that collects inside the stem of an opium pipe; it may be collected and then resold. [synon. Chinese *yí-yín*; note GEE n.[6] (1)]

geez n.[1] (*also* **geeze**) [1960s–70s] (*drugs*) an injection of narcotics. [GEEZE v. (1)]

geez n.[2] [1960s–70s] a man, a fellow, a 'bloke'. [abbr. GEEZER n.[1] (1)]

geez! *excl. see* JEEZ! excl.

geeze v. (*also* **geez**) (*drugs*) **1** [1960s+] to inject narcotics. **2** [2000s] to inhale cocaine. [GEEZER n.[3] (1); given the date of the root n., Spears, *Slang and Jargon of Drugs and Drink* (1986), is surely right to suggest 'this may be much older than the attestations suggest']

geezed adj. **1** [1900s–10s] (*US*) drunk. **2** [1930s–50s] (*US drugs*) (*also* **geezed up**) intoxicated by drugs. [(2) GEEZE v. (1) which suggests (1), although both predate cits. for v.]

geezer n.[1] **1** [late 19C+] (*also* **geeser, geyser, gheeser**) a man, a 'bloke'; occas. a woman. **2** [late 19C+] (*US*) an old man, occas. woman; often as *old geezer*. **3** [1910s+] a term of address to a man. **4** [1940s–50s] in fig. use of (2), staleness, tiredness. **5** [1950s] a well-dressed, stylish man. **6** [1970s] a confidence trickster's victim; a prostitute's client. **7** [1970s] (*UK gay*) a young male prostitute's older client. **8** [1970s+] an authority figure. **9** [2000s] (*UK Black*) one who fails to achieve the standards of the 'street' lifestyle, the opposite of a 'brother'. [dial. pron. of 15C *guiser*, a mummer (*OED*); E.P. wonders if Wellington's troops might not have picked it up from the Basque *giza*, a man, during the Peninsular War (1808–14)]

geezer n.[2] [1910s–40s] (*US*) a drink of whisky or strong alcohol. [Lincolnshire dial. *geezer*, a state of drunkenness]

geezer n.[3] (*US drugs*) **1** [1920s+] (*also* **geeser**) an injection of a narcotic drug. **2** [1920s+] the equipment with which one injects. **3** [1960s+] a heroin addict. [? ext. of GEE n.[6] (1), although this predates]

geezer! *excl.* [1990s+] an excl. of greeting or joy. [GEEZER n.[1] (3)]

geezo n. [1930s] (*US prison*) a convict. [GEEZER n.[1] (1) + -O sfx (4)]

geggy n. [2000s] one who wears spectacles. [GEGS n.]

gegor n. [mid–late 19C] a beggar. [? GAGGER n.[1] (3) although this predates; ? pron. of SE *beggar*]

gegs n. [2000s] spectacles. [GIG-LAMPS n. (1)]

gehuncled adj. [1920s–60s] (*US*) crippled. [? Ger. *gehunkelt*, hobbled]

geize v. [1980s+] (*US campus*) to drive or run extremely fast. [ety. unknown]

gek adj. [mid-19C+] (*S.Afr.*) foolish, obsessed, insane. [Du. *gek*, mad]

geke n. *see* GEEK n.[1] (1).

gel v. *see* JELL v.

geld/geldt n. *see* GELT n.

gellie/gelly n. *see* JELLY n.[4] (1).

gelly n. *see* JELLY n.[5].

gellyhead n. (*also* **jellyhead**) [1990s+] (*N.Z.*) a fool (cf. APPLEHEAD n.). [SE *jelly* + -HEAD sfx (1)]

gel on v. [1980s+] (*US campus*) to break an appointment. [ext. of JELL v.]

gelt n. (*also* **geld, geldt, gelter, ghelt**) [late 17C+] money (cf. CANARY n.[5]). [Yid. *gelt*, money or Ger. *gelt*, gold; note S.Afr. colloq. *geld*, money f. Du.]

gem n. [19C+] something greatly prized, a 'jewel', a 'treasure'. [note Williams refers to 17C use of *gem* for the male genitals, a woman, the maidenhead and a venereal sore]

gemini! *excl.* (*also* **jeminy!**) [late 17C–1920s] a euph. for JESUS! excl. and used as such in oaths (cf. JIMINY! excl.). [? Ger. excl. *jemine*, oh dear!, gracious! = Lat. Jesu domine]

gemmie n. [1960s] (*Scot.*) a tough, ruthless young man. [GAME adj.[1] (4)]

gemors n. [1970s+] (*S.Afr.*) **1** a mess, a confusion. **2** an insulting form of address. [synon. Afk.]

gen n.[1] [mid-19C] a shilling (12d/5p). [? abbr. *argent*, silver, or abbr. GENERALIZE n., a supposed backsl. formation of *shilling*]

gen n.[2] [1940s+] information, facts; thus *gen up*, to inform; *genned up*, well informed. [? RAF *gen(eral information)* for all ranks]

gendarme n. **1** [20C+] a policeman; also as v., to police. **2** [1950s] (*Aus.*) a large, tough man employed to keep order in a club. [Fr. *gendarme*, policeman]

gender-bender *n.* [1980s+] **1** a synon. for a transvestite or a transsexual, bending or eroding the line between the 2 sexes; thus *v. gender-bend.* **2** an act or example of something that bends the line between the 2 sexes; thus *adj. gender-bending.* [SE + ? a pun on FENDER-BENDER n.; the term was popularized during the rise to fame of the pop star Boy George, whose outrageous clothes and ostentatious make-up managed to disturb many observers]

gender-fuck *n.* [1970s+] **1** a man who shocks the heterosexual world by openly adopting women's clothes, thus destroying the assumptions about male/female separatism; similarly a woman doing the opposite. **2** an act of destroying such assumptions. [SE *gender* + FUCK n.[1] (1)/-FUCK sfx; extreme ext. of GENDER-BENDER n.]

genderfuck *adj.* [2000s] of something that is completely blurring/destroying the boundaries between male and female. [GENDER-FUCK n. (2)]

gender-fuck *v.* [1960s+] (*gay*) of a man, to shock the heterosexual world by openly adopting women's clothes, blurring (or destroying) the assumptions about male/female separatism. [SE *gender* + FUCK v.[1]]

general *n.*[1] **1** [late 19C–1910s] a *general* servant, a maid-of-all-work. **2** [1900s] a *general* stores. [abbr.]

general *n.*[2] **1** [1950s+] a non-specific term of address to a man whose name one does not know. **2** [1950s+] (*W.I. Rasta*) a smart man, a 'cool operator'. **3** [1970s+] (*S.Afr. Und.*) a high rank in a prison gang. [SE]

general *n.*[3] [1960s+] (*US*) the penis.

General Booth *n.* [20C+] a tooth. [rhy. sl.; ult. the founder of the Salvation Army, '*General' William Booth* (1829–1912)]

generalize *n.* [late 19C] a shilling. [backsl.; note GEN n.[1]]

generalize *v.* [mid–late 19C] (*UK middle class*) to give or lend a shilling; usu. in phr. *can you generalize?* [GENERALIZE n.]

General Smuts *n.* [20C+] the testicles (cf. CHEESE AND CRACKERS n.). [rhy. sl. = NUTS n.[2] (1); ult. S.Afr. *General Jan Christian Smuts* (1870–1950)]

generating place *n.* [19C] the vagina (cf. BABY CHUTE n.). [SE *generate,* to procreate]

generating tool *n.* (*also* **generating tube, generation tool**) [mid-17C–19C] the penis. [SE *generate,* to procreate + TOOL n.[1] (1)]

generic *n.* [1990s+] (*US*) a derog. term for a Black person (cf. ALLIGATOR BAIT n.[2]). [SE *generic,* not marked with the producer's brandname, and available at a lower price because of plain, cheap packaging]

Gene Tunney *n.* [1960s+] (*Aus./N.Z.*) **1** money (cf. BEES (AND HONEY) n.). **2** a lavatory (cf. ANGUS ARMANASCO n.). [rhy. sl.; (2) = DUNNY n.; ult. US boxer *Gene Tunney* (1898–1978)]

Gene Tunney *adj.* [1980s] (*Aus.*) sunny. [rhy. sl.; for ety. *see* prev.]

Geneva print *n.* [17C–mid-18C] gin; thus *read Geneva print,* to drink gin; *been at Geneva,* drunk. [pun on *Geneva,* the kind of type used in a Geneva bible, the English translation of the Bible first printed at Geneva in 1560 + *Genever,* Dutch gin]

genial *adj.* [1990s+] excellent, first-rate, the best. [? borrowed fr. synon. Fr. sl. *genial*]

genials *n.* [1960s+] the genitals. [mispron.]

genitrave *n. see* GENNITRAF n.

genned up *adj. see* GEN n.[2].

gen net *n.* (*also* **net gen**) [mid-19C] 10 shillings (50p). [backsl.; GEN n.[1] + NET n.]

gennitraf *n.* (*also* **genitrave**) [late 19C] a farthing. [backsl.]

genol *adj.* [mid–late 19C] long. [backsl.]

gen out *v.* [1940s] (*US*) to figure out, to plan. [GEN n.[2]]

gent *n.*[1] **1** [late 18C+] (*orig. US*) a *gent*leman, a man, a fellow. **2** [mid-19C+] a *gent*leman, but only when 'applied derisively to men of the vulgar and pretentious class who are supposed to use the word, and as used in tradesmen's notices' (*OED*); thus *adj. gentish.* [abbr.; note SE *gent,* genteel, noble, of good rank]

gent *n.*[2] [mid–late 19C] a mistress; usu. as *my gent.* [abbr. Fr. (*une femme*) *gentille,* a gentlewoman]

gent *n.*[3] [mid-19C+] (*Ling. Fr./Polari*) money, usu. silver. [Ital. *argento,* silver]

gentle annie *n.*[1] [mid-19C+] an incline or small hill found on a small road or track. [? lyrics to a contemporary popular song]

gentle annie *n.*[2] [1980s+] (*N.Z.*) a barmaid.

gentleman *n.* [late 18C–19C] (*US Und.*) a crowbar (cf. ALDERMAN n.[2]).

gentleman commoner *n.* [late 18C–early 19C] an empty bottle. [orig. Oxford University use; the Oxford version of Cambridge's FELLOW COMMONER n.; commoners, as opposed to scholars, were seen as empty-headed]

gentleman in black (pantaloons), the *n.* [mid–late 17C] the Devil.

gentleman in blue *n.* [mid–late 19C] a policeman (cf. BABY-BLUES n.[2]). [the uniform]

gentleman in brown *n.* [late 19C] a bedbug.

gentleman in red *n.* [late 18C] a soldier.

gentleman of fortune *n.* [late 19C] a pirate. [pun on SE]

gentleman of four outs *n. see* GENTLEMAN OF THREE OUTS n.

gentleman of the back door *n.* (*also* **usher of the back door**) [late 18C–19C] a sodomite. [SE *gentleman* + BACK DOOR n. (1)]

gentleman of the brush *n.* [early 19C] an artist, a painter.

gentleman of the drop *n.* [late 18C] (*UK Und.*) confidence tricksters who prey on naïve countrymen, persuading them that they can win money by playing cards with a supposedly drunk person – who of course is a confederate.

gentleman of the first head *n.* (*also* **gentleman of the first house**) [early–mid-17C] an upstart. [ety. unknown]

gentleman of the green-baize road *n.* [mid-19C] a card-sharp. [the baize that covers card-tables]

gentleman of the pad *n.* **1** [18C] a highwayman. **2** [early–mid-19C] a street-robber. [SE *gentleman* + PAD n.[1] (1)]

gentleman of the quill *n.* [19C] a writer. [var. on BROTHER OF THE QUILL n./KNIGHT OF THE QUILL n.]

gentleman of the road *n.* **1** [19C] a highwayman. **2** [1920s–50s] (*N.Z./US*) (*also* **man of the road**) a tramp.

gentleman of the round *n.* [late 16C–early 17C] a discharged or invalided soldier who makes his living by begging. [play on SE *gentleman of the round,* 'a gentleman soldier, but of low rank […] whose office it was to visit and inspect the sentinels, watches, and advanced guard. It was, therefore, an office of some trust, though little dignity' (Nares) + pun on one who 'does the rounds']

gentleman of the short staff *n.* [mid-19C] a constable. [his truncheon]

gentleman of the swag *n.* [1940s–50s] (*N.Z.*) a tramp. [SWAG n.[1] (9)]

gentleman of three ins *n.* [late 18C] 'In debt, in gaol, and in danger of remaining there for life; or, in gaol, indicted and in danger of being hanged in chains' (Grose, 1796).

gentleman of three outs *n.* (*also* **gentleman of four outs**) [late 18C–19C] 'Without money, without wit, and without manners; some add another out, i.e. without credit' (Grose, 1785). [vars. include 'out of pocket, out of elbows, and out of credit' (Bulwer-Lytton, *Paul Clifford*, 1830); *...of the four outs,* 'without wit, without money, without credit and without manners' (Hotten, 1864)]

gentleman outer *n.* [early 18C] a highwayman.

gentleman's *n.* [1920s+] (*W.I.*) a euph. for any form of venereal disease. [abbr. GENTLEMAN'S COMPLAINT n.]

gentleman's companion *n.* [late 18C–19C] a louse.

gentleman's complaint *n.* [1920s+] (*W.I.*) a euph. for gonorrhoea.

gentleman's disease *n.* [late 16C–17C] venereal disease.

gentleman's gent *n.* (*also* gent's gent) [1920s–30s] a valet.

gentleman's master *n.* [18C] a highwayman. [his temporary ascendancy over his social betters]

gentleman's pleasure-garden *n.* [late 19C–1900s] the vagina (cf. ADAM'S OWN (ALTAR) n.; BEAUTY SPOT n.).

gentleman usher *n.* **1** [17C] a woman's male companion. **2** [early 18C] the penis. [? pun on SE *gentleman usher of the Black Rod*; note Williams: 'gentleman usher [...] a male attendant on a lady, sometimes providing a sexual or pimping service']

gentleman who pays the rent *n.* [late 19C] (*Irish*) a pig.

gentlemen's walk *n.* [late 19C] a men's lavatory.

gently Bentley! *excl.* [1940s–60s] a general excl. of restraint, hang on! take it easy! not too fast! etc. [BBC radio's weekly comedy *Take It From Here* (1940–60), used as a catchphrase by Jimmy Edwards (1920–88), addressed to Dick *Bentley*]

gentoo *n.* (*also* jentoe, jintoe) [late 19C+] (*S.Afr.*) a prostitute; thus *gentoo house*, a brothel, usu. entertained by a Malay band. ['named for the *Gentoo*, a ship which arrived at Cape Town in the mid-19th century with a group of women passengers who became prostitutes; the countries of origin of the women and the ship, and the circumstances of their arrival at the Cape, are obscure and in dispute' (*DSAE*). The main theories point to the UK, whose authorities sent out 46 women spec. recruited for the task, or the French]

gentry cove *n.* (*also* gentry cofe, gentry cuffin) [mid-16C–1900s] (*UK Und.*) a nobleman, a gentleman. [SE *gentry* + COVE n. (1)/CUFFIN n. (1)]

gentry cove's ken *n.* (*also* gentry cove ken, gentry ken) [mid-16C] (*UK Und.*) a nobleman's or gentleman's house. [GENTRY COVE n. + KEN n.¹ (1)]

gentry mort *n.* [mid-16C–mid-19C] (*UK Und.*) a noblewoman, a gentlewoman. [SE *gentry* + MORT n.]

gents *n.* [1930s+] the *gent*leman's lavatory (cf. LADIES n.). [abbr.]

gent's gent *n. see* GENTLEMAN'S GENT n.

genuffel *v.* [1930s+] (*S.Afr.*) to flirt. [? backsl. = 'loving']

gen up *v. see* GEN n.².

gen up? *phr.* [1990s+] do you mean it? are you telling the truth? [SE *genuine*]

Geoff Hurst *n.* [1990s+] a first-class university degree (cf. DESMOND (TUTU) n.). [rhy. sl.]

Geoffrey Chaucer *n.* [20C+] a saucer. [rhy. sl.; ult. *Geoffrey Chaucer* (*c*.1343–1400), author of *The Canterbury Tales*]

geography *n.*¹ [1920s+] the vagina (cf. ANTIPODES n.). [one 'explores' it]

geography *n.*² [1920s+] the lavatory. [euph.]

Geordie *n.* **1** [mid-19C+] a Tynesider; thus *Geordie-land*, Tyneside. **2** [1910s+] (*Aus./N.Z.*) a Scot. **3** [1940s+] the Tyneside dialect and accent. [proper name]

George *n. see* GRANDMA (GEORGE) n.

George! *excl. see* BY GEORGE! excl.

george *n.*¹ **1** [late 16C–17C] a noble (worth 6s 8d (33p) or ⅓ of a pound). **2** [mid-17C–mid-19C] a half crown, 2s 6d (12½p). **3** [early 18C] a guinea; a pound. **4** [early 19C] a penny (cf. GEORGIE n.). **5** [1990s+] money in general. [the image of St *George* or (4) George IV engraved on the coin]

george *n.*² **1** [early–mid-19C] (*N.Z.*) a generic term for a Maori. **2** [1900s–40s] (*US*) a generic term for a Black male. **3** [1920s–50s] (*Can./US*) a generic name for an otherwise nameless Black Pullman porter. [note RAF jargon *George*, a familiar form of address to any stranger; 1920s+ air crew jargon *George*, the automatic pilot in milit. and civil aircraft; N.Z. WW2 milit. *George*, an Egyptian; note Rowse, *Doughboy Dope from A to Z* (1918), p.25: 'The mysterious George, who did the things you didn't do yourself on the outside, doesn't seem to have enlisted in this man's army']

george *n.*³ [1940s+] (*US*) a $1 bill (cf. ABE n.²). [the portrait of *George* Washington (1732–99), 1st President of the US, printed on the notes]

george *n.*⁴ [1940s+] (*W.I.*) a sore or swollen leg or foot; elephantiasis. [ety. unknown; but note the habit of giving pet names to parts of one's body, usu. the genitals]

george *n.*⁵ [1970s] (*US prison*) a 1-year prison sentence; thus 1 of anything. [ety. unknown]

george *adj.* **1** [1900s–10s] (*US Und.*) wise, in the know; thus *be george*, to understand. **2** [1930s–70s] (*US*) acceptable, satisfactory. [? var. on JERRY adj. (1)]

george *v. see* GEORGIA v.

George and Ringo *n.* [1960s] bingo. [rhy. sl.; ult. The Beatles members *George* Harrison (1943–2001) and *Ringo* Starr (b.1940)]

George Bernard Shaw *n.* [1940s–50s] a door. [rhy. sl.; ult. the Irish-born playwright *George Bernard Shaw* (1856–1950)]

George Blake *n.* [1960s] a snake. [rhy. sl.; ult. Soviet spy *George Blake* (b.1922)]

George Bohee *n.* (*also* bohee) [1900s–40s] tea. [rhy. sl.; the name of a once well-known banjo player, but note *bohea*, the best variety of black tea, from the Wu-i hills in north Fukien]

George called *phr. see* GRANDMA (GEORGE) n.

George Gerrard *n.* [20C+] (*Aus.*) a gross exaggeration. [the proper name of *George Gerrard*, a well-known (and presumably big-talking) character]

George Plateroon *n.* [mid-17C–early 18C] (*UK Und.*) 'silver' plate that is in fact mainly copper with a thin silver coating.

George Raft *n.* [1930s+] **1** a draught. **2** a banker's draft. **3** hard work, i.e. GRAFT n.¹ [rhy. sl.; ult. film star *George Raft* (1895–1980)]

George Robey *n.* [1910s–30s] (*UK tramp*) the road. [rhy. sl. = TOBY n.² (2); ult. comedian Sir *George Robey* (1869–1954)]

george (smack) *n.* [1960s–70s] (*US drugs*) high-quality heroin. [GEORGE adj. (2) + SMACK n.⁶ (1)]

George Spelvin *n.* [20C+] (*US*) an actor's pseudonym when playing a minor role; thus female equivalent *Georgina Spelvin*. [created by the actor Edward Ables in 1906, when playing in *Brewster's Millions* on Broadway]

George Street backblocker *n.* [1910s] (*Aus.*) a business man who owns land in the outback but rarely if ever visits. [George Street, a major artery in Sydney, thus generic for urban life and concerns + SAusE *backblocks*, the remote interior]

George the Third *n.* [1980s+] **1** a third-class degree (cf. DESMOND (TUTU) n.). **2** a piece of excrement (cf. ALI OOP n.). [rhy. sl.; (2) = TURD n. (1)]

Georgette *n.* [1980s] (*US camp gay*) a term of address to a fellow homosexual male (cf. ABIGAIL n.).

George Washington *n.*¹ [1900s] (*Aus./US*) a 'tall tale'. [Washington's legendary assurance that 'I cannot tell a lie']

George Washington *n.*² [1930s+] (*US*) **1** a $1 bill (cf. ABE n.²). **2** in pl., money, in unspecified sums. [the portrait of *George Washington* (1732–99), 1st President of the US, printed on the notes]

georgia *n.* [1960s+] (*US Black*) a swindle, esp. one worked by a prostitute on a customer. [abbr. carnival use *Georgia scuffle*, a form of confidence trick]

georgia *v.* (*also* george, georgy) [1960s+] (*US Black*) **1** to play a confidence trick on a person who has newly arrived from the South and is thus naïve as regards the Northern, urban world. **2** to be seduced into a sexual liaison by a woman. **3** (*also* send to Georgia) of a prostitute's client, to accept her services but to renege on payment. [GEORGIA n.]

Georgia bacon *n.* [1950s] a turtle. [the availability of turtles in the state]

Georgia buggy *n.* [1910s+] (*orig. US Black*) a wheelbarrow.

Georgia chicken *n.* [1970s] (*US*) salt pork.

Georgia ham *n.* [1940s–70s] (*US*) watermelon. [its popularity in Georgia + the pinkness of both foodstuffs]

Georgia ice-cream *n.* [1970s+] (*US*) grits.

Georgia overdrive *n. see* MEXICAN OVERDRIVE *n.*

Georgia peach *n.* [1970s+] (*US gay*) a Black man.

Georgia skin *n.* (*also* **skin**) [1930s+] (*US Black*) a kind of card-game. [abbr. *Georgia skin game*, a card-game]

georgie *n.* (*also* **georgy**) [early 19C] **1** (*orig. UK Und.*) a quartern loaf. **2** a penny (cf. GEORGE *n.*¹). [(1) BROWN GEORGE *n.* (1); (2) the picture of George IV on the coin]

Georgie Best *n.* [1960s+] **1** a guest. **2** a (drunken) pest. **3** a female breast (cf. BRACE AND BITS *n.*). [rhy. sl.; ult. soccer star and fabled drinker *George Best* (b.1946)]

georgie bundle *n.* [20C+] (*W.I.*) **1** a small bundle that nonetheless can hold all one's few possessions. **2** a collection of odds and ends. [ety. unknown; ? anecdotal]

Georgie Moore *n. see* RORY O'MOORE *n.* (1).

Georgina Spelvin *n. see* GEORGE SPELVIN *n.*

georgium sidus *n.* [late 19C] London south of the Thames, trad. less fashionable than the north. [pun on Lat. *georgium sidus*, the planet Uranus, so named by its discoverer Sir William Herschel (1738–1822) in honour of George III; Uranus was then the furthest planet from the Earth and thus from 'civilization']

georgy *n. see* GEORGIE *n.*

georgy *v. see* GEORGIA *v.*

geranium *n.* [late 19C] a red nose.

gerbil *n.* [1980s+] (*US*) a stupid, insignificant or unpleasant person.

gercha! *excl.* (*also* **gertch! gertcha! gertcher!**) [1920s+] a mocking response, either aggressive or affectionate. [abbr. GET ALONG (WITH YOU)! *excl.* (2)/GET AWAY (WITH YOU)! *excl.* (1)]

gerdoing!/gerdoying! *excl. see* KERDOING! *excl.*

gere *n.*¹ *see* GEAR *n.*¹ (1).

gere *n.*² *see* JERE *n.*¹.

geri *n.* (*also* **gerri, gerry**) [1970s+] a term for the old (and middle-aged). [abbr. SE *geriatric*]

geriatricks *n.* [1950s+] (*gay*) ageing or old homosexuals. [pun on SE *geriatric* + TRICK *n.*¹ (4)]

germ *n.* (*also* **jerm**) [1940s+] (*US*) a contemptible person.

Germaine Greer *n.* [1990s+] (*Aus.*) a beer. [rhy. sl.; the Aus. feminist and writer *Germaine Greer* (b.1939)]

German *n.*¹ [late 19C] a German sausage, a wurst.

German *n.*² [1940s+] (*W.I.*) a poor White. [the early 19C settlement of German immigrants near Seaford Town, Westmoreland; their descendants still live there]

German *n.*³ [1990s+] (*US drugs*) a Dominican cocaine dealer. [negative stereotyping]

German aunt *n.* [20C+] (*US*) a fat, frumpish woman. [racial stereotyping]

German (bands) *n.* [1910s+] the hands. [rhy. sl.]

German comb *n.* [late 19C+] (*US*) the hand. [the supposed lack of sophistication in German immigrants, who prefer their fingers to a comb]

German doggies *n.* [late 19C+] (*N.Z.*) the rolling of stones down a hill so as to persuade sheep to move down the hill. [? derog. ref. to German shepherding methods]

German duck *n.*¹ [late 18C–mid-19C] half a sheep's head boiled with onions. [the popularity of the dish among the German sugar-bakers of London's East End]

German duck *n.*² [mid-19C] a bedbug. [orig. Yorks. dial.; ? racial stereotyping]

German flutes *n.* [mid-19C–1960s] a pair of boots. [rhy. sl.]

German goitre *n.* [20C+] (*US*) a beer belly, a noticeable paunch. [the stereotyped German capacity for beer]

German gospel *n.* [late 19C] vain boasting, megalomania, self-aggrandizement. [a speech delivered in November 1897 by Prince Henry of Prussia to his brother Kaiser Wilhelm II (1859–1941), which was full of such fulsome phrs. as: 'The gospel that emanates from your Majesty's sacred person…']

German helmet *n.* [1950s+] (*orig. gay*) the glans penis.

German marching pills *n.* [1950s+] (*gay*) amphetamines, esp. Methedrine, a German invention (cf. A *n.*²). [used by Ger. soldiers, among others, in WWII and later conflicts]

German silver *n.* [late 19C+] anything that is sham, fake. [SE *German silver*, a white alloy consisting of nickel, zinc and copper]

germs *n.* [2000s] (*US prison*) cigarettes.

Geronimo *n.* [1980s+] (*drugs*) a mixture of alcohol and barbiturates. [it leads one to excesses, supposedly similar to those of an Apache warrior (*see next*)]

Geronimo! *excl.* [1940s+] (*US, orig. milit.*) a cry made when leaping or about to start a fight. [proper name *Geronimo*, nickname of Apache leader, Goyathlay ('One Who Yawns') (1829–1909); note *New York Herald Tribune* 19/5/1941: ' The use of "Geronimo" dates back to the early days of the 501st Parachute Battalion, 'way back in last October. Two sergeants got into an argument about being afraid, when the first left the plane. One said that to prove he was not scared stiff he would yell something as he jumped. When he left the plane the only thing that came to mind was the name of the famous Indian chief. So he hollered out "Geronimo!"']

gerook *n.* [1960s+] (*S.Afr.*) intoxicated by drink or a drug, usu. cannabis. [Afk. *gerook*, smoked]

gerri *n. see* GERI *n.*

Gerry *n. see* JERRY *n.*

gerry *n.*¹ [mid-16C] excrement. [ety. unknown; E.P. suggests Lat. *gero*, I carry. Note Devon dial. *gerred*, bedaubed, filthy]

gerry *n.*² *see* GERI *n.*

gerry *v. see* JERRY *v.*¹ (2).

gerry gan! *excl.* [mid-16C] lit. 'shit in your mouth', thus shut up! be quiet! [GERRY *n.*¹ + GAN *n.*]

gerry riddle *n.* [1930s+] (*Aus.*) an act of urination (cf. ANGEL'S KISS *n.*). [rhy. sl. = PIDDLE *n.* (2)]

gersha *n.* [2000s] (*Irish*) a young girl. [? fem. of GARSOON *n.*]

gert and daisy *adj.* [20C+] lazy. [rhy. sl.; ult. characters created on BBC radio in the 1930s by comediennes Elsie (d.1990) and Doris Waters (d.1978)]

gertch!/gertcha!/gertcher! *excl. see* GERCHA! *excl.*

Gertie *n.* **1** [1910s+] a prostitute, a promiscuous woman (cf. BABY JANE *n.*). **2** [1930s+] (*camp gay*) a general term of address to a fellow homosexual man (cf. ABIGAIL *n.*). **3** [1970s+] (*S.Afr. gay*) a heterosexual woman.

Gertie Gitana *n.* [20C+] a banana. [rhy. sl.; ult. music-hall star *Gertie Gitana* (1888–1957)]

gertrude *n.* [1940s] (*US milit.*) a clerk. [? generic use of female name as derog.]

Gerty Lee *n.* [1910s+] (*bingo*) the number 33 (cf. ALDERSHOT LADIES *n.*). [rhy. sl.; ult. late 19C actress *Gertie Lee*]

gerund-grinder *n.* [early 18C–19C; 1940s] a schoolteacher, esp. a pedant; thus *gerund-grinding*, instruction in Lat. grammar, pedantic instruction generally; *gerund-grindery*, a classical school; *gerund-stone*, the imaginary grindstone of a *gerund-grinder*.

gerver *n.* [1910s–20s] (*US Und.*) a safe-breaker. [var./mispron. of GOPHER *n.*² (3)]

geseech *n.* [late 19C–1900s] the face. [? Yid. *gesicht*, face]

gessein *v.* [1940s–50s] (*UK prison*) to trick, to hoax, to dupe; thus *gesseiner*, valuables, belongings. [? Yid., but note Scot. *gess*, to leave clandestinely]

gessump *v.* [1940s–50s] (*UK prison*) to acquire anything by fraud or a confidence trick. [GAZUMP *v.* (1)]

gestapo *n.* (*also* **gestaps**) **1** [1950s+] (*US Black*) the police. **2** [1980s+] (*Aus. prison*) the security section. [fig. use of Ger. *Geheime Staatspolizei*, the *Gestapo*, the internal police force used by the German Nazi regime 1933–45; note WW2 UK milit. use *gestapo*, military police]

gesuip *adj.* [1980s] (*S.Afr.*) drunk. [Afk. *suip*, to drink, used of an animal]

get *n.*¹ **1** [18C+] (*also* **gett**) a bastard child, thus a term of abuse;

often ext. in Ireland to *whore's get*. **2** [1920s+] any creature or object. **3** [1930s+] (*also* **gett, ghet**) an idiot, a fool; an unpleasant person. [orig. 16C SE *get*, bastard, brat; (1) the term lapsed into sl. by 18C]

get n.² [late 19C] a swindle, a trick, a means of defrauding a victim. [GET v.² (1)]

get n.³ [late 19C–1950s] (*Aus.*) an escape; usu. in phr. *do a get*. [GET v.¹ (2)]

get n.⁴ [1940s–60s] (*US*) the profit, the take, the booty of a robbery. [i.e. what the robbers 'get'; SE 14C–17C]

get v.¹ **1** [mid-18C+] to start, to commence, with an implication of urgency, e.g. 'get moving', 'get walking' etc, esp. as GET! excl. **2** [mid-19C+] (*orig. US*) (*also* **git**) to go away.

get v.² **1** [mid-19C+] (*orig. US*) to trick, to cheat, to victimize. **2** [mid-19C+] (*orig. US*) to attract, to enthral, to excite. **3** [late 19C] (*US*) to surpass. **4** [late 19C+] (*orig. US*) to succeed in killing for retribution, to 'do for'. **5** [late 19C+] (*orig. US*) to get even with, to take vengeance on, e.g. *I'll get you, just wait and see*. **6** [late 19C+] to have sexual intercourse. **7** [20C+] (*orig. US*) (*also* **get a body**) to kill, to wound. **8** [20C+] (*orig. US*) to annoy, to irritate; esp. in phr. *that's what gets me*. **9** [20C+] to corner someone, to get hold of, to track down. **10** [1920s+] (*orig. US*) to attack, to hit. **11** [1990s+] to tease, to make someone look foolish. **12** [1990s+] (*US Black/campus*) to meet, to make contact with.

get v.³ [mid-19C+] (*orig. US*) to puzzle, to astound.

get v.⁴ [late 19C] to eat a meal.

get v.⁵ [1910s–30s] to be punished, to get one's deserts. [abbr. SE *get one's deserts*]

get v.⁶ [1910s+] **1** to notice, to look at; usu. as a derog. imper. e.g. *get him!* look at him (isn't he stupid). **2** (*US*) to perceive.

get! excl. [mid-19C+] get moving! start walking! go away! [GET v.¹]

get a bang (out of) v. [1920s+] (*orig. US*) to enjoy, to derive pleasure from, to get a thrill. [BANG n.⁷ (1)]

get a beat on v. [mid-19C+] (*US*) to have at a disadvantage. [BEAT v.¹ (1)]

get a bee in one's bonnet v. (*also* **have a bee in one's bonnet**) [19C+] to become obsessed by a particular topic.

get a belly v. (*also* **grow a belly**) [20C+] (*US/W.I.*) to become noticeably pregnant.

get a belly-bumper/-buster v. *see* GO BELLY-BUMPING v.

getabit n. [1900s–20s] a thief.

get a bit v.¹ (*also* **get one's bit**) [late 19C–1900s] to obtain money. [BIT n.¹ (1)]

get a bit v.² [20C+] to seduce. [BIT n.³]

get (a bit of) a pot v. [1920s+] to become obese. [POT n.⁹]

get aboard v. *see* ABOARD adv.

get a body v. *see* GET v.² (7).

get about v. [late 19C] of a man, to enter a woman.

get above oneself v. **1** [1910s+] to act in an arrogant manner, to be self-satisfied. **2** [1960s] (*US Black*) to brag, to attack verbally. [ABOVE ONESELF phr.]

get a bug up one's ass v. *see* HAVE A BUG UP ONE'S ASS v.¹.

get a buzz on v. *see* HAVE A BUZZ ON v.

get a can on v. (*also* **pin a can on, tie...**) [1920s–50s] (*US*) to go on a drinking spree. [? SE *can*, a container for beer when taken home from a bar or public house]

get a c.b. v. *see* HAVE A C.B. v.

get a clue v. **1** [1960s+] (*US Black*) (*also* **find a clue**) to become aware. **2** [1980s+] (*US campus*) to think sensibly or logically, not to be stupid or naïve.

get a crack at v. *see* HAVE A CRACK AT v.

get a cropper v. *see* COME A CROPPER v.

get across v. [1910s+] **1** to irritate, to annoy. **2** (*US Black*) to succeed. **3** to seduce. **4** to acquire status.

get a curve on v. [1910s] (*US*) to hurry up, to act at once.

get a cut v. [20C+] (*Aus.*) to obtain a job as a sheep-shearer.

get a d.c.m v. [1990s+] (*Aus.*) to be dismissed from one's job, i.e. *don't come Monday*.

get a derry on v. *see* HAVE A DERRY ON v.

get a drive on someone v. [late 19C] (*US campus*) to make a joke at someone else's expense.

get a fall v. *see* TAKE A FALL v.

get a fall out of v. *see* TAKE A FALL OUT OF v.

get a fifty v. [20C+] (*Irish*) to be rebuffed, rejected or 'stood up' by a woman. [Gaelic football, a form of penalty]

get a glow on v. (*also* **have a glow on**) [late 19C–1970s] (*orig. US*) to become intoxicated by drink or drugs. [the reddening of some drinkers' faces]

get a good ready v. [mid–late 19C] (*US*) to be ready to start something.

get a grip v. [late 19C+] (*orig. US campus*) to act in a responsible way, to take control of oneself; often as an imper.

get a grip on things v. [1990s+] to masturbate. [pun]

get a hair up one's ass v. [1950s+] **1** to be in a bad temper (cf. HAVE A BUG UP ONE'S ASS v.¹). **2** to have an obsession (cf. HAVE A BUG UP ONE'S ASS v.²).

get a handful of sprats v. (*also* **have a handful**) [late 19C+] to grope a woman's genital area. [FISH n.¹ (1) and similar terms meaning the vagina]

get a handle v. [1960s+] (*US*) to calm down, to take control of oneself; usu. in imper. [? abbr. phr. *get a handle and turn yourself off* or synon. with GET A GRIP v.]

get a handle on v. [1950s+] (*orig. US*) to understand, to work out, to gain control of a situation.

get a hand on it v. [mid-19C+] to fondle a woman's genitals.

get a hard-on v. [1940s] (*US Und.*) to draw a pistol. [pun on HARD-ON n. (1)]

get a hump on v. [late 19C+] (*US*) to hurry, to exert oneself. [one *humps* one's back with effort]

get a hustle on v. [1900s–30s] (*US*) to get moving, to get going, to get on with the job etc. [HUSTLE v. (4)]

get a jerk on v. [1920s–40s] to hurry up.

get a jig on v. [1900s] (*Aus.*) to hurry up. [fig. use of SE *jig*]

get a job phr. [1950s+] (*US campus*) find something constructive to do with yourself.

get a jump on (someone) v. *see* GET THE JUMP ON (SOMEONE) v.

get a kick out of v. [1920s+] to enjoy, to appreciate. [KICK n.⁵ (3)]

get a knob v. [1950s–60s] (*orig. milit.*) to catch a venereal disease. [i.e. the unpleasant effect on one's KNOB n.¹ (3)]

get a leg in v. [1900s–10s] (*Aus.*) **1** to gain someone's confidence, to win over. **2** to win an advantage.

get a leg up v. *see* GIVE SOMEONE A (CLEAN) LEG UP v.

get-a-life adj. [2000s] describing someone whose preoccupations are considered pitiful. [GET A LIFE! excl.]

get a life! excl. [1980s+] a dismissive excl. used in any context where the speaker wishes to show disdain for the previous speaker and their ideas, suggestions or opinions.

get a line on v. [late 19C+] (*orig. US*) to understand, to acquire information about; thus *give a line on*, to impart information or knowledge. [LINE n.¹ (4)]

get all over v. [late 19C] to examine physically; to manhandle.

get a load of v. (*also* **take a load of**) [1920s+] (*orig. US*) to notice, to look at deliberately.

get a load of that! excl. (*also* **get a load of this!**) [1930s+] (*orig. US*) a demand that one's audience listen to something or notice an event; usu. in a sexual context and between men of a woman. [GET A LOAD OF v.]

get-along n. [1920s+] (*US*) a leg; esp. in phr. a *hitch in one's get-along*, a limp.

get along v. [1930s+] to leave.

get along (with you)! excl. (*also* **go along (with you)!**) [late

18C+] **1** go away! **2** in fig. use, don't be silly! don't try to fool me!

get a manual! *excl.* [1990s+] (*US campus*) an admonition to find out what is going on. [computer imagery]

get among (a woman's) frills *v.* (*also* **get up someone's frills**) [late 19C–1910s] to seduce a woman.

get among it *v.* [1910s+] (*Aus.*) **1** to make a large amount of money. **2** to seduce a woman.

get a move on *v.* [late 19C+] (*orig. US*) to start moving, to hurry up; usu. as imper.

get an eyeful *v.* [1910s+] to have a good look at, to stare; often in the challenging phr. *got your eyeful?* aimed at one who is seen to be gazing over-intently at oneself or a (female) companion; a follow-up is 'Want a picture?' [EYEFUL n. (1)]

get a nut *v.* (*mainly US*) **1** [1950s+] to have an orgasm. **2** [1960s+] to have sexual intercourse. [SE *get* + NUT n.⁹]

get any *v. see* GET SOME v. (1).

get anything *v.* [mid-19C+] to catch a venereal disease.

get a packet *v. see* COP A PACKET v.

get a penn'orth of paradise *v.* (*also* **have a penn'orth of paradise**) [mid-19C–1910s] to have a drink, usu. of gin. [the contemporary cost of a shot of gin, and its anaesthetic effects]

get a piece *v.*¹ (*also* **get a piece of ass, …of tail**) [1940s+] of a man, to seduce a girl or woman, to have sexual intercourse. [PIECE n.¹ (1)/PIECE OF ASS n./PIECE OF TAIL n.]

get a piece *v.*² *see* BEG FOR A PIECE v.

get a rat *v.* (*also* **have a rat**) [1900s–20s] (*Aus./N.Z.*) to act crazily in an eccentric manner. [RATS IN THE ATTIC phr.]

get a rod on *v.* [1960s] (*US*) to have an erection. [ROD n.¹ (1)]

get a scatter on *v.* [1940s+] (*Aus.*) to lose touch with someone. [SE *scatter*, to become dispersed]

get a set on *v.* [late 19C–1910s] (*Aus.*) to take against someone, to attack someone. [DEAD SET n. (2)]

get a shift on *v.* [1970s+] to hurry up.

get a shot of crack *v.* [20C+] (*US*) to have sexual intercourse. [SHOT n.⁵ (1) + CRACK n.⁶ (1)]

get a shot of leg *v.* [1970s+] (*US Black*) to have sexual intercourse. [SHOT n.⁵ (1) + SE *leg*]

get a shove in the blind eye *v. see* BLIND EYE n. (2).

get a skinful *v.* (*also* **have a skinful**) [late 18C+] to get drunk. [SE *skinful*, as much as one can drink]

get a slant on *v.* [1930s+] to form an opinion of/about someone. [fig. use of SLANT n.²]

get a smell of *v.* [late 19C] to get a chance, to approach. [hunting imagery]

get a spark up *v.* [1930s+] (*N.Z.*) to strengthen one's spirits by taking a drink.

get at *v.* **1** [late 19C–1920s] (*US*) to begin, to start work on, to turn one's attention to. **2** [late 19C+] to attack, usu. verbally. **3** [late 19C+] to tease, to banter. **4** [late 19C+] to corrupt, to bribe, to tamper with; thus *got at*, bribed, corrupted, subverted. **5** [late 19C+] to hint, to imply; usu. in phr. *what are you getting at?* **6** [1990s+] (*US campus*) to get in touch. **7** [2000s] (*US Black*) to invite to fight.

get a time with *v.* [20C+] (*W.I.*) to seduce a woman.

get a touch on *v. see* TOUCH v.³.

get at the gee *v.* [1920s–30s] to fool, to hoax. [GEE (UP) v. (3)]

get a waggle on *v. see* GET A WIGGLE ON v.

getaway *n.* **1** [mid-19C–1960s] a sudden dash, esp. from the starting point in a game or sport. **2** [mid-19C+] (*orig. UK Und.*) an escape. **3** [mid-19C+] the mode of escape, i.e. a road or alley. **4** [mid-19C+] (*US Und.*) a train or vehicle used for escape. **5** [late 19C–1900s] (*US*) the very start. **6** [20C+] an excuse. **7** [1900s] (*US Und.*) a successful act of robbery.

getaway car *n.* [1930s+] (*US*) a car used by criminals escaping from a crime. [GETAWAY n. (2)]

get away (with) *v.* [late 19C+] **1** to get the better of, to beat.

2 to carry off successfully, to attain one's goal (with the implication of slight underhandedness).

get away with (blue) murder *v.* [1910s+] to flout all proprieties with absolute success, to achieve the otherwise unacceptable.

get away with the baggage *v.* [late 19C] (*US*) to commit a crime or some form of wrong-doing and escape undetected.

get away (with you)! *excl.* (*also* **get on with you! go away (outta that)!**) [mid-19C+] **1** don't try to fool me! don't tell lies! don't make me laugh! (cf. GO ON! excl.). **2** you amaze me!

get a wet bottom *v. see* DO A WET BOTTOM v.

get a wiggle on *v.* (*also* **do a wiggle, get a waggle on**) [late 19C+] to bustle, to hurry, to 'look lively'.

get a wriggle on *v.* [1910s–60s] (*Aus.*) to move fast, to 'get a move on'. [var. on prev.]

get-back *n.* [20C+] (*US*) revenge. [GET BACK (AT) v.]

get back *v.* [1980s] (*US Black*) to think again.

get back! *excl.* [mid-19C; 1980s+] (*UK Und./US campus*) an expression of admiration. [the image of holding back people crowding to view something special]

get back (at) *v.* (*also* **get one's own back, have it back upon**) [late 19C+] (*orig. US*) to retaliate (against).

get back in your box! *excl.* [late 19C+] (*orig. US*) a general excl. of rebuke, be quiet! I don't want to know! that's quite enough of that!

get beans *v.* [late 19C–1910s] (*orig. US*) to be punished, to suffer. [? SE *bangs, hits*]

get beautiful *v.* [1980s+] (*drugs*) to use narcotics and enjoy the effects. [the illusory but alluring euphoria of drugs]

get before oneself *v.* [late 19C+] to boast, to threaten, to act angrily.

get behind *v.*¹ [late 19C] (*US*) to start smoking or drinking.

get behind *v.*² **1** [1900s; 1960s+] to make a commitment to an idea, a job, a person etc. **2** [1970s+] to understand, to enjoy, to appreciate. [the image of putting one's weight behind]

get behind oneself *v.* [late 19C+] to become forgetful.

get bent! *excl.* [1950s+] (*US campus*) a general excl. of dismissal or contempt.

get brusher *v.* [1900s–30s] (*Aus.*) to be rejected, to be snubbed. [BRUSH-OFF n.]

get business *v.* [1980s] (*US Black*) to be successful.

get busy *v.* **1** [early 19C; 1960s+] (*US Black/teen*) to have sexual intercourse. **2** [mid-19C+] to steal. **3** [late 19C+] (*orig. US*) to become active. **4** [1990s+] (*US Black/teen*) to eat. **5** [2000s] to interfere. [(1) early 19C cit. is Nares, who links this to BRUSH-OFF n.]

get-by *n.* [1950s] (*US*) a way of life, usu. a difficult one. [GET BY v. (2)]

get by *v.* **1** [20C+] to avoid, to evade. **2** [1910s+] to manage, to be acceptable to, to get away with. **3** [1920s+] to survive without working.

get catch *v.* (*also* **get ketch**) [20C+] (*W.I.*) of an unmarried girl or woman, to become pregnant. [CATCH v.³]

get Chinese *v.* [1980s+] (*US campus*) to succumb heavily to a drug, usu. marijuana. [CHINESE adj.; the implication is of the 'skewed' aspect of the Chinese stereotype, rather than the effects of a drug]

get chockers *v.* [1960s] to have sexual intercourse. [CHOKKA adj. (1); but note CHOCK-A-BLOCK adj. (2)]

get clear *v.* [1960s+] to work out a situation to its logical conclusion. [scientology jargon *clear*, the ultimate state of those who subject themselves to a scientology course]

get cold feet *v.* (*also* **get cold tittie, have cold feet**) [late 19C+] to become scared, to back down on a previous promise or statement; the cold comes when one 'tests the water' of a situation and finds it chilly. [note WW1 Aus. milit. *coldfooter*, one who was afraid to enlist for active service]

get cracking v. [1920s+] **1** to start work, to get on with anything speedily and efficiently. **2** to go away. [cracking a whip over one's team of horses]

get dead v. see KNOCK COLD (AS A MONKEY WRENCH) v. (2).

get deep in someone's ass v. [1980s] (US Black) to fight, to beat up.

get dirty v. see PLAY DIRTY v.

get-down, the n. (also **the git-down**) [1990s+] (US) the start, the beginning; the crux of a matter.

get-down adj. [1970s] (US) committed to enjoying oneself. [GET DOWN v.[2] (2)]

get down v.[1] [late 19C+] (US) to place a bet. [the 'putting down' of one's wager]

get down v.[2] **1** [1910s+] (orig. US) to commit oneself, to make a serious effort. **2** [1950s+] (orig. US) to dance, to have a good time. **3** [1950s+] (orig. US) to have sexual intercourse. **4** [1960s+] (orig. US) to concentrate. **5** [1960s+] (US Black) to establish oneself, to work. **6** [1960s+] (orig. US) (also **get down with one's bad self**) to do something especially well. **7** [1960s+] (US Und.) of a prostitute, to start work for the night; thus GIT-DOWN TIME n. **8** [1970s+] to make something happen, to reach a successful conclusion. **9** [1970s+] to join in with, to take part in. **10** [1970s+] (US Black) to fight. **11** [1980s] (US Black) to attempt seduction. [abbr. SE phr. get down to business]

get down v.[3] (also **get down on**) [1930s] (US) to perform fellatio or cunnilingus (cf. AUSSIE KISS n.).

get down v.[4] [1950s+] (US) to take a narcotic or other recreational drug, usu. heroin.

get down! excl. [1960s+] an excl. of encouragement, usu. in the context of a musical performance, whether live or created by a DJ playing records/tapes. [GET DOWN v.[2] (2)]

get down dirty v. (also **get down fonky, ...shitty**) [1970s+] (US Black) to become abusive, to cause trouble. [GET DOWN v.[2] (10) + SE dirty/FONKY adj.[2]/SHITTY adj.[1] (3)]

get down from the Y v. see GO FROM THE FISTS v.

get down heavy v. [1960s] (US Black) to enjoy oneself, to enter wholeheartedly into the spirit of an occasion. [GET DOWN v.[2] (2) + HEAVY adv. (3)]

get down on v.[1] [late 19C+] (US) to develop a dislike for or grudge against, to be hostile or oppressive to. [DOWN ON phr. (2)/var. GET DOWN v.[2] (10)]

get down on v.[2] [20C+] (Aus./N.Z.) to steal; to get hold of. [SE get down; i.e. bending down to pick something up]

get down on v.[3] see GET DOWN v.[3].

get down shitty v. see GET DOWN DIRTY v.

get down to (brass) tacks v. (also **come down to (brass) tacks, get down to brass nails**) [late 19C+] to approach the facts, to deal with the real heart of the matter. [BRASS TACKS n.]

get down to cases v. (also **come down to cases**) [late 19C+] to come to the crux of a matter.

get down to hard-pan v. see HARD-PAN n.

get down to (it) v. [20C+] **1** to start committing oneself seriously, usu. to one's work. **2** to start talking about the crux of a topic. [GET DOWN v.[2] (1)]

get down to tacks v. see GET DOWN TO (BRASS) TACKS v.

get down to the ground (and move it round and round) v. [1980s] (US Black) to have sexual intercourse.

get down to the natural thing v. see DO THE NATURAL THING v.

get down to the nitty-gritty v. [1950s+] (orig. US Black) to get down to essentials, to get back to basics. [SE get down to + NITTY-GRITTY n.]

get down to tin tacks v. (also **come down to tin tacks**) [1920s–40s] to approach and deal with the central issues of a situation. [TIN TACKS n.; this phr. coined by the critic and playwright George Bernard Shaw (1856–1950)]

get down with one's bad self v. see GET DOWN v.[2] (6).

get down wrong v. [1970s] (US Black) to misbehave.

get 'em v. (also **get them**) [20C+] **1** to suffer delirium tremens. **2** to be mad. **3** to be frightened. [them are the SHAKES, THE n. (1)]

get 'em off v. see GET IT OFF v.[1].

get-'em-up adj. [1930s] used of people involved in hold-ups with a gun.

get even (with) v. [mid–late 19C+] to get revenge, to get one's own back. [SE in 20C+]

get fits v. [late 19C–1900s] **1** to become angered by defeat. **2** to be criticized harshly; to be humiliated. [SE fit, a seizure]

get fixed v. [1940s–50s] (US) to have sexual intercourse. [the image of 'fixing' or curing one's sexual frustration]

get flack/flak v. see CATCH FLACK v.

get fucked v. [1960s+] to have sexual intercourse, used of both men and women. [FUCK v.[1]]

get fucked! excl. [1910s+] a general excl. of dismissal or contempt; thus also euph. get intercoursed! [fig. use of FUCK v.[1]]

get funny (with) v. **1** [late 19C+] to provoke, to annoy. **2** [20C+] to reveal that one has been offended. **3** [20C+] to act in an offensive manner; thus the threat don't get funny with me! **4** [20C+] to make sexual advances towards. [FUNNY adj.[2] (1)]

get gay (with) v. **1** [late 19C–1900s] to be aggressive; to behave unpleasantly. **2** [late 19C+] (mainly US) to tease, to provoke, to be flippant or cheeky. **3** [1900s–50s] to go into action, to get on with things. **4** [1940s] (US drugs) to take drugs, to get intoxicated. [GAY adj.[2] (2)]

get ghost v. [1990s+] (US Black) **1** to act quietly, to 'keep a low profile'. **2** to leave.

get giddy with v. [late 19C–1900s] (US) to treat in a bizarre manner.

get gip v. see GIVE GYP v.

get-go, the n. see GIT-GO, THE n.

get going v. (also **have going, set going**) [late 19C+] **1** to drive someone into a temper, to make someone lose control through teasing. **2** to excite someone sexually. **3** to excite someone. **4** to worry or unnerve someone. **5** of a rumour or piece of gossip, to persuade someone of its veracity. **6** to start someone talking, usu. in an angry or neurotic manner.

get good to someone v. [1990s+] (US Black) to be carried away by one's enthusiasm while performing a task.

get gravel for one's goose v. [1930s+] (US) to have sexual intercourse.

get gyp v. see GIVE GYP v.

get hat! excl. [1970s] (US Black) go away! [GET ONE'S HAT v. (1)]

get head v. (also **get skull**) [1990s+] to receive oral sex, thus to be fellated (cf. BRAIN n.[2]). [HEAD n.[10]/SKULL n.[7]]

get hell v. see CATCH HELL v.

get hep v. (also **get hip**) [20C+] (orig. US) to see one's own interest, to learn what is going on, to become aware. [HEP adj. (1)/HIP adj. (1)]

get her! excl. [1950s+] (orig. camp gay) an excl. of derision, mockery (both affectionate and otherwise). ['her' orig. being a gay man acting exceptionally affectedly; now general use]

get-high n. [1980s+] (US Black) any form of drug. [GET HIGH v. (2)]

get high v. **1** [mid-19C+] to drink, to be drunk. **2** [1930s+] (drugs) to experience a drug. [HIGH adj.[1]]

get high behind v.[1] [1930s+] (US) **1** to hurry up, to get off to work. **2** to become impatient, to get angry.

get high behind v.[2] [1950s+] (drugs) to experience a drug. [GET BEHIND v.[1] + HIGH adj.[1] (2)]

get hip v. see GET HEP v.

get hold of the wrong end of the stick v. (also **get hold of the wrong end of a thing, get the wrong end of the stick, grab..., have...**) [mid-19C+] **1** to have the facts wrong, to interpret a situation incorrectly; thus the reverse, get the right *end of the stick*, to get things right, to grasp the essence of the situation. **2** to be treated unfairly. [HAVE THE WORSE END OF THE STAFF v.]

get home v. [late 19C] **1** to bring a woman to orgasm. **2** to impregnate.

get home on v. [1900s–10s] (*Aus.*) to take advantage of; to steal from.

get home (to) v. [early 19C+] to make an impression on. [orig. boxing use, but latterly an emotional impression too]

get horizontal v. (*orig. US*) **1** [late 19C; 1990s+] to drink or drug oneself into a stupor. **2** [1980s+] to have sexual intercourse. **3** [1990s+] to lie down, to go to sleep.

get horrors v.[1] *see* DIG HORRORS v.[1].

get horrors v.[2] *see* DIG HORRORS v.[2].

get hot on v. [1920s] (*US*) to get busy, to put in an extra effort. [HOT adj.[1] (5)]

get hot under the collar v. (*also* **get hot about the collar, …around the collar**) [late 19C+] to become increasingly ill-tempered or emotional. [HOT adj.[1] (4)]

get hunk with v. [mid-19C–1950s] (*US*) to get even with. [HUNK adj.]

get ideas in(to) one's head v. (*also* **have ideas in one's head**) [mid-19C+] to fantasize, esp. about matters that are 'above one's station' or beyond one's abilities (often sexual).

get ignorant v. [20C+] (*W.I.*) to lose one's temper, to be rude; thus *get someone ignorant*, to enrage, to infuriate. [IGNORANT adj. (1)]

get in v.[1] [late 19C+] to hit; usu. as *get in a couple of right-handers* etc. [SE *get a blow in*]

get in v.[2] *see* GET INTO v.[2].

get in a dog corn-piece v. *see* GET IN(TO) A DOG CORN-PIECE v.

get in a gar hole v. [20C+] (*US*) to have bad luck. [angling jargon; a gar swims above the holes in which other, larger fish live; thus an angler who *gets in a gar hole* is fishing for a better fish but is having his bait intercepted by a gar]

get in bad (with) v. [1910s+] (*orig. US*) to earn disfavour, to get into trouble (cf. GET IN GOOD (WITH) v.). [IN BAD phr. (1)]

get in deep v. [mid-19C+] to become heavily involved, usu. in either crime or love. [DEEP adv. (1)]

get in for it v. [1920s–30s] to establish oneself in a situation.

get in good (with) v. [1920s+] (*orig. US*) to find favour with (cf. GET IN BAD (WITH) v.).

get in line v. (*also* **get into line**) [1920s+] to conform. [IN LINE phr.]

get inside and pull the blinds down! excl. [late 19C] a mocking shout aimed at a poor horseman or woman.

get inside someone's pants v. *see* GET INTO SOMEONE'S PANTS v.

get in someone's ass v. (*also* **put oneself in someone's face**) [1950s+] **1** (*US*) to annoy, to irritate. **2** (*US Black*) to hit. [ASS n. (5)]

get in someone's ear v. [1970s] (*Aus.*) to ask questions.

get in someone's eye v. [1970s+] (*US Black*) **1** to beat up. **2** to crowd, to encroach on someone's personal space. **3** to shout at someone from close quarters. **4** to hit someone in the face or eye; also fig. use, to throw or pass something.

get in someone's game v. [1970s] (*US Black*) to interfere in someone else's business. [GAME n.[2] (7)]

get in someone's hair v. [mid-19C+] to annoy, to irritate. [the image is of lice]

get intercoursed! excl. *see* GET FUCKED! excl.

get in the buggy v. (*also* **get in the car**) [1920s] (*US*) to comply with requirements, to act as ordered. [SE *buggy*, a coach or carriage/*car*]

get in the cactus/crap v. *see* GET IN THE SHIT v. (2).

get in the collar v. [20C+] (*US*) to start working, to work hard.

[SE *collar*, the neckpiece of a draft harness; the comparison is to a hard-working draft horse]

get in there! excl. [1920s+] a general exhortation; in post-1980s UK, typically by a man's friends who are watching his approaches to an unknown woman; often ext. as *get in there, my son!*

get in the ropes with v. [20C+] (*W.I.*) to start a quarrel, an argument. [boxing imagery]

get in the shit v. **1** [1940s+] to become involved in a situation; spec. (*US milit.*) to join a firefight or arrive on the front-line. **2** [1960s+] (*also* **get in the cactus, get in the crap**) to get into trouble. [SHIT n.[3] (1)]

get in the wind v. [1950s–70s] (*orig. US Black*) to leave, to depart quickly; often as imper.

get into v.[1] **1** [late 18C; 1960s+] to become aware of, to understand. **2** [1920s+] to enjoy, to become involved in. **3** [1940s+] to develop in, to happen in; usu. in phr., *what's got into you/him/her?* **4** [1950s+] to argue about. **5** [1960s+] to grow close to.

get into v.[2] (*also* **get in**) [late 19C+] to penetrate either the vagina or anus; in weak sense, to seduce.

get into v.[3] **1** [1910s+] (*orig. N.Z.*) to attack, both lit. (in a fight etc) and fig. (food, a task etc). **2** [1920s+] (*US*) to defraud, to become indebted to.

get in(to) a dog corn-piece v. [1910s+] (*W.I.*) to get into difficulties. [*dog* is synon. with a guard or watchman, and if he catches you in his *corn-piece* or corn-field you are in trouble]

get into gear v. (*also* **put it into gear**) [1980s+] (*US*) to get going, to get busy.

get into it v. **1** [1960s+] (*US*) to fight with, to argue with. **2** [2000s] to have sexual intercourse.

get into line v. *see* GET IN LINE v.

get into shit v. *see* HIT SOME SHIT v.

get into someone's pants v. (*also* **get inside someone's pants, get into someone's knickers**) [1940s+] to seduce.

get into someone's ribs v. **1** [1900s] to lay a bet on credit. **2** [1920s–30s] to borrow money. [a wallet is carried in a pocket near the ribs]

get into trouble v. **1** [mid-19C+] a euph. for suffering a variety of legal penalties, arrested, imprisoned, fined etc. **2** [1930s+] to get pregnant.

get in wrong v. **1** [1910s+] to irritate, to annoy. **2** [1920s–50s] to blunder, to get oneself into trouble.

get it v. **1** [early 19C] to be assaulted or beaten up. **2** [mid-19C+] (*US*) to be shot, wounded or killed. **3** [mid-19C+] to be punished or reprimanded. **4** [late 19C+] to be subjected to abuse or nagging. **5** [1930s+] usu. of a man, to have sexual intercourse; usu. of a woman, to be subjected to intercourse. **6** [1940s] to catch a venereal disease. **7** [1940s+] (*US*) to go at great speed. **8** [1960s+] (*US*) to be pleasing, attractive, used in negative contexts, e.g. *Sorry, but he just doesn't get it.*

get it! excl. [1980s+] (*US campus*) an excl. of encouragement.

get it all v. *see* DO IT ALL v.

get it down v. [1990s+] (*US*) to master, e.g. a job of work.

get (it) down fine v. [late 19C+] (*US*) to become skilful or knowledgeable.

get it down one's neck v. [20C+] to consume food or drink.

get it down the spout v. *see* HAVE ONE'S TEAPOT MENDED v.

get it hot (and strong) v. **1** [mid-19C–1920s] to be punished (lit. or fig.) severely (cf. COP IT HOT v.). **2** [late 19C–1910s] to be scolded with great venom. [HOT adv. (1)/HOT AND STRONG adv.]

get it in v. [1920s+] **1** of a man, to enter a woman before sexual intercourse. **2** to seduce. ['it' being the penis; (2) is fig. use of (1)]

get it in one v. (*also* **get there in one**) [1930s+] to succeed in doing, in understanding etc at the first try, esp. in a sexual context.

get it in the ass v. (*also* **get it in the arse, get it up the**

arse/ass) [1940s+] (*orig. US*) to be attacked, victimized, killed; also in fig. use.

get it in the neck *v.* (*also* **get it in the back, ...collar button, ...guts**) [late 19C+] **1** to be punished severely, to suffer badly, to be harshly criticized. **2** (*orig. US*) to be killed or badly wounded.

get it in the nose *v.* [1910s] to be punished, lit. and fig.

get it off *v.*[1] (*also* **get 'em off, get one off**) [1930s+] (*US*) to reach orgasm, to copulate, to derive pleasure. [GET OFF v.[5] (5)]

get it off *v.*[2] *see* HAVE (IT) OFF v.

get it off one's chest *v.* [20C+] to confess, to unburden oneself.

get it off with *v.* [1970s+] of a man, to have sexual intercourse with. [var. HAVE IT OFF (WITH) v.]

get-it-on *adj.* [1970s] active, motivated, energetic. [GET IT ON v. (2)]

get it on *v.* **1** [20C+] (*US*) to start a fight, to fight; both lit. and fig. **2** [1950s+] (*orig. US Black*) to start, to take positive action. **3** [1970s] to get an erection. **4** [1970s+] to enjoy oneself. **5** [1970s+] (*also* **get it on with**) to seduce, to have sexual intercourse.

get it on! *excl.* [1970s+] (*orig. US*) a shout of encouragement, enthusiasm, e.g. directed at a musician. [GET IT ON v. (2)/GET IT ON v. (4)]

get it on the whisper *v.* [1920s–50s] to buy on hire purchase. [the shame such purchases induced among those who were yet to succumb to life 'on the never-never']

get it on with *v. see* GET IT ON v. (2).

get it together *v.* [1960s+] (*orig. US Black*) **1** to start a sexual relationship. **2** to make a decision, to take action. **3** to pull oneself together, to stop vacillating.

get it up *v.*[1] [late 19C+] to harass, to target for unkindness, to tease.

get it up *v.*[2] (*orig. US*) **1** [1930s+] (*also* **get one up**) to achieve an erection; occas. in fig. use of a woman. **2** [1970s+] in fig. use, to maintain enthusiasm for an idea, situation etc.

get it up *v.*[3] [1950s] (*US Und.*) to amass and produce a sum of money, e.g. in payment of an outstanding debt.

get it up for *v.* [1920s+] **1** to concoct evidence against, to frame. **2** to provoke.

get it up one's nose *v.* [1920s+] to be obsessed by something or someone. [? a Wodehouse nonce-word, but note HAVE ONE'S NOSE OPEN v. (2)]

get it up the arse/ass *v. see* GET IT IN THE ASS v.

get it wet *v.* **1** [1950s+] of a man, to have sexual intercourse (cf. BURY IT v.). **2** [1960s+] to be fellated.

get it where Maggie wore the beads *v.* [1900s–20s] to be hit or hurt, to suffer in the worst place, or fig. in the worst poss. way given the context. [i.e. GET IT IN THE NECK v. (1)]

get it where the chicken got the axe *v.* [late 19C–1910s] to suffer in the worst possible way, according to context. [i.e. GET IT IN THE NECK v. (1)]

get Jack in the orchard *v.* [19C] to penetrate a woman. [JACK n.[3] (1) + ORCHARD n.]

get jesse *v. see* GIVE (SOMEONE) JESSE v.

get joined! *excl.* [1930s–70s] a dismissive, derisive excl. [euph. for GET FUCKED! excl.]

get kailed up *v.* [1920s–30s] to get drunk. [KALIED adj.]

get ketch *v. see* GET CATCH v.

get knocked *v.* [1930s+] (*Aus.*) **1** to suffer a setback, a disappointment or defeat. **2** to be killed. [KNOCK v.[1] (5)]

get knotted! *excl.* [1950s+] go away! stop bothering me! [euph. for GET FUCKED! excl.]

get laid *v.* [1930s+] (*orig. US*) to have sexual intercourse; thus *unlaid*, used of those who have not had intercourse. [LAY v.[1] (1)]

get Laurence *v. see* LAZY LAURENCE n.

get left *v. see* LEFT adv.

get legal *v.* [1990s+] (*US Black/drugs*) to be involved in the use of and selling of crack cocaine. [? irony]

get loose *v.* [1970s+] **1** to relax. **2** to throw some punches; usu. as *get loose on*. **3** to dance, to have fun.

get lost *v.* [20C+] to vanish, to disappear; the implication is of stopping causing trouble.

get lost! *excl.* [1940s+] a general excl. of dismissal, go away! be off! [Yid. *ver farvalgert*, disappear, move on, go away]

get low *v.*[1] [1980s+] (*US campus*) to smoke marijuana. [a reverse pun on the usu. GET HIGH v. (2) with other drugs, due to the relaxing effects of marijuana]

get low *v.*[2] *see* LOWRIDE v.

get lucky *v.* [1930s; 1980s+] of (usu.) a man, to seduce, to have sexual intercourse.

get medieval on someone's ass *v.* [1990s+] (*US Black/teen*) to attack with extreme violence. [coined in Quentin Tarentino's film *Pulp Fiction* (1994)]

get mines *v. see* GO FOR MINES v.

get money at the best *v.* [19C] to live as a professional criminal.

get more butt than ashtrays *v.* [1990s+] (*US Black*) of a man, to lead an active sexual life, to have sexual prowess. [pun on BUTT n.[1] (1)/BUTT n.[2] (1)]

get naked *v.* [1970s+] (*US*) to enjoy oneself uninhibitedly.

get next to *v.* **1** [late 19C–1910s] (*US*) to get for oneself. **2** [late 19C–1950s] (*US*) to become suspicious, to work something out. **3** [late 19C+] (*US*) to make a good impression, to curry favour with, to win over. **4** [1920s+] (*US Black*) to become lovers, to seduce. **5** [1950s–70s] (*US Black*) to feel friendly towards, to tolerate. **6** [1970s] to become business partners with. **7** [1970s+] (*US Black*) to embarrass, to annoy, to anger. [all have image of drawing (too) close]

get no change out of *v. see* NOT GET ANY CHANGE OUT OF v.

get no forrarder *v.* (*also* **not get any forrarder**) [late 19C+] to make no progress. [SE *forward*]

get nowhere (with) *v.* (*also* **not get anywhere, get nowhere fast**) [1920s+] (*orig. US*) to fail (with someone), despite one's best efforts, to get no satisfaction (from), to make no headway (with someone).

get-off *n.* [early 19C] (*US*) an excuse. [GET OFF v.[1] (1)]

get off *v.*[1] **1** [19C+] (*also* **get it off**) to get away with. **2** [mid-late 19C] to let off, to excuse; to be excused. **3** [mid-19C+] to help someone else escape punishment (or a portion thereof). **4** [late 19C+] to desist from harassing, to stop annoying.

get off *v.*[2] [early–mid-19C] to succeed in marrying off one's daughter(s).

get off *v.*[3] [mid-19C+] (*Aus./US*) to deliver a speech, to make a joke, a witticism, e.g. *get off a good one*.

get off *v.*[4] [late 19C] (*US*) to steal.

get off *v.*[5] **1** [20C+] to gain satisfaction. **2** [1920s+] (*US Black*) to achieve one's object. **3** [1930s+] (*US*) to improvise or play music skilfully. **4** [1930s+] (*orig. US Black*) to enjoy, to be stimulated by. **5** [1930s+] (*orig. US*) to achieve orgasm. **6** [1970s+] to bring one's partner to orgasm. **7** [1970s+] to masturbate (cf. BALL OFF v.[2]). **8** [1990s+] to please or stimulate someone.

get off *v.*[6] [1950s+] to succeed in getting a child to go off to sleep.

get off *v.*[7] **1** [1950s+] (*drugs*) to quit a drug (or alcohol) addiction. **2** [1950s+] (*drugs*) (*also* **get off on**) to experience the effects of a drug. **3** [1950s+] (*drugs*) to inject oneself with a drug. **4** [1970s] to get drunk.

get off *v.*[8] *see* GET OFF (WITH) v.

get off! *excl.* **1** [late 19C+] a general excl. of disbelief, don't talk nonsense! **2** [1950s+] stop it! **3** [1970s] (*US campus*) an expression of admiration.

get off at Edge Hill *v.* (*also* **get off at Broadgreen, ...Clapham, ...Gateshead, ...Haymarket; ...Hillgate, ...Paisley, ...Redfern, get out at...**) [1970s+] to perform coitus interruptus, i.e. withdrawal well before ejaculation. [the idea of getting off at the smaller station before the main station of one's final destination; *Edge Hill* is the station before Liverpool Lime Street; *Broadgreen* is the station before Edge Hill; *Clapham Junction* before London Victoria; *Gateshead* before Newcastle-upon-Tyne; *Haymarket* before Edinburgh; *Hillsgate* is a notional place, poss. playing on *hill* = the *mons veneris*, and *gate*, i.e. the entry to the vagina; *Paisley* before Glasgow; *Redfern* before Sydney Central]

get off it! *phr.* [1910s+] stop teasing! stop exaggerating!

get off my ear! *excl. see* GET (UP) ON ONE'S EAR v.

get off on v.[1] [1940s+] to enjoy, to be stimulated by, esp. sexually. [the image is of 'rising above' normal life]

get off on v.[2] [1970s+] **1** to defeat in a fight. **2** to insult, to get angry with.

get off on v.[3] *see* GET OFF v.[7] (2).

get off one's bike v. [1930s+] (*Aus./N.Z.*) to lose one's temper.

get off some leg v. *see* GET SOME LEG v.

get off someone's back v. [1940s+] to stop annoying someone, to stop nagging at or otherwise irritating someone; usu. as imper. [ON SOMEONE'S BACK phr.]

get off someone's shit v. [1970s] (*US*) to cease bothering someone; usu. as *get off my shit*, leave me alone. [SHIT n.[3] (2)]

get off steam v. *see* BLOW OFF STEAM v.

get off the bra v. (*also* **get off the jock strap**) [1980s] (*US Black*) to have sexual intercourse.

get off the bucket *phr.* [1970s] a phr. of general dismissal. [abbr. SHIT OR GET OFF THE POT phr.]

get off the button v. [1930s] (*US*) to experience orgasm, to relieve sexual tension. [the pressing of a button to trigger some kind of activity]

get off the dime v. [1920s+] (*US*) to move from a stationary position, esp. of a dancer; to stop idling, to start; also in fig. use: to stop acting/talking in a given manner. [the image of a person being stuck on a small spot, i.e. one the size of a *dime* or *nickel* coin]

get off the earth! *excl.* [late 19C] (*US*) an excl. of dismissal, i.e. GO TO HELL! excl.

get off the grass! *excl.* [1980s+] (*N.Z.*) an excl. of dimissal or contempt.

get off the jock strap v. *see* GET OFF THE BRA v.

get off the natural v. [1960s] (*US drugs*) to become intoxicated.

get off the pot (or shit) *phr. see* SHIT OR GET OFF THE POT phr.

get off the rag! *excl.* [1970s] a dismissive excl.; the implication is that the addressee is lit. or fig. suffering from menstrual ill temper. [fig. use of RAG n.[8] (1)]

get off the squash v. [1930s] (*US*) to have sexual intercourse.

get off (with) v. **1** [1910s+] to seduce, to pick up and poss. go to bed with. **2** [1990s+] to indulge in a session of heavy kissing (occas. petting), but not in intercourse.

get-on n. [1900s–50s] (*US Und.*) the entrance to a streetcar.

get on v.[1] [early 19C+] to relate to a person either positively or negatively, e.g. *get on well, get on badly*.

get on v.[2] **1** [late 19C+] to have sexual intercourse, orig. of a man. **2** [1970s] to physically attack. [(1) his 'mounting' of his partner]

get on v.[3] [late 19C+] to grow older. [abbr. SE *get on in years*]

get on v.[4] [20C+] to leave, to depart. [abbr. SE *get on one's way*]

get on v.[5] **1** [1940s+] (*orig. US Black*) to take drugs, to become intoxicated; to get addicted. **2** [1960s–70s] (*US Black*) to get drunk. **3** [1980s+] (*Aus. prison*) to buy drugs.

get on v.[6] [1970s+] (*orig. US Black*) to pursue a goal or aim.

get on (at) v. [1910s+] to abuse, to scold, to nag. [var. GO ON AT v.]

get on dixie v. [20C+] (*W.I.*) to quarrel noisily, to become very angry. [the energy and noise associated with *Dixieland* jazz]

get one v. [1910s] to lose emotional control. ['one' is a fit]

get one at it v. [1940s+] to tease, to drive into a fury.

get one down v. [late 19C+] to make someone depressed. [DOWN adj.[2] (1)]

get one in v. (*also* **get them in**) [20C+] to order and pay for

a drink or round of drinks; esp. as excl. *get them in!* [ONE n.[4] (1)]

get one off v. *see* GET IT OFF v.[1].

get one on v. (*US*) **1** [1910s] to become very excited. **2** [1970s] of a man, to have an erection.

get one over (on) v. *see* PUT ONE OVER (ON) v.

get one's v. (*also* **have one's**) **1** [late 19C+] (*orig. US*) to suffer in some way. **2** [20C+] (*orig. US*) to be killed, to die, usu. by accident or through violence. **3** [20C+] (*orig. US Black*) to get one's share, usu. of material pleasures, to get what one deserves; usu. as *get mine*. **4** [1960s] (*US*) to get sexual satisfaction.

get one's act together v. [1960s+] (*orig. US Black*) to calm down, to plan sensibly, to state a goal and aim for it.

get one's agates cracked v. *see* AGATES n.

get one's a into g v. [1970s+] (*N.Z.*) to get on with things, to hurry up. [abbr. of GET ONE'S ARSE IN(TO) GEAR v., with added element of trying to calculate something]

get one's arse in(to) gear v. (*also* **get one's ass in gear**, **...balls in gear**, **...rear in gear**) [1950s+] to stop wasting time, to put some effort and commitment into one's activities, to start doing something useful and positive. [fig. uses of ARSE n.[1] (1)/ASS n. (2)/REAR n.[1]/BALLS n.[1] (1)]

get one's ashes hauled v. (*also* **get one's rocks hauled**) [late 19C+] to have sexual intercourse (cf. GET ONE'S AXLE GREASED v.; GET ONE'S BANANA PEELED v.; GET ONE'S BATTERIES CHARGED v.; GET ONE'S COOKIES v.; GET ONE'S CORN GROUND v.; GET ONE'S DIPPER WET v.; GET ONE'S END AWAY v.; GET ONE'S END IN v.; GET ONE'S G ON v.; GET ONE'S GROOVE ON v.; GET ONE'S GUTS UP v.; GET ONE'S LANCE WAXED v.; GET ONE'S LEG OVER v.; GET ONE'S POLE VARNISHED v.; GET ONE'S ROCKS OFF v.; GET ONE'S SWERVE ON v.; GET ONE'S THINGS v.). [? mispron. of ARSE n.[1] (1)/ASS n. (2)]

get one's ass in a crack v. (*also* **get one's tail in a crack/trap**, **have one's tail in a crack**) [1920s+] (*US*) to get into difficulties, esp. in a criminal context. [ASS n. (2)/TAIL n.[2] (1)]

get one's ass in an uproar v. [1950s+] (*US*) to get excited, to become emotionally overwrought. [ARSE n.[1] (1)/ASS n. (2)]

get one's ass in a sling v. (*also* **get one's butt in a sling**, **put one's ass in a sling**) [1940s+] (*US*) to get into bad trouble, physical or otherwise. [ASS n. (2)]

get one's ass in gear v. *see* GET ONE'S ARSE IN(TO) GEAR v.

get one's ass on one's shoulders v. [1940s+] (*US*) to become haughty, angry or excited but with no proper cause, to put on airs. [ASS n. (2); the shrugging gesture, which raises one's shoulders and thus fig. one's posterior + ? ext. of GET ONE'S ASS UP v.]

get one's ass out of joint v. [1950s] (*US*) to lose one's temper. [ASS n. (2)]

get one's ass up v. [late 19C; 1970s] (*US*) to lose one's temper, to be annoyed or infuriated. [ASS n. (2)]

get one's axle greased v. [1940s] (*US*) of a man, to have sexual intercourse (cf. GET ONE'S ASHES HAULED v.).

get one's back up v. (*also* **set one's back up**) [late 17C+] to become annoyed (cf. GET SOMEONE'S BACK UP v.). [the feline habit of bristling the fur when annoyed or frightened]

get one's bait back v. [1920s–50s] (*US*) to succeed in fathering a son. [fishing imagery]

get one's balls in an uproar v. (*also* **get one's balls in a knot**, **get one's nuts in an uproar**) [1910s+] to become excited or agitated (cf. GET ONE'S BOWELS IN AN UPROAR v.). [BALLS n.[1] (1)/NUTS n.[2] (1)]

get one's balls in gear v. *see* GET ONE'S ARSE IN(TO) GEAR v.

get one's balls off v. [1970s+] (*orig. US*) of a man, to achieve orgasm (cf. GET ONE'S NUTS OFF v.). [GET OFF v.[5] (5) + BALLS n.[1] (1)]

get one's banana peeled v. [1960s] (*orig. US*) of a man, to have sexual intercourse (cf. BURY IT v.; GET ONE'S ASHES HAULED v.). [BANANA n.[2] (1)]

get one's batteries charged v. [1930s+] (US) of a man, to have sexual intercourse (cf. GET ONE'S ASHES HAULED v.).

get one's bird in a splint v. see BIRD n.[8] (1).

get one's bit v. see GET A BIT v.[1].

get one's bitters v. [early–mid-19C] (US) to get one's deserts. [SE *bitter end*]

get one's boots on v. [1940s] (US Black) to come up to date.

get one's bowels in an uproar v. (also **get one's pants in an uproar**) [1930s+] to become excited or agitated (cf. GET ONE'S BALLS IN AN UPROAR v.).

get one's cards v. [1930s+] to be dismissed from work; thus to *give someone one's cards*, to dismiss. [the cards in question are insurance cards, P45 forms etc]

get one's checks v. [late 19C] (US) to die (cf. CASH (IN) ONE'S CHECKS v.). [gambling imagery]

get one's cherry busted v. [1950s+] (US) to lose one's virginity, both lit. and fig. use. [CHERRY n.[1] (4) + BUST v.[1] (7)]

get one's chump v. (also **provide one's chump**) [mid-19C–1910s] (UK Und.) to earn one's living. [? CHUMP n.[1] (3)]

get one's clock cleaned v. (also **get one's clock fixed**) [1950s] to be beaten up, to be killed.

get one's cock caught in a zipper v. (also **have one's cock caught in a zipper**) [1970s+] to be in very bad trouble, to get into extreme difficulties. [COCK n.[2] (1)]

get one's collar felt v. (also **have one's collar felt**) [1940s+] (UK Und./police) to be arrested.

get one's cookies v. [1960s+] **1** to have sexual intercourse; thus *get one's cookies off*, to come to orgasm (cf. GET ONE'S ASHES HAULED v.). **2** in fig. use, to enjoy oneself. [COOKIES n.[2] (1)]

get one's corn ground v. (also **have one's corn ground**) [early 19C] (US) to have sexual intercourse (cf. GET ONE'S ASHES HAULED v.).

get one's crap hot v. [1950s] (US) to lose one's temper. [CRAP n.[3] (1)]

get one's dander up v. [mid-19C+] (orig. US) **1** to lose one's temper (cf. GET SOMEONE'S DANDER UP v.). **2** to be energized. **3** to be unnerved. [DANDER n.]

get one's dandruff up v. [20C+] (US) to lose one's temper. [joc. corruption of prev. + image of flecks of dandruff rising as one gesticulates with rage]

get one's dick away v. see GET ONE'S END AWAY v.

get one's dipper wet v. [1980s+] (US) of a man, to have sexual intercourse (cf. BURY IT v.; GET ONE'S ASHES HAULED v.).

get one's ears back v. [1930s] (US) to get excited.

get one's ears chewed down v. (also **get one's ears knocked down**) [20C+] (US) to be scolded severely.

get one's ears lowered v. [20C+] (US) to get a haircut.

get oneself a banner v. [1940s–50s] (US Und.) to move from the general prison population into protective solitary confinement. [SE *banner* = *flag*, a notation on one's prison file]

get oneself a cook v. [20C+] (US) of a man, to get married.

get oneself harnessed v. [20C+] to get married.

get oneself together v. [1960s+] (orig. US) **1** to mend one's ways; to pull oneself together. **2** to amass a sum of money. **3** to sort out one's emotions.

get oneself up v. **1** [mid–late 19C] to dress up. **2** [1970s] to prepare oneself emotionally.

get one's end away v. (also **get one's dick away**) [1910s+] to have sexual intercourse (cf. GET ONE'S ASHES HAULED v.). [END n.[1] (1)/DICK n.[4] (1); note milit. use *ends away*, having intercourse]

get one's end in v. [1930s+] to have sexual intercourse (cf. GET ONE'S ASHES HAULED v.). [END n.[1] (1)]

get one's eyes together v. [20C+] (Ulster) to have a nap.

get one's face in a knot v. [20C+] (Aus.) to get angry, excited or over-emotional.

get one's feet muddy v. [1960s+] to be in criminal trouble.

get one's feet under the table v. **1** [1920s+] to establish friendly relations with someone, to start to settle in. **2** [1990s+] of a man, to start living with a woman (occas. vice versa).

get one's feet wet v. [1960s] (US Und.) to become involved, e.g. in a money-making scheme.

get one's finger out (of one's ass) v. (also **get one's thumb out of one's ass, have one's finger out**) [1940s+] (orig. US) to stop dawdling and lazing about and begin some constructive activity (cf. PULL ONE'S FINGER OUT v.).

get one's fingers nipped v. (also **get one's fingers burned**) [late 19C+] to get into trouble.

get one's freak on v. [1990s+] (US) to get into a particular mood, usu. with ref. to sex. [FREAK n.[2]]

get one's front uptight v. [1970s] (US Black) to assemble the 'props' required to present oneself in a desired manner, usu. expensive material possessions. [FRONT n.[1] (4)]

get one's gage up v. (also **get one's gauge up**) [1930s+] (US) to excite or stimulate oneself, esp. from smoking marijuana or drinking alcohol. [GAGE n.[2]; pun on GAUGE n.[1]]

get one's gallon v. [1960s+] (Irish) to be dismissed from a job. [SE *gallon*, a container used by manual labourers for holding drinks]

get one's game together v. [1960s+] (orig. US Black) **1** to be in full control of a situation. **2** in a pimping context, to define one's image by a variety of material/symbolic 'props'. [GAME n.[2] (9)]

get one's gauge up v.[1] see GAUGE n.[1].

get one's gauge up v.[2] see GET ONE'S GAGE UP v.

get one's G on v. [2000s] (US teen) to have sexual intercourse (cf. GET ONE'S ASHES HAULED v.; GET ONE'S GROOVE ON v. (2)].

get one's groove on v. [1990s+] **1** to dance. **2** (US Black) to have sexual intercourse (cf. GET ONE'S ASHES HAULED v.).

get one's gun (off) v. (US) **1** [1910s+] of a man, to ejaculate, to reach orgasm (cf. FIRE v.[1]; GET SOMEONE'S GUN (OFF) v.). **2** [1940s+] in fig. use, to excite, to invigorate, to stimulate, to satisfy. [GUN n.[1] (2)]

get one's guts in a knot v. [1910s+] (Aus.) to become angry. [GUTS n.[1] (2)]

get one's guts up v. [1970s] (Aus.) to have sexual intercourse (cf. GET ONE'S ASHES HAULED v.). [GUTS n.[1] (2)]

get one's hair cut v. [late 19C] of a man, to visit a woman for the purpose of sexual intercourse. [HAIR n.[1] (1); euph. with overtones of an adulterer's excuse]

get one's hair off v. see KEEP ONE'S HAIR ON v.

get one's hat v. (also **check one's hat, grab a hat, make one's hat**) **1** [1940s+] (US Black) to leave, esp. to leave quickly. **2** [1950s] (US prison) to be released from prison.

get one's head bad v. [1960s–80s] (US Black) to get drunk, to become intoxicated by drugs.

get one's head down v. [1940s+] **1** to have some sleep. **2** (Aus.) to plead guilty in court. [(2) one nods an assent to the charge]

get one's head (on) straight v. [1970s+] (US) to think clearly; to sort oneself out.

get one's head out (of one's ass) v. [1940s+] (US) stop being stupid or acting stupidly.

get one's head read v. (also **need one's head read**) [20C+] to be very stupid, very eccentric; also in first person, meaning that one has been very stupid; thus GET YOUR HEAD READ! excl.

get one's head right v. [1950s+] **1** to get drunk or intoxicated by drugs. **2** to come to one's senses. [SE *right*/RIGHT adj.[2]]

get one's head tight v. [1940s–60s] (US Black) to take drugs. [var. on GET ONE'S HEAD RIGHT v. but note TIGHT adj.[5]]

get one's head up v. **1** [1960s+] (US drugs) (also **get one's head uptight**) to take a drug, usu. cannabis. **2** [1970s+] (US) to cheer up.

get one's hips up (on one's shoulders) v. (also **get one's hips in a sling**) [1920s–40s] (US Black) to get upset, annoyed or hurt.

get one's hole v. [1960s+] (*Scot./Irish*) of a man, to have sexual intercourse. [HOLE n.¹ (2)]

get one's holler on v. [2000s] (*US Black*) to talk to a woman with the intent of seduction. [HOLLER v. (5)]

get one's hooks on v. (*also* **get one's hooks into**) [20C+] to grasp, to grab, to obtain, esp. when the object is most desired or currently held by a rival. [HOOK n.¹ (1)]

get one's hump (up) v. [mid-19C; 1950s] to get in a temper, to become irritated. [the way a cat arches its back when angry or threatened]

get one's jollies v. [1950s+] **1** to enjoy oneself. **2** to have sex. [JOLLY n.⁶]

get one's jones off v. [1960s+] (*orig. US Black*) to reach orgasm; also fig. to enjoy. [JONES n.²]

get one's kicks v. [1930s+] (*orig. US Black*) to enjoy oneself. [KICKS n.³]

get one's kicks off v. [1920s+] (*US*) **1** to enjoy oneself. **2** to come to orgasm. [KICKS n.³]

get one's kit off v. [1970s+] to take off one's clothes, to strip. [KIT n.⁴; widely popularized by the spread of 1990s 'lad culture' and the magazines that pander to it]

get one's knickers in a twist v. (*also* **get one's panties in a bunch, ...up one's crack**) [1960s+] **1** to become excessively agitated over a problem or situation, to worry to extremes; thus *don't get your knickers in a twist*, stop getting so worried; *knicker-twisting*, agonizingly worrying; thus occas. used of other objects (cf. GET ONE'S TITS IN A TWIST v.). **2** to make a mistake, to be under a misapprehension, to 'get the wrong end of the stick'.

get one's lance waxed v. [1980s] of a man, to have sexual intercourse (cf. BURY IT v.; GET ONE'S ASHES HAULED v.). [LANCE n. (1)]

get one's laundry in a bundle v. [1960s+] (*US campus*) to get into an emotional state, to get upset. [var. on GET ONE'S KNICKERS IN A TWIST v.]

get one's learn on v. [2000s] (*US Black*) to educate oneself.

get one's leg lifted v. *see* LIFT ONE'S LEG v.

get one's leg over v. (*also* **get one's leg across, have one's leg over**) [1970s+] of a man, to seduce, to have sexual intercourse (cf. GET ONE'S ASHES HAULED v.).

get one's licks v. [mid-19C+] (*US*) to get one's chance, to get one's way. [LICKS n. (1)]

get one's lines crossed v. *see* GET ONE'S WIRES CROSSED v.

get one's lumps v. *see* TAKE ONE'S LUMPS v.

get one's mad up v. [mid-19C+] (*US*) to get very angry (cf. GET OUT ONE'S MAD v.).

get one's marching orders v. (*also* **receive one's marching orders**) **1** [late 19C+] to be dismissed, to be sent away. **2** [1920s] (*US tramp*) for a vagrant to be thrown out of a town by the local authorities. **3** [1940s] to be given instructions (as to a task or job).

get one's mind right v. [1950s–60s] to think clearly, to agree with.

get one's monkey up v. (*also* **have one's monkey up**) [mid-19C–1900s] to lose one's temper, to get into a bad temper; thus *my monkey's up*, I am very annoyed (cf. GET SOMEONE'S MONKEY UP v.). [MONKEY n.⁷]

get one's neck wet v. [1930s] (*US*) to become nervous.

get one's nigger up v. [20C+] (*US*) to lose control, to lose one's temper. [NIGGER n.³]

get one's nose cold v. [1970s+] (*drugs*) to sniff cocaine. [the drug has a numbing quality, esp. if, as more than likely, it has been adulterated with procaine or Novocaine]

get one's nose open v. *see* HAVE ONE'S NOSE OPEN v.

get one's nose painted v. *see* NOSE PAINT n.

get one's nuff v. (*also* **have one's nuff**) [late 19C–1910s] (*orig. milit.*) to be drunk. [SE *enough*, i.e. too much]

get one's nuts in an uproar v. *see* GET ONE'S BALLS IN AN UPROAR v.

get one's nuts off v. [1930s+] (*orig. US Black*) to achieve orgasm, poss. through masturbation (cf. GET ONE'S BALLS OFF v.). [GET OFF v.⁵ (5) + NUTS n.² (1)]

get one's oats v. [1920s+] to gain sexual release. [OATS n.¹]

get one's own back v. *see* GET BACK (AT) v.

get one's panties in a bunch/up one's crack v. *see* GET ONE'S KNICKERS IN A TWIST v.

get one's pants in an uproar v. *see* GET ONE'S BOWELS IN AN UPROAR v.

get one's picture v. [1920s–40s] to be dismissed from a job. [? a picture on an identity card]

get one's pole varnished v. [1980s+] to have sexual intercourse; different from VARNISH ONE'S POLE v. (cf. GET ONE'S ASHES HAULED v.).

get one's rag out v. (*also* **get one's rag up, let one's rag out**) [late 19C+] to lose one's temper (cf. GET SOMEONE'S RAG OUT v.). [RAG n.³ (2)/RAG v.¹ (2)]

get one's rear in gear v. *see* GET ONE'S ARSE IN(TO) GEAR v.

get one's rocks hauled v. *see* GET ONE'S ASHES HAULED v.

get one's rocks off v. [1940s+] **1** to have sexual intercourse, to experience orgasm (cf. GET ONE'S ASHES HAULED v.). **2** to enjoy oneself. **3** to obtain any form of satisfaction; thus *get someone's rocks off*, to satisfy, to please (cf. GIVE SOMEONE ROCKS v.). **4** to masturbate. **5** (*drugs*) to binge pleasurably on drugs. [lit./fig. uses of ROCKS n.⁴ (1)]

get one's roll on v. [2000s] (*US teen*) to drive an expensive car. [ROLL v.³ (3)]

get one's rug beat v. [1940s] (*US Black*) to have a haircut. [RUG n.¹ (3)]

get one's screws into v. *see* PUT THE SCREWS ON v.

get one's shirt out v. [mid-19C–1920s] to become angry; thus *get someone's shirt out*, to make another angry. [the disarrangement of one's clothes that may follow a fit of arm-brandishing fury]

get one's shit blown away v. (*also* **get one's shit blown backwards**) [1960s+] (*US*) to be killed. [SHIT n.⁶]

get one's shit together v. [1970s+] (*orig. US Black*) **1** to calm down, to plan sensibly, to work out one's life. **2** to be competent. [SHIT n.⁶]

get one's shoes full v. (*also* **get the shoes on**) [20C+] to become drunk. [the drink 'overflows']

get one's skates on v. (*also* **have one's skates on, put one's skates on**) [late 19C+] (*orig. milit.*) to hurry up, to stop wasting time; often as imper. [note SKATE v.¹ (1)]

get one's skull swelled v. *see* HAVE A SWELLED HEAD v. (2).

get one's snout in the trough v. *see* HAVE ONE'S SNOUT IN THE TROUGH v.

get one's soul in soak v. [early 19C] to become very drunk (cf. DAMP adj.).

get one's swerve on v. [1990s+] (*US Black/campus*) **1** to dance. **2** to have sexual intercourse (cf. GET ONE'S ASHES HAULED v.). **3** to perform well, to achieve something positive. **4** to send a prostitute out to work. **5** to drink.

get one's tail down v. [mid-19C+] to act in a dejected manner, to lose heart. [reverse anthropomorphism]

get one's tail-feathers up v. (*also* **get one's tail up**) [mid-19C+] (*US*) to get annoyed, to lose one's temper; thus *get someone's tail-feathers up*, to annoy someone else. [reverse anthropomorphism]

get one's tail in a crack/trap v. *see* GET ONE'S ASS IN A CRACK v.

get one's tank filled v. [late 19C] (*US*) to become drunk.

get one's thing off v. [1970s+] (*US Black*) to gain pleasure from any act. [THING n.⁵ (3)]

get one's things v. [1970s–80s] (*UK Black*) of a man, to have sexual intercourse (cf. GET ONE'S ASHES HAULED v.). [THING n.²]

get one's thing together v. [1970s+] to sort out one's way of life, one's business.

get one's thumb out of one's ass v. see GET ONE'S FINGER OUT (OF ONE'S ASS) v.

get one's tits in a twist v. (also **get one's tits in a knot, …tangle**) [1970s+] (US) to be upset (cf. PUT SOMEONE'S TITS IN A TANGLE v.). [var. on GET ONE'S KNICKERS IN A TWIST v.]

get one's tits out v. [1990s+] to act in an uninhibited manner; usu. of a woman, but not necessarily so. [the image of a woman revealing her breasts both as a gesture of her own lack of inhibition and as a display for male delectation, esp. in phr. 'get your tits out for the lads!']

get one's water hot v. [1940s] (US) to get over-excited, to lose one's temper.

get one's wings v.[1] [1960s+] (Hell's Angels) to be initiated into an outlaw motorcycle club. [play on USAF/RAF jargon get one's wings, to be commissioned as a pilot]

get one's wings v.[2] see WINGS n.

get one's wires crossed v. (also **get one's lines crossed**) [1930s+] to make a mistake in communication, to misunderstand. [telephonic imagery]

get one's wires straight v. [1960s] (US Black) to obtain accurate information.

get one's work in v. [late 19C] (US) to succeed in a course of (criminal) action. [WORK n.[1] (1)]

get one up v. see GET IT UP v.[2] (1).

get on it v. [1950s+] (orig. N.Z.) to go out on a drinking spree.

get on like a bushfire v. [1940s] (Aus.) to get on well with someone, to make friends fast. [the speed with which a bushfire spreads]

get on like a house on fire v. **1** [mid-19C+] to do very well. **2** [1920s+] to become very close friends. [i.e. as fast as a house would burn, very fast or vigorously]

get on one's back v. [1930s+] **1** (UK Und) to work as a prostitute. **2** of a woman, to have sexual intercourse.

get on one's bike v. [1980s+] to busy oneself, to get down to work. [popularized by a speech given by right-wing Employment Secretary Norman Tebbit (b.1931) at the Conservative Party Conference on 15 October 1981, in which he pointed out that his unemployed father – unlike that year's inner-city rioters – had not rioted in the 1930s but had 'got on his bike and looked for work']

get on one's ear v. see GET (UP) ON ONE'S EAR v.

get on one's elbows v. [1940s] (US) to get angry.

get on one's hind legs v. (also **stand on one's hind legs**) [late 19C+] **1** to rise to speak, usu. in a formal context. **2** to get angry, to lose one's temper. [a dog 'walking' on its back legs or a rearing horse]

get on one's horse v. [1940s+] (US) to get moving.

get on one's job v. (also **get on one's j.o.b.**) [1980s] (US Black) to concentrate on one's life, involvements, pursuits.

get on one's own tail v. [1910s+] (Aus.) **1** to become angry. **2** to become scared.

get on someone's ass v. (also **get someone's ass**) [1950s+] (orig. US) **1** to annoy. **2** to pressurize, to harass, to nag. [ASS n. (2)]

get on someone's back v. [1920s+] (orig. Aus.) **1** to annoy, to harass. **2** to tell off, to scold.

get on someone's brain v. see GET ON SOMEONE'S NERVES v.

get on someone's ear v. [1920s] (US) to shout, to talk loudly and effusively.

get on someone's goat v. see GET SOMEONE'S GOAT v.

get on someone's nerves v. (also **get on someone's brain, …neck**) [late 19C+] to annoy, to irritate.

get on someone's prick v. [1940s+] to annoy, to infuriate someone. [PRICK n. (2)]

get on someone's quince v. [1920s+] (Aus.) to annoy. [QUINCE n. (4)]

get on someone's tit(s) v. (also **get on someone's teats**)

[1930s+] **1** to infuriate, to annoy. **2** (US) to pursue sexually (used by a woman of a pursuing man). [TIT n.[3] (1)]

get on someone's tripe v. [1930s+] (Aus.) to annoy or irritate someone.

get on someone's wheel v. [1960s+] (Aus./US) to irritate, to pester someone.

get on someone's wick v. [1930s+] to irritate, to annoy. [HACKNEY WICK n.]

get on someone's works v. [1940s+] (Aus.) to annoy.

get on some stiff time v. [1930s–70s] (US Black) to succeed, esp. in an illicit, but profitable occupation. [ety. unknown]

get on stink v. [20C+] (W.I.) to behave badly, to start a noisy argument.

get on that v. [late 19C–1940s] (Aus.) to understand, to look at.

get on the cars v. [late 19C] (US campus) to start. [SE streetcar]

get on the case v. [1970s+] to get down to work, to occupy oneself with what needs to be done.

get on the firm v. [1980s] to charm, to please, to seduce.

get on the good foot v. [1970s+] (US Black) **1** to correct what needs improving. **2** to do one's best, to 'put one's best foot forward'.

get on the old fork v. [late 19C–1900s] of a man, to have sexual intercourse. [SE fork, the fork of the body, where the legs divide from the torso]

get on the pole v. [late 19C–1900s] to be approaching drunkenness. [UP THE POLE phr.[1] (2)]

get onto v.[1] [late 19C+] **1** to suspect. **2** (US) to understand, to work out. **3** to interrogate, to pressurize. **4** to look (at), to observe.

get onto v.[2] [1910s+] (Aus.) to join in, to participate.

get on with you! excl. see GET AWAY (WITH YOU)! excl.

get-out n. [1940s–50s] (US Black/N.Z.) an outfit, a suit of clothes. [worn when one 'gets out' of the house]

get out v.[1] [early 18C+] to leave; usu. in imper.

get out v.[2] [late 19C–1910s] to lengthen, e.g. nights are getting out. [note the synon. 'nights are drawing in']

get out! excl. [early 18C+] an excl. of dismissal, expressing one's disbelief or scepticism.

get out at Edge Hill v. for this and all other combs. see GET OFF AT EDGE HILL v.

get out from under v. [mid-19C+] (orig. US) to get away from a dangerous or awkward situation.

get out of here! excl. [1910s+] (orig. US Black) a general excl. of disbelief, dismissal, I don't believe you! you must be joking! don't be silly! who do you think you're fooling?

get out of it! excl. [mid-19C+] an excl. of dismissal or disdain, go away! don't be silly! don't make me laugh!

get out of one's pram v. (also **jump out of one's pram**) [1950s+] to lose one's temper.

get out of someone's face v. (also **get out of someone's ass**) [1920s+] (orig. US Black) to stop pestering, to leave alone, esp. as imper.

get out of someone's hair v. [1930s+] to stop pestering someone; to leave them alone.

get out of the rain v. [mid-19C] to leave at any sign of trouble.

get out of town! excl. [1980s+] (orig. US Black/campus) a general excl. of disbelief, dismissal.

get out on v. [1930s] to get away with.

get out one's mad v. [1920s+] (Aus.) to lose one's temper (cf. GET ONE'S MAD UP v.).

get outside v. **1** [mid-19C+] (orig. US) (also **get outside of, put onself outside**) to consume, to swallow, esp. a drink, e.g. get outside a pint. **2** [late 19C+] (US) to understand, to learn, to master. **3** [late 19C+] of a woman, to have sexual intercourse.

get-over n. [1980s] (US campus) a lucky benefit. [GET OVER v.[1] (1)]

get over v.[1] **1** [mid-19C+] to take advantage of, to get around. **2** [late 19C–1910s] to astonish, to impress. **3** [1910s+] (US) to achieve a goal, to do well, to prosper. **4** [1940s+] (*Aus.*) to intimidate. **5** [1970s+] (*US Black/prison*) (*also* **get over on**) to improve one's own image/reputation by putting someone else at a disadvantage. **6** [1990s+] (*US drugs*) to help someone in need of drugs. **7** [1990s+] (*US drugs*) to take the regular dose of drugs that sustains an addiction.

get over *v.*[2] [late 19C; 1970s+] (*US Black*) to seduce, to have sexual intercourse. [the physical act of 'mounting' a woman]

get over a fast one *v. see* PULL A FAST ONE V.

get over her garter *v.* (*also* **get over the garter**) [mid-17C–18C; 1940s] to caress a woman sexually. [note D'Urfey, *Pills to Purge Melancholy* (1719–20): 'The Barn's a brave place to steal garters': 'The Maid she held her Legs so wide, / The Young man slipt between, / Such tying of a Garter, / You have but seldom seen']

get over it *phr.* [1980s] (*US campus*) calm down, forget it.

get over on *v. see* GET OVER V.[1] (5).

get over the garter *v. see* GET OVER HER GARTER V.

get over the hump *v.* [1950s+] (*US Black*) to overcome a difficulty, to move through a bad period in one's life.

get ox-tail soup *v.* [mid–late 19C] (*Irish*) to maim cattle by cutting off their tails. [one of the ways in which Irish Fenians attacked English landowners]

get paddywhack the drumstick *v.* [late 19C+] (*Aus.*) to get a spanking. [ext. PADDYWHACK V.]

get paid *v.* [1980s+] **1** (*US campus*) to have sexual intercourse. **2** (*US Black*) to obtain money, not necessarily by working for it.

get past oneself *v.* [1910s–70s] to get into a peevish, fractious mood; to get over-excited.

get past (with) *v.* [1910s+] to get away with, to escape (moral) censure.

get plunked *v. see* PLUNK A BABY V.

get points *v.* (*also* **have points**) [late 19C+] to have an advantage.

get props *v.* [1990s+] (*US Black*) to gain respect, admiration. [PROPS N.[3]]

get rats *v.* (*also* **have rats, see rats**) (*Aus./N.Z.*) **1** [mid–late 19C] to feel unwell, 'out of sorts'. **2** [mid-19C+] to be very drunk. **3** [1900s] to act in a cowardly manner. [RATS IN THE ATTIC phr.]

get real *v.* [1960s+] (*orig. US*) to face facts, to abandon one's unreal fantasies.

get real! *excl.* [1970s+] (*US campus*) an admonition to be serious, act maturely. [GET REAL V.]

get religion *v.* (*orig. US*) **1** [late 18C+] to succumb to religious belief. **2** [20C+] in fig. use, for one who was previously less than wholly honest to abandon their old ways and espouse the truth/ethical behaviour.

get right *v.* **1** [late 19C+] (*US*) to pull oneself together. **2** [1930s+] (*US Black*) to become drunk or intoxicated by drugs. **3** [1980s] (*US campus*) to get ready. [SE *right*/RIGHT adj.[2]]

get ripped! *excl.* [1940s+] (*Aus.*) a general excl. of dismissal, be quiet! go to hell!

get rooted! *excl.* [1950s+] (*Aus.*) a strongly dismissive excl., euph. for GET FUCKED! excl. [ROOT V.[3] (1)]

get round *v.* **1** [mid-19C+] (*orig. US*) to trick, to fool. **2** [mid-19C+] to persuade, to 'con'. **3** [late 19C+] to escape from an obligation or activity; to arrange events as one prefers them.

get rubber *v. see* BURN RUBBER V.

get run *v. see* HIT A HOME RUN V.

gets *n.* [1950s] (*US Und.*) an escape from prison. [abbr. GETAWAY n. (2)]

get set *v.* [late 19C+] to buckle down to one's work.

get shet of *v. see* GET SHUT OF V.

get shit of *v.* [20C+] to get rid of something or someone. [var. on GET SHUT OF V.]

get shot in the tail *v.* [late 17C–early 18C] of a woman, to have sexual intercourse (cf. CATCH AN OYSTER V.). [SE *shot* + TAIL n.[2] (3)]

get shut of *v.* (*also* **get shet of, get shot of, get shut on**) [late 16C+] to get rid of something or someone.

get skins *v. see* GET (SOME) SKINS V.

get skull *v. see* GET HEAD V.

get sloppy *v.* [1980s+] (*US Black/campus*) **1** to get drunk. **2** to have sexual intercourse.

get slops *v.* [1900s] (*Aus.*) to be punished.

get sloughed up *v.* [1940s–50s] (*US Und.*) to move from the general prison population into protective solitary confinement. [SLOUGHED (UP) adj.]

get smart *v.* [20C+] **1** to act in an arrogant manner; usu. in phr. *don't get smart with me*. **2** to become aware, to act intelligently.

get some *v.* (*orig. US*) **1** [1930s+] (*also* **get any**) to have sexual intercourse; thus *get none*, to be deprived of sex (cf. GET SOME BOOTY V.; GET SOME COCK V.; GET SOME DUKE V.; GET SOME HOOTER V.; GET SOME LEG V.; GET SOME PANTS V.; GET SOME PINK V.; GET SOME PUSSY V.; GET SOME ROD V.; GET (SOME) SKINS V.; GET SOME SWEET V.; GET SOME TAIL V.; GET SOME TRIM V.). **2** [1970s] to be physically beaten. **3** [1970s+] to fight hard; to kill. [SOME n. (2)/SE *some*/ANY n.]

get some! *excl.* [1960s+] (*US*) a cry of encouragement, esp. to a participant in a fight or firefight. [as used by US troops in the Vietnam War (1964–75)]

get some big leg *v. see* GET SOME LEG V.

get some booty *v.* (*also* **get some boody**) [1980s+] **1** (*US Black*) of a male, to have sexual intercourse (cf. GET SOME V.). **2** to have homosexual anal intercourse (cf. ASK FOR THE RING V.). [BOOTY n.]

get some brown eye *v. see* BROWN EYE n. (2).

get some brown (sugar) *v.* [1970s+] **1** of a male, whether hetero- or homosexual, to have anal intercourse (cf. ASK FOR THE RING V.). **2** (*US Black*) to have heterosexual intercourse. [BROWN n.[3] (1)/BROWN SUGAR n. (1)]

get some cock *v.* [1970s+] (*US Black/Southern*) of a man, to have sexual intercourse (cf. GET SOME V.). [COCK n.[6] (1)]

get some cold comfort *v.* [1980s+] to have sexual relations with a corpse.

get some duke *v.* [1970s+] **1** of a male homosexual, to have someone's fingers or fist pushed into one's anus. **2** (*US Black*) of a male, to have anal intercourse (cf. ASK FOR THE RING V.). **3** (*US Black*) to have sexual intercourse (cf. GET SOME V.). [DUKE n.[3] (1)/DUKE n.[4] (4)]

get some hooter *v.* [1980s] (*US campus*) to have sexual intercourse (cf. GET SOME V.). [? HOOTER n.[3] (2)]

get some ink *v.* [1930s+] to receive coverage in the printed media for one's actions, speech etc. [INK n.[1] (3)]

get some kick *v.* [1940s] (*US Black*) to obtain some money. [KICK n.[2] (2)]

get some leg *v.* (*also* **get some big/soft leg, get off some leg**) [1960s+] (*US Black*) usu. of a man, to have sexual intercourse (cf. GET SOME V.).

get some mud for the duck *v. see* STICK ONE'S DUCK IN THE MUD V.

get some of this *v.* [1990s+] (*US Black*) to participate, to take a share of; usu. as imper. *get some of this!*

get someone at it *v.* [1950s+] to tease.

get someone away *v.* [late 19C] (*Aus. Und.*) to trick, to hoax.

get someone in *v.* [1920s+] (*Aus.*) to fool, to trick.

get someone in a line *v. see* LINE n.[1] (2).

get someone in a string *v.* [late 19C] (*orig. US*) to deceive someone over a period of time.

get someone in the cold *v.* [late 19C] (*orig. US*) to have at one's mercy, to have at a disadvantage.

get someone off one's hands *v.* [early 19C+] to get rid of a person who is a responsibility, esp. an unmarried daughter.

get someone round the corner *v.* [early–mid-19C] to infuriate someone on purpose.

get someone's angora v. [1920s–40s] (US) to annoy, to irritate. [a pun on GET SOMEONE'S GOAT v. (1)]

get someone's ass v. see GET ON SOMEONE'S ASS v.

get someone's back v. see WATCH SOMEONE'S BACK v.

get someone's back up v. (also **get up someone's back**) [late 18C+] to annoy, to irritate, to infuriate. [GET ONE'S BACK UP v.]

get someone's dander up v. [late 19C+] (orig. US) to annoy someone. [GET ONE'S DANDER UP v.]

get someone set v. [20C+] (Aus.) to bear a grudge against someone, to have a score to settle with someone.

get someone's goat v. (also **get on someone's goat**) [20C+] **1** to annoy someone; thus goat-getting, deliberate provocation to gain a psychological advantage. **2** to impress, to move emotionally. **3** to render nervous. [SE get/GET v.² (8) + SE goat; ? the goat's propensity to butt when in a bad temper]

get someone's guinea up v. [1930s] to make angry. [GUINEA n. (1); stereotyping of Italians as excitable]

get someone's gun (off) v. **1** [1940s+] to delight someone. **2** [1960s] (US Black) to give someone an orgasm (cf. FIRE v.¹; GET ONE'S GUN (OFF) v.). [lit./fig. uses of GUN n.¹ (2)]

get someone's hackles up v. [19C+] to infuriate, to annoy. [SE hackles, the long, prominent feathers on the tail of a fighting cock]

get someone's measure v. (also **take someone's measure**) [mid–late 17C; mid-19C+] to assess someone's character.

get someone's monkey up v. (also **put someone's monkey up**) [mid-19C–1920s] to annoy someone, to infuriate someone (cf. GET ONE'S MONKEY UP v.). [MONKEY n.⁷]

get someone's nanny (goat) v. [1900s–40s] to annoy someone, to infuriate someone. [var. on GET SOMEONE'S GOAT v.]

get someone's number v. see HAVE SOMEONE'S NUMBER v.

get someone's nut v. [2000s] to tease, to 'wind up'. [NUT n.¹ (2)]

get someone's pratt v. [1950s] (US prison) to annoy someone, to drive someone to lose their temper. [fig. use of PRAT n.¹ (1)]

get someone's rag out v. [late 19C+] to make someone angry. [GET ONE'S RAG OUT v.]

get someone's rattle up v. [20C+] (Ulster) to infuriate. [dial. rattlie, a child's rattle]

get someone's rocks off v. see GET ONE'S ROCKS OFF v. (3).

get someone's shirt out v.¹ (also **have someone's shirt (out)**) [mid-19C–1930s] to cause someone to lose all their money (through gambling). [the idea of losing one's shirt to someone else (cf. LOSE ONE'S SHIRT v.)]

get someone's shirt out v.² see GET ONE'S SHIRT OUT v.

get someone's steam up v. see STEAM v.¹ (2).

get someone's tail-feathers up v. see GET ONE'S TAIL-FEATHERS UP v.

get someone straight v. (also **get something straight**) [1920s+] to explain something to someone, to make things clear.

get someone told v. [1930s–50s] (US Black) to reprimand someone, to upbraid someone, to tell someone off.

get someone wet v. [1920+] (N.Z.) to gain an advantage over someone. [the image of dunking them in water]

get someone wrong v. [1910s+] (orig. US) to misunderstand a person's meaning or intentions, to misinterpret someone.

get some pants v. [1960s] (US Black) of a man, to have sexual intercourse (cf. GET SOME v.).

get some pink v. [2000s] (US) to have sexual intercourse (cf. GET SOME v.). [PINK n.¹ (3)]

get some pussy v. [1950s+] (US/Aus.) of a male, to have sexual intercourse (cf. GET SOME v.). [PUSSY n. (2)]

get some rod v. [1990s+] (US campus) of a woman, to have sexual intercourse (cf. CATCH AN OYSTER v.; GET SOME v.). [ROD n.¹ (1)]

get some scrumptious v. [1980s+] (US campus) usu. of a woman, to enjoy sexual relations with someone.

get (some) skins v. [1990s+] (US Black) to have sexual intercourse (cf. GET SOME v.).

get some soft leg v. see GET SOME LEG v.

get some stanky on the hang-low v. see HANG-LOW n.

get some sweet v. [1980s] (US Black) of a woman, to have sexual intercourse (cf. CATCH AN OYSTER v.; GET SOME v.).

get some tail v. [1970s+] (US) of a man, to have sexual intercourse (cf. GET SOME v.). [TAIL n.² (3)]

get something from v. [1940s] (US Black) to attack someone physically, esp. with a knife.

get something on one's brain v. (also **have something on one's brain/mind**) [20C+] to be obsessed with.

get something on someone v. [1910s+] (orig. US) to find out incriminating or otherwise negative information about someone, to gain an advantage over someone.

get something straight v. see GET SOMEONE STRAIGHT v.

get some tight eye v. see BROWN EYE n. (2).

get some trim v. [1940s+] of a man, to have sexual intercourse (cf. GET SOME v.). [TRIM n. (2)]

get somewhere v. [1930s+] to succeed, to gain one's desires. [opposite of GET NOWHERE (WITH) v.]

get straight v.¹ [late 19C+] to overcome a temporary problem, usu. financial. [STRAIGHT adj.¹ (1)]

get straight v.² **1** [1940s+] (orig. US Black) to sober up, from either drink or drugs, esp. when overcoming an addiction; also in fig. use. **2** [1960s+] (drugs) for a heroin addict to inject the drug, thus relieving the pain of withdrawal symptoms. **3** [1960s+] (drugs) to consume a narcotic, whether or not one is addicted/suffering withdrawal. [STRAIGHT adj.²]

get string v. see GET WOOD v.

get stuck in v. [1930s+] **1** to begin, esp. of a meal or a job. **2** to fight, to act in an aggresive manner, esp. in sporting context.

get stuck into v. [1910s+] (orig. Aus./N.Z.) **1** to start any form of activity; the implication is one of enthusiasm and activity. **2** to start a fight. **3** to abuse verbally.

get stuffed! excl. [1940s+] a general excl. of dismissal. [STUFF v.¹ (1), i.e. var. on GET FUCKED! excl.]

get stupid v. [1990s+] (US Black/teen) **1** to attend a party. **2** to become drunk or intoxicated by drugs. [STUPID adj. (1)]

gett n. see GET n.¹.

getter n. **1** [late 19C–1920s] (US Und.) a thief; thus stone-getter, a diamond thief. **2** [1940s] (UK Und.) a criminal who steals letters for forgery gangs.

get that! excl. see GET THIS! excl.

get the air v. [20C+] (US) to be dismissed or rejected, esp. in the context of a love affair (cf. GIVE SOMEONE THE AIR v.).

get the apple v. [1970s] (US) to blunder, to make mistakes.

get the ass v. [1960s+] (US Black/campus) to lose one's temper, to become annoyed. [abbr. GET THE RED ASS v.]

get the bass out of one's voice v. [1990s+] (US prison) to stop acting aggressively. [one trad. lowers one's voice when one is being verbally threatening]

get the belt v. [1920s+] to be rejected, to be jilted. [for ety. see GIVE SOMEONE THE BELT v.]

get the best of it v. see GIVE SOMEONE THE BEST OF IT v.

get the (big) bird v. **1** [early 19C+] (orig. and mainly theatrical) to be jeered, mocked etc (cf. GIVE (SOMEONE) THE BIRD v.). **2** [late 19C+] to be dismissed, usu. from a job. [BIRD n.⁵ (1); orig. 16C; the hissing noise that geese, and an unappreciative audience, can make]

get the big head v. [late 19C+] to become arrogant. [BIG HEAD n.¹ (1)]

get the big one v. [1920s] (US) to die.

get the bird v. see GET THE (BIG) BIRD v.

get the bitch on v. [1990s+] (US campus) to yell at someone, to criticize, to nag. [BITCH v.² (6)]

get the blue envelope v. [1900s–30s] (US) to be dismissed from one's job. [the packaging of a note of dismissal + ? BLUE adj.[1] (4)]

get the boat *v.* [late 19C] to be sentenced to transportation overseas or a severe form of penal servitude. [BOAT n.[2] (1)]

get the bolt *v.* [mid–late 19C] to be sentenced to penal servitude. [the *bolt* on one's cell door]

get the book *v.* [1940s+] (*UK prison*) to become religious. [SE *book*, i.e. the Bible]

get the boost *v.* [1900s] (*US*) to be rejected, dismissed. [var. on BOOT, THE n.]

get the bounce *v.* [late 19C+] to be thrown out, to be ejected, to be dismissed, to be jilted (cf. GIVE SOMEONE THE BOUNCE *v.*). [BOUNCE, THE n.]

get the breeze up *v.* (*also* **have the breeze up, put...**) [1910s+] to worry, to disturb.

get the bulge on *v. see* HAVE THE BULGE ON *v.*

get the bullet *v.* [mid-19C+] to be thrown out, both of a place or of one's employment (cf. GIVE SOMEONE THE BULLET *v.*). [BULLET n.[2] (1); one is fig. 'shot']

get the bull's feather *v.* [early–mid-18C] to be cuckolded, to be betrayed by one's lover or spouse. [phr. *a new feather made of an old horn*]

get the chase *v. see* CHASE *v.*[1] (2).

get the chop *v.* (*also* **get the chopper**) [1940s+] **1** to be killed (cf. GIVE SOMEONE THE CHOP *v.*). **2** to be dismissed from one's job, or from a sports team. **3** to be jilted or rejected in a love affair. [SE *chop*, to remove (one's head)]

get the chuck *v.* **1** [late 19C+] to be dismissed, to be rejected (cf. GIVE SOMEONE THE CHUCK(-UP) *v.*). **2** [1970s] of a criminal, to be found not guilty in court. [CHUCK n.[2] (2)]

get the chutes *v.* [late 19C–1910s] (*US*) to be dropped, to be dismissed. [play on SE *parachute*]

get the clincher *v. see* CLINCHER n.[1] (1).

get the deadwood (on) *v. see* HAVE THE DEADWOOD (ON) *v.*

get the dirty water off one's chest *v.* [20C+] **1** to masturbate. **2** to have sexual intercourse.

get the done *v.* [20C+] (*W.I. teen*) to be jilted or rejected by a lover (cf. GIVE THE DONE *v.*). [SE *done*, over, finished]

get the drawers *v. see* GET (TO) THE DRAWERS *v.*

get the drop on *v.* [mid-19C+] (*orig. US*) to obtain an (unfair) advantage over someone; orig. spec. with a gun (cf. HAVE THE DROP ON *v.*). [DROP n.[2]]

get the empty *v.* [late 19C] to be dismissed from one's job. [play on GET THE SACK *v.* (1), which is seen as empty of contents]

get the eye *v.* [1990s+] to be stared at.

get the fat off *v. see* FAT n.[1].

get the flick *v.* [1980s] (*Aus.*) to be dismissed from one's job (cf. GIVE IT THE FLICK *v.*). [a dismissive flick of the fingers]

get the fuck *v.* [1990s+] (*Aus.*) to be dismissed from one's job. [FUCK *v.*[2] (8)]

get the fuck (out)! *excl.* [1950s+] **1** intensifier of 'go away!' **2** intensifier of GET OUT OF HERE! excl.or similar phrs. of (joc.) disbelief.

get the fuck out my face! *excl.* [1990s+] (*US Black teen*) go away! [comb. of GET THE FUCK OUT (OF) *v.* and GET OUT OF SOMEONE'S FACE *v.*]

get the fuck out (of) *v.* [1940s+] to leave, to go away; the use of *fuck* intensifies the urgency.

get the fuck out of Dodge *v. see* GET THE HELL OUT OF DODGE *v.*

get the g *v.* [20C+] (*W.I.*) to understand, to 'get the hang of'. [ety. unknown; ? the initial 'g' of *get*]

get the gate *v.* [1910s+] (*US*) to be ejected, to be dismissed (cf. GIVE SOMEONE THE GATE *v.*).

get the g.b. *v.* [late 19C–1910s] (*US*) to be snubbed, to be ignored. [*get the g*o *by* or grand *bounce*]

get the gimmes *v.* [1920s+] to be greedy, to be covetous. [SE *give me*]

get the glory *v.* [1940s–50s] (*UK prison*) to become suddenly and fervently religious while serving a prison sentence. [Tempest (1950) suggests that, far from actual faith, such prisoners 'imagine that by crawling' round the chaplain or priest they will get preferential treatment']

get the glow *v.* [late 19C–1900s] to blush.

get the gooner *v.* [1920s–30s] to be dismissed from a job (cf. GIVE SOMEONE THE GOONER *v.*). [SE *gone* or GONER n.[1] (3)]

get the grapes *v.* [1920s] (*US*) to enjoy the good things in life; to have good luck.

get the gun *v.* **1** [1900s] (*US*) to die. **2** [1950s] (*Aus.*) to be dismissed from one's job.

get the hang of *v.* [mid-19C+] to work out, to learn the use of, to become familiar with. [orig. spec. to the use of tools]

get the hard end *v.* [1900s–30s] (*US*) to suffer, to be victimized, to be placed in an invidious position.

get the hard-nose *v. see* HARD-NOSE n. (1).

get the hare's foot to lick *v.* [19C] to get very little or nothing whatsoever. [the lack of meat on the hare's foot]

get the harpoon *v. see* GET THE SPEAR *v.*

get the heels on *v.* (*also* **have the heels on**) **1** [mid-18C; late 19C] (*US*) to succeed, to conquer. **2** [mid-19C–1910s] (*also* **have the heels of**) to outpace. [Ware suggests the habit of sitting with one's feet proprietorially on a desk or table; but ? SE phr. *hard on someone's heels*]

get the hell out (of) *v.* [20C+] (*orig. US campus*) to leave, to depart, e.g. *if you don't want to stay here, then get the hell...*, usu. with a place-name.

get the hell out of Dodge *v.* (*also* **get the fuck out of Dodge**) [1960s+] to leave, usu. at speed; usu. as imper. [GET THE HELL OUT (OF) *v.*/GET THE FUCK OUT (OF) *v.*; the clichéd dialogue of a variety of Western films/TV series in which the 'baddie' is given this order]

get the home *v.* [1940s] (*UK prison*) to be sentenced to preventive detention.

get the hoof *v.* [late 19C+] to be thrown out, both of a place or one's employment. [HOOF *v.* (3)]

get the hook *v.* [late 19C–1920s] (*US*) **1** to be ejected. **2** in fig. use, to take second place; to suffer a rejection. [the long pole or *hook* used to drag unpopular performers off stage; introduced in 1903 at Harry Minor's Bowery Theatre, New York City]

get the hook up *v.* [2000s] (*US teen*) for a situation to surpass one's expectations; to enjoy a satisfactory sexual relationship. [lit./fig uses of HOOK UP (WITH) *v.*[1] (2)]

get the horn to *v.* [1970s] (*US*) to pressurize.

get the horse laugh *v. see* GIVE SOMEONE THE HORSE LAUGH *v.*

get the hot end of (the stick) *v.* [20C+] (*US*) to be victimized, to be given a hard time. [HOT adj.[2] (2) but also the image of a brand-iron]

get the hump *v.* [late 19C+] **1** to be depressed, miserable (cf. GIVE SOMEONE THE HUMP *v.*). **2** to be over-sensitive or 'touchy', thus angry. [HUMP n.[1]]

get the Indian sign on *v. see* PUT THE INDIAN SIGN ON *v.*

get the juice *v. see* JUICE n.[4] (1).

get the jump on (someone) *v.* (*also* **get a jump on (someone), have the...**) [20C+] (*orig. US*) to gain a lead on, to get an advantage over (someone). [JUMP n.[4] (1)]

get the kick *v.* [late 19C–1910s] to be dismissed from a job (cf. GIVE SOMEONE THE KICK(OUT) *v.*). [KICK n.[3]]

get the knickers *v.* [1930s+] **1** (*US prison*) to get a life sentence. **2** (*UK prison*) to get penal servitude. [the *knickbocker* suits once worn by convicts]

get the knock *v. see* TAKE THE KNOCK *v.*

get the laugh on *v. see* HAVE THE LAUGH ON *v.*

get the lead *v.* [late 19C–1900s] to be shot. [LEAD n.[1] (1)]

get the lead out (of one's ass) *v.* (*also* **get the lead out of one's pants/tail**) [1910s+] (*orig. US*) to make an effort, to 'get a move on', to stop being lazy; usu. as imper. hurry up! stop dawdling! [SE *lead* weighs one down]

get the length of someone's foot *v.* (*also* **know the length of someone's foot**) [late 16C–19C] to understand, to have worked out, to 'get the measure of'.

get the loan of *v.* (*also* **have a lend/loan of**) [20C+] (*Aus.*) to play a trick on, to treat like a fool. [dial. *take the lend of*, to take advantage of, to cajole]

get them *v. see* GET 'EM *v.*

get the message *v.* [1950s+] to appreciate, to understand. [orig. jazz use, but now general]

get them in *v. see* GET ONE IN *v.*

get the miseries *v.* [1990s+] **1** (*US*) to be tetchy, to be irritated. **2** (*US Black*) to be in pain, to be ill.

get the mitten *v.* **1** [mid-19C] (*US campus*) to be expelled from a college. **2** [mid–late 19C] (*US*) to be turned down as a suitor, to be rejected (cf. GIVE SOMEONE THE MITTEN *v.*). [MITTEN n. (2); in this case the handshake is of farewell]

get the nark *v. see* NARK n.¹ (4).

get the narkies on *v.* [20C+] to become domineering, arrogant and bossy. [NARK n.¹ (4)]

get the needle *v.* [mid-19C+] to be extremely annoyed. [NEEDLE n.³]

get the net! *excl.* [1980s+] a teasing comment aimed at someone whose behaviour is seen as strange or eccentric. [the image of the 'men in white coats' brandishing a net with which they capture the 'mad' person]

get the order of the boot *v.* [late 19C+] to be sacked from work (cf. GIVE SOMEONE THE ORDER OF THE SACK *v.*). [ORDER OF THE BOOT n.]

get the pedal *v.* [1930s] to be dismissed from a job.

get the picture *v.* [20C+] to understand, to appreciate.

get the pinchers into *v.* [1920s] (*N.Z.*) to pressurize. [SE *pinch*]

get the pip *v.* **1** [mid-19C+] to feel depressed, out of sorts, ill, fed up (cf. GIVE SOMEONE THE PIP *v.*). **2** [1910s] to become obsessed with. [PIP n.¹ (1)]

get the poke *v.* [late 19C+] (*Scot.*) to be dismissed from one's job. [SE *poke*, a small bag or sack, i.e. GET THE SACK *v.* (1)]

get the pox out (of) *v.* [1970s] a euph. for GET THE FUCK OUT (OF) *v.* [POX n.¹ (1)]

get the pricker *v.* [1940s–60s] (*Aus./N.Z.*) to get angry, to lose one's temper. [SE *pricker*, that which pricks or pierces]

get the rap *v.* [1970s+] to be scolded, to be told off, to be blamed. [RAP n.⁴ (1)]

get-there *n.* [late 19C] (*US*) ambition, energy. [GET THERE *v.* (2)]

get there *v.* **1** [mid-19C+] of a man, to have sexual intercourse, esp. to deflower. **2** [late 19C+] (*US campus*) to achieve an aim. **3** [1980s+] to achieve orgasm. **4** [1990s+] to become intoxicated by drink or drugs. [fig. uses of SE]

get the red ass *v.* [1960s+] (*orig. US*) to bear a grievance. [RED ARSE n. (2)]

get there Eli *v.* (*also* **get there Ely**) [19C] to do something well, to succeed in a notable manner. [a racehorse named *Eli* or *Ely*]

get there in one *v. see* GET IT IN ONE *v.*

get there with both feet *v.* [late 19C+] (*US*) to do something well, to succeed in a notable manner.

get the run *v.* [late 19C–1950s] to be dismissed from a job.

get the run on *v.* [mid-19C] (*US*) to have at a disadvantage, to be in a position to laugh at.

get the sack *v.* **1** [mid-19C+] to be dismissed from a job (cf. GIVE SOMEONE THE SACK *v.*). **2** [1930s+] to be rejected by one's lover or sweetheart. [SACK, THE n. (1)]

get the sads *v.* [late 19C] to have 'a fit of the vapours', to become depressed. [SE *sad*]

get the shaft *v.* [1950s+] (*orig. US*) **1** to treat unfairly or harshly.

2 to cheat, to deceive. **3** to take advantage of. **4** to slight, to reject. [SHAFT n.²]

get the shillings ready *v.* [late 19C] to get ready to hand out some money. [the mass of charities that took advantage of Queen Victoria's Diamond Jubilee in 1897, esp. the *Daily Telegraph*'s shilling lists, designed to help the London Hospital meet its debts]

get the shits (with) *v.* [1990s+] (*Aus.*) to become annoyed (with someone) (cf. GIVE SOMEONE THE SHITS *v.*). [SHITS, THE n. (3)]

get the shoes on *v. see* GET ONE'S SHOES FULL *v.*

get the shoot *v.* [mid-19C–1900s] to be dismissed from a job. [SE *shoot*]

get the shove *v.* **1** [late 19C+] to be dismissed from a job (cf. GIVE SOMEONE THE SHOVE *v.*). **2** [1900s] to be rejected by a lover. [SHOVE, THE n.]

get the show on the road *v.* [1940s+] to start off, to set things in motion. [show business imagery]

get the slingers *v.* [1950s–60s] to be thrown out, to be dismissed from a job. [SE *sling*, to throw]

get the spear *v.* (*also* **get the harpoon**) [late 19C–1960s] (*Aus.*) to be dismissed from a job. [SPEAR n.¹]

get the spike *v.* [late 19C+] to be extremely annoyed; thus *give someone the spike*, to render annoyed.

get the spirit *v.* [early 19C+] (*US Black*) **1** to become extremely religious. **2** to have an intense emotional experience.

get the sticky end *v.* [1920s] (*US*) to do badly, to be treated unfairly.

get the swerve *v.* [1970s] (*US*) to be deceived, to be let down. [baseball imagery]

get the tom-tits *v.* (*also* **have the tom-tits**) [1950s+] to become annoyed (cf. GIVE SOMEONE THE TOM-TITS *v.*). [fig. use of TOM TITS n.]

get the upshoot *v.* [late 16C] of a woman, to receive a man's ejaculation.

get the whole menu *v.* [1990s+] (*US*) to find out everything one needs to know.

get the wind up *v.* (*also* **have the wind up**) **1** [mid-19C; 1910s+] to become nervous. **2** [1910s] to make others nervous. [abbr. *get the wind up one's trousers*]

get the wire *v.* [1910s+] (*US*) to find out, to be informed. [WIRE n.² (1)]

get the woolies *v.* [1980s] (*US*) to become bored, nervous. [? WILLIES n.]

get the works *v.* **1** [1920s–50s] to suffer, to be punished, to be killed. **2** [1920s+] (*US prison*) to receive a death sentence, to receive a very long sentence. **3** [1990s+] (*US prison*) to serve one's entire sentence, without deductions for good behaviour. [WORKS, THE n. (1)]

get the wrong end of the stick *v. see* GET HOLD OF THE WRONG END OF THE STICK *v.*

get the wrong pig by the ear *v.* (*also* **get the wrong pig by the tail, ...wrong sow by the ear, have the wrong pig/sow by the ear**) [mid-16C–1900s] to make a mistake.

get the zig *v.* [2000s] to become angry. [? fig. use of ZIG-ZIG n., i.e. 'fucked (off)']

get this! *excl.* (*also* **get that!**) [20C+] now listen! take note! this is amazing!

get through *v.* [1970s+] (*drugs*) to obtain drugs.

get through to *v.* [1950s+] to make oneself understood, esp. by someone who is 'slow on the uptake'.

getting any (lately)? *phr.* [1940s+] (*orig. Aus.*) a popular greeting between men (cf. CLIMBING TREES TO GET AWAY FROM IT *phr.*; KNOCKING IT BACK WITH A STICK *phr.*). [ANY n.]

getting much? *phr.* [1920s+] (*US*) a male-to-male greeting. [the 'much' is sex]

getting place, the *n.* [late 19C–1930s] (*US Black*) an abstract 'place' used in answer to a child's question, 'where did you get such-and-such?'

getting the job done *phr.* [1990s+] masturbating.

get to *v.* **1** [late 19C] to start doing something. **2** [late 19C+] to effect, to influence emotionally, to worry. **3** [20C+] to corrupt, to bribe, to influence. **4** [1910s+] (*N.Z.*) to attack physically. **5** [1920s] (*US Und.*) to gain or posess information about. **6** [1960s+] to listen; thus *get to this*, listen to this. **7** [1960s+] to watch.

get toco for yam *v.* (*also* **nap toco for yam**) [19C] to be punished; opposite of GIVE COCO FOR YAM *v.* [TOCO *n.*; *for* in this context equals 'instead of']

get to fuck (out of it)! *excl.* (*also* **get to hell (out of here/it)!**) [1920s+] a harsh demand telling someone to go away, leave one alone. [note synon. Scot. *awa' tae fuck!*]

get-together *n.* **1** [1910s+] a meeting, gathering, an informal conference, esp. an informal social gathering. **2** [1980s] in ext. use, sexual intercourse.

get together *v.* **1** [late 19C+] to act in concert, to help one another. **2** [1950s+] (*US campus*) to have sexual relations, with or without intercourse. **3** [1970s] (*US Black*) to improve one's appearance.

get to hell (out of here/it)! *excl. see* GET TO FUCK (OUT OF IT)! *excl.*

get tongue-pie *v.* (*also* **get tongue**) [1900s–20s] to receive a scolding. [TONGUE PIE *n.* (1)]

get tonked *v.* [1910s+] **1** to get punched. **2** to be completely defeated. [TONK *v.* (3)]

get to onest *v.* [late 19C] (*US*) to run off, to escape. [SE *honest*; i.e. once one has escaped one is 'honest']

get tore in *v.* [1940s+] (*Scot.*) to fight vigorously. [TEAR INTO *v.* (2)]

get (to) the drawers *v.* [20C+] (*US Black*) to have sexual intercourse. [abbr. *get the drawers off*]

get to the joint *v.* (*also* **go to the joint**) [late 19C–1930s] (*US*) to come to the point, to achieve one's aim, esp. in a criminal context.

get tough (with) *v.* [1920s+] (*orig. US*) esp. of the criminals or the police, to act in an aggressive, harsh manner towards someone or something.

get under one's neck *v.* [1930s+] (*Aus.*) to defeat or outwit someone. [horseracing]

get under the tide *v.* [late 19C–1900s] (*US*) to become very drunk.

get under the wire *v.* [1940s] (*US Black*) to obtain something, e.g. money.

get-up *n.*[1] [mid-19C+] one's dress, esp. when special or 'best'.

get-up *n.*[2] (*also* **git-up**) [mid-19C+] (*US*) energy, spirit.

get-up *n.*[3] [1900s–50s] lies, a ruse, a subterfuge, a false charge. [something 'got up' to allay suspicions or enquiries]

get-up *n.*[4] [1920s+] (*US prison*) the date of one's release as given by a parole board. [the day on which one 'gets up' in prison but goes to bed free]

get-up *n.*[5] [1930s+] an amount of heroin, used in the morning to prevent withdrawal symptons.

get up *v.*[1] **1** [mid-17C; 19C+] to penetrate sexually (whether the vagina or anus). **2** [1990s+] (*Aus.*) to beat, to defeat.

get up *v.*[2] [late 19C] to dress up. [GET-UP *n.*[1]]

get up *v.*[3] [1930s] (*US prison*) to reach the end of one's sentence. [GET-UP *n.*[4]]

get up! *excl.* [1980s+] (*US campus*) an expression of admiration or disbelief.

get up and dust *v.* [mid-19C–1910s] (*US*) to act energetically; to run off quickly. [DUST *v.*[2] (1)]

get up and get *v.* (*also* **get up and git**) [mid-19C+] (*US*) to leave in a hurry, to move rapidly; to act energetically.

get up and go *n.* (*also* **get up and get, get up and hustle**) [late 19C+] (*orig. US*) energy, spirit, ambition, drive.

get up and go *v.* [20C+] (*orig. US*) to move fast, to get moving.

get up early (in the morning) *v.* [mid-18C+] to be clever, to be aware.

get up in *v.* [1980s+] (*US Black/prison*) to intefere in, to force oneself upon, to fig. enter where one is unwelcome/forbidden.

get up in a bunch *v.* [1980s+] (*US*) to get over-excited about something.

get up in someone's ass *v.* [1990s+] (*US Black*) to assault. [GET UP IN *v.* + ASS *n.* (5)]

get up in someone's business *v.* [1990s+] (*US*) to interfere in someone's privacy. [GET UP IN *v.*]

get up in someone's face *v.* [1990s+] (*orig. US Black*) to argue, to confront face-to-face. [GET UP IN *v.*]

get up in someone's shit *v.* [1980s] (*US*) to get angry with someone else. [GET UP IN *v.* + SHIT *n.*[6]]

get up (off) *v.* [1930s–70s] (*US Black*) **1** to experience the effects of a drug. **2** to resist a way of doing things. **3** to give up something important or valuable. **4** to refrain from gossiping about a third party.

get up off the shoulder *v.* [1990s+] (*US Black gang*) to fight with one's fists.

get up on *v.* [1960s+] (*US Black*) to get excited by, to become interested in; thus imper. meaning to become aware or (with *n.*) to act.

get (up) on one's ear *v.* (*also* **go off on one's ear**) [late 19C+] (*US*) to lose one's temper, to become violently angry, to get embarrassed; thus *get off my ear!* leave me alone!

get up someone's back *v. see* GET SOMEONE'S BACK UP *v.*

get up someone's frills *v. see* GET AMONG (A WOMAN'S) FRILLS *v.*

get up someone's nose *v.* (*also* **get up someone's shirt**) [1910s+] (*orig. US*) to annoy, to irritate.

get up someone's pipe *v.* [1990s+] to annoy, to infuriate, to provoke. [BROWN PIPE *n.* or the idea of close pursuit in a car, thus an exhaust *pipe*]

get up steam *v.* **1** [mid-19C–1910s] to act energetically, to become interested in. **2** [late 19C] to become sexually excited. **3** [late 19C] to excite sexually.

get up there *v.* [20C+] (*US*) to grow old.

get up the yard! *excl.* [20C+] (*Irish*) **1** an invitation to have sexual intercourse. **2** a general dismissive excl.

get up to *v.* (*also* **get up to dickens**) [late 19C+] to perform an action, usu. mischievous, of dubious legality or in a sexual context.

get up to tricks *v.* [late 19C] to work as a prostitute. [GET UP TO *v.* + TRICK *n.*[1] (1) + play on SE]

get up with *v.* [1970s+] (*US Black/campus*) **1** to meet someone. **2** to have a romantic encounter; to have sexual intercourse.

get up your pole! *excl.* [1900s] (*Aus.*) an excl. of dismissal.

get weaving *v.* [1940s+] (*orig. RAF*) to stop wasting time, to hurry up; to leave, to be off.

get well *v.* [1900s] (*US Und.*) to improve one's financial position; to amass money.

get wet *v.*[1] **1** [late 19C–1950s] (*Aus.*) to lose one's temper, to become angry. **2** [1900s–40s] (*Aus./N.Z.*) to gain the upper hand over, to have at one's mercy. [? one gets wet with sweat]

get wet *v.*[2] [1970s+] **1** to murder, to kill. **2** to be wounded, to be stabbed. [the blood that, fig. at least, gets on one's hands; thus KGB, CIA, MI6 jargon *get wet*, to kill]

get wise (to) *v.* (*also* **get wise on**) [late 19C+] (*orig. US*) **1** to become aware, to learn about. **2** to come to one's senses. [WISE *adj.* (1)]

get wise (with) *v.* [1930s+] **1** to act in a cheeky, 'smart' manner. **2** to make a sexual pass (at someone). [WISE *adj.* (1)]

get with *v.* **1** [1930s+] (*orig. US Black*) to understand, to join in, to accept the party line; esp. as imper. *get with it*, join in, stop standing aside. **2** [1940s–50s] (*US Black campus*) to enjoy oneself, usu. as *get with it*. **3** [1950s+] (*orig. US*) to have sexual intercourse. **4** [1990s+] to associate with, to join forces with.

get with it! *excl.* [1950s+] (*orig. US teen/campus*) stop acting stupidly! [WITH IT adj.]

get with the program *v.* (*also* **go with the program**) [1960s+] (*orig. US milit.*) **1** to act in a mature or responsible way, often as imper. **2** to accept the majority rules. [the various '12-Step Programs', e.g. that promoted by Alcoholics Anonymous]

get wood *v.* (*also* **get string**) [1990s+] to achieve an erection. [WOOD n.⁴ (2)]

get worked! *excl.* [20C+] (*Aus.*) a general excl. of dismissal or contempt.

get x-rated *v.* [2000s] (*US Black*) to have sexual intercourse.

get you! *excl.* [1940s+] a teasing, mocking phr., used to deflate someone who is seen as showing off, overdressing etc; thus *get me!* teasing oneself; the tone is usu. stereotypically effeminate/homosexual.

get your head read! *excl.* [1910s+] (*Aus.*) a general derisive excl. [GET ONE'S HEAD READ v.]

gevalt *n.* [1930s+] (*orig. S.Afr.*) a noisy argument, a row. [Yid. excl. *oi gevalt!*, ult. f. Ger. *Gewalt*, powers, force]

gey *adj. see* GAY adj.³.

geycat *n. see* GAYCAT n. (4).

geycat *v. see* GAYCAT v.¹ (1).

geyser *n.*¹ [1900s] (*Aus.*) a talker of nonsense, of empty words. [play on SPOUT v.¹]

geyser *n.*² *see* GEEZER n.¹ (1).

geyser *adj.* [1900s] (*US*) old, old-fashioned. [GEEZER n.¹ (2)]

gezeybo *n. see* GAZABO n.

gezump/gezumph/gezzump *v. see* GAZUMP v.

g.f. *n.* [1920s–50s] (*US*) girlfriend; used by either gender. [abbr.]

g.f.o. *n.* (*also* **g.f.u**) [1940s+] (*orig. US milit.*) a lazy, incompetent individual (cf. S.N.A.F.U. n.). [abbr. *general fuck-off, general fuck-up*]

G-girl *n.* [1930s] (*US*) a female government employee (cf. G-GUY n.). [G adj. + SE *girl*; fem. of G-MAN n.¹ (1)]

G-guy *n.* [1930s] (*US*) an agent of the FBI (cf. G-GIRL n.). [G adj. + GUY n.² (1); var. on G-MAN n.¹ (1)]

g.h. *n.* [1900s] stale or irrelevant news. [orig. printers' jargon *George Horne*, stale news; supposedly the name of a compositor given to recounting such irrelevances]

g'hal *n.* [mid-19C] (*orig. US*) the female companion of a 'lad', a young rowdy. ['Irish' pron. of GAL n. (1); for background *see* B'HOY n.]

'Ghan *n.* [20C+] (*Aus.*) **1** an Afghan; a term that is ext. to cover Turks and Arabs; thus *Ghan Town*, an area primarily populated by *'Ghans*. **2** as *the Ghan*, a train running between Port Augusta and Oodnadatta on the Central Australian Railway, its main passengers being Afghan camel teamsters, heading for their jobs; suspended in 1984, it was relaunched on an ext. track in 2004, joining the cities of Darwin and Adelaide. [abbr.]

ghanja *n. see* GANJA n.

ghastly *adj.* [mid-19C+] of people, objects and circumstances, horrible, shocking, unpleasant, distasteful. [weak ext. of SE use]

G-heat *n.* [1930s–60s] (*US*) trouble from, or agents of, federal law enforcement agencies. [G adj. + HEAT n.³ (1)]

ghedis *n. see* GEETUS n.

ghee *n.*¹ [20C+] (*US*) a man, a fellow. [SE *guy*]

ghee *n.*² *see* GUEE n.

gheeser *n. see* GEEZER n.¹ (1).

ghelt *n. see* GELT n.

gherkin *n.* [1930s+] (*Aus. prison*) the penis; usu. in JERK ONE'S GHERKIN v.

ghet *n. see* GET n.¹ (3).

ghetto *adj.* [1990s+] (*US*) **1** second-rate, old-fashioned, inferior. **2** superior, first-rate. **3** tough, aggressive, confrontational. [SE

ghetto; (1) negative connotations; (2) bad = good model; (3) perceived positive connotations]

ghetto bird *n.* [1990s+] (*US Black*) a police helicopter. [the use of police surveillance helicopters above ghetto areas]

ghettoblaster *n.* (*also* **ghetto box, ghetto buster, ghetto guitar**) [1980s+] a large stereo tape recorder-cum-radio carried by youths. [its orig. link to Black ghetto youths; thus derog. stereotyping; SE *ghetto* + *blaster*/BOX n.⁵ (7)/*buster*/*guitar*]

ghetto booty *n.* [2000s] (*US Black*) attractive female buttocks. [GHETTO adj. (2) + BOOTY n. (2)]

ghetto champagne *n.* [2000s] (*US Black*) cheap, potent liquor.

ghettofabulous *adj.* [1990s+] (*US Black*) referring to anything of quality and related to the ghetto. [SE *ghetto*/GHETTO adj. (2) + SE *fabulous*]

ghetto guitar *n. see* GHETTOBLASTER n.

ghetto onion *n.* [2000s] (*US Black*) a large, well-rounded pair of buttocks. [GHETTO adj. (2) + ONION n.¹ (4)]

ghetto sled *n.* [1990s+] (*US Black*) a large, 70s-model automobile. [SE *ghetto*/GHETTO adj. (1) + SLED n. (1)]

ghetto star *n.* [1990s+] (*US Black gang*) a leading gangster. [*ghetto*/GHETTO adj. (2) + SE *star*/STAR n.² (7)]

ghetto thing *n.* [1990s+] (*US Black*) anything pertaining to Black cultural identity. [SE *ghetto*/GHETTO adj. (2) + THING n.⁵ (5)]

ghinny *see under* GUINEA.

ghinzo *n. see* GINZO n.

ghoef *see under* GOEF.

ghomey *n. see* GOM n.².

ghost *n.*¹ **1** [mid-19C] (*US*) a photograph. **2** [late 19C+] an individual who does the work on behalf of the person who is publicly credited. **3** [1900s–30s] (*US*) a paymaster or cashier. **4** [1950s+] (*US*) (*also* **phantom**) a fictitious name created for fraudulent purposes. **5** [1960s+] (*drugs*) LSD (cf. A n.³). **6** [1970s+] (*US Black*) a White person.

ghost *n.*² **1** [1920s–50s] (*US drugs*) an opium smoker. **2** [2000s] a crack cocaine addict.

ghost *n.*³ [1930s] (*US Und.*) a beggar who simulates the symptoms of tuberculosis in order to excite sympathy.

ghost *n.*⁴ [1960s] (*Aus.*) a creditor. [they give bad debtors an unpleasant fright when they appear]

ghost *n.*⁵ [1970s+] (*US campus*) an absentee, someone who has opted out of normal social life.

ghost *v.*¹ [late 19C+] (*orig. US*) to shadow, to follow surreptitiously.

ghost *v.*² (*US*) **1** [1920s+] to write a book or article for someone else who takes the credit. **2** [1980s+] to share lodgings or a hotel room with someone, unbeknown to the proprietor.

ghost *v.*³ **1** [1960s] (*US prison*) to escape from jail. **2** [1970s+] (*US/UK prison*) to move a prisoner from one prison to another during the night, both departure and arrival taking place when the other prisoners are locked in their cells; thus *ghosting*, the late-night/early-hours transfer of prisoners from one prison to another with the intention of avoiding riots, frustrating external investigations etc. **3** [2000s] (*US Black*) to leave, to go somewhere. [(2) such prisoners are 'spirited away']

ghostbusting *n.* [1980s+] (*drugs*) when taking a drug, usu. heroin, cocaine or crack cocaine, searching for every particle of it. [play on film title *Ghostbusters* (1984)]

ghost job *n.* [1950s+] (*US*) material written by a ghost writer. [GHOST v.² (1) + JOB n.⁴]

ghost-story *n.* [late 19C–1960s] (*US tramp*) a fanciful or lying story; esp. a romantic story of tramp life.

ghost train *n.* [1970s+] (*UK/US prison*) the transfer of prisoners, under cover of night, from one jail to another. [GHOST v.³ (2) + SE *train*]

ghost turds *n.* [1960s+] (*US*) fluff that collects under beds and furniture. [SE *ghost* + TURD n. (1)]

ghost walks, the *phr.* [early 19C+] (*orig. theatre*) a phr. indicating that weekly salaries are about to be given out. [the *ghost* is a joc. ref. to that of Hamlet's father]

ghoul *n.* **1** [mid-19C–1920s] (*US Und./police*) a man who attempts to blackmail a woman who is deceiving her husband. **2** [late 19C] (*US*) a grave robber. **3** [1900s] (*Aus.*) an undertaker. **4** [1900s–10s] (*Aus.*) a morgue attendant. **5** [1940s–70s] (*US*) an unattractive-looking woman.

ghoul *v. see* GOAL *v.*

ghoulie *n.* [1960s+] (*US*) a low-budget horror film depicting excessive violence. [SE *ghoul*]

ghow *n. see* GOW *n.*[1].

g.i. *v.* [1940s+] to extinguish a cigarette before it is fully smoked, so that it can be re-lit later. [the practice of US soldiers or GIs]

giant-killer *n.* [1930s–40s] (*US*) whisky. [its illusory effects]

giant powder *n.* [late 19C–1940s] (*US*) a brand of dynamite. [the orig. brandname]

gib *n.* [late 19C] a prison. [abbr. *Gibraltar*, orig. a convict settlement to which prisoners were transported up until 1875]

gibber *n.*[1] [mid-18C] a horse dealer. [? SE *jib*, of a horse, to back away, to refuse to go forward]

gibber *n.*[2] *see* JIBBER *n.*[1].

gibble-gabble *n.* [17C; 1910s–20s] nonsense. [GABBLE *n.* (1) + redup.]

gibbs *n. see* JIB *n.*[1] (4).

gibby *n.* [1960s] (*US Black*) a reckless, foolhardy person. [Los Angeles use; ? dial. *gib*, a tom-cat]

gibface *n.* [mid-late 19C] an ugly person, esp. one with a heavy lower jaw. [Hotten (1860) states 'properly the lower lip of a horse' but this is not in *OED* or *EDD*; poss. mistake for dial. *gib*, the upper lip of a fish; note also dial. *gib*, a hook, thus *gib-nosed*, hook-nosed]

giblets *n.* **1** [mid-16C] the male genitals. **2** [mid-late 19C] (*also jiblets*) the intestines; thus an obese man. **3** [1990s+] the vagina, esp. with pronounced labia.

gibroney *n.* [1960s] (*US*) an Italian (cf. DAGO *n.*). [? JIBONE *n.* (3)]

gibs *n.*[1] [1980s] (*US prison*) the buttocks, the anus. [SE *giblets*]

gibs *n.*[2] *see* JIB *n.*[1] (4).

gib teenuck *n.* [mid-19C+] a large vagina, lit. 'big cunt'. [backsl.]

gib teesurbs *n.* [mid-19C+] big breasts, usu. said of a passing woman. [backsl.]

GI bug *n. see* GIs *n.*

gick *n.* **1** [1950s] (*US*) viscous matter. **2** [1990s+] (*Irish*) anything disgusting, esp. excrement; thus *give someone the gick*, to disgust. [var. on GUCK *n.*]

gicker *n.* [2000s] (*Irish*) the buttocks or anus. [GICK *n.* (2)]

gicky *adj.* [1990s+] (*Irish*) disgusting. [GICK *n.* (2)]

GI craps *n. see* GIs *n.*

giddie *n.* [1990s+] (*US campus*) **1** sexual activity. **2** something pleasing, attractive. [? it makes one SE *giddy*]

giddyack *n.* [2000s] (*US Black*) one's own area.

giddyap *n.* (*also* **giddyup**) [1920s–30s] (*US*) a racehorse. [SE *giddyap!* a sound made to urge a horse forward]

giddy goat *n.*[1] [20C+] a fool (cf. AIREDALE *n.*). [backform. f. PLAY THE GIDDY GOAT *v.*]

giddy goat *n.*[2] [1920s+] (*Aus.*) the Totalizator. [rhy. sl. = TOTE, THE *n.* (1)]

giddy gout *n.* [20C+] (*Aus.*) a boy scout. [rhy. sl.; note popular juv. rhyme 'Giddy, giddy gout, your shirt is hanging out!']

giddy kipper *n.* [late 19C–1910s] a young man about town. [SE *giddy*, frivolous, excitable; thus an essentially ludicrous persona]

giddyup *n. see* GIDDYAP *n.*

giddy whilk *n. see* WHILK *n.*

giddy young whelp *n.* (*also* **giddy young whelk**) [late 19C–1910s] a young man about town. [SE *giddy*, frivolous, excitable + *whelp*, a child; *whelk* is a play on *whelp*]

gidget *n. see* GADGET *n.*

gidgy *n.* [1950s–60s] (*US*) **1** an affectionate tickling under the

chin or caressing, usu. directed at an infant. **2** romantic caressing. ['baby talk' *gidgy, gidgy, gidgy*; (2) f. (1)]

gietus *n. see* GEETUS *n.*

gieve *n.* [1930s] (*US Black/prison*) talk, esp. when misleading. [JIVE *n.*[1] (2)]

gieve *v.* [1930s] (*US Black/prison*) to deceive; to confide in. [JIVE *v.*[1] (2)]

giffed *adj.* [1970s+] tipsy, drunk. [abbr. *t.g.i.f.*, thank God it's Friday, i.e. time to stop work and go out for pleasure]

giffle gaffle *n.* [mid-19C] nonsense. [? dial. *jiffle*, shuffling, confusion]

giffy *n. see* JIFFY *n.*

gift *n.* **1** [mid-19C] in ext. use of (3), used of a person. **2** [mid-19C] (*UK Und.*) anything that has been stolen and then is sold off cheaply. **3** [mid-19C+] anything seen as especially easy, requiring no effort to perform or obtain.

gifted *adj.* [1920s+] (*Can.*) homosexual. [an ironic use of the common suggestion that 'despite' being gay, so-and-so is 'very gifted']

gift of the gab *n.* (*also* **gift of the gob, gift o' gab**) [mid-17C+] articulacy, charm, persuasiveness. [GAB *n.* (1)/GOB *n.*[1] (1); *gob* appears to have come first]

gift that keeps on giving, the *phr.* [1980s+] (*US campus*) venereal disease. [joc. use of an advertising slogan]

gig *n.*[1] (*also* **gigg**) **1** [late 14C–19C] a flighty young woman. **2** [mid-17C–early 19C] the female genitals. **3** [1950s] (*Aus.*) a young woman. [ME *gig*, a foolish, coquettish, or lewd young woman + ? SE *gig*, a light carriage; thus something one 'rides']

gig *n.*[2] (*also* **gigg**) **1** [mid-17C–early 19C] the nose. **2** [mid–19C] the mouth. [ety. unknown]

gig *n.*[3] (*also* **gige, gigg**) [18C–mid-19C] a door. [GIGGER *n.*[1] (1)]

gig *n.*[4] **1** [late 18C–mid-19C] a term of disparagement. **2** [1940s+] (*Aus.*) (*also* **gighead**) a fool, an idiot; thus *act the gig*, to pretend to be a fool when caught in a criminal act. [UK dial. *gig*, a flighty fellow, a trifler]

gig *n.*[5] **1** [late 18C+] (*Irish*) a joke, fun. **2** [20C+] (*orig. US*) business, state of affairs. **3** [20C+] (*orig. US*) a musical performance or act at a particular venue. **4** [1940s+] a job, an occupation. **5** [1950s+] (*US teen*) an event, a party. **6** [1950s+] (*US Black*) a jazz party or jam session. **7** [1950s+] (*US*) a trick or swindle. **8** [1950s+] (*US Und.*) a criminal job; a criminal charge. **9** [1960s] (*Aus.*) a successful coup. **10** [1960s+] (*US*) one's special interest, practice or plan. **11** [1980s] any event. **12** [1980s+] (*US campus*) a brief sexual entanglement. [*HDAS* sees (1), and thus subseq. defs., as development of gambling use at GIG *n.*[7]]

gig *n.*[6] [mid-late 19C] a farthing. [? GRIG *n.*[1]]

gig *n.*[7] [mid-19C–1960s] (*US*) **1** a set of 3 numbers forming a bet in 'policy' or 'numbers' gambling. **2** by ext., any set of 3. [ety. unknown]

gig *n.*[8] **1** [late 19C] one who wears spectacles. **2** [1920s] (*US*) an eye. **3** [1920s+] (*Aus.*) a look, a glance. **4** [1970s+] (*Aus.*) an inquisitive person, a 'busybody'. [abbr. GIG-LAMPS *n.*]

gig *n.*[9] (*also* **giggy**) [20C+] the anus. [ety. unknown; ? link to GIG *n.*[1] (2) + note late 17C *gig*, a hole in the ground for drying flax or gig]

gig *n.*[10] **1** [1900s–40s] (*US*) a goading or gibing. **2** [1970s] (*US campus*) a disciplinary report. [ety. unknown]

gig *n.*[11] **1** [1920s+] (*US*) a gigolo. **2** [1950s] (*Aus.*) one who watches others working. **3** [1980s+] (*US campus*) a dedicated womanizer. [abbr. SE *gigolo*]

gig *n.*[12] **1** [1930s+] (*Aus.*) an informer. **2** [1930s+] (*Aus.*) a detective, an intrusive person; an eavesdropper. **3** [1950s+] (*Aus. prison*) a visitor, esp. a busybody. **4** [1970s] (*Aus.*) a visitor, a stranger. [abbr. FIZGIG *n.*[2]]

gig *n.*[13] [1950s] (*W.I.*) a dumpling that resembles a top. [SE *gig*, a whipping top]

gig *v.*[1] **1** [18C; 1950s+] to look at, to stare. **2** [1920s+] (*Aus.*) (*also*

gig about) to look on when one ought to be working. [GIG n.[8] (3); (1) 1950s+ Aus.]

gig v.[2] [mid-18C] to have anal intercourse. [ety. unknown; but note GIG n.[1] (2) and GIG n.[9]]

gig v.[3] [late 18C–early 19C] to hamstring (an animal). [ety. unknown]

gig v.[4] [late 19C+] (Aus./US) to mock, to tease; to irritate, to annoy. [? SE gig, to fool, to hoax]

gig v.[5] [1910s–60s] (US) to cheat or swindle. [? SE gig, to spear with a gig, a form of fish-spear]

gig v.[6] **1** [1930s+] (also gig around) orig. music business, to play at a particular venue, to perform. **2** [1970s] (US campus) to give a party. **3** [1970s] (US) to work, esp. at a number of short-lived jobs. **4** [1990s+] to go to a musical performance. **5** [2000s] to socialize. [GIG n.[5] (3)]

gig v.[7] [1980s+] (US campus) to have a single night's sex with someone. [GIG n.[11]/GIG n.[5] (12)]

gig about v. see GIG v.[1] (2).

gig around v. see GIG v.[6] (1).

gige n. see GIG n.[3].

gigg see also under GIG.

gigg n. see JIG n.[2] (1).

gigger n.[1] **1** [mid-16C–19C] a door. **2** [18C–early 19C] (UK Und.) (also jigger) a whipping post. [JIGGER n.[1] (1)]

gigger n.[2] [late 19C] one who wears spectacles. [GIG-LAMPS n. (1); the locus classicus was its use as the bespectacled Rudyard Kipling's schoolboy nickname and used as such for his fictional alter ego, 'Beetle', in Stalky & Co. (1899)]

gigger out! excl. [2000s] (US prison) a shout of warning.

giggle n. **1** [20C+] (also giggles) anything amusing, enjoyable, esp. if frowned upon. **2** [1940s–60s] a group of children or girls. [note Cotgrave, Dict. French and English Tongues (1611): Gadrouillette, minx, gigle, flirt]

giggle adj. [1970s] (Aus.) ridiculous, comical.

giggle academy n. (also giggling academy) [1940s+] (US) a psychiatric institution.

giggle and titter n. (also chirrup and titter, laugh…, smile…) [20C+] bitter beer. [rhy. sl.]

giggle bin n. [1980s] (Aus.) a psychiatric institution.

gigglebox n. [1960s] (US) a girl or child who is prone to giggling.

giggle dust n. [1990s+] (US drugs) cocaine (cf. BIRDIE POW-DER n.).

giggle-factory n. [1910s+] (Aus./N.Z.) a psychiatric institution.

giggle-grass n. see GIGGLEWEED n.

giggle-house n. [1910s+] (Aus./N.Z.) a psychiatric institution.

giggle-juice n. [1930s–40s] (Aus./US) alcohol.

gigglemug n. [late 19C] a face that is always smiling. [MUG n.[1] (2)]

giggler n. [early 18C–19C] (UK Und.) a young woman, esp. a prostitute. [SE giggle or ? GIG n.[1] (1)]

giggles n. see GIGGLE n. (1).

giggle-smoke n. see GIGGLEWEED n.

giggle-soup n. [1930s–40s] (US) strong alcohol.

gigglestick n.[1] [20C+] (orig. US) the penis (cf. BAT n.[7]). [rhy. sl. (although not the rhy. sl. format of full phr.) = PRICK n. (2); the word may be equally placed among the various terms that equate the penis with 'weapon' or laughter]

gigglestick n.[2] **1** [1920s+] (Aus.) a swizzlestick, used for stirring cocktails. **2** [1930s+] cannabis; a cannabis cigarette (cf. BAT n.[8]; BOMB n.[4]). [one of the effects of alcohol or cananbis is to improve (or so it appears) one's sense of humour; (2) STICK n.[9] (3)]

giggle-water n. [1920s+] (orig. US) **1** alcohol, esp. whisky or gin. **2** champagne.

giggleweed n. (also giggle-grass, giggle-smoke) [1930s+] (drugs) cannabis (cf. AFRICAN BUSH n.; BOMB n.[4]). [one of the drug's effects is to improve (or so it appears) one's sense of humour]

giggling academy n. see GIGGLE ACADEMY n.

giggling gas n. [1940s–50s] (US Black/teen) nitrous oxide.

giggling gear n. [1960s] the mouth.

giggling-pin n. [20C+] (US) the penis. [PIN n.[1] (1) + the ability of the penis to make both partners 'giggle' during sex]

giggly-guts n. [1970s+] (US) a giggly person. [SE giggle + -GUTS sfx]

giggy n. see GIG n.[9].

gighead n. see GIG n.[4] (2).

GI gin n. [1960s+] (orig. US milit.) cough syrup with a high alcohol content popular with addicts when heroin supplies are short.

gig-lamps n. (also gigs, jig-lamps) **1** [mid-19C+] spectacles; thus as a nickname for one who wears them. **2** [late 19C–1900s] (US) jewellery; thus gig-lamped, wearing jewellery. **3** [1900s] one who wears spectacles. **4** [1900s–30s] eyes. [SE gig-lamps, the 2 lights placed to either side of a gig or light carriage]

giglet n. (also goglet) [mid-16C–18C] a young woman, esp. a prostitute. [14C SE giglet, a lewd, wanton woman]

giglot n. [mid-16C–17C] a prostitute. [14C SE giglot, a giddy, laughing, romping girl haberdasher]

gigo phr. [1960s+] a phr. implying that one cannot expect poor input to produce, by some magic, excellent output. [computer jargon; abbr. garbage in, garbage out; pron. 'gyego']

gigolo v. [1980s+] (US Black) **1** to steal a friend's lover, to cheat on one's lover or partner. **2** to fool, to hoax, to deceive. [SE gigolo, a professional male dancing-partner or escort; a 'kept' man. Formed c.1920 as a masc. version of the French gigole, a tall, thin woman and hence a woman of the streets or public dancehalls. One 'who lives off women's money […] one of those incredible and pathetic male creatures, who, for ten francs, would dance with any woman wishing to dance in the cafés, hotels, and restaurants of France' (Woman's Home Companion, 1922)]

gigs n. see GIG-LAMPS n.

gigster n. [1990s+] (teen) **1** one who attends a rock concert or similar event. **2** one who performs at concerts. [GIG v.[6] + -STER sfx]

gigunda adj. (also gigundo, gigundus) [1970s] (US campus) gigantic. [cod Lat.]

GI haircut n. [1940s+] (US) a very short haircut, imported into civilian life by former soldiers.

GI Jane n. [1940s+] (US) a female member of the armed forces. [SAmE GI + generic use of Jane]

GI Joe n. [1930s+] (US) an American soldier. [SAmE GI + generic use of Joe]

gil n. see GILL n.[1] (2).

Gilbey's gin n. [1990s+] the chin. [rhy. sl.]

gilded moonshine n. [early 19C] sham IOUs or other bills of credit that have no actual financial backing. [MOONSHINE n. (1)]

gilder n. [1900s] (UK Und.) a sixpence gilded so as to counterfeit a half-sovereign.

Giles's breed n. see ST GILES'S BREED n.

gilgadget n. see GILLGADGET n.

gilhickie n. [1930s+] anything for which one has forgotten the name. [naut. use gilguy, a gadget + DOHICKEY n.[1] (1)]

gilkes (for the jigger) n. [17C] skeleton keys or picklock tools. [? GILT n.[2] (2) (+ JIGGER n.[1] (1))]

gill n.[1] **1** [late 16C–1950s] a gullible person. **2** [19C–1910s] (also gil) a general term for a man. **3** [early 19C] an interfering person. **4** [late 19C] (UK Und.) oneself.

gill n.[2] **1** [20C+] (W.I.) a penny; then 3 farthings. **2** [1950s] (US) a dollar.

gill n.[3] see JILL n.

gill v. [early 18C] to flirt, to tease. [GILL-FLIRT n.]

gill-ale n. [late 17C–early 18C] ale used for medicinal purposes. [SE gill, a quarter of a pint, would be a suitably small measure]

Gillette v. [1930s] (US) to adulterate whisky. [play on the Gillette safety razor which cuts/CUT v.[10] (1)]

gill-flirt n. (also gill-flurt, jill-flirt) [late 16C–19C] **1** a flirt, a tease; a prostitute. **2** a proud, vain woman. [SE *gill*, a lass, a wench + *flirt*]

gillgadget *n.* (*also* **gilgadget**) [1930s+] (*US*) anything for which one has forgotten the name. [? naut. jargon *gilguy*, a gadget]

Gillian *n. see* JILL n.

gillie *n. see* GILLY n.

gillie potters *n.* [1950s+] **1** pig's trotters. **2** the human feet. [rhy. sl.; (2) = TROTTER n.¹ (1); ult. proper name of comedian *Gillie Potter* (1887–1975)]

gilliflower *n. see* GILLYFLOWER n.

gilligan (hitch) *n.* (*also* **gilligan guzzler**) [1930s–50s] (*US Und.*) a stranglehold. [US naut. jargon *gilligan hitch*, an out-of-the-ordinary or speedily tied knot/GUZZLE n.¹ (1); Ersine, *Underworld and Prison Slang* (1933), suggests 'Mr. *Gilligan*, an old-time strong-arm actor']

gills *n.* **1** [17C+] (*also* **gils**) the cheeks; often in phrs., e.g. *red/pink in the gills*, embarrassed; GREEN ABOUT THE GILLS phr. **2** [early–late 19C] the corners of a stand-up shirt-collar. **3** [mid–late 19C] (*US*) the mouth. [SE *gill*, a fish's breathing apparatus, situated on each side of the neck]

gilly *n.* (*also* **gillie**) [late 19C–1930s] (*US*) a yokel or simpleton; also attrib. (cf. BLOOTER n.). [? GILL n.¹ (1)]

gillyflower *n.* (*also* **gilliflower**) [early 19C] a man who wore a yellow handkerchief round his neck. [SE *gillyflower*, the clove-pink (*Dianthus caryophyllus*); note Williams for refs. to 17C use of *gillyflower* as a metaphor for prostitute]

gilpin *n.*¹ [1930s] (*US*) a stupid or gullible person. [GILLY n.]

gilpin *n.*² *see* JOHN GILPIN n.

gils *n. see* GILLS n. (1).

gilt *n.*¹ [late 16C–19C] gold, money (cf. CANARY n.⁵). [SE *gilt*, silver plate, ult. Ger. *gelt*, although this means gold]

gilt *n.*² (*UK Und.*) **1** [early 17C–early 19C] a burglar. **2** [late 17C–mid-19C] a skeleton key. [ety. unknown]

gilt *n.*³ [late 17C–early 18C] 'a slut or light housewife' (B.E.). [? SE *gilt*, a young sow or female pig]

gilt dubber *n.* **1** [late 17C–early 19C] (*UK Und.*) an expert picklock. **2** [late 19C] (*US Und.*) a hotel thief. [GILT n.² (2) + DUBBER n.¹]

gilt-edged *adj.* [mid-19C+] first-rate, absolutely dependable. [lit. 'with gilded edges']

gilter *n.* [late 17C–mid-19C] a house-breaker who employs a skeleton key. [GILT n.² (2)]

gilt-horn *n.* [18C] a complacent cuckold. [GILT n.¹ + HORN n.¹ (1); presumably he is paid for the 'use' of his wife]

gim *v.* [1940s] (*US Black*) to stare at. [? *give me the eye*]

gimbal-jawed *adj.* (*also* **gimber-jawed**) [mid-19C] very talkative. [SE *gimbal*, 'a contrivance by means of which articles for use at sea (esp. the compass and the chronometer) are suspended so as to keep a horizontal position. It usually consists of a pair of rings moving on pivots in such a way as to have a free motion in two directions at right angles, so as to counteract the motion of the vessel' (*OED*)]

gimblet-eyed *adj.* [late 18C–early 19C] squinting.

gimcrack *n.* **1** [early 17C–early 19C] a fop, an affectedly showy person. **2** [late 17C–mid-19C] a pert young woman. **3** [19C] the female genitals. [SE *gimcrack*, a showy but insubstantial trifle]

gi' me breeze *n.* [1950s+] (*W.I.*) ragged, torn, old work clothes (through which the wind blows).

gimix *n.* [1920s–40s] (*US*) a gadget. [SE *gimmicks*]

gimme *n.*¹ [1930s–60s] (*Aus.*) an acquisitive, greedy woman. [SE *give me*]

gimme *n.*² (*also* **gimmie**) **1** [1960s+] something given away for free. **2** [2000s] (*UK Und.*) a bribe.

gimme *phr.* [late 19C+] (*orig. US*) give me. [mispron./sp. of SE *give me*]

gimme cap *n.* [1970s+] (*US*) a baseball cap carrying the logo of a sports team, manufacturer or other commercial institution.

[GIMME phr.; the practice of emblazoning objects with a logo and offering them free in order to spread the brandname began with cigarette papers, which were given away free with the purchase of loose tobacco. Buyers demand: *give me...a pack of papers, a cap or whatever is on offer*]

gimme girl *n.* [1990s+] (*US*) a greedy, materialistic young woman. [GIMME phr. + SE *girl*]

gimmer *n.* [late 18C–19C] an old woman. [Scot. *gimmer*, a derog. term for a woman; ult. a young female sheep]

gimmers *n. see* GIMS n.

gimme's, the *n.* [1910s–60s] **1** greediness. **2** (*US Black*) (*also* **gimmies**) an irritable mood, usu. of women, thus a menstrual period. [GIMME phr.]

gimmick *n.* **1** [1910s+] a tricky or ingenious device, gadget, idea, esp. one adopted for the purpose of attracting attention or publicity. **2** [1920s–30s] (*US*) a foolish person. **3** [1920s+] (*orig. US*) a gadget; spec. a contrivance for dishonestly regulating a gambling game or an article used in a conjuring trick. **4** [1920s+] (*US Und.*) that which helps to implement a criminal scheme. **5** [1930s] (*US tramp*) a lame person. **6** [1940s] (*US*) affairs, business. **7** [1960s] (*US*) the penis (cf. BAUBLE n.). [ety. unknown, but note US journal *Words* (November 1936): 'The word gimac means "a gadget". It is an anagram of the word magic, and is used by magicians the same way as others use the word "thing-a-ma-bob"']

gimmick *v.* [1960s] (*US*) to adapt, to alter the function, typically of an electronic component. [GIMMICK n. (3)]

gimmicks *n.* [1960s+] (*drugs*) the equipment used for injecting a narcotic drug.

gimmicky *adj.* [1950s+] foolish, esp. in the context of pursuing the current fashions. [GIMMICK n. (1)]

gimmie *n. see* GIMME n.².

gimmies *n. see* GIMME'S, THE n. (2).

gimming *n.* [1940s] (*US Black*) staring at, gazing at. [GIMS n.]

gimp *n.*¹ [late 19C+] **1** (*US*) courage, bravery, spirit. **2** (*Irish/US*) swagger, elegance. [Scot. *gimp*, slender, neat]

gimp *n.*² **1** [1920s+] a cripple, esp. a crippled beggar. **2** [1920s+] a limp. **3** [1920s+] a fool. **4** [1970s+] (*orig. US campus*) a weakling, an inadequate. **5** [1990s+] a person dressed head to toe in a leather or rubber bondage suit, usu. with a zip over the mouth. **6** [1990s+] (*UK juv.*) a fool; a toady. [? GAMMY n.²; note letter passed on by Terence Blacker, 13 June 2000: 'When I lived in Adelaide, Australia, in 1986 the word "Gimp" was slang for a mentally retarded person or with the advent of political correctness now known as someone with learning difficulties. It derived from the acronym for The Glenelg Institute for Mental Patients and had expanded to encompass all those South Australians perceived to have some form of mental aberration']

gimp *adj. see* GIMPY adj.².

gimp *v.* **1** [1920s+] to limp. **2** [1960s] to cripple. **3** [1970s+] (*US campus*) (*also* **gimp up**) to ruin, to spoil. [GIMP n.² (1)]

gimped in *adj.* [1970s+] (*US campus*) irregularly shaped, dented. [north. dial. *gimp*, to give a scalloped or indented outline to]

gimped out *adj.* [1990s+] messed-up. [GIMP v. (3)]

gimped up *adj.* **1** [1940s+] (*US*) crippled, disabled. **2** [1970s+] (*US campus*) confused, at a loss, mixed up. [GIMP v.]

gimper *n.* (*also* **gimpster**) [1970s+] (*US*) a disabled person. [GIMP n.² (1); note newspaper jargon *gimper*, a human interest 'sob' story featuring illness, invalidity etc]

gimp-legged *adj.* [1960s] (*US*) limping. [GIMP n.² (1) + SE *legged*]

gimp pram *n.* [1990s+] a wheelchair. [GIMP n.² (1) + SE *pram*]

gimpster *n. see* GIMPER n.

gimp stick *n.* [1930s] (*US*) a crutch or walking-stick. [GIMP n.² (1) + SE *stick*]

gimpty *adj.*¹ *see* GIMPY adj.¹.

gimpty *adj.*² *see* GIMPY adj.² (1).

gimp up *v. see* GIMP v. (3).

gimpy *n.* [1920s+] **1** a cripple, often as a nickname. **2** a fool, someone who is inadequate in some manner. [GIMP n.²]

gimpy *adj.*¹ (*also* **gimpty**) [mid-19C+] (*US*) spritely, brave, energetic. [GIMP n.¹ (1)]

gimpy *adj.*² (*also* **gimp**) **1** [1920s+] (*also* **gimpty**) crippled. **2** [1970s] botched, second-rate. **3** [1980s+] in ext. use of (1), a general term of abuse. **4** [2000s] homosexual. [GIMP n.² (1)]

gims *n.* (*also* **gimmers**) [1940s] (*US Black*) the eyes. [? misprint GLIM n.¹ (4)/GLIMMERS n. (1)]

gin *n.*¹ [19C+] (*Aus.*) **1** (*also* **blackgin**, **ginny**) a Black woman. **2** any woman. [Dharuk *diyin*, woman; also (quite coincidentally) the abbr. for *Aborigine*]

gin *n.*² [1960s+] (*US Black*) a street fight; thus *gin time*, time to fight. [GIN v.² (2)]

gin *n.*³ [1970s+] (*drugs*) cocaine. [? play on SE *gin*, an engine; cocaine makes one 'work' faster]

gin *n.*⁴ *see* GUINEA n.

gin *v.*¹ [mid-19C+] to drink gin.

gin *v.*² **1** [1910s–60s] (*US Black*) to thrash, to beat. **2** [1930s+] to fight, to scuffle. **3** [1940s–60s] to engage in sexual intercourse. [the threshing action of a cotton *gin*]

ginal *n.* (*also* **ginnal**, **jinal**, **jinnal**) [1920s+] (*W.I., Jam.*) a trickster, a confidence man. [an ironic play on SE *general*]

ginal *adj.* (*also* **ginnal**, **jinal**, **jinnal**) [1920s+] (*W.I., Jam.*) sharp, able to find quick efficient solutions to problems; thus *ginalism*, a philosophy that basically says that the end justifies any means, fair or foul. [? GINAL n. or abbr. SE *original*]

gina la salsa *n.* [1950s+] (*camp gay*) an Italian male effeminate homosexual. [ext. of camp gay nickname *gina* + Sp. *salsa*, sauce]

gin and fog *n.* [late 19C–1940s] a hoarse or broken-down voice. [? rhy. sl. = *frog* (in the throat)]

gin and French *n.* (*also* **gin and it**) [1930s+] gin and French or Italian vermouth. [abbr.]

gin and fuck-it *n.* [1960s] a woman, usu. a foreign au pair or tourist, who can allegedly be seduced for the price of a drink in pubs where such young women congregate.

Gin and Gospel Gazette *n.* [mid–late 19C] the *Morning Advertiser* newspaper. [its preoccupations]

gin and it *n. see* GIN AND FRENCH n.

gin and jag *n.* [1950s+] (*UK Und.*) a crime committed in an upmarket area. [GIN AND JAG BELT n.]

gin and Jag belt *n.* (*also* **gin and Jaguar belt**) [1960s+] (*UK Und.*) the wealthy Home Counties areas around London, esp. ripe for robbery; thus *gin and Jaguar bird*, a louche, raffish woman of this background, presumed, while prob. married, not to be averse to something 'on the side'. [SE *gin* + JAG n., both popular with the wealthy]

gin and lime *n.* [1940s] the number 9. [rhy. sl.]

gin-and-tatters *n.* [late 19C] a heavy drinker whose clothes have been reduced to rags.

gin and tidy *adj.* [late 19C] neat. [SE *gin* + SE *tidy*]

gin-banger *n.* [1910s] (*Aus.*) a man who sexually exploits Aborigine women. [GIN n.¹ (1) + BANG v.¹ (2)]

gin barrel *n.* [mid-19C] (*US*) a drunk.

gin blossom *n.* [1930s+] (*US*) a red nose or blotches resulting from drinking alcohol.

gin-bottle *n.* [late 19C] a 'dirty, abandoned, flabby, debased woman, generally over thirty; the victim of alcoholic abuse, within an ace of inevitable death' (Ware).

gin-bud *n.* [early 19C] a facial spot or ulcer resulting from excessive gin-drinking.

gin-burglar *n.* [1940s+] (*Aus.*) a man who sexually exploits Aborigine women; thus *gin-burglary*, having sex with an Aborigine. [GIN n.¹ (1) + *burglar*]

ginch *n.* **1** [1930s+] an attractive woman, esp. when seen as a sex object. **2** [1950s+] the vagina; thus the act of sexual intercourse.

3 [1970s] (*gay*) an attractive young man. [ety. unknown, but note dial. *ginch*, a small piece]

ginchy *adj.* [1950s+] attractive, sexy. [GINCH n. (1) + sfx -*y*]

gin-crawl *n.* [late 19C] a tour of public houses for the purpose of drinking a series of gins. [SE *gin* + CRAWL n. (2)]

gin-cuddler *n.* (*also* **gin-dozzler**) [1950s–70s] (*Aus.*) a man who sexually exploits Aborigine women. [GIN n.¹ (1) + SE *cuddler* (+ *dozzler*, ety. unknown; ? SE *dazzle* or DO v.¹ (1))]

giner *n.* [2000s] (*US campus*) the vagina. [clipping of SE *vagina*]

ging *n.* [20C+] (*Aus.*) a catapult. [it 'gingers up' its targets]

gingambobs *n.* [late 18C–19C] **1** toys, baubles. **2** the testicles (cf. BAUBLES n.; NICK-NACKS n.; THING n.²; THINGUMABOBS n.; THINGUMMIES n.; WHIBLIN n.; YOU KNOW WHERE n.). [SE *jiggumbob*]

ginge minge *n.* [1990s+] ginger female pubic hair. [abbr. SE *ginger* + MINGE n. (1)]

ginger *n.*¹ **1** [late 18C–early 19C] a cock with reddish plumage. **2** [late 19C+] a red-haired or sandy-haired person.

ginger *n.*² **1** [early–mid-19C] a showy, fast horse. **2** [mid-19C+] high spirits, verve, vigour.

ginger *n.*³ (*also* **ginger-cake**, **gingerer**, **ginger girl**) **1** [mid-19C–1900s] (*UK Und.*) a girl, poss. (2). **2** [1940s+] (*Aus.*) a prostitute who robs her customer of his wallet. **3** [1940s+] (*Aus.*) the act of robbing a prostitute's client; thus *gingering joint*, a brothel where such practices are common; *work a ginger*, for a prostitute to rob her customer. [? backform. f. SE *gingerly*, with extreme caution, i.e. the caution necessary to effect the theft]

ginger *n.*⁴ *see* GINGER (BEER) n.

ginger *v.* [1940s+] (*Aus.*) of a prostitute, to rob a client. [GINGER n.³ (2)]

ginger! *excl. see* SUGAR! excl. (2).

ginger ale *n.* [20C+] **1** (*Aus./US*) a jail. **2** (*Aus./N.Z.*) (*also* **steak and ale**) bail. **3** (*Aus.*) a tail. **4** (*Aus.*) the mail. [rhy. sl.]

ginger (beer) *n.* [1940s+] a male homosexual; also as adj. [rhy. sl. = QUEER n. (4)]

ginger beer *n.* (*Aus.*) **1** [1940s+] an engineer, in both civilian and milit. contexts. **2** [2000s] an ear. [rhy. sl.]

ginger (blue)! *excl.* [late 19C–1920s] (*US*) an excl. used to mock one who is seen as behaving in a socially unacceptable way.

gingerbread *n.*¹ [late 17C–mid-19C] money; thus *have the gingerbread*, to be rich (cf. BATTER n.⁴; CANARY n.⁵). [the gold colour]

gingerbread *n.*² *see* GINGER-CAKE n.¹.

gingerbread *n.*³ [1930s] the head. [rhy. sl.]

gingerbread-office *n.* [17C] a privy (cf. HOUSE OF OFFICE n.; LITTLE OFFICE n.; OFFICE n.²). [the colour of excrement/urine]

ginger-cake *n.*¹ (*also* **gingerbread**) [19C+] (*US*) a mulatto. [the ginger-toned shade of the person's skin]

ginger-cake *n.*² *see* GINGER n.³.

gingerer/ginger girl *n. see* GINGER n.³.

ginger-hackled *adj.* [late 18C] red-haired. [cock-fighting jargon, *ginger*, a red cock]

ginger-nob *n.* [20C+] a red-headed person. [NOB n.¹ (1)]

ginger-peachy *adj.* [1950s–70s] (*US*) splendid, usu. ironic. [ext. of PEACHY adj.]

ginger-pop *n.* [late 19C] a policeman (cf. BOTTLE (AND STOPPER) n.). [rhy. sl. = COP n.¹ (1)]

gingersnap *n.* [1940s–50s] (*US Black*) a Black person. [the colour]

ginger up *v.* [mid–late 19C] to enliven, to put spirit into. [SE f. 1890; f. the 18C technique of placing ginger in a horse's anus to make it more lively]

gingery *adj.* [1940s+] pertaining to homosexuals or homosexual culture. [GINGER (BEER) n.]

gingham *n.* [mid-19C–1910s] an umbrella, esp. one that is covered in gingham cloth.

gingleboy *n.* (*also* **jingleboy**) [17C] **1** a sovereign (£1 sterling); thus any gold coin (cf. CHING n.²). **2** one who possesses gold coins. [the noise it makes in one's pocket]

gingler *n. see* JINGLER n.¹.

gingumbob *n.* [late 17C–mid-19C] a trifle.

ginhead *n.* [1920s+] (*orig. US*) a gin drinker. [SE *gin* + -HEAD sfx (3)]

gin her up *v.* [late 19C] (*US*) to work hard, to infuse with energy. [SE *gin*, engine or var. GINGER UP v.]

gin-hunter *n. see* GIN-MASHER n.

ginicomtwig *v.* [late 16C–early 17C] to have sexual intercourse (cf. ARRIVE AT THE END OF THE SENTIMENTAL JOURNEY v.). [like THINGUMABOB n. it could also mean a 'nameless item' and is thus also a euph.]

ginigog *n. see* GUINEA BIRD n.[2] (2).

ginj *v.* [1940s] (*W.I.*) to fill with lies. [dial. *ginj*, to strangle, using a piece of wire; ult. fishing use *ginj*, to protect the line near the hook by twisting a piece of wire around it; thus, in turn, SE synon. *gange*]

gin-jockey *n.* [1950s+] (*Aus.*) a White man who enjoys sexual relations with Aborigine women. [GIN n.[1] (1) + SE *jockey*, i.e. play on RIDE v.[1] (1)]

gink *n.*[1] **1** [20C+] (*orig. US*) a useless, stupid person. **2** [1910s–20s] (*US tramp*) a tramp who worked seasonally or occasionally. **3** [1910s–60s] (*US*) a fellow, a person (not pej.); also as joc./affectionate address. **4** [1910s+] (*orig. US*) a peasant. **5** [1920s] (*US Und.*) a traitor. **6** [1940s+] (*US*) an East Asian (cf. BROWNIE n.[2]). [? link to Scot. *gink*, trick]

gink *n.*[2] [1950s+] (*Aus.*) a look, a glance. [? GIG n.[8] (3)]

gin ken *n.* [mid-18C–mid-19C] a gin shop. [SE *gin* + KEN n.[1] (1)]

ginky *adj.* [1960s–70s] (*US*) unfashionable or stupid-looking. [GINK n.[1] (1)]

gin lane *n.* [mid–late 19C] the mouth; the throat. [presumably acknowledging William Hogarth's celebrated engraving of 1751]

gin-masher *n.* (*also* **gin-hunter**) [1900s] (*Aus.*) a man who sexually exploits Aborigine women. [GIN n.[1] (1) + MASHER n.[1] (3)/SE *hunter*]

gin-mill *n.* **1** [mid-19C+] (*US*) (*also* **whiskey-mill**) a bar or nightclub, orig. a speakeasy specializing in cheap, and prob. adulterated, liquor; thus *gin-millist*, a bartender. **2** [1960s] a liquor store. [SE *gin* + *mill* + pun on *gin*, a type of mill]

ginnal *see under* GINAL.

ginned up *adj.*[1] (*also* **ginned**) [20C+] (*US*) drunk, tipsy (cf. ALED UP adj.). [SE *gin*]

ginned up *adj.*[2] [1920s] (*US*) dressed up. [ety. unknown; ? GINGER UP v. or the image of one who frequents 'gin palaces']

ginnery *n.* [mid-19C] a public house dedicated to the sale of gin.

ginney *see under* GUINEA.

ginnified *adj.* [late 19C] intoxicated by gin, or any other liquor.

ginning-up *n.* [1960s+] (*Can.*) a scolding, a telling-off. [fig. use of GIN v.[2] (1)]

ginny *n.*[1] [late 17C–early 19C] (*UK Und.*) 'an instrument to lift up a Grate, the better to Steal what is in the window' (B.E.). [JEMMY n.[3] (1), but note SE *gin*, engine, machine + dial. *ginny*, a simple form of crane]

ginny *n.*[2] [1980s] (*US Black*) the vagina. [abbr.]

ginny *n.*[3] *see* GIN n.[1] (1).

ginny *n.*[4] *see* GUINEA n.

ginny *adj.* **1** [late 19C] of the liver or kidneys, adversely affected by excessive gin drinking. **2** [20C+] very keen on gin. **3** [1920s+] (*US*) tipsy; also in fig. use. [SE *gin*]

ginny gall *n.* (*also* **guinea gall, jimmy gall**) [1900s–50s] (*US Black*) anywhere considered far away, unpleasant and culturally alien. [proper name *Guinea*, a region in West Africa]

gin-palace *n. see* GIN-TRAP n.

gin-shepherd *n.* [20C+] (*Aus.*) **1** a man who sexually exploits Aborigine women; thus *gin-shepherding*, searching for Aboriginal women for sexual purposes; also in fig. use. **2** a White man who attempts to prevent miscegenation between his peers and Aborigine women. [GIN n.[1] (1) + SE *shepherd*]

gin-shop/-sling *n. see* GIN-TRAP n.

gin-slinger *n.* [late 19C] (*US*) a bartender. [SE *gin* + SLINGER n.[1] (1)]

ginso *n. see* GINZO n.

gin-soak *n.* [1930s+] (*US*) an alcoholic, a gin-drinker. [SE *gin* + SOAK n.[1] (1)]

gin-spinner *n.* [late 18C–19C] **1** a distiller. **2** a dealer in spirits. **3** a wine-vault.

gin-stealer *n.* [1900s–20s] (*Aus.*) a man who sexually exploits Aborigine women. [GIN n.[1] (1) + SE *stealer*]

gin-trap *n.* (*also* **gin-palace, gin-shop, gin-sling**) [early 19C; 1950s] the mouth. [SE *gin* + SE *trap*/TRAP n.[3]/SE *palace*/*shop*/ SLING n.[1]]

gin-tub *n.* [mid-19C] a drunkard.

gin up *v.*[1] [late 19C–1920s] (*US*) to drink alcohol.

gin up *v.*[2] [1970s+] (*US*) to stir up, to enliven, to make ready. [fig. use of GIN v.[2]]

ginzo *n.* (*also* **ghinzo, ginso, guinzo, guinzola**) [1930s+] (*US*) **1** a derog. term for an Italian person or their language; also adj use (cf. DAGO n.). **2** any worthless person. [GUINEA n. (1)]

Giorgio Armani *n.* [1990s+] a sandwich. [rhy. sl. = SARNIE n.; ult. fashion designer *Giorgio Armani* (b.1935)]

gip *see also under* GYP.

gip! *excl.* [mid-17C] 'an expression of surprise, derision, or contempt addressed to a person = 'get out', 'go along with you' (*OED*).

gipe *n.* (*also* **gype**) [20C+] (*Ulster*) **1** a fool. **2** a clumsy, awkward person. **3** a person with long legs. **4** a foolish young woman. [Scot. *gipe*, an awkward person, a fool]

GI pill *n. see* GIs n.

gippo *see under* GYPO.

gippy *n.* **1** [1900s] an Egyptian cigarette. **2** [1910s+] an Egyptian, esp. an Egyptian soldier. **3** [1910s+] a gypsy. [pron./abbr.]

gippy *adj. see* GYPO adj.

gippy tummy *n. see* GYPPY TUMMY n.

gipsy *see also under* GYPSY n. and its combs.

gipsy *n.* **1** [mid-17C–early 18C] a hussy. **2** [19C] a term of address to a woman, esp. one with a dark, i.e. 'gypsy', complexion.

giraffe *n.* [mid-19C] the swindle, the deception; thus *come/play the giraffe*, to fool someone. [US milit. *giraffe*, a form of game]

giraffe *v.* [mid-19C] (*US*) to hoodwink. [GIRAFFE n.]

girl *n.*[1] **1** [mid-17C–19C] a (street-walking) prostitute (cf. AWAYDAY GIRL n.). **2** [late 18C+] one's sweetheart or girlfriend. **3** [19C+] (*US*) any Black woman, irrespective of age. **4** [late 19C+] (*US*) used in direct address to a man, without homosexual implication. **5** [20C+] a male homosexual, esp. a prostitute; also used in direct address as an insult. **6** [20C+] (*US Black*) a general form of address between 2 women, neither of whom need be a girl in terms of age. **7** [1940s+] (*gay*) used as an affectionate term of address between 2 homosexual men. **8** [1950s–60s] (*US*) a queen of any suit in cards. **9** [1990s+] (*US*) an insult aimed at a heterosexual male.

girl *n.*[2] [1950s+] (*drugs*) **1** cocaine (cf. AUNT NORA n.; BERNICE n.; CHARLOTTE n.; CORINNE n.; DAMA BLANCA n.; GIRLFRIEND n.[2]; GOLDEN GIRL n.[2]; HER n.[2]; JANE n.[3]; LADY n.[3]; LADY SNOW n.[2]; MAMA COCA n.; MARY JANE n.[2]; MISSY n.[2]; NITE NURSE n.; OLD LADY WHITE n.; OLD MADGE n.[2]; SOPHISTICATED LADY n.; WHITE GIRL n.; WHITE LADY n.[2]; WITCH, THE n.). **2** heroin. [the image of cocaine as a 'feminine' drug, the injecting of which gives a sexual thrill (although heroin, too, has that effect on some users), as opposed to heroin or BOY n.[7] (1), a 'masculine' drug, i.e. one that 'knocks you down'; (2) may be a misreading]

girl abductor *n.* [1900s–1910s] (*Aus.*) a tram conductor. [rhy. sl.]

girl about town *n. see* WOMAN ABOUT TOWN n.

girl and boy *n.* **1** [mid-19C–mid 20C] a saveloy. **2** [20C+] a toy. [rhy. sl.]

girl-boy *n.* **1** [late 16C; late 19C+] (*orig. US*) a feminine young man, an effeminate homosexual boy; also as general insult (cf.

BOY-GIRL n.[1]). **2** [1960s+] (*US prison*) a heterosexual prisoner who engages in homosexual acts.

girl-catcher *n.* [19C] the penis.

girl-deb *n. see* DEB n.[2].

girlery *n.* [19C] a brothel. [SE *girl* + sfx *-ery*, the place where an occupation is carried on]

girlesk *n.* (*also* **girlesque**) [1930s–50s] (*US*) a show featuring striptease women. [SE *girl* + *burlesque*]

girl Friday *n.* (*also* **gal Friday**) [1930s+] (*orig. US*) a female secretary or personal assistant. [*Man Friday*, Crusoe's servant in Daniel Defoe's *Robinson Crusoe* (1719) and thus fig. a male assistant]

girlfriend *n.[1]* **1** [1950s+] (*S.Afr. prison*) the male lover of another prisoner. **2** [1970s+] (*US Black*) a form of address from a man to a woman, not necessarily known. **3** [1980s+] a form of address between lesbians, not necessarily in a relationship. **4** [1980s+] a form of address between homosexual men. **5** [1990s+] (*orig. and mainly US Black*) a form of address between women. **6** [1990s+] (*US gay*) any friend, irrespective of gender/sexuality; a lesbian. **7** [1990s+] (*US Black*) a woman.

girlfriend *n.[2]* [1970s+] (*US Black*) cocaine. [ext. GIRL n.[2] (1)]

girl-getter *n.* [late 19C–1900s] an effeminate male. [? *girl-begetter*, an effeminate man would be unable to produce 'macho' boys]

girlie *n.* [late 19C+] a girl, irrespective of age although orig. young, usu. as a term of endearment.

girlie *adj.* (*also* **girl-girl**, **girlie-girlie**, **girly**) **1** [1910s+] (*orig. US*) used of a young woman employed in some form of the sex industry; thus *girlie book*, *girlie-magazine*, *girlie rag*, a pin-up magazine; *girlie-show*, a strip show; *girlie bar*, a bar or 'nightclub' at which the hostesses may double as prostitutes. **2** [1960s+] of a woman, sexually alluring. **3** [1990s+] of a man, effeminate.

girl of the town *n. see* WOMAN ABOUT TOWN n.

girlometer *n.* [mid–late 19C] the penis.

girl out *v.* [2000s] (*US*) of a man, to make another man into a 'female' homosexual. [GIRL n.[1] (5)]

girls, the *n.* **1** [early 19C+] a generic term for prostitutes considered as a group. **2** [1960s+] a generic term for male prostitutes. [GIRL n.[1] (1)/GIRL n.[1] (5)]

girls and boys *n.* [20C+] noise. [rhy. sl.]

girls are bandy at Urandangie, the *phr.* [1960s+] (*Aus.*) a phr. used to denote an unsatisfactory situation. [assonance]

girl's blouse *n. see* BIG GIRL'S BLOUSE n.

girl scout *n.* [1970+] (*US camp gay*) a soldier on leave and looking for sex.

girl-shop *n.* [late 19C] a brothel (cf. BANGING-SHOP n.). [GIRL n.[1] (1) + SE *shop*/SHOP n.[1] (1)]

girl show *n.* [late 19C] a ballet or review, usu. featuring chorus girls in revealing costumes.

girls together *phr.* (*also* **all girls together**) [1930s+] a phr. used to suggest that a woman is on close friendship terms with another woman or women.

girl-trap *n.* [late 19C] a dedicated womanizer.

girly *adj. see* GIRLIE adj.

girlyboy *n.* [2000s] a male homosexual (cf. BOY-GIRL n.[1]). [GIRL-BOY n. (1)]

GIs *n.* (*also* **GI bug**, **GI craps**, **GI trots**) [1940+] (*US*) diarrhoea; thus the *GI pill*, a pill designed to combat the malady (cf. AZTEC HOP n.). [i.e. the food poisoning to which soldiers posted abroad might be susceptible; SAmE *GI*, an American soldier + BUG n.[6] (3)/CRAP n.[3] (5)/TROTS, THE n.[2]]

gism *n. see* JISM n.

gismo *n. see* GIZMO n.

git *n.* [1920s+] a fool, a worthless person. [var. GET n.[1] (3)]

git *v. see* GET v.[1] (2).

git! *excl.* [mid-19C+] (*US*) go away! [GET v.[1] (2)]

gitbox *n.* (*also* **git**, **git flip**, **gitter**, **gitter box**) **1** [1930s+] (*US*) a guitar. **2** [1950s] (*US Black*) a juke box. [orig. jazz jargon]

gitch *n.* [1990s+] (*Can.*) male underpants. [ety. unknown; ? link to SE *breech(es)*]

git-down, the, *n. see* GET-DOWN, THE n.

git-down time *n.* [1960s+] (*US*) the start of a prostitute's working 'day', when she *gets down to business*. [GET DOWN v.[2] (7)]

git-'em-up guy *n.* [1930s] a hold-up man, a robber. [GET-'EM-UP adj., i.e. his demand *get your hands up!*]

gitfiddle *n.* [1930s+] (*US*) a guitar. [*git* (get) *your fiddle and play*]

git flip *n. see* GITBOX n.

git-go, the *n.* (*also* **the get-go**) [1960s+] (*orig. US Black*) the beginning, esp. in phr. *from the git-go*, from the beginning. [SE *get going*]

gitlet *n.* [1920s+] (*US Black*) an illegitimate child. [SE *get* + dimin. sfx *-let*]

gitney *n. see* JITNEY n.

GI trots *n. see* GIs n.

gitter *n. see* JITTER n.

gitter (box) *n. see* GITBOX n.

gitty-gap *n.* [1970s+] (*US campus*) a thing. [ety. unknown; ? a nonsense word, like the synon. THINGUMABOB n.]

git-up *n. see* GET-UP n.[2].

give *v.[1]* [mid-19C+] to allow someone a specified, limited period of time, e.g. *I'll give you 10 minutes*.

give *v.[2]* [mid-19C+] used as a reprimand in angry retorts, to indicate one's displeasure at the previous statement, e.g. *I'll give you 'forgot'*.

give *v.[3]* [late 19C] (*US*) to renege on one's debts or bills.

give *v.[4]* **1** [late 19C+] to impart information, esp. in dismissive phrs. *what are you giving me?* or *don't give me that*. **2** [1930s+] (*orig. US*) of a young woman, to be willing to engage in sexual intercourse; thus GIVE OUT v.[2] (2). **3** [1930s+] (*US*) to give up, to surrender.

give *v.[5]* [1930s+] (*orig. US*) to happen; usu. in phr. *what gives (with)...?*

give *v.[6]* [1950s] (*US Und.*) to be an active 'masculine' homosexual.

give! *excl.* **1** [late 19C+] (*orig. US*) explain! confess! **2** [1920s] an excl. of contempt.

give a belly *v.* [mid-17C; 20C+] (*W.I.*) to make a woman pregnant.

give a bit of hard for a bit of soft *v. see* GIVE HARD FOR SOFT v.

give a black eye *v.* [late 18C+] to finish off. [GIVE A BOTTLE A BLACK EYE v.]

give a blow *v.* [1960s+] (*drugs*) to blow marijuana smoke directly from the cigarette into someone else's mouth, achieved by reversing the joint in one's own mouth and blowing. [SE *blow*]

give a bottle a black eye *v.* [late 18C–early 19C] to drink a bottle almost to the bottom. [i.e. SE *finish*/FINISH v.]

give a cat's ass *v.* [1990s+] to care about someone or something, usu. in negative, e.g. *like I give a cat's ass*.

give a damn *v.* (*also* **give a dam**, **give a dang**) [1930s+] to care, usu. in negative use, e.g. *who gives a damn?* [backform. f. NOT GIVE A DAMN v.]

give a dig about *v.* [1910s–20s] to mock, to tease. [SE *dig*, a poke, a jab]

give a ducat to chapel *v.* [2000s] (*US prison*) to set up a victim to be killed. [DUCAT n. (1) + SE *chapel*, i.e. the funeral service]

give a fart *v. see* GIVE A FUCK v.

give a for instance *v.* [1950s] (*orig. US*) to give an example.

give-a-fuck *n.* (*also* **give-a-shit**) [1970s+] (*US*) the desire to do something, the state of being motivated towards or enthusiastic for. [GIVE A FUCK v./GIVE A SHIT v.]

give a fuck *v.* (*also* **give a fart**, **...a rusty fuck**, **...two fucks**) [1930s+] (*orig. US*) to care about, to be concerned, usu. in negative use, e.g. *who gives a fuck?* or *like I give a fuck*. [backform. f. NOT GIVE A FUCK v./NOT GIVE A FART v.]

give a gudgeon *v. see* GUDGEON n.

give a hoot *v.* (*also* give a hoot in hell, …two hoots, care a hoot, …two hoots) [1930s+] to care, usu. in negative use, e.g. *who gives a hoot?* [backform. f. NOT GIVE A HOOT v.]

give a hot poultice for the Irish toothache *v.* [late 19C] of a woman, to have sexual intercourse (cf. CATCH AN OYSTER v.). [SE *hot poultice* + IRISH TOOTHACHE n. (1)]

give a kick at *v.* [1970s] to look at, to ogle. [synon. Yid. *geb a kook*]

give a line on *v. see* GET A LINE ON v.

give a man's head the bastinado *v.* [early 17C] of a man, to cuckold a husband. [SE *bastinado*, to beat, to cudgel; 'the lover's penis is the cudgel and the bumps that it "raises" on the unsuspecting husband's head are the cuckold's horns' (Henke, *Gutter Life and Language*, 1988)]

give and get *n.* [1990s+] a bet. [rhy. sl.]

give and take *n.* [20C+] **1** a cake. **2** a bundle of notes. [rhy. sl.; (2) is fig. use of (1), i.e. a 'cake' of notes]

give a packing-penny *v.* [late 16C] to dismiss, to 'send packing'.

give a pass *v. see* PASS v.[1].

give a play to *v. see* MAKE A PLAY FOR v.

give a Remington *v.* [1970s] to have 2 penises in one's mouth. [a *Remington* double-barrelled shotgun]

give a rusty fuck *v. see* GIVE A FUCK v.

give-a-shit *n. see* GIVE-A-FUCK n.

give a shit *v.* [1960s+] (*orig. US*) to care, usu. in negative use, e.g. *who gives a shit?, I could give a shit.* [backform. f. NOT GIVE A SHIT v.]

give a stuff *v.* [1990s+] (*Aus./N.Z.*) to care, usu. in negative use, e.g. *who gives a stuff?* [backform. f. NOT GIVE A STUFF v.]

give a toss *v.* (*also* care a toss) [1990s+] (*orig. US*) to care, usu. in negative use, e.g. *who gives a toss?* [backform. f. NOT GIVE A TOSS v.]

give attitude *v. see* THROW ATTITUDE v.

give-away *n.*[1] [late 19C+] a betrayal of something, usu. a secret. [GIVE AWAY v. (1)]

give-away *n.*[2] [1930s+] (*US*) free samples and prizes.

give-away *adj.* [late 19C+] obvious, unmistakable. [GIVE-AWAY n.[1]]

give away *v.* **1** [mid-19C+] to betray. **2** [late 19C+] (*Aus.*) to give up, to abandon, to forsake.

give beans *v. see* GIVE SOMEONE BEANS v.

give bed-service *v.* [20C+] (*W.I., Bdos*) for a woman to take part in a sexual relationship in return for material support.

give beef *v. see* CRY (HOT) BEEF v.

give birth (to a copper) *v.* (*also* give birth to it) [1990s+] (*Aus.*) to defecate. [fig. use of COPPER n.[3] (1)]

give bondi *v.* (*also* give boondie, …bundi, …bundy) [late 19C–1950s] (*Aus.*) to attack savagely. [SE *bondi*, a heavy Aboriginal club]

give both barrels *v.* [1910s+] (*US*) to act or deal with in a very positive, uncompromising manner.

give brusher *v.* [late 19C+] (*Aus.*) **1** to obtain or borrow something (esp. money) and fail to return it; to fail to pay one's bills. **2** to abandon a task. **3** to run away (from). [BRUSH-OFF n.]

give bundi/bundy *v. see* GIVE BONDI v.

give chi-ike with the chill off *v.* [mid–late 19C] to scold, to reprimand. [CHI-IKE n. (2) + *with the chill off*, i.e. HOT adj.[1] (4)]

give coco for yam *v.* [mid-19C] (*W.I.*) to give as good as one gets; opposite of GET TOCO FOR YAM v. [SE *coco(nut)* + *yam*]

give cone *v.* [1980s] (*US teen*) to fellate. [the image of licking an ice-cream cone]

give cunt licks *v. see* CUNT-LICK v.

give curried hell *v. see* GIVE SOMEONE CURRY v.

give cuts *v.* [1980s+] (*US campus*) to let someone into a queue or line; thus *have cuts*, to get into the queue in a favourable position. [SE *cut in*]

give 'em hell! *excl.* [20C+] a general excl. of encouragement.

give five *v.* (*also* give someone five) [1950s+] (*orig. US*) to slap hands in order to seal a bargain or to greet a friend; occas. ext. as *give ten*, to slap both hands; often as GIVE ME FIVE! excl. [the 5 fingers]

give France *v.* [1920s+] (*W.I.*) **1** to quarrel very bitterly. **2** to cause a good deal of trouble for someone. [FRANCE n.]

give gammon *v.* [early 18C] (*UK Und.*) to stand next to a person while an accomplice picks their pocket. [GAMMON n.[1]]

give gas *v.* **1** [mid-19C+] to beat. **2** [mid-19C+] (*US*) to scold, verbally abuse or ridicule. [GAS n.[1] (1)]

give gip *v. see* GIVE GYP v.

give good *v.* [20C+] (*W.I.*) to berate, to scold severely, to tell off.

give good — *v.* (*also* give great —) [1970s+] (*US*) used with a sing. n. as a generic, e.g. *give good spiel*, to be notable for talking. [on model of orig. comb. *give good head* (GIVE HEAD v.)]

give green rats *v.* [19C] to slander someone in their absence, to backbite. [the link of *green* to envy/jealousy]

give gyp *v.* (*also* give gip, give jip) [late 19C+] to pain, to cause pain or trouble, to admonish; usu. as *give someone gyp* or *give one gyp*; thus *get gip/gyp*, to receive such pain. [? OED implies contraction of GEE UP n. in dial. but note Yorks. dial. *jip*, a sound thrashing, heavy punishment]

give hard for soft *v.* (*also* give a bit of hard for a bit of soft) [late 19C] of a man, to have sexual intercourse (cf. BURY IT v.; GIVE SOFT FOR HARD v.). [SE *bit* + HARD n.[3]/SE *hard* + SE *soft*]

give head *v.* (*orig. US*) **1** [1950s+] to perform oral sex, usu. to fellate (cf. BRAIN n.[2]). **2** [1960s+] to give flattering comments, usu. with sexual innuendo. [HEAD n.[10]]

give her a tail *v.* [1960s+] of a man, to have sexual intercourse (cf. DO HER JOB FOR HER v.). [TAIL n.[2] (6)]

give her one *v.* [1940s+] **1** of a man, to have sexual intercourse (cf. DO HER JOB FOR HER v.). **2** to kiss. [ONE n.[3] (2)]

give her the gas *v. see* GIVE (IT) THE GAS v.

give her the jampot *v.* [1980s] (*US Black*) of a man, to have sexual intercourse (cf. DO HER JOB FOR HER v.).

give her the time *v.* [1950s] of a man, to have sexual intercourse (cf. DO HER JOB FOR HER v.).

give him a hole to hide it in *v.* (*also* lend him a hole to hide it in) [late 19C+] of a woman, to permit sexual intercourse. [HOLE n.[1] (2) + IT n.[1] (2)]

give horrors *v.* [20C+] (*W.I.*) to annoy, to infuriate, to disgust.

give hot beef *v. see* CRY (HOT) BEEF v.

give it a bash *v. see* BASH v.[2] (1).

give it a (bit of a) nudge *v.* [1950s+] (*Aus.*) to drink to excess; thus *nudge (the turps)*, to drink heavily, often with a specified drink, e.g. *nudge the nelly*, to drink too much cheap wine.

give it a bone! *excl.* [late 19C+] shut up! stop talking! [the silencing of a dog by giving it a bone; 20C+ use mainly N.Z.]

give it a burl *v.* [1910s+] (*Aus.*) **1** (*also* give it a birl) to give something a try, to make an attempt (cf. GO FOR A BURL v.). **2** to stop doing something. [Scot. *birl*, to spin, to twist, i.e. SPIN n.[3] (1); (2) ? a misreading]

give it a fly *v.* [1910s+] (*Aus.*) to give something a try.

give it a go *v. see* GIVE SOMETHING A GO v.

give it all that *v.* [1990s+] to boast, to show off. [ALL THAT (AND THEN SOME) adj. (3)]

give it an airing! *excl.* [late 19C+] **1** take it away! **2** be quiet!

give it a name *v.* [20C+] (*Aus./US Black*) to speak with absolute candour or honesty; thus [1990s+] (*US Black*) as a general phr. of affirmation.

give it a name *phr.* [mid-19C–1950s] a phr. used when one is buying a round of drinks and asks the company what they would like.

give it a nudge *v. see* GIVE IT A (BIT OF A) NUDGE v.

give it a pull *v.* [20C+] (*Aus.*) to stop, to desist. [? the pull on the reins that halts a horse]

give it a rest! *excl.* [late 19C+] shut up! stop talking! [GIVE SOMEONE A REST v.]

give it a tug *v.* [1950s+] to masturbate. [var. TUG *v.* (2)]

give it a tumble *v.* [1910s+] to try out, to experiment. [fig. use of GIVE SOMEONE A TUMBLE *v.*[1] (1)]

give it a twirl *v. see* GIVE SOMETHING A WHIRL *v.*

give it away *v.* [1940s+] **1** (*Aus.*) to stop, to give up, to abandon. **2** (*US*) of a woman or male or female prostitute, to permit sexual intercourse.

give it a whirl *v. see* GIVE SOMETHING A WHIRL *v.*

give it hot (and strong) *v.* [late 19C+] **1** to castigate severely. **2** to attack and/or punish severely. [HOT AND STRONG *adv.*]

give it lip *v.* [late 19C+] **1** (*also* **give some lip, give lip**) to be cheeky. **2** (*Aus.*) to speak out loud. [LIP *n.*[1] (1)]

give it loads *v.* [1990s+] to make a fuss. [LOADS OF *n.*]

give it one's best shot *v.* [20C+] to make one's best efforts. [SHOT *n.*[5] (1)]

give it one upon the rush *v.* [early–mid-19C] to make an intense effort to leave or escape a place.

give it some welly *v.* [1970s+] **1** to apply more force, energy or effort. **2** to reject, to get rid of. [WELLIE *n.*; an extra image is from the 'wellie-chucking' contests that have become popular]

give it the big one *v.* [1990s+] **1** to act in a verbally aggressive manner. **2** to celebrate, to act in an excessive manner.

give it the boot *v.* [1990s+] to accelerate. [one pushes down on the accelerator with a boot or shoe]

give it the flick *v.* **1** [20C+] (*Aus.*) to throw something away. **2** [1990s+] (*UK juv.*) to end a relationship (cf. GET THE FLICK *v.*). [SE *flick*]

give (it) the gas *v.* (*also* **give her the gass**) [1940s+] (*US*) to move fast, to accelerate.

give it the gun *v.* [1920s+] (*orig. US*) to accelerate, to drive a car or other vehicle fast. [GUN *n.*[3]]

give it the nod *v. see* NOD THE NUT *v.*

give it to *v.*[1] **1** [late 18C–mid-19C; 1930s+] to shoot, poss. to kill. **2** [19C] (*UK Und.*) to rob. **3** [19C] to deceive, to take advantage of credulity. **4** [19C+] to hit, to beat, to stab. **5** [mid-19C+] to admonish severely. **6** [late 19C+] to punish severely. **7** [20C+] of a man, to have sexual intercourse (cf. BURY IT *v.*). **8** [1920s+] of a woman, to permit intercourse. **9** [1920s+] (*US Und.*) to murder, to execute. **10** [1970s] to tease, to provoke.

give it to *v.*[2] *see* HAND IT TO *v.*[1].

give it toes *v.* [1990s+] to run away, to escape.

give it up *v.* **1** [1940s+] to explain, to impart information. **2** [1960s+] (*orig. US*) to accede to seduction or forced intercourse. **3** [1960s+] to surrender oneself to pleasure (non-sexual). **4** [1970s+] to hand over, usu. money, but also drugs etc. **5** [1990s+] to applaud; usu. in phr. *let's give it up for…*

give it up! *excl.* [1970s+] **1** an aggressive demand from one male that another accept his advances, esp. in prison. **2** the same demand for sex, made from a man to a woman. [GIVE IT UP *v.* (2)]

give jaro *v.* [20C+] (*N.Z.*) to scold. [? Maori]

give jesse *v. see* GIVE (SOMEONE) JESSE *v.*

give jiggs *v.* (*also* **give jiggers**) [1910s–60s] (*US*) to keep a lookout. [JIGGER! *excl.*[2]]

give jip *v. see* GIVE GYP *v.*

give juice for jelly *v.* [19C] of a woman, to have sexual intercourse (cf. CATCH AN OYSTER *v.*). [JUICE *n.*[2] (1) + JELLY *n.*[1] (1)]

give jute (to) *v.* [1980s+] (*N.Z.*) to tease. [? link to Scot. *jute*, a derog. term for a woman]

give laldie *v.* (*also* **give laldy**) [late 19C+] (*Scot.*) **1** to be punished, to be beaten. **2** to do something energetically, enthusiastically. [Scot. *laldy*, to punish]

give lamb and salad *v.* [mid-19C–1900s] to beat, to thrash. [pun on LAM *v.*[1] (1)]

give laugh for peas-soup *v.* [20C+] (*W.I.*) **1** for a visitor to act in a sufficiently entertaining manner to win an invitation to a meal. **2** to chat or gossip instead of getting on with

one's work, thus using one's wit and charm to hide one's actual laziness.

give law *v.* [late 18C–mid-19C] to give someone a chance. [sporting jargon *give law*, to give a hunted animal a chance of escape]

give leg bail (and land security) *v. see* LEG BAIL *n.*

give lip *v. see* GIVE IT LIP *v.* (1).

give love *v.* [1990s+] (*US/UK Black*) to respect, to praise.

give me a break! *excl.* [1920s+] (*orig. US*) an ironical excl. of resignation and/or supplication delivered when faced with a statement or event deemed unacceptable, irritating etc. [GIVE SOMEONE A BREAK *v.*]

give me five! *excl.* (*also* **slip me five!**) [1920s+] (*orig. US Black*) let's slap hands to seal the deal or bargain; also as *give me five on the sly*, to slap hands behind one's back so as not to alert onlookers; *give me five on the black-hand side/the soul side*, to slap hands on the back (darker) side or the palm side of the hand. [GIVE FIVE *v.*]

give Moses *v. see* BASH THE LIVING MOSES OUT OF *v.*

give mutton for beef *v.* [19C] of a woman, to have sexual intercourse (cf. CATCH AN OYSTER *v.*). [MUTTON *n.*[1] (3) + BEEF *n.*[1] (1)]

given! *excl.* [1990s+] (*US campus*) an expression of agreement. [SE *given*, something that is automatically accepted, 'taken as read']

give nature a fillip *v.* [late 17C–18C] to indulge in hedonistic pleasures, notably women and wine.

give off *v.* [20C+] (*Irish*) to make a fuss. [fig. use of phr. *give out the hour*]

give on a man *v.* (*also* **give upon a man**) [20C+] (*W.I.*) for a woman to surrender herself to male advances.

give one hell *v.* [1960s+] **1** to cause pain. **2** of an inanimate object, to prove difficult. [GIVE SOMEONE HELL *v.*]

give one's arse a salad *v.* [early 18C] to have sexual intercourse outdoors.

give one's bit *v.* [1900s] (*Aus.*) to do anything in one's power. [? BIT *n.*[1]/SE *bit*]

give one's bum an airing *v.* [1940s–50s] to visit the lavatory. [BUM *n.*[1] (1)]

give oneself a head-butt *v.* [1980s+] (*Aus. prison*) to masturbate.

give oneself a low five *v.* [1980s+] to masturbate (cf. AUDITION THE FINGER PUPPETS *v.*). [play on the raised-arm, palm-slapping rituals of the HIGH FIVE *n.*[1]]

give oneself a rope necklace *v.* [1970s+] (*US Black*) to commit suicide by hanging.

give one's gravy *v.* [19C] **1** of a man, to reach orgasm. **2** of a man, to bring a partner to orgasm (presumably simultaneously with his own ejaculation). **3** to hit, to beat. [GRAVY *n.*[1] (2)]

give one's guts *v. see* COME ONE'S GUTS *v.*

give one's left nut *v.* [1950s+] (*US*) to yearn for, to desire. [fig. use of NUTS *n.*[2] (1)]

give or take *phr.* [1950s+] a phr. implying an estimation, usu. of time, number or weight, e.g. *give or take half an hour, give or take a couple of kilos.*

give out *v.*[1] [19C+] (*Irish*) to make a fuss, to complain.

give out *v.*[2] **1** [1930s+] (*US Black*) to talk emotionally, to talk with great feeling. **2** [1930s+] of a young woman, to make herself available for sexual intercourse. **3** [1940s] as *give out with*, to speak in a given manner. **4** [1940s+] to play music, to sing. **5** [1950s] to scream. **6** [1980s+] to be reprimanded, criticized, attacked. [fig. uses of SE]

give out *v.*[3] [1950s+] to make out, to imply, to pretend.

give out shite *v.* [1990s+] (*Irish*) to criticize, to scold. [fig. use of SHITE *n.* (1)]

give out the pay *v.* [1940s+] (*Irish*) to make a fuss.

give out with *v. see* GIVE OUT *v.*[2] (3).

give over! *excl.* [late 18C+] (*mainly northern*) stop it! shut up!

give pap with a hatchet *v. see* FEED PAP WITH A HATCHET *v.*

give points to *v.* [late 19C] to permit an advantage to.

give props *v.* (*also* give propers) [1970s+] (*US Black*) to applaud, to praise, to acknowledge as good (cf. GET PROPS *v.*). [PROPS n.[3]]

giver *n.* [1970s+] (*US gay/prison*) an active prison homosexual.

give rats *v.* [late 19C–1910s] (*Aus.*) to drive someone mad. [RATS, THE n.]

give roast meat and beat with the spit *v.* [late 17C–18C] to offer an apparent compliment and then to abuse its recipient.

give rounders *v.* [20C+] (*W.I., Trin.*) to be evasive, to deceive, to deal with in an annoying manner. [SE *go round in circles*]

give six *v.* (*also* keep six) [1970s+] (*Can. prison*) to keep a lookout. [SE *give* + SIX! excl.]

give skin *v. see* GIVE SOME SKIN *v.*

give skin-teeth *v.* [20C+] (*W.I.*) **1** to smile falsely when one actually feels furious or embittered. **2** to laugh cynically. [fig. use of 'the skin of one's teeth' to mean superficiality]

give sky-high *v. see* BLOW SKY HIGH *v.* (1).

give snaps *v.* [1990s+] (*US teen*) to give (someone) credit.

give soft for hard *v.* [19C] of a woman, to have sexual intercourse. (cf. GIVE HARD FOR SOFT *v.*).

give some body *v.* (*also* give some dick) [1960s+] to accede to sexual advances. [BODY n. (3)/DICK n.[4] (3)]

give some curry *v. see* GIVE SOMEONE CURRY *v.*

give some flesh *v.* [20C+] (*W.I.*) ritual palm-slapping that forms a greeting between Blacks or between Blacks and knowledgeable Whites.

give some jive *v. see* JIVE *v.*[1] (2).

give some lip *v. see* GIVE IT LIP *v.* (1).

give someone a baker's dozen *v.* [mid-19C] to beat up, to thrash. [fig. use of SE *baker's dozen*, 13]

give someone a bell *v.* [1930s+] to call on the telephone.

give someone a bent nail *v.* [1950s] (*US*) to make an unclear, misleading statement.

give someone a bit of hurry-up *v.* [20C+] (*Aus.*) to stimulate, to encourage to act more energetically.

give someone a bit of one's mind *v.* (*also* ...a piece of one's mind) [early 18C; mid-19C+] to scold, to reprimand, to tell off, to speak forcefully.

give someone a black eye *v.* [late 19C–1940s] to injure someone's or something's reputation. [fig. 'hurting' of the reputation]

give someone a blow *v.* [1930s] to make contact, to communicate.

give someone a bone *v.* [1990s+] of a man, to have sexual intercourse (cf. BURY IT *v.*). [BONE n.[1] (1)]

give someone a break *v.* (*also* cut someone a break, give something a break) [1920s+] (*orig. US*) to give someone or something a chance, to let off, to excuse, to give an opportunity; esp. as GIVE ME A BREAK! excl. [BREAK n.[1] (1)]

give someone absence without leave *v.* [early 19C] to dismiss from employment. [play on milit. use]

give someone a burst *v.* [1940s+] to complain, to criticize, to remind strongly. [SE *burst of fire*]

give someone a buzz *v.*[1] [1920s+] **1** to call someone on the telephone. **2** to look up, to call at one's house. [BUZZ n.[1] (3)]

give someone a buzz *v.*[2] [1950s+] to excite, to thrill (usu. sexually). [BUZZ n.[3] (2)]

give someone a chalk *v.* [mid-19C+] to cheat, to swindle, to get the better of. [? SE *chalk up*]

give someone a chubby *v.* [1980s+] (*UK juv.*) to pinch or twist someone's nipples.

give someone a (clean) leg up *v.* (*also* give someone a leg) [mid-19C+] to help someone (occas. something) over an obstacle, wall etc, both physically and fig., esp. to help someone advance themselves professionally; thus **get a leg up**, to gain such an advantage.

give someone a coating *v.* **1** [1930s+] to beat up, to thrash. **2** [1970s] (*UK Und.*) to give someone a reprimand. [COAT *v.*]

give someone a dose *v.* **1** [19C] (*UK Und.*) (*also* dose) to kill, to beat up. **2** [1930s] (*US*) to shoot. [the idea of TAKE ONE'S MEDICINE *v.* (3)]

give someone a dry shave *v.* [1930s] (*US*) to defraud, to hoax. [DRY SHAVE *v.*[1] but poss. fig use of DRY SHAVE *v.*[2]]

give someone a fill *v.* [1900s] (*UK Und.*) to deceive.

give someone a go *v. see* GIVE SOMETHING A GO *v.*

give someone a hard time *v.* [1950s+] (*US*) to harass.

give someone a hot time (of it) *v.* [mid-19C+] to make someone unhappy, to punish, to reprimand; to cause problems for.

give someone a hurting *v. see* PUT A HURTING ON *v.*

give someone a jacket *v.* [20C+] (*W.I., Jam.*) for a married woman to conceive and bear a child by her lover and pass it off as her husband's. [JACKET n.[2] (1)]

give someone a jolly *v.* [mid-late 19C] **1** to applaud, to give someone a cheer. **2** to deceive, to tell a tale in order to trick someone.

give someone a jump *v.* [20C+] of a man, to have sexual intercourse. [JUMP n.[3] (1)]

give someone a kyrie eleison *v.* (*also* sing someone a kyrie eleison) [16C–early 17C] to scold, to 'tell off'. [Gk *kyrie eleison*, Lord, have mercy]

give someone aleck *v.* [mid-19C] (*US*) to thrash, to beat. [? pun on GIVE SOMEONE (A LICK WITH) THE ROUGH SIDE OF ONE'S TONGUE *v.*]

give someone a leg (up) *v. see* GIVE SOMEONE A (CLEAN) LEG UP *v.*

give someone (a lick with) the rough side of one's tongue *v.* [late 19C+] to attack verbally. [pun on SE *lick*, a blow/*lick*, an act of licking]

give someone a lift *v.* [late 19C–1900s] to give someone a short, swift kick. [the victim's body is 'lifted' through the air; note Grose (1785): 'to give one a lift, to assist']

give someone a little leg *v.* (*also* give someone the leg) [1960s+] to confuse, to tell tales. [var. on PULL SOMEONE'S LEG *v.* (1)]

give someone a miss *v.* (*also* give something a miss) [20C+] to avoid seeing someone or doing something.

give someone a mouthful of moonshine *v. see* MOONSHINE n. (1).

give someone an eye *v.* [1900s] (*Aus.*) to blacken someone's eye. [abbr. SE *black eye*]

give someone a pain in the arse *v.* [1930s+] to irritate; thus PAIN IN THE ARSE n. [later more explicit var. on next]

give someone a pain (in the neck) *v.* (*also* give someone a pain in the guts) [late 19C+] to irritate; thus PAIN (IN THE NECK) n.[1].

give someone a pair of gloves *v.* [late 18C–early 19C] to give someone a bribe.

give someone a pay *v.* [1970s–80s] (*N.Z. prison*) to reprimand, to criticize harshly.

give someone a perm *v.* [1980s+] (*US campus*) to perform oral sex. [SE *permanent wave*, a hairstyle (achieved by a blowdryer) + pun on BLOW JOB n. (1)]

give someone a piece *v.* [1940s+] (*W.I.*) of a woman, to permit casual sexual intercourse. [PIECE n.[1] (3)]

give someone a piece of one's mind *v. see* GIVE SOMEONE A BIT OF ONE'S MIND *v.*

give someone a play *v. see* GIVE SOMEONE SOME PLAY *v.*

give someone a pull *v.* [1950s+] **1** to tell off, to reprimand. **2** to arrest. [PULL n.[3] (2)/PULL n.[3] (4)]

give someone a rest *v.* (*also* give something a rest) [late

19C+] (*orig. Aus.*) to leave someone or something alone; to abandon an obsession or interest.

give someone a rev *v.* [1990s+] (*Aus. Und.*) to warn, to inform. [? abbr. of SE *revelation*]

give someone a rise in the world *v.* [1920s+] (*Aus.*) to kick someone's buttocks. [pun]

give someone arseholes *v.* [1960s] (*N.Z.*) to harass, to berate (cf. GIVE SOMEONE THE ARSEHOLE v.). [fig. use of ARSEHOLE n. (1)]

give someone a rub *v.* (*also* **give someone the rub**) [1940s] to tease. [RUB UP THE WRONG WAY v.]

give someone a run for their money *v.* (*also* **give someone a run for it**, **give someone a run for their marbles**) [late 19C+] to provide satisfaction, to give someone their 'money's worth', usu. fig. [note earlier racing sl. *have a run for one's money*, to have some kind of return or satisfaction for one's expenditure or exertions]

give someone a shot *v.* [19C+] of a man, to have sexual intercourse. [SHOT n.²]

give someone a shout *v.* [1970s+] **1** to get in touch with, usu. by telephone. **2** (*W.I./US*) to pay a casual visit.

give someone a snake *v.* [late 19C–1920s] to annoy, to irritate.

give someone a song and dance *v.* [late 19C+] (*orig. US*) to tell fanciful tales for the purpose of confusing or tricking the listener. [SONG AND DANCE n.¹ (1)]

give someone a thrill *v.* [1920s+] **1** to bring to orgasm. **2** of a man, to have sexual intercourse. [THRILL n. (2)]

give someone a toothache *v.* [1990s+] to be excessively 'sweet' (cf. GIVE SOMEONE DIABETES v.). [pun; but note TOOTHACHE n.]

give someone a touch of them *v.* [1920s+] (*Aus.*) to infuriate. [fig. use of TOUCH OF 'EM n. (2)]

give someone a tumble *v.*¹ **1** [late 19C+] to have sexual intercourse. **2** [1920s] in fig. use, to do someone a favour, to give a present. [TUMBLE n.²]

give someone a tumble *v.*² [1920s+] (*US*) to recognize, to acknowledge. [TUMBLE n.³]

give someone a wide *v.* [20C+] to avoid. [SE *give a wide berth*]

give someone beans *v.* **1** [mid-19C+] (*orig. US*) to scold; to deal severely with, to punish heavily. **2** [late 19C] to bore. **3** [late 19C+] of a man, to have sexual intercourse with. [? SE *bangs*, hits]

give someone best *v.* (*also* **give something best**) [late 19C–1950s] to leave, to abandon.

give someone big rocks to hold *v.* [20C+] (*W.I., Bdos*) for a woman to make a date with a man when she has no intention of keeping it, thus to trick a suitor in any way.

give someone blue devil *v.* [1980s+] to be angry with someone. [fig. use of BLUE DEVILS n.¹ (1)]

give someone cards and spades *v.* [late 19C–1930s] to allow someone else an advantage. [card-playing imagery]

give someone cavities *v. see* GIVE SOMEONE DIABETES v.

give someone chalks on *v.* [late 19C+] to acknowledge someone else's superiority. [? *chalk up*]

give someone change *v.* **1** [early–late 19C] to make a suitable response in verbal badinage. **2** [mid–late 19C] to punish someone. [CHANGE n.¹; the idea of doing someone a service, paying someone back, whether physically or mentally]

give someone curry *v.* (*also* **give curried hell**, **give some curry**) [1930s+] (*Aus.*) to attack (verbally or physically), 'to make things hot' for someone. [SE *curry* is seen as 'hot', but note mid-19C Aus. pidgin *give one kurrajong*, to hang with a rope made from kurrajong fibre]

give someone diabetes *v.* (*also* **give someone cavities**) [1980s+] (*US campus*) to be excessively 'sweet' (cf. GIVE SOMEONE A TOOTHACHE v.). [SE *diabetes* results from an excess of sugar in the blood; tooth *cavities* from eating too many sweet things]

give someone down the banks *v.* (*also* **give someone down the country/river**) [late 19C; 1960s+] (*orig. US/Irish*) to scold, to reprimand. [ety. unknown]

give someone fits *v.* (*orig. US*) **1** [mid-19C–1900s] to inflict a humiliating defeat on, to crush. **2** [mid-19C–1920s] to scold vigorously, to reprimand. **3** [20C+] to frighten.

give someone five *v. see* GIVE FIVE v.

give someone fuck *v. see* GIVE SOMEONE HELL v.

give someone ginger *v.* [1920s] to treat brusquely, to make someone 'jump'.

give someone grief *v.* [1960s+] to make miserable, to harm in any way. [GRIEF n.¹ (1)]

give someone gruel *v.* [mid-19C] to kill or defeat. [GRUEL n. (1)]

give someone haemorrhoids *v.* [1980s+] (*US campus*) to bother, to pester, to irritate. [pun on GIVE SOMEONE A PAIN IN THE ARSE v.]

give someone hell *v.* (*also* **give someone fuck**, **give someone heck**, **play hell**) (*orig. US*) **1** [mid-19C+] to give someone a 'hard time', to scold severely. **2** [20C+] to hurt, to inflict punishment on.

give someone it tight *v.* [1990s+] to constrain someone, to limit someone's freedom.

give (someone) jesse *v.* (*also* **give someone jessie/jessy**) [mid-19C–1940s] to punish, to beat, to scold soundly; sometimes used with other verbs, such as *administer*; thus *catch/get jesse*, to be punished. [play on Isa. 11:1 'There shall come forth a rod out of the stem of Jesse']

give someone lanty *v. see* LANTY v.

give someone larry dooley *v.* [1940s+] (*Aus.*) to beat someone, to punish; thus *larry-doo*, a thrashing, a disturbance. [Larry Foley, late 19C Aus. boxer; the phr. began by using the proper name, but soon replaced *Foley* by *dooley*]

give someone Moll Doyle *v.* [mid-19C+] (*Irish*) to scold, to reprimand, usu. of a wife to a husband. [*Moll Doyle's daughters*, a clandestine agrarian society, pitted against rapacious landlords and similar figures]

give someone oatmeal *v.* [mid-18C–early 19C] to punish, to reprimand. [? OATMEAL n.]

give someone once-round *v.* [1900s] (*Aus.*) to scold.

give someone one *v.* **1** [mid-19C+] to hit. **2** [late 19C+] to have sexual intercourse, to kiss etc. [ONE n.¹/ONE n.³ (2)]

give someone one in the eye *v.* (*also* **give someone one on the nose**) [late 19C+] to hit, to reprimand; also in fig. use. [ext. of GIVE SOMEONE ONE v. (1)]

give someone one's cards *v. see* GET ONE'S CARDS v.

give someone onions *v.* [late 19C–1900s] to attack physically. [one's watering eyes]

give someone pants *v.* [1960s] (*US Black*) of a woman, to allow sexual intercourse.

give someone rats *v.* [mid-19C+] (*US*) to give someone a hard time, to berate, to rebuke. [the negative image of the rodent]

give someone rocks *v.* [1950s+] (*US*) to excite sexually, spec. to make a man have an erection (cf. GET ONE'S ROCKS OFF v.). [fig. use of ROCKS n.⁴ (1)]

give someone's arse a chance *v.* (*also* **give someone's ears a chance**) [20C+] a comment aimed at a talkative person, usu. prefaced by *Why don't you shut up and…*

give someone scissors *v.* [mid-19C–1900s] to treat someone badly, to pay someone back (for a slight or injury). [one fig. 'cuts them up']

give someone shit *v.* [1960s+] (*orig. US*) **1** to cause trouble for someone. **2** to nag, to criticize. [SHIT n.³ (2)/SHIT n.³ (8)]

give someone snuff *v.* [late 19C–1920s] to punish, to reprimand. [SE *snuff*; the image is of beating someone to powder]

give someone some (meat) *v.* [1970s+] of a man, to have sexual intercourse (cf. BURY IT v.). [MEAT n. (2)]

give someone some play *v.* (*also* **give someone a play**) [1930s+] (*US Black*) **1** to express sexual interest in, to flirt with. **2** to give someone a chance; to make a deal with. **3** in fig. use, to frequent (and spend money).

give someone (some) stick v. (*also* give something (some) stick) [1960s+] to threaten, to criticize roughly, to beat up, to assault, both lit. and fig. [STICK n.10 (1)]

give someone something for themself v. [late 19C] to thrash, to beat. [ironic]

give someone that v. [1910s+] to acknowledge the other person's point, e.g. *I'll give you that.*

give someone the air v. [20C+] (*orig. US*) to dismiss, to reject, esp. when ending a love affair (cf. GET THE AIR v.).

give someone the arries v. [1980s] to get rid of. [? fig. use of ARRIS n. (2)]

give someone the arse v. [1950s+] (*Aus.*) to treat with contempt. [ARSE n.1 (1); ? turning one's back, and thus one's buttocks, to someone]

give someone the arsehole v. [2000s] to infuriate (cf. GIVE SOMEONE ARSEHOLES v.). [fig. use of ARSEHOLE n. (1)]

give someone the atmosphere v. [1930s] (*US*) to turn down, to reject. [var. on GIVE SOMEONE THE AIR v.]

give someone the avaunt v. [late 16C–early 17C] to send someone away. [SE excl. *avaunt*, be off!]

give someone the bag v. (*also* give someone the pike, ...road) [late 16C–19C] 1 to depart suddenly. 2 to dismiss, usu. from a job. 3 to jilt or reject a suitor, to end a relationship. [the handing over of a fig. bag of problems, responsibilities etc; SE *give + bag*, i.e. of possessions/SE *pike/road*; Nares defines phr. as 'to cheat']

give someone the belt v. (*also* give someone the Lonsdale (belt)) [1930s+] (*orig. Aus.*) to get rid of, to throw out, to dismiss, to reject (cf. GET THE BELT v.). [the *Lonsdale belt*; thus a pun on BELT n.1 (1)/BELT v.1 (1); the belt itself, given to a boxing champion, is named after Hugh Cecil Lowther, 5th earl of Lonsdale (1857–1944)]

give someone the berries v. *see* GIVE THE BERRIES TO v.

give someone the best of it v. [late 19C–1940s] (*Aus./US*) to allow someone an advantage, typically in a gambling game; thus *get the best of it*, to gain such an advantage.

give (someone) the bird v. [late 19C+] 1 to express one's disapproval vocally, esp. by hissing; also in fig. use (cf. GET THE (BIG) BIRD v.). 2 to reject, to dismiss. [the hissing is supposed to resemble that of a goose; orig./usu. theatrical, where the phr. began as GET THE (BIG) BIRD v., but also in general use]

give someone the boak v. [1980s+] to make sick. [SE *bolk*, to belch; see also BOKE v.]

give someone the boot v. [late 19C+] 1 to dismiss from a job, to throw out; to end a relationship. 2 (*also* give someone the boots, ...heel) to give someone a kicking; also in fig. use. [BOOT, THE n.]

give someone the bounce v. [late 19C+] (*US*) 1 to jilt, to reject (cf. GET THE BOUNCE v.). 2 to send away, to dismiss from a job. [BOUNCE, THE n.]

give someone the breeze v. [1930s+] (*orig. US*) to dismiss, to reject, esp. when ending a love affair. [var. on GIVE SOMEONE THE AIR v.]

give someone the brown-trouser treatment v. [1980s] to terrify. [the soiling of one's trousers through fear]

give someone the brush(-off) v. [1920s+] (*orig. US*) to ignore, to snub. [BRUSH-OFF n.]

give someone the bucket v. [mid-19C] to dismiss from a job. [var. on SACK v.2 (1)]

give someone the bullet v. [mid-19C+] 1 to dismiss from employment, to throw out (cf. GET THE BULLET v.). 2 to jilt, to terminate a relationship. [BULLET n.2 (1)]

give someone the business v. [1930s+] (*orig. US*) 1 to kill. 2 to beat up, to assault. 3 to have sexual intercourse. 4 to tease, to taunt, to put at a disadvantage by one's own actions. 5 to deceive, to bamboozle. 6 to interrogate. 7 to cast flirtatious glances (at). 8 to frustrate sexually. 9 to brag, to boast. [BUSINESS n.1]

give someone the buzz v. [1930s+] to get away from someone, to lose someone. [BUZZ v.2]

give someone the chop v. [1940s+] 1 (*also* give someone the old chop-chop) to kill or otherwise dispose of a person (cf. GET THE CHOP v.). 2 to dismiss from a job. 3 to destroy, to abandon, to stop, to cut off. [SE *chop*, to remove (one's head)]

give someone the chuck(-up) v. [late 19C+] to dismiss from a job, to get rid of, to end a relationship (cf. GET THE CHUCK v.). [CHUCK n.2 (2)/CHUCK UP v.2 (1)]

give someone the clouts v. [1910s] to hit, to beat up.

give someone the cock v. [20C+] (*W.I.*) 1 to outsmart, to outwit by trickery or other unfair means. 2 to cause someone unexpected trouble. [COCK n.2 (1)]

give someone the cold shake v. [late 19C–1900s] (*US*) to reject or snub someone (cf. GIVE SOMEONE THE SHAKE v.). [abbr. SE *cold handshake/cold shoulder*]

give someone the crock v. [late 19C] to admit defeat, to award a victory. [SE *crock*, a jug, i.e. to award a fig. cup as in a sporting victory]

give someone the cross hop v. [late 19C] (*US tramp*) to betray; to double-cross.

give someone the dead hand v. 1 [late 19C] (*US campus*) to betray. 2 [1970s] (*US*) to grope a woman in a crowd, e.g. on a tube train.

give someone the deep six v. [1920s+] (*US*) to kill, to murder. [DEEP SIX n.]

give someone the dinky-dink v. [late 19C] to reject; to dismiss.

give someone the dirty eyeball v. [1990s+] (*Aus.*) to stare at aggressively.

give someone the double v. [19C] to give the slip, to evade by stratagem. [SE *double*, to trace a winding, tortuous path; to evade]

give (someone) the drop v. [late 19C] (*US tramp*) to pass on information. [? DROP n.2 (1)]

give someone the dust-off v. *see* DUST OFF v.1 (3).

give someone the east and west v. [1910s] (*US*) to look someone over, to appraise.

give someone the eye v. (*also* give the eye to) 1 [late 19C+] to stare at. 2 [20C+] to appraise sexually. 3 [1940s–50s] to give a signal, to 'tip the wink'.

give someone the fall v. [mid-17C–18C] of a man, to lay a woman down preparatory to sexual intercourse.

give someone the finger v. (*orig. US*) 1 [late 19C+] in fig. use of (2), to mock. 2 [1940s+] (*also* do the finger, finger, flip the finger) to make a manual gesture (the raised middle finger in the US, the V-sign in the UK) to imply derision and disdain; also in fig. use. [FINGER, THE n. (also note there comment on dating)]

give someone the fish-eye v. [20C+] (*US*) to stare at (in a hostile manner). [the wide, round eyes of a fish]

give someone the foot v. [20C+] (*US*) 1 to throw out, to oust, to reject. 2 to kick. [var. on GIVE SOMEONE THE BOOT v.]

give someone the gate v. [20C+] (*US*) to dismiss, to reject, to get rid of (cf. GET THE GATE v.).

give someone the glad eye v. [1910s+] to give someone a glance that implies sexual attraction. [GLAD EYE n. (1)]

give someone the go v. (*also* give something the go) [1900s; 1980s+] (*Aus./N.Z.*) to reject a suitor, to give up a job, leave a country etc. [var. on GIVE SOMEONE THE GO-BY v.]

give someone the go-around v. (*also* give something the go-around) [late 19C+] to reject, to avoid, to jilt, of a person or thing. [var. on GIVE SOMEONE THE GO-BY v.]

give someone the go-by v. (*also* give something the go-by) 1 [late 17C+] to reject, to avoid, to jilt, of a person or thing. 2 [early 19C] to surpass. 3 [early 19C+] to overtake, to pass.

4 [early 19C+] to allow, to turn a blind eye. [SE *go-by*, the action of going]

give someone the go-bye *v.* [1930s–60s] to reject someone, to end a relationship. [var. on GIVE SOMEONE THE GO-BY *v.* (1)]

give someone the good word *v.* [2000s] to pass on information, to 'tip off'.

give someone the gooner *v.* [1920s–30s] **1** to dismiss someone from a job (cf. GET THE GOONER *v.*). **2** to jilt, to terminate a relationship. [SE *gone* or GONER n.[1] (3)]

give someone the go-sign *v.* [1950s–60s] (*US*) to dismiss, to reject, to brush off. [SE *go away*]

give someone the guy *v.*[1] *see* GUY n.[1] (1).

give someone the guy *v.*[2] *see* GUY n.[3].

give someone the handkerchief *v.* [1980s] to give someone a signal.

give someone the hard ass *v.* [1970s+] (*US*) to give a hard time. [HARD-ASS n.]

give someone the head *v.* [1960s] to headbutt (cf. GIVE SOMEONE THE NUT *v.*).

give someone the heel *v. see* GIVE SOMEONE THE BOOT *v.* (2).

give someone the highball *v.* [1960s+] (*US*) to reject, to brush off, esp. to end a relationship or love affair. [? railroad jargon *highball*, a fast train; thus the individual who ends the affair is fig. 'taking a fast train' out]

give someone the hook *v.* [1900s] (*US*) **1** to imprison. **2** to betray, to double-cross. **3** to punish, to treat unkindly. [HOOK *v.*[3] (1)]

give someone the horse laugh *v.* [late 19C–1950s] (*US*) to mock, to tease; also *take/get the horse laugh*. [SE *horse laugh*, a loud coarse laugh]

give someone the hump *v.* [late 19C+] to annoy, to irritate (cf. GET THE HUMP *v.*). [HUMP n.[1]]

give someone the icy mitt *v. see* GIVE SOMEONE THE MITT *v.*

give someone the irrits *v.* [20C+] (*Aus.*) to annoy, to irritate. [abbr. SE *irritate*]

give someone (their) running shoes *v.* [1930s+] (*orig. Aus./N.Z.*) to dismiss from a job, as a lover etc. [US use added post 1960s]

give someone the jerks *v.* [1910s–30s] to tease, to hoax. [? fig. use of JERKS n.[1] (2) or ? predecessor to JERK SOMEONE AROUND *v.*]

give someone the jolts *v.* [1970s] (*US*) to execute in the electric chair. [SE *jolts*, electric shocks]

give someone the kick(out) *v.* [late 19C–1910s] to dismiss from a job (cf. GET THE KICK *v.*). [KICK *v.*[3]]

give someone the laugh *v.* (*also* **give something the laugh**) [late 19C–1930s] (*US*) to jeer, to pour scorn.

give someone the leather *v.* [1930s] **1** to kick a person. **2** to beat with the fist, to punch. [the leather of (1) shoes, (2) boxing gloves]

give someone the leg *v. see* GIVE SOMEONE A LITTLE LEG *v.*

give someone the length of one's tongue *v.* [late 19C+] to attack verbally.

give someone the licks of Lisbon *v.* [20C+] (*W.I., Guyn.*) to berate, to scold severely, to tell off. [SE *lick*, a blow; + ? ref. to Port. colonialism]

give someone the Lonsdale (belt) *v. see* GIVE SOMEONE THE BELT *v.*

give someone the miller *v.* [mid–late 19C] to pelt someone with flour, grease or other rubbish.

give someone the mitt *v.* (*also* **give someone the icy mitt**) **1** [late 19C] to say goodbye. **2** [late 19C–1940s] (*US*) to reject, esp. in the context of a proposal of marriage. [MITT n. (3)/ICY MITT n.; var. on GIVE SOMEONE THE MITTEN *v.*]

give someone the mitten *v.* [mid-19C–1900s] (*US*) to reject a proposal of marriage, to end a relationship (cf. GET THE MITTEN *v.*). [MITTEN n. (2)]

give someone the monkeys *v.* [1930s] to annoy, to distress.

give someone the nark *v. see* NARK n.[1] (4).

give someone the needle *v.* **1** [late 19C+] to irritate. **2** [1920s] (*US*) to cuckold. **3** [1940s–60s] (*US*) to criticize. **4** [1990s+] (*US*) to kill.

give someone the nut *v.* [mid-19C+] to hit with one's head (cf. GIVE SOMEONE THE HEAD *v.*). [NUT n.[1] (2)]

give someone the office *v.* [19C+] **1** to tip off, to give a warning. **2** to inform, to tell, with no implication of warning. **3** (*UK prison*) to initiate a new prisoner into the rules and regulations, official and unofficial, of prison life. [OFFICE n.[3]]

give someone the old boracic *v.* [1950s+] to deceive, to tell tales. [? POKE (THE) BORAK *v.*; ult. SE *barrack*, to jeer]

give someone the old chop-chop *v. see* GIVE SOMEONE THE CHOP *v.* (1).

give someone the order of the sack *v.* (*also* **give someone the order of the boot**) [mid-19C+] to dismiss, to relieve of one's job, to throw out (cf. GET THE ORDER OF THE BOOT *v.*). [joc. amplification of SACK *v.*[2] (1)/BOOT *v.*[1] (2)/ORDER OF THE BOOT n.]

give someone the peppermint drops *v.* [1900s] to trip someone up. [ety. unknown]

give someone the pike *v. see* GIVE SOMEONE THE BAG *v.*

give someone the pip *v.* [late 19C+] to annoy, to infuriate (cf. GET THE PIP *v.*). [PIP n.[1] (1)]

give someone the prod *v.* [1950s] (*Aus.*) to warn, to give an order.

give someone the rap *v.* [1930s+] (*US*) **1** to murder, to kill. **2** to blame. [SE *rap*, a blow]

give someone the rinky-dink *v.* [1900s–40s] (*US*) to cheat, to swindle. [RINKY-DINK n.]

give someone the road *v.*[1] [1910s+] (*US/US Black*) to avoid, to ignore.

give someone the road *v.*[2] *see* GIVE SOMEONE THE BAG *v.*

give someone the rounds of the kitchen *v.* [late 19C+] (*Aus.*) to tell off, to scold.

give someone the rub *v.*[1] [1960s] (*US*) to murder, to assassinate. [RUB(-OUT) n.]

give someone the rub *v.*[2] *see* GIVE SOMEONE A RUB *v.*

give someone the rub of the thumb *v.* [mid–late 19C] to impart information to someone. [the gesture of rubbing one's thumb against the forefinger]

give someone the rush *v.* [mid-19C–1910s] to sponge off someone for a lengthy period and top it off by successfully requesting a loan. [RUSH n.[1] (4)]

give someone the sack *v.* **1** [early 19C+] to dismiss from a job (cf. GET THE SACK *v.*). **2** [mid-19C–1920s] to reject (as a former lover or sweetheart). [SACK, THE n. (1)]

give someone the shake *v.* (*also* **give something the shake**) **1** [late 19C+] to run off, to leave someone (cf. GIVE SOMEONE THE COLD SHAKE *v.*). **2** [1900s] to abandon, to give up.

give someone the shits *v.* [1960s+] to annoy, to infuriate someone (cf. GET THE SHITS (WITH) *v.*). [SHITS, THE n. (3)]

give someone the shove *v.* (*also* **give the shove to**) [late 19C+] to dismiss from a job, to jilt or reject a lover (cf. GET THE SHOVE *v.*). [SHOVE, THE n.]

give someone the sick(s) *v.* [mid-19C–1950s] to disgust.

give someone the sign *v.* [1950s] to make a gesture of recognition, usu. indicating that all is well, 'the coast is clear'.

give someone the slip *v.* [19C] to die. [SE *give the slip*, to elude, to run off]

give someone the spike *v. see* GET THE SPIKE *v.*

give someone the spur *v. see* SPUR *v.*

give (someone) the ta-tas *v.* [1960s+] (*N.Z.*) to make a derisive gesture, to 'give the finger'. [TA-TA n.]

give someone the tee-hee *v.* [1900s] (*US*) to laugh at.

give someone the threepennies *v.* [late 19C+] to annoy, to irritate someone. [fig. use of THREEPENNY BITS n. (1)]

give someone the tom-tits v. [1950s+] to annoy someone (cf. GET THE TOM-TITS v.). [fig. use of TOM TITS n.]

give someone the treatment v. 1 [1960s+] to have sexual intercourse. 2 [1970s+] to beat up, to torture, usu. in order to elicit information. 3 [1970s+] to submit someone to some form of verbal interrogation or telling-off.

give someone the V v. (also **give something the V**) [2000s] to make the obscene gesture known as the 'V-sign'.

give (someone) the whisper v. see SLING (SOMEONE) THE WHISPER v. (1).

give someone the wind v. [1930s] to get rid of someone.

give someone the works v. 1 [1920s–40s] (also **tell the works**) to reveal everything. 2 [1920s+] to harm, ranging from actual murder to beating up. 3 [1920s+] to put all one's efforts into communicating something, typically a sermon or political oration, or doing something, criticizing or selling something etc. 4 [1930s] (US tramp) to be forced to work. 5 [1930s+] to make sexual advances towards. 6 [1930s+] to engage in sexual intercourse. 7 [1940s] (also **hand the works to**) to spoil someone's chances. [WORKS, THE n. (1)/WORKS, THE n. (5)]

give someone tone v. [1950s] (W.I./UK Black) to tease.

give someone turnips v. [early–mid 19C] to abandon or jilt, esp. heartlessly, ruthlessly. [pun on TURN (SOMEONE) UP v. (1)/SE turnip; note Suffolk dial. give someone cold turnips, to turn down a proposal of marriage/love]

give someone what-for v. 1 [late 19C+] (also **give someone what's what**) to reprimand severely, to inflict severe pain or chastisement, esp. on an errant child. 2 [late 19C+] to beat up. 3 [1950s+] of a man, to have sexual intercourse. [WHAT-FOR n./ SE what's what]

give some skin v. (also **give skin, give some plank/splib, slip some skin**) [1930s+] (orig. US Black) the ritual palm-slapping that forms a greeting between Blacks or a Black and a knowledgeable White; thus the greeting give/slip me some skin. [SE skin/plank/SPLIB n. (1). The practice is of African origin; thus Temme botme-der, put skin and/or Mandingo i golo don m bolo, place your hand in my hand]

give something... see also under GIVE SOMEONE...

give something a go v. (also **give it a go, give someone a go**) [20C+] (orig. Aus.) to try something or someone out, to take a chance on, to make an attempt. [GO n.³ (6)]

give something a whirl v. (also **give it a twirl/whirl, take a whirl**) [late 19C+] (orig. US) to try something out.

give teeth v. [1990s+] to smile.

give ten v. see GIVE FIVE v.

give the arm v. see PUT THE ARM ON v. (1).

give the berries to v. (also **give someone the berries**) [1920s–30s] (US) to deride, to insult. [RASPBERRY n.¹]

give the bird v. see GIVE (SOMEONE) THE BIRD v.

give the boys a treat v. [late 19C+] for a girl or woman inadvertently to reveal more of her body than would otherwise be seen, such as cleavage by leaning over, or upper thighs or underwear when getting out of a vehicle or bending down to pick something up.

give the cheer v. [late 19C] to greet, to welcome.

give the chuck-up v. see GIVE SOMEONE THE CHUCK(-UP) v.

give the crow(s) a pudding v. [late 16C–early 19C] 1 to hang on a gibbet. 2 to die. [SE crow + SE pudding, entrails, i.e. the crow will eat the entrails of the corpse]

give the dirty sign v. see DIRTY adj.¹ (5).

give the ditch v. see DITCH v.¹ (3).

give the dog a bone v. [1980s+] to have sexual intercourse (cf. BURY IT v.). [DOG n.⁴ (2) + BONE n.¹ (1)]

give the dog a swim v. [20C+] (Aus./S.Afr.) to have an excuse for doing something, to use an action as an excuse, I'm just off to give the dog a swim.

give the done v. [20C+] (W.I., UKVI) to end a relationship (cf. GET THE DONE v.). [SE done, over, finished]

give the drummer some v. [1950s+] (US Black) to perform the ritual palm-slapping that is a greeting between Blacks or Blacks and knowledgeable Whites. [the drumming of one hand upon another]

give the eye to v. see GIVE SOMEONE THE EYE v.

give the fan v. see FAN v.¹ (4).

give the fence a run v. [1970s+] (N.Z.) to fulfil one's sexual urges. [the image of a bull smashing through or jumping over a fence on the way to a cow]

give the fig v. [late 16C–early 19C] to stick one's thumb up between 2 forefingers as a gesture of derision. [FIG (OF SPAIN) n.]

give the four-eleven v. (also **give the 411**) [1990s+] (US Black) to give out information, to instruct. [? telephone code for directory enquiries]

give the glad hand v. see GLAD-HAND v.

give the heat v.¹ [1930s+] to murder, to kill. [HEAT n.⁴]

give the heat v.² see HEAT n.¹ (1).

give the ig v. see IG v.

give the knock v. see KNOCK v.¹ (2).

give the knock to v. [late 19C] to knock down.

give the man the play v. [1970s+] (US Black) to inform. [MAN, THE n. (1) + PLAY n.¹ (3)]

give them away with a pound of tea v. [late 19C+] 1 a phr. used to deride something, or someone, considered of little or no value; e.g. Expensive? He gives them away... 2 an ironic reply by a criminal to questions referring to the origins of obviously stolen goods in his possession, e.g. Stolen goods, officer? No. Give them away...

give the old man his supper v. [late 19C] of a woman, to make herself available for sex. [pun on OLD MAN n.¹ (1)/OLD MAN n.¹ (3)]

give the rib v. see RIB v. (2).

give the shove to v. see GIVE SOMEONE THE SHOVE v.

give the show away v. [mid-19C+] to betray a secret, to reveal one's or another's plans.

give the snap away v. [late 19C] to betray plans, to 'give the game away'. [? the snap of a finger that launches an action]

give the tin ear v. see HAVE A TIN EAR v. (2).

give tongue-pie v. (also **give tongue**) [1900s–20s] to give a scolding, to harangue. [TONGUE PIE n. (1)]

give 'tude v. see THROW ATTITUDE v.

give two fucks v. see GIVE A FUCK v.

give two hoots v. see GIVE A HOOT v.

give-up n. [1970s+] 1 (US Und.) a payment made under duress. 2 (US) submission, surrender. 3 (US Und.) a robbery or hijacking in which the driver is in league with the hijackers. 4 (Aus. prison) an informer. [GIVE UP v.]

give up v. 1 [mid-19C+] (Aus./US Und.) to betray, to inform against. 2 [late 19C+] (US Und.) to pay money, esp. under duress. 3 [late 19C+] (US Und.) to reveal, to explain.

give up on v. [1970s+] to lose one's faith, trust or belief in.

give upon a man v. see GIVE ON A MAN v.

give up one's face v. [1960s+] to permit oneself to indulge in oral intercourse at the insistence of a partner. [FACE n.² (8)]

give up rhythm v. [1960s+] (US Black) of a woman, to indicate her sexual availability to a man with whom she is walking or dancing, through her body language.

give up the ass v. [1970s+] (US) to accede to seduction, usu. of a woman. [ASS n. (3)]

give up the gold v. [2000s] (US teen) for a girl to lose her virginity prior to marriage.

give up the ship v. [late 19C–1930s] to die. [Captain James Lawrence's famous dying words, 'Don't give up the ship' at the taking of the Chesapeake, 1 June 1813]

give up the store v. [20C+] to surrender, to give in.

give — what-for v. [20C+] to talk eloquently about a given topic. [WHAT-FOR n.]

give with v. see MAKE WITH v.

give your can a chance! excl. [1910s] (Aus.) stop talking! [CAN n.[1] (2)]

giving it phr. [late 19C+] acting in a specific manner, e.g. giving it the old emotion.

gixie n. 1 [late 16C–early 17C] an affected, posing woman. 2 [17C] a prostitute. [SE gixie, a woman]

giz n. 1 [1940s] (US) any small thing for which one has temporarily forgotten the correct name. 2 [1970s+] (US) the vagina. 3 [1990s+] an annoying thing, which is impossible to get rid of. [abbr. of GIZMO n.]

gizmo n. (also gismo) [1940s+] 1 (orig. US) any (small) thing for which one has temporarily forgotten the correct name, a gadget, a thingumijig. 2 (US drugs) the paraphernalia used for injecting narcotics. 3 (US) the vulva or vagina (cf. ARTICLE n.). 4 (US) the penis (cf. BAUBLE n.). 5 (US) a foolish man. [ety. unknown]

gizz n. (also gizzard) [1940s] (US Black) a general form of greeting between men. [Mezzrow & Wolfe, Really the Blues (1946): 'Gizzard has a subtle overtone here: a gizzard is stuffed, and stuff means jive or kidding in hip talk, so the implication is: don't come up with no stuff, in other words, don't kid me, make sure that you pay me']

gizzard n. 1 [mid-17C+] the stomach, the solar plexus. 2 [mid-19C+] the heart. 3 [20C+] (US) courage. 4 [1920s+] the throat. [10C SE gizzard, animal or insect stomachs; ult. Lat. gicerium, the cooked entrails of a fowl]

gizzard v. [1950s] to cut out someone's guts. [GIZZARD n. (1)]

gizzem/gizzum n. see JISM n.

glad adj. 1 [mid-18C+] tipsy, drunk (cf. ABOUT RIGHT phr.[1]). 2 [late 19C–1900s] foolish; cheeky.

glad-and-sorry system n. [1910s+] hire purchase. [the emotions it sequentially creates]

glad bag n. [1980s+] (US) a body bag. [play on tradename Glad Bags]

glad clothes n. see GLAD RAGS n.

gladdie n. (also gladi) [1960s+] (orig. Aus.) a gladiolus. [abbr.]

glad eye n. 1 [20C+] (also glad glance) a glance of sexual interest; thus GIVE SOMEONE THE GLAD EYE v. 2 [1910s] a look of entreaty, of pleading, of friendliness.

glad hand n. (also glad mitt) [late 19C+] an expression of effusive if insincere greeting or welcome. [SE glad + hand/MITT n. (3)]

glad-hand v. (also give the glad hand) [late 19C+] to welcome enthusiastically, even excessively and very likely insincerely; often used of politicians and similar professional charmers; thus glad-handing, the act of so doing. [GLAD HAND n.]

glad-hander n. (also gladhand-shaker) [20C+] an enthusiastic, friendly but totally insincere person. [GLAD-HAND v.]

gladi n. see GLADDIE n.

gladiator school n. (also gladiator camp, kindergarten) [1960s+] (US prison) 1 a maximum–security prison (cf. BIG SCHOOL n.). 2 a prison with a notably harsh regime and a violent atmosphere. [? Irish gladiaathor, a fighting quarrelsome man]

glad lad n. [1940s] (US teen) an attractive boy.

glad mitt n. see GLAD HAND n.

glad pad n. [1940s] (US Black) a nightclub, a dancehall or similar establishment. [SE glad + PAD n.[2] (2)]

glad rag n. [1960s+] (US drugs) 1 a rag soaked with an intoxicating chemical, the fumes of which one inhales. 2 one who sniffs such inhalants. [the use of a proprietary Glad Bag for holding the liquid inhalant]

glad rags n. (also glad clothes) [late 19C+] (orig. US) one's best and prob. gaudiest clothes. [SE glad + RAGS n. (1)]

Gladstone n. [mid–late 19C] cheap claret. [Prime Minister William Gladstone's reduction, in 1860, of the duty on French wine]

gladstonize v. [late 19C] to evade and prevaricate. [the alleged characteristics of Prime Minister William Gladstone (1809–98)]

glad stuff n. [1950s+] (drugs) any form of hard or narcotic drug. [STUFF n.[3] (2) + the effects]

glad-time girl n. [1980s+] (W.I.) a promiscuous woman. [var. on SE good-time, of a woman, promiscuous]

glad weeds n. [1970s] (US) formal dress wear. [SE glad + WEEDS n.[1]]

gladys n. [1990s+] an act of defecation (cf. ANDY CAPP n.). [rhy. sl.; Gladys Knight = SHITE n. (2); ult. US singer Gladys Knight (b.1944)]

glahm v. see GLOM v.

glaik see under GLEEK.

glam v. see GLOM v.

glamity n. [1980s+] (W.I./UK Black teen) 1 the vagina. 2 sexual intercourse. 3 the 'ability' of a vagina, i.e. a woman's sexual prowess. [W.I. dial. glami, sticky and elastic; ult. SE clammy, wet, moist, sticky]

glamour boy n. (also glamour girl) [1930s+] a glamorous young man or woman. [orig. used of RAF, esp. flying crews]

glamour butch n. [1990s+] (US gay) a masculine lesbian or homosexual who wears formal clothes. [SE glamour + BUTCH n.[4] (3)/BUTCH n.[4] (5)]

glamour fart n. [1980s+] (Aus. prison) a woman, esp. when attractive. [rhy. sl. = TART n.[1] (1); but note GLAMOUR PANTS n.]

glamour girl n. see GLAMOUR BOY n.

glamour pants n. [1930s–70s] an attractive young woman, occas. a man.

glamour puss n. (also glamour pussy) [1940s+] an ostentatiously well-dressed, lavishly made-up etc (young) person, usu. a woman.

glamour up v. [1950s+] (US) to glamorize.

glands n. (US) 1 [1910s–20s] the testicles. 2 [1970s+] the breasts.

glanthem n. [late 18C] money.

Glasgow kiss n. [20C+] a headbutt (cf. CHELSEA SMILE n.).

Glasgow magistrate n. (also Glasgow baillie) [mid-19C–1930s] a salt herring. ['When George IV visited Scotland, a wag placed some salt herrings on the iron guard of the carriage belonging to a well-known Glasgow magistrate, who made one of a deputation to receive his Majesty' (Hotten, 1867). The Scots Magazine (December 1950) attributes the term to Walter Gibson, 'a merchant of Glasgow and Provost of that city in 1688']

Glasgow Rangers n. (also Glasgows) [1920s+] strangers, esp. as used by lookout men working with unlicensed street pitchmen. [rhy. sl.; ult. the football team]

glasheen n. (also glawsheen) [20C+] (Irish) a small glass of strong drink. [SE glass + dimin. sfx -een]

glasier n. (also glazier, glazyer) 1 [mid-17C–mid-19C] (UK Und.) a thief who breaks into houses after removing an accessible window, or into shops by smashing the shop window. 2 [mid-18C] (UK Und.) a window. [SE glasier]

glasiers n. (also glaziers) [mid-16C–early 19C] the eyes. [SE glass]

glass n.[1] 1 [late 14C+] a glass of alcohol. 2 [1980s+] (Irish) a half-pint of stout or beer.

glass n.[2] 1 [20C+] (US Und.) a diamond; thus genuine glass, a very high-quality diamond; fake glass, a worthless diamond. 2 [1940s+] (UK Und.) any form of jewellery.

glass n.[3] [1940s+] (drugs) a hypodermic needle. [early syringes were made of glass]

glass n.[4] [1940s+] the penis. [one 'blows' glass to make it larger]

glass n.[5] (drugs) 1 [1970s+] methamphetamine (cf. BOMBITA n.). 2 [1980s+] heroin. [the shininess of the powder]

glass adj. [1910s+] (US, orig. boxing) used of any weak or vulnerable part of the body, e.g. a glass chin or GLASS JAW n. (1).

glass v. [1930s+] to hit in the face with a (broken) glass. [abbr. USE THE GLASS v.]

glass case n. [mid-19C] a face. [rhy. sl.]

glass dick n. [1990s+] (drugs) a pipe for smoking crack cocaine. [SE glass + fig. use of DICK n.⁴ (1)]

glass eyes n.¹ (also **glasseye**) [late 18C–1950s] one who wears spectacles.

glass eyes n.² (also **glassy eye**) [1940s–50s] (drugs) a drug user. [the effect on one's eyes]

glass gun n. [1940s+] (drugs) a hypodermic needle. [early syringes were made of glass + they give one a SHOT n.⁶ (2)]

Glass House, the n. [1960s+] (US) the Los Angeles County Jail. [the design]

glasshouse n.¹ **1** [1910s+] a milit. prison or guardroom (cf. BANDHOUSE n.). **2** [1960s+] a police station. [the glass-roofed North Camp milit. prison at Aldershot]

glasshouse n.² [1990s+] (drugs) a place where crack cocaine can be sold and/or smoked. [GLASS DICK n. + SE house]

glass jaw n. **1** [1910s+] (US, orig. boxing) a conspicuously weak jaw, which breaks or fractures when hit and loses its possessor their fights. **2** [1920s+] (US campus) a coward. [GLASS adj.]

glass legs n. see HOLLOW LEG n. (1).

glass of beer n. [20C+] an ear. [rhy. sl.]

glass of lunch n. (also **glass of steak**) [1960s] (Aus.) a drink, a 'liquid lunch'. [GLASS n.¹ (1)]

glass of plonk n. [20C+] the nose. [rhy. sl. = CONK n.¹ (3)]

glass of water n. [1950s] (US) a tall, thin person. [such a person is seen to lack strength, as does water when compared to alcohol]

glassy (alley), the n. (also **the agate, the glassy agate**) [20C+] (Aus.) the best, the favourite, the most admired; thus JUST THE GLASSY (MARBLE) phr. [SE glassy, of a surface, smooth, unruffled, absolutely flat + glass alley, a specially prized type of marble/SE agate, both used for marbles]

glassy (eye) n. [1910s+] (Aus.) a cold, disdainful stare. [dead fish, lying on the slab have 'glassy' eyes]

glassy eye n. see under GLASS EYES n.².

glaum see under GLOM.

glaver v. [late 17C] to fawn, to flatter. [orig. dial.]

glawsheen n. see GLASHEEN n.

Glaxo baby n. [1930s] (N.Z.) a young member of the special police used against strikers in Auckland. [brandname Glaxo, a proprietary babyfood popular among the parents of these mainly middle-class young men]

glaze n. **1** [late 17C–19C] a window; thus on the glaze, robbing jewellers' shops after smashing the windows; mill a glaze, to smash a window. **2** [late 18C] (US Und.) a bottle. **3** [late 18C–early 19C] a mirror. **4** [early 19C] a lantern. [SE glaze, a vitreous composition used for glazing pottery etc]

glaze the donut v. [1990s+] of a woman, to masturbate (cf. APPLY LIP GLOSS v.; BEAT ONE'S MEAT v.). [DOUGHNUT n.² (2)]

glazier see under GLASIER.

glazyer n. see GLASIER n.

gleaming adj. [1990s+] (US campus) first-rate, excellent.

glean v. [mid–late 19C] a euph. for to steal. [SE glean, to gather, to harvest]

gleaner n. **1** [mid–late 19C] a thief. **2** [1920s] in weak use, a sponger. [GLEAN v.]

gleat n. (also **gleet**) **1** [late 17C+] urethritis. **2** [1940s+] (Aus.) venereal infection in the rectum. [OF glette, slime, filth, purulent matter]

gleef n. [1960s] (US) an idiot. [GLEEP n.]

gleek n. (also **glaik**) [1930s+] (Irish) a glance, a quick look. [Scot. glee, a squint, a look behind]

gleek v. (also **glaik**) [1930s+] (Irish) to glance quickly. [GLEEK n.]

gleep n. [1940s+] (US campus) an odd or stupid person. [ety. unknown; HDAS suggests 'perhaps intended to represent a Chinese speaker's pron. of CREEP n. (3)'; but note Time, 25 August

1947, 74: 'Britain's first pile [...] began operation last week. Officially it is a gleep (graphite low energy experimental pile)']

gleep v. [1950s+] (US Und.) orig. of a motorcycle gang, to steal; often gleep a cage, to steal a car. [ety. unknown; ? link to CLIP v.¹ (4)]

gleet n. see GLEAT n.

glengorm n. [20C+] (Ulster) dirt, filth. [ety. unknown]

Glenn Hoddle n. [1970s+] something very easy. [rhy. sl. = DODDLE n.; ult. soccer star and later England team manager Glenn Hoddle (b.1957)]

glib n. (also **glibb**) **1** [mid-18C–early 19C] a ribbon. **2** [19C–1900s] loquacity, verbosity. **3** [mid-19C–1930s] the tongue; thus slacken your glib, loosen your tongue. [(3) resemblance to (1) but note SE glib, voluble but essentially trivial]

glibe n. see GYBE n.

glick adj. (also **glic**) [1980s+] (Irish) cunning, clever. [Irish glic, cunning, crafty]

glide v. **1** [late 19C] (Aus.) to die. **2** [late 19C+] (later use US Black) to walk, to move, to arrive.

glim n.¹ (also **glym**) **1** [early 17C; late 19C–1960s] a look, a glimpse. **2** [late 17C–1940s] a lantern, esp. a dark lantern used by thieves (later a flashlight or torch); thus DOUSE THE GLIM v. **3** [late 17C+] a candle; any form of light. **4** [late 18C–1950s] (also **glimm**) the eye. **5** [19C] a fake account of a dramatic fire, as sold in the streets. **6** [mid-19C–1900s] (also **shade-glim**) a window. **7** [late 19C–1940s] a match. **8** [1930s] (US tramp) an eyeglass. **9** [1940s] a lighter. [SE gleam]

glim n.² [mid-18C] a fiery drink. [fig. use of GLIM n.¹ (5)]

glim n.³ [mid–late 19C] a venereal disease. [GLIM n.¹ (2), on pattern of FIRE n.¹, i.e. it 'burns']

glim v. **1** [late 17C–early 19C] (UK Und.) to burn on the hand, to brand. **2** [late 19C–1960s] (also **glimb**) to see, to catch sight of. **3** [20C+] (UK Und.) to beg. **4** [1910s–20s] (US Und.) to illuminate, to light. **5** [1950s] (US) to know, to realize. [GLIM n.¹]

glim-dropper n. [1940s–50s] (US Und.) a confidence trick whereby a trickster allegedly drops an artificial eye in a shop. He offers a reward if it is found. The merchant cannot do so, but a second con-man arrives, only to find the eye. He then says he will claim the reward, until the merchant, who also wants it, buys it off him. There is no reward. [GLIM n.¹ (4) + DROPPER n.⁶]

glim-fenders n. (UK Und.) **1** [late 17C–mid-19C] andirons. **2** [19C] handcuffs. [(2) puns on (1) as 'hand irons']

glimflashy adj. (also **glimflashly, grimflushly**) [late 17C–mid-19C] angry, impassioned. [one fig. flashes a GLIM n.¹ (2)]

glim-gibber n. (also **glim-glibber**) [mid-19C] a particular jargon or professional slang. [? fig use of GLIM n.¹ (2) as a generic for underworld + SE gibber, to mutter, to talk incomprehensibly]

glim jack n. [late 17C–mid-19C] **1** (also **glym jack**) a link boy. **2** (UK Und.) a thief who works only at night. [GLIM n.¹ (2) + generic proper name Jack]

glim lurk n. [19C] (UK Und.) the pleading for alms after suffering a supposed fire. [GLIM n.¹ (5) + LURK n. (1)]

glimm n. see GLIM n.¹ (4).

glimmer n. (also **glimmar, glymmer**) **1** [mid-16C–early 19C; 1940s] (UK Und.) fire; thus a lantern etc. **2** [late 17C–mid-18C] venereal disease. **3** [19C–1960s] the eye. **4** [late 19C] (US) a match, a locomotive headlight, a kerosene lamp. **5** [1910s] (US) a cut gem. **6** [1930s] a person who watches vacant motorcars. **7** [1930s] (US) a black eye. **8** [1930s–70s] an electric light, a torch. **9** [1940s–70s] a beggar, esp. one who claims to have lost all his possessions in a fire. **10** [1960s] (US) a sight, a view. [SE glimmer, to shine; ult. Du./Ger. glimmer, to shine]

glimmerer n. (also **glimmering mort, glymmerer**) **1** [late 16C–early 19C] a beggar who claims to have lost all their possessions as the result of a fire. **2** [mid-17C] a person, usu. a woman, who gains entry to a house on the pretext of getting a light for the fire and, while inside, steals whatever she can. **3** [mid-17C–mid-18C] one who deliberately sets fire to a house, hoping to take advantage of the confusion in order to steal. [GLIMMER n. (1) (+ MORT n.)]

glimmers n. **1** [19C+] the eyes. **2** [1930s–60s] (US Und.) spectacles. [GLIMMER n. (3)]

glimming n. [late 19C–1940s] **1** (US Black) watching, observing. **2** (UK Und.) watching out for cabs etc for wealthy people, in return for a tip. [GLIM v. (2); note London cab-driver jargon glim, to look for a cab]

glimpse n. [1950s+] (W.I.) an albino. [albinos tend to have poor eyesight]

glimpses n. [1910s] the eyes.

glims n. [mid-19C–1940s] (mainly US) spectacles, eye-glasses; thus (Aus.) glim-faking, selling spectacles at inflated prices. [GLIM n.¹ (4)]

glimstick n. (also glym stick) [late 17C–mid-19C] (UK Und.) a candlestick; thus rum glimstick, a silver candlestick; queer glimstick, a brass or pewter candlestick. [GLIM n.¹ (3) + SE stick]

glint n. [20C+] a look, a glimpse; thus have/take a glint at, to observe, to glance at.

glisten n. [mid-19C] (US) a collective term for diamonds.

glistener n. [early 19C–1920s] a gold coin (cf. BRASS n.¹). [the coin's shine]

glister n. [late 19C] a glass, a tumbler; thus a glister of fish-hooks, a glass of Irish whisky. [SE glister, a bright light, brilliance, lustre]

glister-pipe n. see CLYSTER-PIPE n. (2).

glitch n. [1960s+] a hitch, a snag, a malfunction. [Ger. glitschen, to slip, via Yid. glitshen, to slide or skid; orig. mainframe computer jargon glitch, 'a sudden interruption in electric service, sanity, continuity, or program function' (New Hacker's Dictionary, 1992). This was adopted c.1960 by astronauts, who gave it the more general def., and it moved into mainstream sl. with the spread of the personal computer]

glitter n. **1** [1900s–10s] (Aus.) money (cf. BRASS n.¹). **2** [1940s] (US Und.) (also glitters) cheap or imitation jewellery. **3** [1950s+] (US prison) salt. **4** [1960s–70s] (US gay) powdered Methedrine. **5** [1970s] (US) a collective term for diamonds. [all sparkle or shine]

glitterati n. [1940s+] (orig. US) those fashionable writers, academics and sundry critics etc who have transcended their usual obscurity into the dubious limelight of the New York and London gossip columns. [SE glitter + literati]

Glitter Gulch n. [1950s+] (US) the Las Vegas downtown casino area. [the lurid neon signs etc of the original entertainment area, before The Strip developed]

glitters n. see GLITTER n. (2).

glittery n. [1970s] (US) gold.

glitz n. [1950s+] (orig. US) an extravagant but superficial display. [backform. f. GLITZY adj. (1)]

glitz up v. [1950s+] to make flashy, showy, to get dressed gaudily. [GLITZ n.]

glitzy adj. **1** [1950s+] fashionable, sophisticated, glamorous. **2** [1970s] (US campus) very capable. [Ger. glitzern, glittering; or comb. of SE glitter + RITZY adj. (1)]

g.l.o. phr. [1990s+] guest list only, used to describe an event so unappealing that one would go only if on the guest list, as it would not be worth paying for admission. [abbr.]

gloak n. (also gloach, gloke, gloque) [mid-18C–mid-19C] a man, a fellow. [Shelta gloch, ? cognate with Irish loach, hero]

gloak v. [1920s–30s] (UK tramp) to induce pity by one's tale. [ety. unknown]

glob n. (also globber) **1** [1930s] (US) a plain sundae. **2** [1950s+] a mass or lump of some liquid or semi-liquid substance. **3** [1960s] (US campus) in pl., a great deal, a large quantity. [? SE blob + GOB n.² (1)]

globber n. [1990s+] foolish talk. [? GLOB n.]

globber v. [1990s+] to talk incoherently. [GLOBBER n.]

globe n. **1** [18C–early 19C] a round, pewter pot. **2** [late 19C] a bowler hat.

globes n. **1** [late 17C] the testicles (cf. BALLS n.¹). **2** [mid-19C+] the female breasts (cf. BAGS n.¹). **3** [1970s+] the buttocks.

globetrotter n. [1960s] (drugs) a narcotics addict who is continually on the move, usu. in search of supplies.

globular adj. [18C] drunk. [? the sufferer is 'going round in circles']

glock n. [mid–late 19C] a fool. [Irish gloichd, a fool]

gloik n. [1910s+] (Aus.) a fool, a simpleton. [GLOCK n.]

gloke n. see GLOAK n.

glom n.¹ [1930s+] (US) a fool. [? echoic of the solidity/dullness of the individual]

glom n.² (also glaum) (US) **1** [1930s+] a hand. **2** [1940s+] a look. [GLOM v.]

glom v. (also glahm, glam, glaum, glomm, glom onto, gloom, glum) **1** [late 19C+] (US) to grab, to steal. **2** [1910s+] (US) to arrest. **3** [1910s+] (US) to get, to obtain, to seize upon. **4** [1910s+] (US) to look, to see, to realize. **5** [1920s+] (US Und.) to pick fruit or crops. **6** [1930s+] (US) to eat, usu. to eat greedily. **7** [1970s+] (US) to stick, to entangle. [Scot. glaum, to snatch, to grab, to seize with the jaws, to eat greedily]

glomp v. [1980s] to grab, to suck up. [? GLOM v.]

gloom n. (also gloom bug/shedder) [1910s–30s] (US) a depressed and/or depressing individual; thus adj., gloomed up. [GLOOMS n. (+ SE shedder/BUG n.⁵ (2))]

gloom v. see GLOM v.

glooms n. (also glums) [1910s+] a bad mood, depression. [SE gloomy/glum]

gloom shedder n. see GLOOM n.

gloomy-drawers n. see GRUMPY-DRAWERS n.

gloomy gus n. [20C+] (US) a very unhappy, pessimistic person. [created c.1904 as a comic-strip character in Happy Hooligan by Frederick Burr Opper (1857–1937)]

gloop n. see GOOP n.².

gloopy adj. [1960s+] **1** viscous, sticky. **2** stupid. [GLOOP n.]

glop n. **1** [1940s+] a liquid or viscous substance or mixture. **2** [1940s+] unappetizing food. **3** [1950s+] (US) silly nonsense. [onomat. of such a substance falling onto a hard surface; coined by cartoonist Elzie Segar (1894–1938) as a sound made by the baby Swee'pea in the cartoon Popeye the Sailor]

gloque n. see GLOAK n.

Gloria Gaynors n. [1990s+] trainers. [rhy. sl.; ult. US pop singer Gloria Gaynor (b.1947)]

glorioski! excl. [1950s+] (US) an excl. used to express surprise. [GLORY (BE)! excl. + -SKI sfx]

glorious adj. [late 18C–1900s] very drunk (cf. ABOUT RIGHT phr.¹).

gloriously adv. [late 18C+] extremely; usu. in phr. gloriously drunk.

glorious sinner n. [mid-19C; 1930s–40s] dinner. [rhy. sl.]

glory be n. [1990s+] tea. [rhy. sl.]

glory (be)! excl. [19C+] a euph. for God!; also used in a variety of mild oaths and excls.

glory-grinding n. [late 19C] (Aus.) preaching.

glory hole n.¹ **1** [mid-19C] a small, holding cell in the court buildings, in which prisoners are kept during their trial. **2** [late 19C–1900s] a meeting place used by the Salvation Army. **3** [20C+] (Irish) the space under the stairs, or similar confined place (a place of punishment for badly behaved children). **4** [1960s+] (US) a bar frequented by homosexuals. [SE glory hole, anywhere in which things are heaped together without any attempt at order; ult. Scot. glaur, to make muddy; (4) plays on GLORY HOLE n.² (2)]

glory hole n.² **1** [1920s+] (orig. US) the vagina (cf. BLACK HOLE n.¹). **2** [1940s+] (gay) a hole cut in the side of a public toilet cubicle; one man pushes his penis through while another anonymous man fellates him. [SE glory, splendour, magnificence, esp. as pun on go to glory, to ascend to heavenly bliss + hole]

glory pole *n.* [1950s] (*US*) the penis. [SE *glory* + POLE n.]

glory roll *n.* [1930s–40s] (*US Black*) a large bankroll, produced as often as possible in order to impress one's acquaintances (cf. CALIFORNIA BANKROLL n.). [SE *glory* + ROLL n.[2]]

glossy *n.* **1** [1950s+] a glossy magazine, esp. expensive women's fashion magazines, such as *Vogue* or *Harpers & Queen* (which has called itself 'the non-drip glossy', punning both on DRIP n.[2] and on gloss paint). **2** [1970s+] (*US*) a sexy picture of young women, esp. ones that are posted outside bars, clubs etc to allure customers; also later of men such as film actors.

glossy *adj.* [1900s] (*US*) very pleasant, enjoyable.

glouter *n.* [20C+] **1** a sticky mess. **2** tapioca pudding (cf. FISHEYES n.). [? Scot. *cloiter*, a vile wet mess]

glove *n.*[1] [17C] some form of unspecified drinking vessel. [the term is used in Thomas Dekker's book of 'manners', *The Guls Hornebooke* (1609), in a list of similar containers: 'hoopes, cans, half-cans, Gloues, Frolicks, and flap-dragons']

glove *n.*[2] [1950s+] (*Aus./US*) a condom. [note Williams for 17C use of *glove* as metaphor for vagina]

glow *n.* [1960s] the euphoric state of being intoxicated by drugs.

gluck *n. see* GUCK n.

glucose-slinger *n.* [late 19C] (*Aus.*) a publican. [? nonce-word; + SLINGER n.[1] (1)]

glue *n.*[1] **1** [mid-19C] gonorrhoea. **2** [late 19C] semen (cf. BOLLOCK SNOT n.). **3** [late 19C+] thick soup. **4** [1920s–40s] (*US*) beer. **5** [1940s] (*US*) alcohol. **6** [1960s] (*US*) blood. **7** [1980s+] (*Aus. prison*) porridge. [appearance; (3) E.P. says 'it sticks to the ribs']

glue *n.*[2] [late 19C–1940s] (*US*) money. [? one wishes to 'stick onto it']

glue *v.* [1920s–70s] (*orig. US*) **1** to steal. **2** to arrest.

glued *adj.*[1] [late 19C] (*US campus*) enthusiastic about.

glued *adj.*[2] [1940s–60s] (*US*) drunk. [GLUE n.[1] (4) + the lassitude of a drunkard's speech and movements]

glued *adj.*[3] [1980s+] (*orig. US campus*) stable, sane. [HAVE ONE'S HEAD GLUED ON v.]

gluehead *n. see* GLUEY n.

glueneck *n.* (*also* **gluepot**) [1920s–70s] (*US*) a dirty prostitute; thus *adj.*, **gluenecked**. [GLUE n.[1] (2)]

gluepot *n.*[1] **1** [late 18C–early 19C] a parson. **2** [late 19C–1930s] a part of the road so muddy that vehicles stick in it. **3** [late 19C–1930s] (*S.Afr.*) a particularly pleasant public house. **4** [1920s–40s] (*US Und.*) a post office. **5** [1920s–60s] (*US*) an old horse. [(1) he 'joins together' married couples; (3) one wishes to be 'stuck' there; (5) suggested by use of horse carcasses in glue manufacture]

gluepot *n.*[2] [20C+] the vagina (cf. ALL QUIET n.[1], BAG n.[1]). [rhy. sl. = TWAT n. (1); but note GLUE n.[1] (2)]

gluepot has come unstuck *phr.* [late 19C] used of someone who smells of semen or recent intercourse. [GLUE n.[1] (2)]

gluey *n.* (*also* **gluehead**) [1960s+] (*drugs*) a person who sniffs glue. [SE *glue* + sfx -*y*/-HEAD sfx (3)]

glug *n.* [1970s+] (*orig. US*) a swig, a swallow. [echoic]

glug *v.* [1980s+] (*orig. US*) to swig, to swallow. [GLUG n.]

gluggar *n.* [20C+] (*Irish*) a general term of abuse. [Irish *ubh ghluagir*, a rotten egg]

glum *n. see* GLOM v.

glum-pot *n.* (*also* **glum-bum**) [late 19C+] a miserable, sulky person. [SE *glum* + -POT sfx]

glumpy *adj.* [late 18C–19C] unhappy. [SE *glum*]

glums *n. see* GLOOMS n.

glunch *v.* [1910s+] (*Ulster*) to grumble, to complain. [Scot. *glunch*, to grumble, to frown]

glut *n. see* GLUTTON n. (3).

glutes *n.* [1980s+] (*US*) the buttocks. [medical Lat. *gluteus maximus*, one of the large muscles that form the buttock; ult. Gk *glutos*, the rump]

glutton *n.* **1** [early–mid-19C] an enthusiast; in boxing, one who

is a 'glutton for punishment'. **2** [mid-19C] enthusiasm, ardour, greediness. **3** [1940s+] (*gay*) (*also* **glut**) a man obsessed with sex to the exclusion of other considerations. [SE *glutton* but ? link to Suffolk dial. *glutton*, a glut (of commodities) or Scot. *gluther*, to swallow voraciously]

glutton for punishment *n.* [1940s+] (*gay*) a fellator who continues sucking the penis even when orgasm has been reached.

glybe *n. see* GYBE n.

glym *see under* GLIM and its combs.

glype *n.* [20C+] (*Irish*) a fool. [synon Scot. *glype*]

g.m. *n.* [late 19C–1950s] (*Aus./US*) a.m., the morning. [abbr. *good morning*]

G-man *n.*[1] (*US*) **1** [1920s+] (*also* **G**) an FBI agent, lit. 'Government-man' (cf. G-WOMAN n.). **2** [1940s+] a garbage man. [abbr.; (1) G adj.; note pre-US use as a political detective in pre-independence Ireland]

G-man *n.*[2] [1990s+] (*drugs*) a cocaine dealer. [G n.[1] (3)]

g.m.b.u. *n.* (*also* **g.m.f.u.**) [1940s+] a disaster, utter chaos (cf. S.N.A.F.U. n.). [abbr. *grand military balls-up/fuck-up*]

G-money *n.* [2000s] (*US Black/teen*) a term of affectionate address. [G n.[3] (1) + MONEY n.[4] (3)]

'gnac *n.* [1990s+] (*US Black*) cognac. [abbr.]

gnarlatious *adj. see* GNARLY adj. (2).

gnarler *n.* (*also* **gnawler**) [early 19C; late 19C–1920s] **1** a small watchdog. **2** an informer. [SE *gnarl*/GNARL (UPON) v.]

gnarl (upon) *v.* [late 18C–early 19C] (*UK Und.*) to spy on, to inform against; thus *gnarling*, likely to act as an informer. [SE *gnarl*, to snarl]

gnarly *adj.* [1980s+] **1** (*US*) a general term of disapproval, disappointment, disgust. **2** (*US campus*) (*also* **gnarlatious, knarly, narly**) on bad = good model, wonderful, first-rate. **3** (*US campus*) bizarre, frightening, amazing. [SE *gnarly*; popularized by the film *Fast Times at Ridgemont High* (1982)]

gnashers *n.* [1960s+] the teeth.

gnasp *v.* [early–mid-18C] to annoy. [16C SE *gnasp*, to snap at]

gnat *n.* [1940s+] (*US campus*) an unattractive male who pesters women. [characteristic of the insect]

gnatbrain *n. see* BEETLEBRAIN n.

gnat butter *n.* [1900s–40s] (*US*) **1** semen (cf. BABY GRAVY n.). **2** smegma. **3** decayed skin tissue.

gnat's eyebrow *n.* (*also* **gee hair, gnat's balls, ...bristle, ...ear, ...elbow, ...eye, ...hair, ...heel, ...nip, ...prick, ...toenail**) [mid-19C+] (*US*) something very small; esp. in phrs., e.g. *down to a gnat's eyebrow*, to the finest detail; *sharp enough to split the hair on a gnat's ass*, extremely fine.

gnat's liver *n.* [1930s] (*US Black*) an unattractive woman.

gnat's piss *n.* (*also* **gnat's pee/widdle**) [1920s+] a derog. description of any liquid, but esp. alcohol, that is weak, thin, tasteless etc (cf. BUFFALO PISS n.). [note Minnesota college *squaw piss*, weak beer]

gnat's prick/toenail *n. see* GNAT'S EYEBROW n.

gnaw *v.* [1980s+] (*N.Z.*) to kiss.

gnawler *n. see* GNARLER n.

gnaw the bone *v.* [1990s+] to perform fellatio (cf. BASKET LUNCH n.). [SE *gnaw* + BONE n.[1] (1)]

gnaw the 'nana *v.* [1960s+] to perform fellatio (cf. BASKET LUNCH n.). [SE *gnaw* + BANANA n.[2] (1)]

gnof *n. see* GONNOF n.

gnome *n.*[1] [1950s–60s] an international (esp. Swiss) banker. [coined on 12 November 1956 by Labour politician Harold Wilson (1916–95), referring to the economic problems that had plagued Britain in the wake of the Suez Crisis of earlier that year; he blamed them on the machinations of Swiss bankers and financiers, who could manipulate the economies of nations, seemingly at will]

gnome *n.*[2] [1950s+] (*US*) an insignificant person, esp. a low-level employee.

gnomon *n.* [late 16C–early 19C] the nose. [SE *gnomon*, 'object which serves to indicate the time of day by casting its shadow upon a marked surface; esp. the pin or triangular plate used [...] in an ordinary sun-dial' (*OED*)]

gnostic *n.* [early–mid-19C] a 'knowing one', thus a cheat or sharper; thus *gnostically*, knowingly, artfully. [SE *gnostic*, an intellectual, one who possesses esoteric spiritual knowledge]

G-note *n.* [1930s+] (*US*) a $1000 note. [G n.¹ (1) + SE *note*]

go *n.*¹ **1** [late 18C–1970s] a measure (of alcohol), e.g. a *go of gin*; thus a vessel that contains such a measure, esp. a 3-halfpenny bowl of gin and water, available at a *go shop*. **2** [late 19C–1900s] (*Aus.*) a helping of food. **3** [1930s–50s] (*US drugs*) a measure of drugs; an injection of a given drug.

go *n.*² **1** [late 18C+] the height of fashion. **2** [early 19C] a dandy, a fashionable man. [SE *go*, spirit, energy, dash]

go *n.*³ **1** [late 18C+] an event, circumstances, a state of affairs; esp. as *rum go*, an odd situation; thus *what goes?* what's happening? **2** [late 18C+] a success; thus MAKE A GO OF v. **3** [early 19C+] an enjoyable time, a spree. **4** [early 19C+] a portion, a 'time'. **5** [mid-19C] a wonderful person, esp. an attractive woman. **6** [mid-19C+] an attempt, a try, e.g. *have a go (at)*. **7** [mid-19C+] a turn in a game, an opportunity to do something, a chance; thus *at/in one go*, at/in one attempt; *have a go*, take a turn. **8** [late 19C–1930s] a bargain, an agreement, a 'deal'; usu. in phr. *it's a go*, that's settled. **9** [late 19C+] a contest, a fight, esp. a boxing-match or a street fight. **10** [1930s] a bet. **11** [1950s+] an argument; a verbal attack; usu. in phr. *have a go at (someone)*. **12** [1960s+] (*Aus.*) news, information. **13** [1960s+] (*Aus./US*) the important, relevant thing. **14** [1980s+] (*Aus. prison*) a plan.

go *n.*⁴ [20C+] (*Aus.*) a goanna. [abbr.]

go *n.*⁵ **1** [1930s] (*US drugs*) a very small quantity of drugs wrapped in paper. **2** [1980s+] (*drugs*) cocaine. **3** [2000s] (*drugs*) amphetamine (cf. A n.²).

go *v.*¹ [17C–18C] to have an orgasm.

go *v.*² [mid-17C+] usu. of a woman, to perform sexual intercourse; usu. in interrog. phr. used between 2 men, *does she go?*

go *v.*³ **1** [late 17C; mid-19C+] to be acceptable, to be permitted. **2** [late 17C+] to succeed, to win approval or applause; thus *goingest*, best. **3** [late 19C+] (*orig. US*) to be accepted or carried into effect, to have authority or effectiveness, to be obeyed without question; esp. in phr. *what I say goes*. **4** [late 19C+] to deal with, to find appealing or acceptable, to like or prefer. **5** [1920s+] (*US*) to choose, esp. to become a member of, e.g. *go Catholic*. **6** [1950s] to characterize, to explain, to make sense of.

go *v.*⁴ **1** [mid-18C+] to bet, to wager. **2** [mid-19C] to bet on. **3** [mid-19C+] to pay for.

go *v.*⁵ **1** [mid-19C+] to tolerate, to bear, to put up with. **2** [late 19C+] to eat or drink, e.g. *I could go a couple of beers*.

go *v.*⁶ **1** [mid-19C+] (*US*) to be killed; to die. **2** [1950s] (*US prison*) to be executed. **3** [1960s+] (*US*) to go to prison. **4** [2000s] to collapse, to fall down.

go *v.*⁷ [late 19C+] to match, to get along. [a pair of matched horses]

go *v.*⁸ [late 19C+] for something to work out in a specific way, esp. of a political contest, e.g. *go Labour, go Republican*.

go *v.*⁹ [20C+] to *go* to the lavatory, used euph., esp. by children, e.g. *Miss, I've got to go!* [abbr.]

go *v.*¹⁰ **1** [20C+] (*Aus./US*) to attack, verbally or physically. **2** [1940s] (*US Black*) in fig. use, to attack.

go *v.*¹¹ [1920s+] to say, to talk, e.g. *I go 'How are you?', and he goes 'Lousy'*.

go a bomb *v.* [1960s+] to be very keen on or enthusiastic for.

go-about *n.* [1910s–30s] (*US*) a tramp.

go about the bush *v. see* BEAT ABOUT THE BUSH v.

go abroad *v.* **1** [19C] to be transported. **2** [1940s] (*US Und.*) to be imprisoned. [ironic euph.]

go a bundle on *v.* [1930s+] to support wholeheartedly, to be very fond of. [fig. uses of GO v.⁴ (1) + BUNDLE n.¹ (2)]

go a-crash of *v.* [20C+] to assault. [SE *go* + pfx *a-* (implying motion) + *crash* (into)]

go a cropper *v. see* COME A CROPPER v.

go across the river *v.* [19C+] to die; thus *gone across*, dead. [the mythological River Styx across which dead Greeks were supposedly ferried by Charon on their way to Hades]

goad *n.* [16C–early 18C] (*UK Und.*) a decoy at a horse-fair. [SE *goad*, a spur]

goadie *n. see* GODY n.

go a fairy *v.* [late 19C] to toss coins to see who buys a round of halfpennyworths of gin. [GO v.⁴ (1) + SE *fairy*, very small]

go a-gallin *v. see* GAL v.

go aggro *v.* [1980s+] (*US campus*) to become aggressive. [AGGRO n. (3)]

go-ahead *n.* [mid-19C+] (*orig. US*) **1** progress, ambition, energy; thus adj. *goaheaditive*; n. *goaheaditiveness*. **2** a command or permission to do something; esp. in phr. *give it/someone the go-ahead*. [GO-AHEAD adj.]

go-ahead *adj.* [mid-19C+] (*orig. US*) progressive, enthusiastic to do well.

go ahead *v.* [mid-19C+] to authorize an action or a person to perform an action. [GO-AHEAD adj.]

go ahead like a whale *v.* [late 19C] to throw oneself into something wholeheartedly. [ext. GO AHEAD v.; the size of a whale]

go ahead up *v.* [1970s+] (*US Black*) to take part in some form of activity with another person. [GO AHEAD v.]

goak *n.* [mid-19C–1930s] (*Aus.*) a prank, a practical joke. [SE *joke* + dial. *gowk*, a fool]

goal *v.* (*also* **ghoul**, **gool**) [1910s–30s] (*US*) to knock down, to stun, to defeat; thus *knock someone for a goal*, to astonish. [SE *goal*; *ghoul/gool* are dial. prons.]

go all off *v. see* GO OFF (ON) v. (1).

go all out *v.* [1920s+] to make one's best effort. [SE *go* + *all out*, completely]

go all over town with *v.* [1940s+] to lick and suck the partner's body, including the genitals and sometimes the anus. [the tongue 'travels' around the body; usu. used by a prostitute as part of the 'menu' of paid services she can offer; a 'localized' var. of AROUND THE WORLD n.]

go (all) round the houses *v.* [1960s+] to take a circuitous route; also in fig. use.

go all the way *v.* (*also* **go the whole way**) **1** [1920s+] of a man, to have sexual intercourse; of a woman, to be willing to permit this. **2** [1940s+] to commit oneself completely; to be totally successful. **3** [1960s] of a male prostitute, to take on the 'active' role in oral intercourse.

go all the way to Cockfosters *v.* [1990s+] to have sexual intercourse. [*Cockfosters* is the last station on London Underground's Piccadilly line]

go all unnecessary *v. see* COME OVER ALL UNNECESSARY v.

go aloft *v.* [19C+] of a person, to die; of an object or situation, to cease exisiting. [i.e. to heaven]

go alone *v.* [early 19C–1900s] to be wary or cautious, to be experienced.

go-along *n.*¹ (*also* **go-alonger**) [early–mid-19C] (*UK Und.*) a fool. [he 'goes along' when someone orders him]

go-along *n.*² [mid-19C] a thief.

go along (with you)! *excl. see* GET ALONG (WITH YOU)! excl.

goamey *n. see* GOM n.

go a million *v.* (*Aus./N.Z.*) **1** [1910s] to love very much. **2** [1910s+] to be utterly lost, in a totally hopeless position, at a total disadvantage. [fig. uses of GO v.⁴ (1), i.e. one has wagered and presumably lost 'a million']

go and...! *excl. see also under* excls. without 'and', e.g. for *go and boil your head! see* GO BOIL YOUR HEAD! excl.

go and bark up a tree! *excl.* [1900s] a generally dismissive excl., a euph. for GO TO HELL! excl.

go and eat coke! *excl. see* GO (HOME) AND EAT COKE! excl.

go and get cut! *excl.* [20C+] (*Aus.*) a general excl. of dismissal or disdain.

go and have a roll! *excl.* [1940s+] go away! get lost!

go and kiss your aunt! *excl.* [1920s] a general excl. of contempt or dismissal.

go and look at the crops *v. see* GO LOOK AT THE CROPS v.

go and scrape yourself! *excl.* [late 19C–1900s] a general excl. of dismissal or contempt.

go and sing 'sweet violets' *v.* [late 19C+] to defecate. [euph.]

go and take a run (against the wind)! *excl.* [mid-19C+] (*Anglo-Irish.*) a general excl. of dismissal or contempt.

go and take a running jump at yourself! *excl.* [20C+] a general excl. of dismissal and distaste.

go animal *v.* [1960s] (*US*) to lose one's emotional control. [ANIMAL n.[1] (8)]

goanna *n.*[1] [late 19C] (*Aus.*) ? a virile man.

goanna *n.*[2] [1910s+] (*Aus.*) a piano. [rhy. sl.; note pron. 'pianer']

goanna oil *n.* [1950s] (*Aus.*) any supposedly remarkable medicinal cure.

go a-padding *v. see* PADDING n.[1] (2).

go ape *v.* (*also* go apeshit, go ape wild) **1** [1950s+] (*orig. US*) to lose control, esp. of one's temper. **2** [1960s+] (*orig. US*) to malfunction. [APE adj. (2)/APESHIT adj. (1); the alleged 'craziness' of the animal. The specific ref. is prob. to the fictitious *King Kong*, created for the film in 1933]

go ape for *v.* (*also* go ape over) [1960s+] to be obsessed with. [GO APE v. (1)]

go a peg lower *v.* [late 19C] to drink heavily. [PEG n.[5]; the pegs that were once driven into a public house tankard to mark the amount drunk]

go a raker *v.* (*Aus.*) **1** [late 19C] place a heavy bet. **2** [late 19C+] to fall heavily. [GO v.[4] (1)/SE *go* + RAKER n.[2]]

go around *v.* [1940s] (*US*) to argue, to fight.

go around in circles *v.* (*also* run around in circles, rush around in circles) [1930s+] (*orig. US*) to move or act aimlessly or inconclusively.

go around the block *v.* [1940s+] (*orig. US*) to gain experience; esp. in phr. *X has been around the block* (*a few times*), X is experienced, esp. sexually.

go around the tower *v.* [late 17C–early 19C] (*UK Und.*) to clip money. [proper name *Tower of London*, one of London's criminal centres]

go around with *v. see* GO ROUND WITH v.

go as if she cracked nuts with her tail *v.* [late 17C–early 18C] of a woman, to be sexually enthusiastic. [GO v.[2] + TAIL n.[2] (3)]

go a snack *v. see* GO SNACKS v.

goat *n.*[1] **1** [late 16C+] a womanizer, a lecher; usu. as *old goat*; thus *goatish*, lecherous. **2** [17C; late 19C+] a dupe, a fool (cf. AIREDALE n.). **3** [late 19C] (*US Und.*) a Catholic priest. **4** [1910s] (*US*) a slow or worthless horse. **5** [1910s+] (*US*) an offensive (old) man, occas. woman. **6** [1940s] the buttocks. **7** [1960s] (*US campus*) a student being initiated into a fraternity, a fraternity pledge; thus *goat room*, the room used for initiation. [the trad. characteristics of the animal, i.e. lechery, stubbornness etc]

goat *n.*[2] (*US*) **1** [late 19C+] a goatee beard. **2** [1910s+] a scapegoat. [abbr.]

goat *n.*[3] [1900s–60s] (*US*) a racehorse.

goat *n.*[4] [1910s] (*US*) temper. [backform. f. GET SOMEONE'S GOAT v. (1)]

goat *n.*[5] [1960s+] (*US*) a Pontiac GTO automobile. [pron./reversal of GTO; note HOT-ROD n. jargon *goat*, an old racing car, generally used when speaking of a driver 'herding his goat']

goat *n.*[6] [1980s] a caddy.

goat *v.* [mid-19C–1900s] to beat, to thrash. [? to butt like a *goat*]

goat-and-galah *adj.* [1920s–50s] (*Aus.*) used of a small hotel, town or other place to indicate the lack of amenities. [the main inhabitants are *goats* and *galahs*]

goat breath *n.* [1980s] (*US campus*) a derog. term of contempt. [SE *goat*/GOAT n.[1] (5) + SE *breath*]

goatees *n.* [1970s] (*US gay*) the testicles. [? GONADS n. (1) + ref. to goatish lechery]

goat-fuck *n.* (*also* goat-rope, goat-screw) [1970s+] (*orig. US milit.*) a fiasco, a mess, chaos, confusion. [such a coupling is seen as an epitome of chaos]

goat-fucking *adj.* [1960s] a euph. for MOTHERFUCKING adj. (1).

go at full bang *v.* [1910s–20s] to go at full speed.

goat-getting *n. see* GET SOMEONE'S GOAT v. (1).

goat-hair *n.* [1900s–60s] (*US Black*) homemade or bootleg liquor.

goat hill *n.* (*also* goat's gulch, goat town, goat woods) [20C+] (*US*) an area of town where a certain class of people live, usu. the poor, but sometimes the better-off. [note one such *goat's gulch* in Kansas was gentrified and re-nicknamed *Angora Heights*]

goat house *n.* [mid–late 19C] a brothel (cf. ACCOMMODATION HOUSE n.). [GOAT n.[1] (1) + HOUSE n.[1] (1)]

go at it baldheaded *v. see* BALD-HEADED adv.

go at it hammer and tongs *v.* (*also* go at it shovel and tongs, go hammer and tack) [early 18C+] to approach an activity with maximum effort and energy; modern use esp. refers to sexual intercourse. [imagery of a blacksmith using a hammer to beat a piece of metal extracted with tongs from a furnace]

goatmilker *n.* [mid-19C] **1** the vagina. **2** a prostitute (cf. COCKATRICE n.). [GOAT n.[1] (1) + SE *milker*; note SE *goatmilker*, *goatsucker*, a name given to the bird *Caprimulgus europœus*, f. a belief that it sucks the udders of goats]

goat-mouth *n.* [20C+] (*W.I.*) the ability that certain individuals supposedly possess to cause problems or frustrate the efforts of others; thus *put goat-mouth on*, to cause such problems; *goat-mouth bite you?* a question asked of one who seems unhappy or worried.

goat-rope *n. see* GOAT-FUCK n.

goat roper *n.* [20C+] (*US*) a peasant, a rural person, an unsophisticated person (cf. ACORN-CRACKER n.). [their stereotypical occupation]

goat-screw *n. see* GOAT-FUCK n.

goat's genolickers *n.* [1940s–50s] (*Irish*) the real thing, the ultimate example. [var. on DOG'S BALLOCKS n. (2)]

goat's gulch *n. see* GOAT HILL n.

goat's jig *n.* [late 17C–18C] sexual intercourse. [the perceived sexuality of the goat]

goat skin *n.* [1970s] (*US gay*) a long foreskin.

goat's nest *n.* [1950s] (*US*) a dirty, untidy place.

go at something baldheaded *v. see* BALD-HEADED adv.

goat town/woods *n. see* GOAT HILL n.

goaty *adj.* (*US*) **1** [1910s–50s] sexually frustrated. **2** [1910s–70s] irritated. [characteristics of the SE *goat*]

go-away *n.* **1** [mid-19C] (*US Und.*) a railroad train. **2** [late 19C] (*UK society*) the dress in which a bride departs from her reception to begin her honeymoon. **3** [1920s+] (*Aus.*) a train, a tram, a bus.

go away *v.* [20C+] to go to jail?. [AWAY adj.[1] (1)]

go away (outta that)! *excl. see* GET AWAY (WITH YOU)! excl.

gob *n.*[1] (*also* gub) **1** [mid-16C+] (*orig. UK Und.*) the mouth. **2** [mid-19C+] verbosity. **3** [late 19C] the face. **4** [1960s] a blow to the mouth. [orig. northern dial.]

gob *n.*[2] **1** [mid-16C+] a lump or clot of some slimy substance. **2** [early 17C; 19C+] a lump, a mouthful. **3** [late 19C] (*UK Und.*) a theft carried out by a thief who spits on a man's coat, alerts him to the problem then robs him while pretending to 'help' him clean up. **4** [1910s] (*UK public school*) a person who makes one feel sick. **5** [1930s+] a lump. **6** [1970s] spit.

gob *n.*[3] [19C+] a large amount; esp. as *gobs* (*of*). [16C SE *gob*, a large amount of money]

gob *n.*⁴ [late 19C+] **1** a coastguard or a quarterdeck man. **2** (*US*) (*also* **gobshite**) any sailor. [GOB n.² (1); 'When a meeting takes place the men indulge in a protracted yarn and a draw of the pipe. The session involves a considerable amount of expectoration all round, whereby our friends come to be known as gobbies' (F&H)]

gob *n.*⁵ *see* GOBSHITE n.¹ (3).

gob *v.* **1** [early 19C] to hit in or on the mouth. **2** [late 19C+] to spit. **3** [1990s+] to swallow in large mouthfuls, to 'choke down'. [GOB n.¹ (1)/GOB n.²]

gob! *excl.* [20C+] a euph. for *God!*

go-back *n.* [20C+] **1** (*Aus.*) a reply, a retort. **2** (*US Und.*) a second (or subseq.) attempt at the same crime.

go back *v.* [20C+] (*US Black*) for processed hair to return to its normal state. [SAmE *go back*, to retreat to a wild state]

go back on *v.* [mid-19C+] (*orig. US*) to reverse one's position, to break a promise.

go back to Africa *v.* [20C+] (*W.I., Guyn.*) for a light-skinned man to marry a woman whose complexion is much darker than his own.

go back to square one *v.* [1930s+] to start again at the beginning. [? such board games as ludo or snakes and ladders where an unlucky throw of the dice can send one 'back to square one'; an alternative suggestion refers to the game of hopscotch, also based on squares]

go backwards *v.* [18C] to visit an outdoor privy. [the position of the anus + the usu. siting of the privy at the back of the house]

go bag your head! *excl.* [mid–19C+] (*US/Aus.*) a general dismissive excl., give in! back off! admit defeat! be quiet! [BAG ONE'S HEAD v.]

go bail *v.* (*also* **go baill**) [mid-19C+] to be absolutely certain, to 'put one's money where one's mouth is'. [the presumption that one will only go bail for a person in whom one has faith]

go bald-headed at/for/into *v. see* BALD-HEADED adv.

go ballarat *v.* [late 19C–1920s] (*Aus.*) to drink alone. [? the minimal population of the town *Ballarat*]

go ballistic *v.* [1980s+] (*orig. US*) **1** to lose one's temper. **2** to do very well. **3** of a situation, to escalate out of control.

go ballocking *v.* [19C+] to have sexual intercourse (cf. GO BEARD-SPLITTING v.; GO BED-PRESSING v.; GO BELLY-BUMPING v.; GO BIRDS-NESTING v.; GO BITCHING v.; GO BUM-FAKING v.; GO BUM-FIGHTING v.; GO BUSH-RANGING v.; GO BUTTOCKING v.; GO BUTTOCK-STIRRING v.; GO COCKFIGHTING v.; GO CUNNY-CATCHING v.; GO DOODLING v.; GO FACEMAKING v.; GO FLASHING IT v.; GO FLESHMONGERING v.; GO GOOSING v.; GO JOCK-HUNTING v.; GO JUMMING v.; GO LEATHER-STRETCHING v.; GO MOTTING v.; GO PILE-DRIVING v.; GO PRICK-SCOURING v.; GO QUIM-STICKING v.; GO RUMPING v.; GO RUMP-SPLITTING v.; GO STAR-GAZING (ON ONE'S BACK) v.; GO STRUMMING v.; GO TAIL-TICKLING v.; GO TROMBONING v.; GO TUMMY-TICKLING v.; GO TWAT-FAKING v.; GO TWATTING v.; GO UNDER-PETTICOATING v.; GO VAULTING v.; GO WENCHING v.). [BALLOCK n. (1)]

gobaloon *n. see* GABBERLOONEY n.

go bananas *v.* [1960s+] (*orig. US*) **1** to lose emotional control, to become obsessed by. **2** to delight in something absolutely; usu. as *go bananas over.* [image of an over-ripe banana that 'goes soft']

go bang *v.* [1920s+] (*Aus.*) of a man, to have sexual intercourse. [BANG n.² (2) + the 'explosion' of ejaculation]

go banzai *v.* [2000s] to lose emotional control. [SE *banzai*, 'a reckless attack by Japanese servicemen' (*OED*)]

gobber *n.* [1920s–30s] the mouth. [GOB n.¹ (1)/GOB v. (2)]

gobberloony *n. see* GABBERLOONEY n.

gobble *n.* [1930s+] an act of fellatio; both hetero- and homosexual (cf. BASKET LUNCH n.). [GOBBLE v.¹ (2)]

gobble *v.*¹ **1** [mid-19C–1900s] (*US*) to grab, to steal, to apprehend. **2** [1910s+] (*also* **gobble off**) to fellate (cf. BASKET LUNCH n.). [SE *gobble*, to eat food greedily, thus (2) play on EAT v.³ (1)]

gobble *v.*² [1930s–40s] (*US*) **1** to chatter. **2** to talk incoherently. [SE *gabble* + ? the turkey's *gobbling*]

gobble *v.*³ [1970s] (*US*) to fail in the entertainment business. [i.e. to act like a TURKEY n.³ (1)]

gobble box *n.* [1970s] (*US campus*) a television set. [var. on GOGGLE (BOX) n.]

gobbledygoo *n.*¹ (*also* **gobblegoo**) [1930s–40s] (*US*) **1** a prostitute who performs fellatio (cf. COCKATRICE n.). **2** fellatio (cf. BASKET LUNCH n.). [GOBBLE THE GOO v.]

gobbledygoo *n.*² (*also* **gobblegoo**) [1940s+] (*US*) pretentious or nonsensical speech. [*gobbledegook*, coined in 1944 by Maury Maverick, chairman of US Smaller War Plants Committee in Congress, who suggested a link to the *gobbling* noises of a turkey; the term began as sl. but very quickly mutated into SE]

gobble-gobble *n.* [1940s] (*US Black*) talk, chatter. [GOBBLE v.² (1) + redup.]

gobble-gut *n.* [early–mid-17C] a glutton. [SE *gobble* + *gut*]

gobble off *v. see* GOBBLE v.¹ (2).

gobble pipe *n.* [1930s] (*US*) a saxophone.

gobbleprick *n.* [late 17C–18C] a sexually active woman. [SE *gobble*/GOBBLE v.¹ (2) + PRICK n. (2)]

gobbler *n.*¹ **1** [mid-16C–18C] a duck. **2** [1910s] (*Aus.*) a Turkish soldier. [despite its appearance in Grose (1785), and in Bailey, *Universal Etymological English Dict.* (1721 et seq.), as 'cant', *gobbler*, a turkey-cock, is SE, thus (2) is play on that use]

gobbler *n.*² **1** [19C] the mouth. **2** [mid-19C+] a voracious eater. **3** [1920s+] (*US*) (*also* **bone-gobbler**) an individual who performs oral sex. [SE *gobble*/GOBBLE v.¹ (2)]

gobbler's knob *n.* (*also* **gobbler hill**) [1930s–60s] (*US*) a generic nickname for anywhere considered far away.

gobble someone's bird *v. see* BIRD n.⁸ (1).

gobblestick *n. see* GOB-STICK n. (2).

gobble the goo *v.* (*also* **gobble the gook, ...goop, ...goose, ...gravy**) [1910s+] (*orig. US*) to fellate (cf. BASKET LUNCH n.). [GOBBLE v.¹ (2) + GOO n.¹ (1)/GOOK n.³ (1)/GOOP n.² (1)/SE *goose*/GRAVY n.¹ (2)]

gobble up *v.* [mid-19C+] (*US*) to seize upon, to snatch up, to lay hold of. [ext. GOBBLE v.¹ (1)]

gob-box *n.* [late 18C–early 19C] the mouth. [GOB n.¹ (1) + SE *box*]

gobby *n.*¹ [late 19C–1920s] **1** a sailor. **2** a coastguardsman. [GOB n.⁴]

gobby *n.*² [1920s] (*US*) a socially unacceptable person.

gobby *adj.* [late 19C+] talkative. [GOB n.¹ (1)/GAB v. + sfx *-y*]

gob-crockery *n.* [1980s] (*Aus.*) false teeth. [GOB n.¹ (1)]

gobdaw *n.* (*also* **daw**) [1940s+] (*Irish*) a gullible simpleton. [Irish *gabhdán*, a gullible person]

go beard-splitting *v.* [18C] of a man, to have sexual intercourse (cf. GO BALLOCKING v.). [BEARD-SPLITTER n. (1)]

go beat your meat! *excl.* [1940s+] (*US*) a general excl. of dismissal. [BEAT ONE'S MEAT v. (1)]

go Bedford *n.* [mid-19C] a rich, throaty chuckle. [the contemporary actor Paul *Bedford* who issued such a trademark chuckle accompanied by the words 'I believe you my boy', a phr. he used in the hit melodrama *The Green Bushes*]

go bed-pressing *v.* [19C] to have sexual intercourse (cf. GO BALLOCKING v.).

gobeen *n.* [late 19C–1930s] (*Irish*) a general term of abuse. [Irish *gob*, a beak + dimin. sfx *-een*]

go behind *v.* [1940s] (*US Black*) to argue with, to contradict.

go belly-bumping *v.* [19C] to have sexual intercourse; thus *get a belly-bumper/belly-buster*, to become pregnant (cf. BELLY BUMP v.; GO BALLOCKING v.).

go belly-up *v.* (*also* **go belly-side up**) **1** [20C+] of a thing, an event, a situation, to collapse, to fail, to come to an end. **2** [1920s+] to go bankrupt. **3** [1970s] to abandon one's defences. **4** [1980s] of a person, to die. [the image of a dead fish, floating belly up, or of a dog, rolling on its back as a gesture of defeat]

go bent v. [1950s+] (*UK Und./prison*) **1** for a witness to retract a previous statement (which would have helped the prosecution). **2** to become corrupt. **3** to turn to criminality. **4** for one's girlfriend to take up with someone else. [BENT adj. (3)]

go bent on v. [1950s+] (*UK Und.*) to let down, to desert. [BENT adj.]

Go-between, The n. [late 19C] St Alban's Church, Holborn, London WC1. [a court case of 1897 when a witness, asked what denomination this church was, replied 'It ain't Roman Catholic, and yet it's very High. It's a go-between' (Ware)]

go between the moon and the milkman v. [late 19C] to abscond from a house or flat, taking one's furniture and possessions, but avoiding payment of any outstanding rent, utility bills etc. [i.e. to leave the house at or just prior to dawn]

go beyond v. [mid-19C] (*Anglo-Irish*) to suffer judicial transportation. ['beyond' the world one knows]

gobful n. see MOUTHFUL n.

gob-gobbler n. [1980s+] (*US gay*) a gay man who specializes in sailors as partners. [GOB n.⁴ (2) + GOBBLER n.² (3)]

gobhawk n. [late 19C–1900s] (*Irish*) an uncouth person. [GOB n.² (1) + SE *hawk*, to spit]

go big v. [1900s–70s] (*US*) **1** to like very much, to enthuse over. **2** to go well. **3** to embark on a major project.

go binting v. see BINT n. (1).

go birds-nesting v. [20C+] to have sexual intercourse (cf. ARRIVE AT THE END OF THE SENTIMENTAL JOURNEY v.; GO BALLOCKING v.). [euph.; BIRD n.¹ (2) + NEST n.¹]

gob-iron n. [1950s+] a mouth organ. [GOB n.¹ (1) + SE *iron*]

go bitch v. [1990s+] (*US Und.*) of a man, to act in a cowardly or effeminate manner. [BITCH n.¹ (5)]

go bitchcakes v. [2000s] (*US campus*) to be angry, to act aggressively. [ext. of BITCHY adj. (2)]

go bitching v. [late 17C–mid-19C] of a man, to have sexual intercourse, esp. with a prostitute (cf. GO BALLOCKING v.). [BITCH n.¹ (1)]

gob job n. [1980s+] **1** fellatio (cf. COCKSUCK n.). **2** (*US gay*) fellatio performed on a sailor. [GOB n.¹ (1) + JOB n.⁴; (2) adds pun on GOB n.⁴ (2)]

go blah v. [20C+] to have one's mind go momentarily blank. [SE *blah*, echoic of a nonsensical noise]

goblet of jam n. [1960s] (*US drugs*) marijuana. [transl. of Arabic, *m'jun-i akbar*]

goblin n. [late 19C–1920s] a sovereign. [abbr. JEMMY O'GOBLIN n.]

go blind v. [20C+] to masturbate. [mockery of the Puritan warning that those who masturbate will go blind]

goblin juice n. [1960s–70s] (*US*) whisky. [SE *gobble* + *juice*]

gob-lock n. [1990s+] a fool. [GOB n.¹ (1) + SE *lock*; their inarticulacy]

go blooey v. (*also* **go blooie**) [1920s+] to explode suddenly, to go wrong, to fail, to break down. [BLOOEY! excl.]

gob off v. [2000s] to talk (loudly). [GOB n.¹ (1)]

gob off! excl. [1990s+] go away! [euph.]

go boil your head! excl. (*also* **go and boil your head! go boil yourself!**) [late 19C+] a generally dismissive excl., a euph. for GO TO HELL! excl.

go Bondi v. see SHOOT THROUGH LIKE A BONDI TRAM v.

go bong v. see GO BUNG v.

goboon n. (*also* **gaboon**) [1930s–40s] (*US*) a spittoon. [GOB v. (2) + sfx *-oon*]

gob-organ n. [1930s] (*Aus.*) a mouth organ. [GOB n.¹ (1)]

go Borneo v. [1970s+] (*US campus*) to get crazily drunk. [the presumed antics of the 'Wild Man of Borneo']

go both ways v. **1** [1960s+] to be a bisexual. **2** [1970s] to take either role in sado-masochistic sex.

go-boy n. (*Can./Irish*) **1** [1940s+] a young hoodlum, a juvenile delinquent. **2** [1970s] an escapee, successful or otherwise.

gobshite n.¹ **1** [late 19C–1910s] (*US*) an expectorated wad of tobacco. **2** [20C+] (*also* **gabshite**) a fool, a dupe (cf. DIPSHIT n.). **3** [1960s+] (*also* **gob**) a general term of abuse. **4** [1990s+] nonsense, rubbish; also as adj., stupid. **5** [1990s+] one who talks nonsense. [lit. and fig. uses of GOB n.¹ (1) + SHITE n.]

gobshite n.² see GOB n.⁴ (2).

gobsmacked adj. (*also* **gobstruck**) [1950s+] flabbergasted, amazed, speechless. [orig. northern dial.; lit. SE *smacked* in the GOB n.¹ (1)]

gob-stick n. **1** [late 18C–19C] (*US*) usu. in pl., (silver) forks or spoons. **2** [1920s–50s] (*orig. US*) (*also* **gobblestick**) a clarinet or fife. [GOB n.¹ (1) + fig. use of SE *stick*]

gobstopper n. **1** [1920s+] a large, spherical sweet that one sucks, gradually reducing the size. **2** [1990s+] the penis (cf. BUTT-PLUNGER n.). [used to stop someone's GOB n.¹ (1); (2) pun on (1)]

gob string n. see GAB STRING n.

gobstruck adj. see GOBSMACKED adj.

gob the knob v. [1990s+] (*US*) to perform fellatio (cf. COCKSUCK n.). [GOB v. (3) + KNOB n.¹ (3)]

go buck v. [1990s+] (*US Black*) to act in an outrageous, often destructive and aggressive manner. [BUCK-WILD adj.]

go bum-faking v. [late 19C] to have sexual intercourse (cf. GO BALLOCKING v.). [BUM-FAKE v.]

go bum-fighting v. (*also* **go bum-tickling, -working**) [late 19C–1900s] to have sexual intercourse (cf. GO BALLOCKING v.). [BUM n.¹ (1) + SE *fight*/SE *tickle*/SE *work*]

go bung v. (*Aus./ N.Z.*) **1** [mid-19C+] (*also* **go bong**) to die. **2** [late 19C+] to become bankrupt. **3** [late 19C+] to collapse, to break down, to fail. [Aboriginal *bong*, dead]

go bung into v. [late 19C] to smash into, to hit hard. [SE *bung*, into the very heart of things]

go bush v. [20C+] (*Aus.*) **1** to go wild, to go mad. **2** to seek the solitude and privacy of the bush. **3** of farm animals, to run free. **4** to escape from prison and vanish. [SE *bush*, uncleared or untilled areas that are still in a state of nature]

go bush-ranging v. [19C] to have sexual intercourse (cf. GO BALLOCKING v.). [pun on SE + BUSH n.² (1)]

go bust v. [late 19C+] of an individual firm or company, to lose one's money, to become bankrupt. [BUST adj.]

go buttocking v. [18C] to have sexual intercourse (cf. GO BALLOCKING v.).

go buttock-stirring v. [19C] to have sexual intercourse (cf. GO BALLOCKING v.).

goby n. [1970s] a middleman in criminal dealings, an underworld fixer. [SE *go-between*]

go by hand v. [1920s–50s] (*US tramp*) to travel on foot (as opposed to train).

go-by-the-ground n. [late 18C–early 19C] a short person.

go by the number eleven bus v. [late 19C] to walk. [the 2 legs resemble the figure 11]

go by walker's bus v. [late 19C] to go on foot. [pun on SE *walk*]

go by way of Lothbury v. [mid-16C–mid-17C] to hate, to dislike. [pun on *Lothbury* in the City of London/SE *lo(a)the*]

go caflooey v. see GO KERFLOOEY v.

go-cart n. [1910s–70s] (*US*) a car.

go case v. (*also* **come case, go case-o, have a case (on)**) **1** [1900s–50s] to have a semi-permanent relationship with. **2** [1910s+] to sleep with. [CASE n.⁶ (1)/CASE n.³ (1)]

go caso v. [1900s–30s] to work as a genteel prostitute, from a flat, rather than walking the streets. [CASE n.³ (1)]

go catch a horse v. [20C+] to urinate (cf. BURN THE GRASS v.). [euph.]

go chase yourself! excl. see CHASE v.¹ (2).

go chew on a chitlin! excl. [1960s] a generally dismissive excl., a euph. for GO TO HELL! excl.

go chicken v. see CHICKEN (OUT) v.

go chock-a-block (with) v. [1970s] (Aus.) to have sexual intercourse (with). [CHOCK-A-BLOCK adj. (2)]

gock n. [1970s] (US) any form of sticky substance, ointment, cream. [var. GOOK n.³ (1)]

go climb up your thumb! excl. (also **go climb a tree/the chain!**) [1930s–40s] (US) a general excl. of dismissal.

go cockfighting v. [19C] to have sexual intercourse (cf. GO BALLOCKING v.). [COCK n.² (1)]

go coconuts n. [1990s+] to go wild, crazy. [? one is off/out of one's COCONUT n.¹]

go cold at v. [1920s+] (Aus.) to scold, to blame, to reprimand.

go cold on v. [1920s+] to lose one's initial enthusiasm for a proposition, activity etc.

go comb your wig! excl. [early 19C] a general excl. of dismissal.

go commando v. [1970s+] (orig. US campus) to go without underwear. [? tough commandos need no such 'soft' apparel]

go commercial v. [1940s–60s] (orig. US Black) to become a prostitute.

go conk v. [1920s+] (Aus.) **1** usu. of machinery, to collapse, to break down, to malfunction. **2** to die. **3** to fall asleep. [CONK (OUT) v.]

go crackers v. [1920s+] to go mad, insane, eccentric. [CRACKERS adj.]

go crawl back in your hole! excl. [20C+] a hostile excl. used when requesting someone to be quiet and go away.

go crawl up a hole! excl. [1940s+] (Aus.) a general excl. of dismissal or contempt.

go critical v. [1990s+] to explode with emotion or rage. [nuclear physics; go critical, for the fissile material placed in a reactor or bomb to reach the minimum mass or size required to produce a chain reaction]

go crook (on) v. (Aus.) **1** [20C+] to act dishonestly; of an honest person, to join the underworld. **2** [1910s+] to lose one's temper (with); to assail. **3** [1910s+] to break down, to stop working, to deteriorate. **4** [1910s+] of people, to experience difficulties. **5** [1910s+] to become ill. [CROOK adj.]

go cunny-catching v. [18C] of a man, to have sexual intercourse (cf. GO BALLOCKING v.). [CONYCATCH v.¹]

God n.¹ [late 17C+] used in a number of oaths that, when coined, had a good deal more resonance, given their blasphemous context, e.g. GOD-AWFUL adj. (cf. GOD'S...! excl.).

God n.² [1990s+] (US Black) a term of address to a male friend.

god n. [late 19C; 1980s+] (US campus) an exceptionally attractive male.

God almighty n. [1990s+] a nightie, a nightdress. [rhy. sl.]

God-almighty adj. [mid-19C+] a general intensifier.

God-awful adj. [late 19C+] (orig. US) especially appalling; thus superlative god-awfullest.

God-awful adv. [1930s+] appallingly. [GOD-AWFUL adj.]

god-bird n. [1950s] (W.I.) the much-loved and petted 'baby' of the family. [dial. god-bird, the youngest bird in a nestful]

God-blasted adj. [20C+] a general oath.

God-blessed adj. [1960s+] (US) a euph. for GOD-DAMN adj. (1).

God bless the duke of Argyle phr. [mid-19C] a remark made on observing one's companion shrug their shoulders; the insinuation is that they have lice. [a row of iron posts erected in Glasgow by the contemporary duke. Grateful lice-ridden citizens were able to use them as scratching-posts. Another version suggests that the posts were erected around the duke's various estates; primarily for the benefit of sheep, they were adopted by verminous shepherds]

God-blind-me n. [1950s] (W.I.) flashy footwear. [the ironic excl. by one who sees them]

God blind old Reilly! excl. [1940s–50s] a general oath of annoyance, incredulity etc.

God-botherer n. [1920s+] (orig. milit.) an evangelist. [note RMC

Duntroon (Aus.) God-botherer, a college padre or chaplain; God-botherers, any group of overtly religious cadets or of religious people in general]

God-bothering n. [2000s] religious ceremonies, esp. when excessively and sanctimoniously pious. [GOD-BOTHERER n.]

God-bothering adj. [1960s+] unctuously pious. [GOD-BOTHERER n.]

God-box n. **1** [1910s+] a church. **2** [1930s+] an organ.

Goddam n. [late 18C–19C] as used by a foreigner, an English person. [the stereotyped English propensity for the oath GOD-DAMN! excl.; note more recent French les fuckoffs, the English, coined for similar reasons]

God-dam! excl. see GOD-DAMN! excl.

goddam n. see GOD-DAMN n.¹.

goddamit adj. (also **goddammit**) [1960s+] (US) a general intensifier. [GOD-DAMN IT! excl.]

God-dam-me n. see DAMME-BOY n.

God-damn n.¹ (also **goddam**, **goddem**) [18C+] a DAMN n.; thus NOT GIVE A GODDAM v.

God-damn n.² [1990s+] jam. [rhy. sl.]

God-damn adj. **1** [17C+] (also **God-damned**) a general intensifier, lit. 'most damnable'; thus superlative God-damnedest. **2** [mid-19C+] (US) exasperating, most strange. **3** [1940s+] as an infix, e.g. ABSOGODDAMLUTELY adv. **4** [1980s] as a term of affection, admiration; usu. as God-damnedest.

God-damn v. **1** [17C+] a general curse. **2** [1910s–30s] to swear.

God-damn! excl. (also **God-dam!**) [17C+] a generally pej. excl. expressing anger, astonishment etc. [note WW1 Aus. milit. goddam-guy, an American]

God-damned adj. see GOD-DAMN adj. (1).

God-damn it! excl. [mid-19C+] a general excl. of exasperation.

God-dang adj. (also **God-darn**) [1910s–60s] a euph. for GOD-DAMN adj. (1).

goddem n. see GOD-DAMN n.¹.

goddess n. [1980s+] (US campus) an ambitious, successful woman.

goddess Diana n. [mid-19C] a sixpence (2½p). [rhy. sl. = TANNER n.]

godfather n. **1** [late 16C–early 19C] (also **godfather-in-law**) a juryman. **2** [late 18C–early 19C] one who pays the bill after a meal or a session of drinking; thus will you stand godfather and we will take care of the brat, you pay now and we will repay you later.

godfer n. [late 19C] a badly behaved child. [SE godforsaken]

God forbid n. [1930s–70s] a hat. [rhy. sl. = LID n.¹ (1)]

God-forbids n. **1** [late 19C+] (also **gawd-forbids**, **gord-forbids**, **lord-forbids**) children. **2** [1960s+] Jews. [rhy. sl.; (1) = KID n.¹ (1); (2) = YID n.¹]

Godfrey n. (also **Gadfrey**) [mid-19C+] (orig. US) a euph. for God and used as such in various mild oaths, e.g. by Godfrey! Godfrey mighty! (cf. BOB n.².)

God-help-us see under GAWDELPUS.

God-hopper n. [1940s–50s] (US) an evangelist or very religious person.

go ding-a-ling v. [1990s+] to go mad. [DINGALING adj.]

God in heaven n. [20C+] the number 7 (cf. GOD'S IN HEAVEN n.). [rhy. sl.]

God love her n. [1970s] one's mother. [rhy. sl.]

go dog on v. [late 19C–1950s] (Aus.) to let down; to betray, to inform against. [DOG n.³ (1)]

go doodling v. [late 19C–1900s] to have sexual intercourse (cf. GO BALLOCKING v.). [DOODLE v.¹]

go-down n. **1** [mid-17C–early 18C] a drink. **2** [1940s+] (orig. US Black) a basement flat or apartment (cf. GO-UP n.). [both the the liquor in (1) and the human dweller or visitor in (2) 'go down']

go-down adj. [1960s] used of one who enjoys giving oral sex. [GO DOWN v.⁶ (1)]

go down v.[1] [17C+] to be accepted by, to be approved, to be allowed; usu. in phr. go down well/badly with.

go down v.[2] [late 19C–1910s] (UK Und.) to rob, to steal from. [go down into the pockets]

go down v.[3] [late 19C–1930s] to lose one's money, e.g. in a wager; to become bankrupt.

go down v.[4] (also **go down below**) [20C+] **1** to be sent to prison; to be punished while in prison. **2** (W.I.) to be admitted to a mental hospital. [for ety. see UP THE STAIRS phr.]

go down v.[5] [1900s–20s] to give birth. [? the child goes down from the womb; the mother goes down to the hospital]

go down v.[6] (also **go down on**) **1** [1910s+] (orig. US) (also **go down south**) to perform fellatio or cunnilingus (cf. AUSSIE KISS n.). **2** [1950s+] (US) to copulate readily.

go down v.[7] **1** [1940s+] (orig. US Black) to happen, to take place, often of a fight or other dramatic encounter. **2** [1950s] (US gang) (also **come down, go down on**) to attack a rival gang.

go down v.[8] [1970s+] (US) to die.

go down below v. see GO DOWN v.[4].

go down for the gravy v. [1950s+] to perform cunnilingus (cf. BOX LUNCH n.). [GO DOWN v.[6] (1) + GRAVY n.[1] (1)]

go down in flames v. [1910s+] to fail to complete a task, despite one's best efforts. [the image of a downed aircraft]

go down in (food) v. [20C+] (W.I., Bdos) to eat ravenously.

go down like a dinner v. [1940s+] to be extremely popular, also used ironically.

go down like a lead balloon v. see LEAD BALLOON n.

go down like a pork chop at a Jewish wedding v. see LIKE A PORK CHOP AT A JEWISH WEDDING phr. (1).

go down like flies v. [20C+] to collapse in the face of weapons, disease or adversity.

go down like hot cakes v. [late 19C+] to prove extremely popular or acceptable. [GO DOWN v.[1]]

go down on v.[1] see GO DOWN v.[6].

go down on v.[2] see GO DOWN v.[7] (2).

go down one v. [late 19C] to fail, to be conquered, to be beaten. [school use, where one goes down a place or class]

go down south v. see GO DOWN v.[6] (1).

go downstairs for breakfast v. [1970s] (Aus.) to perform cunnilingus (cf. AUSSIE KISS n.; BOX LUNCH n.). [ext. of GO DOWN v.[6] (1) + play on EAT v.[3] (1)]

go down the bay v. [late 19C–1900s] (US) to spend heavily. [? earlier synon. for SPLASH OUT (ON) v.]

go down the chute(s) v. (also **go down the garbage can, ...the mine, shoot the chutes**) [late 19C+] (US) to be ruined, to meet with disaster.

go down the crapper v. see GO DOWN THE TOILET v.

go down the drain v. see GO DOWN THE PLUGHOLE v.

go down the line v. [1950s] to make an effort, to commit oneself.

go down the mine v. see GO DOWN THE CHUTE(S) v.

go down the pan v. see GO DOWN THE TOILET v.

go down the plughole v. (also **go down the drain, ...pipe**) [1930s+] to be wasted, to be lost for ever. [the image of an emptying bath]

go down the river v. [1900s–40s] (US, Southern) to go to the state prison in Mississippi. [the practice of selling an errant slave to a Mississippi sugar-cane plantation. The journey to the plantation, where work was especially hard, meant a trip 'down the river']

go down the road v. [1960s+] to pursue a policy or a course of action, even if it is unpleasant.

go down the Swanee v. (also **go up the Swanee**) [1970s+] to be ruined, to become bankrupt. [generic use of UP THE RIVER phr. to imply any form of trouble + ref. to the Al Jolson song 'Swanee']

go down the toilet v. (also **go down the crapper, ...pan,**

...sewer) [1960s+] to collapse, to end in failure. [SE/CRAPPER n.[3] (2)]

go down the tube(s) v. [1960s+] (orig. US) to fail badly, to collapse completely.

go down the weather v. [17C] to become bankrupt. [one suffers an 'ill wind']

go down the wind v. [late 17C–early 19C] to be unfortunate. [one suffers an 'ill wind']

go down to v. [1900s] (Aus.) to fall asleep.

go down to the ground v. [17C] to defecate.

go down with v. [1980s] (US Black) **1** to help a friend. **2** to fight.

go down with a smacker v. [late 19C] to fall flat on one's face or posterior. [one 'smacks' into the ground]

God permit n. [late 18C–mid-19C] a stage-coach. [such coaches were advertised as starting 'if God permit']

go drabbing v. see DRAB v.

God's...! excl. [16C+] an excl. used to express astonishment or annoyance, used in combs. e.g. God's bread! ...fast! ...foot! ...grease! ...guts! ...hats!...lid! ...knockers! ...precious! ...sides! ...teeth! ...wounds!

God save n. (also **God saves**) [1900s–30s] the British national anthem. [it starts 'God save our gracious king/queen']

God save the queens n. [20C+] vegetables. [rhy. sl. = SE greens]

God's flesh n. [1950s+] (drugs) psilocybin/psilocin. [popular translation of Nahuatl teonanacatl, lit. teotl, God + nancatl, mushroom]

gods for clods n. [1970s+] (US campus) a course in basic comparative religion.

God's green apple n. [20C+] (US) the Earth.

God's in heaven n. [1940s+] (bingo) the number 7 (cf. ALDERSHOT LADIES n.; GOD IN HEAVEN n.). [rhy. sl.]

God slot n. [1970s+] that period of early Sunday evening TV viewing set aside by law for mandatory, if marginal, religious broadcasting.

God's medicine n. see GOD'S (OWN) MEDICINE n.

God's mercy n. [19C] a dish of bacon and eggs served in a country inn. [the grace that preceded eating it]

Godsown n. (also **Godzone, Gordzone**) **1** [1910s+] (N.Z.) New Zealand. **2** [1970s+] (Aus.) Australia; or one's own country. [abbr. SE God's own country]

God's own — adj. [1920s+] a general intensifier, e.g. God's own row.

God's (own) medicine n. [1930s+] (drugs) opium, morphine, heroin (cf. APOSTLE n.; AUNTIE EMMA n.).

God squad n.[1] [1960s+] any form of proselytizing religious group (often evangelical), esp. as found within a university or similar institution.

God squad n.[2] [1980s+] (Aus. prison) prison officers responsible for security.

God squad n.[3] [1990s+] (US) the Endangered Species Committee. [they are accused of 'playing God' with nature]

God's quantity n. [1910s–20s] a large amount, an abundance.

God's time n. [20C+] (US) time as measured before the introduction during WW1 of Daylight Saving Time. [DST was ordained by the government, God's time by the passage of the sun]

God's trousers! excl. [1900s–50s] (Aus.) a mild oath.

god-thumper n. see BIBLE-THUMPER n. (1).

go due north v. [mid-19C] to become bankrupt. [the purpose-built debtor's prison, Whitecross Street Prison, is sited in what was then north London; its site is now covered by the Barbican development]

go Dutch v.[1] [1910s+] (orig. US) to share expenses, esp. of a meal. [DUTCH adj.[2]; racial stereotyping of the Dutch]

go Dutch v.[2] see DUTCH ACT n.

gody n. (also **goadie**) [20C+] (W.I.) a hugely swollen testicle, due to a rupture; known in medical jargon as a *hydrocele*, a water tumour. [? SE *gourd*, a water carrier]

godzillion *n.* [1980s+] (*US*) an indescribably large number. [SE *God*/GOD'S QUANTITY n. + ZILLION n.]

Godzone *n. see* GODSOWN n.

go easy *v.* [20C+] **1** to act cautiously, to proceed with caution. **2** to deal with someone kindly, to resist acting cruelly; usu. as *go easy on/with*. **3** to use sparingly; usu. as *go easy on*.

go eat pussy! *excl.* [1950s+] (*US Black*) go away! leave me alone! [SE *eat*/EAT v.[3] (1) + PUSSY n. (2)]

goef *n.* (*also* **ghoef, goof**) [1960s+] (*S.Afr.*) a swim. [synon. Afk.]

goef *v.* (*also* **ghoef, goof**) [1960s+] (*S.Afr.*) to swim. [GOEF n.]

goer *n.* **1** [mid-19C] a dancer. **2** [mid-19C+] an expert, a practitioner. **3** [mid-19C+] anything or anyone dependable, which can be counted on to work or succeed. **4** [20C+] an enthusiastic if not always competent amateur. **5** [1910s] a flirt. **6** [1920s+] a promiscuous, sexually available woman. [SE *go*; (6) GO v.[2]]

goers *n.* [19C] the feet. [they make one *go*]

goey *adj.* [1900s] enthusiastic, keen. [SE *go* + sfx -*y*]

go eyes out *v.* [mid-19C+] (*Aus./N.Z.*) to weep excessively. [SAusE/SNZE *eyes out*, at top speed, at full stretch]

go facemaking *v.* [late 18C–early 19C] to have sexual intercourse (cf. GO BALLOCKING v.). [the *face* is that of a newly conceived child]

go fall on yourself! *excl.* [late 19C] (*US*) a dismissive excl.

go fanti *v.* (*also* **go fantee**) [late 19C–1930s] to go crazy, to lose control, to go on the rampage. [SE *go fantee*, for a White man to 'go native'; ult. *Fante*, the inhabitants of Ghana]

go-fast *n.* (*also* **go-faster**) [1960s+] (*drugs*) methcathinone. [its effects]

go feel around! *excl.* [late 19C] (*US*) a dismssive excl.

gofer *n.* (*also* **gopher**) [1930s+] (*orig. US*) an assistant, errand boy or girl, anyone who is told to *go for...* some requirement.

gofer *v.* (*also* **gopher**) [1960s+] (*orig. US*) to run errands, to go out for something. [GOFER n.]

g off *v.* [1990s+] (*US drugs*) to make $1000 in a day's drug dealing. [G n.[1] (1)]

goffel *n.* [1970s] (*S.Afr.*) an ageing prostitute.

goffer *n.* [late 19C–1910s] a blow, a punch. [? fig. use of RN *goffer*, mineral water or lemonade, orig. that manufactured by *Goffe* & *Sons Ltd*. The image is of an angry person who is excited in the way that the bubbles in aerated water are. The mineral water use is extant in Aus.]

goffer *v.* [late 19C–1900s] to pull or crush a person's hat over their eyes, thus temporarily blinding them. [GOFFER n.]

goffo *n.* [1950s+] (*Irish*) a free ride on the back bumper of a car, van or lorry, unknown to the driver. [ety. unknown; ? SE *go for* (*a ride*)]

go fight city hall *v. see* YOU CAN'T FIGHT CITY HALL phr.

go fish *v.* (*gay, orig. US*) **1** [1940s+] for an effeminate gay man to take the 'feminine', passive role during sex. **2** [1960s+] of a male homosexual or lesbian, to give cunnilingus (cf. BOX LUNCH n.). **3** [1970s+] to become coy, fluttery. [FISH n.[1] (6)/FISH n.[1] (7)]

go fishing *v.* [mid-19C+] to go out looking for a sexually obliging woman. [FISH n.[1] (3)]

go flashing it *v.* (*also* **go fleshing it**) [mid–late 19C] to have sexual intercourse (cf. GO BALLOCKING v.).

go fleshmongering *v.* [17C] to have sexual intercourse (cf. GO BALLOCKING v.). [FLESHMONGER n. + sfx -*ing*]

go flip *v. see* FLIP n.[3] (4).

go flooey *v.* [1920s+] (*US*) to go wrong. [FLOOEY! excl.]

go flop *v. see* FLOP v. (9).

go flouch *v. see* FLOUSH v.

go fly a kite *phr.* [1910s+] a phr. used to suggest that an unwanted person should go away.

go for *v.*[1] [mid-19C+] **1** to attack physically. **2** to attack verbally. **3** (*orig. US*) to make an attempt.

go for *v.*[2] **1** [mid-19C+] (*orig. US*) to enthuse over, to be keen on. **2** [late 19C+] to find sexually or otherwise attractive or appealing. **3** [late 19C+] to be willing to give or invest. **4** [1930s+] to accept, to believe, to be deceived.

go for *v.*[3] **1** [20C+] to be worth, to amount to. **2** [1940s+] to cost.

go for *v.*[4] **1** [1920s+] to resemble, to 'pass' as. **2** [1970s] (*US Black*) 'a pseudorelationship in which two persons agree to present themselves and act toward each other in this relationship' (Roberts, *The Third Ear*, 1971).

go for *v.*[5] [1950s+] to be in one's favour, to be favourable or advantageous to; esp. in phr. *have something going for one*.

go for a burl *v.* [1980s] (*Aus.*) to go out joy-riding in the family car, esp. when one falls foul of the police (cf. GIVE IT A BURL v.). [play on Scot. *birl*, to spin/GO FOR A SPIN v.]

go for a Burton *v.* [1940s+] (*orig. UK milit.*) **1** to die, also in fig. use. **2** to fail, to malfunction. [the precise ety. remains unknown but there are a number of suggestions. First is the elision of SE *burnt 'un*, i.e. a burning aircraft (and its pilot). E.P. (*DSUE*, 1970), and Paul Beale (*DSUE*, 1984) suggest: (1) a euph., going for a glass of Burton ale; (2) *Burton-on-Trent* as rhy. sl. for 'went', as in 'went west' (cf. GO WEST v.); (3) Burton ale is heavy, as is a burning aircraft as it crashes to the ground; (4) the tailors Montague Burton; (5) during WW2 the RAF used a number of billiard halls, invariably sited above Burton shops, as medical centres, and those who attended such centres had 'gone for a Burton'. Other suggestions include the inter-war advertising campaign for Burton ales, bearing the copy line: 'He's gone for a Burton.' Another claim states that Burton's halls were used for Morse aptitude tests, not medical check-ups, thus the phr. meant failing such a test. Finally seafarers' jargon *burton*, the notoriously unsafe stowing of a barrel athwart rather than fore and aft, thus *going for a Burton* meant risking death]

go for a bust *v.* [1930s] to spend extravagently. [BUST n.[3] (1)]

go for a ride *v. see* TAKE FOR A RIDE v.[1] (1).

go for a skate *v.* [1950s+] (*N.Z.*) **1** to fail. **2** to be brought up in court. [ext. of SKATE v.[1]]

go for a spin *v.* (*also* **take a spin**) [20C+] to go out for a drive in a motor vehicle, or a ride on a bicycle. [the spinning wheels]

go for a taco *v.* [1990s+] (*US teen*) to move one's face between a woman's thighs preparatory to performing cunnilingus (cf. BOX LUNCH n. *see* TACO n.; ? ult. the shape]

go for a walk *v.* [1950s+] to be stolen. [euph.]

go for a walk with a spade *v.* [20C+] to defecate in the open air.

go for breaks *v.* [1970s–80s] (*N.Z. prison*) to make excuses; to tell lies. [BREAK n.[1] (3)]

go-for-broke *adj.* [1970s+] absolute, committed, unreserved. [GO FOR BROKE v.]

go for broke *v.* [1950s+] (*orig. US*) to commit oneself unreservedly, esp. in a gambling or betting context. [GO v.[4] (1) + BROKE adj.[1]]

go for channa *v.* [20C+] (*W.I., Guyn.*) to be absolutely wasted, esp. of money. [Hind. *chanaa*, chick-pea; thus the invested money has fig. turned into chick-peas]

go for it *v.* **1** [late 19C+] to commit oneself wholeheartedly. **2** [1920s+] of a woman, to be sexually enthusiastic. **3** [1970s+] to make an effort, to overcome one's fears, to get on energetically. **4** [1970s+] (*US campus*) to seduce. [GO FOR v.[2]]

go for mines *v.* (*also* **get mines, take care mines**) [1990s+] (*US Black teen*) to look after oneself, to indulge one's own interests. [Black var. on SE *mine*]

go for one's life *v.* [1920s+] (*Aus.*) to engage in an activity with vigour and enthusiasm.

go for one's quoits *v.* (*also* **go for the lick of one's coit**) [1920s+] (*Aus.*) to run fast, to work hard, to make one's best effort. [fig. use of QUOIT n.]

go for one's tea *v.* [20C+] to die.

go for pink slips v. [1950s+] (US) to race cars with the winner gaining the loser's vehicle. [the *pink* insurance *slip* that is proof of ownership]

go for six v. [1940s+] **1** to die; usu. as *gone for six*. **2** to be knocked down or knocked across a room. **3** to be punished. [cricketing imagery, one is 'knocked out of the ground']

go for someone scone-hot v. *see* GO SCONE-HOT AT v.

go for soul v. [1930s–40s] (US Black) to be deeply moved.

go for sushi v. [1990s+] (US campus) to kiss passionately. [TONGUE SUSHI n.]

go for the big spit v. [1950s+] (Aus.) to vomit. [BIG SPIT n.]

go for the doctor v. (also **look for the doctor**) [1940s+] (Aus./N.Z., orig. racing/gambling) **1** for one rider and his mount to move significantly ahead of the field. **2** to bet all one's money. **3** to go full tilt at something. [the image of rushing for (and paying a large fee to) a doctor]

go for the lick of one's coit v. *see* GO FOR ONE'S QUOITS v.

go for the long gallop v. [1960s] to look at the long-term prospects of a situation and act accordingly.

go for the whole shot v. [20C+] to make an absolute commitment, to indulge oneself completely. [GO FOR v.[1] (3) + SHOT n.[5] (1)]

go for veg v. [1970s] (US campus) to become drunk. [i.e. to enter a *vegetative* state]

go-forwards n. [20C+] (W.I.) a thong sandal that, if one does not keep walking forwards, is liable to fall off the foot.

go four v. [1910s] (Aus.) to support, to back up. [card-playing imagery]

go from sugar to shit v. [1960s] of a place and its standards, to decline severely.

go from the fists v. (also **go from the shoulders/the Y, get down from the Y**) [1970s+] (US Black) to fight. [SE *go from*/GET DOWN v.[2] (10) + SE *fists/shoulders/Y*, i.e. the shape of the arms and the trunk]

go fuck a duck! excl. [1930s+] (orig. and mainly US campus) an excl. of dismissal or disbelief.

go fuck your mother! excl. [1930s+] an all-purpose dismissive excl., generally seen as a supremely offensive remark.

go fuck yourself! excl. (also **fuck yourself! go and fuck yourself! go jump….! go screw…!**) [20C+] (orig. US) a general excl. of dismissal (cf. FUCK YOU! excl.). [FUCK v.[1]/JUMP v.[1] (1)/SCREW v.[2] (1)]

go full sesh v. *see* DO THE FULL SESH v.

gog n. [16C+] a euph. for *God*, and used as such as in oaths (cf. BOB n.[2]).

go gaflooey v. *see* GO KERFLOOEY v.

go gay v. **1** [16C] to commit adultery. **2** [late 19C] to pursue a career as a prostitute. **3** [1930s] to become homosexual. **4** [1940s–60s] (Aus.) to have sexual intercourse. [GAY adj.[1]]

go-getter n. **1** [1910s] (US) an attractive person or thing. **2** [1910s+] (orig. US) an active, enterprising person, an attractive person; also of animals.

go-getting adj. [1920s+] ambitious. [GO-GETTER n.]

gog-eye n. [20C+] (Aus. juv.) a catapult. [? SHANGHAI n.[1]]

gogga n. (S.Afr.) **1** [20C+] an insect, a 'creepy-crawly'. **2** [20C+] a term of affection aimed at a child or a small adult. **3** [1930s+] something menacing or frightening, a dangerous person or thing. [Nama *xo xo*, an insect]

goggle (at) v. [late 16C+] to stare at. [earlier use SE]

goggle (box) n. [1950s+] the television. [GOGGLE (AT) v.+ SE *box*/BOX n.[5] (6)]

goggle-eye n. (also **google-eye**) [mid-19C; 1920s] a person that is in a daze, staring. [GOGGLE-EYED adj.]

goggle-eyed adj. **1** [16C–17C] having prominent, staring eyes. **2** [early 18C; mid-19C+] (US) (also **google-eyed**) wearing spectacles. **3** [late 19C–1930s] (US) (also **goggly, google-eyed,**

googly-eyed) drunk (cf. ARSEHOLED adj.). **4** [20C+] (Aus.) (also **google-eyed**) dazed. [(1) SE after 17C]

goggler n. **1** [early–mid-19C] an eye. **2** [late 19C] a person with bulging 'goggle' eyes. **3** [late 19C+] one who stares. [GOGGLE (AT) v./GOGGLE-EYED adj. (1)]

goggles n. **1** [mid-17C] one who stares. **2** [18C–1910s] the eyes; in sing. the white of the eye. **3** [early 19C+] spectacles, esp. when round. **4** [20C+] the nickname of someone who wears spectacles. [GOGGLE (AT) v.]

goggly adj. *see* GOGGLE-EYED adj. (3).

goggy n. [1980s+] a schoolchild who has been rejected by their peers. [? GOGGLES n. (4)]

go girling v. [late 18C–1930s] to go out looking for female companionship and possible seduction. [SE *girl*]

goglet n. *see* GIGLET n.

go glimmering v. [late 19C–1940s] (US) to die away, to die out, to vanish. [SE *glimmer*, to give a weak, intermittent light]

gogo n. [1940s] (US) the buttocks. [Louisiana-French]

go goosing v. [late 19C] to have sexual intercourse (cf. GO BALLOCKING v.). [GOOSE v.[3] (1)]

go gorilla (on) v. [1980s] to attack physically, to beat up. [GORILLA n.[1] (1)]

go great guns v. [20C+] to have a run of success, to advance rapidly towards success. [SE *go* + GREAT GUNS adv.]

go Greek v.[1] *see* GREEK n.[3].

go Greek v.[2] *see* GREEK n.[4] (1).

go grungy v. [1980s] (US campus) to not bother showering. [GRUNGY adj. (1)]

go grunts v. [1960s] to defecate. [the noise of the effort required]

go hairless v. [1980s] to get mad, to go crazy. [? one tears one's hair out with rage]

go halves v. (also **cry halves, go halfsies, go halvers, go halvsies**) [mid-17C+] to share, to divide equally, to be partners; thus [1920s+] (Aus.) *on the halves*, sharing equally. [SE *halves*/HALVERS n.]

go hammer and tack v. *see* GO AT IT HAMMER AND TONGS v.

go hang v. **1** [early 17C] of a plan, to collapse, to go wrong, to fail. **2** [1900s] to allow to fail or die.

go hang! excl. [late 16C+] a dismissive excl.; a euph. for GO TO HELL! excl.; thus *tell someone to go hang!, go hang crepe on oneself.*

go hatstand v. [1990s+] to lose emotional control, to go mad.

go have a roll! excl. [1950s] (Aus.) a euph. for GO TO HELL! excl.

go head on v. [1930s] (US Black) to stop trying to fool someone, usu. as imper.

go head up v. [1980s] (US Black) to take part in some form of activity with another person.

go Hollywood v.[1] [1940s+] (US) to sodomize. [the presumption that such 'excesses' are quotidian pleasures in the movie capital]

go Hollywood v.[2] [1990s+] (US campus) to lose emotional control, to act hysterically. [the image of Hollywood as a centre of excessive (if faked) emotion]

go home v.[1] **1** [early 19C–1910s] to die. **2** [1920s+] of an article of clothing, to wear out. [note SE phr. *go to one's last home*, to die]

go home v.[2] [20C+] (W.I., Gren.) to defame a member of one's own or someone else's family.

go (home) and eat coke! excl. [late 19C+] a general excl. of contempt or dismissal. [? punning on Marie Antoinette's supposed (but fictional) dismissal of the starving Paris mob, *Let them eat cake*]

go home by beggar's bush v. [late 16C–18C] to be ruined. [to be reduced, like a beggar, to sleeping under a bush]

go home by Woodcock's cross v. [17C] to regret one's actions, to fail badly; thus *go crossless home by Woodcock's cross*, to repent and then to be hanged. [ety. unknown; ? anecdotal]

go hop in the bowl! excl. [1920s] (US, mainly juv.) a general excl. of dismissal or abuse.

go hostile at v. (also **go hostile on**) [1930s+] (Aus.) to become angry with. [orig. Aus./N.Z. milit. use]

gohuddy v. [2000s] (US Black) to go fast, to accelerate. [ety. unknown]

go-in n. 1 [mid-19C] a share of. 2 [mid-19C–1900s] an attack or onslaught upon; also, a spell of work upon. 3 [late 19C] (Aus.) an attempt; a try at. 4 [late 19C+] (Aus. Und.) a criminal attack or onslaught upon, e.g. an act of bush-ranging; also in fig. (non-criminal) use. 5 [1930s] (UK Und.) an escape (attempt).

go in v. [mid–late 19C] to attempt; usu. as go in and win, to try.

go in a buster v. [mid-19C–1920s] to spend regardless of the expense; similarly of unrestrained physical effort. [BUSTER n.³]

go in a perisher v. [mid–late 19C] (Aus.) to pursue one's course of action with maximum enthusiasm. [i.e. to the extent that one might SE perish]

go in (at) v. [mid-19C] to attack.

go in for v. (orig. US) 1 [mid–late 19C] of a man, to court a woman. 2 [mid-19C+] to approve of, to favour. 3 [mid-19C+] to specialize in. 4 [late 19C+] to attempt to obtain, to choose to wear.

going high n. [1960s] a state of 'full' intoxication.

going-over n. (orig. US) 1 [late 19C+] a scolding, a telling-off. 2 [1910s+] an inspection. 3 [1930s–40s] petting, sexual caressing. 4 [1930s+] treatment, doctoring. 5 [1930s+] a thrashing, a beating. 6 [1940s+] a police interrogation, thus any interrogation. [SE go over, to inspect, in lit. or fig. uses]

go in lemons v. see LEMONS adv.

go in on v. [mid-19C] (US) to attack physically. [var. GO IN (AT) v.]

go in the brown v. see DO IT UP BROWN v.

go in the skin v. see SHOOT SKIN v.

go in the tank v.¹ (also **go in the water**) [1910s+] 1 to surrender, to give up, esp. when such a surrender is by no means necessary. 2 to collapse, to go badly wrong. [fig. use of boxing jargon go in the tank, to lose a fight deliberately; ult. SE tank, a swimming pool, thus synon. with TAKE A DIVE v. (1)]

go in the tank v.² see TANK v.¹ (1).

go in the toilet v. [1960s+] (US) to fail, usu. in a show business context.

go in the water v. see GO IN THE TANK v.¹.

go into v. [1950s] to take advantage of, to obtain money from.

go into a flat spin v. [1910s+] to lose perspective and orientation, to become very confused. [flying use]

go into a huddle v. [1920s+] to hold a secret conference to consult specially about something. [US football use]

go into one v. [1980s+] 1 to lose one's temper, to lose emotional control. 2 to launch into a speech or diatribe. [? 'one' being a rage, a tantrum]

go into the kitchen v. [late 19C] to drink one's tea out of the saucer. [the vulgarity of such a way of drinking tea – seen as a servants' habit]

go it v. 1 [late 17C; mid-19C+] to move at great speed. 2 [late 18C+] (also **go it hot**) to indulge to a reckless extent. 3 [early 19C+] to commit oneself fully, usu. to a course of self-indulgent pleasure or as in a fight. 4 [late 19C+] (Aus.) to accept, to believe in.

go it! excl. [mid-19C+] a general excl. of encouragement; often ext. to go it you cripples, crutches are cheap! [GO IT v. (1)]

go-it-alone adj. [mid-19C+] characterized by independent action. [GO IT ALONE v.]

go it alone v. [mid-19C+] to act by oneself, without support or assistance.

go it blind v.¹ [mid-19C–1900s] (US) to enter on an undertaking without proper preparation or planning.

go it blind v.² [late 19C+] to drink heavily; usu. of alcohol. [BLIND adv.¹]

go it, boots! excl. [mid-19C–1910s] (US) a general cry of encouragement.

go it hot v. see GO IT v. (2).

goitre n.¹ [1970s] (UK Und.) a bulging wallet full of notes. [SE goitre, a swelling, sometimes very pronounced, of the thyroid gland]

goitre n.² [1980s+] (drugs) small 'sticks' of tobacco, which interfere with the quality of one's smoke when rolled together with cannabis. [SE goitre; they make a bulge in the cigarette]

go it strong v.¹ (also **go it thick**) [mid-19C+] to speak frankly, forcefully. [GO IT v. (3)]

go it strong v.² see COME IT STRONG v. (1).

go jagging v. [20C+] (Aus./N.Z.) to go visiting for the purpose of exchanging gossip. [? dial. jag, a journey; but note dial. jag, to tear roughly, i.e. the gossips 'tear someone to pieces']

go jesse v. [1950s+] (US) to act energetically, to be skilful, to 'go great guns'. [adoption of jesse, as in GIVE (SOMEONE) JESSE v., to mean vigour, strength]

go jock-hunting v. [late 19C–1900s] to have sexual intercourse (cf. GO BALLOCKING v.). [JOCK n.¹ (1)]

go jottling v. see DO A JOTTLE v.

go jumming v. [17C] to have sexual intercourse (cf. GO BALLOCKING v.). [JUMM v.]

go jump in the lake (and pull the chain)! excl. (also **go and jump in the lake!**) [1910s+] a general excl. of dismissal or disdain.

go jump yourself! excl. see GO FUCK YOURSELF! excl.

go kerflooey v. (also **go caflooey**, **go gaflooey**) [1910s+] to go to pieces, to break down. [KERFLOOEY adj.]

go lay an egg! excl. [1920s–30s] (US campus) an excl. of dismissal.

golblamed adj. [1920s] (US) a euph. for GOD-DAMN adj. (1).

gold n.¹ [late 19C+] money (cf. CANARY n.⁵).

gold n.² (drugs) 1 [1940s–50s] a hypodermic syringe. 2 [1960s+] marijuana (cf. BLACK DOMINA n.). 3 [2000s] crack cocaine (cf. BASE n.). 4 [2000s] heroin (cf. BLACK n.³). [? its value]

gold and silver adj. [1980s] bisexual. [the 'opposite' metals]

goldarn adj. (also **goldang**, **goldurn**) [mid-19C+] (US) a euph. for GOD-DAMN adj. (1).

goldarn! excl. (also **goldang! goldurn!**) [early 19C+] a euph. for GOD-DAMN! excl.

goldarned adj. (also **galdarned**, **gaul darned**) [mid-19C+] a euph. for GOD-DAMN adj. (1). [GOLDARN adj.]

gold-backed ones n. (also **gold-backed 'uns**) [mid–late 19C] body lice.

gold-badge man n. [1950s] (US) a city detective (cf. BADGE n.²).

Goldberg n. (also **Goldstein**) [1950s+] (US Black) any Jew, esp. the shopowners of Harlem and other ghettos (cf. ABE n.¹). [the stereotyped 'Jewish' surname and as such usu. derog.]

gold braid n. [1930s+] a collective n. for a number of senior military or prison officers. [the gold braid that adorns their caps]

goldbrick n. 1 [late 19C+] (also **bat**) a confidence game in which the victim buys a 'gold' (actually gold-painted lead) brick. 2 [1900s] (US campus) an unattractive, dull girl. 3 [1900s–40s] (US Und.) a swindle; anything bogus. 4 [1900s–50s] (also **goldbricker**) a swindler. 5 [1910s+] (US) (also **goldbricker**) a shirker, a loafer, a lazy person. 6 [1970s] one who obtains money without working for it; thus goldbricking, swindling, cheating. [subseq. uses from (1); the scheme was originated by one Reed Waddell who, in 1880, sold his first brick for $4000 and thereafter never dropped his price below $3,500 – making an alleged $250,000 in 5 years]

goldbrick v. (US) 1 [1900s–30s] to swindle. 2 [1910s+] to shirk, to loaf, to act lazily. [GOLDBRICK n.]

goldbricking n. [1930s–50s] (US) wasting time, loafing, avoiding work. [GOLDBRICK v.]

goldbricking adj. [1910s–50s] lazy, shirking. [GOLDBRICK v. (2)]

goldbug n. [late 19C+] (US) a gold speculator. [SE gold + BUG n.⁵ (2)]

gold-dig v. [1920s+] usu. of a woman, to obtain money and other gifts in exchange for sexual favours. [backform. f. GOLD-DIGGER n. (2)]

gold-digger n. **1** [1910s–20s] (US) a prostitute (cf. ASS PEDDLER n.). **2** [1910s+] (orig. US) a young woman, orig. typically from the chorus line, who swaps sexual favours for the monetary and material gifts of a (usu.) older lover. **3** [1920s+] anyone, of either gender, who seeks money through advantageous relationships. [(2) faltered after WW2 but has been revived in US Black use]

gold-digging n. [1920s+] of a (young) woman, swapping sexual favours for material comforts. [GOLD-DIGGER n. (2)]

gold-digging adj. [1920s+] seeking monetary and other material benefits from an advantageous, if not especially enjoyable relationship. [GOLD-DIGGER n. (2)]

gold-drop n. [late 18C] a gold coin.

gold-dropper n. (also **dropper, money-dropper**) [late 17C–19C] (UK Und.) a rogue who specializes in dropping something supposedly valuable where it will be found by a potential victim, who is either lured into a game or persuaded to buy the 'valuable', while the con-man claims that although they should, by rights, share the profits, he will sell his share and let the victim have the whole benefit; alternatively the victim is introduced to some of the sharp's friends, who propose a game of cards or dice, in which they rob him.

gold dust n. (US drugs) **1** [1930s+] cocaine (cf. BIRDIE POWDER n.; BLANCA n.). **2** [1970s] heroin (cf. BLACK n.³). [the high price of narcotics + ref. in (1) to the colour of, presumably, the Chinese (brown) variety]

gold duster n. [1960s] (US drugs) a cocaine user. [GOLD DUST n. (1)]

gold dust twins n. [20C+] (US) close friends. [the twin Black boys who featured in advertisements for Gold Dust washing powder, c.1900; the slogan declared: 'Let the Gold Dust twins do your work']

golden adj. **1** [late 19C; 1950s+] (orig. US campus) fine, successful, secure. **2** [1980s+] (US) lucrative.

golden ballocks n. [2000s] a wonderful, successful, admirable person. [BALLOCKS n.¹ (1); note 'Golden Balls', nickname of UK footballer David Beckham, punning on the SE balls he kicks + BALLS n.¹ (1)]

golden boy n. [1970s] (US) a gold-shield police detective (cf. BADGE n.²).

golden chub n. [early 18C] a dupe, a fool. [a pun on the fish name; SE golden + CHUB n.¹ (1)]

golden cream n. [late 19C] (UK Und.) rum. [its colour]

gold-end man n. [17C] an itinerant jeweller, a buyer of gold and silver.

golden doughnut n. [1970s] the vagina (cf. APPLE n.⁶).

golden eagle n. [1990s+] (drugs) a far stronger form of MDMA, properly known as DOB.

golden gate n. [1980s] £800. [rhy. sl.]

golden girl n.¹ [1960s+] (US Black) a very attractive woman. [the positive perception of blonde hair on White women]

golden girl n.² **1** [1970s+] (drugs) heroin (cf. BLACK n.³). **2** [1980s] particularly high grade cocaine (cf. BLANCA n.). [GIRL n.² (1)/GIRL n.² (2); note heroin is more usu. BOY n.⁷ (1), presumably the golden, i.e. brown, colour is more pertinent here]

golden googie n. [1900s] (Aus./N.Z.) a golden coin, a sovereign. [SE golden + GOOG n.¹ (1); ? ref. to 'the goose that laid the golden eggs']

golden grease n. [19C] a bribe. [SE golden, resembling gold in value + fig. use of grease/GREASE n.¹ (1)]

golden handcuffs n. [1970s+] (orig. US) financial perks that keep employees attached to a firm.

golden handshake n. [1960s+] **1** a tip, a monetary hand-out. **2** a bonus given as compensation for dismissal or compulsory retirement.

golden hello n. [1980s+] a signing-on bonus, given when starting a new job.

golden hind adj. [20C+] blind. [rhy. sl.; ult. the name of the ship in which Francis Drake circumnavigated the globe in 1577–80]

golden leaf n. [1920s+] (drugs) top-quality marijuana (cf. AFRICAN BUSH n.; BLACK DOMINA n.). [SE golden, resembling gold in value + SE leaf; note later LEAF n.¹ (4)]

golden rain n. see GOLDEN SHOWER n.

golden rivet n.¹ [1940s–50s] the anus.

golden rivet n.² [1960s] (US gay) the penis.

golden screw n. [1970s+] (US gay) anal intercourse culminating in urination rather than ejaculation. [SE golden, yellow-coloured + SCREW n.¹ (2)]

golden shower n. (also **golden rain**) **1** [1940s+] urolagnia, i.e. the act of urinating on one's partner as part of sexual experimentation (cf. BROWN SHOWER n.). **2** [1970s] (US gay) one who displays contempt for other people, i.e. he 'pisses on' them. [SE golden, yellow-coloured + shower; note 17C use of golden shower as a euph. for copulation, the image coming the from Greek myth of Danawe, who was seduced by Zeus in the form of a shower of gold]

golden shower queen n. (also **GSQ**) [1960s+] a homosexual who enjoys being urinated on. [GOLDEN SHOWER n. (1) + QUEEN n.² (1)/QUEEN sfx (2)]

goldfinch n. **1** [17C–mid-19C] one who always has money in his pocket or purse, thus a target of thieves. **2** [late 17C–early 19C] a golden guinea or sovereign. [play on the bird species]

goldfinch's nest n. [19C] the vagina (cf. AGREEABLE RUTS OF LIFE n.).

gold-finder n. **1** [early 17C–19C] a latrine cleaner. **2** [mid-18C] a confidence trickster. [the colour of faeces]

goldfish n.¹ [1900s] (Aus.) a man suitable to be made into one's husband. [? its role as a pet]

goldfish n.² **1** [1900s–40s] (Aus./US) any form of canned fish. **2** [1940s–70s] (US Black) sliced, canned peaches. [orig. milit. use goldfish, herrings]

goldfish n.³ **1** [1920s–40s] (US) a beating of a prisoner to extract a confession; also the rubber hose used in such beatings. **2** [1930s] (US Und.) a prisoner standing in an identification line-up. **3** [1950s–60s] (US Black) a married woman, esp. one who is ripe for seduction; thus fish for goldfish, to seduce married women. [fig. uses of SE; (1) and (2) the prisoner is the isolated goldfish, the interrogators gather round; (3) the goldfish is trapped in its bowl, but apparently yearning for the world beyond]

goldfish bowl n. (also **goldfish room**) **1** [1930s–60s] (US) an interrogation room in a police station. **2** [1970s] any small room where a discussion takes place. [GOLDFISH n.³ (1); the isolation of the prisoner among their interrogators]

gold-hunters n. [mid–late 19C] (US) Californians. [the Gold Rush of 1849]

Goldie Hawn n. [1990s+] a prawn. [rhy. sl.; ult. US film star Goldie Hawn (b.1945)]

goldies n. [1910s] (Aus.) the teeth.

goldilocks n. [1990s+] venereal disease. [rhy. sl. = POX n.¹ (2)]

gold ring n. [20C+] a king. [rhy. sl.]

gold seal n. [1970s+] (drugs) top-quality hashish (cf. AFGHAN n.). [the block is stamped with a gold seal]

goldskin n. [late 19C–1930s] (US gay) a young light-skinned Black male prostitute.

gold star n. (also **gold shield, gold tin**) [1960s+] (US) a gold-shield police detective (cf. BADGE n.²).

gold star lesbian n. [1990s+] (US gay) a lesbian who will absolutely never have sex with a man or a bisexual.

Goldstein n. see GOLDBERG n.

gold tin n. see GOLD STAR n.

gold-tooth n. [1950s] (US) a derog. term for a Puerto Rican (cf. BATO n.).

goldurn see under GOLDARN.

gold watch *n.* [20C+] Scotch whisky. [rhy. sl.; the orig. ref. was to the Waterbury watch]

go leather-stretching *v.* [late 18C–19C] of a man, to have sexual intercourse (cf. GO BALLOCKING v.). [LEATHER n.[2] (1) + SE *stretch*]

go lemony at *v.* (*also* **go lemony with**) [1940s–50s] (*Aus./N.Z.*) to lose one's temper with. [SE *go* + LEMONY adj.]

golfed *adj.* [1990s+] (*US campus*) drunk. [? GOOF n.[2] (1)]

golgotha *n.* [mid-19C] a hat. [a pun on Gk *Golgotha*, the place of skulls]

go lickety-split *v.* (*also* **come lickety-split**) [1990s+] to give oral sex to a woman. [SE *lick* + SPLIT n.[3] (1) + pun on SE phr.]

go like a bastard *v.* [1990s+] (*Aus.*) to commit oneself unstrainedly. [SE *go* + LIKE A BASTARD adv.]

go like a bat out of hell *v.* (*also* **go like a bat through hell**) [1910s+] (*orig. US*) to move exceptionally fast.

go like a bird *v.* [1920s+] of an automobile, or any vehicle, to go fast and smoothly with no mechanical problems.

go like a bomb *v.*[1] [1950s+] to go very fast.

go like a bomb *v.*[2] [1950s+] to work out very successfully. [BOMB n.[1] (4)]

go like a cut cat *v.* [1960s+] (*N.Z.*) to leave or run off at speed. [SE *cut*, castrated]

go like a dingbat *v.* [1950s+] to go very fast. [DINGBAT n.[2] (2)]

go like a rabbit *v.* (*also* **go like a herd of turtles**) [1940s+] of a woman, to copulate enthusiastically (cf. FUCK LIKE A BUNNY v.). [GO v.[2]]

go like a train *v.* [20C+] **1** to go very fast. **2** of a woman, to be a very enthusiastic sexual partner. [(2) GO v.[2]]

go like a wanker's elbow *v.* [1990s+] to be extremely busy.

go like hell *v.* (*also* **go like the devil**) [18C+] to go very fast.

go like hot cakes *v.* (*also* **go like hot cross buns**, **...like frozen Daiquiris in hell**) [late 19C+] (*orig. US*) **1** of a product or commodity, to sell out quickly. **2** of anything, to occur quickly, plentifully.

go like the clappers *v.* [1940s+] (*orig. RAF*) to run very fast; a euph. for GO LIKE HELL v. [rhy. sl.; *clappers = bell = hell*; note RAF jargon *like the clappers of hell*, very fast]

go like the devil *v. see* GO LIKE HELL v.

go like the hammers of hell *v.* (*also* **go like the hammers of fuck**) [1930s+] to go very fast.

go like three tin kettles at the tail of a mad cougar *v.* [mid-19C] (*US*) to rush in a dangerous and erratic manner.

goll *n.*[1] [17C; early 19C] the hand. [ety. unknown; ? link to Irish *gabhlach*, a forked instrument used in fishing, used in modern Irish sl. as *golly-fishing*]

goll *n.*[2] [late 19C–1900s] in a variety of oaths, a synon. for God.

goll bing me! *excl.* [late 19C] (*US*) a euph. for *God damn me!* [GOLL n.[2]]

gollier *n.* (*also* **gollyer**) [1930s+] (*Irish*) a lump of phlegm (cf. GOLLION n.; GOLLY n.[2]). [GOLLY v.]

gollion *n.* [1930s+] (*Aus.*) **1** a lump of phlegm (cf. GOLLIER n.). **2** a term of abuse. [GOLLY v.]

golliwog *n.*[1] [1920s+] (*Aus.*) a large, hairy caterpillar. [it supposedly resembles the child's toy]

golliwog *n.*[2] [1930s+] a receiver of stolen property.

golliwog *n.*[3] [1990s+] fog. [rhy. sl.]

golliwog *n.*[4] *see* GOLLY n.[1].

golliwogs, the *n.* [1920s–70s] greyhound racing. [rhy. sl. = DOGS, THE n.]

golliwogs! *excl.* [1950s] (*mainly UK juv.*) an excl. of surprise, disappointment etc.

gollop *n.* (*also* **gollup**) **1** [19C+] (*US*) an amount, a portion. **2** [20C+] a gulp. **3** [1920s] (*US*) a fool. [GOLLOP v.]

gollop *v.* [19C+] to swallow down greedily or hastily. [SE *gulp* + *gobble*]

gollumpus *n.* [late 18C–early 19C] a large, loutish, uncoordinated person. [? Scot. *golamus*, ungaily, large, unshapely]

gollup *n. see* GOLLOP n.

golluptious *adj. see* GOLOPSHUS adj.

golly *n.*[1] (*also* **golliwog**) [1950s+] a derog. term for a Black person (cf. ALLIGATOR BAIT n.[2]). [SE *golliwog*; for the problems of Robertson's jam/marmalade see my *Words Apart* (1996)]

golly *n.*[2] [1960s–70s] (*Aus.*) a lump of phlegm (cf. GOLLIER n.). [GOLLY v.]

golly *v.* [1930s+] (*Aus.*) to spit; thus *golly-gum*, chewing gum; *golly-pot*, a spittoon. [? Scot. *golly*, to shout hoarsely; ult. Scot. *gollar*, to utter loud but thick and scarcely articulate sounds, to shout]

golly! *excl.* (*also* **gaully! great golly! golly Moses!**) [mid-18C+] (*mainly US/UK juv.*) an extra-mild euph. for *God!* [E.P. suggests a Black origin, but the *OED* cit. (G. White, *Journals*, 1775) reads: 'Golly, a sort of jolly kind of oath, or asseveration much in use among our carters, & lowest people']

gollybuster *n. see* GOLLYWHOPPER n.

gollyer *n. see* GOLLIER n.

golly Moses! *excl. see* GOLLY! excl.

gollywhopper *n.* (*also* **gollybuster, gollysocker**) [20C+] (*US*) an outstanding example of its kind. [GOLLY! excl. + WHOPPER n. (1)/BUSTER n.[1] (4)/SOCK v.[1] (1)]

gollywobbles *n.* [1940s+] (*US*) feelings of tension, fear or sickness, usu. seen as stemming from the stomach. [var. on COLLYWOBBLES n. (1)]

gol-mol *n.* [mid-19C] (*Anglo-Ind.*) a disturbance, a commotion. [Hind. *golmaul*, confusion, disorder]

go loc *v.* [2000s] to prepare onself for a drive-by shooting by putting on dark glasses and any other form of disguise. [LOCS n.[2]]

go-'long *n.* (*US Black*) **1** [20C+] consequences, inevitable developments, circumstances; thus *caught in the go-'long*, to be a victim of circumstances. **2** [1920s–40s] the police truck in which arrested people are taken to the local cells. [one has no choice but to fig. or lit. *go along*]

go look at the crops *v.* (*also* **go and look at the crops**) [20C+] a euph. excuse when one wishes to leave the room and urinate, e.g. *I've just got to go...* (cf. BURN THE GRASS v.).

golopshus *adj.* (*also* **galluptious, galophus, galoptious, galumptious, golluptious, goloptious, goluptious**) [mid-19C–1930s] delicious, flavoursome, luscious.

goloss *n.* [1960s] dialect, slang, patois.

golpe *n.* [1970s+] (*drugs*) heroin. [Sp. *golpe*, a jolt, a blow]

golumptiously *adv.* [late 19C] wonderfully, delightfully. [GOLOPSHUS adj.]

goluptious *adj. see* GOLOPSHUS adj.

g.o.m. *n.*[1] [late 19C+] grand old man. [coined for Prime Minister William Ewart Gladstone (1809–98) but used more generally]

g.o.m. *n.*[2] [1940s+] (*drugs*) opium, morphine (cf. APOSTLE n.; AUNTIE EMMA n.). [abbr. GOD'S (OWN) MEDICINE n.]

gom *n.*[1] [early–mid-19C] a euph. synon for *God*, and as such used in mild oaths (cf. BOB n.[2]). [Lancashire dial.]

gom *n.*[2] (*also* **gam, gaum, gawm, ghomey, goamey, gomey, gommouge, gorm**) [mid-19C+] (*orig. Irish*) a painfully stupid or gullible person, a fool. [Irish *gamal*, a simpleton]

gom *n.*[3] (*also* **gommie**) [1960s+] (*S.Afr.*) a fool, an idiot; thus *gommy*, stupid, vulgar. [GOMTOR n.]

goma *n.* [1960s] (*drugs*) opium; black tar heroin (cf. APOSTLE n.). [Sp. *goma*, gum/GUM n.[3]]

goma de moto *n.* [1980s+] (*drugs*) hashish (cf. AFGHAN n.). [Sp. *goma de moto*, gum of dust]

gombay *n.* [1940s+] (*W.I.*) a very dark-complexioned Black person. [dial. *gombay*, drum or drummer; ult. Kongo *nboma*, a goatskin drum]

gome *n.* [1980s+] (*US campus*) a devotedly hard worker. [GOMER n.[2]]

go mental *v.* **1** [1960s+] to become insane, to have a mental breakdown or outburst. **2** [2000s] to have an uproarious time. [SE *go* + MENTAL adj. (1)]

gomer *n.*[1] [1900s] (*Irish*) a measure of drink. [poss. 'a large pewter dish' (E.P.)]

gomer *n.*[2] [1960s+] (*US*) a fool, a rustic simpleton (cf. ALVIN *n.*). [the proper name *Gomer Pyle*, a fictional TV comic yokel character; apparent link to GOM *n.*[2] may be coincidental]

gomer *n.*[3] [1960s+] an old, dirty, difficult or chronically ill hospital patient, usu. male; thus *gomere*, the female equivalent. [? abbr. *get out of my* emergency room; note email from Doug Wilson to *American Dialect Society-List* (Internet, 21 July 2001): 'The acronym-etymology is spurious, I think; another bogus candidate is "Grand Old Man of the Emergency Room". I think the origin is related to the other "gomer" – like in "Gomer Pyle" [...] maybe the original form was "old gome" or so, and maybe "gome" = "man" (from OE "guma" or so; cf. "gome" [and "gomerel"] in OED) [...] Probably reinforced [...] by "gummer" = "one who gums (i.e., chews without having any teeth)" and maybe by "gnome"']

gomeral *n.* (*also* **gomeril**) [19C–1910s] (*Irish*) a lout. [Irish *gomaral, gamal*, a lout, a boor; *gomeril* is also found throughout dial.]

gomer pyle *n.* [1980s+] (*US*) a fool, a yokel (cf. ALVIN *n.*). [for ety. *see* GOMER *n.*[2]]

gomey *n. see* GOM *n.*[2].

gommie *n. see* GOM *n.*[3].

gommouge *n. see* GOM *n.*[2].

gommy *n.* [19C] a dandy. [Fr. argot *gommeux*, pretty, fashionable]

gommy *adj. see* GOM *n.*[3].

go molrowing *v. see* MOLROWING *n.* (1).

go motting *v.* [late 19C] of a man, to have sexual intercourse (cf. GO BALLOCKING *v.*). [MOT *n.* (5)]

gomtor *n.* [1960s+] (*S.Afr.*) an uncouth or common loutish person. [synon. Afk.]

go much on *v.* [20C+] (*orig. US*) to like, to enjoy; often in negative forms, e.g. *I don't go much on that*.

go mulga *v. see* MULGA *v.*

gomus *n.* [mid-19C–1910s] (*Anglo-Irish*) a fool (cf. DOOFUS *n.*). [GOM *n.*[2]]

gon *n.*[1] (*also* **gonny**) [1930s–70s] (*US*) gonorrhoea. [pron./abbr.]

gon *n.*[2] *see* GONNOF *n.*

gonads *n.* **1** [1910s+] (*orig. US*) the testicles; thus *have someone by the gonads*, to be in a controlling position. **2** [1970s] (*US*) courage. [SE *gonads*, any organ in an animal (as a testis or an ovary) that produces gametes]

gonaff *n. see* GONNOF *n.*

go nap (on) *v.* **1** [mid-19C+] to commit oneself fully. **2** [1900s] to choose. **3** [1910s+] (*Aus.*) to like very much. [racing use; orig. cards, *nap*, to take all 5 tricks in the game of *nap*]

go native *v.* [20C+] to adopt the habits, dress etc of local people when in a foreign country; also in fig. use.

gonce *n.* (*also* **gons**) [late 19C–1930s] (*Aus.*) money. [? Yid. *gunz*, the lot]

gondola *n.* **1** [1920s–50s] (*US tramp*) a railroad coal car. **2** [1930s–50s] (*US Und.*) a large stolen automobile.

gondolas *n.* [1920s–70s] (*US*) large clumsy shoes. [resemblance]

gone *adj.*[1] **1** [mid-16C+] (*US*) used of someone or something considered to be a lost cause, a hopeless case. **2** [17C; late 18C+] of a person or animal, dead or doomed; both usu. in combs., e.g. GONE BEAVER *n.*; GONE CHICKEN *n.*; GONE COON *n.*; GONE GOOSE *n.*; GONER *n.*[1] (3). **3** [late 19C+] worn-out, exhausted; old. [fig. uses of SE *gone*, lost]

gone *adj.*[2] [late 16C; 19C+] pregnant. [abbr. *gone with child*]

gone *adj.*[3] **1** [mid-17C+] drunk, intoxicated by a drug; also in fig. use. **2** [mid-19C; 1990s+] dead. **3** [mid-19C+] insane, crazy, bizarre. **4** [1920s+] (*US*) a general intensifier, both positive and negative, extraordinary or thoroughly; thus *n., goner*. **5** [1940s+] (*orig. US Black*) weird and wonderful, lost in music, drugs etc; esp.

in *gone cat, gone chick*. **6** [2000s] (*US campus*) asleep. [abbr. *gone out of this world*]

gone *adj.*[4] *see* GONE (ON) *adj.*

gone *phr.* [1990s+] (*US campus*) goodbye.

gone across *adj. see* GO ACROSS THE RIVER *v.*

gone a million *phr.* [20C+] (*Aus.*) in a hopeless state. [? coined by the profligate John Scadden, Prime Minister of Western Australia, 1911–16]

gone and forgotten *adj.* [20C+] (*Aus.*) rotten. [rhy. sl.]

gone beaver *n.* [mid-19C] (*orig. US*) one who is utterly doomed, without hope of escape. [GONE *adj.*[1] (2) + SE *beaver*]

gone chicken *n.* (*also* **gone chick**) [mid-19C+] (*US*) a doomed person, a 'lost soul'. [GONE *adj.*[1] (2) + CHICKEN *n.*[6] (2)]

gone coon *n.* (*also* **gone ginny, gone sucker**) [mid-19C+] (*orig. US*) one who is utterly doomed, without hope of escape. [GONE *adj.*[1] (2) + COON *n.* (4)/GUINEA *n.* (3)/SUCKER *n.*[3] (1)]

gonef *n. see* GONNOF *n.*

gone goose *n.* (*also* **gone gander, gone gosling**) [mid-19C+] (*orig. US*) a person or thing that is beyond all hope. [GONE *adj.*[1] (2) + SE *goose/gander/gosling*; note 19C naut. jargon *gone-goose*, a ship deserted or given up in despair]

gone in *adj.* [mid–late 19C] (*US*) exhausted.

gone off one's dip *phr.* [late 19C–1910s] insane, eccentric. [? DIPPY *adj.* (1)]

gone (on) *adj.* **1** [late 19C–1900s] impressed by. **2** [late 19C+] obsessed by, esp. when in love; usu. with an intensifying adv.

gone overboard *adj.* [20C+] **1** dead. **2** (*W.I., St Kitts*) pregnant, the implication is unintentionally.

goner *n.*[1] (*also* **gonner**) **1** [mid-19C] a failure, an impossibility. **2** [mid-19C+] one who is dead, or something that is ruined. **3** [mid-19C+] a doomed person, anyone who cannot avoid an unpleasant fate, one on the verge of death; also in fig. use. **4** [mid-19C+] an obsessed person, i.e. one who is 'gone' on something or someone. **5** [late 19C] in weakened form of (2), one who is very ill. **6** [1900s] (*Aus.*) one who has departed. **7** [1940s] a sucker, a pushover. [GONE *adj.*[1]]

goner *n.*[2] *see* GONE *adj.*[3] (4).

gonest *adj.* [1940s–50s] (*orig. US Black*) the most extraordinary, the most bizarre. [GONE *adj.*[3] (5)]

gonesville *adj.* **1** [1950s+] knocked out, lit. and fig. **2** [1990s+] vanished, escaped, gone. **3** [2000s] dead. **4** [2000s] eccentric, insane. **5** [2000s] in weaker form of (4), emotionally carried away. [SE *gone*/GONE *adj.*[3] + -VILLE *sfx*[1]]

gone to buggery *phr.* [1960s+] of a person, completely defeated; of an object, wrecked beyond repair. [TO BUGGERY *adv.*]

gone to Gowings *phr.* [1990s+] (*Aus.*) useless, wrecked. [the mail-order male clothing firm and self-styled 'blokatorium' *Gowings* of Sydney; the phr. was popularized in the late 1940s when the well-known criminal Darcy Dugane escaped from jail and left a note on his cell wall reading 'Gone to Gowings!']

gone to hell *phr. see* ALL TO HELL *phr.*

gone to Moscow *phr.* [1910s+] (*Aus.*) in pawn. [pun on *mosk*, to pawn]

gone to pot *phr.* **1** [mid-18C; mid-19C+] of a person, fallen in status, leading a degenerate life, dead. **2** [mid-19C+] of a thing, broken down, not functioning properly or well. [GO TO POT *v.*]

gone to Rotisbone *phr.* (*also* **gone to Rot-His-Bone**) [late 18C–early 19C] dead. [pun on the religious colloquy or Diet of Ratisbon + lit. *rot his bone*]

gone to the dogs *phr.* [mid-19C+] in social decline, run-down, dirty, poss. living as a tramp. [GO TO THE DOGS *v.* (1)]

gone to the pack *phr.* [1910s+] (*Aus./N.Z.*) **1** in social decline, run-down, dirty, poss. turned into a tramp. **2** drunk. [SE *pack of hounds*; thus var. on GONE TO THE DOGS *phr.*]

gone to visit his uncle *phr.* [late 18C–early 19C] of a man who has deserted his wife soon after the marriage. [ironic euph.]

gone up *adj.* [mid–late 19C] **1** dead. **2** finished, defeated. **3** unfashionable. [as in *gone up* to heaven]

goney *n. see* GOONEY n.

gong *n.*[1] [11C–16C] the privy. [OE *gang*, the act of walking or going; thus it is, however remotely, an ancestor of the child's plaint, 'I've got to go']

gong *n.*[2] (*US drugs*) **1** [1910s–50s] an opium pipe. **2** [1930s–50s] opium (cf. APOSTLE n.). **3** [1950s+] marijuana. [? transliteration of a Chinese word]

gong *n.*[3] [1910s+] (*orig. milit.*) a medal; thus any form of award, e.g. a knighthood, an OBE. [Anglo-Ind. *gong*, a metal disc, not musical, used for striking the hour, thus imported by Indian Army veterans]

gong *n.*[4] [1920s–40s] the bell (later replaced by a siren) on a police car.

gong *n.*[5] [1960s–70s] (*US campus*) the penis (cf. GONGS n.). [supposed resemblance]

gonga *n.*[1] [1930s–50s] (*US prison*) marijuana.

gonga *n.*[2] *see* GUNGA n.[1].

gonga *adj.* [1930s] (*US Und.*) intoxicated by opium. [GONG n.[2] (2)]

gong-beater *n. see* GONG-KICKER n.

gonger *n.* [1910s+] (*US drugs*) **1** an opium pipe; thus the dimin. *gongerine*, a small pipe. **2** an opium addict. **3** opium; thus *up against the gonger*, addicted to opium (cf. APOSTLE n.). **4** any form of opium derivative. [GONG n.[2]]

gongers *n.* [1930s–40s] police patrolling in cars. [GONG n.[4]]

gong farmer *n.* [mid-15C–16C] a cleaner-out of privies, a nightsoil man. [GONG n.[1] + SE *farmer*]

gong girl *n.* [1930s] a woman who is picked up by a motorist, presumably for sex. [? *gonged*, of a motorist, pulled up by the police on some matter of road safety]

gong house *n.* [11C] a privy (cf. BACKHOUSE n.). [GONG n.[1]]

gong-kicker *n.* (*also* gong-beater) **1** [1930s–70s] (*US*) an opium smoker. **2** [1950s] a marijuana smoker. [GONG n.[2]]

gongola *n.* [1930s–60s] (*drugs*) an opium pipe. [ext. GONG n.[2] (1)]

gongs *n.* [1950s] (*US gay*) the testicles (cf. BANGERS n.; GONG n.[5]). [they 'clang' together + ? GONADS n. (1)]

gonicles *n.* [1950s] (*US*) testicles. [GONADS n. (1)]

gonie *n.* [1960s+] (*S.Afr.*) a knife. [Angoni (Nyasaland) *goni*, to stab]

gonies *n.* [1990s+] the male genitals. [GONADS n. (1)]

gonif *see under* GONNOF.

gonk *n.* **1** [1960s+] (*UK juv.*) a fool. **2** [1960s+] a contemptuous description of a prostitute's client. **3** [2000s] an obsessive, an eccentric. [the large cuddly homunculoid dolls briefly popular in the 1960s; but note milit. use *gonk*, to sleep]

gonkulator *n.* [1990s+] a word used in place of the actual technical term for a mechanical device. [onomat. noise *gonk* + *calculator*]

gonner *n. see* GONER n.[1].

gonnof *n.* (*also* ganef, ganov, gnof, gon, gonaff, gonef, gonif, goniff, gonnif, gonnofer, gonoph, gonof, gonoff, gonoph, gonov, gonovim, gunnif) **1** [mid-19C–1960s] a scoundrel, fool. **2** [mid-19C+] a thief, an 'amateur pickpocket' (Hotten, 1859). [Heb. *gannabh*, thief; Hotten (1860) suggests that the word is 'as old as Chaucer's time', but his ref. is to *gnoff*, a peasant, a lout, which comes from East Frisian *knufe*, lump and *gnuffig*, thick, rough, coarse, ill-mannered; note S.Afr. *goniva*, a stolen diamond]

gonnof *v.* (*also* gonif, gonoph) [mid-19C–1910s; 2000s] to steal, to rob, to deceive; thus *gonnofing/gonophin*, stealing, deception. [GONNOF n. (2)]

gonny *n. see* GON n.[1].

gonof(f) *n. see* GONNOF n.

gonoph *see under* GONNOF.

go north *v.* [1970s] (*US Black*) to leave.

gonov(im) *n. see* GONNOF n.

go nowhere *v.* [1920s+] to be worthless, to be grossly inadequate.

gons *n. see* GONCE n.

gonsel *n.* (*also* gonsil, gonzel, guncel, gunsel, gunshel) **1** [late 19C+] (*US tramp*) a youth, a naïve boy. **2** [1910s–40s] (*US tramp/prison*) a young, homosexual sidekick who accompanies a tramp or acts as a lover to a masculine prisoner. **3** [1930s–70s] (*US*) a stupid or contemptible man. **4** [1940s+] an informer, a criminal, a gunman. [Ger. *gänslein*, a little goose, thence Yid. *genzel*, a man's young male lover, a catamite; the *locus classicus* is as the description of Elmer, the young, inadequate hoodlum of Dashiell Hammett's *The Maltese Falcon* (1930, film 1941); given that he is also a criminal's sidekick, the term is often mistranslated as 'gunman'. However, while Raymond Chandler is convinced of this, *HDAS* still quotes *The Maltese Falcon* as a source for *gunsel*, 'a gunman; thug', suggesting a root in GUN n.[9], SE *gunman* or GUN-SLINGER n. (1)]

gonski *adj.* [2000s] gone, in the sense of not working properly. [SE *gone* + -SKI sfx]

gonus *n.* [mid-19C+] (*US campus*) a fool, a stupid person (cf. DOOFUS n.). [GOONEY n. (2)]

go nuts *v. see* NUTS adj. (2).

gonzel *n. see* GONSEL n.

gonzo *n.* [1970s+] (*orig. US*) an anarchic eccentric. [GONZO adj.[1] (1)]

gonzo *adj.*[1] [1970s+] **1** eccentric, bizarre, extraordinary, groundbreaking; esp. in comb. *gonzo journalism*, a form of extreme 'New Journalism', in which reporters, rather than taking the typical distanced, neutral position, interpolate their thoughts, emotions and actions into the story. **2** out of control. **3** crazy about. **4** psychotic, crazy. **5** in the sex industry, unrestrained, extreme. [GONE adj.[1] (2)/GONE adj.[3] (5) + CRAZO n. or cod Ital. sfx -zo + pun on GUNG-HO adj.; coined and pioneered as a journ. form by US writer Hunter S. Thompson (1939–2005) in *Rolling Stone* magazine 1970]

gonzo *adj.*[2] [1970s+] **1** finished, defeated, useless. **2** (*US*) drunk (cf. ADDLED adj.). [ext. of GONE adj.[1]/GONE adj.[3] (1)]

gonzoed *adj.* [1980s] (*US*) very drunk or intoxicated (cf. ADDLED adj.). [GONZO adj.[2] (2)]

Gonzo (the Great) *n.* [1990s+] a state (usu. of drunken excess). [rhy. sl.; ult. the *Muppet Show* character]

goo *n.*[1] **1** [20C+] (*orig. US*) anything sticky or viscid, e.g. blood, semen, glue (cf. BOLLOCK SNOT n.). **2** [1920s+] sickly sentimentality, esp. in speech or writing. [? abbr. BURGOO n.]

goo *n.*[2] [1990s+] (*Irish*) a glimpse, a look. [ety. unknown]

goo *v.*[1] (*also* goob) [20C+] (*Aus.*) to spit out a lump of phlegm. [GOO n.[1] (1)]

goo *v.*[2] [2000s] (*US Black*) to feel stupid, angry, stuck. [GOO n.[1] (1)]

goob *n. see* GOOBER n.[2].

goob *v. see* GOO v.[1].

goober *n.*[1] [mid-19C+] (*US*) an inhabitant of North Carolina, Arkansas or Georgia. [SAmE *goober*, a peanut, an important crop in these states]

goober *n.*[2] (*also* goob, goobette) **1** [mid-19C+] an idiot, a fool, an incompetent, a country bumpkin; also affectionate use; thus *goob*, to act irritatingly; GOOB OUT v. (cf. BUCKWHEAT n.). **2** [1920s+] (*US*) the penis. **3** [1940s] the testicles (cf. ACORNS n.). **4** [1960s+] (*Aus./N.Z./US*) a gob of phlegm. **5** [1970s+] (*US campus*) a small child. **6** [1970s+] (*US campus*) a small mole, spot or similar skin blemish. **7** [1980s+] (*US campus*) someone not attuned to the peer group norms. [fig. uses of SAmE *goober*, a peanut, thus an insignificant object; ult. f. African languages]

gooberbrain *n.* [1960s+] (*US*) a silly person. [SAmE *goober*, a peanut + sfx -*brain*]

goober-grabber *n.*[1] (*also* gauber-grubber, goober-grubber, gruber-grubber) [mid-19C+] (*US*) an inhabitant of North Carolina, Arkansas or Georgia. [SAmE *goober*, the peanut, grown widely in all 3 states; the term means lit. 'one who grabs or digs peanuts']

goober-grabber n.² **1** [1950s] (US, Southern) a sexually voracious woman. **2** [1990s+] (US) a male homosexual (cf. BONE-EATER n.). [GOOBER n.² (2) + SE *grabber*]

gooberhead n. [1980s+] (US) a general derog. term, typically describing an eccentric, a fussy person, one who drives badly. [SAmE *goober* + -HEAD sfx (1)]

goob out v. [1980s+] (US campus) to disgust, to repel. [GOOBER n.² (1)]

gooby n.¹ [late 19C] a fool, a dullard. [GABY n.]

gooby n.² [1940s–50s] (US prison) food. [GOO n.¹ (1)]

gooch v. [1970s] (US campus) to kiss. [GOO n.¹ (1) + SMOOCH v.¹ (1)]

good n.¹ [early 19C] (UK Und.) a place or person that can be robbed easily; thus *good upon the crack*, easily broken into.

good n.² **1** [mid–late 19C] (orig. US) alcohol; thus *get good*, to get drunk. **2** [1970s+] (drugs) phencyclidine (cf. ACE n.⁴). **3** [2000s] heroin.

good adj.¹ **1** [late 16C; late 19C+] solvent, able to pay for or lend; usu. as *good for*. **2** [late 19C+] able to sustain a given situation.

good adj.² [late 19C+] worthless or dead, esp. of an enemy or a criminal. [orig. used on frontier as *good Indian*, a dead Indian]

good and bad n. [20C+] one's father, i.e. 'dad'. [rhy. sl.]

good a piece as ever strode a pot n. [19C] an admirable woman, as good as one might find. [a woman bestrides a chamberpot to urinate]

good as all get-out phr. [mid-19C+] (orig. US) excellent, wonderful, first-rate. [ALL GET OUT phr.]

good as caz phr. [early 19C] (UK Und.) easy, simple, referring to any projected fraud or robbery, or a person who is to be made a victim of either. [CAZ n. (see CASSAN n.)]

good as ever pissed phr. [mid-17C–18C] of a person, as good as there has ever been. [PISS v.¹ (1)]

good as ever twanged phr. [17C–early 18C] **1** of women, as good as one might wish, esp. in the sexual context. **2** of the male genitals, as good as one might wish. [TWANG v.¹]

good as pie phr. see NICE AS PIE phr. (1).

good as shit phr. [1970s] (US campus) very good.

good at the game n. (also **good at it**) [19C] an enthusiastic, skilful lover. [SE + GAME n.¹ (1)/IT n.¹ (1)]

good bet n. [1920s+] a dependable person, idea or object.

good bite n. see BITE n.¹ (4).

good biz! excl. [late 19C–1910s] wonderful! excellent! also as adj. [abbr. SE *good business!*]

good buddy n. **1** [1950s+] the popular form of address among users of Citizen's Band radios; also in general use. **2** [1950s+] a CB radio user. **3** [1980s+] (US) a homosexual. [SE *good* + BUDDY n. (1)]

good butt n. [1960s+] (drugs) a marijuana cigarette. [SE *good* + BUTT n.² (2)]

goodbye Charlie phr. (also **goodbye McGinnis**) [1930s–40s] (US) the end, the finish; usu. in phr. *and it's goodbye, Charlie* (cf. GOODNIGHT phr.).

goodbye John phr. [late 19C–1900s] (US) the end, 'it's all over'.

good cess to you! excl. see BAD CESS TO YOU! excl.

good Christmas! excl. [1920s+] a euph. var. of *good Christ!*

good deal! excl. [1940s+] (US) an expression of approval or congratulation, well done! that's wonderful!

good doer n. [1910s+] a smart person, one who 'knows a thing or two'; thus *good-doing*, smart, knowledgeable. [a play on *do-gooder*]

good dud n. [1980s+] (US campus) an unamusing joke. [SE *dud*, a failure, a 'flop']

good eating n. [1920s+] (Aus.) an attractive young woman. [the image is of food; the sexual use of EAT v.³ (1) is coincidental]

good egg n. (also **nice egg**) [20C+] **1** an admirable person; thus

good-eggishness, the quality of being such a person. **2** a good thing. [EGG n.¹ (1)]

good egg! excl. [20C+] that's good! that's lucky! [GOOD EGG n.]

gooden n. [2000s] (US Black) a very fat woman. [ety. unknown]

good enough for gundy phr. see NO GOOD TO GUNDY phr.

goodfellas n. [1990s+] (drugs) fentanyl. [ety. unknown; ? link to the film *Goodfellas* (1990)]

good fellow n. see GOOD PEOPLE n. (1).

good-for n. [late 19C] (S.Afr.) an IOU. [it is GOOD adj.¹ (1) for the debt]

good form n. [late 19C+] (UK society) anything or anyone that is seen as 'proper' or socially acceptable. [horseracing use *form*, the state of a horse's health etc]

good for you! excl. (also **good for him/her!**) [mid-19C+] well done!

good future! excl. [1980s+] (US campus) a sarcastic response to the speaker's announcement of some form of menial employment, i.e. what a good job! aren't you lucky!

good-gal n. [1930s] (US) a girlfriend.

good Germans n. [1940s+] (US) law-abiding, respectable, unquestioning people, irrespective of actual racial origins. [stereotype of Germans as law-abiding people who do not question authority]

good giggles n. [1970s] (drugs) marijuana (cf. BOMB n.⁴). [its effect]

good girl n. (also **good one**) [17C–18C] a prostitute, a wanton (cf. AWAYDAY GIRL n.). [ironic + she is *good for* sex]

good go n. [1950s–70s] (drugs) the proper amount of drugs for the money paid. [SE *good* + GO n.¹ (3)]

good gosh! excl. see GOSH! excl.

good gravy! excl. [mid-19C+] (Aus.) a mild expeletive.

good grief! excl. (also **spare my grief!**) [20C+] a general excl. of surprise and/or dismay. [dial.]

good guts n. [1910s+] (Aus.) the facts, the essential information. [SE *good* + GUTS n.¹ (3)]

good guy n. [1920s+] a friendly individual, male or female, esp. if on one's side; usu. in pl. as in phr. *one of the good guys*.

good hair n. [20C+] (US Black) straight, soft hair. [*good* as in superior, more acceptable, i.e. 'White']

good head n. **1** [19C+] an expert. **2** [1920s–70s] (orig. US Und.) a trustworthy, admirable person.

good heavens! excl. see HEAVENS! excl

good humour, be in a v. [mid-18C] (US) a euph. for to be drunk (cf. ABOUT RIGHT phr.¹).

goodie n.¹ (also **goody**) **1** [late 18C–19C] a moralizer, a religious hypocrite. **2** [late 19C+] (orig. US) a good person, esp. in a film or story (cf. BADDIE n.).

goodie n.² (also **goody**) [mid-19C+] a good thing; esp. in phr. OLDIE BUT GOODIE n.

goodie n.³ (US) **1** [1950s+] the vagina. **2** [1970s] the female breast and/or nipple.

goodie and baddie n. [20C+] an Irish person (cf. SHOVEL (AND PICK) n.). [rhy. sl. = PADDY n. (1)]

goodies n. **1** [mid-19C+] sweetmeats, latterly any form of tasty food. **2** [mid-19C+] objects, things, presumably beneficial. **3** [1950s+] drugs. **4** [1960s] (US) sexual intercourse. **5** [1960s] (US campus) alcohol. **6** [1960s+] possessions. **7** [1960s+] (US) the genitals, the female breasts (cf. APPLES n.¹).

good ink n. [1910s+] (Aus./N.Z.) something agreeable, pleasant; usu. in phr. *that's good ink*. [? journ. imagery]

good iron phr. (Aus.) **1** [mid-19C–1900s] a general phr. of approval, congratulations. **2** [1900s] an expression of incredulity. [quoits jargon *good iron*, a good throw]

good job! excl. [1940s+] (Aus.) well done!

good jump n. [20C+] usu. of a woman, a sexually satisfying partner. [JUMP n.³ (1)]

goodle n. [1950s+] (Ulster) a lot. [SE *good deal*]

good-looker *n.* [late 19C+] (*orig. US*) an attractive person, usu. a woman.

good luck *n. see* LUCK *n.*

goodman *n.* **1** [late 16C–early 19C] a boon companion, a roisterer; an admirable person, defined according to context. **2** [18C] a gaoler.

goodman turd *n.* (*also* **goodman fool**) [late 16C–early 17C] a derog. description of another person. [GOODMAN *n.* (1) + TURD *n.* (2)/SE *fool*]

goodness Agnes! *excl.* (*also* **goodness godness Agnes!**) [1940s–60s] (*US*) a general excl. of surprise and/or pleasure. [? *agnus dei*, the lamb of God and thus a euph. for God or Christ]

good news *n.* [1970s+] a general term of approval, whether of people, things or events.

goodnight *phr.* [late 19C+] used to indicate incipient trouble or one's resignation in the face of a problem or disaster; thus also ext. in phrs., e.g. *goodnight Irene*; *goodnight nurse*; *goodnight Vienna*; (*N.Z.*) *goodnight McGuinness*; (*Irish*) *goodnight Joe Doyle* (cf. GOODBYE CHARLIE *phr.*). [fig. uses of SE, although for Vienna note *Good Night, Vienna*, a romantic operetta by Eric Maschwitz and George Posford (1929)]

goodnight kiss *n.* [20C+] urination (cf. ANGEL'S KISS *n.*). [rhy. sl. = PISS *n.* (2)]

good-o *adj.* (*also* **good-oh**) [20C+] (*orig. Aus./N.Z.*) excellent, wonderful, as it should be.

good-o *adv.* (*also* **good-oh**) [20C+] (*Aus.*) very well, excellently.

good-o! *excl.* (*also* **good-oh!**) [1910s+] (*orig. Aus./N.Z.*) an excl. of approbation or assent. [usu. associated with somewhat dated schoolboy use]

good oil *n.* [1910s+] (*Aus.*) the honest truth, true facts. [OIL *n.*[2] (3)]

good old *pfx* [mid-19C+] a general pfx of approval and affection, sometimes ironic.

good old boy *n.* (*also* **good ole boy, old boy**) **1** [1940s+] (*US*) a man who embodies the trad. values of the Southern White male country-dweller; used neutrally by those so defined (although there may be a slight implication of tolerable rascality), but usu. derog. or as *good ole boy* at least ironic by outsiders for whom it is often a synon. for bigot/racist; also attrib. **2** [1960s+] an acceptable person, 'one of the gang'. **3** [1980s] (*US preppie*) a student who is considered of the 'right type' by his peers. [GOOD OLD pfx + SE *boy*]

good old brown *n.* [20C+] (*Can.*) sodomy. [GOOD OLD pfx + BROWN *n.*[3] (2)]

good old sort *n. see* GOOD SORT *n.*

good ole boy *n. see* GOOD OLD BOY *n.*

good one *n.*[1] (*also* **good 'un**) [late 18C+] **1** a joke; usu. as *that's a good one*. **2** an implausible statement, thus a lie.

good one *n.*[2] [mid-19C+] a hard blow.

good one *n.*[3] [late 19C] a gullible fool, a SUCKER *n.*[3] (1).

good one *n.*[4] *see* GOOD GIRL *n.*

good on the fang *phr.* (*also* **good on the tooth**) [1940s+] (*Aus.*) a phr. used of someone known as an enthusiastic eater.

good on the star *phr.* (*also* **good on the crack**) [early–mid-19C] (*UK Und.*) easy to open, usu. of a window. [the 'starring' of the window when one breaks the glass]

good on you! *excl.* [20C+] (*Aus./Irish*) a general expression of approbation, thanks etc; also abbr. to *good!* [invariably linked to Aus., the term is equally common in Ireland. Share suggests that the origin lies in Irish *rinne sé mhaith orm*, lit. 'he made/did his good on me']

good pay, be *v.* [early 18C+] to be trustworthy, esp. as regards paying one's debts.

good people *n.* **1** [late 19C+] (*also* **good fellow**) an admirable individual; a member of one's peer group. **2** [20C+] (*US Und.*) spec. former criminals who have retired from their various specialities. **3** [1920s+] a leading criminal, irrespective of speciality.

Goodrich game *n.* [mid-19C] (*US Und.*) pretending to have

been robbed to avoid paying one's bill. [? a contemporary confidence man; note Asbury, *Sucker's Progress* (1938): 'According to [anti-gambling writer Jonathan] Green, the [*Secret Band of*] *Brothers* were a great organization of gamblers, robbers and counterfeiters, formed in 1798 at Hanging Rock, in the western part of Virginia, with one Goodrich at the head of the band']

goods *n.* **1** [18C; 1910s+] the female body, usu. in the context of prostitution. **2** [1920s+] the male genitals. **3** [1930s+] drugs.

goods, the *n.*[1] (*orig. US*) **1** [late 19C+] the real thing, the ideal thing or person; thus DELIVER (THE GOODS) *v.* **2** [1900s–20s] accurate information, the truth. **3** [1910s+] information, usu. to be used in an unfriendly manner towards its subject; thus *get/have the goods on someone*, to have or acquire information or to put in a difficult position. **4** [1980s] sexual intercourse.

goods, the *n.*[2] [20C+] (*US Und.*) stolen goods, contraband; usu. in phr. *catch someone with the goods*, to catch someone in the act.

good shake *n. see* EVEN SHAKE *n.*

good ship Venus *n.* [20C+] the penis (cf. ALMOND *n.*). [rhy. sl.; ref. to the eponymous 'rugby song']

good shit *n.* [1960s+] (*orig. US*) anything of high quality, esp. drugs. [SHIT *n.*[3] (6)/SHIT *n.*[5] (1)]

good shot *n.* [mid-18C+] a good try, even though one may have failed. [SE *shot*/SHOT *n.*[5] (1)]

good show! *excl.* [1930s+] a general excl. of approval or pleasure.

good sick *n.* [1950s+] (*drugs*) the short-lived bout of vomiting that can follow an injection of heroin. [SICK *n.* (2)]

good sort *n.* (*also* **good old sort**) **1** [mid-19C+] a generally admirable person or creature. **2** [1920s+] a very pretty woman. **3** [1940s+] (*Aus.*) one who is attractive to the opposite sex; thus *extra sort*, one who is extremely attractive; DRACK SORT *n.* [SORT *n.*]

good stuff *n.* **1** [early 19C; 1960s] hard liquor. **2** [1960s+] (*US drugs*) (*also* **bad stuff**) effective, high-quality, pleasant drugs. **3** [1970s–80s] (*US Black*) sexual sophistication. **4** [1980s] success in a confidence trick, in deception. [SE *good* + STUFF *n.*[3]; (2) BAD *adj.* (1)]

good thing *n.* **1** [early 19C+] an advantageous opportunity, usu. in business or in horserace gambling. **2** [20C+] (*Aus./US*) one who can easily be duped, a 'sucker'. [orig. horseracing use, a certain winner]

good time *n.*[1] (*US Und.*) **1** [late 19C+] time off for good behaviour. **2** [1970s+] a jail sentence that is suffered without any particular problems. [SE *good* + TIME *n.*[1]]

good time *n.*[2] [1920s+] (*US Black*) an especially acceptable, likeable person.

good time *n.*[3] [1960s+] the penis. [its role in sex]

good-time Charlie *n.* [1920s+] a playboy, a dissolute man; occas. of a woman. [SE *good time* + CHARLIE *n.*]

good-time-Charlie *v.* [1920s–50s] (*US*) to act in a jovial, (over-)friendly manner. [GOOD-TIME CHARLIE *n.*]

good-time Jane *n.* [1940s–60s] (*US*) a sexually promiscuous woman. [SE *good time* + JANE *n.*[2] (1)]

good to go *phr.* [1990s+] (*US Black teen*) said by males when referring to a woman they presume to be sexually available; often as *babe's good to go*; also as a positive reply to 'How are you?'

good 'un *n.*[1] (*also* **good one**) **1** [19C+] a dependable, trustworthy, admirable person or creature. **2** [1920s+] used similarly of an object or situation.

good 'un *n.*[2] *see* GOOD ONE *n.*[1].

good voice to beg bacon *n.* [late 17C–early 19C] a very unmelodious singing voice and therefore good only for begging.

good warrant *n.* (*also* **great warrant**) [20C+] (*Irish*) a good bet, a certainty. [SE *warrant*, a surety]

good woman *n.* (*also* **quiet woman, silent woman**) [late 18C–mid-19C] a common public house sign representing a woman without a head (cf. HONEST LAWYER *n.*). [the implication is that her 'goodness' stems from the fact that bereft of a head she cannot scold]

good-woolled *adj.* [mid-19C] used of a plucky, spirited person. [Lincolnshire dial. *good-woolled*, said of a sheep that has a good fleece]

goody *see also under* GOODIE.

goody! *excl.* (*also* **goody-goody!**) [20C+] (*orig. Aus.*) a general excl. of approval, pleasure, satisfaction.

goody-box *n.* [1970s] a safe-deposit box. [GOODIES n. + BOX n.² (4)]

goodyear *n.*¹ [late 16C–early 17C] venereal disease, esp. gonorrhoea. [? *gouge*, a slattern, a soldier's companion; ult. Fr. argot *gouge*, a slut; the link between Fr. *goujère*, a hypothetical derivative of 'the French word gouje, which signifies a common Camp-Trull' is considered 'curiously plausible,' by the OED but, it adds, 'there is no evidence that the definite meaning of 'pox' was really intended by any of the writers who used the word; and the alleged etymology is [thus] utterly inadmissible']

goodyear *n.*² [1960s+] the ring of excess flesh around a portly stomach that may be seen in a kinder light by those who appreciate the Rubenesque figure. [the *Goodyear* Rubber Company; thus pun on SPARE TYRE n. (1)]

goody-goody *n.* (*also* **goody-good**) [late 19C+] a law-abiding, respectable person. [GOODY-GOODY adj.]

goody-goody *adj.* (*also* **goody-good**) [mid-19C+] overly well-intentioned, pious, law-abiding.

goody-goody! *excl. see* GOODY! excl.

good young man *n.* [late 19C] a hypocrite. [a lyric by music-hall star Arthur Roberts (1852–1933)]

goody two-shoes *n.* [mid-19C; 1930s+] (*orig. US*) a self-righteous person. [fairy-tale character]

gooey *n.* **1** [20C+] (*Aus.*) a lump of phlegm. **2** [20C+] a man of weak character. **3** [1980s+] a pretty girlfriend. [GOOEY adj.]

gooey *adj.* **1** [1900s] (*US campus*) bizarre, strange. **2** [1910s+] sentimental, mawkish. **3** [1910s+] sticky, viscid. **4** [1930s] distasteful and distressing. [fig. uses of GOO n.¹ (1) + sfx -*y*]

goof *n.*¹ **1** [20C+] a fool, a blunderer. **2** [1910s] a form of derog. address. **3** [1910s+] an eccentric, crazy person. **4** [1950s] (*US*) something very unpleasant. **5** [1950s] (*US*) an unsophisticated rustic (cf. BLOOTER n.). **6** [1960s+] (*US*) a mistake. **7** [1970s+] (*US*) a joke, a surprise; thus *goofs*, fun. [dial. *goof*, a fool, a clown, an oaf]

goof *n.*² **1** [1940s] (*US*) alcohol, a drinker. **2** [1940s–50s] (*US drugs*) (*also* **goof burner**) a marijuana smoker. **3** [1940s–60s] (*US drugs*) psychotropic drugs, esp. marijuana or barbiturates; thus *on the goof*, drowsy from the effects of a drug (cf. BARBIT n.). **4** [1950s–60s] (*US drugs*) the relaxed state that follows the taking of a drug, usu. marijuana or a barbiturate. [GOOF v.²]

goof *n.*³ *see* GOEF n.

goof *v.*¹ (*also* **goof around**, **goof on**) **1** [1910s+] to fool (with), to play around; thus *goof time*, a period of relaxation. **2** [1940s+] (*Aus./US*) to gawk, to stare mindlessly, esp. at the television; thus *goof box*, a TV set. **3** [1940s+] (*also* **goof it**) to blunder, to make a mistake; thus *goof oneself*, to get into trouble. **4** [1950s+] to dawdle, to waste time, to avoid work. **5** [1950s+] (*US*) to mistreat, to victimize. **6** [1960s+] to make a mess of. **7** [1970s] of an object, a machine, to malfunction. **8** [1980s+] to give oneself up.

goof *v.*² [1940s+] (*US*) **1** to take drugs; thus *goofed up*, *on the goof*, under the influence of drugs. **2** in fig. use, to be addicted to or obsessed with, usu. a person. **3** to render someone into a state that approximates that which follows drug use. **4** to relax, to go to sleep under the influence of drugs, usu. heroin. **5** to become drunk. [GOOF v.¹ (1), i.e. the effects]

goof *v.*³ *see* GOEF v.

goofball *n.*¹ **1** [1930s–50s] (*drugs*) marijuana. **2** [1940s+] (*drugs*) a barbiturate, a tranquillizer (cf. BARBIT n.). **3** [1950s+] (*Aus.*) a

knockout drop. **4** [1950s+] (*drugs*) a combination of cocaine and heroin. [GOOF v.² (1); ult. GOOF v.¹ (1)]

goofball *n.*² [1940s+] (*US*) a silly, amusing, eccentric or insane person. [GOOF n.¹ (3) + -BALL sfx]

goofball *adj.* [1940s+] crazy, eccentric (cf. GOOFY adj.). [GOOFBALL n.²]

goofbang *n.* [1950s] casual sex. [GOOF v.¹ (1) + BANG n.² (2)]

goof box *n. see* GOOF v.¹ (2).

goof burner *n. see* GOOF n.² (2).

goof butt *n.* (*also* **goofy butt**) [1940s+] (*drugs*) a marijuana cigarette. [GOOF n.² (3) + BUTT n.² (2)]

goofed (up) *adj.* **1** [1930s] (*US*) made a fool of. **2** [1940s+] (*US*) ruined, messed up. **3** [1940s+] (*US*) drunk (cf. ADDLED adj.). **4** [1940s+] (*S.Afr./US*) intoxicated by a drug, esp. cannabis or barbiturates. **5** [1950s–60s] crazy, infatuated or bewildered. [GOOF v.¹/GOOF v.²]

goofer *n.*¹ (*also* **goopher**) [1910s+] (*US*) a lout, an oaf, a clumsy fool. [GOOF n.¹ (1)]

goofer *n.*² **1** [1940s–70s] one who 'plays around' with drugs, esp. amphetamines or barbiturates. **2** [1960s+] (*also* **goofers**) a barbiturate. [GOOF v.² (1) + GOOFBALL n.¹ (2)]

goofer *n.*³ [1940s+] a homosexual prostitute who takes active roles in fellatio or anal intercourse. [fig. use of GOOF n.¹ (3)]

goofer dust *n.* [1920s+] (*US Black*) any form of dust or powder used in the casting of spells; usu. based on graveyard dirt plus pulverized red/black pepper, powdered snail or snake etc. [Ki-Kongo *kufwa*, to die]

goofer feathers *n.* (*also* **goopher feathers**) [1920s–40s] (*US*) nonsense (cf. BULLFEATHERS n.). [GOOFER n.¹ + SE *feathers*]

goofers *n. see* GOOFER n.² (2).

go-off *n.* [mid-19C+] the starting time, at the start; usu. in phr. the *first go-off*.

go off *v.*¹ **1** [late 17C–19C] to die. **2** [mid-18C–19C] of a woman, to be married. **3** [early 19C+] to happen, to take place, esp. of a fight, a riot. **4** [mid-19C] to be disposed of, whether of persons or objects. **5** [late 19C–1910s] (*UK society*) to not take place, to fail to happen. **6** [20C+] to pass out, to go to sleep.

go off *v.*² **1** [mid-18C; 1920s+] to have an orgasm. **2** [mid-19C+] (*also* **go off pop**) to lose emotional control. **3** [1970s+] (*US Black*) to do something exceptionally well. **4** [1970s+] (*US*) to talk about. **5** [1980s+] (*US campus*) to become foolish or silly. **6** [1980s+] (*US campus*) to act intensely. **7** [1980s+] (*US campus*) to move from topic to topic while talking.

go off *v.*³ [late 19C+] to lose freshness, to become increasingly rotten, usu. of fruit, meat or milk; also in fig. use.

go off *v.*⁴ (*Aus.*) **1** [1910s+] to be sent to prison. **2** [1920s+] to suffer a police raid, usu. because a hotel or public house is breaking local drinking laws. **3** [1940s+] to be fined.

go off *v.*⁵ [1930s+] to find a person or object unappealing, distasteful or tedious, usu. when one's feelings have been more positive before.

go off at *v.* [1930s+] (*mainly Aus./N.Z.*) to lose one's temper, to attack verbally, usu. at length (cf. GO OFF (ON) v.).

go off at half-cock *v.* (*also* **go off half-cocked**) **1** [early 19C+] to speak or act prematurely. **2** [early 19C+] to talk foolishly, esp. when under the influence of one's emotions or of drink or drugs. **3** [mid-19C] to work badly or inadequately. **4** [late 19C+] to ejaculate prematurely (cf. FIRE v.¹). [SE *half-cock*, to put (a gun) at half-cock; (4) adds pun on COCK n.² (1)]

go off at the deep end *v. see* FLY OFF AT THE DEEP END v.

go off at the fall of the leaf *v. see* GO OFF WITH THE FALL OF THE LEAF v.

go off at the nail *v.* [early 18C+] (*Ulster*) to become confused or flustered. [the image of 2 parts of a pair of scissors flying apart when the nail that links them snaps or falls out]

go off half-cocked *v. see* GO OFF AT HALF-COCK v.

go off like a two-bob watch *v.* (*also* **go off like a tin of**

bad fish) [1960s+] (*Aus.*) of a woman, to be highly sexed. [pun on SE *go off*/GO OFF v.² (1)]

go off (on) v. [1960s+] (*mainly US Black*) **1** (*also* **go all off**) to lose one's temper, to attack verbally, usu. at length (cf. GO OFF AT v.). **2** to attack physically.

go off one's brain v. see OUT OF ONE'S BRAIN phr.

go off one's burner v. [late 19C–1910s] to go mad.

go off one's dot v. [late 19C–1920s] to go mad. [DOTTY adj. (2)]

go off one's face v. see OFF ONE'S FACE phr. (2).

go off one's napper v. see NAPPER n.² (2).

go off one's nut v. [late 19C+] to go mad, to lose emotional control. [NUT n.¹ (2)]

go off on one's ear v. see GET (UP) ON ONE'S EAR v.

go off pop v. see GO OFF v.² (2).

go offside v. [2000s] to disappear.

go off the bat v. (*also* **go to bat**) [1980s+] (*Aus. prison*) to masturbate.

go off the boil v. [20C+] **1** to lose impetus, to lose enthusiasm. **2** to calm down. **3** of a woman, to lose her enthusiasm for sex.

go off the deep end v. see FLY OFF AT THE DEEP END v.

go off the handle v. [mid-19C+] **1** to lose one's temper, to lose emotional control (cf. FLY OFF (THE HANDLE) v.). **2** to die.

go off the hooks v. [mid–late 19C] to die. [OFF THE HOOKS phr.⁴]

go off the side v. [1930s–40s] (*UK Und.*) to abscond, e.g. when a criminal runs off with a gang's spoils.

go off twanging v. see TWANGING adj.

go off with the fall of the leaf v. (*also* **go off at the fall of the leaf**) [late 18C–19C] to be hanged. [a pun on the leaves or hinged panels of the drop and the dead leaves that fall from a natural, rather than judicial 'tree'. Grose (1796) notes that 'criminals in Dublin being turned off from the outside of the prison by the falling of a board, propped up, and moving on a hinge, like the leaf of a table'; Griffiths (1884) notes that the adoption of the gallows in England followed the invention of the Dublin 'engine of death'; George Parker, *Life's Painter* (1789): '*Fall of the leaf.* The new mode of hanging. The culprit is brought out upon a stage, and placed upon a leaf, when the rope is fixed about his neck the leaf falls, and the body immediately becomes pendant']

goofie n. see GOOFY n.¹.

goofily adv. [1930s+] foolishly. [GOOF n.¹ (1)]

goofiness n. [1920s+] stupidity, foolishness. [GOOFY adj. (3)]

goof it v. see GOOF v.¹ (3).

goof-off n. **1** [1940s+] (*US*) a loafer, an idler. **2** [1960s+] (*US*) an error or blunder. **3** [1980s] a joker. [GOOF OFF v. (1)]

goof off v. **1** [1930s+] (*orig. milit.*) to act lazily, to mess around instead of working. **2** [1930s+] (*orig. milit.*) to blunder, to wreck. **3** [1940s] to go mad. **4** [1940s–60s] (*US drugs*) to go to sleep, esp. under the influence of drugs. **5** [1950s] (*US*) to leave. **6** [1960s] (*US*) to gain pleasure from, to be enthralled by. **7** [1970s] to chat, to socialize. **8** [1980s] to turn down an invitation, to avoid a meeting. [ext. GOOF v.¹ (1)]

goof on v.¹ (*also* **goof over**) **1** [1940s+] (*US*) to laugh at, to find amusing. **2** [1950s] to get excited by. [ext. GOOF v.¹ (1)]

goof on v.² see GOOF v.¹.

goof oneself v. see GOOF v.¹ (3).

goo food n. [1990s+] (*US campus*) Oriental food. [? GOOK n.² (1) or ? GOO n.¹ (1), i.e. a ref. to consistency of some dishes]

goof out v. [1980s+] (*US*) to trick or fool. [GOOF v.¹ (1)]

goof over v. see GOOF ON v.¹.

goof pill n. (*also* **goofy**) [1950s–70s] (*drugs*) a barbiturate (cf. BARBIT n.). [var. GOOFBALL n.¹ (2)]

goof-proof adj. [1970s+] (*US*) foolproof. [GOOF n.¹ (1) + SE *proof*]

goofs n. see GOOF n.¹ (7).

goof up n. [1950s+] (*US*) **1** a blunder. **2** a person who blunders or messes up, causing trouble for themself. [GOOF UP v.]

goof up v. [1940s+] (*US*) to blunder, to spoil, to injure. [ext. GOOF v.¹ (3)]

goofus n. [1910s+] (*US*) an idiot (cf. DOOFUS n.). [GOOF n.¹ (1)]

goofy n.¹ (*also* **goofie**) [1920s–30s] (*US campus*) a fool. [GOOFY adj. (3)]

goofy n.² see GOOF PILL n.

goofy adj. [1910s+] **1** uncoordinated, inept. **2** drunk (cf. ADDLED adj.). **3** (*also* **goofy-ass**) silly, foolish; thus GOOFINESS n. **4** mad (cf. GOOFBALL adj.). **5** (*US*) obsessed, keen on. **6** incomprehensible. **7** disorientated, confused. **8** (*US drugs*) suffering from narcotics withdrawal. [GOOF n.¹ (1) + sfx *-y*; the personification of the term (albeit anthropomorphic) is the eponymous Disney character]

goofy butt n. see GOOF BUTT n.

goog n.¹ **1** [20C+] (*Aus.*) (*also* **googie**, **googy**) an egg. **2** [1980s] a fool. [Scot. *goggie*/Irish *gogaí*, nursery term for an egg]

goog n.² [1920s–30s] (*US*) a black eye. [GOOGS n.]

goog v. [1950s] to stand around; to watch others. [GOGGLE (AT) v.]

googeen adj. [20C+] (*Irish*) fidgety, usu. of a woman. [synon. Irish *guaigin*]

googiana n. [1990s+] (*UK juv.*) sexual intercourse. [ety. unknown]

googie n.¹ (*also* **googy**) [1930s+] a fool. [GOO-GOO n.⁴]

googie n.² see GOOG n.¹ (1).

google-eye n. see GOGGLE-EYE n.

google-eyed adj. see GOGGLE-EYED adj.

googlum n. see GOOZLUM n.

googly n. [1940s+] anything that poses a tough problem, esp. an awkward question that a person would rather not answer. [cricket jargon *googly*, an off-break that is delivered with what appears to the batsman as a leg-break action. Invented by the English bowler B.J.T. Bosanquet (1877–1936), it is also known as a *bosie* in Australia]

googly-eyed adj. see GOGGLE-EYED adj. (3).

goo-gobs n. [1970s+] (*US Black*) a very large or infinite amount. [ety. unknown; note SE *googol*, 10 to the 100th power]

googons n. see GOOGS n.

goo-goo n.¹ (*US*) **1** [late 19C–1950s] (*also* **gu-gu**) a derog. term for an Asian or dark-skinned foreigner, esp. a Filipino; also attrib. (cf. BROWNIE n.²). **2** [1970s] an unintelligible foreign language. [? echoic of a supposedly unintelligible language]

goo-goo n.² [late 19C+] (*US*) a supporter of political reform. [SE *good government* + GOODIE n.¹ (1)]

goo-goo n.³ [1910s] (*orig. US*) anything sticky or viscid, e.g. blood, semen, glue (cf. BOLLOCK SNOT n.). [redup. of GOO n.¹ (1)]

goo-goo n.⁴ [1910s+] (*US*) a silly fool; thus as adj., foolish;, mawkish, sentimental. [? *goo-goo* noises of stupidity]

goo-goo v. [1900s–40s] (*US*) to make eyes at someone. [GOO-GOO EYES n.]

goo-goo eyes n. (*also* **goo-goo**, **goo-goo lamp**, **goo-goos**, **googy eyes**, **oogle eyes**) [late 19C+] an amorous glance directed at a loved, or hopefully soon to be loved, one. [? GOGGLE (AT) v. + the double 'o' is reminiscent of 2 rounded eyes; *goo-goo* is also a classic piece of 'baby-talk' and as such reflects the infantility of such glances]

goo-goo watch n. [1930s–40s] (*US Black*) dawn and the period just preceding it. [ety. unknown]

googs n. (*also* **googons**) [1920s–50s] (*US Und.*) spectacles. [GOGGLES n. (3) or ? play on GOO-GOO EYES n.]

googy n.¹ see GOOG n.¹ (1).

googy n.² see GOOGIE n.¹.

googy eyes n. see GOO-GOO EYES n.

googy-googy adj. [1960s] given to playing pranks, fooling around. [GOOGIE n.¹]

gooi n. [1940s+] (*S.Afr.*) a fling, a spree, a party. [GOOI v.]

gooi v. [1940s+] (*S.Afr.*) to throw, to fling, to give someone something. [Afk. *gooi*, to throw; fling]

gooi ankers v. [1980s+] (S.Afr.) to brake suddenly. [GOOI v. + Afk. sl. *ankers*, the brakes]

gooi a spasm v. [1980s+] (S.Afr.) to react with joy or enthusiasm. [GOOI v. + SE *spasm*]

gooi a Uie v. [1980s+] (S.Afr.) to make a U-turn. [GOOI v. + U-IE n.]

gooi grief v. [1940s+] (S.Afr.) to annoy someone. [GOOI v. + SE *grief*]

gooi pomp v. [1980s+] (S.Afr.) to have sexual intercourse. [GOOI v. + POMP v.]

gooi tackie v. [1980s+] (S.Afr.) to accelerate. [GOOI v. + SAfrE *tackie*, a tyre]

gook n.[1] [mid-19C–1910s] a street-walker. [? GOWK n. (2), although this predates]

gook n.[2] [1910s+] (orig. US milit.) **1** a derog. term for any foreigner esp. Oriental, e.g. (in chronological order of use) Filipino, Japanese, Korean, Vietnamese; thus *Gookland*, Vietnam (cf. BROWNIE n.[2]). **2** any foreigner, other than an Oriental. **3** any foreign language. [ety. unknown; ? GOO-GOO n.[1] (1); or ? *goo-goo*, baby-talk, a ref. to the incomprehensibility of Oriental languages in Western ears; or ? nursery excl. of disgust, *gucchh!* denoting Western distaste for the omnivorousness of some Oriental cuisines; neither seems very likely]

gook n.[3] (US) **1** [1940s+] slimy, sticky, dirty viscid matter, also distasteful food. **2** [1980s+] anything unpleasant; nonsense. [ext. of GOO.[1] (1)]

gook n.[4] see GOWK n. (1).

gook adj. [1920s+] (US) Italian, Oriental, by late 20C+ usu. Korean or Vietnamese. [GOOK n.[2] (1)]

gook car n. see GOOK WAGON n.

gook-eyed adv. [1950s] (US) stupidly, foolishly, vacantly. [GOWK n. (1) + SE -*eyed*]

gook up v. [1950s] to smear with GOOK n.[3] (1).

gook wagon n. (also **gook car**) [1950s–60s] (US) an inferior car over-decorated with chrome and accessories. [GOOK n.[2] (1), i.e. as synon. with a taste for gaudiness and excess]

gooky adj. [1960s+] (US) **1** unpleasantly sticky. **2** in fig. use, awkward. [GOOK n.[3] (1) + sfx -*y*]

gool v. see GOAL v.

goola n.[1] [1940s] (US) the anus (cf. GOUL n.). [Ital. *culo*, the anus]

goola n.[2] [1930s–50s] (US Black) a piano. [ety. unknown]

goola box n. [1930s–50s] (US Black) a jukebox or 'nickarola'. [GOOLA n.[2] + SE *box*]

goolies n. **1** [late 18C+] testicles; thus *have someone by the goolies*, to have the upper hand (cf. BALLS n.[1]). **2** [1940s+] (US/Aus.) (also **goonies**) small stones or pebbles. [? Hind. *golí*, a bullet, ball or pill; or ? dial. *gullies*, marbles; given the common equation of the male genitals with weaponry, one might also note dial. *gully*, a large knife, although that would more properly represent the penis; also note New South Wales Aborigine *goolie*, a stone]

goom n. [1960s+] (Aus.) **1** methylated spirits, as an alcoholic's drink. **2** (also **goomy**) a drinker of methylated spirits. [? Jagara *goom*, water]

gooma n. [1990s+] (US Und.) in US Mafia, a mistress. [synon. Ital.]

goombah n. (also **gumba(h)**) **1** [1950s+] (US, orig. US Ital.) a close male friend. **2** [1950s+] (US) a stupid person. **3** [1950s+] (US) an Italian-American (cf. DAGO n.). **4** [1960s+] (US) a thug, a gangster; spec. a member of an organized crime syndicate, usu. the US Mafia. **5** [1970s+] (US Und.) in the US Mafia, a patron, lit. a 'godfather'. **6** [1990s+] (US campus) an outsider, a social outcast. [Italian *compare*, godfather, one of the names (see Mario Puzo, *The Godfather*, 1969) used for a leader of the Italian-American Mafia]

goom-bye phr. (also **goomba**) [1900s–70s] (US) goodbye.

goomer n. [1960s+] (US) a fool, a failure. [GOMER n.[2]]

goomp n. see GUMP n.[1] (1).

goomy n. see GOOM n. (2).

go on v.[1] [early 19C+] (orig. US) to like, to approve; thus negative phr. *not go much on*, to disapprove.

go on v.[2] (also **go on about**) [mid-19C+] to talk continuously, repetitively and often tediously; thus *going on (about)*, talking in this manner.

go on v.[3] [1940s+] to use as a basis for one's opinions, calculations; usu. in phr. *something/nothing to go on*.

go on! excl. (also **gahn! garn!** and **go on with you! g'wan!**) **1** [late 19C+] an excl. used to imply incredulity (cf. GET AWAY (WITH YOU)! excl.). **2** [1970s+] (US campus) an excl. of admiration. [*garn!* etc is Cockney pron.]

goon n.[1] (orig. US) **1** [20C+] (also **goony**) a stolid, stupid person. **2** [1930s+] a thug. **3** [1930s+] non-union labour used for strike breaking, intimidation etc. **4** [1930s+] a policeman. **5** [1940s] a derog. term for a Black person (cf. ALLIGATOR BAIT n.[2]). [? cartoon character Alice the *Goon* from the comic *Thimble Theatre* (1919) by E.C. Segar (1894–1938). Given the implication of stupidity, note GOONEY n. (2); note *Independent Review*, 25 October 1999, suggests link to a 'family saying' by F.L. Allen in *Harper's Mag.*, December, 121/1: (title) 'The Goon and his Style'. Ibid. 121/2: 'A goon is a person with a heavy touch as distinguished from a jigger, who has a light touch. While jiggers look on life with a genial eye, goons take a more stolid and literal view']

goon n.[2] (also **goon crystal, goon dust**) [1970s+] (drugs) phencyclidine (cf. ACE n.[4]). [its effects may turn the user into a GOON n.[1] (1)]

goon n.[3] [1980s] (Aus.) a flagon of cheap wine. [? mispron./abbr. SE *flagon* or ? GOOM n.]

go on about v. see GO ON v.[2].

go on a date with handrea and palmela v. [1990s+] to masturbate (cf. CONVERSE WITH HARRY PALM v.). [ironic use of DATE n.[1] (2) + puns on female names *Andrea/Pamela* and *hand/palm*]

go on a lark v. (also **have a lark, take a lark**) [early 19C–1900s] to have fun, esp. at the expense of others. [LARK n.[1] (2)]

go on and on v. [late 19C+] to nag. [ext. of GO ON v.[2]]

go on at v. [late 19C+] to scold, to abuse, to nag; thus *going on at*, nagging, telling off. [note W.I. use *go on*, to argue fiercely]

go on a tear v. see GO (OUT) ON A TEAR v.

go on circuit v. [1900s] (Aus.) of a prostitute, to tour diggings and camps selling her services.

goon crystal/dust n. see GOON n.[2].

gooned (out) adj. [1960s+] (US) intoxicated on drugs or by alcohol. [made into a GOON n.[1] (1)]

go one-on-one v. [1970s+] (orig. US) to have a direct confrontation with another person. [ONE-ON-ONE adv.]

gooner n. [1990s+] (US prison) a member of the GOON SQUAD n. (3).

go one's death v. [mid-19C] (US) to do one's utmost for, to risk one's all on, to bet to the limit. [GO v.[4] (1)]

gooney n. (also **goney, goonie**) **1** [mid-19C] (UK Und.) a newly arrived prisoner, esp. one who is not of the criminal underworld. **2** [mid-19C+] (US) a fool, an idiot. **3** [1920s+] (US) (also **gooner**) a foreigner, an enemy, esp. a Chinese communist soldier. [OE *ganian*, to gape]

goon from Saskatoon n. [1950s] (US Black) a metaphorical fool, an unsophisticated person. [GOON n.[1] (1) + assonance]

goonhead n. [1980s+] (US) a fool. [GOON n.[1] (1) + -HEAD sfx (1)]

go on Hobbes's voyage v. [late 17C] to have sexual intercourse. [pun on the last words of the political philosopher Thomas Hobbes (1588–1679): 'I am about to take my last voyage, a great leap in the dark']

goonie n. see GOONEY n.

goonies n. see GOOLIES n. (2).

go on one's face v. see RUN ONE'S FACE (FOR) v.

goon squad n. **1** [1930s+] a group of thugs, usu. organized for a specific purpose – strike-breaking, extortion etc. **2** [1940s] (US

Black) the police. **3** [1960s+] (*US prison*) a squad of prison guards used to quell riots or any other form of trouble. [GOON n.[1] (3)/GOON n.[1] (2)+ SE *squad*]

goon suit *n.* [1990s+] (*US*) army surplus clothing. [GOON n.[1] (2)]

go on the brag *v.* [1990s+] to boast. [SE *brag*]

go on the drag *v.* [late 18C] to follow a cart or wagon in order to rob it. [SE *drag*, a wheeled vehicle]

go on the dub *v.* [late 17C–18C] (*UK Und.*) to break into a house using a picklock or skeleton key. [DUB n.[1] (1)]

go on the dummy *v.* [1930s–70s] (*US*) to stop talking, to be quiet. [DUMMY n.[1] (1)]

go on the hop *v. see* PLAY THE HOP v.

go on the lap *v. see* LAP n.[2] (2).

go on the letter Q *v.* [early 19C] (*UK Und.*) to work as a confidence trickster. [synon. for ON THE BILLIARD SLUM phr. and thus a pun on Q/(billiard) cue]

go on the lob *v.* [late 18C–early 19C] to play a confidence trick on shopkeepers by asking for change for a high-value coin but then switching coins to make a profit. [LOB n.[1] (3)]

go on the missing list *v.* [1970s] to abscond.

go on the nod *v.* [1950s] (*US*) to die.

go on the piss *v.* [1910s+] to go out drinking. [ON THE PISS phr.]

go on the sneak *v.* [late 17C–19C] (*UK Und.*) to go out working as a sneak-thief or petty pilferer. [SNEAK n.[1] (1)]

go on the stitch *v. see* STITCH v. (1).

go on the top *v.* [early 18C] (*UK Und.*) to break into houses using entry via an upper window.

go on, twist my arm *phr.* [1950s+] a joking pretence that the speaker has to be persuaded into doing something (esp. taking a drink) that is, in fact, very appealing and will require no second thoughts about doing it.

go on with you! *excl. see* GO ON! excl.

goony *n. see* GOON n.[1] (1).

goony *adj.* [1930s+] (*US*) silly, crazy. [GOON n.[1] (1) + sfx *-y*]

goop *n.[1]* (*also* **gooper, goopy**) [20C+] (*orig. US*) a fool, an idiot, a boor. [coined by Gelett Burgess (1866–1951) in 1900 for a 'race' of fantasy childlike creatures; ? ult. var. on GOOF n.[1] (1)]

goop *n.[2]* (*also* **gloop**) **1** [1910s+] (*US*) any slimy, sticky viscous matter, esp. hair oil, sticky sweets, cosmetics. **2** [1940s+] (*US, orig. milit.*) napalm. **3** [1960s] (*US*) gelignite, nitroglycerine. [var. GOO n.[1] (1)]

goop *v.[1]* [1950s] (*N.Z.*) to stare. [GAWP v. + ? link to GOOP n.[1]]

goop *v.[2]* [1960s+] (*US*) to perform fellatio or cunnilingus. [ext. of GOO n.[1] (1)]

gooper *n. see* GOOP n.[1].

goop-gobbler *n.* [1960s–70s] (*US gay*) a fellator or fellatrix. [GOOP n.[2] (1) + GOBBLER n.[2] (3)]

goopher *n.[1] see* GOOFER n.[1].

goopher *n.[2] see* GOPHER n.[2] (2).

goopher feathers *n. see* GOOFER FEATHERS n.

goopy *n. see* GOOP n.[1].

goopy *adj.* (*US*) **1** [1910s+] sticky. **2** [1910s+] lacking in energy, exhausted. **3** [1950s+] silly. [GOOP n.[2] (1)/GOOP n.[1] + sfx *-y*]

goorie *n.* (*also* **goory**) [1930s+] (*N.Z.*) a general term of abuse. [Maori *goorie*, a mongrel dog; var. on KURI n.]

goose *n.[1]* **1** [mid-16C+] a fool (cf. AIREDALE n.). **2** [1960s] (*US campus*) an effeminate man. **3** [1960s–70s] (*US campus*) a socially unacceptable person. **4** [1970s] (*Aus. Und.*) a shopkeeper; a shop assistant.

goose *n.[2]* [17C–1920s] a tailor's iron. [the shape of its neck]

goose *n.[3]* **1** [mid-19C–1920s] a scolding, a reprimand. **2** [1940s–50s] an instruction, a warning to act in the required manner. [theatrical use, *get the goose*, to be hissed]

goose *n.[4]* [late 19C–1940s] a Jew (cf. FAST-TALKING CHARLIE n.). [? pron. of *goose* as *joose*, i.e. Jews; *HDAS* suggests the link of Jews to tailoring, thus GOOSE n.[2]]

goose *n.[5]* **1** [1930s+] a poke into the genital area with a finger or some form of implement. **2** [1940s] anal intercourse. [GOOSE v.[3] (2)]

goose *n.[6] see* GOOSE (AND DUCK) n.

goose *n.[7] see* WINCHESTER GOOSE n.

goose *v.[1]* **1** [mid-19C] to ruin, to spoil. **2** [mid-late 19C] to make a fool of; to hiss like a goose at a play. [GOOSE n.[1] (1)]

goose *v.[2]* [late 19C] to repair or enlarge boots by putting in or adding pieces of leather (a process known as 'footing'). [ety. unknown]

goose *v.[3]* **1** [late 19C+] to pursue women, to womanize. **2** [20C+] to poke or tickle a person in the genital or anal area, usu. by a man to a woman. **3** [20C+] (*US*) of emotions, to press, to push, to provoke, to enliven. **4** [1910s+] of a person, to push, to poke. **5** [1930s+] (*US*) to accelerate a car; thus *goose up*, to move forward a short distance. **6** [1940s] to perform anal intercourse (cf. ASK FOR THE RING v.). **7** [1940s+] to have sexual intercourse (cf. BANG v.[1]). **8** [1960s] (*US*) to grab. **9** [1960s+] to increase the volume on a radio, sound system or TV. **10** [1970s] (*US campus*) to grasp someone's testicles from behind, as a prank. **11** [1970s+] to improve, to cajole into progress. **12** [2000s] to excite sexually.

goose (and duck) *n.* [late 19C+] sexual intercourse. [rhy. sl. = FUCK n.[1] (1)]

gooseberries *n.* [20C+] a small boy's testicles (cf. ACORNS n.). [supposed resemblance]

gooseberry *n.[1]* [19C] a fool (cf. APPLEHEAD n.). [punning on the popular dessert, *gooseberry fool*, which is also SOFT adj. (1)]

gooseberry *n.[2]* (*also* **gooseberry bush**) [mid-19C–1940s] (*US tramp*) laundry hanging on a washing-line, and which is thus vulnerable to theft. [from the era when clothes were draped over bushes to dry]

gooseberry *n.[3]* (*also* **gooseberry-picker**) [mid-19C+] an unwanted chaperon(e), esp. a third party who is not wanted by or feels uncomfortable being with the couple. [? *gooseberry-fool* or ? their excuse for following the couple round a garden: 'I'm just picking gooseberries'; but note GOOSEBERRY PUDDING n. (1), an (older) woman, who might well be an unwanted chaperone]

gooseberry *n.[4]* [1940s] (*US*) a small piece of excrement around the anus (cf. CLAGNUT n.). [var. on DINGLEBERRIES n. (1)]

gooseberry *v.* [1910s–40s] (*US Und.*) to steal clothes from a clothes-line. [GOOSEBERRY n.[2]]

gooseberry bush *n.[1]* [19C] pubic hair. [ext. of BUSH n.[2] (1); it is this bush, of course, rather than the fruiting variety, beneath which a child is allegedly born]

gooseberry bush *n.[2] see* GOOSEBERRY n.[2].

gooseberry-eyed *adj.* [late 18C–19C] having eyes that look like boiled gooseberries, grey and lifeless.

gooseberry grinder *n.* [late 18C–19C] the buttocks; esp. in phr. *ask Bogey the gooseberry grinder*, a euph. for 'ask my arse'. [ety. unknown; ? ref. to the effect on the digestion and thus defecation of unripe gooseberries]

gooseberry lay *n.* (*also* **gooseberry picking**) [mid-19C–1940s] (*UK/US Und.*) the stealing of linen drying in the open air by tramps and thieves. [GOOSEBERRY n.[2]+ LAY n.[4] (1)]

gooseberry-picker *n.[1]* [1940s] (*US tramp*) one who steals from clotheslines. [GOOSEBERRY n.[2]]

gooseberry-picker *n.[2] see* GOOSEBERRY n.[3].

gooseberry picking *n. see* GOOSEBERRY LAY n.

gooseberry pudding *n.* (*also* **gooseberry pudden**) **1** [mid-19C–1950s] a woman; esp. as *old gooseberry*, one's wife. **2** [1920s–40s] a promiscuous woman. [rhy. sl.; *pudding* pron. 'pudden']

gooseberry ranch *n.* [1930s–70s] (*US*) a brothel (cf. BIRDCAGE n.[1]). [var. GOOSING RANCH n.]

gooseberry tart *n. see* RASPBERRY TART n.

gooseberry wig *n.* [late 18C–early 19C] a large, frizzled wig. [? its resemblance to a gooseberry bush]

goose-bumper *n.* [1980s+] (*US*) a horror film (cf. GOOSE-FLESHER n.). [the tension gives watchers GOOSE-BUMPS n.]

goose-bumps *n.* (*also* **goose-creeps**) [mid-19C+] gooseflesh, the rough pimply condition that can be produced by cold or a sudden attack of nerves. [skin in such a condition supposedly resembles the flesh of a plucked goose]

goose-cap *n.* [late 16C–mid-19C] a fool, an idiot, a numbskull. [GOOSE *n.*[1] (1) + SE *cap*, head. Coined in the UK, it had lapsed by the 18C but was picked up in the US during the 19C]

goosed *adj.* **1** [mid-19C+] ruined, finished. **2** [1990s+] (*US*) drunk (cf. ANNIHILATED *adj.*). [GOOSE *v.*[1] (1)]

goose-drownder *n.* (*also* **goose-drowner**) [1920s+] (*US*) very heavy rain.

goose egg *n.*[1] (*also* **egg, gooser**) [mid-19C+] zero, nothing. [the shape of the egg resembles a zero; note cricket jargon a *duck('s egg*), a score of nothing]

goose egg *n.*[2] [1940s+] (*US*) a large bruise or swelling that comes up on the head after striking it or being struck a blow. [joking resemblance]

goose egg *n.*[3] (*also* **gooser**) [1970s] (*US*) an illegitimate child. [euph.]

goose flat *n.* *see* GOOSE TOWN *n.*

gooseflesher *n.* [1940s] a thriller, a detective/mystery story (cf. GOOSE-BUMPER *n.*). [its exciting story gives one *gooseflesh*]

goose girl *n.* [1910s] a lesbian. [synon. Fr. argot *gousse*; ? ult. Fr. argot *gousser*, to eat; but note GOOSE *n.*[1] (2)]

goosegog *n.* (*also* **goosegob**) [mid-19C+] a gooseberry. [abbr.]

goose-grease *n.* [late 19C] vaginal secretions (cf. BINDERJUICE *n.*). [pun on SE + GREASE *n.*[3] (2)]

goosehead *n.* [mid-17C–1910s] (*US*) an idiot (cf. AIREDALE *n.*). [GOOSE *n.*[1] (1) + -HEAD sfx (1)]

goose-headed *adj.* [1900s] (*US*) foolish (cf. AIRHEADED *adj.*). [GOOSEHEAD *n.*]

goosehole *n.* [1970s+] (*US gay/prison*) the anus (cf. A-HOLE *n.*).

goose hollow/nibble *n.* *see* GOOSE TOWN *n.*

gooser *n.*[1] [mid-19C] **1** a knockout blow. **2** in fig. use, a waste, a failure. **3** the end, a goner. [? such a blow would COOK SOMEONE'S GOOSE *v.*]

gooser *n.*[2] **1** [late 19C] the penis. **2** [20C+] (*Can.*) a pederast. [GOOSE *v.*[3] (1)/GOOSE *v.*[3] (2)]

gooser *n.*[3] *see* GOOSE EGG *n.*[1].

gooser *n.*[4] *see* GOOSE EGG *n.*[3].

goose's gazette *n.* [early–mid-19C] a foolish story. [GOOSE *n.*[1] (1) + SE *gazette*]

goose shearer *n.* [18C–19C] (*UK Und.*) a beggar; thus a confidence trickster. [such a villain 'shears' a gullible GOOSE *n.*[1] (1)]

goose's neck *n.*[1] [late 19C] the penis; thus *have a bit of goose's neck*, to have sexual intercourse (cf. ANTEATER *n.*). [supposed resemblance]

goose's neck *n.*[2] [20C+] a cheque. [rhy. sl.]

goose town *n.* (*also* **goose flat, ...hollow, ...nibble**) [20C+] (*US*) the poor part of town. [geese might be running free in such an area]

goose tracks *n.* [mid-19C+] (*US*) illegible handwriting. [resemblance to geese's scratchy prints]

goosey *adj.*[1] **1** [20C+] (*also* **goosy**) nervous, jittery, on edge. **2** [1930s+] foolishly excited.

goosey *adj.*[2] [1920s+] effeminate or homosexual. [predates but implied by GOOSE *n.*[1] (2)]

goosie *n.* [1960s+] (*S.Afr. prison*) **1** the passive, 'female' partner of a homosexual couple. **2** a girl, a girlfriend. [GOOSE *n.*[1] (1)/ GOOSE *n.*[1] (2)]

goosing ranch *n.* [1920s–40s] (*US*) a brothel (cf. BIRDCAGE *n.*[1]). [GOOSE *v.*[3] (1)/GOOSE *v.*[3] (7) + SE *ranch*]

goosing slum *n.* [mid–late 19C; 1950s] (*orig. UK Und.*) a brothel-cum-low saloon (cf. BIRDCAGE *n.*[1]). [GOOSE *v.*[3] (1)/GOOSE *v.*[3] (7) + SLUM *n.*[1] (1)]

goosy *adj.* *see* GOOSEY *adj.*[1] (1).

goot *n.* [2000s] (*US Black*) something pleasant. [? Ger. *gut*, good]

gooter *n.* [1980s+] (*Irish*) the penis. [ety. unknown]

go-out *n.* [1930s] (*US Und.*) a death, a murder. [GO OUT *v.*[2] (1)]

go out *v.*[1] **1** [early 19C] (*UK Und.*) to work as a thief. **2** [1980s+] (*US Black*) to act, to behave. [fig. uses of SE]

go out *v.*[2] **1** [late 19C+] (*Aus./US/US prison*) to die. **2** [1920s+] to escape from prison. **3** [1930s+] (*orig. US*) to faint, to lose consciousness; esp. in phr. *go out like a light*. [(1) note Moore, *Tom Crib's Memorial to Congress* (1818): 'For a lad who *goes into the world*, DICK, like me, / Should have his neck tied up you know [...] / Almost as tight as *some* lads who *go out of it*']

go out foreign *v.* [late 19C] (*UK Und.*) to emigrate under suspicious circumstances.

go out like a sucker *v.* [1980s+] (*US Black*) to die as a result of one's involvement in gangs, drug use or similar activities. [GO OUT *v.*[2] (1) + SUCKER *n.*[3] (1); the implication, little heeded, is that involvement in such activities is pointless]

go (out) on a tear *v.* [mid-19C+] (*orig. US*) to go out on a spree. [TEAR *n.* (2)]

go out the back door *v.* [1950s+] (*US prison*) to back down under pressure.

go out with the blades *v.* [1950s–60s] (*Aus.*) to become obsolete. [shearing jargon *blades*, hand-held shears, discarded by most shearers in the early 20C]

go over *v.*[1] **1** [late 19C–1900s] to rob, after running one's hands over and through the victim's clothes. **2** [1910s] (*UK Und.*) to commit a robbery. **3** [1910s+] to inspect.

go over *v.*[2] [late 19C–1920s] (*US Und.*) to be sent to prison.

go over *v.*[3] [20C+] (*orig. US*) to succeed.

go over *v.*[4] [1940s+] (*Aus.*) of a man, to become a homosexual. [fig. to *go over to the other side* in one's sexuality; note mid-19C clerical use *go over*, to convert to Roman Catholicism]

go over *v.*[5] [2000s] (*drugs*) to overdose.

go over big *v.* [1910s+] (*orig. US*) **1** to be notably successful. **2** to make a good impression. [ext. of GO OVER *v.*[3]]

go overboard *v.* **1** [20C+] to behave immoderately, to display excessive enthusiasm. **2** [1930s+] to commit oneself completely; often as *go overboard for*.

go over like a lead balloon *v.* *see* LEAD BALLOON *n.*

go over like a million bucks *v.* [1990s+] to succeed absolutely, to do very well. [ext. of GO OVER *v.*[3]+ BUCK *n.*[3] (1)]

go over the fence *v.* [1950s] (*Aus.*) to be unreasonable.

go over the highside *v.* [1960s+] (*US*) **1** to lose control, to lose one's composure. **2** to show off. **3** of riding a motorcycle, to slide to the side when driving fast round a corner. [HIGHSIDE *v.*]

go over the hill *v.*[1] [1910s+] **1** (*US prison*) to escape. **2** (*US milit.*) to abscond. [orig. escaping outdoor work gangs, using hills as cover from one's pursuers]

go over the hill *v.*[2] [1950s+] (*US*) to get married. [image of couple vanishing from everyday 'single' life into the world of matrimony]

go over the hill *v.*[3] [1960s] (*US*) to go mad.

go over the hump *v.* **1** [1940s] to finish a job. **2** [1940s+] (*US*) to pass one's prime, to decline in ability. **3** [1950s] (*US drugs*) to get intoxicated on drugs (cf. BLOW ONE'S HUMP *v.*). [OVER THE HUMP *phr.*]

go over the range *v.* [late 19C–1940s] (*Aus./US*) to die.

go over the score *v.* (*also* **have a few over the score**) [mid-18C+] to drink too much. [SE *score*, a line, thus a limit]

go over the top *v.* [1920s+] to do something dangerous or remarkable, esp. to get over-excited or angry. [WW1 imagery; the 'top' was that of a trench]

go over the wall *v.* **1** [1910s] to go to prison. **2** [1930s+] (*orig. US*) to escape from prison. **3** [1940s+] (*also* **jump/leap over the wall**) to leave a religious order; also in fig. use, to gain sexual experience. **4** [1960s+] to go mad. **5** [1970s] to defect to another country. [lit. and fig. uses of SE]

goozer *n.*[1] [1980s+] (*Irish*) a kiss. [? GUZZLE *v.*[2] (5)]

goozer n.[2] [1990s+] (UK juv.) one who attempts to join a group in which they are not numbered and/or welcome. [? GOOSEBERRY n.[3]]

goozie n. (also **gozzie**) [late 19C+] (Aus.) a gooseberry. [abbr.]

goozle n. (also **goozlem, goozle pipe, goozler, gozzle**) [late 19C+] (US) usu. of an animal, the windpipe; of a human, the throat, the Adam's apple. [GUZZLE n.[1] (1)]

goozlum n. (also **googlum**) [20C+] (US) any viscous, treacly substance, often describing a food. [ext. of GOO n.[1] (1)]

go pear-shaped v. [1990s+] of plans or schemes, to fail, to collapse. [the image of a solid rectangle 'slipping down' into a pear shape, thus 'the bottom drops out']

go peddle your fish! excl. [1930s] (US) an excl. of disdainful dismissal.

gopher see also under GOFER.

gopher n.[1] (US) **1** [mid-19C] a louse. **2** [mid-late 19C] a primitive form of plough. **3** [mid-19C+] an Arkansan. **4** [mid-19C+] a Floridian. **5** [mid-19C+] a Minnesotan. **6** [mid-19C+] an offensive or stupid person, a country bumpkin. [SE gopher, a burrowing rodent of the genera Geomys and Thomomys, native to these states; the other images are of the animal's burrowing or its role as vermin]

gopher n.[2] (US Und.) **1** [late 19C–1960s] a member of a notorious New York City street gang; thus a generic term for any thug or gangster. **2** [late 19C–1960s] (also **goopher**) a safe. **3** [late 19C–1960s] a robber who specializes in safes, strongboxes or bank vaults; thus gopher racket, safe-cracking; gopher worker, a safe-breaker. **4** [1920s–40s] a robber who tunnels to his target; thus gopher gang/mob, a gang who works in this way. [(1) the Gophers, whose 'turf' encompassed New York's 'Hell's Kitchen' (the West Side between 42nd Street and 14th Street), used the area's cellars and basements as their preferred hideouts]

go phut v. (also **go pfft, go phffft**) [late 19C+] to come to an abrupt end; esp. of a couple, to divorce. [echoic of the noise of air escaping from a deflated, popped balloon]

go pile-driving v. [late 19C] to have sexual intercourse (cf. GO BALLOCKING v.).

go pill n. [1950s–60s] (US) a pill or capsule of amphetamine (cf. A n.[2]). [amphetamines give one energy and 'go']

go piss up a rope! excl. [1930s+] (orig. US) a general excl. of dismissal; thus piss-up-a-rope, of a person or mood, belligerent, dismissive. [PISS v.[1] (1) + SE rope]

go places v. (also **go place**) [1920s+] (orig. US) **1** to succeed, to do well. **2** to wander about, to travel; thus go places and see things. **3** to visit a lavatory (cf. DO ONE'S BUSINESS v.).

go plait your shit! excl. [1960s] a general excl. of dismissal.

go plop v. [1930s] to collapse.

go pop v. [1900s–10s] **1** to die. **2** to lose one's temper.

go postal v. [1990s+] (US teen) to lose one's temper, to lose control of one's emotions. [POSTAL adj.]

goppy adj. [1970s] (US) sentimental, tearful.

go prick-scouring v. [late 19C] of a man, to have sexual intercourse (cf. GO BALLOCKING v.). [PRICK n. (2) + SCOUR v.[2] (3)]

gops n. (also **gopse**) [1960s+] (S.Afr.) **1** the backwoods, a backward, rural area. **2** an uncouth or common loutish person. [ety. unknown]

go queueing v. [1940s] to live as a homosexual. [Q adj.]

go quim-sticking v. (also **go quim-wedging**) [19C] of a man, to have sexual intercourse (cf. GO BALLOCKING v.). [QUIM n. (1) + SE stick v. (cf. QUIM-STICKER v.; QUIMWEDGE v.)]

gor n. [17C+] a euph. for God and as such used in a variety of oaths (cf. BOB n.[2]).

gorb n. (also **gorby-guts**) [20C+] (Irish) a glutton. [dial. gorb, a gluttonous person or animal; ? ult. Scot. gorb, an unfledged bird; note also SE gorbelly, a (person with) a fat stomach]

Gorbachev! excl. [1990s+] (US campus) a response to a sneeze. [a play on the trad. Gesundheit + a ref. to the former USSR leader Mikhail Gorbachev (b.1931)]

Gorbals kiss n. [1930s+] a headbutt (cf. CHELSEA SMILE n.). [ironic use of SE]

gorblimeries n. [late 19C] Seven Dials, London WC2. [its Cockney/villainous population, for whom GORBLIMEY! excl. is a stereotyped excl. Note a parallel use as an adj.: 'the Gorblimey aspect of history, the feelings of the ordinary man on the spot at the time' (Oxford Magazine, 27 February 1958)]

gorblimey n. [1910s+] a rakish cap. [orig. milit. use; ult. GORBLIMEY! excl.; note Fraser & Gibbons, Soldier & Sailor Words & Phrases (1925): 'A "Gorblimey" was the common colloquial term for an unwired, floppy, field-service cap worn by a certain type of subaltern in defiance of the Dress Regulations. Lines from a song, popular before the War, ran: "He wears Gorblimey trousers/An a little Gorblimey 'at"']

gorblimey adj. [20C+] **1** uncouth. **2** indicative of a working-class background. [GORBLIMEY! excl.]

gorblimey! excl. (also **cor blimey! gorblimey O'Reilly!**) [late 19C+] a mild, euph. oath, lit. 'God blind me!' [GOR n./COR! excl.]

gorby-guts n. see GORB n.

gor damn n. (also **gah damn**) [late 19C–1910s] jam. [rhy. sl.]

gordelpus see under GAWDELPUS.

gord-forbids n. see GOD-FORBIDS n. (1).

Gordon & Gotch n. [20C+] a watch. [rhy. sl.; ult. the firm of book and periodical importers]

Gordon Bennett! excl. [20C+] a euph. for GORBLIMEY! excl. [either f. James Gordon Bennett (1795–1872), the founding editor of the New York Herald, or his similarly named son (1841–1918); or Gordon Bennett, promoter of motor- and air-races before 1914]

Gordon Hutter n. [1930s–40s] (N.Z.) butter. [rhy. sl.; ult. the contemporary racing and wrestling commentator Gordon Hutter]

Gordzone n. see GODSOWN n.

gore n. [1920s–30s] (US) juicy gossip, scandal. [SE gore, blood]

gore v. [1980s] (UK Black) to stab, to slash with a knife. [SE gore, to stab with a sharp weapon]

goree n. (also **gory**) [late 17C–early 19C] money (cf. CANARY n.[5]). [proper name of Fort Goree, on the Gold Coast, a centre for slave-trading and gold]

gore-stained adj. [1900s] (Aus.) a euph. for BLOODY adj.[1] (1) (cf. GORY adj.).

gorge n. **1** [late 19C–1900s] a heavy meal, a feast. **2** [1920s] a glutton. [SE gorge, that which has been swallowed + gorge, to eat to excess]

gorge out v. [1960s+] (US campus) to commit suicide by jumping from a high cliff. [SE gorge, a ravine with rocky walls]

gorger n.[1] **1** [early 19C] any man, irrespective of appearance. **2** [early–mid-19C] a dandy, an exceptionally well-dressed man. [Rom. gorgio, a non-Romany; (2) + ? SE gorgeous]

gorger n.[2] [mid-19C] an employer. [? SE gouge, to cheat, to impose upon]

gorgon n. [1950s+] **1** (W.I. Rasta) outstanding dreadlocks. **2** (W.I.) a thug, a ruffian. [the mythical Gorgon, whose hair was made of writhing snakes]

gorgonzola adj. [1940s+] (Aus.) very good. [play on CHEESE, THE n. (1)]

goric n. [1950s–70s] (drugs) opium (cf. APOSTLE n.). [SE paregoric elixir, a camphorated tincture of opium flavoured with aniseed and benzoic acid; opium and heroin addicts use paregoric when stronger drugs are unavailable]

gorill n. (US) **1** [mid-19C] a guerrilla. **2** [1930s–40s] a thug. [abbr.; (2) GORILLA n.[1] (1)]

gorill v. see GORILLA v.

gorilla n.[1] **1** [mid-19C+] (US) a thug, a ruffian, a violent person. **2** [1960s–70s] a person. **3** [1970s] (US) a prostitute's customer who likes to beat up the prostitute. **4** [1970s] (US campus) an unattractive, often overweight young woman. **5** [1980s+] (US) something or someone irresistible or posing difficulty; often modified as *600-pound gorilla, 800-pound gorilla* etc. **6** [1990s+] a monster success, a smash hit. [the image of the animal as a brutal monster; (5) note the conundrum: Where does a 500-pound gorilla sleep? Anywhere it wants to]

gorilla *n.*[2] [1950s+] (*US drugs*) a severe heroin addiction. [SE *gorilla*, i.e. the size of the primate, a huge MONKEY *n.*[12] (1)]

gorilla *n.*[3] [1970s] £1000, A$1000 (cf. FOAL *n.*). [i.e. twice the size of a MONKEY *n.*[8]]

gorilla *adj.* [1920s+] (*US*) aggressive, menacing, thuggish. [GORILLA *n.*[1] (1)]

gorilla *v.* (*also* **gorill**) [1950s+] (*US Black/Und.*) to use violence, to intimidate; to rape. [GORILLA *n.*[1] (1)]

gorilla biscuits *n.* (*also* **gorilla tabs**) [1970s+] (*drugs*) phencyclidine (cf. ACE *n.*[4]; GORILLA PILLS *n.*). [? the drug turns the user into a GORILLA *n.*[1] (1)]

gorilla burger *n.* [1990s+] cunnilingus. [? GORILLA IN THE WASHING MACHINE *v.*]

gorilla dick *n.* [2000s] (*US*) a large handgun. [fig. use of SE *gorilla* + DICK *n.*[4] (1)]

gorilla game *n.* [1960s] (*US Und.*) the forcing of a woman into prostitution. [GORILLA *n.*[1] (1)]

gorilla in the washing machine *v.* [1970s] (*US Black*) to perform cunnilingus.

gorilla milk *n.* [2000s] (*US Black*) a Black man's semen (cf. BABY GRAVY *n.*).

gorilla pills *n.* [1960s+] (*drugs*) barbiturates (cf. BARBIT *n.*; GORILLA BISCUITS *n.*). [? the drug turns a user into a GORILLA *n.*[1] (1)]

gorilla pimp *n.* [1960s+] (*US Black*) a pimp who controls his prostitutes by threats and actual violence (cf. CANDYMAN *n.*). [GORILLA *n.*[1] (1) + SE *pimp*]

gorilla salad *n.* [1970s+] (*US gay*) pubic hair, esp. if luxuriant.

gorilla tabs *n. see* GORILLA BISCUITS *n.*

gork *n.* [1960s+] (*US campus*) an inadequate, an incompetent?. [GEEK *n.*[1] (1) + DORK *n.* (2); note hospital jargon *gork*, an imbecile or comatose patient, f. acronym *God only really knows*]

gorked (out) *adj.* [1970s+] (*US*) mindless, dumb. [GORK *n.*]

gorm *n.*[1] [1920s–30s] (*UK tramp*) chewing tobacco. [? GORM *v.*/SE *gourmandize*]

gorm *n.*[2] *see* GOM *n.*[2].

gorm *v.* [late 19C–1920s] (*orig. US*) to eat heartily. [SE *gourmandize*]

gormagon *n.* [18C] a man on horseback with a woman riding side-saddle behind him. [? SE *gorgon* + *dragon*; the nonsense word was supposedly 'Chinese'. 'A monster with six eyes, three mouths, four arms, eight legs, five on one side and three on the other, three arses, two tarses, and a **** [cunt] upon its back' (Grose, 1785). Note mid-18C secret society, the Gormogons, a short-lived imitation of the Freemasons]

gormed *adj.* [mid–late 19C] a euph. for GOD-DAMN *adj.* (1). [coined by Charles Dickens for Mr Peggotty in *David Copperfield* (1850)]

gormy-ruddles *n.* [19C] the stomach, the intestines. [SE *gormy ruttles*, 'the strangles', i.e. horses' quinsies or tonsillitis]

gornet *n.* [20C+] (*Ulster*) a fool. [fig. use of SE *gurnard*]

go rocky *v.* [late 19C+] to go wrong. [ROCKY *adj.* (2)]

go roll in it! *excl.* [1970s] (*US*) a dismissive retort. [abbr. of *go roll in the shit*]

go roll your hoop! *excl.* [late 19C+] (*US*) a disdainful excl. of dismissal.

go-round *n.* [late 19C+] a fight.

go round *v.* [late 19C] to go out on the town.

go round the corner *v.* [late 19C+] to visit the lavatory (cf. DO ONE'S BUSINESS *v.*). [euph.]

go round the houses *v. see* GO (ALL) ROUND THE HOUSES *v.*

go round the tower *v.* [late 17C–18C] (*UK Und.*) to clip money. [play on the *Tower* of London, where money was minted, and a *tour* around the circumference of the coin]

go round the traps *v.* [1930s–60s] (*Aus.*) to make a tour of inspection. [the image is of a farmer, gamekeeper or poacher touring the traps set to catch game]

go round with *v.* (*also* **go around with**) **1** [1950s+] to have a relationship with. **2** [1970s] to fight with, physically or verbally.

gorp *v.* [1930s] (*US*) to eat noisily, greedily. [? onomat.]

gorrel *n.* [1980s+] (*S.Afr.*) the throat. [Afk. *gorrel-(pyp)*, the throat]

gorry *n.* (*also* **gorree**) [mid-19C+] (*orig. US*) a euph. for *God* and used as such in various mild excls., e.g. *gorry mighty!* (cf. BOB *n.*[2]).

Gor Save *n.* [1900s] (*Aus.*) the British National Anthem: 'God save the King/Queen'.

gorsoon *n. see* GARSOON *n.*

go rubber walls *v.* [1960s–70s] (*gay*) to go mad. [the *rubber walls* used in padded cells]

go rude at *v.* [1970s+] (*N.Z.*) to insult, to attack verbally.

go rumping *v.* [19C+] of a man, to have sexual intercourse (cf. GO BALLOCKING *v.*).

go rump-splitting *v.* [19C] of a man, to have sexual intercourse (cf. GO BALLOCKING *v.*).

gory *n.*[1] [early 19C] a person, a fellow. [ety. unknown]

gory *n.*[2] *see* GOREE *n.*

gory *adj.* [late 19C–1900s] (*Aus.*) a euph. for BLOODY *adj.*[1] (1) (cf. GORE-STAINED *adj.*).

gos *n.*[1] (*also* **gosse**) [mid-16C–early 17C] a term of address. [SE *gossip*, a friend, a chum]

gos *n.*[2] *see* GOSS *n.*[1].

go scone-hot at *v.* (*also* **go (for) someone scone-hot**) [1930s+] (*Aus.*) to lose one's temper with; to tell off severely. [SCONE-HOT *adv.*]

go scrape! *excl.* [early 17C] go away! [? trans. of Fr. *envoyer au grat*, to dismiss from employment, lit. 'to send grazing']

go screw yourself! *excl. see* GO FUCK YOURSELF! *excl.*

go see a man *v. see* SEE A MAN ABOUT A DOG *v.* (2).

gosh *n.* [mid-18C+] a euph. for *God*; usu. in combs. e.g. GOSH-AWFUL *adj.*, GOSH-DARNED *adj.*; or excl., e.g. BY GOSH! *excl.*, GOSH! *excl.*, MY GOSH! *excl.* (cf. BOB *n.*[2]).

gosh! *excl.* (*also* **good gosh!**) [mid-18C+] an mild euph. for *God!* [GOSH *n.*; by 20C+ usu. juv. use]

gosh all! *excl.* [mid-19C+] (*US*) a euph. for *God almighty!* usu. in combs, e.g. *gosh all fish-hooks! gosh all hemlock(s)! gosh all Potomac! gosh all Tarnation!* [GOSH *n.*]

gosh almighty! *excl.* [19C+] a euph. used in excl. and mild oaths, lit. 'God almighty!' [GOSH *n.*]

gosh-awful *adj.* [20C+] (*orig. US*) especially appalling; a euph. for GOD-AWFUL *adj.* [GOSH *n.*]

gosh-awfulness *n.* [1920s+] appallingness. [GOSH-AWFUL *adj.*]

gosh-blamed *adj. see* GOSH-DARNED *adj.*

gosh-damned *adj.* (*also* **gosh-damn**) [20C+] (*US*) a euph. used in excl. and mild oaths, lit. GOD-DAMN *adj.* (1). [GOSH *n.*]

gosh-dang! *excl. see* GOSH-DING! *excl.*

gosh-darn! *excl.* (*also* **gosh-darnit!**) [20C+] (*US*) a euph. used in excl. and mild oaths, lit. GOD-DAMN! *excl.* [GOSH *n.*]

gosh-darned *adj.* (*also* **gosh-blamed, gosh-danged, gosh-darn, gosh-darnit, gosh-derned**) [mid-19C+] (*US*) a euph. for GOD-DAMN *adj.* (1). [GOSH *n.*]

gosh-ding! *excl.* (*also* **gosh-dang!**) [mid-19C+] (*US*) a mild oath, a euph. for GOD-DAMN! *excl.* [GOSH *n.*]

gosh-dinger *n.* [1910s] (*US*) an outstanding example of its kind. [GOSH-DING! *excl.*]

gosher *n.* [late 19C–1910s] a heavy punch. [? it makes the recipient say GOSH! *excl.*]

go shit in your hat! *excl.* [1940s+] (*US*) a general term of abuse; an ext. version is *go shit in your hat, pull it over your head and call it flowers*.

go sideways *v.* [late 19C] (*UK Und.*) to commit a crime.

go sit on a tack! *excl.* (*also* **go sit on a tap!**) [1930s+] (*US campus*) an excl. of dismissal.

go sixteen annas v. [1900s–30s] (*Anglo-Ind.*) to go very fast, at full speed. [*16 annas* make a full rupee]

go slops v. [1970s+] (*Aus.*) of a man, to be one of the last to participate in the multiple rape of or intercourse with a woman. [SLOPPY SECONDS n. (1)]

go-slow n. [1980s+] (*Aus. prison*) the punishment cells.

go smash v. see SMASH v.[1] (2).

go snacks v. (*also* go a snack, go snucks) [late 17C–mid-19C] to divide up, to hand over a share of the loot.

go snip v. [mid-17C–early 18C] to share, to divide up. [SE *snip*, to cut]

go soak your head! excl. [late 19C+] an abusive, dismissive excl.

go social v. [1960s] (*US gang*) to maintain a truce.

go solid v. [late 19C–1940s] (*US*) to unite, to act together.

go some v. [20C+] (*orig. US*) **1** to go fast, to work hard, to do well. **2** to be excessive. [SOME adv.]

go someone scone-hot v. see GO SCONE-HOT AT v.

go south v.[1] [20C+] (*orig. US*) **1** to be defeated, to lose. **2** to abscond with, to run off. **3** of a person, to exhaust. **4** to collapse, to malfunction, to break down; of events, to go wrong. **5** to be killed. **6** to squander, to waste.

go south v.[2] (*also* go way down south in Dixie) [1930s+] (*US*) to perform cunnilingus or anilingus (cf. AUSSIE KISS n.; AUSTRALIAN n.). [*south* being 'down' the body + fig. use of DIXIE n.]

go spare v. [1940s+] to lose one's temper, to act crazily. [SPARE adj. (2)]

go sparrow-catching v. [19C] to work as a prostitute. [? the Cockney *sparrow*]

gospel n. [late 16C+] the absolute truth. [abbr. SE *gospel truth*]

gospel according to St Jeames n. [late 19C] (*UK society*) snobbery. [William Thackeray's character *Jeames* Yellowplush, a servant noted for his crawling to his social superiors and the narrator of *The Yellowplush Papers* (1837–8)]

gospel bird n. (*also* gospel fowl) [1930s–60s] (*US Black/tramp*) a chicken. [the practice of rewarding itinerant preachers with a chicken dinner]

gospel-cove n. [1900s–10s] (*Aus.*) a clergyman. [SE *gospel* + COVE n. (1)]

gospel gab n. [late 19C] supposedly pious, but actually empty, hypocritical talk about religion. [SE *gospel* + GAB n. (2)]

gospel-grinder n. (*also* gospel-gent, -hawk, -peddler, -postillion, -shark, -sharp, -shooter, -slinger, -whanger) **1** [late 18C+] (*US*) a preacher. **2** [mid-19C–1910s] an evangelistic missionary or tract-distributor, a Sunday School teacher. **3** [20C+] an unctuous, self-satisfied, smug person. **4** [1910s] (*US*) a well-behaved, law-abiding person.

gospel-gun n. [late 19C] (*Aus.*) a preacher.

gospel mill n. (*also* gospel shop) [late 18C–1910s] (*US*) a chapel, a church; thus adj., pious, moralistic, censorious. [SE *gospel* + *mill*, a place where a given industry is performed/*shop*]

Gospel Oak n. [1990s+] a joke. [rhy. sl.; ult. area of London, NW5]

gospel of gloom n. [late 19C] (*UK society*) the Aesthetic Movement, whose advocacy of drab interior decoration was regarded by its critics as distinctly gloomy.

gospel of the tub n. [mid-19C–1910s] (*UK society*) the mania for cold baths that afflicted Britain in the 19C and has not yet, in certain quarters, been properly abandoned.

gospel-peddler n. see GOSPEL-GRINDER n.

gospel-pipe n. [1910s–20s] (*US*) the penis. [it 'preaches' to the vagina]

gospel-postillion/-shark/-sharp/-shooter n. see GOSPEL-GRINDER n.

gospel shop n. see GOSPEL MILL n.

gospel-slinger/-whanger n. see GOSPEL-GRINDER n.

goss n.[1] (*also* gos) [mid-19C–1910s] (*orig. US*) punishment; thus

give goss, to beat, to dole out punishment; *get/catch goss*, to receive punishment or a beating. [? Virginia dial. *give gorse*, to thrash]

goss n.[2] (*also* gozz) [1980s+] news, information, *gossip*. [abbr.]

goss n.[3] see GOSSAMER n.

goss n.[4] see GOSSE n.[1].

goss v. (*also* gozzy) [1990s+] (*UK juv.*) to spit. [? Devon dial. *goss*, to guzzle or drink]

gossamer n. (*also* goss) [mid-19C–1910s] a hat. [SE *gossamer hat*, fashionable c.1830 and costing 4s 9p (23½p); such hats were made of *gossamer* silk]

gosse n.[1] (*also* goss) [mid-16C] a euph. for *God*, used in mild oaths (cf. BOB n.[2]).

gosse n.[2] see GOS n.[1].

gossip pint-pot n. [late 16C] a hard drinker. [SE *gossip*, a friend, a companion + *pint-pot*]

gossled adj. see GUZZLED adj.[1].

gossoon n. see GARSOON n.

go star-gazing (on one's back) v. **1** [late 18C–mid-19C] (*also* study astronomy on one's back) of a woman, to have sex in the open air. **2** [1990s+] of a woman, to have sexual intercourse (cf. CATCH AN OYSTER v.; GO BALLOCKING v.). [the earlier use, which had languished, has recently reappeared, although without any 'open air' implications]

go steady v. (*also* keep steady) [20C+] (*orig. US*) to maintain a regular relationship.

go steady with one's right hand v. [1970s+] (*US*) to masturbate (cf. CONVERSE WITH HARRY PALM v.). [ironic use of GO STEADY v.]

goster n. [20C+] (*Irish*) chat, conversation; also as v., to chat. [Irish *gastaire*, a chatterer; note UK-wide dial. *gauster*, *goster*, to gossip, to talk, to waste time chatting]

go stiff v. [late 19C] (*Aus.*) to lose (a race) deliberately.

go straight v. **1** [mid-19C] to behave honourably or honestly. **2** [late 19C+] to start living a respectable life. **3** [late 19C+] to give up crime. **4** [1950s–60s] (*gay*) to abandon homosexuality. **5** [1970s+] to give up drugs. [STRAIGHT adj.[1]/STRAIGHT adj.[2]]

go street v. [1990s+] (*US Black/drugs*) to be involved in the use of and selling of crack cocaine.

go strumming v. [19C] to have sexual intercourse (cf. GO BALLOCKING v.). [STRUM v. (1)]

go tail-tickling v. (*also* go tail-twitching) [late 17C–early 18C] of a man, to have sexual intercourse (cf. BELLY BUMP v.; GO BALLOCKING v.). [TAIL n.[2] (3) + SE *tickle/twitch*]

gotcha n. [1950s+] (*orig. US*) a sudden humiliation, esp. the inadvertent exposure of the buttocks or genitals; also in fig. use. [GOTCHA! excl. (2)]

gotcha! excl. (*also* gotcher!) **1** [1920s+] I understand! OK! **2** [1930s+] I have got you! [SE *got you!*; (2) the *locus classicus* is the 1981 *Sun* newspaper headline *Gotcha!* on the drowning of the crew of the Argentine warship *Belgrano*]

gotcha back phr. [1990s+] (*US campus*) an expression of support. [lit. 'I've got your back']

gotcha covered phr. [1950s+] (*US campus*) an expression of support. [lit. 'I've got you covered']

gotcher! excl. see GOTCHA! excl.

gotch-gutted adj. [18C–early 19C] pot-bellied. [dial. *gotch*, a pot-bellied jug]

got 'em bad phr. [late 19C+] used of one who is suffering from bad nerves, intense (if irrational) terror or delirium tremens.

goth n. **1** [mid-19C] a fool. **2** [1980s+] a subgroup of rock fans who dress in austere black, usu. with black make-up, and enjoy correspondingly austere music. [SE *Goth*, one who behaves like a barbarian; a rude, uncivilized or ignorant person]

go the biff v. see BIFF n.[1] (1).

go the big figure v. see COME THE BIG FIGURE v.

go the big spit v. [1960s+] (*Aus.*) to vomit.

go the bundle v. [20C+] (*orig. US*) **1** to bet heavily, to bet one's entire funds. **2** to be very fond of. **3** fig. use of (1), to commit oneself completely. [GO v.⁴ (1) + BUNDLE n.¹ (1)]

go the complete swine v. (also **go the complete unicorn**, ...**entire animal/swine**, ...**whole animal**) [mid-19C–1920s] to do thoroughly, to go all the way, to commit oneself unreservedly. [var. on GO THE WHOLE HOG v.]

go the distance v. **1** [1910s+] to commit oneself wholeheartedly. **2** [1950s+] to have sexual intercourse. [boxing/horseracing imagery]

go the grope v. see COME THE GROPE v.

go the grouter v. [1980s+] (Aus. prison) to grope a woman.

go the hang-out road v. [1970s+] to tell the complete truth. [LET IT ALL HANG OUT v.]

go the hops v. [1940s–50s] (Aus.) to enjoy drinking beer (cf. HOPS n.¹).

go the jump v. see JUMP n.¹ (4).

go the knock on v. [1910s+] (Aus.) to steal. [KNOCK v.¹ (2)]

go the knuckle(s) v. see KNUCKLE n.².

go the length of a... v. [late 19C] to lend, the amount being specified at the end, e.g. go the length of a quid.

go the limit v. **1** [20C+] to commit oneself unreservedly. **2** [1920s+] to have or permit sexual intercourse.

go the other way v. **1** [1960s+] (US) to be bisexual or homosexual. **2** [1970s] to alter one's position, to back down on a promise. **3** [1970s] of a judicial verdict, to find against the plaintiff.

go the pace v. [early 18C; mid-19C+] to proceed with reckless vigour of action, to indulge in dissipation.

go the rat v. [1990s+] (Aus.) to act without restraint.

go there! excl. [1980s] (UK Black) an excl. of approval.

go the route v. [20C+] (US) to commit oneself completely.

go the shits v. [1970s] (Aus.) to sulk. [SHITS, THE n. (3)]

go the way of all flesh v. see WAY OF ALL FLESH phr.

go the whole animal v. see GO THE COMPLETE SWINE v.

go the whole critter v. (also **go the whole coon**) [mid–late 19C] (US) to do thoroughly, to go all the way, to commit oneself unreservedly. [var. on GO THE WHOLE HOG v.]

go the whole figure v. see COME THE BIG FIGURE v.

go the whole hog v. [mid-19C+] (orig. US) to do thoroughly, to go all the way; vars. include whole-hogger, -hoggery, -hogging, -hoggism, -hoggite. [? to eat a complete pig]

go the whole shoot v. [mid-19C] to commit oneself whole-heartedly. [slighly earlier var. on WHOLE BANG SHOOT, THE n.]

go the whole shot v. [1960s+] (orig. US) to commit oneself unreservedly. [WHOLE SHOT, THE n.]

go the whole way v. see GO ALL THE WAY v.

gothic adj. [18C] ill-behaved, uncouth. [SE Goth, a barbarian]

go thorough-stitch (with) v. [late 18C–1900s] to perform something thoroughly, to carry it out completely. [tailors' jargon go thorough-stitch, to finish a job that has been begun]

go through v.¹ **1** [mid-19C–1900s] (orig. US) to search. **2** [mid-19C+] (US) to thrash, to beat up; lit. and fig. **3** [mid-19C+] (US) to suffer, to be defeated. **4** [mid-19C+] (US/Aus.) to rob, after searching the victim's clothes. **5** [late 19C+] (Aus.) (also **go through on**) to rob; lit. and fig. **6** [1900s] (US Und.) to fool, to trick. **7** [1920s+] (Aus.) (also **go through on**) to give up, to desist. **8** [1940s+] (orig. milit.) to desert one's responsibilities, to shirk one's work.

go through v.² **1** [late 19C+] of a man, to have sexual intercourse, sometimes ext. to go through like a dose/packet of salts (cf. BANG v.¹). **2** [1940s] (Aus.) to defeat soundly.

go through v.³ [1900s] (US) to work out, to succeed.

go through Hades with one's hat off v. [late 19C] (US) to act courageously, to show no fear. [SE Hades, hell]

go through on v.¹ [1930s+] (Aus.) **1** to leave, esp. without giving prior warning. **2** to go absent without leave. **3** to escape from prison or abscond while on bail.

go through on v.² see GO THROUGH v.¹.

go through someone for a short cut v. [1980s+] (Irish) to criticize severely.

go through the card v. [1960s+] to cover comprehensively and completely, e.g. to order extensively from a menu. [fig. use of GO v.⁴ (1), i.e. to bet on every horse in a race]

go through the hackles v. [20C+] (US) to suffer, to endure an excess of bad luck. [SE hackle, a flax-comb, an instrument set with parallel steel pins for splitting and combing out the fibres of flax or hemp]

go through the motions v. [1920s+] to make a pretence of enthusiasm, effort, commitment etc when performing a tedious or unappealing task. [orig. milit. when men being trained without proper equipment, e.g. a rifle, were told to 'go through the motions']

go through the ox house to bed v. [late 17C–early 19C] of an old man, to marry a young girl (and thus to risk cuckoldry). [phr. used of an old man with a young wife, ox refers to the cuckold's HORNS n.]

go through the ring v. [mid-19C] to become bankrupt. [one fig. jumps through a ring or hoop]

go through the roof v. [1950s+] to lose one's temper.

go through without a water-bag v. [1940s–50s] (Aus.) to rush, to be in a very great hurry.

got it bad phr. [1910s+] used of one who is sexually infatuated. [HAVE IT BAD v. (1)]

go to Abney Park v. [late 19C–1920s] to die. [Abney Park cemetery in Stoke Newington, north London. Founded in 1840, it succeeded Bunhill Fields as the centre for Nonconformist burials. Among those buried there is General William Booth (1829–1912), founder of the Salvation Army]

go to balls! excl. [1960s] a general excl. of dismissal. [BALLS! excl. (1)]

go to Bannagher! excl. [1910s] (US) a euph. for GO TO HELL! excl. [for ety. see BEAT BANAGHAN v.]

go to bat v.¹ (also **come to bat**) **1** [late 19C+] to take action, to involve oneself with a specific task or job, to take a stance. **2** [20C+] to take one's turn. **3** [1920s+] to be prosecuted in court, to receive a jail sentence. [cricket/baseball imagery]

go to bat v.² see GO OFF THE BAT v.

go to bat for v. [1910s+] (US) to act in support of, to back up. [baseball imagery]

go to Bath v. [mid-17C–19C] to take up life as a beggar; thus go to Bath (and get your head shaved)! go away! you're insane! [the rich pickings that were supposedly to be obtained from Bath's fashionable wealthy population. Bath, with its spas, attracted the mad as well as the rich and their parasites]

go to bed in one's boots v. [late 19C–1900s] to be very drunk.

go to Bible class v. [late 19C] to get a pair of black eyes. [orig. printing f. the rowdiness and horseplay of a printer's chapel or workshop]

go to bits v. see GO TO PIECES v. (3).

go to blazes v. [mid-19C+] to decline, to collapse. [BLAZES n. (1)]

go to blazes! excl. [mid-19C+] an excl. of dismissal, both of the person and of their opinion or statement. [BLAZES n. (1), i.e. euph. for hell, where the fires of perdition burn]

go to blows v. [1970s+] (US Black) to fight.

go to buck v. [early 18C] of a woman, to have sexual intercourse (cf. CATCH AN OYSTER v.). [BUCK v.¹]

go to Buenos Aires v. (also **take the road to Buenos Aires**) [1900s–30s] to become a prostitute. [the association of 'White slavery' with South America]

go to buggery! excl. [late 19C+] a general excl. of dismissal.

go to Chicago v. [late 19C] (US) to run away, esp. to avoid one's debts. [New York businessmen who found themselves in trouble tended to run to Chicago or at least announce it as their destination]

go to Copenhagen v. (*also* **go to Denmark**) [1950s+] (*gay*) to have a sex change operation. [for ety. *see* COPENHAGEN CAPON n.]

go to Europe with Ralph and Earl in a Buick v. *see* RIDE THE BUICK v.

go to foreign parts v. [early 19C] to be transported as a convict. [euph.]

go to France! excl. [20C+] (*W.I.*) a general excl. of dismissal; a euph. for GO TO HELL! excl. [FRANCE n.]

go to fuck! excl. *see* GO TO HELL! excl.

go to glory v. 1 [early 19C+] to die; to disappear; of inanimate objects, to be destroyed. 2 [1910s] (*also* **slip to glory**) to make a serious error.

go to grass v. 1 [19C+] (*US*) (*also* **come to grass**) to be knocked down, to collapse. 2 [mid-19C] to vanish suddenly, to disappear, to be dismissed. 3 [mid-19C–1900s] of a limb, to waste away. 4 [mid-19C+] (*US*) to die, to be ruined, to retire. 5 [late 19C] to lose (a competition). [fig. uses of SE *go to grass*, of an animal, to be put to pasture; (1) adds a lit. image of falling to the grass on which open-air prizefights were held]

go to grass! excl. [19C+] (*US*) a dismissive excl. either demanding that the subject leaves or suggesting that their statement is nonsense; often ext. as *go to grass and eat hay!* [? a comparison of the subject with a farm animal or with King Nebuchadnezzar, whose madness was denoted by his appetite for grass; Hotten (1859) suggests 'a corruption of "go to GRACE," *grace* being written *gras* in olden times']

go to grass with one's teeth upward v. [19C] 1 to be buried. 2 to die.

go to Hairyfordshire v. [mid–late 19C] to have sexual intercourse. [HAIRYFORDSHIRE n.]

go to Halifax v. [1900s] to go the long way round. [HALIFAX n.]

go to Halifax! excl. [mid-17C–19C] a euph. for GO TO HELL! excl. [HALIFAX n.]

go to Hanover! excl. [18C] a general dismissive excl., a euph. for GO TO HELL! excl. [the 18C dislike of its Hanoverian monarchs]

go to heaven in a handbasket v. *see* GO TO HELL IN A (HAND)BASKET v.

go to heaven in a string v. [late 16C–mid-18C] to be hanged; thus *feel like going to heaven in a string*, to be so deliriously happy that one does not mind even the possibility of imminent death. [orig. applied in 16C to the Jesuits whose faith could bring them judicial death]

go to heaven in a wheelbarrow v. [mid-17C] to go to hell. [the popular image of the Devil taking away a scolding wife in a wheelbarrow]

go-to-hell adj. [1910s+] outrageous, extreme. [GO TO HELL! excl.]

go to hell v. [mid-19C+] 1 to go wrong, to fail. 2 to become useless, unimportant.

go to hell! excl. (*also* **go to fuck!**) [mid-18C+] a general excl. of dismissal.

go to hell across lots! excl. [mid-19C–1940s] (*US*) a general excl. of dismissal; the implication is that they should go with speed. [GO TO HELL! excl. + ACROSS LOTS phr. (1)]

go to hell and help your mother make bitch-pie! excl. [mid-18C–19C] an intensified version of GO TO HELL! excl.

go to hell and pump thunder! excl. [late 19C] an excl. of derision and dismissal.

go to hell, Hull and Halifax! excl. [16C+] a general excl. of dismissal. [the 16C prayer 'from hell, Hull and Halifax Good Lord deliver us', which refers to the Halifax Gibbet Law under which a prisoner was executed first and his guilt or innocence ascertained afterwards; for an eyewitness account *see* Taylor, *News from Hell, Hull and Halifax* (1639)]

go to hell in a (hand)basket v. (*also* **go to hell in a hack**, **...handcar, ...wheelbarrow**) [mid-19C+] (*US*) to come to a bad end; thus [mid–late 19C] the antithesis, *go to heaven in a handbasket*, i.e. something to be desired, if never attained.

go to hell or Connaught! excl. [mid-17C–19C] an excl. of aggressive dismissal, go where you want but don't expect me to be bothered! [a law, passed in 1654, forcing Irish landowners out of Ulster, Munster and Leinster]

go to it v. (*also* **hop to it**) 1 [17C+] to get on with things, to get to work. 2 [mid-17C–early 18C; 1960s] to have sexual intercourse, to pet. [(2) IT n.[1] (1)]

go to Jericho v. [mid-18C–early 19C] to become drunk. [fig. use of *Jericho* as a place of exile]

go to Jericho! excl. [late 19C–1920s] an excl. of dismissal.

go to Jerusalem v. [mid-18C–early 19C] to get drunk. [? drunkenness being 'the promised land']

go to market v. [late 19C+] (*Aus.*) to lose one's temper, to behave irritably, to make a fuss, to let off steam.

go to Mary's room v. (*also* **go to visit Mary**) [1980s] (*Aus.*) to use the lavatory (cf. AUNTIE n.[1]). [euph.]

go-to-meeting adj. [late 18C+] one's Sunday best; usu. in phr. *go-to-meeting clothes* but also describing other objects, e.g. *go-to-meeting bags*, best hat. [church *meetings*]

go-to-meetings n. [19C] (*US*) one's best clothes. [GO-TO-MEETING adj.]

go to noggin-staves v. [mid–late 19C] to be ruined financially. [SE *noggin*, a vessel made of wood (holding nearly a quart/1.14 litres), ult. synon. Irish *noigin* + *stave*, a piece of wood used in the making of a barrel]

go to Paul's for a wife v. *see* GO TO WESTMINSTER FOR A WIFE v.

go to Peckham v. [early–mid-19C] to sit down to eat. [pun on *Peckham* in south London/PECK v.[1] + SE *ham*]

go to Peg Trantum's v. [late 17C–early 19C] to die. [note East Anglian dial. *peg trantum*, a tomboy]

go to pieces v. 1 [mid-19C] to become bankrupt. 2 [mid-19C–1900s] to give birth. 3 [mid-19C+] (*also* **go to bits**) to collapse emotionally. 4 [late 19C+] to fail, to go badly. 5 [1930s+] to break down in health, cleanliness etc.

go to pigs and whistles v. [late 18C–mid-19C] (*Scot.*) to be ruined financially. [Scot. *pigs and whistles*, a mass of foolish, inconvenient furniture or nick-nacks' (*EDD*)]

go to pot v. 1 [mid-17C+] to fall on hard times, to be ruined economically or morally, voluntarily or otherwise. 2 [mid-18C–mid-19C] to die. 3 [mid-19C+] to collapse, to stop working properly. [fig. uses of SE *pot*; (1) the cutting up of whole pieces of meat for the stewing pot; (2) 'the classic custom of putting the ashes of the dead in an urn' (Hotten, 1867)]

go to pot! excl. [late 17C+] a general excl. of dismissal. [GO TO POT v. (1)]

go to Putney (on a pig)! excl. [mid-19C; 1990s+] a dismissive excl., as in GO TO JERICHO! excl. [*Putney*, SW London]

go to quat v. (*also* **quat**) [19C] to defecate. [? SE *squat*]

go to rack and manger v. *see* LIE AT RACK AND MANGER v.

go to rest in a horse's nightcap v. *see* DIE IN A HORSE'S NIGHTCAP v.

go to roost v. [19C–1920s] to go to bed.

go to St Paul's for a wife v. *see* GO TO WESTMINSTER FOR A WIFE v.

go to Salt River v. *see* ROW UP SALT RIVER v. (2).

go to school at Bromley v. [1920s] (*W.I.*) not to go to school at all and thus become a rough, ignorant person. [the celebrated 1920s Bromley dance band, based in Bridgetown and named for its leader, and its association with hedonistic fun]

go to school in August v. [20C+] (*W.I.*) to be uneducated, to display one's ignorance. [*August* is a school holiday]

go to (see) the doctor v. (*also* **have a doctor's appointment**) [1980s+] (*US campus*) to drink alcohol. [the supposedly restorative effects of alcohol]

go to shit v. [1970s+] to decline, to collapse. [SHIT n.³ (1)]

go to shut-eye land v. [1940s] (W.I.) to die. [SHUT-EYE n. (1)]

go to sleep v. [20C+] to die. [perhaps the ultimate of such euphs. and equally popular when *putting an animal to sleep*]

go to smash v. (*also* go to smashes) [mid-19C+] **1** to ruin one's life. **2** to blunder, to err, to fail. [SMASH n.³]

go to someone's chest v. [1900s–20s] of objects or events, to irritate, to annoy.

go to sticks (and) staves v. [mid-19C] to be ruined financially.

go to the bad v. [mid-19C+] to adopt a life of crime or at least one that is seen as outside society's acceptable norms.

go to the Bahamas v. [1990s+] (US Und.) to be sent to solitary confinement. [the distance of the Bahamas from the mainland]

go to the basket v. [early 17C–early 18C] to go to prison; thus *brought to the basket*, sent to prison. [the *alms-basket* on which poor prisoners in the public prisons were mainly dependent for food]

go to the bow-wows/bugs/cats v. *see* GO TO THE DOGS v.

go to the cleaners v. [20C+] (*orig. US*) to lose badly, esp. in sport, gambling or business. [TAKE SOMEONE TO THE CLEANERS v.]

go to the country v. [late 19C] (Aus. Und.) to be imprisoned.

go to the devil v. (*also* go to the deuce, go to the dickens) [mid-17C+] to fall into disreputable habits; often as imper. excl. *go to the devil!*

go to the diet of worms v. [late 18C–early 19C] to die. [pun on the proper name *Diet of Worms*, the meeting (1521) between Emperor Charles V and Martin Luther that effectively launched the Protestant Reformation + the action of worms on the dead body]

go to the doctor v. *see* GO TO (SEE) THE DOCTOR v.

go to the dogs v. (*also* go the the bow-wows, …bugs, …cats) **1** [mid-18C+] to decline socially, to become run-down and dirty, to turn into a tramp. **2** [mid-19C+] to fail. [the sending of run-down horses to the knackers, thence to become dogs' meat]

go to the grass v. [1900s] (N.Z.) to run off, to abscond. [i.e. the countryside]

go to the joint v. *see* GET TO THE JOINT v.

go to the kaffirs v. [1980s+] (S.Afr.) to deteriorate, to decline socially. [KAFFIR n.¹ (2), i.e. derog. var. on GO TO THE DOGS v. (1)]

go to the mattress v. (*also* hit the mattress(es)) [1930s+] (*orig. US Und.*) to hide, to take refuge, esp. when under siege from another gang. [the practice of sleeping on mattresses in one's hideout, rather than in one's bed at home. Orig. a US Mafia usage, the phr. was widely popularized by the success of Mario Puzo's book *The Godfather* (1969) and the films that followed]

go to the pack v. **1** [1910s+] (Aus.) to decline socially, economically etc. **2** [1960s] (Aus.) to give up. **3** [1980s] (N.Z.) to fail continually.

go to the pot v. [18C–1900s] to die; also as dismissive excl.

go to the races v. [20C+] to die. [euph.]

go to the ranch v. [1990s+] (US gay) to go crazy. [the ranch-style 'homosexual healing centres' advocated by anti-gay campaigner Anita Bryant]

go to the ropes v. [1900s] (US) to suffer. [boxing imagery]

go to the school of placebo v. *see* AT THE SCHOOL OF PLACEBO, BE v.

go to the scriveners (and learn to make indentures) v. [mid-17C] to get drunk. [ety. unknown]

go to the spot v. [mid-19C–1920s] to suit the circumstances, to be absolutely satisfactory in the context.

go to the woods v. [1910s] (Aus.) to get drunk.

go to town v. (*also* go to town on/with) **1** [1930s+] (*orig. US*) to do something to an extreme extent, to go 'all out'. **2** [1960s] (US) to enjoy greatly. **3** [1960s+] (*orig. US*) to make a great fuss about, to concentrate on. **4** [1970s] (US gay) to have sexual intercourse. [a rural sensibility that equates such activities with urban life]

got out of pawn adj. [20C+] born. [rhy. sl.]

go to visit Mary v. *see* GO TO MARY'S ROOM v.

go to visit one's uncle v. [late 18C–early 19C] to abandon one's wife shortly after the marriage ceremony. [euph; but note RAF jargon *go uncling*, to pursue a married woman; her children call the suitor 'uncle']

go to Westminster for a wife v. (*also* go to St Paul's for a wife) [late 16C–early 19C] to visit a brothel. [16C pvb 'Who goes to Westminster for a wife, to St Paul's for a man or to Smithfield for a horse, may meet with a horse, a knave and a jade.' Despite the supposed difference indicated in the proverb, Old St Paul's Cathedral was also well-known for the raffish individuals who frequented its purlieus]

go to work on v. [mid-19C+] to attack.

Gotrocks n. [1930s+] (US) a rich person, used as a 'surname', e.g. *Mr Gotrocks*. [SE *got* + ROCKS n.¹ (1) + link to the millionaire Rockefeller family]

go tromboning v. [20C+] to have sexual intercourse (cf. GO BALLOCKING v.). [the physical action]

go trumpet-cleaning v. [late 19C–1910s] to die. [the trumpeter in question being the angel Gabriel]

gotta love that phr. (*also* gotta like that) [1980s+] (US campus) an expression of approval of another's good fortune.

gotter-dam-merung n. [mid-late 19C] (UK society) coarse swearing. [a pun on Richard Wagner's *Ring* cycle of operas, first performed in London in 1862]

got the arse at Bulli Pass phr. [1960s+] (Aus.) a phr. used to denote an unsatisfactory situation. [ARSE n.³]

gotto n. [1940s] (W.I.) a rope-soled shoe. [? SE *got to*, i.e. poverty dictates that one has no choice but to buy such cheap footwear]

got to swim underwater to dodge it phr. *see* CLIMBING TREES TO GET AWAY FROM IT phr.

go tummy-tickling v. [mid-late 19C] to have sexual intercourse (cf. BELLY BUMP v.; GO BALLOCKING v.).

got-up n. [late 19C–1910s] an upstart. [he has 'got up' in the world]

got up adj. **1** [mid-19C+] dressed up particularly smartly for some occasion; thus ext. in phrs. *got up regardless, got up to kill, got up to the knocker, got up to the nines*. **2** [late 19C] of an object, of good quality. [GET UP v.²]

got up like a dog's dinner phr. *see* DRESSED UP LIKE A DOG'S DINNER phr.

got up like a pox-doctor's clerk phr. *see* DONE UP LIKE A POX DOCTOR'S CLERK phr.

got up to kill phr. *see* DRESSED TO KILL phr.

go turtles (over) v. [1970s] to fall in love with, to become sexually obsessed with. [TURTLE (DOVE) v.]

go twat-faking v. (*also* go twat-raking) [1900s–20s] of a man, to have sexual intercourse (cf. GO BALLOCKING v.). [TWAT n. (1) + FAKE v.¹ (2)/RAKE v.¹ (1)]

go twatting v. [1900s–20s] of a man, to have sexual intercourse (cf. GO BALLOCKING v.). [TWAT n. (1)]

got your eyeful? phr. [1950s+] a phr. addressed to someone who is staring, with the undoubted suggestion that they should stop at once; it can be followed with 'Want a picture?'

gouch (out) v. [1980s+] to fall asleep or collapse, whether through exhaustion or an excess of drink or drugs. [ety. unknown; ? GOUCHY adj. or ? link to GOW n.¹ (2) or joc. ref. to the clichéd image of a sleeping *gaucho*]

gouchy adj. [20C+] (Scot.) depressed. [? Scot. *gowk*, to stare vacantly]

gouda, gouda, gouda n. [1990s+] (US campus) an unappealing, unpopular person. [SE *gouda*, a popular Dutch cheese; thus one who is CHEESY adj.² (1)]

gouge n. (US) **1** [mid-late 19C] a swindle, a cheat. **2** [1920s] swindling, cheating. [SE *gouge*, to cheat]

gouge v. [mid-19C+] (*orig. US*) to take something from another person, to cheat out of, to insult; thus excl. *gouge!* uttered after a successful insult or theft. [SE *gouge*]

gouger *n.*[1] (*also* **gouge**) [19C+] a swindler, a cheat. [SE *gouge*/GOUGE v.]

gouger *n.*[2] [19C+] (*Irish*) a thug, a lout. [SE *gouger*, one who gouges out another's eye in a fight]

Goughed *adj.* [mid-19C] (*US*) drunk. ['J. B. Gough, "the temperance spouter", had recently gone missing; it was found that he had been on a bender' (G. A. Thompson, personal correspondence)]

gouk *n. see* GOWK n. (1).

goul *n.* [1960s–70s] (*US*) the anus (cf. GOOLA n.[1]). [Ital. *culo*, the anus]

goulash *n.* **1** [1920s] a fool (cf. APPLEHEAD n.). **2** [1920s–50s] (*US*) nonsense. **3** [1920s+] (*UK Und.*) prison stew (which is not goulash), also as in any institution. [? bridge use *goulash*, a re-deal of unshuffled cards after the hands have been thrown in without bidding, thus fig. a mess]

go under *v.* **1** [19C+] (*orig. US*) to die. **2** [mid-19C+] (*orig. US*) to go bankrupt. **3** [1900s] (*Aus.*) in fig. use, to fail, to be defeated. **4** [1980s+] (*Aus. Und.*) to be imprisoned.

go under-petticoating *v.* [19C] to have sexual intercourse (cf. GO BALLOCKING v.).

go under someone's neck *v.* [1950s+] (*Aus.*) to take someone's prerogative, to steal someone's idea, to stop someone's intended actions. [horseracing imagery]

go under the house *v.* [1940s–70s] (*US Black/gay*) to perform cunnilingus (cf. AUSSIE KISS n.).

go under the South Pole *v.* [late 16C] to suffer from syphilis or some other venereal disease. [the belief that those who went on long sea voyages suffered from fevers]

go-up *n.* [1940s] (*US Black*) an upstairs flat or apartment (cf. GO-DOWN n.).

go up *v.*[1] [early–mid-19C] to be killed or hanged, to die, to be done for; esp. in phr. *to be gone up*.

go up *v.*[2] **1** [mid-19C] to be unavailable (through lack of funds). **2** [mid-late 19C] (*US*) to be ruined, to be destroyed, to become bankrupt. **3** [1920s] (*US*) to surrender one's money in a hold-up.

go up *v.*[3] **1** [mid-19C+] (*orig. US*) to go to prison. **2** [1900s–50s] (*Aus.*) to be punished (in a non-custodial manner). [abbr. GO UP THE RIVER v.]

go up *v.*[4] [late 19C–1920s] to become explosively angry.

go up *v.*[5] [1960s+] (*US drugs*) to become intoxicated by psychotropic drugs. [one gets HIGH adj.[1] (2)]

go up against (the collar) *v.* [19C+] (*US*) to work hard, esp. in a difficult or inconvenient situation. [SE *collar*, the neckpiece of a draft harness; the comparison is to a hard-working draft horse]

go up a log *v.* [1910s+] (*Aus.*) to hide. [the activity of a snake or lizard]

go up a tree *v.* **1** [mid-19C] to be hanged. **2** [1910s+] (*Aus.*) to fall off one's horse.

go up-country *v.* (*Aus.*) **1** [1910s–40s] to go to prison. **2** [1920s] to die. [euph.]

go up Green River *v.* [mid-19C–1940s] (*US*) to die; thus *send up Green River*, to kill. [the *Green River* brand of knife, made in Texas]

go up her petticoats *v.* (*also* **raise her petticoats**) [late 19C] of a man, to have sexual intercourse (cf. DO HER JOB FOR HER v.).

go up in a balloon *v.* [mid-late 19C] (*US*) to be ruined, to come to nothing.

go up in that fire *v.* [2000s] (*US prison*) to have AIDS.

go up in the air *v.* (*US*) **1** [20C+] to lose one's temper. **2** [1900s] to fail, to collapse. **3** [1900s–10s] to lose one's senses, to become over-excited.

go up one! *excl.* [late 19C] a general compliment. [school use, whereby the successful pupil goes up a place or class]

go upon the kid *v.* [late 18C] (*UK Und.*) to steal a parcel from

an errand boy by promising to hold it while he makes another delivery. [KID n.[1] (1)/KID (AROUND) v. (2)]

go upon the top *v.* [18C] (*UK Und.*) for one thief to jump onto a partner's shoulders to climb through a window.

go up Salt River *v.* [1920s–40s] (*US Black*) to die. [? the salty tears of the mourners and/or the bitterness of death]

go upside someone's head *v.* [1950s+] (*US Black*) to hit in the face, to beat up.

go upstairs out of the world *v.* [late 17C–early 18C] to be hanged. [? the steps to mount the gallows]

go upstate *v.* [2000s] (*US Und.*) to die by assassination. [euph.]

go up the chute *v. see* CHUTE n.[2].

go up the council *v. see* COUNCIL GRITTER n.

go up the escape *v.* [1900s] (*US*) to die.

go up the flue *v.* [late 19C] (*US campus*) to die. [SE *flue* or FLUE n.[1] (2)]

go up the flume *v.* [mid-late 19C] (*US*) **1** to suffer a disaster. **2** to be exhausted, to be worn out, to be dead. [mining jargon *flume*, an artificial stream that brings water to a mine]

go up the ladder to bed *v.* [late 16C–19C] to be hanged.

go up the old dirt road *v.* [1930s+] to perform anal intercourse (cf. ASK FOR THE RING v.). [DIRT ROAD n.[2]]

go up the rainbow *v.* [1970s] to reach orgasm. [the end of the *rainbow* as being supposedly heaven]

go up the river *v.* [mid-19C+] to go to prison; thus fig., to get oneself into trouble. [the Hudson *River*, which leads to Sing-Sing, New York State's main prison]

go up the Swanee *v. see* GO DOWN THE SWANEE v.

go up the wall *v.* [1950s+] **1** to lose one's temper. **2** to be terrified.

gourd *n.*[1] [mid-16C–18C] (*UK Und.*) a crooked die, which has been hollowed out to affect the throw. [the hollow centre of the plant or OF *gourd*, a swindle]

gourd *n.*[2] **1** [mid-19C; 1960s+] (*esp. drugs*) the head; thus OUT OF ONE'S GOURD phr. (1). **2** [1970s] (*US campus*) a stupid, empty-headed person.

gourd-head *n.* [mid-19C–1970s] (*US*) a blockhead, a fool; thus *make gourds*, make a fool of. [SE *gourd*/GOURD n.[2] (1) + -HEAD sfx (1)]

Gourock ham *n.* [mid-19C] a salt herring. [*Gourock*, on the Clyde 40km (25 miles) from Glasgow, was once a fishing port]

gouster *n. see* GOWSTER n.[2].

gov *n.* **1** [mid-19C+] (*US*) a state governor. **2** [late 19C–1910s] one's father (cf. GUV n.). **3** [1930s+] one's boss, or anyone higher up the social order than oneself. **4** [1940s+] a prison officer. **5** [1990s+] (*US*) the government. [abbr.; (2), (3) and (4) abbr. GOVERNOR n.]

go vaulting *v.* [late 16C–17C] to have sexual intercourse (cf. GO BALLOCKING v.).

governess *n.* [1960s+] a dominatrix.

government beef *n.* (*also* **government cow**, **...yearling**, **governor's beef**) [20C+] (*US*) a deer that has been illegally shot by poachers.

government cheese *n.* [2000s] (*US Black*) welfare payments and similar hand-outs. [SE *government* + CHEESE n.[1]]

government grapes *n.* [1990s+] temazepam. [their being issued on a National Health Service prescription and the similarity of the pills to grapes]

government house *n.* [late 19C–1950s] (*Aus./N.Z.*) the house of a plantation or estate owner or manager.

government-inspected meat *n.* [1960s+] (*US gay*) a homosexual man serving in the US armed forces. [MEAT n. (1)/MEAT n. (2)]

government man *n.* [19C] a prisoner.

government rag *n.* [mid-19C] (*N.Z.*) a paper currency worth 5 shillings, issued in 1844 by Governor Fitzroy. [SE *government* + RAG n.[1] (3)]

government securities *n.* [mid–late 19C] handcuffs or fetters. [pun]

government signpost *n.* [mid-19C] the gallows. [it points the way to the next world]

government stroke *n.* [mid-19C+] (*Aus.*) **1** lazy working. **2** relief work, subsidized by the state. [the deliberately minimal rate of work put out by convict labourers]

government yearling *n. see* GOVERNMENT BEEF n.

governor *n.* **1** [19C+] an employer, a superior. **2** [early 19C+] a father. **3** [early 19C+] a general term of address to any strange man. **4** [mid-19C; 1950s] (*UK Und.*) a crime boss, usu. of a local area. **5** [1950s+] a publican. **6** [1970s+] an acknowledged expert.

Governor Green *n.* [1920s] (*US prison*) freedom, the state of having escaped.

governor's beef *n. see* GOVERNMENT BEEF n.

govo *n.* (*also* **gubbo**) [1980s] (*Aus.*) a member of a home for disadvantaged or delinquent children. [SE *government*, i.e. the administrator of the home + -o sfx (4)]

govy *n.* (*also* **govey**) [1900s] a governess. [abbr.]

gow *n.*[1] (*also* **ghow**) (*US drugs*) **1** [1900s] alcohol. **2** [1920s+] opium, heroin or morphine (cf. APOSTLE n.; AUNTIE EMMA n.). **3** [1930s–50s] an opium pipe. **4** [1940s] a pleasurable drug experience. [Chinese *yao-kao*, opium; ult. *yao*, drug + *kao*, an oily, fatty substance, esp. an unguent]

gow *n.*[2] [1900s–40s] (*US*) a prison. [abbr. HOOSEGOW n. (1)]

gow *n.*[3] [1960s] (*US prison*) sauce. [? GOO n.[1] (1)]

gow *n.*[4] [1970s] (*Aus. teen*) a derog. term for a Black or Oriental person (cf. DAPTO DOG n.; BROWNIE n.[2]). [backsl. = WOG n.[1] (1)]

gow *v.*[1] [1930s] (*US drugs*) to remove opium residue from the pipe. [GOW n.[1] (2)]

gow *v.*[2] [1930s] (*US Und.*) to arrest, to imprison. [GOW n.[2]]

go walkies *v.* (*also* **go walkabout**) [1950s+] to disappear, to vanish.

go walking *v.* [20C+] to go rotten. [the foodstuff is not walking, but the maggots are]

go wax a gaza *phr.* [20C+] (*Irish*) a dismissive phr. [lit. 'go climb a gas lamp']

go way down south in Dixie *v. see* GO SOUTH v.[2].

gowed (up) *adj.* [1930s+] (*US*) very intoxicated by narcotics. [GOW n.[1] (2); note 1910s USN *gowed*, intoxicated by liquor]

go wenching *v.* [early 17C–early 18C] to have sexual intercourse (cf. GO BALLOCKING v.). [ext. of SE *wenching*, associating with common women]

Gower Street dialect *n.* [mid-19C] a form of sl. whereby the user transposes the initial letters of adjacent words. [for ety. *see* MARROWSKY n.]

go west *v.* [1910s+] to die, to end, to collapse; thus *gone west*, dead. [the image of the setting sun, going down in the west + the drive west that took a condemned criminal along Holborn from Newgate prison to the 'triple tree' at Tyburn (today's Marble Arch); note 'A Budg and Snug Song' (1676): 'With a kiss we part, and westward part, / To the nubbing cheat in a cart']

go whack *v.* [mid-19C–1940s] to take or offer a share. [WHACK n.[2] (1)]

gowhead *n.* [1930s–50s] (*US*) a drug addict, usu. of opium. [GOW n.[1] (2) + -HEAD sfx (3)]

go when the wagon comes *v.* [1940s] (*US Black*) of a situation, to be out of control. [the only solution will be when the metaphorical police wagon arrives and all concerned are arrested]

go where the big knobs hang out *v.* [1960s–70s] (*Aus.*) to urinate. [play on KNOB n.[1] (3)/NOB n.[2] (3)]

go with *v.* **1** [mid-19C+] to have an affair or relationship with someone, to have sexual intercourse with. **2** [late 19C+] to go around with, to be friends with. **3** [1960s+] to accept and act upon a plan or suggestion.

go with a roar *v.* [mid-19C–1900s] to be extremely or conspicuously successful.

go with a swing *v.* [1970s+] of a party, show or entertainment, to pass off highly successfully and enjoyably.

go without a passport *v.* [mid-19C] (*US*) to commit suicide. [the 'passport' is presumably the funeral ritual]

go with the birds *v.* [1930s] (*US tramp*) to go south for the winter.

go with the flow *v.* [1960s+] to accept a situation and make no attempt to alter it, to act passively. [a mass popularization of the more complex dictum of US psychologist Carl Rogers (1902–87), who saw life as 'floating with a complex streaming of experience']

go with the program *v. see* GET WITH THE PROGRAM v.

gow job *n.* [1940s] **1** (*US*) a HOT-ROD n. car modified for high performance. **2** (*US campus*) a flashily dressed young woman. [? SE *go* or fig. use of GOW n.[1] (2) + JOB n.[4]]

gowk *n.* **1** [late 19C+] (*UK Und.*) (*also* **gook, gouk**) a naïve, gullible individual, a fool, thus a generic term for a countryman. **2** [1900s–30s] a tramp. [Scot. *gowk*, a fool; (1) 20C+ use is US]

gowl *n.* [1990s+] (*Irish*) **1** the vagina. **2** a fool. [Irish *gabhal*, a fork, a junction]

go working the double oracle *v.* (*also* **go working the dumb oracle, go working the hairy oracle, work the...**) [late 18C–mid-19C] to have sexual intercourse. [SE *work* + DUMB ORACLE n./HAIRY ORACLE n.]

gowster *n.*[1] [1930s–60s] (*US drugs*) an opium addict or habitual user of marijuana, heroin etc. [GOW n.[1] (2) + -STER sfx]

gowster *n.*[2] (*also* **gouster**) [1970s] (*US Black*) a young man dressed in bell-bottom trousers and a wide-lapelled jacket. [ety. unknown]

goy *n.* (*also* **goyisher, goyus**) [late 19C+] a gentile, a non-Jew; thus pl. **goyim**. [Heb. *goy*, a nation, thence Yid.]

goy *adj.* (*also* **goyish, goyisher**) [late 19C+] gentile. [GOY n.]

goynk *n.* [1940s–50s] (*US drugs*) narcotics, esp. opium. [? JUNK n.[5] (1)]

goyno *n. see* GUINO n.

goyus *n. see* GOY n.

gozz *n. see* GOSS n.[2].

gozzie *n. see* GOOZIE n.

gozzle *n. see* GOOZLE n.

gozzle *v.* [1940s–50s] (*US*) to throttle. [GOOZLE n.]

gozzy *n.* [1990s+] (*UK juv.*) saliva or phlegm, in the context of spitting. [GOSS v.]

gozzy *v. see* GOSS v.

G.P. *n.* [1980s+] (*Aus. prison*) a person serving an indeterminate sentence by reason of insanity, usu. for murder. [the sentence is determined at the Governor's Pleasure]

g.p. *n.* **1** [1940s+] (*US Black*) general principles. **2** [1950s] (*UK juv.*) grand passion. **3** [1980s] (*US campus*) good plan. [abbr.]

G-pack *n.* [1990s+] (*US drugs*) a wholesale purchase of 100 vials of crack cocaine, which can be merchandised for $1000. [G n.[1] (1) + PACKAGE n.[1] (3)]

g.q. *adj.* [1980s+] (*US campus*) fashionably dressed. [ref. to *GQ* or *Gentleman's Quarterly* magazine]

graal *n.* (*also* **grawl**) [20C+] (*Ulster*) a growing boy, a large young lad. [fig. use of Scot. *grawl*, a young salmon]

grab *n.* **1** [mid-18C+] an arrest. **2** [19C+] a robbery, an act of theft; thus *put the grab on*, to steal or kidnap. **3** [early 19C] a thief. **4** [mid–late 19C; 1950s] a policeman (cf. BEAT-POUNDER n.). **5** [mid-19C–1900s] (*US*) a 'go', a 'time', a 'handful'. **6** [1900s–30s] (*US*) a hand. **7** [1940s–50s] (*UK prison*) one's pay.

grab *v.*[1] **1** [18C+] to steal, to take or obtain for oneself. **2** [mid-18C+] (*also* **grab off**) to arrest. **3** [1900s–60s] (*US*) to grasp, to comprehend. **4** [1910s+] to appeal to; esp. as *how does that grab you?*, how do you like that? **5** [1920s+] (*US*) to capture, to kidnap, to abduct (other than in a judicial context). **6** [1920s+] (*US*) to catch some form of transport, usu. a train or taxi. **7** [1960s] (*US*) to irritate. **8** [1970s+] (*US*) to make a turn in a vehicle. **9** [1980s] (*US campus*) to have sexual relations. [fig. uses of SE]

grab *v.*[2] *see* GRAB (ON) *v.*

grab a cloud *v. see* GRAB SKY *v.*

grab a handful of *v.* (*also* grab an armful of) [1910s+] **1** (*US tramp*) to steal a ride. **2** (*US*) to take, to steal, to secure for oneself.

grab a hat *v. see* GET ONE'S HAT *v.*

grab air *v. see* GRAB SKY *v.*

grabalicious *adj.* (*also* grabilicious) [1970s–80s] (*W.I. Rasta/UK Black*) greedy, grabby, covetous (cf. GRAVALICIOUS adj.). [SE grab + -LICIOUS sfx]

grab-all *n.* **1** [late 19C] a bag to carry odds and ends. **2** [late 19C+] (*Aus./US*) a greedy person.

grab a root *v.* [mid-19C+] (*US*) to hold tight, to get busy, to go ahead.

grab a sit-down *v.* [1970s–80s] (*US Black*) to take a seat, often as an invitation to a guest or visitor.

grab-ass *n.* [1940s+] (*US*) fighting, fooling around. [SE grab + ASS n. (2)]

grab-ass *v.* [1950s+] (*US*) to play around, to mess about, esp. in a sexual context; thus *grab-assing*, fooling around. [GRAB-ASS n.]

grabasstic *adj.* [2000s] (*US Black*) used of one who persistently harasses others, esp. in a sexual manner. [GRAB-ASS v.]

grab-bag *n.* [late 19C+] a random collection of items, ideas, people etc. [orig. US carnival *grab-bag*, the equivalent of 'lucky dip', a bag containing various articles, into which one may dip on payment of a small sum]

grabber *n.* **1** [mid–late 19C] (*UK Und.*) a garrotter. **2** [mid-19C–1940s] (*US Und.*) a thief, spec. (*Irish*) a cattle thief. **3** [mid-19C+] a hand, often in pl. **4** [1910s–20s] a pickpocket. **5** [1940s+] (*US*) a selfish or greedy person. **6** [1960s+] (*US*) something that seizes the attention.

grabbers *n.*[1] [mid-19C] boots.

grabbers *n.*[2] [1980s] (*Aus.*) the teeth.

grabble *v.* [late 18C–19C] to snatch, to grab, to seize; thus *grabble the bit*, to snatch someone's money. [OED lists it as SE (ult. synon. Du. *grabbelen*), although it cites Grose (1796)]

grabbling irons *n. see* GRAPPLING IRONS n. (2).

grabby *n.* [mid-19C–1910s] (*orig. RN*) an infantryman. [? SE *grubby*, or their propensity to *grab*, i.e. loot]

grabby *adj.* [1910s+] greedy, avaricious. [SE grab + sfx -*y*]

grabhooks *n.* [1910s–40s] (*US*) the hands or fingers. [SE grab/GRAB v.[1] (1) + HOOK n.[1] (1)]

grabilicious *adj. see* GRABALICIOUS adj.

grab-it-and-growl *n.* (*also* grab-it-and-gallop) [1930s+] (*US*) a diner, a lunch counter. [SE grab, i.e. the speed of one's eating]

grab joint *n.* [1940s+] (*US*) a snack bar, a cafeteria. [SE grab + JOINT n.[4] (3)]

grab off *v. see* GRAB v.[1] (2).

grab (on) *v.* [1960s+] (*US campus*) to make sexual advances towards, to neck. [ext. of GRAB v.[1] (1)]

grab on *v.* [mid-19C] to survive, to get along. [GRAB v.[1] (1)]

grab one's dick *v.* (*also* grab one's balls) [1980s+] (*US Black*) to boast, to brag. [fig. use of GRAB v.[1] (1) + DICK n.[4] (1)/BALLS n.[1] (1)]

grab sky *v.* (*also* claw sky, grab a cloud, grab air, reach for a cloud, ...the moon, ...the roof, ...the sky, ...the stars) [20C+] (*US*) to put one's hands in the air; usu. as an imper.

grab the flab *v.* (*also* grab the slab) [1990s+] to masturbate.

grab the wrong end of the stick *v. see* GET HOLD OF THE WRONG END OF THE STICK *v.*

grace before meat *n.* [late 19C] a kiss (presumably as a preliminary to sexual intercourse). [SE grace + MEAT n. (1)]

grace-card *n.* [mid-19C] **1** (*Irish*) in cards, the 6 of hearts. **2** the ace of hearts. [ety. unknown]

Gracemans *n.* [17C] (*UK Und.*) 'Gracious' (Gracechurch) Street market, the corn and hay market of medieval London. [abbr. *Gracechurch* + -MANS sfx]

gracing *n.* (*also* greycing) [1920s+] greyhound racing. [contraction of SE]

gracious Miss Agnes! *excl.* [20C+] (*US*) a general excl. of surprise and/or pleasure. [? *agnus dei*, the lamb of God and thus a euph. for God or Christ]

gracious to goodness *adj.* [late 19C+] (*US Black*) excessive, far too much.

grad *n.* [late 19C+] (*orig. US*) a *grad*uate, lit. or fig.; also attrib., e.g. *grad student*. [abbr.]

grade A *n.* [1930s–50s] (*US*) an order of milk in a snack bar. [the US division of milk into 3 classes: Grade A for infants and children; Grade B for adults only; Grade C for cooking purposes only]

grade A *adj.* (*also* A-grade) [1920s+] (*orig. US*) the very best.

gradoo! *excl.* [1970s] (*US campus*) an excl. of frustration or disgust. [according to Eble, *Campus Slang*, 2 November 1973: 'literally bird faeces', although in what lang. is not stated]

graduate *n.* **1** [late 19C] an up-market prostitute. **2** [late 19C] a clever, cunning man. **3** [1920s–40s] (*US Und.*) one who has served a sentence.

graduate *v.* **1** [late 19C+] to increase, through knowledge and sophistication, one's status within the ranks of one's peers in the streets and the criminal milieu. **2** [1920s–40s] (*US prison*) to complete one's sentence. **3** [1970s+] (*drugs*) to stop using drugs altogether or to progress to stronger drugs. [(1) modern use mainly US Black]

graf *n.* [1990s+] *graf*fiti; also attrib. [abbr.]

graf-head *n.* (*also* graffer) [1980s+] (*orig. US Black*) a graffiti artist. [GRAF n. + -HEAD sfx (4)]

graft *n.*[1] [mid-19C+] efforts, hard work, usu. physical, labouring work. [? fig. use of SE *graft*, the depth of earth that may be thrown up at once with a spade]

graft *n.*[2] **1** [mid-19C+] any form of illicit, underhand – but not necessarily criminal – money-making. **2** [mid-19C+] (*UK Und.*) one's criminal speciality. **3** [late 19C+] corruption. **4** [late 19C–1940s] (*US*) an easy job or sinecure. **5** [late 19C] (*US Und.*) an act of theft. **6** [late 19C+] work, esp. in the context of working to take up or waste time. **7** [20C+] the proceeds of corruption, political bribery etc. **8** [1910s–20s] influence. [? link to GRAFT n.[1] or fig. use of SE *graft*, to insert or fix in or upon something]

graft *v.*[1] [late 16C–18C] **1** to cuckold. **2** to have sexual, or anal, intercourse. [SE *graft*, to fix onto; in (1) the cuckold's HORNS n.]

graft *v.*[2] [mid-19C+] to work hard, to make an effort, to struggle. [GRAFT n.[1]]

graft *v.*[3] **1** [mid-19C+] to acquire (money) through trickery, fraud. **2** [mid-19C+] to steal; thus *grafting pal*, one with whom one forms a team of thieves. **3** [20C+] to live as a professional criminal. **4** [20C+] to acquire political gain though bribery or extortion. **5** [20C+] to fool, to hoax. **6** [1910s] to take bribes. **7** [1910s] to live as a parasite. **8** [1930s–50s] (*US*) to bribe. **9** [1950s] in a non-criminal context, to pretend, to fake. [GRAFT n.[2]]

graft china *n.* [1940s–50s] (*UK prison*) a companion with whom one works regularly, as opposed to a SNOUT CHINA n. [GRAFT n.[1] + CHINA (PLATE) n. (1)]

grafted *adj.* [late 17C–early 19C] cuckolded. [GRAFT v.[1] (1)]

grafter *n.*[1] **1** [mid-19C+] a pickpocket, a thief. **2** [late 19C–1920s] a parasite. **3** [late 19C+] a swindler, esp. one who works at a fair, carnival, mock auction etc. **4** [20C+] one who is involved in corruption. **5** [1930s+] a street salesman, a hawker. [GRAFT v.[3]]

grafter *n.*[2] [20C+] a hard worker, one who perseveres. [GRAFT v.[2]]

grafty *adj.* [20C+] (*US Black*) mean, stingy, miserly. [? GRAFT n.[2] (3) + sfx -*y*]

g-rag *n.* [1950s–60s] (*drugs*) a cloth wrapped round an opium pipe. [? abbr. of GUM n.[3]/GOW n.[1] (2) + SE *rag*]

graham cracker *n.* [2000s] (*US Black*) one who is mixed-race, usu. Black and White. [the tan-coloured sweet cracker (biscuit) invented by Sylvester Graham (1795–1851), a promoter of temperance, vegetarianism and wholewheat flour]

grain *n.* [2000s] (*US teen*) money (cf. ACTUAL, THE n.). [var. on CORN n.[1]]

gram *n.* **1** [late 19C–1960s] a tele*gram*. **2** [1900s–70s] a *gramo*phone. [abbr.]

gram-fed *adj.* [late 19C] (*Anglo-Ind.*) getting the best of everything, living 'in the lap of luxury'. [SE *gram*, chick-pea, usu. as *gram-flour*, an ingredient of Indian cooking]

grammel *v.* [20C+] (*Irish*) to grope for, to fumble at. [? SE *grope* + *fumble*]

gramp *n.* (*also* **grampa, gramps, grampy**) [late 19C+] a grandfather. [dial.]

granary *n.* [mid-19C] the stomach.

grand *n.*[1] (*also* **gran, grands**) [1910s+] (*orig. US*) 1000, usu. dollars or pounds.

grand *n.*[2] *see* GRANDSTAND PLAY n.

grand *adj.*[1] [early 19C+] a general term of approval, magnificent, splendid.

grand *adj.*[2] [20C+] (*W.I.*) proud but impoverished, unwilling to take charity no matter how much it might be needed.

grand *v. see* GRANDSTAND V.

grand *adv.* **1** [mid-19C–1900s] in an excellent, well-funded manner. **2** [late 19C+] to a great extent.

grand bag *n.* [1940s–70s] (*gay*) a large scrotum (cf. BALL-BAG n.). [SE *grand* + BAG n.[1] (1)]

grand bounce, the *n. see* BOUNCE, THE n.

Grand Canyon *n.* (*also* **Lincoln Tunnel**) [1970s+] (*US gay*) a loose anus; thus *Grand Canyon Suite*, noisy, sloppy-sounding anal intercourse. (cf. ALLEY WAY n.).

Grand Central Station *n.* [1960s+] (*US gay*) the scarred arm of a long-term heroin user. [pun on the numerous SE *tracks*/TRACKS n.[2]]

grand charge *n.* [20C+] (*W.I.*) an empty bluff, loud but hollow boasting. [Fr. *grand*, great, big + *charge*, exaggeration]

grand charge *v.* (*also* **make grand charge**) [20C+] (*W.I./UK Black*) to present a false but self-aggrandizing image. [GRAND CHARGE n.]

granddad *n.* (*also* **grandpa**) [20C+] any old man, there is no need for a blood relationship.

grand-daddy *n.* [20C+] the extreme example, the most outstanding (of a kind). [ext. of DADDY n. (6)]

grand duchess *n.* [1950s+] (*gay*) **1** a heterosexual woman who occupies pride of place in a homosexual male coterie. **2** an experienced, older, sophisticated homosexual man (cf. DUCHESS n.[1]). [on the model of QUEEN n.[2] (1)]

grandfather *n.*[1] (*also* **grandmother**) [late 19C+] a general intensifier, added to a n.; thus *a grandmother of a...*

grandfather *n.*[2] [20C+] the penis (cf. ALMOND n.). [rhy. sl.; *grandfather clock* = COCK n.[1] (1)]

grandies *n.* [1990s+] (*N.Z.*) *grand*parents. [abbr.]

grandma *n.*[1] [1940s+] (*US*) the lowest gear of a vehicle. [the image of a slow-driving grandmother]

grandma *n.*[2] [1970s+] (*US gay*) an old(er) homosexual; thus *grandpa*, an ageing lesbian (cf. AUNTIE n.[2]).

grandma change *n.* [1930s–40s] (*US Black*) a very rich person.

grandma (George) *n.* (*also* **George**) [1950s+] (*US*) menstruation; thus *grandma's coming*; *George called*; *George is visiting*. [euph.]

grandmother *n.*[1] [1960s] the vagina.

grandmother *n.*[2] *see* GRANDFATHER n.[1].

grandpa *n.*[1] *see* GRANDDAD n.

grandpa *n.*[2] *see* GRANDMA n.[2].

grandpappy *n.* (*also* **granpappy**) [1940s] a grandfather.

grand quay *n.* [mid-19C–1910s] (*US Und.*) a state prison. [? SE *dock*]

grands *n. see* GRAND n.[1].

grand slam *n.* [2000s] simultaneous vomiting and defecation.

grandstand *n. see* GRANDSTAND PLAY n.

grandstand *v.* (*also* **grand**) [20C+] to make oneself conspicuous, to show off. [GRANDSTAND PLAY n.]

grandstand-artist *n.* (*also* **grandstand-jockey, -player**) [1920s+] (*US*) an exhibitionist, a show-off. [GRANDSTAND v. + ARTIST sfx/JOCKEY n.[3] (2)/SE *player*]

grandstand play *n.* (*also* **grand, grandstand, grandstand eye**) [late 19C+] (*US*) a conspicuous, often ostentatious, action. [sporting imagery: one 'plays' to the audience in the grandstand]

grand strut *n.* [mid-19C] used of various fashionable promenading areas of London, e.g. Rotten Row or the Broad Walk in Hyde Park or Bond Street, W1. [SE *grand* + *strut*]

grand theft *n.* [1960s] (*US Black*) a large amount of (stolen) money. [US legal jargon *grand theft* synon. for *grand larceny*, the theft of sums exceeding a figure established by local penal codes]

grand tour *n.* [1980s+] (*US campus*) the trad. tour undertaken by recently graduated US college students in Europe. [SE *grand tour*, a similar tour undertaken, esp. during 18C–19C, by England's young aristocrats]

grand Turk *n.* [mid-19C] a boastful, arrogant person. [SE *Grand Turk*, the Sultan of Turkey]

granger *n.* [late 19C–1930s] (*US*) a farmer or countryman. [SAmE *Granger*, a member of the Patrons of Husbandry (a farmers' organization)]

granite boulder *n.* [late 19C+] a shoulder. [rhy. sl.]

granite-boy *n.* [mid-19C+] a native of New Hampshire, known for its granite quarries.

granite jug *n.* [1930s–50s] Dartmoor prison, west Devon. [SE *granite* + JUG n.[2] (1)]

granite-rocked *adj.* [late 19C] totally penniless. [STONE BROKE adj.]

grannam *n.*[1] [mid-16C–early 19C] corn. [SE *grain*/*granary*]

grannam *n.*[2] (*also* **grannum**) [17C–early 19C] a grandmother; thus a term of address to an old woman. [SE *grand-dam*]

grannam-gold *n.* (*also* **grannam's gold**) [late 17C–mid-19C] old, hoarded coin. [GRANNAM n.[2] + SE *gold*, lit. 'grandmother gold']

grannie *see under* GRANNY.

grannies *adj.* [1960s] (*Aus.*) all right, satisfactory; usu. in phr. *she'll be grannies*, it will be all right. [*Granny Smith*, a brand of apple; originated in Aus. and named for Maria Ann 'Granny' Smith (d.1870); thus synon. APPLES adj.]

grannum *n. see* GRANNAM n.[2].

Granny *n.* [late 19C+] (*Aus.*) the *Sydney Morning Herald*. [? its style and attitudes]

granny *n.*[1] (*also* **grannie**) **1** [late 18C–mid-19C; 1950s+] an old woman. **2** [late 18C–1900s] (*Aus.*) nonsense, rubbish, 'old wives' tales'; usu. in MY GRANNY! excl. **3** [mid-19C+] (*orig. naut.*) a badly tied knot which will not hold. **4** [20C+] a fussy person, not necessarily old or female. **5** [1920s+] a grandmother. **6** [1940s–50s] (*UK Und.*) a legitimate business that serves only as a front for criminal activities. **7** [1950s+] (*US*) menstruation; thus (*Aus./US*) *granny's coming*, a woman is menstruating. **8** [1970s+] (*US*) the lowest (thus slowest) gear of a vehicle. [all based on the stereotyped characteristics of a SE *granny*/*grandmother*]

granny *n.*[2] (*also* **grannie**) [mid-19C+] (*US*) a dollar. [ety. unknown]

granny *n.*[3] **1** [mid-19C] knowledge, importance, pride; thus *take the granny off*, to humiliate, to 'bring down a peg', thus to make dirty. **2** [late 19C] a knowledgeable person. [? the supposed experience of a grandmother, or phr. *teach your grandmother to suck eggs*]

granny *n.*[4] [2000s] (*UK Und.*) the essence, the 'guts', e.g. *bash the granny out of*.

granny *v.*[1] **1** [mid-19C] to swindle, to cheat. **2** [20C+] to defeat comprehensively, to allow one's opponent no score at all. **3** [1910s–20s] to disguise oneself. [the wolf's disguise in the story of 'Little Red Riding Hood']

granny v.[2] [mid-19C] **1** to recognize, to understand. **2** (*UK Und.*) to survey, to look over (prior to a robbery).

granny chills n. see GRANNY GRUNT n.[2].

granny-dodger n. [1960s–70s] **1** (*US Black*) a contemptible person. **2** (*US prison*) a rapist of elderly women. [GRANNY n.[1] (5) + SE *dodge*, as a euph. for MOTHERFUCKER n. (1); on pattern of MAMMY-DODGER n.; (2) extrapolated backwards f. (1)]

granny-dodging adj. [1960s–70s] contemptible. [GRANNY-DODGER n. (1)]

granny grunt n.[1] [20C+] a fussy, irritating person, although not necessarily female or old. [rhy. sl. = CUNT n.[2] (1)]

granny grunt n.[2] (*also* **granny chills**) [20C+] (*US*) a stomach ache, menstruation.

granny grunt n.[3] [1930s–40s] (*US Black*) a mythical figure to whom otherwise unanswerable questions are referred.

granny-jazzer n. [1970s–80s] (*US*) a euph. for MOTHERFUCKER n. (1). [GRANNY n.[1] (5) + JAZZ v.[1] (1)]

granny-jazzing adj. [1960s] (*US*) a euph. for MOTHERFUCKING adj. (1). [GRANNY-JAZZER n.]

granny lane n. [1970s+] (*US*) the right or slow lane of a highway. [the stereotyped cautious driving of old women]

granny rag n. [1950s+] (*US*) homemade sanitary towels, made of pieces of cloth. [GRANNY n.[1] (7)]

granny's coming phr. see GRANNY n.[1] (7).

granny's wrinkle n. [20C+] a winkle (a form of crustacea). [rhy. sl.]

granola(-groid) n. [1980s+] (*US campus*) (*also* **granola-head**) a natural-looking person who pursues a healthy lifestyle; an environmentalist; used derog. to indicate one who pursues a 1960s-style lifestyle, a HIPPIE n.[2] (3) (cf. CRUNCHY (GRANOLA) n.). [the supposedly healthy US cereal *Crunchy Granola*]

granpappy n. see GRANDPAPPY n.

grape n.[1] **1** [17C+] (*also* **grapes**) wine. **2** [late 19C+] any form of liquor.

grape n.[2] [1970s+] (*US prison*) an alcoholic.

grape n.[3] see GRAPEVINE n.[1].

grape-cat n. [1940s] (*US Black*) an alcoholic who prefers wine to other drinks; thus the female version, *grape-chick*. [GRAPE n.[1] (1) + CAT n.[11] (4)/CHICK n.[4] (2)]

grapefruit n. [1960s–80s] usu. in pl., the female breasts (cf. APPLES n.[1]). [resemblance]

grape juice n. (*also* **juice of the grape**) [mid-19C+] (*orig. US*) wine.

grape-monger n. [early 17C] a wine-drinker.

grape-nut n. [1980s+] (*US campus*) one who identifies with the styles and concerns of the 1960s. [the healthiness of the breakfast cereal, *Grape-Nuts*]

grape on the business n. [1940s+] (*Aus.*) **1** a puritan. **2** a bore, one who depresses or irritates the company by their presence. [? SE phr. *sour grapes*]

grape parfait n. [1970s+] (*drugs*) LSD (cf. A n.[3]). [when packaged in purple pills]

grapes n.[1] **1** [1950s–70s] (*Aus./US Black*) haemorrhoids. **2** [1980s] the female breasts (cf. APPLES n.[1]). **3** [1990s+] the testicles (cf. ACORNS n.[1]). [resemblance]

grapes n.[2] [1960s–70s] (*US Black*) money (cf. ALFALFA n.; BANANAS n.[3]). [the colour/the 'richness' of wine]

grapes n.[3] [2000s] (*US prison*) gossip. [it grows on the GRAPEVINE n.[1]]

grapes n.[4] see GRAPE n.[1] (1).

grapeshot adj. [19C] drunk (cf. ALED UP adj.). [play on SE and GRAPE n.[1] (1) + pattern of CUPSHOT adj.]

grape society n. [1930s–50s] (*US Black*) an ironic dignification of a group of wine-drinkers standing around on a street corner. [GRAPE n.[1] (1) + play on SE *great society*]

grapes of wrath n. [1940s] (*US Black*) wine. [GRAPE n.[1] (1); the

biblical use + the then-recent publication of John Steinbeck's novel *The Grapes of Wrath* (1939)]

grape-stomper n. [1940s+] any person of Mediterranean origin, e.g. Italian, French, Spanish, Portuguese, Greek (cf. DAGO n.). [the viticulture practised in these countries]

grapevine n.[1] (*also* **grape**) [mid-19C+] a network of unofficial sources, rumours, half-truths etc, which seems to spread the news around a circle or group faster than any sanctioned announcement; coined during US Civil War and abbr. of 'a despatch by grape-vine telegraph'.

grapevine n.[2] [20C+] a washing-line. [rhy. sl.]

grapevine cinch n. [late 19C] (*US*) a certainty. [GRAPEVINE n.[1]+ CINCH n.[1] (1); however, somewhat pardoxical given the innate unreliability of such communications]

grapevine telegraph n. [mid-19C–1970s] (*US*) a network of unofficial communications. [GRAPEVINE n.[1] + BUSH TELEGRAPH n. (2)]

grapevine wireless n. [1930s] (*US*) a network of unofficial communications. [GRAPEVINE n.[1] + SE *wireless*]

grapey adj. [mid-19C] (*US*) grumpy. [? through an excess of the GRAPE n.[1] (1)]

graph n. [1970s+] (*US*) a para*graph*. [abbr.]

grappler n. (*also* **mug-grappler**) [mid-19C] a hand; thus *grapplers*, fingers. [SE *grapple*]

grapples n. [mid–late 19C] the hands. [SE *grapple*]

grapple the rails n. [18C–early 19C] (*Irish*) a glass of rough whisky. [its effects; one hangs on to keep upright]

grappling hooks n. [late 19C+] (*US*) fingers or hands. [SE *grapple* + HOOK n.[1] (1)]

grappling irons n. **1** [early–mid-19C] handcuffs. **2** [mid-19C–1910s] (*also* **grabbling irons**) the fingers. **3** [late 19C] (*US*) spurs. [(3) note synon. use in WW1 Aus. milit.]

grap up v. [2000s] to spray graffiti. [? pron. of GRAF n. used as a v.]

grass n.[1] **1** [early 18C; mid-19C+] pubic hair. **2** [1910s–50s] hair; thus *cut the grass*, to cut one's hair. [note *double entendre* in D'Urfey, *Pills to Purge Melancholy* (1719–20): 'But what if my Nag [i.e. penis] should chance to slip in, / [...] / Then catch hold of the Grass that grows on the brim']

grass n.[2] [mid-19C+] green vegetables, esp. asparagus. [asparagus use SE in 18C]

grass n.[3] [late 19C–1900s] sexual intercourse. [var. on GREENS n.[2]]

grass n.[4] [1920s+] an informer. [rhy. sl.; *grasshopper* = SHOPPER n.; note GRASSHOPPER n.[3]]

grass n.[5] [1930s+] marijuana (cf. AFRICAN BUSH n.). [note WW1 Aus. milit. *grass*, Army issue tobacco]

grass v.[1] **1** [19C] (*orig. boxing*) (*also* **send to grass**) to knock down. **2** [mid-19C–1900s] to kill, to defeat. [i.e. to knock onto the *grass* (boxing orig. took place on grass)]

grass v.[2] (*also* **grass someone up**) [1930s+] to inform, to tell tales, to betray. [GRASS n.[4]]

grass v.[3] [1940s+] (*US Black*) to have sexual intercourse outdoors, esp. lit. on the grass.

grassback n. [1960s] (*US campus*) a promiscuous young woman, or one who has been branded as such (cf. GRASS SANDWICH n.; GREEN GOWN n.). [her supposed propensity for alfresco intercourse]

grass before breakfast n. [mid-18C–mid-19C] (*Irish*) a duel. [? *grace before breakfast* or GO TO GRASS v. (1)]

grass-eater n. [1970s+] (*US*) a policeman who accepts small bribes; thus *grass-eating*.

grasser n. [1940s+] an informer. [GRASS v.[2]]

grass-fighter n. [1950s+] (*Aus.*) **1** a bare-knuckle boxer; thus *grass-fighting*, bare-knuckle boxing. **2** one who fights in public rather than in the prize-ring. **3** anyone known for losing their temper and brawling in public. [fighting on the grass rather than on canvas; note John Healy's book *The Grass Arena* (1988)]

grasshead *n.* [1960s+] (*drugs*) a regular smoker of marijuana. [GRASS n.[5] + -HEAD sfx (3)]

grasshopper *n.*[1] **1** [mid-19C–1910s] a waiter at a tea-garden. **2** [20C+] (*Aus.*) a waiter at a picnic. [he 'hops across the grass']

grasshopper *n.*[2] [late 19C] a thief. [? he 'hops' from theft to theft]

grasshopper *n.*[3] **1** [20C+] a policeman (cf. BOTTLE (AND STOPPER) n.). **2** [1940s+] an informer. [rhy. sl.; (1) = COPPER n.[3] (1); (2) = SHOPPER n.; (1) note WW1 milit. *grasshopper*, a military policeman; (2) note earlier GRASS n.[4]]

grasshopper *n.*[4] [1930s+] a marijuana user. [GRASS n.[5] + pun]

grasshopper *n.*[5] [1950s+] (*Aus.*) a tourist, esp. one who is visiting Canberra. [they descend on a town or tourist site like a plague of hungry insects]

grasshopper crusher *n. see* BEETLE-CRUSHER n. (2).

grasshopping *adj.* [1940s–50s] tale-telling, informing, thus *grasshopper*, to inform on. [GRASSHOPPER n.[3] (2)]

grass in the park *n.* [1990s+] an informer. [rhy. sl. = NARK n.[1] (1) but note GRASS n.[4]]

grass sandwich *n.* [1910s–50s] (*US*) an alfresco act of sexual intercourse (cf. GRASSBACK n.).

grass-seed *n. see* HAYSEED n.

grass someone up *v. see* GRASS v.[2].

grassville *n.* [late 19C] the countryside. [SE *grass* + -VILLE sfx[1]]

grass widow *n.* **1** [late 17C–19C] a discarded mistress. **2** [18C+] (*orig. Anglo-Ind.*) a woman whose husband is temporarily absent. **3** [mid-19C] an unmarried mother. [(1) A mistress is one who is enjoyed on a temporary straw-mattress or actually in/on the grass, rather than in the feather-filled matrimonial bed; *widow* is ironic, although it denotes that her 'husband' has gone; (2) phr. *out to grass*]

grass widower *n.* [mid-19C+] a man whose wife is temporarily absent. [male var. GRASS WIDOW n. (2)]

grassy *adj.* [1950s] (*Und.*) likely to become an informer. [GRASS n.[4]]

gratters *n.* [1900s–60s] (*school/campus*) congratulations. [abbr. SE + -ER sfx]

graum *v.* [1950s] (*US*) to worry; thus *the graums*, worries, depression, 'the blues'. [ety. unknown]

gravalicious *adj.* [1950s+] (*W.I. Rasta*) covetous (cf. GRABALICIOUS adj.). [SE *greedy* + *avaricious*/-LICIOUS sfx]

grave-bait *n.* [1940s] a young girl, flirtatious and sexy, but linked to a powerful and dangerous man.

grave-digger *n.*[1] [late 19C] (*Anglo-Ind.*) strong drink. [alcohol often proved fatal to White men in India]

grave-digger *n.*[2] [late 19C+] the spade suit in cards. [resemblance; var. on DIGGER n.[1] (3)]

grave-digger *n.*[3] [1910s+] a Black person. [rhy. sl. = NIGGER n.[1] (1) + ref. to SPADE n.]

gravel *n.* **1** [1900s–30s] (*US*) granulated sugar. **2** [1980s+] (*drugs*) crack cocaine (cf. BASE n.). [consistency; (2) plays on ROCK n.[3] (4)]

gravel *v.* **1** [late 16C–mid-17C; 19C] to confound, to confuse. **2** [18C; mid-19C+] (*orig. US*) to annoy, to irritate. [the rubbing action of *gravel* e.g. on the bottom of a boat]

gravel-agitator *n.* (*also* **gravel-grinder**, **gravel-walloper**) [late 19C+] (*US*) an infantryman. [his marching and drilling]

gravel-crusher *n.* **1** [mid-19C+] (*also* **mud-crusher**) an infantryman; thus *gravel-crushing*, marching. **2** [late 19C+] (*Anglo-Irish*) a tramp. **3** [20C+] (*Anglo-Irish*) a heavy boot, typically worn by a farmer or agricultural worker.

gravel-digger *n.* [mid-19C] an agile dancer.

gravel-grinder *n.*[1] [mid-19C] a drunkard, esp. one who has a drunken fall and scratches their face. [their drunken falling to the ground]

gravel-grinder *n.*[2] *see* GRAVEL-AGITATOR n.

gravelled *adj.* [20C+] drunk. [lit. falling on the *gravel* but note STONED (OUT) adj. (1)]

gravel-path *n.* [1900s] (*Aus.*) the human hair. [the SE *gravel-path* is raked, the hair is combed; both for neatness]

gravel rash *n.* [mid-19C–1940s] abrasions caused by a fall on a gravely or uneven surface, esp. in the context of drunkenness.

gravel tax *n.* [mid-19C] (*UK Und.*) the proceeds of street robbery.

gravel train *n.* [1910s–30s] **1** (*US Und.*) (*also* **gravel wagon**) a go-between for lobbyists who buy up legislators. **2** (*US*) a sugar bowl. [(2) GRAVEL n. (1)]

gravel-walloper *n. see* GRAVEL-AGITATOR n.

grave noddy *n.* [early 18C] an unpleasant person. [SE *grave*, serious + NODDY n.[1]]

graves *n.* [1910s–20s] long, dirty fingernails. [they are filled with dirt]

Gravesend bus *n.* [late 19C–1910s] a hearse. [pun on the town of *Gravesend*/the grave is at 'the end of the line']

Gravesend sweetmeats *n.* [mid-late 19C] shrimps. [*Gravesend*, a town on the Thames estuary]

Gravesend twins *n.* [mid-19C] solid pieces of excrement. [the sewerage outfall at *Gravesend*]

gravestones *n.* [20C+] (*US*) **1** prominent front teeth. **2** false teeth. [resemblance]

graveyard *n.*[1] [19C–1930s] the mouth. [the supposed resemblance of the teeth to tombstones]

graveyard *n.*[2] [1980s+] (*US*) the least desirable seats in a restaurant. [they represent social 'death']

graveyard *n.*[3] *see* GRAVEYARD SHIFT n.

graveyarder *n. see* CHURCHYARD COUGH n.

graveyard juice *n.* [1940s–50s] (*US*) whisky. [the fatal effects of excessive drinking]

graveyard shift *n.* (*also* **graveyard**, **graveyard trick**) [20C+] the overnight shift, the late shift; the personnel who work that shift. [usu. in the context of paid employment, but also used of gamblers, prostitutes and any other late-night 'workers']

graveyard stew *n.* (*also* **graveyard poultice**, **graveyard soup**) [late 19C–1940s] (*US*) milk toast. [such toast is generally given to the ill; thus the idea that once his or her appetite has been reduced to such a meal the sufferer has nowhere to go but the graveyard]

graveyard widow *n.* [20C+] (*US*) an actual widow, whose husband is dead.

graviers *n.* [mid-16C–early 17C] (*UK Und.*) crooked dice. [perhaps f. Fr. *grave*, heavy, given that the weight of crooked dice was generally affected in one way or another; however, the *OED* suggests poss. alternative sp. of *graniers* (cited in Thomas Dekker, *The Bellman of London*, 1608), which offers no obvious origin]

gravney *n.* [mid-late 19C] a ring. [ety. unknown]

gravy *n.*[1] **1** [late 17C–early 18C; 1920s+] vaginal secretions; thus *gravy bowl*, the vagina (cf. BINDERJUICE n.). **2** [18C+] semen; thus GRAVY-GIVER n.; *gravy-receiver*, the vagina (cf. BABY GRAVY n.). **3** [mid-19C] blood (cf. BADMINTON n.). **4** [1970s] sweat.

gravy *n.*[2] **1** [late 19C+] money, esp. profit when easily acquired, a tip or bonus, that comes 'on top of' something that is already very good. **2** [1910s+] (*orig. US*) extras, perquisites, the best. **3** [1910s+] good fortune. **4** [1930s+] (*US*) emotional stimulation. **5** [1940s+] (*Aus.*) any form of tinned food.

gravy *n.*[3] **1** [1960s+] (*drugs*) the mix of blood and heroin solution that is created in a hypodermic syringe before it is reinjected into the vein; it can coagulate while in the syringe and, when this happens, must be heated before the injection; usu. in phr. SHOOT GRAVY v. **2** [1980s+] heroin.

gravy *adj.* (*also* **gravy noodles**) [1930s+] a general term of approbation, easy, privileged, wonderful, perfect.

gravy boat *n.* (*also* **gravy case**) [1940s+] (*US*) a sinecure, a simple, substantially profitable situation from which one can benefit easily. [var. on GRAVY TRAIN n.]

gravy-eyed *adj.* [late 18C–19C] bleary-eyed, having mucus-filled eyes.

gravy-giver *n.* (*also* **gravy-maker**) [19C] **1** the vagina. **2** the penis. [GRAVY n.¹ (1)/GRAVY n.¹ (2) + SE *giver*]

gravy noodles *adj. see* GRAVY adj.

gravy-rider *n.* [1920s–50s] (*US*) a person with an easy job. [GRAVY TRAIN n.]

gravy ring *n.* [20C+] (*Ulster*) a doughnut. [resemblance to a ring of gravy staining a cloth]

gravy street *n.* [1970s] (*US*) an easy, profitable or successful situation. [GRAVY TRAIN n. + EASY STREET n. (2)]

gravy strokes *n. see* VINEGAR STROKES n.

gravy train *n.* [late 19C+] (*orig. US*) a sinecure, a simple, substantially profitable situation from which one can benefit easily; thus RIDE THE GRAVY TRAIN v. [GRAVY n.² (1) + SE *train*; Dillard, *Lexicon of Black English* (1977) suggests the image of a gambler who is in the 'gravy' and thus pursued by a 'train' of those who wish to benefit]

grawl *n. see* GRAAL n.

gray/grey the sp. of gray/grey remains debatable; according to the *OED* there have been various choices over the years, but there seems to have been little real consistency. For the purposes of this dictionary, and based as far as possible on the pre-eminent style of the respective countries, 'gray' is used for US terms and 'grey' for UK/Aus./Irish and other 'Commonwealth' uses.

gray *n.* (*also* **grey**) **1** [1940s+] (*US Black*) a White person. **2** [1980s] (*US campus*) a Black person who behaves like and associates with White people.

gray *adj.* (*also* **grey**) [1940s+] (*orig. US Black*) used of a White person, esp. when racist; usu. in combs., e.g. *gray cat*, a White man; *gray broad*, a White woman; also by 1980s also ext. to a Latino or Chicano. [colour, but also f. what Blacks perceive as the 'colourless' behaviour and character of Whites, esp. the middle classes]

grayback *n.* (*US*) (*also* **graycoat**) **1** [early 19C] a professed Christian. **2** [mid–late 19C] a Confederate soldier in the US Civil War. **3** [mid–late 19C] an unreliable or worthless person. **4** [mid-19C+] a head or body louse. [colour of the (1) dress, (2) uniform or (4) body; (3) fig. use of *grayback*, a treasury note issued by the Confederate government]

graybar hotel *n.* (*also* **greybar hotel**) [1940s+] (*US*) a prison (cf. BOARDING HOUSE n.). [its *grey* walls and steel *bars*]

grayboy *n.* (*also* **gray boy, grey boy**) [1950s+] (*US Black*) a derog. term for a White person. [GRAY adj.+ SE *boy* + conscious counter to the racists' 'black boy']

graycoat *n. see* GRAYBACK n.

gray dog *n.* [1970s+] (*US Black*) the police. [GRAY adj. + DOG n.³ (15)]

gray gal *n.* (*also* **grey chick**) [1950s+] (*US Black*) a White woman. [GRAY adj. + GAL n. (1)/CHICK n.⁴ (2)]

Gray Goose *n.* [1970s+] (*US Und.*) a converted Greyhound bus, painted gray, that is used for transporting prisoners securely between jails, courts etc.

grayhair *n.* (*also* **grayhaired**) [1980s+] (*US campus*) an old person.

gray house *n. see* GRAYSTONE COLLEGE n.

graymail *n.* [1960s+] (*US*) a threat to reveal classified information in court as a form of legal blackmail. [on pattern of *gray imports*, imports that are not illegal as such but that sidestep a country's customs duties]

graymite *n.* [late 19C] (*US*) a vegetarian. [abbr. of *Graham-ite*, from Sylvester Graham (1794–1851), an advocate of vegetarianism]

gray mule *n.* [1900s–10s] (*US*) corn whisky or gin. [MULE n.³ (1)]

grays *n. see* SCOTCH GREYS n.

graystone college *n.* (*also* **gray house, gray-rock hotel,**

graystone hotel, greystone college) [1930s–60s] (*US Und.*) prison (cf. BIG SCHOOL n.).

graze *n.* [1960s+] (*S.Afr.*) food.

graze *v.* **1** [mid-18C; 1950s] (*US prison*) to eat prison food. **2** [1960s+] to eat.

grazer *n.* [1990s+] **1** a person who snacks. **2** (*UK Und.*) a tramp who rifles through rubbish bins for food. [GRAZE v. (2)]

grazie *phr.* [1950s+] (*US campus*) thanks. [synon. Ital.]

greapha *n. see* GREEFO n.

grease *n.¹* **1** [19C+] money, esp. when given as a bribe or paid as protection money. **2** [mid-19C+] flattery, persuasion. **3** [1940s+] (*US*) political influence. [GREASE v.¹ (1)]

grease *n.²* [1910s–50s] (*US drugs*) opium; thus *hit the grease*, to smoke opium; *in the grease pit*, smoking opium (cf. APOSTLE n.). [the viscosity of the drug (cf. GUM n.³)]

grease *n.³* **1** [1910s–60s] (*orig. US campus*) butter or margarine. **2** [1920s+] (*US Black*) vaginal secretions (cf. BINDERJUICE n.). **3** [1950s+] (*gay*) any form of lubricant – KY Jelly etc – that facilitates anal intercourse. [dial. use referring to rancid or second-rate butter; (1) there is no pej. in Aus. use]

grease *n.⁴* [1920s–70s] (*US Black*) a Black man.

grease *n.⁵* [1920s+] (*US Und.*) nitroglycerine.

grease *n.⁶* [1950s+] (*US Black/campus*) a meal, food.

grease *n.⁷* [1960s+] **1** motorcycle riders (Rockers, as opposed to Mods); also collectively as *the grease*. **2** (*US*) a working-class White youth, a member of a HOT-ROD n., motorcycle or teenage gang. [abbr. GREASER n.⁴ (2)]

grease *n.⁸* [1960s+] (*US*) death. [GREASE v.⁵]

grease *v.¹* **1** [mid-16C+] to corrupt, to bribe. **2** [17C] to cheat, to deceive. **3** [20C+] to smooth over problems, esp. from authorities. **4** [20C+] to curry favour with, to toady to. **5** [20C+] to embellish, to add to.

grease *v.²* [1920s–50s] (*US drugs*) to smoke opium. [GREASE n.²]

grease *v.³* [1930s–50s] (*US Und.*) to open a safe using nitroglycerin. [GREASE n.⁵]

grease *v.⁴* (*US*) **1** [1930s+] (*also* **grease down**) to eat. **2** [1940s] in fig. use, to fellate.

grease *v.⁵* [1960s+] (*orig. US milit.*) to kill.

grease *v.⁶ see* GREASE (DOWN) v.

grease *v.⁷ see* GREASE (OFF) v.

grease a man in the fist *v.* [late 16C–early 19C] to bribe someone. [ext. GREASE v.¹ (1)]

grease and lease *v.* [1960s+] (*gay*) to have anal intercourse (cf. ASK FOR THE RING v.). [GREASE n.³ (3)]

greaseball *n.* **1** [1910s+] (*orig. US milit.*) (*also* **greaseball grunt**) a short-order cook, a kitchen worker. **2** [1910s+] (*US*) any filthy or offensive person; thus the lowest category of tramp. **3** [1920s+] (*orig. US*) a derog. description of any Latin race, Italians, Greeks, Puerto Ricans, various South Americans etc (cf. BATO n.; DAGO n.). **4** [1930s+] (*US*) an automobile factory worker; a garage mechanic. **5** [1950s+] (*orig. US*) a derog. term of address to a Latin. [SE *grease* + -BALL sfx]

greasebox *n.* [1990s+] the vagina (cf. BAG n.¹). [GREASE n.³ (2)]

greaseburger *n.* (*also* **greasebomb**) [1960s+] (*US*) a very greasy or unappetizing hamburger.

grease-burner *n.* (*also* **burner**) [1920s–60s] (*US*) a cook.

greased *adj.* [1920s–50s] (*US*) drunk.

greased mitt *n.* [1920s–40s] (*US*) anyone who has been bribed. [GREASE v.¹ (1) + MITT n. (3)]

grease down *v. see* GREASE v.⁴ (1).

grease (down) *v.* [1980s+] (*US campus*) to have sexual intercourse. [GREASE n.³ (2); vaginal secretions and/or semen]

grease-gun *n.* [1940s+] an automatic weapon. [it goes as fast as 'greased lightning']

grease gut *n.* [1960s] (*US*) a derog. term for a Mexican or Mexican-American (cf. BATO n.). [var. on GREASEBALL n. (3)]

grease-hand *n.* (*also* **grease-palm**) [1970s] (*W.I.*) a bribe. [GREASE n.[1] (1)/GREASE v.[1] (1) + SE hand/palm]

greasehound *n.* [1910s–40s] (*US*) a mechanic. [SE grease + HOUND sfx]

grease job *n.*[1] [1940s+] (*US*) **1** a bribe. **2** insincere flattery. [GREASE n.[1] + JOB n.[4]]

grease job *n.*[2] [1950s+] anal intercourse using Vaseline, KY Jelly or a similar lubricant. [GREASE n.[3] (3) + JOB n.[4]]

grease joint *n.* [1910s+] (*US*) **1** a cheap or inferior restaurant. **2** a hamburger or hot dog stand. [SE grease + JOINT n.[4] (3)]

grease-man *n.* [1970s] (*US Und.*) a safe-blower who uses nitroglycerine. [GREASE n.[5] + SE man]

grease monkey *n.* (*also* **grease-monk**) [1920s+] a mechanic. [SE grease + MONKEY n.[2] (3)]

grease (off) *v.* [mid-19C–1920s] **1** (*also* **do a grease**) to slip away. **2** to go away.

grease one's chops *v.* [1920s–70s] (*US Black*) to eat, esp. to eat very greasy food. [SE grease/GREASE v.[4] (1) + CHOPS n.[1] (1)]

grease one's gills *v.* (*also* **grease the gills**) [late 19C–1900s] to eat heartily and substantially. [SE grease/GREASE v.[4] (1) + GILLS n. (1)]

grease one's mitts *v.* [20C+] (*US*) to accept/solicit bribes (cf. GREASE SOMEONE'S PALM v.). [SE grease/GREASE v.[1] (1) + MITT n. (3)]

grease one's throat *v.* (*also* **grease one's tonsils**) [1900s–10s] (*US*) to drink alcohol.

grease-palm *n. see* GREASE-HAND n.

grease parlor *n.* [1940s] (*US Black*) a hairdresser's, a beauty parlour.

grease patty *n.* [1990s+] (*US prison*) prison-cooked, chicken-fried steak.

grease pit *n.* **1** [1950s–70s] (*US drugs*) anywhere a drug seller sets up their business. **2** [1960s] an unpleasant place. **3** [1960s+] a cheap restaurant. [(1) GREASE n.[2]; (2) SE; (3) GREASE n.[6]]

grease pot *n.* [1910s–60s] (*US*) a cook, orig. and usu. in a prison or camp.

grease-pusher *n.* [1950s] (*US*) a mechanic.

greaser *n.*[1] **1** [mid-19C+] (*orig. US*) a derog. term for a Mexican, orig. as an inhabitant of Spanish California and thus a member of another Latin race (cf. BATO n.). **2** [late 19C+] a Spaniard, or an object pertaining to Spain, e.g. a vessel. **3** [1900s] the Spanish language. **4** [1970s+] a native of the Middle East or the Indian subcontinent (cf. ABDUL n.). [note RMC Duntroon (Aus.) *greaso*, an Italian or Greek; note Asbury, *The Barbary Coast* (1933): 'According to Hubert Howe Bancroft in his *California Pastoral* [1888], this term was first applied by the Spaniards to the American and English traders who bought hides and tallow. The traders promptly transferred the appellation to the Spaniards who sold these products, and it soon became a term of contempt applied to all Spanish-Americans, and particularly to Mexicans']

greaser *n.*[2] **1** [late 19C+] (*US*) an objectionable person. **2** [20C+] a sycophant. **3** [1960s] (*US campus*) a person who studies a great deal. [GREASE v.[1]]

greaser *n.*[3] [1930s–70s] (*US Black*) an enthusiastic eater, esp. of soul food. [GREASE v.[4] (1)]

greaser *n.*[4] **1** [1950s+] a 1950s Teddy boy, his hair styled with Brylcreem or a similar unguent. **2** [1960s+] (*orig. US*) a member of a motorcycle gang or (*Calif.*) a HOT-RODDER n. **3** [1970s+] (*US campus*) an old-fashioned person, whose style harks back to 1950s youth cults. [the greasiness of the youths' hair (and the motors with which they tinker)]

greaser *n.*[5] [1950s+] (*N.Z.*) a fall, a setback; esp. in phr. **come a greaser**, to fall (lit. or fig.).

greaser *n.*[6] [1960s] a finger.

greaser *adj.* [mid-19C+] (*US*) a derog. ref. to a Mexican/Latin person or culture. [GREASER n.[1] (1)]

greaser yacht *n.* [1980s] (*orig. US*) a large flashy car, as driven by Mexicans. [GREASER n.[1] (1) + SE yacht]

grease someone's duke *v.* [late 19C] **1** to hand over money. **2** to give a bribe. [GREASE v.[1] (1) + DUKE n.[3] (1)]

grease someone's hide *v.* [late 19C] (*US*) to whip someone.

grease someone's palm *v.* (*also* **grease someone's fist, …mitt, grease the palm**) [late 17C+] to bribe (cf. GREASE ONE'S MITTS v.). [GREASE v.[1] (1) + SE/MITT n. (3)]

greasespot *n.* [mid-19C+] (*US*) **1** an infinitesimally tiny quantity. **2** the fig. state to which one is reduced either after losing a violent fight or suffering extremely hot weather.

grease stop *n.* [1980s+] (*US*) a stop for refreshment during a bus or car journey. [var. GREASE JOINT n.]

grease the gash *v.* [20C+] of a woman, to masturbate (cf. APPLY LIP GLOSS v.). [SE grease v. + GASH n.[1] (1)]

grease the gills *v. see* GREASE ONE'S GILLS v.

grease the palm *v. see* GREASE SOMEONE'S PALM v.

grease the rails *v.* (*also* **grease the track**) [1910s–40s] (*US*) to be run over by a train; to commit suicide by throwing oneself on the tracks. [ironic use of SE]

grease the weasel *v.* [1990s+] (*US teen*) to have sexual intercourse (cf. BURY IT v.). [SE grease + WEASEL n.[3]]

grease the wheel *v.* [mid-19C–1900s] to have sexual intercourse.

grease-trap *n.* [1980s] (*US*) a lunch counter.

grease-trough *n.* [1940s] (*US*) a lunch counter.

grease up *v.* [1970s+] (*Aus. prison/US gay*) to prepare with a lubricant for anal sex. [GREASE n.[3] (3)]

grease-wagon *n.* [1960s] (*US*) a cheap restaurant or mess-hall.

greasies *n.* [1960s] (*N.Z.*) fish and chips or some form of take-away fast food.

greasy *n.*[1] (*Aus./N.Z./US*) **1** [late 19C+] a cook, esp. in an institution. **2** [1920s–30s] a butcher. **3** [1960s+] a seller of fast or take-away food.

greasy *n.*[2] [1930s+] a shearer. [SE greasy, wool that has not yet been cleaned]

greasy *n.*[3] *see* GREASY (MOP) n.

greasy *adj.*[1] [1960s–70s] (*US Black*) anything that is simultaneously appalling and appealing. [fatty food is both tasty and bad for one's health]

greasy *adj.*[2] [1970s] (*US drugs*) anything concerning drugs and their sale. [GREASE n.[1] (1)]

greasy as a butcher's apron *phr.* (*also* **greasy as bad bacon**) [late 19C; 1940s–60s] (*Aus./N.Z.*) very greasy or slippery.

greasy bag *n.* [1970s] (*US drugs*) a bag in which heroin is transported and/or sold. [GREASY adj.[2] + BAG n.[11] (1)]

greasy chin *n.* **1** [mid-18C–early 19C] a treat given to parish officers in recompense for registering the birth of a bastard. **2** [mid-19C] a dinner. [the effects of the treat or dinner]

greasy corner *n.* [20C+] (*US*) any poor area or settlement, esp. that occupied by Blacks and poor Whites. [SE greasy, i.e. the stereotypically pork-based diet of such impoverished groups]

greasy fingers *n.* [1930s–40s] (*US Black*) a pickpocket. [objects 'stick' to such fingers]

greasy grind *n.* [late 19C+] (*US campus*) one who is seen by their peers as overly hard-working and as such socially unacceptable.

greasy guts *n.* [1940s] (*US*) a fat person. [SE greasy + -GUTS sfx]

greasy junkie *n.* [1960s] (*US drugs*) a heroin addict who maintains their own supplies by running errands for dealers or by prostitution. [SE greasy, i.e. they 'slither around' + JUNKIE n. (1)]

greasy Mac *n.* [1980s] (*US*) any fast-food restaurant. [proper name *McDonalds*, purveyors of fast-food; development of GREASY SPOON n.[1]]

greasy (mop) *n.* [20C+] (*Aus.*) a policeman (cf. BOTTLE (AND STOPPER) n.). [rhy. sl. = COP n.[1] (1)]

greasy spoon *n.*[1] (*also* **dirty spoon**) [1910s+] a cheap café or restaurant. [the state of its cutlery and the texture of its product; note RMC Duntroon (Aus.) *greasy*, a shop that sells GREASIES n.]

greasy spoon n.[2] [1980s+] (*Aus. prison*) a lout or hooligan. [rhy. sl. = HOON n. (2)]

great adj.[1] [late 17C+] (*Irish*) close, very friendly; thus *great with*, close to, esp. of lovers; *great as shirt and shitten arse*, very intimate indeed.

great adj.[2] [late 18C+] wonderful, excellent. [SE 20C+]

great adj.[3] [20C+] (*W.I.*) proud but impoverished, unwilling to take charity however much it might be needed. [abbr. POOR-GREAT adj.]

great adv. [late 19C+] excellently.

great! excl. [late 19C+] an excl. of approval, often in ironic use. [GREAT adj.[2]]

great as shirt and shitten arse phr. see GREAT adj.[1].

great balls of fire! excl. [20C+] (*orig. US*) an excl. of surprise, amazement.

great bounce n. [late 19C] (*US*) death. [SE *great* + BOUNCE, THE n.]

great Caesar! excl. (*also* **great Caesar's ghost!**) [mid-19C+] a mild oath, a euph. for *great God!*

great divide, the n. **1** [20C+] the vagina (cf. ANTIPODES n.). **2** [1930s+] (*Aus.*) the cleavage between a woman's breasts. [pun on the *Great Divide*, in the Blue Mountains, or the US equivalent in the Rocky Mountains, cited in the celebrated poem 'Eskimo Nell']

greatest, the adj. [1940s+] (*US*) excellent.

great gas n. [1910s+] (*Irish*) something, or someone, extremely enjoyable. [SE *great* + GAS n.[3]]

great golly! excl. see GOLLY! excl.

great gun n. **1** [19C+] an important, powerful, influential person, usu. a man. **2** [mid-19C] a successful enterprise. **3** [1910s–20s] a cheerful rogue.

great guns adv. [19C+] energetically, successfully, violently, loudly; esp. in phr. GO GREAT GUNS v. and, in ref. to gale-force winds, to BLOW GREAT GUNS v.

great guns! excl. [19C+] (*US*) a general excl. of surprise or annoyance.

great heavens! excl. see HEAVENS! excl.

great house n. [mid-19C] the workhouse. [its size in comparison with the homes its inmates might have had]

great I am, the n. (*also* **the big I am**) **1** [mid-19C+] a self-important person. **2** [1920s–30s] (*W.I.*) God; also as excl. [the *locus classicus* is in the career of the US confidence trickster Guy Ballard, who set up a whole cult under the title 'The Great I Am', which mulcted the deserving gullible of hundreds of thousands of dollars of 'love gifts' in 1934–9]

great joseph n. [18C–early 19C] (*UK Und.*) an overcoat. [ext. JOSEPH n. (1); the biblical *Joseph*'s 'coat of many colours']

great Kiwi clobbering machine see CLOBBERING MACHINE n.

great national indoor game n. see NATIONAL INDOOR GAME n.

great on adv. [mid–late 19C] expert in, knowing a great deal about. [var. on SE *great at/in*]

great pip! excl. [1900s–60s] an excl. of surprise or irritation.

great priest n. [18C–19C] (*Scot.*) constipation. [Scot. *priest*, a strong but ineffectual desire to defecate; ? ult. SE *pressed* or ? link to QUAKER n.]

great scott! excl. [19C+] a mild oath. [? euph. for *great satan* or *good God!*; but note *Out West*, October 1911, 241: 'The expression 'Great Scott' dates back to the Mexican war in which General Winfield Scott distinguished himself and is an example of the tenacity with which a phrase clings to our vocabulary long after the sense has departed from it']

great seizer n. [late 19C–1950s] (*US*) a sheriff. [the sheriff 'seizes' wrongdoers; a pun on GREAT CAESAR! excl.]

great shakes adj. (*also* **great shucks, some shakes**) [early 19C+] very good, admirable, usu. in negative *no great shakes, not any great shakes* etc.

great snakes! excl. [19C+] (*orig. US*) a mild oath.

great tobacco n. [20C+] (*drugs*) opium (cf. APOSTLE n.).

great warrant n. see GOOD WARRANT n.

great whipper-in n. [mid-19C–1920s] a personification of death. [hunting jargon *whipper-in*, a huntsman's assistant who keeps the hounds from straying by whipping them back into the pack]

great white chief n. (*also* **big white chief**) [1910s+] (*orig. US*) the senior figure in any business, institution or organization, any important man (cf. BIG INJUN n.). [a play on the 19C Native American name for the US president; orig. applied to a Civil Service head of department]

great white father n. [1930s–50s] (*US Black*) an ironic description of any White authority figure, esp. the US president. [19C SE *white father*, a White man, esp. in Africa, who controls and/or protects members of a Black race]

Great White Way n. [20C+] (*US*) Broadway, New York City, esp. its theatrical district around Times Square. [SE *great* + *white way*, a street lit with electric lights. The first *white way* was a stretch of Broadway between 14th Street and 23rd Street, on which electric lights were introduced on 20 December 1880. As used with its qualifying adj., the term was coined by Oscar Gude, a New York advertising man who pioneered the use of electrical advertising, starting with a sign erected over Madison Square in 1892 and began erecting signs in Times Square (then Longacre Square) in 1900. His first use of the term came in 1901. Alternatively, and as claimed by Barry Popik orig., it derives f. the title of Albert Bigelow Paine's novel, *The Great White Way* (1901), although this story, set in the Antarctic, referred not to light but to snow; the link, supposedly, came when a reporter, Shep Friedman, viewed midtown Broadway under a blanket of snow]

grebo n. (*also* **greb, greebo**) [1980s+] a British youth cult featuring a cultivatedly sordid appearance, a boorish manner and a devotion to heavy metal music. [? *greb*, a general term of abuse used in north of England schools since 1930s; note GREEBY adj.]

Grecian n. [mid-17C; 19C+] an Irish immigrant; thus *Grecian accent*, the brogue. [GREEK n.[1] (2)]

Grecian v. [1940s] (*W.I.*) for a woman to walk in a self-consciously 'stylish' manner, either arrogantly or proudly. [? GRECIAN BEND n.[1] (1)]

Grecian bend n.[1] **1** [19C] a particular, stooping style of walking adopted by fashionable women (*c.*1872–80), in which the body bends forward from the hips. **2** [mid-19C] (*US*) a bustle; thus *Grecian bender*, one who wears a bustle. **3** [1900s] in fig. use, that which resembles a bustle. [orig. Eton College sl., referring to a typically scholarly stoop]

Grecian bend n.[2] (*also* **Grecian bender**) [late 19C] a revolver. [ety. unknown]

Grecian bend n.[3] [late 19C] 'the bends' or caisson disease. [play on GRECIAN BEND n.[1]]

greebo n. see GREBO n.

greeby adj. [1940s–60s] (*US teen*) ugly, unattractive. [? var. on SE *grubby*; note GREBO n.]

greed n. [late 19C] (*Aus.*) money.

greedhead n. [1970s+] (*US*) an avaricious person. [SE *greed* + -HEAD sfx (1)]

greedy adj. [1990s+] bisexual. [i.e. one who is 'not satisfied' with attraction to 1 sex]

greedy-gut n. (*also* **greedy-guts, greedy-gutz**) [mid-16C+] a glutton, a selfish person. [SE *greedy* + *gut*/-GUTS sfx (18C+); US use is 19C+]

greefo n. (*also* **greapha, greefa, grefa, griefo, grifa, griffa, griffo, grifo**) [1920s+] marijuana. [Mex. Sp. sl. *grifo*, under the influence of marijuana; the original use of *grifo* is tangled or frizzy hair; thus the image of mental fuzziness/frizziness]

Greek n.[1] **1** [16C+] a cunning, sly individual, esp. a gambler or swindler. **2** [mid-17C; 19C+] a derog. term for an Irish immigrant to the US or UK. **3** [mid-19C] a newcomer. [the use of *Greek* as a generic for a 'foreigner', in the UK an automatically suspect figure; 20C+ use of (1) is derog.]

Greek *n.*[2] [late 16C+] unintelligible language, esp. cant or sl.; esp. in phr. *it's all Greek to me*, suggesting that something is incomprehensible; occas. of actions or ideas.

Greek *n.*[3] (*also* **Greek freak**) [1930s+] (*US campus*) a member of a college fraternity or sorority; thus **go Greek**, to join a college fraternity or sorority. [the use of *Greek* letters as the names of such societies]

Greek *n.*[4] [1930s+] **1** a person who engages in anal intercourse, not necessarily but usu. a homosexual; thus **go Greek**, to have anal intercourse. **2** anal intercourse; often used on a prostitute's 'bill of sale'. [GREEK *adj.*[2]]

Greek *adj.*[1] [mid-19C] Irish. [GREEK *n.*[1] (2)]

Greek *adj.*[2] [late 19C+] **1** (*also* **Persian**) a generic term for homosexual. **2** pertaining to anal intercourse. [the identification of Greeks with homosexuality]

Greek *v.*[1] [early 19C] to cheat at cards. [GREEK *n.*[1] (1)]

Greek *v.*[2] [1970s+] (*gay*) to engage in anal intercourse. [GREEK *n.*[4]]

Greek back *n. see* MEDITERRANEAN BACK n.

Greek culture *n.* [1960s+] anal intercourse, usu. in homosexual advertisement use. [the ethnic cliché that categorizes all (ancient) Greeks as sodomites + GREEK *adj.*[2] (2)]

Greek fashion *n. see* GREEK WAY n.

Greek fire *n.* [late 19C] (*UK Und.*) bad whisky. [burning sensation; SE *Greek fire*, a highly combustible composition used in warfare]

Greek freak *n. see* GREEK *n.*[3].

greeking *n.*[1] [early 19C] cheating at cards. [? racial stereotyping]

greeking *n.*[2] *see* GREEK WAY n.

Greek lightning *n. see* JEWISH LIGHTNING n.

Greek love *n.* [1930s+] **1** (*gay*) pederasty. **2** anal intercourse, irrespective of age. [GREEK *adj.*[2] (2)]

Greek's, the *n.* [1930s+] (*orig. Aus.*) a generic term for any small café. [Greek immigrants, who specialize in such establishments]

Greek sauna *n. see* DUTCH OVEN n. (2).

Greek shop *n.* [1920s+] (*S.Afr.*) a local corner store, often owned by an immigrant Greek family. [the equivalent of the stores owned by Koreans in the US and by exiled Ugandan Asians in the UK]

Greek side *n.* [1930s+] (*gay*) the buttocks. [GREEK *adj.*[2] (2) + SE *side*]

Greek trust *n.* [20C+] (*US*) an absolute lack of trust. [Virgil's maxim *Timeo Danaos et dona ferentis* ('I fear the Greeks bearing gifts') + GREEK *n.*[1] (1)]

Greek way *n.* (*also* **Greek fashion, ...style, greeking**) [1960s+] **1** (*gay*) pederasty. **2** anal intercourse. [GREEK *adj.*[2] (2)]

green *n.*[1] [19C] an unsophisticated, naïve person. [SE *green*, naïve]

green *n.*[2] **1** [late 19C+] (*US*) (*also* **green certificates, welcome green**) money, dollar bills (cf. ALFALFA n.). **2** [1990s+] (*US prison*) (*also* **green money**) US currency, forbidden in prison and used for illegal transactions. [the colour of the notes]

green *n.*[3] (*US drugs*) **1** [1950s+] marijuana, esp. of inferior quality (cf. AFRICAN BUSH n.; BLACK DOMINA n.). **2** [1970s+] phencyclidine (cf. ACE n.[4]). **3** [1980s+] ketamine.

green *n.*[4] [1990s+] **1** (*US Black*) a bottle of beer. **2** (*Aus.*) Victoria bitter beer. [the colour of the glass]

green *adj.*[1] [mid-19C+] of money, liquid or in funds. [SE *green*, ripe, but note GREEN n.[2] (1)]

green *adj.*[2] [1960s+] (*US*) out of order, in a mess. [? the image of something going green with mould]

green *v.* [late 19C] to deceive, to hoax, to swindle, to render gullible. [SE *green*, naïve]

green *adv.* [1910s+] (*US*) utterly.

green about the gills *phr.* (*also* **green around the gills, blue about/around..., pale..., white...**) [mid-19C+] feeling and looking sick, esp. from an excess of alcohol. [GILLS n. (1); the colour of one's complexion, lit. or fig.]

green and blacks *n.* [1960s–80s] (*UK prison/drugs*) librium capsules. [the colour]

green and greasy *n.* [1920s] (*US Und.*) banknotes. [the colour and texture of well-used dollar bills]

green and yellow fellow *n.* [late 19C] a male homosexual. [GREENERY-YALLERY *adj.*, i.e. affected]

green apple *n.* [1960s–70s] (*US*) a naïve person. [SE *green*, naïve]

green apple quickstep *n.* (*also* **green apple nasties, ...trots, ...two-step**) [1950s+] (*US*) diarrhoea (cf. APPLE-BLOSSOM TWO-STEP n.). [the result of eating sour fruit + pun on SE *trot*/TROTS, THE n.[2]]

green apron *n.* [mid-17C–mid-18C] a lay preacher. [female Quaker preachers wore a *green apron*]

green around the gills *phr. see* GREEN ABOUT THE GILLS phr.

green ashes *n.* (*also* **green mud**) [1930s–50s] (*US drugs*) opium residue.

green as owl-shit *adj.* [1970s] (*US*) naïve, inexperienced.

green-ass *adj.* [1940s+] (*US*) naïve, inexperienced. [SE *green* + -ASS sfx]

greenback *n.*[1] [late 18C–19C] a frog.

greenback *n.*[2] **1** [mid-19C+] (*US*) (*also* **g.b.**) a $1 bill, usu. in pl. (cf. BLUE-BACKS n.). **2** [1950s+] (*Aus./UK/Irish*) a £1 note. [colour]

greenback *v.* [1970s] (*US*) to pay, esp. a bribe. [GREENBACK n.[2] (1)]

greenback *adv.* [1970s] (*US*) in cash. [GREENBACK n.[2] (1)]

green bag *n.* [late 17C–19C] a lawyer; thus [19C] *what's in the green bag?*, what is the charge to be preferred against me? [the green cloth that was trad. used to make lawyers' bags, used to carry briefs and other documents. 'These gentlemen carry their clients' deeds in a green bag; and, it is said, when they have no deeds to carry, frequently fill them with an old pair of breeches [...] to give themselves the appearance of business' (Grose, 1785). *Green bags* were replaced by *blue bags* (barristers) and *red bags* (King's or Queen's Counsel)]

green banana *n.*[1] [1940s] (*US Black*) a young, light-skinned woman. [SE *green*, naïve + BANANA n.[2] (2)]

green banana *n.*[2] *see* BANANA n.[2] (1).

green bean *n.*[1] [1950s+] (*US*) a naïve person. [SE *green*, naïve]

green bean *n.*[2] (*also* **greenfly**) [1980s+] (*S.Afr.*) a township municipal policeman (cf. BABY-BLUES n.[2]). [colour of the uniform]

green bean *n.*[3] *see* BEAN n.[1] (3).

green belly *n.* [1950s] (*US*) a novice, an unsophisticated person, esp. a new arrival in the city from the country. [SE *green*, naïve]

green boys *n.* [mid-19C] paper money, notes (cf. ALFALFA n.). [the colour of dollar bills/GREEN n.[2] (1)]

greenbud *n.* [1980s+] (*US drugs*) marijuana that is green, usu. of a superior quality (cf. AFRICAN BUSH n.; BLACK DOMINA n.). [SE *green* + BUD n.[4] (1)]

green cart *n.* [1930s+] (*Aus.*) a vehicle, actual or metaphorical, in which people are taken to a mental hospital.

green certificates *n. see* GREEN n.[2] (1).

green cloth *n.* [late 19C] a billiards/snooker table. [abbr. *board of green cloth*, the green baize with which it is covered]

green death *n.* [1960s–70s] (*US campus*) sickness and diarrhoea, supposedly caused by student canteen food. [play on SE *Black Death*]

green door *n.* [1910s–70s] (*US Und.*) the door of the execution chamber in New York state prisons (cf. GREEN ROOM n.). [the colour of the door in question]

green dragons *n.* (*drugs*) **1** [1930s+] heroin (cf. BLACK n.[3]). **2** [1970s+] barbiturates (cf. BARBIT n.). **3** [1970s+] amphetamines (cf. A n.[2]). **4** [1980s+] LSD (cf. A n.[3]). [(1) a stamp on the box; (2) and (3) the colour of the pills; (4) a type of LSD distributed on squares of blotter stamped with a *green dragon*]

greener n.[1] **1** [late 19C] an inexperienced workman used as a strike-breaker. **2** [late 19C+] (orig. US) a novice, an innocent, one who has newly arrived. **3** [1940s] (UK prison) (also **greeney**) a young or new prison inmate. [SE green, naïve]

greener n.[2] see GREENIE n.[2].

greenery n. **1** [1970s] (US Black) money (cf. ALFALFA n.). **2** [1990s+] (UK Black) marijuana (cf. AFRICAN BUSH n.).

greenery-yallery adj. [late 19C–1940s] (UK society) pertaining to the Aesthetic Movement whose preferred colours were green and yellow. [thus W.S. Gilbert, Patience (1880) 'A greenery-yallery, Grosvenor Gallery, Foot-in-the-grave young man!']

greeney n. see GREENER n.[1] (3).

greenfinch n. [mid-19C] a member of the Pope's Irish guard. [green being the national colour of Ireland]

greenfly n. see GREEN BEAN n.[2].

green folding n. see FOLDING GREEN n.

greengages n. (also **greens**) [1930s+] wages. [rhy. sl.]

green goddess n. [1930s–50s] (US drugs) marijuana (cf. AFRICAN BUSH n.; BLACK DOMINA n.). [the colour of the marijuana leaves and the pleasure of the drug]

green gold n. [1980s+] (drugs) cocaine (cf. BLANCA n.). [? SE green gold, an alloy of gold and silver; high-quality cocaine sparkles]

green goods n. **1** [late 19C–1950s] (US Und.) counterfeit banknotes; thus green goods game/racket, selling counterfeit money as 'real' money allegedly made from a plate stolen from the government; green goods man, a counterfeiter. **2** [1910s+] paper currency. [the colour of the bills]

green goose n. [late 16C–early 17C] a young, innocent girl, soon to be made into a prostitute (cf. ALLEY CAT n.). [SE green goose, a gosling, a young goose; a simpleton or SE green + GOOSE n.[1] (1)]

green gown n. (also **green mantle**) [late 16C–19C] the loss of one's virginity, usu. out of doors; occas. just sex outdoors; often in phrs. get/take a green gown, to lose one's virginity; give someone a green gown, to remove someone's virginity in this way (cf. GRASSBACK n.). [pun on SE green, with its general meanings of both countryside and innocence + the green stains that come from rolling on the grass; dial. get on the green gown, however, means to be buried]

greengrocer n. [late 18C] a prostitute (cf. ASS PEDDLER n.). [play on legit. bumboating, selling provisions to ships and BUM n.[1] (2)]

greengrocery n.[1] [early 19C] an illicit bar or 'speakeasy'. [euph.]

greengrocery n.[2] [mid-19C] **1** the vagina (cf. CABBAGE n.[7]). **2** a brothel (cf. BANGING-SHOP n.). [lit. the seller/provider of GREENS n.[2] + the potential of the vagina as a money-maker]

green grove n. [late 19C] pubic hair. [GREENS n.[2]]

green handshake n. [1970s] (US) a bribe, a tip, a bonus. [GREEN n.[2] (1)]

greenhead n. [late 18C–1910s] an inexperienced young man. [SE green, naïve + -HEAD sfx (1)]

greenhorn n. **1** [late 17C+] a novice, an unsophisticated person, esp. a new immigrant or a new arrival in the city from the country. **2** [late 19C] a virgin, a sexual novice. [15C SE greenhorn, a young animal, spec. an ox with 'green' or young horns. The term is first used in a milit. sense, describing a new recruit. Grose (1785) defines it as 'an undebauched young fellow, just initiated into the society of bucks and bloods'. Its post-19C use has been mainly US]

greenhorn adj. [1980s] (US) virginal. [GREENHORN n. (2)]

green hornet n. **1** [1940s–70s] (US drugs) amphetamine (cf. A n.[2]). **2** [1960s] (US) a New York City police patrol car, suggested by colour scheme of the time. **3** [1960s] (Can. Und.) a Toronto motorcycle policeman (cf. BABY-BLUES n.[2]). [the colour + ref. to the NBC radio series The Green Hornet]

greenhouse n.[1] [1900s–70s] (Irish) a public lavatory (cf. BACKHOUSE n.).

greenhouse n.[2] [1980s+] (drugs) a place known for selling drugs, esp. marijuana. [GREEN n.[3] (1) + pun on SE]

greenie n.[1] (also **greeny**) [mid-19C+] a novice, an unsophisticated person, esp. a new arrival from the country. [abbr. GREENHORN n. (1)]

greenie n.[2] (also **greener**) **1** [1920s–70s] (US) a $1 bill; thus greenies, money (cf. ALFALFA n.). **2** [1970s+] (S.Afr.) (also **green tiger**) a 10-rand note. [the colour]

greenie n.[3] [1980s+] (US/N.Z. campus) beer, spec. Heineken lager, which comes in green cans or green-labelled bottles.

greenie n.[4] [1980s+] (Aus./N.Z./UK) an environmentalist, a conservationist, a supporter of ecological issues. [the Green party]

greenie n.[5] see GREENY n.[1].

greenies n.[1] [1960s] (US) envy. [one is 'green with envy']

greenies n.[2] (drugs) **1** [1960s+] amphetamines (cf. A n.[2]). **2** [1990s+] MDMA (cf. ECSTASY n.).

greenies n.[3] [1970s] (US) green vegetables. [SE greens]

green-lamp house n. [1900s] (US) a police station.

Greenland n. **1** [mid-19C] the fig. world of innocence; thus greenlander, a gullible, innocent person; from Greenland, used of an unsophisticated, ignorant person. **2** [mid-late 19C] (US) Ireland; thus Greenlander, an Irish person. [SE green, naïve + SE land; (2) adds green, Ireland's national colour]

green leaves n. [1980s+] (drugs) phencyclidine (cf. ACE n.[4]). [the parsley with which PCP is often smoked (cf. PARSLEY n.[3])]

green light n. **1** [1930s+] a positive response, permission; usu. in phr. give someone the green light or get the green light (cf. RED LIGHT n.[3]). **2** [1970s+] (US prison) one who has been targeted for death.

green light v. **1** [1940s+] to give or get permission, to allow or be allowed. **2** [1970s+] (US prison) to target someone for death. [traffic lights/railway signals imagery]

green-light hotel n. (also **green light, green lights**) [1910s–40s] (US) a prison or police station (cf. BOARDING HOUSE n.). [the green light that marks its address]

green man n. [20C+] a public house urinal. [the common pub name + the common painting of such urinals green]

greenmans n. [early 17C] fields, countryside. [SE green + -MANS sfx]

green mantle n. see GREEN GOWN n.

green meadow n. [mid-19C] the vagina (cf. BEAUTY SPOT n.; CABBAGE n.[7]). [GREENS n.[2]]

green money n. see GREEN n.[2] (2).

Green Mountain boy n. [late 18C+] (US) a native of Vermont. [lit. meaning of Vermont, France verts monts, green mountains]

green mud n. see GREEN ASHES n.

green nigger n. [20C+] (US) an Irishman (cf. BOG ARAB n.). [similar inferior status to a Black NIGGER n.[1] (1) but green, i.e. Irish from the national colours]

green one n.[1] **1** [1910s] (US) a $1 bill (cf. ALFALFA n.). **2** [1930s–80s] a £1 note. [the colour; (2) was demonetized in 1988]

green one n.[2] [1990s+] a piece of phlegm, in the context of spitting (cf. GREENY n.[1]).

green pea n. **1** [1910s–70s] (US) a naïve person. **2** [1950s–70s] a key. [(1) SE green, naïve; (2) rhy. sl.]

green pill n. see BLACK PILL n.

Green Pop n. [1940s] (US) Rolling Rock beer. [SE green + POP n.[2] (1); the predominantly green glass bottle]

green room n. [1950s+] (US prison) the gas chamber (cf. GREEN DOOR n.). [its green-painted walls]

greens n.[1] [18C–early 19C] chlorosis. [abbr. of the synon. nickname green sickness; 'A disease mostly affecting young females about the age of puberty, characterized by anæmia, suppression or irregularity of the menses, and a pale or greenish complexion; green sickness']

greens n.[2] [mid-19C+] sexual intercourse; thus get/have one's greens, to have sexual intercourse; give one's greens, to consent to sexual intercourse (cf. CABBAGE n.[7]). [GREEN GOWN n.]

greens *n.*[3] (*also* **green stuff**) [mid-19C+] paper currency, notes. [the colour]

greens *n.*[4] (*also* **collard greens, turnip greens**) [1970s+] (*Black drugs*) marijuana (cf. AFRICAN BUSH n.). [play on the popular soul food]

greens *n.*[5] [1980s+] (*Aus. prison*) prison uniform; thus **green**, adj. used to describe prisoner activities. [the colour]

greens *n.*[6] see GREENGAGES n.

greens and brussels *n.* [20C+] muscles. [rhy. sl.]

green shit *n.* [1950s–70s] (*US Black*) money (cf. ALFALFA n.; CHAFF n.[2]). [SE *green* + SHIT n.[3] (6); the apparent synon. with terms based on money = excrement, e.g. CRAP n.[1], is coincidental]

Green Sod *n.* see OLD SOD n.

green stamp *n.* (*US*) **1** [1950s+] a $1 bill; thus **green stamps**, money (cf. ALFALFA n.). **2** [1970s] a traffic offence summons. [play on *Green Shield* trading stamps, issued in 1960s]

green stuff *n.*[1] **1** [late 19C–1900s] (*US*) absinthe. **2** [1940s+] (*US Black*) marijuana (cf. AFRICAN BUSH n.; BLACK DOMINA n.).

green stuff *n.*[2] see GREENS n.[3]

green tea *n.* **1** [1950s] (*US drugs*) marijuana, esp. of inferior quality (cf. AFRICAN BUSH n.; BLACK DOMINA n.). **2** [1980s+] (*drugs*) phencyclidine (cf. ACE n.[4]). [(1) SE *green*/GREEN n.[3] (1) + TEA n.[2] (1); (2) ? rhy. sl. or the common mixing of the drug with parsley, which may resemble (1)]

green thumb *n.* **1** [1960s] (*US gay*) the penis. **2** [1970s+] (*US Black*) one who has the knack of making money (cf. ALFALFA n.). [(2) GREEN n.[2] (1) + play on the more usual gardeners' 'green fingers']

green tiger *n.* see GREENIE n.[2] (2).

green 'un *n.* [mid-19C–1900s] (*Aus.*) a naïve or gullible person. [SE *green*, gullible]

green verbs *n.* [20C+] (*W.I.*) poorly spoken, ungrammatical English, esp. when used by one who would be expected to speak correctly. [SE *green*, unripe, immature, thus unsophisticated]

green wedge *n.* [1970s+] (*drugs*) LSD (cf. A n.[3]). [? packaging]

green weenie *n.* **1** [1940s+] (*US, orig. milit.*) anything bad; thus *eat/get/have had the green weenie*, to be killed. **2** [1960s–70s] (*US campus*) the act of breaking a date or ending a relationship. **3** [1980s] (*US campus*) a Heineken beer. [(1) SE *green*, of food, decaying, 'off'; (2) f. (1); (3) colour + WEENIE n.[1] (5)]

green wellies *n.* see WELLIES n.

green welly brigade *n.* [1970s+] the rural upper classes. [SE *green* + WELLIE n. + BRIGADE n., i.e. the green wellingtons (rather than the more common black variety) that such people tend to wear]

Greenwich barber *n.* [late 18C–early 19C] a seller of sand from the Greenwich sandpits. [such retailers 'shaved' the sand for their product]

Greenwich goose *n.* [late 18C–19C] a pensioner of Greenwich Royal Naval Hospital, founded in 1692 by Queen Mary. [proper name *Greenwich* + SE *goose*]

greeny *n.*[1] (*also* **greenie, gremlin, grolly**) [1960s+] (*UK juv.*) a lump of phlegm, usu. in the context of spitting (cf. GREEN ONE n.[2]).

greeny *n.*[2] [1990s+] (*US drugs*) the best grade of marijuana (cf. AFRICAN BUSH n.; BLACK DOMINA n.). [GREEN n.[3] (1)]

greeny *n.*[3] see GREENIE n.[1]

greeper *n.* [1990s+] (*US drugs*) withdrawal symptoms. [? SE *gripper*]

greet *n.* [20C+] (*US*) a *greeting*; thus **greets**, greetings. [abbr.]

greeter *n.* (*also* **greta**) [1940s–60s] (*drugs*) marijuana. [? misreading of GREEFO n.]

greetin' fou *adj.* [late 17C+] very drunk, lit. 'crying drunk'. [Scot. *greet*, to cry + FOU adj.[1]]

grefa *n.* see GREEFO n.

greg *v.* (*also* **grig**) [mid-19C+] (*Irish*) to tease, to fool. [Irish *griog*, to tease]

grego *n.* [mid-19C] a rough greatcoat, with a hood. [SE *grego*, a coarse jacket with a hood, worn in the Levant; ult. Lat. *Graecus*, Greek]

gregorian tree *n.* [mid-17C–early 19C] the gallows. [for ety. see next]

gregory *n.* [early 17C] a hangman. [*Gregory* Brandon, who worked as executioner under James I (1601–25), to be succeeded by his son Richard, better known as 'Young Gregory']

Gregory Peck *n.* [1950s+] **1** the neck. **2** a cheque. [rhy. sl.; proper name of US actor *Gregory Peck* (1916–2003)]

Gregory Pecks *n.* [1950s+] (*Aus.*) spectacles, glasses. [rhy. sl. = SPECS n. (1); ult. see prev.]

gregory peg *n.* [20C+] (*Aus.*) the leg. [rhy. sl.; pun on GREGORY PECK n. + SE *peg-leg*]

gremlin *n.*[1] [1910s+] an unidentified source of trouble or malfunctioning. [? SE *goblin*; orig. use in 1929 refers to troublesome or unimportant officers. Popularized through WW2 RAF use, where the meaning was as above, although one cit. claims the term was invented in WW1 by the Royal Flying Corps]

gremlin *n.*[2] see GREENY n.[1]

greng-greng *n.* [20C+] (*W.I., Trin.*) coarse, short hair. [Twi *greng*, rough, rugged, coarse]

gret *n.* see GRETTE n.

gret *v.* [1960s] (*US campus*) to smoke, possess or obtain a cigarette. [GRETTE n.]

greta *n.* see GREETER n.

grette *n.* (*also* **gret**) [1960s–70s] (*US campus*) a cigarette; thus **grette**, to ask for a cigarette (cf. GRIT n.[5]; RETTE n.). [abbr.]

Greville Starkey *n.* [1990s+] a derog. term for a Black person (cf. DAPTO DOG n.). [rhy. sl. = DARKIE n.[1] (1); ult. UK horseracing trainer *Greville Starkey* (b.1939)]

grey/gray see also under GRAY/GREY.

grey *n.* **1** [early 19C+] (*also* **gray**) a halfpenny or other coin having 2 heads or 2 tails, esp. as used in cheating games. **2** [mid-19C] money in general. [(1) Rom. *gry*, a horse, thus linked to PONY n.[1] (3); 20C+ use mainly Aus.; (2) the colour of 'silver' coins once they have been some time in circulation]

greyback *n.*[1] (*also* **grey-backed 'un**) [late 18C–1950s] a louse.

greyback *n.*[2] [1970s–80s] (*UK Black*) an old person.

greybeard *n.* [late 18C–19C] an earthenware jug used in public houses. [such jugs had the figure of a man with a large beard stamped on them. The name was also used for Dutch earthenware jugs, used for smuggling gin along the east coast]

grey biscuit *n.* [1990s+] (*drugs*) MDMA (cf. ECSTASY n.). [the colour of the tablet]

grey bomber *n.* see GREY GHOST n.

greycing *n.* see GRACING n.

greycoat *n.* [1900s] (*Aus. Und.*) a prisoner. [the prison uniform]

grey-coat/-coated parson *n.* see GREY PARSON n.

grey death *n.* [1950s+] (*Aus. prison*) weak prison stew; similarly porridge.

greyers *n.* see GREYS n.[1]

grey ghost *n.* (*also* **grey bomber**) [1970s+] (*Aus.*) a parking policeman in New South Wales; the same officer in Victoria is a **grey meanie** (cf. BABY-BLUES n.[2]). [the colour of the uniform]

greyhound *n.*[1] [1970s+] (*N.Z.*) a very thin hand-rolled cigarette. [SE *greyhounds* are very thin dogs]

greyhound *n.*[2] [1990s+] a very short skirt. [it is only an inch from the 'hare']

greyhound *v.*[1] [1940s–50s] (*US Black*) to run fast.

greyhound *v.*[2] [1970s] (*US Black*) to pursue White sexual partners. [GRAY adj. + SE *hound* v.]

grey jock *n.* see BLACK JOCK n. (2).

grey mare *n.* [1930s–50s] the fare. [rhy. sl.]

grey matter *n.* (*also* **gray matter**) [19C+] the human brain, intelligence. [its colour]

grey meanie *n.* see GREY GHOST n.

grey nurse *n.* [1960s+] (*Aus.*) a purse, a wallet. [rhy. sl.]

grey parson n. (also **grey-coat parson**, **grey-coated parson**) [late 18C–19C] a farmer who rents out the tithes normally due to a vicar or rector. [grey as 'light black' in an adj. use of 'black', referring to matters clerical. The use of grey to mean amateur or partial is similar to 20C+ grey import, an unofficial, but not actually illegal import, typically of computer hardware manufactured elsewhere that has yet to become available in the country in which it is sold]

grey puss n. [1950s+] (W.I.) an albino. [GRAY adj. + PUSS n.[5]]

greys n.[1] (also **greyers**) [1900s–40s] grey flannel trousers, once a staple of the 'off-duty' uniform of the British middle-class male. [SE grey (+ -ER sfx)]

greys n.[2] [1960s] by HIPPIE n.[2] (3) standards, disenchanted, negative individuals, unwilling to encompass new ideas.

greys n.[3] see SCOTCH GREYS n.

greys, the n. [late 18C–1920s] a fit of yawning, a feeling of laziness, lassitude.

grey suit n. see SUIT n.[4] (2).

grey-white nigger n. [1950s] (W.I.) a mulatto. [GRAY adj./SE white + NIGGER n.[1] (1)]

greyworld n. [1960s] the conventional world, as opposed to that of the hippies. [GREYS n.[2]]

gribber n. [1970s] small pieces of excrement adhering to the anal hairs (cf. CLAGNUT n.). [? UK dial. gribble, to remove matted wool and dung from the tails of sheep; ult. dial. gribble, a small pellet or grain]

grick n. [early 19C] a farthing. [var. on GRIG n.[1]]

grid n.[1] **1** [1910s] a football field. **2** [1920s+] a bicycle. **3** [1950s] a car. **4** [1950s] a piano. [abbr. GRIDIRON n.[3]/SE gridiron, as a generic term for a machine; (2) post-1940s use mainly Aus.]

grid n.[2] [2000s] the human face. [? SE grid, a form of grating, in this context the teeth or a griddle, which is round]

grid n.[3] [2000s] (US) the rows of dialling buttons on a modern telephone.

griddle n. (also **grid**) [late 19C–1900s] a violin. [? rhy. sl. = fiddle]

griddle v. (also **gridle**) [mid-late 19C; 1930s] to beg, to peddle, to scrounge, esp. as a street singer. [ety. unknown; 20C+ use is US]

griddler n. **1** [mid-late 19C; 1950s] a street singer who performs without benefit of a lyric sheet. **2** [1930s] a wandering tinker, a gypsy tramp. [GRIDDLE v.]

griddling homey/polone n. [late 19C+] a male or female violinist. [Polari; GRIDDLE n. + OMEE n. (3)/POLONE n. (1)]

g-ride n. [1990s+] (US Black) any type of automobile favoured by teen gangs, usu. stolen. [G n.[3] (1) + RIDE n.[2] (1)]

gridiron n.[1] [early 19C] (Anglo-Irish) a public house sweetheart. [? she is 'hot stuff']

gridiron n.[2] [mid-19C] in London, a county court summons. [the arms of the City of Westminster, which resemble a gridiron]

gridiron n.[3] **1** [late 19C] the bars on a prison-cell window. **2** [late 19C–1940s] (US) a football field. **3** [1930s–50s] a bicycle. [resemblance to SE gridiron; (2) post-WW2 use is SE]

gridle v. see GRIDDLE v.

grief n.[1] **1** [mid-19C+] misery, problems, troubles; thus COME TO GRIEF v., GIVE SOMEONE GRIEF v. **2** [1970s+] (US gay) a homophobic thug.

grief n.[2] [1970s+] (Aus. drugs) marijuana. [abbr. GREEFO n.]

grief v. [1970s+] (US campus) to trouble, to bother, to annoy. [GRIEF n.[1] (1)]

griefer n. [1930+] (US drugs) a habitual marijuana user. [GREEFO n.]

griefo n. see GREEFO n.

grievous n. [1940s–50s] (Aus.) grievous bodily harm. [abbr.]

grifa n. see GREEFO n.

griff n.[1] see GRIFFIN n.[2].

griff n.[2] see GRIFFIN n.[4].

griff v.[1] [mid-19C–1920s] (Anglo-Ind.) to cheat, to fool. [GRIFFIN n.[1] (1)]

griff v.[2] [2000s] (US Black) to fight. [? pickpocket jargon griff, to jostle one's way through a crowd, picking pockets]

griffa n. see GREEFO n.

griffin n.[1] **1** [18C–19C] a fool; thus griffinish, foolish. **2** [early 19C–1920s] a menacing woman, a 'gorgon'. [SE griffin, a mythical animal usu. represented as having the head and wings of an eagle and the body and hind-quarters of a lion]

griffin n.[2] (also **griff**) [late 18C–19C] (Anglo-Ind.) **1** a cadet newly arrived from the UK to join the Indian Army or Civil Service. **2** any novice or newcomer. [Y&B notes an actual Admiral Griffin 'who commanded in the Indian seas from November 1746 to June 1748, and was not very fortunate', but they also note a 1624 use, again meaning a novice, by Beaumont and Fletcher]

griffin n.[3] [mid-19C] an umbrella. [ety. unknown; as used by 'fast' young men in London]

griffin n.[4] (also **griff**) [late 19C+] news, reliable information, a tip (in betting), a hint; esp. as straight griffin. [? pun on GRIFFIN n.[2] (2); in modern use mainly as Liverpool dial.]

griffmetoll n. [mid–late 18C] (UK Und.) a sixpence. [ety. unknown]

griffo n. see GREEFO n.

griff sense n. [1940s+] a pickpocket's ability to assess a potential victim's personality. [? GRIFFIN n.[4], i.e. news of a potential victim; or ? GRIFFIN n.[1] (1); + SE sense]

grifo n. see GREEFO n.

grift n. **1** [20C+] (US Und.) any crime that depends not upon violence or coercion but on 'lightness of touch and quickness of wit' (Maurer, The Big Con, 1940), e.g. professional confidence trickery, pickpocketing, professional gambling, circus/carnival work; thus the grift, the world of such crimes. **2** [1920s–50s] corruption; the proceeds of corruption, political bribery etc. **3** [1930s] (US Und.) the proceeds of a theft. **4** [1930s–40s] a plan, a scheme, an intention. **5** [1950s] an opinion. [GRAFT n.[2]]

grift v. **1** [1910s+] to work as a confidence trickster or petty thief; thus grifting, confidence trickery, swindling. **2** [1930s–50s] to trick, to hoax. **3** [1950s+] to steal. **4** [1990s+] (US campus) to scrounge off other people. [GRIFT n.]

grifter n. **1** [1910s+] (US Und.) (also **grift**) a confidence trickster; any form of non-violent criminal, living primarily on his or her wits. **2** [1910s+] (US Und.) a small-change swindler, thus any small-time gambler. **3** [1910s+] (US Und.) a thief. **4** [1930s–50s] a worker, a struggler. **5** [1990s+] (US campus) a scrounger, someone living off other people. [GRIFT v.]

grig n.[1] [mid-17C–mid-19C] a farthing; in pl. money, cash. [ety. unknown, but all meanings of SE grig (a dwarf, a short-legged hen etc) imply small size. Johnson, Dictionary (1755), suggests that its orig. meaning was 'anything below the natural size']

grig n.[2] [1990s+] anything or anyone which the speaker dislikes or does not require. [ety. unknown]

grig v. see GREG v.

gril n.[1] [1970s+] (S.Afr.) a shiver, a shudder, 'the creeps'. [Afk. gril, shudder]

gril n.[2] [1990s+] (US campus) an affectionate term of address between women. [play on SE girl]

grill n.[1] **1** [1940s] (US Black) the stomach. **2** [1980s+] (US Black/teen) the face or mouth; thus one's personal space, esp. in phr. all up in one's grill; thus bust someone's grill, to beat up, to hit in the mouth. **3** [1990s+] (also **grille**) the teeth.

grill n.[2] [1950s+] (Aus.) a southern European immigrant, esp. a Greek. [the near-monopoly of Greeks on the running of small cafés]

grill v. **1** [late 19C+] to interrogate; thus on the grill, under close interrogation. **2** [2000s] (US Black) to stare at; to menace.

grille n. see GRILL n.[1] (3).

grilled cheese n. [1980s+] (US drugs) cannabis. [? a supposed similarity in smell]

grilling n. 1 [20C+] an interrogation. 2 [1960s] a scolding. [GRILL v. (1)]

grimacious adj. [1980s+] (Irish) unpleasant, terrible. [SE grim; on pattern of BODACIOUS adj. (1)]

grim and gory n. [20C+] (Aus.) a story. [rhy. sl.]

grimbo n. [1980s+] (US campus) a contemptible or unattractive person. [SE grim + BIMBO n. (3)/DUMBO n. (1)]

grimmy n. [1960s–70s] a middle-aged woman. [? SE grim-faced]

Grimsby Docks n. [1990s+] socks. [rhy. sl.; ult. place in UK]

grin n.¹ [early 19C] an inquisitive, challenging stare. [note Egan, Life in London (1821): 'A low slang term made use of in opposition to the stylish phrase of QUIZ. It is considered rather an unpleasant circumstance to persons entering a splendid ball-room who are not accustomed to it. At all times it should be executed in a graceful manner']

grin n.² [1960s+] (US) amusement; thus for grins, for fun.

grin, the n. [early 19C] an interrogation. [SE grin, a snare]

grinagog (the cat's uncle) n. [mid-16C–18C] a simpleton who has a fixed grin on his face. [SE grin + agog]

grin at the daisy roots v. [late 19C] (Anglo-Ind.) to be dead. [one is 'looking upwards' at the soil that covers one's coffin]

grincum/grincom/grincombe/grincome/grincum n. see CRINKUM n.

grind n.¹ 1 [mid-19C–1920s] (US) a swindle. 2 [late 19C] (US campus) a satirist. 3 [late 19C–1930s] (US campus) a joke, usu. personal. 4 [1930s] (US tramp) patter used to lure customers into a sideshow or similar attraction. 5 [1930s–50s] (US Und.) the 'salestalk' that is used to persuade a confidence man's victim.

grind n.² 1 [mid-19C+] hard, continuous, wearing work, esp. academic work; thus ON THE GRIND phr. 2 [late 19C–1900s] (US campus) a demanding instructor. 3 [late 19C–1900s] (US campus) a demanding course. 4 [late 19C+] (US campus) a student who studies constantly. 5 [late 19C+] anything wearing, monotonous, exhausting, debilitating; also attrib.; thus on the grind, nagging, complaining. 6 [1900s] (US campus) a tiring or boring person or task. 7 [1910s–50s] a hard worker, a daily worker.

grind n.³ 1 [mid-19C+] an act of sexual intercourse; thus do/have a grind; [2000s] get one's grind on, to have sexual intercourse. 2 [late 19C] a person (female or gay male) regarded as a sex object, further qualified as a good grind, bad grind. 3 [1930s+] the rubbing of one's body, esp. the genital area, against one's partner while dancing; thus similar movements by a solo dancer or singer, esp. in phr. bump(s) and grind(s). 4 [1940s–50s] (orig. US Black) a striptease performance. 5 [1970s] masturbation. [GRIND v.¹ (1)]

grind v.¹ 1 [mid-16C+] to have sexual intercourse. 2 [1920s+] (US) to rotate the hips in a sensuous manner while dancing. 3 [1940s+] to rub one's body, esp. the genital area, against one's partner while dancing. 4 [1970s] (also **grind off**) to masturbate (cf. BOFF v.).

grind v.² 1 [early 19C+] to work hard, esp. at an unrewarding but necessary task; thus grinding, hard-working, dedicated. 2 [mid-19C+] to devote an unreasonable amount of time and effort to one's studies. 3 [late 19C–1900s] to tire, to exhaust, to annoy. 4 [late 19C–1900s] to cause someone to work hard. 5 [1920s–30s] (US) to tout a carnival sideshow. 6 [1930s] (US Und.) of a confidence man, to devote a great deal of time to persuading a potential victim.

grind v.³ [late 19C–1900s] to ridicule, to satirize. [GRIND n.¹ (3)]

grind v.⁴ [1980s+] (US campus) to eat, to have some food. [SE grind one's teeth]

grindage n. [1990s+] (US teen) food. [GRIND v.⁴ + -AGE sfx]

grind coffee v. [1920s–60s] (US) 1 to rotate one's hips during intercourse. 2 to rotate one's hips in a manner suggestive of copulation. [ext. of GRIND v.¹ (2)]

grinder n.¹ [late 16C+] a tooth; usu. in pl. [their function + 14C+ SE grinder, a molar; the term moved into sl., nearly always in pl.]

grinder n.² [19C] a private tutor. [GRIND v.² (1)]

grinder n.³ [mid–late 19C] a coarse gesture, which involves placing the tip of one's thumb on one's nose and using the other hand to work an imaginary coffee-grinder; the gesture is used to refute what the subject feels is an unjustified attack on their credulity.

grinder n.⁴ [late 19C] a highly diligent student. [GRIND v.² (2)]

grinder n.⁵ [20C+] (Aus.) a small coin. [ety. unknown; ? link to GRIND v.² (4)]

grinder n.⁶ [1920s–30s] (US tramp) a sideshow tout. [GRIND v.² (5)]

grinder n.⁷ 1 [1940s] (US) a penis. 2 [1940s–60s] (US) a vagina. 3 [1950s+] (US) a striptease artist. 4 [1960s+] (US) a sexually promiscuous or powerful male. [SE grind/GRIND v.¹]

grinder n.⁸ [1950s+] (US) a large sandwich made of 2 slabs of bread cut lengthwise from the loaf and containing a variety of ingredients. [? the need to grind one's teeth as one chews into the over-sized sandwich]

grinder n.⁹ [1960s+] (US, Midwest) a Slovenian. [dial. griner, greiner, ult. Ger. Krainer, a Slovenian inhabitant of Carniola in the former Austria-Hungary]

grind house n.¹ 1 [1920s+] a cinema that shows continuous performances; generally second-rate venues, rarely showing any first-run feature films, often screening pornography. 2 [1930s+] (orig. US Black) a strip club. [SE grind, i.e. the physical turning of the early projectors, similar to the rotation of the arm of a coffee grinder; also the second-rate films, which a studio simply 'grinds out'; (2) GRIND v.¹ (2)]

grind house n.² see GRIND JOINT n.¹.

grind house n.³ see GRIND JOINT n.².

grinding n. [1990s+] (US Black teen) selling drugs of any kind on the street. [SE grind (it) out]

grinding gear n. [1970s] the penis.

grinding-house n.¹ [17C–18C] a house of correction. [SE grind; a ref. to the work one did as part of one's punishment]

grinding-house n.² [19C] a brothel (cf. ACCOMMODATION HOUSE n.). [GRIND v.¹ (1) + HOUSE n.¹ (1)/SE shop, a place of business or work]

grinding mill n. [1930s] (US Black) the vagina. [GRIND v.¹ (1)]

grinding tool n. [19C] the penis; thus grind one's tool, to copulate. [GRIND v.¹ (1) + TOOL n.¹ (1)]

grind joint n.¹ (also **grind house**) [1920s+] (US) 1 an entertainment establishment that uses a front-man to solicit customers and runs continuous performances. 2 a third-rate casino. [SE phr. grind it out + JOINT n.⁴ (3)/SE house]

grind joint n.² (also **grind house**) [1960s+] (US) a brothel (cf. BADGER-CRIB n.). [GRIND v.¹ (1) + JOINT n.⁴ (3)/HOUSE n.¹ (1)]

grindoff n. (also **grindo**) [late 19C] a miller. [name of a character in Pocock's play The Miller and His Men (1813); ult. SE grind]

grind off v. see GRIND v.¹ (4).

grind one's coffee v. [1920s] (orig. US Black) to have sexual intercourse. [GRIND v.¹ (1) + pun]

grind one's tool v. see GRINDING TOOL n.

grinds n. [1980s+] (US campus) food. [GRIND v.⁴]

grind show n. [1920s–50s] (US) an entertainment show that runs continuously. [SE grind + show]

grindsman n. [20C+] (W.I. Rasta) one who displays great prowess in bed. [GRIND v.¹ (1)]

grind someone's jaw v. see TIGHTEN SOMEONE'S JAWS v.

grindstone n. [mid-19C+] the vagina. [GRIND v.¹ (1) + pun]

gringo gallop n. [1960s] (US) diarrhoea suffered by tourists (cf. APPLE-BLOSSOM TWO-STEP n.; AZTEC HOP n.). [pun on SE trot/TROTS, THE n.²]

gringy adj. see GRUNGY adj.

grin in a glass case v. [late 18C–19C] to be anatomized. [many criminals were dissected after their execution and their skeletal remains preserved under glass in hospitals]

grin in the canyon v. see YODEL IN THE CANYON (OF LOVE) v.

grinkcome/grinkum *n. see* CRINKUM n.

grin like a basket of chips *v.* (*also* **smile like a basket of chips**) [late 18C–1900s] to grin broadly. [SE *basket* + *chips*, small pieces of wood sawn or chiselled off by a carpenter; ult. Shropshire saying, *smile like a basket of chips*]

grin like a cheese-gash *v.* [late 19C] (*Aus.*) to grin broadly.

grin like a street-knocker *v.* [mid-19C+] to grin broadly. [? one's teeth shine like a well-polished knocker]

grin like a wanking jap *v.* [1990s+] to grin broadly. [WANK v. (1) + JAP n.]

grinning bear *n.* [1950s–60s] (*US*) the vulva. [ext. BEAR n.⁶]

grinny bin *n.* [1970s] (*US*) a psychiatric institution. [the inmates whose fixed smiles fail to reflect their inner turmoil]

grip *n.*¹ **1** [mid-19C] (*US Und.*) something that is easy to achieve or obtain. **2** [1900s–50s] (*Aus.*) a steady job, regular employment. **3** [1970s+] (*US Black*) an expense, a problem. **4** [1990s+] (*US Black*) money; a sum of money. **5** [1990s+] (*US campus*) (*also* **gripa**) a substantial amount, a lot of. **6** [1990s+] (*US campus*) a long time. **7** [1990s+] (*US Black*) the male genitals. **8** [2000s] (*US Black*) a weapon. **9** [2000s] (*US Black*) talent. [one either grips onto it or it has one in its grip]

grip *n.*² [late 19C–1900s] a place, a town or city. [ety. unknown]

grip *n.*³ [late 19C+] (*orig. US*) a small, hand-held bag or case. [abbr. GRIPSACK n.]

grip *v.*¹ [1960s] (*US Black*) to boast and then retreat from one's claims. [? GRIPE v.]

grip *v.*² [1960s+] (*US prison*) to curry favour with a more powerful inmate or with the authorities.

grip *v.*³ [2000s] to apprehend and arrest.

gripa *n. see* GRIP n.¹ (5).

gripe *n.*¹ (*also* **griper**) **1** [mid-16C–early 17C] (*UK Und.*) any cheating gamester, spec. the member of a team who makes bets with the victim. **2** [mid-17C–19C] (*UK Und.*) a miser. **3** [late 18C] (*Irish*) a hand. [SE *gripe*, the act of grasping]

gripe *n.*² [1920s+] (*US*) a complaint or tedious person or thing; thus *gripe session*, an airing of complaints. [SE *gripe*, to grip, to grasp]

gripe *v.* **1** [1900s–30s] (*US*) to disgust. **2** [1920s+] (*orig. US*) to complain, to make a fuss. **3** [1940s+] (*US*) to anger, to annoy. [SE *gripes*, the pains of colic, of which one complains]

griped *adj.* [1920s–60s] (*US*) angry. [GRIPE v. (3)/GRIPE v. (2)]

gripe-fist *n.* (*also* **gripe-penny**) [19C] a moneylender, a miser. [ext. GRIPE n.¹ (2)]

griper *n.*¹ (*US*) **1** [late 18C] an annoying thing. **2** [1930s] (*also* **gripes, gripster**) a moaner, a complainer. [SE *gripe*/GRIPE v.]

griper *n.*² (*also* **gripper**) [early 19C+] (*Irish*) a bailiff. [SE *griper*, one who grasps]

griper *n.*³ *see* GRIPE n.¹.

gripes *n.*¹ [late 17C–18C] a miser, a banker, a usurer. [SE *gripe*, to grasp; ? underpinned by SE *gripe*, a vulture]

gripes *n.*² [late 17C+] of humans, stomach-ache. [SE *gripe*, a spasm of pain]

gripes *n.*³ *see* GRIPER n.¹ (2).

gripe someone's soul *v.* [1930s+] (*US campus*) to anger or disgust greatly; also with vars., e.g. *grip someone's shit*. [GRIPE v. + SE *soul*]

grip it *v. see* GRIP THE PENCIL v.

gripper *n.*¹ [late 19C] a miser.

gripper *n.*² *see* GRIPER n.².

gripper *n.*³ *see* GRIPS n.

grippers *n.* **1** [1940s] (*US Black*) shoes, esp. new ones (cf. GROUND GRIPPERS n.). **2** [1980s] (*US campus*) men's briefs.

gripples *n.* [1980s] (*US Black*) the anus. [*gripple*, a small ditch or trench; ult. synon. 11C *grip*]

grips *n.* [2000s] sideburns; thus *gripper*, one who has sideburns. [abbr. BUGGER'S GRIPS n.]

gripsack *n.* [late 19C–1940s] (*US*) a holdall, a traveller's handbag.

gripster *n. see* GRIPER n.¹ (2).

grip the pencil *v.* (*also* **grip it**) [1970s] to masturbate. [PENCIL n. (2)/IT n.¹ (2)]

gris *n. see* GRISTLE n.

grisly *adj.* [1910s+] (*US teen*) awful, disgusting, generally distasteful.

gristle *n.* (*also* **gris, grist**) [mid-17C+] the penis; thus [2000s] (*US Black*) *give someone the gristle*, of a man, to have sexual intercourse. [SE *gristle-bone*, any part of the body consisting of gristle]

gristle-gripper *n.* **1** [1980s] (*Aus.*) a masturbator. **2** [1990s+] the vagina. [GRISTLE n. + SE *gripper*]

gristle hammer *n.* [2000s] the penis (cf. AX n.²). [ext. GRISTLE n.]

grit *n.*¹ [19C+] (*US*) solidity or strength of character, spirit, pluck, stamina; thus *be the grit*, to be the 'right sort', the 'genuine article'.

grit *n.*² [mid-late 19C] (*US*) land or property. [SE *grit*, the ground; SE in 20C+]

grit *n.*³ [1940s–70s] (*orig. RAF*) food (cf. GRITS n.¹). [orig. RAF, but likely SAmE *hominy grits*, a staple of Black and White food in the US South]

grit *n.*⁴ (*also* **gritty**) **1** [1960s+] (*orig. US Black*) a White person, esp. a Southerner or redneck. **2** [1980s] (*US campus*) a working-class White student. [for ety. *see* GRIT n.³]

grit *n.*⁵ [1980s+] (*US campus*) a cigarette (cf. GRETTE n.). [abbr.]

grit *n.*⁶ [1980s+] (*US drugs*) crack cocaine (cf. BASE n.). [its consistency]

grit *v.*¹ [1970s] (*US prison*) to stop talking to another inmate.

grit *v.*² *see* GRIT (IT) v.

gritch *v.* [1960s+] (*US campus*) to nag, to complain. [GRIPE v. (2) + BITCH v.² (1)]

gritchy *adj.* [1970s+] (*US campus*) irritable, grouchy. [GRITCH v. + sfx -*y*]

grit (it) *v.* [1960s–70s] (*US Black/campus*) to eat; thus *gritting place*, a restaurant. [GRITS n.¹]

grit on *v.* [1970s] (*US Black*) to stare in a rude manner. [SE *grit*, coarse, tiny particles of stone or sand; one's stare grates on its target]

grit out *v.* [1980s+] (*US*) to endure hardship. [GRIT n.¹]

grits *n.*¹ [1950s+] (*US Black*) any form of food; thus *get one's grits*, to enjoy something (cf. GRIT n.³). [lit. + fig. uses of SE *grits*, coarse oatmeal, a trad. African-American food]

grits *n.*² [1970s+] **1** anything seen as a necessity, e.g. money or sex. **2** one's business. [NITTY-GRITTY n.]

gritty *n.*¹ *see* GRIT n.⁴.

gritty *n.*² *see* NITTY-GRITTY n.

gritty *adj.*¹ [mid-19C–1950s] (*US*) determined, firm, plucky. [GRIT n.¹ + sfx -*y*; subseq. use is SE]

gritty *adj.*² **1** [late 19C] impoverished, penniless. **2** [1950s+] in 'straitened circumstances'. [one is 'down in the grit', i.e. dirt]

grizzle *n.* **1** [late 17C–early 18C] a grumbler, a whinger. **2** [20C+] a fit of whingeing, grumbling or sulking, a peevish mood. [GRIZZLE (ONE'S GUTS) v.]

grizzle-guts *n.* [1940s+] (*Aus.*) a grumbler, a whinger. [GRIZZLE n. (1) + -GUTS sfx]

grizzle (one's guts) *v.* [mid-19C+] to whine, to cry slightly but continually, usu. of a child. [despite the lack of cits. (the first is in a ballad recorded in 1842), the v. is prob. orig. contemporary with GRIZZLE n. (1)]

grizzler *n. see* STREET-GRIZZLING n.

grizzly *n.* **1** [mid–late 19C; 1990s+] (*US*) a brute. **2** [late 19C] a Russian; the Russian people. **3** [1970s] (*US Black*) an unattractive woman. [SE *grizzly bear*; (2) BEAR n.²; (3) BEAR n.¹ (3)]

groady *adj. see* GRODY adj.

groak *n.* (*also* **growk**) [20C+] (*Ulster*) a child who sits watching others eating, in the hope of being asked to join them. [synon. Scot. *groak*]

groan and grunt *n. see* GRUMBLE (AND GRUNT) n.

groan-box *n.* [1920s–50s] (*orig. US Black*) a musical instrument, esp. an accordion, radio or juke box.

groaner *n.*[1] [late 18C–19C] (*UK Und.*) a pickpocket who specializes in robbing members of a church congregation. [his exaggeratedly enthusiastic, albeit completely spurious devotions, which draw the congregants' attention away from his actual purpose]

groaner *n.*[2] [1980s+] (*US*) a bad pun or joke. [the groan from the person told the joke]

groatable *adj.* [early 18C] (*US*) drunk. [? SE *groats*, hulled and/or crushed grain of various kinds; poss. used in brewing; or ? SE *groat*, 4 pence, the price of a drink]

groaty *adj.* [1960s] (*US teen/campus*) disgusting, unpleasant. [SE *grotesque*]

grob *adj.* [1940s+] (*S.Afr.*) unpleasant, coarse. [Ger./Yid. *grob*, loutish, vulgar, coarse]

groceries *n.*[1] (*also* **grocery**) [mid-19C–1910s] sugar, esp. when added to a hot alcoholic drink.

groceries *n.*[2] **1** [1960s+] (*US gay*) the male genitals. **2** [1980s] the vagina (cf. APPLE *n.*[6]; CABBAGE *n.*[7]). **3** [1980s] the breasts (cf. APPLES *n.*[1]). [? link to GREENS *n.*[2]]

grocer's cart *n.* [20C+] (*Aus.*) the heart. [rhy. sl.]

grocer's shop *n.* [1970s] an Italian (cf. DAGO *n.*). [rhy. sl. = WOP *n.*[1] (1)]

grocery *n.*[1] [mid-18C–early 19C] small change. [? its suitability for buying groceries]

grocery *n.*[2] [mid-19C–1940s] a liquor store or small bar; a speakeasy.

grocery *n.*[3] [2000s] (*US Black*) a large amount. [? SE *gross*]

grocery *n.*[4] *see* GROCERIES *n.*[1].

grocery boy *n.* [1930s–50s] (*US drugs*) an addict, in the throes of withdrawal, whose appetite has returned. [he is a constant visitor to his local grocery]

grock *n.* [1990s+] a nightclub or bar doorman. [GROCKLE *n.*]

grockle *n.* [1960s+] **1** a tourist. **2** (*UK society*) an outsider, with overtones of unpleasantness and boorishness. [the term originated in the West Country, spec. in Torbay, where a local remarked that the stream of visitors to the town resembled little Grocks (the celebrated clown *Grock*, real name Charles Adrien Wettach, 1880–1959) but spread throughout Britain's holiday resorts where the local people thus derided the flocks of annual visitors to their area; however, note Michael Quinion, *World Wide Words* (Internet, 14 July 2000): 'GROCKLE An interesting note has arrived from Dr Jeremy Marshall, an associate editor of *The Oxford English Dictionary*. The OED has worked on the word, preparatory to writing the entry for it (which will not, however, appear for some years). "The word was popularized because of its use in the film *The System* in 1962, the script-writer having picked the word up from the locals during filming in Torquay. According to research by a local journalist in the mid-1990s, the word in fact originated from a strip cartoon in the comic *Dandy* entitled 'Danny and his Grockle'. (The grockle was a magical dragon-like creature.) A local man, who had had a summer job at a swimming pool as a youngster, said that he had used the term as a nickname for a small elderly lady who was a regular customer one season. During banter in the pub among the summer workers, the term then became generalized as a term for summer visitors. I have the impression that this had occurred in, or only shortly before, the summer in which *The System* was filmed: we know of no instances of the word from the 1950s, or indeed from before the release of *The System*"']

grody *adj.* (*also* **groady, grodie**) [1960s+] **1** (*US teen*) disgusting, unpleasant; often ext. as *grody to the max*. **2** (*US campus*) noisy, vulgar, e.g. of a party. [GROTTY adj., ult. SE *grotesque* (+ TO THE MAX phr.)]

groe *n.* [1990s+] (*US*) a derog. term for a Black person (cf. ALLIGATOR BAIT *n.*[2]). [abbr. SE *Negro*; esp. New England use]

grog *n.*[1] **1** [late 17C+] (*also* **Mr Grog**) alcohol, orig. rum but soon a generic term for any intoxicating liquor, whether beer or spirits. **2** [late 19C] a party at which alcohol is drunk. **3** [1950s] (*Aus.*) a drink of beer. **4** [1950s] (*mainly UK juv.*) tea. [abbr. SE *grogram*, a coarse fabric of silk, of mohair and wool, or of these mixed with silk. Orig. applied as a nickname to Admiral Vernon, known as 'Old Grog', from the fact of his wearing a grogram cloak. The name was transferred to the mixture of rum and water, which in August 1740 he ordered to be served out instead of the RN's usual issue of neat spirit; however, note cit. 1672–85 in *The Roxburghe Ballads*, which would seem to overturn this otherwise accepted ety.]

grog *n.*[2] [1990s+] (*Scot. juv.*) spittle. [? Shetland Isles *grog*, sediment, grounds]

grog *v.*[1] [early 19C+] (*Aus.*) to drink; thus *grog on*, to drink for a lengthy period; *grog up*, to drink excessively; *grogging*, drinking. [GROG *n.*[1] (1)]

grog *v.*[2] [1990s+] (*Scot. juv.*) to spit. [GROG *n.*[2]]

grogan *n.* [1990s+] (*orig. Aus.*) a large piece of excrement. [ety. unknown; used at RMC Duntroon as a derog. for a woman]

grogans *n.* [1900s–20s] (*US*) muttonchop sidewhiskers. [generic Irish family name *Grogan*. Such whiskers were popular among Irish-Americans]

grog artist *n.* [1990s+] (*Aus./N.Z.*) a heavy drinker, a drunkard. [GROG *n.*[1] (1) + ARTIST sfx]

grog blossom *n.* [late 18C+] a red face caused by the bursting of blood-vessels through excessive, long-term drinking. [GROG *n.*[1] (1) + SE *blossom-faced*, having a red, bloated face; note 1960s US campus *blossom*, a pimple]

grog-den *n. see* GROG-SHOP *n.*

grog-fight *n.* [mid–late 19C] (*orig. milit.*) a drinking party. [GROG *n.*[1] (1) + SE *fight*]

grogged *adj.* [mid–late 19C] tipsy. [GROG *v.*[1]]

groggery *n.* [early 19C+] (*US/N.Z.*) a saloon, a public house. [GROG *n.*[1] (1)]

groggified *adj. see* GROGGY *adj.* (1).

grogging *n.* [late 19C] adulteration. [SE *grogging*, extracting spirits from an empty cask by soaking the interior with hot water; ult. GROG *n.*[1] (1), i.e. watered-down rum]

groggist *n.* [late 19C] (*Aus.*) the landlord of a public house. [GROG *n.*[1] (1) + sfx -*ist*]

groggy *n.* [late 19C] (*US*) **1** an alcohol seller. **2** an opponent of prohibition. [GROG *n.*[1] (1) + sfx -*y*]

groggy *adj.* **1** [mid-18C+] (*also* **groggified**) drunken, tipsy. **2** [19C+] weak, unsteady, semi-conscious. [GROG *n.*[1] (1) + sfx -*y*; (2) f. (1)]

grogham *n.* [late 18C–19C] (*UK Und.*) a horse. [ety. unknown]

groghead *n.* [1960s] (*US*) a drunkard. [GROG *n.*[1] (1) + -HEAD sfx (3)]

grog-hole *n.* [mid-19C] (*US*) a public house. [GROG *n.*[1] (1) + SE *hole*]

grog-mill *n.* [1940s] (*US*) a rough or illicit drinking place. [GROG *n.*[1] (1) + pattern of GIN-MILL *n.* (1)]

grog-on *n.* (*also* **grog-up**) [1950s+] (*Aus./N.Z.*) a drinking session, a party. [GROG *v.*[1]]

grog-shanty *n.* [mid-19C–1930s] (*US/Aus./N.Z.*) a public house. [GROG *n.*[1] (1) + SE *shanty*]

grog-shop *n.* (*also* **grog-den**) [late 18C+] a public house. [GROG *n.*[1] (1) + SE *shop*]

grog's talking *phr. see* IT'S THE BEER TALKING *phr.*

grog-up *n. see* GROG-ON *n.*

grog watch *n.* [late 19C] (*US*) a watch set forward in time, thus closer to the next drinking hour. [GROG *n.*[1] (1)]

groid *n.* [1970s+] (*US Southern campus*) a derog. term for a Black student (cf. ALLIGATOR BAIT *n.*[2]). [abbr. *Negroid*]

groin *n.* (*also* **growne, groyne**) [1910s+] (*UK Und.*) any ring containing a gemstone, esp. a diamond. [ety. unknown; OED links it to the body's physical *groin*, but the link seems unlikely]

grok *v.* [1960s+] in popular HIPPIE *n.*[2] (3) and mystic use, to appreciate, to understand and experience completely, usu. in phr. *grok the fullness.* [coined by SF author Robert Heinlein (1907–88) in *Strangers in a Strange Land* (1961), where it was 'Martian' for 'to drink']

grollies *n.* [2000s] testicles. [? var. on GOOLIES *n.* (1)]

grolly *n. see* GREENY *n.*[1].

grommet *n.*[1] [late 19C–1940s] (*US*) **1** the vagina. **2** the anus. **3** sexual intercourse. [SE *grommet*, a ring of rope, a washer]

grommet *n.*[2] [1990s+] (*Aus.*) a surfer. [surfing use *grommet*, a novice]

gronk *n.* **1** [1960s] (*US campus*) dirt between the toes. **2** [1980s+] (*Aus. prison*) (*also* **gronkster**) a thug, a bully. **3** [1990s+] an act of defecation. **4** [1990s+] a contemptible person.

gronk *adj.* [1990s+] of a person, disgusting, contemptible. [GRONK *n.* (4)]

gronked *adj.* [1960s+] (*US*) drunk, passed out, tired out, fast asleep (cf. ADDLED adj.). [? echoic of snoring]

gronkster *n. see* GRONK *n.* (2).

grooby *adj.* [1940s–60s] (*US*) wonderful, excellent, first-rate. [GROOVY adj.[2] (1)]

groodies *n.* [1990s+] (*US teen*) the female breasts. [coined by Anthony Burgess in *A Clockwork Orange* (1962)]

grooh *adj. see* GRUESOME adj.

grool *n.* [1950s] a sinister person, thus fig. an ugly person. [GROOLY adj.]

grooly *adj.* [1920s–70s] sinister. [SE *gru(esome)* + *(gris)ly*]

groom *v.* [1930s] (*US tramp*) to beat (with a weapon). [play on SE *groom*, to tidy, and as such cognate with RUB DOWN WITH AN OAKEN CUDGEL/TOWEL v.]

groomed to zoom *phr.* [1970s+] (*US campus*) well-dressed.

grooner *n.* [2000s] a drunken tramp. [? SE *gurn*, to pull faces]

grootbek *n.* [1940s+] (*S.Afr.*) a braggart, a boaster. [Afk. *groot*, big + *bek*, mouth]

groot krokodil *n.* [1980s+] (*S.Afr.*) **1** anyone considered to be acting in a ferocious or relentless manner. **2** the nickname of Prime Minister P.W. Botha (b.1916). [Afk. *groot krokodil*, great crocodile, and as such parodying the reverse-anthropomorphic titles given to African chiefs]

grootpraat *n.* [1940s+] (*S.Afr.*) boasting, bragging. [Afk. *groot*, big + *praat*, talk]

groove *n.*[1] [late 19C–1960s] (*later use US Black*) the vagina (cf. AGREEABLE RUTS OF LIFE *n.*). [physiognomy + latterly play on IN THE GROOVE phr.]

groove *n.*[2] **1** [1900s; 1930s+] a way of life, a way of thinking and dealing with people, events etc. **2** [1930s+] the rhythm, both lit. and fig. **3** [1940s+] a delight, a pleasure, anything enjoyable; thus *bust someone's groove*, to annoy someone. **4** [1950s–60s] an amusing or attractive person. **5** [1960s+] a party. [widely popularized by and generally ascribed to US jazz]

groove *n.*[3] [1960s+] (*US*) a record or cassette recording.

groove *v.* **1** [1930s+] (*US*) to play jazz or (latterly) rock music. **2** [1950s+] to enjoy oneself, e.g. at a party, to give pleasure; thus *grooved*, happy; *grooviness*, pleasure, enjoyment. **3** [1960s+] to travel along, to move. **4** [1960s+] to have sexual intercourse. **5** [1960s+] (*also* **groove with**) to accomodate oneself to, to get along with. **6** [1960s+] to dance; to enjoy music. [GROOVE *n.*[2]]

groove behind *v. see* GROOVE ON v.

groove on *v.* (*also* **groove behind**) [1950s+] to enjoy or appreciate a situation or other stimulus. [ext. of GROOVE v. (2)]

groover *n.* [1960s+] a person, neutral when coined in the 1960s but by 1980s+ usu. slightly derisory, since the term, and by ext. the person described, is de facto old-fashioned (cf. GROOVY adj.[2]). [GROOVE v. (2)]

groove with *v. see* GROOVE v. (5).

grooving *n.* [1960s+] **1** (*orig. US*) enjoying oneself generally.

2 (*drugs*) having an enjoyable time while using a drug. [GROOVE v. (2)]

groovy *n.* [1960s–70s] (*Scot.*) a scar. [SE *groove*]

groovy *adj.*[1] **1** [late 19C–1910s] staid, conservative. **2** [1960s+] (*US campus*) (*also* **grooving**) not using drugs; not fashionable. [SE *groove*, a routine life, also a 'line', thus pun on STRAIGHT adj.[1] (5)/STRAIGHT adj.[1] (13)/STRAIGHT adj.[2] (3)]

groovy *adj.*[2] **1** [1930s–60s] delightful, wonderful, pleasant, enjoyable etc. **2** [1940s–70s] intoxicated by a drug, usu. marijuana. **3** [1940s+] fashionable. **4** [1960s+] attractive. **5** [1980s+] (*US teen*) passé, out of date, esp. when referring to the tastes and styles of the 1960s (cf. GROOVER *n.*). [Mezzrow & Wolfe, *Really the Blues* (1946): 'He's groovy, the way musicians are groovy when they pool their talents instead of competing with each other, work together and slip into the same groove']

groovy *adv.* [1960s+] a general positive intensifier, e.g. *groovy cool*. [GROOVY adj.[2] (1)]

groovy! *excl.* [1960s+] a general excl. of approval, pleasure. [GROOVY adj.[2] (1)]

grope *n.* [late 18C+] (*US*) a welcome or unwelcome fondling or handling of the breasts, buttocks or genitals. [GROPE v. (1)]

grope *v.* **1** [14C+] (*also* **grople**) to fondle or touch the breasts, buttocks or genitals of someone, esp. a potential partner in order to assess the response to one's advances. **2** [20C+] to kiss passionately. **3** [1980s] (*US campus*) to act in a clumsy manner. [SE *grope*]

grope for Jesus *v.* [late 19C] to pray in public. [SE *grope*; the Salvation Army's early prayer meetings, when congregants were urged to 'grope for Jesus!']

grope for trout in a peculiar river *v.* [early 17C] to have sexual intercourse. [coined by Shakespeare in *Measure for Measure* (1603)]

gropehole *n.* [early 18C] the anus (cf. A-HOLE *n.*).

groper *n.*[1] **1** [late 17C–mid-19C] a blind man, both actually and in the game of Blind Man's Buff. **2** [18C–19C] a midwife. **3** [late 19C] (*US*) a blind beggar. [SE *grope*]

groper *n.*[2] [late 18C–mid-19C] a pocket. [one gropes in it for money]

groper *n.*[3] [late 19C+] (*Aus.*) a Western Australian; thus *Groperland*, Western Australia; *Groperlander*, an inhabitant of West Australia; *Groperdom*, West Australia. [abbr. SAND-GROPER *n.*]

groper *n.*[4] [1980s+] (*US drugs*) a deep inhalation of cannabis from a pipe. [it tends to be followed by a coughing fit as one's lungs grope for air]

groperess *n.* [mid-19C] a blind woman. [GROPER *n.*[1] (1) + fem. sfx -*ess*]

Groperland(er) *n. see* GROPER *n.*[3].

gropers *n.* [early 19C] the hands.

groping *n.* [1940s+] sexual stimulation, often unwanted. [GROPE v. (1)]

grople *v. see* GROPE v. (1).

gropus *n.* [mid-19C] a coat pocket. [var. GROPER *n.*[2]; one has to grope into its depths to find small items]

gross *adj.* [1920s; 1950s+] (*orig. US teen/campus*) disgusting. [SE *gross*, of huge size]

gross! *excl.* [1950s+] (*mainly US teen/campus*) disgusting! [GROSS adj.]

grossed (out) *adj.* [1960s+] (*US campus*) disgusted, repelled, appalled. [GROSS OUT v.]

grosser *n.* [1970s+] (*US*) a disgusting or ugly person. [GROSS adj.]

gross-out *n.* [1960s+] **1** (*orig. US*) something or someone disgusting. **2** (*US campus*) a contest between students to see who can be most disgusting. [GROSS OUT v.]

gross-out *adj.* [1970s+] disgusting, repellent, shocking. [GROSS OUT v.]

gross out *v.* [1960s+] (*orig. US campus*) to disgust, to shock; thus excl. *gross me out!* that really disgusts me! [GROSS adj.]

grostulation n. [1990s+] (*US*) the contractions of the rectum during anal sex. [? GROSS adj.]

grosvenor squares n. [1970s] flares (flared trousers). [rhy. sl.]

grot n.[1] **1** [1940s+] (*N.Z.*) a lavatory; thus an act of defecation or a piece of excrement. **2** [1960s+] (*Aus./US*) a dirty, untidy person. **3** [1980s+] dirt, detritus. [(1) SE *grot*, i.e. *grotto* or *grotesque*; (2) and (3) GROTTY adj.]

grot n.[2] *see* GROTTO n.

grot adj. *see* GROTTY adj.

grote n. [late 19C–1910s] an informer. [ety. unknown]

groth n. [1990s+] (*UK juv.*) spittle. [? echoic]

grotto n. (*also* **grot**) [early 18C; 19C–1900s] the vagina (cf. AGREEABLE RUTS OF LIFE n.).

grotty adj. (*also* **grot**) [1960s+] disgusting, unattractive. [SE *grotesque*; esp. popular during the Beatlemania era of the early 1960s as it was used in the film *Hard Day's Night* (1964) by The Beatles and allegedly coined by them (or more likely the writer of the screenplay Alun Owen although he has claimed that it was existing Liverpool sl.)]

grouce adj. *see* GROUSE adj.

grouch n. [late 19C+] (*orig. US*) **1** a bad temper; thus *have a grouch on*, to feel hostile towards someone or something. **2** a grumpy, complaining person or creature. [? backform. f. GROUCHY adj.]

grouch v. [1910s+] (*orig. US*) to mope, to grumble, to complain. [GROUCH n.; note OF *groucier*, to murmur, grumble (cf. GROUSE v.[1])]

grouch-bag n. **1** [20C+] a hidden pocket or purse, in which money can be secured. **2** [1910s] the money hidden in it; thus *grouch money*, savings. [the image, among the actors who coined the term, of one who saved as a GROUCH n. (2)]

grouch-box n. (*also* **grouch-pot**) [late 19C+] (*US*) a grumpy, irritable person. [GROUCH n. (2) + SE *box/-POT* sfx]

groucho n. [1950s+] an electrician. [rhy. sl.; *Groucho Marx* = SPARKS n.[2] (2)); ult. US comedian *Groucho Marx* (1890–1977)]

grouchy adj. (*also* **grouched**) [late 19C+] ill-tempered, sour. [? *OED* suggests a root in GROUCH n. (1), but *HDAS* prefers the reverse and roots *grouchy* in SE *grudge*, synon. dial. *grutch* or Yorks./US dial. *grouty*, grumpy]

grounation n. [1950s+] (*W.I. Rasta*) a large, island-wide meeting-cum-celebration for Rastas. [? ety. unknown; ? Fr. *grosnation*, a great nation or fig. use of SE *groan*, i.e. shout out + sfx *-ation*]

ground n. [1950s+] (*W.I. Rasta*) one's home.

ground v. (*also* **house**) [1950s+] (*orig. US*) to restrict someone, usu. an errant teenager, from enjoying their regular social life as a punishment for some real or perceived misdemeanour; usu. as *grounded*; thus in fig. use, dismissed from work; also dead. [SE *ground*, for an aircraft to not be able to fly]

ground angel n. [1940s] (*US Black*) a pretty young woman.

ground apple n. [1930s–40s] (*US Black*) a rock, a stone.

ground biscuit n. [1920s+] (*US*) a brick or stone when used as a missile.

ground control n. (*also* **ground man**) [1960s+] (*drugs*) a guide or caretaker during a hallucinogenic experience; such a person is either not taking the drug or a veteran user (cf. GUIDE n.; GURU n.). [SE *ground control*, a ground-based individual who communicates with an astronaut]

grounded adj. *see* GROUND v.

grounder n.[1] **1** [late 19C] a knock-down blow. **2** [1970s+] (*US drugs*) a barbiturate (cf. BARBIT n.). [they lit. and fig. *knock one to the ground*]

grounder n.[2] [1930s; 1990s+] (*US*) a cigarette that is picked up from the ground to be smoked.

ground grippers n. (*also* **ground grabbers**) [1910s–60s] (*US Black*) shoes, esp. new ones (cf. GRIPPERS n.).

ground-hog n.[1] [1910s–50s] (*US*) a frankfurter, a hot dog.

ground-hog n.[2] **1** [1910s+] (*US*) any worker whose occupation keeps them on the ground. **2** [1920s+] (*US*) a caisson worker,

working under compressed air, digging and laying the foundations of bridges etc. **3** [1960s+] (*Can.*) a meteorologist.

groundhog case n. [late 19C–1950s] (*US, Western*) a tight corner, an inescapable situation. [imagery of the trapped animal]

ground man n. *see* GROUND CONTROL n.

groundnut n. (*also* **ground-seed**) [mid-19C] (*US*) a rock or stone.

groundpads n. (*also* **groundpad bags**) [1930s–40s] (*US Black*) **1** feet. **2** shoes. **3** socks.

groundpad spade n. [1940s] (*US Black*) a shoehorn. [GROUNDPADS n. (2) + SE *spade*]

ground-parrot n. [late 19C] (*Aus.*) a small farmer. [play on COCKATOO n.[3]]

ground-pounder n. [1940s+] (*US*) an infantry soldier.

ground rations n. (*also* **under rations**) [1930s+] (*US Black*) sexual intercourse. [pun; note also UNDER n.]

grounds n. [1960s] (*drugs*) the residue left after an injection of heroin.

ground-seed n. *see* GROUNDNUT n.

ground smashers n. [1950s] (*US Black*) feet; shoes.

ground-sweat n. [late 17C–mid-19C] a grave; thus *take a ground-sweat*, to be buried.

ground zero n. [1950s+] (*orig. milit.*) the basic position, the start, the essentials.

grouper *see under* GROUPIE.

grouper trooper n. [1980s] (*US*) a member of the Florida state marine patrol. [SE *grouper*, 'One of several species of the genus *Epinephelus* of serranoid fishes, inhabiting West Indian waters and the Mexican gulf and used extensively for food' (*OED*) + *trooper*]

group grope n. **1** [1960s+] an orgy. **2** [1970s+] (*US campus*) in fig. use, an encounter group, esp. one that stresses physical contact. [SE *group* + GROPE n.]

groupie n.[1] (*also* **grouper**) [1960s+] a devotee of group sex. [SE *group*, a collection of people]

groupie n.[2] (*also* **grouper**, **groupy**) **1** [1960s+] a young girl or woman who associates herself with rock bands, offering her body in return for a share of their celebrity. **2** [1970s+] anyone, male or female, who is an obsessive fan; the adoration need not run to sex, nor are the subjects necessarily rock stars. [SE *group*, a pop/rock band]

group portrait n. [1970s] an orgy.

grouse n.[1] [mid-19C+] a young woman; hence a generic term for sexual intercourse. [SE *grouse*, the small game bird]

grouse n.[2] [1910s+] a complaint; thus *grouser*, a complainer. [GROUSE v.[1]]

grouse n.[3] [1960s–70s] (*Aus. Und.*) a tailormade, rather than prison-issue cigarette. [GROUSE adj.]

grouse, the n. [1920s+] (*Aus./N.Z.*) the best, the ultimate, the ideal. [GROUSE adj.]

grouse adj. (*also* **grouce**) [1930s+] (*Aus./N.Z.*) wonderful, attractive, excellent, an all-purpose term of approval. [ety. unknown; ? UK dial. *crouse*, happy, lively, pleased]

grouse v.[1] [late 19C] (*orig. milit.*) to grumble, to complain; thus *grousy*, ill-tempered, complaining. [? OF *groucier*; to murmur, grumble (cf. GROUCH v.)]

grouse v.[2] [1950s+] (*US*) to engage in sexual activity. [GROUSE n.[1]]

grouse gear n. [1950s+] (*Aus. teen*) a particularly attractive woman. [GROUSE adj. + GEAR n.[1] (2); but note GEAR n.[2] (1)]

grouser n. *see* GROUSE n.[2]

grout-bag n. [1910s] (*UK teen*) a very hard worker. [SAmE *grout*, to grumble, to sulk + -BAG sfx]

grouter n. [20C+] (*Aus.*) a piece of good luck, an unfair advantage; esp. in phr. *come in on the grouter*, *run the grouter*; occas. as excl. [ety. unknown; ? Yorks. dial. *grout*, to rummage or root about]

grouter v. [20C+] (*Aus.*) to get hold of something through luck rather than judgement, to take unfair advantage of a situation. [GROUTER n.]

grouthead *n.* [late 16C–mid-17C; mid-19C–1900s] a fool, a simpleton. [16C–mid-17C use UK; later use US; SE *grout*, lit. coarse meal, taken as something large and rough and/or SAmE *grout*, grumble + -HEAD sfx (1)]

groutnoll *n.* [early–mid-17C] a fool. [SE *grout*, lit. coarse meal, taken as something large and rough + *noll*, head]

grouty *adj.* [mid-19C–1910s] (*US*) grumpy, irritable; thus *the grouties*, ill temper. [SAmE *grout*, to grumble, to sulk]

Grove, the *n.* [1950s+] (*orig. UK Black*) Ladbroke *Grove*, London W11/W10. [abbr.]

grovel *v.* [1980s+] (*US campus*) to neck, to enjoy sexual relations, esp. with someone who is not one's regular partner.

grove of eglantine *n.* [19C] pubic hair. [SE *eglantine*, the sweetbriar]

grove of Venus *n. see* VENUS'S HIGHWAY n.

grover *n.* [1980s] (*US*) $1000 bill (cf. ABE n.[2]). [the picture of US President *Grover* Cleveland (1837–1908), printed on the bills]

grow a belly *v. see* GET A BELLY v.

grow a tail *v.* [1990s+] to be ready to defecate.

grow hay in one's nose *v.* [1920s–30s] (*US*) to be an unsophisticated, rural person, a peasant. [play on HAYSEED n.]

grow horns *v.*[1] [17C–18C] to become the victim of cuckoldry.

grow horns *v.*[2] [1970s+] (*US campus*) to become angry. [the horns are those of a bull rather than of a cuckold]

growk *n. see* GROAK n.

growl *n.* [1930s] (*US*) food, a snack (cf. GROWLER n.[6]). [? the growling of one's stomach or ? the growling sounds of eating]

growl (and grunt) *n. see* GRUMBLE (AND GRUNT) n.

growl at the badger *v.* [1970s+] to perform cunnilingus. [SE *growl* + BADGER n.[5] (2); note RMC Duntroon *growl out*, to perform cunnilingus]

growl-biter *n.* [late 19C+] one who performs cunnilingus. [GROWL (AND GRUNT) n. + SE *bite*]

growl-biting *n.* [late 19C+] cunnilingus. [GROWL-BITER n.]

growler *n.*[1] **1** [early 19C+] a dog. **2** [early 19C+] a cannon. **3** [1910s] a horse. **4** [1960s] (*US*) a police car siren; the car itself. **5** [1970s] a lion. **6** [1990s+] (*UK juv.*) a nagging female. [they all 'growl']

growler *n.*[2] [mid-19C–1910s] a 4-wheeled cab. [either a pun on SE *sulky* (although this was a 1-horse, 2-wheeled vehicle) or the creaks and rattles of the cab or the stereotypically poor temper of the driver]

growler *n.*[3] **1** [late 19C–1930s] a whisky flask. **2** [late 19C–1940s] (*US*) a container, usu. a covered pail with a carrying handle, in which beer was purchased at a tavern, then brought home for consumption; thus *growler money*, *growler boy*, *growler bag*. **3** [1920s–50s] (*US prison*) any form of container, e.g. used for coffee, conveying illicit homebrewed alcohol etc. [ety. unknown; ? the growling, grating noise of the can in (2) as it slid, full of beer, across the bar, or the 'growling' or grumbling of the children who were sent on the errand, or the drunken arguing that ensued among recipients of the liquor; for full discussion *see* Cohen (ed.), *Studies in Slang* VI (1999) pp.1–20]

growler *n.*[4] (*US*) **1** [1940s–70s] a lavatory, usu. as in a prison cell. **2** [1980s] a prison. [the noise, either of someone straining to defecate or of incarcerated prisoners]

growler *n.*[5] [1990s+] the vagina; thus an attractive young woman. [GROWL (AND GRUNT) n.]

growler *n.*[6] [2000s] food (cf. GROWL n.). [? the growling of one's stomach or ? the growling sounds of eating]

growler *n.*[7] [2000s] (*UK prison*) a menacing prison inmate who resists using physical violence. [he *growls* instead of fighting]

growler-shover *n.* [late 19C–1910s] a cab driver. [GROWLER n.[2] + SE *shove*]

growlery *n.* [mid–late 19C] a private sitting-room, a 'den'. [coined by Charles Dickens in *Bleak House* (1852–3)]

growlies *n.*[1] [1980s+] **1** (*US*) a craving for food in general. **2** (*US drugs*) spec. the craving for food while smoking marijuana. [one's stomach rumbles or 'growls']

growlies *n.*[2] [2000s] (*US campus/teen*) ill temper, a bad mood. [SE *growl*]

grown-ass *adj.* (*also* **grown-assed**) [1930s] (*US Black*) adult, mature, grown-up. [SE *grown* + -ASS sfx]

growne *n. see* GROIN n.

grownies *n.* [1970s+] adults. [SE *grown-ups* + *groan*]

grow up! *excl.* [1910s+] used contemptuously to anyone, adult or child, who is behaving immaturely.

groyne *n. see* GROIN n.

grrl *n.* [1990s+] (*US gay*) a young lesbian, reasonably but not wholly masculine in style.

grub *n.*[1] [mid-17C; mid-19C+] (*US campus*) a hard worker, one who works to the exclusion of other interests. [he 'grubs up' facts]

grub *n.*[2] **1** [mid-17C+] food; thus [early 19C] *in grub*, employed (i.e. with the means to eat); [1990s+] (*US Black*) *get one's grub on*, to eat, esp. voraciously. **2** [1940s+] a meal; thus *grub palace*, a restaurant. [one has 'grubbed it up']

grub *n.*[3] **1** [mid-18C+] a dirty, unkempt person, esp. a child, any obnoxious person. **2** [1960s] (*US campus*) a student kitchen worker. [SE *grub*, the larva of an insect]

grub *n.*[4] [1950s] (*Aus.*) tuberculosis. [SE *grub*, the larva of an insect]

grub *adj.* [1990s+] of food, tasty. [GRUB n.[2] (1)]

grub *v.*[1] **1** [18C+] to eat. **2** [19C–1920s] to provide with food. [GRUB n.[2] (1)]

grub *v.*[2] [mid-19C] (*UK Und.*) to walk (unsteadily). [dial. *grub*, to potter about]

grub *v.*[3] [mid-19C+] (*US campus*) to study hard.

grub *v.*[4] [late 19C+] to beg, to scrounge; thus phr. *on the grub*. [SE *grub up*, to uproot, in this case whatever can be begged]

grub *v.*[5] **1** [1960s+] to kiss passionately. **2** [1960s+] to have sexual intercourse. [? GRUB n.[2] (1); or ? SE *grubby*]

grub! *excl.* [1900s] (*Aus.*) a mild excl. [ety. unknown]

grub along *v.* [late 19C+] to subsist, to struggle along. [GRUB v.[4]]

grub and bub *n.* (*also* **bub and grub**) [19C] food and drink. [GRUB n.[2] (1) + BUB n.[1]]

grubbed up *adj.* [1960s] (*US*) unkempt, dirty. [GRUB n.[3] (1)]

grubber *n.*[1] (*US*) **1** [late 18C–1940s] a beggar. **2** [1930s] a working man. [(1) GRUB v.[4]; (2) GRUB ALONG v.]

grubber *n.*[2] **1** [19C] a promiscuous woman. **2** [1920s+] (*US*) a disgusting person. [GRUB n.[3] (1); (2) note Yid. *grobber*, a coarse or rude person]

grubber *n.*[3] [mid-19C–1900s] an eater; thus *heavy grubber*, an enthusiastic, if unmannered, eater. [GRUB v.[1] (1)]

grubber *n.*[4] [late 19C] (*US campus*) a diligent student. [GRUB v.[3]]

grubber *n.*[5] [20C+] a vagrants' casual night shelter or workhouse. [GRUB ALONG v. + SE *grub*, an insect larva, thus a disease]

grubbery *n.* [19C] **1** food. **2** a public meal. **3** a cookshop; an eating house. **4** a dining room. **5** the stomach. **6** (*UK Und.*) a workhouse. [GRUB n.[2] (1)]

grubbies *n. see* GRUBS n.

grubbiken *n.* [mid-19C] a workhouse where one was fed without performing the usual mandatory labour. [GRUB n.[2] (1) + KEN n.[1] (1)]

grubbing *n.*[1] [19C] eating. [GRUB v.[1] (1)]

grubbing *n.*[2] *see* GRUBBINS n.

grubbing-crib *n.* (*also* **grubbing-ken**) [mid-19C] **1** a cookshop; thus *grubbing-crib fencer*, the proprietor of an eating house. **2** a workhouse. [GRUBBING n.[1] + CRIB n.[1] (1)/KEN n.[1] (1)]

grubbins *n.*[1] [mid-19C] (*US*) food. [GRUB n.[2] (1)]

grubbins *n.*[2] (*also* **grubbing**) [1910s] (*UK/US Und.*) money. [GRUB v.[4]]

grubble v. [1960s] (orig. US) to rummage around, to search at random. [GRUB v.[4] + SE scrabble]

grubby n. [1940s] (US campus) an ostracized student. [GRUB n.[1]]

grub-cadging n. see CADGING n.

grub-crib n. [mid-19C] an eating house. [GRUB n.[2] (1) + CRIB n.[1] (1)]

gruber-grubber n. see GOOBER-GRABBER n.[1].

grub hooks n. [1920s+] (US) fingers or hands. [GRUB n.[2] (1) + SE hooks/HOOK n.[1] (1)]

grub-liner n. (also **grub-rider**) [1900s–60s] (US) an itinerant, out-of-work cowboy who subsists on hand-outs; thus RIDE THE GRUB LINE v. [GRUB n.[2] (1) + fig. use of cowboy jargon line, the boundary of a ranch]

grub-mill n. [late 19C] (US) the mouth. [GRUB n.[2] (1) + SE mill]

grub on v. (also **grub out**) [1980s+] (US campus) to eat. [GRUB v.[1] (1)]

grub palace n. see GRUB n.[2] (2).

grub-pile n. [late 19C–1940s] (US, Western) a meal. [GRUB n.[2] (1) + SE pile]

grub-rider n. see GRUB-LINER n.

grubs n. (also **grubbies**) [1960s+] (US campus) old or comfortable, informal clothes. [SE grubby]

grubshite v. [late 18C–early 19C] to foul, to make dirty. [SE grubby + SHITE v.]

grub-shop n. [mid-19C] 1 an eating house. 2 the mouth. [GRUB n.[2] (1) + SE shop]

grub-slinger n. [1910s] (US) 1 a cook. 2 a waiter or waitress. [GRUB n.[2] (1) + SE sling/SLINGER n.[1] (1)]

grub-spoiler n. [late 19C–1950s] (US) a cook. [GRUB n.[2] (1) + SE spoiler]

grubstake n. 1 [mid-19C+] (orig. US) enough money to buy one a meal; ext. to any form of deposit or any form of advance that allows one to work. 2 [1900s–40s] (also **grubstakes**, **grubsteaks**) food, rations. [GRUB n.[2] (1) + SE stake, the sum of money one places on a bet; immediate root is US mining jargon grub stake, 'the outfit, provisions etc furnished to a prospector on condition of participating in the profits of any find he may make; a lay-out' (Century Dict., 1889)]

grubstake v. [late 19C+] (orig. US) to provide one with sufficient money with which to eat, live etc. [GRUBSTAKE n. (1)]

grub station n. [1900s] (US) a restaurant. [GRUB n.[2] (1)]

grubsteaks n. see GRUBSTAKE n. (2).

Grub Street news n. [late 17C–early 19C] rumours, lies; thus Grub Street philosopher, one who spreads such rumours; Grub Street crew, the gossips. [proper name Grub Street, the notional home of hack journalism. There actually was a Grub Street, poss. named for a Mr Grubbe, near Moorfields in the City of London; it was renamed Milton Street in 1830; Andrew Marvell coined the phr. to epitomize the world of hackery. Grub Street, according to Johnson, Dictionary (1755), was 'much inhabited by writers of small histories, dictionaries, and temporary poems']

grub thirst n. [late 19C] (US) hunger, appetite. [GRUB n.[2] (1)]

grub-trap n. [mid–late 19C] the mouth. [GRUB n.[2] (1) + SE trap/TRAP n.[3]]

grub up v. [1920s+] to eat. [GRUB v.[1] (1)]

grub up! excl. [1950s+] an excl. denoting that it is time to eat, the food is ready. [GRUB n.[2] (1)]

grub warehouse n. [mid-19C] the stomach. [GRUB n.[2] (1)]

grudge fuck n. [2000s] (US) an act of intercourse undertaken simply as a result of a grudge, e.g. against an absent partner. [GRUDGE-FUCK v.]

grudge-fuck v. [1970s+] usu. of a woman, to make intercourse unsatisfying or even impossible. [SE grudge + FUCK v.[1]]

grue adj.[1] (also **gruey**) [1920s+] nervous, afraid. [SE gruesome]

grue adj.[2] see GRUESOME adj.

gruel n. 1 [late 18C–1900s] punishment; thus have/get one's gruel, to receive one's punishment, to get killed; take one's gruel, to receive and accept punishment; GIVE SOMEONE GRUEL v. 2 [late 19C] (US) sentimental, 'thin' poetry. [the thin, unpalatable gruel one receives in prison]

gruel v. [late 19C] to ejaculate (into). [for ety. see prev.]

grueller n. 1 [mid-19C] a problem. 2 [late 19C] a knock-down blow, a 'floorer'. [SE gruel, to punish, to exhaust]

gruesome adj. (also **grue**, **grooh**) [1930s+] (US) awful, unattractive.

gruesome and gory n. [20C+] the penis (cf. ALMOND n.). [rhy. sl. = CORIE n.]

gruesome twosome n. [1940s+] (orig. US) 1 a couple in a steady relationship. 2 a pair of individuals, esp, when unpopular, e.g. 2 teenage girls sharing a very close friendship, a lesbian couple.

gruey adj. see GRUE adj.[1].

gruff-nut n. [1990s+] (UK juv.) 1 faecal matter sticking to the anal hairs. 2 a general insult.

grulch n. [20C+] (Irish) a small stocky person, usu. somewhat uncouth and less than amicable. [synon. Scot. grulsh]

grumble v. [1920s] (US tramp) to pray.

grumble (and grunt) n. (also **groan and grunt**, **growl (and grunt)**) [1930s+] 1 the vagina (cf. ALL QUIET n.). 2 a generic term for women. 3 sexual intercourse. [rhy. sl. = CUNT n.[1] (1)]

grumble and mutter n. [20C+] a bet. [rhy. sl. = FLUTTER n.[2] (2)]

grumble-guts n. (also **grumble-gizzard**) [late 18C+] a habitual complainer. [SE grumble + -GUTS sfx; orig. Yorks. dial.; note synon. Lancashire dial. grumble-belly]

grumble in the gizzard v. [late 17C–early 19C] to be annoyed, but to keep one's feelings to oneself.

grumbler n. [early 19C] 4 pennyworth of grog. [the landlord grumbles at the customer's economy or the drink makes one's stomach grumble]

grumbles, the n. [mid–late 19C] bad temper, sulkiness; thus be all on the grumbles, to be in a bad mood.

grumbletonian n. [late 17C–mid-19C] a constant grumbler, esp. as regards the 'state of the country'. [a pun on 2 17C religious sects, the Muggletonians (founded 1651 by Lodowicke Muggleton) and the Grindletonians (? the Yorks. village of Grindleton); the term was used first as specific political jargon c.1690 when the 'Court Party' apostrophized as grumbletonians their 'Country Party' rivals, who, they claimed, resented their personal ambitions being thwarted]

grummet n. (also **grummit**) 1 [mid–late 19C] the vagina. 2 [mid–late 19C] sexual intercourse. 3 [1960s+] (orig. N.Z. surfing) a woman, esp. as a sex object. 4 [1980s+] (N.Z. juv.) someone or something disliked. [SE grummet, a ring of rope, a washer]

grummy adj. [1920s] (US) unhappy, depressed. [ety. unknown]

grump n. 1 [mid-19C+] (also **grumps**) ill temper. 2 [20C+] a bad-tempered, surly person. [dial.]

grumper n. [1970s] (US) the buttocks. [? SE rump]

grumpus n. [1960s] (US) a bad-tempered person. [SE grumpy]

grumpy-drawers n. (also **gloomy-drawers**) [1980s+] (mainly UK juv.) an ill-tempered, depressive person.

grundies n. [1980s+] (Aus./N.Z./UK) underwear (cf. REG GRUNDYS n.). [rhy. sl. = UNDIES n.; ult. Aus. media executive Reg Grundy (b.1923)]

grundle n. [1990s+] (US) the perineum. [ety. unknown; ? link to 16C grundy, a short person, and thus, here, a short distance]

grundy n.[1] [late 16C] usu. of men, a short, fat person. [? Du. grundje, groundling]

grundy n.[2] [1990s+] (UK juv.) a school 'game' whereby the waistband of the victim's underwear is grasped and pulled up hard, thus causing them pain. [GRUNDIES n.]

grunge n. (orig. US) 1 [1960s+] sticky, dirty, unpleasant substances. 2 [1960s+] a general term of abuse, a repugnant, odious, dirty or boring person or thing. 3 [1970s+] a form of rock music, epitomized by the work of the Seattle band Nirvana, but first used in relation to the New York Dolls, c.1973 (also known, among many rivals, as the 'godfathers of PUNK n.⁴'). **4** [1980s+] the clothing style that developed out of and surrounds (3).

grunge v. [1960s+] **1** to whine, to complain. **2** to assault, to attack, to terrify. [? GRIPE v. (2) + SE *whinge*]

grunged-out adj. [1980s+] (*US*) dirty, messy, unappetizing, unappealing. [GRUNGY adj. (1)]

grungehole n. [1980s] (*US*) a dirty room or place. [GRUNGE n. (1) + HOLE n.² (2)]

grungey adj. see GRUNGY adj.

grungie n. [1980s] (*US*) an unconventional person. [GRUNGE n. (3)]

grungies n. [1980s+] (*US campus*) dirty laundry. [GRUNGE n. (1)]

grungy adj. (*also* **gringy, grungey**) **1** [1960s+] dirty, messy, unappetizing, unappealing. **2** [1990s+] dressed in the style of GRUNGE n. (3). [SE *grubby* + SE *dingy*]

grunt n.¹ (*US*) **1** [20C+] an ill-tempered, constantly complaining person. **2** [1970s+] a stupid or unpleasant person. [GRUNT v.¹ (1)]

grunt n.² **1** [1920s–40s] (*US*) the bill, usu. for food or drink. **2** [1920s+] (*US*) a slice of ham or pork; bacon. **3** [1970s+] (*also* **grunts**) food, esp. snack food. [GRUNTER n.¹ (1)/SE *grunt*, i.e. the sound of eating]

grunt n.³ (*US*) **1** [1920s+] any person doing menial work; an assistant. **2** [1960s+] a combat soldier, a marine soldier or a non-flying Air Force officer. [(1) SE *grunt*, the noise; ? (2) the soldier's endless complaining; the Vietnam era successor to the DOUGHBOY n.¹, thus used in civilian senses]

grunt n.⁴ **1** [1940s+] (*US*) (*also* **grunties**) excrement; thus fig 'the daylights', the essence. **2** [1960s] (*US Black*) a bowel movement. [the sounds of defecation]

grunt n.⁵ [1990s+] an extremely unattractive woman. [play on PIG n.¹ (3)]

grunt n.⁶ see GRUNTER n.¹ (1).

grunt v.¹ **1** [late 18C+] to complain. **2** [1930s–40s] (*US*) to do menial work. [SE *grunt*/GRUNT n.³]

grunt v.² **1** [1960s] (*US*) to defecate. **2** [2000s] (*UK juv.*) to break wind. [GRUNT n.⁴ (1)]

grunter n.¹ **1** [early 17C–1950s] (*also* **grunt, gruntler**) a (sucking) pig. **2** [1900s] (*Aus.*) A Boer soldier.

grunter n.² **1** [late 18C–early 19C] a shilling (5p). **2** [mid–late 19C] a sixpence (2½p). [play on HOG n.¹]

grunter n.³ [early 19C; 1990s+] a policeman (cf. ANIMAL n.¹). [pun on PIG n.¹ (1)]

grunter n.⁴ **1** [1900s–20s] an automobile, a steam engine. **2** [1930s+] (*US*) a professional wrestler. [the noise]

grunter n.⁵ [1940s+] (*Aus.*) a prostitute; a promiscuous girl or woman. [? the (simulated) grunts of passion with which she embellishes her services]

grunter n.⁶ [1980s+] an old person out of sympathy with current youth enthusiasms. [their grunts of complaint]

grunter's gig n. [late 18C–19C] the flesh of a smoked pig's face. [GRUNTER n.¹ (1) + GIG n.² (1)]

grunt horn n. (*also* **grunt iron**) [1920s–30s] (*US*) a tuba.

grunties n. see GRUNT n.⁴ (1).

grunting-cheat n. (*also* **grunting-chete, gruntling-cheat/-chete**) [mid-16C–mid-19C] (*UK Und.*) a pig, pork. [SE *grunt* + CHEAT n. (1)]

grunting peck n. [mid-17C–mid-19C] pork, bacon or any pigmeat. [SE *grunting* + PECK n.¹ (1)]

grunt iron n. see GRUNT HORN n.

gruntler n. see GRUNTER n.¹ (1).

gruntling n. [late 17C–early 18C] a pig.

gruntling-cheat/-chete n. see GRUNTING-CHEAT n.

grunt work n. [1970s+] (*US*) menial work, drudgery. [SE *grunt*/GRUNT n.³ (1)+ SE *work*]

grush v. (*also* **grushie**) [1920s+] for children to scramble for a handful of small change tossed to them, typically after a wedding. [synon. Scot. *grush*]

gruts n. [early 19C] tea. [ety. unknown]

G-shot n. [1960s+] (*drugs*) a small dose of drugs used to hold off withdrawal symptoms until a full dose can be taken. [it SE *gees* one up + SHOT n.⁶ (2)]

G-smack n. [2000s] (*US Black*) the police. [G n.³ (1) + SMACK v.¹ (2)]

GSQ n. see GOLDEN SHOWER QUEEN n.

G-ster n. see GANGSTA n.

G-string n. [1970s+] **1** (*US Black*) any device – a tampon, towel etc – used to staunch the flow of menstrual blood. **2** (*US gay*) an athletic supporter, a jockstrap. [SE *G-string*, the minimal 'loin-cloth' worn by striptease artists etc]

g.t.a. phr. see G.T.T. phr.

g.t.f.o.! excl. (*also* **g.t.f.o.o.m.w.!**) [1990s+] get the fuck out; often ext. to *get the fuck out of my way.* [abbr. of GET THE FUCK (OUT)! excl.]

g.t.h.! excl. [1910s] (*US*) go to hell! [abbr.]

g-thang n. (*also* **g-thing**) [1990s+] (*US Black*) **1** anything that is seen as a male preserve, a 'guy thing'. **2** anything that concerns a street thug, a 'gangster thing'. **3** anything that is seen as a female preserve, a 'girl thing'.

G-town n. [1980s+] (*US*) Georgetown, Washington, D.C. [abbr.]

g.t.t. phr. (*also* **g.t.a**) [mid-19C–1900s] (*US*) gone to Texas/ Arkansas; the sign affixed to the door of an absconding businessman's. [abbr.]

Guam n. [late 19C+] a generic term for any very distant place. [orig. naut. use]

guaranfuckingtee v. (*also* **guarandamntee**) [1940s+] an intensified form of *guarantee*. [SE *guarantee* + FUCKING adj. (4)/DAMN adj. (3)]

guardhouse lawyer n. see BARRACK-ROOM LAWYER n.

guard's van n. [1990s+] the last man of those taking part in gang-rape or group intercourse. [play on PULL A TRAIN v. (1)]

Guat n. [1990s+] a Guatemalan. [abbr.]

guava n.¹ [1970s+] (*S.Afr.*) the buttocks, the posterior. [resemblance]

guava n.² [1980s] (*S.Afr.*) a South African version of the YUPPIE n. [abbr. grown/growing up and very ambitious]

gub n.¹ (*also* **gubbah, gubber, Mr Gub**) [1970s+] (*Aus. Aborigine*) a term for a White man, usu. derog. [? SE *garbage* or SE *government*; note Seal, *The Lingo* (1999): 'The origins of the word [...] may derive from GOVERNMENT BLANKET, widely pronounced [...] as GUBMENT BLANKET, sometimes GUBBY BLANKET. Such blankets were often identified with a red stripe or other device sewn along them. It is said that Aboriginal people would spend many hours unpicking these stitches and over the years this hated symbol of dependence on white handouts has been honed to its present usage'; note 1887, *Bulletin* (Sydney) 15 October 12/3: 'At La Perouse, Sydney, there lives a black who goes by the exalted and sacred name of "The Gubnor"']

gub n.² see GOB n.¹.

guban n. [20C+] (*Irish*) a general term of abuse, esp. an unpleasantly negative critic whose attacks are not based in actual expertise or knowledge. [Irish *gobán*, an old-fashioned incompetent tradesman]

gubbah/gubber n. see GUB n.¹.

gubberigine n. [1980s+] (*Aus. prison*) an Aborigine who is considered by his peers to have sold out to White society. [GUB n.¹ + SE *Aborigine*]

gubbins n. **1** [1900s–50s] a fool, a simpleton. **2** [1910s+] a term for any nameless object. [SE *gubbins*, fragments, esp. of fish; fish-parings]

gubbo n. see GOVO n.

gubbrow v. [late 19C] (*Anglo-Ind.*) to bully, to confuse, to worry. [Hind. *gabrao*, to dumbfound]

Gucci queen n. [1970s] (*US gay*) an affected, fashion-conscious older homosexual. [brandname *Gucci* + QUEEN n.² (1)/QUEEN sfx (2)]

guck *n.* (*also* **gluck**) [1950s+] (*orig. US*) any form of sticky substance, ointment, cream. [echoic]

gucky *adj.* [1960s+] (*UK society*) of an event or person as much as of food or drink, sickening, likely to make one vomit. [GUCK n.+ sfx -*y*]

gud *n.* [late 17C–mid-18C] God, as used in oaths.

guddha *n.* [mid-19C–1900s] (*Anglo-Ind.*) a fool. [synon. Hind. *gadhā*]

gudgeon *n.* [late 16C–1920s] a gullible person, one who will 'swallow' anything; thus *gape for gudgeons/give a gudgeon*, to be fooled. [SE *gudgeon*, a small freshwater fish, often used as bait]

gudgeon *v.* [late 18C–early 19C] to render oneself gullible, to become a victim. [GUDGEON n.]

guee *n.* (*also* **gee, ghee**) [mid-19C–1940s] (*US*) a derog. term for a Portuguese person. [abbr.]

Guernsey highball *n.* [1940s] (*US*) milk. [Guernsey cows]

guerrilla *n.* [mid–late 19C] (*US*) a swindler, a crooked gambler.

guesser *n.* [1900s] (*N.Z.*) a dishonest racing tipster, hired by bookmakers to persuade punters to bet on useless horses.

guessing-gear *n.* [1900s] (*Aus.*) the head, the brain.

guessing-stick *n.* (*also* **guess stick**) [1930s–40s] a slide-rule.

guest of the cross-legged knights, be *v.* [18C–early 19C] to go without one's dinner. [the effigies of such knights in the Round Church in the Temple, London]

guff *n.*[1] **1** [mid-19C+] (*also* **guffery**) lies, nonsense, twaddle. **2** [late 19C+] insolence. **3** [20C+] talk. [SE *guff*, a puff, a whiff]

guff *n.*[2] [1980s+] a fart. [dial. *guff*, an offensive smell]

guff *v.*[1] [late 19C] (*US*) to chat. [GUFF n.[1] (3)]

guff *v.*[2] [1980s+] to break wind. [GUFF n.[2]]

guff *v.*[3] *see* GUFF (OFF) v.

guffery *n. see* GUFF n.[1] (1).

guffin *n.* [mid–19C–1960s] a clumsy fool. [northern dial.]

guff (off) *v.* [20C+] (*Aus.*) to shirk, to act lazily. [? dial. *guff*, to talk nonsense, to babble]

guffoon *n.* [late 19C] (*Irish*) a clumsy fool.

guffy *n.* [1900s] a fool, one who 'talks guff'. [GUFF n.[1] (1)]

gugag *n. see* HEWGAG n.

gugga *adj. see* GAGA adj.

guggle *n.* [late 17C] the windpipe, the throat. [SE *guggle*, to make a gurgling sound, like that of water pouring from a narrow-necked bottle]

guggy *n.* [20C+] (*Irish*) an egg. [Irish *gogaí*, nursery term for an egg]

gu-gu *n. see* GOO-GOO n.[1] (1).

Guguland *n.* [1900s] (*US*) the Philippines. [GOO-GOO n.[1] (1) + SE -*land*]

guide *n.* [1960s] (*drugs*) a guide or 'caretaker' during a hallucinogenic experience; such a person is either not taking the drug or a veteran user (cf. GUIDE n.).

guided missile *n.* [1970s+] (*US Black*) the erect penis (cf. AX n.[2]).

guide-post *n.* [late 18C–1900s] a clergyman. [he is supposed to guide the congregation to heaven]

guido *n.* **1** [1970s] (*US*) an Italian; thus fem. var. *guidette* (cf. DAGO n.). **2** [1980s+] (*US campus*) someone acting in an ostentatiously masculine (or feminine) manner. **3** [1990s+] a MULLET n.[2] hairstyle. [Ital. proper name *Guido*; the initial ref. was to the young working-class Italians who live outside Manhattan and come into the city for their entertainment]

guilderhead *n.* [1970s+] (*Ulster*) a stupid, clumsy person. [Scot. *guldie*, 'a tall, black-faced, gloomy-looking man' (*EDD*) + -HEAD sfx (1)]

guin *n. see* GUINEA n.

Guinea *n.*[1] [late 19C+] (*US*) a euph. for *hell*, e.g. *go to Guinea*. [the far distance of African Guinea]

Guinea *n.*[2] [1930s–60s] (*US*) a euph. for *God*, e.g. *swear to Guinea!* (cf. BOB n.[2]). [the initial G]

guinea *n.* (*also* **ghinny, gin, ginney, ginny, guin, guinny**) (*US*) **1** [late 19C+] an Italian person, usu. an immigrant to the US. **2** [1910s+] various other non-Anglo nationalities, usu. Mediterranean, e.g. a Greek, a Portuguese, a Jew (cf. DAGO n.). **3** [1910s+] a foolish, gullible or insignificant man. **4** [1940s] a Japanese person, a Pacific native (cf. BUDDHAHEAD n.). **5** [1950s–60s] the Italian language. [18C *guinea*, a Black. The original guineas were Black slaves from the Guinea Coast of Africa, and the term gradually evolved to mean anyone with a notably dark complexion, although it is rarely if ever used to mean a Black in 20C+ other than in the SE *Guinea Negro*, a mixed-race group native to Maryland, Virginia and West Virginia, who call themselves *Our People* or *Melungeons*]

guinea *adj.* (*also* **ghinny, ginney**) [20C+] (*US*) used of an Italian person or culture. [GUINEA n. (1)]

guinea bird *n.*[1] [17C; mid-19C] a prostitute (cf. ALLEY CAT n.). [? her price]

guinea bird *n.*[2] (*W.I.*) **1** [early 19C] an African-born Black person; so called by the Creoles, who were born in the West Indies. **2** [1980s] (*also* **ginigog**) someone who is superior in some way, either positively or negatively. [the state of Guinea + BIRD n.[2] (1)]

guinea cadillac *n.* [1970s] (*US*) a powered tricycle used in the construction industry to convey concrete on a building site. [GUINEA adj. + ironic use of SE *Cadillac*; many big city construction workers are Italians]

guinea-dropper *n.* [late 17C–early 18C] a confidence trickster who drops counterfeit guineas to ensnare the gullible.

guinea football *n.* [20C+] (*US*) a large firecracker; a homemade bomb. [GUINEA adj.+ SE *football*; the popularity of fireworks in the Italian community]

guinea gall *n. see* GINNY GALL n.

guinea gold *adj.* [18C] sincere, perfect. [the golden guineas of the 18C, which were made from Guinea gold]

guinea hen *n.* [17C–early 18C] a courtesan, a prostitute (cf. ALLEY CAT n.). [pun on SE *guinea hen*/SE *guinea* + HEN n.[1] (2), i.e. a girl who costs a guinea]

guinea pig *n.*[1] **1** [mid-18C–19C] a general term of opprobrium. **2** [early 19C] anyone whose fee comes to a guinea, e.g. a doctor. **3** [mid-19C] (*UK Und.*) a man who receives a guinea for talking up a second-rate horse. **4** [late 19C–1930s] anyone working only part-time, e.g. a company director who only attends board-meetings, a clergyman serving as a deputy etc. **5** [1980s] (*US Und.*) an informer, a stool pigeon. [all puns on SE with ref. to their availability for money]

guinea pig *n.*[2] [1990s+] a wig. [rhy. sl.]

guinea red *n.* [1930s+] (*US*) cheap red wine, poss. homemade. [GUINEA adj. + SE *red* (*wine*); the making of wine by Italian immigrants (and their descendants)]

guineas *n.* **1** [19C] money of any denomination. **2** [1970s] (*US campus*) money. [SE *guinea*, a pre-decimal coinage sum worth £1 1s (£1.05p)]

guinea ship *n.* [1920s+] (*W.I.*) a crowd, a large number of people. [SE *Guinea ship*, a ship bringing slaves – in terribly crowded conditions – from West Africa]

guinea stinker *n.* [late 19C+] a cheap, malodorous cigar supposedly preferred by Italian-Americans. [GUINEA adj.+ STINKER n.[1] (3)]

guinea to a gooseberry *n.* (*also* **guinea to a goosegog**) [late 19C–1920s] the longest possible odds, thus an absolute certainty (cf. ALL THE WORLD TO A CHINA ORANGE phr.). [var. on LOMBARD STREET TO A CHINA ORANGE phr.]

guinea trade *n.* [early 19C] the work of anyone acting as a deputy or locum. [pun on SE *Guinea trade*]

guinny *n. see* GUINEA n.

guino *n.* (*also* **goyno**) [1920s–50s] (*Irish*) money. [? SE *guinea*]

guinzo/guinzola *n. see* GINZO n.

Guitar Town *n.* [1970s] (*US*) Nashville, Tennessee. [the 'home of country music']

guiver *n.*[1] (*also* **guyver, gyver**) (*mainly Aus./N.Z.*) **1** [mid-19C+] insincerity, pretension; flattery. **2** [1900s–10s] a lie. [ety. unknown]

guiver *n.*[2] [late 19C] a hairstyle affected by Cockney dandies, in which the hair was brushed forward over the forehead; thus *guiver-lad*, a working-class dandy. [note WW1 milit. *guyvo*, a dandy]

guiver *adj.* [mid-19C] fashionable, smart. [GUIVER *n.*[2]]

guiver *v.* **1** [late 19C] to cheat, to trick. **2** [20C+] (*Aus./N.Z.*) to pretend, to put on airs. [GUIVER *n.*[1] (1)]

gulder *n. see* GAULDER *n.*

gulf *n.* [mid-16C–mid-18C] the vagina (cf. AGREEABLE RUTS OF LIFE *n.*).

gulf of Venus *n. see* VENUS'S HIGHWAY *n.*

gull *n.* [late 16C–17C; early 19C] a trickster, a cheat. [GULL *v.*; note that *gull*, simpleton, dupe, despite inclusion in Grose (1785), is SE]

gull *v.* [late 16C–18C] to deceive, to fool. [? SE *gull*, a fledgling; thus an innocent. The image is compounded by that of the feeding of the open-mouthed young bird, voraciously swallowing whatever is offered, which in turn echoes SE *gull*, to swallow hungrily; 19C+ use is SE]

gulley-raker *n.* (*also* **gully-raker**) [19C] **1** the penis. **2** a man having sexual intercourse. **3** a womanizer. [? GULLY (HOLE) *n.* (2) + SE *raker*; or ? GULLY-RAKER *n.*[1]]

gull-finch *n.* [17C] a simpleton, a fool (cf. AIREDALE *n.*). [SE *gull*, a simpleton, a dupe + *finch*]

gull-groper *n.* [17C–early 19C] (*UK Und.*) a moneylender who specializes in lending money – often to gamblers – and then defrauding them by avoiding repayment when due, but rather entrapping them in a legal suit, the only resolution of which is the handing over not of the original loan, but of land or valuables that are worth much more. [SE *gull* + *grope*; 19C naut. jargon has *gull-sharper*]

gull-groping *n.* [16C–18C] the swindling of a fool or innocent. [SE *gull* + *grope*]

gullion *n.*[1] [20C+] (*Ulster*) a muddy hole, an open sewer. [Irish *góilin*, a creek]

gullion *n.*[2] *see* SLUMGUDGEON *n.* (1).

gullivers *n.* [1980s] (*Aus.*) diarrhoea. [the sufferer 'travels' to the lavatory for relief]

gully *n.* [1990s+] (*Black*) a woman. [pron. of *girlie* but note GULLY (HOLE) *n.* (2)]

gully *v.* [mid-19C–1900s] to trick, to fool. [GULL *v.*]

gully dirt *n.* [1960s+] (*US*) a worthless, contemptible person, one who fails to fit the local norms; esp. in phr. *sorry as gully dirt*.

gully-groper *n.* [late 19C] (*Aus.*) a long cattle-whip. [var. on GULLY-RAKER *n.*[1] (1)]

gully-gut *n.* [mid-16C–17C; 1930s+] a glutton. [20C+ use is US Black; one can pour food and drink down someone]

gully (hole) *n.* (*also* **gulley (hole)**) [19C] **1** the throat. **2** the vagina (cf. BLACK HOLE *n.*[1]). [(1) food and drink pour down the throat, as they might down a gully; (2) one of many terms equating the vagina with a hole]

gully-jumper *n.* [20C+] (*US*) a farmer, a peasant (cf. ACORN-CRACKER *n.*).

gully-raker *n.*[1] [mid-19C–1950s] (*Aus.*) **1** a long whip used to drive cattle. **2** a cattle thief; thus *gully-raking*. [the *gullies* or narrow valleys where the cattle he steals collect]

gully-raker *n.*[2] *see* GULLEY-RAKER *n.*

gully-raking *n.* [mid-19C–1950s] (*Aus.*) cattle-rustling. [GULLY-RAKER *n.*[1] (2)]

gully-washer *n.* [20C+] (*US*) a heavy downpour of rain.

gully-whumper *n.* [1950s] (*US*) a surprising example. [SE *gull* + WHOMP *v.* (1), i.e. something that will shock a fool]

gulpin *n.* (*also* **gulp**) [early 19C+] a fool. [he will 'gulp down' anything; orig. naut. jargon for a Royal Marine; note Irish *guilpin*, a lout, Scot. *gulpin*, a simpleton, a gullible fool]

gulpy *adj.* [late 19C–1900s] gullible. [GULPIN *n.*/SE *gull* + *gulp*]

gum *n.*[1] **1** [mid-18C–mid-19C] impertinent, abusive talk, chatter; thus one who talks impertinently. **2** [mid-19C] (*US*) a trick or deception; thus COME THE GUM (GAME) OVER *v.* [SE *gum*]

gum *n.*[2] [19C+] a euph. for *God* and used in various phrs.; esp. BY GUM! excl. (cf. BOB *n.*[2]). [*God*, or abbr. *God almighty*]

gum *n.*[3] (*also* **guma**) [late 19C+] (*drugs*) opium; thus *chewing the gum*, using/addicted to opium (cf. APOSTLE *n.*). [its stickiness (cf. GREASE *n.*[2])]

gum *n.*[4] [1980s+] (*Irish*) a taste for, desire. [Scot. *gum*, the palate]

gum *v.*[1] [mid-19C] (*US*) to cheat, to delude, to humbug. [GUM *n.*[1] (2)]

gum *v.*[2] [1980s+] (*US gay*) for a person using dentures to remove them before performing fellatio.

gum *v.*[3] *see* GUM (UP) *v.*

gum! *excl. see* BY GUM! excl.

guma *n. see* GUM *n.*[3].

gum action *n.* [1940s] (*US Black*) conversation, talk. [SE *gum* + ACTION sfx]

gumba(h) *n. see* GOOMBAH *n.*

gumball *n.* (*also* **gumball light, gumball machine**) [1970s+] (*US*) **1** the flashing light on a police car. **2** a police car. [joc. equation of the shape]

gum-beat *n. see* GUM-BEATING *n.*

gum beat *v.* (*US Black*) **1** [1940s] to tell, to recount. **2** [1940s+] to chatter. [BEAT (UP) ONE'S GUMS *v.*]

gum-beater *n.* [1940s–70s] (*US*) a chatterer or complainer; a braggart. [GUM BEAT *v.* (2)]

gum-beating *n.* (*also* **gum-beat**) [1930s+] (*orig. US*) incessant, frivolous, tedious chatter. [GUM BEAT *v.* (2)]

gumbler *n. see* KNULLER *n.*

gumboil *n.* [1940s–50s] a person, used either antagonistically or affectionately. [? a P.G. Wodehouse nonce use]

gumbook *n. see* GUMBRAIN *n.*

gumboot *n.*[1] [1990s+] (*N.Z.*) rough, forthright, mainly rural language, i.e. that of fishermen, roustabouts etc. [the SE *gumboots* they are seen as wearing]

gumboot *n.*[2] *see* GUMSHOE *n.* (1).

gumbrain *n.* (*also* **gumbook, gumhead**) [1950s+] (*US*) an idiot (cf. BAKEBRAIN *n.*). [GUM (UP) *v.* (1) + sfx -*brain*]

gum-bumping *n. see* GUM-FLAPPING *n.*

gumby *n.*[1] [1980s+] a fool, an idiot. [the green character, *Gumby*, a toy, portrayed by Eddie Murphy on the US TV show *Saturday Night Live* and/or the character in BBC TV's *Monty Python's Flying Circus* (1969–74); echoic of his monosyllabic incoherence]

gumby *n.*[2] [1980s] (*US campus*) a large quantity. [ety. unknown]

gumbyhead *n.* [1980s+] (*US campus*) someone who does something stupid. [GUMBY *n.*[1] +-HEAD sfx (1)]

gum-chum *n.* [1940s] an American soldier stationed in the UK. [his plentiful supplies of chewing gum]

gum-digger *n.* [1910s+] (*Aus./N.Z.*) a dentist; thus *gum-digging*, dentistry (cf. GUM-PUNCHER *n.*; GUM-SMASHER *n.*; GUM-TICKLER *n.*[2]).

gumdrop *n.*[1] [late 19C] **1** (*US campus*) a boyfriend or girlfriend. **2** (*US Und.*) a person, esp. one to be duped.

gumdrop *n.*[2] [1970s+] (*drugs*) **1** a barbiturate, esp. Seconal (cf. BARBIT *n.*). **2** any kind of drug available in pill or capsule form (cf. PILL *n.*[4]).

gumdrop *adj.* [late 19C] (*US*) sweet and silly. [play on SE]

gum-flapping *n.* (*also* **gum-bumping**) [1990s+] empty, boastful chatter, argument. [GUM BEAT *v.* (2)]

gumfoot *see under* GUMSHOE.

gumfudgeon *n.* [mid-19C] (*US*) nonsense. [ety. unknown]

gum game *n.* [mid-late 19C] (*US*) a trick or dodge; thus COME THE GUM (GAME) OVER *v.* [the activity of the opossum, which, in its efforts to elude the hunter, climbs to the very top of a gum tree, thus taking itself beyond the hunter's reach and, since it was hunted at night, beyond his eyesight]

gum-gardening *n.* [1990s+] working as a dental hygienist.

gumhead *n. see* GUMBRAIN *n.*

gum heel *n.* [1930s+] (*US prison*) a policeman (cf. FLATFOOT n.[1]).

gumjob *n.* [1980s+] (*US*) fellatio (cf. COCKSUCK n.). [var. on BLOW JOB n.]

gummagy *adj.* (*also* **gummidgy**) [late 19C–1920s] used of peevish, self-pitying and pessimistic people. [*Mrs Gummidge*, a character in Dickens's *David Copperfield* (1850)]

gummed *adj.* [late 19C] (*US*) old, geriatric. [old people tend to lose their teeth]

gummed up *adj.* [1940s] (*US*) in trouble; out of favour.

gummer *n.*[1] **1** [mid–late 19C] an old, toothless pit-bull or other fighting dog. **2** [1900s–30s] a toothless person. **3** [1990s+] (*US*) an act of fellatio from an old, toothless person (cf. COCKSUCK n.).

gummer *n.*[2] *see* GAMMY n.[4].

gummers *n. see* GUMS n.[2] (1).

gummidgy *adj. see* GUMMAGY *adj.*

gummy *n.*[1] **1** [19C–1940s] a fool, a tedious person. **2** [late 19C–1910s] a toothless person or animal.

gummy *n.*[2] [late 19C] a dandy, a swell. [Fr. *gommeux*, dandy]

gummy *adj.*[1] [mid-18C–mid-19C] puffy, swollen, esp. of the ankles of a horse or human, also of a clumsy drunkard. [orig. dial.; ult. ety. unknown]

gummy *adj.*[2] [1920s–40s] (*US*) dubious, untrustworthy.

gummy *adj.*[3] [1950s+] (*US drugs*) used of one who has become lethargic after smoking cannabis. [the rubberiness of their movements]

gummy! *excl.*[1] [mid-19C–1920s] a mild oath. [var. on BY GUM! excl.]

gummy! *excl.*[2] [1980s] (*W.I., Jam.*) a general excl. of praise, excellent! wonderful!

gump *n.*[1] **1** [early 19C+] (*also* **goomp, gumph, gump-head**) a fool; thus *gump-headed*, foolish. **2** [1910s+] (*US*) nonsensical or cheeky talk. **3** [1980s+] (*US prison*) a passive homosexual, the target of predatory prison homosexuals. [Yorks. dial. *gump*, homely, parochial, awkward, well-meaning; the role of a pathetic *gump* was adopted as a trademark by the 20C+ UK comedian Norman Wisdom (b.1915)]

gump *n.*[2] [late 19C+] (*US*) a chicken, a fowl, esp. a sick or dying chicken given by a dealer to a begging tramp. [? its innate stupidity; ? link to Scot. *gump*, an overgrown child]

gump *n.*[3] [1920s–60s] intelligence, native wit. [abbr. GUMPTION n. (1)]

gumph/gump-head *n. see* GUMP n.[1] (1).

gumption *n.* **1** [early 18C+] intelligence, natural wit, shrewdness; thus *gumptioner*, one who possesses such faculties; *gumptious*, in possession of gumption. **2** [mid-19C+] enterprise, drive; courage. **3** [1990s+] (*W.I.*) a woman's ability to intensify the pleasures of intercourse. [18C dial. *gawm*, understanding, thus ? *gawmtion* (*gawm* also gives *gormless*, stupid, doltish) or Scot. *rumgumption/rumblegumption*, common sense]

gumptious *adj.* **1** [19C+] ambitious, aggressive. **2** [mid-19C] proud, conceited. **3** [1910s] excellent, first-rate. [GUMPTION n.]

gum-puncher *n.* [1950s+] (*Aus.*) a dentist (cf. GUM-DIGGER n.).

gums *n.*[1] **1** [17C; 19C; 1930s–40s] the eyes. **2** [1940s] (*US Black*) the lips, the mouth.

gums *n.*[2] (*US*) **1** [mid-19C–1900s] (*also* **gummers**) rubber-soled shoes. **2** [1900s] suspenders, braces. [*elastic gum*, India rubber]

gumshoe *n.* (*also* **gumshoer**) **1** [20C+] (*also* **gumboot, gumfoot**) a private detective or police officer (cf. FLATFOOT n.[1]). **2** [1900s–40s] (*US*) a sneak-thief or prowler. **3** [1950s] (*US*) a hanger-on. [lit. or fig. rubber-soled shoes used for creeping around, whether as investigator or as thief]

gumshoe *adj.* [20C+] (*US*) **1** describing a private detective, e.g. *gumshoe man, gumshoe guy,* GUMSHOE WORKER n. **2** of an action, surreptitious, undercover; pertaining to being a private detective. [GUMSHOE n. (1)]

gumshoe *v.* [20C+] **1** (*also* **gumfoot**) to investigate, esp. used of policemen or private detectives. **2** to walk softly, to creep around. [GUMSHOE n. (1)]

gumshoe artist *n.* **1** [late 19C–1900s] a sneak-thief, a street robber. **2** [1930s+] (*US*) a plain-clothes detective (cf. FLATFOOT n.[1]). [SE *gumshoe*/GUMSHOE n. + ARTIST n. (1)/ARTIST sfx]

gumshoer *n. see* GUMSHOE n.

gumshoe worker *n.* [1900s–50s] (*US Und.*) **1** a sneak-thief. **2** an informer. [GUMSHOE n. (1)/GUMSHOE adj. (1) + WORKER n.[1] (1)]

gum-smasher *n.* [late 19C–1920s] a dentist (cf. GUM-DIGGER n.).

gumsuck *v.* [late 19C–1920s] (*US*) to humbug or deceive. [SE *gum + suck*]

gum-sucker *n.* (*Aus.*) **1** [mid-19C–1940s] a European native Australian (esp. one from Victoria) or Tasmanian. **2** [1900s–50s] a fool or simpleton. [the proliferation of gum trees]

gum-sucking *n.* (*also* **jowl-sucking**) [late 19C] (*orig. US campus*) kissing (esp. in public and thus seen as excessive).

gum-tickler *n.*[1] [early–mid-19C] (*US*) an alcoholic drink.

gum-tickler *n.*[2] [late 19C] (*orig. US*) a dentist (cf. GUM-DIGGER n.).

gum (up) *v.* **1** [20C+] (*US*) to mess up, to spoil; thus *gum the game*; GUM (UP) THE WORKS v. **2** [1930s+] to talk nonsense.

gum (up) the works *v.* (*also* **gum up the job**) [1910s+] to make a mess, to cause an obstruction. [GUM (UP) v. (1)]

gun *n.*[1] **1** [mid-17C] the vagina. **2** [mid-17C+] the penis; thus *shoot one's gun*, to ejaculate, to masturbate (cf. AX n.[2]; FIRE v.[1]). **3** [20C+] (*US drugs*) a hypodermic syringe; thus *gun-toter*, one who uses such a syringe. **4** [20C+] an important person. **5** [1910s–20s] a general pej. term, e.g. a 'rascal', a 'terror'; thus *great gun*, a cheery scamp. **6** [1910s+] (*US*) throttle power; thus *give her the (full) gun*, to accelerate; *cut the gun*, turn off the motor. **7** [2000s] (*US prison*) any form of edged weapon.

gun *n.*[2] [mid-17C–18C] a flagon of ale; thus IN THE GUN phr.[2]. ['perhaps from an allusion to a vessel called a gun, used for ale in the universities' (Grose, 1785)]

gun *n.*[3] [late 17C–18C] a strange and unaccountable story. [E.P. prefers def. 'a lie']

gun *n.*[4] [18C–early 19C; 1960s] a tobacco pipe.

gun *n.*[5] [early 19C; 1910s–30s] (*UK/US Und.*) a view, a look, an observation; taking notice.

gun *n.*[6] **1** [mid-19C] a fool, a bungler. **2** [mid-19C–1960s] a thief. **3** [mid-19C–1960s] a pickpocket; thus *on the gun*, working as a pickpocket. **4** [1900s–20s] (*Aus.*) a confidence trickster. [abbr. GONNOF n.; note Sutherland, *The Professional Thief* (1936): 'The term "cannon" is used to designate the pickpocket and also the racket of picking pockets. The theory of the origin of this term is that the pickpocket some centuries ago was called a *gonnif*, which is the Jewish word for thief. This term was then abbreviated to "gun"; later someone in a moment of smartness referred to a pickpocket as a "cannon" to designate a big gun, and the term "cannon" then became general. The term "gun" is still used to refer to pickpockets, and the female pickpocket who operates upon men is called a "gun-moll"']

gun *n.*[7] [late 19C+] gonorrhoea. [abbr./pron.]

gun *n.*[8] **1** [late 19C+] (*Aus./N.Z.*) the fastest shearer in a shed (usu. 200+ sheep per day); also attrib. **2** [1980s] a first-rate person. [he SE *shoots down* the sheep]

gun *n.*[9] [1920s+] (*US*) a gunman, a gangster; esp. in *hired gun*, a professional gunman who kills, wounds or merely intimidates as required by his employer. [metonymy]

gun *n.*[10] [1980s] (*US*) the arm.

gun *v.*[1] **1** [early 19C+] (*UK/US Und.*) to stare at, to look over, to examine; to look out for; thus *on the gun*, on the lookout. **2** [1940s+] (*orig. US Black*) to stare aggressively or pointedly. **3** [1950s] to stare with sexual interest or intent. **4** [2000s]

(*UK teen*) to insult. [the aggression of the stare equates with a pointed gun]

gun *v.*[2] **1** [mid-19C–1930s] (*UK Und.*) to steal; thus *on the gun*, to be engaged in theft. **2** [late 19C+] (*US*) to shoot someone. **3** [1920s] (*US Und.*) to work as a swindler, a confidence trickster. **4** [1930s+] (*US Black*) to attack, physically or verbally. **5** [1980s] (*US campus*) to have sexual intercourse (cf. BANG v.[1]). **6** [1980s] (*US Black*) to look for trouble, to start a fight. **7** [1990s+] (*drugs*) to inject a drug. [lit. or fig. use of a weapon]

gun *v.*[3] [1920s+] to rev an engine hard; thus to accelerate. [GUN n.[1] (6)]

gun *v.*[4] *see* GUN (IT) v.

gun after *v. see* GUN FOR v. (1).

gun artist *n.* [1920s] (*US*) a Western gun-fighter. [SE *gun* + ARTIST sfx]

gun baggage *n.* [1990s+] underage gangsters who carry weapons for adults.

gunboat *n.*[1] **1** [late 19C] (*US*) an armed stage-coach. **2** [1930s–40s] (*US tramp*) a steel coal wagon.

gunboat *n.*[2] [1920s–70s] (*US tramp*) a water bucket made from a gallon can. [its unwieldiness]

gunboat *n.*[3] [1940s] (*US*) a river-boat being used as a brothel. [GUN n.[1] (2) + SE *boat* + pun]

gunboats *n.* [mid-19C+] (*US*) big shoes. [SE *gunboat*, considered oversized and awkward by sailors, as are the shoes]

gun boss *n.* [1940s] (*US*) the leader of a gang of Western gunmen.

gun bull *n.* [1920s–60s] (*US prison*) an armed guard who surveys the prison yard from a guntower. [SE *gun* + BULL n.[10] (5)]

gun-case *n.* [mid–late 19C] a judge's tippet, a scarlet cloth from the right shoulder to the left side, held in by the sash or girdle. [resemblance to the way in which one wears a SE *gun-case*]

guncel *n. see* GONSEL n.

gunch *n.* [1960s] (*US gay*) a male homosexual. [GUNCH v.]

gunch *v.* [1960s–70s] (*US gay*) to fellate. [? SE *gay* + ? MUNCH v.[1] (2)]

Gundaroo bullock *n.* [late 19C] (*Aus.*) cooked koala meat. [*Gundaroo*, a town in southeast New South Wales]

gundiguts *n.* [late 17C–early 19C] a fat person. [Scot. *gundie*, greedy + -GUTS sfx]

gun dog *n.* [1940s–50s] (*US*) a Western gun-fighter. [SE]

gun down *v.* [1960s+] (*US*) to reject a suitor or to refute facts.

gun-fanner *n.* [1900s] (*US*) a Western gun-fighter. [gun-fighters supposedly 'fanned' the hammer of their pistol to increase the speed of shooting]

gun-fanning *adj.* [1900s] (*US*) usu. in Westerns, toting a gun.

gun-fighter *n.* (*US*) **1** [1950s+] a wild, undisciplined fighter. **2** [1960s+] an aggressively forceful political candidate or campaigner.

gun-flint *n.* [late 19C] (*US*) a native of Rhode Island. [trad. nickname]

gun-foot *n.* [1940s] (*W.I.*) long trousers, esp. narrow ones. [the narrow, tubular trousers, reminiscent of a shotgun barrel]

gun for *v.* (*orig. US*) **1** [late 19C+] (*also* **gun after**) to look for someone, or something, with the intent of creating some form (violent or otherwise) of confrontation. **2** [1910s+] to be sexually interested in a person. **3** [1940s+] to criticize negatively. **4** [1980s+] to aim for, to desire, usu. in the context of provoking/promoting violence. [the image of a Western gun-fighter pursuing a victim or rival]

Gunga *n.* [1910s] (*Aus.*) a generic term for an Indian. [Rudyard Kipling's poem 'Gunga Din' (1892)]

gunga *n.*[1] (*also* **gonga, gunger**) **1** [1940s+] (*Aus./N.Z.*) the anus. **2** [1960s] (*US campus*) an unattractive woman. **3** [1980s] (*Aus./N.Z.*) the vagina. [? GONG n.[1], but note Rudyard Kipling's poem 'Gunga Din' (1892): 'though I've belted you and flayed you', i.e. on the backside]

gunga *n.*[2] *see* GANJA n.

Gunga Din *n.* [20C+] **1** the chin. **2** (*Aus.*) gin (and water). [rhy.

sl.; ult. *Gunga Din*, water carrier in poem by Rudyard Kipling (1865–1936)]

gun gang *n.* [1970s+] (*US Und.*) the chain gang or any gang of workers who are taken outside the prison and are thus supervised by armed guards. [they work 'under the gun']

gunge *n.*[1] **1** [20C+] (*Ulster*) sweets, cakes, desserts. **2** [1950s+] a sticky mess, poss. when in the form of gravy or sauce, but equally often merely resembling such foods. **3** [1960s+] (*US*) a skin irritation of the male genitals, a mythical disease believed to make a man rot from his genitals outwards, prevalent among soldiers in Vietnam.

gunge *n.*[2] [1970s+] (*US drugs*) **1** potent marijuana. **2** heroin. [abbr. GUNGEON n.]

gunge *v.* [1960s+] to clog up with a sticky or messy substance, to become clogged up. [GUNGE n.[1] (2)]

gungeon *n.* (*also* **gungion, gungun, gunion**) [1940s+] (*drugs*) potent marijuana, usu. from Mexico or Africa. [? GANJA n.]

gunger *n. see* GUNGA n.[1].

gung-ho *n.* [1980s+] (*Aus. prison*) an enthusiastic prison guard. [GUNG-HO adj.]

gung-ho *adj.* (*also* **gungy**) [1940s+] (*orig. US*) often of soldiers or sportsmen, enthusiastic, usu. aggressively so; thus as v., to do something in an aggressive manner. [Chinese *keng ho*, awe-inspiring (lit. 'more fiery'). The term was initially popularized as the motto of the US Marine Corps Second Raider Battalion, introduced there in 1942 by Lieut. Col. Evans F. Carlson]

gung-ho *adv.* [1940s+] enthusiastically, vigorously. [GUNG-HO adj.]

gungion/gungun *n. see* GUNGEON n.

gungy *adj.*[1] [1950s+] **1** sticky, messy, slimy. **2** second-rate, inferior; of food, spoilt. **3** revolting. [GUNGE n.[1] (2)]

gungy *adj.*[2] *see* GUNG-HO adj.

gun hand *n.* [1950s+] (*US*) a gun-fighter. [on model of SE *farm hand*]

gun-happy *adj.* [1950s+] (*US*) prone to frequent shooting of guns. [SE *gun* + -HAPPY sfx (2)]

gunhawk *n.* [1940s+] (*US*) an expert gun-fighter.

gun in her baggy *phr.* [1990s+] (*W.I.*) a woman with venereal disease.

gunion *n. see* GUNGEON n.

gun (it) *v.* [1990s+] (*Aus./US drugs*) to maintain a heroin addiction. [GUN n.[1] (3)]

gunja *n. see* GANJA n.

gunjie *n.* [1990s+] (*Aus. Aborigine*) a White person, by ext. a policeman. [ety. unknown]

gunk *n.*[1] **1** [20C+] (*Ulster*) an unpleasant shock, a major disappointment; thus *gunked*, disappointed. **2** [1940s+] (*US*) nonsense. **3** [1960s+] (*US*) a fool, a dullard. **4** [1990s+] a school-child who has been rejected by their peers. [? Irish *gonc*, to snub, to rebuff]

gunk *n.*[2] [1930s+] (*orig. US*) a viscous or liquid substance. [orig. a proprietary name registered in 1932 by A.F. Curran Co. for 'liquid soaps and liquid cleaners for hard surfaced materials or articles']

gunk up *v.* [1960s+] (*orig. US*) to mess up with viscous or liquid substances. [GUNK n.[2]]

gunky *adj.* [1970s+] (*US*) sticky, viscous; messed up with or looking like gunk. [GUNK n.[2] + sfx -y]

gun-maker *n.* [1900s–30s] (*US Und.*) an older thief who instructs young criminals, esp. pickpockets. [GUN n.[6] (3) + pun]

gun mob *n.* [1910s–50s] (*US Und.*) an expert pickpocketing team. [GUN n.[6] (3) + MOB n.[2] (3)]

gun moll *n.* (*US Und.*) **1** [20C+] a female, gun-carrying gangster or female accomplice of a gun man. **2** [1900s–40s] a female pickpocket. [SE *gun*/GUN n.[6] (3) + MOLL n.[1] (1)]

gun-mouth (pants) *n.* [20C+] (*W.I.*) a (young) man's trousers that are too short and narrow.

gunner n.[1] (*also* **gunster**) [early 18C] one who spreads malicious rumours. [GUN n.[3]]

gunner n.[2] [late 19C] a 1-eyed person.

gunner n.[3] [late 19C] (*UK Und.*) a thief. [GUN n.[6] (2)]

gunner n.[4] (*US campus*) **1** [1920s–60s] a zealous woman-chaser; a sexual athlete. **2** [1970s+] an ambitiously competitive student. [GUN FOR v. (2)]

gunner n.[5] [1930s–50s] the person who is throwing the dice in a game of craps. [var. on SHOOTER n.[1] (2)]

gunner n.[6] [1970s] (*US Und.*) a gunman.

gunner n.[7] [1990s+] **1** (*US drugs*) a heroin addict. **2** a term of abuse. [GUN n.[1] (3)]

gunner n.[8] [2000s] (*US prison*) a prisoner who masturbates while looking at a female warder. [GUN v.[1] (3)]

gunnif n. see GONNOF n.

gunny n.[1] [1930s+] (*US*) a gunman, a gangster. [SE *gun*]

gunny n.[2] [1960s+] (*drugs*) marijuana. [GUNGEON n.]

gunny adj. [1980s] (*N.Z.*) first-class, superior. [GUN n.[8] (2)]

gun opera n. see HORSE OPERA n. (2).

gunpoke n. (*also* **gunpoker**) [1900s–30s] (*US*) a gun-fighter. [on model of *cowpoke*]

gunpowder n.[1] [late 17C–early 19C] (*UK Und.*) an old woman. [presumably a cantankerous one who 'goes off with a bang'. In *Henry IV Pt 1* Shakespeare uses the term in such a manner to describe the irascible 'gunpowder Percy']

gunpowder n.[2] **1** [mid-18C] a fiery drink; prob. gin. **2** [1900s–30s] (*US Black*) gin. [the short-lived 18C UK use was revived in US Black use]

gunpowder n.[3] (*US drugs*) **1** [1970s] opium (cf. APOSTLE n.). **2** [1990s+] cocaine (cf. BIRDIE POWDER n.). [it makes the user 'go off with a bang']

gunpowder tea n. [mid-19C] (*US*) gunfire. [note British Army sl. *gunfire*, an early morning cup of tea served out to troops before going on first parade]

guns n. [1980s+] **1** (*US prison*) fists. **2** (*US campus*) biceps. **3** (*US Black*) the female breasts (cf. BAGS n.[1]).

gunsel n.[1] [1960s+] (*US prison*) a (young) troublemaker. [misreading of GONSEL n.]

gunsel n.[2] see GONSEL n.

gun-sharp n. (*also* **gun-shark**) **1** [1900s] an artillery expert. **2** [1930s+] (*US*) an expert gun-fighter. [on model of SE *card-sharp*/SHARK n.[1] (1)]

gunshel n. see GONSEL n.

gunshot n. **1** [1920s] (*Irish*) a strong rough whisky. **2** [1980s+] reversing a cannabis cigarette, placing the lit end between one's lips, then exhaling the smoke into another person's mouth.

gunslick n. [1930s–50s] (*US*) an expert gun-fighter. [SE *gun* + SLICK adj. (1)]

gun-slinger n. **1** [1920s+] (*US*) a gunman, esp. in the (fictional) 'Wild West'. **2** [1960s] (*US Black*) a sexually powerful male. **3** [1990s+] (*US campus*) a woman who rejects a man's attention rudely. **4** [1990s+] an employee dedicated to troubleshooting. [all 'shoot down' their target]

gunsmith n. **1** [mid-19C] a thief. **2** [1930s] (*US*) an older thief who trains young criminals. [GUN n.[6] (2)]

gunster n. see GUNNER n.[1].

gunstick n. [mid-17C] a penis (cf. BAT n.[7]).

gunt n. [1990s+] (*Can.*) a fat woman. [SE *gut* + CUNT n.[1] (1)]

gun talk n. [1920s] (*US*) thieves' cant. [? GUN n.[6] (2) or the language of those who carry *guns*]

gunterpake n. [20C+] (*Ulster*) a fool. [ety. unknown; ? link to Scot. *gant*, to gape]

gun-thrower n. (*also* **gun-tosser**, **gun-toter**) [1910s–50s] (*US*) a gun-fighter as found in the real/fictional 'Wild West'.

guntz n.[1] [1950s+] the whole lot. [synon. Ger. *ganz*]

guntz n.[2] [1980s] (*US*) a worthless person. [abbr. GONSEL n.]

gun up v. [1980s+] (*US prison*) to get oneself ready for a fight. [GUNS n. (1), although many fights employ some form of knife]

gun-wadding n. [1910s–50s] (*US*) soft white bread.

gun-work n. [1920s] (*US Und.*) robbery (with violence). [GUN n.[6] (2)/SE *gun* + SE *work*]

gunyah n. [late 19C+] (*Aus.*) a White person's hut or house. [SAusE *gunyah*, an Aboriginal hut or other dwelling; as sl. the term is thus derisively racist]

gunzel v. (*also* **gunzle**) [1980s] (*US Black*) to fight. [? misreading of GONSEL n.]

gup n.[1] (*also* **gup-gup**) [mid-19C–1950s] (*orig. Anglo-Ind.*) gossip. [Hind. *gap*, prattle, which borrowed in turn from the Turkish *gep* or *geb*, word, saying or talk and the Persian *guftan* or *guptan*, to say. The word made its way to the UK *c.*1868, the year in which a highly critical account of South Indian society was published, under the pseudonym of 'Gup']

gup n.[2] [1930s–40s] (*Aus.*) a fool, a simpleton. [? GUP n.[1] or SE *gulp*]

gup v. [1930s] to chat, to gossip. [GUP n.[1]]

gup-gup n. see GUP n.[1].

guppie n. [1980s+] **1** (*US gay*) a gay urban professional, i.e. the gay equivalent of a YUPPIE n. **2** (*US*) a grown-up urban professional, i.e. one who has transcended the YUPPIE n. phase. [abbr.]

guppy adj. [1930s+] (*orig. Aus.*) silly, foolish. [GUP n.[2]]

guppy-gobbler n. [1960s] (*US*) a Catholic. [the former Catholic 'fish-day' of Friday]

gurgle n. [1940s+] (*Aus./US*) liquor, a drink. [SE *gurgle*, to swallow]

gurk v. **1** [1920s] to belch. **2** [1940s] (*Aus.*) to break wind. [echoic]

gurly adj. [20C+] (*Ulster*) boisterous, ill-tempered. [synon. Scot.]

gurrawaun n. [mid-19C] (*Anglo-Ind.*) a coachman. [Hind. *gari*, a cart or carriage]

gurrell n. [mid-19C] a fob, a small pocket either in the waistband of the breeches or, latterly, in the waistcoat. [? link to dial. *gorrell*; *gurrel*, a glutton, a fat-stomached person]

gurrier n. [1950s+] (*Irish*) a street urchin. [? Fr. *guerrier*, a fighter; ? link to Fr. argot *guéri*, free; ? *gur-cake*, a fruit pastry slice popular with poor Dublin children]

guru n. **1** [1960s] (*drugs*) a guide or caretaker during a hallucinogenic experience; such a person is either not taking the drug or a veteran user (cf. GUIDE n.). **2** [1980s] (*US campus*) an expert. [Hind. *guru*, a holy man]

gush n.[1] **1** [mid-19C] a whiff, a smell. **2** [mid–late 19C] (*US*) a good deal of a commodity. [both 'gush out']

gush n.[2] [mid-19C+] an objectionably effusive or sentimental display of feeling, esp. as spoken. [GUSH v.]

gush v. [mid-19C+] to speak in a cloying sentimental manner; thus *gushing*, an extravagant display of feeling or sentiment.

gusher n. (*also* **gusheress**) **1** [mid–19C–1940s] one who talks to excess, uttering usu. insincere and sentimental remarks. **2** [1990s+] a crying fit. [(1) GUSH v.; (2) SE *gusher*, an well from which the oil flows without pumping]

gusset n. [17C; 1990s+] **1** a woman; esp. as considered collectively as sex objects. **2** the vagina. [SE *gusset*, a triangular piece of material sewn into garments to make it easier to move, typically at the armpit or the crotch]

gusseteer n. [19C] a womanizer. [GUSSET n.]

gusset-nuzzler n. [1990s+] a lesbian (cf. CARPET-BITER n.).

gusset of the arse n. [late 18C–early 19C] the cleft of the buttocks.

gusset typing n. [1990s+] female masturbation; thus *gusset typist*, a woman who masturbates.

gussie n. [late 19C+] (*Aus./US*) a weak, effeminate man, thus a male homosexual. [proper name *Augustus*, seen as stereotypically effeminate]

gussies n. [1950s] women's lace underwear. [the tennis player 'Gorgeous *Gussie*' Moran, who favoured such knickers]

gussy (up) v. [1910s+] to smarten up, to dress up; esp. as *gussied* *up*, of people, dressed up, esp. for a night out; of objects, ornamented, disguised. [GUSSIE n.; the implication is usu. of excessive smartness and, in a man, effeminacy]

gusto *n.*[1] [1960s+] (*orig. US Black*) beer. [SE *gusto* as used in the 1966 advertising slogan for Schlitz beer, 'Schlitz. Grab for the gusto!' an abbr. of the orig. line 'You only go around once in life, so grab for all the gusto you can']

gusto *n.*[2] [1980s+] (*US Black*) money. [ety. unknown]

Gut, the *n.* [1940s+] Strait Street, Valetta, the centre of Malta's red-light district. [? SE *gut*, i.e. the fig. centre of the island]

gut *n.*[1] **1** [19C] gluttony. **2** [1910s–60s] (*US Und.*) (*also* **redgut**) a sausage.

gut *n.*[2] **1** [1910s+] (*US campus*) an easy course; thus *gut gunner*, one who succeeds in such a course. **2** [1920s] (*US*) a certainty. **3** [1970s+] (*US*) an easy task. **4** [2000s] (*US*) a gut feeling. [GUT adj.]

gut *n.*[3] [1920s+] (*US*) the main street; thus SHOOT THE GUT v. [SE *gut*, a narrow passage or lane]

gut *n.*[4] *see* GUTS n.[2] (1).

gut *adj.* **1** [1910s+] (*US campus*) easy. **2** [1950s+] (*orig. US*) based on instinct, feeling. **3** [1960s+] of fundamental importance. [SE *gut*, i.e. the use of the instincts rather than the brain, one knows 'in one's guts']

gut *v.*[1] **1** [17C–1900s] to eat like a glutton. **2** [late 17C–1900s] to empty; esp. in phr. *gut a quart pot*, to drink the pot to the dregs; *gut a house*, to empty a house of its furnishings.

gut *v.*[2] **1** [1940s] (*US*) to display one's courage. **2** [1960s+] (*US Black*) to punch in the stomach; lit. and fig. use. [GUTS n.[2] (1)/GUTS n.[1] (1)]

gut-ache *n.* (*also* **guts-ache**) **1** [late 18C+] a stomach-ache. **2** [1950s] (*UK juv.*) a greedy person. [SE *gut*]

gut bomb *n.* [1960s+] (*US*) a very greasy hamburger or similar food. [SE *gut*; its deleterious effects]

gut-bracer *n. see* GUT-WARMER n.

gutbucket *n.*[1] **1** [1920s+] (*orig. US Black*) a very basic, raw, unsophisticated style of jazz; thus ext. to rock music; also attrib. **2** [1930s–60s] (*US Black*) a bucket used to carry food or drink, thus inferior liquor. **3** [1940s–50s] (*US Black*) a low place or dive. **4** [1960s+] (*US*) a washtub bass. **5** [1970s] a jazz musician. [lit. + fig. derivations of saloon use *gutbucket*, the small bucket to catch drippings or 'gutterings' from the barrels that is found in cheap bars and saloons; (1) such jazz was played in these 'low' saloons]

gutbucket *n.*[2] (*US*) **1** [1930s+] a (pompous) fat person. **2** [1940s] a toilet. **3** [1950s+] the belly.

gut-burner *n. see* GUT-WARMER n.

gut-buster *n.* **1** [1930s] a funny person. **2** [1930s+] something powerful and dramatic; thus *gutbusting*, powerful, energetic, overwhelming. **3** [1950s+] (*N.Z.*) a very steep hill. **4** [1980s+] (*US*) something very funny, e.g. a joke or performance. [it 'busts one's guts']

gut-butcher *n. see* GUT-REAMER n.

gut check *n.* [1970s+] (*US*) a quick reassessment of strategy and stiffening of morale. [orig. sporting use]

gut-eater *n.* [1920s–60s] (*US, Western*) a Native American. [their taste for offal, despised by Whites]

gut-eating *adj.* [1940s–60s] (*US, Western*) used derog. of a Native American. [GUT-EATER n.]

gut entrance *n.* [19C] the vagina (cf. BELLY ENTRANCE n.).

gutfatty *n. see* FAT-GUTS n.

gut foot *n.* [1930s–40s] (*US Black*) fallen arches, i.e. flat feet. [ety. unknown]

gut-foundered *adj.* [mid-17C–18C] extremely hungry. [SE *gut + founder*]

gut-fucker *n.* (*also* **gut-monger**, **gut-sticker**) [late 19C–1900s] a sodomite. [SE *gut +* FUCKER n. (1)/sfx *-monger*/SE *sticker*]

gutful *n. see* GUTSFUL n.

guthammer *n.* [2000s] the penis (cf. ARSE-OPENER n.).

gut-head *n.* [early 17C] one who is stupefied by an excess of food. [GUT n.[1] + -HEAD sfx (1)]

gut-heater *n. see* GUT-WARMER n.

gut-hooks *n.* [1930s+] (*US*) spurs. [they stick into the stomach of the horse]

gut it *v.* **1** [1910s+] (*US campus*) to stay up all night working without any amphetamine for stimulation but purely through strength of will and character. **2** [1960s+] (*US*) (*also* **gut (it) out**, **gut (it) through**) to be strong, tough, in the face of adversity. [GUTS n.[2] (1)]

gutless *adj.* [20C+] cowardly; thus GUTLESS WONDER n.

gutless *adv.* [1980s+] as a general intensifer, to a very great extent, in a very intense manner etc.

gutless wonder *n.* [1930s+] a coward. [GUTLESS adj.]

gut-monger *n. see* GUT-FUCKER n.

gut out *v. see* GUT IT v. (2).

gut-piece *n.* [1960s] (*US*) the abdomen.

gut plunge on butch *n.* [1920s–30s] (*US*) an act of scrounging for meat from a butcher's shop by a tramp. [SE *gut + plunge +* abbr. *butcher*]

gut pudding *n.* [late 16C–19C] a sausage. [sausages were orig. encased in animal gut]

gut-puller *n.* [mid–late 19C] a poulterer.

gut-reamer *n.* (*also* **gut-butcher**, **gut-stretcher**, **gut-stuffer**) [1920s–70s] (*US*) a pederast.

gut-ripper *n.* [1940s] (*US*) any kind of knife used as a weapon.

gut-robber *n.* [20C+] (*US*) a cook, esp. a bad one. [orig. logging jargon]

gutrot *n.* **1** [1910s+] cheap wine or spirits. **2** [1930s+] unpalatable drink or food, also fig. use. [its presumed effect on one's innards]

guts *n.*[1] **1** [early 16C] the stomach. **2** [mid-16C+] one's insides, the contents. **3** [late 16C+] a notably fat person; thus *tub of guts*, a grossly obese person. **4** [mid-19C+] a glutton.

guts *n.*[2] **1** [mid-17C+] (*also* **gut**) courage, bravery, staying power. **2** [mid-18C+] energy, vigour, power in performance. **3** [1910s–50s] cheek, audacity, 'nerve'.

guts *n.*[3] **1** [late 19C; 1960s+] the source of true feelings; thus *at gut level*, instinctively. **2** [20C+] the essence of a matter, the underlying meaning. **3** [1910s+] (*orig. Aus.*) the facts, the information, esp. as GOOD GUTS n.

guts *n.*[4] [1910s–30s] (*US Und.*) the undercarriage of railroad trains on which tramps hitched a ride.

guts *n.*[5] [1920s] (*US tramp*) a sausage.

guts *n.*[6] [1950s] (*Aus.*) in the game of two-up, the centre of the betting circle into which betted money is tossed.

guts *v. see* GUTS (UP) v.

-guts *sfx* [late 16C+] a person; used in combs. to describe a defining characteristic (cf. BLABBERGUTS n.; DOUBLE GUTS n.; DOUGHGUTS n.; FAT-GUTS n.; FORTY-GUTS n.; FULL-GUTS n.; GABBY-GUTS n.; GIGGLY-GUTS n.; GREASY GUTS n.; GREEDY-GUT n.; GRIZZLE-GUTS n.; GRUMBLE-GUTS n.; GUNDIGUTS n.; GUZZLE GUTS n.; LUSTY-GUTS n.; MISERYGUTS n.; POSSUM-GUTS n.; POT-GUTS n.; PUFF GUTS n.; ROUGH-GUTS n.; RUSTYGUTS n.; SHEEP-GUTS n.; WIMP-GUTS n.; WORRYGUTS n.). [metonymy]

guts-ache *n. see* GUT-ACHE n.

guts and garbage *n.* [late 18C–early 19C] a very fat person.

guts ball *n.* [1960s+] (*US*) **1** any kind of fiercely aggressive and competitive ball game. **2** any action requiring aggression, courage and determination. [GUTS n.[2] (1)]

gutsball *adj.* [1960s+] (*US*) plucky, courageous. [GUTS BALL n. (2)]

gut-scraper *n.* [early 18C+] a fiddle-player, a violinist. [the violin's catgut strings]

gutser *n.*[1] (*also* **gutzer**) [1910s+] a greedy person. [GUTS n.[1] (4)]

gutser *n.*[2] (*also* **gutzer**) [1910s+] (*Aus*) **1** in lit. or fig. use, a heavy fall, a collision; thus *come a gutser*, to trip over and fall; *bring* *someone a gutser*, to engineer someone's downfall. **2** a disappointment, a let-down; a misfortune. [note WW1 milit. use 'to get into serious trouble'; orig. Scot. for suffering a 'bellyflop']

gutser *v.* [1950s] to be beaten or overcome, to lose. [GUTSER n.² (1)]

gutsful *n.* (*also* **gutful**) [1920s+] (*orig. Aus./N.Z.*) a sufficiency, quite as much of anything as one wants or cares to take; often as *have a gutful*. [GUTS n.¹ (1) + SE *full*]

gutsful of grunts *n.* [1910s+] (*Aus.*) an unpleasant person.

guts high *adj. see* GUTS UP adj.

gut-shoot *v.* [1930s+] (*US*) to shoot in the stomach; thus *gut-shot*, wounded in the stomach. [SE *gut*]

gutso *n.* [1950s+] a fat person. [GUTS n.¹ (3) + -o sfx (1)]

gutstick *n.* [late 19C; 1970s+] the penis (cf. BAT n.⁷).

gut-sticker *n. see* GUT-FUCKER n.

gut-stretcher *n. see* GUT-REAMER n.

gut-struggle *n.* [1920s] (*US*) a dance that involves the partners being physically very close.

gut-stuffer *n. see* GUT-REAMER n.

guts up *adj.* (*also* **guts high**) [1950s–60s] (*US*) fearless. [GUTS n.² (1)]

guts (up) *v.* [late 19C+] (*Aus.*) to overeat. [GUTS n.¹ (4)]

gutsy *adj.* **1** [late 19C+] tough, spirited, brave; thus *gutsiness*, courage, spirit. **2** [1950s] greedy, very hungry. [GUTS n.² (1)/GUTS (UP) v. + sfx -y]

gutta-percha *n.¹* [late 19C–1910s] (*Aus.*) an inhabitant of the state of Victoria. [? the prevalence of the gutta-percha tree (*Isonaudra Gutta*) in the state]

gutta-percha *n.²* [1920s] (*US*) the foreskin. [the use of a *gutta-percha* leaf as a covering]

gutted *adj.¹* [early 19C–1900s] impoverished, without money. [SE *gut*]

gutted *adj.²* [1960s+] deeply disappointed, sick and tired, fed up, utterly depressed, very upset. [abbr. of phr. *sick to one's guts*, the term originated in prison use, but has become widespread since mid-1970s]

gutter *n.¹* [late 19C] the vagina (cf. AGREEABLE RUTS OF LIFE n.).

gutter *n.²* [1930s+] (*drugs*) a vein into which a drug is injected.

gutter alley *n.* [17C–19C] the throat.

gutter-blood *n.* [mid-19C] **1** a lout, a hoodlum. **2** a parvenu, a vulgar man who puts on airs. [SE *gutter*, low class + BLOOD n.¹]

gutter-chaunter *n.* [mid–late 19C] a street-singer. [SE *gutter* + CHANTER n. (1)]

guttered *adj.* [1950s+] very drunk (cf. AFFLICTED adj.). [the image of falling into a *gutter*]

gutter-gripper *n.* [1950s+] (*Aus.*) a motorist who drives with one hand stuck through the open window, gripping the gutter that runs around the car's roof.

gutter hotel *n.* [late 19C] (*UK tramp*) the open air.

gutter hype *n.* (*also* **gutter hyp, …junkie**) [1920s–50s] (*drugs*) a very low-level narcotics user. [SE *gutter*, low class + HYPE n.² (2)/JUNKIE n. (1)]

gutter-kid *n.* [late 19C] a street urchin.

gutter lane *n.* [late 17C–19C] the throat. [? proper name *Gutter Lane*, a small street in 17C London and the source of phr. *go down Gutter Lane*, to be a drunkard or glutton. E.P., however, suggests links to Lat. *guttur*, the throat, and to Devon dial. *gutter*, to eat greedily, as well as to GUTTLE v. and GUZZLE v.¹]

gutter merchant *n.* [1900s–20s] an itinerant street salesman. [SE *gutter* + MERCHANT n.]

gutter-prowler *n.* [19C] a small-time thief.

gutter snipe *n.* [late 19C] (*UK tramp*) a derog. term for a male servant.

gut through *v. see* GUT IT v. (2).

guttie *n.* (*also* **gutty**) **1** [19C] a glutton. **2** [19C+] a very fat person. **3** [1910s+] (*Irish*) one who has no redeeming features, a street urchin; thus adj., *guttiest*. [SE *gut*]

gutties *n.* [20C+] (*Ulster*) plimsolls, trainers. [SE *gutta-percha*, a

---

tree (*Isonaudra Gutta*), the juice of which is used in their manufacture]

guttle *v.* [late 17C] to eat or drink heartily. [synon. dial.]

gutty *n. see* GUTTIE n.

gutty *adj.¹* [1940s+] tough, spirited, brave. [var. on GUTSY adj. (1)]

gutty *adj.²* [1950s–60s] (*US Black*) raw, unsophisticated. [SE *gutter*, thus the lifestyle of those who lived 'in the gutter']

gut-wagon *n.* [1920s+] (*US*) a truck that carries cattle carcasses.

gut-warmer *n.* (*also* **gut-bracer, gut-burner, gut-heater**) [1940s+] (*US*) a strong alcoholic drink.

gut-winder *n.* [mid-19C] (*US*) a bullet wound in the abdomen. [SE *gut*]

gut-wrench *n.* [1940s+] (*US*) the penis (cf. ARSE-OPENER n.). [SE *gut*]

gutzer *see also under* GUTSER.

gutzer! *excl.* [1910s] (*Aus.*) an excl. of dismissal.

guv *n.* **1** [late 19C+] a general term of address, usu. to someone seen as or actually higher in the social order (cf. GOV n.). **2** [1900s] one's father.

guvnor *n.* (*also* **gov'nor, guv, guvner, guv'nor**) [mid-19C+] **1** a boss, an important, influential person. **2** a general term of address. **3** (*also* **my old guvnor**) one's father. [pron. GOVERNOR n.]

guvnor *adj.* [1970s] the most important. [GUVNOR n. (1)]

guy *n.¹* **1** [19C+] a fool; thus *give someone the guy*, to make a fool of someone, to tease. **2** [early–mid-19C] a dark lantern; thus *stow the guy*, to cover or douse the lantern. **3** [mid-19C] an ugly or badly dressed person. **4** [mid-19C] a crimp, one who tricked men into joining the navy. **5** [mid-19C–1910s] (*US*) a comical fellow, a SMART ALEC(K) n. **6** [mid-19C–1910s] (*US*) a trick or hoax, a joke. **7** [late 19C–1950s] an act of running off, of leaving surreptitiously; usu. in phr. *do a guy, give the guy to*, to slip away. [fig. uses of the negative image of *Guy* Fawkes (1570–1606), leader of the Gunpowder Plot of 1605]

guy *n.²* **1** [late 19C+] (*orig. US*) a man or boy; thus MAIN GUY n. **2** [1910s+] a general term of address, repopularized in 1970s+ among young UK Blacks, and now in general teen use. **3** [1910s+] (*US*) a woman. **4** [1960s] a boyfriend, a lover. **5** [1970s+] a person, irrespective of gender. **6** [1970s+] (*US*) an animal. **7** [1980s+] (*US campus*) in ironic reversal, an incompetent, an inadequate. **8** [1980s+] (*US*) an object, a thing.

guy *n.³* [late 19C+] a walk, thus an expedition or journey; thus *give someone the guy*, to run away. [rhy. sl.; *Guy Fawkes* = walk; ult. for ety. *see* GUY n.¹]

guy *n.⁴* [1940s+] (*US*) a euph. for *God* (cf. BOB n.²).

guy *adj.* [1990s+] (*US*) particularly or only of interest to men; thus *it's a guy thing*. [GUY n.² (1)]

guy *v.¹* [mid-19C+] to tease, to fool, to mock. [GUY n.¹ (1)]

guy *v.²* *see* GUY-A-WHACK v.

guy-a-whack *n.* [20C+] (*Aus.*) a defaulting bookmaker. [GUY-A-WHACK v.]

guy-a-whack *adj.* [20C+] (*Aus.*) useless, incompetent. [GUY-A-WHACK v.]

guy-a-whack *v.* (*also* **guy**) [late 19C–1910s] (*Aus.*) to run off, to leave quickly. [ety. unknown; AND suggests ext. of GUY n.³/GUY (OFF) v. + *a-whack* as a var. on SE *away*]

guyess *n.* [2000s] a woman or girl. [GUY n.² (1)]

guy (off) *v.* [late 19C–1930s] (*UK Und.*) to run away, to escape.

guy-rope *n.* [1990s+] the frenum.

guyver *n. see* GUIVER n.¹.

guzinter *n.* [1940s–50s] (*Aus.*) a schoolteacher. [basic maths, e.g. answering 'how many times does 2 *go into* 4?']

guzinters *n.* [1910s+] (*Aus.*) an animal's innards. [*goes into* the animal]

guzunder *n.* [20C+] a chamberpot. [it *goes under* the bed]

guzzle *n.¹* **1** [mid-17C+] the throat. **2** [mid-17C+] liquor; thus *guzzling*, drinking heavily. **3** [late 17C] beer. **4** [mid-19C] the eating of a meal. **5** [1920s+] a swig, a gulp. [? OF *gosiller*, to vomit or to chatter + OF *gosier*, throat]

guzzle *n.*[2] [18C–1960s] (*US*) a drink.

guzzle *v.*[1] [17C+] to drink (greedily); to eat voraciously.

guzzle *v.*[2] **1** [late 18C] to lie. **2** [mid–late 19C] to swindle. **3** [late 19C+] to strangle, to throttle, to murder; thus *guzzler*, one who employs this method. **4** [1930s] (*UK Und.*) to arrest; to interrogate. **5** [1930s] to indulge in sexual foreplay, to 'neck'. [lit. + fig. uses of GUZZLE *n.*[1] (1)]

guzzle crib *n. see* GUZZLE SHOP *n.*

guzzled *adj.*[1] (*also* **gossled**) [late 19C–1930s] drunk. [GUZZLE *v.*[1]]

guzzled *adj.*[2] [1920s–30s] (*US*) killed. [GUZZLE *v.*[2] (3)]

guzzle guts *n.* **1** [late 18C+] a drunkard. **2** [1950s] (*UK juv.*) a greedy person. [GUZZLE *v.*[1] + -GUTS sfx]

guzzler *n.*[1] [18C+] a heavy drinker, a voracious eater. [GUZZLE *v.*[1]]

guzzler *n.*[2] [1920s] (*US*) an insignificant person, i.e. one who eats scraps.

guzzler *n.*[3] *see* GAS-GUZZLER *n.*

guzzle shop *n.* (*also* **guzzle crib**, **guzzlery**) [late 19C+] (*US*) a cheap saloon or bar. [GUZZLE *v.*[1] + SE *shop*/CRIB *n.*[1] (2)]

guzzle the grass *v.* [1980s] (*Aus.*) to vomit.

guzzling *n.* [1930s] kissing and cuddling. [GUZZLE *v.*[2] (5)]

g.v. *n.* [1900s–10s] a *governor*. [abbr.]

gwaai *n.* [1980s+] (*S.Afr.*) **1** tobacco. **2** a cigarette, a 'smoke'. [Zulu *ugwayi*, tobacco, snuff]

gwaan! *excl.* [20C+] (*W.I./UK Black teen*) a term of encouragement or appreciation, i.e. go ahead! get going! [lit. *go on!*]

g'wan! *excl. see* GO ON! excl.

gweeb *n.* (*also* **gweebo**, **gweep**) [1980s+] (*US campus*) a person entirely lacking in social skills and style. [var. on DWEEB *n.*]

gweva *n.* [1960s+] (*S.Afr. township*) a bootlegger. [Xhosa *igweva*, an illicit diamond buyer]

G-woman *n.* [1980s+] (*US*) a female FBI agent (cf. G-MAN *n.*[1]). [G adj.]

gybe *n.* (*also* **glibe**, **glybe**, **jibe**, **jybe**) [mid-16C–mid-19C] (*UK Und.*) a written paper, esp. a counterfeit pass or licence, carried by many of the mendicant villains. [ety. unknown; E.P. suggests Ger. *schreiben*, a writing; if so then also ? SE *scribe*]

gybe *v.* [late 17C–18C] to whip, to beat; thus *gybed*, whipped. [SE *gybe*, for a sail to swing from one side to the other]

Gyle *n.* [late 19C] the A*rgyle* Rooms, Windmill Street, London W1. [abbr.]

gylrig *n.* [1950s] (*UK gay*) **1** a desirable person. **2** sexual activity. [Polari; ? backsl. of SE *girl* or *girly*]

gym *v.* [1930s] (*UK Und.*) to travel to or gain admission to, usu. a racecourse, without paying the full charge. [? dial. *gan*, to walk]

gymnasium *n.* [17C] the vagina.

gym rat *n.* [1970s+] (*US*) a sports enthusiast; usu. one who frequents gyms and training grounds; anyone fanatically pursuing a course of activity, a career etc. [SE *gym* + RAT *n.*[2] (6)]

gynae *n.* (*also* **gynie**) [1940s+] **1** *gynae*cology. **2** a *gynae*cologist. [abbr.]

gyno *n.* [1960s+] a gynaecologist.

gyp *n.* (*orig. US*) **1** [mid-19C+] (*also* **gip**) a thief. **2** [1910s+] (*also* **jip**) an act of deception, a fraud or hoax. **3** [1930s+] a cheat, a swindler; one who fails to pay his due debts. [abbr. SE *gypsy* and as such an ethnic slur]

gyp *adj.* [1920s–40s] cheating, deceitful. [GYP *v.* (1)]

gyp *v.* (*also* **gip**, **gypsy**, **jip**) (*orig. US*) **1** [late 19C+] to cheat, to deceive, to renege on one's debts. **2** [1910s–40s] to steal; to rob from. **3** [1920s–30s] to disappoint. **4** [1970s] to play truant from school. [GYP *n.*]

gyp artist *n.* [1940s+] a swindler. [GYP *n.* (2) + ARTIST *n.* (1)/ARTIST sfx]

gype *n. see* GIPE *n.*

gyp joint *n.* (*also* **gyp flat**) [1920s+] (*US*) anywhere, esp. a club, bar etc, where the unwary will be swindled. [GYP *v.* (1) + JOINT *n.*[4] (3)]

gyp moll *n.* [20C+] (*US*) a female swindler. [GYP *v.* (1) + MOLL *n.*[1] (1)]

gypo *n.* (*also* **gippo**, **gyppo**, **gyppy**, **jippo**) **1** [late 19C–1960s] an Egyptian. **2** [late 19C+] a gypsy, usu. derog. **3** [1920s–70s] (*US*) contract work, a sub-contractor, a piece-worker. **4** [1990s+] (*UK juv.*) an impoverished, badly dressed schoolchild. [abbr.; the implication of (3) is that like a gypsy the worker fulfils the contract then moves on. Note UK services sl. *gyppo*, gravy, grease, stew; S.Afr. milit. *gyppo*, to shirk duty]

gypo *adj.* (*also* **gippo**, **gippy**, **gyppo**) **1** [1910s–40s] Egyptian. **2** [1930s+] pertaining to a gypsy or gypsy culture. [GYPO *n.*]

gyppery *n.* [20C+] (*US*) dishonest activity, swindling. [GYP *v.* (1) + sfx -*ery*]

gyppo *see also under* GYPO.

gyppo gut *n. see* GYPPY TUMMY *n.*

gyppy *n. see* GYPO *n.*

gyppy tummy *n.* (*also* **gippy tummy**, **gyppo gut**) [1940s+] stomach troubles, diarrhoea; orig. that contracted in Egypt, but now ext. to any such problems that UK tourists experience abroad or in ethnic restaurants at home (cf. AZTEC HOP *n.*). [GYPO *n.* (1)]

gyp racket *n.* [20C+] (*US*) swindling, fraud. [GYP *v.* (1) + RACKET *n.*[1] (1)]

gyp sheet *n.* [1970s] (*US*) a crib sheet. [GYP *v.* (1) + SE *sheet*]

Gypsie Lee *n.* [1930s+] (*Aus.*) tea. [rhy. sl.]

gypsy *n.* (*also* **gipsy**) [1950s+] (*US*) **1** an independent trucker or the truck he owns. **2** an independent cab-driver or taxi-cab. **3** a prostitute who travels around for trade or lives in a trailer park.

gypsy *adj.* (*also* **gipsy**) **1** [20C+] (*W.I.*) interfering, irritatingly inquisitive. **2** [1980s+] independent of any organization, legal or otherwise. [the negative image of the Romanies]

gypsy *v. see* GYP *v.*

gypsy queen *n.* [2000s] a homosexual. [play on SE + QUEEN *n.*[2] (1)]

gypsy's deal *n.* (*also* **gipsy's deal**) [1990s+] (*US*) a business deal that never actually materializes. [negative stereotyping]

gypsy's ginger *n.* (*also* **gipsy's ginger**) [20C+] a pile of human excrement found out of doors. [negative stereotyping]

gypsy's (kiss) *n.* (*also* **gipsy's**) [1970s+] urination (cf. ANGEL'S KISS *n.*). [rhy. sl. = PISS *n.* (2)]

gypsy's leave *n.* (*also* **gipsy's leave**) [20C+] departure without warning and without settling one's debts. [negative stereotyping]

gypsy's warning *n.*[1] (*also* **gipsy's warning**) [20C+] morning; also as 'good morning'. [rhy. sl.]

gypsy's warning *n.*[2] (*also* **gipsy's warning**) [20C+] no warning at all. [negative stereotyping]

gypsy switch *n.* [1950s] (*US Und.*) a form of criminal sleight of hand in which a high-denomination note is palmed and swapped for a low-denomination one.

gyrene *n.* [late 19C+] (*US*) a US marine. [ety. unknown; HDAS rejects popular ety. GI + *marine*; suggests Gk *gyrinos*, tadpole, pollywog, as ref. to the Marine's 'amphibious' role]

gytch *v.* [1950s] (*US*) to steal. [ety. unknown]

gyte *n.* [19C] (*Scot.*) a derog. term for a child. [pron. of SE *goat*]

gyve *n.* [1930s–50s] (*drugs*) a marijuana cigarette. [JIVE *n.*[2] (1)]

gyvel *n.* [late 18C–19C] (*Scot.*) the vagina. [SE *gyve*, a shackle, a fetter]

gyver *n. see* GUIVER *n.*[1]

gyvo *n.* [1930s+] (*Aus.*) flattery, insincerity, pretence. [GUIVER *n.*[1] (1)]

gyzm *n. see* JISM *n.*

H

H *n.*[1] [mid-19C+] (*orig. US*) *h*ell. [abbr.]

H *n.*[2] (*also* **aitch, the H**) **1** [1920s+] (*drugs*) heroin (cf. BIG H *n.*). **2** [1950s] a *h*ypodermic syringe. **3** [1980s+] (*US drugs*) *h*ashish. [abbr.]

ha *n. see* HA-HA *n.*[2].

hab *n.* [20C+] (*Can.*) a derog. term for a share-cropper, a tenant farmer. [Fr. *habitant*, an inhabitant. The name was adopted deliberately by the Montréal Canadians, to display their pride as French, rather than British, Canadians]

habdabs *n. see* ABDABS *n.*

habe *n.* [1970s+] *habe*as corpus, an order compelling its subject to attend court. [abbr. legal jargon]

haberdasher of (nouns and) pronouns *n.* [late 17C–early 19C] a schoolmaster, a tutor. [the expanded version is 17C–18C only]

habit *n.* **1** [late 19C+] (*drugs*) drug addiction; thus *get the habit off*, to take enough of a narcotic to stop the pain of withdrawal; *bend the habit*, to decrease one's narcotics intake in an attempt to withdraw from addiction. **2** [20C+] ext. to other addictions. **3** [1920s–30s] (*drugs*) withdrawal symptoms; thus *have a habit*, to be suffering from withdrawal symptons. [note that earliest cits. are more SE than sl., e.g. in 1887, 'May he continue to wage war against Chinese opium dens until the habit has been swept entirely out of existence'; the term was adopted by drug users in the 1910s. Note 'William Lee', *Junkie* (1953): 'A junk habit. It takes at least a month of daily use to get a needle habit, two months for a smoking habit, four months for an eating habit']

habitch *n.* [1950s] a habitual criminal. [abbr./pron. SE *habitual*]

habitual *n.* [late 19C+] a *habitual* criminal, drunkard etc. [abbr.]

hab-nab *adv.* (*also* **hab-nabs, hab or nab**) [mid-16C–early 19C] at random, hit or miss. [ME *habbe*, have and *nhabbe*, have not. The *OED* offers this ety., but notes that while the phonology seems correct 'there is a long gap in the history, between the general disappearance of the *habbe* forms of the verb in ME and the first examples of *hab-nab*']

hache *n.* [1950s+] (*drugs*) heroin (cf. BIG H *n.*). [Sp. *hache*, the letter H/H *n.*[2] (1)]

hachi *n.* (*also* **hotchee, hotchie**) [1950s+] (*orig. US milit.*) the penis; thus *eat/suck a hachi!* go to hell! [Jap. *shakuhachi*, 50cm (20in); imported by US veterans of the Korean War (1950–3); but note HATCHI *n.*]

hack *n.*[1] **1** [late 17C–1910s] (*also* **hackman**) the driver of a hackney carriage. **2** [19C+] a reporter, a journalist, formerly derog. but recently popular, if tongue-in-cheek. **3** [mid-19C+] (*US*) a taxi-cab. **4** [late 19C] a prostitute; one who is sexually experienced (cf. BANBURY *n.*). **5** [1930s+] (*Aus./US*) a taxi-driver. **6** [1950s–70s] anyone who acts as a 'yes-man', esp. in politics. **7** [1950s+] an incompetent, an inadequate. **8** [1960s] (*N.Z.*) a customer, as in a pub. **9** [1990s+] a worker of any type, the image is of monotonous 'grind'. [abbr. SE *hackney* carriage/cab-driver; non-vehicular refs. reflect the idea of being available 'for hire'; note

Ned Ward, *The London Spy* (1699): 'His beard [...] was as well-grown as a *Hackney-Writers* in the middle of a *Long Vacation*'; note 'A Pembrochian', *Gradus ad Catabrigiam* (1803): 'HACK, a hack preacher "the common exhibitioners of St. Mary's, employed in the service of defaulters and absentees"']

hack *n.*[2] [19C+] **1** an embarrassment, an embarrassing situation. **2** an annoying characteristic. [SE *hackneyed*, banal, lacking novelty]

hack *n.*[3] [mid-19C–1920s] (*US*) an attempt, a try. [SE *hack*, to chop (at)]

hack *n.*[4] (*US*) **1** [late 19C–1960s] a hearse. **2** [1910s–60s] an ambulance. **3** [1910s–60s] an old, dilapidated boat. **4** [1920s–30s] a car. **5** [1960s+] a motorcycle sidecar. [SE *hackney carriage*]

hack *n.*[5] **1** [1910s–50s] (*US/Can. Und.*) a night watchman. **2** [1920s+] (*US*) a policeman. **3** [1930s] (*US Black*) a generic term for any White person. **4** [1930s+] (*US/Can. Und.*) a prison guard. **5** [1950s–60s] a bodyguard. [SE *hack*, a night watchman; or HAWK *n.*[2] (1)]

hack *v.*[1] **1** [late 19C+] (*US campus*) to socialize, to waste time, to idle. **2** [1940s–60s] (*US*) to neck, to kiss, to engage in sexual activity. [? SE *hack*, to chop]

hack *v.*[2] **1** [late 19C+] (*also* **hack off, hell-hack**) to irritate, to annoy. **2** [20C+] (*US campus*) to tease gently. [SE *hack*, to chop]

hack *v.*[3] [late 19C+] (*US*) to ride in or drive a hackney coach or taxi-cab. [HACK *n.*[1]]

hack *v.*[4] [1910s] (*US Und.*) to work as a night watchman. [HACK *n.*[5] (1)]

hack *v.*[5] (*US*) **1** [1950s+] to accomplish; thus HACK IT *v.* (1). **2** [1970s] to understand. [SE *hack*, to cut through]

hack *v.*[6] (*orig. computing*) **1** [1960s+] to tinker with a computer system for pleasure and as a proof of one's expertise. **2** [1980s+] to gain unauthorized access to a computer system (and poss. use that access for illegal activities). [SE *hack*, to chop, cut through]

hack *v.*[7] [1970s] (*US campus*) to vomit (cf. BARF *v.*). [SE *hack*, to cough]

hack *v.*[8] *see* HAWK *v.*[2].

hack around *v.* (*also* **hack about/off**) **1** [1920s+] (*US campus*) to socialize, to fool about. **2** [1950s–70s] (*US*) to joke, to tease. **3** [1960s+] (*US*) to waste time. [HACK *v.*[1] (1)]

hacked (off) *adj.* (*orig. US*) **1** [late 19C–1910s] exhausted. **2** [1930s+] very angry. **3** [1950s+] grumpy, bored. [HACK *v.*[2] (1)]

hackems *n.* [1960s+] (*Aus.*) hostilities, conflicts. [SE *hack*, to chop (at)]

hacker *n.*[1] [1930s–60s] (*US*) a taxi-driver. [HACK *n.*[1] (3)]

hacker *n.*[2] [1960s] (*US campus*) an idler, a time-waster. [HACK *v.*[1] (1)]

hacker *n.*[3] (*orig. computing*) **1** [1960s+] one who uses their skill with computers to try to gain unauthorized access to computer systems. **2** [1970s+] an enthusiast for programming or using computers as an end in itself. [HACK *v.*[6]]

hacker *n.*[4] [1970s] (*US*) one who perseveres in the face of challenges, a survivor. [HACK IT v. (1)]

hacker *n.*[5] [1970s+] a run-of-the-mill, average person. [HACK n.[1] (7); the implication is of a 'jack-of-all-trades']

hacker *n.*[6] [1990s+] (*US prison*) a prison guard. [HACK n.[5] (4)]

hackette *n.* [1970s+] a female journalist. [HACK n.[1] (2) + SE fem. sfx *-ette*]

hack hand *n.* [1940s] (*US*) a commercial truck-driver. [HACK n.[1] + HAND n.[1]]

hackie *n.* (*also* **hacky**) [late 19C+] (*US*) a taxi-driver. [HACK n.[1] (3)]

hacking *n.* (*orig. computing*) **1** [1960s+] the unauthorized accessing of computer systems. **2** [1970s+] the use of a computer for the sheer pleasure in computing. [HACK v.[6]]

hack it *v.* [1950s+] **1** to manage, to tolerate, to bear a difficulty, to solve a problem, to succeed; thus *hack it out, hack it over*, to work out, to make a plan. **2** (*US*) (*also* **hack up**) to achieve, to succeed in a task. [HACK v.[5]]

hackle *n.* [mid-19C] courage, pluck; thus *show hackle*, to be willing to fight. [SE *hackles*, the long, shining feathers on the necks of certain birds, typically the domestic cockerel]

hackle *v.* [1950s+] (*W.I. Rasta*) to bother, to worry, to trouble. [? HASSLE WITH v. (2) + ? SE *get one's hackles up*]

hackle up *adj.* [20C+] (*W.I.*) **1** of people, physically deformed. **2** of things, torn, damaged, untidy. [? SE *hacked*, chopped up]

hackle up *v.* [20C+] (*W.I., Baha.*) to beat up. [? SE *hack*, to chop up]

hackling *n.* [1950s+] (*W.I. Rasta*) bothering, worrying, troubling. [HACKLE v.]

hackman *n. see* HACK n.[1] (1).

hackney *n.* **1** [mid-15C–18C] (*also* **hackney jade/lady, hackster**) a prostitute (cf. BANBURY n.). **2** [early 16C] a pimp (cf. ABBOT ON THE CROSS n.). [14C SE *hackney horse*, a run-of-the-mill horse, i.e. not a warhorse or hunter, which was used for everyday riding and subseq. typified as the sort of horse available for hire]

hackney *v.* [mid-18C] to work as a prostitute. [HACKNEY n. (1)]

hackneyed *adj.* [early 17C–mid-18C] pertaining to prostitution. [HACKNEY n. (1)]

hackney jade/lady *n. see* HACKNEY n. (1).

Hackney marsh *n.* [20C+] **1** a glass (of alcohol). **2** in pl., spectacles, glasses. [rhy. sl.]

Hackney wick *n.* (*also* **wick**) [20C+] the penis (cf. ALMOND n.). [rhy. sl. = PRICK n. (2)]

hack off *v.*[1] *see* HACK v.[2] (1).

hack off *v.*[2] *see* HACK AROUND v.

hack one's mack *v.* [20C+] to masturbate. [SE *hack*; to chop + assonance]

hack pusher *n.* (*also* **hack pilot**) [1930s–60s] (*Aus./US*) a taxi-driver. [HACK n.[1] (5) + SE *pusher/pilot*]

hack rack *n.* [1970s] (*US*) a taxi-cab stand. [HACK n.[1] (3) + SE *rack*]

hackslaver *v.* [19C] to stutter. [SE *hack*, to stammer + *slaver*, to salivate]

hackster *n. see* HACKNEY n. (1).

hack the hog *v.* [1960s+] to masturbate (cf. BEAT ONE'S HOG v.). [SE *hack* + HOG n.[6]]

hackum *n.* [late 17C–early 18C] a braggart. [SE *hack*, i.e. he fig. *hacks about* him]

hack up *v. see* HACK IT v. (2).

hacky *n. see* HACKIE n.

had *adj.*[1] [late 17C; early 19C+] seduced. [HAVE v.[1]]

had *adj.*[2] [late 18C+] tricked, hoaxed, deceived. [HAVE v.[3]]

ha'd *n.* (*also* **ha-d, ha-dee**) [mid-19C–1960s] a halfpenny (pron. 'hay-dee'). [SE *half* a d. (a penny)]

haddit *adj. see* HAD IT adj.

haddock *n.* **1** [early–mid-19C] a purse; thus *haddock stuff'd with beans*, a purse full of guineas. **2** [mid-19C] (*US*) money. [the once popular belief that assigned the dark marks on the shoulders of a haddock to the impression left by St Peter's finger and thumb, when he took the tribute-money out of the fish's mouth at Capernaum. Note 16C pvb 'to bring haddock to paddock', to spend or lose everything]

haddock and bloater *n.* [1950s+] a *motor*-car. [rhy. sl.]

haddock and cod *n.* [20C+] **1** an irritating person. **2** an affectionate name for a child. [rhy. sl. = SOD n.[1] (1)/SOD n.[1] (3)]

haddock stuff'd with beans *n. see* HADDOCK n. (1).

haddums *n.* (*also* **had 'em**) [mid-17C–18C] venereal disease. [the punning phr. 'been at had 'em and come home by Clapham' (cf. CLAP n.)]

ha-dee *n. see* HA'D n.

Hades *n.* [late 19C+] a euph. for *hell*, in all senses. [the underworld in Greek mythology]

had it *adj.* (*also* **haddit**) [1960s+] (*N.Z.*) useless, second-rate. [HAVE HAD IT v. (2)]

hadland *n.* [late 16C–early 17C] one who has lost land that they once possessed.

had your pennorth or do you want a ha'penny change? *phr.* [1920s+] a phr. addressed to a person one feels is staring rudely.

haematoid *adj.* [1920s] a consciously 'clever' euph. for BLOODY adj.[1]. [SE *haematoid*, resembling blood, characterized by the presence of blood]

haemorrhage *n.* [1940s] (*US*) tomato ketchup. [SE *haemorrhage*, a flow of blood]

haemorrhage *v. see* HAVE A HAEMORRHAGE v.

haemorrhoid *n.* (*also* **hemo**) **1** [1970s+] (*US campus*) an annoying person. **2** [1980s+] (*Aus. prison*) a prison officer. [pun on a PAIN IN THE ARSE n.]

haemorrhoid hitman *n.* [1990s+] a homosexual man (cf. BROWN ARTIST n.). [SE *haemorrhoid* + fig. use of HIT MAN n.]

haffie *n.* [1970s] (*S.Afr.*) a 375ml half-bottle of spirits or wine. [SE *half*]

haffies *n. see* HALVIES n.

hag *n.* **1** [1920s–60s] (*US campus*) an unattractive or sexually promiscuous young woman; thus derog. *hag party*, a party for women. **2** [1980s] an unattractive (older) homosexual man. [SE *hag*, an ugly old woman]

hag *v.* (*US*) **1** [19C] to provoke, to annoy. **2** [19C] to bring bad luck upon. **3** [1940s] to complain, to discuss critically. [SE *hag*, to torment or terrify as a hag]

hagarian *adj.* [1940s+] (*W.I.*) oafish, uncouth, rough. [SE *hog*]

haggard *n.* [late 16C] (*UK Und.*) a potential dupe who refuses to fall into the trap that has been prepared. [SE *haggard*, an intractable person (esp. a woman) who refuses to abandon their own desires. Orig. applied to a wild falcon that would not be tamed]

haggerawator *n. see* AGGERAWATOR n.

Haggisland *n.* [late 19C+] Scotland. [SE *haggis*, the 'national' dish, which was once equally popular in England]

haggy *adj.* [20C+] (*US*) of a woman, possessing the attributes of a hag. [SE *hag*, an ugly old woman]

hagsmash *n.* [20C+] (*Ulster*) a botched, inadequate piece of work. [SE *hog* + *smash*]

ha-ha *n.*[1] (*also* **hah-hah**) [late 19C–1960s] (*US*) a laugh of ridicule or derision; thus *give someone the ha-ha*, to laugh at, to ridicule and take advantage of. [the sound of a laugh]

ha-ha *n.*[2] (*also* **ha, haha**) [1970s+] (*US campus*) beer. [abbr. BREWHA n.]

ha-ha *n.*[3] [1970s+] (*drugs*) marijuana (cf. MARI-HA-HA n.). [abbr./pron. mari*juana*]

ha-ha pigeon *n.* [1940s+] (*Aus.*) a kookaburra or laughing jackass. [the distinctive call of the bird, which resembles laughter]

hah-hah *n. see* HA-HA n.[1].

hail *n.* **1** [1930s–50s] (*US*) ice cubes, as in a drink. **2** [1980s+] (*drugs*) crack cocaine (cf. BASE n.). [resemblance]

hail! *excl.* [1950s+] (*W.I. Rasta*) a general excl. of greeting.

hail and rain *n.* [1920s] a train. [rhy. sl.]

hail Columbia *n.* (*also* **hail Columbus**) (*US*) **1** [mid-19C] America. **2** [mid-19C–1960s] a euph. for *hell*. **3** [mid-19C+] a punishment, a telling-off, a scolding. [*Hail Columbia*, a patriotic song publ. in 1798 by Joseph Hopkinson (1770–1842)]

hailer *n.* [1920s+] (*Irish*) the prayer 'Hail Mary'.

hail Mary *adj.* [1990s+] (*US*) desperate, last-ditch. [a Catholic prayer for spiritual help. Note 1980s+ football/basketball jargon *hail Mary*, of a pass or throw, very long, often the last of the game, only likely to succeed through divine intervention]

hail smiling morn *n.* [1980s+] an erection. [rhy. sl. = HORN n.[2] (3)]

hailstorm *n.* [mid-19C] (*US*) any cocktail made with crushed ice. [HAIL n. (1) + SE *storm*]

hail up *v.* [late 19C–1900s] (*Aus.*) to stay at an inn or similar lodging. [but, given Ware's confusion of *hail up*, 'an order by a bushranger – an intimation to throw up the hands', ? misreading of BAIL UP v. (1)]

haim *n.* (*also* **hame**) [1940s+] (*US Black*) a job, usu. tedious or unpleasant. [ety. unknown; orig. jazz use *hame*, a job other than in the music business]

haincty *see under* HINCTY.

Haines! *excl.* [mid-19C–1900s] (*orig. US*) a warning shout. [MY NAME IS HAINES phr.]

hain'ting *adj.* (*also* **ain'ting**, **hain'ting ain'ting**) [20C+] (*US*) rustic, uneducated. [rustic pron. of SE *hasn't* as *hain't* and *isn't* as *ain't*]

hair *n.*[1] **1** [mid-19C–1920s] pubic hair. **2** [mid-19C–1950s] a generic for the female sex; thus AFTER HAIR phr.; BIT OF HAIR n.; HAIR-MONGER n.; *plenty of hair*, large numbers of women; *put down some hair*, of a man, to have sexual intercourse.

hair *n.*[2] [mid-19C–1970s] (*US*) the scalp, as a trophy; usu. in phrs. *lift hair* or *raise hair*.

hair *n.*[3] [mid-19C+] (*US*) a curative drink for a hangover. [abbr. HAIR OF THE DOG (THAT BIT US) n.]

hair *n.*[4] [20C+] (*Ulster*) a hair-pulling fight between women.

hair *n.*[5] **1** [1910s+] composure. **2** [1950s+] (*US campus*) courage, masculine prowess; thus HAIR OUT v. [the image of the hairy-chested macho man. Note 1960s US sports use *show hair*, for a sportsman to play aggressively and well]

hair about the heels *adj.* (*also* **hairy about the fetlocks/ heels**) [late 19C–1930s] of poor breeding, socially inferior. [bloodstock use]

hair and hide *phr.* (*also* **hair hoof and hide**, **hide and hair**, **hide and tallow**, **hilt and hair**) [mid-19C+] everything, entirely, completely. [butcher/slaughterhouse jargon, the whole animal]

hairbag *n.* (*US*) **1** [1950s+] a veteran police officer. **2** [1970s+] an unpleasant, disgusting person. [SE *hair* + -BAG sfx; ? the disgusting image; ? var. on HAIRBALL n.]

hairball *n.* [1980s+] a general term of derision for a situation or person. [SE *hairball*, a mass of hair found in the stomachs of various animals, e.g. a cat]

hairburger *n.* [1970s–80s] (*US*) the female genitals. [HAIR n.[1] + sfx -*burger*]

hairburner *n.* (*also* **hair bender**) [1960s–80s] (*US gay*) a gay male hairdresser.

hair court *n.* [19C] female pubic hair. [SE *hairy* + *court*]

hair-curler *n.* [mid-19C] (*US*) alcohol. [its effects]

haircut *n.*[1] [late 19C] (*US*) a blow over the head. [SE *hair* + CUT n.[4]]

haircut *n.*[2] **1** [1940s] (*US Black*) a week. **2** [1940s+] (*UK prison*) a short term of imprisonment, in a local prison from a few weeks up to 2–3 months or in a convict prison for 3–5 years. [(1) the notional cutting of one's hair on a weekly basis; (2) the relatively short period and the cutting of one's hair on arrival in prison]

haircut *n.*[3] [1960s] (*US Und.*) a verbal telling off. [the image is of diminishing someone, cutting someone down to size]

haircut *n.*[4] [1960s+] (*US drugs*) marijuana. [ety. unknown; ? euph.]

haircut band *n.* [1980s+] a band that is mocked for being more interested in style than music.

hair-divider *n.* (*also* **hair-splitter**) [mid-19C+] the penis (cf. ARSE-OPENER n.). [HAIR n.[1] + SE *divider*]

haired up *adj.* (*also* **haired off**) [20C+] (*US*) annoyed, furious, upset. [GET A HAIR UP ONE'S ASS v.]

hair fairy *n.* [1960s–70s] (*US*) an effeminate male homosexual, with long or styled hair. [SE *hair* + FAIRY n.[3]]

hairhead *n.* [1970s] (*US*) a long-haired man, a HIPPIE n.[2] (3). [SE *hair* + -HEAD sfx]

hairhead *adj.* [1970s] long-haired, HIPPIE adj. [HAIRHEAD n.]

hair hoof and hide *phr. see* HAIR AND HIDE phr.

hair-hopper *n.* [1980s+] (*US*) a woman who frequently changes her hairstyle. [she *hops* from style to style]

hair in the butter *n.* [20C+] (*US*) a delicate situation. [var. on SE *fly in the ointment*]

hair-monger *n.* [late 19C] a womanizer. [HAIR n.[1] (2)]

hair of the dog (that bit us) *n.* [mid-16C+] a hangover cure that consists of drinking more of the alcohol that created the hangover; occas. ext. to drugs.

hair out *v.* [1990s+] to be fearful. [HAIR n.[5] (2)]

hair pie *n.* (*also* **hairy pie**) **1** [1930s+] (*orig. US*) cunnilingus (cf. BEARD RIDE n.; BOX LUNCH n.). **2** [1950s+] (*orig. US*) the vagina (cf. APPLE n.[6]). **3** [1970s] (*US*) the penis in the context of fellatio. [HAIR n.[1] (1) + SE *pie* (which one can EAT v.[3] (1)), plus pun on SE *hare pie*; one of many sl. examples of equating sex with food]

hairpin *n.* **1** [late 19C+] (*US*) a fool, a simpleton. **2** [1920s–60s] (*US*) a woman. **3** [1950s] (*US*) a thin person. **4** [1950s–70s] (*US gay*) a homosexual; thus *drop hairpins*, to hint that one is homosexual.

hair-raiser *n.* [20C+] an exciting or terrifying adventure story or film.

hair-shifter *n.* [1900s] (*Aus.*) a barber.

hair-shirt *n.* [1940s] (*US teen*) a prude. [alluding to the shirts of hair worn by some extreme religious penitents]

hair-splitter *n. see* HAIR-DIVIDER n.

hair to sell *phr.* [late 19C] used of a woman who is willing to prostitute herself. [HAIR n.[1] (2)]

hairy *n.*[1] [1920s+] (*Scot.*) a woman, esp. (*Glasgow*) a poor woman. [the premise is that a better-off woman would wear a hat and hide her hair]

hairy *n.*[2] [1950s+] (*drugs*) heroin. [pron. of SE as 'hair-o-in']

hairy *n.*[3] (*also* **hairyback**) [1960s+] (*S.Afr.*) an Afrikaner. [a hairy back is seen as an image of animality]

hairy *adj.*[1] [mid-19C–1960s] desirable, sexy; thus *feel hairy*, to feel sexually inclined. [HAIR n.[1] (2)]

hairy *adj.*[2] **1** [mid-19C+] difficult. **2** [late 19C] excellent, first-rate. **3** [1910s+] wary, sharp. **4** [1910s+] dangerous, exciting. **5** [1920s–50s] (*orig. Irish*) impressive, sometimes used as a general intensifier. **6** [1940s+] (*US*) bad or unsatisfactory. **7** [1960s–70s] (*US*) stylish, excellent. **8** [1960s+] weird, complicated. [ety. unknown]

hairy *adj.*[3] [1900s–40s] ill-bred, bad-mannered. [HAIR ABOUT THE HEELS adj.]

hairy *adj.*[4] [1910s–70s] annoyed, furious, upset. [GET A HAIR UP ONE'S ASS v.]

hairy *adj.*[5] *see* HAIRY-ARSED adj. (1).

hairy about the fetlocks/heels *adj. see* HAIR ABOUT THE HEELS adj.

hairy ape *n.* [1970s–80s] (*N.Z. prison*) rape. [rhy. sl.]

hairy-arsed *adj.* (*also* **hairy-ass, hairy-assed**) **1** [1940s+] (*also* **hairy**) overtly, aggressively masculine. **2** [1960s+] veteran, mature. [SE *hairy*/HAIRY adj.[2] + -ASSED sfx]

hairy axe wound *n.* (*also* **hairy cheque book**) [1990s+] the female genitals. [SE *hairy* + AX n.[2] + SE *wound/cheque-book*]

hairyback *n. see* HAIRY n.[3]

hairy-bank *n.* [1990s+] (*W.I.*) the vagina (cf. BANK n.[1]). [SE *hairy* + *bank*; Francis-Jackson, *Official Dancehall Dict.* (1995), 'a man who is generous to his girlfriend by giving gifts of jewellery, cash, etc. is said to be making deposits at hairy-bank']

hairy-belly *n.* (*also* **hairy-guts**) [1910s+] (*Aus.*) a sycophant.

hairy bit *n.* [mid-19C+] a sexually attractive woman. [HAIRY adj.[1] + BIT n.[2] (1)]

hairy buffalo *n.* [1960s–80s] (*US*) a strong mixed alcoholic drink, esp. when used to relax the inhibitions of women at parties. [ety. unknown]

hairy cheque book *n. see* HAIRY AXE WOUND n.

hairy clam *n.* [2000s] the vagina (cf. BEARDED CLAM n.). [SE *hairy* + CLAM n.[1] (2)]

hairy crunchy *n. see* CRUNCHY (GRANOLA) n. (3).

hairy cup *n.* (*also* **hairy goblet**) [1990s+] the vagina (cf. BAG n.[1]). [SE *hairy* + *cup*, i.e. the idea of drinking from it]

hairy doughnut *n.* [1990s+] the vagina (cf. APPLE n.[6]). [SE *hairy* + DOUGHNUT n.[2] (2)]

hairy eyeball *n.* [1960s+] (*US*) a hostile look. [HAIRY adj.[2] (3) + EYEBALL n.[2] (1)]

hairyfordshire *n.* [mid-19C+] the vagina (cf. ANTIPODES n.). [pun on UK county *Herefordshire* and the pubic HAIR n.[1] (1); *ford* also points to those words that equate the vagina with a stream or river (cf. DAMP n.)]

hairy goblet *n. see* HAIRY CUP n.

hairy-guts *n. see* HAIRY-BELLY n.

hairy-heeled *adj.* **1** [1900s] of racehorses, fast. **2** [1930s+] of people, of poor breeding, socially inferior. [bloodstock use; (2) spec. HAIR ABOUT THE HEELS adj.]

hairy Mary *n.[1]* [1960s+] (*US gay*) a masculine homosexual (cf. ABIGAIL n.). [SE *hairy* + MARY n.[2] (1)]

hairy Mary *n.[2]* (*also* **hairy Molly**) [1960s+] (*Irish*) the female genitals. [SE *hairy* + assonance; a logical 'naming' of the vagina]

hairy oracle *n.* [late 18C–mid-19C] female pubic hair; the vagina. [SE *hairy* + ORACLE n.[2]]

hairy oyster *n. see* HIRSUTE OYSTER n.

hairy pie *n. see* HAIR PIE n.

hairy ring *n.* [late 19C] the female genital area. [SE *hairy* + RING n.[1] (1)]

hairy sausage *n.* [1990s+] the penis (cf. BACON n.[1]). [SE *hairy* + SAUSAGE n.[1] (1)]

hairy wheel *n.* [mid-19C+] **1** (*Aus.*) the female genital area. **2** the male genitals.

Haiti *n.* [19C+] (*US*) that area of a town where the Black population lives. [proper name]

ha-ja *n. see* HALF-JACK n.[2].

hakim *n.* [mid-19C] (*Anglo-Ind.*) a doctor. [Arabic *hakim*, wise, learned, a philosopher, a physician; ult. f. *hakama*, to exercise authority; thus to know, be wise or learned]

halal *n.* [1990s+] a derog. term for a Muslim, esp. a Pakistani immigrant. [Arabic *halal*, lawful; in this context ritually slaughtered meat, eaten by Muslims]

halari *n.* [20C+] (*W.I.*) a low-class woman given to fighting. [*halari*, a noisy brown bird]

hale and hearty *n.* [1970s+] a party. [rhy. sl.]

half *n.* **1** [mid-19C] (*US*) 50 cents. **2** [late 19C+] a ½ pint (280ml) of beer, a ½ gill (70ml) of spirits; esp. in phr. *a swift half* (of beer). **3** [1920s+] £50 or $50. **4** [1930s–70s] 10 shillings (50p). **5** [1940s+] (*drugs*) ½oz (14g) of a drug. [abbr.]

half *adv.* [mid-19C+] nearly, almost.

half-a-bar *n.* (*also* **half-bar**) [20C+] a half-sovereign (10 shillings, 50p). [SE *half* + BAR n.[2] (1)]

half-a-bean *n.* (*also* **half-bean**) **1** [late 18C–19C] a half-sovereign. **2** [20C+] (*US*) 50 cents. [SE *half* + BEAN n.[1]]

half-a-bill *n.* [1940s–60s] (*US*) $50, a $50 note. [SE *half* + BILL n.[2] (1)]

half-(a-)borde *n.* [late 16C–18C] (*UK Und.*) a sixpence (2½p). [SE *half* + BORD n.]

half-a-brewer *phr.* [mid-19C] drunk.

half-a-buck *n.* [1940s–50s] (*US*) 50 cents. [SE *half* + BUCK n.[3] (1)]

half-a-bull *n.* (*also* **half-bull, half-bull white**) [late 18C–1900s] half-a-crown, 2s 6d (12½p). [SE *half* + BULL n.[4] (1)]

half a button *n.* [1970s] (*US Und.*) a criminal who is on the fringe of full membership of the US Mafia. [SE *half* + BUTTON MAN n./BUTTON n.[8]]

half-a-C *n.* (*also* **half-C**) [1930s+] (*orig. US Und.*) a $50 note (cf. HALF-A-G n.). [SE *half* + C n.[1] (2)]

half-a-case *n.* **1** [mid–late 19C] a counterfeit half-crown. **2** [1940s–50s] (*US Und.*) (*also* **half-a-slug, half-case**) 50 cents. [SE *half* + CASE n.[5]]

half-a-caser *n.* (*also* **half-caser**) [late 19C–1950s] (*Aus.*) half-a-crown, 2s 6d (12½p). [SE *half* + CASER n.[1] (1)]

half-a-century *n. see* HALF-CENTURY n.

half-a-cock *n.* [1950s+] £5 (cf. BEEHIVE n.[2]). [rhy. sl.; SE *half* + COCK AND HEN n. (1)]

half-a-couter *n. see* HALF-COUTER n.

half-a-crack *n.* [1930s–50s] half-a-crown, 2s 6d (12½p). [SE *half* + corruption of SE *crown*]

half-a-crown *n.* [1940s+] (*bingo*) the number 26 (cf. ALDER-SHOT LADIES n.). [SE *half-a-crown*, in pre-decimal coinage 2s 6d (12½p)]

half-a-crowner *n.* (*also* **half-crowner**) **1** [late 19C] any publication costing 2s 6d. **2** [late 19C–1950s] one who pays half-a-crown for a seat at a show. [SE *half-a-crown*, in pre-decimal coinage 2s 6d (12½p)]

half-a-dollar *n.[1]* [late 19C+] a collar. [rhy. sl.]

half-a-dollar *n.[2] see* HALF-DOLLAR n.[1].

half-a-foot *n.* [1920s+] (*W.I.*) a person with a wooden leg.

half-a-G *n.* (*also* **half-a-grand, half-G**) [1930s+] (*US Und.*) $500. [SE *half* + G n.[1] (1)]

half-a-grunter *n. see* HALF-GRUNTER n.

half-a-hog *n.* (*also* **half-hog**) [late 17C–19C] sixpence. [SE *half* + HOG n.[1] (1)]

half-a-idiot *n. see* HALF-IDIOT n.

half-a-job *n.* [late 17C–18C] a half-guinea. [SE *half* + JOB n.[2]]

half-alligator *adj.* [mid–late 19C] aggressive, tough, rambunctious. [abbr. HALF-HORSE, HALF-ALLIGATOR adj.]

half a man *n.* [1970s+] (*US Black*) a passive homosexual (cf. BOY-GIRL n.[1]).

half-a-man *n.[1]* [1960s] 50 cents. [SE *half* + MAN n.[3] (2)]

half-a-man *n.[2] see* HALF-MAN n.

half a mo *n.[1]* [late 19C+] a very short time, lit. 'half a moment'; often used as HALF A MO phr. [SE *half* + MO n.[2] (1)]

half a mo *n.[2]* [1910s–30s] a cigarette. [? the delaying excuse, 'Half a mo, I'm just having a fag']

half a mo *phr.* [late 19C+] wait a moment, hang on. [HALF A MO n.[1]]

half a mongrel *n.* [1990s+] (*Aus.*) a semi-erect penis. [SE *half* + ? DOG n.[4] (1)]

half and between *phr.* [20C+] (*Ulster*) **1** of a person, slightly mad, eccentric. **2** neither one thing nor another.

half-and-half *n.[1]* **1** [mid-18C+] a mixture of ale and porter. **2** [early 19C–1960s] a mixture of wine and whisky.

half-and-half *n.[2]* **1** [19C+] (*US*) a half-breed, a person of mixed race. **2** [1930s–60s] (*US Black*) a hermaphrodite. **3** [1960s] (*Irish*) a homosexual man. [(1) half-Black/half-White; (2) and (3) half-man/half-woman]

half-and-half n.[3] 1 [1930s+] as offered by a prostitute, fellatio plus full intercourse. 2 [1970s+] (*US gay*) fellatio plus anal intercourse.

half-and-half adj. 1 [early 19C–1900s] (*UK Und.*) (*also* **half-and-half-and-half, half-half-and-half**) drunk, tipsy. 2 [mid-19C] second-rate. 3 [1900s] married. 4 [1970s+] (*US campus*) bisexual.

half-and-half coves n. (*also* **half-and-half boys/men**) [early–mid-19C] would-be dandies who fail to make the grade. [SE *half-and-half* + COVE n. (1)/SE *boys/men*]

half-and-halfer n. [late 19C+] a person or object that cannot easily be categorized, 'neither one thing nor the other'.

half-an-hour n. [20C+] (*Aus.*) flour. [rhy. sl.]

half-a-nick(er) n. *see* HALF-NICKER n.[1].

half-a-nicker n. (*also* **half-nicker**) [20C+] a vicar. [rhy. sl.]

half-a-note n. (*also* **half-note**) [late 19C–1970s] (*Aus./Irish*) a 10-shilling note, 10 shillings. [abbr. *half a pound-note*]

half-an-ounce n. [early 18C–early 19C] half-a-crown, 2s 6d (12½p). [the contemporary measurement of silver at 5s an ounce]

half-a-pint n. *see* HALF-PINT n.

half-a-quid n. (*also* **half-quid**) [early 19C+] 10 shillings; latterly 50p. [SE *half* + QUID n. (2)]

half-a-quid adj. [early 19C+] worth 10 shillings or 50p. [HALF-A-QUID n.]

half-arse/-arsed adj. *see* HALF-ASSED adj.

half-arsed adv. *see* HALF-ASSED adv.

half-a-shake n. [20C+] (*N.Z.*) a moment, a very short time.

half a sheet n. [1930s–50s] (*UK prison*) a punishment for wardens, usu. a fine. [based on HALF-A-NOTE n.]

half-a-slug n. *see* HALF-A-CASE n. (2).

half-ass n. [1920s+] (*US*) a stupid, incompetent person. [SE *half* + ASS n. (1)/HALF-ASSED adj.]

half-assed adj. (*also* **half-arse, half-arsed, half-ass**) [mid-19C+] (*orig. US*) careless, inadequate, incompetent, second-rate. [SE *half* + ARSE n.[1] (1)/ASS n. (2)]

half-assed adv. (*also* **half-arsed, half-ass**) 1 [1920s+] (*orig. US*) carelessly, incompetently. 2 [1960s+] not seriously. 3 [1970s+] reasonably. [HALF-ASSED adj.]

half-assed-backwards adj. [1960s+] (*US*) back-to-front.

half a stretch n.[1] (*also* **half stretch**) [mid-19C+] (*UK Und.*) 6 months' imprisonment; also used by criminals for any period of 6 months. [SE *half* + STRETCH n.[1] (2)]

half a stretch n.[2] [1940s] (*US Black*) the distance of half a city block; usu. with *away*. [SE *half* + *stretch*, a distance]

half-a-surprise n. [late 19C–1900s] a single black eye. [Charles Coborn's song lyric (c.1886), 'Two lovely black eyes/Oh what a surprise']

half-a-thick n. *see* HALF-THICK n.

half a tick n. (*also* **half a tic**) [late 19C+] a very short time. [SE *half* + TICK n.[4] (2)]

half a tick phr. [1910s+] wait a bit, hang on. [HALF A TICK n.]

half-a-ton n. 1 [1940s+] £50. 2 [1960s+] (*bingo*) the number 10 (cf. ALDERSHOT LADIES n.). [SE *half* + TON n.[1]]

half-a-tosheroon n. (*also* **half-a-tusheroon**) [mid–late 19C] half-a-crown, 2s 6d (12½p). [SE *half* + TOSHEROON n.]

half-away adj. [20C+] (*Ulster*) insane. [on the model of NOT ALL THERE phr.]

half-a-yard n. (*also* **half-yard**) 1 [1920s+] (*US*) $5. 2 [1960s] $50 (worth of heroin). [SE *half* + YARD n.[3]]

half-bake n. [1940s–60s] a fool, an inadequate. [HALF-BAKED adj.]

half-baked n. [late 19C+] (*Aus.*) an immature person. [HALF-BAKED adj.]

half-baked adj. 1 [early 16C; early 19C+] incompetent, inadequate, below standard. 2 [early 19C+] silly, foolish.

half-bar n. *see* HALF-A-BAR n.

half-bean n. *see* HALF-A-BEAN n.

half-brass n. [1940s+] a woman who associates with the

prostitute milieu but is not a 'working girl' herself. [SE *half* + BRASS (NAIL) n.]

half-bull (white) n. *see* HALF-A-BULL n.

half-C n. *see* HALF-A-C n.

half-canned adj. [1920s+] tipsy rather than wholly drunk. [SE *half* + CANNED adj.[1]]

half-case n. *see* HALF-A-CASE n. (2).

half-caser n. *see* HALF-A-CASER n.

half-century n. (*also* **half-a-century**) [late 19C–1940s] 1 £50. 2 (*US*) a $50 note. [SE *half* + CENTURY n. (1)]

half-cocked adj.[1] [late 18C+] drunk.

half-cocked adj.[2] [20C+] (*orig. US*) second-rate, not fully capable, unfinished. [SE *half* + *cock*, to pull back the hammer on a gun; GO OFF AT HALF-COCK v.]

half-copper n. [20C] 1 (*N.Z.*) a halfpenny. 2 (*US*) a half-cent. [SE *half* + COPPER n.[2]]

half-couter n. (*also* **half-a-couter**) [mid–late 19C] a half-sovereign, 10 shillings. [SE *half* + COUTER n.[1]]

half-cracked adj. [late 19C+] slightly insane, not wholly balanced. [SE *half* + CRACKED adj.[2] (1)]

half-crowner n. *see* HALF-A-CROWNER n.

half-cut adj.[1] [19C] (*US*) crude, uncultivated. [SE *half-cut quality*, those who look down on everyone, other than those who look down on them]

half-cut adj.[2] 1 [19C+] more than mildly drunk but not yet incapable. 2 [late 19C+] (*Aus.*) foolish, silly. [SE *half* + CUT adj.[1]]

half-dollar n.[1] (*also* **half-a-dollar**) [late 18C+] half-a-crown, 2s 6d (12½p). [a period when £1 sterling was worth around $4, i.e. 5 shillings (25p) to a dollar]

half-dollar n.[2] [1970s] (*US prison*) one who is serving 50 years in jail. [SE *half* + fig. use of SE *dollar* to mean 100]

halfer n. [1930s–40s] (*US*) a half-dollar coin.

half-fonged adj. *see* FONGED (UP) adj.

half-foolish adj. [mid-19C] ridiculous.

half-G n. *see* HALF-A-G n.

half-go n. [late 19C–1900s] 3 pennyworth of spirits, usu. mixed with water. [SE *half* + GO n.[1] (1)]

half-gone adj. 1 [19C] simple, stupid. 2 [late 19C+] drunk (cf. ADDLED adj.). 3 [1940s] (*US milit.*) hungry. [SE *half* + GONE adj.[3] (1)]

half-grunter n. (*also* **half-a-grunter**) [mid-19C] a sixpence. [SE *half* + GRUNTER n.[2] (2)]

half-half-and-half adj. *see* HALF-AND-HALF adj. (1).

half-hard adj. [20C+] 1 of the penis, semi-erect. 2 in fig. use, not very intelligent. [SE *half* + *hard*, of a penis, erect]

half-high adj. [1960s–70s] (*US*) tipsy, mildly drunk (cf. ELEVATED adj.). [SE *half* + HIGH adj.[1] (1)]

half-hipped adj. [1940s] (*orig. US Black*) ill-informed, unsophisticated. [SE *half* + HIPPED adj.[2] (2)]

half-hitch v. [1970s+] (*N.Z.*) to steal. [rhy. sl. = SNITCH v. (2)]

half-hog n. *see* HALF-A-HOG n.

half-horse, half-alligator adj. [19C+] (*US*) a notably tough man, esp. a river-boatman; also used of a woman. [characteristics of the animals]

half-hour gentleman n. [late 19C] (*UK society*) a parvenu, one in whom breeding is at best an affectation. [he can only sustain the act of being a gentleman for half an hour]

half-hundred n. [1970s+] (*N.Z.*) a £50 note.

half-idiot n. (*also* **half-a-idiot**) [20C+] (*W.I., Bdos*) a complete fool.

halfie n.[1] [1910s–60s] (*Aus.*) a half-caste.

halfie n.[2] [1990s+] a half-brick.

halfies n. *see* HALVIES n.

half-inch n. [1950s+] (*W.I.*) an inferior workman. [HALF-INCH adj.]

half-inch adj. [1950s+] (*W.I.*) inadequately equipped for a job. [? ref. to the size of one's penis]

half-inch v.[1] **1** [20C+] to steal. **2** [1990s+] to arrest. [rhy. sl. = PINCH v.]

half-inch v.[2] [1910s+] (N.Z.) to approach slowly. [ext. of SE *inch forward*, to move very slowly]

half in two v. [late 19C–1930s] (US Black) to break in two.

half-iron n. **1** [1940s+] a man who enjoys the company but not the specific predilections of homosexuals. **2** [1980s+] a bisexual. [SE *half* + IRON (HOOF) n.]

half-jack n.[1] [mid–late 19C] 10 shillings (50p), half a sovereign. [SE *half* + JACK n.[11]]

half-jack n.[2] (also **ha-ja**) [1960s+] (S.Afr.) **1** a 375ml half-bottle of spirits or wine. **2** brandy.

half-jack n.[3] see JACK n.[11].

half-James n. (also **half-jane**) [mid–late 19C] 10 shillings (50p). [SE *half* + JAMES n.[3]/JANE n.[1]]

half jim n. see JIM n.[3].

half-load n. (also **half-lo**) [1960s+] (US drugs) 15 packs of heroin, each weighing approx. 1g and thus equivalent to ½oz (14g) in total, a typical purchase made by a small pusher. [SE *half-load*; LOAD n.[7] (3)]

half-man n. (also **half-a-man**) [1930s–40s] (US Black) a half-bottle of spirits, esp. whisky. [Scot. *halfman*, half a bottle of spirits; MAN n.[4]]

half-moon n.[1] **1** [early 17C–19C] the female genital area. **2** [18C–19C] a wig; also occas., a head. **3** [1970s] a patch of sweat under the arm. [resemblance]

half-moon n.[2] [1970s+] (drugs) **1** a piece of hashish moulded in a half-moon shape. **2** a piece of peyote cactus. [resemblance]

half-mourning n. see MOURNING n.

half-nab adv. (also **half-nap**) [18C–early 19C] 'hit or miss', haphazardly. [SE *half* + HAB-NAB adv.]

half-ned n. **1** [late 18C–19C] 10 shillings (50p). **2** [mid-19C] (US) a $5 gold piece. [SE *half* + NED n.[1]]

half-nelson adj. [1910s–20s] half-drunk. [? pun on BLIND DRUNK adj. and the blind eye of British admiral Lord Nelson (1758–1805)]

half-nibs n. see NIB n.[2] (1).

half-nicker n.[1] (also **half-a-nick**, **half-a-nicker**) [20C+] a 10-shilling note (50p). [SE *half* + NICKER n.[2] (1)]

half-nicker n.[2] see HALF-A-NICKER n.

half-note n. see HALF-A-NOTE n.

half-off adj. (also **half-on**) [late 19C] tipsy, semi-drunk.

half of marge n. [1980s+] (UK Und.) a police sergeant. [rhy. sl. = SARGE n.]

half-one n. [20C+] (Irish) a small glass of whisky.

half-ounce v. [20C+] **1** to cheat, to short-change. **2** to beat up. [rhy. sl. = (1) BOUNCE v.[1] (6); (2) BOUNCE v.[1] (17)]

half-ounce of baccy n. [1970s+] a derog. term for a person of Indian, Pakistani, Bangladeshi or Ugandan Asian blood (cf. HEDGEHOG n.[2]; HERE AND NOW n.; JOE DAKI n.; OUNCE OF BACCY n.). [rhy. sl. = PAKI n.]

half-ouncer n. [20C+] a security man at a nightclub, dancehall or similar place. [rhy. sl. = BOUNCER n.[2] (5)]

half-Oxford n. [late 19C] half-a-crown, 2s 6d (12½p). [SE *half* + OXFORD (SCHOLAR) n. (1)]

half past a colored man phr. [1940s–50s] (US) half past midnight; usu. said in answer to one who asks what time it is. [i.e. midnight is pitch black]

half past a monkey's ass phr. [1970s] (US Black) half past midnight; usu. said in answer to one who asks what time it is. [i.e. midnight is pitch black]

half past eight phr. [1980s] (US) sneaky, shady. [ety. unknown]

half past kissing time (and time to kiss again) phr. [late 19C–1920s] a catchphrase used in answer to the query, 'What time is it?'

half past nines n. [late 19C–1900s] women's outsize footwear. [a size that was then considered large, even for a man's foot]

half past two n. [20C+] a Jew (cf. BILLY THE KID n.). [rhy. sl.]

half-pay n. [1940s] (Irish) a general term of derision. [SE *half-pay*, an officer, currently unemployed and thus receiving only half-pay]

halfpenny dip n. [mid-19C+] a ship. [rhy. sl.]

halfpenny howling swell n. [late 19C] an imitation dandy, a pretentious man. [SE *halfpenny* + HOWLER n.[1] (2) + SWELL n. (1)]

halfpenny stamp n. [20C+] a tramp. [rhy. sl.]

half-pie adj. [1910s+] (Aus./Can./N.Z.) imperfect, mediocre. [SE *half* + ? Maori *pai*, good]

half-pie adv. [1910s+] (Aus./N.Z.) partially, vaguely. [HALF-PIE adj.]

half-piece n. [1930s+] (drugs) ½oz (14g) of heroin or cocaine. [SE *half* + PIECE n.[6] (1)]

half-pint n. (also **half-a-pint**, **half-pinter**) [late 19C+] (orig. US) a short person or child.

half-pint adj. **1** [20C+] small, undersized. **2** [1930s+] (US) of a child, short; thus *quarter-pint*, even smaller. [HALF-PINT n.]

half-portion n. [1900s–40s] a short person.

half-portion adj. [20C+] tiny; usu. of a person. [HALF-PORTION n.]

half-quarter n. [1980s+] (US drugs) an ⅛oz (4g) of cannabis. [SE *half* + QUARTER n.[2] (2)]

half-quid n. see HALF-A-QUID n.

half-rats adj. [late 19C] tipsy, mildly drunk. [DRUNK AS A RAT phr.]

half-rinsed adj. [1910s+] (Aus./N.Z.) tipsy, semi-drunk (cf. DAMP adj.). [SE *half* + RINSE v.[2]]

half-rocked adj. [mid-19C–1910s] incompetent, inadequate, foolish. [? one who has not been fully rocked in the cradle and is thus still infantile]

half saw n. [mid-19C+] (US Und.) $5. [SE *half* + SAW n.[1]]

half seas over phr. [late 17C+] **1** drunk. **2** in fig. use, intensely emotional, whether with joy, love etc. [either naval imagery, an unstable boat is more likely to ship water, or Du *op-zee zober*, overseas strong beer (cf. UPSEE adj.)]

half-section n. [1950s+] (S.Afr.) a friend. [orig. UK services]

half set n. [1950s–60s] (mainly drugs) an unacceptable offer, usu. in the context of a drug deal. [presumably from SET n.[3], with SE *half* indicating the dissatisfaction]

half-shot adj. [mid-19C+] (orig. US) tipsy, mildly drunk. [SE *half* + SHOT adj. (1); note CUPSHOT adj.]

half-slewed adj. [early 19C+] tipsy, half-drunk. [SE *half* + SLEWED adj. (1)]

half-smart adj. (also **half-slick**) [1920s–60s] (US) stupid or reckless.

half-snack n. (also **half-snags**) [late 17C–19C] half-shares in something. [SE *half* + *snag*, to catch onto]

half-square n. (also **half-squarie**) [1920s–60s] (Aus.) a sexually experienced woman, positioned in the contemporary moral spectrum between an all-out prostitute and a respectable woman. [SE *half* + SQUARE n.[1] (2)]

half-stamp n. [20C+] a tramp. [rhy. sl.]

half-step v. **1** [1940s+] to loaf, to idle, to go slowly. **2** [1980s+] (US Black/Und.) to make a feeble effort, to act in an inappropriate or ineffectual manner. **3** [1980s+] (US Black) to make promises, e.g. of sexual favours, that are not carried through. **4** [1990s+] (US Black) to sneak up on. [milit. *half-step*, a form of slow marching]

half-stepper n. [1950s+] (orig. US prison) one who promises things, but never properly achieves them, thus one who cannot be depended upon. [HALF-STEP v.]

half-stepping adj. [1950s+] (US Black/Und.) unreliable, untrustworthy. [HALF-STEP v.]

half-strainer n. (also **half-way strainer**) [late 19C–1910s] (US, Southern) a social climber. [dial. *half-strain*, a mongrel, *half-strained gentry*, shabby-genteel individuals]

half stretch n. see HALF A STRETCH n.[1].

half the bay over *phr.* [late 19C] drunk. [var. on HALF SEAS OVER phr. (1)]

half-there *adj.* **1** [20C+] simple, stupid. **2** [1950s] (*Aus.*) tipsy, semi-drunk (cf. ADDLED adj.). [var. on NOT ALL THERE phr. (2)]

half-thick *n.* (*also* **half-a-thick, half-thick 'un**) [late 19C–1900s] (*N.Z.*) a half-sovereign, 10 shillings. [SE *half* + THICK 'UN n. (1)]

half-tiz *n.* [late 19C–1900s] (*N.Z.*) 3 pence. [SE *half* + TIZZY n.[1]]

half-tore *adj.* [20C+] (*Ulster*) tipsy, half-drunk. [SE *half* + TORE UP adj. (2)]

Half-Way House *n.* [1930s] (*UK Und.*) Parkhurst prison, Isle of Wight (cf. ABBOTT'S PRIORY n.). [the volume of mentally disturbed inmates, making it a 'half-way house to Broadmoor' (the UK's main prison for the criminally insane)]

half-way house *n.* [1940s+] (*bingo*) the number 50 (cf. ALDERSHOT LADIES n.). [there are 100 numbers available to the caller]

half-way strainer *n. see* HALF-STRAINER n.

half-wheel *n.* [1960s] (*N.Z.*) half-a-crown, 2s 6d (12½p). [SE *half* + WHEEL n.[1] (2)]

half-wide *adj.* **1** [16C] immoral. **2** [19C+] reasonably intelligent, aware of what goes on and thus, in certain contexts, corruptible. [SE *half* + WIDE adj. (1)]

halfy *n.* [1910s–60s] (*US*) a legless beggar. [he has only 'half' his body]

half-yard *n. see* HALF-A-YARD n.

half-yenork *n.* [mid-19C–1900s] half-a-crown, 2s 6d (12½p). [SE *half* + YENORK n.]

half your luck! *excl.* [1930s+] (*Aus.*) signifying envy, jealousy of the person addressed, i.e. *I wish I had…*

Halifax *n.* [17C+] a euph. for *hell*; often as GO TO HALIFAX! excl. [GO TO HELL, HULL AND HALIFAX! excl.]

Halifax *v.* [17C–19C] **1** to kill, thus to send to hell. **2** to beat. [HALIFAX n.]

Halifax mutton *n.* [late 19C+] (*W.I.*) salt codfish. [as imported from *Halifax*, Nova Scotia]

Hall, the *n.* [mid-19C] Leaden*hall* Market. [abbr.; orig. used as the market for 'foreigners', i.e. out-of-Londoners, the Hall burnt down in 1666 and was rebuilt as a meat, poultry, fish and vegetable market. The current buildings date f. 1881]

hall *n. see* JOHN HALL n.

hallan shaker *n.* (*also* **halland shaker**) [16C–18C] a 'sturdy' or able-bodied and poss. violent beggar. [Scot. *hallan*, the partition of a cottage wall, esp. when it cut off the front door from the fire + SE *shaker*]

hallelujah *n.* **1** [20C+] (*US*) a euph. for *hell*. **2** [1930s] (*UK tramp*) a Salvation Army hostel for the homeless.

hallelujah *adj.* [late 19C–1950s] pertaining to the Salvation Army; or a religious group.

hallelujah garment *n.* [late 19C] (*Aus.*) a swallow-tailed morning coat (as typically worn by a preacher).

hallelujah-hawking *n.* [1910s–50s] (*Aus.*) working as a door-to-door evangelist. [SE *hallelujah* + *hawk*, to peddle]

hallelujah lass *n.* (*also* **hallelujah maid, lulyah lass**) [late 19C–1950s] a young woman Salvationist. [HALLELUJAH adj. + SE *lass*]

hallelujah-peddlar *n.* [1920s–30s] (*US*) a Salvation Army or any other affiliation of preacher. [HALLELUJAH adj. + SE *peddlar*]

hallelujah stew *n.* [20C+] the stew served out at Salvation Army hostels. [HALLELUJAH adj. + SE *stew*]

Halley's comet *n.* [1990s+] (*Aus.*) vomit (cf. HARVEY DREW n.; UP AND UNDER n.v.; WALLACE AND GROMIT v.). [rhy. sl.]

halliballoo *n. see* HULLABALLOO n.

halligator *n.* [late 19C–1900s] a herring. [var. on ALLIGATOR n.[1] (2)]

hall of fame *n.* [late 19C–1910s] (*US Und.*) a rogues' gallery.

halloo-wach *n.* [1980s+] (*drugs*) amphetamine (cf. A n.[2]). [*Halloo-*

Wach, brandname of a German drug sold over the counter as a stimulant, like Pro Plus]

halter *n.* [16C+] the noose used in a judicial hanging. [20C+ use is US]

halter *v.* [16C+] to hang someone. [HALTER n.]

halter-broke *adj.* [1910s–60s] (*US*) timid, submissive, unadventurous. [SE *halter broken*, of a horse, accustomed to the halter]

halter-sack *n.* [late 16C–early 17C] a villain whose destination will be the gallows. [the noose is the *halter*, the condemned felon's body the *sack*]

halvers *n.* [19C+] equal shares; usu. as *halvers!* I demand half! (cf. GO HALVES v.). [SE *half*]

halvies *n.* (*also* **haffies, halfies, halvsies**) [20C+] equal shares. [SE *half*]

ham *n.*[1] **1** [mid-19C+] an incompetent, esp. one who poses as more expert than his performance – often in sport – shows him to be. **2** [late 19C+] an over-theatrical or incompetent performer. **3** [1930s+] (*US*) an inexpert or over-theatrical performance. [theatrical use *ham*, a melodramatic, ranting, over-acting actor; ult. abbr. *hamfatter*, a second-rate and thus impoverished actor who was forced to rub hamfat over their face, as a base for the powder that was then applied, rather than being able to afford sweeter smelling oils; *Century Dict.* (1889) suggests an origin in a Black song 'The Ham-Fat Man'; hamfat was also used by old-time jazzmen to grease the slides of their trombones – thus the 1930s band The Harlem Hamfats; note U. of Missouri (in 1931) *ham*, 'one of unpolished manners' and Baker et. al., *College Undergraduate Slang Study* (1967–8) 'a person who always fools around'; note ref. to a *lard actor* 'an early professional version of "ham actor"', in a Federal Writers' Project (1939) essay on Vaudeville, suggesting that lard, rather than hamfat was a substitute for cold cream as a basis for make-up]

ham *n.*[2] [late 19C–1920s] (*US*) an incompetent boxer, a poor fighter. [HAM n.[1] (1)/SE *ham-fisted*]

ham *n.*[3] [1910s–40s] (*US*) the hand. [backform. f. *ham-fisted*, plus shape and mispron.]

ham *n.*[4] (*also* **radio ham**) [1910s+] a student or amateur telegraphist, subseq. an amateur radio operator, i.e. one who makes a hobby of picking up and transmitting radio messages. [? SE *amateur* + *ham-fisted*]

ham *n.*[5] [1940s+] the penis (cf. BACON n.[1]). [HAMBONE n.[3] (1)]

ham *n.*[6] [1980s] home. [rhy. sl.]

ham *adj.* **1** [1920s–60s] clumsy, ineffective, incompetent. **2** [1920s+] theatrical, melodramatic. [HAM n.[1]]

ham *v.*[1] [1910s–60s] (*US Und.*) to walk. [the trad. HAM n.[1] (2), an actor whose company gets stranded on the road, forcing him to walk to the city]

ham *v.*[2] (*also* **ham it up**) [1930s+] (*orig. US*) to act in an exaggerated manner, to ruin a situation by foolishly excessive behaviour. [HAM n.[1]]

ham and *n.* [late 19C–1940s] (*US*) an order of ham and eggs.

ham and beef *n.*[1] [1940s–50s] (*Aus.*) a corner shop. [the purchases made there]

ham and beef *n.*[2] [1940s+] (*UK prison*) the *chief* officer. [rhy. sl.]

ham and cheesy *adj.* [2000s] easy; in fig. use, willing. [rhy. sl.]

ham and egg *adj.* [20C+] **1** (*US*) unskilled. **2** (*orig. US*) second-rate. [HAM AND EGGER n.]

ham and egger *n.* [20C+] (*US, orig. boxing*) an ordinary, run-of-the-mill person or a mediocre individual. [SE *ham and eggs*, the image is of its commonness]

ham and eggs *n.* [1920s+] legs. [rhy. sl.]

ham-bags *n.* [late 19C–1910s] women's knickers. [SE *ham*, the back of the thigh and buttock + *bags*]

hambo *n.* [1920s–50s] (*US*) a posing incompetent, esp. on stage. [HAM n.[1] + HAMBONE n.[1]]

hambone *n.*[1] **1** [late 19C–1910s] (*US*) a bad 'nigger minstrel'.

2 [late 19C+] a second-rate actor. **3** [late 19C+] a second-rate performance. **4** [1950s+] (*US*) a show-off. [var. on HAMFATTER n.]

hambone *n.*[2] **1** [20C+] a telephone. **2** [1930s] (*US*) a trombone. [rhy. sl.]

hambone *n.*[3] [1920s–70s] (*US Black*) **1** the penis (cf. BACON n.[1]). **2** the vagina. [the idea of meat + BONE n.[1] (1)]

hambone *n.*[4] [1960s+] (*orig. US Black*) **1** shorthand for the Black cultural experience. **2** a Black person. [the stereotyped Black diet is pig-based]

hambone *adj.* [1960s+] referring to Blacks. [HAMBONE n.[4]]

hambone *v.*[1] (*US*) **1** [1920s+] to live as a travelling performer. **2** [1940s+] to live frugally. **3** [1960s+] to show off. [HAMBONE n.[1]]

hambone *v.*[2] [1960s+] (*Aus.*) of a man, to strip off his clothes in public, usu. at a drunken party. [? SE *hams*, the buttocks and back of the thighs]

hambone *v.*[3] [1960s+] (*US*) to trick, to cheat. [HAMBONE n.[1]]

hambones *n.* [1900s–60s] (*US*) the knees. [SE *hams*, the buttocks, the thighs]

ham buggy *n.* [1970s+] (*US Black*) a hamburger. [pron.]

Hamburg *n.* [late 19C–1900s] (*Anglo-Ind.*) a 'bazaar' rumour. [the role of Hamburg as a trading entrepôt and thus centre of gossip]

hamburger *n.*[1] [1930s+] (*US*) a stupid or worthless individual, e.g. *he has no more brains than a....*

hamburger *n.*[2] [1940s+] (*US*) mangled flesh, remains. [note Hamburger Hill, the Vietnam War battle of Ap Bia (1969), thus nicknamed because large numbers of US troops were killed or wounded]

hamburger *n.*[3] [1980s+] (*drugs*) MDMA (cf. ECSTASY n.). [? the round shape of the tablet]

hamburgerhead *n. see* HAMHEAD n.

hamburger heaven *n.* [1940s–60s] (*US*) any small diner serving hamburgers. [the name of a chain of New York City restaurants]

hamburger helper *n.* [1990s+] (*drugs*) **1** heroin. **2** crack cocaine (cf. BASE n.). [the resemblance to SE *hamburger helper*, i.e. MSG (monosodium glutamate), which looks like white crystals]

hamburger shot *n.* [1990s+] close-up photographs of the vagina, as displayed in 'men's magazines' (cf. BACON SANDWICH n.). [the supposed resemblance of the vagina to raw meat]

ham-cases *n.* [late 18C–19C] breeches, trousers. [? Rom. *hamyas*, knee breeches or SE *ham*, the back of the thigh and buttock + *cases*; HAMS n.]

hame *n. see* HAIM n.

hamfat *n.*[1] [late 19C–1940s] (*US*) a derog. term for a Black person (cf. ALLIGATOR BAIT n.[2]). [the stereotypical pig-based Black diet]

hamfat *n.*[2] [1900s–50s] (*US Black*) a mediocrity, whether a person or thing. [ext. of HAM n.[1]]

hamfat *n.*[3] [1950s] (*US Black*) a euph. for *hell*.

hamfat *adj.* [1900s–70s] mediocre, second-rate. [HAMFAT n.[2]]

hamfatter *n.* **1** [late 19C] (*US*) a vociferous, but non-participating critic. **2** [late 19C–1950s] (*US*) an ineffective actor or performer, a mediocre jazz musician. **3** [1900s] (*US Und.*) a second-rate confidence trickster. **4** [1930s] a loudly dressed and loudly decorated dandy. [for ety. see HAM n.[1]]

hamhead *n.* (*also* **hamburgerhead**) **1** [1910s–50s] (*US*) a fool (cf. APPLEHEAD n.). **2** [1950s] (*US Und./prison*) a police officer. [SE *ham/hamburger* + -HEAD sfx (1)]

ham-hock *n.* [1980s+] (*US*) a Black person. [stereotypical Black food]

ham-hocks *n.* **1** [20C+] the legs. **2** [1930s–80s] (*US Black*) the female legs or ankles. [SE *hams*, the buttocks, the thighs + HOCK n.[1]]

ham howitzer *n.* [1990s+] the penis (cf. BACON n.[1]). [HAM n.[5] + SE *howitzer*; on lines of PORK SWORD n.]

hamilton *n.* [1940s+] (*US*) a $10 note (cf. ABE n.[2]). [the portrait of US politician Alexander *Hamilton* (1755–1804) printed on the notes]

haming *n.* [1960s] (*US Black*) working, having a non-criminal job. [? HAM v.[1], idea of working hard for a living]

ham it up *v. see* HAM v.[2].

hamlet *n.* **1** [late 17C–mid-19C] (*UK Und.*) a high constable. **2** [mid-19C] (*US Und.*) a police captain. [note Yorks. dial. *play Hamlet with*, 'play the devil with']

hamma *n.* (*also* **hammer**) [1960s+] (*US Black*) a very attractive Black woman, occas. ext. to men (cf. NAIL n.[5]). [? they 'knock one on the head'; but note HAMMERS n.]

ham-match *n.* [late 19C–1900s] a stand-up luncheon. [SE *ham* + fig. use of *match*, a contest]

hammer *n.*[1] **1** [late 16C–mid-19C; 1930s+] the penis; thus HOW'S YOUR HAMMER HANGING? phr. (cf. AX n.[2]). **2** [late 18C] the testicles. [later use of (1) is US Black]

hammer *n.*[2] [19C] (*also* **hammer man**) a strong puncher. **2** [19C+] a bodyguard, a thug.

hammer *n.*[3] **1** [mid–late 19C] an unashamed lie. **2** [late 19C+] an unjust or carping criticism. [play on KNOCK v.[1] (2)]

hammer *n.*[4] **1** [1970s+] (*US*) the accelerator (cf. PUT THE HAMMER DOWN v.). **2** [2000s] (*Irish*) a turn, e.g. *take a right-hand hammer*.

hammer *n.*[5] *see* HAMMA n.

hammer *n.*[6] *see* HAMMER (AND TACK) n.

hammer *v.*[1] **1** [late 16C; mid-19C+] to copulate (vigorously) with (cf. BANG v.[1]). **2** [early 19C+] to beat up, to hurt physically, to defeat comprehensively; thus *hammering*, a comprehensive beating, also used fig. **3** [20C+] to assail, to pressurize. **4** [2000s] to masturbate. [(2) note Egan, *Book of Sports* (1832) describing a prize-fight: 'It was blacksmith work, complete hammering']

hammer *v.*[2] **1** [late 19C+] (*Aus./US*) to drive at maximum speed. **2** [1980s+] (*US campus*) to drink fast, usu. beer. **3** [2000s] to take a large amount of a drug, usu. cocaine. [SE *hammer*; note HAMMER n.[4] (1)]

hammer *v.*[3] [1960s–70s] (*US Und.*) to solicit money for drinking. [SE *hammer* (*away*), to persist; cf. PUT THE HAMMER ON v. (2)]

hammer *v.*[4] *see* HAMMER (AND NAIL) v.

hammer a job *v.* [1940s+] (*Irish*) to have sexual intercourse. [HAMMER v.[1] (1) + JOB v.[1] (1)]

hammer and discus *n.* [1990s+] whiskers. [rhy. sl.]

hammer and jack *n. see* HAMMER AND TACK n. (5).

hammer (and nail) *v.* [20C+] to follow. [rhy. sl. = TAIL v.[2]]

hammer and saw *n.* [1920s] (*US*) a policeman (cf. BOTTLE (AND STOPPER) n.). [rhy. sl. = SE *officer of the law*]

hammer and sickles *n.* [1990s+] (*drugs*) MDMA (cf. ECSTASY n.). [the pattern imprinted on the pills]

hammer (and tack) *n.* **1** [late 19C+] (*Aus./N.Z.*) a sixpence. **2** [1920s+] (*Aus.*) a road. **3** [1930s+] (*Aus./US*) the human back. **4** [1980s] (*Aus.*) dismissal from a job. **5** [1980s+] (*Aus./N.Z. drugs*) (*also* **hammer and jack**) heroin (cf. SALISBURY CRAG n.; TOM MIX n.; UNCLE MAC n.). [rhy. sl.; (1) = ZAC n. (1); (2) = SE *track*; (4) = SACK, THE n. (1); (5) = SMACK n.[6] (1)]

hammer and tack *adv.* [1990s+] back (in time). [rhy. sl.]

hammered *adj.* **1** [1950s+] very drunk (cf. ANNIHILATED adj.). **2** [1980s+] (*US drugs*) extremely intoxicated by a drug. **3** [1990s+] (*US campus*) of a car, loaded up with accessories. [fig. uses of SE *hammer*]

hammered down *adj.* [1910s–60s] (*US*) stunted, short, squat, insignificant. [the image is of one who has been pounded down]

hammer-handle *n.* (*also* **hoe-handle**) [1920s–50s] (*US*) the penis (cf. AX n.[2]). [supposed resemblance]

hammerhead *n.*[1] [16C–17C; 20C+] (*US*) anyone stupid and obstinate, often used of a horse. [SE *hammer* + -HEAD sfx (1); but note HAMMER n.[1] (1) thus cf. DICKHEAD n.]

hammerhead *n.*[2] [1990s+] the penis (cf. AX n.[2]). [joc. use of SE or HAMMER n.[1] (1) + -HEAD sfx (1)]

hammerheaded *adj.* [17C; 20C+] stupid, stubborn (cf. AIRHEADED adj.). [HAMMERHEAD n.[1]]

hammering *n. see* HAMMER v.[1] (2).

hammerish *adj.* **1** [mid-18C] (*US*) drunk. **2** [early–mid-19C] very well aware. [fig. use of SE *hammer*]

hammer lane *n.* [1970s+] (*US*) the left, or overtaking, traffic lane. [HAMMER n.[4] (1) + SE *lane*]

hammer man *n.*[1] [1920s–70s] (*US Black*) an authoritarian figure.

hammer man *n.*[2] *see* HAMMER n.[2] (1).

hammer on *v.* [late 19C–1920s] to reiterate, to nag.

hammers *n.* [1960s+] (*US Black*) a woman's thighs. [SE *ham*, the back of the thigh and buttock]

hammock *n.* [1990s+] (*UK juv.*) a sanitary towel. [the hammock is for a 'lazy cunt': 'lazy' because it is not available for intercourse]

hammy *adj.* [late 19C+] **1** incompetent, second-rate. **2** typical of bad acting. **3** sentimental, false, bogus. [HAM n.[1]]

ham-on-ham *n.* [1990s+] 2 women enjoying mutual cunnilingus (cf. BOX LUNCH n.). [presumably SE *ham*, the back of the thigh and buttock; ? ref to HAMBONE n.[3] (2)]

hamps *n.*[1] [1990s+] (*US Black/drugs*) a Hav-a-Tampa cigar. [abbr.; as used for rolling marijuana cigarettes]

hamps *n.*[2] *see* HAMPSTEAD HEATH n.

Hampshire hog *n.* [early 18C+] a nickname for an inhabitant of Hampshire. [the popularity of hogs in the county, which was thus also known as *Hoglandiad*]

Hampstead donkeys *n.* [mid–late 19C] lice. [ety. unknown]

Hampstead Heath *n.* (*also* **hamps, Hampsteads**) [late 19C+] the teeth. [rhy. sl.]

Hampstead Heath sailor *n.* [late 19C] a very poor sailor, no sailor at all. [apart from the Round Pond and a number of bathing pools, the Heath is dry land]

Hampton Court *n.* [20C+] salt. [rhy. sl.; Cockney pron.]

Hampton rock *n.* [late 19C+] the penis (cf. ALMOND n.). [rhy. sl. = COCK n.[2] (1)]

Hampton (Wick) *n.* **1** [20C+] the penis (cf. ALMOND n.). **2** [1960s+] a fool (cf. BEECHAM'S PILL n.; CHOAD n.). [rhy. sl. = PRICK n.]

hams *n.* **1** [late 16C–mid-19C; 1940s+] the legs. **2** [mid-17C–mid-19C] breeches, trousers. [(1) obs. UK use revived by US Black]

ham sandwich *n.*[1] [1970s] (*US*) nothing. [the absolute insignificance thereof]

ham sandwich *n.*[2] [2000s] (*US Black*) a Cadillac Brougham. [pun on abbr.]

ham scram *n.* (*also* **ham scam**) [1920s–40s] (*US Black*) a tough time, a difficult period in one's life. [HAM adj. (1) + SE *scram*/SCAM n.[1]; note dial. *hamstram*, a difficulty]

ham shank *n.*[1] [1940s+] an American. [rhy. sl. = YANK n.]

ham shank *n.*[2] [1990s+] an act of masturbation. [rhy. sl. = WANK n.[1] (1)]

ham shank *n.*[3] [2000s] a third-rate, insignificant person. [HAM SHANKER n.]

ham shank *v.* [1990s+] to masturbate (cf. BEAT ONE'S MEAT v.; COTTON WOOL v.). [rhy. sl. = WANK v. (1)]

ham shanker *n.* [1990s+] **1** a masturbator. **2** an unpleasant, stupid, despised person. [rhy. sl. = WANKER n.]

ham-snatcher *n.* [1960s+] (*US Black*) a looter, breaking into stores during urban riots. [lit. to steal hams]

ham-stealer *n.* [1950s] (*US Black*) one who robs for no more than subsistence. [note Wepman et. al., *The Life* (1976): 'Ham stealing: stealing just to eat, rather than for profit. A ham stealer is thus the lowest-status player in the Life']

hanced *adj.* [17C] tipsy. [SE *enhanced*]

hancock *n.* [1920s] (*US*) one's personal signature. [abbr. JOHN HANCOCK n.]

hancock *v.* [1920s] (*US*) to sign, to affix one's personal signature. [HANCOCK n.]

hand *n.*[1] **1** [mid-18C+] an expert, usu. combined with a defining adj., e.g. *old Africa hand, poor hand at computing*. **2** [early 19C+] a person, as in COOL HAND n., *loose hand*. [metonymy]

hand *n.*[2] [20C+] (*Irish*) a butt, a victim. [dial.]

hand *n.*[3] [1960s+] (*S.Afr. drugs*) a small measure of marijuana. [SE *handful*]

hand *adj.* [1990s+] (*US campus*) best, ultimate, superlative. [? link to HAND IT TO v.[1]]

hand *v.*[1] [late 19C–1950s] (*US*) to inflict a blow, to impress upon, to conquer. [one hits with the hand]

hand *v.*[2] [late 19C+] (*US*) to tell with intent to deceive, e.g. *hand someone a line of nonsense/bull*.

hand! *excl.* [1990s+] (*US campus*) an excl. used to wish that someone will *have a nice day*. [abbr.]

hand and pocket shop *n.* [late 18C–mid-19C] an eating house where one must pay cash and credit is not available. [one must put one's *hand in one's pocket*]

hand artillery *n.* (*also* **hand cannon**) [1920s+] (*US*) a pistol.

handbag *n.* [2000s] one's wife or girlfriend.

handball *n.*[1] **1** [1970s+] (*US gay*) fondling one's own testicles from the comfort of one's pocket. **2** [1980s+] (*US gay*) the insertion of one's hand and forearm into a partner's anus or vagina. [SE *hand* + BALL v.[2] + pun on SE *handball* and BALLS n.[1]]

handball *n.*[2] [1980s+] (*drugs*) crack cocaine (cf. BASE n.). [ety. unknown]

hand-basket portion *n.* [late 18C–mid-19C] a woman whose family continually gives money to her husband. [note 16C SE *handbasket sloy*, a unpleasant epithet for a woman]

handbook *n.* [late 19C–1970s] (*US*) a small bookmaker or illegal betting establishment. [SE *hand* + BOOK n.[2]]

H & C *n.* [1960s+] (*drugs*) heroin and cocaine. [H n.[2] (1) + C n.[2] (1)]

hand cannon *n. see* HAND ARTILLERY n.

hand crank *n. see* CRANK n.[5] (2).

handcuff *n.* [1920s–40s] (*US*) **1** an engagement, a wedding. **2** an engagement or wedding ring. [a negative view of marriage; note RMC Duntroon (Aus.) *handbrake*, a girlfriend, one's wife]

-handed *sfx* [mid-19C+] (*UK Und.*) describing the size of a gang of criminals, which can be *two-, three-, four-handed* etc; thus MOB-HANDED adv.; TEAM-HANDED adv.; also used of any group, e.g. police. [HAND n.[1] (2)]

hander *n.* [1960s+] (*Scot./Aus. prison*) a helper, an assistant. [one who gives a *hand*]

hand fucking *n.* [1960s+] (*US Black*) male masturbation.

handful *n.*[1] [17C] (*UK Und.*) a long penis, the unit of measurement of a penis.

handful *n.*[2] [late 19C+] **1** a difficult person, usu. a child. **2** a difficult thing.

handful *n.*[3] [1930s+] (*UK Und.*) **1** a 5-year prison sentence. **2** a £5 note or cheque for £5; thus *two-handful*, £10. [the hand's 5 fingers]

handful of gimme and a mouthful of much obliged *phr.* [1940s+] (*US*) a phr. used of one who expects generosity but offers little or insincere thanks in return.

hand-gallop *n.* [1970s+] an act of masturbation. [SE *hand-gallop*, an easy gallop]

hand gallop *v.* [1970s+] to masturbate (cf. AUDITION THE FINGER PUPPETS v.).

hand gig *n.* [1940s+] (*gay*) **1** a homosexual prostitute who specializes in masturbating his clients or joining in mutual masturbation with them. **2** mutual masturbation.

hand gig *v. see* HAND JOB v.

handicap *n.* [20C+] venereal disease. [rhy. sl. = CLAP n.]

handicap chase *n.* [1990s+] the face. [rhy. sl.]

handicapped *adj. see* PARALYSED adj.

hand in one's checks *v.* (*also* **hand in one's cards/part**) [mid-19C+] (*US*) to die (cf. CASH (IN) ONE'S CHECKS v.). [faro imagery]

hand in one's chips *v.* [late 19C+] to die (cf. CASH (IN) ONE'S CHECKS v.). [var. on CASH IN ONE'S CHIPS v. (3)]

hand in one's dinner pail *v.* (*also* **pass/turn in one's dinner**

pail) **1** [1920s+] to die. **2** [1930s+] to resign from one's job; to stop what one is doing.

hand in one's part v. see HAND IN ONE'S CHECKS v.

hand it out v. [1920s–40s] (US) to harm, to kill.

hand it to v.[1] (also **give it to**) [20C+] (orig. US) to accept someone else's achievements (esp. when one has no real respect for the individual concerned and the acceptance is reluctant), usu. in phr. *I've got to hand it to…*

hand it to v.[2] **1** [1900s–40s] to tell off, to reprimand. **2** [1900s–40s] to tease. **3** [1910s–50s] (orig. US Black) to shoot at someone.

hand jig n. (also **three-fingered hand jig**) [1930s–70s] (US prison) masturbation, usu. of 1 prisoner by another. [SE *hand* + *jig*, a fidgety movement]

hand jig v. [1930s–70s] to masturbate (cf. AUDITION THE FINGER PUPPETS v.; DANCE WITH JOHNNIE ONE-EYE v.). [HAND JIG n.]

hand jive n. [1970s+] an act of masturbation. [SE *hand* + JIVE n.[1] (1)]

hand jive v. (US) **1** [1950s+] to move and slap the hands in time to the rhythm of music. **2** [1970s+] to masturbate, usu. someone else (cf. AUDITION THE FINGER PUPPETS v.; DANCE WITH JOHNNIE ONE-EYE v.). [SE *hand* + JIVE v.[1] (3)/JIVE v.[1] (1)]

hand job n. **1** [1930s+] an act of masturbation, performed by a partner; often offered as such in a prostitute's price list. **2** [1970s+] (US) an act of insincere flattery. **3** [1970s+] any form of deceit, misinformation. **4** [1980s+] (US) an obnoxious person. [SE *hand* + JOB v.[1] (1)]

hand job v. (also **hand gig**) [1960s+] to masturbate (cf. AUDITION THE FINGER PUPPETS v.). [HAND JOB n. (1)]

handkerchief-head n.[1] (US Black) **1** [1940s+] a subservient, role-playing, White-stereotyped Black woman, the female version of an UNCLE TOM n. (1). **2** [1940s+] a middle-class Black person, irrespective of gender. **3** [1970s+] one who has straightened or 'processed' hair, worn under a headscarf. [the covering of one's expensively straightened hair with a handkerchief. Black militants of the 1960s, who advocated the AFRO n.[2] as a symbol of emancipation, saw such hairstyles as selling out to White standards]

handkerchief-head n.[2] [1970s+] (US) a derog. term for an Arab or a man who wears a turban (cf. ABDUL n.). [SE *handkerchief* + -HEAD sfx (2); the *keffiyeh* head-dress worn by Arabs; along the lines of TOWEL-HEAD n.]

handle n.[1] **1** [16C–early 18C; 1960s+] the penis. **2** [late 18C–1940s] the nose. [(1) is US 1960s+]

handle n.[2] [early 19C+] a name, a nickname, a title (esp. as spoken rather than written); thus *a handle to one's name*, a title, an honorific.

handle n.[3] (US) **1** [late 19C; 1960s+] an influence on; a role in. **2** [1980s+] a reference to, a clue; an understanding of.

handle n.[4] [1940s+] (Aus./N.Z.) a glass of beer with a handle (as opposed to a 'straight' glass).

handle v. **1** [19C] to masturbate (cf. BOFF v.). **2** [19C; 1970s] to have sexual intercourse (cf. ARRIVE AT THE END OF THE SENTIMENTAL JOURNEY v.). **3** [1910s–40s] (US) to manhandle.

handlebars n. see LONG HANDLEBARS n.

handle cranker n. [1980s+] (Aus. prison) a masturbator. [rhy. sl. = WANKER n. (1)]

handle it! excl. [1970s] (US Black) a general exhortation, differing as to context.

handles n. **1** [1910s] (US Und.) side-whiskers. **2** [1980s+] (US campus) a ring of excess fat around one's stomach, a 'spare tyre' (cf. BAR HANDLES n.). **3** [1980s+] (US) the female breasts.

handle the pots v. [1970s] (US Black) to cook; to eat.

handle the ribbons v. [19C] to drive a coach and horses. [SE *ribbons* as reins]

handle to one's name, a n. see HANDLE n.[2].

handle up (on) your business v. [2000s] (US prison) to fight.

handle with kid gloves v. [20C+] to treat carefully, gently. [SE *handle* + *kid gloves*, gloves made f. soft goat leather]

hand like a foot n. [early 18C] clumsy, badly shaped handwriting. [SE *hand*, a style of writing]

handmade adj. (also **hand-raised**, **hand-reared**) [1960s–70s] (US) of the penis, bent noticeably in one direction or another or particularly large. [idea that masturbation has changed its shape]

hand-me-downs n. [mid-19C+] second-hand clothes, either given free (often inherited from an elder sibling) or bought at a second-hand shop, also by ext., poor-quality clothes. [such clothing is 'handed down' from one owner to the next]

hand-me-down shop n. [mid-19C–1910s] an illicit pawnbrokers. [HAND-ME-DOWNS n.]

hand-mucker n. [1930s+] a card cheat who specializes in palming cards, then holding them out of the game until they become useful to him. [MUCK v.[1] (1)]

hand-out n. **1** [late 19C+] (orig. US) food or money given to a beggar. **2** [1920s+] in ext. use, any food or meal. **3** [1950s+] (US Und.) a bribe.

hand out v. [late 19C–1930s] (US) to impart information that is insincere or aiming to impress.

hand (out) a line v. [20C+] to deceive through a cunning story or excessive charm. [SE HAND OUT v. + LINE n.[1] (3)]

hand out the b.a. v. [1950s] (US school/campus) to display one's naked buttocks. [B.A. v.]

hand over v. [late 18C–mid-19C] (UK Und.) to pay a bribe so as to have a case dropped; to drop an argument, to abandon a court case.

hand over fist adv. **1** [early 19C+] (also **hand over hand**) very quickly. **2** [late 19C+] in large quantities, usu. of the making of money. [naut. jargon, referring to the pulling on, or climbing of, ropes]

hand queen n. [1960s+] (US gay) someone who prefers masturbating a partner or being masturbated to other forms of sex. [SE *hand* + QUEEN n.[2] (1)/QUEEN sfx (2)]

hand-raised/-reared adj. see HANDMADE adj.

hands n.[1] [20C+] (a piece of) meat. [rhy. sl.; *hands and feet* = meat]

hands n.[2] [1980s+] (US campus) the female breasts. [euph.]

hand-saw n. [mid-19C] a street seller of cutlery, razors and knives. [E.P. suggests that -FENCER sfx, i.e. seller, should be assumed]

handsell v. [mid-19C] to hawk goods in the street; thus *handseller*, a street or open-air seller.

handshake v. [1910s–60s] (US) to curry favour. [HANDSHAKER n.]

handshaker n. **1** [late 19C] (US) a swindler. **2** [late 19C–1930s] (US) an insincere person. **3** [1930s–50s] a toady, a sycophant. [SE *shake hands*]

hand shandy n. [1980s+] the act of masturbation. [SE *shandy*, a fizzy drink combining beer and lemonade]

hand shandy v. [1980s+] to masturbate (cf. AUDITION THE FINGER PUPPETS v.; BEAT ONE'S MEAT v.). [HAND SHANDY n.]

hand shoe n. [late 19C–1970s] (US) a glove.

hands-off adj. [20C+] a way of doing things that distances the performer from the subject of the action. [opposite of SE *hands on*]

hands off (your) cocks, feet in (your) socks phr. [1910s+] a joc. wake-up cry, orig. RAF, but general in the services, institutions and similar sites of dormitory accommodation.

hand solo n. (also **han solo**) [1990s+] masturbation. [pun on the character Han Solo in the *Star Wars* films]

handsome n. [1930s+] (orig. US) (also **hansome**) a general term of address, the subject may or may not actually be attractive.

handsome adj. **1** [mid-16C+] of money, substantial. **2** [17C+] decent, kind, useful; thus *do the handsome (thing)*, to behave in the decent, honourable way.

handsome adv. [mid-19C+] satisfactorily, as required or desired.

handsome! excl. [1970s+] a general term of approval, excellent, wonderful. [16C SE *handsome*, becoming, courteous, gracious]

handsome harry n. [1930s+] a womanizer, esp. one whose seductive 'line' cannot be trusted.

hand someone something on a (silver) platter *v.* [1910s+] to give someone something (concrete or fig.) without calling for any effort on the receiver's part.

hand someone the cold and frosty *v.* [1920s+] to treat disdainfully. [i.e. to treat coldly]

hand someone the hat *v.* [1910s+] to reject, to dismiss.

hand someone the ice-bowl *v.* [1900s] to offer a rejection, to fail to pay a debt. [i.e. to treat coldly]

hand someone the kick-along *v.* [1930s] (*UK tramp*) to refuse someone something.

hand someone the lemon *v. see* LEMON *n.*[1] (3).

hand someone the mitt *v.* (*also* **hand someone the mitten**) [1910s–20s] (*US*) to reject, to turn down, to dismiss. [SE *hand* + MITT *n.* (3)]

handsome ransome *n.* [1930s] (*US Black*) a large sum of money.

hand something to someone on a plate *v.* [1920s+] to give someone something (concrete or fig.) without calling for any effort on the receiver's part.

handstaff *n.* [mid-19C+] the penis (cf. BAT *n.*[7]). [SE *handstaff*, the handle of a flail]

hand's turn *n.* [early 19C–1910s] a stroke of work; thus *at every hand's turn*, often, frequently, continually. [SE *hand* + *turn*, a stroke of work]

hands up *n.* [1920s] (*Irish*) a bottle of Allsop ale. [the bottle has the Red Hand of Ulster on its label]

handsupper *n.* [1940s+] (*S.Afr.*) a traitor. [those Boers who surrendered, i.e. *put their hands up*, at the end of the Anglo-Boer Wars (1880–1, 1899–1902)]

hand the works to *v. see* GIVE SOMEONE THE WORKS *v.* (7).

hand to fist *phr.* [mid-17C–early 19C] intimately, right up close to each other.

hand-to-gland combat *n.* [1990s+] masturbation. [pun on SE *hand-to-hand combat*; note US Air Force Academy *hand to gland*, unarmed combat]

hand-to-hand *phr.* [1950s+] of drugs, delivered immediately.

hand trouble *n.* [1950s] (*US teen*) from a female point of view, a boy's desire to become excessively intimate.

hand-warmers *n.* [1920s+] (*Aus.*) the female breasts.

hand work *n.* (*also* **handy work**) [1990s+] masturbation.

handy *adj.* **1** [mid-19C+] useful, admirable. **2** [1990s+] (*Irish*) easy, as in phr. *take her handy*, take it easy. [var. on SE]

handyman *n.* [1940s+] a man who, unable to bring his partner to orgasm through intercourse, uses his fingers to bring her to the desired climax. [SE *hand* + *man*; but pun on HANDY *adj.* (1)]

handy wagon *n.* [1920s–30s] (*US*) a police patrol car. [its SE *handiness* for making arrests]

handy work *n. see* HAND WORK *n.*

hang *n.*[1] [mid-19C+] a euph. for DAMN *n.*; thus NOT CARE A HANG *v.* [HANG! excl.]

hang *n.*[2] [1950s] (*US*) a hangover. [abbr.]

hang *n.*[3] [1950s+] (*US Black*) a job, esp. one that may not be ideal but supports one's living. [SE *hang*, to hold on to]

hang *n.*[4] (*orig. US campus*) **1** [1980s+] a loiterer, someone who spends a lot of time at a place. **2** [1980s+] (*also* **hang spot**) a place where one goes 'hangs out'. **3** [1990s+] a social occasion, a rock or other concert, a party. **4** [1990s+] time spent relaxing, loitering. [HANG *v.*[4]]

hang *v.*[1] [late 16C+] a euph. for TO HELL WITH —! excl.

hang *v.*[2] [mid–late 19C] to be in difficulties; thus *hanging*, in great difficulties. [sporting jargon a *hanging man* is one who is facing great problems, usu. in the form of debts]

hang *v.*[3] [20C+] (*US*) to impose upon, to blame, to make a criminal charge against (cf. HANG SOMETHING ON *v.*). [SE *hang*, to kill with a noose/*hang*, to put on a hook]

hang *v.*[4] [1920s+] to loiter, to stand around aimlessly, to relax. [HANG AROUND *v.*]

hang *v.*[5] [1930s+] (*US*) to behave, usu. in combs., e.g. HANG LOOSE *v.*; HANG TOUGH *v.*

hang *v.*[6] [1950s–70s] (*Aus./US drugs*) **1** to be under the influence of drugs. **2** to be in need of some drugs.

hang *v.*[7] [1950s+] (*US*) **1** to murder. **2** to beat up.

hang *v.*[8] [1960s+] (*orig. US*) to turn a corner in a motorcar, as in *hang a left/right*.

hang *v.*[9] [1980s+] **1** to endure, to suffer, to handle pressure. **2** to leave somebody waiting. [abbr. HANG IN *v.*; HANG TIGHT *v.*]

hang *v.*[10] *see* HANG UP *v.*[6].

hang! *excl.* [late 16C+] a general excl. (cf. HANG ME! excl.). [SE *hang*]

hang a b.a. *v.* [1990s+] (*US campus*) to expose one's buttocks. [B.A. *v.*]

hang a bootie! *excl.* [1980s+] (*US campus*) **1** good luck! **2** wait! [(2) joc. pron. of HANG ABOUT! excl.]

hang about *v. see* HANG AROUND *v.*

hang about! *excl.* [1960s+] wait a minute! hold on!

hang a hat on someone *v. see* PUT A HAT ON SOMEONE *v.*

hang a jacket on *v.* [1950s+] (*US prison*) for one inmate to accuse another of informing. [HANG *v.*[3] + JACKET *n.*[3] (2)]

hang a lilly *v.* [1960s+] to turn left. [HANG *v.*[8] + the initial letter of *lilly*]

hang a louie *v.* (*also* **hang a louis**) [1960s+] to turn left. [HANG *v.*[8] + LOUIE *n.*[2]]

hang an arse *v.* [late 16C–early 18C] to hang back, to be afraid to go forwards.

hang a pin *v.* [1930s] (*US*) to give one's girlfriend one's fraternity pin to wear as a sign of an engagement or exclusive dating relationship.

hang a pinch on *v.* [1930s–50s] (*US*) to arrest, to have someone arrested. [HANG *v.*[3] + PINCH *n.*[2] (2)]

hangar *n.* [1970s] (*US*) the fly of the trousers. [the image of the penis as a 'flying machine']

hangara *adj. see* HANG OF A *phr.*

hang a ralph *v.* (*also* **hang a ralphie**) [1960s+] to turn right. [HANG *v.*[8] + RALPHIE *n.*; compare HANG A LOUIE *v.*]

hang a rap on *v.* (*also* **hang the rap on**) [1920s–50s] (*US Und.*) of police or other authorities, to charge a criminal (fairly or otherwise). [HANG *v.*[3] + RAP *n.*[4] (1)]

hang a rat *v.* [2000s] (*Can.*) for a (teenage) man to press his bared genitals against the window of an automobile. [? visual similarity]

Hangar Lane *n.* [20C+] pain. [rhy. sl.]

hang-around *n.* [20C+] an aimless person, a loiterer. [HANG AROUND *v.*]

hang around *v.* (*also* **hang about**) [late 18C+] (*orig. US*) to wait about, to linger in one place.

hang a Sam *v.* [1960s] (*US*) to go straight on. [HANG *v.*[8] + initial letter of *Sam*]

hang a shanty on *v.* [1940s] (*Aus.*) to give someone a black eye. [SE *hang* + *shanty*, a bruised eye]

hangashun *adj.* [1920s+] (*Aus./N.Z.*) a general intensive, meaning something extreme or large. [phonetic sp. of nonce-form *hangation*]

hang a U-ie *v.* (*also* **hang a U-ey, ...Ulysses, ...yewie, ...youee**) **1** [1960s+] (*orig. Aus.*) to make a U-turn. **2** [1990s+] to urinate. [(1) HANG *v.*[8] + U-IE *n.*; (2) is pun on (1) as well as initial letter of SE *urinate*]

hangava *adj.* [1940s+] (*Aus./N.Z.*) a general intensive, describing something extreme or large of its kind. [SE *hang of a*, thus euph. for HELLUVA *adj.*]

hang black *v.* [20C+] (*US Black*) to associate primarily, if not wholly, with one's Black peers. [HANG OUT *v.*[1] (5) + SE *black*]

hang bluff *n.* [mid-19C] snuff. [rhy. sl.]

hang chilly *v. see* CHILLY *adj.*[2] (1).

hang cool *v. see* HANG (OUT) COOL *v.*

hang dog *adj.* [1940s+] (*W.I.*) plentiful. [? US phr. *till the last dog is hung*, till everything is used up]

hang-doodle *adj.* [1950s] a large amount; a general intensifier.

hang-down *n.* [1970s+] the penis. [its flaccid posture]

hang easy! *excl. see* HANG (IT) EASY! excl.

hanged! *excl. see* I'LL BE HANGED! excl.

hanger *n.* [1920s+] (*US Und.*) a wallet protruding from a pocket or purse, thus ripe for pickpocketing. [SE *hang*, to dangle]

hangers *n.* **1** [late 16C–early 17C] the testicles (cf. BANGERS n.). **2** [late 19C–1910s] gloves, esp. when unworn but held in the hand for ornamental purposes. **3** [1930s+] (*Aus./US*) the female breasts (cf. BOBBER n.[2]).

hang five! *excl.* [1990s+] (*Aus.*) wait a moment! [i.e. 5 seconds]

hang forth *v.* [late 19C] (*US*) to live.

hang-house *n.* [1940s] (*UK prison*) the room or building that holds the gallows.

hang in *n.* [1930s+] (*US*) influence.

hang in *v.* (*also* **hang in there**, **hang on in (there)**) **1** [1930s+] to stay, to maintain a position, usu. with implication of pressures to surrender. **2** [1970s+] to exist, to survive, to be living.

hangin', bangin' and slangin' *phr.* [1990s+] (*US Black gang*) a phr. used to describe the GANGSTA n. (2) lifestyle: associating with one's friends and fellow gangsters, fighting with other gangs and selling drugs. [HANG OUT v.[1] (5) + BANG v.[1] (1) + SLANG v.[3]]

hang-in-chains *n.* [late 18C–early 19C] a villain, a desperate-looking person. [the corpses of villains were trad. hung in chains as an 'awful warning' to passers-by]

hanging *n.* [mid–late 19C] (*Aus.*) a perquisite, a bonus, an 'extra'. [such extras fig. 'hang' off the primary task, occupation etc]

hanging *adj.[1]* **1** [late 19C+] (*Irish*) drunk. **2** [1960s+] (*US campus*) feeling ill, esp. hungover.

hanging *adj.[2]* [2000s] **1** of a woman, very unattractive. **2** of food, disgusting. [the image of hanging game until it has become 'high']

hanging *adj.[3] see* HANG v.[2].

hanging bee *n.* [early 19C–1940s] (*US*) a public hanging.

hanging cheat *n.* [16C–19C] the gallows. [SE *hanging* + CHEAT n. (1); lit. 'hanging thing']

hanging johnny *n.* [late 19C+] the flaccid penis (cf. ABRAHAM n.[1]). [SE *hanging* + JOHNNIE n.[5]]

hanging out *phr.* [1980s+] (*N.Z. drugs*) suffering from withdrawal symptoms. [HANG OUT v.[2] (2)]

hanging party *n.* [1950s] (*US*) a hanging, usu. an illicit, impromptu lynching.

hangin' on the leg *phr.* [1990s+] (*US prison*) of a prisoner, to fraternize with the prison authorities; thus *leg-hanger*, one who pursues such acquaintances.

hang in the bellropes *v.* [mid-18C] to postpone marriage even after the banns have been read in church.

hang in the hedge *v.* [late 17C–early 18C] to be undecided, usu. of a lawsuit.

hang in there *v. see* HANG IN v.

hang in there! *excl.* [1980s+] used as a farewell. [HANG IN v.]

hang it (all)! *excl.* [late 16C+] a general excl. of frustration, annoyance. [HANG! excl.]

hang it all on one's back *v.* (*also* **put it all on one's back**) [20C+] of a woman, to display wealth through extravagant dress and jewellery.

hang (it) easy! *phr.* [1950s–60s] (*US*) take it easy!

hang it in your ass! *excl.* [1950s+] (*US*) an excl. of contempt, often accompanied by a gesture, the right forefinger being hooked over the left thumb, which in turn makes a circle with the left forefinger.

hang it in your ear! *excl.* [1960s+] (*US campus*) don't bother! forget it!

hang it on *v.[1]* [early 19C] **1** to protract, to put into abeyance. **2** to cohabit with a woman, to form a temporary sexual relationship. [image of hanging something on a peg and forgetting it]

hang it on *v.[2]* [1910s] (*US*) to hit hard.

hang it on the limb *v.* (*also* **hang it on a bush**) [1920s–50s] (*US prison*) to escape from prison or from a chain gang. [ety. unknown; ? image of a member of a work gang removing his prison uniform and hanging it from a tree or bush before running]

hang it out *v.* **1** [late 19C–1940s] (*Aus.*) to endure. **2** [1960s+] (*US*) to run a risk, to risk one's life, to go to extremes. [(1) HANG OUT v.[1] (3); (2) euph. for HANG ONE'S ASS OUT v.]

hang it up *v.[1]* **1** [mid-19C+] to stop doing something. **2** [1950s+] to give up trying, to accept defeat, to acknowledge that a target will never be achieved. [the image of hanging up something that is no longer in use]

hang it up *v.[2]* [1950s] (*US Und.*) to escape from prison. [HANG IT ON THE LIMB v.]

hang it up *v.[3] see* HANG UP v.[1] (1).

hang-loose *adj.* [1950s+] (*orig. US*) very informal. [HANG LOOSE v.]

hang loose *v.* [1950s+] (*orig. US*) to relax, to take things as they come (cf. STAY LOOSE v.). [HANG v.[5] + SE *loose*; note personal correspondence from Paul Kunino Lynch (Sydney, Aus., 1999) 'Boswell remarks that he had never heard of an occasional contributor to literary journals of the time named F Lewis. Then he overheard Johnson describe him to an acquaintance: "He lived in London and hung loose on society."']

hang loose! *excl.* [1950s+] (*orig. US*) an imper. excl. relax! enjoy yourself! don't worry! [HANG LOOSE v.]

hang-low *n.* [1990s+] (*US Black*) the penis; thus *get some stanky on the hang-low*, to have sexual intercourse.

hangman *n.* [mid-19C+] (*N.Z./W.I.*) a reprobate, a ruffian. [i.e. one who ought to be hanged]

hangman's wages *n.* [late 17C–19C] 13½ pence, 1s 1½d. [the equivalent of a Scot. mark, the sum instituted as the executioner's fee by James VI and I (1566–1625). It was divided into 1 shilling for the execution and 3 halfpence for the rope]

hang me! *excl.* [late 16C+] a general excl. [HANG! excl.]

hangnail *n.* [1990s+] a snail, i.e. a slow, shambling person. [rhy. sl.]

hang of a *phr.* (*also* **hangara**, **hangura**) [1940s+] (*orig. N.Z./S.Afr.*) a general intensifier, e.g. *a hang of a headache*. [along lines of HELL OF A, A phr.]

hang on! *excl.* [1940s+] a general excl. requesting a pause in either activity or speech.

hang on by one's eyelids *v.* **1** [late 18C–mid-19C] to persevere despite every difficulty, to be extremely tenacious. **2** [20C+] to be very near death, ruin or defeat.

hang one on *v.[1]* **1** [20C+] to hit someone, to have a fight; also in fig. use. **2** [1910s] to impose a task or burden. **3** [1970s] (*US*) to have an affair. [deliver a punch, a blow]

hang one on *v.[2]* [1940s+] to be drunk. ['one' is a drunken spree]

hang one's ass out *v.* (*also* **hang one's fanny out**) [1940s+] (*US*) **1** to run a risk, to risk one's life; usu. in phr. *have one's ass hanging out*. **2** to work hard. [SE *hang* + ASS n. (2)]

hang one's bugle in an invisible baldrick *v.* [late 16C] of a man, to have sexual intercourse (cf. BURY IT v.). [play on SE *bugle* as the penis + SE *baldric*(k), a sword-belt]

hang oneself out *v.* [1990s+] (*US Black*) to take a risk. [the image of hanging out over a long drop]

hang one's fanny out *v. see* HANG ONE'S ASS OUT v.

hang one's hat *v.* (*also* **hang one's socks**) **1** [late 19C+] to make a commitment towards, to rely on. **2** [20C+] (*also* **hang up one's hat**) to live, to stay.

hang one's hat up *v.* [mid-19C–1950s] to become engaged; thus *hang one's hat up to*, to propose to a woman; *hanging one's hat up*, engaged.

hang one's jib *v.* [late 18C–19C] to look miserable, lit. to 'hang one's underlip'. [obs. SE *jib* = lower lip]

hang one's latchpan *v.* [late 19C–1900s] to look miserable;

to pout. [SE *latchpan*, a pan to catch the drippings from roasting meat. In this context the 'drippings' are presumably tears]

hang one's lip *v.* [20C+] (*US*) to be in a bad temper, to sulk. [the position of the pouting lower lip]

hang one's meat *v.* [1900s–10s] (*US*) of a man, to urinate. [SE *hang* + MEAT n. (2)]

hang one's mouth where the soup drips *v.* [20C+] (*W.I.*) to curry favour with whichever political party is currently in power, irrespective of one's own political beliefs (if any). [the image of collecting whatever hand-outs are on offer]

hang one's socks *v. see* HANG ONE'S HAT v.

hang on in (there) *v. see* HANG IN v.

hang on like grim death *phr. see* LIKE GRIM DEATH adv.

hang on someone's bra strap *v.* [1990s+] (*US Black*) of a woman, to impose upon or bother another woman.

hang on someone's door *v.* [1950s] (*UK prison*) to place blame on someone. [HANG v.³]

hang onto your hat! *excl.* (*also* **hold onto your hat!**) [1910s+] (*orig. US*) be prepared for a shock!

hang-out *n.*¹ **1** [mid-19C] (*US campus*) a party, a celebration. **2** [mid-19C+] a lodging, a place of residence. **3** [late 19C+] a place where a group tends to meet. [HANG OUT v.¹]

hang-out *n.*² [1960s+] **1** the penis. **2** (*also* **hing-oot**) a general term of abuse, applied equally to either sex (cf. BELL END n.).

hangout *adj.* [1960s+] pertinent to those with whom one associates regularly. [HANG OUT v.¹ (4)]

hang out *v.*¹ **1** [early 19C+] to live, to make one's home. **2** [mid-19C] (*UK/US campus*) to treat. **3** [late 19C–1940s] (*Aus.*) to endure, to survive. **4** [late 19C+] to meet, to collect together at a regular venue, to frequent. **5** [late 19C+] to idle away time with friends. **6** [20C+] to exist, to be situated, to be available, to happen. **7** [1980s+] to lie in wait.

hang out *v.*² **1** [1960s+] to be desperate for something. **2** [1980s+] (*Aus./N.Z. drugs*) of an addict, to be desperate for drugs. [i.e. have one's tongue hanging out for]

hang out big bootie *v.* [1980s+] (*US campus*) to be in the way, esp. to park one's car in such a way that it causes an obstruction. [pun on the car *boot*/BOOTY n. (2)]

hang (out) cool *v.* [1970s+] (*US*) to remain calm, to relax. [HANG OUT v.¹ (5) + COOL adj.¹ (2)]

hang out one's shingle *v.* (*also* **hoist one's shingle, put out one's shingle, stick out one's shingle**) [mid-19C+] (*US*) to establish oneself in business by hanging up or otherwise affixing a nameplate or signboard (cf. PULL IN ONE'S SHINGLE v.). [SAmE *shingle*, a small signboard]

hang out the broom *v.* [17C] of a man, to admit to one's being cuckolded. [the tradition of hanging out a broom to announce that one's wife was absent and thus advertise for a temporary housekeeper]

hang out the flag of distress *v.* [mid-19C] **1** to advertise a list of charges for board and lodging in one's home. **2** to be in poverty. **3** to have one's shirt hanging out. **4** to live in furnished accommodation. **5** to be a street prostitute. [var. uses of FLAG OF DISTRESS n.]

hang paper *v.* [1930s+] (*US Und.*) to pass counterfeit cheques or similar financial documents.

hang-slang about *v.*¹ [mid-19C–1900s] to attack verbally. [SLANG v.¹ (2) + assonance; note SE *sling*, to throw]

hang-slang about *v.*² [1920s] to loiter with illicit intent. [HANG ABOUT v. + assonance; note SE *sling*, to throw, in this case to throw oneself around]

hang someone out to dry *v.* (*also* **hang someone up to dry, leave someone out to dry, leave someone up to dry**) [1920s+] (*orig. US*) to treat particularly harshly; to make an example of someone.

hang someone's ass *v.* [1960s+] (*US*) to defeat thoroughly, to trounce. [HANG v.⁷ (2) + ASS n. (2)]

hang someone to the wall *v.* [20C+] to punish severely. [SE *hang*, the victim is tied against a wall for a beating; also HANG v.⁷ (2)]

hang someone up *v.* [1950s+] (*orig. US*) **1** to put at a disadvantage. **2** to depress.

hang someone up to dry *v. see* HANG SOMEONE OUT TO DRY v.

hang something on *v.* [1920s+] (*US*) to bring a charge against a criminal, where justified or not, to allot, to blame, often as *hang one on* (cf. PUT SOMETHING ON v.). [HANG v.³]

hang spot *n. see* HANG n.⁴ (2).

hang the moon *v.* [1950s+] (*US*) to be very important; thus *think one hung the moon*, to think very highly of oneself. [only someone very important, e.g. God, could have *hung the moon* in the sky]

hang the rap on *v. see* HANG A RAP ON v.

hang tight *v.* [1940s+] (*US*) to sit, to wait, esp. under pressure. [HANG v.⁵ + TIGHT adj.⁴ (2)]

hang together *v.* [1990s+] (*US Black*) to survive.

hang tough *n.* [1960s+] a tough character. [HANG TOUGH v.]

hang tough *adj.* [1960s+] stubborn. [HANG TOUGH v.]

hang tough *v.* [1930s+] (*orig. US*) to behave in an aggressive, tough manner, to persist in a course of action whatever the problems; thus *hang tough tit*, to stick to a decision; thus as imper.: wait a minute, bear with me. [HANG v.⁵ + TOUGH adj. (1)]

hang-up *n.*¹ **1** [mid-16C–mid-17C] one who is to be hanged. **2** [late 19C] one who is in serious trouble, whether criminal or financial. **3** [1970s] (*US prison*) a suicide.

hang-up *n.*² **1** [1940s+] (*orig. US*) a problem, a delay. **2** [1950s+] a neurosis, an obsession. **3** [1960s] (*US drugs*) an addiction. **4** [1960s] (*US*) a boring, irritating person. [one's mind gets fig. 'hung up' on the problem or emotion]

hang up *v.*¹ **1** [early 18C+] (*also* **hang it up**) to leave a bill unpaid at a public house; to buy on credit (with the intention of defrauding the creditor). **2** [late 19C] (*US*) to pawn. **3** [late 19C–1950s] (*US*) to charge someone an exorbitant price. [the placing of records of debt on a piece of paper nailed to a tavern or shop wall]

hang up *v.*² **1** [mid-19C–1910s] to rob in the street, to garrotte, to 'mug'. **2** [1940s–50s] (*US*) to place under arrest. **3** [1950s+] to distress, to annoy. **4** [1980s] (*US Black*) to insult.

hang up *v.*³ [mid-19C] (*Aus.*) to tether one's horse; lit. and fig., i.e. to pause. [one hangs the reins on a hitching post. Note UK taxi jargon *hanging it up*, loitering around a theatre or similarly lucrative place waiting for a fare]

hang up *v.*⁴ (*US*) **1** [mid-19C+] to stop work, to retire, to quit. **2** [late 19C] to be quiet, to stop talking. [(2) HANG UP ONE'S HAT v.¹ (2)]

hang up *v.*⁵ [late 19C+] to delay, to hold up.

hang up *v.*⁶ (*also* **hang**) [1910s+] to end a telephone call. [one *hangs up* the receiver]

hang up one's... *v.* [1940s+] used in a variety of phrs., usu. linked to the occupation in question, to mean to retire; thus fig. to die; *see* combs. below. [image of hanging up on a peg the item required for the job]

hang up one's boots *v.* [20C+] **1** to die. **2** to retire. [HANG UP ONE'S... v. + SE *boots*]

hang up one's fiddle *v.* [mid-19C–1930s] (*US*) **1** to stop what one is doing. **2** to retire. **3** to die. [HANG UP ONE'S... v. + SE *fiddle*]

hang up one's harness *v.* (*also* **hang up one's tackle/irons**) [late 19C–1910s] **1** (*also* **drop one's harness**) to retire. **2** to die. [HANG UP ONE'S... v. + SE *harness/tackle/irons*, stirrups]

hang up one's hat *v.*¹ [mid-19C–1910s] **1** to die. **2** to retire. [HANG UP ONE'S... v. + SE *hat*]

hang up one's hat *v.*² *see* HANG ONE'S HAT v. (2).

hang up one's irons *v. see* HANG UP ONE'S HARNESS v.

hang up one's jock v. [1980s+] (*US*) **1** to retire, to give up. **2** to be killed. [HANG UP ONE'S... v. + JOCK n.¹ (2)]

hang up one's tackle v. see HANG UP ONE'S HARNESS v.

hang up the gloves v. [1920s+] (*US*) **1** to retire from one's profession. **2** to give up. **3** to die. [HANG UP ONE'S... v. + SE *gloves*; orig. prize-fighting jargon]

hang up the ladle v. [18C] to get married. [the bride brings kitchen implements to hang in her new home]

hang up the spikes v. [1940s] (*US*) to retire from baseball, football etc. [HANG UP ONE'S... v. + SE *spikes*; the spiked shoes worn by such athletes]

hangura adj. see HANG OF A phr.

hang with v.¹ [1930s+] (*US*) to associate with, to spend time with. [HANG v.⁴]

hang with v.² [1970s+] (*US*) to handle a situation, to endure. [HANG v.⁹ (1)]

hank n.¹ [late 18C–mid-19C] the baiting of an animal; thus *Smithfield hank*, an ox 'rendered furious by over-driving and barbarous treatment,' (Grose, 1785), *hanker*, one who takes part in a baiting (cf. HANK v.¹). [? SE *hank*, a restraint, a power of check or dial. *hank*, a cluster, a gang]

hank n.² [19C] a break from work, usu. gained by pretending to be feeling unwell or some other similar small lie. [dial. *hank*, a hook, a loop; i.e. one is fig. 'hung on a hook', rather than moving back to work]

hank n.³ (*also* ank) [late 19C–1950s] nonsense. [ety. unknown; ? dial. *be in a hank*, to be confused, mixed up; based on HANK n.²]

hank n.⁴ (*also* hank of hair) **1** [1940s+] (*US Und./campus*) a slut, a promiscuous woman. **2** [1960s+] (*US campus*) an unpopular person. **3** [1960s+] (*US gay*) the penis; thus TAKE ONE'S HANK v. [SE *hank* of hair]

hank v.¹ [early 19C–1910s] to tease, to bait, to persecute. [HANK n.¹]

hank v.² [late 19C–1940s] to hesitate, to draw back. [SE *hank*, a restraining or curbing hold]

hank freak n. [1960s] (*US prison*) a compulsive masturbator. [? the masturbator ejaculates into a *hand*kerchief]

hankie-head n. [1970s+] a derog. term for an Arab (cf. ABDUL n.). [SE *hankie* + -HEAD sfx (2); the *keffiyeh* head-dress]

Hank Marvin adj. [2000s] starving. [rhy. sl.; ult. the guitarist *Hank B. Marvin* (b.1941), best known as a member of Cliff Richard's band The Shadows]

hank of hair n. see HANK n.⁴.

hanktelo n. [late 16C–early 19C] a fool, a simpleton. [ety. unknown]

hankty adj. see HINKY adj.

hankypanky n. (*also* hanky pank) **1** [mid-19C+] trickery, deceit, esp. of a sexual nature. **2** [late 19C+] a carnival game. **3** [20C+] (*US*) silly talk. **4** [20C+] sexual intercourse; thus *play hanky-panky*, to have sexual intercourse. **5** [20C+] kissing and cuddling. [? Rom. *hakk'ni panki*; or ? redup. of the *hanky* (handkerchief) used by a conjuror in some tricks; thus note theatrical jargon *hank-panky bloke*, a conjuror]

hankypanky adj. **1** [20C+] (*Aus.*) cranky, silly. **2** (*US*) (*also* hanky-pank) counterfeit or obtained through trickery or deceit. [HANKYPANKY n.]

hanky-spanky adj. [mid-19C–1910s] stylish, fashionable, well cut. [HANKYPANKY n. + SPANKING adj. (1)]

Hannah n. (*US*) **1** [late 19C–1910s] a proper name used as the generic subject of various phrs., e.g. *that's what's the matter with Hannah*, a general phr. of agreement or certainty; *since Hannah died*, *since Hannah was a rag doll*, for a very long time; *dead as Hannah Emerson*, totally dead; *he/she doesn't amount to Hannah*, referring to a worthless individual. **2** [20C+] a euph. for *God* and used in various mild oaths, such as *so help me Hannah!* (cf. BOB n.²). **3** [1930s] an opinion, information. [note Texas prison use, *Hannah*, the sun]

hannah cook phr. [19C+] (*US*) a general phr. implying unimportance or insignificance, e.g. *not give a hannah cook*, *not worth a hannah cook*. [naut. jargon *hand* or *cook*, a lowly-ranked seaman who had no specific job or qualification and could thus be used either as a crewman or a cook, according to the captain's wishes]

Hannibal Lecter n. [1990s+] a ticket inspector. [rhy. sl.; ult. fictional character *Hannibal Lecter*, in *Silence of the Lambs*, the novel by Thomas Harris (1988) and film (1991)]

Hanover jack n. [late 19C–1910s] an imitation sovereign. [? counterfeit sovereigns produced in Germany and bearing the head of James II or *Jac(obus)*); they were infiltrated into England and circulated during the reign of William III (r.1689–1702)]

Hans n. **1** [late 16C–17C] a Dutchman. **2** [late 19C+] a German. [the common name]

Hans Carvel's ring n. [mid-18C–19C] the vagina. ['Hans Carvel, a jealous old doctor, being in bed with his wife, dreamed that the Devil gave him a ring, which, so long as he had it on his finger, would prevent his being made a cuckold, waking, he found he had got his finger the Lord knows where' (Grose, 1785)/ RING n.¹ (1)]

hansel and gretel n. [20C+] a kettle. [rhy. sl.; ult. the fairy-tale characters]

hanseller n. [mid–late 19C] a street salesman, a 'cheap jack'. [SE *handseller*]

Hans-en-Kelder n. (*also* Hans in kelder) [early 17C–early 19C] an unborn child, often used as a drinking toast. [joc. use of Du. *Hans-en-Kelder*, Jack in the cellar]

han solo n. see HAND SOLO n.

hansom cab n. [20C+] (*Aus.*) a scab, a non-unionist. [rhy. sl.]

hansom cabs n. (*also* hanson cabs) [20C+] body lice. [rhy. sl. = CRAB n.²]

hansome n. see HANDSOME n.

hans wurst n. [mid-19C+] (*US*) a fool, an idiot (cf. APPLEHEAD n.). [Ger. proper name *Hans* + *wurst*, a sausage or salami]

hanus adj. see HEINOUS adj.

hap n.¹ (*also* haps) [1960s+] (*US Black*) happening; thus *what's the haps?* used as a greeting; *no haps*, no indeed; *the haps*, something good. [abbr.]

hap n.² [1970s+] (*S.Afr.*) a bite, a mouthful, a morsel. [synon. Afk.]

hapas capas n. see HAPUS CAPUS n.

ha'penny n. [20C+] the female genital area. [usu. middle-class euph.]

ha'penny boy n. [1960s+] (*Irish*) a worthless, unimportant person.

ha'penny place n. [1960s+] (*Irish*) a worthless, unimportant place, position or status.

hap-harlot n. **1** [mid-16C–mid-18C] a rug. **2** [19C] women's undergarments. [SE *hap*, to cover + *harlot*, a knave, a rascal]

ha'porth of liveliness n. **1** [mid-19C] any musical entertainment. **2** [late 19C] an idler, a dawdler.

happa n. [1980s+] (*US campus*) a person who is half-Asian. [Jap. *hampa*, half]

happen v.¹ **1** [1940s+] (orig. *US music industry*) to attract publicity and be successful. **2** [1960s+] (*US*) to appear, to function, to work.

happen v.² [1950s+] (*drugs*) used euph. in a variety of questions, e.g. *anything happening?* do you have any drugs; *nothing happening*, I have no drugs/there are no drugs around.

happening adj. [1960s+] fashionable, chic, up-to-the-minute. [rarely used 1980s + other than ironically/historically]

happenings n. [1950s+] **1** (*US*) goings–on, esp. those of an intimate nature. **2** (*US drugs*) any illicit narcotics. **3** (*US Black*) in fig. use, women.

happy n. [1990s+] a pleasurable feeling. [coined in late 1990s US TV show *Buffy the Vampire Slayer*]

happy adj. [late 18C+] drunk (cf. ABOUT RIGHT phr.¹). [euph.]

-happy sfx [1930s+] (orig. *milit.*) **1** slightly insane as a result of a circumstance, e.g. *bomb-happy*; DEMOB-HAPPY adj. **2** obsessed with.

happy as a bastard on father's day *phr.* [1950s+] (*Aus.*) very unhappy.

happy as a black in a barrel of treacle *phr.* [1900s] extremely happy.

happy as a boxing kangaroo in fog time *phr.* [20C+] (*Aus.*) very discontented, very unhappy.

happy as (a box of) birds *phr.* [late 19C+] (*Aus./UK*) in very high spirits. [the chirping of birds]

happy as a bug in a rug *phr.* (*also* happy as a bug on a hot stove) [1910s+] (*US*) very happy.

happy as a clam *phr.* (*also* happy as a clam at high tide/water, ...a cricket, ...a horned toad, ...a sand-bag) [mid-19C+] (*US*) very happy, totally satisfied. [the full phr. *happy as a clam at high tide* explains the 'happiness']

happy as a dog with two tails *phr.* (*also* happy as a dog with a bellyful of soup and a streetful of lamp-posts, ...with a tin tail, ...with two dicks) [1950s+] very happy.

happy as a flea at a dog show *phr.* (*also* happy as moths in a best blanket) [20C+] (*N.Z.*) very happy.

happy as a hophead *phr.* [1940s] (*US*) very happy. [HOPHEAD n.¹ (1)]

happy as a nun weeding the asparagus *phr.* [1910s+] (*Can.*) very cheerful (with obvious sexual overtones given the 'phallic' asparagus).

happy as a pig in shit *phr.* (*also* happy as pigs in clover, ...in muck, ...in mud, ...in shit) [19C+] extremely happy.

happy as a sick eel on a sandspit *phr.* (*also* happy as a hooked fish) [1940s] (*N.Z.*) very unhappy.

happy as Larry *phr.* (*also* happy as Harry) [20C+] (*orig. Aus.*) perfectly happy, quite content. [ety. unknown; 'possibly but not certainly commemorating the noted Aus. pugilist Larry Foley (1847–1917)' (Baker, *The Australian Language*, 1945)]

happy bag *n.* 1 [1970s+] (*UK Und.*) the bag in which a shotgun is carried on an armed robbery; the gun makes the victim 'happy' to pass over his money. 2 [2000s] (*US*) the scrotum. [(2) BAG n.¹ (1)]

happy box *n.* [1980s+] (*S.Afr.*) wine sold in 2½- or 5-litre (4½–8¾-pint) containers, placed in a cardboard box.

happy camper *n.* [1980s+] (*orig. US campus*) one who is perfectly satisfied with their life and the circumstances in which they find themselves, often ironic; also in negative, *not a happy camper*, a dissatisfied, unhappy person; the deliberate levity of the term may hide a genuinely deep unhappiness/dissatisfaction. [SE *happy* + CAMPER n.²]

happy cigarette *n.* (*also* funny cigarette) [1970s+] (*drugs*) a marijuana cigarette (cf. AFRICAN WOODBINE n.; BOMB n.⁴).

happy clam *n.* [1990s+] (*US*) a very cheerful, satisfied person. [HAPPY AS A CLAM phr.]

happy-clappies *n.* [1980s+] (*orig. S.Afr.*) members of an evangelical church, whose services involve a good deal of 'audience participation', e.g. singing, responding, clapping the hands. [a derog. term that emphasizes the differences between the lower- and lower-middle-class evangelicals and the middle- and upper-class Church of England]

happy-clappy *adj.* [1980s+] naïve, gullible; typical of the evangelical church and its devotees. [HAPPY-CLAPPIES n.]

happy days *n.* [1920s–30s] a mixture of strong ale and beer. [? its effect]

happy days! *excl.* [1910s+] a common toast before drinking.

happy dosser *n.* [late 19C–1900s] a homeless person. [SE *happy* + DOSSER n. (1); ironic; such a down-and-out was, unless fuelled by a good deal of alcohol, far from 'happy']

happy-drugs *n.* [1960s+] anti-depressants.

happy dust *n.* 1 [1910s+] (*orig. US drugs*) cocaine; thus *happy duster*, a cocaine user or seller (cf. BIRDIE POWDER n.). 2 [1920s+] morphine (cf. AUNTIE EMMA n.). 3 [1930s+] heroin. [SE *happy* + DUST n.⁵]

happy Eliza *n.* [late 19C–1900s] a female Salvationist. [the relentless good humour of such individuals; *Eliza* is generic for a Salvation Army girl]

happy endings *n.* [2000s] (*US*) a massage that concludes with masturbation of the male client.

happy farm *n.* [1960s+] (*US*) a psychiatric institution. [var. on FUNNY FARM n.]

happy gas *n.* 1 [1930s] marijuana (cf. BOMB n.⁴). 2 [1940s] (*US*) heroin. 3 [2000s] (*US*) laughing gas or nitrous oxide.

happy grass *n.* [1960s+] (*US drugs*) marijuana (cf. AFRICAN BUSH n.; BOMB n.⁴). [SE *happy* + GRASS n.⁵; among its effects is the promotion of laughter]

happy half-hours *n. see* HAPPY HOURS n.

happy-hand *v.* [1950s] (*US*) to make unwanted physical advances to a woman. [HAPPYHANDS n.]

happyhands *n.* [1950s] (*US*) a young man who is rebuffed for making unwanted physical advances to a woman.

happy herb *n.* [1980s+] (*Aus. drugs*) cannabis (cf. AFRICAN BUSH n.; BOMB n.⁴). [SE *happy* + HERB n.² (3); among its effects is the promotion of laughter]

happy home *n. see* HAPPY HOUSE n.

happy hour *n.*¹ [1950s+] (*orig. US*) a period, 1 or poss. 2 hours, when a pub or bar offers drinks at half price, usu. about 6pm; the assumption is that those customers who arrive for the cheap drinks will become sufficiently tipsy to stay on for the more expensive ones. [orig. US Navy term for a scheduled period of time for entertainment and refreshment]

happy hour *n.*² [1950s+] (*Aus.*) a shower. [rhy. sl.]

happy hours *n.* (*also* early hours, happy half-hours) [20C+] flowers. [rhy. sl.; f. use by Covent Garden Market porters]

happy house *n.* (*also* happy home) [1960s+] a psychiatric institution.

happy hunting grounds *n.* (*orig. US*) 1 [mid-19C+] death. 2 [late 19C] the vagina. [Native American imagery]

happy juice *n.* [1920s–50s] (*US*) good humour, usu. resulting from alcohol or drug intoxication.

happy pill *n.* [1950s+] a tranquillizer or stimulant.

happy powder *n.* [1940s+] (*drugs*) 1 cocaine (cf. BIRDIE POWDER n.). 2 heroin; morphine (cf. AUNTIE EMMA n.).

happy returns *n.* [late 19C–1950s] (*Aus.*) the act of vomiting. [pun]

happy shack *n.* [1970s+] (*US Black*) a liquor store. [HAPPY adj.]

happy shop *n.* [1960s–70s] (*US Black*) a liquor store. [HAPPY adj.]

happy shopper *n.* [1990s+] a bisexual. [SE *happy shopper*, a cheap grocery store, with the idea of being indiscriminate]

happy sticks *n.* (*US drugs*) 1 [1950s+] marijuana (cf. BOMB n.⁴). 2 [1980s+] marijuana laced with phencyclidine.

happy stuff *n.* [1920s+] (*US*) cocaine.

happy trail *n.* (*also* the divine line, snail trail, treasure trail) [1990s+] (*US*) a line of chest hair down the middle of a man's torso leading from the navel to the penis.

happy valley *n.*¹ 1 [20C+] the female genitals. 2 [1960s+] (*US gay*) the cleft of the buttocks. [note milit. use *happy valley*, first an area of the Somme battlefield and, later, anywhere that is suffering heavy bombing]

happy valley *n.*² [1930s+] (*Aus.*) an area of shanty towns.

happy wagon *n.* [1950s–60s] (*US*) a prison or police van. [ironic]

happy water *n.* [1950s–60s] (*US*) alcohol, liquor. [HAPPY adj.]

haps *n. see* HAP n.¹.

hapus capus *n.* (*also* hapas capas) [1940s–50s] (*US prison*) a prison inmate who has made himself into a self-taught lawyer, in order to pursue his own case, combat prison corruption or help his fellow inmates. [a speedy, lazy pron. of Lat. *habeas corpus*, thou (shalt) have the body (in court). The prerogative writ *habeas corpus ad subjiciendum* requires the body of a person restrained of liberty to be brought before the judge or into court so that the lawfulness of the restraint may be investigated and determined.]

This writ is seen as the basis of all open, honest and democratic legal systems]

haramzada *n.* (*also* **haramzadeh**) [mid–late 19C] (*Anglo-Ind.*) a scoundrel. [Pers. *haramzada*, misbegotten, 'son of the unlawful']

harbour light *phr.* [late 19C+] all right; usu. as phr. *all harbour*. [rhy. sl.]

harbour master *n.* [1990s+] a successful womanizer.

harbour (of hope) *n.* [late 17C–1900s] the vagina (cf. ADAM'S OWN (ALTAR) *n.*; AGREEABLE RUTS OF LIFE *n.*). [idea of sheltering]

harbour shark *n.* [1990s+] (*W.I.*) a greedy person.

harch off *v.* [1940s+] (*Aus.*) to abandon, to leave. [orig. milit. use; ? parade-ground pron. of 'march' as 'harch']

hard *n.*[1] **1** [late 17C–early 19C] sour or stale beer. **2** [mid-19C+] plug tobacco. **3** [mid-19C+] (*also* **the hard**) hard cider or whisky. **4** [late 19C–1950s] hard labour in prison. **5** [1960s+] (*US/ N.Z. drugs*) hard drugs, i.e. cocaine and heroin. [(3) 20C+ use is US]

hard *n.*[2] [mid-19C+] (*UK Und.*) coins (as opposed to notes). [HARD adj. (1)]

hard *n.*[3] [late 19C+] an erection; thus *on the hard*, of a penis, being erect. [abbr. HARD-ON *n.* (1)]

hard *n.*[4] [late 19C+] a thug, a hoodlum. [abbr. HARD CASE *n.* (2)]

hard, the *n. see* HARD *n.*[1] (3).

hard *adj.* **1** [18C+] cash, coins, change (as opposed to notes). **2** [19C+] tough, aggressive, violent. **3** [1930s+] (*orig. US Black/teen*) excellent, fashionable, admirable, on bad = good model. **4** [1950s+] (*drugs*) of narcotics, usu. heroin. **5** [1980s+] (*US*) of clothing, in a tough style, rugged.

hard *adv.* **1** [19C+] to a great extent, in a zealous manner. **2** [mid-19C–1920s] very, extremely. **3** [late 19C–1950s] in a painful, problematic manner, e.g. of a prison sentence. **4** [1980s+] (*US Black*) in an aggressive, hostile manner; intensely. [note George Parker, *Life's Painter* (1789): 'He went off at the *fall* of the *leaf*, at tuck 'em fair — he died d—d hard, and was as *bad* as *brass*'; (4) is late 20C US Black usage of (2)]

hard act to follow *n.* (*also* **tough act to follow**) [1960s+] (*orig. US*) anything or anyone seen as difficult to emulate or rival, usu. in the context of performing an activity directly after an impressive performance.

hard as lard *phr.* [1940s–60s] (*US Black*) excellent, wonderful, as good as one could desire. [assonance]

hard-ass *n.* (*also* **hard-arse**) **1** [1960s+] (*orig. US*) a tough person, a thug. **2** [1990s+] (*US*) an insensitive nature; a 'thick skin.' [HARD-ASS *v.*]

hard-ass *adj.* (*also* **hard-arse, hard-arsed, hard-assed**) **1** [late 19C; 1960s+] tough, no-nonsense, uncompromising. **2** [1960s+] mean, miserly. [HARD adj. (2) + -ASS sfx]

hard-ass *v.* [1940s] (*US*) **1** to bully, to treat severely. **2** to endure, to tough it out. [one has, fig. a *hard* ARSE *n.*[1] (1)]

hard as the hobs of hell *phr.* (*also* **hard as the hinges of hell, ...hubs of Hades, ...hugs of hell**) [19C+] (*US*) **1** very hard. **2** very tough or dangerous (cf. HOT AS THE HINGES OF HELL *phr.*). [orig. in a song detailing the miserable life endured by Irish immigrant quarrymen in the US; the *hobs of hell* refers to the bread baked by the boss's wife]

hard-back *adj.* [20C+] (*W.I.*) **1** approaching middle-age or older. **2** used of one who ought to know better. [the onset of back problems with advancing age]

hard-baked *adj.* **1** [mid-19C] (*orig. US*) stern, unrelenting. **2** [mid–late 19C] constipated.

hardball *n.*[1] [1970s+] (*US*) aggressive tactics. [the hard balls used in professional baseball, as opposed to softball]

hardball *n.*[2] [1980s+] (*US drugs*) **1** a mixture of heroin and cocaine. **2** crack cocaine (cf. BASE *n.*). [HARD adj. (4) + SPEEDBALL *n.*[1] (3)]

hardball *adj.* [1970s+] (*US*) aggressive, intimidatory. [HARD-BALL *n.*[1]]

hardball (it) *v.* [1970s+] (*orig. US*) to act aggressively towards, to coerce or intimidate. [HARDBALL *n.*[1]]

hard bargain *n.* [mid–late 19C] a lazy person, one who cannot be disciplined.

hard bit *n.*[1] [late 19C+] an erect penis.

hard bit *n.*[2] [1960s+] (*US prison*) an unpleasant experience of prison, as a result of one's personality, one's crime (which may alienate other prisoners) or one's inability to adapt etc. [SE *hard* + BIT *n.*[5]]

hard body *n.* [1980s+] (*US*) a physically trim, sexually attractive person.

hard-boiled *adj.* [20C+] tough, mean, unpleasant. [HARD-BOILED EGG *n.*]

hard-boiled collar *n.* [1920s–50s] a stiff, starched, detachable collar.

hard-boiled egg *n.* [late 19C–1960s] (*US*) a tough man, esp. a boxer. [they 'can't be beat']

hard-boiled hat *n.* [1900s–60s] (*US*) a stiff hat.

hard-boiled shirt *n.* [1910s–30s] (*US*) a stiff, starched detachable shirt-front. [ext. of BOILED SHIRT *n.*]

hard bop *n.* [1950s–60s] (*orig. US*) a variety of jazz that links blues to bop and resembles the earlier form, hot jazz; thus *hard bopper*, a fan of the form.

hard candy *n.* [1960s+] (*drugs*) heroin. [HARD adj. (4) + CANDY *n.*[4] (4)]

hard case *n.* **1** [mid–late 19C] (*US*) a native of Oregon. **2** [mid-19C+] (*orig. US*) a tough, ruthless person. **3** [late 19C+] (*Aus./N.Z.*) a cheeky or amusing person. **4** [late 19C+] (*Aus./N.Z.*) a sexually available woman. **5** [20C+] (*Aus.*) an indefatigable person, who struggles on irrespective of any obstacle. [HARD adj. (2) + CASE *n.*[4] (4)]

hard-case *adj.* [1940s+] tough, ruthless. [HARD CASE *n.* (2)]

hard chaw *n.* (*also* **hardjaw**) [20C+] (*Irish*) **1** a tough person. **2** an irrepressible joke. [SE *hard* + *chaw*, chew/SE *jaw*]

hard cheese *n.* (*also* **hard Cheddar, hard fodder, stiff cheddar, stiff cheese, tough Cheddar**) [late 19C+] bad luck; usu. in (unsympathetic) phrs. *hard cheese (on/for)*, meaning that's bad luck for someone.

hardcore *n.*[1] [1950s+] one who is considered the most serious, the most dedicated.

hardcore *n.*[2] [1960s+] the strongest varieties of pornography, usu. featuring uncensored still or moving pictures of intercourse, plus such personal choices as paedophile shots, bestiality, extreme sado-masochism etc.

hardcore *n.*[3] [1970s+] the US branch of PUNK *n.*[4] (1) rock; other similar rock music genres include *thrashcore, grindcore, dancecore*. [HARDCORE *n.*[1]; 'If you worship nonsense Heavy Metal bands, like whacking out 30-minute long songs with wind down riffs and useless guitar wanking, plus crave to be "hip" and have journos licking your scrotum, call yourself grindcore; ...grunge-core...much the same as [grindcore] with absolutely zero musical skill and unwashed underwear' ('Britcore', *The Street Suss Encyclopedia*, 1990)]

hardcore *adj.*[1] **1** [1960s+] (*orig. US*) a general term of approval, serious, experienced, committed, full-time; the implication is that the word, act or person thus qualified is the ultimate of the type. **2** [1980s+] substantial in quantity. **3** [1990s+] aggressive, criminal. **4** [2000s] (*US campus*) difficult. [HARDCORE *n.*[1]]

hardcore *adj.*[2] [1970s+] pertaining to the more extreme forms of pornography. [HARDCORE *n.*[2]]

hardcore *adj.*[3] [1990s+] (*US teen*) true to what you believe. [HARDCORE adj.[1] (1)]

hardcore *adv.* [2000s] (*US campus*) to a great extent, intensely.

hard-cutting *adj.* [1940s] (*US Black*) extremely good, fashionable. [var. on HARD-HITTING adj.]

hard daddy *n.* [1960s+] (*orig. US prison*) a masculine, 'butch' lesbian. [HARD adj. (2) + DADDY *n.* (12)]

hard dick n. [1970s+] (*US*) a tough guy. [SE *hard* + DICK n.¹ (1)]

hard doer n. [20C+] (*Aus.*) **1** a character, an eccentric, one who never gives up despite any circumstances. **2** an amusing fellow, a 'good sport'. [ext. of DOER n.² (2)]

hard-down adj. [1930s] (*US Black*) truthful, genuine, dependable.

hard-down adv. [1930s–70s] (*US Black*) really, truly, genuinely. [HARD-DOWN adj.]

hard drink n. [late 16C–early 18C] stale, sour drink. [HARD n.¹ (1)]

hard dumpling n. [mid-19C] in boxing, a fist.

hard-ears n. [late 19C+] (*W.I.*) disobedience. [HARD-EARS adj.]

hard-ears adj. [late 19C+] (*W.I.*) obstinate, stubborn.

hardegat n. [1950s+] (*S.Afr.*) an obstinate person. [HARDEGAT adj.]

hardegat adj. [1950s+] (*S.Afr.*) stubborn. [Afk. *harde*, hard + GAT n.²]

hard egg n. *see* TOUGH EGG n.

harder than pulling a soldier off your sister phr. [1930s+] very difficult indeed.

hard-eye v. [1980s] (*US*) to stare aggressively. [HARD EYES n.]

hard eyes n. [1950s+] (*US*) unpleasant look, disapproving stare.

hard fodder n. *see* HARD CHEESE n.

hard guy n. **1** [1910s+] (*US*) a criminal character, a 'tough guy'. **2** [1980s+] (*US campus*) a difficult person. [HARD adj. (2) + SE *guy*]

hard hair n. [1950s+] (*US Black/W.I.*) a Black person's naturally kinky hair.

hard hat n.¹ [1930s–40s] (*US*) a bowler hat.

hard hat n.² [1940s+] (*US*) a construction worker. [the essential part of his 'uniform']

hardhead n.¹ [mid-19C–1960s] (*US*) **1** a White native of rural Tennessee or Kentucky. **2** a Dutchman. **3** a German. **4** an Englishman. **5** a primitive Baptist. [the stereotyped hard-headedness, whether emotional or physical, of all these groups]

hardhead n.² **1** [1930s+] (*US Black*) a rebellious, non-conformist Black person, a hot-tempered person. **2** [1940s+] (*US*) an extremely zealous person. **3** [1950s+] (*Aus.*) a villain, a criminal. **4** [1960s] (*US*) an intransigent, uncompromising person. **5** [1980s+] (*US*) a fool. [HARDHEADED adj.; such a name reinforces the White cliché that one can never knock out or hurt a Black man by hitting him on his head because it is too solid to damage]

hardheaded adj. [1920s+] (*US Black*) stubborn, rebellious, hot-tempered.

hard hit n. [1970s+] an act of defecation (cf. ANDY CAPP n.). [rhy. sl. = SHIT n.¹ (3)]

hard-hitter n. (*also* **hard-knocker**) [late 19C+] (*Aus./N.Z.*) a bowler hat.

hard-hitting adj. [1940s] (*US Black*) smart, fashionable. [ext. of HARD adj. (3)]

hard horse n. [early 19C–1920s] (*US*) a brutal, tyrannical person.

hard hustle n. [1950s+] (*US*) any form of complex, and thus potentially highly lucrative, confidence trick. [SE *hard* + HUSTLE n. (1)]

hardjaw n. *see* HARD CHAW n.

hard John n. [1930s–40s] (*US Black*) an FBI agent. [SE *hard* + JOHN n.⁴]

hard knock n. [1980s] a tough, aggressive individual. [SCHOOL OF HARD KNOCKS n.]

hard-knocker n. *see* HARD-HITTER n.

hard knut n. *see* HARD NUT n. (1).

hard labour n. [20C+] a neighbour. [rhy. sl.]

hard leg n. (*also* **hard legs**) (*US Black*) **1** [1940s+] a tough man or boy. **2** [1940s+] a man who devotes all his time and energies to pursuing the street life and the world of strictly male endeavour – pimping, HUSTLING n. etc. **3** [1960s+] an ugly woman, esp. an old, worn-out prostitute. [HARD adj. (2) + SE *leg*]

hard-leg adj. (*US Black*) **1** [1940s+] of a male, tough, aggressive.

2 [1940s+] devoted to pursuing the street life and the world of strictly male endeavour – pimping, HUSTLING n. etc. **3** [1960s+] of a woman, ugly, esp. of an old, worn-out prostitute. [HARD LEG n.]

hard lines n. (*also* **tough lines**) [early 19C+] bad luck, misfortune; thus *easy lines*, good fortune. [? biblical use of *lines* as one's 'lot in life', i.e. Ps. 16:6: 'The lines are fallen unto me in pleasant places; yea, I have a goodly heritage']

hard log n. *see* HARD NUT n. (1).

hard lot n. [mid-19C–1900s] (*US*) a rough, aggressive individual. [HARD adj. (2) + SE *lot*, a person]

hard mack n. [1970s+] a tough, aggressive, brutal pimp. [HARD adj. (2) + MACK n.¹ (1)]

hard man n. **1** [20C+] one who has a high opinion of his own powers, usu. physical. **2** [1930s+] a thug, a professionally violent person. **3** [1960s+] (*Irish*) a term of affection. [HARD adj. (2) + SE *man*]

hard money n. [1940s] (*US Und.*) counterfeit money. [pun on HARD adj. (2) and SE *hard*, difficult]

hard morris n. [1940s+] (*W.I.*) a tough fighter. [? anecdotal, i.e. proper name *Morris*; or ? SE *morris* (dancing), i.e. the 'dancing' around of a fighter]

hardmouth n. [20C+] (*W.I.*) one who argues and resists when it is time to repay a loan or to pay a bill.

hardmouth v. [1960s+] to attack verbally, to slander.

hard mouthful n. [1980s] the erect penis, presumably in the context of fellatio.

hard neck n. [1950s+] **1** cheek, impudence. **2** an impudent person. [i.e. to be able to STICK ONE'S NECK OUT v. because it is so hard; but note NECK n.² (1)]

hard-nose n. **1** [1930s+] (*orig. US*) a mean, unpleasant person; thus *get the hard-nose*, to become angry or irritated. **2** [1960s+] (*Aus.*) an indefatigable person, who will struggle no matter what the odds.

hard-nose adj. (*also* **hard-nosed**) [1960s+] tough, uncompromising. [HARD-NOSE n. (2)]

hard-nose v. [1950s+] to get angry with someone, to become nasty. [HARD-NOSE n. (1)]

hard nut n. [late 19C+] **1** (*also* **hard knut/log**) a tough person, a dangerous enemy. **2** something that is difficult to achieve. **3** an incorrigible person. [abbr. phr. *hard nut to crack*]

hardo n. [2000s] a 'tough guy'. [HARD adj. (2) + -O sfx (2)]

hard oil n. [1910s–40s] (*US*) butter, margarine, lard. [*hard oil*, any form of grease, used for lubrication, that will not flow; orig. used in WW1 for butter]

hard-on n. **1** [late 19C+] an erection. **2** [1940s+] passionate, lustful feelings. **3** [1940s+] an obsession, usu. hostile, aggressive feelings towards. **4** [1940s+] (*US*) a bad temper, irrespective of gender. **5** [1950s+] (*US*) used as a term of address, usu. sarcastic and referring to someone's high self-esteem. **6** [1960s+] (*US*) a despicable individual, a tough, aggressive person. **7** [1960s+] in fig. use of (1), a sense of excitement. **8** [1980s+] (*US*) a difficult task.

hard-on adj. **1** [late 19C+] sexually aroused. **2** [1950s+] tough, aggressive. [HARD-ON n.]

hard one n.¹ [1920s] (*US tramp*) $1.

hard one n.² [1930s] a strong drink. [SE *hard*, intoxicating]

hard-pan n. [mid-19C–1950s] (*US*) the most basic part of something; thus *get down to hard-pan*, to get down to basics, to come down to fundamentals. [SE *hardpan*, hard compacted soil or subsoil]

hard-pan adj. [late 19C–1900s] (*US*) fundamental, conservative. [HARD-PAN n.]

hard-pay man n. [1950s] (*W.I.*) a bad debtor, either through his inability or unwillingness to pay.

hard-puncher n. [mid–late 19C] a fur cap typically worn by a London tough. [his wearing it identifies him as a thug]

hard-pushed adj. [mid-19C–1920s] in poor economic circumstances, in difficulties.

hard rock n. [1910s+] (US Black) a tough person, both emotionally and physically.

hardrock adj. (US) 1 [1910s+] (also **hardrocks**) craggy, physically tough. 2 [1960s+] a general term of approval. [HARD ROCK n.]

hardrocker n. [1970s+] (US) a thug, a tough person. [HARD ROCK n.]

hard-rock hotel n. (also **hard-rock city**) [1940s–70s] (US) a prison (cf. BOARDING HOUSE n.). [the stones from which it is built + ? the rocks that prisoners are made to break]

hardrocks adj. see HARDROCK adj. (1).

hard root n. [1920s+] (Irish) a tough, devil-may-care individual. [SE hard + ? ROOT n.²]

hard-run adj. [late 18C–mid-19C] in poor financial circumstances. [one is exhausted by a fig. SE hard run]

hards n. [early 19C] hard times. [abbr.]

hardscrabble adj. [19C+] (US) tough, challenging. [SE hard + scrabble, a difficult struggle for survival; hardscrabble is often used as the fig. name for any barren location, where survival is achieved only through the greatest efforts]

hard scran! excl. [mid-19C–1940s] (Aus.) bad luck (to you)! [fig. use of SCRAN n. (2)]

hard-shell n. (US) 1 [mid-19C–1930s] a member of the primitive Baptist Church; thus softshell, Baptists who are less severely fundamentalist. 2 [mid-19C–1970s] an uncompromising conservative person. [SE hard + shell, having a hard shell, e.g. a clam, a crab]

hard-shell adj. [mid-19C+] 1 (US) pertaining to Baptists, of the primitive Baptist Church. 2 (orig. US) uncompromising, fundamentalist, unswervingly conservative. [HARD-SHELL n.]

hard shot n. (also **hard thing**) [late 19C+] (Aus./N.Z.) 1 a tough but still witty and amusing daredevil. 2 a sexually available woman. [HARD CASE n.]

hard shot adj. [late 19C+] (Aus./N.Z.) 1 tough, uncompromising, incorrigible. 2 of a woman, sexually available. [HARD SHOT n.]

hard skull-fry n. [1940s–50s] (US Black) a straightened or 'processed' hairdo that is covered in hair-oil or cream. [the hot lye that is placed on the head to straighten one's hair]

hard sledding n. see TOUGH SLEDDING n.

hard spiel n. [1930s–40s] (US Black) 1 Black slang, jive talk. 2 interesting, persuasive patter. [SE hard + SPIEL n.]

hardstep n. [1990s+] a kind of music originating out of London and combining rave and ragga.

hard stuff n.¹ [late 18C–1940s] money in the form of coins, as opposed to notes (cf. SOFT STUFF n.). [HARD adj. (1) + STUFF n.⁴]

hard stuff n.² 1 [mid-19C+] spirits, as opposed to beer. 2 [1950s+] (drugs) drugs like narcotics, rather than tranquillizers, cannabis etc. [(1) SE hard; (2) HARD adj. (4) + STUFF n.³]

hard tack n. 1 [early 19C–1940s] inadequate rations. 2 [1910s] (Aus.) hard work. 3 [1960s+] (Irish) spirits, as opposed to beer. [SE hard, stiff/difficult/intoxicating + TACK n.²; (1) naval use, ship's biscuits, coarse food]

hardtail n. (US) 1 [1910s–80s] a mule. 2 [1930s–70s] an experienced man. [SE hard + tail/TAIL n.² (1)]

hard talk v. [20C+] to employ pressure tactics in a sales pitch.

hard thing n. see HARD SHOT n.

hard thomas n. [1950s] (W.I.) a stubborn man. [? biblical doubting Thomas]

hard ticket n. 1 [late 19C+] (US) a ruthless, uncompromising, tough person. 2 [20C+] (US) a difficult situation. 3 [1960s+] (Irish) a humorist, an eccentric.

hard time n. [20C+] (orig. UK Und.) 1 a long or severe prison sentence. 2 having trouble serving a sentence, suffering while in jail (whether from the regime or from self-inflicted problems). 3 on the railways, third class. [SE hard + TIME n.¹]

hard time v. [1960s–70s] to give someone a hard time, to irritate them or scold them.

hard-timer n. [20C+] 1 a prisoner. 2 a prisoner who suffers in

prison (whether from the regime or from self-inflicted problems). [HARD TIME n.]

hard times n. [mid-19C–1950s] (US) a cheap, poor-quality fabric, which resembles heavy wool but is not much better than cotton shoddy and used for the cheapest of clothes; thus hard times party, someone who wears worn-out or seedy clothes. [SE hard times, a period of poverty]

hard titty n. see TOUGH TITTY n.

hard-up n.¹ [mid-19C–1930s] 1 tobacco that is made of broken-up cigar stumps or cigarette ends. 2 a collector of cigar or cigarette ends which are dried and sold as tobacco to the very poor. 3 a smoker of cigar or cigarette ends. 4 a cigarette or cigar end. [the collectors/smokers are HARD-UP adj.¹]

hard-up n.² [mid-19C–1960s] an impoverished person. [HARD-UP adj.¹ (1)]

hard-up n.³ [late 19C+] an erection. [var. on HARD-ON n. (1)]

hard-up adj.¹ 1 [19C+] impoverished, thus [mid-19C+] hardup-ness, hardup(p)ishness, poverty. 2 [late 19C+] in fig. use, at a loss, desperate, in need of something.

hard-up adj.² 1 [late 19C] drunk. 2 [20C+] (W.I.) unable to attract a steady partner. 3 [1930s+] (US) in need of sexual gratification, sexually frustrated. [ext. of HARD-UP adj.¹, but in (3) note HARD-UP n.³]

hard walk n. [late 19C–1910s] a swaggering walk affected by New York's 'Bowery Boys' (and girls). [HARD adj. (2) + SE walk]

hardware n. 1 [early 19C–1960s] strong liquor, whisky. 2 [mid-19C–1960s] (US) coins, cash. 3 [mid-19C+] (orig. UK Und.) guns, ammunition, safe-cracking equipment and other 'tools of the trade'. 4 [1930s–50s] jewellery. 5 [1990s+] (drugs) isobutyl nitrite (cf. AIMIES n.).

hardware bloke n. [late 19C–1900s] (UK Und.) a native of Birmingham, known for its manufacture of pots, pans and other hardware; thus Hardware Village, Birmingham. [SE hardware + BLOKE n.]

hardware shop n. (also **hardware store**) [1950s+] a male homosexual brothel (cf. BANGING-SHOP n.). [pun on HARD n.³ + SE shop/SHOP n.¹ (1)]

hard way n. 1 [20C+] (gambling) the making of an even point in a dice game by throwing a pair rather than 2 separate numbers; thus in pool, the making of a pot through a difficult rather than easy shot; thus also in fig. use. 2 [1980s] (UK prison) a sentence served without remission.

hard word n. 1 [mid-19C–1910s] (Anglo-Irish) a tip-off, a warning; thus give someone the hard word, to warn. 2 [1910s] (Aus.) an outrageous request.

hare n. [mid-16C–mid-19C] a prostitute; a promiscuous woman (cf. ALLEY CAT n.). [a poss. link to the dial. puss, a hare and CAT n.¹ (1) + a play on SE (pubic) hair]

hare and hound n. [20C+] a round or order of drinks. [rhy. sl.]

hare-finder n. [late 16C–mid-18C] a womanizer, a lecher. [HARE n. + SE finder; a play on SE hare-finder, a man whose job it is to find hares]

hare it v.¹ [late 19C] to retrace one's steps. [the zigzag, backwards-and-forwards course of a hare when attempting to elude a pursuer]

hare it v.² (also **hare off**) [1920s+] to run or move very fast. [the animal's speed]

harelip v. [1960s+] (US) to destroy, to disfigure, to discomfit; esp. in phrs. harelip the government/governor. [SE harelip in the general sense of disfigurement]

haricot n.¹ [late 19C+] the penis (cf. BANANA n.²). [SE haricot bean + BEAN n.⁴ (1)]

haricot n.² [1960s+] (Aus.) a male homosexual. [rhy. sl.; haricot bean = QUEEN n.² (1)]

harker n. [mid–late 19C] (US) an ear. [SE hark, to listen]

hark-from-the-tomb n. [mid-19C] (US) a severe scolding, a telling-off, a reprimand. [such an admonition fig. comes from grim spirits of the afterlife]

hark-ye v. [late 17C–early 19C] to borrow money. [the image is of drawing one's target to one side and whispering a request for a loan]

Harlem adj. [late 19C+] (US) used in derog. senses to emphasize the negative stereotypes of Afro-Americans as lazy, larcenous, stupid, vulgar etc; see also combs. below. [proper name Harlem, the centre of New York City's Black community]

Harlem credit card n. (also **Mexican credit card**) [1950s+] (US) a piece of hose used to siphon petrol from another car into the tank of one's own. [HARLEM adj. + SE credit card, negative racial stereotyping]

Harlem oil n. [late 19C–1960s] (US) a medicine based on a mixture of kerosene or petroleum and sugar and used for children. [HARLEM adj. + SE oil]

Harlem sunset n. [1940s; 2000s] (US) blood pouring from razor slashes. [HARLEM adj. + SE sunset, the stereotyped use of razors in Black-on-Black fights]

Harlem taxi n. [1960s] (US police) a large, fin-tailed, brightly coloured car. [HARLEM adj. + SE taxi]

Harlem toothpick n. [1930s–40s] (US Black) a knife. [HARLEM adj. + TOOTHPICK n.[1] (2)]

harlequin n. [late 19C] (orig. theatre) a sovereign (cf. BRASS n.[1]). [SE Harlequin, a character in English pantomime who wears particoloured, bespangled tights; the shininess, and thus the colours reflected in it]

harlequin Jack n. [late 19C–1900s] a show-off, both in manner and in dress. [SE Harlequin + JACK n.[2]]

harman n. (also **harman-beck**) [mid-16C–1920s] (UK Und.) a constable. [ety. unknown; ? OED suggests elision of SE hard-man; E.P. prefers ha-man, i.e. one who shouts ha! stop!; ult. dial. har! stop! + SE beck, beak]

harmans n. (also **hartmans**) [mid-16C–mid-19C] (UK Und.) the stocks. [fig. use of HARMAN n. or ? SE hard + -MANS sfx, thus lit. a 'hard state of being']

Harmony hair spray n. [1970s+] the act of ejaculating into a woman's hair. [the brandname of the popular hair spray]

Harmy n. [late 19C–1900s] (Aus.) the Salvation Army. [rhy. sl.]

harness n. 1 [early 17C+] (US) clothes, esp. a uniform; thus Sunday harness, one's best clothes; harness up, to get dressed. 2 [mid-19C] (UK Und.) a watchman, a constable, a policeman. 3 [1920s–40s] the settings that hold jewels, e.g. a gold ring surrounding a diamond.

harness bull n. (also **harness cop**, **…gent**, **…guy**, **…man**) [20C+] (US Und.) a uniformed police officer. [SE harness, i.e. the Sam Browne belt some forces in the US favour + BULL n.[10]]

Harold Holt n. [1970s+] (Aus.) 1 salt. 2 a bolt, an act of absconding; thus do a Harold Holt, to abscond. [rhy. sl.; ult. Aus. Prime Minister Harold Holt (1908–67), who died in mysterious circumstances, apparently drowned in the Bass Strait]

Harold (Lloyd) n. see LLOYD n.

Harold Macmillan n. [1960s+] a villain. [rhy. sl.; ult. Prime Minister Harold Macmillan (1894–1986)]

Harold Pinter n. [1960s+] a splinter. [rhy. sl.; ult. UK playwright Harold Pinter (b.1930)]

harolds n. [20C+] (Aus.) 1 trousers. 2 knickers. [rhy. sl.; Harry Taggs = BAGS n.[2]]

harp n.[1] 1 [late 18C+] (Irish) the 'tail' (reverse side) of a coin; thus a halfpenny. 2 [late 19C+] (US) an Irish person (cf. BOG ARAB n.). [the 'national instrument' of Ireland; the reverse of a coin once pictured Hibernia and her harp]

harp n.[2] 1 [late 19C+] (orig. US) a harmonica, a mouth organ. 2 [1930s–40s] (US) a vibraharp or vibraphone. [abbr. MOUTH HARP n.]

harp adj. [1970s] (US) Irish. [HARP n.[1] (2)]

harper n. [late 16C–17C] (Irish) a penny. [the Irish coin had a harp on it]

harpic adj. [1930s+] crazy, insane (cf. CLEAN AROUND THE BEND phr.). [the eponymous lavatory cleaner, which uses the advertising slogan 'clean around the bend']

harpoon n. 1 [late 19C–1950s] (US) ridicule or victimization. 2 [20C+] the penis (cf. AX n.[2]). 3 [1930s–60s] a hypodermic syringe, as used by drug addicts. [(1) and (2) often in THROW THE HARPOON IN(TO) v.]

harpoon v. (US) 1 [mid-19C+] to ridicule, to criticize, to victimize. 2 [1960s] to copulate with a woman. [HARPOON n.]

harp six adv. [20C+] (Ulster) head-over-heels; esp. to go down harp six, to fall head-over-heels. [the harp engraved on the reverse of Irish coins]

harpy n. [1940s+] (US Black) an old woman. [SE harpy, 'A fabulous monster, rapacious and filthy, having a woman's face and body and a bird's wings and claws, and supposed to act as a minister of divine vengeance' (OED); in Homer the Harpies personified hurricanes and whirlwinds]

harriet lane n. [late 19C–1920s] (Aus.) chopped meat. [proper name Harriet Lane, the victim and wife of the murderer Henry Wainwright (executed 1875); coincidentally the USS Harriet Lane, launched 1857, was commanded by one Jonathan Wainwright who was killed on board her during the US Civil War; the ship, however, was named after the niece of President James Buchanan]

Harrington n. [early–mid-17C] a farthing. [Sir John Harington (1561–1612) obtained a patent from James I to mint farthings]

harris n. see ARRIS n.

harris tweed n. [1950s] a weakling. [rhy. sl. = WEED n.[3] (2)]

harry n.[1] 1 [early 18C–1950s] a countryman, a peasant. 2 [late 19C–1910s] a Cockney lad. [proper name, used as a generic; note TOM, DICK AND HARRY n.]

harry n.[2] (also **Harry Jones**) [1930s+] (drugs) heroin (cf. BIG DADDY n.; BIG H n.). [initial letters; also note heroin is a 'masculine' drug, see BOY n.[7] (1)]

harry v. [1960s] (US campus) to vomit (cf. BARF v.; CALL CHARLES v.). [echoic]

harry bluff n. [mid–late 19C] snuff. [rhy. sl.]

harry-carry n. [1970s+] hari-kari; thus an act of suicide. [ult. Jap. hara-kiri, belly cut]

harry common n. [late 17C–18C] a womanizer. [generic use of proper name Harry + SE common]

harry dash n. [2000s] a glimpse. [rhy. sl. = FLASH n.[4] (3)]

harry dash adj. [1990s+] showy, ostentatious. [rhy. sl. = FLASH adj.[1] (1)]

Harry — -ers phr. [1940s–50s] a verbal style, orig. in services, affected in 1950s by society and then widespread, although now obs., in which various words are prefixed by Harry and suffixed by -ers, e.g. Harry flakers, tired out, Harry crashers, asleep etc. [? HARRY FREEMAN'S n. + -ER sfx; note 19C Cambridge University harry sophs, students who kept all terms required to become Bachelor of Law, f. harisophs, a corruption of Gk herisophos, erudite]

harry fat n. see FAT n.[2].

harry freeman's n. see FREEMAN'S n.

harry-harry n. [1940s+] (W.I.) rum. [ety. unknown]

Harry High Pants n. [2000s] (Aus.) an unfashionable man or boy. [alluding to a person who unfashionably wears his trousers or jeans above the hips]

harry high school n. see HIGH SCHOOL HARRY n.

harry holt n. [1980s+] (Aus. prison) an escape. [rhy. sl. = BOLT n.[1]]

harry huggins n. [20C+] a fool, an idiot (cf. BEECHAM'S PILL n.). [rhy. sl. = MUGGINS n.[1] (4)]

Harry James n. 1 [1950s] the nose. 2 [1970s] (US prison) Bugler smoking tobacco. [the trumpet played by US bandleader Harry James (1916–83)]

Harry Jones n. see HARRY n.[2].

Harry Lauder n. [20C+] a prison warder. [rhy. sl.; ult. the Scot. music-hall star *Harry Lauder* (1870–1950)]

Harry Lime n. [1950s–90s] time (of day). [rhy. sl.; ult. *Harry Lime*, the anti-hero of the film *The Third Man* (1949)]

harry monk n. [2000s] semen. [rhy. sl. = SPUNK n. (4)]

harry nash n. [20C+] cash. [rhy. sl.]

Harry Randall n. [20C+] **1** a handle. **2** a candle. [rhy. sl.; ult. the music-hall comedian *Harry Randall* (1860–1932)]

harry ronce n. *see* CHARLIE RONCE n.

Harry's hideaway n. [1980s+] (*Aus. prison*) isolation cell.

Harry Tate n. **1** [1910s+] (*bingo*) the number 8 (cf. ALDERSHOT LADIES n.). **2** [1910s+] a plate. **3** [1920s+] a state of nerves. [rhy. sl.; ult. comedian *Harry Tate* (1872–1940); note also WW1 milit. use *Harry Tate's Cavalry*, the Yeomanry (cf. FRED KARNO'S ARMY n.), *Harry Tate's Navy*, the Royal Naval Volunteer Reserve, the Fleet Auxiliary and the Motor Boat Reserve]

Harry Tate adj. [20C+] **1** late. **2** incompetent, disorderly, amateur. [rhy. sl.; (2) = in a STATE n. (1); *see* HARRY TATE n. for ety.]

Harry Tates n. [1950s+] Player's Weights cigarettes. [rhy. sl.; see HARRY TATE n. for ety.]

harry, tom and dick adj. [20C+] sick. [rhy. sl.]

Harry Wragg n. [1930s–70s] a cigarette. [rhy. sl. = FAG n.[4] (3); ult. *Harry Wragg*, the jockey and trainer whose career peaked in the 1930s]

harsh adj. **1** [1970s+] (*US campus/teen*) very unpleasant, exceptionally rude, ill-mannered, extremely bad. **2** [1980s+] (*US drugs*) used of marijuana that, whether through strength or dryness, makes one cough.

harsh v. **1** [1970s+] (*US campus*) to mistreat, to be very unfair towards; thus *harsh me out!* that's very unfair! **2** [1990s+] (*US*) to ruin, to damage. [HARSH adj.]

harsh on v. [1980s+] (*US campus*) to criticize, to belittle. [ext. HARSH v. (1)]

hartmans n. *see* HARMANS n.

harum scarum n. [20C+] (*US*) a reckless, unreliable person. [HARUM-SCARUM adj.]

harum-scarum adj. [mid-18C+] wild, reckless, careless. [HARUM-SCARUM adv.]

harum-scarum adv. [late 17C+] wildly, giddily, uncontrollably. [SE *hare*, to run wildly + *scare*]

Harve n. *see* HARVEY NICHOL n.

harvest v. **1** [late 19C–1900s] to guard, to watch over. **2** [1920s–30s] (*US Und.*) to arrest a group of criminals.

harvest buzzard n. [1920s] (*US tramp*) a thief who robs seasonal workers. [SE *harvest* + BUZZARD n.[1] (9)]

harvest moon n. [20C+] a derog. term for a Black person (cf. DAPTO DOG n.). [rhy. sl. = COON n. (5)]

harvest the cherries v. *see* CHERRY n.[1] (3).

harvey drew n. [1990s+] (*Aus.*) vomit (cf. HALLEY'S COMET n.). [rhy. sl. = SE *spew*]

Harvey (Nichol) n. [1930s–70s] a problem, a difficult situation; thus personified as a man or woman who acts in a stupid or naïve fashion; sometimes abbr. as *Harve*. [rhy. sl. = PICKLE n.[1] (2); ult. the store, *Harvey Nichols*, in Knightsbridge, London SW3]

Harvey Nichols n. [20C+] pickles, the condiments. [rhy. sl.; ult. the store in Knightsbridge, London SW3]

harvy n. [mid-19C] (*US campus*) a *Harv*ard student. [abbr. proper name *Harvard* + sfx *-y*]

has-beens n. [20C+] (*mainly UK prison*) greens, any kind of vegetables. [rhy. sl.]

hasbian n. [2000s] (*US gay*) a woman who used to be a lesbian but is now heterosexual. [SE *has been* + *lesbian*]

hash n.[1] **1** [mid-18C+] a mess; esp. in *make a hash of*, to make a mess, often of one's speech. **2** [mid-19C+] food or a meal; often of reheated left-overs. [SE *hash*, a mess or jumble]

hash n.[2] [1940s+] (*drugs*) hash*ish* (cf. AFGHAN n.). [abbr.]

hash n.[3] *see* HESH n.

hash v.[1] [late 19C+] **1** to work as a waiter/waitress in a café. **2** to provide, to serve up. [HASH n.[1] (2)]

hash v.[2] [1910s+] to make a mess. [HASH n.[1] (1)]

hash-bash n. [1990s+] (*drugs*) an evening spent sitting around smoking hashish. [HASH n.[2] + BASH n.[2] (4)]

hash bazaar n. *see* HASH FACTORY n.

Hashbury n. [1960s–70s] (*US*) the Haight-Ashbury area of San Francisco. [HASH n.[2] + elision of *Haight-Ashbury*]

hash-cake n. [20C+] a cake of any sort into the ingredients of which hashish has been mixed; such cakes, thanks to the cooking process, render the hashish a good deal more potent than simply smoking it. [HASH n.[2] + SE *cake*]

hash dispensary n. [late 19C–1900s] a boarding house. [HASH n.[1] (2) + SE *dispensary*]

hashed out adj. [1970s] heavily intoxicated by smoking hashish. [HASH n.[2]]

hash emporium n. *see* HASH FACTORY n.

hasher n. [late 19C+] (*Aus./US*) a waiter or waitress. [HASH n.[1] (2)]

hashery n. *see* HASH-HOUSE n.

hash factory n. (*also* **hash bazaar**, **...emporium**, **...foundry**) [late 19C–1940s] (*Aus./N.Z./US*) a cheap café or restaurant, a 'greasy spoon'. [HASH n.[1] (2) + SE *bazaar/emporium/factory/foundry*]

hash girl n. (*also* **hesh girl**) [1970s+] (*S.Afr.*) a woman who frequents shebeens (drinking clubs) to rob the male patrons. [? Zulu *héshe*, swooping onto, or *heshe*, a hawk]

hash-head n. [1950s+] (*US*) a habitual user of hashish. [HASH n.[2] + -HEAD sfx (3)]

hash hook n. [1910s–20s] (*US*) a fork. [HASH n.[1] (2) + SE *hook*]

hash hound n. [1910s–40s] (*US*) anyone notably keen on their food, a glutton. [HASH n.[1] (2) + HOUND sfx]

hash-house n. (*also* **hashery**, **hash hotel/joint**) (*US/Aus.*) **1** [mid-19C+] a cheap café or restaurant. **2** [late 19C–1930s] a boarding house, a cheap hotel. [HASH n.[1] (2) + SE *house*]

hash-house Greek n. [20C+] (*US*) the jargon of US fast-food restaurants and cafés. [HASH-HOUSE n. (1) + GREEK n.[2]; such jargon included SLAUGHTER IN THE PAN n., RED MIKE AND (A BUNCH OF) VIOLETS n., *two of a kind*, fishballs and a *sheeny funeral with two on horseback*, roast pork and boiled potatoes]

hashmagandy n. [late 19C–1940s] (*Aus./N.Z.*) a basic stew, served on sheep stations and in the army. [HASH n.[1] (2) + ? SE *salmagundi*, a dish composed of chopped meat, anchovies, eggs, onions with oil and condiments]

hashman n. [late 19C] (*US*) a restaurant owner. [HASH n.[1] (2) + SE *man*]

hash-monster n. [1980s+] (*US drugs*) a crumb of hashish burned on the point of a pin; the smoke is trapped in a container and then inhaled through a straw. [HASH n.[2] + MONSTER sfx]

hashover n. [1960s+] the after-effects of an evening's heavy indulgence in smoking hashish. [HASH n.[2] + play on the drinkers' *hangover*]

hash over v. [1900s] (*US*) to ponder, to think about. [HASH n.[1] (2); idea is to CHEW (IT) OVER v.]

hash rat n. [2000s] a smoker of hashish. [HASH n.[2]]

hash-slinger n. [mid-19C+] (*US*) **1** a short-order cook or waiter/waitress. **2** a college student waiter in a mountain resort hotel. [HASH n.[1] (2) + SLINGER n.[1] (1)]

hash-trap n. [1940s+] (*US*) the mouth. [HASH n.[1] (2) + SE *trap/*TRAP n.[3]]

hash-up n. [late 19C+] (*orig. US*) **1** a meal, usu. of whatever ingredients are available, or of reheated, recooked left-overs. **2** in fig. use, anything that has been speedily thrown together or reworked. [HASH n.[1]]

hash up v. [20C+] (*US*) **1** to fashion, to create. **2** to plan. **3** to spoil, to ruin, to make a mess of. [HASH n.[1] (1)]

hashy n. [1940s] (*UK drugs*) hashish (cf. AFGHAN n.). [HASH n.[2]]

hashy fag n. [1940s] (UK drugs) a cigarette blending tobacco and hashish. [HASHY n. + FAG n.⁴ (3)]

hasie n. [1960s+] (S.Afr.) a male homosexual. [Afk. haas, hare]

hasikara n. [20C+] (W.I.) a noise, a commotion; thus make hasikara, to cause an argument, to make trouble, to make a noise. [? Hind. hasiikar, ludicrous, ridiculous]

hassle n. (also hass, hassel) [1940s+] (orig. US) a dispute, a quarrel, a problem, a nuisance, anything requiring irritating effort. [? Cumbrian dial. hassle, to hack or cut at with a blunt edge, using a sawing motion]

hassle v.¹ [1950s+] **1** (orig. US) to annoy, to nag, to pressurize. **2** (US) to quarrel. [HASSLE n.]

hassle v.² [1960s] to sell. [HASSLE v.¹ (1)]

hassle with v. (also hassle out) [1960s+] (US) **1** to sort something out through discussion, to argue. **2** to worry about, to be bothered with. [HASSLE v.¹]

hassling n. [1960s+] nagging, pestering. [HASSLE v.¹ (1)]

hasta phr. [1980s+] (US campus) goodbye, see you later. [Sp. hasta la vista, see you later; ? popularized by the use of 'Hasta la vista' (usu. after an act of extreme violence) by film star Arnold Schwarzenegger in Terminator 2 (1991)]

hasta la bye-bye phr. [1980s+] (US) see you later. [Sp. hasta la vista + SE bye-bye]

hasta la pasta phr. [1980s+] (US campus) see you later, goodbye. [play on Sp. hasta la vista]

haste! excl. [1950s+] (Aus.) stop it! look out!

haste it up! excl. [1940s] (Aus.) shut up! hurry up and finish – what you're saying is boring!

hasty banana phr. [1940s+] (US) goodbye. [a play on Sp. hasta manana]

hasty pudding n.¹ [mid-late 17C] a bastard, an illegitimate child. [pun; the couple have been 'hasty', the child is the 'pudding']

hasty pudding n.² [late 18C–19C] a muddy road. [SE hasty pudding, a pudding made of flour stirred into boiling milk or water to the consistency of a thick batter]

has your bottle fallen out? phr. see BOTTLE n.² (2).

has your mother sold her mangle? phr. [late 19C] an all-purpose teasing phr., aimed at a passer-by. [note 1990s TV comedy character 'Arthur Atkins' (the comedian Paul Whitehouse), the cod 1930s music-hall comic with his catchphrase 'Where's my washboard?']

hat n.¹ **1** [mid-18C–mid-19C] the vagina. **2** [early 19C–1900s] a prostitute. **3** [late 19C+] (US) a general term for sexual intercourse. **4** [1940s–50s] (US prison) a male homosexual. **5** [1940s–60s] (US Black) a woman, esp. a wife or sweetheart (cf. WEAR A HAT v.). [abbr. OLD HAT n.; it too is 'frequently felt' (Grose, 1796)]

hat n.² [late 19C–1910s] a condition, a 'state'; thus get into a hat, to get into difficulties; deuce of a hat, a bad situation.

hat n.³ (US) **1** [1970s] the head. **2** [1990s+] hair.

hat n.⁴ [1980s+] (US) a contraceptive sheath. [note Yid. Schmeckeldecke, a condom, lit. 'cock ceiling']

hat n.⁵ [1990s+] (US campus) a fraternity member. [the 1990s fashion of wearing baseball caps]

hat v.¹ [mid-19C+] (Aus.) to live by oneself in a remote area.

hat v.² see HAT (UP) v.

hata n. see PLAYER HATER n.

hat and coat n. [20C+] a boat, esp. a refrigerated cargo ship. [rhy. sl.]

hat and feather n. [20C+] weather. [rhy. sl.]

hat and scarf n. [20C+] a bath. [rhy. sl.]

hatch n.¹ (US) [20C+] a psychiatric institution; thus HATCH UP v. **2** [1900s–30s] (also hatch house) a prison.

hatch n.² [1920s+] (US, orig. naut.) the throat or mouth; thus DOWN THE HATCH! excl.

hatchet n.¹ **1** [mid-19C+] (US) the female genitals. **2** [late 19C–1930s] an ugly or debauched woman.

hatchet n.² see HATCHET MAN n.

hatchet-face n. **1** [late 17C–early 20C] a long, thin face. **2** [mid-19C+] an ugly person, usu. used of a woman.

hatchet-faced adj. [mid-17C+] ugly, plain, usu. of a woman. [HATCHET-FACE n.]

hatchet job n. **1** [1940s+] (orig. US) a particularly vicious piece of criticism, slanderous gossip etc. **2** [1970s] (US campus) a broken date.

hatchet man n. (also hatchet) [1940s+] (orig. US Und.) **1** a man who is used to punish, or even murder, selected victims on the orders of his boss; also in fig. use. **2** anyone who takes on, or is told to take on, unpleasant tasks, such as, in a company, firing members of staff, broaching distasteful but necessary topics etc. **3** a person who is willing to perform a HATCHET JOB n. in support of a cause or political party. [SE hatchet man, a Chinese assassin, who uses a hatchet]

hatchet-thrower n. [1930s–40s] (US Black) a derog. term for a Spanish-speaking man living in Harlem. [Hispanic 'Indians' were equated with Native Americans]

hatch house n. see HATCH n.¹ (2).

hatchi n. [1960s+] (lesbian) the vagina. [? SE hatch]

hatching jacket n. [1960s–70s] (US) a maternity garment.

hatch up v. [1970s] to commit to a psychiatric institution. [HATCH n.¹ (1)]

hatchway n. (orig. naut.) **1** [early–mid-19C] the mouth. **2** [mid–late 19C] the vagina.

hate on v. [1990s+] to do something bad to somebody else.

hater n.¹ [1990s+] (US gang) an informer.

hater n.² see PLAYER HATER n.

hate someone's guts v. (also hate someone's gizzard/hide) [1920s+] to loathe, to detest.

hat job n. see HEAD JOB n.

hat peg n. (also hat holder) [mid-19C; 1940s–60s] the head. [upon which one 'hangs one's hat'; the obs. UK use was revived by US Black use; cf. HAT RACK n.]

hat rack n. **1** [20C+] (Aus./US) a scraggy animal, usu. a horse. **2** [1920s–60s] the head.

hat size n. [1990s+] (US Black) one's self-image, usu. the implication is of an exaggerated one.

hatstand n. [1930s] (US) the head.

hatter n.¹ [mid-19C+] (Aus.) an eccentric individual, esp. one who lives and works alone; occas. of an animal. [? mining jargon hatter, a miner who works independently rather than in a partnership, but note MAD AS A HATTER phr.]

hatter n.² see BROWN-HATTER n.

hat time n. [1970s] (US Black) the end of a day's work; thus a synon. for goodbye. [note prison farm jargon hat time, the moment when the captain takes off his hat and waves it to signal the end of the chain gang's working day]

hat trick n. [1950s+] a remarkable achievement, usu. involving 3 consecutive successes. [orig. a 19C cricket term, adopted by other sports]

hatty n. (also hutty) [19C] (Anglo-Ind.) an elephant. [Hind. hathi, an elephant, lit. a hand, with ref. to the trunk which is used to pick up objects]

hat (up) v. [1970s+] (US Black) to leave, to exit. [one puts on one's hat]

hat up! excl. [1970s] (US Black) go away!

haugh n. see HOUGH n.

haul n. **1** [late 18C+] (orig. US) a large amount of loot or profit. **2** [mid-19C+] (US) a robbery. **3** [late 19C–1930s] a round-up of suspects, criminals (cf. HAUL IN v.).

haul v.¹ **1** [late 17C–mid-18C] to pester, to irritate. **2** [late 19C–1910s] to call to account, to bring up for a reprimand. **3** [1970s] to beat. [(1) and (3) fig. use of SE haul, to pull with violence; (2) abbr. colloq. phr. haul over the coals]

haul v.² see HAUL ASS v.

haul a cly *v. see* HAUL-CLY *n*.

haul and pull *adj.* [20C+] (*W.I.*) messy, confused, upset. [HAUL AND PULL *v.*]

haul and pull *v.* [20C+] (*W.I.*) to upset, to make a mess of, to confuse.

haul ashes *v.* [1930s] to leave, to run off. [euph. for HAUL ASS *v.* (1)]

haul ass *v.* (*also* **haul, haul arse, ...bottom, ...buns, ...butt, ...feet, ...freight, ...hindparts, ...hiney, ...leg, ...plug, ...tail, tail ass**) (*orig. US*) **1** [1910s+] to leave, to escape, to run off; as excl. *haul ass!* let's go, hurry up! get out of here! the phr. has created several euphs. **2** [1960s+] to move fast, to rush. **3** [1970s+] to increase one's efforts, to work harder. **4** [1990s+] to be extremely successful. [SE *haul* + ASS *n.* (2)/ARSE *n.*[1] (1)/SE *bottom*/BUNS *n.* (2)/BUTT *n.*[1] (2)/SE *feet*/SE *freight*/SE *hindparts*/HINEY *n.*/SE *leg*/? SE *plughole*/TAIL *n.*[2] (1)]

haul back *v. see* HAUL OFF *v.* (2).

haul buggy *v.* **1** [1970s+] to leave, to escape, to run off. **2** [1990s+] to increase one's efforts, to work harder. [euph. for HAUL ASS *v.*]

haul buns/butt *v. see* HAUL ASS *v.*

haul-cly *n.* [18C] a pickpocket; thus *haul a cly*, to pick a pocket. [SE *haul* + CLY *n.* (2)]

haul-devil *n.* [mid-19C–1900s] a clergyman.

haul feet *v. see* HAUL ASS *v.*

haul freight *v.* [late 19C+] a euph. for HAUL ASS *v.*

haul hindparts/hiney *v. see* HAUL ASS *v.*

haul in *v.* [1910s+] (*US*) to arrest.

haul it *v. see* HAUL ONESELF *v.* (2).

haul leg *v. see* HAUL ASS *v.*

haul off *v.* **1** [mid-18C+] to get ready to leave; often as *haul off and...* **2** [mid-19C+] (*orig. US*) (*also* **haul back**) to prepare to strike a blow. **3** [1900s] (*Aus.*) to restrain oneself. **4** [1950s+] to give, to deliver. [the image is of drawing back slightly before acting]

haul one's ashes *v.* (*also* **shake one's ashes**) [1920s+] (*US*) to have sexual intercourse. [GET ONE'S ASHES HAULED *v.*]

haul oneself *v.* (*also* **haul one's ass, ...one's skin, ...one's tail**) **1** [20C+] (*W.I.*) to leave, esp. as imper., *haul yourself!* get the hell out! **2** [1940s] (*also* **haul it**) to move. [SE *haul* + ASS *n.* (2)/SE *skin*/TAIL *n.*[2] (1)]

haul one's own ashes *v.* [2000s] (*US*) to masturbate. [HAUL ONE'S ASHES *v.*]

haul plug/tail *v. see* HAUL ASS *v.*

haul the mail *v.* (*also* **tote the mail**) [20C+] (*US*) to go or run fast. [the image of the indomitable US mailman]

haul-up *adj.* [20C+] (*W.I.*) unhealthy-looking, sick-looking. [the position of one's arms and shoulders, huddled against the pain or cold]

haul up *v.*[1] [early 19C+] to round-up wrong-doers, usu. suspects or criminals.

haul up *v.*[2] [1940s–50s] to run off.

haul up one's slacks *v.* [1910s–30s] to pronounce vehemently on a topic. [? poss. a Wodehouse nonce-creation]

haul up stakes *v. see* PULL UP *v.*[1].

haul yourself! *excl. see* HAUL ONESELF *v.* (1).

havage *n.* [early–mid-19C] a family or group of criminals. [southwest dial. *havage*, a lineage, a family tree]

have *n.*[1] [mid-19C+] one who 'has' something, usu. money.

have *n.*[2] **1** [late 19C–1900s] a swindle, a hoax. **2** [20C+] a disappointment. [HAVE *v.*[3]]

have *v.*[1] [16C+] to seduce, usu. a woman; to have sexual intercourse.

have *v.*[2] (*orig. US*) **1** [late 16C+] (*also* **have it**) to have received punishment. **2** [early 19C+] to capture; to arrest. **3** [late 19C+] to harm, to beat, to punish. **4** [20C+] to kill, to injure, used in passive only. **5** [20C+] to rob.

have *v.*[3] (*also* **have on**) [19C+] to deceive, to trick, to cheat.

have *v.*[4] **1** [early 19C+] to make an incontrovertible point in an argument or dispute, to confound. **2** [early 19C+] to place in a situation from which there is no escape. **3** [late 19C+] to accept, e.g. a point of view, a situation. **4** [late 19C+] (*UK Und.*) to recognize. **5** [late 19C+] to understand, to see through a deception.

have *v.*[5] [1920s+] to represent as doing something.

have *v.*[6] [1990s+] **1** (*orig. US Black*) to protect. **2** to have something covered. [HAVE SOMEONE'S BACK *v.*]

have a... *v. see* DO A... *v.*

have a baby *v.* [1930s+] to experience fright, shock or fury. [var. on HAVE KITTENS *v.*]

have a bad cold *v.* **1** [mid-19C–1910s] to be in debt; thus *have a very bad cold*, to leave one's lodgings without paying the rent. **2** [mid-19C+] to have a venereal disease. [euph.]

have a bag *v.* [1960s–70s] (*US Black*) to have a problem; thus *have a bag and a half*, to have a very great problem. [fig. use of BAG *n.*[10]]

have a ball *v.* (*orig. US*) **1** [1920s+] to enjoy oneself. **2** [1990s+] to masturbate.

have a banana with *v.* [1910s+] to have sexual intercourse. [lines from the song *Berlington Bertie*, 'When they ask me to dine I say "No./I've just had a banana with Lady Diana."/I'm Berlington Bertie from Bow.' Whether the *double entendre*, with its ref. to socialite goddess Lady Diana Cooper, was deliberate is unknown]

have a bar on *v.* [20C+] to have an erection. [BAR *n.*[3]]

have a bash *v. see* BASH *v.*[2] (1).

have a beat *v.* [1980s] (*Aus.*) **1** to masturbate (cf. BANG THE BISHOP *v.*). **2** in fig. use, to waste time, to mess about. [BEAT OFF *v.*[2] (1)]

have a beat on *v.* [20C+] to have an erection.

have a bee in one's bonnet *v. see* GET A BEE IN ONE'S BONNET *v.*

have a beer in *v.* [1900s] (*N.Z.*) to be very drunk.

have a belly like a poisoned pup's *v.* [1920s–50s] to be pot-bellied. [the dead animal swells up]

have a belly rash *v.* [1990s+] (*Aus.*) to be a sycophant.

have a Bex *v.* [1980s+] (*Aus.*) to relax. [*Bex*, a tranquillizing drug]

have a bird *v.* [1980s] (*US*) to become very angry. [BIRD *n.*[5] (3)]

have a bit in *v. see* HAVE A BIT ON *v.* (1).

have a bit of beef *v.* (*also* **do a bit of beef**) [late 19C] to have sexual intercourse (cf. BIT *n.*[3]). [BEEF *n.*[1]]

have a bit of bum *v.* [20C+] to have sexual intercourse (cf. BIT *n.*[3]). [BIT OF BUM *n.*]

have a bit of cauliflower *v.* [18C] to have sexual intercourse (cf. BIT *n.*[3]). [*cauliflower*, a large white wig 'such as is worn by the dignified clergy'; it came to mean vagina, according to Grose (1785), after a woman used the term in court and was duly reproved by the Judge 'saying she might as well call it artichoke. Not so my lord replied she; for an artichoke has a bottom but a **** and a cauliflower have none']

have a bit of cock *v.* [late 19C+] to have sexual intercourse (cf. BIT *n.*[3]). [COCK *n.*[2] (1)]

have a bit of cunt *v.* [late 18C+] to have sexual intercourse (cf. BIT *n.*[3]). [CUNT *n.*[1] (1)]

have a bit of curly greens *v.* [late 19C+] to have sexual intercourse (cf. BIT *n.*[3]). [GREENS *n.*[2]]

have a bit off *v. see* HAVE IT OFF (WITH) *v.*

have a bit of fish (on a fork) *v.* [mid-19C+] to have sexual intercourse (cf. BIT *n.*[3]). [FISH *n.*[1] (1)]

have a bit off the chump end *v.* [late 19C] to have sexual intercourse. [SE *chump-end*, the thick end of a loin of mutton]

have a bit of fun (with) *v.* [late 19C+] to have sexual intercourse (cf. ARRIVE AT THE END OF THE SENTIMENTAL JOURNEY *v.*). [euph.]

have a bit of giblet pie *v. see* DO A BIT OF GIBLET PIE *v.*

have a bit of goose's neck *v.* [late 19C–1900s] to have sexual intercourse (cf. CATCH AN OYSTER *v.*).

have a bit of gutstick v. [late 19C; 1970s+] of a woman, to have sexual intercourse (cf. BIT n.³; CATCH AN OYSTER v.). [GUTSTICK n.]

have a bit of jam v. [late 19C+] to have sexual intercourse (cf. BIT n.³). [JAM n.³ (2)]

have a bit of meat v. [late 19C+] to have sexual intercourse (cf. BIT n.³). [MEAT n. (1)]

have a bit of mutton v. [mid-19C+] to have sexual intercourse (cf. BIT n.³). [MUTTON n.¹ (3)]

have a bit of pork v. [18C+] to have sexual intercourse (cf. BIT n.³). [PORK n.¹ (1)]

have a bit of quimsy v. [19C] to have sexual intercourse (cf. BIT n.³). [QUIM n. (1)]

have a bit of rabbit pie v. see LIVE RABBIT n.

have a bit of rough v. [mid-19C+] to have sexual intercourse (cf. BIT n.³). [BIT OF ROUGH n.¹]

have a bit of sharp and blunt v. [late 19C–1900s] of a man, to have sexual intercourse (cf. BIT n.³). [SHARP AND BLUNT n.]

have a bit of skirt v. see DO A BIT OF SKIRT v.

have a bit of someone v. [1900s] (Aus.) to assault; to fight with.

have a bit of split mutton v. [18C–1900s] to have sexual intercourse (cf. BIT n.³). [SPLIT MUTTON n.]

have a bit of sugar stick v. [19C] of a woman, to have sexual intercourse (cf. BIT n.³; CATCH AN OYSTER v.). [SUGAR-STICK n.]

have a bit of summer cabbage v. [19C] to have sexual intercourse (cf. BIT n.³). [CABBAGE n.⁷ (1) + play on GREENS n.²]

have a bit on v. (also **have something on**) 1 [late 19C–1930s] (also **have a bit in**) to be drunk. 2 [late 19C+] to make a bet, to wager money on. [(2) BIT n.¹ (1)]

have a blow-through v. [20C+] to have sexual intercourse.

have a blue fit v. [1940s+] (N.Z.) to lose emotional control. [SE blue fit, an apoplectic fit]

have a bottom-wetter v. see DO A BOTTOM-WETTER v.

have a brick in one's hat v. [mid–late 19C] (orig. US) to be extremely drunk. [the image of being top heavy]

have a bug on v. [1930s–70s] (US) to be in a bad temper. [BUG n.⁵ (3)]

have a bug up one's ass v.¹ (also **get a bug up one's ass, have a bug in one's ass, have a roach up one's ass**) [1940s+] (US) 1 to be acting nervously, to fidget. 2 to be in a bad mood. [SE bug, an insect]

have a bug up one's ass v.² (also **have a bug up one's behind/tail**) [1950s+] (US) to be obsessed by something. [SE bug/BUG n.⁵ (3)]

have a bun in the oven v. (also **have a bun in the club, have a pudding in the oven**) [1950s+] 1 to be pregnant. 2 of a man, to impregnate one's partner. [SE bun/one/PUDDING n.¹ (4) + OVEN n. (3)]

have a bun on v. (also **get a bun on, put a bun on**) [late 19C+] (US prison) to be drunk or under the influence of a drug. [BUN n.³ (1)]

have a burr up one's ass v. [1960s+] (US) to be very short-tempered.

have a busy foot v. [1920s+] (Aus.) of a horse, to be a fast mover.

have a butcher's (at) v. (also **take a butcher's (at)**) [1930s+] to look at, to inspect. [BUTCHER'S (HOOK) n.]

have a buzz on v. (also **get a buzz on**) (orig. US) 1 [1930s+] to be drinking and mildly intoxicated but not drunk. 2 [1960s+] to be slightly intoxicated from drugs. [BUZZ n.³]

have a cab v. [late 19C–1900s] to be drunk. [the phr. is used to the drunkard, advising him not to try walking home]

have a calf v. [1970s] (US) to lose control, to have an emotional fit. [CALF n.¹ (1)]

have a canary v. 1 [1940s+] (US) to be mentally unstable; for one's brain to be injured or damaged. 2 [1960s+] (Irish) to have an emotional outburst.

have a case (on) v. see GO CASE v.

have a c.b. v. (also **get a c.b.**) [1980s+] (US campus) of a woman, to get extremely excited sexually or otherwise. [abbr. clitoris BONER n.⁴ (1)]

have a chicken dinner v. [1970s+] (US gay) to fellate an underage boy (cf. BASKET LUNCH n.). [CHICKEN DINNER n. (2)]

have a Chinaman on one's back v. [1930s–50s] to be addicted to narcotics, esp. heroin. [CHINAMAN n.⁴]

have a chip at v. [1910s–20s] to tease, to make fun of. [CHIP v.¹ (1)]

have a chip on one's shoulder v. see CARRY A CHIP ON ONE'S SHOULDER v.

have a clear-out v. [1920s+] to defecate. [the implication is subseq. to a bout of constipation]

have a cob on v. [1930s+] to be in a bad temper, to be annoyed; thus cobby, angry. [? dial. cob, to strike or cob, a lump, a large piece, thus cf. CARRY A CHIP ON ONE'S SHOULDER v.]

have a collar on v. [late 19C–1900s] to put on airs. [working-people rarely wore collars on an everyday basis]

have a colt's tooth v. [late 14C–19C] to have youthful desires that belie one's real age. [SE colt's tooth, the first set of a horse's teeth]

have a conversation with the one-eyed trouser snake v. [1990s+] to masturbate (cf. BEAT ONE'S HOG v.). [ONE-EYED TROUSER-SNAKE n.]

have a cook v. [20C+] to have a look. [COOK n.²]

have a cookie in the oven v. [1960s] (US) to be pregnant. [var. on HAVE A BUN IN THE OVEN v.]

have a cork eye v. [1930s+] (Aus.) to stare aggressively at someone. [ety. unknown; ? link to CORKED adj.]

have a crack at v. (also **get a crack at, take a crack at**) [late 19C+] (orig. US) to attempt, to have a try, to 'have a shot'. [CRACK n.¹⁰ (1)]

have a crow's eye v. [1940s] (Aus.) to be cunning, underhand.

have a crumb in one's beard v. [18C] to be drunk.

have a cup of tea v. [1970s+] (US gay) to have sex in a public lavatory.

have a cut (at) v. [late 19C+] (Aus.) to try, to make an attempt. [SE cut, a blow]

have a cut off the joint v. [20C+] of a man, to have sexual intercourse. [CUT OFF THE JOINT n.]

have a dash v. [early 19C+] to try, to make an attempt. [DASH n.⁵ (1)]

have a dash (of) lavender v. [1940s+] to be marginally homosexual. [LAVENDER adj.]

have a date with fisty palmer v. [1990s+] to masturbate (cf. CONVERSE WITH HARRY PALM v.). [ironic use of DATE n.¹ (2) + play on SE fist + palm]

have a dead and done-for look v. [late 19C] to look utterly miserable.

have a derry on v. (also **get a derry on**) [mid-19C+] (orig. UK Und.) to be prejudiced against. [late 19C+ mainly Aus. use; abbr. derry down = DOWN ON phr. (2)]

have a dirty nose v. [late 16C–mid-17C] to be a good drinker.

have a doctor's appointment v. see GO TO (SEE) THE DOCTOR v.

have a dog tied up v. [1910s–40s] (Aus./N.Z.) to be indebted, esp. at a hotel. [the image of having left one's dog while moving on elsewhere]

have a dose of the balmy v. see BALMY, THE n.

have a drop in one's eye v. [late 17C–mid-19C] to be tipsy.

have a dumpling on v. [late 19C–1900s] to be pregnant.

have a face as long as a fiddle v. (also **have a face as long as a yard measure**) [18C–1910s] to look dismal.

have a face as long as a Lurgan spade v. (also **have a face as long as a crowbar**) [late 19C+] (Irish) to look miserable. [Irish lorgán spáid, spade handle]

have a face like a badger's arse v. [1960s–70s] (Scot.) to be very unattractive.

have a face like a busted sandshoe v. [1990s+] (Aus.) to be very unattractive.

have a face like an undertaker's horse v. (also **have a face like a goanna**) [1900s–40s] (Aus./US) to look miserable.

have a face like a wet week v. see LIKE A WET WEEK phr.

have a face like the north end of a cow going south v. [1910s–40s] to look awkward.

have a face on one v. **1** [20C+] to be ugly, e.g. she's got a face on her like... **2** [1980s+] to be in a troubled, nervous mood.

have a few v. (also **have a few in, have one or two in**) [20C+] (orig. Aus.) to have a few drinks; thus have a few too many, to be drunk. [FEW, A n. (2)]

have a few of one's pages stuck together v. [20C+] to be stupid, to be foolish.

have a few over the score v. see GO OVER THE SCORE v.

have a field day v. **1** [early 19C+] to have a task or problem turn out to be infinitely simple. **2** [20C+] to have great and unopposed success. [milit. field day, a military review, military exercises]

have a fit (in the arm) v. [late 19C–1900s] to aim a punch or blow. ['one Tom Kelly' who was tried for striking a woman; 'his defence before the magistrate took the shape of a declaration that "a fit had seized him in the arm"' (Ware)]

have a fly at v. [1910s+] (Aus.) to have a try, to make an attempt.

have a foot in the dish v. [late 17C–18C] to get a share of, to become involved in. ['(? like a pig in the trough)' OED]

have a foot up one's ass v. [1960s] (US Black) to be treated unfairly, to be victimized.

have again v. [20C+] (W.I., Gren.) to have as much as one desires.

have a game at pully-hawly v. (also **play at pully-hawly**) [late 18C–19C] to have sexual intercourse. [colloq. pully-hawly, a rough and tumble]

have a gecko at v. [1970s+] (US) to take a look at, to glance at. [play on DEKKO v. + ? TAKE A GANDER (AT) v.]

have a glow on v. see GET A GLOW ON v.

have a go v. [late 19C+] **1** to fight; usu. with at. **2** to attack verbally. **3** to pick a fight. [GO n.³ (9); the image is that one is trying to defeat an opponent, whatever the result]

have a go at the creamstick v. [late 19C–1900s] to have sexual intercourse. [CREAMSTICK n.]

have a good innings v. (also **have a long innings**) [mid-19C+] **1** to be lucky, to make plenty of money. **2** to live a long time. [cricketing imagery]

have a good marble v. [1920s–60s] (Aus.) to be in an advantageous position. [horseracing, to be in a good position at the starting gate; ult. MAKE ONE'S MARBLE GOOD v.]

have a good nose v. [late 17C–early 18C] to arrive at a house in time for a meal.

have a grape on v. (also **be a grape on**) [1920s+] (Aus.) to feel hostile towards someone or something. [? SE sour grapes]

have a guest in the attic v. (also **have toys in the attic**) [20C+] **1** to be eccentric, to be insane, to be simple or childlike. **2** to be drunk (cf. ADDLED adj.).

have a gut like a crane v. [1920s+] (Aus.) to be very thirsty. [the bird's habits]

have a haemorrhage v. (also **haemorrhage**) [1920s+] (US) to become furious.

have a hair across one's ass v. (also **have a hair in one's ass, have a hair up one's prat**) [1960s+] (US) to be irritable, to complain. [fig. use of ASS n. (2)/PRAT n.¹ (1)]

have a hair crossed v. [20C+] (US) to be over-sensitive, to be touchy.

have a hair on one's ass v. see HAVE HAIR ON ONE'S CHEST v.

have a hair up one's prat v. see HAVE A HAIR ACROSS ONE'S ASS v.

have a hairy canary v. [1950s+] (US) to have a temper tantrum, an emotional outburst. [euph. var. on GET A HAIR UP ONE'S ASS v.]

have a half-nelson on v. [late 19C–1950s] (US) to be in firm control of. [wrestling jargon half-nelson, a hold in which one arm is thrust under the corresponding arm of the opponent and the hand placed on the back of his neck]

have a handful v. see GET A HANDFUL OF SPRATS v.

have a hank on v. [late 17C–early 19C] to have the advantage over; the implication is of potential blackmail. [SE hank, a restraining or curbing hold]

have a hate on v. [1940s+] (Aus./US) to dislike intensely.

have a head full of proclamations v. [late 17C–18C] to have one's head full of nonsense.

have a head like a robber's dog v. (Aus.) **1** [1940s+] (also **have a head like a beaten favourite, ...like a drover's dog, ...like a half-sucked mango**) to be suffering a very bad hangover. **2** [1960s+] (also **have a head like a twisted sandshoe**) to be ugly or unattractive. [(1) HEAD n.⁵ (1)]

have a head on v. [late 19C–1950s] **1** to have a hangover. **2** to be aware, to be alert. [(1) HEAD n.⁵ (1); (2) SE have a (smart) head on one's shoulders]

have a heart! excl. [1910s+] have pity! don't be cruel! be reasonable!

have a hearty-choke for breakfast v. [early 17C–19C] to be hanged; also ext. as have a hearty-choke for breakfast and/with caper sauce; thus artichoke and an oyster, a pre-hanging breakfast. [pun on SE artichoke/caper/hoist]

have a hop of v. see HOP OFF v.² (2).

have a hot back v. [late 16C] to be sexually aroused or available. [HOT adj.¹ (1) + SE back]

have a hot-mouth v. [20C+] (W.I., Guyn.) to answer cheekily, to talk back.

have a hot pudding for supper v. see HAVE A LIVE SAUSAGE FOR SUPPER v.

have a hot stomach v. [late 18C–early 19C] to pawn one's clothes to get money for buying liquor; also ext. as have so hot a stomach as to burn the clothes off one's back. [one is warm enough without the pawned garments and one's stomach is HOT adj.¹ (5) for drink]

have a hummer going v. [1960s–70s] (US) to be drunk. [HUMMER n.⁸]

have a hump in one's back v. [1990s+] (US Black) of a man, to be in the middle of sexual intercourse. [the physical movement of 'missionary position' intercourse]

have air and exercise v. **1** [late 18C+] to be whipped at the cart's tail as a judicial punishment; to be similarly punished in prison. **2** [early 19C] to be placed in the pillory.

have a jack (nohi) v. [1970s+] (N.Z.) to take a look. [JACK NOHI n. (2)]

have a joey in the pouch v. [1950s–60s] (Aus.) to be pregnant. [SE joey, a baby kangaroo]

have a keg on board v. [late 19C] (US) to be drunk.

have a kill v. see KILL v.⁴.

have a knocker on the front door v. [late 19C–1900s] to achieve respectability.

have a lam on v. [1990s+] to be in a bad temper. [? LAM n.²]

have a lark v. see GO ON A LARK v.

have a lash (at) v. (Aus.) **1** [late 19C+] to attack, to fight (with). **2** [1940s+] to try, to make an attempt. [LASH n.¹/SE lash, a whip-crack]

have a lend of v. see GET THE LOAN OF v.

have a line on v. [20C+] to understand, to know what is happening. [racing jargon the line, the daily details of the horses running and the odds on them]

have a live sausage for supper v. (also **have a hot pudding for supper, have a live sausage for breakfast**) [19C] of a woman, to have sexual intercourse (cf. CATCH AN OYSTER v.). [LIVE SAUSAGE n.]

have all one's buttons on v. (*also* **know one's buttons**) [late 19C–1960s] to be 'sharp', to know what is going on, to be impervious to hoaxers.

have all one's chairs (in a straight line) v. [1960s+] to be sane, to be rational, to be 'all there'.

have (all) one's work cut out v. [mid-19C+] to be forced to make a great effort, to be occupied with as much as one can handle.

have all that one can carry v. (*also* **have more than one can carry**) [mid-18C+] to be very drunk.

have a long innings v. *see* HAVE A GOOD INNINGS v.

have a loose connection v. [1970s] (*US*) to be eccentric, to be mad.

have a loose leg v. [20C+] (*Irish*) to be free to live one's life without restraint.

have a lot on one's plate v. [1920s+] to be overburdened with duties, worries, responsibilities etc.

have a lump of jaw on v. [late 19C–1900s] to be talkative.

have a mad on v. [mid-19C+] (*orig. US*) to be annoyed with, to be charged up emotionally. [SE *mad*]

have a maggot in one's tail v. [late 17C–early 18C] of a woman, to be venereally diseased.

have a moustache v. [1940s] to perform cunnilingus (cf. BEARD RIDE n.). [MOUSTACHE n. (2)]

have a mouth like a cow's cunt v. [late 19C+] to be very talkative.

have a mouth like the bottom of a bird-cage v. (*also* **have a mouth like the bottom of a parrot-cage, look like the bottom of a bird cage**) [1920s+] to be suffering the physical results of a night's drinking; also as *one's mouth feels like...* [the filthiness of the cage]

have a mouth like the inside of an Arab's armpit v. (*also* **have a mouth like a Greek wrestler's jockstrap, ...like an Arab's underpants**) [1940s+] to be suffering ghastly physical feelings as are concomitant with a hangover. [stereotyping of Arabs as dirty]

have a mouth on one v. [late 19C+] to be foul-mouthed or abusive, to be aggressively cheeky.

have an aching tooth v. **1** [16C] to desire, usu. sexually. **2** [mid-18C] to be angry with. [pun; note TOOTHACHE n.]

have an Anglo-Indian back v. [20C+] (*Can.*) of a young woman, to have leaves adhering to her back after a stroll in the woods with her boyfriend. [the idea of 'Red Indians' having sex in the open-air]

have an egg in the nest v. [20C+] (*US Black*) to be pregnant.

have an Elvis year v. [2000s] (*orig. US*) to be successful. [ult. the successful US singer *Elvis Presley* (1935–77)]

have a nibble v. *see* NIBBLE v.[2].

have a nickel in that dime v. [1970s+] (*US Black*) to have an interest in a state of affairs. [i.e. to invest 5 cents (a *nickel*) in a larger investment of 10 cents (a *dime*)]

have an in v. *see* IN n.

have an itch in the belly v. [mid-17C–19C] of a woman, to feel amorous.

have an itchy back v. [1920s+] (*Aus.*) of a woman, to desire sexual intercourse (presumably in the 'missionary' position). [a common female means of initiating sex is to request 'scratch my back']

have a nose of wax v. [19C] to be gullible, to be impressionable. [SE *nose of wax*, an impressionable person]

have a nose on v. [1900s–70s] (*Aus./N.Z.*) to bear a grudge against someone, to take offence.

have another think coming v. (*also* **have another guess coming**) [20C+] (*US*) to be wrong, to be mistaken.

have a notice to quit v. [19C] to have a terminal illness.

have ants in one's pants v. (*also* **have ants in one's britches**) [1930s+] (*orig. US*) to be restless, nervous, twitchy, (sexually) excited.

have a packet v. *see* COP A PACKET v.

have a pain on one's forehead v. [early 17C] to be cuckolded. [one is suffering from growing HORNS n.]

have a paper asshole v. [1940s+] **1** (*US*) to be a weakling, to be a coward. **2** (*also* **have a paper ass**) to talk excessively, esp. when meaningless; usu. *talk like you have a paper asshole*. **3** to do anything excessively. [SE *paper* + ASSHOLE n.[1] (1)/ASS n. (2)]

have a pelt at v. [1920s] to have a try at, to make an attempt at. [SE *pelt*, an act of throwing]

have a penn'orth of paradise v. *see* GET A PENN'ORTH OF PARADISE v.

have a peppermint in one's speech v. [late 19C–1910s] to stammer, to stutter. [the idea of one's speech being impeded by the sucking of a large peppermint + the 'stutter' implicit in *pepper*]

have a period v. [1980s+] to become emotional, agitated. [SE *period*, menstruation]

have a piece (of) v. [1940s+] of a man, to seduce a woman, to have sexual intercourse. [PIECE n.[1] (1)]

have a plaster for every sore v. [20C+] (*W.I.*) to have an excuse ready for any situation.

have a plum in the mouth v. [1920s+] to speak in what is considered an affected, upper-class British accent; thus *plum-in-the-mouth*, affectedly upper-class in speech.

have a pop (at) v. *see* TAKE A POP (AT) v.

have a pot in the pate v. [mid-17C–mid-18C] to be drunk. [lit. a 'tankard in the head']

have a potion v. [2000s] to have sexual intercourse.

have a pudding in the oven v. *see* HAVE A BUN IN THE OVEN v.

have a puff v. [1990s+] (*drugs*) to smoke cannabis.

have a put-in v. [19C] to have sexual intercourse. [the insertion of the penis]

have a rag on every bush v. [mid-19C+] of a man, to pursue a number of women at the same time.

have a rat v. *see* GET A RAT v.

have a rattle v. [20C+] of a man, to have sexual intercourse. [RATTLE v.[1] (2)]

have a rear v. *see* REAR v.

have a ring through one's nose v. **1** [1960s] (*US gambling*) to bet heavily when losing badly, hoping to get even. **2** [1960s+] (*US Black/campus*) to be obsessed, to the point of foolishness, with one other person, usu. a lover, by whom one can be led. [image of a bull or similar animal being led by means of a rope tied to a ring through the beast's nose]

have a roach up one's ass v. *see* HAVE A BUG UP ONE'S ASS v.[1].

have a roll on v. [late 19C–1910s] (*UK teen*) to swagger, to put on airs.

have a San Francisco accent v. [1990s+] (*US gay*) to be homosexual. [*San Francisco* has a large homosexual population]

have a screw loose v. (*also* **have a wheel loose, have screws loose**) **1** [early 19C] to be unwell. **2** [early–late 19C] to be on bad terms. **3** [early 19C–1920s] to have something wrong in the condition of things; a dangerous weakness in some arrangement; also of a person and their behaviour. **4** [early 19C+] to be eccentric, insane or retarded.

have a set on v. (*also* **take a set on**) [mid-19C+] (*Aus./N.Z.*) to bear a grudge against, to have a score to settle with. [SE *set against*]

have a sheet short v. [1910s+] (*Aus.*) to be mentally deficient; also *short of a sheet of bark*. [the *sheets* of bark used to roof early dwellings]

have a shot at v.[1] [early 19C+] (*Aus.*) to make a sneering remark in someone's direction, to try to provoke. [SHOT n.[3] (1)]

have a shot at v.[2] [late 19C+] to make an attempt, to have a try. [SHOT n.[5] (1)]

have a shy for v. [1920s+] (Aus.) to search for. [SE shy, as throw, thus an attempt to hit]

have a skinful v. see GET A SKINFUL v.

have a slap at v. [late 19C+] to make an attempt, to have a try. [SLAP n.¹ (2)]

have a slate loose v. see HAVE A TILE LOOSE v. (1).

have a slide up the board v. [late 19C] of a man, to have sexual intercourse.

have a smell of oneself v. [20C+] (Irish) to have a high opinion of oneself.

have a smell of the barman's apron v. (also have a sniff…, have a whiff…, …of the barmaid's apron) [1920s+] to be drunk.

have as much idea (of it) as a donkey has of Sunday v. [late 19C] to have no idea at all.

have as much wit as three folks, two fools and a madman v. [late 17C–early 19C] **1** to be a fool. **2** to be clever.

have a sniff of the barman's apron v. see HAVE A SMELL OF THE BARMAN'S APRON v.

have a snout on someone v. (also take a snout on someone) [20C+] (Aus./N.Z.) to bear a grudge against someone, to take offence. [SE snout, nose; they get 'up one's nose']

have a sore eye v. [mid-19C] (US Und.) to weep with laughter.

have a sosh on v. [1900s] to be drunk. [? SLOSHED adj.]

have a soul above buttons v. (also have a soul above socks) [late 18C–1900s] to see oneself realistically or otherwise as superior to the situation in which one currently exists. [orig. use by George Colman in New Hay at Old Market (1795): 'My father was an eminent Button-maker…but I had a soul above buttons…I panted for a liberal profession']

have a spark in one's throat v. [early 18C–early 19C] **1** to be continually thirsty. **2** to be keen on, to be enthusiastic.

have a spiral swallow v. [1920s] to have a large capacity for alcohol. [water runs down a plughole in a spiral]

have a splash v. [20C+] of a man, to urinate.

have a spur in one's head v. [late 18C] to act bravely, with courage.

have a stick up one's ass v. [1960s+] to be totally and irredeemably boring; such a stick would render one physically, and thus mentally, rigid. [SE stick + ASS n. (2)]

have a sticky palm v. [mid-19C+] **1** to be a habitual thief. **2** to be susceptible to bribes.

have a stomach on one's chest v. [late 19C] to have something, presumably food, lying heavily on one's stomach.

have a swelled head v. (also have a swollen head) [late 19C+] **1** to feel tipsy, drunk. **2** (also get one's skull swelled) to be arrogant, conceited.

have a thing about v. (also have a thing for) [1930s+] (orig. US) **1** to be obsessed with, esp. to be sexually obsessed. **2** to dislike intensely.

have a thing on v. [1910s+] to compare with.

have a thing (with) v. (also have a thing going) **1** [1940s+] to have a love affair with (cf. HAVE SOMETHING GOING v.). **2** [1960s+] (US) to have a complaint, a criticism of someone.

have a tile loose v. (also have a slate loose) **1** [mid-19C+] to be eccentric or foolish. **2** [1910s] (US) to be drunk.

have a tin ear v. [1920s+] **1** to have no ear for music, to be tone deaf. **2** (US tramp) (also give someone the tin ear) to ignore.

have a tip on v. [1900s–20s] to be drunk. [TIP n.¹]

have a tongue v. (also have a tongue in one's head/have a tongue on (one)) [late 19C+] to be sarcastic. [SE have a sharp tongue]

have a tongue too long for one's teeth v. (also have a tongue too long for one's mouth) [mid–late 19C] to be indiscreet.

have a toot v. [1930s–40s] to take a drink. [TOOT n.¹ (4)]

have a trial at Stafford Court v. [early 17C] to be beaten, to be thrashed. [pun on SE staff]

have a trout in the well v. [1940s+] (Irish) to be pregnant.

have a tug v. [1950s+] to masturbate. [SE tug]

have a turn v. [late 19C] to fight.

have a vacancy on the top floor v. [1970s+] (US) to be stupid. [i.e. NOT ALL THERE phr.]

have a vacant spot v. [late 19C–1900s] to be stupid [i.e. NOT ALL THERE phr.]

have a very bad cold v. see HAVE A BAD COLD v. (1).

have a wet arse and no fish v. [late 19C+] to have been out on a fruitless errand. [the image of fishing; successful or not, one is still likely to get wet]

have a wetty v. [1940s+] (Aus.) to work oneself up into a rage. [GET WET v.¹ (1)]

have a whack at v. (also take a whack at) [mid-19C+] (orig. US) to make an attempt or attack upon. [WHACK n.² (3)]

have a wheel loose v. see HAVE A SCREW LOOSE v.

have a whiff of the barman's apron v. see HAVE A SMELL OF THE BARMAN'S APRON v.

have a white coat v. [late 19C–1900s] to be drunk. [ety. unknown; ? joc. ref. to the white coats of those who 'take away' sufferers from delirium tremens]

have a white feather v. [late 18C–19C] to be a coward (cf. SHOW THE WHITE FEATHER v.). [cock-fighting jargon; a white feather denoted that a cock was not of the true gaming breed]

have a white swelling v. [late 18C–early 19C] to be pregnant. [18C medical jargon white swelling, a watery tumour found on a joint]

have a wink in one's eye v. [mid-19C–1900s] (Aus.) to feel sleepy.

have a wolf in the stomach v. [late 18C–19C] to suffer the pangs of intense hunger.

have a woman on one's dick v. see HAVE WOMEN ON ONE'S DICK v.

have bad typee for v. [20C+] (W.I., Guyn.) to be sexually obsessed with. [Carib.E. typee, an infatuation, an obsession]

have balls on one like a scoutmaster v. [1930s+] (Can./N.Z.) to have large testicles. [BALLS n.¹ (1); the popular image of the infinitely rampant paedophile scoutmaster]

have bats in the belfry v. [late 19C+] to be eccentric, to act crazily. [the image is of infestation of the brain]

have beans up one's nose v. [20C+] (US) to have ulterior motives, to act in a deceptive or dishonest manner.

have been after the girls v. [mid–late 19C] to have contracted a venereal disease. [euph.]

have been around v. **1** [1920s+] to be experienced in life. **2** [1950s+] to be experienced sexually; if used of a woman, usu. derog.

have been around the block v. see GO AROUND THE BLOCK v.

have been around the track v. [1950s+] to be experienced; usu. spec. sexually experienced; if used of a woman (the usu. form) derog.

have been in a storm v. [18C] to be drunk.

have been in the sunshine v. see HAVE THE SUN IN ONE'S EYES v.

have been to Barking creek v. (also have been to Barkshire) [early–mid-19C] to have a very bad cough. [pun]

have been to Blackwall v. [mid–late 19C] to have suffered a black eye. [pun]

have beetles in one's arcade v. [1910s] (Aus.) to lose one's senses, to be mad.

have blood like gnat's piss v. [1900s–10s] to be extremely frightened. [the insect's blood is seen as weak]

have boiled pig at home v. [late 18C–early 19C] to be the master in one's own home. [according to Grose (1785), an allusion to a 'well-known' (but unspecified) poem and story]

have breath strong enough to carry coal v. [late 19C–1900s] (orig. US) to be very drunk.

have broken knees v. [late 19C] of a girl or woman, to have been deflowered or seduced. [euph.]

have bugs (in the head) v. (also **have bugs in one's head**) [20C+] (orig. US) to be mentally unstable. [BUG n.⁵ (3)]

have business on both sides of the way v. [18C] to be drunk.

have but a mile to midsummer v. [mid–late 15C] to be eccentric, to be verging on insane. [the popular image of 'midsummer madness']

have buttered eggs in one's breeches v. [mid-17C–18C] to soil one's trousers through a sudden attack of terror.

have cavities v. [1980s+] (US campus) to consider something or someone extremely sweet.

have claws for breakfast v. see CLAW OFF v.

have cobwebs v. [1980s+] (US campus) to have lived a celibate life for a long time.

have cog-wheels v. [1910s] (Aus.) to be demented.

have cold feet v. see GET COLD FEET v.

have corns in the head v. [mid-18C–mid-19C] to be drunk (cf. ALED UP adj.). [play on SE corns/corn as used in brewing]

have cramp in one's kick v. [late 19C] to be mean. [SE cramp + KICK n.⁴]

have crap in one's blood v. [1940s–50s] (US) to be a coward. [CRAP n.³ (1)]

have cuts v. see GIVE CUTS v.

have death adders in one's pocket v. [1940s] (Aus.) to be a miser, to spend only reluctantly.

have donkey in one's throat v. [late 19C] to have phlegm caught in one's throat.

have down cold v. (also **have down chill**) [20C+] (US) to know something thoroughly. [COLD adv.¹ (1)/CHILL adv.]

have drunk of sauce's cup v. (also **have eaten sauce**) [late 15C–16C] to be abusive. [SE saucy, insolent]

have ears v. [1940s+] (orig. US Black) to listen, to be aware.

have egg on one's face v. [1940s+] (US) to be embarrassed, to look foolish.

have everything v. [1920s+] to possess every kind of attraction, advantage, requirement etc.

have eyes (for) v. [20C+] (US) to desire, to wish for; usu. sexually.

have eyes for fluff v. [1960s+] (gay) for a 'masculine' lesbian to be looking for a 'feminine' partner. [HAVE EYES (FOR) v. + FLUFF n.¹ (3)]

have eyes like a shithouse rat v. [1910s+] to have shifty, but acute eyes.

have eyes like cod's ballocks v. [20C+] to have popping eyes.

have fat nuts v. [1980s+] (US Black) to use violence, to be a violent person. [NUTS n.² (1)]

have feathers in one's hair v. [20C+] (US) to be sleepy. [FEATHER n.²]

have fireworks on the brain v. [late 19C–1900s] to be emotionally disturbed.

have fish-hooks in one's pockets v. [1910s+] (US) to be particularly mean and miserly. [one's pockets are lined with fish-hooks but note FISH-HOOKS n.]

have five minds to v. [20C+] (W.I.) to be strongly inclined to do something (usu. rash). [var. on SE be in two minds]

have five on v. [1990s+] (US campus) to help. [the lit./fig. use of one's 5 fingers]

have foot v. [1930s] to have an advantage in a chase.

have glass eyes v. [18C] to be drunk (cf. ARSEHOLED adj.).

have go-go in one's eyes v. [1990s+] (US prison) to wish to escape.

have going v. see GET GOING v.

have got knock in the cradle v. [mid-17C–18C] to be stupid; thus occas. knock in the cradle, a fool.

have got something on someone v. see HAVE SOMETHING ON SOMEONE v. (1).

have got something on the winkle v. [1920s+] to be obsessed by something. [fig. use of WINKLE n.¹]

have got them (all on) v. [late 19C] to be very well-dressed, often to excess.

have gravy on one's grits v. [1930s+] (US Black) to be enjoying a materially successful life. [the image of a brimming plate, grits being coarsely ground grain]

have gum-leaves growing out of one's ears v. [1920s+] (Aus.) to be a countryman; thus to be naïve, foolish, gullible. [the plentiful gum-trees found in the outback]

have guts in one's brains v. [mid-17C–early 19C] to be sensible, to show some intelligence. [SE guts, courage, spirit]

have had enough phr. [mid-18C+] drunk, e.g. you've had enough.

have had it v. **1** [19C+] to have been seduced. **2** [1930s+] to have failed, to have broken down, to have collapsed, to have died; often ext. with in a big way. **3** [1930s+] to be in trouble; esp. in the minatory phr. you've had it, you're in serious trouble.

have had it up to here v. (also **have had it up to the hairline**) [1940s+] to be exasperated, to have lost all one's patience.

have had it (with) v. (also **have had someone**) [1940s+] (orig. N.Z.) to have finished with, to have had a surfeit of, to be tired or bored of, to have lost one's patience; often ext. as HAVE HAD IT UP TO HERE v.

have had more — than — has had hot dinners v. [1930s+] a general phr. used to imply the expertise of the named person in a certain area of life; esp. of sexual experience.

have had one or two v. [late 19C+] to be drunk. [a euph. understatement]

have (had) one's chips v. [20C+] **1** to have died; lit. or fig. (cf. CASH (IN) ONE'S CHECKS v.). **2** to have been rejected, dismissed. [gambling use]

have had someone v. see HAVE HAD IT (WITH) v.

have had the claw v. (also **have had the Dic, ...Richard, ...sword**) [1980s] (Aus.) to have failed, to have broken down. [HAVE HAD IT v.]

have had the cotton v. [1970s] (US) to be doomed. [ety. unknown]

have hair on it v. [20C+] of a joke or anecdote, to be old, to be out of date, no longer to be amusing or pertinent. [the way mould appears on ancient, rotting fruit or vegetables, but note SE hoary, white with age, musty and mouldy]

have hair on one's chest v. (also **have a hair on one's ass, have wild hair**) [20C+] to be brave, to be plucky.

have heads on them like boils v. (also **have heads on them like mice**) [1940s+] (Aus.) of a hand at cards, of a succession of good throws of the dice or of a group of important and powerful people, to be strong.

have his brains in his ballocks v. [early 19C] to be stupid, to be a fool. [BALLOCKS n.¹ (1)]

have hot balls v. [1980s+] (US campus) to be drunk, usu. as —'s balls are hot. [SE eyeballs]

have hot pudding for supper v. see PUDDING n.¹ (1).

have ideas in one's head v. see GET IDEAS IN(TO) ONE'S HEAD v.

have in one's mouth v. [1960s] to talk about something or someone.

have in (some) liquor v. (also **have in (some) rum**) [20C+] (W.I.) to be drunk (cf. ALED UP adj.).

have it v.¹ **1** [late 17C+] (also **have one**) to have sexual intercourse. **2** [mid-19C+] to have a fight. [note music hall song 'A Little of What You Fancy...': 'I always hold with having it if you fancy it, / If you fancy it, that's understood... / 'Coz a little of what you fancy does you good']

have it *v.*[2] *see* HAVE V.[2] (1).

have it all over someone *v. see* HAVE IT ON SOMEONE V.

have it away *v.* (*also* **have it, have it away on one's toes, have it on one's toes, take it on one's toes**) [1950s+] **1** to escape; usu. from prison or impending arrest (cf. HAVE IT ON ONE'S DANCERS v.). **2** to walk, to leave, to exit. **3** to go to, to visit.

have it away (with) *v.*[1] [1920s+] to steal an object.

have it away (with) *v.*[2] [1960s+] to have sexual intercourse; sometimes ext. as *have it away together*.

have it back upon *v. see* GET BACK (AT) V.

have it bad *v.* (*also* **have them bad**) **1** [late 19C+] to be experiencing something intensely, e.g. illness, sexual obsession, love, delirium tremens. **2** [1960s+] to be sexually frustrated.

have it coming *v.* [late 19C+] to deserve, to merit; usu. 'it' is unpleasant.

have it covered *v.* (*also* **have someone covered**) [1950s+] (*orig. US Black*) **1** to have a situation well under control. **2** to understand a person and accept their position.

have it for *v.* [1930s–60s] (*US*) to be in love with.

have it going on *phr.* [1990s+] (*US Black*) living in the swing of things, being chic or fashionable.

have it in *v.* [late 19C+] to have sexual intercourse.

have it knocked *v.* [late 19C+] to have a problem, and esp. life in general, absolutely under control. [KNOCK v.[2] (2)]

have (it) off *v.* (*also* **get it off**) **1** [mid-19C+] (*UK Und.*) to carry out a successful crime. **2** [1930s+] to be successful in any area, but in a specific task. **3** [1950s+] (*UK Und.*) of police, to make a successful raid and arrest. [HAVE v.[2]]

have it off (with) *v.* (*also* **have a bit off**) [1930s+] to copulate (with). [HAVE v.[1]]

have it on one's dancers *v.* [1950s+] (*UK Und.*) to run away, to escape (cf. HAVE IT AWAY v.). [DANCERS n. (2)]

have it on one's toes *v. see* HAVE IT AWAY V.

have it on someone *v.* (*also* **have it all over someone**) [20C+] (*Aus./US*) to have someone at a disadvantage; to feel superior towards.

have (it) out *v.* **1** [mid-18C+] to fight. **2** [early 19C+] to have a frank, argumentative discussion, to air an otherwise 'difficult' topic. [imagery of exposing the problem to fig. 'open air']

have it out of someone *v.* [late 19C+] to punish, to exact compensation from.

have it so good *v.* [1940s+] (*orig. US*) to have a variety of advantages; usu. in negative use. [the *locus classicus* is British Prime Minister Harold Macmillan's speech on 20 July 1957: 'Let's be frank about it. Most of our people have never had it so good. Go around the country, go to the industrial towns, go to the farms, and you'll see a state of prosperity such as we have never had in my lifetime – nor indeed ever in the history of this country. What is beginning to worry some of us is "Is it too good to be true?" or perhaps I should say "Is it too good to last?"']

have (it) taped *v.* [1910s+] (*orig. milit.*) to have something worked out, assessed fully etc. [SE *tape*, to measure with a tape]

have it together *v. see* KEEP IT TOGETHER V.

have it up *v.* [late 19C+] to have sexual intercourse.

have kangaroos in one's top paddock *v.* [20C+] (*Aus.*) to be eccentric, to be mentally unstable.

have kidney trouble *v.* [1940s+] (*gay*) to frequent public lavatories for sex. [one's excuse for making so many visits to the lavatory]

have kittens *v.* [20C+] to worry to excess, to throw a fit, to succumb to one's emotions, to lose one's temper, often through worry or fear. [the nervousness of a pregnant cat]

have larks for breakfast *v.* (*also* **have larks for supper**) [1910s] (*Ulster*) to be especially eloquent. [larks are trad. good singers]

have Laurence on one's back *v. see* LAZY LAURENCE n.

have lead in one's pencil *v.* [1920s+] (*orig. US*) **1** to be potent.

2 to have an erection. **3** in fig. use, to feel emotionally/physically strong.

have legs on one's belly *v.* [1940s+] (*Aus./N.Z.*) to be a sycophant, to be a toady. [the legs facilitate one's 'crawling']

have long eyes *v.* (*also* **have raw eyes**) [20C+] (*W.I.*) to be covetous for.

have long pockets and short arms *v.* [1970s] (*Aus.*) to be miserly, to be mean.

have lunch downtown *v.* [1920s+] to engage in cunnilingus (cf. BOX LUNCH n.). [LUNCH n.[3] (1) + DOWNTOWN n.[1]]

have marbles in one's head *v.* [1950s] (*US*) to be insane, eccentric, foolish.

have mind *v.* [20C+] (*W.I.*) to possess courage, to be brave.

have missile lock *v.* [1980s+] (*US campus*) to target another person, either though love or hate. [milit. jargon *missile lock*, to aim a missile electronically so that it follows a specific target until its destruction; popularized through the film *Top Gun* (1986)]

have more kid in them than a goat in the family way *v.* [1930s+] (*Aus.*) to be an incurable joker or 'kidder'. [pun on KID n.[2] (2)/KID n.[1]]

have more than one can carry *v. see* HAVE ALL THAT ONE CAN CARRY V.

have mousetraps in one's pocket *v.* (*also* **have scorpions..., have snakes...**) [1920s+] (*Aus.*) to be extremely mean. [one dare not, therefore, put one's hand in one's pocket to extract money]

have ne'er a face but one's own *v.* (*also* **have never a face but one's own**) [late 17C–early 18C] to be penniless. [the 'faces' are those on coins]

have negative clues *v.* [1980s+] (*US campus*) to have no idea of what is going on, to be totally devoid of common sense.

have no butter in one's eyes *v.* [early–mid-19C] to be well aware, to have no illusions.

have no ink in one's pen *v.* [mid-16C] to be impotent.

have no lead in one's pencil *v.* [1920s+] to be impotent. [HAVE LEAD IN ONE'S PENCIL v. (cf. the earlier HAVE NO INK IN ONE'S PEN v.)]

have no life *v.* [1980s+] (*US campus*) to exist in an aimless manner, to have no purpose in life.

have no more wit than a coot *v. see* COOT n.[1].

have no skin on one's face *v.* [20C+] (*Irish*) to have no shame. [? without skin one cannot blush]

have-not *n.* [mid-19C+] one who is materially unsuccessful.

have no tale *v. see* AIN'T GOT NO TALE phr.

have no time for *v.* [1910s+] to be intolerant of, to be uninterested in.

have off *v.* [1930s+] (*orig. US Black*) **1** to berate, to attack verbally. **2** to attack. **3** to defeat, to beat up. [HAVE v.[2] (3)]

have-on *n.* [late 19C–1930s] a swindle, a hoax. [var. on HAVE n.[2] (1)]

have on *v. see* HAVE v.[3].

have one *v. see* HAVE IT v.[1] (1).

have one foot in the funny farm *v.* [1980s] to be slightly mad, eccentric.

have one foot in the grave *v.* [early 17C+] to be dying.

have one for the worms *v.* [late 19C–1930s] to have a drink of alcohol. [the assumption that drinking will, eventually, prove fatal]

have one in the box *v.* [late 19C+] to be pregnant. [? BOX n.[1] (1)]

have one more wrinkle in one's arse *v.* [late 18C–mid-19C] to have gained a fresh piece of knowledge. ['Every fresh piece of knowledge being supposed by the vulgar naturalists to add a wrinkle to that part' (Grose, 1796); note *wrinkle*, a tip, a clever trick, a short-cut]

have one mother too many *v.* [20C+] to be illegitimate. [a bastard should not have any mother at all, i.e. should have been left unconceived]

have one on the city *v.* [19C+] (*US*) to have a drink of water. [the city-run water supply]

have one or two in *v. see* HAVE A FEW *v.*

have one's *v. see* GET ONE'S *v.*

have one's act together *v.* (*also* **have one's act down**) [1960s+] (*orig. US Black*) to be in full control of a situation, whether emotional, social, sexual, financial etc.

have one's ass hanging out *v. see* HANG ONE'S ASS OUT *v.* (1).

have one's ass in the wind *v.* [1960s+] (*US*) to be exposed to trouble or danger.

have one's back scratched *v.* [late 19C+] to suffer a judicial flogging. [one is *scratched* by the cat-o'-nine-tails]

have one's back teeth afloat *v.* (*also* **have one's back teeth awash, have one's back teeth under water, have one's teeth swimming**) (*orig. US*) **1** [late 19C+] to be very drunk. **2** [20C+] (*also* **have one's kidneys afloat**) to be desperate to urinate.

have one's back teeth underground *v.* [1900s–10s] to have eaten to satiation or excess.

have one's ballocks in the right place *v.* [20C+] to be deserving of praise, commendation, approval by one's fellows. [BALLOCKS *n.*[1] (1)]

have one's balls in the fire *v.* [1960s] (*US*) to be in serious trouble.

have one's balls twisted *v.* [1970s] to be stupid but outspoken. [BALLS *n.*[1] (1)]

have one's balls under one's chin *v.* [1930s–60s] (*US*) to be terrified. [a coarser version of SE *have one's heart in one's mouth*]

have one's barrel full *v.* [late 19C] (*US*) to be drunk (cf. ALED UP *adj.*).

have one's beer goggles on *v.* [1980s+] (*US campus*) to find someone attractive because of the influence of alcohol. [BEER GOGGLES *n.*]

have one's belly boil *v.* [20C+] (*W.I., Gren.*) to be very frightened.

have one's belly full *v.* [late 18C–19C] to be pregnant.

have one's belly touching one's back *v.* [20C+] (*W.I.*) to be absolutely starving.

have one's boots on *v.* (*also* **have one's boots laced**) [1930s–70s] (*US Black*) to be wise, sophisticated, intelligent. [one is thus ready to confront the world]

have one's bottle fall out *v.* [1950s] to be frightened, to act in a cowardly manner. [BOTTLE *n.*[2] (2)]

have one's chips *v. see* HAVE (HAD) ONE'S CHIPS *v.*

have one's clock stopped *v.* [late 19C–1900s] to have been denied credit. [pun on no more TICK *n.*[3] (1)]

have one's cock caught in a zipper *v. see* GET ONE'S COCK CAUGHT IN A ZIPPER *v.*

have one's cock on the block *v.* [1970s+] (*orig. US*) to be facing serious problems, to be prepared to take a risk or a stand that may be dangerous. [COCK *n.*[2] (1)]

have one's collar felt *v. see* GET ONE'S COLLAR FELT *v.*

have one's corn ground *v. see* GET ONE'S CORN GROUND *v.*

have one's cut *v.* [late 19C+] of a man, to have sexual intercourse. [CENTRAL CUT *n.*]

have one's dick in the dirt *v.* [2000s] (*US*) to be in serious trouble. [DICK *n.*[4] (1)]

have one's ducks in a row *v.* [1930s+] (*US*) to have one's affairs in order. [? image of the mother duck and her attendant ducklings]

have oneself *v.* **1** [1920s+] to indulge oneself, to provide for oneself; usu. in phrs., e.g. *have oneself a good time, have oneself some fun*; often as HAVE ONESELF A TIME *v.* **2** [1970s+] (*US gay*) to be excited. **3** [1980s+] (*US Black*) to masturbate.

have oneself a time *v.* [1930s+] to enjoy oneself, to go out on a spree. [HAVE ONESELF *v.* (1) + SE *time*]

have one's eye in a sling *v.* [late 19C+] to be depressed, crushed, defeated.

have one's eye on the ball *v.* [20C+] to be alert and aware. [sporting imagery]

have one's eyes opened *v.* [20C+] to be drunk (cf. ARSEHOLED *adj.*). [one's wild, unfocused stare]

have one's face at half-past eight *v.* (*also* **have a face like half-past six**) [late 19C+] to look miserable. [the corners of the mouth point down, as would the hands of the clock]

have one's face made of a fiddle *v.* [late 18C] to be irresistibly charming.

have one's fighting clothes on *v.* [20C+] (*US*) to be ready to quarrel, to be spoiling for a fight.

have one's finger on the trigger *v.* [1990s+] to pose a threat, i.e. one is prepared to shoot if necessary.

have one's finger out *v. see* GET ONE'S FINGER OUT (OF ONE'S ASS) *v.*

have one's finger up one's arse *v.* (*also* **have one's finger up one's ass**) [1940s+] to idle, to loiter, to stand around doing nothing. [ARSE *n.*[1] (1); PULL ONE'S FINGER OUT *v.*]

have one's foot in the road *v.* [20C+] (*US*) to spend a good deal of time away from home, to travel frequently.

have one's foot on the rail *v.* [20C+] (*US*) to drink heavily. [the 'rail' is that of a bar]

have one's game uptight *v.* (*also* **have one's game together, …program together**) [1960s+] (*orig. US Black*) to be in full control of a situation. [GAME *n.*[2] + UPTIGHT *adj.*[3] (3)]

have one's garret unfurnished *v.* (*also* **have one's upper storey unfurnished**) [late 18C] to be a fool.

have one's glasses on *v.* [1930s–40s] (*US Black*) to pose as an intellectual, to lay down the law. [stereotyped association of spectacles with intelligence]

have one's glue *v.* [1960s+] (*Irish*) used in phrs. to indicate disdain.

have one's hand in someone's pocket *v.* [1920s–40s] to be in receipt of bribes.

have one's hand out *v.* **1** [late 19C+] to beg, to scrounge. **2** [20C+] to be amenable to a bribe.

have one's hat nailed to the ceiling *v.* [1910s–30s] (*US*) to be fellated. [the excitement so produced]

have one's head glued on *v.* [20C+] to be mentally balanced, emotionally controlled.

have one's head on *v. see* KEEP ONE'S HAIR ON *v.*

have one's head screwed on *v.* (*also* **have one's head screwed on right, …the right way**) [early 19C+] to be aware, to understand, to know what's what.

have one's head up one's arse *v.* (*also* **have one's head (stuck) up one's ass**) [1940s+] (*orig. US*) **1** to be completely and deliberately stupid. **2** to be obsessed with oneself and one's own interests. **3** to ignore what is happening.

have one's head wedged *v.* [1960s+] (*US*) to be very stupid. [it is wedged 'up one's ASS *n.* (2)']

have one's heart in one's mouth *v.* [mid-16C+] to be terrified, to be very apprehensive.

have one's hip boots on *v.* [1930s–60s] to be sophisticated, aware. [pun on SE *hip*/HIP *adj.* (1) + SE *boots*]

have one's jawing-tackle on board *v.* [early 19C–1910s] to be impudent, to be cheeky. [JAW *v.*[1] (1)]

have one's kidneys afloat *v. see* HAVE ONE'S BACK TEETH AFLOAT *v.* (2).

have one's leg over *v. see* GET ONE'S LEG OVER *v.*

have one's legs open *v.* [1930s+] (*US Black*) of a woman, to behave in a promiscuous manner.

have one's little hat on *v.* [18C] to be drunk.

have one's mind in the mud v. [1900s–40s] (US Black) to be thinking vulgar or lustful thoughts.

have one's monkey up v. see GET ONE'S MONKEY UP v.

have one's mouth full of pap v. [late 18C–early 19C] to act in a childish manner. [SE *pap*, baby food]

have one's mouth on v. [1930s+] (US Black) to gossip, to criticize someone in their absence.

have one's mouth paved v. [early 18C] to have a mouth inured to hot food or drink.

have one's name on v. (also **have one's number on**) [1910s+] to be destined or intended for someone, orig. used of a bullet.

have one's nightcap on v. [18C] to be drunk.

have one's nose in parenthesis v. [late 18C–early 19C] to have one's nose pulled. [SE *parenthesis*, an interlude, a hiatus]

have one's nose in the air v. [20C+] to act in a snobbish or superior manner. [the tilted nose intends to avoid noxious smells]

have one's nose in the manger v. [mid-19C–1920s] to eat heartily.

have one's nose open v. (also **get one's nose open**) [1950s+] (US Black) **1** to produce sexual excitement in another person (cf. OPEN SOMEONE'S NOSE v.). **2** to be infatuated with another person. **3** to be under someone's control (other than sexually). **4** to be excited, in a non-sexual context. **5** to be angry. **6** to anger. [all uses imply heavy breathing]

have one's nose up someone's arse v. (also **have one's nose up someone's ass**) [1970s+] to act sycophantically, to toady.

have one's nuff v. see GET ONE'S NUFF v.

have one's number on v. see HAVE ONE'S NAME ON v.

have one's nuts in a knot v. [1990s+] to be in a state of confusion and worry. [NUTS n.² (1) + SE *knot*]

have one's pots on v. [19C–1940s] to be drunk (cf. ALED UP adj.).

have one's program together v. see HAVE ONE'S GAME UPTIGHT v.

have one's sails high v. [1940s+] (US Black) to be drunk (cf. ELEVATED adj.).

have one's shirt on v. see PUT ONE'S SHIRT ON v.

have one's shite v. [late 19C+] (Irish) an indication of rejection, i.e. one is due to suffer. [fig. use of SHITE n.]

have one's shit together v. (also **have one's shit down, have one's shit in one bag**) [1960s+] (orig. US Black) to be in full control of a situation. [SHIT n.⁶]

have one's shutters up v. [late 19C–1900s] to act in a surly manner.

have one's sitting breeches on v. (also **wear one's sitting breeches**) [late 18C–early 19C] to outstay one's welcome.

have one's skates on v. see GET ONE'S SKATES ON v.

have one's snout in the trough v. (also **get one's snout in the trough, put...**) [1940s+] **1** to act greedily and selfishly. **2** to drink beer or ale rather than spirits.

have one's spike up v. [1940s] to be in a bad temper.

have one's tail in a crack v. see GET ONE'S ASS IN A CRACK v.

have one's tail in the water v. [mid-19C–1900s] to be well-off, to be thriving. [ety. unknown]

have one's tail out v. [late 19C–1910s] to be angry. [the waving of a cat's tail, which supposedly denotes aggression]

have one's tail over the line v. [1910s] to act stubbornly.

have one's teapot mended v. (also **get it down the spout**) [late 19C] (UK prison) to regain the privilege – earned by good behaviour – of replacing the usual gruel with tea.

have one's teeth swimming v. see HAVE ONE'S BACK TEETH AFLOAT v.

have one's tit (caught) in a wringer v. [1960s+] (US) to be in difficulties, to be foolish. [TIT n.³ (1)]

have one's tit in a tight crack v. [1920s+] (Can.) to find oneself in trouble, in an unpleasant situation. [TIT n.³ (1)]

have one's tongue hanging out v. [late 19C+] to be eagerly expectant.

have one's upper storey unfurnished v. see HAVE ONE'S GARRET UNFURNISHED v.

have one's whack v. (also **take one's whack**) [mid-19C+] to have or take one's share. [WHACK n.²]

have one's wires crossed v. [20C+] to act in an eccentric or unstable manner, to be confused, to misunderstand. [electrical imagery]

have one's work cut out v. see HAVE (ALL) ONE'S WORK CUT OUT v.

have one too many v. [20C+] to be drunk. [euph.]

have one up v. [1960s] of a woman, to be pregnant.

have only fifty cards in one's deck v. see NOT PLAYING WITH A FULL DECK phr.

have on one's high-heeled shoes v. (also **have on one's high-heeled boots**) [mid-19C–1910s] (US) to be arrogant, self-important, snobbish. [HIGH-HEELED adj.]

have on the raws v. [early 19C] to tease, to touch an emotionally sensitive spot. [SE *raw*]

have on the stick v. [late 19C–1910s] to make fun of. [? the image of a toy 'monkey on a stick']

have paper(s) on v. [1940s+] (US Black) to be legally married. [one's marriage certificate]

have pepper in the nose v. [late 14C–17C] to act in a super-cilious, arrogant and rough manner.

have plenty of stir on v. (also **have plenty to stir on**) [late 19C–1900s] to be very well-off. [? dial. *stir/stirabout*, a stew, i.e. one is well fed; or SE *stir*, a commotion, i.e. one is busy with making money]

have points v. see GET POINTS v.

have rats v. see GET RATS v.

have raw eyes v. see HAVE LONG EYES v.

have red-eye for v. (also **look with red-eye (at), red-eye after, red one's eye**) [20C+] (W.I.) to become obsessed with someone at first sight and thus to desire to possess them immediately. [the red eyes that are trad. associated with madness]

have red sails in the sunset v. [1930s+] of a woman, to be menstruating. [the 1935 song 'Red Sails in the Sunset', a hit for Bing Crosby, Nat King Cole etc; however, nothing in the lyrics implies a link to menstruation, other than the *red* of menstrual blood]

haverel n. (also **haveril**) [20C+] (Irish) an ignorant man, a slatternly woman. [synon. dial. *haverel*; ult. SE *haver*]

have rheumatism in the shoulder v. [early 19C] to be arrested. [the pain engendered by the hand that grasps one's shoulder]

have rocks in the head v. [20C+] (Aus./US) to be stupid.

have scales (on one's belly) v. [1910s] (Aus.) to be a syco-phant. [idea of being a snake or fish that crawls + CRAWL v.¹ (1)]

have scorpions in one's pocket v. see HAVE MOUSETRAPS IN ONE'S POCKET v.

have screws loose v. see HAVE A SCREW LOOSE v.

have seen the cheque v. [late 19C] to have exact knowledge of something, to have proof.

have seen the French king v. [17C–mid-18C] to be drunk.

have shit in one's blood v. [1970s] (US) to be a coward.

have shit on one's liver v. [1930s+] (Aus.) to be in a bad temper. [SE *liverish*, testy]

have smallpox v. [20C+] (US Und.) to be wanted on an arrest warrant.

have snakes in one's pocket v. see HAVE MOUSETRAPS IN ONE'S POCKET v.

have snaps on v. [2000s] (US Black) to claim for oneself, or to claim a share in.

have so hot a stomach as to burn the clothes off one's back v. see HAVE A HOT STOMACH v.

have someone beat v. (also **have something beat**) [20C+] (US) to defeat intellectually, to get the better of, to baffle, to confuse. [BEAT v.[1] (2)]

have someone bent v. [2000s] (US teen) to misinterpret, to 'read' incorrectly.

have someone by the balls v. (also **have something by the balls, have someone/something by the bollocks**) [late 19C+] to have someone or something at one's mercy, at a complete disadvantage. [NUTS n.[2] (1)]

have someone by the jalino v. see JALINO n.

have someone by the joint v. [1970s] of a woman, to have sexually enslaved a man. [JOINT n.[1]]

have someone by the short and curlies v. (also **have someone by the short hair(s), …by the shorts, …by the wool**) 1 [late 19C+] to have someone at an extreme disadvantage, to control completely. 2 [1920s+] (Aus.) to know a subject extremely well. 3 [1930s+] (US) to annoy. [the image of grasping the victim's pubic hair]

have someone cold v. [1910s+] (orig. US) to have at one's mercy, to have at a disadvantage. [COLD adv.[1] (1)]

have someone covered v. see HAVE IT COVERED v.

have someone for breakfast v.[1] [mid–late 19C] (US, Western) to discover a murdered body when one wakes in the morning. [ironic]

have someone for breakfast v.[2] (also **eat someone for breakfast**) [20C+] to be able to achieve a task, to defeat a rival, to terrify or overwhelm a lesser figure, to have at a complete disadvantage.

have someone going v. [1910s–20s] to excite sexually, to render infatuated.

have someone in v. [1940s+] (orig. US) to swindle, to cheat, to deceive.

have someone in your craw v. [20C+] (W.I.) to harbour ill-feeling towards someone. [SE craw, the throat]

have someone mapped v. [20C+] to have someone completely and accurately assessed, to work out another's movements and attitudes.

have someone on v.[1] [mid-19C+] to tease, to hoax, to engage someone's attention with the longer term intention of deceiving them; thus to swindle, to cheat.

have someone on v.[2] (Aus./N.Z.) 1 [1940s–60s] to accept sexually. 2 [1940s+] to prepare oneself to fight, to accept a challenge. 3 [1950s+] to attack physically. [dial.]

have someone on a string v. 1 [late 19C+] to hoax, to trick, to fool. 2 [20C+] to have in a dependent relationship. 3 [1920s+] to keep in suspense.

have someone on the ropes v. [1910s+] to have someone at a disadvantage. [boxing imagery]

have someone on toast v. [late 19C+] to have at a complete disadvantage. [the victim becomes no more than a fig. 'mouthful' to be chewed up at the aggressor's leisure, like a mouthful of toast]

have someone over v. [1970s+] 1 to deceive, to defraud, to trick. 2 to seduce. [abbr. of HAVE SOMEONE OVER A BARREL v.; (2) is fig.]

have someone over a barrel v. (also **put someone over a barrel**) [late 19C+] to put at a great disadvantage, to inconvenience deliberately. [? 19C barrel punishment, lashing someone across a barrel and whipping them]

have someone pegged v. [1910s+] (US) to categorize (properly), to form an (accurate) opinion of. [PEG v.[4] (2)]

have someone right v. [1940s] (US Und.) to buy protection from an official.

have someone's arse v. (also **have someone's ass**) [1950s+] to reprimand severely, to punish. [ARSE n.[1] (1)/ASS n. (2)]

have someone's back v. [1980s+] to take care of, to look after. [the image of guarding someone's back from attack]

have someone's balls (for a game of pool) v. (also **have someone's balls for breakfast**) [1960s+] to treat very harshly, to punish comprehensively.

have someone set v. [20C+] (Aus.) to have someone marked down for punishment or revenge. [abbr. SE set down]

have someone's guts for garters v. (also **have someone's guts for a garter, wear someone's guts for earmuffs**) [late 16C; late 18C; 1930s+] to punish comprehensively, to hurt.

have someone's number v. (also **get someone's number, know…, take…**) (orig. US) 1 [mid-19C+] to understand another person absolutely, for all their possible evasions and excuses. 2 [1920s+] to be aware, to be alert, to see through someone's pretences.

have someone's nuts in a sling v. [1990s+] to have someone at one's mercy, lit. or fig. [NUTS n.[2] (1) + SE sling]

have someone's shirt (out) v. see GET SOMEONE'S SHIRT OUT v.[1].

have someone's weights up v. [1970s+] (N.Z.) to have the measure of a person. [horseracing imagery]

have someone to the bad v. [1900s] (US) to put at a disadvantage.

have someone waxed v. [1900s] to have someone at a disadvantage.

have some rabbit in one v. [1980s] (US Black/Und.) 1 to be a habitual absconder from institutions or situations. 2 to be sexually active. [both meanings derive f. the alleged obsessions of rabbits]

have something v. [1910s+] to have a valid point or opinion; thus you have something there, you may well be right.

have something beat v. see HAVE SOMEONE BEAT v.

have something by the balls/bollocks v. see HAVE SOMEONE BY THE BALLS v.

have something down v. [1910s+] to be aware of the situation, to know what is going on. [DOWN adj.[1] (1)]

have something going v. [1960s+] 1 to be involved in a close relationship (usu. sexual). 2 to be conducting business (often illicit). 3 to be pursuing some form of plan.

have something going for oneself v. [1960s+] to be in a good situation, to have circumstances working in one's favour.

have (something) off v. [1970s+] (UK Und./police) to be involved in criminal activity.

have something on v. see HAVE A BIT ON v.

have something on one's brain/mind v. see GET SOMETHING ON ONE'S BRAIN v.

have something on someone v. [20C+] (orig. US Und.) 1 (also **have got something on someone**) to have someone at a disadvantage; usu. through incriminating or negative information. 2 to be popular with. 3 to be better than; although usu. in negative.

have sweaters on one's teeth v. [1980s+] (US campus) to have a dry mouth accompanying a hangover from excess alcohol.

have swollen balls for v. [1980s+] (US prison) to lust after.

have taken ugly pills v. [1950s+] (Can.) to be unpleasant, aggressive, unattractive etc.

have the bags (off) v. [mid–late 19C] to be well-off, to be rich.

have the ball at one's feet v. [19C+] to have a thing or situation in one's power. [soccer imagery]

have the better end of the staff v. [mid-16C–19C] to be treated fairly (cf. HAVE THE WORSE END OF THE STAFF v.).

have the big one v. [1970s] (US) to die of a heart attack. [euph.]

have the bot v. [1940s+] (Aus./N.Z.) to be ill, to be out of sorts, moody or disagreeable. [N.Z. medical jargon bot, a germ, a sufferer from tuberculosis; ult. bot(t), 'a parasitical worm or maggot; now restricted to the larvae of flies of the genus Oestrus' (OED)]

have the breeze up v. see GET THE BREEZE UP v.

have the Britts (up) v. [1940s] (Aus.) to be in a nervous state. [abbr. JIMMY BRITTS n.]

have the bulge on v. (*also* **get the bulge on**) [mid-19C+] (*US*) to have an advantage over, to be in a superior position. [BULGE n.]

have the cheek-ache v. [late 19C–1900s] to blush.

have the darling pea v. [late 19C–1910s] (*Aus.*) to act eccentrically. [SAusE *Darling pea*, a variety of *Swainsona*, a herb that can cause cattle to suffer from stiffness of limbs, muscle tremor and uncoordination]

have the dead needle v. *see* HAVE THE NEEDLE v.

have the deadwood (on) v. (*also* **get the deadwood (on)**) [mid-19C+] (*US*) to have at a disadvantage, to control, esp. through the possession of incriminating information (cf. HAVE THE WOOD ON v.). [logging use, where a skilled axeman would cut a tree in such a way that he spared himself work by ensuring that any dead wood broke off by itself when the tree fell; alternate ety. suggests the shooting in the back of Marshall James Butler 'Wild Bill' Hickok in the town of Deadwood, South Dakota on 2 August 1876; note in 10-pin bowling, if after 1 pitch a single pin is left lying in front of those that have not been knocked down, hitting that 'dead wood' will knock it into the others, successfully knocking them all down]

have the decorators in v. [mid-19C+] of a woman, to be menstruating. [euph.; the colour they 'paint' is of course blood-red]

have the dick v. [1950s+] (*Aus.*) to be finished, to be permanently damaged. [DICKED adj.[1] (1)]

have the drop on v. [mid-19C+] to place someone else at a disadvantage, in any confrontation, physical, mental, financial etc. [DROP n.[2] (1); *see also* GET THE DROP ON v.]

have the flags out v. [20C+] of a woman, to be menstruating. [the flag in question is, presumably, that indicating quarantine]

have the frost v. [late 19C–1910s] to be unemployed. [FROST n.[1]]

have the grindstone on one's back v. [18C–19C] of a man, to fetch the nurse for one's wife's confinement.

have the heels of/on v. *see* GET THE HEELS ON v.

have the hots for v. [1940s+] (*orig. US*) **1** to desire, usu. sexually. **2** in fig. use, to want something. **3** to become enthusiastic, excited. [HOTS, THE n.]

have the inside track v. [mid-19C–1950s] to be privy to exclusive information; to be in an advantageous position. [1960s+ use is SE; note racing jargon *inside track*, the truth]

have the jump on (someone) v. *see* GET THE JUMP ON (SOMEONE) v.

have the laugh on v. (*also* **get the laugh on, have the laugh over**) [20C+] to outwit, to get the better of.

have the lid off v. [1910s] of a situation, to be out of control.

have the loan of v. *see* GET THE LOAN OF v.

have them v. *see* SEE THEM v.

have them bad v.[1] [late 19C–1910s] to be suffering from delirium tremens.

have them bad v.[2] *see* HAVE IT BAD v.

have the monkies v. [1910s] feelings of irritation. [MONKEY n.[7]]

have the morbs v. [late 19C] to feel depressed. [SE *morbid*]

have the needle v. (*also* **have the dead needle**) [20C+] to be very angry.

have the painters in v. [20C+] of a woman, to be menstruating. [euph.]

have the pants v. [late 19C–1900s] to be exhausted. [one *pants* when out of breath through exertion]

have the perpetual v. [late 19C–1900s] usu. of young men, to be vigorous, go-getting. [SE *perpetual motion*]

have the pot on v. [1960s] (*US prison*) to have (homosexual) sexual intercourse.

have the rabbits v. [late 19C+] (*Aus.*) to be exceptionally stupid. [the assumed stupidity of rabbits]

have the rag on v. **1** [1940s+] of a woman, to be menstruating.

2 [1960s+] to act foolishly or eccentrically, to be annoyed. [(1) JAM RAG n.]

have the Richard v. [1960s+] (*Aus.*) to be finished or exhausted, to be irreparably damaged. [theatrical rhy. sl.; *Richard III* = BIRD n.[5] (3)]

have the screaming uglies v. [1980s+] (*US campus*) to look very messy, bad. [SCREAMING adj. (3) + SE *ugly*]

have the shiners for v. *see* TAKE A SHINE TO v.

have the shits v. [1970s+] to be worried, frightened. [SHITS, THE n. (2)]

have the skids put under v. *see* PUT THE SKIDS TO v. (3).

have the slows v. **1** [mid-19C+] to suffer some form of imaginary disease to which one attributes lassitude, inactivity etc. **2** [1970s+] (*drugs*) to be very intoxicated, at which point life outside one's head seems to crawl by.

have the stick v. [1950s+] (*Aus.*) (*also* **have the sword**) to be finished, to be permanently damaged.

have the sun in one's eyes v. (*also* **have been in the sunshine**) [mid–late 19C] to be drunk (cf. ARSEHOLED adj.). [a euph. play on BLIND DRUNK adj.]

have the sweetest end of the stick v. [1970s] to be successful, living a satisfactory life (cf. FUZZY END OF THE LOLLIPOP n.).

have the sword v. *see* HAVE THE STICK v.

have the tiger by the tail v. **1** [20C+] to wade in, to take control of a situation even if it seems impossible. **2** [1900s–40s] to endure, to survive.

have the tom-tits v. *see* GET THE TOM-TITS v.

have the ups on v. [1940s] (*US Black*) to have an advantage over. [abbr. of SE *upper hand*]

have the wind up v. *see* GET THE WIND UP v.

have the woefuls v. [late 19C–1900s] to feel miserable or depressed.

have the wood on v. [1920s+] (*Aus./N.Z.*) to have the upper hand over, to hold at a disadvantage. [abbr. HAVE THE DEADWOOD (ON) v.]

have the worse end of the staff v. [mid-16C–19C] to be treated unfairly (cf. FUZZY END OF THE LOLLIPOP n.; GET HOLD OF THE WRONG END OF THE STICK v.; HAVE THE BETTER END OF THE STAFF v.).

have the wrong end of the stick v. *see* GET HOLD OF THE WRONG END OF THE STICK v.

have the wrong pig/sow by the ear v. *see* GET THE WRONG PIG BY THE EAR v.

have the X on v. [1920s] (*US*) to prove superior to, to place at a disadvantage. [note US carnival use *X*, the exclusive right to work a particular novelty or type of concession]

have tickets on v. [20C+] (*Aus.*) to be very fond of someone; thus *have tickets on oneself*, to be vain, to be conceited. [i.e. one would pay to see them/oneself]

have-to n. [1950s+] (*US*) anything inescapable, esp. something that is forced upon one by social convention; also as adj., thus *have-to wedding*, a wedding that is arranged after the putative bride is found to be pregnant. [SE *have to*]

have tongue enough for two sets of teeth v. [late 18C–mid-19C] to be overly talkative.

have to rights v. [mid-19C+] to settle with, to get even with, to conquer.

have toys in the attic v. *see* HAVE A GUEST IN THE ATTIC v.

have two hands alike v. [20C+] (*Irish*) to fail to pay one's way. [? neither is in one's pocket]

have two left shoes v. [1980s] (*US Black*) to be absolutely wrong.

have two penn'orth of rope v. [early 19C–1930s] to have this bare minimum of sleeping accommodation. [TWOPENNY ROPE n.]

have two shirts and a rag v. [late 17C–18C] to be reasonably well-off, to be comfortable.

have under one's belt v. **1** [early 19C] to have in one's stomach. **2** [1930s+] (orig. Aus.) to have to one's credit, to have stored away. [the image is of eating a good meal and storing energy]

have up v. [mid-18C+] to arrest, to put on trial.

have what it takes v. [1920s+] to possess the requisite characteristics, commodities, money etc.

have wheels (in one's head) v. [late 19C–1930s] (US) to be insane, eccentric. [fig. use of SE ride, e.g. an eccentric idea]

have whiskers on (it) v. [1920s+] of a thing, a situation, an idea etc, to be very old, very dated.

have wild hair v. see HAVE HAIR ON ONE'S CHEST v.

have wind in one's jaws v. [1950s–70s] (US Black) to be extremely annoyed.

have windmills in the head v. [early 17C–early 19C] to entertain crazy notions, to fantasize. [Don Quixote's 'tilting at windmills']

have women on one's dick v. (also **have a woman on one's dick**) [1980s+] (US) of a man, to be sexually successful. [DICK n.^{4} (1)]

havey cavey adj. (also **havy cavy**) [late 18C–early 19C] **1** higgledy-piggledy, confused, doubtful; thus on the havey-cavey, questioning, doubting. **2** drunken. [dial.]

havil n. [early 18C–mid-19C] (UK Und.) a sheep. [ety. unknown; dial. havil, a small crab]

Hawaii n. [1990s+] (also **Hawaiian**) £50. [TV series Hawaii Five-O]

Hawaiian n. [1970s+] (drugs) marijuana grown in and exported from Hawaii (cf. ACAPULCO (GOLD) n.).

Hawaiian disease n. [1980s+] **1** the lack of female company. **2** (gay) being homosexual, i.e. the lack of women. [(2) f. (1) but also Hawaii's large homosexual population]

Hawaiian eye n. [1970s+] (gay) the anus. [play on the eponymous 1960s television programme but note EYE sfx]

Hawaiian sunshine n. [1970s+] (drugs) LSD (cf. A n.^{3}).

Hawaiian time n. [1970s+] (US) flexible time, a general disregard for punctuality (cf. AFRICAN (PEOPLE'S) TIME n.). [racial stereotyping]

hawbuck n. [19C] a country bumpkin, a lout (cf. ACORN-CRACKER n.). [? SE haw, hedge + buck, a man]

Hawcubite n. (also **Hawkubite**) [early 18C] one of a band of dissolute young men infesting the streets of London at this period; a street-bully, a ruffian. [? SE hack about; but note Brewer, Dict. of Phrase and Fable (1894): 'The succession of these London pests after the Restoration was…The Muns, the Tityre-Tus, the Hectors, the Scourers, the Nickers, then the Hawkubites (1711–14), and then the Mohocks – most dreaded of all. (Hawkubite is the name of an Indian tribe of savages)']

haw-haw v. see HEE-HAW v.^{1}.

haw-haw toff n. (also **haw-haw, haw-haw fellow**) [mid-19C–1920s] a dandy, an aristocrat. [his 'haw-haw' laugh + TOFF n. (2)/SE fellow]

hawk n.^{1} **1** [late 17C–19C] a card-sharp, a confidence trickster. **2** [1970s+] (US) a robber or mugger. [HAWK v.^{1}; 'pouncing upon [their victims] mercilessly' (Bee)]

hawk n.^{2} **1** [late 18C+] a bailiff, a constable, a police officer; thus WARE (THE) HAWK! excl., a cry of warning. **2** [20C+] (US Black) a prison officer. **3** [1940s+] (US prison) one who looks out for the arrival of the authorities, e.g. a prison inmate, a carnival worker.

hawk n.^{3} [1940s+] (US Black) chilly winter winds, esp. as experienced in Northern cities; often as the hawk.

hawk n.^{4} [1960s–70s] (drugs) **1** LSD (cf. A n.^{3}). **2** an LSD user. **3** an LSD seller.

hawk n.^{5} [1960s+] **1** (US) a person (esp. one in public office, government or business) who advocates an aggressive policy. **2** (US) an older male homosexual with a preference for young boys. **3** (Irish) any person; often as QUEER HAWK n. **4** (S.Afr.) a 'masculine' male homosexual. **5** (US campus) an unattractive woman. **6** (US campus) a very hard worker. **7** (US gay) a lesbian who picks women up in the street.

hawk adj. [1960s+] politically aggressive; also fig. [HAWK n.^{5} (1)]

hawk v.^{1} [mid-19C–1900s] **1** to act as a decoy, esp. for a card-sharp or a cheapjack. **2** to pounce upon, to capture, esp. of a criminal seizing upon a victim.

hawk v.^{2} (also **hack**) **1** [late 17C+] (US Black) to keep a suspicious and close watch on. **2** [late 19C+] (US) to pilfer, to steal. **3** [1960s–70s] to walk quickly. **4** [1970s+] (UK Black) to greet, to speak to. **5** [1990s+] to stare someone down.

hawk v.^{3} [20C+] to irritate, to annoy. [var. on HACK v.^{2}]

hawk v.^{4} [1960s] (US campus) to work hard.

hawk v.^{5} [1960s+] (orig. US Black) to participate in an athletic activity for fun.

hawk and pigeon n. [late 19C] a sharper and his victim. [HAWK n.^{1} (1) + PIGEON n.^{1} (1)]

hawker n. [1970s+] (US) a gob of expectorated phlegm (cf. HOCKER n.; HONKER n.^{5}). [SE hawk, to spit, to cough up]

hawker v. [1970s+] (US) to cough up phlegm. [HAWKER n.]

Hawkesbury duck n. [1980s] (Aus.) little or nothing to eat. [SE Hawkesbury duck, an ear of maize or a corncob with the kernels intact, which road gang convicts used to steal from fields when hungry]

Hawkesbury rivers n. (also **Hawkesburies, Hawksbury rivers**) [1940s+] (Aus.) the cold shivers. [rhy. sl.]

hawkeye n.^{1} [mid-19C+] (US) a native or inhabitant of Iowa, popularly called the Hawkeye State.

hawkeye n.^{2} [1980s+] (Aus. prison) a prison officer.

hawkeye v. [1970s] (US Black) to keep watch.

Hawkins n.^{1} [late 19C–1900s] a severe disciplinarian. [the 'hanging judge' Sir Frederic Hawkins]

Hawkins n.^{2} (also **'Awkins**) [late 19C–1900s] a superior costermonger. [the line by music hall star Albert Chevalier (1862–1923): 'And 'Enery 'Awkins is a first-class name']

Hawkins n.^{3} (also **Mister Hawkins**) [1930s+] (US Black) very cold weather. [HAWK n.^{3}]

hawk it v. [late 19C+] to work as a street prostitute. [abbr. HAWK ONE'S FORK v.]

hawk off v. [late 19C] to carry away, to arrest. [16C–18C SE hawk after (for), to hunt after, to endeavour to catch]

hawk one's brawn v. [1970s+] **1** (Aus.) to work as a prostitute. **2** (UK Und.) to work as a male prostitute. [SE hawk, to sell + brawn, a form of potted pork]

hawk one's brown v. [1960s+] to work as a male prostitute. [SE hawk, to sell + BROWN n.^{3} (1)]

hawk one's brownie v. see BROWNIE n.^{4} (3).

hawk one's fork v. [1970s+] (Aus.) to work as a prostitute; the 'fork' is the juncture of the legs and thus the vagina. [SE hawk, to sell + fork, the crutch]

hawk one's greens v. [1930s] to work as a prostitute. [SE hawk, to sell + GREENS n.^{2}]

hawk one's mutton v. [mid-19C+] of either sex, to work as a prostitute. [SE hawk, to sell + MUTTON n.^{1} (3)]

hawk one's pearly v. [1970s+] to act in a promiscuous manner, to offer one's body for sexual enjoyment. [SE hawk, to sell + rhy. sl., pearly king = RING n.^{1} (1)]

hawks n. [mid-19C] an advantage.

Hawksbury rivers n. see HAWKESBURY RIVERS n.

hawkshaw n. [20C+] (US/W.I.) a detective. [Hawkshaw the Detective created by Henry Cecil Bullivant in such books as The Ticket-of-Leave Man (1935), itself taken f. The Ticket-of-Leave Man (1863), a play by the English dramatist Tom Taylor (1817–80); also in the comic strip Hawkshaw the Detective by the US cartoonist Gus Mager (d.1956)]

hawkshaw v. [1940s] to investigate, as a policeman or detective. [HAWKSHAW n.]

Hawkubite *n. see* HAWCUBITE *n.*

haw maws *n.* [1960s–70s] (*Scot.*) the testicles (cf. CHEESE AND CRACKERS *n.*). [rhy. sl. = *baws*, i.e. *balls*/BALLS *n.*[1] (1)]

hay *n.*[1] [20C+] a bed, also in the context of a place for sexual intercourse; thus *great in the hay*, an above-average sexual performer. [the use of hay for stuffing mattresses]

hay *n.*[2] [1920s+] **1** a small sum of money; usu. in phr. THAT AIN'T HAY phr. **2** in fig. use, something worthy of notice.

hay *n.*[3] [1930s+] **1** (*US*) tobacco; cigarettes. **2** (*US drugs*) marijuana (cf. AFRICAN BUSH *n.*). [note Kipling 'The Taking of Lungtungpen' (1880): "Tis no good [...] fillin' my pouch wid your chooped hay. Canteen baccy's like the Army. It shpoils a man's taste for moilder things']

Hay and Hell and Booligal *n.* (*also* Hay, Hell and Booligal) [late 19C+] (*Aus.*) a mythical place that is beyond all the bounds of civilization and devoid of any proper comforts. [*Booligal*, a town in western New South Wales]

haybag *n.* [mid-19C+] (*US*) a fat old woman, often a slovenly drunkard; thus ext. as *old haybag*. [US milit. jargon *haybag*, a camp-follower]

hayband *n.* [mid-19C] a second-rate cigar. [SE *hay*, the supposed content + the cigar-band]

hay burner *n.*[1] **1** [20C+] (*Aus./US*) a horse. **2** [1940s] (*US*) a Western film. [the animal's food]

hay burner *n.*[2] [1920s–40s] (*US*) a tobacco pipe.

hay burner *n.*[3] [1930s+] (*US*) a smoker of marijuana. [HAY *n.*[3] (2) + BURN *v.*[3] (1)]

hay butt *n.* [1940s+] (*drugs*) a marijuana cigarette. [HAY *n.*[3] (2) + BUTT *n.*[2] (2)]

hay eater *n.* [late 19C–1930s] (*US Black*) a White person. [? derog. ref. to White farmers]

hayfoot *n.* (*also* **strawfoot**) [late 19C–1950s] (*US*) a farmer; also as a term of derision, a peasant, a rustic (cf. ACORN-CRACKER *n.*).

hay-footed *adj.* [late 19C–1950s] (*US*) rustic, unsophisticated. [HAYFOOT *n.*]

hayhead *n.* [1940s–70s] (*US*) a smoker of marijuana. [HAY *n.*[3] (2) + -HEAD sfx (3)]

Hay, Hell and Booligal *n. see* HAY AND HELL AND BOOLIGAL *n.*

hay-kicker *n. see* HAYMAKER *n.*[2].

hay lee *n.* [1940s–50s] tea. [rhy. sl.]

haymaker *n.*[1] (*also* **old haymaker**) [mid-19C–1920s] (*US*) the sun. [its beneficial effect on crops]

haymaker *n.*[2] (*also* **hay-kicker**) [mid-19C–1950s] (*US*) a farmer. [his job]

haymaker *n.*[3] [20C+] a swinging, roundhouse punch, which counts more on energy and ire than on skill and direction. [the image of a man swinging a scythe to cut hay]

Haymarket hector *n.* [mid-17C–19C] a pimp (cf. ABBOT ON THE CROSS *n.*). [proper name *Haymarket*, the centre of contemporary London prostitution + HECTOR *n.*[1]]

Haymarket ware *n.* [late 19C] prostitutes in general. [London's Haymarket, a centre of 19C prostitution]

hayneck *n. see* HAYSEED *n.*

haypile *n.* [1900s–30s] (*US*) a bed or mattress. [HAY *n.*[1]]

hay-pitcher *n.* [late 19C–1940s] (*US*) a farmer, a peasant (cf. ACORN-CRACKER *n.*).

hay-pounder *n.* (*also* **hay-shagger/-shaker**) [20C+] (*Aus./N.Z./US*) a farmer, a simple peasant (cf. ACORN-CRACKER *n.*).

hay rube *n. see* RUBE *n.*[1].

Hays! *excl.* [mid-19C] used as a warning among thieves, to cut and run. [*Hays*, the name of a High Constable at the time]

hayseed *n.* (*also* **appleseed**, **grass-seed**, **hayneck**, **hayseeder**) [mid-19C+] (*Aus./N.Z./UK/US*) a farmer, a simple peasant, a novice (cf. BUCKWHEAT *n.*). [naut. phr. *he hasn't got the hayseed out of his hair*]

hayseed *adj.* (*also* **hayseedy**) [mid-19C+] (*Aus./US*) rustic, unsophisticated. [HAYSEED *n.*]

hay-shagger/-shaker *n. see* HAY-POUNDER *n.*

haystack *n.* [20C+] the *back* of a building etc. [rhy. sl.]

haystack agreement *n.* [1920s+] (*US*) a secret agreement or understanding. [the participants fig. retiring behind a haystack to converse in secret]

haystack game *n.* [1900s] (*US Und.*) a card-game played on an unsophisticated level.

haystack kid *n.* [1960s] (*US*) an illegitimate child. [such a child is conceived in a haystack]

haytie twaity *adj. see* HOITY-TOITY *adj.* (1).

hay-tosser *n.* [1900s–10s] (*US*) a farmer.

haywire *adj.* [1920s+] **1** (*orig. US*) obsessed, crazy, out of control; usu. as *go haywire*, to lose control, to go mad. **2** (*US*) out of order, impaired, ruined. [(1) SE *hay wire*, which flails around when cut; (2) the baling wire used by US farmers to mend malfunctioning implements]

hazard-drum *n.* [mid-19C] a casino, a gambling house. [SE *hazard*, a gambling game + DRUM *n.*[3] (7)]

haze *n.* **1** [1970s+] (*drugs*) LSD (cf. A *n.*[3]). **2** [1990s+] (*drugs*) a kind of marijuana (cf. BOMB *n.*[4]). [abbr. PURPLE HAZE *n.* (1) + its effect]

hazel *n.* (*also* **Aunt Hazel**, **witch hazel**) [1930s–50s] (*drugs*) heroin (cf. BIG H *n.*; BLACK *n.*[3]). [the shared initial *H* + the hazel-brown colour of some heroin; note also WITCH, THE *n.*]

hazeler *n.* [20C+] (*Irish*) a countryman. [the *hazel* rods used to drive cattle]

hazel-gild *v.* (*also* **hazel-geld**) [late 17C–early 19C] to beat with a hazel rod. [B.E. has sp. *hazel-geld*, but this may be a printer's error]

hazel oil *n.* (*also* **oil of hazel**) [late 17C–19C] a beating; often as *anoint with oil of hazel*, to beat. [a variety of sap supposedly contained in a green hazel rod, which adds vigour to a beating]

hazy *adj.* **1** [early 19C–1910s] tipsy, drunk (cf. ADDLED *adj.*). **2** [1950s] under the influence of a drug.

h.b. *n. see* HIGHBALL *n.*[1].

h.b.i. *n.* [mid-19C+] (*UK Und.*) house breaking implements. [abbr.]

H caps *n.* [1960s+] (*drugs*) heroin (cf. BIG H *n.*). [H *n.*[2] (1) + CAP *n.*[4] (1)]

h.c.l. *phr.* [1910s+] (*US*) high cost of living. [abbr.]

h.d. *n.* [1980s+] (*US campus*) a man who lives off a woman. [abbr. *husband dependent*]

he *n.* (*also* **him**) **1** [17C+] the penis. **2** [1960s] (*US gay*) used by lesbians in the same way as male homosexuals refer to each other as 'she'. [the dating is almost random, as E.P. says, this personification is 'prob. almost immemorial']

Heab *n. see* HEBE *n.*

head *n.*[1] [19C+] a lavatory, a privy. [naut. jargon *head* or *heads*, the ship's lavatory, which was orig. sited at the 'head' of a ship, near the bowsprit]

head *n.*[2] **1** [mid-19C; 1950s+] (*orig. US drugs*) a regular user of any kind of drug; orig. of alcohol. **2** [1930s+] a user, a performer. **3** [1950s+] a drug-induced state. **4** [1960s+] a state of mind, other than drug-influenced. **5** [1980s+] (*Aus. prison*) high-grade marijuana. [nominalization of -HEAD sfx (3)]

head *n.*[3] [mid-19C–1920s] a postage stamp. [the monarch's head appears on UK stamps]

head *n.*[4] [mid-19C+] (*US*) the mouth, as source of offensive language; only in combs., e.g. RUN ONE'S HEAD *v.*; SHOOT ONE'S HEAD OFF *v.*; SHUT ONE'S HEAD *v.* [metonymy]

head *n.*[5] **1** [late 19C+] a hangover, e.g. *I've got an awful head this morning*. **2** [1940s] a sickness resulting from contaminated homemade alcohol. [abbr. SE *headache*]

head *n.*[6] (*orig. Aus.*) **1** [late 19C+] a professional gambler. **2** [20C+] a long-term prisoner. [? HARDHEAD *n.*[2] (3)]

head *n.*[7] **1** [20C+] the end of the penis. **2** [1950s+] (*US*) the erect penis.

head *n.*[8] [1920s–30s] (*US Und.*) an illegal immigrant. [? such immigrants were counted as 'heads']

head n.[9] (*US*) **1** [1930s+] a young woman. **2** [1970s+] a sexually appealing young woman.

head n.[10] (*also* **head play**) [1930s+] oral intercourse, usu. fellatio, but also cunnilingus; usu. as GIVE HEAD v. (1) or GET HEAD v. (cf. BRAIN n.[2]; FACE n.[2]). [note synon. RMC Duntroon (*Aus.*) *head job, heady*]

head n.[11] **1** [1930s+] (*US*) a person. **2** [1980s+] (*US Black*) a White person, seen as a potential victim of street crime. **3** [1990s+] (*Irish*) a form of address, e.g. *Howaya head*? [ext. of HEAD n.[2]]

head n.[12] [1960s+] (*US*) facial appearance; usu. constructed with 'bad', e.g. *she's got great tits, but that's a bad head.*

head n.[13] [1970s+] (*US campus*) beer.

head n.[14] [1980s] (*US Black*) a belligerent, aggressive person. [abbr. HARDHEAD n.[2]]

head v.[1] [late 19C+] (*Aus.*) **1** to play the game of two-up. **2** to throw 'heads' in a game of two-up. [the betting on 'heads or tails']

head v.[2] [1980s+] to fellate (cf. BRAIN n.[2]). [HEAD n.[10]]

head *sfx* **1** [16C+] in a variety of combs. in which *-head* is linked to a n. to create a term meaning fool or idiot; the implication is that the head is shaped like or otherwise resembles the n.; also less frequently used with an adj. (cf. AIRHEAD n.; APEHEAD n.; APPLEHEAD n.; ASSHEAD n.; BALLOON-HEAD n.; BANANAHEAD n.; BAPHEAD n.; BEAN-HEAD n.; BEEF-HEAD n.; BEETLE-HEAD n.; BLOCKHEAD n.[1]; BLUBBER-HEAD n.; BLUNDERHEAD n.; BOMBHEAD n.[1]; BONEHEAD n.[1]; BOOFHEAD n.; BOTTLEHEAD n.; BOWHEAD n.; BOXHEAD n.; BRASS-HEAD n.; BUBBLEHEAD n.; BUCKETHEAD n.; BUFFLEHEAD n.; BULLET-HEAD n.; BULL-HEAD n.[1]; BURRHEAD n.; BUSH-HEAD n.[2]; BUTTERHEAD n.; BUTTHEAD n.; CABBAGE-HEAD n.; CEMENT-HEAD n.; CHEESEHEAD n.; CHICKENHEAD n.[1]; CHOWDER-HEAD n.; CHUCKLEHEAD n.; CHUGGERHEAD n.; CLOTH-HEAD n.; CLUCKHEAD n.[1]; CLUNKHEAD n.; COCKHEAD n.; COCONUT HEAD n.[2]; CORKHEAD n.; COTTONHEAD n.; CRACKHEAD n.; CRAPHEAD n.; CRAZYHEAD n.; CRUDHEAD n.; CUNTHEAD n.; DACEHEAD n.; DEADHEAD n.[1]; DICKHEAD n.; DIDDLEHEAD n.; DIPHEAD n.; DOPEHEAD n.[2]; DORKHEAD n.; DOSSHEAD n.; DOUGH-HEAD n.; DOUGHNUT-HEAD n.; DUDHEAD n.; DULLHEAD n.; DUMBHEAD n.; DUNCEHEAD n.; DUNDERHEAD n.; DUNGEON HEAD n.; EGGHEAD n.[1]; FART-HEAD n.; FAT-HEAD n.; FEATHERHEAD n.; FENDERHEAD n.; FOOLHEAD n.; FUCKHEAD n.; GELLYHEAD n.; GOOBERHEAD n.; GOONHEAD n.; GOOSEHEAD n.; GOURD-HEAD n.; GROUTHEAD n.; GUMBYHEAD n.; HAMHEAD n.; HAMMERHEAD n.[1]; HARDHEAD n.[2]; HOLLOWHEAD n.; HOSEHEAD n.; HULVERHEAD n.; IRONHEAD n.[1]; JARHEAD n.[1]; JERKHEAD n.; JOLTERHEAD n.; JUGHEAD n.[1]; KNOTHEAD n.; LAMEHEAD n.; LARDHEAD n.; LEADHEAD n.; LEATHERHEAD n.[1]; LIGHT-HEAD n.[1]; LOGGERHEAD n.; LUGHEAD n.; LUMPHEAD n.; LUNKHEAD n.; MALLETHEAD n.; MARBLEHEAD n.[2]; MEATHEAD n.; MELONHEAD n.; MOLLYHEAD n.; MOTORHEAD n.; MUDDLE-HEAD n.; MUD-HEAD n.[2]; MUFFIN-HEAD n.; MULLETHEAD n.; MUMMYHEAD n.; MUSCLEHEAD n.; MUSH-HEAD n.; MUTTHEAD n.; MUTTON-HEAD n.; NAILHEAD n.[1]; NIBHEAD n.; NIT-HEAD n.; NOODLEHEAD n.; NODDY HEAD n.; NUMBHEAD n.; NUTHEAD n.; NYAAMS HEAD n.; ONIONHEAD n.[1]; PECKERHEAD n.; PESTLEHEAD n.; PIGHEAD n.; PINHEAD n.[2]; PISS-HEAD n.[2]; POINTY-HEAD n.; POO-HEAD n.; POOPHEAD n.; POTATO-HEAD n.; POTHEAD n.[1]; PRAWNHEAD n.; PRICKHEAD n.; PROPELLER HEAD n.; PUDDING-HEAD n.; PUMPKIN HEAD n.; PUPPET-HEAD n.; PUTTY-HEAD n.; ROCK-HEAD n.[1]; RUBBLEHEAD n.; SAP-HEAD n.; SAPPYHEAD n.; SCUMHEAD n.; SHITHEAD n.; SHOVELHEAD n.; SHREWD-HEAD n.; SMEGHEAD n.; SOTHEAD n.; SPACKAHEAD n.; SPLAY HEAD n.; SPUNK-HEAD n.; SQUAREHEAD n.[1]; STUPE-HEAD n.; STUPID-HEAD n.; TACKHEAD n.; THICKHEAD n.; TIMBER-HEAD n.; TOOLHEAD n.; WEATHERHEAD n.; WETHEAD n.). **2** [mid-19C+] (*US derog.*) a person of a specific (and alien) ethnic origin (cf. BUDDHAHEAD n.; CABBAGE-HEAD n.; CHILE-HEAD n.; HANDKERCHIEF-HEAD n.[2]; HANKIE-HEAD n.; MARBLEHEAD n.[1]; POPEHEAD n.; RAG-HEAD n.[1]; TACO-HEAD n.; TOWEL-HEAD n.). **3** [20C+] a habitual user of a drug or a particular drink (cf. ACID-HEAD n.; A-HEAD n.; BASE-HEAD n.; BEERHEAD n.; BLOCKHEAD n.[2]; BOOZE-HEAD n.; BOTTLEHEAD n.;

BUDHEAD n.; CLUCKHEAD n.[2]; COKEHEAD n.; CRACKHEAD n.; CUBEHEAD n.; DOPEHEAD n.[2]; DOWN-HEAD n.; DRUGHEAD n.; GARBAGE HEAD n.; GINHEAD n.; GOWHEAD n.; HASH-HEAD n.; HAYHEAD n.; HEAT-HEAD n.; HIT-HEAD n.; HOPHEAD n.[1]; HORSE-HEAD n.; JAKEHEAD n.; JARHEAD n.[2]; JICKHEAD n.; JUGHEAD n.[2]; JUICE-HEAD n.; JUNKHEAD n.; LIQUORHEAD n.; LUSH-HEAD n.; METH-HEAD n.; MUGGLEHEAD n.; PILL-HEAD n.; PIPE-HEAD n.; PISS-HEAD n.[1]; POTHEAD n.[2]; SMACK-HEAD n.; TEA-HEAD n.; WEEDHEAD n.; WHISKYHEAD n.). **4** [1950s+] a fan or devotee of a particular thing, e.g. a certain type of music (cf. BREADHEAD n.; CHIPHEAD n.; GRAF-HEAD n.; GEARHEAD n.; HAIRHEAD n.; METALHEAD n.; PETROL-HEAD n.).

headache n. **1** [1920s+] (*orig. US*) a problem, a cause of anxiety, a worry. **2** [1930s] (*US*) one's wife or girlfriend.

headache man n. [1940s–50s] (*US drugs*) a federal narcotics agent.

head-acher n. [mid-19C] in boxing, a blow to the head.

headache stick n. [1910s–70s] (*US Black*) a stick used as a club, a policeman's baton or truncheon.

head and heels n. [1970s] (*US gay*) a young, inexperienced homosexual. [one has to lift the boy by his *head and heels* to position him for sex]

head artist n. [1970s] (*US*) a fellator or fellatrix. [HEAD n.[10] + SE *artist*]

headbang v. [1970s+] to shake one's head violently when watching or listening to heavy metal music; thus *headbanging music.*

headbanger n.[1] **1** [1960s+] a psychotic person, a randomly and obsessively violent person, someone who cannot control their temper. **2** [2000s] in weak use, a 'crazy' person, often affectionate.

headbanger n.[2] [1970s+] in the music business, a fan of loud, monotonous, 'heavy metal music'; usu. a youth who plays a make-believe (or even cardboard) guitar and shakes his head violently as he watches or listens to his heroes. [HEADBANG v.]

headbanging adj. [1990s+] psychotic, emotionally unstable. [HEADBANGER n.[1] (1)]

headbeater n. (*also* **headbreaker, headbuster**) **1** [1950s+] (*US Black*) a brutal police officer. **2** [1980s+] (*US*) a thug who works for a ruthless criminal.

headbeating adj. (*also* **headbusting**) [1950s–70s] of police officers, brutal, in full strength.

head-beetler n. [mid–late 19C] **1** 'the bully of the workshop, who lords it over his fellow-workmen by reason of superior strength, skill in fighting &c' (Hotten, 1864). **2** a foreman, not a derog. term. [SE *beetle*, any implement used in a variety of industrial processes for crushing, bruising, beating, flattening or smoothing]

headbin n. [20C+] (*Ulster*) an unstable person, an eccentric. [var. on HEADCASE n.]

headbone n. [1930s+] (*US Black*) the skull.

headbreaker n. see HEADBEATER n.

head buck-cat n. [1960s–70s] (*Irish*) a person in authority. [Irish *buc*, he-goat]

head bully of the pass n. (*also* **head bully of the passage bank, head cully of the pass/the passage bank**) [late 17C– early 19C] a gang boss or top criminal who levies a tax on all games of chance in the area of which he is in control. [BULLY n.[1] (2)/CULLY n. (3) + PASS-BANK n.]

head bummaroo n. (*also* **head bummer**) [mid-19C–1940s] the chief, the person in charge. [? BUMPER n.[1] (2)]

headbuster n. see HEADBEATER n.

headbusting adj. see HEADBEATING adj.

head-candler n. [1950s–60s] (*US*) a psychotherapist; thus *head-candling,* psychotherapy. [SE *head + candle,* to test an egg for freshness]

headcase n. [1950s+] **1** an eccentric, bizarre person. **2** someone undergoing, or in need of, psychiatric treatment. **3** a violent person, a psychotic person. **4** a state of psychosis. **5** a clever person, or one who believes themselves to be so. [SE *head* + CASE n.[7]]

headcheese n.[1] [20C+] an important, powerful influential person. [SE *head* + BIG CHEESE n.]

headcheese n.[2] [1940s+] smegma. [CHEESE n.[2] (1); its odour and its appearance near the *head* of the penis]

headcheese n.[3] [1950s+] (*US Black*) pork luncheon meat. [SE *headcheese*, brawn]

head-chick n. [1930s–40s] (*US Black*) a female lover, a favourite girlfriend, one's wife, esp. an expert fellatrix. [SE *head*, chief/HEAD n.[10] + CHICK n.[4] (2)]

head cook and bottle-washer n. *see* CHIEF COOK AND BOTTLE-WASHER n.

head cully of the pass/the passage bank n. *see* HEAD BULLY OF THE PASS n.

head devil n. [mid-19C–1910s] (*US*) the boss.

head doctor n. **1** [1950s+] (*US*) a psychiatrist, a psychotherapist. **2** [2000s] (*drugs*) a drug dealer.

head drugs n. [1960s+] (*drugs*) amphetamines (cf. A n.[2]). [they affect the head (although so do all drugs)]

header n.[1] **1** [early 19C] a blow to the head. **2** [mid-late 19C] in fig. use of (3), a bet, usu. spontaneous and unthought-out. **3** [mid-19C+] a head-first dive, usu. into water. **4** [1990s+] one who jumps, usu. for the purposes of suicide, off a high building, bridge etc.

header n.[2] [1960s+] (*Irish*) a psychotic, an unstable or bizarre person.

header n.[3] [1970s+] (*US*) an act of oral copulation. [HEAD n.[10]]

head-feeler n. [1940s] (*US*) a psychotherapist.

headfuck n. [1990s+] **1** a severe depression or that which causes it. **2** the extreme effects of a drug, usu. strong cannabis. **3** something that causes problems, a worry. [HEADFUCK v.]

headfuck adj. [2000s] pertaining to a depression. [HEADFUCK n.]

headfuck v. [1970s+] (*orig. US*) to confuse, to mislead, to disorientate. [SE *head* + FUCK v.[2] (3)]

headfucker n. [1970s+] (*drugs*) a particularly powerful drug, esp. a hallucinogen. [HEADFUCK v.]

head game n. [1970s+] (*orig. US*) psychological trickery and manipulation, usu. hostile or negative in intent; usu. in pl.

head gasket n. [1960s+] (*US*) a condom. [HEAD n.[7] + SE *gasket*]

head hen n. [1930s–50s] (*US Black*) a landlady.

head hunt v. [1920s+] (*US Black*) to look for trouble, to start a fight.

head hunter n.[1] **1** [1920s] (*US*) a person who tracks down wanted criminals. **2** [1960s+] (*US*) a policeman who reports on another policeman. **3** [1980s+] (*Aus. Und.*) a criminal who specializes on preying on other, successful and thus wealthy criminals. **4** [1980s+] (*US*) an aggressively selfish and single-minded individual.

head hunter n.[2] [1970s+] (*US*) one who performs oral sex, esp. in exchange for drugs. [HEAD n.[10] + SE *hunter*]

headie n. [1940s+] (*Aus.*) in the game of two-up, a bettor who favours 'heads' (cf. TAILIE n.).

heading n. [1940s–50s] using the top of the head to butt someone in a fight.

head job n. (*also* **hat job**) [1960s+] (*orig. US*) an act of oral intercourse, usu. fellatio (cf. BRAIN n.[2]). [HEAD n.[10] + JOB n.[4]; SE *hat* plays on the idea of the mouth 'putting a hat' on the penis]

head jockey n. [1950s+] a man who performs cunnilingus. [HEAD n.[10] + SE *jockey*]

headkicker n. [1990s+] (*Aus.*) a person in authority who is aggressive.

head knock n. [1940s–50s] (*US Black*) **1** God, Jesus. **2** an important, outstanding person. [the image of the deity 'knocking' and summoning one to heaven/hell]

head knocker n. (*US*) **1** [late 19C+] a boss, a manager. **2** [1960s+] a thug, a violent person. **3** [1960s+] a brutal policeman (cf. BEAT-POUNDER n.).

head-knocking adj. [1960s+] (*US*) violent.

headlamps n.[1] **1** [mid-late 19C] the eyes. **2** [1950s+] (*US*) spectacles.

headlamps n.[2] [1960s+] the female breasts.

head lar n. [20C+] (*Irish*) the man in charge. [SE *head* + LAIR n.]

headlight n.[1] **1** [late 19C–1950s] a large and ostentatious tiepin, usu. a diamond one. **2** [1910s–40s] a large diamond ring.

headlight n.[2] [1930s+] (*US*) a light-skinned Black person. [the golden colour]

headlight v. [late 19C+] (*US*) to focus one's eyes on. [HEADLIGHTS n. (1)]

headlights n. **1** [late 19C+] (*US*) the eyes. **2** [late 19C+] (*orig. US*) a precious stone, usu. a diamond. **3** [20C+] (*also* **searchlights**) the female breasts, esp. when prominent and well shaped. **4** [20C+] (*Aus./US*) spectacles, glasses, esp. tinted or dark glasses. **5** [1920s–40s] (*US*) eggs. [supposed resemblance]

headliner n. [20C+] (*orig. US*) esp. in show business, an important, powerful, influential person.

head nigger in charge n. (*also* **big nigger in charge, black nigger in charge, boss nigger in charge, nigger in charge**) [1960s+] (*US Black*) a sarcastic ref. to any Black authority figure. [the implication being that, given institutional racism, the authority lies in the title not in the actual job. According to Darryl Pinckney (*New York Review of Books*, December 1995), the phr. was coined for the authoritarian Black rights campaigner Booker T. Washington (1856–1915)]

head off at the pass v. *see* CUT OFF AT THE PASS v.

head over teakettle phr. (*also* **head over tincup/tinkettle**) [1940s+] head-over-heels.

head over turkey phr. (*also* **head over tuck**) [20C+] (*Aus./N.Z.*) head-over-heels. [SE *head* + *turkey*, the plucked bird here seen as resembling the shape of the buttocks]

head-peeper n. [1980s] (*US*) a psychotherapist. [SE *head* + *peep*, to look]

head-piece n. **1** [late 16C+] the head, the mind. **2** [early 18C] a cuckold's horns. **3** [late 19C–1900s] (*US tramp*) a hat. **4** [20C+] (*Irish*) an intelligent person; thus *have the head-piece on one*, to be intelligent.

head play n. *see* HEAD n.[10].

headquarters n. [1920s–50s] (*US Black*) a person with a particularly prominent skull. [pun]

head queen n. [1940s–70s] (*US gay*) a male homosexual who frequents public toilets in search of sex. [HEAD n.[10] + QUEEN n.[2] (1)/QUEEN sfx (2)]

head rails n. (*also* **muzzle rails, nob rails**) [mid-18C–1930s] the teeth. [Grose (1785) cites it as a 'sea phrase']

head robber n.[1] [mid-late 19C] a boxer, a prize-fighter. [he 'takes your head off']

head robber n.[2] [mid-late 19C] a butler. [SE *head*, chief + *robber*; used by those with a low opinion of servants]

heads n.[1] [1990s+] (*US Black*) one's children.

heads n.[2] [1990s+] (*Aus. drugs*) marijuana. [the *heads* of the marijuana plants]

heads and tails n. **1** [late 18C–1950s] (*Aus.*) the act of SIXTY-NINE n. (1). **2** [late 19C+] for 2 people to sleep in the same single bed lying in the opposite direction to each other.

head-serag n. (*also* **head-serang**) [mid-19C–1900s] (*Anglo-Ind.*) a (Bengali) overseer, a foreman. [Pers. *sarhang*, a commander, an overseer]

head-set n. [1970s+] (*US*) a state of mind, a mood. [var. on SE *mind-set*]

head shop n.[1] [1960s+] (*orig. US*) a shop specializing in drug paraphernalia. [HEAD n.[2] + SE *shop*. The first such emporium was San Francisco's Psychedelic Shop, opened in January 1966]

head shop n.[2] [1980s] (*US*) a pornographic bookshop. [HEAD n.[10] + SE *shop*]

headshot n. [1990s+] (*US Black/teen*) **1** a shot to the head from any firearm. **2** in rap music, freestyle rapping.

head-shrinker n. (*also* **headshrink**) [1950s+] (*orig. US*) a psychoanalyst, a psychotherapist, a psychiatrist; thus *head-shrinking*, psychoanalysis, psychotherapy.

head smack n. [1960s+] (*US*) a dose of morphine or heroin inhaled through the nose. [SE *head* + SMACK n.[6] (1), playing on SMACK n.[1] (3)]

head smack v. [1960s+] (*US*) to inhale heroin through the nose. [HEAD SMACK n.]

headsman's daughter n. [early 19C] the guillotine.

head space n. [1990s+] (*US*) a state of mind, a mood.

headsplitter n. [mid-19C+] (*US*) strong whisky, esp. when illegally distilled.

headstaggers n. [20C+] (*Irish*) mental illness or instability. [SE *head* + *staggers*, a disease of horses and sheep]

heads up n. [1990s+] **1** information, facts. **2** (*US Black*) a greeting.

heads-up adj. [1930s+] (*US*) **1** alert and skilful, esp. in sport. **2** of a fight, one-on-one; thus open, honest.

heads up phr. [1930s] (*US*) **1** honestly. **2** used to indicate affirmation. [HEADS UP! excl.]

heads up! excl. [1910s+] **1** a shout by lookouts for illegal street traders or street gamblers to warn of an approaching policeman. **2** a warning.

head-the-ball n. [1990s+] (*Irish/Scot./Welsh*) **1** a fool. **2** a usu. derog. term of address. **3** a violent psychotic. [the image of one who has headed the ball so often that their brains are scrambled]

head-to-head n. [1980s+] (*US*) a private conversation.

head-to-head phr. [1970s+] at close-quarters.

head-top n. [1970s–80s] (*UK Black*) the hair.

head-topper n. [mid–late 19C] a wig.

head trip n. (*also* **h.t.**) **1** [1960s+] (*orig. US drugs*) a drug-induced fantasy, reverie. **2** [1970s+] (*US*) something requiring challenging thought. **3** [1980s+] (*US*) deception or flattery. [SE *head* + TRIP n.[4]/TRIP n.[5] (1)]

head trip v. [1960s+] (*orig. US*) **1** to daydream, usu. under the influence of drugs. **2** to confuse, to deceive. [HEAD TRIP n.]

head-tripper n. **1** [1970s+] (*US*) a psychotherapist. **2** [1990s+] a day-dreamer. [HEAD TRIP v.]

head up v. [1980s+] (*US Black gang*) to start a fight. [HEAD-UP adv.]

head-up adv. [1980s+] in direct confrontation.

headwhipper n. [1950s+] (*US Black*) a police officer.

headwing n. [1900s] (*Aus.*) an ear.

head-worker n. [1910s+] (*US gay*) a fellator. [HEAD n.[10] + SE *worker*]

headwrecker n. (*also* **headwreck**) [1990s+] something, or someone, which causes a great deal of anxiety or unhappiness.

heady adj.[1] [mid-19C–1910s] drunk. [SE *heady*, intoxicating, stupefying]

heady adj.[2] [20C+] **1** (*mainly Aus./N.Z.*) ingenious, shrewd. **2** (*US*) arrogant, opinionated. [the contents of one's head]

Healtheries, the n. [late 19C] the Health Exhibition, held in London in 1884.

heap n.[1] [17C+] a large amount, often of money. [SE *heap*, a pile; note also the earlier SE *heap*, a great company of people]

heap n.[2] **1** [early 19C+] a woman; usu. with some derog. adj., e.g. *lazy heap, fat heap*. **2** [1920s+] a man. **3** [1920s+] (*orig. US*) an old or unreliable vehicle. **4** [1940s+] (*US*) an old aeroplane. [abbr. *heap of scrap, heap of junk*; (2) note HEAP OF COKE n.]

heap n.[3] [1950s–60s] (*Aus./US Und.*) a large prison.

heap adv. (*also* **a heap**) [mid-19C+] (*orig. US*) very, much. [supposedly a representation of the speech of Native Americans]

heap-clouting n. [1950s+] (*US Und.*) stealing automobiles. [HEAP n.[2] (3) + CLOUT v.[2] (1)]

heaped adj. [17C] involved in sexual intercourse. [SE *heap*, to pile on top]

heap of coke n. (*also* **heapy**) [mid-19C+] (*US*) a man. [rhy. sl. = BLOKE n.]

heaps n. [late 16C+] a large quantity, many, an abundance.

heap sight n. [late 19C–1910s] (*US*) a great deal.

heapy n. see HEAP OF COKE n.

hear v. [1930s+] (*US*) to understand, to agree with someone completely; often as I HEAR YOU phr. [SE *hear*, with an implication, the product of drugs/New Age philosophizing, of a deeper understanding than the pure SE implies]

hear a bird sing v. [late 16C–early 17C] to discover a secret.

hearing cheats n. [mid-16C–mid-19C] (*UK Und.*) the ears. [SE *hearing* + CHEAT n. (1)]

hear it on the street v. [20C+] to pick up a rumour, to hear the latest gossip.

hearse n.[1] (*US*) **1** [late 19C] a police patrol wagon. **2** [20C+] an ambulance. **3** [20C+] a large automobile.

hearse n.[2] (*also* **hearse-driver**) [late 19C] (*US*) a pessimistic person. [the popular image of undertakers]

hearse-chaser n. [1930s–50s] (*US Und.*) one who preys on the relatives of newly deceased people, esp. by claiming there are outstanding bills to be paid.

hearsed adj. [1990s+] (*US Black*) killed.

hearse-driver n. see HEARSE n.[2].

hearseman n. [1930s] (*US prison*) a convicted murderer.

hear someone's horn v. [1940s+] (*US*) to hear and acknowledge the importance of what someone is saying.

hear something knock v. [mid-19C] to take a hint.

heart n. [1930s+] (*orig. US Und.*) courage, bravery, spirit. [metonymy]

heart adv. [1900s] (*Ulster*) very, extremely.

heart and dart n. [mid-19C–1920s] a fart. [rhy. sl.]

heart and lung n. (*also* **liver and lung**) [1920s–30s] (*US*) the tongue. [rhy. sl.]

heartbalm n. [1920s–30s] (*US*) alimony. [cynical use of SE *heart-balm*, that which soothes a person's emotions]

heartbeat n. [1930s] (*US campus*) a love- or sex-object, a HEART-THROB n.

heartbreaker n. [mid-17C–19C] a curled love-lock. [its supposed effect on the opposite sex]

heartbreak hotel n. [1980s+] (*US*) a prison (cf. BOARDING HOUSE n.). [suggested by 1956 song 'Heartbreak Hotel' by Elvis Presley]

heartburn n. [late 19C–1920s] a bad cigar. [its effects]

heart check n. [2000s] (*US prison*) the act of giving a member of a prison gang a mission, such as a murder, to test his loyalty. [HEART n. + SE *check*]

hearthrug n. [1910s+] **1** a fool, a simpleton (cf. BEECHAM'S PILL n.). **2** a drinking mug. **3** a bedbug. [rhy. sl.; (1) = MUG n.[2] (1)]

hearthrug pie n. [1950s+] sexual intercourse on the sitting-room floor. [SE *hearthrug* + PIE n.[1] (1)]

hearthstone n. [late 19C–1900s] butter, as spread on a thick slice of bread (cf. DOORSTEP n.).

heart of oak adj. (*also* **hearts of oak**) [20C+] out of funds, impoverished. [rhy. sl. = BROKE adj.[1]; ult. *Hearts of Oak* Benefit Society]

heart of the roul n. (*also* **heart of the rowl**) [1940s+] (*Irish*) the best person. [? Scot. *rail, raul*, a line; ? corruption of SE *royal*; ? the brand of tobacco called Irish Roll, the centre being the freshest, manufactured by Messrs. T.P. & R. Goodbody, Co. Offaly, in 1843]

heart-on n. [1980s+] (*drugs*) an inhalant. [play on HARD-ON n. (1) + the stimulating effect on the heart]

hearts n. [1960s–70s] (*drugs*) amphetamine; Dexedrine (cf. A n.[2]). [abbr. PURPLE HEARTS n.]

hearts-and-flowers n. [1930s+] (*orig. US*) mawkish sentimentality. [? the sentimental tune 'Hearts and Flowers' played by the pianists accompanying silent movies]

heartsease *n.* [mid-17C–early 19C] **1** a 20-shilling piece. **2** a measure of gin. [both 'ease the heart' in their separate ways]

hearts of oak *adj. see* HEART OF OAK *adj.*

heart-starter *n.* [1960s+] (*Aus.*) the first alcoholic drink of the day.

heart-throb *n.* (*also* **throb**) [1910s+] someone (of either sex) who thrills the heart, a lover; esp. used of film stars and other entertainers.

heart-to-heart *n.* [1910s+] (*orig. US*) an intimate talk. [HEART-TO-HEART *adj.*]

heart-to-heart *adj.* [late 19C+] intimate.

hearty *n.* [mid-19C–1910s] strong drink.

hearty *adj.* [mid-19C–1910s] drunk (cf. ABOUT RIGHT *phr.*[1]). [HEARTY *n.*]

heat *n.*[1] (*US*) **1** [17C–18C; 1920s–60s] sex appeal, pornography; thus *give the heat*, to make sexual advances. **2** [1980s+] popularity. **3** [1980s+] anger, excitement. **4** [1990s+] excessive emotion, e.g. enthusiasm, terror. [(1) HOT *adj.*[1] (1); note Shakespearian *heat*, sexual or amatory enthusiasm; ? (2) f. (1); (3) HOT *adj.*[1] (12); (4) HOT *adj.*[1] (5)]

heat *n.*[2] **1** [1900s–60s] (*US*) drunkenness. **2** [1900s–60s] (*US*) a drink. **3** [1920s–70s] (*US tramp*) the crude alcohol that is drunk in solution as a substitute for alcohol. **4** [1950s] an intoxication from drugs; usu. as *have a heat on.* **5** [1970s+] (*drugs*) the heating of powdered heroin before smoking it. **6** [1990s+] electricity.

heat *n.*[3] **1** [1920s+] (*orig. US Und.*) intense police activity of any kind; pressure, esp. on criminals from the police. **2** [1920s+] pressure, irrespective of its source. **3** [1930s] physical violence. **4** [1930s] (*US Und.*) a police record. **5** [1930s+] a police officer, or the police in general. **6** [1930s+] gunfire. [? they 'cast light' on things or 'warm things up'; HOT *adj.*[2] (1)]

heat *n.*[4] [1920s+] (*US*) weapons, arms.

heat *n.*[5] [1930s+] (*US*) **1** problems, difficulties, trouble, bad feeling. **2** blame, sarcasm, intense criticism.

heat, the *n.*[1] [1940s] (*US Und.*) the electric chair.

heat, the *n.*[2] [1980s+] (*US campus*) the best, the most attractive.

heat *adj.* [1980s] (*US campus*) very attractive.

heated *adj.* [1980s+] (*US campus*) drunk. [HEAT *n.*[2] (1)]

heated up *adj. see* HET UP *adj.*

heater *n.* **1** [1910s–30s] (*US*) an overcoat. **2** [1910s+] (*US*) a cigar. **3** [1920s+] (*also* **heatrola**) a pistol, a revolver. **4** [1930s–60s] (*US*) the female genitals.

heat-head *n.* [1920s+] (*US*) a consumer of crude alcohol. [HEAT *n.*[2] (3) + -HEAD sfx (3)]

heathen chinee *n.* [late 19C–1950s] (*US*) a Chinese person (cf. AH CABBAGE *n.*). [coined 1871 by US writer Bret Harte (1836–1902) in his poem 'Plain Language from Truthful James', better known, from this coinage, as 'The Heathen Chinee': 'For ways that are dark / And for tricks that are vain, / The heathen Chinee is peculiar']

heathen philosopher *n.* [late 17C–early 19C] a ragged vagrant, whose flesh can be seen through his garments. [image of Greek philosophers who trad. scorned the niceties of dress]

heather *n.* [1980s+] (*US campus*) a superficial young woman, pretty but lacking in intelligence. [film *Heathers* (1988)]

heather c *n.* [1990s+] a fat, ugly person who stutters. [? film *Heathers* (1988)]

heat-packer *n.* [1940s+] (*US Und.*) a gunman, an armed gangster. [PACK HEAT *v.*]

heatrola *n. see* HEATER *n.* (3).

heat-seeking (moisture) missile *n.* [1980s+] (*US campus*) the penis (cf. AX *n.*[2]).

heat's on *phr.* [1950s+] the police are exerting exceptional pressure on the community. [HEAT *n.*[3] (1)]

heat up *v.* **1** [1930s+] (*US Und.*) to bring pressure upon someone. **2** [1930s+] (*US Und.*) for the victim of a confidence trick to make a fuss or call in the authorities. **3** [1930s+] (*US Und.*) for pressure

of discovery or suspicions to intensify. **4** [1930s+] (*orig. US Und.*) to infuriate, to annoy. **5** [2000s] (*US*) of a restaurant, to become busy. [HEAT *n.*[3] (2)]

heave *n.*[1] [19C] a flagrant attempt to deceive, to swindle, to persuade.

heave *n.*[2] *see* HEAVE-HO *n.*

heave *v.*[1] [mid-16C–mid-19C] to rob. [SE *heave*, lift and carry away]

heave *v.*[2] [mid-19C+] to vomit (cf. BLOW *v.*[3]). [the sensation in one's stomach]

heave a bough *v.* (*also* **heave a booth**) [mid-16C–early 19C] (*UK Und.*) to rob or rifle a booth; thus *booth-heaver*, one who performs such a robbery. [HEAVE *v.*[1] + SE *bough*, booth]

heave a case *phr.* [18C–early 19C] to rob a house. [HEAVE *v.*[1] + CASE *n.*[3] (1)]

heave-ho *n.* (*also* **heave**, **heavus**) **1** [1930s+] rejection, ejection; often as *the old heave-ho.* **2** [1940s+] (*US*) an act of vomiting. [naut. jargon *heave-ho!*, a sailor's cry when hauling on the anchor cable, pulling in sails and performing similar strenuous tasks; (1) in this case the task was that of the BOUNCER *n.*[2] (5), who grasped his victim by the scruff of the neck and the seat of the trousers and tossed him through the saloon door]

heave it into *v.* [late 19C–1900s] (*US*) to persuade, to impose a story upon.

heaven *n.* [19C–1900s] the vagina.

heaven dust *n.* (*drugs*) **1** [1930s+] cocaine (cf. BIRDIE POWDER *n.*). **2** [1940s+] heroin; morphine (cf. AUNTIE EMMA *n.*). [SE *heaven*, i.e. the effects + DUST *n.*[1]]

heaven-eleven *n.* [1960s+] (*US gambling*) the point of 11 in craps dice (cf. ADA FROM DECATUR *n.*). [SE *heaven*, since if the shooter throws 11 on the first throw the bet is won]

heavenly *adj.* [late 19C+] wonderful, splendid.

heavenly bliss *n.* [1930s–40s] (*US*) a kiss. [rhy. sl.]

heavenly blue *n.* [1970s] (*US drugs*) LSD (cf. A *n.*[3]).

heavenly plan *n.* [late 19C+] (*Aus.*) a man. [rhy. sl.]

heaven reacher *n.* [1920s] (*US tramp*) a preacher. [rhy. sl.]

heavens! *excl.* (*also* **heavens alive! good heavens! great heavens!**) [late 16C+] a mild oath.

heavens to Betsy! *excl.* (*also* **heavens to Murgatroyd!**) [late 19C+] (*US*) a general excl. of shock, horror, surprise. [ety. unknown; note George Cole on *American Dialect Society-List* (Internet, September 2001): 'It's possible that Betsy Ross might have inspired the exclamation. Like "Goodness gracious me" (probably elliptical for "May Goodness (i.e., God) be gracious to me"), "Heavens to Betsy" might have been elliptical for "May the heavens be gracious to Betsy."']

heaver *n.*[1] **1** [late 17C–early 19C] (*UK Und.*) the female breast (cf. BOBBER *n.*[2]). **2** [18C–19C] a person in love. **3** [mid-19C] the male chest. **4** [1980s+] (*US Black*) a self-styled great lover, esp. of the more earthy, animalistic type. [the cliché, the breast *heaves* with emotion]

heaver *n.*[2] [mid-18C–early 19C] (*UK Und.*) a thief who specializes in stealing tradesmen's shop books.

heaver *n.*[3] *see* COAL (HEAVER) *n.*

heaves *n.* [mid-19C+] stomach cramps.

heave up Jonah *v.* (*also* **throw up Jonah**) [mid-19C–1910s] (*US*) to be violently sick. [the biblical story of Jonah and the whale]

heavies *n.*[1] [1970s+] (*UK Und.*) the Special Branch. [abbr. HEAVY MOB *n.*]

heavies *n.*[2] **1** [1970s+] emotional intensity, usu. depressing. **2** [1980s+] (*N.Z.*) threats. [(1) HEAVY *v.* (2); (2) HEAVY *v.* (1)]

heaving *adj.* [1960s] a general intensifier. [? euph. for FUCKING *adj.* (1)]

heavus *n. see* HEAVE-HO *n.*

heavy *n.*[1] **1** [late 19C–1940s] (*US*) (*also* **heavy merchant**) an actor playing a serious or tragic part in a melodrama; occas. of an actress. **2** [late 19C+] a heavyweight boxer. **3** [1910s–20s] (*US campus*) a girlfriend, a boyfriend, an important date. **4** [1910s+] a thug, a villain, esp. a violent criminal (also as portrayed in cinema and theatre); also in fig. use, e.g. a moralizer. **5** [1920s–40s] (*US*) a large, fat man. **6** [1920s+] violent crime, armed robbery. **7** [1920s+] (*US*) an important or powerful person. **8** [1930s–50s] (*US Und.*) a bank robber; thus *on the heavy*, working as a bankrobber. **9** [1940s+] (*US/Aus.*) hard work, heavy labour. **10** [1950s+] (*drugs*) a hard drug (heroin, cocaine) rather than a soft one (cannabis etc). **11** [1960s] (*Aus.*) a detective (cf. BEAT-POUNDER n.). [(4) note B.E. (1698): 'A heavy Fellow, a dull Blockish Slug']

heavy *n.*[2] *see* HEAVY WET n.[1].

heavy *adj.*[1] **1** [mid-19C+] respectable. **2** [mid-19C+] (*US*) of an object or idea, remarkable in a positive or negative way. **3** [mid-19C+] (*US*) of a person, powerful, wealthy, influential, popular. **4** [mid-19C+] ponderously dignified, stern, repressive, unbending; esp. as *heavy father*, *heavy uncle*. **5** [mid-19C+] thuggish, violent, unpleasant. **6** [20C+] of money, substantial. **7** [1920s+] intense, urgent. **8** [1920s+] shocking, frightening, threatening. **9** [1920s+] meaningful, important, emotionally strong; a general intensifier, esp. loved by late 1960s hippies and radicals, varying as to context. **10** [1970s+] menacing. **11** [1970s+] of a crime, important, large-scale. **12** [1970s+] in sex, pertaining to sado-masochism. **13** [1980s+] of a jail sentence, substantial, lengthy.

heavy *adj.*[2] **1** [mid-19C+] (*US*) in possession of a great deal of a commodity, usu. money. **2** [1990s+] armed. [the weight of one's purse or wallet; or the gun]

heavy *adj.*[3] **1** [1920s] (*W.I.*) enthusiastic. **2** [1930s+] (*W.I./US*) physically attractive, sexy. **3** [1930s+] intellectual, highbrow. **4** [1940s+] (*US Black*) wonderful, amazing, admirable. **5** [1940s+] very passionate, either physically or emotionally. **6** [1960s+] (*US Black*) highly intelligent.

heavy *adj.*[4] [1950s] (*US drugs*) **1** in possession of drugs. **2** referring to a narcotic drug rather than a soft drug such as cannabis. [the fig. 'weight' of the drugs]

heavy *v.* **1** [1950s+] to threaten, to menace. **2** [1990s+] to render depressing, to 'bring down'. [(1) HEAVY n.[1] (4)]

heavy *adv.* **1** [20C+] to a large extent. **2** [1920s+] of money, possessing or spending a large amount. **3** [1930s+] keenly, enthusiastically.

heavy-arse *n.* [late 19C+] a lazy person. [HEAVY-ARSED adj.]

heavy-arsed *adj.* [17C–18C] apathetic, lazy. [SE *heavy* + ARSE n.[1] (1); thus pamphlet, *Shove to Heavy-Arsed Christians* by Richard Baxter (1615–91)]

heavy baggage *n.* [late 18C–19C] women and children. [they weigh down the man who is in pursuit of pleasure or focused on work]

heavy cavalry *n.* (*also* **heavy dragons**, ...**dragoons**, ...**horse-men**) [mid-19C–1930s] bedbugs, lice etc.

heavy cheer *n.* [early–mid-19C] a mixture of porter and beer. [SE *heavy* + *cheer*, happiness, contentment, esp. as a result of drinking alcohol]

heavy date *n.* [20C+] a more than usu. important meeting with one's boy- or girlfriend.

heavy dragons/dragoons *n. see* HEAVY CAVALRY n.

heavy-duty *adj.* **1** [1930s+] (*orig. US*) intense, serious, committed. **2** [1970s+] (*US*) tough, unpleasant. **3** [1970s+] (*US*) terrific, first-rate. **4** [1980s+] (*US*) deeply committed, heavily involved. **5** [1980s+] (*US drugs*) strongly addictive. [SE *heavy-duty*, hard-wearing]

heavy-foot *n.* [1930s–40s] (*US Und.*) a plain-clothes detective (cf. BEAT-POUNDER n.). [identified as such by his shoes]

heavy game *n.* (*also* **strong game**) [1970s] (*US Black*) a well-conceived, well-executed plan of action. [HEAVY adj.[1] (9)/SE *strong* + GAME n.[2]]

Heavy Gang, the *n.* [1980s+] (*Irish*) a special, extra-tough section of the Garda Síochána.

heavy gee *n.* [1930s–40s] (*US Und.*) a safe-blower.

heavy gun *n.* (*also* **heavy guy**) [1930s–40s] (*US Und.*) a criminal gang leader.

heavy guy *n. see* HEAVY MAN n.[1] (1).

heavy heat stretch *n.* [1940s] (*US Black*) summer.

heavy hen *n.* [1940s] (*US Black/Harlem*) a mature woman (as opposed to a young girl).

heavy hitter *n.* **1** [1970s+] an important, influential person, esp. in the worlds of business, politics or crime. **2** [1970s+] (*US*) a violent criminal, a hired thug. **3** [1980s+] (*US*) an alcoholic. [baseball imagery + (3) HIT THE BOOZE v.]

heavy horsemen *n.*[1] [mid-19C] Thames thieves who pose as dock-hands to enter ships and steal the cargoes.

heavy horsemen *n.*[2] *see* HEAVY CAVALRY n.

heavy job *n.* [1900s–30s] (*US Und.*) a violent crime.

heavy lard *n.* [1940s] (*US Black*) **1** any impressively, convincingly told story. **2** a 'tall story', a dramatic but unfeasible story.

heavy lump *n.* [1940s] the fashionable area of contemporary Harlem, New York City, otherwise known as Coogan's Bluff, between Amsterdam and Edgecombe Avenues, between 138th and 155th Streets. [pun on SUGAR HILL n. (1)]

heavy man *n.*[1] (*US Und.*) **1** [1910s+] (*also* **heavy guy/worker**) a safe-breaker. **2** [1930s] a bank robber; thus *on the heavy*, working as a bankrobber. **3** [1930s+] a thug, a criminal who is prone to use violence. [HEAVY n.[1] (4)]

heavy man *n.*[2] [1990s+] (*W.I.*) an influential man. [HEAVY n.[1] (7)]

heavy manners *n.* [1970s+] (*orig. W.I., later UK Black*) any form of oppression or repression experienced by Blacks (esp. at the hands of the police); thus *under heavy manners*, under strict discipline. [HEAVY adj.[1] (4) + SE *manners*; also used by the authorities to denote their own firm measures in the fight against crime]

heavy manners *v.* (*also* **manners**) [1980s] (*UK Black*) to dictate, to bully. [HEAVY MANNERS n.]

heavy merchant *n. see* HEAVY n.[1] (1).

heavy metal! *excl.* [1970s+] (*Ulster*) an excl. of surprise or amazement. [? SE *heavy metal* music or a euph. for *Holy Mother!*]

heavy mob *n.* [1950s+] (*UK Und.*) **1** (*also* **heavy squad**) a gang of thugs. **2** physically tough police or prison officers used in violent situations. **3** officers from the Flying Squad and, formerly, the Special Patrol Group.

heavy number *n.* [1970s+] anything or anyone seen as serious, important etc. [HEAVY adj.[1] (9) + NUMBER n.[3] (1)]

heavy plodder *n.* [mid-19C] (*UK Und.*) a stockbroker.

heavy rackets *n.* [1900s–40s] (*US Und.*) those forms of crime that depend on violence or coercion for their success.

heavy roller *n. see* HIGH ROLLER n. (1).

heavy sledding *n.* [1920s] (*US*) in a social situation, hard going.

heavy soul *n.* [1950s] (*drugs*) heroin. [its long-term effects]

heavy squad *n. see* HEAVY MOB n. (1).

heavy stuff *n.* [1960s] (*drugs*) drugs like narcotics, rather than tranquillizers, cannabis etc. [HEAVY adj.[4] (2) + STUFF n.[3] (2); as opposed to LIGHT STUFF n. (1)]

heavy sugar *n.* [1920s+] (*orig. US*) a large amount of money; thus *heavy sugar guy*, a big spender; *heavy sugar papa*, a sweet old man with a fat purse. [HEAVY adj.[1] (6) + SUGAR n.[1] (1)]

heavy swell *n.* (*also* **howling swell**) [mid-19C–1910s] a dandy, an aristocrat or one who tries to pose as one; thus *heavy swelldom*, the world of such individuals. [HEAVY adj.[1] (3)/HOWLING adj. + SWELL n. (1)]

heavyweight *n.* **1** [late 19C+] an important person with power and influence. **2** [1910s] (*US Und.*) a thief. **3** [1910s+] (*US Und.*) a violent criminal. **4** [1970s] (*US*) a fat person, esp. a fat woman. **5** [1970s+] (*US gay*) the possessor of a larger-than-average penis. **6** [1970s+] (*US campus*) a heavy drinker.

heavyweight *adj.* [20C+] important, influential. [HEAVYWEIGHT n. (1)]

heavy wet *n.*[1] (*also* **heavy, heavy whet**) **1** [early 19C] a heavy drinking bout. **2** [early 19C+] malt liquor; also a mixture of porter and beer. [(2) 'Heavy wet, malt liquor, because the more a man drinks of it, the heavier and more stupid he becomes' (Hotten, 1867); (1) f. (2)]

heavy wet *n.*[2] [1930s–40s] (*US Black*) a downpour, a rainstorm.

heavy worker *n. see* HEAVY MAN *n.*[1] (1).

Hebe *n.* (*also* **Heab, Hebie, Heeb**) [1920s+] (*orig. US*) a derog. term for a Jew (cf. ABE *n.*[1]). [abbr. SE *Hebrew*, a Jew]

hebe *n.* [18C] pubic hair. [*Hebe*, the mythological goddess of youth and spring and cup-bearer of Olympus; note SE *Hebe*, a barmaid]

hebe *adj.* [1920s+] Jewish. [HEBE n.]

hebe-jebes *n. see* HEEBIE-JEEBIES *n.*

Hebie *n. see* HEBE *n.*

he-blow *n.* [1980s+] (*US gay*) a gay Jewish man. [a pun on SE *Hebrew* + BLOW *v.*[2] (3)]

Hebrew *n.* [18C–19C] unintelligible language.

Hebrew hoppers *n. see* AIR HEBREWS *n.*

he can put his shoes under my bed any time *phr.* [1920s+] a complimentary ref. by a woman about an attractive man; occas. vice versa.

heck *n.* [late 19C+] a euph. for *hell.*

heck! *excl.* (*also* **by heck!**) [early 19C+] a euph. for HELL! excl.

hecka *adv.* [1980s+] (*US campus*) very. [HECK n.]

heck-of-a-no! *excl.* [1990s+] (*US teen*) a statement of absolute rejection, an emphatic negative, esp. when one is being pressurized to do something against one's will. [HECK n.]

heckuva *adj. see* HELLUVA adj.

he-coon *n.* [late 19C–1970s] (*US*) an important, powerful man. [SE *he* + COON *n.* (3)]

he could make me write bad checks *phr.* [1980s+] (*US campus*) a comment made by a woman about an especially attractive man.

he could sleep on a clothes-line *phr.* [mid-19C+] a phr. used to describe someone who is capable of dealing with difficult or challenging circumstances. [note George Orwell's refs. to the ropes slung across rooms in tramps' lodgings, on which impoverished men could lean and thus, if fortunate, sleep]

hectic *adj.* [20C+] exciting, disturbing, in a state of feverish excitement or activity.

hector *n.*[1] (*also* **bully-hector**) [mid-17C–mid-19C] a blustering, swaggering bully, a thug, a bouncer, esp. of a brothel. [an ironic use of the Trojan hero *Hector*, son of Priam and Hecuba, husband of Andromache, 'the prop or stay of Troy'; thus note Shadwell, *The Squire of Alsatia* (1688): 'They are all of them as stout as Hector']

hector *n.*[2] [20C+] (*US*) the proper name used in a variety of phrs., e.g. *dead as Hector, mad as Hector, meaner than Hector*. [? a euph. for SE *hell*]

hector *v.* [mid-17C+] to bluster, to swagger.

he'd drink the stuff if he had to drain it through a shitty cloth *phr.* [1920s+] (*Can.*) a phr. used of an unregenerate drunkard.

he'd fuck anything... *phr. see* ANYTHING ON TWO LEGS *n.*

hedge *n.*[1] [20C+] (*UK Und.*) the crowd that gathers around illicit street traders or gamblers.

hedge *n.*[2] **1** [1900s] (*US*) a moustache. **2** [1980s+] pubic hair.

hedge *adj.* [late 16C–1950s] a general pej., used in a number of compounds, e.g. HEDGE-BIRD n.; HEDGE-CREEPER n.; HEDGE-PRIEST n.; HEDGE-WHORE n. [SE *hedge*, implying dirty, inferior, lit. plying one's trade beneath a hedge]

hedge and ditch *n.*[1] **1** [late 19C] a market pitch. **2** [1910s+] a cricket or football pitch. [rhy. sl.]

hedge and ditch *n.*[2] *see* HEDGE-BIT n.

hedge-bird *n.* [17C–mid-19C] a general derog. term, esp. for a tramp or vagrant, i.e. one who lives or might as well live in a hedge, or for a low-grade prostitute who plies her trade in the open air. [HEDGE adj. + SE *bird*/BIRD *n.*[2] (1)]

hedge-bird trull *n.* [mid-17C] a prostitute who plies her trade in the open air (cf. ALLEY CAT n.). [HEDGE-BIRD n. + TRULL n. (1)]

hedge-bit *n.* [late 17C–mid-19C] (*also* **hedge and ditch**) a low-grade prostitute who carries on operations in the open air. [HEDGE adj. + BIT n.[3]]

hedge-creeper *n.* (*UK Und.*) **1** [late 16C–early 19C] a petty thief who steals laundry from the hedges on which it is laid to dry; a term of abuse. **2** [mid-19C] (*also* **hedge-prowler, hedge ranger**) a prostitute, presumably working in the countryside. [obs. SE *hedge-creeper*, a sneak thief, a creeping rogue]

hedge-docked *adj.* [19C] seduced, esp. deflowered, in the open air. [SE *hedge* + DOCK *v.*[1]]

hedgehog *n.*[1] [mid-19C] veal. [the 2 meats are supposedly not dissimilar when cooked]

hedgehog *n.*[2] [20C+] a derog. term for a foreigner, esp. a Black or Asian person (cf. DAPTO DOG n.; HALF-OUNCE OF BACCY n.). [rhy. sl. = WOG n.[1]]

hedgehog *n.*[3] [1970s] an unattractive woman.

hedge-hopping *n.* [1910s+] flying an aeroplane as close as possible to ground and 'hopping' over the trees.

hedge off *v.* [mid-19C] to run off, to escape.

hedge on the dyke *n.* [19C] female pubic hair. [*dyke* is SE; there is no ref. to lesbianism]

hedge-popping *n.* [mid–late 19C] shooting small birds perched on hedges, the pursuit of boys only and considered unsportsmanlike in adults; thus *hedge-popper*, one who shoots in this manner. [SE *hedge* + POP *v.*[1] (2)]

hedge-priest *n.* (*also* **hedge-parson**) [late 16C–early 19C] (*UK Und.*) a priest, or a beggar who poses as such, who works in rural areas, ministering to other beggars and the local peasantry; the implication is that such clergy were not true priests. [HEDGE adj. + SE *priest*]

hedge-prowler *n. see* HEDGE-CREEPER n. (2).

hedger *n.* [mid–late 19C] one who 'hedges' or secures their bets.

hedge ranger *n. see* HEDGE-CREEPER n. (2).

hedge-tavern *n.* [late 17C–mid-19C] a low tavern, often the home of criminals, card-sharps and similar underworld figures. [HEDGE adj. + SE *tavern*]

hedge-whore *n.* [late 16C+] a prostitute who plies her trade in the open air. [HEDGE adj. + SE *whore*]

Heeb *n. see* HEBE n.

heebie-jeebies *n.* (*also* **hebe-jebes, heebies, heebs**) **1** [1920s+] (*orig. US*) unpleasant fantasies, nameless terrors, anything the mind can conjure up to produce nerves and fear. **2** [1920s+] (*US*) a hangover, delirium tremens. **3** [1980s+] the physical and mental symptoms that accompany heroin or cocaine withdrawal. [? ety. unknown, although the *heebie-jeebie*, a dance popular *c.*1926, was alleged to have taken its name f. the incantations of an Indian witch-doctor before making a human sacrifice. More likely it is a nonce coinage by the US cartoonist Billy Derbeck and first noted in his strip *Barney Google* in the *New York American* on 26 October 1923]

heefus *n.* [1950s–60s] (*US*) sexual intercourse. [ety. unknown; ? SE *heave*]

hee-haw *n.* **1** [mid-19C+] a donkey. **2** [20C+] (*US*) loud, offensive laughter, esp. if scornful. **3** [20C+] derision, nonsense. [the trad. transliteration of the donkey's bray]

hee-haw *v.*[1] (*also* **haw-haw**) [20C+] (*US*) to laugh scornfully. [HEE-HAW n.]

hee-haw *v.*[2] *see* HEM-HAW v.

hee-haw shoes *n.* [1960s] large, clod-hopping shoes, the sort a donkey-riding rustic would choose.

heel n. [1910s+] **1** (orig. US) a petty criminal; thus on the heel, working as a criminal, spec. till-tapping. **2** (orig. US) a general derog. term, a dishonest, untrustworthy person, esp. one who treats women badly. **3** (US Und.) an informer. [? SE down-at-heel or the image of an unwanted person, continually at one's heels; note Asbury, Sucker's Progress (1938): 'An extraordinary number of the terms, technical and otherwise, which were employed by Faro players in the palmy days of the game have passed into the language [...] and are commonly used by millions who never heard of Faro. Here are some of them: [...] Heeled bets—Wagers which played one card to win and another to lose. Heeler or heel— A player who consistently makes heeled bets']

heel, the n. [1900s–30s] (US Und.) 'The racket of stealing by sneaking' (Sutherland, The Professional Thief, 1936). [HEEL v.³ (3)]

heel v.¹ **1** [mid-19C+] (US) (also **heel it**) to run away, to escape, to walk quickly. **2** [1910s–60s] (US Und.) to walk stealthily, to stalk, to steal sneakily, to leave without paying one's bill. [SE heel]

heel v.² **1** [late 19C+] (also **heel up**) to arm oneself with a firearm. **2** [1900s–40s] (US) to lend money. [cock-fighting jargon heel, to arm a game-cock with a gaff or spur]

heel v.³ **1** [late 19C+] (US) to court, to flatter for personal advantage. **2** [1920s+] (US Und.) to rob a store using an accomplice to distract the clerk or cashier. **3** [1930s+] (US) to cheat a hotel or similar establishment by sneaking in another person without registering. [HEEL n.]

heel-and-toe n. [late 19C+] (US) the act of running or walking quickly; thus take it on the heel-and-toe, to escape. [HEEL-AND-TOE v. (1)]

heel-and-toe v. **1** [early 19C+] (US) to run or walk quickly. **2** [late 19C] to have sexual intercourse where the man's strokes are very long, deep into the vagina and then almost all the way out. [(2) the idea of the 2 extremes]

heel-and-toe boy n. (also **heel-and-toe man/walker**) [20C+] one who walks speedily, one who runs away or escapes. [HEEL-AND-TOE v. (1)]

heel-ball n. [1990s+] (Irish) **1** a busy, energetic person; as adj., business-like. **2** a term of abuse. [SE heel-ball, a shoemaker's tool]

heeled adj.¹ (also **well-heeled**) [mid-19C+] (orig. US) armed. [SE heeled, used of a fighting cock, which had sharpened spurs tied to its heels]

heeled adj.² **1** [late 19C+] (orig. US) prepared, well provided for, wealthy, rich. **2** [1950s+] intoxicated by or in possession of drugs. [abbr. SE well-heeled]

heeler n. **1** [mid-19C–1950s] (US Und.) a criminal's unskilled accomplice, a hired thug. **2** [late 19C–1920s] a lurch to one side. **3** [late 19C–1960s] (US) a hanger-on who performs tasks for a politician or political party in the hope of personal aggrandizement. **4** [1910s+] (US Und.) a sneak-thief. [SE heel, of a dog, to follow at the heels; note ety. at HEEL n.]

heel-grifter n. [1940s+] (US Und.) a small-time or second-rate con-man. [HEEL n. (1) + GRIFTER n. (1)]

heel it v. see HEEL v.¹ (1).

heel-licker n. [20C+] (US) a toady, a sycophant. [var. on ARSE-LICKER n. (1)]

heel on v. [1910s+] (US Black) to leave, to depart.

heeltap n. **1** [late 18C–1930s] the liquor left at the bottom of a glass; thus [late 18C+] no heeltaps! no bootheels! [mid-18C–mid-19C] take off your heeltap! drain your glasses! **2** [1930s] knockout drops. [SE heel-tap, a layer of leather used in making a shoe heel]

heel-thief n. (also **shoe thief**) [1930s–70s] (US) a petty criminal.

heel up v. see HEEL v.² (1).

heesh n. [1940s+] (US drugs) hashish (cf. AFGHAN n.). [abbr.]

heezie n. [2000s] (US teen) a house, a home. [dimin./pron. of SE house]

he-fluesy n. see FLOOZIE n.

heft n. [19C–1920s] the bulk, the mass, the main part. [SE heft, weight, heaviness, ponderousness]

he-he boy n. [1930s] a homosexual man.

heifer n. **1** [late 16C–early 17C; 1920s+] a promiscuous woman, a prostitute; thus HEIFER DEN n. **2** [mid-19C+] (also **effie**) a woman, a girl. **3** [late 19C+] (later use US Black) an unattractive, obese woman. **4** [1960s+] (US Black) an immoral woman, esp. one who chooses to defy the current moral codes.

heifer den n. [1920s+] (US tramp) a brothel (cf. BIRDCAGE n.¹). [HEIFER n.]

heifer-dust n. **1** [1920s–40s] (US) Bull Durham brand tobacco. **2** [1920s+] (US) nonsense, rubbish. **3** [1920s+] (Aus.) a girl or woman. [SE heifer + dust, rubbish, garbage; (2) euph. for BULLSHIT n. (2)]

heifer-dust act n. [1920s] (US) an arrest and interrogation by the police. [HEIFER-DUST n. (2) + SE act]

heifer-paddock n. [late 19C–1950s] (Aus.) a girls' school. [HEIFER n. (2) + SE paddock]

heigh-ho n. [mid-19C] (UK Und.) stolen yarn. [the SE excl. heigh-ho! was used to indicate to a potential buyer that such yarn was on offer]

height n. [1900s] type, as in phr. not one's height.

heighty-toity n. see HIGHTY-TIGHTY n.

heiney n. see HEINIE n.².

Heinie n.¹ [20C+] (also **Hiney**) a derog. term for a German. [Ger. proper name, Heinz, but note HEINIE n.² (1)]

Heinie n.² [1970s+] (US) a bottle or can of Heineken lager beer. [abbr.]

heinie n.¹ [20C+] (US) a very short haircut. [? the popularity of crewcut hair among Germans; the hairless HEINIE n.² (1)]

heinie n.² (also **heiney, heiny**) **1** [1920s+] (US) the buttocks; thus from head to heinie, from top to bottom. **2** [1970s+] (US campus) a woman, for sexual purposes. **3** [1970s+] (US campus) a handsome man. [euph. dimin. of SE hind end or hinder parts]

heinie highway n. (also **heinie hideout**) [20C+] (US) the anus (cf. ALLEY WAY n.). [HEINIE n.² (1)]

heinous adj. (also **hanus, heinous crime**) **1** [1970s+] (US campus) terrible. **2** [1990s+] (US teen) fantastic. [intensified use of SE]

Heinz n. (also **Heinz dog, Heinz 57**) **1** [1920s+] (orig. US) a mongrel. **2** [1940s+] (bingo) the number 57 (cf. ALDERSHOT LADIES n.). **3** [1940s+] (gambling) any combination bet. **4** [1940s+] anything, e.g. a concert, that combines a variety of disparate items. [the 57 varieties offered by H.J. Heinz]

heir castle n. [1900s–20s] (US Und.) a form of confidence trick based on an estate fraud.

heirhead n. [1980s+] a rich, hedonistic, stupid young woman, due to inherit a large fortune; occas. of a man. [play on SE heir + AIRHEAD n. (1)]

heist n.¹ [1930s+] (US Und.) **1** (also **heist job, hyste**) a robbery. **2** the site of a robbery or break-in. [HEIST v. (1)]

heist n.² see HOIST n.².

heist v. (also **hist, hyst**) **1** [1920s+] (US Und.) to steal, to hold up; thus HEIST ARTIST n., heisting, burglary. **2** [1940s] to increase, e.g. of a sum of money. [var. on HOIST v.² (1)]

heist artist n. (also **heist guy**) [1930s+] (US) a robber, a 'stick-up man'. [HEIST n.¹ (1) + ARTIST sfx/GUY n.²]

heister n. (also **heist man, hister**) **1** [1920s+] a robber, a hold-up man. **2** [1970s] a car thief. [HEIST v. (1)]

heist job n. see HEIST n.¹ (1).

hel-bat n. [mid-19C] a table. [backsl.]

Helen! excl. [20C+] (US) a euph. for HELL! excl. and used in various mild oaths.

helen n. [1970s+] (drugs) heroin (cf. BIG H n.). [the initial letter]

helitywhoop adv. see LICKETY-SPLIT adv.

helium-brain n. (also **helium-head**) [1930s+] (US campus) a silly person (cf. AIRBALL n.). [SE helium + sfx -brain/-HEAD sfx (1)]

helium heels n. [1990s+] (US) a woman who seduces a succession of increasingly important men.

hell *n.*[1] [late 16C+] the vagina (cf. BLACK HOLE *n.*[1]). [misogyny + phr. PUT THE DEVIL INTO HELL *v.*]

hell *n.*[2] **1** [mid-17C] Bridewell prison. **2** [late 17C–early 18C] a debtor's prison near Westminster for the King's debtors, who were never freed. **3** [early 19C+] a casino, a gambling house. **4** [1910s] (*Aus.*) an opium den. [the puritan terror of such places; note also Taylor, *News from Hell, with a short description of the Hell at Westminster* (1639), which describes a 17C tavern: 'Within this *Hell* is good content and quiet, / Good entertainment, various sorts of diet' etc]

hell *n.*[3] [1920s+] (*US Black*) an expert, an admirable or impressive person. [HELL *adj.*]

hell *adj.* [late 19C+] very good. [on bad = good model]

hell *v.* **1** [mid-17C] to place in hell or in a situation similar to hell, to cause someone to experience their hell. **2** [mid-17C] to make into a hell. **3** [mid-17C–1930s] to scold, to reprimand, to 'give someone hell'. **4** [late 19C+] to hurry, to go 'hell for leather', to fly around (esp. in some activity disapproved of by the speaker). **5** [late 19C+] to cause a commotion, to 'raise hell'; often as HELL AROUND *v.*

hell, the *phr.*[1] **1** [mid-19C+] a general intensifier, used to express anger, annoyance, impatience, also (ironically) disbelief or contempt; used to dismiss another speaker's assertion. **2** [late 19C+] (*also* **hell**) a general intensifer implying quantity, intensity (cf. BEAT (THE) HELL OUT OF *v.*).

hell, the *phr.*[2] [mid-19C+] (*orig. US*) used to intensify a variety of preps., such as *how, what, when, where, who, why.*

hell! *excl.* [late 16C+] a general expletive (cf. HELL NO! *excl.*; HELL YES! *excl.*).

hella *adv.* [1980s+] (*US campus*) **1** very, extremely, really. **2** a lot (of), many. [abbr. HELLUVA *adj.*]

hellabad *adj.* (*also* **helluvbad**) [1990s+] amazing, excellent.

hellacious *adj.* (*also* **hellashus**) [1920s+] (*US*) **1** wonderful, amazing, extraordinary. **2** difficult, demanding. [HELL *adj./SE hell* + BODACIOUS *adj.*]

hellafied *adj. see* HELLIFIED *adj.*

hell-all *n.* (*also* **hell-in-all**) [1930s+] (*US*) absolutely none, nothing whatsoever. [var. on DAMN-ALL *n.*]

hell-a-mile *adj.* [late 19C–1930s] (*US*) terrible, hellish.

hell-a-mile! *excl.* [1930s] (*US*) a general excl., the meaning varying as to context.

hell and gone *phr.* (*also* **from here to hell and gone**) (*US*) **1** [mid-19C+] far away, godforsaken. **2** [1910s+] increased in value.

hell and maria! *excl. see* HELL AND TOMMY! *excl.*

hell and scissors *n.* [20C+] (*W.I., Guyn.*) any form of dramatic, exciting, threatening or frightening situation, typically an argument.

hell and tommy *n.* (*also* **devil and tommy, thunder and tommy**) [mid-19C+] a general intensifier, usu. meaning utter destruction; esp. as *play hell and tommy*, to cause absolute chaos. [? proper names Henry VIII ('Hal') (r.1509–47) and Thomas Cromwell ('Tommy') (c.1485–1540), the chief engineers of the English Reformation, or SE *hell and torment*]

hell and tommy! *excl.* [mid-19C+] (*also* **hell and maria!**) a general excl. [ext. of HELL! *excl.*]

hell a-popping *phr. see* HELL'S A-POPPING *phr.*

hell-around *adj.* [1960s] (*US*) trouble-making. [HELL AROUND *v.*]

hell around *v.* [late 19C+] (*US*) to cause trouble or a disturbance. [HELL *v.* (5)]

hellashus *adj. see* HELLACIOUS *adj.*

hell-a-tootin' *adv. see* HELL-TO-SPLIT *adv.*

hell beating tanbark *phr.* (*also* **devil beating tanbark**) [mid-19C–1900s] (*US*) a general intensifier, usu. meaning very fast; in phrs. such as *quicker than hell beating tanbark*.

hell-bender *n.* (*also* **hell bending fool**) **1** [19C+] (*US*) a formidable, outrageous thing or individual. **2** [late 19C] a drinking

bout. [fig. use of US dial. *hellbender*, the American salamander or alligator; (2) ext. of BENDER *n.*[2] (1)]

hell-bending *adj.* **1** [late 19C+] (*US*) hellish, arduous. **2** [1910s+] (*Can.*) hellfire evangelistic preaching.

hellbent *adj.* [mid-19C+] (*orig. US*) determined, stubborn. [lit. 'determined on hell']

hellbent for breakfast *adv. see* HELL FOR BREAKFAST *adv.*

hellbent for election *adv.* (*also* **hellbent for Georgia/Sunday**) [late 19C+] (*US*) hurriedly, recklessly. [HELLBENT *adj.* + fig. uses of *election/Georgia/Sunday*; the enthusiasm of politicians for the fruits of power/workers for their day of rest]

hellbent for leather *adv. see* HELL FOR LEATHER *adv.*

hell-box *n. see* BOX *n.*[5] (3).

hell-broth *n.* [mid-19C–1910s] liquor, whether actually 'off' or seen as morally evil by teetotallers. [SE *hell-broth*, 'a decoction of infernal character or prepared for an infernal purpose' (*OED*)]

hell buster *n.* [1910s–30s] (*orig. US*) an amazing, riotous or violent thing or person.

hell-cart *n.* [mid–late 17C] a hackney carriage. [? its lack of comfort]

hell-cat *n.* (*also* **hell-kite**) [late 17C+] a lewd bawdy person; also a mischievous young boy, a lively animal, a spiteful person. [SE when used of a woman, and dating to early 17C, despite its inclusion by Grose (1785)]

hell-clinking *adj. see* CLINKING *adj.*

hell-dodger *n.* [20C+] (*US*) a sanctimonious Christian.

hell-driver *n.* **1** [late 17C] a coachman, presumably one who drives recklessly. **2** [1940s] a similarly inclined car-driver.

hell dust *n.* [1930s+] (*drugs*) heroin. [SE *hell* + DUST *n.*[5] (1)]

heller *n.* **1** [late 19C+] one who lives an unfettered, undisciplined and adventuresome life. **2** [late 19C+] (*US*) a very difficult, formidable or exciting thing or person. **3** [1960s+] (*US campus*) an exciting, dramatic party. [SE *hell*/HELL OF A, A *phr.*]

hellfire club *n.* [1980s] (*US gay*) a club for devotees of hardcore sado-masochism. [presumably inspired by the original 18C *Hellfire Club*, a coterie of aristocratic debauchees, although not known for sado-masochism]

hell-fired *adj.* (*also* **hell-fire**) **1** [mid-18C+] (*orig. US*) a general intensifier, extreme, extensive, great. **2** [1950s] as an infix.

hell-fired *adv.* (*also* **hell-fire**) [mid-18C+] (*orig. US*) a general intensifier, very, extremely, extensively.

hell for *adv.* (*US*) **1** [mid-19C+] intent on, insistent upon. **2** [1940s+] as a general intensifier, exceedingly.

hell for breakfast *adv.* (*also* **hellbent for breakfast**) [20C+] rushed, hurriedly, at top speed. [var. on HELLBENT FOR ELECTION *adv.*]

hell-for-leather *adj.* [20C+] rip-roaring. [HELL FOR LEATHER *adv.*]

hell for leather *adv.* (*also* **hellbent for leather, pelt for leather**) **1** [late 19C+] very fast, at top speed, rip-roaringly. **2** [20C+] vehemently. [the leather refers to the phr.'s origin in riding and refers to the harness]

he'll fuck anything... *phr. see* ANYTHING ON TWO LEGS *n.*

hell-hack *v. see* HACK *v.*[2] (1).

hellified *adj.* (*also* **hellafied**) [1960s+] (*US Black*) extreme, excessive.

hellifying *adj.* [1970s] (*US*) wonderful or very bad.

hell-in *n.* [1960s+] (*S.Afr.*) a fury, a temper.

hell-in *adj.* [1960s+] (*S.Afr.*) furious, angry.

hell in, the *adv.* [1960s+] (*S.Afr.*) furiously, angrily, e.g. *he's going the hell in on everyone today.*

hell-in-all *n. see* HELL-ALL *n.*

helling *n.* [1930s–40s] carousing, causing a disturbance, living a hedonistic lifestyle.

hellish *adj.* **1** [early 17C+] a general intensifier, terrible, awful. **2** [1990s+] on bad = good model, first-rate, excellent. [SE *hell*]

hellish *adv.* (*also* **hellishly**) [early 17C+] a general intensifier, terribly, very. [HELLISH *adj.*]

hellishing *adj.* (*also* **hellishun**) [1930s+] (*mainly Aus./N.Z.*) a general intensifier.

hell is popping *phr.* (*also* **hell pops**) [late 19C+] (*US*) all hell is breaking out.

hellite *n.* [mid-19C] a professional gambler. [HELL n.² (3)]

hellity-split *adv. see* LICKETY-SPLIT adv.

hell-kite *n. see* HELL-CAT n.

hell-master *n.* [1980s+] (*US campus*) an over-bearing, bullying person. [i.e. a fig. 'devil']

hell night *n.* [1940s+] (*US campus*) the night of initiation into a fraternity or sorority. [the initiatory rituals, known as hazing, that accompany such an event]

hell no! *excl.* [1930s+] an excl. of denial, absolutely not! (cf. HELL YES! excl.). [HELL! excl. + SE *no*]

hello! *excl.*¹ (*also* **hello Mary!**) [20C+] (*US*) a euph. for HELL! excl. or *hail Mary!*

hello! *excl.*² **1** [20C+] (*also* **hullo!**) a general response to someone making a comment; there is no inference of greeting. **2** [20C+] (*also* **hullo!**) a general excl. of surprise and disbelief, I don't believe this! what's happening? **3** [1980s+] (*US teen*) a dismissive excl., implying that the individual at whom it is aimed should stop talking foolishly, or saying things in which they patently do not believe.

hello! *excl.*³ (*also* **hello Mary!**) [1950s+] **1** a cry of surprise to no one in particular when a beautiful woman is seen. **2** (*Aus.*) used by a woman to announce the sighting of an attractive man.

hell of a, a *phr.* (*also* **one hell of a, the hell of a**) **1** [late 18C+] hellish, awful; often abbr. to HELLUVA adj. **2** [mid-19C+] (*orig. US*) extraordinary, surprising (as often positive as negative). **3** [mid-19C+] to a very great extent. [SE *hell*]

hell of a note *n.* [late 19C+] (*US*) very bad news. [HELL OF A, A phr. + SE *note*]

hello-girl *n.* [late 19C+] (*US*) a female telephone operator. [she answers all calls with *hello*]

hello Mary! *excl.*¹ *see* HELLO! excl.¹.

hello Mary! *excl.*² *see* HELLO! excl.³.

hell on *phr.* **1** [mid-19C–1960s] (*US*) very fond of. **2** [1920s+] difficult or problematic for. **3** [1940s+] (*US*) very hard on, opposed to.

hello nurse! *excl.* [1990s+] (*US teen*) a comment made on seeing an attractive member of the opposite sex.

hell on wheels *n.* [mid-19C+] (*orig. US*) anyone or anything regarded as the equivalent of hell, usu. referring to character, speed or enthusiasm. [SE *hell* + ON WHEELS phr.]

hellova *adj. see* HELLUVA adj.

hellpig *n.* [1980s+] (*US campus*) an unattractive, fat woman. [SE *hell* + PIG n.¹ (1)]

hell pops *phr. see* HELL IS POPPING phr.

hell-raiser *n.* [1910s+] one who deliberately causes trouble. [RAISE HELL v.]

hell-raising *n.* [1910s+] making trouble. [RAISE HELL v.]

hell-raising *adj.* [1920s+] trouble-making. [RAISE HELL v.]

hell-raker *n.* [19C+] a violent, forceful or exuberant person or thing. [HELL-RAKING adj.]

hell-raking *adj.* [17C+] dramatically violent, chaotic. [backform. f. SE *rakehell*]

hell-roarer *n.* [late 19C+] (*US*) a wild, uncontrolled individual or situation. [HELL-ROARING adj.]

hell-roaring *adj.* (*also* **hell-tearing**) [late 19C+] (*US*) wild, out of control.

hell-robber *n.* [1930s+] (*US*) a Christian evangelist.

hell's a-popping *phr.* (*also* **hell a-popping, hellzapoppin'**) [late 19C+] (*orig. US*) a general phr. of intensification, implying aggression, chaos, forcefulness.

hell's bells *n.*¹ [mid–late 19C+] (*US*) 'the daylights', 'the stuffing', as in *I'll knock hell's bells out of you!*

hell's bells *n.*² [1980s] (*US campus*) somewhere considered very far away.

hell's bells *adv.* [1920s+] (*US*) headlong, at great speed.

hell's bells! *excl.* (*also* **hell's fire! hell's flames! hell's teeth!**) [mid-19C+] a general mild excl., usu. implying irritation or disappointment.

hell's bottom *n.* (*also* **hell's hollow, hell's point**) [20C+] (*US*) any disreputable or out-of-the-way area. [SE *hell* + BOTTOM n.³/HOLLOW n.²]

hell's delight *n.* [early 19C+] pandemonium, chaos; often in phr. *play hell's delight* (*with*), to cause chaos.

hell's fire/flames! *excl. see* HELL'S BELLS! excl.

hell's front porch *n.* (*also* **devil's front porch**) [1990s+] (*US prison*) prison.

hell's half acre *n.* [mid-19C+] (*orig. US*) any disreputable area or place, esp. the slum area of a town or a low-class dancehall or bar; thus *all around/over hell's half-acre*, all over the place, everywhere.

hell's hollow *n. see* HELL'S BOTTOM n.

hell's kitchen *n.* (*orig. US*) **1** [mid-19C+] any very unpleasant or dangerous place. **2** [late 19C+] a generic term for any urban slum area, esp. one that serves also as a working-class entertainment centre, or any dangerous or seedy place. [proper name *Hell's Kitchen*, the Irish-Black slum area that covered part of the West Side of New York City from *c.*1850 to 1910, bounded by the Hudson River and 8th Avenue, it ran from 39th Street to 59th Street. The name may have applied initially only to a single tenement or it may have been picked up from the name of a saloon in the red-light area of Corlear's Hook. The toughest part of Hell's Kitchen was known, at least to the writer O. Henry, as the *stovepipe*, a narrow enclave running along 11th and 12th Avenues]

hell's mint of *phr.* [late 19C–1910s] (*US*) a large quantity.

hell's own *adj.* [late 19C+] (*orig. US*) used as a general intensifier.

hell's point *n. see* HELL'S BOTTOM n.

hell's teeth! *excl. see* HELL'S BELLS! excl.

hell-stick *n.* [20C+] (*US*) a sulphur match.

hell-tearing *adj. see* HELL-ROARING adj.

hell to pay (and no pitch hot) *phr.* [19C+] serious consequences will follow; usu. as *there'll be hell to pay*. [the myth of the 'Faustian bargain' (cf. DEVIL TO PAY phr.)]

hell-to-split *adv.* (*also* **hell-a-tootin', hell to toot**) [19C+] (*US*) at breakneck speed.

helluva *adj.* (*also* **heckuva, hellova**) [1920s+] a general intensifier. [mispron. of HELL OF A, A phr.]

helluvbad *adj. see* HELLABAD adj.

hell week *n.* [1930s+] (*US campus*) the period of initiation for pledges to a college fraternity.

hell west and crooked *phr.* (*also* **hell west and winding**) [late 19C+] (*orig. US*) in all directions, disarray, confusion.

hell with it!, the *excl.* (*also* **the hell with…!**) [20C+] a mild oath of annoyance or dismissal.

hell with the lid off *n.* [late 19C+] (*US*) something extremely difficult or hard to bear.

helly! *excl.* [1960s] synon. with HELL! excl.

hell yes! *excl.* (*also* **hell yeah!**) [1960s+] an affirmative excl. (cf. HELL NO! excl.). [HELL! excl. + SE *yes*]

hellza *adj.* [1990s+] a lot of. [var. on HELLUVA adj.]

hellzapoppin' *phr. see* HELL'S A-POPPING phr.

helmet *n.* **1** [1950s+] the glans penis. **2** [1970s+] a haircut. **3** [1980s] (*US Black teen*) a condom. **4** [1980s+] a woman. [(3) and (4) are things that go on the penis]

helo *n.* [1960s+] (*US*) a *hel*icopter. [abbr.]

helpa *n.* [mid-19C] an apple. [backsl.]

helpers *n.* [1960s] (*US drugs*) amphetamine pills (cf. A n.²). [? the Rolling Stones' song 'Mother's Little Helper' (1966)]

helpless *adj.* [mid-19C+] very drunk.

helter-skelter *n.* **1** [1940s] an air-raid shelter. **2** [1950s+] a bus shelter. [rhy. sl.]

helter-skelter *adv.* (*also* **hilter-skilter**) [late 16C+] in disordered haste; confusedly, tumultuously, pell-mell. [echoic, i.e. 'a jingling expression vaguely imitating the hurried clatter of feet rapidly and irregularly moved, or of many running feet' (*OED*)]

he-male *n.* [late 19C–1900s] a manly man.

hem-haw *v.* (*also* **hee-haw, hem and haw, hum and haw**) [late 15C+] (*US*) to mutter, to mumble, to be indecisive. [SE *hem* + *haw*, representations of a speaker clearing their throat]

hemo *n. see* HAEMORRHOID *n.*

hemp *n.* [late 19C+] (*drugs*) marijuana (cf. AFRICAN BUSH *n.*). [the lit. name of *cannabis sativa*, generally used in the context of textiles rather than intoxication]

hemp *v.* [mid-17C–19C] to hang, to choke to death; thus *hemp office*, the condemned cell. [19C use is US]

hempen casement *n.* [late 18C–mid-19C] (*UK Und.*) a hangman's noose. [SE *hempen*, made of hemp + *casement*]

hempen circle *n. see* HEMPEN CRAVAT *n.*

hempen collar *n.* [late 16C–1940s] a hangman's noose. [SE *hempen*, made of hemp + *collar*]

hempen consummation *n.* [early 19C] death by judicial hanging. [SE *hempen*, made of hemp + *consumption*]

hempen cravat *n.* (*also* **hempen circle, ...garter, ...halter, ...hornpipe, ...knot, ...necktie, ...whood, ...wings, hemp necktie**) [late 16C–1940s] a hangman's noose; thus *frisk in a hempen cravat*, to be hanged. [SE *hempen*, made of hemp + *cravat*]

hempen fever *n.* [18C–early 19C] a judicial hanging. [SE *hempen*, made of hemp + *fever*]

hempen fortune *n.* (*also* **hempen furniture**) [late 18C–mid-19C] (*UK Und.*) money paid to thief takers and others involved in the conviction of felons. [SE *hempen*, i.e. the resulting hanging]

hempen garter *n. see* HEMPEN CRAVAT *n.*

hempen habeas *n.* [early 19C] a hangman's noose. [SE *hempen*, made of hemp + pun on *habeas corpus*, lit. 'thou shalt have the body'; a writ whereby an accused and imprisoned person must be brought before the court and the reason for his imprisonment justified]

hempen halter/hornpipe/knot/necktie *n. see* HEMPEN CRAVAT *n.*

hempen quinsy *n.* (*also* **hempen-squincy**) [mid-17C–mid-19C] death by hanging. [SE *hempen*, made of hemp + *quinsy*, a form of tonsillitis]

hempen string *n.* **1** [early 16C–mid-19C] (*also* **hempen line, ...rope, ...snare, ...twister**) a hangman's noose. **2** [mid-17C] (*also* **hemp-string**) as a term of abuse, a thief. [SE *hempen*, made of hemp + *string*]

hempen tippet *n.* [late 16C–early 17C] a hangman's noose. [SE *hempen*, made of hemp + *tippet*, a loose scarf]

hempen whood *n. see* HEMPEN CRAVAT *n.*

hempen widow *n.* [late 17C–1940s] a woman whose husband has been hanged. [SE *hempen*, made of hemp + *widow*]

hempen wings *n. see* HEMPEN CRAVAT *n.*

hemp fever *n.* [late 18C–1930s] execution by hanging. [the hangman's noose is made from *hemp*]

hemp necktie *n. see* HEMPEN CRAVAT *n.*

hemp office *n. see* HEMP *v.*

hemp party *n.* (*also* **hemp stretching**) [late 19C] (*US*) a hanging, esp. a lynching. [the hangman's noose is made from *hemp*]

hemp roller *n.* [1950s] (*US drugs*) one who smokes marijuana cigarettes. [HEMP *n.* + SE *roller*]

hempseed *n.* [late 16C–18C; 1940s] one who is destined to hang. [the hangman's noose is made from *hemp*]

hemp's grown for you, the *phr.* [17C–mid-19C] a warning phr. implying that the person in question is bound to end on the gallows if they pursue their current lifestyle. [the hangman's noose is made from *hemp*]

hemp stretching *n. see* HEMP PARTY *n.*

hemp string *n. see* HEMPEN STRING *n.* (2).

hems *n.* [1980s] haemorrhoids. [abbr.]

hen *n.*[1] **1** [late 16C+] a woman, usu. over 30. **2** [17C–early 19C] a prostitute (cf. ALLEY CAT *n.*). **3** [early 17C–19C] a mistress, a girlfriend, a wife. **4** [late 19C+] (*Scot.*) (*also* **hinny**) a term of address to a woman. **5** [20C+] (*US campus*) a female student. **6** [20C+] (*W.I., Tob.*) a male homosexual. **7** [1920s+] (*US Black*) an unkempt, unattractive woman, esp. with messy hair.

hen *n.*[2] [late 19C] a quart pot (cf. CAT *n.*[5]; KITTEN *n.*[1]). [a large CHICKEN *n.*[5] (a quart is 2 pints)]

hen *adj.* [late 18C+] pertaining only to women; female. [HEN *n.*[1]]

hen *v.* [19C] to act cautiously; to back down. [the timidity of the fowl]

hen apple *n.* (*also* **hen berry**) [1930s–60s] (*US*) an egg.

hencackle *n.* [1940s+] (*N.Z.*) a trifle, anything unimportant. [mountaineering jargon *hencackle*, an easy climb]

hench *n.* [2000s] (*UK teen*) **1** a large, muscular person. **2** a friend. [SE *henchman*/HENCHMAN *n.*]

henchman *n.* [1950s–60s] (*US*) a friend.

hen college *n.* [1920s+] (*US*) a women's college. [HEN *n.*[1] (5)]

hen-coop *n.* **1** [early 19C] (*also* **hen-roost**) a brothel (cf. BIRDCAGE *n.*[1]). **2** [1900s] (*US campus*) (*also* **hen-roost, hennery**) a women's dormitory. **3** [1920s] (*US*) a beauty parlour. [HEN *n.*[1]]

hen-fest *n.* [1940s+] (*US*) a women-only party or gathering. [HEN *n.*[1] (1) + -FEST sfx]

henfire *n.* [1920s] (*US Black*) used in a variety of phrs. as a euph. for hell or damnation; including *how the henfire, I'll be henfired!*, *hen-fired.*

hen frigate *n. see* HEN HOUSE *n.*[1].

hen fruit *n.* (*also* **hen's fruit**) [mid-19C+] (*US*) chicken's eggs.

heng-pan-nail *n.* [20C+] (*W.I.*) **1** unpressed clothes; thus a general term of abuse. **2** ready-made clothes, rather than individually tailored garments. [W.I. pron. of SE *hang upon a nail*, whether in one's house or in the shop]

hen-headed *adj.* (*also* **hen-witted**) [20C+] (*US*) stupid, foolish, scatter-brained (cf. AIRHEADED *adj.*). [characteristics of the barnyard fowl]

hen-hearted *adj.* [16C–mid-19C] cowardly. [early var. on CHICKEN-HEARTED *adj.*]

hen house *n.*[1] (*also* **hen frigate**) [late 18C–early 19C] any house where the wife rather than the husband rules. [note naut. jargon *hen frigate*, a ship where the captain's wife travelled with her husband]

hen house *n.*[2] **1** [late 19C–1900s] a woman's hostel or lodging house. **2** [1900s] a prison in general. **3** [1900s–40s] (*US prison*) a women's prison; the women's section of a prison (cf. BANDHOUSE *n.*). [note US Army *hen house*, the Officers Club, 'where all the chicken hangs out']

hen-hussy *n.* [late 19C–1940s] (*US*) a man who is seen to be overly involved in household affairs and similar 'women's concerns'; thus an effeminate man. [dial. *hen hussy*, a woman who looks after the poultry]

hen is on, a *phr.* [late 19C–1940s] (*US*) something important is about to happen.

Henley Regatta *n.* [1990s+] a chat, a gossip. [rhy. sl. = NATTER *n.*]

hen mill *n.* [1960s] (*US Und.*) a women's prison.

hennery *n. see* HEN-COOP *n.* (2).

hen night *n. see* HEN PARTY *n.*

Henny *n.* [1990s+] (*US Black*) Hennessey brandy.

hen of the game *n.* (*also* **hen of the walk**) **1** [early 17C–19C] a prostitute (cf. ALLEY CAT *n.*). **2** [late 19C] a stalwart working-class woman. [HEN *n.*[1] (1) + GAME *n.*[1] (1)/SE *walk*]

hen party *n.* (*also* **hen night/picnic**) [late 19C+] a women-only get-together. [HEN *n.*[1] (1) + SE *party/night/picnic*]

henpeck *n.* **1** [mid-18C+] a nagged husband. **2** [early 19C] a wife who nags her husband. **3** [mid-19C+] (*also* **henpeckery**) the condition of being nagged. [backform. f. HENPECKED adj.]

henpeck *v.* [late 17C+] of a woman or wife, to dominate her partner. [backform. f. HENPECKED adj.]

henpecked *adj.* [late 17C+] used of a man who is persecuted by the woman with whom he lives, usu. his wife.

henpeckery *n. see* HENPECK n. (3).

hen pen *n.* **1** [20C+] (*US Und.*) a woman's prison. **2** [1960s] (*Aus.*) a women-only room in a local hotel, i.e. public house. [HEN n.[1] (1) + PEN n.[2]]horse fun

hen picnic *n. see* HEN PARTY n.

henrietta *n.* [1990s+] a letter. [rhy. sl.]

Hen-Rock *n.* [1990s+] Hennessey brandy.

hen-roost *n. see* HEN-COOP n.

henry *n.*[1] [20C+] (*US*) a Ford automobile. [*Henry* Ford I (1863–1947), the patriarch of the automobile assembly line]

henry *n.*[2] [1950s+] (*drugs*) heroin (cf. BIG DADDY n.; BIG H n.). [initial letter; also note heroin is a 'masculine' drug, *see* BOY n.[7] (1)]

henry *n.*[3] *see* HENRY VIII n.

henry berry *n.* [1990s+] (*Aus.*) sherry. [rhy. sl.]

Henry Fonda *n.* [1990s+] a Honda 90 motorcycle, esp. as used by trainee taxi-drivers or 'knowledge boys'. [rhy. sl.; ult. US film star *Henry Fonda* (1905–82)]

henry halls *n.* [1950s+] the testicles (cf. CHEESE AND CRACKERS n.). [rhy. sl. = BALLS n.[1] (1); ult. popular UK bandleader *Henry Hall* (1898–1989)]

Henry Hase *n.* [early 19C] a banknote, usu. defined as to its amount, e.g. *a £10 Henry Hase* (cf. ABE n.[2]). [the signature of the banking official]

henry nash *n.* [20C+] cash. [rhy. sl.]

henry neville *n.* (*also* **Henry Nevil, Henry Neville**) [late 19C–1920s] the Devil. [rhy. sl.; ult. the G.R. Sims ballad 'Tottie' (1887): 'What the Henry Neville / Do you think you're doing there?'; ? elision of *henry neville* = hell]

Henry VIII *n.* (*also* **henry**) [2000s] (*drugs*) ⅛oz (4g) of a drug, e.g. cannabis or cocaine [rhy. sl. = EIGHTH n.]

Henry III *n.* (*also* **Henry the Third**) **1** [1950s+] a piece of human excrement (cf. ALI OOP n.). **2** [1980s+] a word. [rhy. sl.; (1) = TURD n.]

hens and chickens *n.* [1930s] (*US gambling*) large or small stakes. [fig. use of HEN n.[2] + CHICKEN n.[5]]

hen's fruit *n. see* HEN FRUIT n.

hen-skin *n.* [1900s–50s] (*US*) a cowboy's blanket or underwear, usu. filled with feathers.

hen's race *n.* [20C+] (*Ulster*) a very short distance.

hen toy *n. see* HOP TOY n.

hen track *v.* [1940s] (*US Black/Harlem*) to sign one's name.

hen tracks *n.* **1** [late 19C–1970s] (*US*) illegible handwriting. **2** [1940s] (*US Black*) a signature.

hen-whipped *adj. see* PUSSY-WHIPPED adj. (1).

hen-witted *adj. see* HEN-HEADED adj.

hep *n.*[1] **1** [1910s] understanding. **2** [1930s+] (*US*) someone who is aware of the situation, esp. within non-establishment circles. [HEP adj. (1)]

hep *n.*[2] [1960s+] *hepatitis.* [abbr.]

hep *n.*[3] *see* JOE HEP n.

hep *adj.* **1** [20C+] aware, sophisticated, in the know; thus GET HEP v. HEPPED (ON) adj. **2** [1940s+] fashionable. [first used among jazz fans of the 1940s (although not orig., as some claim, by jazz musicians: Gold, *A Jazz Lexicon* (1964), suggests that the fans simply heard a Black inflexion of HIP adj. (1) and says that musicians only use it 'derisively'), but rooted in the 19C SE *hep*, shrewd, which comes in turn from *Hep!*, the exhortation of the ploughman or driver urging his horses to 'Get up!' and get lively]

hep *v. see* HIP v.[2].

hep-cat *n.* (*also* **hip-cat**) **1** [1920s+] (*also* **hep bird**) an aware, sophisticated person. **2** [1930s+] (*US Black*) a jazz or swing fan.

3 [1950s+] a general term for a Black person. [HEP adj. (1) + CAT n.[11] (2); note Gold, *A Jazz Lexicon* (1964) pp.143–4: 'though frequently represented as jazz slang…jazzmen have never used this term in speech except derisively. Its etymology…is based on a Northern white hearing a Southern negro speak *hip* with a diphthongized vowel sound']

hepkitten *n.* [1970s] (*US*) a young woman who is a fan of swing music. [joc. dimin. of HEP-CAT n. (2)]

hepped (on) *adj.* [1930s+] (*US*) enthusiastic about, keen on. [HEP adj. (1)]

hepped up *adj.* (*US*) **1** [1930s+] agitated, excited. **2** [1940s+] intoxicated by drugs or alcohol. [HEP adj. (1)]

hepster *n.* [1930s–50s] a jazz or swing fan. [HEP-CAT n. (2)]

hep to the jive *phr.* (*also* **hep to the groove, hep with**) [1940s+] aware, informed, sophisticated, in the know. [HEP adj. (1) + JIVE n.[1] (4)]

her *n.*[1] (*also* **herself**) [1950s+] the wife.

her *n.*[2] [1960s+] (*drugs*) cocaine. [note cocaine is a 'feminine' drug, *see* GIRL n.[2] (1)]

her and him *n.* [20C+] (*Aus.*) a hymn; often in pl. as *hers and hims.* [partial rhy. sl.]

Herb *n. see* HERBERT n.

herb *n.*[1] [1950s] a character, also used of children. [? abbr. *Herbert*, a common Cockney name]

herb *n.*[2] (*also* **herba, herbs**) **1** [1960s] (*US campus*) a cigarette. **2** [1960s–70s] (*US Black*) a marijuana cigarette. **3** [1960s+] (*US Black/W.I. Rasta/drugs*) marijuana (cf. AFRICAN BUSH n.). [orig. used in Jamaica, the religious role of marijuana for Rastafarians is emphasized in the 'natural' image of *herb*, also known as the 'herb of meditation' + a poss. ref. to Ps. 104:14: 'He causeth the grass to grow for the cattle, and herb for the service of man'; (2) f. (3)]

herb *n.*[3] **1** [1990s+] (*US Black*) an unsophisticated person, one who has no knowledge of street life; thus *herbette*, the female equivalent. **2** [2000s] (*US campus*) homosexual. [(1) an early 1990s Burger King commercial featuring a pathetic character named Herb; but note HERB n. as abbr. of HERBERT n.]

herbal *n.* [1990s+] (*US drugs*) a pure marijuana cigarette, as opposed to one that has been laced with cocaine or another drug (cf. AFRICAN BUSH n.).

herbalist *n.* [1970s–80s] (*UK Black*) a drug seller. [HERB n.[2] (3)]

herbalz *n.* [1990s+] (*US Black*) **1** marijuana (cf. AFRICAN BUSH n.). **2** semen. [(2) ety. unknown]

herb and al *n.* [1980s+] (*drugs*) marijuana and alcohol. [HERB n.[2] (3) + abbr.]

Herbert *n.* (*also* **'erbert, Herb**) [1930s+] a simple person; thus *Herbert music*, music hall jokes mixed with rock music.

herbette *n. see* HERB n.[3] (1).

Herbie Hides *n.* [1990s+] trousers. [rhy. sl. = STRIDES n. (1); ult. heavyweight boxer and former WBO champion *Herbie Hide* (b.1973)]

Herbie's bonnet *n.* (*also* **beetle bonnet**) [1990s+] the female genital area, esp. when shaved. [*Herbie*, the star of the eponymous films (1968–80) was a Volkswagen 'Beetle'; the similarity of the car's curving smooth bonnet]

herbs *n.*[1] [1930s+] (*Aus.*) **1** a car's speed, power, responsiveness to the accelerator; thus *give it/someone the herbs*, to accelerate a car or fig. to give someone power. **2** enthusiasm, praise, 'wind-up'. **3** beer. [ety. unknown; ? fig. use SE *herbs*, which 'spice up' a dish or ? given to horses]

herbs *n.*[2] *see* HERB n.[2].

herd *v.* [1930s+] (*US*) to drive a car or other vehicle.

herder *n.* [20C+] (*US prison*) a prison guard who works in the prison yard, controlling the prisoners. [SE *herd*, to drive and control animals]

herd (of camels) *n.* [1930s–40s] (*US Black*) a pack of Camel cigarettes. [pun]

here and now *n.* [1990s+] (*Aus.*) a derog. term for an Oriental person (cf. HALF-OUNCE OF BACCY n.). [rhy. sl. = CHOW n.]

here and there *n.* **1** [1930s] (*Aus.*) hair. **2** [1930s+] (*orig. US*) a chair. [rhy. sl.; never truncated]

here-and-thereian *n.* [late 18C–early 19C] a wanderer, a nomad. [they wander *here and there*]

Herefordshire weed *n.* [mid-19C] an oak tree. [the commonness of the tree in that county]

here goes! *excl.* **1** [early 19C+] an excl. voiced on starting to do something, esp. if the action is potentially dangerous or risky. **2** [20C+] (*also* **here's a go!**) a popular toast before drinking.

here's how! *excl.* [20C+] a popular toast before drinking.

here's looking at you! *excl.* [late 19C+] a toast before drinking. [immortalized (and clichéd) after Humphrey Bogart's rendition in the film *Casablanca* (1941)]

here's looking up your kilts! *excl.* [1940s] (*Aus.*) a facetious toast before drinking. [HERE'S LOOKING AT YOU! excl.; spec. the immortalized toast 'Here's looking at you kid!' spoken by Humphrey Bogart in the film *Casablanca* (1941)]

here's mud in your eye! *excl.* (*also* **mud in your eye(s)!**) [1920s+] a toast when drinking. [orig. milit. use, thus ? ref. to the muddy trenches of WW1]

here's off *phr.* [1900s] (*Aus.*) goodbye.

her highness *n. see* HER (ROYAL) HIGHNESS n.

her indoors *n.* [1970s+] one's wife. [coined by Leon Griffiths in the *Minder* series on Thames TV, 1979; note Jap. *uichinomono*, wife, lit. 'the one inside']

herkin' the gherkin *n.* [20C+] masturbation. [var. on JERK ONE'S GHERKIN v.]

herky-jerky *adj.* (*also* **herky-jerk**) [1940s+] (*US*) awkward, uneven, foolish.

her ladyship *n.* (*also* **his lordship**) **1** [late 19C+] an ironic term for any individual; the social status is irrelevant. **2** [20C+] one who sees himself or herself as a superior being.

Her Majesty's... *see also under* HIS MAJESTY'S...

Her Majesty's carriage *n.* (*also* **His Majesty's...**) [late 19C] a prison van (cf. ANOTHER DAY UP THE QUEEN'S ARSE phr.).

Her Majesty's naval police *n.* (*also* **His Majesty's...**) [late 19C–1900s] sharks. [by swimming near warm-water ports they prevent sailors from attempting to desert ship by swimming ashore]

Her Majesty's pictures *n.* [late 17C] money (cf. ABE n.²).

Her Majesty's School for Heavy Needlework *n.* (*also* **His Majesty's...**) [1940s+] prison (cf. ANOTHER DAY UP THE QUEEN'S ARSE phr.).

Herman *n.* [1910s–40s] (*Aus.*) a German. [rhy. sl. + the Germanic-style name]

Herman (the one-eyed German) *n.* **1** [1970s] (*US*) a large breast. **2** [1990s+] (*US campus*) the penis (cf. ABRAHAM n.¹).

hermit *n.* [mid-19C] (*gypsy*) a highwayman.

Her Mope-Eyed Ladyship *n.* [late 17C–early 18C] fortune, chance, 'Lady Luck'. [SE *mope-eyed*, shortsighted or blind in 1 eye]

herms *n.* [1980s+] (*drugs*) phencyclidine (cf. ACE n.⁴). [ety. unknown]

hernandies *n.* [1970s+] (*US gay*) the buttocks. [play on song title 'Hernando's Hideaway' (1954): 'I know a dark, secluded place…']

her nibs *n. see* HIS NIBS n.

hero *n. see* HERO (SANDWICH) n.

hero/heroina *n. see* HERO (OF THE UNDERWORLD) n.

heroin-head *n.* [1940s] (*US Und.*) a heroin addict. [SE *heroin* + -HEAD sfx (3)]

herone *n.* [1970s+] (*drugs*) heroin. [? Sp.]

hero (of the underworld) *n.* (*also* **heroina**) [1950s+] (*drugs*) heroin.

hero (sandwich) *n.* [1930s+] (*US*) a large sandwich made of 2 slabs of bread cut lengthwise from the loaf and containing a variety of ingredients. [? the idea that one need be a hero to eat one, or an ironic comment on the qualities (eating rather than fighting) of an 'Italian hero']

herp *n.* [1970s+] (*US*) genital *herpes*. [abbr.]

herped *adj.* [1970s+] (*US*) carrying the virus for herpes. [HERP n.]

herring *n.*¹ [late 16C+] (*US*) a foolish, offensive or inconsequential person. [? the commonness of the fish]

herring *n.*² [1930s–40s] (*US*) $1. [play on FISH n.² (2)]

herring-brook *n. see* HERRING POND n.

herring choker *n.* [late 19C+] **1** (*Can.*) a nickname for a native or inhabitant of the Maritime Provinces. **2** (*US*) a Scandinavian-born immigrant. [their consumption of herrings]

herring destroyer *n.* [late 19C+] (*US*) a Scandinavian-born immigrant.

herring-faced *adj.* [early 17C+] worthless. [HERRING n.¹]

herring farm *n.* [1930s] (*US*) a mountain resort.

herring-gut *n.* [1910s] (*Aus.*) a thin man. [backform. f. HERRING-GUTTED adj. (1)]

herring-gutted *adj.* **1** [early 18C–1940s] used of a thin person. **2** [late 19C+] cowardly, 'gutless'.

herring-Jew *n.* [1960s] (*W.I.*) a derog. term for a Jewish or Syrian immigrant, who founded their fortunes on peddling salt-fish.

herring pond *n.* (*also* **herring-brook**) [late 17C+] the sea, esp. the Atlantic; thus *be sent across the herring pond* or *cross the herring pond at the King's expense*, to be transported (albeit to Botany Bay, Australia, rather than America).

herring snapper *n.* [late 19C+] (*US*) a Scandinavian-born immigrant.

her (royal) highness *n.* [late 19C+] used by a man as a sarcastically 'respectful' description of his wife; the implication is of laziness (cf. HIS (ROYAL) HIGHNESS n.).

hers and hims *n. see* HER AND HIM n.

herself *n. see* HER n.¹.

Hershey *adj.* [1970s+] (*US*) used in refs. to the anus and thus male homosexuality; usu. in combs. below. [brandname of *Hershey Bars*, a popular US chocolate bar; thus link to CHOCOLATE adj. (2)]

Hershey highway *n.* (*also* **Hershey bar highway, Hershey Road**) [1970s+] (*US*) the anus (cf. ALLEY WAY n.; BOURNEVILLE BOULEVARD n.). [HERSHEY adj.]

Hershey squirt *n.* (*also* **Hershey squirts**) **1** [1970s+] (*US*) diarrhoea. **2** [1980s+] (*US campus*) (*also* **Hershey stains**) faecal stains on one's underwear due to liquid emitted when breaking wind or through a badly cleaned anus. [HERSHEY adj.]

Hertfordshire kindness *n.* [late 17C–early 19C] a favour that is granted in return for a favour received, repaying one positive gesture with another; the phr. particularly refers to an exchange of congratulatory toasts. [apparently a custom among Hertfordshire people]

Hertz *v.* [1960s] (*US*) to travel in a hired car. [*Hertz* car hire company]

he-say-she-say *n.* (*also* **he-said-she-said**) [1960s–80s] (*US Black*) gossip, chatter, loose talk.

hesh *n.* (*also* **hash**) [1930s+] a male homosexual (cf. BOY-GIRL n.¹). [SE *he + she*]

he-she *n.* **1** [late 19C; 1960s+] a transvestite, transsexual or homosexual person (cf. BOY-GIRL n.¹). **2** [1960s+] a 'masculine' lesbian.

hesher *n.* [1980s+] (*US campus*) a fan of heavy metal music. [? *heavy metal + thrash*]

hesh girl *n. see* HASH GIRL n.

hesitation marks *n.* **1** [1960s+] scars on one's wrist denoting a failed or insufficiently committed suicide attempt. **2** [1970s] (*US gay*) excessive weight. [(2) f. (1) in the sense that extra weight is enough to make gay men suicidal]

hessian *n.* [20C+] (*US*) **1** a troublesome, mischievous person, esp. a fussy woman. **2** a mischievous, ill-behaved child. [SE *Hessian*, a

Hessian mercenary employed by the British during the War of Independence (1775–83); thus a general term of derision. Note also the *hessian fly*, supposedly imported by the Hessian troops, the larvae of which devastate wheat crops]

hessle *n.* [20C+] (*drugs*) heroin. [? HASSLE n.; i.e. the problems involved in buying it, the addiction etc]

het *n.* [1970s+] a *het*erosexual. [abbr.]

hetero *n.* (*also* **heter**) [1950s+] *hetero*sexual. [HETERO adj.]

hetero *adj.* [1930s+] *hetero*sexual. [abbr.]

heterosex *adj.* [1950s] *heterosexual.*

het up *adj.* (*also* **heated up**) [late 19C+] (*orig. US*) tense, nervous, angry, excited. [SE *heat*, thus lit. 'heated up'; in general use 14C–16C but subseq. in dial. or sl. only]

hevethee *n.* [late 19C–1920s] a thief. [centre slang; created by rearranging the syllables or constituent parts of a word]

he went mad and they shot him *phr.* [1940s+] (*Aus.*) a general answer to the question, 'Where is X?'

hewgag *n.* (*also* **gugag**, **hugag**) **1** [mid-19C+] (*US*) a bugle or trumpet. **2** [late 19C] (*US campus*) something for which one has no specific name. **3** [1970s+] (*US*) a battle cry. [SE *hewgag*, a toy musical instrument; ult. origin unknown; ? *gewgaw*, a jew's-harp; (3) f. (1)]

he-whore *n.* **1** [mid-17C–early 18C; 1970s+] a male homosexual, usu. a prostitute. **2** [2000s] a promiscuous man.

he who smelt it, dealt it *phr.* [1950s+] a phr. used to disclaim all responsibility for having farted; often used as a rejoinder to the query WHO CUT THE CHEESE? phr.

he wouldn't go out to a dog-tucker's picnic *phr.* [1980s+] (*N.Z.*) a phr. used to describe a dedicated recluse. [DOG-TUCKER n. + SE *picnic*]

he wouldn't say 'shit' even if he had a mouth full of it *phr.* (*also* ...**even if he had his mouth full of it**) [20C+] (*Can.*) a phr. used of an especially mealy-mouthed, hypocritical person.

he wouldn't work in an iron lung *phr.* [1940s+] (*Aus.*) a phr. said of someone who is totally lazy. [the purpose of an iron lung is to perform the patient's breathing for them]

he would skin a turd *phr.* [late 19C+] (*Can.*) a phr. said of a particularly mean person. [SE *skin* + TURD n. (1)]

hex *n.* [late 19C+] a curse, a spell. [HEX v.]

hex *v.* [mid-19C+] (*orig. US*) to curse, to cast a spell against. [Pennsylvania Ger./Yid. *hexe*, a witch]

hexed *adj.* [1990s+] stupid, confused. [as if somebody had put a HEX n. on you]

hey *n.* [1960s+] (*US*) a synon. for *hell*; thus *what the hey!* what the hell! [euph. + SE *hey!*]

hey! *excl.* [late 19C; 1980s+] used as a form of intimacy, suggesting a complicity between addressee and addressed. [SE *hey!* a greeting]

hey-diddle-diddle *n. see* HI-DIDDLE-DIDDLE n.

hey gammer cook *n.* (*also* **gammer cook, hey gaffer cook, hey gamer cook, high gammer cook**) [late 17C–mid-18C] sexual intercourse; often as *play...* [? dial. *gammocks*, wild play]

hey-hey *n.* **1** [1930s] (*US*) a 'good-time girl'. **2** [1930s] (*US*) problems, controversy, action. **3** [1940s–60s] (*orig. US Black*) sexual intercourse.

hey-hey *adj.* [1930s] of a woman, promiscuous. [HEY-HEY n. (1)]

hey-nonny-no *n.* [late 16C–mid-18C] the vagina (cf. ARTICLE n.). [used in SE as a chorus in various songs/ballads + SE *nonny-no*, a trifle, a 'nothing']

hey Rube! *excl.* [late 19C+] a call for help. [SE *hey!* + RUBE n.[1] (1); *Hey Rube!* was the trad. rallying cry of circus or carnival employees when faced with any trouble from locals]

heyrube *n.* [late 19C+] a fight, orig. between circus or carnival people and local townspeople. [HEY RUBE! excl.]

hey-wow *n.* [1980s+] (*US campus*) someone who clings to the styles of the 1960s. [mockery of the hippie's cries of 'Hey, wow, man, can you dig that...' etc]

H/H *n.* [1960s+] used in sex contact advertisements, *h*igh *h*eels.

hi! *excl.* (*also* **hiya!**) [mid-19C+] (*orig. US*) hello!

hi-ball *n. see* HIGHBALL n.[1].

hic *n. see* HICK n.[1] (2).

hiccius (doccius) *adj.* [18C] drunk. [SE *hiccius doccius*, a juggler; ult. ? real Lat. *hicce est doctus*, this or here is the learned man, or cod Lat. formula used, like the conjuror's *abracadabra* to accompany a juggling trick. Note SE *hiccup*]

hice yourself! *excl.* [20C+] (*W.I.*) get up and get out! [Scot. *hoise*, to lift up, to raise]

hick *n.*[1] **1** [late 17C+] any inhabitant of the countryside, a peasant, a farmer (cf. ALVIN n.). **2** [late 17C+] (*also* **hic**) a potential victim, a gullible simpleton. **3** [1960s+] (*US*) a Puerto Rican (cf. BATO n.). **4** [1960s+] (*US campus*) one who lacks social and/or academic abilities. [popular corruption of the personal name *Dick*, seen as generic]

hick *n.*[2] [1920s] (*US Und.*) $1.

hick *adj.* [20C+] **1** rural, countrified. **2** (*US*) unsophisticated, naïve. [HICK n.[1] (1)]

hick and hack *v.* [late 16C] to pursue and have sexual intercourse with women.

hickery-pickery *n.* (*also* **hicra-picra, higry-pigry**) [19C] a nickname for the plant *Hiera picra*, 'a purgative drug composed of aloes and canella bark, sometimes mixed with honey and other ingredients' (*OED*).

hickey *n.*[1] [20C+] (*N.Z./US*) any small, otherwise nameless object; occas. an unknown person. [ety. unknown]

hickey *n.*[2] (*also* **hicky**) **1** [1910s+] (*US*) a pimple, a boil. **2** [1940s+] (*orig. US*) a love bite, usu. on the neck. **3** [1940s+] (*US*) the penis (cf. BAUBLE n.). **4** [1950s+] (*US*) a bruise, a bump. [ety. unknown; ? HICKEY n.[1]]

hickey *n.*[3] [1940s+] (*Aus.*) any inhabitant of the countryside, a peasant, a farmer; with derog. implication. [HICK n.[1] (1)]

hickey *adj.*[1] [late 18C–19C] drunk, tipsy. [SE *hiccup*]

hickey *adj.*[2] *see* HICKY adj.

hickey hockey *n.* [1920s+] (*Aus.*) a jockey. [rhy. sl.]

hickory *v.* [mid-19C] (*US*) to whip, to thrash. [SE *hickory*, a walking-stick of hickory wood]

hickory-dock *n.* (*also* **hickory-dickory**) [1930s+] (*Aus./US*) a clock. [rhy. sl.]

hickory oil *n.* (*also* **hickory tea**) [early 19C–1950s] (*US*) a whipping. [SE *hickory* (*stick*) + joc. use of *oil/tea*]

hickory towel *n.* [mid-19C] (*US*) a hickory switch.

hicksius doxius *adj.* (*also* **hictius-doctius**) [late 18C–early 19C] drunk. [var. on HICCIUS (DOCCIUS) adj.]

hickster *n.* [1990s+] a gullible, unsophisticated person. [HICK n.[1] (1) + -STER sfx]

Hicksville *n.* [1920s+] (*US*) a generic term for any small, rural town. [HICK n.[1] (1) + -VILLE sfx[1]]

Hicksville *adj.* [1920s+] (*US*) rustic, rural. [HICKSVILLE n.]

hick town *n.* [20C+] (*US*) a small town. [HICK n.[1] (1) + SE *town*]

hicky *n. see* HICKEY n.[2].

hicky *adj.* (*also* **hickey**) [1940s+] (*US*) countrified, rural, unsophisticated. [HICK n.[1] (1)]

hicra-picra *n. see* HICKERY-PICKERY n.

hictius-doctius *adj. see* HICKSIUS DOXIUS adj.

hid *adj.* [1980s+] (*US campus*) very ugly. [abbr. SE *hideous*]

hidden forest *n.* [2000s] (*US Black*) the vagina of a fat woman (cf. BEAUTY SPOT n.).

hidden magic *n.* [1960s+] (*US gay*) a penis that is substantially larger than expected when erect.

hidden treasure *n.* [20C+] **1** the vagina. **2** the landlady's husband, who never appears. [both are 'hidden' and valuable]

hiddy *adj.* [1980s+] (*US campus*) drunk. [SE *hideously*]

hide *n.*[1] **1** [17C+] the human skin, thus one's life; esp. in phrs. *save one's hide* etc. **2** [20C+] a person. **3** [1930s–60s] (*US*) a horse.

4 [1930s–70s] (*jazz*) drums (cf. HIDES n.). **5** [1930s+] (*US*) a wallet. [(1) SE 11C–16C]

hide *n.*[2] **1** [18C] the female genitals. **2** [20C+] (*US*) a woman, usu. considered as a sex object. **3** [20C+] (*US*) an old crone, a hag, an ugly old woman. **4** [1940s–50s] (*US*) an effeminate male homosexual. [SE *hide*/HIDE n.[1] (1), the human skin]

hide *n.*[3] [late 19C+] (*mainly Aus./N.Z.*) impudence, effrontery, cheek. [fig. use of SE *hide*/HIDE n.[1] (1), the human skin]

hide *v.*[1] [late 18C] (*W.I.*) to murder, dismember and bury secretly. [a practice carried out on 18C plantations to discipline rebellious slaves]

hide *v.*[2] [mid-19C–1900s] to thrash, to flog. [SE *hide*/HIDE n.[1] (1), the human skin]

hide and hair *phr. see* HAIR AND HIDE phr.

hide and seek *n.* [20C+] cheek, insolence. [rhy. sl.; never truncated]

hide and tallow *phr. see* HAIR AND HIDE phr.

hideaways *n.* [1930s–40s] (*US Black*) pockets. [one *hides* one's money etc]

hide-beater *n.* [1930s–40s] (*US*) a drummer. [HIDE n.[1] (4) + SE *beater*]

hided *adj.* [19C; 1990s+] beaten up. [SE *give a hiding*]

hi-de-hi *n.* [1930s] (*US*) the exemplar; the very best.

hi-de-hi...ho-de-ho *phr.* [1930s+] a popular style of greeting and the requisite response. [orig. used by US bandleader Cab Calloway in 'The Hi-De-Ho Man' but popularized in the BBC-TV situation comedy, *Hi De Hi!* (1970s–80s), which was set in a 1950s holiday camp]

hideous nightmare *n. see* NIGHTMARE n.

hides *n.* [1930s–50s] (*US Black*) drums. [HIDE n.[1] (4)]

hide the baloney *v.* [1930s+] (*US*) to have sexual intercourse (cf. BURY IT v.). [BALONEY n.[2]]

hide the salami *v.* (*also* **hide the hot dog/the tubesteak**) [1980s+] (*US*) to have sexual intercourse; usu. in phr. PLAY HIDE THE SALAMI v. (cf. BURY IT v.). [SALAMI n.]

hide the sausage *v.* [1940s+] (*Aus.*) to have sexual intercourse (cf. BURY IT v.). [SAUSAGE n.[1] (1)]

hide the weenie *v.* (*also* **hide the wienie**) [1910s+] (*US*) to have sexual intercourse (cf. BURY IT v.). [WEENIE n.[1] (4)]

hide-up *n.* [1920s+] (*Aus.*) a hideout.

hide won't hold hay *phr.* (*also* **hide won't hold shavings, hide won't hold shucks**) [20C+] (*US*) a phr. used as a threat; usu. as *beat him so his hide...*

hidey! *excl.* [1920s+] (*Aus.*) a general greeting, how are you? how do you do? [HI! excl. + HOWDY DOODY! excl.]

hi-diddle-diddle *n.* (*also* **hey-diddle-diddle**) [1950s+] **1** the middle. **2** urination (cf. ANGEL'S KISS n.). **3** a fiddle. [rhy. sl.; (2) = PIDDLE n. (2)]

hi-diddle-diddle *v.* [20C+] (*Aus.*) to urinate (cf. APPLE AND PIP v.). [rhy. sl. = PIDDLE v. (1)]

hiding *n.* [early 19C+] a thrashing; thus fig. a severe sporting defeat. [HIDE v.[2]]

hieser *n.* [1920s] (*US tramp*) a tramp.

hiez-haad *adj.* [20C+] (*W.I. Rasta*) thick-skulled, stubborn, unwilling or unable to hear. [pron. of *ears-hard*]

hifalutin *see under* HIGHFALUTIN.

hig *adj.* [1980s+] (*US campus*) disgusting, ugly. [HID adj. + SE *ugly*]

high *n.*[1] (*also* **highness**) **1** [1940s+] (*drugs*) the euphoric, pleasurable state induced by taking drugs; also the emotional, undrugged equivalent; thus *hold one's high*, to maintain control while intoxicated. **2** [1960s+] (*US*) a drink, a drug or anything that induces an intoxicated state. **3** [1970s] on the lines of *a drunk*, a person when intoxicated by drugs. **4** [1970s+] a general feeling of well-being, esp. in phr. *on a high*, feeling very happy and positive. [HIGH adj.[1]]

high *n.*[2] *see* HIGHBALL n.[1].

high *adj.*[1] **1** [17C+] intoxicated with drink or poss.

religious/spiritual enthusiasm. **2** [1930s+] (*drugs*) intoxicated with drugs. **3** [1930s+] very enthusiastic about or taken with something; often as HIGH ON phr. **4** [1930s+] exhilarated; experiencing the sensation of drugs but without having taken any. **5** [2000s] in fig. use, successful. [(5) in the manner of DOPE adj.[2] (2)]

high *adj.*[2] **1** [mid-18C–1940s] (*US*) impressive, attractive, splendid (cf. HOW'S THAT FOR HIGH? phr.). **2** [late 19C; 2000s] (*orig. US*) expensive. **3** [1940s] (*US*) exaggerated.

high *adj.*[3] [late 19C] often of a prostitute, suffering from venereal disease. [SE *high*, of meat, slightly tainted but still desirable]

high *adj.*[4] [1950s] (*W.I.*) fashionable, stylish.

high *adj.*[5] [1950s–60s] (*drugs*) pure. [such a drug has a *high* percentage of the stated drug, rather than being cut]

high *adv.* [mid-19C+] intensely, forcefully, to a great extent.

high and dry *n.* [mid-19C–1900s] belonging to the Church of England, Anglican. [abbr. *High Church*]

high and dry *adj.* [1910s] (*Aus.*) imprisoned.

high and goodbye *n.* [1950s+] (*US Black*) an unreliable person. [? HI! excl. + SE *goodbye*]

high as a cat's back *phr. see* HIGHER THAN A CAT'S BACK phr.

high as a fiddler's fist *phr.* [1950s–60s] (*US*) drunk. [HIGH adj.[1] (1)]

high as a Georgia pine *phr.* (*also* **higher than a Georgia pine**) [1920s+] (*US Black*) very drunk. [pun on SE *high*/HIGH adj.[1] (1)]

high as a kite *phr.* **1** [20C+] very happy. **2** [1930s+] very drunk. **3** [1930s+] intoxicated by a drug. [play on SE *high*/HIGH adj.[1] + (2) rhy. sl. = TIGHT adj.[5]]

high as Lindbergh *phr.* [1930s–40s] (*US*) drunk. [pun on SE *high*/HIGH adj.[1] (1); Charles *Lindbergh* (1902–74), the first person to fly solo from the US to the UK]

high as ninety *phr.* [mid-19C] (*US*) drunk. [HIGH adj.[1] (1); the use of *ninety* may be ext. of trad. image of *nine* as a lucky number]

high-ass *adj.* (*also* **high-assed**) [1930s+] (*US*) haughty. [SE *high* + ASS n. (2)]

highball *n.*[1] (*also* **h.b., hi-ball, high, highboy**) [late 19C+] (*US*) whisky and soda. [? the tall or *high* glass in which it is served]

highball *n.*[2] [late 19C+] (*US*) a signal, orig. used by railroads, meaning 'proceed'. [HIGHBALL v.[2]]

highball *v.*[1] [1910s+] (*US*) **1** to leave at high speed. **2** to call urgently. **3** to drive fast. **4** to speed things up. [HIGHBALL n.[2]]

highball *v.*[2] (*US Black*) **1** [1920s] to summon. **2** [1930s–50s] to make a gesture with one's hand. [railway use *highball*, to give a signal to proceed]

highball *v.*[3] *see* EYEBALL v. (1).

highballer *n.* [1910s+] (*US*) one who moves fast, one who works hard. [HIGHBALL v.[1]]

highbeams *n.* [1980s+] **1** (*drugs*) the wide eyes of a person on crack cocaine. **2** (*US campus*) prominent nipples. [SE *highbeams*, automobile headlights when they are not dipped]

high bicycle *n.* [1930s] (*US*) a famous or self-important person.

highbinder *n.* **1** [early 19C+] (*US*) a rowdy person, a vandal. **2** [early 19C] (*UK/US prison/Und.*) a criminal; a prison inmate. **3** [late 19C–1950s] (*US*) a member of a secret society supposedly existing among the Chinese in the US for the purpose of black-mailing, extortion and murder. **4** [late 19C–1950s] (*US*) a criminal or fraudulent politician. **5** [20C+] (*US*) a gangster, a thug. **6** [20C+] a snobbish person. [SE *high*, haughty, pretentious, arrogant + BENDER n.[2], a hard drinker or drinking spree. Note, however, *high-binder*, an early 19C New York City gang, composed orig. of butchers' boys and simultaneously known as the *Hide-binders*; and the similarly named late 19C Chinese secret society, supposedly terrorizing fellow-Chinese throughout the US in the late 19C to early 20C, *see* (3)]

high blood *n.* [1950s+] (*US Black*) *high blood* pressure. [abbr.]

high blower *n.* [late 18C–mid-19C] a broken-down horse. [its heavy breathing]

high boy *n.* [18C] a High Churchman, and thus usu. a supporter of Jacobitism.

highboy *n. see* HIGHBALL *n.*[1].

highbrow *n.* [20C+] (*orig. US*) a clever person, an intellectual; depending on context there is often a nuance of jealous attack. [HIGHBROW *adj.*]

highbrow *adj.* (*also* **high-browed**) [20C+] intellectual; often with pej. overtones. [a large forehead supposedly indicates great intelligence]

high brown *n.* (*also* **Vaseline brown**) [1910s+] (*US*) a mulatto, usu. a woman or girl.

high-brown *adj.* **1** [1910s+] (*US*) mulatto. **2** [1930s] (*US Black*) classy, sophisticated. [HIGH BROWN *n.*]

high class *n.* [2000s] (*US prison*) hepatitis C.

high cockalorum *n.* [late 19C–1940s] (*orig. US*) an important person. [for ety. *see* next]

high cockalorum! *excl.* [early 19C–1960s] a general excl. ['an ejaculation or exclamation; also a boy's game in which one set of players jump astride the others (who present a chain of 'backs'), calling out Hey cockalorum, jig, jig, jig! (Hey cockalorum jig! is given as refrain of a popular song c 1800)' (*OED*)]

high collar and short shirt *n.* [late 19C] an imitation dandy.

high cotton *n.* (*also* **tall cotton**) [1930s+] (*orig. US Black*) the good life, the materially successful life. [the wealth that comes from a high cotton crop]

high-daddy *adj.* [late 19C+] (*US*) slick, deceptive, excellent, pleasing. [SE *high* + DADDY *n.* (6)]

high dive *v.* [1930s+] (*US*) to pickpocket. [SE *high* + DIVE *v.*[1]]

high diver *n.*[1] [1930s+] (*US*) a pickpocket. [HIGH DIVE *v.*]

high diver *n.*[2] [1930s+] a person who performs cunnilingus. [DIVE *v.*[2]]

high drag *n.* [1960s] (*US gay*) formal clothing of the opposite sex. [SE *high* + DRAG *n.*[8] (2)]

high Dutch *n.* [17C–mid-19C] nonsense, unintelligible gibberish. [presumably fig. use not of 'Dutch' but *Hochdeutsch*, High German, the German spoken in the southern part of the country]

high eating *n.* [late 18C–early 19C] 'eating skylarks in a garret' (Grose, 1796). [? no more than Grose's punning joke]

high-end *adj.* [1960s+] (*US*) expensive or first-class.

higher than a cat's back *phr.* (*also* **high as a cat's back**) (*US*) **1** [mid-19C+] very tall, very high. **2** [late 19C+] in fig. use, referring to financial limits in gambling. **3** [20C+] very expensive. **4** [1960s] drunk. [pun on SE *high*/HIGH *adj.*[1] (1)]

higher than a Georgia pine *phr. see* HIGH AS A GEORGIA PINE *phr.*

higher than Gilderoy's kite *phr.* (*also* **as high as Gilderoy**) [mid-19C–1900s] (*US*) extremely high. [phr. *to be hung higher than Gilderoy's kite*, to be punished more savagely than one's fellow-criminals. The 17C Scot. robber *Gilderoy* of whom a ballad notes: 'Of Gilderoy sae fraid they ware / They bound him mickle strong, / Tull Edenburrow they led him thair, / And on a gallows hong; / They hong him high above the rest'; so high that he resembled 'a kite in the air']

higher-up *n.* [20C+] a person in authority; one who holds a superior rank (to oneself).

highfalutin *n.* (*also* **hifalutin**) [mid-19C–1950s] (*Aus.*) snobbery, pomposity. [HIGHFALUTIN *adj.*]

highfalutin *adj.* (*also* **hifalutin, high-fallootin', highfaluten, highfaluting, hiki-fallootin'**) [mid-19C+] (*orig. US*) snobbish, pompous. [SE *high* + unknown *falutin*; ? f. *floating, flighting* or *flown*; Hotten (1860) suggests Du. *verlooten*, to go and cast lots; other poss. etys. include Yid. *hifelufelem*, extravagant, boastful talk; Cohen (ed.), *Studies in Slang* II (1989), suggests US milit. jargon *high saluting*, saluting in accordance with milit. training

(crisply, with a sharp snap of the wrist) rather than the somewhat lackadaisical salute of everyday milit. practice]

highfalutin *adv.* [1900s] (*US*) snobbily, pompously.

high femme *n.* [1990s+] (*US gay*) a very feminine lesbian (cf. LOW FEMME *n.*). [SE *high* + FEMME *n.* (3)]

high five *n.*[1] [1980s+] a greeting or celebratory gesture that takes the form of raising the arm and ritualistically slapping each other's palm (cf. LOW FIVE *n.*). [the number of fingers on a hand and the height of the gesture]

high five *n.*[2] [2000s] (*US teen*) HIV, AIDS. [the letters of HIV = abbr. of SE *high* + *V*, roman numeral for 5]

high five *v.* **1** [1980s+] to greet someone by raising the arm and ritualistically slapping the other's palm. **2** [1990s+] to slap hands as a form of celebration, affirmation, congratulation etc. [orig. used in sports as a greeting or sign of congratulation]

high fly *n.* [late 19C–1910s] showing off, acting in a superior, arrogant manner.

high-flyer *n.*[1] (*also* **flier, high-flier**) **1** [late 17C–19C] a daring adventurer. **2** [late 17C+] a pretentious or fashionable strumpet, a promiscuous woman. **3** [18C] a patron of the gallery at a theatre. **4** [18C–19C] a piece of hurried revision. **5** [late 18C–1910s] a pretentious or exaggerated statement. **6** [19C] a genteel beggar or swindler. **7** [19C] a 'swell' beggar, who poses as a fashionable gentleman; thus HIGH FLYING *n.*, ON THE HIGH FLY *phr.* **8** [mid-19C+] (*US*) an important person or one who poses as such. **9** [late 19C] a begging-letter writer. **10** [late 19C–1900s] a gentleman who has fallen on hard times. **11** [20C+] (*US Black*) one who lives well, one who enjoys material success. [(2) 20C+ use is US]

high-flyer *n.*[2] (*also* **high-flier**) [late 17C–early 19C] a High Churchman, a Tory, a Jacobite.

high flying *n.* **1** [19C] the practice of posing as a fashionable gentleman to swindle the gentry (cf. ON THE HIGH FLY *phr.*). **2** [20C+] (*US*) immorality, hedonism, extravagance. [(1) HIGH-FLYER *n.*[1] (7); (2) HIGH-FLYER *n.*[1] (11)]

high-flying *adj.* **1** [late 18C–1910s] of a statement, pretentious. **2** [mid-19C+] (*US*) arrogant, pretentious. [(1) HIGH-FLYER *n.*[1] (5); (2) HIGH-FLYER *n.*[1] (8)]

high gammer cook *n. see* HEY GAMMER COOK *n.*

high gazabo *n.* [1930s] an important or superior person. [SE *high* + GAZABO *n.*]

high-go *n.* [early 19C] a frolic, a spree. [SE *high* + GO *n.*[3] (1)]

high-grade *adj.* [20C+] (*US*) first-rate, excellent, superior.

high Greek *n.* [1960s+] (*gay*) homosexual anal intercourse. [as opposed to LOW GREEK *n.*, but note GREEK *n.*[4] (1)]

high guy *n.* [late 19C+] (*US*) an important person. [SE *high* + GUY *n.*[2] (1)]

high-gyve *v. see* HIGH JIVE *v.*

high hard yard *n.* [1940s] (*US Black*) a high stiff collar.

high hat *n.*[1] **1** [late 19C–1950s] (*US drugs*) a large opium pill (cf. APOSTLE *n.*). **2** [1900s–50s] a glass of whisky and soda. [? its supposed resemblance]

high hat *n.*[2] (*also* **high hatter**) [1920s+] (*orig. US*) **1** a member of the social élite. **2** an arrogant, superior person, a snob. **3** a slight, a snub; usu. as *give someone the high hat*, or *put on the high hat*, to put on airs. [the *high hat* or top hat they were presumed to wear]

high-hat *adj.* [1920s+] of items and individuals, snobbish, pertaining to the upper class. [note Philip 'Vaudeville' (in Federal Writers' Project, 1939): '"High hat," another term used in the same sense, is quite obvious. For example: John Juggler, who has been performing in white flannels, or other cheap costume, appears in new wardrobe presenting his act in a full dress suit and top hat, i. e. – a "high hat." This new ensemble indicates greater prestige, apparent prosperity, and a professional advance. Other vaudevillians, upon commenting upon it might remark: "I see John has gone high hat"']

high hat v. (also **hi-hat**) [1920s+] (orig. US) to act in a superior manner towards others, to snub. [HIGH HAT n.²]

high-hat adv. [1960s] arrogantly. [HIGH-HAT adj.]

high hatter n. see HIGH HAT n.².

high-hatty adj. (also **high-hatted**) [1920s+] (orig. US) snobbish, stuck up. [HIGH HAT n.²]

high-headed adj. [20C+] (US) arrogant, haughty, self-important. [orig. used of horses, referring to the way a horse carries its head high]

high-heeled adj. [mid-19C–1910s] (US/Aus.) arrogant; mostly in HAVE ON ONE'S HIGH-HEELED SHOES v. [wearing high-heeled shoes is a sign of superiority]

high-heeled time n. [20C+] (US) an exciting or enjoyable time. [wearing high heels denotes a special evening out]

high-heeler n. [1920s] (US Und.) a female beggar. [? SE high + HEELER n.]

high in tooth phr. [late 19C] arrogant, boastful. [? the 'long teeth' of the old, whose gums have shrunken and whose tones may tend to the superior]

high iron n. [1930s–60s] (US tramp) the railroad, esp. as regards the main rather than branch lines.

highjacker n. [1930s] (US Und.) a criminal or tramp who robs other criminals or tramps. [HIJACK v. (1)]

high jinks n. [late 17C–mid-19C] a gambler who drinks with his victim in order to render the latter more malleable. [SE high jinks, any form of game, usu. involving some form of forfeit, that is played by drinkers]

high jive v. (also **high-gyve**) [1930s+] (US) to tease, to provoke. [ext. of JIVE v.¹ (4)]

high jump n. 1 [late 19C–1940s] the gallows. 2 [20C+] serious problems. 3 [1960s+] (Aus.) the criminal court. [horseracing imagery]

high kick n. see KICK n.¹ (1).

high-kicker n.¹ [late 19C+] (US) a dissolute person. [image of a troublesome horse that kicks out]

high-kicker n.² [1900s] (Aus.) a chorus girl. [the focal point of her performance]

high-kilted adj. [19C] (Scot.) indecorous. [wearing the kilt or petticoat high or tucked up]

highland n. [1970s] (US Black) the northern, often Black area of a city.

highland fling n.¹ 1 [20C+] (Aus.) string. 2 [20C+] a (wedding) ring. 3 [1960s+] in cards, the king. [rhy. sl.]

highland fling n.² [1980s+] (Aus. prison) masturbation.

highland fling v. [1950s+] to sing; thus **highland flinger**, a singer. [rhy. sl.]

highland flute n. see FLUTE n.⁴.

Highland frisky n. [late 19C] whisky. [rhy. sl. + its effects on the drinker]

highlands n. [20C+] (US) the prosperous parts of a town, where the wealthy élite live. [the way in which the wealthy gravitated to the high ground in an era when the lowlands, usu. near the river, had a higher incidence of disease]

high law n. [mid-16C–early 17C] (UK Und.) highway robbery. [SE highway + LAW n.¹]

high lawyer n. [late 16C–early 17C] a highwayman. [HIGH LAW n.]

high living n. [late 18C–early 19C] esp. of a thief, living in a garret or cockloft, i.e. a very small room immediately above the garret. [pun]

high lonesome n. [late 19C+] (US) a solo drinking spree; thus **hit the high lonesome**, to go out alone.

high-lows n. [early–late 19C] laced boots that reach the ankles. [such footwear stands between low shoes and high boots]

highmadandy n. [20C+] (Ulster) someone who has more money than brains. [SE high + dandy]

high maggie n. see HIGH NELLIE n.

high maintenance adj. [1980s+] (US) emotionally (or otherwise) demanding. [popularized by the film When Harry Met Sally (1989)]

high men n. [mid-16C–early 18C] crooked dice that will always produce a high number.

high mob n. (also **high mobsmen**) [late 19C] (UK Und.) leading criminls.

high muck-a-muck n. (also **big mucky-muck, high mickey-doodle, high monkey-muck, high muckety-muck, high muckty-muck, high mucky-muck**) [mid-19C+] (US) a superior or important person, whether actually or through pretension. [Chinook jargon hiu, plenty + muckamuck, food; MUCK-A-MUCK n.]

high nellie n. (also **high maggie**) [20C+] (Irish) an old-fashioned ladies' bicycle.

highness n. see HIGH n.¹.

high noon n. [1950s+] a spoon. [rhy. sl.; ult. the film High Noon (1952)]

high-noon v. [1980s+] (US) to challenge someone to one-on-one combat. [the Western High Noon (1952) which climaxes with such a confrontation]

high nose n. [20C+] (US) arrogance, snobbery. [HIGH-NOSED adj.]

high-nosed adj. [late 18C–1940s] arrogant, supercilious; intellectual, pretentious. [the subject's sticking of their nose in the air]

high octane n. [1990s+] (US) 1 very strong alcohol. 2 strong caffeinated coffee. [HIGH-OCTANE adj.]

high-octane adj. 1 [1980s+] dynamic, high-powered. 2 [1990s+] of alcohol, highly intoxicating. 3 [1990s+] of coffee, strong, highly caffeinated (cf. LOW-OCTANE adj.). [SE high octane, of gasoline]

high off the hog phr. see HIGH ON THE HOG phr.

high (old) time n. (also **big old time**) [mid-19C+] (US) an uproarious time, a spree.

high on phr. [1930s+] (orig. US) 1 enthusiastic about. 2 in ample possession of (cf. LOW ON phr.). [HIGH adj.¹ (3)]

high one n. [late 19C–1910s] (US) a large drink.

high on the hog phr. (also **high off the hog**) [1940s+] (orig. US) living a comfortable, secure and well-off life; often as live high on the hog. [that area of the animal from which come the choicest cuts of pork and its by-products]

high pad n. (UK Und.) 1 [mid-16C–early 17C] the highway. 2 [mid-17C–mid-19C] (also **high-padsman**) a highwayman; thus high-padding, highway robbery. [SE high + PAD n.¹ (3)]

high pike n. [mid-19C] an exorbitantly high price. [SE pike, the toll paid at a turnpike]

high-play v. [1960s] (US Und.) to act in an ostentatious manner.

highpockets n. (also **high pocket**) [1910s+] (orig. US) a tall man; thus a nickname.

high power n. 1 [1940s+] (US prison) the maximum security section. 2 [1970s] (Aus./UK/US prison) a convict who, on the grounds of good behaviour and trustworthiness, is allotted a privileged position in prison; a TRUSTY n.².

high-powered adj. [1930s+] (US Black) stylish.

high pressure n. [1920s] (US) a boss, a powerful man. [HIGH-PRESSURE v.]

high-pressure adj. [1940s] coerced, forced. [HIGH-PRESSURE v.]

high-pressure v. [1920s+] to pressurize, to intimidate.

high prime v. [late 19C–1920s] (US Black) to show off.

high-rent adj. [1970s] 1 (US campus) moral. 2 sophisticated, superior. [opposite of LOW-RENT adj.]

high-rented adj.¹ [late 19C] hot.

high-rented adj.² [late 19C] (UK Und.) of a villain, extremely well known to the police. [HIGH-RENTED adj.¹; pun on SE hot/HOT adj.² (3)]

high-rider n. [1980s+] (US) a young, esp. working-class, man whose car is modified in such a way that its rear is higher than the front.

high roll v. (orig. US) **1** [20C+] to spend money freely. **2** [1900s] to act boldly or aggressively. [HIGH ROLLER n.]

high roller n. **1** [late 19C+] (orig. US) (also **heavy roller**) one who spends extravagantly, one who gambles for high stakes. **2** [20C+] (US) an expensive prostitute. **3** [1920s] (US) one who behaves outrageously. **4** [1930s] (US Black) a type of hat worn by gamblers. **5** [1980s+] (W.I./UK/US Black teen) a materially successful person, usu. a rich ghetto drug dealer; as used by the Los Angeles gang, the Crips. **6** [1990s+] (US) a senior manager. [SE high + roller, a dice-player]

high-rolling adj. [late 19C+] (orig. US) **1** extravagant, betting or spending heavily. **2** in ext. use, important, influential. [HIGH ROLLER n.]

high Russian n. [1960s+] (gay) simultaneous anal and oral sex.

highs n. [1970s+] (US) high-topped sneakers or trainers.

high school harry n. (also **harry high school**) [1950s+] (US campus) an immature male student.

high seas n. [1920s+] (US) the knees. [rhy. sl.]

high-season brown n. [1900s–60s] (US Black) a beautiful, brown-skinned woman.

high-shoe n. (also **high shoon**) [mid-17C–early 19C] a rustic, a peasant (cf. BOGHOPPER n.). [? the heavy footwear favoured by country-dwellers]

high-shoed adj. [late 17C–early 19C] countrified, gullible. [HIGH-SHOE n.]

high shot n. [1920s+] (orig. US) a superior person or one who claims to be superior. [var. on BIG SHOT n.]

highside v. [1960s+] (US Black) to behave in an arrogant, boastful manner, to show off.

highsider n. [1990s+] an arrogant person, a person who shows off their material wealth. [HIGHSIDE v.]

high-siding n. [1960s+] (US Black) showing off, bragging, often in the ostentatious display of jewellery, expensive clothes, cars etc. [HIGHSIDE v.]

high sign n. **1** [late 19C+] (orig. US) a warning, a recognition signal, a secret sign, esp. when denoting one's membership of a group; a signal that the 'coast is clear'. **2** a sign to leave, a rejection; as give someone the high sign.

high sign v. **1** [1920s+] (US) to warn, to give a sign of recognition, to signal that there is no danger. **2** [1970s+] (US Black) to show off, to upstage somebody. [HIGH SIGN n.]

high-sniffing adj. [mid-19C+] arrogant. [the sniffing nose is also 'in the air']

high spicer n. [late 18C–mid-19C] (UK Und.) a highwayman. [SE high + SPICER n.]

high-spice toby n. see HIGH-TOBY SPICE n.

high steam adj. [1940s] (W.I.) very good, superior. [? SE high esteem]

high-step v. [1910s–20s] (Aus.) to feel pleased with oneself, to feel self-satisfied.

high-stepper n.[1] (also **stepper**) **1** [late 19C–1930s] a fashionably dressed or smoothly mannered person; a hedonist. **2** [1920s–60s] (US Black) a tough, resilient person. [(1) 20C+ use is SE; orig. of a horse that lifts its feet high when walking or trotting]

high-stepper n.[2] [1910s–60s] pepper. [rhy. sl.]

high-stepping adj. [1910s+] (Aus./US Black) aristocratic, smart; thus boastful, arrogant, showing off. [HIGH-STEPPER n.[1] (1)]

high-stomached adj. [mid-16C–18C; 1900s] haughty, arrogant.

High Street, China phr. [1930s+] a far-away, fantasy place.

highstrikes n. [mid-19C–1930s] hysterics. [mispron.]

hightail v. (also **hightail it, hi-tail**) [1910s+] (orig. US) to leave quickly, to run off, to escape. [reverse anthropomorphism]

high tec n. [2000s] (drugs) alkyl nitrites. [play on SE high tec(hnology)]

high tide n. [late 17C–mid-19C] a state of financial security.

high tober n. [late 18C–mid-19C] (UK Und.) an élite highway-man. [note E.P. suggests a misreading of HIGH-TOBY n. and thus misdefinition]

high-toby n. **1** [late 18C–19C] the highway, the main road. **2** [late 18C–1940s] highway robbery; thus on the high-toby, living the 'high' life, usu. of a gambler.

high-toby-gloak n. (also **high-tober-gloak, high-toby gloque**) [19C] a mounted highwayman. [HIGH-TOBY n. + GLOAK n.]

high-toby-man n. [19C] a highwayman. [HIGH-TOBY n. + SE man]

high-toby spice n. (also **high-spice toby, high-toby splice, high-toby spree**) [late 18C–19C] **1** the highway, the road. **2** highway robbery. [HIGH-TOBY n. + SPICE n.[1]]

high-tone n. (also **high-toner**) [late 19C+] (US) an important person, a pretentious person. [HIGH-TONE adj.]

high-tone adj. (also **high-toned, high-toney**) **1** [late 18C+] superior, high-quality. **2** [late 19C+] stand-offish, snobbish; upper-class.

high tone v. [1910s–20s] (US) to snub, to ignore. [HIGH-TONE adj. (2)]

high toner n. see HIGH-TONE n.

high-top fade n. [1980s+] a style of haircut favoured by young Blacks. [SE high + top + FADE n.[4]]

high-topper n. [mid–late 19C] a dandified thief. [fig. use of SE]

highty-tighty n. (also **heighty-toity, hity-tity**) **1** [late 17C–18C] a promiscuous girl. **2** [early 19C–1920s] an aloof, snobbish person. [first cited in B.E. (1699) – who spells it 'hightetity'; although HOITY-TOITY n. is earlier, OED notes the contemporary pron of 'oi' as 'igh', as in oil = ile, boil = bile, and thus sees it as no more than 'a variant']

highty-tighty adj. [early 19C–1920s] aloof, snobbish, supercilious. [HIGHTY-TIGHTY n.]

highty-tighty adv. [early 19C–1920s] aloofly, superciliously. [HIGHTY-TIGHTY adj.]

highty-tighty! excl. [early 19C–1920s] an excl. of disdain, annoyed surprise, infuriation. [HIGHTY-TIGHTY adj.]

high-up n. [1930s+] (orig. US) the boss, the leader, anyone senior to or more powerful than the speaker. [HIGH-UP adj.]

high-up adj. [1910s+] (orig. US) influential, important.

high up in the pictures phr. see IN THE PICTURE phr. (1).

high water n. [late 18C–mid-19C] financial security. [the image is, however, of impermanence – like the real high water, such an economic 'tide' will ebb in time]

highwater adj. [mid-19C+] (US) too short, usu. of trousers, occas. of other clothing or hair (cf. HIGHWATERS n.).

high-water mark n. (also **tidemark**) [late 19C+] the line of dirt, usu. on the neck, that shows the limit to which a person has washed.

high waters n. [1980s+] (US Black) an erection.

highwaters n. [1950s+] (US) trousers that are too short. [HIGHWATER adj.]

highway n. [20C+] the vagina (cf. ALLEY n.[1]).

high, west and crooked phr. [19C+] (orig. US) in all directions, disarray, confusion.

high, wide and handsome phr. [20C+] (orig. US) happy, pleasant, carefree, performing well and easily; esp. with v. ride.

high yellow n. (also **deep yellow, high yalla, high yaller, yalla**) [1920s+] a mulatto woman or girl; occas. a man. [HIGH-YELLOW adj.]

high-yellow adj. (also **high-yaller**) (US) **1** [1920s+] mulatto. **2** [1970s+] arrogant, superior. **3** [2000s] in colour, light brown. [SE high + YELLOW adj.[2] (1); the colour of the complexion; (2) f. (1) i.e. considered better than Black]

higrade v. [1920s] (US tramp) to obtain something illegally.

higry-pigry n. see HICKERY-PICKERY n.

hi-hat v. see HIGH HAT v.

hijack n. **1** [late 19C–1920s] (US) the robbery of tramps as they sleep in the 'hobo jungles'; the individual who does this. **2** [late

19C+] (*orig. US*) a hold-up followed by the theft of goods (often exercised by one criminal upon another). **3** [1920s] a robber who uses violence. [according to Cohen, *Studies in Slang* II (1989), based on *high jack*, zinc ore, a term used *c.*1899 in the mines of Webb City, Missouri, then the world's greatest lead/zinc mine. This zinc ore was more valuable than the basic lead among which it was found, and miners would steal it to further enrich themselves. The term was virtually SE by 1900, as are the later meanings referring to the holding up of vehicles, including aircraft, and the killing or ransoming of their occupants]

hijack *v.* **1** [1900s–20s] (*US tramp*) to rob another tramp as they sleep in the 'hobo jungles'; later, to rob a fellow criminal. **2** [1920s+] (*US*) to subject to extortion. **3** [1920s+] (*US gay/prison*) to rape another man. **4** [1920s+] (*US*) to remove or move a person against their will. **5** [1930s] (*US prison*) to rob a fellow prisoner, with violence. [HIJACK n.]

hi jimmy knacker *n.* [20C+] tobacco. [rhy. sl.; ult. the name of an old street game]

hijo! *excl.* [1950s+] (*US*) a general excl. [Sp. *hijo*, son (of a —)]

hijo de puta *n.* [1950s+] (*US/P.R.*) a general term of abuse; lit. 'son of a whore'. [Sp.]

hike *n.*[1] [mid-19C+] a vigorous or laborious walk; a tramp or march, a long journey by car.

hike *n.*[2] [late 19C] (*US*) a derog. term for an Italian immigrant (cf. DAGO n.). [? comb. of HUNKY n. (1) + KIKE n. (1)]

hike *v.* **1** [mid-19C+] to raise. **2** [mid-19C+] to drag, to pull. **3** [1900s–30s] to carry. **4** [1940s] to store up, to put away, esp. a valuable object. **5** [1950s] to send away. **6** [1950s–60s] to take someone for a walk, with the implication being that they will be assaulted or killed. [dial.]

hike off *v.* **1** [early 18C+] (*UK Und.*) (*also* **hike**, **hike out**) to leave, to go home. **2** [mid–late 19C] (*UK Und.*) to arrest. **3** [1950s] (*US*) to trick or cheat. [dial. *hike*, to run off with, to snatch]

hiker *n.*[1] (*US*) **1** [1900s] a countryman. **2** [1930s–40s] a small-town marshal.

hiker *n.*[2] [1910s–20s] (*US*) a leg.

hiki-fallootin' *adj. see* HIGHFALUTIN adj.

hikori *n.* (*also* **hikuli**) [20C+] (*drugs*) peyote. [? Amerindian]

hilda handcuffs *n.* [1980s+] (*camp gay*) a policeman.

hilding *n.* [late 16C–early 18C] a prostitute. [SE *hilding*, a contemptible, worthless person of either sex; a good-for-nothing]

hill *n.* (*also* **marble hill**, **still hill**) [20C+] (*US*) a cemetery.

hill and dale *n.* [1940s+] confidence trickery. [rhy. sl. = TALE n.[1] (1)]

hillbilly heroin *n.* [2000s] (*US drugs*) oxycontin. [SAmE *hillbilly*, used as a general derog. adj. + SE *heroin*]

hilljack *n.* [20C+] (*US*) a hillbilly, a country yokel (cf. BOONIE n.[1]). [SE *hill* + JACK n.[2]]

hillman hunter *n.* [20C+] a customer. [rhy. sl. = PUNTER n.[1] (4); ult. the motorcar *Hillman Hunter*]

hillocks *n.* [1970s+] (*US gay*) the buttocks.

hill of beans, a *n.* (*also* **a row of beans/pins**) [mid-19C+] an insignificant or useless thing, nothing; often in phr. *not amount to a hill of beans*.

hill of Venus *n. see* VENUS'S HIGHWAY n.

hill-top literature *n.* [late 19C] good advice. [the warnings that, in the early days of cycling, were posted at the top of hills, warning cyclists of the incline and/or dangerous curves ahead]

hilt and hair *phr. see* HAIR AND HIDE phr.

hilter-skilter *adv. see* HELTER-SKELTER adv.

him *n.*[1] [1960s+] (*drugs*) heroin (cf. BIG DADDY n.). [heroin is a 'masculine' drug, *see* BOY n.[7] (1)]

him *n.*[2] *see* HE n.

him and his boy *n. see* BOY n.[2].

himbette *n.* [2000s] a younger, and perhaps more attractive HIMBO n.; the male equivalent of a BIMBETTE n. [HIMBO n. + SE fem./dimin. sfx *-ette*]

himbo *n.* [1980s+] a gigolo. [*him* + BIMBO n. (5); allegedly coined in *Tatler* magazine]

himmer *n.* [1950s–70s] a male homosexual (cf. BOY-GIRL n.[1]). [SE *him*; poss. f. an old joke, the punchline of which puns on SE *hymn/him*]

hinaki *n.* (*also* **hinake**) [1940s+] (*Aus./N.Z.*) prison. [Maori slang *hinake*, eel trap]

hinchinarfer *n.* [late 19C] a grumpy, gruff-voiced woman. [SE *inch and a half*, the supposed length of her husband's penis – her grumpiness is due to sexual frustration]

hincty *n.* (*also* **hinckty**, **haincty**) (*US Black*) **1** [1920s+] a snob, an arrogant, self-opinionated person. **2** [1960s+] a White person. [HINCTY adj.[1]]

hincty *adj.*[1] (*also* **haincty**, **hinckty**) (*US Black*) **1** [1920s+] snobbish, pretentious, putting on airs. **2** [1960s+] a derog. ref. to any Black abandoning racial pride for attempts to ape White manners or styles. [ety. unknown; a suggestion that the word is an elision of HANDKERCHIEF-HEAD n.[1] has no linguistic backing and this is earlier anyway; ? note Lincolnshire dial. *hinch*, meanness, miserliness]

hincty *adj.*[2] *see* HINKY adj.

hind *n.* [1930s+] (*US Black*) the buttocks, the posterior (cf. ARSE-END n.). [abbr. BEHIND n. (1)]

hind coach-wheel *n.* [late 17C–early 19C] a 5-shilling piece (25p), a crown. [the 'hind' or rear coach-wheels are larger than the front ones]

hind fist *n.* [1900s] (*Aus.*) a leg, a foot.

Hindoo *n.* (*also* **Hindu**) **1** [19C] (*S.Afr.*) Europeans who came from India to recuperate. **2** [1900s–10s] (*US*) a person with special ability, a wizard. **3** [1950s] a spell. [facetious uses of SE *Hindoo/Hindu*, a follower of Hinduism and thus, broadly, an Indian]

hind paw *n.* [18C–19C] a foot, a leg.

hind-shifters *n.* [early 19C] the feet or heels; esp. as *a pair of…*

hindside *n.* (*also* **hind-quarter**, **hind sights**) [mid-19C+] the buttocks, the posterior (cf. ARSE-END n.). [SE *behind/backside*; note HIND n.]

hindside-backaways *adv.* (*also* **hindside-backwards**) [20C+] (*US*) back to front.

hindside-before *adv.* (*also* **hindside-first**) **1** [20C+] (*US*) back to front. **2** [1930s] in fig. use, confused.

hindside of nowhere *n.* [20C+] (*US*) a particularly out-of-the-way place.

hind sights *n. see* HINDSIDE n.

Hindu *n.*[1] [1930s] (*US Und.*) one who cannot be bribed. [play on the 'untouchable' caste (properly *harijan* or *dalit*)/TOUCH v.[1]]

Hindu *n.*[2] *see* HINDOO n.

Hindustani jig *n.* [1960s+] (*gay*) anal intercourse. [? a supposed predilection of Hindus for sodomy]

Hiney *n. see* HEINIE n.[1].

hiney *n.* [1920s–50s] (*US Black*) the buttocks, ext. to one's self. [abbr. SE *hind-quarters*]

hinge *n.* [1930s+] (*US*) a look.

hinge-jaw *n.* [20C+] (*US*) one who talks too much.

hinges *n.*[1] [19C+] (*US*) used in general phrs. of intensification, e.g. BLACK AS THE HINGES OF HELL phr., HOT AS THE HINGES OF HELL phr. [SE *hinge*]

hinges *n.*[2] [20C+] (*US*) the joints of the human body; thus *one's hinges are creaking*, one is getting old.

hing-oot *n. see* HANG-OUT n.[2] (2).

hink *n.* [1950s] suspicious information or rumour, suspicious activity. [HINKY adj. (1)]

hinked *adj.* [1950s] frightened of, nervous about. [HINKY adj. (2)]

hinkie *adj. see* HINKY adj.

hink (out) *v.* [1950s–60s] (*US*) to become or appear nervous, frightened. [HINKY adj. (2)]

hinky *n.* [1920s] (*US*) something or somewhere cheap and unsophisticated. [HINKY adj. (3) although this predates]

hinky *adj.* (*also* **hankty, hincty, hinkie, hinkty**) **1** [1920s+] (*US police*) suspicious. **2** [1950s+] (*US*) scared, jumpy, nervous. **3** [1960s] (*US*) very cheap, petty. [Scot. *hink*, a hesitation, a misgiving]

hinky-dinky *adj.* (*US*) **1** [1900s–30s] excellent. **2** [1900s–40s] little, short in stature. [the nickname of Michael 'Hinky Dink' Kenna (1858–1946), alderman and politician of Chicago]

hinny *n. see* HEN n.¹ (4).

hinterland *n.* [late 19C] the buttocks, the posterior.

Hip, the *n.* [1920s] the *Hipp*odrome, New York. [abbr.]

hip *n.*¹ [1910s] (*US Und.*) a burden, a problem. [ON ONE'S HIP phr. (1); but note also HIP, THE n.]

hip *n.*² (*also* **hipness**) [1940s+] (*orig. US Black*) sophistication, the prevailing fashion. [HIP adj. (1)]

hip *n.*³ [1950s] (*drugs*) a narcotics user. [from lying on one's hip when partaking of opium; ON THE HIP phr.²]

hip, the *n.* (*also* **hipp, hipps, hips, hyps**) [18C–19C] neuroses, misery, esp. when brought on by excessive drinking (cf. HIPPED adj.¹; HIPPY adj.). [SE *hypochondria*]

hip *adj.* (*also* **hip to**) **1** [20C+] (*also* **hip on**) sophisticated, aware, in tune with events, ideas and situations (cf. HIPPED adj.²). **2** [1920s+] (*US*) infatuated, excited. **3** [1940s–50s] (*US*) insolent, cheeky. **4** [1940s+] (*US Black*) splendid, enjoyable. **5** [1960s+] (*US Black*) in possession of or able to supply drugs. [HEP adj. (1) or the posture of the opium smoker, reclining on his *hip* and the idea that the term, e.g. 'are you hip?', was used as a form of recognition between smokers; a link to Wolof *hepi*, to see or *hipi*, to open one's eyes has been posited. As abbr. for HIPSTER n. the word had a more specific meaning to jazz buffs/beatniks of the 1950s, but now the general use is predominant]

hip *v.*¹ [mid–late 19C] to depress. [HIP, THE n.]

hip *v.*² (*also* **hep, hip on, hip to, hyp**) **1** [1910s+] (*orig. US Black*) to explain, to initiate into. **2** [1930s+] to inform, to tell about. **3** [1950s] as interrog., to understand. [Décharné, *Straight from the Fridge* (2000), notes that *hep* can be found in this sense in A.H. Lewis, *Apaches of New York* (1912)]

hip *adv.* [1950s+] smartly, fashionably. [HIP adj. (1)]

hip-and-drop *v.* (*also* **hop-and-drop**) [20C+] (*W.I.*) to limp, either because of a temporary injury or a permanent deformity.

hip at the clinch *n.* [20C+] (*Ulster*) one who has a limp.

hip-cat *n. see* HEP-CAT n.

Hip City *n.* [20C+] (*US Black*) Cleveland, Ohio. [? HIP adj.]

hip deep to a tall Indian *phr.* [20C+] (*US*) very deep; often used of water, snow.

hip-disease *n.* [1920s+] (*Aus.*) the habit of carrying a hip-flask.

hipe *n. see* HYPE n.¹ (1).

hip-flipper *n.* [1920s–50s] (*US*) an Oriental dancer. [coined by columnist Walter Winchell (1897–1972)]

hip-hitter *n.* [1970s] (*gay*) a male homosexual. [the physical movements of anal intercourse]

hip-hop *n.* [1970s+] (*orig. US Black*) the singing or chanting of the lyrics of a RAP n.⁵ song against a heavy bass line, usu. produced by a drum machine or synthesizer. [coined either by DJ Hollywood, who pioneered the hip-hop style of singing at Club 371 in Harlem, New York, spec. in the scat-rap 'Hip hop de hippy hop the body rock' or by DJ Kool Herc in 1968 (Alex Pate *USA Weekend* magazine 1993) or 1975 (*George*). While the terms *hip-hop* and RAP n.⁵ are used interchangeably, the former will often feature a more elaborate, even dominant backing track; note William Shaw, *Westsiders* (2000): 'For the most part the terms rap and hip-hop are interchangeable. But purists insist that hip-hop refers to the whole culture, not just the MC-ing [...] Hip-hoppers look down on mere rappers'; Shaw also notes that hip-hoppers tend be middle class while rappers are working-class]

hip-hop *adj.* [1970s+] (*orig. US Black*) pertaining to the hip-hop/rap lifestyle and attitudes. [HIP-HOP n.]

hipidity *n.* [1970s] (*US campus*) a usu. young person, preaching a philosophy of 'love and peace', backed by a wide spectrum of drug use, esp. cannabis and hallucinogens. [HIPPIE n.² (3)]

hip inside *n.* [mid-19C] (*UK Und.*) an inside coat pocket (cf. HIP OUTSIDE n.).

hip-layer *n.* [1930s–50s] (*US drugs*) an opium smoker.

hip Michael, your head's on fire! *excl.* [mid-18C–early 19C] an excl. aimed at any passing red-headed man.

hipness *n. see* HIP n.².

hip-nipper *n.* [1970s] (*Aus.*) girls' bikini underpants.

hip on *adj. see* HIP adj. (1).

hip on *v. see* HIP v.².

hip one's ship *v.* [1950s] (*US Black*) to make clear, to explain. [HIP v.² + assonance]

hip outside *n.* [mid-19C] (*UK Und.*) an outside coat pocket (cf. HIP INSIDE n.).

hipp *n. see* HIP, THE n.

hipped *adj.*¹ **1** [early 18C+] (*also* **hippish, hypped**) miserable, unhappy, in low spirits. **2** [mid-19C+] angry, irritated. **3** [late 19C–1940s] (*US campus*) impoverished. **4** [1900s–30s] (*US*) defeated, done for. [HIP, THE n.]

hipped *adj.*² (*also* **hipped on**) **1** [late 19C+] obsessed with, convinced of. **2** [1920s–70s] (*US Black*) aware, well-informed; often ext. as *hipped to the play*, *hipped to the jive*. [HIP adj. (1)]

hipped *adj.*³ [1920s–40s] (*US Und.*) **1** carrying a weapon. **2** carrying a hip-flask. [SE *hip*]

hip-peddler *n.* [1900s–40s] (*US*) a prostitute (cf. ASS PEDDLER n.).

hipped on *adj. see* HIPPED adj.².

hippie *n.*¹ [20C+] (*W.I., Guyn.*) a half-bottle. [a bottle small enough to be kept in one's hip pocket]

hippie *n.*² (*also* **hippy**) **1** [1950s–60s] (*US Black*) one who poses (with little or no success) as a HIPSTER n. **2** [1950s–70s] (*orig. US*) a sophisticated, cool, 'hip' person. **3** [1960s+] (*orig. US*) a (usu.) young person, preaching a philosophy of 'love and peace', backed by a wide spectrum of drug usage, esp. of cannabis and hallucinogens. [like many terms, *hippie* crossed from the Black to White worlds; unlike most, however, it altered its meaning, in this case from negative to, in peer-group eyes at least, positive. Since the 1960s/early 1970s the negative image has returned, although not as a failed *hipster* but as a 1960s throwback]

hippie *adj.* (*also* **hippy**) [1960s+] pertaining to the style or fashion of the 1960s lifestyle. [HIPPIE n.² (3)]

hippie crack *n.* [1980s+] (*drugs*) nitrous oxide. [HIPPIE n.² (3) + CRACK n.¹³]

hippies *n.* [1940s–50s] (*N.Z.*) male swimming briefs. [SE *hip*]

hippins *n.* [1930s] (*US tramp*) a mattress.

hippish *adj. see* HIPPED adj.¹ (1).

hippo *n.*¹ [1970s+] (*S.Afr.*) an armoured police vehicle. [abbr. SE *hippopotamus*]

hippo *n.*² *see* HYPO n.¹.

hippodrome *n.* [late 19C–1900s] (*US sporting*) any race or sporting contest in which the result has been fixed in advance. [SE *hippodrome*, a course or circus for horseraces and chariot-races]

hippodrome *v.* [late 19C–1940s] (*US sporting*) to fix a sporting competition. [HIPPODROME n.]

hipps *n. see* HIP, THE n.

hippy *see also under* HIPPIE.

hippy *adj.* [late 19C] miserable, low-spirited. [HIP, THE n.]

hippy-dippy *adj.* **1** [1960s] (*US Black*) immature, juvenile. **2** [1960s+] eccentric with added overtones of hippiedom. [HIPPIE adj. + DIPPY adj. (1); note Cooper, *The Scene* (1960): 'Hippy-dippy, sometimes kiddy, cry for your bottle when you want your titty' used to berate one who is acting childishly]

hippy-trippy *adj.* (*also* **trippy-hippie**) [1970s+] eccentric with added overtones of hippiedom. [HIPPIE adj. + TRIPPY adj. (2)]

hips n.[1] [1920s] bad luck, a misfortune. [HIP, THE n.]

hips n.[2] see HIP, THE n.

hipsidoodle n. [1990s+] (US) a HIPPIE n.[2] (3), or someone who resembles one.

hipster n. [1930s+] (orig. US Black) one who espouses the fashionable Bohemian stance of the period; the essence was a conscious downplaying of emotional display, a stance poss. facilitated by heroin addiction. [HIP adj. (1) + -STER sfx; Black use dropped by 1940s]

hipsy hoy n. [20C+] a boy. [rhy. sl.]

hip to adj. see HIP adj.

hip to v. see HIP v.[2]

hip-tosser n. [1950s] a male homosexual.

hip to the tip phr. [1950s] (US Black) to the greatest extent, e.g. dressed up in one's best clothes.

hip up v. [1970s] (US) to understand, to appreciate. [HIP adj. (1)]

hiram n. 1 [1910s] (US Und.) an initiate into criminality; a thief. 2 [1930s+] (US) a rustic, a peasant (cf. ALVIN n.). [(1) a metaphor taken from freemasonry; (2) the proper name, used in the Old Testament and thus popular among Puritan immigrants]

hiray n. (also **hirey**) [20C+] money. [? SE hire]

hired gun n. [1950s+] (orig. US) in business, an executive who is hired for the performance of a particularly tough task. [the imagery of cinema Westerns; the task performed, he may well 'ride off into the sunset'; GUN n.[9]]

hi-res adj. [1930s+] (US) fine, satisfactory, admirable. [abbr. SE high resolution, used to define image quality on a video monitor]

hirey n. see HIRAY n.

hirsute oyster n. (also **hairy oyster**) [1980s+] the vagina. [play on BEARDED CLAM n.]

his balls are bigger than his brains phr. [1940s+] said of a man who rushes into situations without thinking. [BALLS n.[1] (1)]

his blue serge n. [1920s] (US) a sweetheart.

his dibs n. [1920s–30s] a wealthy person. [a pun on HIS NIBS n. (3) + DIBBS n. (1)]

his feathers n. [1900s] (US) an important person, or one who believes that they are. [FEATHERS n.[1] (1)]

his gills n. [late 19C–1910s] (Aus.) a self-important person, an authority, on the model of HIS NIBS n. (1).

his highness n. see HIS (ROYAL) HIGHNESS n.

hi si n. [1950s] (US) high society. [phonetic abbr.]

his knabs/knobs n. see HIS NABS n.

his knibbs n. see HIS NIBS n.

his lordship n. see HER LADYSHIP n.

His Majesty's... see also under HER MAJESTY'S...

His Majesty's bad bargain n. (also **Her Majesty's bad/hard bargain, king's bad/hard bargain, Q.H.B., queen's bad/hard bargain, queen's bad shilling**) [late 18C–1900s] a worthless soldier; a malingerer; a soldier jailed in a civilian prison (cf. ANOTHER DAY UP THE QUEEN'S ARSE phr.). [his service does not justify his pay]

his morning and evening song do not agree phr. [late 18C–early 19C] his statements are inconsistent.

his nabs n. (also **his knabs, his knobs, his nobs**) [late 18C–1930s] himself. [? NEB n.[1]]

his nibs n. (also **her nibs, his knibbs, his nobs**) 1 [mid-19C+] himself. 2 [late 19C+] an employer, a superior. 3 [late 19C+] an important, impressive person. 4 [late 19C+] (also **his nabs**) a self-important person. [NIBS n. (2)]

his (royal) highness n. [late 19C+] used by a woman as a sarcastically 'respectful' description of her husband; the implication is of laziness, or someone considered to be pompous, overbearing (cf. HER (ROYAL) HIGHNESS n.).

his shoe pinches him phr. 1 [mid-18C–19C] he is drunk. 2 [20C+] he (probably) has a large penis. [euphs.; (2) the premise that large feet or a large nose equate with a large penis]

his stockings belong to two parishes phr. [late 18C–early 19C] said of one who is wearing odd stockings.

hissy (fit) n. [1970s+] (US) a tantrum, an outburst of bad temper. [? SE hysterical or hiss]

hist adj. [1980s+] (US campus) finished, over. [SE history]

hist v. see HEIST v.

hist phr. [1980s+] (US campus) goodbye. [abbr. SE history]

hister n. see HEISTER n.

historical adj. [late 19C] (UK society) old-fashioned, unfashionable, e.g. of clothes.

history of the four kings, the n. (also **the book of the four kings**) [mid-18C–19C] a pack of cards; thus study the history of the four kings, to play cards.

his whiskers n. see WHISKERS n.[1] (1).

his wife keeps the key phr. [late 19C] a phr. used of one who has to sneak out to the pub surreptitiously.

hit n.[1] 1 [18C+] a successful coup of any sort, usu. based on crime. 2 [18C+] a success, usu. in show business. 3 [early 19C+] (US gambling) a winning series of numbers in gambling. 4 [20C+] a good impression.

hit n.[2] 1 [19C+] an attempted crime, esp. a robbery. 2 [1950s+] (UK Und.) a murder, esp. a gangster killing. 3 [1950s+] (US Und.) the target/victim of an assassination. 4 [1960s+] (US Und.) an attack against a rival gang or gang member.

hit n.[3] 1 [20C+] a single drink of alcohol. 2 [20C+] a swig of liquid, a measure of anything. 3 [1910s+] the effect that follows the taking of any drug or drink. 4 [1930s+] (drugs) a purchase of a drug. 5 [1950s+] (drugs) a puff on a cigarette, marijuana cigarette or pipe. 6 [1950s+] (drugs) a portion of any drug; a tablet of amphetamine or barbiturate, an injection or a line of heroin or cocaine, a 'trip' of LSD etc (cf. PILL n.[4]). 7 [1960s+] (drugs) the act of injecting a narcotic drug; the injection itself. 8 [1980s+] (drugs) a puff on a crack cocaine pipe. 9 [1990s+] in fig. use, a stimulus. [HIT v.[3]]

hit n.[4] (US Und.) 1 [1940s–60s] a prison sentence or denial of parole. 2 [1960s+] an arrest. [HIT v.[5]]

hit n.[5] 1 [1970s+] (US) an instance, an attempt or time. 2 [1980s+] in gambling, a single card. [(2) HIT v.[9] (2)]

hit n.[6] see HIT AND MISS n. (1).

hit adj. [1910s] (US) in love.

hit v.[1] 1 [late 16C–17C; 1920s+] (orig. US) to have sexual intercourse with a woman (cf. BANG v.[1]). 2 [1920s+] to rob, to hold up; lit. and fig. uses. 3 [1950s+] to kill, to assassinate. 4 [1960s] to seduce. 5 [1960s+] to attack. 6 [2000s] (US) to sodomize.

hit v.[2] 1 [late 16C+] to arrive at something in one's mind, to discover, to guess correctly, as in hit it. 2 [20C+] to take. 3 [1960s] to make some money.

hit v.[3] 1 [mid-17C] for an aphrodisiac to take effect. 2 [mid-19C+] (drugs) to use or consume drugs or alcohol. 3 [late 19C+] (US campus) to use. 4 [1920s+] to inject narcotics. 5 [1920s+] for a (narcotic) drug to take effect; occas. of alcohol. 6 [1940s+] to give someone an injection of narcotics. 7 [1940s+] (drugs) to take a puff of a cigarette or marijuana cigarette. 8 [1960s+] (drugs) to adulterate drugs before selling them.

hit v.[4] 1 [mid-18C; late 19C+] (US) (also **hit for**) to beg, to ask for a loan, to accost. 2 [1950s+] to charge money, e.g. as rent. 3 [1990s+] (US Black/drugs) to call someone on a pager.

hit v.[5] 1 [19C+] (US) to send to prison. 2 [1950s+] to raid an establishment, usu. of police.

hit v.[6] 1 [early 19C] to succeed, to work out. 2 [late 19C–1920s] to defeat, to overcome. 3 [20C+] to succeed, to do well. 4 [1910s+] to make a successful bet. 5 [1930s+] (US Black) to work hard. 6 [1940s+] for a bet to prove successful.

hit v.[7] 1 [late 19C+] to go to, to visit; to arrive at; of people but also objects (cf. HIT FOR v.[2]). 2 [1920s+] to do something, usu. involving motion.

hit $v.^8$ [late 19C+] (*US campus*) to pass an exam with a high grade.

hit $v.^9$ (*orig. US*) **1** [late 19C+] to pay, to hand over money, to bet. **2** [1920s+] to deal out a card, esp. in HIT ME! excl. (1). **3** [1930s+] to give someone a drink, esp. in HIT ME! excl. (2).

hit $v.^{10}$ [1940s+] to switch on or off, to apply, e.g. the lights or the brakes of a vehicle.

hit a 180 *v.* [1990s+] to make an abrupt reversal; to change one's mind. [180 degrees]

hit a big one *v.* [1940s] (*US*) to wander unintentionally into trouble.

hit a home run *v.* (*also* **get run, score a home run**) [1980s+] (*US campus*) to have sexual intercourse. [HOME RUN n.]

hit a house *v.* [20C+] (*US prison*) to search a cell. [HIT $v.^5$ (2) + HOUSE $n.^1$ (6)]

hi-tail *v. see* HIGHTAIL v.

hit a knot *v.* [20C+] (*US*) to snore. [the sound made when a saw hits a knot while cutting timber]

hit a lick *v.* [2000s] (*US prison*) **1** to come into money. **2** to masturbate (cf. BANG THE BISHOP v.). **3** to commit armed robbery. [? HIT A LICK (AT A SNAKE) v.]

hit a lick (at a snake) *v.* (*also* **hit a tap**) [1920s+] (*US*) to make an effort; usu. in negative combs. implying laziness on behalf of the subject of the phr., e.g. *He hasn't hit a lick all week.* [SE *hit* + LICK $n.^2$ (1)]

hit and miss *n.* (*also* **hit or miss**) [1930s+] **1** (*also* **hit**) a kiss. **2** urine. **3** urination (cf. ANGEL'S KISS n.). [rhy. sl.; (2) = PISS n. (1), (3) = PISS n. (2)]

hit and miss *v.* [1980s] (*Aus.*) to urinate. [HIT AND MISS n. (3)]

hit and missed *adj.* [1960s+] drunk (cf. ADRIAN (QUIST) adj.). [rhy. sl. = PISSED adj.[1]; unlike most rhy. sl. this phr. is always used in full]

hit and run *n.* [1990s+] the sun. [rhy. sl.]

hit and run *adj.* [20C+] cheated, deceived. [rhy. sl. = DONE adj.[1] (2)]

hit a switch *v. see* HIT SWITCHES v.

hit a tap *v. see* HIT A LICK (AT A SNAKE) v.

hitch $n.^1$ **1** [mid-19C+] (*US*) a period of time, esp. of employment of any sort. **2** [20C+] (*US milit.*) a term of enlistment in one of the US armed forces. **3** [1920s+] (*US*) a prison sentence. [SE *hitch*, a temporary fastening, as with a loop or knot]

hitch $n.^2$ [1920s+] an act of hitchhiking, e.g. *I got a hitch up to London.* [HITCH $v.^2$]

hitch $v.^1$ [late 19C–1920s] (*US Black*) to start fighting. [? abbr. *hitch up one's sleeves*]

hitch $v.^2$ [1920s+] to *hitch*hike. [abbr.]

hitch $v.^3$ *see* HITCH (UP) v.

hitch a ride *v. see* DRIVE THE CAR v.

hitched (up) *adj.* [mid-19C+] (*orig. US*) married, in a relationship; thus *unhitched*, divorced; *hitching-on*, a marriage ceremony. [HITCH (UP) v.]

hitcher up *n. see* HITCH (UP) v. (1).

hitches *n.* [1950s] (*US drugs*) punctures and scar tissue from injections that accumulate along the veins of a regular heroin addict.

hitchhike *v. see* DRIVE THE CAR v.

hitchhiker on the Hershey highway *n.* [20C+] (*US*) a homosexual man (cf. BROWN ARTIST n.). [SE *hitchhiker* + HERSHEY HIGHWAY n.]

hitch horses (together) *v.* [19C] (*US*) **1** to agree upon, to get along well. **2** to marry. [hitching 2 horses to the same post]

hitching-on *n. see* HITCHED adj.

hitch it *v.* [1910s] (*Aus.*) to get married. [var. on HITCH (UP) v.]

hitch on *v. see* HITCH (UP) v.

hitchpussy *n.* [1980s+] (*US gay*) a gay hitchhiker. [HITCH $v.^2$ + PUSSY n. (9)]

hitch teams *v.* (*also* **hitch one's wagon, hitch tackle**) [mid-19C–1900s] to get married. [rural imagery]

hitch (up) *v.* (*also* **hitch on**) **1** [mid-19C+] to establish a relationship with, to marry; thus *rehitch*, to remarry; *hitcher up*, one who is getting married. **2** [20C+] to join in marriage. [SE *hitch*, to fasten, esp. in a temporary way]

hitch-up *n.* [19C] (*US*) **1** a marriage. **2** a married couple.

hitch up *v.* [late 19C–1900s] (*US*) to start, to set off. [the *hitching up* of one's team to a wagon or coach before setting off on a journey]

hitch up the reindeers *v.* (*drugs*) **1** [1930s–50s] to prepare the needle etc for an injection of cocaine. **2** [1930s+] to inhale cocaine; occas. of other narcotics. [play on the relationship of reindeer to SNOW $n.^2$ (1)]

hitey-titey *adj.* [1950s+] (*W.I. Rasta*) aloof, snobbish, supercilious. [HIGHTY-TIGHTY adj.]

hit for $v.^1$ **1** [20C+] to purchase, esp. drugs. **2** [2000s] to cost, e.g. *how much did it hit you for?* [(1) HIT $v.^9$ (1); (2) HIT $v.^4$ (1)]

hit for $v.^2$ [1900s–50s] (*US*) to travel towards. [HIT $v.^7$ (1)]

hit for $v.^3$ *see* HIT $v.^4$ (1).

hit-head *n.* [1980s+] a user of crack cocaine. [HIT $n.^3$ (6) + -HEAD sfx (3)]

hit her up *v.* [1920s–30s] (*US*) to accelerate, to go fast. [? HIT IT UP v. (2)]

hit house *n.* **1** [1930s] (*US Black*) an illegal bar that sells contraband liquor. **2** [1950s+] (*drugs*) a house where users go to inject narcotics and leave the owner drugs as payment. [HIT $n.^3$ + SE *house*]

hit in the high places *v. see* HIT THE HIGH SPOTS v. (2).

hit it $v.^1$ **1** [early 19C+] to have a given experience, usu. with a combining adj. that implies some form of success. **2** [1970s+] (*US gay*) to perform to the best of one's ability. [HIT $v.^2$ (1)]

hit it $v.^2$ **1** [1920s+] (*US/N.Z.*) to drink (heavily). **2** [1970s+] to smoke cannabis. **3** [1980s+] to smoke crack cocaine or heroin. [HIT $v.^3$ (2)]

hit it $v.^3$ **1** [1980s+] (*US Black*) to have sexual intercourse. **2** [2000s] (*US prison*) to masturbate; to have anal sex (cf. BANG THE BISHOP v.). [HIT $v.^1$ (1)]

hit it $v.^4$ *see* HIT $v.^2$ (1).

hit it $v.^5$ *see* HIT THE BOOKS v.

hit it $v.^6$ *see* HIT THE ROAD v. (1).

hit it! *excl.* [1960s] (*US prison*) be quiet!

hit it off $v.^1$ (*also* **hit it, hit off**) [mid–late 19C] **1** to establish a relationship, to become friendly, to get on well. **2** to be successful. [20C+ use is SE]

hit it off $v.^2$ [1920s] (*US*) to leave, to depart.

hit it (up) *v.* **1** [late 19C+] to act positively, to succeed, to do something. **2** [1920s] (*US*) to get on with, to establish good relations. [dial. *hit it*, to agree]

hit it up *v.* (*also* **hit things up**) [20C+] **1** to get drunk. **2** to behave in an aggressive, noisy manner. [ext. of HIT IT (UP) v. (1)]

hit it with *v.* [20C+] (*Aus.*) to get on with, to establish good relations.

hit lady *n. see* HIT WOMAN n.

hit leather *v. see* LEATHER $n.^3$ (7).

Hitler boot *n.* [1940s] (*W.I.*) a shoe made from old automobile tyres and very common during WW2. [Adolf *Hitler* (1889–1945), dictator of Nazi Germany]

hit list *n.* [1970s+] (*US*) **1** a list of those scheduled for assassination. **2** any list that details tasks that are to be carried out. [HIT $v.^1$ (3) + SE *list*]

hit man *n.* **1** [1930s+] (*US Und.*) a hold-up man. **2** [1950s+] (*orig. US*) a hired or 'contract' killer. **3** [1990s+] one who performs non-lethal violence for money. [HIT $v.^1$ (3) + SE *man*]

hit me! *excl.* **1** [1930s+] (*orig. US gambling*) an invitation to the dealer to give one another card. **2** [1940s+] (*orig. US*) an invitation to a bartender to pour one another drink. [(1) HIT $v.^9$ (2); (2) HIT $v.^9$ (3)]

hitmeister *n.* [1980s+] (*US drugs*) a small pipe made from 3mm

($^1/_8$in) brass fittings used for burning roaches and small chunks of marijuana. [HIT n.^{3} (5) + -MEISTER sfx]

hit off v. see HIT IT OFF v.^{1}.

hit on v. **1** [20C+] to ask, to approach, e.g. for help. **2** [1950s+] (orig. US Black) to make advances, to make attempts to seduce. **3** [1960s+] (US) to attempt to swindle or victimize. **4** [1960s+] in pimp use, to attract a woman to one's team of prostitutes. **5** [1970s+] (US) to rob. **6** [1990s+] (US) to enjoy, to indulge in. [ext. HIT v.^{4} (1) but note HIT v.^{1}]

hit on all (four) cylinders v. (also **hit on all six**) [1910s+] to work properly. [SE hit + automobile imagery]

hit one's head on the ceiling v. [1970s] (US campus) to make a mistake.

hit one's hobbles v. [1950s+] (Aus.) to make a comeback. [racing use hit the hobbles, for a horse to keep galloping despite a hobble chain]

hit on the master vein v. [late 16C] to become pregnant (cf. PRICK THE MASTER VEIN v.). [SE hit + master-vein, a major vein, usu. the carotid artery or jugular vein]

hit or miss n. see HIT AND MISS n.

hit paydirt v. (also **hit pay clay**, **strike paydirt**) [1950s+] (US) to be successful. [gold-mining imagery]

hit pussy v. [2000s] (US) to have sexual intercourse with a woman. [HIT v.^{1} (1) + PUSSY n. (1)]

hit red v. [1960s+] (US drugs) to draw blood into the syringe, where it mixes with the water/narcotic solution prior to injection. [HIT v.^{3} (4) + SE red]

hit skins v. [20C+] to have sexual intercourse. [note Papua New Guinea Tok Pisin paitim bun, to have sex, lit. 'hit bones']

hit someone off v. [1990s+] (US Black) to give someone (something).

hit someone on the hip v. [1990s+] (US Black) to page someone. [the wearing of a pager on one's belt; HIT v.^{4} (3)]

hit someone up v. [1980s+] (US Black) to attack physically. [ext. SE hit]

hit someone with v.^{1} [1950s] to approach someone with a plan.

hit someone with v.^{2} [1950s+] to give someone something, often used of money but occas. of something less desirable.

hit someone with the book v. [1940s] to discipline heavily, to reprimand severely. [var. on THROW THE BOOK AT v.; the 'book' is the 'book of rules' that one has contravened]

hit some shit v. (also **get into shit**) [1970s+] (US Black) to encounter problems. [SE hit, encounter + SHIT n.^{3} (2)]

hit some z's v. see BUST SOME Z'S v.

hitsville n. [1960s+] the fig. world of success. [HIT n.^{1} + -VILLE sfx^1]

hit switches v. (also **hit a switch**) [2000s] (US Black) to have sexual intercourse.

hitter n.^{1} **1** [1950s+] a thug, esp. a hired killer. **2** [1960s+] a success, a star, an influential individual; usu. with overtones of violence or criminality. **3** [1980s+] one who derives their sexual satisfaction from beating a partner. [(1) HIT v.^{1} (3); (2) HIT n.^{1}; (3) HIT v.^{1}]

hitter n.^{2} [1980s+] (drugs) **1** a user of crack cocaine. **2** a small crack pipe, designed for a single puff. [HIT v.^{3} (2)]

hit the air v. [1920s–50s] (US) to leave, to depart.

hit the ball v.^{1} [20C+] (US) to leave quickly. [SE hit + railway jargon highball, a signal directing the train to go at full speed; thus highball, to go fast]

hit the ball v.^{2} [1910s+] (US) **1** to work hard, to be diligent at a job. **2** to travel or move fast. [sporting imagery]

hit the books v. (also **hit it**) [1920s+] (US campus) to study hard.

hit the booze v. (also **hit the bottle**, **...flask**, **...jug**, **...piss**) [late 19C+] (orig. US) to drink heavily. [SE hit + BOOZE n./SE bottle/flask/jug/PISS n. (4)]

hit the breeze v. [late 19C+] (N.Z./US) to depart, to travel, to run fast.

hit the bricks v. (orig. US) **1** [20C+] to exit, to leave for the street, to start walking. **2** [1930s+] to be discharged from a prison sentence. **3** [1940s] to go on strike. **4** [1960s+] to walk the streets all night, through homelessness.

hit the bumpers v. [1910s] (US) to ride for free on a freight train.

hit the bung v. [1930s] (US) to get drunk. [HIT v.^{3} (2) + BUNG n.^{3} (3)]

hit the button v. [20C+] of a person, to talk aptly or pertinently; of a thing, to be pertinent.

hit the ceiling v. **1** [20C+] (orig. US) to increase to a new level, usu. of prices. **2** [20C+] (orig. US) to become shocked. **3** [1900s] (US campus) to fail an examination. **4** [1910s+] (orig. US) to lose one's temper. **5** [1950s] (US drugs) to smoke opium or marijuana.

hit the deck v.^{1} **1** [1910s+] to get up from one's bed. **2** [1920s+] to fall down. **3** [1920s+] to throw oneself deliberately to the ground. **4** [1920s+] to go to bed. **5** [1930s+] to be poor. [SE hit + DECK n.^{1} (2); (2) orig. naut.]

hit the deck v.^{2} [1950s+] (Aus.) to pay for a round of drinks.

hit the dirt v. [20C+] (US) to throw oneself to the ground.

hit the dust v. [1910s] (US) to set off, to get going.

hit the fan v. (US) **1** [1940s+] of trouble or scandal, to erupt, to become public; thus the egg has hit the fan, the trouble has started. **2** [1970s] to get enraged. [SHIT HITS THE FAN, THE phr.]

hit the flask v. see HIT THE BOOZE v.

hit the gas v. [1920s+] (US) to accelerate in a motorcar. [HIT v.^{1} (5) + SAmE gas(olene)]

hit the gate v. [1990s+] (US Und./prison) to leave prison, to be released.

hit the gong v. (also **hit the gonger**) [1930s+] (drugs) to smoke opium. [HIT v.^{3} (2) + GONG n.^{2} (2)]

hit the gow v. [1930s+] (drugs) to smoke opium. [HIT v.^{3} (2) + GOW n.^{1} (2)]

hit the grit v. (also **hit the turf**) **1** [20C+] (US) to leave, to get moving, to travel fast. **2** [1950s+] (US Und.) to resume a criminal career after leaving prison.

hit the ground v. [1920s–60s] (US) to be given a parole or to be released from prison.

hit the hard stuff v. [1950s+] to drink spirits rather than beer or wine. [SE hit + HARD STUFF n.^{2} (1)]

hit the hay v. **1** [20C+] to go to bed; thus in the hay, asleep. **2** [1900s–20s] (also **beat the hay**) to sleep. **3** [1940s+] to have sexual intercourse, to 'go to bed with'. [SE hit + HAY n.^{1}]

hit the headlines v. [1930s+] (US) to become famous.

hit the high spots v. **1** [1900s–20s] to go to excess or extremes, to rise to a very high level. **2** [1900s–50s] (Can.) (also **hit in the high places**) to tackle only superficial issues. **3** [1910s+] to go out for an evening's dining and dancing.

hit the hump v. see HIT THE WALL v.

hit the jackpot v. [1930s+] (orig. Aus./N.Z.) to have very good luck, esp. when unexpected.

hit the jug v. see HIT THE BOOZE v.

hit the kellicks v. [1940s+] (Aus.) to put the brakes on. [SE hit + killick, an anchor; orig. a stone on a rope used to anchor a boat in place]

hit the mainline v. (also **bust the mainline**, **hit the main vein**) [1930s+] (drugs) to inject a drug. [SE hit/BUST v.^{1} (4) + MAINLINE n.^{2} (1)]

hit the mattress(es) v. see GO TO THE MATTRESS v.

hit the mud v. see MUD n.^{3} (2).

hit the needle v. [1920s+] (drugs) to inject a drug. [the hypodermic needle]

hit the number v. [1930s+] **1** to make a successful bet on the numbers game. **2** to be successful, in a non-gambling context.

hit the pavement v. [1930s+] **1** to be ejected, esp. from a nightclub or other place of entertainment. **2** to be released from prison. **3** to be dismissed from one's job.

hit the pike *v.* [1900s] (*US*) **1** to leave. **2** to leave one's job. [SE *hit* + PIKE n.² (3)]

hit the pipe *v.*¹ (*US drugs*) **1** [late 19C+] to smoke opium; thus *pipe-hitter*, an opium smoker. **2** [1980s+] (*also* **crack the pipe**) to smoke crack cocaine. [note Burnett, *Little Caesar* (1929): 'Hit the pipe, drinking'; presumably the author's error]

hit the pipe *v.*² *see* PIPE v.¹ (1).

hit the piss *v. see* HIT THE BOOZE v.

hit the pit *v.* [20C+] **1** (*US Und.*) to be imprisoned. **2** (*N.Z.*) to go to bed.

hit the pot *v.* [1900s–30s] (*US*) to drink excessively. [SE *hit* + *pot*, a tankard]

hit the rack *v. see* HIT THE SACK v.

hit the road *v.* [late 19C+] (*orig. US*) **1** (*also* **hit it**) to leave, to set out on a journey; thus imper. *hit the road (Jack)*, get out, go away. **2** to leave prison. **3** to take up a life of crime.

hit the rods *v.* (*also* **hop the rods**) [1920s–50s] (*US*) **1** to ride freight trains as an itinerant worker or tramp. **2** to leave, to run off. [SE *hit* + ROD n.²]

hit the roof *v.* [1920s+] to explode with temper, to become extremely annoyed. [var. on HIT THE CEILING v.]

hit the round brown *v. see* DO IT UP BROWN v.

hit the ruby *v.* [late 19C] (*US*) to drink heavily, to be drunk.

hit the sack *v.* (*also* **hit the rack**) **1** [1920s+] to go to sleep. **2** [1960s+] (*US/US gay*) (*also* **hit the springs**) to have sexual intercourse. [SE *hit* + SACK n.³ (1); note synon. RMC Duntroon (Aus.) *hit the rack*]

hit the sauce *v.* [1920s+] (*orig. US*) to drink to excess. [HIT v.³ (2) + SAUCE n.² (5)]

hit the sheets *v.* [1960s+] **1** (*US*) to go to bed. **2** (*US*) to have sexual intercourse. **3** (*US lesbian*) to be passive to the overtures of another woman.

hit the shucks *v.* [20C+] (*US*) to go to bed, to go to sleep. [dial. *shuck*, a corn husk, with which old mattresses were sometimes filled]

hit the sidewalks *v.* [20C+] (*US*) to walk the streets searching for a job.

hit the silk *v.* **1** [1940s–50s] (*US*) to bail out of an aeroplane using a parachute. **2** [1940s+] (*orig. US*) thus, to bail out of any situation. [the silk that makes the parachute canopy]

hit the skids *v.* [1920s+] (*orig. US*) to enter into a period of economic or emotional decline. [ON THE SKIDS phr.]

hit the slit *v.* [20C+] of a woman, to masturbate (cf. APPLY LIP GLOSS v.). [SLIT n.¹ (1)]

hit the smoky trail *v. see* HIT THE TRAIL v.

hit the spot *v.* [20C+] to suit the circumstances, to be absolutely satisfactory in the context.

hit the springs *v. see* HIT THE SACK v. (2).

hit the steel *v. see* HIT THE TIES v.

hit the stem *v.* **1** [1920s–50s] (*US tramp*) to beg on the main street. **2** [1930s–40s] (*US drugs*) to smoke opium.

hit the street *v.* **1** [1950s+] (*orig. US*) to leave, to go out for the night. **2** [1960s+] (*US prison*) to return to free society.

hit the stuff *v.* **1** [1910s+] (*US*) to drink alcohol. **2** [1930s–50s] (*drugs*) to smoke opium. **3** [1950s] to use narcotics. [(1) STUFF n.³ (1); (3) STUFF n.³ (2)]

hit the switch *v.* [1990s+] (*US Black*) to have sexual intercourse.

hit the tarpot *v. see* TARPOT n.¹.

hit the tick *v.* [20C+] (*US*) to go to bed, to go to sleep. [SE *hit* + *tick*, a mattress cover]

hit the ties *v.* (*also* **hit the steel**) [1900s–30s] (*US*) to walk along railway tracks, esp. after quitting one's job in a work camp; also in fig. use. [SE *tie*, a railway sleeper]

hit the toe *v. see* TAKE TO THE TOE v.

hit the trail *v.* [late 19C+] (*orig. US*) to leave; as *hit the smoky trail*, leave by a railroad.

hit the turf *v. see* HIT THE GRIT v.

hit the wall *v.* (*also* **hit the hump**) **1** [1940s+] (*US prison*) to make an escape. **2** [1980s+] (*Aus. prison*) to make an unsuccessful escape.

hit the white *v.* [1950s] (*Aus.*) to succeed.

hit the wind *v.* (*also* **split the wind**) [mid-19C+] (*US/US Black*) to leave quickly, to run away.

hit things up *v. see* HIT IT UP v.

hitting up *n.* [1940s+] (*drugs*) (*also* **hitting it**) injecting drugs. [HIT UP v.⁴ (1)]

Hittite *n.* [early 19C] those who fought in and patronized the Prize Ring. [pun on SE *hit/Hittite*]

hit under the wing *phr.* [mid-19C] drunk.

hit up *v.*¹ **1** [late 19C–1920s] (*US*) to drink. **2** [1900s] to buy (a round of drinks). [HIT v.³ (2)]

hit up *v.*² **1** [late 19C+] (*US*) (*also* **hit up for**) to visit. **2** [1970s+] (*US*) to make affectionate and/or sexual advances towards. **3** [2000s] (*US campus*) to contact by mobile phone.

hit up *v.*³ [1900s–30s] to perform.

hit up *v.*⁴ **1** [1950s+] (*orig. US*) to inject oneself with a drug. **2** [1980s+] to inject someone else with a drug. [HIT v.³ (4)]

hit up *v.*⁵ [1990s+] **1** (*US Und.*) to rob, to mug. **2** (*US*) to win a bet.

hit up (for) *v.* [late 19C+] (*orig. Aus./N.Z.*) to ask someone for something, usu. money. [HIT v.⁴ (1)]

hit up for *v. see* HIT UP v.² (1).

hit with a lily *v.* [1950s] (*US Und.*) to kill.

hit with the stupid stick, be *v.* [1970s+] (*US Black*) to be stupid.

hit woman *n.* (*also* **hit lady**) [1970s+] (*US*) a female hired killer. [fem. version of HIT MAN n.]

hit-your-back *n.* [20C+] (*US*) a native of Virginia. [the supposed hospitality of Virginians, an attitude that is underlined by their constantly slapping one another's backs in camaraderie]

hity-tity *n. see* HIGHTY-TIGHTY n.

hive *n.* [mid–late 19C; 1970s] the vagina (cf. BAG n.¹). [as a receptacle for HONEY n.² (2); see Williams for 17C metaphorical uses]

hive off *v.* [1910s+] (*Aus.*) to leave. [SE *hive off*, to break away from a group]

hiver *n.*¹ [late 19C] (*US, Western*) a travelling bawd, usu. in pl. [SE *hive (off)* of bees, to swarm; the image is of prostitutes 'swarming like bees' to the newly settled Western towns]

hiver *n.*² [1980s+] a derog. term for a person with AIDS. [SE *HIV* (human immuno-deficiency virus)]

hiya! *excl. see* HI! excl.

hizzo *n.* [2000s] (*US Black*) an extremely promiscuous woman. [HO n.¹ (4) + -IZ- ifx]

H.M.I.C. *n.* [1970s+] (*US*) the dominant figure in a given situation or institution. [*head motherfucker in charge*]

HMP *n.* [1990s+] prison, time in prison. [the legal phr. 'detained at *Her Majesty's Pleasure*']

h.n. *n. see* HOUSE NIGGER n.

h.n.i.c. *n.* (*also* **b.n.i.c., h.n., n.i.c.**) [1960s+] (*US Black*) a sarcastic ref. to any Black authority figure. [abbr. HEAD NIGGER IN CHARGE n.]

ho *n.*¹ (*also* **hoe, whoe**) **1** [1950s+] (*orig. US Black*) a prostitute. **2** [1960s+] (*also* **who**) a generic term describing any woman. **3** [1970s+] (*US gay*) a passive sexual partner. **4** [1980s+] (*US Black/campus*) a promiscuous or seductively dressed young woman. **5** [1980s+] a girlfriend. **6** [1980s+] a person indiscreet in sexual matters. **7** [1980s+] (*US Black*) a sexually promiscuous man. **8** [1990s+] an unfriendly person, either male or female. **9** [1990s+] (*US Black*) a coward, i.e. a man who acts like (2). **10** [2000s] (*US campus*) as a form of friendly address. [Black pron.

of SE *whore*. (2) is ostensibly neutral, but the undertones of its ety. still make it controversial]

ho *n.*[2] [2000s] (*drugs*) cannabis. [? HO n.[1] (1), it is available to anyone with the money; it is a soft, thus 'feminine' drug compared to harder, 'male' narcotics]

ho *v.* 1 [1950s+] (*US Black*) to work as a prostitute. 2 [1980s+] (*US Black teen*) to sell out, to prostitute oneself. [HO n.[1] (1)]

hoag *see under* HOGO.

hoagie *n.* 1 [1950s+] (*US*) a large sandwich consisting of a sliced French loaf filled with a variety of fillings. 2 [1990s+] the penis. [as named in Pennsylvania and New Jersey]

ho-ass *adj.* [1990s+] (*US Black*) a general term of address, used of a man. [HO n.[1] (9) + -ASS sfx]

hoax *n.* [late 18C–early 19C] a deception, a fraud, a 'tease'. [? SE *hocus*, to trick. Although this ety. seems highly likely, there are no 18C cits. and thus 'no direct evidence of connection' (*OED*). Subseq. use is SE]

hoax *v.* [late 18C–19C] to deceive, to ridicule; thus *hoax a quiz*, to tease an eccentric person. [HOAX n.]

hob *n.* [17C–mid-19C] a rustic, a simpleton; often found as a generic proper name (cf. ALVIN n.). [early use is SE. Corruption of proper name *Robin* or *Robert*]

ho-bag *n.* [1990s+] (*US*) a derog. term for a woman. [HO n.[1] + -BAG sfx]

hob and nob *v.* 1 [mid-18C–19C] to invite to drink, and then to clink glasses. 2 [mid-19C–1910s] (*also* **hobnob**) to fraternize, to be on intimate terms. [lit. 'to lay heads together']

hob a nob *n. see* HOB NOB v.

hobbes! *excl.* [1980s+] (*US campus*) a general excl., really! honest! on my honour! [? joc. ref. to the US comic strip *Calvin and Hobbes* (1980s)]

hobbinol *n.* (*also* **hobbinal**) [17C–early 19C] a rustic, a simpleton. [HOB n. + NOLL n.; orig. a character in Spenser' *Shepherd's Calendar* (1579)]

hobbit *n.* 1 [1980s+] (*US campus*) a socially unappealing, studious student. 2 [2000s] (*UK prison*) a compliant prisoner. [the country-dwelling creatures created by J.R.R. Tolkien in his books *The Hobbit* (1937) and *Lord of the Rings* (1954)]

hobble *n.* 1 [late 18C–1940s] a difficult situation, from which it is hard to extricate oneself. 2 [1950s] (*Irish*) a troublesome person, a term of abuse. [Scot. *habble*, a difficulty, a perplexity]

hobble *v.* 1 [18C–early 19C] (*UK Und.*) to steal. 2 [18C–early 19C] (*UK Und.*) to arrest. 3 [late 19C–1900s] (*US*) to restrain. 4 [1980s+] (*US campus*) to have sexual intercourse. [SE *hobble*, orig. of an animal, to restrain]

hobbled *adj.* [late 18C–mid-19C] arrested, committed to trial; thus *hobbled upon the legs*, transported, sent to the hulks. [HOBBLE v. (2)]

hobbledegee *n.* (*also* **hobbledejee**) [late 18C–early 19C] a jog trot, a pace between a walk and a run. [SE *hobble*, to limp, to walk unsteadily]

hobby *n.* [mid-19C] (*US*) a translation of a text, classical or otherwise, for the illegitimate use of students (cf. ANIMAL n.[3]). [play on PONY n.[3]]

hobby bobby *n.* [1980s] a special constable. [SE *hobby* + BOBBY n. (1)]

hobby horse *n.*[1] [late 16C–early 17C] a fool, a jester. [SE *hobby horse*, the performer, in a morris dance, who manipulates, with much capering, the wicker horse that is part of the trad. 'cast']

hobby horse *n.*[2] [late 16C–18C] a prostitute, a promiscuous woman; a mistress (cf. ALLEY CAT n.; BANBURY n.). [SE *hobby horse*, a small horse; she can be 'ridden' by all and sundry]

hobby horse man *n.* [early 17C] a womanizer, an adulterer. [HOBBY HORSE n.[2]]

hobey-man *n. see* HO-BOY n.

ho-bitch *n.* [1990s+] (*US campus*) a general negative when applied to any woman. [HO n.[1] (1) + BITCH n.[1] (1)]

hob-job *n.* [mid-late 19C] an unskilled job, an odd job, e.g. holding horses, carrying parcels; also as *v.* [HOB n. + SE *job*]

hob-jobber *n.* [mid-late 19C] a man or boy walking the streets on the lookout for small jobs. [HOB-JOB n.]

hobnail *n.* (*also* **hopnail**) [late 16C–19C] a rustic, a simpleton (cf. BOGHOPPER n.). [the heavy footwear, studded with hobnails, used by country-dwellers]

hobnailed *adj.* [late 16C–19C] rustic, boorish. [HOBNAIL n.]

hobnail express *v.* [1950s+] (*N.Z.*) to walk, to travel by foot.

hobnob *v. see* HOB AND NOB v. (2).

hob nob *v.* [late 18C–mid-19C] to invite to drink and then to clink glasses; thus as *hob (a) nob*, a toast before drinking. [according to Grose (1785), the custom dates to the late 16C: 'When great chimnies were in fashion, there was at each corner of the hearth … a small elevated projection, called the *hob*, and behind it a seat. In winter time the beer was placed on the hob to warm; and cold beer was set on a small table, said to have been called the *nob*, so that the question, Will you have hob or nob, seems only to have meant Will you have warm or cold beer?' Skeat opts for AS *hab*, have and *nabban*, not have, thus 'take it or leave it', i.e. the choice is yours]

hobnobs *n.* [1960s+] (*Scot./Irish*) members of the upper classes. [NOB n.[2] (1)]

hobo *n.*[1] [late 19C–1960s] (*US*) the penis. [fig. use of HOBO n.[2] (1); i.e. it 'wanders around']

hobo *n.*[2] (*US*) 1 [late 19C+] a tramp, a vagrant, an itinerant worker, often using the US rail system as a means of free transport. 2 [1900s–20s] the vagrant cell. 3 [1970s+] someone whose poverty renders them effectively a tramp. [ety. unknown; claims have been made for *hoe-boy*, a migrant farm-worker, and the cry *Ho, boy!* used regularly by northwestern railway mail handlers *c.*1880–90; note Mencken, *The American Language* (3rd edn, 1936): 'Tramps and hoboes are commonly lumped together, but in their own sight they are sharply differentiated. A *hobo* or *bo* is simply a migratory laborer; he may take some longish holidays, but soon or late he returns to work. A *tramp* never works if it can be avoided; he simply travels. Lower than either is the *bum*, who neither works nor travels, save when impelled to motion by the police'; note WW1 milit. *hobo*, a cadger, a useless person]

hobo *adj.* [late 19C+] (*US*) pertaining to tramps or their culture; used lit. and fig. [HOBO n.[2] (1)]

hobo *v.* [late 19C+] (*US*) 1 to live or travel as a tramp. 2 in fig. use. [HOBO n.[2] (1)]

hobo cell *n.* (*also* **hobo cage**) [1900s–20s] (*US*) the iron cage in a prison for locking up minor offenders. [HOBO n.[2] (2)]

hobo cocktail *n.* [1940s] (*US*) a glass of water, esp. when requested (rather than alcohol) in a restaurant. [HOBO n.[2] (1) + SE *cocktail*]

hobo jungle *n. see* JUNGLE n.[1] (4).

Hoboken *n.* [20C+] (*US*) 1 an insignificant, out-of-the-way place. 2 hell. [proper name of *Hoboken*, New Jersey; poss. f. an imagined identification with HOBO n.[2] (1) although the name is, in fact, Indian]

ho boots *n.* [1970s+] (*US Black*) ostentatiously sexy, tight, high-heeled woman's boots. [HO n.[1] (1) + SE *boots*]

hobo's delight (on a rainy night) *n.* [2000s] (*US*) a throw of 12 in craps dice (cf. ADA FROM DECATUR n.). [HOBO n.[2] (1)]

hobosex *n.* 1 [1970s+] (*US gay*) a sexual partner who performs badly or whose anus is not as tight as it once was. 2 [1990s+] sex with a number of strangers in a short period of time; thus *hobosexual*, one who enjoys such random adventuring. [HOBO n.[2] (1) + SE (*hetero*)*sexual*]

hobo soup *n.* [1990s+] (*US*) ketchup mixed with hot water. [HOBO n.[2] (1) + SE *soup*]

ho-boy *n.* (*also* **hobey-man**) [19C] (*US*) a nightsoil carrier. [SE *hautboy*, *hoboy*, an oboe, humorously applied to a clyster-pipe or enema]

Hob's Knob n. [20C+] (US) the smart, rich area of a town. [? pun on HOB NOB v. or HOB AND NOB v.]

hobson's (choice) n. [20C+] the human voice. [rhy. sl.; ult. SE *Hobson's choice*, no choice at all. Named for Tobias Hobson or Jobson (d.c.1630), the Cambridge carrier (commemorated by John Milton (1608–74) in 2 epitaphs), who let out horses and is said to have compelled customers to take the horse that happened to be next to the stable-door or to go without; orig. *Hodgson's choice* and cited as such by Weekley, *Etymological Dict. of Modern English* (1921), as occurring in 1617, 13 years before Hobson's death]

ho cake n. [1990s+] (US Black) the vagina (cf. APPLE n.⁶). [HO n.¹ (1) + SE *cake*; it is something to EAT v.³ (1)]

ho-catcher n. [1970s] (US Black) a smart suit. [HO n.¹ (1) + SE *catcher*]

hoch n.¹ [1910s] (Aus.) a German. [Ger. excl. *hoch!*]

hoch n.² see HOUGH n.

hochmagandy n. see HOUGHMAGANDY n.

hock n.¹ [late 18C+] the foot, or the foot and ankle; usu. in pl. as *hocks* (cf. CURBY HOCKS n.; HAM-HOCKS n.). [SE *hock*, a joint in the back leg of a quadruped, between the knee and the fetlock, which points backwards]

hock n.² [late 19C+] the state of being pawned; usu. as IN HOCK phr. [Du. *hok*, hutch, hovel, prison; but note HOCKELTY n. and see Asbury, *Sucker's Progress* (1938), 15–16: '*In hock*—The last card in the box was said to be *in hock*. Originally it was known as the *hockelty card*, and in the early days of Faro, when it counted for the bank, a player who had bet on it was said to have been caught *in hock*. Also, a gambler who had been trimmed by another sharper was said to be *in hock* to his conqueror; and as late as the middle 1880's, in the underworld, a man was *in hock* when he was in jail. The phrase is now principally used in reference to pawnshop pledges, but it seems to have acquired that meaning in recent years']

hock n.³ [1950s+] a male homosexual. [rhy. sl. = COCK n.² (1)]

hock n.⁴ see HOCKER n.

hock v.¹ **1** [late 19C+] (orig. US) to pawn. **2** [1930s–70s] (US) to steal. **3** [1950s+] to sell. **4** [1960s] (N.Z.) to get hold of, to obtain. [HOCK n.²]

hock v.² [1970s] (US) to kick. [? HOCK n.¹]

hock-dockies n. [mid-19C] shoes. [HOCK n.¹ + redup.]

hockelty n. [mid-late 19C] (US gambling) in faro, the last card remaining in the box after the deal has been made. [ety. unknown; see also ety. at HOCK n.²]

hocker n. (also **hock**) [1960s+] (US teen) a gob of phlegm or spit (cf. HAWKER n.). [SE *hawk*, to clear one's throat of phlegm]

hockey see also under HOCKIE.

hockey adj. (also **hocky**) [late 18C–early 19C] drunk, spec. with strong, stale beer known as *old hock*. [such beer was trad. served at harvest-homes or harvest-suppers, celebrating the successful completion of the annual harvest. The beer was sold cheap to the farmer]

hockey box n. [1970s–80s] (US) the buttocks. [HOCKIE n. (1) + SE *box*/BOX n.¹ (4)]

hockey head n. see MULLET n.².

hockey puck n. [1960s+] (US) a stupid person. [the rubber disc used instead of a ball in ice hockey; coined in 1963 by US comedian Don Rickles]

hockey stick n. [1940s+] (N.Z.) a mutton chop.

hockie n. (also **hockey, hocky**) **1** [late 19C+] excrement, both human and animal. **2** [1930s+] (US) in fig. use, nonsense, lies. [? CACKY n.]

hockie adj. (also **hocky**) [1970s] (US campus) unpleasant, nasty. [HOCKIE n.]

hockie v. (also **hockey, hocky**) [20C+] to excrete. [HOCKIE n. (1)]

hock-pintled adj. (also **hock-pointed**) [18C–19C] suffering

from penile strabismus, lit. 'a squint of the penis', i.e. a condition in which the penis is painfully bent out of shape. [SE *hock* + PINTLE n. (1)]

hocks n. see HOCK n.¹.

hock sheet n. [1990s+] (US police) a list of stolen goods that may have been pawned. [HOCK n.²]

hock shop n. **1** [late 19C+] a pawnbroker's shop. **2** [1950s] a prison. [HOCK n.² + SE *shop*]

hocky see also under HOCKIE.

hocky adj. see HOCKEY adj.

hocus n.¹ **1** [mid-17C–early 18C] a juggler, a magician, a charlatan. **2** [mid-17C–18C] juggling, imposture. **3** [20C+] lies, criminal deception. [abbr. HOCUS-POCUS n.¹]

hocus n.² **1** [early 19C–1900s] drugged liquor. **2** [1930s+] (US drugs) heroin, morphine or cocaine in solution, prepared for injection (cf. AUNTIE EMMA n.). **3** [1930s+] (drugs) (also **hokus**) opium, morphine, heroin or cocaine (cf. APOSTLE n.). **4** [2000s] (drugs) marijuana. [HOCUS v. (1); fig. use of HOCUS n.¹]

hocus n.³ see HOCUS-POCUS n.².

hocus adj. [early 18C–19C] drunk. [abbr. HOCUS-POCUS adj.]

hocus v. **1** [early 19C+] to drug a person with a mixture of opium or snuff and beer before robbing them; also of animals, e.g. racehorses. **2** [1940s–50s] (US gambling) to make dice crooked. [SE *hocus*, to confuse]

hocus-pocus n.¹ **1** [early 17C–18C] a juggler. **2** [mid-17C+] a juggler's trick; thus any form of imposture, trickery. **3** [early 18C] an astrologer. [SE *hocus-pocus*, nonsense incantation used by jugglers to accompany a trick or piece of sleight of hand; itself, according to Archbishop Tillotson (1630–94), Lat. *hoc est corpus*, this is the body: 'In all probability those common juggling words of hocus pocus are nothing else but a corruption of hoc est corpus, by way of ridiculous imitation of the priests of the Church of Rome in their trick of Transubstantiation' (Sermons xxvi., 1742). About 1620 a popular juggler worked under the name of Hocus Pocus, accompanying his tricks with the line 'Hocus pocus, tontus talontus, vade celeriter jubeo']

hocus-pocus n.² (also **hocus**) [mid-17C; 1930s–50s] (US Und.) a purse or wallet. [joc. play on POKE n.² (2)]

hocus-pocus n.³ **1** [19C] drugged alcohol. **2** [1980s+] marijuana. [fig. uses of HOCUS-POCUS n.¹; they all 'confuse' the mind]

hocus-pocus adj. **1** [mid-17C+] deceitful. **2** [18C] drunk. [(1) HOCUS-POCUS n.¹ (2)]

hocus-pocus v. [late 18C–1900s] to employ tricks or trickery, to 'magic'. [HOCUS-POCUS n.¹ (2)]

hod n. see BROTHER HOD n.

hodad n. (also **ho-daddy, hodag**) [1960s+] (US) a stupid, obnoxious person. [surfing jargon *hodad*, a non-surfer, thus a fool; ult. ety. unknown; poss. greeting *Ho! Dad*]

hoddie n. [1950s+] (Aus.) a bricklayer's mate, a hod-carrier. [the *hod* he carries]

hoddy-doddy n. **1** [mid-16C–early 19C] a short, squat person; thus rhy. phr. *hoddy doddy, all arse and no body*. **2** [late 16C–18C; 20C+] a fool, a simpleton. [dial. *hoddy-doddy*, a snail; (2) 20C+ use is US]

hoddy peak n. **1** [16C] a fool, a simpleton. **2** [late 16C–17C] (also **hoddy-peel**) a cuckold. [dial. *hoddy-doddy*, a snail; in (2) the snail's horns become those of the cuckold + SE *peak*, head]

hodedor n. [1970s] (US/P.R.) a thug, a hoodlum, a gangster. [phonetic pron. of Sp. *jodedor*, one who makes a mess of something, who fouls up]

hodge n. [late 16C–1940s] a rustic, a simpleton (cf. ALVIN n.). [corruption of proper name Roger]

hodmandod n. (also **hodmedod, hodmendod**) **1** [early 17C–19C] a snail. **2** [mid-17C–18C] a crippled or deformed person; thus adj. *hodmandod*, short and clumsy. [SE *hodmandod*, any form of shelled snail]

hod of mortar n. [mid-19C] a pot of porter. [rhy. sl.]

hoe *n. see* HO n.[1].

hoe check *n.* [2000s] (*US prison*) a beating given to a prison inmate to see how he will react. [HO n.[1] + SE *check*]

hoe-handle *n. see* HAMMER-HANDLE n.

hoe into *v.* (*Aus.*) **1** [late 19C+] to begin a task with energy and enthusiasm. **2** [1950s+] to use enthusiastically. [agricultural imagery]

hoe jockey *n.* [2000s] (*US Black*) a successful pimp or womanizer (cf. BOSS PLAYER n.). [HO n.[1] (1) + JOCKEY n.[3] (4)]

hoe on the pink allotments *v.* [1990s+] to be a male homosexual.

hoe train *n.* [2000s] (*US Black*) a group of prostitutes who accompany their pimp on the street (cf. BROTHER-IN-LAW n.). [HOE n. + SE *train*]

hoffing *n.* [1970s] (*US Black*) a fight. [? HUFF v.[1]]

hog *n.*[1] **1** [mid-17C–1930s] a shilling (5p); thus *hog and a kye*, one shilling and sixpence (1s 6d/7½p). **2** [18C–early 19C] a sixpence (2½p). **3** [mid-18C–1900s] half-a-crown, 2s 6d (12½p). **4** [mid-19C–1940s] (*US*) a 10-cent piece. **5** [1940s–50s] (*US*) (*also* **hoggie**) $1. [picture of a pig engraved on the coins]

hog *n.*[2] **1** [late 17C+] a miser, a mean person; a generally foolish person. **2** [1900s–10s] (*Aus.*) an unpleasant person, situation or object. **3** [1950s+] (*drugs*) anyone who uses more drugs (orig. narcotics, but later ext. to cover cannabis) than the speaker does. [HOG v.[2] (3)]

hog *n.*[3] (*also* **hog-train**) [late 19C] (*US tramp*) the world of tramping. [abbr. of ON THE HOG (TRAIN) phr.]

hog *n.*[4] **1** [late 19C+] (*US*) an engine used for hauling freight cars. **2** [20C+] (*later use US Black*) any large automobile, esp. a Cadillac. **3** [1960s+] (*orig. Hell's Angels*) a motorcycle (usu. a Harley-Davidson) modified and cut down for outlaw gang use. **4** [1970s+] (*US*) any large vehicle or aircraft that uses quantities of fuel. [fig. ref. to the size and power of a *hog*; (2) note *Hy Lit's Unbelievable Dict. of Hip Words* (1968): 'the reasons it's called a HOG is because it eats up all your bread through monthly payments to the finance company'; also *Current Slang* IV (1970): '1956 or 1958 Cadillac']

hog *n.*[5] [1940s+] (*US*) a derog. term for a policeman; usu. as *the hogs*, the police (cf. ANIMAL n.[1]). [development of PIG n.[3] (1); note 'Sayers' and Heenan's Great Fight' in Hindley, *Curiosities of Street Literature* (1871): 'So those heroes were surrounded / By a lot of Hampshire hogs', ref. to the police breaking up a prizefight in 1860]

hog *n.*[6] [1960s+] (*US*) the penis (cf. ANTEATER n.). [HOG v.[1]]

hog *n.*[7] **1** [1960s+] (*US campus*) (*also* **boo-hog**) a male term for an unattractive woman, occas. a woman's term for a man. **2** [1980s] (*US campus*) a male who epitomizes good looks, intelligence and sexual prowess.

hog *n.*[8] [1960s+] **1** (*US prison*) a tough prisoner who survives hardship stoically. **2** (*US*) similarly, in a non-prison context. [the toughness of the animal]

hog *n.*[9] [1970s+] (*drugs*) phencyclidine (cf. ACE n.[4]). [the original use of phencyclidine (PCP) as an animal tranquillizer, often of pigs]

hog *adj.* [1960s] (*US*) large, heavyweight, substantial. [HOG n.[4]]

hog *v.*[1] **1** [19C] to have sexual intercourse. **2** [1960s–70s] (*US prison*) (*also* **sell a hog**) to subject to assault, esp. homosexual rape. [the puritan image of 'swinishness' allied to sex]

hog *v.*[2] **1** [mid–late 19C] (*US*) to defraud, to cheat. **2** [mid-19C+] (*US*) to steal. **3** [late 19C+] (*orig. US*) to grab for oneself, to act greedily or selfishly. [the negative image of the animal]

h.o.g. *n.* [late 19C–1900s] (*US*) high old genius. [abbr.; a satire on such honorifics as G.O.M., *g*rand *o*ld *m*an, coined for Prime Minister W.E. Gladstone (1809–98) but also a nudge towards SE *hog*]

hog-age *n.* [mid-19C–1900s] (*US*) male adolescence. [the behaviour of the young men concerned]

hogan *n. see* HOGAN-MAGAN n.

hog and a kye *n. see* HOG n.[1] (1).

hog and hominy *n.* [late 18C+] (*US*) pork with hominy grits or cornbread; thus fig. as the basics of existence.

hogan-magan *n.* (*also* **hogan, hogen-mogen**) **1** [mid-17C–mid-18C] an important person or one who presumes himself to be one. **2** [late 17C–early 18C] a Dutchman. [Du. *Hoogmogendheiden*, lit. 'High Mightinesses', the title of the States-General]

hogan-magan *adj.* (*also* **hogen-mogen**) **1** [mid-17C–mid-18C] pretentious, high and mighty. **2** [mid-17C–mid-18C] of drink, strong. **3** [late 17C–early 18C] Dutch. [HOGAN-MAGAN n.]

hogan-mogan rug *n.* [mid-17C] a strong drink. [HOGAN-MAGAN adj. (2) + 17C SE *rug*, a strong drink]

hogans *n.* [1960s+] (*US*) **1** the female breasts. **2** in sing., a mouthful, used as a unit of measurement when describing the size of a woman's breasts, thus often found in pl. **3** a young woman. [? fig. use of SE *hog*, to eat greedily; Dr Walter Bergdorf suggests: 'don't you think this comes from the name for a Navaho stone and dirt house, now used mainly for ceremonial purposes. They are dome-shaped and easily visualized as breasts']

hogan's alley *n.* [20C+] (*US*) a mess. [? the cartoon series *Hogan's Alley* (generally known as The Yellow Kid) created by R.F. Outcault (1863–1928); the storyline is set in the Manhattan slums]

hogan's ghost! *excl.* [20C+] (*Aus.*) a general expression of amazement. [? an unknown anecdote]

Hogan's goat *phr.* [1950s+] (*Irish*) a kept woman. [a fanciful animal owned by a fictitious Irishman]

hog at *v.* (*also* **hog up**) [20C+] (*W.I.*) **1** to speak roughly to, to humiliate verbally. **2** to eat ravenously.

hog-caller *n.* (*US*) **1** [1940s–60s] a loudspeaker. **2** [1940s–60s] one who makes themselves heard, with complaints, arguments, orders etc. **3** [1940s+] a loud and piercing scream, akin to those used by farmers calling their pigs.

hog dollar *n.* [20C+] (*US*) $1. [the picture of a pig engraved on the coin]

hog-drunk *adj.* [1950s–60s] (*US*) very drunk. [the negative image of the animal]

hogen-mogen *see under* HOGAN-MAGAN.

hoger *adj. see* HOGO adj.

hog-eye *n.* (*also* **hog's eye**) **1** [1900s] (*US*) a hamlet or small village. **2** [1910s+] (*US*) the female genitals. **3** [1930s+] (*US Und.*) a lock. **4** [1990s+] the anus. **5** [1990s+] the urethral hole in the head of the penis. [supposed resemblance; (4) EYE sfx]

hog-eye man *n.* [mid–late 19C] (*US*) a sailor, often Black, who manned the 'hog-eye boats', running between Cape Horn and San Francisco at the time of the Californian Gold Rush.

hog-fat *n.* [1920s+] (*Aus.*) a useless person, a parasite, a 'good-for-nothing'; lit. very fat.

hog feed *n.* [mid-19C+] (*US*) food considered unfit for human consumption, whether on grounds of taste or actual rottenness.

hog for *v.* [1910s] (*Aus.*) to desire intensely.

hoggenheimer *n.* [1910s] (*S.Afr.*) a generic name for the stereotypical Jewish capitalist (esp. as found in Johannesburg); thus *Hoggie*. [a 1902 stage character, amplified into a cartoon character created *c*.1913 by D.C. Boonzaaier of *Die Burger*]

hogger *n.*[1] [late 19C+] (*Irish*) a street-corner idler. [the image of the lazy *hog*]

hogger *n.*[2] [1910s–50s] (*US tramp/railroad*) a locomotive engineer. [HOG n.[4] (1)]

hogger *n.*[3] [1960s+] (*US campus*) a fat, homely young woman. [HOG n.[7] (1)]

hogger *n.*[4] **1** [1960s+] (*US campus*) a sexual athlete. **2** [1980s+] (*US*) the penis (cf. ANTEATER n.). [HOG n.[6]]

hogger *n.*[5] *see* HOG-HEAD n.

hoggers *n.* [1990s+] (*Scot.*) Hogmanay. [SE *Hogmanay* + -ER sfx]

Hoggie *n. see* HOGGENHEIMER n.

hoggie *n. see* HOG n.[1] (5).

hoggins n. (also **oggins**) [20C+] a due share in pleasure, usu. sexual pleasure. [SE *hoggings*, i.e. a pig's portion]

hoggish adj. (also **hoggy**) [20C+] (*US*) **1** greedy, avaricious. **2** stupid. [the negative image of the animal; *hoggish*, rude or filthy, is SE despite inclusion by Grose (1785)]

Hoggishland n. [mid-18C] Scotland. [? SE *Hogmanay*]

hog-grubber n. [late 17C–mid-19C] a mean, miserly, sneaking person. [HOG n.²/fig. use of SE *hog*, a disgusting person + GRUBBER n.¹ (1)]

hoggy adj. see HOGGISH adj.

hog-head n. (also **hogger**, **hogshead**) [1910s–40s] (*US tramp*) a railroad engineer. [HOG n.⁴ (1) + -HEAD sfx (4)]

hog heaven n. [1940s+] (*US*) a state of bliss or blissful ignorance. [the stupidity of the animals]

hog in armour n. [mid-17C–19C] a well-dressed lout, of either sex. [SE *hog*]

hog in togs n. [mid-19C] (*US*) a man about town, a loafer with no visible means of support but an endless appetite for good clothes, parties and places of entertainment. [SE *hog* + TOGS n. (1); such a man lived by his wits, often off foolish women, and worked, if at all, as a ROPER n. (2) or SHILL n.² (3) for a gambling house or similar establishment]

hog island n. (also **hog town**, **hog waller**) [late 19C+] (*US*) a generic term for any small, impoverished, out-of-the-way settlement, also in adj. use *hog-wallowing*, to refer to an inhabitant of such. [i.e. a 'pig sty']

hog it v. [1910s–40s] to sleep deeply, esp. when accompanied by snores. [the snores resemble a hog grunting]

hog-killing n. [late 19C–1910s] (*US*) an unexpected or large financial profit. [the *hog*, born on the farm, costs nothing; *killing* it provides food etc]

hog-killing (time) n. (also **hog wallow**) [mid-19C–1950s] (*US*) a boisterous party, a celebration. [trad. throwing of a party to coincide with the annual killing of a farm's hogs]

hogleg n. (also **hog's leg**) (*US*) **1** [1910s+] a large handgun; occas. a shotgun. **2** [1940s] the penis (cf. ANTEATER n.; ARM n.¹). [resemblance; the nickname of the Colt Single-Action Army, also known as the *Peacemaker* and launched in 1870]

hogmagundy n. [late 18C–19C] (*Scot.*) sexual intercourse. [? HOG v.¹ (1) + SE *salmagundi*]

hogmanay n. [late 19C] (*Scot.*) a promiscuous woman. [? the New Year's celebrations on Hogmanay or the *Hogmanay cake*, trad. given away at Scot. New Year]

hogmarket somebody n. [late 19C] (*W.I.*) an ill-mannered person. [they have porcine manners]

hogo n. (also **hoag**) [mid-17C+] a stench. [HOGO adj.]

hogo adj. (also **hoag**, **hoger**) [late 18C–mid-19C] stinking, esp. of rotting meat. [20C+ use Ulster only; Fr. *haut goût*, a 'high' flavour, thus also SE *high*]

Hogopolis n. see PORKOPOLIS n.

hog out v. [1980s+] (*US*) to overeat massively. [var. on PIG OUT v. (2)]

hog pen n. [1920s–60s] (*US Black*) a disgusting or filthy place.

hog ranch n. [late 19C+] (*US*) a brothel (cf. BIRDCAGE n.¹). [derog. use of SE; ? an actual brothel thus named]

hog-rich adj. [1980s] (*US*) very wealthy. [one has had one's 'snout in the trough'; see HAVE ONE'S SNOUT IN THE TROUGH v. (1)]

hog-rubber n. [17C] a rustic, an ignorant peasant, a disgusting, filthy person (cf. ACORN-CRACKER n.). [lit. 'one who rubs hogs']

hogs n. see HOG n.⁵.

hog's eye n. see HOG-EYE n.

hogshead n. see HOG-HEAD n.

hog-shearing n. [late 17C–18C] futile labour, much effort and little reward. [pvb 'Great cry and little wool, as the man said when he sheared his hogs']

hog's leg n. see HOGLEG n.

hog-stomp n. see HOG-WRESTLE n.

hogstye of Venus n. [19C] the vagina (cf. ADAM'S OWN (ALTAR) n.). [the 'hoggishness' of sexual intercourse]

hogswash n. see HOGWASH n. (2).

hog-thomas n. [20C+] (*W.I.*) a crude, loud person. [SE *hog* + THOMAS n.²]

hog town n. see HOG ISLAND n.

hog-train n. see HOG n.³.

hog up v. see HOG AT v.

hog waller n. see HOG ISLAND n.

hog wallow n. see HOG-KILLING (TIME) n.

hog-wallowing adj. see HOG ISLAND n.

hogwash n. **1** [late 17C–1960s] thick and bad beer; occas. inferior wine, or tea. **2** [late 19C+] (also **hogswash**) nonsense, rubbish. [fig. uses of 15C *hogwash*, the swill of a brewery, which was given to the pigs]

hogwash! excl. [late 19C+] rubbish! [HOGWASH n. (2)]

hog-whimpering adj. [20C+] (*orig. US*) extremely drunk.

hog-wild adj. [20C+] (*US*) out of control.

hog-wrestle n. (also **hog-stomp**) [20C+] (*US*) a noisy, inelegant, low-class dance.

ho-gya adj. [mid–late 19C] (*Anglo-Ind.*) in trouble, confused, lost for words; esp. in anglicized phr. *that won't hogya*, that won't do. [ety. unknown; ? Hind.]

hoha n. [1970s] (*N.Z.*) an annoying person. [HOHA adj.]

hoha adj. [1970s+] (*N.Z.*) irritated, tetchy, 'fed up'. [synon. Maori]

h.o.h.a. phr. [20C+] (*Irish*) a street challenge, esp. from a weaker to a stronger person or group. [abbr. *hit one*, *hit all*; pron. 'haitch-oh-haitch-ay']

ho-hum adj. [1960s+] non-committal, inconclusive, dull. [SE *ho-hum!*, an excl. of boredom]

hoick v.¹ [late 19C+] **1** to lift or hoist, with a jerk or snatch. **2** to drag (out of). [? SE *hike*, drag]

hoick v.² [20C+] (*Aus.*) to spit. [SE *hawk*]

hoist n.¹ **1** [early 18C+] (*UK Und.*) (also **hoys**) the act of shoplifting or breaking into houses. **2** [late 18C+] (*UK Und.*) a shoplifter. **3** [late 18C+] a pickpocket. **4** [1930s+] (*US*) a hold-up or hijacking. **5** [1930s+] any form of robbery (cf. HEIST n.¹). **6** [1960s+] (*US*) the proceeds of a theft. [HOIST v.²]

hoist n.² (also **heist**, **hyst**) [mid-19C–1960s] (*US*) a kick, a prod, a fall.

hoist v.¹ **1** [late 18C–19C] (*UK Und.*) to turn a man upside down and shake him until the money falls out of his pockets. **2** [late 19C–1910s] (*US*) to kick or thrash someone. **3** [late 19C–1910s] (*US gambling*) to raise one's opponent's bet in poker. **4** [1970s] (*US gambling*) to defeat soundly. **5** [2000s] (*UK Und.*) to be arrested. [SE *hoist*, to raise]

hoist v.² **1** [19C+] (*UK/US Und.*) to shoplift; in weak use, to steal. **2** [mid-19C+] to break into, to rob. **3** [1920s+] (*US Und.*) to commit an armed robbery or a hold-up. [HOIST n.¹]

hoist v.³ [mid-19C+] to drink; thus *hoist a few*, to have a few drinks; *on the hoist*, out drinking; HOIST ONE v. [one *hoists* one's elbow]

hoister n.¹ **1** [18C+] (*UK Und./tramp*) (also **hoyster**, **hyster**) a shoplifter; thus female *hoister mot*. **2** [19C+] (*orig. UK Und.*) a pickpocket. **3** [1980s+] (*Aus. prison*) one who steals from warehouses. [HOIST n.¹]

hoister n.² [late 19C–1900s] a drunkard. [HOIST v.³]

hoist-in n. [mid-19C–1910s] a drink. [HOIST v.³]

hoisting n. [19C+] shoplifting. [HOIST v.² (1)]

hoisting engineer n. [1910s–30s] (*US*) a drunkard. [HOIST v.³ + pun]

hoist-lay n. [19C] **1** shoplifting. **2** robbing a man by holding him upside down and shaking the money out of his pockets. [HOIST v.² (1)/HOIST v.¹ (1) + LAY n.⁴ (1)]

hoist merchant n. [19C] a shoplifter. [HOIST n.¹ (2) + MERCHANT n.]

hoist one v. [mid-19C+] to have a drink. [HOIST v.³]

hoist one's shingle *v. see* HANG OUT ONE'S SHINGLE v.

hoist tail *v.* [1940s] (*US*) to get going, to set off. [reverse anthropomorphism]

hoist the blue flag *v.* [late 18C] to take on the running of a public house. [the blue apron trad. worn by the publican]

hoitch *n.* [1980s+] (*US campus*) an unpopular, unpleasant woman. [HO n.¹ (1) + BITCH n.¹ (1)]

hoity-toity *n.* **1** [mid-17C–early 19C] an immodest, lively woman, a 'romping girl'. **2** [18C] sexual play or joking. [SE *hoity-toity*, giddy behaviour, flightiness; *see also* ety. of HIGHTY-TIGHTY n.]

hoity-toity *adj.* **1** [mid-17C+] (*also* **haytie twaity, hoighty-toighty**) aloof, snobbish (cf. HIGHTY-TIGHTY adj.). **2** [1910s] (*US*) irritable. **3** [1950s] dull, formal, staid. [SE *haughty* + redup., although Weekley, *Etymological Dict. of Modern English* (1921), notes that the synon. mid-17C phr. *upon the hoyty-toyty* has poss. link to walking on a high wire]

hoity-toity! *excl.* [late 17C–1900s] an excl. to express surprise or disdain. [HOITY-TOITY adj.]

Ho-Jo *n.* (*US*) **1** [1960s+] a *Howard Johnson's* motel. **2** [1980s+] a take-away meal from a *Howard Johnson's* restaurant. [abbr.]

hoke *n.* **1** [1920s] (*US*) a fool. **2** [1920s–50s] sentimental melodrama; thus nonsense. [HOKUM n.]

hoke *v.* [1920s+] (*US*) to flatter, to string along, to hoax. [abbr. HOKUM n.]

hoke up *v.* [1920s+] (*US*) to embellish, to render fraudulent.

hokey *n.*¹ [late 19C–1910s] a prison (cf. BUCKET n.²). [? rhy. sl. on CHOKEY n. (1)/POKEY n.² (1)]

hokey *n.*² **1** [1950s–60s] (*US*) a fool. **2** [1960s+] nonsense. [HOKUM n.]

hokey *adj.* [1920s+] (*US*) fake, false. [HOKUM n.]

hokey cokey *n.* [1990s+] karaoke. [rhy. sl.; note also the song]

hokey-dokey *see under* OKEY-DOKE.

hokey-pokey *n.*¹ **1** [mid–19C+] swindling and other illicit activities. **2** [late 19C+] nonsense. **3** [1940s] an unspecified object. [HOCUS-POCUS n.¹ (2)]

hokey-pokey *n.*² [late 19C+] **1** a cheap kind of ice-cream, sold by street vendors. **2** (*N.Z.*) a toffee-like sweet. [street cry 'hokey-poky, a penny a lump!' The ices were sold by Italian organ-grinders at 1 penny or a halfpenny each, but despite the popular ety., it does not come f. Ital. *o che poco!* 'o how little!']

hokey-pokey *n.*³ [1910s+] (*US*) a local or county prison. [HOKEY n.¹ + POKEY n.² (1)]

hokey-pokey *adj.* [mid–late 19C] duplicitous, untrustworthy, swindling. [HOKEY-POKEY n.¹ (1)]

Hokitika swindle *n.* [1930s+] (*N.Z.*) a bar game, based on betting on a sequence of numbers, e.g. on a £1 note, to determine who will buy the round of drinks. [proper name *Hokitika*, a town on the west coast of New Zealand + SE *swindle*]

hokum *n.* **1** [20C+] nonsense, flattery, lying. **2** [1910s+] (*orig. theatre*) sentimental or melodramatic speechifying or 'business'. [? HOCUS-POCUS n.¹ + BUNKUM n. Orig. theatrical jargon *hokum*, to use comedy or sentimentality to appeal to an unsophisticated audience]

hokum *adj.* (*also* **hokumy**) [20C+] sentimental, melodramatic, nonsense. [HOKUM n. (2)]

hokum snivey *n. see* HOOKEM-SNIVEY n.

hokum-snivvy *n.* [20C+] (*US*) a stew or boiled dinner made of unspecified ingredients. [fig. use of HOOK AND SNIVEY, WITH NIX THE BUFFER n.]

hokumy *adj. see* HOKUM adj.

hokus *n. see* HOCUS n.² (3).

ho layer *n.* [1980s+] (*US Black*) **1** one who conducts most (or all) of his sex-life with prostitutes. **2** a womanizer, a ladies' man. [HO n.¹ (1) + LAY v.¹ (1)]

hold *v.*¹ [late 19C+] (*US*) to restrain someone, esp. from speech, e.g. *that'll hold you*, that will keep you quiet.

hold *v.*² **1** [late 19C+] to be in possession of money, usu. large sums. **2** [1930s–60s] (*US drugs*) for a supply of drugs to suffice an addict for a given period of time. **3** [1930s+] (*US drugs*) to be in possession of drugs, esp. for selling. **4** [1970s–80s] (*UK Black*) to take, to steal. **5** [1970s+] (*US Und.*) to be armed. **6** [1970s+] to be in possession of anything.

hold a bowling ball *v. see* TENPIN v.

hold a candle to the devil *v.* [mid-15C–mid-19C] to be civil to someone out of fear. [the tale of the old woman, who, not knowing whether she was destined for heaven or hell, lit tapers to both St Michael and to the Devil in the hope of making friends in both place]

hold aces *v.* (*also* **hold an ace full, hold every ace**) [late 19C+] (*US*) to be in total control. [poker use]

hold a fresh *v.* [1990s+] (*W.I.*) to take a shower.

hold a tangi *v.* [1940s] (*N.Z.*) to analyse, to hold a 'post mortem'. [Maori *tangi*, a formal lamentation, a dirge]

hold big rocks *v.* [20C+] (*W.I.*) to be left waiting for someone who does not turn up.

hold court in the street *v.* [1960s+] (*US*) to engage in a gun battle on the street (with the implication that one would rather die than face prison).

hold-door trade *n.* [late 16C–early 17C] the world of prostitution. [prostitutes standing around brothel doorways in the hope of attracting passing trade]

hold down *v.*¹ **1** [late 19C–1910s] (*US tramp*) to ride atop a freight car, despite it being known by the crew. **2** [late 19C+] to keep a job for some time, to occupy. **3** [1980s+] (*US campus*) to wait, esp. as imper. *hold down!*

hold down *v.*² [20C+] (*W.I.*) **1** of a woman, to control one's partner, esp. to stop him from having other sexual relationships. **2** of a man, to assault a woman sexually.

holder *n.* [1990s+] (*US prison*) an inmate entrusted with keeping a gang's supply of drugs. [HOLD v.² (3)]

hold every ace *v. see* HOLD ACES v.

hold everything! *excl. see* HOLD IT! excl.

hold foot *v.* [20C+] (*Ulster*) to sustain, fig. to keep up with.

hold hard *v.* (*also* **hold on**) [mid-18C+] to stop, usu. in imper. *hold hard!/hold on!* [orig. referring to holding a horse's reins]

hold heavy *v.* [20C+] to have a good deal of money (cf. HOLD LIGHT v.). [HOLD v.² (1) + SE *heavy*]

holding *adj.* **1** [late 19C+] being in possession of money, funds. **2** [1930s+] (*drugs*) in possession of drugs, for dealing, selling. **3** [1980s] (*US campus*) of dress, attractive. [fig. use of SE *hold*/HOLD v.²]

hold it! *excl.* (*also* **hold everything! hold it right there!**) [20C+] stop what you're doing! be quiet! etc. [the subject is supposed to freeze in position. E.P. suggests orig. painters' jargon]

hold it down! *excl.* [1940s+] be quiet! calm down!

hold jiggers *v. see* STAND JIGGERS v.

hold light *v.* [20C+] to have only a little money, to be out of pocket (cf. HOLD HEAVY v.) . [HOLD v.² (1) + SE *light*]

hold me down *n.* [late 19C] (*US tramp*) a regular job. [HOLD DOWN v.¹ (2)]

hold no weight *v. see* WEIGHT n.¹ (1).

hold on *v. see* HOLD HARD v.

hold one's ass *v.* [1960s+] (*US*) to be patient. [fig. use of ASS n. (2)]

hold one's clack *v.* [mid-17C] to stop talking, usu. as imper.

hold one's cool *v. see* KEEP ONE'S COOL v.

hold one's copper *v. see* BLOW ONE'S COPPER v.

hold one's corner *v.* **1** [mid-19C+] to stay in one's personal space, as opposed to invading somebody else's, to hold one's own. **2** [1980s] (*UK Black*) to wait. [boxing imagery]

hold one's gob *v.* (*also* **hold one's gab/mug**) [19C+] to be quiet, often as imper.

hold one's hair on *v. see* KEEP ONE'S HAIR ON v.

hold one's head v. [20C+] (US Black) to be patient, to restrain oneself. [? the holding of a horse's head]

hold one's high v. see HIGH n.[1] (1).

hold one's horses v. [mid-19C+] (orig. US) to slow down, to show restraint, often as excl.

hold one's jaw v. (also **stop one's jaw**) [mid-18C+] to be quiet; often as imper. hold/stop your jaw! [JAW n. (1)]

hold one's mud v. [1960s+] 1 (US Black) to keep one's own counsel, to keep quiet. 2 (US drugs) to be courageous. [a job that one has to do oneself]

hold one's mug v. see HOLD ONE'S GOB v.

hold one's noise v. (also **hold one's row, shut one's noise**) [mid-19C+] to stop talking, esp. as imper. hold your noise! shut your noise! shut up!

hold one's own v. [20C+] to masturbate. [pun]

hold one's pecker up v. see KEEP ONE'S PECKER UP v.

hold one's rag v. [1990s+] to keep one's temper. [opposite of LOSE ONE'S RAG v.; SE hold + RAG n.[3]]

hold one's row v. see HOLD ONE'S NOISE v.

hold one's water v. [20C+] to be patient, to remain calm, esp. in imper. [fig. ref. to restraining oneself from urinating]

hold onto the slack v. [mid-19C] to be lazy, to skulk around. [naut. imagery, holding the slack of a sail requires no real effort]

hold onto your hat! excl. see HANG ONTO YOUR HAT! excl.

hold-out n. [20C+] (US) an act of evasion; something that has been held back, e.g. money; thus an individual who 'holds out'; also attrib. [HOLD OUT (ON) v.]

hold out v. [mid-19C+] (US) to live, to reside.

hold-out artist n. [1950s+] a gambler or cheat who will never admit how much money they have made out of a game. [SE hold out + ARTIST n. (2)/ARTIST sfx]

hold out (on) v. [20C+] (orig. US) to withhold something from someone; to resist.

hold over someone v. [mid–late 19C] (US) to have an advantage over someone.

hold someone's hand v. [1930s+] to give comfort or moral support to someone, to back someone up.

hold sticks to v. (also **hold sticks with**) [19C] to compete on equal terms.

hold still for v. see STAND STILL FOR v.

hold that mule! excl. [20C+] be patient! remain calm!

hold the baby v. (also **carry the baby**) [late 19C+] to be left to clear up a problem, to take an unpleasant responsibility.

hold the bag v. 1 [mid-18C+] to take responsibility. 2 [20C+] to be in a disadvantageous position. 3 [20C+] (UK Und.) for a villain to be left with full responsibility for a crime in which his associates have not been legally involved. 4 [1960s+] (drugs) to be in possession of a quantity of drugs, to deal drugs. [SE bag, but in (4) note BAG n.[11] (1); the 18C–mid-19C use is properly 'give someone the bag to hold' but the meaning is identical]

hold the belt v. [late 19C–1910s] (Aus.) to be the outstanding example, the 'champion'. [boxing imagery]

hold the blow! excl. [18C+] be quiet! [BLOW v.[1] (1)]

hold the bold v. [1990s+] to masturbate. [SE hold + assonance]

hold the can v. [1920s+] to take responsibility, usu. unwanted. [var. on CARRY THE CAN (FOR) v./HOLD THE BABY v.]

hold the flute v. see FLUTE v.[1].

hold the fort v. (also **mind the fort**) [20C+] to look after, to take care of, esp. in another person's absence.

hold the lady down v. [1930s] (US tramp) for a tramp to ride on the 'gunnels' or 'rods' beneath the wagons while a fast train is passing over a bumpy stretch of track.

hold the line! excl. [1920s–30s] wait a minute! [telephone imagery]

hold the phone v. [1970s+] (US) to wait, to delay, to 'hang on'; esp. as imper. hold the phone! [telephone imagery]

hold the sausage hostage v. [1990s+] to masturbate (cf. BEAT ONE'S MEAT v.).

hold tight! excl. 1 [1910s+] stop! don't move! 2 [1960s+] (W.I.) calm down! [orig. a bus- or tram-driver's shout]

hold-up n. 1 [late 19C+] (orig. US) an armed robbery. 2 [late 19C+] (orig. US) (also **hold-up man**) an armed robber. 3 [1900s–50s] (US) an instance of extortion; lit. or fig. [HOLD UP v.[1]]

hold up v.[1] 1 [mid-19C+] to commit an armed robbery. 2 [late 19C–1950s] to cheat, to blackmail. 3 [late 19C–1960s] (US) to demand, esp. to charge an exorbitant price. [the demand that victims should hold up their hands]

hold up v.[2] [mid-19C+] in joc. use, to lean against, to support. [the pretence of 'holding up' the structure against which one leans]

hold up! excl. [20C+] a general excl. requesting a pause in either activity or speech.

hold-up man n. see HOLD-UP n. (2).

hold up one's clothes at v. (also **hold up one's dress at**) [20C+] (W.I.) of a woman, to raise her skirts and expose her buttocks as a gesture of derision.

hold with v. [late 19C+] to agree with; to approve of.

hold your...! see also under HOLD ONE'S...

hold your kitties! excl. [20C+] be patient! remain calm!

hold your mag! excl. [1900s] (Aus.) be quiet! shut up! [SE hold + MAG n.[2] (1); var. on HOLD YOUR MOUTH! excl.]

hold your mouth! excl. [18C+] be quiet!

hold your pants on! excl. [20C+] be patient! remain calm!

hold your potato! excl. [mid-19C+] (orig. US) slow down! show restraint! [ety. unknown]

hold your shirt! excl. [20C+] calm down!

hole n.[1] 1 [late 14C+] the anus (cf. A-HOLE n.). 2 [late 16C+] the vagina (cf. BLACK HOLE n.[1]). 3 [mid-19C+] the mouth; esp. in SHUT ONE'S HOLE v. 4 [20C+] the buttocks. 5 [20C+] sexual intercourse; thus GET ONE'S HOLE v. 6 [1940s+] (US) a (promiscuous) woman or a prostitute. 7 [1970s+] (US) a passive homosexual man, esp. when promiscuous. 8 [2000s] an underage girl used for paedophile exploitation.

hole n.[2] 1 [mid-16C+] (orig. UK prison) the punishment cells. 2 [18C+] a derog. description of any small, dirty, clandestine place, presumably one where illegal occupations were planned or carried out; thus (US) rum hole, a squalid drinking place. 3 [1920s+] (US campus) a student's room. 4 [1930s–50s] (US Und.) a hideout. 5 [1930s+] (US) the subway or one of its stations. 6 [1940s+] (US) a space or slot, a position, e.g. in a race. 7 [1990s+] (US Und.) a railroad side track. 8 [1990s+] (Aus./US) a prison. [the orig. Hole was found in the Counter or Compter debtors' prison in Wood Street, London, where it was the nickname for that cell, a notably squalid one, in which the poorest prisoners were confined. The rich enjoyed the 'masters' side', while the middle classes went to the 'knights' side'; all were entered in the prison's Black Book. William Fennor's Counter's Commonwealth (1617) gives an extensive survey of life within the prison. A similar form of dungeon, not apparently sl., was the hell, cited by the OED and Nares, who suggests it was 'something worse than the hole']

hole n.[3] [late 18C+] a difficult situation, a fix, a scrape, a mess.

hole n.[4] [1930s] (UK tramp) a shilling (5p).

hole, the n. [20C+] (US) a euph. for hell.

hole v.[1] [late 19C] 'to effect intromission' (F&H); thus holing, womanizing, whoring.

hole v.[2] see HOLE (UP) v.

hole and corner business n. [late 19C] (UK Und.) something surreptitious, hidden from the authorities.

hole and corner work n. [mid–late 19C] sexual intercourse. [HOLE n.[1] (2) + pun]

hole card n. [1920s+] (orig. US) a secret, which can be either a weakness that, once discovered, can be exploited, or a hidden strength; thus PEEP SOMEONE'S HOLE-CARD v. [poker jargon *hole card*; the card that, in 5-card stud, is dealt face down]

holed *adj.* [late 19C+] of a man, enjoying sexual intercourse. [HOLE n.¹ (2)]

hole in my shoe *n.* [1960s+] (*bingo*) the number 82 (cf. ALDERSHOT LADIES n.).

hole in one! *excl.* [1970s+] absolutely correct! [golf imagery]

hole in the ground *n.* [20C+] £1 sterling (cf. CHERRY-PICKER n.⁵). [rhy. sl.]

hole in the wall *n.* **1** [mid-17C] a brothel. **2** [mid-19C–1930s] (*US*) an illicit liquor store or bar; *see also* (6) below. **3** [mid-19C–1950s] a small shop. **4** [mid-19C+] (*US*) (*also* **hole in the road**) a small, insignificant, remote place. **5** [late 19C+] a tiny, cramped apartment. **6** [1910s+] (*US*) a bar. **7** [1920s–40s] a restaurant. **8** [1980s+] an automatic teller machine (ATM), installed in the external wall of a bank or building society branch. [either f. the holes in the walls of English debtors' prisons, through which the inmates could obtain supplies and money to alleviate their situation, or f. the small shops and similar establishments found in the broad stone walls of fortified medieval cities. *Hole in the wall* became a generic term, although the US West had its *Hole in the Wall*, an outlaw hideaway in the gorges and cliffs that straddle the Wyoming, Colorado and Utah state lines (a sometime refuge for Butch Cassidy and the Sundance Kid and the real-life Wild Bunch), while 1860s New York City boasted the *Hole in the Wall* on Water Street, where its proprietor, Gallus Meg (a monstrous Englishwoman), bit the ears off ill-behaved customers and preserved her trophies in a pickle jar displayed behind the bar]

hole in the wall *adj.* [mid-19C+] (*orig. US*) second-class, inferior. [HOLE IN THE WALL n.]

holemonger *n. see* HOLER n.

hole nervous *n.* [1970s] (*US Und.*) the nervousness that arises from a lengthy period spent in hiding or keeping a low profile. [HOLE n.² (4)]

hole of content *n.* [19C] the vagina (cf. ADAM'S OWN (ALTAR) n.; BLACK HOLE n.¹). [HOLE n.¹ (2); pun on SE *whole of content*]

hole of holes *n.* [19C] the vagina (cf. ADAM'S OWN (ALTAR) n.; BLACK HOLE n.¹). [HOLE n.¹ (2)]

hole out in one *v.* [1910s+] (*Aus.*) to become pregnant after one's first sexual intercourse, esp. one's marriage night. [golfing imagery]

holer *n.* (*also* **holemonger**) **1** [16C+] a womanizer, a successful seducer. **2** [19C] a male prostitute. **3** [19C] a pimp (cf. ABBOT ON THE CROSS n.). **4** [late 19C] a prostitute. [13C–15C SE *holour*, a fornicator or whoremonger and, as such, applied to men only; HOLE n.¹ (2) + SE sfx *-monger*]

-holer *sfx* [1940s+] (*US*) applied to an outside lavatory or privy and denoting the number of seats available, e.g. *one-holer, two-holer* etc.

holes and poles *n.* [1960s+] (*US campus*) sex education classes. [HOLE n.¹ (2) + POLE n.]

hole time *n.* [20C+] (*US prison*) time spent in the punishment cells. [HOLE n.² (1) + TIME n.¹]

hole up *n.* [late 19C+] a hideout. [HOLE (UP) v. (2)]

hole (up) *v.* [late 19C+] **1** to settle. **2** to take up residence, with a possible but not invariable implication of hiding away or taking refuge. [SE *hole up*, (of an animal) to retire to a hole for hibernation or security]

holey dollar *n. see* HOLY DOLLAR n.

holiday *n.* [late 19C] a prison sentence. [i.e. a *holiday* from normal life]

holier-than-thou *adj.* (*also* **better-than-thou**) [1910s+] sanctimonious.

holing *n. see* HOLE v.¹.

hol' it dung! *excl.* [1980s+] (*W.I./UK Black teen*) keep it a secret! keep it quiet! take care! [Black pron. of HOLD IT DOWN! excl.]

holla-balloo *n. see* HULLABALLOO n.

holla boys, holla *n. see* HOLLER BOYS, HOLLER n.

H.O.L.L.A.N.D. *phr.* [1940s+] an affectionate message, written on envelopes of love letters. [abbr. *hope our love lives/lasts and never dies*]

holland *n.* [late 16C] the anus. [play on 'hole-land' (i.e. HOLE n.¹ (1)) + NETHERLANDS n. (2)]

hollanders *n.* [late 19C] (*south London*) a pointed waxed moustache. [Mr W. Holland, lessee of Covent Garden, who had 'the finest pair of black-waxed sheeny moustaches ever beheld' (Ware)]

Holland tape *n.* (*also* **hollands**) [mid-18C–19C] gin. [SE *Holland* + TAPE n.]

Hollard Street *n.* [1940s–70s] (*S.Afr.*) the Johannesburg Stock Exchange. [its address]

holler *n.* [late 19C+] **1** (*US*) a complaint, a fuss. **2** (*UK Und.*) information given to the police. [SE *holler*/HOLLER v. (2)]

holler *v.* **1** [mid-19C–1920s] (*US*) to surrender, to admit defeat. **2** [1940s+] to confess, to betray one's criminal associates. **3** [1960s] to sing. **4** [1980s+] (*US Black*) to ridicule, to abuse. **5** [2000s] (*US Black*) to demand, to ask for. **6** [2000s] (*US teen*) to greet. **7** [2000s] (*US campus*) to phone or talk to someone. [SE *holler*, to scream, shout or complain]

holler *adv. see* HOLLOW adv.

holler (bloody) murder *v.* (*also* **yell (bloody) murder**) [mid-19C+] (*US*) to raise an outcry, to make a fuss. [SE *holler/yell* + *bloody* + *murder*]

holler boys, holler *n.* (*also* **holla boys, holla**) [20C+] a (stiff) collar. [rhy. sl.]

holler calf-rope *v.* (*also* **say calf-rope, yell...**) [19C] (*US, orig. Western/Southern*) to give in, to surrender, to admit defeat, esp. in children's games. [HOLLER v. (2)]

holler copper *v.* (*also* **holler cop, squeal copper, yell copper**) [1930s+] to inform (cf. CALL COPPER v.). [SE *holler*/SQUEAL (ON) v./SE *yell* + COPPER n.³ (1)]

holler New York *v.* [1960s+] (*US*) to vomit (cf. CALL CHARLES v.). [echoic]

holler uncle *v. see* CRY UNCLE v.

holliers *n.* [1940s+] (*Irish*) holidays.

hollow *n.*¹ [early 19C] poultry, when served for a meal. [the hollow cavity within a cooked bird]

hollow *n.*² [late 19C+] (*US*) in a variety of combs., describing an area of a town; usu. combined with a ref. to poor or foreign groups, e.g. *dead man's hollow, frog hollow, Irish hollow, piggy hollow, punkin hollow, skunk hollow, sleepy hollow, smoky hollow, snuff hollow.*

hollow *adv.* (*also* **holler**) [mid-17C+] completely, utterly, esp. in phr. *beat hollow* or *knock hollow*, to trounce completely.

Holloway *n.* **1** [mid-19C–1920s] the vagina (cf. ANTIPODES n.). **2** [1930s] the throat. [pun on 'hollow way']

Holloway Castle *n.* (*also* **the Castle, royal palace of Holloway**) [late 19C–1930s] Holloway prison (cf. ABBOT'S PRIORY n.; NORTH CASTLE n.; RAT CASTLE n.). [before its mid-20C+ remodelling, the gateway of the original Holloway prison (now England's main women's prison) had 'castellated' architecture, copied in part from Caesar's Tower, Warwick Castle. The pub across the road is still called the Holloway Castle]

Holloway, Middlesex *n.* [mid-19C–1900s] the stomach. [Holloway, London N7/N19; puns on both words]

hollowhead *n.* [mid-19C+] (*US*) an idiot (cf. AIRBALL n.). [SE *hollow* + -HEAD sfx (1)]

hollow leg *n.* **1** [20C+] (*orig. US*) (*also* **glass legs**) a capacity for heavy drinking, a heavy drinker; occas. of over-eating. **2** [1920s+] a person who can indulge to a great extent.

hollow-legged *adj.* [20C+] used of a serious drinker. [HOLLOW LEG n. (1)]

hollow log *n.* **1** [1960s+] (*Aus.*) a derog. term for any non-White person. **2** [1970s+] (*Aus.*) a (racing) dog. **3** [1980s+] (*Aus. prison*) an informer. [rhy. sl.; (1) = WOG n.[1]; (3) = DOG n.[3] (7)]

holly-bag *n.* [1990s+] a holiday.

Hollyweird *n.* [1950s+] (*US*) Hollywood, California. [the negative image of the film capital]

Hollywood *adj.* [1950s+] (*US*) used generically to imply luxury, self-indulgence etc; occas. disparagingly so.

Hollywood eyes *n.* [1950s] (*US Black*) an attractive woman.

Hollywood hustler *n.* [1970s+] (*US*) a male homosexual prostitute. [SE *Hollywood*, seen as a 20C+ 'Sodom' + HUSTLER n. (7)]

Hollywood stew *n.* [20C+] (*US prison*) creamed cod fish. [the 'luxury' of the dish]

Hollywood stop *n. see* CALIFORNIA STOP n.

Hollywood swoop *n.* [1970s+] (*US Black/West Coast*) an automobile manoeuvre whereby one cuts in front of another vehicle, stopping one's own car and thus forcing the other vehicle to halt. [such manoeuvres are reminiscent of, or learned from, film or TV police chase sequences]

holmes *n.* (*also* **holm slice**) [1970s+] (*US campus*) an affectionate dimin. of HOMEBOY n. [pun on HOMES n.; Larry *Holmes* (b.1949), heavyweight champion; also note NO SHIT, SHERLOCK! excl.]

hols *n.* [20C+] holidays. [abbr.]

holstein cow *n.* [1950s+] (*Can.*) a black and white police car. [the colours of *Holstein* cattle]

holus-bolus *adv.* [early 19C–1900s] in a mess, jumbled up. [cod Lat. or a ponderous pun on Gk *holos bolos*, the whole lump]

holy *adj.* **1** [mid-19C+] a general intensifier. **2** [1990s+] (*UK juv.*) excellent, best.

holy...! *excl.* [mid-19C+] used in combs., a mild excl. of surprise, dismay, alarm; as well as those combs. below, *holy balls! ...Biddy! ...bilge water! ...cats! ...Egypt! ...frost! ...gee! ...ginger! ...gosh! ...hailstones! ...heck! ...hell! ...hokey! ...hoptoads! ...Jack the Ripper! ...monkey! ...pretzel! ...snakes!* [despite the use of *holy*, none is blasphemous]

holy alls *n.* [20C+] (*Irish*) the end result.

Holy City *n.* [late 19C–1910s] (*Aus.*) Adelaide, South Australia; thus *Holy State*, South Australia. [the city's many churches; thus the alternative nickname the *city of churches*]

Holy Cod *n.* [late 19C–1920s] Good Friday. [a mockery of religious fish-eating; note Fr. equivalent *La Sainte Morue*]

holy cow! *excl.* [1930s+] (*orig. US*) an excl. of surprise or disappointment.

holy crap! *excl.* [1930s+] (*US*) a general excl. of amazement, surprise, annoyance etc. [SE *holy* + CRAP n.[3] (1)]

holy crow! *excl.* [1960s+] (*US*) an excl. of amazement, surprise.

holy dollar *n.* (*also* **holey dollar**) [mid–late 19C] (*Aus.*) a silver dollar out of which a circle has been punched.

holy dooley! *excl.* [1940s+] (*Aus.*) a general expression of surprise. [? link to GIVE SOMEONE LARRY DOOLEY v.]

holy father *n.* [late 18C–19C] 'A butcher's boy of St Patrick's Market, Dublin or any other Irish blackguard' (Grose, 1785). [SE *holy father*, the Pope, used as an excl. by such boys]

Holyfield's ear *n.* [1990s+] a year. [rhy. sl.; Evander *Holyfield* (b.1962), the boxer whose ear was bitten by Mike Tyson in a boxing match in 1997]

holy fly! *excl.* (*also* **holy flyback!**) [20C+] (*Aus./Irish*) a mild oath.

holy friar *n.* [late 19C+] a liar. [rhy. sl.; never truncated]

holy fuck! *excl.* [1940s+] (*orig. US*) a general excl. used to express surprise, astonishment. [SE *holy* + FUCK! excl.]

holy ghost *n.* **1** [20C+] (*Aus.*) the post, the mail. **2** [1940s] the post, i.e. the start-line for a horserace. **3** [1950s+] toast. [rhy. sl.]

holy ghosts *n.* [20C+] (*Aus.*) fence posts. [rhy. sl.]

holy ghost shop *n.* [late 19C–1900s] a church.

holy ground *n. see* HOLY LAND n.

holy herb *n.* (*also* **holy weed**) [1960s+] marijuana (cf. AFRICAN

BUSH n.). [the use of marijuana as sacramental by Rastafarians; HERB n.[2] (3)/WEED n.[1] (4)]

holy horror *n. see* HOLY TERROR n.

holy Joe *n.* **1** [mid-19C+] a clergyman, esp. in the services or in a prison. **2** [late 19C+] anyone of a religious bent. **3** [late 19C+] (*also* **holy Josie**) a prudish, sanctimonious, narrow-minded puritan; thus *holy joeism*. [orig. naut. jargon]

holy Joe! *excl.* [20C+] an excl. of surprise.

holy jumping...! *excl.* [late 19C+] a general excl.; ext. of JUMPING...! excl.; usu. with *jimminy, jemima* etc and other words beginning with *j*, but also can be used with any other n. Common ones include *mother of god, beans, cats*.

holy lamb *n.* [late 18C–19C] (*Irish*) a complete and utter villain. [a pun on Lat. *agnus dei*, the lamb of God, used as the first words of the Catholic mass. The term lamb was given to the particularly violent troops led by the soldier of fortune Colonel Percy Kirke in 1684–6. Their flag carried an image of the paschal lamb, known in heraldry as the *holy lamb*, and the troops were known as 'Kirke's lambs'. Lambs also referred to gangs of thugs used to intimidate voters at 19C elections, e.g. the 'Nottingham lambs', which flourished 1860–70]

holy land *n.* (*also* **holy ground**) **1** [19C] (*orig. US*) a red-light district or slum. **2** [19C] the area around St Giles, London WC2, including Seven Dials. **3** [late 19C+] any area of a city populated by or frequented by Jews. **4** [late 19C+] (*Aus.*) Tasmania. [SE *holy ground/land*, an area within church jurisdiction in which villains or persecuted people could gain sanctuary. The slums and criminal ghettos were often impervious to the law; St Giles is the patron saint of beggars; Ribton-Turner, *A History of Vagrants* (1887), notes: 'An old *fancy* chaunt [that] ends every verse thus: "For we are the boys of the holy ground / And we'll dance upon nothing and turn us around"]

holy mackerel! *excl.* (*also* **holy mac!**) [late 19C+] an excl. of surprise, shock, wonder or amazement.

holy Mary *n.* [1950s+] (*Irish*) of men or women, a religious hypocrite, one who pretends to great and showy religiosity.

holy moly! *excl.* (*also* **holy moley!**) [1920s+] (*orig. US juv.*) a general excl. of amazement or shock. [var. on HOLY MOSES! excl. The catchphrase favoured by the comic-book character Captain Marvel]

holy Moses *n.* [early 17C] a cuckold. [paintings of Moses displaying him with a part-halo, the curves of which resemble horns protruding from his head]

holy Moses! *excl.* [mid-19C+] a general excl. of amazement or shock.

holy nail *n.* [late 19C+] legal bail. [rhy. sl.]

holy piss! *excl. see* HOLY SHIT! excl.

holy poker *n.* [mid-19C+] the penis.

Holy Roller *n.* (*US*) **1** [mid-19C+] (*also* **Roller**) a member of a Pentecostal church. **2** [1940s+] a sanctimonious person or a religious fundamentalist. [their physical twitchings and 'rollings' at the height of their apparent religious ecstasy]

holy-rolling *n.* [1920s] (*US*) religious fervour.

holy-rolling *adj.* [1940s+] (*US*) sanctimonious. [HOLY ROLLER n. (2)]

holy shit! *excl.* (*also* **holy piss!**) [1960s+] a general excl. of surprise or astonishment. [SHIT n.[1] (1)]

holy show *n.* (*also* **holy spectacle, show**) [mid-19C+] (*Aus./Irish*) the cause of a scandal or embarrassment; esp. in phr. *make a holy show of oneself*, to make an exhibition of oneself.

holy smoke *n.* [20C+] **1** coke, the fuel. **2** Coke, the drink Coca-Cola. [rhy. sl.]

holy smoke! *excl.* [late 19C+] an excl. of surprise, shock, wonder or amazement.

holy spectacle *n. see* HOLY SHOW n.

Holy State *n. see* HOLY CITY n.

holy terror *n.* (*also* **holy horror**) [late 19C+] **1** a person of exasperating habits or manners. **2** an exasperating event or situation. [HOLY adj. (1)]

holy wars! *excl.* [1900s–10s] a general excl.

holy water *n.*[1] [20C+] water that has been laced with whisky.

holy water *n.*[2] [20C+] a daughter. [rhy. sl.]

holy-water sprinkler *n.* (*also* **holy-water stick**) [19C] a spiked club, a 'morning star'. [it sprinkled not water but blood]

holy weed *n. see* HOLY HERB n.

holy week *n.* **1** [1960s] (*US*) the time of menstruation. **2** [1970s] (*gay*) any time one abstains from sex, e.g. when one has VD.

holy Willie *n.* [late 19C+] a sanctimonious, hypocritically pious person. [the subject of Robert Burns's poem 'Holy Willie's Prayer' (1785)]

hom *n.* [1990s+] used as a term of abuse. [abbr. SE *homosexual*]

homa *n. see* OMEE n. (1).

hombre *n.* (*also* **ombrey**) **1** [mid-19C+] a man. **2** [late 19C+] as a term of address. **3** [1990s+] (*orig. US campus*) a male friend. [Sp. *hombre*; widely popularized through 20C+ spread of the Hollywood Western film]

hombrecitos *n.* [1970s+] (*drugs*) psilocybin. [Sp. *hombrecitos*, little men; ? those that one sees after taking the hallucinogen]

hombug *n. see* HUMBUG n.[1].

Home *n.* [late 19C–1940s] (*US Und.*) St Paul, Minnesota. [apparently criminals were welcome to use this as a base as long as they did not operate locally]

home *n.* **1** [1940s+] (*orig. US Black*) a friend, often used in direct address. **2** [1970s+] (*US campus*) a person from the same home town, a friend. [abbr. HOMEBOY n.]

home and dried *phr.* (*also* **home and dry**) [late 19C+] **1** safe and sound. **2** accomplished without having to have made any real effort. [image of a person arriving home safe and sound]

home and fried *phr.* [1910s] (*Aus.*) safe and sound. [play on HOME AND DRIED phr.]

home and hosed *phr.* (*also* **home with a rug on**) [1940s+] (*Aus./N.Z.*) **1** safe and sound. **2** accomplished without having to have made any real effort.

homebake *n.* (*also* **bake**) [1980s+] (*Aus./N.Z. drugs*) the manufacture of homemade heroin or morphine from codeine phosphate. [HOMEBAKE v.]

homebake *v.* (*also* **bake**) [1980s+] (*Aus./N.Z. drugs*) to manufacture homemade heroin or morphine from codeine phosphate; thus *homebaker*, one who does this; *homebaking*, the process. [the use of heat in the manufacturing process]

homebird *n.* **1** [mid–late 19C] a hen-pecked husband. **2** [1950s+] (*orig. US*) one who prefers their home to venturing anywhere more exciting or challenging.

home biscuit *n.* [1980s+] (*US campus*) a friend. [SE *home* + *biscuit*]

homeboy *n.* **1** [late 19C+] (*also* **home-buddy**) someone who stays mainly at home. **2** [late 19C+] a neighbourhood person. **3** [late 19C+] a good friend (cf. LANDSMAN n.). **4** [late 19C+] a naïve person, newly arrived in the city from the countryside. **5** [1910s+] (*S.Afr./US*) someone who has come to the city from the same rural or provincial area as oneself (cf. HOMEGIRL n.). **6** [1950s–60s] (*Irish*) an ex-inmate of a religious institution. **7** [1970s+] (*US Black*) a young Black or Hispanic member of a street gang. **8** [1980s+] (*US Black*) a fellow Black person. [now almost exclusively a Black term, *homeboy* origated in the South *c.*1930 and was used by all races before it migrated, with the Black population, to the urban ghettos]

homebrew *n. see* BREW n.[1] (7).

homechicken *n.* [1980s] (*US campus*) a male or female homosexual.

homechop *n.* [1980s+] (*US campus*) a friend, usu. of the opposite sex. [? SE *home* + *lambchop*]

home cooking *n.*[1] [1930s–40s] (*US Black*) anything outstanding, wonderful or first-rate. [the presumed excellence of home cookery]

home cooking *n.*[2] [1960s] (*US*) sexual intercourse, usu. from a man's point of view with his wife.

home dirt *n. see* HOME SLICE n. (1).

homee *n. see* OMEE n.

home folks *n.* [19C+] (*US*) **1** one's immediate or extended family. **2** people from the area in which one grew up, from one's home community.

homegirl *n.* (*orig. US Black*) **1** [1910s+] a woman from one's home town or neighbourhood. **2** [1980s+] a woman. **3** [1980s+] a close female friend. **4** [1980s+] a female gang member. [var. on HOMEBOY n.]

homegrown *n.*[1] [1970s+] (*drugs*) marijuana that has been grown at home. [such marijuana was usu. seen as inferior before the introduction of new techniques, e.g. hydroponics, that have revolutionized the former cottage industry over the last 20 years]

homegrown *n.*[2] [1990s+] (*US prison*) a 'masculine' lesbian.

home guard *n.* [20C+] **1** (*US*) a regular worker, one who stays on one job in one locality rather than a transient. **2** (*US*) a beggar or tramp who stays in one place. **3** (*US Und.*) a con-man's victim who lives in the same city/town in which he is fleeced. **4** (*US Und.*) a local, as opposed to an itinerant confidence man.

homeland *n.* [1960s–70s] (*US Black*) the Black area of a city.

homely as a basket of chips *phr.* (*also* **homely as a hedge fence, ...as a mud fence, ...as a pig head three, ...as a stump fence, ...enough to fade a carpet, ...enough to sour milk, ...enough to stop a clock/train**) [early 19C+] (*US*) plain.

homemade *n.* [1940s–60s] (*US*) a homemade pistol, a 'zip gun'.

homemade shit *n.* [1970s] (*US campus*) unpleasant, depressing feelings. [SE *homemade* + SHIT n.[3] (1)]

home of rest *n.* [1910s] a prison.

home on the pig's back *phr. see* ON THE PIG'S BACK phr.

home on the range *n.* [20C+] (*Aus.*) small change. [rhy. sl.]

home on the range *adj.* [1990s+] strange. [rhy. sl.]

home piece *n.* [1970s+] **1** (*US prison*) a fellow inmate who was already a friend before imprisonment. **2** (*US*) a friend.

homer *n.*[1] (*US*) **1** [late 19C+] in sports, a referee who favours the home team. **2** [1980s+] a friend.

homer *n.*[2] [1980s+] (*US campus*) a penis. [? it goes for a HOME RUN n.]

homer *n.*[3] *see* HOME RUN n.

homer *n.*[4] *see* OMEE n. (1).

home rule *n.* [late 19C–1900s] Irish whisky. [play on FENIAN n.[1]]

home rulers *n.* [late 19C] **1** baked potatoes, cooked and sold in the street. **2** (*Irish*) pint bottles of stout. [? the stereotypical Irish diet of potatoes. The period saw a major agitation by the Fenians in favour of Irish Home Rule]

home run *n.* (*also* **homer**) [1960s+] (*US*) sexual intercourse (cf. FIRST BASE n.). [baseball imagery]

homes *n.* [1970s+] (*orig. US Black*) an affectionate dimin. of HOMEBOY n., usu. as a term of address, e.g. *Hey, homes...* (cf. HOLMES n.).

home skillet *n.* [1980s+] (*orig. US Black*) a fellow Black person. [var. on HOMEBOY n. (8)]

home slice *n.* **1** [1980s+] (*US campus/prison*) (*also* **home dirt**) someone from one's town, area, state; ext. to any friend. **2** [1990s+] (*US Black teen*) a fellow Black person. [(1) var. on HOMEBOY n. (5); (2) var. on HOMEBOY n. (8)]

home squeeze *n.* [1970s+] **1** (*orig. US*) one's most favourite person, usu. a lover. **2** (*orig. US Black*) one's wife or regular partner. [SE *home* + SQUEEZE n.[7]]

homestone *n.* [1980s+] (*US drugs*) marijuana grown on private premises. [SE *home* + STONED (OUT) adj. (2)]

home sweet home *n.*[1] [late 19C–1920s] the vagina.

home sweet home *n.*[2] [1980s] (*Aus.*) a comb. [rhy. sl.]

home with a rug on *phr. see* HOME AND HOSED phr.

homework *n.* [1930s+] (*orig. US*) **1** petting, necking. **2** a girl-friend.

homey *n.*[1] (*also* **homie**) [1920s+] (*Aus./N.Z.*) an Englishman; a British immigrant, esp. one newly arrived or still nostalgic for the UK. [SE *home country*]

homey *n.*[2] (*also* **homie**) **1** [1940s+] (*orig. US Black*) an affectionate dimin. of HOMEBOY *n.*; also used as a term of address; also attrib. **2** [1990s+] (*US campus*) a partner in a casual sexual relationship. **3** [1990s+] a relative.

homey *n.*[3] *see* HOMIE *n.*[1].

homey *n.*[4] *see* OMEE *n.*

homey *adj. see* HOMY *adj.*

homey don't play dat *phr.* [1990s+] (*US campus*) a phr. indicating one's refusal to cooperate with, consent to or accept something. [the catchphrase of the character Homey the Clown in the TV show *In Living Color*]

homicide *n.* **1** [1950s] (*US*) someone or something formidable. **2** [1990s+] (*US drugs*) a cocktail of heroin and/or cocaine plus various prescription drugs, including scopolamine, used to increase the heart-rate, a sea-sickness remedy and dextromethorphan, usu. used as a cough medicine. The effects are generally negative, including paranoia, hallucinations and memory loss, and can lead to death, usu. by heart attack. [play on MURDER *n.* (1)/SE *murder*]

homie *n.*[1] (*also* **homey**) [1940s+] (*US*) a homosexual. [abbr.]

homie *n.*[2] [1990s+] (*Aus.*) a person who wears expensive brands of sportswear. [HOMEY *n.*[2]]

homie *n.*[3] *see* HOMEY *n.*[1].

homie *n.*[4] *see* HOMEY *n.*[2].

homie *n.*[5] *see* OMEE *n.*

homie *adj.* [1960s] homosexual. [HOMIE *n.*[1]]

hominy gazette *n.* [1910s+] (*Aus. prison*) internal prison rumours. [the main constituent of prison meals. Note Aus. prison sl. *hominy bus*, the bus that runs between Darlinghurst Prison and Long Bay Prison; *hominy pimples*, an itchy rash, prevalent in summer, which prisoners ascribe to the monotonous diet; *hominy cock/prick*, a substitute 'penis' made by stuffing a sock with hominy and used by women prisoners for masturbation]

homi-polone *n. see* OMEE-POLONE *n.*

homo *n.*[1] [early 19C–1920s] a man. [Ling. Fr.]

homo *n.*[2] **1** [1920s+] a male *homo*sexual. **2** [1960s+] gay pornography. **3** [1970s+] (*US campus*) a weakling, an inadequate. [abbr. of SE; (3) no specific sexuality is implied]

homo *adj.* [1920s+] *homo*sexual. [HOMO *n.*[2] (1)]

homo heaven *n.* [1960s] (*US gay*) any public area where homosexuals meet, pick each other up etc. [HOMO *n.*[2] (1) + SE *heaven*]

homoney *n.* [18C] **1** a woman. **2** a wife. [Lat. *homo*, man]

ho-monga *n.* [2000s] (*US teen*) a male who has a number of girlfriends at the same time. [US Black pron. of archaic SE *whoremonger*, a lecher, a fornicator]

homosexual *adj.* [1980s+] (*US campus*) eccentric, odd, strange. [no specific sexuality is implied, although the negative stereotype remains central]

homy *adj.* (*also* **homey**) **1** [mid-19C] feeling like home, thus comfortable, secure. **2** [1920s+] homely, conventional, dominated by 'family values'.

hon *n.* [20C+] (*US*) a general term of endearment, affection. [abbr. HONEY *n.*[1] (4)]

honch *n.* [1970s] (*US drugs*) heroin.

honcho *n.* **1** [1940s+] (*orig. US*) a leader, employer, boss, the head person of any job or other situation. **2** [1960s+] (*US*) a fellow man. **3** [1990s+] a well-built, attractive man. [Jap. *han'cho*, group leader; imported to West by US forces in Korea]

honcho *v.* [1950s+] (*orig. US*) to lead, to direct others in a task or plan. [HONCHO *n.*]

hondoo *n.* [1910s–60s] (*US*) the vagina. [Sp. *honda*, 'the eye or eyelet on the loop of a rope through which the main line is passed to form a loop for roping' (Logsden, *Whorehouse Bells Were Ringing*, 1989)]

hone *n.* [18C] the vagina. [SE *hone*, a whetstone used to grind knives]

hone *v.* [20C+] (*US*) **1** to pine for, to yearn after. **2** to look for, to search out. [OF *hogner, hoigner*, to grumble, mutter or murmur, to whine like a child, or dog]

hone out *v.* [1980s+] (*US campus*) to eat voraciously. [? one has *honed* the edge of one's appetite]

honest Injun *adj.* [20C+] honourable. [HONEST INJUN! excl.]

honest Injun! *excl.* (*also* **honest Indian!**) **1** [mid-19C+] (*orig. US*) on my honour!; also as interrog. *really?* **2** [20C+] really! definitely! [the term was orig. sarcastic (Indians being seen as essentially dishonest) but became used at face value, esp. by children]

honest john *n.* **1** [late 19C+] (*US*) (*also* **honest Joe**) an honest citizen, a hard-working person. **2** [1930s] (*US prison*) a naïve person who does not care to 'work the system'. [SE *honest* + JOHN *n.*[1] (1)]

honest lawyer *n.* [mid-19C] a public house sign showing a headless man dressed in lawyer's robes (cf. GOOD WOMAN *n.*). [the implication being that his honesty is only possible since, headless, he is bereft of the chance to speak (i.e. lie)]

honest-to-God *adj.* (*also* **honest-to-Christ, -to-goodness, -to-gosh, -to-holy-cripes**) [1910s+] genuine, sincere, proper; also as excl. of affirmation.

honest-to-Hannah *adj.* [1950s–60s] genuine, pure. [euph. var. on HONEST-TO-GOD *adj.*]

honest-to-John *adj.* (*also* **honest-to-Pete**) [1940s+] (*US*) genuine, sincere, proper; also as excl. of affirmation. [a euph. var. on HONEST-TO-GOD *adj.*]

honest to Pete *adv.* [1910s] (*US*) honestly, sincerely.

honest trout *n.* [early 18C] an honest, respectable woman. [SE *honest* + TROUT *n.*[1] (1)]

honey *n.*[1] **1** [mid-14C+] (*also* **honey-chops**) a term of endearment, whether male to female or vice versa; occas. to a child of either sex. **2** [late 14C+] a sweetheart, a lover. **3** [early 19C+] (*orig. US*) anyone or anything good of its kind. **4** [1920s+] an attractive young woman. **5** [1920s+] (*US*) a female term for an endearing, attractive man. **6** [1930s+] (*orig. US*) ironic use of (3), something problematical.

honey *n.*[2] **1** [late 17C+] semen (cf. BABY GRAVY *n.*). **2** [18C+] vaginal secretions (cf. BINDERJUICE *n.*).

honey *n.*[3] [19C+] (*US*) one whose personality makes them hard to associate with but who has no appreciation of the fact. [abbr. *she's a honey but the bees don't know it*]

honey *n.*[4] [mid-19C+] (*US*) money (cf. BEES (AND HONEY) *n.*). [rhy. sl.; *pot o' honey* = money]

honey *n.*[5] **1** [1900s] (*US Und.*) a Black person. **2** [1920s+] (*US*) (*also* **honeydew**) human excrement; thus *honey-pit, honey-vat*, a cesspit; *honey gatherer, honeyman*, a cesspit cleaner. [the colour]

honey (around) *v. see* HONEY UP *v.*

honey-baby *n.* [1920s–50s] a general term of affection, usu. for a girl or woman.

honey-bucket *n.* (*also* **honeypot**) [1930s+] a bucket used for night-soil. [HONEY *n.*[5] (2)]

honey-bum *n.* [1940s–50s] (*Aus.*) a passive homosexual. [SE *honey* + BUM *n.*[1] (1)]

honey-bun *n.* (*also* **honey-bunch, honeypie**) [20C+] a general term of affection (cf. HONEY-BUNNY *n.*).

honey-bunny *n.* [1990s+] (*US*) a pretty girl. [ext. of HONEY *n.*[1] (4)]

honey-cart *n.* (*US*) **1** [1920s+] a vehicle for collecting human excrement. **2** [1950s+] a portable outdoor toilet. [HONEY *n.*[5] (2); the term has been adopted by airlines, railway companies and other owners of public transport that provide mobile lavatory facilities]

honey-chile *n.* (*also* **honey child**) [1920s+] (*US*) a general term of affection, usu. in Southern and/or Black use. [SE *honey-child*]

honey-chops *n. see* HONEY n.[1] (1).

honey-cooler *n.* [mid-19C–1900s] (*US*) an extraordinary person or thing. [ety. unknown]

honeydew *n.*[1] (*also* **honey dip**) [20C+] (*US*) whisky.

honeydew *n.*[2] *see* HONEY n.[5] (2).

honeydew *n.*[3] *see* HONEY-DO n.

honey-digger *n. see* HONEY-DIPPER n.

honey dip *n.*[1] [1990s+] (*US Black*) a pretty young woman with a golden-brown complexion. [HONEY n.[1] (4); the idea is of having been dipped in honey]

honey dip *n.*[2] *see* HONEYDEW n.[1].

honey-dipped *adj.* [1990s+] (*US Black*) of a young woman, having a golden-brown complexion. [HONEY DIP n.[1]]

honey-dipper *n.* (*also* **honey-digger**, **honey-dripper**) [1920s+] a latrine cleaner; thus *honey-dipping*, the removal of excrement or sewage; thus a term of abuse. [HONEY n.[5] (2)]

honey-do *n.* (*also* **honeydew**) [1990s+] (*US*) a household chore. [domestic imperatives, starting with *Honey, do...*]

honey-dripper *n.*[1] [1960s+] (*US Black*) a sexual partner. [HONEY n.[2]]

honey-dripper *n.*[2] *see* HONEY-DIPPER n.

honeyfackle *v. see* HONEYFUGGLE v.

honey-fall *n.* [mid-19C] a piece of good luck.

honeyfogle *v. see* HONEYFUGGLE v.

honeyfoogler *n. see* HONEYFUGGLER n.

honeyfuck *n.* [1970s+] **1** a very sexy woman. **2** a prepubescent girl, viewed as a sex object. [HONEYFUCK v.]

honeyfuck *v.* [1960s+] (*US*) **1** to have sexual intercourse in innocent or idyllic circumstances. **2** to have sex with a prepubescent girl. [HONEY n.[1] (4) + FUCK v.[1]]

honeyfuggle *v.* (*also* **honeyfackle, honeyfogle, honeyfugle**) (*US*) **1** [early 19C–1940s] to swindle, to trick, to fool. **2** [mid-19C–1940s] a fig. version of (3), to 'sweet talk', to flatter, to entice. **3** [mid-19C+] to cuddle up to. **4** [mid-19C+] to have sex, esp. with a prepubescent girl. [dial. *connyfogle*, to entice by flattery, to hoodwink, or dial. *gallyfuggle* to deceive or trick]

honeyfuggler *n.* (*also* **honeyfoogler, honeyfugler**) [mid-19C–1940s] (*US*) a flatterer; one who makes alluring but empty promises. [HONEYFUGGLE v. (2)]

honey gatherer *n. see* HONEY n.[5] (2).

honey hill *n.* [20C+] (*US*) the poor area of a town. [? HONEY n.[5]]

honey house *n.* [20C+] (*US*) a privy or outside lavatory (cf. BACKHOUSE n.). [HONEY n.[5] (2) + SE *house*]

honey it up *v. see* HONEY UP v.

honeyman *n. see* HONEY n.[5] (2).

honeymoon cystitis *n.* [1960s+] a vaginal infection that supposedly stems from intensive intercourse, which, in turn, is supposedly the staple of honeymooning couples.

honeymoon (stage) *n.* [1930s+] (*drugs*) the early use of heroin, before actual addiction, during which period the user can stop without any real physical or mental pain.

honeypie *n. see* HONEY-BUN n.

honey-pit *n. see* HONEY n.[5] (2).

honeypot *n.*[1] **1** [late 17C+] the vagina (cf. APPLE n.[6]; BAG n.[1]). **2** [1930s+] (*also* **nectar pot**) an attractive woman; also as term of address. [Puxley, *Cockney Rabbit: A Dick 'n' Arry of Rhyming Slang* (1992), suggests rhy. sl. *honey pot* = TWAT n. (1); D'Urfey, *Pills to Purge Melancholy* (1719–20) credits the lines to the poem 'To chuse a Friend, but never Marry' by the Earl of Rochester, but offers no date]

honeypot *n.*[2] [1930s+] (*Aus.*) jumping into a swimming pool with one's knees drawn up and one's hands clasped around them.

honeypot *n.*[3] *see* HONEY-BUCKET n.

honeypot *adj.* [1930s] of a woman, attractive. [HONEYPOT n.[1] (2)]

honey-thighs *n.* [1940s+] (*orig. US*) a general term of affection from a man to a woman; occas. vice versa.

honey up *v.* (*also* **honey, honey around, honey it up**) [mid-19C+] to cajole, to flatter, to sweet talk; as adj., affectionate. [abbr. HONEYFUGGLE v. (2)]

honey-vat *n. see* HONEY n.[5] (2).

honey-wagon *n.* (*US*) **1** [1920s+] a manure cart used for cleaning out barns. **2** [1920s+] a garbage wagon. **3** [1920s+] a vehicle used to spread manure on a field. **4** [1920s+] a vehicle for collecting human (occas. animal) excrement. **5** [1940s+] a portable toilet. [HONEY n.[5] (2) + SE *wagon*]

Hongers *n. see* HONKERS n.

Hong Kong *n.* [20C+] a smell. [rhy. sl. = PONG n.[1]]

Hong Kong *adj.* [1990s+] wrong. [rhy. sl.]

Hong Kong dog *n.* [20C+] diarrhoea or any form of stomach problem picked up by visitors to Hong Kong (cf. AZTEC HOP n.).

honk *n.*[1] [1920s+] (*orig. Aus.*) an unpleasant smell. [? Maori *haunga*, ill-smelling]

honk *n.*[2] **1** [1940s–60s] a wild, uproarious party. **2** [1970s+] (*US*) country and western or honky-tonk music. [abbr. HONKY-TONK n.[1] (1)]

honk *n.*[3] [1960s–70s] (*US*) the penis. [? HONKER n.[1] (2)]

honk *n.*[4] [1980s+] (*US drugs*) an inhalation of cocaine or heroin. [HONK v.[4]]

honk *n.*[5] *see* HONKIE n.

honk *v.*[1] **1** [20C+] (*US*) (*also* **honk on**) to talk loudly in a boastful manner. **2** [1960s+] to vomit (cf. BARF v.). [SE *honk*, to make a honking noise]

honk *v.*[2] **1** [1920s+] (*orig. Aus.*) to smell unpleasant, to stink; intensified as *honk like a gaggle of geese*. **2** [1970s+] (*US campus*) to be very offensive or unattractive. [HONK n.[1]]

honk *v.*[3] **1** [1940s+] to have sexual intercourse, to seduce. **2** [1970s+] (*US campus*) to be sexually aroused. **3** [1970s+] (*US Und.*) to kill someone.

honk *v.*[4] [1960s–70s] (*US*) to inhale or snort a narcotic. [HONKER n.[1] (2)]

honk *v.*[5] [1970s+] (*US*) to squeeze the penis or breast. [the image of squeezing or 'honking' an old-fashioned horn or hooter]

honk *v.*[6] *see* HONK (IT ON) v.

honkatonk *n. see* HONKYTONK n.[1].

honked (off) *adj.* [1950s+] (*US campus*) angry. [HONK OFF v.]

honked up *adj.* [1960s+] (*US campus*) excited. [HONK v.[1] (1)]

honker *n.*[1] **1** [mid-19C+] (*US*) a goose. **2** [1940s+] the nose. **3** [1960s+] (*US*) a player of a brass instrument. [SE *honk*, nose]

honker *n.*[2] [1960s+] (*US*) a very fast vehicle. [HONK (IT ON) v.]

honker *n.*[3] [1970s+] **1** a large penis. **2** (*US*) in pl., the female breasts, esp. if large. [HONK v.[5]]

honker *n.*[4] **1** [1970s+] (*US campus*) an offensive or unattractive person. **2** [1980s+] (*US teen*) anyone considered odd or eccentric. [HONK v.[2] (2)]

honker *n.*[5] [1980s+] (*US*) a gob of phlegm (cf. HAWKER n.). [HONK v.[1] (2)]

Honkers *n.* (*also* **Hongers**) [1920s+] Hong Kong, usu. among UK expatriates stationed or working in the Far East. [*Hong Kong* + -ER sfx]

honkers *n.* [1940s] (*US Black*) the buttocks.

honkers *adj.* [1950s+] drunk. [HONK v.[1] (2)]

honk, honk! *excl.* [1930s] a toast when drinking.

honkie *n.* (*also* **honk, honkey, honky**) **1** [1940s+] (*US Black*) a White person, occas. a light-skinned Latino. **2** [1940s+] an ice-cream bar. **3** [1970s] a phoney person. **4** [1980s+] a man, usu. derog. and used by any race. [abbr. BOHUNK n. (1); the Black use is a development of the White HUNKY n. (1), the orig. name for Poles who worked in Chicago stockyards. The change of the White 'u' to the Black 'o' supposedly accentuates the Black desire, embodied in the Black militants of the 1960s, to distance themselves as far as possible from the object of their hate]

honkie *adj.* (*also* **honky**) [1940s+] (*orig. US Black*) **1** a derog. term for White or pertaining to White lifestyle/culture. **2** fake, pseudo, second-rate. [HONKIE n.]

honkietown *n.* [1970s] (*US Black*) the predominantly White area of a town. [HONKIE n. (1)]

honking *adj.*[1] [1940s+] very drunk. [HONK v.[1] (2)]

honking *adj.*[2] [1980s+] (*US campus*) enormous, huge. [? var. on HULKING *adj.*]

honking brown *n.* [1940s] (*US Black*) an ostentatious tan-coloured suit of clothes. [HONK v.[1] (1)]

honk (it on) *v.* [1960s+] (*US*) to drive or go at top speed. [? the *honking* of the horn that accompanies such a progress]

honk job *n.* [1970s] (*US*) the act of squeezing someone's penis or breast. [HONK v.[5] + JOB n.[4]]

honk like a gaggle of geese *v. see* HONK v.[2] (1).

honkoe *n.* [1930s–60s] (*Aus.*) a general term of abuse. [? HONKIE n., but with no racial overtones, or HONK v.[2]]

honk off *v.* [1950s+] (*US campus*) to anger, to annoy. [HONK v.[2]]

honk on *v.*[1] (*also* **honk off**) [1970s] (*US campus*) to go away, to leave one alone. [? HONK (IT ON) v.]

honk on *v.*[2] *see* HONK v.[1] (1).

honky *see also under* HONKIE.

honky *n. see* HUNKY n. (2).

honky-dooley *adj. see* HUNKY-DORY adj. (1).

honkymobile *n.* [1970s] (*US Black*) any car seen as unfashionable and thus driven only by Whites. [HONKIE n. (1) + -MOBILE sfx]

honkytonk *n.*[1] (*also* **honkatonk**) **1** [late 19C+] (*orig. US*) a seedy bar which may also offer music, gambling, prostitutes. **2** [1980s+] (*US*) a small town. [the *honkytonk* piano that was often a feature of such establishments and thus the *honkytonk* music itself. The UK comedian Dick Emery (1918–83) used 'hello honky-tonk/ tonks' as a catchphrase, but it has not survived his death, other than in the context of his career]

honkytonk *n.*[2] [20C+] (*Aus.*) cheap wine. [rhy. sl. = PLONK n.[1]]

honkytonk *adj.* (*also* **honky-tonky**) [1920s+] (*orig. US*) seedy, sordid, run-down, mediocre. [HONKYTONK n.[1] (1)]

honky-tonk *v.* [1950s+] (*US*) to go out on the town. [HONKY-TONK n.[1] (1)]

honour (bright) *phr.* [early 19C+] a phr. used to confirm the honesty or sincerity of one's statement.

honyock/honyocker *n. see* HUNYAK n.

hoo *n. see* HOOHA n.

hooa *n. see* HOOER n.

hooch *n.*[1] (*also* **hootch**) **1** [late 19C+] (*orig. US*) alcohol, liquor. **2** [late 19C+] any inferior alcoholic drink (esp. whisky) in Alaska and the Can. northwest. **3** [late 19C+] (*orig. US, esp. prison*) illicitly distilled liquor, often made from surprisingly unorthodox ingredients. [*hoochinoo*, an alcoholic liquor made by Alaskan Indians, esp. the Hoochinoo people]

hooch *n.*[2] (*also* **hoochie**) [1970s+] (*US drugs*) cannabis. [adoption of HOOCH n.[1] (1)]

hooch *n.*[3] *see* HOOCHIE n.[1] (1).

hooch *n.*[4] *see* HOOTCHY-KOOTCHY n.

hooch *v.* [1900s] to drink alcohol. [HOOCH n.[1] (1)]

hooch dog *n.* [1980s+] (*US campus*) a marijuana cigarette. [HOOCH n.[2]]

hooched (up) *adj.* [1920s+] (*US/S.Afr.*) tipsy. [HOOCH n.[1] (1)]

hooch hound *n.* **1** [1930s] a Prohibition agent. **2** [1940s–60s] (*orig. US Black*) a drunkard. [HOOCH n.[1] + HOUND sfx]

hoochie *n.*[1] (*US Black*) **1** [1940s+] (*also* **hooch, hoochie mama, hootchie, hootchie mama, hootchy mama**) a promiscuous girl or woman. **2** [1990s+] an affectionate term of address. [HOOTCHY-KOOTCHY n. (2)]

hoochie *n.*[2] *see* HOOCH n.[2].

hoochie *n.*[3] *see* HOOTCHY-KOOTCHY n.

hoochie-coocher *n.* [1930s–40s] (*orig. US Black*) a striptease artist. [HOOTCHY-KOOTCHY n.]

hoochie-coochie *n. see* HOOTCHY-KOOTCHY n.

hoochie-coochie man/woman *n.* (*also* **hootchie-cootchie…, hootchy-cootchy…**) [late 19C+] (*US Black*) a practitioner of voodoo. [HOOTCHY-KOOTCHY adj. + SE *man/woman*]

hoochie mama *n. see* HOOCHIE n.[1].

hoochie-pap *n.* [1920s] (*US Black*) **1** the buttocks, the posterior. **2** copulation. [? the exaggerated movement of the buttocks when dancing the HOOTCHY-KOOTCHY n. (1)]

hoochy(-coochy) *n. see* HOOTCHY-KOOTCHY n.

hood *n.*[1] **1** [late 19C+] (*US*) a gangster, a thug. **2** [20C+] (*Aus.*) the police. **3** [20C+] a street ruffian. [abbr. HOODLUM n.]

hood *n.*[2] [1950s+] (*W.I. Rasta*) the penis. [? its foreskin]

hood *n.*[3] **1** [1960s+] (*US Black*) the area in which one lives, one's home ground; thus *from the hood*, being a member of a neighbourhood gang. **2** [1980s+] (*US prison*) a friend who has come from one's own neighbourhood. [abbr. SE *neighbourhood*]

hoodickie *n.* (*also* **hoodackie**) [1940s+] (*N.Z.*) an otherwise nameless object, often a gadget. [DOHICKEY n.[1] (1)]

hoodie *n.* (*also* **hoody**) [1980s+] (*orig. US*) a *hood*ed sweatshirt, as worn by many young people, esp. those involved in rap music, as a semi-uniform. [abbr.]

hoodle *v.* [20C+] (*US*) to cobble together, to botch up, to perform a bad job. [Ger. *hudeln*, to do something incompetently]

hoodledoo *n. see* HOODOO n. (2).

hoodle-hoodle wagon *n. see* HOODLUM WAGON n.

hoodlelacky *n.* (*also* **hoojacky, hoojay, hoojit, howdzacky**) [1940s+] (*N.Z.*) an otherwise nameless object, often a gadget.

hoodlum *n.* [late 19C+] (*orig. US*) **1** an unpleasant person or a street ruffian. **2** a thug or gangster. [ety. unknown. The term was coined in San Francisco *c.*1870–2 and spread across the US by the end of the decade, generating a number of popular etymologies. Among them, according to H.L. Mencken (1880–1956), is the idea of a local newspaperman who, keen to coin a term to describe the street gangs that were plaguing the city's streets, decided simply to reverse the name of a leading gangster, one Muldoon. This created *noodlum*, and a printer's error, substituting 'h' for 'n', did the rest. Other theories include a ref. to a gang rallying-cry, 'Huddle 'em!', and to roots in the Bavarian dial. term *Hodalump*, which carries exactly the same meaning, in various terms in Spanish and among US Indian languages. There is also the wonderfully unlikely linkage put forward by B&L that the term is based on the pidgin English *hood lahnt*, lazy. It is tempting to bring in the near-synon. SE *hooligan*, but that word was British and was noted only when it began appearing in London police reports *c.*1898; see Asbury, *The Barbary Coast* (1933), pp.150–3 for possible etys. and his persuasive opting for the 'huddle 'em' theory]

hoodlum *adj.* [late 19C+] lowlife, criminal, frequented by unpleasant characters.

hoodlum wagon *n.* (*also* **hoodle-hoodle wagon**) [late 19C–1960s] (*US*) a police patrol wagon. [note cowboy jargon *hoodlum wagon*, the bed wagon]

hoodman *adj.* **1** [18C–early 19C] blind. **2** [19C] drunk; thus *hoodman blind*, very drunk. [*hoodman*, the blinded player in a game of *hoodman-blind*, the older name of *blind man's buff*]

hoodoo *n.* (*US*) **1** [late 19C] a party or celebration. **2** [late 19C+] (*also* **hoodledoo**) a curse, a jinx, a run of bad luck. [SE *hoodoo*, the practice of witchcraft]

hoodoo *adj.* [late 19C–1940s] jinxed, cursed. [HOODOO n.]

hoodoo *v.* (*also* **hoodoodle**) [late 19C+] (*US*) to cheat, to deceive, to take advantage of; to suffer or give bad luck. [HOODOO n. (2)]

hood rat *n.* [1990s+] **1** (*US Black teen*) an unattractive and/or promiscuous woman. **2** (*US Black teen*) a young person living in a (Black) neighbourhood or part of a gang, usu. spec. female. **3** (*US campus*) a gangster, a thug. [(2) HOOD n.[3]/(3) HOOD n.[1] (1) + SE *rat*]

hoods n. [1970s+] (*US gay*) dark glasses. [*hoods* for one's eyes]

hoody n. see HOODIE n.

hoody adj. [1960s+] (*US*) acting in a thuggish manner; resembling a thug. [HOOD n.¹]

hooer n. (*also* **hooa, hoor, hua, huer**) [1950s+] (*Aus.*) a term of general disapproval, applied to either sex. [SE *whore*]

hooey n. **1** [1910s+] rubbish, nonsense. **2** [1980s+] (*US*) excrement. [? Rus. (transliteration) *hooey*, sl. for penis, i.e. COCK n.² (1), thus load of old COCK n.⁵ (2)]

hooey! *excl.* [1920s+] nonsense! [HOOEY n. (1)]

hoof n. **1** [late 16C+] the human foot; thus BEAT IT ON THE HOOF v.; ON THE HOOF phr. **2** [1960s+] a shoe.

hoof v. (*also* **hoof it, huff it**) **1** [mid-17C+] to walk, to go on foot. **2** [late 19C+] to run. **3** [20C+] to kick, also in fig. use. **4** [1920s+] to dance. **5** [1950s] (*US*) to work hard. **6** [1980s+] (*US campus*) to hurry. **7** [1990s+] to engage enthusiastically in something. [HOOF n. (1)]

hoof-and-mouth-disease n. [1940s–60s] (*US*) the act of talking too much. [var. on FOOT-IN-MOUTH DISEASE n.]

hoofball n. [1910s] (*Aus.*) Australian Rules Football.

hoof-covers n. (*also* **hoof-coverings**) [late 19C] (*US*) a boot or shoe. [HOOF n. (1) + SE *covers*]

hoofer n. [1910s+] (*US*) a dancer of either sex; a chorus–girl or chorus–boy. [HOOF n. (1)]

hoofery n. [1940s–60s] (*orig. US Black*) a dance hall. [HOOF v. (4)]

hoofing n. **1** [late 17C+] travelling on foot. **2** [20C+] (*orig. US*) dancing. [(1) HOOF v. (1); (2) HOOF v. (4)]

hoof it v.¹ [2000s] (*US prison*) to hide contraband in one's rectum. [? fig. use of HOOF v. (3), with the idea of kicking someone up the arse]

hoof it v.² see HOOF v.

hoofler n. [20C+] (*Irish*) a general term of abuse. [HUFFLE v.]

hoof out v. [late 19C+] to throw out, to expel. [one is kicked with the HOOF n. (1)]

hoof the pad v. [mid-19C–1920s] (*Aus.*) to live as a tramp, to go on the tramp. [HOOF v. (1) + PAD n.¹ (1)]

hoogie n. (*also* **hoogy**) [1970s+] (*US Black*) a derog. term for a White person, esp. a racist. [? HOOJAH n./HOOSIER n. (6)]

hooha n. (*also* **hoo, hoohah**) **1** [1930s+] an uproar, commotion. **2** [1970s+] (*orig. milit.*) nonsense, rubbish, twaddle. **3** [1980s+] (*US*) an important or self-important person. [Yid. *hu-ha*, a hullabaloo]

hoohah n. [1920s+] a lavatory. [? fig. use of HOOHA n., although chronology mitigates against it and E.P. notes a suggestion that brackets the *hoo* of effort and the *ha* of relief that accompany defecation]

hoo-has/hoo-hoos, the n. see HOO-JAHS, THE n.

hoojacky n. see HOODLELACKY n.

hoojah n. (*also* **hoojer**) [1920s+] (*US Black*) a derog. term for a White person.

hoo-jahs, the n. (*also* **the hoo-has, the hoo-hoos**) [1930s+] (*Aus./US*) delirium tremens.

hoojay n. see HOODLELACKY n.

hoojer n. see HOOJAH n.

hoojit n. see HOODLELACKY n.

hook n.¹ **1** [late 18C+] a finger; usu. in pl. as *hooks*, thus a hand; thus *toss the hooks*, to box. **2** [mid-19C+] (*also* **breech hook**) the pickpocket who actually steals the wallet, money etc rather than his various accomplices; thus *lady hook*, a female pickpocket. **3** [late 19C] in fig use, one's skill, one's ability. **4** [late 19C+] (*Aus.*) any expert thief, esp. a pickpocket. **5** [1940s+] (*Irish*) a confidence trickster, a cheat. **6** [1940s–50s] an arrest. **7** [1970s] (*US Und.*) a key. **8** [2000s] (*US Black/Und.*) the police.

hook n.² [late 19C+] **1** a catch, a drawback. **2** a gimmick or angle. **3** an imposture. [late 20C+ use is US Black]

hook n.³ **1** [late 19C+] (*orig. Aus.*) a spur, usu. in pl. **2** [1910s–60s] (*US prison*) a straight razor used as a weapon.

hook n.⁴ [1930s+] (*US*) **1** an influential patron or contact; political influence. **2** any form of influence, e.g. blackmail.

hook n.⁵ [1940s+] (*US campus*) the telephone. [one 'hangs it up'; early models had a hook on which the receiver was hung]

hook n.⁶ **1** [1940s+] (*US*) a jack or 7 in poker. **2** [1960s+] (*US campus*) the grade C; thus *hook and a half*, the grade C+ (cf. ACE n.⁶). [the shape of the letter or number]

hook n.⁷ [1950s+] (*drugs*) an addiction. [HOOK v.⁵]

hook n.⁸ [1960s+] (*US Black*) a derog. term for a Jew (cf. BIGNOSE n.). [the popular stereotype of hook-nosed Semites]

hook n.⁹ [1980s] (*Aus.*) a prison.

hook n.¹⁰ see HOOKER n.¹.

hook n.¹¹ see HOOKER n.³.

hook adj. [1980s+] (*US Black*) physically attractive.

hook v.¹ **1** [early 17C–19C] to steal, to pilfer, esp. by cutting a hole in a shop window and 'fishing' for its contents with a hook on a string. **2** [late 18C+] to steal, to rob; to pick a pocket. [SE *hook*]

hook v.² **1** [18C+] to fool, to practise a confidence trick upon, to swindle. **2** [20C+] to (over)charge. **3** [1990s+] (*US Black*) to cost. [SE *hook*, ensnare]

hook v.³ **1** [early 18C+] (*US*) to arrest, to catch in a crime. **2** [early 19C+] to attract, esp. into marriage. **3** [late 19C+] to attract, to catch the eye of.

hook v.⁴ (*also* **hook it**) **1** [late 18C] to run off, to escape; also as phr. *take one's hook* (cf. SLING ONE'S HOOK v.²). **2** [mid-19C+] to go about one's own business. **3** [20C+] (*US*) to play truant. [SE *hook*, move with a sudden twist or turn]

hook v.⁵ [20C+] (*drugs*) to addict someone to drugs.

hook v.⁶ [1910s+] (*Aus./US*) to punch, to fight.

hook v.⁷ **1** [1930s+] (*US, orig. tramp*) to steal a ride on a train or other vehicle, to hitchhike. **2** [1980s+] to catch a train, a bus etc. **3** [1980s+] (*US campus*) to engage in love-making. **4** [1980s+] (*US Black*) to search for. **5** [1990s+] (*US drugs*) to find or obtain something. [HOOK ONTO v.]

hook v.⁸ [1940s+] to engage in prostitution. [HOOKER n.³ (1); while there appears to be no evidence of this use before the 1940s, it seems likely that the word was in unrecorded use as much as a century earlier]

hook v.⁹ [1950s] (*drugs*) to inject narcotics.

hook v.¹⁰ [1970s+] (*US campus*) to get a grade C. [HOOK n.⁶ (2)]

hook v.¹¹ [1990s+] (*UK juv.*) to vomit (cf. BARF v.). [SE *hawk*, to spit]

hook v.¹² see HOOK UP (WITH) v.¹ (8).

hook and a half n. see HOOK n.⁶ (2).

hook-and-eye n. [1920s] a villain, a criminal. [? rhy. sl. = CROOK n.² (2), although rhyme is uncharacteristically on the first element]

hook-and-eyes n. (*also* **hook-and-eye Baptists, hook-and-eye Dutch, hook-and-eyers, hookers**) [late 19C+] (*US*) a nickname for the Amish, whose beliefs forbid them the use of buttons.

hook and snivey/snivvy see under HOOKEM-SNIVEY.

hook and snivey, with nix the buffer n. [late 18C–early 19C] (*UK Und.*) a criminal trick designed to feed a dog and an additional man for nothing, when food has to be purchased per head.

hook down v. [20C+] to swallow.

hooked adj.¹ [late 17C+] tricked, fooled, deceived, ensnared; usu. in the context of a confidence trick or blackmail. [HOOK v.² (1)]

hooked adj.² **1** [mid-19C+] (*also* **hooked on**) in fig. uses, e.g. *hooked on someone*, obsessed with someone. **2** [1910s] married. [HOOK v.³]

hooked adj.³ [1920s+] addicted (usu. to a narcotic drug). [HOOK v.⁵]

hooked adj.⁴ **1** [1980s] (*US campus*) sorted out, taken care of. **2** [1990s+] (*US Black/campus*) physically attractive.

hooked into adj. [1970s+] (*US*) involved with.

hooked on *adj. see* HOOKED *adj.*[2] (1).

hooked on *phr.* [20C+] (*Aus.*) of a woman, 'picked up' in the street or in some other informal situation.

hooked up *adj.*[1] [1910s+] (*US*) dating, 'going steady'. [SE *hook up*, to join with]

hooked up *adj.*[2] [1920s] dead. [one has been *hooked up* to heaven]

hooked up *adj.*[3] [1970s+] (*US*) **1** well-dressed. **2** intelligent, culturally aware. [*hooked up* with what is fashionable, interesting]

hookem-snivey *n.* (*also* **hokum snivey**, **hook and snivey**, **hook and snivvy**, **hook 'em snivey**, **hookem-snivvy**, **hookum-snivey**, **hookum-snivvy**) **1** [late 18C] (*Irish*) a blow. **2** [late 18C–19C] a trick or deceit, spec. a contrivance for undoing the bolt of a door from the outside; a device to help with putting on boots. **3** [late 19C] nobody. [abbr. of HOOK AND SNIVEY, WITH NIX THE BUFFER n.]

hookem-snivey *adj.* (*also* **hook and snivey**, **hook and snivvy**, **hook 'em snivey**, **hookem-snivvy**, **hookum-snivey**, **hookum-snivvy**) [mid-19C–1930s] deceitful, tricky. [HOOKEM-SNIVEY n. (2)]

hookem-snivey *v.* (*also* **hook and snivey**, **hook and snivvy**, **hook 'em snivey**, **hookem-snivvy**, **hookum-snivey**, **hookum-snivvy**) [mid–late 19C] to deceive, esp. by faking an illness. [HOOKEM-SNIVEY n. (2)]

hooker *n.*[1] (*also* **hook**) **1** [mid-16C–18C] a thief, orig. one who uses a pole with a hook at one end to 'fish' items from open windows, unguarded market stalls, passing carts etc (cf. CANTING CREW n.). **2** [late 19C–1950s] a pickpocket, esp. of watches. [HOOK v.[1]]

hooker *n.*[2] [17C] a confidence trickster. [HOOK v.[2] (1)]

hooker *n.*[3] (*also* **hook**) **1** [mid-19C+] (*orig. US*) a prostitute. **2** [1990s+] (*US campus*) in fig. use, as a term of abuse, an idiot, a stupid person. [SE *hook*, to catch, to lure, to entice. One popular ety. suggests the denizens of *Corlear's Hook*, known as *The Hook*, a red-light area on the New York City waterfront. The view is sanctified by Bartlett's *Dict. of Americanisms* (1859), which defines *hooker* as 'a resident of The Hook, i.e. a strumpet, a sailor's trull'. Also note claim by Nell Kimball [1854–1934], 'My Life as Madam': 'The moniker hooker came about in the Civil War... General Joe Hooker, a handsome figure of a man, was a real quif-hunter, and he spent a lot of time in the houses of the redlight district, so that people began to call the district Hooker's Division.' However, the term is attested as early as 1835 thus the ety. is prob. the SE, but with strong reinforcement f. the geographical ref.; ? also poss. link to 19C SE *hooker*, a sailor's affectionate term for a vessel and thus synon. with various terms equating a prostitute with a ship, e.g. LAND CARRACK n.; PINNACE n.]

hooker *n.*[4] [mid-19C+] (*US*) a drink, a measure of liquor. [Scot. dial.]

hooker *n.*[5] [1930s–40s] (*US Und.*) a warrant for an arrest. [HOOK v.[3] (1)]

hooker *n.*[6] [1960s+] (*US*) a trick or concealed drawback. [HOOK n.[2] (1)]

hookers *n. see* HOOK-AND-EYES n.

hooker shop *n. see* HOOK SHOP n.

hookety *adj. see* HOOKITY adj.

hookey *n.* [late 19C] the nickname of a hook-nosed man, thus a Jew (cf. BIGNOSE n.). [the popular stereotype of hook-nosed Semites]

hookey *adj. see* HOOKY adj.

hookey walker! *excl.* (*also* **with a hook!**) [early 19C–1900s] **1** an expression of incredulity, nonsense! rubbish! **2** go away! be off!; thus *play Hookey Walker*, to run off. **3** fig. use of (1), meaning bad luck, trouble. [? according to Bee, the proper name of *John Walker*, 'an outdoor clerk' at Longman, Clementi and Co. in Cheapside; Walker had a hooked or crooked nose and was used by

the 'nobs of the firm' to spy on his fellow employees. Those upon whom he spied naturally declared that his reports were nonsense and since there were more of them than him, they tended to prevail. Hotten (1867) offers an alternative view, and a third can be found in *Notes & Queries* iv. 425]

hookface *n. see* HOOKNOSE n.

hook house *n.* [late 19C+] (*US*) a brothel (cf. ACCOMMODATION HOUSE n.). [HOOK n.[11] + HOUSE n.[1] (1)/SE *house*]

hookie bookie *n.* [2000s] (*US Black*) time-wasting, acting as a parasite. [HOOKY n.[2] + assonance]

hook in *v.* **1** [19C+] (*US*) to get introduced to or put in touch with, to entice. **2** [late 19C+] to associate oneself with. **3** [20C+] (*Aus./US*) to get involved in.

hook it *v. see* HOOK v.[4].

hook it up *v.*[1] [1990s+] (*US*) to finish, to bring to a conclusion.

hook it up *v.*[2] [2000s] (*US Black*) to be a prostitute or to act like one. [HOOK v.[8]]

hook it up *v.*[3] *see* HOOK UP (WITH) v.[2].

hookity *adj.* (*also* **hookety**) [1900s] (*Aus.*) dubious, unacceptable.

hook jack *v.* [late 19C–1910s] (*US*) to play truant. [HOOK v.[4] (3)]

hooknose *n.* (*also* **hookface**) [mid-19C+] a derog. term for a Jew; also a derog. term of address (cf. BIGNOSE n.). [physiological stereotyping; also note Folb, *Runnin' Down Some Lines* (1980): 'Whites who display characteristics associated with what is seen as Jewish behavior or looks are often labeled as such. I heard a variety of non-Jewish people, such as Italians, Armenians, and Greeks, being called by these terms because they showed stereotypic Jewish features or they behaved in some manner associated with Jews']

hook off *v.*[1] [late 19C] to steal. [HOOK v.[1]]

hook off *v.*[2] [1930s+] (*N.Z.*) to escape, to run off. [HOOK v.[4] (1)]

hook one's bait *v.* (*also* **hook one's mutton**) [1920s+] (*Aus./N.Z.*) to escape, to run off. [HOOK v.[4] (1)]

hook onto *v.* **1** [late 19C+] to attach oneself to someone, to follow about. **2** [20C+] to discover.

hook-pointed *adj.* (*also* **hook-pintled**) [19C] of the penis, semi-erect. [the curved shape; *pintled* is Scot. use]

hook shop *n.* (*also* **hooker shop**) [mid-19C+] a brothel (cf. BANGING-SHOP n.). [HOOK n.[11] + SE *shop*/SHOP n.[1] (1)]

hookum-snivey/-snivvy *see under* HOOKEM-SNIVEY.

hook-up *n.*[1] **1** [1900s] a fight. **2** [1900s–50s] a connection (between one person and another). **3** [1910s+] a connection (between one thing and another). **4** [1980s+] (*US campus*) an ability to get proper connections with certain people or things, e.g. drugs. **5** [1980s+] (*US drugs*) a place where drugs are sold. **6** [1980s+] (*US*) a sexual or romantic relationship or the person with whom one has a relationship. **7** [2000s] (*US prison*) a story made up by a prison officer to cause trouble for a prisoner.

hook-up *n.*[2] [2000s] (*US prison*) **1** various items purchased from the commissary. **2** (*US Black*) a suit of clothes, an outfit.

hook up (with) *v.*[1] **1** [20C+] to meet. **2** [20C+] to form a relationship with, sexual or otherwise. **3** [20C+] to get married. **4** [1910s+] (*US*) to corrupt, to suborn. **5** [1940s+] to introduce, to bring 2 parties together in a commercial transaction, to connect. **6** [1950s+] (*US Und.*) to involve a fellow criminal in or to advise of a potentially lucrative scheme. **7** [1970s] (*US Und.*) to work as a prostitute. **8** [1970s+] (*also* **hook**) to have a sexual encounter with someone, whether kissing or having sex. **9** [1980s+] (*US campus*) to give, to hand over, to provide. **10** [1980s+] to obtain drugs for someone. **11** [1990s+] (*US Black*) to create something according to one's own taste, e.g. clothing, house decoration, holiday plans. **12** [1990s+] (*US*) to take an academic course. **13** [2000s] (*US prison*) to get an address and phone number.

hook up (with) *v.*[2] (*also* **hook it up**) [1990s+] (*US teen*) to get more than one is entitled to, to get something for free. [one is 'hooking up to' fashionable people, occupations etc]

hooky *n.*[1] [1930s] (*US Und.*) a thief. [HOOK n.[1] (2)]

hooky n.[2] [1940s+] (US) truanting. [backform. f. PLAY HOOKY v.]

hooky n.[3] **1** [1950s] a Jew (cf. BIGNOSE n.). **2** [1970s] (US Black) a White person. [popular stereotype of hook-nosed Semites; (2) may be a generic or euph. form of (1)]

hooky adj. (also **hookey**) [1940s+] illegal. [HOOK v.[1] + pun on BENT adj. (3)]

hooky v. [1960s+] to play truant. [HOOKY n.[2]]

hooky house n. [1990s+] (US teen) anywhere that teenagers gather outside the supervision/control of their parents. [HOOKY n.[2] + SE house]

hooky party n. [1990s+] (US Black) a group of teenagers who skip school to drink malt liquor or liquid crack cocaine. [HOOKY n.[2] + SE party]

hooley n.[1] **1** [late 19C–1900s] a fur-lined and fur-collared overcoat. **2** [1960s] (US) a worthless person. [Mr Hooley, a noted millionaire; his luck ran out in 1898 when he was declared bankrupt and the term, initially admiring, became more ironic]

hooley n.[2] (also **hoolie**) [late 19C+] (orig. Irish) a rip-roaring party. [? Irish ceilidh, a gathering for the playing of music, telling of tales and general conversation (pron. 'kayley'). Share, however, opts for Anglo-Ind. hooly, ult. Hind. holi, the Hindu spring festival in honour of Krishna]

hooley v. [late 19C] to prosper, to follow success with success. [for ety. see HOOLEY n.[1]]

hoolie n.[1] [2000s] a hooligan. [abbr.]

hoolie n.[2] see HOOLEY n.[2].

hoolihan n. [1930s+] (US) a riotous event, a boisterous party; thus throw the hoolihan, to celebrate riotously. [Hoolihan, an Irish surname, thus the stereotyped image of the riotous Irish + ? SE hooligan]

hoolihan v. [1940s+] (US) to have a very good time, esp. of a cowboy going out on the town. [HOOLIHAN n.]

hoon n. **1** [1930s+] (Aus./N.Z.) a pimp, a procurer of prostitutes, whether to 'his' specific prostitute (or prostitutes) or simply as a general procurer. **2** [1930s+] (Aus./N.Z.) a show-off with limited intelligence; a flashy lout or hooligan. **3** [1930s+] (Aus./N.Z.) one who drives in a dangerous, showing-off manner. **4** [1980s+] (N.Z.) an exploit that involves 'hoonish', i.e. exhibitionist, loutish behaviour. [ety. unknown; Baker, The Australian Language (1945) suggests, esp. for (2), a contraction of Jonathan Swift's houyhnhnm (the anthropomorphic horses of Gulliver's Travels, 1726), but they are seen as intelligent beings. It is their human slaves, the yahoos, who are the fools – and noted as such in dictionaries. Note also N.Z. WW2 use by religiously motivated conscientious objectors to describe those with political or humanitarian agendas]

hoon v. **1** [1970s] to exploit, to take advantage of. **2** [1980s+] to behave in a loutish manner. [HOON n.]

hoon bin n. [1980s+] (N.Z.) an enclosure where drunken sports supporters are detained during a match. [HOON n. (2) + SIN BIN n.[1] (1)]

hoonchaser n. [1980s+] (N.Z.) a policeman (cf. BEAT-POUNDER n.). [HOON n. (1)/HOON n. (2) + SE chaser]

hoondom n. [1980s+] (N.Z.) the world of loutish exhibitionists. [HOON n. (2) + sfx -dom]

hoonery n. [1980s+] (N.Z.) loutish behaviour. [HOON n. (2) + sfx. -ery]

hoonish adj. [1980s+] (N.Z.) of a person or their behaviour, exhibitionist, loutish. [HOON n. (2)]

hoon it up v. [1980s] (N.Z.) to have a noisy, boisterous party. [HOON n. (2)]

hoop n.[1] [mid-19C–1960s] a ring, e.g. a wedding ring. [SE 16C–19C]

hoop n.[2] [1930s+] **1** the vagina. **2** the anus. **3** (US prison) sodomy.

hoop n.[3] [1930s+] (Aus.) a jockey. [the hooped 'colours' worn by some jockeys]

hoop n.[4] (also **hoops**) [1970s+] (US) the game of basketball. [the basketball hoop, thus the basketball film Hoop Dreams (1994)]

hoop n.[5] [1990s+] (Aus. drugs) the tourniquet that isolates a vein prior to injecting a narcotic drug.

hoop v.[1] [mid-18C–1900s] to beat. [fig. SE put through the hoop]

hoop v.[2] [mid-19C; 1980s] (US) to vomit (cf. BARF v.). [echoic]

hoop v.[3] (also **hoop down, hoop it, hoop out**) [1970s+] (US) to play basketball. [HOOP n.[4]]

hoop v.[4] [2000s] (US Black) to steal.

hoopdee/hoopdie n. see HOOPTIE n.

hoopdie swoop v. [1970s+] (US Black) to move in on and pick up a man or woman with great speed and efficiency. [? SE hoopla! + swoop]

hoop down v. see HOOP v.[3].

hooped adj. (also **hoopsy coopsy**) [mid-18C; 1940s+] (N.Z.) drunk. [? ref. to a barrel hoop]

hoop it v.[1] [mid–late 19C] (Aus./UK Und./US) to run away, to escape.

hoop it v.[2] see HOOP v.[3].

hoopla n. [late 19C+] fuss, commotion. [SE hoop-la! an expression accompanying a sudden movement, esp. of some trick on stage or in a circus ring; ult. Fr. houp-là!]

hoopla adj. [1910s–30s] crazy, wild, confused. [HOOPLA n.]

hoople n.[1] [1920s–30s] (US Und.) a ring. [Du. hoepel, a hoop, orig. used in New York City]

hoople n.[2] **1** [1920s+] (US) a fool, an idiot. **2** [1970s] (US Black) a White person. [? Major Hoople, a US cartoon strip character]

hoop one's barrel v. [18C] to beat. [HOOP v.[1] + SE barrel]

hoop out v. see HOOP v.[3].

hoops n. see HOOP n.[4].

hoop-stick n. [late 19C] the arm.

hoop stretcher n. [1990s+] a male homosexual (cf. ANAL ASTRONAUT n.). [HOOP n.[2] (2) + SE stretcher]

hoopsy coopsy adj. see HOOPED adj.

hoop-te-doodle n. [1920s] (US) anything for which one has no specific name.

hooptie n. (also **hoopdee, hoopdie, hoopty**) **1** [1960s+] (US, orig. Calif.) a car, esp. the latest model. **2** [1990s+] (US Black) a worn-out, falling-to-pieces automobile. [? the noise the car makes]

hoop up v. see WHOOP IT UP v.

hoopy adj. [1980s] crazy. [? SE hoop, i.e. var. on LOOPY adj.]

hoor n. see HOOER n.

hoorah see also under HURRAH.

hoorah n. **1** [1960s+] (US Black) loud talking, noise. **2** [1980s] (US) a DAMN n. [SE excl. hoorah!]

hooraw v. see HURRAH v.

hooray n. (also **hoorah, hoorah Henry, hooray Henry, whooray**) [1930s+] (orig. US) a rich young man given to much public exhibitionism, drunkenness and similar anti-social activities, all based on an excess of snobbish self-esteem. [despite the term's virtually invariable appearance in a UK context, note its US coinage]

hooray adj. (also **hurray**) [1960s+] noisily and affectedly upper-class. [HOORAY n.]

hooray fuck! excl. [1940s+] (N.Z.) used as a farewell to someone one dislikes or has just been insulting. [SE hooray + FUCK! excl.]

hooray Henry n. see HOORAY n.

hooride n. [1980s+] (US Black) a run-down automobile. [RIDE n.[2] (1)]

hooride v. [1980s+] (US Black) **1** to act in a rowdy manner. **2** to shoot, to assassinate. [SE excl. hoorah!]

hooroo! excl. **1** [1900s–50s] hoorah! hooray! **2** [1910s+] (Aus.) goodbye! [SE excl. hoorah!]

hooroosh n. (also **hurroo, hurroosh**) [20C+] (orig. US) an uproar, a great fuss. [SE hurrish, hurroosh. 'To drive with the cry "hurrish!" or "hurroosh!"' (OED). ? ult. hooray!]

hoosegow n. (also **hoosgow, hoozegow, house-gow**) [20C+] (US) **1** a prison. **2** any form of institution to which inmates are sent rather than volunteer for entrance. **3** an outhouse, a privy. [Sp. *juzgado*, a tribunal or court of justice]

hoosegow *v.* [20C+] to imprison. [HOOSEGOW n. (1)]

hoosey *adj. see* HOOSIER adj.

hoosgow *n. see* HOOSEGOW n.

hoosh *n.* **1** [1900s–20s] a form of thick soup, as eaten by Arctic explorers. **2** [1910s+] (*Can.*) corned beef hash. [? Inuit term]

hoosh *v.* **1** [mid-19C+] to shove up, to lift, to give a leg up. **2** [late 19C+] to deride. **3** [1900s–40s] of animals and people, to herd, to drive. **4** [1950s] to rush around. [*hoosh!*, excl. used when driving animals]

hoosheroon *n. see* HOOSIEROON n.

hooshgoo *n.* [20C+] (*Can.*) a cook. [HOOSH n. + SE *God*]

hooshierina *n. see* HOOSIERINA n.

hooshta *n.* (*also* **hooshter**) [1910s] (*Aus.*) a camel. [cry of *hooshta!* used to urge the camel forward]

hoosier *n.* **1** [19C+] (*US*) (*also* **hosier, hoozier**) a peasant, a rustic simpleton. **2** [19C+] (*US*) a native of Indiana. **3** [mid-19C+] (*US Und.*) a gullible person. **4** [late 19C+] (*US tramp*) a 'farmer'. **5** [late 19C+] (*US*) an amateur, novice or incompetent. **6** [20C+] (*US Black*) a White person, esp. a racist. **7** [1910s] (*US Und.*) a local small-town policeman. **8** [1930s–40s] (*US prison*) a prison visitor. [Cumbrian dial. *hoozer*, something large of its kind; ? a ref. to the size of the corn-fed country farm-boys]

hoosier *adj.* (*also* **hoosey, hoosiery**) [late 19C–1960s] peasant, rustic, simple. [HOOSIER n. (1)]

hoosier *v.* [20C+] (*US*) to cheat, to make someone a victim of trickery. [HOOSIER n. (3)]

hoosier (fiend) *n.* [1930s–50s] (*US drugs*) an inexperienced or naïve drug user, one who is in the early days of their addiction to narcotics. [HOOSIER n. (5) + FIEND n.[2] (1)]

hoosierina *n.* (*also* **hooshierina**) [mid–late 19C] (*US*) a female native of Indiana. [HOOSIEROON n.]

hoosieroon *n.* (*also* **hoosheroon**) [mid–late 19C] (*US*) a native of Indiana. [HOOSIER n. (2)]

hoosier up *v.* [1920s] (*US tramp*) to act like a simpleton. [HOOSIER n. (1)]

hoosiery *adj. see* HOOSIER adj.

hoot *n.*[1] (*also* **hootoo, hout, hutu**) [mid-19C+] (*Aus./N.Z.*) money, esp. money as paid in return for something, e.g. work. [Maori *utu*, money paid as recompense]

hoot *n.*[2] [late 19C; 1940s+] (*US*) a party. [abbr. HOOTENANNY n. (4)]

hoot *n.*[3] [late 19C+] **1** (*orig. US*) (*also* **two hoots**) a very small amount; esp. in phr. NOT GIVE A HOOT v. **2** (*orig. US*) anything or anyone considered unimportant, insignificant. **3** (*US*) a tot of liquor, a drink. **4** (*US*) a euph. for *hell*. [? fig. use of SE *hoot*, an abrupt, sharp cry]

hoot *n.*[4] (*orig. US*) **1** [late 19C+] a laugh; thus *give someone the hoot*, to laugh at. **2** [1920s+] a most amusing experience. **3** [1920s+] a very amusing person. [HOOT v.[1] (1)]

hoot *v.*[1] **1** [late 19C+] to laugh loudly. **2** [20C+] (*US*) to talk loudly and to excess. **3** [20C+] (*US*) to cough. **4** [20C+] (*orig. Aus.*) to smell badly, to stink. [SE *hoot*, to shout, to call out]

hoot *v.*[2] [1960s+] to have a good time, to carouse. [HOOT n.[4]]

hoot-and-holler *n.*[1] [20C+] (*US*) an out-of-the-way place. [pun on *holler/hollow* as a name + the need to *hoot and holler* to make oneself heard from an out-of-the-way place]

hoot-and-holler *n.*[2] [20C+] (*US*) a nickname for a HOLY ROLLER n. [their noisiness]

hootch *n.*[1] [1960s+] (*orig. US milit. in Vietnam*) any form of shelter, from a peasant hut to a bunker or an office building; now a general word. [SE *hutch*]

hootch *n.*[2] *see* HOOCH n.[1]

hootchie *n. see* HOOCHIE n.[1] (1).

hootchie-cootchie man/woman *n. see* HOOCHIE-COOCHIE MAN/WOMAN n.

hootchie mama *n. see* HOOCHIE n.[1] (1).

hootchy-cootchy man/woman *n. see* HOOCHIE-COOCHIE MAN/WOMAN n.

hootchy-kootchy *n.* (*also* **hooch, hoochie, hoochie-coochie, hoochy, hoochy-coochy, hootchie-kootchie, hootchy**) **1** [late 19C+] (*orig. US*) a form of highly suggestive belly-dance, usu. performed at carnivals. **2** [1980s+] (*US*) sexual activity. [ety. unknown; perhaps no more than a showman's idea of an 'exotic' or 'Oriental' name, the vowels of which suggest the sinuous gyrations of the dancer]

hootchy-kootchy *adj.* [20C+] (*orig. US*) erotic, suggestive, sexy. [HOOTCHY-KOOTCHY n. (1)]

hootchy mama *n. see* HOOCHIE n.[1]

hooted (up) *adj.* [late 19C–1930s] (*US*) drunk. [HOOT n.[3] (3)]

hootenanny *n.* (*orig. US*) **1** [1920s+] an imaginary object; something for which one cannot remember the name. **2** [1920s+] a general term of abuse. **3** [1920s+] nonsense, rubbish, anything insignificant; a euph. for DAMN n. and used similarly, e.g. *I don't give a hootenanny*. **4** [1940s+] a party. **5** [1950s+] a performance of folk music. **6** [1980s+] a commotion. [ety. unknown]

hooter *n.*[1] [mid-19C–1900s] (*US*) an insignificant amount. [HOOT n.[3]]

hooter *n.*[2] [late 19C] (*US*) a drink.

hooter *n.*[3] **1** [1950s+] the nose. **2** [1970s+] the female breast; usu. in pl. (cf. BAGS n.[1]). **3** [1980s+] (*US*) a woman with large breasts. [the supposed resemblance to an old-fashioned automobile *hooter*]

hooter *n.*[4] [1960s] (*N.Z.*) the lavatory.

hooter *n.*[5] [1970s–80s] (*US*) a telephone.

hooter *n.*[6] [1980s+] (*US*) a breaking of wind. [HOOT v.[1]]

hooter *n.*[7] **1** [1980s+] (*drugs*) a marijuana cigarette (cf. BONE n.[11]). **2** [1980s+] (*N.Z. drugs*) a tube (generally of rolled cardboard) used to inhale smoke from heated drops of cannabis oil.

hooter *n.*[8] [1990s+] (*Ulster*) a person who boasts.

hooter *n.*[9] [2000s] (*US Black*) a police officer.

hoot him! *excl.* [1920s–30s] (*Aus.*) a derisory cry at a passer-by deemed worthy of verbal attack.

hoot in hell *n.* [late 19C+] (*US*) the least bit. [ext. of HOOT n.[3] (1)]

hootoo *n. see* HOOT n.[1]

hooty *adj.*[1] [1930s–40s] (*US*) angry. [HOOT v.[1] (2)]

hooty *adj.*[2] [1970s+] (*US campus*) crazy. [HOOT n.[4]]

hoover *n.* [1930s] (*US*) an outside lavatory, a privy. [US President Herbert *Hoover* (1874–1964), during whose administration (1929–33) the US suffered the worst privations of the Depression]

hoover *adj.* [1930s–70s] (*US*) a generic adj. used in a variety of combs., all referring to events or objects engendered by the poverty that accompanied the Great Depression, e.g. *Hooverville*, a shanty town; *Hoover blankets*, newspapers used to wrap up in for warmth; *Hoover flush*, an unfinished flush in poker. [for ety. see HOOVER n.]

hoover *v. see* HOOVER (UP) v.

hoover buggy *n.* (*also* **hoover cart/wagon**) [1930s–70s] (*US*) any makeshift vehicle horsedrawn and dedicated to hauling hay. [HOOVER adj. + SE *buggy, cart, wagon*]

hoover dust *n.* [1930s] (*US*) cheap tobacco. [HOOVER adj. + SE *dust*]

hoover flags *n.* [1930s] (*US*) empty pockets turned inside out. [HOOVER adj. + SE *flag*]

hoover gravy *n.* [1930s–70s] (*US*) particularly thick gravy, often virtually all a family had to eat. [HOOVER adj. + SE *gravy*]

hoover hog *n.* [1930s+] (*US*) **1** a wild rabbit. **2** an armadillo, a cheap form of meat for poor farmers during the Depression. [HOOVER adj. + SE *hog*]

hoover pork *n.* [1930s–50s] (*US*) **1** sow belly. **2** rabbit meat. [HOOVER adj. + SE *pork*]

hoover's ham *n.* [1930s–40s] (*US*) salt pork. [HOOVER adj. + SE *ham*]

hoover (up) v. **1** [1970s–80s] (*UK Black*) to smoke a (cannabis) cigarette. **2** [1980s+] (*orig. US*) to inhale drugs. **3** [1980s+] (*orig. US*) to eat or drink, esp. greedily. **4** [1980s+] (*orig. US*) to snatch, esp. greedily. **5** [1980s+] (*orig. US*) to fellate vigorously (cf. CLEAN SOMEONE'S PIPE v.). **6** [2000s] (*US Black*) to follow someone around, to be clingy. **7** [2000s] (*US teen*) to obtain an abortion. [suggested by the brandname of *Hoover* vacuum cleaners, used generically as meaning to vacuum, thus to 'suck up']

hoover wagon n. see HOOVER BUGGY n.

hoozegow n. see HOOSEGOW n.

hoozie n. (*also* **hosie**) [1970s] (*US*) a sexually promiscuous woman or prostitute. [SE whore/HO n.[1] (1) + FLOOZIE n.]

hoozier n. see HOOSIER n. (1).

hoozy adj. see WOOZY adj.

hop n.[1] **1** [late 17C+] (*also* **hopser**) a dance; thus HOP MERCHANT n.[1]. **2** [19C] a dancing academy. **3** [20C+] (*US*) an organized dance, held in a dancehall and frequented by working-class young people. [note *Sinks of London* (1848) defines such dances as 'a sixpenny, a dancing room where sixpence is the price of admission']

hop n.[2] (*also* **hops**) **1** [late 19C+] opium; thus *hop-smoker*, an opium user (cf. APOSTLE n.). **2** [20C+] heroin. **3** [1920s–40s] morphine (cf. AUNTIE EMMA n.). **4** [1920s–50s] a regular drug user. **5** [1920s+] any type of illicit drugs; thus *on the hop*, using narcotics; *hop (someone) up*, to give an injection (of legal or illegal drugs). **6** [1940s] in fig. use referring to anything addictive. [ety. unknown; ? Chinese term; (2) note Mezzrow & Wolfe, *Really the Blues* (1946): 'A patent product called Wampole's Mixture that was supposed to help you taper off the stuff. What you did was you took a toy (a tin) of hop and shook it up with this medicine in a bottle and kept taking it every day. As the bottle got empty you kept filling it up with more of the medicine, so the amount of hop kept going down, and finally you were taking practically straight medicine'; note Burnett, *Little Caesar* (1929): 'Hop, beer', presumably the author's lack of knowledge, although note next]

hop n.[3] [1910s+] (*US/Aus./N.Z.*) beer. [SE *hops*, the main constituent of beer]

hop n.[4] [1920s+] (*UK/Aus.*) a policeman. [abbr. JOHN HOP n.]

hop n.[5] (*also* **hopper**) [1930s+] (*US*) a hotel porter. [abbr. BELLHOP n.]

hop v.[1] **1** [late 19C] to 'go', to fare, used as a general greeting in phr. *how hops it?* **2** [late 19C+] (*US*) to jump onto (occas. off) a moving vehicle, esp. a train, to get a lift or ride, to catch a train or aeroplane. **3** [late 19C+] to depart. **4** [late 19C+] (*US*) to assault. **5** [1910s–40s] to make someone jump, to admonish and thus frighten someone. **6** [1920s–60s] (*US Black*) to dance, to cavort, to play. **7** [1920s+] to move from place to place. **8** [1920s+] (*US*) of a man, to engage in sexual intercourse. **9** [1950s+] (*orig. US Black*) of a place, e.g. a party or club, to pulsate with excitement.

hop v.[2] [1910s] (*US*) to give a horse some form of drug to alter its natural performance. [HOP n.[2] (5)]

hop along! excl. see HOP IT! excl.

hop-and-drop v. see HIP-AND-DROP v.

hop bail v. [1900s–50s] (*US*) to forfeit one's bail by fleeing. [HOP v.[1] (3)]

hop bells v. [1920s–60s] (*US*) to work as a hotel porter. [backform. f. BELLHOP n.]

hopeful n. [early 18C+] an optimist; thus *young hopeful*, a neophyte, a beginner, often used ironically.

hope-to-die adj. (*orig. US Black*) **1** [1960s+] absolute, total. **2** [1980s+] closest, most trusted, best. [abbr. *hope to die if...*]

hope to hell v. see WISH TO HELL v.

hope to my die! excl. [1920s–30s] (*US*) a strong excl. used to underline the veracity or sincerity of the speaker's statement. [*hope to die + I hope I may die*]

hope to tell you! excl. [20C+] (*US*) a strong excl. used to underline the speaker's statement.

hop fiend n. [late 19C–1940s] a drug user. [HOP n.[2] + SE *fiend*]

hop-fighter n. [1910s] (*US drugs*) an opium smoker. [HOP n.[2] (1) + SE *fighter*]

hop gun n. [1930s–50s] (*US drugs*) a hypodermic syringe. [HOP n.[2] (2) + GUN n.[1] (3)]

hop harry n. [1920s–40s] (*Aus.*) a bowler hat. [play on SE *hop*, to move/*bowl*, to move]

hophead n.[1] [20C+] (*drugs*) **1** an opium, morphine or heroin addict; thus *hophead house*, a place where addicts buy and take narcotics. **2** a cocaine addict. **3** a user of any drug. **4** a marijuana smoker. [HOP n.[2] + -HEAD sfx (3)]

hophead n.[2] **1** [1940s+] (*US/N.Z.*) a drunkard or a beer-drinker; an alcoholic. **2** [1940s+] (*N.Z.*) a wild, eccentric person. **3** [1970s+] (*US*) a German-American. [HOP n.[3]/SE *hops* + -HEAD sfx (3); (3) -HEAD sfx (2)]

hophead adj. (*also* **hopheaded**, **hopheads**) [20C+] **1** (*drugs*) addicted to a narcotic drug, usu. opium or heroin; pertaining to that addiction. **2** as a general insult, implying mental deficiency. [HOPHEAD n.[1] (1)]

hophead house n. see HOPHEAD n.[1] (1).

hop in for one's chop v. [1960s+] (*Aus.*) to seize one's opportunity. [SE *hop in* + CHOP n.[3]]

hop in(to) v. (*Aus.*) **1** [1930s+] to start, to begin, e.g. *hop into the grub*, to start eating, often used as an invitation or imper. **2** [1940s–50s] to fight, to attack.

hop into bed with v. (*also* **hop in the hay**, **hop into the sack**) [1950s+] to have casual or spontaneous sexual intercourse with.

hop it v. **1** [20C+] to leave, to run off. **2** [1950s+] to die (cf. HOP OFF v.[1]). [HOP IT! excl.]

hop it! excl. (*also* **hop along!**) [20C+] go away! run along! etc.

hop it and scram n. [20C+] ham. [rhy. sl.]

hop-jockey n. see JOCKEY n.[3] (8).

hop joint n.[1] [late 19C+] a room or apartment where patrons gather to smoke opium or, more recently, to take heroin. [HOP n.[2] + JOINT n.[4] (3)]

hop joint n.[2] [late 19C+] (*US*) a saloon bar. [HOP n.[3] + JOINT n.[4] (3)]

hop juice n. [late 19C] (*US*) beer. [HOP n.[3]/SE *hops* + JUICE n.[3]]

Hopkins n. see MR HOPKINS n.

hop layout n. see LAYOUT n.[4].

hop merchant n.[1] **1** [late 17C–mid-19C] a dancing master. **2** [19C] a fiddler. [HOP n.[1] (1) + MERCHANT n.]

hop merchant n.[2] [1910s] (*US Und.*) a drug peddler. [HOP n.[2] + MERCHANT n.]

hopnail n. see HOBNAIL n.

hop off v.[1] **1** [late 18C–1920s] to die or kill (cf. HOP IT v.). **2** [20C+] to leave.

hop off v.[2] [20C+] **1** (*Ulster*) to beat, to thump violently. **2** (*Irish*) to tease; thus *have a hop of*, to make fun of.

hop off v.[3] [1970s] to happen, to transpire.

hopola n. [1990s+] (*US Black*) a woman. [HOP ON v. (1) + -OLA sfx]

hop on v. [20C+] **1** to have sexual intercourse. **2** to put pressure on. **3** to attack, to beat up.

hop on a babe v. [1990s+] (*US campus*) to have sexual intercourse; the implication is that the man, lacking greater finesse, has made a pounce (prob. when drunk) to initiate the activity. [HOP ON v. (1) + BABE n. (1)]

hop one's frame v. [1910s–40s] (*N.Z.*) to move, to make a sudden journey.

hop-out n. [1910s] (*Aus.*) argument, controversy. [HOP OUT v.]

hop out v. [20C+] (*Aus.*) to challenge someone to a fight.

hop out! excl. [20C+] (*Aus.*) are you ready to fight? [HOP OUT v.]

hop-over n. [1910s] (*Aus.*) a riotous convivial celebration. [WW1 Aus. milit. *hop-over*, a battle, an assault]

hop pad *n.* [1920s–40s] (*drugs*) a room or apartment where patrons gather to smoke opium or to take heroin. [HOP n.² + PAD n.² (2)]

hop party *n.* [1920s+] (*US drugs*) a party where drugs of some sort are consumed. [HOP n.² + SE *party*]

hopped out *adj.* [1980s+] (*N.Z.*) drunk. [HOP n.³]

hopped to the gills *phr.* [1920s+] completely intoxicated by a drug, esp. opium or heroin. [HOPPED (UP) adj. (1) + TO THE GILLS adv.]

hopped (up) *adj.* **1** [1910s+] (*US drugs*) under the influence of drugs. **2** [1920s+] (*US*) in fig. use, excited, impatient. **3** [1930s+] (*US*) crazy. **4** [1940s–50s] (*US*) embellished, 'jazzed up.' **5** [1940s+] (*US*) of a car, improved beyond its basic specifications. [lit. + fig. uses of HOP n.²]

hopper *n.*¹ **1** [mid-19C–1910s] the mouth. **2** [1950s+] (*US*) a toilet.

hopper *n.*² [late 19C+] (*Irish*) a flea.

hopper *n.*³ [1990s+] (*US Black*) a young Black man. [SE *hip-hopper*]

hopper *n.*⁴ *see* HOP n.⁵.

hopper arse *n.* (*also* **hopper breech/hips**) [early 16C–1950s] large buttocks. [HOPPER-ARSED adj.]

hopper-arsed *adj.* (*also* **hopper-hipped, hopper-rumped, hopper-tailed**) [early 16C–1950s] large-buttocked. [SE *hopper* + -ARSED sfx¹]

hopper-dockers *n.* [early 19C] shoes. [ety. unknown; ? var. on HOCK-DOCKIES n.]

hopper hips *n. see* HOPPER ARSE n.

hopper-rumped/-tailed *adj. see* HOPPER-ARSED adj.

hop-picker *n.* [late 19C] a prostitute. [? euph.]

hopping *n.* [late 19C] dancing. [HOP n.¹ (1)]

hopping *adj.* **1** [late 19C–1920s] (*US*) furious. **2** [1970s+] (*Irish*) crazy. [abbr. SE *hopping mad*]

hopping around like a gin at a christening *phr.* [1960s+] (*Aus.*) on one's best behaviour, esp. when slightly nervous, socially uncomfortable. [SE *hopping around* + GIN n.¹ (1)]

hopping Giles *n.* [late 18C–19C] a lame, limping person. [proper name *St Giles*, the patron saint of cripples]

hopping Jesus *n.* [mid-19C–1920s] a limping person.

hopping pot *n.* [late 19C+] the lot. [rhy. sl.]

hopping wife *n.* [late 19C] a prostitute.

hoppin' john *n.* [mid-19C+] (*US*) a dish of pork, rice and peas seasoned with chilli.

hop-pole *n.* [mid-19C] a tall, thin person.

hoppy *n.*¹ **1** [mid–late 19C] a dancing master. **2** [late 19C] a fiddler. [HOP n.¹ (1)]

hoppy *n.*² [mid-19C+] (*US*) a lame person. [they *hop* along]

hoppy *n.*³ [1900s–50s] (*drugs*) a drug addict, orig. an opium addict. [HOP n.²]

hoppy *n.*⁴ [1960s+] a flea; usu. in pl.

hoppy *adj.*¹ **1** [mid-19C+] lame, limping. **2** [1930s+] lively, full of movement.

hoppy *adj.*² [1940s] (*US drugs*) characteristic of, or relevant to, drugs or drug-taking. [HOP n.²]

hoppy *adj.*³ [1940s–50s] (*US drugs*) **1** well-supplied with narcotics, esp. opium. **2** smelling of opium. [HOP n.²]

hops *n.*¹ **1** [mid-19C+] beer (cf. GO THE HOPS v.). **2** [1900s] (*US prison*) tea. [SE *hops*; later use of (1) is Aus./N.Z./US Black]

hops *n.*² [1990s+] (*US Black*) the ability to jump high during a game of basketball.

hops *n.*³ *see* HOP n.².

hopscotch *n.* [1990s+] a watch. [rhy. sl.]

hopscotch *v.* (*US Und.*) **1** [1910s–40s] to move frequently from place to place. **2** [1940s] to take a confidence game on the road.

hopser *n. see* HOP n.¹ (1).

hop-shop *n.* [late 18C] a tavern. [HOPS n.¹ (1) + SE *shop*]

hop-smoker *n. see* HOP n.² (1).

hop someone's bones *v.* [1950s] to have sexual intercourse.

hopster *n.* [1940s–50s] (*US drugs*) an opium addict. [HOP n.² (1)]

hop stick *n.* [1930s] (*US drugs*) **1** an opium pipe. **2** a cannabis cigarette (cf. BAT n.⁸). [HOP n.² + SE *stick*/STICK n.⁹]

hop talk *n.* [late 19C+] (*US*) foolish or exaggerated talk. [HOP n.² (1) + SE *talk*; the implication is that such talk is promoted by opium smoking]

hop the ball *v.* [20C+] (*Irish*) to make a provocative remark. [Gaelic football *hop the ball*, to set the game in motion]

hop the charley *v.* [late 19C] to run off, to decamp. [var. on HOP THE WAG v./PLAY THE CHARLEY WAG v.]

hop the coop *v.* [mid-19C+] to escape from any form of confinement, not necessarily prison. [SE *hop* + COOP n.¹]

hop the perch *v.* [early 19C+] to die.

hop the rattler *v. see* JUMP THE RATTLER v.

hop the rods *v. see* HIT THE RODS v.

hop the twig *v.* (*also* **jump the twig**) **1** [late 18C–1900s] (*UK Und.*) to run away. **2** [late 18C+] to die.

hop the wag *v.* [mid-19C+] to play truant from school. [dial *wag*, to move, to go]

hop to it *v. see* GO TO IT v.

hop toy *n.* (*also* **hen toy**) [late 19C–1950s] **1** (*drugs*) a container for opium, and part of the opium LAYOUT n.⁴ (2). **2** in fig. use, any unnamed object. [HOP n.² + SE *toy*]

horchin *n.* [20C+] (*Ulster*) an unpleasant person. [SE *urchin*]

hori *n.* [1940s+] (*N.Z.*) a semi-derog. term for a Maori. [lit. Maori transcription of 'George']

horie *n. see* HORRIE n.

horizontal *n.* **1** [late 19C–1950s] (*also* **horizontalist**) an up-market prostitute, a kept woman. **2** [late 19C+] (*US*) sexual intercourse; usu. as *do a horizontal* (cf. DO A PERPENDICULAR v.). [Fr. *grande horizontale*; she is, of course, 'horizontal' on a bed or *chaise longue*]

horizontal dancing *n.* (*also* **horizontal barn-dancing**, ...**bop**, ...**folk-dancing**, ...**mambo**, ...**polka**, ...**polo**, ...**rhumba**, ...**rumble**, ...**tango**, ...**twist and shout**) [1940s+] sexual intercourse. [all modern vars. on HORIZONTAL REFRESH-MENT n.]

horizontalize *v.* [1980s+] (*US*) to have sexual intercourse. [HORIZONTAL n. (2)]

horizontal jogging *n.* (*also* **horizontal exercise**) [1950s+] sexual intercourse.

horizontal mambo/polka/polo *n. see* HORIZONTAL DANC-ING n.

horizontal refreshment *n.* [late 19C+] sexual intercourse.

horizontal relaxation *n.* [1940s+] (*Aus./N.Z.*) sexual intercourse.

horizontal rhumba/rumble *n. see* HORIZONTAL DANCING n.

horizontals *n.* [1920s–30s] (*US*) sexual intercourse. [HORIZONTAL n. (2)]

horizontal tango/twist and shout *n. see* HORIZONTAL DANCING n.

horizontal worker *n.* [late 19C+] (*US*) a prostitute. [HORIZONTAL n. (1) + SE *worker*]

hork *v.*¹ [1980s+] (*US campus*) to steal, to take without permission, to borrow without asking. [? HOICK v.¹]

hork *v.*² [1990s+] (*US*) to spit. [SE *hawk*, to clear the throat of phlegm, to spit]

hormone *n.* [1980s+] (*US campus*) a sexually aggressive person, whether verbally or physically.

hormone fix *n.* [1980s+] (*US campus*) any form of sexual encounter, from the most marginal to full intercourse. [SE *hormone* + FIX n.⁴ (5)]

hormone queen *n.* [1960s–70s] (*US*) a male transvestite who takes oestrogen. [SE *hormone* + QUEEN n.² (1)]

hormones *n.* [1980s] (*US*) audacity, cheek, impudence.

Horn, the *n.* [late 17C] the Compter prison, in London (cf. ABBOTT'S PRIORY n.).

horn *n.*¹ **1** [mid-15C+] a cuckold, cuckoldry. **2** [20C+] (*W.I.*)

adultery; thus *take a horn*, to accept that one's partner is having/ has had an affair without making an issue out of it. [HORNS n.]

horn *n.*[2] **1** [late 16C+] the penis. **2** [late 17C+] sexual excitement or lust; thus *on the horn*. **3** [late 18C+] an erection. **4** [1960s] (*US campus*) a male sexual athlete. [resemblance to an SE *horn*]

horn *n.*[3] [19C+] (*US*) a drink. [SE *horn*, a drinking vessel made from a horn]

horn *n.*[4] **1** [mid-19C+] the nose. **2** [1930s+] an ear. **3** [1940s+] (*US*) a telephone.

horn *n.*[5] [1930s+] (*orig. jazz*) **1** a trumpet. **2** a trombone. **3** any kind of wind instrument.

horn *v.*[1] [mid-16C+] to cuckold. [HORN n.[1]]

horn *v.*[2] [1950s+] (*US drugs*) to inhale a narcotic. [HORN n.[4] (1)]

hornbag *n.* [1980s+] an attractive woman. [HORN n.[2] (2) + BAG n.[4] (1)/SE *bag*, a receptacle for HORN n.[2] (1)]

hornbug *n.* [1950s] (*US*) a sex maniac. [HORN n.[2] (2) + BUG n.[5] (2)]

horn-child *n.* [20C+] (*W.I.*) the offspring of an adulterous relationship. [HORN n.[1] (2) + SE *child*]

horn colic *n.* [late 18C–1950s] **1** an involuntary erection. **2** male sexual frustration. [HORN n.[2] (2) + SE *colic*]

horndog *n.* [1980s+] (*US campus*) a sexually aggressive person. **2** a sexually frustrated person. [HORN n.[2] (2) + DOG n.[3] (8)]

horndog *v.* [1980s+] (*US campus*) to pursue sexually. [HORNDOG n.]

horned-up *adj.* [1940s+] (*orig. US*) sexually excited. [HORN n.[2] (2)]

horner *n.* [16C+] an adulterer. [HORN n.[1]]

horner-man *n.* [20C+] (*W.I.*) an adulterer. [HORNER n.]

hornet *n.* [mid-18C] (*UK Und.*) a policeman (cf. ANIMAL n.[1]).

horney *n.*[1] [mid-18C] (*UK Und.*) a member of the watch, an officer of the law. [? OLD HORNIE n. (2)]

horney *n.*[2] [early 19C] the nose. [its shape]

horney-steerer *n. see* HORNY n.[2].

horn fair *n.* [mid-17C–early 19C] the state of being cuckolded; a fig. gathering of cuckolds. [Horn Fair was a real occasion, held annually from the 12C until 1768 at Charlton, Kent on St Luke's day, 18 October; St Luke, bearing the evangelistic sign of the Ox, was thus portrayed as wearing horns; so, on St Luke's Day, processions of revellers, all wearing horns and sometimes masks, walked from Cuckold's Point near Deptford, to Charlton. For an extensive discussion of the actual Horn Fair see Ned Ward 'A Frolic to Horn-Fair' in *Writings* (1704), pp.194–222 (esp. pp.211–13 in which he attributes the custom to a dalliance of King John); Grose (1785, 1796) and Ebsworth, *Roxburghe Ballads* (1890; vol. VII pt. 1, pp.195–6)]

horn-grower *n.* (*also* **horn-merchant**) [18C–19C] a married man. [HORNS n.; he is likely to 'wear the horns' of cuckoldry]

horn-headed *adj.* [18C] cuckolded. [HORNS n.]

hornies, the *n.* [1920s+] (*US*) sexual desire. [HORNY adj.]

hornified *adj.* [late 18C–19C] cuckolded. [HORNS n.]

hornify *v.* [17C–19C] to cuckold. [HORNS n.]

horn in (on) *v.* [20C+] (*orig. US*) to intrude, to interfere. [SE *horn*]

horniness *n.* [1960s+] sexual excitement, lust. [HORNY adj. (1)]

horn-mad *adj.* **1** [late 16C–19C] extremely jealous, esp. as a victim of cuckoldry. **2** [late 16C–1950s] lecherous, maddened by lust; thus *horn-madness*, the condition of lustfulness; *horn-madded*, lustful. [SE *horn-mad*, enraged, the image is a horned beast that is ready to gore anyone in its way, but note HORNS n. and HORN n.[2] (2)]

horn-maker *n.* [late 16C–17C] one who cuckolds. [HORN n.[1] (1) + SE *maker*]

horn-merchant *n. see* HORN-GROWER n.

horn movie *n.* [1950s+] a pornographic film. [HORN n.[2] (2)]

horn off *v.* (*also* **horn out**) [mid-19C–1910s] (*US*) to impose upon, to force someone. [fig. to use one's horns]

horn of plenty *n.* [1990s+] (*bingo*) the number 20 (cf. ALDERSHOT LADIES n.). [rhy. sl.]

horn out *v.*[1] [1910s] (*US*) to escape.

horn out *v.*[2] *see* HORN OFF v.

horn-pills *n.* [20C+] aphrodisiacs or supposed ones. [HORN n.[2] (2) + SE *pills*]

hornpipe *n.* [late 16C–18C] **1** sexual intercourse, often adultery; usu. as *dance the hornpipe*. **2** a penis. [HORN n.[2]]

horns *n.* [mid-16C+] a generic term for cuckoldry. [the obvious link is to HORN n.[2] (1), the penis, but the term apparently comes from an old German farming practice of grafting the spurs of a castrated cock on the root of the severed comb. These transplants would grow into horns, sometimes several inches long. The German word *hahnreh* or *hahnrei*, meaning cuckold, orig. meant capon, a castrated cock; an older theory took the posture of 'missionary position' intercourse, in which the man represented a head and the woman's legs, spread and raised, were his horns; thus note Ned Ward, 'The Dancing School' (1700): 'I should hate a Husband with horns, were they even of my own grafting']

horn smoker *n.* [2000s] a fellator or fellatrix. [HORN n.[2] (1)]

hornsmoking *n.* [2000s] fellatio. [HORN SMOKER n.]

horn-sticks *n.* [1960s+] celery. [HORN n.[2] (2); the theory that celery is an aphrodisiac]

horns-to-sell *n.* [18C–19C] **1** a promiscuous wife. **2** a cuckold. [HORNS n. + SE *sell*]

hornswoggle *n.* [19C+] (*US*) nonsense, humbug; thus *hornswoggler*, a fraud, a cheat. [HORNSWOGGLE v. (2)]

hornswoggle *v.* (*US*) **1** [19C+] to embarrass, to confuse, to disconcert. **2** [late 19C+] (*also* **horn-swaggle**) to cheat, to swindle. [ety. unknown]

hornswoggled *adj.* (*also* **cornswoggled, onswoggled**) [19C+] (*US*) a euph. for DAMNED adj. [HORNSWOGGLE v.]

hornswoggler *n. see* HORNSWOGGLE n.

hornswoggling *n.* [mid-19C+] (*US*) cheating, deceiving. [HORNSWOGGLE v. (2)]

horn-thumb *n.* [mid-16C–early 17C] a cut-purse. [the sheath of horn worn by a cut-purse to protect his thumb from the knife-blade]

horn with *v.* [20C+] (*W.I.*) to be unfaithful to one's husband, wife or lover by having sex with or dating another person. [the cuckold's HORNS n.]

horn work *n.* [early 17C–mid-19C] cuckoldry. [HORNS n.]

horny *n.*[1] [18C] a cuckold. [HORNS n.]

horny *n.*[2] [20C+] (*Aus.*) a cow, a bullock; thus *horney-steerer*, a bullock-driver; thus used generically for the beef interest. [orig. Scot.]

horny *n.*[3] [1970s] (*US*) one who is sexually excited, desirous of sex. [HORNY adj. (1)]

horny *adj.* **1** [early 19C+] sexually eager, aroused. **2** [1930s+] sexually arousing, erotic, pornographic, e.g. a *horny picture*. [HORN n.[2] (2)]

horrible *n.* **1** [1920s–50s] (*Aus.*) a rascal, a villain; a Bohemian, one who acts without regard for social convention. **2** [1960s] (*US campus*) an unattractive female.

horrid *adj.* [late 18C] semi-drunk, tipsy.

horrid *adv.* (*also* **horridly**) [mid-17C+] offensively, exceedingly.

horrid horn *n.* [mid–late 19C] (*Anglo-Irish*) a fool. [Erse *omadhun*, a fool]

horrie *n.* (*also* **horie**) [1980s] (*Aus.*) a derog. term for an Asian (cf. BROWNIE n.[2]). [HORI n.]

horries *n.* (*S.Afr.*) **1** [1950s+] delirium tremens. **2** [1970s+] a phobia, a visceral fear. [Afk. *horries*, DTs, but note HORRORS, THE n.]

horrorbag *n.* (*also* **horrorhag, horrorhead**) [1980s] (*Aus.*) a girl or woman, usu. unattractive. [SE *horror* + -BAG sfx; note WHOREBAG n.]

horrors, the *n.* **1** [mid-18C+] a fit of depression, unpleasant worries. **2** [mid-19C+] delirium tremens; often as *in the horrors* (cf. BLUE HORRORS n.; CAST-IRON HORRORS n.; STONEWALL HORRORS n.). **3** [mid-19C+] a hangover. **4** [1920s+] unpleasant reactions suffered during the withdrawal from narcotic drugs. **5** [1950s+] unpleasant experiences (usu. paranoid fantasies) brought about occas. by the effects of smoking cannabis, opium or from taking a hallucinogen.

horrorshow n. (also **horror smash**) [1950s+] (*US*) a disgusting or embarrassing person, thing or situation (cf. HORRORBAG n.). [note RMC Duntroon (Aus.) *horror show*, an ugly woman]

horrorshow adj. [1990s+] (*US teen*) extremely good. [on *bad = good* model, HORRORSHOW n., but note use in Anthony Burgess, *A Clockwork Orange* (1962), where it means excellent and is based on Rus. *horosho*]

horry n. [1940s+] (*Aus./N.Z.*) sexual intercourse. [abbr. HORIZONTAL n. (2)]

hors d'oeuvre n. [1960s] (*Aus.*) a paedophile. [rhy. sl.; PERV n. (1)]

hors d'oeuvres n.[1] [1970s+] (*drugs*) barbiturates or amphetamines (cf. A n.[2]; BARBIT n.). [SE *hors d'oeuvres*, the first dish of a meal, usu. of mixed items and intended to whet the appetite; a prelude to stronger, more exotic pleasures]

hors d'oeuvres n.[2] [1990s+] nerves. [rhy. sl.]

Horse, the n. (also **the Old Horse**) **1** [mid-19C] Horsemonger Lane prison, Southwark, London (cf. ABBOTT'S PRIORY n.). **2** [mid-19C] Bridge Street prison, Blackfriars. [(1) erected 1799 as a model prison, it lasted until 1880s. It was outside this prison on 13 November 1847 that Charles Dickens witnessed the public hanging of the murderers Frederick and Maria Manning]

horse n.[1] **1** [mid–late 18C] a lottery ticket that is hired out by the day. **2** [late 19C] (*US*) a queen in cards. **3** [late 19C–1930s] (*US gambling*) a selection of 4 numbers to be played simultaneously. **4** [1950s] (*US*) gambling in general.

horse n.[2] [late 18C–mid-19C] work charged for before it is executed. [abbr. HORSEFLESH n.]

horse n.[3] **1** [19C] a £5 note (cf. FOAL n.). **2** [1960s] (*Irish*) a half-crown. [? play on PONY n.[1] (2)]

horse n.[4] (also **hoss**) **1** [19C+] (*US*) a strong, athletic man or an admirable, good fellow. **2** [mid-19C] (*US*) one's husband. **3** [mid-19C+] (*US*) (also **cholly hoss**) a form of address by one man to another. **4** [mid-19C+] a fine specimen, usu. constructed with *of*. **5** [late 19C–1910s] (*US campus*) an exceptionally able student. **6** [1980s+] (*US*) a large, ungainly woman.

horse n.[5] (also **hoss**) **1** [late 19C–1910s] (*US campus*) horseplay, fun. **2** [late 19C+] (*US*) a joke, esp. a joke at someone else's expense. **3** [1900s–40s] (*US*) nonsense, rubbish. [? SE *horse laugh*]

horse n.[6] [late 19C–1910s] (*US campus*) **1** a translation of a text, classical or otherwise, for the illegitimate use of students (cf. ANIMAL n.[3]). **2** help in an examination. [play on PONY n.[3]]

horse n.[7] (also **embalmed horse**) [1900s–10s] (*US campus*) corned beef.

horse n.[8] (also **hoss**) [1930s+] (*drugs*) heroin (cf. BIG H n.). [the initial letters]

horse n.[9] [1940s–60s] (*US*) a motorcycle.

horse n.[10] [1950s+] (*US*) a prostitute, one of a group of women working for a pimp (cf. ALLEY CAT n.; BANBURY n.; BROTHER-IN-LAW n.). [she is part of his STABLE n. (2); but also similar pron. to SE *whore*]

horse n.[11] [1950s+] (*US prison*) a visitor or prison warder who is willing to smuggle contraband in and out of prison. [var. on MULE n.[4]]

horse n.[12] [1960s+] venereal disease, spec. gonorrhoea. [rhy. sl.; *horse and trap* = CLAP n. but note HORSE-POX n.]

horse n.[13] see CHARLEY (HORSE) n.

horse v.[1] [late 16C–17C; 1930s+] to have sexual intercourse (cf. RIDE v.[1]).

horse v.[2] [late 17C–19C] to flog, to whip; thus *horsed*, held on another person's back before receiving a flogging. [the victim is placed across a wooden frame or 'horse']

horse v.[3] [19C+] (*US*) to yearn for, to want eagerly, to lust after. [? a horse straining at the bit or dial. *horse*, for a mare to be in heat]

horse v.[4] **1** [mid-19C] to work very hard, to work harder than another person. **2** [20C+] (*US*) to haul or drag with great effort. **3** [1920s] to move energetically. [the animal's strength]

horse v.[5] **1** [mid–late 19C] to swindle, to cheat. **2** [late 19C–1960s] (*US*) to trick, to deceive, to tease.

horse v.[6] [late 19C–1900s] (*US campus*) to amaze.

horse v.[7] [late 19C–1910s] (*US campus*) to study with the help of a translation (cf. CRIB v.[2]). [HORSE n.[6] (1)]

horse v.[8] [1930s+] (*US*) in a vehicle or plane, to change direction abruptly.

horse v.[9] see HORSE AROUND v. (1).

horse v.[10] see HORSE (IT) v.

horse and carriage n. [20C+] a garage. [rhy. sl.]

horse and cart n. **1** [late 19C–1900s] the heart. **2** [20C+] (*Aus.*) the start. **3** [1960s+] a tart. **4** [1970s+] a breaking of wind. [rhy. sl.; (4) FART n. (1)]

horse and cart v. [1970s+] to break wind. [rhy. sl. = FART v. (1)]

horse and dog show n. see DOG AND PONY SHOW n.

horse and donk n. [1960s+] (*Aus.*) cheap wine. [rhy. sl. = PLONK n.[1]]

horse and foal n. [20C+] (*Aus.*) unemployment benefit (cf. BLESS MY SOUL n.). [rhy. sl. = SE *dole*]

horse and horse phr. (also **hoss and hoss**) [mid-19C–1950s] (*US*) dead even, esp. in gambling. [horseracing imagery]

horse and trap n. **1** [20C+] venereal disease, spec. gonorrhoea. **2** [1950s+] excrement (cf. ALI OOP n.). [rhy. sl.; (1) = CLAP n.; (2) = CRAP n.[3] (1)]

horse and trough n. [20C+] a cough. [rhy. sl.]

horse apple n. (also **horse bean, …biscuit, …doughnut, …dumpling, …plum**) [mid-17C; early 19C+] a piece of horse manure found lying in the road (cf. ALLEY APPLE n.[2]). [SE *horse* + APPLE n.[1]]

horse apples n. [1910s+] (*US*) nonsense. [HORSE APPLE n.; a euph. for BULLSHIT n.]

horse around v. **1** [20C+] (also **horse**) to joke, to mess about. **2** [1920s+] (*US*) to make sexual advances to, to indulge in sexual horseplay. **3** [1950s+] (*US*) to be keen on becoming married. **4** [1950s+] (*US*) to sleep around, to philander.

horse-ass adj. [1950s] (*US*) stupid, incompetent (cf. CLAY-ASSED adj.). [SE *horse* + -ASS sfx]

horseback adj. [late 19C+] (*US*) of an opinion or judgement, casual, off-hand, tentative. [a man estimating the extent of his land by riding round it on horseback but making no accurate measurements]

horse bean/biscuit n. see HORSE APPLE n.

horse blanket n.[1] (also **monkey blanket**) [late 19C+] (*US Black, orig. milit.*) an overcoat.

horse blanket n.[2] (also **money blanket, saddle blanket**) [20C+] (*US*) a griddle cake.

horsebreaker n. see PRETTY HORSE BREAKER n.

horseburger n. see HORSESHIT n. (2).

horse buss n. [late 18C–early 19C] **1** a loud smacking kiss. **2** a bite. [SE *horse* + *buss*, a kiss, ult. earlier *bass*]

horse chaunter n. [mid-19C] a crooked horse dealer; thus *horse chaunting*, crooked horse dealing.

horsechips n. [1960s] (*US*) nonsense. [SE *horse chips*, horse droppings]

horsecock n.[1] [1920s–50s] (*US*) **1** an idiot, a fool (cf. LOBCOCK n.; NOD COCK n.; WOODCOCK n.[1]). **2** nonsense. [SE *horse* + COCK n.[5] (2)]

horsecock n.[2] (*US*) **1** [1940s+] a sausage, a salami. **2** [1990s+] a large penis (cf. ANTEATER n.). [SE *horse* + COCK n.[2] (1)]

horsecocked adj. [2000s] having a large penis. [HORSECOCK n.[2] (2)]

horse-collar *n.* **1** [late 19C+] the vagina, esp. when considered larger than average. **2** [1900s–10s] (*US*) a zero, esp. in sport. **3** [1920s–50s] (*Can./US*) a clerical or man's high collar. [supposed resemblances]

horsecollar! *excl.* [1920s+] (*US*) nonsense!

horse cop *n.* [1940s+] (*US*) a police officer riding a horse. [SE *horse* + COP *n.*[1] (1)]

horsecrap *n.* [1930s+] (*US*) nonsense. [SE *horse* + CRAP *n.*[3] (3)]

horsed *adj. see* HORSE *v.*[2].

horse dookie *n.* [1970s+] (*US*) nonsense. [SE *horse* + DUKIE *n.*[2] (1)]

horse doughnut/dumpling *n. see* HORSE APPLE *n.*

horsed out *adj.* [1980s+] (*drugs*) intoxicated on heroin. [HORSE *n.*[8]]

horsed up *adj.* [1950s+] (*US*) of a woman, showy, overdressed, over made-up. [ASTOR'S PET HORSE *n.* (1)]

horse-faker *n.* [late 19C] a horse dealer. [SE *horse* + FAKER *n.*]

horsefeathers *n.* (*also* **feathers**) [1920s+] (*orig. US*) nonsense, rubbish (cf. BULLFEATHERS *n.*). [a euph. for HORSESHIT *n.*; supposedly coined by the comic strip artist William de Beck]

horseflesh *n.* [late 17C] work that is charged for before it is actually done. [ult. SE phr. *dead horse*, anything that is beyond saving or use and cannot be revived. The work, which will bring in no further money, is no more use than a 'dead horse']

horse-fly *n.* (*also* **hoss-fly**) [mid-19C–1930s] (*US*) a fellow.

horse frocky *n. see* HORSE HOCKEY *n.*

horsefuck *v.* [1970s+] sexual intercourse with the man using rear entry. [SE *horse* + FUCK *v.*[1]]

horse-fucking *adj.* [1960s] (*US*) very large.

horse godmother *n.* [late 18C–mid-19C] a large masculine woman, 'a gentlemanlike kind of lady' (Grose, 1785).

horse-head *n.* [1950s+] (*US*) a heroin addict. [HORSE *n.*[8] + -HEAD *sfx* (3)]

horse heads *n.* [1970s+] (*drugs*) amphetamines (cf. A *n.*[2]). [? packaging or like the celebrated severed horse's head in a film-maker's bed in the book/film *The Godfather* (1969), the drug makes one 'jump out of bed']

horse heavy *n.* [1940s] (*US Black*) a fat person.

horse-high, bull-strong, pig-tight *phr.* [late 19C+] (*US*) totally secure, esp. used of financial dealings. [19C agricultural jargon referring to the qualities required of a 'lawful fence'; it required 5 strands of wire, must be too high to be jumped by a horse, too strong to be butted down by a bull and too tight to be wormed through by a pig. Some versions added *goose-proof*, many substitute *hog* for *pig*]

horse hockey *n.* (*also* **horse frocky**) [1950s+] (*US*) nonsense. [SE *horse* + HOCKIE *n.* (2)]

horse hooey *n.* [1980s+] (*US*) nonsense. [SE *horse* + HOOEY *n.* (1)]

horse-hung *adj. see* HUNG LIKE A HORSE phr.

horse (it) *v.* **1** [late 19C–1960s] (*US*) (*also* **hoss it**) to walk fast. **2** [20C+] to work hard. [the strength and stamina of the animal]

horse-jockey *n. see* JOCKEY *n.*[3] (8).

horse joint *n.* [1950s] (*US Und.*) a bookmaker's 'office'. [SE *horse* + JOINT *n.*[4] (3)]

horse kiss *n.* [late 17C–18C] a rough, heavy kiss. [the image is of a horse's mouth, with large teeth and lips]

horse-leech *n.*[1] **1** [late 16C–mid-18C] (*also* **horse-leach**) a quack doctor. **2** [17C; 1900s] a general term of abuse. [SE *horse-leech*, a veterinary surgeon]

horse-leech *n.*[2] [mid-17C] a prostitute (cf. ALLEY CAT *n.*). [SE *horse-leech*, a sucking worm]

horseman *n.*[1] [18C+] **1** a promiscuous man, a philanderer (cf. BANBURY *n.*). **2** the penis. [HORSE *v.*[1]; his 'riding' of women]

horseman *n.*[2] [20C+] **1** (*Can. Und.*) a Mountie, a member of the Royal Canadian Mounted Police (RCMP). **2** (*US Und.*) a corrupt policeman. **3** (*US campus*) a habitual cheat, one who 'rides' on the efforts of their fellow students.

horse manure *n.* [1910s+] (*US*) nonsense, rubbish; also as excl. [euph.]

horse-marine *n.* [mid-19C–1900s] an awkward person. [trad. sailors' disdain for the poor seamanship of the Royal Marines]

horsemeat *n.*[1] [1920s] (*US*) corned beef. [the low opinion in which the meat is held]

horsemeat *n.*[2] [1980s+] (*US gay*) a large penis. [HUNG LIKE A HORSE phr.]

horse-milliner *n.* [19C] a saddle and harness maker.

horse-nails *n.* [mid-19C] money (cf. ACTUAL, THE *n.*). [SE *horse-nail*, a nail used to secure a horseshoe]

horse of another colour *phr.* [late 18C–1920s] a very different topic.

horse opera *n.* **1** [mid-19C–1940s] (*US*) a show featuring trained horses. **2** [1920s+] (*orig. US*) (*also* **gun opera, hoss opry**) a Western, whether on film or television. [on model of SOAP OPERA *n.* (1) although this predates]

horsepad *n. see* FOOTPAD *n.*

horse parlour *n. see* HORSE ROOM *n.*

horse piss *n.* (*also* **horse pee**) [20C+] (*US*) weak coffee or weak beer; any unpleasant tasting food (cf. BUFFALO PISS *n.*). [SE *horse* + PISS *n.*]

horseplayer *n.* [1930s+] (*US*) a person who bets on horseracing.

horse plum *n. see* HORSE APPLE *n.*

horse-pox *n.* [mid-17C–18C] an especially severe strain of venereal disease, esp. as used in excl.

horse-protestant *n.* [20C+] (*Irish*) **1** the country gentry. **2** in pl., Protestants in general. [as opposed to the Catholic peasantry]

horse pucky *n.* [1970s+] (*US*) nonsense; also as excl. [SE *horse* + PUCKEY *n.*]

horseradish *n.* [1910s+] (*US*) nonsense; also as excl. [euph.]

horse room *n.* (*also* **horse parlour**) [1940s–50s] (*US*) a book-making establishment.

horses *n.* [20C+] horsepower. [abbr.]

horses! *excl.* [1920s] (*US*) an excl. used to express anger or disappointment. [abbr. HORSESHIT *n.*]

horses and asses *n.* [2000s] (*Irish*) drinking glasses. [rhy. sl.]

horses and carts *n.* [20C+] darts. [rhy. sl.]

horse's ass *n.* (*also* **horse's arse, ...behind, ...can, ...patootie**) [mid-19C+] **1** a fool, an idiot (cf. AIREDALE *n.*; ASSHEAD *n.*; HORSE'S PATOOT *n.*). **2** a general term of abuse. [SE *horse* + ASS *n.* (2)]

horse's handbrake *n.* [1990s+] the erect penis (cf. ANTEATER *n.*).

horse's hangdown *n.* [20C+] a fool, an idiot (cf. CHOAD *n.*). [SE *hangdown*, i.e. the animal's penis, on the model of PRICK *n.*]

horse-shed *v.* [mid-19C–1910s] (*US*) to attempt to influence another person's opinion, esp. in political matters; thus *horse-shedder*, one who tries to influence opinions. [SE *horse-shed*, into which a political campaigner might take a potential supporter for a chat and poss. a quiet drink or even the passing of a small bribe]

horseshit *n.* **1** [1920s+] horse dung. **2** [1920s+] (*also* **horse-burger, horseshite**) rubbish, nonsense. **3** [1940s] (*US*) a DAMN *n.*, e.g. *that isn't worth horseshit*. [SE *horse* + SHIT *n.*[1] (1)]

horseshit *adj.* [1930s+] (*US*) contemptible, offensive, worthless. [HORSESHIT *n.*]

horseshit *v.* [1950s+] (*US*) to lie, to flatter. [var. on BULLSHIT *v.*]

horseshit! *excl.* [1920s+] (*US*) an excl. of disgust, disappointment, disbelief. [HORSESHIT *n.*]

horseshite *n. see* HORSESHIT *n.* (2).

horseshit luck *n.* [1970s] (*US*) surprising and exceptional good luck. [the superstition that stepping in horse manure betokens good luck]

horseshoe *n.*[1] [18C–1900s] the female genitals. [? resemblance but F&H note Ger. phr. 'she has lost a horseshoe', she has been seduced]

horseshoe n.[2] [1910s–20s] (US) **1** a propensity for good luck. **2** in nickname *horseshoes*, a very lucky person. [the trad. association of horseshoes and luck]

horseshoe v. [1900s] (Aus.) to disparage, to criticize harshly.

horse's hoof n. [1950s+] a male homosexual. [rhy. sl. = POOF n. (1)]

horse-skinner n. [1920s–50s] (Can.) one who drives horse teams.

horse's meal n. [late 18C–mid-19C] a meal that has no accompanying drink, alcoholic or otherwise. [cf. synon. Scot. and Yorks. dial. *horse-feast*]

horse's neck n.[1] [20C+] (orig. US) ginger ale flavoured with lemon peel, with or without whisky, brandy or gin. [ety. unknown; *HDAS* suggests a link to HORSE'S NECK n.[2] or to HORSE'S ASS n. (1), but gives no reason]

horse's neck n.[2] [1920s–70s] (US) a fool, an idiot, a general term of abuse. [a partial euph. for HORSE'S ASS n.]

horse's necklace n. [late 19C–1930s] (Aus. prison) the hangman's noose.

horse's nightcap n. [late 16C–1930s] the cap pulled over the condemned man's head before his death; thus the noose itself.

horse's ovaries n. [1930s–70s] (US) hors d'oeuvres. [intentional malapropism]

horse sovereign n. [late 19C] a sovereign coin decorated by Benedetto Pistrucci (1784–1855) with effigies of St George and the Dragon.

horse's patoot n. (also **horse's patootie**) [1980s+] (US) a fool, an idiot, a general term of abuse. [a partial euph. for HORSE'S ASS n.]

horse's rug n. [1980s] (Aus.) a fool (cf. BEECHAM'S PILL n.). [rhy. sl. = MUG n.[2] (1)]

horse thief n. [1910s+] (US) a dishonest person.

horse tranquillizer n. (also **pig tranquillizer**) [1970s+] (drugs) phencyclidine (cf. ACE n.[4]). [the legitimate use of the drug as an animal tranquillizer]

horsewoman n. [1940s+] a masculine lesbian. [they 'ride' their partner]

horsey adj. [20C+] (US) **1** amorous, lustful, frolicsome. **2** impatient, rude, peremptory. [(1) HORSE v.[1]]

hortical adj. [1950s+] (W.I./UK Black teen) genuine, sincere, respected. [? SE *exhort*]

hortical don n. [1970s+] (W.I. Rasta) a respected, acclaimed person. [HORTICAL adj. + DON n.[3]]

hortus n. [18C] the vagina. [Lat. *hortus*, a garden]

hose n.[1] **1** [1920s+] (US) the penis, usu. large. **2** [1940+] (UK Und.) sexual intercourse. **3** [1960s] (US) a prostitute's pimp. **4** [1980s] (US campus) a boyfriend. [joc. uses of SE; but (2) ? link to HO n.[1] (1)]

hose n.[2] [1980s] (US campus) a difficult test or examination. [HOSE v.[3]]

hose n.[3] [1980s+] (US campus) a promiscuous woman. [? HO n.[1] (1) or HOSE v.[2] (2)]

hose v.[1] **1** [1910s+] to fire at, orig. with a machine gun. **2** [1920s+] (US orig. police/Und.) to beat with a rubber hose, to punish. **3** [1940s+] (US) to cheat, to victimize. **4** [1970s+] (US campus) to defeat. **5** [1990s+] to lie. [SE *hose* (down)]

hose v.[2] **1** [1920s] (US campus) to curry favour with. **2** [1930s+] (also **hose down**) to copulate with (always from a man's point of view). **3** [1960s+] (gay) to sodomize. **4** [1980s+] (US campus) of a woman, to search for a sexual partner. **5** [1990s+] to urinate on. [HOSE n.[1]; (1) note RMC Duntroon (Aus.) *hosing*, to ingratiate oneself with those in authority; *hoser*, a sycophant]

hose v.[3] [1980s+] (US campus) **1** to fail, to do badly, to be rejected. **2** to have too much work to do.

hosebag n. **1** [1970s+] (orig. US campus) a promiscuous woman. **2** [1980s+] (US campus) an unattractive person, often female. [ext. HOSE n.[3] + -BAG sfx; ? + pun, she is a 'bag' for the male HOSE n.[1] (1)]

hosebeast n. [1990s+] (US) a sexually promiscuous person. [HOSE n.[1] + SE *beast*]

hosed adj. **1** [1980s] (US campus) drunk (cf. ANNIHILATED adj.). **2** [1990s+] (US Black) in trouble, in difficulties. [HOSE v.[1] (3)]

hosed out adj. [1960s] (US) exhausted. [SE *hose*]

hose down v.[1] [1910s+] (orig. milit.) to fire at, usu. with automatic weapons or aircraft weapons. [HOSE v.[1] (1)]

hose down v.[2] see HOSE v.[2] (2).

hosehead n. [1980s+] (US campus) a stupid person. [SE *hose* + -HEAD sfx (1)]

hose in v. [1980s+] (N.Z.) to win easily.

hose job n. [1970s+] (US) fellatio. [HOSE n.[1] (1) + JOB n.[4]]

hoseman n. [1970s] (US) an exceptionally virile man. [HOSE n.[1] (1) + sfx -*man*]

hose monster n. [1980s+] (US) a sexually promiscuous person, usu. a woman. [HOSE n.[1] (1) + MONSTER sfx]

hose off v.[1] [1950s+] (N.Z.) to annoy, to infuriate.

hose off v.[2] [1980s+] (US) to get out, to send off. [? play on PISS OFF v.]

hose off! excl. [1980s+] (US) go away! be off! [HOSE OFF v.[2]]

hose one's hole v. [20C+] of a woman, to masturbate (cf. APPLY LIP GLOSS v.). [? by using the stimulating qualities of a shower head]

hose-out n. [1930s+] (US campus) a useless person. [HOSE n.[1] (1) on model of PRICK n. (3); or the image of a hose that is out of water]

hose out v. [1970s+] (N.Z.) to beat comprehensively.

hose queen n. [1980s+] (US campus) a sexually promiscuous woman. [HOSE n.[1] (1) + QUEEN sfx (1)]

hoser n. (Can./US campus) **1** [1960s+] a promiscuous man or woman. **2** [1980s+] a fool, an idiot, an uncultured, boorish person. [HOSE n.[1] (1)]

ho shit n. [1990s+] (US Black teen) women's clothing that is seen as overtly sexy. [HO n.[1] (4) + SHIT n.[6]; not necessarily pej.]

hosie n. see HOOZIE n.

hosier n. see HOOSIER n. (1).

hosing n. **1** [1930s+] sexual intercourse. **2** [1960s+] (gay) sodomy. [HOSE v.[2]]

hospital game n. [late 19C] soccer or football. [the broken limbs that accompany it; note N.Z. rugby *hospital pass*, passing the ball to a player about to be heavily tackled]

hospital heroin n. [1980s+] (drugs) Dilaudid. [a synthetic opiate used in hospitals as a substitute for heroin]

hoss see also under HORSE and its combs.

hoss n. [1980s] (US campus) a successful womanizer.

hossie n. [1960s–70s] (Aus.) a hospital. [abbr.]

hostie n. [1960s+] (Aus.) air hostess. [abbr.]

ho stroll n. [1960s+] (US Black pimp) the street or streets in a town or city where prostitutes work regularly. [HO n.[1] (1) + STROLL n. (3)]

hot n.[1] [late 18C–19C] beer mixed with gin, plus egg and spices. [George Parker, *Life's Painter* (1789): 'a mixed kind of liquor, of beer and gin, with egg, sugar and nutmeg, drank mostly in night-houses, but when drank in a morning, it is called flannel']

hot n.[2] [20C+] (US) a hot meal; thus THREE HOTS AND A COT phr. [abbr. SE *hot meal*]

hot n.[3] [1910s–20s] (US) sexual intercourse. [HOT adj.[1] (1)]

hot n.[4] see HOT PROPERTY n.

hot n.[5] see HOT-SHOT n.[1] (2).

hot adj.[1] **1** [14C+] sexually aroused, sexually available. **2** [mid-16C+] urgent, pressing, poss. dangerous. **3** [late 16C+] unpleasant, usu. in phr. *make it hot (for)*. **4** [late 16C+] furious, extremely angry. **5** [late 16C+] zealous, eager, enthusiastic. **6** [mid-17C+] of people, reckless, boisterous. **7** [18C+] lively, energetic; spec. (US Black) of jazz. **8** [mid-19C+] (orig. US) highly amusing, esp. if ironic, ludicrous (cf. HOT ONE n.). **9** [mid-19C+] attractive, pleasurable, a general term of approval. **10** [mid-19C+] severe. **11** [late 19C+] of books, films etc, erotic, sexually arousing; thus of language, obscene. **12** [late 19C+] in constant use; busy, hectic. **13** [late 19C+] current, of the moment, up-to-date. **14** [late 19C+] (*US*) (*also* **warm**) fast or powerful. **15** [late 19C+] orig. applied by men to women, sexy, sexually attractive. **16** [20C+] very promising, potentially useful, thus commercially successful. **17** [20C+] in the context of gunfire etc, dangerous. **18** [1920s+] tense. **19** [1940s+] healthy. **20** [1950s+] of a bullet, loaded into the weapon's chamber; of a gun, loaded. **21** [1980s+] (*US campus*) lucky.

hot *adj.*² **1** [late 16C+] (*orig. UK Und.*) dangerous, thus unsafe for criminal activity. **2** [17C+] of people, in difficulties (other than criminal). **3** [mid-19C+] (*orig. UK Und.*) of people or objects, known to or wanted by the police, suspect. **4** [20C+] (*mainly US Und.*) of goods, stolen. **5** [1920s–60s] (*US Und.*) of a house or place, occupied while being robbed. **6** [1920s+] (*US Und.*) of money or documents, forged or counterfeit. **7** [1930s] (*US Und.*) marked for death. **8** [1930s+] (*US prison*) smuggled. **9** [1940s–50s] (*US Und.*) of dice (etc), crooked. [(1) orig. SE]

hot *adj.*³ **1** [17C–19C] suffering from venereal disease or pubic lice. **2** [17C+] (*US*) drunk; usu. in combs., e.g. *hot as a red wagon, hotter than love in haying-time, hotter than a skunk* (cf. AFFLICTED adj.). **3** [1930s+] (*US drugs*) of an injection or drug, likely to cause death. **4** [1930s+] (*US*) electrified. **5** [1940s+] (*US*) radioactive. **6** [1950s+] (*US*) of a part of body, an organ, seriously physically infected.

hot *adj.*⁴ **1** [mid-19C+] (*US*) first-rate; later used ironically as NOT SO HOT phr. **2** [mid-19C+] very adept, skilful. **3** [20C+] of a sportsman, playing well, on top form; also used fig. of any contestant, in business, a show business performer etc.

hot *v.*¹ **1** [1920s] to tell off, to reprimand. **2** [1930s] (*Irish*) to beat. **3** [1990s+] to unmask, to cause trouble for. [to cause HEAT n.³ (2)]

hot *v.*² [1990s+] to indulge in joy-riding of stolen cars; thus HOTTING n.

hot *adv.* **1** [mid-19C+] ardently, eagerly, violently, severely, angrily. **2** [1930s+] well, much. [HOT adj.¹]

hot about *adv. see* HOT FOR adv.

hot air *n.*¹ (*also* **hot water**) [late 19C+] (*orig. US*) nonsense, rubbish, empty chatter; thus *hot-air artist, hot-air merchant*, one who indulges in talk of this kind.

hot and cold *n.*¹ [20C+] gold. [rhy. sl.]

hot and cold *n.*² [1970s–80s] (*US drugs*) a combination of heroin and cocaine. [initial letters, plus fig. ref. to the effects of the drugs]

hot and heavy *adv.* [mid-19C+] intense, intensely.

hot and heavy like a tailor's goose *phr.* [late 17C–18C] a phr. applied to a passionate lover. [SE *goose*, a tailor's iron, the neck of which supposedly resembles that of the bird; + ? the hissing noise it makes when the heated iron meets the dampened cloth]

hot-and-nice *n.* [1940s] (*W.I.*) a meat patty.

hot and strong *adv.* [late 19C+] severely, intensely; usu. in phrs. GET IT HOT (AND STRONG) v.; GIVE IT HOT (AND STRONG) v. [HOT adv. (1) + STRONG adv. (1)]

hot-arsed *adj.* (*also* **hot-ass, hot-assed, hot-bummed, hot-cunted**) [late 17C+] of a woman, lecherous, lascivious. [HOT adj.¹ (1) + ARSE n.¹ (2)/BUM n.¹ (2)/CUNT n.¹ (1)]

hot as a fire-cracker *phr.* [1910s+] **1** (*Can.*) sexually promiscuous. **2** (*US*) sexually aroused. **3** (*US*) under suspicion, liable to arrest. [HOT adj.¹ (1)/HOT adj.² (3)]

hot as a fresh-fucked fox in a forest fire *phr.* (*also* **hot as a hen laying a goose egg, hot as hell's kitchen, hotter than...**) [1930s+] (*US*) extremely hot, whether as to temperature or sexuality; plus vars. [SE *hot*/HOT adj.¹ (1)]

hot as a (three-dollar) pistol *phr.* (*also* **hotter than...**) [20C+] (*US*) **1** very hot. **2** (*also* **hot as July jam, hot as mustard**) very angry. **3** very popular or successful. **4** (*also* **hot as a 45**)

suspicious, wanted by the police. [play on SE *hot*/HOT adj.¹ (4)/HOT adj.⁴ (3)/HOT adj.² (3)]

hot-ass *adj.*¹ [1960s+] a general superlative. [SE *hot* + -ASS sfx]

hot-ass *adj.*² *see* HOT-ARSED adj.

hot ass *v.* [1970s] (*US*) to go out drinking and enjoying oneself.

hot-assed *adj. see* HOT-ARSED adj.

hot as the hinges of hell *phr.* **1** very tough or dangerous. **2** of temperature, very hot (cf. HARD AS THE HOBS OF HELL phr.).

hot baby *n.* [late 19C–1910s] **1** (*US campus*) (*also* **warm baby**) a student who excels in a certain subject. **2** (*US*) (*also* **warm baby**) any person who excels in something. **3** (*US campus*) a promiscuous person. [HOT adj.⁴/HOT adj.¹ (1) + BABY n.³ (1)]

hot baby! *excl.* [1920s] (*US*) an excl. of surprise.

hot-backed *adj.* [17C] of a woman, promiscuous, sexually voracious. [HOT adj.¹ (1)]

hotbed *n.* [1930s+] (*US*) **1** a bed in a cheap rooming-house that could be hired for 25 cents for 8 hours. **2** a cheap rooming-house. **3** a cheap brothel. [the beds are continually occupied]

hot beef *n.* (*also* **hot meat/mutton**) [19C] a promiscuous woman. [HOT adj.¹ + BEEF n.¹/MEAT n. (1)/MUTTON n.¹]

hot beef! *excl.* (*also* **beef!**) [late 17C–1930s] a cry of alarm, synon. with and rhyming on SE 'stop thief!'; thus CRY (HOT) BEEF v.; SING OUT BEEF v.; WHIDDLE BEEF v.

hot beef incision/injection *n. see* BEEF INJECTION n.

hot belly *n. see* PEPPER BELLY n.

hot biscuit *n.* [1980s+] (*US*) something exciting.

hot blanketer *n.* (*also* **hot blanketeer**) [late 19C–1900s] one who pawns their blankets on a daily basis to provide money for food. [the blankets are still *hot* from being slept in]

hot book *n.* [1940s+] (*US*) a pornographic magazine or book. [HOT adj.¹ (11) + SE *book*]

hot-bot *n.* (*also* **lady hot-bot**) [20C+] a promiscuous, sexually voracious woman. [HOT adj.¹ (1) + SE *bottom*]

hot box *n.*¹ [late 19C–1900s] (*US*) **1** a difficult situation. **2** a tantrum. [HOT adj.² (2)/HOT adj.¹ (4) + SE *box*]

hot box *n.*² [1900s] **1** a crematorium, the actual cremator. **2** [1960s] a battery used for applying torture by electricity. [SE *hot*/HOT adj.³ (4) + SE *box*]

hot box *n.*³ (*US*) **1** [1940s–60s] a sexually promiscuous woman. **2** [1960s+] the female genitals. [HOT adj.¹ (1) + BOX n.¹ (1)]

hot box *v.* **1** [1940s+] (*drugs*) to hold onto a marijuana cigarette for too long before passing it. **2** [1980s+] (*US drugs*) to fill a small sealed room with the smoke of cannabis or crack cocaine. **3** [1980s+] to take a deep draw on a cigarette.

hot boy *n.* [late 19C+] (*orig. US Black*) a fashionable young man, a 'young blood'. [HOT adj.¹ (9)/HOT adj.¹ (13) + SE *boy*]

hot-bummed *adj. see* HOT-ARSED adj.

hot buns *n.* **1** [1970s] (*US prison*) a prison homosexual. **2** [1980s+] (*US gay*) the buttocks, esp. when attractive (cf. BAKERY GOODS n.). [HOT adj.¹ (15) + BUNS n. (2)]

hot burglary *n.* [1970s] (*US Und.*) aggravated burglary.

hot button *n.* [1970s+] (*US*) something that affects someone, provoking a response.

hot-button *adj.* [1970s+] of a topic or issue, important, sensitive, engendering debate. [HOT BUTTON n.]

hot cack *adj.* [20C+] (*Aus.*) very good. [SE *hot* + CACK n.² (1); ? a euph. of SHIT-HOT adj.]

hot card *n.* [late 19C–1920s] (*US*) a provocative, lively person. [HOT adj.¹ (7) + CARD n.² (2)]

hotch *v.* [20C+] to swarm with, to burst with. [Scot. *hotch*]

hotcha *n.* **1** [1930s+] (*orig. US*) hot jazz music, any flashy, exciting entertainment. **2** [1940s+] (*US*) an exciting, attractive young woman. [HOTCHA! excl.]

hotcha *adj.* [1930s+] (*US*) sexy. [HOTCHA n.]

hotcha! *excl.* [1920s+] (*orig. US*) an excl. of enthusiasm, approval or excitement; esp. in phr. *with a hey nonny-nonny and a hotcha-cha*. [onomat.]

hot chair n. (also **hot stool**) [1920s+] (US) the electric chair. [HOT adj.³ (4)]

hotchee/hotchie n. see HACHI n.

hot chocolate n. (also **sweet chocolate**) [1980s] (US) a Black woman. [SE hot chocolate punning on CHOCOLATE n.¹ (3)]

hot cock n. [1950s+] (Aus./US) nonsense, rubbish. [SE hot + COCK n.⁵ (2)]

hot cock adj. [1970s] (US) of a woman, sexually voracious. [HOT adj.¹ (1) + COCK n.² (1)]

hot coffee n. [late 19C–1900s] (Aus.) something problematic. [SE hot coffee/HOT adj.² (2)]

hot coffee adj. [1900s] (Aus.) in a temper. [HOT COFFEE n.]

hot coppers n. [mid-19C–1900s] a mouth and throat parched through excessive drinking or (sometimes) through excessive talk; thus, a hangover. [SE hot + copper, a large saucepan used for boiling either food or laundry]

hot corner n. [mid-19C–1900s] a difficult situation in which one finds oneself threatened, bullied or otherwise under attack. [HOT adj.² (2) + SE corner]

hot crate n. [1930s+] (Aus./US) a stolen car. [HOT adj.² (4) + CRATE n.¹ (3)]

hot cross bun n. [20C+] (Aus.) the sun. [rhy. sl.]

hot cross bun phr. [1950s+] on the run. [rhy. sl.]

hot-cunted adj. see HOT-ARSED adj.

hot cup of tea n. [late 19C–1910s] a sexually attractive woman. [SE hot cup of tea, punning on HOT adj.¹ (1)]

hot damn! excl. [1920s+] (US) a general excl., usu. implying pleasure rather than fury. [var. on GOD-DAMN! excl.]

hot deal n. see BIG DEAL n. (2).

hot diggety (dog)! excl. [20C+] (US) a general excl. of pleasure or surprise.

hot dinner n. [20C+] a winner. [rhy. sl.]

hot-dish adj. (also **hot-slop**) [late 19C] (US campus) attractive, fashionable. [HOT adj.¹ (9) + DISH n.¹ (4)]

hot dog n.¹ (orig. US) **1** [late 19C+] a spiced, heated sausage or frankfurter, served on a split roll and trad. garnished with sauerkraut and mustard. **2** [1920s+] the penis (cf. BACON n.¹). **3** [1990s+] a piece of canine excrement. [SE since c.1939, when (1) was served under that name by the Coney Island Chamber of Commerce to President Franklin D. Roosevelt and his guests, King George VI and Queen Elizabeth of England, the hot dog started life as sl. It prob. comes from heavy-handed mid-19C humour focusing on the supposed use of horse- and dog-meat as sausage filling, a concept that was accentuated by the 1843 scandal concerning the use of dog-meat for human consumption. The image was intensified by the use (c.1860) by German immigrants of *Hundewurst*, dog sausage, to mean smoked frankfurter sausages (larger sausages were *Pferdwurst*, horse baloney). The dachshund, of course, is a 'sausage dog'. The term originated c.1895 at the Yale Club (as well as at Harvard, Cornell and other US 'Ivy League' colleges) where lunch wagons were known as 'dog wagons' and frankfurters known as 'hot dogs']

hot dog n.² (orig. US campus) **1** [late 19C+] one who is particularly proficient at an occupation or activity, esp. a successful gambler. **2** [late 19C+] a show-off. **3** [1960s+] in ironic use, an unpleasant or incompetent person. **4** [1960s+] something exciting, amusing. [HOT adj.⁴ + DOG n.² (1)]

hot dog adj.¹ **1** [late 19C+] (orig. US campus) good, excellent. **2** [1920s+] (US) showy, flamboyant. [HOT DOG n.²]

hot dog adj.² [1960s–70s] (US prison) pornographic. [HOT DOG n.¹ (2), punning on HOT adj.¹ (11)]

hot dog v.¹ **1** [1950s] to prioritize, to find important. **2** [2000s+] to grab for oneself.

hot dog v.² **1** [1960s+] to show off. **2** [1990s+] (US) to perform very well. [HOT DOG n.²]

hot dog! excl. [20C+] (orig. US campus) an expression of delight or strong approval.

hot-dogger n. [20C+] (US teen/campus) **1** a show-off, a braggart. **2** a successful, talented individual. [HOT DOG n.²]

hot duke v. [1970s+] (Aus.) to fool, to take advantage by trickery. [HOT adj.¹ + DUKE n.³]

hote n. [1900s] (US) a cheap lodging house. [abbr. of SE hotel]

hotel n. **1** [19C] the vagina. **2** [early 19C+] (orig. US) a prison (cf. BOARDING HOUSE n.). **3** [1930s] (US) a brothel.

hotel beat n. [late 19C–1900s] one who stays in hotels and then leaves without paying the bill. [SE hotel + BEAT v.¹ (1)]

hotel crowbar n. [1920s+] (Can.) a local prison (cf. BOARDING HOUSE n.). [you need a crowbar to leave]

Hotel de Garvie n. (also **Hotel de Garvey**) [1900s] (N.Z.) the Wellington prison (cf. ABBOTT'S PRIORY n.; BOARDING HOUSE n.). [its governor, one *Garvey*]

hotel de gink n. [1910s+] (US, orig. tramp) a lodging house; subseq. used for transient officers' quarters in US forces. [SE hotel + GINK n.¹; the orig. *Hotel de Gink* was founded in Seattle in 1913 and flourished until 1915, a chain of similarly named hotels were then founded across the US]

hotel-de-loose n. [late 19C] (US) a brothel. [pun on hotel de luxe/the loose women]

hotel warming-pan n. [19C] a hotel chambermaid. [her supposed sexual availability]

hot enchilada n.¹ see HOT TACO n.

hot enchilada n.² see HOT TAMALE n. (3).

hot end n. [late 19C] (US) problems. [HOT adj.² (2); SE end, with the idea of a lollipop]

hot enough to fuck phr. [1960s+] (US) very angry, furious. [HOT adj.¹ (4), punning on HOT adj.¹ (1) + FUCK v.¹]

hot fat injection n. [1930s–50s] (Aus./US) sexual intercourse. [SE hot + FAT n.⁴ + INJECTION n. (2)]

hot flannel n. (also **warm flannel**) [18C–19C] heated gin and beer with nutmeg, sugar and spices. ['a play on the old name "lambswool"' (Hotten, 1874)]

hot-fling n. [20C+] a particularly active bout of sex, esp. with a new partner. [HOT adj.¹ (1) + SE fling, a fit of self-indulgence. Note 16C fling, to wriggle the buttocks during sex]

hot foot n.¹ [mid-19C+] (orig. US) speedy action, a quick movement or journey; as phr. on the hot foot. [HOT FOOT v.]

hot foot n.² (US) **1** [late 19C+] the act of beating the soles of someone's feet or shoes, e.g. of a rough sleeper by a policeman. **2** [1930s–50s] a malicious trick played on an unsuspecting sleeper. Matches are thrust end-first into the gap between the upper and sole of the shoe (or between naked toes if vulnerable); the matches are lit, and the shoe 'catches fire' or the flesh is painfully singed. **3** [1940s–50s] in fig. use, an unpleasant surprise.

hot foot v. (also **hot foot it**, **hot heel**) **1** [mid-19C+] (orig. US) to rush around, to hurry, to run. **2** [20C+] to escape from. **3** [1910s–20s] to chase away.

hot foot adv. (also **with hot feet**) [mid-19C+] quickly. [HOT FOOT v.]

hot for adv. (also **hot about**, **hot on**, **hot over**, **hot to**, **hot upon**) [18C+] (orig. US) enthusiastic, keen on, esp. sexually. [HOT adj.¹ (5)]

hot hay n. [1930s] (US drugs) marijuana (cf. AFRICAN BUSH n.). [SE hot + HAY n.³ (2)]

hot head n. [1970s] (US prison) a prison homosexual.

hot-headed adj. **1** [late 17C] hungover. **2** [18C] drunk (cf. ARSEHOLED adj.).

hot heel v. see HOT FOOT v.

hot in the biscuit phr. [1940s–50s] (US) very angry, furious. [HOT adj.¹ (4) + BISCUIT n.² (2)]

hot in the pants phr. see HOT PANTS adj.

hot in the tail phr. (also **light in the tail**, **warm in the tail**) **1** [late 17C–early 18C] wanton, promiscuous. **2** [1930s–50s] zealous; sexually eager. [HOT adj.¹/LIGHT adj.¹/WARM adj.¹ + TAIL n.² (3)]

hot iron *n. see* HOT-ROD n. (1).

hot item *n.* [1980s+] (*US*) a couple having a romantic relationship. [SE *hot* + ITEM n. (3)]

hot joint *n.* (*also* **hot slough**) [1920s–60s] (*US tramp*) somewhere that is robbed while the owners are in occupation. [HOT adj.² (5) + JOINT n.⁴ (3)]

hot-knife *v.* [1980s+] (*drugs*) to smoke cannabis from a heated knife; the fumes are sucked up through a broken-off milk-bottle neck.

Hotlanta *n.* (*also* **Hot Town**) [1970s+] (*US*) Atlanta, Georgia. [the city's actual and fig. temperature]

hot-lips *n.* [1920s+] (*US*) a nickname applied to someone with a reputation for passionate kissing. [HOT adj.¹ (1) + SE *lips*]

hotload *n.* [1970s+] (*US*) a powerful firearm cartridge.

hot lot *n. see* HOT MEMBER n.

hot lot it *v.* [1970s] (*US*) to go at great speed.

hot-making *adj.* [1930s–50s] embarrassing. [SE *hot* + -MAKING sfx; one's cheeks 'burn']

hot mama *n.* (*also* **hot mamma, hot momma, red hot, red-hot mama**) [1920s+] **1** (*US*) a flighty young woman. **2** (*orig. US Black*) (*also* **hot papa**) a large, hedonistic woman, often an habitué of saloons, bars and nightclubs; occas. used of men. **3** (*US*) a sexy woman, irrespective of her figure. [HOT adj.¹ (15) + MAMA n. (1); note the entertainer Sophie Tucker (1884–1966), who billed herself as 'the last of the red hot mamas']

hot mama *v.* [1920s] (*US*) to flirt. [HOT MAMA n.]

hot meat *n.*¹ [1940s] (*US*) exposed female flesh. [HOT adj.¹ (1) + MEAT n. (1)]

hot meat *n.*² *see* HOT BEEF n.

hot meat injection *n.* [1930s+] sexual intercourse. [SE *hot* + MEAT n. (2) + INJECTION n. (2)]

hot meds *n.* [2000s] (*US prison*) controlled *medication*.

hot member *n.* (*also* **hot lot**) **1** [late 19C] a debauchee, a degenerate; in weak use, one who lives for pleasure. **2** [late 19C–1900s] one who flaunts convention. **3** [late 19C–1900s] a troublesome, bad-tempered, quarrelsome person. **4** [late 19C–1910s] (*US*) the penis (cf. DEAREST MEMBER n.). **5** [late 19C–1940s] (*US*) a sexually attractive woman, also a prostitute. [HOT adj.¹ (1) + SE *member/lot*; (4) MEMBER n.¹]

hot milk *n.* [late 19C; 1970s] semen (cf. BABY GRAVY n.).

hot minute *n.* (*also* **hot second**) [1930s+] (*US*) a moment.

hot momma *n. see* HOT MAMA n.

hot mutton *n. see* HOT BEEF n.

hotnot *n.* [1940s+] (*S.Afr.*) a derog. term for a Black person (cf. AFRICAN APE n.). [SE *Hottentot*]

hot number *n.* [late 19C+] a sexually attractive woman, also her telephone number, esp. if written on the wall of a phone booth. [HOT adj.¹ (15) + NUMBER n.¹ (1) + pun on telephone number]

hot nuts *n.* [1930s+] (*US*) usu. of a man, strong sexual desire. [HOT adj.¹ (1) + NUTS n.² (1)]

hot oil *n.*¹ [1960s] (*US*) a predicament. [var. on HOT WATER n.¹]

hot oil *n.*² [1980s] (*US Black*) a self-opinionated person, an important person.

hot-on *n.* [1960s] **1** (*US Black*) lust; lustful feelings. **2** (*US campus*) an unpleasant person. [HOT adj.¹ (1)]

hot on *adv.*¹ [late 19C+] very severe towards. [HOT adj.¹ (10)]

hot on *adv.*² [1930s+] very skilful at. [HOT adj.⁴ (2)]

hot on *adv.*³ *see* HOT FOR adv.

hot one *n.* **1** [mid-19C–1900s] a violent blow. **2** [late 19C] a promiscuous woman. **3** [late 19C+] an admirable individual, a good example, usu. with sexual overtone. **4** [late 19C+] a 'difficult' person. **5** [late 19C+] (*gambling*) a winning tip. **6** [20C+] something shocking, surprising, exciting or funny. **7** [1940s+] something or someone appealing. **8** [1970s] a good idea or plan. [HOT adj.¹ (9) + ONE n.⁵ (1)]

hot on someone's tail *phr. see* ON SOMEONE'S TAIL phr.

hot over *adv. see* HOT FOR adv.

hot pants *n.* **1** [1920s+] (*US*) strong sexual desire; often as *have hot pants for*. **2** [1930s+] a sexually eager woman. **3** [1960s–70s] (*US*) extreme keenness. **4** [1960s+] a term of address to a sexually eager woman (or one who is seen as such). [HOT adj.¹ (1) + SE *pants*]

hot pants *adj.* (*also* **hot in the pants**) **1** [1920s+] sexually eager. **2** [1960s+] sexy, provocative. [HOT PANTS n.]

hot papa *n.*¹ [1920s] (*US Und.*) a womanizer; a dandy. [HOT adj.¹ (1) + SE *papa*]

hot papa *n.*² *see* HOT MAMA n. (2).

hot paper *n.* [1940s–50s] (*US Und.*) any form of fraudulent document, esp. of a financial nature, e.g. a fake cheque. [HOT adj.² (6) + PAPER n.¹]

hot patootie *n.* [1910s+] (*US*) an attractive young woman. [var. on HOT POTATO n.³]

hot patsy *n.* [1900s] a funny person, entertaining. [HOT adj.¹ (8) + PATSY n.]

hot pepper belly *n. see* PEPPER BELLY n.

hot pillow (joint) *n.* [1950s+] (*US*) a room in a cheap hotel or motel that is rented out to lovers or to a prostitute and her client. [SE *pillow* + JOINT n.⁴ (3)]

hot place *n.* [mid-19C+] (*US*) a euph. for *hell*.

hot plate *n.* [1940s] (*US Und.*) the electric chair. [HOT adj.³ (4) + SE *hot plate*]

hot pockaroo *n.* (*also* **potcharooney**) [1960s+] (*US gay*) the buttocks.

hotpoint *v.* [1970s+] (*Aus.*) to fool, to take advantage by trickery; thus *hotpointer*, one who does this. [the trickster *points out* something that is supposedly HOT adj.¹ (16)]

hot poop *n.* [1950s+] the latest news or gossip. [HOT adj.¹ (13) + POOP n.⁴ (1)]

hot pot *n.*¹ [late 17C–early 19C] a hot drink made of ale and brandy.

hot pot *n.*² [1920s–30s] (*US Black*) a sexually promiscuous woman. [HOT adj.¹ (1); she is always 'on the boil']

hotpot *n.* [20C+] (*Aus.*) in horseracing, the favourite.

hot potato *n.*¹ (*also* **hot potato jacket**) [mid-19C+] (*orig. US*) a problem, a difficult person, a trying situation, anything those concerned would prefer not to handle.

hot potato *n.*² [late 19C–1900s] a waiter. [rhy. sl.; Cockney pron. 'pertater']

hot potato *n.*³ [late 19C+] (*US*) an admirable, clever or energetic person. [HOT adj.¹ (9) + POTATO, THE n.]

hot potato *adv.* [2000s] (*Aus.*) later. [rhy. sl.; Aus. pron. 'pertater']

hot potato jacket *n. see* HOT POTATO n.¹.

hot property *n.* (*also* **hot**) [1950s+] a success, a sensation.

hot pup *n. see* PUP n.² (1).

hot rail *n.* [2000s] (*US prison*) an instance where a group of inmates stand around a particular prisoner during visiting time so that he can have sex with his partner.

hotrock *adj.* [1940s–50s] flashy, arrogant, aggressive.

hot rock *v.* [1980s+] (*drugs*) to drop burning lumps of cannabis from a cigarette onto one's clothes. [HOT ROCKS n.²]

hotrock *adv.* [1940s–50s] absolutely, intensely.

hot rocks *n.*¹ **1** [1920s] (*US campus*) someone or something splendid. **2** [1940s+] (*US*) esp. of a man, strong sexual desire. **3** [1950s] (*US*) as a form of address, usu. ironically. [HOT adj.¹ (1) + ROCKS n.⁴]

hot rocks *n.*² [1980s+] (*Irish/Aus. drugs*) hot ash that drops from a joint or is sucked through a pipe and burns one's throat.

hot-rod *n.* **1** [1940s+] (*also* **hot iron, hot-up, rod**) a car modified for speed and flashiness. **2** [1930s+] (*US*) an aggressive, unruly young man. [HOT adj.¹ (14) + SE piston *rod*/? ROD n.¹]

hot-rod *adj.* [1950s+] (*US*) energetic, aggressive. [HOT-ROD n. (2)]

hot-rodder *n.* [1950s+] a person who drives or races a car that has been modified for speed and flashiness. [HOT-ROD n. (1)]

hot roller *n.* [1970s+] (*US police*) a stolen car, esp. while being driven. [HOT adj.[2] (4)]

hot roll with cream *n.* [late 19C+] sexual intercourse. [HOT adj.[1] (1) + ROLL n.[4] + CREAM n.[1] (1); pun on SE]

hots *n.* [1970s+] (*US campus*) electric hair rollers. [abbr. SE *hot rollers*]

hots, the *n.* [1940s+] **1** sexual desire. **2** in fig. use, any form of excitement. [HOT adj.[1] (1)]

hot school *n.* [1910s] (*Aus.*) a dramatic, challenging environment.

hot scone *n.* [1920s+] (*Aus.*) a policeman, a detective (cf. BOTTLE (AND STOPPER) n.). [rhy. sl. = JOHN n.[4]]

hot seat *n.* (*also* **hot squat, seat**) **1** [1920s+] (*US*) the electric chair. **2** [1930s–40s] any situation in which the subject, consciously or not, is exposed, esp. for the purposes of a confidence trick. **3** [1950s+] an unpleasant situation, esp. in a courtroom or public enquiry; esp. as *in the hot seat*. **4** [1950s+] the seat in an interrogation room on which the prisoner sits. **5** [1960s+] any form of interrogation, in a non-official context. [(1) HOT adj.[3] (4); (5) note Val Davis, *Phenomena in Crime* (1941): 'So called because the hooked "mug" is on tenterhooks re the materialization of the investments he has handed over to the crooks']

hot seat *v.* [1940s] (*US*) to be subjected to the electric chair. [HOT SEAT n. (1)]

hot seat man *n.* [1930s] (*UK Und.*) (*also* **hot seat boy**) a superior variety of confidence man, specializing in long-term, elaborate schemes. [HOT SEAT n. (2) + SE *man*]

hot second *n.* see HOT MINUTE n.

hot session *n.* [1920s+] (*US*) a good time (orig. sexual intercourse). [HOT adj.[1] (1) + SE *session*]

hot sex on a platter *n.* [1990s+] (*US Black teen*) **1** a very sexy woman. **2** overtly or excessively sexy clothes. [HOT adj.[1] (15)]

hot sheet *n.* **1** [1920s+] (*US police*) a list of stolen property and of crimes under investigation. **2** [2000s] (*US Black*) the list of members of opposite gangs that are considered serious enemies. [the items that are HOT adj.[2] (3)]

hot-sheet hotel *n.* (*also* **hot-sheet house, hot-sheet motel**) [1930s+] (*US*) a hotel that rents out some or all of its rooms to prostitutes, adulterous couples and others who wish to use the beds for short periods rather than for overnight accommodation. [such beds are in near-continuous occupation and thus stay warm]

hot shit *n.* (*also* **that hot shit**) [1950s+] (*orig. US*) **1** that which is important, vibrant, exciting, fashionable etc. **2** an important person or someone who thinks they are. [HOT adj.[4] (1) + SHIT n.[2]]

hot-shit *adj.* [1960s+] (*orig. US*) **1** splendid. **2** offensively self-conceited. [HOT SHIT n.]

hot shit! *excl.* [1940s+] (*US*) an expression of excitement, enthusiasm.

hot-shit for *phr.* [1970s+] (*US*) keen or enthusiastic. [HOT SHIT! excl.]

hot-shot *n.*[1] **1** [17C] a sexual athlete, used of either sex. **2** [early 19C+] (*orig. US*) (*also* **hot**) an important, influential person or one who believes that they are. **3** [1950s+] an ironic use of (1); usu. as an address. [(1) HOT adj.[1] (1); note 17C *hot-shot*, one who discharged his firearm too enthusiastically]

hot-shot *n.*[2] [late 19C–1920s] (*US*) a cutting or sarcastic remark. [HOT adj.[1] + SHOT n.[3] (1)]

hot-shot *n.*[3] [1920s–30s] (*US tramp*) **1** a fast freight train. **2** a stolen car.

hot-shot *n.*[4] [1930s+] (*drugs*) the substitution of cyanide, strychnine or battery acid for white powdered heroin; when injected by the addict, it causes instant death and leaves no trace; also as *v.*, to sell or take such a preparation. [HOT adj.[3] (3) + SHOT n.[6] (2)]

hot-shot *n.*[5] [1960s] (*US*) bad homemade liquor, bootleg whisky.

[whisky distilling jargon *hot shot*, the first drops of distilled liquor in a batch to be produced]

hot-shot *adj.* [1920s+] (*orig. US*) **1** conceited, self-opinionated, ostentatious. **2** first-rate, excellent. [HOT-SHOT n.[1] (2); a truck-freighting term from *c.*1920, rapid, offering through or non-stop service]

hotshot charlie *n.* [1940s–70s] (*US*) a nickname for a brash, egotistical young man. [HOT-SHOT adj. (1) + CHARLIE n.[1]; coined in Milton Caniff's comic strip 'Terry and the Pirates' (1940s+)]

hot sketch *n.* (*also* **sketch**) [1900s–30s] (*US*) **1** an attractive person, usu. a young woman. **2** an amusing person or thing. **3** an eccentric person. [HOT adj.[1] + SKETCH n.[2]]

hot-slop *adj.* see HOT-DISH adj.

hot slough *n.* see HOT JOINT n.

hotsmoke *n.* [1980s+] (*drugs*) the smoking of crack cocaine.

hot spit *n.* [1930s+] (*US*) anything good, exciting, sexually attractive.

hot spot *n.* **1** [20C+] a dangerous or difficult situation. **2** [1900s–20s] (*US Und.*) an area where there is likely to be a good deal of police presence or similar security. **3** [1920s+] (*US*) a popular, fashionable nightclub or bar. [HOT adj.[2] (1) + SPOT n.[8]]

hot squat *n.* see HOT SEAT n.

hot stepper *n.* [20C+] (*W.I./UK Black teen*) a prison-breaker, a fugitive from prison or a penal institution. [he runs off 'as if his feet were on fire']

hot stick *n.* [1950s+] (*drugs*) a marijuana cigarette (cf. BAT n.[8]). [HOT adj.[2] + STICK n.[9]]

hot-stopping *n.* [mid-19C] hot spirits and water.

hot stuff *n.*[1] (*US*) **1** [mid-19C+] spiced rum, strong alcohol. **2** [1920s–30s] coffee.

hot stuff *n.*[2] **1** [late 19C+] (*orig. US*) something or someone considered first-rate, excellent or particularly intelligent or capable. **2** [late 19C+] (*orig. US*) an attractive woman. **3** [late 19C+] (*orig. US*) something or someone pornographic or sexy. **4** [1930s] (*UK Und.*) fraudulent literature used in financial swindling. [HOT adj.[1] + SE *stuff*]

hot stuff *n.*[3] [1920s+] (*US*) stolen goods. [HOT adj.[2] (4) + SE *stuff*]

hot stuff! *excl.* [late 19C+] (*orig. US*) a form of address, often implying that the person in question has a higher opinion of him or herself than does the audience. [HOT STUFF n.[2] (1)]

hot supper *n.* [1960s] (*US Black*) a switch-blade knife or flick-knife. [? used for robberies it will obtain one the money for food]

hotsy-totsy *n.* (*also* **hotsy**) [1920s–40s] (*US*) a pretty young girl.

hotsy-totsy *adj.* **1** [1920s] of a place, sophisticated. **2** [1920s+] (*orig. US*) excellent, satisfactory, just right. [ext. of HOT adj.[1] (9); coined by cartoonist William 'Billie' de Beck, *c.*1925]

hot taco *n.* (*also* **hot enchilada**) [1970s] (*US*) a passionate young woman, esp. Hispanic. [one of several terms that equate women with food; HOT adj.[1] (1) + SE *taco*, a Mexican food stuff]

hot-tailed *adj.*[1] [late 17C–18C] infected with venereal disease. [HOT adj.[3] (1) + TAIL n.[2] (3)]

hot-tailed *adj.*[2] [1960s+] of a woman, lecherous, lascivious. [HOT adj.[1] (1) + TAIL n.[2] (3)]

hot tamale *n.* (*also* **tamale**) **1** [late 19C–1930s] (*US*) a clever person, often used ironically. **2** [late 19C+] (*US*) an attractive, sexy, young woman. **3** [1920s+] (*US gay*) (*also* **hot enchilada**) a Hispanic homosexual man. [HOT adj.[1] (9)/HOT adj.[1] (15) + Sp. *tamale*, a Mexican dish consisting of corn husks wrapped around a variety of fillings]

hot tamale! *excl.* [1940s+] (*US*) an excl. of excitement, pleasure. [HOT TAMALE n.]

hotted-up *adj.* [1950s+] (*US*) of a car engine, customized. [HOT (UP) v.]

Hottentot *n.* **1** [18C–1910s] a fool, a simpleton. **2** [18C+] (*S.Afr.*) a derog. term for a Black person (cf. AFRICAN APE n.). **3** [late 19C–1910s] used in the East End of London to denote a stranger; thus the cry *Hottentots!* strangers coming! [proper name Hottentot, poss. meaning 'stutterer' or 'stammerer'. 'One of the two sub-races of the Khoisanid race (the other being the Sanids or Bushmen), characterized by short stature, yellow-brown skin colour, and tightly curled hair. They are of mixed Bushman-Hamite descent with some Bantu admixture, and are now found principally in South-West Africa' (*OED*). Since 18C the term has been used abusively, to describe someone 'uncivilized' and of inferior intelligence and culture]

Hottentot apron *n.* [20C+] elongated labia. [the physical characteristics of 'Hottentot' women]

Hottentots *n.* [20C+] the buttocks. [the nakedness of African tribespeople]

Hottentots! *excl. see* HOTTENTOT *n.* (3).

hotten up one's copper *v.* [1940s] (*N.Z.*) to have something warm to eat and drink.

hotter than... *see also under* HOT AS...

hotter than a little red wagon *phr.* (*also* **hotter than a bitch-wolf**) [1970s] (*US*) of a woman, sexually voracious. [HOT adj.[1] (1)]

hot ticket *n.* [1960s+] (*US campus*) a person, event or object that is currently fashionable or stylish. [orig. theatre use, a successful show or performer]

hot ticket! *excl.* [1990s+] (*US campus*) an excl. of affirmation. [HOT TICKET *n.*]

hottie *n.*[1] [20C+] (*orig. Aus.*) a *hot*-water bottle. [abbr.]

hottie *n.*[2] (*also* **hotty**) [1990s+] (*US Black/campus*) a good-looking or attractive member of the opposite sex; occas. used of a promiscuous person. [HOT STUFF *n.*[2] (2)]

hottie *n.*[3] [2000s] (*drugs*) hashish or marijuana smoked off a hot knife.

hottie *adj.* (*also* **hotty**) [1990s+] (*US*) very attractive. [HOTTIE *n.*[2]]

hot tiger *n.* [mid-19C] a mixture of hot-spiced ale and sherry. [originated at Oxford University]

hotting *n.* [1990s+] the vogue term for what used to be known, prosaically, as *joy-riding*, or, in legal parlance, *taking and driving away*. [HOT v.[2]; the 'hotter' steals a high performance car, drives it off and, often to the cheers of an appreciative crowd, puts it, and his own driving skills through their paces, emphasizing skids, spins and hand-brake turns – the stuff of film car chases]

hot to *adv. see* HOT FOR *adv.*

hot toddy *n.* [20C+] a body. [rhy. sl.]

hot tomato *n.* 1 [1920s–30s] (*US*) a clever person. 2 [1950s] (*US Und.*) a passionate or tough woman.

hot tongue *n.* [1920s–30s] (*US tramp*) a sexually passionate woman. [HOT adj.[1] (1) + SE *tongue*]

hot topic *n.* [1990s+] one who has a far-reaching reputation.

Hot Town *n. see* HOTLANTA *n.*

hot trap *n.* [1930s–50s] (*US Und.*) a stolen car. [HOT adj.[2] (4) + ? SE *trap* or TRAP *n.*[4]]

hot tuna! *excl. see* TUNA *n.* (3).

hotty *see under* HOTTIE.

hot 'un *n.* 1 [mid-19C] a gulp of liquor. 2 [mid-19C+] a painful, punishing blow. 3 [late 19C–1900s] a debauchee, a degenerate. [HOT adj.[1] + SE *one*]

hot-up *n. see* HOT-ROD *n.* (1).

hot up *v.* 1 [late 19C+] to heat up, to warm up. 2 [20C+] of events, to become more exciting, more dramatic.

hot upon *adv. see* HOT FOR *adv.*

hot water *n.*[1] [mid-16C+] difficulties, problems; usu. as *in hot water*.

hot water *n.*[2] [late 19C] (*US*) in a restaurant, a cup of tea.

hot water *n.*[3] *see* HOT AIR *n.*

hot water! *excl.* [2000s] (*US prison*) a warning that an officer is coming. [HOT WATER *n.*[1]]

hot Willie (dog) *adj.* [late 19C] (*US campus*) smart, fashionable, showy.

hot wire *n.* [1900s–50s] (*US prison*) information.

hot-wire *v.* 1 [1950s+] (*orig. US*) (*also* **wire**) to start a car without an ignition key by making the required connection between 2 wires. 2 [1980s+] to connect illegally to the electricity supply. [the electric spark thus produced is 'hot']

hot with *n.* [mid-19C] a drink of *hot* spirits and water *with* sugar (cf. WARM WITH *n.*).

hot ziggety! *excl.* (*also* **hotzickity!**) [1900s–50s] (*US*) an excl. used to express excitement, enjoyment. [var. on HOT DIGGETY (DOG)! excl.]

Houdini *n.*[1] [1920s+] (*US*) someone who avoids something, usu. work (cf. PULL A HOUDINI v.). [joc. ref. to Harry *Houdini* (1874–1926), US conjuror and escape artist]

Houdini *n.*[2] (*also* **houbini**) [1980s+] (*US drugs*) marijuana (cf. AUNT MARY *n.*[2]). [US escapologist Harry *Houdini* (1874–1926); the smoker 'escapes' reality]

Houdini *v. see* PULL A HOUDINI v.

hough *n.* (*also* **haugh, hoch, huff**) [20C+] 1 a thigh. 2 a mess. [SE *hough*, the hollow part of the human knee joint; the adjacent section of the thigh]

houghmagandy *n.* (*also* **hochmagandy**) [18C+] (*Ulster/Scot.*) (adulterous) sexual intercourse. [? *hough*, the hollow part of the human knee joint; the adjacent section of the thigh + *canty*, cheerful, lively, brisk or *gundy*, a push; but note ? fig. use of HASHMAGANDY *n.* or SE *hogmanay*; the balad collector Ebsworth prefers an interpretation of *gandy* as a variant pron. of 'go over gaudy', extra-marital intercourse 'over the broomstick']

hou jou bek! *excl.* [1910s+] (*S.Afr.*) shut your mouth! [Afk. *bek*, an animal's mouth, when used of a human it is sl.; note Fr. *ferme ta gueule*, shut your mouth, in which *gueule*, usu. of an animal, is sl. when used of a human]

hoult *n.* [20C+] (*Irish*) 1 a sexually attractive woman, often qualified as a *fine/great/good hoult*. 2 sexual intercourse. [pron. of SE *hold*]

hound *n.*[1] [mid-19C+] an unpleasant person; a gangster, a hoodlum. [the negative characteristics of a dog]

hound *n.*[2] 1 [late 19C+] a general derog. description. 2 [1930s+] (*Aus.*) a lazy, good-for-nothing person. 3 [1960s] (*US*) a coward. 4 [1980s+] (*Aus. prison*) an informer. 5 [1980s+] an unattractive woman. [play on DOG *n.*[3]]

hound *n.*[3] [1910s+] (*US*) an enthusiast, a devotee. [HOUND sfx]

hound *n.*[4] [1920s+] (*US Black*) an indiscriminatingly promiscuous man. [play on SE]

hound *n.*[5] [1950s+] (*US Black*) a Greyhound Corporation bus. [abbr.]

hound *n.*[6] [1960s] (*US*) 'the daylights', 'the stuffing'; thus *kick/ knock the hound out of*.

hound *adj.* [1960s] (*US prison*) cowardly. [HOUND *n.*[2] (3)]

hound *v.* [1980s+] (*US Black/campus*) 1 to have sex with. 2 to go out looking for sex. [HOUND *n.*[4]]

hound *sfx* [1910s+] an enthusiast, usu. for 'pleasures of the flesh' (cf. ASS-HOUND *n.*; BOOZE HOUND *n.*; COCK-HOUND *n.*; COKEHOUND *n.*; CUNT-HOUND *n.*; DICKHOUND *n.*; GASH-HOUND *n.*; HASH HOUND *n.*; LUSH HOUND *n.*; PUSSY-HOUND *n.*; SAUCE-HOUND *n.*; SMOKE-HOUND *n.*; SMUT-HOUND *n.*; TEA-HOUND *n.*[2]).

hound dog *n.*[1] [20C+] (*US*) a person of mixed race. [dial. *hound dog*, a mongrel]

hound dog *n.*[2] [20C+] (*US*) one who hangs around when he or she is not wanted.

hound-dog *v.* [1990s+] to go out looking for a (sexual) companion. [HOUND v. (2)]

houndish *adj.* [20C+] (*W.I., Guyn.*) shamelessly gluttonous. [SE *hound*, a glutton, but the n. form is rarely found]

hound pudding *n.* [1950s] (*mainly UK juv.*) mince.

Hounslow Heath *n.* [mid-late 19C] the teeth. [rhy. sl.]

hour-grunter *n.* [late 17C–early 18C] a watchman. [watchmen patrolled the streets, calling out the time]

hours *phr.* [1980s] (*UK Black*) an expression of farewell.

House, the n. [late 19C] the London Stock Exchange.

house n.[1] **1** [17C+] a whore-house, a house of ill-repute, a brothel (cf. ACCOMMODATION HOUSE n.). **2** [mid-17C–1920s] a public house, a hotel, an illegal drinking house. **3** [mid-19C–1900s] a poor-house, a workhouse. **4** [late 19C–1930s] (*UK society*) a group of guests at a ball or dance who sit, eat and dance within their own circle only. **5** [20C+] (*US Und.*) a police station. **6** [1920s+] (*US Und.*) a single prison cell; thus *house time*, a sentence in jail. **7** [1940s–70s] (*US Black/teen*) a prison (cf. BANDHOUSE n.).

house n.[2] [1980s+] the most popular form of contemporary dance music, originated at Chicago's Warehouse Club and spread across the Western world; a direct descendant of disco, it features what critics dismiss as similarly mindless rhythms and banal lyrics, with the sole difference that electronic special effects (synthesizers, sampling, drum machines) have replaced the original instrumental playing.

house n.[3] *see* BRICKHOUSE n.[2] (2).

house v.[1] **1** [1980s+] (*US*) to outdo, to defeat. **2** [1990s+] (*US*) to attack someone violently. **3** [1990s+] (*US Black*) to take over, to exert one's authority. [abbr. of ROUGHHOUSE v.]

house v.[2] **1** [1980s+] (*US Black*) to take for oneself, to steal. **2** [1990s+] (*US Black*) to go, to come or to move towards. **3** [1990s+] (*US teen*) to give, to take or to bring. [SE *house*, to take into a house]

house v.[3] [1980s+] (*US Black*) in rap music, to excite and impress an audience. [? SE *bring down the house*]

house-a-blazes adv. [1940s] (*W.I.*) utterly, completely.

house ape n. [1960s+] (*US*) a small child.

house-bit n. (*also* **house-keeper, house-piece**) [mid-19C–1910s] a servant who doubles as a lover. [SE *house(maid)* + BIT n.[2]/PIECE n.[1] (1)]

house-broad n. [1940s] (*US*) a prostitute who lives and works in a hotel. [SE *house* + BROAD n.[2] (2)]

house connect n. [1990s+] (*US drugs*) a drug dealer who works from his or her home, rather than from the street. [SE *house* + CONNECTION n.]

housed adj. [2000s] (*US campus*) drunk.

house dog n. [1930s] (*US tramp*) one who takes jobs in private houses.

house-farmer n. *see* HOUSE-KNACKER n.

house fee n. [1980s+] (*drugs*) a fee charged for entry into a room or apartment where one can smoke crack cocaine. [CRACK HOUSE n. (1) + SE *fee*]

house for rent n. [18C–19C; 1930s] **1** a widow's weeds. **2** the widow herself. [a widow becomes 'vacant' for a new (male) 'tenant']

house-gow n. *see* HOOSEGOW n.

house hop n. [20C+] (*orig. US Black*) a party at which the guests buy their refreshments to help pay the rent (cf. FISH-FRY n.). [SE *house* + HOP n.[1]]

house in a state n. [1960s] (*bingo*) the number 78 (cf. ALDERSHOT LADIES n.).

house-keeper n.[1] **1** [late 18C–1940s] (*US Und.*) a madame. **2** [1930s–70s] a kept mistress. [euph.]

house-keeper n.[2] *see* HOUSE-BIT n.

house-knacker n. (*also* **house-farmer**) [late 19C] a landlord who rents third-rate accommodation to the poor. [SE *house-knacker*, one who buys old houses to strip out their materials or to convert them for profitable use]

housemaid's knee n. [1970s] the sea. [rhy. sl.]

houseman n. [1900s–40s] (*US*) a burglar. [his specializing in house-breaking rather than safe-cracking etc]

house mother n. [1950s+] in the sex industry, a madame. [HOUSE n.[1] (1) + SE *mother*]

house nigger n. (*also* **h.n.**) [1970s+] (*US Black*) **1** a Black person employed, often as the 'token nigger', i.e. token Black worker, in a mainly White organization. **2** a Black person who is seen as

preferring White friends and opinions to those of their own community. **3** a subservient person, a 'yes-man' irrespective of race. [the slavery-era division between 'house' and 'field niggers', i.e. those who worked as indoor servants and those who worked in the fields; the former were seen as 'softer' than the latter]

house of civil reception n. [mid-18C–early 19C] a brothel (cf. ACCOMMODATION HOUSE n.). [HOUSE n.[1] (1) + SE *civil reception*]

House of Commons n. [late 18C–mid-19C] a privy, a lavatory (cf. BACKHOUSE n.). [HOUSE OF EASEMENT n. + COMMONS n.; + pun on *House of Commons*, UK Parliament]

house of conveniency n. [18C] a brothel (cf. ACCOMMODATION HOUSE n.). [SE *house*/HOUSE n.[1] (1) + SE *conveniency*]

house of countless drops n. [1930s–40s] (*US Black*) a bar that sells grilled food as well as the usual liquor.

house of D n. [1960s+] (*US prison*) a *house of* detention (cf. BANDHOUSE n.). [abbr.]

house of delight n. (*also* **house of entertainment/pleasure**) [18C] a brothel (cf. ACCOMMODATION HOUSE n.). [SE *house*/HOUSE n.[1] (1) + *delight/entertainment/pleasure*]

house of easement n. (*also* **house of ease, office of ease**) [17C–19C] a privy (cf. BACKHOUSE n.). [euph.]

house of fraser n. [20C+] a razor, either as a weapon or for shaving. [rhy. sl.; usu. as 'howser'; ult. *House of Fraser*, a department store company]

house of knowledge n. *see* KNOWLEDGE BOX n. (2).

House of Lords n.[1] [early 19C+] a urinal.

House of Lords n.[2] [20C+] corduroy trousers. [rhy. sl. = *cords*]

house of many slammers n. [1940s+] (*US*) a prison (cf. BANDHOUSE n.).

house of noodles n. [mid-19C] the House of Lords. [SE *house* + NOODLE n.[1] (2)]

house of office n. [17C–mid-19C] a privy (cf. BACKHOUSE n.; GINGERBREAD-OFFICE n.).

house of pain n. [1940s] (*US Black*) the dentist's.

house of profession n. [17C] a brothel (cf. ACCOMMODATION HOUSE n.). [SE *house*/HOUSE n.[1] (1) + SE *profession*]

house of resort n. [late 16C–early 17C] a brothel (cf. ACCOMMODATION HOUSE n.). [SE *house*/HOUSE n.[1] (1) + SE *resort*]

house of sale n. [late 16C–early 17C] a brothel (cf. ACCOMMODATION HOUSE n.). [HOUSE n.[1] (1) + SE *sale*]

house of state n. [17C] a brothel (cf. ACCOMMODATION HOUSE n.).

house of waste n. [late 18C–early 19C] a tavern. [the moral standpoint]

house of wax n. [2000s] (*Irish*) the lavatory (cf. ANGUS ARMANASCO n.; BACKHOUSE n.). [rhy. sl. = JACKS n.]

house party n. [20C+] (*US Black*) a party held in a private house, for which an admission fee (to cover food and drink) is paid.

house-piece n. *see* HOUSE-BIT n.

house-plant n. [1910s+] (*US*) an indolent person who does nothing but sit around.

house rat n. [1960s] (*US*) a child.

house-rent party n. (*also* **house-rent shake, …stomp, …strut**) [20C+] (*US Black*) a party held in a private house, for which an admission fee is paid.

house that Jack built n.[1] [late 19C–1930s] a prison (cf. BANDHOUSE n.). [the generic hangman *Jack Ketch*]

house that Jack built n.[2] [1920s+] (*Aus.*) the Government Savings Bank in Sydney, opened in 1928.

house time n. *see* HOUSE n.[1] (6).

house to let n.[1] [1930s] (*UK Und.*) a bet. [rhy. sl.]

house to let n.[2] *see* APARTMENT TO LET n.

house-trashing n. [1980s+] (*N.Z.*) a party held by tenants who are leaving a house or flat, in which the fixtures and fittings are deliberately destroyed.

house under the hill n. [late 19C+] the vagina. [the image of the vagina as being 'down there' and beneath the fig. *hill*, or pubic mound; note Aubrey Beardsley's title for his sole and unfinished erotic novel *Under the Hill* (1898)]

housewife *n.* [late 19C] the female genitals. [metonymy, but note poss. play on 18C *housewife*, a small (pocket-sized) case for needles, thread, scissors etc]

housewife's hour *n.* [1960s+] (*US gay*) the afternoon, esp. as used for masturbation since nothing else is happening.

house without chairs *n.* [1920s–40s] (*US Black*) a temporarily unfurnished apartment or house; usu. as used for parties.

housewives' choice *n.* [1950s+] a voice. [rhy. sl.; ult. the BBC radio programme]

housework *n.* [1900s–20s] (*US Und.*) burglary; thus *house-worker*, a burglar.

housey-housey *adj.* [20C+] lousy, i.e. unwell. [rhy. sl.]

hout *n.*[1] *see* HOOT n.[1].

hout *n.*[2] *see* HOUTKOP n.

houthern *n.* [20C+] (*Ulster*) a slovenly, untidy woman.

houtkop *n.* [1950s+] (*S.Afr.*) a blockhead, a fool, thus a general term of abuse for a Black person; often abbr. to *hout, houtie*. [Afk. *hout*, wood + *kop*, head]

how? *phr.* [19C] (*US*) used as a synon. for 'what?' when one fails to hear a statement properly.

how about my forty-five up your ass? *phr.* [1990s+] (*US Black teen*) a rejoinder to the threat HOW ABOUT MY NINE IN YOUR FACE? phr. [FORTY-FIVE n. + ASS n. (2)]

how about my nine in your face? *phr.* [1990s+] (*US Black teen*) a threat, demanding either obedience or silence. [NINE n. (2) + SE *face*]

how about that (then)? *phr.* (*also* **how's about that?**) [1930s+] an interrog. phr. calling for agreement that something is worthy of praise or approval.

how are the bots biting? *phr. see* BOT n.[1] (3).

how (are) they hanging? *phr.* (*also* **how are they coming? ...rolling?**) [1910s+] a joc. man-to-man greeting. ['they' are testicles; the popular answer is 'One in front, for speed'; *see also* HOW'S IT HANGING? phr.]

how (are) they hitting? *phr. see* HOW (ARE) YOU HITTING THEM? phr.

how are they stacking up? *phr.* [1900s–30s] (*US*) a greeting.

how are you! *excl.* [1910s+] (*Irish*) an expression of disbelief, a dismissive retort.

how are you blowing? *phr.* [1900s–20s] (*Irish*) a general term of informal greeting.

how (are) you bumping? *phr. see* BUMP v.[3] (2).

how are you diddling? *phr.* [1970s] a general term of informal greeting. [? DIDDLE v.[1]]

how are you going? *phr.* (*also* **how are you coming up?**) [1910s+] (*orig. and mainly Aus.*) a general phr. of greeting.

how (are) you hanging? *phr. see* HOW'S IT HANGING? phr.

how (are) you hitting them? *phr.* (*also* **how (are) they hitting?**) [late 19C+] (*US*) a phr. of greeting, how are you? [sporting imagery]

how are you off for soap? *phr.* [mid–late 19C; 1990s+] a general phr. of greeting, how are things? how are you doing?

how are you popping (up)? *phr.* [late 19C–1940s] (*Aus.*) a general phr. of greeting, how are you doing? how are you feeling?

how are your poor feet? *phr.* [mid–late 19C] a general interrog. aimed at a passing person.

how came you so *phr.* (*also* **Lord how came you so**) [late 18C–19C] drunk. [? a blasphemous ref. to a biblical quotation]

how come? *phr.* [mid–19C+] (*US*) why?

how-come-ye-so *phr.* (*also* **how-come-you-so**) 1 [late 18C+] slightly tipsy, mildly drunk. 2 [19C–1910s] (*US*) pregnant.

how-de-do *n. see* HOW-DO-YOU DO n.

how does that grab you? *phr.* [1960s+] what do you think of that? [a slightly aggressive implication, a challenge is assumed]

how does that hang? *phr.* [1980s+] (*US Black*) what do you think?

how-do-you do *n.* (*also* **how-de-do, howdy-do, how-d'ye-do**) 1 [19C] (*US*) a thrashing. 2 [mid-19C+] a problem, a difficulty, a fuss; usu. as *a fine/pretty how-do-you do*. 3 [1930s] a shoe. 4 [1930s] trousers. 5 [1930s] (*US*) ladies' underwear, pyjamas. [rhy. sl.; (2) = STEW n.[1]]

how do you like them apples? *phr.* (*also* **how do you like them onions? how do you like your eggs done?**) [1910s+] (*US*) an ironic, rhetorical demand, 'What do you think of that then and what are you going to do about it?' The implication is that whatever one thinks, one can do nothing.

how do you sell your string? *phr.* [mid-19C] a phr. used to disabuse someone who appears to be taking the speaker for a fool.

howdy-do *n. see* HOW-DO-YOU DO n.

howdy (doody)! *excl.* [late 19C+] (*US*) a general greeting. [SE *how do you do?* + the NBC-TV puppet *Howdy-Doody*, launched 27 December 1947]

how-d'ye do *n. see* HOW-DO-YOU DO n.

howdzacky *n. see* HOODLELACKY n.

how fare ye *phr.* [mid-19C] (*US*) drunk. [var. on HOW-COME-YE-SO phr. (1)]

how goes (it)? *phr.* [mid-19C+] a general phr. of greeting.

how goes the enemy? *phr. see* ENEMY n.[1].

how high is a Chinaman? *phr.* [1950s+] the answer to a statement or question which the speaker considers to be absurd or unanswerable. [pun on the supposed Chinese name *How Hi*]

how hops it *phr. see* HOP v.[1] (1).

how in (holy) hell? *phr. see* WHAT IN HELL? phr.

how is it (there)? *phr.* [1910s–40s] a phr. of greeting.

how is that for (a) high? *phr. see* HOW'S THAT FOR HIGH? phr.

howitzer *n.* (*US*) 1 [late 19C–1960s] a large pistol or revolver. 2 [2000s] a large female breast (cf. BAGS n.[1]). [SE *howitzer*, a light cannon]

howl *n.* 1 [late 19C+] (*US*) a noisy objection, a complaint. 2 [1910s] a miserable person. 3 [1930s+] a highly amusing story, situation, experience or person.

howl *v.* 1 [20C+] (*US*) to celebrate wildly. 2 [20C+] (*US*) to complain. 3 [1980s] (*US preppie*) to mock, to tease. [fig. use of SE; (3) the 'howls of derision' that accompany such teasing]

howler *n.*[1] 1 [late 19C] a boisterous lout. 2 [late 19C–1910s] a dandy, a fop, a fashionable dresser. 3 [late 19C–1930s] an expert. [his clothes and personality 'howl' for attention]

howler *n.*[2] [late 19C] a heavy fall, a bad accident; thus *come/go a howler*. [one 'howls' with pain]

howler *n.*[3] [late 19C+] a notable blunder (esp. in an examination), a gross error, a social solecism. [such errors 'howl out' for notice]

howler *n.*[4] [1950s+] (*US*) a siren.

howling *adj.* [mid-19C+] great, extreme, pronounced.

howling bags *n.* [mid-19C] 'trousers of an extensive pattern, or exaggerated fashionable cut...when the style has been very "loud"' (Hotten, 1860). [SE *howl* + BAGS n.[2]]

howling rags *adj.* [1910s] (*Aus.*) very drunk. [HOWLING adj. + ? clothes awry]

howling-stick *n.* [mid–late 19C] a flute. [SE *howl* + *stick*]

howling swell *n. see* HEAVY SWELL n.

howling thing *n.* [late 19C–1900s] (*US*) a particularly exciting individual. [HOWLING adj. + SE *thing*]

howl on *v.* [1990s+] (*Aus. Und.*) to complain about.

how low can you go? *phr.* [1990s+] (*US Black*) a general teasing taunt, i.e. how good a lover are you? how long can you last?

how many f's are there in 'go away'? *phr.* [1990s+] (*US teen*) a remark indicating that someone should leave. [a euph. for FUCK OFF! excl. (1)]

how much? *excl.* [mid-19C+] an excl. of incredulity, a demand for further detail or information, esp. when what has been offered seems unbelievable; it need have no ref. to price, but is delivered in response to what the listener considers to be a far-fetched statement.

how rudeness! *excl.* [1980s+] (*US campus*) how rude!

hows *n.* [20C+] (*drugs*) morphine (cf. AUNTIE EMMA n.). [? coded enquiry: 'How's you going to act? do you have any drugs?']

how's about that? *phr. see* HOW ABOUT THAT (THEN)? phr.

how's by you? *phr.* [1960s] (*US*) a greeting.

how's happening? *phr. see* HOW'S IT GOING? phr.

how's high? *phr.* [late 19C] (*US*) how are you?

how's it bouncing? *phr.* [1990s+] (*US*) a general phr. of greeting.

how's it going? *phr.* (*also* **how's happening? how's it? how's she going?**) [20C+] a general phr. of greeting.

how's it hanging? *phr.* (*also* **how (are) you hanging? what's hanging?**) [1970s+] a man-to-man greeting, what are you up to? how are you? ['it' being the penis; note earlier HOW (ARE) THEY HANGING? phr.]

how's it shaking? *phr. see* WHAT'S SHAKING? phr. (1).

how's she cutting? *phr.* [1970s+] (*Irish*) a general phr. of greeting. ['she' being some form of agricultural implement]

how's she going? *phr. see* HOW'S IT GOING? phr.

how's that for high? *phr.* (*also* **how is that for (a) high?**) [19C+] (*US*) a phr. synon. with *what do you think of that?*

how's the body? *phr.* [1940s–50s] (*Irish*) how are you?

how's the boy? *phr.* (*also* **how's the girl?**) [1910s–30s] a phr. of greeting, how are you?

how's the way? *phr.* [20C+] (*N.Z.*) a phr. of greeting.

how's things? *phr.* [late 19C+] how are you?

how's tricks? *phr.* [20C+] a phr. of greeting.

how's-yer-father *n.*[1] (*also* **how's-your-father**) **1** [20C+] sexual intercourse; often as *bit of how's-yer-father*. **2** [20C+] used of anything for which one either does not know the name or prefers not to mention. **3** [20C+] nonsense, rubbish. **4** [20C+] occas. used as a general euph., *swear like how's yer father*, i.e. swear 'like fuck'. **5** [1990s+] petty criminality. **6** [1990s+] a condom. [coined in a music-hall sketch performed by the comedian Harry Tate (1872–1940) and popularized by the services during WW1]

how's-yer-father *n.*[2] [20C+] a state of excitement. [rhy. sl. = SE *lather*]

how's your ass? *phr.* [1950s+] (*US*) a general phr. of greeting. [ASS n. (2)]

how's your bird? *phr. see* BIRD n.[8] (1).

how's your bod? *phr.* [1970s+] (*orig. US*) how are you (feeling)? [BOD n. (3)]

how's your box? *phr.* [1930s] (*US Black*) a general phr. of greeting.

how's your (dirty) rotten form? *phr.* [1950s+] (*Aus.*) a phr. used to someone who has just proved themselves successful, had a piece of luck etc.

how's-your-father *n. see* HOW'S-YER-FATHER n.[1].

how's your hammer hanging? *phr.* [1930s+] (*US*) a phr. used to inquire about someone's state of well being; the typically facetious answer being: 'A little to the left and in the dirt.' [HAMMER n.[1] (1)]

how the devil! *excl. see* WHAT THE DEVIL! excl.

how they...? *see under* HOW (ARE) THEY...?

how you...? *see under* HOW (ARE) YOU...?

howzit? *excl.* [1930s+] hello, how are you?; thus *howzit for/with something?* how about something? i.e. may I have something? shall we do something? [HOW IS IT (THERE)? phr.]

hoxter *n.* [19C] an inside pocket. [SE *oxter*, the armpit]

hoy *n.* [1910s] (*US*) in lit. and fig. uses, rubbish, nonsense. [HOOEY n. (1)]

hoy *v.*[1] (*Aus.*) **1** [1920s+] to drag, to take. **2** [1930s+] to get rid of, to discard. [dial. *hoy*, to throw, to heave/SE *haul*]

hoy *v.*[2] [1950s+] (*Aus.*) to call. [excl. *hoy!*]

hoys *n. see* HOIST n.[1] (1).

hoyster *n. see* HOISTER n.[1] (1).

hozzy *n.* [1990s+] a hospital. [abbr.]

h.p. *n.* [1990s+] (*US Black teen*) the Hunter's Point area of San Francisco. [abbr.]

h.q. *n.* [1980s+] (*US drugs*) ⅛oz (4g) of cannabis. [abbr. *half-quarter*]

h.r.n. *n.* [1950s+] (*drugs*) heroin. [abbr.]

h.t. *n.*[1] [1940s] (*US Black campus*) a *h*eart *t*hrob. [abbr.]

h.t. *n.*[2] *see* HEAD TRIP n.

h town *n.* **1** [1970s+] (*US*) any town whose name begins with H. **2** [2000s] (*US Black*) Harlem, New York City.

hua *n. see* HOOER n.

Hub, the *n.* [mid-19C+] Boston; thus *Hubite*, a Bostonian. [self-styled as the 'hub of the solar system/universe']

hub *n. see* HUBBY n.

hubba *n.*[1] [1980s+] (*US campus*) an attractive man. [HUBBA HUBBA! excl.]

hubba *n.*[2] [1980s+] (*drugs*) crack cocaine (cf. BASE n.). [fig. use of HUBBA HUBBA! excl. to denote its energizing effect]

hubbaboo *n. see* HULLABALLOO n.

hubba-hubba *n.* **1** [1940s] (*US*) nonsense. **2** [1940s+] a lively, energetic spirit.

hubba hubba! *excl.* [1940s+] (*US teen*) a term of approval, esp. when directed at a passing girl. [SE *hubba! hubba!*, a college cheer; according to posting on *American Dialect Society-List* (Internet): 'At one of the WWII training bases in the U.S. there was a sergeant who was known for shouting "A HUB A HUB A HUB" and who was thereby nicknamed Sergeant Hubba Hubba. One day two soldiers were in the town near the base (the author of the account and a friend). They became temporarily separated, when the author of the account spotted two beautiful, charming women walking in his direction. The author wanted to call his friend immediately to take a look at the two women, but he did not want to do so in an obvious and socially gauche manner. So he shouted out something that his friend would understand but would mean nothing to the civilians: HUBBA HUBBA. Later they told the story of this incident about the beautiful women to their buddies back at the base. And HUBBA HUBBA became a local expression on the base in reference to seeing a beautiful woman. A few months later Bob Hope was scheduled to perform at the base, and his advance men (as they always did) visited the base beforehand to pick up anything of local interest that could be used by Bob Hope in his act. They picked up the story about HUBBA HUBBA and gave it to Hope, who did use the expression in his act. That was the seal of approval']

hubbie *n. see* HUBBY n.

hubble *n.* [20C+] (*Ulster*) fuss and bother. [? abbr. HUBBLE-BUBBLE n.]

hubble-bubble *n.* [mid-18C–1900s] confusion, chaos; thus *hubble-bubble fellow*, a fool. [SE *hubble-bubble*, the confused noise emanating from a person talking so fast as to be incomprehensible; rhy. sl. = SE *trouble*]

hubble de shuff *adv.* [late 18C–19C] confusedly, chaotically. [milit. jargon *fire hubble de shuff*, fire quickly and irregularly. ? the orig. root of both is 16C northern dial. *hubbleshow*, a hubbub, a disturbance]

hubbly-bubbly *n.* [1960s+] a water pipe, used for smoking cannabis. [the noise of the bubbling liquid]

hubby *n.* (*also* **hub, hubbie**) **1** [late 17C+] a husband. **2** [1980s] (*US campus*) (*also* **husband**) a steady boyfriend. [abbr./corruption of SE]

hubcap biter *n.* [1980s] (*Aus.*) a woman who chooses the men she goes after on the basis of their cars.

Hubite *n. see* HUB, THE n.

hubshi *n.* [mid-19C+] (*Anglo-Ind.*) anyone or anything with tight kinky hair, esp. a Black person, but also used of animals. [Arab. *habashi*, an Abyssinian, an Ethiopian, a Black person in general]

huck *n.* **1** [late 19C–1910s] (*US*) a person. **2** [1920s+] a Black person. [? proper name *Huckleberry Finn*, hero of Mark Twain's novel *The Adventures of Huckleberry Finn* (1884)]

huckle *n.* [20C+] (*US*) an effeminate male homosexual. [? dial. *huckle*, to bend the body; he 'bends over' for penetration]

huckle *v.*[1] [late 17C–18C] to chatter, to gossip. [? dial. *huckle*, to bend the body, as one might during intimate conversation]

huckle *v.*[2] [1950s+] to be seized or arrested. [? dial. *huckle*, to stoop, to bend the body]

huckle and buff *n. see* HUCKLE-MY-BUFF *n.*

huckleberry *n.*[1] (*US*) **1** [mid-19C+] a fellow, a boy. **2** [late 19C+] the person who suits one's wishes. **3** [late 19C+] a person of little importance. **4** [1920s+] a nickname for a Black person. [SE *huckleberry*, a sweetheart. (2) and (3) influenced by proper name *Huckleberry Finn*, hero of Mark Twain's novel of 1885]

huckleberry *n.*[2] [mid-19C+] (*US*) a small amount, degree or extent.

huckleberry *n.*[3] [2000s] (*US drugs*) a very compact marijuana bud, 5cm (2in) or less in length (cf. AFRICAN BUSH *n.*). [resemblance to the fruit]

huckleberry, the *n.* [late 19C+] (*US*) bad treatment.

Huckleberry Finn *n.* [20C+] (*Aus.*) gin. [rhy. sl.; ult. the novel *The Adventures of Huckleberry Finn* (1884) by Mark Twain]

huckleberry hound *n.* [1960s+] (*Aus. prison*) a punishment cell; solitary confinement. [rhy. sl. = pound]

huckle-my-buff *n.* (*also* **huckle and buff, huckle-my-butt, huckle-my-muff**) **1** [mid-18C–early 19C] a mixture of gin and ale. **2** [late 18C–early 19C] a drink made by heating beer, eggs and brandy together. **3** [20C+] (*US*) bourbon and milk poured over crushed ice, recommended as a hangover cure. [dial. *huckle*, to jog along, thus lit. 'jog my skin/buttocks']

huddle *v.* [18C–19C] to have sexual intercourse. [dial. *huddle*, to hug]

hue *v.* (*UK Und.*) **1** [late 17C–mid-19C] to beat, to whip. **2** [19C] to hit with a cudgel. [SE *hue*, colour (of the flesh after a beating), *hue*, to assail, to drive, or *hew*, to cut with blows]

huer *n. see* HOOER *n.*

huey *n.*[1] (*also* **hughey**) [mid–late 19C] (*UK tramp*) a town or village. [? SE *hue*, to chase with shouts, or *hue and cry*; since such fates might befall a hapless tramp]

huey *n.*[2] [mid-19C–1920s] (*UK/US Und.*) a newspaper that lists stolen articles; spec. the National Police Gazette (NY). [SE *hue and cry*]

huey *n.*[3] *see* HUGHIE *n.*

huff *n.*[1] [mid-16C–mid-19C] **1** a blusterer, a bully. **2** a state of blustering. [HUFF *v.*[1]]

huff *n.*[2] **1** [late 16C+] a bad temper; thus *take the huff*, to lose one's temper, to take offence. **2** [mid-19C] a dodge or trick. [SE *huff*, to puff, to blow up]

huff *n.*[3] *see* HOUGH *n.*

huff *n.*[4] *see* HUFFCAP *n.*

huff *v.*[1] **1** [late 16C–early 19C] to swagger. **2** [late 17C–early 19C] to scold, to reprove, to bully. **3** [18C+] to annoy, to offend. [SE *huff*, to blow]

huff *v.*[2] [early 19C] to throw one's arms over a victim's shoulders and then take the money from his pockets; the assault requires 2 partners, one to grab and one to rifle the clothes. [SE *huff*, to bully, to hector; note 1910s–20s milit. sl. *huff*, to kill]

huff *v.*[3] [1960s+] (*drugs*) to sniff solvents or similar volatile substances; thus *huffing*, inhaling. [? the opposite of SE *huff*, to blow]

huff! *excl.* [late 15C–16C] 'an exclamation attributed to a swaggerer or bully, esp. when introduced on the stage' (OED). [imitative of a blast of air through some form of orifice]

huffa! *excl.* [early 16C–early 17C] a general excl.

huff and ding *v.* [late 17C–early 18C] to swagger and boast. [HUFF *v.*[1] + DING *v.*[1]]

huffcap *n.* (*also* **huff**) **1** [late 16C–19C] a form of strong ale. **2** [early 17C–early 18C] a swaggerer, a blusterer. [(2) HUFF *v.*[1] (1) + SE *cap*, i.e. that which raises the cap. The bully set his cap at a swaggering angle]

huffer *n.*[1] [mid-17C–18C] a bully, a braggart, a boaster. [HUFF *v.*[1]]

huffer *n.*[2] [1960s+] (*drugs*) an inhalant abuser. [HUFF *v.*[3]]

huffily *adv. see* HUFFY *adj.*

huffing *n. see* HUFF *v.*[3]

huff it *v. see* HOOF *v.*

huffle *v.* [late 17C–18C] to fellate; to frottage with the armpit (cf. BLOW *v.*[2]). [SE *huff*, to blow; 'a piece of bestiality too filthy for explanation' (Grose 1785)]

huff-snuff *n.* [late 16C–mid-18C] a bully, a braggart. [his swaggering, threatening presence; Urquhart in his translation of Rabelais translates Fr. *Lifrelofres*, synon. used for Germans or Swiss; the editor adds 'Here it is a buffooning term for an impertinent philosopher']

huffy *adj.* [late 17C+] angry, bad-tempered; thus *adv. huffily*. [HUFF *n.*[2] (1)]

hufty-tufty *n.* (*also* **huftie-tuftie, hufty**) [17C] a swaggering, boastful individual. [HUFTY-TUFTY *adj.*]

hufty-tufty *adj.* [late 16C–17C] swaggering, boastful. [HUFF *v.*[1] (1) + redup.]

hug, the *n.* [mid-19C] (*UK Und.*) the act of garrotting; thus *hugging*, garrotting; *put on the hug*, to garrotte. [SE *hug*, to grasp tightly]

hugag *n. see* HEWGAG *n.*

hug-booby *n.* [late 17C–18C] a pej. term for a married man. [SE *hug* + BOOBY *n.*[1]]

hug brown bess *v. see* MARRY BROWN BESS *v.*

hug centre *n.* [late 19C–1900s] (*orig. US*) anywhere popular for public love-making, e.g. Hyde Park. [love-making in the 19C rather than 20C+ sense]

hug drug *n.* [1980s+] (*drugs*) MDMA (cf. ECSTASY *n.*). [its effects; the drug makes users want to touch everyone around them]

huge *adj.* [mid-19C; 1950s+] (*US*) wonderful, great, impressive. [note RMC Duntroon (Aus.) *huge!* wonderful! marvellous! fantastic!]

hugging *n. see* HUG, THE *n.*

huggle-my-buff *n.* [mid-18C] a form of mixed, hot drink.

huggy-bear *n.* [1960s+] (*US*) a cuddly person.

hughey *n. see* HUEY *n.*[1]

hughie *n.* (*also* **huey**) [1950s+] (*US/Aus.*) the act of vomiting. [echoic]

hugh prowler *n.* [16C] a generic nickname for a small-time thief. [generic use of proper name *Hugh* + SE *prowler*]

hugmatee *n.* [late 17C–early 18C] a type of ale. [? SE *hug me t'ye*, hug me to you]

hug-me-tight *n.* [mid-19C+] (*Ulster*) **1** a woollen vest. **2** a shawl that can be fastened across the body.

hugs and kisses *n.* [20C+] one's wife. [rhy. sl. = MISSIS *n.*]

hugsome *adj.* [late 19C+] sexually attractive. [SE *hug* + sfx *-some*]

hug the hog *v.* [1990s+] to masturbate (cf. BEAT ONE'S HOG *v.*). [SE *hug* + HOG *n.*[6]]

hug the porcelain god(ess)/the throne *v. see* KISS THE PORCELAIN GOD(DESS) *v.*

hula raider *n.* [1990s+] a male homosexual (cf. ANAL ASTRONAUT *n.*). [abbr. SE *hula-hoop* + *raider*; thus cf. HOOP STRETCHER *n.*]

hulk *n.* **1** [early 19C–1920s] (*US*) the body, the torso. **2** [1940s+] (*US*) a large, muscular man. [SE *hulk*, a big, unwieldy person; popularized by the 1962 comic-book character, the *Incredible Hulk*, created by Stan Lee and Jack Kirby]

hulk *v.* [mid-19C] to hang about in the hope of an invitation.

hulked *adj.* [1980s+] (*US campus*) angry, furious. [the *Incredible Hulk* would turn into his superhero form only when emotionally aroused; note HULK *n.*]

hulking *adj.* (*also* **hulky**) [late 17C+] unwieldy, heavy, lumpish. [SE *hulk*, a big, unwieldy person]

hull *n.* [1910s–30s] (*US*) a saddle. [SE *hull*, that which encases, e.g. a peapod]

hullaballoo *n.* (*also* **halliballoo, holla-balloo, hubbaboo**) [mid-18C–19C] uproar, confusion, noisy chaos. [SE in 20C+; redup. *halloo-baloo*. Ware suggests an origin in Fr. *hurluberlu* and *OED* notes, but rejects, another Fr. use, the hunting cry *bas le loup!* bring down the wolf!]

hull-cheese *n.* [17C] malt liquor and water; thus *eat hull-cheese*, to become drunk. [orig. Yorks. dial. *hull-cheese*, 'the strong ale of Hull' (*EDD*)]

hullo! *excl. see* HELLO! *excl.*[2].

hully *n.* [1970s+] (*US Black*) an especially fat person.

hully-gully *n.* [1960s+] (*W.I.*) **1** a young ruffian. **2** a playboy. [SE *hully-gully*, a form of dance, based on the *frug*; thus a fan of the dance]

hulverhead *n.* [17C–early 19C] a fool. [Norfolk dial. *hulver*, holly; the wood of a holly bush is notably hard]

hulver-headed *adj.* [17C–early 19C] stupid (cf. AIRHEADED *adj.*). [HULVERHEAD *n.*]

hum *n.*[1] [17C–18C] strong beer. [abbr. HUMMING ALE *n.*]

hum *n.*[2] [early 18C+] speed, energy, enthusiasm. [HUM *v.*[1]]

hum *n.*[3] **1** [mid-18C–19C] nonsense, a trick, a hoax; a whispered lie. **2** [mid-19C] (*UK Und.*) a liar. **3** [late 19C] something unpleasant. **4** [1910s–30s] (*Aus.*) a cadger, a scrounger; thus *on the hum*, begging, cadging. [abbr. SE *humbug*; (2) also HUM-BOX *n.*]

hum *n.*[4] [late 18C–mid-19C] a member of a church congregation (cf. HUMS *n.*). [? their mumbling or 'humming' of prayers, hymns or responses]

hum *n.*[5] [late 19C+] an unpleasant smell. [HUM *v.*[3]; note ballad 'The Fart' in D'Urfey, *Pills to Purge Melancholy* (1719–20) which has the chorus 'With a hum, hum, hum, hum']

hum *n.*[6] [1940s+] (*US*) a euph. for *hell*.

hum *n.*[7] [1960s+] (*US*) fellatio (cf. BLOW *v.*[2]). [HUM *v.*[5]]

hum *n.*[8] [1970s+] (*US drugs*) a mild intoxication from drug use.

hum *v.*[1] [early 18C+] to be active, to be getting about one's business energetically, to go fast. [HUMMER *n.*[2] (1)]

hum *v.*[2] **1** [mid-18C–mid-19C] to trick, to hoax, to humbug; thus *humming*, teasing, hoaxing, fooling. **2** [late 19C+] (*Aus.*) to scrounge, to borrow with no intention of giving back. [HUM *n.*[3]]

hum *v.*[3] [late 19C+] to smell disgusting; lit. and fig. ['the humming of fermentation in an active manure heap' (Ware)]

hum *v.*[4] [1960s] (*US Und.*) to arrest on false charges. [HUMMER *n.*[6]]

hum *v.*[5] [1960s+] to give fellatio (cf. BLOW *v.*[2]). [abbr. HUMMER *n.*[9]]

hum and haw *v. see* HEM-HAW *v.*

humangous *adj. see* HUMONGOUS *adj.*

humble *n.* **1** [1940s+] (*US Und.*) an arrest on false or petty charges. **2** [1950s+] (*US Black*) (*also* **humbolt**) a self-defeating act; any situation that puts one at a disadvantage. [var. on HUMMER *n.*[6]]

humble as a dead nigger *phr.* [mid–late 19C] (*US*) totally subservient, utterly cowed.

hum-box *n.* [early 18C–mid-19C] a pulpit. [the preacher's droning tones]

hum-box patterer *n.* [mid-19C] a preacher. [HUM-BOX *n.* + ironic use of PATTERER *n.* (2)]

humbug *n.*[1] (*also* **hombug**) **1** [mid-18C+] a trick, a hoax, an imposture. **2** [early 19C+] nonsense; esp. moralizing hypocrisy. **3** [early 19C+] the person who employs such ploys, a hypocrite. [ety. unknown. 'The facts as to its origin appear to have been lost, even before the word became common enough to excite attention' (*OED*). Hotten (1859) traces the first use back to *c*.1735, finding it in Ferdinando Killigrew's *The Universal Jester* (the *OED* dates this edn to 1754), where it is cited in list of 'merry conceits, facetious drolleries, &c., clenchers, closers, closures, bon-mots and humbugs'. He also notes that the mid-18C radical Orator Henley was sometimes nicknamed 'Orator Humbug'. As to ety.,

he suggests either *hum* or the German town of Hamburg 'from which town so many false bulletins and reports came during the war in the last century'. After 1800 its use spread 'in periodical literature, and in novels not written by squeamish or over-precise authors'. However, note HUMMER *n.*[1], an obvious lie, is earlier]

humbug *n.*[2] **1** [mid-19C+] (*US, later use US Black*) anything worrying, complicated, unpleasant, offensive, troublesome; any misunderstanding, esp. if trivial. **2** [1960s+] (*US Black*) a fight. **3** [1970s] (*US Black*) a gang. [fig. uses of HUMBUG *n.*[1]]

humbug *n.*[3] [1970s+] (*US Und.*) a false arrest on trumped-up charges. [var. on HUMMER *n.*[6]]

humbug *v.*[1] **1** [mid-18C+] to cheat, to delude, to deceive; thus *humbuggery*, cheating, deception. **2** [mid-19C] to waste time talking. [HUMBUG *n.*[1]]

humbug *v.*[2] [1960s+] (*US Black*) to fight, to act tough; thus *humbugger*, a thug, a fighter; *humbugging*, fighting, brawling. [HUMBUG *n.*[2] (2)]

humbug! *excl.* [early 19C+] nonsense! rubbish! [HUMBUG *n.*[1] (2)]

humbug about *v.* [19C] to play the fool (cf. ACT THE ANGORA *v.*). [HUMBUG *v.*[1]]

humbugger *n.* [mid-18C–19C] **1** a cheat. **2** a hoaxer. **3** one who 'plays about' all the time. [HUMBUG *v.*[1]]

humbugging *adj.* (*also* **humbuggery**) [mid-18C+] hoaxing, swindling, deceiving. [HUMBUG *v.*[1] + sfx *-ing*]

humbug into *v.* [19C+] to persuade into doing something. [HUMBUG *v.*[1] (1)]

humbug of *v.* [mid-18C–mid-19C] to cheat out of. [HUMBUG *v.*[1] (1)]

hum cap *n.* [late 17C–19C] very old, very strong beer.

humdinger *n.* [20C+] (*orig. US*) a remarkable and excellent object, event or person. [? HUMMER *n.*[2] (2) + DINGER *n.*[3]; note the earliest (print) use includes a hyphen, i.e. *hum-dinger*]

humdinging *adj.* [20C+] extraordinary, excellent, remarkable. [HUMDINGER *n.*]

humdrum *n.* **1** [17C–early 19C] a wife, a husband. **2** [18C–19C] a parson. [SE *humdrum*, a dull, monotonous person; ult. SE *hum*, to murmur on]

humdudgeon *n.* (*also* **humdurgeon**) [late 18C–mid-19C] any imaginary illness, low spirits; thus *humdurgeoned*, annoyed. [? HUMBUG *n.*[1] (1) + SE *dudgeon*, ill humour]

humgumptious *adj.* **1** [early–mid-19C] artful, cunning, knowing. **2** [1910s] (*US*) fine, grand, pretentious. [fanciful formation]

hum job *n.* [1960s+] (*US*) an act of fellatio which is intensified by the fellator humming as he/she sucks (cf. BLOW *v.*[2]; HUMMER *n.*[9]). [HUM *v.*[5] + JOB *n.*[4]]

Hummer *n.* [1990s+] (*US*) a Humvee military vehicle, also produced for civilian use.

hummer *n.*[1] [late 17C–early 19C] an obvious lie. [HUMMING *adj.* (2)]

hummer *n.*[2] **1** [late 17C+] a very energetic or lively person, a powerful lively thing. **2** [late 19C+] something or someone exceptional. [? the speed makes it hum; (2) f. (1)]

hummer *n.*[3] [mid-18C–early 19C] a cheat, an imposter. [HUMBUG *n.*[1] (1)]

hummer *n.*[4] [1900s] one who smells. [HUM *v.*[3]]

hummer *n.*[5] **1** [1910s–40s] (*Aus.*) a scrounger. **2** [1960s–70s] (*US campus*) a stupid or inconsequential person. [HUM *v.*[2] (2)]

hummer *n.*[6] [1930s+] (*US Und.*) an arrest on false or petty charges. [HUMMER *n.*[1]]

hummer *n.*[7] [1950s–70s] (*US Black*) something deceptive, a minor or insignificant mistake. [HUMBUG *n.*[2] (1)]

hummer *n.*[8] [1960s+] (*US*) a heavy drinking session; thus HAVE A HUMMER GOING *v.* [? link to HUM *n.*[1] or HUMDINGER *n.*]

hummer *n.*[9] [1970s+] (*US*) fellatio, esp. when the testicles are held in the mouth and the woman hums; thus in fig. use (cf. BLOW *v.*[2]; HUM JOB *n.*).

humming *n. see* HUM *v.*[2] (1).

humming *adj.* **1** [mid-17C–mid-19C] of liquor, strong, frothing; thus HUMMING ALE n. **2** [mid-17C+] notably large or active, energetic, intense. [? SE *hum*; (1) causes a humming in the drinker's head; (2) is so big it virtually hums]

humming *adv.* [18C] exceedingly, very.

humming ale *n.* (*also* **humming beer, ...bub, ...liquor, ...punch, ...stuff, ...tipple**) [mid-17C–mid-19C] strong beer. [HUMMING adj. (1) + SE *ale/beer/*BUB n.[1]/SE *liquor/*STUFF n.[3] (1)/TIPPLE n. (1)]

humming bird *n.* [late 19C–1930s] [US prison] **1** a type of torture using electricity. **2** the electric chair. [electricity hums]

humming October *n.* [early 18C–19C] very strong ale, made from the new season's hops. [HUMMING adj. (1) + SE *October*]

humming punch/stuff/tipple *n. see* HUMMING ALE n.

hummum *n.* [late 17C–early 19C] a brothel. [Arabic *hammamm*, a hot or Turkish bath. The original *Hummum* was set up in Covent Garden in 1631; it later became a hotel]

humongous *adj.* (*also* **humangous, humongoid, humungo, humungous**) [1960s+] (*orig. US*) enormous, outsized, huge. [suggested by SE *huge/monstrous/tremendous*]

Hump, the *n.* [1920s–30s] (*US tramp*) the Rockies; thus *go over the hump*, to cross the Rockies on one's trek from East Coast to West.

hump *n.*[1] [late 19C+] a fit of bad-humour, a sulk; thus GET THE HUMP *v.*; GIVE SOMEONE THE HUMP *v.* [abbr. SE phr. *hump the back*, to sulk]

hump *n.*[2] [20C+] (*US*) a euph. for DAMN n., e.g. *I don't give a hump*.

hump *n.*[3] [1910s+] (*US Und.*) the midpoint of one's prison sentence. [for ety. *see* HUMP DAY n.]

hump *n.*[4] **1** [1910s+] (*orig. US*) an act of sexual intercourse; thus *on the hump*, engaging in sexual intercourse; *throw someone a hump*, to have sexual intercourse. **2** [1920s+] (*orig. US*) a person considered purely as a sexual object, usu. of a woman. **3** [1940s–50s] (*US prison*) a (passive) male homosexual. [HUMP *v.*[1]]

hump *n.*[5] **1** [1910s+] (*Aus.*) a camel. **2** [1920s+] (*US*) a Camel (brand) cigarette. [the animal's defining aspect]

hump *n.*[6] [1950s+] **1** a contemptible person, esp. a man. **2** a general term for a person, basically a peasant or manual worker. [? HUMP *v.*[2]]

hump *n.*[7] *see* HUMP DAY n.

hump *v.*[1] [mid-17C+] to have sexual intercourse. [the *hump* in the man's back, when in the 'missionary position'. The term starts in the UK, dies out by the early 19C, then to the US early 20C, and back to the UK mid-20C+]

hump *v.*[2] **1** [mid-19C–1920s] (*US*) to take pride in oneself, to fancy oneself. **2** [mid-19C+] (*US*) to exert oneself, to work hard; as imper. *hump yourself!* get on with it! **3** [mid-19C+] (*US*) to travel fast, of people or objects. **4** [mid-19C+] (*US/Aus.*) to carry heavy objects; esp. in milit. use, patrolling with a heavy pack, weapon, supplies etc. **5** [late 19C+] (*orig. Aus.*) to tramp, to trudge, to go on foot; also in fig. use. [lit. + fig. uses of SE *hump*, to make a hump in one's back, f. effort etc]

hump *v.*[3] **1** [mid–late 19C] to botch, to spoil. **2** [late 19C] (*US*) to beat up. **3** [20C+] (*US*) to act lazily, to loaf around, to be idle. **4** [1940s+] used as an expletive, like FUCK *v.*[3]. **5** [1950s+] to make someone else suffer, to exploit, to harm. **6** [1960s+] to suffer. [fig. uses of HUMP *v.*[1] on the model of FUCK *v.*[2]]

hump *v.*[4] [20C+] to take offence. [HUMP n.[1]]

hump day *n.* (*also* **hump, hump night**) [1950s+] (*US*) Wednesday, the middle of the week. [SE *hump*, the critical point of an undertaking. Once Wednesday has passed one is coasting 'downhill' towards the weekend]

hump 'em and dump 'em *phr.* [1980s+] a popular male catchphrase suggesting that seduction and then abandonment are the best ways of relating to women. [HUMP *v.*[1] + DUMP *v.*[1] (5)]

humper *n.*[1] [early 19C; 1970s+] a seducer. [HUMP *v.*[1]]

humper *n.*[2] **1** [1900s] (*Aus.*) a vagrant. **2** [1960s+] a carrier of heavy objects, esp. in rock music use to describe those who lift a band's equipment. **3** [1970s+] (*US*) an irritating thing. **4** [1970s+] (*US*) a hard-working person. [HUMP *v.*[2]]

hump house *n.* [1920s] (*US*) a brothel (cf. ACCOMMODATION HOUSE n.). [HUMP *v.*[1] + HOUSE n.[1] (1)]

humping *n.* [1950s+] sexual intercourse. [HUMP *v.*[1]]

humping *adj.* **1** [1940s+] (*US*) a general intensifier, positive or negative according to context. **2** [1980s+] (*US Black*) very attractive. [HUMP *v.*[1]; thus a euph. for FUCKING adj.]

hump it *v.* **1** [20C+] to leave. **2** [1920s] to die. [HUMP *v.*[2]]

hump-me pumps *n. see* FUCK-ME SHOES n.

hump night *n. see* HUMP DAY n.

hump-nutty *adj.* [1920s] (*US*) obsessed with sex. [HUMP *v.*[1] + NUTTY adj.[2] (1)]

hump one's drum *v.* (*also* **hump one's bluey, ...swag**) [late 19C+] (*Aus./N.Z.*) to walk from place to place carrying a pack on one's back, to be a tramp. [HUMP *v.*[2] + DRUM n.[4]/BLUEY n.[2] (1)/SWAG n.[1] (9)]

hump one's hose *v.* [20C+] to masturbate. [HUMP *v.*[1] + HOSE n.[1] (1)]

humps and grumps *n.* [mid-18C] slights and snubs. [dial. but note GRUMP n.]

humpsome *adj. see* HUMPY adj.[2] (2).

hump the horn *v.* [20C+] to masturbate. [HUMP *v.*[1] + HORN n.[2] (1)]

humpty *n.*[1] (*also* **humpty-bump, humpty-dumpty, humpty-hump**) [1980s+] sexual intercourse; thus *do the humpty-hump*, to have sexual intercourse. [HUMP *v.*[1]]

humpty *n.*[2] *see* HUMPTY-DUMPTY n.[2] (2).

humpty *adj.*[1] [1980s+] sexually excited. [HUMPTY n.[1]]

humpty *adj.*[2] [1990s+] irritated, tetchy. [HUMP n.[1]]

humpty *adj.*[3] *see* HUMPTY-DUMPTY adj.

humpty-bump *n. see* HUMPTY n.[1].

humpty-doo *adj. see* UMPTY-DOO adj.

humpty-dumpty *n.*[1] [late 17C–mid-19C] (*also* **humty dumty**) a hot drink made of ale and brandy boiled together. [redup.; the 2 liquors are 'humped together']

humpty-dumpty *n.*[2] **1** [late 18C–19C] a short, squat person. **2** [1920s+] (*US*) (*also* **humpty**) an outright failure, an incompetent person, esp. in sport. [abbr. the nursery-rhyme character *Humpty-Dumpty*, who despite his posturing 'fell off a wall']

humpty-dumpty *n.*[3] *see* HUMPTY n.[1].

humpty-dumpty *adj.* (*also* **humpty**) **1** [mid-19C] of a person, short and thick. **2** [late 19C+] (*US*) generally down on one's luck, tiresome, incompetent, foolish, ridiculous, ill. [HUMPTY-DUMPTY n.[2]]

humpty-hump *n. see* HUMPTY n.[1].

humpy *n.*[1] **1** [mid-18C+] a hunchback; also used as a derog. name. **2** [1930s–40s] (*Aus.*) a camel. [their defining physical characteristic]

humpy *n.*[2] **1** [1920s] a sexually attractive woman. **2** [1970s+] (*US gay*) a good-looking man. [HUMP *v.*[1]]

humpy *adj.*[1] [late 19C+] (*US*) hunchbacked. [HUMPY n.[1] (1)]

humpy *adj.*[2] **1** [late 19C+] depressing. **2** [1900s–10s] (*also* **humpsome**) depressed, miserable. [HUMP n.[1]]

humpy *adj.*[3] [1970s+] (*US gay*) good-looking, sexually attractive; often as *humpy number*. [HUMP *v.*[1]]

hump yourself! *phr. see* HUMP *v.*[2] (2).

humpy-pumpy *n. see* RUMPY-PUMPY n.

hums *n.* [late 18C–mid-19C] **1** a parson. **2** a church congregation (cf. HUM n.[4]). [(1) his droning sermons]

humty-dumty *n. see* HUMPTY-DUMPTY n.[1].

humungo/humungous *adj. see* HUMONGOUS adj.

Hun *n.* **1** [late 19C+] a derog. term for a German, the German army. **2** [1960s] a Hell's Angel. **3** [1990s+] (*Scot.*) a Roman Catholic. **4** [1990s+] (*Scot.*) Glasgow Celtic FC. [Ger. *Hunnen*, one of an Asiatic race of warlike nomads, who invaded Europe *c*.375, and under their leader Attila (*c*.406–453), overran much of Europe *c*.445. The original Huns were the Chinese *Hiong-nu* or *Han*. The modern use originated during WW1 and stemmed directly from the speech made by Kaiser Wilhelm II to German troops setting sail for China on 27 July 1900: 'No quarter will be given, no prisoners will be taken. Let all who fall into your hands be at your mercy. Just as the Huns a thousand years ago ... gained a reputation in virtue of which they still live in historical tradition, so may the name of Germany become known in ... China that no Chinaman will ever again even dare to look askance at a German']

Hun *adj.* [1910s+] German. [HUN n.¹ (1)]

hun n.¹ [late 19C] an attractive, wonderful thing or person. [abbr. HONEY n.¹]

hun n.² [late 19C+] a *hundred*, \$100. [abbr.]

hunch *n.* [mid-19C+] (*US*) a hint, a suggestion, a premonition, a guess; also as v., to point out. [20C+ use effectively SE]

hunch *v.* [1940s–50s] (*US*) to betray, to double-cross.

hunch up *v.* [1900s] to work things out, to think. [HUNCH n.]

hunchy *n.* [1910s–30s] (*Aus.*) a camel. [its hump]

hundred n.¹ [1990s+] (*Aus. drugs*) A\$100 of heroin.

hundred-pounder *n.* [1980s] (*US drugs*) a 100mg tablet of Demerol.

hundred to eight *n.* [1990s+] a plate. [rhy. sl.]

hundred to thirty *adj.* [1970s+] dirty. [rhy. sl.]

hung *adj.*¹ **1** [mid-17C; 1930s+] having a large penis; often in combs. *hung like a —*, for which see below; thus *underhung*, having a small penis. **2** [1950s+] having large breasts.

hung *adj.*² [1940s+] (*US*) suffering from a minor illness, e.g. a hangover. [SE *hungover*]

hung *adj.*³ (*orig. US*) **1** [1940s+] depressed or upset. **2** [1950s] drunk. **3** [1950s+] obsessed with or infatuated by. **4** [1960s+] in trouble, facing problems. [HUNG UP adj.]

hung *adj.*⁴ *see* HUNG FOR adj.

hungarian *n.* [17C] a hungry person, a glutton. [pun on SE *hungry* + racial slur]

hungarian *adj.* **1** [late 17C–early 18C] thievish, marauding, needy, beggarly. **2** [1990s+] (*US campus*) hungry. [for ety. *see* HUNGARIAN n.]

Hungarian champagne *n.* [1990s+] (*Aus.*) soda water. [racial slur]

hung beef *n.* [early 19C] a dried bull's penis, esp. when used as a whip.

hunger street *n.* (*also* **hunger lane, hungry-go-naked place, hungry gulch, ...hill, ...hollow, ...ridge, ...street**) [20C+] (*US*) the poor area of a town. [SE + HOLLOW n.²]

hung for *adj.* [1950s+] (*US teen*) in need of, lacking; thus *hung for bread*, in need of cash.

hung like a bull *phr.* [1960s+] possessing a large penis. [HUNG adj.¹ (1) + SE *bull*]

hung like a donkey *phr.* see HUNG LIKE A (JACK) DONKEY phr.

hung like a doughnut *phr.* [1960s+] (*US gay*) a woman, i.e. one who has a vagina (a hole). [play on HUNG LIKE A HORSE phr./SE *doughnut*]

hung like a (field) mouse *phr.* [1960s+] possessing an extremely small penis. [play on HUNG LIKE A HORSE phr.]

hung like a hamster *phr.* [2000s] possessed of a very small penis. [HUNG adj.¹ + SE *hamster*]

hung like a hoover hose *phr.* [1960s+] possessing a large penis. [HUNG adj.¹ (1) + *Hoover*, brandname]

hung like a horse *phr.* (*also* **horse-hung, hung like a stallion, ...stud, ...stud-horse**) [1960s+] possessing a large penis. [HUNG adj.¹ + SE *horse/stallion/stud/stud-horse*]

hung like a humming bird *phr.* [1970s+] possessing a very small penis. [HUNG adj.¹ + SE *humming bird*]

hung like a (jack) donkey *phr.* (*also* **hung like a mule**)

[1960s+] possessing a large penis (cf. HUNG LIKE AN ASS phr.). [HUNG adj.¹ + SE *donkey*]

hung like a mosquito *phr. see* HUNG LIKE A (STUD) MOSQUITO phr.

hung like a mouse *phr. see* HUNG LIKE A (FIELD) MOUSE phr.

hung like an ass *phr.* [17C] possessing a large penis (cf. HUNG LIKE A (JACK) DONKEY phr.). [HUNG adj.¹ + SE *ass*]

hung like a show dog *phr.* [1960s+] possessing a large penis. [HUNG adj.¹ (1) + SE *show dog*]

hung like a (stud) mosquito *phr.* [1960s+] (*US*) possessing a very small penis. [HUNG adj.¹ + SE *stud mosquito*]

hung low *adj.* [1990s+] (*US Black*) equipped with a notably large penis. [HUNG adj.¹ + SE *low*]

hung on *adj. see* HUNG UP adj. (5).

hung out *adj.* **1** [1960s+] (*US campus*) obsessed with, fascinated by. **2** [1980s+] (*US drugs*) addicted. [(1) HUNG adj.³ (3)]

hungries *n.* [1970s+] (*US*) an appetite, esp. one developed after smoking marijuana. [SE *hungry*]

hungry *adj.* **1** [mid-19C+] ambitious, enthusiastic, driven. **2** [20C+] (*Aus.*) mean, grasping, stingy, obsessed with money; often used as a nickname, e.g. Hungry Scott. **3** [20C+] (*US campus*) sexually excited. [intensified version of SE *hungry*, 'Having or characterized by a strong desire or craving' (*OED*)]

-hungry *sfx* [20C+] keen, desperate for. [HUNGRY adj. (1)]

hungry-belly *adj.* [20C+] (*W.I.*) esp. of children, starving, malnourished.

hungry croaker *n.* [1950s+] (*drugs*) a doctor who, for one reason or another, is willing to prescribe drugs for any user who asks for them. [HUNGRY adj. (1) + CROAKER n.⁵ (1)]

hungry enough to eat the arse out of a dead skunk *phr.* [1950s+] (*Can.*) very hungry; and vars.

hungry-go-naked place *n. see* HUNGER STREET n.

hungry gulch/hill/hollow *n. see* HUNGER STREET n.

hungry mile *n.* [1930s–70s] (*Aus.*) a stretch of Sussex Street, Sydney, frequented by dockers in search of work.

hungry ridge/street *n. see* HUNGER STREET n.

hungry track *n.* [late 19C+] (*Aus.*) a section of the road on which a vagrant finds it hard to find either food or work.

hung to *adj.* [1950s–60s] (*US Black*) obsessed with. [HUNG adj.³ (3)]

hung up *n.* [2000s] (*US prison*) a prisoner who tries to hang himself. [SE *hang* but poss. inference of HUNG UP adj.]

hung up *adj.* **1** [late 19C+] (*orig. UK society*) self-obsessed, snobbish. **2** [late 19C+] delayed or hindered. **3** [20C+] desperate, poor, in trouble. **4** [1940s+] (*orig. US*) unhappy, depressed, neurotic, anxious. **5** [1940s+] (*orig. US*) (*also* **hung on**) obsessed or infatuated. **6** [1940s+] (*US drugs*) intoxicated. **7** [1940s+] (*US drugs*) addicted.

hung up on *adj.* [1940s+] **1** obsessed with, esp. in love with someone. **2** (*US drugs*) addicted to. [ext. of HUNG UP adj. (5)/HUNG UP adj. (7)]

hunk n.¹ **1** [19C+] (*US*) a country bumpkin, a peasant, a farmer. **2** [late 19C+] a dull, slow, stupid person. **3** [1930s+] (*US*) sexual intercourse, thus a sexual partner, usu. a woman. **4** [1940s+] (*also* **hunker**) a large man or woman. **5** [1940s+] (*US*) a sexually attractive woman. **6** [1940s+] (*US*) an attractive, rugged, well-built man, poss. somewhat unintelligent. [19C US dial. *hunk*, bulk; a large body; (6) appears to have been coined as a description of the film star Victor Mature (1915–99), first described as a 'beautiful hunk of a man' and a 'wonderful hunk of a man' by Sheilah Graham in a syndicated column on 3 April 1941]

hunk n.² [late 19C+] (*US*) an immigrant from Central Europe, i.e. a Hungarian, Lithuanian, Slav, Pole; thus *hunky town*, the area of a town in which such immigrants congregate. [abbr. SE *Hungarian* as generic for all Central European immigrants]

hunk n.³ *see* HUNKY n. (2).

hunk adj. [mid-19C–1930s] (US) satisfactory, fine. [SAmE *hunk*, in a safe or good position or condition, all right; ult. East Frisia *hunk*, corner, nook, retreat, home in a game]

hunk v. [1990s+] (US) to vomit.

hunker n.[1] [mid-19C–1930s] (US) a political conservative. [SAmE *hunker*, a curmudgeon; also *see* 1888 M. Lane *Political Catch-Words* 15: 'Hunkers.—A division of the New York Democracy that arose in opposition to Governor Wright in his disagreement with President Polk [...]. By sharp management the administration faction packed the state convention and nominated a complete ticket for their faction; or, as a Wright man said, took the whole "hunk." [i.e. of the political spoils] From this expression they took the name of 'Hunkers.']

hunker n.[2] *see* HUNK n.[1] (4).

hunker v. [20C+] (*Ulster*) to act as a parasite, to curry favour with. [one fig. *hunkers* down awaiting orders]

hunker-slider n. [20C+] (US/Irish) one who acts deceitfully. [HUNKER-SLIDING n.]

hunker-sliding n. [20C+] (US/Irish) acting unfairly, deceitfully. [Scot. *hunkersliding*, dishonourable or shifty conduct]

hunkey adj. *see* HUNKY adj.[1] (1).

hunkey-dorey/hunkidori adj. *see* HUNKY-DORY adj. (1).

hunkie *see under* HUNKY.

hunking adj. [1980s+] **1** (US *campus*) large. **2** attractively well-built. [HUNK n.[1]]

hunko adj. [1950s+] (US) of someone's physique, short, stocky. [HUNKY adj.[4]]

hunk of arse/ass n. *see* PIECE OF ASS n.

hunk of meat n. *see* PIECE OF MEAT n. (1).

hunk of tail n. *see* PIECE OF TAIL n. (2).

hunk of work n. *see* PIECE OF WORK n.[1] (2).

hunks n. **1** [17C–1920s] a miser, also a surly person. **2** [19C–1920s] (US) a worthless, good-for-nothing person. [ety. unknown; ? *Hunks*, the name of a well-known bear, kept in 17C London for baiting; bearlike, the miser 'hugs' his money and a *bear* (cf. BEAR WITH A SORE HEAD n.) is a grumpy person]

hunkum-bunkum adj. [mid-19C–1910s] (US) excellent. [? HUNKY adj.[1] (1)]

hunky n. (*also* **hunkie**) **1** [late 19C+] (US) an immigrant from Central Europe, i.e. a Hungarian, Lithuanian, Slav, Pole; thus *Hunky Town*, the area of a town in which such immigrants congregate (cf. HUNYAK n.). **2** [1920s+] (US) (*also* **honky, hunk**) a derog. term for a Black person (cf. ALLIGATOR BAIT n.[2]). **3** [1950s+] (US *Black*) a derog. term for a White person (cf. HONKIE n.). [HUNK n.[2]]

hunky adj.[1] **1** [mid-19C+] (US) (*also* **hunkey**) excellent, satisfactory, lucky, pleasurable, in good condition, 'safe and sound'. **2** [late 19C–1910s] (US) friendly, ingratiating. [abbr. HUNKY-DORY adj. (1)]

hunky adj.[2] (*also* **hunkie**) [20C+] pertaining to an immigrant from Central Europe, i.e. a Hungarian, Lithuanian, Slav, Pole. [HUNKY n. (1)]

hunky adj.[3] [1930s] (US) aggressive.

hunky adj.[4] [1970s+] of a man, good-looking, well-built. [HUNK n.[1] (6)]

hunky chunk v. [mid-19C] (US *Und.*) to steal food.

hunky-doke adj. [1940s] in good/proper order; functioning as required. [HUNKY-DORY adj. (1) + OKEY-DOKE adj.[1]]

hunky-doodle adj. [1900s] (US) fine, satisfactory. [var. on HUNKY-DORY adj. (1)]

hunky-dory adj. (*orig.* US) **1** [mid-19C+] (*also* **honky-dooley, hunkey-dorey, hunkidori**) wonderful, excellent, first-rate. **2** [1980s+] close, cosy, intimate. [Du. *hunk*, home (in a game), which was first used by youngsters in New Amsterdam and thence New York; thus giving the adv. *hunk*, in a safe position, all right; *dory*, ety. unknown; ? redup. Note Michael Quinion, *World Wide Words* (Internet, 27 November 1999): 'HUNKY-DORY Subscriber

Robert Burns wrote to point out gently that if I had consulted the authoritative Random House Historical Dictionary of American Slang, I would have found a more likely (and more interesting) origin for the word. The suggestion is that the term was introduced in America about 1865 by a popular variety performer named Japanese Tommy. Mr Burns reports that it is said to have been sailors' slang for a street in Yokohama named Honki-Dori, whose inhabitants "catered for the pleasures of sailors", as he puts it. The word was a play on the existing word 'hunky' for something that was fine, splendid or satisfactory, which itself probably derives from the adjective 'hunk' with much the same sense. That can be traced back to the 1840s and has links to another reduplicated term, 'hunkum-bunkum'']

hunky-dory adv. [20C+] in an excellent manner. [HUNKY-DORY adj. (1)]

hunky-dunky adj. [1950s+] (US) fine, excellent. [var. on HUNKY-DORY adj. (1)]

hunky-fucking-dory adj. [1970s+] (US *Black*) wonderful, excellent, first-rate. [HUNKY-DORY adj. (1) + FUCKING adj. (4); according to Major, *Juba to Jive: A Dict. of Afro-American Slang* (1994), Black users prefer this augmented version of the basic White term]

hunky-peroodlum adj. [1900s] attractive, sexually inviting.

Hunky Town n. *see* HUNKY n. (1).

hunt v. **1** [20C+] (*Aus.*) to drive away, to chase off. **2** [1970s+] (US *campus/gay*) to search for a partner for romance or sex.

hunt-about n. [mid-19C–1920s] **1** a prostitute. **2** an interfering, meddlesome gossip.

hunt a gowk n. [20C+] (*Ulster*) one who can be sent on a fool's errand. [SE *hunt* + SE *gowk*, a cuckoo, a fool]

hunt a tavern fox v. [mid–late 17C] to get drunk. [pun on SE *fox*/FOXED adj.]

hunter n. [19C] the penis.

hunter-pitching n. [mid–late 19C] the game of cock-shy, a fairground game, which involved throwing broomsticks at a cock; if the thrower could knock the cock over and then grab it before it regained its feet he would win the bird.

hunt grass v. [mid–late 19C] (US) **1** to be knocked down. **2** to be extremely confused.

hunting n. (*also* **squirrel hunting**) [late 17C–19C] (UK *Und.*) searching for a victim whether for a theft, a confidence trick etc.

hunting licence n. [20C+] (US *prison*) a commitment to kill an inmate, often ordered by a gang leader.

hunt leather v. *see* LEATHER n.[3] (7).

hunt one's hole v. [mid-19C–1960s] (US) to run away, to seek refuge.

hunt-smock n. *see* SMOCK HUNTER n.

hunt the anchovy v. [1960s+] to perform cunnilingus (cf. BOX LUNCH n.).

hunt the dummy v. [19C] to steal pocketbooks. [SE *hunt* + DUMMY n.[2]]

hunt the fox v. [late 16C–17C] to be drunk. [pun on SE *fox*/FOXED adj.]

hunt the same old coon v. [late 19C] (US) to persist in doing the same thing.

hunt the squirrel v. [late 18C–19C] for 2 coachmen to attempt to upset each other's vehicles as they race along a public road; typically one being a hackney coach, the other a stage. [the coaches veer from side to side as does a frightened squirrel]

hunt up a cow v. *see* CHASE (UP) A COW v.

hunyak n. (*also* **honyock, honyocker, hunyok**) (US) **1** [20C+] an immigrant from central or eastern Europe, e.g. a Hungarian or Pole (cf. HUNKY n.). **2** [1920s+] an ignorant, inexperienced or unsophisticated person, esp. a rustic, a peasant. [? *Hun(garian)* + (*Pol*)*ack*]

hura n. [1960s+] (US) the police. [Sp.]

Hurdy-Gurdy, the n. [1940s] (US *Und.*) Cedar Rapids, Iowa.

[pickpockets caught in the town were obliged to leave by swimming the Cedar River]

hurdy-gurdy *n.* (*also* **hurdy**) [mid-19C+] (*US*) a dancehall, a dancer in a dancehall; thus *hurdy-gurdy house, hurdy-gurdy girl*. [SE *hurdy-gurdy*; onomat. f. the sound of the instrument]

hurdy-gurdy *adj.* [1970s] noisy, brash, bright; all mimicking the image of a thronging dancehall. [HURDY-GURDY n.]

hurkaru *n.* [mid-19C] (*Anglo-Ind.*) a messenger. [Hind. *harkara*, messenger, emissary, spy]

hurkle *v.* [20C+] (*Ulster*) to look on rather than offer help when others are working. [dial. *hurkle*, to crouch, to squat, to shrink from the cold]

hurl *v.* [1950s+] (*Aus./S.Afr.*) **1** to vomit (cf. BLOW v.³). **2** in fig. use, to enrage, to make sick.

hurl a monkey wrench into the machinery *v. see* THROW A MONKEY WRENCH INTO THE MACHINERY v.

hurler *n.* [20C+] (*Irish*) a measure of whisky. [? SE *hurl*, to toss, i.e. what is tossed into the glass]

hurley foot *n.* [20C+] (*Irish*) a club-foot. [? Irish game of *hurley/hurling*, in which the ball is hit with a stick or club]

hurrah *n.* (*also* **hoorah**) [mid-19C+] (*US*) a boisterous party, a ruckus, uproariousness; thus *on a (great) hurrah*, on a spree. [SE *hurrah!*]

hurrah *adj.* (*also* **hoorah**) [late 19C+] (*US*) **1** wild and disorderly. **2** boisterous, noisy. [HURRAH n.]

hurrah *v.* (*also* **hoorah, hooraw**) [20C+] (*US*) **1** to tease someone, to harass. **2** to cause a commotion, to raise a ruckus. [HURRAH n.]

hurrah boys *n.* [mid-19C–1920s] (*US*) **1** supporters, fans. **2** college students. [the ritualized college cheers popular among students]

hurrah clothes *n.* [20C+] (*orig. US*) one's best clothes, one's 'Sunday suit'. [SE *hurrah!*; i.e. the wearing of such clothes to events at which one may applaud]

hurrah's nest *n.* [early 19C+] (*US*) a confused, tangled or disorderly mess, a state of confusion or disorder. [*hurrah*, an imaginary bird]

hurray *adj. see* HOORAY adj.

hurricane *n.* [mid-18C–early 19C] (*UK society*) a crowded, fashionable assembly held in a private house.

hurricane deck *n.* [mid-19C+] (*US*) the back of a horse or mule. [SE *hurricane-deck*, a light upper deck on a steamer]

hurricane lamp *n.* [20C+] tramp. [rhy. sl.]

hurroo(sh) *n. see* HOOROOSH n.

hurry-buggy *n.* [1920s–40s] a police van. [it 'hurries' one to prison]

hurry-come-up *n.* [1930s–40s] (*W.I.*) a parvenu, esp. with overtones of a bad reputation.

hurry-up *n.¹* **1** [20C+] anything or anyone that goes fast. **2** [20C+] an emergency, anything urgent. **3** [1970s–80s] (*N.Z. prison*) a reprimand, a telling-off.

hurry-up *n.²* [20C+] (*US*) **1** a request for money; thus *on the hurry-up*, begging. **2** a romantic proposition.

hurry-up *adj.* [20C+] (*US*) urgent, in emergency.

hurry up the cakes *v.* [mid-late 19C] (*US*) to go quickly.

hurry-up (wagon) *n.* (*also* **hurry-up van**) [19C+] (*US*) a police van or car. [the speed with which it is driven]

hurry-whore *n.* [early-mid-17C] a street-walker. [the speed with which she deals with a customer]

hurt *adj.* **1** [1960s+] (*US Black/campus*) unattractive. **2** [1980s] (*US Black/drugs*) extremely intoxicated by a given drug or hungover from alcohol excess.

hurt *v.¹* **1** [1900s] to be anxious or impatient. **2** [1910s+] (*US*) of an inanimate object, to cause problems for, to injure. **3** [1940s] (*US*) to complain. **4** [1950s] (*UK Und.*) to wound severely, to kill. **5** [1960s+] of a person, to suffer.

hurt *v.²* [1950s+] (*drugs*) of a drug addict, to suffer the lack of their drug of choice.

hurt dance *n. see* HURTING DANCE n.

hurt for *v.* [1940s+] to want something desperately, usu. to alleviate current unhappiness. [HURT v.¹]

hurtin' for certain *phr.* [1950s+] (*US Black*) **1** distressed, in trouble. **2** ugly, very unattractive. **3** in great need, esp. of drugs or sex. [HURTING adj.]

hurting *adj.* (*also* **hurting for**) **1** [1940s+] (*US*) short of money. **2** [1950s+] (*US*) generally miserable or in trouble. **3** [1950s+] (*drugs*) urgently needing narcotics to sustain one's regular dosage. **4** [1980s+] (*US campus*) drunk; thus *hurtin' cowboy*, a person who is very drunk (cf. AFFLICTED adj.). **5** [1980s+] (*US campus*) bad, out of condition. [HURT v.¹]

hurting dance *n.* (*also* **hurt dance**) [1950s+] (*orig. US*) sadness, frustration, jealousy, usu. in a relationship in which one person has another *doing a hurting dance*. [HURT v.¹ (5)]

hus *see under* HUSS.

husband *n.¹* [1930s+] the supposedly 'aggressive' partner of a homosexual couple (cf. AUNTIE n.²).

husband *n.²* *see* HUBBY n. (2).

husband and wife *n.* [20C+] (*US*) a knife. [rhy. sl.]

husband game *n.* [mid-19C] (*US Und.*) a confidence trick where a prostitute has her 'husband' knock on the door after she has been paid but before she has performed.

husband's tea *n.* [mid-19C] very weak tea. [? a husband's inadequacy as opposed to that of a lover]

hush *n.* **1** [early 18C; 1930s–40s] a bribe. **2** [20C+] silence, quietness, calm; esp. in phr. *let's have a bit of hush*, used to quieten a crowd or audience; also imper., *hold your hush!* be quiet!

hush *v.* [early 18C–mid-19C] (*UK Und.*) to murder. [SE *hush*, to silence]

hush-crib *n. see* HUSH-SHOP n.

hush dough *n. see* HUSH MONEY n.

hush-house *n.* [1920s–40s] (*US*) a speakeasy. [coined by columnist Walter Winchell (1897–1972) but note HUSH-SHOP n.]

hush-hush *n.* [1930s–60s] **1** (*US Und.*) a pistol with a silencer. **2** (*US*) secrecy. **3** (*US*) a secret. [SE *hush-hush*, most secret, undercover + ref. to HUSH v.]

hush money *n.* (*also* **hush dough**) [18C+] a bribe paid to ensure that embarrassing facts are concealed. [SE *hush*, silent]

hush mouth *n.* [1940s] (*US Black*) a sip of whisky. [it shuts the drinker up]

hush-mouth *adj.* [1920s] (*US Black*) secret, silenced.

hush puppy *n.* [1980s+] a YUPPIE n. [rhy. sl.]

hush-shop *n.* (*also* **hush-crib**) [mid-late 19C] an unlicensed beer or liquor shop. [the sales are made 'on the hush']

hush-up *n.* [1920s] (*US*) a 'cover-up' of a crime. [SE *hush*]

husk *v.* [1940s] (*US Black*) to undress, to strip. [SE *husk*, to remove a shell]

huskings *n.* [1940s] (*US Black*) a pile of clothes, esp. those discarded immediately after undressing. [HUSK v.]

Husky *n.* (*also* **husky**) [mid-19C–1940s] (*US*) **1** a derog. term for an Inuit. **2** a derog. term for the Inuit language. [SE *husky*, an Eskimo/Inuit dog]

husky *n.* [mid-19C+] (*US*) a large, tough man.

husky *adj.* **1** [mid-19C+] large, tough. **2** [late 19C] in fig. use, self-satisfied, arrogant. [HUSKY n.]

huskylour *n.* [late 17C–19C] (*UK Und.*) a guinea. [SE *husky*, dry (as a corn husk) + LOUR n.; thus lit. 'dry money', i.e. hard cash]

huss *n.* (*also* **hus**) (*US Black*) **1** [1950s] a fellow, a man, also used in direct address. **2** [1960s] a smart, stylish man's suit. [abbr. HUSTLER n.]

huss *adj.* (*also* **hus**) [1960s] (*US Black*) smart, fashionable, stylish. [HUSS n. (2)]

hussle *v. see* HUSTLE v.

hussy *n. see* HUZZY n.

hustle *n.* **1** [1940s+] (*orig. US Und.*) a swindle, a hoax, a get-rich-quick scheme. **2** [1940s+] (*US*) any means of survival, often providing little more than subsistence. **3** [1940s+] (*US Black*) a job, a means of earning a living. **4** [1940s+] (*US Black*) work as a pimp, prostitute or tramp. **5** [1970s+] (*US*) flattery, deception. **6** [1970s+] (*US*) a means of seduction, a pass. **7** [1970s+] (*US*) a criminal scheme or activity. [HUSTLE v.]

hustle *v.* (*also* **hussle**) **1** [19C] to have sexual intercourse. **2** [mid-19C+] to practise swindling or petty theft. **3** [mid-19C+] (*orig. US*) to use initiative to obtain or secure; to live by one's wits. **4** [late 19C+] (*US*) to work hard, to make an effort. **5** [late 19C+] (*US*) to sell goods, esp. in an aggressive manner, to promote; thus in combs. *hustle hash*, to work as a waiter or waitress; *hustle shoes*, to work as a shoe-shine; *hustle sheets*, to sell newspapers. **6** [late 19C+] (*US*) to work as a prostitute. **7** [20C+] to urge someone to work harder. **8** [20C+] to obtain money or some other commodity through begging. **9** [1930s+] (*orig. US*) to deceive or to con. **10** [1940s+] (*US*) to make sexual advances. **11** [1960s+] to work as a male prostitute. **12** [1970s] to pimp. **13** [1970s+] (*drugs*) to attempt to obtain drug customers, to sell drugs. [SE *hustle*, to push around or against, to jostle; ult. Du. *husselen, hutselen*, to shake, to toss]

hustle-buggy *n.* [1920s–30s] (*US*) a police car. [SE *hustle* + *buggy*]

hustle one's bustle *v.* **1** [1930s+] to work as a prostitute. **2** [1970s+] to hurry.

hustler *n.* **1** [19C] (*US Und.*) a member of a pickpocket gang. **2** [late 19C–1930s] (*US*) a racetrack tout. **3** [late 19C+] (*US*) a hard-working, ambitious person, also an energizer, one who exhorts his fellows to harder work, greater commitment. **4** [late 19C+] anyone who makes a living through their wits and ingenuity, rather than accepting the restraints of a conventional job; their occupations are often, but not invariably, criminal or virtually so. **5** [20C+] (*W.I.*) a confidence man, a well-dressed beggar. **6** [1910s+] (*US Und.*) a pimp. **7** [1920s+] (*US*) a prostitute of either sex (cf. ASS PEDDLER n.). **8** [1930s+] (*US gay*) a male prostitute with homosexual clients. **9** [1930s+] a gambler or player of pool, bowling etc, who uses skill and poss. cheating to make a living against lesser opponents. **10** [1960s+] (*US campus*) a man who succeeds in seducing women, a womanizer. **11** [1960s+] a tout. [HUSTLE v.]

hustlers don't call showdowns *phr.* [1960s+] (*US Black*) one who is on the receiving end of a hand-out does not cause trouble because that might terminate the flow of free gifts. [HUSTLER n. + SE *showdown*]

hustling *n.* **1** [early 19C+] street robbery; bag-snatching. **2** [late 19C+] selling objects, ideas, one's services etc, esp. in an aggressive manner. **3** [late 19C+] living by one's wits; also as adj. **4** [1920s+] working as a prostitute. **5** [1960s] (*US Black*) making a nervous sign at somebody. **6** [1960s+] cadging, begging. [HUSTLE v.]

hustling-ass *adj.* [1980s+] (*US Black*) aggressively self-aggrandizing, hard-working, self-promoting etc. [HUSTLE v. + -ASS sfx]

hustling broad *n.* (*also* **hustling dame, …girl, …woman**) [1930s+] (*US Und.*) a female prostitute (cf. ASS PEDDLER n.). [HUSTLE v. (6) + BROAD n.² (2)/SE *girl/woman*]

hut *n.* **1** [1900s] (*US*) an apartment, a dwelling place; one's home. **2** [1920s+] (*US prison*) a cell.

hutch *n.* **1** [1900s–10s] (*Aus.*) a home, a house. **2** [1930s+] (*US*) an office, usu. small. **3** [1950s] (*US*) a nightclub.

hutty *n. see* HATTY n.

hutu *n. see* HOOT n.¹

huxter *n.* [20C+] (*Ulster*) a decaying, dilapidated house or property. [SE *huckster*, a middleman, a small businessman, one who will cheat to make money]

huzzy *n.* (*also* **hussy**) [18C–early 19C] a small container of needles, thread and similar useful items. [SE *housewife*; note synon. naval jargon *huzzif*]

Hyde Park *n.* [20C+] an informer. [rhy. sl. = NARK n.¹ (1)]

Hyde Park railings *n.* [late 19C–1900s] a breast of mutton. [the row of bones that make up such a breast resemble the fencing of the London park]

hydrant *n.* [1900s–40s] (*US*) tears, weeping.

hydraulic *n.* [1960s+] (*Aus.*) a light-fingered person, who will 'lift anything that isn't nailed down'. [pun on SE *hydraulic jack*]

hydraulic *adj.* [1960s+] (*Aus.*) used of a petty thief or shoplifter. [HYDRAULIC n.]

hydraulics *n.* [1990s+] nonsense, rubbish. [rhy. sl. = BALLOCKS n.² (2)]

hydro *n.* [1980s+] (*US drugs*) **1** *hydro*ponically grown marijuana. **2** crack cocaine (cf. BASE n.). **3** amphetamine. [(1) abbr.; (2) ? the chemical process used in manufacturing crack]

hydroplug *n.* [1980s+] (*US drugs*) a pipe for smoking marijuana. [HYDRO n. (1)]

hyena *n.* [mid-19C–1950s] (*US*) a lazy or stupid person.

hygelo *n.* [1930s–50s] (*US drugs*) a narcotics addict.

hyke *v.* [late 19C–1900s] to attract someone's attention, to shout after someone. [CHI-IKE v. (2)]

hykey *n.* [mid-late 19C] pride. [? fig. use of HIKE v. (1)]

hymenally challenged *adj.* [1990s+] being a virgin.

Hymie *n.* [20C+] (*orig. US*) **1** a derog. term for a Jew (cf. ABE n.¹). **2** a derog. nickname for a German. [the stereotypical Jewish name *Hyman*/Ger. name *Herman*]

Hymie *adj.* [1970s+] (*orig. US*) used derog. of a Jew.

hymie *n.* **1** [1930s] (*US gay*) the anus. **2** [1930s–40s] (*US tramp/gay*) an adolescent who doubles as a lover and cook. **3** [1950s] (*US tramp*) sexual intercourse.

Hymietown *n.* [1980s+] (*US*) a derog. nickname for New York City. [HYMIE n. (1) + SE *town*]

hymns and prayers *n.* [late 19C+] usu. unmarried men and women. [SE *hims and hers* but note pun on the woman who is 'praying' for a husband]

hymnslinger *n.* [late 19C] (*Aus.*) a preacher, a clergyman. [SE *hymn* + SLINGER n.¹ (2)]

hyp *n.*¹ (*also* **hyp man**) [1950s+] (*drugs*) a narcotics addict. [SE *hypodermic* (syringe)]

hyp *n.*² *see* HYPO n.¹ (1).

hyp *v. see* HIP v.².

hype *n.*¹ **1** [1910s+] (*US Und.*) (*also* **hipe**) a short-change swindle in which the criminal persuades a shopkeeper that he has paid with a larger denomination note than he actually has, thus gaining extra change. **2** [1920s+] (*US*) a swindle, a confidence trick, fraud, lies or exaggeration; thus *drop a hype*, to air one's opinions, to tell one's story. **3** [1920s+] (*US Und.*) a confidence trickster; a 'short-change artist'. **4** [1920s+] (*US*) an exorbitant increase in prices. **5** [1930s+] any contrived situation or scheme designed to fleece a victim. **6** [1950s+] publicity, promotion, esp. wild statements guessing about something's nature (whether positive or negative); thus *throw hype*, to talk in a self-aggrandizing manner. [SE *hyperbole*]

hype *n.*² **1** [1910s+] (*US drugs*) a hypodermic syringe or injection. **2** [1920s+] (*US drugs/Und.*) a heroin or morphine addict. **3** [1970s] (*US pimp*) a prostitute who works simply to support her narcotic addiction. **4** [1990s+] (*US drugs*) narcotic drugs. **5** [1990s+] (*US campus*) a regular user of marijuana. [abbr. SE *hypodermic* (syringe)]

hype *adj.*¹ [1950s–60s] (*US*) pertaining to narcotics and narcotic users. [HYPE n.²]

hype *adj.*² **1** [1970s] (*US*) fraudulent. **2** [1980s+] (*US campus*) uptight, upset, jittery, nervous, worried. **3** [1980s+] (*US Black*) splendid, exciting, cool or attractive. [HYPE n.¹]

hype *v.*¹ **1** [1910s+] (*US Und.*) to operate a short-change racket, to swindle, to cheat. **2** [1910s+] to work up one's emotions, to become stimulated, to make more exciting. **3** [1930s+] (*US Black*) to fool or cajole, to outsmart. **4** [1940s+] (*orig. US*) to promote a person or commodity through an excess of overzealous, grandiose publicity, esp. in rock or show business use. **5** [1940s+] to excite. **6** [1960s+] (*US campus*) to annoy. [HYPE n.[1]]

hype v.[2] (*also* **hype up**) [1930s+] (*drugs*) to inject a drug. [HYPE n.[2]]

hyped (up) adj. **1** [1910s+] intense, excited. **2** [1930s+] intoxicated by narcotic drugs, or a stimulant. **3** [1960s] artificial, fake, all HYPE n.[1] and no substance. **4** [1970s+] tense, nervous. [HYPE v.[1]]

hyper n. **1** [1910s–50s] (*US Und.*) one who works the short-change racket. **2** [1940s] (*US Black*) a persuasive talker. **3** [1960s] a publicist. [HYPE n.[1]]

hyper adj. **1** [late 19C; 1940s+] tense, over-emotional, 'wired'. **2** [1940s+] betraying one's feelings, esp. towards an attractive person. [abbr. SE *hyperactive*]

hyper v. [mid-19C–1950s] (*US*) to hurry, to run. [abbr. SE *hyperactive*]

hyper down v. [1980s+] (*US*) to calm down. [abbr. SE *hyperactive*]

hyperdrive whore n. [1980s+] (*US campus*) a highly promiscuous woman. [SE *hyperdrive*, an SF coinage to indicate ultra-fast speeds + *whore*]

hyperjacks n. [1980s+] (*drugs*) ampoules of heroin. [HYPE v.[2] + JACK (AND JILL) n. (4)]

hype stick n. [1910s] (*US drugs*) a hypodermic needle. [HYPE n.[2] + STICK v.[4] (3)]

hype up v. *see* HYPE v.[2].

hyp man n. *see* HYP n.[1].

hypnotist n. [1980s+] (*US campus*) an eccentric. [HYPE v.[1] (2) + pun]

hypo n.[1] **1** [18C+] (*also* **hippo, hyp**) a feeling of mild depression, of being out of sorts. **2** [mid-18C+] (*also* **hippo, hypps**) a hypochondriac. [abbr. SE *hypochondriac*]

hypo n.[2] (*drugs*) **1** [late 19C+] (*also* **hypo-smecker**) a drug addict. **2** [20C+] a hypodermic syringe. **3** [20C+] a hypodermic injection. [HYPE n.[2]/abbr. SE *hypodermic*]

hypo n.[3] [1950s] encouragement, excitement. [HYPE n.[1]]

hypo v.[1] [1920s+] to administer a hypodermic injection. [HYPE v.[2]/abbr. SE *hypodermic*]

hypo v.[2] [1930s] (*US Und.*) to 'load' a pair of dice.

hypo v.[3] [1930s+] (*US*) to promote or enhance, to stimulate enthusiasm. [HYPE v.[1]]

hypocon n. (*also* **hyppocon**) [early 18C] hypochondria. [abbr.]

hypogastrian cranny n. [mid-17C] the vagina (cf. ADAM'S OWN (ALTAR) n.; AGREEABLE RUTS OF LIFE n.). [the Greek *hypogastrium*, that section of the body below the belly and above the privates]

hypo-smecker n. *see* HYPO n.[2] (1).

hypped adj. *see* HIPPED adj.[1] (1).

hyppocon n. *see* HYPOCON n.

hypps n. *see* HYPO n.[1] (2).

hyps n. *see* HIP, THE n.

hyst n. *see* HOIST n.[2].

hyst v. *see* HEIST v.

hyste n. *see* HEIST n.[1] (1).

hyster n. *see* HOISTER n.[1] (1).

I

I *n.* [mid-19C+] (*US, mainly Southern/Midwest*) used in a variety of combs. to express *God* or *Jesus*, e.g. *I golly! I Godfrey!*

i *n.* [1910s–20s] (*US*) an idea. [abbr.]

iah *n.* [1990s+] (*W.I.*) a term of address to a friend. [JAH n. (2) + Rastafarian use of pfx *i-* to imply the spirituality that encompasses all humans, thus obviating the need for individual personal pronouns]

I ain't coming (on that tab) *phr.* [1930s–40s] (*US Black*) a phr. rejecting another person's suggestion. [TAB n.⁵]

I ain't no joke *phr.* [1990s+] (*US Black teen*) a minatory phr. designed to warn any possible attacker of one's own powers. [NO JOKE phr.]

I am sure *phr.* (*also* **I'm sure**) [mid-19C+] (*US teen*) a phr. meaning I am sure that you are wrong or that I don't want to do what you suggest etc; intensified as *I am so sure*, a phr. used at the end of a sentence to imply either 'I don't know' or 'I am sure of that'.

I and I *n.* [1960s+] (*W.I./UK Black teen*) a Rastafarian.

I and I *pron.* [1960s+] (*W.I./UK Black teen*) us, we; you and I.

Ian Rush *n.* [1980s] a brush. [rhy. sl.; ult. UK footballer *Ian Rush* (b.1961)]

I ask you *phr.* [mid-19C+] a phr. implying one's distaste for what has just been said or done; often prefixed by *well…*

i.b.m. *n.* [1960s+] (*US*) a small penis. [abbr. *itty bitty meat*; MEAT n. (2)]

I can't hardly wait *phr.* (*also* **I can hardly wait**) [1930s+] an ironic phr. used to imply one's distaste for something that is going to happen in the future.

I caught that ill vibe *phr.* [1990s+] (*US Black teen*) I was tricked. [CATCH v.² (2) + ILL adj. (2) + VIBE n. (1)]

ice *n.¹* (*US*) **1** [late 19C+] money in general. **2** [late 19C+] profit from the illegal sale of tickets for the theatre, cinema etc. **3** [20C+] protection money, bribes. **4** [2000s] failure to pay a debt.

ice *n.²* **1** [late 19C+] (*US*) a cool reception, a BRUSH-OFF n.; often in phr. *give someone the ice*, to snub someone. **2** [1990s+] (*US Black*) an emotionless person, one who has no qualms about saying and doing whatever they want. [COOL adj.¹ (1)]

ice *n.³* [late 19C+] (*orig. US*) jewellery, esp. diamonds.

ice *n.⁴* [1960s+] (*US Black*) something or someone excellent. [COOL adj.¹ (6)]

ice *n.⁵* [1970s] (*US prison*) solitary confinement. [abbr. SE *isolation*]

ice *n.⁶* [1970s+] (*US drugs*) **1** cocaine. **2** methamphetamine (cf. BOMBITA n.). [supposed resemblance]

ice *n.⁷* [1990s+] (*US Black*) courage, ruthlessness. [COOL adj.¹]

ice *adj.* [1970s+] (*US Black*) **1** a synon. for COOL adj.¹ (2). **2** a synon. for COOL adj.¹ (3).

ice *v.¹* [20C+] to ensure victory, orig. in a sporting contest.

ice *v.²* [1930s+] (*US*) to pay bribes, to pay protection money. [ICE n.¹ (3)]

ice *v.³* **1** [1930s+] (*US*) (*also* **ice out**) to snub, to treat coldly. **2** [1930s+] (*US Und.*) (*also* **ice down**) to imprison. **3** [1930s+] (*US*

prison) to place in solitary confinement. **4** [1940s+] to murder; to kill. **5** [1960s+] (*US Black*) to reject, to turn down, to cease; often as *ice that!* **6** [1970s+] in fig. use, to harm, to cause trouble for. **7** [1980s+] to break an appointment with, to abandon or cancel a plan or scheme. **8** [1990s+] to hide. [fig. uses of PUT ON ICE v.]

ice *v.⁴* (*also* **ice off**) [1980s+] to complete, to round off. [SE *to put the icing on the cake*]

iceberg *n.* **1** [mid-19C+] an unemotional person. **2** [1930s+] (*Aus.*) anyone who enjoys an early morning swim in the icy ocean waters.

iceberg act *n.* [1950s] (*US Black*) an act of rejection, esp. between lovers. [var. on COLD SHOULDER n.]

iceberg slim *n.* [1960s] (*US Black*) a pimp (cf. CANDYMAN n.). [the street name of Robert *Iceberg Slim* Beck (1918–92), one-time pimp and author of a series of autobiographical books; such gangsta rappers as Ice T (real name Tracy Morrow, b.1959) took their names from his]

icebox *n.¹* [late 19C+] (*US*) an unemotional person, esp. a sexually unresponsive woman.

icebox *n.²* **1** [1920s+] (*Can./US prison*) a solitary confinement cell. **2** [1920s+] (*US prison*) the morgue. **3** [1930s–40s] (*US prison*) a life sentence. **4** [1930s+] (*US*) a prison. **5** [1970s+] a coffin. [the lack of amenities but note SE *isolation*]

icebox *n.³* [1930s+] (*US*) the vagina (cf. BAG n.¹).

icebox *n.⁴* [1940s] (*US Und.*) a safe.

ice-cream *n.¹* **1** [1920s+] (*US drugs*) cocaine, morphine, heroin, crack cocaine (cf. AUNTIE EMMA n.; BASE n.). **2** [1980s] (*US campus*) alcoholic drink. [the pleasure they give; (1) also the whiteness of the drugs]

ice-cream *n.²* [1960s+] semen (cf. BABY GRAVY n.).

ice-cream *n.³* [1970s] (*UK Black teen*) a White person; usu. in pl.

ice-cream *n.⁴* *see* ICE-CREAM (FREEZER) n.

ice-cream *adj.* [2000s] (*US*) perfect, as desired. [var. on APPLE PIE adj.]

ice-creamer *n.* [1930s+] an Italian (cf. DAGO n.). [the stereotyped occupation of Italian immigrants]

ice-cream (freezer) *n.* **1** [1950s+] a man. **2** [1980s] someone who can be easily tricked. **3** [1980s] (*US campus*) a form of address to a good friend. [rhy. sl. = GEEZER n.¹]

ice-cream habit *n.* [1930s+] (*drugs*) the irregular use of an otherwise addictive drug. [SE *ice-cream* + HABIT n. (1); on the premise that one likes ice-cream but doesn't want it all the time]

ice-cream machine *n.* [1960s+] the penis. [ICE-CREAM n.²]

ice-cream man *n.* **1** [1950s] a dealer in narcotics. **2** [1990s+] (*US Black/drugs*) a seller of crack cocaine. [ICE-CREAM n.¹ (1) + pun]

ice-cream pants *n.* [1900s–50s] (*US*) lightweight, light-coloured summer trousers. [the colour]

ice-cream suit *n.* [late 19C+] (*orig. Aus./US*) a white linen suit. [the colour]

ice-cube *n.* [1930s+] a diamond.

iced *adj.¹* **1** [1930s+] (*US prison*) placed in the punishment block, in solitary confinement. **2** [1970s+] (*US Black*) isolated, ignored. [(1) ICE v.³ (3) + chilly conditions in the cells; (2) ICE v.³ (1)]

iced *adj.*² (*also* **iced down/out**) [1950s+] (*US*) wearing jewellery, esp. diamonds. [ICE n.³]

iced *adj.*³ **1** [1950s] (*US*) drunk. **2** [1970s+] (*drugs*) intoxicated by (crack) cocaine. [(1) fig.; (2) ICE n.⁶ (1)]

iced *adj.*⁴ [1980s+] (*US campus*) abandoned, let down. [ICE v.³ (1)]

iced down/out *adj.* see ICED adj.².

ice down *v. see* ICE v.³ (2).

iced to the eyebrows *phr.* [1950s] extremely drunk (cf. ARSEHOLED adj.). [ICED adj.³ (1)]

ice-house *n.* [1930s+] (*US Und.*) a jewellery store. [ICE n.³]

ice jack *n.* [1910s–20s] an ice-cream salesman. [SE *ice* + generic use of proper name]

ice job *n.* [1960s] (*US gay*) an act of fellatio in which the fellator has ice cubes in his/her mouth. [SE *ice* + JOB n.⁴]

ice maiden *n.* [1950s+] an unemotional or unresponsive woman. [ICE n.² (2)]

iceman *n.*¹ [1920s+] (*US Und.*) a diamond thief. [ICE n.³ + sfx *man*]

iceman *n.*² [1940s+] an emotionless person. [ICE n.² (2) + sfx *man*]

iceman *n.*³ [1940s+] a paid killer. [ICE v.³ (4) + sfx *-man*]

iceman *n.*⁴ [1960s+] **1** one, e.g. a corrupt policeman, who is given bribes by gangsters etc. **2** the frontman who pays or receives protection money on behalf of illegal gamblers or the authorities. [ICE n.¹ (3) + sfx *-man*]

ice-o *n.* [1920s+] (*Aus.*) an iceman. [SE *ice* + -o sfx (4)]

ice off *v. see* ICE v.⁴.

ice out *v. see* ICE v.³ (1).

ice palace *n.* **1** [1920s–30s] (*US Und.*) an upmarket saloon or brothel. **2** [1940s+] (*US Black*) a jewellery store. [ICE n.³ + SE *palace*]

ice queen *n.* [1980s+] an unemotional or unresponsive woman. [var. on ICE MAIDEN n.]

ice-tong doctor *n.* [1930s–50s] (*US drugs*) a doctor who is happy to supply illegal drugs. [*ice tongs*, i.e. a nickname for the tools used by an illegal abortionist, who often compunded one crime with another]

ice wagon *n.*¹ [late 19C–1950s] (*US*) a slow-moving person or vehicle; thus *wagonish*, slow.

ice wagon *n.*² *see* WATER-WAGON n.

ichiban *n.* [20C+] (*US*) the best. [Jap. *ichiban*, number 1, picked up by US troops serving in the Korean War (1951–3)]

icing expert *n.* (*also* **icing queen**) [1940s+] (*gay*) a fellator. [ICE-CREAM n.² + SE *expert*]

ick *n.*¹ (*also* **ickaroo**) [1930s+] (*US Black*) a fool, a sucker. [ICKY n. (1)]

ick *n.*² [1940s+] anything disgusting, e.g. greasy dirt. [backform. f. ICKY adj. (3)]

ick *adj.* [1960s+] (*US*) sickly, over-sentimental, distasteful. [abbr. ICKY adj. (1)]

ickaroo *n. see* ICK n.¹.

icky *n.* [1930s–50s] (*US Black*) **1** a stupid person, a person who is conventional. **2** a member of the upper classes. [ICKY adj. (1); thus lit. one who likes only 'bad' (from a Black perspective) jazz]

icky *adj.* (*also* **icky-boo, icky-poo**) **1** [1920s+] (*orig. US*) of a person or an object (typically a film or play), sickly, over-sentimental. **2** [1920s+] (*mainly US teen*) usu. of food, sticky, sweet, unpleasant. **3** [1920s+] (*mainly teen*) (*also* **yicky**) distasteful, nauseating, unpleasant. **4** [1960s] (*US drugs*) feeling sick as part of heroin withdrawal. [echoic of SE *sticky/sick* + 'baby-talk' sfx *-boo/poo*]

ickyness *n.* [1960s+] (*US teen*) disgust. [ICKY adj. (3)]

icod! *excl. see* ECOD! excl.

I could care less *phr. see* I COULDN'T CARE LESS phr.

I could do her a favour *phr.* (*also* **I could do that a favour**) [1930s+] remark made by a man of a passing female. [the 'favour' would, of course, be sexual]

I could do that with my prick out *phr.* [1930s+] a phr. used to emphasize the ease of a task. [PRICK n. (2)]

I could do with *phr.* [late 18C+] I would be glad to have, I need.

I could eat a baby's arse through the bars of a cot *phr.* (*also* **I could eat a baby's bottom through the monkey cage in the zoo, ...a farmer's arse (through a hedge)**) [20C+] I am extremely hungry.

I could eat a horse (and chase the jockey) *phr.* (*also* **...and chase the rider**) [20C+] (*Aus./US*) I am extremely hungry.

I could eat the hind leg off a donkey *phr.* (*also* **I could eat the hind leg of a boudie**) [20C+] I am extremely hungry.

I couldn't care less *phr.* (*also* **I could care less**) [1940s+] (*UK/US*) a statement of absolute indifference, although the opposite sentiment, albeit hidden, may be the true one; sometimes ext. as (*N.Z.*) *I couldn't care less if the cow calves or breaks a leg*.

I could shit through the eye of a needle *phr.* [late 19C+] a phr. used by someone suffering from diarrhoea.

I could struggle *phr.* [late 19C] a phr. indicating that one would like a drink. [joc. understatement of one's enthusiasm]

I could use her shit for toothpaste *phr.* (*also* **I'd crawl three miles over broken glass to use her shit for toothpaste**) [1950s+] a hugely exaggerated phr. implying the extent of one's infatuation.

icy *adj.* [1910s+] (*US*) emotionless. [ICE n.² (1)]

icy-blues *n. see* BABY-BLUES n.¹.

icy eye *n. see* COLD-EYE n.

icy mitt *n. see* FROZEN MITT n.

icy pop *n.* [1990s+] (*US campus*) beer. [SE *icy* + POP n.² (4)]

i.d. *n.*¹ [1940s+] **1** identification. **2** an identification photograph or card. [abbr.]

i.d. *n.*² [1950s+] (*US*) the penis. [abbr. SE *identification*; a pun on the phr. *Let's see your I.D.*]

i.d. *v.* [1940s+] (*orig. US*) to identify. [abbr.]

Idaho rainstorm *n.* (*also* **Idaho brainstorm, ...rain, ...shower**) [1930s+] (*US*) a dust storm.

i.d.b. *n.* [1920s] a general insult. [abbr. *ignorant Dutch bastard*]

i.d.b. *phr.* [1980s+] used by privileged young men to describe their occupation. [abbr. *in daddy's business*]

I'd crawl three miles over broken glass to use her shit for toothpaste *phr. see* I COULD USE HER SHIT FOR TOOTHPASTE phr.

idea!, the (very) *excl.* [20C+] an excl. implying one's (supposed) shock or disgust on hearing a proposition (usu. accredited to women, esp. working-class or lower middle-class women).

idea box *n.* (*also* **idea pot**) [late 18C–19C; 1930s+] the brain, the head, knowledge. [1930s+ use is US Black]

ideal home *n.* [1950s+] a comb. [rhy. sl.]

I'd eat my chips out of her knickers *phr.* [1970s+] a statement of absolute (sexual) devotion. [var. on I COULD USE HER SHIT FOR TOOTHPASTE phr.]

I declare *n. see* I DON'T CARE n.

identity *n. see* OLD IDENTITY n.

I desire *n.* [mid-19C–1940s] a fire. [rhy. sl.]

I'd have done it for half a farthing *phr.* [late 19C–1920s] it would have taken very little persuasion to make me do it.

I didn't come down in the last shower (of rain) *phr.* [20C+] (*Aus.*) I'm not stupid, don't take me for a fool.

I didn't fall off a Christmas tree *phr.* [1940s+] I'm not stupid, don't take me for a fool.

idiot box *n.* (*also* **idiot, idiot's lantern**) **1** [1950s+] (*orig. US*) the television, implying that TV watchers are less than normally intelligent (cf. IDIOT TUBE n.). **2** [1990s+] a computer. [BOX n.⁵ (6); note TV jargon *idiot girl*, the girl who holds up cue cards for an announcer or other performer; *idiot card*, a cue card]

idiot fringe *n.* [late 19C–1920s] a popular hairstyle for girls and young women.

idiot juice *n.* [1970s+] (*US drugs*) a mixture of nutmeg and water, used mainly in prisons. [its effects]

idiot light *n.* [1960s+] a warning light, usu. red, that goes on when a fault occurs in a mechanical or electrical device.

idiot oil *n.* [1980s+] **1** alcohol. **2** a fig. 'liquid', immersion in which renders one stupid. [(1) its effects]

idiot pills *n.* [1960s+] (*drugs*) barbiturates, any strong sedatives (cf. BARBIT *n.*). [their effects]

idiot-proof *adj.* [1980s+] of a machine or a mechanical process, supposedly designed to be comprehensible to even the least technologically minded person.

idiot's lantern *n. see* IDIOT BOX *n.*

idiot spoon *n.* [1940s–60s] (*US*) a shovel. [the supposed level of intelligence of those that wield them]

idiot stick *n.* [1930s+] (*US*) **1** a shovel. **2** a hoe. [for ety. *see* IDIOT SPOON *n.*; note also use by US army in Vietnam to mean (1) a rifle, (2) a wooden yoke used by Vietnamese to carry 2 baskets or water buckets etc]

idiot tool *n.* [1980s+] (*US*) a shovel. [for ety. *see* IDIOT SPOON *n.*]

idiot tube *n.* [1960s+] (*US*) the television, implying that TV watchers are less than normally intelligent (cf. IDIOT BOX *n.*). [SE *idiot* + TUBE *n.*[3] (2)]

idjeet/idjit/idjut *n. see* EEJIT *n.*

Idle Hall *n.* [20C+] (*W.I.*) a notional place used fig. to mean a state of unemployment; thus *work at Idle Hall*, to be unemployed.

idle jubbie *n.* [1990s+] (*W.I.*) a young unemployed person. [SE *idle* + JUBBIE *n.*]

idles, the *n.* [17C] laziness, esp. in the guise of an illness; often as *sick of the idles*.

idleset *n.* [20C+] **1** (*Ulster*) a fat stomach. **2** (*Scot.*) unemployment. [(1) evidence of one's idleness]

I don't care *n.* (*also* **I declare**) [1930s–40s] (*US*) a chair. [rhy. sl.]

I don't make the fries *phr.* [1990s+] (*US teen*) a phr. used to express the fact that one does not have any influence on the outcome of life. [the image of a worker in a junk-food restaurant]

I don't think *phr.* [mid-19C+] an ironic phr. used at the end of a declaratory statement as a means of negating whatever has just been said, e.g. *She's a real sweetie. I don't think!*

idrin *n.* [1950s+] (*orig. W.I. Rasta*) one's fig. 'brothers'. [W.I. pron. of SE *brethren*]

iez-haad *adj.* [1950s+] (*W.I. Rasta*) thick-skulled, stubborn, unwilling or unable to hear. [W.I. pron. 'ears-hard']

I feel you *phr.* [1990s+] (*US Black*) a phr. of affirmation, agreement. [FEEL *v.* (2)]

if ever! *excl.* [early 19C+] would you believe it? is it possible?

iffy *adj.* (*also* **iffey**) [1930s+] (*orig. US*) **1** marginal, not wholly acceptable, unpalatable. **2** involved with criminality. **3** difficult. **4** ambiguous. [SE *if* + sfx *-y*]

if his cap be made of wool *phr.* [17C–18C] certainly, without any doubt. [? the common use of woollen caps; Hindley, *The Old Book Collector's Miscellany* (1871–3), suggests that woollen caps (the wearing of which was enforced by law in 1571) were the mark of a superior citizen, implying a def. 'however grand you are', but usage tends to override this]

if his/her brains were dynamite, there wouldn't be enough to blow his/her nose off *phr.* (*also* ...head off) [1920s+] a statement underlining the absolute stupidity or inadequacy of the person so assailed. Vars. include [1920s+] *if his brains were bells, they wouldn't make his ears ring*; [1970s] (*US Black*) *if his brains were gas, they couldn't power a flea's motorcycle around the inside of a Cheerio*; [1990s+] (*US Black*) *if his brains were made of elastic, there wouldn't be enough to make a garter for a canary's leg.*

if I'm lying I'm dying *phr.* (*also* **if I'm lying I'm flying**) [1930s+] (*US Black*) a phr. implying the speaker's absolute honesty and good faith.

if it ain't you, it's somebody else *phr.* (*also* ...someone else) [1930s+] (*US Black*) a phr. in which the speaker indicates a belief that trouble is imminent.

if it had been a bear it would have bit you *phr.* (*also* ...a snake...) [17C+] a phr. used to ridicule someone who can't see something that is right in front of them.

if it were raining pea soup I'd get hit on the head by a fork *phr.* [1920s+] (*Aus.*) a general expression of continual bad luck.

if my aunt had been a man, she'd have been my uncle *phr.* [mid-17C+] a phr. used as a rejoinder to a speaker who has just finished a long and laborious explanation of the obvious.

if the cat went a pound *phr.* [1990s+] (*Irish*) an expression of impossibility. [GO *v.*[4] (1); i.e. the unlikely event of a cat betting]

if they're big enough, they're old enough *phr.* [1910s+] a phr. used among men to suggest that, whatever actual age a girl is, if she has reached puberty biologically (menstruation, body shape etc), she is old enough for intercourse.

if they're old enough to bleed, they're old enough to fuck *phr.* (*also* if they're old enough to bleed, they're old enough to butcher; if they're big enough to bleed...) [1960s+] a phr. used among men to suggest that if a girl is old enough to menstruate she is old enough for intercourse; similarly used by homosexuals of young boys.

if you can't be good, be careful *phr. see* BE GOOD *phr.*

if you can't do the time, don't do the crime *phr.* [1960s+] (*orig. US Und.*) don't take an action if you cannot deal with the concomitant responsibilities. [TIME *n.*[1]; orig. Und. but used fig. in the wider world]

if you don't mind *phr.* [late 17C+] a phr. used as a form of reproof, esp. to someone who barges in, pushes one aside etc.

if your aunt had balls, she'd be your uncle *phr.* [20C+] a phr. used as a rejoinder to a speaker who has just finished a long and laborious explanation of the obvious. [BALLS *n.*[1] (1)]

ig *n.* (*also* **igg**) [1960s–70s] (*US Black*) a snub, a rejection. [IG *v.* (1)]

ig *v.* (*also* **give the ig, igg**) [1930s+] (*orig. US Black*) **1** to ignore a person deliberately, to snub. **2** to overlook something, to ignore the facts. [abbr. SE *ignore*]

igaree *v.* (*also* **iggery, iggry, igri**) [1910s] to hurry up, to go quickly. [IGAREE! *excl.*]

igaree! *excl.* (*also* **iggry!**) [1910s] hurry up! quickly! [Arabic *igaree*, quick]

igaretsay *n.* [1940s+] (*orig. US*) a cigarette. [cod Lat.]

iggy *adj.* [1910s] (*US*) ignorant. [abbr. + sfx *-y*]

ight *phr. see* A-IGHT *phr.*

ig man *n.* [20C+] (*US Black*) an ignorant *man*, a fool. [abbr.]

ignant *n.* [1940s+] (*US Black*) an ignorant, stupid person. [abbr./pron. of SE *ignorant*]

ig'nant oil *n. see* IGNORANT OIL *n.*

ignite (oil) *n.* [1980s+] (*US Black*) whisky. [it sets the drinker 'on fire']

igno *n.* [1970s+] (*US*) a fool (cf. BOBO *n.*[1]). [abbr. SE *ignoramus*]

ignorance *n.* [1940s+] (*W.I.*) extreme anger that threatens the other person. [IGNORANT *adj.* (1)]

ignorant *adj.* [1940s+] (*W.I./UK Black*) **1** angry, irascible, short-tempered. **2** arrogant, ill-natured, bullying. [dial. *ignorant*, uncouth, ill-mannered]

ignorant as Paddy's pig *phr.* [1970s+] (*N.Z.*) very stupid. [PADDY *n.* (1); thus negative racial stereotyping]

ignorant oil *n.* (*also* **ig'nant oil**) [1960s+] (*US Black*) alcohol. [its effects]

ignorant stick *n.* [1950s+] (*US*) a shovel. [var. on IDIOT STICK *n.*, i.e. the lack of intelligence of those that wield them]

I got it like that *phr.* [1980s+] (*US Black teen*) a phr. indicating that one is doing well.

igri *see under* IGAREE.

I guess *phr.* [mid-19C+] (*orig. US*) I imagine, I assume, I am fairly certain; often in reply to a question as 'I suppose you are right'.

I guess yes! *excl.* [late 19C+] (*US*) yes indeed! absolutely!

I guess you laid that *phr.* [1930s] (*US Black*) a compliment to a person who has just made a clever retort. [LAY v.⁴]

igxagxa *n.* [1950s+] (*S.Afr. Black*) **1** a poor White. **2** one who falls between 2 ethnic cultures. [Xhosa *ukugxagxa*, one who has become poor and squalid]

I hate it *phr.* (*also* **I hate that**) [1980s+] (*US campus*) a sarcastic expression of pleasure.

I heard that! *excl.* [1980s] (*US campus*) an excl. of agreement. [HEAR v.]

I hear you *phr.* [1930s+] an emphatic way of saying I understand, 'yes'. [HEAR v.; note jazz use of *hear*, to become emotionally involved with the music, to concentrate absolutely on what one is hearing]

I hope to spit! *excl.* [1910s–20s] (*US*) an excl. of agreement.

ijet/ijit/ijjit/ijut *n. see* EEJIT n.

ijuwishi *n.* [1960s+] (*S.Afr. Black*) expensive clothing. [var. on JEWISH n.]

Ike *n.* (*US*) **1** [late 19C+] (*also* **country ike**) an ignorant rustic male (cf. ALVIN n.). **2** [20C+] a self-important, pretentious person; esp. as *wise Ike*. **3** [20C+] a derog. term for a Jew (cf. ABE n.¹). [abbr. of the 'rural' or Jewish name *Isaac*; (1) + COUNTRY adj.]

ike *v.* [2000s] (*US Black*) to lose one's temper. [musician *Ike* Turner's (b.1931) notoriously bad relations with his former wife, the singer Tina (b.1939)]

ikey *n.*¹ **1** [early 19C+] a nickname for a Jew or one who has 'Jewish' features (cf. ABE n.¹). **2** [mid-19C] (*UK Und.*) a Jewish receiver of stolen goods. **3** [mid-19C+] a derog. term for a Jew. **4** [late 19C+] one who plays a duplicitous, 'sharp' trick. **5** [20C+] a pawnbroker (irrespective of racial origin). **6** [20C+] a moneylender. [abbr. IKEY-MO n.; lit. or fig. refs. to stereotyped Jewish characteristics]

ikey *n.*² *see* IKEY-MO n. (5).

ikey *n.*³ [1910s+] (*S.Afr.*) a student of the University of Cape Town; thus *Ikeys*, the university itself. [proper name *Isaac*, f. the large Jewish enrolment; thus ? f. IKEY-MO n.; despite the obvious racial implication, the term is regularly used in sports reports without further comment]

ikey *adj.* **1** [late 19C+] Jewish. **2** [late 19C+] funny. **3** [late 19C+] extraordinary, showy. **4** [late 19C+] smart, cunning. **5** [late 19C+] (*US*) (*also* **iky**) impertinent, cheeky. **6** [late 19C+] melodramatic, done for effect (the image of the over-emotional Jew). **7** [1900s] (*Aus.*) large in amount. [IKEY n.¹ (1)]

ikey *v.* (*also* **iky**) [1930s–60s] (*US*) to cheat financially. [IKEY n.¹]

ikey-mo *n.* **1** [early 19C+] a derog. term for a Jew; thus the various stereotypes (cf. ABE n.¹). **2** [early 19C+] a Jewish receiver, moneylender, pawnbroker, peddler. **3** [mid-19C+] a loafer, a layabout. **4** [mid-19C+] a tip, information. **5** [mid-19C+] (*Aus.*) (*also* **ikey, mo, moses**) a bookmaker. **6** [20C+] (*Aus.*) a mean person. [SE *Isaac* + *Moses*, 2 typical Jewish given names; note Kentish dial. *ikey*, proud; 'probably popularised by the *Ikey Mo* who was partner in the nefarious doings of the original Ally Sloper, the first British strip-cartoon 'character', in the series which started in *Judy* magazine, 1867, and ran for many years' (E.P.)]

ikey-mo *adj.* **1** [late 19C+] Jewish. **2** [late 19C+] artful, crafty, knowing. **3** [late 19C+] having a good opinion of oneself, stuck-up. **4** [1960s] dandified. [IKEY-MO n.]

ikeyness *n.* [late 19C+] Jewishness and the derog. stereotypes associated with it, i.e. artfulness, craftiness, greed, financial chicanery etc (the subject need not be a Jew). [IKEY n.¹ + sfx -*ness*]

I kid you not *phr.* [1950s+] (*orig. US*) a phr. implying that the speaker is being absolutely serious. [KID (AROUND) v. (2)]

iky *see under* IKEY.

ilie *adj.* [1950s] (*W.I. Rasta*) describes something valuable, exalted, sacred. [lit. use of SE *highly*]

Ilie Nastase *n.* [1990s+] the lavatory (cf. ANGUS ARMANASCO n.). [rhy. sl. = CARSEY n. (4); ult. Romanian tennis player *Ilie Nastase* (b.1946)]

I like it, but it doesn't like me *phr.* [late 19C+] a phr. that refers to food or drink that, while delicious, has a deleterious effect on the consumer.

ilk *adj.* [2000s] (*US Black*) unpleasant, bizarre, distasteful. [ILL adj. (2)]

ill *adj.* (*US Black/teen*) **1** [1900s; 1980s+] angry, frustrated. **2** [1970s+] aggressive, offensive, bad. **3** [1980s+] wonderful, first-rate; on the bad = good model. **4** [1990s+] bizarre, surprising. **5** [1990s+] unattractive. [fig. uses of SE *ill*, unwell]

ill *v.* (*orig. US Black teen*) **1** [1980s+] to act crazily, aggressively, wildly. **2** [1990s+] to do something very well. [(1) ILL adj. (2); (2) ILL adj. (3)]

Illadelphia *n.* [2000s] (*US Black*) Philadelphia, PA. [ILL adj. (3)]

I'll be! *excl. see* I'LL BE DAMNED! excl.

I'll be a... *see also under* I'M A...

I'll be a dirty motherfucker *phr.* (*also* **I'm a motherfucker**) [1960s+] an excl. of commitment, usu. followed by 'if' and some form of negative. [MOTHERFUCKER n. (3)]

I'll be a dirty word! *excl.* (*also* **I'll be a dirty name!**) [20C+] a mild oath. [SE *dirty word*, i.e. euph. for I'LL BE DAMNED! excl.]

I'll be a (lowdown) son of a bitch! *excl.* [20C+] an excl. of surprise or annoyance. [LOWDOWN adj. + SONOFABITCH n.]

I'll be a marble (upon your taw) *phr. see* I'LL BE ONE UP ON YOUR TAW PRESENTLY phr.

I'll be a monkey's uncle! *excl.* [1920s+] a general expression of surprise.

I'll be a rat's ass! *excl.* [1960s–70s] a general excl. of surprise.

I'll be blowed! *excl.* (*also* **blowed! I'm blowed!**) [mid-19C+] a general excl. of surprise, shock etc. [euph. for I'LL BE DAMNED! excl.]

I'll be cow-kicked! *excl.* [20C+] (*US*) a euph. for I'LL BE DAMNED! excl.; often ext. as *cow-kicked by a jackass/mule*.

I'll be damned! *excl.* (*also* **damned! I'll be! I'm damned!**) [mid-18C+] an excl. of annoyance, surprise etc; usu. as *I'll be damned if...*. [DAMNED adj.]

I'll be darned! *excl.* (*also* **I'm darned!**) [19C+] a mild oath, a euph. for I'LL BE DAMNED! excl. [DARNED adj.]

I'll be dicked! *excl.* [1960s] (*US*) a general excl. of surprise, amazement. [DICKED adj.¹ (1)]

I'll be doggoned! *excl.* [mid-19C+] (*US*) a general excl. of surprise, amazement. [DOGGONE adj.]

I'll be fucked! *excl.* [1940s+] a general excl. of surprise, anger etc. [fig. use of FUCKED adj.¹ (4)]

I'll be hanged! *excl.* (*also* **hanged! I'm hanged!**) [late 16C+] a general excl. of surprise, annoyance etc. [SE *hang*]

I'll be jiggered! *excl.* [mid-19C+] a general excl. of surprise, irritation etc. [JIGGER v.¹ (2)]

I'll be jitterbugged! *excl.* [1930s] (*US Black*) an excl. of surprise. [nonsense use of JITTERBUG v. (1)]

I'll be john browned! *excl.* [20C+] (*US*) a joc. euph. for I'LL BE HANGED! excl. [JOHN BROWN v.]

I'll be one up on your taw presently *phr.* (*also* **I'll be a marble (upon your taw), I'll be one marble...**) [late 18C–19C] a threatening phr. meaning I'll deal with you in due course. [marbles imagery; SE *taw*, the large marble with which a player shoots]

I'll be photographed! *excl.* [1940s] (*Aus./N.Z.*) a general excl. of anger, surprise or astonishment. [euph. for I'LL BE FUCKED! excl.]

I'll be pick-axed! *excl.* [1910s] (*Aus.*) a strong expression of denial or refusal.

I'll be seeing you *phr.* [1940s+] goodbye.

I'll be shot! *excl.* (*also* **I'll see you shot first!**) [mid-18C–1920s] a general excl. of surprise; also as *I'll be shot if…*, a strong expression of denial or refusal.

I'll be switched! *excl.* [mid-19C–1940s] an excl. of irritation, surprise, denial. [SE *switch*, to thrash]

I'll bet *phr.* [late 19C+] a phr. used to imply (depending on context) the speaker's enthusiastic or sceptical response to what they have just heard.

I'll be there *n.* [20C+] a chair. [rhy. sl.]

I'll buy that *phr. see* BUY v. (1).

I'll eat my hat *phr.* [late 18C+] a statement of utter disbelief, e.g. *if such and such is true/happens, I'll eat my hat.*

illegim *n.* [1900s] (*Aus.*) an *illegim*itimate child. [abbr.]

illegit *adj.* [1910s+] *illegit*imate, criminal. [abbr.]

illegitimate *n.*[1] [19C] (*Aus.*) a free, i.e. non-convict, Australian settler. [paradoxically, a *legitimate* settler was a criminal who had been sentenced to transportation]

illegitimate *n.*[2] [early 19C] a counterfeit sovereign; thus *young illegitimate*, a counterfeit half-sovereign.

illegitimate *n.*[3] [mid-19C] a poor class of costermonger looked down on by the mainstream costers, selling pea soup, sweetmeats, spice-cakes etc.

ill fortune *n.* [late 17C–early 19C] a ninepence coin. [unfortunate in that it is not a whole shilling]

I'll give you Jim Smith! *excl.* [late 19C] a threat to give someone else a beating. [*Jim Smith* was a contemporary pugilist]

I'll go he! *excl.* [1950s+] (*N.Z.*) an excl. of surprise.

I'll go hopping to hell! *excl.* (*also* **I'll go hopping! I'll go hopping to hell backwards!**) [20C+] an excl. of amazement, approval or admiration.

illing *adj.* (*also* **illin'**) [1980s+] **1** (*orig. US Black/teen*) acting or thinking wildly, aggressively, crazily. **2** (*US campus*) annoyed, unhappy. **3** (*US campus*) in a difficult or unpleasant situation, under severe stress. **4** (*US campus*) drunk (cf. AFFLICTED adj.). **5** (*US campus*) unattractive, old-fashioned. [ILL v. (1)]

I'll knock out your eight eyes *phr.* [late 18C–early 19C] a threat, commonly used by Billingsgate fishwives. ['a common Billingsgate threat from one fish nymph to another: every woman, according to the naturalists of that society, having eight eyes, viz. two seeing eyes, two bub-eyes [cf. BUBBIES n.], a bell-eye [SE *belly*], two popes-eyes [f. SE *pope's eye*, the lymphatic gland in a leg of mutton, regarded as a delicacy; here presumably the urinal and anal orifices], and a ***-eye' (Grose, 1796); the censored term remains mysterious, it is, presumably, a ref. to the vagina]

I'll make you sing (o-be-joyful on the other side) *phr.* [late 18C–19C] a general threat of violence. ['o-be-joyful' implies hymn-singing; phr. mimics but predates 'I'll make you laugh on the wrong/other side of your face']

ill piece *n.* [1950s+] (*gay*) an unattractive and therefore unpopular homosexual. [SE *ill* + PIECE n.[1] (4)]

I'll say (so) *phr.* [1910s+] (*orig. US*) absolutely, definitely, I couldn't agree more.

I'll see you shot first! *excl. see* I'LL BE SHOT! excl.

I'll tickle your tail *phr.* [late 19C+] a threat of violence, although often teasing or joc.

illuminated *adj.* [20C+] drunk. [play on LIT (UP) adj. (1)]

illustrated shirt *n.* [mid-19C] a coloured shirt, as favoured by costermongers.

ill-willie *adj.* [20C+] (*Ulster*) uncooperative. [SE *ill will*]

illy *n.* [1980s] (*drugs*) marijuana. [ILL adj. (3)]

illywhacker *n.* [1940s+] (*Aus.*) a professional confidence man, esp. an itinerant following fairs and country shows. [*AND* offers no ety.; Baker, *The Australian Language* (1945), offers: 'the following terms for sharpers and those who live by their wits:

spieler, eeler-spee, eeler-whack and *illywhacker* (the last three are formed by transposition and mutilation of the first']

I.L.U.V.M. *phr.* [20C+] *I love u* (=you) *very much*; written on the envelopes of love letters. [abbr.]

I'm (a)… *see also under* I'LL BE (A)…

I'm a coon *phr.* (*also* **I'm a coyote/nigger**) [mid-19C+] a phr. used to refute a suggestion or hypothesis, and as an excl. of astonishment. [COON n. (5)/COYOTE n. (2)/NIGGER n.[1] (1)]

I'm a Dutchman *phr.* (*also* **I'm a Chinaman, …a bishop …a Chink, …a tinker, …a Turk, …Dutch, I'll be a Chinaman/Dutchman**) [late 18C+] a phr. used to refute a suggestion or hypothesis, usu. preceded by *If that's…then I'll be…*

I'm afloat *n.* **1** [mid-19C–1940s] (*UK/US*) a boat. **2** [late 19C+] (*also* **armour float**) a coat. [rhy. sl]

image *n.* [mid-19C+] a person attracting amused, affectionate or contemptuous glances, a 'sight'; esp. qualified as *old/little image.*

i-man *pron.* [1950s+] (*W.I. Rasta*) I, me, mine.

I'm a nigger *phr. see* I'M A COON phr.

I'm a tinker/Turk *phr. see* I'M A DUTCHMAN phr.

I'm a wreck *n. see* NERVOUS WRECK n.[2].

imbo *n.* [1950s–70s] (*Aus.*) a fool, a simpleton (cf. BOBO n.[1]). [SE *imbecile* + -O sfx (4)]

imbuggerance *n.* [1960s+] (*Aus.*) irrelevance. [phr. *I don't give a bugger*]

imby *n.* [1980s] (*US*) a fool, a simpleton (cf. BOBO n.[1]). [SE *imbecile*]

I'm chest not breast! *excl.* [1940s–60s] (*US Black/teen*) an excl. expressing one's masculinity, used to deny suggestions that one is weak or effeminate.

I'm Dutch *phr. see* I'M A DUTCHMAN phr.

I'm easy *phr.* [1940s+] (*orig. Aus.*) I don't mind, I'm satisfied whatever the outcome.

imey-wimey *n.* [1920s–30s] (*US Black*) a meek-sounding, whining voice. [? SE *whine* or elision of *I…me…why me?* + onomat.]

I'm from Missouri *phr.* [late 19C+] (*US*) a phr. used to denote one's scepticism and suspicions; usu. ext. with some form of *so you'll have to show me!* [orig. *I come from Missouri. You have got to show me*; the image is of the cautious countryman refusing to fall for the wiles of the city slicker. The phr. was popularized, although not actually coined, by Missouri Congressman Willard D. Vandiver (1854–1932) – see Cohen (ed.), *Studies in Slang* V (1997), pp105–28 for a detailed discussion]

I'm ghost *phr.* [1990s+] (*US Black*) I've left, I'm leaving. [SE *ghost*/GHOST n.[5]]

I'm history *phr.* [1980s+] goodbye; thus *make history!* go away! [SE *history*]

I'm in the wind *phr.* [1970s] goodbye. [IN THE WIND phr.[2] (1)]

imma *n.* (*also* **immy**) [1920s+] a marble. [SE *immy*, a choice marble made in imitation, as of a cornelian or an agate; ult. SE *imitation*]

immense *adj.* [mid-18C–1930s] extremely good, splendid.

immense *adv.* [mid-18C–mid-19C] splendidly, well. [IMMENSE adj.]

immensikoff *n.* [late 19C–1900s] a bulky, fur-lined overcoat. [coined by the music-hall star Arthur Lloyd (1840–1904), who called himself *Immensikoff* and appeared on stage in such a coat to sing, c.1868, his hit 'The Shoreditch Toff']

immensikoff *adj.* [late 19C–1900s] splendid, esp. as regards one's dress. [IMMENSIKOFF n.]

immies *n.* [1940s+] (*US*) **1** the game of marbles. **2** the eyes. [SE *immy*, a highly rated marble, made to resemble a semi-precious stone, e.g. cornelian, agate]

immigrant chic *n. see* PORTAGEE COLONIAL n.

I'm missing *phr.* [1990s+] a phr. meaning I'm leaving.

immo *adj. see* IMO adj.

immortal *adj.* **1** [mid-16C–mid-17C] superhuman, inhuman, excessive. **2** [mid-19C–1900s] (*US*) wonderful, excellent.

immortally *adv.* [late 19C] (*US*) infinitely, superlatively. [IMMORTAL adj.]

immy *n. see* IMMA n.

I'm not crying *phr.* [1960s] (*US Black*) a phr. used to respond to a greeting, such as how are you? how are things? etc.

I'm not so green as I'm cabbage-looking *phr.* (*also* **I'm not so soft...**) [late 19C+] don't take me for a fool, I may look stupid but I'm not. [SE *green*, naïve]

imo *adj.* [1940s+] (*US Black/campus*) *im*itation, counterfeit. [abbr. SE *imitation*]

imoogie *adj. see* MOEGIE adj.

I'm outtie *phr.* (*also* **I'm out**) [1990s+] (*US teen*) I'm leaving. [lit. *I'm out of here*]

impale *v.* [19C] to have sexual intercourse (cf. BANG v.¹).

imperence *n.* [mid-18C–19C] impudence, impertinence; thus *imperent*, impudent; also in direct address. [SE *impudence*]

imperial pop *n.* [late 19C–1900s] ginger beer. [POP n.² (1) + the fact that the Emperor Napoleon III (r.1852–70) declared it to be his favourite drink]

impimpi *n.* [1960s+] (*S.Afr.*) a police informer. [SE *pimp* or Zulu *umbimbi*, a conspiracy or *iphimpi*, a species of cobra]

impixlocated *adj.* [1930s] tipsy. [SE *intoxicated* + PIXILLATED adj. (2)]

implement *n.* [late 17C–18C] a fool who is persuaded to take part in a dangerous or foolhardy enterprise.

import *n.* [1920s+] (*US campus*) a date or partner brought from elsewhere (outside the college town itself) to attend a party or dance.

importance *n.* [mid-17C–1910s] one's wife. [abbr. COMFORTABLE IMPORTANCE n. (2)]

impos *adj.* [1900s–20s] *impos*sible. [abbr.]

impost-taker *n.* [late 17C–early 19C] one who lends money to losing gamblers, taking advantage of their desperate need for new funds to extort the highest possible interest. [SE *impost*, a tax or customs levy + *taker*]

impot *n.* [late 19C–1920s] (*UK juv.*) a (public) school punishment, usu. writing 'lines'. [abbr. SE *imposition*]

impudence *n.* [mid-18C–19C] the penis.

impudent stealing *n.* [18C–19C] 'cutting out the backs of coaches and robbing the seats' (Grose, 1796).

impure *n.* [late 18C–19C] a prostitute.

I'm saying doe *phr.* [2000s] (*US Black*) a phr. of agreement, affirmation.

imshee *v.* (*also* **imshi, imshy**) [1910s+] (*orig. milit.*) 1 to go away, to vanish. 2 to hurry someone along. [IMSHEE! excl.]

imshee! *excl.* (*also* **imshi!**) [1910s+] (*orig. milit.*) go away! [Arab. *imshi*, go away, adopted by WW1 troops serving in the Middle East]

I'm so (frisky) *n.* [late 19C+] whisky. [rhy. sl.]

I'm so hungry I could eat a shit sandwich – only I don't like bread *phr.* [1950s+] (*Aus.*) a phr. implying the intensity of one's hunger. [SHIT n.¹ (1)]

I'm straight *phr.* [2000s] (*US teen*) I'm fine.

I'm sure *phr. see* I AM SURE phr.

I'm sure I don't know *phr.* [mid-19C+] a phr. used assertively, i.e. to add emphasis to one's earlier statement.

I'm talking to the butcher, not the block *phr.* [20C+] a dismissive phr. used to put a stop to an intervention by someone the speaker does not consider worthy of an audience; and other dismissive examples, such as *I want to see the butcher, not the block* (cf. TALK TO THE ENGINEER, NOT THE OILY RAG v.; TALK TO THE ORGAN-GRINDER, NOT THE MONKEY v.).

I'm there *phr.* [1970s+] (*US campus*) an expression of support.

I must break you *phr.* [1990s+] (*US Black teen*) a general phr. used to threaten an opponent or rival.

I'm willing *n.* [20C+] a shilling. [rhy. sl.]

in *n.* [1920s+] (*orig. US*) a means of infiltrating otherwise closed groups, usu. those holding power and influence; often in phr. *have an in*.

in *adj.*¹ 1 [late 18C–19C] in pawn. 2 [19C+] in prison. 3 [20C+] (*US*) facing trouble, under scrutiny. 4 [1970s] in debt.

in *adj.*² 1 [19C+] (*UK Und.*) being part of a closed or influential group, often through the payment of bribes, wielding of influence etc. 2 [mid-19C] in season. 3 [mid-19C] fashionable. 4 [late 19C+] (*US Und.*) being a member of a confidence trick team, or, as a 'civilian', aware and tolerant of their activity. 5 [20C+] guaranteed of success in a given project, e.g. sexual seduction. 6 [20C+] socially acceptable. 7 [20C+] partaking in a game, e.g. of cards or pool. 8 [1950s+] (*US*) being a member of one of the armed services. 9 [1960s+] (*drugs*) connected with drug suppliers. 10 [1960s+] limited to a small circle, e.g. a shared sense of humour. 11 [1980s+] being a member of the police force.

in a bad loaf *phr. see* IN BAD BREAD phr.

in a bad skin *phr.* [late 18C–1910s] bad-tempered, 'out of sorts'.

in a bad way *phr.* 1 [late 19C+] suffering problems, difficulties. 2 [20C+] drunk. 3 [1960s] (*US campus*) sexually frustrated.

in a bag *phr. see* IN THE BAG phr.² (1).

in a big way *adv.* [late 19C+] (*orig. US*) very much, extremely, intensely.

in a box *phr.* [mid-19C+] in difficulties, in a confused state of mind, in a quandary; thus *in the same box*, sharing the same problems.

in a bull's arse! *excl.* [1960s] completely impossible! absolutely not! I don't believe you! go away! [var. on IN A PIG'S ASS! excl.]

in a cat's ass! *excl.* [1940s] (*orig. US*) completely impossible! absolutely not! I don't believe you! go away! [var. on IN A PIG'S ASS! excl.]

in a crack *phr.* [early 18C–19C] very soon, in a moment.

in a cross *phr.* [1950s–60s] (*US Black*) in trouble, at a disadvantage; usu. as *put in a cross*, to put into a difficult situation.

in a difficulty *phr.* [19C] drunk. [euph.]

in a good skin *phr.* (*also* **in a whole skin**) [mid-18C–1910s] good-humoured, cheerful.

in a hobble *phr.* [18C–19C] 1 in trouble, perplexed. 2 committed for trial. [Scot. dial. *habble*, a difficulty, a perplexity]

in a hole *phr. see* IN THE HOLE phr.

in a horn *phr.* [mid-19C+] (*US*) a general phr. of dismissal. [? dial. *in a horn*, expression of incredulity]

in a kick *phr.* [mid-19C] in a moment, very soon. [KICK n.⁷ (1)]

in alt *adj.* [mid-18C–early 19C] haughty, arrogant. [musical jargon *in alt*, in the octave above the treble stave, i.e. a high tone]

in a man's beef, be *v.* [late 18C–early 19C] to wound a man with a sword. [BEEF n.¹ (3)]

in a minute *phr.* [1970s+] (*US Black*) goodbye, see you later.

in and in *adv.* [1920s] (*US*) participating positively.

in-and-out *n.*¹ 1 [mid-17C–mid-19C] (*also* **in-and-to**) the penis. 2 [mid-17C+] (*also* **in-and-in, in-out, outs and ins**) sexual intercourse; thus attrib. and fig. as a euph. for FUCK v.¹.

in-and-out *n.*² [late 19C] a pauper who alternates between living in a workhouse and street begging. [*in* and *out* of the workhouse]

in-and-out *n.*³ [20C+] 1 the nose. 2 a cigarette. 3 a bottle of stout. 4 a tout, a racecourse tipster. 5 gout. 6 (*Aus.*) the throat. [rhy. sl.; (1) = SE *snout*; (2) = SNOUT n.² (2); (6) = SE *spout*]

in-and-out boy *n. see* IN-AND-OUT MAN n. (1).

in-and-outer *n.*¹ 1 [late 19C–1950s] (*US*) an incompetent, esp. in sport. 2 [1950s] (*US Und.*) a second-rate, petty criminal. 3 [1970s] (*US Und.*) a criminal who is arrested, but never actually charged and jailed. [in and out of success/prison/the police station]

in-and-outer *n.*² *see* IN-AND-OUT-OF n.

in and out like a fiddler's elbow *phr.* [20C+] 1 engaged in rapid and enthusiastic copulation. 2 (*Aus.*) extremely active without actually achieving anything.

in-and-out man *n.* 1 [1920s–50s] (*also* **in-and-out boy**) a second-rate criminal, i.e. one whose life alternates between being in and out of prison. **2** [1950s+] (*UK Und.*) an opportunist thief. [(1) in and out of prison; (2) one who goes quickly in and out of the house he is robbing]

in-and-out-of *n.* (*also* **in-and-outer**) [1940s] (*US Black*) a door.

in-and-out shop *n.* [20C+] a shop in a corridor along which are displayed the items for sale.

in-and-to *n. see* IN-AND-OUT *n.*[1] (1).

in a pickle *phr.* **1** [17C+] (*also* **in a pepper-pot**) in a mess, in difficulties. **2** [18C–early 19C] drunk. [PICKLE *n.*[1] (1)]

in a pig's ass! *excl.* (*also* **in a pigs!** **in a pig's arse!** ...**butt!** ...**ear!** ...**eye!** ...**gizzard!** ...**hole!** ...**neck!** ...**poke!** ...**snout!** ...**tit!** ...**tonsil!** ...**valise!** ...**wig!**) [mid-19C+] (*orig. US*) completely impossible, absolutely not! I don't believe you! go away! (cf. PIG'S ARSE! excl.). [US rural catchphrase *in the pig's ass*, referring to bestiality and, as such, the subject of a variety of coarse jokes, which depend on the mistaken orifice (the anus rather than the vagina) and the mistaken object of affection (the pig rather than the woman)]

in a pig's whisper *phr.* [early 19C; 1970s] very quickly, immediately.

in arsehole street *phr. see* UP ARSEHOLE STREET *phr.*

in a sling *phr.* [1940s–60s] (*US*) in difficulties.

in a stew *phr.* [late 19C–1910s] sweating heavily.

in a sweat *phr.* **1** [late 19C] keen. **2** [late 19C+] anxious, worried.

in a tight place/spot/squeeze *phr. see* TIGHT adj.[2] (1).

in a whole skin *phr. see* IN A GOOD SKIN *phr.*

in a zone *phr.* **1** [1980s+] (*US campus*) out of touch with reality, daydreaming or drunk. **2** [1990s+] confident, self-assured.

in bad *phr.* [20C+] (*US*) **1** out of favour. **2** in trouble.

in bad bread *phr.* (*also* **in a bad loaf**) [late 18C–early 19C] in trouble, in a difficult situation.

in bed with *phr.* (*also* **in bed together**) [1970s+] (*orig. US*) allied or associated with, usu. implying nefarious activities.

in-between *n.* [20C+] (*Aus.*) a male homosexual (cf. BOY-GIRL *n.*[1]). [rhy. sl. = QUEEN *n.*[2] (1)]

in-betweens *n.* [1970s+] (*drugs*) a mixture of amphetamines and barbiturates.

in bits over *phr.* [late 19C+] obsessed with.

in bondage *phr.* [20C+] (*US Black*) indebted to, under the control of, with a biblical implication.

in Bushey Park *phr. see* AT BUSHEY PARK *phr.*

in cack street *phr. see* IN SHIT STREET *phr.*

in cahoots (with) *phr.* (*also* **cahoots, in cahoot**) [early 19C+] (*orig. US*) in partnership (with), usu. implying a slightly disreputable or surreptitious alliance. [? Fr. *cahute*, cabin, or *cohorte*, company; other suggestions include US *cahot*, a pothole, or KER- pfx + *hoot*, albeit the latter remains inexplicable]

Inca message *n.* [1980s+] (*drugs*) cocaine (cf. ANDES CANDY *n.*). [the relation of cocaine to South America]

Incandescent District, the *n.* [1920s–50s] (*US*) Broadway, New York City.

inch *n.* [17C+] the penis. [it *inches* in]

inch *v.* [1990s+] (*US campus*) to steal. [abbr. HALF-INCH *v.*[1]]

in chancery *phr.* [19C–1900s] in an awkward situation. ['the tenacity and absolute control with which the Court of Chancery holds anything, and the certainty of cost and loss to property "in chancery"' (*OED*)]

inch and pinch *v.* [20C+] (*Ulster*) to live frugally.

in check *phr.* [1990s+] (*US teen*) under control. [SE *check*, to restrain]

incident *n.* [late 19C–1900s] (*orig. US*) an illegitimate child. [euph.]

in clover *phr.* [early 18C+] in comfort. ['to live luxuriously; clover being extremely delicious and fattening to cattle' (Johnson, *Dictionary*, 1755)]

in co *phr.* [early 19C–1910s] (*orig. US*) along with, *in* company with. [abbr.]

incog *adj.*[1] [late 17C–1930s] *incog*nito. [abbr.]

incog *adj.*[2] [19C] drunk. [Scot. dial. *cogue*, a drinking vessel or dram]

incognita *n.* [mid–late 19C] a courtesan, a high-class prostitute. [Lat. *incognita*, an unknown woman]

in collar *phr.* [mid-19C–1900s] employed. [the image is of a horse in its working harness]

in Crab Street *phr.* [early 19C] annoyed, irritated. [CRAB *v.*[1] (1)]

incubator *n.* [1900s] (*Aus., Sydney*) a wife.

inde *adj.* [1960s] *inde*pendent. [abbr.]

in deadly suspense *phr.* [late 18C–early 19C] hanged. [pun]

in decent nick *phr. see* IN GOOD NICK *phr.*

in deep shit *phr. see* IN (THE) SHIT *phr.*

indescribables *n.* [late 18C–19C] trousers (cf. DON'T-KNOW- WHAT-TO-CALL-'EMS *n.*).

index *n.* **1** [early 19C] the nose. **2** [early–mid-19C; 1930s–40s] the face. [(2) 20C use is US Black]

india *n.* [1950s–70s] (*camp gay*) a plain man, with homely, peasant features. [Sp. *india*, a peasant woman]

India man *n. see* INDIA WIPE *n.*

Indian *n.*[1] (*US*) **1** [mid-19C+] an uncouth, rowdy person, irrespective of actual race. **2** [mid-19C+] a person; esp. as *big Indian*, an influential, important person. **3** [late 19C+] a quick temper; esp. in *get one's Indian up*, to lose one's temper. [note B&L differentiate: 'to say that one has his "*Indian*" up" implies a great degree of vindictiveness, while *Dutch* wrath is stubborn but yielding to reason']

Indian *n.*[2] [late 19C] (*US*) a cent. [a picture of a Native American was engraved on the reverse]

Indian *v. see* INJUN *v.*

Indian charm *n.* [1990s+] the arm. [rhy. sl.]

Indian coffee *n.* [mid-19C+] (*US*) coffee made from reheated grounds. [the assumption being that 'Red Indians' deserved nothing better]

Indian giver *n.* (*orig. US*) **1** [mid-18C+] one who when giving, expects a gift in return; thus *Indian gift* and *Indian giving*. **2** [20C+] one who first gives, then takes back a gift. [the racist stereotype of the untrustworthy 'Red Indian']

Indian haircut *n.* [20C+] (*US*) scalping. [the stereotype of the warlike 'Red Indian', tomahawk in hand]

Indian hay *n.* [1930s+] (*drugs*) marijuana; thus *burn Indian hay/an Indian*, to smoke marijuana (cf. ACAPULCO (GOLD) *n.*; AFRICAN BUSH *n.*). [SE *Indian hemp* + HAY *n.*[3] (2)]

Indian hunting *n.* [19C] (*US*) a fight between 2 men. [ety. unknown]

indian joe *n.* [2000s] (*Irish*) a toe. [rhy. sl.]

Indian liquor *n.* (*also* **Indian rum/whisky**) [late 18C–19C] (*US*) the lowest-quality spirits. [the assumption that anything could be palmed off on 'Red Indians']

Indian pow-wow *n.* [early 19C+] (*US*) a noisy discussion or gathering. [racist stereotyping]

Indian rug *n.* [1960s+] (*gay*) a cheap wig done in braids. [SE *Indian* + RUG *n.*[1] (1)]

Indian rum *n. see* INDIAN LIQUOR *n.*

Indian side *n.* [1920s+] (*US, mainly Western*) **1** the right-hand side, esp. of a horse; in fig. use as 'correct'. **2** the wrong way of going about things. [the Indian practice of mounting a horse from the right, as opposed to Whites who mounted from the left]

Indian time *n.* [1960s+] (*US, mainly Western*) unpunctuality, a relaxed attitude to time-keeping (cf. AFRICAN (PEOPLE'S) TIME *n.*). [racial stereotyping]

Indian whisky *n. see* INDIAN LIQUOR *n.*

India wipe *n.* (*also* **India man**) [late 18C–early 19C] a handker-chief made of Indian (Asian) cotton.

Indie, the *n.* [1980s+] an abbr. for the *Independent* newspaper; thus *the Sindie*, the *Independent on Sunday*.

indie *n.* [1920s+] an independent (record label, film company etc).

indispensables *n.* [mid-19C] trousers (cf. DON'T-KNOW-WHAT-TO-CALL-'EMS n.). [note 20C+ Romanian *indispensabili*, underpants]

indispensible *n.* [early 19C] a small satchel or bag worn by a woman.

Indo *n.* **1** [1960s–70s] (*orig. Aus.*) *Indo*nesia. **2** [1980s+] (*drugs*) marijuana (cf. ACAPULCO (GOLD) n.). [abbr.]

in dock *phr.* **1** [late 18C+] out of work, out of circulation. **2** [late 18C+] in hospital. **3** [1920s+] of an object, usu. a car, undergoing repair. [fig use of SE *dry dock* where ships are laid up for repairs]

Indonesia *n.* [1980s+] (*US drugs*) **1** (*also* **Indonesian bud**) marijuana (cf. ACAPULCO (GOLD) n.). **2** the state of intoxication caused by marijuana, irrespective of origin. [SE *Indonesia*, the origin + BUD n.⁴ (1)]

indoor aviator *n.* [1920s–40s] (*US*) an elevator operator.

indoor golf *n.* [1920s–50s] (*US*) the game of craps dice (cf. ABYSSINIAN POLO n.).

indoor money *n.* [1960s+] (*UK Und.*) a reserve of cash for use in day-to-day life rather than the proceeds of a robbery.

indoor sledging *n.* [20C+] sexual intercourse.

indorse *v.* [18C–19C] to sodomize. [SE *in* + *dorse*, the back]

indorser *n.* [early 18C–19C] a male homosexual. [INDORSE v.]

indorse with a cudgel *v.* [late 18C–19C] to thrash, to beat with a stick. [SE *indorse*, stamping the flesh of one's victim]

in duck's guts, be *v.* [20C+] (*W.I.*) to be in a hopeless situation, to be in irretrievable difficulties.

indulge *v.* **1** [early 18C+] to eat or drink (to excess). **2** [1990s+] to have sexual intercourse.

industrial *adj.* [1980s+] (*US campus*) extremely masculine. [the image of an industrial worker as a 'real man']

industrial debutante *n.* [1980s+] (*US*) a prostitute who specializes in attending US business conventions.

in dutch *phr.* [early 19C+] (*US*) in trouble, out of favour. [one who has fig. succumbed to the DUTCH ACT n.]

ineffable *n.* [mid-19C] a supreme dandy.

ineffable, the *n.* [19C] the vagina (cf. ARTICLE n.). [lit. the 'unspeakable']

ineffables *n.* [19C] trousers (cf. DON'T-KNOW-WHAT-TO-CALL-'EMS n.).

in effect mode *phr.* [1980s+] (*US Black teen*) in a relaxed, stress-free state of mind.

inexpressibles *n.* (*also* **innominables, insuppressibles**) [late 18C–1900s] trousers (cf. DON'T-KNOW-WHAT-TO-CALL-'EMS n.).

i-ney! *excl.* [1950s+] (*W.I. Rasta*) a greeting. [ety. unknown]

infantry *n.* [19C] children. [pun on SE *infant*; SE in 17C–18C]

in feather *phr. see* IN FULL FEATHER phr.

inferior half *n.* (*also* **other half, worse half**) [late 19C+] one's wife or partner, usu. in joc. use. [var. on BETTER HALF n.]

infernal *adj.* [17C+] a general term of abuse or condemnation. [euph. for SE *hellish*]

infernal *adv.* (*also* **infernally**) [17C+] detestably, confoundedly. [INFERNAL adj.]

in fine twig *phr.* (*also* **in good twig, in prime twig**) [19C] splendidly, stylishly; in high spirits or good order. [SE *fine* + TWIG n.¹]

in flaggers *phr.* [1920s–60s] (*Aus.*) *in flagrante delicto*. [abbr.]

in flagrante *adv.* [early 17C+] (caught) in the act, usu. of sexual intercourse. [Lat. *in flagrante delicto*, lit. 'in flagrant lust']

info *n.* [20C+] information. [abbr.]

in for (it) *phr.* **1** [mid-17C–18C] in trouble, facing punishment. **2** [18C] drunk. **3** [mid-19C+] willing, committed to, eager. **4** [1910s–20s] pregnant. [(1) SE post-1800]

in for one's chop *phr.* [1920s+] (*Aus./N.Z.*) out for oneself, for one's own profit or advantage. [CHOP n.³ (3)]

in for patter *phr.* [mid-19C] facing trial. [PATTER n. (2); the *patter* is that of the judge, counsel, witnesses etc, dismissed as such by the prisoner]

in for the plate *phr.* [late 18C–early 19C] suffering from venereal disease. [a rather laboured derivation f. horseracing jargon. Horses that qualify for the *plate* (the main race) have first won the *heat*; symptoms of VD include inflammation, i.e. *heat*]

in front *adj. see* UP FRONT adj.

in front *adv. see* UP FRONT adv.

in full dig *phr.* [mid-19C–1900s] earning one's full pay. [one 'digs' out one's pay]

in full effect *phr.* [1990s+] (*orig. US Black*) present, going on, happening.

in full feather *phr.* (*also* **in feather**) **1** [late 18C–19C] (*US*) in one's best clothes. **2** [early 19C–19C] rich. **3** [early 19C+] in top condition, very cheerful.

in full fig *phr.* [mid-19C+] dressed up. [SE *fig out*, to dress up]

in full paint *phr.* [1900s] (*Aus.*) dressed up.

ing-bing *n.* [1920s–40s] (*US*) a fit, an emotional outburst. [? var. on WING-DING n. (2)]

ingler *n.* [late 18C–mid-19C] a horse thief who toured country fairs looking for victims. [? dial. *ingle*, to fondle; thus he 'fondles' the horse to persuade it to go with him. Note SE *ingle*, a catamite]

in goat heaven and kiddie kingdom, be *v.* (*also* **be in hog heaven and john crow paradise**) [20C+] (*W.I., Bdos*) to be in a state of absolute bliss.

ingogo *n.* [1970s+] (*S.Afr.*) a cheap prostitute (cf. DOLLAR-WOMAN n.). [Zulu *ingogo*, a half-crown or 25 cents]

in good nick *phr.* (*also* **in decent nick, in nick**) [20C+] of a person or thing, in good condition. [orig. dial.]

in good twig *phr. see* IN FINE TWIG phr.

ingoted *adj.* (*also* **ingotted**) [mid–late 19C] very rich. [SE *ingot*, a brick of gold or silver]

in great shape *phr.* [late 19C+] in excellent condition, either physically or emotionally.

in great snuff *phr. see* IN HIGH SNUFF phr.

in great spout *phr.* [late 18C] in high spirits.

in grub *phr. see* GRUB n.² (1).

in guts gully *phr.* [20C+] (*W.I.*) in serious difficulties.

inhale *v.* [late 19C+] **1** to eat very fast, to gobble up. **2** to drink.

inhale the oyster *v. see* OYSTER n.² (2).

in harness *phr.* [mid-19C+] employed, in work; including working for a pimp. [working horse imagery]

in heat *phr.*¹ [1910s+] (*US gambling*) on a winning streak. [var. on HOT adj.⁴ (3)]

in heat *phr.*² *see* ON HEAT phr.

in her beef *phr.* (*also* **in her mutton**) [late 18C–mid-19C] having sexual intercourse with a woman. [BEEF n.¹ (2)/MUTTON n.¹ (3)]

in high feather *phr.* [early 19C–1920s] rich, very cheerful.

in high snuff *phr.* (*also* **in great snuff, in mighty snuff**) **1** [late 17C; mid-19C–1930s] elated, very happy. **2** [early 19C] of dress, showy, stylish. **3** [mid-19C–1930s] healthy, in good shape. [SE *snuff*, a fit of temper, emotion]

in his Sunday best *phr. see* OLD MAN HAS HIS SUNDAY CLOTHES ON, THE phr.

in hock *phr.* **1** [mid-19C–1950s] in prison; thus the reverse, *out of hock*. **2** [late 19C+] indebted to, owing both money and metaphorical debts; thus the reverse, *out of hock*; thus *on the hocks*, impoverished. **3** [late 19C+] in pawn; thus the reverse, *out of hock*. [for ety. *see* HOCK n.²]

in hog heaven and john crow paradise, be *v. see* IN GOAT HEAVEN AND KIDDIE KINGDOM, BE v.

in holts *phr.* [1900s–20s] (*Aus.*) in conflict. [orig. dial. *holt*, a grip, a grasp + link to SE *hold*, i.e. in wrestling]

in huckster's hands *phr.* [late 16C–early 19C] in a bad way, in difficulties. [SE *huckster*, a small trader; the sufferer presumably owes money to such a trader]

Iniskillen men *n.* [late 17C–18C] a derog. term for the militia. [the original *Iniskillen* regiment distinguished itself in Ireland; the militia was less impressive, 'soon raised, as soon set down' (B.E.)]

in'it *n.* [1990s+] (*UK Asian*) a teenage gang. [the ubiquitous INNIT! excl.]

in it *phr.* **1** [early 19C+] (*mainly Aus.*) agreeing to participate, taking a share. **2** [late 19C] at the heart of society. **3** [late 19C+] worthy of notice, conforming to one's ideas and attitudes, often as NOT IN IT phr. **4** [late 19C+] in trouble. **5** [late 19C+] (*US*) aware, alive. **6** [1960s+] (*Aus.*) having sexual intercourse.

iniversal *adj.* [1960s+] (*W.I./UK Black teen*) universal. [the substitution by Rastafarians of 'i' for 'you' or the sound 'u']

in jail at Innisfail *phr.* [1960s+] (*Aus.*) a phr. used to denote an unsatisfactory situation. [assonance]

injection *n.* **1** [mid-18C] semen, at the point of ejaculation. **2** [late 19C] sexual intercourse, the intromission of the penis. [see Williams for metaphorical use in 17C]

in jigtime *adv.* [20C+] very quickly.

Injun *n.* (*also* **Injen, Injin, Injunn**) [early 19C+] (*US*) a Native American.

Injun *v.* (*also* **Indian**) [19C+] (*US*) to sneak up without alerting one's target, to spy. [racial stereotyping of *Indian*/INJUN n.]

ink *n.*[1] **1** [20C+] (*Aus./N.Z./US*) cheap red wine. **2** [1920s–40s] strong, bitter coffee. **3** [1930s+] publicity; a mention in the newspapers. **4** [1980s+] a tattoo. **5** [1990s+] (*US*) a police or prison record. [colour, although *DNZE* suggests (1) is rhy. sl. = SE *drink*]

ink *n.*[2] (*also* **ink face**) [1910s–40s] (*US*) a derog. term for a Black person, esp. with a very dark complexion (cf. BLACKBELLY n.). [the blackness of SE *ink*]

ink *v.* **1** [1940s+] (*orig. US*) to sign a contract. **2** [1970s+] to take fingerprints. **3** [1980s+] (*US*) to tattoo. [SE *ink*; (3) note INK n.[1] (4)]

ink-bottle *n.* [late 19C–1900s] a clerk. [note RN jargon *ink-slinger*, the purser's clerk]

inkbug *n.* [mid-19C] (*US*) a derog. term for a Black person (cf. BLACKBELLY n.).

inked *adj.* [late 19C+] (*Aus./N.Z.*) drunk. [SE *ink*, i.e. the dark colour of wine or whisky]

ink face *n. see* INK n.[2].

ink-flinging *n.* [late 19C] journalism, writing.

in kinks *phr.* [20C+] (*Irish*) doubled up with hysterical laughter.

ink-jerker *n.* [mid-19C–1910s] (*US*) a writer, esp. a journalist. [Farmer, *Americanisms Old New* (1889), has the lesser known synon. *adjective-jerker*]

inkos *n.* [late 19C] (*S.Afr.*) a White man. [Xhosa/Zulu *inkosi*, chief]

ink-pot *n.* [1910s–50s] (*US Und.*) a place where criminals gather.

ink-slinger *n.* (*also* **ink-walloper**) **1** [mid-19C+] (*orig. US*) a writer, esp. a journalist; thus *ink-slinging*, the profession of writing or journalism. **2** [1910s–60s] a clerk. **3** [1930s] a musician who arranges music.

ink-spiller *n.* (*also* **ink-shedder, ink-splasher, ink-waster**) [mid-19C–1910s] a writer, usu. a journalist or clerk.

inkspot *n.* [1910s–60s] (*US*) a Black person, usu. derog. (cf. BLACKBELLY n.).

inkwell *n.* [1970s] (*US*) the vagina (cf. BAG n.[1]; BLACK HOLE n.[1]). [SE *ink* as a euph. for semen]

inky *adj.* (*also* **inky-poo**) [1900s–60s] (*orig. Aus.*) drunk. [INKED adj.]

inky blue *n.* [1970s+] influenza. [rhy. sl. = SE *flu*]

inky-dink *n.* [1900s–40s] (*US Black*) a particularly dark-skinned person. [note the popular fictional schoolboy Billy Bunter's Indian rajah friend, nicknamed *Inky*]

inky-poo *adj. see* INKY adj.

inky smudge *n.* [late 19C–1970s] (*UK Und.*) a judge. [rhy. sl.]

inlaid *adj.* (*also* **inlayed, well-inlaid, well-inlayed**) [late 17C–early 19C] rich, well-off. [SE *inlaid*, ornamented, usu. with precious metals]

in lavender *phr.* **1** [mid-17C; mid-19C–1930s] hidden from the police. **2** [late 18C] in a charity hospital. **3** [mid-19C–1940s] (*US Und.*) in prison. **4** [1930s] (*US Und.*) dead. [LAY UP IN LAVENDER v.]

in licker *phr. see* LIQUORED (UP) adj.

in like Flynn *phr.* [1940s+] (*orig. US*) a dead certainty, esp. in areas of sexual conquest. [the alleged sexual prowess of the actor Errol Flynn (1909–59); however, note Michael Quinion, *World Wide Words* (Internet, 1999): 'Reference books almost universally assert that this set phrase, an American expression meaning to be successful emphatically or quickly, especially in regard to sexual seduction, refers to the Australia-born actor Errol Flynn […] the phrase is said to have been coined following his acquittal in February 1943 for the statutory rape of a teenage girl. This seems to be supported by the date of the first example recorded, in *American Speech* in December 1946, which cited a 1945 use in the sense of something being done easily. The trouble with this explanation is that examples of obviously related expressions have now turned up from dates before Flynn's trial. Barry Popik of the American Dialect Society found an example from 1940, as well as this from the sports section of the *San Francisco Examiner* of 8 February 1942: "Answer these questions correctly and your name is Flynn, meaning you're in, provided you have two left feet and the written consent of your parents". To judge from a newspaper reference he turned up from early 1943, the phrase could by then also be shortened to "I'm Flynn", meaning "I'm in". It's suggested by some writers that the phrase really originated with another Flynn, Edward J. Flynn – "Boss" Flynn – a campaign manager for the Democratic party during FDR's presidency. Flynn's machine in Chicago was so successful at winning elections that his candidates seemed to get into office automatically. The existence of the examples found by Mr Popik certainly suggest the expression was at first unconnected with Errol Flynn, but that it shifted its association when he became such a notorious figure']

in line *phr.* [1920s+] not breaking any rules, law-abiding; often in phr. GET IN LINE v.

in liquor *phr. see* LIQUORED (UP) adj.

in lug *phr.* [mid-19C] in pawn. [LUG v.[1] (1)]

in lumber *phr.* **1** [early 19C+] (*mainly Aus.*) jailed, in prison. **2** [1930s+] in trouble; often ext. to *in dead lumber*. [fig. uses of LUMBER n.[1]]

in lust *phr.* [1960s+] (*US*) sexually attracted to another's body, rather than in love.

in Mexico *phr.* [1910s–50s] (*US Und.*) in prison.

in mighty snuff *phr. see* IN HIGH SNUFF phr.

in more strife than a pork chop at a synagogue *phr. see* LIKE A PORK CHOP AT A JEWISH WEDDING phr.

in Morocco *phr.* [mid-19C] stripped, naked. [prob. nonce-word; coined as supposed 'gypsy slang' by H.W. Longfellow (1807–82); ? a pun on *buff*, which can refer, like *morocco*, to leather and can also mean naked in the phr. *in the buff*]

in my bollocks *phr.* (*also* **in my arse, ...belt, ...bollix, ...boot, ...brown, ...hole, ...ring, ...wick, in your tailboard, on my pratt**) [1920s+] a general intensifier, usu. negating the previous statement. [ARSE n.[1] (1)/SE *belt*/BOLLIX/SE *boot*/BROWN n.[3] (1)/HOLE n.[1] (1)/RING n.[1] (2)/WICK n.[1]/SE *tail-board*, the rear gate of a truck/PRAT n.[1] (1)]

in my eye *phr. see* ALL MY EYE phr.

inna *prep.* [20C+] (*W.I./UK Black teen*) inside, in the, in.

inner man *n.* [mid-19C–1910s] the stomach, one's appetite.

inner tube *n. see* RUBBER CHEQUE n.

in nick *phr. see* IN GOOD NICK phr.

innie *n.* (*also* **insy**) [1970s+] an indented navel, as opposed to an OUTIE *n.*[2].

innit! *excl.* [1940s+] an all-purpose, otherwise meaningless term, used at the end of sentences. [SE *isn't it*]

innocent *n.*[1] **1** [mid-19C–1930s] (*US Und.*) a prisoner. **2** [late 19C+] (*UK Und.*) a sentence passed on an innocent man. [(2) since the prisoner is locked up they cannot be accused of any subseq. crimes until release; Irwin suggests the near universal claim by criminals that they are innocent]

innocent *n.*[2] [1960s] (*US Black*) an ironic ref. to White liberals wishing to become involved in the Black struggle. [the usual liberal disavowals of racism, prejudice, the responsibility for slavery etc]

innominables *n. see* INEXPRESSIBLES n.

in on *phr.* [late 19C+] involved with, esp. a plan or scheme.

in on a good thing, be *v.* [1970s+] to be placed advantageously as regards a plan or business deal. [GOOD THING n. (1)]

in once *adv.* [late 19C–1900s] at the first attempt.

in one's *phr.* [mid-19C–1940s] (*US*) in one's life, e.g. *none of that in mine*, no thank you.

in one's ackee *phr.* (*also* **in one's salt**) [1940s+] energetic, cheerful. [these positive emotions arise from being well-fed on *ackee*, a popular W.I. fruit of the *Blighia sapida* tree, usu. accompanied by saltfish]

in one's airs *phr.* **1** [mid-18C] emotional, hysterical. **2** [late 19C] distant, stand-offish. **3** [1930s] drunk.

in one's ale *phr.* (*also* **in one's ales/beer**) [late 16C–18C] drunk (cf. ALED UP adj.).

in one's altitudes *phr.* [17C–early 19C] drunk (cf. ELEVATED adj.).

in one's armour *phr.*[1] [17C–early 19C] drunk (cf. POT-VALIANT adj.).

in one's armour *phr.*[2] [early 18C–early 19C] using a condom; thus *fight in armour*, to have intercourse using a condom.

in one's attitudes *phr.* [18C] drunk.

in one's beer *phr. see* IN ONE'S ALE phr.

in one's blood *phr.* [20C+] (*W.I.*) in hot pursuit.

in one's book *phr.* (*also* **by one's book**) [1950s+] in one's opinion, to one's way of thinking.

in one's brown *phr.* [1980s+] (*Irish*) a phr. of dismissal, contempt, general negation, e.g. *'I mean it, I really do', 'Bollocks!, you do in your brown!'.* [BROWN n.[3] (1)]

in one's corner *phr.* [1920s+] (*orig. US*) on one's side. [boxing imagery]

in one's cups *phr.* [late 16C+] drunk; often as *deep in one's cups* (cf. ALED UP adj.).

in one's element *phr. see* ELEMENT n.

in one's gears *phr.* [late 17C–early 18C] **1** dressed, ready. **2** ready to get to work. [SE *gear*, apparel or dress]

in one's glory *phr.* **1** [late 19C–1950s] extremely happy and satisfied. **2** [1970s+] displaying one's genitals. [SE *in one's glory*, in a state of magnificence or prosperity]

in one's grannie's *phr.* (*also* **in one's granny's**) [20C+] (*Irish*) in a state of absolute comfort, both physical and psychological.

in one's jeans *phr.* [late 19C–1960s] in one's trouser pockets.

in one's mouth *phr.* [2000s] (*US prison*) eavesdropping.

in one's nip *phr.* (*also* **in the nip**) [20C+] (*Irish*) stark naked. [? NIPPY adj.[2], i.e. one suffers from the cold]

in one's pots *phr.* [early 17C] drunk (cf. ALED UP adj.). [SE *pot*, a tankard]

in one's puff *phr. see* ON ONE'S PUFF phr.

in one's royal *phr.* [20C+] (*W.I.*) very drunk. [? Carib.E *royal/rial*, arrogant, high and mighty]

in one's salt *phr. see* IN ONE'S ACKEE phr.

in one's skin *phr.* [early–mid-18C] a non-committal answer when asked where someone is.

in on one's fourth, be *v.* [late 19C–1900s] to be very drunk. [? one's fourth glass]

in orbit *phr.* (*also* **into orbit**) (*orig. US*) **1** [1960s+] in a state of high excitement, whether of delight or of anger. **2** [1960s+] doing very well. **3** [1970s+] in a state of intoxication from drugs or alcohol (cf. ELEVATED adj.). [one is extremely HIGH adj.[1] + ref. to the Sputnik of 1957 and subseq. circumnavigations of the earth]

in-out *n. see* IN-AND-OUT n.[1] (2).

in Paris, be *v.* [late 19C–1900s] (*UK society*) to have eloped. [Paris was a popular destination for such romantic flights]

in pickle *phr.* [late 16C–18C] venereally diseased. [the contemporary cure for VD, which involved sitting in a 'sweating tub']

in pig *phr.* [1940s+] pregnant. [joc. use of SE, which refers only to swine]

in plant *phr.* [early–mid-19C] (*Aus.*) hidden away. [PLANT v.[1] (1)]

in pleats *phr.* [1990s+] reduced to hysterical laughter. [? play on *in stitches*]

in pod *phr.* [late 19C+] pregnant.

in prime twig *phr. see* IN FINE TWIG phr.

in pull *phr. see* PULL v.[2] (1).

in queer *phr.* [late 19C+] in trouble with the authorities. [abbr. QUEER STREET n.]

in quick sticks *adv.* (*also* **quick sticks**) [mid-19C+] hurriedly, quickly.

in rag order *phr.* (*also* **in rags**) [1940s+] (*Irish/Aus.*) in dire straits, in a mess. [SE *ragged*]

ins *n.* **1** [1930s+] (*US*) informations. **2** [1950s+] (*US*) interests. **3** [1990s+] (*US campus*) money. [abbr.; (3) money is an IN n.]

insane *adj.*[1] [mid-19C+] idiotic, utterly senseless, irrational, obsessive, e.g. *insane lust for…*

insane *adj.*[2] [1940s+] (*orig. US Black*) wonderful, admirable, excellent. [on bad = good model]

insangu *n.* [2000s] (*S.Afr. drugs*) marijuana. [synon. Xhosa *intsangu*/Zulu *insangu*]

in schtook *phr. see* IN SHTUCK phr.

insects (and ants) *n.* [20C+] **1** trousers. **2** knickers, i.e. underwear. [rhy. sl.; (1) = PANTS n.[1] (2); (2) = SE *pants*]

in shape *phr.* [1960s] in possession of drugs. [euph., based on IN GREAT SHAPE phr.]

in shit *phr. see* IN (THE) SHIT phr.

in shit street *phr.* (*also* **in cack street, up cack street, up shit street**) [1920s+] (*orig. US*) in difficulties, facing problems. [SHIT n.[3] (1)/fig. use of CACK n.[2] (1)]

in short pants *phr.* [1960s] (*US*) impoverished, out of work. [what children wear]

in shtuck *phr.* (*also* **in schtook, in shtook, in stook**) [1940s+] in trouble. [Yid. *shtook*, difficulties]

Inside, the *n.* [late 19C+] (*Aus.*) central Australia; thus *insider*, one who lives there.

inside *n.*[1] (*also* **insides**) [mid-18C+] the stomach, the intestines.

inside *n.*[2] [late 18C–1900s] one who rides inside a passenger coach or similar vehicle.

inside *n.*[3] (*also* **insides**) [late 19C+] (*US*) information, esp. when privileged.

inside *adj.*[1] **1** [mid-19C+] (*also* **on the inside**) in prison. **2** [1940s] in a psychiatric hospital.

inside *adj.*[2] [late 19C+] of information, privileged, intimate; thus *on the inside*, privy to such information.

inside and outside! *excl.* [early–mid-19C] a popular toast when drinking. [abbr. *inside of a cunt and outside of a jail!*]

inside job *n.* [late 19C+] a crime that has been committed with the aid or cognizance of an employee of the company or servant of the house in question. [INSIDE adj.[2] + JOB n.[3] (1)]

inside kid *n.* [1920s–30s] one who has privileged information or knowledge. [INSIDE adj.[2] + KID n.[1] (5)]

inside lining n. [mid-19C–1930s] a meal or the eating of any foodstuff. [INSIDE n.[1] + SE *lining*]

inside man n. **1** [late 19C] (*UK Und.*) a police spy. **2** [20C+] (*orig. UK Und.*) anyone involved in a crime, usu. a large-scale robbery of a firm or private house, who is employed on site and helps the robbers with information etc. **3** [1930s+] (*orig. UK Und.*) a tipster who locates prospects for robbers or safe-blowers. **4** [1930s+] (*orig. UK Und.*) in a 3-card trick team, an accomplice who poses as a normal bettor but acts only to encourage the real victims of the game. **5** [1930s+] (*US Und.*) in any confidence trick, that member of the team who takes the lead role in tricking the victim; the ROPER n. (1) or OUTSIDE MAN n. (2) brings the victim to the *inside man*. [INSIDE adj.[2] + SE *man*]

inside of prep. [mid 19C+] within a period of time, during, e.g. *inside of a week*, before a week has passed.

insider n. see INSIDE, THE n.

inside right adj. [1990s+] mean, grasping. [rhy. sl. = TIGHT adj.[4] (1)]

insides n. see INSIDE n.[1].

inside the walls phr. see BEHIND THE WALLS phr.

inside wire n. [1960s] privileged, 'inside' information, esp. in the context of a crime. [INSIDE adj.[2] + WIRE n.[2] (2)]

in smoke phr. [1910s+] (*Aus.*) in hiding. [the obscurity cast by a pall of smoke]

in soak phr.[1] **1** [mid–late 19C] in prison. **2** [mid-19C+] in pawn. [(2) SOAK v.[2] (1)]

in soak phr.[2] [late 19C] (*Aus.*) drunk (cf. DAMP adj.). [SOAK v.[1] (1)]

in soft phr. [1910s] (*US*) enjoying a comfortable situation.

in someone's ass, be v. [1960s–70s] (*US*) to nag or scold someone. [ASS n. (5)]

in someone's crack phr. [1980s+] (*US campus*) inquisitive, over involved. [CRACK n.[6] (4)]

in someone's face phr. (*also* **in someone's business**) [1950s+] (*orig. US Black*) in a confrontational manner, used of one who forces their attentions on another; thus *get in someone's face*, to confront, to provoke (cf. IN-YOUR-FACE adj.). [basketball use, when a defensive player crowds his opposite number. The term, while ostensibly unappealing, is considered positive by its primary users, the young; note also FACE v. (2)]

in someone's gunga phr. [1950s] (*Aus.*) directly, openly. [fig. use of GUNGA n.[1], i.e. 'up someone's arse']

in someone's skin phr. [20C+] (*W.I.*) harassing, nagging.

in spades adv. [1920s+] (*orig. US*) to the greatest extent, very much, extremely, any form of intensifier; thus *you can say that in spades*, you couldn't be more right. [SE *spade* but note in many card-games, *spades* are the highest suit]

inspector n. [1930s–40s] (*US*) an itinerant worker. [he moves from job to job, 'to see what they are like']

inspector of city buildings n. [1920s+] (*Aus.*) one who is unemployed and not especially keen on finding work. [for ety. see INSPECTOR n.]

inspector of manholes n. (*also* **manhole inspector**) [1930s+] a male homosexual, usu. the active partner. [pun on SE *manhole/man hole*, i.e. the male anus; note MANHOLE n.[1] (2)]

inspector of public buildings n. [late 19C–1910s] an unemployed person. [for ety. *see* INSPECTOR n.]

inspector of the pavement n. (*also* **inspector of pavements**) **1** [late 18C–mid-19C] (*also* **surveyor of the pavement**) one who stands in the pillory. **2** [1940s] (*US Und.*) a tramp. [(1) the posture one has to adopt]

inspired adj. [late 19C+] drunk (cf. ABOUT RIGHT phr.[1]). [euph.]

instant boot camp n. [1970s+] (*US campus*) the act of vomiting. [BOOT v.[9] + pun on milit. *boot camp*, a notably vile environment]

instant zen n. [1960s+] (*drugs*) LSD (cf. A n.[3]). [the contemplative world of *Zen* Buddhism]

in stook phr. see IN SHTUCK phr.

in stout with phr. [1930s] (*US*) intimate with, on good terms with. [play on SOLID adv.[1] (1); ext. of IN WITH phr. (1)]

instrument n. [1900s–50s] (*US Und.*) the member of a pick-pocketing team who actually takes the object from the victim.

instrument (of generation) n. (*also* **instrument of propagation**) **1** [16C+] the penis. **2** [late 16C–17C] the vagina (cf. BABY CHUTE n.). **3** [mid-17C] in pl., the testicles. [euph.]

insuppressibles n. see INEXPRESSIBLES n.

in Swell Street phr. [early 19C–1900s] (*UK Und.*) living a prosperous, respectable, secure life. [SWELL adj. + SE *street*]

insy n. see INNIE n.

in synch phr. (*also* **in sync**) [1970s+] happening or doing something at the same time or in the same way, as if linked. [SE phr. *in synchronization*, of sound, usu. in films]

intended n. [mid-18C+] one's future husband or wife.

intense adj. (*US campus*) **1** [1970s+] very good, excellent. **2** [1980s+] very difficult.

intense! excl. [1980s+] (*US campus*) a general excl. of approval. [INTENSE adj. (1)]

intensive care adj. [1970s] of a place, subject to saturation policing.

interior n. (*also* **interiors**) [late 19C+] the internal parts of the body, esp. the digestive system.

interior decorating n. [1980s+] (*UK society*) sexual intercourse during the day.

international bitch n. [1960s] (*US Black*) a female INTERNATIONAL NIGGER n. [BITCH n.[1] (1)]

international milk thief n. [1970s+] (*UK police*) an ironic term for any petty villain.

international nigger n. [1950s–70s] (*US Black*) a person who dresses in expensive, imported clothes. [SE *international* + NIGGER n.[1] (10)]

interplanetary mission n. [1990s+] (*drugs*) going around from one CRACK HOUSE n. (1) to another in the hope of getting some drugs. [a term from *Star Trek*, the 'mission' here being to get HIGH adj.[1] (2)]

in the altogether phr. [late 19C+] naked. [abbr. SE *altogether naked/nude*]

in the arms of murphy phr. [mid-19C–1920s] asleep. [a pun on the classically based *arms of Morpheus*, the Greek god of sleep or dreams]

in the bag phr.[1] (*orig. US*) **1** [20C+] secured, made certain. **2** [1910s+] of a criminal, arrested, caught. **3** [1930s+] of a situation, e.g. a trial or a sporting contest, whose outcome has been made certain by the giving of bribes, doping of one or more contestants, horses etc. **4** [1980s+] committed to a cause. [? BAG v.[2]]

in the bag phr.[2] **1** [1910s+] (*also* **in a bag**) in trouble, facing difficulties. **2** [1920s+] (*orig. US*) in debt. [? BAG v.[1]]

in the bag phr.[3] (*also* **in the wrapper**) **1** [1940s+] (*orig. US*) (*also* **out of one's bag**) drunk; thus *half in the bag*, beginning to become drunk. **2** [1960s] (*US campus*) feeling ill. [BAG n.[9] (1)/SE *wrapper*]

in the ball-park phr. see BALL-PARK adj.

in the barrel phr. (*US*) **1** [1930s+] in debt, bankrupt. **2** [1980s+] dismissed or likely to be dismissed from one's job. [ety. unknown]

in the basket phr. [early 19C] confused, nonplussed.

in the beads phr. [1970s+] (*US gay*) at the mercy of the fates. [rosary beads/BEADS n.[2]]

in the black phr. [late 19C+] in credit, financially secure. [the pre-computer-era practice of writing up credit accounts in *black* ink and debits in *red* ink]

in the blowing of a match phr. [late 19C] immediately.

in the blue phr.[1] [1920s–40s] **1** far away, off in the distance. **2** (*US*) in the clear, not guilty. [SE *the wild blue yonder*]

in the blue phr.[2] [1920s+] (*Aus.*) **1** in debt, in difficulties. **2** out of control. [BLUES n.[1]; note WW1 milit. *in the blue*, referring to troops who were in difficulties, e.g. from a failed attack]

in the blue jigs *phr. see* IN THE JIGS phr.

in the blues *phr. see* BLUE DEVILS n.[1].

in the book *phr.* [1950s+] recorded, in existence. [the *Book of Life*]

in the box seat *phr.* [20C+] (*Aus.*) in full control, in a position of dominance. [SE *box seat*, the driving seat in a horse-pulled coach]

in the briers *phr.* [16C–18C] in trouble, in difficulties. [SE *brier*, a thorny, prickly bush, thus implying difficulty]

in the broth *phr. see* IN THE SOUP phr.

in the bucks *phr.* [1940s–50s] (*US*) well-off, wealthy. [BUCK n.[3] (3)]

in the butter *phr.* [1950s] in difficulties.

in the cactus *phr.* [1950s+] (*Aus./N.Z.*) in difficulties.

in the car *phr.* [20C+] (*US prison*) on good terms. [CAR n.]

in the cart *phr.* **1** [late 19C] aware, in the know. **2** [late 19C+] (*also* **carted**) in trouble, in difficulties; thus *put someone in the cart*, to trick, to deceive.

in the cellar *phr.* **1** [mid-18C] drunk. **2** [20C+] in sports, at the bottom of a league or similar points table. **3** [1900s] in trouble. **4** [1950s] miserable, feeling low, 'down in the dumps'. [note P.G. Wodehouse (1881–1975) coinage 'down among the wines and spirits']

in the chair *phr.* [1930s+] buying a round of drinks. [SE *in the chair*, acting as chairperson of a meeting]

in the chips *phr.* [1930s+] (*orig. US*) financially secure, well-off. [CHIPS n.[2]]

in the clarts *phr.* [1970s] **1** suffering from diarrhoea. **2** in trouble, lit. 'in the shit'. [CLART n.]

in the class *phr.* [1920s–30s] well-to-do. [the *upper* class]

in the clear *phr. see* CLEAR adj.[1].

in the closet *phr.* [1970s+] (*orig. US*) **1** used of a gay man/woman who has yet to reveal their sexuality in public. **2** hidden away. [(1) CLOSET n.[2]]

in the club *phr.* [1940s+] pregnant. [the club in question is the PUDDING CLUB n.]

in the clutch *phr.* [1940s–60s] (*US*) in the final assessment, 'when push comes to shove'. [SE *clutch*, i.e. when one finally 'grasps' and deals with a situation]

in the cold *phr.* [1910s+] (*Aus.*) in prison.

in the cooler *phr.* [late 19C–1900s] (*US*) in reserve. [SAmE *cooler*, refrigerator]

in the crapper *phr.* [1940s+] (*US*) finished, failed, rejected, abandoned, rendered useless. [fig. use of CRAPPER n.[3] (2)]

in the crown office *phr.* [late 17C–18C] tipsy. [play on SE *crown* (of the head), which suffers]

in the cut *phr.* (*US Black*) **1** [1960s+] in a location or neighbourhood that is far away, hidden or removed for some reason; thus LAY IN THE CUT v. **2** [1990s+] present, in place, on hand. [CUT n.[7]]

in the dark *n.* [late 19C–1940s] (*US*) black coffee. [the colour of the coffee]

in the days of Queen Dick *phr.* (*also* **in the reign of Queen Dick**) [late 18C+] never. [*Dick*, i.e. Richard, being a man, there could not be a *Queen Dick*]

in the death *phr.* [1950s–60s] in the end.

in the ditch *phr.* (*US*) **1** [1970s+] impoverished, at the bottom of the social ladder. **2** [1980s+] extremely drunk. [(2) the image of a drunk driver steering off the road and into a ditch]

in the dogbox *phr.* [1950s+] (*N.Z.*) out of favour, in disgrace. [SE *dogbox*, a dog-kennel; var. on IN THE DOGHOUSE phr.]

in the doghouse *phr.* [1930s+] (*orig. US*) in trouble, out of favour. [SAmE *doghouse*, a dog kennel; i.e. in disgrace and so consigned to the dog's kennel rather than one's own home]

in the dough *phr.* (*also* **doughy**) [1910s+] well-off, prospering, rich. [DOUGH n.[1] (1)]

in the dumper *phr.* [1980s+] **1** out of favour, rejected, thrown away. **2** lost, ruined, good for nothing. [fig. use of DUMPER n.[1] (1)]

in the dwang *phr.* [1990s+] (*S.Afr.*) in trouble, in difficulties, constrained. [Afk. *dwing*, to force; but note dial. Scot. *dwang*, to struggle, to oppress]

in the familiar way *phr.* [mid–late 19C] pregnant. [play on IN THE FAMILY WAY phr.]

in the family way *phr.* [mid-18C+] pregnant.

in the flue *phr.* (*also* **up the flue**) **1** [19C–1900s] in pawn. **2** [mid-19C] in trouble. **3** [mid-19C–1900s] dead. **4** [1920s] physically or mentally run-down. **5** [2000s] pregnant. [the FLUE n. (2) or SE *spout* (cf. UP THE SPOUT phr.), a lift used in pawnbrokers' shops, up which the articles pawned were taken for storage; all subseq. defs. are fig. uses of (1)]

in the frame *phr.* [20C+] (*UK Und./police*) **1** under suspicion, usu. with some grounds, of having committed a crime. **2** involved in a situation. [racetrack use, the *frame* holds the numbers of the winning horses in a race + FRAME(-UP) n. (2)]

in the gears *phr.* [1970s] in trouble, in difficulties.

in the glue *phr.* [1960s+] (*US*) in trouble, in difficulties.

in the grease *phr.* [1910s–60s] (*US*) in serious trouble.

in the groove *phr.* [1930s+] (*orig. US*) **1** carried away by music. **2** perfect, ideal. [the *groove* on a record]

in the gun *phr.*[1] [late 17C–early 19C] drunk, tipsy. [GUN n.[2]]

in the gun *phr.*[2] (*Aus.*) **1** [1910s–20s] facing dismissal from one's job. **2** [1910s+] unpopular, of ill repute, in trouble, likely to attract criticism or punishment; thus *get someone in the gun*, to get someone in trouble. [one is 'under fire']

in the hat *phr.* [2000s] (*US prison*) targeted for death.

in the hay *phr. see* HIT THE HAY v. (1).

in the hole *phr.* (*also* **in a hole**) [mid-19C+] (*orig. US*) **1** in debt, owing, usu. connected with gambling. **2** in difficulties.

in the hospital *phr.* [1900s–20s] (*US*) in prison. [euph.]

in the house *phr.* [1980s+] **1** lit. present and fig. aware, 'on the ball' etc. **2** (*orig. US Black/teen*) excellent.

in the jigs *phr.* (*also* **in the blue jigs**) **1** [1940s+] very drunk. **2** [1950s+] very frightened. [(2) JIGGERED adj.[1] (3)]

in the know *phr.* [late 19C+] **1** privy to secret, privileged information. **2** fashionable, up-to-date.

in the lime *phr.* [1940s] (*Aus.*) conspicuous, popular, heavily advertised. [abbr. SE *in the limelight*]

in the long grass *phr.* [1940s+] lying low, esp. of someone one hasn't seen for some time; thus *wait for someone in the long grass*, to lie low, to maintain a 'low profile'.

in the lurch *n.* [20C+] (*Aus.*) a church. [abbr. LEFT IN THE LURCH n.]

in the market *phr.* **1** [1930s] (*US Black*) in prison. **2** [1940s] rich, well-off, usu. as the result of gambling or crime.

in the middle *phr.* [1920s+] (*orig. US*) in trouble, in a dangerous or difficult situation.

in the mix *phr.* [1980s+] **1** (*US Black*) involved, esp. in gang activities. **2** (*US prison*) in prison. [record industry jargon]

in the money *phr.* [1930s+] rich, successful in a wager. [*run in the money*, a racing term for those horses that finish 1–2–3, thus paying out to those who bet on them]

in the mood *n.* [20C+] food. [rhy. sl.]

in the nack *phr.* [1990s+] in the nude, naked. [? NACKERS n./pron. of SE *naked*]

in the never-never *phr.* [1960s] naked.

in the nick *phr.*[1] [1940s+] (*N.Z.*) naked, esp. in the context of swimming. [? SE *naked*]

in the nick *phr.*[2] *see* NICK n.[1] (2).

in the nip *phr. see* IN ONE'S NIP phr.

in the nooer *phr.* [1970s] (*Aus.*) in difficulties. [SE *manure*]

in the nuddy *phr.* (*also* **in the nud**) [1940s+] (*orig. Aus.*) naked. [SE *nude*; a coy euph. used by those who find any sexual ref. embarrassing]

in the nude *n.* [1970s+] food. [rhy. sl.]

in the ozone *phr.* (*also* **ozoned**) [1970s+] (*US*) dazed; or intoxicated by drugs or drink. [SE *ozone*, i.e. one is HIGH adj.¹ (2)]

in the pan *phr.* [1930s–60s] (*US*) in difficulties, facing problems. [i.e. the SE *lavatory pan*; thus euph. for IN (THE) SHIT phr.]

in the park *phr. see* AT BUSHEY PARK phr.

in the peek *phr.* [1940s–50s] (*UK prison*) in an observation cell, into which prisoners are placed if, for instance, they have smashed up their cells or shown other signs of instability.

in the picture 1 [mid-19C+] important, successful; usu. in phr. *high up in the pictures*. **2** [20C+] aware of what is happening; often as *put someone in the picture*, to inform.

in the pig's a.h. *phr. see* A.H. n.

in the pink *phr.* [late 18C+] extremely fit, well and cheerful. [abbr. *in the pink of condition*; ult. SE *pink*, the finest example of excellence, extending the colloq. 'flower of excellence/perfection', itself based on SE *pink*, the *Dianthus plumarius*, a popular garden flower]

in the poo *phr.* [1960s+] (*Aus.*) in difficulties. [POO n.¹ (2)]

in the pool *phr. see* POOL v.

in the pot *phr.* [early 19C] in trouble.

in the rats *phr. see* RATS, THE n. (2).

in the raw *phr.* [1930s+] (*orig. US*) naked.

in the raz *phr.* [1940s+] (*Aus.*) naked. [var. on IN THE RAW phr.]

in there *phr.* **1** [1930s–60s] (*orig. US Black*) involved, aware, informed; doing well, prospering. **2** [1940s+] (*US Black*) looking attractive. **3** [1950s+] sexually successful; thus phr. *you're in there*, you'll find no problems with seduction. **4** [1950s+] (*US campus*) pleased and excited.

in the red *phr.* **1** [1920s+] in debt; thus *out of the red*, out of debt. **2** [1930s] rich. **3** [1950s] in difficulties. [the inking of old accounts, *red* for profit, *black* for loss]

in the reign of Queen Dick *phr. see* IN THE DAYS OF QUEEN DICK phr.

in the right ball-park *phr. see* BALL-PARK adj.

in the ruck *phr.* [1980s+] (*Aus. prison*) involved. [football imagery]

in the sack *phr.* [1940s+] in bed for the purpose of sex. [SACK n.³ (1)]

in the saddle *phr.* **1** [mid-18C; 20C+] engaged in sexual intercourse. **2** [1950s+] in charge, in control. **3** [1990s+] menstruating.

in the shade *phr.* [1910s] (*US Und.*) in prison.

in (the) shit *phr.* [1920s+] in serious trouble; often ext. as *in deep shit*. [SHIT n.³ (1)]

in the skies *phr.* [1900s] intoxicated by a drug. [the image is cognate with FLY v.⁴ (1)/HIGH adj.¹ (2) but predates both]

in the snore *phr.* [2000s] **1** in bed. **2** in fig. use, friendly with, 'in bed with'.

in the soup *phr.* (*also* **in the broth**) [late 19C+] (*orig. US*) in trouble, in difficulties; thus *out of the soup*, out of trouble.

in the spoon *phr.* [20C+] (*drugs*) using drugs. [SPOON n.³]

in the spud line *phr.* [1930s+] pregnant.

in the straight *phr.* [20C+] out of one's difficulties, e.g. after financial struggles. [*the straight and narrow* rather than *the straight* in horseracing]

in the straw *phr.* (*also* **in the strummel**) [mid-17C+] pregnant, in labour, giving birth. [18C SE *straw* as the stuffing of a bed, but note the defunct practice of laying straw in the street outside the house of a woman in labour in order to quieten the passing traffic; 20C+ use mainly Aus.]

in the street *adv.* [1960s+] (*US Black*) openly, publicly.

in the stretch *phr.* [20C+] almost complete, near the end. [horseracing term *the stretch*, the last part of the course]

in the strummel *phr. see* IN THE STRAW phr.

in the suds *phr.* **1** [17C–mid-19C] in trouble, in a disagreeable situation. **2** [mid-18C–early 19C] tipsy. [SE *suds*, filth, muck]

in the swim *phr.* **1** [mid–late 19C] moving in smart, fashionable circles. **2** [mid-19C–1900s] keeping out of the hands of the police.

3 [late 19C] (*UK Und.*) involved in some form of transaction. **4** [late 19C–1910s] in the fig. game, situation etc. [(1) SE f. 1900]

in the switches *phr.* [1940s–50s] (*US*) confused, undecided. [SE *switch*, i.e. an image of indecision]

in the tank *phr.* [1970s+] drunk. [SE *tank*, a swimming pool; one is 'sodden' with liquor]

in the tin *phr.* [1940s–50s] (*Aus.*) in trouble, in a tight spot. [fig. use of SE *tin can*]

in the toilet *phr.* [1980s+] (*US*) in difficulties, undergoing problems, in debt.

in the toot *phr.* [1960s+] in trouble, facing problems. [fig. use of TOOT n.³ (1)]

in the wind *phr.*¹ [1960s] in the end. [WIND-UP n.¹]

in the wind *phr.*² [1970s+] (*orig. US prison*) **1** freed from prison; absenting oneself. **2** of money, being used for a transaction, rather than held in a wallet, bank etc.

in the wombats *phr.* [1960s] (*Aus.*) having halucinations, seeing things which are not there. [WOMBAT n.¹]

in the works *phr.* [1940s+] about to happen, in process.

in the wrapper *phr. see* IN THE BAG phr.³.

in the wrong box *phr.* **1** [mid-16C+] out of one's element, incorrect. **2** [1900s] injured, losing. [? a mix-up among an apothecary's boxes]

intimate *n.* [19C] (*US Und.*) a shirt. [the shirt's proximity to one's body]

in Tip Street *phr.* [mid–late 19C] well-off, generous. [SE *tip*, a gratuity]

into *prep.*¹ [mid-19C+] fighting or attacking. [abbr. *pitch into* etc]

into *prep.*² [late 19C+] (*orig. US*) **1** owing money to. **2** having taken a payment for a job.

into *prep.*³ **1** [late 19C+] (*Aus.*) sexually involved with. **2** [1930s+] involved in a money-making scheme of some form, esp. criminal. **3** [1980s+] of the police, pursuing, investigating.

into *prep.*⁴ [1960s+] aware of, interested in, involved with, attracted by; thus *be into*. [abbr. *deeply into* or similar; a HIPPIE n.² (3) phr. that emerged during the late 1960s and thence proceeded to general speech as well as use in a variety of New Age therapies; ult. from 19C SE *into*, 'involved with']

into orbit *phr. see* IN ORBIT phr.

into smash *phr. see* ALL TO SMASH phr. (1).

in tow *phr.* [1980s+] (*Aus. prison*) susceptible to bribery.

into whack *phr.* [1930s] into the correct order, position, etc (cf. OUT OF WHACK phr.). [SE *whack*, to hit a blow, i.e. a ref. to that which has been knocked home properly]

in town *phr.* **1** [early 19C] well-off, having plenty of money. **2** [1960s] (*US campus*) acceptable.

in town for the weekend *phr.* [1970s] (*US campus*) homosexual.

intro *n.* [1910s+] an *introduction*, whether to a person or to a piece of writing, music etc. [abbr.]

introduce Charley *v.* (*also* **introduce Charlie**) [20C+] of a man, to have sexual intercourse (cf. BURY IT v.). [CHARLEY n.³]

introduce her to Fagan *v.* (*also* **introduce her to Fagin**) [1950s+] of a man, to have sexual intercourse (cf. DO HER JOB FOR HER v.). [FAGAN n.]

introduce the shoemaker to the tailor *v.* [late 19C–1900s] to kick someone on the seat of their trousers.

in trouble *phr.*¹ [mid-16C; late 19C–1900s] serving a sentence in prison. [euph.]

in trouble *phr.*² [late 19C+] of a woman, pregnant and unmarried. [euph.]

intro up *v.* [2000s] to *introduce*. [abbr. + SE *up*]

in tucks *phr.* [20C+] reduced to helpless laughter.

in two ups *adv.* [1930s+] (*Aus.*) very quickly. [the game of *two-up*, based on tossing coins; the image of the time taken to make a couple of tosses]

invasion *n.* [1980s+] (*US campus*) in comb. with a relevant n., denoting a quantity, a large number, e.g. *hunk invasion*, a lot of handsome boys.

Inventories *n.* [late 19C] the Inventions Exhibition, London 1885.

invertebrated *adj.* [1980s+] (*US campus*) drunk (cf. AFFLICTED *adj.*). [SE *invertebrate*, without a backbone, i.e. one has collapsed]

invigorator *n.* [mid-19C] **1** a drink. **2** an oyster.

invite *n.* [mid-17C+] an *invitation*. [abbr.]

in with *phr.* **1** [late 17C–18C] intimate with. **2** [mid-19C–1900s] suspicious of, getting even with. **3** [mid-19C+] fashionable, socially aware. **4** [late 19C] in comparison with, compared with. [(1) SE post-1800]

in with the boot *phr. see* PUT THE BOOT IN v. (1).

in wrong *phr.* (*US*) **1** [1900s–50s] in trouble, unpopular. **2** [1910s–20s] wrong, erroneous. **3** [1920s] wronged.

in you go says Bob Munro *phr.* [1950s+] (*N.Z.*) a general phr. of encouragement at the outset of a project, competition etc. [ety. unknown; ? anecdotal or simply assonant]

in your arse *phr.* [20C+] (*W.I.*) a phr. used to add emphasis to what has been said, a synon. with 'by God', 'for God's sake'. [ARSE n.¹ (1)]

in your boot! *excl.* [1960s] (*Aus.*) an excl. of dismissal, rejection.

in your dipper! *excl.* [1920s+] (*N.Z.*) a general excl. of rejection, dismissal. [? ref. to sheep dip]

in your eye! *excl.* [late 19C+] (*US*) an excl. of general derision, dismissal, contempt. [sl. *in a pig's eye!* (*see* IN A PIG'S ASS! excl.)]

in your face! *excl.* [1950s+] a dismissive rejoinder. [IN SOMEONE'S FACE phr.]

in-your-face *adj.* [1970s+] (*orig. US*) **1** aggressive, intense, confrontational. **2** unashamed. [IN SOMEONE'S FACE phr.]

in your hat! *excl.* [1930s–50s] a dismissive retort.

in your hole! *excl.* (*also* **in your pants! in your shite!**) [1970s+] a dismissive rejoinder. [HOLE n.¹ (1)/PANTS n.¹ (3)/SHITE n. (1)]

in your tail-board *phr. see* IN MY BOLLOCKS phr.

in your teeth! *excl.* [late 17C–mid-18C] a dismissive rejoinder.

ipsal dixal *n.* [mid-19C–1900s] an unsupported statement. [Lat. *ipse dixit*, an unproved statement, a dictum, lit. 'he himself said it']

ipse *n.* [early 18C] a variety of ale. [Lat. *ipse*, itself; thus 'the very thing'. Note the Umbrian wine *Est! Est! Est!*, lit. 'It is! It is! It is!', i.e. it is the best/the thing]

ipsydinxy *n.* (*also* **ipse dixit**) [late 18C–mid-19C] whisky. [? echoic of the slurred tones of a drinker; ? poss. challenge to a drunkard to say the Lat. phr. *ipse dixit*]

I.Q. *n.* [1960s] (*US*) a signature. [play on I.D. n.¹ (1)]

I.R.A. *adj.* [1980s] (*Aus.*) homosexual. [rhy. sl. = GAY adj.¹ (3)]

ira *n.* [1970s] (*gay*) hair. [E.P. suggests 'centre slang', but ? mis-sp. of RIAH n.]

irey *adj.* (*also* **irie**) [1950s+] (*W.I. Rasta*) pleasing, powerful, euphoric; orig. in the context of the sensations that followed smoking cannabis; thus used as an affirmative greeting. [HIGH adj.¹ (2)]

Irish *n.*¹ [mid-19C+] (*orig. US*) temper; esp. as *get one's Irish up*.

Irish *n.*² *see* IRISH ARMS n.

Irish *adj.* [18C+] a general negative racial epithet; usu. in combs. below. [the stereotypical Irishman or woman is stupid, short-tempered, violent (whether on the street or in the home), addicted to potatoes, keen on brawling and usu. employed in a menial, labouring task, often rural; all these traits are reflected in the combs. that follow, and all combs. with *Irish* should be assumed to be derog. (if seen as joc. by the coiner/speaker) unless otherwise stated]

Irish ambulance *n.* [1910s–30s] (*US*) a wheelbarrow.

Irish apple *n.* [late 18C+] a potato. [stereotype of the potato as an Irish staple]

Irish applesauce *n.* [1960s] (*US*) mashed potatoes. [ext. of IRISH APPLE n.]

Irish apricot *n.* (*also* **Irish wall-fruit**) [late 18C+] a potato.

Irish arms *n.* (*also* **Irish**) [mid-18C–mid-19C] thick legs. [racial stereotyping]

Irish assurance *n.* [late 18C–19C] boldness, shamelessness. [like the Greek myth, which proclaims that being dipped in the River Styx gives a child invulnerability, 'so it is said, that a dipping in the River Shannon totally annihilates bashfulness' (Grose, 1785)]

Irish baby buggy *n.* [1910s+] (*US*) a wheelbarrow.

Irish banjo *n.* (*also* **Irish spoon**) [mid-19C+] a spade, a shovel.

Irish beauty *n.* [late 18C+] a woman with a pair of black eyes.

Irish bouquet *n.* [1960s–70s] (*US*) any form of projectile, usu. a stone or brick.

Irish buggy *n.* (*also* **Irish pluggy**) [1920s+] (*US*) a wheelbarrow.

Irish by birth but Greek by injection *phr.* [1960s+] a phr. said of a male homosexual. [GREEK adj.² (2) + INJECTION n. (2)]

Irish cabbage *n.* [1960s] (*US*) the trad. St Patrick's Day meal of corned (salt) beef, cabbage and Irish potatoes.

Irish caviar *n.* [1930s] (*US*) a meat stew.

Irish channel *n.* [1900s] the throat. [down which alcohol flows]

Irish chariot *n.* [1940s] (*US*) a wheelbarrow.

Irish cherry *n.* [1930s+] (*US*) a carrot.

Irish chicken *n.* [1920s–30s] (*US*) pork.

Irish clubhouse *n.* **1** [20C+] (*US*) a police station. **2** [1960s+] (*US gay*) a sophisticated, expensive brothel (cf. ACCOMMODATION HOUSE n.). [(1) plays on SE *club*, association/*club* to hit, i.e. police violence]

Irish coat of arms *n. see* IRISHMAN'S COAT OF ARMS phr.

Irish cocktail *n.* [1980s] (*US*) a drink containing a substance that causes unconsciousness. [play on MICKEY FINN n.]

Irish comics *n.* (*also* **Irish funnies, …sports pages**) [1970s+] the obituary columns in a newspaper. [supposed Irish illiteracy]

Irish compliment *n.* [mid-19C+] a back-handed compliment.

Irish confetti *n.* (*US*) **1** [20C+] (*also* **confetti**) bricks, esp. as thrown during riots. **2** [1980s+] an ejaculation of semen that is outside the vagina. [IRISH adj. + pun on SE *confetti*. (1) From c.1832, in the era before asphalt, New York streets were paved with bricks]

Irish curtains *n.* [1960s+] (*Aus./US*) cobwebs.

Irish dip *n.* [1960s+] (*gay*) sexual intercourse. [? derog. stereotyping based on large size of Catholic families]

Irish disease *n.* [1990s+] having a small penis.

Irish dividend *n.* **1** [mid-19C+] (*US*) a non-existent or fictitious profit, a deficit, a stock assessment. **2** [1920s] (*US Und.*) a shakedown by the police.

Irish draperies *n.* **1** [late 19C+] cobwebs. **2** [1980s+] drooping female breasts.

Irish evidence *n.* **1** [late 18C–19C] a perjuring witness. **2** [1960s] (*gay*) pendulous breasts.

Irish fan *n.* [1920s+] (*US*) a spade, a shovel.

Irish flag *n.* [1960s] (*US*) a diaper, a nappy.

Irish football *n.* [1970s] (*US*) a potato.

Irish fortune *n.* [19C] the vagina (cf. BANK n.¹).

Irish funnies *n. see* IRISH COMICS n.

Irish goose *n.* [mid-19C] cooked codfish.

Irish grape *n.* [1940s–70s] (*US*) a potato.

Irish hint *n.* [mid-18C+] (*US*) a very broad hint. [the supposed stupidity of the Irish]

Irish hoist *n.* [mid-19C+] a kick in the behind. [the stereotypically boorish, brawling Irishman]

Irish horse *n.* **1** [mid-18C+] tough, undercooked salt beef. **2** [1950s+] (*gay*) an impotent penis (cf. ANTEATER n.).

Irish inch *n.* [1970s–80s] (*US*) the erect penis. [a slur on Irish penis size]

Irish jig *n.* [20C+] **1** wig. **2** a cigarette. [rhy. sl.; (2) = CIG n.]

Irish karate *n.* [1990s+] (*Aus.*) the use of a shotgun.

Irish king *n.* [1960s] (*N.Z.*) something one needs; usu. in phr. *buggered for the want of an Irish King.* [? something unattainable]

Irish lace *n.* [1950s+] a spider's web. [var. on IRISH DRAPERIES n. (1)]

Irish lasses *n.* [20C+] glasses. [rhy. sl.]

Irish legs *n.* [late 18C+] heavy female legs.

Irish lemon *n.* [late 19C+] (*US*) a potato.

Irish local *n.* **1** [1900s] a railway hand-car, propelled by pushing a handle backwards and forwards. **2** [1930s+] (*US*) a wheelbarrow. [SAmE *local*, a local train]

Irishman's buggy *n.* [1920s] (*US*) a wheelbarrow.

Irishman's coat of arms *phr.* (*also* **Irish coat of arms**) **1** [mid-18C+] a black eye. **2** [early 19C] (*US*) 2 black eyes and a bleeding nose.

Irishman's dinner *n.* [19C+] a fast. ['a smoke and a visit to the urinal' (Hotten, 1874) + ref. to Irish Famine 1845–6]

Irishman's harvest *n.* [19C] the orange season. [used by London costermongers; indigent Irishmen presumably picked up rotten oranges]

Irishman's pocket *n.* [20C+] (*US*) a pocket that is both large and empty.

Irishman's rest *n.* [late 19C–1900s] mounting a ladder carrying a hod of bricks.

Irishman's rise *n. see* IRISH RISE n.

Irishman's sidewalk *n.* (*also* **Irish sidewalk**) [mid-19C–1930s] (*US*) the street. [racial stereotyping; either the loathed Irish ought to walk in the street, rather than on the pavement where more civilized people walked, or they were too stupid to know the difference]

Irishman's turkey *n.* [1910s+] (*US*) corned beef and cabbage.

Irish marathon *n.* [20C+] a lengthy session of sexual intercourse.

Irish mike *n. see* PAT AND MIKE n.[1].

Irish mile *n.* [late 19C+] a 'country mile', i.e. a mile that twists and turns and thus seems much further.

Irish nachos *n.* [1990s+] (*US*) fried potato wedges and (refried) beans.

Irish necktie *n.* [late 19C] (*US*) a rope.

Irish nightingale *n.* [mid-19C–1940s] (*US*) a bullfrog (cf. CAMBRIDGE NIGHTINGALE n.).

Irish pasture *n.* [20C+] (*US*) a fainting fit, esp. a fake one. [? SE *posture*]

Irish pluggy *n. see* IRISH BUGGY n.

Irish potato *n.* [1990s+] (*W.I.*) a young man who is 'kept' by an older woman. [? play on SPUD n.[2] (3)/STUD n.[1] (7)]

Irish promotion *n.* **1** [late 19C+] a cut in one's pay. **2** [20C+] (*gay*) masturbation.

Irish rifle *n.* [19C] a small comb.

Irish rise *n.* (*also* **Irishman's rise**) **1** [mid-19C] (*US/UK*) (*also* Irish raise) a cut in one's pay. **2** [late 19C+] sexual detumescence.

Irish root *n.* **1** [19C+] the penis. **2** [mid-19C] a potato.

Irish rose *n.*[1] [20C+] the nose. [rhy. sl.]

Irish rose *n.*[2] [1930s] (*US*) a stone, for throwing.

Irish screwdriver *n.* [20C+] a hammer.

Irish shave *n.* [1920s+] an act of defecation.

Irish shift *n.* (*also* **Irish switch**) [1960s+] (*US*) political hypocrisy. [the supposed propensity of Irish politicians to blow with the prevailing wind. Given the year of first use – 1960 – the Irish in question may have been the Kennedys, whose scion John was elected president that year]

Irish sidewalk *n. see* IRISHMAN'S SIDEWALK n.

Irish spoon *n. see* IRISH BANJO n.

Irish sports pages *n. see* IRISH COMICS n.

Irish stew *adj.* [20C+] **1** true; esp. in the phr. *too Irish stew.* **2** blue. [rhy. sl.]

Irish switch *n. see* IRISH SHIFT n.

Irish toothache *n.* (*also* **i.t.a.**, **Paddy's toothache**) **1** [19C+] an erection. **2** [20C+] pregnancy.

Irish toothpick *n.* **1** [1920s] (*US*) a pickaxe. **2** [1980s+] (*US gay*) the erect penis.

Irish toyle *n.* [16C–18C] (*UK Und.*) a mendicant villain who posed as a tinker or peddler to fool their victims. [IRISH adj. + SE *toil*, a net or trap]

Irish tumble-dryer *n.* [1980s] a cement mixer.

Irish turkey *n.* [mid-19C+] (*US*) corned (salt) beef and cabbage. [popularized by its use in the *Jiggs and Maggie* comic strip]

Irish twins *n.* [1960s+] (*US*) 2 siblings born within a 12-month period. [the stereotypical fecundity – and lack of contraceptive practice – of Irish families]

Irish virgin *n.* [20C+] (*US*) one who is a virgin and is likely to remain one. [? pious Irish virgins who become nuns]

Irish wake *n.* [mid-19C+] any boisterous occasion, not necessarily a wake.

Irish wall-fruit *n. see* IRISH APRICOT n.

Irish wash *n.* [1960s+] (*US*) the turning or reversing of a garment or other object to hide rather than actually remove the dirt.

Irish way *n.* [1970s+] heterosexual anal intercourse. [the belief that pious Catholics used anal intercourse as their sole means of contraception]

Irish wedding *n.* (*also* **wedding**) **1** [late 18C–19C] a brawl, 'where black eyes are given instead of favours' (Grose, 1796). **2** [19C] the emptying of a cesspool. **3** [20C+] (*gay*) masturbation.

Irish whist *n.* [19C] sexual intercourse; thus *play (at) Irish whist*, to have sexual intercourse; often ext. by *...where Jack takes the ace.*

Irishy *n.* [late 19C] (*Aus.*) an Irish immigrant to Australia.

iris out *v.* [1960s–70s] to leave unobtrusively. [film jargon *iris out*, to contract the picture to the dimensions of a small dot and thence a blank screen; prob. a Wodehouse coinage/nonce-word]

iron *n.*[1] [16C–early 18C; 1930s+] the penis (cf. AX n.[2]). [later use is US]

iron *n.*[2] **1** [late 18C–1920s] money (cf. BRASS n.[1]). **2** [1900s–10s] (*US*) $1 in cash. [the metal coins]

iron *n.*[3] **1** [early 19C–1920s] (*US*) bullets or shells. **2** [mid-19C+] (*US*) (*also* **piece of iron**) a gun; thus *carry iron*, to go armed, esp. as a gangster's bodyguard. **3** [1920s] (*US Und.*) a drill bit. **4** [1920s+] (*US prison*) handcuffs. **5** [1930s+] (*US*) a discontinued model of motor car, a run-down, dilapidated car. **6** [1940s] a house-breaker's implement, a crowbar. **7** [1960s–70s] (*US*) a motorcycle. **8** [1960s+] (*US*) weights, as used in body-building exercises; usu. as PUMP IRON v. **9** [1970s+] a knife.

iron *n.*[4] [mid-19C; 1990s+] courage; thus as adj., courageous, fearless.

iron *n.*[5] [1980s+] (*W.I.*, *Jam.*) a thug, a gangster.

iron, the *n. see* IRON HORSE n.[2].

iron *v.* **1** [late 19C+] to kill. **2** [1950s+] (*Aus.*) to defeat in a fight. **3** [1970s+] (*Aus.*) to get drunk.

iron bar *v.* (*also* **bar**) [1980s+] (*Aus. prison*) to make a surprise attack (irrespective of the weapon used).

iron ben *n.* [1940s] (*US Und.*) a bullet-proof vest.

iron-bound *n.* [late-19C–1910s] a hard-baked pie.

iron-bound hat *n.* [late 18C–early 19C] a silver-laced hat.

iron boy *n.* [1910s–20s] (*US*) $1.

iron butterfly *n.* (*also* **butterfly**) [1950s+] an old-fashioned hypodermic syringe made of metal and glass. [shape; the curved finger-holes are the 'wings' of the butterfly]

iron cross *n.* [1960s+] (*US Black*) extremely unfavourable circumstances from which it is hard to extract oneself. [SE *cross*, a burden]

iron cunny *n.* [1950s] (*W.I.*) a tough sugar candy, extremely hard to chew. [SE *iron* + *candy*]

iron cure *n.* (*also* **steel and concrete cure**) [1930s–50s] (*US drugs*) a 'cure' for addiction given in prison; the prisoner is deprived of drugs and forced to withdraw in his cell. [the *iron bars of the cell*]

iron dollar *n.* [1900s–20s] (*US*) $1 in cash.

iron doublet *n.* [17C–early 19C] a prison.

iron duke *n.* [late 19C+] a lucky chance. [rhy. sl. = FLUKE n.² (1); the orig. *Iron Duke* was the Duke of Wellington (1769–1852)]

iron eye, the *n.* [1940s] (*US*) a hard and hostile stare.

iron feed *n.* [1940s] (*W.I.*) corn meal cooked with rice. [such a starchy dish is very 'hard']

iron freak *n.* [1960s] (*US*) a weight-lifting enthusiast. [IRON n.³ (8) + FREAK sfx]

iron gaiters *n.* (*also* **iron garters**) [mid-18C–mid-19C] leg-irons.

iron girder *n.* [1990s+] murder; usu. in fig. uses, *get away with iron girder, there'll be iron girder if…* [rhy. sl.]

iron hat *n.* [1910s–30s] (*US*) a derby hat. [note WW1 US milit. *iron derby*, a steel helmet]

ironhead *n.*¹ [1910s+] (*US*) a fool. [the hardness of iron]

ironhead *n.*² [1940s] (*Aus.*) a German soldier. [the German soldier's helmet]

ironhead *n.*³ [1990s+] (*US prison*) one who works out with body-building weights. [IRON n.³ (8)]

ironheaded *adj.* [1940s] stupid (cf. AIRHEADED adj.). [IRONHEAD n.¹]

iron (hoof) *n.* [1930s+] a male homosexual. [rhy. sl. = POOF n. (1)]

iron hoop *n.* [late 19C–1910s] soup. [rhy. sl.]

iron horse *n.*¹ [1920s] (*US Und.*) prison.

iron horse *n.*² **1** [1930s+] (*also* **the iron, the ironing**) a toss of a coin (note Cockney pron. *torss*). **2** [1950s+] a racecourse. [rhy. sl.]

iron horse *n.*³ [1970s+] (*US Black*) the subway. [the original *iron horse* was the mid-19C railroad]

iron horse *v.* [20C+] to toss a coin. [IRON HORSE n.² (1)]

iron house *n.* **1** [1910s+] (*US Und.*) (*also* **iron hotel**) a prison (cf. BANDHOUSE n.). **2** [1990s+] a punishment cell.

ironing, the *n. see* IRON HORSE n.²

iron jaws *n.* [1970s+] (*US gay*) an exceptionally competent fellator.

iron louie *n.* [late 19C] (*US*) $1.

iron lung *n.* **1** [1940s] a deep shelter in the London underground, used as an air raid shelter. **2** [1950s] the Central Line, in its extension from Shoreditch to Essex. **3** [1960s+] (*Irish*) an aluminium keg of beer, usu. Guinness. **4** [1970s+] an open-air urinal.

iron man *n.* **1** [20C+] (*US*) $1; usu. in pl. **2** [1940s–60s] (*US*) $1000. **3** [1940s–70s] (*orig. Aus.*) £1 note. **4** [1960s] (*US*) $100. [the metal coins]

iron Mike *n.* [1940s+] **1** a bicycle. **2** (*US Und.*) brass knuckles. [(1) rhy. sl. = *bike*]

ironmongery *n.* [20C+] firearms, weapons.

ironmongery department, the *n.* [1940s+] prison. [the iron bars; pun]

iron out *v.* [20C+] **1** to correct a situation, to put things right. **2** to overwhelm in a fight. **3** of money, to spend freely. **4** to kill, to murder. [fig. uses of SE; ? (4) IRON n.³ (2)]

iron parenthesis *n.* [early 19C] a prison. [it provides a *parenthesis* in one's on-going life]

iron pile *n.* [20C+] (*US Und.*) **1** a prison. **2** (*also* **weight pile**) the weight-lifting and body-building facilities in a prison. [the SE *iron bars*/IRON n.³ (8) + SE *pile*]

irons *n.*¹ **1** [early 19C+] (*US*) handcuffs; thus adj. *ironed*, handcuffed. **2** [1980s+] knuckledusters. [SE *iron*; (1) compare IRON n.³ (4)]

irons *n.*² [1920s+] eating utensils, a knife and fork. [abbr. EATING IRONS n.]

iron tank *n.* [1910s+] a bank. [rhy. sl.]

iron theatre *n.* [1920s–30s] (*US Und.*) a prison.

iron-whip *v.* [1970s] (*US Und.*) to pistol-whip. [IRON n.³ (2)]

irrigate *v.* [mid-19C–1900s] (*Aus./US*) **1** to drink. **2** to give a drink to someone else.

irrigate one's canal *v.* [late 18C+] to drink.

irrigation *n.* [mid-late 19C] alcoholic refreshment. [IRRIGATE v.]

irvine *n.* (*also* **irv**) [1970s+] (*US Black*) the police. [? joc. use of proper name]

Isaac *n.* [late 17C] a fool (cf. BEN n.¹). [? generic use of *Isaac* as a rural, thus 'foolish' name]

isabella *n.* (*also* **isabeller**) [mid-19C+] an umbrella. [rhy. sl.]

isadora *n.* [1960s–70s] (*camp gay*) a long scarf. [the demise of dancer *Isadora* Duncan (1878–1927), who was throttled to death when her long scarf was caught in a car's rear wheel]

is all *phr.* [1940s+] (*orig. US*) abbr. of *that is all*.

is a pig's pussy pork? *phr.* (*also* **is a pig's ass pork?**) [1960s+] (*US*) the response to a question to which the answer is definitely in the affirmative.

I say! *excl.* [early 19C+] a general excl. of surprise, disagreement or to attract attention.

isda *n.* [1970s+] (*drugs*) heroin. [? Sp.]

ish, the *n.* [1990s+] (*US Black*) **1** something bad. **2** the very best, the ultimate. [SHIT, THE n.¹]

ish *adj.* (*also* **tish**) [1980s+] (*UK juv.*) a general negative, use varying as to context. [? abbr. CUNTISH adj. but poss. backsl. = SHIT n.¹]

i-shence *n.* (*also* **ishen**) [1950s+] (*W.I. Rasta*) marijuana, often particularly potent strains. [SE *essence*]

ish kabibble *phr.* [1910s+] (*US*) it is of no importance to me, I don't care. [for ety. *see* ABIE KABIBBLE n.]

ishkimkisk *adj.* [18C–19C] (*tinker*) drunk. [mispron. of Shelta *misgeach*]

I shot him lightly and he died politely *phr.* [1930s–50s] (*US Black*) a phr. implying that the speaker has had the better of an opponent, verbally or physically.

I should be so lucky! *excl.* [20C+] an excl. intimating envy on behalf of a speaker who has just been informed of another's luck, also used ironically. [the word-pattern implies a Yid. origin]

I should blush to murmur *phr.* [late 19C] (*US*) a phr. of affirmation.

I should cocoa! *excl.* [1930s+] you must be joking! don't make me laugh! [rhy. sl.; COFFEE AND COCOA phr. = *say so*; esp. popular in BBC Radio's *Billy Cotton Bandshow* in the 1950s]

I should smile *phr.* [mid-19C–1920s] (*US*) an ironic response to an implausible suggestion.

I should snicker to smile *phr.* [late 19C] (*US teen*) a phr. of affirmation, you are absolutely right.

I should talk *phr.* [1970s+] a phr. used to stress that one speaker is in no position to criticize another.

I should worry *phr.* [20C+] I don't care. [Yid.]

is it? *phr.*¹ [1910s+] a general challenging phr.

is it? *phr.*² [1960s+] (*S.Afr.*) a non-committal colloq. expression used to convey polite disbelief, astonishment, really? you don't mean to say?

is it buggery! *excl.* (*also* **is it fuck/hell/shit!**) [20C+] an excl. used to stress one's disbelief, derision and general negative attitude.

Island, the *n.* **1** [mid-19C+] Riker's Island prison, near New York (cf. ABBOTT'S PRIORY n.). **2** [late 19C–1930s] (*US Und.*) Blackwell's Island Asylum, New York City. **3** [20C+] the Isle of Wight, and thus the prisons of Parkhurst and Camp Hill, both of which are situated on the island.

island nigger *n.* [1980s+] (*US*) a derog. term for a Puerto Rican (cf. BATO n.). [SE *island* + NIGGER n.¹ (1); the premise being that, as foreigners and non-Whites, Puerto Ricans are *de facto* niggers]

isle of fling *n.* [late 19C–1900s] a coat. [ety. unknown; ? one 'flings' it over one's shoulders]

isle of France *n.* [mid-19C–1900s] a dance. [rhy. sl.]

Isle of Man *n.* [20C+] a pan. [rhy. sl.; never shortened]

Isle of Wight *n.* [1950s+] **1** the right side. **2** right, permission. [rhy. sl.]

Isle of Wight *adj.* [20C+] **1** light. **2** tipsy. **3** all right. **4** mean, grasping. [rhy. sl.; (2) = TIGHT adj.[5]; (4) = TIGHT adj.[4] (1)]

ism *n.* (*also* **izm**) [1980s+] (*US drugs*) marijuana. [ety. unknown]

ism and skism *n.* (*also* **ism and schism**, **isms and skisms**) [1970s+] (*W.I./UK Black teen*) a phr. that denotes society's ways, class consciousness, sub-systems and/or classifications. [? coined by Bob Marley]

isn't that special *phr.* [1980s+] (*US campus*) a dismissive phr. implying that 'that' is not special at all.

iso *n.* [1930s] (*US prison*) the *iso*lation cells. [abbr.]

Isro *n.* (*also* **Izro**) [1970s+] (*US*) a bushy hairstyle worn by White people, often curly-headed Jews. [SE *Israel* + AFRO n.[2]]

Issey *n. see* IZZY n.

issue *n.* [1910s+] (*Aus.*) everything, the lot, all there is; often as *the whole issue.*

issue *v.* [1990s+] (*US drugs*) to cheat; to sell fake drugs.

I.S.T. *n.* [1990s+] (*US*) a lack of punctuation. [abbr. *Indian Stretchable Time*; cultural/national stereotyping]

is the pope a Catholic/guinea? *phr. see* DOES A BEAR SHIT IN THE WOODS? IS THE POPE A CATHOLIC? phr.

I suppose *n.* [mid-19C+] the nose. [rhy. sl.]

I swan! *excl.* [early–mid-19C] (*US*) an excl. of asseveration, I declare!

is your father a glazier? *phr.* (*also* **your father's a glazier?**) [mid-18C–1950s] a rude phr. used to embarrass someone who is obstructing one's view.

it *n.*[1] **1** [17C+] sexual intercourse. **2** [mid-17C+] the male or female genitals. **3** [19C] a chamberpot. **4** [late 19C+] (*US*) a fool or an unpleasant person, a term of contempt. **5** [late 19C+] (*orig. US*) the acme of fashion, the ultimate, usu. when applied to a person, e.g. *he really thinks he's it.* **6** [20C+] (*US*) money. **7** [20C+] a coverall for such special qualities that are required for social or professional success. **8** [20C+] sex appeal. **9** [1910s+] a person. **10** [1920s] ejaculation. **11** [1930s] (*US*) excrement. **12** [1930s] (*US Und.*) death. **13** [1930s+] a ref. to a casual, picked-up partner as opposed to a lover. **14** [1930s+] sexually available women. **15** [1940s+] virginity. **16** [1950s] (*US*) a dose of an addictive drug. **17** [1950s+] (*US Black*) the quintessence of Black spirit, sensitivity etc. **18** [1970s] masturbation. [(8) although the term was popularized in Elinor Glyn's *It* (1927), note R. Kipling 'Mrs Bathurst' (1904): 'Tisn't beauty, so to speak, nor good talk necessarily. It's just It. Some women'll stay in a man's memory if they once walk down a street.' Cited as such in the *OED*, and by Andrew Lycett in *Rudyard Kipling* (1999), who adds 'Possibly he gleaned this idea from Lord Milner, who had courted Glyn']

it *n.*[2] [late 19C+] as an indefinite object, used with a v., e.g. *walk it, cab it.*

i.t.a. *n. see* IRISH TOOTHACHE n.

ital *adj.* (*also* **i-tal**) **1** [1950s+] (*orig. W.I. Rasta*) essential, basic, *echt* Rastafarian. **2** [1950s+] (*W.I. Rasta*) vital, organic, natural, wholesome, referring both to a way of cooking and of life. **3** [1960s+] (*W.I./UK Black teen*) of food, natural, unprocessed (fresh vegetables, fruits etc) or prepared without salt. [SE *vital* + Rastafarian use of pfx *i-*]

Italian *n.* [1990s+] (*US*) anger, bad temper. [stereotyping]

Italian *adj.* **1** [late 16C–17C; 1900s–30s] (*also* **Italick**) devoted to hetero- or homosexual anal intercourse. **2** [17C] in fig. use, referring to anything 'backward' or reversed. **3** [mid-17C] pertaining to syphilis. [(1) seen as a 'dirty' and 'foreign' practice; Wardroper uses alternative and more pertinent title: 'A Relation of a Quaker that to the Shame of his Profession Attempted to Bugger a Mare near Colchester']

Italian airlines *n.* [1950s+] (*gay*) walking. [the stereotyped inefficiency of Italian air companies]

Italian fence climbers *n.* [1990s+] (*US*) shoes, boots. [SE *Italian*, i.e. the leather]

Italian football *n.* [1940s–80s] (*US Und.*) a bomb. [derog. stereotyping, ? based on Mafia]

Italian hero *n.* [20C+] (*US*) a large sandwich made of 2 slabs of bread cut lengthwise from the loaf and containing a variety of ingredients. [its 'heroic' size, or ? f. stereotype of Italians as placing sexual – the phallic sandwich – above martial prowess]

Italian lock *n. see* SPANISH PADLOCK n.

Italian mean time *n.* [2000s] unpunctuality (cf. AFRICAN (PEOPLE'S) TIME n.).

Italian padlock *n. see* SPANISH PADLOCK n.

Italian perfume *n.* [1940s] (*US*) garlic.

Italian quarrel *n.* [late 19C–1900s] death, murder, poisoning, treachery. [stereotyping; the image is of the corrupt Borgia family]

Italian salute *n.* [1950s+] (*US*) an obscene gesture of contempt or derision; one arm is bent and the fist and forearm thrust upwards while the other hand grasps the forearm or bicep. [the gesture originated in Italy and was imported by immigrants]

Italian sin *n.* (*also* **Italian tricks**) [17C] hetero- or homosexual anal intercourse. [ITALIAN adj. (1)]

Italian special *n.* (*also* **Italian straws**) [20C+] (*US*) pasta, spaghetti.

Italian tune-up *n.* [1990s+] (*US*) driving one's car into the desert and speeding at 100mph to check that everything works. [SE *tune-up*, service for a car]

italist *n.* [1990s+] (*W.I.*) one who leads a natural 'organic' lifestyle; often of Rastafarians. [ITAL adj.]

it all depends *phr.* (*also* **that all depends**) [late 19C+] a temporizing phr. for perhaps, possibly, probably; thus *it all depends what school you went to,* used by those who are unsure as to the proper pronunciation of a (foreign) word and thus offer both variations.

I.T.A.L.Y. *phr.* [1940s+] *I trust and love you,* written on envelopes of love letters (cf. B.O.L.T.O.P. phr.). [abbr.]

itch *n.* (*also* **itching**) **1** [17C+] sexual excitement. **2** [1950s+] (*drugs*) an addiction to narcotics.

itch and scratch *n.* [1910s+] a match. [rhy. sl.]

itcher *n.* [19C] the vagina. [ITCH n. (1)]

itching *n. see* ITCH n.

itching jenny *n.* [19C] the vagina. [ITCH n. (1); note JENNY n.[3] (2) despite dates]

itchland *n.* **1** [late 17C–early 18C] Wales. **2** [18C–mid-19C] Scotland; thus *Itchlander,* a Scot. [derog. stereotyping of Wales and Scotland as a land of overt sexuality or of infestations of body-lice; thus early 18C ballad 'The Curse of Scotland': 'So God keep me from Scotland, and all that mangy race / For it is a nasty, mangy, lousy, itchy, dirty place']

itchy eye *n.* [1990s+] (*US*) haemorrhoid. [SE *itchy* + EYE n.[1] (2)/ROUNDEYE n. (1); a typical symptom is an itching sensation of the sphincter]

Ite *n. see* EYETIE n.

item *n.* **1** [19C–1900s] (*US*) a hint, an inkling, a piece of information. **2** [1940s+] (*US*) a person. **3** [1940s+] (*orig. US*) a couple. [(2) and (3) the exploits of such fashionable individuals provide items for newspaper gossip columnists]

item *v.* [19C] to pass on information to a confederate. [ITEM n. (1)]

Itie *see under* EYETIE.

-itis *sfx* [20C+] used humorously to create imagined 'diseases', e.g. *Zeppelinitis,* a fear of aerial bombardment during WW1; *danceitis,* an obsession with dancing; *workitis,* a pathological dislike of work. [SE *-itis,* used with the proper n. to create the name of a disease, often an inflammation of the part in question, e.g. arthritis, nephritis]

it is to laugh *phr.* [late 19C–1960s] (*US*) it is very ironic.

it'll cost ya! *excl. see* COST YA! excl.

it must be jelly, 'cos jam don't shake like that *phr.*
[1920s+] (*US Black*) a phr. used between males to express their
appreciation of an especially attractive female.

it's a bastard *phr.* (*also* **it's a proper bastard**) [20C+] (*orig.*
Aus.) a phr. for anything considered unpleasant, excessively
challenging etc.

it's a case of spoons with them *phr.* [mid-19C–1920s] a phr.
used of a couple who are obviously in love. [SPOON v.¹ + ? CASE
n.⁶ (1) + a pun on the *case of spoons* one might receive as a
wedding gift]

it's a dog's life *phr.* [20C+] said of an unpleasant situation or
of one's whole wretched existence.

it's a fair old bugger *phr.* (*also* **it's a proper bugger, ...right
bugger, ...right old bugger**) [mid-19C+] said of anything
considered unpleasant, excessively challenging etc.

it's a fine day for travelling *phr.* [1950s+] (*Aus.*) a phr. used
in the outback to signify that one has received notice to quit.
[ironic use of SE]

it's a gas *phr.* [1960s+] (*US/UK teen*) a phr. indicating that
everything is fine, it's all wonderful. [GAS n.³ (1)]

it's a go *phr. see* GO n.³ (8).

it's a new one on me *phr.* [20C+] that's the first I have heard of
it, I've never seen, heard or experienced that before.

it's an idea *phr.* (*also* **that's an idea**) [1910s+] that is an idea
worth considering.

it's an old — custom *phr.* [1930s+] a phr. used to justify a
practice, usu. in the workplace, that would otherwise be
condemned, abandoned etc had it not been established over a
long period; usu. *an old Spanish custom*, earlier *an old Southern
custom*.

it's a peg *phr.* [1930s+] (*Aus.*) a phr. used to indicate pleasure,
that's wonderful. [ety. unknown]

it's a proper bastard *phr. see* IT'S A BASTARD phr.

it's a proper/right (old) bugger *phr. see* IT'S A FAIR OLD
BUGGER phr.

it's been real *phr.* [1970s+] (*orig. US campus*) a farewell, an
acknowledgement of what has just been experienced, e.g. a
meeting; also used ironically.

it's dogged as does it *phr.* [mid-19C+] a phr. stating that
persistence always wins through in a given endeavour. [SE *dogged*,
persistent, obstinate, stubborn]

it's my way or the highway *phr.* [1980s+] (*US*) do as I say
or you will suffer. [the image of a boy tossing a girl out of his car,
some way from home, after she has refused to have sex]

it's no hanging matter *phr.* [late 19C+] an assurance that
something is unimportant.

it's not the bull they're afraid of, it's the calf *phr.* [20C+]
(*Aus.*) of women, it's not intercourse they dislike, it's the thought
of possible pregnancy.

it's one o'clock (at the button factory) *phr.* (*also* **it's two
o'clock..., it's three o'clock..., ...at the waterworks**) [20C+]
advice to a man that his fly is open.

it's the beer talking *phr.* (*also* **beer's talking, drink's...,
grog's..., liquor's..., whisky's...**) [20C+] **1** the excuse, usu. in
a public house, for breaking wind. **2** an excuse for any excessive
talk or actions when drunk, either at the time or when sober on
reflection (cf. RUM TALKING phr.).

it's your little hip pocket *phr.* [1950s+] (*US Black*) you're in
great trouble. [the position of the hip pocket over the buttocks;
thus one is about to receive a KICK IN THE PANTS, A n.]

it takes one to know one *phr.* [late 19C+] a phr. upbraiding
someone for possessing the exact characteristics they are
criticizing in another.

it takes two to tango *phr.* **1** [1930s+] a phr. meaning that
sexual intercourse, esp. adulterous, requires 2 people, not just a
lustful male. **2** [1960s+] applied to a situation where one party
is getting the blame but both are equally responsible.

it won't wash *phr.* [mid-19C+] that won't work, that won't
stand proper investigation. [dyeing imagery, when a poor or
badly applied dye will vanish in the wash]

it would make a cat laugh *phr. see* ENOUGH TO MAKE A CAT
LAUGH phr.

itzy house *n.* [1930s] (*US*) a psychiatric institution. [? DITZY adj.¹
(1)]

IV *v.* [1990s+] (*US drugs*) to inject a drug intravenously. [abbr.]

Ivan *n.* [1940s+] **1** a generic for a Russian; thus a Communist. **2** a
generally stupid east European person. [*Ivan*, a stereotypical
Slavic/Russian name]

I've got the time if you've got the money *phr.* [1910s+] a
joc. phr. delivered to one who asks 'Have you got the time?' [the
supposed conversation between a streetwalker and her client
who has asked, as a way of initiating their relationship, 'Do you
have the time?']

ivory *n.* **1** [late 18C+] a tooth; usu. in pl. **2** [mid-19C+] in pl.,
dice; thus *rattle the ivories*, to throw dice. **3** [mid-19C+] a piano.
4 [late 19C–1930s] (*US*) in pl., poker chips. **5** [late 19C–1950s] in
pl., billiard balls. **6** [late 19C+] (*US Black*) in pl., piano keys; thus
TICKLE THE IVORIES v. [lit. or fig. uses of SE *ivory*, used in
manufacturing all these items]

ivory *adj.* [1930s+] (*US*) White, Caucasian. [the whiteness]

ivory-bender *n.* [1920s] (*US*) a piano-player. [IVORY n. (3) + SE
bend]

ivory box *n.* [19C+] the mouth. [IVORY n. (1) + SE *box*]

ivory-carpenter *n.* (*also* **ivory-picker, -puller, -snatcher**)
[1940s–50s] (*US*) a dentist. [IVORY n. (1) + image of pulling teeth]

ivory dome *n.* **1** [20C+] a bald-headed person. **2** [1910s–30s]
(*US*) a fool; thus *ivory-domed, solid ivory*, stupid. [DOME n. (1)]

ivory float *n.* [1920s–50s] (*US*) a coat. [rhy. sl.]

ivory gate *n.* [19C] the vagina (cf. BELLY ENTRANCE n.).

ivory hound *n.* [1930s] (*US*) a piano-player. [IVORY n. (3)
+ HOUND sfx]

ivory pearl *n.* [1930s] a girl. [rhy. sl.]

ivory-picker *n. see* IVORY-CARPENTER n.

ivory-pounder *n.* [20C+] (*US*) a piano-player. [IVORY n. (3) + SE
pound]

ivory-puller/-snatcher *n. see* IVORY-CARPENTER n.

ivory-thumper *n.* [1920s+] (*US*) a piano-player. [IVORY n. (3)
+ SE *thump*]

ivory-tickler *n.* [1910s+] (*US*) a piano-player (cf. TICKLE THE
IVORIES v.; TICKLER n.⁶). [IVORY n. (3) + SE *tickle*]

ivory-turner *n.* [early–mid-19C] a skilful dice-player. [IVORY n.
(2) + pun]

ivy cottage *n.* [late 19C+] an outside lavatory (cf. BACKHOUSE
n.).

I want to know! *excl.* [mid-19C–1920s] an excl. of interest,
amazement, 'well, well!'

I want to see the butcher, not the block *phr. see* I'M
TALKING TO THE BUTCHER, NOT THE BLOCK phr.

I Won't Work *n.* [1900s–20s] (*US*) a derog. term for a member of
the Industrial Workers of the World (IWW). [pun on initial letters]

I wouldn't be in it *phr.* [1940s+] (*Aus.*) I wouldn't join in, take
part.

I wouldn't fuck her with a borrowed prick *phr.* (*also* **I
wouldn't fuck her with your prick**) [20C+] a general term
of masculine distaste, spoken on seeing what is considered an
unattractive or unpleasant woman. [FUCK v.¹ + PRICK n. (2)]

I wouldn't kick her out of bed *phr.* [1920s+] referring to
an attractive woman; a comment usu. made by one of a group
of young men observing a passing woman.

I wouldn't piss on them if they were on fire *phr.*
[1960s+] a phr. implying the speaker's absolute contempt or
loathing for the person thus decried.

I wouldn't shit you, you're my favourite turd *phr. see*
WOULD I SHIT YOU? YOU'RE MY FAVOURITE TURD phr.

I wouldn't trust... *phr.* used in a variety of contexts to imply one's absolute lack of faith in the person who is its object; e.g. [early 19C] *they may be trusted alone*, the implication being '...but I wouldn't trust them in company'; [mid-19C+] *I wouldn't trust them as far as I could fling a bull by the tail*; [late 19C+] *I wouldn't trust them as far as I could throw them*; [20C+] *I wouldn't trust them as far as I could throw an anvil in a swamp*; [20C+] *I wouldn't trust them with a kid's money-box* (with an added ref. to financial improbity); [20C+] *I wouldn't trust them with our cat* (with an added ref. to sexual perversion).

ixnay *adv.* [1920s+] (*US*) no. [cod Lat., the reverse of *nix*]

-iz- *ifx* [1930s+] (*US Black*) used as a general infix, e.g. in BIZALLS n., BIZNATCH n., HIZZO n., SHIZNIT n. etc. [note the earlier use of an infix *-eas* found in a number of terms used by US carnival workers, e.g. *ceasarnie* (carnie), *measark* (a mark), *heasar* (here), *neasix* (nix) etc]

izm *n. see* ISM n.

Izro *n. see* ISRO n.

Izzy *n.* (*also* **Issey**) [20C+] a nickname for a Jew (cf. ABE n.[1]). [Jewish name *Isaac*]

J

J *n.*[1] *see* JAVA n.

J *n.*[2] *see* JAY n.[3]

j *n.* (*also* **jay, jaybird, j-bo**) [1960s+] (*drugs*) a cannabis cigarette (cf. AFRICAN WOODBINE n.). [abbr. JOINT n.[5] (3)]

j.a. *n.* 1 [1970s] (*W.I.*) a Jamaican. 2 [1990s+] (*US*) a Japanese-American. [abbr.]

j.a. *adj.* [1990s+] (*US*) Japanese-American. [J.A. n. (2)]

Ja *n.* (*also* **JA**) [20C+] (*W.I. Rasta*) Jamaica (cf. JAMDUNG n.). [abbr.]

jaap *n.* (*also* **japie**) (*S.Afr.*) 1 [1940s+] an Afrikaner. 2 [1950s+] a peasant, a rustic, an unsophisticated person (cf. ALVIN n.). [Afk. *jaap*, f. proper name *Jacob*, a typical 'country' name. *DSAE* claims that 'no examples of the word in use by non-South Africans have been found', but cf. YARPIE n., common in Aus., albeit transliterated]

jab *n.*[1] [20C+] (*US*) an attempt, a try.

jab *n.*[2] [1910s+] 1 (*orig. milit.*) an inoculation, any form of injection, esp. against diseases such as TB and polio. 2 (*drugs*) an injection of a narcotic drug. [note earlier JAB v.[1]]

jab *n.*[3] 1 [1970s+] (*US/Irish*) an act of copulation. 2 [2000s] (*Irish*) a woman's breast; usu. in pl. [(1) note earlier JAB v.[2]]

jab *v.*[1] [20C+] (*drugs*) to inject drugs.

jab *v.*[2] [1960s+] (*US campus*) of a man, to have sexual intercourse (cf. BANG v.[1]).

jaba *n.* [2000s] (*US teen*) marijuana. [? JABBER n.[1] (1)]

ja-baas *n.* [1960s+] (*S.Afr.*) a servile, subservient Black. [Afk. *ja baas*, 'yes, master']

jabber *n.*[1] (*also* **jabbering**) 1 [18C+] unrestrained talking, completely unintelligible, incomprehensible talk. 2 [1930s–40s] gossip. [JABBER v.]

jabber *n.*[2] 1 [1900s–40s] (*US prison*) a prize-fighter. 2 [1910s+] any person who is prone to fighting. [one who SE *jabs*]

jabber *n.*[3] [1930s–50s] (*US drugs*) a drug addict. [JAB v.[1]]

jabber *v.* 1 [late 15C+] to talk in an incomprehensible or nonsensical manner. 2 [mid-16C+] to talk a foreign language. 3 [mid-19C+] to gossip. [the sound]

jabberknowl/jabbernowl *see under* JOBBERKNOWL.

jabez *v.* [1910s–20s] to play an underhand trick. [*Jabez*, a typical rural name; thus peasant cunning]

jabfest *n. see* GABFEST n.

jab job *v.* [1950s+] (*drugs*) to inject a drug. [JAB v.[1] + JOB n.[4]]

jaboff *n.* (*also* **jabpopp, jabpoppo**) [1930s–50s] (*US prison*) an injection of drugs; the sensation that follows it. [JAB v.[1] + SE -*off*/POP n.[7] (1)]

jabone/jaboney *n. see* JIBONE n.

jabongoes *n.* [1960s] (*US*) the female breasts. [nonce-word; var. on BAZONGAS n.]

jabonie *n. see* JIBONE n.

jabooby *n.* [1950s+] (*drugs*) marijuana. [? play on JOINT n.[5] (3)]

jabpopp/jabpoppo *n. see* JABOFF n.

jabronie *n. see* JIBONE n.

jab trotters *v.* [1900s] (*Aus.*) to travel with a pack. [fig. use of SE *jab* + TROTTER n.[1] (1)]

Jabus! *excl. see* JAPERS! excl.

Jack *n.*[1] 1 [late 17C–mid-18C] a *Jacob*ite, i.e. an adherent of James II of England after his abdication (1688), or of his son, the Old Pretender (James Stuart), or grandson, the Young Pretender (Charles Edward Stuart). 2 [mid-19C] (*US*) a *Jack*sonian Democrat, i.e. a supporter of Andrew Jackson, the 7th President of America (1767–1845). [abbr.]

Jack *n.*[2] (*also* **Jack D, Jack's**) [1970s+] (*US*) *Jack* Daniel's brand of whisky.

Jack *n.*[3] *see* JACK KETCH n.

Jack *pfx* [18C] a *pfx* used to denote a nationality, e.g. *Jack French*.

jack *n.*[1] [late 14C–17C; 20C+] a fool (cf. BEN n.[1]). [abbr. SE *jackass*]

jack *n.*[2] [late 15C+] a man or boy, a commoner as distinct from a gentleman. [later 20C+ usage is US Black]

jack *n.*[3] 1 [17C; 19C] the penis (cf. ABRAHAM n.[1]). 2 [late 19C+] an erection; thus phr. *on jack*, erect; thus often as sexual desire. 3 [1950s+] copulation. 4 [1980s+] an act of masturbation. [SE *jack*, a device for lifting things]

jack *n.*[4] 1 [late 17C–mid-19C] a farthing. 2 [late 19C+] (*US*) money. 3 [1980s+] £5 (cf. BEEHIVE n.[2]). [(1) and (2) ety. unknown; (3) abbr. of JACK'S (ALIVE) n.]

jack *n.*[5] (*also* **jackie, jackshite, jacky**) [late 17C+] a sailor. [abbr. JACK TAR n.[1] (1)]

jack *n.*[6] [mid-18C+] a general term of address to a man. [20C+ use primarily US]

jack *n.*[7] [late 18C–19C] a lavatory. [JAKES n.]

jack *n.*[8] 1 [late 18C+] (*US*) a donkey or *jack*ass. 2 [19C] (*US*) a flap*jack*. 3 [19C] a *jack*-boot. 4 [late 19C] a *jack*al. 5 [20C+] (*US/Can.*) a lumber*jack*. 6 [1900s–10s] (*US*) a *jack*pot. 7 [1960s] a *jack*et. [abbr.]

jack *n.*[9] (*also* **jack lamp, jack lantern, jacklight**) [19C+] (*orig. US*) a light used for hunting by night. [the light momentarily stuns the prey, giving the hunter time to shoot; also used in fishing, when the powerful light shines through the water to the fish below]

jack *n.*[10] [early 19C] a post-chaise, a travelling carriage seating 2 or 4, with the coachman or postilion riding one of the horses. [ety. unknown, but note SE *jack*, used for a variety of machines]

jack *n.*[11] (*also* **half-jack**) [mid-19C] a counter, similar in size and shape to a sovereign or half-sovereign, used in gambling houses and casinos. [strangely enough, *jack* and *half-jack* are gambling counters worth a whole/half a sovereign, and HALF-JACK n.[1] contemporaneously means a half-sovereign, but *jack* alone never seems to equal a whole sovereign]

jack *n.*[12] [mid-19C] (*UK Und.*) a low-ranking prostitute (cf. BABY JANE n.).

jack *n.*[13] [mid–late 19C] (*Anglo-Ind.*) a native soldier. [*Jack-Sepoy*, the name is 'kindly, rather than otherwise' (Y&B)]

jack n.[14] **1** [mid-19C+] (*Aus.*) a black*jack* or cosh. **2** [1930s] (*US*) the card-game black*jack*. [abbr.]

jack n.[15] (*also* **country jack**) [mid-19C+] (*US*) a rustic, a simpleton (cf. ALVIN n.). [JAKE n.[1] (1) (+ COUNTRY adj.); note JACK n.[1]]

jack n.[16] **1** [mid-19C+] (*US*) illegally distilled liquor, based on various fruits and vegetables and usu. specified as such, e.g. *tater jack* (potatoes), *prune jack, raisin jack*. **2** [20C+] (*W.I.*) illegally distilled rum. **3** [1930s+] methylated spirits, used as a drink; thus *jack man*, one who habitually drinks meths.

jack n.[17] [late 19C–1920s] (*US*) a *Jacqueminot*, a variety of tea-rose. [abbr.]

jack n.[18] (*also* **jacko, jacky**) [late 19C–1950s] (*Aus.*) a kookaburra. [SE *laughing jackass*]

jack n.[19] [late 19C+] **1** a detective (cf. DICK n.[6]). **2** a policeman (cf. BILLY n.[6]). [orig. northern dial.]

jack n.[20] [late 19C+] the anus. [abbr. JACKSIE n.[1]]

jack n.[21] [20C+] (*Aus.*) in the gambling game of two-up, a double-headed coin (the game is based on tossing 2 coins and betting on heads or tails), produced by filing down standard coins and welding them together (cf. KNOB n.[2]). [? JACK n.[4]]

jack n.[22] [1900s] horseflesh that has been salted and washed to remove its 'horsey' flavour. [ety. unknown; ? joc. ref. to the JACK n.[5] who will be eating it]

jack n.[23] [1900s–40s] (*US campus*) an illegitimate translation of a text, or hidden notes (cf. ANIMAL n.[3]). [? play on SE *jackass*, i.e. the sort of student who requires a crib]

jack n.[24] [1920s+] (*US*) a mugger, a thief; thus *jack-racket*, mugging. [abbr. JACK ROLLER n.[1]]

jack n.[25] [1940s] (*US milit.*) a corporal.

jack n.[26] [1940s+] (*Aus.*) a non-union labourer, a strike-breaker, spec. a member of the Permanent and Casual Waterside Workers' Union. [rhy. sl.; *Jack McNab* = SCAB n. (4); ? ult. anecdotal]

jack n.[27] *see* JACK (AND JILL) n.

jack n.[28] *see* JACK (IN THE BOX) n.

jack n.[29] *see* JACKSHIT n.

jack, the n. [1940s+] (*Aus.*) venereal disease. [abbr. JACK (IN THE BOX) n.]

jack adj.[1] [late 19C+] (*Aus.*) aware (of).

jack adj.[2] [1980s+] (*US Black*) flashy, ostentatious. [NEW JACK n.]

jack v.[1] (*also* **jack-light**) [mid-19C+] (*US*) to hunt deer at night, illegally, with the aid of a light; thus *jacker*, one who hunts in this way. [JACK n.[9]]

jack v.[2] [1900s] (*US campus*) to use a translation or hidden notes to pass an examination (cf. CRIB v.[2]). [JACK n.[23]]

jack v.[3] **1** [1910s+] (*US Und.*) to beat with a blackjack. **2** [1940s+] to masturbate (cf. BOFF v.). **3** [1950s+] (*US prison*) to serve a prison sentence. **4** [1970s+] (*US prison*) to stun a fellow inmate with a blackjack before raping. **5** [1980s+] to stab or punch; usu. in passive as JACKED adj.[1] (4). [note JACK UP v.[6]]

jack v.[4] **1** [1930s+] (*orig. US*) to steal (from), to hijack, to take forcibly. **2** [1990s+] (*drugs*) to steal someone else's drugs. **3** [1990s+] (*US*) to search.

jack v.[5] [1980s+] (*N.Z.*) to take charge of, to get ready. [ety. unknown]

jack v.[6] *see* JACK (AROUND) v.

jack v.[7] *see* JACK (IT) (IN) v.

jack v.[8] *see* JACK (UP) v.[2].

jack act v. [1920s+] (*Irish*) to play the fool (cf. ACT THE ANGORA v.). [SE *jackass*]

Jack Adams n. [late 17C–19C] a fool; thus *Jack Adams's parish*, Clerkenwell. [? anecdotal]

jack (a) dandy n. [mid-19C] brandy. [rhy. sl.]

jack-a-dandy n. (*also* **jack of dandy**) [early 17C–19C] an insignificant person, a fop. [SE pfx *jack*, a person, esp. in derog. or contemptuous contexts + *dandy*]

jackal n. [19C] **1** (*US Und.*) a steamboat thief, spec. the thief who actually removes the booty. **2** a moneylender's tout.

jackal v. [1990s+] (*US*) to masturbate (cf. BOFF v.). [var. on JACK OFF v.[1]]

jack an' danny n. (*also* **jacky danny**) [1990s+] **1** the vagina (cf. ALL QUIET n.). **2** nonsense, time-wasting, prevarication. [rhy. sl.; (1) = FANNY n.[1] (1); (2) = FANNY n.[2]; ? ult. *Jack Torrence* and his son *Danny*, characters in the film *The Shining* (1980)]

jack (and jill) n. **1** [1930s+] a hill. **2** [1930s+] a bill. **3** [1930s+] a till. **4** [1970s+] a pill, esp. of heroin; usu. in pl; thus *the Jack*, a birth control pill. **5** [1970s+] (*Aus.*) a fool (cf. BEECHAM'S PILL n.). [rhy. sl.; (5) *jack and jill* = DILL n.]

Jack and Joan phr. [1990s+] on own's own. [rhy. sl.]

jack and shit n. *see* JACKSHIT n.

jackanory n. [1970s+] **1** a story. **2** a lie, i.e. a 'tall story'. [rhy. sl.; f. the UK children's TV programme, *Jackanory*, which involved stories being read aloud]

jackaroo n. (*also* **jackeroo**) [late 19C+] (*Aus.*) **1** a White man living beyond the bounds of 'civilization'. **2** a man newly arrived from Britain to gain experience in the bush. **3** a young hired hand. [(1) Jagara *dhugai-tu*, a wandering White man; (2) Baker, *The Australian Language* (1945) suggests Queensland Aborigine *tchaceroo*, the shrike, which 'talks' a great deal, orig. applied to a group of German missionaries settled near Brisbane and thence all Whites; a corruption of JACKY RAW n.; JACK n.[18] + SE *kangaroo*]

jackaroo v. (*also* **jackeroo**) [late 19C+] (*Aus.*) to pick up experience. [JACKAROO n. (2)]

jack (around) v. [1960s+] **1** to mess about. **2** to mess about, with sexual, adulterous overtones. **3** (*US campus*) to tease. **4** (*US*) to treat badly, with deceit or contempt.

jack ashore phr. [late 19C–1900s] larky, excited, tipsy. [JACK TAR n.[1] and his habits when in port]

jackass n. [1920s–40s] (*US*) home-distilled liquor, e.g. brandy or corn whisky. [JACK n.[16] (1) + it turns the drinker into a SE *jackass*]

jackass adj. [mid-19C+] large, substantial. [? SE *jackass*, used of things that are gross and stupid]

jackass brandy n. [1920s–70s] (*US*) home-distilled brandy. [US Western *jackass*, second-rate, irregular]

jackass rope n. [1950s+] (*W.I., Jam.*) home-grown tobacco, twisted into a rope.

jack-at-a-pinch n. **1** [late 17C–mid-19C] a temporary clergyman, hired when the regular incumbent is absent. **2** [mid-19C] one whose assistance is required only in an emergency. [generic use of SE *jack*, a man, usu. derog. + phr. *at a pinch*]

Jack Benny n. [1930s+] a penny. [rhy. sl.; ult. US comedian *Jack Benny* (1894–1974)]

jack blunt n. [late 19C–1910s] a blunt person. [generic use of SE *jack*, a man + *blunt*]

jack boots n. [early 19C] the 'boots' or bootboy at an inn. [generic use of SE *jack*, a man + *boots*]

jack boy n.[1] [early 19C] a postilion, one who rides one of a carriage's leading horses rather than riding on the box. [JACK n.[10] + SE *boy*]

jack boy n.[2] [1980s+] (*US police*) an armed robber. [JACK n.[24] + SE *boy*]

jack bragger n. (*also* **jack brag**) [mid–late 16C] a boaster, a braggart. [generic use of SE *jack*, a man + *bragger*]

jack bumps n. [1960s+] (*US*) acne, allegedly caused by masturbation. [JACK OFF v.[1] (1)]

Jack Catch n. *see* JACK KETCH n.

Jack D n. *see* JACK n.[2].

jackdaw n. [mid-19C+] a jaw. [rhy. sl.]

Jack Dee n. [1990s+] an act of urination (cf. ANGEL'S KISS n.). [rhy. sl. = PEE n.[1] (2)/WEE n.[1]; ult. UK comedian *Jack Dee* (b.1961)]

jack-deuce adv. [1930s] (*US*) at an angle or slanted.

jack drum's entertainment n. (*also* **John Drum's entertainment, Tom Drum's entertainment**) [late 16C–early 19C] a rough reception, esp. the throwing out of an unwelcome guest. [they are 'drummed out' of the house]

jacked *adj.*[1] **1** [late 18C–19C] of a horse, spavined. **2** [late 19C+] (*Aus.*) angry, annoyed, fed up. **3** [1960s+] (*US campus*) physically broken down. **4** [1980s+] stabbed, attacked. [(4) JACK v.[3] (5)]

jacked *adj.*[2] [2000s] (*US campus*) muscular.

jacked off *adj.* [1980s+] (*US*) enthusiastic, very keen. [fig. use of JACK OFF v.[1] (1)]

jacked out *adj.* [1970s+] (*US campus*) annoyed, irritated, angry. [JACKED adj.[1] (2)]

jacked (up) *adj.*[1] [1930s+] (*US drugs*) suffering (usu. negatively) from the effect of a given drug and/or alcohol. [JACK (UP) v.[2]]

jacked (up) *adj.*[2] [1970s+] **1** (*US*) excited, exhilarated, happy. **2** (*US gay*) sexually excited. [JACK UP v.[5]]

jacked up *adj.*[1] **1** [mid–late 19C] ruined, given up, abandoned. **2** [1900s–10s] (*US*) pregnant. [? JACK UP v.[2] (1)]

jacked up *adj.*[2] [20C+] (*Aus.*) infected (usu. with venereal disease). [JACK (IN THE BOX) n.]

jacked up *adj.*[3] [1950s+] (*US Und.*) charged with an offence, esp. while already serving a sentence. [JACK UP v.[6] (4)]

jacked up *adj.*[4] [1960s+] (*N.Z.*) arranged, sorted out, 'fixed'. [JACK (UP) v.[1] (2)]

jacked up *adj.*[5] [1960s+] **1** (*US teen*) upset, anxious, waiting anxiously for time to pass. **2** (*US campus*) unfair. [JACKED adj.[1] (2) or fig. use of JACKED (UP) adj.[1]]

jackeen *n.* (*also* **Dublin jackeen**) [mid-19C+] (*Anglo-Irish*) **1** a Dubliner, as opposed to a country person. **2** a self-assertive but worthless person. [generic use of SE *jack*, a man + dimin. sfx *-een*]

jacker *n.* **1** [1960s+] (*US*) a hijacker. **2** [2000s] a street robber, a thief. [JACK v.[4] (1)]

jacker-off *n. see* JACK-OFF n. (1).

jackeroo *see under* JACKAROO.

jackery *n.* [late 19C–1900s] (*Aus.*) a popular station-hand; usu. in pl. [JACKAROO n. (3)]

jackery-pokery *n. see* JIGGERY-POKERY n.

jacket *n.*[1] [17C–19C] (*US*) the human skin; usu. in phrs. such as WET ONE'S JACKET v.; LINE ONE'S JACKET v.

jacket *n.*[2] [20C+] (*W.I.*) **1** a child fathered by a woman's lover rather than by her husband. **2** any child who has no 'official' father; thus *wear a jacket for*, for a husband to accept the child as his own. **3** a man who accepts the role of father to a child he knows is not his. [the image is of a jacket 'dressing up' a man and thus conferring respectability on the child]

jacket *n.*[3] [1930s+] (*US Und.*) **1** a record of a criminal's previous convictions etc, a criminal record. **2** a reputation, usu. bad; thus *fruit jacket*, a reputation as a homosexual. **3** a military service record. **4** a jail sentence. **5** a witness to a crime.

jacket *n.*[4] [1960s+] (*US*) a condom.

jacket *v.*[1] **1** [19C] to 'remove a man by underhand and vile means from any birth or situation he enjoys, commonly with a view to supplant him' (Vaux). **2** [1960s] (*W.I.*) to seduce someone else's lover.

jacket *v.*[2] [mid–late 19C] to beat, to thrash. [Lincolnshire/Sussex dial.]

jacket *v.*[3] **1** [mid-19C–1930s] (*US Und.*) to be identified or caught in the act. **2** [1970s+] (*US prison*) to be labelled untrustworthy or given any form of bad reputation by fellow prisoners. [get a JACKET n.[3] (1)/JACKET n.[3] (2)]

jacket *v.*[4] [late 19C–1900s] to threaten someone with confinement in a lunatic asylum. [the threat is of the *strait-jacket*]

jacket and vest *n.* [1930s] the *West End* of London. [rhy. sl.]

jacketing *n.* [mid-19C–1900s] a thrashing, a beating; also of verbal abuse. [JACKET v.[2]]

jacket job *n.* [1990s+] something, or someone, liable to drive one crazy; thus a mad or insane person. [SE (*strait*) *jacket* + JOB n.[4]]

jackets *n.* [1950s+] (*drugs*) Nembutal, a tranquillizer. [abbr. YELLOW JACKETS n.]

jackey *n.* [late 18C–mid-19C] gin. [? name of a gin distiller]

jack flash *n.* [1960s+] (*Aus.*) hashish (cf. AFGHAN n.; BOB HOPE n.). [rhy. sl. = HASH n.[2]; + ? ref. to Rolling Stones' song 'Jumping Jack Flash' (1968)]

jack fool *n.* [17C] a foolish person. [SE *jack*, generic for a man + *fool*; the term survived in 1940s Kansas dial.]

jack-gagger *n. see* JOCKUM-GAGGER n.

jack gentleman *n.* [late 17C–18C] a man of low birth or manners who has pretensions to be a gentleman, an insolent fellow, an upstart. [SE *jack*, generic for a man, esp. derog. + *gentleman*]

jack gentlewoman *n.* [late 18C] a large masculine woman. [var. on JACK GENTLEMAN n.]

jackhammer *n.* [1970s+] (*US gay*) the erect penis (cf. AX n.[2]). [play on SE; note HAMMER n.[1] (1)]

jackhandle *n.* [1960s] (*US*) the erect penis.

jack horner *n. see* JOHNNY HORNER n.

jackhouse *n. see* JAKEHOUSE n.

jackhunt *v. see* JACKROLL v.[1].

jack-hunter *n.* [late 18C+] (*US*) someone who hunts by night, using a light to stun the prey; thus *jack-hunt* and *jack-hunting*. [JACK n.[9]]

jackie *n. see* JACK n.[5].

Jackie (Dash) *n.* [1990s+] an act of urination (cf. ANGEL'S KISS n.). [rhy. sl. = SLASH n.[3]; ult. UK dockers' leader *Jack Dash*]

Jackie Howe *n.* (*also* **Jacky Howe, Jimmie Howe, Jimmy Howe**) [1930s+] (*Aus./N.Z.*) a navy blue or black woollen singlet worn by Aus. and N.Z. shearers and bushmen. [proper name of *Jackie Howe* (1855–1922), an Aus. shearer who in 1892 established a world shearing record by shearing 321 merino sheep with hand shears in 8 hours 40 minutes]

Jackie Robinson *n.* (*US Black*) **1** [1940s+] any Black person who is the first to gain entry to a profession. **2** [1950s] the penis (cf. ABRAHAM n.[1]). [proper name of *Jackie Robinson* (1919–72), who in 1947 became the first Black man to play in major league baseball (for the Brooklyn Dodgers); (2) note JACK ROBINSON n.]

jackies *n.* [1910s] American sailors. [JACK TAR n.[1] (1)]

Jackie Trent *adj.* [1990s+] corrupt, untrustworthy. [rhy. sl. = BENT adj. (3); ult. singer/songwriter *Jackie Trent* (b.1940)]

jack in *v. see* JACK (IT) (IN) v.

jack in a box *n.* [late 16C–mid-19C] a cheat, spec. a thief who deceives tradesmen by the substitution of identical boxes: his own filled with gold pounds, the one that the tradesman finds himself left with filled with silver shillings. [E.P. claims prob. from JACK IN THE BOX n.[1]]

jacking off *n.* [20C+] (*gambling*) **1** racking up the pool balls. **2** shaking dice with a movement that might be seen as resembling masturbation. [JACK OFF v.[1] (1)]

jack-in-office *n.* [late 17C–1930s] an officious petty official, their assumed power of inverse proportion to the actual importance of their job (cf. JACK OUT OF OFFICE n.). [SE *jack*, generic for a man, usu. derog. + *office*]

jack in the bean stack *n.* [1950s–70s] (*US Black*) an adventurous, daredevil person. [assonance/play on the fairy-tale character *Jack in the Beanstalk*]

jack (in the box) *n.* [20C+] venereal disease. [rhy. sl. = POX n.[1] (2)]

jack in the box *n.*[1] [mid-16C–17C] the consecrated host. [a blasphemous joke]

jack in the box *n.*[2] (*also* **jack in a box**) [late 17C–early 18C] (*UK Und.*) a street peddler, usu. one who doubles as a confidence trickster. [the box of goods that is carried]

jack in the box *n.*[3] [late 19C+] the penis. [it 'pops up']

jack in the box *n.*[4] [20C+] (*US Und.*) breaking and entering a house or apartment.

jack in the box *n.*[5] [20C+] socks. [rhy. sl.]

jack in the box *n.*[6] [1960s+] (*US Black*) the state of having one's penis inside one's partner's vagina. [JACK n.[3] (1) + BOX n.[1] (1)]

jack in the (low) cellar n. [late 18C–early 19C] an unborn child. [trans. of Du. HANS-EN-KELDER n.]

jack in the pulpit n. [19C] a pretender, an upstart. [SE *jack*, generic for a man, usu. derog. + *pulpit*, i.e. one who sets themselves up as a preacher, lit. or fig.]

jack in the water n. [mid–late 19C] a waterman's attendant, who helps passengers on and off boats. [SE *jack*, generic for a man, usu. derog. + *water*]

jack iron n. [20C+] (*W.I.*) a form of unlicensed and very potent rum, distilled secretly in the countryside.

jack it v. [late 19C–1900s] to die. [fig. use of JACK (IT) (IN) v.]

jack (it) (in) v. (*also* **jag it in**) [late 19C+] to stop doing something, to give in, to abandon, to resign; thus *jacked in*, abandoned, given up. [? dial. *jack*, to give up suddenly, to relinquish, to abandon or throw away]

jack it up someone's ass v. [1960s+] (*US*) to punish or victimize someone. [SE *jack*, to force up + ASS n. (2)]

jack job n. [1970s+] (*US campus*) unfair treatment. [JACKSHIT n.]

jack (jones) adj. [20C+] alone; usu. in phr. ON ONE'S JACK (JONES) phr. [rhy. sl.]

Jack Ketch n. (*also* **Jack, Jack Catch, John Ketch, Master Ketch, Mr Ketch**) **1** [mid-17C+] (*orig. UK Und.*) a hangman. **2** [late 19C] ext. to anyone chosen to carry out a death sentence. **3** [late 19C+] a jail sentence. [proper name of the common executioner *Jack Ketch* (c.1663–86). Partly on account of his barbarity at the executions of Lord Russell, the Duke of Monmouth and other political offenders, and partly perhaps f. the obvious links with SE *catch*, his name became widely known. When it was given to the hangman in the puppet-play of *Punchinello*, which arrived from Italy shortly after his death, his immortality was assured; (2) rhy. sl. = STRETCH n.[1] (3)]

Jack Ketch's certificate n. [early 19C] a judicial flogging. [JACK KETCH n. (1); it is 'given under his hand']

Jack Ketch's kitchen n. [18C–19C] that room in Newgate prison where the hangman boiled the quarters of those dismembered for high treason. [JACK KETCH n. (1) + SE *kitchen*]

Jack Ketch's necklace n. [early 19C] a hangman's noose. [JACK KETCH n. (1) + NECKLACE n. (2)]

Jack Ketch's pippin n. [late 17C–19C] a candidate for the gallows. [JACK KETCH n. (1) + PIPPIN n. (2)]

Jack Ketch's warren n. [19C] the slum area in and around Turnmill Street, Clerkenwell. [JACK KETCH n. (1) + SE *warren*]

jack-knife face n. [mid-19C+] (*US*) a thin, pointed face.

jack lamp n. see JACK n.[9].

Jack Lang n. (*also* **old Jack Lang**) [1960s+] (*Aus.*) slang; spec. rhyming slang.

jack lantern n. see JACK n.[9].

jack lattin n. (*also* **jack latten**) [20C+] (*Irish*) a threat of punishment. [*John Lattin* of Morristown House, Co. Kildare, won a bet after dancing, as wagered, a distance of over 32km (20 miles), changing his dance-step every furlong]

jackleg n. (*US*) **1** [mid-19C+] an incompetent, unskilled or unprincipled worker or professional person, esp. a quack doctor, a crooked lawyer or a hypocritical preacher. **2** [20C+] an itinerant preacher. [JACKLEG adj. (1)]

jackleg adj. (*also* **jack-legged, jakeleg**) (*US*) **1** [mid-19C+] untrained, unprofessional, dishonest. **2** [20C+] thrown-together, makeshift. [US dial. *jackleg*, unskilled, ult. UK dial. *jack-a-legs*, a large clasp knife, as used by a second-rate carpenter]

jackleg v. [mid-19C+] (*US*) to act in an incompetent, unskilled or unprincipled way. [JACKLEG adj. (1)]

jacklight n. see JACK n.[9].

jack-light v. see JACK v.[1].

jackman n. [mid-16C–mid-19C] (*UK Und.*) a mendicant villain who used his abilities of reading and writing to forge counterfeit begging licences. [apparently derived f. a mis-sp. of JARKMAN n. as printed in the 1575 edn of Awdeley, *Fraternitie of Vagabondes*]

jack Mormon n. **1** [mid-19C+] a non-Mormon who sympathizes with the Mormons. **2** [20C+] an apostate Mormon. [(2) ? JACKLEG adj. (1) + *Mormon*]

jack mum n. [20C+] (*Irish*) a discreet person; esp. in the phr. *between you and me and jack mum*. [SE *jack*, generic for a man, esp. derog. + MUM n.[1]]

jack nasty n. [mid–late 19C] a sneaking, slovenly person. [SE *jack*, generic for a man, usu. derog. + *nasty*]

jack nasty face n. [19C] the vagina. [punning on the general use, 'a dirty fellow, seldom seen' (Bee). Note merchant navy jargon *jack nasty face*, a cook's assistant, or anyone considered ugly]

jack nohi n. (*N.Z.*) **1** [1940s+] an inquisitive person, a 'nosey parker'. **2** [1970s+] (*also* **jack**) a look-round, a glance; often as HAVE A JACK (NOHI) v. [Maori pron. of NOSEY adj.]

jack 'n' the beanstalk v. [1990s+] to masturbate. [pun on JACK OFF v.[1] (1) + fairy-tale *Jack and the Beanstalk*]

jacko n. (*Aus.*) **1** [1910s] (*also* **jacky**) a Turkish soldier. **2** [1940s] a kookaburra.

jack of adj. [late 19C+] (*Aus.*) bored with, tired of; usu. as *get jack of*, to resent, to grow tired of. [JACK UP v.[1]]

jack of clubs n. [19C] (*US*) a good fellow or man. [generic use of proper name + SE *club*, a social centre; also play on SE]

jack of dandy n. see JACK-A-DANDY n.

jack of Dover n. [late 14C–17C] a sole. [play on SE *jack*, generic for a man + *Dover sole*]

jack-off n. [1930s+] (*US*) **1** (*also* **jacker-off**) a general insult, lit. a masturbator. **2** an act of masturbation; thus fig., something worthless or pointless. **3** a term of derog. address. **4** in fig. use, a hoax, a confidence trick. [JACK OFF v.[1] (1)]

jack-off adj. [1930s+] **1** pertaining to the act of masturbation. **2** in fig. use, a general term of abuse, disdain.

jack off v.[1] **1** [1910s+] (*also* **jack oneself (off)**) to masturbate (cf. BALL OFF v.[2]). **2** [1930s+] to masturbate someone else. **3** [1940s–60s] in fig. use, to blink, i.e. to move up and down fast. **4** [1940s+] (*US*) to fool around, to do nothing. **5** [1960s+] (*US*) to take advantage of, to deceive or tease someone. **6** [1990s+] (*US*) to fantasize. [JACK n.[3] + JERK OFF v.[1]/JERK SOMEONE OFF v.]

jack off v.[2] [1930s–60s] (*UK tramp*) to leave.

jack off v.[3] [1950s+] (*drugs*) to pump backwards and forwards with the plunger of the hypodermic without finally injecting the blood and heroin mix into the arm. [JACK OFF v.[1]; the up-and-down gesture of masturbation and the fig. 'jacking off' instead of reaching a climax]

jack off one's jaw v. see JACK ONE'S JAW(S) v.

jack of legs n. [late 18C–19C] **1** a tall, long-legged man. **2** an outsize clasp-knife. [folk legend of *Jack of Legs*, a supposed giant, some 3m (14ft) tall, who is allegedly buried in the churchyard at Weston, Hertfordshire. A large thigh bone, excavated in the graveyard, was given to the naturalist Sir John Tradescant (1608–62)]

jack of the clockhouse n. [17C] (*UK Und.*) a confidence trickster, specializing in selling supposedly purpose-written pamphlets, poems etc, which flatter the vanity of the purchaser but which are, in fact, mass-produced with a personalized dedication tacked on. [SE *jack of the clockhouse*, which 'goes upon screws, and his office is to do nothing but strike'; the actual *jack* was a figure of a man which strikes the bell on the outside of a clock]

jack oneself (off) v. see JACK OFF v.[1] (1).

jack oneself up v. [1920s+] **1** (*N.Z.*) to settle in; thus to make oneself or someone else at home. **2** (*US*) to pull oneself together. [JACK (UP) v.[1] (2)]

jack one's jaw(s) v. (*also* **jack off one's jaw, jerk one's jaw(s)**) [1960s+] (*US*) to chatter at length (and aimlessly).

jack one's jizz v. [1930s+] to masturbate. [JACK OFF v.[1] + JIZZ n.]

jack out v. [mid–late 19C] (*US*) to knock unconscious. [JACK v.[3] (1)]

jack out of doors *n.* [late 16C–17C] a vagrant, one who has been thrown out of his house. [SE *jack*, generic for a man, usu. derog.]

jack out of office *n.* (*also* **jack out of service, john out of office**) [mid-16C–17C] one who has been dismissed from his job (cf. JACK-IN-OFFICE *n.*). [SE *jack*, generic for a man, usu. derog. + SE *doors* + SE *office/service*]

Jack Papish *n.* (*also* **Jack Priest**) [early 18C–mid-19C] a derog. term for a Roman Catholic.

jack poke *n.* [1930s–40s] (*US*) a slow, listless person. [SE *jack*, generic for a man, usu. derog. + POKE ALONG *v.*]

jackpot *n.* [late 19C+] (*Can./US*) **1** a dilemma, a difficult situation, trouble. **2** an arrest. [sources claim a link to poker's *jackpot*, a large 'pot' of money, but there seems no real proof]

jackpot *v.*[1] [20C+] (*US prison*) to fight, usu. with fists. [JACKPOT *n.* (1)]

jackpot *v.*[2] [1970s+] (*US Und.*) to chat, to gossip, to reminisce. [abbr. of gambling *cut up jackpots*, to reminisce over card-games]

Jack Priest *n. see* JACK PAPISH *n.*

jack pudding *n.* [mid-17C–1910s] a jester or clown, travelling with a 'mountebank' or itinerant quack. [SE *jack*, generic for a man, usu. derog. + innate humour of a *pudding*]

jackrabbit *n.*[1] **1** [late 19C–1960s] (*US*) a mule. **2** [1970s+] (*US prison*) an escaped convict.

jackrabbit *n.*[2] [1980s+] (*Aus. prison*) narcotics addiction. [rhy. sl. = HABIT *n.* (1)]

jackrabbit *n.*[3] [1990s+] (*Aus.*) the penis (cf. ANTEATER *n.*).

jackrabbit *v.* [1970s+] (*Can./US*) to run, to escape. [JACKRABBIT *n.*[1] (2)]

jackrabbit parole *n.* [1970s+] (*US prison*) an escape from prison. [JACKRABBIT *n.*[1] (2)]

jack-racket *n. see* JACK *n.*24.

Jack Randall *n.* (*also* **jack randle, jerry randle, johnny randle, ron randell**) [mid-19C+] a candle. [rhy. sl.; ult. noted pugilist *Jack Randall* (Hotten, 1873)]

jack-ready *adj.* [1970s] (*US*) absolutely ready, ready and waiting.

jack rec *v.* [2000s] (*US prison*) to waste time, to mess up recreation by causing a disturbance. [JACK (AROUND) *v.* + REC *n.*]

jack rees *n.* [20C+] (*Aus.*) fleas. [rhy. sl.]

jack robinson *n.* [19C] the penis (cf. ABRAHAM *n.*[1]). [BEFORE ONE CAN SAY JACK ROBINSON phr.; Grose (1785) suggests a real 'Jack Robinson […] a very volatile gentleman of that appellation, who would call on his neighbours, and be gone before his name could be announced']

jackroll *v.*[1] (*also* **jackhunt**) [1910s+] to rob a victim (often one of one's own companions) while they are drunk or sleeping. [SE *jack*, generic for a man + ROLL *v.*[4] (1)/SE *hunt*]

jackroll *v.*[2] [1990s+] (*S.Afr.*) to abduct then rape a woman, usu. a schoolgirl, to gang-rape; thus *jack-rolling*, abducting and raping. [despite logical link to JACKROLL *v.*[1], *DSAE* suggests a song by Womack & Womack, with lyrics 'Love is just a ballgame, sometimes you lose – jackroll']

jack roller *n.*[1] [1920s+] (*US*) a robber who specializes in stealing from drunk, drugged or otherwise incapacitated victims. [JACKROLL *v.*[1]]

jack roller *n.*[2] [1990s+] (*S.Afr.*) an individual, usu. one of a gang, who abducts and rapes women. [JACKROLL *v.*[2]]

Jack's *n. see* JACK *n.*[2].

jacks *n.* (*also* **jax, jaxx**) [1940s+] (*Irish*) the lavatory. [JAKES *n.*]

jack's (alive) *n.* (*also* **jax**) [1910s+] **5**, esp. a £5 note (cf. BEEHIVE *n.*[2]). [rhy. sl.]

jack sauce *n.* [mid-16C–early 18C] a saucy or impudent fellow. [SE *jack*, generic for a man + *sauce*]

jack scratches *n.* [20C+] (*Aus./US*) matches. [rhy. sl.]

jack's delight *n.* [mid-19C–1930s] a prostitute (cf. BABY JANE *n.*). [JACK *n.*[5] + SE *delight*]

jacksey *n. see* JACKSIE *n.*[1].

jack shea *n.* (*also* **jack shay**) [late 19C+] (*Aus.*) a tin container, holding a quart (2 pints/1 litre) of liquid, used for brewing tea and, when empty, containing a smaller vessel for drinking the tea. [? rhy. sl. = tea (in Irish pron. 'tay')]

jackshit *n.* (*also* **jack, jack and shit**) **1** [1960s+] (*orig. US*) absolutely nothing, always used with a qualifying negative *v.*, e.g. *you don't know jack shit about…* **2** [1970s+] (*US*) nonsense. **3** [1970s+] (*US*) a stupid, contemptible person. [JACK *n.*[1] + SHIT *n.*[3] (3)]

jackshite *n. see* JACK *n.*[5].

jacksie *n.*[1] (*also* **jacksey, jacksy**) [late 19C+] the anus; thus *up your jacksie*, a derog. response to an unpalatable idea or opinion. [ety. unknown]

jacksie *n.*[2] [20C+] (*Aus.*) a brothel. [? link to JACK *n.*[3]]

jacksie *n.*[3] [1940s] a taxi. [rhy. sl.]

jack smithers *n.* (*Aus.*) **1** [1900s–40s] a drink taken by one who is drinking alone. **2** [1930s+] a solitary drinker. [? anecdotal]

Jackson *n.* [1930s+] (*US*) a form of address, usu. between men. [ext. of JACK *n.*[6]]

jackson *n.* [mid-19C+] (*US*) a $20 bill; thus money in general (cf. ABE *n.*[2]). [the portrait of Andrew *Jackson* (1767–1845), 7th President of America, printed on the bills]

Jackson Pollocks *n.* [2000s] **1** the testicles (cf. CHEESE AND CRACKERS *n.*). **2** nonsense, rubbish. [rhy. sl.; (1) = BALLOCKS *n.*[1] (1); (2) = BALLOCKS *n.*[2] (2); ult. the abstract expressionist painter *Jackson Pollock* (1912–56)]

jack sprat *n.*[1] [late 16C–19C] a small person, a dwarf. [the name survives mainly in the nursery rhyme, which itself post-dated it. Its first appearance in print was *c.*1570, while the nursery rhyme was first publ. in 1639]

jack sprat *n.*[2] [20C+] **1** fat (on meat). **2** a brat, an irritating small child. [rhy. sl.]

jack squat *n.* [1980s+] (*US*) a partial euph. for JACKSHIT *n.*

jack stickler *n.* [mid-16C–mid-17C] a meddlesome or interfering person, a busybody. [SE *jack*, generic for a man, usu. derog. + *stickler*]

Jack Straw *n.* (*also* **jackstraw**) [late 16C–17C] a nonentity, lit. a 'man of straw'. [SE *jack*, generic for a man, usu. derog. + *straw*, and ref. to *Jack Straw*, leader of the failed Peasants' Revolt, 1381]

Jack Straw's Castle *n.* [19C] the vagina (cf. ANTIPODES *n.*). [JACK STRAW *n.*; the image of the vagina as a trifle, a nothing, is common in sl.]

jack surpass *n.* [mid-19C] a glass. [rhy. sl.]

jacksy *n. see* JACKSIE *n.*[1].

jacksy jockey *n.* [1990s+] an aficionado of anal sex, whether hetero- or homosexual (cf. ANAL ASTRONAUT *n.*). [JACKSIE *n.*[1] + JOCKEY *n.*[3] (2)]

jacksy-pardo *n.* (*also* **jacksy-pardy, jaxey, jaxie**) [mid-19C+] the anus. [vars. on JACKSIE *n.*[1]]

jack tar *n.*[1] **1** [18C+] a sailor. **2** [19C] a hornpipe. [SE *jack*, generic for a man + *tar*, i.e. the 17C naut. practice of smearing canvas breeches with tar to provide a primitive form of waterproofing. The term gradually evolved into SE during the 19C]

jack tar *n.*[2] **1** [20C+] a bar (in a public house). **2** [1960s] 10 shillings. **3** [2000s] a bar (in a jail cell). [rhy. sl.; (2) = HALF-A-BAR *n.*]

Jack the Bear *n.* [1940s–60s] (*US Black*) a general derog. term, a failure, a fool; occas. used positively to mean a success; often abbr. to just *the Bear* (cf. AIREDALE *n.*). [rhy. sl.; Mezzrow & Wolfe, *Really the Blues* (1946): 'When you're *like Jack the Bear*, you ain't nowhere, because for a good part of the year a bear is just huddled snugly in a hole, oblivious to the world. His brother, *No Fu'er*, is in the same sorry predicament, far from alert']

jack the contract *v.* [1910s+] (*Aus.*) to give up or leave a job when it proves too difficult. [JACK (IT) (IN) *v.* + SE *contract*]

jack the corn *v.* [1990s+] to masturbate (cf. BEAT ONE'S MEAT *v.*). [JACK OFF *v.*[1] (1)]

jack the dancer *n.* [20C+] (*Aus.*) cancer. [rhy. sl.]

jack the dog *v.* [1940s] (*US*) **1** to waste time, to loaf on the job. **2** to bungle, to blunder. [JACK OFF v.¹ (4) + SE *dog*]

Jack the Jew *n.* [19C] a receiver of stolen goods, usu. of the least valuable type. [racial stereotyping]

jack the joystick *v.* (*also* **jam the joystick**) [1990s+] to masturbate. [JACK OFF v.¹ + JOYSTICK n.¹]

jack the lad *n.* [1970s+] **1** a show-off, anyone particularly pleased with themself and keen to ensure that everyone knows it. **2** a priapic 'robot' made from a cigarette packet, the packet is folded in such a way that the 'robot' appears to have an erection. [SE *jack*, generic for a man + SE *lad*; note Egan in *Captain Macheath* (1842): 'For sounding, frisking any clie, / Jack was the lad, and never shy']

jack the lad *adj.* [20C+] bad. [rhy. sl.]

jack the painter *n.* [mid-19C–1940s] (*Aus.*) a strong, coarse green tea, which stained the drinker's lips. [the stain it leaves on the cup or teapot or its smell, supposedly similar to paint]

Jack the Ripper *n.* **1** [20C+] a kipper. **2** [2000s] a stripper. [rhy. sl.; ult. *Jack the Ripper*, the late 19C mass-killer. (1) like his victims, kippers are slit open]

jack the sack *v.* [1990s+] to masturbate. [JACK OFF v.¹ (1) + SACK n.¹ (3)]

jack the slipper *n.* [late 19C] a prison treadmill.

jack (up) *v.¹* **1** [20C+] (*orig. US*) to raise, to increase, e.g. to raise rents. **2** [1920s+] (*N.Z.*) to arrange, to organize, to put right, to spruce up.

jack (up) *v.²* (*orig. US drugs*) **1** [1930s+] to inject narcotics; usu. as JACKED (UP) adj.¹. **2** [2000s] in non-drug contexts, e.g. to drink coffee.

jack-up *n.¹* [1940s+] (*Aus.*) an argument, a dispute, a refusal to cooperate, esp. at work or in the office. [JACK UP v.³ (2)]

jack-up *n.²* [1980s+] (*Aus./N.Z.*) a 'frame-up', an act of calculated deception. [JACK n.²¹]

jack-up *n.³* [1990s+] a confrontation; violent or otherwise. [JACK UP v.⁶ (1)]

jack up *v.¹* [late 19C–1910s] to give up, esp. a love affair, to abandon, to leave. [note dial. uses; to give up anything in a bad temper (Sussex); to become bankrupt or insolvent (Leicester); later mainly JACK (IT) (IN) v.]

jack up *v.²* **1** [late 19C+] to collapse, either physically or financially, to be completely exhausted. **2** [2000s] (*US campus*) to fail to work, to be injured.

jack up *v.³* **1** [late 19C+] to ruin, to exhaust completely, to mess up. **2** [late 19C+] (*Aus.*) to refuse to carry out an instruction, to refuse to work, to offer resistance. **3** [20C+] (*UK Und./Aus.*) to plead 'not guilty'.

jack up *v.⁴* [late 19C+] (*US*) **1** to criticize, to rebuke, to discipline or call to account. **2** to suspend in disgrace, to take disciplinary action.

jack up *v.⁵* (*US*) **1** [1910s–60s] to urge, to incite. **2** [1960s+] to excite, to stimulate.

jack up *v.⁶* [1960s+] (*US Black*) **1** to assault, to beat up, to hold up, to mug; usu. in a group. **2** (*also* **jack**) to have sexual intercourse (cf. BANG v.¹). **3** of the police, to interrogate, to stop and search. **4** to arrest, to be charged, to be jailed. **5** to take aside for a conversation.

jack up *v.⁷* [1990s+] (*US*) to vomit.

jack up (on) *v.* [20C+] to show disapproval, to withdraw one's cooperation; thus *jacked up (on)*, annoyed (with), disenchanted.

jack weight *n.* [late 18C–19C] a fat man. [SE *jack*, generic for a man, usu. derog. + SE *weight*]

jack-whore *n.* **1** [mid-18C–mid-19C] a large, tough prostitute (cf. BABY JANE n.). **2** [mid-19C–1920s] a womanizer. [SE *jack*, generic for a man, usu. derog. + SE *whore*]

jack with *v.* [1960s] (*US*) **1** to annoy, to irritate, to 'mess around'. **2** to become involved with. [var. on JACK (AROUND) v.]

jacky *n.¹* [late 18C–1920s] gin. [? a gin distiller]

jacky *n.²* *see* JACK n.⁵.

jacky *n.³* *see* JACKO n. (1).

jacky *n.⁴* *see* JACKY JACKY n.

jacky danny *n. see* JACK AN' DANNY n.

Jacky Howe *n. see* JACKIE HOWE n.

jacky jacky *n.* (*also* **jacky**) [mid-19C+] (*Aus./N.Z.*) **1** a White man's derog. name for an Aborigine, the 'typical' Aborigine. **2** a coconut. [generic use of SE *jack* + redup.]

Jacky Lancashire *n.* [1900s] (*Aus.*) a handkerchief (pron. 'hankercher'). [rhy. sl.]

jacky raw *n.* (*also* **jimmy raw**) [20C+] (*Aus.*) a new immigrant. [generic use of SE *jack* + *raw* + ? JACKAROO n.]

jacky rue *n.* [20C+] (*Aus.*) a squatter. [? JACKY RAW n. + JACKAROO n.]

jacob *n.¹* **1** [mid-18C] (*UK Und.*) a thief who uses a ladder. **2** [mid-18C–1970s] (*UK Und.*) a ladder. **3** [19C+] the penis (cf. ABRAHAM n.¹). [the biblical story of *Jacob*'s ladder; (3) the penis 'climbs up' the vagina]

jacob *n.²* [late 18C–19C] a fool. [pun on 16C SE *jay*, a simpleton]

jacobite *n.* [late 17C–mid-19C] a shirt collar, a fake shirt. [? the 'false' claims of the *Jacobites* to the British throne]

Jacob's (crackers) *n.* [1980s+] testicles. [rhy. sl. = KNACKERS n.; ult. *Jacob's cream crackers*, a brand of biscuits]

Jacob's crackers *adj. see* CREAM CRACKERED adj.

jacob's ladder *n.* [19C] **1** (*orig. theatre*) a 'ladder' in a pair of tights or stockings. **2** the vagina. [one 'climbs' up it]

jacobus *n.* [early 17C–18C] a guinea. [the Lat. name *Jacobus*, (King) James I (r.1603–25) inscribed on it]

jacque's *n. see* JAKES n.

Jacques Cousteau job *n.* [1980s+] in football, a dive. [*Jacques Cousteau* (1910–97), the aquanaut + JOB n.⁴]

jacum-gag *n. see* JOCKUM GAGE n.

jade *n.* [mid-19C+] (*Aus.*) a prison sentence of between 4 and 12 months. [? one becomes SE *jaded*]

jadrool *n.* (*also* **jadroney**) [1960s+] (*US, esp. US Ital.*) a stupid or unpleasant person. [ety. unknown]

jaffa *n.* [1990s+] (*UK juv.*) a male who has notably large testicles. [the size of a *Jaffa* orange]

jaffle *n.* [1960s+] (*Aus.*) a toasted sandwich. [brandname of a sandwich toaster, reg. in 1965 by Hi-Craft Manufacturing Co. Pty. Ltd]

Jag *n.* [1950s+] a *Jag*uar motorcar. [abbr.]

jag *n.¹* **1** [late 17C+] a drunken spree; thus *have/get a jag on*, to be drunk; *on a jag*, on a spree. **2** [late 19C–1940s] a drunkard. **3** [late 19C+] a drink. **4** [late 19C+] (*drugs*) the taking of a drug, usu. narcotic, but also cannabis or LSD. **5** [20C+] in fig. use, the experience of taking a specific drug. **6** [1930s] a hangover. [dial. *jag*, as much liquor as one can hold, a 'load'. Note 'What a Jag is', *S.F. Alta*, 4 August 1889: 'An inquirer asks us the meaning of "Jag" applied to inebriety. It is a new slang. In the rural districts the cargo of a wagon that is hauling wood, when all that the wagon can carry, is called a "load." When it is less than up to the full capacity it is called a "Jag." Therefore, when a man is less then dead drunk he has not a load on but merely a Jag']

jag *n.²* **1** [late 19C+] a foolish notion. **2** [20C+] (*US*) a strange or stupid person. [JACK n.¹ or ? fig. use of JAG n.¹ (2)]

jag *n.³* [20C+] **1** (*US*) a period of indulgence, a fit, a spree of any kind. **2** (*orig. US*) a breakdown, an emotional collapse; often as *crying jag*, lengthy and profound sobbing. [fig. use of JAG n.¹]

jag *v.¹* [mid-19C+] (*S.Afr.*) to hunt, to chase. [Du. *jagen*, to hunt]

jag *v.²* **1** [late 19C] to vaccinate. **2** [late 19C–1900s] to assault with a knife. **3** [1960s] (*US*) to copulate with a woman (cf. BANG v.¹). **4** [1960s–70s] to make pregnant. **5** [1980s+] (*drugs*) to inject oneself or someone else. [dial. *jag*, to cut roughly; (5) note JACK (UP) v.² (1)]

jag *v.³* [20C+] (*N.Z.*) to depress, to irritate. [JAG n.³ (2)]

jag *v.*[4] [1950s+] (*drugs*) to maintain one's drugged or drunken state. [JAG n.[1]]

jagabat *n.* **1** [20C+] (*W.I.*) a prostitute or notably promiscuous woman. **2** [1990s+] (*W.I.*) (*also* **jagga-bite**) people of the lowest class and style of behaviour. [? Hind. *jaggery*, sugar, sweet + *bat*, language]

jagamaree *n. see* JIGAMAREE n.

jag-feeder *n.* [late 19C–1900s] (*US*) a drink. [JAG n.[1] (2) + SE *feeder*]

jagga-bite *n. see* JAGABAT n. (2).

jagged *adj.*[1] **1** [mid-18C+] drunk; also in fig. use. **2** [1930s+] (*also* **jagged up**) intoxicated by drugs. [JAG n.[1]]

jagged *adj.*[2] [20C+] (*N.Z.*) tired, depressed; irritating. [JAG v.[3]]

jagger *n.*[1] [mid-19C] a gentleman. [Ger. *Jäger*, a sportsman]

jagger *n.*[2] [2000s] a heroin user. [JAG v.[2] (5)]

Jagger's lips *n.* [1990s+] chips. [rhy. sl.; ult. rock singer *Mick Jagger* (b.1943), noted for his large lips]

jag it in *v. see* JACK (IT) (IN) v.

jag-off *n.* [1930s+] (*US*) a masturbator, thus an idiot, a dolt. [JACK-OFF n. (1)]

jag-off *adj.* [1980s] (*US*) stupid. [JAG-OFF n.]

jag off *v.* **1** [1950s–60s] (*US drugs*) to inject a narcotic, esp. slowly. **2** [1960s+] (*US*) to masturbate (cf. BALL OFF v.[2]). **3** [1970s+] (*US*) to fool around, to mess about. **4** [1970s+] (*US*) to tease or deceive someone. [JACK OFF v.[1]/JACK OFF v.[3]]

jags *adj.* [20C+] (*S.Afr.*) randy, lecherous. [Afk. *jags*, of an animal, in season, on heat]

jag snakes *n.* [late 19C] (*US*) hallucinations from delirium tremens. [JAG n.[1] (1) + SE *snakes*]

jague *n.* [mid-17C–mid-19C] (*UK Und.*) a ditch. [? JAKES n., since both are seen as repositories of filth]

Jah *n.* [1950s+] (*W.I./UK Black teen*) **1** God, as used by Rastafarians. **2** a term of address, emphasizing the innate divinity of humanity. [contraction of SE *Jehovah*]

jail *see also under* GAOL and its combs.

jail *v.* [1960s+] (*US*) to spend time in prison, spec. to create the best possible situation for oneself given the overriding circumstances; usu. as JAILING n. (1).

jailbait *n.* **1** [1930s+] (*US*) a young person who is a troublemaker and thus likely to be sent to prison. **2** [1930s+] (*orig. US*) (*also* **penitentiary bait**) a young person, usu. a girl, who is under the age of sexual consent; having sex with such an individiual is to invite a jail sentence. **3** [1960s–70s] (*US*) a charge of statutory rape. [SE *jail* + BAIT n.[3] (1)]

jailbait *adj.* [1950s+] (*orig. US*) dangerous; of people, attractive but dangerous. [JAILBAIT n. (2)]

jailhouse bitch *n.* [1990s+] a wife or grilfriend who pays regular visits to her partner while he is in jail. [SE *jailhouse* + BITCH n.[1] (18)]

jailhouse daddy *n.* [1950s–60s] (*US prison*) a dominating male homosexual prisoner who exploits or protects his partner. [SE *jailhouse* + DADDY n. (15)]

jailhouse lawyer *n.* (*also* **gaolhouse lawyer**, **jail lawyer**) [1920s+] (*US Und.*) a prison inmate who has made themself into a self-taught lawyer, either to pursue their own case, combat prison corruption or help fellow inmates.

jailhouse pussy *n. see* JAIL TAIL n.

jailhouse salute *n.* [1970s] (*US*) an obscene gesture.

jailhouse turnout *n.* (*also* **j.t.**, **j.t.o.**) [1960s–70s] (*US*) a prisoner who is forced to engage in homosexual practices or who becomes a homosexual while in prison. [TURN (SOMEONE) OUT v. (1)]

jailic *n.* [1970s+] (*Irish*) Irish as learned while imprisoned in the prison at Long Kesh, Belfast. [SE *jail* + *Gaelic*]

jailing *n.* (*US prison*) **1** [1960s+] accustoming oneself to life in jail and adapting one's lifestyle to make one's time there as tolerable as possible. **2** [1990s+] wearing one's trousers in such a way that a few inches of one's underwear is visible; such a

fashion was very popular among Black youth and their White imitators in the 1990s. **3** [2000s] serving time in the punishment cells. **4** [2000s] of one's family or friends, visiting a prisoner. [JAIL v.; (2) the removal of prisoners' belts]

jail lawyer *n. see* JAILHOUSE LAWYER n.

jail tail *n.* (*also* **jailhouse pussy**) [1960s] (*US gay*) a young boy who is below the age of sexual consent, with whom sex would mean prison. [var. on JAILBAIT n. (2)]

jail wireless *n. see* BUSH RADIO n.

jaina *n.* [1960s+] (*US*) a girlfriend. [Sp.]

jajazy *n. see* JASEY n.

jakalorum *adj.* [1900s] (*Aus.*) as required, satisfactory, in order. [JAKE adj.[1] (2) + -ALORUM sfx]

jake *n.*[1] (*also* **country jake**) [mid-19C+] (*US*) a farmer, a rustic (cf. ALVIN n.). **2** [1980s+] (*US campus*) an unsophisticated person, a misfit, a fool. [the 'rural' proper name *Jacob* (+ COUNTRY adj.)]

jake *n.*[2] [20C+] a toilet. [JAKES n.]

jake *n.*[3] [1910s] (*Can./US*) an admirable example. [JAKE adj.[1] (2)]

jake *n.*[4] [1920s–40s] (*orig. US Black*) a general term of address.

jake *n.*[5] (*also* **jakers**, **jakey**) **1** [1920s+] (*US*) Jamaica ginger, a drink with intoxicating properties. **2** [1920s+] (*US*) methylated spirits, or surgical spirits, used as an alcoholic drink; thus *jake-drinker*, a meths drinker; thus JAKELEG n. **3** [1930s–70s] (*US prison*) a drunkard. [abbr. *Jamaica*; (1) was esp. popular during Prohibition (1919–33)]

jake *n.*[6] **1** [1970s] (*US*) coffee. **2** [1980s+] (*US*) a New York City police patrolman. [? (1) from JAKE n.[5] or elision of JAMOKE n.[1]; note JOE n.[5]; ? (2) drinks a lot (1)]

jake *n.*[7] *see* JAKELEG n.

jake *adj.*[1] **1** [1910s–20s] (*US Und.*) aware, in the know. **2** [1910s+] (*Aus./N.Z./US*) satisfactory, as required; esp. in phr. *she's/she'll be/we're jake*, it's fine, it/things will be fine, we are fine. [? SE *chic*]

jake *adj.*[2] [2000s] (*US Black*) unsatisfactory, disappointing.

jake *v.* [1990s+] (*US campus*) to cancel an appointment without prior notice, to drop out of an arrangement. [? SE *jerk* oneself out of]

jakealoo/jake-a-pie *adj. see* JAKELOO adj.

jaked *adj.* [1980s+] (*US campus*) **1** excited, happy, thrilled. **2** drunk. [JAKE adj.[1] (2)]

jake-drinker *n. see* JAKE n.[5] (2).

jake flake *n.* [1950s+] (*US Black*) anyone interested in themselves above anything or anyone else. [JAKE n.[1] (1) + FLAKE n.[2] (1)]

jakehead *n.* (*also* **jakehound**) [1920s–30s] (*US*) an addict of Jamaica ginger. [JAKE n.[5] (1) + -HEAD sfx (3)/HOUND sfx]

jakehouse *n.* (*also* **jackhouse**) [1900s–10s] a privy, a lavatory (cf. BACKHOUSE n.). [JAKE n.[2] + SE house]

jakeleg *n.* (*also* **jake**) [1930s–70s] paralysis of the leg or legs caused by an excess of JAKE n.[5] (2); thus *jakeleg liquor/whisky*, 'bad' liquor or whisky (which may well cause paralysis); *jake-legged*, paralysed.

jakeleg *adj. see* JACKLEG adj.

jake leg *v.* [1990s+] (*US*) to tease, to deceive playfully. [Tennessee dial. *jack leg*, the loss of motor control of the limbs caused by drinking poisonous bootleg liquor; note Polito, *Savage Art* (1995): 'As a Texas roughneck recalled, "I've seen a lot of 'em that had jake leg. You can't walk straight, and you have to have crutches and walking canes, and then whenever you step, why, your leg goes to trembling. Your feet goes to trembling. And they're mighty near jerked out from under you."']

jakeloo *adj.* (*also* **jakealoo**, **jake-a-pie**, **jakerloo**) [1910s+] (*Aus./N.Z.*) excellent, wonderful, very good. [JAKE adj.[1]]

Jakers! *excl. see* JAPERS! excl.

jakers *n. see* JAKE n.[5].

jakes *n.* (*also* **jacque's**) [mid-16C+] a lavatory. [? *jack's* or *jack's place*, using SE *jack* as generic for a man. Note synon. 1930s + Virginia dial. *jack-house*; note also Nares: 'Its etymology is uncertain, unless we accept the very bad pun of Sir John, who derives it (in jest indeed) from an old man who, at such a place, cried out *age akes, age akes*, meaning that age causes aches']

jakes-farmer *n.* (*also* **jakes-barreller**) [late 16C–mid-17C] a man employed to clean out privies. [JAKES n. + SE *farmer*, one who cleanses]

jake the rape *v.* [1980s+] (*Aus. prison*) to escape. [rhy. sl.]

jakey *n.*[1] [1960s] (*US gay*) the penis (cf. ABRAHAM n.[1]).

jakey *n.*[2] [1980s+] a beggar, an alcoholic vagrant. [JAKE n.[5] (2)]

jakey *n.*[3] *see* JAKE n.[5].

jakey *adj.* [1950s+] (*US*) unsophisticated, gauche, rustic, characteristic of a country person. [JAKE n.[1] (1)]

jakkitch *n.* [late 19C–1900s] (*provincial*) a general pej. [? proper name of the hangman JACK KETCH n.]

jalino *n.* [1940s] (*US*) a disadvantage; usu. as *have someone by the jalino*. [ety. unknown]

jalobies *n.* [1960s+] nipples. [ety. unknown]

jalopy *n.* (*also* **jalop, jaloppy, jollopi, joppy, loppy**) [1920s+] (*orig. US*) **1** a decrepit car. **2** a worthless or unattractive person or object. [ety. unknown; ? Sp.; echoic of the car's unsteady progress]

Jam *n.* [1970s+] a *Jamaican*. [abbr.]

jam *n.*[1] **1** [19C–1920s] (*US*) a social gathering or party, a crowd. **2** [1930s+] (*US Black*) swing or other popular music. **3** [1950s+] (*US Black*) a party with music. **4** [1960s+] music in general, a song, a record, a performance of jazz, rock or rap music (orig. with a dance routine). **5** [1970s+] (*US gay*) a spontaneous party that ends in an orgy or a big fight. **6** [1990s+] (*W.I.*) a crowd in a venue that is at full capacity. [SE *jam*, a crush. Note 19C SE *crush*, a party; Wolof *jama*, a crowd, a gathering; by 1860s a gathering of slaves getting together for pleasure and dancing]

jam *n.*[2] **1** [mid-19C+] anything easy. **2** [mid-19C+] profit, an advantage. **3** [mid-19C+] something very enjoyable. **4** [1920s–40s] (*US Und.*) small stolen articles, e.g. personal jewellery. [orig. sporting jargon *real jam*, anything exceptionally good]

jam *n.*[3] [late 19C+] **1** an attractive woman. **2** sexual intercourse with a woman. **3** (*later use US Black*) the vagina (cf. APPLE n.[6]). [JAM TART n. (2)]

jam *n.*[4] **1** [late 19C+] a problem, a difficult situation. **2** [20C+] (*US*) a disagreement or a fight. [SE *jam*, a crush]

jam *n.*[5] [20C+] (*Aus.*) **1** affectation, pretentiousness; thus *put on the jam, show jam*, to act in an affected manner. **2** toadying. [the image of spreading jam on bread]

jam *n.*[6] (*also* **jammie**) **1** [1930s–50s] (*US drugs*) an overdose. **2** [1970s+] (*US Black/drugs*) cocaine. **3** [1970s+] (*US drugs*) amphetamine (cf. A n.[2]). ['it gets you in a jam' (Spears, *Slang and Jargon of Drugs and Drink*, 1986)]

jam *n.*[7] **1** [1940s+] (*US gay*) faeces; often in the context of homosexual foreplay. **2** [1960s+] menstrual blood. **3** [1960s+] (*US Black*) semen (cf. BABY GRAVY n.). **4** [1990s+] vaginal secretions (cf. BINDERJUICE n.). [resemblance]

jam *n.*[8] [1960s+] (*gay*) a heterosexual man. [abbr. *just a m*an, but this may be a camp joke and the real ety. is unknown; ? JAM n.[7] (2)]

jam *n.*[9] [1980s+] (*Ulster*) a second-rate teacher. [abbr. *junior assistant mistress*]

jam *n.*[10] [2000s] parole. [abbr. JAM ROLL n. (1)]

jam *n.*[11] *see* JAM JAR n.[1].

jam *n.*[12] *see* JEM n.[1].

jam *adj. see* JAM(-UP) adj.

jam *v.*[1] [mid-18C–early 19C] to hang; usu. as JAMMED adj.[1]. [one's head is 'jammed' into the noose; ? ref. to the original method of hanging, jamming the neck into a forked piece of wood]

jam *v.*[2] **1** [mid-19C+] to injure, to damage by striking or crushing. **2** [mid-19C+] to strike hard and suddenly. **3** [mid-19C+] to cause trouble for, to put in danger; often as JAM UP v. **4** [1920s] (*US*) to persist forcefully. **5** [1960s+] (*US Black*) to confront, to fight, to overcome or defeat. **6** [1970s+] to threaten, to harass, to arrest. **7** [1980s+] (*US Black*) to defeat verbally.

jam *v.*[3] **1** [1930s+] (*W.I./US Black*) to play or, of an instrument or of music in general, to be played so as to encourage vigorous dancing; thus *jamming*, dancing in an abandoned manner. **2** [1930s+] (*orig. US*) of musicians, to play together without set scores or arrangement for the pleasure and the spontaneous music thus created. **3** [1970s+] (*US Black*) to talk forcefully, esp. in a group. [JAM n.[1]]

jam *v.*[4] [1940s+] (*orig. US Black/W.I.*) to have sexual intercourse. [JAM n.[3] (2)]

jam *v.*[5] **1** [1950s+] (*US Black/campus/drugs*) (*also* **jam down**) to have fun, to have a good time, also by taking drugs. **2** [1970s+] (*US Black/campus*) (*also* **jam back**) to dance. **3** [1980s+] (*US campus*) to do very well. [ext. of JAM v.[3]]

jam *v.*[6] [1960s–70s] (*US Black*) to sniff cocaine. [JAM n.[6] (2)]

jam *v.*[7] [1960s+] (*US teen*) to leave, to exit fast. [? SE *jam* one's foot on the accelerator]

jam *adv.* [mid-19C] (*US*) comfortably, easily. [JAM n.[2] (1)]

Jamaica discipline *n.* [1960s+] (*gay*) a wife's denial of sexual favours to her husband. [? pun on *do you make her*]

Jamaican coat-of-arms *n.* [1940s+] (*W.I.*) a dish of rice and peas. [rice and peas is the Jamaican national dish]

Jamaica rum *n.* [20C+] a thumb. [rhy. sl.]

jam and fritters *n.* [late 19C] a real treat. [JAM n.[2] (3) + SE *fritters*]

jamas *n.* [1910s–50s] py*jamas*. [abbr.]

jam back *v. see* JAM v.[5] (2).

jambas *n.* [1960s+] (*US*) theft, robbery. [Sp.]

jamberoo *n.* [late 19C–1950s] (*Aus.*) a drunken spree. [var. on JAMBOREE n. (1)]

jambo *n.* [1980s+] (*Scot.*) a supporter of the football club Heart of Midlothian. [JAM TARTS n.]

jambone *adj.* [1980s] (*US*) worthless, contemptible. [? var. on JIBONE n.]

jamboree *n.* **1** [mid-19C+] (*orig. US*) a spree, a noisy revel. **2** [late 19C–1950s] (*US*) a disturbance or fight. [best known in 20C+ as a SE description of any large Boy Scout rally, the first of which, the International Rally of Boy Scouts, was held in 1920]

jamboree *v.* [1920s] to go on a spree. [JAMBOREE n. (1)]

jambox *n.* [1980s+] (*US campus*) a portable stereo. [JAM n.[1] (4) + BOX n.[5] (7)/SE *box*]

jam butty *n. see* JAM SANDWICH n.

jam cecil *n.* [1970s+] (*drugs*) amphetamine (cf. A n.[2]). [? JAM n.[6] (3) + CECIL n.[2]]

Jam Down *n. see* JAMDUNG n.

jam down *v. see* JAM v.[5] (1).

jam duff *n.* [20C+] a male homosexual. [rhy. sl. = PUFF n.[3] (1)]

Jamdung *n.* (*also* **Jam Down**) [1950s+] (*W.I., Jam.*) Jamaica (cf. JA n.) [SE *jam*, press + *dung* (W.I. pron.), down; refers to oppression of the Jamaican proletariat]

james *n.*[1] [19C–1950s] a house-breaker's implement. [play on the nickname *Jemmy*/JEMMY n.[3] (1)]

james *n.*[2] [early–late 19C] a cooked sheep's head. [JEMMY n.[1] (2)]

james *n.*[3] (*also* **jemmy**) [mid–late 19C] a sovereign. [orig. use as 16C *James Royal*, a Scot. silver coin of James VI of Scotland (r.1567–1603), the sword dollar]

james *n.*[4] *see* JOHN n.[8] (1).

james bong *n.* [1980s+] (*US drugs*) that person in a group who is the most intoxicated or most visibly intoxicated by a drug, usu. cannabis. [pun on BONG n.[1] and the fictional spy *James Bond*]

James Crow *adj. see* JIM CROW adj.

james crow *n. see* JIM CROW n.[2].

james earl dog *n.* [1980s+] (*US campus*) a marijuana cigarette. [? ref. to *James Earl Ray* (1928–98), the alleged killer of Martin Luther King in 1968]

James Hunt *n.* [20C+] **1** audacity, cheek. **2** the vagina (cf. ALL QUIET n.). [rhy. sl.; (1) = FRONT n.[1] (1); (2) = CUNT n.[1] (1); ult. UK motor racing champion *James Hunt* (1947–93)]

jamette *n.* [20C+] (*W.I.*) **1** a prostitute (cf. KURVE n.; POULE n.; PUT n.²; PUTO n.; TRUG n.; TRULL n.). **2** a woman widely recognized to be promiscuous. [? Fr. sl. *jeanette*, a prostitute, or Fr. *diamètre*, diameter, i.e. the line between 2 halves of the social world]

jam fag *n.* [1940s+] a homosexual with no sexual interests other than semen (cf. BONE-EATER n.). [JAM n.⁷ (3) + FAG n.⁵ (1)]

jam foutre *n. see* JEAN FOUTRE n.

jam house *n.* [1970s] (*US Black*) a place where cocaine can be both purchased and then snorted in convivial surroundings. [JAM n.⁶ (2) + SE *house*]

jamie duff *n.* [mid–late 19C] a professional mourner. [? an undertaker's name]

jam it *v.* [1960s+] to drive a car or bike fast. [JAM v.⁷]

jam it! *excl.* [1950s+] (*Aus./US*) a threatening excl. [abbr. *jam it up your ass!*]

jam jar *n.*¹ (*also* **jam**) [1910s+] initially a tram car, a motor car. [rhy. sl.]

jam jar *n.*² [1950s] a farthing. [near rhy. sl. = *far*, i.e. abbr.]

jammed *adj.*¹ [mid-18C–19C] (*UK Und.*) hanged, murdered, killed. [JAM v.¹]

jammed *adj.*² **1** [mid-19C; 1920s] (*US*) drunk or intoxicated. **2** [late 19C+] (*US Und.*) in trouble with the law, arrested. **3** [1910s] subject to discipline. **4** [1970s+] (*US*) troubled, upset. [JAM n.⁴ (1)]

jammed out *adj.* [early 19C–1940s] (*US*) dressed up. [JAM(-UP) adj.]

jammed up *adv.* **1** [1920s+] in a difficult situation, in trouble. **2** [1960s] having taken an overdose of drugs. [(1) JAM n.⁴ (1); (2) JAM n.⁶]

jammer *n.*¹ [1980s+] (*US*) a player of music. [JAM v.³]

jammer *n.*² [2000s] (*Irish*) a stolen car. [JAM IT v.]

jammie *n.*¹ *see* JAM n.⁶.

jammie *n.*² *see* JAMMY n.¹.

jammies *n.* [1940s+] pyjamas. [abbr.]

jammiest bits of jam *n.* [late 19C] extremely attractive young women. [JAM n.³ (1)]

jammin' *n.* [1960s+] (*W.I. Rasta*) having a good time, dancing calypso/soca. [JAM v.⁵]

jamming *n.*¹ [20C+] (*W.I.*) severe verbal criticism, physical assault. [JAM v.²]

jamming *n.*² [2000s] menstruation. [JAM n.⁷ (2)]

jamming *adj.* [1980s+] (*orig. US Black*) exciting, pleasing, excellent, best; also as excl. of pleasure. [JAM v.⁵]

jammiwam *n.* [1990s+] a difficult situation, a problem. [JAM n.⁴ (1); note use in Anthony Burgess, *A Clockwork Orange* (1962), where it means SE *jam*]

jammy *n.*¹ (*also* **jammie**) [1960s+] (*S.Afr.*) a motorcar. [abbr. JAM JAR n.¹ + dimin. sfx *-ie*]

jammy *n.*² [1980s+] (*US Black*) **1** the penis. **2** a handgun, a pistol. [? JIMMY n.⁵ (1)]

jammy *n.*³ [1980s+] a tampon. [abbr. JAM RAG n.]

jammy *n.*⁴ [1990s+] (*US Black*) a film. [? in non-specific use meaning a 'thing' f. JAMMY n.² (1); on model of JOINT n.¹/JOINT n.⁷ (2)]

jammy *adj.*¹ [late 19C+] easy, simple, lucky, profitable. [JAM n.² (2)]

jammy *adj.*² [1900s] (*Aus.*) pretentious. [JAM n.⁵ (1)]

jammy *adj.*³ [1960s+] (*Aus.*) unwashed. [lit. covered in jam]

jammy client *n.* [2000s] (*Irish*) a fool.

jammy dodger *n.* [1990s+] an act of sexual intercourse. [rhy. sl. = ROGER n.² (3); ult. SE *jammy dodger*, a type of biscuit]

jam off *v.* [2000s] to ejaculate. [JAM n.⁷ (3)]

jamoke *n.*¹ (*also* **jamoch, jamocha, jamoka, jomoke**) [late 19C+] (*US*) coffee. [*Java* + *Mocha* coffee beans]

jamoke *n.*² (*also* **jamouche**) [1940s+] (*US*) a stupid or objectionable fellow. [a WW1 soldier's nickname]

jamoke *n.*³ [1960s] (*US*) the penis. [ety. unknown; ? ext. of JAMOKE

n.² on pattern of DORK n. etc, where the term means both a fool and a penis]

jam on your egg *phr.* [2000s] (*Irish*) wishful thinking. [? SE *do you want jam on it?* a phr. meaning to stop complaining/being so demanding]

jamouche *n. see* JAMOKE n.².

jam out *v.* [1980s+] (*US campus*) **1** to listen to music. **2** to play music intensely. [JAM v.³]

jam pies *n.* [1990s+] the eyes. [rhy. sl.]

jampot *n.*¹ [late 19C–1950s] (*Aus.*) a high collar. [resemblance]

jampot *n.*² [late 19C+] the vagina (cf. APPLE n.⁶; BAG n.¹). [JAM n.³ (3)]

jampot *n.*³ [1940s+] (*US Black/gay*) the anus (cf. BAKERY GOODS n.). [JAM n.⁷ (1)]

jam rag *n.* [1960s+] a tampon, a sanitary towel. [JAM n.⁷ (2) + RAG n.⁸ (1)]

jam roll *n.* **1** [1970s+] (*UK prison*) parole. **2** [1990s+] unemployment benefit, the dole (cf. BLESS MY SOUL n.). **3** [2000s] the anus; thus a general pej. description (cf. BAKERY GOODS n.; BOTTLE AND GLASS n.). [rhy. sl.; (3) = ARSEHOLE n. (1)/ARSEHOLE n. (2)]

jams *n.*¹ [late 19C–1910s] delirium tremens, a hangover. [abbr. JIM-JAMS n.¹ (1)]

jams *n.*² [1960s+] **1** pyjamas. **2** long and baggy shorts or swimming trunks. [abbr.; (2) are seen as pyjama-like]

jam sandwich *n.* (*also* **jam butty**) [1980s+] a police car. [the fluorescent coloured stripe running round the middle of the car]

jam session *n.* **1** [1920s+] (*orig. US*) an informal gathering, a get-together, esp. of musicians, a group discussion. **2** [1930s+] (*W.I./UK Black*) 'any event in which there is a large noisy crowd' (Allsopp). [jazz use *jam session*, an impromptu concert. The first session, according to Mezzrow & Wolfe, *Really the Blues* (1946), took place in late 1927 at 22 North State Street, Chicago, in the cellar of the Three Deuces speak-easy. Among those playing were Bix Beiderbecke, Bing Crosby and Mezzrow himself. 'I think the term "jam session" originated right in that cellar. Long before that, of course, the colored boys used to get together and play for kicks, but those were mostly private sessions, strictly for professional musicians, and the idea was usually to try and cut each other, each one trying to outdo the others and prove himself best. Those impromptu concerts of theirs were generally known as "cuttin' contests." Our idea [...] was to play together, to make our improvisation really collective [...] to see could we fit together and arrive at a climax all at once. Down in that basement concert hall, somebody was always yelling over to me, "Hey Jelly, what you gonna do?" [...] and almost every time I'd cap them with, "jelly's gonna jam some now," just as a kind of play on words. We always used the word "session" a lot, and I think the expression "jam session" grew up out of this playful yelling back and forth']

jam someone up *v.* (*US Black*) **1** [1960s+] to rape. **2** [1960s+] to beat, to overpower. **3** [1970s+] to talk forcefully, to challenge, to confront. [SE *jam*, to press, to squeeze, to push]

jam tart *n.* **1** [mid–late 19C] a mart. **2** [mid-19C+] (*also* **tamtart**) a sweetheart, a girlfriend. **3** [20C+] the heart, whether anatomically or as a playing-card suit. [rhy. sl.]

jam tart *v.* [1980s] (*Aus.*) to fart. [rhy. sl.]

Jam Tarts *n.* [1990s+] (*Scot.*) Hearts, i.e. Heart of Midlothian F.C. [rhy. sl.]

jam the joystick *v. see* JACK THE JOYSTICK v.

jam(-up) *adj.* **1** [early 19C+] (*orig. US*) splendid, fine, excellent, first-rate. **2** [mid-19C–1940s] thorough; as adv., totally, keenly. [image of SE *jam*, e.g. on bread in addition to butter, as conferring extra pleasure; note JAM n.²]

jam up *v.* **1** [mid-19C+] (*US*) to cause trouble, to put someone or oneself in a difficult position. **2** [1990s+] (*US prison*) to confront, to question. [ext. of JAM v.²]

jam-up and jelly-tight *phr.* (*also* **jelly-tight**) [1960s+] (*US

Black) splendid, first-rate. [JAM(-UP) adj. + JELLY n.¹ (2); the overall implication is sexual]

jan *n.* [17C] (*UK Und.*) a purse. [ety. unknown; ? Rom.]

janasmug *n. see* JANUSMUG *n.*

jancro *n. see* JOHN CROW *n.*

Jane *adj.* [1920s] (*Scot.*) of a woman, smart, sophisticated. [JANE n.² (1)]

jane *n.*¹ [mid-19C–1900s] a sovereign. [SE *jane*, a small silver coin from Genoa, introduced into England towards the end of the 14C]

jane *n.*² **1** [late 19C+] a woman, a sweetheart, a girlfriend. **2** [1940s–70s] an effeminate or homosexual man (cf. ABIGAIL n.). **3** [1950s+] (*US*) a women's lavatory. **4** [1950s+] (*camp gay*) the embodiment of one's feminine side. [generic use of the proper name]

jane *n.*³ (*US drugs*) **1** [1970s+] marijuana (cf. AUNT MARY n.²). **2** [1990s+] cocaine (cf. AUNT NORA n.). [abbr. MARY JANE n.²; (2) note cocaine is a 'feminine' drug, *see* GIRL n.²]

jane *n.*⁴ *see* JEAN n.

Jane Crow *n.* [1970s] discrimination against women. [after JIM CROW n.]

Jane Doe *n.* [1970s+] the female version of JOHN DOE n.

ja-nee! *excl.* (*S.Afr.*) **1** [1940s+] a non-committal excl. used when one wishes to avoid controversy. **2** [1970s+] an excl. used to express resignation, reluctant acquiescence. **3** [1970s+] an excl. used to express emphatic approval, that's a fact! I'll say that is! that's right! **4** [1970s+] an excl. used to indicate the contradictory, paradoxical nature of a situation. **5** [1980s+] an excl. used to indicate that one understands but disagrees with the previous speaker. [Afk. *ja*, yes + *nee*, no]

Jane Q Public *n.* (*also* **Jane Q Citizen**) [1970s+] (*US*) the average, typical woman.

Jane Russell *n.* [20C+] a mussel. [rhy. sl.; ult. *see* next]

Jane Russell special *n.* [1990s+] (*US*) 2 poached eggs on toast. [the voluptuous Hollywood film star *Jane Russell* (b.1921)]

Jane Shore *n.* **1** [18C–1930s] a prostitute (cf. BOAT AND OAR n.). **2** [mid–late 19C] the floor. [rhy. sl.; (1) = SE *whore*; ult. *Jane Shore* (d.1527), mistress of Edward IV]

janet *n.* [1980s+] (*drugs*) ¼oz (7g) of cannabis. [rhy. sl.; *Janet Street-Porter* = QUARTER n.² (2); ult. UK journalist and TV personality *Janet* Street-Porter (b.1944)]

janey (mack)! *excl.* [1920s+] (*Irish*) a general excl., a euph. for JESUS (CHRIST)! excl. (cf. GAWNEY (MAC)! excl.).

janga-manga *n.* [1940s] (*W.I.*) a person of the lowest class. [? *jangga*, a river prawn, eaten by poor peasants + *manga* = Fr. *manger*, to eat]

jangle *v.* [1960s+] **1** to speak ill of someone, to gossip. **2** to unnerve. [SE *jangle*, to squabble]

jank *v. see* GANK v.

jankie *n.* (*also* **janky**) [1990s+] (*US Black*) bad luck. [? SE *Yankee*, i.e. a negative comment on White people]

janky *adj.* [1990s+] (*US Black teen*) **1** second-rate, inferior, unpleasant. **2** stupid. [JANKIE n.]

jannie *n.* [1980s+] (*US drugs*) a meticulously rolled, large cannabis cigarette that burns smoothly. [? abbr. JANE n.³]

jannock *adj.* (*also* **jonic**, **jonnick**, **jonnock**) [mid-19C+] sociable, fair-dealing, honest; thus *die jannock*, to die bravely. [dial. *jannock*, fair, straightforward]

janny *n.* [1920s] (*US*) a janitor. [abbr.]

janusmug *n.* (*also* **janasmug**) [mid-19C–1940s] (*UK Und.*) one who works as the intermediary between a thief and a receiver of stolen goods. [*Janus*, the Roman god with 2 faces + MUG n.¹ (2)]

Jap *n.* [mid-19C+] a derog. term for a Japanese person (cf. BUDDHAHEAD n.). [abbr.]

Jap *adj.* [mid-19C+] pertaining to Japan or Japanese lifestyle or culture.

jap *n.* **1** [late 19C+] (*US*) a derog. term for a Black person

(cf. ALLIGATOR BAIT n.²). **2** [1940s] (*US gang*) a sneak, a spy. **3** [1950s–70s] (*US gang*) a surprise attack by a teenage gang. **4** [1960s+] (*US campus*) an unexpected test, a bad surprise. [(2), (3) and (4) JAP n.; the lingering dislike of the Japanese as America's 'trad. enemy', esp. in the context of the surprise attack on Pearl Harbor in WW2]

jap *v.* **1** [1940s+] (*US*) to attack, esp. of street gangs. **2** [1950s+] (*US*) to undermine someone's plans or efforts, to surprise. **3** [1960s] (*US campus*) to steal. **4** [1960s+] (*also* **jap out**) to back down, to renege on an appointment. **5** [1960s+] to swindle, to be cheated. [JAP n.]

j.a.p. *n.* [1970s+] (*US*) a rich, spoiled Jewish girl. [abbr. JEWISH-AMERICAN PRINCESS n.]

japan *n.* [mid-19C–1900s] in prize-fighting, the skin. [fig./journ. use of SE *Japan*, varnish, veneer]

japan *v.* **1** [mid-18C–19C] to ordain a priest. **2** [1930s] (*US Und.*) to force the truth from someone. [(1) SE *japan*, to make black and glossy. The ref. is to the black clerical garb. Note Aus./US prison use *japanned*, said of a convict who has been converted by the chaplain]

Japanee *n.* [mid-19C+] (*US*) a derog. term for a *Japanee*se person. [abbr.]

Japanese knife-trick *n.* [late 19C–1900s] eating from one's knife, esp. peas. [the image is of chopsticks]

Japanese roller skate *n.* [1970s] (*US*) a small car of Japanese manufacture.

japanning *n.* [1900s] (*Aus.*) stealing cash-boxes. [the *japanned* surface of such a box]

Jap crock *n.* [late 19C] (*UK society*) Japanese porcelain. [abbr. *Jap*anese *crock*ery]

jape *v.* **1** [late 14C–16C] to seduce a woman. **2** [mid-15C–16C] to have sexual intercourse. [in 1598 *jape* appears in Florio, *World of Wordes*, alongside the first ever listing of *fuck*. Note its survival in 20C+ in certain US states, esp. North Carolina, West Virginia and Virginia, and in the Appalachians]

japers! *excl.* (*also* **Jabus! Jakers!**) [late 19C+] (*Irish*) a general excl., a euph. for JESUS! excl.

Jap hash *n.* [20C+] (*US*) chow mein. [*chow mein*, itself an ersatz form of Chinese food, invented for Western consumers, has nothing to do with Japanese cuisine]

japie *n. see* JAAP n.

Jap moll *n.* (*also* **Asian moll**) [1970s+] (*N.Z.*) a prostitute who specializes in Asian or Japanese customers. [JAP n./SE *Asian* + MOLL n.¹ (2)]

jap out *v. see* JAP v. (4).

jappa-jappa *adj.* [20C+] (*W.I.*) rough, indifferent, esp. of work or personal appearance. [? Yoruba *jaba-jaba*, higgledy-piggledy, Krio *jagbajagba*, worthless stuff]

Jappy *n.* (*also* **Jappo**) [1900s–50s] (*Aus./US*) a derog. term for a Japanese person (cf. BUDDHAHEAD n.). [JAP n. + sfx -*y*]

Jappy *adj.* [1900s–10s] (*Aus.*) Japanese, in a Japanese style. [JAP n. + sfx -*y*]

Jap safety boots *n.* [1980s+] (*Aus. prison*) sandals, thongs.

Jap scrap *n.* [1980s+] (*US campus*) a motorcycle or appliance made in Japan, slightly derog. [JAP adj. + SE *scrap*]

Jap's eye *n.* [1990s+] the male urethral opening at the end of the penis. [its resemblance to a 'slit eye' and thus racial stereotyping]

Jap-slap *v.* [1980s+] (*US*) to slap someone suddenly; also in fig. use. [racist stereotyping of the Japanese as specialists in surprise attacks, e.g. Pearl Harbor]

Japstick *n.* [1950s+] (*gay*) the penis of an Asian man (cf. BAT n.⁷). [JAP n. + STICK n.¹ (1) + pun on the brandname *Chapstick*]

Jap wise *adj.* [20C+] (*US*) partially or insufficiently informed. [JAP n. + -WISE sfx (1); ult. ? stereotype of Japanese stealing Western skills and reproducing the form but still lacking the innate knowledge that helped create them]

jar n.[1] **1** [20C+] (*Anglo-Irish*) a stone hot-water bottle. **2** [1920s+] a glass of beer; thus phr. *with a few jars on*, drunk.

jar n.[2] [1940s–70s] fake jewellery, usu. so well made that it can pass for real; thus DO A JAR UP v. [? SE *jargoon*, a zircon or fake diamond]

jar n.[3] [1960s+] (*drugs*) a quantity of pills, usu. 500 or 1000. [the amount in the jars supplied to pharmacists]

jar v. [mid-19C+] to drink.

jarboni n. *see* JIBONE n.

jarbox n. (*also* **jawbox**) [20C+] (*Ulster*) the kitchen sink. [Scot.]

jarg adj. [2000s] illegal, stolen, counterfeit. [SE *jargoon*, a zircon, thus a counterfeit precious stone]

jargonelle n. [18C–19C] the penis. [SE *jargonelle*, an early-ripening brand of pear, orig. limited to what gardeners condemned as a second-rate variety. It may be pure coincidence that in Fr. the fruit is known as *Cuisse Madame*, lady's thigh]

jargoozle v. [late 19C–1900s] to confuse, to trick. [SE *jargogle*, to confuse + BAMBOOZLE v. (1)]

jarhead n.[1] (*US Black*) **1** [1930s–40s] a Black man. **2** [1940s+] a fool, a slow, stupid person. [US dial. *jarhead*, a mule; ult. pron. of *jawhead*]

jarhead n.[2] [1930s+] an alcoholic, a heavy drinker. [SE *jar* (of liquor) + -HEAD sfx (3)]

jarhead n.[3] [1930s+] (*US*) a US marine. [JARHEAD n.[2]]

jark n. **1** [mid-16C–19C] (*UK Und.*) (*also* **jarke, jerke**) a seal. **2** [19C] any trinket worn on a watch-chain. **3** [19C] (*UK campus*) a safe-conduct pass. **4** [19C] a watch. [ety. unknown]

jark v. [18C] to seal. [JARK n. (1)]

jark it v. [mid-19C] to run away. [? fig. use of SE *jerk*]

jarkman n. (*also* **jarkeman**) [mid-16C–mid-19C] (*UK Und.*) a mendicant villain who used his abilities of reading and writing (Latin) to forge counterfeit begging licences (cf. CANTING CREW n.). [JARK n. (1) + -MANS sfx]

jar loose v. [late 19C+] (*US*) to let go, to leave, to hand over.

jaro n. (*also* **jyro**) [late 19C+] a telling off, a scolding. [Maori *whauran*, to scold]

jar of jam n. **1** [20C+] a pram. **2** [1930s+] a tram. [rhy. sl.]

Jarrahland n. [20C+] (*Aus.*) the state of Western Australia; thus *jarrah-jerker*, anyone who works in the bush. [SAusE *jarrah*, a type of eucalyptus found in Western Australia]

jarred adj.[1] [1930s+] **1** drunk (cf. ALED UP adj.). **2** in fig. use, in a mess. [JARHEAD n.[2]]

jarred adj.[2] [1990s+] (*orig. US teen*) emotionally disturbed, upset. [SE *jar*]

jarsey n. *see* JASEY n.

jar someone's frame v. *see* CLIMB SOMEONE'S FRAME v. (2).

J. Arthur (Rank) n. **1** [1940s+] a bank. **2** [1970s+] masturbation. **3** [1970s+] a fool (cf. BEECHAM'S PILL n.). [rhy. sl.; (2) = WANK n.[1] (1); (3) = WANK n.[1] (3); ult. *J. Arthur Rank*, later Lord Rank (1888–1972), the British flour producer turned film magnate who dominated the British film business in the 1930s–40s]

jar up v. *see* DO A JAR UP v.

jarvel n. [early 19C] (*US Und.*) a jacket.

jarvey n. (*also* **jarvis, jervis, jervy**) **1** [late 18C+] a hackney coachman; thus *jervis' upper benjamin*, a coachman's greatcoat. **2** [19C; 1950s] the coach itself. **3** [19C] (*US*) a waistcoat. [proper name *Jarvis*]

jarvey v. [early 19C] to drive a hackney coach. [JARVEY n. (1)]

jasbo n. *see* JAZZBO n.

jasey n. (*also* **jajazy, jarsey, jazey**) [late 18C–1930s] a wig, esp. one made of worsted; thus *bloke with the jasey*, a judge. [? proper name *Jersey*, a type of flax used in the making of a certain type of wig]

jasm n. [mid–late 19C] (*US*) spirit, energy. [var. on JISM n. (1)]

jason's fleece n. (*UK Und.*) **1** [17C] the gold pieces that are used to trap the victim in a money-switching fraud. **2** [late 17C–early 19C] a citizen who has been swindled of their money. [the Greek myth, where *Jason* stole the Golden Fleece + pun on SE *fleece*, to strip someone of their money or possessions]

JASP n. [1970s] (*US*) a Jew who has assimilated into the Anglo-Saxon elite culture. [SE *J*ewish + WASP n.]

jasper n. **1** [late 19C+] (*US*) a man, esp. a rustic, a peasant (cf. ALVIN n.). **2** [1910s+] (*US*) a Black person. **3** [1950s+] (*US prison/Black*) a lesbian (cf. AMY-JOHN n.). [the male proper name]

jasper adj. [1950s–60s] (*US*) lesbian, pertaining to the world of lesbians.

Jasper Carrot n. [1990s+] a parrot. [rhy. sl.; ult. UK comedian *Jasper Carrot* (b.1945)]

jass v. *see* JAZZ v.[1].

jassack n. (*also* **jass-onkey**) [mid-19C+] (*US*) a mule. [SE *jackass* (+ *donkey*)]

jaul n. *see* JOL n.

java n. (*also* **J, jay**) [mid-19C+] (*US/Can.*) coffee. [*Java* coffee beans]

javin n. [late 18C] (*US Und.*) a jacket.

jaw n. **1** [mid-18C+] talk, conversation, a speech; thus HOLD ONE'S JAW v. [19C–1910s] a lecture, a speech. **2** [19C–1910s] a lecture, a speech. **3** [early 19C–1950s] a telling-off, ridicule. **4** [1940s] braggadocio. **5** [1970s] (*US*) sexual intercourse. [SE *jaw*]

jaw v.[1] **1** [mid-18C+] to talk, to argue. **2** [19C+] to address censoriously or abusively, to scold or lecture. **3** [mid-19C] (*US*) to yell. [JAW n.]

jaw v.[2] [mid–late 19C] to go. [? Rom. *java*, I go or Hind. *jao*, go]

jaw-ass v. [1960s+] (*US*) to talk at length. [JAW v.[1] + -ASS sfx]

jaw at the jibs v. *see* RUN ONE'S JIBS v.

jawaub n. (*also* **juwaub**) [mid-19C] (*Anglo-Ind.*) a dismissal, a rejection. [Hind. *jawaub*, an answer]

jawbation n. [17C–early 19C] a tedious scolding; thus *jawbatious*, tedious, argumentative, ill-humoured; a noisy argument that takes place in the street.

jawblock v. [1940s] (*US Black*) to talk. [one 'blocks one's jaw' with words]

jawbone n.[1] [mid-19C] (*US*) **1** a castanet, usu. in pl. **2** a Jew's harp.

jawbone n.[2] **1** [mid-19C–1970s] (*orig. Can./US*) credit. **2** [late 19C+] (*US*) empty talk, exaggerated promises that are not kept. **3** [1960s+] (*US*) political persuasion. [the verbal persuasiveness required to get goods on credit, to make political speeches etc]

jawbone adj. [mid-19C–1970s] (*orig. Can./US*) on credit. [JAWBONE n.[2] (1)]

jawbone v. **1** [late 19C–1970s] to persuade someone into extending credit, to sell or buy on credit. **2** [1950s+] to talk, to chatter. **3** [1960s+] (*US*) to persuade, esp. in politics. [JAWBONE n.[2]]

jawbone breaker/doctor n. *see* JAWBREAKER n.[2].

jawbone time n. [1940s+] (*US Und.*) time spent in jail awaiting sentencing. [JAWBONE n.[2] (1); i.e. 'credit' towards one's jail time]

jawboning n. [1960s+] (*US*) a political or industrial tactic whereby a negotiator or leader attempts to talk 2 warring sides out of making unreasonable demands. [JAWBONE v. (3)]

jawbox n. *see* JARBOX n.

jawbreaker n.[1] (*also* **jawcracker, jaw-twister**) [mid-19C+] a word that the speaker considers so long or complex that its pronunciation threatens to be harmful.

jawbreaker n.[2] (*also* **jawbone breaker/doctor, jawbuster, jawcracker, jaw puller**) [1920s+] (*US*) a dentist.

jaw-breaking adj. (*also* **jaw-cracking**) [mid-19C+] of words and speech, hard to pronounce. [JAWBREAKER n.[1]]

jaw cove n. [mid-19C] (*US Und.*) **1** a lawyer. **2** an auctioneer. [JAW v.[1] (1) + COVE n. (1)]

jawelnofine phr. [1980s+] (*S.Afr.*) a general response (usu. ironical and resigned) to any form of information, fair enough, what can I say? that's life. [Afk. *ja*, yes + SE *well* + *no* + *fine*; coined by R.J.B. Wilson, broadcaster with South African Broadcasting Association]

jawer *n.* [1900s] (*Aus.*) one who nags. [JAW v.¹ (2)]

jawfest *n.* [1910s+] (*US*) a long chat or talking session. [JAW n. (1) + -FEST sfx]

jaw-flapping *n.* [1940s+] (*US*) empty chatter; thus *jawflaps*, a talkative person. [JAW n. (1) + SE *flap*]

jawing *n.* **1** [late 18C+] talk, a conversation, often when seen as pointless. **2** [19C+] a telling-off, a scolding. [(1) JAW v.¹ (1); (2) JAW v.¹ (2)]

jawing-tackle *n.* [late 18C–19C] (*US*) the mouth, the tongue, as used in talking. [JAW v.¹ (1)]

jaw-jack *v.* [1960s+] (*US Black*) to talk excessively, loudly or inconsequentially. [US Black pron. of *jaw-jerking/-jerking off*, i.e. 'verbal masturbation']

jaw-jaw *n.* [1950s+] conversation, chatter. [JAW n. (1) + redup.; note Prime Minister Harold Macmillan's dictum delivered at Canberra, 30 January 1958: 'Jaw-jaw is better than war-war']

jaw-jaw *v.* [1950s+] to talk, to converse, to discuss. [JAW-JAW n.]

jawkins *n.* [mid-19C–1900s] a club bore. [used in clubs and taken f. William Thackeray's *Book of Snobs* (1848), where it is the name of one such character]

jawl *n. see* JOL n.

jaw-mag *n.* [late 19C–1900s] talk, conversation, a speech. [JAW n. (1) + MAG n.⁴ (1)]

jaw-me-dead *n.* (*also* **jaw-me-dad**) [late 18C–1900s] a chatterer. [JAW v.¹ (1); lit. someone who will talk one to death]

jaw-music *n.* [1920s] (*US*) conversation, chatter, esp. when verbose or tedious. [SE *jaw*, but note JAW n.]

jawn *n.* [1980s+] (*US campus*) an indiscriminate term, usu. used of something or someone that causes happiness, joy or excitement; also used as adj. [ety. unknown]

jaw puller *n. see* JAWBREAKER n.².

jaws *n.* [1940s+] (*US*) the vaginal labia (cf. CUNT-LIPS n.). [the myth of the *vagina dentata*]

jaws, the *n.* [1960s+] (*US*) anger. [? the grinding of one's teeth]

jawsing *n.* [2000s] (*US teen*) lying. [? JAW v.¹]

jawsmith *n.* (*US*) **1** [late 19C+] a talkative person, a demagogue. **2** [1930s–40s] a dentist.

jawsome *adj.* [late 19C] talkative, verbose. [JAW n. + SE sfx *-some*]

jaw someone's head off *v. see* TALK SOMEONE'S HEAD OFF v.

jaw-tackle (fall) *n.* [mid–19C–1910s] (*US*) the mouth, the tongue, as used in talking. [JAW v.¹ (1) + SE *tackle*]

jaw-twister *n. see* JAWBREAKER n.¹.

jaw-work *n.* [mid-18C–19C] talk, conversation. [SE *jaw*, but note JAW n.]

Jax *n.* [1920s+] (*US*) *Jacks*onville, Florida. [abbr.]

jax *n.¹ see* JACKS n.

jax *n.² see* JACK'S (ALIVE) n.

jaxey/jaxie *n. see* JACKSY-PARDO n.

jaxx *n. see* JACKS n.

jaxy *n.* (*also* **joxy**) [20C+] the female genitals. [? JACKSIE n.¹]

jay *n.¹* [early 16C–early 17C] a cheeky chatterer. [SE *jay* (*Garrulus glandarius*), a bird noted for its noisiness]

jay *n.²* (*also* **jaybird**) [late 16C–17C; late 19C+] a showy woman, a prostitute (cf. ALLEY CAT n.). [SE *jay* (*Garrulus glandarius*), a bird noted for its noisiness and bright colouring; late 19C+ use is US, mostly Black]

jay *n.³* (*also* **J**) **1** [late 19C–1920s] (*US campus*) a person who does something disagreeable or foolish. **2** [late 19C+] (*orig. US*) (*also* **country jay**) a rustic, a simpleton, a novice, a newcomer (cf. BLOOTER n.). [16C SE *jay*, a simpleton; ult. SE *jay* (*Garrulus glandarius*), a bird that is typified as noisy and boorish towards other birds]

jay *n.⁴ see* J n.

jay *n.⁵ see* JAVA n.

jay *adj.¹* [late 19C] (*US campus*) enjoyable.

jay *adj.²* [late 19C–1910s] (*US*) naïve, worthless, unsophisticated. [JAY n.³ (2)]

jay *v.* [1990s+] (*US*) to steal. [JAYHAWK v.]

jaybee *n. see* J.B. n.².

jaybird *n.¹* [late 19C+] (*US*) a rustic, a simpleton, a novice, a newcomer (cf. BLOOTER n.). [JAY n.³ (2)]

jaybird *n.² see* J n.

jaybird *n.³ see* JAY n.².

jaybird *adj.* [late 19C+] (*US*) inferior, contemptible. [JAYBIRD n.¹]

jaybird(-naked) *adj. see* NAKED AS A JAYBIRD phr.

jayhawk *n.* (*US*) **1** [20C+] a rustic, a simpleton, a novice, a newcomer (cf. BLOOTER n.). **2** [1910s+] a mythical bird used as an emblem of Kansas. **3** [1930s+] a native of Kansas. [JAYHAWKER n.; (3) combines (1) and (2)]

jayhawk *v.* [mid-19C+] (*US, esp. milit., orig. Civil War*) to raid, to plunder, to steal, to operate as a guerrilla soldier. [negative image of SE *jay*, the bird]

jayhawker *n.* (*US*) **1** [mid-19C+] a native of Kansas, spec. in the context of murderous activities carried on before and during the Civil War. **2** [late 19C–1950s] a rustic, a simpleton (cf. BLOOTER n.). [the alleged similarity of Kansans – raping and pillaging during the US Civil War (1861–5) – to the SE *jay*, noted for its aggressive, bullying relations with other birds; Schele de Vere, *Americanisms* (1872), claims the term was imported from Aus. convicts]

jayhoo *n. see* JEHU n.².

jay-naked *adj. see* NAKED AS A JAYBIRD phr.

jay-o *v. see* J.O. v.

Jays *n.* [20C+] (*Irish*) members of the Society of Jesus, the Jesuits. [initial letter]

jay smoke *n.* [1960s+] (*drugs*) marijuana. [J n. + SMOKE n.³ (3)]

jaytown *n.* [late 19C–1920s] (*US*) a small town. [JAY n.³ (2) + SE *town*]

jazbo *n. see* JAZZBO n.

jazey *n. see* JASEY n.

Jazuz! *excl. see* JESUS (CHRIST)! excl.

jazz *n.¹* **1** [1910s–60s] (*orig. US Black*) sexual intercourse. **2** [1910s+] (*US*) spirit, energy, excitement. **3** [1930s+] (*US*) semen. **4** [1960s+] (*US*) a thrill, a moment of pleasure. [the ety. of *jazz* remains one of the most fiercely debated and heavily researched; roots in Fr., in West Africa, in African-American sex slang and elsewhere have been suggested, and abandoned; while the current position links the term to JISM n. (1). Its first use has been traced to players on the 1913 San Francisco Seals baseball club, as reported by one 'Scoop' Gleason in the San Francisco *Bulletin*. The first use of (2), on 3 March, runs: 'Everybody has come back to the old town full of the old "jazz" and they promise to knock the fans off their feet with their playing [...] What is the "jazz"? Why, it's a little of that "old life," the "gin-i-ker," the "pep," otherwise known as the enthusiam.' The progress from baseball to music is uncharted, but examples of the latter usage appear almost contemporaneously. For an extensive study of the ety. see Cohen (ed.), *Comments on Etymology* 32:4–5 (December/January 2002–03)]

jazz *n.²* **1** [1910s+] (*orig. US*) misleading, untrue, empty or pretentious talk, nonsense. **2** [1910s+] (*US*) anything, stuff. **3** [1950s+] fighting, confrontation. **4** [1960s+] (*US drugs*) heroin. [fig. use of JAZZ n.¹]

jazz *v.¹* (*also* **jass**) **1** [1910s+] (*orig. US Black*) to have sexual intercourse. **2** [1910s+] (*US*) to enliven, to inspire, to excite. **3** [1920s+] to enjoy oneself, to be inspired or excited. **4** [1980s+] (*Aus. prison*) to sodomize. [JAZZ n.¹; note Pierre Guiraud in his *Dictionnaire érotique* (Paris 1978, 1984, 1993) has 'jaser = coiter' and gives as a quotation 'Tu as les genoux chauds, tu veux jaser' (La Comedie des proverbes XVIe s.) As his source he gives *Glossaire érotique de la langue francaise depuis son origine jusqu'à nos jours* by Louis de Landes, Bruxelles 1861; this cit. is used in Farmer, *Vocabula Amatoria* (1896)]

jazz *v.²* **1** [1910s+] (*US*) to mess up, to confuse. **2** [1920s+] (*US*) to tease. **3** [1940s+] to lie, to deceive. [JAZZ n.² (1)]

jazz around v. [1910s+] **1** to fool about, to be idle, to lead a fast life, mainly in pursuit of sex. **2** to squander money. [JAZZ v.[2] + SE *around*]

jazz baby n. [1910s–40s] a flighty young girl, usu. middle-class, in her late teens or very early 20s, who sported short, bobbed hair, lipstick, skimpy dresses and generally led a lifestyle as far as possible removed from that of her parents. [SE *jazz*/JAZZ n.[1] + BABY n.[3] (1); whether the jazz refers to sex or music, or to something of both, remains debatable. Note Merrill and Jerome's popular US song 'Jazz Baby' (1919)]

jazzbo n. (*also* **jasbo, jazbo**) **1** [1910s–20s] in vaudeville, slapstick comedy. **2** [1910s–20s] a Black vaudeville performer, esp. in a 'black and white minstrel' show. **3** [1910s–20s] syncopated music. **4** [1910s–60s] a Black person, esp. a soldier. **5** [1910s+] (*US*) a fellow, a man, esp. a fashionable young man. **6** [1920s+] (*US/US campus*) a fool, an idiot (cf. BOBO n.[1]). [? proper name *Jasper* or SE *jazz*/JAZZ n.[1] + SE *boy*; (6) ? BOZO n.[1] (3)]

jazzbo adj. [1910s+] stylish, up to date. [JAZZBO n. (5)]

jazzed (up) adj. **1** [1910s–60s] (*US*) intoxicated by drugs or alcohol. **2** [1910s+] (*US campus*) excited, thrilled, pleased; thus *unjazzed*, depressed. **3** [1930s+] augmented, embellished (esp. in a flashy, vulgar manner). **4** [1940s–50s] of a woman, overtly sexual. **5** [1940s+] ostentatious, showy. [JAZZ v.[1] (2)/JAZZ UP v.]

jazzer n.[1] (*also* **jazzist**) [1910s+] (*orig. US*) **1** a jazz musician. **2** a jazz fan. [SE *jazz*]

jazzer n.[2] [1920s+] (*Irish*) one who has sexual intercourse. [JAZZ v.[1] (1)]

jazzhound n.[1] [1920s] (*US*) a sexually promiscuous man. [JAZZ n.[1] (1) + HOUND sfx]

jazzhound n.[2] [1920s] (*US*) a jazz enthusiast. [SE *jazz* + HOUND sfx]

jazz house n. [1920s] (*US*) a brothel (cf. ACCOMMODATION HOUSE n.). [JAZZ n.[1] (1) + HOUSE n.[1] (1)]

jazzing n.[1] [1920s–50s] (*US*) having sexual intercourse. [JAZZ v.[1] (1)]

jazzing n.[2] [1910s+] **1** (*US*) playing jazz music. **2** (*Scot.*) competitive dancing. [SE *jazz*]

jazzist n. *see* JAZZER n.[1].

jazz joint n. [1920s] (*US Black*) a brothel (cf. BADGER-CRIB n.). [JAZZ n.[1] (1) + JOINT n.[4] (3)]

jazz mag n. [1990s+] a pornographic magazine. [JAZZ n.[1] (3) + colloq. SE *mag*, a magazine]

jazz talc n. [1990s+] (*drugs*) cocaine (cf. BIRDIE POWDER n.). [JAZZ v.[1] (2) + abbr. SE *talcum-powder*]

jazz up v. [1910s+] of people, places or objects, to brighten up, to improve, to make more gaudy, to pep up. [JAZZ v.[1] (2)]

jazz water n. [1920s] (*US*) bootleg alcohol. [JAZZ v.[1] (2) + SE *water*]

jazzy adj.[1] (*US*) **1** [1910s+] bright, lively, exciting. **2** [1920s+] ostentatious, brash. [SE *jazz*; both defs. refer to the music and its image rather than to the sl. use]

jazzy adj.[2] [1920s+] (*US Black*) sexy. [JAZZ n.[1] (1)]

jazzy-ass adj. [1970s] flashy, ostentatious, vulgar. [JAZZY adj.[1] (2) + -ASS sfx]

j.b. n.[1] [1930s–40s] a hat made by the John B. Stetson Company. [abbr.]

j.b. n.[2] (*also* **jaybee**) [1940s+] (*US*) a Black person. [abbr. *jet black*; also a pun on *j.c.* or *jaycee*, a respectable, middle-class White person]

j-bo n. *see* J n.

J. Carroll Naish n. [1970s+] urination (cf. ANGEL'S KISS n.). [rhy. sl. = SLASH n.[3] (1); ult. US actor *J. Carroll Naish* (1900–73)]

j.c.l. n. [1940s+] (*US*) a novice. [abbr. JOHNNY-COME-LATELY n.]

j.c.o. n. [1940s] (*US*) a newly arrived immigrant. [*abbr.* just come over]

j.d. n. **1** [1950s+] (*US*) a juvenile *d*elinquent. **2** [1970s] (*US Und.*) an anonymous person, a pseudonym. **3** [1990s+] (*also* **JD**) Jack Daniel's whisky. [abbr.; (2) JOHN DOE n.]

j.d. v. [1960s] (*US*) to behave as a juvenile delinquent. [J.D. n. (1)]

jeah! excl. [2000s] (*US Black*) an excl. of satisfaction. [play on SE *yeah!*]

jeames n. [mid-19C] the *Morning Post* newspaper. [deliberately tortured pron. of proper name *James* and thus a generic term for a footman or a pej. for a flunkey. This in turn based on Thackeray's servant *Jeames* in the *Diary of C. Jeames de la Pluche, Esq.* (1846). Until it was swallowed up by the *Daily Telegraph* (in 1937), the ultra-conservative *Morning Post* was the paper of choice for the British upper classes]

jeames adj. [1910s] (*Aus.*) of journalism, snobbish. [JEAMES n.]

jean n. (*also* **jane**) [1960s+] (*US*) a female prostitute's female client. [the female equivalent of a JOHN n.[8] (4)]

jean v. [1910s] (*US Und.*) to place (a wallet) into a pocket. [IN ONE'S JEANS phr.]

jean-baptiste n. [late 19C+] a French Canadian. [the 'typical' name]

jean crapeau n. *see* JOHNNY CRAPOSE n.

jean foutre n. (*also* **jam foutre**) [mid-17C–18C] a Frenchman. [stereotypical Fr. excl. *je m'en foutre!* the fuck with it!]

jean potage n. [19C] (*US*) a French-born immigrant. [Fr. *Jean potage*, John(ny) soup]

jeasley/jeasly adj. *see* JEEZLY adj.

Jebby n. [1940s+] (*US*) a *Je*suit. [abbr.]

jeckle adj. *see* JEKYLL (AND HYDE) adj.

'jects adj. [1990s+] (*US Black teen*) cheap, rubbishy. [abbr. of housing pro*jects*, considered to be the lowest form of housing]

Jedburgh justice n. (*also* **Jeddart justice, Jedwood justice**) [18C–early 19C] the execution of someone before or without a trial, as such severe and often arbitrary justice was administered by petty local magistrates. [the level of *justice* meted out in the courts of *Jedburgh*]

J. Edgar n. [1970s+] (*US Black*) the police. [*J. Edgar* Hoover (1895–1972), head of the FBI]

jee v. *see* GEE v.[1].

jee! excl. *see* GEE! excl.

jeebies n. (*also* **jeeby**) [1930s+] (*US*) unpleasant fantasies, nameless terrors, anything the mind can conjure up to produce nerves and fear. [abbr. HEEBIE-JEEBIES n.]

jee gee n. [1970s+] (*drugs*) heroin. [? DUJI n.]

jeek adj. [1980s+] (*US campus*) smartly dressed, stylish, fashionable. [pron. of GQ or *Gentleman's Quarterly* magazine]

jeems! excl. [mid-19C–1910s] (*US*) used in mild oaths as a euph. for JESUS! excl. (cf. BEJABERS! excl.).

jeep n.[1] **1** [1930s–50s] (*US campus*) a greedy, materialistic girl. **2** [1930s+] (*US*) a stupid, inept or inexperienced person. **3** [1940s] (*US Black*) a drunkard. [Eugene the *Jeep*, an animal with amazing powers, created in 1936 by E.C. Segar (1894–1938) and incorporated in his cartoon *Popeye*]

jeep n.[2] [1940s+] any 4-wheeled vehicle. [abbr. *general purpose vehicle*; but supposedly influenced by E.C. Segar's cartoon character, Eugene the *Jeep* (*see* JEEP n.[1])]

jeep n.[3] [1960s] (*drugs*) a paper 'collar' used by a drug user to secure the needle to an eye-dropper before injecting the heroin/water solution. [var. on GEE n.[7]]

jeep v. [2000s] (*US Black*) to steal.

jeepers (creepers)! excl. [1920s+] (*orig. US*) a mild oath, a euph. for JESUS (CHRIST)! excl.

jeer *see under* JERE.

jees(e)! excl. *see* JEEZ! excl.

jeesunk n. *see* JUNK n.[5] (1).

jeeter n. [1930s–60s] (*US*) a rustic, a peasant (cf. ALVIN n.). [*Jeeter* Lester, the poor White peasant protagonist of Erskine Caldwell's novel *Tobacco Road* (1932)]

jeetled adj. [20C+] (*Ulster*) exhausted, worn-out. [Scot. *jeetle*, to delay, to idle]

jee up *n. see* GEE UP n. (2).

jeez! *excl.* (*also* **geez! jees(e)!**) [1920s+] (*orig. US*) a mild excl., a euph. for JESUS! excl.

jeezer *n.*[1] [1970s] (*US*) a man, a fellow. [GEEZER n.[1] (1)]

jeezer *n.*[2] [1980s] (*US*) something remarkable. [it makes one exclaim JESUS! excl.]

jeezly *adj.* (*also* **jeasley, jeasly**) (*US*) **1** [1930s+] a euph. for DAMNED adj. **2** [1990s+] inferior. [var. on JESUSLY adj.]

jef *n. see* JIFFY n.

jefe *n.* [1990s+] (*US drugs*) a senior cocaine dealer. [Sp. *jefe*, boss, chief]

jeff *n.* **1** [1930s–40s] a dull, stupid person, a pest. **2** [1930s–60s] (*US Black*) a derog. term for a White rustic, a peasant, esp. a Southerner (cf. ALVIN n.). **3** [1950s] an admirable person. **4** [1950s–60s] a White person, esp. if a racist. **5** [1960s+] a Black person who is obsequious towards Whites. [abbr. proper name *Jefferson Davis* (1808–89), president of the Confederate States 1861–5. Note mid-19C circus jargon *tight-jeff*, a tight-rope, *slack-jeff*, a slack rope]

jeff *v.* [1960s+] **1** (*US Und.*) to lie, to work a confidence trick, to fool a victim; usu. as *jeffing*. **2** (*US prison*) to tease, to joke with. **3** (*US Black*) to talk, to chatter, esp. to seduce, to fool or deceive with a 'line'; thus *tight jeff*, well-rehearsed patter; *slack jeff*, spontaneous ad-libbed chatter. **4** (*US Black*) to behave obsequiously, esp. towards Whites, to humiliate oneself. [abbr. proper name *Jefferson Davis* (1808–89), president of the Confederate States during the US Civil War 1861–5]

jeff artist *n.* [1960s+] **1** (*US*) a liar, a confidence trickster. **2** (*US Black*) a Black person who behaves subserviently towards Whites. [JEFF v. + ARTIST n. (1)/ARTIST sfx]

Jeff Davis *n.* (*US Black*) **1** [1940s] a rustic, a peasant, usu. from the South (cf. ALVIN n.). **2** [1960s+] a Black person who behaves subserviently towards Whites. [abbr. proper name *Jefferson Davis* (1808–89), president of the Confederate States 1861–5]

jeffer *n.* [1960s+] (*US Black*) a rustic, a peasant (cf. ALVIN n.). [JEFF n. (2)]

jefferson airplane *n.* [1960s+] (*US drugs*) a split match that is used as an improvised holder for the last fraction of a marijuana cigarette. [*Jefferson Airplane*, one of the most successful 'psychedelic' bands of the 1960s]

jeffey *n. see* JIFFY n.

jeffy *n. see* JIFFY n.

Jehoshaphat! *excl.* (*also* **Jehosaphat!**) [mid-19C+] used in a variety of mild oaths as a euph. for JESUS! excl.

jehu *n.*[1] **1** [mid-17C–1920s] a coachman. **2** [mid-19C–1950s] a cab-driver. **3** [mid-19C+] any form of driver. [II Kings 9:20: 'The driving is like the driving of Jehu the son of Nimshi, for he driveth furiously']

jehu *n.*[2] (*also* **jayhoo**) [1900s–40s] (*US*) a rustic, a simpleton (cf. ALVIN n.). [? the 'rustic' name *Jehu* + JAY n.[3] (2)]

jejo *n. see* YEYO n.

jekyll *n.* [1930s–40s] (*S.Afr.*) a brandy and Coca-Cola. [*Dr Jekyll and Mr Hyde* (1866), the story by R.L. Stevenson; the phr. reverses the actual tale, where Dr *Jekyll* is the good figure, i.e. the soft drink, and Mr Hyde is the villain, i.e. the alcohol]

Jekyll (and Hyde) *adj.* (*also* **jeckle**) [1920s+] crooked, fake, spurious, counterfeit. [rhy. sl. = SNIDE adj. (1); ult. *Dr Jekyll and Mr Hyde* (1866) by R.L. Stevenson]

Jekyll and Hydes *n.* [20C+] (*Aus.*) trousers. [rhy. sl. = STRIDES n.; ult. *see* prev.]

jel *n.* (*also* **jell**) [1980s+] (*US teen*) an appalling, unacceptable person. [abbr. JELLO-BRAIN n.]

jel *adj.* [1990s+] (*US*) jealous. [abbr.]

jeldi/jeldy *adv. see* JILDI adv.

jell *n.*[1] [1950s+] (*Aus.*) a coward. [SE *jelly*]

jell *n.*[2] *see* JEL n.

jell *v.* (*also* **gel, jell around, jell out, jelly, jelly around**)

[1930s+] (*US campus*) to relax, to waste time, to hang about, esp. at a soda fountain or café. [SE *gel*/SAmE *jel*, to solidify into a jelly-like substance; the image is of a jelly slowly melting; to turn into *Jell-O*/*jelly*]

jellhead *n.* (*also* **jelly**) [1990s+] (*UK drugs*) a habitual drug user, whose mental faculties have been, it is implied, thus impaired. [JELLY n.[6]]

jellied *adj.* [1980s+] under the influence of tranquillizers. [JELLY BEAN n.[3] (1)]

jellied eels *n.* [20C+] transport. [rhy. sl. = WHEELS n.[1]]

jellied out *adj.* [1930s] (*US campus*) dressed up. [JELLY BEAN n.[1] (4)]

jellies *n. see* JELLY n.[6].

jell (it) *v.* [1950s+] (*Aus.*) to act in a cowardly way. [JELL n.[1]]

jello *v. see* JELLY v. (3).

jello-brain *n.* (*also* **bag of jello, jello**) (*US campus*) **1** [1960s+] a foolish, scatterbrained person. **2** [1960s+] an older person. **3** [1980s+] a drug user. [someone whose brain is like jelly; *Jell-O*, the brandname of a gelatine dessert + SE sfx *-brain*; (3) also ref. to JELLY n.[6]/JELLY BEAN n.[3] (1)]

jello-brained *adj.* [1960s+] stupid, foolish (cf. AMOEBA-BRAINED adj.). [JELLO-BRAIN n. (1)]

jello squad *n.* [1970s+] (*US campus*) an imaginary gathering or club of all those students considered beyond the social pale of their peers on campus. [JELLO-BRAIN n. + SE *squad*]

jell out *v. see* JELL v.

jelly *n.*[1] **1** [17C+] semen (cf. BABY GRAVY n.). **2** [1920s+] (*US Black*) the penis or the vagina (cf. APPLE n.[6]). **3** [1920s+] (*US Black*) sexual intercourse. **4** [1940s] (*US Black*) male sexual prowess, sexuality. **5** [1940s] (*US Black*) a tough, virile man. [SE *jelly*; subseq. defs. f. (1)]

jelly *n.*[2] [late 19C+] a buxom, pretty young woman. [she 'wobbles']

jelly *n.*[3] [1930s–40s] (*US Black*) anything given free.

jelly *n.*[4] **1** [1930s+] (*orig. Aus.*) (*also* **gellie, gelly**) gelignite. **2** [1970s+] napalm. [(1) abbr./pron.; (2) form of chemical]

jelly *n.*[5] (*also* **gelly**) [1960s+] (*US*) a close friend, esp. a girlfriend or boyfriend. [abbr. of JELLY ROLL n.[1] (2)]

jelly *n.*[6] [1980s+] (*drugs*) temazepam; usu. in pl. as *jellies*. [the gel-like content of the capsules]

jelly *n.*[7] *see* JELLHEAD n.

jelly *v.* **1** [1930s–50s] (*US*) to dance. **2** [1940s] (*US*) to walk provocatively. **3** [1950s–60s] (*also* **jello**) to have sexual intercourse. **4** [1970s–80s] (*US gang*) to beat someone up.

jelly (around) *v. see* JELL v.

jelly ass *v.* [1930s–60s] (*US*) to dance. [JELLY v. (1) + ? the shaking of one's ASS n. (2)]

jelly baby *n.* [1920s+] secretions from the anus or vagina during or after intercourse. [JELLY n.[1]]

jelly bag *n.* [17C–19C] **1** the scrotum. **2** the vagina (cf. APPLE n.[6]; BAG n.[1]). [JELLY n.[1] (1) + BAG n.[1] (1)/SE *bag*]

jelly ball *n.* [1970s] (*US*) a weak-willed person. [SE *jelly*, which 'wobbles' + -BALL sfx]

jelly bean *n.*[1] **1** [1910s–60s] (*US*) a sweetheart. **2** [1910s+] (*US*) a foolish, inept, dishonest or effeminate person. **3** [1920s–30s] one who is devoted to pleasure rather than work, esp. used of a high-school student. **4** [1920s–30s] a fashionably dressed young man, a womanizer. **5** [1930s+] a pimp. **6** [1960s+] (*US Black*) a term of address.

jelly bean *n.*[2] [1960s] (*US gay*) a small penis.

jelly bean *n.*[3] **1** [1960s+] (*drugs*) any type of drug in pill form, e.g. a barbiturate, an amphetamine (cf. PILL n.[4]). **2** [1990s+] (*US campus*) a painkiller. [the drugs resemble sweets]

jelly bean *adj.* [1990s+] (*Aus.*) unpleasant, lying. [JELLY BEAN n.[1] (2)]

jelly beans *n.* [1990s+] **1** (*drugs*) crack cocaine (cf. BASE n.). **2** (*US campus*) painkillers. [JELLY BEAN n.[3]; although there is no actual similarity of crack cocaine to sweets]

jelly-bellied *adj.* **1** [late 19C+] fat. **2** [1930s+] (*Aus./US*) (*also* jelly-belly*) cowardly. [JELLY BELLY n.]

jelly belly *n.* **1** [mid-19C+] a fat person. **2** [1930s+] (*Aus./US*) a coward.

jelly box *n.* [1950s+] (*orig. US*) the vagina (cf. APPLE n.[6]; BAG n.[1]). [JELLY n.[1] (1) + SE *box*/BOX n.[1] (1)]

jelly-date *n.* (*also* **bean-date, cake-date, coke-date**) [1920s–40s] (*US campus*) **1** a date to take a girlfriend to the soda fountain or similar, where one sits and chats. **2** the person who is one's date in that situation. [the relevant SE food + DATE n.[1] (1); note JELL v.]

jelly-dog *n.* [late 19C] a harrier; thus *jelly-dogging*, hunting with a harrier. [the dog's use in hunting hares, which, when caught, killed and cooked, are served with redcurrant jelly]

jellyfish *n.* [20C+] a weak, ineffectual, cowardly person. [SE *jellyfish*, which has no backbone]

jellyfish *adj.* [1900s–10s] (*US*) common, ordinary.

jellyhead *n. see* GELLYHEAD n.

jelly jewellery *n.* [1990s+] ejaculated semen, covering the face and throat of one's partner. [JELLY n.[1] (1)]

jelly roll *n.*[1] (*orig. US Black*) **1** [20C+] sexual intercourse. **2** [1910s+] a lover, a spouse. **3** [1910s+] the female genitals. **4** [1970s+] a sanitary napkin. [? JELLY n.[1] (2)/(3), although this predates; ? SAmE *jelly roll*, a doughnut, which has a hole at its centre]

jelly roll *n.*[2] [1950s] (*US*) a male hairstyle, popular in the 1950s.

jelly roll *v.* [1920s+] (*orig. US Black*) to have sexual intercourse. [JELLY ROLL n.[1] (1)]

jelly roller *n.* [1920s–60s] (*US Black*) a womanizer, a seducer. [JELLY ROLL v.]

jelly sandwich *n.* [1970s+] (*US Black*) a sanitary towel. [JELLY n.[1] (2) + SE *sandwich*]

jelly snatchers *n.* [1970s] (*US Black*) the hands. [JELLY n.[1] (2) + SE *snatchers*]

jelly-tight *adj. see* JAM-UP AND JELLY-TIGHT phr.

jem *n.*[1] (*also* **jam**) [18C–1900s] (*UK Und.*) a jewel, a gold ring; thus *rum-jem*, a diamond ring. [SE *gem*]

jem *n.*[2] (*also* **jembo**) [1940s+] (*Irish*) a generic name for a Dubliner. [abbr. JEMMY n.[2] (1)]

jemima *n.*[1] **1** [late 19C] a servant girl. **2** [late 19C–1900s] a chamberpot. **3** [late 19C–1920s] a dressmaker's dummy. [generic use of proper name; the removal of (2) is one of the tasks of (1)]

jemima *n.*[2] [1950s+] (*gay*) the Black female genitals. [AUNT JEMIMA n., the stereotypical Black 'mammy']

jemima! *excl.* [mid-19C+] (*US*) a euph. for JESUS! excl.; used in a variety of mild oaths and in comparisons, e.g. *nice as Jemima*.

jemimas *n.* [1900s–30s] elastic-sided boots. [ety. unknown; ? a brandname or link to JEMMY adj.[1] (3)]

jeminess *n. see* JEMMY adj.[1].

jeminy! *excl. see* GEMINI! excl.

jeminy-o! *excl.* [mid-19C–1900s] a general excl., a euph. for JESUS! excl. (cf. BEJABERS! excl.).

jem mace *n.* (*also* **jim mace**) [20C+] face. [rhy. sl.; ult. the prize-fighter *Jem Mace* (1831–1910)]

jemmily *adv. see* JEMMY adj.[1].

jemmy *n.*[1] (*also* **jimmy**) **1** [early 17C] a fool (cf. BEN n.[1]). **2** [mid-18C–1910s] a sheep's head. **3** [mid-late 19C] a large human head. [ety. unknown; Bee suggests an actual butcher *Jemmy* Lincomb, who lived near Scotland Yard]

jemmy *n.*[2] **1** [mid-17C–early 19C] (*also* **jemmy fellow**) a dandy. **2** [mid-late 18C] a light cane, as carried by a dandy. **3** [mid-19C–1910s] a shooting coat, a great coat. [16C SE *gim*, smart, spruce and thus ? linked to Scot. *jimp*, slender]

jemmy *n.*[3] (*also* **jemmy rook, jenny, London jemmy, London jimmy**) **1** [late 17C+] (*UK Und.*) a house-breaker's short crowbar. **2** [mid-18C] a walking stick.

jemmy *adj.*[1] **1** [mid-late 18C] clever, 'sharp'. **2** [mid-18C–mid-

19C] dandified, e.g. a *jemmy fellow*, a smart, well-turned-out, dandified man; thus *jemminess*, neatness, smartness; *jemmily*, smartly. **3** [mid-19C] smart, of superior class. [JEMMY n.[2] (1)]

jemmy *adj.*[2] (*also* **jimmy**) [mid-19C–1900s] nonsensical, rubbishy.

jemmy *v.* [late 19C+] to break open with a crowbar. [JEMMY n.[3] (1)]

jemmy jessamy *n.* [mid-18C–mid-19C] a smart, well-turned-out fellow. [JEMMY adj.[1] (2) + JESSAMY n.]

jemmy jessamy *adj.* [mid-18C–mid-19C] smart, well turned-out. [JEMMY JESSAMY n.]

Jemmy O'Goblin *n.* (*also* **Jimmy O'Goblin**) [late 19C–1930s] (*orig. theatre*) a sovereign; in pl., money (cf. BEES (AND HONEY) n.). [rhy. sl.]

jemmy rook *n. see* JEMMY n.[3].

jemson *n.* (*also* **jimmison**) [1930s–50s] (*US, Ozarks*) the penis. [? SE *jimsonweed*, i.e. the penis also grows]

jeng-jeng *n.* [20C+] (*W.I., Jam.*) **1** anything considered worthless, a useless collection of bits and bobs. **2** of things or of personal appearance, a general state of confusion. [? Carib.E. *jege*, rags, tatters + Ngombe *jengé*, disorder]

jeng-jeng *adj.* [20C+] (*W.I., Jam./Bel.*) disreputable, unpleasant. [JENG-JENG n.]

jenny *n.*[1] [late 18C+] a donkey. [post-18C uses are US]

jenny *n.*[2] [late 19C–1920s] a hot-water bottle. [? abbr. SE, it *gen*erates warmth; note TV/film jargon *jenny*, a generator]

jenny *n.*[3] **1** [late 19C–1950s] (*US*) a young woman. **2** [1990s+] the vagina. [dial. *jenny*, a country girl]

jenny *n.*[4] (*also* **jenny-ass, jinny, jinny-ass, jinny-wing**) [1930s+] (*Irish/US Black*) an effeminate man; also as adj. [the female name]

jenny *n.*[5] *see* JEMMY n.[3].

jenny *v.*[1] [late 19C–1900s] (*UK Und.*) to understand. [ety. unknown; ? link to JERRY v.[1] (2)]

jenny *v.*[2] (*also* **jinny**) [20C+] of a woman, to nag, to henpeck. [SE *jenny*, used as a pfx denoting the female sex]

jenny-ass *n. see* JENNY n.[4].

jenny darby *n.* [mid-19C] a policeman (cf. BILLY n.[6]). [Fr. *gendarmes* + ref. to DARBIES n. (1)]

jenny hill *n.* [late 19C] a pill; usu. in pl. [rhy. sl.; ult. UK music-hall star *Jenny Hill* (1851–96)]

jenny lee *n.* (*also* **jenny lea**) **1** [late 19C+] a flea. **2** [1930s–60s] a key. **3** [1930s+] tea. [rhy. sl.; (2) and (3) ult. Baroness *Lee* of Asheridge (1904–88), Scottish Labour politician]

Jenny Lind *n.* [20C+] wind, either in the context of weather or the human stomach; thus *Jenny Lindy*, windy. [rhy. sl.; ult. Swedish singer *Jenny Lind* (1820–87)]

Jenny Linda *n.* (*also* **jenny linder**) [mid-late 19C] a window. [rhy. sl.; for ety. *see* JENNY LIND n.]

jenny off *v.* [1990s+] of a woman, to masturbate (cf. APPLY LIP GLOSS v.; BALL OFF v.[2]). [female version of JACK OFF v.[1]]

jenny riddle *n. see* JIMMY RIDDLE n.

jenny wine *n.* [20C+] (*Irish*) a non-drinker, a teetotaller. [? JENNY n.[4]]

jenny wren *n.* [20C+] *Ben* Truman beer. [rhy. sl.]

jentoe *n. see* GENTOO n.

jere *n.*[1] (*also* **gere, jeer**) [mid-16C–17C] (*UK Und.*) a piece of human excrement. [Rom. *jeer*, excrement]

jere *n.*[2] (*also* **jeer**) [20C+] a homosexual. [? rhy. sl. = QUEER n. (4)]

jeremiah *n.* [1930s+] a fire. [rhy. sl.]

jeremiah *v.* [late 19C–1930s] to complain. [proper name *Jeremiah*, the biblical prophet]

jeremiah-mongering *n.* [late 19C–1900s] (*UK society*) needless pessimism. [JEREMIAH v. + -MONGER sfx; coined to describe those who proclaimed that after the fall of Khartoum in 1885 all was over for the Empire and thus Britain]

Jeremy Beadle *n.* [1990s+] irritation, annoyance. [rhy. sl. = NEEDLE n.[3]; ult. UK TV entertainer *Jeremy Beadle* (b.1948)]

jeremy diddler *n. see* DIDDLER *n.*[2].

jericho *n.* **1** [mid-17C–1920s] a place of retirement, banishment or concealment, a far-distant place; esp. in phr. *let someone go to jericho*. **2** [mid-18C–19C] a privy, an outside lavatory. [anecdote in 2 Sam. 10:5 when David ordered his servants to stay in that city until their beards were grown]

jerk *n.*[1] [1930s+] **1** (*US*) a male masturbator. **2** (*orig. US*) a general term of abuse, a fool, an idiot, a failure. [JERK OFF *v.*[1]; (1) may be earlier]

jerk *n.*[2] (*US*) **1** [1940s+] a soda-fountain clerk. **2** [1960s+] an ice-cream soda. [abbr. SAmE *soda jerk*; (2) f. (1)]

jerk *n.*[3] *see* JERKWATER TOWN *n.*

jerk *adj.*[1] [late 19C–1940s] (*US*) small-time, second-rate, mediocre; of a railroad, secondary. [abbr. of JERKWATER *adj.*; as in SAmE *jerk line*, branch railroad]

jerk *adj.*[2] [1930s+] foolish, stupid. [JERK *n.*[1] (2)]

jerk *v.*[1] [17C–18C] (*UK Und.*) to counterfeit.

jerk *v.*[2] **1** [mid-17C–mid-19C] to accost; to beat. **2** [late 17C–18C; 1970s] to copulate. **3** [late 18C–19C] to write; to utter. **4** [20C+] (*US*) to dismiss, to disqualify, to withdraw. **5** [1980s+] (*US*) to cheat, to mistreat. **6** [1980s+] (*US campus*) (*also* **jerk over**) of a person, to mess around, to annoy deliberately, to harass; of a situation, to make a mess, to interfere with.

jerk *v.*[3] (*US*) **1** [mid-19C] to take, to snatch. **2** [mid-19C+] to draw a gun or weapon. **3** [late 19C+] to draw beer, soda etc from a tap.

jerk *v.*[4] [late 19C+] to masturbate (cf. BOFF *v.*; JERK ONE'S GHERKIN *v.*; JERK ONE'S JELLY *v.*; JERK ONE'S JOYSTICK *v.*; JERK SOMEONE'S JOINT *v.*). [abbr. JERK OFF *v.*[1]]

jerk across the Jordan *v.* [1910s] (*Aus.*) to be executed by hanging (cf. JERK TO JESUS *v.*). [SE *jerk* + River Jordan, fig. used as a place that had to be crossed in death]

jerk a gybe *v.* [mid-17C–mid-18C] (*UK Und.*) to forge a licence. [JERK *v.*[1] + GYBE *n.*]

jerk a knot *v.* [1940s+] (*US*) to hit or punch someone. [SE *knot*, a lump or bruise]

jerk around *v.* [1960s+] (*US campus*) to waste time, to fool around. [JERK SOMEONE AROUND *v.*]

jerk-ass *n.* [1960s+] (*US*) a contemptible idiot (cf. ASSHEAD *n.*). [JERK *n.*[1] (2) + -ASS sfx]

jerk bald-headed *v.* (*also* **snatch bald**, **snatch bald-headed**) [mid-19C–1970s] (*US*) **1** to treat roughly, to manhandle. **2** in fig. use, to overwhelm emotionally. [the idea of being hanged]

jerke *n. see* JARK *n.* (1).

jerked *adj.* (*also* **jerked off/up**) [1950s+] (*US*) exceedingly stupid. [JERK *n.*[1] (2)/JERK-OFF *adj.* (2)]

jerker *n.*[1] (*US*) **1** [late 19C+] (*also* **soda-juggler**) a soda-fountain clerk; usu. as *soda-jerker*. **2** [1930s] a drinker; often as BEER-JERKER *n.*[1]. **3** [1950s+] a bartender; in combs. such as *whiskey-jerker* or BEER-JERKER *n.*[2]. [JERK *v.*[3] (3)]

jerker *n.*[2] **1** [1940s+] a masturbator, esp. one who frequents striptease shows or similar. **2** [1990s+] (*US Black*) in fig. use, one who talks nonsense. [JERK OFF *v.*[1]]

jerkface *n.* [1970s+] (*US campus*) a foolish, dull person. [JERK *n.*[1] (2) + SE sfx -*face*]

jerkhead *n.* [1950s+] (*US*) a stupid, contemptible person. [JERK *n.*[1] (2) + -HEAD sfx (1)]

jerking *n.*[1] [late 19C+] masturbation. [JERK *v.*[4]]

jerking *n.*[2] [2000s] (*UK prison*) a thrusting attack with a sharp object by one prisoner at another. [SE *jerk*]

jerk-nod *n. see* YEKNOD *n.*

jerko *n.* [1940s+] (*US*) a stupid, contemptible person. [JERK *n.*[1] (2) + -o sfx (1)]

jerk-off *n.* (*US*) **1** [1920s+] an act of masturbation. **2** [1930s+] a useless, despised person, a lazy incompetent. **3** [1970s+] a fraud, a pretence. [JERK OFF *v.*[1]]

jerk-off *adj.* [1930s+] (*US*) **1** pertaining to masturbation. **2** stupid, worthless, despicable. [JERK OFF *v.*[1]]

jerk off *v.*[1] **1** [mid-19C+] to masturbate (cf. BALL OFF *v.*[2]; JERK SOMEONE OFF *v.*). **2** [1960s+] (*orig. US*) in fig. use, to waste time or energy, to work at a pointless task, to mess around. **3** [1960s] (*US*) to get out, to go away, often in imper.

jerk off *v.*[2] [late 19C] (*Aus.*) to do quickly and perfunctorily, esp. in the context of writing. [var. on KNOCK OFF *v.*[4] (1)]

jerk off *v.*[3] [1950s+] (*US drugs*) to inject a drug, pumping the blood/heroin/water mixture in and out of the vein. [fig. use of JERK OFF *v.*[1] (1)]

jerk one's bird *v. see* BIRD *n.*[8] (1).

jerk one's gherkin *v.* [1930s+] to masturbate (cf. BEAT ONE'S MEAT *v.*). [JERK *v.*[4] + GHERKIN *n.* + assonance]

jerk one's jaw(s) *v. see* JACK ONE'S JAW(S) *v.*

jerk one's jelly *v.* (*also* **jerk one's juice**) [20C+] to masturbate (cf. BEAT ONE'S MEAT *v.*). [JERK *v.*[4] + JELLY *n.*[1] (1)/JUICE *n.*[2] (1)]

jerk one's joystick *v.* (*also* **jerk one's joystick, ...mutton, ...rod, ...rope, ...turk, ...turkey**) [20C+] to masturbate. [JERK *v.*[4] + JOYSTICK *n.*[1]/MUTTON *n.*[3]/ROD *n.*[1] (1)/SE *rope*/TURKEY NECK *n.*]

jerk over *v. see* JERK *v.*[2] (6).

jerks *n.*[1] **1** [19C] a hangover. **2** [late 19C; 1940s] (*US*) delirium tremens, acute anxiety or religious fervour.

jerks *n.*[2] [20C+] (*Aus.*) the pieces of cork that are suspended from a hat to distract flies. [abbr. FLY JERKS *n.*]

jerks, the *n.* [1900s] (*US*) the physical writhings that are evinced by one who is supposedly possessed of the Holy Spirit.

jerk-silly *adj.* (*also* **jerk-simple**) [1930s+] (*US*) mentally unbalanced, supposedly from chronic masturbation. [JERK *v.*[4]]

jerk someone around *v.* [1930s+] (*US*) to treat badly, to tease, to mess someone about (cf. JERK AROUND *v.*). [JERK OFF *v.*[1] (1)]

jerk someone off *v.* **1** [1920s+] to masturbate a partner (cf. JERK OFF *v.*[1]). **2** [1960s+] (*US*) to tease someone, to treat someone badly, to infuriate, to interfere maliciously with someone or something.

jerk someone's chain *v.* [1960s+] to annoy, to distract forcefully, to taunt. [SE *jerk*, as an owner drags on a dog's lead to control it]

jerk someone's joint *v.* [1990s+] to masturbate someone else, e.g. of a prostitute and her client. [JERK *v.*[4] + JOINT *n.*[1]]

jerk the cat *v.* [early 17C] to vomit. [var. on WHIP THE CAT *v.*[2] (2)]

jerk the tinkler *v.* [mid-19C] to ring a bell. [SE *jerk* + TINKLER *n.*[2]]

jerk to Jesus *v.* [late 19C–1930s] (*US*) to execute by hanging (cf. JERK ACROSS THE JORDAN *v.*).

jerk town *n.* [late 19C–1950s] (*US*) a small provincial or rural town. [abbr. JERKWATER TOWN *n.*]

jerk up *v.* (*US*) **1** [mid-19C–1940s] to arrest. **2** [20C+] to reprimand. **3** [1990s+] to impose upon, to mess someone around. [fig. uses of SE; but note JERK SOMEONE OFF *v.* (2)]

jerkwad *n.* [1990s+] (*US*) a masturbator, a general term of abuse. [JERK *v.*[4] + -WAD sfx]

jerkwater *n.* [1950s+] (*US*) a fool, an idiot. [JERKWATER *adj.* (2)]

jerkwater *adj.* **1** [late 19C+] (*US*) small-time, second-rate, mediocre. **2** [1950s+] (*US*) stupid, foolish. [railroad use, as *jerkwater railroad*, a small remote rural location where trains didn't stop except to pick up water. These places had a trackside water tower and a trough from which a train could scoop or *jerk water* from between the tracks without actually stopping. An alternative ety., based on earlier railroad practice, suggests that the crew had actually to leave the train and *jerk* the *water* in buckets from local wells, then run with it to the waiting locomotive. A further suggestion cites buckets that were attached to the locomotive by a leather strap and that were used to *jerk* the *water* from streams running alongside the track]

jerkwater town *n.* (*also* **jerk**, **jerkwater**) [20C+] (*US*) a small, insignificant town. [JERKWATER *adj.* (1)]

jerkweed *n.* [1990s+] (*US*) a stupid, contemptible person. [JERK *n.*[1] (2) + DICKWEED *n.* (1)]

jerky *adj.* [1930s+] (*US*) silly, idiotic. [JERK n.¹ (2)]

jerm *n. see* GERM n.

jeroboam *n.* [mid–late 19C] a chamberpot. [SE *jeroboam*, an outsize winebottle, containing the equivalent of 12 75cl bottles]

jerrawicke *n.* [mid-19C] (*Aus.*) Australian-brewed beer. [? dial. *jerry beer*, second-rate beer]

jerri *n. see* JERRY n.⁶.

jerried *adj.* **1** [late 19C+] in fig. non-building use, botched. **2** [1920s] injured. [JERRY n.⁸]

Jerry *n.* (*also* **Gerry**) [1910s+] a derog. name for a German. [abbr.; Brophy & Partridge, *Songs and Slang of the British Soldier* (1930), suggest this was the preferred WW1 term subseq. to 1915]

Jerry *adj.* [1910s+] German. [JERRY n.]

jerry *n.¹* [19C] (*UK Und.*) a fog, a mist. [ety. unknown]

jerry *n.²* [mid-19C] (*US*) a spree. [JERRY n.⁴]

jerry *n.³* [mid-19C] a pessimist, a complainer. [SE *Jeremiah*]

jerry *n.⁴* [mid–late 19C] a cheap tavern. [abbr. TOM AND JERRY (SHOP) n.]

jerry *n.⁵* [mid–late-19C] a round felt hat. [abbr. SE *jerry hat*]

jerry *n.⁶* (*also* **jerri**) **1** [mid-19C+] a chamberpot. **2** [1980s] a lavatory. [abbr. SE *jeroboam*, a double magnum of wine]

jerry *n.⁷* [late 19C–1930s] (*UK Und.*) a watch; thus *jerry-getting*, *jerry-nicking*, *jerry-stealing*, stealing watches. [? link to JERRY n.⁵/JERRY n.⁶, they are all round]

jerry *n.⁸* [late 19C+] a second-rate builder who erects badly built houses with inferior materials; usu. in phr. *jerry built*. [abbr. SE *jerry builder*, itself ? a Merseyside building firm]

jerry *n.⁹* [1920s] the penis (cf. ABRAHAM n.¹).

jerry, the *n.* [1910s] (*UK Und.*) the police.

jerry *adj.* **1** [20C+] (*orig. US*) (*also* **jerry to**) aware, knowledgeable; often as *get jerry (on/to)*, to understand. **2** [1900s–30s] (*US*) good, fine. **3** [1980s] (*Aus.*) (*also* **jerry to**) interested in. [JERRY v.¹ (2)]

jerry *v.¹* **1** [mid–late 19C] to tease, to chaff, to sneer at. **2** [late 19C+] (*also* **gerry**) to understand, to work out, to recognize, to discern. [? abbr. JERRYCUMUMBLE v. (2)]

jerry *v.² see* JERRYCUMUMBLE v.

jerry built *adj. see* JERRY n.⁸.

jerry-come-tumble *n.* [mid–late 19C] a lavatory. [JERRY n.⁶ (1) + JERRY-GO-NIMBLE n.]

jerrycumumble *v.* (*also* **jerry, jerrymumble**) **1** [early 18C–19C] to shake about, to tumble. **2** [20C+] to understand, to work out. [? rhy. sl.; (1) = SE *tumble*; (2) = TUMBLE v.²/RUMBLE v.² (1)]

jerry-diddle *n.¹* [20C+] a violin. [rhy. sl. = SE *fiddle*]

jerry-diddle *n.²* [20C+] (*Aus.*) a drink 'on the house'. [? rhy. sl. = FIDDLE v.² (2); the implication that the publican is 'fiddling' himself out of a profit]

jerry-getting *n. see* JERRY n.⁷.

jerry-go-nimble *n.* [mid–late 19C] diarrhoea (cf. APPLE-BLOSSOM TWO-STEP n.). [JERRY n.⁶ (1) + SE *go nimble*; + pun on SE *trot*/TROTS, THE n.²]

jerry lynch *n.* [mid-19C–1900s] a poor-quality pickled pig's head. [? anecdotal]

Jerry McNabs *n.* [1930s] (*US*) bugs. [rhy. sl. = CRAB n.²]

jerrymumble *v. see* JERRYCUMUMBLE v.

jerry-nicking *n. see* JERRY n.⁷.

Jerry O'Gorman *n.* [20C+] a Mormon. [rhy. sl.]

jerry randle *n. see* JACK RANDALL n.

jerry riddle *n. see* JIMMY RIDDLE n.

jerry rumble *v.* [1900s] (*N.Z.*) to discover, to understand. [JERRY adj. (1) + RUMBLE v.² (1); ? rhy. sl. = TUMBLE v.²]

jerry shop *n.* [early–late 19C] **1** a cheap tavern. **2** a pawnbroker's shop. [for ety. *see* TOM AND JERRY (SHOP) n.]

jerry sneak *n.¹* [late 18C–19C] a hen-pecked husband; thus *jerry-sneakery*, henpecking. [*Jerry Sneak*, a character in *The Mayor of Garratt* (1764) by Samuel Foote, who is dominated by his wife]

jerry sneak *n.²* [19C] a thief who specializes in stealing watches. [JERRY n.⁷ + SNEAK n.¹ (2)]

jerry sneak *adj.* [early 19C] underhand, deceitful. [JERRY SNEAK n.²]

jerry-stealing *n. see* JERRY n.⁷.

jerry to *adj. see* JERRY adj.

jerry wag *n.* [early–mid-19C] a tipsy individual, out on a spree; thus *jerry-wag shop*, a coffee stall, much frequented by such people. [JERRY n.² + SE *wag*]

Jersey *n.* [1940s] (*US*) milk.

jersey *n.* [late 19C–1940s] (*Aus.*) a red-headed person. [Cheshire dial. *jersey*, 'a contemptuous term for a head of hair' (*EDD*)]

Jersey (City) *n.* [1930s–70s] (*US*) a female breast; often in pl. *jerseys* (cf. BRACE AND BITS n.). [rhy. sl. = TITTY n.¹ (1)]

Jersey eagle *n.* (*also* **Jersey bird**) [1900s–30s] (*US*) a mosquito. [the abundance of mosquitoes in New Jersey]

Jersey highball *n.* [1940s] (*US Black*) cow's milk. [SE *Jersey (cow)* + HIGHBALL n.¹]

Jersey lightning *n.* [mid-19C–1960s] (*US*) a strong kind of applejack, peach brandy or illicitly distilled whisky. [made in New Jersey]

jerseys *n. see* JERSEY (CITY) n.

Jersey side *n.* [1940s] (*US Black*) the wrong side, the inferior type etc. [the position of New *Jersey*, the 'wrong' side of the Hudson River from Manhattan]

Jersey side of the snatch play *phr.* [1940s] (*US Black*) over 38 years old. [JERSEY SIDE n. + SNATCH n.¹ (3) + SE *play*; lit. on the wrong side of one's sexual peak]

Jerusalem *n.* [19C] a donkey (cf. JERUSALEM PONY n.). [Egan, *Real Life in Ireland* (1821), footnote p.91: 'Donkeys and their riders are so called in honour to a late entry into Jerusalem by some female crusaders against common decency']

Jerusalem *adj.* [mid-19C–1920s] a euph. for DAMNED adj.

Jerusalem! *excl.* [mid-19C+] used in a variety of mild oaths; a euph. for JESUS! excl.

Jerusalem artichoke *n.* [late 19C–1930s] a donkey. [rhy. sl. = MOKE n.¹ (1)]

Jerusalem artichokes! *excl.* [1940s] a euph. for JESUS (CHRIST)! excl.

Jerusalem-by-the-sea *n. see* JERUSALEM THE GOLDEN n.

Jerusalem cuckoo *n.* **1** [1910s–40s] a mule. **2** [1920s] (*Irish*) a Jew. [its 'hee-haw' bray is presumably reminiscent of the cuckoo's 'cuc-oo']

Jerusalem Ford *n.* [1930s] (*US*) a mule or donkey. [JERUSALEM n. + *Ford*, the brand of car]

Jerusalem parrot *n.* [20C+] a flea.

Jerusalem pony *n.* [19C+] a donkey (cf. JERUSALEM n.). [according to the Bible, Christ rode into Jerusalem on a donkey]

Jerusalem screw *n.* [1920s+] (*Aus.*) an extremely harsh prison warder. [SCREW n.² (3); WW1, when the Aus. military police based in Jerusalem were taught by the British Army the best methods of breaking even the most recalcitrant prisoners]

Jerusalem slim *n.* [1920s–70s] (*US tramps*) Jesus Christ. [proper name *Jerusalem* + nickname *slim*]

Jerusalem the Golden *n.* (*also* **Jerusalem-by-the-sea**) [late 19C+] Brighton. [the large number of Jews who retire to Brighton and other towns along Britain's south coast]

jerve *n.* (*also* **jerv**) **1** [mid-19C–1950s] (*US Und.*) a waistcoat or waistcoat watch pocket; thus *jerver*, a pickpocket. **2** [1910s] (*US Und.*) in a pickpocket team, the one who actually does the stealing. [abbr. JERVIS n.]

jervis/jervy *n. see* JARVEY n.

jessamy *n.* (*also* **jessimy**) [late 17C–mid-19C] a fop or dandy. [SE *jessamine*, jasmine. Lit. a man who scents himself with perfume or who wears a sprig of jessamine in his buttonhole; the implication is of effeminacy as well as dandyism. The term forms part of an ascending scale of fashionableness, notably the 'Greenhorn, Jemmy, Jessamy, Smart, Honest Fellow, Joyous Spirit, Buck, and Blood', cited as such by the editor and essayist John Hawkesworth (1715–73) in his journal *The Adventurer* (1753)]

jesse *n.* (*also* **jessie**) [1910s–30s] (*US Und.*) a bluff or threat. [? US outlaw *Jesse James* (1847–82); note also GIVE (SOMEONE) JESSE v.]

Jesse James *n.* [1960s] a dangerous, hardened criminal. [US outlaw *Jesse James* (1847–82)]

Jesse James killer *n.* [1940s] (*US Black*) any heavy, sticky hair pomade, usu. with a distinctive smell. [? Robert Ford, killer of the outlaw *Jesse James* (1847–82), was a former member of his gang; thus a traitor and a 'slimy' figure]

jessie *n.*[1] (*also* **jessie-boy**) **1** [1920s+] a male homosexual (cf. ABIGAIL n.). **2** [1930s+] a weakling, an ineffectual person; thus *woman-jessie*, a weak man who physically abuses women. [use of generic female name]

jessie *n.*[2] [1940s] (*US Black*) a red-haired girl or woman. [JERSEY n.]

jessie *n.*[3] *see* JESSE n.

jessie-boy *n. see* JESSIE n.[1].

jessimy *n. see* JESSAMY n.

jesta *n. see* DIGESTER n.

jester *v.* [1970s] (*W.I.*) to play the fool (cf. ACT THE ANGORA v.). [SE court *jester*]

Jesuit *n.* [mid-17C–early 19C] a male homosexual; thus *the Jesuits' fraternity*, the world of homosexuality; *Jesuit box*, to masturbate. [the contemporary suspicion of Jesuits, who were thus branded with a suitably derog. image]

Jesus, the *n. see* BEJAZUS, THE n.

Jesus *adj.* (*also* **Jesus Christ**) [1920s+] (*US/W.I.*) a general intensifier, e.g. *not one Jesus shilling*, not one DAMNED adj./cursed shilling.

Jesus! *excl. see* JESUS (CHRIST)! excl.

Jesus boots *n.* (*also* **Jesus gliders**, **...shoes**, **...slippers**, **...weejuns**) [1940s+] (*orig. US*) footwear, orig. boots, now usu. sandals. [Christ is trad. portrayed as wearing sandals]

Jesus Christ *adj. see* JESUS adj.

Jesus (Christ)! *excl.* (*also* **by Jesus! Christ Jesus! Jazus!**) [late 14C+] a general and blasphemous oath (cf. CHRIST! excl.).

Jesus Christ on a raft! *excl.* (*also* **Jesus Christ on a bicycle! ...crutch! ...pogo stick!**) [1940s+] a mild excl. (cf. CHRIST ON A BIKE! excl.).

Jesus freak *n.* [1960s+] (*orig. US*) a fervent or evangelical Christian; usu. used contemptuously. [*Jesus (Christ)* + FREAK sfx]

Jesus guy *n. see* MISSION STIFF n. (3).

Jesus H Christ! *excl.* (*also* **Jesus H! Jesus X Christ!**) [late 19C+] a mild oath. [JESUS (CHRIST)! excl.; the H is redundant other than for rhythm, although *DARE* suggests a link to *IHS*, the monogram for Jesus; note Michael Quinion, *World Wide Words* (Internet, 5 August 2000): 'There have been various theories, but the one that seems most plausible is that it comes from the Greek monogram for Jesus, 'IHS' or 'IHC'. This is formed from the first two letters plus the last letter of His name in Greek (the letters iota, eta, and sigma; in the second instance, the C is a Byzantine Greek form of sigma). The H is actually the capital letter form of eta, but churchgoers who were unfamiliar with Greek took it to be a Latin H']

jesusly *adj.* [19C] (*US*) a general intensifier. [JESUS adj.]

Jesus, Mary and Joseph! *excl.* [20C+] a mild oath; an excl. of surprise.

Jesus screamer *n.* [1950s+] (*US*) a street preacher.

Jesus shit! *excl.* [1970s+] an excl. of exasperation or astonishment. [JESUS (CHRIST)! excl. + SHIT! excl.]

Jesus shoes/slippers *n. see* JESUS BOOTS n.

Jesus stiff *n.* [1920s–50s] **1** (*US Und.*) a religious tramp. **2** (*US prison*) a prisoner who adopts religious beliefs while serving a sentence. [*Jesus (Christ)* + STIFF n.[2] (4)]

Jesus tonight! *excl.* [20C+] (*Irish*) a general excl., a euph. for JESUS (CHRIST)! excl.

Jesus weejuns *n. see* JESUS BOOTS n.

Jesus wept! *excl.* [1920s+] a general and blasphemous oath.

Jesus X Christ! *excl. see* JESUS H CHRIST! excl.

jet *n.*[1] [early 18C–19C] a lawyer. [the *jet* black gown]

jet *n.*[2] [1980s+] (*drugs*) ketamine. [its effect on the mental process]

jet *v.* [1950s+] (*US Black/campus/teen*) **1** to leave in a hurry, to move very fast. **2** to excite someone. [SE *jet*, to travel by jet aircraft; note 16C–17C SE *jet*, to move along jauntily, to caper]

jet one's juice *v.* [late 19C–1970s] of a man, to achieve orgasm (cf. BLOSH v.). [SE *jet* + JUICE n.[2] (1)]

jeune siècle *n.* [late 19C–1900s] (*UK society*) those who are considered *fin de siècle*, i.e. advanced, modern or decadent in their behaviour. [Fr. *jeune siècle*, 'young century']

Jew *n.* **1** [17C+] a mean person, a skinflint. **2** [1900s] (*Aus.*) a bookmaker. **3** [1940s–50s] (*US Black*) the boss, irrespective of their actual religion. **4** [1950s+] (*W.I.*) any rich person, presumably White but with no religious overtones, other than the worldwide derog. stereotype.

Jew *adj.* (*also* **Jewish**) [17C+] in sl., reflecting centuries of Christian teaching, the Jew is grasping, avaricious, wealthy, untrustworthy, deceitful and mean (as well as circumcised and abstaining from pork). Thus virtually all combs. below with *Jew/Jewish* are derog. and play on these stereotypes.

jew *v. see* JEW (DOWN) v.

Jew baby *n.* [1910s–50s] a derog. term for a Jew (cf. ARAB n.[2]).

Jew bagel *n. see* BAGEL n.[1] (1).

Jew bail *n.* (*also* **Jew's bail**) [late 18C–19C] insufficient bail. [the belief that while Jews will offer bail in any situation, they will not be there to pay it if the criminal absconds]

Jew boy *n.* **1** [late 18C–19C] a young Jewish man. **2** [20C+] a derog. term for a male Jew, irrespective of age (cf. ARAB n.[2]). [the term was not initally derog. (although note the US use of *boy* to address Blacks)]

Jew buggy *n. see* JEW CANOE n.

Jewburg *n.* [1900s–50s] (*S.Afr.*) Johannesburg; thus *Jewburger/ Jewburgher*, a rich Johannesburg merchant. [the city's large Jewish population + a pun on the usual nickname, *Jo'burg*]

Jew butter *n.* [late 19C] (*US*) goose or chicken dripping. [the popularity among Jews of *schmaltz*, fat, as a spread]

Jew canoe *n.* (*also* **Jew buggy, Jewish submarine**) **1** [1970s+] (*US*) a Cadillac. **2** [1980s+] (*UK society*) a Jaguar. [SE *Jew* + CANOE n.[2]]

Jew cheque *n.* [1980s+] (*US*) any form of cheque that is obtained through fraud, e.g. on Social Security. [the stereotyping of Jews as devious money-makers]

Jew chum *n.* **1** [1930s–50s] (*Aus.*) a Jewish refugee from Germany or central Europe. **2** [1940s–50s] (*US*) a tramp. [(1) pun on NEW CHUM n.; (2) rhy. sl. = BUM n.[3] (1)]

jew (down) *v.* (*also* **jew out/up**) [early 19C+] to cheat financially; also to haggle. [racial stereotyping; the cheater need not be Jewish]

jewel *n.* (*also* **jewel case, jewels**) **1** [late 15C+] the male genitals. **2** [mid-16C–19C] (*also* **jewelery**) the vagina. **3** [late 18C–1950s] (*US/US Irish*) a fellow, a man, often as a term of address.

jewel *adj.* [2000s] (*US Black*) excellent, first-rate.

jewel box *n.* **1** [1960s] the vagina (cf. BAG n.[1]). **2** [1970s] (*US gay*) the scrotum. [JEWEL n.]

jewel case *n. see* JEWEL n.

jewelery *n. see* JEWEL n. (2).

jeweller *n.* [1990s+] one who ejaculates, esp. on the face of their partner. [someone who makes a PEARL NECKLACE n.]

jewellery *n.* [late 19C–1940s] (*US prison*) handcuffs, shackles, chains.

jewelry *n. see* FAMILY JEWELS n. (1).

jewels *n. see* JEWEL n.

Jewey *n. see* JEWY n.

Jew-fencer *n.* [mid-19C] a Jewish street-seller. [SE *Jew* + -FENCER sfx]

Jew flag *n. see* JEWISH FLAG n.

Jew food *n.* [20C+] ham. [in mockery of the Jewish dietary prohibition on all pork products]

Jewhannesburg *n.* [1900s] (*Aus.*) Johannesburg, South Africa. [its large Jewish population]

Jewie *n. see* JEWY n.

jewie louie *n. see* JEWY LOUIS n.

Jewish *adj. see* JEW adj.

jewish *n.* [1960s+] (*S.Afr. Black*) smart, expensive clothing. [racial stereotyping of the invariably rich Jew]

jewish *adj.*[1] [1940s] (*US*) odd, abnormal.

jewish *adj.*[2] [1960s+] (*S.Afr. Black*) of clothes or other material objects, smart, expensive, chic. [JEWISH n.]

jewish *v.* [1960s+] (*S.Afr. Black*) to dress someone up in smart clothes. [JEWISH n.]

Jewish airlines *n.* [1960s+] (*gay*) walking. [Jews are too mean to pay airfares]

Jewish Alps *n.* (*US*) **1** [20C+] Washington Heights, New York City, home of many successful Jews. **2** [1960s+] the Catskill Mountain resort area, patronized by Jewish New Yorkers.

Jewish-American princess *n. see* JEWISH PRINCESS n.

Jewish bonfire *n. see* JEWISH LIGHTNING n.

Jewish by hospitalization *phr.* [1950s+] (*gay*) circumcised but not Jewish.

Jewish champagne *n.* [1930s] (*US*) celery tonic.

Jewish compliment *n. see* JEW'S COMPLIMENT n.

Jewish corned beef *n.* [1960s+] a circumcised penis (cf. BACON n.[1]; CLIPDICK n.). [BEEF n.[1] (1)]

Jewish fire sale *n. see* JEWISH LIGHTNING n.

Jewish flag *n.* (*also* Jew flag) [1910s+] (*US*) a currency note. [the avaricious Jew has no nation, only money; the same image as the Communist derog. phr. 'rootless cosmopolitans']

Jewish foreplay *n.* [1950s+] (*US*) a situation where the man pleads for sex, his partner refuses all physical contact. [the supposed frigidity of the JEWISH PRINCESS n.]

Jewish forest *n.* [20C+] in poker, 3 threes. ['mittel-European' pron. 't'ree t'rees']

Jewish joanna *n.* (*also* Jew joanna) **1** [20C+] a taximeter. **2** [1960s+] a cash register. [SE *Jewish* + JOANNA n. = JEWISH PIANO n.]

Jewish lightning *n.* (*also* Greek lightning, Jewish bonfire, Jewish fire sale) [20C+] deliberate arson in order to gain the insurance on an otherwise unprofitable business.

Jewish muscles *n.* [1940s] shoulder pads.

Jewish national *n.* [1950s+] (*US gay*) a circumcised penis (cf. CLIPDICK n.). [the ref. is to the *Hebrew National* brand of kosher salami]

Jewish nightcap *n.* [late 19C–1950s] a foreskin.

Jewish overdrive *n.* (*also* Portagee overdrive) [20C+] (*US*) freewheeling down hills to save petrol. [the stereotyped meanness of Jews or poverty of Port. immigrants]

Jewish Oxo *n.* [1960s+] money. [*Oxo*, the brandname of a beef extract. Like the kitchen stand-by, money makes 'gravy']

Jewish penicillin *n.* [1960s+] (*US*) chicken soup. [despite its essentially humorous content, the term has some medical reality, as the effect of hot soup on the mucous membranes is to make them work harder and thus help clear the nose of the blocking that comes with a cold]

Jewish piano *n.* (*also* Jewish pianola) **1** [20C+] a taximeter. **2** [1930s+] a cash register. [racial stereotyping]

Jewish prince *n.* [1980s+] (*US*) a (middle-class) Jewish man who is spoiled or dominated by his mother (cf. ARAB n.[2]).

Jewish princess *n.* (*also* Jewish-American princess) [1970s+] (*US*) a young, conceited (middle-class) Jewish woman (cf. ARAB n.[2]).

Jewish renaissance *n.* [1950s+] (*gay*) over-elaborate furniture in doubtful taste.

Jewish screwdriver *n.* (*also* Yiddish screwdriver) [20C+] a hammer. [the supposed inability of stereotypically cerebral/ entrepreneurial Jews to perform manual tasks]

Jewish sidewalls *n.* [1950s–60s] (*US*) white rubber sidewalls, glued onto otherwise black tyres in an attempt to make them look more fashionable. [stereotyped Jewish meanness]

Jewish (standard) time *n.* (*also* j.s.t.) [1930s+] (*US*) unpunctuality; derog. only if used by a non-Jew (cf. AFRICAN (PEOPLE'S) TIME n.). [the supposed propensity of Jews to arrive late for any meeting or appointment]

Jewish submarine *n. see* JEW CANOE n.

Jewish waltz *n.* [1980s+] (*US*) deal-making, haggling. [racial stereotype]

Jewish windbreaker *n.* [1960s] (*US*) a mink coat.

Jew joanna *n. see* JEWISH JOANNA n.

Jew joint *n.* [20C+] (*US*) a second-hand clothes store. [SE *Jew* + JOINT n.[4] (3)]

jewlark *v.* [mid-19C+] (*US*) to flirt, to court. [SE *gill/jill*, a girl or woman + LARK v.]

jewlarker *n.* (*also* jewlarky) [late 19C+] (*US*) **1** [late 19C–1900s] a dandy. **2** a sweetheart. [JEWLARK v.]

Jewman *n.* [20C+] (*Irish*) a moneylender. [var. on JEW BOY n.]

jew out *v. see* JEW DOWN v.

Jew's *n.* [1970s] (*US Black*) a pawnbroker's shop. [the fact that most Harlem pawnbrokers were Jews; note 1887, *Bulletin* (Sydney), 5 November 8/3: 'The Red Sea was divided and held back as a wall on either hand for the ancient pawn brokers to pass over']

Jew's bail *n. see* JEW BAIL n.

Jew's Bentley *n.* (*also* Jew's Rolls Royce) [1930s–60s] a Jaguar motorcar. [the stereotyped association of Jaguars and *nouveaux riches* Jews]

Jew's compliment *n.* (*also* Jewish compliment, Judische compliment) **1** [mid-19C+] of a man, having a large penis but no money or presents. **2** [1950s+] (*gay*) a circumcised penis (cf. CLIPDICK n.). [the premise of (1) is that the penis is free, but to the stereotypically mean Jew, presents involve losing money]

Jew's eye *n.* [late 16C–1900s] something valuable or desirable; usu. as *worth a Jew's eye*. [? Ital. *gioie* or Fr. *joaille*, a jewel or, given the prevailing stereotype, the medieval practice of extorting money from the Jewish community on pain of threatened torture, which may or may not have involved blinding]

Jew shave *n.* [1930s] (*US*) covering one's face with talcum powder instead of shaving. [traces of a beard that still remain on some swarthy Jewish men's faces despite their shaving]

Jew sheet *n.* [1950s+] (*gay*) an account, often imaginary, of money lent to friends.

Jew's lance *n.* [1950s+] (*gay*) a Jewish circumcised penis (cf. CLIPDICK n.).

Jew's poker *n.* [late 19C] the gentile who, in religious households, is brought in to light the fires on the Sabbath. [the lighting of fires (and in more recent years, the turning on of electric lights), is among many prohibitions against 'work' on the Sabbath. The Yid. term for the same individual is *shabbas goy*, Sabbath gentile]

Jew's Rolls Royce *n. see* JEW'S BENTLEY n.

Jew's typewriter *n.* [20C+] a cash register. [racial stereotyping]

Jew town *n.* [late 19C+] (*US*) a Jewish community within an urban area.

jew up *v. see* JEW (DOWN) v.

Jewy *n.* (*also* Jewey, Jewie) [late 19C+] an 'inevitable' nickname for a Jew, esp. when surnamed *Moss*; a derog. name for a Jew.

Jewy Louis *n.* (*also* Jewie Louie) [1970s+] (*UK society*) a flashy, vulgar style of interior decoration, poss. featuring (fake) Louis XV or Louis XVI furniture.

Jew York n. [20C+] a derog. term for New York City; thus *Jew Yorker*. [the large Jewish population in that city]

jeysey ears adj. [1970s] (*W.I.*) of a person, dirty, filthy.

jezabel n. [19C] the penis. [proper name *Jezabel*, wife of Ahab king of Israel, in SE a wicked, impudent or abandoned woman]

J-hole n. [2000s] (*US campus*) a contemptible person. [coined on the US TV show *Saturday Night Live*]

jib n.[1] (*also* **jibb**) **1** [mid-19C] (*UK tramp*) the tongue. **2** [mid-19C] the face or expression. **3** [mid-19C+] (*orig. US Und.*) speech, impudent talk. **4** [20C+] (*US Black*) (*also* **gibbs, gibs, jibs, jibbs**) the mouth. **5** [1950s–60s] (*US Black*) a tooth; usu. in pl. [Rom. *chib*, *jib*, the tongue; Hind. *tschib*, language; (4) dial. *jib*, the underlip, thus the mouth]

jib n.[2] [late 19C–1900s] (*UK society*) an opera hat, i.e. 'flat-folding "chimney-pot" hat, closed by springs set in centre of vertical ribs' (Ware). [proper name *Gibus*, the Fr. inventor]

jib n.[3] *see* JIBBER n.[1].

jib v.[1] **1** [mid-19C+] to depart quietly, to slip away. **2** [20C+] to leave behind, to abandon. [? JIBBER n.[1]]

jib v.[2] (*also* **jibb**) [mid-19C+] to talk, to chatter, esp. at length and without meaning. [JIB n.[1] (3)]

jib v.[3] *see* JIBB (IN) v.

jiba n. (*also* **jibba, juba**) [19C+] (*US Black*) left-overs. [SE *giblets*; the slave term for left-overs from the White masters' table]

jibb *see also under* JIB.

jibb n. [1990s+] (*US drugs*) a gram of hashish (cf. AFGHAN n.). [ety. unknown; ? SE *jib*, the 'arm' of a crane; thus pun on getting one HIGH adj.[1] (2)]

jibba n. *see* JIBA n.

jibba-jabba n. [1950s+] (*US Black*) excessive conversation. [JIB v.[2] + JABBER n.[1]]

jibber n.[1] (*also* **gibber, jib**) [mid-19C–1960s] a worn-out horse, an uncooperative horse. [SE *jib*, of a horse, to back away, to refuse to go forward]

jibber n.[2] [20C+] (*orig. Irish*) a coward. [fig. use of JIBBER n.[1]]

jibber the kibber v. [late 18C–early 19C] to set up a device on land in order to wreck ships deliberately for the potential plunder. [a lantern is tied to a horse's neck and the horse itself has one foot tied; the movement this produces appears, from out on a dark sea, to resemble a moving ship's light. Ety. unknown; E.P. suggests *jibber*, to confuse, but it does not appear until 1824; *jib*, for a horse to move in fits and starts, is also 19C; ? 7C dial. *jibby-horse*, a flashy, showy woman is East Anglian, but Grose (1785) links such wrecking to 'our western coasts'; *kibber* may be redup. or it may relate to Cornish dial. *kib*, to steal]

jibbery adj. [late 19C] uncooperative. [JIBBER n.[1]]

jibb (in) v. (*also* **jib**) [1960s+] to gain admission to an event or service (e.g. a bus ride) without a ticket and without paying. [? JIB v.[2], the idea of talking oneself in, or GYP v.]

jibbs n. *see* JIB n.[1] (4).

jibe n. *see* GYBE n.

jib-jibe n. (*also* **ji-jibe**) [1960s+] (*US Black*) talk that goes in one ear and out the other, unimportant chatter. [JIB v.[2]]

jiblet n. [1960s+] (*drugs*) barbiturate (cf. BARBIT n.). [ety. unknown]

jiblets n. *see* GIBLETS n. (2).

jibone n. (*also* **jabone, jaboney, jabonie, jabronie, jarboni, jiboney, jumbloney, shaboney**) **1** [1920s+] (*US*) a novice, an innocent, a newly arrived immigrant, a fool. **2** [1920s+] (*US*) a heavy, a thug, a muscleman, as which (1) was often used. **3** [1950s] (*US Und.*) an Italian (cf. DAGO n.). [? Milanese *giambone*, ham, cf. JAMBONE adj.]

jibs n.[1] **1** [1950s+] (*US Black*) the buttocks. **2** [1980s+] (*US*) a woman's breasts (cf. BAGS n.[1]). [SE *jib*, a protruding sail at the bow of the ship]

jibs n.[2] [1910s+] (*US*) clothes.

jibs n.[3] *see* JIB n.[1] (4).

jick n. [1920s–40s] (*US Black*) alcohol, esp. illicitly distilled alcohol. [JIGGER n.[2]]

jickajog n. [17C–mid-19C] a shoving, a commotion. [echoic of the action]

jickhead n. [1930s–70s] (*US Black*) a drunkard. [JICK n. + -HEAD sfx (3)]

jidder n. [1910s] (*Aus.*) a woman, a girl. [? JUDY n.[1] (1)]

jiffy n. (*also* **giffy, jef, jeffey, jeffy, jif, jiff, jiffey, jiffin**) [late 18C+] a moment, a very short time; almost invariably in phr. *in a jiffy*, occas. *in a jiff*, also intensified as *half a jiffy*. [the vars. *jeffey*, *jeffy* are 19C only]

jig n.[1] **1** [17C–18C] sexual intercourse. **2** [1980s] (*US campus*) a promiscuous man.

jig n.[2] **1** [17C+] (*also* **gigg**) a trick, a swindle; thus [late 18C+] *the jig is up*, the game is up. **2** [1910s] (*US Und.*) a problem, a mistake. [late 16C SE *jig*, a comical performance, usu. given in the interval or at the conclusion of a play]

jig n.[3] [18C–19C] a joking, mocking nickname for a person. [SE *jig*, a lively dance; a general name for a mechanical device]

jig n.[4] [18C–early 19C] a lock or door.

jig n.[5] (*also* **jigg, swamp jig**) (*orig. US*) [1920s+] a derog. term for a Black person, thus not derog. (cf. ALLIGATOR BAIT n.[2]). [abbr. JIGABOO n.]

jig adj. [1920s+] (*US*) referring, in a derog. manner, to a Black person or the Black lifestyle and culture. [JIG n.[5]]

jig v.[1] [17C–18C] to have sexual intercourse. [JIG n.[1] (1)]

jig v.[2] [1960s] (*Aus.*) to play truant.

jig v.[3] [1960s+] (*US*) to bother, to irritate.

jig v.[4] [1980s+] (*US*) to prod with a knife, to stab.

jigaboo n. (*also* **jigabo, jiggaboo, zigabo, zigaboo, ziggerboo**) **1** [1920s+] (*orig. US*) a derog. term for a Black person (cf. ALLIGATOR BAIT n.[2]). **2** [1920s+] as used by a Black person, thus not derog. **3** [1940s] (*US Black campus*) a crazy person. **4** [1950s] (*US*) an unsophisticated peasant, a farmer. [either SE *jig*, a dance, ult. Fr. *giguer*, to leap, to gambol, to frolic (the classic 19C Black stereotypes); or modelled on SE *bugaboo*, which, in the 13C, was the name of a demon, and since the 18C, the fear of demons in general; or Bantu *tshikabo*, a meek and servile person, used as derog. by slaves. Paradoxically, the first approximate use of *jigaboo* – in the song 'I've got rings on my fingers' by Weston, Barnes & Scott – appears to have referred to Asians. Certainly the lyrics are set in India, although the ref. to 'Mistress Mumbo Jumbo Ji-jiboo J O'Shea' would imply that the writer was of the 'they all look alike to me' persuasion]

jigaboo (cig) n. [1990s+] (*US drugs*) a cannabis cigarette (cf. AFRICAN WOODBINE n.). [JIGABOO n. (1) + CIG n.]

jigaboo joy shop n. [1920s–50s] (*US*) an automobile supply store specializing in cheap but ostentatious chrome accessories. [JIGABOO n. (1); stereotyping of the tastes of Black car buyers]

jig-a-jig n. (*also* **jig-a-jog, jig-jig**) [17C; late 18C+] sexual intercourse, often found in pidgin slangs. [redup. indicative of the movements of copulation; note JIG n.[1]]

jig-a-jig v. [20C+] to have sexual intercourse. [JIG-A-JIG n.]

jigamaree n. (*also* **jagamaree, jiggamaree**) **1** [early 19C+] (*US*) a thing, a gadget, a fanciful contrivance. **2** [mid-19C] anything the speaker considers ridiculous or worthless. **3** [mid-late 19C] a cunning trick. [var. on JIGGUMBOB n.]

jig around v. **1** [20C+] to wander around, to loiter. **2** [1960s] to prance, to strut, to swagger.

jig-chaser n. [1920s–40s] (*US*) a White person who pursues the company of Blacks. [JIG n.[5] + SE *chaser*]

jig cut n. [1920s–70s] (*US*) a razor or knife slash. [JIG n.[5] + SE *cut*; the stereotype of the knife-wielding Black]

jigg n. *see* JIG n.[5].

jigga n. [2000s] (*US teen*) a womanizer (cf. JIGGER n.[10]). [? JIG v.[1]]

jiggaboo n. *see* JIGABOO n.

jiggalorum *n.* [early 17C; 1920s] a trifle, a fanciful thing. [on pattern of JIGGUMBOB n.]

jiggamaree *n. see* JIGAMAREE n.

jiggambob *v. see* JIGGER v.¹ (1).

jiggam-bob *n. see* JIGGUMBOB n.

jigged *adj.* 1 [20C+] (*Aus.*) broken, useless. 2 [1900s–50s] (*US*) a euph. for DAMNED adj. [JIGGERED adj.¹]

jigger *n.*¹ 1 [mid-16C–19C] (*UK Und.*) a door. 2 [late 18C–19C] a doorkeeper. 3 [early-late 19C] (*UK Und.*) a key. [? link to Lancashire dial. *jigger*, a narrow entry between houses, although the cant very likely preceded it; Ribton-Turner, *A History of Vagrants* (1887), suggests Welsh *gwddor*, a gate]

jigger *n.*² 1 [early-late 19C] (*also* **chigger**) a clandestine, illicit still. 2 [early-late 19C] (*UK Und.*) one who operates an illicit still and sells the liquor. 3 [early-late 19C] illicitly distilled liquor. 4 [mid-late 19C] a drink of spirits, a dram. 5 [mid-19C+] a small glass or metal cup, a measure used in mixing cocktails. 6 [mid-19C+] a whisky cocktail. [SE *jig*, to shake + idea of JIGGER n.¹, i.e. under lock and key; (4) SE in 20C+]

jigger *n.*³ 1 [mid-late 19C] the penis. 2 [mid-19C–1940s] the vagina. [? JIGGER n.¹ or JIGGER n.⁴ (1) or SE *jig*, to move up and down]

jigger *n.*⁴ (*also* **jiggie**, **jiggus**) 1 [mid-19C+] (*US*) a thing, a gadget, any small, mechanical contrivance. 2 [1950s+] (*Aus. Und.*) an improvised radio receiver, used in prison. [ety. unknown; ? fig. uses of SE *jig*, to dance]

jigger *n.*⁵ (*also* **jiggers**) [late 19C–1930s] (*US*) a policeman. [JIGGER! excl.²]

jigger *n.*⁶ (*also* **jiggers**) 1 [late 19C–1940s] (*US tramp*) a fake sore, wound or bandage to elicit sympathy. 2 [1900s] (*US*) a tattoo. 3 [1900s–10s] (*US*) a scoop of ice-cream.

jigger *n.*⁷ [late 19C+] a person; often a foolish person. [euph. for BUGGER n.¹]

jigger *n.*⁸ [late 19C+] a prison or cell. [JIGGER n.¹ (1); 20C+ uses are US]

jigger *n.*⁹ 1 [1900s–20s] a bicycle. 2 [1910s] a motorcycle. 3 [1910s–20s] a car. [ext. of JIGGER n.⁴ (1)]

jigger *n.*¹⁰ [1920s] (*US*) a young man who frequents soda fountains in the hope of picking up women (cf. JIGGA n.).

jigger *n.*¹¹ [1920s+] (*orig. US*) a derog. term for a Black person (cf. ALLIGATOR BAIT n.²). [JIGABOO n. (1)]

jigger *n.*¹² (*also* **jigger man**) [1920s+] (*US prison/Und.*) a lookout man. [JIGGER! excl.²]

jigger *n.*¹³ [2000s] (*US Black*) a Jew (cf. ARAB n.²). [initial letter on model of NIGGER n.¹ (1)]

jigger *n.*¹⁴ *see* GIGGER n.¹ (2).

jigger *v.*¹ 1 [mid-19C] (*also* **jiggambob**) to shake or jerk rapidly. 2 [mid-19C+] to break, to destroy, to ruin. 3 [late 19C–1930s] (*US*) to fool, to cheat, esp. in passive. [SE *jig*, to move around]

jigger *v.*² 1 [late 19C–1920s] to lock up, to imprison. 2 [1970s] to unlock. [JIGGER n.¹]

jigger *v.*³ [late 19C–1930s] a euph. for DAMN v.

jigger *v.*⁴ 1 [1900s] (*US*) to tattoo. 2 [1910s–30s] (*US Und.*) to deface, to mar (the flesh), thus to create a fake sore. [(1) JIGGER n.⁶ (2); (2) JIGGER n.⁶ (1)]

jigger *v.*⁵ [1960s] (*US prison/Und.*) to act as a lookout. [JIGGER n.¹²]

jigger! *excl.*¹ (*also* **jiggers!**) [early 19C+] used as a vaguely indecent oath, e.g. as *by jiggers! jigger it!* etc. [? a euph. for JESUS (CHRIST)! excl., although usu. used in v. forms]

jigger! *excl.*² (*also* **jiggeroo! jiggers!**) [1910s+] (*US*) a warning that someone hostile, e.g. the police, a teacher, one's parents, is coming. [? euph. of JESUS (CHRIST)! excl.]

jigger-dubber *n.* (*also* **gigger-dubber**) [late 18C–19C] a turnkey. [JIGGER n.¹ (1) + DUB v.¹]

jiggered *adj.*¹ 1 [mid-19C+] a euph. for DAMNED adj., with some feeling of confusion; thus I'LL BE JIGGERED! excl. 2 [mid-19C+] exhausted, worn-out; often as *jiggered up*. 3 [1920s–40s]

drunk (cf. ADDLED adj.). 4 [1990s+] in fig. use, unstable. [JIGGER v.¹ (2)]

jiggered *adj.*² [late 19C] 1 contraband, smuggled. 2 secret. [JIGGER n.²]

jigger-foot market *n.* [1940s+] (*W.I.*) a market popular among the very poorest people. [Carib.E *jigger-foot*, a foot infested with *jiggers* or larval mites, which lay their eggs beneath the skin. The poor are often prone to such infestation]

jiggering *adj.* [late 19C–1930s] a mild pej. [JIGGER! excl.¹]

jigger man *n. see* JIGGER n.¹².

jiggeroo! *excl. see* JIGGER! excl.².

jiggers *see under* JIGGER.

jigger stuff *n.* [early-mid-19C] liquor made at a secret still. [JIGGER n.² (3) + STUFF n.³ (1)]

jigger-worker *n.* 1 [mid-19C–1900s] a seller of illicitly distilled spirits. 2 [late 19C] a drinker of such illegal spirits, esp. whisky. [JIGGER n.² (3) + SE *worker*/WORKER n.¹ (1)]

jiggery-pokery *n.* (*also* **jackery-pokery, jiggery**) [late 19C+] tricks, lies, underhand activities in general. [? ult. Scot. *joukery-pawkery*, a trick]

jiggie *n. see* JIGGER n.⁴.

jiggle *adj.* (*also* **jiggly**) [20C+] of a woman, amorously inclined. [JIGGLE v.]

jiggle *v.* [mid-19C–1940s] to have sexual intercourse.

jiggle and jog *n.* [1970s+] a French person. [rhy. sl. = FROG n. (2)]

jiggler *n.* [1980s] (*US*) a female breast (cf. BOBBER n.²).

jigglers *n.* [1940s+] (*UK Und.*) skeleton keys for use on pin tumbler locks. [SE *jiggle*, i.e. using the sleight of hand required to turn the lock, but note JIGGER n.¹]

jiggling bone *n.* [19C] the penis. [JIGGLE v. + SE *bone*/BONE n.¹ (1)]

jiggly *adj. see* JIGGLE adj.

jiggly bits *n. see* DANGLY-BITS n.

jigglywhack *adj.* [2000s] (*US Black*) eccentric, extreme.

jiggs *n.*¹ [1940s] (*US*) corned beef and cabbage. [popularized in the *Jiggs and Maggie* comic strip]

jiggs *n.*² [2000s] (*US Black*) a fellow Black person. [JIG n.⁵]

jiggumbob *n.* (*also* **jiggam-bob**) 1 [17C; 1920s] (*US*) something strange, peculiar, unknown. 2 [mid-17C] a euph. for the vagina (cf. ARTICLE n.). [var. on THINGUMABOB n.]

jiggus *n. see* JIGGER n.⁴.

jiggy *n.* [1990s+] (*US Black*) the police. [JIGGER n.⁵]

jiggy *adj.* 1 [1920s+] (*US*) crazy, nervous, fidgety. 2 [1990s+] (*orig. US Black*) sexually excited or exciting. 3 [1990s+] (*US Black*) acting in a sophisticated, moneyed manner and looking the part. [SE *jig*, to move around]

jiggy-jig *n.* [19C–1930s] (*Anglo-Ind.*) sexual intercourse. [E.P. quotes 'a Hindi-English dictionary', which defines it as an 'exclamation of delight used by Indian women during sexual intercourse']

jig is up, the *phr. see* JIG n.² (1).

jig-jagging *n.* [1900s–20s] (*US Black*) dancing with absolute abandonment. [SE *jig* v.]

jig-jig *n. see* JIG-A-JIG n.

jig juice *n. see* JIG WATER n.

jig-lamps *n. see* GIG-LAMPS n.

jiglets *n.* [late 19C–1910s] (*US*) oneself, as in *his jiglets*. [ety. unknown; ? fig. use of SE *giblets*, i.e. generic use of one's innards as one's whole being]

jigs! *excl.* [1920s–40s] (*US*) a cry of warning. [var. on JIGGER! excl.²]

jig shop *n.* [1920s] (*US Und.*) a blacksmith's. [pun on JIG n.⁵]

jigs on the green *phr. see* WIGS ON THE GREEN phr.

jig town *n.* [1920s+] (*US*) a Black community within an urban area. [JIG n.⁵ + SE *town*]

jigwalker *n.* (*also* **jigwawk, jigwalk**) [1920s–60s] (*US*) a derog.

term for a Black person, unless used by Blacks (cf. ALLIGATOR BAIT n.²). [JIG n.⁵ + play on SE *jaywalker*]

jig water n. (*also* **jig juice**) [late 19C+] (*US*) alcohol, spirits. [JIG n.⁵ + SE *water/juice*; stereotyped fondness of Blacks for alcohol]

ji-jibe n. see JIB-JIBE n.

jildi n. (*also* **jildy, juldee**) [late 19C+] haste, speed, a hurry; esp. in phrs. *move a jildi*, *get a jildi on*, to hurry up. [Hind. *jaldi*, quickness]

jildi adj. [late 19C+] quick, speedy. [JILDI n.]

jildi v. (*also* **juldi**) [late 19C+] to hurry up, to smarten up, to improve; often as excl. *jildi!* hurry up! [JILDI n.]

jildi adv. (*also* **jeldi, jeldy, on the jildi, on one's jildy**) [late 19C+] in a hurry, quickly. [Hind. *jaldi*, quickness]

jildy n. see JILDI n.

jill n. (*also* **gill, Gillian**) [late 15C+] (*US*) a young woman. [note B.E. (*c*.1698): 'Gill…a homely Woman. Every Jack must have his Gill']

jillaroo n. [1940s+] (*Aus.*) **1** a White woman newly arrived in Australia, a White woman living in the bush. **2** a land girl. [play on JACKAROO n.]

jill-flirt n. see GILL-FLIRT n.

jillion n. [1940s+] (*orig. US*) an indefinite, extremely large number; thus *jillionaire*, an extremely wealthy person. [on model of SE *million, trillion*]

jill off v. [1980s+] (*orig. US gay*) of a woman, to masturbate; thus *jilling*, female masturbation (cf. APPLY LIP GLOSS v.; BALL OFF v.²). ['feminized' version of JACK OFF v.¹ (1)]

jills n. [mid-19C–1900s] the self, used with possessive pron., e.g. *my jills*, I, *his jills*, he. [Shelta; used mainly in show business]

jilt n.¹ [early 17C–19C] a prostitute. [SE *jilt*, 'a woman who gives her lover hopes, and deceives him' (Johnson, *Dictionary*, 1755); ult. *gillet/jillet*, a loose or wanton woman]

jilt n.² **1** [mid-18C] a thief who robs travellers staying in taverns or alehouses. **2** [mid-19C–1900s] a crowbar, house-breaking tools in general. [GILT n.² (1)]

jilt v. [mid-19C–1900s] (*orig. US*) to break into a house, to enter a building under false pretences for the purpose of theft. [JILT n.²]

jilter n. [mid-19C+] (*orig. US*) a sneak-thief. [JILT v.]

jiltish adj. [late 17C] flirtatious. [JILT n.¹]

jil to woodrus v. [1930s] to go crazy, to lose control. [? Scot. *woodrum*, a state of confusion]

Jim n. **1** [late 19C+] (*US, esp. Black*) a title for a fellow man (usu. Black), usu. used as shorthand for making a gesture of friendship (cf. ALLIGATOR BAIT n.²). **2** [late 19C+] (*S.Afr.*) a derog. all-purpose generic name for Black men. **3** [1910s] (*Aus.*) a generic name for the average Australian.

jim n.¹ [19C+] jewellery, diamonds. [SE *gem* or a play on TOM n.⁸]

jim n.² [1900s] (*US campus*) a urinal. [play on JOHN n.¹⁰]

jim n.³ [1900s–20s] (*Aus.*) £1; thus *half-jim*, 10 shillings. [? abbr. JIMMY O'GOBLIN n.]

jim n.⁴ [1910s] (*US Und.*) something second-rate, worthless. [abbr. *Jim Crow* and thus CROW adj.]

jim n.⁵ [1970s+] a man who likes to watch prostitutes at work (or just a 'dirty old man' who frequents 'adult' bookshops, stripshows etc) but offers no actual sexual threat. [generic use of proper name; based on JOHN n.⁸ (4)]

jim v.¹ [1900s] (*US campus*) to urinate. [JIM n.²]

jim v.² see JIM (UP) v.

jim adv. [1920s] (*US Black/W.I.*) an intensifier, completely.

jimber-jawed adj. (*US*) **1** having a projecting lower jaw. **2** [20C+] lopsided, askew. [SAmE *gimbal-jawed*]

Jim Britts n. see JIMMY BRITTS n.

jim brown n. [late 19C+] town, the West End of London; or any city. [rhy. sl.]

jimbrowsky n. (*also* **jim browski, jimbrowski**) [1980s+] (*US Black*) the penis. [? JIMMY n.⁵ (1)]

jimbugg n. [mid-19C] (*Aus./N.Z.*) a sheep. [Aboriginal *jombok*, a sheep]

jimcrack n. [1900s–50s] (*US*) **1** a fop, an affectedly showy person. **2** a fool. **3** a lie. [GIMCRACK n. (1)]

jimcracker n. (*also* **jimcrack, jimcracky**) [mid-19C–1970s] (*US*) a remarkable person or thing. [GIMCRACK n. (1)]

Jim Crow n. **1** [early 19C+] a complaisant, subservient Black person. **2** [mid-19C] (*Irish*) a Black person. **3** [mid-19C+] (*also* **Jim Crowism**) White racist discrimination against Blacks and the *Jim Crow* laws that embody it; usu. attrib. as JIM CROW adj. (4). **4** [late 19C] (*US*) a small touring theatrical company. [early 19C Kentucky plantation song with the chorus 'Jump *Jim Crow*' and the 'black face' entertainer Thomas Dartmouth Rice (1808–60), who first performed it in Louisville in 1828; its popularity in the UK followed Rice's appearance at the Adelphi theatre in 1836, in a 'farcical Burletta' entitled 'A Flight to America, or, Twelve Hours in New York'; for details see Hindley, *The Life and Times of James Catnach* (1878), pp.267ff.; note also Schele de Vere, *Americanisms* (1872): 'We have no ballad and no song that can be called American. The nearest approach […] was the dramatic song *Jim Crow*, brought out about the year 1835 by an enthusiastic Yankee on the boards of a theatre in New York; it created a sensation, for it was new in form and conception, and no doubt rendered still more attractive by the strange guise in which it was presented. It was quickly followed by several other songs of the same kind, such as *Zip Coon, Longtailed Blue, Ole Virginny nebber tire, Settin' on a Rail*, etc. […] For a time this African inroad drove nearly every other song from the publisher's store and the drawing-room']

Jim Crow adj. (*also* **James Crow**) **1** [mid-19C] (*US*) a derog. adj. describing a Black person (cf. ALLIGATOR BAIT n.²). **2** [mid-19C–1960s] small-time, incompetent, fraudulent. **3** [mid-19C+] (*US*) (*also* **jim-crowed**) for use by Blacks only, segregated, e.g. *Jim Crow car*. **4** [mid-19C+] (*US*) describing legislation that is racially prejudiced against Blacks; hence racist in general. [JIM CROW n.]

Jim Crow v. [20C+] (*US Black*) to treat a Black person in a patronizing and authoritative manner, to discriminate against Black people. [JIM CROW n. (3)]

jim crow n.¹ **1** [mid-19C] a soft felt hat with a broad brim and low crown. **2** [late 19C–1900s] (*US Black*) a small card, resembling a currycomb, used by Black people in rural areas. [JIM CROW n. (1)]

jim crow n.² (*also* **james crow**) [mid–late 19C] a street clown (with no racial inference). [rhy. sl. = *saltimbanco*, a street clown]

jim dandy n. [late 19C+] (*US*) an excellent person or thing. [? 1844 song 'Dandy Jim ob Caroline'. The song, apparently written by a Black rather than White author, trumpets the admirable qualities of this especially 'dandy nigger'. Alternatively, dial. *gim/jim*, neat, spruce + DANDY adj.; *gim* ult. ? Scot. *jimp*, slender, delicate, graceful. Cohen (ed.), *Studies in Slang* II (1989), suggests that the popularization of the term may have come through its use in baseball *c*.1890s]

jim-dandy adj. [late 19C+] (*US*) of a thing or situation, excellent, satisfactory; of a person, first-rate, admirable. [JIM DANDY n.]

jim fish n. [1930s+] (*S.Afr.*) a derog. term of address to a Black man (cf. ALLIGATOR BAIT n.²). [? the character *Jim Fish*, who was used in miners' training films in the 1940s as an example of what not to do]

jim gerald n. [20C+] (*Aus.*) *The Herald* newspaper. [rhy. sl.]

jim-hickey n. **1** [late 19C–1900s] an excellent or admirable person or thing. **2** an intensifier, HELL OF A, A phr. [? JIM DANDY n. + DOHICKEY n.¹ (1)]

Jim Hill n. [1930s] (*US tramp*) a freight wagon. [? anecdotal]

jiminetty! excl. [20C+] (*US*) a var. on JIMINY! excl.

jiminy! excl. [mid-19C+] a euph. for JESUS! excl. and used as such in mild oaths (cf. GEMINI! excl.). [? Ger. excl. *jemine*, oh dear! gracious! = Lat. *Jesu domine*]

jiminy cricket n. [1980s] (Aus.) a ticket. [rhy. sl.]

jiminy cricket(s)! excl. (also **jiminy criminy!**) [mid-19C+] (orig. US) a euph. for JESUS (CHRIST)! excl. [? Ger. excl. jemine, oh dear! gracious! = Lat. Jesu domine + cricket = euph. for Christ]

jim-jam n. 1 [mid-16C–19C] a fanciful or trivial article, a knick-knack. 2 [1990s+] (Aus.) nonsense, rubbish. [ety. unknown, but of similar pattern to FLIM-FLAM n.[1] and WHIM-WHAM n.[1]]

jim-jam v. [1940s–50s] (US Black) to sing, dance and play music, to have a lively party. [? JIM CROW n. (1) + JAM v.[3] (1)]

jimjam adv. [1960s] (US Black) jumpily.

jim-jams n.[1] (also **jim-jims**) 1 [mid-19C–1960s] (orig. US) delirium tremens, a hangover. 2 [late 19C–1920s] odd manners, personal peculiarities. 3 [late 19C+] a sense of fear, apprehension, a fit of depression. [ety. unknown]

jim-jams n.[2] [20C+] pyjamas, usu. children's use. [abbr. + redup.]

jimkwim n. see DR JIM n.

jim mace n. see JEM MACE n.

jimmey n. see JIMMY n.[2].

jimmied up adj. [1900s] (US) in a mess, in chaos.

Jimmie Howe n. see JACKIE HOWE n.

jimmies n.[1] 1 [20C+] a sense of fear, apprehension, a fit of depression. 2 [1900s–30s] delirium tremens, a hangover. [abbr. JIM-JAMS n.[1] (1)/JIM-JAMS n.[1] (3)]

jimmies n.[2] (US) 1 [20C+] pyjamas. 2 [1940s+] candy that is sprinkled on ice-cream. [(1) abbr. JIM-JAMS n.[2]]

jimmies n.[3] see JIMMY BRITTS n.

Jimmie Valentine n. [1920s] (US Und.) a safe-cracker. [the anti-hero of an O. Henry short story 'Jimmie Valentine' (1910)]

jimmison n. see JEMSON n.

jimmunt n. see DR JIM n.

Jimmy n.[1] [20C+] (mainly Scot.) used as a term of address to a person whose actual name one does not know. [generic use of the name]

Jimmy n.[2] see JIMMY HIX n.

jimmy n.[1] 1 [mid-19C–1930s] a guinea. 2 [late 19C–1910s] a sovereign (£1). [abbr. JEMMY O'GOBLIN n.; note ety. at JACOBUS n.]

jimmy n.[2] (also **jimmey**) [mid-19C+] (mainly US Und.) a short house-breaker's crowbar. [var. on JEMMY n.[3] (1)]

jimmy n.[3] [1930s+] an act of urination. [abbr. JIMMY RIDDLE n.]

jimmy n.[4] [1940s+] (US) a vehicle manufactured by the General Motors Corporation. [abbr./pron. initial letters]

jimmy n.[5] 1 [1980s+] the penis (cf. ABRAHAM n.[1]). 2 [1990s+] (US Black/campus) a condom. [? JIMMY v.[1] (4); note that (2) is not considered authentic by rap aficionados since it appeared to have been coined by a White and thus 'fake' rapper, Vanilla Ice]

jimmy n.[6] see JEMMY n.[1].

jimmy n.[7] see JIMMY GRANT n.

jimmy adj.[1] [mid-19C–1920s] (US) exact, fit, stylish, fashionable. [? JEMMY adj.[1] (2); 16C SE jump, exact, precise, coinciding]

jimmy adj.[2] see JEMMY adj.[2].

jimmy v.[1] 1 [late 19C+] (US Und.) to break into, using a small crowbar. 2 [1900s–50s] to gain access to something whether mental or physical, but without violence, to 'wriggle' into or out of something. 3 [1910s–50s] (US Und.) to injure, wound or spoil. 4 [1910s–60s] (US) to copulate. 5 [1920s–30s] (US) to steal from, to extract from someone, to cajole or cheat. 6 [1970s+] to get in without paying. [JIMMY n.[2]]

jimmy v.[2] [1930s+] to urinate. [JIMMY RIDDLE n.]

Jimmy Boyle n. [2000s] (drugs) kitchen foil, as used for smoking heroin or to CHASE THE DRAGON v. [rhy. sl.; ult. ex-convict and writer Jimmy Boyle (b.1940)]

Jimmy Britts n. (also **Britts, Jim Britts, jimmies**) [1940s+] (orig. Aus.) 1 diarrhoea (cf. BANANA (SPLITS) n.). 2 in fig. use, nerves, fear. [rhy. sl.; (1) = SHITS, THE n. (1); (2) = SHITS, THE n. (2); ult. proper name of Jimmy Britt (1879–1940), a US-born boxer who toured Australia during WW1]

jimmy cap n. (also **gym hat, jimmy hat**) [1980s+] (US Black) a condom. [JIMMY n.[5] (1) + SE cap]

jimmy dancer n. [20C+] (Aus.) cancer. [rhy. sl.]

jimmy dog n. 1 [20C+] (Irish juv.) the penis (cf. ANTEATER n.). 2 [1980s+] (US campus) a marijuana cigarette. [ety. unknown]

jimmy gall n. see GINNY GALL n.

jimmy Gee! excl. see JIMMY JEE! excl.

jimmy grant n. (also **jimmy, jimmy grunt**) [mid-19C–1960s] (Aus./N.Z./S.Afr.) an immigrant. [rhy. sl.]

jimmy green (on) phr. [20C+] naïve, gullible, e.g. I was jimmy green on that. [SE green, naïve; note Jimmy, an 'inevitable' nickname (also 'Dodger' or 'Shiner') for men surnamed Green in the British Army/Royal Navy]

jimmy hat n. see JIMMY CAP n.

jimmy-heel n. [1920s] (US) a worthless, despicable person.

Jimmy Hill n. [20C+] a pill. [rhy. sl.; ult. UK TV soccer pundit Jimmy Hill (b.1928)]

Jimmy Hix n. (also **Jimmy, Jimmy Hicks, Sister Hicks**) 1 [1910s+] (US gambling) a point of 6 in craps dice (cf. ADA FROM DECATUR n.). 2 [1950s+] (UK Und.) an injection of narcotics. [rhy. sl.; (2) = FIX n.[4] (1)]

jimmy hope n. [1910s+] (US prison) soap. [rhy. sl.]

Jimmy Howe n. see JACKIE HOWE n.

Jimmy Jee! excl. (also **Jimmy Gee! Jimmy Jesus!**) [1900s–40s] (Aus.) a mild excl., a euph. for JESUS (CHRIST)! excl.

jimmy joint n. [1980s+] (US Black) the penis. [JIMMY n.[5] (1) + JOINT n.[1]]

jimmy lee n. [20C+] (Aus.) tea. [rhy. sl.]

Jimmy Logie n. [1950s+] a piece of nasal mucus. [rhy. sl. = BOGEY n.[3] (1); ult. footballer Jimmy Logie, who played for Arsenal 1939–55]

jimmy low n. [late 19C] (Aus.) a timber-tree, eucalyptus resinefera. [? a local New South Wales 'character']

Jimmy Mason n. [20C+] a basin. [rhy. sl.; ult. James Mason, Hollywood film star (1909–84)]

Jimmy Nail adj. [1990s+] stale. [rhy. sl.; ult. UK actor Jimmy Nail (b.1954)]

Jimmy O'Goblin n. see JEMMY O'GOBLIN n.

Jimmy Prescott n. see CHARLIE PRESCOTT n.

jimmy protector n. [1980s+] (US Black) a condom. [JIMMY n.[5] (1) + SE protector]

jimmy raw n. see JACKY RAW n.

jimmy riddle n. (also **jenny riddle, jerry riddle, J.R.**) [1930s+] an act of urination; and also used as a request to use the lavatory (cf. ANGEL'S KISS n.). [rhy. sl. = PIDDLE n.; often abbr. to JIMMY n.[3]]

jimmy rollocks n. see TOMMY ROLLOCKS n.

jimmy rounds n. [early 19C–1900s] Frenchmen. [Fr. je me rends, the cry supposedly offered by hapless French sailors when faced with the might of the RN]

jimmy sangster n. [1980s] (Aus.) a gangster. [rhy. sl.]

jimmy skinner n. (also **jim skinner, joe…, johnny…, ned…**) [late 19C+] dinner. [rhy. sl.]

jimmy-swing n. [1940s+] (W.I.) a poor, common young man. [note Captain Swing, 'the Kent rick-burner', who terrorized farmers c.1830 in an attempt to put off the spread of farm machinery that was seen as a threat to farm-workers' livelihoods]

Jimmy Wilde n. [20C+] mild beer. [rhy. sl.; ult. world flyweight boxing champion Jimmy Wilde (1892–1969)]

jimmy woodser n. (also **jimmy woods, johnny woods, johnny woodser, woodser**) (Aus./N.Z.) 1 [late 19C+] anyone who drinks alone, a drink that is taken by oneself; thus jimmy woodsing, drinking by oneself; similarly one of a group who pays only for his own drink. 2 [1900s–10s] a drink that one buys for oneself, despite being in company. 3 [1900s–50s] a solitary person, an orphan. [a character in a poem by B.H.T. Boake, publ. in The Bulletin (7 May 1892): 'At the thought the heart beats quicker / Than an old

Bohemian's should ... / I'll go and have a liquor / With the genial "Jimmy Wood".' Poss. a genuine person, a loner named Jim Wood]

jimmy woodser v. [1900s–60s] (*Aus.*) to drink by oneself. [JIMMY WOODSER n.]

Jimmy Young n. [1990s+] **1** a bribe. **2** the tongue. [rhy. sl.; (1) = BUNG n.¹ (4); ult. UK singer turned radio personality *Jimmy Young* (b.1923)]

jimplecute n. see JIMSECUTE n.

jim-rags n. [late 19C] (*Aus.*) tiny pieces, shreds; esp. in the phr. *kick someone to/knock someone into jim-rags.* [dial. *jamrags*, tatters, rags]

jims n. [late 19C–1930s] (*Aus./US*) **1** delirium tremens. **2** a sense of fear, apprehension, a fit of depression. [abbr. JIM-JAMS n.¹]

jimscreech v. [1980s+] (*UK Black*) to con, to gain entry.

jim-screechy adj. [1990s+] (*W.I.*) underhand, deceitful.

jimsecute n. (*also* **jimplecute**) [mid–late 19C] (*US, Southern*) a sweetheart. [? dial. *jimpsey*, neat, smart, pretty + SE *cute*]

jim skinner n. see JIMMY SKINNER n.

Jimson n. [1950s] (*US Black*) a term of address to a man.

jimswinger n. (*also* **jimswigger**) [late 19C–1940s] (*US, mainly Southern Black*) a tailcoat. [? JIM n., a generic Black name + the swinging of the coat's tails]

jim time n. [1950s] (*US Black*) 'good connections, good time' (Durst, *The Jives of Dr Hepcat*, 1953).

jim town n. [late 19C–1960s] (*US*) **1** a shanty town. **2** the poor (thus often Black or Hispanic) part of a town. [? JIM n.]

jim (up) v. [20C+] (*US*) **1** to spoil, ruin or botch. **2** to fool around, to mess someone around. [? JIM n., if so, a racist slur; cf. AFRICAN ENGINEERING n.]

jim-whizzed adj. [late 19C] (*US*) a euph. for DAMNED adj.; usu. in phr. *jim-whizzed!* [fanciful; ? link to JESUS (CHRIST)! excl.]

jin n. [1940s] (*US Black*) a Native American. [abbr. INJUN n.]

jinal see under GINAL.

jing n. [1970s+] (*US campus*) money (cf. CHING n.²). [it 'jingles' in one's pocket]

jing-bang n. [1940s+] (*W.I.*) **1** a noisy, dirty crowd. **2** a low-class, rough, noisy person. **3** a promiscuous woman. [echoic of the noise and crush of the crowd/the careless lifestyle of the individuals]

jing-jang n. [1940s+] (*US gay*) **1** the penis. **2** the vagina. **3** sexual intercourse. [echoic of the movements of sex]

jingle n.¹ [mid-19C] (*US*) spirit, energy.

jingle n.² [late 19C–1920s] (*US*) an alcoholic drink. [? the rattle of ice-cubes in one's glass]

jingle n.³ [20C+] (*orig. Aus.*) money (cf. CHING n.²). [its noise in one's pocket]

jingle n.⁴ [1940s+] (*US*) a telephone call.

jingle adj. see JINGLE-BRAINED adj. (2).

jingle v. [1990s+] to sell. [JINGLE n.³]

jingleberries n. [1930s] (*US*) a wealthy person. [JINGLE n.³]

jingleberry n. [1930s–50s] (*US*) a testicle (cf. ACORNS n.). [var. on DINGLEBERRY n. (1)]

jingle-box n. [late 17C–early 19C] a leather drinking vessel, decorated with silver bells, popular among heavy drinkers.

jingleboy n. see GINGLEBOY n.

jingle-brained adj. **1** [1920s] (*US*) foolish (cf. AMOEBA-BRAINED adj.). **2** [1930s+] (*also* **jingle**) intoxicated. [JINGLE-BRAINS n.]

jingle-brains n. (*also* **jingle-brain**) [late 17C–early 19C] a fool, a dunce (cf. BAKEBRAIN n.).

jingled adj. [1900s–30s] (*US*) drunk. [JINGLE n.²]

jingler n.¹ (*also* **gingler**) [17C–early 19C] a crooked horse-dealer. [SE *jingle*; thus the noise of the harness, but perhaps more f. a further SE meaning, 'to play with words', verbal facility being the stock-in-trade of the horse-trader]

jingler n.² [late 19C–1920s] (*US*) usu. pl., money, coins (cf. CHING n.²). [GINGLEBOY n.]

jingling johnny n.¹ [late 19C–1940s] (*Aus./N.Z.*) **1** hand shears. **2** a hand-shearer. [the clicking noise of the shears]

jingling johnny n.² [20C+] the musical instrument known as a Chinese pavilion or Chinese crescent. [it 'consists of a pole, with several transverse brass plates of some crescent or fantastic form, and generally terminating at top with a conical pavilion or hat. On all these parts a number of very small bells are hung which the performer causes to jingle' (*Grove's Dictionary of Music*). A later Aus. version, which uses bottle tops tacked loosely onto an old broomstick, is the *lagerphone*]

jingo n. [1980s+] (*drugs*) a cannabis cigarette. [play on JOINT n.⁵ (3)]

jings! excl. [late 18C+] (*orig. and mainly Scot.*) used as a mild oath. [euph. for JESUS! excl.]

jink n.¹ [mid-19C–1900s] money (cf. CHING n.²). [the noise of one coin hitting another]

jink n.² [1960s+] (*US Black*) a disabled person, anyone seen as bizarre, unpleasant. [SE *jink*, to move jerkily; note dial. *jinked*, hurt in the loins or back]

jink v. [1920s+] (*Aus.*) to swindle. [Scot. *jink*, to dodge]

jink one's tin v. [mid-19C–1900s] **1** to pay out money. **2** to rattle one's change. [SE *jink*, to rattle with a metallic sound + TIN n.¹ (1)]

jinks the barber n. [mid-19C] (*UK middle class*) a secret informant, a gossip. [the stereotype of the chatty barber]

jinky adj. [1950s–80s] (*US Black*) difficult, problematical, unpleasant. [SE *jinx*]

jinnal see under GINAL.

jinna rumble n. [1940s] (*W.I.*) makeshift crutches, made of sticks and used to help walking. [ety. unknown]

jinnit n.¹ [20C+] (*Irish*) a mule. [Sp. *jinete*, a light horseman]

jinnit n.² [1930s+] a cocktail of gin and Italian vermouth. [abbr./pron. of GIN AND IT n.]

jinny see also under JENNY.

jinny n. [1920s–40s] (*US*) a speakeasy or unlicensed drinking place. [the SE *gin* available there]

jinny-ass/-wing n. see JENNY n.⁴.

jintoe n. see GENTOO n.

jip n.¹ [mid-19C–1940s] (*US*) a derog. term for a woman, esp. a Black woman. [? US sporting jargon *gyp*, a bitch (dog); ult. abbr. *gypsy*, used as a popular dog's name]

jip n.² [1940s+] (*Aus.*) energy, 'pep'. [? GIVE GYP v.]

jip n.³ [2000s] (*Irish*) semen.

jip n.⁴ see GYP n. (2).

jip adj. (*also* **jip-job**) [20C+] (*Ulster*) badly done, poorly produced, botched. [dial. *jip*, to trick, to cheat]

jip v. see GYP v.

jippo n. see GYPO n.

jirk-nod n. see YEKNOD n.

jis v. see JIZ v.

jislaaik! excl. [1950s+] (*S.Afr.*) a general excl., the meaning of which varies as to context and the speaker's mood, usu. surprise, but also annoyance, grievance, dismay. [? euph. for JESUS! excl.; pron. 'yis-like']

jism n. (*also* **gism, gizzem, gizzum, jiss, jiz, jizz, jizzum**) **1** [mid-19C+] (*orig. US*) energy, spirit. **2** [late 19C+] (*orig. US*) semen. **3** [1930s–40s] (*US, mainly Southern*) gravy. **4** [1990s+] (*orig. US*) an ejaculation, lit. and fig. an emission. [ety. unknown; ? Ki-Kongo *dinza*, the life force; note northeast US dial. *jasm*, energy]

jiss v. see JIZ v.

jit n.¹ [1910s] (*Aus.*) a cigarette. [? JIT n.², i.e. the price]

jit n.² [1910s+] (*US*) a nickel, a 5-cent coin. [JITNEY n. (1)]

jit n.³ **1** [1930s–40s] (*US*) a Black person (cf. ALLIGATOR BAIT n.²). **2** [1990s+] (*US Black*) a derog. term for a young person, anyone inexperienced, foolish or annoying. [? fig. use of JIT n.², i.e. a virtually worthless person]

jit n.[4] [1970s] (*US campus*) semen. [? var. on JISM n. (2); or the SE *jet* of ejaculated semen]

jit n.[5] *see* JITTERBUG n. (3).

jitbag n. [1990s+] **1** a condom. **2** a general term of abuse. [JIT n.[4] + SE *bag*/BAG n.[7]/-BAG sfx]

jitney n. (*also* **gitney**) **1** [20C+] (*US*) a 5-cent piece, a nickel. **2** [1910s+] (*US*) a small, cheap car or vehicle. **3** [1910s+] (*US*) (*also* **jitney bus**) a bus charging a fixed fare. **4** [1940s–50s] (*US Black*) a cab. [the 5-cent fare charges on the original *jitney* omnibuses. *DARE* quotes a source claiming *jitney* to be 'Jewish slang', but there is no evidence]

jitney adj. [1910s+] anything cheap, improvised or ramshackle; thus *jitney dance*, a pay-per-dance or 'taxi-dance' dancehall. [JITNEY n. (1)]

jitney v. [1910s+] (*US*) to travel by bus or small vehicle. [JITNEY n.]

jitney bus n. *see* JITNEY n. (3).

jitney girl n. [1950s–60s] (*US*) a prostitute who drives around in her own car soliciting customers (cf. AWAYDAY GIRL n.). [JITNEY n. (2) + SE *girl*]

jits n. [1930s+] (*US*) anxiety, nervousness. [abbr. of JITTERS, THE n.]

jitter n. (*also* **gitter**) [1980s+] (*UK teen*) a fan of 'heavy metal' music. [? JITTERBUG n. or the movement of dancing to such bands]

jitter box n. [1940s] (*US*) a guitar.

jitterbug n. **1** [1930s–60s] (*orig. US*) a nervous person. **2** [1930s+] a fan of swing music. **3** [1940s+] (*US*) (*also* **jit**) an adolescent who is naïve or foolish. **4** [1960s+] (*US Black*) a voluble, indiscreet person, a chatterer. **5** [1960s+] (*US Black*) a youth who lives a street life but is not necessarily a criminal. [JITTERS, THE n. + BUG n.[5] (4); apparently coined in 1934 by US band leader Cab Calloway (1907–94); note *jitterbug*, the dance and a dancer, is SE]

jitterbug v. **1** [1940s–70s] (*US*) to fool around. **2** [1940s–70s] (*US Black*) to saunter, to swagger. **3** [1950s–70s] (*US*) (*also* **jitterhop**) to participate in gang fighting. [JITTERBUG n.]

jitterdoll n. (*also* **jitterjane**) [1940s] (*US Black*) a woman who loves to dance. [for ety. *see* JITTERBUG n.]

jitter joint n. [1940s–50s] (*US*) a cheap dancehall. [JITTERBUG n. (2) + JOINT n.[4] (3)]

jitters, the n. **1** [1920s+] extreme nervousness, a state of emotional and often physical tension, agitation. **2** [1930s–40s] (*US*) a hangover, delirium tremens. [supposedly f. the Spoonerism 'bin and jitters' for 'gin and bitters' and orig. used of one who has drunk too much of that mixture]

jittery n. [1950s] a nervous, unstable person. [JITTERY adj.]

jittery adj. [1930s+] nervous, tense, 'on edge'. [JITTERS, THE n.]

jive n.[1] [1920s–70s] (*US Black*) sexual intercourse; also a sexual partner. **2** [1920s+] (*orig. US Black*) nonsense, rubbish, insincere, deceitful or pretentious talk. **3** [1930s+] (*US*) Afro-American slang, esp. as coined in Harlem and thence used by jazz musicians (cf. JIVE TALK n.). **4** [1930s+] (*US*) any thing, stuff, goings-on, any situation. **5** [1960s–70s] one's personality or material posessions. **6** [1970s] a proposition, a suggestion. [? Wolof *jev*, gossip, false talk, trickery or SE *jibe*, to scoff, to sneer; (2) note Burley: 'Jive is a distortion of that staid, old, respectable English word "jibe" — jibber — speak fast and inarticulately, chatter. [...] Jibberish — unintelligible speech, meaningless sounds, jargon, blundering or ungrammatical talk'; he dates it to Chicago, 1921; also note Mezzrow & Wolfe, *Really the Blues* (1946): 'The word *jive* probably comes from the old English word *jibe*, out of which came the words *jibberish* and *gibberish*, describing sound without meaning, speech that isn't intelligible'; Mezzrow further suggests, quoting Black journalist Earl Conrad, that 'Jive talk may have been originally a kind of "pig Latin" that the slaves talked with each other, a code – when they were in the presence of whites'. Note that *jive*, swing music, is SE]

jive n.[2] (*drugs*) **1** [1930s+] marijuana. **2** [1950s+] heroin. **3** [1990s+] recreational drugs in general. [fig. uses of JIVE n.[1] (4)]

jive n.[3] [1950s+] (*US Black*) **1** a deceitful, arrogant or pretentious person. **2** an unsophisticated person. [abbr. JIVE-ASS n.[1] but note the earlier JIVE ARTIST n.]

jive adj. (*orig. US Black*) **1** [1940s+] a generally negative term, applicable to a range of dubious actions, fake, phoney, deceitful, unappealing, hypocritical, insincere etc. **2** [1960s+] unimportant, trivial, foolish. [JIVE n.[1] (2)]

jive v.[1] (*orig. US Black*) **1** [1920s+] to engage in sexual intercourse. **2** [1920s+] (*also* **jive up**) to talk nonsense, to deceive, trick or flatter by apparently empty chatter; thus *jive about with, give some jive*, to play with, to mess around. **3** [1930s+] to play or dance to jive music, to have a good time. **4** [1930s+] to tease, to make fun of. **5** [1940s–70s] to converse, to talk JIVE n.[1] (3). **6** [1960s+] to saunter, to swagger, to dodge. **7** [1970s] to idle, to loaf about. [JIVE n.[1]; Burley suggests that the original use of *jiving* was as a synon. for the DOZENS n.]

jive v.[2] [1940s+] to fit in, to make sense, to agree, esp. in negative uses, e.g. *that don't jive*, that doesn't make sense. [SE *jibe*]

jive and juke v. [1970s+] (*US campus*) to have a very good time. [JIVE v.[1] (3) + JUKE v.[3] (2)]

jive around v. (*US*) **1** [1930s+] to tease, to make fun of, to fool around. **2** [1960s+] to tell lies, to deceive. [JIVE v.[1] (4)/JIVE v.[1] (2)]

jive artist n. [1930s] (*orig. US Black*) a pretentious person. [JIVE n.[1] (2) + ARTIST sfx]

jive-ass n.[1] (*also* **jive nigger**) [1950s+] (*orig. US Black*) a deceitful, arrogant or pretentious person. [JIVE-ASS adj. (1)]

jive-ass n.[2] [1960s+] (*US*) one who loves fun or excitement. [JIVE v.[1] (3) + -ASS sfx]

jive-ass adj. (*orig. US Black*) **1** [1950s+] (*also* **jive-end**) deceitful, pretentious, arrogant, insincere. **2** [1960s+] a general derog. [JIVE n.[1] (2) + -ASS sfx]

jive-ass v. [1960s+] (*orig. US Black*) to talk nonsense, to swagger, to boast. [JIVE-ASS adj. (1)]

jive-bomber n. [1940s] (*US teen*) a good dancer. [JIVE v.[1] (3) + ? BOMB v.[3] (1); or ? play on SE *dive-bomber*]

jive-end adj. *see* JIVE-ASS adj. (1).

jive hand n. [1970s+] (*US Black*) an undesirable situation that puts one person at an unfair disadvantage, one is dealt 'a bad hand'. [JIVE adj. (1) + SE *hand*, the cards that one has been dealt]

jive-nigger n. *see* JIVE-ASS n.[1].

jiver n.[1] [1920s–60s] (*US Black*) a trickster, a deceiver, a flatterer, an insincere person. [JIVE v.[1] (2)]

jiver n.[2] **1** [1940s–50s] a jazz fan. **2** [1970s] a rock musician. [JIVE v.[1] (3)]

jive someone out of v. [1960s] to deceive, to trick, to cheat. [JIVE v.[1] (2)]

jive stick n. [1950s+] (*drugs*) a marijuana cigarette (cf. BAT n.[8]). [JIVE n.[2] (1) + STICK n.[9] (3)]

jive talk n. [1940s+] (*orig. US Black*) slang-talking. [JIVE n.[1] (3)]

jive-talk v. [1960s+] (*orig. US Black*) to talk slang. [JIVE TALK n.]

jivetime adj. [1960s+] (*US Black*) insincere, dishonest, stupid. [JIVE n.[1] (2) + ? pun on the radio daypart *drivetime*]

jive turkey n. [1970s+] (*US Black*) an insincere, deceitful, dishonest person. [JIVE adj. (1) + TURKEY n.[3]]

jive up v. *see* JIVE v.[1] (2).

jivey adj.[1] [1940s+] (*US*) redolent of jive music, lively, aware. [SE *jive*, swing music]

jivey adj.[2] [1960s+] (*US*) pretentious, insincere, phoney, hypocritical etc. [JIVE adj. (1)]

jiz n. *see* JISM n.

jiz v. (*also* **jis, jiss, jizz, jizz up**) [1970s+] (*orig. US*) to ejaculate. [JISM n.]

jizrag n. (*also* **jizz rag**) [1990s+] a handkerchief or similar piece of material into which one masturbates. [JIZ n./JIZZ n. + SE *rag*]

jizz n. *see* JISM n.

jizz v. see JIZ v.

jizzbag n. (also **jizzbucket**) [1980s+] **1** a contraceptive sheath. **2** a general term of abuse. [JIZZ n. + SE bag/bucket/BAG n.[7]/-BAG sfx]

jizzbags n. [1990s+] the testicles. [JIZZ n. + SE bag/BAG n.[1] (1)]

jizzer n. [2000s+] an ejaculator. [JIZ v.]

jizzlob v. [1990s+] to masturbate. [JIZZ n. + SE lob, to throw]

jizz rag n. see JIZRAG n.

jizz rocket n. [2000s] (US) the penis (cf. AX n.[2]). [JIZZ n. + SE rocket]

jizzum n. see JISM n.

jizz up v. see JIZ v.

jizzwater n. [2000s] semen (cf. BABY FLUID n.). [JIZZ n. + SE water]

j.k. phr. [2000s] just kidding. [abbr.]

j.o. n.[1] [1970s+] **1** an act of masturbation. **2** a general term of abuse. [abbr. JERK-OFF n.]

j.o. n.[2] [1990s+] (US Black) a job. [abbr.]

j.o. v. (also **jay-o**) [1950s+] to masturbate, esp. in sex industry use. [abbr. JERK OFF v.[1] (1)/JACK OFF v.[1] (1)]

jo v. **1** [early 19C] (US) to spoil. **2** [1930s] (US) to be exhausted. **3** [1980s] (US gambling) to rig a game. [? abbr. SE joke]

joan n.[1] [16C–1930s] a homely woman. [the commonness of the proper name]

joan n.[2] (also **darby and joan**) [18C–19C] a fetter. [play on DARBIES n. (1)/SE Darby and Joan (see DARBY AND JOAN n.[1])]

joan v. (also **jone**) **1** [1970s+] (US Black) (also **joan on**) to indulge in a session of ritualized mutual insults. **2** [1980s+] (US campus) to be idle while pretending to be busy. **3** [1990s+] (US teen) to gossip (maliciously). [JOANING n.]

Joan Baez n. [1980s] the eyes. [rhy. sl.; ult. US folk singer Joan Baez (b.1941)]

joanie n. [1980s+] (US teen) an out-of-date, unfashionable girl. [? the character Joanie in the sitcom Happy Days, set in late 1950s and early 1960s; note JOAN n.[1]]

joaning n. (also **joning**) [1930s+] (US Black/Southern) indulging in a ritualized exchange of insults. [ety. unknown, but note dial. Joan Blunt, an outspoken woman]

joanna n. (also **joanner**, **joanno**) [late 19C+] a piano. [rhy. sl.]

Joan of Arc n.[1] **1** [20C+] a park. **2** [20C+] a lark, a situation; thus sod this for a Joan of Arc. **3** [1940s–50s] (Aus.) a shark. [rhy. sl.; ult. Joan of Arc (c.1412–31)]

Joan of Arc n.[2] [1950s–80s] (camp gay) an ostentatious, camp homosexual (cf. ABIGAIL n.). [pun on FAGGOT n.[2] (3)/the SE faggots with which St Joan (c.1412–31) was burned]

job n.[1] (also **jobe**) **1** [17C] a tedious scolding. **2** [mid-19C–1920s] a hen-pecked husband. [the biblical proper name Job, who received a lengthy telling-off from his supposed 'comforters']

job n.[2] [late 17C–mid-19C] a guinea, a pound. [? 15C SE job, a small compact portion of some substance; a piece or lump; cf. THICK 'UN n.]

job n.[3] **1** [late 17C+] (orig. UK Und.) any form of criminal activity, esp. a robbery, often with a qualifying name, e.g. the Barclays Bank job. **2** [late 19C–1910s] (US) a trick, a hoax. **3** [late 19C–1910s] (US) a jab; a blow. **4** [1940s] an effort, a problem. **5** [1960s] (US) a way of life.

job n.[4] [late 18C; late 19C+] a type, a variety or a procedure, e.g. the desk was a teak-oiled job, his moustache was a bushy brown job, a boob job, a nose job.

job n.[5] [mid-19C+] a bowel movement; thus DO A JOB v.[2].

job n.[6] **1** [1920s+] (orig. US) a person of either sex, a type of person; usu. with adj., e.g. cute little job, 14-year-old job. **2** [1930s+] (Aus.) a drunkard. **3** [1930s+] (Aus.) a fool, a poor worker. **4** [1940s+] (N.Z.) a prostitute.

job n.[7] [1920s+] (orig. US) an aircraft, a motorcar or any other vehicle; of a vehicle, a brand, a make, a style.

job n.[8] see BLOW JOB n. (1).

job v.[1] **1** [mid-16C+] to have sexual intercourse; thus jobbing,

sexual intercourse (cf. BANG v.[1]). **2** [late 19C+] (Aus.) to hit, to beat up. **3** [1970s+] (drugs) to inject a narcotic. [SE job, to pierce, to thrust something into]

job v.[2] (also **jobe**) [late 17C–1900s] to scold, to tell off. [JOB n.[1]; Grose (1796) suggests 'Cambridge term']

job v.[3] [mid-19C+] to finish. [SE job, to do a piece of work]

job v.[4] **1** [late 19C+] to cheat, to betray, to 'frame up'. **2** [1960s] (US) to steal.

jo-bag n. [1960s+] a condom. [JOHNNIE n.[5] + SE bag/BAG n.[7]]

jobanjeremiah n. [late 19C–1900s] an especially depressed, and depressing, person. [biblical figures Job and Jeremiah, both synon. with misery and complaint]

jobation n. [mid-18C–19C] a tedious scolding, esp. when following a minor offence. [JOB n.[1] (1); the lengthy scolding given to Job by his supposed 'comforters'; + ? link to JAW n.]

jobbard n. (also **jobard**) [15C–16C] a fool, a simpleton. [Fr. jobard, a fool, jobe, silly]

jobbed adj.[1] [mid-19C] concluded, finished; usu. in phr. (that) job's jobbed. [JOB v.[3]]

jobbed adj.[2] [1900s–40s] (UK Und.) accused or 'framed' on false evidence. [JOB v.[4] (1)]

jobber n. [1900s–70s] (US) a job, employment, a difficult chore.

jobber knot n. [mid-19C] a tall man. [? misreading of JOBBERKNOWL n.]

jobberknowl n. (also **jabberknowl**, **jabbernowl**, **jobbernowl**) **1** [mid-16C–mid-19C] (UK Und.) a fool, a blockhead; physically, the head of a fool. **2** [late 16C–early 19C] (also **jobbernole**) the head. [? JOBBARD n. + OE noll, the crown of the head]

jobberknowl adj. (also **jabberknowl**, **jabbernowl**, **jobbernowl**) [mid-17C–19C] stupid, blockheaded. [JOBBERKNOWL n.]

jobbie n.[1] **1** [1900s–30s] (US) a man or woman. **2** [1950s+] (US) (also **jobby**) a thing. **3** [1990s+] a job. [(1) JOB n.[6] (1); (2) JOB n.[4]; (3) SE job + sfx -ie]

jobbie n.[2] (also **jobby**) **1** [1980s+] (orig. Scot.) a piece of excrement, a turd; often as do a jobbie. **2** [1980s+] a general term of abuse. [JOB n.[5] + sfx -ie]

jobby jouster n. (also **jobby jabber**) [1990s+] a male homosexual. [JOBBIE n.[2] + joc. use of SE jouster]

job description n. [1990s+] (US) personal responsibility, usu. in negative contexts, that's not my job description.

jobe n. see JOB n.[1].

jobe v. see JOB v.[2].

job-off n. [1970s+] (drugs) an injection of a narcotic. [JOB v.[1] (3)]

job of work n. [19C] any form of criminal enterprise. [JOB n.[3] (1)]

job out v. [19C] (US Und.) to distribute counterfeit money to criminal associates and dealers. [JOB n.[3] (1)]

Job's ward n. [late 18C–early 19C] the venereal disease ward at St Bartholomew's Hospital in London. [the suffering therein]

Job's wife n. (also **Job's comforter**) [19C–1930s] a scolding, promiscuous woman. [the biblical story of Job]

jobsworth n. [1960s+] a minor factotum whose only status comes from enforcing petty regulations. [the inevitable rejoinder, It's more than my job's worth to…]

Joburg n. [late 19C+] (orig. milit.) Johannesburg, South Africa. [abbr.]

Jocelyn n. (also **Jozlin**) [1990s+] (UK juv.) a male homosexual (cf. ABIGAIL n.). [the perceived 'effeminacy' of the name]

Jock n. **1** [mid-18C–19C] a Northcountry seaman, esp. a crewman of a collier. **2** [mid-18C–19C] (also **Jockey**, **Jockie**, **Jocky**) a generic term for a Scotsman. **3** [late 19C+] as a term of address to a Scot. [the stereotypical Scot. given name Jock, f. John]

Jock adj. [1980s+] Scottish. [JOCK n. (2)]

jock n.[1] **1** [mid-18C+] (also **jocum**) the genitals, both male and female; also in fig. use. **2** [1920s+] an athletic support or 'jock strap'. **3** [1940s+] (US campus/sporting) (also **jocko**, **jockstrap**) a sportsman, esp. an assiduously keen one; thus *jockette*, the female equivalent. **4** [1960s+] (*US campus*) a politically conservative, White, middle-class young man. **5** [1960s+] (*US campus*) as ext. of (3), a devoted and diligent student, e.g. *math jock, computer jock*. **6** [1980s+] (*US*) a stupid, unimaginative person, a nerd. [(1) JOCKUM n.; subseq. defs. fig. ext. of (1); (1) the word vanished from the mainstream but remains in US Black use late 20C+]

jock n.² **1** [early 19C+] a *jockey*. **2** [1940s+] (*orig. US*) a disc *jockey*. [abbr.]

jock n.³ [1960s+] (*US*) a worker, an operator, e.g. *construction jock, elevator jock*. [abbr. JOCKEY n.³ (2)]

jock adj. **1** [1960s] (*US Black*) of a woman, having an attractive figure. **2** [1960s+] (*US*) athletic, sporty. [(2) JOCK n.¹ (3)]

jock v.¹ [late 17C–early 19C; 1960s+] to have sexual intercourse (cf. BAGAGA v.). [JOCK n.¹ (1)]

jock v.² [1960s+] (*US*) to engage in athletics. [JOCK n.¹ (3)]

jock v.³ [1980s+] (*US Black*) **1** to steal, either an object or a person, e.g. a lover. **2** to copy, e.g. song lyrics. [? JACK v.¹]

jock v.⁴ **1** [1980s+] (*US Black*) to imitate, to irritate, to be ON SOMEONE'S JOCK (STRAP) phr. **2** [1980s+] (*US Black teen*) to idolize, to pay someone lots of attention, trying to impress them. **3** [1990s+] to toady to, to act sycophantically. [(2) and (3) fig. use of JOCK n.¹ (3) as an object of desire]

jockam n. see JOCKUM n.

jock and boxer n. [20C+] (*gay*) a young man and his older friend. [the names of 2 varieties of underwear]

jock and doris n. (*also doc and doris, dock-and-doris, dockin doris*) [20C+] a drink, usu. of whisky. [Scot. *deoch-an-doris*, a parting drink or stirrup cup, which, by ancient custom, must be taken standing and need not be paid for]

jocker n.¹ (*US*) **1** [late 19C+] a tramp who has a younger partner working for him and poss. acting as his catamite (cf. PRUSHUN n.). **2** [20C+] (*also jocky*) a male homosexual, the 'husband' of the couple. **3** [1910s+] (*also joko*) a predatory homosexual, esp. in the context of prison, who forces his attentions on younger/weaker men or boys. **4** [1960s–70s] a lecher. [JOCK v.¹]

jocker n.² [2000s] an athletic support, a 'jock strap'. [JOCK n.¹ (2)]

jockette n. see JOCK n.¹ (3).

Jockey n. see JOCK n. (2).

jockey n.¹ [17C; 1920s–30s] the penis. [JOCKUM n.; note *double entendre* on a man's name in D'Urfey, *Pills to Purge Melancholy* (1719–20): 'You've been ranting, playing the Wanton, / Keeping of Jockey Company']

jockey n.² [mid–late 19C] (*UK Und.*) the expert, the exemplar.

jockey n.³ **1** [mid-19C–1940s] an accomplice or assistant, usu. of a driver of a cab or utility vehicle. **2** [mid-19C+] a worker in a particular job, e.g. *swab jockey*, a washer-up; *pump jockey*, a petrol pump attendant; *grunt-and-squeal jockey*, a stock hauler; *juice jockey*, a gasoline-truck driver; *suicide jockey*, a nitro-glycerine hauler; *disc jockey*. **3** [1900s–30s] (*US Und.*) a horse thief. **4** [1930s] a pimp. **5** [1930s] (*UK Und.*) ? a gang member. **6** [1930s+] any form of driver, esp. of cabs or buses. **7** [1930s+] a prostitute's client. **8** [1950s–70s] a user of drugs or one who is habituated, e.g. *hop-jockey*, drug addict; *horse-jockey*, heroin user. [SE *jockey*, one who rides racehorses]

jockey n.⁴ [1940s+] (*US*) **1** a homosexual tramp. **2** a masculine lesbian.

jockey n.⁵ [1950s] (*gypsy*) a general term of address.

jockey v.¹ [mid-18C+] to struggle for a place, esp. the lead in a race, to force into a position, to persuade. [racecourse use]

jockey v.² [early–late 19C] (*US Und.*) to trick, to defraud. [one 'rides' the victim in a required direction]

jockey v.³ **1** [1930s+] to do a job of work. **2** [1940s–60s] (*US Black/teen*) to drink. **3** [1940s+] (*US*) to drive a vehicle, to pilot a plane.

jockey around v. [1900s–70s] (*US*) to move from place to place, job to job.

jockeying n. [late 19C] racing carriages along the streets of London.

jockey's breakfast n. [1990s+] (*Irish*) sexual intercourse and a slice of bacon (cf. BARBER'S BREAKFAST n.). [SE *jockey*, who has to keep his weight down]

jockey's (whip) n. **1** [1940s–50s] a bed, a sleep. **2** [1960s+] in pl., potato chips. [rhy. sl.; (1) = KIP n.¹ (2)]

jock-gagger n. see JOCKUM-GAGGER n.

Jockie n. see JOCK n. (2).

jock itch n. see JOCK ROT n.

jock major n. [1960s+] (*US campus*) a student who majors in physical education. [JOCK n.¹ (3)]

jocko n.¹ (*US*) **1** [1910s+] a stupid or contemptible man or boy; also a term of address. **2** [1950s+] a friendly form of address. [generic use of name *Jock* but note dial. *jockey*, a peasant, a countryman]

jocko n.² see JOCK n.¹ (3).

jock-piece n. [1920s] (*US*) the penis. [JOCK n.¹ (1) + SE *piece*]

jock rot n. (*also jock itch*) [1960s+] (*US*) a skin infection of the genital area. [JOCK n.¹ (1) + SE *itch/rot*]

jocks n.¹ [late 19C–1920s] (*US*) used in mild oaths, typically *by jocks!* [euph. for JESUS! excl.]

jocks n.² [1950s+] (*Aus./US*) men's underwear. [abbr. SE *jockey shorts*]

jocksniffer n. [1960s+] (*US*) a (presumably male) sports groupie who likes to hang around sports stars. [joc. use of JOCK n.¹ (2) + SE *sniffer*; note reported 2003 US Army use, a civilian who is very wrapped up in military affairs]

jock someone's style v. [2000s] (*US Black*) to imitate. [JOCK v.⁴ (1) + STYLE n.]

jockstrap n.¹ [1960s+] (*US*) a stupid, insignificant fellow. [SE *jockstrap*]

jockstrap n.² see JOCK n.¹ (3).

jockum n. (*also jockam*) [mid-16C–1900s] the penis. [ety. unknown]

jockum cloy v. [late 17C–early 19C] of a man, to have sexual intercourse (cf. BURY IT v.). [JOCKUM n. + fig. use of CLOY v.]

jockum gage n. (*also jacum-gag*) [late 17C–early 19C] (*UK Und.*) a chamberpot; thus *rum jockum gage*, a silver chamberpot. [JOCKUM n. + GAGE n.¹ (2)]

jockum-gagger n. (*also jack-gagger, jock-gagger*) [late 18C–early 19C] a man who lives on his wife's prostitution, a pimp (cf. ABBOT ON THE CROSS n.). [JOCKUM n./JOCK n.¹ (1) + GAGGER n.¹ (3), lit. 'penis-beggar']

Jocky n. see JOCK n. (2).

jocky n.¹ [mid–late 17C] the penis. [JOCKUM n.]

jocky n.² see JOCKER n.¹ (2).

jocum n. see JOCK n.¹ (1).

Jodrell (Bank) n. [1950s+] **1** masturbation. **2** a tired-out old prostitute (cf. BOAT AND OAR n.). [rhy. sl. = WANK n.¹; ult. the *Jodrell Bank* observatory]

jods n. [1950s+] *jod*hpurs. [abbr.]

jody n. (*also jodie*) **1** [1940s+] (*US*) used derisively by US troops, prisoners and other isolated men, the lover who takes the 'girl you've left behind'. **2** [1940s+] (*US*) used derog. by soldiers, a male civilian; thus *jody clothes*, men's civilian clothes. **3** [1970s+] (*US gay/prison*) a homosexual prison's younger lover (cf. ABIGAIL n.). [pron. of JOE THE GRINDER n.]

Joe n. [1960s+] (*gambling*) a point of 4 in craps dice (cf. ADA FROM DECATUR n.). [JOEY n.¹ (1)]

joe n.¹ **1** [early 18C–early 19C] (*Scot.*) a friend. **2** [mid-19C+] a generic name for a person, e.g. *joe average, joe citizen*, the average man in the street; also one who has a job or position, e.g. *joe plainclothes*, a plain-clothes policeman; *working joe*, one who is employed etc. **3** [1910s+] (*US*) a (likeable) person, often used in direct address. [*The Swell's Night Guide* (1846) defines *joe* as 'an imaginary person, nobody']

joe n.[2] (*Aus.*) **1** [mid-19C] a policeman (cf. BILLY n.[6]). **2** [mid-late 19C] a term of abuse hurled at anyone who was not a miner. [(1) *Joe!/Joe-Joe!* a cry of warning issued by a miner at the approach of police; (2) Victorian goldfield jargon *joe*, a trooper enforcing the regulations laid down by Gov. Charles *Joseph* LaTrobe (1801–75); *AND* adds a cit. noting that LaTrobe himself was not actually unpopular]

joe n.[3] (*also* **joe house**) [mid-19C–1940s] (*US campus*) a privy; thus v., to use a lavatory; *joe-wad*, toilet paper. [supposedly f. the burning of the privies at Hamilton College on one Nov. 5, following the refusal of the president, Joseph Penney, to have them cleaned]

joe n.[4] **1** [mid-19C+] (*W.I.*) a sixpence; 5 cents. **2** [1930s] (*N.Z.*) a penny. [? JOEY n.[1]]

joe n.[5] [1910s+] (*US*) coffee. [initial letter of JAVA n.; ? elision of JAMOKE n.[1]; or ? play on Stephen Foster song 'Old Black Joe']

joe n.[6] [1920s] (*US*) a fit, occasioned by drug withdrawal or alcoholic excess. [? JOE BLAKES n.]

joe n.[7] [1960s] (*US*) a Navajo Indian. [abbr. of proper name]

joe n.[8] [1960s+] (*Can.*) a French Canadian. [generic use of proper name]

joe n.[9] [1970s+] (*US campus*) beer. [the *Joseph* Schlitz Brewing Co. of Milwaukee]

joe n.[10] *see* JOE BLAKE n.

joe n.[11] *see* JOE GURR n.

joe n.[12] *see* JOE (HUNT) n.

joe n.[13] *see* JOE MILLER n.

joe n.[14] *see* JOEY n.[1] (1).

joe adj.[1] (*US*) **1** [1900s–20s] aware, in the know. **2** [1950s–60s] used for anything exceptionally strong, large or extraordinary. [ety. unknown, but note northern dial. *to be joe*, to be the master, presumably a generic use of the name]

joe adj.[2] [1990s+] (*US*) tedious or inconsequential. [? JOE n.[1] (2)]

joe v.[1] (*also* **joey**) [mid-late 19C] (*Aus./N.Z.*) **1** to warn. **2** to abuse. [JOE n.[2] (1); goldfields' jargon, thus a cry of *joe!/joey!* warned that a trooper was approaching]

joe v.[2] [1980s] to steal from handbags.

Joe Baxi n. [1980s+] a taxi. [rhy. sl.; ult. US heavyweight boxer *Joe Baksi* (*fl.*1940s)]

joe blake n. (*also* **joe**) **1** [20C+] cake. **2** [20C+] (*Aus.*) a snake. **3** [1930s+] (*Aus./US*) steak. **4** [1980s+] (*Aus.*) a stake, a bet. [rhy. sl.]

joe blakes n. [late 19C+] (*Aus./N.Z.*) the shakes, delirium tremens. [rhy. sl. = SE *shakes*/SNAKES (IN ONE'S BOOTS) n.]

Joe Blake the Bartlemy v. [mid-19C] to visit a prostitute. [? rhy. sl. *joe blake* = FAKE v.[1] (2) + *Bartlemy* = Bartholomew Fair]

joe bloggs n. [1940s+] a generic name used for any otherwise unnamed man.

joe blow n. (*also* **joe bloe**) **1** [1920s+] (*Aus./US*) any man. **2** [1930s] (*US Und.*) a drugs carrier. [orig. the horn player in a band, who 'blows']

joe bonce n. [1930s+] a pimp (cf. ALPHONSE n.[2]). [rhy. sl. = PONCE n. (1)]

joe brown n. [late 19C+] town. [rhy. sl.]

joe buck n. [1930s+] (*Aus.*) an act of copulation. [rhy. sl. = FUCK n.[1] (1); note the heterosexual male prostitute hero of the novel *Midnight Cowboy* (1965), 'Joe Buck']

joe chink n. [1970s] (*US drugs*) a heroin addiction. [JOE n.[1] (2) + CHINK n.; ult. the link of heroin (or properly opium) to the Orient]

joe college n. (*also* **kid college**) [1930s+] (*US*) a college boy, esp. one who is self-satisfied and self-indulgent; also attrib. [JOE n.[1] (2) + SE *college*]

Joe Cool n. (*also* **Johnny Cool, Mr Cool**) [1960s+] one who is, or more likely sees themselves, as sophisticated, wordly etc. [JOE n.[1] (2) + COOL adj.[1] (3); note character 'Joe Cool' in Burnett, *Asphalt Jungle* (1949)]

Joe Cotton n. [1910s] (*US*) the point of 8 in craps dice (cf. ADA FROM DECATUR n.). [JOEY n.[1] (1)]

joe crap n. *see* JOE SHIT (THE RAG MAN) n.

joe daki n. [1990s+] a derog. term for a British Asian (cf. HALF-OUNCE OF BACCY n.). [rhy. sl. = PAKI n.]

joe dandy n. [late 19C–1940s] an excellent person or thing. [var. on JIM DANDY n.]

joe darter n. [1900s] (*US*) an outstanding example of its kind.

joe de grinder n. *see* JOE THE GRINDER n.

joe doakes n. [1920s+] (*US*) any anonymous man. [circus jargon *Joe Doakes*, the ringmaster; note JOHN DOE n.]

joe erk n. [1950s+] a fool, a general term of abuse (cf. BEECHAM'S PILL n.). [rhy. sl. = BERK n.]

joe gardiners n. [1950s] (*Aus.*) boots. [proper name of *Joe Gardiner Ltd*, a boot and shoe maker of Sydney]

Joe Goss n. [20C+] (*Aus./US*) **1** the boss; thus a political boss. **2** a policeman (cf. BOTTLE (AND STOPPER) n.). [rhy. sl.; ult. ? *Joe Goss*, a late 19C US prize-fighter]

Joe Gurr n. (*also* **joe, joe ghirr**) [1930s+] prison (cf. BUCKET n.[2]). [rhy. sl. = STIR n.[1]; ult. *Joe Gurr*, Amelia Earhart's radio consultant on her 1937 round-the-world flight]

joe heath's mare n. [20C+] (*W.I.*) a workhorse; thus *like joe heath's mare*, exerting oneself, behaving in an excited manner. [ety. unknown; presumably anecdotal]

joe hep n. (*also* **hep, joe hept, joe hip**) [20C+] (*US*) an aware, wise person. [JOE n.[1] (2) + HEP adj. (1)/HIP adj. (1)]

joe hep adj. (*also* **joe hept, joe hip, johnny hep**) [1900s–40s; 1980s] (*US*) smart, aware, knowledgeable. [JOE HEP n.]

joe hoke n. *see* JOE ROKE n.

joe hook n. **1** [1930s+] a villain, a crook; as adj., untrustworthy. **2** [1950s+] a book. [rhy. sl.]

joe hope n. [20C+] (*Aus.*) soap. [rhy. sl.]

joe house n. *see* JOE n.[3].

joe (hunt) n. (*also* **joey (hunt)**) [20C+] a fool, a general derog. term (cf. BEECHAM'S PILL n.). [rhy. sl. = CUNT n.[2] (1)]

joe job n. [1980s+] (*US campus/teen*) a menial, low-paid task. [JOE n.[1] (2) + SE *job*]

Joe Jorgensen n. [1950s] (*Aus.*) one who kicks while fighting. [proper name *Joe Jorgensen*, a well-known goal kicker for Balmain Aus. Rules Football team]

Joe Loss n. [20C+] a toss, as in a DAMN n. [rhy. sl.; ult. UK bandleader *Joe Loss* (1909–90)]

Joe Louis n. [1940s–50s] **1** (*W.I.*) a large, solid cake. **2** (*W.I., Jam.*) home-distilled rum. **3** (*US*) 'bad' or homemade liquor. [proper name of US heavyweight champion *Joe Louis* (1914–81); the size of (1); the strength of (2) and (3)]

joe lunchpail n. (*also* **joe lunchbox, joe lunchbucket**) [1960s+] (*US*) an ordinary working man. [JOE n.[1] (2) + SE *lunchpail/lunchbox/lunchbucket*]

Joe McGee n. **1** [1920s–70s] (*US*) a stupid, unreliable person. **2** [1930s] a mean person, spec. a non-tipping hotel guest. [? anecdotal]

Joe McGee adj. [1930s] (*US*) fake. [JOE McGEE n.]

Joe McNab v. [1970s–80s] (*N.Z. prison*) to stab. [rhy. sl.]

Joe Manton n. (*also* **manton**) [19C] a fowling-piece. [proper name *Joe Manton* (d.1837), a celebrated London gunsmith]

joe marks n. [1930s–40s] (*Aus.*) sharks. [rhy. sl.]

joe maxi n. (*also* **jo maxi**) [1990s+] (*Irish*) a taxi. [rhy. sl.]

Joe Miller n. (*also* **joe**) **1** [late 18C–1900s] a joke-book. **2** [early 19C+] (*also* **Joe Millerism**) a joke, esp. an 'old chestnut'; thus *I don't see the Joe Miller of it*, I don't see what's funny about it. **3** [mid-19C+] a joke-teller, a humourist. [proper name of *Joe Miller* (1684–1738), a comedian whose name was attached to the bestselling *Joe Miller's jests, or the Wit's Vade-mecum*, written by John Mottley and publ. in 1739, after Miller's death]

joe morgan n. [1940s] (*Aus.*) an organ. [rhy. sl.]

joe morgans n. [1920s] (*N.Z.*) delirium tremens. [? anecdotal]

joe muggins *n. see* MUGGINS n.[1] (1).

Joe O'Gorman *n.* [late 19C+] a foreman. [rhy. sl.]

joe poke *n.* [late 19C–1910s] a *J*ustice of the *P*eace. [a play on the initial letters.]

joe public *n.* [1930s+] (*orig. US*) the general public. [JOE n.[1] (2) + SE *public*]

joe rail *n.* [1900s] (*Aus.*) a hard-luck story aimed at obtaining money. [rhy. sl. = TALE n.[1]]

joe rocks *n.* (*also* **tommy rocks**) [20C+] socks. [rhy. sl.]

joe roke *n.* (*also* **joe hoke**) [1920s+] (*US*) a smoke. [rhy. sl.]

joe ronce *n. see* CHARLIE RONCE n.

joe rook *n.* **1** [1930s+] a bookmaker. **2** [1950s+] a crook. [rhy. sl.; (1) = BOOK n.[2] (3)]

joe rookie *n.* [1990s+] a bookmaker. [rhy. sl. = BOOKIE n. (1)]

joe rourke *n.* **1** [1930s] (*UK Und.*) a thief. **2** [1950s+] a fork. [rhy. sl.; (1) = FORK n.[1] (2)]

joes *n.*[1] [1910s+] (*Aus.*) **1** a fit of depression. **2** an attack of nerves. [abbr. JOE BLAKES n.]

joes *n.*[2] [2000s] (*US prison*) cigarettes.

joe sad *n.* [1920s+] (*US Black*) a miserable or unpopular person. [JOE n.[1] (2) + SE *sad*/SAD adj. (2)]

joe savage *n.* [mid-19C] a cabbage. [rhy. sl.]

joe schmo *n.* (*also* **joe schmoe, joe shmo, joe shmoe**) [1940s+] (*orig. US*) anyone, 'Mr. Average'. [JOE n.[1] (2) + SCHMO n.]

joe shit (the rag man) *n.* (*also* **joe crap**) [1940s+] (*US*) an extremely contemptible person, a nobody. [JOE n.[1] (2) + SHIT n.[2] (1)/CRAP n.[3] (7)]

joe six-pack *n.* [1970s+] (*US*) an ordinary, beer-drinking man. [JOE n.[1] (2) + SE *six-pack*]

joe skinner *n. see* JIMMY SKINNER n.

joe soap *n.* **1** [1930s+] a self-description, e.g. *joe soap here…* **2** [1930s+] a fool, a gullible individual. **3** [1980s+] any man. [rhy. sl. = DOPE n.[2]]

Joe Strummer *adj.* [1970s+] unpleasant, disappointing. [rhy. sl. = BUMMER adj.; ult. *Joe Strummer* (1952–2002), leader of punk band *The Clash*]

joe the grinder *n.* (*also* **joe de grinder**) [1930s+] (*US Black*) the mythical seducer, who specializes in married women or those with boyfriends; the lover who takes the 'girl you've left behind', as used by US troops, prisoners and other isolated men. [generic use of proper name *Joe* + GRIND v.[1] (1)]

joey *n.*[1] **1** [mid–late 19C] (*also* **joe**) a fourpenny piece, a groat. **2** [1900s–50s] a threepenny bit. [radical politician *Joseph Hume* MP (1777–1855), who encouraged the introduction of the coin. The term was coined by the London cabbies, who lost money by the coin's invention, when the *joey* replaced the sixpence as the usual payment for shorter journeys]

joey *n.*[2] (*Aus.*) **1** [mid–late 19C] in the goldfields, an outsider. **2** [mid-19C+] a policeman; in WW1 a military policeman (cf. BILLY n.[6]). [JOE n.[2]]

joey *n.*[3] **1** [mid-19C–1940s] a hypocrite. **2** [20C+] an excuse, a small 'white' lie. [? HOLY JOE n.]

joey *n.*[4] [late 19C–1940s] a circus clown. [abbr. proper name *Joseph Grimaldi*, the British clown (1779–1837)]

joey *n.*[5] [late 19C+] (*Aus.*) a child, usu. a White child. [SAusE *joey*, a young kangaroo]

joey *n.*[6] **1** [20C+] (*Aus.*) a sodomite, an active male homosexual (cf. ABIGAIL n.). **2** [1970s] (*Aus. gay*) a young male prostitute or the young lover of an older man. [SAusE *joey*, a young kangaroo]

joey *n.*[7] [20C+] the menstrual period. [euph.]

joey *n.*[8] [1910s+] (*Aus.*) a worthless cheque. [like SAusE *joey*, a young kangaroo, it 'bounces']

joey *n.*[9] [1940s–50s] (*US Black*) a White person. [ety. unknown; ? generic use of proper name]

joey *n.*[10] **1** [1940s+] (*UK prison*) any form of contraband, letters, parcels etc, smuggled into a prison. **2** [2000s] (*drugs*) a drug addict who works as a drug mule. [ety. unknown; ? link to JOEY n.[2] (2)]

joey *n.*[11] [1970s+] (*N.Z.*) a condom.

joey *n.*[12] (*also* **deacon**) [1980s+] a general derog. term implying physical inadequacy and used on the pattern of SPASTIC n. [proper name *Joey Deacon*, a disabled child who featured on *Blue Peter* in the 1980s; but note also JOEY (HUNT) n.]

joey *n.*[13] [2000s] (*drugs*) £10 worth of heroin. [? JOEY n.[10] (2)]

joey *v. see* JOE v.[1].

joey (hunt) *n. see* JOE (HUNT) n.

Joeys *n.* (*also* **Johies, Jozi**) [1970s+] (*S.Afr.*) Johannesburg. [abbr./pron.]

joe zilch *n.* (*also* **joe zilsch**) [1920s+] (*US*) the average, otherwise unnamed man. [JOE n.[1] (2) + ZILCH n.[1] (2)]

jo-fired *adj.* [early–mid-19C] (*US*) a general intensifier, complete, absolute, total, utter; occas. as adv. [var. on ALL-FIRED adv.]

jog *v.*[1] [late 16C–19C] (*UK Und.*) to move, to leave. [SE *jog*]

jog *v.*[2] **1** [17C–mid-19C] of a man, to have sexual intercourse. **2** [1970s] of a homosexual man, to have anal intercourse (cf. ASK FOR THE RING v.).

jogar *n.* (*also* **jogah**) [1920s+] a busker. [JOGAR v.]

jogar *v.* (*also* **jogger**) [late 19C+] (*Ling. Fr./Polari*) to sing, to play, to entertain. [Ital. *giocare*, to play]

jogari omee *n.* (*also* **jogari polone, joggering omee/polone**) [late 19C+] an entertainer, a busker. [JOGAR v. + OMEE n./POLONE n.]

jogue *n.* (*also* **jug**) [early 19C–1900s] (*UK Und.*) a shilling. [the term survives in 20C+ market traders' jargon *joag*]

jogul *v.* [mid-19C] to play a game, esp. a card-game. [Sp. *jugar*, to play]

Johies *n. see* JOEYS n.

john *n.*[1] **1** [17C+] a generic term for a man. **2** [18C–1900s] a male servant. **3** [mid-19C+] a general term of address, orig. of White men by immigrants etc, irrespective of actual name, e.g. *Hello John, got a new motor?* etc. **4** [late 19C+] (*S.Afr.*) a generic term for any male Black servant. [commonness of the name; note police/legal jargon *John Doe*, any anonymous male suspect, victim etc (cf. JOHN DOE n.)]

john *n.*[2] [early 19C–1900s] (*US*) an Englishman. [abbr. JOHN BULL n.]

john *n.*[3] [mid-19C–1940s] a derog. term for a Chinese man (cf. AH CABBAGE n.). [abbr. JOHN CHINAMAN n.]

john *n.*[4] (*also* **johndarm, john darme**) [mid-19C+] a policeman (cf. BILLY n.[6]). [abbr./mispron. of Fr. *gendarme*]

john *n.*[5] [mid-19C] (*US*) money. [abbr. JOHN DAVIES, THE]

john *n.*[6] [20C+] a skilled, professional tramp. [ext. of JOHN n.[1] (1); such a top-class tramp is well dressed and thus resembles a 'normal' citizen]

john *n.*[7] [1900s–50s] (*US*) in poker, a jack. [punning on the name *Jack*]

john *n.*[8] **1** [1900s–60s] (*US Und.*) (*also* **james**) an easy victim, a sucker; a free spender. **2** [1910s] (*Aus.*) a boyfriend. **3** [1910s+] (*US Und.*) any law-abiding man. **4** [1910s+] (*orig. US*) a female or male prostitute's client. **5** [1940s–60s] (*US Black*) a gullible White man. **6** [1980s] (*US Black*) a man susceptible to feminine trickery. [ext. of JOHN n.[1] (1)]

john *n.*[9] [1910s+] the penis (cf. ABRAHAM n.[1]). [abbr. JOHN THOMAS n. (1)]

john *n.*[10] [1930s+] (*orig. US college*) the lavatory, usu. for men. [? abbr. CUZ JOHN n.]

john *n.*[11] **1** [1950s+] (*gay*) an older man who supports a younger one without actually sharing a long-term relationship with him. **2** [1960s+] (*US gay*) among lesbians, a man who associates with female homosexuals. [ext. use of JOHN n.[1] (1)]

john *n.*[12] [1950s+] an arrest. [rhy. sl.; *John Bull* = PULL n.[3] (2)]

john *n.*[13] [1960s+] a condom. [? JOHN n.[9]; note JOHNNIE n.[11]]

john *n.*[14] [1960s+] (*US*) one's personal signature. [abbr. JOHN HANCOCK n.]

john *n.*[15] [1970s] (*US*) the menstrual period. [var. on JOEY n.[7]]

john n.[16] [1990s+] (*US drugs*) heroin (cf. BIG DADDY n.). [fig. use of JOHN n.[1] (1), based on BOY n.[7] (1) and the idea that heroin is a 'masculine' drug]

john among the maids n. [19C] a whoremonger, a promiscuous man. [JOHN n.[1] (1) + SE *maid*]

john-and-joan n. [late 18C–mid-19C] a hermaphrodite. [the proper names]

john audley phr. **1** [mid-18C] (*UK Und.*) quietly. **2** [late 19C] stop doing that. **3** [1920s] quickly, to be quick. ['Ex. the actor-manager John Richardson (d.1837), who used to ask 'Is John Audley here?' whenever another 'house' was waiting, though tradition (H., 1864) has it that John Audley or Orderly taught him the wheeze' (E.P.)]

john b n. [1930s] (*US*) a hat made by the *John B.* Stetson Company. [abbr.]

John Bates n. *see* MR BATES n.

john bluebottle n. [20C+] a policeman (cf. ANIMAL n.[1]; BABY-BLUES n.[2]; BILLY n.[6]). [JOHN n.[4] + BLUEBOTTLE n. (2)]

John Bradbury n. *see* BRADBURY n.

John Brown n. (*also* **John D, John Esquire, John Handle, John Q, John Rogers, John Smith, John Willy**) [1960s] (*US*) one's signature. [all vars. on JOHN HANCOCK n.]

John Brown v. [mid–late 19C] (*US*) to execute by hanging; thus phr. *be john-browned*, to be hanged. [the abolitionist *John Brown* (1800–59), who was hanged for his part in the attack on Harper's Ferry, Virginia]

John Bull n. **1** [early 18C+] (*also* **Bull, Johnnie Bull, Johnny Bull**) an Englishman, the British, Great Britain. **2** [1900s] (*also* **Miss Bull**) an English woman. [first used to name a character in John Arbuthnot's *The History of John Bull* (1712), in which he also coined *Nic Frog + Louis Baboon*, for a Dutchman and a Frenchman respectively]

John Bull adj. (*also* **Johnny Bull**) [late 18C+] characteristically English. [JOHN BULL n. (1)]

john bull n. [20C+] **1** a pull, a tug. **2** an arrest. **3** a seduction, or the hope of it; thus *go out on the john bull*, to go out looking for sex. [rhy. sl.; (2) = PULL n.[3] (2); (3) = PULL v.[2] (5)]

john bull adj. [1960s+] (*Aus.*) drunk (cf. ADRIAN (QUIST) adj.). [rhy. sl. = FULL adj.[1] (1)]

John Bull's bastard n. [1940s–50s] (*Irish*) an Englishman. [JOHN BULL n. + SE *bastard*]

john canoo v. *see* CANOE v.[1].

john catcher n. [1950s] (*US*) a prostitute (cf. COCKATRICE n.). [JOHN n.[8] (4) + SE *catcher*]

John Chinaman n. (*also* **China John, Johnnie/Johnny Chinaman, Johnnie/Johnny Chinee**) [early 19C–1940s] a derog. term for a Chinese man (cf. AH CABBAGE n.). [assonance]

John Cleese n. [2000s] cheese. [rhy. sl.; ult. UK writer of and actor in Monty Python, *John Cleese* (b.1939)]

john crappo n. *see* JOHNNY CRAPOSE n.

john crow n. (*also* **jancro**) [1940s+] (*W.I.*) a general derog. description of a person. [*john crow*, the carrion crow]

John D n. *see* JOHN BROWN n.

johndarm/john darme n. *see* JOHN n.[4].

john davies, the [late 19C] (*US*) money in general. [ety. unknown; ? anecdotal]

john dillon n. [1930s+] (*N.Z.*) a shilling (5p). [rhy. sl.]

John Doe n. [20C+] an anonymous person, a pseudonym. [18C+ police/legal jargon *John Doe*, any anonymous male suspect, victim etc]

john dory n. [1990s+] (*Aus.*) a story. [rhy. sl.]

john drum's entertainment n. *see* JACK DRUM'S ENTERTAINMENT n.

john dunn n.[1] [late 19C–1900s] (*Aus.*) £1 (cf. CHERRY-PICKER n.[5]). [rhy. sl. = one]

john dunn n.[2] [1910s+] (*Aus.*) a policeman (cf. BILLY n.[6]). [mispron. of Fr. *gendarme*; note JOHNDARM/JOHN DARME n.]

john elbow n. [20C+] a policeman (cf. BILLY n.[6]). [he grabs one by the elbow]

John Esquire n. *see* JOHN BROWN n.

john farmer n. [1900s–70s] (*US*) an ordinary farmer. [JOHN n.[1] (1) + SE *farmer*]

john fortnight adj. [late 19C–1900s] the tallyman, who visits debtors every fortnight to pick up their regular down-payment on goods purchased on credit.

john gilpin n. (*also* **gilpin**) [1950s] (*W.I.*) a large cutlass with a curved back and flared blade. [? tradename, but note the 'trusty sword' carried by the eponymous hero of William Cowper's poem 'John Gilpin' (1783)]

John Hall n. (*also* **Dr Hall, hall**) [1920s–30s] (*US tramp*) alcohol. [rhy. sl. or ? brandname]

John Hancock n. (*also* **hancock**) [late 19C+] (*US*) one's signature, esp. on some form of legal or otherwise official document. [the particularly large signature of *John Hancock* (1737–93) on the US Declaration of Independence, 1776]

John Hancock v. [1960s+] (*US*) to sign one's name. [JOHN HANCOCK n.]

John Handle n. *see* JOHN BROWN n.

john henry n.[1] [late 19C–1940s] (*US Black*) a hard-working Black man, tough and indomitable in the face of appalling challenges; thus *play john henry*, of a man, to make advances towards a woman. [the mythical hero of a popular 19C work song; note Texas prison *john henry*, a snack lunch eaten in the field]

john henry n.[2] [late 19C+] the penis (cf. ABRAHAM n.[1]). [var. on JOHN THOMAS n. (1)]

john henry n.[3] [1910s+] (*US*) one's personal signature, esp. on some form of legal or otherwise official document. [var. on JOHN HANCOCK n.]

john-hold-my-staff n. [17C] a servile attendant. [note JOHN n.[1] (2)]

john hop n. (*also* **hop, johnny hop, johnny hopper**) [20C+] (*Aus.*) a policeman (cf. BOTTLE (AND STOPPER) n.; BILLY n.[6]). [rhy. sl. = COP n.[1] (1)]

john-house n. *see* JOHNNY HOUSE n.

john is dead phr. (*also* **johnny's dead**) [1950s+] (*US teen*) a warning to a woman that her slip is showing. [var. on CHARLIE'S DEAD phr.]

John Ketch n. *see* JACK KETCH n.

John Knox n. [1960s–70s] (*Scot.*) venereal disease. [rhy. sl. = POX n.[1] (2); ult. Scottish religious reformer *John Knox* (1505–72)]

john law n. [20C+] (*orig. US Und.*) a policeman, esp. a senior one (cf. BILLY n.[6]). [JOHN n.[4]/JOHN n.[1] (1) + SE *law*]

johnnie *see also under* JOHNNY and its combs. Note that wherever I have source material, I have given alternative spellings; in those cases where there is a single sp., I have given only the one I found. The alternative may, none the less, exist.

johnnie n.[1] (*also* **johnny**) [late 17C–1900s] a sweetheart, a lover.

johnnie n.[2] (*also* **johnny**) **1** [18C+] a generic term for a man. **2** [mid-19C+] used in direct address to any man whose name is unknown. **3** [late 19C–1940s] an idle, vacuous young aristocrat, a smart young man about town; thus *johnniedom*, the world of such young men.

johnnie n.[3] (*also* **johnny**) **1** [19C] (*mainly Aus.*) a new immigrant. **2** [late 19C+] an inexperienced youngster, a raw recruit, a new hand. [abbr. JOHNNY RAW n.]

johnnie n.[4] (*also* **johnny**) **1** [mid-19C] (*US*) a Confederate soldier. **2** [mid-19C–1940s] a soldier in the Indian Army. **3** [late 19C–1910s] a Gurkha. **4** [1910s–20s] a Turk. **5** [1910s–40s] an Arab (cf. ABDUL n.). **6** [1950s+] an onion-seller from Brittany. **7** [1980s] (*S.Afr. Black*) a soldier. [(1) abbr. JOHNNY REB n.; generic (and slightly contemptuous) use of proper name]

johnnie n.[5] (*also* **johnny**) [mid-19C+] the penis (cf. ABRAHAM n.[1]). [abbr. JOHN THOMAS n. (1)]

johnnie n.[6] (*also* **johnny**) [mid-19C+] (*Anglo-Irish.*) a half-glass of whisky. [synon. Scot. use]

johnnie n.[7] (*also* **johnny**) [20C+] the corner, esp. a public house on a corner. [abbr. JOHNNY HORNER n.]

johnnie n.[8] (*also* **johnny**) [20C+] (*Aus.*) a kookaburra.

johnnie n.[9] (*also* **johnny**) [1930s] a sanitary towel. [? JOEY n.[7]]

johnnie n.[10] (*also* **johnny**) [1930s] (*US*) in poker, a jack. [var. on JOHN n.[7]]

johnnie n.[11] (*also* **johnny**, **johnny bag**) [1960s+] a condom. [? JOHNNIE n.[5]/JOHN n.[13]]

johnnie n.[12] *see* STAGE-DOOR JOHNNIE n.

Johnnie Bates n. *see* MR BATES n.

Johnnie Chinaman/Chinee n. *see* JOHN CHINAMAN n.

johnniedom n. *see* JOHNNIE n.[2] (3).

johnnie nab n. [1940s] (*US Black*) a policeman (cf. BILLY n.[6]). [JOHNNY n.[2] + NAB v.[1] (2)]

johnnie rollocks n. (*also* **johnnie rollox**) [late 19C] nonsense; something fraudulent. [rhy. sl. = BALLOCKS n.[2] (2)]

johnny *see also under* JOHNNIE and its combs.

Johnny n. (*also* **Johnnie**) [1950s+] *Johnny* Walker whisky; differentiated as *Johnny Red*, *Johnny Black*, denoting labels/strength.

johnny n.[1] [mid-19C–1900s] a rustic simpleton or fool (cf. ALVIN n.).

johnny n.[2] [mid-19C+] a policeman; a prison guard (cf. BILLY n.[6]). [JOHN n.[4]]

johnny n.[3] (*also* **johnnie**) [mid-19C; 1930s+] (*US*) a lavatory. [var. on JAKES n./JOHN n.[10]]

johnny n.[4] [2000s] (*US prison*) a sandwich in a sack.

johnny n.[5] *see* JOHNNY (GOVERNMENT) n.

johnny v. [late 19C] to realize, to understand.

johnny pfx (*also* **john**) [19C+] used as a pfx, as in *johnny-darkie, johnny-gyppo* etc; occas. as a sfx. [modern use tends to be facetious/ironic]

johnny all sorts n. [mid-19C–1910s] (*Aus.*) a general dealer, usu. in second-hand goods. [JOHNNY pfx + SE *all sorts*]

Johnny Armstrong n. *see* CAPTAIN ARMSTRONG n.

johnny-at-the-rat-hole n. [1900s–30s] (*US*) an exceptionally enthusiastic, greedy person; thus *play johnny-at-the-rat-hole*, to eavesdrop, to interfere in other people's affairs. [JOHNNIE n.[2] (1) + RATHOLE n.]

johnny bag n. *see* JOHNNIE n.[11].

johnny-bait n. [1960s] an under-age, and thus illegal, sexual partner; used of either sex, although more often of teenage girls. [? JOHNNIE n.[5]/JOHNNY n.[2] + SE *bait*]

johnny-be-good n. [1970s–80s] (*US Black*) the police. [JOHNNY n.[2] + play on rock song 'Johnny B. Goode' (1958)]

johnny bliss n. (*also* **arthur bliss**, **micky bliss**, **mike bliss**) [20C+] (*Aus./UK*) an act of urination; also in fig. use as in phr. 'take the piss' (cf. ANGEL'S KISS n.). [rhy. sl. = PISS n.]

Johnny Bull n. *see* JOHN BULL n.

johnny bum n. [late 18C–early 19C] a donkey. [a euph. for SE *jackass*]

johnny cake n. **1** [mid-19C–1930s] (*US*) a countryman, esp. a New Englander. **2** [20C+] (*US/Can.*) a French-born immigrant. [a cornmeal bread made by Indians and early settlers]

Johnny Cash n. **1** [1960s+] urination (cf. ANGEL'S KISS n.). **2** [1960s+] (*Aus.*) hashish (cf. AFGHAN n.; BOB HOPE n.). **3** [1980s+] (*Aus. prison*) a hiding place. [rhy. sl.; (1) = SLASH n.[3]; (2) = HASH n.[2]; (3) = STASH n.[2] (3); ult. US country singer *Johnny Cash* (1932–2003)]

Johnny Chinaman/Chinee n. *see* JOHN CHINAMAN n.

johnny-come-lately n. [mid-19C+] a novice, an unsophisticated person, a recent arrival or recruit. [JOHNNIE n.[2] (1) + SE *come lately*]

johnny congress n. [early 19C] (*US*) the US Congress. [JOHNNY pfx + SE *Congress*]

Johnny Cool n. *see* JOE COOL n.

johnny cotton adj. (*also* **dolly cotton**) [1930s+] rotten. [rhy. sl.]

johnny crapose n. (*also* **jean crapeau**, **john crappo**, **johnny croppi**, **johnny crapeau**, **...crapaud**, **...crapo**, **...crappo**, **...croppo**) [19C–1930s] a Frenchman. [JOHNNY pfx + Fr. *crapaud*, a toad]

johnny darbies n. [mid-19C+] handcuffs. [DARBIES n. + JOHNNY DARBY n.]

johnny darby n. [mid-late 19C] a policeman (cf. BILLY n.[6]). [JOHNNY n.[2]; added pun on Fr. *gendarme*, a policeman]

johnny foreigner n. (*also* **johnny wop**) [20C+] any foreign person. [JOHNNY pfx + SE *foreigner*]

johnny gallagher n. [20C+] (*US*) a policeman (cf. BILLY n.[6]). [JOHNNY n.[2] + the trad. association of the police with the Irish]

johnny gee n. [1930s] (*N.Z.*) methylated spirits, as drunk by alcoholics. [? GEE (UP) v. (1)]

johnny giles n. *see* FARMER GILES n.

johnny (government) n. [1900s] (*Aus.*) the government, esp. as a tax-gatherer. [JOHNNY pfx + SE *government*]

johnny grab n. [mid-19C] (*US Und.*) an executioner. [JOHNNIE n.[2] (1) + ? GRAB v.[1] (2)]

johnny green n. [mid-late 19C] a naïve person. [JOHNNIE n.[2] (1) + SE *green*]

johnny ham n. [1930s+] (*US*) a detective (cf. DICK n.[6]). [JOHNNY n.[2] + play on PIG n.[3] (1)]

johnny hep adj. *see* JOE HEP adj.

johnny hop/hopper n. *see* JOHN HOP n.

johnny horner n. (*also* **charlie horner**, **jack horner**) [late 19C+] the corner, esp. a public house on a corner. [rhy. sl.]

johnny house n. (*also* **john-house**) [1930s+] (*US*) an outside lavatory (cf. BACKHOUSE n.). [JOHNNY n.[3]/JOHN n.[10] + SE *house*]

johnny-jump-up n. [20C+] (*Irish*) a bottle of cider, or mix of beer and cider. [joc. ref. to its effects]

johnny-just-come n. (*also* **just-come**) [20C+] (*W.I.*) a newcomer. [JOHNNIE n.[2] (1) + SE *just come*]

johnny law n. [1920s+] (*US*) a policeman (cf. BILLY n.[6]). [JOHNNY n.[2] (1) + LAW n.]

johnny newcome n. (*also* **johnny newcomer**) **1** [early 19C–1940s] a newcomer or novice. **2** [mid-late 19C] a newborn child. [JOHNNIE n.[2] (1) + SE *new come/newcomer*]

johnny no-stars n. [2000s] a fool. [JOHNNIE n.[2] (1) + the rating of fast food restaurant personnel]

Johnny O'Keefe n. [1980s+] (*Aus. prison*) the teeth. [rhy. sl.; ult. the Aus. rock and roll singer *Johnny O'Keefe* (1935–78)]

johnny-on-the-spot n. [late 19C+] (*US*) a reliable, punctual or decisive person or thing (cf. CHARLIE-ON-THE-SPOT n.). [JOHNNIE n.[2] (1) + SE *spot*]

johnny pea-soup n. *see* PEA-SOUP n.[1] (2).

johnny-popper n. [1990s+] a form of high-powered, if rudimentary catapult, based on a rubber condom taped to a plastic bottle, which, with its bottom cut out, forms a basic barrel; a small stone or slug is placed in the condom, which is pulled back and fired, at high speed, through the plastic 'barrel'. [JOHNNIE n.[11] + POP v.[1] (2)]

Johnny Pry n. *see* PAUL PRY n.

johnny-pump n. [1970s] (*US*) a water hydrant.

johnny randle n. *see* JACK RANDALL n.

johnny rann n. [20C+] food. [rhy. sl. = SCRAN n. (2)]

johnny raper n. [1980s+] **1** (*Aus.*) a newspaper. **2** (*Aus. prison*) a cigarette paper. **3** (*Aus. prison*) a caper, a criminal exploit. [rhy. sl.]

johnny raw n. (*also* **johnnie raw**, **raw**) **1** [19C] a rustic, an unsophisticated country dweller (cf. ALVIN n.). **2** [19C; 1960s] an inexperienced youngster, a raw recruit, a new hand, a novice. **3** [late 19C+] (*mainly Aus.*) a new immigrant. [JOHNNIE n.[2] (1) + SE *raw*]

johnny raw adj. [19C] inexperienced, naïve. [JOHNNY RAW n. (2)]

johnny ray *adj.* [1980s] (*Aus.*) homosexual. [rhy. sl.]

johnny reb *n.* (*also* **johnny, johnny red**) [mid-19C+] (*US*) a Southerner, esp. a fighter for the Confederacy. [JOHNNIE n.² (1) + abbr. SE *rebel*]

johnny rocks *n.* [1920s] (*Irish*) syphilis. [rhy. sl. = POX n.¹ (1)]

johnny ronce *n. see* CHARLIE RONCE n.

johnny rowsers *n.* (*also* **charlie rousers, jolly rousers**) [1920s–60s] (*US*) trousers. [rhy. sl.]

Johnny Russell *n.* [20C+] (*Aus.*) bustle, hustle; esp. in the phr. *on the johnny russell*, bustling about. [rhy. sl.; ult. ? politician Lord *John Russell* (1792–1878)]

johnny rutter *n.* [1930s+] butter. [rhy. sl.]

johnny's dead *phr. see* JOHN IS DEAD phr.

johnny skinner *n. see* JIMMY SKINNER n.

johnny tapp *v.* [1980s+] (*Aus. prison*) to defecate (cf. BOB AND HIT v.). [rhy. sl. = CRAP v.² (1)]

johnny tinplate *n.* [1910s–20s] (*US*) a rural sheriff. [a mocking allusion to his badge]

johnny veg *n. see* YEGG n.

johnny walker *n.* [20C+] **1** a garrulous person. **2** an informer. [rhy. sl. = SE *talker*; ult. *Johnnie Walker*, a brand of whisky]

johnny warder *n.* (*Aus.*) **1** [late 19C] a drunken layabout. **2** [1910s–30s] anyone who drinks alone, a drink that is taken by oneself. [proper name of *John Ward*, who kept a public house in Sussex Street, Sydney, in which he allowed such people to drink]

johnny wet-bread *n.* [20C+] (*Irish*) a teasing rather than aggressive term of mockery. [anecdote of a Dublin beggar who moistened his bread in the city's fountains]

Johnny whop-straw *n. see* WHOP-STRAW n.

johnny woods/woodser *n. see* JIMMY WOODSER n.

johnny wop *n. see* JOHNNY FOREIGNER n.

Johnny wopstraw *n. see* WHOP-STRAW n.

John O'Brien *n.* (*US*) **1** [1900s–50s] a freight train or one of its boxcars; a side-door Pullman. **2** [1910s] an empty safe. **3** [1920s] a hand-car. [ety. unknown; ? anecdotal]

John O'Groat *n.* [20C+] a coat. [rhy. sl.; *John O'Groats*, the northernmost town in mainland Britain]

John O'Groats *n.* [1920s+] sexual satisfaction. [rhy. sl. = OATS n.¹; ult. *see* prev.]

john out of office *n. see* JACK OUT OF OFFICE n.

john palace *n.* (*also* **john house**) [1900s] (*Aus.*) a police station. [JOHN n.⁴ + SE *palace*]

John Pigtail *n. see* PIGTAIL n.⁴ (2).

john plush *n.* [mid-19C–1920s] a footman. [his *plush* uniform]

John Prescott *n. see* CHARLIE PRESCOTT n.

John Q *n. see* JOHN BROWN n.

john q law *n.* [1980s+] (*US*) a policeman (cf. BILLY n.⁶). [JOHN LAW n. + JOHN Q PUBLIC n.]

john q public *n.* (*also* **john q citizen, john q voter**) [1930s+] the average, law-abiding citizen. [JOHN n.¹ (1) + ? ref. to US President *John Q(uincy) Adams* (1767–1848)]

John Roberts *n.* [late 19C] enough alcohol to last a drinker from Saturday night to Sunday night. [*John Roberts*, MP, the author of the Sunday Closing Act, which was applied to Wales]

John Rogers *n. see* JOHN BROWN n.

john roper's window *n.* [mid-16C] a hangman's rope. [pun]

john roscoe *n. see* ROSCOE n.

john sap *n. see* SAP n.².

John Selwyn *n.* [1980s] **1** an unpleasant reaction to drugs. **2** any unpleasant experience or person. [rhy. sl.; *John Selwyn Gummer* = BUMMER n.⁴; ult. *John Selwyn* Gummer (b.1939), UK Conservative politician]

John Smith *n. see* JOHN BROWN n.

johnson *n.*¹ **1** [mid–late 19C; 1960s+] the penis (cf. ABRAHAM n.¹). **2** [1970s] (*US*) a dildo. [analogous with JOCK n.¹ (1) or JACK n.³ (1); (1) 1960s+ use mainly US Black and ? linked to boxing champion Jack *Johnson* (1878–1946)]

johnson *n.*² [1950s+] a pimp; a man living off a prostitute's earnings. [JOHNSONS n.¹ + ? ref. to JOHN n.⁸ (4)]

johnson *n.*³ **1** [1970s] (*US*) a thing. **2** [1980s] the buttocks. [generic use of the common surname]

johnson *n.*⁴ (*US drugs*) **1** [1970s+] marijuana (cf. AUNT MARY n.²). **2** [1980s+] crack cocaine (cf. BASE n.). [ext. of JOHNSON n.³ (1)]

johnson bar *n.* (*US*) **1** [1920s+] a penis. **2** [1960s–70s] a dildo. [? railroad jargon *johnson bar*, the reverse bar of an early 20C locomotive; note JOHNSON n.¹]

johnson rod *n.* [1950s+] (*US*) an imaginary part of an engine, as in a car, blamed for a malfunction. [? railroad jargon *johnson bar*, the reverse bar of an early 20C locomotive; also note JOHNSON n.³ (1)]

johnsons *n.*¹ (*also* **johnson boys, …brothers, …family, …man**) [1920s+] (*US*) a generic term for the world of professional criminals. [? the commonness and thus potential anonymity of the name; or ? railroad jargon *johnson bar*, the reverse bar of an early 20C locomotive, used as a weapon or cosh]

johnsons *n.*² [1970s] (*US*) a woman's breasts. [ety. unknown; ext./misreading of JOHNSON n.¹ (1)]

john stagger-back *n.* [20C+] (*W.I.*) a variety of codfish fritter, so tough and chewy that one 'staggers back' when one bites it.

John T Henry *n.* (*also* **O Henry, Paul Henry, Sam Henry**) [1960s+] one's signature. [on pattern of JOHN HANCOCK n.; despite *O. Henry* (the writer) these are generic uses of fictional names]

john thomas *n.* **1** [late 17C+] (*also* **john thomson, Sir Thomas**) the penis (cf. ABRAHAM n.¹). **2** [mid–late 19C] a liveried servant. [? like the former, the latter 'stands' in the presence of a lady]

johnwalker *n.* [1970s] (*US Und.*) a security man in a brothel. [JOHN n.⁸ (4) + SE *walk*, i.e. to remove]

John Wayne *n.*¹ [1960s+] (*US*) anything or anyone seen as heroic, macho, manly. [suggestive of heroic film characters played by the Hollywood actor *John Wayne* (1907–79)]

John Wayne *n.*² [1990s+] a train. [rhy. sl.; ult. *John Wayne* (*see* prev.)]

John Wayne *adj.* [1960s+] (*US*) heroic, macho, manly. [JOHN WAYNE n.¹]

John Wayne *v.* [1960s+] (*US*) to act decisively, daringly, in an aggressive manner; often in ironic use. [JOHN WAYNE n.¹]

john willie *n.* [1930s+] the penis (cf. ABRAHAM n.¹). [var. on JOHN THOMAS n. (1); note WILLIE n.⁵]

John Willy *n. see* JOHN BROWN n.

John Woo *v.* [2000s] (*US Black*) to shoot with a pistol in each hand. [the trademark of Hong Kong/Hollywood film director *John Woo* (b.1946)]

john yegg *n.* [1900s] (*US Und.*) the leader of a gang of criminal tramps. [real-life criminal *John Yeager*, who led such a gang]

join *n.* [20C+] (*Ulster*) a pool or 'kitty' of money to provide a round of drinks.

join-boy *n.* [1940s+] (*S.Afr.*) a newly recruited miner. [? Fanakalo *joyin*, a contract + SE *boy*]

joined *adj.* [late 19C] married. [note JOIN GIBLETS v.]

joiner *n.* [late 19C+] (*orig. US*) one who delights in joining a number of societies, groups and other organizations.

join giblets *v.* (*also* **mix giblets**) **1** [18C–19C] to have sexual intercourse (cf. BELLY BUMP v.). **2** [late 18C–early 19C] to cohabit without being married. [SE *join giblets*, to marry]

join out *v.* [late 19C–1920s] **1** (*US tramp*) for 2 or more tramps to become companions on the road; to be hired. **2** (*US Und.*) to join a criminal gang.

join paunches *v.* [mid-17C–18C] to have sexual intercourse (cf. BELLY BUMP v.).

joint *n.*¹ [17C; mid-19C; 1930s+] (*US*) the penis. [? the physical connection or joining that is basic to sexual intercourse]

joint *n.*² [late 19C–1900s] a wife. [JOINED adj.]

joint *n.*[3] [late 19C–1950s] (*Aus.*) a person, a fellow, a 'chap'. [briefly Cockney in the late 19C; ? the 'other half' of JOINT n.[2]]

joint *n.*[4] **1** [late 19C–1950s] (*US drugs*) (*also* **pipe joint**) an opium den. **2** [late 19C+] (*orig. US Und.*) a swindling set-up or a place to be robbed. **3** [late 19C+] (*orig. US*) any place, esp. a bar or club, a brothel, a gambling establishment (cf. BADGER-CRIB n.). **4** [20C+] (*orig. US tramp*) a meeting place. **5** [1910s] a factory. **6** [1910s+] one's house or home. **7** [1910s+] a country, a geographical area, a town, a city. **8** [1920s+] (*US*) prison; also as *the joint*. **9** [1920s+] (*Aus./US carnival*) any 'sideshow' devoted to gambling. **10** [1940s] the profits of a confidence trick. **11** [1960s] (*US*) a police station. **12** [1980s] (*US*) a detoxification facility. **13** [1990s+] in fig. use, any kind of object or place, often unspecified. **14** [2000s] (*US Black/prison*) a prison sentence. [according to the *OED* the orig. use applied spec. to Chinese-run opium dens and thence to illicit saloons; in both cases the *joint* was seen as a gathering place for criminals, a low-life nuance that remains with the word, even in its more general sl. use]

joint *n.*[5] (*orig. US drugs*) **1** [1930s+] an opium pipe or hypodermic syringe and other drug paraphernalia; thus *crack a joint*, to smoke an opium pipe. **2** [1950s] a cigarette laced with paregoric. **3** [1950s+] a marijuana or hashish cigarette (cf. AFRICAN WOOD-BINE n.). [(1) the 'joining' of the opium and its pipe; (2) the 'joining' of the drug with tobacco to make the cigarette; by the 1990s the drug ref. had become sufficiently common for the word to be used almost without comment or identifying quotation marks]

joint *n.*[6] [1940s+] (*US*) a gun. [? fig. use of JOINT n.[1]]

joint *n.*[7] (*orig. US Black*) **1** [1970s+] something excellent, as in the phr. *the serious joint*, the real thing. **2** [1980s+] an artistic creation, typically a record or film. [? JOINT n.[4] (13); (2) popularized by film-maker Spike Lee (b.1956) who credits his films 'Another Spike Lee Joint'; now used by many HIP-HOP n./RAP n.[2] artists to describe their records]

join the angels *v.* [19C+] to die.

join the bird family *v.* [1940s] (*US Black*) to leave fast, to run away. [to 'fly' away]

join the crowd! *excl.* [1970s+] an excl. used to make it clear to one who is complaining that their problems are by no means theirs alone.

join the gang *v.* [late 19C] to become a professional thief.

join the great majority *v.* [18C+] to die (cf. LEAVE THE MINORITY v.). [to die, thereby joining all the dead of thousands of years of humanity]

join the household brigade *v.* [late 19C] of a man, to get married. [pun]

jointman *n.* [1920s+] (*Can./US prison*) any prisoner who toadies to the authorities. [JOINT n.[4] (8) + SE *man*]

joint of beef *n.* [20C+] the chief, i.e. the boss. [rhy. sl.]

joint-togs *n.* [1950s] (*US Und.*) the clothes worn by a prostitute in a brothel. [JOINT n.[4] (3) + TOGS n. (1)]

jointwise *adj.* [1930s–50s] (*US prison*) well-adjusted to prison life, capable of sustaining one's existence in prison. [JOINT n.[4] (8) + -WISE sfx (1)]

jojee *n.* [1960s+] (*drugs*) heroin. [var. on DUJI n.]

jo-jo *n.*[1] **1** [late 19C–1900s] (*Aus.*) a man with a very heavy beard and side-whiskers. **2** [20C+] (*US*) a funny character. [proper name *Jo-Jo* of (1) a Russian 'dog-man' who was exhibited as a sideshow freak in Melbourne, *c*.1880; (2) a dog-faced boy exhibited by P.T. Barnum (1810–91)]

jo-jo *n.*[2] [1960s+] (*Can. prison*) a bulky coat without pockets. [ety. unknown]

jojo *n.* [1960s+] (*US Black*) the penis. [? JOHN n.[9]; ? JOHNSON n.[1] (1)]

jo-jo book *n.* [1990s+] (*US*) a pornographic book. [JOJO n.]

joker *n.*[1] **1** [early 19C+] (*orig. Aus.*) a man, a person, usu. with implications of incompetence. **2** [mid-19C+] (*US*) any thing or situation that poses a problem, a hidden catch, a surprise.

3 [20C+] (*W.I.*) anyone who is given authority but performs their work with irritating incompetence, thus 'a disgrace to one's profession'. **4** [1920s] a Black person. **5** [1950s] (*US gay*) a masculine homosexual. [they make a joke of the situation; (2) is playing-card imagery]

joker *n.*[2] [1920s–50s] (*US drugs*) **1** a hypodermic syringe. **2** an injection of morphine.

joko *n. see* JOCKER n.[1] (3).

jol *n.* (*also* **jaul, jawl**) (*S.Afr.*) **1** [1950s+] a good time, merry-making, enjoyment, entertainment. **2** [1970s+] a party, a festival or other social occasion. **3** [1980s+] a joke, a stunt, a game. **4** [1980s+] a holiday, a trip taken for pure enjoyment. [Afk. *jol*, a dance, a party]

jol *v.* (*also* **jaul, jawl**) (*S.Afr.*) **1** [1940s+] to go out. **2** [1940s+] to stroll, to run, to depart, to look for some fun or entertainment. **3** [1960s+] to have an affair with, to flirt, to 'carry on'. **4** [1970s+] to tease, to joke. **5** [1970s+] to play, to frolic, to have fun, to 'party'. [JOL n.]

jola *n.* [1950s+] (*W.I.*) an over-sized handbag. [Carib.E *jola*, a large jute sack]

joller *n.* (*S.Afr.*) **1** [1960s+] a hedonist. **2** [1960s+] one who frequents 'unsavoury' bars, dancehalls and similar places of low-life entertainment. **3** [1980s+] one who attends a party, concert or social gathering. **4** [1980s+] a player of a game. [JOL v.]

jollier *n.* (*also* **jolly**) [late 19C–1930s] (*UK Und.*) a card-sharp's accomplice, who pretends to be a member of the public.

jollies *n. see* JOLLY n.[6] (1).

jolling *n.* (*S.Afr.*) **1** [1960s+] flirting. **2** [1980s+] merry-making, 'partying'. [JOL v. + sfx -*ing*]

jollo *n.* [20C+] (*Aus.*) **1** a party, a celebration, usu. involving drinking. **2** intense activity, not necessarily pleasurable. [SE *jollification* + -O sfx (4)]

jollocks *n.* (*also* **jollock, jollux**) **1** [mid-18C–early 19C] a fat person. **2** [late 18C–19C] a parson. [SE *jolly*, but note dial. *jollus*, fat, fleshy, *jollock*, jolly, hearty]

jollop *n.*[1] **1** [late 19C+] a purgative, a medicine. **2** [1920s+] strong liquor or a measure of liquor. [SE *jalap*, a purgative drug obtained from the tuberous roots of *Exogonium* (*Ipomoea*) *purga*]

jollop *n.*[2] [1990s+] (a gob of) semen (cf. BOLLOCK SNOT n.). [dial. *jollop*, a wet mess (of food)]

jollopi *n. see* JALOPY n.

jollux *n. see* JOLLOCKS n.

jolly *n.*[1] [late 18C–mid-19C] the head. [abbr. JOLLY NOB n.]

jolly *n.*[2] [early–mid-19C] an accomplice. [? they 'jolly one along']

jolly *n.*[3] [early 19C–1940s] a marine; thus *tame jolly*, a militiaman; *royal jolly*, a royal marine. [*OED* suggests n. use of SE *jolly*, cheerful, gallant, brave etc, but Bowen (*Sea Slang*, 1929) and Fraser & Gibbons (*Soldier & Sailor Words & Phrases*, 1925), say it was adapted from the nickname of the City Trained Bands, a 'Tame Jolly' (which may also have come from SE)]

jolly *n.*[4] **1** [mid-19C] praise, esp. when spoken for an ulterior and/or criminal purpose. **2** [mid–late 19C] a cheer. **3** [mid–late 19C] a sham purchaser, who praises up inferior goods in order to facilitate their sale to an innocent buyer; similarly used for a fairground stallholder's or crooked gambler's accomplice. [JOLLY v.]

jolly *n.*[5] **1** [mid-19C] (*UK Und.*) an aggressive complaint or warning. **2** [mid–late 19C] a ruckus, a fracas. **3** [mid–late 19C] the person who encourages or initiates a ruckus. **4** [mid-19C–1910s] a deception or hoax. **5** [mid-19C+] (*US*) light-hearted teasing, bantering; often as *the jolly*. [(1) and (2) f. (5)]

jolly *n.*[6] **1** [late 19C+] (*also* **jollies**) a thrill of pleasure or excitement. **2** [1960s+] (*US*) an orgasm. **3** [1990s+] sexual play, whether or not including intercourse.

jolly *n.*[7] [late 19C+] a party, a merry-making. [SE *jollification*]

jolly *adj.*[1] [mid-14C+] used as an admiring intensive, splendid, good, pleasant; also in ironic use.

jolly adj.[2] [mid-17C+] tipsy, drunk (cf. ABOUT RIGHT phr.[1]).

jolly adj.[3] [mid-17C+] big, great, plump.

jolly v. 1 [mid-19C] to make a sham bid at an auction. 2 [mid-19C–1920s] to tease roughly, to chaff, to abuse, to trick. 3 [mid-19C+] (also **jolly along, jolly for, jolly up**) to treat someone in an agreeable manner, with the intention of keeping them happy and/or obtaining a favour from them. 4 [late 19C] to cheer. 5 [late 19C] (US campus) to have a good time.

jolly adv. 1 [mid-16C+] extremely, very, esp. when used ironically. 2 [late 19C+] a euph. for BLOODY adv. [SE 14C–19C]

jolly pfx see JOLLY (OLD) pfx.

jolly bag n. [1980s+] (US) a condom. [JOLLY n.[6] (2) + SE bag/ BAG n.[7]]

jolly beans n. (also **jolly pills**) [1960s+] (drugs) amphetamine pills (cf. A n.[2]). [JOLLY n.[6] (1) + SE beans/pills]

jolly boys n. [late 19C] 'a group of small drinking vessels connected by a tube, or by openings one from another' (F&H). [the effect of using such a vessel]

jolly cod n. see LUSTY COD n.

jolly d! excl. [1940s+] (UK juv.) wonderful, excellent, fantastic. [? abbr. SE jolly delightful/decent; note D adj.]

jolly dog n. [18C–19C] a boon companion; thus jolly-doggy-ness. [SE jolly + DOG n.[2] (1); later use is SE]

jolly for polly phr. [20C+] sexually available. [SE jolly + rhy. sl. polly = LOLLY n.[4]]

jolly joker n. [20C+] a poker. [rhy. sl.]

jolly member n. [19C] the penis (cf. DEAREST MEMBER n.). [MEMBER n.[1]]

jolly nob n. [late 18C–mid-19C] the head. [SE jolly + NOB n.[1] (1)]

jollyo n. [1970s] a celebration. [JOLLY n.[7] + -O sfx (1)]

jolly (old) pfx [1920s+] a pfx of affection, dear (old).

jolly pills n. see JOLLY BEANS n.

jolly roger n. [20C+] a lodger. [rhy. sl.]

jolly rousers n. see JOHNNY ROWSERS n.

jolly stick n. [1970s] the penis (cf. BAT n.[7]). [SE jolly + STICK n.[1]]

jolly tit n. [early 18C] a pleasant companion. [SE jolly + TIT n.[2] (2)]

jolly-up n. 1 [1900s–20s] a drinking bout, a spree. 2 [1920s] an informal dance, a party. 3 [1920s–50s] a good time. [JOLLY n.[7]]

jolly utter adj. [late 19C–1900s] appalling, unspeakable. [JOLLY adv. (1) + SE utter; coined by W.S. Gilbert in Patience (1881), his satire on the Aesthetic Movement]

Jolson story n. [1970s–80s] the penis (cf. ALMOND n.). [rhy. sl. = CORIE n.; ult. The Jolson Story, a biopic of the singer Al Jolson (1886–1950), released in 1946]

jolt n.[1] 1 [20C+] (US drugs) a measure of a drug as taken by a user, esp. an injection of a narcotic; occas. of a non-recreational drug. 2 [20C+] a stiff drink of spirits, esp. brandy, whisky or bourbon. 3 [1920s+] (US) the immediate effect of a drug or alcohol.

jolt n.[2] 1 [1910s+] (US Und.) a prison sentence, usu. with the number of years specified, e.g. a seven-year jolt. 2 [1940s] (US) a job.

jolt n.[3] [1960s] (US) a train.

jolt v.[1] 1 [17C–18C] to have sexual intercourse. 2 [mid-19C+] (orig. US) (also **pass someone a jolt**) to hit someone. 3 [1910s+] (US) (also **jolt up**) to drink. 4 [1950s+] (US drugs) to inject a drug. 5 [1960s–70s] (Scot.) to abscond.

jolt v.[2] [1920s–30s] (US Und./prison) to sentence to prison. [JOLT n.[2] (1)]

jolter n. [1910s] (drugs) a drug user. [JOLT n.[1] (1)]

jolterhead n. (also **jolter-pate, jolthead**) [late 16C–19C] a fool, a stupid person. [dial; ult. ? SE jowl, a bump on the head]

jolter-headed adj. (also **jolt-headed**) [late 16C–19C; 1980s+] stupid, foolish (cf. AIRHEADED adj.). [JOLTERHEAD n.]

jolt up v. see JOLT v.[1] (3).

jomer n. [mid-late 19C] a girlfriend; occas. any woman (cf. BLOWER n.[1]). [? Rom./Polari]

jomoke n. see JAMOKE n.[1].

jonah n. 1 [mid-19C+] one who brings bad luck; thus jonahness; also of objects. 2 [late 19C+] one who suffers severe misfortune. 3 [1960s] (US prison) a misfortune. [the biblical story of Jonah and the Whale]

jonah v. 1 [late 19C+] to bring bad luck. 2 [1960s] (US Black) to trick, to swindle. [JONAH n.]

jonah's whale n. [late 19C–1910s] a tail. [rhy. sl.]

jonathan n. 1 [late 18C–mid-19C] (US) a New Englander. 2 [late 18C–1900s] (orig. US) an American; thus fem. Jonatheena. [abbr. SAmE Brother Jonathan, a generic for the US and for its people; note Bartlett, Dict. Americanisms (1848): 'When General Washington [...] came to Massachusetts to organize it and make preparations for the defence of the country, he found a great want of ammunition and other means necessary to meet the powerful foe he had to contend with [...] On one occasion at that anxious period, a consultation of the officers and others was had, when it seemed no way could be devised to make such preparation as was necessary. His Excellency, Jonathan Trumbull the elder, was then Governor of the State of Connecticut, on whose judgment and aid the General placed the greatest reliance, and remarked, "We must consult 'Brother Jonathan' on the subject." The General did so, and the Governor was successful in supplying many of the wants of the army. When difficulties afterwards arose, and the army was spread over the country, it became a by-word [...] The term Yankee is still applied to a portion, but "Brother Jonathan" has now become a designation of the whole country, as John Bull has for England'; there is no evidence for this popular story, however, in Washington's papers]

Jonathan Aitken n. [2000s] eggs and bacon. [rhy. sl.; ult. Jonathan Aitken (b.1942), former Conservative MP and convicted perjurer]

Jonathan Ross n. [1980s+] **1** a drink, spec. beer. **2** a TOSS n.[1] (1). [rhy. sl.; ? (1) = SE toss (it back) or play on TOSSER n.[1]; ult. Jonathan Ross, UK TV personality (b.1960)]

Jonathan Simonizer n. [1930s–40s] (US campus) a toady, a sycophant. [var. on APPLE-POLISHER n.; Jonathan, a kind of apple + Simonizer, a brand of wax]

jone v. see JOAN v.

jones n.[1] **1** [1960s+] (US drugs) (also **Mr Jones**) drug addiction, esp. to heroin. **2** [1960s+] (US drugs) a heroin addict. **3** [1960s+] (US drugs) heroin. **4** [1960s+] the symptoms of heroin withdrawal. **5** [1970s+] pleasurable drug-induced feelings. **6** [1970s+] (US) a strong craving or habit, whether for cigarettes, food, a person or anything, e.g. a love jones, a chocolate jones. [the common family name; its link to craving remains unexplained; note Hip-Hop Connection (December 1999): 'According to our colleagues at the Online Rap Dictionary, it comes from Jones Alley in Manhattan where junkies, with their ever-present longing, used to live']

jones n.[2] [1960s+] (US Black) **1** the penis (cf. ABRAHAM n.[1]). **2** sexual intercourse. [? JOHNSON n.[1] (1)]

jones n.[3] [1970s+] (US Black) a Black person. [generic use of surname]

jones n.[4] [1980s] (US drugs) a marijuana cigarette.

jones v. **1** [1970s+] (drugs) to suffer from narcotics addiction or the withdrawal symptoms that accompany it. **2** [1980s+] in fig. use, to be obsessed by, to be dependent on. **3** [1980s+] to want very much. **4** [1980s+] (US campus) to intrude in order to try to prevent someone who is attempting to seduce another. **5** [1990s+] (US campus) to do wrong, to cause someone to be unhappy. [JONES n.[1]]

jones boy n. see JONES MAN n.

joneser n. [1980s+] (US) an addict, esp. of cocaine. [JONES n.[1] (1)]

jonesing adj. [1980s+] (US campus) boring. [fig. use of JONES v. (1)]

jonesing (out) n. [1970s+] (US drugs) withdrawal from an addictive drug, with the symptoms that accompany this. [JONES v. (1)]

jones man n. (also **jones boy**) [1970s+] (US Black/drugs) a heroin dealer. [JONES n.¹ (3) + SE man/boy]

Jones's locker n. see DAVY JONES'S LOCKER n.

jong n.¹ (S.Afr.) **1** [early 17C–19C] a Black servant. **2** [early 19C] an informal mode of address, irrespective of sex. **3** [20C+] a derog. term for a Black man (cf. ALLIGATOR BAIT n.²). [Cape Du. jongen, a young lad]

jong n.² [1920s–50s] (US) the penis. [? JOHN n.⁹ + SCHLONG n. (1)]

jong! excl. [1950s+] (S.Afr.) an excl. of surprise, delight, exasperation, approval etc. [? JONG n.¹/JONG n.²]

jon-hop n. (also **john-hop, jonn, jonna, jonnop, jonop**) [20C+] (Aus.) a policeman. [rhy. sl. = COP n.¹ (1)]

jonic adj. see JANNOCK adj.

joning n. see JOANING n.

jonn/jonna n. see JON-HOP n.

jonnick/jonnock adj. see JANNOCK adj.

jonnop/jonop n. see JON-HOP n.

jont n. [2000s] (US prison) a thing, an object. [var. on JOINT n.⁴ (13)]

joog v. see JUKE v.¹.

joogie n. [1970s–80s] (US Black) a Black person; occas. in derog. use. [? JUKE n.¹ (1) + BOOGIE n.²]

jook see also under JUKE.

jook n. see JUK n.

jook v. (also **jog, joog, jug**) [1970s+] (US gay) to sodomize. [JUKE v.² (3)]

jookass n. [1920s] (US Black) a jackass. [pron.]

jook-halter n. [19C+] (Ulster) one who has only just escaped hanging. [Scot. jouk, to trick + SE halter]

jook house/joint n. see JUKE n.¹ (1).

jook out someone's eye v. [1950s+] (W.I.) to cheat in a business deal. [fig. use of JUKE v.² (1)]

jooks n. [1990s+] (Black) a fool. [JUKE v.¹ (2)]

jook-the-beetle n. [20C+] (Ulster) **1** a bad cook. **2** a lump in mashed potatoes or porridge. [fig. use of Scot. jouk, to trick + beetle, a hammer, in this case a masher for the vegetables]

jook-the-bottle n. [20C+] (Ulster) a teetotaller. [fig. use of Scot. jouk, to trick + SE bottle]

joppy n. see JALOPY n. (1).

joram n. (also **jorum**) [mid-18C+] a drinking vessel, thus the drink it contains. [joram, a drinking bowl; ? ult. the biblical name Joram who 'brought with him vessels of silver, and vessels of gold, and vessels of brass' (2 Sam. 8:10)]

jordan n.¹ (also **jordain, jurden**) [late 14C–1970s] a chamberpot. [ety. unknown; one theory suggested that the term is an abbr. of Jordan-bottle – a bottle of water brought from the River Jordan by crusaders or pilgrims – but this ignores the orig. form of the word, as found in Promptuarium Parvulorum (1440), jurdanus, which has no links to Jordanes, the contemporary Lat. for the Jordan. An earlier SE use was a kind of pot or vessel formerly used by physicians and alchemists; such pots might often have held urine for analysis; thus leading to the sl. term]

jordan n.² (also **jordain**) [late 17C–mid-19C] (UK Und.) a blow with a staff. [ety. unknown; ? f. use of 'go over the Jordan' as euph. for die; such a blow might kill the recipient]

jork n. [1990s+] (US campus) an idiot, a fool. [JERK n.¹ (2) + DORK n. (2)]

jorum n. see JORAM n.

j.o. scene n. [1960s+] (gay) **1** masturbation. **2** mutual masturbation. [J.O. n.¹ (1) + SCENE n. (6)]

José n. [1970s+] (US) a term for a Puerto Rican, usu. derog. (cf. BATO n.). [a common given name among Hispanics]

Joseph n. **1** [mid-17C–mid-19C] a (usu. woman's) overcoat or cloak; thus rum Joseph, a first-rate overcoat. **2** [mid-17C–19C] a bashful young man. **3** [1950s] (UK juv.) a dreamer. [all are biblical:

(1) Joseph's 'coat of many colours'; (2) Joseph who fled from Potiphar's wife; (3) Joseph's dream]

joseph adj. [1900s–20s] (US) aware, in the know; thus as n., one who is aware. [ext. of JOE adj.¹ (1)]

Josh n. [mid-19C–1900s] (US) a rustic, simpleton (cf. ALVIN n.). [JOSKIN n.]

josh n. [late 19C+] (US) a good-natured joke or piece of banter. [JOSH v.]

josh adj. [1990s+] of a person, horrible, unpleasant, stupid. [? JOSH n.]

josh v. (also **put the josh on someone**) [mid-19C+] (US) to tease or engage in banter with someone; thus n. joshing; also as adj. josh, amusing. [proper name Josh Billings, the pen name of American humorist Henry Wheeler Shaw (1818–85)]

josh! excl. [mid-19C] (US) a cry of encouragement. [JOSH n.]

josher n.¹ [late 19C–1920s] (US) a teaser. [JOSH v.]

josher n.² [late 19C–1940s] (Aus.) an immoral old woman. [? JOSH v. or play on Suffolk dial. josh, an old cow]

josies n. [1970s+] (Irish) women's breasts.

joskin n. **1** [early 19C+] a country bumpkin (cf. BLOOTER n.). **2** [late 19C] a foreigner, esp. one from the British Colonies. [dial. joss, bump + SE bumpkin; 20C+ use is US]

joss n. **1** [late 19C–1950s] (Aus./US) a derog. term for a Chinese person (cf. AH CABBAGE n.). **2** [late 19C+] luck; thus good joss, bad joss. [pidgin joss, a Chinese god; ult. Port. deos and Javanese dejos]

josser n.¹ **1** [late 19C] an ageing roué. **2** [late 19C–1900s] a swell, a grandee. **3** [late 19C–1940s] (Aus.) a clergyman, a minister. [pidgin joss, a Chinese god or idol; ult. Port. deos and Javanese dejos]

josser n.² [late 19C–1910s] one who begs for loans, a 'sponger'. [var. on PROSSER n.]

josser n.³ [late 19C–1920s] a simpleton, a fool. [? JOSSER n.⁴]

josser n.⁴ [late 19C–1950s] an outsider. [Polari]

josser n.⁵ **1** [late 19C+] a man, a fellow; usu. in old josser, with the implication of crotchety old age. **2** [1900s] as a term of address. [? a 'beggar' i.e. JOSSER n.²]

joss-house n. [late 19C–1930s] (Aus.) a church. [JOSSER n.¹ (3)]

jossop n. [mid-19C+] gravy. [ety. unknown; ? link to JOLLOP n.¹; ? ult. ME jussell, a broth]

joss-pidgin-man n. (also **joss-house-man**) [late 19C–1920s] a clergyman, esp. a missionary. [SE joss-man, a priest of a Chinese religion, ult. joss, a Chinese idol or image; thus luck (f. Pidgin version of Port. deos, god). Note RN use jossman, Plymouth gin, which carried a picture of a monk on the bottle]

joss temple n. [late 19C] (US) an opium den. [pidgin joss, a Chinese god]

jostle v. **1** [late 18C–1960s] (UK Und.) to cheat. **2** [1960s+] (US Und./police) to pickpocket; thus jostle operation, pickpocketing. **3** [1990s+] to masturbate (cf. BOFF v.).

jostler n. [1920s–60s] (US Und./police) a pickpocket or petty thief. [JOSTLE v.]

joto n. [1970s+] (US gay/prison) a male homosexual, esp. the passive/effeminate member of a couple. [Sp.]

jots n. [1930s–60s] (US) bread. [ety. unknown]

joukoutoo pron. [20C+] (W.I.) a derog. pron., even you, unimportant you; thus, as adj., insignificant, unimportant. [Fr. jusqu'à vous, as far down (socially) as you]

jounce v. **1** [19C] of a man, to have sexual intercourse (cf. BANG v.¹). **2** [2000s] (US campus) to punch. [SE jounce, to shake]

jour n. [19C] a journeyman worker, e.g. a printer, a cabinet-maker. [abbr.]

journey n. [late 19C–1930s] a spell of work, a time or occasion.

journeyman soul-saver n. [mid–late 19C] a scripture-reader.

journo n. [1960s+] (orig. Aus.) a journalist. [abbr. + -O sfx (4)]

Jove n. [late 16C+] used in mild oaths and excls. as a euph. for the otherwise blasphemous God (cf. BOB n.²). [the Latinized version of the Greek Zeus, 'king of the gods']

jow v. [mid–late 19C; 1980s] to go away, to leave; usu. as imper. *jow!* go away! be off! [Hind.]

jowl-sucking n. see GUM-SUCKING n.

joxer n. [20C+] (*Irish*) **1** an idler. **2** one who is out of work. [? northern dial. *jock*, a seaman]

joxy n. see JAXY n.

Joy, the n. [late 19C+] (*Anglo-Irish*) Mount*joy* prison, Dublin (cf. ABBOTT'S PRIORY n.). [abbr.]

joy n. (*drugs*) **1** [1940s+] marijuana (cf. BOMB n.⁴). **2** [2000s] heroin. [the effects]

joy bang n. [1950s+] (*drugs*) an occasional injection of a narcotic by anyone who is not addicted. [SE *joy* + BANG n.⁶; such an injection would usu. be subcutaneous rather than intravenous]

joy bone n. [1980s+] (*US*) the penis. [SE *joy* + SE *bone*/BONE n.¹ (1)]

joy box n. **1** [1940s–60s] (*US Black*) a radio or a piano. **2** [1970s] (*US*) the vagina (cf. BAG n.¹). [SE *joy* + BOX n.⁵/BOX n.¹ (1)]

joy boy n. **1** [1920s+] (*US*) a foolish joker, or (ironically) a bad-tempered person. **2** [1960s+] a male homosexual. **3** [1960s+] a homosexual prostitute. **4** [1990s+] (*US*) a drug addict. [note *Mr Joyboy*, the US mortician, in Evelyn Waugh's *The Loved One* (1948)]

joy button n. (*also* **joy buzzer**) [1970s+] (*US*) the clitoris (cf. BABY IN THE BOAT n.). [SE *joy* + BUTTON n.¹ (3)]

Joyce n. [2000s] (*Irish*) £10 (cf. DANNY BOY n.). [the picture on the pre-Euro note is of Irish writer *James Joyce* (1882–1941)]

joy dust n. [1930s+] (*US drugs*) heroin, morphine or cocaine (cf. AUNTIE EMMA n.; BIRDIE POWDER n.). [SE *joy* + DUST n.⁵]

joy flakes n. [1940s+] (*US drugs*) heroin, morphine or cocaine (cf. AUNTIE EMMA n.). [SE *joy* + FLAKE n.¹]

joy girl n. (*also* **joy lady**) [1910s–70s] (*US*) a prostitute (cf. AWAYDAY GIRL n.).

joy hemp n. (*also* **joy roots**) [1940s] (*US Black*) marijuana (cf. AFRICAN BUSH n.; BOMB n.⁴).

joy hole n. [1930s+] (*US*) the vagina (cf. BLACK HOLE n.¹). [SE *joy* + HOLE n.¹ (2)]

joy house n. [1910s–70s] (*US*) (*also* **joy club/shop**) a brothel (cf. ACCOMMODATION HOUSE n.). [SE *joy* + HOUSE n.¹ (1)]

joy jelly n. (*also* **joy jell**) [1970s+] (*US*) fruit-flavoured vaginal lubricant jelly.

joy joint n. [late 19C–1960s] (*US*) a saloon bar. [SE *joy* + JOINT n.⁴ (3)]

joy juice n. **1** [20C+] (*US*) liquor, alcohol. **2** [1950s] (*US*) rubbing alcohol. **3** [1950s+] (*US Black/campus*) beer. **4** [1950s+] (*US drugs*) liquid amyl nitrite (cf. AIMIES n.). **5** [1960s+] (*US drugs*) chloral hydrate. **6** [1960s+] (*US drugs*) a depressant. [SE *joy* + JUICE n.³]

joy knob n. (*US*) **1** [1940s–70s] a knob screwed to a vehicle's steering wheel, to facilitate steering with 1 hand. **2** [1950s+] the penis. [SE *joy* + SE *knob*/KNOB n.¹ (3)]

joy lady n. see JOY GIRL n.

Joynson-Hicks n. [1920s] (*bingo*) the number 6 (cf. ALDERSHOT LADIES n.). [rhy. sl.; ult. *William Joynson-Hicks* (1865–1932), Conservative Home Secretary 1924–9]

joy of my life n. [20C+] one's wife. [rhy. sl.]

joy pop n. [1930s+] (*drugs*) an occasional injection of a narcotic by anyone who is not addicted. [JOY POP v.]

joy pop v. [1930s+] (*drugs*) to inject narcotic drugs occasionally, without becoming addicted. [SE *joy* + POP v.⁴ (1)]

joy-popper n. **1** [1930s+] (*drugs*) an occasional user of illegal drugs, esp. injectable narcotics. **2** [1960s+] a delight. [JOY POP v.]

joy-popping n. [1930s–70s] (*drugs*) the occasional use of drugs. [JOY POP v.]

joy powder n. [1920s+] (*US drugs*) heroin, morphine or cocaine (cf. AUNTIE EMMA n.; BIRDIE POWDER n.).

joy prong n. [1910s–70s] the penis. [SE *joy* + PRONG n. (1)]

joy ride n. [1940s–60s] (*US*) sexual intercourse.

joy-rider n.¹ [1920s–30s] (*US*) a legless beggar who transports themself on a wheeled platform.

joy-rider n.² [1930s–60s] (*US drugs*) an occasional narcotic drug user.

joy roots n. see JOY HEMP n.

joy shot n. [1920s] (*drugs*) an occasional injection of a narcotic by anyone who is not addicted. [SE *joy* + SHOT n.⁶ (2); note later JOY POP n., JOY BANG n.]

joy smoke n. [1930s–60s] (*drugs*) marijuana (cf. BOMB n.⁴). [SE *joy* + *smoke*/SMOKE n.³ (3)]

joystick n.¹ (*also* **gear stick**) [1910s+] (*orig. US*) the penis (cf. BAT n.⁷). [play on SE *joystick*; Puxley, *Cockney Rabbit: A Dick 'n' Arry of Rhyming Slang* (1992), suggests rhy. sl. = PRICK n. (2), but this is unlikely]

joystick n.² **1** [1930s–50s] (*drugs*) an opium pipe. **2** [1960s+] a marijuana cigarette (cf. BAT n.⁸; BOMB n.⁴). [SE *joy* + STICK n.⁹ (3)]

joy trail n. [1970s+] the vagina (cf. ALLEY n.¹).

joy water n. **1** [1900s–30s] alcohol. **2** [1910s] (*Aus.*) champagne.

joy weed n. [1930s–40s] (*US drugs*) marijuana (cf. AFRICAN BUSH n.; BOMB n.⁴). [SE *joy* + WEED n.¹ (4)]

Jozi n. see JOEYS n.

Jozlin n. see JOCELYN n.

J school n. [1950s+] (*US campus*) a *school* of journalism. [abbr.]

j.s.t. n. see JEWISH (STANDARD) TIME n.

j.t. n. [20C+] the penis. [abbr. JOHN THOMAS n.]

j.t./j.t.o. n. see JAILHOUSE TURNOUT n.

juanita n. (*also* **juana**) [1930s+] (*drugs*) marijuana (cf. AUNT MARY n.²). [play on the Sp. name *marijuana*, lit. 'Mary Jane']

juba n. see JIBA n.

jubbie n. [1990s+] (*W.I.*) a friend, a girlfriend. [? JUBBIES n.]

jubbies n. (*also* **jubblies, jumblies**) [20C+] breasts. [? SE *chubby*]

jubes n. see JUJUBES n.

jubilee n. [late 19C] the buttocks, the posterior. [coined by *The Sporting Times* at the time of Queen Victoria's Golden Jubilee (1887) + a play on the 'arse-end' of the century]

jubilee mutton n. [late 19C–1920s] (*Irish*) very little, a very small portion. [the meagre portions of *mutton* that were distributed in 1897 as part of Queen Victoria's Diamond *Jubilee* celebrations]

Judaic superbacy n. [late 19C] a Jew dressed in 'all the glory of his best clothes' (Ware). [the implication is of flashiness and vulgarity]

Judas! excl. see JUDAS PRIEST! excl.

judas n.¹ [mid-19C+] (*US Und.*) the spyhole set into a solid cell door. [SE *judas-hole, judas-slit*, a peep-hole; ult. the biblical *Judas*, the betrayer of Christ]

judas n.² [1960s] (*Irish*) an unexpected blow, delivered from behind.

judas-haired adj. [mid-19C] **1** red-haired. **2** deceitful. [the biblical *Judas* was supposedly red-haired]

Judas Priest! excl. (*also* **Judas! Judast!**) [late 19C+] (*orig. US*) euph. for JESUS (CHRIST)! excl.

jude n. **1** [late 19C] a prostitute (cf. BABY JANE n.). **2** [late 19C] (*US*) a good-looking and thus, as an insult, effeminate man. **3** [late 19C–1910s] a woman. **4** [1910s] (*Aus.*) a man. [JUDY n.¹]

jude adj. [late 19C] (*US*) of a man, good-looking, thus effeminate. [JUDE n. (2)]

judge n.¹ **1** [early–mid-19C] (*UK Und.*) an experienced criminal. **2** [1950s+] (*S.Afr.*) a senior figure in a prison gang, among whose tasks is to authorize the assassination of a fellow prisoner.

judge n.² [mid-late 19C] (*US*) used in direct address to a man whose real name is unknown.

judge n.³ [1960s+] (*Aus.*) a manual labourer who shirks on the job. [such a person is 'always sitting on a case']

judge v. [1950s+] (*W.I. Rasta*) to wear one's everyday or ordinary clothes or shoes in the yard or in the bush. [ety. unknown; ? the idea of a judge refusing to relinquish their robes]

Judge Dredd *n.* (*also* **Judge Dread**) [1990s+] the head. [rhy. sl.; ult. the comic book hero]

Judge Lynch *n.* [mid-19C–1940s] (*US*) lynch law. [SE *lynch law*, ult. the court held by *Captain William Lynch* (1742–1820) of Pittsylvania in Virginia *c.*1776–80]

judgin' *adj.* [20C+] (*W.I. Rasta*) used to describe everyday or ordinary clothes or shoes worn in the yard or in the bush, as in *judgin' boot.* [JUDGE v.]

Judi Dench *n.* [1990s+] a stench, a stink. [rhy. sl.; the UK actor Dame *Judi Dench* (b.1934)]

Judische compliment *n. see* JEW'S COMPLIMENT n.

judy *n.*[1] **1** [19C+] (*orig. UK Und.*) a generic term for a woman. **2** [19C+] (*orig. UK Und.*) a promiscuous woman or prostitute (cf. BABY JANE n.). **3** [mid-19C+] (*orig. UK Und.*) a girlfriend or wife. **4** [20C+] a ludicrous-looking woman. **5** [1960s] (*Aus.*) a feminine lesbian (cf. AMY-JOHN n.). **6** [1980s+] (*US campus*) a fat woman. [Punch's wife *Judy* in the puppet-show 'Punch and Judy'; 20C+ use mainly in Liverpool dial. + Aus.]

judy *n.*[2] [early 19C–1940s] (*orig. US*) a fool (cf. BEN n.[1]). [? *Punch and Judy*]

judy *n.*[3] (*also* **jupe balls**) [20C+] (*US prison*) a particularly unappealing item of food served to prisoners in solitary confinement; the meal consists of a ground patty, approx. 10 × 10 × 8cm (4 × 4 × 3in), which is composed of the entire meal's ingredients put together through a blender; it is trad. burned on the outside and raw within. [ety. unknown]

judy and punch *n.* [20C+] lunch. [rhy. sl.]

judy-slayer *n.* [late 19C–1900s] a successful ladies' man. [JUDY n.[1] (1) + SE *slayer*; play on SE *lady-killer*]

Judy with the big booty *n.* [1970s+] (*US Black*) a fat woman. [JUDY n.[1] (1) + BOOTY n. (2)]

jued up *adj. see* JUICED adj.[1].

juff *n.* [late 19C+] the buttocks, the posterior. [? Fr. *joues*, cheeks]

jug *n.*[1] [early 18C–late 19C] the buttocks, the posterior. [abbr. DOUBLE JUGG n.]

jug *n.*[2] **1** [early 19C+] prison; thus as *the jug*, solitary confinement; *jugged*, in prison. **2** [mid-19C] the mouth, esp. as a receptacle for alcoholic drink. **3** [mid-19C+] (*orig. UK Und.*) a bank. **4** [mid-19C+] (*US*) a safe; thus *shoot the jug*, to blow open a safe. **5** [1920s+] (*US*) a bottle of whisky or wine. **6** [1930s] (*UK Und.*) a forged cheque. **7** [1930s+] a drink, esp. a pint of beer; thus *knock a jug*, to buy a drink. **8** [1930s+] a female baby. **9** [1970s] (*US drugs*) a bottle of a drug in liquid form.

jug *n.*[3] [late 19C–1950s] a fool, a gullible person. [17C uses SE *jug*, pet name for Joan, generic for the quintessential country girl; late 19C use is abbr. JUGGINS n.]

jug *n.*[4] [1940s+] (*US*) a carburettor. [resemblance]

jug *n.*[5] *see* JOGUE n.

jug *v.*[1] [mid-19C+] to imprison, to incarcerate. [JUG n.[2] (1)]

jug *v.*[2] **1** [late 19C–1960s] to deceive, either jokingly or through some form of illegality. **2** [2000s] (*US prison*) to provoke, to harass. [JUKE v.[1]]

jug *v.*[3] [1930s] (*UK Und.*) to rob someone as they leave a bank. [JUG n.[2] (3)]

jug *v.*[4] (*also* **juge, jugg**) [1960s] (*US Black*) to have sexual intercourse. [JUKE v.[2] (3)]

jug *v.*[5] [1970s+] (*N.Z.*) to hit or slash with a beer bottle. [SNZE *jug*, a litre bottle of beer]

jug *v.*[6] *see* JUKE v.[1].

jug and pail *n.* [20C+] jail. [rhy. sl.]

jug-bitten *adj.* (*also* **jug-broke**) [early 17C] drunk (cf. ALED UP adj.).

jugelow *n.* [early 19C] (*UK Und.*) a dog. [Rom. *guggal*, a dog; note market traders' jargon *juck, juckle*, a dog]

jug-fuck *n.* [1980s+] (*US*) an awful mess or terrible situation. [such an image, copulation with a jug, is seen as absurd]

jugged *adj.* **1** [early 19C+] imprisoned. **2** [1920s+] (*US*) (*also*

jugged up) drunk (cf. ALED UP adj.). [(1) JUG n.[2] (1); (2) JUG n.[2] (5)]

jugger *n.* **1** [1910s–30s] (*US Und.*) a banker. **2** [1920s–60s] (*US Und.*) a bank robber. **3** [1960s–70s] (*US*) a drunk. [(1) and (2) JUG n.[2] (3); (3) JUG n.[2] (5)]

jugging *n.* [2000s] (*UK prison*) a form of punishment inflicted on sex offenders by other prisoners, involving scalding with hot water and sugar. [JUG UP v. (2)]

jugging law *n.* [late 16C] (*UK Und.*) criminality as it pertains to the corrupt practice of certain games, e.g. dicing or skittles. [? unknown use of SE *jug* (sl. uses are too late) + LAW n.[1]]

juggins *n.* [late 19C–1950s] a fool, a dupe, esp. someone who is so foolish that they can be prevailed upon to buy every round of drinks. [var. on MUGGINS n.[1] (4); note Henry Ernest Schlesinger Benzon, better known to London's sporting fraternity as the *Jubilee Juggins*. Benzon, the son of a Birmingham umbrella frame-maker, went through an inheritance of £250,000 (a massive sum at the time) in less than 2 years. His last pennies went in 1887, the year of Queen Victoria's Golden Jubilee, thus earning him his nickname. Only the kindness of his fellow patrons of the raffish Romano's Restaurant in the Strand, who established a fund that sustained him on £7 a week for life, saved him from absolute penury]

juggins' boy *n.* [late 19C–1900s] 'the sharp and impudent son of a stupid and easily ridiculed father' (Ware). [JUGGINS n. + SE *boy*]

juggins-hunting *n.* [late 19C–1900s] looking for someone who will pick up one's bar bill. [JUGGINS n. + SE *hunting*]

juggle *v.* **1** [mid-16C–early 18C] to have sexual intercourse. **2** [late 19C–1930s] (*US*) to manhandle, esp. large things. **3** [1960s+] (*US drugs*) to sell drugs, esp. to support one's own habit. **4** [1990s+] (*W.I./UK Black*) to do any form of illicit business. [SE *juggle*]

juggler *n.*[1] **1** [mid-16C–early 18C] a fornicator, a womanizer. **2** [1950s] someone who keeps many relationships going at the same time. [JUGGLE v. (1)]

juggler *n.*[2] **1** [1960s+] (*drugs*) an addict who sells drugs to help finance their own addiction. **2** [1980s+] a street dealer, orig. of marijuana, latterly of crack cocaine. [JUGGLE v. (3)]

juggler *n.*[3] [1970s] (*US Und.*) an expert at fraudulent manipulation of accounts. [14C SE *juggler*, one who deceives by trickery; a trickster]

juggler's box *n.* [mid-17C–early 19C] (*UK Und.*) a machine used to brand criminals on the hand.

juggs *n. see* JUGS n.

jug-handles *n.* (*also* **jug lugs**) [20C+] sticking-out ears. [joc. use of SE *jug* + *handle*/LUG n.[1]]

jughead *n.*[1] (*US*) **1** [late 19C+] a fool, a general term of abuse. **2** [1910s+] a mule or a horse. [? JUGGINS n.; orig. use denoted a horse or mule with a large chunky head; such a head supposedly denoted stubbornness and stupidity]

jughead *n.*[2] [1940s–70s] a drunkard. [JUG n.[2] (5) + -HEAD sfx (3)]

jugheaded *adj.* [1930s+] (*US*) stupid (cf. AIRHEADED adj.). [JUGHEAD n.[1] (1)]

jug-heavy *n.* [1920s–40s] (*US Und.*) a safe-cracker. [JUG n.[2] (4)]

jug heel *n.* [1900s–30s] (*US Und.*) a bank robber. [JUG n.[2] (3) + HEEL n. (1)]

jug-heistman *n.* (*also* **jug heister**) [1940s–50s] (*US Und.*) a bank robber. [JUG n.[2] (3) + HEISTER n. (1)]

jughouse *n.* [1930s–60s] (*US*) a prison (cf. BANDHOUSE n.). [JUG n.[2] (1) + SE *house*]

jug-loops *n.* [mid–late 19C] loops of hair brought forward over the temples and curled. [such loops resemble the handle of a jug]

jug-lugs *n. see* JUG-HANDLES n.

jugman *n.* [1920s–50s] (*US Und.*) a bank robber. [JUG n.[2] (3) + SE *man*]

jugrooter n. [1930s] (*US Und.*) a bank robber. [JUG n.² (3) + ROOTER n.⁴]

jugs n. (*also* **juggs, milk jugs**) [1950s+] (*orig. US*) the female breasts, esp. when large (cf. BORDENS n.). [abbr. SE *milk jugs*]

jug-steamed adj. [mid-19C] (*US*) drunk (cf. ALED UP adj.). [JUG n.² (5)]

jug touch n. [1900s–30s] (*US Und.*) robbing people as they come out of banks. [JUG n.² (3) + TOUCH n.¹ (3)]

jug-up n. [1960s+] (*Can. prison*) mealtime. [JUG UP v. (1)]

jug up v. **1** [1960s+] (*US prison*) to eat prison food. **2** [2000s] (*UK prison*) (*also* **jug**) to attack a fellow inmate with a jug of scalding water. [(1) JUG n.² (1)]

juice n.¹ **1** [early 16C–early 17C] the profits of a profession or office. **2** [late 17C; 1920s+] money, esp. from bribery, corruption, loan-sharking. **3** [1930s–50s] protection money. **4** [1930s+] (*US*) political or criminal influence, anything involving corruption, pay-offs, favours. **5** [1950s+] (*US gambling*) a bookmaker's percentage. **6** [1960s+] recognition, publicity, respect. **7** [1970s+] (*US*) interest on a debt or loan. [money's 'lubricant' properties; (2) 1920s+ use US]

juice n.² **1** [mid-17C+] semen or vaginal fluid (cf. BABY FLUID n.; BINDERJUICE n.). **2** [18C+] energy, spirit, vitality, usu. sexual. **3** [20C+] (*orig. US*) blood (cf. BADMINTON n.). **4** [1940s–60s] (*US Black teen*) vomit. **5** [1970s] (*US gay*) sweat. **6** [1970s+] (*US*) 'the daylights', or a fig. use of urine, i.e. PISS n., e.g. *knock the juice out of someone*. **7** [1980s+] (*US Black*) sexual intercourse. [despite chronology seems likely that (2) came first as it does with JISM n.]

juice n.³ **1** [mid-17C+] alcohol, wine. **2** [20C+] (*US Und.*) any form of alcohol illicitly made inside a prison. **3** [20C+] (*US*) whisky or any other strong liquor. **4** [20C+] any form of drugs, esp. heroin or methadone in liquid, phencyclidine, crack cocaine; in prison use, the tranquillizer Largactil. **5** [1960s] (*US*) beer. **6** [1970s+] (*S.Afr.*) methylated spirits, as drunk by alcoholics. **7** [1970s+] steroids.

juice n.⁴ **1** [late 19C+] electricity; thus *get the juice*, to be executed in the electric chair. **2** [20C+] petrol. **3** [1910s] (*US*) mercury, as in a thermometer. **4** [1920s–60s] (*US Und.*) nitroglycerine. **5** [1950s] energy. **6** [1990s+] gas. **7** [1990s+] of a vehicle, power. [fig. use of JUICE n.² (2)]

juice n.⁵ [1920s–60s] (*Irish*) 2 pence. [pron. of DEUCE n.¹ (2)]

juice n.⁶ (*US*) **1** [1930s–60s] flattering talk. **2** [1960s+] gossip. [both 'lubricate' communication]

juice n.⁷ [1930s+] gunfire, the power of a weapon. [fig. use of JUICE n.¹ (4)]

juice n.⁸ [1980s+] enjoyment, satisfaction, stimulation. [JUICE v.⁴ (4)]

juice adj. [1990s+] (*US*) privileged, pleasant, convenient. [JUICY adj.¹]

juice v.¹ **1** [late 19C+] (*US*) (*also* **juice (it) up**) to drink alcohol, to get drunk. **2** [1910s–70s] (*US*) to milk a cow, also used facetiously. **3** [1920s–30s] to rain. **4** [1950s] to render someone drunk. [JUICE n.³]

juice v.² **1** [1920s+] (*US*) to electrocute, to kill or torture with electricity. **2** [1940s+] (*orig. US*) (*also* **juice up**) to increase the power of a machine, usu. an automobile. **3** [1960s+] (*US Black*) to intensify, to augment, to liven up, to excite. **4** [1970s–80s] (*US*) to attack with a weapon, to fire a gun. **5** [2000s] to provide with electrical power. [JUICE n.⁴; (4) JUICE n.⁷]

juice v.³ **1** [1950s] to bribe, esp. in the context of organized crime paying off the authorities. **2** [1950s+] to add interest to a loan or debt. **3** [1990s+] to extort money, through threats or trickery. [JUICE n.¹ (2)]

juice v.⁴ **1** [1970s+] (*US Black/campus*) to have sexual intercourse. **2** [1970s+] (*US gay*) of a man, to sweat, esp. during sex. **3** [1980s+] (*US*) to dampen with vaginal secretions. **4** [1980s+] (*US*) in fig. ext. of (3), to get excited. [(1), (3) and (4) JUICE n.² (1); (2) JUICE n.² (5)]

juice a woodie v. to masturbate. [JUICE n.² (1) + WOODIE n.²]

juice box n. (*also* **juice can**) [1940s–60s] (*US*) a battery. [JUICE n.⁴ (1) + SE *box/can*]

juiced adj.¹ (*also* **jued up, juiced up**) **1** [late 19C+] (*orig. US*) drunk or intoxicated by drugs; ext. as *juiced to the skin* (cf. ALED UP adj.). **2** [2000s] energized, hyperactive. [(1) JUICE v.¹; (2) JUICE v.² (3)]

juiced adj.² (*also* **juiced up**) **1** [1970s+] (*US*) excited, nervous. **2** [1980s+] of a woman, sexually aroused. [JUICE v.⁴]

juice-freak n. [1970s] (*US campus*) a person who drinks, as opposed to taking drugs. [JUICE n.³ + FREAK sfx]

juice harp n. [mid-19C–1920s] a harmonica, a Jew's harp. [pron.]

juice-head n. (*also* **juice-hound**) [1950s+] (*US*) a heavy drinker, an alcoholic. [JUICE n.³ + -HEAD sfx (3)/HOUND sfx]

juice house n. [1920s+] (*US Black*) a liquor store. [JUICE n.³ + SE *house*]

juice it up v. *see* JUICE v.¹ (1).

juice joint n.¹ [1920s+] (*US*) a tavern, a bar, any establishment selling liquor. [JUICE n.³ + JOINT n.⁴ (3)]

juice joint n.² [1940s+] (*US gambling*) a crooked gambling establishment operating electronically controlled games. [JUICE n.¹ (2) + JOINT n.⁴ (3)]

juice man n.¹ [1920s–50s] (*US*) an electrician. [JUICE n.⁴ (1) + SE *man*]

juice man n.² [1950s+] (*US Und.*) the collector of loans for an illegal moneylender. [JUICE n.¹ (2) + SE *man*]

juice man n.³ [1970s] (*US*) an influential person. [JUICE n.¹ (4)]

juice of the grape n. *see* GRAPE JUICE n.

juiceoline n. [1970s] (*US*) petrol. [JUICE n.⁴ (2) + SE *gasoline*]

juice one's fruit v. [1980s+] to masturbate (cf. BEAT ONE'S MEAT v.). [brandname *Juicy Fruit*, a popular variety of chewing gum; JUICE n.² (1)]

juice one's joystick v. [1910s+] to masturbate. [JUICE n.² (1) + JOYSTICK n.¹]

juicer n.¹ [1920s+] (*US*) an electrician. [JUICE n.⁴ (1)]

juicer n.² [1940s] (*US*) one who chews rather than smokes tobacco. [the saliva created]

juicer n.³ [1960s+] (*US*) a heavy drinker, an alcoholic. [JUICE n.³]

juicer n.⁴ [1980s+] (*drugs*) a woman who barters sex for drugs, esp. crack cocaine. [JUICE n.³ (4)]

juice road n. [1930s] (*US tramp*) an electric railway. [JUICE n.⁴ (1)]

juicery n. [mid-late 19C] a drinking house. [JUICE n.³]

juice the plum v. [1990s+] to masturbate (cf. BEAT ONE'S MEAT v.). [JUICE n.² (1)]

juice up v.¹ [1990s+] **1** to become damp with sexual arousal. **2** to stimulate one's female partner sexually. [JUICE n.² (1)]

juice up v.² *see* JUICE v.¹ (1).

juice up v.³ *see* JUICE v.² (2).

juicily adv.¹ [1910s+] vigorously, excellently. [JUICY adj.¹ (3)]

juicily adv.² [1960s+] suggestively. [JUICY adj.² (1)]

juicy adj.¹ **1** [early 17C–1950s] wealthy; financially rewarding. **2** [early 17C+] intellectually stimulating. **3** [late 19C+] excellent, first-rate. **4** [20C+] pleasant, enjoyable. [in all cases the implication is of being 'suitable for sucking dry']

juicy adj.² **1** [late 17C+] suggestive, racy, sexy. **2** [1920s+] dramatic, exciting. [JUICE n.²]

juicy adj.³ [late 17C+] secreting vaginal fluids, ready for sex.

juicy adj.⁴ [mid-late 19C] of weather, raining, very wet.

juicy adj.⁵ [late 19C–1930s] painful.

juicy about phr. [1920s+] (*Aus.*) aware of. [fig. use of JUICY adj.²]

juicy fruit n.¹ [1930s+] (*Aus./US Black*) a male homosexual. [JUICY adj.² (1) + FRUIT n.² (2); also a pun on the eponymous chewing gum brandname]

juicy fruit n.² [1950s+] (*Aus.*) sexual intercourse. [rhy. sl. = ROOT n.¹ (5)]

juicy-spicy n. [mid-19C] (*US, Texas*) a boyfriend, the object of a young woman's affections. [JUICY adj.² + SPICY adj. (3)]

ju-ju *n.* (*drugs*) **1** [1940s+] a marijuana cigarette, marijuana. **2** [1980s+] any drugs in capsule form (cf. PILL n.[4]). [SE *ju-ju*, a charm, an amulet, a fetish; the image is of the exoticism of drugs + (1) abbr. SE *marijuana*]

jujubes *n.* (*also* **jubes**) [1960s+] the female breasts (cf. APPLES n.[1]). [SE *jujube*, a suckable lozenge, flavoured so as to represent the jujube fruit (*Ziziphus vulgaris*). Jujube is a very much altered form of the orig. Gk *zizuphon*]

juk *n.* (*also* **jook**) [1940s+] (*W.I.*) **1** a stab. **2** a hypodermic injection. [JUKE v.[2] (1)]

juk *v. see* JUKE v.[2]

juke *n.*[1] (*also* **jook**) **1** [1930s+] (*orig. US Black*) (*also* **jook house/joint, juke house/joint**) any establishment offering drink, food, music or dancing. **2** [1930s+] (*orig. US Black*) cheap, raucous music played at similarly inclined roadhouses, cafés and brothels. **3** [1940s+] (*US*) (*also* **juker**) a jukebox. [? Gullah *jook/joog house*, a disorderly house, a house of ill-repute; ? ult. Bambara (dial. of Mandingo) *jugu*, wicked; Bambara (dial. of Mandingo) *jugu*, wicked, violent]

juke *n.*[2] [1970s+] a trick, a dodge, whether physical or mental. [JUKE v.[1] (1)]

juke *n.*[3] *see* DUKE n.[3] (1).

juke *v.*[1] (*also* **jook, joog, jug, jugg**) **1** [mid-19C+] to evade, to dodge, to avoid, to hide. **2** [mid-19C; 1980s+] (*US/Ulster*) to trick, to cheat, to victimize. **3** [20C+] (*Ulster*) to play truant. [? Scot. *jouk*, to trick, esp. for (2) and (3)]

juke *v.*[2] (*also* **jook, joog, jug, jugg, juk**) (*orig. W.I./US Black*) **1** [late 19C+] to pierce or stick, as with a needle, thorn or a long pointed stick; to stab. **2** [late 19C+] to hit, to beat up. **3** [1930s+] (*also* **joop**) to have sexual intercourse, often quick and casual when the man is keen but the woman is reluctant (cf. BANG v.[1]). **4** [1990s+] to shoot. [? Fulani *jukka*, to poke, to knock down, to spur; note South Carolina dial. *joog/jook*, to prick, to poke, to stab]

juke *v.*[3] (*also* **jook, joog, jug, jugg**) [1930s+] (*orig. US Black/campus*) **1** to dance, to party, to play music, to frequent dancehalls etc. **2** to have a good time. **3** (*also* **juke up**) to boost, to improve. [? Bantu *juka*, Wolof *dzug*, thence to Gullah *juke, joog*, disorderly, wicked]

juke house/joint *n. see* JUKE n.[1] (1).

juker *n. see* JUKE n.[1] (3).

juke up *v. see* JUKE v.[3] (3).

jukey *n.* [1990s+] a *jukebox*. [abbr.]

juk-maka *n.* [1940s] (*W.I.*) a cunning person. [JUKE v.[2] (1) + SE *maker*. He is 'sharp enough to prick a thorn' (Cassidy & LePage, *Dict. of Jamaican English*, 1967, 1992)]

jukrum *n.* [late 17C–early 19C] **1** a seal. **2** a licence. [JARK n.]

juldee *n. see* JILDI n.

juldi *v. see* JILDI v.

julip *n.* [2000s] (*US prison*) homemade alcohol, usu. some kind of fermented juice. [SE (*mint*) *julep*, 'a mixture of brandy, whisky, or other spirit, with sugar and ice and some flavouring, usually mint' (*OED*)]

Julius Caesar *n.*[1] [mid-19C–1910s] the penis (cf. ABRAHAM n.[1]).

Julius Caesar *n.*[2] [20C+] **1** a cheeser, i.e. 'cheesecutter' cap. **2** a freezer. [rhy. sl.]

julk *v.* [mid–late 19C] of a caged songbird, to sing. [? link to East Anglian dial. *julk*, to make a sound like liquor shaken in a cask that is not quite full]

jum *n.* (*drugs*) **1** [1980s+] an outsize vial or rock of crack cocaine. **2** [2000s] a sealed plastic bag containing crack cocaine. [JUMBO n.[3]]

jumbie *n.* (*also* **jumbee, jumby**) [mid-19C+] (*W.I.*) a ghost or spirit, a duppy. [? one of several Bantu languages incorporating *nsmabi*, God or Devil]

jumble *n.*[1] **1** [early 18C–mid-19C] a bumpy ride in a coach or carriage. **2** [mid–late 19C] a kind of cake. [SE *jumble*, a confused or disorderly mixture]

jumble *n.*[2] [1950s–60s] a White person. [pron. of *John Bull*; used by West African immigrants/students in UK and popularized in the books of Colin MacInnes (1914–76)]

jumblefuck *v.* [1930s] (*US*) to participate in an orgy or group sex. [CLUSTERFUCK n. (3)]

jumble-giblets *n.* [17C–19C] the penis; thus *do/perform a jumble-giblets*, to have sexual intercourse.

jumble-gut lane *n.* [late 17C–early 19C] a rough, badly maintained road.

jumbler *n.* [17C–18C] a womanizer, a promiscuous man. [JUMBLE (UP) v.]

jumble (up) *v.* [late 16C–19C] to have sexual intercourse.

jumbloney *n. see* JIBONE n.

jumbo *n.*[1] **1** [early 19C+] a large and clumsy person. **2** [1940s+] (*N.Z.*) the buttocks, the posterior. **3** [1940s+] a fool, a simpleton (cf. BOBO n.[1]). [? *Mumbo-Jumbo*, a West African (Mandingo) deity. Popular ety. links the term to *Jumbo*, the celebrated elephant of the Regent's Park Zoo, sold to Barnum and Bailey's Circus in 1881. However, the Zoo opened in 1828 and Jumbo and a female, Alice, did not arrive until 1863. *OED*'s first cit. for (1) is from *Badcock* in 1823 and thus the term was initially applied to people rather than, as is assumed, to the elephant]

jumbo *n.*[2] [late 19C–1930s] the Elephant and Castle public house in south London. [*Jumbo*, as applied to elephants; for ety. *see* JUMBO n.[1]]

jumbo *n.*[3] **1** [1950s] (*US drugs*) a large capsule of heroin. **2** [1980s+] (*US drugs*) an outsize vial of crack cocaine. **3** [1980s+] (*US*) a quart (2 pints/1 litre) bottle of beer. [JUMBO adj.]

jumbo *adj.* [late 19C+] very large. [JUMBO n.[1] (1)]

jumbo! *excl. see* JESUS! excl.

Jumbo's trunk *adj. see* ELEPHANT'S (TRUNK) adj.

jumbuck *n.* [mid-19C+] (*Aus./N.Z.*) **1** a sheep; thus used generically for the sheep-farming interest. **2** a fool, a simpleton. [Native Aus. *jombok*, a sheep; *DNZE* prefers mispron. of SE *jumpup*]

jumby *n. see* JUMBIE n.

jumm *adj.* [1990s+] (*Ulster*) used of something that is large but unwieldy and as such virtually worthless. [Scot. *jumm*, a clumsily built, awkward-looking house]

jumm *v.* [17C] to have sexual intercourse. [abbr. JUMBLE (UP) v.; but note dial. *jum*, a sudden jolt]

Jump, the *n.* [early 19C] the Black Jack Tavern, Portugal St, London WC2.

jump *n.*[1] (*UK Und.*) **1** [late 16C–early 17C] a robbery carried out around dusk by a number of rogues, who mill about, walking slowly along a street and opening every accessible window, grabbing whatever they can reach and moving on. **2** [late 18C] a robbery carried out by a man posing as a lamp-lighter, who can lean his ladder against a house without suspicion, climb it and enter through any window he can open. **3** [19C] a ground-floor window. **4** [19C] a robbery that involves breaking in through a ground-floor back window; thus *jump the glaze*, to open the window; *go the jump*, to effect such a robbery. **5** [late 19C] an escape, whilst committing a burglary.

jump *n.*[2] **1** [late 19C–1910s] (*US*) liveliness, energy. **2** [late 19C+] (*orig. US*) a journey, esp. from coast to coast or city to city; thus (*US tramp*) a free trip on a train or a boat. **3** [1930s+] (*orig. US Black*) a party where the guests buy their refreshments to help pay the rent (cf. FISH-FRY n.). **4** [1940s–80s] (*US gang/Black*) a dance party. **5** [2000s] (*US prison*) homemade alcohol. [SE *jump*]

jump *n.*[3] **1** [20C+] an act of sexual intercourse. **2** [1930s–40s] (*US*) a sexually promiscuous woman. **3** [1950s+] (*US*) a gang fight. **4** [1970s+] (*US gay/prison*) gang-rape. [JUMP v.[1]]

jump *n.*[4] **1** [20C+] an ambush, an attack, a surprise, an advantage; esp. in GET THE JUMP ON (SOMEONE) v. **2** [20C+] a head start. **3** [1980s] a start. [JUMP v.[1] (4)]

jump *n.*[5] [1970s] (*US gay*) one's home. [JUMP v.[6] (1)]

jump *n.*[6] **1** [1970s+] (*orig. Western Aus.*) a public house bar.

2 [1980s+] (*Aus.*) a barmaid. **3** [1990s+] a shop counter. [one 'jumps up' to buy something]

jump, the *n.* [mid-19C+] (*US*) the beginning, the outset; thus *at/from/on (the) jump*, from the start.

jump *v.*[1] **1** [17C+] to have sexual intercourse (cf. BANG v.[1]). **2** [late 18C–mid-19C] to break into, for the purpose of robbery. **3** [late 18C–19C] (*UK Und.*) to cheat, to defraud. **4** [mid-19C+] to ambush, to attack, esp. in a surprise attack. **5** [mid-19C+] (*US, orig. Western*) to rob, to take possession of another's property unlawfully etc. **6** [late 19C] (*S.Afr.*) to seize goods wrongfully. **7** [late 19C] (*Aus.*) of a convict, to become a prison warder. **8** [late 19C–1960s] (*US Und.*) of police, to raid. **9** [late 19C+] (*US*) to rebuke, to criticize. **10** [late 19C+] to stop and question, as of the police. **11** [1900s] (*US campus*) to punish. **12** [1900s] (*US*) to accuse. **13** [1920s+] (*Aus./US/UK Black*) to arrest. **14** [1930s] (*US*) to inform. **15** [1940s+] to beat up. **16** [1940s+] to rape. **17** [1960s+] (*US Black/campus*) to seduce, to make determined or aggressive sexual advances.

jump *v.*[2] **1** [mid-19C+] (*US*) to leave, to abscond, to quit, from one's duty or to avoid payment. **2** [late 19C–1930s] (*US*) to leave without paying one's bill; often as JUMP ONE'S BILL v. **3** [late 19C+] (*US campus*) to miss a class; to drop a course. **4** [1920s+] (*US*) to leave a job. [SE *jump ship*]

jump *v.*[3] [20C+] (*W.I.*) to startle, to surprise. [SE *make* (one) *jump*]

jump *v.*[4] [1910s+] (*Aus.*) to understand, to work out. [? play on SE *jump to a conclusion*]

jump *v.*[5] (*also* **bust a light**) [1930s+] to fail to stop at a red traffic light or stop signal; usu. in phr. *jump the lights*.

jump *v.*[6] **1** [1930s+] (*orig. US Black*) of a place of entertainment, e.g. a nightclub, to pulsate with energy, to be full of excitement; usu. as *jumping*, esp. in phr. *the joint is jumping*. **2** [1940s+] (*US Black*) to dance, to have fun. [? JUMP n.[2]; ult. SE *jump*]

jump *v.*[7] (*US Black*) **1** [1930s+] to act, to behave, in combs. such as JUMP SALTY V., JUMP SMART V. or JUMP STINK V. **2** [1940s+] to occur, to happen (cf. JUMP OFF v.[2]).

jump *v.*[8] [1950s+] (*Ulster*) to convert from Catholicism to Protestantism for the material advantages such a change would confer.

jump *v.*[9] *see* JUMP THE GUN v.

jumpabout *n.* [1980s] (*Aus.*) a ticket. [rhy. sl.]

jump all over *v.* [20C+] (*orig. US*) to attack verbally, to berate. [note synon. US dial. uses *jump out*, *jump up*]

jump-and-jive *n.* [1940s] (*W.I.*) a shoe made from old automobile tyres, very common during WW2. [SE *jump* + JIVE v.[1] (3)]

jump at *v.* **1** [mid-19C+] to grab an opportunity enthusiastically and speedily. **2** [late 19C] to guess.

jump back! *excl.* [1960s+] (*US Black/campus*) an expression of astonishment.

jump bad *v.* [1940s–70s] (*orig. US Black*) to misbehave. [JUMP v.[7] (1) + SE *bad*]

jump bail *v.* [mid-19C+] (*orig. US*) to disappear (usu. by leaving the country) and thus avoid a possible prison sentence while remanded on bail before trial. [JUMP v.[2] (1) + SE *bail*]

jump city *n.* [1980s+] (*US*) the start; esp. in phr. *from jump city*, from the very beginning. [JUMP, THE n. + CITY sfx]

jump-down *n.* [late 19C–1900s] (*Can.*) somewhere at the very extreme of 'civilization'. [? where one *jumps down* from the wagon at the end of one's journey]

jump down someone's throat *v.* (*also* **jump someone's neck**) [mid-19C+] to become furious with someone, often for no apparent reason.

jumped in port *phr.* [1930s–40s] (*US Black*) newly arrived.

jumper *n.*[1] (*UK Und.*) **1** [late 18C–early 19C] a thief who enters a house through a window. **2** [1980s+] a thief who steals from offices. [JUMP n.[1]]

jumper *n.*[2] [early–mid-19C] a Scot. coin, worth 10 pence. [the image of a man on horseback carried on 1 face of the coin]

jumper *n.*[3] **1** [early 19C–1930s] a flea. **2** [20C+] a travelling bus or rail inspector. **3** [1960s+] (*US*) someone who makes or attempts a suicide jump from a height. **4** [1980s+] (*US*) someone who attempts or makes a suicide jump onto the subway tracks. [SE *jump*]

jumper *n.*[4] **1** [mid-19C–1940s] (*Can.*) a light buggy, a basic form of sledge. **2** [1990s+] (*US Black*) an expensive bicycle, esp. when stolen. [it *jumps over* the bumps]

jumper *n.*[5] [mid-19C–1940s] (*Aus.*) one who jumps a mining claim. [JUMP v.[1] (5)]

jumper *n.*[6] [1940s+] one who absconds while on bail. [JUMP v.[2] (1)]

jumper *n.*[7] [1990s+] (*US drugs*) an injection or portion of a narcotic drug, esp. the first of the day. [it gets one 'up and jumping']

jumpers *n.* [1960s–70s] (*US Black*) gym shoes. [their use in basketball]

jump in *v.* [1980s+] (*US Und.*) **1** to initiate someone into a street gang. **2** to be initiated into a street gang. [JUMP v.[1] (15); the initiation involves the new member being beaten up by one or more of their putative peers]

jumping *adj.* [1940s+] (*orig. US*) lively, energetic, exciting. [JUMP v.[6] (1)]

jumping...! *excl.* [early 19C+] (*orig. US*) used as the first half of a number of combs. that make up mild, euph. oaths, e.g. *jumping beans!* ...*butterballs!* ...*catfish!* ...*cats!* ...*fire!* ...*fish hooks!* ...*gee whillikers!* ...*grasshoppers!* ...*hyenas!* ...*jacks!* ...*Jehovah!* ...*Jehu!* ...*jemima jane!* ...*jenny!* ...*Jerusalem!* ...*jews!* ...*jews harps!* ...*Joseph!* ...*Judas!* (cf. HOLY JUMPING...! excl.; JUMPING JEHOSHAPHAT! excl.; JUMPING JESUS! excl.; JUMPING MOSES! excl.).

jumping beans *n.* [1930s] (*US*) dice.

jumping cat *n.* [1950s+] (*US Black*) **1** a sophisticated, poised older person. **2** anyone successful in their occupation, legitimate or criminal. [JUMPING adj.[2] + CAT n.[11] (4)]

jumping china *n.* [1980s+] (*UK Und.*) someone with whom one is escaping. [JUMP v.[2] (1) + CHINA (PLATE) n.]

jumping jack *n.* [20C+] the *black* ball in snooker. [rhy. sl.]

jumping Jehoshaphat! *excl.* [20C+] one of a variety of phrs. that euphemizes the once blasphemous JESUS (CHRIST)! excl. [JUMPING...! excl.]

jumping Jesus! *excl.* [1920s+] a mildly blasphemous oath or intensifier. [JUMPING...! excl.]

jumping Moses! *excl.* [mid-19C+] (*US*) a mild oath, great heavens! [JUMPING...! excl.]

jumping powder *n.* [early–mid-19C] a stimulant, esp. that taken (usu. in liquid form) by huntsmen or steeplechasers.

jump in someone's shit *v.* [1960s+] (*US*) to scold, to reprimand. [JUMP v.[1] (9) + SHIT n.[6]]

jump (in) the box *v.* [1960s+] (*Aus.*) to give evidence. [one 'jumps' into the witness box]

jump in the sack *n.* [1990s+] an act of casual sexual intercourse. [JUMP n.[3] (1) + SACK n.[3] (1)]

jump it *v.* [1960s] to desert, to run off. [JUMP v.[2] (1)]

jump Jim Crow *v.* [mid-19C–1930s] to become agitated, to 'hop around'. [for ety. *see* JIM CROW n.]

jump jobber *n.* [1940s–60s] (*US*) a pimp. [JUMP n.[3] (1) + SE *jobber*, 'one who does jobs or odd pieces of work; one employed to do a job' (*OED*)]

jump joint *n.* [1930s+] **1** (*orig. US Black*) a party where the guests buy their refreshments to help pay the rent (cf. FISH-FRY n.). **2** (*US*) a cheap roadhouse or brothel, esp. an establishment providing food, drink and music for dancing. [JUKE n.[1] + JOINT n.[4] (3)]

jumpo *n.* [1950s] (*US*) the penis. [JUMP n.[3] (1) + -O sfx (7)]

jump-off, the *n.* [1910s+] (*orig. US/Can. milit.*) the outset, the beginning. [JUMP, THE n.]

jump off *v.*[1] **1** [mid-19C+] to begin, e.g. of a military attack. **2** [late 19C] (*US*) to leave. [(1) JUMP, THE n.; (2) JUMP v.[2] (1)]

jump off *v.*[2] **1** [1930s+] to happen, to start happening. **2** [1970s] of a person, to start doing something. [JUMP *v.*[7] (2)]

jump off the perch *v.* [1990s+] to commit suicide.

jump on *v.*[1] (*also* **jump upon**) [mid-19C+] to attack, verbally or physically, someone who is seen to have exposed themselves to such an assault by their behaviour or their weakness.

jump on *v.*[2] *see* STEP ON *v.*

jump one's bill *v.* (*also* **jump one's board**) [late 19C–1930s] (*US*) to abscond, esp. from a hotel or lodging, without paying one's bill. [JUMP *v.*[2] + SE *bill/board*]

jump one's horse over the bar *v.* [late 19C–1900s] (*Aus.*) to barter one's horse for liquor.

jump (on) someone's bones *v.* **1** [early 19C+] of a man, to have sexual intercourse. **2** [1980s] to attack. [JUMP *v.*[1] + SE *bones*]

jump on someone's program *v. see* PROGRAM *n.* (2).

jump-out *n.* [20C+] (*Aus.*) the outset, the beginning. [var. on JUMP-OFF, THE *n.*]

jump out *v.*[1] [1900s] (*US Und.*) to steal.

jump out *v.*[2] **1** [1960s+] (*US Und.*) to throw out (of a place). **2** [1980s+] (*US Black*) to be unfaithful. **3** [1990s+] (*US Und.*) to expel from a street gang, a ritual that involves beating up the departing member. [JUMP *v.*[2] (1); (3) is the opposite of JUMP IN *v.*]

jump-out boy *n.* [1990s+] (*US*) one who performs an ambush. [SE *jump out*]

jump out of one's pram *v. see* GET OUT OF ONE'S PRAM *v.*

jump over the wall *v. see* GO OVER THE WALL *v.* (3).

jumps, the *n.* **1** [late 19C–1950s] (*orig. US*) delirium tremens. **2** [20C+] (*US*) nervousness. **3** [1920s] excitement, 'the fidgets'. [fig. uses of SE]

jump salty *v.* (*also* **fly salty**) [1930s+] (*orig. US Black*) to be annoyed or irritated, to take offence. [JUMP *v.*[7] (1) + SALTY *adj.*]

jump ship *v.* [1930s+] (*US*) to quit, to renege. [SE *jump ship*, for a sailor to leave the ship (at a port) before the voyage has finished]

jump smart *v.* [1970s] (*US Black*) to act in a foolishly 'clever' manner. [JUMP *v.*[7] (1) + SE *smart*]

jump someone's bones *v. see* JUMP (ON) SOMEONE'S BONES *v.*

jump someone's hand *v.* [1970s+] (*US Black*) to threaten or victimize someone. [JUMP *v.*[1] + fig. use of SE *hand* (*of cards*)]

jump someone's neck *v. see* JUMP DOWN SOMEONE'S THROAT *v.*

jump steady *n.* [1930s+] (*US Black*) alcohol, which ensures that one keeps 'jumping'.

jump steady *v.* [1930s–50s] (*US Black*) to act properly, to be honest, usu. in the context of a sexual relationship. [JUMP *v.*[7] (1) + SE *steady*]

jump stink *v.* [1940s+] (*US*) to attack, to turn hostile. [JUMP *v.*[7] (1) + SE *stink*]

jump street *n.* [1970s+] (*US*) the start; esp. in phr. *from jump street*, from the very beginning. [JUMP, THE *n.* + SE *street*]

jump the box *v. see* JUMP (IN) THE BOX *v.*

jump the fence *v.* [1930s+] (*US prison*) to make an escape. [JUMP *v.*[2] (1) + SE *fence*]

jump the glaze *v. see* JUMP *n.*[1] (4).

jump the gun *v.* (*also* **beat the gun, jump**) **1** [1930s+] to act prematurely. **2** [1940s+] of an engaged couple, to have sexual intercourse (and for the woman to become pregnant) before their wedding (cf. BEAT THE STARTER *v.*). [sporting jargon; in a false start a competitor will set off before the starting pistol has been fired]

jump the joint *v.* [1910s–50s] (*Aus.*) to take command. [ext. use of SAusE *jump*, to take possession of a parcel of land, esp. in a deceitful or illegal manner + JOINT *n.*[4] (3)]

jump the lights *v. see* JUMP *v.*[5].

jump the rails *v.* [20C+] to lose control, to disappear. [horseracing imagery]

jump the rattler *v.* (*also* **hop the rattler**) [late 19C+] (*orig. Aus.*) to travel on the railway without paying.

jump the twig *v. see* HOP THE TWIG *v.*

jump the wrong stump *v. see* BARK UP THE WRONG TREE *v.*

jump through one's ass *v.* [1960s+] (*US*) to panic, to lose control, to be terrified. [SE *jump* + ASS *n.* (2)]

jump through one's asshole *v.* [1970s] (*US*) to throw a tantrum. [SE *jump* + ARSEHOLE *n.*]

jump to (it) *v.* [1910s+] to obey at once, to act smartly. [orig. milit. use]

jump-up *n.*[1] [mid-19C–1940s] (*Aus.*) a paste made of flour, water and sugar. [? it jumps in the pan]

jump-up *n.*[2] [late 19C] (*Aus.*) the witness box. [one *jumps up* there]

jump-up *n.*[3] [1940s+] (*UK Und.*) hijacking a lorry and/or stealing its contents. [JUMP UP *v.* (2)]

jump-up *n.*[4] [1950s+] (*W.I.*) a wild dancing party. [orig. held as a funeral wake, but now in general use; note US *jump-up/jump-up song*, a lively song with ad hoc lyrics, often extemporized from various pvb sayings]

jump-up *n.*[5] [1970s+] (*US Black*) sexual intercourse. [JUMP UP (AND DOWN) *v.*]

jump up *v.* (*also* **jump up on**) **1** [mid-19C–1900s] to criticize harshly. **2** [1940s+] to steal a lorry and/or its contents. **3** [1960s] (*US*) to arrest. [JUMP *v.*[1]]

jump up (and down) *v.* [1970s+] (*US Black*) to have sexual intercourse.

jump-up merchant *n.* (*also* **jump-up man**) [1940s+] one who steals from lorries, trucks etc. [JUMP UP *v.* (2) + MERCHANT *n.*/SE *man*]

jump up my ass! *excl.* [1970s] (*US*) a coarse, derisive retort.

jump up on *v. see* JUMP UP *v.*

jump upon *v. see* JUMP ON *v.*[1].

jump up someone's ass/butt *v.* [1970s+] (*US*) to attack, verbally or physically. [SE *jump* + ASS *n.* (2)]

Junction, the *n.* [1970s+] the area of south London near Clapham Junction railway station.

june around *v.* [late 19C–1900s] (*US campus*) to make a great deal of apparent effort, without any concrete accomplishment.

junebug *n.* [mid-19C–1950s] (*US Black*) a boy who is named after his father. [SE *junior boy*]

june too-too *n.* [late 19C] Queen Victoria's Diamond Jubilee, 22 June 1897. [apart from the spelling out of *22*, there is a dig at the contemporary Aesthetic Movement, which was *too-too* sensitive]

jungle *n.*[1] **1** [late 19C–1920s] (*US*) the backwoods, the suburbs. **2** [20C+] (*W.I.*) an area in West Kingston, Jamaica. **3** [20C+] (*US*) a prison. **4** [1910s+] (*US*) (*also* **hobo jungle**) that area of a town or city, often outside the city limits, where criminals, tramps and vagrants congregate. **5** [1930s] (*UK tramp*) a very cheap London lodging house for tramps.

jungle *n.*[2] [1930s+] (*US*) **1** a derog. term for a Black person (cf. AFRICAN APE *n.*). **2** the Black area of a town or city. [racist stereotyping]

jungle *n.*[3] [1990s+] (*W.I./UK Black teen*) a kind of music originating in London and combining *rave* and *ragga*, with emphasis on a very fast drum beat.

jungle *adj.* [1930s+] (*US*) **1** pertaining to the Black area of a town or city. **2** used, orig. derog., in ref. to Black people or culture. [JUNGLE *n.*[2]]

junglebird *n.* [1920s–30s] (*US*) a tramp. [JUNGLE *n.*[1] (4) + BIRD *n.*[2] (1)]

jungle blaster *n.* [1990s+] (*US*) a large, portable stereo. [JUNGLE *n.*[2] (2) + GHETTOBLASTER *n.*]

jungle bunny *n.* [1950s+] (*US*) a derog. term for a Black person; also attrib (cf. AFRICAN APE *n.*). [racist stereotyping]

jungle buzzard *n.* (*also* **jungle bum/buzzer**) [1910s+] (*US tramp*) a parasite on other tramps; a tramp who robs his fellows. [JUNGLE *n.*[1] (4) + BUZZARD *n.*[1] (9)/BUM *n.*[3] (1)]

jungle fever *n.* **1** [1960s+] (*US*) (*also* **black fever**) the desire of Whites (usu. men) to have sex with Black partners. **2** [1990s+]

(*US Black*) the desire of Blacks to have White partners. [the term, generally outlawed as racist in White use, changed its emphasis with the release of Spike Lee's film *Jungle Fever* in 1991]

jungle juice *n.* **1** [1940s+] (*orig. Aus.*) any form of strong, home-distilled liquor, often made of jungle-grown fruits and plants, herbs etc by soldiers with no 'regular' drinks. **2** [1950s] (*mainly UK juv.*) tea. **3** [1970s] (*US*) men's aftershave that supposedly enhances virility and sexual appeal. **4** [1990s+] (*US campus/UK juv.*) semen or vaginal secretions (cf. BABY FLUID n.; BINDERJUICE n.). [SE *jungle* + JUICE n.³/JUICE n.² (1)]

jungle meat *n.* [1960s+] (*gay*) a Black man or his penis (cf. BACON n.¹). [JUNGLE n.² (1) + MEAT n.]

jungle mouth *n.* [1970s+] (*US campus*) bad breath. [on pattern of SE *jungle rot*, US milit. *jungle mouth*, very bad halitosis suffered by soldiers patrolling in the jungle]

jungle sex *n.* [1990s+] an intense, rough and speedy bout of sexual intercourse. [the image of 'Black natives' and their lusts; thus racial stereotyping]

jungle stiff *n.* (*also* **jungle-wallah**) [1920s–40s] (*US tramp*) one who frequents that area of a town or city where criminals, tramps and vagrants congregate. [JUNGLE n.¹ (4) + STIFF n.² (4)]

jungle telegraph *n.* [1940s+] a network of gossip and rumour that brings news (often inaccurate) before the official sources.

jungle up *v.* **1** [1910s+] (*US tramp*) to share a campsite with other tramps, to live in a tramps' encampment, to cook up a meal. **2** [1960s] to gather together, in a non-tramp context. **3** [1960s] to be allies, to work together. **4** [1960s] (*US gay*) to share a bed with many people, to cuddle up. **5** [1970s+] (*US gay/tramp*) to have homosexual anal intercourse (cf. ASK FOR THE RING v.). [JUNGLE n.¹ (4)]

jungli *adj.* [1900s–60s] (*Anglo-Ind.*) uncouth, unsophisticated. [Urdu *jungli*, of the jungle]

junglist *n.*¹ [20C+] (*W.I., Jam.*) someone who comes from the area in West Kingston, Jamaica known as JUNGLE n.¹ (2).

junglist *n.*² [1990s+] (*W.I./UK Black teen*) a lover of JUNGLE n.³ music.

jungly *adj.* [1980s+] (*UK society*) disorganized, chaotic, less than smart. [racist stereotyping]

junior *n.* [1950s–80s] (*US Black*) a socially and/or sexually inept male.

junior jumper *n.* [1990s+] (*US Black*) a juvenile (under 16) who commits rape and robbery. [SE *junior* + JUMP v.¹ (1)]

Junior Walker and the All Stars *n.* [1970s+] (*US Black*) the police. [R&B star *Junior Walker*, stage name of Autry DeWalt II (b.1942), and his band]

juniper *n.*¹ [late 19C–1940s] (*US*) a rustic (cf. BUCKWHEAT n.).

juniper *n.*² (*also* **juniper ale/juice**) [18C+] gin. [SE *juniper*, its primary constituent]

juniper lecture/letter *n.* [late 19C–early 19C] a severe reprimand, a 'telling-off'. [the sharpness of the juniper berry]

junjo *n.* [1990s+] (*W.I.*) a term of abuse.

junk *n.*¹ **1** [mid-18C–1930s] (*also* **salt junk**) salt beef. **2** [mid-19C+] poor or indigestible food. [naut. jargon *junk*, old or second-rate cable or rope; + ? overtones of SE *junk*, a lump, a chunk]

junk *n.*² [mid–late 19C] (*UK prison*) oakum (loose fibre, obtained by untwisting and picking old rope), the 'picking' of which provided the main cell task for 19C prisoners.

junk *n.*³ **1** [mid-19C+] (*orig. US*) possessions, stuff or any unspecified objects that may be recyclable but equally poss. worthless; also used dismissively of objects that are in fact sound but that the speaker no longer likes. **2** [20C+] (*Aus.*) the dregs of a bottle or glass of alcohol. **3** [20C+] (*US Und.*) jewellery. **4** [20C+] (*US*) rubbish, nonsense. **5** [1900s] (*US*) money (cf. CHAFF n.²). **6** [1920s+] a run-down vehicle. **7** [1990s+] (*US*) cheap or inferior liquor. **8** [1990s+] (*US campus*) the male genitals.

junk *n.*⁴ [1910s–20s] (*US*) a mean, despicable man.

junk *n.*⁵ (*drugs*) **1** [1910s+] (*also* **jeesunk**) opiates, esp. heroin;

thus *on the junk*, addicted to narcotics (cf. CACA n.). **2** [1910s+] non-recreational drugs in general. **3** [1950s–60s] cannabis. **4** [1960s] amphetamine, Benzedrine (cf. A n.²). [SE *junk*, rubbish (cf. SHIT n.¹) + ref. to SE *junk*, a form of Chinese sailing boat]

junk *n.*⁶ [1950s+] (*Aus.*) a heroin addict. [abbr. JUNKIE n.]

junk, the *n.* [1990s+] (*US campus*) the very best. [JUNK n.³ on bad = good model; or JUNK n.⁵ on image of being the ultimate in drugs]

junk *adj.*¹ [1960s] (*drugs*) pertaining to heroin or the hard drug culture. [JUNK n.⁵ (1)]

junk *adj.*² (*also* **junky**) [1960s+] rubbishy, second-rate, inferior. [JUNK n.³ (4)]

junk *v.* [late 19C+] to reject, to throw away, to abandon. [JUNK n.³ (1)]

junk box *n. see* JUNKER n.².

junk buzzard *n.* [1970s+] (*US*) an extremely contemptible person, usu. a drug addict. [JUNK n.⁵ + BUZZARD n.¹]

junked *adj.* (*also* **junked up**) [1930s+] (*drugs*) intoxicated by drugs. [JUNK n.⁵]

junker *n.*¹ [1920s+] (*US drugs*) **1** a drug addict. **2** a drug seller. [var. on JUNKIE n.]

junker *n.*² (*also* **junk box**) [1940s+] (*US*) a near-derelict but just drivable second-hand car, or motorcycle, one step from the junkyard. [JUNK n.³ (6)]

junket around *v.* [20C+] (*Aus.*) to play the fool (cf. ACT THE ANGORA v.). [SE *junket*, to go on an excursion, a spree]

junket-brain *n.* (*also* **junket-head**) [1950s] (*Aus.*) a general term of abuse. [SE *junket*, whey, + SE *brain/head*, thus 'soft brain']

junkette *n.* [1960s+] (*drugs*) a young female heroin addict. [JUNKIE n. (1) + SE fem. sfx *-ette*]

junk food *n.* (*also* **junk snacks**) [1970s+] **1** the products of the burgeoning world of 'fast-food' restaurants such as McDonalds, Burger King, KFC etc. **2** anything considered as lacking in 'nutrition', usu. cultural. [JUNK n.³ (1) + SE *food*; the implication, and to many palates, the actuality, is that such food is indeed *junk*, i.e. rubbish]

junk hawk *n.* [1970s+] (*US drugs*) a heroin user whose entire existence centres on the drug. [JUNK n.⁵ + SE *hawk*]

junkhead *n.* [1950s+] (*US drugs*) a drug addict or drug dealer. [JUNK n.⁵ + -HEAD sfx (3)]

junkheap *n.* **1** [1920s+] a disgusting, filthy place. **2** [1940s+] an old, battered automobile. [JUNK n.³ (1) + SE *heap*]

junk hog *n.* [1930s–50s] (*US drugs*) a drug addict who is seen as excessive in their consumption.

junk hound *n.* [1930s] (*US drugs*) a narcotics addict. [JUNK n.⁵ (1) + HOUND sfx]

junkhouse *n.* [2000s] (*US drugs*) a place – an apartment, a house – used for the consumption of narcotics, crack cocaine etc. [JUNK n.⁵ (1) + SE *house*]

junkie *n.* (*also* **junkey, junkster, junky**) **1** [1920s+] (*drugs*) a heroin addict. **2** [1950s–70s] (rare) a heroin seller. **3** [1960s+] a user of any drug. **4** [1970s+] in fig. use, an addict of any sort, e.g. *vinyl junkie*, a collector of vinyl (rather than cassette or CD) recordings. [JUNK n.⁵; (4) f. (1)]

junkie *adj.* **1** [1950s+] (*drugs*) (*also* **junkey**) used of one who is addicted to narcotics; pertaining to the world of narcotics. **2** [1970s+] addicted to anything. **3** [1970s+] addictive. [JUNKIE n.]

junkie fold *n.* [1950s] (*drugs*) a method of folding a square of paper, one end tucking into the other, and the top folding into the resulting 'slot', in which a measure of narcotics can be held. [JUNKIE n. (1)]

junk in the trunk *phr.* (*also* **junk in one's trunk**) [1990s+] (*US Black*) having large buttocks. [JUNK n.³ (1) + SAmE *trunk*, the 'boot' of a car]

junkman *n.* (*also* **junk guy**) [1940s+] (*US drugs*) **1** a heroin dealer. **2** a cocaine dealer. [JUNK n.⁵ (1) + SE *man*]

junko n. [1970s+] (US) a drug addict. [JUNK n.⁵]

junkster n. see JUNKIE n.

junk tank n. [1960s+] (US police) a cell reserved for drug abusers and alcoholics. [JUNK n.⁵ + TANK n.² (5); pun on DRUNK TANK n.]

junky n. see JUNKIE n.

junky adj.¹ [1960s] (US) nonsensical, absurd. [JUNK n.³ (4)]

junky adj.² see JUNK adj.².

junkyard dog n. [1980s+] (US) a politician who is adept at investigating corruption. [SE phr. meaner than a junkyard dog]

junta n. [1970s] a playboy, a womanizer. [? rhy. sl. = cunter]

jupe balls n. see JUDY n.³.

Jupiter! excl. (also **by Jupiter!**) [17C+] a general excl. [mainly literary use until mid-19C]

jurden n. see JORDAN n.¹.

jurk n. [19C] a seal, a licence. [var. on JARK n. (1)]

jury leg n. [mid-18C–early 19C] a wooden leg. [ety unknown; ? on pattern of naut. jargon jury-rigged or jury-mast, temporary rigging or a temporary mast, a short-term arrangement that replaces equipment swept away in a gale or after a battle]

jury nobbling n. see NOBBLE v.² (4).

just adv. [late 19C+] absolutely, definitely, very.

just as cheap phr. [1950s+] (W.I. Rasta) just as well.

just as I feared n. [20C+] a beard. [rhy. sl.; ult. the Edward Lear limerick (1846): 'There was an old man with a beard / Who said "It is just as I feared! / Two owls and a hen / Four larks and a wren / Have all built their nests in my beard"']

just a tick phr. [late 19C+] wait a moment. [TICK n.⁴ (2)]

just-come n. see JOHNNY-JUST-COME n.

just come up phr. [20C+] naïve, gauche, inexperienced, stupid. [the image is of a young plant's first shoots; cf. SE green]

just fallen off the cabbage/turnip truck phr. [1980s] (US) very naïve, unsophisticated. [play on SE green, naïve]

just like a bear('s daughter), ain't got a quarter phr. (also **just like the bear's brother, Jim, his pickings are slim**) [1920s–40s] (US Black) miserable, out of sorts, dejected.

just nicely phr. [1930s+] tipsy (cf. ABOUT RIGHT phr.¹). [abbr. SE just nicely drunk]

just one's speed phr. see SPEED n.¹ (1).

just quietly phr. [1910s+] (Aus./N.Z.) just between you and me, confidentially.

just-raped look n. [1980s+] of a woman, a sluttish, provocative style of dressing.

just the glassy (marble) phr. [1900s–50s] (Aus.) wholly satisfactory, just as required. [GLASSY (ALLEY), THE n.]

just the hammer phr. (also **just the gears, that's the hammer**) [1910s+] ideal, perfect, exactly what is wanted. [Stock Exchange/auction-house imagery]

just the job phr. see JUST THE TICKET phr.

just the shiny (bob/shilling) phr. (also **just the shiner/shining**) [20C+] (Aus.) a general term of approval.

just the shot phr. see SHOT n.⁵ (3).

just the ticket phr. (also **just the job**) [20C+] perfect, ideal, exactly as desired and required. [? a winning lottery ticket, or SE ticket, the list of candidates put forward by a political party/SE job]

justum n. [16C; 19C] the vagina (cf. ARTICLE n.). [Lat. 'a suitable thing']

jutland n. [18C–mid-19C] the buttocks. [their 'jutting out' from the body]

juve n. (also **juvey, juvie**) **1** [1930s–50s] (US) a juvenile, e.g. on stage. **2** [1930s+] (US) (also **juve delinq**) a juvenile delinquent. **3** [1960s+] (US) a juvenile court or detention establishment. **4** [1960s+] (US) Juvenile Hall, reform school. **5** [1960s+] pornography featuring supposed 'juveniles'. [abbr.]

Juvember n. [1940s] (US) an undetermined, but not too distant date.

juvie adj. [1970s+] (US Und./police) pertaining to juvenile crime. [JUVE n.]

juwaub n. see JAWAUB n.

jybe n. see GYBE n.

jyro n. see JARO n.

K

K *n.*[1] [20C+] a knighthood. [abbr.]

K *n.*[2] **1** [1940s+] a kilometer. **2** [1960s+] 1000, esp. as $1000 or £1000 (cf. C *n.*[1]; G *n.*[1]). **3** [1990s+] (*US campus*) money. [abbr.; (2) SE pfx kilo-, 1000; (3) f. (2); since 1980s *K* has replaced the equivalent G *n.*[1] (1) in popularity]

K *n.*[3] [1960s+] a homosexual. [abbr.; deliberately illiterate 'kweer', i.e. QUEER *n.* (4)]

K *n.*[4] (*drugs*) **1** [1970s+] a kilogram of any illicit drug. **2** [1980s+] ketamine hydrochloride, a mildly hallucinogenic drug, developed as a battlefield anaesthetic, associated chemically with phencyclidine and often used as a legal substitute for MDMA. **3** [1980s+] phencyclidine.

K! *excl. see* KAY! excl.

ka- *pfx see* KER- pfx and its combs.

kaalgat *adj.* [1960s+] (*S.Afr.*) naked. [Afk. *kaal*, bare + GAT *n.*[2]]

kaalvoet *adj.* [late 19C+] (*S.Afr.*) barefoot. [synon. Afk.]

KaaPee *n.* [1980s+] (*S.Afr.*) the Conservative Party. [Afk. *Konserwatiewe Party*]

kaartjie *n.* [1950s+] (*S.Afr. drugs*) a very small measure of cannabis. [Afk. *kaartjie*, a ticket, a card, in turn f. UK *card*, a small measure of opium or Mex. Sp. *cachucha*, a capsule of drugs, which is f. Chilean sl. *cachucha*, a small comet]

kaaskop *n.* [1970s+] (*S.Afr.*) a Dutchman. [Afk. *kaas*, cheese + *kop*, head]

kabac genals *n. see* KABGNALS *n.*

kaba-kaba *n.* [20C+] (*W.I.*) a low-class, worthless, rough person. [KABA-KABA *adj.*]

kaba-kaba *adj.* [20C+] (*W.I.*) **1** of people, slovenly, ill-kempt, boorish-looking. **2** of animals and things, cheap, worthless. [Yoruba *kaba-kaba*, orig. used of speech to mean haltingly, then second-rate, of inferior quality]

kabayo *n. see* CABALLO *n.*

kabeezer *n.* [1960s+] (*US*) **1** the head. **2** the face. [CABEZA *n.*]

kabgnals *n.* (*also* **kabac genals**) [late 19C] backslang. [the word itself is *backslang* spelt backwards and its use – spoken very quickly – is a coded way of asking, 'Do you understand backslang, and shall we use it for this conversation?']

kabillion *n.* (*also* **kajillion, kazillion**) [1980s+] (*US*) an uncountable large number. [KER- pfx + play on SE (*m*)*illion*]

kabitz *n. see* KIBITZ *n.*

kabitzer *n. see* KIBITZER *n.*

kablooey!/kablooie! *excl. see* KABOOM! excl.

kaboolies *n.* [2000s] (*US*) the female breasts.

kaboom *n.* [1940s+] a loud bang or noise. [KABOOM! excl.]

kaboom! *excl.* (*also* **kablooey! kablooie!**) [1940s+] an onomat. term indicating a loud noise or explosion. [KER- pfx + BOOM! excl. (1)/BLOOEY! excl. (1)/echoic]

kabosh *n. see* KIBOSH *n.*

kabuki *n.* [1980s+] (*drugs*) a crack cocaine pipe made from a plastic rum bottle and a rubber spark-plug cover (cf. LAMBORGHINI *n.*; MASERATI *n.*). [? *Kabuki*, style of Japanese theatre]

kabump! *excl.* [1970s+] an onomat. term indicating the noisy landing of one object or person on another. [KER- pfx + SE *bump*; note US *belly-cabump*, to throw oneself face-down onto a sled preparatory to sliding down a hill]

kaching! *excl.* [1960s+] an onomat. term indicating the noise of a metal object striking another and giving a sharp, bell-like note. [KER- pfx + SE *ching*]

kack *n.* (*US Black*) **1** [1900s–50s] an important person. **2** [1920s] a Black person. **3** [1920s–40s] a snobbish person. [CACK *n.*[3] (1)]

kacky-hander *n.* [1980s] (*Aus.*) a clumsy person. [CACK-HANDED *adj.*]

kadi *n.* (*also* **kadie, kady, katy**) [late 19C+] a hat (cf. CADY *n.*). [? Rom. *stadi*, a hat]

kadoodle *v.* [late 19C] (*US*) to hang around, to frequent, to wander about. [KER- pfx + TODDLE *v.*]

kadooment *n.* [20C+] (*W.I.*) **1** noise, confusion. **2** usu. as *Kadooment*, open-air fun and excitement. [dial. *'k*, look + *do(o)ment*, 'doings', disturbance, entertainment; thus lit. 'look, excitement!']

kadoova *n.* [late 19C] (*Aus.*) the head.

kady *n. see* KADI *n.*

kafferboetie *n. see* KAFFIRBOETIE *n.*

kafferpak *n.* [1930s+] (*S.Afr.*) a thorough beating, a thrashing, a comprehensive defeat. [Afk. *kaffer*, KAFFIR *n.*[1] + *pak*, a hiding]

kaffir *n.*[1] (*orig. S.Afr.*) **1** [mid-19C–1900s] a pimp, an unpleasant person. **2** [mid-19C+] a derog. term for a Black person (cf. AFRICAN APE *n.*). [Arab *kefir*, an infidel; orig. a Xhosa-speaking African and by extension, any African; orig. (18C) seen as a simple description of a given ethnic group, the term became insulting and abusive and its use is now actionable]

kaffir *n.*[2] *see* CAFFER *n.*

kaffir *adj.* **1** [late 18C+] (*S.Afr.*) used in a wide variety of combs. to mean of or pertaining to Black people, all of which are *de facto* insulting, including [late 18C+] *kaffir corn*, a form of sorghum; [early 19C+] *kaffir bread*, the Encephalartos (a form of mollusc); [mid-19C+] *kaffir dog*, a species of long-tailed, sharp-muzzled, lean dog, popular among indigenous Africans; [mid-19C+] *kaffir sheeting*, a coarsely woven, thick cotton fabric used for clothes or cheap curtains; [late 19C] *kaffir beer*, a drink made from fermented prickly pears and honey; [late 19C+] *kaffir piano*, the mbila or 'thumb piano'. **2** [1930s–60s] bad, unreliable. [for ety. *see* KAFFIR *n.*[1]]

kaffir appointment *n.* [1950s+] (*S.Afr.*) an appointment for which one fails to arrive on time. [KAFFIR *adj.* (1) + SE *appointment*]

kaffirboetie *n.* (*also* **kafferboetie**) [1930s+] (*S.Afr.*) a White sympathizer with Black causes. [KAFFIR *n.*[1] (2) + BOET *n.*]

Kaffirland *n.* [mid-19C] the Cape provinces; latterly South Africa. [KAFFIR *n.*[1] (2)]

kaffir's tightener *n.* [mid-19C] (*S.Afr.*) a large, heavy meal. [KAFFIR *n.*[1] (2) + TIGHTENER *n.*; such a meal supposedly satisfies even an African]

kaffir taxi *n.* [1980s+] (*S.Afr.*) brandy plus Coca-Cola or some other sweet fizzy drink. [KAFFIR adj. (1) + SE *taxi*; ? it 'gets you going']

kaffir tobacco *n.* [1960s+] (*S.Afr. drugs*) marijuana (cf. ACAPULCO (GOLD) n.). [KAFFIR adj. (1) + SE *tobacco*]

kafooster *n.* [1970s+] (*US*) useless talk, idle chatter. [KER- pfx + ? PHOOEY! excl.]

kagg *n. see* CAG n.

kagou *adj.* [20C+] (*W.I., Trin.*) looking miserable, unenthusiastic, 'sorry for oneself'. [Fr. *cagot*, sanctimonious]

kahoonas *n.* (*also* **cahoonas, kazooms**) [1970s+] the female breasts, esp. if large (cf. BAZONGAS n.). [joc. use of KAHUNA n.]

kahuna *n.* [1980s+] (*US*) a large or important person or thing; often in phr. *the big kahuna*. [Hawaiian *kahuna*, priest or wise man, orig. used for an expert surfer]

kaifa *n. see* KYFER n.

kai-kai *see under* KIKI.

Kaintuck *n. see* KENTUCK n.

kaiser baby *n.* [1920s–30s] (*US Black*) a woman who leaves home and returns married to a successful, wealthy (and usu. White) husband. [SE *kaiser*, a metaphor for power]

kajees *n.* [1980s+] (*drugs*) cannabis. [ety. unknown]

kajillion *n. see* KABILLION n.

kak *n. see* CACK n.[2].

kak *adj.* [1970s+] (*S.Afr.*) unpleasant, nasty. [CACK n.[2]]

kak *v.* **1** [1960s+] (*US*) to vomit. **2** [1970s+] (*S.Afr.*) to defecate (cf. CACA v.). [(2) CACK n.[2] (1)]

ka-ka/kaka *n. see* CACA n.

kaka queen *n.* [1950s–70s] (*gay*) one whose sexual preferences involve excrement, a coprophage. [CACA n. + QUEEN n.[2] (1)/QUEEN sfx (2)]

kaker *n.* **1** [1930s+] anything, or anyone, unpleasant or distasteful. **2** [1960s+] cannabis. [Yid. *kaker*, excrement]

kakker-boosah *n.* [19C] prematurely voided excrement. [CACA n. (1)/CACK n.[2] (1) + *boosah*, ety. unknown]

kakpot *n.* [1970s+] (*S.Afr. Und.*) a latrine. [CACK n.[2] (1) + SE *pot*]

kaks *n.* [20C+] (*Irish*) the testicles. [ety. unknown; ? link to KECKS n.]

Kalahari wishing well *n.* [1970s+] (*S.Afr.*) an outdoor privy. [the *Kalahari* desert, with the idea of digging a hole]

kale (seed) *n.* [20C+] (*US*) money (cf. ALFALFA n.). [its greenness connotes the vegetable, but ? note COLE n.]

kali *n.* (*also* **cooly**) [1950s+] (*W.I. Rasta*) marijuana. [ety. unknown; ? link to COOL adj.[3] (1) or Carib.E *coolie weed*, a variety of fern and thus a play on WEED n.[1] (4)]

kalied *adj.* (*also* **kaylied**) [1930s+] drunk (cf. ALED UP adj.). [? SE *alcohol* + *alkali*]

kali-water *n.* [1970s+] champagne. [KALIED adj.]

kalumpus! *excl.* [mid-19C] an onomat. term indicating the noise made when an object falls onto a hard surface. [KER- pfx + SE *lump*]

kamma *adj.* [20C+] (*S.Afr.*) fake, trumped up, spurious, esp. of emotions or illness. [Nama *khamo*, like, similar]

Kanacka *n. see* CANUCK n.

Kanaka *n.[1]* (*also* **Canaka**) [mid-19C+] (*orig. Aus.*) **1** a Pacific Islander, esp. one brought to Australia as an indentured labourer on the Queensland cotton or sugar plantations. **2** (*also* **Kanock**) a Hawaiian, sometimes derog. [Hawaiian *kanaka*, man]

Kanaka *n.[2] see* CANUCK n.

Kanakaland *n.* [late 19C–1940s] (*Aus.*) Queensland. [KANAKA n.[1] (1)]

Kanakalander *n.* [late 19C–1940s] (*Aus.*) a Queenslander. [KANAKALAND n.]

kanakas *n.* [20C+] (*Aus.*) the testicles. [a play on KANAKA n.[1] + KNACKERS n.]

kanga *n.[1]* **1** [1950s] (*UK prison*) (*also* **kangar**) chewing tobacco. **2** [1950s+] (*Aus.*) money (cf. BEES (AND HONEY) n.). [rhy. sl.; abbr. *kanga*roo = (1) CHEW n. (1); (2) SCREW n.[6] (1)]

kanga *n.[2]* [1970s] (*orig. Aus.*) a pneumatic drill. [abbr. SE *kangaroo*, which also 'jumps up and down']

kanga *n.[3]* [1980s] (*Aus.*) a White child. [the TV series *Skippy, the Bush Kangaroo*]

kangaroo *n.[1]* [mid-19C+] (*US*) an Australian; an Australian soldier.

kangaroo *n.[2]* [late 19C–1900s] a thin, slope-shouldered person. [the supposed resemblance to the animal]

kangaroo *n.[3]* (*also* **kanga**) **1** [20C+] (*Aus./US*) a shoe. **2** [1920s+] a Jew (cf. BILLY THE KID n.). [rhy. sl.]

kangaroo *n.[4]* (*also* **kanga**) [1920s+] a prison warder. [rhy. sl. = SCREW n.[2] (3)]

kangaroo *v.[1]* **1** [20C+] (*US*) to convict unjustly, orig. as in a 'kangaroo court'. **2** [1910s] (*US*) to beat up. **3** [1950s–60s] (*US Black*) to make one hyperactive, often used of a drug. **4** [1970s+] of a car, to jerk along rather than run smoothly; thus *kangaroo start*, a jerky, shuddering start, typically that of a learner driver. [the bounding motion of the animal]

kangaroo *v.[2] see* KANGAROO (IT) v.

kangaroo (court) *n.* [mid-19C+] (*US*) an irregular court, esp. one set up by prisoners or strikers.

kangaroo feathers *n.* [1910s] (*Aus.*) an impossible thing, often an unlikely story (cf. BULLFEATHERS n.). [kangaroos don't have feathers]

kangaroo hop *n.* [late 19C] (*Aus.*) a short-lived feminine affectation in which the hands were held palm-down at the breast, a pose reminiscent of the kangaroo.

kangaroo (it) *v.* [1950s+] (*Aus.*) to defecate in a squatting position, usu. with one's feet on the seat. [SAusE *kangaroo*, to hop in the manner of the animal]

Kangarooland *n.* [1900s–50s] (*Aus.*) Australia.

kangaroo shit *n.* [1940s+] (*Aus.*) defecation in a squatting position. [KANGAROO (IT) v.]

kangarooster *n.* [1920s+] (*Aus.*) an amusing or eccentric person. [SE *kangaroo* + sfx *-ster*]

kangaroo straight *n.* [1950s+] (*US*) a poker hand which resembles a straight but has a card or cards missing, thus a worthless hand. [suggested by the gaps or 'jumps']

Kangaroo Valley *n.* [1960s+] Earls Court, London, base for many expatriate Australians. [KANGAROO n.[1]]

kango *n.* [1940s+] an Australian. [abbr. SE *kangaroo*]

kangol *n.* [1990s+] (*US Black/teen*) a beret. [the brandname of a popular make]

kangse *n.* (*also* **koks, konks**) [20C+] (*W.I.*) a light blow, usu. given to a child and usu. on the head. [? dial. *conk*, a blow on the nose]

kangse *v.* [20C+] (*W.I.*) to hit lightly. [KANGSE n.]

kani *n.* [1940s+] (*W.I.*) **1** a bad cough, usu. with a temperature. **2** a person who is suffering from this. [SE *consumption*, 19C name for tuberculosis]

kanits *n.* [mid-19C] a stink. [backsl.]

kanitseno *n.* [mid-19C] a stinker, lit. 'stinking one'. [backsl.; KANITS n.]

kanker *n.* (*also* **canker**) [1930s+] a Jew (cf. BILLY THE KID n.). [abbr. KANGAROO n.[3] (2)]

Kanock *n. see* KANAKA n.[1] (2).

Kansas City (bank)roll *n. see* CALIFORNIA BANKROLL n.

Kansas City workout *n.* [1970s+] (*US gay*) watching men go by.

Kansas neck-blister *n.* [late 19C–1900s] (*US*) a Bowie knife.

Kansas yummy *n.* [1960s+] (*US*) a young woman who proves hard to seduce; she need not necessarily come from Kansas, but the implication is of small-town or rural innocence and morality. [*Kansas* + YUMMY n.]

Kanuck/Kanuk *n. see* CANUCK n.

kanurd *adj.* (*also* **kenird, kennurd**) [mid-19C–1930s] drunk. [backsl.]

kapello *n.* [mid-19C+] (*Ling. Fr./Polari*) a coat. [Ital. *capello*, a coat]

kapok-cruncher *n.* [1980s] (*Aus.*) a male homosexual. [play on PILLOW-BITER n.; some pillows being stuffed with SE *kapok*]

kapow! *excl.* (*also* **kapowie!**) [1930s+] an onomat. term indicating a sudden noise or shock, typically an imitation of a handgun firing. [KER- pfx + SE *pow!* echoic of a blow or sudden noise]

kappa *n.* [1990s+] (*UK juv.*) a disabled person; thus a general insult. [abbr. SE *handicapped*]

kappie *n.* [1980s+] (*S.Afr.*) a member of the *Kappie Kommando*, an ultra-conservative Afrikaner women's organization. [Afk. *kappie*, a large cloth sunbonnet, part of the trad. wear of Afk. women]

kaps *n.* [1970s+] (*drugs*) phencyclidine (cf. ACE n.[4]). [? SE *capsules*]

kapswalla *v.* [late 19C–1900s] (*US Und.*) to steal. [orig. Native American use, 'adopted from the original by American thieves' (Ware)]

kaput *adj.* [1910s+] **1** out of order, utterly ruined or exhausted, thus *get the kaput*, to be rejected, dismissed. **2** dead, finished. [Ger. *kaputt* and Fr. (*être*) *capot*, (to be) without tricks in the card-game of piquet]

karibat *n.* [mid-19C] (*Anglo-Ind.*) food. [Hind. *karibat*, curry and rice, thus generic term for food]

kark *v. see* CARK v.

karma *n.* [1960s+] (*US*) an emotional or spiritual state of being, either good or bad, orig. used by hippies, from Hindu and Buddhist beliefs but latterly very little to do with religion. [Skrt *karma*, fate, action]

karsey/karzee/karzey/karzi/karzie/karzy *n. see* CARSEY n.

kaschnickered *adj.* [1970s+] (*US Black*) drunk, intoxicated. [KER- pfx + ? SHICKERED (UP) adj. (1)]

kashoom! *excl.* [1970s+] an onomat. term indicating speedy movement. [KER- pfx + SE *shoot/zoom*]

kasj *adj. see* CAS adj.

kas-kas *n.* [1950s+] (*W.I.*) rumour-mongering. [? CUSS-CUSS n.]

kass kass *n.* (*also* **kas-kas**) [1940s+] (*W.I. Rasta*) a quarrel or contention. [SE *curse/cuss* + redup. or Twi *kasa kasa*, to dispute verbally]

kat *n. see* CAT n.[1] (1).

Kate, the *n.* [late 19C+] the British army. [abbr. KATE CARNEY, THE n.]

kate *n.[1]* [16C–1930s] (*Scot.*) a prostitute (cf. BABY JANE n.). [generic use of proper name; Irwin, *American Tramp and Und. Slang* (1931), also suggests Du. *kat*, 'a wanton']

kate *n.[2]* [mid-17C–mid-19C] **1** a skeleton key. **2** a picklock. [the dimin. of the SE name *Katherine*, and on the model of other burglars' tools, e.g. BETTY n.[1], JEMMY n.[3]]

kate and sidney *n.* (*also* **kate and sydney**) [20C+] steak and kidney. [rhy. sl.]

Kate Carney, the *n.* (*also* **Kate Karney, Kate Kearney**) [20C+] the British army. [rhy. sl.; ult. music-hall singing star *Kate Carney* (1869–1950)]

kate moss *v.* [1990s+] to toss, to throw. [rhy. sl.; ult. fashion model *Kate Moss* (b.1974)]

kath *n. see* KATHLEEN MAVOURNEEN n.[1].

Katharine Docks *n.* [20C+] socks. [rhy. sl.; ult. *St Katharine's Docks* in London]

kathleen maroon *n.* [1910s+] (*Aus.*) a 3-year prison sentence. [KATHLEEN MAVOURNEEN n.[1] (2)]

kathleen mavourneen *n.[1]* (*also* **kath**) **1** [20C+] (*Aus.*) an indeterminate period of time. **2** [1910s+] (*Aus.*) a prison sentence of indeterminate time. **3** [1910s+] (*Aus.*) a habitual criminal. **4** [1910s+] (*US*) a promise, usu. in the context of paying back a loan. **5** [1920s] (*Aus.*) a pack. [the song 'Kathleen Mavourneen', the chorus of which runs 'It may be for years, it may be forever'; (5) presumably refers to the way a vagrant carries his pack]

kathleen mavourneen *n.[2]* [20C+] the morning. [rhy. sl.; for ety. *see* prev.]

kathleen mavourneen system *n.* (*also* **cathleen mavoureen system**) [1920s–80s] (*Aus.*) hire purchase. [business jargon *Kathleen Mavourneen*, a defaulting debtor; ult. KATHLEEN MAVOURNEEN n.[1] (1)]

katonk *n.* (*also* **kotonk**) [1940s+] (*US, Hawaiian*) a Japanese-American from the USA rather than from Hawaii (cf. BUDDHAHEAD n.). [the theory, propounded by Hawaii-born Japanese, that tapping their heads would give the sound *katonk* like that of a coconut]

katoo *v.* [late 19C] (*Aus.*) to act as a sycophant. [SE *kowtow*]

katootin'! *excl.* [1920s+] (*US*) a general intensifier, as in *durn katootin' right*. [KER- pfx + TOOTING adj. (1)]

katowse *n.* [mid-19C] (*US*) a row, a rumpus. [Ger. *getöse*, a rumpus]

katterzem *n.* [late 19C–1900s] (*Scot.*) a parasite, a hanger-on; 'a man willing to go out dining at a moment's notice' (Ware). [Fr. *quatorzième*, 14th (the 14th at table is there purely to stop there being an unlucky 13 people and is thus socially dispensable)]

Katy *n.* [late 19C–1960s] (*US*) the Missouri, Kansas and Texas Railroad. [initial letters]

katy *n. see* KADI n.

Katy-bar-the-door *phr.* (*also* **Katy-bar-the-gate, Katie...**) [20C+] (*US*) used as a warning, to indicate impending danger. [adoption of a popular US fiddle tune, thus entitled]

katzenjammer *n.* (*US*) **1** [mid-19C+] a hangover or its symptoms. **2** [20C+] anxiety or jitters. **3** [1940s] a catsuit. [Ger. *Katzen*, cats + *Jammer*, distress, wailing]

kawhallop *see under* KERWHALLOP.

kay *n.* [1980s+] (*S.Afr.*) 1 kilometre. [K n.[2] (1)]

kay! *excl.* (*also* **K!**) [1950s+] all right, in order. [abbr. OK! excl.]

kaya *n.* [1980s+] (*drugs*) marijuana. [orig. Jam. use; ety. unknown; ? link to Carib.E. *kayakiit*, a form of medicinal herb, thus note HERB n.[2] (3)]

kaycuff foe! *excl.* [20C+] go away! [backsl. = FUCK OFF! excl.]

kayf *n. see* CAF n.

kaylied *adj. see* KALIED adj.

kayo *see under* K.O.

Kay See *n. see* K.C. n.

kaze *n. see* CASE n.[2].

kazi *n. see* CARSEY n.

kazillion *n. see* KABILLION n.

ka-zip *n.* (*also* **kerzip**) [1900s–30s] the head.

kazoo *n.* [1960s+] the anus, the buttocks, the vagina or penis; thus *up the kazoo*. [? KEISTER n. (7) or SE *kazoo*, a rudimentary wind instrument]

kazooms *n. see* KAHOONAS n.

kazoonie *n.* [1950s] (*US prison*) a child. [KAZOO n.]

kazotski *n.* [1980s] (*US*) an act of sexual intercourse. [Rus. *kozatchok*, a Slavonic dance with a quickening tempo]

k.b. *n.[1]* [20C+] **1** (*UK prison*) a rejection, esp. of parole. **2** any form of rejection. [abbr. KNOCKBACK n.]

k.b. *n.[2]* [1960s+] (*S.Afr.*) kaffir beer (a form of beer brewed with malted sorghum millet). [abbr.; the initials are preferred to the offensive term at KAFFIR adj. (1)]

k.b. *n.[3]* [1990s+] (*US Black/drugs*) top-quality marijuana. [abbr. KIND, THE n. (2) + BUD n.[4] (1)]

k.b. *v.* [20C+] to reject. [abbr. KNOCK BACK v.[3]]

k.b.o. *phr.* [1940s] keep *b*uggering *o*n, i.e. persevere, stick to the job. [abbr.]

K-boy *n.* [1940s+] (*US*) a king in cards. [SE *k(ing)* + *boy*]

K.C. *n.* (*also* **casey, Kay See**) [late 19C+] (*US*) Kansas City, Missouri. [initial letters]

k.c. brown *n. see* CASEY BROWN n.

kcirp *n. see* CURP n.

k'daar *n. see* KY'DAAR n.

keaster *n. see* KEISTER *n.*

keck *n.* (*also* **keek**) [late 19C–1910s] (*US*) a pocket. [KICK n.[4]]

keck-handed *adj.* (*also* **keck-fisted**) [late 19C+] left-handed. [dial.; note SE *cack-handed*, maladroit]

kecks *n.* (*also* **kaks, keks, kex**) **1** [late 19C+] trousers. **2** [1960s+] knickers, underpants. [orig. Liverpool var. OF KICKS n.[1]]

kedger *n.* [19C] a beggar who gains money for performing small jobs; thus *kedger's coffee-house/hotel*, a centre for beggars. [Cockney pron. of SE *cadger*]

kee *n. see* KEY n.[3].

keebler *n.* [1990s+] (*US Black*) a White person. [ety. unknown]

keech *n.* (*also* **keegh, keek**) [1970s+] **1** excrement. **2** something distasteful, disgusting. **3** nonsense, rubbish. [Scot. *keech*, excrement]

keechter *n.* [1990s+] the posterior, the buttocks. [KEECH n. (1)]

keed *n.* [1920s+] (*US*) a person, used in direct address. [pron. of KID n.[1] (4)]

keef *n. see* KIF n.

keegh/keek *n. see* KEECH n.

keek *n. see* KECK n.

keek-cloy *n.* [early 19C] (*UK Und.*) a trouser pocket. [? KECKS n./KICKS n.[1] + CLY n. (2)]

keel *n.* [late 19C+] the buttocks. [naut. imagery; SE *keel*, the bottom of a boat]

keeler *n. see* KEELIE n.

keel-haul *v.* [early 19C+] to treat badly, to punish, to beat, to ruin. [naut. jargon *keel-haul*, 'To haul (a person) under the keel of a ship, either by lowering him on one side and hauling him across to the other side, or, in the case of smaller vessels, lowering him at the bows and drawing him along under the keel to the stern' (*OED*)]

keel-hauling *n.* [mid-19C; 1940s+] a flogging. [20C+ use is W.I.; KEEL-HAUL V. + joc. use of KEEL n.]

keelie *n.* (*also* **keeler**) [mid-19C+] (*Scot.*) a thief; latterly a street thug, esp. from Glasgow. [Scot. *keelie*, a kestrel]

keel off *v.* (*also* **keel out**) [20C+] (*W.I.*) **1** to collapse. **2** to die. [var. on KEEL OVER v.]

keel over *v.* (*also* **keel up**) **1** [mid-19C–1900s] (*US*) to knock down or to kill. **2** [mid-19C+] (*orig. US*) to collapse, to fall over. [naut. jargon *keel over*, for a boat to capsize and thus reveal her keel]

keen *adj.* [late 19C+] (*US*) splendid, competent, sharply dressed etc; thus *keen society*, high society. [SE *keen*, eager or shrewd]

keener *n.* (*also* **keenie**) **1** [mid-19C+] (*US*) a hard bargainer, a cheat, a card-sharp. **2** [2000s] (*Can. juv.*) a toady, a sycophant. [SE *keen* + sfx -*er*]

keen gear *n.* [1990s+] (*US teen*) something good or fabulous. [KEEN adj. + GEAR n.[1] (2)]

keeno *adj.* [1910s+] excellent, wonderful, first-rate. [KEEN adj. + -O sfx (3)]

keen on *phr.* [late 19C+] interested in, esp. in pursuit of love or sex.

keen society *n. see* KEEN adj.

keep *n.* **1** [1940s] (*US Black/Harlem*) a housekeeper. **2** [1960s] (*US*) a barman. [abbr.; (2) SAmE *barkeep*]

keep *v.*[1] [19C] to live at, to dwell. [SE 15C–18C; SE *keep*, to stay or remain in or at a place]

keep *v.*[2] [early 19C] to remain a virgin.

keep a cart on the wheel *v.* [late 19C–1920s] to sustain a situation.

keep a fuss *v.* [20C+] (*W.I.*) **1** to make a noise or a disturbance. **2** to quarrel loudly.

keep a nestling *v.* [late 17C–early 18C] to be restless, uneasy. [imagery of a worried mother bird]

keep-a-nigger *adj.* [1990s+] (*US Black*) intended to maintain a relationship, e.g. used of a child deliberately conceived by a woman with the intention of keeping a lover who had only desired a brief relationship.

keep an ironmonger's shop by the side of a common *phr.* (*also* **...where the sheriff sets up**) [late 18C–early 19C] to be hanged in chains.

keep a stiff lip *v.* [1970s+] (*US Black*) to keep quiet, to maintain a secret. [SE *keep a stiff upper lip*]

keep a straight face *v.* [late 19C+] to restrain oneself from laughing.

keep a swannery *v.* [late 18C–early 19C] to boast, to boost one's own achievements. [the mocking phr. 'all his geese are swans']

keep a tab on *v. see* KEEP TABS ON v.

keep a tight asshole *v.* (*also* **keep a tight hole**) [1940s+] (*orig. US milit.*) to maintain emotional control. [ASSHOLE n.[1] (1); the propensity of intense fear to loosen one's bowels]

keep at the stick's end *v.* [late 19C–1920s] to snub, to keep 'at arm's length'.

keep a weather eye open *v. see* KEEP ONE'S EYE PEELED v.

keep banker's hours *v.* [20C+] to act lazily. [the relatively brief periods during which banks remained open for public business]

keep cases on *v.* [late 19C–1930s] (*US*) to watch closely. [CASE v.[1] (1)]

keep cave *v.* (*also* **keep cavvy**) [mid-19C+] (*UK juv.*) to keep a lookout. [Lat. *cave*, beware; but Ware suggests *K.V.* as in *on the qui vive*, on the lookout]

keep chick *v.* (*also* **keep chickie, lay chic, lay chick, lay chickie**) [1930s+] (*US*) to maintain a lookout (during a crime). [SE *keep* + CHICK! excl.]

keep company (with) *v.* [mid-19C+] to associate with, esp. as a lover.

keep cool *v.* (*also* **stay cool**) **1** [mid-19C+] (*orig. US Black*) to keep calm, to restrain one's emotions. **2** [1940s] (*US Black campus*) to stay in one's place. [SE *keep* + COOL adj.[1] (2)]

keep dark *v.* (*also* **keep it dark**) [mid-19C+] to keep secret, to hide away (esp. of information).

keep dick *v.* [20C+] (*Ulster*) to keep a lookout. [DICK v.[1]]

keep dog *v.* [1980s+] to keep a lookout. [SE *watchdog*]

keep doggo *v. see* LIE DOGGO v.

keep down *v.* [20C+] (*Aus.*) to maintain one's job despite the problems entailed. [SE *hold down*]

keeper *n.* [20C+] any form of weapon. [SE, i.e. it keeps one safe]

keep in a tow-line *v. see* KEEP IN TOW v.

keep in gammon *v.* [early 19C] (*UK Und.*) to engage a person's attention while a confederate is robbing them. [SE *keep* + GAMMON v.]

keeping cully *n.* [late 17C–early 19C] **1** 'one that maintains a mistress and parts with his money very generously to her' (B.E.). **2** 'one who keeps a mistress, as he supposes, for his own use, but really for that of the public' (Grose, 1785). [SE *keep* + CULLY n. (2)]

keeping the passover *phr.* [late 19C] (*W.I.*) spreading out one's clothes for an airing. [orig. known as *hold a Rag Fair* or *hold a Monmouth Street*. The association of Jewish old-clothes sellers with Monmouth Street led to the introduction of *Passover*, the Jewish spring festival commemorating the Exodus from Egypt; presumably + added ref. to the 'passing over' of the fresh air]

keep in the pin *v.* [mid-19C] to abstain from drinking. [SE *keep* + *pin*, one of a set of pegs fixed on the inside of a large drinking vessel, poss. used to indicate the amount each drinker is allowed as the vessel is handed from person to person]

keep in tow *v.* (*also* **keep in a tow-line, keep on a string**) [early 19C–1900s] (*UK Und.*) to keep someone in suspense.

keep in with *v.* [late 16C+] to remain on good terms with.

keep it between the ditches *phr.* [1990s+] (*US*) a phr. of farewell; 'it' being a metaphorical vehicle.

keep it dark v. see KEEP DARK v.

keep it greasy phr. [2000s] (US Black) a farewell, 'stay cool'.

keep it in one's pants v. see KEEP ONE'S DICK IN ONE'S PANTS v.

keep-it-real adj. [1990s+] honest, dedicated to one's roots. [KEEP IT REAL v.]

keep it real v. (also **keep one's shit real**) [1990s+] to maintain one's honesty, to stick to one's roots.

keep it together v. (also **have it together**) [1980s+] (orig. US Black) **1** to maintain a satisfactory lifestyle. **2** to keep emotional control.

keep it under one's hat v. (also **keep things under one's hat**) [20C+] to act discreetly, to keep a secret; esp. in imper. keep it under your hat!

keep it up v. [late 18C–1900s] to live a fashionable life; to prolong a debauch. [pun on SE keep it up, to maintain an erection]

keep-miss n. (also **keep-woman**) [20C+] (W.I.) a kept woman. [SE keep + miss/woman]

keep mum v. [19C+] to keep quiet; thus [1940s] exhortation to secrecy, be like Dad, keep Mum. [SE keep + MUM adj.]

keep nikko v. (also **keep nick**) [1940s+] (Irish) to keep a lookout. [? link to NICK v.[3], i.e. prepared to run off]

keep nit v. [20C+] (Aus.) to act as lookout; thus NIT KEEPER n. [var. on KEEP NIX v.; note NIT! excl.[2]]

keep nix v. [mid-19C+] to keep a lookout. [SE keep + NIX! excl.; 20C+ use is mainly juv.]

keep off the grass v. [late 19C–1930s] **1** to act cautiously. **2** as imper., keep away, do not disturb (me).

keep on and on v. [1970s+] to nag.

keep on a string v. see KEEP IN TOW v.

keep one's cock up v. [1970s] (US) to stay cheerful, despite possible adversity; often as imper. [COCK n.[2] (1)]

keep one's cool v. (also **hold one's cool**) [1950s+] (orig. US) to remain calm, despite circumstances to the contrary. [COOL n.[2] (1)]

keep one's dick in one's pants v. (also **keep it in one's pants**) [1980s+] to act calmly, in sexual contexts or otherwise; often as imper. keep your dick in your pants! [DICK n.[4] (1)]

keep one's drawers on v. see KEEP ONE'S PANTS ON v.

keep one's ears skinned v. see KEEP ONE'S EYE SKINNED v.

keep one's ear to the ground v. [1940s+] (orig. US) to be on the lookout, to take note of developments.

keep one's end up v. (also **keep one's tail up**) [late 19C+] to do one's duty, to carry out one's share. [? cricket imagery or ? f. helping lift a heavy weight]

keep one's eye on the ball v. [20C+] to stay alert and aware. [sporting imagery; note mid-19C cant keep up to the ball, to live and be jolly]

keep one's eye peeled v. (also **keep a weather eye open**, **keep one's eyes peeled**, **skin one's weather eye**) [mid-19C+] (orig. US) to keep on one's guard, to act cautiously.

keep one's eye skinned v. (also **keep one's ears skinned**) [mid-19C+] (orig. US) to pay the closest attention to what is happening. [var. on KEEP ONE'S EYE PEELED v.]

keep one's feet in one's pants v. [1960s] (US Black) to keep calm, to restrain one's emotions.

keep one's foot in someone's ass v. [1960s] (US Black) to pressurize someone, to treat someone badly.

keep one's game tight v. see TIGHTEN (UP) ONE'S GAME v. (2).

keep one's hair on v. (also **have one's head on**, **hold one's hair on**, **keep one's skin on**, **keep one's wool on**) [late 19C+] to keep calm, to keep one's temper; thus get one's hair off, to lose one's temper. [? the image of tearing out one's hair when in a rage, or (though prob. a folk ety. at best) the need of members of US pioneering wagon trains to keep calm in the face of an Indian attack (were they to panic, they might well be scalped, thus losing their hair)]

keep one's hand in v. [early 18C–19C] to maintain one's skills (in a job). [20C+ use is SE]

keep one's head cool v. (also **keep one's head right**) [1980s+] (US Black) to keep control of oneself, both emotionally and physically.

keep one's head down v. [1950s+] **1** to be careful. **2** to maintain a 'low profile'.

keep one's lips at home v. [mid-19C] (US) to be quiet, to stop being impertinent.

keep one's nose clean v. **1** [mid-19C–1940s] (orig. milit.) to avoid alcohol. **2** [late 19C+] (also **keep one's snout clean**) to lead a law-abiding, upright life. **3** [1920s+] to resist interfering in things that are not one's business. **4** [1930s+] of a criminal, to avoid being implicated in something illegal.

keep one's nose in someone's ass v. [1960s+] (US) to toady to, to be sycophantic towards.

keep one's nose to the grindstone v. [20C+] to work long and hard. [KEEP SOMEONE'S NOSE TO THE GRINDSTONE v.]

keep one's pants on v. (also **keep one's drawers on**, **keep one's pants up**) [1920s+] (orig. US) to act in a sensible, calm manner, to keep one's temper.

keep one's pecker up v. (also **hold one's pecker up**) [mid-19C+] to stay cheerful, despite possible adversity; often as imper. keep your pecker up! [PECKER n.[2] (1); despite chronological impossibility, popular ety. usu. links phr. to PECKER n.[2] (2)]

keep one's shirt on v. (also **keep one's jumper on**, **keep one's shirt in**) [mid-19C+] to keep one's temper, to stay calm; esp. as imper.

keep one's shit real v. see KEEP IT REAL v.

keep one's skin on v. see KEEP ONE'S HAIR ON v.

keep one's snout clean v. see KEEP ONE'S NOSE CLEAN v. (2).

keep one's tache on v. [late 19C–1910s] (Anglo-Ind.) to keep calm, to keep one's temper. [E.P. ingeniously suggests roots in Hind., in Welsh gypsy jargon and a ref. to a hair-restorer ('Tatcho'); the prosaic reality of the root is much more likely an abbr. of SE moustache]

keep one's tail quiet v. [20C+] (W.I.) to stay where one is, to keep quiet, to stay out of trouble. [TAIL n.[2] (1)]

keep one's tail up v. see KEEP ONE'S END UP v.

keep one's tits on v. [1990s+] (US) to be patient. [TIT n.[3] (1); var. on KEEP ONE'S HAIR ON v.]

keep one's trap shut v. [20C+] to be quiet. [TRAP n.[3]]

keep one's wig cool v. (also **keep one's wig on**) [1910s+] to remain calm.

keep one's wool on v. see KEEP ONE'S HAIR ON v.

keep on keeping on v. [1910s+] (orig. US Black) to persist in one's efforts.

keep out of the rain v. [late 19C+] (orig. Aus.) to avoid trouble.

keep schtum v. see KEEP STUM v.

keep shady v. [mid–late 19C] (UK Und.) to act discreetly, to keep oneself hidden.

keep sheep by moonlight v. [late 18C–early 19C] to hang in chains. [the gibbet was often on a heath or moorland where sheep might be wandering; the corpse provided a fig. 'shepherd']

keep shoatie v. [20C+] (Scot.) to keep a lookout. [presumably SHUT-EYE n., but rather than closing the eyes, one is keeping them wide open; note also Scot. shut-eye, a trick or swindle; or link to shotgun, i.e. one who backs up, lit. or fig., a protagonist]

keep shtoom v. see KEEP STUM v.

keepsies! excl. [1950s+] (US, mainly juv.) an excl. claiming the right to keep something found or won.

keep six v. see GIVE SIX v.

keep someone guessing v. [20C+] (orig. US) to keep someone in a state of uncertainty.

keep someone on the jump v. [20C+] to keep someone in a state of uncertainty, esp. as regards their employment. [SE keep + ON THE JUMP phr.]

keep someone's nose to the grindstone v. [17C+] to make someone work hard, to treat someone harshly (cf. KEEP ONE'S NOSE TO THE GRINDSTONE v.).

keep steady v. see GO STEADY v.

keep stum v. (also **keep schtum, ...shtoom, ...stumm**) [1950s+] to keep quiet, to say nothing. [SHTUM adj.]

keep tabs on v. (also **keep (a) tab on**) [late 19C+] (orig. US) to keep under surveillance, to take note of. [TAB n.³ (1)]

keep the ball rolling v. [mid-19C+] to maintain the progress of a situation. [sporting imagery; note late 18C–19C cant *keep up to the ball*, to live and be jolly]

keep the block v. see DO ONE'S BLOCK v. (1).

keep the bone green v. [20C+] (Ulster) **1** to postpone settling an argument. **2** to confront someone.

keep the cap on the bottle v. [1970s+] to suppress the publication of facts or information deleterious to oneself.

keep the cork on v. [20C+] to maintain control of one's emotions.

keep the doctor v. [late 19C–1930s] to sell adulterated alcohol. [SE *doctor*, to adulterate + ? implication that one's customers will require a *doctor*]

keep the door v. [late 18C–mid-19C] to run a brothel. [euph.]

keep the faith v. [1960s+] (US Black) to stay loyal, to keep struggling with. [KEEP THE FAITH! excl.]

keep the faith! excl. [1960s+] (orig. US Black) stay loyal! don't desert us! [best known in the slogan *keep the faith, baby*, popularized by the controversial US Congressman Adam Clayton Powell Jr (1908–72)]

keep the lid on v. [20C+] (orig. US) to keep something secret. [SE *keep* + LID, THE n.]

keep the line v. [early–mid-19C] to behave properly. [hunting jargon *keep one's own line*, to ride straight]

keep the lines open v. [20C+] to maintain communication. [telephone imagery]

keep the log rolling v. see KEEP THE BALL ROLLING v.

keep the peg in v. [1900s] (Aus.) to refrain from drinking. [? the peg in the keg]

keep things under one's hat v. see KEEP IT UNDER ONE'S HAT v.

keep tout v. [early–mid-19C] to spy on, to keep a lookout. [TOUT n.¹ (3)]

keep-up n. [1970s+] (US Black) anyone who looks after the home, esp. a maid. [SE *keep up appearances*]

keep up to the collar v. **1** [mid–late 19C] to stay hard at work, or to make someone else stay hard at work. **2** [1910s–20s] to be overwhelmed by one's work. [the *collar* is that of a horse, linked to a cart]

keep up with the Joneses v. [1930s+] to maintain one's social position, to ensure that one does not let one's neighbours or peers 'get ahead'. [generic use of *Jones* as anyone else]

keep-woman n. see KEEP-MISS n.

keep your hair on! excl. (also **keep your britches on! ...knickers on! ...pants on! ...shirt on! ...wool on!**) [late 19C+] calm down! don't lose (emotional) control!

keep your hand on your ha'penny (till the right man turns up) phr. [20C+] a phr. advising a young woman to retain her virginity until the advent of 'Mr Right'. [HA'PENNY n.]

keep your syrup on! excl. (also **keep your wig on!**) [1980s+] relax! calm down! [SYRUP (OF FIGS) n. (1); var. on KEEP YOUR HAIR ON! excl.]

keep your teeth! excl. [mid-19C] calm down!

keep your wool on! excl. see KEEP YOUR HAIR ON! excl.

keep yow v. [1940s+] (Aus.) to keep a lookout, esp. in a criminal context. [*yow*, onomat. for a cry of alarm]

keeshkas n. see KISHKES n.

keester n. see KEISTER n.

keeva adj. [1990s+] (US campus) excellent, worthy of admiration. [ety. unknown]

kef n. see KIF n.

keffal n. (also **keffel**) [late 17C–mid-19C] (UK Und.) a horse. [Welsh *ceffyl*, a horse; its use often implied that the horse was second-rate]

keg n.¹ (also **beer keg**) [late 19C+] (US) the stomach.

keg n.² **1** [1940s+] (Aus./N.Z.) beer, a barrel of beer. **2** [1970s] (US drugs) 5 lbs. of marijuana. [(1) abbr. SE *beer keg*; (2) ? the amount of marijuana that would fill a beer keg]

keg v.¹ [late 18C–mid-19C] (US) to abstain from drinking alcohol. [SE *keg*; the image is of leaving the beer in the keg]

keg v.² see CAG v.

keg fly n. [1980s+] (US campus) someone who hovers around the beer keg at parties. [on pattern of BAR-FLY n.]

kegger n. **1** [1910s+] (N.Z.) a person who buys beer legally to drink it in a teetotal or 'dry' area of the country. **2** [1960s+] (US campus) (also **X kegger**) a party featuring a large supply of beer. [SE *keg*]

kegging n.¹ (N.Z.) **1** [1910s+] buying alcohol legally, and then taking it to a teetotal or 'dry' area of the country for consumption. **2** [1970s+] indulging in a keg-party, i.e. a party where kegs of beer are consumed. [SE *keg*]

kegging n.² [1990s+] stripping as part of sexual bullying by boys.

kegging adj. [1990s+] (US campus) excellent, worthy of admiration.

keg it up v. [1990s+] (N.Z.) to drink, usu. in a party or public house. [KEG n.² (1)]

keg-legs n. [1990s+] (UK juv.) an insult aimed at a girl with fat thighs or esp. calves. [SE *keg*, a beer-barrel]

kegmeg n. **1** [mid-19C] tripe; thus *kegmeg shop*, a tripe shop. **2** [late 19C] an intimate conversation. [SE *kegmeg*, rotten meat or a tough old goose; (2) ? pun on TRIPE n.¹ or a moral disapproval of the 'rotten-ness' of gossip]

keifer n. see KYFER n.

keister n. (also **keaster, keester, keyster, kiester, kister**) **1** [late 19C+] (US) a suitcase, a satchel, a handbag, a salesman's sample case. **2** [late 19C+] (US Und.) a burglar's bag of safe- or house-breaking tools. **3** [1910s+] (US Und.) a safe, a strongbox (often within a safe). **4** [1930s–40s] (US) the female genitals. **5** [1930s–60s] (US) sexual intercourse with a woman. **6** [1930s–60s] (mainly US prison) anal copulation. **7** [1930s+] (orig. US) the anus, the buttocks; thus *grease someone's keister*, to sodomize; [1960s] (US prison) *keister-stashed*, hidden in the anus. **8** [1940s–60s] (US) a prison. **9** [1960s+] (US) one's self. [Ger. *kiste*, a box, a case + Ger. sl. the rump; (4), (5) and (6) f. (7)]

keister v. (also **keester**) (US, esp. prison) **1** [1930s+] (also **ass-keister**) to hide something in the rectum; thus KEISTER PLANT n. **2** [1930s+] to sodomize. **3** [1960s+] to betray, to harm. [KEISTER n. (7); (3) is fig. use of (2)]

keister bandit n. [1930s+] (US prison) a 'masculine' male homosexual; by ext., a womanizer, a rapist (cf. ANAL ASTRONAUT n.). [KEISTER n. (7) + BANDIT sfx (2)]

keister bunny n. [1990s+] (US prison) an inmate who places contraband items – tobacco, drugs – in his rectum. [KEISTER n. (7) + SE *bunny*]

keisterman n. [1930s–50s] (US Und.) a thief who specializes in stealing suitcases on railway stations. [KEISTER n. (1) + SE *man*]

keister plant n. [1930s–70s] (US drugs) a cache of drugs hidden, usu. in some from of hollow metal container, in the rectum. [KEISTER n. (7) + PLANT v.¹ (1)]

keister shafting n. [1980s+] (US gay) anal intercourse. [KEISTER n. (7) + SHAFT v. (1)]

keister stab v. [1980s+] (US gay) to have anal intercourse (cf. ASK FOR THE RING v.). [KEISTER n. (7) + STAB v.]

keister stash n. [1960s] (US Und.) any slim, hollow item, e.g. a biro tube, that can be placed in the anus and used to transport money, drugs etc. [KEISTER n. (7) + STASH n.²]

Keith Moon n. [1960s+] an eccentric, a loon (cf. BREAD AND BUTTER n.²). [rhy. sl.; ult. drummer of the rock band The Who, Keith Moon (1947–78)]

keks n. see KECKS n.

kelch n. see KELT n.

kelder n. see HANS-EN-KELDER n.

kell n. [20C+] (Ulster) a ring of dirt that reveals an unwashed neck. [northern dial. kell, the equivalent of SE caul]

kelly n.¹ [20C+] (Aus.) an axe; thus swing kelly, to swing an axe. [brandname of Kelly Axe Manufacturing Co., Charleston, West Virginia]

kelly n.² [20C+] a crow. [Cumbrian dial. kelp, a young crow]

kelly n.³ [1900s–70s] (US) a man's hat. [pun on a Derby hat; ? rhy. sl. DARBY KELLY n.]

kelly n.⁴ [1940s–50s] (Aus.) a bus or tram inspector. [the bushranger Ned Kelly (1855–80); like him the inspectors pounce suddenly on their victims]

Kelly gang n. see NED KELLY n.¹ (1).

kelly ned n. [20C+] (Aus./US) the head. [rhy. sl.; ult. the bushranger Ned Kelly (1855–80)]

kelly's eye n. [20C+] (bingo) the number 1 (cf. ALDERSHOT LADIES n.). [? a lost anecdote]

kelp n.¹ (also calp) [mid-18C–mid-19C] a hat. [Turkish calpac, a Turkish and Tartar felt cap]

kelp n.² [20C+] a self-conscious, awkward teenager, usu. a girl. [? Scot. gilpp, a growing girl]

kelp v. [early–mid-19C] to raise one's hat to an acquaintance. [KELP n.¹]

kelper n. [1960s+] a Falkland Islander. [the kelp (large seaweeds) found on the islands + sfx -er]

kelsey n. [1930s–70s] (US Black) **1** a prostitute (cf. BABY JANE n.). **2** straight hair: a popular hairstyle favoured by many prostitutes. [(2) orig. carnival use; presumably a punning ref. to TIGHT AS KELSEY'S NUTS phr. (see next)]

Kelsey's nuts n. [1930s+] (US Und.) used alone to imply the best, the absolute; used in phrs. as a superlative to mean extremely, the most, e.g. tight as Kelsey's nuts, very mean, stingy. [punning ref. to the US Kelsey Wheel Company, founded in 1910 to produce automobile wheels. The need for nuts and bolts to be exceptionally tight fitting to preclude wobbly wheels gave rise to the saying]

kelt n. (also kelch, kelsey, keltch, keltz) [1910s+] (US Black) **1** a White person. **2** used to mean a light-skinned Black person, in phrs. such as three-quarter kelt. [? Scot. kelt, a homespun cloth, usu. of black and white wool mixed, once used for outer garments by country people]

kelter n. [late 18C–mid-19C] money, cash. [northern dial.]

kembla (grange) n. [1950s+] (Aus.) small change. [rhy. sl.; ult. Kembla Grange, an area of Wollongong, New South Wales]

kemels n. [1940s] (US Black) shoes. [? brandname]

kemesa n. see CAMESA n.

kemo sabe n. [1930s+] (US) a friend, used in direct address. [according to scriptwriter Frank Striker, the 'Native American' term 'trusty scout' applied to the loyal Indian companion, Tonto, in the Lone Ranger radio and television series created by George Trendle in 1933; for some of the alternative theories behind the phr., see www.write101.com/kemosabe.htm]

kemp n. (also kimp) [1950s] (US) a car. [ety. unknown]

ken n.¹ (UK Und.) **1** [16C+] (also kennel) a house, a home, a room. **2** [17C–1920s] a low drinking room. [poss. abbr. SE kennel (in a non-canine mode) or f. Hind. khan(n)a, a house or room, which is also found in combs., e.g. buggy-khanna (coach house) or bottle-khanna (drinking house); Hotten (1867) attributes it to 'Gypsy and Oriental' and notes that 'all slang and cant words which end in -ken are partly of Gypsey origin' on which basis E.P. opts for

a root in Rom. tan, a place; the term vanished from sl. c.1860, but has survived in market-traders' jargon]

ken n.² [1990s+] (Aus.) a cleaning implement for a barbecue. [BARBIE n.²; punning on Ken and Barbie, the fashion dolls]

ken n.³ [1990s+] (US campus) a painstakingly fashionably dressed and groomed man. [the popular male companion for Barbie]

ken n.⁴ see FENCING KEN n.

ken a handsaw from a hog v. see KNOW A DEVIL FROM A JACKDAW v.

ken-burster n. [early–mid-19C] a house-breaker. [KEN n.¹ (1) + SE burster]

ken cove n. see COVE OF THE KEN n.

ken-cracker n. [late 18C–19C] a house-breaker. [KEN n.¹ (1) + SE cracker]

Ken Dodd n. [1960s+] a large roll of banknotes. [rhy. sl. = WAD n.¹ (1); ult. comedian Ken Dodd (b.1931)]

Ken Dodds n. [1960s+] the testicles (cf. CHEESE AND CRACKERS n.). [rhy. sl. = CODS n.¹ (1); for ety. see prev.]

kenird adj. see KANURD adj.

ken-miller n. [mid-17C–mid-19C] a house-breaker. [KEN n.¹ (1) + MILL v.¹ (1)]

kennedy n. **1** [early 19C–1900s] a poker. **2** [early 19C–1900s] a blow inflicted with a poker. **3** [1980s+] the penis (cf. ABRAHAM n.¹). [proper name Kennedy, a man who allegedly suffered thus in London's St Giles slums; (3) fig. use of (1)]

kennedy v. [mid-19C] to strike or beat to death with a poker. [KENNEDY n.]

kennedy rot n.¹ [20C+] (Aus./US) a sot. [rhy. sl.]

kennedy rot n.² see BARCOO ROT n.

kennedy swoop n. [1970s+] (US Black) a hairstyle in which Black hair is straightened, then brushed to one side in a manner loosely resembling the hairstyles of John Kennedy (1917–63) and Robert Kennedy (1925–68).

kennel n.¹ [late 17C–19C] the vagina (cf. BAG n.¹; BEST IN CHRISTENDOM n.). [SE kennel, a gutter]

kennel n.² [1900s–20s] (US tramp) a house. **2** [1920s] (US) a booth, any small structure reminiscent of a dog kennel.

kennel raker n. [19C] the penis. [KENNEL n.¹ + SE raker; SE kennel-raker, 'a raker of the gutter; a scavenger; also used as a term of abuse' (OED)]

kennetseeno adj. [mid-19C] putrid, stinking, 'off'. [backsl.]

kennick n. [mid–late 19C] a mixture of criminal cant and the slang talked in a lodging house. [KEN n.¹ (1) ? + model of Celtic]

Kennington Lane n. [20C+] pain. [rhy. sl.; ult. Kennington Lane, a south London thoroughfare]

kennuck n. (also kenuck) [mid–late 19C] a penny. [? KILKENNY n.²]

kennurd adj. see KANURD adj.

keno! excl. [mid-19C–1930s] (US) used to express excitement or success. [used in game of keno to describe a winning set of numbers]

kenobe n. [mid-19C] (UK Und.) a thief.

Kenso n. [1940s+] (Aus.) **1** Kensington, a suburb of Sydney. **2** the University of New South Wales at Kensington. [Kens(ington) + -o sfx (4)]

Kent n. [19C] any variety of coloured handkerchief; thus also kent clout, kent rag. [ety. unknown; ? as favoured in Kent, the UK county]

Kentish Town n. [20C+] a penny. [rhy. sl. = BROWN n.² (1)]

kentry n. [late 19C] (US Und.) a gang's territory.

Kent Street ejectment n. (also Kent Street distress) [late 18C–19C] the removal of the front door when tenants are more than 2 weeks in rent arrears. [Kent Street, Southwark, a very poor area in 16C London, where the practice originated]

Kentuck n. (also Kaintuck) [early 19C+] (US) a Kentuckian, Kentucky; also as adj. [abbr.]

Kentucky n. see KENTUCKY (TREAT) n.

Kentucky *adj.* [early 19C] (*US*) pertaining to violence. [geog. stereotyping]

Kentucky argument *n.* [late 19C] (*US*) a dispute which escalates to the drawing of firearms. [geog. stereotyping]

Kentucky bite *n.* [mid-19C] (*US*) a cutting bite to the ear or nose during a fight. [regional stereotyping]

Kentucky blue *n.* [1960s+] (*drugs*) a variety of marijuana grown in Kentucky (cf. ACAPULCO (GOLD) *n.*). [joc. ref. to *Kentucky blue grass*]

Kentucky breakfast *n.* [late 19C+] (*US*) **1** popularly defined as 'three cocktails and a chew of terbacker' (cf. BARBER'S BREAKFAST *n.*). **2** a bottle of bourbon, a 3-pound steak and a setter dog; the dog is there to eat the steak. [the supposed favourite breakfast of the classic 'Southern gentleman']

Kentucky loo *n. see* FLY LOO *n.*

Kentucky oysters *n.* [late 19C+] (*US, mainly Black*) chitterlings, pig intestines. [regional stereotyping]

Kentucky (treat) *n.* [1910s–50s] (*Aus./US*) a supposed 'treat' for which everyone present has to contribute. [regional stereotyping]

kenuck *n. see* KENNUCK *n.*

kenwood *n.* [2000s] a gentile woman. [rhy. sl.; *Kenwood mixer* = SHIKSA *n.* (1); ult. the brand of food processor]

kenz *adj.* [20C+] (*W.I., USVI*) gullible, simple-minded, easily fooled. [Scot. *kensy*, a general term of abuse for a rough, rude person]

keo *n.* (*also* **keo-boy**) [20C+] (*Ulster*) **1** an entertaining, if less than respectable, individual. **2** a term of abuse, a contemptible person. **3** a womanizer. **4** a trickster. [Scot. *kiow-ow*, a trifle in speech or conduct]

keptie *n.* [1930s–60s] (*US*) a mistress, a kept woman. [SE *kept* + fem. sfx *-ie*]

ker- *pfx* (*also* **ca-, co-, ka-**) [mid-19C+] (*orig. US*) a pfx used in a wide variety of combs. to indicate the sound of falling, collision or movement; as well as the main vars. above, other synon. pfxs include *che-, com-, con-, cor-, cul-, cur-, ga-, ger-, k'-, ke-, ki-, ko-, ku-*. [most dictionaries (*OED*, Webster, F&H) link the pfx to onomat., but beyond that the precise meaning of *ker-* becomes more problematical. A range of possibilities is listed by Cohen, whose detailed analysis is recommended for further study (*Studies in Slang* I, 1985, pp.1–28): (i) f. simple onomat.; (ii) f. Ger. past participle pfx *ge-*; (iii) f. dial. *cur-/car-* and Gaelic *car-*, wrongly, confusedly; ult. f. Gaelic *car*, a twist, a turn; (iv) the initial *crrr-* pron. of words such as *crash* and *crunch* (Cohen's own belief)]

kerb *see under* CURB.

kerbam! *excl.* [20C+] an onomat. term indicating a sudden noise or sharp shock. [KER- pfx + SE *bam*]

kerb and gutter *n.* [20C+] (*Aus.*) butter. [rhy. sl.]

kerbang! *excl.* [late 19C+] an onomat. term indicating a sudden sharp noise or explosion. [KER- pfx + SE *bang*]

kerb boy *n.* [20C+] a street-seller of trifles, e.g. combs, thread etc.

kerb-crawler *n.* [1950s+] a man who tries to pick up prostitutes by driving a car slowly along the edge of the pavement in areas where prostitutes are known to operate.

kerbiff! *excl.* [late 19C+] an onomat. term indicating a sudden blow. [KER- pfx + BIFF *n.*[1] (1)]

kerbim! *excl.* [mid-19C] an onomat. term indicating a sudden blow. [KER- pfx + echoic *bim*]

kerblam! *excl.* [late 19C+] an onomat. term indicating a sudden shock or explosion. [KER- pfx + SE *blam*]

kerblinketyblank! *excl.* [late 19C] an onomat. term indicating annoyance, irritation. [KER- pfx + BLANKETY-BLANK phr.]

kerblip! *excl.* [20C+] an onomat. term indicating the noise of something hitting the (soft) ground. [KER- pfx + echoic *blip*]

kerblump! *excl.* [1940s+] an onomat. term indicating the noise of a solid object hitting the (soft) ground. [KER- pfx + echoic *blump*; var. on KERPLUMP! excl.]

kerbolluxed *adj.* [20C+] messed up, confused, with overtones of attendant noise. [KER- pfx + BALLOCKSED (UP) *adj.* (1)]

kerbonk! *excl.* [1980s+] an onomat. term indicating the noise of a solid object hitting (or being hit by) another one. [KER- pfx + BONK *n.* (1)]

kerbside virginia *n.* [20C+] a cigarette rolled from discarded cigarette ends.

kerbstone *see also under* CURBSTONE and its combs.

kerbstone jockey *n.* [1980s+] (*N.Z.*) a safe job.

kerbstone language *n.* [1900s] (*N.Z.*) coarse language, i.e. that 'of the gutter'.

kerchew! *excl.* (*also* **kachew!**) [20C+] an onomat. term indicating the sound of a sneeze. [KER- pfx + SE (*ti*)*shoo*]

kerchug! *excl.* [20C+] an onomat. term indicating the sound of an ailing motor engine turning over. [KER- pfx + SE *chug*]

kerchunk! *excl.* (*also* **cachunk! cochunk!**) [mid-19C+] an onomat. term indicating the sound of a solid object hitting the ground or 2 solid objects colliding. [KER- pfx + echoic]

kerdap! *excl.* [1930s] (*US*) an onomat. term echoic of something liquid hitting a solid surface. [KER- pfx + echoic *dap*]

kerdash! *excl.* [mid-19C] (*US*) an onomat. term indicating the sound of an object hitting a liquid. [KER- pfx + ? SE *splash*]

kerdiff! *excl.* [mid-19C] (*US*) an onomat. term indicating a sudden shock or noise. [KER- pfx + *diff*, echoic of a sudden noise]

kerdoing! *excl.* (*also* **gerdoing! gerdoying! kerdoink! kerdoying!**) [1950s+] an onomat. term indicating a sudden noise. [KER- pfx + echoic *doing*]

kerel *n.* (*S.Afr.*) **1** [early 19C+] a chap, a fellow. **2** [early 19C+] a boyfriend. **3** [early 19C+] a tricky, cunning person. **4** [late 19C+] a term of address to a man. **5** [1970s+] the police. [OE *ceorl*, a countryman, a common man]

kerflap! *excl.* [20C+] an onomat. term indicating a sudden shock or gesture. [KER- pfx + SE *flap*]

kerflip! *excl.* [1930s+] an onomat. term indicating the sound of a solid body hitting a soft one or hitting liquid. [KER- pfx + SE *flip*]

kerflooey *adj.* (*also* **caflooey, kerfluey**) [1910s+] crazy, chaotic, disorganized; usu. in phr. GO KERFLOOEY *v.* [KERFLOOEY! excl.]

kerflooey! *excl.* (*also* **kaflooey!**) [1910s+] an onomat. term indicating a sudden explosion. [KER- pfx + FLOOEY! excl.]

kerflop! *excl.* [late 19C+] an onomat. term indicating the sound of a solid body hitting a soft one or hitting liquid. [KER- pfx + SE *flop*]

kerfluey *adj. see* KERFLOOEY *adj.*

kerflummox *v.* (*also* **kerflumix, kerflummux**) (*US*) **1** [mid-19C–1900s] to confound, to flabbergast. **2** [late 19C–1900s] to fall heavily or noisily. [KER- pfx + FLUMMOX *v.*[1]]

kerflummox *adv.* (*also* **kerflumix**) [mid-19C–1900s] (*US*) of falling, heavily or noisily, with a thump. [KERFLUMMOX *v.*]

kerflunk! *excl.* (*also* **kaflunk!**) [1980s+] an onomat. term indicating something solid falling to the ground. [KER- pfx + echoic *flunk*]

kerfuffle *n.* (*also* **cufuffle, curfuffle**) [early 19C+] (*orig. US*) a fuss, a row, a confusion. [Scot. *curfuffle*, a fuss, a row]

kerfuffle valve *n.* [1970s+] (*Aus.*) a make-believe 'valve' within the human body, supposedly under stress when one lifts heavy objects. [joc. use of KERFUFFLE *n.* + SE *valve*]

kerlaraping *n.* [late 19C] (*US*) cavorting, jumping around excitedly. [KER- pfx + ? *larrup*, to thrash]

kerlumpus! *excl. see* KERPLUMPUS! excl.

Kermit the Frog *n.* [1970s+] **1** a lavatory (cf. ANGUS ARMANASCO *n.*). **2** sexual caressing, stopping short of intercourse. [rhy. sl.: (1) = BOG *n.*[1]; (2) = SNOG *n.*; ult. *Kermit the Frog*, a character in *The Muppet Show* (1976–81)]

kero *n.* [1930s+] (*Aus.*) **1** kerosene. **2** beer. [abbr. SE *kerosene*; (2) implies a form of 'fuel']

kerosene tin push *n.* [1900s] (*Aus.*) a flock of goats. [the joc.

story that goats are fed on kerosone tins; thus *Bulletin*, 11 January 1906, 15/1: 'What a multiplicity of uses the kerosene tin is put to in the bush [...] Houses are made of it in some parts and I have heard they feed the goats on kerosene tins about Byrock, but I cannot vouch for that']

kerp *n. see* CURP n.

kerplooey! *excl.* (*also* **kaplooey!**) [1930s+] an onomat. term indicating the noise made by the explosion of something soft and messy, e.g. a large fruit or a living body. [KER- pfx + echoic *plooey*; var. on KERFLOOEY! excl.]

kerplop! *excl.* [late 19C+] an onomat. term indicating the sound of a solid body falling, usu. into liquid, or of a bubble bursting in liquid. [KER- pfx + SE *plop*]

kerplump! *excl.* [1930s+] an onomat. term indicating the sound of a solid body hitting a soft surface. [KER- pfx + echoic *plump*]

kerplumpus! *excl.* (*also* **kerlumpus!**) [mid-19C] an onomat. term indicating the sound of a solid body hitting a soft surface. [ext. of KERPLUMP! excl.]

kerplunk! *excl.* [late 19C+] an onomat. term indicating one object hitting another with a dull thump, or a solid object falling into liquid. [KER- pfx + echoic *plunk*]

kerpoomph! *excl.* [1950s] an onomat. term indicating the sound of a solid body hitting a soft surface. [KER- pfx + echoic *poomph*]

Kerry Packered *adj.* (*also* **kerried**) [1970s+] exhausted, tired out. [rhy. sl. = KNACKERED adj. (1); ult. Aus. media magnate *Kerry Packer* (b.1937)]

Kerry security *n.* [late 18C–early 19C] any form of bond or oath that has been sworn in return for money. [? stereotyping of Kerrymen as corrupt]

Kerry witness *n.* [late 18C] a witness who is happy to swear to anything (for a price). [? stereotyping of Kerrymen as corrupt]

kershewey! *excl.* [1940s+] (*US*) a euph. excl., the equivalent of BY CHRIST! excl. or BY JESUS! excl. [KER- pfx + ? *Jesus*]

kershlunk! *excl.* [1940s+] an onomat. term indicating the clandestine, slinking movement of an animal or human, e.g. *the cat went kershlunk into the bushes*. [KER- pfx + *slunk/slink*]

kerslam! *excl.* [late 19C–1900s] an onomat. term indicating a sudden noise or action. [KER- pfx + SE *slam*]

kerslap! *excl.* [mid-19C+] an onomat. term indicating a sudden noise or, usu., action. [KER- pfx + SE *slap*]

kerslash! *excl.* [mid-19C] (*US*) an onomat. term indicating a sudden crash, as caused by tripping over an object. [KER- pfx + SE *slip/crash*]

kerslesh! *excl.* [mid-19C] (*US*) an onomat. term indicating movement at speed. [KER- pfx + SE *slash*]

kerslosh! *excl.* (*also* **caswash! kersplosh! kerswash! kerswosh!**) [mid-19C+] an onomat. term indicating movement through a wet or soft substance, or the falling of a solid object into such a substance, e.g. viscous mud. [KER- pfx + echoic]

kerslung! *excl.* (*also* **kersling!**) [mid-19C] an onomat. term indicating a sudden movement. [KER- pfx + echoic]

kersmack! *excl.* [1930s+] an onomat. term indicating a sudden movement or a sharp blow. [KER- pfx + SMACK v.¹ (2)]

kersmash! *excl.* (*also* **ca-smash! co-smash!**) [mid-19C+] an onomat. term indicating a sudden crash or collision. [KER- pfx + SE *smash*]

kersouse! *excl.* (*also* **kasouse! kesouse!**) [mid-19C] an onomat. term indicating a fall into liquid. [KER- pfx + SE *souse*]

kersplash! *excl.* (*also* **ca-splash!**) [mid-19C+] an onomat. term indicating a fall into liquid. [KER- pfx + SE *splash*]

kersplat! *excl.* (*also* **kasplat!**) [1980s+] an onomat. term indicating a fall onto a soft surface, esp. with concomitant mess, e.g. a stunt-man's dive into a stall of soft fruit and vegetables. [KER- pfx + SPLAT! excl.]

kersplosh! *excl. see* KERSLOSH! excl.

kerswallop! *excl.* (*also* **kerswollop!**) [mid-19C] (*US*) an onomat. term indicating a fall or flop. [KER- pfx + echoic]

kerswash! *excl. see* KERSLOSH! excl.

kerswop! *excl.* [mid-19C] an onomat. term indicating a fall into liquid. [KER- pfx + echoic]

kerswosh! *excl. see* KERSLOSH! excl.

kerteever/kerterver *see under* CATEVER.

kertever cartzo *n.* [mid-19C] venereal disease. [Ling. Fr. *cattivo cazzo*, lit. 'bad cock']

kerthud! *excl.* [1940s+] an onomat. term indicating the dull noise of a solid object landing on a solid surface. [KER- pfx + SE *thud*]

kerthump! *excl.* [late 19C+] an onomat. term indicating a sudden dull noise. [KER- pfx + SE *thump*]

kertish *n.* [late 19C–1900s] (*US*) dollars, money. [ety. unknown]

kerumph! *excl.* (*also* **kerump!**) [20C+] an onomat. term indicating an excl. or sudden shock. [KER- pfx + echoic]

kerwallux! *excl.* (*also* **cawallux! cawhalux!**) [mid-19C] (*US*) an onomat. term indicating the sound of a slap or a box on the ear. [KER- pfx + SE *wallop*]

kerwhackety! *excl.* [1940s+] an onomat. term indicating noisy, stumbling, erratic progress. [KER- pfx + SE *whack/racket*]

kerwhallop *v.* (*also* **cowhallop, cowollap, keswollup**) [mid-19C+] to hit hard and suddenly, to smack. [KER- pfx + SE *wallop*]

kerwhallop *adv.* (*also* **co-wallop**) **1** [mid-19C] (*US*) precisely, exactly. **2** [20C+] indicating suddenness, or a fall. [KERWHALLOP v.]

kerwhammy! *excl.* [1940s+] an onomat. term indicating the sound of a sudden collision. [KER- pfx + WHAM! excl.]

kerwhop! *excl.* (*also* **cawhop!**) [mid-19C+] an onomat. term indicating the noise of a solid body falling onto a solid surface. [KER- pfx + echoic]

kerwoosh! *excl.* [20C+] an onomat. term indicating speedy movement. [KER- pfx + SE *whoosh*]

kerzip *n. see* KA-ZIP n.

keskydee *n. see* KISKEEDEE n.

kesouse! *excl. see* KERSOUSE! excl.

keswollup *v. see* KERWHALLOP v.

ket *n.* [2000s] (*drugs*) ketamine. [abbr.]

ketchup *n.* **1** [20C+] (*Aus.*) beer. **2** [1950s–70s] (*US*) blood (cf. BADMINTON n.). [(1) the colour of 'brown sauce'; (2) the colour of tomato ketchup]

kettle *n.*¹ [17C–19C] the vagina; thus *get one's kettle mended*, of a woman, to have sexual intercourse (cf. BAG n.¹). [the image of a vagina as a receptacle; note the repertoire of bawdy songs in which wandering tinkers 'mend' ladies' *kettles*]

kettle *n.*² **1** [early 19C–1930s] (*US*) a steam engine. **2** [mid-19C+] a pocket watch; thus *red kettle*, a gold watch; *white kettle*, a silver watch; *dummy kettle*, a toy watch. **3** [1920s+] a wrist watch. [(1) the steam; (2) the original large circular pocket watches resembled kettles]

kettle *n.*³ *see* KETTLE (ON A HOB) n.

kettle *v.* [1920s–30s] (*US*) esp. of a horse, to frighten or become frightened. [? dial. *kittle*, to arouse, to stimulate, to prick]

kettlebelly *n.* [late 19C–1920s] (*US*) a fat person.

kettle brandy *n.* [late 19C–1900s] tea, esp. as drunk at tea parties.

kettled *adj.* [1990s+] drunk.

kettle-de-benders *n. see* KITTLY-BENDERS n.

kettledrum *n.* [mid–late 19C] an afternoon tea party on a large scale. [a play on the omnipresent tea kettle + *drum*, 'an assembly of fashionable people at a private house, held in the evening, much in vogue during the latter half of the 18th and beginning of the 19th century [...] later, an afternoon tea party, formerly sometimes followed by the larger assembly' (*OED*)]

kettledrums *n. see* CUPID'S KETTLEDRUMS n.

kettle (on a hob) *n.* **1** [late 19C+] a shilling (5p). **2** [20C+] a pet name for someone called *Bob*. [rhy. sl.; (1) = BOB n.⁴ (1)]

Kevin *n.* (*also* **Kev**) [1980s+] (*UK upper and middle classes*) a derog. name for lower-middle- or working-class youths, whom they regard as overly flashy and socially unacceptable; a male SHARON n. [the commonness of the name]

kevork v. [1990s+] to kill. [*Jack Kevorkian* (b.1928), US doctor who assisted patients to commit suicide and was imprisoned for 10–25 years in 1999]

kew n. [mid-19C–1900s] a week; thus *skew*, weeks. [backsl.]

kewl adj. [1990s+] (*US teen*) a general term of approval. [COOL adj.[1]]

kewpie n. **1** [1920s] (*US*) a fool, an unsophisticated person. **2** [1920s–40s] (*US Und.*) a child. **3** [1990s+] (*Aus.*) a prostitute (cf. BOAT AND OAR n.). [abbr. *kewpie doll*; (3) rhy. sl. = MOLL n.[1] (2)]

kex n. see KECKS n.

key n.[1] [17C+] the penis. [the complement to KEYHOLE n.; see *double entendres* in D'Urfey, *Pills to Purge Melancholy* (1719–20), e.g. 'Ne'er hope to keep a find Cabinet lock'd, / When every Furr'd Gown has a Key, Sir' and 'To have her stock, / So close kept Lock'd, / And put a Key to her Till']

key n.[2] (*also* **keys**) [20C+] (*US prison*) a prison warder. [metonymy SE *key*, which they carry]

key n.[3] (*also* **kee, keye, ki**) **1** [1960s+] (*drugs*) a *ki*lo of marijuana, hashish or any other drug. **2** [2000s] £1000. [abbr.; (2) SE *kilo-*, a thousand]

key n.[4] [1990s+] (*W.I.*) a friend.

key n.[5] [2000s] (*US prison*) a pack of cigarettes. [? its role as a means of exchange, i.e. it 'opens doors']

key, the n. [1910s+] (*Aus./N.Z.*) a declaration that one is a habitual criminal, thus the indefinite detention that, following the Habitual Criminals Act (1905), was mandatory for such individuals, who would first serve a specified sentence, then, subject to behaviour etc, would begin the indefinite 'key'. [SE *throw away the key*]

key adj. [1970s+] (*US campus*) excellent, admirable. [SE *key*, central, vital]

key v. [1980s+] (*orig. US campus*) to scratch an automobile with a key or other pointed object.

keyed adj. **1** [1910s–30s] (*US*) drunk (cf. ABOUT RIGHT phr.[1]). **2** [1990s+] (*US Black*) intoxicated by a drug. [? KEYED (UP) adj.]

keyed (up) adj. [late 19C+] (*US*) intense, emotional, fired up.

keyhole n. [17C; 1920s] the vagina (cf. BAG n.[1]; BLACK HOLE n.[1]). [KEY n.[1] + SE *hole*/HOLE n.[1] (2)]

keyhole a round-tripper v. [1930s–40s] (*US Black*) to witness a remarkable event; to gaze at an exceptional individual. [SE *keyhole* suggests seeing + ety. unknown]

keyhole-whistler n. (*also* **keyhole-whisperer**) **1** [mid-19C–1920s] one who sleeps in barns or outhouses, thus a tramp or vagrant. **2** [1930s] (*US Und.*) a criminal in hiding. [those inside the adjacent house hear whispering/whistling through the keyhole]

keyholing n. [1950s–60s] singing and playing at public house doors.

key in v. [1950s+] to focus on. [film jargon; the *key light* focuses directly on a single actor]

key man n. **1** [1960s+] (*Aus.*) a habitual criminal. **2** [1970s+] (*UK Und.*) the member of a criminal gang who clinches the deal. [(1) KEY, THE n.; (2) SE *key*, essential]

keynod n. see YEKNOD n.

key of the door n. [1950s+] (*bingo*) the number 21 (cf. ALDERSHOT LADIES n.). [the trad. year of 'coming of age' and getting one's own front-door key]

key on v. [1980s+] (*US*) to instruct, to teach.

keys n. see KEY n.[2].

keyster n. see KEISTER n.

Keystone n. [1910s+] a policeman. [Hollywood's *Keystone Cops*, a group of comical, incompetent policemen created by director Mack Sennett (1884–1960) in 1912; they featured in a number of films made by his Keystone Studios]

Keystone cop n. [1990s+] a chop (pork, beef etc.). [rhy. sl.; for ety. see KEYSTONE n.]

key winder n. [1910s] (*US*) a girl; thus *stem-winder*, a boy. [SE *key winder*, a watch that is wound up with a key (ref. to KEY n.[1]); *stem winder*, a watch that requires no key]

k.f. n. see KID n.[1] (10).

k-foot n. [1940s+] (*W.I.*) knock-knees.

K.G. n. see COUSIN JACK n.

k.g. n. [1970s+] (*US Und.*) a known *g*ambler. [abbr.]

khabbar n. see KUBBER n.

khaki n.[1] [late 19C] pease pudding; thus *cannon and khaki*, a globular steak pudding and a lump of pease pudding on the side. [the colour of the food]

khaki n.[2] [1940s+] (*S.Afr.*) a non-Nationalist White South African, usu. of English background. [Boer War sl. *khaki*, an English soldier]

khaki n.[3] [1960s] (*N.Z.*) a Maori. [colour]

khaki n.[4] [1970s+] **1** (*US*) a county policeman (cf. BABY-BLUES n.[2]). **2** (*Irish*) a lifeguard. [the *khaki*-coloured uniform]

khaki pussy n. [1970s+] (*US gay*) a soldier. [SE *khaki*, the colour of the uniforms + PUSSY n. (11)]

khakis n. [1990s+] *khaki* shorts or clothes. [abbr.]

khaki-wacky adj. [1940s+] (*US*) of a woman, enamoured of men in military uniform. [SE *khaki* + WHACKY adj.]

kharzi/khazi n. see CARSEY n.

khazi v. [2000s] to be infuriated. [KHARZI/KHAZI n.; play on SHIT ONESELF v.]

K-hole n. [1980s+] (*drugs*) a period of confusion that follows the use of ketamine. [K n.[4] (2); the 'hole' in one's life]

khubber n. see KUBBER n.

Khyber (Pass) n. (*also* **kiber, kyber**) **1** [late 19C] a glass. **2** [20C+] the buttocks (cf. ALA n.). **3** [1960s+] the anus (cf. ALLEY WAY n.; BOTTLE AND GLASS n.). **4** [1970s+] the rear, e.g. of a car. [rhy. sl.; (2), (3) and (4) = ARSE n.[1] (1)]

khyfer see under KYPHER.

khypher n. see KYFER n.

ki n.[1] [1940s–70s] (*UK prison*) cocoa. [orig. naut. use; supposedly dial. *kyish*, muddy-looking, brown, but *EDD* has no listing]

ki n.[2] see KEY n.[3].

kiaora n. [1980s+] (*Aus. prison*) a male homosexual who plays both active and passive roles in anal intercourse. [*Kiaora*, a brand of drink that claims to contain 50 percent fruit (i.e. FRUIT n.[2] (2)) juice]

kibbitz v. see KIBITZ v.

kibbitzer n. see KIBITZER n.

kibbled adj. [1990s+] (*US*) crushed, in bits and pieces. [KIBBLES & BITS n. (2)]

kibbles & bits n. [1980s+] **1** (*US Black*) cheap food. **2** (*drugs*) small crumbs of crack cocaine (cf. BASE n.). **3** a description of a man who has small genitals. [the brandname of a petfood]

kiber n. see KHYBER (PASS) n.

kibitz n. (*also* **kabitz**) [1930s+] (*US*) tedious chatter, unwanted advice. [KIBITZ v. (1)]

kibitz v. (*also* **kibbitz**) [1920s+] **1** to watch (a gambling game) and comment/advise but not participate. **2** to chat, to gossip, to pester, to cajole. [Ger. *Kiebitz*, a lapwing or peewit, a noisy and inquisitive bird; thus *kiebitzen*, to look over a card-player's shoulder; popularized by Yid. speakers]

kibitzer n. (*also* **kabitzer, kibbitzer**) [1920s+] **1** one who looks over a card-player's shoulder, advising and interfering with the game. **2** anyone who butts in or meddles, offering usu. unwanted advice. [KIBITZ v. (1)]

kibo n.[1] [1900s] (*US*) an overwhelming success. [PUT THE KIBOSH ON v.]

kibo n.[2] see KYBO n.

kibosh n. (*also* **kabosh, kiboshery, kybosh**) **1** [mid-19C+] a bad accident, a defeat; usu. in PUT THE KIBOSH ON v.; thus *give someone the kibosh*, to destroy or defeat someone. **2** [mid-19C;

1930s–70s] 18 pence, i.e. 1s 6d pre-decimalization. **3** [mid-19C+] rubbish, nonsense, humbug. **4** [late 19C] the height of fashion. **5** [1940s–50s] an 18-month prison sentence. [? Heb. or Yid. *kabas, kabasten,* to suppress (B&L, but rejected by Rosten, *The Joys of Yiddish,* 1968); but note intensifying KER- pfx + BOSH n.[1]; KYE n. + BOSH n.[1], i.e. 18 pence, and thus synon. with a FOURPENNY (ONE) n. (see E.P., *DSUE,* 8th edn, Appendix, for further theories); however, note Irish Gaelic *ceip bàis,* death cap, i.e. the black cap used in court; note also Dolan (1998): 'Irish *caidhp (an) bháis* or *caidhpín (an) bháis,* "cap of death", the black cap or judgment cap worn by judges when pronouncing sentence of death']

kibosh v. (*also* **kybosh**) [mid-19C+] to finish off, to destroy; thus *on the kibosh,* ruined. [KIBOSH n. (1)]

kick n.[1] (*also* **kicky**) **1** [late 17C–19C] the current fashion; thus *all the kick,* the present vogue; *high kick,* the height of fashion. **2** [mid-19C] a fashionable garment. **3** [1940s+] a fashion, a fad, with comb. adj./n.; thus *on a/the — kick,* e.g. *on a writing kick, on the religion kick* etc. **4** [1950s+] one's attitude or opinion. [ety. unknown; ? fig. use of SE *kick,* with the image of the sharp impact thereof]

kick n.[2] **1** [18C+] a sixpence; thus *two-and-a-kick,* half-a-crown (25p). **2** [20C+] money in general. [rhy. *six = kick,* but not rhy. sl. as such]

kick n.[3] **1** [19C–1900s] a chance, a 'go'. **2** [1910s+] (*US*) something ironic or elusive, a twist. **3** [1940s+] a trick, a 'line'.

kick n.[4] (*also* **kicker**) [mid-19C+] a pocket, esp. in trousers. [Ware suggests Und. only]

kick n.[5] **1** [mid-19C+] a stimulating or intoxicating effect, usu. from alcohol or drugs; also as v., to feel the effects of a drug. **2** [20C+] (*Aus.*) a spree, a party. **3** [1910s+] (*orig. US*) a thrill, amusement or excitement; usu. as GET A KICK OUT OF v. **4** [1920s–50s] energy, vitality. **5** [1930s] an amusing, surprising or stimulating person. **6** [1950s–60s] the sensation any place, situation or thing produces.

kick n.[6] (*orig. US*) **1** [mid-19C+] a complaint; thus *make a kick,* to raise an objection, to complain. **2** [late 19C+] trouble. **3** [1930s+] a worry or concern. [i.e. a 'kick against the pricks']

kick n.[7] **1** [mid-19C+] a moment. **2** [1950s+] (*US Black*) generally any little thing or situation.

kick n.[8] **1** [1940s] (*US drugs*) addiction. **2** [1940s–50s] an injection or shot of heroin. **3** [1950s] (*W.I.*) gin or whisky. **4** [1950s+] (*US drugs*) any kind of psychotropic drug. **5** [1990s+] (*drugs*) withdrawal from drug addiction. [KICK n.[5] (1)]

kick n.[9] [1950s–60s] (*US*) a fit, as in *a laughing kick.* [one 'kicks up one's legs']

kick n.[10] [1950s+] (*orig. US Black*) the beat or rhythm in music.

kick n.[11] [1990s+] (*US Black*) death, a murder. [KICK v.[8] (2)]

kick n.[12] *see* KICKBACK n.[1] (2).

kick, the n.[1] [late 19C–1900s] a dismissal, 'the sack'; thus *get/give the kick,* to be dismissed or to dismiss. [SE *kick;* one is lit./fig. 'kicked out'; var. on BOOT, THE n.]

kick, the n.[2] [1920s] (*US Und.*) a beating, during interrogation, by the police.

kick adj.[1] [1950s+] (*US drugs*) describing anything relating to coming off an addiction, e.g. *kick pad* or *kick ward,* a hospital ward reserved for recovering addicts. [KICK v.[7] (1)]

kick adj.[2] [1990s+] (*US teen*) unfashionable. [? they should be kicked out]

kick v.[1] [18C+] to leave, to walk, to wander aimlessly. [the image is of kicking stones etc; the use is more usu. in combs. from the early 19C+]

kick v.[2] **1** [late 18C–mid-19C] to ask for money, work etc. **2** [late 18C–mid-19C] to appeal to, to obtain something by asking. **3** [1930s] (*US Und.*) to rob a safe or cash box.

kick v.[3] **1** [19C–1940s] to rid oneself of something, to reject someone, esp. a lover. **2** [1920s+] (*Aus.*) to dismiss from a job. [abbr. SE *kick out*]

kick v.[4] **1** [mid-19C] (*UK Und.*) to put in one's pocket. **2** [mid-19C–1960s] by ext., to make money, often in comb. with a qualifying n., e.g. *kick some dough.* [KICK n.[4]]

kick v.[5] [mid-19C+] to die. [? abbr. KICK THE CLOUDS v./KICK v.[1]]

kick v.[6] (*US*) **1** [late 19C–1900s] to amuse or entertain one's audience. **2** [1930s+] to perform well or with energy, usu. of music. **3** [1950s+] to delight, to please. [KICK n.[5]]

kick v.[7] (*orig. US drugs*) **1** [1920s+] to stop taking an addictive drug. **2** [1960s+] to stop any form of addiction. [abbr. KICK THE HABIT v.]

kick v.[8] **1** [1950s] (*US prison*) of a prison sentence, to deal with, to manage. **2** [1990s+] (*US Black/Und.*) to kill, to murder.

kick v.[9] [1980s+] (*US Black*) in rap music, to raise the volume or level of something. [one fig. *kicks* the volume etc upwards]

kick v.[10] [1990s+] (*US Black*) to empty, to finish, e.g. a bottle of beer.

kick v.[11] [2000s] (*US Black*) to have sexual intercourse (with) (cf. BANG v.[1]).

kick v.[12] *see* BOOT v.[8] (1).

kick v.[13] *see* KICK (AT) v.

kick v.[14] *see* KICK DOWN (TO) v. (2).

kick v.[15] *see* KICK IN v.[2].

kick v.[16] *see* KICK IN (WITH) v.

kick v.[17] *see* KICK IT v.[2] (2).

kick about v.[1] [mid-19C+] (*orig. US*) to make a fuss, to complain. [KICK (AT) v. (1)]

kick about v.[2] *see* KICK AROUND v.

kick a brown dog v. *see* CHUCK A BROWN DOG v.

kick (a goal) v. [1980s+] (*Aus. prison*) to succeed, to win an advantage.

kick along v. [1970s+] (*Aus.*) to survive reasonably easily, to get along well.

kick and buck n. [1920s] (*W.I.*) a water tank or cistern made of clay that has been *kicked* and *bucked* (pounded) until it is absolutely water-tight.

kickapoo (juice) n. (*also* **kickapoo joy juice, kikipoo**) [1940s+] (*US*) strong alcohol, esp. home-brewed or prison-brewed alcohol. [coined in 1941 by cartoonist Al Capp in his strip *L'il Abner,* in ref. to patent medicines of 1900s named after the *Kickapoo,* the Algonquian Indians; the ingredients, according to the strip, included 'a barr'l o' kerosene, two dozen chicken haids, a bucket o' somethin' sloppy we swiped off a passin' truck, a motorman's glove, three pairs o' old socks, a dash o' axlegrease, turpentine']

kick around v. (*also* **kick about**) **1** [mid-19C+] (*orig. US*) to hang about, to wander aimlessly. **2** [late 19C+] to exist. **3** [1940s+] (*orig. US*) to discuss or consider a topic or idea. **4** [1960s+] to put into circulation, to distribute. [sporting imagery]

kick-ass adj. (*also* **kick-arse, kick-butt**) (*orig. US*) **1** [1970s+] powerful, aggressive, stimulating, thuggish or violent. **2** [1980s+] terrific, exciting. [KICK ASS v.]

kick ass v. (*also* **kick A, ...arse, ...behind, ...butt**) **1** [1950s+] (*orig. US*) to beat someone up, to fight; also in fig. use. **2** [1970s+] (*US campus*) to have a good, if boisterous, time. **3** [1980s+] (*orig. US campus*) to do well, to make a successful effort. [lit. + fig. uses of KICK SOMEONE'S ASS v.; + ARSE n.[1] (1)/BUTT n.[1] (2)]

kick (at) v. **1** [mid-19C+] (*US*) to complain or protest. **2** [1980s+] (*US campus*) to be difficult, to prevail over something or someone. [SE *kick,* to resist, to rebel]

kick away the prop v. [18C] to suffer execution by hanging. [the removal of the ladder, cart, stool etc on which the victim stands]

kickback n.[1] **1** [1910s+] (*US*) a repercussion, usu. negative. **2** [1920s+] (*orig. US Und.*) (*also* **kick**) a payment (prob. illegal) made to a person who has facilitated a deal, a transaction, someone's appointment to a job etc. **3** [1930s+] a portion of one's profits that is handed over as 'protection money'. **4** [1940s+] a commission on a payment made by the payee to the customer, usu. a genteel euph. for a bribe. **5** [2000s] (*US*) a response. [KICK BACK v.[1]]

kickback *n.[2]* [1930s–60s] (*US drugs*) a return to addiction despite efforts to abandon drug use.

kickback *n.[3]* [1990s+] (*orig. US Black*) a period of relaxation, relaxing. [KICK BACK v.[2]]

kickback *adj.* [1980s+] (*US*) relaxing, calm, low-key. [KICK BACK v.[2]]

kick back *v.[1]* **1** [1910s+] (*US*) to return something, such as money or stolen goods, to the original owner. **2** [1930s+] to pay a bribe or a commission.

kick back *v.[2]* [1970s+] (*orig. US Black*) to laze around, to relax. [KICK v.[1] + LAID-BACK adj.]

kick back *v.[3]* [1980s+] (*US*) to drink.

kickback place *n.* [1990s+] (*US Black gang*) anywhere one can relax, away from the stresses and threats of the streets. [KICK BACK v.[2] + SE *place*]

kick brass *v.* (*also* **kick dust**, **...hell**, **...sands**) [20C+] (*W.I.*) to make a fuss, to cause a commotion. [? var. on KICK ASS v.]

kick butt *v. see* KICK ASS v.

kick down (to) *v.* (*also* **kick down with**, **kick out with**) **1** [20C+] to go to, to arrive, to visit, to wander. **2** [1980s+] (*US*) (*also* **kick**) to give something to, to hand over. **3** [1980s+] (*US Black*) to set a person up in the drug business. [? KICK v.[1]]

kick dust *v. see* KICK BRASS v.

kicked *adj.* [1940s+] (*drugs*) having withdrawn from narcotic addiction. [KICK v.[7] (1)]

kicked back *adj.* [1990s+] (*US*) relaxing, lazing around. [KICK BACK v.[2]]

kicked up *adj.* [1930s] intoxicated on a drug. [? KICK n.[5] (1)]

kicker *n.[1]* [mid-19C] a dancing master.

kicker *n.[2]* [late 19C+] (*US*) in poker, a high card, such as an ace, retained in the hope of matching the pair or as a bluff. [? KICK n.[4], i.e. if the bluff works one will fill one's pockets]

kicker *n.[3]* [late 19C+] (*US*) one who complains or grumbles. [KICK (AT) v. (1)]

kicker *n.[4]* [1940s+] (*US*) a thrill. [KICK n.[5] (3)]

kicker *n.[5]* [1940s+] (*US*) a consequence or hidden twist. [KICK n.[3] (2)]

kicker *n.[6]* [1950s] (*US*) a cache of money, a find. [KICK n.[4]]

kicker *n.[7]* **1** [1950s+] a culminatory action. **2** [1970s+] (*orig. US*) the last, most problematical piece of information. [it *kicks* the rest along]

kicker *n.[8]* [1990s+] (*US*) a chaser, usu. pertaining to drugs rather than drinks. [the added KICK n.[5] (1) it gives]

kicker *n.[9] see* SHITKICKER n. (3).

kickeraboo *v.* [late 18C–mid-19C] (*W.I.*) to die. [pron. of KICK THE BUCKET v.]

kickers *n.* **1** [mid-19C+] the feet. **2** [1940s+] shoes. **3** [1940s+] (*US*) boots with pointed toes, made from rare or exotic reptile skins (e.g. armadillo, alligator, snake); such boots are used spec. for dancing.

kick flavor *v.* [1990s+] (*orig. US*) to perform rap music. [KICK v.[9] + FLAVOR n.[2] (1)]

kick game *v.* [1980s+] (*US Black*) to use any means whereby one attempts to gain economic, psychological or other advantages over a rival or victim. [KICK v.[10] + GAME n.[2] (3)]

kick hell *v. see* KICK BRASS v.

kick hell out of *v. see* BEAT (THE) HELL OUT OF v.

kick-in *n.[1]* [1900s] (*US Und.*) a form of robbery whereby one member of a gang kicks in the front of a shop, and steals the contents while the remainder of the gang stand outside and keep any interference at bay. [SE *kick in*]

kick-in *n.[2]* [1930s–50s] (*US*) a commission on a payment made by the payee to the customer, usu. a genteel euph. for a bribe. [KICK IN (WITH) v.]

kick in *v.[1]* (*US*) **1** [20C+] to die. **2** [1910s+] to give up, to abandon. [ext. of KICK IN v.[5]]

kick in *v.[2]* (*also* **kick**) **1** [20C+] to do what is required, to join in. **2** [20C+] to begin, to start to happen. **3** [1970s+] to (make something) start working, to accelerate an action, usu. of mechanical objects. **4** [1980s+] of drugs, to take effect, to start to work; also of alcohol. [? KICK v.[6]]

kick in *v.[3]* [1910s+] (*US*) to speak up, to tell the truth.

kick in *v.[4]* **1** [1910s+] (*US Und.*) to smash one's way through a door, to break in and burglarize. **2** [1990s+] (*US Black*) to start a fight.

kick in *v.[5] see* KICK IN (WITH) v.

kicking *adj.[1]* [late 19C] (*US*) complaining. [KICK (AT) v. (1)]

kicking *adj.[2]* (*also* **kickin'**, **kickin' hard**) **1** [1960s+] excellent, wonderful, first-rate. **2** [1980s+] (*US campus*) difficult, unpleasant. [KICK n.[5]]

kicking (it) *n.* (*also* **kickin' (it)**) [1980s+] (*orig. US Black/teen*) lying around, wasting time, relaxing, socializing. [KICK IT v.[2]]

kick in someone's gallop, a *phr.* [20C+] (*Ulster*) a weakness of character; thus *put a kick in someone's gallop*, to ruin someone's plans, to 'put a spoke in their wheel'. [riding imagery]

kick in the arse, a *n.* (*also* **a kick of the arse**) [1990s+] a very small distance, lit. or fig.; a short space of time.

kick in the arse/ass/butt *v. see* KICK IN THE TAIL v.

kick in the guts, a *n.* **1** [mid-18C–early 19C] a dram of gin or any other spirit. **2** [1920s+] a setback or disappointment.

kick in the pants, a *n.* (*also* **a kick in the arse**, **...ass**, **...balls**, **...bollocks**, **...head**, **...nuts**, **...tail**) **1** [1920s+] a setback, a grave disappointment. **2** [1920s+] a salutory punishment. **3** [1920s+] a joke, a laugh (often used ironically). **4** [1950s+] anything that urges one on to greater effort, commitment.

kick in the tail *v.* (*also* **kick in the arse**, **...ass**, **...butt**, **...pants**) [1910s+] to kick hard, lit. or fig.

kick into dry goods *v. see* DRY GOODS n.[2] (1).

kick in (with) *v.* (*also* **kick**) [20C+] (*US*) to hand over money. [var. on KICK BACK v.[1]]

kick it *v.[1]* [late 19C+] to die. [abbr. KICK THE BUCKET v.]

kick it *v.[2]* **1** [1930s+] (*also* **kick out**) to play music. **2** [1980s+] (*orig. US Black*) (*also* **kick**) to chatter, to gossip, to relax. **3** [1980s+] (*US Black*) to act, to do something. [KICK IT AROUND v.[1]]

kick it *v.[3]* [1950s+] (*US*) to leave. [KICK v.[1]]

kick it *v.[4]* [1970s+] (*US*) to accelerate a vehicle. [put one's foot on the gas pedal]

kick it *v.[5]* [1990s+] **1** (*US*) to get on well with someone. **2** (*US*) to associate with someone. **3** (*US*) to have an affair over and above one's primary, monogamous relationship. **4** (*US Black/prison*) to have sexual intercourse (cf. BANG v.[1]). **5** (*US*) of a man to a woman, to make suggestive comments. [KICK v.[6]]

kick it! *excl.* [1990s+] (*US campus*) pay attention!

kick it around *v.[1]* [1930s–40s] (*US*) to carouse, to have a good time. [KICK AROUND v. (1)]

kick it around *v.[2] see* KICK THE GONG AROUND v.[1].

kick it live *v.* [1980s+] (*US Black*) to have a good time, to talk, to chatter, to gossip. [KICK IT v.[2] (2)]

kick (it) off *v.* [1970s+] to argue, to fight. [? KICK OFF v.[2] (1)]

kick it to *v.* [1990s+] (*US Black*) **1** to give something to someone, 'to let someone have it'. **2** to inform, to explain the facts. **3** to do something in a committed manner. [var. on SOCK IT TO v.]

kick loose *v.* [1930s+] to release, to make available, to let go. [var. on KICK BACK v.[2] + LOOSE adj.[1] (2)]

kick mud *v.* [1950s–70s] (*US Black*) **1** to perform hard, dirty work. **2** to work as a street prostitute. [backform. f. MUD-KICKER n.]

kick-off *n.* [late 19C+] the beginning, the start. [soccer imagery; Gold, *A Jazz Lexicon* (1964), notes the 'signal for the musicians to play by the leader's stamping his foot several times in the desired tempo']

kick-off *adj.* [1930s] (*US*) first. [KICK-OFF n.]

kick off *v.*[1] **1** [20C+] to die. **2** [1910s–20s] (*US*) to kill. **3** [1910s+] to leave.

kick off *v.*[2] **1** [1910s+] (*orig. US*) to begin, to start, to set in motion. **2** [1970s] of a club or bar, to open. [KICK-OFF n.]

kick off *v.*[3] [1940s–60s] (*US*) to delight, to excite. [KICK n.[5] (1)]

kick off *v.*[4] [1950s] (*US drugs*) to sleep off the effects of drugs.

kick off *v.*[5] *see* KICK (IT) OFF v.

kick of the arse, a *n. see* KICK IN THE ARSE, A n.

kick on *v.* **1** [1940s+] (*Aus.*) to struggle on despite the unfavourable odds. **2** [1980s] (*Aus.*) to continue drinking once somebody has found some money to buy another round with. **3** [2000s] to enjoy oneself.

kick one's heels *v.* (*also* **kick one's ass off, knock one's heels**) [mid-18C+] to be kept waiting.

kickout *n.* **1** [late 19C+] a dismissal, a discharge; thus also as phr. *give the kickout.* **2** [1960s+] one who has been ejected from a job or from their education. [KICK OUT v.[1] (1)]

kick out *v.*[1] **1** [late 17C+] to eject, to force to leave. **2** [late 19C+] to die. **3** [20C+] to run away. **4** [1910s] (*US Und.*) to appear suddenly. **5** [1910s+] to get out of bed. [(2) late 20C+ use only W.I.]

kick out *v.*[2] (*US*) **1** [1920s+] to pay up. **2** [1930s] to work something out. **3** [1970s+] to play music. **4** [1980s+] to fail. **5** [1990s+] to produce, to create.

kick out *v.*[3] *see* KICK IT v.[2] (1).

kick out a hind leg *v.* [late 18C–early 19C] to bow in an unsophisticated, 'rustic' manner.

kick out with *v. see* KICK DOWN (TO) v.

kick over *v.* **1** [1920s–30s] (*US Und./police*) to raid an establishment or place. **2** [1930s] to rob.

kick rocks *v.* [2000s] (*US prison*) to go away.

kicks *n.*[1] [late 17C–1930s] breeches, thus trousers. [ety. unknown; ? link to UK dial. *kecks*, the (dried) hollowed-out stem of an umbelliferous plant, e.g. a teazle; such stalks were used as candlesticks, water-pipes etc, and the link to trousers, themselves 'hollow stalks', seems feasible]

kicks *n.*[2] (*also* **kicksees, kicksies**) [late 18C+] (*US Black/campus*) shoes; in later usage, athletic shoes.

kicks *n.*[3] [1920s+] (*orig. US*) thrills, pleasure. [KICK n.[5] (3)]

kick sands *v. see* KICK BRASS v.

kicksees/kickseys *n. see* KICKSIES n.

kick seven kinds of shit out of *v. see* THUMP SEVEN KINDS OF SHIT OUT OF v.

kick-shoe *n.* [19C] a dancer, a buffoon.

kick-sick *n. see* SICK n. (2).

kicksies *n.* (*also* **kicksees, kickseys, kicksters, kixes**) [18C–1910s] trousers; thus *kicksies-builder*, a tailor. [for ety. *see* KICKS n.[1]]

kicksing *n.* [1920s+] (*W.I.*) making fun of, not taking seriously. [KICKS n.[3]]

kick someone for *v.* [late 18C–mid-19C] to ask someone for money, to borrow money. [KICK v.[2] (1)]

kick someone into touch *v.* [1970s+] to reject, to dismiss, to throw away. [rugby imagery]

kick someone's ass *v.* (*also* **kick someone's arse, ...butt, ...guts, ...pants, belt someone's arse/ass**) **1** [1920s+] (*orig. US*) to give someone a beating, to defeat someone. **2** [1970s+] to exhaust, to wear out. **3** [1970s+] (*US Black*) to impress, to overwhelm. **4** [1970s+] (*US Black*) to defeat intellectually. [SE *kick* + ASS n. (2)]

kick someone's lung out *v.* [late 19C–1900s] to criticize harshly, to attack verbally.

kick start *v.* [1950s+] to set going with an initial sudden impetus. [from the kick-starting of a motorcycle]

kickster *n.* [20C+] (*W.I.*) a jester, a joker, an irresponsible person. [KICKS n.[3]]

kicksters *n. see* KICKSIES n.

kick stick *n.* [1960s] (*drugs*) a marijuana cigarette (cf. BAT n.[8]). [KICK n.[5] (1) + STICK n.[9] (3)]

Kickstone & Co. *n.* [20C+] (*W.I.*) a notional firm or business, used fig. to mean a state of unemployment. [KICK STONES v.]

kick stones *v.* [20C+] (*W.I.*) to be unemployed. [one is idly 'kicking stones' around]

kick-sweat *n.* [1990s+] (*drugs*) the sweating that is one of the symptoms of withdrawal from narcotic drugs use. [KICK v.[7] (1) + SE *sweat*]

kicksy *adj.* [mid-17C; mid-19C] troublesome, disagreeable. [Ger. *keck*, bold or SE *kick*]

kick the air *v. see* KICK THE CLOUDS v.

kick the arse out of *v.* [1990s+] to surpass, to defeat comprehensively. [SE *kick* + fig. use of ARSE n.[1] (1)]

kick the beam *v.* [1920s] to experience an intense emotion, to reach orgasm. [Gifford, *Ulysses Annotated* (1988): '"Kick the beam" means literally that one arm of a scale is so lightly weighted that it strikes the beam or frame of the scales; hence, figuratively, to be light in weight, and in slang, to experience sudden emotion or orgasm']

kick the bucket *v.* [late 18C+] to die. [the contemporary method of slaughtering a pig, in which the animal is suspended from a beam by the insertion of a piece of bent wood (a 'bucket') behind the tendons of its hind legs; the dying animal naturally kicks out at the bucket. Alternatively, and rather less likely, the story of an ostler working at an inn on the Great North Road who killed himself by hanging; to gain the necessary drop he stood on a bucket, kicking it away as required]

kick the cat *v.* [late 19C–1950s] to vent one's frustrations. [the cat being the 'lowest' member of the household and thus most likely to suffer such abuse]

kick the clouds *v.* (*also* **kick the air/wind**) [late 16C–1940s] to be hanged; often ext. as *...before the hotel door*. [SE + HOTEL n. (2); public hangings were performed outside the prison where the malefactor had been held]

kick the crap out of *v. see* KICK THE SHIT OUT OF v.

kick the dust out of *v.* [1910s] (*Aus.*) to beat up.

kick the fuck out of *v. see* KICK THE SHIT OUT OF v.

kick the gong around *v.*[1] (*also* **boot the gong around, kick it around, kick the pipe around, ...rag around, ...toy around**) **1** [late 19C–1950s] (*drugs*) to use drugs, esp. opium, heroin or morphine. **2** [1940s+] (*US Black*) in fig. use, to behave, to do something, to fool around. **3** [1940s+] to gossip, to chat. **4** [1950s] (*drugs*) to smoke marijuana. [GONG n.[2] (1)]

kick the gong around *v.*[2] [1970s+] (*US*) to masturbate. [play on KICK THE GONG AROUND v.[1]; the image is of fantasies, as enjoyed with opium]

kick the habit *v.* **1** [1920s+] (*drugs*) to stop taking an addictive drug, usu. heroin (cf. KICK v.[7]). **2** [1950s+] in fig. use, to stop doing something. [SE *kick* + HABIT n.]

kick the hell out of *v. see* KICK THE SHIT OUT OF v.

kick the hound out of *v. see* HOUND n.[6].

kick the mooch around *v.* [1950s] (*US drugs*) to smoke opium. [MOOCH n.[5]]

kick the pipe around/rag around *v. see* KICK THE GONG AROUND v.[1].

kick the shit out of *v.* (*also* **kick the crap out of, ...fuck out of, ...hell out of, ...piss out of**) [1920s+] to beat (a person) severely; also in fig. use, to defeat. [SHIT, THE n.[2]/CRAP n.[3] (6)/FUCK n.[2] (2)/HELL, THE phr.[1]/PISS, THE n.]

kick the stuffing out of *v.* [20C+] to maltreat, to beat up severely. [STUFFING n.[1]]

kick the tin *v.* [1960s+] (*Aus.*) to make a financial contribution, esp. to buying a round of drinks. [fig. use of SE *kick* + *tin*]

kick the toy around *v. see* KICK THE GONG AROUND v.[1].

kick the wind *v. see* KICK THE CLOUDS v.

kick through (with) *v.* [1910s+] (*US*) to pay up, to come across with. [KICK IN (WITH) v.]

kick to *v. see* KICK IT TO v.

kick to the curb *v.* [1990s+] (*US Black*) to reject someone, esp. to bring a relationship to an end.

kickumbob *n.* [mid-17C] anything for which one has no proper name.

kick-up *n.* **1** [late 18C–1910s] (*orig. US*) a dance, a party. **2** [late 18C–1950s] an argument, a disturbance, esp. a prison riot. [KICK UP v.¹]

kick up *v.¹* **1** [mid-18C+] to cause trouble, to react unfavourably; usu. in combs., e.g. *kick up a fuss, kick up a lark, kick up a riot, kick up a row, kick up a shindy, kick up a stick*. **2** [mid-19C+] to create, to make something happen. **3** [1970s+] to raise the volume, e.g. on a stereo. **4** [1990s+] (*US*) to start.

kick up *v.² see* KICK UP ONE'S HEELS v.¹.

kick up a breeze *v.* (*also* **raise a breeze**) [late 18C+] to make a fuss, to cause trouble. [KICK UP v.¹ + BREEZE n.¹]

kick up a dido *v. see* CUT UP A DIDO v. (2).

kick up a fuss *v. see* KICK UP v.¹ (1).

kick up (a) murder *v.* [1920s–60s] to make a great fuss. [KICK UP v.¹ + BLUE MURDER n.]

kick up bobsy-die *v.* [19C+] (*N.Z.*) to make a fuss, a commotion. [KICK UP v.¹ + dial. *bobs-a-dying*, a great fuss, pandemonium]

kick up hell's delight *v.* [20C+] (*Can.*) to cause a great deal of trouble or disturbance. [KICK UP v.¹ + HELL'S DELIGHT n.]

kick up (high) jack *v. see* CUT UP JACK v.

kick up merry hell *v.* [1920s+] to cause a great deal of fuss. [KICK UP v.¹ + MERRY adj. + SE *hell*]

kick up murder *v. see* KICK UP (A) MURDER v.

kick up one's heels *v.¹* (*also* **kick up, lay up one's heels, topple up one's heels, turn up one's heels, wag one's heels**) [late 16C+] to die; to kill.

kick up one's heels *v.²* [mid-19C+] to enjoy oneself, to have a good time. [the image of dancing, or of a horse freed from its harness]

kick up sand *v.* [1950s–60s] (*US Black*) to make a fuss, to complain. [? the famous 'Charles Atlas' advert, in which the bully kicks sand into the weakling's face]

kick up shit *v.* [1940s+] to cause a commotion, to cause trouble. [KICK UP v.¹ + SHIT n.³ (2)]

kick upstairs *v.* [late 19C+] to promote an official or executive who cannot actually be dismissed but whose value in their current role is no longer useful to the organization.

kick with *v.* [1990s+] (*US Black*) to associate with; to be part of a gang.

kick with the left foot *v.* (*also* **dig with the left foot**) [1950s+] (*N.Z.*) to be a Roman Catholic (cf. DIG WITH THE...FOOT v.). [LEFT-FOOTER n.¹ + rugby imagery]

kicky *n. see* KICK n.¹.

kicky *adj.¹* [mid-19C+] (*orig. US*) notable for complaints, filled with complaints. [KICK (AT) v. (1)]

kicky *adj.²* [1940s+] (*US*) exciting, lively. [lit. providing or creating a KICK n.⁵ (3)]

kicky-wicky *n.* [early 17C] the penis. [? Fr. *quelquechose*, something]

kid *n.¹* **1** [late 16C–18C] (*also* **kidd**) a child. **2** [mid-18C–19C] (*UK Und.*) a child of either sex, esp. a juvenile thief, known as 'the kid — ' (their surname). **3** [late 18C] (*UK Und.*) a member of a confidence team. **4** [late 18C+] (*also* **kyd**) a person, usu. young. **5** [mid-19C+] a friend or fellow, often used in direct address. **6** [late 19C–1930s] a tramp's young companion. **7** [late 19C+] (*US*) a young person, usu. a woman, used affectionately, esp. in direct address. **8** [late 19C+] (*orig. US*) as *one's kid*, one's younger sibling. **9** [1910s+] used self-referentially, i.e. 'the kid — '. **10** [1910s+] (*US prison*) a catamite, an underage or young

homosexual boy; thus *kid fruit, k.f.*, an older man who prefers sex with such boys. **11** [1970s] (*US Black*) a sophisticated person. [SE *kid*, a young goat; (1) SE f. 19C]

kid *n.²* **1** [mid-19C–1900s] (*UK Und.*) persuasive talk, aimed at effecting a confidence trick, interrogating a prisoner etc. **2** [mid-19C+] teasing, mockery, chaff; thus *on the kid*, bantering, teasing. **3** [20C+] nonsense, rubbish; usu. as *no kid*, I am not telling a lie (*see* NO KIDDING phr.). [KID (AROUND) v.]

kid *n.³ see* KIDS n.

kid *adj.* (*orig. US*) **1** [late 19C+] younger, as in *kid brother*. **2** [20C+] pertaining to or fit for children, as in KID STUFF n.¹. **3** [20C+] (*US*) childish. [KID n.¹ (1)]

kidalidaloo *n.* [1980s] (*Aus.*) a small child, old enough to walk.

kid along *v.* [1910s+] **1** to tease, esp. with a long and apparently feasible story. **2** (*also* **kid up**) to deceive, to hoax. [ext. of KID (AROUND) v.]

kid (around) *v.* **1** [19C–1900s] to persuade. **2** [19C+] to tease, to pretend, to fool; used in phrs. *I'm not kidding*; NO KIDDING phr.; I KID YOU NOT phr.; *who do you think you're kidding?* who do you think you're fooling (because it certainly isn't me)? [? to treat as a KID n.¹ (1) or to COD v.]

kid blister *n.* [20C+] (*Aus.*) a sister. [KID adj. (1) + rhy. sl.]

kid-bouncing *n.* [late 19C] (*UK Und.*) to frighten simpletons by telling frightening stories.

kid-catcher *n.* [late 19C] a truant officer, employed by the London School Board to track down those refusing to attend school. [KID n.¹ (1) + SE *catcher*]

kid college *n. see* JOE COLLEGE n.

Kid Creole *n.* [2000s] unemployment benefit, the dole (cf. BLESS MY SOUL n.). [rhy. sl.; ult. rock band *Kid Creole* and the Coconuts]

kidd *n. see* KID n.¹ (1).

kidded *adj.* [late 19C–1900s] pregnant. [KID n.¹ (1)]

kiddeliwink *n.* [mid-19C] a village store or small shop, an aleshop.

kidden *n.* [mid-19C] a low lodging house for boys.

kidder *n.¹* **1** [late 18C–early 19C] (*also* **crocker**) a tradesman's tout. **2** [late 19C+] a teaser, a joker, a hoaxer; thus ext. as (*Aus.*) *kidder from Kidderville*. **3** [2000s] a general term of address. [KID (AROUND) v.]

kidder *n.²* **1** [mid-19C+] *Kidder*minster. **2** [late 19C] a carpet made in *Kidder*minster. [abbr.]

kiddey *n. see* KIDDY n.¹.

kiddie *adj. see* KIDDY adj.².

kiddiefiddler *n.* [1990s+] a paedophile. [KIDDY n.¹ (2) + FIDDLE v.¹ (2)]

kiddier *n.* [mid-19C] a pork butcher. [? SE *kidney*]

kiddiess *n.* [mid-19C] (*UK Und.*) a well-dressed young woman.

kiddily *adv.* [early–mid-19C] fashionably or showily; thus *kiddily togged*, smartly dressed. [KIDDY n.²]

kidding *n.* [mid-19C+] (*US*) teasing, joking. [KID (AROUND) v. (2)]

kiddish *adj.* [late 19C+] childish. [KID n.¹ (1)]

kiddiwink *n.* [20C+] a young child. [ext. of KID n.¹ (1)]

kiddken *n. see* KIDKEN n.

kiddleywink/kiddliwink *n. see* KIDLYWINK n.

kiddo *n.* **1** [late 19C+] (*orig. Aus./N.Z.*) a child, esp. as a greeting, *Hey, kiddo*. **2** [20C+] a person. **3** [20C+] (*also* **kiddoo**) a general term of address to an adult, sometimes derog. **4** [1910s] a girlfriend. [KID n.¹ (1) + -O sfx (1)/-O sfx (4)]

kiddy *n.¹* (*also* **kiddey, kiddie**) **1** [late 18C-mid-19C] a fashionable, flashy young man, a rake, a pimp or a thief; thus [early 19C] *rolling kiddy*, a dandy-cum-thief, or a dandy who dresses like a smart thief. **2** [19C+] a child. **3** [19C+] a man. **4** [mid-19C] a stagecoach driver. **5** [mid-19C–1900s] a pimp (cf. ABBOT ON THE CROSS n.). **6** [mid-19C+] (*later use US Black*) a friend or fellow, a person. **7** [1920s+] as *the kiddy/kiddie*, the most important person.

8 [1970s] (*US Black*) one who is seen as less important than the speaker. [fig./joc. uses of KID n.[1]]

kiddy n.[2] [mid-19C] a hat fashionable among small-time but dandified thieves. It featured a broad ribbon passing through a large buckle at its front. [KIDDY n.[1] (1)]

kiddy adj.[1] [late 18C–mid-19C] **1** well-dressed, fashionable, flashy. **2** skilful, esp. in a criminal context. [KIDDY n.[1] (1)]

kiddy adj.[2] (*also* **kiddie**) [1930s+] pertaining to, or fit for children. [KIDDY n.[1] (2)]

kiddy v. [mid-19C] to hoax, to humbug, to subject to confidence trickery. [KID (AROUND) v. or KIDDY n.[1] (1)]

kiddyish adj. **1** [early 19C–1910s] stylish, showily dressed. **2** [mid-19C] frolicsome, jovial. [KIDDY n.[1] (1)]

kideo n. see KIDVID n.

kidflick n. [1970s+] (*orig. US*) a film or video recording aimed at the child audience. [KID n.[1] (1) + FLICK n.[3] (1) + play on SKIN FLICK n.]

kid fruit n. see KID n.[1] (10).

kidger n. [late 19C+] (*Irish*) a term of endearment to a young boy, occas. to an animal. [KID n.[1] (5) + var. on CODGER n. (1)]

kid glove n. [late 19C–1920s] (*US Und.*) an elite tramp or criminal.

kidken n. (*also* **kiddken**) [mid-19C] a lodging house frequented by young criminals. [KID n.[1] (1) + KEN n.[1] (1)]

kid lamb n. see LAMB n. (2).

kid lay n. [late 17C–mid-19C] (*UK Und.*) robbery that involves waylaying messenger boys and similar youngsters, and defrauding them of the goods they are carrying by offering them money to run a quick errand and promising, during their absence, to look after the goods; thus *work the kid*. [KID n.[1] (1) + LAY n.[4] (1)]

kid leather n. [mid-late 19C] a very young prostitute; a generic term for the world of very young female prostitution. [KID n.[1] (1) + LEATHER n.[2] (1)]

kidlet n. [late 19C+] a small child or an affectionate term for a young woman; often in pl. [KID n.[1] (1) + dimin. sfx *-let*]

kidling n. **1** [early 19C] a young thief, esp. if the father is already 'in the trade'. **2** [late 19C] a baby, an infant. [KID n.[1] (1) + dimin. sfx *-ling*]

kidlywink n. (*also* **kiddleywink**, **kiddliwink**) **1** [mid-19C] 'a woman of unsteady habits' (Hotten, 1864). **2** [1980s] a small child. [KID n.[1] (1)]

kidman's blood mixture n. (*also* **kidman's joy**) [1930s–40s] (*Aus.*) treacle. [proper name of Sir Sidney *Kidman* (1857–1935), a large-scale grazier]

kidment n. [mid-late 19C] **1** a handkerchief that is attached to the pocket from which it is protruding, so that a pickpocket, however careful, alerts the handkerchief's owner when an attempt is made to remove it. **2** any inducement to dishonesty or crime. **3** a fictitious story or any form of statement written with the intent of deception. **4** a begging letter. [KID (AROUND) v. (1) + sfx *-ment*]

kidnap v. [late 17C–mid-19C] to steal children, esp. for use as servants or labourers on the plantations; thus *kidnapper*, one who kidnaps. [KID n.[1] (1) + NAP v.[2] (1); SE by mid-19C]

kidney n. [1980s] (*US Black*) the womb.

kidney-bruiser n. (*also* **kidney-buster**, **-crusher**, **-rider**, **-rotter**) [1940s+] (*Aus./N.Z.*) a frameless pack that, without any support, bangs on one's back and kidneys.

kidney-buster n. (*US*) **1** [1920s+] (*also* **kidney-cracker**, **kidney disturber**) a large penis (cf. ARSE-OPENER n.). **2** [1930s–40s] a vehicle that gives a bumpy ride.

kidney-foot n. [mid-19C–1930s] (*US*) a flat-footed person. [resemblance]

kidney-pie n. [1930s+] (*Aus./N.Z.*) flattery, humbug, deceit. [pun on SE *kidney*/KID (AROUND) v.]

kidney-prodder n. [1930s+] (*US*) a large penis; thus *prod someone's kidneys*, of a man, to have sexual intercourse (cf. ARSE-OPENER n.).

kidney punch n. [20C+] lunch; usu. as a *bit of kidney*. [rhy. sl.]

kidney-rider/-rotter n. see KIDNEY-BRUISER n.

kidney-scraper n. [2000s] a man with an extra-large penis (cf. ARSE-OPENER n.).

kidney-wiper n. (*also* **kidney-wash**) [late 19C+] (*US*) a large penis (cf. ARSE-OPENER n.).

kidology n. [1970s+] the art of teasing or fooling a victim, esp. with the intent of obtaining something from them. [KID (AROUND) v. + sfx *-ology*; thus note the nonce-word coined by Terry Pratchett (b.1948), *headology*, using one's head rather than force to get what one wants]

kid on v. [mid-19C+] **1** to encourage someone else to do something. **2** to tease, to deceive.

kid oneself (up) v. [mid-19C+] to delude or fool oneself. [KID (AROUND) v.]

kid-rig n. [late 18C–mid-19C] (*UK Und.*) the robbery of children (occas. adults) sent out on errands (their parcel or the money with which they have been entrusted is taken either by guile or by force). [KID n.[1] (1) + RIG n.[2] (2)]

kids n. [mid–late 19C] kid gloves. [abbr.]

kids, the n. [1960s+] a generic term for the youth of the moment. [KID n.[1]]

kid's eye n. [early–mid-19C] 5 pence. [orig. Scot.]

kid-simple adj. [1920s+] (*gay*) of an older homosexual male, obsessed with young boys; less common for a heterosexual paedophile whose obsession is for young girls. [KID n.[1] (1) + SE *simple*]

kidsman n. [mid–late 19C] (*UK Und.*) one who trains boys to steal and pick pockets. [KID n.[1] (1) + SE *man*]

kid's shit! excl. [1970s] (*US*) an excl. of disappointment.

kid's stuff n. see KID STUFF n.[1].

kidstakes n. [1910s+] (*Aus./N.Z.*) flattery, insincerity, deceit, nonsense; in sing., a fake. [rhy. sl. = SE *fake*; or KID n.[2] (3) + SE *stake*, a wager]

kid stretcher n. [19C] a paedophile. [KID n.[1] (1) + SE *stretcher*]

kid stuff n.[1] (*also* **kid's stuff**) [20C+] (*orig. US*) anything considered childish and/or insignificant. [KID adj. (2) + SE *stuff*]

kid stuff n.[2] [1980s+] **1** pornography that features the sexual exploitation of young children. **2** the children who are exploited in such pornography. [euph. use of KID STUFF n.[1] but note KID STUFFER n.]

kid stuffer n. [1980s+] (*Aus. prison*) a child molester. [KID n.[1] (1) + STUFF v.[1] (1); but note KID STUFF n.[2]]

kid the pants off v. [1930s+] to tease mercilessly. [KID (AROUND) v. + PANTS, THE n.]

kidult n. [1980s+] **1** (*orig. US*) any form of entertainment, usu. film, videotape or television, geared to attract both child and adult audiences. **2** an adult person who indulges in this cross-over entertainment. [KID n.[1] (1) + SE *adult*]

kidult adj. [1980s+] appealing to children and adults simultaneously. [KIDULT n.]

kid up v. see KID ALONG v.

kidvid n. (*also* **kideo**) [1950s+] (*orig. US*) children's TV or videos. [KID n.[1] (1) + abbr. SE *video*]

kid-walloper n. (*also* **brat-whacker**, **kid-whacker**) [late 19C–1950s] a schoolmaster; thus v. *kid-whack*. [KID n.[1] (1) + SE *walloper*/*whacker*, Yorks. dial.; 20C+ use mainly Aus.]

kidwy n. [early–mid-19C] (*UK Und.*) a thief's child. [KID n.[1]]

kief see under KIF.

kielbasa n. [1970s+] (*US*) a penis. [Polish *kiełbasa*, a highly seasoned garlicky sausage, usu. poached before it is eaten]

kiester n. see KEISTER n.

kif n. (*also* **keef**, **kef**, **kief**) [1950s+] (*drugs*) a variety of hashish produced in Morocco (cf. AFGHAN n.). [Arabic *kaif*, the state of bliss reached after smoking hashish]

kif adj. (*also* **kief**, **kiff**) [1970s+] (*S.Afr.*) a general term of approval, wonderful, first-rate, excellent. [fig. use of KIF n.; note Afk. *gif*, poison; the similarity in pron. has led to POISON adj., and the nickname for marijuana, DURBAN POISON n.; note WW1 milit. *all kiff*, all right]

kife *n.* [late 19C+] a bed. [? var. on KIP n.¹ (2)]

kife *v.* **1** [late 19C+] to have sexual intercourse. **2** [1930s+] (*US*) to cheat or to steal. [KYFER n.]

kife/kifer *n. see* KYFER n.

kiff *adj. see* KIF adj.

kiffed *adj.* [1960s] (*drugs*) intoxicated on hashish. [KIF n.]

kiffle *v.* [20C+] (*Ulster*) to procrastinate, to act hesitantly, to potter about. [? Scot. *kiffle*, a slight cough]

kike *n.* (*also* **kyke**) [20C+] **1** (*orig. US*) a derog. name for a Jew, esp. an East European late 19C immigrant to US rather than the older, German immigrants of earlier decades (cf. ARAB n.²). **2** (*US Und.*) a Jewish thief. **3** a grasping, dishonest if also shrewd person (irrespective of race). [poss. rhyming with the common Jewish name *Ike*, i.e. Isaac (cf. IKEY-MO n. (1)); or f. Yid. *kikel*, a circle, the mark used by some illiterate Jewish immigrants rather than a cross when signing papers at Ellis Island, New York City, *c.*1900; or f. common sfx *-ki, -ski*, which was found in many European Jewish names. P. Tamony (*Maledicta* I:2, 1977, pp.269ff) rejects these, preferring Ger. *kieken*, to peep. In this case the ref. is to the (predominantly Jewish) US clothes manufacturers who 'peeped' at smarter European fashions and produced mass-market knock-offs for poorer customers]

kike *adj.* [20C+] (*orig. US*) Jewish. [KIKE n.]

kike it *v.* [20C+] (*US*) to walk. [KIKE n.; the stereotypically mean Jew prefers not to pay fares]

Kiketown *n.* [1920s] (*US*) the Jewish area of a city. [KIKE n. + SE *town*]

kikey *adj.* [1920s+] (*orig. US*) Jewish. [KIKE n.]

kiki *n.* (*also* **ki-ki**) (*US gay*) **1** [1930s+] a homosexual who is equally happy in active or passive sex roles. **2** [1930s+] a bisexual. **3** [1940s+] a lesbian who takes neither an overtly feminine nor masculine role. **4** [1960s] a male homosexual who engages in oral and genital sex simultaneously. **5** [1960s–70s] sexual intercourse between 2 homosexual men of the same 'type', i.e. passive and passive or active and active. [play on QUEEN n.² (1) or CHI-CHI adj. (1)]

kiki *adj.* (*also* **kai-kai**) [1940s] (*US gay*) describing one who enjoys anal sex.

kiki *v.* (*also* **kai-kai**) [1940s] (*US gay*) to have (anal) sex.

kikipoo *n. see* KICKAPOO (JUICE) n.

kilkenny *n.*¹ [late 17C–early 19C] a frieze coat. [proper name *Kilkenny*, a county and city in Leinster in the Republic of Ireland; *frieze* is a variety of coarse woollen cloth usu. made in Ireland]

kilkenny *n.*² [1930s–60s] a penny. [rhy. sl.]

kill *n.*¹ (*also* **kilo**) [1910s–20s] a *kilometre*. [abbr.]

kill *n.*² **1** [1930s–50s] a murder. **2** [1930s–50s] (*UK Und.*) in fig. use, the actual moment of bringing a confidence trick to a climax. **3** [1940s–50s] (*US Black*) an impressive person or thing. **4** [1980s+] a major coup, esp. in criminal terms. [SE *kill*; (3) abbr. of KILLER n.¹]

kill *n.*³ [1970s+] (*drugs*) high-grade, strong marijuana; thus *smoke some kill*. [abbr. KILL n.³ (1)]

kill *n.*⁴ *see* KILLING n.

kill *adj.* [1980s+] (*US*) fashionable, smart, sophisticated. [abbr. KILLER adj.; on bad = good model]

kill *v.*¹ (*orig. US*) **1** [mid-19C+] to amaze or delight, esp. an audience. **2** [late 19C+] to cause to convulse with laughter, to delight, to bowl over; esp. as *that kills me*; often ironic. [(1) note earlier SE use in 17C–18C, usu. as *kill one with…* or *kill at first sight*]

kill *v.*² **1** [mid-19C+] (*orig. US*) to consume, to eat or drink. **2** [mid-19C+] (*orig. US*) to suppress information, to cancel. **3** [late 19C+] (*orig. US*) to cut the engine of a vehicle or the power on a machine. **4** [1910s+] to turn off in general, to stop, esp. of noise or talking; often as KILL IT v.¹. **5** [1920s+] to turn off lights, esp. in

TV or film studios. **6** [1920s+] to finish, esp. a drink. **7** [1920s+] to use up, to expend, e.g. time. **8** [1940s+] to put out a cigarette. **9** [1990s+] (*US*) to get rid of or remove an item, usu. of clothing or food.

kill *v.*³ (*US campus*) **1** [20C+] to do something very well and easily, esp. pass an exam. **2** [1970s+] to fail, to do badly. **3** [2000s] to punch; also in fig. use, to succeed.

kill *v.*⁴ (*also* **kill it, have a kill**) **1** [1990s+] (*US*) (*also* **kill off**) to masturbate. **2** [2000s] (*US campus*) to have sexual intercourse with (cf. BANG v.¹). [(1) the waste of procreative possibility]

kill a Chinaman *v.*¹ [late 19C+] (*Aus.*) to experience any form of bad luck, to have fig. or lit. done something that will bring about bad luck. [the stereotyping of the Chinese as capable of bringing on ill luck]

kill a Chinaman *v.*² *see* CHINAMAN n.⁴.

kill-a-ho *adj.* [1990s+] (*US Black teen*) used of the lyrical style of rap bands who specialize in extreme misogynism. [lit. *kill a whore*]

kill a number *v.* [1990s+] (*US prison*) to finish one's sentence. [KILL v.² (7) + NUMBER n.³ (5)]

kill a snake *v.* (*also* **kill a tree**) [20C+] to urinate (cf. BURN THE GRASS v.). [the act of urinating in the bush, note also SNAKE n.³]

kill a worm *v.* [1910s] to drink a glass of absinthe.

kill-calf *adj.* (*also* **kill-cow**) [late 16C–mid-18C] murderous. [SE *kill-calf/-cow*, a butcher]

kill-cobbler *n.* [early–mid-18C] gin. [? the propensity of shoemakers for gin-drinking]

kill-cow *n.* [late 16C–19C] an unrestrained braggart. ['I could kill a cow with one blow']

kill-cow *adj. see* KILL-CALF adj.

kill-devil *n.*¹ **1** [mid-17C–19C] (*US*) rum, or newly made rum, also known as *rumbullion*. **2** [mid-19C–1960s] (*US*) strong alcohol, esp. whisky. **3** [1950s] (*US, Ozarks*) very strong tobacco.

kill-devil *n.*² [late 17C–19C] a gun. [late 19C use is US]

killed *adj.* [1980s+] (*US*) intoxicated by drugs or alcohol. [KILL v.¹ (2)]

killed off *adj.* [19C] dragged out from one's recumbent position beneath a table after drinking to excess.

killer *n.*¹ **1** [mid-19C+] (*orig. US*) an outstanding, formidable person, often attractive, occas. menacing. **2** [1910s+] of an object, something exceptional of its type. **3** [1910s+] (*orig. US*) something very difficult to manage. **4** [1930s+] of performers/performances, the very best. **5** [1940s+] (*orig. Aus.*) the 'clincher', the final word in an argument. **6** [1970s+] as a term of address.

killer *n.*² [1940s+] (*Aus./US*) a womanizer. [abbr. LADY-KILLER n.]

killer *n.*³ (*drugs*) **1** [1940s+] (*also* **killer stick**) marijuana, a marijuana cigarette. **2** [2000s] phencyclidine (cf. ACE n.⁴). **3** [2000s] the narcotic drug OxyContin.

killer *adj.* (*orig. US*) **1** [1970s+] terrific, amazing, effective. **2** [1980s+] ghastly, terrible, demanding. **3** [1980s+] extreme, ultimate.

killer *adv.* [1950s+] a general intensifier.

killer beans! *excl.* (*also* **killer boots!**) [1990s+] (*US teen*) a general expression of approval meaning really wonderful, absolutely excellent. [ext. of COOL BEANS! excl.]

killer-diller *n.*¹ [1930s+] (*US*) something considered the very best; also used ironically. [KILLER n.¹ (2) + redup.]

killer-diller *n.*² [1930s+] (*orig. US*) a ladies' man. [KILLER n.² + redup.]

killer-diller *adj.* (*also* **thriller-diller**) [1930s+] (*orig. US*) excellent, wonderful. [KILLER-DILLER n.¹]

killers *n.* [late 18C] the human eyes.

killer stick *n. see* KILLER n.³ (1).

killer weed *n.* [1970s+] (*drugs*) **1** marijuana (cf. AFRICAN BUSH n.). **2** phencyclidine (cf. ACE n.⁴). [SE *killer* + WEED n.¹ (4); orig. a non-sl. epithet applied to discourage use, now used ironically]

kill-grief *n.* [early–mid-18C] gin or rum. [the emotional anaesthesia of the drinks]

killin' fields, the *n.* [1990s+] (*US Black teen*) East Oakland. [the frequency of random killings, usu. gang or drug-related, in the area; ult. the title of the film *The Killing Fields* (1984)]

killing *n.* (*also* **kill**) [mid-19C+] (*US*) a great success, usu. financial; usu. in MAKE A KILLING v. [now SE]

killing *adj.*[1] **1** [mid-18C–1940s] fashionable, stylish. **2** [mid-19C+] (*orig. US*) fascinating, very interesting, wonderful. [17C SE *killing*, captivating, bewitching]

killing *adj.*[2] [mid-19C+] extremely funny. [KILL v.[1] (1)]

killing floor *n.* [1960s+] (*US Black*) **1** anywhere used for the purpose of sexual intercourse. **2** a place where victims are robbed and/or cheated by a confidence trickster.

kill it *v.*[1] [1910s+] (*orig. US*) to stop talking; usu. as imper. [KILL v.[2] (4)]

kill it *v.*[2] *see* KILL v.[4].

killjoy *n.* [1920s–40s] (*US Black*) a policeman or any authority figure (cf. BEAT-POUNDER n.).

kill-me-dead *n.* [1930s] (*UK tramp*) bread. [rhy. sl.]

kill-me-quick *n.* **1** [mid-19C–1900s] (*US*) whisky. **2** [late 19C–1900s] (*Aus.*) a form of fritter. **3** [1940s+] (*S.Afr.*) a form of strong liquor drunk in the townships, made of bread, syrup, brown sugar, yeast and bran. [the effect of such food or drink]

kill off *v. see* KILL v.[4] (1).

kill one's dog *v.* [mid-18C] to be drunk, to drink heavily (cf. LET'S KILL A DOG phr.).

killout *n.* [1930s–40s; 1980s+] (*US Black*) an amazing person, an enthralling topic or thing. [var. on KILLER n.[1]]

kill out *v.* [1930s] (*US Black*) to feel good, to be exhilarated.

kill out oneself *v.* [20C+] (*W.I.*) to exhaust oneself.

killpig *n.* [2000s] an appalling situation.

kill-priest *n.* (*also* **kill-preacher**) [late 18C–19C] port wine; also whisky. [the clergy's supposed partiality to the drink]

kill some babies *v.* [1990s+] (*US*) to masturbate.

kill someone's buzz *v.* (*also* **stomp someone's buzz**) [1980s+] (*US campus*) to depress someone, to destroy someone's enjoyment or pleasure, to disappoint someone. [SE *kill* + BUZZ n.[3] (2)]

kill-the-beggar *n.* [19C] rough whisky.

kill who? *excl.* [late 19C] a defiant response to a threat.

Kilmarnock whittle *n.* [late 19C+] (*Scot.*) a person of either sex who is engaged to be married. [dial. *whittle*, a blanket; thus the term may refer to the practice of *bundling*, unmarried couples sleeping together, albeit fully dressed]

kilo *n. see* KILL n.[1].

kilt *adj.* [19C+] (*Irish*) suffering, whether mentally or physically. [hyperbolic use of SE *killed*]

kilter *n.* [1960s] (*US drugs*) marijuana. [? it puts one *out of kilter*]

kiltie *n.* (*also* **kilty**) [mid-19C+] a Scottish soldier. [his SE *kilt*; Brophy & Partridge, *Songs and Slang of the British Soldier* (1930), claim that it was used 'only mockingly for the purpose of starting a fight']

kimbaw *v.* [late 17C–mid-19C] (*UK Und.*) **1** to cheat, to rob, to deceive. **2** to beat up. [SE *akimbo*, crossed or crooked]

Kimberley *adj.* [20C+] (*Aus.*) a general derog. term used in various combs., e.g. *Kimberley mutton*, roast goat; *Kimberley oyster*, a meat fritter. [*Kimberley*, an area of northwest Australia]

kimble *n.* [1960s+] (*US Black*) an exaggerated, identifiable pimp walk. [? SE (*arms*) akimbo]

kimible *v.* (*also* **kimble**) [1960s+] (*US Black*) to walk in the exaggerated style of a pimp. [KIMIBLE n.]

kimino/kimona *n. see* WOODEN KIMONO n.

kimp *n. see* KEMP n.

kin *n.* [18C] (*UK Und.*) a thief.

kinarkey *n.* [1990s+] (*W.I.*) a woman wearing garish make-up.

kinat *n.* (*also* **canat, kinnat, kinnatt**) [20C+] (*Irish*) an impertinent, conceited youngster. [Irish *cnat*, a gnat]

kinchin *n.* (*also* **kinch, kinchen**) (*UK Und.*) **1** [mid-16C–1900s]

a (small) child. **2** [mid-18C–mid-19C] a young woman. [Ger. *Kindchen*, MDu. *kindeken*, a little child]

kinchin cove *n.* (*also* **kinchen cove**) (*UK Und.*) **1** [mid-16C–early 19C] (*also* **kitchin co, kynchen co**) a child who has been brought up to thieving as a profession (cf. CANTING CREW n.). **2** [late 17C–mid-19C] a little man. **3** [late 18C–mid-19C] a man who steals children for gypsies, beggars etc. [KINCHIN n. + COVE n. (1)]

kinchin lay *n.* (*also* **kynchin lay**) [mid-19C–1900s] **1** stealing money from children in the street. **2** in fig. use, devoting oneself to the topic of children. [KINCHIN n. + LAY n.[4] (1)]

kinchin mort *n.* (*also* **king's mot, kitchin mort**) [mid-16C–mid-19C] (*UK Und.*) **1** a beggar's child. **2** a young, virgin girl, destined to be a prostitute or beggar's companion (cf. CANTING CREW n.). [KINCHIN n. + MORT n.]

kincob *n.* [mid-19C] (*Anglo-Ind.*) uniform, fine clothes, richly embroidered dresses. [Hind. or Gujerati *kamkhâb*, gold brocade; note 13C *camocca*, damasked silk, f. Pers. *kamkha*, ult. Chinese *kin-kha*, gold cloth]

kind, the *n.* **1** [1960s+] (*US*) anything good, such as food, drugs or liquor. **2** [1980s+] (*US drugs*) superior-quality cannabis. [Hawaiian surf sl. *da kine*, anything of which one forgets the precise name]

kind *adj.* [2000s] (*US campus*) of a person, very popular or admirable.

kinda/kinder *adv. see* KIND OF adv.

kinder *n.* (*also* **kinda, kindie, kindy**) [1950s+] (*Aus.*) the *kinder*garten class in a primary school. [abbr.]

Kinder Eggs *n.* [1990s+] (*drugs*) MDMA (cf. ECSTASY n.). [brandname of a popular sweet]

kindergarten *n.*[1] [1950s] (*US Und.*) a reform school.

kindergarten *n.*[2] *see* GLADIATOR SCHOOL n.

Kinder Surprise *n.* [1990s+] (*UK juv.*) a woman who has large breasts, waist and hips but thin legs. [*Kinder Surprise*, a popular egg-shaped sweet]

kindheart *n.* [17C] a dentist.

kindie *n. see* KINDER n.

kind of *adv.* (*also* **kinda, kinder**) [mid-19C+] to some extent, in a way, rather.

kindy *n. see* KINDER n.

'kin'ell! *excl.* [20C+] an excl. of surprise, annoyance, wonder etc. [abbr. FUCKING HELL! excl.]

King *n.*[1] [late 19C+] (*S.Afr.*) King William's Town, Eastern Cape; once capital of the provinces of Queen Adelaide and British Kaffraria.

King *n.*[2] [1990s+] (*US Black*) Burger King. [abbr.]

king *n.*[1] **1** [mid-19C+] (*US campus*) used with a suitable n. or v. to denote the best of something, e.g. *surfer king, toking king* (cf. QUEEN sfx). **2** [20C+] (*Aus./US*) a respected figure, e.g. in a prison, or the leader of a gang of larrikins. **3** [1960s+] (*gay*) a masculine lesbian. **4** [2000s] (*US Black*) a term of address.

king *n.*[2] *see* KING (DEATH) n.

king *adj.* [1960s+] (*Aus.*) excellent, wonderful, perfect.

king *v. see* KING HIT v.

king! *excl.* [1960s+] (*Aus.*) brilliant! wonderful! [KING adj.]

king bee *n.* [mid-19C+] (*orig. US*) the most important person of a group or organization. [KING n.[1] (2); var. on SE *queen bee*]

King Billy *n.* (*also* **Billy**) [late 19C+] (*Aus.*) **1** a generic term for any Aboriginal leader. **2** any Aboriginal singled out from the rest. [King William IV of England (r.1830–7)]

king billy *adj.* [1970s–80s] (*N.Z. prison*) foolish, stupid; mad (cf. COCK-SPARROW adj.). [rhy. sl. = SE *silly*]

king canutes *n. see* DAISY (ROOTS) n.[1]

king daddy *n.* [1990s+] (*US teen*) the very best of a person, place or thing; thus the female counterpart QUEEN MAMA n. [KING n.[1] (2) + DADDY n. (6)]

king (death) *n.* [20C+] (*bad*) breath. [rhy. sl.]

king dick *n.*[1] [late 19C+] a brick; thus *king dickie*, a brickie, a bricklayer. [rhy. sl.]

king dick *n.*[2] [20C+] (*Aus.*) the leader, the boss, the 'guvnor'. [generic use of proper name]

king dick *adj.* [20C+] stupid, dull. [rhy. sl. = THICK adj.[1]]

kingdom come *n.* **1** [20C+] rum. **2** [1970s+] the buttocks (cf. ALA n.). [rhy. sl.; (2) = BUM n.[1] (1)]

King Farouk *n.* [1950s] a book. [rhy. sl.]

kingfish *n.* [1920s+] (*US*) a political leader or 'boss'. [the orig. *Kingfish* was the populist Governor and Senator Huey P. Long (1893–1935) of Louisiana; Long, who declared that he 'looked around at the little fishes present and said "I'm the Kingfish"', and fought his campaigns on the slogan 'Everyman a King but no man wears a crown'. The name was also given to a character in the hit US radio show *Amos 'n' Andy*]

king-hell *adj.* [1960s+] (*orig. US*) formidable, impressive. [extrapolated f. 'KIN'ELL! excl./FUCKING HELL! excl.]

king hit *n.* [1940s+] (*Aus.*) **1** a knockout or knock-down blow. **2** a thug, a bully; thus *king-hit artist, king-hit merchant*, one who specializes in thuggery. **3** a surprise punch. [SE *king*, supreme, extreme + *hit*]

king hit *v.* (*also king*) [1940s+] (*Aus.*) **1** to knock down. **2** to deliver a surprise punch. [KING HIT n.]

King Kong *n.* **1** [1940s–60s] (*US Black*) cheap, potent, homemade whisky. **2** [1970s] (*US drugs*) a strong addiction to a drug. [the name of the fictitious monster ape, who 'starred' in the film *King Kong* (1933)]

King Kong pills *n.* [1960s+] (*drugs*) barbiturates (cf. BARBIT n.). [the film *King Kong* (1933), in which the monster ape is knocked out, albeit by gas, not pills]

King Lear *n.* **1** [1930s+] an ear. **2** [1940s+] a male homosexual. [rhy. sl.; (2) = QUEER n. (4)]

King Lear *adj.* [1940s+] homosexual. [KING LEAR n. (2)]

king muck *n. see* LORD MUCK n.

king of Spain *n.* [20C+] (*Aus.*) **1** rain. **2** a train. **3** a plane. [rhy. sl.]

king of Spain's trumpeter *n.* [late 18C–early 19C] a donkey. [pun on SE *Don Key/donkey*]

kingpin *n.* [mid-19C+] (*orig. US*) the central figure, the most important figure in an organization or team. [SE *kingpin*, synon. with *kingbolt*, the most important or largest bolt in a mechanical structure, itself linked to *kingpost*, the central post that holds up a roof-truss]

kingpin *adj.* [mid-19C+] (*orig. US*) of a person, most important, most central or authoritative in an organization.

kings and queens *n.* [20C+] baked beans; thus *kings on holy ghost*, baked beans on toast. [rhy. sl.]

king's bad bargain *n. see* HIS MAJESTY'S BAD BARGAIN n.

king's books *n.* [mid-17C–early 19C] a pack of cards. [SE *king's books*, taxation lists; gamblers are 'taxed' when they lose]

King's College *n.* [late 18C–early 19C] the King's Bench prison (cf. ABBOTT'S PRIORY n.; ANOTHER DAY UP THE QUEEN'S ARSE phr.; BIG SCHOOL n.).

king's elevator *n. see* ROYAL SHAFT(ING) n.

king's hard bargain *n. see* HIS MAJESTY'S BAD BARGAIN n.

King's Head Inn (in Newgate Street), the *n.* (*also* **Chequer Inn (in Newgate Street)**) [late 17C-mid-19C] Newgate prison (cf. ABBOTT'S PRIORY n.; ANOTHER DAY UP THE QUEEN'S ARSE phr.; BOARDING HOUSE n.).

king shit *n.* (*also king spit*) [1940s+] (*orig. US*) an important person; usu. in negative use, an arrogant, self-opinioned person. [SE *king* + SHIT n.[2] (1)]

kingsize *adv.* [1960s+] (*US*) to a large extent.

kingsman *n.* [mid–late 19C] **1** (*also* **kinsman**) a silk handkerchief in a variety of colours, as worn by costermongers of both sexes. **2** a silk handkerchief with a green base and a yellow pattern; thus *kingsman of the rortiest*, a very gaudy variety.

king's mot *n. see* KINCHIN MORT n.

kings on holy ghost *n. see* KINGS AND QUEENS n.

king's peg *n.* [late 19C+] a champagne cocktail, champagne mixed with brandy. [SE *king* + PEG n.[5]; the ref. is presumably to royalty's appetite for the wine]

king's pictures *n.* [mid-17C-mid-19C] money (cf. ABE n.[2]). [the royal features as engraved or printed on money]

king spit *n. see* KING SHIT n.

king's plate *n.* [early 19C] chains, fetters. [the ult. royal control of the prisons and police]

king's proctor *n.* [20C+] a doctor. [rhy. sl.]

king's throne *n. see* THRONE n.

Kingswood lion *n.* [early 19C] a donkey. [the village of Kingswood, known for the keeping of donkeys by the colliers who lived there]

kinifee *n.* [1950s–60s] (*Aus. teen*) a knife. [exaggerated lit. pron. of SE *knife*]

kink *n.*[1] **1** [late 18C+] (*US*) a whimsical idea, a slight eccentricity. **2** [early 19C–1940s] (*US*) a tricky or surprising aspect of something. **3** [1910s+] (*Aus.*) a good idea, a tip. [SE *kink*, a sudden bend in an otherwise straight line]

kink *n.*[2] (*also* **kinkhead**) [mid-19C–1940s] (*US*) a derog. term for a Black person; thus *come the kink*, to steal a Black slave from the country, and dispose of them in town (cf. BRILLOHEAD n.). [typically 'kinky' (curly) Black hair]

kink *n.*[3] [1910s–60s] (*US Und.*) **1** a criminal, later esp. a car thief. **2** a non-criminal tramp or a criminal who specializes in a style of theft different from that practised by the speaker.

kink *n.*[4] **1** [1920s+] a perversion, esp. in sexual activity. **2** [1960s+] a sexually abnormal person, an eccentric. [KINK n.[1]]

kinked *adj.* [1950s] (*Aus.*) eccentric (cf. KINKY adj.[1]). [KINK n.[1] (1)]

kinked out *adv.* [1990s+] dressed in a sexually perverse manner. [KINK n.[4] (1)]

kinker *n.* [1900s–40s] (*US*) a circus performer.

kinkey *adj. see* KINKY adj.[3].

kinkhead *n. see* KINK n.[2].

kinko *n.* [1960s+] (*US*) **1** an eccentric person. **2** a person with bizarre sexual tastes. [KINK n.[1] (1)/KINK n.[4] (1) + -O sfx (1)]

kinky *n.*[1] [1920s–40s] (*US*) one who has 'kinky' (curly) hair, thus usu. a Black person. [abbr. KINKYHEAD n.]

kinky *n.*[2] [1920s–40s] (*US Und.*) anything that has been obtained dishonestly, esp. a stolen car. [KINKY adj.[2] (1)]

kinky *n.*[3] **1** [1950s+] a sexual eccentric. **2** [1960s+] a film portraying unconventional sexual acts. [KINKY adj.[3]]

kinky *adj.*[1] **1** [mid-19C+] (*US*) odd, bizarre, eccentric (cf. KINKED adj.). **2** [late 19C+] immoral or unladylike. **3** [1900s–50s] (*US*) of livestock, frisky; of people, high-spirited. **4** [2000s] cheeky. [SE *kink*, a bend]

kinky *adj.*[2] **1** [1900s–70s] (*US Und.*) dishonest or criminal. **2** [1920s–50s] (*Und.*) stolen. [var. on BENT adj. (3)/BENT adj. (4)]

kinky *adj.*[3] (*also* **kinkey**) **1** [1940s+] sexually perverse, esp. sadomasochistic; thus *kinky boots*, thigh-high boots, worn by women and associated with the trad. 'dominatrix' figure. **2** [1950s+] in fig. use, almost perversely interested in. **3** [1970s+] as *kinky about/over*, sexually excited by. [KINK n.[4] (1)]

kinkyhead *n.* [mid-19C+] (*US Black*) one who has 'kinky' (curly) hair, thus a Black person. [SE *kink*]

kinky-headed *adj.* [mid-19C+] (*US Black*) of a person, having 'kinky' (curly) hair; thus Black. [KINKYHEAD n.]

kinnat/kinnatt *n. see* KINAT n.

kinney *n.* [2000s] (*US Black/drugs*) very high-quality marijuana. [? KIND, THE n. (2)]

Kinsey 6 *n.* [1950s] (*US gay*) a person who is completely homosexual, as opposed to one with some bisexual inclinations. [the categorization by sexologist Alfred Kinsey in his book *Sexual Behavior in the Human Male* (1947), popularly known as the 'Kinsey Report']

kinsman *n. see* KINGSMAN n. (1).

'kin teet' *adj.* [1950s] (*W.I.*) dead. [pron. of *skin teeth*; the skin has drawn back from the teeth through *rigor mortis*]

'kin teet' *v. see* SKIN (ONE'S) TEETH *v.*

kioodle *n. see* KIYOODLE *n.*

kip *n.*[1] **1** [mid-18C+] a brothel; thus *kip-keeper*, a brothel-keeper, a madame. **2** [mid-19C+] a bed. **3** [late 19C+] the place where one sleeps, one's home. **4** [late 19C+] sleep, a nap. **5** [late 19C+] a lodging house, a hotel room, an institutional home for the homeless. **6** [1920s–40s] (*Anglo-Irish*) a job. **7** [1920s–40s] (*US Und.*) a nightwatchman. **8** [1930s+] any form of place, building. [Danish *kippe*, hut, a low alehouse, *horekippe*, a brothel]

kip *n.*[2] [late 19C+] (*Aus.*) the spatula-like wooden bat used for tossing pennies in the game of two-up.

kip *n.*[3] [1990s+] (*Scot.*) the face. [Scot. *kip*, a promontory on a hill, a turned-up nose]

kip *v.* **1** [early–mid-19C] to play truant. **2** [early 19C+] (*also* **kip down, kipp**) to sleep. **3** [late 19C+] to lodge. **4** [1900s] to sit, to lie. **5** [1950s] to put someone to bed. **6** [1970s+] (*US teen/Und.*) to sleep on the streets. [KIP *n.*[1]]

kip dough *n.* (*also* **kip jack**) [1930s–60s] (*US tramp*) money to pay for one's lodging. [KIP *n.*[1] (2) + DOUGH *n.*[1] (1)/JACK *n.*[4] (2)]

kipe *v.* (*also* **kype**) [1930s+] (*US*) to steal. [? dial. *kip*, to take property through fraud or violence]

kip house *n.*[1] *see* DOSSHOUSE *n.*

kip house *n.*[2] *see* KIP SHOP *n.*[1].

kip-in *adj.* [20C+] easy, undemanding. [KIP *v.* (2); lit. 'sleep-in']

kip in *v.* [late 19C+] **1** to be quiet, to stop talking; esp. as imper. **2** to go to bed. [fig. use of KIP *v.* (2)]

kip jack *n. see* KIP DOUGH *n.*

kip out *v.* [late 19C–1960s] to sleep in the open air.

kipp *v. see* KIP *v.* (2).

kipped *adj.* [1920s–30s] (*US Und.*) of a place, guarded by a nightwatchman who sleeps on the premises. [KIP *v.* (2)]

kipper *n.*[1] **1** [late 19C–1960s] a person, esp. a young or small person, a child. **2** [2000s] one's face. [an affectionate nickname]

kipper *n.*[2] [20C+] anywhere one can sleep, a 'dosshouse', a hotel, one's bed. [KIP *v.* (2)]

kipper *n.*[3] [1940s+] (*Aus.*) an Englishman, an English immigrant. [SE *kipper*, a herring which, after processing, has become 'two-faced with no guts']

kipper *n.*[4] [1950s+] the vagina (cf. BEARDED CLAM *n.*). [the identification of the vagina with FISH *n.*[1] (1)]

kipper *n.*[5] [1960s] a notably wide-ended tie. [the shape supposedly resembled that of the fish]

kipper *v.*[1] [1920s+] to ruin someone else's chances. [? a herring is 'ruined' by kippering; or var. on SCUPPER *v.*]

kipper *v.*[2] [1930s] (*UK tramp*) to get sunburnt.

kipper and bloater *n.* [1970s+] a motor. [rhy. sl.]

kipper and plaice *n.* [20C+] the face. [rhy. sl.]

kipper box *n.* [1990s+] an unwashed vagina (cf. BAG *n.*[1]; BEARDED CLAM *n.*). [the smell + BOX *n.*[1] (1)]

kippered *adj.* [1900s] (*US*) drunk.

kipper feast *n.* [1990s+] cunnilingus (cf. BOX LUNCH *n.*). [KIPPER *n.*[4]]

kipper-licker *n.* [1990s+] a cunnilinguist. [KIPPER *n.*[4] + SE *lick*]

kipping *n.*[1] [1910s] lodging; thus *make one's kippings*, to live. [KIP *v.* (2)]

kipping *n.*[2] [1950s] (*Aus.*) masturbating. [KIP *n.*[2]; like other similarly shaped objects it can be a synon. for the penis]

kipping-house *n.* (*also* **kippings**) [1910s–30s] a common lodging house (cf. DOSSHOUSE *n.*). [KIP *n.*[1]]

kippsie *n. see* KIPSIE *n.*[1].

kippy *adj.* [1910s–80s] (*US*) attractive, striking, lively. [ety. unknown]

kipsey *n. see* KIPSIE *n.*[1].

kip shop *n.*[1] (*also* **kip house**) [1930s+] (*Scot.*) a brothel (cf.

BANGING-SHOP *n.*). [KIP *n.*[1] (1) + SE *shop*/SHOP *n.*[1] (1)/HOUSE *n.*[1] (1)]

kip shop *n.*[2] *see* DOSSHOUSE *n.*

kipsie *n.*[1] (*also* **kipsey**) **1** [mid-18C–19C] (*also* **kypsey**) a wicker basket, usu. to hold cherries. **2** [late 19C] (*UK Und.*) a tramp's bag or container for his provisions and personal property. **3** [1930s] (*UK Und.*) a woman's handbag. [SE *keep*]

kipsie *n.*[2] (*also* **kippsie, kypsey**) **1** [20C+] (*Aus.*) a home, a house. **2** [1910s] (*Aus.*) a dugout, a shelter in WW1. **3** [1910s+] (*Aus.*) a cheap lodging house. [KIP *n.*[1] (3)]

kipsville *n.* [1910s] (*US Und.*) a hotel. [KIP *n.*[1] (3) + -VILLE sfx[1]]

kirb *n.* [mid-19C] a brick. [backsl.]

Kirby *n.* [late 19C] (*Aus.*) an undertaker.

kirk *n.*[1] [early 19C–1910s] (*UK/US Und.*) a church. [Scot. *kirk*, a church]

kirk *n.*[2] *see* CIRQ *n.*

kirk-buzzer *n.* [mid-19C] (*US Und.*) a pickpocket who specializes in the robbery of church congregations. [KIRK *n.*[1] + BUZZER *n.*[1]]

kirker *n.* [late 17C–1900s] (*orig. Scot.*) a member of a church or religious group; thus in spec. combs., e.g. *auld kirker, free kirker*. [Scot. *kirk*, a church]

kirkling *n.* [late 19C] (*UK Und.*) breaking into houses that are temporarily deserted while the occupants are at church. [KIRK *n.*[1]]

kirk pilot *n. see* SKY PILOT *n.*

kisheda *n.* [2000s] (*US Black*) a man who goes with lots of women, usu. ugly ones. [ety. unknown]

kishkes *n.* (*also* **keeshkas, kishka, kishkas**) [20C+] (*orig. US*) **1** the guts, the stomach; also in fig. use. **2** courage, pluck. [Yid. *kishkes*, intestines]

kiskeedee *n.* (*also* **keskydee**) [mid-19C–1950s] (*US*) a French-speaking person. [Fr. *qu'est-ce qu'il dit?* what is he saying?]

kisky *adj.* [mid-19C] drunk, tipsy (cf. ADRIAN (QUIST) *adj.*). [? rhy. sl. = SE *whisky*; or ? Rom. *kushto*, feeling good or happy]

kiss *n.* **1** [1910s–20s] (*US*) a drink from a bottle. **2** [1920s+] (*US teen*) a blow or hit.

kiss *v.*[1] **1** [16C–mid-19C] to have sexual intercourse (cf. ARRIVE AT THE END OF THE SENTIMENTAL JOURNEY *v.*). **2** [19C–1960s] to fellate or perform cunnilingus (cf. COCKSUCK *n.*; CUNT-LICK *v.*). **3** [1910s+] (*US*) to hit or strike hard. [euph.; note Fr. *baiser*, lit. to kiss, in sl. to have sexual intercourse]

kiss *v.*[2] [1970s+] (*US teen*) to reject, to do without etc. [abbr. KISS OFF *v.*/SE *kiss goodbye*]

kiss *v.*[3] [1990s+] to approach, to draw near, e.g. of a birthday or date.

k.i.s.s.! *excl.* [1960s+] (*US*) keep it simple, stupid. [abbr.; orig. milit. usage, later general, also popular in drug rehabilitation circles]

kiss and cuddle *n.* [20C+] a muddle. [rhy. sl.]

kiss-arse *n.* (*also* **kiss-ass**) [1920s+] (*orig. US*) a toady, a sycophant. [KISS-ARSE *adj.*]

kiss-arse *adj.* (*also* **kiss-ass**) [1910s+] (*orig. US*) sycophantic. [KISS SOMEONE'S ARSE *v.*]

kiss arse *v.* (*also* **kiss ass/butt**) [1930s+] (*orig. US*) to be subservient, to toady, to act as a sycophant. [KISS SOMEONE'S ARSE *v.*]

kisscurl *n.* [mid-19C–1900s] a small twisted curl worn on the temple. [SE in 20C+, when it has tended to refer to a single curl worn over the brow]

kisser *n.*[1] **1** [mid-19C+] (*orig. boxing*) the mouth. **2** [late 19C+] the face. **3** [1920s+] (*gypsy*) a baby. **4** [1970s] the anus.

kisser *n.*[2] **1** [20C+] a male homosexual. **2** [1950s+] a toady, a sycophant. [abbr. ARSE-KISSER *n.*; (1) lit.]

kiss goodbye *v.* [20C+] to reject, to do without, to 'say goodbye' to.

kissing cousin *n. see* COUNTRY COUSIN *n.*[1].

kissing-crust *n.* [18C–mid-19C] **1** the soft part of a loaf, where it has been touching another loaf while cooking and has not therefore become crisp. **2** the 'under-crust' in a pudding or pie. [SE *kiss*, to touch]

kissing-trap *n.* [mid–late 19C] (*orig. boxing*) the mouth. [SE *kiss* + TRAP n.[3]]

kiss kiss *phr.* [1990s+] (*US campus*) goodbye. [the kisses offered on saying goodbye]

kiss mary *v.* [1960s] to smoke marijuana. [SE *kiss* + MARY n.[5]]

kiss me hardy *n.* [20C+] a measure of Bacardi rum. [rhy. sl.]

kiss me neck! *excl.* [1940s+] (*W.I. Rasta*) a common excl. of surprise. [euph. for KISS MY ARSE! excl.]

kiss-me-quick *n.*[1] (*also* kiss-me-quick-before-mother-sees-me*) **1** [mid–late 19C] a small hat, worn by women and fixed to the back of the head. **2** [20C+] a small hat sold at the seaside which may even bear the legend *Kiss me quick!* [its size and position presumably left more room for kissing than larger, veiled pieces of millinery]

kiss-me-quick *n.*[2] [1990s+] **1** the penis (cf. ALMOND n.). **2** a fool (cf. BEECHAM'S PILL n.; CHOAD n.). [rhy. sl. = PRICK n. (2)/PRICK n. (3)]

kiss me where the sun don't shine! *excl.* [1940s+] (*orig. US*) a general excl. of derision or dismissal. [semi-euph. for KISS MY ARSE! excl.]

kiss my arse! *excl.* (*also* kiss my ass! …butt! your face and my arse! your face and my ass! your face and my butt!) [early 17C+] a general statement of contempt or dismissal; often ext. as *kiss my ass in Macey's window.* [note Chaucer, *Miller's Tale* (1386): 'But with his mouth he kiste hir naked ers']

kiss-my-arse fellow *n.* (*also* kiss-my-arse man, kiss-my-toe fellow) [late 18C–early 19C; 1960s] a sycophant; as *kiss-my-arse man* in 1960s.

kiss-my-arse *adj.* (*also* kiss-my-ass, kiss-my-back-cheeks) **1** [1960s+] a general pej. **2** [1970s+] arrogant, undaunted, proud.

kiss my foot! *excl.* [mid-19C; 1940s+] (*US/Aus.*) a general statement of contempt or dismissal. [euph. var. on KISS MY ARSE! excl.]

kiss my tail! *excl.* [late 16C–19C] a general statement of contempt or dismissal. [TAIL n.[2] (1); var. on KISS MY ARSE! excl.]

kiss-my-toe fellow *n. see* KISS-MY-ARSE FELLOW n.

kiss my tuna! *excl.* [1980s+] (*US teen*) an all-purpose excl. of rejection. [TUNA (FISH) n. (2); var. on KISS MY ARSE! excl.; thus the implication is that the oral sex that is invited is *de facto* distasteful]

kiss of death *n.* [1940s+] a person or object, contact with whom or which invariably proves fatal – metaphorically if not practically. [the original *kiss of death* is presumed to be that given by Judas to Christ]

kiss-off *n.* **1** [1920s+] (*US*) a dismissal, a rejection. **2** [1930s+] (*US*) a conclusion, a farewell, a termination (usu. with sense of one party compelling it on the other). **3** [1940s+] death. [KISS OFF v.]

kiss off *v.* **1** [1910s+] (*US*) to murder or to die. **2** [1930s+] to reject, to ignore, to spurn, esp. a lover; thus excl. *kiss off!* go away! don't talk rubbish! **3** [1930s+] (*also* kiss out) to bring to an end. **4** [1940s+] to sidetrack someone or something, to marginalize, to slight or disregard. **5** [1950s] to come to an end. **6** [1960s] (*US campus*) to leave, to leave alone. [? billiards use]

kiss of life *n.* [20C+] one's wife. [rhy. sl.]

kiss one's ass goodbye *v.* (*also* kiss one's asshole goodbye) [1970s+] (*US*) to give up completely, to abandon all hope. [ASS n. (2)/ASSHOLE n.[1] (1)]

kiss oneself goodbye *v.* [1980s+] to commit suicide. [var. on KISS ONE'S ASS GOODBYE v.]

kiss out *v. see* KISS OFF v. (3).

kiss someone's arse *v.* (*also* kiss someone's ass, …behind, …brown end, …bum, …tail) [mid-17C+] to fawn, to act the sycophant, to toady.

kiss someone's dick *v. see* SUCK SOMEONE'S DICK v.

kiss someone's ring *v.* (*also* kiss someone's toe/thumb) [19C+] to fawn, to act the sycophant, to toady. [SE *kiss the ring*, to pay homage, but note RING n.[1] (2), thus var. on KISS SOMEONE'S ARSE v.]

kiss someone's tail *v. see* KISS SOMEONE'S ARSE v.

kiss teeth *v.* [1950s+] (*orig. W.I. Rasta*) to make a hissing noise of disapproval, dislike, vexation or disappointment.

kiss the baby *v.* [1990s+] (*US Und.*) to face a certain term of imprisonment. [such a prisoner would have to kiss their baby goodbye]

kiss the baby (in the boat) *v. see* BABY IN THE BOAT n.

kiss the clink *v.* (*also* kiss the counter, kiss Newgate) [mid–16C–18C] to be confined in one of these prisons. [SE *kiss* + CLINK n.[1] (1)/SE *counter*, a prison attached to a city court/*Newgate* prison]

kiss the cross *v.* [1920s+] (*Aus.*) to be knocked out. [SE *cross*, a blow in boxing + pun on religious use]

kiss the dog *v.* [1930s–50s] (*US Und.*) of a pickpocket, to steal from a person while face-to-face.

kiss the dust *v.* [20C+] (*orig. US*) to die. [orig. mid-18C boxing *kiss the dust*, to be knocked down]

kiss the maid *v.* [late 17C–18C] to be executed on a primitive form of the guillotine. [SE *maiden*, a form of early guillotine used at Edinburgh in late 16C; occas. applied to the Halifax gibbet]

kiss the parson's wife *v.* [late 18C–early 19C] to be lucky in the choosing of or betting on horses. [the belief that those who wish for such luck must 'kiss the parson's wife']

kiss the porcelain god(dess) *v.* (*also* bow to the porcelain god(dess), hug…, pray to…, worship…, pray to the enamel god, hug the throne, worship the throne) [1960s+] (*US campus*) to vomit (cf. DRIVE THE (PORCELAIN) BUS v.). [the 'porcelain god/goddess' being the lavatory bowl]

kiss the worm *v.* [1940s+] to fellate (cf. COCKSUCK n.). [SE *kiss* + WORM n.[1]]

kiss-up *n.* [1960s+] a sycophant. [KISS UP TO v.]

kiss up to *v.* [1960s+] to toady to.

kiss wagon *n. see* PASSION WAGON n.

kissy *adj.* **1** [1940s–70s] (*US gay*) attractive, appealing. **2** [1970s–80s] (*US*) sycophantic. [(1) SE *kissable*; (2) KISS ARSE v.]

kissyface *n.* **1** [1950s+] (*orig. US teen/campus*) (*also* kissy-kissy, kissy-poo) the act of kissing; thus *play kissface*, to kiss and cuddle. **2** [2000s] used fig. to describe any intimate meeting, conversation etc.

kissy-kissy *n.* [1980s+] (*US*) sycophantic behaviour. [KISS ARSE v.]

kit *n.*[1] [early 18C–early 19C] a dancing master. [SE *kit*, a small fiddle, esp. popular among dancing-masters; ult. ? Gk *cithara*]

kit *n.*[2] [late 18C–mid-19C] a number of things or persons viewed as a whole, a set, a lot, a collection.

kit *n.*[3] [19C] the penis and testes.

kit *n.*[4] [mid-19C+] clothing; thus GET ONE'S KIT OFF v. [SE *kit*, the uniforms used for various sports]

kit *n.*[5] **1** [1920s+] (*drugs*) the equipment, such as a syringe or a spoon, required for injection of a narcotic. **2** [1930s] (*US Und.*) a safebreaker's equipment. **3** [2000s] (*drugs*) drugs, in the context of dealing.

kit *n.*[6] [1930s] (*US Und.*) fake documents used to back up the credibility of a financial swindler.

kit *n.*[7] [1940s+] (*N.Z.*) a shopping basket.

kit and boiling, the *n. see* WHOLE KIT AND BILING, THE n.

kit and caboodle, the *n. see* WHOLE KIT AND CABOODLE, THE n.

kit and killybang, the *n. see* WHOLE KIT AND CARGO, THE n.

Kitch *n.* [1910s–20s] (*Aus.*) a British soldier. [Lord *Kitch*ener]

kitchen *n.*[1] **1** [late 17C–19C] the vagina. **2** [late 19C+] the stomach. **3** [1910s+] (*Irish*) food, a meal.

kitchen *n.*[2] [1990s+] (*US Black*) the hairs at the nape of one's neck.

kitchen-bitch *n.* (*also* kitchen-crumb, kitchen-key) [20C+]

(*W.I.*) a man who hangs around the kitchen instead of going out and doing 'men's things'.

kitchen mechanic *n.* **1** [late 19C+] (*US*) a cook or washer-up. **2** [1960s] (*US Black*) a prostitute.

kitchen range *n.* [20C+] small change. [rhy. sl.]

kitchen sink *n.* **1** [20C+] a stink. **2** [20C+] a derog. term for a Chinese person (cf. AH CABBAGE n.). **3** [1970s+] (*Aus.*) a drink. [rhy. sl.; (2) = CHINK n. (1)]

kitchen stoves *n.* [20C+] (*Aus.*) cloves. [rhy. sl.]

kitchin co *n. see* KINCHIN COVE n. (1).

kitchin mort *n. see* KINCHIN MORT n.

kite *n.*[1] **1** [mid-16C–19C; 1960s] a despicable person, one who preys on others. **2** [mid-16C–mid-19C; 1990s+] the stomach. **3** [1900s–40s] (*US*) a prostitute or promiscuous woman. **4** [20C+] (*US*) the human face. [SE *kite*, a bird of prey (*Milvus ictinus*); (2) the stomach as an 'eater'; (4) the position of the 'eating' mouth in the face]

kite *n.*[2] **1** [19C+] a cheque. **2** [mid-19C] a promissory note. **3** [mid-19C] (*UK tramp*) paper. **4** [mid-19C+] (*US/Can. prison*) a contraband letter or note smuggled into or out of prison. **5** [mid-19C+] (*US prison*) any form of written document, note, memo etc used within a prison. **6** [mid-19C+] a dud cheque, i.e. one that has insufficient funds to back it. **7** [1930s–60s] (*US Black*) a letter. **8** [1970s] (*US Und.*) a complaint to the police about some form of illegal operation, often from a gambler who has been fleeced. **9** [1970s+] (*Aus. prison*) a newspaper. **10** [1970s+] (*US campus*) an inveterate drug user, who stays HIGH AS A KITE phr. (3). **11** [1980s+] (*UK Und.*) a credit card, usu. stolen. **12** [1990s+] a person involved in some kind of criminal dealings. [SE *kite*, the toy; all things that 'fly away']

kite *n.*[3] [late 19C] a shirt-front.

kite *n.*[4] [20C+] (*Irish*) the anus. [? dial. *kite*, the stomach/KITE n.[1] (2)]

kite *v.*[1] [mid-19C–1900s] to wander around. [SE *kite*, i.e. one is 'gliding' like a kite]

kite *v.*[2] **1** [mid-19C+] to pass a dud cheque; thus *kite-dropper*, one who passes dud cheques. **2** [1920s+] (*UK/US Und.*) to smuggle letters in and out of prison. **3** [1990s+] (*US prison*) to write a letter or note. [KITE n.[2] (6)/KITE n.[2] (4)]

kite around *v.* [mid-19C+] to rush about. [ext. of KITE v.[1]]

kite box *n. see* SNITCH BOX n.

kited *adj.* [1940s] (*US*) drunk (cf. ELEVATED adj.). [one is 'flying high']

kite-dropper *n. see* KITE v.[2] (1).

kite-flyer *n.* [mid-19C+] a passer of dud cheques. [KITE n.[2] (6)]

kite-flying *n.* **1** [early 19C+] raising money by persons colluding in the exchange of accommodation bills or cheques on different banks, in none of which they possess sufficient funds. **2** [mid-19C] raising money by transferring accounts between banks and creating an illusory balance against which one cashes cheques. **3** [mid-19C+] passing forged, stolen or unbacked cheques. [KITE n.[2] (1)/KITE n.[2] (6)]

kite-man *n.* (*also* **kite-merchant**) [1920s+] a criminal who specializes in cheque fraud. [KITE n.[2] (6) + sfx *-man*/MERCHANT n.]

kite mob *n.* [1930s–40s] (*UK Und.*) a gang specializing in passing fraudulent cheques. [KITE n.[2] (6) + MOB n.[2] (3)]

kiter *n.* [1930s+] a criminal who specializes in cheque fraud. [KITE v.[2] (1)]

kite-string *n.* [1970s+] (*N.Z.*) a close attachment, an 'apron-string'.

kite with no string, a *n.* [1930s+] (*US Black*) **1** an airmail letter. **2** a letter, email or other form of communication. [SE *kite*; such a 'kite' flies off into the sky; note KITE n.[2] (7)]

kiting *n.* [1930s+] (*UK/US Und.*) passing dud cheques. [KITE v.[2] (1)]

kiting-book *n.* [1960s] a cheque-book. [KITE n.[2] (1)]

kit-kat *n.* [1960s+] a fool, a general term of abuse (cf. BEECHAM'S PILL n.). [rhy. sl. = PRAT n.[1] (6)]

kit-kat shuffle *n.* [1990s+] female masturbation. [a 2-fingered version of the FIVE-FINGER SHUFFLE n.; the chocolate bar *Kit-Kat*, which comes in 2 or 4 fingers; but note KITTY n.[2] (1)]

kitmegur *n.* (*also* **kitmutgar**) [mid-19C] (*Anglo-Ind.*) an under-butler, a footman. [Hind. *khidmatgar*, an under-butler; lit. 'one who renders service']

kitskonstabel *n.* [1980s+] (*S.Afr.*) a special constable, only partially trained, used to keep order in townships during a state of emergency. [Afk. *kits*, instant + *konstabel*, constable]

kitt *n.* [1980s+] (*drugs*) cannabis. [ety. unknown; ? misuse of KIT n.[5] (1) or KIF n.]

kitted-up *adj.* [1960s+] dressed, clothed. [KIT n.[4]]

kitten *n.*[1] [19C] a pint or half-pint pot (cf. CHICKEN n.[5]; HEN n.[2]). [i.e. a small CAT n.[5]]

kitten *n.*[2] **1** [1900s] (*US Und.*) the junior member of a gang, used to check places susceptible to a robbery etc. **2** [1900s] an attractive young woman. **3** [1920s+] (*US Black*) a young, inexperienced girl. **4** [1930s+] an affectionate term of address to one's girlfriend or child. **5** [1940s+] (*US Black*) a girlfriend. **6** [1990s+] the vagina (cf. BIRD n.[8]). [(1) is dimin. of SE *cat*, but note CAT n.[1] (5); (2) and (3) are dimin. of SE *cat* but also play on CAT n.[1] (2); (5), a jazz-era coinage, plays on CAT n.[11] (4); (6) is a var. on CAT n.[3] (1)]

kitten *v.* [late 19C–1900s] of a woman, to go into labour.

kittens' noses *n.* [1990s+] female nipples. [supposed resemblance; but note CATS AND KITTIES n.]

kitten's vest *n. see* CAT'S PYJAMAS n.

kittie *n.* [16C] a prostitute (cf. ALLEY CAT n.; BABY JANE n.). [the popular name + ref. to CAT n.[1] (1)]

kitties *n.* (*also* **kittys**) [late 18C–mid-19C] one's furniture or household effects. [? SE *kit*; note cit. in Grose (1785) in which kit is defined as 'the whole of a soldier's necessaries, the contents of his knapsack']

kittle pitchering *n.* [late 18C–early 19C] a way of cutting off a boring talker by continually interrupting them with small queries. [Scot. *kittle*, to puzzle with a question, a riddle etc + *pitcher*, to throw in]

kittly-benders *n.* (*also* **kettle-de-benders**) [mid-19C] (*US*) **1** thin ice which bends under one's weight. **2** the sport of running over this. [SE *kittly*, requiring great caution or skill, unsafe to meddle with, risky]

kitty *n.*[1] **1** [19C–1940s] a prison, a lock-up. **2** [late 19C+] the 'pool' in card-games, or any other game of chance. **3** [1920s+] any reserve of money; or any valuable commodity. [Northumbrian dial.; ? f. *kidcote*, the name of the prison in various northern towns, including York and Lancaster; (2) the money is fig. 'imprisoned' while the hand is played, virtually SE 20C+]

kitty *n.*[2] (*also* **kitty-cat**) **1** [late 19C+] the vagina (cf. BIRD n.[8]). **2** [20C+] (*US*) a young, inexperienced girl. **3** [1930s] a pej. nickname, a general term of abuse. **4** [1930s+] the equivalent of a jazz/beatnik CAT n.[11] (4). **5** [1970s+] a woman, esp. in a sexual context. [SE *Kitty*, the dimin. of the female name *Katherine*]

kitty *n.*[3] (*also* **cat**, **kitty-cat**) [1930s+] (*US Black*) a cadillac.

kitty *n.*[4] [1950s–60s] (*US*) a young man. [CAT n.[11] (4)]

kitty-cat *n.*[1] *see* KITTY n.[2].

kitty-cat *n.*[2] *see* KITTY n.[3].

kitty-hop *n.* [1910s] (*US Und.*) any form of scheme whereby the criminal cannot lose.

kitty-ki-wampus *adj. see* KITTYWAMPUS adj.

kitty litter *n.* [1990s+] (*US gay*) used by transsexuals to denote HIV.

kittys *n. see* KITTIES n.

kittywampus *adj.* (*also* **kitty-ki-wampus**) [1940s+] (*US*) aslant, askew. [SAmE *kittycorner*, diagonal, askew + var. on CATAWAMPUS adj. (3)]

kivey *n.* (*also* **kiver**) [19C] a man. [presumably a dimin. of COVE n., though poss. linked to Lat. *civis*, a citizen]

Kiwi *n.* [20C+] a New Zealander. [the national bird]

Kiwi *adj.* [20C+] pertaining to New Zealand or New Zealand culture. [KIWI n.]

kiwi *n.* [2000s] a homosexual. [SE *kiwi*, the soft FRUIT n.² (2)]

Kiwi grace *n.* [1970s+] a name for the excl. '2, 4, 6, 8, bog in, don't wait!'; i.e. an allusion to the New Zealander's enthusiasm/greediness for food. [SE *Kiwi*, generic for N.Z. + *grace* (before meals)]

Kiwi green *n.* [1970s+] (*N.Z. drugs*) locally grown marijuana (cf. ACAPULCO (GOLD) n.; AFRICAN BUSH n.). [SE *Kiwi*, generic for N.Z. + GREEN n.³ (1)]

Kiwi haircut *n.* [1950s+] (*N.Z.*) a 'short-back-and-sides' haircut. [SE *Kiwi*, generic for N.Z. + *haircut*]

kixes *n. see* KICKSIES n.

ki-yi *n.* (*US*) **1** [late 19C–1910s] a noisy dog. **2** [late 19C–1940s] a contemptible fellow, a cur. [echoic]

kiyoodle *n.* (*also* **kioodle, kyoodle**) (*US*) **1** [late 19C+] a small noisy dog. **2** [20C+] a worthless fellow. **3** [1920s] worthless talk. [? echoic; or ? SE *cur*]

klaat! *excl.* [20C+] (*W.I.*) a general excl. of anger. [BLOOD CLAAT n.]

kleenex *n.* [1980s+] (*US*) **1** a juvenile word used for sex, because 'You pick it up, blow, and throw it away'. **2** among paedophiles, a description of those they exploit. [*Kleenex*, a popular brand of paper handkerchief]

kleinhuisie *n.* [1960s+] (*S.Afr.*) an outdoor privy. [Afk. *klein*, small + *huis*, house, lit. 'little house']

klep *n.* (*also* **klepper**) [late 19C–1970s] a thief. [SE *kleptomaniac*]

klep *v.* [late 19C–1970s] to steal. [KLEP n.]

klepto *n.* [1950s+] a *klepto*maniac, an obsessive shoplifter. [abbr.]

klick *n.* (*also* **click, klik**) [1960s+] (*orig. US milit.*) a kilometre. [abbr.]

klingon *n.* **1** [1980s+] (*drugs*) a crack cocaine addict. **2** [1990s+] a piece of excrement *clinging on* to the anal hairs (cf. CLAGNUT n.). **3** [1990s+] an unpleasant person. [play on *cling on* (in (1)) to every morsel of crack); the *Klingons* are the 'bad guys' in the TV series *Star Trek* (from 1966)]

klink *v.* [1930s] (*US Und.*) to hit with a gun or cosh. [echoic]

klinker top *n.* [1950s] (*US Black*) a person with tightly curled 'nappy' hair.

klip *v.* [late 19C] (*S.Afr.*) to place a stone under a vehicle's wheel to stop it running away downhill. [Afk. *klip*, a small rock]

klippy *adj.* [1920s] (*US*) nice and neat.

klobber *see under* CLOBBER.

klondike *n.* [20C+] (*US prison*) the punishment cells. [the *Klondike*, site of the Alaskan gold rush in the late 19C; miners worked alone and in darkness]

klondike *adj.* [late 19C] mad. [the 19C Alaskan gold rush on the *Klondike* river, which rendered diggers mad with greed]

klonkie *n.* [1950s+] (*S.Afr.*) a young Black boy. [Afk. *klein-jong*, servant-boy]

kloof *n.* [1910s] (*US*) a fool.

kloop *n.* [mid–late 19C] an onomat. term describing the sound of a cork being withdrawn from a bottle.

kluck *n. see* CLUCK n.¹ (1).

klucker *n.* (*also* **kluck, kluxer**) [late 19C+] (*US Black*) a member of the racist Ku Klux Klan.

kludge *n.* [1960s+] anything thrown together more by luck than judgement and with little style or sophistication. [computer jargon; note Ger. *kluge*, smart, witty. Coined by J.W. Granholm (*Datamation*, n.d.) and defined by him as 'an ill-assorted collection of poorly matching parts, forming a distressing whole']

klunk *n.* [1930s+] (*US*) a fool. [CLUNK n.¹]

klunker *n. see* CLUNKER n.¹.

klunk out *v.* [1970s+] (*US*) **1** to break down. **2** to faint or fall down. [var. on CONK (OUT) v.]

klutz *n.* (*also* **clutz**) [1950s+] (*orig. US*) a stupid, clumsy, socially inept person. [synon. Yid.; ult. Ger. *klotz*, a log, a lump of wood]

klutz *v.* [1970s+] (*orig. US*) to bungle or botch. [KLUTZ n.]

klutzy *adj.* [1960s+] (*orig. US*) clumsy, inept. [KLUTZ n.]

kluxer *n. see* KLUCKER n.

k.m. *n.* [late 19C–1940s] (*US*) a chef or washer-up. [abbr. KITCHEN MECHANIC n.]

k.m.a.! *excl.* [late 19C–1920s] (*US*) a general statement of contempt or dismissal. [abbr. KISS MY ARSE! excl.]

knabs *n. see* NABS n.

knack *n.* **1** [17C] the vagina (cf. ARTICLE n.). **2** [19C] the penis (cf. BAUBLE n.). [SE *knack*, a trinket]

knack *adj.* [2000s] (*US campus*) horrible, undesirable. [? NAFF adj.¹ + WACK adj. (1)]

knacked *adj.* [1980s+] exhausted, utterly tired-out. [abbr. KNACKERED adj.]

knacker *n.* **1** [mid–late 19C] a worn-out horse, fit only for slaughter. **2** [late 19C] by ext. a worn-out, useless person. **3** [1960s] (*Aus.*) a 2-dollar bill. **4** [1990s+] (*UK juv.*) a general insult aimed at a person. **5** [1990s+] (*UK juv.*) a thief. [SE *knacker*, a horse-slaughterer]

knacker *v.* **1** [mid-19C+] (*Aus.*) to castrate. **2** [late 19C+] to kill, to ruin. **3** [late 19C+] to tire. [KNACKERS n./KNACKER n. (1)]

knacker drinking *n.* [1990s+] (*Irish*) drinking alcohol in the open air. [Irish *knacker*, a tinker]

knackered *adj.* **1** [1930s+] worn-out, exhausted; also in fig. use. **2** [1940s] of a person, dead. **3** [1950s+] of machinery or objects, broken, irreparable. **4** [1950s+] stopped from doing what one wishes, thwarted. **5** [1990s+] drunk (cf. ADDLED adj.). [KNACKER v.]

knackering *adj.* [1950s+] exhausting, debilitating. [KNACKER v.]

knackers *n.* (*also* **knacks**) [mid-19C+] the testicles. [dial.]

knackers! *excl.* [1930s+] a general excl. of derision or dismissal.

knackety *adj. see* NAUKY adj.

knacks *n. see* KNACKERS n.

knacky *adj. see* NAUKY adj.

knap *n.* [mid–late 19C] a mock blow; thus *give/take the knap*. [SE *knap*, to strike]

knap *v.* **1** [late 17C–early 18C] (*UK gambling*) a form of dice cheating. **2** [mid-18C] (*UK Und.*) to swear, to take an oath. **3** [mid-18C] to arrest. **4** [late 18C–19C] (*UK Und.*) to steal, to take, to receive; thus *knap a clout*, to steal a handkerchief; *knap seven penn'orth*, to receive a 7-year sentence; *knap the glim/glue*, to catch venereal disease; *knap the swag*, to grab the plunder. [var. on NAP v.² (1)]

knap a bellowser *v. see* BELLOWSER n.².

knap a jacob from a danna-drag *v.* [early 19C] (*Aus. Und.*) 'This is a curious species of robbery…; it signifies taking away the short ladder from a nightman's cart, while the men are gone into a house, the privy of which they are employed emptying, in order to effect an ascent' (Vaux). [KNAP v. (4) + JACOB n.¹ (2) + DANNA n. + DRAG n.² (2)]

knap of the case, the *n.* [mid-16C] (*UK Und.*) the head of the house. [? SE *knap*, the crest or summit of a hill, but *OED*, which includes it as a derivative, notes 'doubtfully placed here' + CASE n.³ (1)]

knapped *adj.* [early–mid-19C] (*UK Und.*) pregnant. [fig. use of KNAP v.]

knapper *n.*¹ (*also* **knepper**) [mid-18C–mid-19C] the knee. [dial.]

knapper *n.*² *see* NAPPER n.¹ (1).

knapper *n.*³ *see* NAPPER n.² (2).

knapper's poll *n.* (*also* **napper's noll/poll**) [18C–early 19C] (*UK Und.*) a sheep's head. [NAP n.³ + SE *poll*, the head]

knapping-jigger *n.* [mid-19C] (*UK Und.*) a turnpike gate; thus *dub at the knapping-jigger*, to pay at the turnpike gate. [KNAP v. (4) + JIGGER n.¹ (1)]

knapsack descent *n.* [late 19C–1900s] a family in which one or both sides are trad. professional soldiers. [the SE *knapsacks* that soldiers carry]

knap the ding *v.* [early–mid 19C] (*UK Und.*) to take or steal what has already been stolen. [KNAP v. (4) + DING n.¹]

knap the rust *v.* [19C] to lose one's temper. [KNAP v. + SE *rusty*, of horses, refractory]

knap the stoop *v.* (*also* **nab the stoop, nap the stoop**) [late 18C–mid-19C] to be placed in the pillory. [fig. use of KNAP v. + SE *stoop*, the position into which the prisoner is forced]

knark *n.* **1** [mid-19C] 'a hard-hearted or savage person' (Hotten, 1859). **2** [mid-19C+] a police informer. [var. on NARK n.¹]

knarly *adj. see* GNARLY *adj.* (2).

knave in grain *n.* [late 17C–early 19C] a first-rate rogue. [SE *knave* + (*shining*) *grain*, cochineal; note Grose (1785): 'a phrase borrowed from the dyehouse, where certain colours are said to be in grain, to denote their superiority, as being dyed with cochineal, called grain']

knave's grease *n.* [late 16C–early 17C] a flogging.

knawky *adj. see* NAUKY *adj.*

knee *n.* [1950s+] an attack with one's knee, as used to hit an opponent in the testicles. [KNEE v.]

knee *v.* [1920s+] to hit someone in the testicles with one's knee.

kneebangers *n. see* KNEE-KNOCKERS n.

kneecap *v.* **1** [1970s+] to exact an extra-legal 'punishment' esp. beloved of, and poss. introduced by, the IRA, whereby victims are shot through the kneecaps and, while painfully crippled, are not actually killed. **2** [1970s+] to break someone's kneecaps with a stick or similar weapon. **3** [1980s+] in fig. use, to destroy someone's career.

knee-drill *n.* [late 19C–1920s] insincere praying, presumably on one's knees. [esp. the prayers one needed to offer when claiming free food, drink and lodging from the Salvation Army]

knee-high to a flivver *phr.* (*also* **knee-high to the pump handle**) [1930s] (*US*) very short, thus young. [? FLIVVER n.]

knee-knockers *n.* (*also* **kneebangers**) [1960s+] (*US*) knickerbockers or men's knee-length shorts.

kneel at the altar *v.* [1920s+] (*US gay/prison*) **1** to fellate. **2** to sodomize.

kneelo *n.* [1980s] (*Aus.*) a second-rate surfer, lit. one who can only kneel and not stand on the board.

knee pad *v.* [1950s] (*US Black*) to beg.

kneesies *n.* (*also* **kneesie**) [1950s+] (*US*) amorous knee contact, usu. covertly under a table.

knee-slapper *n.* [1960s+] (*US*) an uproarious joke, often used ironically. [such a joke makes the listener slap their knee with delight]

knee-trembler *n.* (*also* **knee-tremble, knee-wobbler**) [20C+] sexual intercourse when both partners are standing up, popular with cheap prostitutes or with couples who have nowhere to lie down; thus *do a knee-trembler*, to have intercourse standing up.

knee-walking *adj.* (*also* **knee-walking drunk**) [1960s+] (*US*) very drunk, often preceded by *falling-down*; also of drugs (cf. ARSEHOLED *adj.*).

knepper *n. see* KNAPPER n.¹

knicker bacon *n.* [1990s+] the labia (cf. BACON STRIPS n.). [note BACON n.¹ (3)]

knickers! *excl. see* KNICKERS (TO YOU)! excl.

knickers and stockings *n.* [1930s] a term of imprisonment. [GET THE KNICKERS v.]

knickers bandit *n.* [1960s+] **1** one who steals from washing lines. **2** a general term for a small-time petty criminal.

knickers (to you)! *excl.* [1970s+] a general excl. meaning rubbish! you must be joking! etc; a general negation of the preceding speaker's opinion, demand etc. [? euph. for KNACKERS n. or use of SE *knickers* as a juv. 'obscenity']

knick-knack *n.*¹ **1** [late 17C; late 19C] the penis (cf. BAUBLE n.).

2 [late 19C] the vagina (cf. ARTICLE n.). **3** [1970s] (*gay*) a small penis. [SE *knick-knack*, a pleasing or curious trifle]

knick-knack *n.*² *see* NICK-NACK n.².

knick-knacked *adj.* [1970s] absolutely exhausted. [KNACKERED adj.]

knick-knacker *n.* [1960s–70s] (*US*) a fussy, officious person. [SE *knick-knack*, one whose mind is limited by their obsession with trivia]

knicks *n.* **1** [late 19C+] *knick*erbockers. **2** [1960s+] *knick*ers. **3** [1990s+] (*Irish*) (*also* **nicks**) sports shorts. [abbr.; (3) f. (2)]

knife *n.* [late 19C–1900s] a shrewish, nagging woman. [like a knife, she is 'into' her victim with 'sharp' remarks]

knife *v.* [late 19C+] (*US*) to attack, either verbally or in print, in an underhand manner; thus n. *knifing.*

knife and fork *n.* [20C+] pork. [rhy. sl.]

knife and pork *v.* [1980s] (*Aus.*) to walk. [rhy. sl.]

knife it! *excl.* [early–mid 19C; 1960s] stop! don't go on! [i.e. cut it short]

knife-man *n.* [1960s] a surgeon.

knifer *n.* [late 19C–1920s] a fraud and cadger.

knife-thrower *n.* [1900s] (*US*) a waiter or waitress. [the laying of tables]

knife up *v.* [1980s] (*Aus.*) to share. [rhy. sl.]

kniff-knaff *n.* [late 17C] a joke, a jest. [? link to Scot. *kniff*, lively, alert]

knight *n.* **1** [16C+] an all-purpose appellation, linked to a variety of occupations; usu. as KNIGHT OF THE... n. **2** [late 18C–mid-19C] (*UK Und.*) 'a poor silly fellow' (*Sinks of London*, 1848).

knight and barrow pig *n.* [late 18C–early 19C] someone with ideas above their station. [one who poses as a knight, but is more of a barrow-pig, i.e. a (castrated) pig; note phr. *more hog than gentleman*]

knight of Hornsey *n.* [mid-17C–early 19C] a cuckold. [HORNS n.]

knight of industry *n. see* KNIGHT OF (THE) INDUSTRY n.

knight of St Nicholas *n.* [late 16C–early 19C] a wandering criminal beggar; thus a highwayman.

knight of the... *n.* (*also* **burgess of the...**) [16C+] 'Various jocular (formerly often slang) phrases denoting one who is a member of a certain trade or profession, has a certain occupation or character etc. In the majority of these the distinctive word is the name of some tool or article commonly used by or associated with the person designated, and the number of such phrases may be indefinitely increased' (*OED*). While the earlier [16C–18C] terms definitely have this occupational basis, the later [19C] ones tend to use the occupation in more of an ironic or joking sense. See combs. below (cf. BROTHER (OF THE)... n.).

knight of the awl *n.* [mid-19C] a cobbler.

knight of the blade *n.*¹ **1** [late 17C–early 19C] (*also* **bully of the blade**) a bully, a thug (cf. BROTHER (OF THE) BLADE n.). **2** [late 18C–mid-19C] a wandering villain, posing as a soldier and living on his wits.

knight of the blade *n.*² (*also* **knight of the blades, ...bright blade, ...shining sword, ...sword**) [late 19C] (*Aus.*) a shearer.

knight of the brush *n.* [late 19C] an artist (cf. BROTHER OF THE BRUSH n.).

knight of the brush and moon *n.* [mid-19C] a drunkard. [? SE *brush* that was once used as the sign of a tavern; or a real or generic public house name]

knight of the burning pestle *n. see* KNIGHT OF THE PESTLE n. (1).

knight of the cleaver *n.* [late 18C–19C] a butcher.

knight of the cloth *n.* [late 18C–mid-19C] a tailor.

knight of the collar *n.* [mid-16C–mid-17C] one who has been hanged.

knight of the cross *n.* [mid-19C] (*UK Und.*) a professional criminal. [CROSS, THE n. (1)]

knight of the cue *n.* [late 18C–19C] a billiard-player; a billiard marker.

knight of the elbow *n.* [late 17C–mid-18C] a card-sharp, a cheating gambler.

knight of the forked order *n.* (*also* **knight of the order of the fork**) **1** [late 16C–17C] a cuckold. **2** [mid-17C–mid-18C] one whose job involves digging with a fork.

knight of the golden grummet *n.* [1930s+] (*US Und.*) one who enjoys anal intercourse. [naut. jargon *grummet*, rope ring + *gold* = excrement]

knight of the grammar *n.* [late 17C–mid-18C] a teacher.

knight of the green cloth *n.* [late 19C–1920s] (*orig. US*) a gambler. [the green baize of card tables]

knight of the gusset *n. see* BROTHER OF THE GUSSET *n.*

knight of the hod *n.* [early–mid-19C] a bricklayer (cf. BROTHER HOD *n.*).

knight of (the) industry *n.* [mid-17C–19C] a cheating gambler. [he 'works' his victims]

knight of the jemmy/jimmy *n.* [late 19C–1920s] (*UK/US Und.*) a burglar.

knight of the knife *n.* [17C] a cut-purse.

knight of the lapstone *n.* [mid–late 19C] a cobbler.

knight of the napkin *n.* [mid-18C–19C] a waiter.

knight of the needle *n.* [late 18C–1900s] a tailor.

knight of the order of the fork *n. see* KNIGHT OF THE FORKED ORDER *n.*

knight of the pad *n.* (*also* **knight of the rumpad**) [mid-17C–mid-19C] a highwayman. [PAD *n.*[1] (1)]

knight of the pen *n.* [mid–late 19C] **1** a clerk. **2** a writer.

knight of the pencil *n.* [late 19C–1920s] a bookmaker.

knight of the pestle *n.* **1** [17C] (*also* **knight of the burning pestle**) someone with a venereal disease, a term of abuse. **2** [17C–19C] an apothecary, esp. one who prescribes for venereal diseases. [(2) prob. came first]

knight of the petticoat *n.* [late 19C–1900s] a man employed as 'muscle' by a brothel.

knight of the pigskin *n.* [late 19C] a jockey.

knight of the pisspot *n.* [late 19C] a doctor, an apothecary.

knight of the pit *n.* [late 19C] a fan of cock-fighting.

knight of the post *n.* (*also* **post-knight**) [late 16C–mid-19C] (*UK Und.*) a notorious perjurer, one who earns a living by giving false evidence. [prob. meaning a whipping-post or pillory; despite entry in *Sinks of London* (1848), E.P. suggests it was SE by 19C; OED has it SE from its 16C coinage]

knight of the quill *n.* [late 17C] an author (cf. BROTHER OF THE QUILL *n.*).

knight of the rainbow *n.* [late 18C–mid-19C] a footman, a waiter. [the colours of the uniform, which would represent those of the person served]

knight of the road *n.* **1** [mid-17C–1900s] a highwayman. **2** [late 19C] (*Aus.*) a bushranger. **3** [late 19C+] a commercial traveller. **4** [late 19C+] (*mainly Aus.*) a tramp. **5** [1930s] someone on a walking or cycling holiday. **6** [1970s] a truck-driver.

knight of the rumpad *n. see* KNIGHT OF THE PAD *n.*

knight of the shears *n.* (*also* **knight of the sheers**) [late 18C–19C] a tailor.

knight of the shining sword *n. see* KNIGHT OF THE BLADE *n.*[2].

knight of the spigot *n.* [early 19C] a publican, an inn-keeper.

knight of the spout *n.* [early 19C] a pawnbroker. [SPOUT *n.*[1]]

knight of the standard *n.* [late 19C] a racecourse bookmaker.

knight of the sword *n. see* KNIGHT OF THE BLADE *n.*[2].

knight of the thimble *n.* [late 18C–19C] a tailor.

knight of the trencher *n.* [late 18C–early 19C] a great eater.

knight of the vapour *n.* [17C] a smoker. [also known, by the coiner John Taylor, 'The Water Poet' (*c.*1578–1653), as *gentlemen of the whiffe, esquires of the pipe*]

knight of the wheel *n.* [late 19C] a cyclist.

knight of the whip *n.* [late 18C–19C] a coachman (cf. BROTHER (OF THE) WHIP *n.*).

knight of the whipping-post *n.* [early–mid-19C] a sharper, a cheating gambler.

knight of the yardstick *n.* [late 19C] (*Aus.*) a draper, a haberdasher.

K-9 *n.* (*US prison*) **1** [1980s+] a dog. **2** [2000s] a corrections officer. [pron. of SE *canine*]

knish *n.* **1** [1930s+] (*US*) the vagina. **2** [1940s+] (*US gay*) the anus. **3** [1960s] a typical housewife on a gambling spree. [Yid. *knish*, 'a dumpling of flaky dough filled with chopped liver, potato, or cheese, and baked or fried' (*OED*); ult. Rus. *knish*, a type of cake]

knit *v.* [1960s–70s] to masturbate.

knits *n.* [1960s–70s] (*US Black*) knitwear, esp. garments expensively imported from Italy.

knit the knot *v. see* TIE THE KNOT *v.* (1).

knitting *n.* [1930s–40s] girls or women considered collectively. [the 'feminine' occupation]

knitting needle *n.* [1960s–70s] the penis.

knitty *adj. see* NITTY *adj.*[1].

knob *n.*[1] **1** [late 17C+] the head. **2** [late 19C+] (*also* **cock-knob**) the head of the penis. **3** [1910s+] the penis. **4** [1930s+] (*also* **knobbies**) a female breast; usu. in pl. **5** [1930s+] (*US*) spec. a woman's nipple; usu. in pl. **6** [1940s+] (*US Black*) the knee; usu. in pl. **7** [1950s+] (*US teen*) a general term of abuse (cf. BELL END *n.*). **8** [1960s] a blow.

knob *n.*[2] **1** [mid–late 19C] a swindling fairground game, also called 'under and over'. **2** [1920s–40s] (*Aus./N.Z.*) a double-headed penny, esp. as used in the game of two-up (a gambling game based on tossing 2 coins and betting on heads or tails), produced by filing down standard coins and welding them together (cf. JACK *n.*[21]). [(2) KNOB *n.*[1] (1)]

knob *n.*[3] [1930s–60s] (*US Black*) stylish, up-to-date shoes with shined toecaps. [? the shape of the toecap]

knob *v.*[1] **1** [early 19C–1950s] (*also* **do the knob**) to hit in the face or head (cf. BAGAGA *v.*). **2** [1990s+] usu. of a man, to have sexual intercourse (cf. BANG *v.*[1]). [KNOB *n.*[1]]

knob *v.*[2] *see* NOB *v.*[2].

knob artist *n.* (*also* **nob artist**) [1990s+] a male homosexual; thus a general term of abuse (cf. BONE-EATER *n.*). [KNOB *n.*[1] (3) + ARTIST *sfx*]

knobber *n.* **1** [1970s+] (*US*) a male homosexual transvestite prostitute. **2** [1980s+] (*US campus*) fellatio. **3** [1990s+] (*US*) a stupid, obnoxious person. [KNOB *n.*[1] (3)]

knobbies *n. see* KNOB *n.*[1] (4).

knobbing *n.* [1990s+] an act of sexual intercourse. [KNOB *v.*[1] (2)]

knobbly-knee *n.* [20C+] a key. [rhy. sl.]

knobby *adj. see* NOBBY *adj.*

knob cheese *n. see* COCK CHEESE *n.*

knob-end *n.* [1990s+] a general derog. term. [KNOB *n.*[1] (3) and SE *end*; lit. the glans penis]

knob-gobbling *n.* [1960s+] fellatio; thus *knob-gobbler*, a fellatrix or fellator (cf. BASKET LUNCH *n.*). [KNOB *n.*[1] (3) + GOBBLE *v.*[1] (2)]

knobhead *n.* (*also* **knobknot**) [1930s+] (*orig. US*) a stupid person. [KNOB *n.*[1] (3) + -HEAD *sfx* (1)/SE *knot*]

knob it! *excl.* [1990s+] a general phr. of dismisssal. [KNOB *v.*[1] (2), as synon. for FUCK IT! *excl.*]

knob-job *n.* [1960s+] (*orig. US*) fellatio. [KNOB *n.*[1] (3) + JOB *n.*[4]]

knob jockey *n.* (*also* **nob jockey**) [1990s+] a general insult, implying that the male subject is a masturbator or a homosexual (cf. BONE-EATER *n.*). [KNOB *n.*[1] (3) + JOCKEY *n.*[3] (2)]

knob-knocker *n.* [1920s] (*US tramp*) a safe-cracker.

knobknot *n. see* KNOBHEAD *n.*

knob polisher *n.* [1960s+] a young male prostitute; thus *knob polish*, to masturbate. [KNOB *n.*[1] (3) + pun]

knobs *n. see* KNOB *n.*[1].

knob-shiner *n.* [1990s+] **1** a masturbator. **2** a general term of abuse. [KNOB n.[1] (3) + SE *shiner*]

knob snot *n.* [1990s+] semen (cf. BOLLOCK SNOT n.). [KNOB n.[1] (3) + SNOT n.[1] (4)]

knobstick *n.* (*also* **nobstick**) [mid-19C–1920s] a strike-breaker. [SE *knobstick*, a club with a rounded head, used by strike-breakers as a weapon]

knob stilton *n. see* COCK CHEESE n.

knob-thatcher *n. see* NOB-THATCHER n.

knob-twister *n.* [1980s] (*Aus.*) a bookmaker. [the knobs on the betting board]

knob yoghurt *n. see* COCK CHEESE n.

knock *n.[1]* **1** [mid-16C–18C; 20C+] sexual intercourse; thus DO A KNOCK WITH v. **2** [18C+] the penis. **3** [1900s–10s] (*US*) a prison sentence. **4** [20C+] a prostitute or promiscuous woman; *on the knock*, working as a prostitute. **5** [1910s] (*Aus.*) a girlfriend. **6** [1990s+] (*US prison*) the crime with which one has been charged; the crime one has committed. [(1) 20C+ use is Aus.]

knock *n.[2]* [late 19C+] **1** a negative opinion, a criticism, an insult. **2** (*also* **knockout**) a setback.

knock *n.[3] see* POSTMAN'S KNOCK n.

knock *v.[1]* **1** [late 16C+] to have sexual intercourse (cf. BANG v.[1]). **2** [early 17C; mid-19C+] (*orig. US*) (*also* **give the knock**) to disparage, to criticize. **3** [mid-18C+] (*UK Und.*) to rob, to steal; thus [late 18C] *knock the lobb*, to break and enter; [1920s+] *knock a peter*, to break into a safe. **4** [mid-19C+] (*US/Aus.*) to kill, to shoot dead; later usage in phr. *knock oneself*, to commit suicide. **5** [mid-19C+] to destroy, to defeat. **6** [late 19C+] (*US*) to complain, to inform on, to betray. **7** [late 19C+] (*US*) to explain, esp. to explain to a confidence trickster's victim that he is being swindled. **8** [1910s+] to cheat, to defraud, esp. to obtain credit which one has no intention of honouring. **9** [1920s+] (*Aus.*) to flirt with a woman. **10** [1920s+] to hit. **11** [1940s–70s] (*US*) to earn. **12** [1940s+] (*US*) to arrest.

knock *v.[2]* **1** [early 18C+] to strike with astonishment, alarm or confusion, to confound. **2** [mid-19C–1900s] to excel, to surpass. **3** [mid-19C+] to impress highly, to elicit great admiration, to make a big impression, esp. of new fashions, entertainments. [(2) subseq. use is SE]

knock *v.[3]* (*US Black*) **1** [late 19C+] to give, to do, to perform. **2** [1920s–50s] to consume. **3** [1940s] to speak. **4** [1940s–70s] to borrow; to ask for. **5** [1960s] to write.

knock *v.[4]* [1910s–20s] (*Aus.*) to give in; to be exhausted.

knock *v.[5] see* KNOCK UP v.[2] (2).

knocka *n. see* KNOCKER n.[10].

knockabout *n.[1]* (*also* **knock-around**) **1** [mid-19C] a drinking spree. **2** [late 19C+] (*Aus.*) a tramp, a vagrant. **3** [late 19C+] (*Aus.*) a layabout, a low criminal or idler. **4** [20C+] (*W.I.*) the lowest type of prostitute. **5** [1910s+] a social 'jack-of-all trades', a 'regular chap'. [KNOCK ABOUT v.[1]]

knockabout *n.[2] see* KNOCKABOUT MAN n. (1).

knockabout *adj.* [late 19C+] (*orig. theatre*) noisy, violent, rambunctious. [SE *knock about*]

knock about *v.[1]* (*also* **knock around**) **1** [early 19C+] to travel around rather than settle down. **2** [mid-19C+] to exist, to be. **3** [mid-19C+] to loaf around, to idle, to waste time. **4** [late 19C+] to associate with.

knock about *v.[2] see* KNOCK BACK v.[2].

knockabout hand *n. see* LUMPER n.[1].

knockabout man *n.* **1** [late 19C–1950s] (*Aus.*) (*also* **knocka-bout**) an unskilled labourer or handyman on a sheep station. **2** [1930s+] a layabout, an idler. **3** [1930s+] a thief, esp. a pick-pocket. [KNOCKABOUT n.[1]]

knock about the bub *v.* [late 18C–mid-19C] to circulate the bottle, to pass the drink around. [SE *knock about* + BUB n.[1]]

knock a broom *v. see* BROOM n.[4].

knock acock *v.* [19C] to amaze, to shock, to 'knock sideways'. [abbr. COCK-EYED adj.[1]; note SE *acock*, defiantly]

knock across *v.* (*also* **knock against**) [late 19C–1920s] to encounter, to meet.

knock a drill *v.* [1940s] (*US Black*) to leave, to walk.

knock a joe *v.* [1900s–40s] (*US Black*) to mutilate oneself in order to escape hard labour in prison or on the chain gang. [ety. unknown]

knock a jug *v.[1]* [1920s–30s] (*US Black*) to get drunk. [KNOCK v.[3] (2)]

knock a jug *v.[2] see* JUG n.[2] (7).

knock a line (with) *v. see* DO A LINE (WITH) v.

knock-all *n.* [1970s] no, none. [euph. for FUCK-ALL n. (1)]

knock all of a heap *v.[1]* [mid-19C+] **1** to overturn, to destroy. **2** to amaze.

knock all of a heap *v.[2] see* STRIKE ALL OF A HEAP v.

knock all to rags *v.* [late 19C] (*US*) to knock senseless.

knock all to sticks *v. see* BEAT ALL TO STICKS v.

knock along *v.* [late 19C+] **1** (*orig. Aus.*) to idle, to wander. **2** to travel around rather than settle down. **3** to manage, to subsist.

knock a nod *v.* [1920s–40s] (*US Black*) to go to sleep. [NOD n.[1] (1)]

knock Anthony *v. see* CUFF ANTHONY v.

knock a peter *v. see* KNOCK v.[1] (3).

knock a piece *v.* [1940s] (*US Black*) to have sexual intercourse (cf. BREAK A BIT OFF v.). [KNOCK v.[1] (1) + PIECE n.[1] (3); var. on KNOCK OFF A PIECE v.]

knock-around *n. see* KNOCKABOUT n.[1].

knockaround *adj.* [1940s+] (*US*) having worldly or criminal experience. [KNOCK AROUND v.[1] (1)]

knock around *v.[1]* (*orig. US*) **1** [mid–late 19C] to wander, to travel aimlessly. **2** [20C+] to associate with. [(1) 20C+ use is SE]

knock around *v.[2] see* KNOCK ABOUT v.[1].

knock a scarf *v.* [1940s–50s] (*US Black*) to eat. [KNOCK v.[3] (2) + SCARF n.]

knock a slice off *v. see* CUT A SLICE (OFF THE JOINT) v.

knock a statue act *v.* [1940s–60s] (*orig. US Black*) to wait.

knock a string of farts out of *v.* [1930s] (*US*) to beat severely.

knock a stroll *v.* [1940s] (*US Black*) to (take a) walk. [KNOCK v.[3] (1) + SE *stroll*]

knock a trot *v.* [1940s] (*US Black*) to escape, to run away. [KNOCK v.[3] (1) + TROT v.]

knock at the door, a *n.* (*also* **a knock on the door**) [20C+] (*bingo*) the number 4 (cf. ALDERSHOT LADIES n.). [rhy. sl.]

knock at the door *v.* [1930s–70s] (*US drugs*) to withdraw from narcotics use.

knockback *n.* **1** [late 19C+] a rejection, a refusal. **2** [1940s+] (*UK prison*) the rejection of one's application for parole. [SE *knock back*]

knock back *v.[1]* **1** [20C+] to cost, e.g. *that'll knock you back a bit*. **2** [1910s+] to fine someone.

knock back *v.[2]* (*also* **bang back, knock about**) [1910s+] to eat, to drink, esp. to finish off one's drink.

knock back *v.[3]* [1930s+] (*orig. Aus./N.Z.*) to reject. [KNOCKBACK n. (1)]

knock-beetle *n.* [20C+] (*Ulster*) one who allows themselves to be victimized. [Scot.]

knock boots (with) *v.* [1980s+] (*US Black/campus*) to have sexual intercourse (with). [SE *knock* + BOOTY n. (1)]

knock cats out of *v.* [1900s] (*Aus.*) to berate.

knock cold (as a monkey wrench) *v.* (*also* **knock dead**) [mid-19C+] **1** to knock unconscious. **2** (*also* **get dead**) to astound, to amaze.

knock cuckoo *v.* (*also* **slap cuckoo**) [1920s–30s] (*US*) to knock out. [SE *knock* + CUCKOO adj.]

knock dog *v.* [20C+] (*W.I.*) to idle, to do nothing. [the image of lying around like a dog]

knock-down n.[1] [late 17C–19C] strong ale or liquor. [its effects]

knock-down n.[2] [mid-18C] something astounding, remarkable, that 'knocks one down'.

knock-down n.[3] [19C+] (US) a fight; also in fig. use, an undeniable argument. [SE *knock down*]

knock-down n.[4] **1** [mid-19C+] (Aus./N.Z./US) an introduction, esp. a formal introduction of a man to a woman in whom he is interested; thus *give someone a knock-down*, to give someone an introduction. **2** [1930s–60s] (US) information.

knock-down n.[5] [1950s] (Aus.) **1** a loan. **2** a profit, usu. illicit. [? abbr. KNOCK-DOWN MONEY n.]

knock-down adj. [19C+] violent, whether lit. or fig. [KNOCK-DOWN n.[3]]

knock down v.[1] [mid-18C–mid-19C] to choose, to nominate someone. [the chairman at a dinner knocking with a hammer before announcing a speaker]

knock down v.[2] [late 18C+] (orig. US) to sell by auction. [the use of the auctioneer's hammer, now SE]

knock down v.[3] **1** [early 19C+] (orig. US) to drink. **2** [mid-19C+] (Aus./N.Z.) to spend money freely, esp. on drink. [(2) abbr. KNOCK DOWN ONE'S CHEQUE v.]

knock down v.[4] **1** [mid-19C+] to lower prices. **2** [mid-19C+] (US) (also **knock down on**) to embezzle, to steal from a firm's takings. **3** [1920s+] (US) to earn or obtain money, usu. for work, or by requesting a loan or gift. **4** [1950s] (US) to accumulate money, usu. through crime.

knock down v.[5] [late 19C+] (Aus.) to make an introduction; thus *knock someone down to*, to introduce, e.g. *knock me down to that daisy*, introduce me to that girl. [KNOCK-DOWN n.[4] (1)]

knock down v.[6] [1950s+] (Can.) to act lazily, to shirk one's work.

knock down v.[7] [1990s+] (US prison) to serve a sentence.

knock down v.[8] [2000s] (US Black) to have sexual intercourse.

knock-down-(and)-drag-out adj. (also **knock-down-and-drag-off, knock-down-and-pull-out**) [early 19C+] lit. or fig., intense, violent. [KNOCK-DOWN (AND) DRAG-OUT (FIGHT) n.]

knock down and drag out v. [early 19C+] to fight violently. [KNOCK-DOWN (AND) DRAG-OUT (FIGHT) n.]

knock-down (and) drag-out (fight) n. [early 19C+] (orig. US) a vicious violent fight; thus fig. an acrimonious but non-violent dispute. [ext. of KNOCK-DOWN n.[3]; one or more participants are knocked unconscious and dragged outside]

knock-down money n. [mid-19C; 1980s+] (US) tips or gratuities. [? SE *knock-down*, a reserve price at an auction]

knock down on v. see KNOCK DOWN v.[4] (2).

knock down one's cheque v. (also **drink out one's cheque, knock down one's money/tin**) [mid-19C+] (Aus./N.Z.) to spend an entire season's pay cheque on a single drinking bout.

knock dust v. [1970s] (US prison) to knock down, to beat up.

knocked adj.[1] [1950s+] under control, at one's mercy, e.g. *I've got it knocked*. [KNOCK v.[1] (5)]

knocked adj.[2] see KNOCKED OUT adj. (3).

knocked adj.[3] see KNOCKED UP adj. (4).

knocked down for (the) crap v. [early–mid-19C] condemned to execution by hanging. [ironic use of KNOCK DOWN v.[1] + CRAP n.[2]]

knocked off adj.[1] [1910s+] stolen. [KNOCK OFF v.[5]]

knocked off adj.[2] [1920s+] killed, murdered. [KNOCK OFF v.[3]]

knocked off one's pins phr. [late 19C+] utterly astounded. [SE *knock off* + PINS n.]

knocked out adj. **1** [late 19C+] (US) bankrupt. **2** [late 19C+] exhausted. **3** [20C+] (also **knocked**) overwhelmed. **4** [1920s+] (US) heavily intoxicated. **5** [1950s+] (US) stylish, excellent. [KNOCK OUT v.[2]]

knocked over adj. [late 19C–1930s] dead, very ill.

knocked up adj. **1** [late 18C+] tired, jaded, used up. **2** [late 18C; 1930s] dead. **3** [19C–1930s] (Irish) drunk (cf. ANNIHILATED adj.).

4 [mid-19C+] (orig. US) (also **knocked**) pregnant. **5** [late 19C] (Aus.) of an animal, angry. **6** [1930s] emotional, floored by emotion. **7** [1960s] defeated, in a difficult situation. [KNOCK UP v.[2]]

knocked with a French faggot-stick phr. see BLOW WITH A FRENCH FAGGOT-STICK n.

knock eleven kinds of stuffing out of v. see KNOCK THE STUFFING OUT OF v.

knock 'em (cold) v. [1910s–20S] to make a success, to score a 'hit', to amaze. [thus music-hall song 'Wotcher!, or Knocked Them in the Old Kent Road']

knock-'em-dead adj. [1930s+] astounding, amazing, overwhelming. [KNOCK COLD (AS A MONKEY WRENCH) v. (2)]

knock-'em-down n. [early 16C] a fiery drink. [its effects]

knock 'em down v. [late 19C] to be given applause.

knock-'em-down business n. [late 19C] the profession of auctioneering. [KNOCK DOWN v.[2]]

knock-'em-downs n. (also **knock-me-downs**) **1** [early 19C] a coconut shy. **2** [mid-19C] skittles, esp. as played in a public house.

knock-'em-stiff n. [mid-19C–1900s] (US) strong whisky. [SE *knock* + STIFF adj.[2] (1)]

knock endways v. (also **knock sky-wise and crooked**) [mid-19C–1930s] to astound, to astonish, to shock profoundly, to overturn (cf. KNOCK SIDEWAYS v.).

knocker n.[1] [17C] a promiscuous man, a whoremonger. [KNOCK v.[1] (1)]

knocker n.[2] **1** [early 17C–19C] an outstandingly attractive person. **2** [late 19C+] (US) the top person, the person in authority; often in combs., e.g. HEAD KNOCKER n., *top knocker*. [KNOCK v.[2] (1); their 'striking' appearance]

knocker n.[3] [mid-17C+] the penis. [KNOCK v.[1] (1)]

knocker n.[4] [early–mid-19C] a form of pendant to a wig, similar to a pigtail. [its similarity to a door-*knocker*]

knocker n.[5] [late 19C–1900s] (Aus.) common sense. [ety. unknown; ? link to Yid. *naches*, pleasure]

knocker n.[6] [late 19C+] (US Und.) an informer or complainant. [KNOCK v.[1] (6)]

knocker n.[7] [late 19C+] (orig. US) **1** a critic, esp. one who relishes making negative comments. **2** a criticism. **3** a disappointment. [KNOCK v.[1] (2)]

knocker n.[8] [1920s–30s] (UK tramp) an arrest.

knocker n.[9] [1920s+] **1** a gambler or prisoner who refuses to pay their debts. **2** one who passes bad cheques, or gains goods on credit and fails to pay the bill. [KNOCK v.[1] (8)]

knocker n.[10] (also **knocka**) [1990s+] (US Black) a fool. [? KNUCKLEHEAD n.]

knocker and knob n. [20C+] a job. [rhy. sl.]

knocker-face n. (also **knocker-head**) [late 19C–1920s] an ugly face, or the person who 'owns' it.

knocker-off n. [1920s+] a thief. [KNOCK OFF v.[5] (1)]

knockers n.[1] [19C] small curls worn flat on the temples, a fashionable hairstyle at that time. [abbr. NEWGATE KNOCKER n.]

knockers n.[2] **1** [late 19C+] the testicles (cf. BANGERS n.). **2** [1930s+] (orig. US) the female breasts; occas. in sing. (cf. BOBBER n.[2]). [they knock against each other/the body]

knocker up n. see KNOCK UP v.[1].

knocker-worker n. [20C+] a door-to-door peddler.

knock fairly silly v. [late 19C] to overcome almost to the point of annihilation. [joc. understatement]

knock flat v. see KNOCK OUT v.[2] (6).

knock for a Burton v. [1940s+] to destroy. [GO FOR A BURTON v. (2)]

knock for a loop v. [1920s+] to astound, to astonish, to devastate; thus THROW FOR A LOOP v. [one is fig. knocked 'head-over-heels']

knock for a row of ashcans v. (also **knock for a gool, knock for a row of flat tires, …latrines, …Mongolian**

whipped cream containers, ...silos, ...sour apple trees, ...stumps, ...totem poles) [1910s+] (*US/N.Z.*) **1** to hit or knock someone senseless. **2** to impress or amaze.

knock fowl soup v. [1950s] (*US Black*) to die.

knock hell/hell's blazes out of v. see KNOCK (THE) HELL OUT OF v.

knock her dead one on the nose each and every double trey v. [1940s] (*US Black*) to get a pay cheque every sixth day (or on the sixth day of every week).

knock hollow v. see HOLLOW adv.

knock-in n. [mid–late 19C] the game of loo; thus a hand at any card-game. [ety. unknown; ? one 'knocks in' or plays one's cards]

knock in v.[1] [mid-19C–1900s] (*costermonger*) to make money. [the money is 'knocked in' to the coster's pocket]

knock in v.[2] [2000s] to beat up.

knocking n.[1] [late 16C+] sexual intercourse. [KNOCK v.[1]]

knocking n.[2] [20C+] negative criticism. [KNOCK v.[1] (2)]

knocking company n. [1940s–60s] a hire-purchase company. [KNOCK v.[1] (8)]

knocking dog adj. [20C+] (*W.I.*) plentiful, in abundance, usu. of cheap items on sale at a market. [ety. unknown]

knocking-house n. see KNOCKING-SHOP n.

knocking it back with a stick phr. [1940s+] (*Aus.*) a phr. used by a man who wishes to boast of the success of his sex life; usu. in answer to a question, e.g. GETTING ANY (LATELY)? phr.

knocking-jacket n. [early 18C–19C] a nightdress. [KNOCK v.[1] (1)]

knocking-joint n. see KNOCKING-SHOP n.

knocking on (a bit) phr. [1930s+] growing older, usu. of a middle-aged or old person.

knockings n. **1** [1950s] the residue of one's funds; also in fig. use as the end of one's life, nearly dying. **2** [1990s+] information, facts. [? (1) KNOCK-DOWN MONEY n.; (2) KNOCK-DOWN n.[4] (2)]

knocking-shop n. (*also* **knocking-house, knocking-joint, knock shop**) **1** [mid-19C+] a brothel (cf. BANGING-SHOP n.). **2** [1910s] (*Aus.*) an untidy or dirty place. [KNOCK v.[1] (1) + SE shop/SHOP n.[1] (1)/HOUSE n.[1] (1)/JOINT n.[4] (3)]

knock in the cradle n. see HAVE GOT KNOCK IN THE CRADLE v.

knock into v. **1** [late 19C+] to run into. **2** [1910s+] (*Aus.*) to fight with.

knock into a cocked hat v. (*also* **fuck into a cocked hat, knock into a coked hat, knock into fits**) [mid-19C+] (*orig. US*) to overturn, to destroy completely, to beat thoroughly or completely.

knock into a mish v. [mid-19C] (*N.Z.*) to overcome, to surpass. [SE mishmash]

knock into horse-nails v. [late 19C–1900s] to defeat heavily.

knock into (the middle of) next week v. (*also* ...next century, ...next month, ...the north end of creation) [early 19C+] (*orig. US*) to overturn, destroy or beat thoroughly or completely.

knock it down v. [late 19C–1900s] to signify one's approval by hammering on the table or stamping on the floor.

knock it off v.[1] [mid-19C+] to stop doing something. [KNOCK OFF v.[1] (1)]

knock it off v.[2] (*also* **knock it cold**) [20C+] to complete or dispose of something easily or quickly. [KNOCK OFF v.[4] (1)]

knock it off v.[3] see KNOCK OFF v.[3] (5).

knock it off v.[4] see KNOCK OFF v.[5] (1).

knock it off! excl. [mid-19C+] stop it! be quiet! shut up! [KNOCK IT OFF v.[1]]

knock it on the head v. [early 19C+] to stop doing something, to finish a task; to bring something to an end. [? the final blow of a hammer that drives in a nail]

knock (it) out v. [1960s+] (*US Black*) **1** to have sexual intercourse. **2** to do anything quickly, with neither style nor concentration.

knock it out (of) the box v. [2000s] (*US Black*) to have sexual intercourse. [? KNOCK DOWN v.[8] + BOX n.[1] (1)]

knockman n. see KNOCKO n.

knock-me n. see KNOCK-ME-SILLY n.

knock-me-down n.[1] [mid-18C–1900s] strong beer or any fiery drink. [var. on KNOCK-'EM-DOWN n.]

knock-me-down n.[2] [mid-19C] something or someone remarkable.

knock-me-down adj. [mid-18C–1920s] violent, aggressive or overpowering.

knock-me-downs n. see KNOCK-'EM-DOWNS n.

knock-me-silly n. (*also* **knock-me**) [20C+] (*Aus.*) a billy (used to boil water). [rhy. sl.]

knocko n. (*also* **knocker, knockman**) [1950s+] (*US Black*) a police officer, esp. a member of the drugs squad. [the knocking at one's door or on one's skull]

knock-off n.[1] (*also* **knocking-off, knock-off time**) [early 19C+] (*orig. US*) **1** time to leave work, the end of the day; the act of ceasing work. **2** a period away from work; a holiday. [KNOCK OFF v.[1] (1)]

knock-off n.[2] **1** [1920s+] (*US Und.*) an underworld killing. **2** [1950s] an act of sexual intercourse. [KNOCK OFF v.[3] (2)/KNOCK OFF v.[3] (5)]

knock-off n.[3] **1** [1930s–60s] (*US drugs*) an arrest. **2** [1930s+] a robbery; thus *on the knock-off*, working as a thief. **3** [1950s] (*US Und.*) a police raid. **4** [1950s+] something that has been stolen or has the potential for theft. [KNOCK OFF v.[5]]

knock-off n.[4] [1960s+] a fake, a copy; used in the fashion trade to describe cheap copies of 'designer' garments, cheap reproductions of antiques etc. [SE knock off; ult. KNOCK OFF v.[4] (1)]

knock-off adj. [1960s+] a cheap version of an originally expensive garment. [SE knock off; ult. KNOCK OFF v.[4] (1)]

knock off v.[1] **1** [mid-17C+] to stop work. **2** [18C+] to die. **3** [late 18C+] to consume, esp. a drink. **4** [early 19C+] to abandon, to cease from. **5** [late 19C+] (*US*) to abstain or give up a habit.

knock off v.[2] **1** [mid-18C–19C] (*orig. US*) to assign to a bidder at auction. **2** [1950s] (*Aus./N.Z.*) to sell, to dispose of. [(1) 20C+ use is SE]

knock off v.[3] **1** [early 19C+] (*US*) to free from work, to stop someone working. **2** [mid-19C+] (*orig. US*) to kill, to murder. **3** [late 19C+] (*N.Z.*) to dismiss from a job. **4** [1920s+] to defeat, to overcome, to destroy. **5** [1930s+] (*orig. US*) (*also* **knock it off**) to seduce, to have sexual intercourse (often commercial, adulterous or purely hedonistic). **6** [1930s+] (*orig. US*) to marry.

knock off v.[4] **1** [early 19C+] to conclude or complete speedily, to do quickly and perfunctorily, esp. in the context of writing. **2** [1920s–40s] (*US*) to acquire money, usu. easily.

knock off v.[5] **1** [1910s+] (*orig. US Und.*) to steal, to burglarize; also as *knock it off*, to break into a premises. **2** [1920s+] (*orig. US police*) to raid, to seize stolen goods or to arrest someone.

knock off a piece v. (*also* **knock off a little**) [1920s+] of a man, to seduce, either a woman or man. [KNOCK OFF v.[3] + PIECE n.[1] (1)]

knock off hen tracks on a rolltop piano v. [1940s] (*US Black*) to use a typewriter to compose a personal letter. [? typewriters were usu. reserved for business use]

knock off one's perch v. (*also* **knock off one's peg/stand**) [mid-19C+] **1** to upset, to displace. **2** to conquer. **3** to kill.

knock off the hooks v. see OFF THE HOOKS phr.[4].

knock one out v. [1990s+] to masturbate (cf. BANG THE BISHOP v.). ['one' is an orgasm]

knock one's can in v. (*also* **knock one's arse in, knock one's end in**) [1910s+] (*Aus.*) to surprise, to worry, to confound, to disconcert.

knock oneself v. see KNOCK v.[1] (4).

knock oneself off v. [1930s+] to kill oneself.

knock oneself out v. [1930s+] (*orig. US*) **1** to have a very enjoyable time, to 'let oneself go', to amaze oneself. **2** to work very hard. **3** to worry.

knock one's nuts out v. [1960s+] (*US*) to make an overwhelming impression, to have a notable effect.

knock one's pipes out v. [1980s] to work oneself to exhaustion.

knock one's wig v. [1940s] (*US Black*) to comb one's hair.

knock on the door, a n. *see* KNOCK AT THE DOOR, a n.

knock on together v. (*also* knock on with) [1950s+] to have an affair.

knockout n.[1] **1** [late 19C+] a person or thing of outstanding quality, attractiveness or excellence. **2** [20C+] a pleasant, gratifying surprise. **3** [20C+] a complete success. **4** [1910s] (*US Und.*) the 'badger game', where a man is blackmailed after being lured into a compromising situation. **5** [1930s–40s] a knockout drug or potion. [KNOCK OUT v.[2]]

knockout n.[2] *see* KNOCK n.[2] (2).

knockout adj. (*orig. US*) **1** [late 19C+] stupefying or liable to cause unconsciousness, orig. of a drug. **2** [20C+] excellent, wonderful, very best. **3** [20C+] very attractive. [KNOCKOUT n.[1]]

knock out v.[1] (*also* bang out) **1** [mid-19C+] to do roughly or quickly, esp. of writing, to create, to make etc. **2** [late 19C+] (*orig. Aus.*) to earn a sum of money, e.g. *knock out £200 per week*; orig. of food, in phr. *knock out tucker*. **3** [late 19C+] to obtain for oneself, e.g. *knock out some sleep*. **4** [20C+] to sell.

knock out v.[2] **1** [late 19C] to make someone bankrupt. **2** [late 19C] to fail an examination candidate. **3** [late 19C–1960s] (*US*) to deprive someone, esp. of money. **4** [late 19C+] to kill someone. **5** [late 19C+] (*orig. US*) to surprise, to overcome or defeat. **6** [late 19C+] (*esp. US Black*) (*also* knock flat) to impress, to overwhelm, to delight. **7** [1930s–40s] (*US Und.*) to arrest. **8** [1940s–70s] to steal, esp. to steal absolutely everything from the place that one is robbing.

knockout adv. [1920s+] completely, utterly. [KNOCKOUT n.[1]]

knock out an apple v. [19C] to father a child. [KNOCK OUT v.[1] (1)]

knockout artist n. [1990s+] a thug.

knockout drops n. **1** [late 19C+] chloral hydrate mixed into a drink to render an innocent victim unconscious. **2** [late 19C+] a soothing linctus, usu. based on laudanum or opium, used to soothe fractious young children. **3** [1900s] in fig. use, something powerful, destructive. **4** [1910s+] (*Aus.*) drugged or adulterated liquor.

knock out of the box v. [late 19C+] (*US*) to defeat, to overcome, to kill. [baseball jargon]

knock out one's link v. [mid-18C] to be very drunk. [? SE *link*, 'a torch...formerly much in use for lighting people along the streets' (*OED*)]

knock-over n. **1** [1920s–30s] (*US Und.*) a police raid. **2** [1920s+] (*US police*) an armed robbery. **3** [1920s+] (*Aus.*) a substantial, if surprising, success. **4** [1970s] (*US*) an easy task. [KNOCK OVER v.[1]]

knock over v.[1] **1** [early 19C+] (*orig. US*) to murder, to kill, orig. animals or birds. **2** [mid-19C; 1970s+] (*US*) to defeat or abuse through violence; to beat up. **3** [1920s] (*US Und.*) to ban. **4** [1920s+] (*orig. US*) to rob or steal, usu. with violence. **5** [1920s+] (*US Und./police*) to arrest. **6** [1920s+] (*US Und./police*) to raid. **7** [1920s+] (*US Und./police*) to get someone into trouble, to punish (a prisoner). **8** [1940s–60s] (*US*) to seduce, to have sexual intercourse. **9** [1940s+] to impress.

knock over v.[2] [mid-19C+] (*US*) to drink, to eat.

knock over a doll v. (*also* knock over the doll) [1950s] (*Aus.*) to take the consequences for an act.

knock persimmons v. *see* RAKE UP THE PERSIMMONS v.

knock rotten v. [1910s+] (*Aus.*) to kill, to stun.

knock round n. [late 19C] a wander, an aimless progress. [KNOCK-AROUND n.]

knock saucepans out of v. (*also* knock smoke out of) (*Aus.*)

1 [late 19C–1900s] to attack aggressively. **2** [1950s] to overcome completely.

knock seven bells out of v. (*also* scare seven bells out of) **1** [mid-19C+] to beat viciously. **2** [1940s+] to terrify. [orig. naut.]

knock shingles in v. (*also* knock the roof in) [1960s+] (*US*) to snore. [the similarity of the noise]

knock shop n. [1950s+] (*Aus.*) a brothel (cf. BANGING-SHOP n.). [var. on KNOCKING-SHOP n. (1)]

knock sideways v. [20C+] to astound, to astonish, to shock profoundly, to overturn. [var. on KNOCK ENDWAYS v.]

knock silly v. (*also* punch silly) [mid-19C+] (*orig US*) to daze or even knock unconscious in a fight; also in fig. use.

knock sky-wise and crooked v. *see* KNOCK ENDWAYS v.

knock slops off v. [1900s] (*Aus.*) to beat thoroughly.

knock smoke out of v. *see* KNOCK SAUCEPANS OUT OF v.

knock someone bandy v. [late 19C+] to astound, to stun with a blow.

knock someone cuckoo v. [1920s] (*US*) **1** to knock someone out. **2** to amaze, to astonish.

knock someone down to v. *see* KNOCK DOWN v.[5].

knock someone down with a feather v. (*also* beat someone down with a feather, knock someone down with a balloon, ...with a sausage roll, ...with a toothpick, ...with half a brick) [mid-18C; mid-19C+] to surprise completely, to astound.

knock someone off the Christmas tree v. [20C+] (*US*) to amaze, to astonish. [ref. to the trad. fairy on the top]

knock someone's balls off v. [1960s+] to astonish, to amaze. [var. on KNOCK SOMEONE'S EYE(S) OUT v.]

knock someone's block off v. (*also* wallop someone's block off) [20C+] to injure someone physically, usu. in the form of a threat, *I'll knock...* [SE *knock* + BLOCK n.[1] (2)]

knock someone's dick in the dirt v. [1970s+] **1** (*US*) to knock down. **2** (*US*) to defeat, to punish. **3** (*US gay*) to share good marijuana with a friend. [DICK n.[4] (1)]

knock someone's eye(s) out v. **1** [late 19C] (*US campus*) to perform one's work well. **2** [20C+] (*US*) of a person, usu. a woman, to be stunningly attractive. **3** [20C+] (*orig. US*) of an object, to delight, to impress.

knock someone's hat off v. [1940s+] to astonish, to amaze.

knock someone sick v. [1900s–20s] to amaze, to astonish.

knock someone's jock off v. (*also* beat someone's jock off) [1950s+] (*US*) to overcome completely. [SE *knock* + JOCK n.[1] (2)]

knock some skin v. [1940s] (*US*) to shake hands.

knock spots off v. (*also* knock spots out of) [mid-19C+] (*orig. US*) to beat thoroughly, to surpass, to excel.

knock stiff v. [mid-19C–1920s] (*US*) **1** to knock unconscious, to shoot. **2** to amaze, to impress. [SE *knock* + STIFF adj.[1] (1)]

knock the ass off v. (*also* knock the arse out of, knock the dick off) [1960s+] (*orig. US*) to thrash severely, to defeat comprehensively. [SE *knock* + ASS n. (2)]

knock the back out of v. [1960s+] used to express a desire to indulge in a sexual act with a member of the opposite sex, e.g. *I'd knock the back out of that!* [KNOCK v.[1] (1) + SE *back*; ult. euph. for FUCK THE ARSE OFF v.]

knock the bottom out of v.[1] [late 19C–1940s] to render invalid, to ruin, to undermine.

knock the bottom out of v.[2] *see* KNOCK THE STUFFING OUT OF v.

knock the corners off v. [20C+] (*N.Z.*) to punish violently.

knock the crap out of v. (*also* beat the crap out of) [1940s+] (*orig. US*) to beat up. [CRAP n.[3] (6)]

knock the dick off v. *see* KNOCK THE ASS OFF v.

knock the dust off the old sombrero v. [20C+] (*US*) to perform oral sex (cf. CLEAN SOMEONE'S PIPE v.).

knock the ears off v. [1930s] (*US*) to beat up comprehensively.

knock the end off v. [late 19C–1920s] to ruin a situation.

knock the filling out of v. see KNOCK THE STUFFING OUT OF v.

knock (the) hell out of v. (also **knock (hell's) blazes out of**) [mid-19C+] (orig. US) to beat severely, to destroy comprehensively.

knock the hindsights out of v. (also **knock the hindsights off**) [19C] (US) to deal a heavy blow to, to beat up, to defeat. [? SE hindsight, the backsight of a rifle]

knock the hound out of v. see HOUND n.[6].

knock the inside out of v. see KNOCK THE STUFFING OUT OF v.

knock the jive out v. [1940s] (US Black) to play the piano. [JIVE n.[1] (3)]

knock the juice out of someone v. see JUICE n.[2] (6).

knock the lard/lining out of v. see KNOCK THE STUFFING OUT OF v.

knock the (living) daylights out of v. see BEAT THE (LIVING) DAYLIGHTS OUT OF v.

knock the lobb v. see KNOCK v.[1] (3).

knock them cold v. (also **knock them dead**) [1920s+] of a performer or performance, to devastate an audience with excellence.

knock them in the aisles v. see LAY THEM IN THE AISLES v.

knock the pad v. [1940s+] (US Black) to have sexual intercourse. [SE knock + PAD n.[2] (1); but note KNOCK v.[1] (1)]

knock the piss out of v. [1970s] to beat up, to assault. [PISS, THE n.]

knock the roof in v. see KNOCK SHINGLES IN v.

knock the socks off v. [mid-19C+] (orig. US) **1** to defeat comprehensively. **2** [1930s+] to cause serious problems for, to overwhelm. **3** [1960s+] (also **blow the socks off**) to astound.

knock the stuffing out of v. (also **knock eleven kinds of stuffing out of, knock the bottom out of, ...filling..., ...inside..., ...lard..., ...lining..., ...wadding..., larrup the lining out of, pound the stuffing out of**) [late 19C+] **1** to beat severely. **2** in fig. use, to destroy. [STUFFING n.[1]]

knock the top off v. (also **knock the head off**) [1980s+] (Aus. prison) to masturbate (cf. BANG THE BISHOP v.).

knock the wadding out of v. see KNOCK THE STUFFING OUT OF v.

knock the wool out of one's head v. [1900s] (N.Z.) to wake up; to think (or make someone else think) clearly.

knock togther v. [1900s] **1** to accumulate, e.g. money. **2** to make, e.g. a meal.

knock under v. **1** [18C–mid-19C] to die. **2** [1900s] (Aus.) to surpass.

knock up v.[1] [17C+] to waken; thus knocker up, one who wakes people up. [knocking on the front or bedroom door]

knock up v.[2] **1** [mid-18C+] to injure, to impair, to wear out, to die, to defeat. **2** [early 19C+] (orig. US) (also **knock**) to impregnate.

knock up v.[3] **1** [early 19C+] to put together spontaneously, to arrange at short notice. **2** [mid-19C+] to earn a living, usu. with a n., e.g. knock up a crust. **3** [late 19C+] to amass.

knock up a cheque v. [late 19C–1940s] (Aus.) to earn money for one's labour. [KNOCK UP v.[3] (2) + SE cheque]

knock-up money n. [1900s–50s] (US Und.) the profit from a crime.

knockwurst n. [1970s+] (US) the penis (cf. BACON n.[1]). [Ger. Knockwurst, a sausage]

knock yourself out! excl. [1940s+] (US) have a good time! [KNOCK OUT v.[2] (6)]

knosh v. see NOSH v.

knot n.[1] [mid-19C+] the swelling at the base of the head of the penis.

knot n.[2] [20C+] (US) the head, esp. one that appears impenetrable by sense. [SE knot, an especially hard mass of wood; later use is US Black]

knot n.[3] [1910s+] (Aus.) a pack; thus carry/hump/push the knot, to travel with a pack, to live as a tramp. [the knot that secures the pack or SWAG n.[1] (9)]

knot n.[4] [1970s+] (US Black) a substantial roll of dollar bills.

K-note n. [1960s] (US) a $1000 bill. [K n.[2] (2)]

knothead n. **1** [1910s+] (US) a mule or stubborn animal. **2** [1920s+] a fool. [SE knot, an imperfection in a piece of wood + -HEAD sfx (1). Such spots are harder than the surrounding wood]

knot-headed adj. (also **knotty-headed**) **1** [1910s+] (US) stupid (cf. AIRHEADED adj.). **2** [1930s] (US Black) having tightly curled hair. [KNOTHEAD n.]

knothole n. [1940s] (US Black) a doughnut.

knotted adj. [1940s] (N.Z.) angry, irritated.

knotty n. see NATTY n.[2].

knotty! excl. [1970s+] (W.I. Rasta) used as a greeting or farewell. [the knotted DREADLOCKS n. that betoken a Rasta-man]

knotty ash n. [1980s+] cash. [rhy. sl.; ult. Knotty Ash, suburb of Liverpool, UK, where comedian Ken Dodd (b.1931) comes from; the ref. is to his problems with taxes]

knotty-headed adj. see KNOT-HEADED adj.

know a devil from a jackdaw v. (also **ken a handsaw from a hog, know a hawk from a handsaw**) [mid-18C–19C] to be fully cognisant of a situation.

know-all n. (also **know-it-all**) [late 19C+] an extremely clever person, esp. one who likes to impress others with their knowledge; often used sarcastically.

know-all adj. (also **know-it-all**) [late 19C+] boastful, self-opinionated. [KNOW-ALL n.]

know a thing or two v. (also **know a thing or six, know a trick or two, see a thing or two, teach someone a thing or two**) [late 18C+] to be aware, to be knowledgeable.

know a trick worth two of that v. [late 16C+] to be cleverer, better informed or more efficient.

know backwards v. [20C+] to know perfectly.

know beans v. (also **know beans when the bag is open/untied**) [mid-19C–1910s] (US) to be well aware, to be very knowledgeable; often in negative, e.g. he doesn't know beans. [abbr. KNOW HOW MANY BEANS MAKE FIVE v.]

know crap from clay v. [1950s] (Aus.) to be astute, not ignorant.

know from nothing v. [1930s+] (US) to be ignorant; usu. as not know from nothing.

know how many beans make five v. [19C+] to be alert, to be aware of facts or information.

know how many go to a dozen v. [late 19C–1900s] to be aware, alert, 'on the ball'.

knowing adj. [late 18C–1900s] stylish, fashionable, i.e. knowing what is in style.

knowing as Kate Mullet phr. [late 19C–1900s] stupid (cf. DUMB AS A BOX OF ROCKS phr.). [Mullet was a murderess, supposedly 'hanged for a fool']

know-it-all see under KNOW-ALL.

know it all v. [late 19C+] to assume one's own perfection and to ignore one's own deficiencies; usu. in phr. he/she knows it all or they know it all.

knowledge box n. **1** [late 18C+] (also **knowledge bag**) the head or the mind. **2** [20C+] (also **knowledge factory, knowledge stash, house of knowledge**) (US) a school. [(1) UK use faded by early 19C but revived in US Black use by 20C+]

know like the back of one's hand v. [1940s+] to know perfectly.

knowmean? phr. see KNOW WHAT I MEAN? phr.[1].

know no more about it than the moon knows about Sunday v. [late 19C] to know nothing whatsoever.

know one's a, b, ab's v. see KNOW ONE'S P'S AND Q'S v.

know one's alphabet v. [mid-19C] to be very aware, to be extremely knowledgeable.

know one's apples/beans *v. see* KNOW ONE'S ONIONS *v.*

know one's book *v.* [late 19C–1900s] **1** to have the correct information; to know what is going on. **2** to make a decision. **3** to see what one can gain.

know one's buttons *v. see* HAVE ALL ONE'S BUTTONS ON *v.*

know one's cucumbers *v. see* KNOW ONE'S GROCERIES *v.*

know one's eggs *v.* [1930s] (*US*) to be intellectually capable. [var. on KNOW ONE'S ONIONS *v.*]

know one's goulash *v.* (*also* **know one's greenpea hash**) [1920s] (*US*) to know one's own business. [var. on KNOW ONE'S ONIONS *v.*]

know one's groceries *v.* (*also* **know one's cucumbers/ vegetables**) [1930s–60s] (*orig. US Black*) to be aware. [var. on KNOW ONE'S ONIONS *v.*]

know one's oil *v.* [1920s] (*US tramp*) to be aware, to know what is going on. [OIL *n.*[2] (3)]

know one's onions *v.* (*also* **know one's apples, …beans, …oats**) [1920s+] (*orig. US*) to be well informed, to be aware.

know one's p's and q's *v.* (*also* **know one's a, b, ab's**) [late 19C+] to be aware of what is going on.

know one's shit *v.* [1990s+] (*US*) to be very competent. [SE *know* + SHIT *n.*[4]]

know one's stuff *v.* (*also* **know one's smoke**) [1910s+] to be accomplished in one's own particular pursuit.

know one's sweet potatoes *v.* [1920s] (*US*) to be knowledgeable, fully aware. [var. on KNOW ONE'S ONIONS *v.*]

know one's vegetables *v. see* KNOW ONE'S GROCERIES *v.*

know someone's number *v. see* HAVE SOMEONE'S NUMBER *v.*

know the dish *v.* [1980s+] (*US Black*) to be aware of the, usu. embarrassing, truth. [DISH *n.*[2] (2)]

know the ins and outs of a duck's bum *v.* (*also* **know the ins and outs of a cat's arsehole, …a nag's arse**) [20C+] to know all the details; thus *want to know the ins and outs…*, to be very inquisitive.

know the length of someone's foot *v. see* GET THE LENGTH OF SOMEONE'S FOOT *v.*

know the pisspot from the handle *v.* [1990s+] (*US tramp*) to be wise.

know the ropes *v.* [19C+] to understand how to do a task. [sailing imagery]

know the score *v.* [1930s+] to understand a situation, to know what is going on; often in negative. [sporting imagery]

know the time of day *v. see* KNOW WHAT TIME (OF DAY) IT IS *v.*

know the words and music *v.* [1940s+] (*gay*) to understand and partake in the gay sub-culture.

know two of that *v.* [late 19C+] to know something much better.

know what day it is *v. see* KNOW WHAT TIME (OF DAY) IT IS *v.*

know what goes *v. see* KNOW WHAT'S WHAT *v.*

know what I mean? *phr.*[1] (*also* **knowmean? know what I'm saying? na mean?**) [1960s+] an almost transparent excl., used as much for punctuation as for explication.

know what I mean? *phr.*[2] *see* NUDGE, NUDGE, WINK, WINK, KNOW WHAT I MEAN, SAY NO MORE *phr.*

know what I mean, Vern? *phr.* [1980s+] (*US campus*) do you understand? [ref. to a nationwide advertising campaign]

know what I'm saying? *phr. see* KNOW WHAT I MEAN? *phr.*[1].

know what o'clock it is/know what's o'clock *v. see* KNOW WHAT TIME (OF DAY) IT IS *v.*

know what's what *v.* (*also* **know what goes, understand what's what**) [early 16C+] to be aware of the facts, to be abreast of a situation.

know what time (of day) it is *v.* (*also* **know the time of day, know what day it is, …what o'clock it is, …what's o'clock**) [early 19C+] to be aware, to know what is going on; often in negative.

know where the bodies are buried *v.* [20C+] to have special

knowledge of a situation, esp. of its less appealing side, giving one power over those who nominally control it. [the threat, rather than the use, of blackmail]

Knuck *n. see* CANUCK *n.*

knuck *n.*[1] **1** [early 19C–1940s] (*also* **nuck**) a pickpocket or thief. **2** [1960s] (*US Black*) a fist fight. [SE *knuckle/knuckles*]

knuck *n.*[2] *see* KNUCKS *n.*

knuck *v.* [mid-19C–1900s] to pick pockets. [abbr. KNUCKLE *v.*[1]]

knucka *n.* [1990s+] (*orig. US Black/teen*) a friend. [? someone you rap knuckles with, plus note MUCKER *n.*[4]]

knuck game *n.* [1960s+] (*US Black*) fist-fighting. [abbr. SE *knuckles*]

knuckle *n.*[1] [late 18C–mid-19C] a pickpocket; thus *go on the knuckle*, to work as a pickpocket. [KNUCKLE *v.*[1]]

knuckle *n.*[2] [1930s+] a fight, violence; thus *go the knuckle(s)*, to fight; *knuckle-boy*, a fighter. [KNUCKLE *v.*[2]]

knuckle *n.*[3] [1990s+] (*US drugs*) a wrap of heroin.

knuckle *v.*[1] [late 18C–mid-19C] to steal, to pick pockets 'after the approved method' (Hotten, 1859); thus *knuckle a wipe*, to steal a handkerchief. [SE *knuckle*; 'the approved method,' according to Vaux, implies the robbery of notes and cash rather than less valuable items]

knuckle *v.*[2] (*also* **knuck, knuckle up**) [mid-19C+] to hit, to fight.

knuckle *v.*[3] *see* KNUCKLE (TO) *v.*

knuckle-boy *n. see* KNUCKLE *n.*[2].

knuckleburger *n.* [1970s+] (*US*) a punch in the mouth. [SE *knuckle* + (*ham*)*burger*; a play on KNUCKLE SANDWICH *n.*]

knuckle-buster *n.* [1940s–60s] (*US*) a crescent wrench (tool). [the hazard of its use]

knuckle-dabs *n.* (*also* **knuckle-confounders**) [late 18C–early 19C] **1** handcuffs. **2** the fists.

knuckle-dragger *n.* [1980s+] **1** a fool, a peasant. **2** a thug; as adj., *knuckle-dragging*, violent.

knuckleduster *n.* **1** [mid–late 19C] a metal instrument, trad. brass, that covers the knuckles, thus strengthening them when delivering a blow. **2** [late 19C+] a large, gaudy, flashy ring. [(1) SE f. 1900]

knucklehead *n.* [1930s+] (*orig. US*) a term of abuse, a description for any foolish, stupid, slow person. [knuckles pressed to the forehead imply the intensity of thought for one who is not overly bright]

knuckleheaded *adj.* (*also* **knucklehead**) [1930s+] (*orig. US*) stupid (cf. AIRHEADED *adj.*). [KNUCKLEHEAD *n.*]

knuckle junction *n.* [1970s+] (*US*) a fist-fight.

knuckleknob *n.* [1950s+] (*US*) a stupid person. [SE *knuckle* + KNOB *n.*[1]]

knuckler *n.* (*also* **knucker, knucksman**) [late 18C–19C] a pickpocket. [KNUCKLE *v.*[1]]

knuckles *n.*[1] [late 18C–early 19C] (*UK Und.*) the top rank of pickpockets. [KNUCKLE *n.*[1]]

knuckles *n.*[2] [mid-19C+] (*US*) a knuckleduster, 'brass knuckles'. [abbr. KNUCKLEDUSTER *n.* (1)]

knuckle sandwich *n.* (*also* **fist sandwich**) [1950s+] (*orig. US*) a blow from a fist, esp. to the mouth.

knuckle shuffle *n.* [1990s+] masturbation.

knuckle soup *n.* [mid-19C] (*US*) a punch in the mouth.

knuckle (to) *v.* [mid-18C–1950s] (*US*) to give in, to confess, to surrender, to accept something one dislikes but is not strong enough to fight. [abbr./var. on SE *knuckle under*]

knuckle-up *n.* [1940s+] (*N.Z.*) a fist fight. [var. on PUNCH-UP *n.*]

knuckle up *v.* [1960s+] (*US Black teen*) to prepare to fight, by closing and raising one's fists; to fight.

knuckling cove *n.* [early 19C] a pickpocket. [KNUCKLE *v.*[1] + COVE *n.* (1)]

knucks *n.* **1** [mid-19C–1950s] (*US*) the knuckles. **2** [late 19C+]

(*orig. US*) (*also* **nucks**) brass knuckles, worn over the fist to ensure victory in a fist fight; rarely in sing. [abbr. (1) SE *knuckle*; (2) KNUCKLEDUSTER n. (1)]

knuller *n.* (*also* **gumbler**) **1** [mid-19C] a chimney sweep who goes from house to house offering his services. **2** [mid-19C–1900s] a clergyman. [OE *cynllan*, to knell; the old-fashioned sweep rang a bell to announce his progress along a street]

knut *n.* (*also* **nut**) [1910s–20s] a dandy, a very well-dressed, fashionable (if not overly intelligent) young man.

k.o. *n.* (*also* **kayo**) (*orig. US*) **1** [1910s+] a *knockout.* **2** [1910s+] in fig. use, death. [abbr.]

k.o. *adj.* (*also* **kayo**) [1910s+] (*US*) all right, in order. [joc. reversal of OK adj.]

k.o. *v.*[1] (*also* **kayo, kyo**) [20C+] to knock out, lit. or fig. [abbr. SE]

k.o. *v.*[2] [1970s+] (*US campus*) to die. [KICK OFF v.[1] (1)]

koala *n.* (*Aus.*) **1** [1940s+] a diplomat, who is immune from Aus. law. **2** [1970s+] an unappreciative man. [(1) the koala is an officially protected creature; (2) a pun on the phr. he 'eats, roots/ROOT n.[3] and leaves']

koboko *n. see* BOKO n.

kochee *n. see* KOOTCH n.

kochonni *n.* [20C+] (*W.I., St Lu./Dmnca*) a piece of junk, anything worthless or useless. [Fr. *cochon*, a pig; note synon. Yid. *chaserei*, lit. 'pig things']

kodak *n.* [late 19C+] **1** a camera. **2** a photograph. [for ety. *see* next]

kodak *v.* **1** [late 19C+] to take visual note. **2** [20C+] (*US*) to pose, as in a photograph. [*Kodak*, a popular brand of camera]

Kodak moment *n.* [1980s+] (*US campus*) the right time to take a photograph. [an advertising campaign]

k.o.'ed *adj.* [1960s–70s] (*US*) very drunk or intoxicated by drugs (cf. ANNIHILATED adj.). [KNOCKED OUT adj. (4)]

koelie *n. see* COOLIE n.[1].

koffie-moffie *n.* [1980s+] (*S.Afr.*) a male flight attendant. [Afk. *koffie*, coffee + MOFFIE n.]

Kofifi *n.* [1950s] (*S.Afr. township*) Sophiatown, a Black residential area of Johannesburg, razed during the 1950s after the forcible removal of its inhabitants. [? Sotho (*le*)*fifi*, darkness, (*se*)*fifi*, corpse or (*bo*)*fifi*, mourning]

Kohen *n. see* COHEN n.

kojak *v.* [1970s+] (*US teen*) to find a parking space in an area where such discoveries are at best rare. [US TV show *Kojak* (1973–7), whose eponymous hero possessed this facility]

Kojak's rollneck *n.* (*also* **Kojak's moneybox**) [1990s+] the glans or 'bell-end' of the penis. [the TV detective *Kojak*, played by bald actor Telly Savalas (1925–94), often sported such clothing]

Kojak with a Kodak *n.* [1970s+] (*US*) a policeman manning a radar speed trap. [the TV show *Kojak* + the make of camera]

kojo *n.* [20C+] (*W.I.*) a tough and violent person, usu. from a rural area. [Fante *Kodwo*, a male born on a Monday]

koki *n.* (*also* **cokey**) [1990s+] (*S.Afr.*) a fibre-tipped colouring pen. [proprietary name *Koki*]

koko *n. see* COCO n. (2).

kokomo *n.* **1** [1930s–50s] (*US drugs*) a cocaine user. **2** [1980s+] (*drugs*) crack cocaine (cf. BASE n.). [play on COKE n.[1] (1)]

koks *n. see* KANGSE n.

kombo *n. see* COMBO n.[2].

komoppo *n.* [1940s] an unattractive woman. [ety. unknown]

komra *n. see* CAMBRA n.

kong *n.* [1930s+] (*US Black*) home-distilled whisky. [the film *King Kong* (1933); thus denoting great strength]

kongkongsa *adj.* [20C+] (*W.I.*) deceitful, hypocritical, biased. [Twi *kongkongsa*, double-dealing, duplicity, betrayal]

kongo *n. see* CONGO n.[1].

koniack *n. see* CONEY n.

koniacker *n.* (*also* **coniacker, coneyacker**) [early 19C–1930s] (*US*) a counterfeiter. [CONEY n.; F&H suggest 'obviously, a play upon COIN, money and HACK, to mutilate']

konk *see also under* CONK and its combs.

konks *n. see* KANGSE n.

konoblin rig *n.* [early 19C] (*UK Und.*) stealing large lumps of coal from coalsheds. [RIG n.[2] (2)]

kooch *n. see* KOOTCH n.

kook *n.* (*also* **cook, kuke**) **1** [1950s+] (*US*) a crazy person, an eccentric, albeit an acceptable one. **2** [1960s] (*US*) a spy. **3** [1960s–70s] (*US/S.Afr.*) a novice. **4** [1960s+] (*orig. US campus*) an annoying or mistaken person. [? CUCKOO n.[1] (2) but popularized following the late 1950s US TV show *77 Sunset Strip* in which the supposedly (by 1958 standards) 'eccentric' character Gerald Lloyd Kookson III ('Kookie'), played by actor Edd Byrnes, became a teenage idol]

kooka *n.* [20C+] (*Aus.*) a *kookaburra.* [abbr.]

kookaboo *n.* (*also* **cuckaboo**) [1950s+] (*US*) a crazy person. [? SE *kookaburra*, the Aus. 'laughing' bird/cuckoo]

kooked-up *adj.* [1950s+] (*US*) crazy, eccentric. [KOOK UP v.]

kookie house *n. see* KOOKY HOUSE n.

koo-koo *adj. see* CUCKOO adj.

kook up *v.* [1950s+] to make eccentric, bizarre. [KOOKY adj.]

kooky *adj.* [1950s+] (*orig. US*) **1** odd, eccentric (often with overtones of charm). **2** infatuated with. [KOOK n.]

kooky house *n.* (*also* **kookie house**) [1950s+] (*US*) a psychiatric institution. [KOOKY adj. + SE *house*]

kool *v.* [mid–late 19C] to look (at). [backsl.]

kool esilop *phr.* [mid–late 19C] (*UK Und.*) a warning cry of 'look police'. [KOOL v. + ESCLOP n.]

kools *n.* [1980s+] (*drugs*) phencyclidine (cf. ACE n.[4]). [play on cigarette brandname *Kool*]

kool toul! *excl.* [mid–19C] look out! [backsl.]

koon *n. see* COON n. (4).

koopa *n.* [2000s] (*US Black*) a close friend. [ety. unknown]

koosh *n. see* CUSH n.[1] (1).

koota *n. see* COOTIE n.[1].

kootch *n.* (*also* **kochee, kooch**) **1** [1920s–70s] (*US*) a form of highly suggestive belly-dance, usu. performed at carnivals; thus *kootcher*, a dancer. **2** [1970s+] the vagina. **3** [1970s+] (*US gay*) the anus. [HOOTCHY-KOOTCHY n.]

kootee *n.* [mid–19C] (*Anglo-Ind.*) a house. [Hind. *kot*, a citadel]

kooti/kootie *n. see* COOTIE n.[1].

kopasetic/kopasette *adj. see* COPACETIC adj.

kopat *v.* [1990s+] (*US teen*) to understand. [Russian *kopat*, to dig (a hole), thus DIG v.[5]; coined by Anthony Burgess in *A Clockwork Orange* (1962)]

kopec *n.* (*also* **kopek**) [late 19C–1930s] (*US*) a dollar; thus money.

kopgee *n.* (*also* **kopje, kop-jee**) [late 19C–1900s] the head. [Du. *kopje*, a mound or low hill]

kopjie-walloper *n.* [late 19C] (*S.Afr.*) a diamond-buyer (often Jewish) who traded directly with miners on their claims; this practice was outlawed by the Diamond Trade Act (1882). [Du. *kopje*, a hill + SE *wallop*, to thrash]

koreegro *n.* [2000s] (*US Black*) an Asian person pretending to be a GANGSTA n. (2). [SE *Korea* + *negro*]

kosh *n. see* COSH n.

kosh *adj.* [late 19C+] honest, legitimate, above-board. [abbr. KOSHER adj.[1] (1)]

kosh *v. see* COSH v.

koshe *adj.* [1980s+] (*US campus*) acceptable, satisfactory, as required. [Yid. *kosher*, according to Jewish dietary laws; pron. rhymes with 'gauche']

kosher *adj.*[1] **1** [late 19C+] honest, legitimate, above-board. **2** [1930s] (*US prison*) not guilty. **3** [1930s+] (*US*) Jewish. **4** [1930s+] clean, pure. **5** [1970s+] safe; thus *unkosher*, dangerous, unsafe. **6** [1970s+] satisfactory, good. [fig. uses of Yid. *kosher*, acceptable according to the Jewish dietary laws; ult. Heb. *kāshēr*]

kosher *adj.*[2] *see* KOSHER (STYLE) adj.

kosher *v.* [1960s] to smuggle.

kosher delicatessen *n.* [1960s+] (*gay*) Israel. [everyone one eats/EAT *v.*[3] (1) will be KOSHER (STYLE) *adj.*]

kosher dill *n.* [1960s+] (*gay*) a circumcised penis (cf. CLIPDICK n.). [KOSHER (STYLE) *adj.*]

kosher nosher *n.* [1970s+] (*US gay*) a coterie of gay Jewish men. [pun on *Cosa Nostra* + Yid. *kosher*, religiously acceptable to Jews + Yid. *nosher*, an eater]

kosher (style) *adj.* [1960s+] (*US gay*) circumcised. [the role of ritual circumcision in Judaism]

kotch *v. see* COTCH *v.*[1].

kote-si-kote-la *n. see* COTE-SI-COTE-LA n.

kotonk *n. see* KATONK n.

kouchie *n. see* CUTCHIE n.

kowabunga! *excl. see* COWABUNGA! excl.

kowtow chow *n.* [1970s+] (*US gay*) the act of performing fellatio while kneeling in front of one's partner (cf. BASKET LUNCH n.). [SE *kowtow*, lit. 'knock the head', 'the Chinese custom of touching the ground with the forehead in the act of prostrating oneself, as an expression of extreme respect, submission, or worship' (*OED*) + CHOW n.[1]]

K.P. *n.* [1910s+] (*US milit.*) kitchen fatigues. [kitchen *parade*]

k.p. *n.* [1940s+] (*Aus.*) a prostitute. [abbr. police jargon *known prostitute*]

kraak *v.* [1950s+] (*S.Afr.*) to speed, to go fast, esp. on a motorcycle. [Afk. phr. *gaan dat dit so kraak*, 'go like the blazes']

krack *v. see* CRACK *v.*[3] (3).

krag *n.* [1950s+] (*S.Afr.*) energy, strength, 'oomph'. [Du. *kracht*, power, strength]

krappy *adj. see* CRAPPY adj. (3).

kratz (up) *v.* [1960s] (*US Und.*) to make a mess, to blunder. [ety. unknown; ? Ger./Yid.]

kraut *n.* **1** [mid-19C+] (*orig. US*) a derog. name for a German. **2** [1940s+] the German language. [*Sauerkraut*, a form of pickled, shredded cabbage, supposedly loved by the nation]

kraut *adj.* [1940s+] pertaining to Germany or things German. [KRAUT n.]

kraut-eater *n.* [mid-19C–1930s] (*US*) a derog. term for a German. [*Sauerkraut*, a form of pickled, shredded cabbage, supposedly loved by the nation + sfx *-eater*]

krauthead *n.* (*also* **kraut stomper**) [1910s+] (*US*) a derog. term for a German. [*Sauerkraut*, a form of pickled, shredded cabbage, supposedly loved by the nation + -HEAD sfx (2); SE *stomper*]

krautland *n.* [1950s+] (*orig. US*) a derog. name for Germany. [KRAUT n. (1) + SE *land*]

krautrock *n.* [1970s+] a style of music, rock with electronic influences, originating in Germay in the 1970s. [KRAUT n. + SE *rock*]

kraut stomper *n. see* KRAUTHEAD n.

krazin *n.* [1960s+] (*US campus*) a load of utter rubbish, absolute nonsense. [ety. unknown; ? play on SE *crazy*]

Kremlin *n.* [1980s+] (*UK Und.*) New Scotland Yard.

kreskin *v.* [1970s+] (*US teen*) to prophesy, to work out intuitively, to foresee. [US TV magician *Kreskin*]

krex *v.* [1930s+] (*US*) to grumble, to fret, to complain. [ety. unknown]

kridel *n.* [1990s+] (*W.I.*) an unattractive woman.

kris' *adj. see* CRIS' adj.

krispy kracker *n. see* CRISPY (CRITTER) n.

krissy *n.* (*also* **kroes, kroesie**) [1940s+] (*S.Afr.*) frizzy hair. [Afk. *kroes*, frizzy]

kroeskop *n.* [1910s+] (*S.Afr.*) one who has frizzy or tightly curled hair, thus a derog. term for Africans in general. [Afk. *kroes*, frizzy + *kop*, head]

kronk *n. see* CRONK n. (1).

krop *n.* [mid–late 19C] pork. [backsl.]

krud *n. see* CRUD n.[1].

kruger-spoof *n.* [late 19C] lying. [the contemporary antipathy to the Boers and their leader Paul *Kruger* (1825–1904) + SPOOF n.[1]]

krunk *n.* [1990s+] (*US*) an all-purpose euph. used in place of an obscenity. [KRUNK v.]

krunk *adj.* [2000s] (*US teen*) wild, uninhibited. [KRUNK v.]

krunk *v.* [1990s+] **1** a euph. for FUCK *v.*[1]. **2** a euph. for FUCK *v.*[2]. **3** to trek, to travel far to somewhere. [joc. use of SE *crunch*]

krunked-up *adj.* [1990s+] **1** a euph. for FUCKED UP adj. (1). **2** a euph. for FUCKED UP adj. (3). [KRUNK v.]

krunking *adj.* [1990s+] a euph. for FUCKING adj. [KRUNK v.]

kryptonite *n.* [2000s] a website. [rhy. sl.; ult. SE *kryptonite*, the mineral that weakens even Superman's powers]

kubber *n.* (*also* **khabbar, khubber**) [mid-19C–1900s] (*Anglo-Ind.*) news. [Hind. *khabar*, news; esp. news of local game suitable for hunting]

ku bomvu *excl.* (*also* **kumbomvu!**) [1970s+] (*S.Afr.*) a warning shout that indicates the presence or proximity of police; usu. used by illicit liquor makers. [Nguni *ku bomvu*, it is red, thus 'red alert']

kuf *n.* [1990s+] (*UK drugs*) cocaine. [ety. unknown]

kuff *n.* [1970s–80s] (*UK Black*) a blow, lit. or fig. [SE *cuff*]

kuff *v.* [1970s–80s] (*UK Black*) to hit, to smash. [KUFF n.]

kuffed up *adj.* [1990s+] (*UK drugs*) experiencing the effects of (crack) cocaine. [KUF n.]

kugel *n.* [1960s+] (*S.Afr.*) the daughter of wealthy parents, whose main interest is her wardrobe, appearance, boyfriend (as an acquisition not a person) and the expenditure of money. Such girls, as the ety. implies, are Jewish; while Black and Boer versions are *ebony-kugel* and *boere-kugel* respectively; thus *kugelese*, the jargon spoken between such young women. [Yid. *kugel*, a sweet or savoury casserole or pudding]

kuh *v.* [1990s+] (*W.I.*) to look at.

kuka *n.* (*also* **kungse**) [20C+] (*W.I.*) a piece of excrement. [var. on CACA n. (1)]

kuke *n. see* KOOK n.

kulu-kulu *adj.* [1990s+] (*W.I.*) abundant, plenty.

kumbomvu! *excl. see* KU BOMVU! excl.

kumquat *n.* [1980s+] (*US*) a young woman. [equation of the fruit with femininity]

kung fu fighter *n.* [2000s] a lighter. [rhy. sl.]

kungse *n. see* KUKA n.

kunker *n. see* CUNKER n.

kunumunu *n.* [20C+] (*W.I.*) a stupid man, esp. one who is controlled by a woman, an imbecile. [Yoruba *kunun*, bashful, lacking in self-confidence]

kuri *n.* [20C+] (*N.Z.*) **1** a mongrel, a badly-behaved dog. **2** a second-rate racehorse. **3** a contemptible, unpopular person. [Maori *kuri*, a dog]

kurl-the-mo *see under* CURL-THE-MO.

kurve *n.* (*also* **kurva**) [late 19C+] a prostitute (cf. JAMETTE n.). [Yid. *kurveh*, a prostitute; ult. Heb. *kurve*, a strange woman who approaches too close]

kush *n.*[1] *see* CUSH n.[1] (1).

kush *n.*[2] *see* CUSH n.[3].

kutcha *adj. see* CUTCHA adj.

kuter *n. see* CUTER n.[2].

kuti *n. see* COOTIE n.[1].

kuzat *n.* [1960s–70s] (*S.Afr. township*) money. [ety. unknown]

kvell *v.* [1960s+] to boast, to feel proud or happy, to gloat, to enjoy oneself. [Yid.; ult. Ger. *quellen*, to gush, to swell]

kvetch *n.* [1950s+] a nag, a whiner, a complainer. [KVETCH v.]

kvetch *v.* [1950s+] (*orig. US*) to complain, to delay, to nag. [Yid. *kvetsh*; ult. Ger. *quetschen*, to squeeze, to press]

kvetchy *adj.* [1950s+] irritable, whiny. [KVETCH v.]

kwaal *n.* [1960s+] (*S.Afr.*) an illness, a complaint. [Afk. *kwaal*, a complaint]

kwan *n.* [2000s] (*US Black*) respect.

Kwang *n.* [1910s] (*Aus.*) a generic term for any Chinese person (cf. AH CABBAGE n.).

kway *n.* [1940s+] (*Aus.*) **1** a general thief, with no real speciality. **2** a man who lives on money taken from a procurer. [? SE *take away*]

kwela-kwela *n.* (*S.Afr. Black*) **1** [1950s+] a police or prison wagon. **2** [1980s+] a minibus taxi. [the shouts of Nguni *kwela! kwela!* get on! get on!; ult. Nguni *kwela*, climb in/on]

kwy *n.* [late 19C–1900s] death. [pron. of Lat. *quietus*, death]

K.Y. *n.* [1960s+] (*US drugs*) the Federal Narcotics Hospital, Lexington, Kentucky. [abbr.]

kyber *n. see* KHYBER (PASS) n.

kybo *n.* (*also* **kibo**) [1970s] (*US*) a privy. [KHYBER (PASS) n.]

kybosh *see also under* KIBOSH.

kybosh *n. see* KYE n.

kyd *n. see* KID n.[1] (4).

ky'daar *n.* (*also* **k'daar**) [1980s+] (*S.Afr.*) a tourist. [Afk. *kyk daar*, look there]

kye *n.* (*also* **kibosh**, **kybosh**) [mid-19C+] **1** shilling and 6 pence. [ety. unknown; E.P. suggests Yid. *kye*, 18; but not cited in Rosen]

kyfer *n.* (*also* **kaifa, keifer, khyfer, kife, kifer, kypher**) **1** [mid-19C+] the vagina. **2** [late 19C+] women regarded as sex objects; thus *kyfer-mashing*, pursuing women; *bit of kyfer*, a woman, a 'bit of skirt'; *have a bit of keifer*, of a man, to have sexual intercourse; by ext. effeminate male homosexuals. **3** money. **4** (*US*) a crooked lawyer. [Arabic *kaif*, absolute enjoyment, perfect contentment, thus 'that which pleases one', one's delight + *keyif*, 'the amiable beauty of a fair woman'; the word is the root of KIF n., a type of hashish, and also meant the pleasure engendered by cannabis]

kyke *n. see* KIKE n.

kylie *n.* [1940s+] (*Aus.*) the small piece of wood used for tossing the coins in the game of two-up.

kynchen co *n. see* KINCHIN COVE n. (1).

kynchin lay *n. see* KINCHIN LAY n.

kyo *v. see* K.O. v.[1].

kyoodle *v. see* KIYOODLE n.

kype *v. see* KIPE v.

kypher *v.* (*also* **khyfer**) [late 19C–1900s] to dress one's hair. [Fr. *coiffeur* OR KYFER n. (2)]

kypsey *n.*[1] *see* KIPSIE n.[1] (1).

kypsey *n.*[2] *see* KIPSIE n.[2].

kyuter *n. see* CUTER n.[2].

L

L *n.*[1] [mid-19C] (*US*) a $50 banknote (cf. C n.[1]). [Roman numeral *L*, 50]

L *n.*[2] [late 19C; 2000s] (*US prison*) a life sentence. [abbr.]

L *n.*[3] (*also* **el**) **1** [1960s+] (*US drugs*) LSD (cf. A n.[3]). **2** [1990s+] marijuana. [abbr.; (2) LOC n.[1]]

L *n.*[4] *see* EL n.

L.A. *n.* [20C+] (*orig. US*) *L*os *A*ngeles. [abbr.; latterly SE]

l.a. *n.* [1990s+] (*drugs*) *l*ong-*a*cting amphetamine (cf. A n.[2]). [abbr.]

la *n. see* LAH n.

la *adj.* [1960s] (*US gay*) effeminate. [? abbr. LA-DI-DAH adj. (2)]

la! *excl. see* LAWK(S)! excl.

laa-dee-laa/la-dee-da *adj. see* LA-DI-DAH adj.

laad-mi-don *n.* [1940s+] (*W.I.*) **1** the poorhouse, the almshouse. **2** a tuberculosis sanatorium. [lit. 'Lord, me done (for)']

laaitie *n. see* LIGHTIE n.

laama *n.* [1940s+] (*W.I.*) clothing worn for celebrations and other special occasions. [lit. 'Lord! Ma'am', the expression uttered on seeing such finery]

laanie *n.* (*also* **lahnee, lani, lanie, larney**) [1970s+] (*S.Afr.*) **1** a boss, an employer. **2** a White person, a rich person. [ety. unknown, but ? Fr. *l'orné*, the ornate one, or Malay/Hind. *rani*, a queen]

laanie *adj.* (*also* **lahnee, lani, lanie, larney**) [1970s+] (*S.Afr.*) **1** showy, arrogant. **2** moneyed. **3** intellectually sophisticated. [LAANIE n.]

lab *n.* **1** [late 19C+] a *lab*oratory. **2** [1950s+] (*orig. Can./US*) a *Lab*rador dog. [abbr.]

laba *n.* (*also* **laba-laba, labba, labba-labba**) [1950s+] (*W.I.*) a chatterbox, a gossip, a talkative person. [BLAB v.; BLABBER n.]

laba-laba *adj.* (*also* **labba-labba**) [1980s] (*UK Black*) verbose, effusive. [LABA-LABA v.]

laba-laba *v.* (*also* **labba-labba**) [1960s] (*W.I.*) to chatter, to gossip, to betray secrets. [LABA n.]

labber-mouth *n.* [20C+] (*W.I.*) a chatterer, a talker. [LABA n. + SE *mouth*; note BLABBERMOUTH n.]

labdick *n.* [20C+] (*Scot.*) a policeman. [abbr. *L*othian *and B*orders Constabulary, and presumably a link to DICK n.[6] (2)]

label *n.* [1910s–50s] (*US*) a person's name.

labes *n.* [1980s+] the labia maiora; also in sing. [abbr.]

lab hound *n.* [1970s+] (*US*) a person who frequently volunteers to be used in psychology experiments. [SE *lab*(*oratory*) + HOUND sfx]

labonza *n.* (*also* **labonz**) (*US*) **1** [1930s+] the pit of the stomach. **2** [1950s+] the buttocks. [? Ital. *la pancia*, the paunch]

labor skate *n.* [1930s–60s] (*US*) a corrupt union official. [SAmE *labor* + SKATE n.]

labour, the *n.* [1920s+] the labour exchange, the employment exchange, the job centre.

labour gone in Maxwell Pond *phr. see* MONEY GONE IN MAXWELL POND phr.

labour leather *v.* [late 19C–1900s] to have sexual intercourse. [SE + LEATHER n.[2] (3)]

labret *n.* [1990s+] in body piercing, a stud through the bottom lip. [SE *labret*, an ornament inserted in the lip]

labrick *n.* (*also* **laverick**) [late 19C–1910s] (*US*) an idiot. [? dial. *laverick*, a lark or a hare]

labrish *n.* [1940s–60s] (*W.I.*) gossip, chatter. [BLAB v.]

labrish *adj.* [1940s–60s] (*W.I.*) talkative, gossipy. [LABRISH n.]

labrish *v.* [1940s–60s] (*W.I.*) to tell tales, to gossip. [LABRISH n.]

labrisher *n.* [1940s–60s] (*W.I.*) a chatterer, a telltale. [LABRISH v.]

lab wretch *n.* [1980s+] (*US*) a person who undertakes unpleasant laboratory tasks. [LAB n. (1) + SE *wretch*]

lac *n.*[1] (*also* **lack, lahk**) [mid-19C] (*Anglo-Ind.*) very many, a great deal; often in pl. [Hind. *lakh*, 100,000 rupees]

lac *n.*[2] (*also* **llac**) [1980s+] (*US Black*) a Cadi*llac*. [abbr.]

lacatan *n.* [1950s] (*W.I.*) a short, stoutish person. [SE *lacatan*, a type of small banana]

lace *n.* [1960s+] (*US gay*) the foreskin; thus LACE QUEEN n. [abbr. LACE CURTAIN n.[2]]

lace *v.* **1** [late 17C+] to beat; thus *lace someone's jacket*, to beat up, to thrash. **2** [1970s] (*US*) to swindle. **3** [1980s+] to shoot. [SE *lace*, to set upon with a whip or lash]

lace curtain *n.*[1] [1930s+] beer, orig. spec. Burton's beer. [rhy. sl.]

lace curtain *n.*[2] (*also* **lace curtains**) [1940s+] (*gay*) a (long) foreskin.

lace-curtain Irish *n.* [1920s+] (*US*) genteel, petit-bourgeois Irish-Americans. [they adorn their windows with such items]

lace curtains *n.*[1] (*also* **chin curtains**) [1900s–30s] (*US*) a beard.

lace curtains *n.*[2] *see* LACE CURTAIN n.[2].

laced *adj.* **1** [late 17C–early 18C] of coffee, sugared. **2** [late 17C–19C] of a drink, mixed or combined with something. **3** [1970s+] of a drug, mixed or combined with something. **4** [1980s+] (*US*) drunk, intoxicated by a drug. **5** [2000s] of music, mixed. [SE *laced*, of a plant, entwined; (2) SE in 20C+; (4) one's blood is *laced* with alcohol]

laced (by the neck) *adj.* **1** [1900s] (*US*) dressed up and bejewelled. **2** [1970s+] (*US Black*) extremely sophisticated. [image of lace-ornamented garments]

laced mutton *n.* **1** [late 16C–mid-19C] a prostitute (cf. BANGTAIL n.[1]; BIT OF MUTTON n.). **2** [early 19C] a woman dressed to appear younger than her years. [SE *lace* + MUTTON n.[1] (1); the lacing is that of stays or corsets, embellishing a young, or disguising an ageing, figure. Poss. a pun on the culinary term 'lacing' (making incisions into) a duck or chicken's breast, but this meaning is slightly later]

lace into *v.* [early 19C+] to attack, to beat, to thrash; also in fig. use. [ext. of LACE v. (1)]

lace queen *n.* [1980s] (*US gay*) a homosexual who prefers uncircumcised partners. [LACE n. + QUEEN n.[2] (1)/QUEEN sfx (2)]

lace someone's jacket *v. see* LACE v. (1).

lacing n. **1** [late 17C+] a judicial flogging, a beating. **2** [1940s+] a verbal attack, criticism. [SE *lace*, to whip; LACE v. (1)]

lack n.[1] [1990s+] (*Irish*) a girlfriend. [abbr. SE *lackey*]

lack n.[2] *see* LAC n.[1].

lackanooky n. (*also* **lakanuki**) [1940s+] (*US*) ill-health caused by lack of sexual activity. [the re-spelling of a Polynesian word + play on SE *lack of* + NOOKIE n. (1)]

lackey-dog n. [1940s+] (*W.I.*) a skulking hanger-on. [ext. of SE *lackey*]

lackin n. (*also* **laken, lakin**) [mid–late 19C] a wife. [ety. unknown]

la cosa n. [1980s+] (*US drugs*) heroin. [Sp. *la cosa*, the thing]

lacy-pants n. [1940s+] (*US*) a flashily dressed person.

Lad, the n. (*also* **bad lad**) [20C+] (*Irish*) cancer. [euph.]

lad n.[1] [20C+] (*Irish*) **1** any inanimate object. **2** a creature. **3** (*also* **large lad**) a penis. **4** a fox.

lad n.[2] *see* CHILD n. (1).

ladder n. **1** [16C] the gallows. **2** [late 19C] the vagina. [metonymy]

laddie n. (*also* **lassie**) [1990s+] (*US gay*) a boy or girl with gay parents.

laddo n. **1** [late 19C+] an affectionate term of address. **2** [1990s+] a hooligan. [SE *lad*]

la-di-dah n.[1] (*also* **la de dah, laudy-daw**) [late 19C+] **1** a snob. **2** (*also* **ladidaism**) snobbishness; upper-class and/or wealthy hedonism. [LA-DI-DAH adj. (1)]

la-di-dah n.[2] **1** [20C+] a car, a tram car. **2** [1960s] a trolley car. **3** [1970s+] (*also* **lardy**) a cigar. [rhy. sl.]

la-di-dah adj. (*also* **laa-dee-laa, la-dee-da, la-di-da, lahdidah**) [late 19C+] **1** stuck up, arrogant, snobbish. **2** effeminate, affected. [? LARDY-DARDY adj.; or the supposed excl. of *La-di-dah!* in the face of information, experience etc]

la-di-dah v. (*also* **la-di-da**) [20C+] to use affected manners or speech. [LA-DI-DAH adj. (1)]

la-di-dah-di n. [1980s] a fantasy.

ladidaism n. *see* LA-DI-DAH n.[1] (2).

ladies n. [1920s+] a *ladies'* lavatory (cf. GENTS n.). [abbr.]

ladies' college n. [18C] a brothel (cf. ACADEMY n.). [euph.]

ladies' delight n. (*also* **ladies' lollipop, ...plaything, ...treasure**) [19C] the penis. [note ety. of DILDO n.]

ladies' tailoring n. [19C] sexual intercourse. [the in-and-out 'sewing' motion of intercourse]

ladies' walk n. [mid–late 19C] a ladies' lavatory.

ladle v. [mid-19C–1910s] to talk slowly and solemnly. [the image of carefully doling out soup]

lad of wax n. [late 18C–19C] **1** a cobbler. **2** a boy, a weak or unimportant man.

lads of the village n. [early 19C] thieves.

Lady, the n. [1980s+] (*US*) the Statue of Liberty.

lady n.[1] **1** [late 17C–19C] a crooked or hunchbacked woman. **2** [late 19C–1900s; 1960s+] (*US*) one's girlfriend, or wife. **3** [1910s+] (*US prison*) one's effeminate homosexual partner. **4** [1930s+] (*US Black*) an independent, high-class prostitute (cf. BANKSIDE LADY n.). **5** [1960s+] (*gay*) as a term of address to a fellow homosexual male. **6** [1970s+] (*US gay*) an effeminate homosexual. **7** [1970s+] (*US*) a prostitute belonging to a specific pimp.

lady n.[2] [late 19C+] a queen in a pack of playing cards.

lady n.[3] [1970s+] (*drugs*) **1** cocaine. **2** the pipe used for smoking base or crack cocaine. [abbr. of LADY SNOW n.[2]/WHITE LADY n.[2] (1); note cocaine is a 'feminine' drug, *see* GIRL n.[2] (1)]

lady abbess n. *see* ABBESS n.

lady and gentleman racket n. [mid-19C] the theft of barnyard fowls.

Lady Berkeley n. [19C] the vagina. [var. on BERKELEY (HUNT) n. (1)]

ladybird n. [late 16C+] a prostitute (cf. BANKSIDE LADY n.). [SE *ladybird*, a sweetheart]

Lady Blamey n. [1940s] (*Aus.*) a drinking vessel made of half a beer bottle with the cut edge rounded by sandpaper. [*Lady Blamey*, widow of Sir Henry Blamey (1884–1951), who taught soldiers how to cut a beer bottle in two by winding a kerosene-soaked string around it, setting the string alight and then plunging the bottle into cold water, where it broke cleanly]

ladyboy n. [1990s+] a transgender or transsexual young man.

lady-cracker n. (*also* **lady-fart, lady-finger**) [1940s+] (*US*) a small firecracker. [image of femininity as small]

Lady Dacre's wine n. [early 19C] gin. [ety. unknown; ? anecdotal]

ladyfied adj. [early 17C–19C] affecting the airs of a fashionable lady. [SE *ladyfy*, to give the title of Lady to someone]

lady-finger n.[1] [1940s–70s] (*US*) a cowardly man. [the softness of female hands]

lady-finger n.[2] *see* LADY-CRACKER n.

lady five fingers n. (*also* **old lady five fingers**) [1960s+] masturbation.

lady flower n. [mid-19C] (*US*) the vagina (cf. ADAM'S OWN (ALTAR) n.; BEAUTY SPOT n.). [euph. coined by Walt Whitman (1819–92)]

lady from Bristol n. (*also* **lady of Bristol**) [20C+] (*orig. Aus.*) a pistol. [rhy. sl.]

lady from the ground up n. [late 19C–1900s] (*US*) a woman who is drunk and disorderly.

Lady Godiva n. [20C+] (*UK/US*) £5/$5 (cf. BEEHIVE n.[2]). [rhy. sl. = FIVER n. (1)]

Lady Green n. [mid-19C] (*UK Und.*) a prison chaplain.

lady hook n. *see* HOOK n.[1] (2).

lady hot-bot n. *see* HOT-BOT n.

Lady Jane n. [mid-19C+] the vagina. [euph. use of proper name]

lady-killer n. (*also* **woman-killer**) [early 19C+] a man who considers himself or is considered to be irresistible to women; thus *lady-killing*, showing off to women.

Lady Laycock n. *see* MISS LAYCOCK n.

lady love v. [1930s+] to engage in lesbian sexual activity. [backform. f. LADY-LOVER n.]

lady-lover n. (*also* **woman-lover**) [1930s+] a lesbian (cf. BEAN FLICKER n.).

Lady Muck n. [1930s+] an arrogant, pretentious woman of any class.

lady of Bristol n. *see* LADY FROM BRISTOL n.

lady of pleasure n. (*also* **woman of pleasure**) [mid-17C+] a prostitute (cf. BANKSIDE LADY n.).

lady of the lake n. [mid–late 17C] a prostitute (cf. BANKSIDE LADY n.). [SE *lake*, to play amorously; ? ult. LARK v.]

lady of the line n. *see* LINE n.[2] (1).

lady of the town n. *see* WOMAN ABOUT TOWN n.

lady's blush n. *see* MAIDEN'S BLUSH n. (1).

lady's finger n. *see* LADY'S WAIST n. (1).

lady's jewels n. [mid-18C] the testicles (cf. AGATES n.). [note JEWEL n. (1)]

lady's low toupee n. [early 18C; 1990s+] pubic hair.

lady snow n.[1] [1950s–80s] (*US Black*) a respected upper-class White woman. [SE *lady* + SNOW n.[3] (3)]

lady snow n.[2] [1960s] (*drugs*) cocaine (cf. BLANCA n.). [SE *lady* + SNOW n.[2] (1); note cocaine is a 'feminine' drug, *see* GIRL n.[2] (1)]

lady's waist n. [1930s+] (*Aus.*) **1** (*also* **lady's finger, lady's wish**) a slender beer glass, with an hour-glass shape. **2** the drink served in such a glass.

lady ware n. **1** [late 16C; 19C] the penis (and testes). **2** [17C] the vagina. [SE *lady* + *ware*, goods]

lag n.[1] **1** [mid-16C–18C] a bundle of clothes for washing; usu. as LAG OF DUDS n. **2** [mid-16C–19C] water, the sea. **3** [17C–19C] urine. **4** [17C–19C] weak liquor or wine. [? OF *l'aige/l'aigue*, water; all f. (2)]

lag n.[2] (*also* **lagg**) **1** [mid-18C–19C] (*US Und.*) a term of transportation or penal servitude. **2** [early 19C+] a convict who has been transported or sentenced to penal servitude. **3** [mid-19C] a convict who has finished his sentence or has been released on parole. **4** [mid-19C+] any convict; thus *Lagland*, the underworld. **5** [1910s+] (*Aus./N.Z./US prison*) any length of sentence. **6** [1930s+] (*Aus. prison*) a 3-month sentence. [LAG v.² (1); note Aus. (Victoria) police jargon *lag*, 'one who informs especially, though not exclusively, against his or her fellow-officers' (Seal, *The Lingo*, 1999)]

lag *n.*³ (*also* **lag-a-bag, lag-lost**) [1910s+] a layabout, ne'er-do-well, a lazy person. [Scot. *lag/lag-a-bag/lag-lost*, a lazy person]

lag *v.*¹ [mid-18C–19C] to urinate. [LAG n.¹ (3)]

lag *v.*² **1** [mid-18C–19C] to sentence to transportation for over 7 years. **2** [early 19C+] to arrest, to apprehend. **3** [mid-19C] (*UK Und.*) to cause trouble for; to lead to an arrest. **4** [mid-19C+] to imprison. **5** [late 19C+] (*Aus.*) to inform on. **6** [1910s+] (*US Und.*) to imprison on trumped up charges and faked evidence. [16C SE *lag*, to carry off, to steal]

lag *v.*³ **1** [1950s+] to talk repetitively and tediously. **2** [1950s+] (*Aus. Und.*) to inform. **3** [1990s+] (*also* **lag off**) to shirk one's duties. [? fig. use of LAG v.¹, i.e. 'pissing around'/'piss on']

lag *v.*⁴ [2000s] to drink. [LAG n.¹ (4)]

lag *v.*⁵ *see* LEG v.⁴.

lag-a-bag *n. see* LAG n.³.

lage *n.* (*also* **lagge**) [mid-16C–19C] (*UK Und.*) water. [LAG n.¹ (2)]

lage *v.* [mid-16C–19C] to wash down or off with water. [LAGE n.]

lager beer *n.* [1960s+] (*Aus.*) an ear. [rhy. sl.]

lag fever *n.* [early 19C] a spurious illness feigned in order to avoid transportation. [LAG n.² (1) + SE *fever*]

lagg *n. see* LAG n.².

lagg *v.* [mid-19C] (*US*) to execute by hanging. [? misreading of LAG v.² (1)]

lagge *n. see* LAGE n.

lagged *adj.*¹ **1** [late 18C+] imprisoned, transported. **2** [1930s] (*US prison*) to be imprisoned with no hope of release. [LAG v.²]

lagged *adj.*² [mid-19C] (*US*) hanged. [LAGG v.]

lagged for one's wind *phr. see* WIND n.².

lagger *n.*¹ [late 18C–mid-19C] a sailor. [? LAG n.¹ (2) or LAG n.² (2) as being transported involved a long trip at sea]

lagger *n.*² **1** [early 19C+] a convict; thus *long-lagger*, a convict serving a long sentence. **2** [mid-19C+] a police informer. **3** [1930s+] an ex-convict. [LAG v.²; 20C+ use of (2) is Aus.]

lagger *n.*³ [20C+] (*Ulster*) anything sticky or greasy, e.g. porridge or mud. [Scot. *lagger*, a muddy place]

lagger *n.*⁴ [1990s+] a layabout, a 'corner boy'. [LAG n.³]

lagging *n.* **1** [early–mid-19C] (*UK Und.*) a sentence of transportation; thus *lagging matter*, any crime punishable by transportation. **2** [mid-19C+] (*UK Und.*) any prison sentence. **3** [mid-19C+] a sentence of more than 3 years' imprisonment. [LAG n.²]

lagging boat *n.* [2000s] a drunkard, an alcoholic. [LAG n.¹ (4) + SE *boat*]

lagging dues *n.* **1** [early–mid-19C] transportation, e.g. *lagging dues will be concerned*, this person is liable to be transported. **2** [late 19C] a sentence of penal servitude. [LAGGING n. + SE *due*]

lagging gage *n.* [18C–19C] a chamberpot. [LAG v.¹ + GAGE n.¹ (2)]

lagging matter *n. see* LAGGING n. (1).

lagging station *n.* [20C+] (*UK prison*) a prison for long-term prisoners. [LAGGING n.]

Lagland *n. see* LAG n.² (4).

lag-lost *n. see* LAG n.³.

lag of duds *n.* [mid-16C–19C] a bundle of clothes for washing. [LAG n.¹ (1) + DUDS n.¹ (1); Harman's orig. definition is 'a buck of clothes', a washtub, and thus a 'washtub's measure of clothes', *buck* contemporaneously meant lye, which would be used in the washing process]

lag off *v. see* LAG v.³ (3).

lag's farewell *n. see* SOLDIER'S FAREWELL n. (1).

lag ship *n.* [early 19C] a ship used for the transportation of convicts to Australia. [LAG n.² (2) + SE *ship*]

Lah *n.* [1970s+] (*US*) Los Angeles. [pron. of L.A. n.]

lah *n.* (*also* **la**) [1990s+] very strong marijuana.

lahdee *adj.* (*also* **lahdi**) [1930s+] smart, fashionable. [abbr. LA-DI-DAH adj.]

lahdidah *adj. see* LA-DI-DAH adj.

lahk *n. see* LAC n.¹.

lah-lah *n. see* LOLLA n.

lahnee *see under* LAANIE.

lahteeache! *excl.* [mid-19C+] all right! [backsl.]

laid *adj.*¹ [1960s+] (*US Black*) intoxicated by alcohol or drugs. [LAID OUT adj.¹]

laid *adj.*² [1970s+] (*US Black*) **1** fashionably dressed. **2** fashionably decorated. **3** worked out.

laid-back *adj.* **1** [1960s+] passive, relaxed, casual. **2** [1960s+] of music, soothing, peaceful. **3** [1970s+] intoxicated by drugs or alcohol.

laid crib *n.* [1970s+] (*US Black*) an attractive, well-furnished home. [LAID adj.² (2) + CRIB n.¹ (1)]

laid out *adj.*¹ [1920s+] (*US*) drunk (cf. ANNIHILATED adj.). [i.e. one is 'dead' drunk]

laid out *adj.*² [1960s+] (*US Black*) **1** of a person, well-dressed; good-looking. **2** of a place, smart, neat. [ext. of LAID adj.²]

laid, relaid and parlayed *phr.* [1950s+] (*US*) **1** having had frequent or protracted sexual intercourse. **2** deceived, cheated. [LAY v.¹ (1) + joc. uses of SE]

laid to the bone *phr.*¹ [1960s–70s] (*US Black*) drunk. [ext. of LAID adj.¹]

laid to the bone *phr.*² [1970s+] (*US Black*) **1** well-dressed. **2** of clothes, cut so well they seem a second skin. [ext. of LAID adj.² (1)]

laid to the natural bone *phr.* [1970s+] (*US Black*) naked. [LAID TO THE BONE phr.² + SE *natural*, unadorned]

laid up in Job's dock, be *v.* [late 18C–early 19C] to be treated in hospital for a venereal disease. [SE *laid up* + JOB'S WARD n.]

laigz *n.* [1940s+] (*W.I.*) **1** a trick. **2** influence. [? fig. use of SE *legs*; or *lag*, used in games as 'a chance, an opportunity']

laimeter *n.* (*also* **lamester, lameter, lamitor**) [20C+] (*Ulster*) one who is feeling unwell. [Scot. *lamiter*, a lame person, a cripple]

lain/laine *n. see* LANE n.

lair *n.* (*also* **lare**) [1920s+] (*Aus.*) a show-off, one who dresses flashily. [backform. f. LAIRY adj. (2)]

lair *v.* (*also* **lair up**) [1920s+] (*Aus.*) **1** to dress flashily, to dress up. **2** (*also* **lairize, lare up**) to act in a showy manner, to brag, to boast. [LAIR n.]

laired up *phr.* (*also* **all laired up**) [1920s+] (*Aus.*) flashily dressed. [LAIR n.]

lairily *adv.* [1990s+] cautiously. [LEERY adj. (2)]

lairize *v. see* LAIR v. (2).

lair up *v. see* LAIR v.

lairy *adj.* (*also* **lary**) **1** [mid-19C+] knowing, conceited, cheeky. **2** [20C+] (*Aus.*) (*also* **leary**) ostentatious, showy. [LEERY adj.]

lairy *adv.* (*also* **leary**) [20C+] (*Aus.*) showily, ostentatiously. [LAIRY adj. (2)]

laka *n.* [1960s] (*US gay*) the penis.

lakanuki *n. see* LACKANOOKY n.

Lake, the *n.* [1920s] (*US Und.*) Salt *Lake* City, Utah. [abbr.]

laken *n. see* LACKIN n.

laker lady *n.* [18C–19C] a prostitute (cf. BANKSIDE LADY n.). [for ety. *see* LADY OF THE LAKE n.]

lakes (of Killarney) *n.* [1910s+] a mad person. [LAKES (OF KILLARNEY) adj. (1)]

lakes (of Killarney) *adj.* [1910s+] **1** (*also* **lakesy**) mad, eccentric (cf. COCK-SPARROW adj.). **2** two-faced, untrustworthy. [rhy. sl; (1) = BARMY adj.; (2) = CARNEY adj. (1)]

Lake Wendouree v. [1990s+] (Aus.) to have just ejaculated. [*Lake Wendouree*, situated at the centre of Ballarat, Australia; the lake is wet, as is one's penis]

lakin n. see LACKIN n.

La-La n. [2000s] (US Black) Los Angeles. [abbr. of LA-LA LAND n.]

la-la n.[1] [1960s+] (Aus.) a lavatory. [abbr./redup.]

la-la n.[2] [1970s] the vagina. [? LOLLA n.]

la-la n.[3] see LOLLA n.

La-La Land n. [1970s+] (orig. US) Los Angeles. [L.A. n., but note LA-LA LAND n.]

la-la land n. [1980s+] (US) a fantasy world; thus *in la-la land*, out of touch with reality, drugged or drunk.

lalapalooza/lalapazaza n. see LALLAPALOOSA n.

lal brough n. (also **lally**) [20C+] snuff. [rhy. sl.; *Lal* = dimin. of *Alice*, the image is of an old lady, 'Lal Brough', taking snuff]

lallah n. see LOLLA n.

lallapaloosa n. (also **lalapalooza, lalapazaza, lallapalooza, lallapaluza, lallypaloozer, lolapaloosa, lollapalo, lollapaloosa, lollapalooza, lollypalooza, lollypaloozer, wollapalooza**) 1 [late 19C+] (orig. US) something or someone out-standingly good, stylish or pleasing of its kind. 2 [1920s] a devastating punch.

lallie n. (also **lallette, lally, lyle**) [1960s+] (Ling. Fr./Polari) a leg, usu. in pl. [? shared initial letters]

lalligag v. see LALLYGAG v.

lall-shraub n. [late 18C–1920s] (Anglo-Ind.) claret, red Bordeaux. [Hind. *lal-sharab*, red wine]

lally n.[1] see LAL BROUGH n.

lally n.[2] see LALLIE n.

lally n.[3] see LULLY n.

lallycooler n. see LOLLYCOOLER n.

lallygag n. (also **lollygag**) 1 [mid-19C+] foolishness, nonsense, empty chatter. 2 [20C+] (also **lollygog**) flirting, love-making; thus *lollygagger*, one who enjoys flirting. 3 [1940s] a wastrel, an irresponsible person. [LALLYGAG v.]

lallygag v. (also **lalligag, lolligag, lollygag**) 1 [mid-19C+] (US) to fool around, to kiss and cuddle. 2 [late 19C] (US campus) to surpass, to take advantage of. 3 [late 19C+] (US) to dawdle, to dally, to fool about. [ety. unknown; ? link to dial. *lolly*, the tongue]

lallypaloozer n. see LALLAPALOOSA n.

lam n.[1] 1 [late 19C+] (US) an escape from prison; thus *do a lam*, to escape (from prison). 2 [1990s+] an escape from work or duty. [LAM v.[2] (1)]

lam n.[2] [1900s–30s] (US) a punch or blow. [LAM v.[1]]

lam v.[1] (also **lamb, lamme**) 1 [late 16C+] to beat or strike; thus *lamming*, a beating; also in fig. use. 2 [mid–late 19C] (US) to defeat in a fight. 3 [late 19C] (Aus.) to swindle. [linked to ON *lemja*, to lame, as a result of a beating]

lam v.[2] (also **lam out**) 1 [late 19C+] (US Und.) to run away, to escape from prison; thus [1940s+] *lam out (on)*, to run away from (someone). 2 [late 19C+] to leave, to go away, without the assumed pressure of (1). 3 [1910s–50s] (US) to chase, to run after. [? early 19C Und. *lammas*, to depart, to leave; or abbr. of SE *slam* or f. LAM v.[1] thus pun on BEAT IT v.; Major, *Juba to Jive: A Dict. of Afro-American Slang* (1994), suggests link to Igbo *lam*, to leave, which would be interchangeable in the eyes of US Black slave owners]

lam v.[3] see LAMP v.[2] (1).

lamaster n. see LAMSTER n.

lamb n. 1 [mid-17C–1960s] a simpleton, a fool, esp. one easily cheated of their money (cf. AIREDALE n.). 2 [1920s–70s] (mainly US prison) (also **kid lamb**) a young homosexual boy, esp. one who accompanies a tramp. 3 [1940s+] (US Black) an innocent. [note Williams for 17C use of *lamb* as a novice prostitute]

lamb v. see LAM v.[1].

lambaste v. [mid-17C–1920s] to beat, to thrash. [LAM v.[1] (1) + SE *baste*, to thrash, to cudgel]

lambasted adj. [1990s+] drunk (cf. ANNIHILATED adj.). [LAMBASTE v.; many words that mean *defeated* also mean *drunk* in sl., e.g. TRASHED(-OUT) adj.]

lamb cannon n. [1990s+] the penis (cf. AX n.[2]).

lamb chop n. [1970s+] a term of affection; usu. of a woman, occas. a man.

lamb down v. [late 19C–1910s] (Aus./N.Z.) 1 to persuade someone to spend all their money on alcohol. 2 to squander one's earnings on drink. 3 to calm someone down. [shearing jargon *lamb down*, to tend ewes at lambing time, usu. used by shearers and other rural workers; but in (1) and (2) note the stereotypical innocence/vulnerability of a lamb]

lambe n. (also **lambiche**) [1960s+] (US) a toady. [Sp. *lambe*, licker]

lamber-down n. [late 19C–1910s] (Aus./N.Z.) a shanty-keeper or landlord who persuades men to spend all their money on drink. [LAMB DOWN v. (1)]

Lambeth v. [late 19C–1900s] to wash. [the well-known public bath-house in Lambeth]

Lambeth Walk n. [1930s+] the chalk used in billiards. [rhy. sl.]

lamb fry n. see LAMB'S FRY n.

lambiche n. see LAMBE n.

lambing-down shanty n. [late 19C–1910s] (Aus.) a rural tavern. [LAMB DOWN v. + SE *shanty*]

lambing-down shop n. [late 19C–1910s] (Aus.) a public house. [LAMB DOWN v. + SE *shop*]

lam black n. see LAMPBLACK n.

lamborghini n. [1990s+] (drugs) a crack pipe made from a plastic rum bottle and a rubber spark-plug cover (cf. KABUKI n.). [fig. use of the make of luxury sports car]

lamb-pie n. [late 17C–early 19C] a beating, a flogging. [a pun on the SE *lamb*/LAM v.[1]]

lamb-pit n. [1950s–70s] the vagina (cf. AGREEABLE RUTS OF LIFE n.; BLACK HOLE n.[1]).

lambsbread n. (also **lamb's breath**) [1950s+] (W.I./Rasta) a form of high-quality marijuana. [? a form of plant, note SE *lamb's lettuce*, corn salad]

lamb's fry n. (also **lamb fry**) [20C+] (Aus./US) 1 a necktie. 2 an eye, usu. used in the pl. [rhy. sl.]

lamb skin-it n. [mid-18C–1910s] the card-game *lansquenet*. [pron.]

lambskin man n. [late 17C–mid-19C] a judge. [the ermine-bordered robes]

lamb's leg n. (also **lamb's tail**) [1950s+] (US) a piece of mucus running from one's nose. [resemblance]

lamb's tongue n. [1930s–40s] (US prison) 1 $1. 2 a $5 bill.

lame n. 1 [1940s+] (US prison) a weakling. 2 [1950s+] (orig. US Black) an unsophisticated person or a fool. 3 [1960s] (US drugs) a tobacco cigarette. 4 [1960s+] (US Und.) a non-criminal and so a possible victim. [LAME adj.]

lame adj. 1 [mid-19C+] (US) bankrupted by gambling. 2 [late 19C+] (also **lame-ass**) naïve, clumsy, socially inept, incompetent; thus LAMENESS n. 3 [20C+] drunk (cf. AFFLICTED adj.). 4 [1950s+] (US Black) contemptible.

lame as a mule phr. [1990s+] (Aus.) utterly useless.

lamebrain n. [1910s+] (orig. US) a fool, a simpleton (cf. BAKEBRAIN n.). [SE *lame* + sfx *-brain*]

lamebrain adj. (also **lamebrained**) [1920s+] stupid, foolish (cf. AMOEBA-BRAINED adj.). [LAMEBRAIN n.]

lame duck n.[1] 1 [mid-18C+] a defaulter on the Stock Exchange; thus anybody who is unable to pay his debts. 2 [early 19C+] any weak, disabled or useless person, and thus falling behind their peers. 3 [mid-19C+] (US orig. political) a defeated politician who is working out a period of office, esp. a president who has been defeated in the presidential election in November but does not leave office – in which all decisions are now *de facto* irrelevant –

until January; this usage can extend to any similarly placed officials. **4** [1940s] (*Aus.*) a rascal.

lame duck *n.*[2] [1940s+] an act of sexual intercourse. [rhy. sl. = FUCK n.[1] (1)]

lame-duck *adj.* [1920s+] weak, useless, inferior. [LAME DUCK n.[1] (2)]

lamehead *n.* [1970s+] (*US*) a fool. [LAME adj. (2) + -HEAD sfx (1)]

lameness *n.* [1990s+] weakness, social ineptitude. [LAME adj. (2)]

lame-o *n.* (*also* **lamo**) [1970s+] (*US campus*) a general term of contempt or disparagement, a weakling, an inadequate, one not attuned to the prevailing styles and priorities. [LAME n. + -O sfx (1)]

lamer *n.* [1950s+] (*US teen*) a general term of contempt or disparagement. [LAME n.]

lameroo *n. see* LAMSTER n.

lames *n.* [1950s+] (*US Black*) a general term of contempt or disparagement; as a term of address. [LAME n.; on pattern of HOMES n.]

lame scene *n.* [1960s] (*US Black*) a disappointing, boring event, typically a tedious party. [LAME adj. (2) + SCENE n.]

lamester *n. see* LAMSTER n.

lamester/lameter *n. see* LAIMETER n.

l.a.m.f. *phr.* [1960s+] (*US gang*) like a motherfucker; when added to a gang name it implies the toughness and aggressiveness of the person so defined. [abbr.]

laminate *n.* [1980s+] (*US campus*) something or someone phoney, false. [pun on PLASTIC adj.]

Lamington *n.* [late 19C–1940s] (*Aus.*) a Homburg hat. ['a soft felt hat with a curled brim and a dented crown, first worn at Homburg, once a fashionable health-resort' (*OED*). Aus. use plays on SAusE *lamington*, a square of sponge cake coated in chocolate icing and desiccated coconut, ult. Baron Lamington (1860–1940), governor of Queensland]

lam into *v.*[1] **1** [late 19C+] to beat up. **2** [late 19C+] to do something aggressively, wholeheartedly. **3** [1970s+] to attack verbally. [ext. of LAM v.[1]; the term began life as UK sl. but crossed the Atlantic to reappear in criminal milieux]

lam into *v.*[2] [1920s] (*US*) to encounter, to run into. [LAM v.[2] (3) + SE *into*]

lamister *n. see* LAMSTER n.

lamitor *n. see* LAIMETER n.

lammas *v.* [mid-19C] (*UK Und.*) to run off. [? var. on LAM v.[2]; ult. SE *Lammas*, harvest festival]

lam-master *n. see* LAMSTER n.

lamme *v. see* LAM v.[1]

Lammermoor lion *n.* [18C–19C] (*Scot.*) a sheep.

lammie *n. see* LAMSTER n.

lamming *n. see* LAM v.[1] (1).

lammister *n. see* LAMSTER n.

lammy *n.* [mid-19C] a blanket. [SE *lambskin*; note naut. jargon *lammy*, a duffel coat]

lamo *n. see* LAME-O n.

lamous *adj.* [1910s] (*US tramp*) **1** cheap, inferior, esp. of jewellery. **2** of a person, harmless. [? the name of a Chicago company that made fake jewellery]

lam out *v.* [late 19C+] to strike out at, to hit. [LAM v.[1] (1)]

lam out (on) *v. see* LAM v.[2] (1).

lamp *n.* **1** [19C+] an eye, usu. in pl.; thus *queer lamp*, a blind, sore or squinting eye; and *smoke (one of) someone's lamps*, to give someone a black eye. **2** [1920s+] (*US*) a look or glance. [(1) note Shakespeare (*Comedy of Errors*, 1590): 'My wasting lampes some fading glimmer left']

lamp *v.*[1] **1** [early 19C+] to beat, to strike, to thrash. **2** [1950s] (*W.I.*) to trick, to deceive. [? LAM v.[1]]

lamp *v.*[2] **1** [20C+] (*orig. US*) (*also* **lam**) to look at, to assess visually. **2** [1950s+] to consider, to think about. **3** [1980s+] (*US Black/campus*) to loiter, to 'hang out', to relax while others panic. [LAMP n.; the image of (2) is watching other people]

lamp along *v.* [mid-19C+] (*Irish*) to go along at a great pace. [a *lamplighter* works quickly]

lampblack *n.* (*also* **lam black**) [1930s–40s] (*US Black*) a very dark-skinned Black person. [? LAM v.[1] (1); thus the bruises make one's skin even darker, or SE *lampblack*, carbon residue, often used for blacking up]

lamper *n.*[1] [1920s–30s] a teasing name for a tall, thin person. [LAMP-POST n. (1)]

lamper *n.*[2] [1950s] (*W.I.*) a confidence trickster. [LAMP v.[1] (2)]

lamp habit *n.* **1** [1930s–40s] (*drugs*) the passive inhalation of opium, which over a period can lead to addiction. **2** [1930s–50s] an opium addiction. [the SE *lamp* at which the opium pipe is lit + HABIT n. (1)]

lampish *adj.* [2000s] like a tramp. [PARAFFIN LAMP n. (1)]

lamp of light *n.* (*also* **lamp of life**) [19C] the penis.

lamp of love *n.* [19C] the vagina (cf. ADAM'S OWN (ALTAR) n.).

lamp oil *n.* [1940s–50s] (*US*) whisky. [? it 'lights you up']

lamp-post *n.* **1** [late 19C+] a teasing name for a tall, thin person. **2** [1920s] (*US*) any large and noticeable piece of jewellery.

lamps *n.*[1] [late 19C–1900s] spectacles. [abbr. GIG-LAMPS n. (1)]

lamps *n.*[2] [1950s] the female breasts (cf. BAGS n.[1]). [joc. abbr. SE *headlamps*]

lamster *n.* (*also* **lamaster, lameroo, lamester, lamister, lammaster, lammie, lammister**) [20C+] (*US Und./prison*) an escapee, a fugitive. [LAM v.[2]]

lam up *v.* [1920s] (*US*) to pick up. [US dial. *lam*, to pick up a small object]

Lancashire lass *n.* [1930s] a drinking glass. [rhy. sl.]

Lancashire lasses *n.* [1930s+] glasses (spectacles). [rhy. sl.]

lance *n.* **1** [late 15C–mid-19C; 1960s+] the penis (cf. AX n.[2]). **2** [1940s–50s] (*US drugs*) a hypodermic needle.

lance *v.* (*US*) **1** [1900s] to charge, to extract money; the inference is of cheating or extorting. **2** [1960s+] of a man, to have sexual intercourse; often ext. in phrs., e.g. *lance with one's pork sword* (cf. BANG v.[1]).

lance-jack *n.* [1910s+] (*orig. UK milit.*) a lance-corporal.

lance-knight *n.* (*also* **lanceman, lance-prigger**) [late 16C–mid-17C] **1** a highwayman. **2** a horse-thief. [? Ger. *Landsknechte*, a mercenary soldier who, when not actually fighting, terrorized civilians]

lance of love *n.* [19C] the penis (cf. AX n.[2]).

lancepresado *n.* (*also* **lanspresado, lansprisado**) [17C–mid-19C] one who comes into company, esp. in a tavern or public house, with only a few pence in their pocket. [Fr. *lancepessade*, 'the meanest officer in a foot-company' (Cotgrave, *Dict. French and English Tongues*, 1611), used in English as a synon. for *lance-corporal*, the lowest rank of non-commissioned officer]

lance-prigger *n. see* LANCE-KNIGHT n.

lance with one's pork sword *v. see* LANCE v. (2).

land *n.*[1] [20C+] (*Irish*) a surprise, usu. a disappointment, a letdown. [SE *land(ed) a blow*]

land *n.*[2] [2000s] (*US Black*) a closed-off area, such as a car, that is a place to smoke marijuana in.

land *v.*[1] **1** [mid-19C–1900s] to win a bet, to win something by betting. **2** [mid-19C+] to help, to aid, to 'set on one's feet'. **3** [mid-19C+] to secure someone, esp. in marriage, or as a potential victim of a confidence trick; to secure something, such as a job. **4** [1910s] to arrest, to capture.

land *v.*[2] (*also* **land out**) [late 19C+] to hit, i.e. to land a blow on; thus *land one on*.

land carrack *n.* [17C] a prostitute. [SE *land* + *carrack*, a large ship; she 'sails' the streets]

landed estate *n.* [late 19C–1910s] **1** a grave; thus (*WW1 milit.*) *become a landowner*, to die. **2** dirt beneath the fingernails.

lander *n.* [late 19C+] a blow. [LAND v.[2]]

landlady *n.* [late 19C+] (*US*) a madam, a proprietress of a brothel. [euph.]

land-leaper n. (also **land-loper**) [mid-14C–mid-19C] a criminal vagabond, subsisting on pilfering and often disguised with fake sores and similar blandishments. [SE *land* + *leap*/Du. *loopen*, to run]

landlord halo n. [1980s+] (*US*) a notably dim light, spec. in the hallway of a slum apartment block but also anywhere.

land-lubber n. (also **land-loper**) [early 17C–mid-19C] a wandering tramp, a vagrant. [SE *land* + LUBBER n.]

land navy n. [mid-19C–1900s] beggars who pose as impoverished seamen.

Land o' Cakes n. [18C–1900s] Scotland.

land o' darkness n. [1930s–40s] (*US Black*) Harlem, New York City; thus the Black district of any city.

land of fruit and nuts n. [1940s+] (*US*) California. [the state's supposed over-representation of homosexuals (FRUIT n.² (2)) and eccentrics (NUT n.⁴ (1))]

land of hope n. [20C+] soap. [rhy. sl.]

land of the wooden hams n. (also **land of the wooden nutmegs**) [19C–1900s] (*Aus.*) America. [the concept of such wooden items (note ety. for NUTMEG (MAKER) n.) as symbols of deceit]

land of twang n. [1900s] (*Aus.*) the United States. [the accent]

land on v. [1910s+] (*US*) to reprimand severely.

land on a pebbly beach v. (also **sight a pebbly beach**) [late 19C–1900s] to be short of money; thus PEBBLE-BEACHED adj. [image of a castaway on such a beach + STONE BROKE adj.]

land one on v. see LAND v.².

land on one's feet v. (also **fall on one's feet**) [1950s+] to survive a difficult situation. [SE *fall on one's feet*, fig. use of a cat always finding its feet when it falls]

Land o' Scots n. [late 19C] heaven. [ety. unknown]

land out v. see LAND v.².

land pike n. [mid-late 19C] (*US*) a wild hog or a more inferior breed of hog.

land-pirate n. 1 [17C–19C] a highwayman, a wandering thief, a gypsy. 2 [early 19C] a thieving prostitute.

landprop n. [1930s–70s] (*US Black*) a landlord or landlady. [? SE *land*lord + *proprietor*]

land-raker n. [late 16C–mid-18C] a vagrant, a tramp. [SE *land* + *rake*, to search]

land-rat n. [late 16C–mid-19C] a term of abuse.

landsakes! excl. [mid-19C+] (*mainly US*) a mild oath. ['Lord's sake!']

land security n. [mid-18C–19C] unauthorized absence.

land's end! excl. [1980s] (*US campus*) an all-purpose excl. [var. on LANDSAKES! excl.]

land-shark n. 1 [17C] a ruffian, a thug. 2 [19C] a policeman (cf. ANIMAL n.¹). 3 [19C] a custom house officer. 4 [early–mid-19C] a lawyer. 5 [mid-late 19C] (*US*) a wild hog. 6 [mid-19C–1930s] a moneylender, a usurer.

landsman n. [early 19C+] a fellow countryman, esp. a fellow Jew. [Yid.]

land someone in the shit v. (also **dump someone in it**) [1950s+] to bring trouble to someone else. [SE *land* + IN (THE) SHIT phr.]

land someone with v. [1950s+] to burden someone with, to pass on responsibility.

Lane, the n. 1 [mid-late 19C] Horsemonger Lane prison. 2 [mid-19C–1900s] Drury Lane Theatre, London WC2. 3 [mid-19C–1910s] Leather Lane, a large street market (London EC1). 4 [mid-19C–1930s] Petticoat Lane Market (Middlesex St, London E1). 5 [1910s] (*US*) The Bowery, New York City.

lane n. (also **lain, laine**) [1930s–60s] (*US Black*) 1 a peasant, a rustic. 2 an unsophisticated person. 3 a male. 4 a new inmate in a prison. [? one who lives in a country lane or var. pron. of LAME n.; the image of (4) is of their lack of knowledge of prison life]

lane, the n. [mid-16C+] the throat.

Lane Cove n. [20C+] (*Aus.*) a stove. [rhy. sl.]

langel n. [20C+] (*Ulster*) a tall, thin person. [dial. *langel*, a tether or rope for restraining an animal]

langer n. [1980s+] (*Irish*) 1 the penis. 2 a contemptible person. [? joc. var. on SE *long one* or link to LANGOLEE n.]

langered adj. (also **langers**) [20C+] (*Irish*) drunk. [Scot. *langer*, weariness]

langolee n. [mid-late 19C] the penis. [Welsh *trangluni*, tools]

langret n. [mid-16C–early 19C] a type of false die, in which one side is fractionally longer than the rest. [15C Eng. and 15C–19C Scot. var. sp. of *lang*, long]

langtries n. [late 19C] attractive eyes. [Lillie *Langtry* (1853–1929), a beauty and popular singer]

language n. [early 19C+] 'bad' language, obscenity; rudeness, argument.

language v. [1900s] (*Aus.*) to use obscene language towards. [LANGUAGE n.]

language! excl. [mid-19C+] be quiet! shut up! [abbr. *Mind your bad language!* or some similar restraint]

language of flowers n. [mid-19C] a fine of 10 shillings or a sentence of 7 days in jail. [a contemporary Bow Street magistrate, Mr Flowers, 'a very popular and amiable magistrate at this court' (Ware), or a play on the SE *language of flowers*, a method of expressing sentiments by means of symbolic flowers]

langulala n. [1940s+] (*W.I.*) a very tall, thin person. [Hausa *langalanga*, a tall, thin person]

lani/lanie see under LAANIE.

lank adj.¹ [late 19C–1930s] (*US*) hungry. [SE *lanky*]

lank adj.² [1970s+] (*S.Afr.*) a general term of approval, usu. from children or young people. [Afk. phr. *lank nie sleg nie*, not bad at all]

lanky n. (also **lank**) [mid-19C+] a nickname for a tall, thin person.

lanky adj. [early 19C+] tall, thin.

Lanna Macree's dog n. (also **Lanty McHale's dog/goat, Larry McHale's dog**) [20C+] (*Irish*) a time-server, one who befriends whoever they happen to be with. [? anecdotal]

lanspresado/lansprisado n. see LANCEPRESADO n.

lantern n. [mid-19C] a bribe.

lantern v. [19C] (*US*) to hang from a lamp-post. [Fr. revolutionary exhortation *à la lanterne!* 'string 'em up!']

lanty v. [20C+] (*Irish/Ulster*) to scold; thus *give someone lanty*, to tell off, to give someone a hard time. [Scot. *lant*, to jeer at, to make a fool of]

Lanty McHale's dog/goat n. see LANNA MACREE'S DOG n.

lap see also under LAP (UP).

lap n.¹ [late 15C–17C] the vagina. [euph.; but note SE *lap*, a fold of flesh]

lap n.² (*UK Und.*) 1 [mid-16C–mid-19C] buttermilk or whey or any thin, non-alcoholic drink. 2 [early 17C–1930s] liquor in general; thus *go on the lap*, to drink a good deal of strong liquor. 3 [mid-17C–mid-19C] soup. 4 [late 18C–1900s] tea. [SE *lap*, to drink]

lap-clap n. [17C–mid-18C] 1 sexual intercourse. 2 conception; thus *get a lap-clap*, to become pregnant. [SE *lap* + *clap*, a blow]

lap-ears n. [mid-19C] (*US campus*) a notably religious student. [SE *lop-ears*, a donkey]

lap feeder n. [late 18C–1900s] a silver tablespoon. [LAP n.² + SE *feeder*]

lapful n. [19C–1920s] 1 a husband; a lover. 2 an unborn child. [LAP n.¹]

lapland n. 1 [late 17C–19C] the vagina; thus *Lapland witch*, a prostitute. 2 [1920s+] the world of women. [LAP n.¹]

lap-lover n. [1970s+] one who enjoys cunnilingus. [LAP n.¹ + SE *lover*]

lapper n.¹ [19C–1900s] (*UK Und.*) alcohol; thus *rare-lapper*, a hard drinker. [LAP n.² (2)]

lapper n.² [mid-19C] (*US*) the tongue. [SE *lap* v.]

lapper n.[3] [1930s+] one who performs oral sex. [LAP (UP) v.[2]]

laprogh n. [late 19C] (*tinker*) a goose or duck; thus a bird of any type. [Shelta]

lap the gutter v. [mid–late 19C] to drink; to get drunk. [SE *lap* v. + either GUTTER ALLEY n. or GATTER n.]

lap (up) n. [late 19C] a tail coat. [SE *laps*, the 'skirts' of a coat]

lap (up) v.[1] **1** [19C+] to drink alcohol, esp. greedily. **2** [late 19C+] to enjoy greatly. **3** [1990s+] to be very fond of. [fig. use of SE *lap* v./LAP n.[2] (2)]

lap (up) v.[2] [1930s+] to perform cunnilingus (cf. CUNT-LICK v.). [LAP n.[1]/CUNT-LAPPER n. (1)]

larceny n.[1] [1920s+] (*US Und.*) an inclination towards theft, a liking for theft; thus *larceny in his heart*.

larceny n.[2] [1940s–60s] (*US Black*) thoughts or feelings, usu. unpleasant or antagonistic; thus *lay one's larceny*, to talk to, to 'chat up'. [use of SE *larceny*, 'taking and carrying away of the personal goods of another with intent to convert them to the taker's use' (*OED*), as a generic for evil]

larceny v. [1940s–60s] (*US Black*) to feel bad towards, to suspect. [LARCENY n.[2]]

larceny shoes n. [1980s+] (*US*) elaborate, high-priced trainers. [such shoes are a status symbol for (orig.) Black teens; thus, this is a racist slur based on the idea that such shoes are allegedly a badge of criminality]

lard n. **1** [mid-19C; 1910s+] (*US*) human fat, often in combs. **2** [1920s–50s] (*US*) butter or margarine. **3** [1970s+] (*Irish*) the essence, the 'daylights'; usu. as BEAT THE LARD OUT OF v. [SE *lard*, the fat of an animal]

lard and pail n. *see* BUCKET AND PAIL n.

lard-ass n. [1910s+] (*orig. US*) **1** (*also* **lard, lard-ball**) an overweight person; often used as a nickname for such a person; thus a lazy, good-for-nothing person. **2** a fat posterior. [LARD n. (1) + ASS n. (2)/-BALL sfx, i.e. someone who sits on their posterior and does nothing but cultivate lard]

lard-assed adj. (*also* **lard-ass**) [1940s+] (*US*) having large buttocks, fat; thus lazy, useless. [LARD-ASS n.]

lard batty n. [2000s] (*UK Black*) a fat person. [LARD n. (1) + BATI n.; var. on LARD-ASS n. (1)]

lard-belly n. [1930s+] (*US*) an obese person. [LARD n. (1) + SE *belly*]

lard-bladder n. [late 19C–1920s] an obese person. [LARD n. (1) + SE *bladder*]

lard-bucket n. [1950s+] a fat person. [LARD n. (1) + SE *bucket*]

lard-butt n. [1960s+] (*US*) an obese person. [LARD n. (1) + BUTT n.[1] (2); var. on LARD-ASS n. (1)]

lard-can n. [1910s+] (*orig. US*) a fat person. [LARD n. (1) + CAN n.[1] (2); var. on LARD-ASS n. (1)]

lardhead n. [1930s+] (*US/Aus.*) a stupid person. [SE *lard* + -HEAD sfx (1)]

lardo n. [1980s+] (*US*) a fat person, usu. used in direct address. [LARD n. (1) + -O sfx (1)]

lard up v. [1990s+] to put on weight. [LARD n. (1)]

lardy n. *see* LA-DI-DAH n.[2] (3).

lardy adj. [1920s+] fat, obese. [LARD n. (1)]

lardy-dardy adj. (*also* **lardy**) [mid-19C+] affected, supercilious, foppish; thus *do the lardy*, to put on airs. [var. on LA-DI-DAH adj. but actually earlier, so ? simply the sound of the speech]

lardy-dardy v. [late 19C] to act in a supercilious manner. [LARDY-DARDY adj.]

lardyface n. [1920s] a derog. description of someone with a fat face. [LARDY adj. + SE *face*]

lare n. *see* LAIR n.

lareover n. (*also* **layer-over, layover**) [late 17C–18C] a word that is substituted for one that is considered indecent. [it is 'laid over' the taboo term]

lare up v. *see* LAIR v. (2).

large n. (*also* **large one**) [1970s+] $1000, £1000; usu. as *15 large*.

large adj. **1** [late 19C–1910s] (*US campus*) enjoyable, fine. **2** [1910s+] (*W.I. Rasta*) respected. **3** [1920s+] (*US Black*) successful, exciting. **4** [1990s+] (*US teen*) impressive.

large adv. [mid-19C+] unrestrainedly, excessively, in a self-indulgent manner (cf. LIVE LARGE v.); thus *dress large*, to dress in an ostentatious manner; *play large*, to gamble heavily; *talk large*, to boast.

large v. *see* LARGE (IT) v.

large dooey n. [1920s–30s] a large cup of tea. [DOOE n.; the 'cuppa' cost 2d., but E.P. notes the typical café menu, 'tea 1d, large do. [i.e. ditto] 2d']

large for adj. [1960s+] (*US*) enthusiastic. [LARGE adj.]

large-head n. [late 19C–1900s] (*US*) a drunkard. [SE *large* + -HEAD sfx (3)]

large house n. [mid–late 19C] the workhouse.

large (it) v. [1990s+] **1** to live extravagantly, in a showy manner. **2** to show off, to act aggressively.

large lad n. *see* LAD n.[1] (3).

large one n. *see* LARGE n.

large order n. *see* TALL ORDER n.

largie n. **1** [1970s+] (*W.I., Bdos*) a 750ml (26fl oz) bottle of rum. **2** [2000s] (*Aus.*) a 750ml (26fl oz) bottle of beer.

larikin n. *see* LARRIKIN n.

lark n.[1] **1** [early 19C] a propensity for fun and games. **2** [early 19C+] a frolic, a game; thus *larkiness*, a propensity for such pleasures; *larkish, larksome, larky*, frolicking around or 'up for' such amusements; *on a lark*, on a spree; also used ironically/negatively. **3** [mid-19C; 1970s] (*also* **larkey**) an amusing person. **4** [20C+] any form of activity, occupation. **5** [1920s+] (*also* **larks**) a criminal scheme. [? north. dial. *lake*, to play (its Yorks. pron. might well have sounded more like 'lark') or SE *skylark*, to play tricks, to indulge in rough horseplay]

lark n.[2] (*also* **larky**) [early–late 19C] (*US*) a fellow, a man. [play on BIRD n.[2] (1)]

lark v. **1** [19C] to masturbate (cf. BOFF v.; PLAY A LITTLE FIVE-ON-ONE v.; PLAY DOLLY UP, DOLLY DOWN, DOLLY SICK v.; PLAY ONESELF OFF v.; PLAY POCKET POOL v.; PLAY SOLITAIRE v.; PLAY STINKY PINKY v.; PLAY TIDDLYWINKS v.; PLAY WITH ONESELF v.; SHUFFLE THE DECK v.). **2** [19C+] (*also* **lark about/around, skylark**) to play tricks, to play around, to enjoy oneself. **3** [mid-19C] to tease. **4** [mid-19C+] to flirt. [LARK n.[1]]

larker n. [mid-19C] one who is given to enjoying themselves at the expenses of others. [LARK v.]

larkery n. [19C] playfulness (whether rough or gentle). [LARK v.]

larkey n. *see* LARK n.[1] (3).

larkin n. [early–mid-17C] a very strong, spiced punch, created in the Raj. [Y&B 'are in the dark' as to the origin; they suggest Robert Larkin (*fl.* early 17C), an employee of the East India Company; a ref. in Hakluyt to '*larnike* = drinke', which takes them to Javan *larih*, to pledge, to invite to drink at an entertainment + Malay *larih-larahan*, mutual pledging to drink]

larkiness n. *see* LARK n.[1] (2).

larking n.[1] **1** [mid-18C–19C] fellatio, cunnilingus. **2** [1970s+] (*UK gay*) experimenting with homosexuality. [Grose included the term in his first edn (1785) as 'a lascivious practice that will not bear explanation'; he omitted it from subseq. edns. It reappears in F&H, who label it 'venery' and define it as 'irrumation'. E.P., in his edition of Grose's 3rd edn (1796), notes its absence and glosses it as 'irrumation, cunnilingism']

larking n.[2] [19C] **1** fun, enjoyment; thus *down to larking*, the excuse offered by one who claims that they were convicted unfairly. **2** masturbation. [LARK v.]

larkish adj. *see* LARK n.[1] (2).

lark rig n. [late 18C] (*UK Und.*) a confidence trick. [LARK v. (2) + RIG n.[2] (2)]

larks n. *see* LARK n.[1] (5).

larksome adj. *see* LARK n.[1] (2).

larky n. see LARK n.[2].

larky adj. see LARK n.[1] (2).

larky-boy n. [20C+] (Irish) a mischief-maker. [LARKY adj. + SE boy]

larney see under LAANIE.

larrikin n. [late 19C+] (orig. Aus.) **1** (also **larikin, larry**) a rascal, a villain, a Bohemian, one who acts without regard for conventions; thus larrikin push, a street gang; larrikiness/larrikina, a female larrikin; larrikinism; also attrib. and in fig. use. [? Warwickshire/ Worcestershire dial. larrikin, a mischievous or frolicsome youth. Other theories include elision of LEERY adj. (1) + KINCHIN n. (1) or dial. larack, to lark/lark about]

larrup v. **1** [early 19C+] to flog, to beat, to thrash; thus larrup, larruping, a sound thrashing. **2** [20C+] (US) to move noisily. [? orig. Suffolk dial., ult. ? lee-rope or a var. on SE lather or leather, to beat + wallop]

larruping adj. (also **tad-larruping**) [1900s] (US) very good, excellent, esp. of food. [fig. use of LARRUP v. (1); cf. LASHINGS n.]

larrup the lining out of v. see KNOCK THE STUFFING OUT OF v.

larry n.[1] (US) **1** [mid-19C–1900s] deception. **2** [1980s+] a failure. [? LAIRY adj.; LEERY adj.; note carnival jargon larry, a cheap or worthless trinket given as a prize at a gambling game]

larry n.[2] [20C+] (Irish) a fool. [Irish learaire, a lounger, an idler]

larry n.[3] [1990s+] (UK juv.) an effeminate or homosexual man. [? the supposed 'effeminacy' of the name]

larry n.[4] see LARRIKIN n.

larry-doo n. see GIVE SOMEONE LARRY DOOLEY v.

Larry Dugan's eye water n. [late 18C–19C] blacking. [Larry Dugan, a well-known Dublin shoe-black]

Larry McHale's dog n. see LANNA MACREE'S DOG n.

larstins n. (also **larstings**) [late 19C–1900s] (Aus.) elastic-sided boots (cf. LAUGHING-SIDED BOOT n.). [? abbr. SE elastics]

lary adj. see LAIRY adj.

las n. [1970s+] (S.Afr.) money, esp. as a loan or a contribution. [colloq. Afk. las, to increase]

lash n.[1] **1** [late 18C] (US) a sword. **2** [1910s+] (Aus.) violence. **3** [1920s+] (Aus.) a trick, a swindle. **4** [1950s+] (Aus./Irish) a try, an attempt; thus give it a lash, to have a try. **5** [2000s] the penis. [SE lash, a whip]

lash n.[2] (also **lasher**) [1980s+] (Aus./N.Z. Und.) a general term of abuse; spec. one who does not pay their debts. [LASH v.[3]]

lash v.[1] **1** [1930s+] (Irish) to rain heavily. **2** [1960s+] (US) to urinate. [(1) as if it is whipping you; (2) f. (1)]

lash v.[2] [1950s+] (W.I.) to have sexual intercourse, esp. in a vigorous manner (cf. BANG v.[1]). [SE lash, to whip]

lash v.[3] [1960s+] (Aus./N.Z. Und.) to fail to honour a debt or obligation. [SE lashes, neglect in the performance of a legal duty]

lash v.[4] [1980s+] (UK Black) to mug, to steal from in the street; thus LASHING n.

lash v.[5] [2000s] to discard, to get rid of.

lashed adj. [1990s+] drunk.

lasher n.[1] [20C+] (Irish) an attractive woman, a beauty. [? SE luscious]

lasher n.[2] [1950s] (W.I.) a womanizer, a sexual athlete. [LASH v.[2]]

lasher n.[3] see LASH n.[2].

lash in v. [20C+] (Irish) to spend money, or provide, without restraint. [SE lash out]

lashing n. [1980s+] (UK Black) a street robbery. [LASH v.[4]]

lashings n. **1** [mid-19C+] (orig. US) lots, an abundance. **2** [1930s+] (Irish) in phr. lashings and leavings, plenty and then some to spare. [16C SE lashing out, lavishing, squandering]

lash larue n. [1950s] (W.I.) a womanizer, a sexual athlete. [LASH v.[2], but also as pun on proper name of US entertainer Lash LaRue 'King of the Bullwhip']

lashool adj. [late 19C] (tinker) pleasant. [Shelta]

lash-up n. [20C+] **1** an object, organization, idea etc that is essentially amateur and homemade, but adequate for the time being. **2** (US milit.) a military organization. [orig. naut.; note WW1 milit. lash-up, a failure, a fiasco]

las mujercitas n. [1970s+] (drugs) psilocybin. [fig. use of Sp. 'little wives'; ? the shape of the mushrooms resembles small breasts]

lassie n. see LADDIE n.

lassitudinarian n. [late 19C] a constitutionally lazy person. [SE lassitude, laziness + pun on valetudinarian]

last n. [early 19C+] the end of one's relationship with someone, or dealings with something; thus you've not heard the last of this…

last bit of the family plate n. [late 19C–1900s] the last silver coin in one's pocket.

last-call look n. [1980s+] (US campus) the desperate, searching look that comes over men who hear the call for 'last orders' in a bar and have still not found a woman to take home.

last card of the pack n. **1** [mid-19C] the human back. **2** [20C+] dismissal from employment. [rhy. sl.; (2) = SACK, THE n. (1)]

last debt n. [17C; 1940s] (US Black) death; thus pay one's last debt, to die.

last farewell n. (also **last goodbye, last muster, last round-up**) [20C+] death.

last heartbeat n. [1940s] (US Black) a lover, a sweetheart. [? an exaggerated phr. of love, i.e. 'I will love you until my last heartbeat']

last mile n. (also **last waltz**) [1930s+] (US prison) the final walk of a condemned man from death row to the execution chamber.

last muster n. see LAST FAREWELL n.

last out n. [1940s] (US Black) death.

last round-up n. see LAST FAREWELL n.

last shake of the bag n. [19C+] one's youngest child. [BAG n.[1] (1) + bingo imagery]

last waltz n. see LAST MILE n.

lasty adj. [20C+] (Irish) lasting, enduring.

lat n. see LATS n.[1].

latch n.[1] [late 18C–mid-19C] (US) a buckle or breast-pin. [i.e. it secures one's clothes]

latch n.[2] [1960s–70s] (US Black) a parasite, a beggar. [SE latch onto + leech]

latch v. **1** [early 18C–19C] (UK Und.) to let in. **2** [1930s+] (US) to get married. **3** [1950s] (US campus) to embrace.

latch for the gate to your front yard n. [1930s–40s] (US Black) fly buttons or a collar pin.

latchico n. [1970s–80s] (Irish) a wastrel, a rogue. [Scot. latch, indolent, idle]

latch-key n. [late 19C] (Irish police) a crowbar. [its use when evicting defaulting tenants]

latchpan n. [mid-19C–1930s] the lower lip; thus HANG ONE'S LATCHPAN v. [SE latchpan, a dripping pan, lit. a 'catching pan']

late adj. [1960s+] describing a woman whose menstrual period has failed to occur at the expected time.

late! excl. **1** [1960s] (US Black) an excl. of amazement, usu. ironic. **2** [1990s+] (US teen) see you later!

late black n. (also **late dark**) [1930s–40s] (US Black) a very dark night, with neither moon nor stars.

late bright n. [1950s] (US Black) the evening.

late night n. [1980s+] (US campus) a party, usu. at a fraternity house, that does not start until after the bars and clubs close, usu. after midnight.

later v. [1980s+] (US campus) to abandon a relationship. [LATER excl./LATER FOR — phr.]

later! excl. (also **later on! laters! lates!**) [1940s+] (orig. US Black) see you later! goodbye!

later for — phr. (also **later on (for) —**) [1940s+] (orig. US) a general phr. of dismissal; a synon. for TO HELL WITH —! excl.; often as later for that.

later for you! *excl.* **1** [1940s+] (*orig. US Black*) shut up! go away! to hell with it! **2** [1980s+] (*US campus*) goodbye. [LATER FOR — phr.]

later on! *excl. see* LATER! excl.

later on (for) *phr. see* LATER FOR — phr.

laters! *excl. see* LATER! excl.

later, tater *phr.* [1970s+] (*US campus*) a farewell.

lates! *excl. see* LATER! excl.

latest *n.* [late 19C+] a person's most recent comment, joke, escapade etc.

late watch *n.* [1940s] the early hours of the morning when prostitutes can solicit more easily.

lath and plaster *n.* [mid-19C] a master, an employer. [rhy. sl.]

lather *n.*[1] [19C–1900s] semen (cf. BOLLOCK SNOT n.).

lather *n.*[2] (*also* **lathering**) [mid-19C–1950s] a scolding, a beating. [LATHER v.]

lather *v.* [late 18C–19C] **1** to thrash. **2** to defeat. [SE in 20C+]

lathered *adj.* **1** [1910s–40s] (*orig. Aus.*) drunk. **2** [1950s] (*US drugs*) intoxicated by a drug. **3** [1970s] (*US*) sexually excited. [SE *lather*, the froth on a liquid, or a state of agitation]

lathering *n. see* LATHER n.[2].

lather-maker *n.* [19C] **1** the vagina. **2** the penis. [LATHER n.[1] + SE *maker*]

lather up *v.* [1930s–40s] (*US*) to show affection, to encourage, to excite; esp. of a woman prior to seduction.

lat-house *n. see* LATS n.[1].

Latin *n.* [mid-17C] alicante wine. [SE *Latin*, one of the communities in Europe, in this case Spain, the manufacturer of *alicante*]

Latin mystery *n.* [20C+] a doctor's prescription. [the medical Lat. in which it was written]

latitat *n.* [mid-16C–mid-19C] an attorney, a lawyer. [Lat. *latitare*, to lie concealed; thus legal jargon *latitat*, 'a writ which supposed the defendant to lie concealed and which summoned him to answer in the King's Bench' (*OED*)]

latro! *excl.* [1990s+] (*US campus*) farewell. ['Italianized' version of LATER! excl.]

lats *n.*[1] (*also* **lat, lat-house**) [1940s+] (*orig. milit.*) a *lat*rine. [abbr.]

lats *n.*[2] [1960s+] the *lat*isimas dorsi muscles.

lattie/latty *n. see* LETTY n.[1].

L.A. turnabouts *n.* [1980s] (*US drugs*) amphetamines (cf. A n.[2]).

laudy-daw *n. see* LA-DI-DAH n.[1].

laugh, the *n.* [late 19C–1900s] (*US*) mockery, teasing.

laugh and joke *n.* [late 19C+] a smoke. [rhy. sl.]

laugh and scratch *v.* [1930s+] (*drugs*) to inject a drug, usu. heroin. [what one does when the injection takes effect]

laugh and titter *n. see* GIGGLE AND TITTER n.

laugh at the ground *v.* (*also* **laugh at the carpet**) [1960s+] (*Aus.*) to vomit.

laughing *adj.* (*also* **away laughing**) [1910s+] (*orig. milit.*) safe, secure; usu. in such phrs. as *you're laughing* or *I'm laughing*.

laughing academy *n.* (*also* **laughing farm, ...house, ...school**) [1940s+] (*US*) a psychiatric institution.

laughing boy *n.* [20C+] **1** an ironic nickname given to someone who seems consistently, or temporarily, miserable and in low spirits. **2** one who laughs complacently prior to encountered Problems. [? Gilbert and Sullivan song 'A Laughing Boy But Yesterday' in *The Yeoman of the Guard* (1888), about a miserable person]

laughing gear *n.* (*also* **laughing tackle**) [1970s+] the mouth. [SE *laughing* + GEAR n.[1] (2)/SE *tackle*]

laughing grass *n.* [1950s+] (*orig. US drugs*) marijuana (cf. AFRICAN BUSH n.; BOMB n.[4]). [SE *laughing* + GRASS n.[5], i.e. its effects]

laughing house/school *n. see* LAUGHING ACADEMY n.

laughing-sided boot *n.* [1930s+] (*Aus.*) an elastic-sided boot (cf. LARSTINS n.). [adopted from Aborigine mispron. of SE]

laughing soup *n.* (*also* **laughing juice/water**) [20C+] (*US*) an alcoholic drink, esp. champagne.

laughing tackle *n. see* LAUGHING GEAR n.

laughing weed *n.* (*also* **laughing tobacco**) [1920s+] (*US drugs*) marijuana (cf. AFRICAN BUSH n.; BOMB n.[4]). [SE *laughing* + WEED n.[1] (4), i.e. its effects]

laugh like a drain *v.* (*also* **laugh like a broken hinge**) [1940s+] to laugh uproariously. [the supposed equivalence of the laughter and the gurgling of water down a drain]

laugh one's ass off *v.* [1970s] to laugh uproariously. [SE laugh + ASS n. (2)]

laughs and smiles *n.* [20C+] (*Aus.*) haemorrhoids. [rhy. sl. = SE *piles*]

laugh that off! *excl.* [1910s+] (*US*) a sarcastic retort meaning that the listener will have to take one seriously.

launch *n.* [late 18C–19C] childbirth, esp. the actual labour. [SE but ? with implication of dial. *launch*, to groan]

launching pad *n.* [1950s–70s] (*US drugs*) a room, flat or house where drug addicts can go to inject. [SE *launch* + PAD n.[2] (2); pun]

launder *v.* [1970s+] to decriminalize money that has been gained through criminal activities by 'washing' it through a legitimate business, such as a casino or bank. [the 'dirty' money is invested or deposited and is withdrawn 'clean' of any association with crime; note Jonson *The Alchemist* (1610): 'I'll bring [...] thy neck within a noose, for laund'ring gold, and barbing it' – the ref. is to 'sweating' gold plate and to clipping money]

laundress *n.* [17C] a prostitute. [euph.]

laundromat *n.* (*also* **laundry**) [1980s+] a business, such as a casino, in which money that has been gained through criminal activities can be decriminalized. [SE *Laundromat*, a 'do-it-yourself' laundry shop; LAUNDER v.]

laundry *n.* **1** [1940s+] (*US*) clothes that are being worn; thus *drop one's laundry*, to undress. **2** [1960s+] (*gay*) the bulge of the genitals under trousers. **3** [1970s] (*US*) women.

laundryman *n.* [late 19C+] (*US*) a Chinese man (cf. AH CABBAGE n.). [the stereotyping in the US of Chinese immigrants as laundry workers]

lauras *n.* [1930s+] (*Can.*) chocolates. [a brand of chocolates made by the firm *Laura* Secord, named after a heroine of the war of 1812]

Laurel and Hardy *n.* [1920s+] Bacardi (rum). [rhy. sl.; ult. comedians Stan *Laurel* (1890–1965) and Oliver *Hardy* (1892–1957)]

Laurence has got me *phr. see* LAZY LAURENCE n.

lav *n.* [1910s+] *lav*atory. [abbr.]

lavender *n.* [mid-19C–1920s] **1** something good, desirable. **2** flattery.

lavender *adj.* [1920s+] (*orig. US*) a euph. for homosexual and anything referring to homosexuality (cf. LILAC adj.; PURPLE adj.).

lavender boy *n.* (*also* **lavender lad/lips**) [1920s+] a male homosexual. [LAVENDER adj. + SE *boy/lad/lips*]

lavender cove *n.* [19C] a pawnbroker. [LAY UP IN LAVENDER v. (1) + COVE n. (3)]

lavender cowboy *n.* [1920s+] an effeminate man; thus a male homosexual. [LAVENDER adj. + SE *cowboy*]

lavender lad *n. see* LAVENDER BOY n.

lavender law *n.* [1920s+] legal issues, practice and study pertaining to the gay and lesbian community. [LAVENDER adj. + SE *law*]

lavender lips *n. see* LAVENDER BOY n.

laverick *n. see* LABRICK n.

la vida loca *n.* [1960s+] (*US gang*) the gangster lifestyle of the Mexican barrios of the US, esp. Los Angeles. [Sp. *la vida loca*, the crazy life; coined by the Mexican immigrant gangs, starting with the *pachucos* of the 1930s–40s and the *cholos* of 1950s–60s, who initiated the gang style, subseq. picked up by Black teens and their elders]

lavo *n.* (*also* **lavvo**) [1920s+] (*Aus./Irish*) the *lav*atory. [abbr. + -O sfx (4)]

la vogue *n.* [1980s+] (*US campus*) a restroom or public lavatory for women. [? *Vogue* magazine, i.e. the use of the restroom for waking up etc]

lavvy *n.* [20C+] (*mainly Scot.*) a lavatory. [abbr.]

law *n.*[1] [mid–late 16C] (*UK Und.*) a type of criminal activity. [OF *lei*; ult. Lat. *legem*, law]

law *n.*[2] **1** [1910s+] a police officer, e.g. *Mark was busted by half a dozen law*; occas. a private detective. **2** [1940s+] (*US prison*) a prison warder. [LAW, THE n.; the article is deliberately omitted]

law, the *n.* **1** [18C+] (*orig. US*) the police. **2** [1920s] (*US prison*) a warder. [metonymy]

law *v.*[1] [1900s–50s] (*US*) to set the law on, to arrest. [abbr. SE *outlaw*]

law *v.*[2] [1940s–50s] (*UK Und.*) to impersonate a policeman.

law! *excl.* [late 16C+] a mild excl. of surprise or amazement. [euph. for SE *Lord!*]

lawbooks *n.* [1940s] a lawyer.

law-car *n.* [1970s] a police car. [LAW, THE n. (1)]

law dog *n.* (*also* **law hound**) [late 19C+] (*US*) a police officer. [SE *law* + *dog*/HOUND sfx; note DOG n.[3] (4)]

lawdy! *excl.* (*also* **lordy!**) [mid-19C+] (*orig. US*) a mild excl. [SE *Lord*]

lawful blanket *n.* [19C] a wife. [SE *lawful* + fig. use of *blanket*]

lawful jam *n.* [late 19C–1900s] one's wife. [SE *lawful* + JAM n.[3] (2)]

lawfully lady *n.* [mid-19C–1920s] (*US Black*) one's legal wife.

lawful picture *n.* [17C–18C] a coin; usu. in pl., money (cf. ABE n.[2]). [the engraving on coins or the picture on notes]

lawful tool *n.* [1950s] (*UK Und.*) a tool used for committing a burglary.

law hound *n.* see LAW DOG n.

lawk(s)! *excl.* (*also* **la!**) [mid-18C+] used as a euph. for SE *Lord!* in a variety of mild oaths; thus LAWKS-A-MUSSY! excl. etc. [var. on LAW! excl.]

lawks-a-mussy! *excl.* (*also* **lawks-a-mercy! laws-a-mercy!**) [late 18C+] a mild oath, lit. 'Lord have mercy!'

lawless *adj.* [20C+] (*W.I.*) **1** irresponsible, troublesome. **2** of a woman, promiscuous, unrestrainedly vulgar. **3** of speech, smutty, dirty. **4** sitting with the legs sprawled apart.

lawless as a town bull *phr.* see TOWN BULL n. (1).

lawman *n.* [1960s+] a law-enforcement officer.

lawn *n.*[1] [early 19C] (*UK Und.*) a white cambric handkerchief. [SE *lawn*, a form of fine linen, resembling cambric]

lawn *n.*[2] **1** [1940s+] a crewcut hairstyle; thus *lawnhead*, a person with a crewcut. **2** [1950s+] (*gay*) pubic hair; thus *mowed lawn*, shaved pubic hair.

lawn mower *n.*[1] [1930s–40s] (*US Und.*) a machine gun.

lawn mower *n.*[2] [1970s+] (*US*) a cunnilinctor. [LAWN n.[2] (2); note MOW THE LAWN v. (4)]

laws! *excl.* [mid-19C+] (*US*) Lord!

law sakes! *excl.* [mid-19C–1900s] (*US*) a mild oath, lit. 'for the Lord's sake!' [LAW! excl.]

law's-a-me! *excl.* [late 19C] (*US*) a mild oath, 'Lord save me!'

law sharp *n.* [late 19C–1940s] (*US*) a lawyer. [SE *law* + SHARP n.[1] (2)]

law-shop *n.* [1970s+] a police station. [LAW, THE n. (1) + SHOP n.[1] (1)]

law station *n.* [1950s] a police station. [LAW, THE n. + SE *station*]

lawt *adj.* [mid-19C] tall. [backsl.]

lax (up) *v.* [2000s] to relax. [abbr.]

lay *n.*[1] [17C] (*UK Und.*) buttermilk. [Fr. *lait*, milk]

lay *n.*[2] [17C–18C] a chance. [SE *lay*, to wager]

lay *n.*[3] **1** [mid-17C; late 18C; 1920s+] a person with whom one has sexual intercourse, or a promiscuous woman; usu. qualified as *a good lay, a bad lay, an easy lay* etc. **2** [1920s+] (*orig. US*) an act of sexual intercourse. [LAY v.[1] (1)]

lay *n.*[4] **1** [mid-17C+] (*UK Und.*) any kind of criminal activity, usu. modified by a participle that denotes the speciality, e.g. CHIVING

LAY n.; CLOUTING LAY n.; CRACK LAY n.; KID LAY n. **2** [18C–1960s] any form of enterprise, business or occupation; often the terms or conditions of such a contract or job. **3** [late 18C–19C] the life and practice of crime, as in *the lay*. **4** [early 19C] stolen goods. **5** [mid-19C–1940s] (*US*) one's (hidden) intention or aim. **6** [mid-19C–1950s] (*UK Und.*) a place considered for robbing. **7** [mid-19C–1950s] (*US*) a state of affairs. **8** [1910s] (*Aus.*) a trick, a deception. [OF *lei*, law, which itself is also the root of the synon. LAW n.[1]]

lay *n.*[5] [mid-19C] **1** a piece, a portion, e.g. a *lay of pannum*, a piece of bread. **2** goods. [? SE *lay*, to place, i.e. that which is laid on the table, counter etc]

lay *n.*[6] **1** [1910s–30s] (*US*) a place to sleep, a bed. **2** [1920s–50s] (*US drugs*) the act of lying down and smoking opium. **3** [1930s] (*US drugs*) a session in an opium den. **4** [1930s] (*US drugs*) a portion of any type of drug.

lay *v.*[1] **1** [17C+] (*also* **lay off**) to have sexual intercourse with; thus GET LAID v. **2** [late 17C; 1950s+] to make oneself available for sexual relations.

lay *v.*[2] (*also* **lie**) [17C+] to watch for, to survey. [abbr. SE *lay in wait*]

lay *v.*[3] **1** [mid-19C–1950s] (*US*) to knock someone unconscious. **2** [1960s+] (*US Black*) to idle, to relax. **3** [1980s+] (*US Black*) to over-indulge in drugs or drink to such an extent that one is laid on one's back.

lay *v.*[4] [1940s+] (*US Black*) an all-purpose v. of action.

lay *v.*[5] see LAY (DOWN) v.

lay *v.*[6] see LAY ON v. (1).

lay a batch *v.* (*also* **lay a patch**) [1960s+] (*US*) to make tyre marks by accelerating fast in a car.

layabout *n.* (*also* **layaround**) [1930s+] a voluntarily unemployed male, usu. involved in some minor criminality.

layabout *adj.* [1950s+] lazy, unemployed. [LAYABOUT n.]

lay about *v.* see LAY INTO v.

lay a cable *v.* see LAY SOME CABLE v.

lay a leg on/over *v.* see LIFT A LEG OVER v.

lay an egg *v.* [1920s+] **1** to fail completely, esp. in show business. **2** (*Aus.*) to worry, to be agitated. [RAF sl. *lay an egg*, drop a bomb. The link with US BOMB n.[1] (6) may be coincidental. Note *Variety* headline the morning after the 1929 Crash, 'Wall Street Lays an Egg']

lay a patch *v.* see LAY A BATCH v.

lay a rap on *v.* [1970s+] (*orig. US*) to persuade. [LAY ON v. (2) + RAP n.[3] (4)]

layaround *n.* see LAYABOUT n.

lay back *v.* (*also* **lay low/up**) **1** [1940s+] to have sexual intercourse. **2** [1960s+] (*US Black*) to relax. **3** [1960s+] to do nothing specific, to pass time (e.g. in prison).

lay back and front shops into one *v.* [late 18C–early 19C] to remove the physical division between the vagina and the anus (cf. LAY PIT AND BOXES INTO ONE v.). [thus described by Grose (1785); presumably, since he refers to 'an operation in midwifery', he means episiotomy, the widening of the vulval orifice to facilitate childbirth]

lay bricks *v.* [1930s] (*US*) to have sexual intercourse. [LAY v.[1] (1) + SE *bricks*]

lay-by *n.* [1920s+] (*Aus.*) a deposit on and the subseq. purchasing by instalments of an article in a shop. [the shop 'lays' the article 'by', i.e. on one side]

lay by the heels *v.* **1** [late 16C–1920s] to arrest, to imprison. **2** [17C] to place in the stocks.

lay cable *v.* see LAY SOME CABLE v.

lay cane upon Abel *v.* [late 17C–early 19C] to beat, to thrash. [pun on the biblical brothers *Cain* and *Abel*]

lay chic/chick/chickie *v.* see KEEP CHICK v.

lay chilly *v.* (*also* **sit chilly**) [1970s+] (*US*) to lie low. [SE *lay/sit* + CHILLY adj.[2] (1)]

lay dead v. **1** [late 19C+] (*US Black*) to wait. **2** [1940s+] to do nothing, to stop everything.

lay-down n.[1] **1** [mid-19C–1950s] a sleep. **2** [late 19C–1900s] (*US*) a refusal or collapse. **3** [1900s–30s] a place to sleep. **4** [1920s–30s] (*US drugs*) an opium den. **5** [1920s–30s] (*US drugs*) the price of admission to enter and smoke in an opium den. **6** [1930s+] (*UK Und.*) a period of remand in prison. [(2) note LAY DOWN v.[1] (2)]

lay-down n.[2] [1930s+] (*US*) a certainty. [one can lay down money on it]

lay (down) v. [1930s–60s] (*drugs*) to smoke opium (cf. LAY (ON) THE HIP v.). [the smoker's recumbent position]

lay down v.[1] **1** [late 19C+] (*US*) to volunteer for defeat. **2** [1910s+] to collapse. **3** [1930s+] to accept, to acquiesce. [boxing imagery]

lay down v.[2] [1930s+] (*US prison*) to place an inmate in the punishment cells. [punishment cells were so cramped there was barely enough room to stand upright]

lay down v.[3] [1940s+] (*US*) to explain, to outline, to present a theory.

lay down! excl. [1920s–50s] (*US*) be quiet! shut up!

lay-down joint n. [1930s+] (*US drugs*) a place to smoke opium. [LAY-DOWN n.[1] (4) + JOINT n.[4] (3)]

lay-down merchant n. [1950s+] a criminal who specializes in the distribution (*laying-down*) of counterfeit banknotes. [LAY PAPER v. + MERCHANT n.]

lay down on v. [late 19C+] (*US*) to abandon someone, to fail in a duty.

lay down one's bone v. [20C+] (*Ulster*) to work very hard. [synon. SE *put one's back into*]

lay down one's knife and fork v. (*also* **chuck in one's knife and fork**) [mid-19C–1930s] to die.

lay down on the job v. (*also* **lie down (on the job)**) [1910s+] (*orig. Aus.*) **1** to act lazily. **2** to do a job badly.

lay down some cow v. [1940s+] (*US Black*) to walk, esp. to walk so much that one's shoes are worn out. [the leather soles]

lay down the law v. [late 19C+] to make dogmatic statements, esp. during an argument.

lay 'em down v.[1] [1930s–40s] (*US*) to die. [one 'lays down' one's body]

lay 'em down v.[2] [1940s+] (*US*) to drive very fast. [the pressing down of the accelerator]

layer n. **1** [1900s–10s] a bookmaker. **2** [1910s] (*US Und.*) one who passes bad cheques. **3** [1930s–50s] (*US*) a currency note.

layer down n. [late 19C–1950s] (*US Und.*) one who passes counterfeit currency. [LAY PAPER v.]

layer-over n. *see* LAREOVER n.

lay five v. *see* SLAP FIVE v.

lay for v.[1] (*also* **lie for**) [17C; late 19C+] (*US*) to wait for someone, invariably with the intention of harming them; to wait to do something; thus *on the lay for*, waiting for. [SE *lay for*, to set an ambush or trap for a person or animal]

lay for v.[2] *see* LAY INTO v.

lay giggy v. [1930s] (*US juv.*) to keep a lookout. [SE *lay* + ? GIG n.[8] (2)]

lay heavy on v. (*also* **lay on the heavy**) [1970s] (*US/Aus.*) to lecture, to sermonize, to reprimand.

lay-in n. [1970s+] (*US prison*) a pass allowing a sick prisoner not to work.

lay in v.[1] **1** [1900s] (*US*) to act as confederates. **2** [1900s] (*US*) to obtain, to 'look out for'. **3** [1920s] (*US*) to stay, esp. in the context of hiding from pursuit. **4** [1930s+] (*US prison*) to stay in one's cell when one might normally be out of it.

lay in v.[2] *see* LAY INTO v.

layin' and playin' phr. [1970s+] (*US Black*) of a man, idling around the house, usu. with one's female partner.

laying hen n. [20C+] a farmer's wife who has a job. [her contribution to the farm economy]

laying out n. *see* LAY OUT v.[1] (6).

lay in the cut v. [1960s+] (*US Black*) **1** to lie in ambush, whether actually or fig. **2** to relax. [IN THE CUT phr. (1)]

lay into v. (*also* **lay about, lay for, lay in, lay on to**) **1** [mid-19C+] to attack physically. **2** [mid-19C+] to start eating in a voracious manner. **3** [1920s+] to attack verbally.

lay it v. [1930s–70s] (*US*) to do something in a noteworthy manner, e.g. to play jazz music well. [LAY v.[4]; note Lincoln University (Oxford, Pennsylvania) use *c.*1934: 'LAY IT. To do something extremely well']

lay it on v.[1] **1** [mid-19C+] to exaggerate; to make an excessive fuss. **2** [1910s+] (*orig. US*) to criticize, to berate. **3** [1930s–70s] (*US Black*) to seek a verbal or physical confrontation, to hit. **4** [1950s+] to inform, to pass on information.

lay it on v.[2] [1930s+] (*US*) to act or work efficiently or energetically.

lay it on someone's hip v. [2000s] (*US Black*) to call someone on their pager. [a pager is often clipped to the belt at hip level]

lay it on the line v.[1] **1** [1930s+] to be absolutely honest, to declare one's feelings, one's attitude. **2** [1940s+] to support, to pledge oneself.

lay it on the line v.[2] [1940s–50s] (*US*) to have sexual intercourse. [ext. of LAY v.[1] (1)]

lay it out v.[1] **1** [1960s+] of a homosexual of either sex, to admit and poss. flaunt one's sexual preference. **2** [1990s+] to offer oneself for intercourse.

lay it out v.[2] *see* LAY OUT v.[2].

lay like a carpet/rug v. *see* LAY (OUT) LIKE A CARPET v.

lay low v.[1] (*also* **lie low/under**) [mid-19C+] to hide oneself away, to keep a low profile.

lay low v.[2] *see* LAY BACK v.

lay me in the gutter n. [1920s+] butter. [rhy. sl.]

lay-off n.[1] (*US*) **1** [late 19C+] a respite from work. **2** [20C+] dismissal from work; retirement. **3** [1930s–40s] a stop-over during a long journey. **4** [1960s+] any kind of respite. [(1) and (2) are now SE]

lay-off n.[2] [1920s] (*US drugs*) a smoke of opium. [var. on LAY-DOWN n.[1]]

lay off v.[1] **1** [mid-19C–1920s] (*orig. US*) to take time off work. **2** [mid-19C+] to leave someone or something alone, to refrain from doing something. **3** [mid-19C+] (*orig. US*) to abstain from using, doing or consuming something. **4** [1910s+] (*US*) to stop being annoying or interfering.

lay off v.[2] *see* LAY v.[1] (1).

lay off! excl. [20C+] a warning to stop doing something. [LAY OFF v.[1] (2)]

lay off to someone v. [1910s–20s] to make an attempt to impress someone.

lay off with v. [1940s–50s] (*Aus.*) to have sex with. [ext. LAY v.[1] (1)]

lay on v. **1** [late 19C+] (*also* **lay**) to give, esp. drugs. **2** [late 19C+] to tell, to impose facts upon. **3** [1900s] (*Aus.*) to assail.

lay on a burn v. [2000s] (*US Black*) to give someone a sexually transmitted disease on purpose. [LAY ON v. (1) + BURN v.[1]]

lay one on someone v. [1930s+] (*US*) to hit or beat someone. [SE *lay* + ONE n.[1] (1)]

lay one's knowledge v. [1940s] (*US Black*) to take advantage of a situation.

lay one's larceny v. *see* LARCENY n.[2].

lay one's racket v. [1930s–40s] (*US Black*) **1** to reveal one's real agenda, usu. a confidence trick or hoax. **2** to tease. [SE *lay(out)* + RACKET n.[1]]

lay on the heavy v. *see* LAY HEAVY ON v.

lay (on) the hip v. [1930s–50s] (*US*) to smoke opium (cf. LAY (DOWN) v.). [the usu. posture for smoking opium is to lie on one's side]

lay on the jack v. [16C] to beat or scold severely. [SE *lay on* + JACK n.[1]]

lay on the shelf v. [late 18C–19C] to pawn something. [an ironic ref. to SE use, to put away for later]

lay on to v. *see* LAY INTO v.

layout n.[1] **1** [mid-19C] an achievement, an activity. **2** [mid-19C–1950s] (*US*) a plan, a scheme. **3** [mid-19C+] (*US*) an apartment, a house, or any place. **4** [late 19C+] a situation, the facts.

layout n.[2] **1** [mid–late 19C] a set of equipment or clothes. **2** [mid-19C+] the table, dice, cards etc required for setting up a gambling club, whether legitimate or as a prop for a confidence trick. **3** [mid-19C+] any form of display, e.g. a showman's stall.

layout n.[3] [mid-19C–1960s] (*US*) an association of persons, such as a gang or team.

layout n.[4] (*also* **hop layout**) **1** [late 19C–1960s] an opium den. **2** [late 19C–1980s] (*drugs*) the various accoutrements – pipe, box, needle etc – required for smoking opium. **3** [1920s+] the syringe, cotton etc required for injecting a narcotic. [the 'kit' is 'laid out' in front of the user before smoking]

lay out v.[1] **1** [early 19C–1950s] (*US*) to defeat or overcome; often ext. as LAY OUT COLD v. **2** [mid-19C–1960s] (*US*) to kill. **3** [mid-19C+] (*orig. US*) to knock someone out in a fight. **4** [late 19C–1900s] (*Aus.*) to indulge oneself to excess, e.g. in drinking. **5** [late 19C–1960s] (*US*) to amaze or astound. **6** [1900s–60s] (*US*) to scold or reprimand; thus *laying out*, a scolding. **7** [1920s–30s] (*US Black*) to stop what one is doing, esp. suddenly. **8** [1920s–30s] (*US Black*) to avoid someone, to step aside.

lay out v.[2] (*also* **lay it out**) [1930s+] to inform, to pass on information, to make something clear; thus *lay it out straight*, to tell all the facts.

lay out v.[3] [1960s+] **1** (*US campus*) to sunbathe. **2** (*Irish*) to deceive sexually.

layout across the drink n. [1940s] (*US Black*) Europe. [LAYOUT n.[1] (3) + DRINK n.[1] (1)]

lay out cold v. [early 19C+] (*orig. US*) **1** to knock out, to defeat. **2** to astound, to amaze. [ext. of LAY OUT v.[1]]

lay out in lavender v. [1940s+] (*US*) to scold severely, to indulge in a verbal battle.

lay (out) like a carpet v. (*also* **lay (out) like a rug**) [1920s–50s] (*US*) to knock unconscious. [ext. of LAY OUT v.[1] (3)]

layover n. *see* LAREOVER n.

lay over v.[1] **1** [mid–late 19C] (*US*) to miss, to allow to pass by, to postpone. **2** [mid-19C+] to wait, to stay somewhere.

lay over v.[2] [mid-19C–1920s] (*Aus./US*) to surpass, to excel.

lay paper v. [20C+] (*US Und.*) to pass counterfeit money or stolen cheques.

lay pipe v. *see* LAY (SOME) PIPE v.

lay pit and boxes into one v. [late 18C–early 19C] to remove the physical division between the vagina and the anus (cf. LAY BACK AND FRONT SHOPS INTO ONE v.). [orig. theatre; 'A simile borrowed from the playhouse, when for the benefit of some favourite player, the pit and boxes are laid together' (Grose, 1785)]

lay rubber v. (*also* **lay tread/wheels**) [1950s+] (*US*) to drive off at speed, spinning the wheels as one accelerates away. [the rubber leaves a mark on the road]

lay some cable v. (*also* **lay (a) cable**) [1970s+] to defecate.

lay some (hot) iron v. [1930s–60s] (*US Black*) to tap-dance, esp. as a professional. [the metal cleats on a tap-dancer's shoes]

lay someone trigging v. [late 18C–mid-19C] to knock someone down. [? SE *trig*, the starting line of a race or that from which bowlers deliver the bowl; or ? SE *trig*, in good physical condition, strong, sound]

lay some on me! excl. [1950s+] (*US Black*) an invitation to swap ritual hand slaps as a form of greeting.

lay (some) pipe v. [1930s+] (*US*) to have sexual intercourse, whether vaginal or anal (cf. BURY IT v.). [PIPE n.[2] (1)]

lay the arm on v. *see* PUT THE ARM ON v. (2).

lay the hip v. *see* LAY (ON) THE HIP v.

lay the leg v. **1** [17C; 1910s+] to have sexual intercourse. **2** [1940s+] (*US prison*) to sodomize. [ext. of LAY v.[1] (1)]

lay the lip v. [1930s–40s] (*US*) to fellate (cf. COCKSUCK n.).

lay the make (on) v. [1960s+] (*US*) to become sexually aggressive. [SE *lay* + MAKE n.[3] (1)]

lay them down v. [mid–late 19C] to play cards.

lay them in the aisles v. (*also* **knock them in the aisles**, **roll them in the aisles**) [1930s+] (*orig. theatre*) to be a great success, to reduce people to uncontrollable laughter.

lay the note v. [1920s–70s] (*US Und.*) **1** to swindle, to short-change. **2** to pay a prostitute.

lay the rod v. [1980s+] (*W.I.*) to have sexual intercourse (cf. BURY IT v.). [LAY v.[1] (1) + ROD n.[1] (1)]

lay the smack down v. [2000s] (*US Black*) to hit someone.

lay the stool's foot in water v. [18C–19C] to prepare for the arrival of guests. [ety. unknown]

lay the track v. [2000s] (*US prison*) to have (presumably homosexual) sexual intercourse. [LAY v.[1] (1) + SE *track*]

lay tight v. [1940s+] (*US Black*) to stay calm, to retain one's grip of a situation.

lay tread v. *see* LAY RUBBER v.

lay two ways v. [1960s–70s] (*US Black*) to short-change, to rob someone in an ostensibly honest exchange of money.

lay-up n. **1** [late 19C] a drink of alcohol. **2** [1930s] a term in jail. **3** [1940s] (*UK Und.*) a hideout. [LAY UP v.[1]]

lay up v.[1] **1** [mid-19C+] to rest, to relax. **2** [late 19C] (*US*) to die. **3** [1920s] to live, to be in a place. **4** [1920s+] (*US*) to hide, to take refuge.

lay up v.[2] *see* LAY BACK v.

lay up in lavender v. **1** [late 16C–19C] to pawn. **2** [17C–19C] to put out of harm's way. **3** [17C–19C] to imprison. **4** [late 17C–19C] to die. [ironic use of SE *lay up in lavender*, to put aside carefully for future use. Lavender was then, as now, kept with stored linen and other fabrics]

lay up one's heels v. *see* KICK UP ONE'S HEELS v.[1].

lay up with v. [1920s+] (*US*) to have sexual intercourse with. [LAY v.[1] (1)]

lay wheels v. *see* LAY RUBBER v.

laziosis n. [20C+] (*W.I., Guyn./Belz.*) laziness. [SE *lazy* + a play on sfx -*osis* used in words that name illnesses, e.g. tuberculosis]

lazy-ass sack of shit n. *see* SAD SACK OF SHIT n.

lazy body n. [1980s+] (*W.I./UK Black teen*) a slob, someone who is averse to physical exercise and exertion.

lazybones n. **1** [mid-16C+] an idler, a loafer. **2** [late 18C–19C] an implement resembling a pair of tongs that old, ill or fat people use to pick things up.

lazyboots n. [19C] a lazy person. [on the pattern of SLYBOOTS n.]

lazy Laurence n. (*also* **lazy Larrence/Lawrence**) [mid-18C–1900s] the embodiment of laziness; thus [19C] *get Laurence*, *Laurence has got me*, I am feeling lazy; *touch of Laurence*, laziness; *have Laurence on one's back*, to be lazy. [the prob. apocryphal tale of the martyred St *Lawrence* who refused to make a sound as he was roasted to death, causing his executioner to suggest that far from being stoic, he was too lazy]

lazy-legs n. [19C] an idler, a loafer.

lazy lob n. [20C+] a semi-erect penis. [SE *lazy* + LOB n.[3]]

lazy-man's load n. [late 18C–19C] an excessively heavy load carried to avoid a second trip.

l.b. n. [1960s+] (*drugs*) one pound in weight. [1*lb*; pron. 'el-bee']

l.b.j. n. [1960s+] **1** (*US drugs*) LSD (cf. A n.[3]). **2** (*US drugs*) phencyclidine (cf. ACE n.[4]). **3** (*US drugs*) heroin. **4** (*US*) a large penis. [? joc. ref. to US President *Lyndon Baines Johnson* (1908–73) or from the nickname for the military prison in Vietnam, *Long Binh Jail*]

l.b.w. n. *see* LEG BEFORE WICKET n.

l.d. n. [1970s+] (*US Black*) a Cadillac *Eldo*rado. [abbr. of pron. 'el-dee']

lead *n.*[1] (*also* **lead plum/sandwich**) (*US*) **1** [19C+] a bullet. **2** [1900s] a gun.

lead *n.*[2] [mid–late 19C] a collection of money, e.g. by a street performer.

lead a gay life *v.* [mid–late 19C] to work as a prostitute, to lead an immoral life. [GAY adj.[1]]

lead apes in hell *v.* [late 16C–mid-19C] to become an old maid; thus APE-LEADER *n.* ['Rather thou shouldest leade a lyfe to thine owne lyking in earthe, than [...] leade Apes in Hell' (John Lyly, *Euphues*, 1579); ult. pvb 'women dying maids lead apes in hell'; *Gentlemans Magazine* (1798) suggests that the image was created 'by the monks to allure young women into the cloisters']

lead balloon *n.* [1950s+] (*US*) a failure; often in phr. *go down/over like a lead balloon.*

lead down the garden path *v. see* LEAD UP THE GARDEN PATH *v.*

leaden capsule *n. see* LEAD PILL *n.*

leaden favour *n. see* LEADEN PILL *n.*

Leadenhall market sportsman *n.* [late 19C] a landowner who sells game to the poulterers of London's Leadenhall Market.

leaden pill *n.* (*also* **leaden favour**) [19C–1900s] a bullet.

leadfoot *n.* (*US*) **1** [1930s+] a fast driver. **2** [1950s] a clumsy person. [SE *lead* + *foot*; (1) refers to the heaviness of a foot on the accelerator; (2) the heaviness that slows one down]

lead foot *v.* (*US*) **1** [1930s+] to drive a vehicle very fast. **2** [1950s] to move slowly and clumsily. [LEADFOOT *n.*]

lead-footed *adj.* (*US*) **1** [1930s+] speeding. **2** [1950s] slow, clumsy. [LEAD FOOT *v.*]

leadhead *n.* [1940s+] (*US*) an idiot. [SE *lead* + -HEAD sfx (1)]

leading article *n.*[1] **1** [mid–late 19C] the nose. **2** [mid-19C–1900s] the vagina.

leading article *n.*[2] [late 19C] the best bargain in the shop, which should lead the buyer onto a more expensive purchase.

leading card *n.* [late 17C+] an example or precedent. [card-playing jargon; the card that is led sets the initial betting standard for a round of play]

lead off *v.* [1910s+] (*orig. milit.*) to lose one's temper.

lead pill *n.* (*also* **leaden capsule**) [mid-19C–1950s] (*US*) a bullet. [LEAD *n.*[1] (1) + SE *pill*]

lead pipe *n.* [1900s–50s] (*US prison*) prison-cooked spaghetti.

lead-pipe cinch *n.* (*US*) **1** [late 19C] a firm grip. **2** [late 19C] (*also* **lead pipe**) an absolute certainty, an easy task. [the solidity of a SE *lead pipe* + CINCH *n.*[1] (1)]

lead plum *n. see* LEAD *n.*[1].

lead poisoning *n.* [late 19C+] (*orig. US*) shotgun shells, revolver bullets, esp. when lodged in a victim's body. [LEAD *n.*[1] (1) + SE *poisoning*]

lead-pusher *n.* (*also* **lead-spitter, lead-squirt**) [20C+] (*US*) a gun.

lead sandwich *n. see* LEAD *n.*[1].

lead sheet *n.* [1930s–40s] (*US Black*) an overcoat or other outer garment. [musical jargon *lead sheet*, a sheet of music containing the melodic line and lyric only; Mezzrow & Wolfe, *Really the Blues* (1946): 'As for *lead sheet*, it's only one sheet of music out of a whole orchestration, with only the melody line on it, and hence thin enough to mean topcoat; whereas the *full orchestration* is, by contrast, thick and bulky, and could only mean a heavy overcoat']

lead sled *n.* [1950s+] (*US*) a slow vehicle.

lead someone by a string *v.* (*also* **lead someone on a string, ...with a string**) [late 19C+] to have someone utterly under one's control.

lead-spitter/-squirt *n. see* LEAD-PUSHER *n.*

lead-swinger *n.* [1910s+] one who shirks their duties, a malingerer.

lead-swinging *n.* [1910s+] the act of shirking one's duties, malingering.

lead towel *n.* **1** [mid-18C–early 19C] a pistol. **2** [early 19C] a bullet.

lead up the garden path *v.* (*also* **lead down the garden path**) [1920s+] to trick, to deceive deliberately, to tease. [the image is of luring a woman up the garden path and so out of sight of the house in order to attempt seduction]

lead with one's chin *v.* [1940s+] (*orig. boxing*) to act incautiously, to act without restraint. [in boxing such a technique would leave one dangerously vulnerable]

leaf *n.*[1] (*US drugs*) **1** [1910s–30s] (*also* **leaf-gum**) crude opium (cf. APOSTLE *n.*). **2** [1930s+] drugs in general. **3** [1940s+] cocaine. **4** [1960s+] marijuana (cf. AFRICAN BUSH *n.*). [the plants from which they are taken]

leaf *n.*[2] (*US*) **1** [1920s–30s] a $100 bill (cf. ALFALFA *n.*). **2** [1920s+] a $1 bill.

leaf freak *n.* (*also* **leaf peeper**) [1960s+] (*US*) a tourist drawn to New England (or elsewhere) in order to enjoy its spectacular autumn leaves. [SE *leaf* + FREAK sfx/SE *peeper*]

leaf-gum *n. see* LEAF *n.*[1] (1).

leafless tree *n.* [early–mid-19C] the gallows; thus *climb the leafless tree/leap from the leafless tree*, to be hanged.

leaf of the old author *n.* (*also* **drop of the old author**) [19C] a drink, esp. of brandy. [? the *old author* being God]

leaf peeper *n. see* LEAF FREAK *n.*

leak *n.*[1] [early 18C–19C] the female genitals.

leak *n.*[2] **1** [1910s+] (*orig. US*) the act of urination; thus TAKE A LEAK *v.* **2** [1910s+] (*orig. US*) a piece of hitherto secret information that has been revealed; thus *turn on the leaks*, to inform, to betray. **3** [1920s+] (*Aus.*) an informer. **4** [1930s+] (*Aus.*) a trick, a dodge.

leak *n.*[3] *see* LEEK *n.*

leak *v.*[1] **1** [late 16C+] to urinate (cf. BLEED ONE'S TURKEY *v.*). **2** [late 19C+] (*US*) to weep. **3** [1900s] (*US*) to rain. **4** [1980s+] (*US*) to bleed.

leak *v.*[2] **1** [mid-19C+] to reveal a secret unintentionally, or intentionally. **2** [late 19C] (*US*) to lie. [(1) is now SE]

leakhouse *n.* (*also* **leakery**) [1940s+] (*Aus.*) a lavatory (cf. BACKHOUSE *n.*). [LEAK *n.*[2] (1) + SE *house*]

leaky *adj.*[1] **1** [late 17C+] unable to keep a secret. **2** [early 19C–1900s] drunk and thus talkative. [SE; but note LEAK *v.*[2] (1)]

leaky *adj.*[2] **1** [early 18C] in need of urination. **2** [20C+] (*US*) tearful, weepy. **3** [1990s+] (*Irish*) of weather, wet. [LEAK *v.*[1]]

leaky bladder *n.* [20C+] a stepladder. [rhy. sl.]

lean *adj.* [late 19C] of employment, unremunerative. [SE *lean*, thin]

lean *v.*[1] [1970s+] (*US Black/West Coast*) to drive a car while leaning out of the window. [the image is supposedly that of a pimp cruising the streets with his prostitutes]

lean *v.*[2] *see* LEAN ON *v.* (1).

lean *adv.* [1980s+] (*US Black*) obviously, strongly.

lean against the engine *v.* [1940s–50s] (*US drugs*) to smoke opium. [the recumbent posture of opium smokers, and the concomitant smoke]

lean and fat *n.* (*also* **leaning fat**) [mid-19C+] a hat. [rhy. sl.]

lean and linger *n.* (*also* **long(ers) and linger**) [1920s+] a finger. [rhy. sl.]

lean and lurch *n.* [mid-19C+] a church. [rhy. sl.]

lean and mean *adj.* [1940s+] (*US*) **1** used to describe something that is plain but efficient. **2** fit, ready for action. [SE *lean* + MEAN *adj.*]

lean-away *n.* [late 19C–1950s] (*Aus.*) a drunkard.

leaned *adj.* [1990s+] (*drugs*) under the influence of cannabis. [? abbr. LEAN AND MEAN *adj.*]

lean green *n.* [1970s+] (*US teen*) money (cf. ALFALFA *n.*). [GREEN *n.*[2] (1)]

leaning fat *n. see* LEAN AND FAT *n.*

leaning house *n.* [1970s+] (*US Black*) a brothel or a place where illicit meetings, drug sales etc take place (cf. ACCOMMODATION HOUSE *n.*). [SE *lean*, i.e. relax + HOUSE *n.*[1] (1)]

lean into v. [20C+] (*Irish*) to pressurize, to threaten.

lean on v. **1** [1910s+] (*also* **lean**) (*orig. US*) to beat up, to strike. **2** [1920s+] (*orig. US*) to pressurize, to persuade, poss. with violence or threats of violence. **3** [1920s+] to depend on. **4** [1960s+] (*US Black*) to disparage or ridicule.

lean over backwards v. *see* BEND OVER BACKWARDS v.

lean-to n. [1940s] a lodging house, night shelter or similar refuge for homeless people.

lean trot n. [1970s+] (*Aus.*) a spell of bad luck or unfortunate experiences. [SE *lean* + TROT n.² (4)]

leap v. [17C–18C] to have sexual intercourse with. [SE *leap*, of an animal, to copulate]

leap and you will receive phr. [1970s+] (*US Black*) a ritual challenge to a fight.

leap at a crust v. [mid-17C–mid-18C] to be starving.

leap at a daisy v. [mid-16C–early 17C] to be hanged. [the grass surrounding the gallows]

leap at Tyburn v. [late 17C–early 19C] to be hanged.

leaper n. (*also* **leapy**) **1** [1930s–70s] (*US drugs*) a cocaine addict. **2** [1960s+] (*drugs*) any form of stimulant, amphetamine etc; usu. in pl. (cf. A n.²). **3** [1960s+] a dud cheque, drawn against inadequate funds. [SE *leap*; (3) note BOUNCE v.² (4)]

leapfrog n. [1970s] a client who hires a number of prostitutes to play leapfrog while he watches.

leapfrog milk n. [1970s+] (*US*) the wine Liebfraumilch. [mispron.]

leaping adj. [1920s–50s] (*US drugs*) under the influence of drugs or alcohol.

leaping dandruff n. *see* GALLOPING DANDRUFF n.

leaping dominoes n. [1920s] (*US*) dice or the game of craps dice (cf. ABYSSINIAN POLO n.).

leaping house n. [late 16C–18C] a brothel (cf. ACCOMMODATION HOUSE n.). [LEAP v. + SE *house*/HOUSE n.¹ (1)]

leaping lena n. [1910s–50s] (*US*) a small car. [its bumpy motion]

leaping lizards! excl. [1920s–70s] (*US*) an excl. expressing surprise. [coined in comic strip *L'il Orphan Annie* by Harold Gray (1894–1968)]

leap in the dark v. (*also* **leap up a ladder**) [18C–19C] to have sexual intercourse.

leap over the wall v. *see* GO OVER THE WALL v. (3).

leaps n. **1** [1920s–60s] (*US drugs*) withdrawal symptoms from cocaine addiction. **2** [1940s–50s] (*US Und.*) nerves, tension. [the fits that may be part of withdrawal]

leap up a ladder v. *see* LEAP IN THE DARK v.

leapy n. *see* LEAPER n.

lea-rigs n. [late 19C] the vagina. [SE *lea-rig*, a ridge left in grass at the end of a ploughed field]

leariness n. *see* LEERY adj. (1).

learn French v. [17C] to become infected with syphilis. [SE *learn* + FRENCH adj. (1)]

learning shover n. [late 19C] a teacher.

learn manners in Seville v. [1910s–20s] to learn acceptable, if rather juv., manners. [pun on *Seville*/SE *civil*]

learn the ropes v. [20C+] to learn the way to do something; to become acquainted with all the dodges. [orig. naut.]

leary *see also under* LAIRY.

leary adj. *see* LEERY adj.

leary bloke n. [mid-19C] a showy dresser. [? LAIRY adj. (2) + BLOKE n. (1)]

leary cove n. [early–mid-19C] one who is well versed in the criminal world. [LEERY adj. + COVE n. (1)]

least n. [1950s] (*US Black*) a mediocre or dull person or event. [the opposite of MOST, THE n.]

leather n.¹ **1** [14C–19C] the skin; thus LOSE LEATHER v. **2** [late 19C] (*US*) liver. **3** [1910s–30s] (*US*) meat. [(1) SE until 18C]

leather n.² **1** [mid-16C+] the vagina. **2** [mid-16C+] a promiscuous woman. **3** [mid-16C+] sexual intercourse; thus LABOUR LEATHER v.;

nothing like leather, there is nothing as good as sex. **4** [1930s+] (*US*) the anus.

leather n.³ **1** [mid-18C+] a wallet, a purse, a bag. **2** [mid-19C+] a leather ball, usu. a cricket ball or football; (*US*) a baseball. **3** [late 19C+] (*US*) a shoe. **4** [1910s–30s] (*US*) a whip. **5** [1920s+] (*US*) a holster. **6** [1920s+] (*US*) a boxing glove. **7** [1920s+] (*US*) a saddle; thus *fork leather*, to ride a horse; *hit leather*, to ride off; *hunt/pull leather*, to grasp the saddle while riding a bucking horse. **8** [1930s] (*US Und.*) a pickpocket. **9** [1930s–40s] (*US*) a brutal kicking with a boot or shoe. **10** [1960s+] a leather coat or jacket.

leather adj. [1960s+] (*orig. US gay*) pertaining to leather fetishism in attire and behaviour.

leather v.¹ [mid-18C+] to beat, to kick. [note LEATHER n.³ (3)]

leather v.² [1930s+] (*gay*) to perform anal intercourse (cf. ASK FOR THE RING v.). [LEATHER n.² (4)]

leather bar n. (*also* **leather lounge**) [1960s+] (*orig. US gay*) a bar frequented by leather fetishists and sadomasochistic male homosexuals. [LEATHER adj. + SE *bar*/*lounge*]

leather-bottom n. (*also* **leatherbum**) [20C+] a civil servant who is totally dedicated to work and thus never leaves their desk.

leather boy n. (*also* **leather man**) [1960s+] (*gay*) a male leather fetishist homosexual. [LEATHER adj. + SE *boy*]

leather-dresser n. [19C] the penis.

leather dyke n. [1990s+] (*gay*) a lesbian leather fetishist. [LEATHER adj. + DYKE n.]

leathered adj. [1990s+] having consumed a large volume of alcohol in a very short time. [fig. use of LEATHER v.¹]

leather-face n. [mid–late 19C] (*US*) an emotionless face or the individual with such a face.

leather freak n. [1960s+] (*US*) a leather fetishist. [LEATHER adj. + FREAK sfx]

leather glommer n. [1930s] (*US*) a pickpocket's assistant. [the pickpocket 'lifts' the LEATHER n.³ (1), while the assistant GLOM v. (1) or grabs it and takes it away]

leatherhead n.¹ **1** [early 17C+] a fool, a stupid person. **2** [mid-19C–1900s] (*US*) an inhabitant of Pennsylvania. [SE *leather* + -HEAD sfx (1)]

leatherhead n.² (*also* **leatherneck**) [mid-19C–1940s] (*US*) a policeman or watchman. [the protective leather helmets worn by the police, or the leather badges that New York's first policemen wore]

leatherhead n.³ [1920s] (*US*) a louse. [their seeming indestructibility]

leather-headed adj. [late 18C–1910s] foolish, stupid (cf. AIRHEADED adj.). [LEATHERHEAD n.¹ (1)]

leathering n. (*also* **leathers**) [late 18C+] a beating, a flogging. [LEATHER v.¹]

leather lane n. [19C] the vagina (cf. ALLEY n.¹; ANTIPODES n.). [LEATHER n.² (1) + pun on the *Leather Lane* market, off Holborn, London]

leather-lane adj. [early 19C] second-rate, poorly made. [the *Leather Lane* market, off Holborn, London EC1]

leather lifter n. [1920s–40s] (*US Und.*) a pickpocket. [LEATHER n.³ (1) + LIFTER n.¹ (1)]

leather lounge n. *see* LEATHER BAR n.

leather man n. *see* LEATHER BOY n.

leather medal n. [early 19C–1940s] (*US*) a fig. medal for failure, laziness, the booby prize. [a 'real' medal is metal]

leathern conveniency n. (*also* **leathern convenience/sanctuary**) **1** [late 17C–mid-19C] a stage-coach. **2** [19C] a purse. [orig. 17C Quaker jargon]

leatherneck n.¹ **1** [late 19C–1960s] (*orig. Aus.*) a roustabout. **2** [20C+] (*US*) a thug, a lout. [the effects of the sun on skin]

leatherneck n.² [20C+] (*UK/US*) a marine. [early US marine uniforms had a leather neckband]

leatherneck n.³ *see* LEATHERHEAD n.².

leathern sanctuary n. *see* LEATHERN CONVENIENCY n.

leather piece *n.* [1960s+] (*US Black*) any garment, esp. a coat, made of leather.

leather-pusher *n.* [1920s] a boxer. [LEATHER n.³ (6) + SE *pusher*]

leather queen *n.* [1960s+] (*orig. US gay*) a male homosexual who likes dressing in leather and may also enjoy sadomasochism. [LEATHER adj. + QUEEN n.² (1)/QUEEN sfx (2)]

leathers *n.*¹ **1** [mid–late 19C] anyone wearing leather leggings or breeches, e.g. a coachman. **2** [1960s+] leather garments, esp. as worn by motorcyclists. **3** [1970s–80s] (*UK Black*) shoes.

leathers *n.*² *see* LEATHERING n.

leatherskin *n.* [mid–late 19C] (*US*) a derog. name for a Native American.

leather-stretcher *n.* [19C] the penis. [LEATHER n.² (1) + SE *stretcher*]

leather worker *n.* [1900s] (*US Und.*) a pickpocket. [LEATHER n.³ (1) + WORKER n.¹ (2)]

leave *v.* [mid-19C+] (*mainly US*) to allow, to permit.

leave before the gospel *v.* [20C+] to practise coitus interruptus. [i.e. before the church service is fully over]

leave for dead *v.* [20C+] to defeat absolutely, to leave far behind in any form of competition. [SE *leave for dead*]

leave go *v.* (*also* **leave hold/loose**) [mid-19C+] to let go of.

leave in the air *v.* [1960s+] to leave unresolved.

leave it out! *excl.* [1970s+] a general excl. of admonition; stop doing that! don't be so stupid! etc.

leave it wet for someone *v.* [2000s] (*US Black*) to have sexual intercourse. [the idea of being with someone else's partner]

leave loose *v. see* LEAVE GO v.

leave off *v.* [mid-19C+] to stop doing something.

leave off! *excl.* [late 19C+] stop it! (esp. in sense of stop telling lies).

leave one's face *v.* [1980s+] (*US campus*) to embarrass oneself, to act in an embarrassing way.

leave shaping *v.* [20C+] (*W.I.*) to outsmart, to fool. [the image is of cricket; a batsman is still *shaping* up to play the ball when it passes the bat and bowls him out]

leave someone cold *v.* [mid-19C+] to fail to excite or interest, to disgust or be uninspiring.

leave someone hanging *v.* [1970s+] (*US Black*) to reject or ignore a proffered handshake or to refuse to indulge in the ritualizing hand-slapping used as a greeting.

leave someone in their glory *v.* [late 19C] to leave someone by themself.

leave someone out to dry *v. see* HANG SOMEONE OUT TO DRY v.

leave someone the bucket *v.* [1940s–50s] (*US prison*) to leave jail. [the bucket used as a chamberpot that prisoners must empty each morning]

leave someone up to dry *v. see* HANG SOMEONE OUT TO DRY v.

leave the dead at someone *v.* [20C+] (*W.I.*) to abandon when in difficulties, to 'leave holding the baby'. [image of abandoning a corpse]

leave the minority *v.* [late 19C] to die (cf. JOIN THE GREAT MAJORITY v.). [i.e. to join the much greater number of dead from thousands of years of humanity]

leave the world with cotton in one's ears *v.* [early 19C] to be hanged. [proper name *Cotton*, a 19C Newgate chaplain who would preach a last sermon to the condemned man]

leave town *v.* [1900s–60s] (*US Black*) to die.

leave yer 'omer *n.* [late 19C] a very attractive man. [one for whom one would 'leave your home']

leaving shop *n.* **1** [mid–late 19C] an unlicensed pawnshop, specializing in lending very small sums on items that mainstream pawnbrokers reject; the usual rate of income was 2 (old) pence on the shilling, i.e. approx. 16.66%. **2** [late 19C] the vagina. [both places where something is left, deposited]

Leb *n.*¹ (*also* **Lebanese**) [1960s+] (*drugs*) Lebanese hashish; usu. qualified as *Red Leb*, *Lebanese Gold* (cf. AFGHAN n.).

Leb *n.*² [1980s+] **1** (*US*) a *Leb*anese person. **2** (*Aus.*) (*also* **lebbo**) an immigrant from the *Leb*anon. **3** *Leb*anon. [abbr.]

leccy *n. see* LECKY n.

lech *see under* LETCH and its combs.

lechery-layer *n.* [late 17C–18C] a prostitute. [SE *lechery* + LAY v.¹ (1)]

lecky *n.* (*also* **leccy**, **lekkie**) [1960s+] **1** electricity, esp. as a utility; thus *fiddle the lecky*, to cheat on one's electricity bill. **2** an electrician. [abbr.]

lecky *adj.* [1960s+] electric; thus *lecky blanket*, *lecky kettle*. [abbr.]

led captain *n.* (*also* **led-friend**) [late 17C–mid-19C] **1** a toady or sycophant, 'an humble dependent in a great family, who, for a precarious subsistence, and distant hopes of preferment, suffers every kind of indignity' (Grose, 1785). **2** a pimp (cf. ABBOT ON THE CROSS n.). [SE *led horse*, a riderless horse that is often seen in the retinues of the rich and powerful, underlining the extent of their possessions, and the fact that they have them, even if they are of no real use; Grose adds that 'the small provision made for officers of the army and navy, in time of peace, obliges many [...] to occupy this wretched station']

ledge, the *n.* [2000s] (*US Black*) the situation, all the facts. [clipping of SE *knowledge*]

leeg *adj.* [1990s+] (*UK juv.*) a general negative. [SE *legitimate*]

lee-gate *v.* [1970s] (*US/P.R.*) to spy on, to act as a peeping Tom. [Sp. sl. *ligando*]

leek *n.* (*also* **leak**) [early 18C] a Welsh person. [a national emblem]

Leekshire *n.* [18C–19C] Wales. [SE *leek*, a national emblem of Wales + sfx *-shire*]

leeky store *n.* [1970s–80s] (*US Black*) liquor store. [pron. of SE]

Lee Marvin *adj.* [1960s+] starving. [rhy. sl.; ult. US film star *Lee Marvin* (1924–87]

leen *n.* [1990s+] (*US Black/drugs*) mescaline. [abbr.]

leer *n.* [late 18C–19C] a newspaper. [? LURE n. or Sp. *leer*, to read]

leerer *n.* [mid-19C] (*UK Und.*) an eye. [? SE *leer*, looking askance, sly]

leery *adj.* (*also* **leary**) **1** [early 18C+] bright, alert, aware; thus *leariness*. **2** [early 18C+] guarded, suspicious of or uneasy about someone or something. **3** [late 19C–1930s] (*US*) hungover, drunk. **4** [20C+] cunning, underhand. **5** [20C+] bad-tempered, disagreeable, cheeky. **6** [1930s] (*US Und.*) of goods, damaged. [? SE *leer*, looking askance, sly]

Lee Van (Cleef) *n.* [1990s+] beef. [rhy. sl.; ult. *Lee Van Cleef* (1925–89), US actor most famous for playing the villains in spaghetti westerns]

left *adv.* [late 19C–1910s] (*US*) at a disadvantage, defeated, abandoned; esp. as *get left*, to be placed at a disadvantage, to be left in a difficult situation.

left and right *n.* [20C+] a fight. [rhy. sl.]

left-field *adj.* [1960s+] (*US*) unorthodox. [baseball imagery]

leftfielder *n.* [1940s–60s] (*US Black/teen*) a criminal. [baseball imagery]

left-footer *n.*¹ (*also* **left-hander**) [1930s+] a Roman Catholic, but used in reverse by Catholics who define themselves as *right-handers*; thus DIG WITH THE...FOOT v.; KICK WITH THE LEFT FOOT v. [? turf-cutting spades, as used by Catholics, having the lugs – that piece upon which the foot presses down – on the left of the haft. Note Pennsylvania use *left-winger*, a Roman Catholic]

left-footer *n.*² [1980s] a male homosexual.

left-footing *n.* [1980s] conducting a homosexual lifestyle. [LEFT-FOOTER n.²]

left-handed *adj.* **1** [early–mid-18C] of sexual relations, extramarital. **2** [late 19C] sly, surreptitious. **3** [late 19C–1910s] (*UK Und.*) second-hand. **4** [late 19C+] undesirable, illicit, evil. **5** [1920s–70s] (*US*) homosexual. **6** [1930s–40s] reverse, back-to-front; also in fig. use. [lit. trans. of Lat. *sinister*]

left-handed batsman *n*. [1990s+] a male homosexual.

left-handed compliment *n*. [late 19C+] an insincere or 'back-handed' compliment, a remark that 'damns with faint praise'. [LEFT-HANDED adj. (4) + SE *compliment*]

left-handed monkey wrench *n*. (*also* **left-handed spanner**) [1920s+] (*US*) an imaginary tool that an inexperienced worker is sent to find as a prank.

left-handed sugar bowl *n*. [1950s+] (*US*) a chamberpot.

left-handed website *n*. [1990s+] a website specializing in pornography. [it causes visitors to use the mouse with their left hand]

left-handed wife *n*. [18C–1930s] a mistress. [anything *left-handed* is *de facto* suspect. Grose (1796) adds the German custom whereby 'when a man married his concubine, or a woman greatly his inferior, he gave her his left hand']

left-hander *n*. *see* LEFT-FOOTER *n*.[1].

leftie *see under* LEFTY.

left in the lurch *n*. [late 19C+] a church (cf. IN THE LURCH *n*.). [rhy. sl.]

left-off *n*. [mid-19C+] a cast-off.

left off! *excl*. [1960s–70s] (*US campus*) a joc. reversal of RIGHT ON! excl.

left over *n*. [1930s] (*US*) mashed potatoes.

left raise *n*. (*US Black*) **1** [1930s–40s] the left-hand side of one's body plus the relevant limbs. **2** [1930s–40s] the left side of anything. **3** [1940s–50s] a pocket, presumably on the left of one's jacket or trousers.

left turn *n*. [1930s] (*US Und.*) a fool.

lefty *n*. (*also* **leftie**) **1** [mid-19C+] (*orig. US*) a left-handed person or a nickname for one who is left-handed; thus adv. *lefty*, with the left hand. **2** [1910s–60s] a person who has lost their limbs on their left side (arm and leg). **3** [1930s+] a left-wing political radical.

lefty *adj*. (*also* **leftie**) **1** [1930s+] left-handed. **2** [1940s+] left-wing, communist. [LEFTY *n*.]

leg *n*.[1] [mid-18C–mid-19C] someone who is to be transported. [LEG *v*.[2] (1)]

leg *n*.[2] **1** [19C–1930s] a bookmaker or professional layer of odds, e.g. in faro. **2** [early–late 19C] a cheating racehorse or cards gambler; thus *leggism*, the characteristics of such a gambler. [abbr. BLACKLEG *n*.[1]]

leg *n*.[3] [mid-19C] the act of running away, escaping.

leg *n*.[4] [mid–late 19C] a round or rubber of a card-game; thus *leg-and-leg*, a situation in which each player in the game has won a leg. [orig. naut. use as 'a run made on a single track' (Webster, 1897)]

leg *n*.[5] **1** [mid–late 19C] a footman. **2** [1970s] (*US*) an errand boy. [metonymy]

leg *n*.[6] [20C+] (*Irish*) influence; thus *have a good/great leg of someone*, to have influence with, to be 'well in' with them.

leg *n*.[7] [1960s+] **1** (*US*) a promiscuous woman. **2** (*US Black/campus*) any woman; women in general. **3** (*US*) female sexuality. **4** (*US*) sexual intercourse. [both metonymic + poss. euph.; DIRTY LEG *n*.]

leg *v*.[1] **1** [17C+] to run. **2** [late 19C] to trip someone up by seizing their leg. **3** [1960s] (*US Und.*) to shoplift by hiding goods between the legs. **4** [1970s] to set a bomb. **5** [1990s+] to chase, i.e. to make someone run (away).

leg *v*.[2] (*UK Und.*) **1** [mid-18C–mid-19C] to be transported. **2** [mid-19C] to be sentenced to prison; thus *legging*, a jail sentence. [the iron on their leg]

leg *v*.[3] [mid-19C–1900s] to run errands. [LEG *n*.[5]]

leg *v*.[4] (*also* **lag**) [1920s+] (*US*) to make or distribute illicitly distilled whisky. [abbr. SE *bootleg*]

leg *v*.[5] (*also* **leg it**) [1970s+] (*orig. US Black*) to have sexual intercourse. [LEG *n*.[7] (4) or GET ONE'S LEG OVER *v*.]

legal beagle *n*. [1940s+] (*orig. US*) a lawyer, esp. an assiduous one. [assonance]

legal eagle *n*. [1930s+] (*orig. US*) a lawyer, with the implication of being an astute one. [rhy. sl., albeit internal]

legal fleagle *n*. [1970s] (*US*) a lawyer.

leg-and-leg *n*. *see* LEG *n*.[4].

leg art *n*. (*also* **leg picture**) [1930s–50s] actual views or pictures of women revealing their legs.

legback *n*. [1970s–80s] (*UK Black*) the female thigh; thus generically, a woman.

leg bags *n*. [late 18C–19C] stockings or trousers.

leg bail *n*. [mid-18C–1940s] unauthorized absence; thus *give/tip leg bail* (*and land security*), to escape, to run off. [SE *leg* + *bail*, security given against the release of a prisoner pending their trial]

leg before wicket *n*. (*also* **l.b.w.**) [20C+] a ticket, both lit. and fig.; thus *not the l.b.w.*, 'not the ticket'. [rhy. sl.; usu. abbr.]

leg-breaker *n*. [1970s+] (*US Und.*) a hired thug.

leg business *n*. **1** [mid–late 19C] (*US*) the ballet. **2** [mid–late 19C] (*US*) any form of entertainment where the focus is on the women's legs. **3** [late 19C–1930s] sexual intercourse.

leg drama *n*. [late 19C] any form of show, whether a musical or full-scale striptease, in which the focus is on a woman's legs.

legem pone *n*. [16C–17C] the payment of money, cash down. [the first 2 words of the fifth division of Ps. 119, which begins the psalms at Matins on the 25th day of the month, associated with 25 March, the year's first quarter day and thus the first major payday of the calendar]

legend *adj*. [1990s+] (*US campus/Black*) amazing, excellent.

leger *n*. [late 16C] (*UK Und.*) **1** a coal merchant who gives short weight. **2** a London coal merchant who buys wholesale in the country and then retails the coal in London, pretending to be from the country himself. [Fr. *lèger*, light; presumably country coal was considered better quality]

legering *n*. [late 16C] (*UK Und.*) the giving of short measure by colliers. [LEGER *n*. (1)]

legged *adj*. [mid–late 19C; 1970s] chained, in irons; thus imprisoned.

legged for groat *phr*. [late 19C] (*UK tramp*) given a jail sentence of 10 years. [LEGGED adj. + ? SE *groat*, fourpence]

legger *n*.[1] **1** [late 18C–1900s] one who pretends to be selling smuggled goods, but is in fact selling old or shop-worn stock, obtained cheaply. **2** [1920s–60s] (*US*) a smuggler of contraband liquor (cf. BOOTLEGGER *n*.). [? he produces such goods from his breeches' pockets or his boot-tops; (2) abbr. BOOTLEGGER *n*.; *OED* cites *legger* as abbr. of *bootlegger*, but (1) predates it]

legger *n*.[2] [20C+] (*Irish*) a departure on foot; usu. as *do a legger*.

legging *n*. *see* LEG *v*.[2] (2).

leggings *n*. [20C+] (*W.I.*) greens and root vegetables used in soup. [Fr. *legume*, a vegetable]

leggins *n*. [1930s+] (*US gay/prison*) copulation when the penis is rubbed between the legs of the sexual partner.

leggism *n*. *see* LEG *n*.[2] (2).

leggner *n*. [1940s–50s] (*UK prison*) a 12-month sentence. [pun on STRETCH *n*.[1] (2)/SE *stretch a leg*]

leggo! *excl*. **1** [late 19C+] (*orig. US*) let go! **2** [late 19C+] a shout of warning, let's go! run for it! [mispron./mis-sp.]

leggo beas' *adj*. [1940s+] (*W.I. Rasta*) wild, disorderly. [LEGGO BEAST *n*.]

leggo beast *n*. [1940s+] (*W.I.*) **1** a tramp. **2** a person, usu. a woman, with loose morals; by ext. a prostitute. [SE *let go*, uncontrolled, without an owner + *beast*]

leggy *adj*. (*orig. US*) **1** [mid–late 19C] of a stage show, featuring the display of female legs. **2** [1920s+] of a woman, having particularly attractive legs; the adj. is esp. loved by tabloid newspapers who offer *leggy lovely* as a n. **3** [1940s+] sexually attractive.

leg-hanger *n*. *see* HANGIN' ON THE LEG *phr*.

leg into *v*. [1990s+] (*Aus. Und.*) to become involved in, to take a share or portion of.

leg it *v.*[1] **1** [mid-19C+] to run away, to walk. **2** [1910s] to wander, to travel. [LEG *v.*[1] (1)]

leg it *v.*[2] *see* LEG *v.*[5].

legit *n.* **1** [late 19C–1950s] in theatre, 'straight' dramatic productions rather than variety etc. **2** [late 19C–1950s] an actor who works in (1). **3** [1920s+] (*UK/US Und.*) a legitimate employment or occupation or person; thus *on the legit*, honest, fair-dealing, trustworthy. **4** [1950s] a legitimate place, usu. of entertainment – as opposed to an 'after-hours' establishment or a speakeasy. [abbr. SE *legitimate*]

legit *adj.* (*also* **ligit**) [1920s+] (*orig. US*) **1** legitimate. **2** of a person, respectable. [abbr.]

legit *adv.* [1930s+] legitimately. [abbr.]

legit! *excl.* [1990s+] (*US teen*) an excl. of approval, acceptance, 'you're OK', 'that's acceptable'. [LEGIT *adj.*]

legitimacy *n.* [19C] the state of emigrating to Australia as a convict. [one had 'legal reasons' for the trip]

legitimate *n.*[1] [19C] (*Aus.*) a settler who arrived in Australia as a transported convict. [such settlers had 'legal reasons' to make the trip]

legitimate *n.*[2] [early 19C] a sovereign (money). [? as opposed to a forgery]

legitimate *adj.* [1970s+] (*US gay*) heterosexual.

legless *adj.* (*also* **footless**) **1** [1940s+] very drunk, drunk to the extent of falling over (cf. ARSEHOLED *adj.*). **2** [1990s+] exhausted.

leg-licker *n.* [1990s+] (*US gay*) a lesbian (cf. CARPET-BITER *n.*).

leg-lifter *n.* [early 18C–19C] a promiscuous man, a womanizer; thus *leg-lifting*, casual sexual intercourse. [LIFT ONE'S LEG *v.*]

leg man *n.*[1] (*orig. US*) **1** [1920s+] a journalist who actively finds the news. **2** [1930s+] one who acts as a go-between for organized crime and its 'customers'. **3** [1940s+] an assistant. **4** [1960s] any form of go-between. [they run errands]

leg man *n.*[2] **1** [1950s+] a man who prefers a woman's legs to any other part of her anatomy (cf. ASS-MAN *n.*). **2** [1970s+] (*US campus*) a womanizer.

leg of beef *n.* [20C+] a thief. [rhy. sl.]

leg of mutton *n.*[1] [mid-19C] a sheep's trotter.

leg of mutton *n.*[2] [20C+] a button. [rhy. sl.]

leg of mutton in a silk stocking *n.* [late 17C–19C] a woman's leg. [SE but note MUTTON *n.*[1] (2)]

leg of pork *n.* [1990s+] a piece of chalk. [rhy. sl.]

leg of the law *n.* [19C] a lawyer. [var. on LIMB OF THE LAW *n.* (1)]

leg-opener *n.* [1950s+] (*orig. Aus.*) a drink given to a woman in the hope of getting her drunk enough for seduction. [on model of EYE-OPENER *n.*[1] (1)]

legover *n.*[1] [20C+] (*Irish*) assistance, help. [image of giving someone a *leg over* a stile or gate]

legover *n.*[2] [1970s+] (*orig. milit.*) sexual intercourse; thus *give/have a bit of legover*, to have sexual intercourse. [backform. f. GET ONE'S LEG OVER *v.*]

leg picture *n. see* LEG ART *n.*

leg piece *n.* **1** [mid–late 19C] any form of stage performance featuring the female leg, e.g. a burlesque show. **2** [1910s–20s] the ballet.

leg pull *n.* (*also* **leg-pulling**) **1** [late 19C–1910s] (*US campus*) a student who is in particular favour with one or more teachers. **2** [late 19C–1980s] a good-natured hoax or tease. [PULL SOMEONE'S LEG *v.*]

leg pull *v.* [1910s+] to make a joke. [LEG PULL *n.* (2)]

leg puller *n.* **1** [late 19C–1910s] a student who behaves sycophantically towards his teachers. **2** [late 19C–1940s] a joker or good-natured hoaxer. [LEG PULL *n.*]

leg-pulling *n. see* LEG PULL *n.*

leg-roped *adj.* [1900s] (*Aus.*) married. [SAusE *leg-rope*, 'a noosed rope used to secure an animal by one hind leg' (AND)]

legs *n.* [mid-19C+] a tall, thin person. [i.e. all *legs*, no body]

leg sacks *n.* [1930s–40s] (*US Black*) socks; stockings.

legs eleven *n.* **1** [20C+] (*bingo*) the number 11 (cf. ALDERSHOT LADIES *n.*). **2** [1910s] (*Aus.*) a tall, thin man. **3** [1950s–60s] £11. [resemblance]

legshake artist *n.* [20C+] (*orig. Aus.*) a pickpocket. [SE *legshake* + ARTIST *n.* (1)/ARTIST sfx]

leg-shaker *n.* [late 19C–1920s] a dancer.

leg shop *n.* [late 19C] (*US*) a theatre devoted to burlesque, i.e. the display of women's legs.

legs right up to her ass *phr.* (*also* **legs right up to her arse/bum**) [1930s+] (*orig. US*) a male description of a woman with exceptionally long and attractive legs. [SE *legs* + ASS *n.* (2)]

legume *n.*[1] [1980s+] (*US drugs*) a piece or 'button' of peyote cactus. [Fr. *legume*, a vegetable]

legume *n.*[2] [1980s+] (*US campus*) a lazy person, one who lies around doing nothing. [Fr. *legume*, a vegetable]

leg work *n.* **1** [late 19C+] (*orig. US tramp*) in terms of a job, a great deal of walking; also in fig. use, a huge amount of research. **2** [1940s+] intercourse between the thighs or the buttocks (without penetration of the anus).

leg worker *n.* [1930s] (*US*) a street prostitute. [LEG WORK *n.* (1) + pun on SE *leg*]

Leicester (Square) *n.* [1990s+] a chair. [rhy. sl.]

leisure hours *n.* [late 19C–1900s] flowers. [rhy. sl.]

lekker *adj.* [mid-19C+] (*S.Afr.*) **1** an all-embracing term of approval. **2** tipsy, slightly drunk. [Du. *lekker*, pleasant, tasty]

lekkie *n. see* LECKY *n.*

lekking *n.* [1990s+] (*S.Afr. juv.*) to play outside the house.

lel *v.* (*also* **lell**) [mid–late 19C] to arrest, to seize. ['It is from the third person indicative present, *lela*; first person, *lava*, I take. This use of the third person for all the others is usual in *posh an' posh* (half and half), or corrupted Romany, and it occurs in Hindustani' (B&L); note market traders' use, to summons, to prosecute]

lem *n.* (*also* **lemon**) [2000s] (*US Black*) marijuana that smells of lemon when smoked. [abbr.]

lem *v.* [1980s+] (*US drugs*) to smoke up and go directly to sleep. [? LEMON *n.*[1] (1), i.e. one who refuses to socialize]

lemac *n.* (*also* **little man**) [2000s] (*US prison*) a Camel cigarette. [backsl.]

lemme *v.* [20C+] (*orig. US*) let me. [mispron./mis-sp.]

lemon *n.*[1] **1** [mid-19C] a person of a sour disposition. **2** [mid-19C+] (*also* **citron, lime**) anything or anyone undesirable, esp. used of a woman. **3** [1910s+] a disappointment, anything worthless or fraudulent, esp. a poor-quality drug purchase; thus *hand someone the lemon*, to dismiss. **4** [1920s+] a defective car; thus the *lemon law*, a law that provides redress for buyers of substandard or defective cars. **5** [1980s+] (*Aus.*) a lesbian. [images of the lit. + fig. sourness of the fruit; (5) also has hints of SE *suck*]

lemon *n.*[2] [20C+] a victim, a fool (cf. APPLEHEAD *n.*). [? pun on SUCKER *n.*[3] (2)]

lemon *n.*[3] [1920s–50s] the head. [the shape]

lemon *n.*[4] [1920s–60s] (*US Black*) a light-skinned Black person. [LEMON *adj.*[2]]

lemon *n.*[5] [1930s] (*US Und.*) an informer. [such a person can be 'squeezed' by an interrogator]

lemon *n.*[6] [1930s+] (*US Black*) **1** female pubic hair. **2** the vagina (cf. APPLE *n.*[6]). **3** the male genitals. [? all can be 'squeezed'; orig. use as euph. in blues lyrics]

lemon *n.*[7] (*also* **lemonade**) [1950s+] (*US drugs*) weak or second-rate narcotics, a diluted or poor-quality drug, esp. poor heroin. [LEMON *n.*[1] (3)]

lemon *n.*[8] *see* LEM *n.*

lemon *n.*[9] *see* LEMON CURD *n.* (1).

lemon *n.*[10] *see* LEMON (DROP) *n.*

lemon *adj.*[1] [1900s–20s] (*US*) useless, second-rate. [LEMON *n.*[1] (3)]

lemon *adj.*[2] [1900s–20s] (*US*) of a Black person, light-skinned. [the colour]

lemon *adj.*[3] [2000s] ostentatious. [rhy. sl.; lemon squash = FLASH adj.[1] (1)]

lemonade *n.*[1] [1970s+] (*US*) urine. [the colour + LEMON n.[6] (3); SQUEEZE ONE'S LEMON v. (2)]

lemonade *n.*[2] *see* LEMON n.[7].

lemonade wallah *n. see* CHAR WALLAH n.

lemon and dash *n.* [1950s+] a public lavatory (cf. ANGUS ARMANASCO n.). [rhy. sl. = SE *wash*/SLASH n.[3]]

lemon and lime *n.* 1 [20C+] time. 2 [1990s+] crime. [rhy. sl.]

Lemon Avenue *n.* (*also* **Lemon Land**) [1910s+] (*Aus.*) the fig. name for the 'spiritual home' of censorious or socially repressive people. [LEMON n.[1] (1); their lips are eternally pursed with disapproval, as if they had just sucked a lemon]

lemon curd *n.* [1960s+] 1 (*also* **lemon**) a piece of excrement (cf. ALI OOP n.). 2 a derog. term for a person. 3 a woman. [rhy. sl.; (1) and (2) = TURD n.; (3) = BIRD n.[1] (2)]

lemon (drop) *n.* [1980s+] a policeman (cf. BOTTLE (AND STOPPER) n.). [rhy. sl. = COP n.[1] (1)]

lemon drop *n.* 1 [1970s] (*US teen*) a contraceptive pill. 2 [2000s] (*US drugs*) a methamphetamine tablet (cf. BOMBITA n.).

lemon-eater *n.* (*also* **lemon-pelter**, **lemon-sucker**) [1960s+] (*US derog.*) an English person. [LEMON n.[1] (1) + SE *eater*/*pelter*, one who skins or peels/*sucker*; the English are seen as sour]

lemoner *n.* [1970s+] (*Irish*) a disappointment, something depressing. [LEMON n.[1] (3)]

lemonfish *n.* [1980s+] (*N.Z.*) shark, as used in fish and chip shops.

lemon flavour *n.* [1990s+] a favour. [rhy. sl.]

lemon-game *n.* [20C+] (*US*) a way of cheating at pool, whereby a victim is enticed into the game and allowed to win; once they are sufficiently confident to bet heavily, their opponent has a 'run of luck' and takes all their money. [LEMON n.[2] + GAME n.[2] (3)]

lemon hand *n.* [1960s] (*US*) a deliberately malicious person. [LEMON n.[1] (1) + HAND n.[1] (2)]

Lemon Land *n. see* LEMON AVENUE n.

lemon law *n. see* LEMON n.[1] (4).

lemon-pelter *n. see* LEMON-EATER n.

lemons *n.* [1930s+] (*US*) the female breasts (cf. APPLES n.[1]).

lemons *adv.* [mid-19C–1940s] (*Aus./US*) energetically, enthusiastically; usu. as *go in lemons*. [the 'sharpness' of the fruit]

lemon spread *n.* [1980s] (*Aus.*) the head. [rhy. sl.]

lemon squash *n.* [20C+] (*Aus.*) a wash. [rhy. sl.]

lemon-squash party *n.* [late 19C] a temperance meeting. [the rejection of any drink but this; orig. Oxford University]

lemon-squeezer *n.*[1] [1920s] (*US*) a subway car.

lemon-squeezer *n.*[2] [1940s+] (*Aus./N.Z.*) a hat with a peaked crown and broad, flat brim worn by Aus. and N.Z. soldiers. [resemblance]

lemon-squeezer *n.*[3] [1970s+] a man. [rhy. sl. = GEEZER n.[1] (1)]

lemon squeezy *adj.* [1990s+] easy. [rhy. sl.; also the rhyme *easy peasy lemon squeezy*]

lemon-sucker *n.*[1] [1920s–60s] (*US*) an effeminate man. [? LEMON n.[6] (2) + SE *sucker*; or his stereotypically pursed lips]

lemon-sucker *n.*[2] *see* LEMON-EATER n.

lemon tart *n. see* APPLE TART n.

lemon tea *n.* [1940s+] an act of urination (cf. ANGEL'S KISS n.). [rhy. sl. = PEE n.[1] (2)]

lemon twist *n.* [1990s+] (*Aus. Und.*) when one gang employs a known police informer to give information about its rivals to the police. [the sweet + ? LEMON n.[2]]

lemony *adj.* [1940s–60s] (*Aus./N.Z.*) angry, irritated; thus GO LEMONY AT v. [the 'sharpness' of the fruit]

lend *n.* [19C+] a loan, e.g. *give us a lend of your barrow.* [16C+ dial.; 20C+ use is Aus.]

lend him a hole to hide it in *v. see* GIVE HIM A HOLE TO HIDE IT IN v.

lend his arse and shit through his ribs *v.* [late 18C–mid-19C] used of anyone who lends money without worrying about a security, e.g. *he would lend his arse and shit through his ribs.*

lend us your breath to kill Jumbo *phr.* [late 19C–1900s] a teasing ref. to another person's bad breath. [*Jumbo*, the London Zoo elephant who arrived in 1863 and proved one of the Zoo's main attractions until he was sold to P.T. Barnum's Circus in 1882]

length *n.*[1] [mid-19C] (*UK Und.*) 6 months' imprisonment. [horse-racing imagery, a *length* is half a STRETCH n.[1] (2)]

length *n.*[2] [1940s+] an act of sexual intercourse; usu. as *give her a length.* [i.e. the 'length' of the penis]

Len Hutton *n.* [1930s+] a button. [rhy. sl.; ult. cricketer *Len Hutton* (1916–90)]

lenny the lion *n.* [1930s+] a homosexual man. [rhy. sl. = IRON (HOOF) n.]

leno *n.* [1950s+] (*US drugs*) marijuana, a marijuana cigarette. [Sp. *leño*, a stick of wood]

lens *v.* (*US*) 1 [1920s] to see, to get to know about. 2 [1980s+] to film a movie.

lens lizard *n.* [1920s+] (*US*) a photographer, a film-maker.

lens louse *n.* [1920s–70s] (*US*) a person who monopolizes the camera; sometimes ext. to someone who monopolizes a conversation.

leo *n.* [1980s] (*Aus.*) a leotard. [abbr.]

Leo Sayer *n.* [1990s+] an all-day drinking session or any other form of party. [rhy. sl. = *all-dayer*; ult. pop star *Leo Sayer* (b.1948)]

leo-time *n.* [2000s] (*US teen*) August. [the astrological sign *Leo*]

leper *n.* [1990s+] (*UK juv.*) a general term of abuse.

Leperland *n.* [late 19C] (*Aus.*) a nickname for Queensland. [its population of lepers]

leper line *n.* [1950s+] (*Aus., Western*) a line running across Western Australia at 20°S. [the W.A. Native Australian Welfare Act (1955), which sought to prevent the spread of leprosy by forcing all sufferers to move to a place south of that parallel]

lepping *n.* [late 19C] a painful throbbing. [fig. use of SE *leap*]

lepping *adj.* [20C+] (*Irish*) angry, keen. [fig. use of SE *leap*]

lepping *adv.* [20C+] (*Irish*) very, hugely. [LEPPING adj.]

leprosy *n.* [1930s–40s] (*Aus.*) cabbage. [ety. unknown]

ler *n.* [2000s] (*US Black, Los Angeles*) a hustler. [abbr.]

leracam *n.* (*also* **lur-a-cham**) [mid-19C] a mackerel. [backsl.]

lerricompoop *v.* [17C] to have sexual intercourse. [? link to LERRICOMTWANG n. or dial. *lerry*, a whim, a caprice; note also SE *liripoop*, the long tail hanging down from a graduate's hood – potentially seen as phallic – and dial. *lerrick*, to beat, to flog]

lerricomtwang *n.* [mid–late 17C] a fool, a simpleton. [the chorus of a contemporary popular song]

les *n.* (*also* **lez**, **lezz**) [1920s+] (*orig. US*) a lesbian. [abbr.]

les *adj.* (*also* **lez**) [1940s+] lesbian. [LES n.]

lesbie *n.* (*also* **lesb**, **lesby**) [1950s+] a lesbian; thus the punning phr. *lesby friends.* [abbr.]

lesbo *n.* (*also* **lezbo**) [1920s+] (*orig. US*) a lesbian.

lesbo *adj.* [1970s+] lesbian. [LESBO n.]

lesby *n. see* LESBIE n.

Lesley Crowthers *n.* [2000s] trousers. [rhy. sl.; ult. UK comedian and TV presenter *Leslie Crowther* (1933–96)]

leslie *n.* (*also* **leslie anne**) [1940s+] (*Aus.*) a lesbian (cf. AMY-JOHN n.). [abbr. + a name that serves for men and women]

leso *n.* (*also* **lezo**, **lezzo**) [1940s+] (*Aus.*) a lesbian. [abbr. + -o sfx (4)]

lessie *adj.* (*also* **leso**, **lezzo**) [1960s+] lesbian.

less it! *excl.* [1970s+] (*UK juv.*) an excl. of prohibition, e.g. *stop that! be quiet!*

less (of your) lip *phr.* (*also* **none of your lip**, **not so much (of your) lip**) [mid-19C+] don't be so cheeky. [LIP n.[1] (1)]

less than nothing *n.* 1 [20C+] (*US Black*) a derog. term for a passive homosexual. **2** [1980s+] (*gay*) a weak gay man, unable to look after himself.

let a brewer's fart grains and all *v.* [late 18C–19C] to foul one's trousers.

let alone *phr.* [early 19C+] not to mention.

letari *n. see* LETTARY *n.*

letch *n.* (*also* lech) **1** [late 18C+] a strong sexual desire. **2** [1940s+] (*orig. US*) a *lecher.* [abbr.]

letch *v.* (*also* lech) [1910s+] to lust, to crave. [LETCH *n.* (1)]

letch about *v.* (*also* lech about) [1960s] to act in a sexual manner. [ext. of LETCH *v.*]

letching-piece *n.* [1910s+] a promiscuous woman. [LETCH *v.* + PIECE *n.*[1] (1)]

letchwater *n.* [19C] **1** semen (cf. BABY FLUID *n.*). **2** vaginal fluid (cf. BINDERJUICE *n.*). [LETCH *n.* (1) + SE *water*]

letchy *adj.* [2000s] lecherous. [LETCH *n.* (1)]

let-down *n.* [mid-19C+] a disappointment.

let down someone's blind *v.* [1910s–20s] to make clear that someone is dead.

let 'em trundle! *excl.* [late 17C–mid-18C] go away! be off!

let fly *v.* **1** [18C] to defecate. **2** [18C–early 19C] to break wind. [SE *let fly*, to fire a missile, a gun etc]

let George do it *phr.* [1910s–40s] (*US*) let someone else do the work or take the responsibility. [GEORGE *n.*[2] (2) + WW2 phr. *let George do it, I can't be bothered*]

let-go *n.*[1] [mid-18C] orgasm, ejaculation. [LET GO *v.*[1] (1)]

let-go *n.*[2] [1980s] (*W.I., Jam.*) a release, a way out (of one's problems).

let go *v.*[1] **1** [late 19C+] to reach orgasm. **2** [1900s] to spend money. **3** [1910s] (*US*) to be quiet; usu. as imper. forget it! **4** [1960s] to urinate. **5** [1990s] (*US campus*) to relax.

let go *v.*[2] *see* LET (ONE) GO *v.*

let go *phr.* [1910s–20s] not to mention, all the more reason, e.g. *let go you didn't even turn up.* [i.e. *let* that fact *go* without comment]

let go a razzo *v. see* RASPBERRY TART *n.* (2).

let go with *v.* [late 19C–1930s] to perform an action, esp. in the context of violence.

let her flicker *phr.* [mid-19C+] (*Aus./US*) a phr. used at the start of some operations; usu. as *OK, let her flicker...* [running a reel of movie film]

let-her-go-Gallagher *adj.* [1910s] naked. [LET HER GO (GALLAGHER) *v.*]

let her go (Gallagher) *v.* [mid-19C+] to allow anything, real or fig., to go at full speed, to remove any impediment to progress. [? assonance of proper name]

let her go (Gallagher)! *excl.* [late 19C–1930s] (*Aus./US*) go ahead! [LET HER GO (GALLAGHER) *v.*]

let her rip! *excl.*[1] (*also* let her roll!) [mid-19C+] (*orig. US*) to allow anything, real or fig., to go at full speed, to remove any impediment to progress. [? steamboat engines that exploded or *ripped* when under excessive pressure. The phr., according to Ware, was common among their captains when urging the crew to put on full steam when racing against a rival boat]

let her rip! *excl.*[2] (*also* let him rip!) [mid-19C+] an excl. of dismissal. [let her/him *rest in peace*]

let her sling! *excl. see* SLING YOURSELF! excl.

let-in *n.* **1** [19C–1920s] a hoax, an act of cheating. **2** [1910s–20s] a robbery. **3** [1910s–20s] an illegal victimization. [LET IN *v.*]

let in *v.* [19C–1900s] to cheat, to defraud, to victimize. [image of falling through ice]

let into *v.* [mid-19C–1900s] to attack physically.

let into the secret *v.* [late 17C–early 19C] to draw a victim into betting on a crooked race or game and then to defraud them.

let it all hang out *v.* [1960s+] (*orig. US Black*) to cast aside any restraints, to do what one wants. [a musicians' term, this migrated to White HIPPIE *n.*[2] (3) use and thence, like a number of similar terms, to the jargon of 'new therapies']

let it go *v.* [mid-19C+] to let something pass, to ignore.

let it ride *v.* [1910s+] to ignore, to forget, to leave a situation as it is, to take no further action. [dice or roulette gambling where a winning bet is not picked up from the table but left to be gambled again]

let it slide *v.* [mid-19C+] to ignore, to dismiss; also as imper. don't bother, it doesn't matter.

let it soak *v. see* SOAK IT *v.*

let it sweat *v.* [1920s+] to stop worrying or interfering, just let things turn out as they will.

let leap a whiting *v.* [mid-16C–19C] to let an opportunity slip. [fishing imagery]

let me hold some change *phr.* [1960s+] (*US Black*) please give me some money.

let-off *n. see* LET-OUT *n.* (1).

let off *v.* [mid-19C; 1920s+] to break wind. [? play on colloq. phr. *let off steam*]

let off a little nigger *v.* [late 19C+] (*US*) a derog. phr. meaning to act in a crazy, uninhibited way, to 'let off steam'. [racist stereotyping]

let off at *v.* [1970s] to shout at, to attack verbally.

let off steam/wind *v. see* BLOW OFF STEAM *v.*

let on *v.* **1** [early 18C+] to admit, to confess. **2** [mid-19C] to suggest, to imply. **3** [mid-19C+] to pretend, to pose. **4** [20C+] to make a fuss. **5** [2000s] to recognize (someone).

let one down for their chimer *v.* [1940s] (*US Black*) to steal a watch. [SE *let one down* + CHIMER *n.* (1)]

let (one) go *v.* (*also* let one fly, let one off, let one rip) [mid-17C; late 19C; 1960s+] to break wind; to burp.

let one's game slip *v.* [1960s+] (*US Black*) to lose control of a situation or plan. [SE *let* + GAME *n.*[2] (3)]

let one's hair down *v.* **1** [1930s+] (*orig. US*) (*also* **take one's hair down**) to relax one's inhibitions. **2** [1930s+] to admit to being gay. **3** [1970s] to 'out' a previously closeted homosexual. [note mid-19C theatre use *let down the back hair*]

let one's horse out of the stable *v.* **1** [1950s–60s] to urinate (cf. FLOG THE LIZARD *v.*). **2** [2000s] to reveal a secret.

let one's rag out *v. see* GET ONE'S RAG OUT *v.*

let-out *n.* **1** [mid-19C–1900s] (*Anglo-Irish*) (*also* **let-off**) a spree, an entertainment, a grand occasion. **2** [1920s] (*US Und.*) money from corruption. **3** [1920s+] an excuse, an alibi.

let out *v.* **1** [early 19C–1900s] to reveal a secret. **2** [late 19C] (*US*) to kill. **3** [late 19C–1950s] (*orig. US*) to exonerate from blame or guilt. **4** [late 19C+] to ride a horse fast. **5** [1910s+] to accelerate or drive a car fast. **6** [1920s] to sing enthusiastically.

let out at *v.* [late 19C+] **1** (*Aus.*) to aim a blow at. **2** to admonish.

let out one's fore room and lie backwards *v.* (*also* lie backwards and let out one's fore room) [late 17C–early 19C] of a woman, to work as a prostitute.

let out one's parlour and lie backwards *v. see* PARLOUR *n.*

let rip *v.* [late 19C+] to 'let fly', to let go, esp. with great energy and force.

let run a milestone *v.* [late 17C] (*gaming*) to let a die roll some distance.

let's be having you! *excl.* (*also* let's have you!) [20C+] time to start work! get out of bed! drink up! etc.

let's boogie *phr.* [1980s+] (*US teen*) let's go, let's be off. [SE *let's* + BOOGIE *v.* (4)]

let's bounce *phr.* [2000s] (*US teen*) let's go.

let's have you! *excl. see* LET'S BE HAVING YOU! excl.

let's kill a dog *phr.* [1900s] (*Aus.*) an invitation to drink. [KILL ONE'S DOG *v.*]

let slide *v.* [mid-19C+] (*orig. US*) to overlook, to forgive.

let slip at *v.* [mid-19C] to attack physically.

let's lose Charley *phr.* [1940s–60s] a term used among intimates who want to get rid of a bore in their company.

let someone down gently v. (*also* **let someone down easily,** ...**easy,** ...**light(ly),** ...**softly**) [mid-19C+] to treat someone kindly and considerately when one has to deliver bad or disappointing news.

let someone have it v. [mid-19C+] (*orig. US*) **1** to hit, to kill, esp. with gunfire. **2** to challenge, to pose a difficult question, to reprimand severely, to criticize.

let someone in for v. [mid-19C+] to involve, usu. in unfortunate circumstances, such as financial ruin or a criminal prosecution.

let someone in on v. [20C+] to impart otherwise secret or privileged information.

let someone off easy v. [20C+] to deal with someone kindly. [var. on GO EASY v. (2)]

let someone off the hook v. [1960s+] to excuse (someone) from punishment.

let's rejoice n. [20C+] (*Aus.*) the voice. [rhy. sl.]

let's vamos! excl. [1980s+] (*US campus*) let's go! [SE *let's* + Sp. *vamos,* let's go]

lettary n. (*also* **letari, letty**) [1900s–30s] (*UK tramp*) a lodging. [Ital. *letto,* a bed]

letter n.[1] [1910s+] (*US*) a letter worn on one's clothing that indicates success in college sports.

letter n.[2] *see* FRENCH LETTER n.

letterbox n. [1990s+] a passive homosexual.

lettered adj. [18C–early 19C] (*UK Und.*) branded on the hand.

letter-fencer n. [late 19C] a postman. [SE *letter* + -FENCER sfx]

letter from home n. **1** [1930s+] (*US*) anything that provokes nostalgia. **2** [1950s–70s] (*US Black*) a watermelon. [the stereotypical link of watermelons and life 'down home']

letter-racket n. [early 19C] (*UK Und.*) the sending of fake begging letters. [SE *letter* + RACKET n.[1] (1)]

let the air out of v. **1** [1940s+] to debunk. **2** [1950s] (*US*) to let down, to deflate emotionally.

let the badger loose v. [1970s+] (*US, Western*) to celebrate wildly, to 'let off steam'. [the 'sport' of badger-baiting]

let the best dog leap over the stile first v. [18C–19C] to allow the best qualified or most suitable person to take the lead. [pvb]

let the daylight into v. (*also* **let the daylight through**) [late 18C–1930s] to shoot, to stab; often ext. as *let the daylight into the victualling department, let the daylight into the luncheon reservoir.*

let the deal go down v. [1940s–60s] (*US Black*) to allow events to proceed without dishonesty or deceit. [card-playing imagery]

let the dog see the rabbit v. [1930s+] to give someone a chance to get on with a task.

let the milk down v. [1970s+] (*US, Southern*) to reveal the facts after withholding them for some time. [breastfeeding imagery]

let the priest say mass phr. [20C+] (*Irish*) a phr. used to reprimand someone who keeps interrupting or offering unwanted suggestions.

let the tail go with the hide v. [20C+] (*US*) to ignore small details while concentrating on the overall picture. [butchers'/slaughterhouse jargon; it implies the throwing in of the relatively worthless tail with the valuable hide]

letting the finger ride the thumb (too often) phr. [19C] getting drunk. [? FINGER AND THUMB n. (1) or ? SUPERNACULUM n. (1)]

lettuce n.[1] [20C+] money in notes; sometimes ext. as *lettuce leaves* (cf. ALFALFA n.). [the colour]

lettuce n.[2] [2000s] (*US prison*) prisoners who perform gang-rapes. [? play on SE *let us*]

lettuce leaf n. [1980s] (*Aus.*) a thief. [rhy. sl.]

lettuce leaves n. *see* LETTUCE n.[1].

letty n.[1] (*also* **lattie, latty**) [mid-19C+] (*Ling. Fr./Polari*) a bed; thus *letties,* lodgings, accommodation. [Ital. *letto,* a bed]

letty n.[2] *see* LETTARY n.

let up on v. [mid-19C+] (*orig. mainly US*) to reject, to snub, to have nothing to do with.

let your father in n. (*also* **Tommy get out and let your father in**) [late 19C] (a glass of) gin. [rhy. sl.]

leucoddy n. [mid-19C+] the human body. [Polari]

levant n. [18C–19C] a bet that is made without sufficient funds to cover one's losses; usu. as *run a levant, come the levant.* [*Levant,* the Middle East. The image is of running off to foreign parts; + ? racial stereotype of the 'oily Levantine'; note the eponymous card-sharp Capt. *Levanter* in Whyte Melville, *Digby Grand* (1853); also note Sp. *levantar,* to lift up]

levant v. **1** [18C–19C] to bet without sufficient funds to cover one's losses. **2** [19C–1920s] (*UK Und.*) to run off, to escape trouble, esp. to avoid gambling debts. [LEVANT n.]

levanter n. [18C–19C] an absconder, esp. one who runs off after placing a losing bet. [LEVANT v.]

level n. *see* LEVEL (BEST) n.

level adj. [late 19C+] (*orig. US*) honest, trustworthy, true.

level v.[1] (*also* **level with**) (*orig. US*) **1** [1910s] to contest. **2** [1910s+] to be honest. **3** [1950s+] to admit, to confess.

level v.[2] [1950s] (*drugs*) to experience the ending of a drug's effects.

level (best) n. (*also* **dead-level best**) [mid-19C+] (*orig. US*) one's very best efforts. [note that *level best* is SE in UK but sl. in US]

leveller n. [19C] a knock-down blow.

level vibes phr. [1980s+] (*W.I./UK Black teen*) a satisfactory situation, peace and quiet. [SE *level* + VIBE n. (1)]

level with v. *see* LEVEL v.[1].

level worst n. [19C] (*US*) one's worst attempt or effort. [reverse of LEVEL (BEST) n.]

leven n. [mid–late 19C] the number 11. [Hotten (1859) credits this to backsl.]

leventy-leven n. *see* ELEVENTY-ELEVEN n.

leven yenneps n. (*also* **leven, nevele yeneps**) [mid-19C] 11 pence. [backsl.; LEVEN n./NEVELE n. + YENNEP n.]

levite n. [mid-17C–mid-19C] a priest or parson. [SE *Levite,* a member of the ancient Hebrew tribe of Levi, one of the 2 tribes authorized to serve as priests in the Temple]

levy n. **1** [19C] (*US*) 12 cents. **2** [mid-19C] a shilling (5p). [abbr. (*e)leven cents,* which was the value of the Spanish *real,* formerly accepted as currency in US]

levy v. [1950s+] to masturbate (cf. BOFF v.). [for ety. *see* LEVY (AND FRANK) n.]

levy (and frank) n. [1950s–70s] an act of masturbation. [rhy. sl. = WANK n.[1] (1); ult. the name of a chain of London restaurateurs, *Levy and Franks*]

lewdie n. [1960s] a married woman who frequents singles' bars looking for brief encounters. [SE *lewd*]

lewd infusion n. [late 19C; 1920s–30s] semen; thus sexual intercourse. [the infusion of semen]

lewinsky n. [1990s+] drinking straight from a bottle. [Monica Lewinsky, the White House intern whose sexual adventures with President Clinton, notably performing fellatio on him, led to his impeachment]

Lewis and Whitty n. **1** [1920s] (*US*) a city. **2** [1940s–50s] (*Aus.*) in pl., the female breasts (cf. BRACE AND BITS n.). [rhy. sl.; (2) = TITTY n.[1] (1); ult. *Lewis and Witty,* a well-known Melbourne department store]

lewis cornaro n. [early 19C] a drinker of water. [the name of a man renowned for his consumption of water]

Lex n. [1950s–60s] (*drugs*) the federal drug habilitation hospital at Lexington, Kentucky. [abbr.]

lex n.[1] [1980s+] (*US Black*) a *Lexus* motorcar, one of the high-status cars preferred by the rap/hip-hop community. [abbr.]

lex n.[2] [1990s+] (*UK Black*) a *Rolex* watch. [abbr.]

lex-luther n. [1990s+] (*US Black teen*) a *Lexus* automobile, a coveted status symbol. [LEX n.[1] + pun on *Lex Luthor,* an enemy of the comic superhero Superman]

lez *see under* LES.

lezbo *n. see* LESBO n.

lezo *n. see* LESO n.

lezz *n. see* LES n.

lezzer *n.* (*also* **lesser, lezza**) [1950s+] (*Aus./Irish/US*) a lesbian. [abbr.]

lezzie *n.* (*also* **lezzy**) **1** [1930s+] a *les*bian. **2** [1990s+] (*mainly UK juv.*) a term of abuse for an unpopular individual. [abbr.]

lezzie *adj.* (*also* **lezzy**) [1960s+] lesbian.

lezzo *see under* LESO.

lezzy *n. see* LEZZIE n.

l.f. *n. see* LONG FIRM n.

l.g.r. *n. see* LITTLE GIRLS' ROOM n.

lib *n.*[1] [17C–18C] a sleep. [LIB v. (1)]

lib *n.*[2] **1** [20C+] a *lib*erty; often in pl.; usu. as *take libs*. **2** [1970s+] (*orig. US*) *lib*eration, usu. in gender political contexts and thus abbr. for 'liberation movement', e.g. *Women's Lib, Gay Lib*. [abbr.]

lib *v.* (*also* **lip, lyp**) (*UK Und.*) **1** [mid-16C–18C] to lie down, to sleep. **2** [late 17C–mid-19C] to sleep together, to have sexual intercourse. [ety. unknown but *see* LIB-BEG n.]

lib-beg *n.* (*also* **libbedge, libbege, libbige, libedge, lybbeg, lybbege**) [mid-16C–mid-19C] (*UK Und.*) a bed. [LIB v. + sfx *-age*; Ribton-Turner, *A History of Vagrants* (1887), suggests Gaelic/Erse *leabadh*, a bed, Manx *lhiabbee*, a bed]

libben *n.* [late 17C–mid-19C] (*UK Und.*) a private house. [LIB v.]

libber *n.*[1] [20C+] (*Irish*) an untidy, slovenly person. [Irish *leadhb*, a strip, a rag, a slovenly person]

libber *n.*[2] (*also* **libbie**) [1970s+] (*orig. US*) **1** a feminist, a member of the Women's Liberation Movement. **2** a member of any liberation group. [LIB n.[2] (2); usu. derog. when used by men]

libbige *n. see* LIB-BEG n.

libb-ken *n. see* LIBKEN n.

libbo *n.* [1950s+] a *lib*erty; usu. as *take libbos*. [abbr.]

libe *n.* [1910s+] (*US campus*) a *lib*rary. [abbr.]

libe *v.* [1910s+] (*US campus*) to study in a library; thus *libe out*, to go to the library. [LIBE n.]

libedge *n. see* LIB-BEG n.

liberate *v.* **1** [1940s+] to steal. **2** [1990s+] to eat or drink. [(1) esp. in 1960s radical use, on the Proudhon principle that 'property is theft' but likewise with a degree of irony/self-mockery given the 1960s obsession with 'freedom' and 'the revolution'. With further irony, the 'radical' use stems f. WW2 'liberating forces' who 'freed' commodities as well as people]

liberty *n.* **1** [1910s–60s] (*US*) money. **2** [1940s] (*US, esp. Black*) a quarter, a 25-cent coin.

libken *n.* (*also* **libb-ken, libkin, lipken, lobkin, lybkin**) [mid-16C–1900s] (*UK Und.*) a house, a lodging. [LIB v. (1) + KEN n.[1] (1)]

library *n.*[1] **1** [mid–late 17C] a drinking club, a friendly gathering. **2** [20C+] a book borrowed from a lending library. **3** [1960s+] (*US*) an 'adult', i.e. pornographic, bookstore.

library *n.*[2] (*also* **outdoor library, reading room, Sears Roebuck library**) [1930s+] (*US*) a privy (cf. ALTAR n.). [the old catalogues, newspapers etc that are often left there as lavatory paper; the common use of old Sears catalogues as lavatory paper]

license *v.* [1960s] (*UK Und./police*) for the police to tolerate a given crime, e.g. prostitution or drug-dealing, in return for bribes.

-licious *sfx* [1970s+] (*orig. US*) a sfx implying excellence, appeal. [SE *delicious* + pattern of BOOTYLICIOUS adj. (2)]

lick *n.*[1] **1** [mid-18C+] a slight and hasty wash, a quick tidy-up. **2** [mid-19C+] a casual amount of work. **3** [mid-19C+] (*orig. US*) a bit, a cursory amount. **4** [mid-19C+] pace, speed; usu. with comb. adj., thus *going at a good lick*. **5** [late 19C+] a portion, e.g. of liquor; a drinking bout. [? East Anglian dial. *lick-up*, a miserably small pittance of any thing]

lick *n.*[2] **1** [mid-18C+] an effort, an attempt at something. **2** [mid-19C+] (*Aus./N.Z./US*) a (short) sprint; intensified as *lick of one's*

life. **3** [mid-19C+] (*US*) a rhythm or pace, spec. on the chain gang. **4** [1910s+] (*later use US Black*) a turn, a 'go', an attempt; thus *one-lick*, once only. **5** [1930s+] (*US Und.*) a theft. **6** [1940s+] (*US Black*) a plan, an idea, a scheme. **7** [1960s+] fig. what one does, an action, one's personal preference. **8** [1970s] (*US Black*) an opportunity. **9** [1990s+] (*drugs*) a puff on a crack cocaine pipe. [SE *lick*, a blow]

lick *n.*[3] [1930s+] (*orig. US*) a particular phrase of music, e.g. a *guitar lick*.

lick *n.*[4] [1960s] (*N.Z.*) an ice-cream.

lick *n.*[5] *see* LICK-ARSE n.

lick, the *n.* **1** [mid-19C+] (*US/US Black/W.I.*) the correct thing, the proper course of action. **2** [1940s+] (*orig. W.I.*) the very best, the supremely fashionable.

lick *v.*[1] **1** [mid-16C+] to beat, to thrash; thus *lick out of*, to change someone's character/beliefs/actions by a threat of violence, to 'knock it out of' someone; also *lick someone's jacket*, to beat. **2** [19C+] to defeat, to overcome, to be victorious. **3** [mid-19C+] (*US*) to move fast; also as *lick it*. **4** [1990s+] to shoot. [SE *lick*, a blow; esp. in W.I. combs., e.g. *lick up*, stir up; *lick down*, knock or fling to the ground; *lick 'way*, strike or cut off (as in a tree branch)]

lick *v.*[2] [1970s+] to fellate or perform cunnilingus; usu. with *dick* for a man or *clit* for a woman (cf. COCKSUCK n.; CUNT-LICK v.). [SE *lick*]

lick about *v.* (*also* **lick around**) [20C+] (*W.I.*) to live an unsettled life. [SE *lick*, a blow]

lick a box *v.* [1990s+] (*orig. W.I., Trin.*) to perform cunnilingus (cf. CUNT-LICK v.). [SE *lick* + BOX n.[1] (1)]

lick and a promise *n.* [mid-19C+] a quick, if not well-performed, piece of work; orig. of a hasty wash.

lick and a smell *n.* [mid-18C+] a very small portion. [the image is of a dog licking its empty bowl]

lick and shine *n.* [2000s] of a man, the act of smoking crack cocaine while a prostitute performs fellatio on him.

lick an' pran *v.* [1950s+] (*W.I.*) to tidy up. [pron. of LICK AND A PROMISE n.]

lick around *v. see* LICK ABOUT v.

lick-arse *n.* (*also* **lick**) [1970s+] (*orig. US*) a toady, a sycophant. [LICK (SOMEONE'S) ARSE v.]

lick arse *v. see* LICK (SOMEONE'S) ARSE v.

lick a shot *v. see* LICK SHOT v.

lick boots *v.* [late 19C+] to act in a servile manner. [note late 18C synon. *lick the shoe*]

lick-box *n.* [1940s+] a male homosexual. [SE *lick* + BOX n.[1] (3); note LICK A BOX v.]

lickdish *n.* (*also* **lick-platter**) [mid-16C–mid-19C] a general term of abuse, the implication is of gluttony.

licked *adj.* **1** [19C+] utterly defeated. **2** [1970s+] exhausted. [LICK v.[1] (2)]

licker *n.*[1] **1** [18C–1930s] anything that is exceptional in size, power etc. **2** [late 19C+] something that proves beyond one's powers. [LICK v.[1] (1)]

licker *n.*[2] [1970s+] **1** (*US Black*) the tongue. **2** (*US gay*) one who, usu. a lesbian, performs oral sex.

licker-head *n. see* LIQUORHEAD n.

lickerish *adj.* [20C+] never satisfied and wanting everything; gluttonous and aggressively greedy, esp. for food. [SE *lick*]

lickety-split *adv.* (*also* **helitywhoop, hellity-split, lickerty-brindle, lickerty-clip, lickerty-cut, lickerty-spit, lickity-split, lick-to-split, linkety-clink**) [mid-19C+] (*orig. US*) fast, with some onomat. overtones. [most alternative forms faded by late 19C]

lick-finger *n.* [late 16C–early 18C] a cook. [note Ben Jonson's *Staple News* (1625): 'Lick-finger, a Master Cooke']

licking *n.* **1** [mid-18C+] a beating. **2** [19C+] a defeat. [LICK v.[1]]

licking *adj.* [late 19C–1900s] a general intensifier, e.g. huge, excellent etc. [LICK v.[1] (1)]

licking-match *n.* [1910s] (*W.I.*) a brawl. [LICK v.[1] (1) + SE *match*]

licking post *n.* (*also* **lick-log**) [mid-19C+] (*US*) **1** a gathering place. **2** the moment of contention or decision; a decision, a pledge. [regional AmE *licking-post*, a salt lick used by cattle]

lick into fits *v.* [late 19C–1910s] to beat comprehensively. [LICK v.[1] (1) + SE *fits*]

lick into shape *v.* (*also* **lick into fashion**) [19C+] (*orig. US*) to prepare, to get ready, esp. if the person or object is far from ready when one starts the 'licking'. [LICK v.[1] (1) + fig. use of SE *shape*]

lick it *v. see* LICK v.[1] (3).

lickity-split *adv. see* LICKETY-SPLIT adv.

lick-log *n. see* LICKING POST n.

lick log *v.* [1990s+] (*US*) to perform fellatio (cf. COCKSUCK n.). [SE *lick* + LOG n.[4]]

lick-me-lug *n.* [1990s+] (*Irish*) a toady, a sycophant. [LUG n.[1]; var. on LICK-ARSE n.]

lickmouth *n.* [20C+] (*W.I.*) cheap, nasty gossip. [LICK ONE'S MOUTH v.]

lick my arse! *excl.* (*also* **lick my ass!**) [late 19C+] a dismissive, abusive excl. [note later LICK (SOMEONE'S) ARSE v.]

lick my froth! *excl.* [1980s] (*US teen*) a general term of abuse or dismissal. [? inference of sexual secretion/fluids]

lick my love pump! *excl.* [1980s+] (*US campus*) a dismissive, abusive excl. [SE *lick* + LOVE PUMP n.; apparently coined for the movie *This Is Spinal Tap* (1982)]

lick of one's life *n. see* LICK n.[2] (2).

lick of the tarbrush *phr. see* TOUCH OF THE TARBRUSH phr.

lick one's mouth *v.* [20C+] (*W.I.*) to carry around or to impart negative gossip. [the participants lick their lips in pleasure]

lick on the whip *v. see* DRINK ON THE WHIP v.

lick out *v.*[1] [1960s+] to perform cunnilingus (cf. CUNT-LICK v.).

lick out *v.*[2] [1990s+] (*W.I.*) to speak out against.

lick out of *v. see* LICK v.[1] (1).

lick-over *n.* [late 19C; 1960s+] (*US*) a quick, cursory clean.

lick pap together *v.* [20C+] (*W.I., UKVI*) to come from the same impoverished background.

lick-platter *n. see* LICKDISH n.

lickpot *n.* [20C+] (*W.I.*) the first finger. [14C–15C SE. Other finger names are *longman* (middle finger), *ring-man* (third or ring-finger), *little man* (little finger) and *big tom* (the thumb)]

licks *n.* **1** [late 18C+] a thrashing. **2** [20C+] orders. **3** [1980s+] verbal abuse. **4** [1990s+] (*US Black*) robbery. [SE *lick*, a blow; (1) and (2) now mainly UK Black]

lick shot *v.* [1980s+] (*W.I./UK Black teen*) **1** to fire a shot from a real or imaginary gun to signal appreciation of music or an event. **2** to fire a gun. [LICK v.[1] (4) + SE *shot*]

lickskillet *n.* [late 19C–1950s] (*US*) a contemptible person. [SE *lick* + *skillet*; note SE *lickspittle*]

licks like fire *n.* [20C+] (*W.I.*) **1** a savage beating. **2** an overwhelming victory. [LICKS n. (1) + SE *fire*]

lick (someone's) arse *v.* [1940s+] to toady, to be a sycophant.

lick someone's jacket *v. see* LICK v.[1] (1).

lick-spigot *n.* **1** [late 16C–17C] a bar-man. **2** [17C–19C] a fellatrix. [SE *lick* + *spigot*/SPIGOT n.]

lick that killed Dick *n.* [1950s–60s] (*US Black*) the final straw.

lick the carpet *v. see* MUNCH THE CARPET v.

lick the chops *v.* [1930s–40s] (*US Black*) of musicians, to tune up before a performance. [pun on SE phr./LICK v.[1] + CHOPS n.[1] (1)]

lick the holy ground *v.* [1990s+] to perform cunnilingus (cf. CUNT-LICK v.).

lick thumbs *v.* [20C+] (*Ulster*) to seal a bargain. [the action thus involved; the equivalent of spitting on one's palm and similar gestures of commitment]

lick tits *v.* [1990s+] (*UK Black*) to run errands and perform small tasks.

lick-to-split *adv. see* LICKETY-SPLIT adv.

lick-twat *n.* [17C–19C; 1990s+] a person who performs cunnilingus. [SE *lick* + TWAT n. (1)]

lick up *adj.* [2000s] (*UK Black*) overcome by drink or drugs. [LICK v.[1]]

lick up (to) *v.* [1960s+] to curry favour, to be obsequious, to grovel shamelessly in return for favours, esteem etc.

licky-licky *n.* [1990s+] (*W.I.*) a parasitical toady. [LICKY-LICKY adj.[1]]

licky-licky *adj.*[1] [1940s+] (*W.I.*) fawning, flattering, obsequious. [LICK (SOMEONE'S) ARSE v.]

licky-licky *adj.*[2] (*also* **likki-likki**, **likky-likky**) [1940s+] (*W.I.*) **1** pernickety, choosy, esp. as to one's food. **2** never satisfied in the sense of greedy, gluttonous. [taking tentative licks rather than bites; (2) f. (1)]

licky-licky *adj.*[3] [1970s–80s] (*UK Black*) alcoholic; drunken.

lick-your-arse *adj.* [1940s] toadying, sycophantic. [LICK (SOMEONE'S) ARSE v.]

licorice stick *n. see* LIQUORICE STICK n.

lid *n.*[1] **1** [mid-19C+] a hat, a cap. **2** [late 19C+] (*orig. US*) the head. **3** [1960s] (*US*) fellatio.

lid *n.*[2] **1** [1910s+] (*US gambling*) a limit. **2** [1920s–60s] (*US Black*) the sky.

lid *n.*[3] [1960s+] (*drugs*) a quantity of marijuana, about 22g (³/₄oz) or 40 cigarettes'-worth, and often considered the equivalent of 1oz (28g). [the quantity of the drug that fills the *lid* of a tin of Prince Albert, a popular brand of tobacco]

lid, the *n.* [20C+] (*orig. US*) a restraint, protection or confidentiality, or the lack of it; usu. in the phr. BLOW THE LID OFF v. (1), KEEP THE LID ON v.

lidder *n.* [1990s+] (*UK juv.*) a fool.

lido *n.* [1980s+] (*US drugs*) crack cocaine (cf. BASE n.). [ety. unknown; ? Sp.]

lid-proppers *n.* (*also* **lid-poppers**) [1960s+] (*drugs*) amphetamines (cf. A n.[2]). [they keep one awake, and 'prop up one's eyelids']

lie *v. see* LAY v.[2].

lie-and-story *n.* [1940s+] (*W.I.*) gossip, slander.

lie at rack and manger *v.* (*also* **go to rack and manger**, **live at...**) [mid-17C–19C] to live hard. [SE *rack and manger*, the frame that holds an animal's food and the stable in which it is kept; thus lit. to live like an animal]

lie backwards and let out one's fore room *see* LET OUT ONE'S FORE ROOM AND LIE BACKWARDS v.

lie by the wall *v.* [15C–17C] to be dead. [SE *lie by the wall*, to lie on one side, remain idle or unused]

lie doggo *v.* (*also* **keep doggo**, **lie doggoh**, **play doggo**) [late 19C+] to remain hidden and quiet, just like a stalking dog.

lie-down *n.* **1** [late 19C+] a rest on a bed or similar object. **2** [1930s+] (*orig. US*) a protest that involves participants lying on the ground and refusing to move. **3** [1980s+] a prison sentence.

lie down (on the job) *v. see* LAY DOWN ON THE JOB v.

lie for *v. see* LAY FOR v.[1].

lie-in *n.* **1** [20C+] an extra portion of sleep, after one would normally have to get up. **2** [1960s+] (*orig. US*) a protest that involves participants lying on the ground and refusing to move. [note milit. sense *lie in*, to remain in one's room when one is supposed to be on leave]

lie in state *v.* [18C–19C] of a man, to lie in bed with 2 or 3 women. [ironic use of SE; the man is 'dead' after his sexual exertions]

lie like a flatfish *v.* [1960s+] to lie skilfully and continually. [pun]

lie like a pig *v.* [20C+] (*Aus.*) to tell plausible lies.

lie like truth *v.* [mid–late 19C] to lie in a plausible manner, often used of cheapjacks and other street salesmen.

lie low *v. see* LAY LOW v.[1].

lie on v. (also **lie upon**) [16C–18C] to have sexual intercourse. [var. on LIE WITH v.]

lie on one's face v. [late 19C–1920s] to drink very heavily until one collapses.

lie out v. [20C+] (*Ulster*) to play truant.

lie rough v. [late 17C–early 19C] to go to sleep without first removing one's clothes.

lieu n. see LOOIE n.[1].

lie under v. see LAY LOW v.[1].

lie upon v. see LIE ON v.

lieuy n. see LOOEY n.[1].

lie with v. [15C+] to have sexual intercourse with, both heterosexual and homosexual.

life, the n. **1** [20C+] (*orig. US*) the world of prostitution. **2** [1910s+] (*UK Und.*) the criminal underworld. **3** [1940s+] (*US Black*) the subculture of crime, pimping, drug dealing etc that makes up the alternative world of the streets. **4** [1950s+] (*US gay*) the world of homosexuality. **5** [1960s–70s] (*US drugs*) the world of drug addiction.

life n. **1** [mid-19C+] imprisonment for a life sentence; thus *life (up)*, to imprison for life. **2** [1970s+] in fig. use, something long-term and permanent outside of a prison context. [abbr. SE *life sentence*]

life and death n. [20C+] breath. [rhy. sl.]

lifeboat n. (also **life liner, lifesaver**) [20C+] (*US prison*) a pardon or the commutation of a sentence.

Lifebuoy soap n. [1980s] (*Aus.*) cannabis. [rhy. sl. = DOPE n.[1] (6)]

Life in London adj. [mid-19C] of a place, e.g. a lodging house, run-down, filthy.

lifejacket n. [1980s+] (*US campus*) a condom.

life liner n. see LIFEBOAT n.

life off v. [2000s] (*UK Und.*) to give someone a life sentence.

life of Larry n. [1960s+] (*Irish*) the good life, a comfortable existence. [? HAPPY AS LARRY phr.]

life of Riley n. (also **life of Reilly, Reilly, Riley**) [1910s+] the good life, a comfortable existence. [? one of a number of late 19C songs. However, the first known use is in 'My Name is Kelly' (1919), written by H. Pease. The relevant line runs 'Faith and my name is Kelly Michael Kelly, / But I'm living the life of Reilly just the same']

life on the instalment plan n. [1910s+] (*US Und.*) a succession of sentences as served, with periods of freedom, by a recidivist.

life preserver n.[1] [mid-19C–1910s] the penis. [SE *life preserver*, a loaded bludgeon]

life preserver n.[2] [1940s] (*US*) a doughnut. [resemblance to SE *life preserver*, a life-buoy]

lifer n.[1] **1** [mid–late 19C] one who has been transported for life. **2** [mid-19C+] a life sentence. **3** [mid-19C+] a prisoner serving a life sentence. **4** [1980s+] (*US campus*) an ironic term for someone who has committed a trivial offence. [SE *life sentence*]

lifer n.[2] (*US, orig. milit.*) **1** [1960s+] a career soldier. **2** [1970s+] a pej. term for anyone who appears excessively keen on discipline and its administration on their peers. **3** [1970s+] a person unwilling to change their way of life, esp. a drug addict. **4** [1970s+] one who intends to stay in the same job or career until retirement. [LIFER n.[1] (3)]

lifer dog n. [1980s+] (*US*) a usu. pej. term for a person who is obsessively committed to their career. [LIFER n.[2] + DOG n.[3]]

lifesaver n.[1] **1** [1930s–40s] (*US Und.*) parole. **2** [2000s] (*Irish*) a condom.

lifesaver n.[2] see LIFEBOAT n.

life's dainty n. [19C] **1** the vagina (cf. ADAM'S OWN (ALTAR) n.). **2** the penis. [euph.]

Liffey water n. [late 19C+] porter (the drink). [rhy. sl.; the orig. ref. was to Guinness, brewed near the River Liffey in Dublin]

lift n.[1] **1** [late 16C–early 19C] (*UK Und.*) a thief of parcels or packages; a shoplifter or pickpocket. **2** [late 16C–1910s] theft, burglary, shoplifting. **3** [late 19C–1900s] a punch. **4** [1950s–60s] (*orig. US*) the effects of intoxication from alcohol or drugs.

lift n.[2] see LIFTER n.[2].

lift v.[1] **1** [late 16C+] (*orig. UK Und.*) to steal. **2** [late 18C+] (*also* **do on the lift**) to shoplift. **3** [mid-19C+] to pick pockets. **4** [1910s+] to arrest. **5** [1910s+] to plagiarize. [orig. SE, esp. for cattle thieving; (4) 1960s+ use esp. Ulster army and police]

lift v.[2] **1** [mid–late 19C] (*US*) to raise someone's bet in a poker game. **2** [1910s+] (*US*) to drink. **3** [1930s–50s] to have an erection.

lift v.[3] (*UK Und.*) **1** [late 19C] to remove or recover one's booty from the place where it has been hidden. **2** [1980s+] to move a prisoner from one jail to another.

lift v.[4] [20C+] (*Ulster*) to understand.

lift v.[5] [1990s+] to give someone a lift (in a car).

lift a leg over v. (also **lay a leg on/over, lift a leg on**) [17C–18C] to have sexual intercourse.

lift arse on v. [20C+] to have sexual intercourse. [SE *lift* + ARSE n.[1] (1)]

lift doesn't reach the top floor phr. [1980s+] a phr. describing a fool, implying that someone is stupid. [var. on NOT ALL THERE phr. (1)]

lifted adj. [1940s+] (*US*) intoxicated by alcohol or drugs.

lifted and laid phr. [20C+] (*Ulster*) favoured unfairly.

lifter n.[1] **1** [17C+] one who steals packages and parcels; a shoplifter; a pickpocket. **2** [early 19C] an act of swindling. [LIFT v.[1]]

lifter n.[2] (also **lift**) [late 17C–early 19C] (*UK Und.*) a crutch.

lifter n.[3] [late 19C] (*US*) a heavy blow. [lit. *lifting* the victim off their feet]

lift hair v. see HAIR n.[2].

lifting law n. [16C–17C] (*UK Und.*) the stealing of parcels or packages. [LIFT v.[1] + LAW n.[1]]

lift-leg n. [late 16C–mid-19C] strong ale. [? its amorous effects (cf. PLAY AT LIFT-LEG v.)]

lift one's hand to one's head v. (also **lift one's hand to one's mouth**) [late 18C–19C] to drink, esp. to excess.

lift one's heels v. [18C–19C] of a woman, to lie down preparatory to sexual intercourse.

lift one's leg v. (also **get one's leg lifted**) [early 18C–19C] of either sex, to have sexual intercourse.

lift pill n. [1960s–70s] (*US drugs*) an amphetamine pill (cf. A n.[2]). [lit. it gives one a 'lift'/LIFT n.[1] (4)]

lifty n. [1930s+] (*Aus.*) a lift attendant.

lig n.[1] [early 18C–mid-19C] a bed. [? dial. *lig*, to lie down or LIB-BEG n.]

lig n.[2] (also **liggety**) [1940s+] (*Ulster*) a fool (*lig* is male, *liggety* female). [Scot. *lug*, a fool]

lig n.[3] see LIGGER n.

lig v. [1990s+] to sponge, to 'freeload', to GATECRASH v. functions or parties, esp. those connected with show business. [backform. f. LIGGER n.]

ligby n. [17C] a mistress. [? LIG n.[1]]

liggen v. [17C] to sleep. [dial. *liggen*, to lie down]

ligger n. (also **lig**) [1960s+] a hanger on, esp. in show business, a 'freeloader'. [ety. debatable; either acronym of *least important guest*; or SE *linger*, to hang around; or Banffshire dial. *lig*, to gossip, to talk too much. Most likely it is dial. *lig*, to lie around. The term became widespread in the early 1970s, but dates at least to 1960 when Colin MacInnes (1914–76) used it in his essay on poncing – 'The Other Man']

liggety n. see LIG n.[2].

light n.[1] **1** [early 19C–1930s] credit; thus *strike a light*, to open a line of credit; *get a light*, to obtain credit; *have one's light put out*, to have one's credit stopped. **2** [20C+] a small amount of money. [orig. printers' use; ? to cast a *light* on one's financial 'darkness']

light n.[2] [1900s] (*US campus*) a bright, clever person.

light n.³ [1950s+] (W.I.) insanity, craziness; thus *have a light*, to be crazy. [? SE *light-headed*]

light adj.¹ [mid-16C–early 19C] of women, promiscuous.

light adj.² **1** [mid-18C; 1930s+] (US) intoxicated, esp. by drugs. **2** [1930s+] (*orig. US Black*) (*also* **light of/on**) short of money. **3** [1960s+] (US Black) stupid. **4** [1960s+] weak. **5** [1990s+] (US) unable to consume large quantities of drink and/or drugs. [fig. uses of SE *light*, as in 'light in the head', 'light in the pocket']

light v. [20C+] (US Black) to enlighten someone with general or specific knowledge. [SE *enlighten*]

light-ale bandit n. [1970s] (UK Und.) one who scrounges drinks in a public house. [SE *light ale* + BANDIT sfx (1)]

light and bitter n. [2000s] the anus (cf. BOTTLE AND GLASS n.). [rhy. sl. = SHITTER n.¹ (1)]

light and dark n. [1930s+] a park. [rhy. sl.]

light a rag v. (*also* **light a shuck**) [late 19C–1970s] (US Und.) to leave at high speed, to run off fast.

light artillery n. [1930s–50s] (US drugs) a hypodermic syringe.

light bird n. *see* BIRD COLONEL n.

light blue n. [19C] gin.

light bread n. [mid-19C+] (US Black) bread made with flour and yeast, as opposed to corn bread or biscuits, occas. mistaken as a term for spec. white bread.

light down on v. *see* LIGHT INTO v.

light drip-drizzle n. [1940s] (US Black) a light spring shower.

lighten the load v. [1980s+] **1** to masturbate. **2** to urinate.

lighten up v. **1** [1940s+] (*orig. US Black*) to calm down. **2** [1960s+] to cease from an action. **3** [1960s+] to act more cheerfully, to cheer up. **4** [1960s+] to reduce verbal or psychological pressure. **5** [1990s+] to act more enthusiastically. **6** [2000s] to diminish one's input of a given substance or activity. [orig. SE 15C]

lighter n. [1950s] (US drugs) a narcotics addict. [? LIGHT adj.² (1)]

light feeder n. [mid-19C–1900s] a silver spoon. [ety. unknown; ? the light reflecting off the silver]

light finger v. [1950s+] (US) to steal, to pilfer. [backform. f. SE *light-fingered* (cited as sl. in Grose, 1785)]

light-food n. [late 19C–1900s] chewing tobacco.

lightfoot n. **1** [20C+] a male homosexual. **2** [1970s–80s] (US Black) a neophyte to the raffish world of the streets, one who leads a sheltered life and does not properly participate in the tougher ghetto world. [i.e. one who does not 'tread heavily' in society + the presumed effeminacy of homosexual men]

light for v. *see* LIGHT OUT v.

light frigate n. [late 17C–19C] a prostitute. [pun on SE *light frigate*, a light, swift vessel + FRIG v. (1)]

light-head n.¹ [19C–1960s] a fool, a simpleton (cf. AIRBALL n.). [SE *light* + -HEAD sfx (1); the supposedly miniscule weight of the fool's brain]

light-head n.² [1950s] (US drugs) one who restricts their drug intake to 'light' drugs, e.g. cannabis.

lightheaded adj. [19C] stupid, foolish (cf. AIRHEADED adj.). [LIGHT-HEAD n.¹]

light heels n. [17C–19C] a promiscuous woman, a prostitute; thus *light-heeled*, promiscuous. [from the 17C fashion for high cork, i.e. lightweight, heels in women's shoes; being fashionable they were seen as encouraging immorality]

light horse n. **1** [17C] a courtesan. **2** [early 18C] a highwayman.

light horsemen n. [mid-19C] '"Light Horsemen" would look out for a lighter having valuable goods on board, and at night, stealing up quietly, would cut her adrift, then following her, as she floated down with the tide, would by-and-by rescue her, and bring her back, claiming salvage' (*Daily News*, 9 January 1899).

lighthouse n. **1** [early 19C] a watch-house. **2** [early 19C] a particularly prominent nose, esp. when reddened by years of drinking. **3** [late 19C–1940s] a lookout man. **4** [1900s–10s] (N.Z.) an illicit dealer in alcohol who carries supplies around and canvasses potential customers. **5** [1910s] (US Und.) those members

of a safecracking team who wait outside while the 'parlor man' lights the fuse to the explosive. **6** [1910s–40s] (US Und.) a lookout man or a person who procures customers for a brothel. **7** [1970s] (UK Und.) one who is skilled at spotting plain-clothes police.

light housekeeping n. [1970s] (US Black) co-habiting.

light housewife n. [mid-16C–18C] a prostitute.

lightie n. (*also* **laaitie, lighty**) **1** [1940s+] (S.Afr.) a child. **2** [1970s+] (S.Afr. Und.) a young man used for sexual purposes by older prisoners. [SE *light-weight*]

light infantry n. [mid–late 19C] fleas.

light in the ass adj. [1990s+] (US Black) second-rate, insubstantial.

light in the loafers adj. (*also* **light on her feet**) [1950s+] (US) homosexual. [the image is of the stereotyped effeminate male, tripping along]

light in the tail phr. *see* HOT IN THE TAIL phr.

light into v. (*also* **light down on**) (*Irish/US*) **1** [mid-19C+] (*also* **light on**) to attack physically. **2** [late 19C+] to attack verbally, to criticize. **3** [late 19C+] to tackle, to attack, whether of food or a task.

light lady n. *see* LIGHT WOMAN n.

lightly and politely phr. (*also* **lightly, slightly and politely**) [1930s–60s] (US Black) smoothly, effortlessly.

lightmans n. (*also* **lightman**) [mid-16C–mid-19C] (UK Und.) the day. [SE *light* + -MANS sfx]

light meat n. *see* WHITE MEAT n.

lightness n. [late 16C–17C] of a woman, wantonness, promiscuity.

lightning n.¹ (*also* **liquid lightning**) **1** [late 18C–mid-19C] gin. **2** [mid-19C+] (Aus./US) (*also* **lightning juice**) whisky or any form of cheap spirits or strong liquor.

lightning n.² **1** [late 19C] (US) electricity. **2** [late 19C] (US) a telegraph. **3** [1970s+] (US drugs) amphetamine or crack cocaine (cf. A n.²; BASE n.).

lightning adj. [mid-19C+] (US) extraordinary, formidable.

lightning jerker n. (*also* **lightning shover, ...slinger, ...squirter, ...wrestler**) [late 19C–1940s] (US) a telegraph operator. [LIGHTNING n.²; the use of electricity in the telegraph system; + JERKER n.¹/SLINGER n.¹ (2)/SE *squirter/wrestler*]

lightning juice n. *see* LIGHTNING n.¹ (2).

lightning rod n. [1970s] (Irish) a penis (cf. BAT n.⁷). [SE *lightning* + ROD n.¹ (1)]

lightning shover/slinger/squirter n. *see* LIGHTNING JERKER n.

lightning water n. [mid-19C+] (US) strong whisky. [LIGHTNING n.¹ (2) + SE *water*]

lightning wrestler n. *see* LIGHTNING JERKER n.

light of adj. *see* LIGHT adj.² (2).

light off v.¹ [late 19C+] to have an orgasm. [SE *light off*, to ignite as an explosive]

light off v.² *see* LIGHT OUT v.

light of love n. [1940s+] (UK prison) a prison governor. [rhy. sl. = abbr. *gov*]

light o' love n. [late 16C–1930s] a prostitute. [euph.; note Nares: 'LIGHT O'LOVE. An old tune of a dance, the name of which made it a pvb expression of levity, especially in love matters']

light on adj. *see* LIGHT adj.² (2).

light on v. *see* LIGHT INTO v. (1).

light on her feet adj. *see* LIGHT IN THE LOAFERS adj.

light out v. (*also* **light for/off**) [mid-19C+] (US) to leave, to escape, to hurry off. [? naut. use *light out*, to move something along, e.g. a sail]

light piece n. [late 19C–1920s] (US tramp) a dime (10 cents) or quarter (25 cents). [the silver, i.e. light, colour of the coins]

lights n.¹ [19C] a fool. [SE *lights*, offal, often considered an inedible piece of the animal]

lights n.² [early 19C+] the eyes. [20C+ usage is usu. US Black]

lights are on but there's nobody home *phr.* [1970s+] insane, mentally deficient, vacant. [ext. of NOBODY HOME *phr.*]

light skirts *n.* [17C; mid-19C] a prostitute.

light someone up *v.* [1940s+] (*drugs*) to supply someone with drugs, usu. marijuana. [LIGHT UP v.[1]]

lights out *n.* [20C+] **1** death. **2** unconsciousness. [a fig. evocation of the end of the day in a dormitory or barracks]

light stuff *n.* **1** [1960s+] (*drugs*) any non-addictive drugs, e.g. cannabis. **2** [1970s+] an unimportant person. [SE *light* + STUFF n.[3] (2)]

light the candle *v.* [1990s+] **1** of a woman, to masturbate (cf. APPLY LIP GLOSS v.). **2** to excite sexually. [the use of a candle as a substitute dildo]

light the lamp *v.* [late 19C–1920s] of a woman, to have sexual intercourse (cf. CATCH AN OYSTER v.).

light-timbered *adj.* [late 17C–mid-19C] **1** of a person, slender, thin. **2** of a person, weak.

light time *n.* [1940s–50s] (*US Und.*) an uneventful time in prison.

light troops *n.* [19C] body lice.

light-up *n.* [1990s+] a marijuana cigarette (cf. AFRICAN WOODBINE n.). [LIGHT UP v.[1] (4)]

light up *v.*[1] **1** [mid-19C+] to light a pipe, cigar or cigarette. **2** [1900s] (*US*) to have a drink; to become drunk. **3** [1920s+] (*US drugs*) to take cocaine. **4** [1930s+] (*US drugs*) to smoke marijuana. **5** [1980s+] to smoke a crack pipe.

light up *v.*[2] [1900s] (*US Und.*) to board a train illegally.

light up *v.*[3] **1** [1940s–60s] to reach orgasm. **2** [1960s] (*US*) to arouse someone sexually. **3** [1960s+] (*US*) to shoot, to destroy with gunfire. **4** [1970s+] (*US Black*) to hit or attack someone. **5** [1980s+] (*US Black*) to dominate, esp. in sports.

light up and say 'tilt' *v.* [1950s+] to register by one's expression or reaction that something is wrong. [pinball imagery; when a player pushes the table too enthusiastically, lights flash, the table 'dies' and a sign declares 'tilt']

light upstairs *adj.* [1970s] (*US Black*) eccentric, insane.

lightweight *n.* **1** [late 19C+] (*orig. US*) (*also* **featherweight**) an insignificant person, a weakling. **2** [1960s] an intellectual mediocrity. **3** [1970s–80s] (*US Black*) one who leads a sheltered life and does not properly participate in the tougher ghetto world. **4** [1980s+] one who cannot equal their peers in the sphere of drinking or taking drugs. [LIGHTWEIGHT adj.]

lightweight *adj.* (*also* **featherweight**) [19C+] (*US*) insignificant, unimpressive. [now SE]

lightweight *adv.* [2000s] (*US Black*) to a certain extent, as opposed to very or completely.

light weight and way late *phr.* [1930s] (*US Black*) fashionable, sophisticated.

light wench *n. see* LIGHT WOMAN n.

light wet *n.* [19C] gin. [SE *light* + WET n.[1] (1)]

lightwit *n.* [1910s] (*US*) a fool (cf. DAMWIT n.).

light woman *n.* (*also* **light lady/wench**) [late 16C–mid-19C] a prostitute (cf. FANCY WOMAN n.).

lighty *n. see* LIGHTIE n.

ligit *adj. see* LEGIT adj.

lig-robber *n.* [1930s–40s] a thief who hides under a bed waiting to rob or assault somebody. [LIG n.[1] + SE *robber*]

like *adv.* **1** [late 18C+] used to express 'kind of', 'in a way' or 'so to speak' when used postpositively, as in *he ran down the road like, and...* **2** [1940s+] (*orig. US Black*) to express 'approximately', 'just about' or poss. to draw attention to the subject matter when used prenominally, as in *it takes like ten minutes; I feel, like, sick.* **3** [1950s+] (*orig. US jazz/teen*) usu. used as an interjection or excl. to introduce or draw attention to what follows, or to indicate uncertainty, or simply as a meaningless filler as in *Like man, it's out of sight; Like he drove so fast...* **4** [1960s+] as if...; the SE used in a derisive sense, denying the validity of the speaker's last statement,

e.g. *like he cares.* **5** [1980s+] referring to one's feelings/speech as recalled when telling an anecdote.

like a... *phr.* [mid-17C+] used in a variety of similes, all of which are fig./joc. uses of SE and of sl.; *see* combs. below.

like a baby's arm with an apple in its fist *phr.* (*also* **like a baby's arm with an orange in its fist**) [1930s+] a phr. used to describe an extra-large penis (cf. ARM n.[1]).

like a baby's bottom *phr.* [1920s+] smooth, featureless.

like a baffled mullet *phr. see* LIKE A STUNNED MULLET phr.

like a bandit *adv.* [1970s+] (*US*) enthusiastically, very fast, very successfully.

like a bastard *adv.* [1910s+] (*orig. US*) a general intensifier; often with *lie* or *work* (cf. AS A BASTARD phr.). [LIKE A... phr. + BASTARD n. (1)]

like a bear on/over hot iron *adv. see* LIKE A HEN ON A HOT GRIDDLE adv.

like a beer bottle on the Coliseum *phr.* [1940s+] (*Aus.*) conspicuous.

like a big dog *phr.* (*also* **like a moose**) [1980s+] (*US campus*) having qualities to do with achievement, success, intensity. [LIKE A... phr. + BIG DOG n. (1)/SE *moose*]

like a blink *adv.* (*also* **like blinko**) [1950s] immediately, very quickly.

like a blue-arsed baboon *adv.* (*also* **like a striped-assed ape**) [1950s+] headlong, very fast (cf. BUZZ AROUND LIKE A BLUE-ARSED FLY v.).

like a bomb *adv.* [1950s+] (*orig. US*) very fast.

like a bugger *adv. see* LIKE BUGGERY adv.

like a bug on a hot frying pan *adv. see* LIKE A HEN ON A HOT GRIDDLE adv.

like a bump on a log *phr.* [mid-19C–1930s] (*US*) stupidly silent or inarticulate.

like a butterfly on heat *phr.* [1970s+] (*orig. gay*) dithering frantically.

like a cat on a hot tin roof *phr.* [20C+] very nervous, very agitated.

like a cat on hot bricks *phr.* [mid-19C+] very nervous.

like a chicken on a hot griddle *adv. see* LIKE A HEN ON A HOT GRIDDLE adv.

like a cock-maggot in a sink-hole *phr.* [late 19C–1920s] very angry, infuriated.

like a dose of salts *adv.* (*also* **like a dose of Epsoms, like a packet of salts**) [mid-19C+] very quickly; usu. as *go through you like a dose of salts.*

like a duck on a dough-pile *adv.* [late 19C] (*US*) heavily, solidly; thus *landed like a duck on a dough-pile.*

like a duck on a hot griddle *adv. see* LIKE A HEN ON A HOT GRIDDLE adv.

like a fart in a bottle *phr.* (*also* **like a fart in a colander/fit**) [late 19C+] twitchy, nervous, agitated.

like a fart in a gale *phr.* (*also* **like a fart in a wind-storm**) [20C+] (*Can.*) utterly useless, helpless.

like a fish on a hook *phr.* [20C+] (*Aus.*) a phr. used to describe one who has been caught or trapped in an inescapable situation.

like a flea in a honeymooner's bed *phr. see* LIKE A POSSUM UP A GUM-TREE phr.

like a fuck *adv. see* LIKE FUCK adv.

like a good 'un *adv.* [mid-19C+] enthusiastically, keenly.

like a gravedigger *phr.* [late 18C–early 19C] extremely busy. [phr. 'up to the a-se in business, and don't know which way to turn' (Grose, 1796)]

like a hen on a hot griddle *adv.* (*also* **like a bear on/over hot iron, like a bug on a hot frying pan, like a chicken/duck on a hot griddle, like a goose/hen on a hot plate**) [mid-19C+] (*US/Irish*) in an agitated or nervous manner.

like a hog on ice *adv.* [late 19C] (*US*) unsteadily, clumsily.

like a hooer at a christening *phr.* (*also* **like an old moll at a christening**) [1960s+] (*N.Z.*) in a state of confusion.

like a knife *adv.* [mid-19C; 1910s] (*US*) very quickly.

like a lily on a dustbin *phr.* (*also* **like a lily on a dirt tin**) [1930s+] (*Aus.*) utterly incongruous or inappropriate.

like all blazes *adv. see* LIKE BLAZES *adv.*

like a lord's bastard *phr.* [1940s] in great luxury, usu. in fig. use.

like a midshipman with money in both pockets *phr.* [mid-19C] extremely unlikely, very odd.

like a mojo *phr.* [1980s+] (*US Black/campus*) a great deal. [LIKE A... *phr.* + MOJO *n.*[1] (1)]

like a monkey on a stick *phr.* [late 19C+] behaving in an eccentric, bizarre manner.

like a monkey with a tin tool *phr.* [mid-19C] impudent, cheeky, self-satisfied.

like a moose *phr. see* LIKE A BIG DOG *phr.*

like a nigger girl's left tit *phr.* [20C+] (*orig. US*) used of something that, punningly, is 'neither right nor fair'. [alternative versions, varying as to chronology, substitute the name of a contemporaneously celebrated Black woman]

like an Irishman's fart *phr.* [1970s] (*US*) of a family, always making a STINK *n.* (1).

like an old moll at a christening *phr. see* LIKE A HOOER AT A CHRISTENING *phr.*

like an owl in an ivy-bush *phr.* [18C–19C] used of a narrow-faced man who has a large wig or very bushy hair, or of a woman with frizzy hair.

like a nun in a knocking shop *phr.* [late 19C+] utterly incongruous.

like a packet of salts *adv. see* LIKE A DOSE OF SALTS *adv.*

like a pakapoo ticket *phr.* (*also* **like a pakapu ticket**) [1940s+] (*Aus.*) said of anything untidy, complex, incomprehensible. [Chinese pidgin *pak-ah-pu ticket*, a form of betting slip used by Chinese gamblers; properly known as *pai-ke-p'iao*, it was a small square of paper marked with 80 Chinese characters; the gambler chose some of these, usu. 10, and, depending on how many matched that day's winning combination, would make a small profit for their 6-penny stake]

like a pearl in a half-storm *phr.* [late 19C] a phr. describing something impossible to find.

like a pork chop at a Jewish wedding *phr.* **1** [1930s+] (*also* **like a baby at a wedding**) superfluous, inappropriate; usu. in phrs. and vars., e.g. *as popular as a..., as useless as a..., as welcome as a..., go down like a..., in more strife than a pork chop at a synagogue.* **2** [1950s+] (*Aus.*) in very great difficulties, in a most embarrassing situation. [the prohibition on pork in orthodox Judaism]

like a possum up a gum-tree *phr.* (*also* **like a flea in a honeymooner's bed**) [late 19C–1950s] (*Aus.*) absolutely content, perfectly happy.

like a rat up a drainpipe *adv.* (*also* **like a rat up a rope**) [1940s+] (*orig. Aus.*) very quickly, fast, usu. used in a sexual context.

like a rope-dancer's pole with lead at both ends *phr.* [late 18C–early 19C] a phr. used of a person considered very stupid and slow (cf. CAN'T SEE THROUGH A LADDER *phr.*).

like arse! *excl. see* LIKE FUCK! *excl.*

like a sailor on a water-cart *phr.* [20C+] useless, inadequate, ineffective.

like a shag on a rock *phr.* [1930s+] (*Aus.*) conspicuous; also used in various phrs. denoting solitariness, e.g. *lonely/miserable as a shag on a rock.* [LIKE A... *phr.* + SE *shag*, a cormorant]

like a shot off a shovel *adv. see* LIKE SHIT OFF A SHOVEL *adv.*

like a snob's cat – all piss and tantrums *phr.* [early–mid-19C] a general phr. of derision or disdain. [LIKE A... *phr.* + SE *snob*, a bootmaker + *cat*]

like a sonofabitch *adv.* [1940s+] very hard, with absolute commitment, to a very great extent. [LIKE A... *phr.* + SONOFABITCH *n.*; var. on LIKE A BASTARD *adv.*]

like a spare prick at a wedding *phr.* (*also* **like a spare dick on a honeymoon**) [1930s+] absolutely useless, often preceded by *standing around...* [LIKE A... *phr.* + PRICK *n.* (2); the assumption is that only the bridegroom is necessary]

like a striped-assed ape *adv. see* LIKE A BLUE-ARSED BABOON *adv.*

like a stunned mullet *phr.* (*also* **like a baffled mullet**) [1950s+] (*Aus.*) dull, stupefied.

like a thousand of brick *adv.* [mid-19C–1910s] of anger or aggression, with full force, violently; thus COME DOWN ON SOMEONE LIKE A TON OF BRICKS *v.*

like a Trojan *adv.* [mid-19C+] in a staunch, determined manner (although moral excellence is not indispensable, as one can *lie like a Trojan*).

like a trooper *adv.* [18C+] vigorously, energetically; thus *swear like a trooper, eat like a trooper, lie like a trooper.* [LIKE A... *phr.* + SE *trooper*]

like a wet week *phr.* [20C+] (*Aus.*) to look depressed; usu. as *have a face like a wet week, look like a wet week.*

like a Whitechapel needle *phr.* [mid–late 19C] very sharp, very fast. [the area's sweatshops]

like a winter's day – short and dirty *phr.* [late 18C–early 19C] a pej. description for an unpopular person.

like barney's bull *phr.* [20C+] (*Aus./N.Z.*) exhausted, tired out. [SE *like* + BARNEY'S BULL *n.*]

like beans *adv.* [mid–late 19C] energetically, very fast.

like billy-o *adv.* (*also* **like billy-ho, ...billy-oh**) [late 19C+] a general intensifier and expression of energy or effort, most enthusiastically, strenuously, speedily. [dial., euph. for 'bloody hell']

like bingo *adv.* [1930s–40s] a general intensifier and expression of energy or effort, most enthusiastically, strenuously, speedily. [SE *like* + BINGO! *excl.*]

like blazes *adv.* [early 19C+] (*also* **like all blazes**) energetically, passionately. [euph. for LIKE HELL *adv.*]

like blinko *adv. see* LIKE A BLINK *adv.*

like bricks *adv.* [mid-19C] energetically, noisily.

like bringer *adv.* [mid-19C] (*US*) energetically.

like buggery *adv.* (*also* **like a bugger**) [1920s+] a general intensifier, usu. negative.

like cow buss rope *adv.* [20C+] (*W.I.*) very angrily, highly enraged. [Carib.E.; *buss* = SE *burst/bust*]

like crap through a goose *phr. see* LIKE SHIT THROUGH A GOOSE *adv.*

like crazy *adv.* [1920s+] **1** intensely, excessively, obsessively, esp. as an answer to 'Do you like...?' 'Sure, like crazy.' **2** as fast as possible.

like daddy-come-to-church *adv.* [1950s] (*US*) to a very great extent, very much, a great deal.

like death to a... *phr.* [19C+] (*US*) a phr. used of someone who is holding on without the slightest weakening, e.g. *he's holding on like death to a...*

like di-wa-didy *adv.* [1920s–60s] uncompromisingly, perfectly, completely.

like Edgware Road *phr.* [1940s+] a phr. describing tight trousers. [because 'that's got no ballroom either'; pun on SE *ballroom* + BALLS *n.*[1] (1)]

like enough *adv.* [mid-16C+] very likely, almost certainly.

like falling off a log *phr. see* EASY AS FALLING OFF A LOG *phr.*

like five hundred *adv.* [mid-19C–1900s] (*US*) to excess, very much so, intensely. [on model of LIKE SIXTY *adv.*]

like forty *adv.* [mid-19C+] (*US*) with great force, with complete and absolute commitment. [on model of LIKE SIXTY *adv.* and LIKE TWENTY *adv.*]

like fuck *adv.* (*also* **like a fuck**) [1960s+] intensely, to a great degree, very much. [FUCK n.⁵]

like fuck! *excl.* (*also* **like arse!**) [late 19C+] an excl. of denial or negation; usu. as *like fuck I will!*

like fuckery *adv.* [2000s] to a very great extent. [LIKE FUCK adv.]

like fucking hell *phr.* [late 19C+] in no way whatsoever, absolutely not.

like fun *adv.* [early 19C+] vigorously, energetically, quickly.

like fun! *excl.* [1910s+] a dismissive excl., implying the absolute unlikeliness of a given event, opinion etc. [euph. for LIKE FUCK! excl.]

like funk on a skunk *phr. see* LIKE STINK ON SHIT *phr.*

like fury *adv.* [early 19C–1910s] (*US*) furiously, earnestly, seriously. [SE *fury*]

like ginger *adv.* [late 19C] to a great extent.

like god-dam *adv. see* LIKE HELL *adv.*

like gravy on rice *adv. see* LIKE WHITE ON RICE *adv.*

like grim death *adv.* [mid-19C+] (*orig. US*) with absolute tenacity; usu. in the phr. *hang on like grim death.*

like grub *adv.* [late 19C] keenly, enthusiastically. [SE *grub*, to dig, to root up]

like hang *adv.* [1960s+] (*Aus./N.Z.*) a general intensive, very much. [euph. for LIKE HELL adv.]

like hang! *excl.* [1960s+] (*Aus./N.Z.*) a general intensive excl. [LIKE HANG adv.]

like hell *adv.* (*also* **like god-dam, like hell for Texas, like merry hell**) [mid-19C+] a general intensifier, recklessly, intensely, very much, very quickly.

like hell! *excl.* [20C+] an ironic excl. of negation and denial; usu. as *like hell I will!*

like hi *phr.* [1990s+] (*US campus*) hello.

like Hunt's dog will neither go to church nor stay at home *phr.* [late 18C–19C] a description of 'discontented and whimsical persons' (Grose, 1785). [a Shropshire labourer by the name of Hunt whose mastiff was neither happy at home where he howled whenever his master left for church or at the church where he refused to enter]

like it or lump it *v.* [late 18C+] to accept a situation, willingly or not; usu. as *you'll have to like it or lump it,* or sometimes the euph. phr. *if you don't like it you'll have to do the other thing.* [SE *like* + LUMP v.¹]

like merry hell *adv. see* LIKE HELL *adv.*

like nuts *adv. see* NUTS adj. (2).

like old boots *adv.* [mid-19C–1920s] a general intensifier, e.g. *fight like old boots,* to fight enthusiastically.

like old gooseberry *adv.* [late 18C–19C] very fast. [SE *like* + OLD GOOSEBERRY n. (1)]

like peas *adj.* [20C+] (*W.I.*) plentiful, abundant.

like peas *adv.* [20C+] (*W.I.*) plentifully, abundantly.

like pie *adv.* [late 19C] energetically, vigorously. [? enthusiastic eating]

liker *n.* [late 19C–1910s] a glance, a look.

like shit *adv.* **1** [1940s+] very fast, enthusiastically. **2** [1970s+] badly, very bad. **3** [1990s+] very much.

like shit! *excl.* [1980s+] a sarcastic retort of dismissal.

like shit off a shovel *adv.* (*also* **like (a) shot off a shovel, like steam on piss**) [1920s+] promptly, very fast, quickly.

like shit on a shoe *adv.* [1980s+] extremely closely.

like shit through a goose *adv.* (*also* **like crap through a goose**) [20C+] extremely fast, quickly.

like shot off a shovel *adv. see* LIKE SHIT OFF A SHOVEL *adv.*

like sixty *adv.* [mid-19C+] (*orig. US*) with great force or vigour, at a great speed. [? SE *like sixty men*; on model of LIKE TWENTY adv. and LIKE FORTY adv.]

like smoke *adv.* [mid-19C–1900s] (*Aus.*) very energetically; very quickly; exceedingly.

like snuff at a wake *adv.* [20C+] (*Irish*) **1** very quickly. **2** in large amounts.

likes of, the *n.* [late 18C+] such (a person) as; often used in a pej. context, e.g. *you shouldn't mix with the likes of him.*

like stank on shit *phr. see* LIKE STINK ON SHIT *phr.*

like steam *adv.* [mid-19C+] very quickly, very easily, energetically. [20C+ use Aus.]

like steam on piss *adv. see* LIKE SHIT OFF A SHOVEL *adv.*

like stink *adv.* (*also* **to stink**) [1920s+] intensely, furiously. [? euph.]

like stink on shit *phr.* (*also* **like funk on a skunk, …stank on shit, …stink on glue**) [1960s+] (*US Black*) very close, extremely intimate.

like St Paul's *phr.* [20C+] (*Aus.*) a phr. used to describe tight trousers. [? because 'there's no standing room inside']

like stupidness *adv.* [1950s] (*W.I./UK Black*) abundantly, in great supply.

like tar *adv.* [1900s] very keenly, very quickly.

like that *phr.* **1** [1910s+] extremely intimate. **2** [1970s+] (*US, mainly Southern*) a euph. for being pregnant. **3** [1970s+] homosexual.

like the cocky on the biscuit tin *phr.* [1980s+] (*Aus.*) useless, impotent, a non-participant. [the old tins of Arnott's biscuits had a picture of a cockatoo, which was thus 'on' the tin but not 'in' it]

like thirty cents *phr.* [late 19C+] (*US*) cheap, worthless; esp. as *feel/look like thirty cents.*

like to meet her in the dark *phr.* [late 19C] a phr. used of a plain woman who presumably has a good figure; usu. as *I'd like to meet her in the dark.*

like twenty *adv.* [mid-19C] (*US*) with great force, with absolute commitment. [on the model of LIKE FORTY adv. and LIKE SIXTY adv.]

like two apples in a bag *phr.* [1950s+] (*orig. US*) a ref. to well-formed buttocks, irrespective of sex.

like two cents *phr.* [1920s–50s] (*US*) worthless.

like two pennorth of tripe *phr.* [20C+] useless, worthless, unpleasant.

like whelks behind a window-pane *phr.* [1900s–10s] a phr. describing the eyes of a person who wears very thick glasses.

like white on rice *adv.* (*also* **like gravy on rice**) [1930s+] (*US Black/P.R.*) very closely. [rice is white itself]

like who shot the cat *adv.* [1930s] (*US*) a general intensifier, e.g. very fast, very successful.

like winking *adv.* (*also* **as winking, before you could say winking, like wink**) **1** [early 19C+] very quickly. **2** [mid-19C–1920s] vigorously, energetically.

like winky *adv.* (*also* **like winkey**) [early 19C–1930s] very quickly. [abbr. LIKE WINKING adv.]

likker *n. see* LIQUOR n.

likkered *adj. see* LIQUORED (UP) adj.

likki-likki/likky-likky *adj. see* LICKY-LICKY adj.².

lil *n.*¹ (*also* **lill**) **1** [early–mid-19C] a book; a pocketbook or wallet. **2** [mid–late 19C] a £5 note (cf. BANK-RAG n.). **3** [mid-19C–1920s] (*UK Und.*) a forged banknote; thus *lil-faker,* a counterfeiter. **4** [1900s] any banknote. [Rom. *lil,* a book, a paper]

lil *n.*² *see* LILY n.¹.

l'il abners *n.* [1940s+] (*US*) square-toed shoes, usu. work shoes. [those worn by the hero of the cartoon strip *L'il Abner* (1934–79), created by Al Capp]

lilac *adj.* [20C+] effeminately homosexual (cf. LAVENDER adj.; PURPLE adj.). [SE *lilac,* a colour seen as stereotypically homosexual]

lilac love lance *n.* [2000s] the penis (cf. AX n.²).

lilacs *n.* [late 19C–1920s] (*US*) sideburns, sideboards. [the supposed similarity of a bushy sideburn to a lilac flower]

lil-faker *n. see* LIL n.¹ (3).

lilies *n. see* LILYWHITES n.

lilies-of-the-valley *n.* [1990s+] (*gay*) haemorrhoids. [supposed resemblance]

lill *n. see* LIL n.[1].

Lilley and Skinner *n.* [1920s+] **1** dinner. **2** a beginner. [rhy. sl.; ult. *Lilley and Skinner*, a London shoe shop (est. 1835)]

lillian *n.* [1970s+] (*gay*) the police. [camp feminization]

Lillian Gish *n.* [1920s+] **1** (*Aus.*) a dish. **2** a fish. [rhy. sl.; ult. US film star *Lilian Gish* (1899–1993)]

Lillian Gished *adj.* [1950s–60s] drunk (cf. ADRIAN (QUIST) adj.). [rhy. sl. = PISSED adj.[1]; for ety. *see* prev.]

lillies *n.* [1910s–60s] (*US*) a White person's hands; thus *lily-presser*, a handshaker.

Lilly *n.* [1970s+] (*drugs*) Seconal. [the manufacturer's name on the pill, branded as *Lilly F-40*]

lilly *n. see* LILY n.[2] (3).

lilly (law) *n. see* LILY LAW n.

lilly white *n. see* LILYWHITE n.[1] (1).

lilt *v.* [20C+] (*Ulster*) to act foolishly or carelessly. [Scot. *lilt*, to dance]

lily *n.*[1] (*also* **lil**) [late 19C–1950s] (*US*) anything or anyone remarkable or particularly outstanding.

lily *n.*[2] **1** [1900s–60s] (*US Und.*) a gullible person. **2** [1920s–30s] (*US*) a virgin. **3** [1920s+] (*also* **lilly**) a derog. term for an effeminate man or a homosexual, esp. one who fears to reveal his sex life. **4** [1930s] the queen in cards. [the purity or innocence of the flower]

lily *n.*[3] [1910s–20s] a livid bruise.

lily *n.*[4] **1** [1940s+] (*US*) a penis, usu. with ref. to urination or masturbation. **2** [1990s+] (*US Black*) the vagina, esp. when loose.

lily *n.*[5] [1950s–80s] (*camp gay*) a proper name used for a variety of camp nicknames for male homosexuals (cf. ABIGAIL n.).

lily *n.*[6] [1960s+] (*US Black*) a White person. [SE *lilywhite*; note 14C SE *lily*, a person or thing of exceptional whiteness, fairness or purity]

lily *n.*[7] *see* LILYWHITE n.[1] (2).

lily-benjamin *n.* [mid-19C] a white greatcoat or overcoat. [SE *lily*, white + BENJAMIN n.[1]]

lily law *n.* (*also* **lilly, lilly law, Miss Lily**) [1940s+] (*orig. US gay*) the police. [female proper name *Lily* + LAW, THE n. (1)]

Lily of Lagoona *n.* (*also* **Lily of Laguna**) [20C+] (*Aus.*) a schooner, which in Aus. is a tall beer glass; thus beer or a glass of beer. [rhy. sl.; ult. 1898 song title 'Lily of Laguna' by Leslie Stuart]

lily-presser *n. see* LILLIES n.

lily-shallow *n.* [early–late 19C] a low-crowned white hat, esp. as worn by a coachman. [SE *lily(white)* + *shallow*, low]

lily's whiskers *n. see* CAT'S WHISKERS n.

lily the pink *n.* [2000s] a drink. [rhy. sl.]

lilywhite *n.*[1] **1** [late 17C–early 19C] (*also* **lilly white**) a chimney sweep. **2** [early 19C] (*also* **lily**) a Black person. **3** [1900s–40s] (*US Black*) (*also* **lilywhiter**) a White person who claims superiority on the grounds of their colour. [(1) and (2) a heavy joke at the expense of the soot-blackened sweep or Black-skinned individual]

lilywhite *n.*[2] [late 19C–1970s] a young male homosexual.

lilywhite *n.*[3] **1** [1950s] (*US*) one who has no connections with any form of crime or corruption. **2** [2000s] (*also* **clean skin**) a drug trafficker who deliberately eschews ostentation to maximize their chances of avoiding arrest.

lilywhite *adj.*[1] [20C+] (*US*) bigoted against or segregated from Black people. [LILYWHITE n.[1] (3)]

lilywhite *adj.*[2] [1960s+] (*Aus./mainly surfing*) cowardly. [? the lack of suntan, but note LILY n.[2] (3)]

lilywhite groat *n.* [mid-19C–1910s] a shilling (5p). [the coin was silver]

lilywhiter *n. see* LILYWHITE n.[1] (3).

lilywhites *n.* (*also* **lilies**) [1930s–70s] **1** (*US Black*) bedsheets. **2** (*orig. US*) a White person's hands.

limb *n.*[1] **1** [17C–19C] the penis. **2** [1990s+] an erection. [euph.]

limb *n.*[2] [early 17C–1920s] a mischievous boy, a 'young rascal'. [abbr. SE *limb of Satan*]

limb *n.*[3] [1930s+] (*Aus.*) a policeman. [abbr. LIMB OF THE LAW n. (2)]

limber dick *n.* [1980s+] (*Aus. prison*) an old prisoner. [SE *limber* + DICK n.[4] (1); his penis is presumed no longer capable of erection]

limber-jack *n.*[1] (*also* **limber-jim**) [mid-19C–1950s] (*US*) a small whip, usu. used to beat children. [SE *limber up*, to make pliant + generic use of proper names]

limber-jack *n.*[2] (*also* **limber-jim**) [1900s–30s] (*US*) a loose-jointed person, a contortionist. [SE *limber*, lithe, nimble + generic use of proper names]

limbie *n.* (*also* **limby**) [1910s+] (*N.Z.*) one who has lost a leg, usu. in battle. [SE *limb*]

limbo *n.*[1] **1** [late 16C–1920s] prison. **2** [late 17C–mid-18C] pawn. **3** [2000s] (*US prison*) time in jail before trial. [SE *limbo*, 'a region supposed to exist on the border of Hell as the abode of the just who died before Christ's coming, and of unbaptized infants' (*OED*)]

limbo *n.*[2] [1970s+] (*drugs*) marijuana from Colombia.

limb of the bar *n.* [early–mid-19C] a barrister. [SE *limb*, an extension, a branch + *bar*, the name given to the bar at which barristers speak in court and thus to barristers in general]

limb of the law *n.* **1** [mid-18C–1920s] a lawyer, spec. a second-rate attorney or any legal functionary, including the police. **2** [1930s+] (*Aus.*) a policeman. [SE *limb*, an extension, a branch + *law*]

limbo room *n.* [1960s+] (*Can. prison*) a place where corporal punishment is administered to prisoners. [SE *limbo* + *room*]

Limburger *n.* **1** [late 19C–1950s] (*US*) a derog. name for a German. **2** [1980s+] (*US campus*) an unpopular or unattractive woman. [note, however, *Limburger* is a Dutch/Belgian cheese, not a German one]

limby *n. see* LIMBIE n.

lime *n.*[1] [1950s+] (*orig. W.I.*) a spontaneous, unorganized social gathering, usu. of young people. Often qualified by its focus, e.g. *beach lime*, a beach get-together; *roti lime*, a gathering to eat roti; thus punning phr. *this lime has no juice*, this get-together is boring. [LIME v.]

lime *n.*[2] *see* LEMON n.[1] (2).

lime *adj. see* LIMEY adj.

lime *v.* (*also* **pick a lime**) [1950s+] (*orig. W.I.*) to sit around and relax with friends or family; thus *liming*, hanging around, chatting. [? LIMEY n. (1), or the groups of US sailors who frequented the Trinidad red-light areas during WW2. Also US teen use in the 1990s; note late 19C Fr. sl. *limer*, 'To take time in the act of kind']

lime acid *n.* [1970s+] (*drugs*) LSD (cf. A n.[3]).

lime-fingered *adj.* [late 16C–17C] light-fingered, given to thieving (cf. BIRDLIME n.[1]). [LIME-TWIG n.]

limehouse *v.* [1910s–30s] to use coarse, abusive language, esp. in a political speech. [the proper name *Limehouse*, then a rough area of East London and one in which the Liberal leader David Lloyd George made a notably acerbic speech on 30 July 1909, in which he attacked the aristocracy, financial magnates etc]

limehouse cut *n.* [20C+] a paunch. [rhy. sl. = SE *gut*]

lime juice *n.* **1** [mid-19C–1900s] (*Aus.*) an immigrant from England; thus phrs. *hasn't got the lime-juice off, smelling of lime-juice* etc, used of newly arrived immigrants. **2** [1950s] (*US*) English, English idiom. [LIME-JUICER n.]

lime juice country *n.* [mid-19C–1900s] (*US*) England. [LIME JUICE n. (1)]

lime-juicer *n.* **1** [mid–late 19C] (*Aus.*) an immigrant from England. **2** [mid-19C–1950s] (*US*) an English or British person or sailing ship. [the former habit of serving sailors lime-juice as a preventative against scurvy on long voyages]

lime-juicer *adj.* (*also* **lime-juice**) [mid-19C–1950s] (*US*) English, British. [LIME-JUICER n.]

limer *n.* [1970s+] (*W.I.*) a layabout, an idler. [LIMEY n. (2)]

lime-twig *n.* [late 16C–17C] a thief (cf. BIRDLIME n.¹). [SE *lime-twig*, a twig smeared with birdlime for catching birds; thus a snare]

lime-twigs *n.* [16C–17C] (*UK Und.*) playing cards, as used by a confidence trickster or card-cheat; thus in fig. use, any snare. [for ety. *see* LIME-TWIG n.]

limey *n.* **1** [1910s+] (*orig. Aus.*) an English person or sailing ship. **2** [1940s+] (*W.I.*) a derog. term for a disreputable working-class White person. **3** [1950s] the English language. [LIME-JUICER n.]

limey *adj.* (*also* **lime**) [1910s+] (*orig. Aus.*) English, British. [LIMEY n. (1)]

limey land *n.* [1910s–70s] (*US*) England. [LIMEY n. (1) + SE *land*]

liming *n. see* LIME v.

limit, the *n.* **1** [late 19C–1940s] (*orig. US*) something splendid or fine. **2** [20C+] (*orig. US*) something or someone considered excessive. **3** [1920s] (*US Und.*) the maximum sentence.

limo *n.* (*also* **limmo, limmie, limou**) [1920s+] (*orig. US*) a *limo*usine. [abbr.]

limo *v.* [1960s] (*US*) to travel in a *limo*usine. [LIMO n.]

limousine liberal *n.* [1970s+] a liberal, the intensity of whose pronouncements on social problems are in direct proportion to their own ability to escape such an existence (cf. BOLLINGER BOLSHEVIK n.).

limp-dick *n.* (*also* **limp-prick**) [20C+] an inadequate person, a weakling. [SE *limp* + DICK n.⁴ (1)/PRICK n. (2)]

limp-dick *adj.* (*also* **limp-prick**) [20C+] inadequate, weak. [LIMP-DICK n.]

limping Jesus *n.* [19C] a lame person.

limpty *n. see* LIMPY n.

limp wrist *n.* (*orig. US*) **1** [1950s+] (*also* **bent wrist, broken wrist, limp wrister**) a male homosexual. **2** [1990s+] a weakling, a social 'liberal'. [his extravagantly effeminate gestures]

limp-wristed *adj.* (*also* **limp-wrist, weak-wristed, wristy**) [1950s+] (*orig. US*) weak, effeminate, homosexual. [LIMP WRIST n.]

limpy *n.* (*also* **limpty**) [1930s–60s] (*US tramp*) a crippled beggar; or any person.

lina *n.* [1990s+] (*drugs*) cocaine. [Sp. *lina*, a line]

Linc *n.* [1970s] (*US*) a *Linc*oln automobile. [abbr.]

Lincoln *n.* [1930s–70s] (*US*) a $5 note (cf. ABE n.²). [the face of Abraham *Lincoln* (1809–65), 16th president of the US, printed on the bills]

lincoln *n.* [2000s] (*US Black*) a bag of drugs that has a small coin in the middle so that it weighs more.

lincoln and bennett *n.* [mid-19C] (*UK society*) a first-class hat. [the makers' name]

Lincoln's Inn *n.* **1** [mid-19C+] a hand. **2** [late 19C+] a £5 note (cf. BEEHIVE n.²). **3** [late 19C+] gin. [rhy. sl.; (1) = FIN n.¹; (2) = FIN n.² (1)]

Lincoln Tunnel *n. see* GRAND CANYON n.

line *n.¹* **1** [mid-17C+] an area of criminal or dubious activity. **2** [early 19C–1930s] a hoax, a trick; thus *get someone in a line*, to mock, to tease. **3** [mid-19C+] (*orig. US*) a smooth verbal style aimed at seduction or at persuading someone else to accept an idea or plan, esp. in sexual or business contexts; thus FEED (SOMEONE) A LINE v.; DO A LINE (WITH) v. **4** [late 19C+] (*orig. US*) a useful tip, a piece of information, usu. acquired confidentially. [fig. use of SE *line* + abbr. *a line of talk*; (1) note SE *line*, an occupation]

line *n.²* **1** [late 19C+] (*US*) a red-light district; thus *lady of the line*, a prostitute; *down the line*, visiting a red-light district in search of sexual intercourse. **2** [late 19C+] the entertainment area of a city. **3** [1930s+] in a brothel, the parade of available girls, thus the girls employed by a single pimp; thus *on the line*, working as a prostitute. [orig. police jargon; lit. a *line* of buildings]

line *n.³* [1930s+] (*US Black*) **1** money. **2** the cost or price of an item. [? BOTTOM LINE n.; Mezzrow & Wolfe, *Really the Blues* (1946): '*Line two* means the price is a dollar; prices, like times of the day, are often doubled so that outsiders won't understand the details']

line *n.⁴* **1** [1930s+] (*drugs*) the main vein in the arm used to inject heroin; thus *take it in the line*, to inject into a vein. **2** [1950s] (*drugs*) injected heroin. **3** [1950s+] (*drugs*) a small marijuana cigarette (cf. BONE n.¹¹). **4** [1960s+] (*drugs*) a portion of heroin or cocaine scraped into a line across a mirror in order for it to be sniffed into the nostril. **5** [1970s+] (*US drugs*) a rough unit of measure used by cocaine dealers. **6** [1970s+] (*drugs*) a portion of any drug which is inhaled.

line *n.⁵* [1930s+] (*Aus.*) a woman, usu. with a defining adj., e.g. *good line, nice line, slashing line*.

line *n.⁶ see* FRONT LINE n.

line *n.⁷ see* LINE-UP n.¹ (1).

line *n.⁸ see* MAINLINE n.¹.

line *v.¹* **1** [16C] to seduce. **2** [1900s] (*Aus.*) to hit. **3** [1940s] (*US*) to copulate, used of both men and animals. [14C SE *line*, to copulate]

line *v.² see* LINE UP v.² (1).

linebacker *n.* [1970s] (*US campus*) an outsider, one who is unsociable and unpopular.

lined *adj.¹* [late 19C–1920s] married. [the couple have signed on the dotted *line*]

lined *adj.²* [1930s+] rich, having money.

line haul *n.* [1930s+] (*US*) a scheduled truck route.

linen armourer *n.* [late 18C–early 19C] a tailor.

linen(-draper) *n.* [mid-19C+] a newspaper. [rhy. sl.]

linen-lifter *n.* [1980s] (*Aus.*) a womanizer.

Linenopolis *n.* [late 19C] Belfast. [its one-time manufacturing base]

line of shit *n.* (*also* **line of bull/crap**) [1920s+] purportedly persuasive nonsense. [SE *line* + SHIT n.³ (4)]

line of the old author *n.* [late 17C–early 19C] a drink, esp. of brandy.

line one's flue *v.* (*also* **line the flue**) [1900s–60s] (*orig. US Western, mainly Black*) to eat.

line one's jacket *v.* [17C–early 19C] to fill one's stomach, either with food or drink. [SE *line* + JACKET n.¹]

line one's kidneys *v.* [1950s] (*Aus.*) to have a drink.

line one's tubes *v.* [1950s] (*Aus.*) to eat.

line out *v.¹* [late 19C–1900s] (*US*) to head for.

line out *v.²* [1920s+] (*US*) to scold, to discipline, to punish; thus *lining out*, a scolding.

liner *n.¹* [20C+] (*Irish*) a substantial meal. [it *lines* one's stomach]

liner *n.²* [1980s+] (*UK Black*) a policeman.

liner *n.³ see* PENNY-A-LINER n.

liners *n.* [2000s] (*US Und.*) money.

lines *n.¹* [19C–1910s] a marriage certificate. [abbr. SE *marriage lines*]

lines *n.²* [1970s+] (*US Black*) **1** words in general. **2** persuasive patter aimed at seduction. [LINE n.¹ (3)]

line-shooter *n.* [1940s+] one who talks pretentiously or boasts. [SHOOT A LINE v.]

line someone up *v.* [1950s] (*orig. US*) to put someone in a given position or situation.

line someone with licks *v.* [20C+] (*W.I.*) to administer corporal punishment. [SE *lick*, a blow]

line stiff n. [1930s] (US tramp) a tramp who spends all day in different bread lines. [SE line + STIFF n.² (4)]

line the flue v. see LINE ONE'S FLUE v.

line-up n.¹ **1** [20C+] (also **line**) a police identification parade. **2** [1910s+] gang-rape or group sex.

line-up n.² [2000s] (US drugs) the consumption in quick succession of a glass of beer, a puff on a marijuana cigarette, a line of cocaine, a shot of whisky and a puff on a cigarette.

line up v.¹ **1** [1900s–70s] (US) to associate, to join up with. **2** [1910s–50s] (Aus.) to accost, to approach.

line up v.² **1** [1910s+] (orig. US) (also **line**) to arrange, to organize, to plan in advance. **2** [1930s–70s] (US) to arrange an illicit and profitable deal.

line up v.³ (US) **1** [1910s+] to subject to or (rare) to be subjected to gang-rape. **2** [1920s–30s] to rob. [LINE-UP n.¹ (2)]

line up v.⁴ [1920s+] (US Und.) to be subjected to a police identification parade. [LINE-UP n.¹ (1)]

line up on v. **1** [1910s+] to gang-rape. **2** [1940s+] (gay) to gang-fellate or sodomize. [ext. of LINE UP v.³ (1)]

line up one's ducks v. [1960s+] (US) to set one's affairs in order.

line up to v. [1920s+] (Aus.) to accost. [ext. of LINE UP v.¹ (2)]

ling n. **1** [17C] a woman, considered as a sexual object. **2** [mid-17C–19C] the vagina or the female sexual odour; thus LING-GRAPPLING n. (cf. BEARDED CLAM n.). **3** [1920s+] (Aus.) a stench. [SE ling, a type of fish; E.P. notes the old music-hall song, c.1835, which tells the tale of a woman attempting to buy a fish, the name of which she has forgotten and runs in part: 'Then the girl shoved her hand 'neath her clothes in a shot / And rubbed it about on a certain sweet spot; / Then, blushing so sweetly, as you may suppose, she put her hand up to the fishmonger's nose. / The fishmonger smelt it, and cried with delight, / [...] "I'll tell you directly, you wanted some ling"']

ling v. [1990s+] (UK juv.) to throw very hard. [? SE line]

ling-grappling n. [19C] womanizing. [LING n. (2) + SE grappling]

lingo n. **1** [18C+] (orig. Ling. Fr./Polari) (also **lingua**) a language, esp. slang. **2** [1920s–50s] (US) insincere talk, a yarn, an excuse. [Ital. lingua, language]

linguist n. [1950s+] (Aus.) a cunnilinguist. [abbr.]

lining out n. see LINE OUT v.².

link adj. [late 19C] (Jewish/Cockney) unorthodox, irreligious. [Ger. links, left, in the sense of left-handed = unorthodox, unnatural]

link v. [early–mid-19C] (UK Und.) to pick a pocket by turning it inside out.

linkboy n. see LINKMAN n.

linkety-clink adv. see LICKETY-SPLIT adv.

link it v. [1900s–40s] to walk arm-in-arm.

linkman n. (also **linkboy**) [17C; late 19C–1900s] a general servant. [ext. of SE linkman, one who carries a link or torch]

links n. (US) **1** [late 19C] sausages. **2** [1940s] handcuffs. [SE link]

Linseed Lancers n. [1910s–40s] (orig. milit.) the Medical Corps.

linthead n. (also **lintbrain**) (US) **1** [1930s–60s] an insignificant or working-class person. **2** [1960s+] a stupid person. [SE linthead, a worker in a cotton mill]

lint-scraper n. (also **lint**) [mid-18C–19C] a junior surgeon. [SE lint, the cotton that bandages are made of]

lion n.¹ **1** [18C] a spy employed by an influential and powerful man. **2** [late 18C–mid-19C] a prosperous citizen or merchant; thus its use in late 18C–early 19C in Oxon. sl. for a visitor to the university (his female companions were lionesses). **3** [mid-19C–1910s] a fashionable person, a man about town. **4** [mid-19C–1920s] a celebrity; by ext., a celebrated place.

lion n.² [1950s+] (W.I. Rasta) an outstanding Rastafarian, a great soul. [the lion of Judah, a central Rasta symbol]

lion v. [mid-19C; 1920s+] (Aus./US) to frighten, to intimidate, to be cheeky. [reverse anthropomorphism]

Lionel Bart n. [1990s+] an act of breaking wind. [rhy. sl. = FART n.; ult. UK composer and lyricist Lionel Bart (1930–99)]

Lionel Blair n. [1970s+] a chair. [rhy. sl.; ult. UK entertainer Lionel Blair (b.1931)]

Lionel Blairs n. [1970s+] flares, flared trousers. [rhy. sl.; for ety. see prev.]

lioness n. **1** [16C] a prostitute (cf. ALLEY CAT n.). **2** [mid-19C–1920s] a female LION n.¹ (4).

lion's lair n. (also **lion's share**) [20C+] a chair. [rhy. sl.]

lion's roar n. [20C+] a snore. [rhy. sl.]

lip n.¹ **1** [19C+] cheek, impertinence; thus have a lip, to be cheeky; LESS (OF YOUR) LIP phr.; GIVE IT LIP v. **2** [1920s+] (US) a lawyer, esp. in criminal practice. **3** [2000s] lies, deception. [(2) plays on (1), i.e. the concept of 'talking back' (as in cheekiness) in defence of a client]

lip n.² **1** [late 19C+] (US) musical ability, esp. of a player of brass instruments. **2** [1980s] a brass-player.

lip v.¹ **1** [late 18C–19C] to sing; thus lip us a chant, sing us a song. **2** [late 18C–1940s] to speak. **3** [late 19C+] to insult, to abuse, to be impudent. **4** [20C+] (Ulster) to eat or drink. **5** [1940s+] to suck on. **6** [1940s+] (US campus) to kiss. [SE lip; (6) note 17C–19C poetic SE lip, to kiss]

lip v.² see LIB v.

lip action n. (also **lip dancing/music**) [1940s+] (US) oral sex. [SE lip + ACTION sfx]

lip and lagging phr. (also **lippin-leggin**) [20C+] (Ulster) full to the brim. [Scot. laggen, the projecting part of the stave at the bottom of a barrel]

lip-burner n. [1930s–40s] (US) a very short cigarette butt.

lip dancing n. see LIP ACTION n.

lip fart n. [1920s+] (US teen) a farting noise made with the lips.

lip fart v. [1920s+] (US teen) to make a rude farting noise with the lips. [LIP FART n.]

lip in v. [late 19C–1950s] (US) to butt into a conversation impolitely. [LIP n.¹ (1)]

lipish adj. (also **lippish**) [mid-19C] impudent, cheeky. [LIP n.¹ (1)]

lipken n. see LIBKEN n.

lip-lock n. [1970s+] (US) **1** a fig. tight hold with the mouth. **2** fellatio (cf. COCKSUCK n.). **3** a passionate kiss.

lip-loyalty n. [late 19C] (Aus.) insincerity. [SE lip service]

lip music n.¹ [1990s+] slangy speech.

lip music n.² see LIP ACTION n.

lip off v. [1950s+] (US) to talk rudely, cheekily or provocatively. [LIP v.¹ (3)]

lipping (the dipper) n. [1930s–40s] (US drugs) sucking the air out of a makeshift syringe.

lippin-leggin phr. see LIP AND LAGGING phr.

lippish adj. see LIPISH adj.

lippy adj. [mid-19C+] cheeky, talkative, loudmouthed. [LIP n.¹ (1)]

lip read v. **1** [1960s] (US) of a lesbian, to perform cunnilingus. **2** [1970s] to kiss.

lip rug n. [1970s+] (US Black) a moustache. [SE lip + RUG n.¹ (1)]

lips n. **1** [1940s+] (US Black) the vagina. **2** [1970s+] (US gay) the anus. [Lat. labia, lips]

lip service n. [1960s] fellatio (cf. COCKSUCK n.).

lip shield n. [1910s] (US) a moustache.

Lipton's n. (also **Lipton tea**) [1960s+] (US drugs) inferior-quality cannabis (cf. AFRICAN BUSH n.). [Lipton's, the cheap brand of tea, pun on TEA n.² (1)]

lip-wrestle v. (also **mouth-wrestle**) [1970s+] (US) to indulge in passionate kissing.

liq n. (also **L.I.Q.**) [1970s+] (US Black) **1** a liquor store. **2** liquor, alcohol. [abbr.]

liquefied adj. (also **liquified**) [1930s+] drunk (cf. DAMP adj.).

liqueur of four ale n. [late 19C–1900s] bitter beer.

liquid n. **1** [1960s+] LSD dissolved into a liquid form (cf. A n.³). **2** [1990s+] a dietary supplement containing furanon di-hydro.

liquidate v. **1** [mid-19C] (US) to pay one's debts. **2** [1930s+] (orig. US) to kill someone. [(1) is SE in UK; (2) euph. used during the Stalinist era in the former USSR]

liquid bread n. [1990s+] (US campus) very cheap beer.

liquid comfort n. [1900s] succour gained through alcohol.

liquid cosh n. [1970s+] (UK prison) major tranquillizers used to calm rebellious or 'difficult' prisoners.

liquid courage n. [1940s+] (US) courage due to the consumption of alcohol.

liquid crack n. [1990s+] (US Black) malt liquor. [SE liquid + CRACK n.¹³; the ref. is to the strength of the drug and of the beer]

liquid crime n. (also **liquid death/fire**) [mid–late 19C] strong, potent alcohol, esp. whisky.

liquid gold n. [1980s+] (drugs) alkyl nitrites.

liquid grass n. [1970s] (US drugs) tetrahydrocannabinol (THC). [SE liquid + GRASS n.⁵]

liquid laugh n. (also **liquid laughter**) [1960s+] (orig. Aus.) vomit.

liquid lightning n. see LIGHTNING n.¹.

liquid lunch n. **1** [1960s+] (orig. Aus.) a meal that consists of alcohol. **2** [1990s+] a self-administered suction enema.

liquid rouge n. [mid-19C] (boxing) blood (cf. BADMINTON n.).

liquid sky n. [1980s] (US drugs) heroin.

liquid stuff n. see STUFF n.³ (1).

liquid sunshine n. [1910s] (Aus.) alcohol.

liquified adj. see LIQUEFIED adj.

liquor n. (also **likker**) **1** [mid-19C–1920s] (US) a drink; thus what's your liquor? what will you have to drink? **2** [late 19C–1900s] the water used by unscrupulous publicans to adulterate beer.

liquor v. see LIQUOR (UP) v.

liquored (up) adj. (also in **licker/liquor, likkered, liquorish**) [19C+] (US) drunk (cf. ALED UP adj.). [LIQUOR (UP) v.]

liquorhead n. [1920s+] (US) (also **licker-head**) a drunkard. [SE liquor + -HEAD sfx (3)]

liquorice stick n. (also **licorice stick**) **1** [1930s+] (US) a clarinet. **2** [1970s+] (US) a Black man. **3** [1970s+] (US gay) a (Black man's) penis (cf. BAT n.⁷). **4** [1980s+] (Aus. prison) a baton. [SE liquorice + STICK n.¹ (1)/PRICK n. (2)]

liquorish adj. see LIQUORED (UP) adj.

liquorize v. see LIQUOR (UP) v.

liquor one's boots v. [late 18C–19C] to drink before leaving on a journey. [note synon. late 18C–19C Roman Catholic jargon 'to deliver extreme unction'; i.e. the anointing with holy oil of one who is at the point of death]

liquor someone's boots v. [18C] to cuckold.

liquor someone's hide v. [late 17C–early 18C] to thrash, to give a beating. [pun on LICK v.¹ (1)]

liquor's talking phr. see IT's THE BEER TALKING phr.

liquor-up n. [mid–late 19C] **1** a drinking spree; a party. **2** (US) a drink. [LIQUOR (UP) v.]

liquor (up) v. (also **liquorize**) **1** [19C+] to ply with drink, to supply with alcohol. **2** [early 19C–1940s] to drink alcohol, to get drunk; thus liquorer, a hard drinker; liquoring, drinking. [(1) SE mid-16C–18C]

lisp and stutter n. [20C+] (Aus.) butter. [rhy. sl.]

lispers n. **1** [18C–mid-19C] (UK Und.) the lips. **2** [late 18C–mid-19C] the teeth.

listen v. [1900s–40s] (US) to sound, e.g. that listens well/good, that sounds promising.

listener n. [early 19C+] (orig. boxing) the ear.

listening flap n. [1900s] (Aus.) the ear.

listen to oneself v. [late 19C–1900s] (Irish) to think.

listing to starboard phr. (also **listing to port**) [19C+] tipsy, drunk. [naut. imagery]

listman n. [late 19C–1930s] a ready-money bookmaker. [the list of prices exhibited]

Lit n. (also **Lith**) [1920s+] (US) a Lithuanian. [abbr.]

Lit adj. [1920s+] (US) Lithuanian. [LIT n.]

lit n. [mid-19C+] literature. [abbr.; note also LIT adj.¹]

lit adj.¹ [late 19C+] literary, esp. in combs. lit. crit., literary criticism; lit. ed., literary editor; lit. supp., literary supplement. [abbr.]

lit adj.² [1960s+] (US Black) having been shot. [? the flash of the shot]

lit adj.³ see LIT (UP) adj.

literature n. [late 19C+] any form of printed material.

Lith n. see LIT n.

little n. [1960s+] (US) **1** petting. **2** sexual intercourse.

little Ada n. see ADA FROM DECATUR n.

little and large n. [1920s+] margarine. [rhy. sl. = SE marge]

Little Barbary n. [late 17C–19C] Wapping, home of the Ratcliffe Highway, once London's tough port area. [for ety. see BARBARY COAST n.]

little barn n. [20C+] (US) an outside lavatory (cf. ALTAR n.). [var. on LITTLE HOUSE n. (1)]

little bitch n. [1970s+] (US prison) an exceptionally long prison sentence. [SE little + BITCH n.¹ (6)]

little bit of all right, a phr. see BIT OF ALL RIGHT, A phr.

little bit of eyes right n. [1910s] (Aus.) a woman, usu. attractive. [milit. play on BIT OF ALL RIGHT, A phr. (1)]

little bit off the top phr. [1910s+] (Aus.) slightly insane. [pun on hairdressing use]

little black book n. **1** [1920s–40s] (US Und.) police files, kept secret. **2** [1930s+] the volume in which every bachelor supposedly keeps lists of available and willing women; also thus any address book.

little black father n. [early 19C] a quart jug.

little bloke n. [1970s] (Aus.) the penis.

Little Bo-Peep n. [late 19C+] sleep. [rhy. sl.; ult. the nursery rhyme]

little boss n. [1980s+] (Aus. prison) a middle-level prison officer.

little boy blue n.¹ [late 19C; 1960s+] the police. [the colour of their uniforms; 1960s+ US Black]

little boy blue n.² [20C+] a prison warder. [rhy. sl. = SCREW n.² (3)]

little boy in the boat n. see LITTLE MAN (IN THE BOAT) n.

little boys' room n. [1930s+] (orig. US) a coy euph. for a men's lavatory (cf. LITTLE GIRLS' ROOM n.).

little breeches n. (also **little britches**) [late 18C+] an affectionate term of address to a small boy; or a term of abuse. [UK use ends and US commences in mid-19C]

little britches n. [1930s+] (US gambling) the point of 3 in craps dice or a 3 in cards (cf. ADA FROM DECATUR n.). [ety. unknown]

little brother n. **1** [mid-19C+] the penis; thus beat one's little brother, to masturbate. **2** [1970s+] (US Black) an affectionate or familiar term of address to a younger man or child.

little brown jug n. [20C+] **1** an electric plug. **2** a bath plug. **3** a tampon. **4** (Aus.) a fool (cf. BEECHAM's PILL n.). [rhy. sl.; (3) is fig. use of SE plug; (4) = MUG n.² (1)]

little casino n. (US) **1** [1900s] a large person. **2** [1900s] any insignificant event or object. **3** [1900s] a term of familiarity, aimed at a woman. **4** [1900s–50s] an insignificant person (cf. BIG CASINO n.). **5** [1930s+] gonorrhoea. [SE casino, a card-game in which the 10 of diamonds, called great casino, counts 2 points, and the 2 of spades, called little casino, counts 1; (2) compares gonorrhoea with syphilis, which would be a 'greater' form of VD]

little charmer n. [late 19C+] an attractive young woman; also in ironic, thus negative use, e.g. she's a right little charmer.

little clergyman n. [late 18C–19C] a young chimney sweep. [blackened clothes]

little conversation n. [late 19C–1900s] violent swearing.

little davy n. [19C+] the penis (cf. ABRAHAM n.[1]).

little deers n. [late 19C–1900s] young women who are involved in some way with the stage. [double pun on *little dear* and *deer* as a fem. version of STAG n.[3] (1), i.e. the single men who frequent the theatre]

little devil n. (*also* **devil**) [17C+] a term of mildly reproving affection.

little Dick n. [1930s+] (*US gambling*) in craps dice, the point of 4 (cf. ADA FROM DECATUR n.). [BIG DICK n. (1)]

little eight n. [late 19C] (*Aus.*) a regular per diem payment.

little end of nothing n. [early 19C+] (*US*) anything very insignificant, utterly unimportant; also intensified as *little end of nothing sharpened/whittled down to a point.*

little end of the horn n. [19C+] (*US*) failure; usu. in the phr. *come out of the little end of the horn;* thus the opposite, *big end of the horn.* [the *Horn of Plenty*, which in mythology was one of the horns of the goat Amalthea by which the infant Zeus was suckled, and hence a symbol of fruitfulness and plenty. Its large end is depicted as pouring forth its bounty]

little eva n. [1950s] **1** (*US Black*) a loud-mouthed White woman. **2** (*US*) used as a term of address to reinforce a negative statement. [(2) f. (1)]

little fish n. [early 19C+] (*US*) an unimportant person. [FISH n.[3]; reverse of BIG FISH n. (1)]

little four n. [20C+] (*US gambling*) the point of 4 in craps dice (cf. ADA FROM DECATUR n.).

little friend n. [1920s+] (*orig. Can./Aus.*) menstruation; thus *my little friend has come*, I am menstruating. [the ref. is to the welcome appearance of a period as a sign that, had one been worried, one was not pregnant]

little gentleman in the black velvet coat n. [18C–19C] a mole. [the Jacobite phr., often used as a toast, referring to the belief that the death in 1702 of William III (their conqueror) was caused by his horse's stumbling over a molehill]

little girls' room n. (*also* **l.g.r.**) [1930s+] a coy euph. for the lavatory (cf. LITTLE BOYS' ROOM n.).

little go n.[1] [late 18C–mid-19C] a private lottery.

little go n.[2] **1** [late 19C–1900s] (*UK Und.*) one's first experience of prison. **2** [1960s] (*US*) an unimportant, unexciting or incomplete attempt at a task or performance. [Oxford University jargon *little go*, the first public examination (usu. taken during or at the end of one's first year and now known as *prelims*) as opposed to finals or *great go*]

little green man n. [2000s] (*Irish*) a small bottle of whisky.

little grey cells n. [1920s+] the human brain. [coined by crime writer Agatha Christie in *The Mysterious Affair at Styles* (1920) and always associated with her fictional sleuth Hercule Poirot]

little grey home in the west n. [1910s–50s] a vest. [rhy. sl.; orig. a song 'Little Grey Home in the West', written in 1911 by Hermann Frederic Löhr and D. Eardley-Wilmot]

little house n. **1** [18C+] a lavatory or privy (cf. BACKHOUSE n.). **2** [1930s+] (*US Und.*) a local prison; a reformatory (cf. BANDHOUSE n.). [(1) 19C+ use is Aus./N.Z./US]

Little India n. [1940s+] Bayswater, west London. [a largely residential area in which many who had retired from colonial posts in India lived in the 1940s; followed by later immigrants]

little in the suds, a phr. [18C] drunk (cf. DAMP adj.).

little Jerusalem n. [1910s+] (*US*) the Jewish area of a town or city.

little jimmy n. [20C+] (*bingo*) the number 1 (cf. ALDERSHOT LADIES n.).

little jobs n. [20C+] (*Aus. juv.*) urination. [euph.]

little Joe n. (*also* **little Joe from Baltimore/Kokomo**) [late 19C+] (*US gambling*) the point of 4 in craps dice (cf. ADA FROM DECATUR n.).

little Joe (in the snow) n. [1920s+] (*drugs*) cocaine (cf. AUNT NORA n.; BLANCA n.). [SNOW n.[2] (1)]

little john n. [1980s+] (*N.Z. drugs*) a cannabis cigarette made from 2 papers. [ety. unknown]

little Josie n. [20C+] (*US gambling*) the point of 4 in craps dice (cf. ADA FROM DECATUR n.). [var. on LITTLE JOE n.]

little madam n. [mid-19C+] a (very) young girl who acts, and considers herself, both older than her years and superior to her peers; often as *proper/right little madam.*

little mama n. [19C+] (*US Black*) an attractive Black woman.

little man n.[1] [1960s+] the penis.

little man n.[2] *see* LEMAC n.

little man (in the boat) n. (*also* **little boy in the boat, little old man in the boat, man in the boat**) **1** [late 19C–1930s] the navel. **2** [late 19C+] the clitoris; thus SINK THE LITTLE MAN IN THE BOAT v. (cf. BABY IN THE BOAT n.). [note LITTLE MAN n.[1]]

little miss big n. [1990s+] (*W.I.*) a precocious young girl.

Little Miss Muffet v. [1930s+] to get rid of, to ignore. [rhy. sl. = STUFF IT! excl.]

Little Miss Roundheels n. [1930s+] a promiscuous woman. [note Robert Greene in *The Blacke Bookes Messenger* (1592): 'the commonest harlot and hackster […] and with the lightnes of hir heeles bring me in the some crownes']

little more! excl. [1950s+] (*W.I. Rasta*) a general excl. of farewell, see you later!

little nell n. [20C+] a bell, usu. a doorbell. [rhy. sl.]

little nigger n. [20C+] (*US*) in poker, a game in which the low spade splits the pot.

little office n. [18C+] the lavatory (cf. GINGERBREAD-OFFICE n.). [SE *little* + OFFICE n.[2]; 20C+ use is Aus./US]

little old pfx [late 19C+] (*US, mainly Southern/Midwest*) a pfx used variously to express contempt, familiarity or affection.

little old man in the boat n. *see* LITTLE MAN (IN THE BOAT) n.

little pal n.[1] [1920s] (*US*) a pretty girl.

little pal n.[2] *see* LITTLE SISTER n.

little peter n. [20C+] a gas or electricity meter. [rhy. sl.; note PETER n.[2]]

little Phoebe n. *see* PHOEBE n.[1].

little pigs on a platter n. [1940s] (*US*) pork sausages.

little ploughman n. [19C] the clitoris (cf. BABY IN THE BOAT n.). [? pun on SE *plough*/PLOUGH v.[1] (1)]

little pretty n. [1960s–80s] (*US Black*) an attractive man.

little red ridings n. [1950s–60s] stolen goods. [rhy. sl. on *Little Red Riding Hoods*]

little red wagon n. **1** [1930s] (*US tramp*) a dump truck. **2** [1930s–70s] (*US Black*) a problem, a difficulty; usu. in the phr. *that's your little red wagon.*

little school n. [1920s–40s] (*US Und.*) a juvenile reformatory. [in contrast to BIG SCHOOL n.]

little shame tongue n. [19C] the clitoris (cf. BABY IN THE BOAT n.). [trans. of synon. Ger.]

little shot n. [1930s+] (*US*) an insignificant person. [reverse of BIG SHOT n.]

little silly n. [1900s] (*Aus.*) a (pretty) girl.

little sister n. (*also* **little pal**) [late 19C–1940s] the vagina.

little smack n. [1900s–20s] a half-sovereign (50p). [? its relatively muted smack into the palm, compared with the full sovereign]

little snakesman n. [late 18C–19C] (*UK Und.*) a small boy in a gang of burglars who is put through a narrow opening into a house, then lets the gang in. [SE *little* + SNAKESMAN n.; the twisting and turning of the boy in his actions]

little stranger n. [20C+] **1** an unborn foetus, esp. one that is illegitimate or of unknown paternity. **2** a newborn child.

little titch n. [20C+] an itch. [rhy. sl.; ult. music-hall comedian Harry Relph (*Little Titch*) (1868–1928)]

little titchy adj. [20C+] itchy. [LITTLE TITCH n.]

little wack n. (also **little whack**) [late 19C] a small measure of spirits. [SE little + WHACK n.[1] (1)]

little wheel n. [1950s] (US) a secondary rank of gang leader; one who has power but remains less important than an actual boss. [play on BIG WHEEL n.]

little woman n. **1** [mid-19C+] one's wife, also as a term of address. **2** [1950s] one's mother.

littlie n. [1960s+] (Aus./N.Z.) a child. [SE little + N.Z. sfx -ie, equivalent of Aus. -o sfx (4)]

lit (up) adj. **1** [late 19C+] (orig. US) drunk (cf. ABOUT RIGHT phr.[1]). **2** [1910s] (Aus.) suffering from a sexually transmitted disease. **3** [1920s] (US) showily dressed up. **4** [1920s+] (US drugs) extremely intoxicated by a drug. **5** [1960s+] (US gang) shot. **6** [1970s+] excited. **7** [1990s+] (US) angry.

lit up like a Christmas tree phr. (also **lit up like a church, ...an ocean liner, ...a pier, ...a sky-rocket, ...a torch, ...a triumphal arch, ...a white way, ...high mass**) [20C+] very drunk; or intoxicated from drugs. [ext. of LIT (UP) adj.]

lit up like Broadway phr. (also **lit up like Main Street, ...Times Square**) [20C+] very drunk. [ext. of LIT (UP) adj. (1)]

litvak n. (also **litvok**) [late 19C+] a Jew whose family come from Lithuania and are therefore considered lower-class by Jews from Poland.

li-un n. see LI-YUEN n.

live adj. **1** [mid-19C+] (orig. US) alert, energetic. **2** [late 19C+] excellent, first-rate, thrilling; thus a live one, an admirable person or object. **3** [20C+] of a potential victim of a confidence trick, willing to be tricked; often as LIVE ONE n. (3). **4** [1930s–50s] of a house, inhabited, occupied, the opposite of DEAD adj.[1] (3). [the image of a live performance]

live at Easy Hall v. [20C+] (W.I.) to live comfortably.

live at rack and manger v. see LIE AT RACK AND MANGER v.

live at the sign of the Queen's Head v. (also **live in Queen Street**) [late 18C–mid-19C] of a man, to be dominated by one's wife.

live at your aunt v. (also **live at your nenne**) [20C+] (W.I.) to find it hard to make enough money to live, to subsist, to suffer great hardship. [W.I. nennen, a godmother]

live bache v. [late 19C–1900s] (UK society) of a man, to live alone, as a bachelor. [abbr.]

live big v. see LIVE LARGE v.

live blanket n. [1990s+] (W.I./UK Black teen) a human body, particularly when covering another, as in sexual intercourse.

live eels n. [mid–late 19C] fields. [rhy. sl.]

live horse n. [mid-19C] work done and not charged for. [antonym of DEAD HORSE n.[1] (1)]

live in a good paddock v. [1950s] (N.Z.) to live comfortably. [farming imagery]

live in Queen Street v. see LIVE AT THE SIGN OF THE QUEEN'S HEAD v.

live in someone's ear v. [20C+] (Irish) to live on very intimate terms.

live-it-up adj. [1960s] happy, having a good time. [LIVE IT UP v.]

live it up v. [1950s+] (orig. US) to have a good time, to enjoy oneself.

live large v. (also **live big**) [1970s+] (US Black) to live extravagantly and ostentatiously. [SE live + LARGE adv./SE big; coined as the motto of 'The Executioner', hero of the action adventure series by Don Pendleton, first publ. 1969]

live low v. [1980s+] (US Black) **1** to have a poor standard of living. **2** to feel depressed.

live meat wagon n. see MEAT WAGON n. (1).

livener n. **1** [late 19C+] a drink used as a 'pick-me-up', usu. the

first drink of the day. **2** [2000s] a small portion of a drug, used for a similar purpose, although the time of day is irrelevant. [SE enliven]

live off the land v. [late 19C+] (Aus.) to live as a tramp.

live off the smell of an oil rag v. (also **live off the smell of an oiled rag, ...oily rag**) [late 19C+] (Aus./N.Z.) to subsist on a bare minimum of material wants.

live-on n. [late 19C–1900s] an attractive young woman. [a husband could live on her earnings; the image is of her (unrealized) potential as a prostitute]

live one n. **1** [late 19C+] (US) a notable, popular or well-respected individual. **2** [20C+] (US) a winning bet. **3** [20C+] (orig. UK Und.) the ideal victim for a proposed hoax, fraud or other deceit. **4** [20C+] (US) a generous and enthusiastic patron of nightclubs, theatres and other places of entertainment (including brothels). **5** [1910s] (US) a success, or one who has the potential so to be. **6** [1940s+] (gay) a generous rich client for a prostitute. **7** [1950s+] an enthusiastic participant in a proposed scheme. **8** [1970s] an eccentric, with implications of homosexuality. **9** [1970s+] someone destined to cause trouble in any situation, usu. challenging authority. [LIVE adj.]

live on someone's eye-top v. [1950s+] (W.I.) to scrounge off someone. [one's continual glancing around for a potential donor]

live on the skin of a rasher v. [20C+] (Irish) to live very frugally.

live out v. [mid–late 19C] (US) to be in domestic service. [one lives out of one's own home]

live out of one's suitcase v. (also **live out of one's boxes/ trunk**) [20C+] to live a peripatetic life, with no opportunity to settle in one place.

live rabbit n. [19C] the penis; thus have a bit of rabbit pie, skin the live rabbit, to have sexual intercourse (cf. ANTEATER n.).

liver and lung n. see HEART AND LUNG n.

liver-chops n. [mid-19C+] large, dark lips; thus a person with thick, dark lips, often used in direct address. [SE liver + CHOPS n.[1] (1)]

liver destroyer n. [late 19C] (UK Und.) brandy. [the effects of excessive drinking on the liver]

liver-disturber n. (also **liver-lifter, liver-turner**) [late 19C] (US) a very large penis (cf. ARSE-OPENER n.).

liver-faced adj. see WHITE-LIVERED adj.

liver-jerker n. [late 19C–1900s] a tricycle.

liver-lifter n. see LIVER-DISTURBER n.

liver-lips n. [1910s+] (US Black) **1** large, dark lips. **2** a person with thick, dark lips, often used in direct address.

liver-pin n. see LIVER-STRING n.

Liverpool kiss n. [1940s+] a blow to the mouth or face. [orig. naut.]

Liverpool leg n. [1980s+] the act of urinating in someone's pocket. [? orig. in crowds at football matches]

liver-shaker n. [late 19C–1910s] a riding hack.

liver-spot n. [1940s+] (W.I.) a mulatto.

liver-string n. (also **liver-pin**) [20C+] (US/W.I., Guyn.) a notional source of one's energy; thus work out one's liver-string, to exhaust oneself through hard labour.

liver-turner n. see LIVER-DISTURBER n.

live sausage n. [mid-17C+] the penis (cf. BACON n.[1]).

live shallow v. [late 19C] for a villain to live quietly, 'in retirement', when wanted by the police.

live square v. [1950s+] (Aus.) to lead a respectable life. [SE live + SQUARE adj. (2)]

livestock n. **1** [late 18C–1910s] lice, fleas, any bodily infestation. **2** [mid-19C] (US) slaves. **3** [1920s–50s] (US) women as objects of sexual interest, or prostitutes.

live tally v. [mid-19C+] (mainly north) to cohabit, to live as man and wife without an actual marriage; thus tally-ho, living in this manner. [SE *tally*, one of 2 corresponding parts; cf. earlier TALLY-HUSBAND n.]

live till they sun you *v*. [20C+] (*W.I.*) to live to a great old age. [the image is of an old person being placed to sit quietly in the sun]

live up to one's blue china *v*. [late 19C–1910s] to live up to or beyond one's means. [the gentility implied by a collection of blue china]

live up to the door *v*. (*also* **live up to the knocker**) [mid-19C–1900s] to live up to one's means.

live wire *n*. [late 19C+] a lively, energetic person; also used ironically. [LIVE adj. (1) + SE *wire*]

live with *v*. (*also* **live wid**) [1930s+] to tolerate, to put up with; usu. with *it*.

livid *adj*. [1920s+] (*orig. US*) furious, overcome with rage.

living color yawn *n. see* TECHNICOLOUR YAWN n.

living end *n*. [1950s+] the extreme, the absolute limit.

living flute *n*. [19C] the penis (cf. ACCORDION n.).

living fountain *n*. [mid-17C–19C] the vagina (cf. DAMP n.).

living Jesus, the *n. see* BEJAZUS, THE n.

living off the tit *phr*. [1960s+] living in luxury, overly protected. [TIT n.³ (1), i.e. 'breast-fed']

living sauce *n*. [1990s+] semen (cf. BABY GRAVY n.). [SE *living* + *sauce*/SAUCE n.² (7)]

livity *n*. [1990s+] (*W.I.*) a healthy attitude to life.

li-yuen *n*. (*also* **li-un**) [late 19C–1950s] (*drugs*) top-grade smoking opium (cf. APOSTLE n.). [var. on PEN YEN n.]

Liz *see also under* LIZZIE.

Liz *n. see* TIN LIZZIE n.

liz *n. see also under* LIZZIE.

lizard *n*.¹ [mid-19C+] an inhabitant of Alabama. [lizards are common in the state]

lizard *n*.² **1** [late 19C+] (*Aus./N.Z.*) a shepherd, a musterer, a mender of boundary fences. **2** [1900s–50s] (*US*) an old or useless racehorse; any horse. **3** [1910s+] a smooth and highly plausible fortune-hunter or womanizer who works his charms in the lounges of hotels, an adventurer. **4** [1910s+] (*US*) a contemptible or unlikeable person. **5** [1980s+] (*US Black*) a young woman.

lizard *n*.³ [1960s+] (*Aus./US*) the penis (cf. ANTEATER n.).

lizard *sfx* [1910s+] (*US*) used in combs. to describe a person with a particular habit or type of behaviour; thus *chow lizard*, a person who eats a lot; *couch lizard*, a person who frequently lies necking with his girlfriends on a couch; LOUNGE LIZARD n.

lizarding *n*. [1970s] (*Aus.*) lazing. [the way a lizard basks in sun]

lizard lap *n*. [1990s+] (*W.I.*) a sexual position. [? centring on oral sex; ? LIZARD n.³]

lizards *n*. [1950s+] (*US Black*) lizard-skin shoes.

lize *n*. [mid-19C] (*US*) a generic name for one of New York's 'Bowery g'hals', the female accomplice/equivalent of MOSE n.¹. [for ety. *see* MOSE n.¹]

lizzie *n*.¹ (*also* **Liz, liz, Lizzie**) **1** [late 19C+] (*orig. US*) (*also* **lizzie boy**) an effeminate youth. **2** [1900s–20s] (*Aus./US campus*) a young woman. **3** [1940s+] a lesbian.

lizzie *n*.² (*also* **Liz, liz, Lizzie**) **1** [1910s] (*US*) an aeroplane. **2** [1910s–50s] (*US*) as *the Lizzie*, the Cunard liner Queen Elizabeth. **3** [1910s+] (*orig. US*) an early Model Ford car, spec. the Model T, known as the TIN LIZZIE n. (1); thus *lizzie stiff*, a tramp who travels by car; *lizzie lice*, policemen in a police car. [affectionate use of the female name]

lizzie *n*.³ (*also* **Lizzie**) [1930s] cheap Portuguese wine. [abbr. *Lisbon*, the capital of Portugal]

lizzie *v*. [1910s+] (*US*) to drive an early Model Ford car, spec. the Model T. [LIZZIE n.² (3)]

lizzie boy *n. see* LIZZIE n.¹ (1).

lizzie up *v*. [1910s–30s] (*US*) to turn gay, to make homosexual; the implication is of raping someone anally. [LIZZIE n.¹ (1)]

L.K. Clark *n*. (*also* **Elkie Clark**) [20C+] the mark, i.e. beginning. [rhy. sl.; ult. *Elkie Clark*, a Glaswegian boxer in the 1920s/30s]

l.l. *n*. [mid-19C–1900s] (*Irish/Dublin*) a superior brand of whisky. [abbr. *lord lieutenant*]

llac *n. see* LAC n.².

llello *n*.¹ [1990s+] (*US Black*) hello. [mispron.]

llello *n*.² *see* YEYO n.

llesca *n. see* YESCA n.

lloyd *n*. (*also* **Harold, Harold Lloyd**) [1950s+] a piece of celluloid used for picking Yale locks. [rhy. sl.; *Harold Lloyd* = LOID n.; ult. silent film star *Harold Lloyd* (1893–1971)]

Lloyd George *n*. [1940s–50s] National Assistance. [the National Assistance Act (1911) introduced by *Lloyd George*'s government]

Lloyd's (List) *adj*. [20C+] drunk (cf. ADRIAN (QUIST) adj.). [rhy. sl. = PISSED adj.¹]

l.m.c. *adj*. [1990s+] lower middle class. [abbr.]

L note *n*. [2000s] (*US prison*) a life sentence. [L n.² + SE *note*]

Lo *n*.¹ (*also* **Mr Lo, Mrs Lo**) [mid-19C+] (*US*) a Native American. [pun on the line 'Lo, the poor Indian' in Pope's *Essay on Man* (1733)]

Lo *n*.² [2000s] Polo, the Ralph Lauren brand of clothing. [abbr.]

'lo *phr*. [1920s+] hello. [abbr.]

load *n*.¹ [late 16C+] a heavy responsibility. [abbr. colloq. phr. 'a load on one's mind']

load *n*.² [late 17C+] drink, usu. in a quantity sufficient to render the drinker drunk; thus a state of drunkenness in phr. *get a load in/on*, *have a load on* (cf. LOAD n.⁷).

load *n*.³ **1** [mid-18C–mid-19C] (*UK Und.*) one's personal possessions or money; also the proceeds of a crime. **2** [1940s+] (*US*) a very fat person.

load *n*.⁴ **1** [mid–late 19C] (*US campus*) a practical joke. **2** [1930s+] (*orig. US*) utter nonsense. **3** [1940s+] (*US*) a stupid, ridiculous or contemptible person. **4** [1970s] (*Aus. Und.*) fabricated evidence. [abbr. *load of garbage*, *load of shit* etc]

load *n*.⁵ **1** [mid-19C+] (*US*) faeces, a bowel movement. **2** [1920s+] (*US*) an ejaculation of semen or an orgasm (of either sex). **3** [1960s+] (*US Black*) a large amount of semen in the testes. **4** [1970s] a large penis. **5** [1980s] (*US Black*) the intense urge to have sex.

load *n*.⁶ [late 19C+] (*orig. Aus.*) a bout of venereal disease. [SE *loaded*, to be burdened with, to be weighed down. Note late 19C use of *load*, measles, smallpox]

load *n*.⁷ (*drugs*) **1** [1920s+] an amount of drugs, e.g. the quantity of heroin required to sustain an addiction; thus *have/get a load on*, to be intoxicated, to take a large amount of drugs. **2** [1920s+] an injection. **3** [1950s+] 25 or 30 packs of heroin held together in a bundle, the equivalent 1oz (28g) weight. [(1) ext. of LOAD n.²]

load *n*.⁸ [1930s+] **1** (*US*) an old, discontinued model or a run-down, dilapidated vehicle, a stolen car. **2** (*orig. US Black*) an automobile.

load *v*.¹ **1** [late 19C] to ply someone with drink. **2** [1960s] (*drugs*) to take drugs. [(1) LOAD n.²; (2) LOAD n.⁷ (1)]

load *v*.² **1** [late 19C–1950s] (*US*) to lie, to deceive. **2** [1900s] (*US campus*) to prepare for an emergency, e.g. an exam.

load *v*.³ [1990s+] (*Aus. Und.*) of police, to plant false evidence.

loaded *adj*.¹ **1** [19C+] of dice, in some way crooked. **2** [1920s+] of anything other than dice, similarly crooked. **3** [1950s] (*US Und.*) prepared to lie on oath. **4** [1970s+] of a boxer, to have one's hands taped with heavy insulating tape, thus rendering one's blows more lethal. **5** [1980s] (*Aus. Und.*) (*also* **loaded up**) 'planted' with incriminating evidence.

loaded *adj*.² **1** [late 19C+] (*orig. US*) (*also* **loaded up**) drunk. **2** [late 19C+] (*orig. US*) (*also* **loaded up**) intoxicated with a drug. **3** [late 19C+] (*orig. US*) (*also* **loaded down**) rich, either in actual cash or simply, esp. in prison use, in possessions such as tobacco; of a place, filled with money or valuables. **4** [1920s+] (*US*) laced with alcohol, drugs or poison. **5** [1920s+] in possession of a large amount of a given commodity, e.g. drugs. **6** [1970s] pregnant. **7** [1990s+] big-breasted. [LOAD v.[1]/LOAD UP v.[1]; (4) note SE *loaded*, of wine, adulterated to appear full-bodied]

loaded (for bear) *adj.* (*also* **loaded for rhino**) (*US*) **1** [late 19C–1950s] holding a good poker hand. **2** [late 19C+] fully prepared for all problems, esp. the hardest ones; thus also fully armed and equipped for conflict. **3** [1940s] drunk. [hunting use, bear-shooting requires heavy armament; (3) plays on LOADED adj.[2] (1)]

loaded gun *n.* [1980s+] (*US gay*) the penis before ejaculation of its 'load' of semen (cf. AX n.[2]). [LOAD n.[5] (2) + GUN n.[1] (2)]

loaded to the gills *phr.* (*also* **loaded to the barrel, ...the earlobes, ...the guards, ...the gunnels, ...the hat, ...the muzzle, ...the Plimsoll Mark, ...the tailgate**) **1** [late 19C+] drunk. **2** [1940s+] (*drugs*) intoxicated by a drug. [LOADED adj.[2] + SE *gills*]

loaded up *adj.[1]* [2000s] of an automobile, customized. [? LOADED (FOR BEAR) adj.]

loaded up *adj.[2]* see LOADED adj.[1] (5).

loaded up *adj.[3]* see LOADED adj.[2].

loadie *n.* [1970s+] (*US campus*) a habitual drinker or drug user. [LOADED adj.[2]]

load in *v.* [late 19C] to drink.

load of *n.* [late 19C+] a great deal of, a lot of; usu. in combs. to form dismissive phrs.; thus *load of crap, load of old cobblers, load of old cods, load of old wank* etc.

load of coal *n.* see COAL n.[1] (1).

load off one's behind *n.* [1920s+] a defecation. [pun on colloq. phr. *load on one's mind*; LOAD n.[1]]

load off one's mind *n.* **1** [1920s+] a haircut. **2** [1960s+] a defecation. **3** [1980s+] (*US gay*) the removal of a penis from the anus. [puns on colloq. phr. *load on one's mind*; LOAD n.[1]]

load of hay *n.* [mid-19C] a day. [rhy. sl.]

load of shit *n.* see CROCK OF SHIT n.

load-on *n.* [1920s+] (*US*) a drunken state. [LOAD n.[2]]

loads *n.* [1990s+] (*US drugs*) a mixture of codeine and Doriden.

loads *adv.* [1920s+] to a very great extent, very much.

loadsamoney *n.* [1990s+] a great deal of money. [ult. the 1980s TV character *Loadsamoney*, created by Harry Enfield]

loads of *n.* [17C+] many, a great quantity, esp. of a desirable commodity.

load-up *n.* [2000s] a shopping spree.

load up *v.[1]* **1** [late 19C] to provide with drink. **2** [late 19C+] to get drunk, to use a drug; also as *load up on* a drink or drug. **3** [late 19C+] to eat heartily. [LOAD n.[2]; LOAD n.[7] (1)]

load up *v.[2]* **1** [late 19C] (*US*) to provide with false information. **2** [1980s+] (*Aus. prison*) to incriminate through perjured evidence. [ext. LOAD v.[2] (1) or LOAD v.[3]]

load up *v.[3]* [1930s+] (*Aus./N.Z.*) to infect with venereal disease. [LOAD n.[6]]

loaf *n.[1]* [mid-19C–1920s] (*orig. US*) **1** the act of loafing, idling; thus *loaf-day*, a day when no regular work is done. **2** one who idles and does not work. **3** any occupation deemed to require minimal if any effort. [LOAF v.[1] (2), but note Sw. *lofdag*, Du. *verlofdag*, a leave-day, a holiday]

loaf *n.[2]* [1980s+] (*Irish*) a headbutt. [LOAF v.[2]]

loaf *n.[3]* see LOAF (OF BREAD) n.

loaf *v.[1]* [mid-19C–1900s] **1** (*US campus*) to steal, to cadge. **2** (*orig. US*) to idle, to relax. [ety. unknown; the posited link to Ger. dial. *lofen*, to run, cannot be sustained; (2) 20C+ SE]

loaf *v.[2]* [1980s+] (*Irish*) to headbutt. [LOAF (OF BREAD) n.]

loaf-day *n.* see LOAF n.[1] (1).

loafer *n.* **1** [mid-19C–1960s] a beggar, a cadger or a ruffian, a tramp. **2** [mid-19C+] (*orig. US*) an idler; thus *loaferess*, the female equivalent. [LOAF v.[1]; note Schele de Vere, *Americanisms* (1872):

'One claims it as a descendant of the Dutch *land-looper*, a vagrant; another traces it back to *loaf*, and sees in it a beggar for bread. Can it be a contracted form of *low-fellow*? asks a third, and still another is sure it owes its origin to Rabelais, who [...] speaks of a certain good-for-nothing person, encountered by Gargantua, as *lipe-lope*. [...] The true origin of the word must, however, be sought in German, where *Läufer* is a term applied by the steady and phlegmatic people to men who are irregular and unsettled in life. Half of Germany pronounces this word with the vulgar sound of *au* as *lofer*, and from this, in all probability, the German term *Lofer* and our *loafer* are derived']

Loaferies, the *n.* [late 19C] the Whitechapel Workhouse. [LOAF v.[1] + sfx *-eries*, the ref. is to the uncharacteristic kindness shown by its staff to those who were forced to live on its charity. Paupers could loaf around, rather than be forced to work, pray or otherwise justify their existence. This extended to their attempt, in 1898, to abandon the pej. name 'Workhouse']

loafing *n.* **1** [mid-19C] begging, cadging. **2** [mid-19C+] lounging, relaxing. [LOAF v.[1]]

loafing *adj.* [mid-19C+] idle, good-for-nothing.

loaf (of bread) *n.* [1910s+] a head, esp. brains, intelligence; thus USE ONE'S LOAF v. [rhy. sl.; note TWOPENNY n.[1]]

loaf of bread *adj.* [1910s–30s] dead. [rhy. sl.]

lo and behold *n.* [20C+] a plunging neckline. [the neckline is *lo(w)* and one *beholds* the breasts]

loaner *n.* [1920s+] (*US*) a temporary replacement for an item being repaired; anything on loan/hire. [SE *loan*]

Loan Land *n.* [1910s] (*Aus.*) Britain. [Aus. debts to 'the mother country']

loan shark *n.* [20C+] a supplier of private loans at maximum interest.

loan sharking *n.* [1910s+] the practice of lending money at usurious rates, esp. by organized crime syndicates.

loap *v.* see LOPE v.

loaver *n.* [mid-late 19C] (*UK Und.*) money. [LOUR n.]

lob *n.[1]* **1** [18C] a snuffbox, any box. **2** [18C–1940s] (*also* **lobb**) a till, a cash register; thus *dip/frisk/pinch/sneak a lob*, to rob a till; *make a good lob*, to take a large amount of money from the till; *lobber*, a till robber. **3** [early 18C] a form of confidence trick, involving confusing a shopkeeper when giving change. **4** [mid-19C–1900s] the head. **5** [mid-19C+] a haul, thus a fortune, a large amount, usu. of money. **6** [1910s–50s] (*Aus./UK prison*) pay, income.

lob *n.[2]* (*also* **lobb**) **1** [mid-19C] (*UK Und.*) an informer. **2** [20C+] a dull, stupid person; thus *lobbish*, stupid. **3** [1910s–20s] (*Aus.*) a policeman, esp. an officious one. **4** [1930s] (*US Und.*) an initiate into criminality. **5** [1990s+] (*US prison*) a deliberate insult implying that the subject is weak and/or homosexual; a spur to a fight. [16C–19C SE/dial. *lob*, a country bumpkin. Note Yid. *lobbes*, rascal + Du. *lobbes*, a clown]

lob *n.[3]* (*also* **lobb**) [late 19C+] the penis, esp. when half- or fully erect. [SE *lob*, something pendulous]

lob *n.[4]* [1920s–30s] (*US*) a waste of time; something fated to fail. [racing *lob*, a horse that is bound to lose]

lob *n.[5]* see LOBBY-GOW n.

lob, the *n.* [20C+] the lavatory. [? ext. of LOB n.[1] (1)]

lob *v.[1]* [early 19C] to droop, to allow to hang heavily. [16C–18C SE]

lob *v.[2]* see LOB (IN) v.

lob around *v.* see LOB (IN) v. (1).

lobb see under LOB.

lobber *n.[1]* see LOB n.[1] (2).

lobber *n.[2]* see LOB (IN) v. (1).

lobbish *adj.* see LOB n.[2] (2).

lobby-gow *n.* (*also* **lob**) [late 19C–1970s] (*US*) **1** (*also* **lobby gob**) a hanger-on, a messenger, a servant, an errand boy, esp. one who frequents or works in an opium den or brothel, or a tourist guide in Chinatown, New York City. **2** a Chinese police informer. **3** in fig. use, an insignificant person. **4** a working-class person, a ruffian. [SE *lobby* + GOW n.¹ (2); Asbury, *Gangs of New York* (1927), suggests Cantonese *Lo Bot Gow*, 'Old White Dog']

lobby louse *n.* (*also* **lobby lizard/tart**) [1930s–60s] (*US*) a person who loiters in hotel lobbies, usu. harassing guests. [SE *lobby* + LOUSE sfx/LIZARD sfx/TART n.¹]

lobby-sneak *n.* (*also* **lobby-thief**) [mid-19C–1920s] (*UK Und.*) a thief who enters a house, takes what is easily available and leaves.

lobcock *n.* [16C–19C] **1** a fool (cf. HORSECOCK n.¹). **2** (*also* **lobprick**) a large, flaccid penis; thus as adj., flaccid, limp. **3** [18C–19C] a penis suffering from penile strabismus. [SE *lob*, a country bumpkin + COCK n.² (1)]

lob-crawler *n.* (*also* **lob-sneak**) [mid-19C–1900s] (*UK Und.*) a thief who specializes in robbing shop tills; thus *lob-crawling/-sneaking*, committing such robberies. [LOB n.¹ (2)]

lobdominion *n. see* LOBSCOUSE n.

lob (in) *v.* [20C+] **1** (*Aus.*) to arrive, to turn up, (of a race horse) to win; thus *lobber*, one who turns up; *lob around*, to wait around. **2** to commence having sexual intercourse. [SE *lob*, to move heavily or clumsily]

lobkin *n.* [late 17C–early 19C] a lodging house. [LIBKEN n.]

loblolly *n.* **1** [late 16C–mid-19C] a thick gruel, both a peasant and a naut. dish, and also used as a simple medicine. **2** [17C–19C] a bumpkin, a peasant, a boor. **3** [early 19C] (*W.I.*) a weakling. **4** [mid-19C–1940s] (*US*) a mud hole. **5** [20C+] (*US*) a fat person. [? echoic but note dial. *lob*, to bubble while boiling, esp. of a thick substance like porridge + Devon dial. *lolly*, broth, soup or other food boiled in a pot]

lobo *n.* [1940s] (*US Black*) an unattractive woman. [SE *lobo*, a grey wolf, thus synon. DOG n.³ (10)]

lob off *v.* [1910s] (*Aus.*) to go away. [? LOB (IN) v. (1)]

lob onto *v.* [1910s+] (*Aus.*) **1** to get hold of or find out through a stroke of luck. **2** to associate oneself with. [? LOB (IN) v.]

lobprick *n. see* LOBCOCK n. (2).

lobs *n.*¹ [mid-19C] (*UK tramp*) talk, conversation. [Rom. *lavaw*, words]

lobs *n.*² [mid-19C] an under-gamekeeper. [? SE *lob*, a country bumpkin]

lobs *n.*³ *see* LOBSTER n.¹ (1).

lobs! *excl.* (*UK juv.*) **1** [mid-19C; 1990s+] a warning shout that heralds an approaching master. **2** [1910s–20s] a call for truce during a game. [ety. unknown]

lobscouse *n.* (*also* **lobdominion**) [18C+] a sailors' dish consisting of meat stewed with vegetables and ship's biscuit, which is the totemic dish of Liverpool.

lob-sneak *n. see* LOB-CRAWLER n.

lob's pound *n.* **1** [late 16C–mid-19C] a prison. **2** [17C] the vagina. **3** [mid-18C–mid-19C] fig. use of (1), i.e. any kind of trouble or difficult situation. [LOB n.¹ (1) + SE *pound*, an enclosure; (2) note LOB n.³]

lobster *n.*¹ **1** [mid-17C–1910s] (*also* **lobs**) a soldier, a marine (who also wears scarlet). **2** [mid-19C] (*UK*) a policeman (cf. ANIMAL n.¹). [(1) orig. f. the full suits of armour worn by the Round-heads in Cromwell's New Model Army (spec. Hazelrigg's cuirassiers); then f. the red coats worn by British soldiers of the period]

lobster *n.*² **1** [mid-19C+] (*US*) a slow-witted, awkward or gullible person; a general term of abuse; esp. of a socially inept or foolish person. **2** [late 19C–1910s] a second-rate racehorse. [the slow movements of the crustacean, but note LOB n.² (2)]

lobster *n.*³ [late 19C–1900s] an older man who gives a younger woman presents and/or money in return for sexual favours. [LOBSTER n.² (1)]

lobster *n.*⁴ [late 19C–1900s] the penis (cf. ANTEATER n.).

lobster *n.*⁵ [1970s–80s] (*US Black*) a rich person. [the role of lobsters as luxury food]

lobster *n.*⁶ [1980s+] (*Aus. prison*) a 20-year jail sentence.

lobster-back *n.* [early–late 19C] a British soldier. [ext. of LOBSTER n.¹ (1)]

lobster-box *n.* **1** [early–mid-19C] a transport ship. **2** [mid-19C] a milit. barracks. **3** [1930s] (*US Und.*) a cell in a police station. [LOBSTER n.¹ + SE *box*]

lobster-palace society *n.* [late 19C–1910s] (*US*) the world of wealth if not of social position. [*lobster-palace*, one of the elegant, expensive new restaurants that emerged in New York City, which specialized in lobsters and attracted the rich and famous]

lobster-pot *n.* **1** [19C] the vagina (cf. BAG n.¹; BEARDED CLAM n.). **2** [1970s+] (*US gay*) a sailor who subjects himself to anal intercourse.

lobster-shift *n.* (*also* **lobster-trick**) [1920s+] (*US*) a late-night work shift. [the slow pace of the crustacean, i.e. such a shift, usu. between 2 a.m. and 9 a.m. is rarely busy]

lobstertails *n.* [1940s–60s] (*US Black*) **1** (*also* **lobstertoes**) a case of venereal disease. **2** a case of body lice.

loc *n.*¹ [1990s+] (*US Black*) marijuana (cf. BOMB n.⁴). [LOCOWEED n.]

loc *n.*² (*also* **lok**) [1990s+] (*US Black*) **1** a street gang member. **2** a friend. **3** a general term of address.

loc *adj.* (*also* **lok**) [1980s+] (*US Black*) **1** crazy, mad, whether because of taking drugs or one's emotional state; thus LOC'D OUT adj. **2** armed. [LOCO adj.; the image of (2) is of one who, once armed, will do something 'crazy']

loc *v.* [1990s+] (*US Black*) to smoke marijuana. [LOC n.¹]

local *n.*¹ [1940s] (*UK Und./police*) a jail sentence of less than 3 years.

local *n.*² [1970s] (*US*) an act of a prostitute masturbating a customer.

local, the *n.* [1930s+] the nearest public house, or that which the speaker uses regularly; thus *my local*.

local *adj.* [1940s+] (*S.Afr.*) eccentric, crazy. [LOCO adj.]

local talent *n.* [1950s+] the attractive women in a neighbour-hood; also used in a homosexual context of young men. [SE *local* + TALENT n. + pun]

local yokel *n.* [1940s+] (*US*) a naïve and foolish small-town or country man.

locating *n.* [1920s] getting prospects.

location joke *phr.* [1980s+] (*US campus*) a phr. meaning you had to be there; said of a joke which can only be appreciated within a subscribed group.

loc'd out *adj.* (*also* **loced out, loqued out**) [1980s+] (*US Black*) **1** crazy, under stress. **2** dressed up in gang clothes. [LOC OUT v.]

loced-assed *adj.* [1990s+] (*US Black*) ultra-aggressive, dangerously unbalanced. [ext. of LOC'D OUT adj. (1)]

lochinvar *n.* [2000s] a brassiere. [rhy. sl. = BRA n.¹]

locie *n.* (*also* **loci, lokey, lokie**) [1930s+] (*Can./N.Z./US*) a locomotive. [abbr.]

lock *n.*¹ **1** [17C–19C] the vagina. **2** [late 17C–mid-19C] (*UK Und.*) a place for storing stolen goods. **3** [late 17C–mid-19C] (*UK Und.*) a receiver of stolen goods. [SE *lock*, an enclosure; (2) f. (1)]

lock *n.*² **1** [early 18C–mid-19C] a chance; thus *stand a queer lock*, to have a poor chance. **2** [late 18C–early 19C] character, e.g. *stand a queer lock*, to bear an indifferent character. **3** [late 18C–mid-19C] an occupation, a way of life; thus *cut a lock*, to conduct a way of life. **4** [early 19C] a scheme, a plan. **5** [1940s+] (*US*) a certainty. **6** [1960s+] (*US*) complete control over something. [SE *lock*, a grip or trick in wrestling]

lock *n.*³ [20C+] (*Ulster*) a small quantity, e.g. of food; thus *brave lock, quare lock*, a substantial amount. [orig. dial.]

lock *n.*⁴ *see* LOCK-UP n. (3).

lock *v.*¹ **1** [1930s+] (*US prison*) to occupy a cell. **2** [1960s+] of a pimp, to ensure a prostitute's fidelity, emotional and economic. **3** [1970s+] (*US Und.*) to imprison.

lock v.[2] [2000s] to arrange one's hair in a Rastafarian dreadlock style. [LOCKS n.]

lock-all-fast n. [late 17C–18C] a receiver of stolen goods.

lock assholes v. (also lock, lock asses) [1950s+] (US) to fight. [SE lock + ASSHOLE n.[1] (1)/ASS n. (2)]

lockdown n. [1970s+] (orig. US prison) an instance of the entire prison population being confined to the cells and deprived of exercise or association.

locked adj. [1970s+] (Irish) drunk. [SE locked, i.e. shut off from coherent thought or action]

locked, cocked and ready to rock phr. see COCKED AND READY TO ROCK phr.

locker n.[1] [mid-18C] (UK Und.) one who leaves goods at a house in the country or a small town and borrows money on them, pretending that they have been made in London, i.e. that they are valuable.

locker n.[2] 1 [19C] the vagina. 2 [mid-19C+] (US) the stomach. 3 [1900s–40s] (US Und.) a safe.

locker room n. [1980s+] (drugs) isobutyl nitrite, amyl nitrite (cf. AIMIES n.). [its association with all-male amusements]

locket n. see LUCY LOCKET n.

lock-in n. [1990s+] a session of drinking that begins after the public house or bar has officially closed for the night.

lock into v. [1960s+] to become part of a plan, a group etc, to join.

lock of (all) locks n. [19C] the vagina (cf. ADAM'S OWN (ALTAR) n.).

lock off v. (also choke-and-rob) [20C+] (W.I.) to put a choke-hold on someone's neck in order to immobilize and then rob them.

lock one's barn door v. [1960s+] (US) to fasten one's trouser fly.

lock on with v. [20C+] (Aus. juv.) to fight.

lock picker n. [1940s] (US Und.) an abortionist. [LOCK n.[1] (1) + SE picker]

locks n. [1950s+] (orig. W.I.) the long knotted hair that is the best-known and typical badge of Rastafarianism. [abbr. DREADLOCKS n. (1)]

locksman n. [1950s+] (orig. W.I.) a Rastafarian. [LOCKS n. + SE man]

locksmith's daughter n. [late 18C–19C] a key.

lock-up n. 1 [19C] (US) a jail. 2 [mid-late 19C] (UK Und.) a prisoners' cell in a magistrates court. 3 [1930s+] (US Und.) (also lock) the punishment cell or cells. 4 [1940s] (US prison) a jailer, a warder. 5 [1990s+] (US) an arrest. [(1) 20C+ use is SE]

lock up v.[1] [1910s+] 1 (US) to be in complete control and thus assured of victory. 2 (US Black) to have under one's complete control, to possess absolutely.

lock up v.[2] [1980s] (US Black) of a pimp, to secure the services of a given prostitute.

lock-up chovey n. [early 19C] a covered cart in which travelling hawkers carry their goods around the country. It can be locked to secure the stock. [SE lock up + CHOVEY n.]

loco n. 1 [mid-19C+] (US) a lunatic. 2 [mid-19C+] (US) madness. 3 [1920s] (US) a car, a locomotive. 4 [1960s+] (US gang) a Mexican-American gang member. 5 [1960s+] (US drugs) marijuana (cf. BOMB n.[4]). [Sp. loco, crazy]

loco adj. [late 19C+] (orig. US) insane, crazy (cf. LOCOED adj.). [abbr. locoweed, a narcotic weed that affects cattle in the Southwest US; ult. Sp. loco, insane, crazy]

loco v. [late 19C+] (US) to drive mad. [LOCO adj.]

loco duds n. (also loco suit) [1940s] (US Und.) a strait jacket. [LOCO adj. + DUDS n.[1] (1)/SE suit]

locoed adj. [late 19C–1940s] mad (cf. LOCO adj.). [LOCO adj.]

locomo v. [1990s+] (US teen) to leave the area. [LOCOMOTE v.]

locomote v. [mid-19C–1910s] (US) to move around from place to place. [backform. f. SE locomotion]

locomotive n.[1] [late 19C–1900s] a winter drink made of Burgundy, curaçao, egg yolks, honey and cloves all heated together. [? play on SE, i.e. it 'gets one moving']

locomotive n.[2] [1900s–50s] (orig. US campus) 'a cheer characterized by a slow beginning and a progressive increase in speed and used esp. at school and college sports events' (Webster, 1966). [SE since the 1960s]

locomotives n. [mid-late 19C] the legs.

locomotive tailor n. [late 19C] a travelling workman.

loco suit n. see LOCO DUDS n.

loc out v. [1980s+] (US Black) to drive crazy, to make exciting. [LOC adj. (1)]

locoweed n. [1920s+] (US drugs) marijuana (cf. AFRICAN BUSH n.; BOMB n.[4]). [Sp. loco, crazy, the erroneously presumed effects of cannabis + locoweed, milkvetch, or any other plant of the genus Oxytropis, which causes erratic behaviour, impaired coordination and poss. lethargy in livestock]

locs n.[1] [1990s+] (US Black) a hairstyle for Black hair that involves natural curls, usu. twisted or braided over months to create the effect. [pron. with a long 'o']

locs n.[2] (also lokes) [1990s+] (orig. US Black) sunglasses. [LOC adj. (1); i.e. the image of the sunglasses-wearer as tough, dangerous and ready for any action – no matter how 'crazy']

loc up v. [2000s] (US Black) to go crazy. [LOC adj. (1)]

locus n. 1 [late 17C] anything stupefying; thus (W.I.) locus-ale, an intoxicating drink made of the scum of sugar-cane. 2 [mid-19C–1950s] (also locust) a drugged drink, using either laudanum or snuff. [? Sp. loco, mad, i.e. the effects of the drink]

locus v. 1 [mid-late 19C] to trick, to fool. 2 [mid-late 19C] to render a victim unconscious with chloroform, usu. to rob them or carry them aboard a ship in need of crew. 3 [mid-19C–1940s] to stupefy with drink; thus locus away, to steal something when the victim is drunk. [? rhy. with hocus, though not proper rhy. sl., or LOCUS n.]

locust n.[1] (US) 1 [mid-19C] a policeman (cf. ANIMAL n.[1]). 2 [mid-19C–1930s] a billy club or stick. [SE locust wood, from which the clubs were made]

locust n.[2] 1 [late 19C–1900s] (UK society) an extravagant person who throws away any left-overs, rather than saving them for possible reuse. 2 [1970s] (Aus.) a tourist.

locust n.[3] see LOCUS n. (2).

loddy n. [early 19C] laudanum or tincture of opium. [abbr.]

lodger n. 1 [mid-late 19C] the penis. 2 [mid-late 19C] an unimportant, insignificant person. 3 [1990s+] a baby in the womb.

lodgers n. [late 19C–1910s] head lice; rats and mice or any kind of vermin.

lodgings n. 1 [19C] the vagina. 2 [1940s–50s] (Aus.) prison.

lodging-slum n. [early 19C] (UK Und.) the hiring of expensive lodgings with the intention of stealing the furniture etc that one finds there. [SE lodging + SLUM n.[2] (3)]

loft n. [1900s] (US) the head.

lofter n. [mid-19C] (US Und.) the very lowest class of prostitute.

lofty n. [20C+] a nickname both for a very tall and a very short man.

log n.[1] 1 [mid-19C+] a stupid person. 2 [1950s] (Aus.) a large person.

log n.[2] 1 [1930s–50s] (US drugs) an opium pipe. 2 [1970s+] a large marijuana cigarette (cf. BONE n.[11]). 3 [1970s+] (US drugs) phencyclidine (cf. ACE n.[4]).

log n.[3] [1930s+] a piece of excrement; thus drop/lay a log, to defecate. [the supposed resemblance]

log n.[4] [1950s+] (US) the penis.

log n.[5] [1960s] (US) a bar counter. [the wood from which it is constructed]

log n.[6] see LOGS, THE n.

log-cabin raider n. [1990s+] a male homosexual (cf. BROWN ARTIST n.). [LOG n.[3] + SE cabin + raider]

log city *n. see* LOG-TOWN n.

loge *n.* [late 17C–mid-19C] (*UK Und.*) a watch. [Fr. *horloge*, watch]

loges *n.* [17C] (*UK Und.*) a faked pass or warrant. [Gk *logos*, a word]

logey *n.* [20C+] (*Irish*) a heavy, fat person. [SE *log*]

loggerhead *n.* [late 16C+] a fool, a dullard; thus *loggerheaded*, dull, stupid. [post-18C use is US, f. SE *logger*, something heavy or clumsy + -HEAD sfx (1)]

logging *n. see* LOG-ROLLING n.

logie *n.* [mid-19C] sham jewellery. [theatre jargon *logie*, prop jewels, made mainly of zinc, invented by one David *Logie*]

logi-logi *n.* (*also* logo-logo) [1950s] (*W.I.*) a stupid, oafish person. [? SE *log*]

log-juice *n.* [mid-19C] a cheap port wine. [the use of SE *logwood* (used in dyeing and in medicine as an astringent) to adulterate port]

log of wood *n.* [mid-19C] (*Aus.*) a dull, stupid person; thus *log of ebony*, a stupid Black person.

logo-logo *n. see* LOGI-LOGI n.

log-pusher *n.* [1990s+] a male homosexual (cf. BROWN ARTIST n.). [LOG n.³ + SE *pusher*]

log-roll *v.* [mid-19C+] to engage in the corrupt giving of mutual aid. [LOG-ROLLING n.]

log-roller *n.* [early 19C–1930s] a politician who engages in the corrupt giving of mutual aid. [LOG-ROLLING n.]

log-rolling *n.* (*also* logging) [early 19C+] (*orig. US*) the corrupt giving of mutual aid, esp. in professional contexts (e.g. a critic consistently pushing a novelist friend). [the habit among early American settlers of communities or neighbours helping one another with the annual heavy tasks occasioned by logging]

logs, the *n.* (*also* log) [late 19C–1920s] (*Aus.*) a lock-up, a prison. [the use of logs in the construction of early Aus. lock-ups]

log-town *n.* (*also* log city) [1950s+] (*US*) a small, insignificant town. [the orig. 19C *log-towns*, made up of buildings constructed of logs]

logy *adj.* 1 [1910s–20s] (*US*) tipsy. 2 [1980s+] (*US drugs*) lethargic after smoking cannabis. [US regional *logy*, slow, lethargic, stupid, ult. synon. dial. *louggy*, *loogy*; but note LOG n.² (2)]

loid *n.* [1950s+] cellu*loid* or a piece of plastic, such as a credit card, used to slip open Yale-style locks when house-breaking. [abbr.]

loid *v.* [1950s+] to open a lock by means of a strip of cellu*loid*. [LOID n.]

loiner *n.* [1940s+] an inhabitant of Leeds, West Yorkshire. [Marples, *University Slang* (1950), suggests a possible corruption of late 19C–1910s *oiner*, f. Gk *oinidzein*, to smell of wine, and as such a term used to disparage 'town' people by students]

loiter *n.* [1970s] (*Aus. Und.*) a charge of loitering with intent to commit a felony.

lok *see under* LOC.

lokes *n. see* LOCS n.².

lokey/lokie *n. see* LOCIE n.

loksh *n. see* LUKSHEN n.

Lola Montez *n.* (*also* Lola Montes) [mid-19C] (*Aus.*) a drink made of Old Tom, ginger, lemon and hot water. [*Lola Montez* (1818–61), an Irish dancer and courtesan, who toured Australia in 1855]

lolapaloosa *n. see* LALLAPALOOSA n.

lolla *n.* (*also* lah-lah, la-la, lallah) [late 19C+] (*US*) something or someone outstanding in some way, whether good, stylish or pleasing; or bad. [ety. unknown; ? abbr. of LALLAPALOOSA n., but note Grose (1785): 'LOLL, a mother's loll, a favourite child']

lollapalo/lollapaloosa/lollapalooza *n. see* LALLAPALOOSA n.

lollie boy *n.* [late 19C] (*Aus.*) someone or something unimportant. [SAusE *lolly boy*, 'one who sells refreshments from a tray at a cinema, sports ground, etc.' (*AND*)]

lollied *adj.* [1960s–70s] informed against, betrayed to the police. [? LOLLIPOP v.¹]

lollies *n.* 1 [mid-19C+] (*Aus.*) all sweets, except for ice lollies. 2 [20C+] the female breasts, which can, like a sweet, be sucked (cf. APPLES n.¹). [abbr. SE *lollipop*]

lolligag *v. see* LALLYGAG v.

lollion *n.* [20C+] (*Ulster*) a fat, clumsy person. [? SE *loll*]

lollipop *n.*¹ 1 [mid-19C–1980s] a woman, esp. an attractive one. 2 [20C+] (*also* lolly) one's special favourite, the prize article in a collection. 3 [1910s+] (*orig. US*) one's sweetheart; usu. used as a term of affection. 4 [1920s+] (*US*) an effeminate man or a homosexual. [all are 'sweet']

lollipop *n.*² 1 [late 19C+] the penis. 2 [1940s+] (*also* pop) the penis or vagina in the context of oral sex (cf. APPLE n.⁶). 3 [1970s] the female breast (cf. APPLES n.¹).

lollipop *n.*³ (*also* lolly, lollypop) [20C+] 1 a policeman (cf. BOTTLE (AND STOPPER) n.). 2 a shop. [rhy. sl.; (1) = COP n.¹ (1)]

lollipop *n.*⁴ 1 [1910s] (*Aus.*) anything easy. 2 [1910s+] (*orig Aus.; later US Black*) a gullible person who has been 'sucked', i.e. taken advantage of. 3 [1950s–60s] an older man who is happy to indulge a younger woman, whether or not he receives any favours in return.

lollipop *n.*⁵ [1910s+] a monetary tip. [rhy. sl. = DROP n.⁶ (1)]

lollipop *v.*¹ (*also* lolly-pop) [20C+] to inform, to betray. [rhy. sl. = SHOP v.³]

lollipop *v.*² [1950s+] (*US Black*) to take advantage of someone. [LOLLIPOP n.⁴ (2)]

lollipop lady *n.* (*also* lollipop man) [1970s+] a man or woman who supervises children crossing the road near a school. [the sign on a pole that they carry; now SE]

lollipop stop *n.* [1980s+] (*US gay*) a lavatory, esp. one where one can get quick, anonymous sex. [LOLLIPOP n.² (2) + SE (*truck*)*stop*]

lollop *n.* [mid-19C–1910s] an insignificant, worthless, lazy person. [LOLLOP v.]

lollop *v.* [mid-18C+] to lounge, to sprawl. [SE *loll*]

lolloper *n.* 1 [late 19C+] a lazy, idle or slow person. 2 [1910s+] (*US*) anything or anyone exceptional in quality, size, character etc; thus *adj. lolloping*. [LOLLOP v.]

lollopy *adj.* [mid-19C+] lazy. [LOLLOP v.]

lollpoop *n. see* LOLPOOP n.

lolly *n.*¹ [early 19C+] the head. [SE *loll*; orig. boxing use]

lolly *n.*² [late 19C] (*US Und.*) a child.

lolly *n.*³ (*Aus. Und.*) 1 [1910s–50s] anything very simple to do or understand. 2 [1930s+] a fool, a dupe.

lolly *n.*⁴ [1940s+] money (cf. BEES (AND HONEY) n.). [? rhy. sl.; *lollipop* = cop = copper]

lolly *n.*⁵ [1960s] (*US*) the anus; esp. in derisive excl. *up your lolly!* [ety. unknown]

lolly *n.*⁶ *see* LOLLIPOP n.¹ (2).

lolly *n.*⁷ *see* LOLLIPOP n.³.

lolly *v. see* LOLLY (UP) v.

lollycooler *n.* (*also* lallycooler) [late 19C+] (*US*) someone or something successful, admirable.

lollygag *see under* LALLYGAG.

lollygog *n. see* LALLYGAG n. (2).

lollypalooza/lollypaloozer *n. see* LALLAPALOOSA n.

lollypop *see under* LOLLIPOP.

lollypop court *n.* [1950s] (*US juv.*) a juvenile court.

lolly scramble *n.* [1960s+] (*N.Z.*) an undignified struggle, for money, power, influence, fame etc. [SNZE *lolly scramble*, the tossing of a handful of *lollies*, i.e. sweets, for children to grab]

lolly (up) *v.* [1930s+] to inform to the police, or prison authorities. [rhy. sl.; *lollipop* = SHOP v.³]

lollywater *n.* [20C+] (*Aus./N.Z.*) a soft, non-alcoholic drink. [SE *lollipop* + *water*]

lo-lo *n.*[1] [1990s+] (*US Black*) **1** a lowrider automobile. **2** a member of a gang. [? LOWRIDER n.[2]]

lo-lo *n.*[2] [2000s] (*US teen*) a state of secrecy. [? DOWN LOW n.]

lolpoop *n.* (*also* **lollpoop**) [late 17C–early 19C] a lazy, idle drone. [SE *loll*]

lolpoop *v.* [late 17C–18C] to idle, to laze around. [LOLPOOP n.]

lombard *n.* [1980s+] *loads/lots of money but a right/real dickhead.* [an acronymic pun on the 17C Lombards, natives of Lombardy who provided Europe, including London, with its leading bankers. One of a rash of acronyms coined during the mid-1980s, *lombard* described many of the newly rich young men who populated the City of London]

Lombard fever *n.* [late 17C–early 19C] idleness, indolence, laziness, 'the idles' (Grose, 1785). [dial. *lomber*, to idle. The *OED* links the term to dial. *fever-lurden, fever-lurgan, fever-lurgy, fever-largie*, all meaning the same. Its first cit. comes from the dialectologist John Ray (1627–1705)]

Lombard Street to a china orange *phr.* (*also* **Lombard Street to a Brummagem sixpence, ...an eggshell, ...ninepence**) [mid-18C+] the longest possible odds, an absolute certainty (cf. ALL THE WORLD TO A CHINA ORANGE phr.). [Lombard Street, a centre of London banking since the 12C + SE *china orange*. The sweet orange (*Citrus aurantium*) was first sold in London in the mid-17C and by the 19C it was used fig. to mean anything of minimal value. The bet wagers the wealth that is available in the street's banks against the almost valueless orange]

lommix *n. see* LUMMOCKS n.

Londonderry *n.* [20C+] sherry. [rhy. sl.]

London fog *n.*[1] [1910s] a dog. [rhy. sl.]

London fog *n.*[2] [1960s+] (*Aus.*) any manual worker who does not perform their share of the work. [such a person 'will not lift']

London ivy *n.* [late 19C] **1** dust. **2** fog. [both tend to obscure what they 'grow on']

London jemmy/jimmy *n. see* JEMMY n.[3].

London ordinary *n.* [mid-19C] Brighton beach, 'where the "eight-hours-at-the-seas-side" excursionists dine in the open air' (Hotten, 1864). [*London* (i.e. trippers) + SE *ordinary*, 'a public meal regularly provided at a fixed price in an eating-house or tavern; also, formerly, the company frequenting such a meal, the "table"' (*OED*)]

London particular *n.*[1] [19C] a type of Madeira wine, imported especially for London merchants.

London particular *n.*[2] [mid–late 19C] a London fog or smog. [? the pale yellow colour of LONDON PARTICULAR n.[1] or f. the image of such a fog appearing only in London]

London smoke *n.* [late 19C–1900s] (*UK society*) a yellowish colour, like the polluted London smogs.

London taxi *n.* [20C+] the anus (cf. BOTTLE AND GLASS n.). [rhy. sl. = JACKSIE n.[1]]

London to a brick *phr.* [1960s+] (*Aus.*) the longest possible odds, an absolute certainty (cf. ALL THE WORLD TO A CHINA ORANGE phr.). [*London* + BRICK n.[4] (1)]

Londrix *n.* [mid-19C] London. [? Fr. *Londres*, London]

lone *v.* [1950s] (*US*) to live or act by oneself.

lone duck *n.* (*also* **lone dove, quiet mouse**) [late 19C–1900s] a former 'kept woman' who is now a common prostitute and works either from her own room or in a house of assignation (cf. ALLEY CAT n.).

lone hand *n.* [1920s–30s] (*US Und.*) a thief who operates alone.

lonely art *n.* [20C+] masturbation. [apart from its obvious connotations, note the pun on 'lonely heart']

lonely as a bastard on Father's Day *phr.* (*also* **solitary as a bastard on Father's Day**) [1960s+] (*Aus.*) extremely lonely.

lonely as a shag on a rock *phr. see* LIKE A SHAG ON A ROCK phr.

lonelyhearts *n.* [20C+] (*US prison*) **1** prisoners who maintain a correspondence with people outside prison. **2** men who write letters to female inmates.

lonely in the weather *n.* [1950s] (*W.I.*) a tall, thin person. [their head is 'in the clouds']

lone man *n.* (*also* **lone woman**) [late 19C–1940s] (*US*) an unmarried man or woman.

lone ranger *n.* [20C+] a chance, an opportunity. [rhy. sl. = SE *danger*]

lonesome pine *n.* [1990s+] (*UK Und.*) a loner with odd ideas.

lone star *n.* [1910s] (*US Und.*) a criminal who works independently of a gang.

lone wolf *n.* [1900s–70s] (*orig. US police/Und.*) a criminal (or 'civilian') who works alone, not necessarily a recluse, but not permitting anyone to penetrate their façade. [thus SE use, a solitary person, usu. male]

lone wolf *v.* [1930s–60s] (*orig. US*) to live or act alone; often with *it*. [LONE WOLF n.]

lone woman *n. see* LONE MAN n.

long *n.*[1] [1930s–40s] (*US*) a long-barrelled revolver; thus *long cut short*, a sawn-off revolver.

long *n.*[2] [1980s+] **1** (*US Black*) money. **2** (*US*) $1000. [abbr. LONG GREEN n. (1)]

long *adj.*[1] **1** [mid-18C+] of numbers, large; thus *long odds*, high odds; *long price*, a high price; *long purse*, riches; *long shillings*, good wages. **2** [mid-19C+] (*orig. US Stock Exchange*) abundant, esp. of money. **3** [mid-19C+] (*UK Und.*) a general intensifier, implying the extreme of a type. **4** [1910s+] (*UK prison*) used to describe a prisoner who still has most of their sentence to serve. **5** [1950s+] (*US drugs*) of a drug addiction, severe; thus *a long jones*, a severe habit. **6** [1990s+] (*US Black*) financially successful.

long *adj.*[2] [mid-19C] of banknotes, in small denominations. [orig. cashiers' jargon, small denominations mean more notes, which take a *longer* time to count]

long *adj.*[3] [1910s–20s] of liquor, watered down. [LONG DRINK n.]

long *adv.* [1990s+] (*US*) abundantly.

long acre *n.* [mid–late 19C] a baker. [rhy. sl.]

long and linger *n. see* LEAN AND LINGER n.

long and narrow, like a Welsh mile *phr.* [late 18C–19C] said of anything that is thus shaped; thus in fig. use, long and boring. [like a country mile, a *Welsh mile* is pvb longer than its actual measure pronounces]

long and short *n.* [20C+] port (wine). [rhy. sl.]

longas *n.* [1950s] (*W.I.*) a very tall man. [? SE *long* + ASS n. (2)]

long bacon *n. see* PULL BACON v.

long beer *n.* [mid-19C+] a glass of beer or of a soft drink, as opposed to wine or spirits.

long belly *n.* (*also* **long gut**) **1** [1920s] (*US*) a hunger for narcotics. **2** [1950s] (*W.I.*) a greedy person.

long-belly *adj.* (*also* **long-guts**) [1950s] (*W.I.*) gluttonous, greedy, usu. of a man or a child. [LONG BELLY n.]

long-bench *n. see* LONG-METER n.

long bit *n.*[1] [mid-19C–1950s] (*US*) 12½ or 15 cents, in contrast to a dime or SHORT BIT n.[1]. [BIT n.[1] (4)]

long bit *n.*[2] [1910s+] (*US Und.*) **1** a sentence of 10 years or more. **2** any term of imprisonment over 38 months that must be completed before becoming eligible for parole. [SE *long* + BIT n.[5]]

long-bow *adj.* [late 19C] untruthful, fantastical. [DRAW A LONG BOW v.]

long-bow man *n.* [late 17C] a liar. [DRAW A LONG BOW v.]

long boy *n.* [1960s+] (*US*) a large sandwich made of 2 slabs of bread cut lengthwise from the loaf and containing a variety of ingredients.

long bread *n.* (*also* **long cash/dough**) [1940s+] (*orig. US Black*) a large amount of money (cf. BATTER n.[4]). [LONG adj.[1] (2) + BREAD n.[1] (2)]

long clay n. [mid-19C] a churchwarden pipe.

long-cock adj. [1960s–70s] (US) of a woman, possessing a large vagina, thus as an insult. [SE long + COCK n.⁶ (1)]

long con n. [1930s+] (orig. US Und.) any confidence trick or cheat that is carefully planned for perfect execution. [opposite of SHORT CON n.]

long cork n. [late 18C–early 19C] claret. [the length of cork used for such wine]

long crown n. [mid–late 19C] a clever person. [pvb 'that caps long-crown, and he capp'd the devil', i.e. one who has a SE long crown, a large skull – and supposedly a large brain]

long dedger n. [mid-19C+] (Ling. Fr./Polari) the number 11. [Ital. undieci, 11]

long dick v. [2000s] (US Black) of a man, to make love very enthusiastically.

long dong silver n. [1980s+] (US) the penis. [DING-DONG n.⁴ + pun on the fictional pirate Long John Silver, the anti-hero of R.L. Stevenson's Treasure Island (1883)]

long dough n. see LONG BREAD n.

long draw n. see DRAW n.² (1).

long drink n. [mid-19C+] a glass of beer or a soft drink, as opposed to wine or spirits. [note Trollope, West Indies (1859): 'A long drink is taken from a tumbler, a short one from a wine-glass']

long drink of water n. [1910s+] a very thin person. [Scot. drink, a lanky overgrown person; ult. ON drengr, a young, unmarried man]

long drop n. [1970s+] (S.Afr.) an outdoor privy.

long drop, the n. see DROP, THE n.

long ear n. 1 [mid-19C] a clever person. 2 [mid–late 19C] (US campus) a sober, religious student. 3 [1930s–50s] (US) an eavesdropper.

long-eared adj. 1 [1910s–50s] stupid (cf. LOP-EARED adj.; THICKLUGGED adj.; TIN-EARED adj.). 2 [1950s] eavesdropping. [a donkey's long ears]

longears n. [late 19C–1960s] (US) a mule, a donkey.

long end n. 1 [1900s–10s] in betting, the favourite. 2 [1900s–40s] (US) the majority, the bulk.

longers n.¹ see LONGIES n. (1).

longers n.² see LONGS n.

long-eye n.¹ 1 [mid–late 19C; 1970s] the vagina. 2 [20C+] (W.I.) a promiscuous woman.

long-eye n.² [20C+] (W.I.) greed, covetousness; thus put one's long eye on, throw long eye on, to covet, to desire for oneself.

long face n. [late 18C+] a miserable or solemn appearance; thus adj. long-faced.

long-faced one n. (also longnosed chum) [late 19C–1920s] a horse.

long fifteen n. [early 17C] 'some class of lawyers' (OED). [ety., or more spec. def., unknown]

long firm n. (also l.f.) [mid-19C+] (UK Und.) a fraudulent scheme whereby a firm is set up, small orders are placed and paid for to establish good credit, then a massive order is made, its contents quickly sold off, often below par, and the firm vanishes, the warehouse is shut down and the debt, this time huge, is never paid.

long foot adj. [20C+] (W.I.) long-legged.

long ghost n. [mid-19C–1900s] a tall, awkward person.

long goodbye n. [1950s+] death. [the title of a Raymond Chandler novel publ. in 1953]

long-grain rice n. [1940s+] (W.I.) a boiled green banana. [similar shape, if different size]

long green n. 1 [late 19C+] (US) money, paper money, esp. in large amounts (cf. ALFALFA n.). 2 [1960s] (US drugs) a kind of marijuana (cf. AFRICAN BUSH n.; BLACK DOMINA n.). [LONG adj.¹ (2) + the colour of dollar bills/marijuana; (2) GREEN n.³ (1)]

long gut n. see LONG BELLY n.

long-guts adj. see LONG-BELLY adj.

longhair n. 1 [mid-19C–1900s] (US, Western) a name for early settlers who wore their hair long. 2 [1920s+] (orig. US) an intellectual or artist. 3 [1930s] (US) a moral reformer. 4 [1930s+] (US) a performer or aficionado of classical music. 5 [1950s+] (US) classical music. 6 [1960s+] (US) a HIPPIE n.² (3) or a politically liberal person. [LONGHAIRED adj.]

longhaired adj. 1 [late 19C+] (orig. US) (also longhair) intellectual, aesthetic, always pej.; thus longhaired music, classical music etc. 2 [1910s–70s] (esp. milit.) of a man, female-looking; as in longhaired bunkie, a longhaired buddy. 3 [1960s+] HIPPIE adj., politically liberal. [stereotyped image of an intellectual as bearded, sandalled and hirsute]

longhaired chum n. (also longhaired one) 1 [late 19C] a horse. 2 [late 19C–1960s] a young woman, a girlfriend. [play on milit. long-eared chum, a mule; note Texas prison longhaired people, one's family and loved ones]

long handlebars n. (also handlebars) [20C+] (US) long underwear.

long-handles n. (also long-handled underwear) [1940s+] (Can./US) long woollen winter underwear, combinations. [late 19C long-handled hose; var. on LONG JOHNS n.]

long-head n. [mid-19C–1900s] (US) an astute, shrewd person. [SE long + head]

long-headed adj. 1 [late 17C+] discerning, shrewd. 2 [late 19C+] obstinate. [LONG-HEAD n.]

long-heel n. [1950s+] (US, mainly Southern) a Black person. [supposed physiological characteristic]

longhorn n. [late 19C–1960s] (US, mainly Western) a tough, Texan old-timer or cowboy (cf. SHORTHORN n.). [the longhorn cattle that were found in Texas]

long house n. [1900s–40s] (US Black) a brothel (cf. ACCOMMODATION HOUSE n.). [a typical brothel of the period had a long central corridor with a number of small bedrooms arranged along either side]

longies n. 1 [1910s+] (also longers) long trousers. 2 [1940s+] (orig. US) long woollen winter underwear, combinations.

long in the arm phr. [late 19C–1910s] a phr. used to describe a habitual thief.

long-jaw n. [1980s] (Aus.) a tourist.

long john n. [1960s+] (US) a sandwich consisting of a small sausage that is put into a much longer bun or roll.

long johns n. [1940s+] (orig. US) long woollen winter underwear, combinations.

long jump n.¹ [1920s–60s] a hanging; thus take the long jump, to be hanged; for the long jump, destined for/in trouble.

long jump n.² see JUMP n.¹ (5).

long lady n. [late 19C] a farthing candle.

long-lagger n. see LAGGER n.² (1).

Long Lane n. [late 17C] a widow, seen in a sexual context. [Long Lane, London EC1, was a contemporary centre for the sale of second-hand clothes]

long lane n. [mid-19C] the vagina (cf. ALLEY n.¹).

long lib n. [17C–18C] death. [SE long + LIB n.¹]

long-lick n. [late 19C–1920s] (Aus./US) molasses.

long meg n. [mid-17C–early 19C] an exceptionally tall woman; thus as long as Meg of Westminster. [proper name of a celebrated 17C woman, Long Meg of Westminster]

long-meter n. (also long-bench) [20C+] (W.I.) a boring, long-winded speaker. [? long meet her, i.e. one who won't go away/one who sits next to you on the bench and will not leave]

long-mouth n. [20C+] (W.I.) a glutton, one who is constantly hungry.

longnebbed adj. see NEB n.¹ (3).

longneck n. [late 19C] (Aus.) a camel.

long nine n. [mid–late 19C] (US) a cigar; also long eighteen (if extra long). [? 9 inches long]

long-nose n. **1** [1900s–40s] a Jew; thus *long-nosed*, Jewish (cf. BIGNOSE n.). **2** [1920s] (*US*) an upper-class person, an aristocrat.

longnosed chum n. *see* LONG-FACED ONE n.

long on *adj.* [20C+] well supplied with, expert in.

long one n.[1] (*also* **long 'un**) [late 19C–1900s] (*Aus.*) a tall glass of beer.

long one n.[2] [late 19C–1900s] (*US*) a horse that is listed at long odds, an outsider. [LONG adj.[1] (1)]

long one n.[3] (*also* **long 'un**) [1970s+] (*UK Und.*) a long prison sentence.

long one n.[4] *see* LONG 'UN n.[3].

long one with many links n. [1940s] (*US Black*) a long key chain, worn with a ZOOT SUIT n. (1).

long out v. [20C+] (*W.I.*) to purse one's lips or stick out one's tongue in a gesture of deliberate rudeness.

long out one's eye on, be v. [20C+] (*W.I.*) to be covetous for.

long paddock n. [1920s+] (*Aus./N.Z.*) the road.

long-pull n. [late 19C–1900s] an over-measure in a public house. [the *pull* is of the handle of the beer pump]

long rod n. [1930s–80s] (*US Und.*) a rifle.

Long's n. [late 19C–1900s] Short's Winehouse, in the Strand opposite Somerset House, London WC2. [joc. reversal]

longs n. (*also* **longers**) [1920s+] long trousers. [the slightly joc. antonym of SE *shorts*]

longs-and-shorts n. [mid-19C] cards purpose-made for cheating.

long shanks n. [late 17C–1910s] a notably tall man.

long-shoe n. [1950s–80s] (*US Black*) a sophisticated, urbane pimp or swindler; thus *long-shoe game*, the profession and lifestyle of pimping (cf. BOSS PLAYER n.). [the style of footwear preferred by US Black pimps at the time]

long-shoe *adj.* [1950s–70s] (*US Black*) pertaining to the world of pimping. [LONG-SHOE n.]

long shoes n. [1950s–80s] (*US Black*) success; thus *wear long shoes*, to be successful.

longshore lawyer n. [early 19C] a corrupt, ruthless lawyer. [SE *longshore*, tough, villainous]

long shot n.[1] [mid-19C+] (*gambling*) a wild guess, an adventurous attempt, a slim chance. [SE *long* + SHOT n.[5] (2); the inaccuracy of shooting at a distant target, thus a bet laid at long odds on an unlikely contender]

long shot n.[2] [1950s–60s] (*UK Und.*) a prostitute's client who spends longer than the usual time – around 15 minutes – with a girl.

long-shot *adj.* [20C+] risky, adventurous. [LONG SHOT n.[1]]

long-sleeved top n. [late 19C–1910s] a silk hat.

long-sleever n. [late 19C+] (*Aus.*) a drinking glass of the largest size. [SE *long* + SLEEVER n. (1); note 1902, *Bulletin* (Sydney), 18 October 14/4 'T.A.D.': 'Anyone know the true derivation of the phrase "long-sleever" as applied to beer. Heard, the other day, that Bishop Barker (consecrated to the Sydney see in 1854) was fond of his long beer. Hence Sydney's barmaids were asked for a "lawn-sleever, please," as a compliment to "His Lordship." That degenerated into "long-sleever." "Long-sleever" comes from the resemblance between a pint-pot and a "long-sleeved hat." A "long beer" used to be called in Sydney a "Bishop Barker" – the bishop was a very tall man']

long spit n. *see* BIG SPIT n.

long stale drunk n. [late 19C] a hangover, the depression that follows a bout of heavy drinking.

long-stem n. [1910s] (*US drugs*) an opium pipe.

long stick n. *see* STICK n.[14].

long stomach n. [late 18C–early 19C] **1** a voracious appetite. **2** a greedy eater.

long-stopper n. [1990s+] (*Aus. Und.*) a lookout.

long streak of misery n. [late 19C+] a very tall person, esp. one with a mournful, depressed air.

long streak of piss n. *see* LONG (THIN) STREAK OF PISS n.

long strokes n. [20C+] the initial stage of sexual intercourse. [as opposed to the SHORT STROKES n.]

long suit n. [late 19C+] anything in which one feels particularly secure or capable. [card-playing imagery, now SE]

long tail n. [20C+] (*Aus.*) treacle. [ety. unknown; ? the slow progress of treacle off the spoon]

long-tail blue n. [early–mid-19C] **1** (*also* **old blue**) a swallowtail jacket, worn by Black dandies. **2** the Black dandy that wore such a coat.

long-tailed *adj.*[1] [early–late 19C] of a coat, having a long tail.

long-tailed *adj.*[2] *see* LONG-TAILED 'UN n.

long-tailed bear n. [late 19C–1900s] a lie. [a bear has no tail]

long-tailed beggar n.[1] [mid-19C] a cat. [the supposed story of a sailor who came home after his first voyage unable to remember the name for a cat and asked his mother 'What's she called, that 'ere long-tailed beggar?'; BEGGAR n. (2)]

long-tailed beggar n.[2] [1900s–20s] a large denomination sterling note. [LONG-TAILED 'UN n. + BEGGAR n. (2)]

long-tailed finnup n. [mid–late 19C] a large denomination sterling note. [LONG-TAILED 'UN n. + FINNIP n.]

long-tailed 'un n. [mid-19C+] a large denomination sterling note, £10, £20, £50; thus *long-tailed*, of more than £5 face value.

long tails n. [1940s] £5 notes.

long tea n. [19C] (*UK juv.*) urine.

long (thin) streak of piss n. **1** [20C+] (*also* **long thin streak of pelican shit**) an unflattering description of a tall, thin person. **2** [1900s–10s] one who over-estimates their own importance or abilities.

long tickey n. (*also* **tickey-wire**) [1970s] (*S.Afr.*) a coin on a thread that can be used to operate a telephone kiosk, then retrieved and used again. [SE *long* + TICKEY n. (1)]

long time no see *phr.* [20C+] (*orig. US*) a general greeting meaning 'I haven't seen you for a long time'.

longtimer n. [20C+] (*US prison*) a prisoner with a very long sentence.

long tog n. [early 19C] (*US Und.*) an overcoat.

long tom n. **1** [mid-19C–1910s] (*Aus./N.Z.*) a long-handled shovel. **2** [late 19C–1900s] the penis. [note naut. *long tom*, a long-barrelled, deck-mounted gun]

long-tongue *adj.* [20C+] (*Irish/W.I.*) talkative, indiscreet. [LONG-TONGUED adj.]

long-tongued *adj.* [late 16C–1900s] of a chatterer, a gossip, one who is unable to keep a secret; thus *as long-tongued as Granny*. ['Granny was an (actual) ideot (*sic*) who could lick her own eye' (Grose, 1796)]

long town n. [19C] (*Anglo-Irish*) London. [? its geographical dimension]

long trot n. *see* TROT n.[2] (4).

long 'un *see also under* LONG ONE.

long 'un n.[1] [mid-19C+] a tall person.

long 'un n.[2] [late 19C–1900s] a pheasant. [the length of its tail]

long 'un n.[3] (*also* **long one**) [1960s+] £100 or £1000. [LONG adj.[1] (1)]

long underwear n. [1930s–60s] (*US*) jazz music popularized for 'easy listening', also classical music. [? play on LONGHAIR n. (5)]

long white roll n. [1940s] (*US Black*) a cigarette.

long-winded *adj.* **1** [late 17C–mid-19C] used of one who takes a long time to do something, e.g. pay a bill or debt. **2** [1940s+] used of a man (or woman) who takes a long time to reach orgasm.

long-winded paymaster n. [late 17C–early 19C] (*UK Und.*) one who extends lengthy credit.

long word n. [mid-19C+] any statement that implies a long time, e.g. *never is a long word*.

lont n. *see* LOON n.[1].

Loo, the n. [1900s–50s] (Aus.) Wooloomooloo, a tough, working-class suburb of Sydney. [abbr.]

loo n.[1] (also **lou**) [late 19C+] the lavatory. [? Fr. l'eau, water. The bordalou, a portable commode, resembling a sauce boat and carried by 18C ladies in their muff; or ? SE leeward, the side of a ship turned away from the wind and as such the side over which one would urinate/defecate; or ? an abbr./pun on Waterloo, whether the station or the battle it commemorates]

loo n.[2] [1960s+] (US) a police or fire lieutenant. [US pron. of loo-tenant]

loo v. [early 19C] (US) to cheat, to defraud. [? the card-game loo]

looby n. (also **loob**) [mid-14C–19C] a fool, a dullard; thus adv. loobily. [dial.]

loocha n. (also **loocher, lootcha**) [19C] (Anglo-Ind.) 'a blackguard libertine, a lewd loafer' (Y&B). [synon. Hind. luchcha]

looder n. [late 19C+] (Irish) a blow. [Irish liúdar/Scot. lowder, a blow]

looey n.[1] (also **lieuy, looie, louie**) [1970s+] (US) 1 a lump of expectorated phlegm (cf. LOOGIE n.). 2 a piece of nasal mucus. [echoic]

looey n.[2] see LOOIE n.[1]

loof-faker n. [mid-19C] a chimney sweep. [backsl. loof = flue + FAKER n. (1)]

loogan n. (also **loogin, lugan**) (US) 1 [1910s–60s] a fool, a newcomer. 2 [1930s–40s] a petty crook or ruffian. 3 [1980s] a gun man. [? typical 'Irish' surname and thus based on negative racial stereotyping]

loogie n. [1980s+] (US) a gob of phlegm (cf. LOOEY n.[1]). [var. on LOOEY n.[1]]

Loogin n. see LUGEN n.

loogin n. see LOOGAN n.

looie n.[1] (also **lieu, looey, louie**) [1910s+] (orig. US milit.) lieutenant. [US pron.]

looie n.[2] see LOOEY n.[1]

lookable adj. [1990s+] (W.I.) of a woman, attractive.

look after number one v. (also **look out for number one, mind number one**) [19C+] to take care of oneself, irrespective of others. [SE + NUMBER ONE n.[1]]

look-a-here! excl. [1910s+] (US) an imper. calling someone's attention, esp. before delivering some reprimand or lecture.

look alive v. (also **come alive**) [mid-19C+] to hurry up, esp. as imper.

look as if one hasn't got the right change v. [late 19C–1900s] to be enraged, to look furious.

look at every woman through the hole in one's prick v. [late 19C+] of a man, to regard every woman as a sex object.

look-at-me n. [2000s] an ostentatious automobile; a limousine.

look at the ceiling v. [late 19C+] of a woman, to have sexual intercourse in the missionary position (cf. CATCH AN OYSTER v.).

look at the maker's name v. (also **read the maker's name**) [19C] to drink heavily. [the name is found on the bottom of an upturned glass]

look at the wall v. [late 17C] of a man, to urinate (cf. BURN THE GRASS v.).

look big v. [late 16C+] to act in what one hopes is an impressive manner.

look blue v. [17C+] 1 to be astonished or surprised. 2 to look miserable, to look nervous. [SE look + BLUE adj.[1]]

look bullets v. [mid-19C] (US) to stare at aggressively. [in style of SE look daggers]

look down one's nose (at) v. 1 [early 19C+] to disdain, to despise, to snub. 2 [1910s–30s] (US) to look unhappy, embarrassed, to give in to someone else. [fig. uses of SE; 'at' is a mid-19C addition. (2) the lowering of one's eyes]

lookee here! excl. (also **looky here!**) [mid-19C+] an imper. calling someone's attention, esp. before delivering some reprimand or lecture.

looker n. (orig. US) 1 [late 19C+] an attractive woman; occas. man. 2 [late 19C+] in combs., that which looks in a certain way. 3 [1970s] a client who wishes only to look at a prostitute, who is usu. naked, and occas. fondle her breasts. 4 [1970s] a voyeur.

lookers n. [20C+] (US) the eyes.

look for a piece v. see BEG FOR A PIECE v.

look for gapeseed v. [19C] to be inattentive, to let one's mind wander. [SE look for + GAPESEED n. (1)]

look for one's swag straps v. [late 19C+] (Aus./N.Z.) to start thinking of leaving one job and going in search of another. [one is about to strap on one's SWAG n.[1] (9) and get moving]

look for what one ain't put down v. [20C+] (W.I.) to be a professional thief.

look goats and monkeys at v. [mid-18C–19C] to gaze lecherously at, to leer. [the trad. propensities of these 2 animals]

look good v. [1910s+] (orig. US) to appear promising.

lookie-lou n. (also **looky-loo**) [1980s+] (US Black/campus) an inquisitive person, a peeping Tom.

look-in n. [mid-19C+] 1 a brief visit. 2 a chance, an opportunity, usu. with the implication of ultimate success.

looking as if one couldn't help it phr. [late 18C–early 19C] looking like a fool or simpleton.

looking glass n.[1] [early 17C–mid-19C] a chamberpot. [one's reflection in the urine, as well, poss., as the attention paid by contemporary physicians to the urine itself; thus the 18C riddle: 'Q. Why is a Chamber-Pot call'd a Looking-Glass? A. 'Because many rarely see their Faces in any other']

looking glass n.[2] [1960s] (US) the buttocks, the posterior (cf. ALA n.). [rhy. sl. = ARSE n.[1] (1)]

looking lively phr. [late 19C+] drunk (cf. ABOUT RIGHT phr.[1]).

look into the whites v. [late 19C–1900s] to be on the verge of fighting. [the 2 adversaries are staring into each other's eyes]

lookism n. [1970s+] (orig. gay) evaluating a stranger purely on the basis of their physical appeal or lack of it. [generally seen as non-politically correct and thus pej.]

look like a kookaburra that has swallowed the kangaroo v. [1930s+] (Aus.) to look elated, to look very happy.

look like a million dollars v. (also **dress like a millon dollars, look like a million, look like a million bucks**) [1910s+] (US) to be extremely attractive, to be extremely smartly or fashionably dressed (cf. FEEL LIKE A MILLION DOLLARS v.).

look like a monkey fucking a football v. [1960s+] (US) to look utterly absurd.

look like a pox doctor's clerk v. [1930s] to be overdressed.

look like a wet week v. see LIKE A WET WEEK phr.

look like Brown's cows v. [1970s] (Aus.) to act in a straggling, uncoordinated manner.

look like bull-beef v. [late 17C–early 19C] to look stern, grim and threatening; thus bluff as bull beef, stern, intimidating.

look like death eating a sandwich v. [1940s+] (US) to look very ill, very emotional or very tired.

look like death warmed up v. (also **look like death warmed over, …shit warmed over**) [1930s+] looking extremely ill, usu. very pale (cf. FEEL LIKE DEATH WARMED UP v.).

look like God's revenge against murder v. [late 18C–early 19C] to look furious; later as abbr. look like murder.

look like hell v. see LOOK LIKE SHIT v.

look like Jock Blunt v. [early 18C–early 19C] for one's face to betray one's disappointment. [SE look like + JACK BLUNT n.]

look like murder v. see LOOK LIKE GOD'S REVENGE AGAINST MURDER v.

look like one lost a pound and found sixpence v. (also **look like one lost a pound and found a halfpenny**) [19C] to look notably downcast.

look like shit v. (also **look like hell**) [1930s+] 1 of a person, to appear extremely unwell, whether through actual illness or through the effects of drink or drugs (cf. FEEL LIKE SHIT v.).

2 of an object, to look in very poor condition. [SE *look like* + SHIT n.[1] (2)]

look like shit warmed over *v. see* LOOK LIKE DEATH WARMED UP v.

look like Sunday *v.* [1910s] to be dressed up.

look like ten bob in the quid *v.* [1960s] (*Aus.*) to look miserable.

look like the ant's pants *v.* [1990s+] (*Aus.*) to be dressed very smartly.

look like thirty cents *v. see* LIKE THIRTY CENTS phr.

look-look *v.* [20C+] (*W.I.*) to gaze about in a furtive manner, to peep.

look (marlin) spikes at *v.* (*also* **look pitchforks**) [19C] to glare at, to 'look daggers' at. [SE *marlin spike*, an iron tool tapering to a point, used to separate the strands of rope in splicing]

look nine ways for Sunday *v.* (*also* **look nine ways at thrice**) [16C+] to squint.

looko *n.* [1950s] (*Aus.*) a glance.

look old *v.* [late 19C–1900s] to act severely or cautiously.

look on with *v.* (*also* **look on over**) [late 19C] to read a book while someone else is reading it.

lookout *n.* [mid-19C+] (*orig. US*) a problem, a responsibility; usu. as *that's their lookout.*

look out for number one *v. see* LOOK AFTER NUMBER ONE v.

look over the spikes *v.* [late 19C] (*Aus.*) to appear in court as a defendant. [the spikes that top the front edge of the dock]

look over the wood *v.* [late 18C–early 19C] to mount the pulpit, to preach. [the wooden pulpit]

look pitchforks *v. see* LOOK (MARLIN) SPIKES AT v.

look round the clock *v.* [late 19C–1900s] (*US*) to look old.

looksee *n.* (*also* **looksie**) **1** [mid-19C+] a glimpse, a glance. **2** [1920s–60s] (*US*) a doctor's licence to practise. [? Pidgin]

looksee *v.* [mid-19C+] (*orig. US*) to make an inspection, to have a look, to glance at.

looksee man *n.* [1920s] (*US*) a tourist or sightseer. [LOOKSEE n. (1) + SE *man*]

look seven ways for Sunday *v.* (*also* **look two ways for Sunday**) [early 19C+] **1** to squint. **2** in fig. use, to be very upset or seriously disturbed. [var. on LOOK NINE WAYS FOR SUNDAY v.]

look sharp *v.*[1] [mid-18C+] to hurry up, to get on with, esp. as imper. [SE *look* + *sharp*, quick-witted]

look sharp *v.*[2] [1920s+] to dress smartly, fashionably. [SE *look* + SHARP adj.]

looksie *n. see* LOOKSEE n.

looks like a wet weekend, it *phr.* [1930s+] (*orig. Aus.*) (*also* **it looks like a wet season**) used by a woman announcing, or registering, the onset of a menstrual period.

looks like he wouldn't piss if his pants were on fire, he *phr.* [20C+] a phr. used of an especially dull, stupid-looking person (cf. CAN'T SEE THROUGH A LADDER phr.).

look slippery! *excl.* [late 19C–1920s] (*orig. RN*) hurry up! get on with it!

look slippy! *excl.* (*also* **look slimy!**) [mid-19C+] hurry up! get on with it!

look snappy (about) *v.* [1920s–40s] to hurry, to 'look smart'.

look spikes at *v. see* LOOK (MARLIN) SPIKES AT v.

look story! *excl.* [20C+] (*W.I.*) a general excl. of dismissal or contempt, how absurd!

look through a glass *v.* [19C] to be drunk.

look through a hempen window *v.* [17C] to be hanged.

look through a rope *v.* [16C] to be hanged.

look through one's fingers *v.* [late 19C–1900s] (*Irish*) to pretend ignorance, to evade one's responsibilities.

look through the wood *v.* [late 18C–mid-19C] to stand in the pillory.

look towards *v.* [mid–late 19C] to drink a health.

look two ways for Sunday *v. see* LOOK SEVEN WAYS FOR SUNDAY v.

look-up *n.* [mid-19C+] a brief visit. [backform. f. LOOK UP v.[1]]

look up *v.*[1] [late 18C+] to visit.

look up *v.*[2] [early 19C+] (*orig. commercial*) usu. of a situation, to improve, to be getting better.

look upon a hedge *v.* [17C; 1930s+] to urinate (cf. BURN THE GRASS v.).

look what the cat's brought in *phr.* (*also* **look what the cat drug in**) [1920s+] a dismissive, disdainful, teasing phr. [SOMETHING THE CAT BROUGHT IN n.]

look what the wind's blown in *phr.* [1920s+] a facetious greeting to a new arrival, or a remark to a companion concerning that arrival.

look who's talking *phr.* [1930s+] a phr. used to stress that one speaker is in no position to criticize another.

look with red-eye (at) *v. see* HAVE RED-EYE FOR v.

looky here! *excl. see* LOOKEE HERE! excl.

looky-loo *n. see* LOOKIE-LOU n.

loolah *n.* [1990s+] a crazy person.

looloo/looly *see under* LULU.

loom *n.* [17C] the vagina. [euph.]

loon *n.*[1] (*also* **lont**) [late 18C+] a fool, an idiot. [SE *lunatic*; ult. Lat. *luna*, moon; such people are supposedly 'moonstruck'. Note mid-15C+ SE *loon*, a worthless person, a rogue, an idler]

loon *n.*[2] [1980s] (*Aus.*) a pimp.

loon (about) *v.* [1960s+] to act crazily or irresponsibly; thus *loon*, a wild time. [LOON n.[1]]

looney *see also under* LOONY and its combs.

looney tune *n.* (*also* **loony tune**) [1960s+] **1** a crazy person, a lunatic. **2** a cartoon. [*Looney Tunes*, the series of film cartoons created for Warner Bros. by the team of Hollywood animators Hanna-Barbera and released 1930–69, then shown on TV from 1950s; the term was popularized by another Hollywood star, Ronald Reagan, to describe such figures as Libyan leader Colonel Gaddaffi]

looney tune *adj.* (*also* **loony tune(s)**) [1960s+] insane, irrational (cf. LOONY adj.). [LOONEY TUNE n.]

loonie *n.*[1] [1980s+] (*Can.*) the Can. $1 coin, introduced in 1987. [the representation of a *loon* or diver on its reverse]

loonie *n.*[2] *see* LOONY n.

loon pants *n.* (*also* **loons**) [1970s+] trousers with enormous flared bottoms, esp. beloved of early 1970s hippies. [LOON (ABOUT) v. + PANTS n.[1] (2)]

loonslate *n.* (*also* **loonslatt**) [late 17C–early 19C] 1 shilling and 1 penny-halfpenny, 1s 1½d. [? LOON n.[1] + SLAT n.[2] (1); lit. 'a fool's half-crown']

loony *n.* (*also* **looney, loonie, lunie, luny**) [mid-19C+] (*orig. US*) a fool, an eccentric, a mad person. [SE *lunatic*; or LOON n.[1]]

loony *adj.* (*also* **looney, luny**) **1** [mid-19C+] (*orig. US*) eccentric, insane, foolish, pertaining to psychiatry (cf. LOONEY TUNE n.). **2** [1970s+] (*US campus*) intoxicated. [LOONY n.]

loony bin *n.* (*also* **looney bin, loony farm**) **1** [1910s+] a psychiatric institution. **2** [1970s+] in ext./fig. use, a chaotic place, a 'madhouse'. [LOONY n. + BIN n. (4)]

loony bird *n.* [1960s–70s] (*US*) a crazy person. [LOONY adj. (1) + BIRD n.[2] (1)]

loony doctor *n.* [1920s+] a psychoanalyst, a psychiatrist. [LOONY n. + SE *doctor*]

loony farm *n. see* LOONY BIN n.

loony house *n.* [1930s+] (*US*) a psychiatric institution. [LOONY n. + SE *house*]

loony pen *n.* [1980s+] (*US*) a psychiatric institution. [LOONY n. + SE *pen*]

loony roost *n.* [1940s+] (*US*) a psychiatric institution. [LOONY n. + SE *roost*]

loony tune *n. see* LOONEY TUNE n.

loony tune(s) *adj. see* LOONEY TUNE adj.

loop *n.*[1] [1940s–50s] (*Aus.*) a fool. [backform. f. LOOPY adj. (1)]

loop *n.*[2] [1980s+] a fig. circle of information; usu. in phr. *in the loop/out of the loop.*

loop *n.*[3] [1990s+] a pornographic film.

loop *n.*[4] [2000s] (*US Black*) sex involving several men and a single woman.

loop *v.*[1] [1920s+] (*US*) to go on a drinking spree; thus *on a loop*, on a drinking spree. [SE *loop*, i.e. one's drunken meandering]

loop *v.*[2] [1980s] to be a caddie. [SE *loop*, to walk around in a circle]

looped (up) *adj.* (*US*) **1** [1930s+] drunk. **2** [1960s+] infatuated with something or someone, or crazy, demented (cf. CLEAN AROUND THE BEND phr.). [one is 'going round in circles']

looper *n.*[1] [1910s] a punch, a blow.

looper *n.*[2] [1980s] a caddie. [LOOP v.[2]]

looper *n.*[3] [1980s+] a crazy, disturbed person. [backform. f. LOOPY adj. (1)]

loopie *n.* (*also* **loopy**) [1970s+] (*N.Z.*) a tourist. [the 'looping' movement used in swatting sand flies + LOOPY adj. (1), i.e. the quality of questions they ask local people]

loop-legged *adj.* [1940s+] (*US*) drunk (cf. ARSEHOLED adj.).

loop off *v.* [early–mid-18C] to run away. [? SE *lope off*]

loop-the-loop *n.*[1] **1** [1920s] (*US*) a ring or hoop. **2** [1940s+] soup. [rhy. sl.]

loop-the-loop *n.*[2] [1960s–70s] mutual oral-genital stimulation.

loopy *n. see* LOOPIE n.

loopy *adj.* (*also* **loopy-loo**) **1** [1920s+] (*orig. naut.*) eccentric, crazy (cf. CLEAN AROUND THE BEND phr.). **2** [1990s+] obsessed with, mad about. **3** [1990s+] drunk or drugged (cf. ADDLED adj.). [? LOOBY n. or Scot. *loopy*, cunning]

loor *n. see* LOUR n.

loose *adj.*[1] **1** [late 19C] of an appointed time, not punctual, round about, e.g. *a loose midday.* **2** [1950s+] (*US*) unperturbed, casual, relaxed; often in phrs. STAY LOOSE v.; HANG LOOSE v. **3** [1960s] (*US Black*) in possession of money.

loose *adj.*[2] **1** [1900s; 1990s+] (*US Black*) out of control. **2** [1910s–30s] crazy (cf. LOOSE IN THE BEAN phr.; LOOSE UP TOP phr.). **3** [1930s+] (*US campus*) drunk.

loose a button *v.* [1940s] (*Irish*) to urinate. [fly buttons]

loose a fiver *v.* [late 19C–1900s] to have to pay heavily for one's pleasures. [SE *loose* + FIVER n. (1)]

loose as a goose *phr.* [1930s+] (*US*) very loose, in any sense.

loose ball *n.* [1970s+] (*Irish*) an opportunity to pick up free drink. [soccer imagery]

loose bit of goods *n.* [late 19C] a flighty young woman who has 'abandoned the proprieties' (Ware). [SE *loose* + BIT OF GOODS n.]

loose-bodied gown *n.* [late 16C–17C] a prostitute. [metonymy; thus Nares: 'This being a very customary dress of abandoned women, was sometimes used as a phrase for such ladies']

loose-box *n.* [mid-19C] a brougham or similar vehicle owned by a kept woman or well-off prostitute. [SE *loose box*, a stall in which a horse can move around freely + pun on euph. *loose woman*/BOX n.[1] (1)]

loose cannon (on a rolling deck) *n.* [1970s+] (*orig. US*) an unstable person, one who may well be dangerous to others.

loose-coat game *n.* [19C] prostitution; thus *play at the loose-coat game*, to have sexual intercourse.

loose end *n.* [late 19C–1920s] a dissolute person. [SE *loose* + pun on *loose end*, of fabric]

loose ends *n.* [1970s+] (*US Black*) spare money available for loans.

loose fish *n.* **1** [early 19C] a prostitute (cf. ALLEY CAT n.). **2** [early–late 19C] one who has no settled way of life. **3** [late 19C] a promiscuous woman. [note whaling jargon *loose fish*, a whale that is fair game for anybody who can catch it]

loose French *v.* [late 19C–1900s] to swear. [SE *loose off* + FRENCH n.[2] (2)]

loose goose *n.* [1950s+] (*US*) a person or thing that is loose, in any sense. [LOOSE AS A GOOSE phr.]

loose house *n. see* LOUSE HOUSE n.

loose-hung *adj.* [19C–1920s] used of an unstable character.

loose in the bean *phr.* (*also* **loose in the canoodle/head**) [1920s–70s] (*US*) eccentric, crazy. [SE *loose*/LOOSE adj.[2] (2) + BEAN n.[5]/SE *head*/? NOODLE n.[1] (1)]

loose in the hilt *phr.* **1** [17C+] suffering from diarrhoea. **2** [mid-17C–early 18C] maritally unfaithful. **3** [mid-18C] drunk.

loose in the rump *phr.* [18C–mid-19C] of a woman, wanton, promiscuous. [SE *loose* + *rump*]

loose-legged *adj.* **1** [19C] suffering from diarrhoea. **2** [1960s] (*US*) promiscuous.

loose link *n.* [1980s+] (*US Black*) an informer.

loosely wired *adj. see* LOOSE-WIRED adj.

loosen *v. see* LOOSEN (UP) v.

loosener *n.* [1900s] (*US*) a giver, usu. of money.

looseners *n.* [1920s–30s] (*US*) prunes. [their trad. role in curing constipation]

loosen someone's hide *v.* [1900s] to thrash, to flog. [SE *loosen* + HIDE n.[1] (1)]

loosen (up) *v.* [late 19C+] (*orig. US*) **1** to relax, esp. as an imper. **2** to start speaking, esp. as an imper. **3** to spend or hand over money. [(1) and (2) fig. use of SE; (3) to loosen one's purse-strings]

loosen up on *v.* [late 19C+] (*orig. US*) to relax one's restraints on another. [LOOSEN (UP) v. (1)]

loose screw *n.* [early 19C+] an eccentric. [HAVE A SCREW LOOSE v. (4)]

loose up top *phr.* [late 19C+] mad, eccentric. [SE *loose*/LOOSE adj.[2] (2)]

loose wig *n.* [1950s] (*orig. US Black*) one who is without inhibitions; one who is open to new ideas.

loose-wired *adj.* (*also* **loosely wired**) [1950s] out of control.

loosey-goosey *adj.* [1960s+] (*US*) very loose, in any sense. [LOOSE AS A GOOSE phr.]

loosies *n.* [1980s+] cigarettes bought unpackaged.

loot *n.*[1] **1** [late 18C+] plunder, booty. **2** [1910s+] money. [(1) SE by late 19C, f. Hind. *lut*, plunder, ult. Skrt *lotra*, plunder. Note also Anglo-Ind. *lootie-wallah*, a plunderer or bandit]

loot *n.*[2] (*also* **Loot, Lute**) [late 19C+] (*Aus./US*) a lieutenant; also used in UK in WW1 to describe the rank, but not to address its bearer. [abbr. pron.]

lootcha *n. see* LOOCHA n.

loothy *n.* [20C+] (*Irish*) a large, ungainly man. [Irish *liútar*, big, ungainly]

lop *n.*[1] (*also* **lophead, loppy**) **1** [20C+] (*US Und.*) a fool. **2** [1970s+] (*US*) a contemptible person. **3** [1990s+] (*US campus*) an uncoordinated person. **4** [2000s] (*US prison*) a second-rate prison officer. [LOB n.[2] (2)]

lop *n.*[2] [1930s+] (*Anglo-Irish*) a penny. [ety. unknown; ? link to dial. *lop*, a flea, i.e. the coin's innate worthlessness]

lop cock *n.* [1930s–40s] (*US*) a circumcised penis (cf. CLIPDICK n.). [SE *lop*, to cut off + COCK n.[2] (1)]

lop down *v.* [mid-19C–1900s] (*US*) to sit down, to lie down. [East Anglian dial. *lop*, to droop]

lope *n.* [2000s] (*US prison*) an envelope. [abbr.]

lope *v.* (*also* **loap**) **1** [late 17C+] to run, to run away; thus *on the lope*, running away, or to run fast. **2** [19C] to steal. [SE *loup*, to leap]

lop-ear *n.* (*also* **flop-ear**) [mid-19C+] (*US*) a nickname for an inhabitant of Oregon. [? the prevalence of rabbits in the state]

lop-eared *adj.* (*also* **flop-eared**) [mid-19C+] (*US*) exceptionally stupid or gullible (cf. LONG-EARED adj.). [the *lop-ears* of an animal, but note LOB n.[2] (2)]

lope one's mule v. [1960s+] (*US*) to masturbate (cf. BEAT ONE'S HOG v.). [MULE n.⁵]

lopes n. *see* MELONS n.

lophead n. *see* LOP n.¹.

loppy n.¹ [late 19C–1940s] (*Aus./N.Z.*) a handyman on a rural station, a roustabout.

loppy n.² *see* JALOPY n. (1).

loppy n.³ *see* LOP n.¹.

loppy cull n. [18C] (*UK Und.*) a drunken man. [? LOP n.¹ + CULL n.¹ (2)]

loppy dust n. [1980s+] (*drugs*) cocaine (cf. BIRDIE POWDER n.). [LOP n.¹ + SE *dust*]

loppy pop n. [2000s] a shop. [rhy. sl.; ? pun on SE *lollipop*]

loqued out adj. *see* LOC'D OUT adj.

lor! excl. [mid-19C+] an abbr. version of *lord!*, used in a variety of excls. and mild oaths.

lor-a-mussy! excl. [mid-19C–1930s] a mild oath, lit. 'Lord have mercy!'

lor blime! excl. [1910s] (*Aus.*) a mild excl.

lor-blimer n. [1910s] (*Aus.*) a vulgar, vociferous person. [those who say LOR BLIME! excl.]

lord n. [late 17C–19C] a hunch-backed or badly crippled man; thus also addressed as *His Honour*. [Gk *lordos*, bent backwards; thus the medical term *lordosis*, anterior curvature of the spine]

lord and lady n. [1970s–80s] (*N.Z. prison*) sexual intercourse.

lord and mastered adj. [1990s+] drunk (cf. ADRIAN (QUIST) adj.). [rhy. sl. = PLASTERED adj.²]

Lord blue me! excl. [late 19C] (*Aus.*) a mild excl.

lord-forbids n. *see* GOD-FORBIDS n. (1).

Lord Harry n. *see* OLD HARRY n. (1).

Lord how came you so phr. *see* HOW CAME YOU SO phr.

Lord John Russell n. [mid–late 19C] a bustle. [rhy. sl.; ult. British politician *Lord John Russell* (1792–1878)]

Lord knows how phr. (*also* **Lord knows what (not)**, **Lord knows where, …who, …why**) [mid-17C+] a phr. implying amazement, incredulity or plain ignorance.

Lord Lovat v. [20C+] to get rid of, to throw away. [rhy. sl. = SHOVE IT! excl.]

lord love a duck! excl. (*also* **gawd love a duck! love a duck!**) [20C+] a mild excl. of surprise etc. [*gawd* is Aus. use]

Lord Lovell n. (*also* **Lord Lovel**) [mid-19C+] a shovel. [rhy. sl.; 20C+ use is mainly US]

lord love me! excl. (*also* **lord love us/you!**) [mid-19C+] a mild oath.

lordlummy! excl. *see* LUMME! excl.

Lord Mansfield's teeth n. [late 18C–early 19C] the *chevaux de frize* or row of spikes embedded into the top of the wall of the King's Bench prison. [*Lord Mansfield* (1733–1821), Lord Chief Justice of the Court of Common Pleas]

lord mayor n.¹ [late 19C–1950s] a large crowbar (cf. ALDERMAN n.²).

lord mayor n.² **1** [1910s–70s] an oath, a 'swear'. **2** [1940s–60s] a chair. [rhy. sl.]

lord mayor v. [1910s–70s] to swear. [rhy. sl.]

lord mayor's coal n. [mid-19C] a piece of slate.

lord mayor's fool n. [mid-19C] 'a personage who likes everything that is good, and plenty of it' (Hotten, 1864). [pvb 'like My Lord Mayor's fool, full of business and nothing to do']

lord muck n. (*also* **king muck**) [20C+] a hypothetical aristocrat, snobbish and conspicuous in his contempt for lesser mortals, but since he is lord of 'muck' he is, in fact, no better than they are.

Lord Northumberland's arms n. *see* NORTHUMBERLAND ARMS n.

lord (of the manor) n. [mid-19C–1970s] a sixpence. [rhy. sl. = TANNER n.]

lord rex n. [1970s–80s] (*N.Z. prison*) sexual intercourse.

lords and peers n. [2000s] the ears. [rhy. sl.]

Lord Sutch n. [1960s+] **1** the clutch. **2** the crotch. [rhy. sl.; ult. popstar/politician *Screaming Lord Sutch* (1940–99), the leader of the maverick UK political party Monster Raving Loony Party]

Lord Wigg n. [1960s+] a pig. [rhy. sl.; ult. UK politician *George Wigg* (1900–83)]

lordy! excl. *see* LAWDY! excl.

lordy me! excl. [late 19C+] a euph. for *Lord help me!*

Loretta Young n. [1990s+] the tongue. [rhy. sl.; ult. Hollywood film star *Loretta Young* (1913–2000)]

lorette n. [mid–late 19C] a euph. term for a prostitute, borrowed from France. [the *lorettes*, a class of courtesan that was based near the Church of Notre Dame de Lorette ('the Paris Pimlico' Barrère) in Paris]

lor lumme! excl. *see* LUMME! excl.

Lorna Doone n. [20C+] a spoon. [rhy. sl.; ult. the novel *Lorna Doone* (1869) by R.D. Blackmore]

lorry up v. (*also* **lurry up**) [1940s+] (*Irish*) to beat, to thrash; thus *lurry into*, to get stuck into, to attack. [Irish *liúradh*, a beating]

Los n. [1910s+] (*US*) *Los* Angeles. [abbr.]

los adj. [1950s+] (*S.Afr.*) usu. of a woman, promiscuous. [Afk. *los*, loose]

los v. [1980s+] (*S.Afr.*) to let go, often as excl. [Afk.]

lose v. **1** [mid-19C+] (*US*) to vomit; usu. in phrs. such as LOSE ONE'S LUNCH v. (cf. BLOW v.³). **2** [mid-19C+] to suffer a miscarriage, to have a still-birth or have one's child die very early in life. **3** [late 19C+] (*US*) to kill. **4** [late 19C+] (*US*) to evade. **5** [1920s+] (*orig. US*) to get rid of, to dispose of. **6** [1990s+] (*US*) of a record, radio etc, to turn off.

lose a cartful and find a waggon-load v. [late 19C–1900s] to become fat.

lose a dinner v. [1950s+] (*Aus./US*) to vomit (cf. BLOW CHOW v.). [LOSE v. (1) + SE *dinner*]

lose a meal v. [1940s+] (*Aus.*) to vomit (cf. BLOW CHOW v.). [LOSE v. (1) + SE *meal*]

lose a screw v. [1960s] to be insane. [HAVE A SCREW LOOSE v. (4)]

lose it v. **1** [1950s+] to lose control temporarily; in an extreme case to have an actual mental breakdown, to go mad. **2** [1970s] to lose one's virginity. **3** [1980s+] (*US campus*) to be surprised, to be shocked. **4** [1980s+] (*US campus*) to vomit (cf. BLOW v.³). **5** [1990s+] to lose one's skills or abilities.

lose leather v. [18C–19C] to become saddle-sore through skin being rubbed off by excessive riding. [SE *lose* + LEATHER n.¹ (1)]

lose move n. [1980s+] (*US campus*) a foolish action. [SE *lose*, to fail, to be defeated + MOVE n. (1)]

lose one's arse v. [late 18C–mid-19C] to be careless; usu. in phr. *they'd lose their arse if it were loose*. [SE *lose* + ARSE n.¹ (1)]

lose one's ass v. [1950s+] (*US*) **1** to fight, to brawl, to argue vehemently. **2** in gambling, to lose heavily. **3** to act irrationally, to lose control of one's life (usu. through drug addiction). [SE *lose* + ASS n. (2)]

lose one's ballast v. [late 19C–1950s] to lose control emotionally. [in a ship the ballast keeps the vessel 'on an even keel']

lose one's bean v. [1910s+] to lose one's temper. [SE *lose* + BEAN n.⁵]

lose one's bird v. *see* BIRD n.¹⁴.

lose one's block v. *see* DO ONE'S BLOCK v.

lose one's bottle v. [20C+] to back down, to turn cowardly. [SE *lose* + BOTTLE n.² (2)]

lose one's britches v. [20C+] to lose a good deal of money, usu. through betting. [var. on LOSE ONE'S SHIRT v.]

lose one's cherry v. (*also* **break one's cherry**) **1** [1920s+] to lose one's virginity. **2** [1970s+] in fig. use, to be initiated into a new experience. [SE *lose* + CHERRY n.¹ (4)]

lose one's cookies v. [1940s+] (US) to lose emotional control. [SE *lose* + COOKIES n.^{2} (2)]

lose one's cool v. [1950s+] (*orig. US*) to lose one's dignity or self-possession, to lose one's temper. [SE *lose* + COOL n.^{2} (1)]

lose one's dash v. *see* DO ONE'S DASH v.^{2}.

lose one's dip v. [20C+] (US) to lose one's composure.

lose one's dog v. [1910s] (US) to lose control of a situation.

lose one's douche bag v. *see* LOSE ONE'S TAMPAX v.

lose one's doughnuts v. [1940s+] (US campus) to vomit (cf. BLOW CHOW v.). [LOSE v. (1) + var. on BLOW DOUGHNUTS v.]

lose one's gender v. [1940s+] (*gay*) to abandon homosexuality to become a heterosexual.

lose one's goat v. [1910s] to lose one's courage, to lose one's ability to fight.

lose one's gourd v. *see* BLOW ONE'S GOURD v.

lose one's grip v. [late 19C+] (*orig. US*) to lose one's composure, to lose one's sanity.

lose one's groceries v. *see* BLOW ONE'S GROCERIES v.

lose one's hair v. [1900s–30s] to lose one's temper.

lose one's jock v. [1960s+] (US) to be fooled. [fig. use of SE *lose* + JOCK n.^{1} (2)]

lose one's knob v. [1910s] (*Aus.*) to go mad, to break down.

lose one's legs v. [mid–late 18C] to be drunk.

lose one's lollies v. *see* TOSS ONE'S LOLLIES v.

lose one's lunch v. (*also* **drop one's lunch**) [1920s+] (*Aus./US*) to vomit (cf. BLOW CHOW v.). [LOSE v. (1) + SE *lunch*]

lose one's nut v. [20C+] to lose emotional control; to act without thinking. [SE *lose* + NUT n.^{1} (2)]

lose one's punch v. *see* DO ONE'S DASH v.^{2}.

lose one's rag v. [1950s+] to lose one's temper. [SE *lose* + RAG n.^{3}]

lose one's rudder v. [18C] to be drunk and thus lose one's sense of direction.

lose one's shirt v. [1910s+] to lose a good deal of money, usu. through gambling or other speculation.

lose one's shit v. [1980s+] (US campus) to experience something frightening or shocking. [SE *lose* + SHIT n.^{1} (1)]

lose one's stopper v. [1940s] (US) to lose one's temper.

lose one's Tampax v. (*also* **lose one's douche bag**) [1960s] (US) to become hysterical.

lose one's vest v. [19C] to lose one's temper.

lose one's wig v. [1960s+] (*drugs*) to lose one's mind from drug intoxication.

lose one's wool v. [early 19C–1940s] to lose one's temper. [SE *lose* + WOOL n.^{2} (1); cf. KEEP ONE'S HAIR ON v.]

lose out (on) v. [mid-19C+] **1** to fail, to miss an opportunity. **2** (*also* **lose out to**) to be fooled, to be swindled.

loser n. **1** [20C+] (*orig. US*) a failure, esp. a socially inadequate person. **2** [20C+] (US) a convicted prisoner, one who served a jail sentence; often ext. by a number that denotes the number of sentences; usu. as THREE-TIME LOSER n. **3** [1920s+] (*orig. US*) a disappointment, a problem, an obstacle, a useless thing or idea.

loser adj. [1970s+] (US) of people or things, second-rate, useless. [LOSER n.]

lose the ball v. [1970s+] to find oneself in an increasingly difficult situation, to lose control of one's life, work, relationships etc. [sporting imagery]

lose the combination v. [late 19C–1910s] to miss the meaning or point.

lose the match and pocket the stakes v. [19C] of a woman, to have sexual intercourse (cf. CATCH AN OYSTER v.). [the male is seen as the 'winner'; the stakes are his ejaculated semen]

lose the number of one's mess v. **1** [early 19C–1930s] to die. **2** [1910s] to lose one's position; to fall from social or professional grace. [naut. imagery]

lose the run of v. **1** [1900s] (*Aus.*) to lose control of someone

else. **2** [1970s+] (*Irish*) to lose one's self-control. [Irish *ná bí ag rith leat féin mar sin*, lit. 'don't be running with yourself like that']

lose work v. [1990s+] (*W.I.*) to lose one's girlfriend.

loskop n. [1950s+] (*S.Afr.*) a forgetful, scatty person. [Afk. *los*, loose + *kop*, head]

loskop adj. [1950s+] (*S.Afr.*) crazy, forgetful, eccentric. [LOSKOP n.]

lossie n. [1950s+] (*S.Afr.*) a promiscuous woman. [LOS adj.]

lost a button phr. [19C+] eccentric, crazy. [var. on NOT ALL THERE phr. (1)]

lost and found n. **1** [1900s] £10 (cf. AYRTON (SENNA) n.). **2** [1960s+] £1 (cf. CHERRY-PICKER n.^{5}). **3** [1970s–80s] (*N.Z. prison*) the punishment block. [rhy. sl.; (3) = POUND n.^{3}]

lost in the suds phr. [1930s] (US Black) totally unaware or unsophisticated.

Lost Wages n. [1960s+] (US) Las Vegas. [an intentional malapropism]

lot n.^{1} [late 17C+] **1** an event, a circumstance, a happening; thus ironic *that was a nice lot, that was*. **2** a person; often as BAD LOT n.

lot n.^{2} [late 19C–1900s] the male genitals. [ext. of LOT, THE n. (1)]

lot, the n. **1** [mid-19C+] all, the complete amount, everything that is/was available, e.g. *he's scoffed the lot*. **2** [1960s+] (*Aus./N.Z. prison*) a life sentence.

loteby n. (*also* **ludby**) [14C–early 18C] a mistress. [SE *lote*, to skulk or hide]

lothario n. [mid-18C+] a libertine, a rake. [in the cast list of Sir William D'Avenant's play *The Cruel Brother* (1627) is a 'Lothario, a frantic young gallant'. The name was used again by Nicholas Rowe in *The Fair Penitent* (1703), and the term's popularity stems from the latter, in which he is characterized as 'The Gay Lothario']

lotion n. [late 19C+] a drink.

lotioned adj. [late 19C] drunken. [LOTION n.]

lot lizard n. [1980s+] (US) a prostitute who works at truck stops (cf. ALLEY CAT n.). [SE (*parking*) lot + LIZARD n.^{2} (5)]

lot of, a adj. [1940s–60s] (US Black) exceptionally good, skilful, esp. of musical ability. [abbr. SE *whole lot of*]

lotsa n. [1920s+] (*orig. US*) very many, a large number. [pron. of SE *lots of*]

Lot's wife n. [1920s] salt. [the biblical story]

lotta n. [1910s+] (*orig. US*) very many, a large number. [pron. of SE *a lot of*]

lotties and totties n. [late 19C] prostitutes as a group. [theatrical jargon *lotties and totties*, out of work young actresses, in turn f. common names]

Lotusland n. [1960s+] (US) California, esp. Los Angeles. [SE *lotus-eating*, i.e. the indolent lifestyle associated with California]

lou n.^{1} *see* LOO n.^{1}.

lou n.^{2} *see* LOUIS n.^{1} (2).

loud adj. **1** [mid-17C+] usu. of smell, strong or foul. **2** [mid-19C+] vulgar, showy; thus *loudness*, vulgarity, showiness. [(1) orig. literary; (2) SE by 20C+]

loud and clear adj. [1990s+] dear, expensive. [rhy. sl.]

loudmouth n. [1920s+] (*orig. US*) **1** a braggart, a boaster. **2** a lawyer. [LOUDMOUTH adj.]

loudmouth adj. (*also* **loudmouthed**) **1** [1910s+] (*orig. US*) boastful, arrogant, vulgar. **2** [1970s] (US) ostentatious, showy.

loudmouth v. [1930s+] **1** (*orig. US*) to brag, to boast. **2** (*US Black*) to speak abusively. [LOUDMOUTH adj.]

loud one n. [late 17C–mid-19C] a gross lie.

loudspeaker n. [1930s] (US) **1** a braggart, a boaster. **2** one's wife.

loudtalk v. [1920s+] (US Black) to talk in a way that confronts or embarrasses one's hearers, that is deliberately antagonistic.

Louie n. (*also* **louie**) [late 19C+] (*orig. US*) $1; in pl., *louis*, money (cf. ABE n.^{2}). [joc. use of proper name, although there appears to be no specific reason]

louie *n.*[1] [1960s+] (*Aus.*) a fly. [the Mortein commercials of 1960s+ which featured *Louie the Fly*]

louie *n.*[2] [1960s+] in driving, a left turn; usu. in phr. HANG A LOUIE *v.* (cf. REGGIE *n.*[2]). [the initial letter]

louie *n.*[3] *see* LOOEY *n.*[1].

louie *n.*[4] *see* LOOIE *n.*[1].

louies *n.* (*also* **louis**) [1980s+] (*US*) the luxury luggage and clothing manufactured by *Louis* Vuitton. [abbr.]

louis *n.*[1] **1** [1920s–30s] (*US*) a pimp. **2** [1990s+] (*US campus*) (*also* **lou**) an unattractive man. [stereotyping of the proper name]

louis *n.*[2] [1980s+] (*UK drugs*) ¹/₁₆th of an ounce of cannabis. [play on French King *Louis* XVI]

louis *n.*[3] *see* LOUIES *n.*

loulou *n. see* LULU *n.*[2].

lounge *n.* [mid-19C; 1940s] (*Aus. Und.*) the dock in a court of law.

lounge lizard *n.* (*also* **lounge serpent/snake**) **1** [1910s+] a fortune-hunter or womanizer who works his charms in the lounges of hotels. **2** [1920s+] a poor or miserly man who would rather court a woman in her own house than take her out on the town. [SE *lounge* + LIZARD sfx but note LIZARD *n.*[2] (3); (2) note University of Missouri (in 1931) synon. *sofa lizard*]

lounge louse *n.* [1930s+] (*Aus./US*) a womanizer, an adventurer; usu. in pl. *lounge lice*. [var. on LOUNGE LIZARD *n.* (1)]

lounge the gag *v.* [early 19C] (*UK Und.*) to beg. [SE *lounge* + GAG *n.* (3)]

lour *n.* (*also* **loor, loure, lower, lowr, lowre, lowrie, lowyer**) [mid-16C–19C] (*UK Und.*) money. [Fr. *louier*, a reward, then 14C SE *lower*, a reward; note Rom. *loor*, to plunder, and *luripen*, booty]

Lou Reed *n.* [1960s+] (*drugs*) amphetamine (cf. A *n.*[2]). [rhy. sl. = SPEED *n.*[2]; ult. rock star *Lou Reed* (b.1942)]

louse *n.* [mid-17C+] an extremely contemptible or untrustworthy individual.

louse *adj.* [1940s+] (*US*) second-rate. [LOUSE *n.*]

louse *v.* [1940s+] (*Aus.*) to pilfer. [LOUSE *n.*]

louse *sfx* [1930s+] (*US*) used in combs. with a qualifying *n.* to refer to a despicable person, a waster, a hanger-on.

louse (around) *v.* [1910s+] (*US*) to idle, to loiter, to waste time. [northern UK dial. *lowse*, stop working]

louse bag *n.* [late 18C–early 19C] a wig or a bag worn over the hair.

lousebound *adj.* [1930s–50s] a general term of abuse, lit. one who is infested with lice.

louse cage *n.* (*also* **louse trap**) (*US*) **1** [late 19C–1940s] a cheap hotel or lodging house; a filthy prison. **2** [late 19C–1960s] a hat. **3** [1920s–60s] a bunkhouse.

loused *adj.* [1950s+] (*drugs*) covered by sores and abscesses from repeated use of unsterile needles.

loused-up *adj. see* LOUSE UP *v.* (4).

louse house *n.* (*also* **loose house**) **1** [late 18C–1930s] a prison (cf. BANDHOUSE *n.*). **2** [1900s–40s] a seedy hotel or lodging house.

louse trap *n.* **1** [late 18C–19C; 1930s] a ladder, i.e. 'a stitch fallen in a stocking' (Grose, 1785). **2** [1920s] a bushy sidewhisker, usu. in pl.

louseland *n.* [late 17C–early 19C] Scotland; thus *Scotch louse-trap*, a comb. [a derog. suggestion that Scotland is infested with vermin]

louser *n.* **1** [1930s+] (*orig. US*) a contemptible individual. **2** [1940s–50s] (*Aus.*) a petty thief. [LOUSE *n.*; also Irish use 1960s+]

louse someone around *v.* [1910s+] (*US*) to mistreat someone. [i.e. to act like a LOUSE *n.*]

louse trap *n.*[1] **1** [mid-18C–mid-19C] a toothcomb. **2** [early 19C] the hair; the head. **3** [20C+] a sideburn or sidewhisker; usu. in pl.

louse trap *n.*[2] *see* LOUSE CAGE *n.*

louse-up *n.* [1970s+] (*US*) a situation or thing that is a mess or that is troublesome. [LOUSE UP *v.* (4)]

louse up *v.* **1** [1910s–60s] to infest with vermin. **2** [1920s] (*US prison*) to wash one's clothes to remove lice. **3** [1930s] to tease. **4** [1930s+] (*orig. US*) to make a mess of, to ruin, usu. deliberately; thus *adj. loused-up*. **5** [1940s+] to blunder, to fail. **6** [1950s+] to cause a person difficulties, to cause trouble for someone. **7** [1950s+] to make a place or situation unpleasant or nasty.

louse walk *n.* [mid–late 19C] a back-hair parting.

lousing *n.* [1960s+] (*Irish*) hanging around on street corners. [LOUSE (AROUND) *v.*]

lousy *n.* [1930s–50s] a despicable person. [LOUSY *adj.*]

lousy *adj.* **1** [late 14C+] a general intensifier, usu. with derog. implications. **2** [late 18C+] (*US*) small, insignificant. **3** [1930s–70s] (*Aus.*) mean, tight-fisted. **4** [1970s] (*US Und.*) corrupt. [fig. use of SE *louse*]

lousy *adv.* [16C; 1930s+] a general intensifier, usu. with derog. implications. [fig. use of SE *louse*]

Lousy Anna *n.* [1920s+] (*US*) a derog. name for Louisiana.

lousy-looked *adj.* [late 17C] a general epithet of abuse. [lit. 'looking lice-ridden']

lousy lou *n.* [20C+] the 'flu, influenza. [rhy. sl.]

lousy with *adj.* (*also* **crabby with**) [mid-19C+] full of, abundant with (a commodity, type of person etc) (cf. FILTHY WITH *adj.*).

love *n.*[1] [early 19C+] any person or thing that is pleasant or attractive, e.g. *it's a real love*.

love *n.*[2] *see* LOVE UP *n.*

love *v. see* LOVE (UP) *v.*

love a duck! *excl. see* LORD LOVE A DUCK! *excl.*

love affair *n.* [1970s+] (*drugs*) a mixture of heroin and cocaine. [pun on BOY *n.*[7] + GIRL *n.*[1]]

loveage *n.* [mid-19C] a drink consisting of the dregs collected from the overflow from the pouring taps, the ends of spirit bottles and similar leavings, which was sold cheaply in gin-shops, particularly to women. [SE *lovage*, a cordial based on the herb lovage (*Ligusticum scoticum*)]

love and hate *n.* [20C+] weight. [rhy. sl.]

love and kisses *n.* [20C+] one's wife. [rhy. sl. = MISSIS *n.*]

love and marriage *n.* [20C+] a carriage. [rhy. sl.]

love apples *n.* [19C; 1980s+] the testicles (cf. ACORNS *n.*). [note Fr. *pomme d'amour*; Ger. *liebesapful*, the fruit of the tomato]

love arm *n.* [1990s+] the penis (cf. ARM *n.*[1]).

love bone *n.* [1960s+] (*US Black*) the penis. [SE *love* + BONE *n.*[1] (1)]

love box *n.* [1980s+] (*US*) the female genitals. [SE *love* + BOX *n.*[1] (1)/SE *box*]

love bug *n.* **1** [20C+] an imaginary virus, the symptoms of which are being in love; thus the disease itself. **2** [1970s+] (*US gay*) a pubic louse. **3** [1980s] a person who is in love with being in love. [SE *love* + BUG *n.*[6]/SE *bug*/BUG *n.*[5]]

love button *n.* [1990s+] (*orig. US*) the clitoris (cf. BABY IN THE BOAT *n.*).

love canal *n.* [1980s+] (*US*) the vagina. [play on SE + pun on 1993 ecological abuse of the *Love Canal*, New York]

love crack *n. see* CRACK *n.*[6] (1).

love-curls *n.* [mid–late 19C] a hairstyle in which the hair is cut short and worn low over the forehead.

love custard *n.* [1990s+] semen (cf. BABY GRAVY *n.*). [note CUSTARD *n.*]

love dart *n.* [late 19C+] the penis (cf. AX *n.*[2]).

loved it! *excl.* [1980s+] (*US campus*) an expression of elation.

love dove *n.* [1990s+] (*drugs*) MDMA (cf. ECSTASY *n.*). [the tablets are branded with a small dove of peace]

love-dove *n. see* LOVEY-DOVEY *n.* (3).

love drug *n.* [1980s+] (*drugs*) MDMA (cf. ECSTASY *n.*). [among the drug's primary effects is a sense of world-embracing benevolence]

loved-up *adj.* [1990s+] **1** intoxicated from love or romance, often used spec. of having had a lot of sex. **2** under the influence of MDMA. [LOVE (UP) *v.*]

love 'em and leave 'em n. [late 19C+] a philanderer, a womanizer. [LOVE 'EM AND LEAVE 'EM phr.]

love 'em and leave 'em phr. [late 19C+] philandering, womanizing, e.g. *he's the love 'em and leave 'em sort.* [SE *love them and leave them*]

love envelope n. [1970s+] (*US gay*) a condom.

love flesh n. [19C] the vagina.

love gap n. *see* PASSION GAP n.

love glove n. [1980s+] (*US*) **1** a condom. **2** a vagina (cf. BAG n.[1]).

love grenades n. [2000s] the testicles (cf. BALLS n.[1]).

love gun n. [1970s+] (*US*) the penis (cf. AX n.[2]). [ext. of GUN n.[1] (2)]

love handles n. (*also* **fuck handles, love rungs**) [1960s+] the excess flesh around a portly stomach that may be seen in a kinder light by those who appreciate the Rubenesque figure. [they provide something to grab hold of]

love hole n. [1980s+] (*US*) the vagina (cf. BLACK HOLE n.[1]).

love-in n. [1960s+] (*orig. US*) **1** a group gathering to express mutually loving feelings; mainly in HIPPIE n.[2] (3) use. **2** an orgy. **3** positive, optimistic relations.

love juice n. [late 19C+] **1** semen (cf. BABY FLUID n.). **2** vaginal secretions (cf. BINDERJUICE n.). [SE *love* + JUICE n.[2] (1)]

love lane n. [mid–late 19C] the vagina (cf. ALLEY n.[1]).

love letter n. [1940s] (*US Black*) **1** a bullet. **2** a stone or rock thrown at someone.

lovelies n. (*also* **lovely, lovely high**) [1970s+] (*US drugs*) marijuana laced with phencyclidine.

lovelips n. [1990s+] (*US*) the labia (cf. CUNT-LIPS n.).

lovely n.[1] [1930s+] a pretty young woman, a word esp. popular with tabloid press, seaside entertainers etc. [SE *lovely* adj.]

lovely n.[2] *see* LOVELIES n.

lovely adj. **1** [early 17C+] delightful, really excellent; often in ironic use. **2** [mid-19C] (*UK Und.*) suitable and ready for criminal action.

lovely adv. [20C+] admirably, enjoyably, well.

lovely drop (of) n. *see* NICE DROP (OF) n.

lovely grub! excl. [1950s+] an excl. implying approval of whatever is being considered, whether actual food or not.

lovely high n. *see* LOVELIES n.

love machine n. **1** [1960s+] (*US*) a sexually virile man, a womanizer. **2** [1980s+] the penis. [(2) note MACHINE n.[1] (2)]

love muffin n. [1980s+] (*US*) a sexually attractive person. [SE *love* + MUFFIN n.[1] (3)]

love muscle n. [1950s+] (*US*) the penis.

love nest n. (*also* **lurve nest**) **1** [1920s+] (*orig. US*) an apartment used by lovers. **2** [1950s] (*US*) a drive-in film, known as a venue for teenage love-making. **3** [1990s+] (*US*) the vagina (cf. AGREEABLE RUTS OF LIFE n.).

love nuts n. *see* LOVER'S NUTS n.

love off v. [20C+] (*W.I., Jam.*) to make obvious sexual advances towards.

love-pot n. [19C] a drunkard.

love pump n. [1980s+] (*US*) the penis. [popularized by the film *This is Spinal Tap* (1984)]

lover n.[1] **1** [20C+] (*US*) a pimp. **2** [1950s] (*US Und.*) a rapist or bigamist. [euph.]

lover n.[2] [1910s+] (*orig. US*) an affectionate general term of address, though no actual love affair need be implied.

lover-boy n. (*also* **lover-man**) **1** [1950s+] a womanizer; the term is often used (esp. by women) ironically. **2** [1960s] (*US gay*) a boyfriend.

lover-girl n. [1950s] the female equivalent of LOVER-BOY n.

lover's nuts n. (*also* **love nuts, lover's balls/knots**) [1950s+] (*US*) aches in the testicles caused by sexual stimulation without ejaculation. [SE *lover* + NUTS n.[2] (1)/BALLS n.[1] (1)/*knots*]

lover's speed n. *see* SPEED FOR LOVERS n.

lover's tiff n. [20C+] venereal disease. [rhy. sl. = SYPH n.]

love rug n. [1990s+] female pubic hair.

lover under the lap n. [1940s–70s] (*Aus.*) a lesbian (cf. CARPET-BITER n.).

love rungs n. *see* LOVE HANDLES n.

love's cabinet n. [18C] the vagina (cf. BAG n.[1]).

love seat n. [late 19C] the vagina.

love shack n. [1960s+] (*orig. US*) **1** a room or apartment that a man keeps for seductions and sex. **2** a lover, an object of sexual desire (and conquest). [(2) is fig. use of (1)]

love's harbour n. [19C] the vagina (cf. ADAM'S OWN (ALTAR) n.; AGREEABLE RUTS OF LIFE n.).

love's paradise n. [19C] the vagina (cf. ADAM'S OWN (ALTAR) n.).

love spuds n. [1990s+] the testicles (cf. ACORNS n.). [SE *love* + SPUD n.[2] (1)]

love staff n. [late 19C] the penis (cf. BAT n.[7]).

lovesteak n. [1980s+] (*US campus*) the penis (cf. BACON n.[1]).

love stick n. [1920s+] (*US*) the penis (cf. BAT n.[7]). [SE *love* + STICK n.[1] (1)]

love torpedo n. [1990s+] the penis (cf. AX n.[2]).

love truncheon n. [late 19C; 1990s+] the penis (cf. AX n.[2]).

love up n. [1950s+] (*US*) a caress, a hug. [LOVE (UP) v. (1)]

love (up) v. **1** [late 19C+] (*orig. US*) to caress, to hug, to embrace; also used fig. **2** [1920s+] to have sexual intercourse. **3** [1990s+] (*drugs*) to render someone intoxicated with MDMA. **4** [2000s] to be very fond of. [(4) backform. f. LOVED-UP adj. (2)]

love weed n. [1930s+] (*US drugs*) marijuana (cf. AFRICAN BUSH n.; BOMB n.[4]). [SE *love* + WEED n.[1] (4)]

lovey-dovey n. **1** [mid-19C+] (*also* **lovey-ducks**) a term of endearment. **2** [20C+] (*also* **lovey-dove**) one's lover, partner. **3** [1920s+] (*also* **love-dove**) (*US*) love-making. [SE *love* + redup. + image of billing and cooing turtle-doves]

lovey-dovey adj. **1** [late 19C+] affectionate. **2** [2000s] maudlin and sentimental. [LOVEY-DOVEY n. (1)]

loving adj. [1940s+] (*US*) used as a euph. for FUCKING adj.

loving it phr. [1980s+] in a positive or pleasing situation. ['it' is life]

low n. **1** [1960s+] (*US drugs*) a bad reaction to a drug, esp. the negative feelings that may follow the 'high'. **2** [1990s+] any form of depression. [opposite of HIGH n.[1] (1), and slightly contrived]

lowball v. [1950s+] (*US*) in negotiating, to make a lower than realistic offer.

lowballer n. [1990s+] (*US*) one who bets – when a spread is on offer – on the assumption of a low score. [LOWBALL v.]

low belly strippers n. *see* STRIPPERS n.

low-bite n. [1990s+] (*W.I.*) an upper-class person who likes working-class pursuits.

lowbrow n. **1** [20C+] (*orig. US*) an uncultured person who is considered to have mass-market, undemanding and non-intellectual tastes. **2** [1910s] (*US*) a thug. [the opposite of HIGHBROW n.]

lowbrow adj. [20C+] (*orig. US*) pertaining to mass-market values. [the opposite of HIGHBROW adj.]

low countries n. **1** [late 16C–17C] the anus. **2** [late 16C–19C] the female genitals. [the 'geography' of the body + a pun on *country*/CUNT n.[1] (1)]

Low Country soldier n. [mid-17C] a good drinking companion. [the characteristics of those who have soldiered in the Low Countries or of Dutch troops]

lowdown, the n. [20C+] (*orig. US*) privileged information, intimate details, 'the inside story'; thus adj. *lowdown*, privileged.

lowdown adj. **1** [mid-19C+] (*US*) mean, contemptible, unpleasant. **2** [late 19C+] (*US*) depressed, impoverished, out of luck. **3** [1920s] (*US*) of a place, run-down. **4** [1920s+] (*US Black*) excellent, impressive.

lowdown *adv.* [late 19C–1910s] meanly, contemptibly, unpleasantly; usu. as PLAY LOW (DOWN) v. [LOWDOWN adj. (1)]

low-downer *n.* [mid-19C–1930s] (*US Black*) a poor White person, esp. a native of North Carolina. [LOWDOWN adj. (2)]

lower *n. see* LOUR n.

lower (a glass) *v.* [late 19C+] to take a drink, to empty a glass (or bottle) by drinking its contents.

lower mouth *n.* [mid-19C] the vagina.

lower one's belt *v.* [1960s] (*US gay*) to be a promiscuous 'feminine' lesbian.

lower than a snake's belly *phr.* (*also* **lower than a snail's belly**, **...snake's hip**) [1930s+] **1** (*Aus.*) as low as one can go. **2** (*orig. US Black*) (*also* **lower than a midget's ass in hell**) depressed.

lower than the belly of a cockroach *phr.* [1940s+] used of a person categorized as the lowest of the low.

lower than whale shit *phr.* [1960s+] (*US*) **1** extremely depressed. **2** of no moral worth.

lower the bomb *v.* [1950s–70s] to speak or act in a decisively negative manner.

lower the boom (on) *v.* (*also* **drop the boom (on)**) [1930s+] **1** (*US*) to hit hard. **2** (*US*) to give up on. **3** (*US*) to take decisive action against. **4** (*US*) to reprimand severely, to put an end to someone's misbehaviour. **5** (*US*) to murder, to kill. **6** (*Aus.*) of a man, to have sexual intercourse (cf. BURY IT v.). [naut. imagery]

lower wig *n.* [19C] pubic hair.

lowey *n.* [1950s–80s] (*Aus.*) a young woman who is dedicated to hedonism, the equivalent and accomplice of a REV-HEAD n. [? LOWHEEL n. (1)]

low femme *n.* (*also* **blue-jeans femme**) [1990s+] (*US gay*) a feminine lesbian but one that is not quite as stereotypically feminine as a HIGH FEMME n. [SE *low* + FEMME n. (3)]

low five *n.* [1980s+] (*US Black*) a palm-/hand-slapping ritual, with the hands held low. [opposite of HIGH FIVE n.[1]]

low five *v.* [1980s+] (*US Black*) to greet someone with a palm-/hand-slapping ritual, where the hands are held low. [opposite of HIGH FIVE v.]

low-flung *adj.* [mid–late 19C] (*US*) of low character or social position.

low forehead *n.* [1900s] (*US*) a foolish person.

low gagger *n.* [late 18C] (*UK Und.*) a confidence trickster who elicits compassion (and money) by pretending to be hurt in some way.

low Greek *n.* [1960s+] (*gay*) heterosexual intercourse (because the vagina is lower than the anus). [SE *low* + GREEK n.[4] (1)]

lowheel *n.* [1930s–60s] **1** a prostitute or promiscuous woman. **2** a down-and-out, a tramp. [the state of one's shoes after constantly walking the streets]

low-heeled *adj.* [1910s] (*Aus.*) tough; ill-bred.

lowie *n.*[1] (*also* **lowy**) [1950s+] (*Aus.*) a prostitute or promiscuous woman. [? LOWHEEL n. (1)]

lowie *n.*[2] [2000s] a depression. [LOW n. (2) + sfx *-ie*]

lowing cheat *n.* (*also* **lowing chete**) [mid-16C–early 17C] (*UK Und.*) a cow, a calf. [SE *lowing* + CHEAT n. (1), lit. 'lowing thing']

lowing rig *n.* [early 19C] (*UK Und.*) the theft of cattle. [SE *lowing* + RIG n.[2] (2)]

low in the lay *phr.* [mid-19C–1910s] extremely poor. [SE *lay low*, to knock down]

low in the saddle *phr.* [20C+] (*orig. US*) drunk and thus slumped over. [cowboy imagery]

low jump *n.* [1960s+] (*Aus.*) a magistrate's court. [play on HIGH JUMP n. (3)]

lowland *n.* [1930s–70s] (*US Black*) the area of a city, usu. the south, where the Black ghetto is generally sited.

lowlands *n.* [late 18C–19C] the female genitals.

lowlife *n.* (*also* **lowlifer**) [1910s+] (*orig. US*) a contemptible person, esp. a criminal. [LOWLIFE adj.]

lowlife *adj.* (*also* **low-lived**) **1** [early 18C+] (*orig. US Black*) unpleasant, contemptible, aggressive, vulgar. **2** [1990s+] in criminal terms, second-rate. [LOWLIFE n.]

low men *n.* [mid-16C–early 19C] fixed dice that will always show low numbers.

low neck and short sleeves *n.* [1940s+] (*gay*) a circumcised penis (cf. CLIPDICK n.). [the foreskin represents the 'sleeves']

low-octane *adj.* [1990s+] of coffee, decaffeinated. [the opposite of HIGH-OCTANE adj. (3)]

low on *phr.* [1940s+] deficient in, short of (cf. HIGH ON phr.).

low on the totem (pole) *phr.* [1940s+] inferior, second-rate, in a junior or uninfluential position at work. [an image of Native American hierarchy]

low pad *n.* [late 17C–early 19C] (*UK Und.*) a footpad; 'a base Sheep-stealing, half-penny Rogue' (Head, *The Canting Academy*, 1674); thus **low-padding**, petty thievery. [SE *low* + PAD n.[1] (3); as opposed to HIGH PAD n. (2)]

low pro *n.* [1990s+] (*US Black*) a low profile. [abbr.]

low quarters *n.* [1930s–70s] (*US Black*) Oxford shoes, with laces over the instep.

lowr *n. see* LOUR n.

low rate *v.* [20C+] (*US Black/Southern*) to attack verbally, to criticize, to denigrate, to ridicule.

lowre *n. see* LOUR n.

low rent *n.* [1960s+] (*US campus*) a worthless individual, or a promiscuous woman who sleeps around. [LOW-RENT adj.]

low-rent *adj.* [1950s+] (*orig. US*) cheap, distasteful, unfashionable.

lowride *n. see* LOWRIDER n.[2] (1).

lowride *v.* [1970s+] (*US*) to cruise the streets in a low-slung, customized car; thus **get low**, to ride in a car so that only one's head is visible. [LOWRIDER n.[2] (1)]

lowrider *n.*[1] [1930s+] (*US Black*) a pimp (cf. CANDYMAN n.). [his fig. 'lowriding' in the area of morals + ethics]

lowrider *n.*[2] (*US*) **1** [1960s+] (*also* **lowride**) a customized car, occas. motorcycle, that has been 'chopped and channelled' to lower the suspension and give it a generally sleeker look. **2** [1960s+] the driver of such a car. **3** [1970s+] a Chicano (amongst whom lowrider cars are popular). [since the driving of such cars is illegal, they are fitted with hydraulic systems to adjust the height of the car while driving, making it appear to bounce]

lowriding *n.* [1970s+] (*US*) cruising the streets in a low-slung, customized car. [LOWRIDE v.]

lowrie *n. see* LOUR n.

low-run *adj.* [1950s+] (*W.I.*) untrustworthy, hypocritical.

low tide *n.* (*also* **low water**) [late 17C–1920s] a state of financial difficulty; thus **be in low tide**. [the image of one's vessel being stranded by low tide]

low-toby *n.* [early–mid-19C] (*UK Und.*) highway robbery by footpads (rather than mounted highwaymen).

low-toby-man *n.* [19C] a footpad.

low water *n. see* LOW TIDE n.

lowy *n. see* LOWIE n.[1].

lowyer *n. see* LOUR n.

lox *n.* [1960s+] (*US*) a fool.

lox jock *n.* (*also* **lox jockey**) [1940s+] (*US*) a Jew (cf. ARAB n.[2]). [Yid. *laks*, thence SE *lox*, smoked salmon, served with cream cheese and bagels, a favourite Jewish dish]

loz *n.* [1990s+] (*drugs*) 1oz (28g) of cannabis. [? misreading of the numeral 1, pron. as the letter 'l' + *oz*, abbr. for 1 ounce]

lozenge *n.* (*also* **lozenger**) [1990s+] (*UK juv.*) the penis; thus a general insult. [? a fellatrix/fellator sucks it]

L.P. *n.* [1990s+] (*US gay*) said of a passing woman who is poss. a lesbian. [abbr. of *lesbian potential*]

L-7 *n.* (*also* **l-seven**) [1950s+] (*US Black/teen*) a conventional, tedious person, unsympathetic to teen interests. [the L and the 7 when put together form a *square* thus pun on SQUARE n.[1] (3); the word can be accompanied by a gesture extending the thumb and forefinger of each hand at right angles, forming an L and a 7, and when both are combined they form a square]

L-7 *adj.* (*also* **l-seven**) [1950s+] (*US Black/teen*) unfashionable, unsophisticated. [L-7 n.]

l.t.r. *n.* [1970s+] a *l*iving *t*ogether *r*elationship, marriage in all but the legalities. [abbr.]

L train *n. see* EL n.

lubber *n.* (*also* **lub**) [mid-14C–1940s] a fool. [? OF. *lobeor*, a swindler or parasite, ult. *lober*, to deceive, to sponge upon or to mock; it is the basis of the 16C naut. *land-lubber*, a landsman or incompetent sailor. The clumsiness implicit in the naut. use implies a further link to SE *lob*, a country bumpkin, ult. from a variety of Teut. forms all meaning heavy or clumsy. Note also 16C–19C SE *lubberland*, an imaginary land of plenty without labour, a land of laziness]

lubber *v.* [mid-19C] to hit. [? SE *belabour*]

lubberly *adj.* [mid-16C–19C; 1930s] stupid.

lube *n.* **1** [1940s+] (*Aus.*) a drink. **2** [1970s+] (*US*) (*also* **lubie**) a lubricated condom. **3** [1970s+] any form of lubricant, e.g. KY Jelly, used to facilitate (anal) sex. **4** [1970s+] (*US gay*) natural lubrication in sex, spec. from pre-semen. [SE *lubrication/lubricant*; note SE *lube*, abbr. of *lubricant*, used on machinery]

lube *v.* **1** [1930s+] to keep happy, to entertain. **2** [1950s] to bribe, to tip. **3** [1970s+] to apply a lubricant, such as KY Jelly, to facilitate (anal) sex. [fig. uses of SE *lubricate*]

lubed *adj. see* LUBRICATED adj.

lube job *n.* [1940s+] (*US*) oral or sexual intercourse. [the fluids thus generated + pun]

lube on *adj.* [1960s] (*US campus*) of a woman, sexually excited. [the lubrication of vaginal secretions]

lubie *n. see* LUBE n. (2).

lubra *n.* [mid-19C+] (*Aus.*) a woman, esp. an Aborigine woman. [Aboriginal *lubra*, a woman]

lubricate *v.* **1** [mid-18C–early 19C] to have sexual intercourse. **2** [late 19C+] to ply with drink. **3** [late 19C+] to drink. **4** [1920s] to bribe.

lubricated *adj.* (*also* **lubed**) [1910s+] (*orig. US*) drunk (cf. DAMP adj.). [LUBRICATE v. (3)]

lubricator *n.* [mid–late 19C] (*US*) a derog. name for a Mexican (cf. BATO n.).

luchini *n.* (*also* **lucci**) [2000s] (*US Black*) money.

luck *n.* (*also* **good luck**) [late 18C–early 19C] stepping into a heap of excrement. [pvb 'Shitten luck is good luck']

luck *v. see* LUCK (IT) v.

luck boy *n. see* LUCKY BOY n.

luck in *v.* (*also* **luck into/onto**) [1920s+] (*orig. US*) **1** to experience good luck. **2** to succeed through good luck.

luck (it) *v.* [1910s+] to take a chance, to succeed or manage something through luck, to come up with a stroke of luck.

luck of a Chow *n. see* CHINAMAN'S LUCK n.

luck of Eric Connolly *phr.* [1940s–60s] (*Aus.*) a description of any lucky person. [proper name of *Eric Connolly* (d.1944), known as an exceptionally lucky gambler]

luck onto *v. see* LUCK IN v.

luck out *n.* [1970s+] (*orig. US*) a piece of good luck. [LUCK OUT v.]

luck out *v.* [1940s+] (*orig. US*) to strike lucky.

luckpenny *n.* [20C+] (*Irish*) a token sum of money handed back to the buyer/seller on the completion of a deal. [on the same principle as that of never giving an empty wallet as a present]

luck through *v.* [1930s+] (*US*) to succeed or manage by good luck.

luck up (on) *v.* [1940s+] (*US Black*) to become lucky.

lucky as a shithouse rat *phr.* [1960s] (*US*) very fortunate.

lucky bag *n.* [19C] the vagina (cf. BAG n.¹). [fairground jargon *lucky bag*, a 'lucky dip']

lucky boy *n.* (*also* **luck boy**) [mid-19C+] (*US*) a crooked professional gambler.

lucky charm *n.* [1990s+] the human arm. [rhy. sl.]

lucky charms *n.* [2000s] (*drugs*) MDMA (cf. ECSTASY n.).

lucky dip *n.* **1** [20C+] a whip. **2** [20C+] in pl., chips, french fries. **3** [1980s+] (*Aus. prison*) LSD (cf. A n.³). [rhy. sl.; (3) = TRIP n.⁴ (2)]

lucky for some *n.* [20C+] (*bingo*) the number 13 (cf. ALDERSHOT LADIES n.).

lucky Pierre *n.* **1** [1940s+] the man in a sexual threesome of 2 women and 1 man; or the woman between 2 men. **2** [1960s+] (*gay*) the middle man in a 'sandwich' of 3 sexually entwined men. [? the punchline of a joke]

lucky shop *n.*¹ [mid-19C] a public house.

lucky shop *n.*² [1970s+] (*Aus.*) a Totalizator Agency Board (TAB) betting shop in Victoria.

Lucozade *n.* (*also* **Luco**, **Luke**) [1950s+] a Black person. [rhy. sl.; the brandname of the tonic drink *Lucozade* = SPADE n.]

lucy *n.*¹ [1950s–60s] (*US gay*) one who has a 'loose asshole'.

lucy *n.*² **1** [1950s+] (*US*) sweet wine. **2** [1950s+] marijuana (cf. AUNT MARY n.²). **3** [1980s+] heroin. **4** [1990s+] (*US Black*) a cigarette. [they all help one become SE *loose*, i.e. less tense, less stressed]

lucy in the sky with diamonds *n.* [1960s+] LSD (cf. A n.³). [the title of a Beatles song (1967), the initial letters (and the psychedelic lyrics) of which left no one in doubt – for all the band's disclaimers – as to its subject]

lucy law *n.* [1960s+] (*gay*) the police.

lucy locket *n.* (*also* **locket**) [1940s+] a pocket. [rhy. sl.]

lud! *excl.* [18C–1940s] a var. on SE *Lord!* and similarly used in mild oaths.

ludby *n. see* LOTEBY n.

lude *n.* (*also* **ludes**, **luds**) [1970s+] (*US drugs*) methaqualone, or other depressant drugs; thus *ludehead*, a habitual user of the drug. [brandname *Quaalude*, manufactured until 1983]

lude out *v.* [1980s+] (*US campus*) to become unable to function, usu. because of drugs. [LUDE n. + SE *out*]

Ludgate bird *n.* [17C] a bankrupt, one who has been imprisoned for bankruptcy. [*Ludgate* prison, which housed mainly debtors]

luds *n. see* LUDE n.

Lud's bulwark *n.* [late 17C–early 19C] Ludgate prison (cf. ABBOTT'S PRIORY n.). [statues of the mythical King *Lud* and his sons used to stand on this old London gate, which the king had supposedly erected in 66BC, but it was more likely a Roman gate. Brewer, *Dict. of Phrase and Fable* (1894) suggests Ludgate comes from OE *ludgeat*, a postern, while E.P. opts for Norse *ludden*, thick, broad]

Lud's unlucky gate *n.* [17C] Ludgate prison, mainly used for debtors (cf. ABBOTT'S PRIORY n.). [for ety. see prev.]

luego *phr.* [1980s+] (*US campus*) goodbye. [Sp. *hasta luego*]

luer *n.* [1930s–50s] (*US drugs*) a hypodermic syringe. [proprietary name *Luer* brand syringe]

luff *n.* [early–late 19C] speech, talk. [echoic of a puff of wind, i.e. that expelled while talking]

l.u.g. *n.* [1990s+] (*orig. US campus*) a female student who is not necessarily a lesbian, but who experiments with feminism and lesbian politics and culture. [abbr. *lesbian until graduation*]

lug *n.*¹ [late 16C+] an ear; thus *lugful*, a sufficiency in being talked to, or in overhearing. [Scot./northern dial.]

lug *n.*² (*orig. US*) **1** [late 19C+] a large, stupid man. **2** [1930s] a lout, a sponger. **3** [1930s+] a general term of abuse. [SE *lug*, to drag, to haul. Such a heavyweight would need to be dragged along, mentally or physically. Note Scot. *luggie*, awkward, sluggish; mid-16C SE *lug*, something heavy and clumsy may be only coincidental]

lug *n.*³ *see* PUT THE LUG ON v.

lug *v.*¹ **1** [19C] to pawn; thus IN LUG *phr.* **2** [20C+] (*orig. US*) to beg. **3** [1930s] (*US*) to extend credit. **4** [1960s+] (*US Black*) to berate, to criticize harshly. [LUG n.[1]; esp. in phr. *bite someone's lug* (see BITE SOMEONE'S EAR v.)]

lug v.[2] **1** [mid-19C+] to escort someone, to bring along a companion. **2** [20C+] to arrest or imprison. **3** [1900s–40s] (*US Und.*) to lure a victim into a confidence game. [SE *lug*, to drag]

lug v.[3] [1950s–70s] (*US Und.*) to beat up. [? LUG n.[1], as in *OED*; however, *HDAS* suggests that this *lug* could poss. be a separate word]

lug v.[4] [1970s+] (*Can./US prison*) to make into a homosexual. [PUT THE LUG ON v. (2)]

Lugan n. see LUGEN n.

lugan n. see LOOGAN n.

lug-bashing n. [1950s] (*Aus.*) talking effusively, preaching. [LUG n.[1]; var. on EARBASHING n. (1)]

lug-bite n. [late 19C–1930s] (*Aus.*) to cadge, to ask for a loan; thus *lug-biter*, a cadger. [LUG n.[1] + SE *bite*]

lug chovey n. [mid–late 19C] a pawnshop. [IN LUG phr. + CHOVEY n.]

luge adj. [1990s+] (*W.I.*) huge, massive.

Lugen n. (*also* **Loogin, Lugan, Lugie, Lugun**) [1940s+] (*US*) a Lithuanian or person of Lithuanian background. [? LOOGAN n. or *Lithuanian*]

lugful n. see LUG n.[1]

luggage n.[1] [late 19C+] the male genitals. [pun on BAG n.[1] (1)]

luggage n.[2] [1970s+] (*US teen*) bags under the eyes. [pun on SE *bags*]

lugger n.[1] [1920s–40s] (*Aus.*) **1** a shameless beggar. **2** a nag, one who criticizes. [LUG v.[1]]

lugger n.[2] **1** [1920s+] (*US Und.*) an accomplice who makes contact with an intended victim or punter, also in a shoplifting team. **2** [1920s+] (*US Und.*) the accomplice (there are usu. 2) who helps the actual thief remove the stolen goods from the store. **3** [1960s+] (*Can. prison*) a smuggler of contraband in or out of the prison. [LUG v.[2] (3)]

luggers n. [mid–late 19C] earrings. [LUG n.[1]]

lugging session n. see WOOFING SESSION n.

lughead n. [1940s+] (*US*) a stupid person. [LUG n.[2] (1) + -HEAD sfx (1)]

lughole n. [20C+] an ear. [dial./LUG n.[1]]

Lugie n. see LUGEN n.

lug out v. **1** [late 17C–mid-18C] to draw a sword. **2** [late 19C] (*US*) to draw a gun. [SE *lug*, to drag (out)]

lugow v. [mid-19C–1930s] (*Anglo-Ind.*) to fasten, to place. [Hind. *lugana*, to attach, to join, to fix]

lugs n. [late 19C–1930s] (*US*) affected manners, posing, pride; usu. in *pile/put on lugs*, to put on airs, to act affectedly.

lug someone's ear v. [20C+] (*Aus.*) to borrow money. [SE *lug*, to drag, to pull]

Lugun n. see LUGEN n.

Luke n. see LUCOZADE n.

luke n. [early–mid-19C] nothing. [? northern dial.]

Luke and Matt Goss n. [1990s+] an infinitesimal amount; nothing whatsoever. [rhy. sl. = TOSS n.[1] (1); ult. *Luke and Matt Goss*, the brothers that made up 1980s pop duo *Bros*]

lukshen n. (*also* **loksh**) [20C+] (*US*) an Italian, as used by Jews (cf. DAGO n.). [Yid. *lokshen*, noodles]

lull n. [mid-17C] ale. [SE *lull*, a soothing drink]

lullaby n. [mid–late 19C] the penis. [it 'puts one to sleep']

lullaby-cheat n. [mid-17C–mid-19C] (*UK Und.*) a child. [SE *lullaby* + CHEAT n. (1), lit. 'lullaby-thing']

lullo-bump n. [1990s+] (*W.I.*) clitoris (cf. BABY IN THE BOAT n.).

lully n. (*also* **lally, lulley**) [mid-17C–19C] (*UK Und.*) **1** wet or drying linen. **2** a shirt. [? SE *laundry* or *lilywhite*]

lully prigger n. [mid-18C–19C] **1** one who steals washing from washing lines or from wherever it has been put out to dry. **2** a thief who catches a child and strips it of its clothing. [LULLY n. + PRIG v.[2] (1)]

lully-prigging n. [mid-18C–19C] (*UK Und.*) the theft of washing. [LULLY n. + PRIG v.[2] (1)]

lulu n.[1] (*also* **looloo, looly, luluh**) **1** [mid-19C–1930s] (*orig. US*) a girlfriend, a gangster's girlfriend. **2** [1950s] a silly young woman. [the proper name, seen as somewhat exotic]

lulu n.[2] (*also* **looloo, looly, loulou**) **1** [mid-19C+] (*orig. US*) anything, or anyone, remarkable, exceptional, wonderful. **2** [late 19C+] (*orig. US*) a disaster, an abject failure or a foolish person. **3** [late 19C+] (*US gambling*) a remarkable poker hand that beats a royal flush. [ety. unknown; (3) is ironic use of (1)]

lulu n.[3] [1930s+] the lavatory. [LOO n.[1]]

lulu n.[4] [1950s] (*US Und.*) a venereally diseased penis; a severe case of gonorrhoea. **2** [2000s] the female genital area.

lulu adj. [1970s+] notable. [LULU n.[2] (1)]

luluh n. see LULU n.[1].

lulyah lass n. see HALLELUJAH LASS n.

lumb adv. [late 18C–early 19C] (*UK Und.*) too much. [? LUMBERED adj.[2] (1)]

lumber n.[1] **1** [early 17C–mid-19C] a pawnshop. **2** [early 17C–mid-19C] the state of being in pawn. **3** [mid-18C] stolen goods. **4** [mid-18C+] a house or room, esp. one used for storing stolen goods. **5** [late 18C–mid-19C] anywhere frequented by confidence tricksters and similar villains. **6** [1940s–80s] the flat from which a prostitute works, but which she does not occupy as a home. [17C SE *Lombard*, a bank, money-changer's or money-lender's office, a pawnshop. The Lombards, or natives of Lombardy, were celebrated bankers; thus the medieval *Lombard Room*, where pawnbrokers and bankers stored their pledges]

lumber n.[2] **1** [1950s] a scheme, usu. criminal, an example of criminal activity. **2** [1960s+] sexual play, petting. **3** [1960s+] (*mainly Scot.*) a prospective sexual partner, a casual pick-up. **4** [2000s] violence, a fight. [? dial. *lumber*, mischief]

lumber n.[3] [1970s+] (*US*) the penis. [pun on WOOD n.[4] (1)]

lumber n.[4] [1970s+] (*US drugs*) unwanted twiggy stems in marijuana (cf. AFRICAN BUSH n.).

lumber n.[5] see LUMBER (SAUCE) n.

lumber v.[1] **1** [19C] to pawn. **2** [early 19C+] (*orig. Aus.*) to arrest, to imprison. [LUMBER n.[1]]

lumber v.[2] **1** [mid-19C+] to court, to 'chat up'; esp. with the intention of robbing the victim; thus LUMBER GAFF n. **2** [1930s+] (*mainly Scot./Ulster*) to fondle sexually, to have intercourse. **3** [1930s+] to take, to escort. **4** [1950s] to steal. [LUMBER n.[2]]

lumber v.[3] [late 19C+] to burden with.

lumber cove n. [late 18C–mid-19C] (*UK Und.*) the landlord of a thieves' meeting-place. [LUMBER n.[1] (5) + COVE n. (1)]

lumbered adj.[1] **1** [early 19C+] pawned. **2** [early 19C+] (*Aus./UK Und.*) arrested. **3** [mid-19C+] imprisoned. **4** [1950s+] short of money, indebted. [LUMBER v.[1]]

lumbered adj.[2] **1** [mid-19C+] burdened with, trapped. **2** [late 19C+] defeated, in trouble. [SE *lumber*, to weigh down, to fill up with; ult. *lumber*, useless, space-consuming objects]

lumberer n.[1] **1** [mid-18C] a poor prostitute. **2** [mid-18C–early 19C] a tramp, a vagrant. [SE *lumber*, i.e. they are forced to sleep on piles of timber]

lumberer n.[2] **1** [mid–late 19C] a pawnbroker. **2** [late 19C] a swindling tipster. **3** [late 19C–1910s] any form of swindler. **4** [1900s–60s] a prostitute or pimp who specializes in robbing her/his clients. [LUMBER v.[1]]

lumber gaff n. (*also* **lumber joint**) [1930s–80s] the flat from which a prostitute works but which she does not occupy as a home. [LUMBER n.[1] (6) + GAFF n.[1] (8)]

lumber house n. (*also* **lumber ken**) **1** [18C–mid-19C] a drinking tavern frequented by confidence tricksters. **2** [mid-19C] a pawnbroker's shop. [LUMBER n.[1] + SE *shop*]

lumberjack n.[1] [1990s+] the human back. [rhy. sl.; pun on SE *lumbar*]

lumberjack n.[2] [1990s+] a homosexual. [Monty Python sketch with the Lumberjack Song, 'I'm a lumberjack and I'm okay', featuring transvestite lumberjacks]

lumber-Jill n. [1940s+] an unattractive woman, with whom one cannot achieve an erection. [a woman that looks like an SE *lumberjack*]

lumber joint n. see LUMBER GAFF n.

lumber ken n. see LUMBER HOUSE n.

lumber out v. [20C+] (*Aus.*) to throw out, to eject. [LUMBER v.[1] + SE *out*]

lumber (sauce) n. [1930s–60s] (*US*) a toothpick. [SE *lumber*, wood]

Lumbo n. [1970s] (*drugs*) Colombian marijuana (cf. ACAPULCO (GOLD) n.). [abbr.]

luminous reader n. see READER n. (2).

lumme! excl. (*also* lordlummy! lor lumme! lummy!) [late 19C+] an excl. of surprise, shock, disbelief. [abbr. LORD LOVE ME! excl.]

lummocks n. (*also* lommix, lummix, lummock, lummokin, lummox, lummux) [mid-19C+] a large, heavy or clumsy person, an ungainly or stupid lout; a fool. [dial. *lummock*, to move heavily or clumsily]

lummy adj. [19C] excellent; thus *lummy lick*, a delicious mouthful; *lumminess*, pleasant things. [Yorks. dial.]

lummy! excl. see LUMME! excl.

Lump, the n. [late 19C–1930s] the workhouse, the casual ward, esp. the Marylebone workhouse; ext. as *Lump Hotel*. [? its occupants are 'lumped together']

lump n.[1] **1** [early 16C+] (*also* lumps) a lot, a large quantity. **2** [early 19C+] (*Irish*) a good size, usu. of a child. [(1) *lumps* is 16C; *lump* late 17C+]

lump n.[2] [mid-19C] (*US*) a gold coin.

lump n.[3] [late 19C–1930s] (*US*) semen; usu. in phrs. *blow one's lump*, *toss one's lump*, to achieve orgasm (also of women) (cf. BOLLOCK SNOT n.).

lump n.[4] [late 19C+] (*US*) a parcel of food given to a tramp or vagrant. [dial. *lump*, a luncheon]

lump n.[5] [1940s+] (*US campus*) a lazy idler. [LUMP v.[4]]

lump n.[6] [1960s] the head.

lump v.[1] [late 18C+] (*orig. US*) to accept something, however grudgingly, that has to be endured; usu. as *lump it*, esp. in phr. LIKE IT OR LUMP IT v. [SE *lump*, to look sulky or disagreeable]

lump v.[2] (*also* lump up) **1** [late 18C+] to beat; to punch, to hit. **2** [1950s] (*US*) to murder. **3** [1950s+] (*US*) to hit someone over the head with a lump of stone or a brick. [SE *lump*, to beat or thresh]

lump v.[3] [mid-19C+] to haul about, to carry a heavy weight. [LUMPER n.[2] (1)]

lump v.[4] (*also* lump up) [1940s+] (*US campus*) to act lazily, to do nothing.

lump v.[5] [1970s+] (*US*) to defecate (cf. CACA v.).

lump and bump n. [late 19C–1930s] a fool, a simpleton (cf. BEECHAM'S PILL n.). [rhy. sl. = CHUMP n.[1] (2)]

lumper n.[1] (*also* knockabout hand) **1** [late 18C–19C] a riverside thief. **2** [late 18C–1940s] the 'lowest order and more contemptible species' of thief who lurk and grab whatever they can, regardless of value. **3** [mid-19C] a seller of goods under false pretences, the old made to look new, the weak strong etc. **4** [1950s] (*US prison*) a convict who is an orderly. [SE *lumper*, a labourer employed in loading and unloading cargoes, esp. timber (cited as sl. in Grose, 1785)]

lumper n.[2] **1** [late 18C+] a contractor or a worker who loads and unloads heavy cargo, orig. ship's cargo. **2** [mid-late 19C] a small contractor, a middleman, an exploitative factory owner.

lumper n.[3] [mid-19C] a militiaman. [his stolidity and/or the weight of his equipment and pack; note dial. *lumper*, of a horse to walk heavily; of a man, to stumble]

lumper n.[4] [1980s+] (*US*) a piece of excrement. [SE *lump*]

lumpers n. [1950s–60s] a lump sum paid as unemployment compensation.

lumphead n. [1910s–60s] (*orig. US*) an absolute fool, an idiot, an incompetent. [SE *lump* + -HEAD sfx (1)]

lumping adj. **1** [late 17C–19C] great, large; often as *lumping bargain* or LUMPING PENNYWORTH n. **2** [mid-19C+] of people or objects, big, heavy, ungainly, unwieldy.

lumping pennyworth n. [late 17C–mid-19C] a good bargain; thus [late 18C–early 19C] *get/have a lumping pennyworth*, to marry a fat woman.

lump of bread n. see LUMP OF LEAD n. (1).

lump of chalk v. see BALL OF CHALK v.

lump of coke n. [mid-19C] a man, a person. [rhy. sl. = BLOKE n. (1)]

lump of ice n. [late 19C–1900s] advice. [rhy. sl.]

lump of lead n. **1** [mid-19C+] (*also* lump of bread) the head. **2** [1950s–60s] a hangover. **3** [2000s] (*Aus.*) bread. [rhy. sl.]

lump of meat n. see MEAT n. (2).

lump of school n. [late 19C–1900s] a fool (cf. BEECHAM'S PILL n.). [rhy. sl.]

lump of soap n. [late 19C–1900s] a woman. [SE *lump* + SOAP n.[4]]

lump of stone n. [late 19C–1900s] (*UK Und.*) a local prison (i.e. one outside London).

lump of stuff n. see BIT OF STUFF n. (1).

lumps n.[1] [1930s+] (*US*) a beating, punishment, blame or criticisms; usu. as *give someone their lumps* or TAKE ONE'S LUMPS v.

lumps n.[2] [1940s+] (*US*) the female breasts (cf. BAGS n.[1]).

lumps n.[3] see LUMP n.[1] (1).

lumps and bumps n. [1980s+] (*Aus. prison*) a convict who loses a lot of fights.

lump the lighter v. [late 18C–19C] to be transported. [fig. use of SE *lump*, to load + *lighter*, a vessel used for loading/unloading ships]

lump up v.[1] see LUMP v.[2].

lump up v.[2] see LUMP v.[4].

lumpus n. [1900s] (*US*) a clumsy person.

lumpy adj. [early 19C–1900s] tipsy, slightly drunk. [dial. *lumpy*, awkward, sluggish]

lumpy chicken phr. [1960s+] (*orig. US milit.*) loud and clear. [initial letters]

lumpy-roar n. [mid–late 19C] a grandee, an aristocrat, 'a swell of the first water' (Ware). [Fr. *l'empereur*, emperor, which gained popularity during the visit to the UK of Napoleon III in 1853]

lumpy work n. [1910s] (*US*) unacceptable behaviour.

lun n. [late 18C–early 19C] Harlequin, the *commedia dell'arte* stock character. [the stagename *Lun* of admired Harlequin-actor John Rich (1692–1761); ? itself f. LOON n.[1]]

lunachick n. [1990s+] (*US campus*) a crazy woman. [pun on SE *lunatic*]

lunan n. [mid–late 19C] (*UK tramp*) a woman. [Rom. *loobni*, a prostitute]

lunar n. [late 19C–1950s] a look, a glance; thus *take a lunar*, to glance at. [abbr. SE *lunar observation*]

lunatic soup n. (*also* lunatic's broth) [20C+] (*Aus./Irish/N.Z.*) **1** cheap alcohol; spec. cheap red wine. **2** methylated spirits as drunk by alcoholics.

lunch n.[1] [1900s] (*US*) a certainty, e.g. in betting.

lunch n.[2] **1** [1900s–10s] (*US*) the stomach. **2** [1910s+] (*US*) the contents of the stomach; as in LOSE ONE'S LUNCH v. **3** [1930s] (*US*) a lunch counter. **4** [1950s+] something/someone who is about to suffer or be physically hurt, or is already ruined. [(4) is only good to serve as food for some large predator]

lunch n.[3] **1** [1920s–30s] cunnilingus (cf. BOX LUNCH n.). **2** [1940s+] the penis. **3** [1970s+] (*US gay*) the bulge of the male genitals under the trousers.

lunch n.[4] (also **lunchie**) [1960s+] (US campus) a dull, stupid person, a fool. [OUT TO LUNCH phr. (2)]

lunch n.[5] [2000s+] a bonus, a profit. [on the pattern of DRINK n.[3] (2)]

lunch n.[6] see BASKET LUNCH n.

lunch adj. **1** [1960s+] stupid, foolish, crazy. **2** [1990s+] good, excellent, admirable. [OUT TO LUNCH phr. (2)]

lunch v.[1] [1950s+] (US campus) to spoil, to ruin, to fail. [LUNCH n.[2] (4)]

lunch v.[2] **1** [1980s+] (US campus) to lack concentration, to be unaware. **2** [1980s+] (US Black/teen) to act in a silly or irrational manner, to overreact; to procrastinate. **3** [1990s+] (US Black) to go insane. [OUT TO LUNCH phr.]

lunch at the lazy Y v. [1950s+] (US) to perform cunnilingus (cf. BOX LUNCH n.). [Y n./the Y of spread legs]

lunchbag n. (also **lunchbox, lunchbucket, lunchpail, lunchsack**) [1950s+] (US campus) a dull, foolish person, an undesirable person. [one who is OUT TO LUNCH phr.; note OnLine Dict. of Playground Slang (2001): 'from people who brought lunch to school in a bag, then went off to sit and eat it alone because no-one liked them', i.e. ext. of BAG n.[10]]

lunch-basket n. (also **lunch-wagon**) [1910s] the stomach.

lunchbox n.[1] [1970s] (US Black) the stomach.

lunchbox n.[2] (also **lunchpack**) [1980s+] the male genitals, esp. when large and prominent beneath tight shorts or trousers. [famously used of the athlete Linford Christie (b.1960)]

lunchbox n.[3] see LUNCHBAG n.

lunchbox lancer n. [1990s+] a male homosexual (cf. BONE-EATER n.). [LUNCHBOX n.[2]/LUNCHBOX n.[1] + SE lancer]

lunchbucket n. see LUNCHBAG n.

lunchbucket adj.[1] [1950s+] (US) working-class, blue-collar. [LUNCHPAIL n.[1]]

lunchbucket adj.[2] [1950s+] (US) stupid, dull, uninspiring. [LUNCHBUCKET n.]

lunchcounter n. (also **lunchpails**) [1960s] (US) the female breasts (cf. BORDENS n.). [their provision of milk]

lunched-out adj. [1970s+] (US) dazed, unaware, stupid. [OUT TO LUNCH phr. (2)]

lunch gut n. [1950s+] (drugs) the vomiting that may follow an injection of heroin.

lunch hooks n. **1** [late 19C–1900s] (US campus) the teeth. **2** [late 19C+] (orig. US) the hand or fingers. [SE lunch hook, a hook used to remove meat from the pot]

lunchie n. see LUNCH n.[4].

lunching adj. [1990s+] crazy, stupid. [LUNCH v.[2]]

lunchmeat n. **1** [1970s+] (US campus) a stupid, contemptible person. **2** [1970s+] (US gay) the bulge of the genitals through the trousers. **3** [1980s+] (US) nonsense. **4** [1990s+] (US) a victim.

lunchpack n. see LUNCHBOX n.[2].

lunchpail n.[1] (also **lunchpailer**) [1950s+] (orig. US) a blue-collar worker. [metonymy]

lunchpail n.[2] see LUNCHBAG n.

lunchpails n. see LUNCHCOUNTER n.

lunchsack n. see LUNCHBAG n.

lunch-wagon n. see LUNCH-BASKET n.

lunchy adj. [1960s+] (US campus) **1** dull, stupid, absent-minded. **2** carefree, light-hearted, jokey. **3** unfashionable, out of style. [OUT TO LUNCH phr.]

lung n. [1980s+] (drugs) a form of pipe used for smoking cannabis. [a 2-litre plastic bottle with a polythene bag attached to the bottom, when the bag is pulled out of the bottle it fills up with smoke]

lung v. [1900s] (US campus) to argue.

lung biscuit n. [1980s] (US campus) a lump of phlegm.

lung-box n. [mid–late 19C] the mouth.

lungbuster n. [1980s+] (Aus./N.Z.) a cigarette.

lung-disturber n. [20C+] the penis (cf. ARSE-OPENER n.).

lung-duster n. [1920s–40s] (US Black) a cigarette.

lunger n. (US) **1** [late 19C+] one who is suffering from lung disease (i.e. tuberculosis) or has been wounded in the lungs. **2** [1940s+] a mouthful of spit, a gob of phlegm.

lungers n. see LUNGS n.[2].

lung hammock n. [1980s+] (US) a brassiere. [LUNGS n.[2] + SE hammock]

lungs n.[1] [late 17C–mid-18C] a powerfully voiced person. [note SE lungs, the fire-blower for a chemist]

lungs n.[2] (also **lungers**) [1930s+] (orig. US) the female breasts; occas. in sing.

lungs, the n. [1950s] (US) tuberculosis.

lung warts n. [1940s+] (US) the female breasts, esp. when small.

lunie n. see LOONY n.

lunk n. (US) **1** [mid-19C+] a fool. **2** [1950s+] an oaf, an ungainly person. [abbr. LUNKHEAD n.]

lunk adj. [late 19C+] (Irish) **1** of weather, close, sultry. **2** of a person, feeling ill. [Scot. lunkie, close; ult. Norwegian lunke, a tepid degree of heat]

lunker n.[1] [mid-19C+] (US) an animal or fish considered more than usu. large for its species. [ety. unknown]

lunker n.[2] [1970s+] (US) a dilapidated motor car. [? CLUNKER n.[1] (1) or LUNKER n.[1]]

lunkhead n. [mid-19C+] (orig. US) an absolute fool, an idiot, an incompetent. [? SE lump + -HEAD sfx (1)]

lunkheaded adj. [late 19C+] slow-witted, foolish (cf. AIRHEADED adj.). [LUNKHEAD n.]

lunky adj. [1940s+] (US) stupid. [LUNKHEAD n.]

luny see under LOONY.

luokal-mediocal n. [1950s] (W.I.) an undependable, untrustworthy person. [W.I. pron. of SE local mediocre]

luppies n. [1990s+] **1** (US gay) lesbian urban professionals, i.e. lesbian yuppies. **2** (US) Latino/Latina urban professionals, i.e. Hispanic yuppies. [abbr.]

luptious adj. [mid-19C–1900s] delicious, luscious, lovely. [SE voluptuous + delicious]

lur-a-cham n. see LERACAM n.

lurch n. [mid-16C+] a cheat or swindle; often ext. as give the lurch; thus in one's lurch, at a disadvantage; have/take at/in lurch, to have at a disadvantage; leave in the lurch, to abandon in difficulty without assistance. [LURCH v.[1]]

lurch v.[1] [mid-16C+] to deceive, to get the better of. [MHGer. lurz, left, wrong, thence lurzen, to deceive. The Ger. appears to have been adopted into Fr. as lourche, the name of a game similar to backgammon, and in its heyday equally popular in Britain, in which a lurch meant a game in which one player defeats an opponent to a score of zero. Those who lose a game of whist without scoring 5 are lurched]

lurch v.[2] [2000s] (Irish) to dance very close together.

lurcher n. [20C+] **1** (Aus.) a rascal, a villain. **2** (Aus.) a Bohemian, one who acts without regard for social convention. **3** (Ulster) one who lurks around waiting for an advantage to present itself. [SE lurcher, a swindler, a rogue; (2) LARRIKIN n.]

lurcher (of the law) n. [18C–early 19C] the lowest rank of bailiff, a 'bum bailiff'. [dial. lurch, to lurk or slink about]

lure n. [late 17C–18C] 'an idle pamphlet' (B.E.). [SE lure, anything that tempts or entices]

lured adj. [20C+] (Ulster) happy, cheerful.

lurgi n. (also **lurgy**) [1940s+] any unspecified but deleterious disease or ailment; esp. as the minatory phr. dreaded lurgi. [popularly attrib. to the writers of The Goon Show (1953–60), but the EDD cites lurgy, idleness, loafing + lurgy-fever, the 'disease' of idleness. The OED adds the synon. fever-lurden, fever-lurgan, ult. SE fever + lurdan, 'a general term of opprobrium, reproach, or abuse, implying either dullness and incapacity, or idleness and rascality; a sluggard, vagabond, "loafer"']

lurid limit n. see DIZZY LIMIT n.

lurk *n.* **1** [early–late 19C] (*UK Und.*) a form of fraud in which one pretends some form of distress in order to raise money from the credulous; thus *go on a lurk*, get money through false pretences. **2** [mid-19C+] a hideaway, a meeting place; thus *servant lurk*, a public house where duplicitous servants meet criminals to plan mutually beneficial robberies. **3** [mid-19C+] (*Aus./N.Z.*) a dodge, racket or scheme; thus *up to all lurks*, wide-awake, cunning. **4** [late 19C+] (*Aus./N.Z.*) a job. **5** [20C+] (*Aus.*) a hanger-on, an eavesdropper. **6** [1950s–60s] (*Aus.*) the best place to meet someone or find some product or whatever. [SE *lurk*, to hide oneself, to lie in ambush, to remain furtively or unobserved about one spot]

lurk *v.* [1960s] (*US Black*) to go riding in a stolen car. [SE *lurk*, i.e. one tends to adopt a 'low profile' while driving in this way]

lurker *n.* **1** [mid–late 19C] a criminal beggar who travels the country showing off various forged certificates referring to losses in fires, shipwrecks or similar disasters and hoping thereby to get financial aid. **2** [20C+] (*Aus.*) a petty criminal. [LURK n.]

lurkie *n.* [1940s+] (*Aus.*) a cunning, knowing, 'wide-awake' person, up to any trick. [LURK n. (3)]

lurking *n.* [mid-19C] (*UK Und.*) **1** stealing. **2** fraudulent begging, following the occupation of a fraudulent beggar. [LURK n. (1)]

lurkman *n.* [mid-19C+] (*Aus.*) a confidence trickster, a petty criminal. [LURK n. (1) + sfx *-man*]

lurkola *n.* [1950s+] (*Aus.*) the practice (ostensibly illegal and generally denied by its practitioners) of bribing (with cash or kind) those with access to the public to tout a product. [LURK n. (1) + -OLA sfx]

lurky *adj.* [1970s+] (*US campus*) seedy, untrustworthy, weird. [SE *lurk*]

lurp *n.* [1990s+] (*US teen*) an extremely clumsy or awkward person. [play on SE *lurch*]

lurpy *adj.* [1990s+] rubbish, looking bad or ugly. [LURP n.]

lurries *n.* (*UK Und.*) **1** [mid-17C–mid-18C] clothes. **2** [mid-17C–early 19C] a quantity of valuables, e.g. watches and rings. [LURRY n.]

lurry *n.* [mid-17C–mid-18C] money. [LOUR n.]

lurry into/up *v. see* LORRY UP v.

lurve nest *n. see* LOVE NEST n.

lus *n.* [1970s+] (*S.Afr.*) a yearning, a longing; thus *be lus for*, to long for. [Afk. *lus vir*, desirous of]

lush *n.*[1] (*also* **lusho**) **1** [late 17C+] alcohol, esp. beer. **2** [mid–late 19C] a drink. **3** [mid-19C+] a drunkard. **4** [mid-19C+] a drinking spree. **5** [2000s] in fig. use, an addict. [? Ger. *Loschen*, strong beer, Shelta *lush*, to eat and drink]

lush *n.*[2] [mid–late 19C] (*US Und.*) money. [? SE *luscious*]

lush *n.*[3] **1** [1940s–50s] (*US gay*) an extremely attractive heterosexual man. **2** [1980s+] (*US campus*) an attractive woman. [SE *luscious*]

lush *n.*[4] [1940s–60s] (*US*) a victim or fool. [fig. use of LUSH n.[1] (3)]

lush *adj.*[1] [early 19C+] drunk (cf. ALED UP adj.). [LUSH v.[1] (1)]

lush *adj.*[2] **1** [1910s+] of a woman, very sexually attractive, esp. if voluptuous, also of a man. **2** [1950s+] good, excellent. [SE *luscious*]

lush *adj.*[3] (*US*) **1** [1930s–40s] wealthy. **2** [1940s+] hedonistic, luxurious. [LUSH n.[2]]

lush *v.*[1] (*also* **lush it**) **1** [19C–1900s] to ply with drink, to make drunk. **2** [early 19C+] to drink. [LUSH n.[1] (1)]

lush *v.*[2] *see* LUSH ROLL v.

lush around *v. see* LUSH (IT) UP v. (1).

lush at Freeman's Quay *v. see* DRINK AT FREEMAN'S QUAY v.

lush betty *n.* [mid-19C] (*US*) a whisky bottle. [LUSH n.[1] (1) + BETTY n.[1] (2)]

lush bint *n. see* BINT n. (1).

lush blowen *n. see* LUSHY COVE n.

lushbum *n.* [1940s] (*US*) an alcoholic tramp. [LUSH n.[1] (1) + BUM n.[3] (1)]

lush cove *n. see* LUSHY COVE n.

lush crib *n.* (*also* **lushing crib**) [19C] a saloon or bar. [LUSH n.[1] (1) + CRIB n.[1] (2)]

lush dip *n. see* LUSH WORKER n.

lush dip *v. see* LUSH ROLL v.

lush diver *n. see* LUSH WORKER n.

lush drum *n.* [mid–late 19C] (*UK Und./US*) a saloon or bar. [LUSH n.[1] (1) + DRUM n.[3] (4)]

lushed *adj.* [19C+] drunk (cf. ALED UP adj.). [LUSH v.[1]]

lushed up *adj.* **1** [1920s+] drunk (cf. ALED UP adj.). **2** [1950s] intoxicated by drugs. [ext. of LUSHED adj.]

lusher *n.*[1] **1** [mid-19C–1950s] (*US*) a heavy drinker, a drunk. **2** [1910s–30s] a prostitute who preys on drunken customers. [LUSH v.[1]]

lusher *n.*[2] *see* LUSH WORKER n.

lushery *n.* [late 19C] a saloon or bar. [LUSH n.[1] (1)]

lush grafter *n. see* LUSH WORKER n.

lush-head *n.* [1930s–60s] (*US*) a drunkard. [LUSH n.[1] (1) + -HEAD sfx (3)]

lush hound *n.* [1930s–50s] a drunkard. [LUSH n.[1] (1) + HOUND sfx]

lush-house *n.* [late 19C–1920s] a bar or saloon. [LUSH n.[1] (1) + SE *house*]

lushie *n. see* LUSHY n.

lushing *n.* [mid-19C+] drinking, usu. to excess. [LUSH v.[1]]

lushing *adj.* [mid–late 19C] used of a person who enjoys drinking. [LUSH v.[1]]

lushing crib *n. see* LUSH CRIB n.

lushing ken *n.* (*also* **lush ken**) [late 18C–1920s] (*UK/US Und.*) an alehouse, saloon or bar. [LUSH n.[1] (1) + KEN n.[1] (1)]

lushing-man *n.* [mid-19C–1900s] (*mainly US*) a drunkard. [LUSH v.[1] + SE *man*]

Lushington *n.* (*also* **alderman Lushington, lushington**) [19C] a drunkard; thus *dealing with Lushington, Alderman Lushington is concerned, voting for the Alderman, Lushington is his master*, to be drinking too much or to be drunk. [either LUSH n.[1] (1), or the proper name *Lushington* (a brewer), or f. 'The "City of Lushington"' which, according to the *OED*, 'was the name of a convivial society (consisting chiefly of actors) which met at the Harp Tavern, Russell Street, until about 189?. It had a "Lord Mayor" and four "aldermen", presiding over "wards" called Juniper, Poverty, Lunacy, and Suicide. On the admission of a new member, the "Lord Mayor" [...] harangued him on the evils of excess in drink.' The society was founded *c.*1750]

lush it *v. see* LUSH v.[1].

lush (it) up *v.* **1** [late 19C+] (*also* **lush around**) to drink, usu. alcohol; to become drunk. **2** [1920s+] to ply with drink. [LUSH v.[1]]

lush ken *n. see* LUSHING KEN n.

lush kick *n.* [1950s] (*US*) a sense of drunkenness; the positive effect of alcohol. [LUSH adj.[1] + KICK n.[5] (1)]

lush merchant *n.* [late 19C+] (*Aus.*) a drunkard. [LUSH n.[1] (1) + MERCHANT n.]

lusho *n. see* LUSH n.[1].

lush-out *n.* [early 19C–1900s] a drinking bout. [LUSH n.[1] (4) + SE *out*]

lushpad *n.* [1940s] (*US Black/Harlem*) a bar. [LUSH n.[1] (1) + PAD n.[2] (2)]

lush panny *n.* [19C] a bar, a saloon, a tavern. [LUSH n.[1] (1) + PANNEY n.[2] (1)]

lush roll *v.* (*also* **lush, lush dip**) [1910s–80s] (*orig. US*) to rob a drunk. [LUSH n.[1] (3) + ROLL v.[4] (1)]

lush roller *n.* [1910s–60s] (*US*) one who specializes in robbing sleeping or passed-out drunks, esp. in subways. [LUSH ROLL v.]

lush stash *n.* [1900s–40s] (*US Black*) a bar, a tavern. [LUSH n.[1] (1) + STASH n.[2] (3)]

lush thrush *n.* [1940s–50s] a very attractive young woman. [LUSH adj.[2] (1) + SE *thrush*]

lush-toucher *n.* [1900s–40s] (*US*) a person who robs a drunk. [LUSH n.[1] (3) + SE *toucher*]

lush trotter *n.* [19C] (*orig. US*) a boy or girl who is sent to the saloon to bring back beer either for their parents or for working men who cannot leave their jobs. [LUSH n.[1] (1) + SE *trotter*, a runner]

lush up *v.*[1] [1960s] to provide with a luxurious standard of living. [LUSH adj.[3]]

lush up *v.*[2] *see* LUSH (IT) UP v.

lush wallower *n.* [late 19C] (*Aus.*) a heavy drinker. [LUSH n.[1] (1) + SE *wallow*]

lushwell *n.* [1960s+] (*US*) a heavy drinker. [LUSH n.[1] (1) + fig. use of SE *well*]

lush worker *n.* (*also* **lush dip, ...diver, ...grafter, lusher**) (*US*) **1** [1900s] one who drinks heavily and/or associates with drunks. **2** [1910s+] one who specializes in robbing sleeping or passed-out drunks, esp. in subways. [LUSH n.[1] (3) + WORKER n.[1] (1)/DIP n.[4] (1)/DIVER n. (2)/GRAFTER n.[1] (1)]

lushy *n.* (*also* **lushie**) [1940s] (*US Black*) a drunkard. [LUSH n.[1] (3)]

lushy *adj.*[1] **1** [early 19C–1950s] drunk, tipsy (cf. ALED UP adj.). **2** [mid-19C] drunken. [LUSH n.[1] (1)]

lushy *adj.*[2] [1980s+] (*US campus*) sexy, voluptuous. [LUSH adj.[2] (1)]

lushy cove *n.* (*also* **lush blowen, lush cove**) [early–late 19C] a drunkard. [LUSH n.[1] (1) + COVE n. (1)]

lust dog *n.* [1970s+] (*US campus*) a male term for an allegedly promiscuous woman. [SE *lust* + DOG n.[3] (8)]

lusty cod *n.* (*also* **jolly cod, rum cod**) [late 17C–early 19C] (*UK Und.*) a substantial sum of money. [SE *lusty*, massive, substantial/*jolly*/RUM adj. (1) + COD n.[4] (2)]

lusty-guts *n.* [late 16C–early 17C] a promiscuous man, a womanizer. [SE *lusty* + -GUTS sfx]

lusty lawrence *n.* [late 16C–17C] a womanizer, a promiscuous man. [? pun on LAZY LAURENCE n.; a balled entitled 'Lusty Laurence' is entered in the Stationers' Register 1594]

Lute *n. see* LOOT n.[2].

lute *n.*[1] [17C–18C] **1** the vagina. **2** the penis; thus *play a lute solo*, to masturbate (cf. ACCORDION n.). [both *doubles entendres*: an 'instrument' upon which one 'plays']

lute *n.*[2] [1950s+] (*US*) a *Lut*heran. [abbr.]

luv, luv *adv.* [2000s] (*US prison*) being wealthy or successful, usu. as *living luv, luv*.

luvvie *n.* (*also* **luvvy**) **1** [1950s+] a general term of affectionate greeting. **2** [1980s+] a slightly derog. synon. for an actor or actress, esp. of the more demonstrative and overtly emotional type. [their stereotyped effusive cries of 'Luvvy! Darling!' on meeting]

lux *v.* [1970s+] (*N.Z.*) to vacuum a carpet etc. [abbr. brandname *Electrolux*]

luzz *v.* [1990s+] (*UK juv.*) to throw.

l.v. *n.* [1990s+] (*US Black teen*) the *L*ake*v*iew area of San Francisco. [abbr.]

L.W.O.P. *n.* [2000s+] (*US prison*) a life sentence with no possibility of parole. [pron. 'el-wop'; abbr. *life without parole*]

lybbeg/lybbege *n. see* LIB-BEG n.

lybkin *n. see* LIBKEN n.

lyesken chirps *n.* [18C–19C] (*tinker*) fortune-telling. [Shelta]

lying in state *phr.* [1920s] (*US prison*) serving time in jail.

L.Y.K.A.H. *phr.* [20C+] (*Irish*) leave your knickers at home, written by men on the back of letters to their loved one (cf. B.O.L.T.O.P. phr.). [abbr.]

lyle *n. see* LALLIE n.

Lymps, the *n.* [mid-19C] the *Olym*pic Theatre, London. [abbr.]

lyp *v. see* LIB v.

lyrebird *n.* [20C+] (*Aus.*) a liar, a mimic. [pun on SE *lyre-bird*]

lyrics *n.* [1980s+] (*UK Black*) **1** fantasies, wild talk. **2** talk, with no overtones.

lyricsing *n.* [1980s+] (*UK Black*) chatting up, sweet-talking.

M

M *n.* (*drugs*) **1** [1910s+] (*also* **em**) morphine (cf. AUNTIE EMMA *n.*). **2** [1950s+] marijuana. **3** [1980s+] MDMA. [abbr.]

ma *pfx* [1930s+] a derog. title put before a man's name to imply his homosexuality.

Maalox moment *n.* [1990s+] (*orig. US campus*) a time of stress. [the proprietary antacid *Maalox*; the phr. was coined for an advertising campaign]

maas *n.* [1990s+] (*W.I.*) money.

maat *n.* (*also* **maatie, maatjie**) [20C+] (*S.Afr.*) a friend, a chum, a pal. [Du. *maat*, a friend]

mab *n.*[1] [late 18C–early 19C] a prostitute; thus *mab up*, to dress carelessly. [SE *mab*, a slattern]

mab *n.*[2] [early–mid-19C] a cab. [rhy. sl.]

mabel *n.* **1** [1950s] (*US*) a girl. **2** [1950s] (*Aus.*) a girlfriend. **3** [1970s+] (*US gay*) a Black man.

Ma Bell *n.* (*also* **Maw Bell**) [1920s+] (*US*) the American Telephone & Telegraph Inc. [SE *ma*, i.e. mother + the earlier firm, the *Bell Telephone Company*]

Mac *n.*[1] (*also* **mac, mack**) **1** [17C+] a Celtic Irishman. **2** [18C+] a Scottish man. **3** [20C+] (*US*) a general term of greeting with no specific ref. to Scottish or Irish men implied. [Irish/Gaelic *mac*, son]

Mac *n.*[2] **1** [20C+] (*Can.*) McMaster University, Hamilton, Ontario. **2** [1990s+] a Mac-10 machine pistol. [abbr.]

Mc- *pfx* (*also* **Mac-**) [1980s+] (*orig. US campus*) used to emphasize the mediocre or mass-market quality of the added *n.*; usu. in the original form McJob *n.* [McJob *n.*]

mac *n.*[1] [late 19C+] (*W.I.*) 1 shilling. [abbr. MACARONI *n.*[3]]

mac *n.*[2] [1970s] a condom. [SE *mac(intosh)*]

mac *n.*[3] *see* MACK *n.*[1].

macadam *n.* [1950s] (*W.I.*) a codfish fritter. [SE *macadam*, a type of road made of compacted layers of stone, invented by *John Loudon McAdam* (1756–1836). The fritter is hard and flat like the road]

macadocious *adj. see* MACKADOCIOUS *adj.*

McAlpine fusilier *n.* [1960s+] a building labourer, a navvy. [*McAlpine*, a leading UK construction company]

mac-and-fip *n.* [1940s+] (*W.I.*) 1 shilling and 3 pence. [MAC *n.*[1] + FIP *n.*[1] (1)]

macaroni *n.*[1] **1** [18C] a jolly fool, esp. an Italian one (cf. APPLEHEAD *n.*). **2** [mid-19C+] (*also* **macaroni bender**) an Italian (cf. DAGO *n.*). [note synon. US regional use *macaroni-smacker*, *macaroni-snapper*]

macaroni *n.*[2] (*also* **maccaroni**) [mid-18C–1930s] a fop, a dandy; thus *macaroni-stake*, a horserace ridden by a 'gentleman jockey'. [the *Macaroni Club*, 'which is composed of all the travelled young men who wear long curls and spying-glasses' (Horace Walpole ed., *Letters of Earl Hertford*, 1764). The travelling, suggests the *OED*, prob. gave the members a taste for foreign foods, hence the name]

macaroni *n.*[3] (*also* **maccarony**) [early 19C+] (*W.I.*) a shilling.

[? the amount of tip commonly proffered by a dandy or MACARONI *n.*[2]]

macaroni *n.*[4] **1** [mid-19C] (*Aus.*) a pony. **2** [mid-19C+] £25; A$25. **3** [1970s+] a piece of human excrement; thus the act of defecation (cf. ALI OOP *n.*; ANDY CAPP *n.*). [rhy. sl.; (2) = PONY *n.*[1]; (3) = PONY (AND TRAP) *n.* (1)]

macaroni *n.*[5] [1920s+] (*Aus.*) nonsense, meaningless talk. [joc. use of SE but note rhy. sl. = PONY (AND TRAP) *n.* (1) = CRAP *n.*[3] (3)]

macaroni *n.*[6] [1970s+] (*US*) the middleman, usu. a pimp, who stands between the client and prostitute. [joc. ext. of MACK *n.*[1] (1)]

macaroni *adj.* [mid-19C+] Italian. [MACARONI *n.*[1] (2)]

macaroni bender *n. see* MACARONI *n.*[1] (2).

macaroni queen *n.* [1980s+] (*US gay*) a non-Italian gay man who prefers Italian partners. [MACARONI *n.*[1] (2) + QUEEN *n.*[2] (1)/QUEEN *sfx* (2)]

macaroon *n.*[1] [early 17C–early 19C] a buffoon, a blockhead, a dolt. [according to Nares these are the only cits., orig. noted in Todd's edn of Johnson's *Dictionary*]

macaroon *n.*[2] [20C+] a Black person. [rhy. sl. = COON *n.* (5)]

McAtah *n.* [1980s] (*W.I.*) mirrored dark glasses. [*McAtah*, a US general at the time]

macca *adj.*[1] [1990s+] (*W.I.*) exceptionally good. [W.I. dial. *macca*, a thorn, thus cognate with SHARP *adj.* (4)]

macca *adj.*[2] [1990s+] (*UK juv.*) very large.

macca-man *n.* [1970s] (*W.I.*) a tough, strong, efficient man. [dial. *macca*, a prick, a thorn, but note MACK MAN *n.*]

maccaroni *n. see* MACARONI *n.*[2].

maccarony *n. see* MACARONI *n.*[3].

McCoy *n.* **1** [1900s–40s] first-rate whisky or beer; often as *clear McCoy*. **2** [1930s–50s] (*US drugs*) medicinal drugs, pure narcotics.

McCoy, the *n. see* REAL MCCOY, THE *n.*

McCoy *adj.* [1920s–60s] (*US*) genuine. [REAL MCCOY, THE *n.*]

McDaddy *n. see* MACK DADDY *n.*

mcdumpster kid *n.* [2000s] (*US Black*) a homeless, starving young person. [the image is of such a person forced to scavenge in the dumpsters or skips that contain refuse from a McDonald's restaurant]

Mace *n.* [late 19C] (*Aus.*) physical violence. [MACING *n.*[1]]

mace *n.* **1** [mid-18C–1930s] a swindle, a fraud, confidence tricks; thus *work the mace*, to swindle. **2** [late 18C–19C] a confidence trickster, a swindler, 'a rogue assuming the character of a gentleman, or opulent tradesman, who under that appearance defrauds workmen, by borrowing a watch, or other piece of goods till one [that] he bespeaks is done [swindled]' (Grose, 1785). [ety. unknown; ? SE *mace*, a club, but con-men do not require violence]

mace *v.* **1** [late 18C+] to sponge, to swindle. **2** [early 19C–1930s] to fail to pay one's debts; thus *give on the mace*, *strike the mace*, *work the mace*, to obtain goods by persuading the shopkeeper to extend credit that one has no intention of paying. **3** [early

19C–1950s] (*US*) to beg or demand money from. **4** [1920s] (*UK Und.*) to avoid paying one's train fare. [MACE n.]

mace-cove *n.* **1** [early–mid-19C] a confidence trickster, a swindler. **2** [late 19C] (*Aus. Und.*) a house-breaker. [MACE n. (1) + COVE n. (1)]

mace-gloak *n.* [early 19C] a confidence trickster, a swindler. [MACE n. (1) + GLOAK n.]

maceman *n.* **1** [19C] a confidence trickster. **2** [mid-19C] one who defaults on their debts. **3** [late 19C] an élite criminal. [MACE n. (1) + sfx *-man*]

macer *n.* **1** [early–mid-19C; 1970s] a swindler. **2** [late 19C; 1970s] a thief, a villain. [MACE v.]

mace the rattler *v.* [late 19C–1930s] to travel by train without buying a ticket. [MACE v. + RATTLER n.[1] (3)]

McFly *n.* [1980s+] (*US campus*) a fool, an empty-headed person; thus **McFly!** wake up! [the character George *McFly* in the *Back to the Future* films (1985, 1989)]

MacGimp *n.* (*also* **McGimp, MacGimper, magimp, M'Gimp**) [1910s–60s] (*US*) a pimp (cf. ALPHONSE n.[2]). [rhy. sl.]

MacGorrey's Hotel *n.* [late 19C–1900s] Chelmsford prison, Essex (cf. ABBOTT'S PRIORY n.; BOARDING HOUSE n.). [the name of a contemporary governor]

MacGuffin *n.* [1950s+] (*US*) a gimmick, key element or a device in a story or plot, from which the whole drama develops. [coined in 1939 by film-maker Alfred Hitchcock to describe an aspect of his technique in creating suspense films]

mach *n.*[1] *see* MACON n.

mach *n.*[2] *see* MECH n.

machine *n.*[1] **1** [early 18C] a prostitute. **2** [mid-18C–19C; 1940s] (*also* **electric machine, spit-fire machine**) the penis. **3** [late 18C–early 19C] a condom. **4** [late 19C–1940s] the vagina.

machine *n.*[2] **1** [late 19C–1940s] (*N.Z.*) a Totalizator (cf. TOTE, THE n.). **2** [20C+] (*US*) an automobile. **3** [1970s+] (*US campus*) a motorcycle.

machine *n.*[3] [1970s] (*drugs*) a hypodermic syringe. [MACHINERY n.[1] (1)]

machine *sfx* [1930s+] (*US*) a combining form that indicates an enthusiast, a devotee, e.g. *sex machine, rap machine*.

machinery *n.*[1] (*US drugs*) **1** [1930s+] the equipment used for injecting a narcotic. **2** [1980s+] marijuana.

machinery *n.*[2] [1980s+] the male genitals. [MACHINE n.[1] (2)]

machinery *n.*[3] [1990s+] a revolver, a pistol.

macing *n.*[1] [19C–1900s] a severe thrashing. [the prize-fighter Jem *Mace* (1831–1910)]

macing *n.*[2] [19C+] cheating, esp. at the 3-card trick. [MACE v.]

McJob *n.* [1980s+] (*orig. US*) a pointless, usu. menial job with no prospects or job satisfaction. [brandname *Mc*Donald's + SE *job*, popularized by Douglas Coupland in his book *Generation X* (1991). The use of McDonald's refers both to the type of job, which epitomizes those available in the fast-food chain, and to what critics see as the disposable, tasteless, non-nutritional quality of the food the chain sells]

mack *n.*[1] (*also* **mac, maque**) **1** [20C+] (*US Und./Black*) a pimp; thus HARD MACK n.; SWEET MACK n. (cf. CANDYMAN n.). **2** [1960s+] (*US Black*) a clever, influential person, a smooth operator; thus *mackdom*, the (fantasy) world of such people. **3** [1990s+] (*US Black*) a person who deceives or tries to charm a member of the opposite sex with seductive words; a successful seducer. [early 15C–mid-17C SE *mackerel*, a pimp, pander or procuress, ult. Fr. *maquereau*, a pimp + ? Du. *makelaar*, a broker; note Jack Black, *You Can't Win* (1952): 'The safety box is also used [...] by race-horse men, gamblers and the moneyed macquereau' (context 1875)]

mack *n.*[2] [1970s] (*US Black*) a French kiss. [? MACK(, THE) n. or abbr. SMACK n.[2] (1)]

mack *n.*[3] *see* MAC n.[1].

mack *adj.* (*US Black*) **1** [1960s] masculine in appearance and behaviour. **2** [1960s+] describing anything pertaining

to a pimp, such as attitude, philosophy, automobile or clothes. [MACK n.[1] (1)]

mack *v.*[1] **1** [late 19C+] to work as a pimp. **2** [1960s–70s] (*US gay*) of lesbians, to act in a masculine manner. **3** [1960s+] (*US Black*) to swagger, to walk rhythmically. **4** [1990s+] (*US Black*) to be successful. [MACK n.[1]]

mack *v.*[2] **1** [1960s] (*US Black*) (*also* **get the mack on**) to talk seductively, to flirt; spec. as a pimp in order to recruit a prostitute. **2** [1970s+] (*US Black*) to lie or exaggerate in order to deceive, exploit or influence someone. **3** [1990s+] to have sexual intercourse. **4** [1990s+] to steal. [MACK(, THE) n.]

mack *v.*[3] **1** [1970s+] (*US campus/Black*) to kiss. **2** [1990s+] (*US campus*) to eat. [MACK n.[2]]

mack(, the) *n.* (*also* **mack talk**) [1940s+] (*US Black*) seductive, persuasive talk, spec. the 'chat-up' line used by a pimp to recruit a new girl. [MACK n.[1]]

macka *n.* [1980s+] (*drugs*) amphetamine (cf. A n.[2]). [ety. unknown; ? var. on MACON n.]

mackadelic *n.* [1990s+] (*US Black*) a first-rate person. [on pattern of MACKADOCIOUS adj.]

mackadocious *adj.* (*also* **macadocious**) [1980s+] (*US Black*) excellent, the very best. [MACK adj. (2) + sfx *-ocious*]

mack daddy *n.* (*also* **McDaddy**) (*US Black*) **1** [1950s+] a successful pimp or criminal (cf. BOSS PLAYER n.). **2** [1990s+] an important, influential Black man, a power in the community, a very successful or skilful man. **3** [1990s+] a handsome, virile man. [MACK n.[1] + DADDY n. (6); thus 'The Great *MacDaddy*', protagonist of an African-American rhyme of 1950s]

mack down *v.* [1970s+] (*US campus*) to eat. [*McDonald's* hamburgers/MACK v.[3] (2)]

macked out *adj.* (*also* **macked up**) [1930s+] (*US*) stylishly or flashily dressed. [MACK v.[1] (1)]

macker *n.*[1] [1930s–40s] (*Aus.*) a pony, a horse. [abbr. MACARONI n.[4] (1)]

macker *n.*[2] [1930s+] (*US Und.*) a pimp. [MACK n.[1] (1)]

mackerel *n.* **1** [15C–19C] (*UK Und.*) (*also* **macquerella**) a madam, a procuress. **2** [16C–17C; 1930s+] a pimp (cf. ABBOT ON THE CROSS n.). **3** [17C–early 19C] a prostitute (cf. ALLEY CAT n.). **4** [mid-19C–1920s] (*US*) a worthless or stupid man. **5** [2000s] a hanger-on, a parasite. [Fr. *maquereau*, a pimp; (2) 1930s+ US Und.]

mackerel-backed *adj.* [mid-17C–19C] long-backed, tall and thin; thus *mackerel-back*, a tall, thin person.

mackerel-snapper *n.* (*also* **mackerel-eater, -gobbler, -smacker, -snatcher**) [mid-19C; 1920s+] (*orig. US*) a Roman Catholic. [the role of fish in the religion]

mackery *n.* [1930s+] (*US*) pimping. [MACK n.[1] (1)]

macking *n.* [1990s+] (*US Black*) working hard. [fig. use of MACK v.[1] (1)]

mack man *n.* (*also* **mac man**) [1950s+] (*US Black*) a pimp (cf. CANDYMAN n.). [MACK n.[1] (1) + SE *man*]

mack on *v.* [1970s+] (*US Black/teen*) to make a verbally forceful attempt to seduce a person, to flirt heavily. [ext. of MACK v.[2] (1)]

mackry *n. see* MONKERY n.

mack talk *n. see* MACK(, THE) n.

mac man *n. see* MACK MAN n.

McMuff *n.* [1990s+] (*US*) the vagina. [MUFF n.[1] (1) + play on Egg *McMuffin*, a McDonald's hamburger chain product]

mcnoon *adj.* [1910s] (*Aus.*) mad. [ANDY McNOON n.]

maco *n.*[1] (*also* **mako**) [20C+] (*W.I.*) **1** a gossip, a busybody. **2** a peeping Tom. [Fr. *ma commère*, lit 'my gossip'; note also Fr. *macommère*, my child's godmother, thus my very good friend]

maco *n.*[2] (*also* **mako**) [20C+] (*W.I.*) **1** an effeminate man. **2** a fool, an idiot (cf. BOBO n.[1]). [? Fr. *maquereau*, a pimp]

maco *adj.* (*also* **mako**) [20C+] (*W.I.*) inquisitive, gossipy, meddlesome; thus *maco-man, maco-woman*. [MACO n.[1]]

maco *v.* (*also* **mako**) [20C+] (*W.I.*) **1** to interfere in other people's affairs. **2** to act as a voyeur. **3** to gossip scandalously. [MACO n.[1]]

macon *n.* (*also* **mach, maconha**) [1960s+] (*drugs*) marijuana. [Brazilian Port. *maconha*, marijuana]

mac on *v.* [1980s+] (*US campus*) to eat. [McDonald's hamburger chain, and its major seller, the *Big Mac*/MACK v.³ (2)]

mac out *v.* [1980s+] (*US teen*) to overeat, to gorge oneself, esp. on JUNK FOOD n. [the *McDonald's* hamburger chain/MACK v.³ (2)]

McPaper *n.* [1980s+] (*US campus*) **1** a sloppily written, poorly researched piece of work. **2** the notoriously banal *USA Today*. [MC- pfx + SE *paper*]

macquerella *n. see* MACKEREL n. (1).

macumeh *n. see* MAKOMÉ n.

mad *adj.*¹ [mid-19C+] (*US/W.I.*) sufficiently aroused to do something drastic. [obs. SE usage]

mad *adj.*² [1940s+] a generally intensifying adj. of approval, whether of objects, e.g. *a mad hat*, or of persons, e.g. *you mad bastard*. [the term received something of a revival in hip-hop/teen use in the 1990s]

mad *adj.*³ [1940s+] **1** absurd. **2** (*UK teen*) good, excellent.

mad *adj.*⁴ (*also* **madd**) [1990s+] (*US Black*) a lot of, very much, e.g. *mad piles of cash*.

mad *v.* [late 16C+] (*UK/US/W.I.*) to exasperate, to drive mad, e.g. with jealousy or worry. [obs. SE usage]

madam *n.*¹ **1** [17C–early 19C] a courtesan, a kept woman, a prostitute. **2** [early 18C+] (*also* **madame**) a bawd; the proprietor of a male or female brothel. **3** [19C] a general term of contempt for a woman, esp. one whose lifestyle does not reflect her self-appraisal. **4** [1970s+] (*US gay*) an older homosexual man (cf. AUNTIE n.²). [? reflecting a prejudice against foreigners, i.e. the adoption of Fr. *madame*]

madam *n.*² [mid–19C–1910s] a handkerchief. [? its ostensible respectability]

madam *n.*³ **1** [1910s–30s] (*UK Und.*) praise, flattery. **2** [1920s+] nonsense, rubbish; esp. in phr. *a load of old madam*. [? the fawning shopkeeper who calls every customer *madam*; or abbr. of MADAME DE LUCE n.]

madam *v.* [1930s+] to tell the tale, to 'pitch a line'. [MADAM n.³ or MADAME DE LUCE n.]

Madam Brown *n. see* MISS BROWN n.

madame *n. see* MADAM n.¹ (2).

madame bishop *n.* [mid-19C–1940s] (*Aus.*) a mixed drink consisting of port, sugar and nutmeg. [? SE *bishop*, mulled and spiced port. The popular ety. based on a link to the proper name of an Aus. hotel-keeper is prob. specious]

Madame de Luce *n.* [20C+] deceptive talk. [rhy. sl. = SPRUCE v.]

Madame Thomasina *n. see* AUNT THOMASINA n.

Madame Tussaud *adj.* [1990s+] bald. [rhy. sl.]

Madam Van *n.* (*also* **Madam Ran**) [late 17C–early 19C] (*UK Und.*) a prostitute (cf. BABY JANE n.). [? a real-life prostitute or madam or (given the contemporary role of the Dutch as 'national enemy') f. the common *van* pfx used in Du. surnames]

mad as (a)... *phr.* [mid-19C+] (*Aus./US*) completely deranged or utterly furious. Other than those listed below, combs. include *mad as a beetle, ...a Chinaman, ...a dingbat, ...a goanna, ...a hornet, ...a tucker.*

mad as a cut snake *phr.* (*also* **mad as snakes, wild as a cut fox**) [1910s+] (*Aus./US*) completely deranged, utterly furious.

mad as a gum-tree full of galahs *phr.* [1940s+] (*Aus.*) insane, eccentric.

mad as a hatter *phr.* [mid-19C+] very mad, utterly insane; in a rage. [the use in 18C of mercurous nitrate in the tanning of felt hats. This was absorbed by the hatters, in whom the effects could produce mental problems]

mad as a maggot *phr.* [1940s+] (*N.Z.*) very crazy.

mad as a (March) hare *phr.* **1** [15C+] very crazy. **2** [18C] lustful. [the hare's sexual excitement, which peaks in March]

mad as a meat axe *phr.* [1920s+] (*Aus./N.Z.*) **1** (*also* **savage as a meat axe**) very angry. **2** completely insane. [MEAT AXE n.¹]

mad as a two-bob watch *phr. see* SILLY AS A TWO-BOB WATCH phr.

mad as a weaver *phr.* [17C] very crazy. [pvb wisdom associates weavers and insanity]

mad as a wet hen *phr.* [early 19C+] extremely angry.

mad as fuck *phr.* (*also* **m.a.f.**) [1990s+] extremely annoyed. [abbr. mad as fuck]

mad as snakes *phr. see* MAD AS A CUT SNAKE phr.

madball *adj.* [1960s+] (*US*) crazy.

mad boner *n. see* BONER n.⁴ (3).

Madchester *n.* [1980s+] Manchester. [the brief but well-publicized period (*c.*1989–92) when Manchester, rather than London, dominated teen fashion, music and choice of drug consumption. *Mad* refers to the use of MDMA (cf. ECSTASY n.), the drug of choice in the city's clubs]

maddi *adj. see* MAD adj.⁴.

madder than a woodheap *phr.* (*also* **madder than a wet hen, ...a wet owl, ...nine hundred dollars, ...seven boiled owls, ...thunder**) [1910s+] very angry.

madder than old rip *phr. see* OLD RIP n.¹ (2).

maddie *n.* [1980s+] (*S.Afr.*) the White mistress of a house, the employer of domestic servants. [abbr. SE *madam*]

maddikin *n.* [late 18C–19C] the vagina. [? MADGE-KEN n.]

maddo *n.* [1910s] (*Aus.*) a lunatic. [SE *madman* + -o sfx (4)]

mad dog *n.*¹ **1** [late 16C–early 17C] strong ale. **2** [1970s+] (*US*) cheap wine, esp. the brand Mogen David 20/20. **3** [1970s+] (*drugs*) phencyclidine (cf. ACE n.⁴). [the effects]

mad dog *n.*² [late 19C+] (*Aus.*) an unsettled debt that the debtor refuses to pay, esp. at a public house.

mad dog *n.*³ **1** [1940s+] (*US*) a violent thug. **2** [1970s+] (*US Black*) a rebel, a non-conformist, one who refuses to accept their role in society. **3** [1990s+] (*US*) a deliberately provocative and aggressive stare. [SE *mad dog* but note MAD DOG v.]

mad-dog *adj.* [1940s+] (*US Black*) violent, thuggish. [MAD DOG n.³ (1)]

mad dog *v.* **1** [1980s+] (*N.Z.*) to nag, to pester. **2** [1990s+] (*US Black/prison*) to stare at intensely and threateningly. **3** [1990s+] (*US campus*) to attack verbally. [such animals fix their targets with an unwavering, aggressive stare; but note MAD DOG n.³]

maddy *n.* [1990s+] (*Scot./Aus.*) a psychologically unstable person, a lunatic. [SE *mad*]

maddy *adj.* [20C+] (*W.I.*) crazy, insane, unstable. [SE *mad*]

made *adj.*¹ [late 17C–19C] (*UK Und.*) stolen. [MAKE v.¹]

made *adj.*² [1930s+] (*US*) recognized, identified. [MAKE v.⁵ (1)]

made *adj.*³ [1940s+] (*US Black*) usu. of girls or women, describing someone who has had their hair straightened. [MAKE v.⁸]

made *adj.*⁴ [1950s+] (*orig. US Und.*) initiated as a member of the US Mafia. [MAKE v.⁹]

made *adj.*⁵ [1950s+] **1** (*US*) cheated, tricked. **2** (*US*) completed succesfully. **3** (*drugs*) satisfactorily supplied/intoxicated with drugs, usu. heroin. [MAKE v.³]

made man *n.* (*also* **made guy**) [1950s+] (*US Und.*) a formally initiated member of the US Mafia. [MADE adj.⁴]

made (up) *adj.* (*orig. Irish*) **1** [1930s+] lucky, secure, well-off. **2** [1980s+] delighted, pleased.

mad for it *phr.* [1940s+] extremely enthusiastic, ready to go mad, UP FOR phr. something. [orig. Scot. local use]

Madge *n.* [1950s–70s] (*camp gay*) a tasteless person. [joc. use of female proper name]

madge *n.*¹ [16C] a woman.

madge *n.*² *see* MADGE HOWLET n.

madge-cove *n.* [late 18C–mid-19C] a homosexual man. [? *Madge*, abbr. Margaret, thus cf. AGNES n. and similar uses of female names to denote male homosexuality + COVE n. (1)]

madge-cull *n.* [late 18C–mid-19C] (*UK Und.*) a homosexual man. [var. on MADGE-COVE n. + CULL n.¹ (4)]

Madge Howlet *n.* (*also* **madge, Madge Howlett**) [17C–19C] the vagina; a prostitute (cf. BABY JANE n.). [dial. *madge howlet*, a barn owl]

madge-ken *n.* [late 18C–mid-19C] the vagina. [MADGE HOWLET n. + KEN n.[1] (1)]

mad haddock *n.* [20C+] (*Aus.*) an exceptionally eccentric person. [? play on ODD FISH n.]

madhatter *n.* [1990s+] (*US teen*) someone who sells drugs. [MAD AS A HATTER phr.]

mad heads *n.* [2000s] (*US Black*) lots of people. [MAD adj.[4] + HEAD n.[11] (1)]

madhouse *n.* [1920s–30s] (*US prison*) a prison with particularly unpleasant conditions (cf. BANDHOUSE n.). [SE *madhouse*, a psychiatric institution]

madison *n.* [1990s+] any form of neck piercing. [ety. unknown; ? anecdotal]

madman *n.* [1970s+] (*drugs*) **1** a notably strong variety of a given drug, e.g. heroin. **2** phencyclidine (cf. ACE n.[4]). [melodramatic assessment of the effects]

madman's broth *n.* [1950s] (*Aus.*) brandy.

madmen *adj.* [1960s] crazy, absurd.

mad mick *n.* [20C+] **1** (*Aus.*) the penis (cf. ALMOND n.). **2** (*Aus./US*) a pick. [rhy. sl.; (1) = PRICK n. (2)]

mad money *n.* **1** [1920s+] (*orig. US*) money carried by a woman for an emergency, such as being abandoned far from home by her boyfriend when she hasn't agreed to sex. **2** [1930s+] (*US*) savings set aside for some spontaneous, unscheduled expenditure, usu. on pleasure. [(1) the 'madness' is in the anger of the boyfriend; (2) it is in the spending]

madonna *n.* [1990s+] in body piercing, a beauty spot stud in the upper lip. [the position of the piercing is usu. the same as the position of the beauty mark on the lip of the pop singer *Madonna* (b.1959)]

mad skills *n.* (*also* **mad skillz**) [1990s+] any admirable quality.

mad Tom *n.* [late 17C–mid-19C] a beggar who counterfeits madness, the 18th rank of criminal beggars. [? a real-life mad beggar or TOM n.[1]]

Mad Town *n.* [1980s+] (*US*) *Madison*, Wisconsin. [abbr.]

mad-up *adj.* [1970s–80s] (*UK Black*) crazy.

madza *n.* (*also* **medza, medzer, midzer**) [mid–late 19C] (*Ling. Fr./Polari*) a half; thus *madza beargured*, half-drunk; *madza round the bull*, half a pound of steak. [Ital. *mezzo*, a half]

madza caroon *n.* [mid–late 19C] half a crown, 2s 6d (12½p). [MADZA n. + CAROON n.]

madza poona *n.* [mid–late 19C] a half-sovereign. [MADZA n. + SE *pound*]

madza saltee *n.* [mid–late 19C] a halfpenny. [MADZA n. + SALTEE n.]

Mae West *n.* **1** [1930s+] a female breast (cf. BRACE AND BITS n.). **2** [2000s] the best (thing). [rhy. sl.; ult. Hollywood star *Mae West* (1892–1980)]

Mae West bonnet *n.* [1940s] (*US milit.*) a steel helmet.

m.a.f. *adj. see* MAD AS FUCK phr.

Maf *n.* [1960s+] (*orig. US*) the (usu. US) *Mafia*. [abbr.]

mafa *n.* [2000s] (*US Black*) an abbr. of MOTHERFUCKER n. (1).

mafficking *n.* [1900s–10s] celebrating in the streets in an uproarious manner, esp. during a national celebration, general street rowdyism. [the lifting of the siege of *Mafeking* on 17 May 1900, a major date in the Boer War]

mafia *n.* [1950s+] (*W.I. Rasta*) big-time criminals. [borrowing of US/Ital. use]

mafias *n.* [2000s] (*US prison*) dark sunglasses. [stereotyping]

mag *n.*[1] [early 18C] (*UK Und.*) a sodomite.

mag *n.*[2] **1** [mid-18C–1910s] a mouth. **2** [late 19C–1910s] the face. [? var. on MUG n.[1] (2)]

mag *n.*[3] **1** [mid-18C–1950s] (*also* **magg, meag, meg**) a halfpenny. **2** [early 19C–1950s] a penny, a cent.

mag *n.*[4] **1** [late 18C+] talk, chatter; thus *tip the mag*, to talk, to

orate. **2** [1910s] nagging. **3** [1910s] (*Aus.*) a lie. **4** [1940s+] a chatterer. [SE *magpie*, post-19C use mainly Aus.]

mag *n.*[5] *see* MAGAZINE n.

mag *n.*[6] *see* MAGSMAN n.[1] (3).

mag, the *n.* [late 19C] (*UK Und.*) confidence trickery, swindling.

mag *v.* **1** [early 19C] (*Scot.*) to steal. **2** [early 19C+] to chatter, to talk, to scold. **3** [mid–late 19C] (*UK Und.*) to cheat, esp. through insincere talk. **4** [20C+] (*Aus.*) to talk at, to nag. [MAG n.[4]]

maga *adj.* [1950s+] (*W.I. Rasta*) thin. [SE *meagre* or Fr. *maigre*, thin]

maga dog *n.* [1950s+] (*W.I. Rasta*) a mongrel; thus as a term of abuse. [MAGA adj. + SE *dog*]

magageba *n.* [1970s+] (*S.Afr. Black*) money. [? Zulu *amakhekheba*, flat, rigid objects]

magazine *n.* (*also* **mag**) [1920s+] (*US Und.*) a 6-month jail sentence (cf. NEWSPAPER n.). [the time it takes an illiterate person to read one]

Magdalen marm *n.* [late 19C] a servant who was recruited from the Magdalen home for 'fallen women' in Blackfriars Road, Southwark. [many employers felt that such servants made only second-rate workers because they had been treated too kindly at the refuge]

mageegle *v.* [20C+] (*Ulster*) to confuse, to bewilder. [Scot. *maggle*, mangle]

mag-flying *n.* [mid–late 19C] playing pitch and toss. [FLY THE MAGS v.]

magg *n. see* MAG n.[3] (1).

maggie *n.*[1] **1** [17C–early 18C; 1930s] (*also* **margaretta, meg**) a prostitute (cf. BABY JANE n.). **2** [19C] a generic term for a woman. [proper name *Maggie*, abbr. Margaret]

maggie *n.*[2] [20C+] (*Ulster*) in cards, the ace or queen of hearts. [proper name *Maggie*, abbr. Margaret]

maggie *n.*[3] [20C+] (*Aus.*) a *mag*pie. [abbr.]

maggie *n.*[4] [1910s] (*US Und.*) an automatic pistol.

maggie *n.*[5] [1940s+] (*W.I.*) a handcuff, a manacle; usu. in pl.

maggie and jiggs *n.* [1930s–60s] (*US*) an outdoor privy. [the 'lead characters' in a long-running US strip cartoon]

maggie ann(e) *n.* (*also* **maggie ryan, maggy ann(e)**) [1910s+] (*orig. milit.*) margarine. [pron.]

maggie mahone *n. see* MIKE MALONE n.

maggieman *n.* [20C+] (*Irish*) a fairground showman. [Irish *margadh*, a fair]

maggie moores *n.* (*also* **maggies**) [20C+] (*Aus.*) women's underpants. [rhy. sl. = SE *drawers*]

maggie rab *n.*[1] (*also* **maggie rob(b)**) [19C] (*Scot.*) a nagging, unpleasant wife. [MAG v. (2) + SE *rob*; play on proper names]

maggie rab *n.*[2] (*also* **maggie rob(b)**) [19C] (*Scot.*) a bad halfpenny. [MAG n.[3] (1) + SE *rob*; play on proper names]

maggie ryan *n. see* MAGGIE ANN(E) n.

maggies *n. see* MAGGIE MOORES n.

maggie's pie *n.* [20C+] (*US Black*) the female genitals. [var. on MAGPIE'S NEST n.]

magging *n.*[1] [early–mid-19C] chattering, talking. [MAG v. (2)]

magging *n.*[2] [mid–late 19C] confidence trickery, swindling. [MAGSMAN n.[1]]

maggot *n.*[1] **1** [late 17C+] a contemptible person. **2** [1980s+] (*US Black*) a White person. **3** [1980s+] (*Aus.*) a general term of abuse, esp. aimed at girls or women. **4** [1980s+] (*US police*) a criminal, esp. a drug dealer. [general loathing of the SE *maggot*; (3) also plays on the image of the *maggot* that 'eats your flesh']

maggot *n.*[2] [20C+] the penis (cf. ANTEATER n.). [a *maggot* burrows into flesh]

maggot *n.*[3] [1920s] (*Irish*) a state of drunkenness.

maggot *n.*[4] [1980s+] (*US campus*) a very lazy person, esp. one who stays in bed all day. [they 'burrow' beneath the sheets]

maggot boiler *n.* [late 18C–early 19C] a tallow chandler. [the maggots that were found in the tallow or animal fat that was used as the basis for candle-making.

maggot-brained *adj.* (*also* **maggot-headed, -pated, -plated**) [late 17C; 20C+] a general epithet of abuse.

maggotish *adj. see* MAGGOTY *adj.*

maggot meat *n.* [1970s] (*US*) a dead person, or one about to be killed.

maggot-pated/-plated *adj. see* MAGGOT-BRAINED *adj.*

maggots! *excl.* [late 19C] an excl. of dismissal.

maggoty *adj.* (*also* **maggotish, maggotty**) **1** [late 17C–19C] eccentric, whimsical. **2** [20C+] (*Aus.*) ill-tempered, irritable. **3** [20C+] (*Irish*) dirty, disgusting. **4** [1920s+] (*US/Irish*) extremely drunk. **5** [1990s+] (*US*) crazy, insane (cf. APEY *adj.*). [the image of a rotting brain]

maggy ann(e) *n. see* MAGGIE ANN(E) *n.*

magic (dust) *n.* [1970s+] (*drugs*) phencyclidine (cf. ACE *n.*[4]). [SE *magic* + DUST *n.*[5] (5)]

magic mushroom *n.* (*drugs*) **1** [1960s+] (*also* **magic**) a psilocybe mushroom, a hallucinogen somewhat milder than LSD; usu. in pl. **2** [1970s] peyote.

magic wand *n.* [1950s–60s] the penis. [either a tribute to masculine power or the myth that sexual intercourse somehow puts an end to quarrels]

magiffer *n. see* MAGOOFER *n.*

magimp *n. see* MACGIMP *n.*

magistrate *n. see* GLASGOW MAGISTRATE *n.*

magistrate's court *n.* [20C+] a measure of spirits, as bought in a public house. [rhy. sl. = SHORT *n.*[1] (2)]

magnet *n.* [18C–19C] the vagina. [its allure]

magnet *sfx* [1960s+] used to imply that a person or object is irresistibly attractive, usu. in a sexual way but not always (cf. BABE MAGNET *n.*; CHICK MAGNET *n.*; COP MAGNET *n.*; FANNY MAGNET *n.*; NERD MAGNET *n.*; PUSSY MAGNET *n.*).

magnificents *n.* [mid-19C] a mood of haughty indignation.

magnolia curtain *n.* [1940s+] (*US Black*) the Mason-Dixon (40°N) line that divides the American north and south. [SE *magnolia*, generic synon. for the South + play on *Iron Curtain*]

magnolious *adj.* [mid-19C+] (*US*) magnificent, splendid, large; thus *magnoliousness*, the fact or quality of being *magnolious*. [elaboration of SE *magnificent*]

magnoon *adj.* (*also* **magnune**) [1910s–40s] (*Aus./N.Z.*) crazy, eccentric. [Arab. *magnoon*, eccentric]

magnum bonum *n.* [early 19C] a bottle holding 2 quarts of wine.

magoo *n.* **1** [1930s+] (*US*) an important person. **2** [1930s+] (*US*) a foolish person. **3** [1980s+] (*US campus*) a driver, usu. old and male, who drives very slowly and thus impedes the faster car behind. [MAGOO, THE *n.*]

magoo, the *n.* (*US*) **1** [1930s–60s] a lie, a trick, a hoax; thus *give the magoo*, to deceive someone. **2** [1930s+] sex appeal. [usage influenced by 1932 Broadway comedy *The Great Magoo* by Hecht and Fowler and the character *Mr Magoo* in UPA Studios cartoon series shown on children's television in the 1970s]

magoofer *n.* (*also* **magiffer**) [1950s–60s] (*US*) a pimp. [var. on MACGIMP *n.*, but note MAGOO *n.*/MAGOO, THE *n.*]

magoozlum *n.* [1920s+] (*US*) rubbish, trash. [? Hollywood jargon *magoo*, the gooey ingredient of 'custard pies']

mag-pie *n.* [late 19C] speech, conversation. [MAG *n.*[4] (1)]

magpie *n.*[1] **1** [early 17C–19C] an Anglican bishop. **2** [mid–late 19C] (*Aus./UK prison*) convict clothing (coloured yellow and black); thus the convict who wears it. **3** [1910s+] (*Aus.*) a nickname for a South Australian. **4** [1980s] (*Aus.*) a half-caste. [(1) the black chimere and white rochet forming his ordinary ceremonial attire; (3) the black and white colouring of the bird, the ref. is to the convict clothes worn by early settlers]

magpie *n.*[2] [mid-19C] a halfpenny. [ext. of MAG *n.*[3]]

magpie's nest *n.* [18C–19C; 1980s] (*US Black*) the female genitals.

magsman *n.*[1] **1** [mid-19C] an assistant for a street swindler or pickpocket. **2** [mid-19C–1900s] the king of the 19C swindlers, a fashionable swell who appeared as sophisticated a figure as those on whom he preyed. **3** [mid-19C+] (*also* **mag**) a street swindler, or thief, esp. one who preys on gullible countrymen. **4** [mid-19C+] a card-sharp or other cheating gamester. [? Yid. *machas*, a great man; Michael Davitt, *Leaves from a Prison Diary* (1885): 'The order of magsmen wil, comprise card-sharpers, "confidence trick" workers, begging-letter writers, bogus ministers of religion, professional noblemen, "helpless victims of the cruel world", medical quacks and various other clever rogues']

magsman *n.*[2] [20C+] (*Aus.*) a chatterbox, a talker. [MAG *v.* (2)]

mag-stake *n.* [mid–late 19C] money obtained by trickery or fraud. [MAGSMAN *n.*[1] (3) + SE *stake*]

maguffy *n.* [20C+] (*W.I.*) **1** one who thinks that they are more important than they really are. **2** anything large and pretentious. [? a real name, but note the film jargon MACGUFFIN *n.*]

mahaha *n. see* MAHULA *n.*

maharishee *n.* [1970s+] (*drugs*) marijuana (cf. AUNT MARY *n.*[2]). [proper name *Maharishi Mahesh Yogi* (b.1911), a popular 1960s guru, espoused by The Beatles and others in search of raised consciousness]

Mahatma Gandhi *n.* [20C+] **1** brandy. **2** shandy. [rhy. sl.; ult. Ind. freedom fighter *Mahatma Gandhi* (1869–1948)]

Mahatma Gandhi *adj.* [2000s] **1** dandy. **2** randy. [rhy. sl.; for ety. *see* prev.]

mahcheen *n.* [mid-19C] (*Anglo-Chinese*) a merchant. [Chinese pron. of SE]

mah jong *n.* (*also* **mahjoun, mahuang**) [1970s] (*drugs*) marijuana. [the Chinese game/pun on pron.]

mahog *n.* (*also* **mahoga**) [1960s+] (*S.Afr. Black*) brandy. [abbr. SE *mahogany*, thus the colour of the wood and the drink]

mahogany *n.*[1] **1** [late 18C–mid-19C] a Cornish drink made of gin and treacle. **2** [mid-19C] a strong mixture of brandy and water. [the colour]

mahogany *n.*[2] **1** [mid-19C+] a table, esp. a dining table. **2** [late 19C+] (*US*) a bar counter; thus *mahogany polisher*, a bartender.

mahogany flat *n.*[1] (*also* **mahogany baxter**) [mid-19C–1930s] a bedbug. [late 19C+ use is US; SE *mahogany* + FLAT-BACK *n.*]

mahogany flat *n.*[2] [1970s–80s] (*US Black*) an expensive, well-furnished and situated apartment or home. [SE *mahogany*, as a symbol of luxury + *flat*]

mahogany gaspipe *n.* [20C+] the intonations of the Irish language, also as one who speaks the language. [a joc. rendering of its sound]

mahogany slosh *n.* [late 19C–1910s] tea from a cook-shop or coffee-stall. [play on SE *mahogany* + SLOSH *n.*[1]; its colour and taste]

mahogany top *n.* [mid–late 19C] a red-headed person. [the colour of the wood/hair]

mahomet *n. see* TURK *n.*[1] (1).

Mahometan gruel *n.* [late 17C–early 19C] coffee. [its origins and popularity in the Middle East]

mahoska, the *n.* [1930s+] (*US Und.*) anything illicit, esp. drugs, money, a weapon, stolen goods etc. [? Irish *mo thosca*, my business; thus cf. *cosa nostra*, 'this thing of ours', a synon. for the Sicilian/US mafia]

mahuang *n. see* MAH JONG *n.*

mahula *n.* (*also* **mahaha, mahoula**) [1900s–40s] (*US*) nonsense. [MAHULA *adj.*]

mahula *adj.* [20C+] (*US*) bankrupt or ruined. [Yid. *mekhule*, Heb. *mechula*, spoiled, bankrupt]

maiden *n.* [mid-19C–1910s] (*Aus.*) cloves; peppermint. [ety. unknown; ? a local plant name]

maiden lane *n.* [late 19C] (*US*) the red-light area of a town.

maiden's blush *n.* **1** [late 19C–1910s] (*also* **lady's blush, maiden's prayers**) port and lemonade. **2** [1940s+] (*Aus.*) ginger beer and raspberry cordial. [the colour]

maiden sessions *n.* [late 17C–early 19C] a legal sessions where no prisoners are sentenced to death. [SE *maiden*, a form of early guillotine]

Maiden Town *n.* [early 18C–19C] Edinburgh. [legend that the maiden daughter of a Pictish king fled there for protection during a civil war]

maiden-wife-widow *n.* [late 17C–18C] **1** a bride, now a widow, whose husband died before consummating their marriage. **2** a prostitute.

Maid Marian *n.* [16C] a prostitute (cf. BABY JANE n.). [the morris-dancing tradition of having that character played by a local prostitute]

maids adorning *n.* [mid-19C] the morning. [rhy. sl.]

maid's meat *n. see* BOY'S MEAT n.

maid's ring *n.* [late 19C] a hymen. [SE *maid* + RING n.¹ (1)/pun on SE *ring*]

Maidstone jailer *n.* [mid-19C] a tailor. [rhy. sl.]

maid's water *n.* [late 19C+] (*Aus.*) any weak drink, esp. tea.

mail *n.*¹ [1940s+] (*S.Afr.*) a carrier for an illicit grog-shop.

mail *n.*² [1960s+] (*Aus.*) a rumour, a report, a racing tip, information on crime.

mail *n.*³ [1990s+] (*US Black teen*) money. [? like the US mail it 'gets through anywhere']

mail *v.* [1950s+] (*S.Afr.*) **1** to send someone to buy liquor illicitly. **2** to act as a go-between in such a purchase. [MAIL n.¹]

mailer *n.* [1950s] (*S.Afr. Und.*) a middleman in the illicit liquor trade. [MAIL v.]

'mailer *n.* [1900s] (*Aus.*) a blackmailer. [abbr.; ? *Bulletin* nonce-word]

mail-order *adj.* [1920s–50s] (*US*) second-rate, inferior.

mail-order cowboy *n.* [1920s–40s] (*US*) a would-be cowboy who has the clothes but is otherwise spurious.

main *n. see* MAINLINE n.².

main *adj.* [late 19C+] (*US*) used to describe a person or thing with power or importance; usu. in combs., e.g. *the main cheese, the main cop* etc.

main *v. see* MAINLINE v.

main alley *n.* [20C+] (*orig. US tramp*) the main street.

main avenue *n.* [19C] the vagina (cf. ALLEY n.¹).

main bitch *n.* (*also* **main girl, ...ho, ...lady, ...stuff, ...who', ...whore, ...woman**) [1960s+] (*US Black*) **1** the favourite prostitute among those a pimp controls. **2** (*also* **main chick**) a man's favourite girlfriend. [MAIN adj. + BITCH n.¹ (1)/CHICK n.⁴ (2)/SE *girl*/HO n.¹ (1)/SE *lady*/STUFF n.⁶ (2)/abbr. SE *whore*/SE *woman*]

main bone *n.* [1970s] the penis. [SE *main* + SE *bone*/BONE n.¹ (1)]

main boy *n. see* MAIN MAN n.¹ (3).

main burg *n. see* BIG BURG n. (1).

main cat *n.* [1960s] the leader, the most important person. [MAIN adj. + CAT n.¹¹ (4)]

main chance *n.* [late 16C+] (*orig. UK Und.*) the principal opportunity one may have for making money, attaining a goal, taking advantage of one's rivals etc; thus one who has an *eye for the main chance*, a smart operator.

main chick *n. see* MAIN BITCH n. (2).

main drag, the *n.* **1** [mid-19C+] the main street of a town or city; thus *buzz/mooch/work the main drag*, to beg along a town's main street. **2** [1930s–40s] (*US Black*) Seventh Avenue in Harlem, New York. **3** [1960s–70s] the main road. [MAIN adj. + DRAG n.⁵ (1), also note *drag* (*oneself along*), to make one's way wearily, tiredly. The term referred orig. to a town or city's centre of tramp or vagrant life but was ext. and then transferred to the main street, whether or not frequented by vagrants. (1) Note despite its almost invariably US use today, the term started in the UK and is cited as such by Mayhew (1861–2)]

main drag of many tears *n.* [1940s] (*US Black*) 125th Street Harlem, New York. [MAIN DRAG, THE n. + SE, the bars and theatres on 125th Street (Harlem's main street) where otherwise depressed and frustrated people can attempt to drown their sorrows]

main event *n.* [1970s] a spectacular action. [sporting imagery]

main finger *n.* [late 19C–1920s] (*US*) the boss. [MAIN adj. + FINGER n.³ (4)]

main girl *n. see* MAIN BITCH n.

main guy *n.* [late 19C+] (*US*) the boss. [MAIN adj. + GUY n.² (1)]

main ho *n. see* MAIN BITCH n.

Mainiac *n.* [mid-19C+] (*US*) a native of Maine. [pun on SE *maniac*]

main kazoo *n.* (*also* **main kazaam**) [20C+] (*US*) a person of importance. [MAIN adj. + play on the self-aggrandizing names of various US societies, esp. the *kleagles* etc of the Ku Klux Klan]

main kick *n.* [1930s–40s] (*US Black*) **1** one's favourite activity. **2** the stage or theatre. **3** an addiction to drugs. **4** alcohol. [MAIN adj. + KICK n.⁵ (3)]

main lady *n. see* MAIN BITCH n.

mainland *n.* [1940s+] (*N.Z.*) the South Island.

mainlander *n.* [1940s+] (*Aus.*) one who lives on the mainland of Australia (rather than Tasmania).

mainline *n.*¹ (*also* **line**) [1930s+] (*US prison*) the prison convict population, excluding those who are detained in punishment cells. [LINE n.²]

mainline *n.*² (*also* **main, mainliner**) (*orig. US drugs*) **1** [1930s+] the vein into which an addict injects narcotics; thus *bust the mainline*, to take an intravenous injection. **2** [1940s+] (*also* **mainline bang**) an injection into the vein; thus *take it main*, to inject narcotics into a vein. **3** [1950s] narcotics (addiction).

mainline *n.*³ *see* MAINLINER n.¹.

mainline *adj.*¹ [1930s+] (*US prison*) pertaining to the main prison population (and the rules to which it is subjected). [MAINLINE n.¹]

mainline *adj.*² [1950s–60s] (*orig. US drugs*) pertaining to narcotics use and addiction.

mainline *v.* (*also* **main**) (*orig. US drugs*) **1** [1930s+] to inject narcotics directly into a vein. **2** [1960s+] to inject intravenously in non-drug use; also fig. [MAINLINE n.²]

mainliner *n.*¹ (*also* **mainline, mainline shooter**) [1930s+] (*orig. US drugs*) a drug addict who injects narcotics into the vein. [MAINLINE v.]

mainliner *n.*² [1940s–50s] (*US prison*) a convict who is part of the main prison population, rather than those held in punishment cells. [MAINLINE n.¹]

main man *n.*¹ (*orig. US Black*) **1** [1920s+] a pimp (cf. CANDYMAN n.). **2** [1940s+] a lover, a sweetheart, a woman's only boyfriend. **3** [1950s+] (*also* **main boy**) one's best friend; an intimate. **4** [1960s+] any important person, e.g. a chief prison warder or a managing director. **5** [1970s] a hero. **6** [1970s] an accomplice, an informer. **7** [1970s+] a leading drug supplier. [MAIN adj. + SE *man*]

main man *n.*² [1960s+] (*S.Afr.*) a local hero, esp. in a school or college. [MAIN MAN n.¹]

main mellow *n. see* MAIN SQUEEZE n. (2).

main momma *n. see* MAIN QUEEN n.

main monkey *n.* [2000s] (*drugs*) addiction to narcotics; the need for narcotics. [MAINLINE n.² (3) + MONKEY n.¹²]

main on the hitch *n.* [1930s–40s] (*US Black*) a woman's favourite man, esp. her husband (cf. MAIN SAW ON THE HITCH n.). [MAIN MAN n.¹ (2) + HITCHED adj.]

main ou *n.* [1970s+] (*S.Afr.*) a local hero, esp. in a school or college. [MAIN MAN n.² + OU n. (2)]

main piece *n. see* MAIN SQUEEZE n. (2).

main queen *n.* (*also* **main momma**) **1** [1940s+] (*US Black*) one's girlfriend or wife. **2** [1960s] (*US*) an attractive and sexually desired male homosexual. [MAIN adj. + SE *queen*/QUEEN n.² (1)]

main saw on the hitch *n.* [1940s] (*US Black*) one's wife (cf. MAIN ON THE HITCH n.). [Mezzrow & Wolfe, *Really the Blues* (1946): 'Your wife is the *main saw on the hitch*; you may have other *saws* to cut your wood, and you might say that you were hitched to them too, but not in such a basic way']

mainsheet n. [late 19C] (*W.I.*) rum and water. [naut. imagery]

main spot n. [mid-18C] the vagina.

main squash n. [1900s] (*US*) the most important person.

main squeeze n. 1 [late 19C+] (*US*) the boss, the foreman, any important person. 2 [1920s+] (*orig. US*) (*also* **main mellow, main piece, number-one squeeze**) one's most favoured person, usu. a lover or most intimate same-sex friend. [SE *main* + SQUEEZE n.⁷]

main stash n. [1940s–60] (*US Black*) one's home. [Mezzrow & Wolfe, *Really the Blues* (1946): '*Main stash* is home, where you and your wife or steady girlfriend live, as distinguished from other secondary "homes" you might have, where other women friends of yours live']

mainstay n. [1980s] (*US drugs*) a dealer's most trustworthy friend or lover. [ext. of SE]

main stem, the n. 1 [late 19C–1930s] (*US*) a person of importance, the boss. 2 [late 19C+] the main street of a town; thus **buzz/mooch/work the main stem**, to be along a town's main street. 3 [20C+] (*US Black*) the elite, the upper class. 4 [1920s–30s] (*US tramp*) the most important street of a town in the context of tramp society and standards. 5 [1920s–50s] Broadway, New York City. [SE *main stem*, the central trunk]

Main Street n. [mid-19C+] (*US*) the 'provinces', a generic term for small-town America. [popularized by the novel *Main Street* (1920), by Sinclair Lewis]

Main Street adj. [1910s+] (*US*) provincial. [MAIN STREET n.; popularized by the novel *Main Street* (1920), by Sinclair Lewis]

Main Streeter n. [1920s+] a provincial, small-town person. [MAIN STREET n.]

main stroll, the n. [1940s] (*US Black*) Seventh Avenue in Harlem.

main stuff n. *see* MAIN BITCH n.

main thrill n. [1930s–40s] (*US Black*) one's drug of choice.

main thrill, the n. [1930s–40s] (*US Black*) the main street, spec. Seventh Avenue in Harlem.

main-toby, the n. [mid-19C] the main road, the highway.

main trill, the n. [1940s] (*US Black/Harlem*) the main street; an avenue. [? pron. of MAIN THRILL, THE n.]

main vein n. [1950s+] the vagina.

main who'/whore n. *see* MAIN BITCH n.

main wire n. [1910s] (*US*) the most important person, the manager, the boss.

main woman n.¹ [1990s+] (*W.I./UK Black*) a man's primary partner, poss. the mother of his children etc.

main woman n.² *see* MAIN BITCH n.

majat n. [1950s+] (*S.Afr. drugs*) the third and lowest grade of marijuana on sale in S.Afr. [? Malay *madat*, opium]

majesty n. [1900s] the penis.

majita n. (*also* **majika**) [1950s+] (*S.Afr. Black*) a streetwise young man, also as a term of address. [the film *The Magic Garden* (1951), which depicts, *inter alia*, the life of such a youth]

majonda n. [1950s+] (*US drugs*) heroin.

major n. [1970s+] (*US gay*) a lesbian.

major-league adj. [1940s+] (*orig. US*) very important, the most powerful, highly impressive (cf. MINOR-LEAGUE adj.). [baseball imagery]

major-league adv. [1990s+] (*US*) extremely.

major nasty adj. [1980s+] (*US Black/teen*) very unpleasant, very difficult. [SE *major* + NASTY adj. (4)]

major operation n. [1930s+] the act of 'cutting someone dead'.

major solde n. [mid-19C] a halfpenny.

major-time adv. [1980s+] (*US campus*) to a great extent, very much.

make n.¹ (*also* **mec**) [mid-16C+] (*UK Und.*) a halfpenny. [Midlands/northern dial.; 20C+ use mainly Dublin]

make n.² 1 [mid-19C–1950s] a successful robbery or swindle. 2 [1910s–60s] (*US Und.*) the proceeds of a theft or robbery. [MAKE v.¹; (1) 20C use is US Und.]

make n.³ 1 [1930s+] a seduction. 2 [1940s+] (*orig. US*) a promiscuous woman or girl, one who can be seduced easily; usu. as EASY MAKE n. 3 [1960s+] (*US*) kissing, necking. [MAKE v.³ (5)]

make n.⁴ [1950s+] (*US*) a description or an identification of a suspect, esp. through fingerprinting, photofit or other forms of police records; thus *put the make to*, to describe. [MAKE v.⁵ (1)]

make v.¹ [late 17C+] to steal (from).

make v.² [mid-19C+] (*US*) to consider, to regard, to estimate as, e.g. *I make it about 10 p.m.*

make v.³ 1 [mid-19C+] to promote, to make successful; usu. as *made*. 2 [20C+] (*US*) to seduce, to have sexual intercourse with. 3 [1910s+] (*US*) to succeed in getting something, constructed with 'for', e.g. *to make a croaker for a reader*, to persuade a doctor to write a prescription for narcotics; *make for a stash*, to steal the drugs another addict has hidden so as to use them oneself. 4 [1920s] (*US Und.*) in weaker form of (3), to entice the potential victim of a confidence trick. 5 [1950s–60s] (*US*) to consume drugs or drink. 6 [1960s] to enjoy, to appreciate. 7 [1960s+] (*US*) to make a drug purchase.

make v.⁴ 1 [mid-19C+] (*US*) to go to, to arrive at, to attend, to pay a visit. 2 [1900s] (*Aus.*) to leave. 3 [1910s+] spec. use of (1), to catch, e.g. *make a plane, make a train*. 4 [1920s+] to attain a goal, e.g. *make the team, make a club*. 5 [1940s+] to appear in the newspaper.

make v.⁵ 1 [20C+] (*orig. US police/Und.*) to witness or observe, to recognize, to identify a suspect; also as *make someone for*, to recognize someone as. 2 [1960s+] to stop and search someone on the street. 3 [1990s+] (*US Und.*) to prove someone guilty in court. [abbr. SE *make an identification*; note earlier MAKE v.²]

make v.⁶ [1910s–60s] (*US*) to understand or to empathize with.

make v.⁷ [1940s+] (*US, mainly Southern*) to distill liquor illegally.

make v.⁸ [1940s+] (*US Black*) to straighten one's hair (cf. CONK v.²).

make v.⁹ [1950s+] (*US*) to enlist someone as an official member of the US Mafia; usu. as MADE adj.⁴.

make v.¹⁰ [1950s+] (*US*) to bear or endure.

make a bad fall v. *see* MAKE A GOOD FALL v.

make a balls of v. [late 19C+] to make a mistake, to get into trouble. [BALLS-UP n.]

make a barney balls of oneself v. [1940s+] (*Irish*) to make a fool of oneself. [ext. of MAKE A BALLS OF v.]

make a big feller of oneself v. (*also* **make a big fellow of oneself**) [1940s+] (*Aus.*) to pose as a generous, magnanimous person.

make a blue blotter of oneself v. [1900s] (*US*) to drink heavily.

make a blue fist of v. [mid-19C] (*US*) to blunder, to make a mess of. [negative and ext. var. on MAKE A GOOD FIST OF v.]

make a bolt (of it) v. (*also* **do a bolt**) [mid-19C–1900s] to run off, to escape. [SE *bolt*]

make a bomb v. [1950s+] to make a great deal of money. [BOMB n.¹ (3)]

make a box of v. [1920s+] (*Aus.*) to make a mess of. [? BALLOCKS n.¹ (2)]

make a break v. [mid-19C+] (*orig. US*) to escape or attempt to escape, usu. from prison. [BREAK n.¹]

make a car v. [1950s+] to break into a parked car in order to steal any valuables left inside it. [MAKE v.³ (3) + SE *car*]

make a chevy v. [mid-19C] (*Irish*) to escape, to run away.

make a cleaning v. *see* MAKE A KILLING v.

make a coffee house of a woman's cunt v. [late 18C] to perform coitus interruptus, i.e. 'to go in and out and spend nothing' (Grose, 1796). [pun; the popularity of SE *coffeehouses* as social centres, rather than places for eating and drinking]

make a cow's of v. [1970s+] to make a mess of. [abbr. *cow's arse*]

make a crush on v. [1920s] (*US*) to impress, to make a good impression on.

make a die of v. [early 17C–19C] to die. [? pun on *make a day of* ('day' = 'die' in Cockney pron.)]

make a do of v. [20C+] (*Aus./N.Z.*) to succeed at, to 'make a go' of.

make a federal case (out) of v. (*also* **make a federal production (out) of**) [1950s+] (*US*) to take very seriously, esp. when the speaker feels that the problem is really minor, 'to make a mountain out of a molehill'. [in the US legal system the federal, rather than state, legislature often implies greater severity]

make a get v. [20C+] (*Aus./N.Z.*) to leave quickly, to run off. [abbr. SE *getaway*]

make a good fall v. (*also* **make a bad fall**) [late 19C–1920s] to have a piece of good or bad luck.

make a good fist of v. (*also* **make a poor out at, …poor fist of**) [early 19C+] to make a good or bad attempt at. [FIST n.¹ (3)]

make a go of v. **1** [1920s+] to succeed (despite odds). **2** [1930s] to put up with, to tolerate. [GO n.³ (2)]

make a hack of v. [late 19C] to wear the same dress every day. [fig. use of SE *hack*, a horse for ordinary riding, as distinguished from cross-country, milit., or other special riding]

make a hames v. (*also* **make a haimes**) [1930s+] (*Irish*) to bungle, to make a mess. [SE *hames*, the 2 pieces of metal placed on each side of a horse's collar; though why then a 'mess'?]

make a hand of v. (*also* **take a hand of**) [20C+] (*Irish*) to tease, to mock, to make fun of. [HAND n.²]

make a hare of v. [mid-19C+] (*Anglo-Irish*) to make someone look foolish; to expose someone's ignorance. [the image of a *hare* as a foolish creature]

make a Hebrew congee v. (*also* **make a Hebrew leg**) [late 17C] to make a formally courteous farewell. [*Hebrew*, i.e. Jewish + SE *congee*, ceremonious dismissal and leave-taking/SE *leg*]

make a hit v. [mid-19C+] (*orig. US*) to make a favourable impression. [SE *hit*]

make a hog of oneself v. *see* MAKE A PIG OF ONESELF v.

make a hole in v.¹ [early 17C+] to use up a great deal of, esp. money or a dish of food. [20C+ use is SE]

make a hole in v.² [1930s] (*US Und.*) to escape from prison.

make a hole in one's manners v. (*also* **put a hole in one's manners**) [mid–late 19C; 1970s+] to behave rudely. [1970s+ use is Aus.]

make a hole in the water v. [mid-19C–1910s] to commit suicide by diving or jumping into water and drowning.

make a hump in one's back v. [1960s] of a man, to have sexual intercourse. [the missionary position]

make a job of v. [20C+] (*Aus.*) to beat up, to defeat severely. [var. on DO A JOB ON v.]

make a joe of oneself v. [1960s] (*N.Z.*) to make a fool of oneself. [JOE (HUNT) n.]

make a Judy (Fitzsimmons) of oneself v. [mid-19C] to be a fool, to make an idiot of oneself. [ety. unknown; ? anecdotal]

make a killing v. (*also* **make a cleaning, make a kill**) **1** [late 19C+] (*orig. US*) to make a profit by gambling, whether at the races, on the stock market, in a casino etc. **2** [1900s] (*US campus*) to answer all of a teacher's questions correctly. [KILLING n.]

make a kirk and a mill of v. [early 18C–19C] (*Scot.*) **1** to make one's best of. **2** to put to whatever use one pleases, to do with however one wishes. [Scot. *kirk*, a church]

make a leg v. [1900s–20s] of a woman, to show one's legs. [a pun on SE *make a leg*, to bow]

make all split v. [late 16C–early 17C] to cause a disturbance, to make a commotion.

make (all) the right noises v. [1950s+] to talk in bland, unaggressive, ameliorative terms, sincerely or otherwise.

make a lobster kettle out of one's cunt v. [late 18C] of a prostitute, to allow a man to have sex without paying.

make a long arm v. [mid-19C–1930s] to stretch out one's arm to grab something.

make a long nose v. [late 19C–1950s] to thumb one's nose. [var. on PULL BACON v.]

make a loose v. [early 18C] to make one's escape.

make a mash v. **1** [late 19C–1920s] (*US*) to seduce someone. **2** [1900s] (*US campus*) to please a teacher. [MASH v.²]

make a May-game of v. [late 17C–18C] to play games with, to trick or deceive. [the trad. Mayday pastimes]

make a meal (out) of v. (*also* **make a mouthful of**) [1950s+] to make a great deal of fuss about, to go into over-elaborate descriptions, esp. of something distasteful; thus *don't make a meal of*, don't make a fuss about.

make a milk run v. [1970s+] (*US gay*) to frequent a men's lavatory looking for sex. [MILK v.²]

make a monkey out of v. [late 19C+] (*orig. US*) to make a fool of, to make someone look stupid.

make a monster of v. [late 16C–early 17C] to cuckold.

make a mouthful of v. *see* MAKE A MEAL (OUT) OF v.

make a napkin of one's dishclout v. [mid-18C–early 19C] **1** to marry one's cook or other servant. **2** to make a foolish, unsuitable marriage. [the cook wields the *dishcloth*, the wife the *napkin*]

make an example v. [late 17C] to get drunk.

make an exhibition of oneself v. [mid-19C+] to make oneself seem stupid by a piece of foolish, ostentatious behaviour.

make an honest woman of v. [early 17C+] to marry. [the assumption is that there has already been some form of 'illicit' (in religious terms) pre-marital relationship]

make a noise v. [1960s] (*Aus.*) to buy a round of drinks.

make a noise like a… phr. [20C+] a phr. meaning pretend to be, a command that is rendered humorous through its impossibility, e.g. *go into the changing room and make a noise like a cricket bat*. [the orig. (perfectly serious) use apparently came in Baden-Powell's *Scouting for Boys* (1908), in which scouts in danger of detection are advised to take cover and 'make a noise like a (say) thrush'; however, note cit. in the *Bismark* (ND) *Daily Tribune*, referring to an incident in 1906 where Capt. Lyons emphasised the necessity of clear commands and overheard a private telling his friends, 'make a noise like an officer'; if true, this appears to predate Baden-Powell]

make a one-eighty v. *see* ONE-EIGHTY v.

make a pass v. (*also* **throw a pass**) (*orig. US*) **1** [20C+] to attempt to harm or attack. **2** [1920s+] to approach with amorous intentions. **3** [1940s+] to approach, usu. with some form of business proposition. **4** [1940s+] to approach, to go near.

make a payday v. [1940s] (*US Black*) to obtain money in any way other than working at a legitimate job. [note RN *make a payday*, to earn extra money by doing odd jobs for other ratings]

make a pearl on the nail v. [late 16C–18C] to upend one's emptied glass onto the left thumbnail, thus proving that one has drunk every drop. [SE *pearl*, a drop of liquid]

make a pig of oneself v. (*also* **make a hog of oneself**) [1920s+] (*orig. US*) to act in a gluttonous manner, to be extremely greedy. [PIG n.¹ (1)/SE *hog*]

make a piss stop v. [1980s+] to visit the lavatory, esp. to stop drinking in order to do so. [PISS n. (2); pun on SE *pit stop*, motor-racing jargon]

make a play v. [20C+] **1** to act in a demonstrative, theatrical manner. **2** to pretend, esp. in an 'obvious' manner.

make a play for v. (*also* **give a play to, make a play with**) [late 19C+] to make sexual advances towards someone, to attempt seduction. [PLAY n.¹]

make a pocket v. [mid-19C] to make money, e.g. as a street-seller.

make a poor fist of v. see MAKE A GOOD FIST OF v.

make a punch v. [1900s–10s] (Aus.) to make a killing in the goldfields, stock market etc; thus *punch*, a killing, a coup.

make a push v. see DO A PUSH v. (1).

make a raise v. **1** [19C] (US Und.) to pick a pocket; to rob. **2** [mid-19C] (US gambling) for fellow-gamblers to fund a peer who has lost all his money. **3** [mid-19C–1930s] (US) to obtain money in a non-criminal manner; to secure something.

make a rendezvous with Mrs Hand v. [1980s+] to masturbate (cf. CONVERSE WITH HARRY PALM v.).

make a rise v. [mid-19C–1940s] (Aus.) to do moderately well, to make a small success.

make a run v. **1** [1950s+] to go out to buy a commodity, esp. drugs, but also groceries, liquor etc. **2** [1970s] to attempt to seduce, to approach with amorous intentions.

make a sale v. [1930s+] (Aus.) to vomit.

make a sandwich v. [1970s+] to make a sexual position in which 2 men are having simultaneous vaginal and anal intercourse with 1 woman (cf. CHOCOLATE SANDWICH n.).

make a scratch v. [1930s] to improve one's status.

make a set v. [mid-17C] to have sexual intercourse. [sporting imagery]

make a shine v. see CUT A SPLASH v.

make a six-fist v. [1990s+] to masturbate. [the enclosed penis being the sixth 'finger']

make a song and dance (about) v. [late 19C+] to make a fuss. [SONG AND DANCE n.[1]]

make a speak v. see SPEAK v.

make a splash v. see CUT A SPLASH v.

make a spread v. [1930s–50s] (drugs) to lay out the equipment used for giving oneself an injection.

make ass v. [1980s+] (US Black) to get going. [MAKE v.[3] (3) + ASS n. (2)]

make a stag v. (also **make someone wear the stag's crest**) [late 16C–mid-17C] of a woman, to cuckold one's husband. [punning use of the stag's horns/HORNS n.]

make a straight coat-tail v. [mid-19C–1920s] (US) to run, to hurry. [one's tails are blown out by the wind of one's progress]

make a strike v. [mid-19C+] to be lucky, to be successful. [skittles/bowling imagery]

make a ten-strike v. [late 19C–1940s] (US) to do well, to succeed. [bowling use *ten-strike*, the knocking over of all 10 pins]

make a time v. [late 19C–1900s] (US) to make a fuss. [? SE difficult/hard time]

make a touch v. [late 19C+] (orig. US) **1** to borrow money, esp. when the donor is less than enthusiastic. **2** to pickpocket. [TOUCH n.[1] (3)]

make a trip v. [late 18C–early 19C] to be mother to a bastard child. [play on BREAK ONE'S ANKLE v.]

make a Tyburn show v. [late 18C–early 19C] to be hanged. [TYBURN n., 18C London's main site of public hangings]

make a welter v. [1910s+] (Aus.) to make a fuss, to make an issue out of something. [dial. *welter*, something exceptionally big or heavy of its kind]

make a wry mouth v. [late 16C–17C] to be hanged. [the rictus of suffocation; ult. SE *make a wry mouth*, to grimace with disapproval]

make babies v. [1950s+] (orig. US) to have sexual intercourse (cf. ARRIVE AT THE END OF THE SENTIMENTAL JOURNEY v.). [a coy euph.]

make bacon v.[1] [1920s] (Irish) to guarantee.

make bacon v.[2] [1970s+] (US) to have sexual intercourse. [the first recorded 'cit.' in 1973 (HDAS) is of a T-shirt picturing copulating pigs, captioned 'Making Bacon'; but note PORK v.[1]; PORK SWORD n. etc]

make bacon v.[3] see PULL BACON v.

make bacon of v. see MAKE MINCEMEAT OF v.

make-bait n. (also **makebate**) [16C–19C] a troublemaker; one who stirs up arguments.

make bank v. [1990s+] (US Black) to make money.

make beef v. [19C] to leave, to run off. [BEEF v.[1]]

make bird v. see BIRD COLONEL n.

make black ink v. [1930s] (US) to make money. [SE *black ink*, as opposed to red ink, denotes the profit side of a ledger]

make bloody carpet bags of v. [late 19C–1900s] (orig. US, then Liverpool) to mutilate with a cut-throat razor, to beat severely, to thrash. [SE *carpet bags* are often red]

make bones v. [20C+] (Irish) to exaggerate, to make a fuss.

make book (on) v. **1** [mid-19C+] to wager (on), to gamble (on); also in fig. use. **2** [1930s+] to run a bookmaking operation.

make bush v. [20C+] (US prison) to escape. [one escapes into the bushes]

make butter and cheese v. [mid-17C] to confound, to bamboozle. [the churning action that turns the former into the latter]

make butter with one's tail v. [mid-17C] of a woman, to have sexual intercourse. [? BUTTER n.[1] (1) + TAIL n.[2] (3)]

make buzzard food of v. [late 19C] (US) to kill.

make caca v. see CACA v.

make cat's meat of v. see MAKE MINCEMEAT OF v.

make change v. [1940s+] (US Black) to work or otherwise obtain money for staying alive.

make children's shoes v. [17C–19C] to fool, to trifle with, to belittle. [Norfolk dial.]

make chip-chip v. see CHIP v.[1] (1).

make cold meat of v. [mid-19C+] (orig. US) to kill. [var. on MAKE MINCEMEAT OF v.]

make crooked spindles v. (also **spin crooked spindles**) [late 16C–early 17C] of a woman, to commit adultery, to cuckold one's husband. [the abandonment of proper wifely tasks]

make dog's meat of v. see MAKE MINCEMEAT OF v.

make ducks and drakes of v. see PLAY DUCKS AND DRAKES WITH v.

make easy v. [late 18C] to kill. [ironic use of SE *easy*, free of care and discomfort]

make faces v. [late 18C–early 19C] to father children; thus *face-making*, sexual intercourse.

make feet for children's shoes v. (also **make feet for children's stockings**) **1** [late 18C–19C] to have sexual intercourse. **2** [1930s+] (US Black) to be pregnant.

make foot v. (also **pick up one's foot, put one's foot in one's hand, take foot, take up one's foot and run**) [late 19C+] (US) to leave, to flee in panic.

make for v. [1940s+] to identify, to connect to. [ext. of MAKE v.[5]]

make for a stash v. see MAKE v.[3] (3).

make four eyes v. [1940s] (W.I.) of 2 people, to gaze at one another.

make free with both ends of the busk v. [late 18C–19C] of a man, to caress a woman intimately. [SE *busk*, a corset, spec. its stiffening and supporting whalebone or other agent]

make fun v. [19C] to drink.

make gallows-apples of v. [early–mid-19C] to hang. [the victim hangs from the TRIPLE TREE n.]

make grand charge v. see GRAND CHARGE v.

make hack v. [1970s] (US Black) to move fast.

make hamburger of/hawk's meat of v. see MAKE MINCEMEAT OF v.

make hay v. [late 19C–1900s] to damage, to break; also in fig. use.

make her grunt v. [20C+] of a man, to have sexual intercourse (cf. DO HER JOB FOR HER v.). [note RMC Duntroon (Aus.) *make the noise*, of a woman, to let out ecstatic cries during intercourse]

make hey-hey v. [1930s] (*US*) to act in a boisterous, celebratory manner.

make ignorant v. [1940s+] (*UK Und.*) to irritate, to annoy. [SE *make* + IGNORANT adj.]

make ill music v. [late 17C–early 18C] to be unwelcome news, e.g. *that makes ill music here*. [SE *ill*, bad + fig. use of *music*]

make it v.[1] **1** [mid-19C+] to subsist, to survive; often in phr. *just barely making it*; also used in greeting, as in *how you making it?* **2** [late 19C+] to achieve (something). **3** [20C+] to be successful; thus *make it big, make it good*. **4** [1910s+] to manage, usu. in the context of movement. **5** [1930s–60s] (*US prison*) to be granted parole. **6** [1940s+] to survive, to stay alive. **7** [1950s+] to get on, to relate.

make it v.[2] **1** [1930s+] to do something, to visit or be at a place, to arrive. **2** [1950s+] to move, to get on, to run off; also as imper. **3** [1980s+] to stop doing something, to abandon.

make it v.[3] [1950s–70s] (*US drugs*) to take drugs, esp. opiates.

make it v.[4] *see* MAKE IT (WITH) v.

make it crisp v. *see* MAKE IT SNAPPY v.

make it hot (for) v. (*also* **make it warm (for)**) [mid-19C+] to punish, to make life difficult for someone. [HOT adj.[1] (3)]

make it hum v. *see* MAKE THINGS HUM v.

make it snappy v. (*also* **make it crisp**) [1910s+] to get on with, to hurry up; usu. as imper. *make it snappy!*

make it (with) v. **1** [1930s+] to have sexual intercourse; either hetero- or homosexual. **2** [1950s+] (*US*) to have an orgasm.

make junk of v. *see* MAKE MINCEMEAT OF v.

make leg v. [mid-19C–1900s] to become prosperous. [var. on MAKE UP ONE'S LEG v.]

make like (a)... v. [late 19C+] (*orig. US*) to imitate, to pretend to be, to behave like or as if; thus *make like a chicken/duck*.

make like a... phr. [1950s+] (*US*) as part of a number of phrs., all of which mean 'go away', 'get lost', e.g. *make like a banana and split*, *...cow pat and hit the trail*, *...dragster and lay rubber*, *...drum and beat it*, *...fart and blow away*, *... paper doll and cut out*, *...rubber and roll on*, *...tree and leave*.

make like a baby and head out v. (*also* **make like a foetus and head out**) [1980s+] (*US campus*) to leave. [MAKE LIKE A... phr.]

make like an alligator and drag ass v. [1950s+] (*US*) to leave. [MAKE LIKE A... phr. + pun on DRAG ASS v. (3)]

make long bacon v. *see* PULL BACON v.

make love to the lav v. (*also* **make love to the loo**) [1960s+] (*Aus.*) to vomit (cf. DRIVE THE (PORCELAIN) BUS v.). [SE *make love* + LAV n.]

make love to the porcelain goddess v. [1960s+] (*US campus*) to vomit (cf. DRIVE THE (PORCELAIN) BUS v.).

make mac with v. (*also* **make mack with**) [1960s+] (*US Black/campus*) to flirt, to pick up a woman. [MACK n.[1] (1)]

make mincemeat of v. (*also* **make bacon of**, *...cat's meat of*, *...dog's meat of*, *...hamburger of*, *...hawk's meat of*, *...junk of*, *...mashed potatoes of*, *...meat of*, *...mince-pie (out) of*, *...small biscuit of*, *...Swiss cheese out of*) [18C+] to beat up, to destroy.

make mutton of v. [mid-19C–1900s] to kill, to murder.

make nice v. (*US*) **1** [1950s+] often as admonition, to be friendly or considerate, to behave oneself. **2** [1990s+] to curry favour, to act in a friendly manner (whether or not one means it). [trans. of Yid./Ger. usage]

make no bones v. (*also* **find no bones**) **1** [mid-16C+] to deal with something promptly, to make no excuses, to find nothing wrong with something. **2** [20C+] (occas. act) frankly and openly. [15C *find no bones*, find no problems, offer no difficulties. The original image was of finding bones in meat jelly or aspic]

make noises about v. [1950s+] to discuss, with the implication that one wishes to take some form of action.

make no knobs v. [late 17C–18C] to act immediately, to resist one's scruples. [var. on MAKE NO BONES v.]

make no never mind v. [1930s+] (*orig. US*) to be utterly unimportant. [NEVER MIND phr.]

make off v. [1940s+] (*US*) to pretend.

make one v. **1** [1970s] (*UK prison*) (*also* **make one out**) to plan and effect an escape. **2** [1970s] (*UK Und.*) to put together plans for a crime, esp. a robbery, and then carry out that crime; thus *make one with*, to commit a crime in partnership with one or more other people. **3** [1970s] to join in with, e.g. for a drink. **4** [2000s] to commit a murder. ['one' is either an escape, a plan, a drink or a murder]

make one right v. (*also* **make oneself right**) [1950s+] (*US Black*) to feel good, esp. as a result of drug use.

make one's alley good v. [1920s+] (*Aus.*) to exploit a situation, to improve one's position. [SE *alley*, a marble; thus orig. marbles jargon]

make one's bird n. [1960s] (*US campus*) to leave. [MAKE LIKE A... phr. + SE *bird*]

make one's bones v. **1** [1950s+] (*US Und.*) to arrange and carry out one's first contracted murder. **2** [1970s+] to achieve a successful course or action, in one's profession or work.

make oneself right v. *see* MAKE ONE RIGHT v.

make oneself scarce v. [late 18C+] to slip away, to hide.

make one's eye(s) pass somebody v. (*also* **take one's eye(s) pass somebody**) [20C+] (*W.I., Guyn.*) to speak disrespectfully to one who ought to be treated respectfully.

make one's hat v. *see* GET ONE'S HAT v.

make one's head v. [late 18C–mid-19C] (*Irish*) to acquire a tolerance or 'head' for drink.

make one's jack v. [late 18C–1900s] (*US*) to prosper, to make one's fortune. [JACK n.[4] (2)]

make one's lucky v. *see* CUT ONE'S LUCKY v.

make one's marble good v. [1920s+] (*Aus./N.Z./S.Afr.*) to make a good impression on someone, to ingratiate oneself, to improve one's position.

make one's move v. [1970s] (*US Black*) to reach an important decision.

make one's tucker v. *see* EARN ONE'S TUCKER v.

make-out n. **1** [1960s+] (*US campus*) one who is good at seducing others. **2** [1970s+] (*US*) romantic and sexual behaviour. [MAKE OUT v.[1] (3)]

make out v.[1] **1** [19C+] to get on with, to socialize with; usu. with adv. meaning well or badly. **2** [mid-19C+] (*orig. US*) (*also* **make**) to get along, to make the grade, to succeed. **3** [1930s+] (*US*) to seduce a woman or man. **4** [1940s–50s] (*US*) to stay, to make one's place. **5** [1940s+] (*US*) to indulge in hetero- or homosexual foreplay or petting but not necessarily intercourse. [SE *make out*, to manage to do something]

make out v.[2] [late 19C+] to arrive at a conclusion; thus *how do you make that out?* how do you reach that conclusion? [SE *make out*, 'to establish by evidence, argument' (*OED*)]

make-out artist n. [1940s+] (*US*) a ladies' man, a successful seducer. [MAKE OUT v.[1] (3) + ARTIST sfx]

make out (like) v. [late 19C+] to pretend, to pose as (if). [ext. of MAKE LIKE (A)... v.]

make out with oneself v. [1950s+] (*US*) to masturbate. [MAKE OUT v.[1] (5)]

make over v. [20C+] (*US Black*) to flatter.

make paper v. [1990s+] (*US prison*) to be granted parole. [MAKE v.[4] (4) + PAPER n.[1] (13)]

make points v. [1960s+] (*US*) to give a good impression, to 'score' with someone. [basketball imagery]

make pots and pans v. [19C] to spend heavily, to use up one's money and start begging. [? the selling of pots and pans by a tinker]

maker n. [19C] a forger, a counterfeiter.

make rab v. [1950s] (W.I.) to make a fuss, to complain. [RAB n.[1]]

make rat v. (also **rat in**) [20C+] (W.I.) to sneak into without paying, to GATECRASH v. [Fr. Creole *faire (le) rat*, to act like a rat; ult. the negative stereotype of the rat]

make rings (a)round v. see RUN RINGS (A)ROUND v.

make roast meat for worms v. [early 17C] to kill.

make small biscuit of v. see MAKE MINCEMEAT OF v.

make someone creak in their shoes v. [late 19C] to terrify, to frighten someone. [? here *creak* = quake]

make someone for v. see MAKE v.[5] (1).

make someone jump v. [20C+] to keep someone in a state of anxiety or fear.

make someone one v. [1960s] (US) to give someone an abortion. [the image of the woman and the embryo being 2 people]

make someone piss v. 1 [late 17C] to annoy, to infuriate, to disgust. 2 [1980s] (Aus.) to beat up, to defeat.

make someone's bristles rise v. [mid-19C–1900s] to irritate, to infuriate. [animal imagery]

make someone scream v. [1980s+] (US campus) to have sexual intercourse with someone. [the screams are of orgasmic bliss]

make someone's hair curl v. see PUT SOMEONE'S HAIR IN(TO) A CURL v.

make someone sit up v. 1 [late 19C+] to astound, to shock, to galvanize someone into action. 2 [1910s] to take one's revenge.

make someone's love come down v. [1930s–60s] (US Black) to stimulate someone sexually, to cause to reach orgasm.

make someone's nipples ache v. [1950s] to irritate, to annoy.

make someone's nose swell v. [mid-18C] to make someone jealous. [SE *put someone's nose out of joint*]

make someone spin v. [20C+] (W.I.) to give someone a hard time, to 'lead someone a dance'.

make someone swim for it v. [mid-19C] (UK Und.) to cheat an accomplice out of his share of the proceeds.

make someone tick v. [1930s+] to stimulate, to motivate. [? TICK v.[1]; or SE *tick* like a clock]

make someone tired v. [late 19C+] (orig. US) to irritate someone, to bore.

make someone wear the stag's crest v. see MAKE A STAG v.

make standing room for v. [late 19C] of a woman, to permit sexual intercourse. [STAND n.[2] (1)]

make streaks v. see STREAK v. (1).

make style v. [20C+] (W.I.) 1 to behave in an exhibitionist manner, to attract attention. 2 to be overly fussy or fastidious.

make Swiss cheese out of v. see MAKE MINCEMEAT OF v.

make the bald man puke v. (also **make the bald man sick**) [1990s+] of a man, to masturbate. [BALD MAN IN A BOAT n.]

make the beast with two backs v. (also **make the two-backed beast**) [17C+] to have sexual intercourse. [the first cited use of the phr. is by Shakespeare, in *Othello* (1604); it also occurs in Fr., where Rabelais uses *faire la bête à deux dos*]

make the big door v. [1950s] (US prison) to be released.

make the blind see v. [1960s+] (US gay) to fellate an uncircumcised penis (cf. DRAW THE BLINDS v.). [BLIND adj.[3]]

make the boast v. [1910s–20s] (US Und.) to obtain a pardon.

make the cheese more binding v. [1910s+] (US) to make matters worse.

make the chimney smoke v. [mid-19C+] of a man, to give one's partner an orgasm.

make the cut v. [1990s+] to succeed. [golf jargon *make the cut*, to score sufficiently well in a preliminary round to proceed to the later stages of a competition; those that fail to make a set figure (the *cut*) are eliminated]

make the fist v. [1960s–80s] (US Black) to give a Black Power salute, with the arm raised at an angle and the fist clenched.

make the grade v. (orig. US) 1 [1920s–40s] to succeed in seducing someone. 2 [1920s+] to succeed in obtaining something.

make the hole v. see WORK THE HOLE v.

make the legal move v. [1950s+] (US teen) to get married.

make the nut v. [1950s+] (US) to achieve a target, to have a sufficiency. [NUT n.[8]]

make the plank v. [1960s] (US gay) to take the passive role in anal sex.

make the riffle v. [mid-19C–1940s] (US tramp) to succeed.

make the right noises v. see MAKE (ALL) THE RIGHT NOISES v.

make the scene v. 1 [1950s+] to understand, to appreciate a situation, to experience something. 2 [1950s+] to go somewhere. 3 [1950s+] to be involved in a particular situation, esp. one that features fashionable, smart people. 4 [1960s–70s] to appear, to be present. 5 [1960s–70s] (US gay) to have sexual intercourse. [SCENE n.]

make the skies look blue v. [mid-17C–mid-18C] to carouse, to enjoy oneself. [blue skies are equated with happiness]

make the turn v. [1980s+] (drugs) to withdraw from drug use.

make the two-backed beast v. see MAKE THE BEAST WITH TWO BACKS v.

make things hum v. (also **make it hum**, **make things talk**) [late 19C+] to excite or stir things up.

make time with v. [1930s+] (US) to make advances, to court, to flirt.

make tortillas v. [1970s] (US prison) to sodomize.

make tracks v. (also **take tracks**) 1 [early 19C+] to run away, to escape. 2 [mid-19C] to travel with. 3 [mid-19C+] to go to, to proceed towards.

make up one's leg v. [late 19C–1900s] (coster) to make money. ['the time of smalls, stockings and buckled shoes, when making up the leg was a necessary prelude to going into society' (Ware)]

make up to v. 1 [late 18C+] to 'make love to', to 'chat up'. 2 [19C+] to curry favour with.

make V v. [early 17C] to make a V-sign with the first and second fingers of the hand, which implies that the target of the gesture is a cuckold. [the V represents the sign of the HORNS n.]

make wallpaper v. (also **be a wall-prop**) [1900s–20s] to be a 'wallflower' at a dance or other social occasion. [one merely provides background for the more enthusiastic participants]

make waves v. 1 [1950s+] to cause trouble, esp. in an otherwise calm situation; thus *don't make waves*, don't make a fuss; (US) *wave-maker*, a person who raises objections or difficult questions. 2 [1990s+] to make an impression.

make wee-wee v. see WEE v.

makeweight n. [late 18C–early 19C] 1 a small candle. 2 a small, slender person.

make whoopee v. [1920s+] 1 to go out on a spree, to enjoy oneself uproariously. 2 to have sexual intercourse. [SE *make* + WHOOPEE n.; the coinage seems to have been in G. Kahn's 1928 song 'Makin' Whoopee': 'Another bride, another June, Another sunny honeymoon, Another season, another reason for making whoopee!']

make with v. (also **give with**) [20C+] (orig. US) to use, to affect, to perform, to pose as. [Yid. *macht mit*, make with]

make yes of it v. [1910s–20s] to agree.

-making sfx [1920s+] used with a variety of nouns, e.g. *blush-making*, *shy-making*, *sick-making*, sometimes prefixed by 'too'. [mainly 1930s and general middle-/upper middle-class use, but disinterred regularly by readers of the novels of Evelyn Waugh, esp. *Vile Bodies* (1930)]

mako see under MACO.

makomé n. (also **macumeh**, **makoumé**) [20C+] (W.I.) an effeminate man. [Carib.E. *makomé*, one's child's godmother, usu. an elderly female friend; ult. Fr. *macommère*]

maku n. [20C+] (W.I.) 1 an effeminate man. 2 a peeping Tom. 3 a fool, an idiot. [? Fr. *maquereau*, a pimp]

Malabar Hilton n. (also **Malabar flats**) [1960s+] (Aus. Und.) Long Bay prison, New South Wales (cf. ABBOTT'S PRIORY n.; BOARDING HOUSE n.).

malady of France *n. see* FRENCH DISEASE n.

malaky *n. see* MALARKEY n.

malalapipe *n.* [1970s+] (*S.Afr.*) a homeless child beggar. [Zulu *umalalepayipini*, 'one who sleeps in a pipe']

malaria *n.* [1980s] (*US Black*) sweat. [SE *malaria*, a disease characterized by a high fever]

malarkey *n.* (*also* **malaky, malarky, mallarkey, mullarkey**) (*orig. US*) **1** [1920s+] nonsense, foolishness, 'messing about'. **2** [1940s+] a fool. [? Irish *mullachán*, a strongly built boy, thus a ruffian]

malavogue *v.* (*also* **malivogue**) [20C+] (*Irish*) to beat, to manhandle. [ety. unknown; a nonce-word]

Malawi grass *n.* [1980s+] (*drugs*) marijuana from Malawi; thus *Malawi cob*, marijuana from Malawi bundled in a shape reminiscent of a cigar (cf. ACAPULCO (GOLD) n.; AFRICAN BUSH n.). [SE *Malawi* + GRASS n.[5]/COB n.[6]]

malazanas *n.* [1960s–70s] (*S.Afr. township*) money. [ety. unknown]

malco *n.* [1980s+] a general term of abuse; also as v., to act in an uncoordinated manner. [abbr. SE *malcoordinated*]

maleesh *phr.* [1910s+] (*Aus./N.Z.*) a phr. used to indicate one's lack of interest in or dismissal of an idea or thing. [Egyptian Arabic *ma'lesh*, no matter, never mind]

male-hustler *n.* [1960s] (*US gay*) a male prostitute, posing as masculine rather than effeminate (cf. ASS PEDDLER n.). [HUSTLER n. (7)]

male-mules *n.* [17C] the testicles. [play on SE; poss. used only in Urquhart's translation of Rabelais]

malflor *n.* [1960s+] (*US*) a lesbian. [Sp.; lit. 'an evil flower']

malformy *n.* [1970s] (*US Black*) a general insult. [? euph. for MOTHERFUCKER n.; SE *malformed*]

malfunction junction *n.* [1970s+] (*US*) a major congestion, usu. a traffic jam.

malhavelins *n. see* MANAVILINS n.

malicious *adj.* [20C+] (*W.I.*) **1** tiresomely inquisitive. **2** offensively meddlesome with the aim of causing harm.

malivogue *v. see* MALAVOGUE v.

malkin *n.* (*also* **mawkin**) **1** [mid-16C–17C] a promiscuous woman. **2** [mid-16C–19C] the vagina (cf. BIRD n.[8]). [Scot. *malkin*, a cat. *Grimalkin* is often the name of a witch's feline familiar, while *malkin* itself also means hare, suggesting a link to the rabbit, a trad. 'sexy' animal, that may or may not be coincidental]

malkin-trash *n.* [late 17C–early 19C] an ill-dressed person. [SE *malkin*, an untidy woman, a slattern]

mallacky *n.* [20C+] (*Irish*) cat excrement. [Irish *meallach*, lumpy, globular]

mallarkey *n. see* MALARKEY n.

mallee root *n.* [1940s+] (*Aus.*) a prostitute. [rhy. sl.; ult. Aboriginal *mallee*, eucalyptus]

mallet *n.*[1] [1970s–80s] (*US Black*) the police. [their image as a repressive agency]

mallet *n.*[2] [1990s+] (*UK juv.*) a boy who lacks pubic hair.

mallet *v.* [late 16C–19C; 1980s+] to hit, to beat, lit. and fig.; latterly spec. to defeat. [SE *mallet*]

mallethead *n.* [1950s+] (*US*) a stupid person. [SE *mallet* + -HEAD sfx (1); note earlier MALLETHEADED adj.]

malletheaded *adj.* [19C] stupid, foolish (cf. AIRHEADED adj.). [SE *mallet*]

malleting bout *n.* [early–mid-19C] a fist-fight. [var. on HAMMER n.[2] (1)]

malley *n.* [mid-19C] (*Anglo-Ind.*) a gardener. [Hind. *mali*, a gardener]

Malley's cow *n.* [1950s–70s] (*Aus.*) one who has left, gone away. [the story of one *Malley* who was supposed to look after a cow. When his boss returned to find Malley but no cow and asked what had happened, he received the reply 'she's a goner']

mall rat *n.* (*also* **mallie, mall punk**) [1980s+] (*US*) a young person who spends the day hanging around shopping malls; young people who dress and behave in a punk fashion. [SE (*shopping*) *mall* + RAT sfx]

malmsey nose *n.* [late 17C–early 19C] a heavily acned nose. [the assumption being that the acned nose is the result of drinking too much *malmsey* wine]

Malt *n.* [late 19C–1960s] a Maltese. [abbr.]

malt *v.* [19C] to drink. [SE *malt*, a component of beer]

malt cove *n.* (*also* **malty cove**) [19C] a beer drinker. [SE *malt* + COVE n. (1)]

malted *adj.* [19C] drunk, tipsy (cf. ALED UP adj.). [MALT v.]

Malteser *n.* [1950s–60s] a Maltese. [the brandname of the popular sweet]

maltooling *n.* [mid–late 19C] of a female pickpocket, stealing from people travelling on buses. [MOLL n.[1] (1) + TOOL n.[2]]

maltoot *n.* (*also* **maltout**) [late 18C–19C] a marine. [? Fr. *matelot*, a sailor]

maltpie *n.* [early 17C] alcohol.

maltworm *n.* [mid-16C–early 17C; mid–late 19C] a heavy drinker. [play on SE *maltworm*, a malt-infesting weevil; note joc. *troll-the-bowl*, a tippler, carouser]

malty *adj.* [early–mid-19C] drunk (cf. ALED UP adj.). [SE *malt*]

malty cove *n. see* MALT COVE n.

mama *n.* (*also* **mamma**) **1** [1910s+] (*orig. US Black*) a woman. **2** [1910s+] (*orig. US Black*) a girlfriend or wife, esp. in direct address. **3** [1940s+] anything considered very powerful, large or admirable. **4** [1940s+] a feminine lesbian. **5** [1950s+] (*US*) an effeminate male homosexual; also as a camp self-description (cf. AUNTIE n.[2]). **6** [1960s+] (*orig. Hell's Angel*) a woman who rides with the Hell's Angels and is available for sex and allied indignities but is distinguished from the *old ladies* (the actual girlfriends of the riders); the term is an abbr. of phr. *let's go make someone a mama*. **7** [1970s] (*US prison*) an inmate who poses as a woman. **8** [1980s] a masculine lesbian.

mama and papa of — *phr. see* FATHER (AND MOTHER) OF — phr.

mama bear *n.* [1970s+] (*US*) a policewoman, esp. in the Highway Patrol (cf. COPESS n.). [SE *mama* + BEAR n.[7]]

mama bitch *n.* [1960s] (*US Black*) the most reliable and experienced of a pimp's STABLE n. (2) of prostitutes.

mamacita *n.* [1970s+] (*US*) an attractive young woman. [Sp.; lit. 'little mother']

mama coca *n.* [1980s+] (*drugs*) cocaine. [lit. 'mother coca'; note cocaine is a 'feminine' drug, *see* GIRL n.[2]]

mama-huncher *n.* [1960s+] a euph. for MOTHERFUCKER n. (1).

mama-jabbing *adj. see* MAMMY-JAMMING adj.

mama-jammer *n. see* MAMMY-JAMMER n.

mama-man *n.* [1940s+] (*W.I.*) **1** a man who does women's work. **2** an unmanly man.

mama's boots *n.* [1930s] (*US gambling*) a pair of threes in craps dice (cf. ADA FROM DECATUR n.).

mama's boss *n.* [1930s–40s] (*US Black*) usu. female usage, a husband or favourite boyfriend.

mamí *n.* [2000s] (*US Black/P.R.*) a woman, usu. Black or Puerto Rican.

mamma *n. see* MAMA n.

mamma-jammer *n. see* MAMMY-JAMMER n.

mammaries *n.* [1970s+] the female breasts. [SE *mammary gland*]

mammock *v.* [mid–late 19C] (*US, mainly Western/Southern*) **1** to beat, to thrash; thus *mammocking*, a thrashing. **2** to mess up, to confuse. [dial. *mammock*, to tear into pieces]

mammy *n.*[1] (*also* **mauma, momma**) [19C+] (*US*) the ideal Black woman as stereotyped by Whites. Such women would typically be employed as nannies or cooks in White households. [SE *mammy*, mother; note Hurston, 'Story in Harlem Slang' (1942), defines it simply as 'a term of insult']

mammy *n.*[2] [1930s+] (*US Und.*) an abundance, a lot; esp. in phr.

money's mammy, a great deal of money. [the image of maternal, i.e. *mammy's* abundance, of love, food etc]

mammy-dodger *n.* [1920s–30s] (*US Black*) a euph. for MOTHERFUCKER n. (1).

mammy-dodging *adj.* [1920s–30s] a euph. for MOTHERFUCKING adj. (1).

mammy-freak *n.* [1950s] (*US*) a prostitute's (White) customer whose sexual tastes demand women who resemble motherly Black women. [MAMMY n.[1] + FREAK n.[1] (6)]

mammyfucking *adj.* [1970s] a synon. for MOTHERFUCKING adj. (1).

mammy-jammer *n.* (*also* **mama-jammer, mamma-jammer, mammy-jabber**) [1950s+] a euph. for MOTHERFUCKER n. (1).

mammy-jamming *adj.* (*also* **mama-jabbing**) [1940s+] a euph. for MOTHERFUCKING adj. (1).

mammy-rammer *n.* [1960s–70s] a euph. for MOTHERFUCKER n. (1).

mammy-ramming *adj.* (*also* **mammy-rammy**) [1960s–70s] a euph. for MOTHERFUCKING adj. (1).

mammy-screwing *adj.* [1960s] a semi-euph. for MOTHERFUCKING adj. (1).

mammy-tapper *n.* [1960s] (*US Black*) a euph. for MOTHERFUCKER n. (1).

mammy-tapping *adj.* [1960s] a euph. for MOTHERFUCKING adj. (1).

mampala *n.* (*also* **mampala-man, maparla, maparla-man**) [20C+] (*W.I.*) an effeminate man, a homosexual man who plays the 'female' role in sex. [Sp. *mampolón*, a cock, but not a fighting cock, thus a weakling]

mampy *n.* (*also* **mampi**) [1990s+] (*W.I.*) a fat woman.

mams *n.* [1970s+] the female breasts. [abbr. SE *mammaries*]

mamzer *n.* (*also* **momser, momza, momzer, momzir**) [20C+] a catch-all term implying everything from great affection to deep dislike. [Heb. *mamzer*, a bastard, adapted in Lat. and thus used throughout the Middle Ages. The modern use, however, is related to Yid., and imported by Jewish immigrants to US and UK]

man *n.*[1] **1** [late 14C+] used emphatically in direct address. **2** [20C+] used in direct address, without emphasis, usu. to acknowledge a shared social or cultural identity (later usage sometimes includes women, children and animals). [Gold, *A Jazz Lexicon* (1964) and Major, *Juba to Jive: A Dict. of Afro-American Slang* (1994), suggest that the term was adopted by US Blacks to counter the common White use of 'boy' when addressing Blacks; note McCall, *Makes Me Wanna Holler* (1994): 'More fights started over one person calling another "boy" than over anything else. To counter that indignity, we addressed each other respectfully as "man", even though we were not adults']

man *n.*[2] [mid-18C–1960s] the penis.

man *n.*[3] **1** [early 19C] the head of a coin. **2** [1910s–60s] (*US*) $1. [the picture, usu. of a male monarch, that was engraved on most coins + IRON MAN n. (1)]

man *n.*[4] [1930s–40s] (*US Black*) a pint bottle of liquor. [Scot. *halfman*, half a bottle of spirits; thus HALF-MAN n.]

man *n.*[5] [1950s+] a fan, e.g. ASS-MAN n.; LEG MAN n.[2] (1).

man, the *n.* **1** [1910s+] (*orig. US*) any man or group in charge of an institution, a commanding officer, esp. a prison warden, a policeman; thus *meet the man*, to go to work. **2** [1920s+] the holder of power, in a non-institutional context, anyone deemed exceptional in ability; thus (*US Black*) *you the man*, a phr. implying one's acceptance of another person's superiority. **3** [1940s+] (*orig. US*) a (major) drug dealer. **4** [1940s+] (*US Black*) the White ruling class. **5** [1950s+] a crime boss, esp. when he masquerades as a respectable businessman. **6** [1950s+] (*US Black*) the US Government. **7** [1960s+] (*US*) (*also* **the Man above**) God. **8** [1970s] (*US Black*) the police. **9** [1990s+] an exemplary person.

man *adj.* [20C+] (*W.I.*) very expensive. [SE *man*, something powerful, strong]

man *v.* **1** [17C] to work as a pimp. **2** [17C–early 19C] to have sexual intercourse.

-man *sfx see* -MANS sfx.

manablins *n. see* MANAVILINS n.

Man above, the *n. see* MAN, THE n. (7).

man a-hanging *n.* [1970s–80s] (*US Black*) a person in trouble.

man alive *n.* [20C+] the number 5. [rhy. sl.]

man and man *n.* [1970s–80s] (*UK Black*) a person. [on pattern of I AND I n.]

man and wife *n.* [1910s+] a knife. [rhy. sl.]

manatee *n.* [1960s–70s] (*US gay*) a 'masculine' lesbian.

manavilins *n.* (*also* **malhavelins, manablins, manarolins, manavalins, manavelings**) [mid–late 19C] odds and ends, bits and pieces, typically of food or small change. [ety. unknown, but note contemp. naut. jargon *manarvel*, to pilfer small stores]

man-better-man *phr.* [20C+] (*W.I.*) a phr. used to issue a definite challenge to fight, with the implication of finding out who is the 'better man'.

man-box *n.* [mid-19C] a coffin.

man-catcher *n.* (*also* **man-getter, -grabber, -hunter, -shark**) [1920s–50s] (*US*) a labour recruiter, an employment agency.

Manchester *n.* [20C+] (*Aus./N.Z.*) household linen; thus the *Manchester department* in shops. [the days when *Manchester* was 'Cottonopolis', the textile capital of the globe]

manchester *n.* [early 19C] the tongue. [? Scot. *mang*, talk and/or Rom. *mag*, to beg]

Manchester-bred *adj.* [mid-19C] physically strong, mentally weak. [the descriptive rhyme 'long in the arms and short in the head']

Manchester Cities *n.* (*also* **Manchesters**) [1950s+] (*Aus./UK*) the female breasts (cf. BRACE AND BITS n.). [rhy. sl.; *Manchester City* = TITTY n.[1] (1)]

Manchester sovereign *n.* [mid-19C–1930s] a shilling (5p). [the implication is of cheapness, from Manchester's reputation for mass production]

mancunt *n.* [1990s+] (*gay*) **1** the anus (cf. MANGINA n.; MANHOLE n.[1]). **2** a passive homosexual. [SE *man* + CUNT n.[1] (1)]

mandarin *n.* [1910s+] a senior civil servant, politician or commentator. [Port. *mandarim*, itself ult. Skrt *mantrin*, counsellor. The term was adopted in China to describe the 9 grades of Chinese officials, each of which was distinguished by a particular kind of 'button']

M and C *n.* [1920s–60s] (*US drugs*) a mixture of mophine and cocaine, the equivalent of the heroin and cocaine SPEEDBALL n.[1] (cf. C AND M n.). [M n. and C n.[2] (1)]

mander *n.* [mid–late 19C] (*UK prison/Und.*) a remand to prison, pending trial. [SE *remand*]

mandingo *n.* [1960s+] (*US Black*) a tough, physically strong, virile African-American man. [proper name *Mandingo*, a member of the peoples of the upper Niger in West Africa, whose ranks supplied many slaves; more immediately a ref. to the book title *Mandingo*, concerning the stereotypical 'Black buck' slave and his effect on women, both Black and White]

M & M *adj.* [2000s] (*US teen*) of a person, just about socially acceptable.

M & Ms *n.* [1960s+] (*orig. US drugs*) barbiturates, amphetamines, drugs available as pills (cf. PILL n.[4]). [the US-originated sweet]

mandozy *n.* [19C] **1** a powerful blow. **2** a term of endearment among London Jews. [the Jewish prize-fighter *Daniel Mendoza* (1764–1836)]

mandrake *n.* **1** [early 17C+] a sodomite, a male homosexual. **2** [mid-17C] a dildo. [SE *mandrake*, 'Any plant of the genus *Mandragora* [...] characterized by very short stems, thick, fleshy, often forked, roots, and fetid lance-shaped leaves. The mandrake is poisonous, having emetic and narcotic properties, and was formerly used medicinally. The forked root is thought to resemble the human form, and was fabled to utter a deadly shriek when plucked up from the ground' (*OED*)]

M and S *n.* (*also* **Marks, Marks and Sparks**) [1930s+] a nickname for the Marks & Spencer group of department stores. [abbr.; note the firm's house magazine is called *Sparks*]

man dumpling *n.* [1950s] (*W.I.*) a very large dumpling. [the implication is either of being as big as a man, or a man-sized portion]

mandy *n.* (*also* **manny**) [1960s+] a Mandrax or methaqualone tablet. [the sp. 'manny' seems to appear only in Fabian & Byrne, *Groupie* (1969), and was coined by them as a deliberate euph.]

man-eater *n.* **1** [mid–late 19C] (*Anglo-Ind.*) a horse that tends to bite people. **2** [20C+] a sexually predatory woman. **3** [1920s] a swindler. **4** [1970s+] a homosexual man; a fellator (cf. BONE-EATER n.). [orig. naut. use, a particularly disciplinarian officer; ult. SE, a man-eating tiger]

maneen *n.* [1910s+] (*Irish*) a little man, a gauche young man. [SE *man* + dimin. sfx *-een*]

maneuvra *v.* [2000s] (*US Black*) to pick up a girl. [SE *manoeuvre*]

mang *n.* [1970s] (*Aus. teen*) a general insult.

mang *v.* [early–mid-19C+] to talk or boast; thus *mangsman*, a lawyer. [Scot. or Rom. *mag*, to beg]

manga *n. see* MUNGER n.

mangarly *n.* (*also* **mangary**) [mid-19C+] (*Ling. Fr./Polari*) food. [Ital. *mangiare*, to eat]

mange *n.* [late 19C–1900s] food. [Ital. *mangiare*, to eat]

mange *adj.* [1990s+] (*W.I.*) unpleasant, impolite. [SE *mangy*]

mange *v.* [1960s+] (*US campus*) to eat. [Ital. *mangiare*/Fr. *manger*, to eat]

man-getter *n. see* MAN-CATCHER n.

mangina *n.* [2000s] **1** (*gay*) the anus (cf. MANCUNT n.). **2** (*US campus*) a reticent, reserved man. [SE *man* + *vagina*]

mangle *n.*[1] [19C] the vagina (cf. BITE n.[2]).

mangle *n.*[2] [1940s+] (*Aus.*) a bicycle. [supposed resemblance]

mangle and wringer *n.* [20C+] a singer. [rhy. sl.]

mangled *adj.* **1** [1920s] worn-out. **2** [1930s] (*US*) hurt, injured. **3** [1980s+] (*US campus*) dishevelled, unkempt. **4** [2000s] (*Irish*) drunk (cf. ANNIHILATED adj.). [as if wrung through a mangle]

mangle the midget *v.* [1990s+] to masturbate.

mango *n.* [1980s+] (*N.Z.*) a NZ$50 note. [the orange colour]

mangoes *n.* [1980s+] (*US*) the female breasts (cf. APPLES n.[1]).

man-grabber *n. see* MAN-CATCHER n.

mangy *adj.* **1** [mid-19C+] contemptible. **2** [20C+] (*Irish*) mean, grasping, avaricious. [SE *mangy*, squalid, shabby, lit. 'scabby']

manhole *n.*[1] **1** [late 19C+] the vagina (cf. BLACK HOLE n.[1]). **2** [1970s+] (*US gay*) the anus (cf. A-HOLE n.; MANCUNT n.). **3** [1970s+] (*US gay*) a passive partner in anal intercourse. [SE *man* + HOLE n.[1] (2)]

manhole *n.*[2] [1970s+] (*US Black*) a bar, a saloon, a club etc. for men only. [SE *man* + HOLE n.[2] (2)]

manhole cover *n.*[1] [20C+] a brother. [rhy. sl.]

manhole cover *n.*[2] [1950s+] (*Aus./US*) a sanitary towel. [MANHOLE n.[1] (1) + SE *cover*]

manhole covers (with custard) *n.* **1** [1940s+] bread pudding. **2** [1950s] (*US short order*) hot-cakes. [supposed resemblance]

manhole inspector *n. see* INSPECTOR OF MANHOLES n.

man-hunter *n. see* MAN-CATCHER n.

manicou-man *n.* [20C+] (*W.I.*) an effeminate man. [? Carib.E. *manicou*, a 'nocturnal, foul-smelling marsupial rodent the size of a cat' (Allsopp); the young of this creature hang onto their mother for transportation]

manifest *n.* [1920s–30s] (*US*) a fast freight train. [the *manifest* of the goods it carries]

man in gray *n.* [1930s–50s] (*US Black*) a postman.

man in the boat *n. see* LITTLE MAN (IN THE BOAT) n.

man in the gap *n.* [20C+] (*Irish*) one who bravely fights for and succeeds in achieving a cause or position.

man in the moon *n.*[1] [mid-17C] a watchman, a constable.

man in the moon *n.*[2] [mid–19C] the nickname for the person, necessarily anonymous and quick to disappear, who pays out bribes at elections.

man in the moon *n.*[3] [20C+] a fool, an eccentric, a crazy person (cf. BREAD AND BUTTER n.[2]). [rhy. sl. = LOON n.[1]]

manjarie *n. see* MANGARLY n.

Mank *n.* [2000s] **1** a Mancunian. **2** Manchester. [abbr.]

man-killer *n.* [late 19C–1900s] porter, stout, any black beer. [the effect of such sweet, heavy beers on one's weight and thus health]

manly-warringahs *n.* [1990s+] (*Aus.*) fingers. [rhy. sl.]

manmanpoul *n.* [20C+] (*W.I.*) **1** a person who fusses excessively. **2** a gullible fool. [Fr. *maman poule*, mother hen]

man muscle *n.* [1970s+] (*US Black*) the penis. [note LOVE MUSCLE n.]

manna from heaven *n.* [2000s] (*US*) the throw of 11 in craps dice (cf. ADA FROM DECATUR n.).

manne die *n.* [1960s+] (*S.Afr.*) a local hero, esp. in a school or college. [Afk. *man(ne)*, man]

manners *v.*[1] [1970s–80s] (*UK Black*) to seduce.

manners *v.*[2] *see* HEAVY MANNERS v.

mannish *adj.* [20C+] (*US/W.I.*) usu. of young people, forward, impertinent. [i.e. a child acting beyond its years]

mannish water *n.* [20C+] (*W.I., Jam.*) goat-head soup, a highly seasoned, peppery soup made from the head and offal of a goat, eaten on festive occasions. The soup is linked to virility in and with placating the spirits of the dead in Tobago. [the association of the soup with virility]

manny *n.*[1] [1970s+] (*US gay*) a lesbian.

manny *n.*[2] *see* MANDY n.

mano *n.* [1960s+] (*US Hispanic*) used in direct address, man.

manoeuvre the apostles *v.* [late 18C+] to manipulate one's accounts to pay off one debt while incurring another. [pun on popular phr. *to rob Peter to pay Paul*]

man of business *n.* [20C+] (*W.I.*) a woman's lover on whom she relies for various favours. [Carib.E. *man of business*, a handyman]

man of remnants *n.* [1910s–20s] a tailor.

man of the road *n. see* GENTLEMAN OF THE ROAD n. (2).

man of the town *n.* [late 17C–early 19C] a debauchee, a libertine.

man of the world *n.* [late 19C] a professional thief, usu. a pickpocket.

man of war *n.* [18C–19C] the Fleet prison, London. [its site, on the east bank of the Fleet River; the image is of an anchored warship]

man on the moon *n.* [1960s+] a spoon. [rhy. sl.]

man outside Hoyt's *n.* [1940s+] **1** (*Aus.*) the source of all rumours; also in phr. *don't know — from the man outside Hoyt's*. **2** (*Aus. Und.*) the source of any stolen property that the police might find with a receiver. [the commissionaire *outside Hoyt's* Theatre, Melbourne, a gorgeously uniformed individual]

man o' war *n.* [20C+] a bore. [rhy. sl.]

man pains *n.* [1990s+] (*US Black teen*) **1** injuries suffered while doing 'manly' things, i.e. lifting a trunk, playing football etc. **2** sexual frustration.

manpower *n.* [1940s+] (*Aus./N.Z., mainly historical*) the organization that conscripts for non-military work, e.g. fruit-picking, as part of the war effort.

manpower *v.* [1940s+] (*Aus./N.Z., mainly historical*) to conscript for non-military work, e.g. fruit-picking, as part of the war effort. [MANPOWER n.]

man root *n.* [19C] the penis.

-mans *sfx* (*also* **-man**) [16C–19C] a state of being or a thing; *see* various combs., e.g. CRACKMANS n., LIGHTMANS n., RUFFMANS n.

etc. [the *OED* cites it as 'unexplained' but E.P. (*DSUE* 8th edn, 1984, *Origins*, 4th edn, 1966) suggests links with Lat. *mens*, mind, Fr. sfx *-ment*, SE *man*, a human being or Skrt *-moni*, mood or mind]

man-shark *n. see* MAN-CATCHER n.

mantalini *n.* [mid–late 19C] a male milliner. [Mr *Mantalini*, the milliner in Charles Dickens's *Nicholas Nickleby* (1839)]

manteca *n.* [2000s] (*US drugs*) heroin.

mantee *n.* [1930s–60s] a masculine lesbian; thus *mantee walk*, to swagger; *mantee voice*, a deep voice. [? link to Fr. *minet*, an effeminate young man]

man thomas *n.* [early 17C–mid-19C] the penis (cf. ABRAHAM n.[1]).

manton *n. see* JOE MANTON n.

mantovani *n.* (*also* **manto**) [1990s+] women, girls. [rhy. sl. = FANNY n.[1]]

man-trap *n.*[1] **1** [late 18C] a widow. **2** [late 18C] (*UK Und.*) the gallows. **3** [late 18C–19C] the vagina (cf. BITE n.[2]). **4** [late 19C] (*Aus.*) a public house. **5** [1910s+] an attractive and available woman.

man-trap *n.*[2] [late 19C–1900s] a piece of excrement (cf. ALI OOP n.). [rhy. sl. = CRAP n.[3] (1)]

manual compliment *n.* (*also* **manual remonstrance, manual subscription**) [mid-18C–19C] a blow. [pun on SE *sign-manual*]

manual labour *n.* [1990s+] masturbation.

manufacture *n. see* ENGLISH MANUFACTURE n.

man upstairs, the *n.* [1940s+] God.

manure *n.* [1920s–70s] (*Can./US*) nonsense. [euph. for BULLSHIT n. (1)]

man walking *phr.* [2000s] (*US prison*) a signal that a prison officer is approaching.

man who rides the screaming gasser *n.* [1930s–40s] (*US Black*) a policeman in a patrol car.

man with a headache stick *n.* [1930s–60s] (*US Black*) a policeman. [his nightstick/truncheon]

man with a paper ass(hole) *n.* [1950s+] (*US Black*) a talkative fool – all talk and little or no action. [ASS n./ASSHOLE n.[1] (1)]

man with no hands *n.* [1940s+] (*Aus.*) a miser.

man with the book of many years *n.* [1940s] (*US Black*) a judge.

man with (the) fuzzy balls *n.* [1950s–80s] **1** (*US Black*) a White man. **2** (*US*) an expert, an accomplished person. [BALLS n.[1] (1); note the theory that FUZZ n.[1] derives from this]

Maori *adj.* [20C+] (*N.Z.*) not a sl. term as such, *Maori* has been stereotyped as an all-purpose shorthand for stupid, lazy or primitive. It is used as such in the combs. that follow.

Maori cannon *n.* [1930s–40s] (*N.Z.*) a badly played shot in billiards or snooker. [racist stereotyping]

Maori car *n.* [1980s] (*N.Z.*) an old or broken-down vehicle. [racist stereotyping]

Maori day off *n.* (*also* **MDO**) [1980s] (*N.Z.*) unauthorized absence from the workplace. [racist stereotyping]

Maori half-crown *n.* [late 19C; 1950s] (*N.Z.*) a penny. [racist stereotyping; the half-crown (12.5p) was worth 30 pennies]

Maori holiday *n.* [1970s+] (*N.Z.*) the day after payday. [racist stereotyping]

Maori mustang *n.* [1970s+] (*N.Z.*) the Mark II Ford Zephyr. [the *Mustang* is a much sought-after sports car; the *Ford* is definitely not]

Maori overdrive *n.* [1970s+] (*N.Z.*) sliding one's car downhill with the engine off and the gears in neutral. [racist stereotyping]

Maori P.T. *n.* [mid-19C+] (*N.Z.*) taking it easy, doing nothing. [racist stereotyping; SE *P.T.*, physical training]

Maori roast *n.* [1970s+] (*N.Z.*) fish and chips or some form of fast food. [racist stereotyping]

Maori time *n.* [1980s+] (*N.Z.*) a flexible attitude to time-keeping (cf. AFRICAN (PEOPLE'S) TIME n.).

Maori weed *n.* [20C+] (*N.Z.*) a wild horse.

map *n.* **1** [20C+] the human face. **2** [1920s] the mouth. **3** [1920s+] (*US Und.*) a bank cheque, usu. a fraudulent one. [? predating in John Taylor, 'The Water Poet', *Works* (1630): 'Being willing to take slender acquaintance of any map whatsoever, viewing, and circumviewing every man's face I met']

map *v.* [1980s+] (*US Black*) to hit, esp. to hit in the face. [MAP n. (1)]

maparla(-man) *n. see* MAMPALA n.

maphepha *n.* (*also* **mephepha**) (*S.Afr.*) **1** [1970s+] a rand. **2** [1970s+] money in general. **3** [1980s+] an official document, 'papers'. [Xhosa *amaphepha*, papers]

map of... *phr.* [1900s–60s] (*US*) a phr. used with the name of a country to refer to typical facial features, e.g. a Jew will have *a map of Jerusalem all over his face.*

map of England *n.* (*also* **map of Africa/Ireland**) [1910s+] semen stain on a sheet, or occas. a garment. [note synon. Fr. *carte de France*; [19C] *cartes de géographie*]

map of Tassie *n.* (*also* **map of Tasmania, map o' Tassie**) [1980s+] (*Aus.*) the female genitals and pubic hair. [the supposed similarity of this shape to the outline of a map of Tasmania]

mapusa *n.* (*also* **mapuza**) [1970s+] (*S.Afr. Und.*) the police. [? Afr. pron. of SE *police*]

maque *n. see* MACK n.[1].

maracas *n.*[1] [1930s+] (*US*) the female breasts (cf. BAGS n.[1]). [? the musical instrument, i.e. one 'plays' on them]

maracas *n.*[2] [1990s+] the testicles (cf. BALLS n.[1]; CHEESE AND CRACKERS n.). [appearance + rhy. sl. = KNACKERS n.]

marathons *n.* [1970s+] (*drugs*) amphetamines (cf. A n.[2]). [their effect on one's stamina]

marble *n.*

marble *v.* [mid–late 19C] (*US*) to leave, to go. [SE *marble*, that rolls along]

marble arch *n.*[1] [mid–late 19C] the vagina (cf. ANTIPODES n.). [lit. euph.]

marble arch *n.*[2] [1990s+] starch. [rhy. sl.]

marble city *n. see* MARBLE ORCHARD n.

marble dome *n. see* MARBLEHEAD n.[2].

marble halls *n.* [20C+] the testicles (cf. CHEESE AND CRACKERS n.). [rhy. sl. = BALLS n.[1] (1)]

marblehead *n.*[1] [19C] a Greek. [the many marble statues of Greece + -HEAD sfx]

marblehead *n.*[2] (*also* **marble dome**) [1910s–60s] (*US*) an idiot. [SE *marble* + -HEAD sfx (1)]

marble heart *n.* [late 19C–1930s] (*US*) a rejection. [play on COLD SHOULDER n.]

marble hill *n. see* HILL n.

marble orchard *n.* (*also* **marble city/town**) [1920s+] (*US*) a cemetery. [note film title *Gardens of Stone* (1987), referring to the Arlington National Cemetery]

marbles *n.*[1] [late 16C–19C] venereal buboes or pocks. [? Fr. *morbilles*, small blisters]

marbles *n.*[2] [mid–late 19C] furniture. [Fr. *meubles*, furniture]

marbles *n.*[3] [mid-19C+] the testicles (cf. AGATES n.). [resemblance, but note MARBLE HALLS n.]

marbles *n.*[4] (*US*) **1** [mid-19C+] personal possessions, esp. money used as gambling stakes. **2** [1930s] pearls. **3** [1940s+] money in general; thus *big marbles*, a large sum of money.

marbles! *excl.* [late 19C] a general excl. of disgust, contempt and negation. [MARBLES n.[3]; pun on BALLOCKS! excl.]

marbles and conkers *adj.* [20C+] eccentric, crazy (cf. COCK-SPARROW adj.). [rhy. sl. = BONKERS adj.]

marbles to manslaughter *phr.* [mid-19C] used of someone who is open to anything, *from marbles to manslaughter*. [the terms are used to symbolize opposite extremes]

marble town *n. see* MARBLE ORCHARD n.

marching money *n.* [1910s+] (*Aus.*) daily travel allowance.

[19C milit. jargon *marching money*, money used to pay for a soldier's meals during a march]

marching powder *n.* (*also* **marching dust**) [1980s+] (*US drugs*) cocaine; as in BOLIVIAN MARCHING POWDER *n.* (cf. BIRDIE POWDER *n.*).

marchioness *n.* [mid-late 19C] a maid-of-all-work. [character in Charles Dickens's *Old Curiosity Shop* (1841)]

Marco Polo *n.* [1980s+] (*US gay*) an Italian gay man. [Ital. explorer *Marco Polo* (1254–1324)]

marcus clark *n.* [20C+] (*Aus.*) a shark. [rhy. sl.; ult. *Sir Marcus Clark* (1883–1953), Aus. retailer (*Marcus Clark's*) and businessman]

mard-arse *n.* [20C+] a sulky person. [dial. *mardy*, sulky, in turn f. dial. *mar*, to spoil or over-indulge a child + *arse*, used as general pej. rather than actual physical description]

mare *n.*[1] 1 [14C–19C] a mistress, a sexually pleasing woman, any woman with sexual overtones. 2 [1920s+] an ill-tempered, unpleasant or spirited woman. 3 [1930s+] an ugly woman. 4 [1940s+] a woman, without pej. overtones. [SE *mare*, a female horse; the orig. sexual connotation being used of a man's partner in copulation, upon whom he 'rides']

mare *n.*[2] [1980s+] a horrendous situation, person or place. [abbr. NIGHTMARE *n.*]

mare's nest *n.* [1950s–70s] (*N.Z.*) a bar set aside for women and their escorts. [SE *mare's nest*, a folly, an impossibility]

mare with two legs *n.* (*also* **mare with three legs**) [17C–mid-19C] a gallows.

marg *n.* [2000s] (*US*) a *marg*arita cocktail. [abbr.]

margaret (rose) *n.* (*also* **mary rose**) [1970s+] the nose. [rhy. sl.]

margaretta *n. see* MAGGIE *n.*[1] (1).

margarine legs *phr.* [1980s] used to describe a promiscuous woman, e.g. *find a woman with margarine legs*. [they are easily spread]

margarine mess *n.* [late 19C–1900s] a yellow cab, running in London in the 1890s.

Margate sands *n.* [20C+] hands. [rhy. sl.]

marge *n.* [1950s+] (*US gay*) a feminine or passive lesbian (cf. AMY-JOHN *n.*). [the proper name]

margery *n.* (*also* **marjorie**) [mid-19C+] a homosexual man (cf. ABIGAIL *n.*). [the proper name]

margery jane *n.* [1900s–10s] margarine.

margery-prater *n.* [mid-16C–early 19C] a hen. ['Here's Grunter and Bleater, / with Tib of the Buttry, / And Margery Prater, / all drest without sluttry' (Richard Brome, *The Joviall Crew*, 1641). *Prater* comes from her constant clucking or 'prating', while *margery* echoes dial. *margery daw*, jackdaw and *margery howlet*, an owl]

margie *n.* 1 [1930s] (*US Und.*) morphine (cf. AUNTIE EMMA *n.*). 2 [1980s+] (*Aus. prison*) marijuana (cf. AUNT MARY *n.*[2]). [the initial letter]

mari *n.* [1930s–50s] (*drugs*) *mari*juana, a *mari*juana cigarette. [abbr.]

Maria *n. see* BLACK MARIA *n.*[1].

maria (monk) *n.* [late 19C+] 1 courage. 2 semen. [rhy. sl. = SPUNK *n.*; ult. *The Awful Disclosures of Maria Monk* (1836)]

maribou stork *n.* [1990s+] the penis (cf. ANTEATER *n.*).

Marie Corelli *n.* [1960s+] television. [rhy. sl. = TELLY *n.*; ult. *Marie Corelli*, pseudonym of romantic novelist Marie Mackay (1855–1924)]

marigold *n.*[1] (*also* **marygold**) 1 [mid-late 17C] a gold coin. 2 [mid-19C] £1 million.

marigold *n.*[2] [1970s] (*drugs*) marijuana (cf. AUNT MARY *n.*[2]; BLACK DOMINA *n.*). [abbr. SE *mari*juana + GOLD *n.*[2]]

mari-ha-ha *n.* [1960s] (*US drugs*) marijuana (cf. AUNT MARY *n.*[2]; HA-HA *n.*[3]; MARIHOOCHIE *n.*; MARIWEEGEE *n.*; MARJORAM *n.*; MA-YO *n.*; MO *n.*[4]; MOHASKY *n.*). [joc. pron.]

marihoochie *n.* (*also* **marihooch, marihootee, marihootie,** **marijooani**) [1970s+] (*drugs*) marijuana (cf. MARI-HA-HA *n.*). [joc. mispron.]

marinate *v.*[1] [late 17C–mid-19C] (*UK Und.*) to transport overseas as a punishment; thus *marinated*, transported to a foreign penal colony. [pun on SE *marine*]

marinate *v.*[2] [1990s+] (*US teen*) to idle, to loaf; thus *marinating*, idling, 'hanging out'. [pun on SE *marinate*, to pickle or tenderize in wine and vinegar, herbs and spices]

marine *n.* [1940s] (*N.Z.*) a pint bottle of beer. [DEAD MARINE *n.*]

marine (officer/recruit) *n. see* DEAD MARINE *n.*

mariner's grave *n.* [1940s–70s] a shave. [rhy. sl.]

Marine Tiger *n.* [1950s] (*US*) a newly-arrived Puerto Rican immigrant (cf. BATO *n.*).

marish and parish *n.* [20C+] (*W.I., Bdos/Guyn./Trin.*) everyone. [SE *marish*, a marsh + *parish*, a local governmental subdivision. Allsopp presumes some lost UK dial. phr. transported to W.I.]

mariweegee *n.* [1970s+] (*drugs*) marijuana (cf. MARI-HA-HA *n.*). [joc. mispron.]

marjie *n.* [1940s+] (*Aus.*) *marg*arine. [abbr.]

marjoram *n.* [1970s] (*drugs*) marijuana (cf. AFRICAN BUSH *n.*; MARI-HA-HA *n.*). [mispron.; also punning on HERB *n.*[2] (3)]

marjorie *n. see* MARGERY *n.*

mark *n.*[1] 1 [mid-18C+] (*orig. UK Und.*) the potential and actual victim of a con-man; a gullible person; thus *make a mark*, to ensnare a victim. 2 [mid-18C+] (*UK Und.*) an item to be stolen, a place to be robbed. 3 [mid-19C+] (*UK Und.*) a pickpocket's target. 4 [mid-19C+] (*Aus.*) a person, usu. in the context of their financial probity, specified as *good mark* or *bad mark*. 5 [late 19C–1930s] (*UK tramp*) a good place to beg. 6 [late 19C–1930s] (*UK tramp*) a generous giver. 7 [1920s] a newcomer to the world of prostitution. 8 [1940s–60s] (*US Black/teen*) (*also* **marko**) as a term of address. 9 [1950s–60s] a drug dealer's customer. 10 [1960s+] (*US Und.*) a prostitute's customer. 11 [1970s+] (*US Black*) the target of a gang assassination. [SE *mark*, to note down, i.e. one who is noted down as a possible victim]

mark *n.*[2] [mid-19C–1930s] a humorist. [? *Mark* Lemon (1809–70), the co-founder and first editor of *Punch* (1841)]

mark *v.* 1 [mid-late 19C] (*UK Und.*) to subject to surveillance, e.g. of criminals by the police. 2 [1910s+] (*US Und.*) to select a prospective victim. 3 [1950s–70s] (*US Black*) to tease, to mock. [MARK *n.*[1]]

marked with a T *phr.* [late 19C] known as a thief. [the ancient habit of branding convicted thieves with a *T*]

marker *n.*[1] 1 [late 16C–early 17C] (*UK Und.*) that member of a pickpocketing or shoplifting team who takes the stolen item from the person who actually picks the pocket. 2 [1950s–70s] (*US Black*) a person engaged in ritual teasing or mocking. 3 [1960s+] (*US Black*) the bait that lures a victim into some form of swindle or other fraud. [MARK *v.*]

marker *n.*[2] 1 [1930s+] (*orig. US*) an IOU for a gambling debt; also used fig. for any form of debt. 2 [2000s] (*US Und.*) money. [it has been 'marked down']

market *n. see* MEAT MARKET *n.*[1] (1).

market dame *n.* [early 18C] a prostitute. [euph., the market being that of Covent Garden]

marketplace *n.* [1960s] (*US*) that area of a city or town where street prostitutes work.

mark foy *n.* [1940s+] (*Aus.*) 1 a boy. 2 a young sexual partner. [rhy. sl.; the name of late 19C London firm of carters or f. a well-known Sydney department store]

marking M *n.* [late 19C–1900s] (*Irish*) rapidity, speed of action. [the Virgin *M*(ary)]

marko *n. see* MARK *n.*[1] (8).

mark of the beast *n.* [18C–19C] the vagina (cf. BLACK HOLE *n.*[1]). [the popular (male) image of the satanic vagina]

mark on *n.* [late 19C–1900s] someone who has a pronounced taste in a commodity or is an expert in an occupation, e.g. *a mark on strawberries*, *a mark on swearing*. [they 'make their mark']

Marks *n. see* M AND S *n.*

marks *n.* [1930s+] (*drugs*) the signs of narcotic injections.

Marks and Sparks *n. see* M AND S *n.*

marksman *n.* [20C+] (*Irish*) one who cannot write and must therefore sign with a mark.

mark someone's card *v.* **1** [1930s+] to watch someone, to place someone under surveillance, to pick someone out as a potential victim. **2** [1940s+] to explain, to point out, to warn. **3** [1960s+] to categorize, usu. either as a good or trustworthy person, or a bad or untrustworthy person, to put someone in a specific position. **4** [1960s+] to realize, to see and understand. [racecourse use, tipsters *mark race-cards* with their selections]

mark up *v.* **1** [1910s+] to bruise, to leave scars after a fight. **2** [1980s+] (*Aus. prison*) to tattoo.

Marlboro country *n.* [1960s+] (*US*) the remote countryside. [suggested by the landscapes featured in advertisements for *Marlboro* cigarettes]

marley *n.* [mid-19C–1950s] a *marble*; usu. in pl. *marlies*. [abbr.]

marley stopper *n.* (*also* **marley-slopper**) [mid–late 19C] one who is splayfooted. [MARLEY *n.* + SE *stopper*]

marmalade *n.* [late 19C] (*Aus.*) popular adulation.

Marmalade Country *n.* [late 19C–1910s] (*orig. music hall*) Scotland. [the popularity of Scot. marmalades]

marmalade madam *n.* (*also* **marmulet madam**) [late 17C–early 18C] a promiscuous woman; a prostitute. [? her gaudy clothes; or ? ironic ref to the 'sweetness' of the preserve; or ? SE *marmalade-eater*, one who has been well brought up + MADAM *n.*[1]]

Marmite driller *n.* (*also* **Marmite miner**) [1990s+] a male homosexual (cf. BROWN ARTIST *n.*). [pun on BROWN *n.*[3] and SE *brown*, the colour of *Marmite*, a popular spread in the UK]

Marmite motorway *n.* [1990s+] the anal passage. [for ety. *see* prev.]

marm poosey *n.* (*also* **marm-puss**) [late 19C] a flashily dressed public house landlady. [SE *ma'am* + PUSSY *n.*; orig. tailors' use *marm-pussy*, one's wife]

marmulet madam *n. see* MARMALADE MADAM *n.*

maroon *n.* [1940s+] (*US*) a stupid person. [SE *maroon*, a former slave]

marquis of Granby *n.* [mid-19C] a bald-headed man. [many public house signs show a bald *Marquis of Granby*]

marquis (of Lorne) *n.* **1** [mid-19C] the penis (cf. ALMOND *n.*). **2** [1960s+] an erection. [rhy. sl. = HORN *n.*[2]]

marquis of marrowbones *n.* [late 16C–17C] a lackey, a servant. [SE *marquis* + MARROWBONES *n.* (1)]

marriage face *n.* [late 19C–1900s] (*UK middle class*) a miserable face. [the bride's tearfulness through leaving her family or at the thought of the married life to come]

marriage gear *n.* [mid-19C] the penis and testes.

marriage music *n.* [late 17C–early 19C] the sound of wailing children.

marriage prospects *n.* [1940s] the penis and testes.

married *adj.* **1** [late 18C–early 19C] used to describe convicts who have been chained together for the purposes of moving them from one place to another, or on board a ship that transports them abroad. **2** [1920s–60s] handcuffed together. **3** [1930s–70s] (*US gay*) in a homosexual relationship. **4** [1980s+] (*US campus*) in a long-term relationship.

marrow *n.* [1990s+] (*US Black*) the penis. [MARROW-PUDDING *n.*[1]]

marrowbone and cleaver *n.* [mid–late 19C] the penis (cf. ARSE-OPENER *n.*). [note Grose (1785): 'marrow bones and cleavers, principal instruments in the band of rough musick; these are generally performed on by butchers, on marriages, elections, riding skimmington, and other public, or joyous occasions']

marrowbones *n.* (*also* **marybones**) **1** [mid-16C–1930s] the knees; thus *bring someone down on their marrowbones*, make someone beg forgiveness. **2** [early 17C–mid-19C] the fists when used as weapons.

marrowbone stage *n.* (*also* **Marylebone stage**) [mid-19C] walking, by foot; usu. as *go/ride in/by the…* [*Marylebone* is simply a mispron. of SE *marrowbone*, itself metonymic for the legs]

marrow-pudding *n.*[1] [late 16C–mid-19C] the penis; thus *marrow*, semen.

marrow-pudding *n.*[2] [mid–late 19C] a foetus; usu. in phr. *bellyful of marrow-pudding*, pregnant.

marrowsky *n.* (*also* **medical Greek, mowrowsky**) [mid-19C–1960s] a form of sl. whereby the user transposes the initial letters of adjacent words; thus *marrowskying*, using this language. [? proper name of a Polish count, poss. Count Joseph Boruwlaski. Popularized by medical students at University College in Gower Street, London]

marry brown bess *v.* (*also* **hug brown bess**) [late 18C–19C] to serve as a soldier. [SE *marry* + BROWN BESS *n.*]

marry come up! *excl.* [late 16C–18C] an excl. used to express indignant or amused surprise or contempt; [late 17C–18C] ext. as *marry come up, my dirty cousin!*, used to tease one who is putting on airs. [synon. with HOITY-TOITY! excl. or the modern GET YOU! excl.]

marry Mistress Roper *v.* [mid-19C] to enlist in the Royal Marines. [the flogging at the 'rope's end' that a recruit would have to endure and because such recruits handle the ships' ropes 'like girls']

marry the Devil's daughter (and live with the old folks) *v.* [late 18C–early 19C] to marry a termagant.

marry the widow *v.* **1** [early 19C] to be hanged. **2** [late 19C–1900s] to make a mess of things. [trans. of Fr. sl. *épouser la veuve*, to be guillotined, lit. 'to marry the widow']

Mars and Venus *n.* [20C+] the penis (cf. ALMOND *n.*). [rhy. sl.]

Mars bar *n.* [1960s+] a scar. [rhy. sl.]

marse *n.* [20C+] (*W.I.*) anyone in authority. [ironic use of the old slave pron. of *master*]

marshall *n.* [late 19C] a £5 note (cf. ABE *n.*[2]). [proper name *Marshall*, chief cashier of the Bank of England, whose name appeared on the notes, *c.*1870]

marshmallow *n.*[1] **1** [1910s–60s] (*US Black*) a White person. **2** [1950s+] (*US*) a soft, weak person or thing.

marshmallow *n.*[2] (*also* **marshmallow reds**) [1970s+] (*drugs*) depressants, barbiturates (cf. BARBIT *n.*). [they soften one's emotions]

marshmallow *adj.* [1960s+] (*US*) sentimental. [MARSHMALLOW *n.*[1] (2)]

marshy *adj.* [1960s] (*US campus*) seedy, unpleasant.

marter *n.* (*also* **martar**) [late 16C] **1** a bargainer. **2** a receiver of stolen goods. **3** a dishonest horse-trader who buys stolen horses and disposes of them at fairs. [SE *mart*, to bargain, to do business]

martian *n.* [1960s+] (*US*) an eccentric person. [SE *martian*, i.e. they come from/live in 'outer space']

martin *n.* [late 16C–mid-17C] the victim of theft, either by a team of confidence tricksters or a highwayman. [? SE *martin*, a species of bird. It is supposedly lucky for a martin to nest in the eaves of one's house; poss. in this case it is the robbers who see the appearance of such a *martin* as lucky for themselves]

martin drunk *adj.* [16C] drunk. [SE *St Martin's evil*, drunkenness]

martingale *v.* [19C] (*gambling*) to double the stakes every time one loses, 'to double stakes constantly, until luck taking one turn only, repays the adventurer all' (Bee). [SE *martingale*, a restraining strap that prevents the horse from rearing or throwing back its head; thus fig. to 'ride one's luck']

Martin-le-Grand *n. see* ST MARTIN'S *n.*

Martin Place *n.* [1930s+] (*Aus.*) the face. [rhy. sl.; ult. proper name *Martin Place*, Sydney]

Martin Place adj. [1930s+] (Aus.) in the context of the city, decadence or corruption, or what is seen as such by country people. [proper name *Martin Place*, Sydney; the image of the 'big city' as *de facto* wicked]

Martin's n. see ST MARTIN'S n.

martooni n. [1950s+] (US) a martini cocktail. [a 'drunken' pron. of SE]

martyr n. [1940s] (Irish) a tormentor. [OF *martire*, to torture]

Marty Wilde n. [1960s+] mild (beer). [rhy. sl.; ult. pop singer *Marty Wilde* (b.1939)]

marv n. [1990s+] (US campus/teen) a highly intelligent person, a scholar. [MARV adj.]

marv adj. (also **marvie**, **marvy**, **marvy-groovy**) [1950s+] (orig. US) wonderful, best, outstanding; also used ironically/ negatively. [abbr. SE *marvellous*]

marvel v. [mid-late 19C] (US) to leave, esp. quickly. [ety. unknown]

marvin n. see MELVIN n.

Marvin (the Arvin) n. [1960s+] (US, orig. milit.) a generic name for any member of the South Vietnam military. [assonance from *Army Republic VietNam*; later use is historical]

marvy(-groovy) adj. see MARV adj.

marwooded adj. [late 19C–1900s] hanged. [the name of a contemporary hangman, *William Marwood* (1820–83). Marwood invented the drop, thus speeding up the execution process by snapping the neck, rather than choking the victim to death]

mary n.[1] **1** [early 19C+] (Aus./N.Z.) (also **meri**) an Aboriginal native woman; thus pidgin *White mary*, a White woman. **2** [1900s–10s] (Aus.) (also **mary ann, mary jane**) a female servant. **3** [1920s–70s] (S.Afr.) an Indian woman, usu. a fruit or vegetable hawker. **4** [1940s+] (S.Afr.) any Black woman, esp. a domestic servant. [generic use of one of the most common of female proper names]

mary n.[2] (US gay) **1** [1920s+] a male homosexual; the most popular camp proper name, used as a term of address; typically in phr. *get you Mary!* (cf. ABIGAIL n.). **2** [1950s+] a gay man's (younger) lover. [the commonness of the name, but also offering a touch of Mariolatry]

mary n.[3] [1940s–50s] (US drugs) morphine (cf. AUNTIE EMMA n.). [the initial letter *M*]

mary n.[4] see MARY JANE n.[1] (3).

mary n.[5] see MARY JANE n.[2].

mary adj. [1960s–70s] (US gay) effeminate, homosexual. [MARY n.[2]]

mary! excl. [1920s+] a clichéd, camp homosexual excl. [MARY n.[2]]

mary and johnny n. [1930s+] (drugs) marijuana (cf. AUNT MARY n.[2]). [play on Sp. which translates as 'mary' and 'jane']

mary ann n.[1] **1** [late 19C–1900s] (Aus.) a girlfriend. **2** [late 19C–1910s] a dressmaker's dummy. **3** [late 19C+] an effeminate male homosexual; a young boy used as a catamite in prison (cf. ABIGAIL n.). **4** [1970s+] (US gay) a US marine. [joc. uses of proper name]

mary ann n.[2] [20C+] **1** a fan. **2** a hand, a fist. [rhy. sl.]

mary ann n.[3] (also **mary anna, maryanne**) [1910s+] (drugs) marijuana; a marijuana cigarette (cf. AUNT MARY n.[2]). [joc. pron.]

mary ann n.[4] [1990s+] female pubic hair. [? MARY JANE n.[1] (1)]

mary ann n.[5] see MARY n.[1] (2).

mary anna/maryanne n. see MARY ANN n.[3].

mary at the cottage gate n. [1980s] (Aus.) the number 8. [rhy. sl.]

mary banger n. [20C+] an extremely plain, dowdy woman.

mary blaine n. (also **mary blaine**) [late 19C] a railway train; as v., to meet a train. [rhy. sl.]

marybones n. see MARROWBONES n.

Mary Decker n. [1980s] (S.Afr. Black) **1** a black taxi. **2** a fast armoured police vehicle. [US athlete *Mary Decker* Slaney (b.1958)]

mary ellen n.[1] see MARY FIST n.

mary ellen n.[2] [1930s] (US Und.) a style of robbery whereby the victim is rendered drunk and then robbed.

mary ellens n. [20C+] the female breasts (cf. BRACE AND BITS n.). [rhy. sl. = MELONS n.]

mary fist n. (also **mary ellen, mary five-fingers, mary palm**) [1940s+] (US) the hand, as used in male masturbation; thus *married to mary fist*, addicted to masturbation (cf. CONVERSE WITH HARRY PALM v.).

mary frances n. [1960s+] a euph. for MOTHERFUCKER n. (1). [euph. using the initial letters]

marygold n. see MARIGOLD n.[1].

mary green n. [20C+] in cards, the queen. [rhy. sl.]

mary hick n. [20C+] a plain, dowdy woman.

mary jane n.[1] **1** [mid-19C–1930s] the vagina. **2** [1960s] (US Black) a sexy skirt with a slit up one side. **3** [1960s+] (US) (also **mary**) a lesbian (cf. AMY-JOHN n.). [generic use of female name]

mary jane n.[2] (also **mary, mary j., mary jonas**) **1** [1920s+] (orig. US drugs) marijuana, cannabis (cf. AUNT MARY n.[2]). **2** [2000s] cocaine (cf. AUNT NORA n.). [lit. trans. of Sp.; note cocaine is a 'feminine' drug, see GIRL n.[2]]

mary jane n.[3] see MARY n.[1] (2).

maryjanes n. [1960s+] (US) round-toed shoes with a strap across the foot. [the schoolgirl sound of the proper name]

mary jo n. [1950s] (US Black) a notably beautiful woman.

mary jonas n. see MARY JANE n.[2].

Marylebone kick n. [mid-19C] a kick to the stomach. [? a speciality of the area's thugs]

Marylebone stage n. see MARROWBONE STAGE n.

marylou n. [20C+] glue. [rhy. sl.]

mary palm n. see MARY FIST n.

mary poppins n. [1960s+] (US) the female breasts. [joc. use of film title *Mary Poppins* (1964)]

mary rose n. see MARGARET (ROSE) n.

mary walkers n. [late 19C] (US) trousers. [Dr *Mary Walker* (1832–1919), US campaigner for rational dress for women who would lecture on her subject wearing men's evening dress]

mary warner n. (also **mary wanner, mary werner**) [1920s–70s] (orig. US drugs) marijuana (cf. AUNT MARY n.[2]). [pron.]

mary weaver n. [1930s–70s] (drugs) marijuana (cf. AUNT MARY n.[2]). [pron.]

mary worthless n. [1940s+] (US gay) an ageing, unattractive male homosexual. [pun on the camp term MARY n.[2] + popular US cartoon *Mary Worth*, launched 1938]

mascot adj. [1950s+] (W.I. Rasta) used of one who is of inferior status. [the small size of a trad. mascot]

maserati n. [1980s+] (drugs) an improvised crack cocaine pipe, using a spark-plug cover and a plastic bottle (cf. KABUKI n.). [fig. use of the make of luxury sports car]

masers n. [1960s+] a *Maserati* car. [abbr.]

mash n.[1] [late 19C–1910s] a dandy. [abbr. MASHER n.[1] (2)]

mash n.[2] **1** [late 19C–1910s] a person with whom one is infatuated; thus *on the mash*, looking for an opportunity for seduction; *make a mash on*, to be the object of someone's infatuation. **2** [late 19C–1920s] (orig. US) an infatuation, a crush on someone; thus *have a mash on*, to make advances towards; MASH NOTE n. **3** [late 19C–1930s] an admirer. **4** [1980s] (US campus) sexual activity that stops short of intercourse, kissing and foreplay. [MASH v.[2]]

mash n.[3] **1** [20C+] mashed potatoes; esp. in phr. *sausage and mash*. **2** [1930s+] (US prison) prison-distilled whisky. **3** [1990s+] (US prison) the ingredients of prison-made alcohol. [abbr.]

mash n.[4] [1910s+] (US/Aus.) sentimental nonsense. [MUSH n.[1] (2)]

mash n.[5] [1920s–30s] (US) a blow, a hit.

mash v.[1] [mid-19C+] (US) to beat someone up; to crush. **2** [1940s+] (US Black) to give someone what is due; thus *mash it on* *me*, give it to me; *mash me a fin*, loan me $5. **3** [1970s] (*US*) to masturbate (cf. BANG THE BISHOP v.; BOFF v.). **4** [1980s] (*US Black*) to pass over stolen or contraband goods. **5** [1990s+] (*US Black*) to work hard, to commit oneself to a task. **6** [1990s+] to fondle the breasts in an aggressive manner. [SE *mash*, to crush, to pulp]

mash *v.²* **1** [late 19C+] (*orig. US theatre*) to make oneself attractive to a member of the opposite sex, to flirt with, to succeed in seduction; thus MASHING n.¹. **2** [1950s] (*W.I.*) to seduce, to rape. **3** [1980s+] (*US campus*) to kiss, to neck. **4** [2000s] (*US Black*) to have sexual intercourse (cf. BANG v.¹). [? SE *mash*, to crush, to pulp, thus to render 'soft'; note Rom. *mash*, to allure, to entice]

mash (and peas) *n.* [2000s] motor neurone disease. [rhy. sl.]

mash dog! *excl.* [20C+] (*W.I.*) a general excl. of irritation and dismissal, get out! get out of my way! [Carib.E. *mash*, a call to a dog, meaning go or walk]

mash down *v.* [20C+] **1** to apply pressure, to press down on. **2** (*W.I. Rasta*) to destroy.

mashed *adj.* **1** [late 19C+] (*US*) drunk (cf. ANNIHILATED adj.). **2** [1970s] drugged. **3** [1980s] (*drugs*) under the influence of cannabis. [SE *mashed*, crushed; but Spears, *Slang and Jargon of Drugs and Drink* (1986), suggests (1) is linked to SE *mash*, the basis of whisky]

mashed (on) *adj.* [late 19C–1950s] **1** infatuated, sexually or romantically obsessed (by). **2** in a non-sexual context. [mash v.² (1)]

mashed potato circuit *n. see* RUBBER-CHICKEN CIRCUIT n.

masheen *n.* [19C] (*tinker*) a cat. [Shelta]

masher *n.¹* **1** [late 19C] an individual, of either gender, who uses charm and beauty to succeed. **2** [late 19C–1910s] a dandy; thus *masher blue*, a shade of blue favoured by such men for their waistcoats. **3** [late 19C+] (*orig. US*) a man who forces his unwanted attentions on women, a 'lady-killer'; thus *masherdom*, *mashery*, the world of mashers. [MASH v.¹; (2) and (3) are often elided]

masher *n.²* [1990s+] (*US Black*) a hard, committed worker. [MASH v.¹ (5)]

masher *adj.* [late 19C–1910s] flashy, dandified, fashionable. [MASHER n.¹ (2)]

mashers *n.¹* [1930s+] (*W.I.*) cheap shoes, sold initially with rope soles, then with pieces of car tyre. [? they 'mash' the ground]

mashers *n.²* [2000s] the female breasts (cf. BOBBER n.²). [they would SE *mash* somebody]

mashers corners *n.* [late 19C–1900s] (*UK society*) the opposite prompt (O.P.) and prompt side (P.S.) entrances to the stalls at the Gaiety Theatre, London. [a MASHER n.¹ (3) or STAGE-DOOR JOHNNIE n. could best ogle the chorus-girls from the front stalls]

mash flat *v.* [1940s] (*W.I.*) to move along, to make room, as in a crowded bus, thus also to accelerate a car. [*mashing* the accelerator pedal]

mash in *v. see* MASH UP v.

mashing *n.¹* [late 19C–1930s] the act of flirting, seducing, making advances. [MASH v.² (1)]

mashing *n.²* [1930s] (*UK tramp*) a portion of tea leaves and sugar, enough for 1 cup of tea.

mash it up *v.* (*also* **mosh it up**) **1** [1950s+] (*W.I. Rasta/UK Black*) to achieve a huge success; to do something well. **2** [1990s+] (*W.I.*) an expression of encouragement.

mashkin-shop *n.* (*also* **motshkin-shop**) [late 19C] a pawnbroker's. [MOSKENEER v. + SE *shop*]

mash letter *n. see* MASH NOTE n.

mash-mash *n.* [1940s–50s] (*W.I.*) small change. [onomat. for the noise it makes in one's pocket]

mash-mouth *adj.* [1990s+] (*W.I.*) toothless. [lit. mashed, i.e. broken mouth]

mash note *n.* (*also* **mash letter**) [late 19C+] (*US*) a love letter. [MASH n.² (2) + SE *note/letter*]

mash one's sore toe *v.* [1950s] (*W.I.*) to embarrass.

mashonisa *n.* [1970s+] (*S.Afr. township*) a moneylender. [? Zulu *mashonisa*, a cause of one's losing heavily]

mash that! *excl.* [late 19C–1900s] be quiet! hold your tongue! [? Fr. *macher*, to chew (on)]

mash the fat *v.* [1970s+] (*US Black*) to have sexual intercourse. [note synon. RMC Duntroon (Aus.) *mash some flesh*]

mash-tub *n.* [19C] a brewer. [note the defunct newspaper the *Morning Advertiser* was known as the 'Morning Mash-tub' because of its brewery interests]

mashugga *see under* MESHUGA.

mash-up *n.* [2000s] a song that is a mix of 2 completely different songs spliced into 1.

mash-up *adj.* [1980s+] (*orig. US/W.I.*) **1** badly broken or bent, damaged beyond repair. **2** in fig. use, e.g. used of someone exhausted or suffering from a hangover. [MASH UP v.]

mash up *v.* (*also* **mash in**) [1920s+] (*orig. US/W.I.*) **1** to destroy, to break, to beat up. **2** (*W.I.*) to get oneself into trouble. **3** (*W.I.*) to cause trouble.

mash with *v.* [1980s+] (*US campus*) to kiss, to neck. [MASH v.² (3)]

mas john *n.* (*also* **Messjohn**) [mid-17C–early 19C] a derog. term for a Scot. Presbyterian minister, as opposed to an Anglican or Roman Catholic. [*Mas*, master; the hostility is underlined by the abbr.]

maskee! *excl.* [mid-19C] (*Anglo-Chinese*) never mind! it's not important! no matter! [? Port. *mas que*]

maso *n.* [1960s] (*US*) a *maso*chist. [abbr.]

mason *n.¹* [mid-18C] one who acquires goods fraudulently by giving a bill that they do not intend to honour. [the stereotyping of Freemasons as dishonest]

mason *n.²* (*also* **mason line**) [19C+] (*US Black*) a town's main street, esp. when it delineates the line between the Black and White communities. [proper name *Mason-Dixon line*, dividing the US north and south along the 40th parallel]

mason *n.³* [1940s–50s] (*US gay*) **1** a 'masculine' male homosexual. **2** a lesbian.

masonics *n.* [late 19C–1900s] (*UK society*) secrets. [Freemasonry, 'not that there are either secrets or rites in Freemasonry – at all events in England – where combined secrets are neither wanted nor expected' (Ware)]

mason line *n. see* MASON n.².

masonry *n.* [mid–late 19C] secret signs and passwords. [the trad. image of 'secretive' Freemasons]

mason's maund *n.* (*also* **mason's mawnd**) [late 17C–early 19C] a fake sore, placed above the elbow and counterfeiting a broken arm caused by a fall from a scaffold. [SE *mason* + MAUND n.]

ma's plaster *n.* [20C+] (*Irish*) a whiner, a whinger. [one who needs a fig. *plaster* from their *ma*, i.e. mother]

mass *n.* [1990s+] (*W.I./UK Black teen*) money, currency. [ety. unknown]

mass *adj. see* MASSIVE adj. (3).

Massa Charley/Charlie *n. see* MR CHARLIE n.

massacre *adj.* (*also* **massacrate**) [1910s] (*Irish*) a general term of abuse, e.g. *that massacree dog!* [SE *massacre*]

massacree *v.* [18C–1920s] (*US*) to massacre, to murder, to victimize or cruelly humiliate.

massa-day *n.* [1960s+] (*W.I.*) **1** the era of slavery. **2** the imperial era between slavery and W.I. independence. [coined by Guyn. P.M. Eric Williams (1911–81) in 1961: 'Massa is the symbol of a bygone age. Massa Day is a social phenomenon. Massa Day Done denotes a political awakening and a social revolution.' Note Papua New Guinea Tok Pisin *taim bilong masta*, the era of imperialism]

massage *v.¹* [1920s+] (*orig. US*) **1** to beat, to injure, to kill. **2** of the police, to beat up a suspect during an interrogation.

massage *v.²* **1** [1960s+] to manipulate initially unpalatable facts or figures to create a required positive impression, profit statement etc. **2** [1970s+] to flatter, to manipulate someone. [(2) SE phr. *massage someone's ego*]

massage someone's tonsils *v. see* WHITEWASH SOMEONE'S TONSILS V.

massa planter *n.* [1960s–70s] (*US Black*) one's boss, esp. when White. [ironic use of 19C *massa*, master]

Massey-Harris *n.* [20C+] (*Aus./Can.*) cheese. [pun on the *Massey-Harris* self-binder (an early combine harvester); the ref. is to the 'binding' effects of cheese on the digestion]

massive *n.* [1980s+] (*W.I./UK Black teen*) a group of people who stick together and have shared social interests, such as a dancehall crowd; often specified by a geographical name, e.g. the *Peckham massive*, the *Tottenham massive*.

massive *adj.* **1** [20C+] a general term of great approval. **2** [1950s+] (*orig. W.I. Rasta*) respected; ext. as *massive large* for emphasis. **3** [1980s+] (*US campus*) (*also* **mass**) large, a lot of.

mass tom *n.* [1940s] (*W.I.*) a shark. [lit. 'master tom'; thus joc. use of proper name]

mast *n.* [1980s+] (*Aus. prison*) the (erect) penis.

Ma State *n.* [1900s–50s] (*Aus.*) New South Wales; thus *ma stater*, a native of New South Wales. [*ma*, mother; thus the 'mother state': New South Wales is the oldest Aus. colony]

master *n.* [20C+] (*US Black*) the absolute best.

master blaster *n.* [1980s+] (*drugs*) a large amount of freebase cocaine. [MASTER n. + BLAST v.⁴ (5)]

mastercan *n.* [18C–19C] a chamberpot. [SE *master* + CAN n.³ (2)]

master-dog *n.* [20C+] (*US Black*) the supreme authoritarian figure (usu. a White man) within an institutional hierarchy.

Master John Goodfellow *n.* (*also* **Master John Thursday**) [17C–19C; 1940s] the penis (cf. ABRAHAM n.¹). [generic use of *John* + SE *goodfellow*, a jovial companion; *John Thursday* was a 17C musician and dancing master, the supposed inventor of a dance known as the 'Hussarde']

Master Ketch *n. see* JACK KETCH n.

master member *n.* [19C] the penis (cf. DEAREST MEMBER n.). [MEMBER n.¹]

master of ceremonies *n.¹* [mid-17C] as a tavern term, 'he that stands upon his strength, and begins new healths', i.e. gets up and proposes a succession of toasts (*The English Liberal Science*, 1650).

master of ceremonies *n.²* [19C] the penis.

master of misrule *n.* [mid-17C] an uproarious drunkard, i.e. 'He that flings Cushions, Napkins, and Trenchers about the room' (*The English Liberal Science*, 1650).

master of the black art *n.* [16C] any beggar, irrespective of their 'speciality'. [E.P., who dates it 16C–17C, notes 'the term is suspect']

master of the mint *n.* [late 18C–mid-19C] a gardener. [a pun on the SE *herb*]

master of the novelties *n.* [mid-17C] a playful drunkard, i.e. 'he that is first to begin new frolicks' (*The English Liberal Science*, 1650).

master of the rolls *n.* [mid-17C–mid-19C] a baker. [pun]

master of the wardrobe *n.* [18C–early 19C] one who pawns their clothes to get money for drink. [pun]

masterpiece *n.* [18C–19C] the vagina. [joc. use of SE + pun on SE *master* + *piece*/PIECE n.¹ (1)]

masterpiece of night work *n.* [late 19C–1900s] a good-looking prostitute (cf. DEADLY NIGHTSHADE n.).

Master Reynard *n.* [19C] the penis (cf. ABRAHAM n.¹). [SE *Reynard*, a nickname for a fox; like the animal the penis 'gets into' a NEST n.¹]

mat *n.¹* [1930s–40s] **1** (*US*) a prostitute or sexually promiscuous woman. **2** (*US Black*) one's regular sweetheart, one's wife. [abbr. SE *mattress*]

mat *n.² see* DOORMAT n.

mat *n.³ see* MOT n.

mat *v. see* CARPET v.

match *n.¹* [1900s] (*US*) a prison. [abbr. MATCHBOX n.¹ (1)]

match *n.² see* MATCHBOX n.².

match *v.* [1950s+] to light a cigarette.

matchbox *n.¹* **1** [1920s+] a very small house, or room. **2** [1960s] a small car. **3** [1980s+] (*UK Und.*) an easily robbed target. [all are flimsy; (1) and (2) are also small]

matchbox *n.²* (*also* **match**) [1940s+] (*US drugs*) **1** $10 worth of marijuana, orig. an actual matchbox full, by 1990s more like a thimbleful. **2** approx. ½oz (14g) of marijuana.

matchstick *n.* [1950s+] a nickname for a very thin person; thus *matchstick with the wood shaved off*, an exceptionally thin person.

mateloe/matelot/matelow *n. see* MATLOW n.

materials *n.* [mid-19C+] (*Irish*) the ingredients of a whisky punch.

maternal *n.* [mid-19C] one's mother. [? abbr. SE *maternal parent*]

matey *adj.* (*also* **maty**) [1910s+] friendly. [SE *mate*]

matic *n.* [1990s+] (*W.I./UK Black teen*) an auto*matic* weapon. [abbr.]

matie *n.* [20C+] (*S.Afr.*) a student at Stellenbosch University in the Western Cape. [MAAT n.]

Matilda *n.* (*also* **matilda**, **tilly**) [late 19C+] (*Aus.*) a tramp's pack; thus *matilda up*, carrying a pack; *matilda-bearer, matilda-carrier, matilda-hawker, matilda-lumper, matilda-man*, a vagrant.

Matilda-waltzer *n. see* WALTZ MATILDA v.

matinée *n.* [1940s+] sexual intercourse (usu. adulterous) in the afternoon. [SE *matinée*, an afternoon theatrical performance]

matineer *n.* [late 19C–1900s] a frequenter of theatrical matinées.

matlow *n.* (*also* **mateloe, matelot, matelow**) [mid-19C+] (*orig. RN*) a sailor. [Fr. *matelot*, a sailor]

mat-man *n.* [1920s+] (*orig. US*) a wrestler. [the SE *mat* on which he fights]

matriculate *v.* [1970s+] (*US campus*) to start on a trip, to go somewhere. [mispron.]

matrimonial *n.* [19C] sexual intercourse in the 'missionary position'. [seen as the usual practice of married couples]

matrimonial peacemaker *n.* (*also* **peacemake**) [mid-17C–19C] the penis.

matrimony *n.* [19C] a mixture of 2 sorts of food or drink. [lit. a 'marriage']

matsakaw *n.* (*also* **matsakow**) [1970s] (*drugs*) heroin. [ety. unknown]

mattress *n.¹* (*US*) **1** [1920s–30s] a beard. **2** [1930s] pubic hair. **3** [1940s] the face.

mattress *n.²* [1960s+] (*Aus./US*) a woman as a sexual partner; a girlfriend. [the man 'lies' on her]

mattressback *n.* **1** [1960s+] (*Aus./US*) a sexually promiscuous woman. **2** [1990s+] (*Aus. prison*) a prisoner who spends a lot of time in their cell.

mattress jig *n.* [19C–1920s] (*US*) sexual intercourse.

mattress job *n.* [20C+] a beating by police to persuade a person to make a confession. The victim is placed under a mattress and then jumped and stamped upon, so no visible marks are left on the victim's body.

mattress-muncher *n.* [1960s+] (*orig. Aus.*) a passive homosexual man. [his response to anal intercourse; var. on PILLOW-BITER n.]

mattress polo *n.* [1930s–60s] (*US*) sexual intercourse.

maty *adj. see* MATEY adj.

matzo *n. see* MOTZER n.¹.

maud *n.* (*also* **maude**) **1** [late 19C–1930s] (*US Black*) a woman. **2** [1940s] a male prostitute (cf. BABY JANE n.). **3** [1960s+] a dowdy or overweight male homosexual (cf. ABIGAIL n.). [play on the female proper name]

maud and ruth *n.* [1970s+] the truth. [rhy. sl.]

mauger *adj.* (*also* **mauga, maugre, mawga, mawgah, mawgar**) [20C+] (*W.I.*) thin, scrawny. [Du. *mager*, lean or Fr. *maigre*, thin]

Maui wowie n. (also **Maui waui/wowee**) [1970s+] (US drugs) a potent variety of marijuana, grown in Maui, Hawaii (cf. ACAPULCO (GOLD) n.). [*Maui*, a Hawaiian island + SE *wow!*, an excl. of pleasure or astonishment]

mauk n. see MAWKES n.

maul v. [late 19C+] (US campus) to have a very passionate petting session.

maul and wedges n. [mid–late 19C] (US) one's possessions, one's goods. [SE *maul*, a hammer]

mauldy adj. [1910s–50s] (Aus.) left-handed. [? MAULEY n. (1)]

mauled adj. [late 17C–mid-19C] very drunk (cf. ANNIHILATED adj.).

mauler n. (also **mawler**) **1** [early 19C+] the hand, the fist. **2** [20C+] (US) a boxer. **3** [1950s] brass knuckles. [SE *maul*, to handle roughly]

mauley n. (also **maulie, mawley, morley**) **1** [late 18C–1950s] the hand, a fist. **2** [mid-19C] a finger, usu. in pl. **3** [mid-19C+] a signature; handwriting. [SE *maul*, to handle roughly; or Shelta *malya*, ult. transposition of Gaelic *lamh*, hand]

mauma n. see MAMMY n.[1].

mauming and glauming n. [mid-18C] pawing in an amorous or sexual manner. [? SE *maul* + Scot. *glaum*, to snatch at]

maund n. [17C] (UK Und.) begging; thus a specific begging ruse, e.g. a fake sore. [MAUND v.]

maund v. (also **mawnd**) [16C–mid-19C] (UK Und.) to ask or require; thus to beg. [? Fr. *mendier/quémendier*, to beg; ult. Lat. *mendicus*, a beggar, the root of the SE *mendicant*. Note Rom. *mang*, to beg]

maund abram v. [17C] to beg while posing as a madman. [MAUND v. + ABRAM n.]

maunder n. (also **maunderer, mawnder**) [17C-mid-19C] (UK Und.) a beggar. [MAUND v.]

maunder v. [early 17C–18C] to beg; thus *maunder on the fly*, to beg in the streets; *maundering*, begging, prone to begging; *maundering tools*, items used to enhance one's begging image and thus gain more sympathy and alms. [MAUND v.]

maundering broth n. [late 17C–early 19C] a scolding. [dial. *maunder*, to grumble, to threaten]

maunding-cove n. [early 17C–18C] a beggar. [MAUND v. + COVE n. (1)]

mause n. [18C] (UK Und.) a bundle.

maut n. see MORT n.

maux n. see MAWKES n.

maven n. (also **mavvin**) [1950s+] (US) an expert, a connoisseur. [Heb. *mavin*, understanding]

maw n. **1** [mid-16C+] the mouth. **2** [1940s+] (US Black) the vagina (cf. BLACK HOLE n.[1]). [SE *maw*, a (usu. animal's) stomach]

Maw Bell n. see MA BELL n.

maw-dicker n. [1960s+] (US, mainly southwest) a general term of extreme dislike. [dial. *maw*, mother + DICK v.[2] (1); euph. for MOTHERFUCKER n.]

mawga adj. see MAUGER adj.

mawgabraw! excl. [20C+] (Irish) a general excl. of abuse, usu. delivered as a parting shot, synon. with GO TO HELL! excl. [Irish *magh go brách*, the field for ever]

mawgah/mawgar/mawgre adj. see MAUGER adj.

mawkes n. (also **mauk, maux**) **1** [late 16C–early 18C] a prostitute. **2** [late 18C–1960s] a slatternly woman. [MALKIN n.]

mawkin n.[1] [17C+] (Ulster) a simpleton. [Scot. *mawkin*, a half-grown girl]

mawkin n.[2] see MALKIN n.

mawkish adj. [early 18C] slatternly. [MAWKES n. (2)]

mawler n. see MAULER n.

mawley n. see MAULEY n.

mawnd v. see MAUND v.

mawnder n. see MAUNDER n.

maw-wallop n. [late 18C–early 19C] a disgusting dish of food, enough to make the eater vomit. [SE *maw*, stomach + *wallop*, a churning and bubbling, a blow]

maw-worm n. [mid-19C+] a hypocrite. [proper name *Mawworm*, a character who epitomized hypocrisy, in Bickerstaffe's play *The Hypocrite* (1769); ult. SE *maw-worm*, a stomach worm]

maw-wormy adj. [mid–late 19C] **1** hypocritical. **2** pessimistic, fault-finding, nagging. [MAW-WORM n.]

max n. **1** [early 18C–19C] (also **maximus, old max**) gin, esp. high-quality gin. **2** [mid-19C] (UK Und.) any form of alcohol. **3** [mid-19C+] (US campus) the maximum score or achievement in an examination; the student who achieves this. **4** [1950s+] (US Und.) the maximum sentence for an offence. **5** [1960s+] (Can./US) a maximum security jail. **6** [1970s+] (US campus) the highest level or degree. **7** [2000s] (drugs) gamma hydroxy butyrate, GBH, dissolved in water and mixed with amphetamine. [all uses of SE *maximum*]

max adj. (also **maximum**) [1960s+] (US) superlative, outstanding.

max v.[1] [mid-19C+] **1** to drink. **2** to treat to a drink. [MAX n. (1)]

max v.[2] **1** [late 19C+] (US campus) to achieve a maximum score or grade in an examination. **2** [1970s+] (US Und.) to serve the full length of a jail sentence. **3** [1970s+] (US) to give one's maximum effort. **4** [1970s+] (US) to exceed the limit. **5** [1980s+] (US Black/campus) to have a very good time, to relax. **6** [1990s+] (US Und.) to give the highest possible sentence for a cited crime. [SE *maximum*]

max adv. (also **maximum**) [1970s+] (US) extremely, at the maximum, at most.

max and relax v. [1980s+] (US Black/campus) to take life easy, to enjoy oneself; esp. in phr. *maxin' and relaxin'*. [MAX v.[2] (5) + SE *relax*]

maxed adj. **1** [mid-19C; 1980s+] drunk or highly intoxicated (cf. ABOUT RIGHT phr.[1]). **2** [1970s+] (US) full to maximum capacity. **3** [1980s+] (US) utterly exhausted, drained of energy. [all fig. use of SE *maximum*; (1) note MAX v.[1]]

maxed out adj. [1980s+] **1** very drunk or highly intoxicated (cf. ABOUT RIGHT phr.[1]). **2** at one's limits, e.g. of strength or weight. [MAX OUT v.; (1) note MAX v.[1]]

Max Factor n. [20C+] an actor, esp. in fig. use, i.e. one who fakes illness or injury, a footballer who 'dives' etc. [rhy. sl.; brandname *Max Factor*, a leading producer of cosmetics and make-up]

max fuckter n. [1950s–70s] (gay) make-up. [brandname *Max Factor*, a leading producer of cosmetics]

maxi n. (also **maxy**) [1940s+] (W.I.) a shilling (5p). [abbr. SE *maximum*; ? an obs. maximum fare on public transport]

maxie n. [mid-19C] (Scot.) a major mistake, a serious blunder. [Lat. *maximus*, the greatest]

maximum see under MAX.

maximus n. see MAX n. (1).

Max Miller n. [1920s+] a pillow. [rhy. sl.; Cockney pron. 'piller'; ult. comedian *Max Miller* (1895–1963)]

max out v. **1** [1970s+] (US prison) to complete one's sentence without gaining any remission for good behaviour. **2** [1970s+] to indulge to extremes. **3** [1970s+] of an object or person, to reach the limit, esp. of a credit card. **4** [1980s+] (US) to succeed. **5** [1980s+] to relax. [MAX v.[2]]

max walls n. [1930s+] the testicles (cf. CHEESE AND CRACKERS n.). [rhy. sl. = BALLS n.[1] (1); ult. comedian *Max Wall* (1908–90)]

Maxwell House n. [1960s+] a mouse. [rhy. sl.; ult. the popular brand of instant coffee]

maxy n. see MAXI n.

maxy adj. [mid-19C] drunk (cf. ABOUT RIGHT phr.[1]). [MAX n.]

mayate n. [1960s+] (US) a Black person. [? Sp.]

Maybelline waste n. [1990s+] (US campus) a disappointing social event. [*Maybelline*, a brandname of cosmetics, i.e. it was not worth getting made-up for]

may I be shot (if...)! excl. (also **may I be hanged (if...)!**) [mid-19C+] a general oath.

may I die! *excl.* [18C] a general oath.

maymay-lippy *adj.* [20C+] (*W.I., Antg.*) talkative, gossipy. [? SE *mama* + LIPPY adj.]

ma-yo *n.* [1970s] (*drugs*) cannabis (cf. MARI-HA-HA n.). [? Chinese or ? joc. pron.]

mayo *n.* [1940s+] (*drugs*) **1** cocaine. **2** heroin; morphine (cf. AUNTIE EMMA n.). [? misreading of MA-YO n.]

mayo *adj.* [2000s] mayonnaise-coloured. [abbr.]

mayonnaise midget *n.* [2000s] (*US Black*) a White man's penis, stereotyped as small.

mayonnaise monkey *n.* [2000s] (*US Black*) a White person.

maypole *n.* [17C–18C] the penis; thus [1960s] (*gay*) *play at maypole*, to indulge in sexual activity. [the shape]

maypop *n.* [1980s+] (*US Black*) a very worn tyre. [pun on SE *may pop*/US dial. *maypop*, the passion flower]

maytag *n.* [1970s+] (*US prison*) a weak male prisoner who is abused by other inmates, forced to do their menial chores and poss. raped; also as v., to rape. [the *Maytag* brand of home appliances]

maytag *v.* [1970s] (*US prison*) to perform anal rape. [MAYTAG n.]

mayvin *n. see* MAVEN n.

may your chooks turn into emus and kick your shithouse down *phr.* [1960s+] (*Aus.*) used to convey one's extreme annoyance with another's actions or words.

may your prick and purse never fail you! *excl.* (*also* **may the two Ps never fail you!**) [early 18C–mid-19C] a popular toast when drinking (cf. BEGGAR'S BENISON! excl.).

mazard *n.* (*also* **mazer, mazzard**) **1** [17C] a drinking vessel. **2** [17C–1920s] the head. **3** [mid-18C–1940s] the face. **4** [early 19C] (*Anglo-Irish*) the 'head' of a coin. [SE *mazer*, a hard wood (usu. but not invariably maple) used as a material for drinking cups]

mazard *v.* (*also* **mazzard**) [early 17C] to hit on the head. [MAZARD n. (2)]

mazarine *n.* [mid–late 18C] a common councilman of London. [the *mazarine* (a deep rich blue) gown he wore]

mazawattee *n.* [20C+] a potty. [rhy. sl.; ult. *Mazawattee*, a brand of tea]

mazda crown *n.* [1930s] (*US*) a bald-headed man. [*Mazda*, a major brand of lightbulb; coined by columnist Walter Winchell (1897–1972)]

Mazda Lane *n.* [1920s–50s] (*US*) Broadway, New York. [*Mazda*, a major brand of lightbulb; coined by columnist Walter Winchell (1897–1972)]

mazeh *n.* (*also* **mazehette**) [1980s+] (*US campus*) a very attractive man or woman. [Heb. *mah ze?* what is this?]

mazer *n. see* MAZARD n.

mazola party *n.* [1960s+] (*US*) a party of 2 or more people who cover their bodies in vegetable oil to engage in sexual activity and intercourse. [*Mazola*, a brand of vegetable oil + SE *party*]

mazoo *n.* (*also* **mazoola**) [1950s–80s] (*US*) money. [abbr. MAZUMA n.]

mazuma *n.* (*also* **mazooboe, mazoom, mazooma, mazume**) [20C+] money. [Yid., ult. Heb. *mazuma*, prepared, ready]

mazuzu *n.* [1960s–70s] (*S.Afr. township*) money. [? an African word or var. on MAZUMA n.]

mazzard *see under* MAZARD.

m.b. *n.* [1930s+] (*Aus.*) Melbourne Bitter; thus *suffer from m.b.*, to be drunk. [abbr. brandname]

m.b. coat *n.* [mid–late 19C] a long coat worn by clergymen. [abbr. *mark of the beast*; the 'beast' in this context was Popery]

mbongo *n.* [1910s+] (*S.Afr.*) a political stooge or apologist, a 'yes-man'. [Nguni *imbongi*, a praise-singer]

m.b. waistcoat *n.* [mid–late 19C] a kind of waistcoat with no opening in front, worn by Anglican clergymen. [orig. worn by Tractarians only, *c.*1840, but later adopted by other clergymen; for ety. *see* M.B. COAT n.]

M.C. *n.* (*also* **emcee**) **1** [1950s+] one who is in charge, a leader, a boss. **2** [1980s+] (*orig. US Black*) the lead singer of a rap band, e.g. *M.C. Noise.* [lit. *master of ceremonies,* orig. 1930s (although note late 19C use)]

m.c. *adj.* [1940s+] middle class. [abbr.]

m.c. *v.* **1** [1930s+] to present a (rock) concert. **2** [1980s+] to perform as a rapper. [M.C. n.]

m.c.p. *n.* [1960s+] (*orig. US*) male chauvinist pig. [abbr.; much beloved by early 1960s–70s feminists but now obs. apart from among tabloid journalists and very late arrivals]

mc² *adj.* [1980s+] (*US campus*) overly studious, over-devoted to books and uninterested in parties, drink, drugs and other forms of pleasure. [the shorthand for Einstein's theory of relativity + pun on SQUARE adj. (8)]

m.d.g. *phr.* [1980s+] (*US campus*) strong physical attraction. [abbr. mutual desire to grope]

m.d.l. *n.* [1990s+] a person, usu. a woman, who dresses younger than her years. [abbr. MUTTON DRESSED AS LAMB n.]

MDO *n. see* MAORI DAY OFF n.

me *pron.* [1950s+] used at the end of a sentence to indicate preference or for emphasis, e.g. *I like lard, me.*

— me *phr.* [1920s+] (*orig. US*) used with a relevant n. to denote an imper., e.g. *pen me,* hand me a pen. [the *locus classicus* comes in the film *The Sweet Smell of Success* (1957) where the venal columnist J.J. Hunsecker confirms his absolute power over the venal, scrabbling press agent Sidney Falco with the command, 'Match me, Sidney', i.e. light my cigarette]

meadow mayonnaise *n.* (*also* **meadow dressing**) [1910s+] (*Aus./US*) nonsense, rubbish. [euph. pun on BULLSHIT n.]

meadow muffin *n.* [1970s+] (*US*) a lump of manure.

meag *n. see* MAG n.³ (1).

mealer *n.* **1** [late 19C] one who pledges to drink alcohol only with meals. **2** [late 19C–1910s] one who has meals at one place but lives elsewhere, a 'table-boarder'.

mealie-muncher *n.* (*also* **mealie**) [1970s] (*S.Afr.*) an Afrikaner. [S.Afr.E. *mealie,* maize + SE *muncher*]

meal-mouth *n.* [late 17C–18C] one who demands money, but in a sly, sheepish manner. [SE *mealy-mouth,* one who fears to speak their mind]

meals on wheels *n.* **1** [1960s+] (*US gay*) teenagers cruising the streets in their cars. **2** [2000s] jellied eels. [(2) rhy. sl.; ult. nickname of social services' food delivery service for the elderly]

meal ticket *n.* **1** [late 19C+] (*orig. US*) anyone good for the price of a meal. **2** [late 19C+] (*orig. US*) anyone who provides money or a livelihood for someone else, who thus needs to make less effort; also the object which earns someone their income, e.g. a guitar if a musician. **3** [late 19C+] (*orig. US*) employment, wages, whatever provides the price of a (fig.) meal. **4** [1950s] (*US*) a personal preference. **5** [1960s+] (*US gay*) as (1), (2) and (3) in homosexual contexts. **6** [1970s] an opportunity.

mealy *adj. see* MEALY-MOUTHED adj.

mealy bustle *n.* [late 19C] (*US short order*) mealy potato.

mealy-mouth *n.*¹ [17C+] an insincere or reticent way of talking. **2** [late 19C] a priggish, censorious, self-righteous person. [backform. f. MEALY-MOUTHED adj. (1)]

mealy-mouth *n.*² [1930s–70s] (*US*) a customer in a café or restaurant who continually makes complaints. [MEALY-MOUTH n.¹ + pun on *meal*]

mealy-mouth *v.* [20C+] to speak in a duplicitous, deceptive, insincere manner. [backform. f. MEALY-MOUTHED adj.]

mealy-mouthed *adj.* (*also* **mealy, mealy-mouth, mealy-mouthy**) **1** [late 16C+] duplicitous, deceptive, insincere. **2** [1930s–70s] (*US*) said of a customer in a café or restaurant, continually complaining. [SE *mealy,* soft-spoken, one who 'minces' matters; ult. SE *meal,* powder; (2) also puns on SE *meal*]

mealy potato *n.* [1900s] (*Aus.*) the right thing.

meamies *n. see* MEEMIES n.

mean *n.* [1980s+] aggressiveness.

mean *adj.* **1** [19C+] (*US*) aggressive, unpleasant. **2** [early 19C+] (*US*) of people and things, poor in quality or condition, comparatively worthless. **3** [mid-19C–1950s] (*US*) unwell, in low spirits. **4** [mid-19C+] (*orig. US*) pettily unpleasant or disobliging; thus *feel mean*, to feel ashamed of one's unpleasant conduct. **5** [1910s+] (*orig. US*) very good, very clever, adroit, with implications of 'so good it's unfair', on the 'outlaw' bad = good model. **6** [1920s+] (*US Black*) exceptionally attractive or stylish. **7** [1980s+] (*drugs*) either very high or very poor in quality.

mean as catshit *phr. see* MEANER THAN CATSHIT phr.

mean as pigshit and twice as nasty *phr.* (*also* **mean as catshit and twice as nasty**) [1930s+] extremely ungenerous. [SE *mean*]

mean-ass *n.* [1950s+] an unpleasant person. [MEAN adj. (1) + -ASS sfx]

mean-ass *adj.* [1950s+] very unpleasant. [MEAN-ASS n.]

mean business *v.* [mid-19C+] to be totally committed, to be utterly earnest.

me and you *n.* [20C+] **1** (*bingo*) the number 2 (cf. ALDERSHOT LADIES n.). **2** sexual intercourse. [rhy. sl.; (2) = SCREW n.¹ (2)]

me-and-you *n.* [1930s–40s] a menu. [a play on words rather than rhy. sl.]

me and you *phr.* [1940s–60s] (*US Black*) an invitation to start fighting; esp. in phr. *it's gonna be me and you.*

mean enough to kill his grandmother *phr.* [20C+] (*US*) a phr. describing a notably unpleasant person; vars. include *mean enough to push his grandmother downstairs; …rob his grandmother's grave; …steal the pennies off his grandmother's eyes; …take the fillings out of his grandmother's teeth.* [MEAN adj. (1)]

mean enough to steal acorns from a blind hog *phr.* [late 19C] (*US Black*) possessing the characteristics of 'poor White trash', i.e. stupid, rustic, unsophisticated. [SE *mean*]

mean enough to steal the pennies off a dead man's eyes *phr.* [mid-19C+] (*US*) a phr. describing a notably ungenerous person. [SE *mean*]

meaner than catshit *phr.* (*also* **mean as catshit, meaner than cat dirt, …cat dung, …cat manure, …cat's tail**) [20C+] (*US*) used to describe a notably unpleasant person. [MEAN adj. (1)]

mean-eye *v.* [1930s] (*US*) to stare at aggressively, in a hostile manner. [MEAN adj. (1)]

mean-hair *adj.* [1960s+] (*gay*) unpleasant, cruel. [MEAN adj. (1) + fig. use of SE *hair*]

mean machine *n.* **1** [1980s+] (*orig. US*) a fast or stylish car. **2** [1990s+] in fig. use, a powerful team or person. [MEAN adj. (6) + MACHINE n.² (2)]

mean-mouth *v.* [1960s+] (*US*) to attack verbally, to slander. [MEAN adj. (1)]

mean potatoes *n. see* SMALL POTATOES n.

mean reds *n.* [1960s+] (*US campus*) a fit of depression. [coined by Truman Capote in *Breakfast at Tiffany's* (1958)]

mean white *n.* [mid-19C–1900s] an extremely poor White person. [SE *mean*]

me arse and Katty Barry! *excl.* [2000s] (*Irish*) an excl. of disbelief. [*Katty Barry* was a shawlie who kept a shebeen, an illicit ale house, in Dublin in 1930s]

measles *n.* [mid-19C] venereal disease, esp. syphilis. [syphilis can also produce a rash]

measure *v.* [1900s–50s] (*US Und.*) to strike hard. [? SE *measure out blows*]

measured for a new overcoat, be *v.* [1930s–40s] (*US*) to be buried. [ref. is to a WOODEN OVERCOAT n.]

measured for a new umbrella, be *v.* [late 19C] (*US*) **1** to appear in new but ill-fitting clothes. **2** to pursue a policy of doubtful wisdom. [joc./fig. uses of SE]

measure out *v.* [late 19C] to knock down. [SE *measure one's length*, to fall prostrate]

measure over the counter *v.* [mid-19C] to die.

measures *n. see* MEDZERS n.

meat *n.* **1** [16C+] a body, usu. a woman's, as an object of sexual pleasure; thus *fond of meat*, amorously inclined; [19C] *hawk one's meat*, to display one's body. **2** [late 16C+] (*also* **lump of meat, piece of meat**) the penis; thus [2000s] (*UK Black*) *bust one's meat*, to ejaculate (cf. BACON n.¹). **3** [17C+] the vagina (cf. BACON SANDWICH n.). **4** [mid-19C+] (*orig. US*) one's body or flesh. **5** [mid-19C+] prey, as in *he's my meat* referring to a potential victim. **6** [late 19C+] a prostitute; thus *fresh meat*, a novice prostitute; *raw meat*, a woman *in flagrante delicto*; the *price of meat*, the cost of a prostitute (cf. BIT OF MUTTON n.). **7** [late 19C+] (*orig. US*) a person of another race as an object of sexual gratification, constructed with a colour; thus *dark meat, White meat*. **8** [late 19C+] (*orig. US*) a person (or thing) that fits the bill, meets one's needs. **9** [20C+] (*US*) a corpse, a wounded person. **10** [1960s+] (*US*) an inferior person, poss. physically robust but mindless or gullible, thus often used to describe sportsmen. **11** [1990s+] (*N.Z.*) a sporty, macho man, who places physical development above intelligence.

meat and drink *n.* **1** [19C] drunken love-making. **2** [late 19C] (*W.I.*) strong drink in general, but spec. liquor thickened with egg yolks.

meat and potatoes *n.* [1950s+] (*US*) the essence, the basics, the 'brass tacks'. [the stereotyped plain meal]

meat-and-potatoes *adj.* [1950s+] (*US*) average, run-of-the-mill, unexciting, basic. [MEAT AND POTATOES n.]

meat and two veg *n.* [1960s+] the penis and testicles (cf. ACORNS n.). [MEAT n. (2)]

meat-and-two-veg *adj.* [20C+] plain, unadorned, 'no-frills'. [the stereotypically basic dish, roast meat, potatoes and cabbage]

meat axe *n.*¹ [mid-19C] (*US*) used in similes, e.g. MAD AS A MEAT AXE phr.

meat axe *n.*² [1970s] (*US*) the penis (cf. AX n.²). [MEAT n. (2)]

meat axe *n.*³ [1990s+] (*Aus./N.Z.*) an eccentric, a mad person. [backform. f. MAD AS A MEAT AXE phr. (2)]

meatbag *n.* [mid–late 19C] the stomach.

meatball *n.*¹ (*US*) **1** [1930s+] a stupid person; thus a potential victim. **2** [1950s+] a prostitute's customer. [fig. ext. of/ref. to MEATHEAD n.]

meatball *n.*² [1940s+] (*US*) **1** an Italian (cf. DAGO n.). **2** an African American. [the stereotyped partiality of Italians for the dish]

meatball *n.*³ [1970s+] (*US Und.*) a minor or false criminal charge. [backform. f. MEATBALL adj.¹]

meatball *adj.*¹ [1940s+] (*US Und.*) used of a criminal charge for a petty crime. [the smallness or commonness, thus unimportance, of the food]

meatball *adj.*² [1960s+] (*US*) stupid. [MEATBALL n.¹ (1)]

meatbeater *n.* [1980s+] a masturbator, esp. one who masturbates excessively; thus a general term of abuse. [BEAT ONE'S MEAT v.]

meatbrain *n.* [1960s+] (*orig. US*) a fool (cf. APPLEHEAD n.; BAKEBRAIN n.).

meat cart *n.* (*also* **meat crate**) [1930s–40s] (*US*) a hearse.

meat-cleaver *n.* [20C+] the penis (cf. ARSE-OPENER n.). [MEAT n. (2) + SE *cleaver*]

meat curtains *n.* [1990s+] the female vaginal lips or labia (cf. BACON STRIPS n.; BEEF CURTAINS n.).

meat-drink-washing-and-lodging *n.* [early–mid-18C] gin. [its image as a universal panacea]

meat-eater *n.* [1970s+] (*US Und.*) a police officer who, not content with the payoffs, bribes and perks that are freely offered, actively compels people to offer him such monies. [ext. of GRASS-EATER n.]

meater *n.* [late 19C–1900s] a coward. ['said of a dog who only bites meat, that is to say, one who will not fight' (Ware)]

meat fancier's *n.* [19C] a brothel. [MEAT n. (1) + SE *fancier*]

meat-flasher *n.* [late 19C–1910s] an exhibitionist, one who exposes themself indecently; thus *meat-flashing*, exhibitionism. [MEAT n. (2) + SE *flasher*]

meat fosh n. [late 19C] hash, stew. [var. on FISH-FOSH n.]

Meat-Freezer n. [1900s] (*Aus.*) a New Zealander. [the export of deep-frozen N.Z. lamb]

meat grinder n. (*US*) **1** [1940s–50s] a car with a loud engine. **2** [1950s+] any tough situation or place in which an elimination process is being carried out, such as training. **3** [1990s+] someone who controls one and renders one's life unpleasant.

meathead n. **1** [1920s+] (*US*) a stupid person. **2** [1940s+] a general term of abuse. [SE *meat* + -HEAD sfx (1), implying that solid flesh, rather than brains, occupies one's skull]

meatheaded adj. [1940s+] stupid, foolish (cf. AIRHEADED adj.). [MEATHEAD n.]

meathook n. **1** [mid–late 19C] a curl on the temple, then fashionable among London cockneys; thus *meathooks*, curls in general. **2** [1910s+] (*Aus./US*) the arm. **3** [1930s+] (*US*) a hand; often in pl. **4** [1970s] (*US*) the penis. [(4) MEAT n. (2)]

meat horn n. [1950s] the penis. [MEAT n. (2)]

meathound n. [1930s–60s] **1** (*US*) a lecher. **2** (*US Black*) one who indulges in oral sex. [MEAT n. (1)/MEAT n. (3) + HOUND sfx; (2) they EAT v.[3] (1) their partner]

meat house n. **1** [late 19C] (*US*) one's body. **2** [late 19C–1960s] (*also* **meat shop**) a brothel (cf. ACCOMMODATION HOUSE n.). **3** [1930s] (*US police*) a morgue. [MEAT n. (1)/MEAT n. (9) + HOUSE n.[1] (1)/SE *house*]

meat injection n. [1980s+] (*orig. US*) an act of penetration by the penis (cf. BACON n.[1]). [MEAT n. (2) + SE *injection*; note synon. RMC Duntroon (Aus.) *flesh injection*]

meat-in-the-pot n. [mid-19C–1940s] (*US, mainly Western*) a rifle, a shotgun, a revolver. [its use in obtaining food]

meat lance n. (*also* **meat spear/stick**) [1970s+] (*US*) the penis (cf. AX n.[2]). [MEAT n. (2) + SE *lance/spear/stick*]

meat mag n. [1970s] (*US*) a magazine of homosexual pornography. [MEAT n. (2) + colloq. SE *mag*, a magazine]

meat market n.[1] **1** [late 19C+] (*also* **market**) a rendezvous for prostitutes of either sex. **2** [1940s+] (*US*) any situation or place where people are regarded as commodities, such as a recruiting agency or a modelling agency. **3** [1950s+] anywhere that people gather for the primary purpose of finding sexual partners, often used in universities to describe first-year parties. [MEAT n. (1); (3) note synon. 1910s US *meet market*]

meat market n.[2] [late 19C+] **1** the female breasts. **2** the vagina (cf. BACON SANDWICH n.). [MEAT n. (1)]

meat-merchant n. [late 19C] a prostitute (cf. ASS PEDDLER n.; BIT OF MUTTON n.). [MEAT n. (3) + SE *merchant*]

meat-mincer n. [mid-19C] in boxing, the mouth.

meat-monger n. [late 18C–19C] a womanizer, a philanderer. [MEAT n. (1) + SE *monger*]

meatpacker n. [1940s] (*US*) an undertaker. [MEAT n. (9); play on SAmE *meatpacker*]

meat pie n. [20C+] **1** a fly. **2** a trouser fly. **3** an eye; usu. in pl. **4** a necktie. [rhy. sl.]

meat pie adj. [1910s+] (*Aus.*) small-time; esp. in *meat pie bookie*, a small-time bookmaker. [the cheapness of SE *meat pies*]

meat puppet n. (*US*) **1** [1980s+] a gullible person. **2** [1990s+] the penis. [MEAT n. (5)/MEAT n. (2) + SE *puppet*, both 'jump up and down']

meat rack n. **1** [1960s+] (*orig. gay*) a place, such as a bar or a particular street, where homosexuals display their charms to potential customers. After the 'singles bar' explosion of the 1970s, the term was ext. to heterosexuality. **2** [1970s] an ambulance, usu. from a morgue. [pun on SE *meat*/MEAT n. (1)/MEAT n. (9)]

meat shop n. *see* MEAT HOUSE n. (2).

meat shot n. (*also* **money shot**) **1** [1960s+] in pornographic still or moving pictures, a close-up of the genitalia, male or female. **2** [1990s+] in fig. use, the big climax. [MEAT n. (2)/MEAT n. (3)/SE

money + SE *shot*; money refers to the commercial potential of such shots + phr. ON THE MONEY phr./MONEY n.[3]; note, however, MONEY n.[1]]

meat skewer n. [late 19C] the penis. [MEAT n. (2)]

meat spear/stick n. *see* MEAT LANCE n.

meat ticket n.[1] [1930s+] **1** anyone good for the price of a meal. **2** anyone who provides money or a livelihood for someone else, who thus needs to make less effort. [var. on MEAL TICKET n.]

meat ticket n.[2] *see* DEAD-MEAT TICKET n.

meat tool n. [1960s+] (*US*) the penis. [MEAT n. (2) + TOOL n.[1] (1)]

meat trap n. [mid-19C+] (*Aus./US*) the mouth. [SE *meat* + SE *trap*/TRAP n.[3]]

meat wagon n. **1** [1910s+] (*US*) (*also* **live meat wagon**) an ambulance. **2** [1940s+] a vehicle used for conveying prisoners to and from court, police stations, prisons etc, a general police van. **3** [1940s+] (*US*) a hearse. **4** [1980s] a large, expensive automobile. [lit. and fig. uses of MEAT n. (9) + SE *wagon*]

meat water n. [1940s+] (*W.I.*) stock, soup.

meat whistle n. [1930s+] (*US*) the penis, esp. as an object of fellatio (cf. BLOW v.[2]). [MEAT n. (2)]

meat-works n. [1940s] (*Aus.*) a brothel. [MEAT n. (1) + SE *works*]

meat wrapper n. *see* FISH WRAPPER n.

meaty n. [1970s+] (*UK juv.*) a lump of spittle containg a proportion of phlegm.

meaty adj. [early 19C+] sexually attractive. [MEAT n. (1)]

mebs n. (*also* **mebbs**) [1990s+] (*Irish*) the testicles.

mec n. *see* MAKE n.[1].

meccano set n. [1950s] (*N.Z. prison*) the portable, silver-painted, steel gallows, moved and erected as and when required. [*Meccano*, a popular construction kit used by children]

mech n. (*also* **mach**) [1910s+] (*orig. RAF*) a *mech*anic. [abbr.]

mechanic n. **1** [early 17C–mid-19C] (*also* **mechanick**) a general term of abuse. **2** [late 19C] (*US gambling*) one who invents methods of cheating. **3** [20C+] (*orig. US*) a professional cheat at cards or dice; occas. as *card/dice mechanic*; thus *mechanic's grip*, a way of holding a deck of cards. **4** [20C+] any notably successful player. **5** [20C+] (*W.I.*) a trick, a contrivance, usu. involving some form of physical activity. **6** [1940s–70s] (*US Und.*) a pickpocket or safe-breaker. **7** [1970s+] a hired killer. [(1) MECHANIC adj.]

mechanic adj. (*also* **mechanick, mechanicke**) [late 16C–early 19C] vulgar, contemptible. [SE *mechanic*, 'pertaining to or involving manual labour' (*OED*)]

mechanical digger n. [20C+] a derog. term for a Black person (cf. DAPTO DOG n.). [rhy. sl. = NIGGER n.[1] (1)]

mechanick n. *see* MECHANIC n. (1).

mechanick/mechanicke adj. *see* MECHANIC adj.

mechanics' avenue n. (*also* **mechanic's alley/street, Mechanicsburg**) [mid-19C–1960s] (*US*) a poor or run-down part of a town or city. [SE *mechanic*, a manual labourer + SE *avenue/ alley/street*]

mechanized dandruff n. *see* GALLOPING DANDRUFF n.

meckem-peckam adj. [1940s+] (*W.I.*) fault-finding, very hard to satisfy. [? SE *make* + *pernickety*]

mecks n. [mid–late 19C] wines and spirits. [ety. unknown]

meddlesome mattie n. [1940s+] (*US*) an interfering, nosy person. [the poem 'Meddlesome Matty' (1804) by Ann Taylor]

meddle (with) v. **1** [1940s+] (*US*) to have sexual intercourse. **2** [1970s] (*US Black*) to be intimate, but not spec. on a sexual level. [14C–17C SE *meddle*, to have sexual intercourse]

meddling duchess n. [late 19C] any interfering upper-class woman who interests herself, doubtless on self-proclaimedly philanthropic grounds, in lives that do not concern her.

Meddy, the n. [1940s] the Mediterranean. [abbr.]

medical Greek n. *see* MARROWSKY n.

medicine n. **1** [mid–late 19C; 1930s+] (*orig. US*) an intoxicating drink. **2** [mid-19C+] punishment, usu. deserved. **3** [mid-19C+]

sexual intercourse. **4** [1910s–30s] (*US*) information, knowledge. **5** [1930s] (*US Black*) semen. **6** [1930s+] drugs.

medicine *adj.* [late 19C–1930s] (*US*) persuasive. [the soothing effects of SE *medicine*]

medicine sharp *n.* [late 19C–1910s] (*US*) a physician. [SE *medicine* + SHARP n.¹ (2)]

medico *n.* **1** [mid-19C+] a doctor; thus *she-medico*, a female doctor. **2** [1940s] a medical student. [SE late 17C–mid-19C]

medieval *adj.* [late 19C+] barbaric, illiberal, cruel; thus phr. [1990s+] *get medieval on someone's ass*, to treat with extreme savagery. [the stereotype of the Middle Ages as symptomatic of such excesses; the phr. was coined in the Quentin Tarantino film *Pulp Fiction* (1993)]

medina *n.* [1990s+] (*US Black*) a nickname for Brooklyn. [? as opposed to Mecca, presumably Manhattan, but note Arab. *medina*, the Arab section of a town; note 1885, *Bulletin* (Sydney), 17 January, 12/1: 'And it is just to hand, the new crack prima donna [...] at a minute's notice, "guyed a whack to her own Medina" – which means London']

meditation *n.* [1960s+] (*US prison*) solitary or segregated confinement. [the loneliness of the punishment]

Mediterranean back *n.* (*also* **Greek back**) [1970s+] (*Aus.*) a supposedly fake illness or incapacity, used to justify malingering, apparently by Italians, Greeks, Yugoslavs and others seen as lazier than 'White' Australians.

medium *n.* (*also* **meejum**) [1930s+] (*Irish*) an indeterminate measure, approx 0.3 litres (a half-pint) of beer.

medium, the *n.* [20C+] (*Irish*) the Irish language. [SE *medium of communication*]

medlar (tree) *n.* **1** [late 16C–19C] the vagina (cf. APPLE n.⁶; BEAUTY SPOT n.). **2** [17C] a promiscuous woman.

med-man *n.* **1** [1930s–40s] (*US*) a quack or a patent *medicine* seller. **2** [1940s+] a doctor. [abbr.; (2) SE *medicine man*]

medza/medzer *n. see* MADZA n.

medzers *n.* (*also* **measures**) [1960s–70s] (*Ling. Fr./Polari*) money. [abbr. MADZA CAROON n.; *measures* is mispron.]

meejum *n. see* MEDIUM n.

me elbow! *excl.* [1910s+] (*Irish*) a general excl. of incredulity, dismissal. [euph. of MY ARSE! excl.]

meemies *n.* (*also* **meamies, meemees, meeyams, mimis**) [1940s+] (*orig. US*) hysteria; usu. as SCREAMING MEEMIES n. [? var. on HEEBIE-JEEBIES n.; note WW2 US milit. sl. *screaming meemie*, the German *nebel-werfer*, a multi-barrelled mortar]

meerschaum *n.* [1930s] (*US*) a saxophone. [SE *meerschaum*, a type of mineral often made into a tobacco pipe]

meet *n.* **1** [mid-19C] (*UK Und.*) a meeting place. **2** [mid-19C+] (*orig. US*) a meeting, an appointment; in [20C+] esp. for illicit purposes such as drug selling. **3** [20C+] (*US*) a gathering for the purpose of an activity, usu. sport, e.g. *a swim meet*; also a conference or convention. [(3) now SE]

meet hell *v.* [20C+] (*W.I.*) to find it hard to make enough money to live, to subsist, to suffer great hardship.

meet mary palm and her five sisters *v.* [1950s+] to masturbate (cf. CONVERSE WITH HARRY PALM v.).

meet rosie hancock *v.* [1950s+] to masturbate (cf. CONVERSE WITH HARRY PALM v.). [pun on name/SE *hand* + COCK n.² (1)]

meet the man *v. see* MAN, THE n. (1).

meet with mother thumb and her four daughters *v.* [20C+] to masturbate (cf. CONVERSE WITH HARRY PALM v.).

meeyams *n. see* MEEMIES n.

meff *n.* [1990s+] a dirty, smelly person, a vagrant. [? pron. of SE *methyl*ated spirits, often drunk by alcoholic tramps]

me for *phr.* [20C+] (*orig. US*) I want.

meg *n.*¹ (*also* **megg**) **1** [late 17C–mid-19C] a guinea. **2** [1910s] (*US*) a dollar. [generic use of MEG n.³ as any coin]

meg *n.*² (*also* **megg, meggie, meggs**) [1940s+] (*drugs*) marijuana (cf. AUNT MARY n.²). [var. on MAGGIE ANN(E) n.]

meg *n.*³ *see* MAG n.³ (1).

meg *n.*⁴ *see* MAGGIE n.¹ (1).

meg *v.* [19C] to swindle; thus *megging*, swindling. [MEG n.³]

mega *adj.* [1960s+] (*orig. US teen*) **1** of an object or person, superlative, excellent, extra-special; usu. as pfx. **2** of an object, huge, enormous, substantial. **3** of a person, very well known or very successful, also later used predicatively e.g. *the movie was mega*. [adopted Greek pfx *mega-*, great]

mega *adv.* [1960s+] extremely, to a great extent. [MEGA adj.]

megablast *n.* [1980s+] (*drugs*) **1** a very deep inhalation of a cannabis cigarette. **2** an act of inhalation from a crack pipe. **3** an extremely exciting, satisfying experience. [MEGA adj. (1) + BLAST n.³]

megg *n. see* MEG n.¹.

megg/meggie/meggs *n. see* MEG n.¹ (1).

megillah *n.* (*also* **megilla**) [1940s+] a long, tedious or complicated story, a complicated state of affairs, a long explanation; esp. in phr. *the whole megillah*, the lot, everything. [Yid. *gantse Megillah*, a whole (tedious) story, ult. Heb. *megillah*, roll, scroll. In standard use the term refers to 5 books of the Old Testament – S. of S., *Ruth*, *Lam.*, *Eccles.* and *Esther* – that are trad. associated with certain Jewish festivals, esp. the Book of Esther, read at Purim]

Meg Ryan *n.* [1990s+] a male homosexual. [rhy. sl. = IRON (HOOF) n.; ult. US film star *Meg Ryan* (b.1962)]

megsman *n.* **1** [mid–late 19C] the king of the 19C swindlers. **2** [mid-19C+] a petty criminal, a cheat. [MEG v.; var. on MAGSMAN n.¹]

mehawn! *excl.* [1930s+] (*Ulster*) nonsense! rubbish! [Irish *mo thón!* my arse!]

meig *n.* [20C+] (*US*) a nickel, a 5-cent coin. [var. on MEG n.¹]

meisensang *n.* [mid-19C] (*Anglo-Chinese*) a missionary. [Chinese pron. of SE *missionary*]

-meister *sfx* [1980s+] (*orig. US campus*) **1** the master, i.e. expert; used in comb. with a relevant n. to denote the leader of a profession, although the praise may often be tinged with irony. **2** used in comb. with a personal name or first syllable of a name. [Ger. *meister*, master, Yid. *meyster*, master]

mejoge *n.* (*also* **midget, midjic**) [mid–18C–1950s] a shilling (5p). [Shelta]

mek-mek *n.* [1940s+] (*W.I.*) **1** a pernickety person, a fault-finder. **2** a quarrel, quarrelling. [SE *make (a fuss)* + redup.]

mek-mek *adj.* [1940s+] (*W.I.*) quarrelsome. [MEK-MEK n. (2)]

mek-mek *v.* [1940s+] (*W.I.*) to hesitate, to be indecisive, to make a half-hearted attempt. [MEK-MEK n. (1)]

mekon *n.* [1990s+] (*UK juv.*) a person with a high forehead. [the evil *Mekon*, the alien villain of the 1950s 'Dan Dare' comic strip in the UK *Eagle* comic]

melancholy hat *n.* [late 16C–early 17C] **1** a mourning hat. **2** a smart, fashionable hat.

Melbourne *n.* [1990s+] a flaccid penis. [ety. unknown]

Melbourne cup *n.* [1980s+] (*N.Z.*) a chamberpot.

melching *n.* [1990s+] sucking the newly ejaculated semen from the vagina (poss. with the aid of a straw). [MINGE n. (1) + FELCH v.]

melia murder! *excl.* (*also* **millia murder!**) [mid-19C+] (*Irish*) a general excl. of surprise, horror, regret. [Irish *míle murdar*, lit. 'a million murders', thus 'horror of horrors!']

melkpens *n.* [1970s] (*S.Afr.*) a young, naïve and inexperienced person. [Afk. *melk*, milk + *pens*, stomach]

mellish *n.* [early 19C] a sovereign. [? Lat. *mel*, honey, thus the image of money as a 'sweetener' and/or the golden colour]

mellow *n.*¹ [late 17C] a smooth drink.

mellow *n.*² **1** [1950s–60s] (*US Black*) a homosexual. **2** [1960s+] (*US Black*) a favourite boyfriend or girlfriend, a good friend of either sex. **3** [1970s+] (*US*) a state of calm relaxation. [MELLOW adj. (5)/MELLOW adj. (6)]

mellow *adj.* **1** [17C+] pleasantly drunk, tipsy (cf. ABOUT RIGHT phr.¹). **2** [late 19C+] (*orig. US Black*) perfect, fine. **3** [1930s+] (*US*

Black) relaxed and comfortable. **4** [1930s+] (*US Black*) attractive, stylish. **5** [1940s+] (*US Black*) of a friend, close, intimate. **6** [1940s+] calm, peaceful, unconcerned with material or painful things, a state often induced by smoking cannabis. **7** [1970s+] of drugs, relaxing.

mellow-back *adj.* [1930s–60s] (*US Black*) fashionable, chic, well-dressed. [MELLOW adj. (5) + BACK adv.]

mellow-Black *n.* [1930s–40s] (*US Black*) an attractive young Black woman. [MELLOW adj. (4) + SE *Black*]

mellow drag with the sag *n.* (*also* **mellow drag that has that sag**) [1930s–40s] (*US Black*) the exaggeratedly long jacket of a ZOOT SUIT n. [MELLOW adj. (4) + DRAG n.[8] (1)]

mellow drug of America *n.* [1960s+] MDA (3,4-methylene-dioxyamphetamine), a hallucinogen that resembles LSD in its effects; it has the same chemical formula as MDMA, but is not identical (cf. ECSTASY n.). [MELLOW adj. (7)]

mellow dude *n.* (*also* **mellow fellow**) [1960s–70s] (*US drugs*) a drug user. [MELLOW adj. (6) + DUDE n. (1)]

mellow man *n.* [1940s] (*US teen*) an attractive boy. [MELLOW adj. (4) + SE *man*]

mellow roof *n.* [1930s–40s] (*US Black*) the human head. [MELLOW adj. (3) + ROOF n. (2)]

mellow yellow *n.*[1] [1950s–60s] (*US Black*) a Mulatto girl or woman, esp. an attractive one. [MELLOW adj. (4) + YELLOW n.[3] + assonance]

mellow yellow *n.*[2] (*also* **yellow**) **1** [1960s–70s] dried banana skins, which, according to contemporary rumour, could be smoked. **2** [1960s+] (*drugs*) a variety of LSD (cf. A n.[3]). ['Mellow Yellow' (1967), a song by HIPPIE n.[2] (3) folk-singer Donovan + MELLOW adj. (6)]

mellow yellow *n.*[3] (*also* **yellow mellow**) [1980s+] (*S.Afr. township*) a CASSPIR armoured truck, used to maintain order in the townships. [the colour of the vehicles, thence the proprietary name of a yellow-coloured soft drink; ult. f. the song, *see* MELLOW YELLOW n.[2]]

mellum *n.* [1930s] (*US*) common sense. [? pron. of MELON n.[1] (1)]

melo *n.* [late 19C+] a *melo*drama on stage or screen. [abbr.]

melodies *n.* [1970s+] the fingers. [rhy. sl; *melody lingers*]

melon *n.*[1] (*Aus./Can./N.Z./US Black*) **1** [mid-19C+] the human head; thus *do one's melon*, to lose one's temper, to become over-excited. **2** [1920s+] a fool (cf. APPLEHEAD n.).

melon *n.*[2] [1910s+] (*US*) a windfall or unexpected profit. [financial jargon *cut a melon*, to announce an extra dividend]

melon-farmer *n.*[1] [1960s] (*US*) an unsophisticated person; a peasant.

melon-farmer *n.*[2] [1980s+] a euph. for MOTHERFUCKER n. (1); often used as the 'equivalent' when dubbing. [coined by Alex Cox, director of *Repo Man* (1984) when re-dubbing the film for television]

melonhead *n.* [1910s+] (*Aus./US*) a fool; thus *melon-headed*, stupid (cf. APPLEHEAD n.). [MELON n.[1] (2) + -HEAD sfx (1)]

melons *n.* (*also* **cantaloupes, honeydews, lopes**) [1940s+] the female breasts, esp. when large (cf. APPLES n.[1]).

melt *n.*[1] [mid-19C] (*US*) one's self. [metonymy of SE *melt*, the spleen]

melt *n.*[2] [20C+] (*Ulster*) the tongue; usu. in phrs. *break someone's melt*, to infuriate beyond reason; *keep in your melt*, hold your tongue; *knock in someone's melt*, to drive mad. [OE *milt*, spleen; the tongue is spleen-shaped]

melt *v.* **1** [late 17C+] to spend money, esp. on drink. **2** [19C] to come to orgasm (cf. BLOSH v.). **3** [early 19C] to beat up. **4** [mid-19C–1920s] to cash a cheque or break a note. **5** [late 19C–1930s] (*Aus./N.Z.*) to spend one season's pay on one extended binge. **6** [1930s+] (*US Black*) (*also* **melt out**) to run out of money, to have no money; often as MELTED OUT adj. **7** [1940s–60s] (*US campus*) to delight, to thrill; to attract someone. **8** [1950s–60s] to leave.

melt! *excl.* [1960s] (*US*) leave! get lost! [MELT v. (8)]

melted *adj.*[1] [20C+] **1** drunk (cf. DAMP adj.). **2** having expended all one's money on drink. [MELT v. (1)]

melted *adj.*[2] [2000s] (*Irish*) tired. [SE *melt*]

melted butter *n.*[1] [18C–19C] semen (cf. BABY GRAVY n.).

melted butter *n.*[2] [1950s–70s] (*US Black*) an attractive woman, esp. a Mulatto. [her 'yellow' skin tone, i.e. YELLOW adj.[2] (1)]

melted out *adj.* [1930s–40s] (*US Black*) without money and thus desperate. [MELT v. (6)]

melting moments *n.* **1** [19C] 2 fat people having sexual intercourse. **2** [late 19C] ardent, intense passion.

melting pot *n.* (*also* **baking pot**) [19C] the vagina (cf. BAG n.[1]). [it 'softens' the penis after ejaculation]

melting pot receiver *n.* [late 18C] (*UK Und.*) a receiver of stolen silver plate who melts down the stolen goods, thus rendering them untraceable.

melt one's grease *v.* [mid-19C] to work very hard.

Melton hot day *n.* [late 19C] (*sporting*) a very hot day. [coined as a pun on SE *melting*, and spec. for 3 June 1885, an excessively hot day (as were those that followed) and one on which the horse *Melton* won the Derby]

melt the wax *v.* [1950s] (*US drugs*) to smoke opium.

melvin *n.* **1** [1950s+] (*Aus./US*) (*also* **marvin, merv, mervin, Uncle Melvin/Merv**) a dull, tedious, socially inept and otherwise distasteful person. **2** [1980s+] (*also* **murphy**) a condition in which clothing gets stuck between the buttocks; thus *give someone a melvin*, to tug someone's underwear up suddenly and roughly; *have a melvin/have melvins/have a murphy*, to receive this. [image of *Melvin* as a 'nerdy' proper name; (2) is seen as a typical problem for (1)]

melvin *adj.* [1980s+] old-fashioned, socially inept, dull, foolish. [MELVIN n. (1)]

melvin *v.* [1980s+] (*US campus*) to tug someone's underwear up suddenly and roughly with the aim of lifting them off the ground. [MELVIN n. (2)]

Melvyn Bragg *n.* [1990s+] **1** sexual intercourse. **2** a promiscuous woman. **3** a cigarette. [rhy. sl.: (1) = SHAG n.[1]; (2) = SLAG n.[1] (5); (3) = FAG n.[4] (3); ult. UK broadcaster and author *Melvyn Bragg* (b.1939)]

Melvyn Bragg *v.* [2000s] to have sexual intercourse. [MELVYN BRAGG n. (1)]

mem *v.* [2000s] to *mem*orize. [abbr.]

member *n.*[1] [18C+] the penis (cf. DEAREST MEMBER n.). [prior use is SE, Lat. *membrum virile*, 'the virile member', i.e. the penis]

member *n.*[2] **1** [mid-19C–1920s] a fellow, a chap; usu. with adj. e.g. *hot member*. **2** [1960s+] (*US Black*) (*also* **club member**) a fellow Black person. **3** [1960s+] (*US gay*) a fellow homosexual. [SE *member* as abbr. of *member of the community* is SE 16C–17C]

member for barkshire *n.* [late 18C–early 19C] one who is suffering from a harsh, persistent cough. [pun on SE *bark*/UK county *Berkshire*]

member for cockshire *n.* [mid-19C] the penis (cf. DEAREST MEMBER n.). [puns on SE *member*/MEMBER n.[1] and *Cock*(shire)/COCK n.[2] (1)]

member for horncastle *n.* [late 18C–early 19C] a cuckold. [punning on SE *member*/MEMBER n.[1] + HORN n.[1]; thus *double entendre* in D'Urfey, *Pills to Purge Melancholy* (1719–20): 'I am a cunning Constable, / And a Bag of Warrants I have here, / To Press sufficient Men and able, / At *Horn-castle* to appear / [...] / Where I miss the Man I'll press the Wife']

member mug *n.* [late 17C–early 19C] a chamberpot. [MEMBER n.[1] + SE *mug*, a drinking vessel]

member of the catch club *n.* [late 18C–early 19C] a bailiff or bailiff's assistant. [they *catch* villains]

member of the union *n.* [1990s+] (*US gay*) a member of the homosexual community.

memo *n.* [late 19C+] a *memo*randum; a *memo*ir. [abbr.]

memory box n. [1990s+] (Aus.) the mind.

Memphis dominoes n. [1940s–70s] (US) dice.

men n. [1990s+] (W.I.) a homosexual. [the pl. of SE *man* implying the homosexuality]

menace n. [1930s+] an unpleasant, irritating person. [esp. used of children, thus the comic character Dennis the *Menace*, star of the *Beano* from 1938]

menavelings n. [mid–late 19C] odd money remaining after the daily accounts are made up at railway offices.

mench *see under* MENSH.

mended adj. [late 19C–1900s] bandaged.

mendic adj. (*also* **mindic**) [1920s+] (Aus.) sick, ill. [Nyungar *mindaik*, sick]

men in blue n. *see* BOYS IN BLUE n.

men in suits n. [1980s+] senior managers, usu. those in finance and administration rather than in creative posts; often abbr. to *suits*.

meno n. [1920s+] the *meno*pause. [abbr.]

meno adj. [1920s+] *meno*pausal. [abbr.]

mensch n. (*also* **mensh**) [1910s+] a 'real man', the implication being of character and integrity rather than sexual or physical prowess. [Yid. *mensch*, Ger. *Mensch*, a person]

mensh n. (*also* **mench**) [1980s+] a *men*tion.

mensh v. (*also* **mench**) [1910s+] to *men*tion; usu. in phr. *don't mensh*, don't mention it. [abbr.]

mental n.[1] **1** [1910s+] an insane, deranged person, a mental patient. **2** [1970s+] intelligence. **3** [1980s+] (Irish) a psychiatric institution. [abbr. SE *mental case/ability*]

mental n.[2] [1970s+] (Aus.) an emotional outburst, a display of ill temper.

mental adj. **1** [late 19C+] insane, crazy, out of one's mind. **2** [1990s+] a general intensifier, meaning wonderful, bizarre, terrifying, according to context. **3** [1990s+] angry.

mental giant n. [1980s+] (US campus) a fool, an idiot.

mental hernia n. [1970s] (US) **1** a fool, an idiot. **2** a mental breakdown.

mentalist n. (*also* **mentaller**) [1990s+] (UK juv.) an eccentric.

mental job n. [1920s+] one who is or potentially might be insane. [SE *mental* + JOB n.[4]]

mental midget n. [1960s+] (US) a stupid person.

mentisental adj. [late 19C–1900s] sentimental. [deliberate mispron./corruption]

mentler n. [1990s+] a crazy person. [pron. of MENTAL adj.]

mentler adj. [1990s+] insane, crazy. [MENTLER n.]

meow n. [1990s+] (US, Brooklyn) an expedition with the aim of causing trouble or shoplifting. [ety. unknown; ? link to TOM CAT v.]

mephepha n. *see* MAPHEPHA n.

Merc n. [1930s+] a *Merc*edes Benz. [abbr.]

merc n. [1960s+] a professional *merc*enary soldier. [abbr.]

Mercedes n. [1970s–80s] (US Black) an elegant woman with good looks and an attractive figure. [the car of the same name and status]

mercer's book n. [late 16C–17C] debt; thus *in the mercer's book*, the state of being in debt. [SE *mercer*, a dealer in luxury textiles + SE *book*. Any Elizabethan gallant worth his name was in debt to his clothier]

merch n. [1950s] the *merch*ant navy. [abbr.]

merchandise n. **1** [late 17C; 1950s+] women as sex objects. **2** [1920s–30s+] contraband liquor. **3** [1930s+] (drugs) drugs. **4** [1970s+] a man, often a male prostitute, as a sex object (cf. ASS PEDDLER n.). [euph.]

merchandise, the n. [1900s] (US) the real thing, the ideal thing, the ideal person. [play on GOODS, THE n.[1]]

merchant n. [mid-16C+] a man, a fellow, esp. as an adept of a particular interest. While [19C] uses are often in comb., [20C+] uses are almost always in a variety of qualifying combs. (cf. BLAG MERCHANT n.; BULL MERCHANT n.; BUN MERCHANT n.; CAPER MERCHANT n.; CON MERCHANT n.; CRAP MERCHANT n.[1]; FANNY MERCHANT n.; FEATHER-MERCHANT n.; GUTTER MERCHANT n.; HOIST MERCHANT n.; HOP MERCHANT n.[1]; HOP MERCHANT n.[2]; JUMP-UP MERCHANT n.; LAY-DOWN MERCHANT n.; LUSH MERCHANT n.; MEAT-MERCHANT n.; MUTTON MERCHANT n.; OIL MERCHANT n.; PETTICOAT MERCHANT n.; PINTLE-MERCHANT n.; READER MERCHANT n.; SKIN-MERCHANT n.; SMOCK MERCHANT n.; TIMBER MERCHANT n.; TOOTLE MERCHANT n.; TURKEY MERCHANT n.; WOOD MERCHANT n.).

merchant banker n. (*also* **Swiss banker**) [1980s+] a masturbator; thus a general term of abuse. [rhy. sl. = WANKER n.]

merchant of capers n. [mid-19C] (UK Und.) a dancing master.

merchant of eel-skins n. [mid-16C–17C] one who only poses as a merchant. [? his slipperiness, the unlikeliness of his supposed commodity]

merck n. (*also* **merk**) [1920s+] (drugs) cocaine. [the *Merck* pharmaceutical company]

mercy! excl. [14C+] a general oath (esp. popular in the 1950s–60s camp gay world, with its overtones of a classic 'Southern belle').

mercy blow through phr. [1910s] (Aus.) thank you. [intentional malapropism of Fr. *merci beaucoup*, thank you very much]

mercy buckets phr. (*also* **messy buckets**) [1930s+] (Aus./US) thank you. [for ety. *see* prev.]

mercy buttercups phr. [1980s+] (US campus) thank you. [for ety. *see* MERCY BLOW THROUGH phr.]

mercy fuck n. (*also* **mercy pussy**) [1960s+] (US) an act of sexual intercourse engaged in out of pity (cf. CHARITY FUCK n.). [SE *mercy* + FUCK n.[1] (1)/PUSSY n. (2)]

mercy mary! excl. [1950s+] (gay) an excl. of surprise. [MERCY! excl. + MARY n.[2]]

mercy percy n. [1930s] (US) an exciting performance.

mercy pussy n. *see* MERCY FUCK n.

mercy seat n. [1940s+] (US) a special pew reserved during a Black church revival for those who wish to be 'saved' and thus receive heavenly mercy.

merde! excl. [1920s+] a coarse excl., lit. *shit!* [SE *merd*, a piece of excrement, ult. Fr. *merde*, shit and Lat. *merda*, dung]

mere circumstance n. (*also* **poor circumstance, remote circumstance**) [mid–late 19C] (US) a person or thing of little or no importance.

meri n. *see* MARY n.[1] (1).

merk n. *see* MERCK n.

merk v. [2000s] **1** (US Black) (*also* **mirk**) to leave. **2** (UK Black) to surpass; in fig. use, to kill. [? MAKE IT v.[2] (1)]

merkin n. **1** [mid-17C–18C] the female genitals. **2** [1990s+] a man who poses as the husband or lover of a lesbian who wishes to hide her real sexual preference. [Early Mod. E *malkin*, a mop, thus the false pubic hair as worn by actors and prostitutes, now SE; (2) is pun on BEARD n.[1] (1)/BEARD n.[2] (3)]

mermaid n. [16C–17C] a prostitute. [the mythical fish-women (based on the Greek sirens) reputed to lure sailors to their doom]

mero chingon, el n. **1** [1950s–60s] (US teen) the leader. **2** [1990s+] (US) an exemplary or admirable person; MAN, THE n. (9). [Sp. sl., lit. the 'biggest fucker']

mero mero n. [2000s] (US Black/teen) **1** God. **2** a gang leader; thus ext. to any important/admirable person. [Sp. lit. 'the biggest biggest']

merry adj. [early 19C+] used in many expressions, e.g. *merry hell*, as an elaboration.

merry and bright n. [20C+] a light; usu. in pl. [rhy. sl.]

merry-arsed Christian n. [19C] a prostitute. [*merry-arsed*, cheerful + joc. reversal of CHRISTIAN n.[1]]

merry-begotten n. [late 18C–19C] a bastard. [i.e. conceived when the parents were *merry*]

merry bit n. (*also* **merry legs**) [19C] a prostitute.

merry-bout n. (*also* **bout**) [late 17C–1900s] sexual intercourse.

merry-go-down n. [16C–17C] a variety of strong ale.

merry-go-round n.[1] [late 19C+] £1 sterling (cf. CHERRY-PICKER n.[5]). [rhy. sl.]

merry-go-round n.[2] (US) **1** [1900s–30s] a racetrack. **2** [1940s] a roulette wheel. [US racetracks are oval]

merry-go-round n.[3] **1** [1920s+] (orig. US) an evasion. **2** [1970s+] (US Black) one who is attempting to deceive or swindle another person. [var. on RUNAROUND, THE n.]

merry-go-round v. [20C+] (US Und.) of a prisoner, to clear all administrative and bureaucratic procedures before being discharged from prison at the end of a sentence.

merry-go-up n. [early–mid-19C] snuff. [? its effects after 'going up' the nose]

merryheart n. [20C+] a sweetheart. [rhy. sl.]

merry legs n. see MERRY BIT n.

merry mac n. [1990s+] (UK drugs) crack cocaine (cf. APPLEJACK n.[3]). [rhy. sl. = CRACK n.[13]]

Merry-macka n. [1990s+] (W.I.) America. [lit. 'merry but thorny'; also mispron.]

merrymaker n. (also merry-man) [19C] the penis.

merry men n. [late 19C+] followers, subordinates. [SE merry men, the followers of a knight or an outlaw chieftain (esp. the mythical Robin Hood)]

merry-merry n. **1** [1900s–20s] (US) a chorus line. **2** [1910s] a song. [i.e. their usual cheeriness]

merry old soul n. [20C+] **1** coal. **2** a hole. **3** the anus (cf. BOTTLE AND GLASS n.). [rhy. sl.; (3) = HOLE n.[1] (1)]

merry snob n. [early 18C] a pleasant companion. [SE merry + generic use of SNOB n. (1)]

merry widow n.[1] [20C+] Veuve Cliquot champagne. [Fr. veuve, widow + pun on The Merry Widow (1906), light opera by Frankz Lehár]

merry widow n.[2] [1920s–30s] (US) a condom. [a popular brand]

merry widow n.[3] [1940s–60s] a foundation garment designed to cinch in a woman's waist.

merv/mervin n. see MELVIN n.

Meryl Streep n. [1990s+] sleep. [rhy. sl.; ult. US actress Meryl Streep (b.1949)]

merzer n. [1980s+] (Aus. prison) a homemade piece of equipment for boiling water. [abbr. immerser]

merzky adj. [1990s+] (US teen) dirty or nasty. [? echoic of a 'myeugh' snort of disgust or Fr. merde + -SKI sfx]

mesc n. (also mezc) [1960s+] (orig. US drugs) mescaline. [abbr.]

mescal n. [1950s+] (drugs) mescaline. [abbr.; note Mex. mescal, a drink made from the fermented juice of the agave plant]

meserole n. see MEZZROLL n.

mesh adj. [1990s+] (W.I.) well-dressed.

meshuga n. (also mashugga, meshuger, meshugga, meshuggah, meshuggener, mishugge) [20C+] a crazy person, an obsessive, an eccentric. [MESHUGA adj.]

meshuga adj. (also mashugga, meshugenah, meshugeneh, meshugener, meshuger, meshugga, meshuggah, meshuggener, mishugge) [late 19C+] crazy, insane, eccentric. [Yid. mushuge, crazy, ult. f. Heb. shagag, to wander, to go astray]

meshugaas n. see MISHEGAAS n.

Mesopotamia n. [mid-19C] Belgravia. [SE Mesopotamia, the land between the rivers Tigris and Euphrates, lit. 'between the rivers', although, much earlier, the Westbourne River once meandered through Belgravia. The implication is less geographical than racist; the Belgravia area was seen as the home of newly rich Jews. Note Oxford University jargon use, referring to that area of Oxford between the rivers Cherwell and Isis, is geographical]

mess n.[1] [early 19C+] (US) a large quantity. [SE mess, a sufficient quantity to make a dish]

mess n.[2] **1** [20C+] excrement, usu. canine or feline; thus make a mess, to excrete on a carpet, floor or similar unsuitable place. **2** [1910s–20s] (US prison) food. **3** [1920s+] (US Black) nonsense, rubbish. **4** [1940s+] (US Black) stuff in general. **5** [1980s+] (US

campus) male or female genitalia. **6** [1990s+] (Irish) foolish behaviour, fun. **7** [1990s+] (US) the daylights, the stuffing. [orig. dial.; all fig. uses of SHIT n.[1]]

mess n.[3] [1920s+] (orig. US) an objectionable, ineffectual or stupid person.

mess n.[4] [1930s–70s] (US Black) something good or praiseworthy, if slightly confusing or disturbing. [SE mess, a state of confusion or muddle]

mess n.[5] [1960s+] semen (cf. CRUD n.[1]).

mess n.[6] [1970s] (US Black/drugs) mescaline. [abbr.]

mess v. **1** [late 19C+] to interfere, to disturb. **2** [20C+] to have sexual intercourse, esp. adulterously (cf. BANG v.[1]). **3** [1910s+] (US) to fight. **4** [1930s+] (US) to defecate (cf. CACA v.). **5** [1980s] (US) to gossip maliciously. **6** [1980s+] to tease, to joke. **7** [1990s+] to masturbate (cf. BOFF v.). [(1) backform. f. MESS WITH v.]

mess! excl. [1910s–20s] a euph. excl. for SHIT! excl. [MESS n.[2] (1)]

mess about v. (also mess around) **1** [late 19C+] to handle roughly, to mistreat, to swindle, to deceive. **2** [late 19C+] to indulge in varying degrees of sexual intimacy; usu. adulterously. **3** [late 19C+] to waste time, to fool around, to wander off the subject, to distract someone's attention. **4** [1920s–30s] (US Black) to dance. **5** [1940s] to be involved with. **6** [1960s] to spend time with, to socialize. [(3) epitomized in Kenneth Williams's catchphrase Stop messing about! used in various Kenneth Horne BBC radio comedy shows and in the UK Carry On... films (1950s–80s)]

message n.[1] [1910s+] (Irish) a small purchase; thus messenger-boy, one who delivers such purchases.

message n.[2] [1950s–60s] (UK Und.) instructions passed on among criminals.

mess-around n. [1940s+] (W.I.) a cake made of flour that must be stirred for a long time.

mess around v. see MESS ABOUT v.

messed adj. [1990s+] extremely intoxicated by a drug or drink. [MESSED UP adj. (2)]

messed up adj. **1** [1910s+] ruined in any sense, physically, emotionally or mentally. **2** [1950s+] (orig. US) extremely intoxicated by a drug or drink; one of a number of terms that equate extreme drunkenness with suffering violence. Many of such terms can also apply to the effects of drugs. **3** [1980s+] (US Black) troubled, suffering bad luck, wrong. **4** [1990s+] (US Black) irrational.

messen n. [20C+] (Ulster) a contemptible person. [Scot. messen, a small dog; thus synon. with SE cur]

messenger n. [late 19C] (N.Z.) a false die, used by a cheat. [it passes the cheat a 'message']

messer n. **1** [20C+] one who makes a mess, a bungler. **2** [1910s+] one who indulges in a number of sexual relationships. **3** [1910s+] an 'amateur prostitute', one who, while not actively swapping sex for cash, will take 'presents' from her admirers. **4** [1930s] (US Und.) a professional thug. **5** [1930s+] (Irish) an extremely incapable or irresponsible person. [MESS ABOUT v.]

messing n. [1990s+] having sexual intercourse.

messjohn n. see MAS JOHN n.

messorole n. see MEZZROLL n.

mess over v. [1960s+] (US Black) to harm, to mistreat, to annoy. [ext. of MESS v. (1)]

mess-up n. **1** [20C+] a blunder, a botch. **2** [1910s] (Aus.) a fight. **3** [1920s+] an inadequate or incompetent person, a person with problems. [MESS UP v.]

mess up v. **1** [20C+] (US) to ruin, to botch. **2** [1910s+] (US) to make a mistake, to get into trouble, to fail. **3** [1910s+] (orig. US) to beat up, to assault. **4** [1930s+] to ridicule. **5** [1930s+] to involve in. **6** [1950s+] to confuse, to make an emotional mess of. **7** [1960s+] (US) to play around, usu. in a sexual manner.

mess up someone's game v. (also mess up someone's action, ...play, ...style) [1970s–80s] (US Black) to interfere in someone else's attempt at seduction. [MESS UP v. (1) + GAME n.² (3)/ACTION n. (2)/ PLAY n.¹/STYLE n.]

mess with v. (*US*) **1** [19C+] to become involved with, to use, to fool around with. **2** [late 19C+] to harass, to annoy, to interfere with. **3** [1980s+] to laugh at, to ridicule, to tease.

mess with nature v. [1970s–80s] (*US Black*) **1** to lose one's potency, esp. through excess use of narcotics or alcohol. **2** to interfere with a couple who are poised to have sexual intercourse. [MESS WITH v. + NATURE n. (2)]

mess with someone's mind v. [1950s+] (*orig. US Black*) to disturb or harm someone emotionally. [MESS WITH v. + SE *mind*]

messy adj.¹ [1920s+] immoral, unethical.

messy adj.² [1930s–60s] (*US Black*) good, first-rate. [MESS n.⁴]

messy attic n. [1950s+] (*US Black*) hair in need of dressing. [SE *messy* + ATTIC n. (1)]

messy buckets phr. see MERCY BUCKETS phr.

mestee n. see MUSTEE n.

Met, the n. **1** [late 19C–1910s] the *Metropolitan* Music Hall, London. **2** [late 19C+] the *Metropolitan* Railway, part of the London Underground system. **3** [late 19C+] (*US*) (*also* **the Mett**) the *Metropolitan* Opera House, New York. **4** [1940s+] (*also* **the Mets**) the *Metropolitan* Police, serving London. **5** [1940s+] the *Meteorological* Office, responsible for weather forecasting; usu. as the *Met Office*; thus *Met man*, a weather forecaster. [abbr.]

metal n.¹ [late 18C+] money (cf. BRASS n.¹). [abbr. *precious metal*]

metal n.² [mid-19C] (*Anglo-Ind.*) sweets. [ety. unknown; ? an Indian language]

metal n.³ [2000s] a pistol, a revolver, a gun.

metalhead n. [1980s+] (*orig. US teen*) a fan of heavy metal music. [SE (*heavy*) *metal* + -HEAD sfx (4)]

metal mouth n. [1970s+] (*US/UK teen/juv.*) a person with orthodontic braces.

mete adj. [20C+] (*W.I.*) meddlesome, interfering. [Sp. *meterse*, to interfere in, to meddle]

meter n. [1930s–40s] (*US Black*) a quarter, 25 cents. [the coin then required to operate a gas *meter*]

meter thief n. [1960s+] (*UK Und.*) a term of contempt for a petty villain. [their targets never rise above gas meters, parking meters etc]

meth n.¹ (*drugs*) **1** [1960s+] *Meth*edrine. **2** [1960s+] *meth*amphetamine (cf. BOMBITA n.). **3** [1980s+] *meth*adone. **4** [1990s+] marijuana. [abbr.]

meth n.² see METHS n.

meth freak n. [1960s–70s] (*US drugs*) **1** a regular user of Methedrine. **2** a regular user of methamphetamine. [METH n.¹ + FREAK sfx]

meth-head n. [1960s+] (*drugs*) **1** a regular user of Methedrine. **2** a regular user of methamphetamine. [METH n.¹ (2) + -HEAD sfx (3)]

meth monster n. [1960s+] (*US drugs*) **1** a person who has a violent reaction to methamphetamine. **2** a Methedrine addict. [METH n.¹ + MONSTER sfx]

metho n.¹ [1940s+] (*Aus.*) a *Metho*dist. [abbr. + -o sfx (4)]

metho n.² (*also* **methy**) [1930s+] (*Aus.*) **1** *methy*lated spirits, beloved by extreme alcoholics. **2** a drinker of *methy*lated spirits; ext. as *metho fiend*. [abbr. (+ FIEND n.² (1))]

Methodist adj. (*US*) used as a synon. for 'puritan'; thus [1930s–40s] *Methodist feet*, religious objections to dancing; [1940s+] *Methodist measure*, a short measure of alcohol; [1960s] *Methodist cocktail*, Coca-Cola. [the supposed levity of dancing and Methodist teetotalitarianism]

Methody n. [mid-19C+] (*Aus./Irish*) a Methodist.

meths n. (*also* **meth**) [1920s+] methylated spirits, usu. as drunk by alcoholic tramps or *meth(s)-drinkers*.

methy n. see METHO n.².

me-too n. [1940s+] (*orig. US*) one who slavishly copies the behaviour of another. [ME TOO! excl.]

me-too v. [1940s+] to follow suit, to join in (slavishly); thus *me-tooing*, following suit, 'climbing on a bandwagon'. [ME TOO! excl.]

me too! excl. [mid-19C+] an excl. signifying one's agreement or one's willingness or desire to share an opinion, experience or object.

met-pot n. [20C+] (*W.I.*) a large pot used for cooking for parties, celebrations or any occasions requiring many servings. [dial. *met*, a gathering, a dance, a fair]

metrop n. [late 19C+] a *metrop*olis, usu. London. [abbr.]

metros n. [1980s] (*US Black*) metropolitan police.

Mett, the n. see MET, THE n. (3).

mettle n. [17C–early 19C] semen. ['the mettle of generation', SE *mettle*, spirit, pluck]

metzel n. [19C] (*US*) a German-born immigrant. [Ger. *Metzelsuppe*, metzel soup, made with sausage]

Mex n. **1** [mid-19C+] (*US*) (*also* **Mexi**) a Mexican. **2** [mid-19C+] (*US*) the Mexican/Spanish language. **3** [late 19C–1950s] (*US*) Mexico or Mexico City. **4** [1900s–10s] (*US*) Mexican money. **5** [1970s+] (*US drugs*) Mexican drugs. [abbr.; note late 19C–1940s US forces use *Mex*, any form of foreign currency, esp. that of the Philippine Islands]

Mex adj. **1** [mid-19C+] Mexican. **2** [late 19C–1900s] (*US*) second-rate, inferior; in measurement, half the length/weight/value etc. [abbr. + derog. stereotyping]

Mexicali revenge n. [1970s] (*US*) diarrhoea, as contracted by travellers in foreign countries (cf. AZTEC HOP n.). [the Mexican town of *Mexicali*]

Mexican n. [1980s+] (*Aus.*) a Victorian as seen from New South Wales, or a native of New South Wales or Victoria viewed from Queensland. [such people come from 'south of the border/Down Mexico way']

Mexican adj. [20C+] (*mainly US*) used in a variety of combs. below to imply cheapness, inadequacy, stupidity, mediocrity and a dependence on donkeys. [the stereotype of Mexicans, esp. in the US, is uniformly negative]

Mexican athlete n.¹ [1910s+] (*US*) a person who exaggerates. [he 'shoots the bull']

Mexican athlete n.² [1930s+] (*US*) an unsuccessful candidate for a college or school sports team.

Mexican bankroll n. [1940s–70s] (*US Und.*) a banknote of high denomination rolled around a large number of notes of small denomination (cf. CALIFORNIA BANKROLL n.).

Mexican Bogner's n. [1950s+] (*US*) jeans worn as ski pants. [*Bogner's*, a fashionable brand of choice in ski-wear]

Mexican boxing glove n. [1990s+] (*Aus.*) a knife.

Mexican breakfast n. [1930s+] (*US, Texas*) a cigarette and a glass of water, i.e. nothing nourishing at all (cf. BARBER'S BREAKFAST n.).

Mexican brown n. (*also* **Mexican tar**) (*US drugs*) **1** [1960s+] high-strength marijuana (cf. ACAPULCO (GOLD) n.). **2** [1970s+] heroin, usu. weak, inferior (cf. CHINA WHITE n.). [SE *Mexico*, i.e. the country of origin + its 'reputation' in the relevant drugs]

Mexican Buick n. [1950s+] (*US*) a Chevrolet. [the respective status of the cars]

Mexican bush n. [1940s] (*US drugs*) an inferior variety of marijuana (cf. ACAPULCO (GOLD) n.; AFRICAN BUSH n.). [SE *Mexican*/MEXICAN adj. + BUSH n.⁵ (1)]

Mexican carriage n. [1950s+] (*US*) a donkey. [stereotyping]

Mexican carwash n. [1950s+] (*US*) washing the car by leaving it out in the rain.

Mexican cashmere n. [1950s+] (*US*) a sweatshirt.

Mexican chrome n. [1950s+] (*US*) **1** aluminium paint used to simulate real (and more expensive) chrome on a car. **2** any form of silver paint.

Mexican cigarette n. (*also* **Mexican cigar**) [1910s+] (*US*) a (poorly made) marijuana cigarette (cf. AFRICAN WOODBINE n.).

Mexican commercial n. [1940s+] (*US drugs*) average strength Mexican marijuana (cf. ACAPULCO (GOLD) n.).

Mexican credit card *n. see* HARLEM CREDIT CARD n.

Mexican dragline *n.* [1960s+] (*US*) a shovel or spade.

Mexican filling station *n.* [1950s+] (*US*) a hose used to siphon petrol from another car into one's own.

Mexican foxtrot *n.* [1950s+] (*US*) diarrhoea, dysentery (cf. AZTEC HOP n.).

Mexican green *n.* [1960s+] (*drugs*) a weak grade and type of marijuana (cf. ACAPULCO (GOLD) n.; AFRICAN BUSH n.). [SE *Mexican*/MEXICAN adj. + GREEN n.³ (1)]

Mexican hairless *n.* [1950s+] an old, hairless tennis ball. [pun on SE *Mexican hairless*, a breed of dog]

Mexican horse *n.* [1970s+] (*drugs*) heroin, presumably from Mexico (cf. CHINA WHITE n.). [SE *Mexican*/MEXICAN adj. + HORSE n.⁸]

Mexican jeep *n.* [1940s+] (*US*) a donkey.

Mexican jelly bean *n.* [1950s+] (*US*) a Chevrolet that has been lowered in the rear and fitted with a Venetian blind in the rear window. [the car bounces up and down on its special suspension]

Mexican jumping beans *n.* [1970s+] **1** (*drugs/gay*) amphetamines (cf. A n.²). **2** (*drugs*) barbiturates, esp. Seconal, made in Mexico (cf. BARBIT n.).

Mexican lightning *n.* [1970s] (*US*) tequila. [SE *Mexican* + LIGHTNING n.¹ (2)]

Mexican lipstick *n.* (*also* **pasata grin**) [1990s+] smears of blood around the mouth of one who has been having cunnilingus with a menstruating woman. [SE; note Ital. *passata*, a tomato sauce]

Mexican look *n.* [1910s] (*US*) a hostile stare.

Mexican Maserati *n.* [1950s+] (*US*) a Mercury car.

Mexican milk *n.* [1970s+] (*US*) tequila.

Mexican motor mount *n.* [1950s+] (*US*) inner tubing used as a shock absorber, rather than the purpose-built material.

Mexican mud *n.* [1980s+] (*US drugs*) heroin (cf. CHINA WHITE n.). [SE *Mexican*/MEXICAN adj. + MUD n.³ (5)]

Mexican muffler *n.* (*also* **cherry-bomb muffler**) [1950s+] (*US*) a homemade silencer made from a tin can stuffed with steel wool that is then attached to the car's exhaust pipe. [SAmE *muffler*, a silencer]

Mexican mushroom *n.* [1960s+] (*drugs*) psilocybin, psilocin. [the psilocybe *mushroom* grows in Mexico]

Mexican nightmare *n.* [1960s+] (*gay*) gaudy ceramic crockery, typical of that sold to tourists in Mexico.

Mexican nose guard *n.* [1950s+] (*US*) an athletic support or jockstrap.

Mexican oats *n.* [1950s+] (*US*) nonsense, rubbish. [euph. for BULLSHIT n. (1)]

Mexican overdrive *n.* (*also* **Georgia overdrive**) [1950s+] (*US*) coasting or freewheeling in order to save petrol.

Mexican promotion *n.* (*also* **Mexican raise**) [1950s+] (*US*) a better job but one that brings no increase in salary.

Mexican quarter-horse *n.* [1960s+] (*US*) a mule.

Mexican red *n.* (*drugs*) **1** [1960s+] a barbiturate (cf. BARBIT n.). **2** [1970s+] a potent variety of Mexican marijuana (cf. ACAPULCO (GOLD) n.).

Mexican rig *n.* [1960s+] (*US*) anything that has been poorly constructed.

Mexican schlock *n.* [1960s+] (*US gay*) any art in poor taste, typically that sold to tourists in Mexico. [MEXICAN adj. + SCHLOCK n. (1)]

Mexican seabag *n.* [1930s+] (*US*) a newspaper or paper bag in which poor sailors carry their belongings.

Mexican shower *n.* [2000s] (*US*) a rudimentary wash, cleaning only the face and armpits.

Mexican sidewalls *n.* [1950s+] (*US*) black tyres painted white to imitate expensive white sidewalls.

Mexican stand-off *n.* **1** [late 19C+] (*orig. US*) a situation in which 2 parties are at a deadlock, with neither party willing to

back down from a stated position and neither party having a superior edge; the result is that both parties give in and walk off. **2** [20C+] (*US*) a partial victory or defeat, but one that still fails to provide a decisive outcome. **3** [20C+] a round in poker when no one is willing to open the betting or no one wins the pot. **4** [20C+] a head-on collision between 2 trains. **5** [1920s–30s] (*US*) execution by firing squad.

Mexican straight *n.* [1950s+] any 5 cards and a knife in poker. [poker jargon *straight*, a run of 5 cards in sequence + the negative stereotyping of the knife-wielding *Mexican*]

Mexican tar *n. see* MEXICAN BROWN n.

Mexican threads *n.* [1950s–60s] (*US*) a stripped bolt that has been forced into a hole to cut new threads.

Mexican time *n.* [1960s+] (*US*) poor timekeeping, unpunctuality (cf. AFRICAN (PEOPLE'S) TIME n.).

Mexican toothache *n.* [1960s+] diarrhoea, often contracted on a foreign holiday (cf. AZTEC HOP n.).

Mexican two-step *n.* [1950s+] diarrhoea (cf. AZTEC HOP n.).

Mexican valve-job *n.* [1950s–60s] (*US*) flushing the carburettor of a running engine with kerosene.

Mexican window-shade *n.* [1950s–60s] (*US*) Venetian blinds in the back window of a car.

mexicoon *n.* [2000s] (*US Black*) a Black man who pursues Hispanic women. [SE *Mexican* + COON n.]

mexx up *v.* [2000s] to join, to form a partnership with. [? SE *mix up*]

mezc *n. see* MESC n.

mezonny *n.* [1930s–50s] (*US drugs*) the act of arranging for and taking the delivery of drugs from one's dealer. [ety. unknown]

mezz *n.* (*also* **mighty mezz**) [1930s+] marijuana, orig. spec. that sold by Milton 'Mezz' Mezzrow. [the jazz musician and marijuana-dealer Milton 'Mezz' Mezzrow (1899–1972)]

mezz *adj.* [1930s–70s] (*US Black*) honest, dependable. [the positive reputation of 'Mezz' Mezzrow (*see* MEZZ n.)]

mezzroll *n.* (*also* **meserole**, **messorole**, **mezz's roll**) [1940s+] (*drugs*) a large, generously filled marijuana cigarette. [MEZZ n. + SE *roll*]

m.f. *n.* [1950s+] (*orig. US*) a euph. for MOTHERFUCKER n. (1). [abbr.]

m.f. *adj.* [1950s+] (*orig. US*) a euph. for MOTHERFUCKING adj. (1). [abbr.]

m'fucka *n. see* MOTHERFUCKER n. (1).

m-fugging *adj. see* MOTHERFUCKING adj.

m.f.u.t.u. *phr.* [1940s] (*US*) a term of abuse, *motherfuck you too* (cf. S.N.A.F.U. n.). [abbr., orig. WW2 milit., inscribed on B-17 bombers with a cartoon of General Hideki Tojo (1885–1948) getting 'the finger']

m.f.w.i.c. *n.* [1970s+] (*orig. US milit.*) a term of abuse, *motherfucker who's/what's in charge*. [abbr.]

m.g.a. *n.* [1970s+] (*Aus.*) Mediterranean *gut-ache*, an 'illness' supposedly contracted by Greek, Yugoslav and similar 'Mediterranean' immigrants to Australia, seen as innately lazier than their Anglo-Saxon counterparts. [abbr.]

M'Gimp *n. see* MACGIMP n.

m.h. *n.* [1990s+] (*US*) a mentally unstable, insane person. [abbr. *mental health*]

miaow! (miaow!) *excl.* [1920s+] used by a third party when overhearing a pair of speakers engaged in malicious gossip. [such a conversation is SE *catty*]

mic *n.*¹ (*also* **mike**) [1940s+] a *mic*rophone. [abbr.]

mic *n.*² (*also* **mike**) [1960s+] (*drugs*) 1 *mic*rogram (1 millionth of a gram), the basic measurement of LSD. An average dose of LSD is approx. 250 *mic*s. [abbr.]

mice *n.* [1950s] (*Aus.*) the girls who accompany the Aus. variety of Teddy boy.

michael *n.*¹ [1910s–30s] (*US*) a hip-flask. [? the 'Irish' name *Michael* and thus stereotype of Irish drinkers]

michael *n.*[2] [1930s+] (*Aus.*) the vagina. [rhy. sl.; *Michael Hunt* = CUNT n.[1] (1); esp. used in joc. phr. 'Has anyone seen Mike Hunt?']

michael *n.*[3] [1940s–50s] (*US*) a knockout drop, as placed in a drink. [abbr./ext. of MICKEY FINN n.]

Michael Caine *n.* [1960s+] (lit. and fig.) a pain. [rhy. sl.; ult. UK actor *Michael Caine* (b.1933)]

Michael Miles *n.* [1990s+] piles. [rhy. sl.; ult. UK TV personality *Michael Miles* (1919–71)]

Michael Schumacher *n.* [1990s+] tobacco. [rhy. sl.; Cockney pron. 'terbaccer'; ult. F1 racing driver *Michael Schumacher* (b.1969)]

Michael Winner *n.* [1990s+] dinner. [rhy. sl.; ult. film director and latterly restaurant critic *Michael Winner* (b.1935)]

Michelin (tyre) *n.* [1950s+] (*W.I.*) **1** a bulla cake. **2** a dumpling. **3** a fat person. [the tyre makers and their 'Michelin man' logo]

Michigan *n.* [1910s] (*US Und.*) a confidence trick.

Michigan roll *n.* (*also* **Michigan, Michigan bankroll, Michigan stake**) [1910s+] (*US*) a fake bankroll, a note of a high denomination around a large number of notes of smaller denomination (cf. CALIFORNIA BANKROLL n.). [ROLL n.[2]]

miching malicho *n.* (*also* **miching mallecho, minchin malacho**) [17C–19C] mischief. [? SE *mitching*, pilfering, skulking, truant-playing, pretending poverty + Sp. *malhecho*, misdeed. The first cit. is in Shakespeare, *Hamlet* (1602), III.ii: 'Marry this is *Miching Malicho*, that meanes Mischeefe']

mick *n.*[1] **1** [mid-19C+] (*orig. US*) an Irish person; usu. but not invariably derog. (cf. DONOVAN n.[1]). **2** [1920s+] (*Aus./US*) a Roman Catholic. **3** [1930s] a labourer on the roads. **4** [1930s+] (*US*) a potato. **5** [1940s] (*US*) an Englishman. [*Michael*, a common Irish (and by stereotype Catholic, labouring and potato-eating) name; note milit. *the Micks*, the Irish Guards, any Irish unit]

mick *n.*[2] [20C+] (*Aus.*) in the game of two-up, the 'tails' side of a coin; thus as v., to spin the coins so that they come up 'tails'.

mick *n.*[3] [1910s+] (*Aus.*) **1** the vagina. **2** the queen in a pack of cards. [abbr. MICHAEL n.[2]/MICKEY n.[6]; ? (2) f. (1)]

mick *n.*[4] [1960s+] (*US campus*) anything easy, esp. an academic class or test. [MICKEY MOUSE adj.[1] (4)]

mick *adj.*[1] **1** [late 19C+] (*orig. US*) Irish. **2** [1920s+] (*Aus./US*) Roman Catholic. [MICK n.[1]]

mick *adj.*[2] [1980s+] (*US campus*) easy. [MICK n.[4]]

Mick Do/Doo/Doolan/Dooley/Doolie/Doolin *n. see* MICKEY DOOLAN n.

Mickey *n. see* MICKEY MOUSER n.

mickey *n.*[1] (*also* **mickie, micky**) **1** [mid-19C+] (*also* **mikey**) (*US*) an Irish person (cf. DONOVAN n.[1]). **2** [1920s+] (*Aus./US*) a Roman Catholic. **3** [1930s+] (*US*) a potato, esp. a roasted sweet potato. **4** [1940s–60s] (*US prison*) a fellow inmate. **5** [1950s–60s] (*US*) a fellow, a person. [fig. uses of MICK n.[1], stereotyping of the Irish as criminal and potato-eating; (5) f. (4)]

mickey *n.*[2] (*also* **micky**) [late 19C+] (*Aus.*) a wild bullock. [? MICKEY n.[1] (1), the stereotyped 'wild Irishman']

mickey *n.*[3] [late 19C+] (*UK tramp*) a casual ward. [rhy. sl.; *mickey* = *mike* = SPIKE n.[2] (1)]

mickey *n.*[4] (*also* **micky**) [20C+] (*Irish*) the penis. [joc. use of proper name]

mickey *n.*[5] [1910s+] (*mainly Can./US Black*) a small bottle of wine or spirits. [MICHAEL n.[1]]

mickey *n.*[6] [1930s+] (*Aus.*) the vagina. [MICHAEL n.[2]]

mickey *n.*[7] [1940s–50s] (*US*) a second-rate, commercial band playing uninspired music. [abbr. MICKEY MOUSE adj.[1] (1) band]

mickey *n.*[8] *see* MICKEY FINN n. (1).

mickey *adj.*[1] (*also* **micky**) [late 19C–1900s] sick. [rhy. sl.]

mickey *adj.*[2] [1950s+] (*US*) something second-rate, corny. [abbr. MICKEY MOUSE adj.[1] (1)]

mickey dazzler *n. see* BOBBY-DAZZLER n.

Mickey Doolan *n.* (*also* **Mickey Do, ...Doo, ...Dooley, ...Doolie, ...Doolin, Mick..., Micky...**) [20C+] (*N.Z.*) an Irish immigrant; a Roman Catholic. [generic Irish name]

Mickey D's (rainbow steakhouse) *n.* (*also* **Mickey Dee's (rainbow steakhouse)**) [1970s+] (*US Black/campus*) a McDonald's hamburger restaurant. [initial letters of McDonald/*Mickey D*]

Mickey Duff *adj.* [1990s+] unwell, 'under the weather'. [rhy. sl. = SE *rough*; ult. UK boxing promoter *Mickey Duff* (b.1929)]

mickey-fickey *n.* (*also* **micky-ficky**) [1990s+] (*US Black*) a euph. for MOTHERFUCKER n. (1).

mickey finn *n.* (*also* **micky finn**) **1** [late 19C+] (*orig. US*) (*also* **mickey, mickey flynn, micky, mike finn**) a knockout drug, poss. chloral hydrate, mixed into an unsuspecting victim's drink; also as v. **2** [1940s] (*Aus.*) in carnival use, the person who goes out and touts for business. **3** [1970s–80s] (*N.Z. prison*) a sleeping pill. **4** [1990s+] (*US drugs*) any form of depressant. [the saloon-keeper *Mickey Finn*, who ran Chicago's Lone Star and Palm Saloons *c.*1896–190?. He, in turn, had supposedly picked up the recipe from voodoo operators in New Orleans; for a detailed history of Finn and his drug, see Asbury, *The Gangs of Chicago* (1940) pp.171–6]

Mickey Mouse *n.*[1] **1** [1930s–70s] (*US Black*) a White person. **2** [1940s–70s] (*US*) a small, silly or inconsequential person. **3** [1940s+] (*US Black*) commercialized music, esp. uninspired jazz music. **4** [1950s+] (*US*) a trivial, petty or unnecessary activity. **5** [1980s+] (*US*) foolish or nonsensical talk. [MICKEY MOUSE adj.[1]]

Mickey Mouse *n.*[2] [1940s+] (*US*) **1** a black and white police patrol car. **2** a police officer. [Disney's *Mickey Mouse* (*see* MICKEY MOUSE adj.) is black and white]

Mickey Mouse *n.*[3] [1950s+] (*US*) a watch. [a line of watches manufactured in 1930s with a picture of *Mickey Mouse* (*see* MICKEY MOUSE adj.) on the face]

Mickey Mouse *n.*[4] [1960s+] (*drugs*) a variety of LSD; squares of blotting-paper overprinted with a picture of *Mickey Mouse* as the Sorcerer's Apprentice, from the film *Fantasia* (1940), are impregnated with a drop of the drug (cf. A n.[3]). [Disney's *Mickey Mouse* (*see* next)]

Mickey Mouse *adj.*[1] **1** [1930s+] (*orig. US*) second-rate, badly made, artificial; thus (*US Black*) *Mickey Mouse music*, commercialized jazz or pop music. **2** [1940s+] small, miniature. **3** [1950s+] (*orig. US*) silly, puerile, contemptible. **4** [1950s+] (*US campus*) easy, facile. [*Mickey Mouse*, Walt Disney's anodyne, albeit hugely successful, cartoon creation, created in 1928; (2) very quickly becomes used primarily as (3)]

Mickey Mouse *adj.*[2] [1960s+] (*Aus.*) excellent, wonderful, the best. [rhy. sl. = GROUSE adj.; ult. *see* prev.]

Mickey Mouse *v.* [1960s+] (*US*) to fool around, to botch; often as *Mickey Mouse around, Mickey Mouse it*. [MICKEY MOUSE adj.[1]]

Mickey Mouse ears *n.* [1970s] (*US campus*) siren lights on a police car. [resemblance, but note MICKEY MOUSE n.[2]]

Mickey Mouse habit *n.* [1980s+] (*drugs*) a limited addiction to or occasional use of heroin. [MICKEY MOUSE adj.[1] (2) + HABIT n. (1)]

Mickey Mouse in the house, and Donald Duck don't give a fuck *phr.* [1950s+] (*US Black*) a phr. used to encourage party guests to move to a new and more abandoned level of self-indulgence. [ult. Disney characters]

Mickey-Mouse money *n.* [1970s+] **1** any unfamiliar currency, including the UK's decimal coins in the immediate aftermath of their introduction. **2** counterfeit money. [MICKEY MOUSE adj.[1] (1) + SE *money*]

Mickey Mouser *n.* (*also* **Mickey**) [2000s] a Liverpudlian. [rhy. sl. = SCOUSER n.]

Mickey Mouse ticket *n.* [2000s] (*US prison*) a disciplinary report.

mickey-muncher *n.* [1980s+] (*Aus.*) a man who performs cunnilingus. [MICKEY n.[6] + SE *muncher*]

Mickey Rooney *n.* **1** [1930s+] macaroni. **2** [1950s+] an eccentric, a mad person (cf. BREAD AND BUTTER n.[2]). [rhy. sl.; (2) = LOONY n.; ult. film star *Mickey Rooney* (b.1920)]

Mickey Rourke *n.* [2000s] the penis (cf. ALMOND n.). [rhy. sl. = FORK n.²; ult. Hollywood film star *Mickey Rourke* (b.1956)]

Mickey Spillane *n.* [1950s+] (*Aus.*) a game. [rhy. sl.; ult. popular novelist *Mickey Spillane* (b.1918)]

mickey T *n.* [1990s+] (*US Black*) a woman who pursues powerful and/or wealthy men only. [ety. unknown; ? anecdotal]

mickey-take *v. see* TAKE THE MICKEY (OUT OF) v.

Mickey the Mouse *n.* [1930s] (*Aus.*) a Roman Catholic priest. [MICKEY n.¹ (2) + play on *Mickey Mouse* (*see* MICKEY MOUSE adj.)]

mickie *n. see* MICKEY n.¹.

Mick O'Dwyer *n.* [late 19C+] a fire. [rhy. sl.]

mickser *n.* [1950s+] an Irishman who has emigrated to the UK (cf. DONOVAN n.¹). [MICK n.¹ (1)]

micky *see also under* MICKEY *and its combs.*

micky bliss *n. see* JOHNNY BLISS n.

micro *n.* (*also* **micro-mini**) [1970s+] a micro-skirt, i.e. a very short mini-skirt.

micro *v.* [2000s] microwave. [abbr.]

micro-chip *n.* [1970s+] a Japanese person (cf. BUDDHAHEAD n.). [rhy. sl. = NIP n. (1) + ref. to Japanese technological expertise]

microdot *n.* [1970s+] (*drugs*) a small dose of LSD, usu. as placed on squares of blotting-paper (cf. A n.³).

mid *n. see* MIDDY n.¹.

midden *n.* [19C+] (*Scot.*) a filthy slattern. [SE *midden*, a dunghill, manure heap, refuse heap]

middle *n.* [1950s–70s] a middle-class person. [abbr.]

middle *v.* [mid-19C] to make a fool of, to cheat. [SE *middle*, to put in the middle, in this context, of an illicit scheme]

middlebrow *n.* [1920s+] a person of average intellectual attainments or conventional taste. [in between HIGHBROW n. and LOWBROW n.]

middlebrow *adj.* [1920s+] pertaining to average intellectual attainments or conventional taste. [in between HIGHBROW adj. and LOWBROW adj.]

middle cut *n.* [1970s+] (*US Black*) the vagina (cf. AXIS n.).

middle finger *n.* [1960s+] a prostitute's trick to ensure that each client arrives at a speedy orgasm so that she can maximize her nightly earning potential.

middle kingdom *n.* [19C] the vagina (cf. AXIS n.). [a pun on SE *Middle Kingdom*, in ancient Egypt, the 11th and 12th dynasties (22C–18C BC), doubtless a back-handed tribute to the Victorian fascination with things Egyptian]

middle leg *n.* (*also* **middle stump**) [late 19C+] the penis (cf. ARM n.¹).

middle name *n.* [20C+] (*orig. US*) something one likes or identifies with strongly; esp. in phr. — *is my middle name.*

middle piece *n.* (*also* **middle-pie**) [mid-19C–1900s] the stomach.

Middlesex clown *n.* [mid-17C–early 19C] an inhabitant or native of the county of Middlesex.

middle storey *n.* [late 17C–18C] the stomach.

middle stump *n. see* MIDDLE LEG n.

middleweight *n.* [1970s] (*US*) a person, usu. criminal, of medium power and influence. [boxing imagery]

middlo *n.* [1990s+] a middle-class person.

middy *n.¹* (*also* **mid**) [19C–1930s] a *mid*shipman. [abbr.]

middy *n.²* (*also* **midi**) [1940s+] (*Aus.*) a measure of beer, approx. 285ml (10fl oz), or the glass that holds it. [SE *middle*; the measure is 'middle sized']

middy screamer *n. see* ONE-POT SCREAMER n.

midge-net *n.* [mid-19C–1900s] a woman's veil. [SE *midge*, a gnat]

midge's knee-buckle *n.* (*also* **midge's dick**) [20C+] (*Ulster*) something infinitesimally small. [SE *midge*, a gnat]

midget *n. see* MEJOGE n.

midget from Harlem *n.* [1930s] (*US/NY short order*) a small chocolate soda.

midi *n.¹* [1970s] a mid-length garment, usu. a skirt, but also a coat.

midi *n.²* *see* MIDDY n.².

midjic *n. see* MEJOGE n.

Midland (bank) *n. see* BARCLAY'S (BANK) n.

midlands *n.* [19C] the vagina (cf. ANTIPODES n.; AXIS n.).

midnight *n.¹* [1910s–50s] (*US*) the point of 12 in craps dice (cf. ADA FROM DECATUR n.). [? link to the DOZENS n.]

midnight *n.²* *see* MIDNIGHT (THE CAT) n.

midnight *adj.* [mid-19C+] (*US*) of people, Black. [MIDNIGHT (THE CAT) n.]

midnight cowboy *n.* **1** [1960s–70s] (*US*) a male prostitute (cf. DEADLY NIGHTSHADE n.). **2** [1980s] (*Aus.*) a man who goes to a male prostitute. [film title *Midnight Cowboy* (1969)]

midnight express *n.* (*also* **midnight mystery tour**) [1980s+] (*Aus. prison*) the sudden night-time transfer of a convict.

midnight lace *n.* [1970s+] (*US gay*) a Black man's penis. [MIDNIGHT adj. + LACE n.]

midnight oil *n.* [1940s–50s] (*drugs*) opium (cf. APOSTLE n.). [play on phr. *burning the midnight oil*]

midnight queen *n.* [1960s+] (*US gay*) a White homosexual man who prefers Black partners. [MIDNIGHT n.² + QUEEN n.² (1)/QUEEN sfx (2)]

Midnight Revue *n.* [1940s–50s] (*US gang*) a prostitute hired by a group of young boys (cf. DEADLY NIGHTSHADE n.).

midnight talk *n.* [1980s+] (*Aus. prison*) the beating of a prisoner by officers. [euph.]

midnight (the cat) *n.* **1** [mid-19C+] (*US*) a Black person. **2** [1950s–80s] (*US Black*) a particularly dark-complexioned Black person.

mid-ocean *n.* [late 19C] (*US*) boiled eggs.

midshipman's watch and chain *n.* [late 18C–early 19C] a sheep's heart and pluck (the liver and lungs).

midway *n.* **1** [late 19C+] (*US*) the main street or streets of a town or city. **2** [1930s+] (*US Black*) a hallway or corridor. [carnival/fairground jargon *the Midway*, the central avenue along which the major shows and amusements are situated. The term originated in 1893, when the Chicago Exposition featured the *Midway* Plaisance]

midwife's friend *n. see* MOTHER'S FRIEND n.

midzer *n. see* MADZA n.

mierda *n.* [1990s+] excrement. [Sp. *mierda*, SHIT n.¹ (1)]

miering *n.* [1960s–70s] (*S.Afr. township*) money. [ety. unknown; ? Afk.]

miesli *v. see* MIZZLE v.

miff *n.¹* [early 17C+] a tantrum, a petty quarrel, a tiff; thus MIFFED adj.; *miffiness*, the propensity to take offence at the slightest justification. [an expression of disgust, i.e. 'Mmmpphh!']

miff *n.²* [1900s] (*US*) a general term of abuse.

miffed *adj.* [early 19C+] annoyed. [MIFF n.¹]

miffy *n.* [18C–19C] the Devil. [? Fr. *maufé*, the Devil]

miffy *adj.* [early–mid-19C] tetchy, cantankerous, likely to take offence. [MIFF n.¹]

mifky-pifky *n.* (*also* **moofky-poofky, moofty-poofty, mufki-pufki**) [1970s+] (*US*) silly behaviour, esp. romantic or sexual. [ety. unknown]

mifty *adj.* [late 17C–mid-18C] apt to take offence for minimal reason. [MIFF n.¹]

mig *n.* [2000s] a milligram. [pron. of the SE abbr. *mg*]

miggle *n.¹* (*also* **miggies, miggles**) [1940s–70s] (*US drugs*) marijuana. [? MEG n.²; ? SAmE *miggle*, a marble, *miggles*, the game of marbles]

miggle *n.²* *see* MUGGLE n.

miggles *n. see* MUGGLES n.².

mighty *n.* [early 19C] a half-pint of ale.

mighty *adv.* [19C+] greatly, exceedingly, very, esp. in ironic use. [SE 14C–18C]

mighty-come-a-tooting *phr.* (*also* **mighty come-a-right, ...-a-shouting, ...-a-whistling, mighty shouting/**

whistling) [20C+] (*US*) quite right; usu. preceded by *you're....* [MIGHTY adv. + SE]

mighty dome *n.* [1930s–40s] (*US Black*) the US Congress building or any similar large, institutional edifice.

mighty joe young *n.* [1960s+] (*drugs*) **1** a depressant. **2** an extremely heavy narcotics addiction. [the film *Mighty Joe Young* (1949)]

mighty mezz *n. see* MEZZ *n.*

mighty mouth *n.* (*camp gay*) **1** [1950s–70s] a fellator. **2** [1950s+] a gossip or one who boasts.

mighty quinn *n.* [1970s] (*drugs*) LSD (cf. A n.³). [the Bob Dylan song 'The Mighty Quinn' (1966), esp. the line 'You ain't seen nothin' like the Mighty Quinn']

mike *see also under* MIC.

mike *n.*¹ **1** [mid-19C–1900s] a labourer, a hod-carrier, esp. when Irish. **2** [1940s–50s] (*Aus.*) a cup of tea. [abbr. *Michael*, the stereotypical Irish forename]

mike *n.*² [late 19C+] (*US*) **1** a familiar term of address to an unknown male. **2** a generic term for an Irishman (cf. DONOVAN n.¹).

mike *v.* **1** [early 19C–1950s] to loiter, to 'hang about'; thus *do/have a mike*, to loiter, to waste time. **2** [1900s–30s] to steal, to make off with. [MOOCH v.¹, but Hotten (1860) notes racial stereotyping (*Mike* is a generic term for an Irishman and Irish labourers were seen as congenitally idle)]

mike bliss *n. see* JOHNNY BLISS n.

mike finn *n. see* MICKEY FINN n. (1).

mike malone *n.* (*also* **maggie mahone**) [1930s–80s] a telephone. [rhy. sl.]

mike malone *adv. see* PAT MALONE adv.

miker *n.* **1** [late 19C+] a loafer, a scrounger. **2** [1920s–30s] a truant. [MIKE v. or Gloucestershire dial.]

mikey *n. see* MICKEY n.¹ (1).

mil *n.* **1** [1960s+] a *mil*lion, usu. of money. **2** [1990s+] a *mil*ligram, usu. of a drug. [abbr.]

milch-cow *n.* [late 17C–early 19C] (*UK prison*) a prisoner who is generous in bribing warders; one who is easily tricked out of money or property. [SE *milch-cow*, a cow 'in milk' + used fig. as an easy source of money]

mild and meek *n.* [20C+] (*Aus.*) a cheek. [rhy. sl.]

mild bloater *n.* [mid-19C–1900s] a second-rate dandy, 'weak young men who keep bull-dogs, and dress in a "loud" stable style, from a belief that it is very becoming' (Hotten, 1864).

mildewed *adj.* **1** [late 19C–1950s] miserable, miserable-looking. **2** [1910s–20s] pitted with smallpox (cf. CRIBBAGE-FACED adj.). [SE *mildewed*, tainted with mildew]

mileage *n.* [1960s+] (*orig. US*) **1** experience of life. **2** a criminal record.

mile-eater *n.* [20C+] a fast driver or traveller.

mile end *n.* [20C+] a friend. [rhy. sl.]

mile high club *n.* [1960s+] (*orig. US*) a notional 'club' of those who have enjoyed sex in an aeroplane. This has now been joined by the *mile-deep club*, those who have had sex while travelling through the Channel Tunnel between UK and France.

miler *n.* (*also* **myla**) [19C–1900s] a donkey, an ass. [Rom. *meila*, a mule; ? ult. Lat. *mulus*]

miles away, be *v.* [1910s+] to be day-dreaming, lost in thought.

miles's boy *n.* [early–late 19C] 'a very knowing lad in receipt of much information' (B&L). [Bee (1823) cites a tax-collector called Miles, who employed a boy to check on people who might be attempting to default on their dues by moving away]

milestone *n.* [early 19C] a country bumpkin. [they stand at the side of the road]

milestone inspector *n.* [1920s–50s] (*UK tramp*) a professional tramp.

milestone-monger *n.* [mid-19C–1910s] (*UK tramp*) a professional tramp.

milf *n.* [2000s] (*US campus*) an attractive (older) woman. [abbr. *mom I would like to fuck*; coined in movie *American Pie* (1999)]

milherm/milihelen *n. see* MILLIHELEN n.

milikers *n.* [late 19C–1900s] the militia. [joking mispron.]

milish *n.* [mid-19C–1910s] (*US*) the militia. [abbr.]

militant *adj.* [1970s+] (*Black*) aggressive, energetic, purposive. [weak use of SE]

military ceremony *n.* (*also* **military wedding**) [1910s+] (*US*) a wedding that is forced on the groom through his girlfriend's (soon to be bride's) pregnancy. [play on SHOTGUN WEDDING n.]

milk *n.*¹ **1** [early 17C+] semen; thus *milk-pail, milk-pan*, the vagina (cf. BABY GRAVY n.). **2** [mid–late 17C] vaginal secretions (cf. BINDERJUICE n.).

milk *n.*² **1** [mid-19C+] (*US*) bourbon or beer. **2** [1990s+] methylated spirits mixed with water and drunk by down-and-out alcoholics. [(2) the resulting white 'milky' colour]

milk *n.*³ [late 19C–1920s] a weakling. [abbr. SE *milksop*]

milk *v.*¹ **1** [16C+] to defraud, to extract money from. **2** [mid-19C–1900s] to intercept telegrams addressed to others. **3** [1930s+] (*Aus.*) to siphon petrol from a car (whether legally or not). [(1) virtually SE now]

milk *v.*² [17C+] to masturbate oneself or someone else, to cause to ejaculate (cf. BOFF v.). [note D'Urfey, *Pills to Purge Melancholy* (1719–20): 'But stupid Honesty; / May teach her how to Sleep all Night / And take a great deal more Delight, / To Milk the Cows than thee'; note MILK n.¹]

milk *v.*³ [late 19C+] to add milk to tea or coffee.

milk *v.*⁴ [1900s; 1990s+] to laze around, to be idle.

milk a duck *v.* [1930s+] (*US*) to attempt the impossible.

milk and honey route *n.* [1910s–30s] (*US tramp*) a rail route that is renowned for good hand-outs, esp. one passing through Mormon parts of Utah.

milk-and-water *adj.* [late 18C+] weak, diluted, adulterated, e.g. *milk-and-water socialism*.

milk and water! *excl.* [late 18C–early 19C] a toast when drinking (cf. BOTH ENDS OF THE BUSK! excl.). [the ref. is to the female breasts and vagina which give, respectively, milk and urine or vaginal juices]

milk bar *n.*¹ [1950s+] the female breasts (cf. BORDENS n.).

milk bar *n.*² [1950s+] (*Aus.*) a corner shop.

milk bar cowboy *n.* [1950s] **1** a person, esp. a motorcyclist, who frequents milk bars. **2** a general term of abuse, usu. aimed at the young.

milk bottle *n. see* MILK CAN n.

milk-bottle bottoms *n. see* COKE BOTTLE GLASSES n.

milk bottles *n.* [1930s+] (*orig. Aus.*) the female breasts (cf. BORDENS n.). [their primary, non-sexual function as dispensers of milk to a baby]

milk can *n.* (*also* **milk bottle**) **1** [late 19C–1900s] a baby. **2** [1970s+] usu. in pl., a female breast (cf. BORDENS n.).

milken *n. see* MILL-KEN n.

milker *n.*¹ [late 19C] the vagina (cf. BAG n.¹). [it 'milks' the penis of semen]

milker *n.*² [late 19C] one who intercepts telegrams addressed to others. [MILK v.¹ (2)]

milker *n.*³ [late 19C+] a masturbator. [MILK v.²]

milker *n.*⁴ [1900s] an idler. [MILK v.⁴]

milkers *n.* [20C+] the female breasts (cf. BORDENS n.).

milker's calf *n.* [late 19C] (*Aus.*) a petted, favourite child, a 'mother's boy'. [SE *milker's calf*, a calf that is still with its mother]

milk factories *n.* [1940s–70s] (*US*) the female breasts (cf. BORDENS n.).

milkie *n.*¹ (*also* **milky**) [late 19C+] **1** a milkman. **2** milk.

milkie *n.*² *see* MILK JUG n.².

milking pail *n.* [early 18C–19C] the vagina (cf. BAG n.¹). [note *double entendre* in D'Urfey, *Pills to Purge Melancholy* (1719–20): 'What Joys are found, / In Russet Gown, / Young, plump and round, / And sweet and sound, / That carry the Milking Pail']

milk in the coconut n. [mid-19C+] (orig. US) a puzzling fact or circumstance, a crux; esp. in phr. that accounts for the milk in the coconut, used to respond to someone's explanation of an event or action.

milk jug n.[1] (also **milk pan**) [late 18C–1900s] the vagina (cf. BAG n.[1]). [MILK n.[1] (1) + SE jug/pan]

milk jug n.[2] (also **milkie**) [1920s+] (Aus.) a fool, a simpleton (cf. BEECHAM'S PILL n.). [rhy. sl. = MUG n.[2] (1)]

milk jugs n. see JUGS n.

milkman n. [late 19C+] **1** the penis. **2** a person who masturbates frequently. [MILK v.[2]]

milkman's horse adj. [late 19C+] cross, annoyed, irritated. [rhy. sl.; Cockney pron. 'crorss']

milko n.[1] (also **milk-oh**) **1** [20C+] (orig. Aus.) a milkman. **2** [1910s] (Aus.) dawn; the very early morning (i.e. milk delivery time). **3** [1940s] (Aus.) a cow-hand. [SE milk + -o sfx (4)]

milko n.[2] [1940s] (UK drugs) a mix of heroin and lactose.

milk pan n. see MILK JUG n.[1].

milkround n. **1** [1940s+] (orig. milit.) a round trip, stopping at a regular list of places, addresses etc. **2** [1970s+] the annual graduate recruitment tour, in which firms send representatives on a trip around universities.

milk route n. [1930s] (US) a female breast (cf. BORDENS n.).

milkshake n. [1990s+] (N.Z.) a mix of bicarbonate of soda, used illegally in the hope of enhancing a racehorse's performance; thus milkshake, to administer such a mixture. [resemblance]

milk shakes n. [1910s–70s] (US) the female breasts (cf. BORDENS n.).

milk shop n. (also **milk walk**) [19C] the female breasts (cf. BORDENS n.).

milk the lizard v. (also **milk the anaconda**, …**maggot**, …**moose**) [20C+] to masturbate (cf. BEAT ONE'S HOG v.). [LIZARD n.[3]/SE anaconda (i.e. SNAKE n.[3])/MAGGOT n.[2]/SE moose]

milk the pigeon v. [late 18C–19C] to attempt an impossible task.

milk wagon n. [1960s+] (US gay) the female breasts (cf. BORDENS n.).

milk walk n.[1] [late 19C] (US Und.) a beggar's 'beat'.

milk walk n.[2] see MILK SHOP n.

milk-woman n.[1] [19C+] (Scot.) a wet-nurse; thus green milk-woman, one who has only recently given birth.

milk-woman n.[2] [late 19C–1900s] a female masturbator. [MILK v.[2] + SE woman]

milky n. see MILKIE n.[1].

milky adj.[1] [mid–late 19C] (UK Und.) white; thus milky duds, white clothes; milky ones, white linen rags; milky tats, white rags.

milky adj.[2] [late 19C+] cowardly. [SE milksop]

Milky Bar kid n. [1980s+] (Aus. prison) a petty criminal. [the child advertising the Milky Bar was known as the Milky Bar Kid]

milky way adj. [1990s+] homosexual. [rhy. sl. = GAY adj.[1] (3)]

milky way (to bliss) n. [mid-17C–mid-19C] **1** the breasts (cf. BORDENS n.). **2** the vagina (cf. ADAM'S OWN (ALTAR) n.).

mill n.[1] **1** [mid-16C–mid-19C] the vagina. **2** [1930s] (US) a woman.

mill n.[2] **1** [17C] a house-breaker. **2** [17C–early 18C] house-breaking. **3** [17C–mid-19C] a chisel. [SE mill, covering a variety of engines and tools]

mill n.[3] [early 19C–1930s] **1** a fight. **2** a prize-fight, a brawl, a fist-fight. [MILL v.[1] (3)]

mill n.[4] **1** [mid–late 19C] a treadmill. **2** [mid-19C–1940s] a prison. **3** [late 19C–1940s] a milit. prison or guardhouse. **4** [late 19C+] any institution that acts to process its affairs by rote, rather than deal with them on their individual merits. **5** [1920s] (US) a Magistrates' Court. **6** [1950s+] (US drugs) anywhere that pure heroin, purchased in bulk, is diluted and packaged for street sales. [(1) abbr. SE; subseq. defs. ext. of (1)]

mill n.[5] [1900s] (US) a bar.

mill n.[6] [1910s+] (US) a typewriter. [it 'grinds out' the words]

mill n.[7] [1910s+] (US) an engine of an aircraft or 'souped up' car; thus turn the mill, start the engine. [Fr. moulin, a mill, thus WW1 Fr. sl. moulin à café, 'coffee-grinder', i.e. a machine gun, operated by a crank handle]

mill n.[8] **1** [1930s+] (orig. US) a million, usu. dollars. **2** [1940s+] (orig. US) a millimetre, esp. in the diameter of a tube or gun barrel. **3** [1960s] (US drugs) $1000 worth of heroin. [abbr.; (2) and (3) Lat. mille, thousand]

mill v.[1] **1** [mid-16C–19C] (UK Und.) to steal, to rob, to break open; thus MILL A KEN v.; [late 18C] mill a go, to succeed in a robbery or theft; [mid-18C–19C] mill a quod, to break out of prison; milling, goods worth stealing. **2** [17C–19C] to smash, to break open, to spoil. **3** [17C+] to thrash, to fight, to overcome. **4** [late 17C–1900s] to kill, to murder. [SE mill, to grind down, to break into small parts]

mill v.[2] [mid-19C] to sentence to the treadmill, to imprison. [MILL n.[4] (1)]

mill a cly v. [early 19C] (UK Und.) to pick a pocket. [MILL v.[1] (1) + CLY n. (2)]

mill a ken v. [mid-16C–mid-19C] (UK Und.) to rob a house. [MILL v.[1] (1) + KEN n.[1] (1)]

mill-clapper n. [late 17C–19C] a (woman's) tongue. [SE mill-clapper, an instrument which by striking the hopper causes the corn to be shaken into the mill-stones]

mill doll n. (also **mill dolly**) [mid-18C–mid-19C] a prison, orig. the Bridewell in Bridge Street, Blackfriars, London. [MILL DOLL v.]

mill doll v. (also **mill-dolly**) [18C–mid-19C] to beat hemp in prison. [MILL n.[4] (2); ? + SE Doll, a woman's name, a woman's job; ? although chronology mitigates against this, f. MILL DOLL n., where doll = woman = play on bride]

millennium dome n. [1990s+] a comb. [rhy. sl.]

miller n.[1] **1** [mid-17C–mid-19C] a house-breaker, a thief. **2** [late 17C–early 19C] (UK Und.) a killer, a murderer. **3** [early 19C] a vicious, intractable horse. **4** [early–mid-19C] a boxer, esp. one who relies on aggression rather than skill. [MILL v.[1]]

miller n.[2] [early 19C–1920s] **1** a joke, esp. an old 'chestnut'. **2** a joke-book. [JOE MILLER n.]

miller n.[3] [1940s+] (Aus.) a cicada. [the grinding of its legs]

miller's daughter n. [1910s–20s] water. [rhy. sl.]

miller's eye n. [mid-late 19C] a lump of flour in a loaf; thus put the miller's eye out, to cut down on one's use of flour when baking.

miller's point n. [1970s–80s] (N.Z. prison) a cannabis cigarette. [rhy. sl. = JOINT n.[5] (3)]

Miller time n. [1970s+] (US) a period of relaxation, the end of the working day. [the advertisements for Miller Lite Beer, which promote the end of the day as Miller time]

milli n. [1990s+] (US Black) a 9 millimetre pistol. [abbr.]

millia murder! excl. see MELIA MURDER! excl.

millihelen n. (also **millihelen**) [1960s+] (US campus) an imaginary unit of measurement to calculate female beauty; thus milherm, used of men. [pun on Helen of Troy whose face 'launched a thousand ships' (Doctor Faustus, 1604, by Christopher Marlowe); or on the Greek god Hermes]

milliner's shop n. [19C] the vagina.

milling n. **1** [mid-16C–early 19C] robbing, stealing. **2** [early 19C] of a horse, kicking. **3** [early–mid-19C] a beating, a thrashing. **4** [early–mid-19C] (also **milling-bout**) boxing for money, prize-fighting. **5** [early 19C–1900s] fighting, usu. with the fists. [MILL v.[1]]

milling-cove n. [early–mid-19C] a prize-fighter. [MILL v.[1] (3) + COVE n. (1)]

milling-panney n. [early 19C] a place where prize-fights are held. [MILLING n. (4) + PANNEY n.[2] (1)]

million n. [1950s+] a sure bet. [abbr. MILLION TO A BIT OF DIRT phr. or SE phr. million to one]

million-dollar adj. [late 19C+] (US) splendid, of great value.

million-dollar wound *n.* [1940s+] (*US milit.*) any wound that guarantees the victim a passage out of a war zone and back to the USA. [equivalent to UK *Blighty one* (*see* BLIGHTY n. (2))]

million to a bit of dirt *phr.* [mid–late 19C] used of a very sure bet.

mill-ken *n.* (*also* **milken**) [mid-17C–19C] a house-breaker. [MILL A KEN v.]

mill lay *n.* [late 17C–early 19C] breaking and entering for the purpose of robbery. [MILL n.² (2) + LAY n.⁴ (1)]

mill one's glaze *v.* [late 18C–early 19C] to knock out one's eye. [MILL v.¹ (3) + GLASIERS n.]

mill on the green *phr. see* WIGS ON THE GREEN phr.

milltag *n.* (*also* **milltog, milltug, milltuig**) [early–late 19C] a shirt. [Shelta *melthog*, a shirt]

mill the glaze *v.* [late 17C–mid-19C] (*UK Und.*) to break a window, esp. as a means of entering a house. [MILL v.¹ (2) + GLAZE n. (1)]

mill town *n.* (*also* **mill village**) [1960s] (*US*) the poor area of a town or city. [the housing built by mill-owners to house their workers]

milltug/milltuig *n. see* MILLTAG n.

Millwall Reserves *n.* [1990s+] nerves. [rhy. sl.; ult. *Millwall* football club, based in Isle of Dogs, London]

milly *n.* [20C+] a shirt. [abbr. MILLTAG n.]

milly *adj.* [1990s+] (*UK Black*) aggressive, pugnacious; thus *get milly*, to become aggressive. [abbr. MILITANT adj.]

miln up *v.* [1940s–50s] (*UK prison*) to lock into a cell. [*Milne*, a well-known firm of locksmiths]

Milquetoast *n. see* CASPAR (MILQUETOAST) n.

milt *n.* [19C] semen (cf. BABY GRAVY n.). [SE *milt*, the roe of the male fish]

milt market *n.* (*also* **milt shop**) [19C] the vagina. [MILT n. + SE *market/shop*]

milton *n.* [mid-19C] an oyster. [? pun on Gray's *Elegy written in a Country Churchyard* (1751): 'mute inglorious Miltons']

miltonian *n.* [mid–late 19C] a policeman. [ety. unknown]

Milton Keynes *n.* [1990s+] **1** beans, usu. baked beans. **2** a homosexual. [rhy. sl.; (2) = QUEEN n.² (1); ult. *Milton Keynes*, town in Buckinghamshire, UK]

milt shop *n. see* MILT MARKET n.

milvad *n.* [mid-19C] a blow. [Scot.]

milvader *v.* [early–mid-19C] to beat, to assault. [MILVAD n.]

Milwaukee cider *n.* (*also* **Milwaukee special/water**) [1950s–60s] (*US*) beer. [the city's many breweries]

Milwaukee goitre *n.* [1930s+] (*US*) a beer belly. [a ref. to, *inter alia*, 'Schlitz, the beer that made Milwaukee famous', as did the many beers brewed for the predominantly Ger. immigrant population]

mimi hill *n.* [1980s+] (*N.Z.*) on a journey, an opportunity to stop and use a lavatory. [Maori *mimi*, to urinate]

mimis *n.*¹ [1990s+] (*US campus*) sleep.

mimis *n.*² *see* MEEMIES n.

min *n. see* MINGE n. (2).

mince *v. see* MINCE (PIE) n.

mince *v.* [1980s+] (*N.Z.*) to work as a prostitute on several different boats in a single night; used by a SHIP-MOLL n.

mince about *v.* [1980s+] (*N.Z.*) to loiter, to 'hang about'.

mince (pie) *n.* (*also* **mincer**) [mid-19C+] an eye; usu. in pl. [rhy. sl.]

minchin malacho *n. see* MICHING MALICHO n.

mind *n.* [1990s+] the human head.

mind *v.*¹ [mid-19C+] (*Ulster*) to remember.

mind *v.*² (*UK Und.*) **1** [20C+] to protect, to act as a bodyguard. **2** [1950s+] to bribe regularly. [backform. f. MINDER n. (1)]

min dae *phr.* [1960s+] (*S.Afr.*) used as a greeting in the S.Afr. army by national servicemen who have 40 or fewer days to serve. [Afk. *min dae*, few days]

mind-bender *n.* (*also* **mind-expander, -explorer, -opener, -spacer, -tripper**) [1960s+] **1** a psychedelic or psychotropic drug. **2** anything that, through the difficulty of its solution or comprehension, fig. 'bends the mind'. **3** a user of hallucinogens. [SE *mind* + *bend/expand/explore/open*/SPACE (OUT) v.¹/TRIP v.¹]

mind-bending *adj.* (*also* **mind-expanding**) [1960s+] amazing, fantastic, remarkable, orig. in the context of hallucinogenic drug use. [MIND-BENDER n.]

mind-blow *v.* [1970s–80s] to shock, to amaze, to surprise. [BLOW ONE'S MIND v.]

mind-blower *n.* (*also* **mind-blow**) [1960s+] **1** something that is astonishing, remarkable. **2** a psychedelic drug. **3** a hallucinogenic drug user. [MIND-BLOWING adj.]

mind-blowing *adj.* [1960s+] astounding, amazing, remarkable, orig. in the context of hallucinogenic drug use. [BLOW ONE'S MIND v.]

mind candy *n.* [1970s+] (*US*) anything light and intellectually undemanding (cf. ARM CANDY n.). [on model of EYE CANDY n.]

mind detergent *n.* [1960s+] **1** a psychedelic or psychotropic drug. **2** anything that, through the difficulty of its solution or comprehension, fig. 'bends the mind'.

minder *n.* **1** [late 19C+] (*orig. UK Und.*) a criminal's bodyguard, a 'strong-arm man', someone who guards stolen property. **2** [1940s+] (*UK Und.*) a pimp. **3** [1970s] (*UK Und.*) a young criminal's patron, who sets up crimes for his protégé to carry out. **4** [1980s+] ext. to a variety of non-criminal milieux, e.g. *governmental minders, journalistic minders*.

mind-expander *n. see* MIND-BENDER n.

mind-expanding *adj. see* MIND-BENDING adj.

mind-explorer *n. see* MIND-BENDER n.

mindfuck *n.* **1** [1960s+] a fantasy copulation. **2** [1960s+] (*orig. US*) an emotionally overwhelming experience, usu. through drugs. **3** [1970s+] (*US campus*) one who delights in manipulating others. **4** [1970s+] a psychotic individual. **5** [1970s+] deception, bafflement, confusion. [SE *mind* + FUCK n.¹ (1)/-FUCK sfx]

mindfuck *v.* [1960s+] (*orig. US*) to manipulate emotionally, to deceive, to tease, esp. while the victim is under the influence of drugs and thus less emotionally stable. [MINDFUCK n. (2)]

mindfucked *adj.* [1980s+] (*orig. US/US campus*) **1** drunk or under the influence of drugs (cf. ADDLED adj.). **2** emotionally overcome. **3** unintelligent. [MINDFUCK v.]

mindfucker *n.* [1960s+] (*orig. US*) a person or event that is totally confusing or amazing. [MINDFUCK v.]

mindfucking *adj.* [1960s+] (*orig. US*) baffling, confusing, amazing. [MINDFUCK v.]

mind game *n.* [1970s+] (*orig. US*) psychological trickery and manipulation, usu. hostile or negative in intent.

mindic *adj. see* MENDIC adj.

mind mice at the crossroads *v.* [20C+] (*Irish*) **1** to do anything undemanding and simple. **2** to undertake a task requiring deviousness and patience.

mind number one *v. see* LOOK AFTER NUMBER ONE v.

mind one's knitting *v. see* STICK TO ONE'S KNITTING v.

mind one's own business *v.*¹ [1990s+] to masturbate. [pun on MIND ONE'S OWN BUSINESS v.²]

mind one's own business *v.*² *see* BUSINESS n.¹ (5).

mind one's own pigeon *v.* [20C+] (*Aus./N.Z.*) to mind one's own business. [corruption of SE *pidgin*, concern, affair]

mind one's p's and q's *v.* (*also* **mind one's q's and p's, watch one's p's and q's**) **1** [late 18C–early 19C] to have an eye for the main chance; thus *on one's p's and q's*, doing this. **2** [late 18C+] to behave oneself, to be careful, to be polite. [? SE abbr. *please* and *thank-you* ('kyou'), shorthand for the basic manners taught to infants]

mind one's step *v. see* WATCH ONE'S STEP v.

mind one's stops *v.* [mid-19C+] to watch one's manners, to behave properly (in front of one's 'elders and betters'); thus [mid-19C] *mind your stops!* be careful! [*mind your full-stops*, said when teaching a child to read, 20C+ use mainly W.I.]

mind one's tune *v.* [1960s] to guard one's behaviour or speech.

mind-opener *n. see* MIND-BENDER n.

mind out! *excl.* [late 19C+] be on your guard! watch out!

mind-spacer *n. see* MIND-BENDER n.

mind the fort *v. see* HOLD THE FORT v.

mind the grease *phr.* [late 19C–1900s] let me pass, please. [the speaker wishes to 'slip past']

mind the paint *phr.* [late 19C–1900s] a phr. used to refer to a passing woman who is considered to be wearing too much make-up. [the sign left by painters to indicate wet paint]

mind the store *v.* (*also* **watch the store**) [1920s+] (*US*) to take care of someone or something.

mind-tripper *n.*[1] [1960s+] (*US campus/teen*) someone seen as eccentric, odd, abnormal. [SE *mind* + TRIPPER n.]

mind-tripper *n.*[2] *see* MIND-BENDER n.

mind your backs! *excl.* [20C+] out of the way! [earlier railway use, coined by porters pushing heavy and thus injurious barrows through the crowds]

mind your eye! *excl.* [mid-19C+] be careful! look out!

mind your own fish *phr.* [20C+] (*Aus.*) mind your own business.

mine *n.* [1900s] (*US Und.*) myself, me.

mine! *excl.* [1980s+] (*US campus*) my fault.

mine arse on a bandbox *phr.* (*also* **my arse on a bandbox**) [18C–early 19C] a phr. used when something offered is inadequate for the purposes required, meaning 'that won't do'. [ARSE n.[1] (1) + SE *bandbox*, a light cardboard box used to contain millinery etc, which would not make a stable seat]

mine-jobber *n.* [late 19C–1900s] a financial fraud. ['When English copper mining became comparatively valueless by reason the import of [...] ore as ballast, all the rascals on change floated mine companies, which had not a chance of success' (Ware)]

mine of pleasure *n.* [mid–late 19C] the vagina (cf. ADAM'S OWN (ALTAR) n.).

minette *n.* [late 19C] fellatio. [Fr. *minette*, a pet name for a cat]

minette *v.* [late 19C] to fellate. [MINETTE n.]

mine uncle('s) *n. see* UNCLE n.[1].

ming *n.*[1] [1980s] a marijuana cigarette made of discarded butts. [MING v. or, given the unpleasant taste, ? ref. to SF character *Ming the Merciless* in the series *Flash Gordon* (from 1936)]

ming *n.*[2] [1990s+] (*Scot.*) a smell, a stench. [MING v.]

ming *v.* [1970s+] (*orig. Scot.*) to stink; in fig. use to be very unattractive. [Scot.]

minga *n. see* MINGER n.

minge *n.* **1** [20C+] the vagina. **2** [1910s+] (*also* **min**) women in general. [Suffolk dial., ult. synon. Rom. *mingra*; note East Anglian *minge*, to drizzle]

minge bag *n.* **1** [1970s+] an unpleasant or disliked woman. **2** [1990s+] a miser, a general term of abuse. [MINGE n. + -BAG sfx]

minge mouse *n.* [1940s–50s] a pubic louse.

minge-muncher *n.* [1980s+] (*N.Z.*) a cunnilinguist. [MINGE n. (1) + SE *muncher*]

minger *n.* (*also* **minga**) **1** [1970s+] one who lit. or fig. smells, a 'stinker'. **2** [1990s+] an unattractive and/or stupid person. [MING v.]

minge wagon *n.* [1980s] a flashy car seen as an adjunct to the seduction of foolishly impressionable young women. [MINGE n. (2) + SE *wagon*]

minging *adj.* [1990s+] **1** a general derog. term, disgusting, ugly, smelly etc. **2** of a person, unattractive. **3** very drunk. [MINGE n. or MING v.]

mingles *n.* [1970s+] (*US*) single and unrelated people who share ownership of a home, usu. for economic benefit. [SE *mingle* + *singles*; a US government coinage, defined as 'mingling for fun, economy or companionship']

mingo *n.* [late 18C–mid-19C] (*US campus*) a chamberpot. [MINGO v.[2]]

mingo *v.*[1] [mid-17C] to have sexual intercourse. [obs. SE *meng*, to have sexual intercourse]

mingo *v.*[2] [mid-18C–mid-19C] (*US campus*) to urinate. [Lat. *mingo*, I make water]

mingra *n.* [20C+] (*costermonger*) a policeman. [? *minch*, to prowl around, to move stealthily]

mingy *n.* [20C+] a mean, ungenerous person. [MINGY adj.]

mingy *adj.* [20C+] mean, tight-fisted, miserly [? SE *mean/mangy* + *stingy*]

mini *n.* [1960s+] a *mini*skirt. [abbr.; orig. created as *the* fashion statement of the 1960s, more recently resurgent in the 1980s and 2000s]

minibennie *n.* [1970s] (*US drugs*) **1** Benzedrine. **2** amphetamine (cf. A n.[2]). [var. on BENNY n.[3]]

Minié rifle *n.* [mid-19C] (*US*) cheap strong bourbon. [the power of its effect; ult. SE *Minié rifle*, named after inventor Claude Étienne *Minié* (1804–79), which fired a 'Minié' (or minnie) ball]

mini-mini *n.* (*also* **minny-minny**) [1950s+] (*W.I.*) small spots that one sees in front of one's eyes, either as a result of a blow to the head, or from the mild hallucinations that may accompany the smoking of cannabis. [Lat. *minimus*, smallest, but note Twi *mini-mínā*, a small, stinging fly + Hausa *míni*, smallness]

Mini Moke *n.* [1990s+] smoke. [rhy. sl.; ult. the once-popular *Mini Moke*, a Mini Minor with a 'jeep'-style body]

minister's coat *n.* [1930s+] (*Irish*) a Garda (police) greatcoat. [coined after a Tipperary woman claimed she had been seduced when a policeman persuaded her to 'lie down on the Minister's coat']

minister's face *n.* (*also* **minister's head/snout, parson's face**) [mid-19C–1950s] (*US*) a boiled or roasted hog's head with the eyes and jowls removed. [anti-clericalism]

mink *n.* **1** [mid–late 19C; 1960s+] (*US Black*) a pretty, sexy young woman. **2** [20C+] (*US*) the vagina. **3** [1900s–70s] (*US*) a lecher or scoundrel. **4** [2000s] (*Irish*) a traveller.

mink and manure belt *n.* [1980s+] (*S.Afr.*) **1** the affluent rural areas that lie between Pretoria and Johannesburg. **2** affluent suburbs, typified by wealth and a love of horses, when found outside any city; their inhabitants can be Black or White.

Minnesota thirteen *n.* [1920s+] (*US*) an illegal brand of bourbon. [? the name of the corn used]

Minnie (Apples) *n.* [1910s+] (*US*) *Minne*apolis, Minnesota. [abbr./pron.]

minnie five fingers *n.* [1920s] (*US*) the hand, as used in male masturbation.

Minnie Mouse *n.* [1940s+] (*Aus.*) the house. [rhy. sl.; ult. the Disney character *Minnie Mouse* (created 1928)]

minnow *n.* [1970s+] (*US campus*) a 340ml (12fl oz) bottle or can of beer. [SE *minnow*, the fish, i.e. a small bottle/can]

minnow-muncher *n.* [1960s+] (*US*) a Roman Catholic. [the habit of eating fish on Fridays]

minny-minny *n. see* MINI-MINI n.

minor *n.* [1990s+] (*UK Black*) an unimportant matter.

minor clergy *n.* [late 18C–19C] young chimney-sweeps. [? the blackness of their sooty clothes]

minor-league *adj.* [20C+] (*orig. US*) small-scale, modest (cf. MAJOR-LEAGUE adj.). [baseball imagery]

minstrel *n.* (*also* **black and white minstrel, nigger minstrel**) [1960s–80s] (*drugs*) Durophet. [the drug's black and white capsules; thus a pun on the popular *Black and White Minstrel Show* (from 1960)]

mint *n.*[1] **1** [16C–mid-19C] (*UK Und.*) a piece of money (cf. ALFALFA n.). **2** [mid-16C–early 19C] (*also* **mynt**) gold. **3** [late 18C+] a great deal of money, thus *minted*, wealthy. **4** [1900s] a great deal. [8C SE *mint*, money. The term was wholly sl. by 16C, although *the Mint*, as a place, remained SE]

mint *n.*[2] [1950s+] (*US gay*) effeminacy; usu. in phr. a *hint of mint*, a trace of homosexual tendencies. [numerous advertisements promoting products with 'a hint of mint'; note earlier MINTY n.]

mint *adj.* [1980s+] (*Can./US/UK teen*) a general term of thorough approval. [SE *mint*, unblemished]

mint *v. see* MINT GOLD v.

mint drops *n. see* BENTON'S MINT DROPS n.

mintee *n. see* MINTY n.

minter *n. see* AFTER-DINNER MINT n.

mint gold *v.* (*also* **mint, mint it, mint money**) [mid-19C+] to make a good deal of money, to profit.

mint hog *n.* [early 19C] an Irish shilling. [? MINT n.[1] + image of the hog as a source of income (cf. GENTLEMAN WHO PAYS THE RENT n.)]

mintie *n.*[1] [1930s+] (*Aus.*) comfort, solace; thus *man with the minties*, a racing tipster; *without a mintie*, without funds. [the advertising slogan, launched by James Stedman-Henderson in 1922, of *Minties*, a peppermint-flavoured sweet, 'It's moments like these you need Minties']

mintie *n.*[2] *see* MINTY n.

mint it *v. see* MINT GOLD v.

mint leaf *n.*[1] [1920s+] (*US*) a banknote, money (cf. ALFALFA n.; BANK-RAG n.). [the colour of dollar bills]

mint leaf *n.*[2] (*also* **mint weed**) [1970s+] (*drugs*) mint or poss. parsley leaves impregnated with phencyclidine for smoking.

mint money *v. see* MINT GOLD v.

mint sauce *n.* [early–mid-19C] money (cf. ALFALFA n.). [laboured pun on SE *mint* + *source*]

mint weed *n. see* MINT LEAF n.[2].

minty *n.* (*also* **mintee, mintie**) [1940s–70s] (*US gay*) **1** an effeminate male homosexual. **2** a masculine lesbian.

minty *adj.*[1] **1** [1950s–60s] (*camp gay*) fading, losing one's attractiveness, said of an ageing effeminate male homosexual. **2** [1950s+] effeminate in mannerism, if not actually homosexual. **3** [1960s] frequented by homosexuals. [MINTY n.]

minty *adj.*[2] [1990s+] (*US campus*) excellent, first-rate.

minus *adj.* **1** [19C] lacking, bereft of. **2** [mid-19C] absent.

minus! *excl.* [2000s] (*US campus*) a negative retort. [var. on NOT! excl.]

minute *n.* [1990s+] (*US Black*) a long time.

mioota *phr.* [1990s+] (*US teen*) see you later. [? Sp./Ital. *minuto*, a minute; or ? 'me outta' (here)]

miraculous *adj.* [19C–1900s] (*Scot.*) very drunk (cf. ABOUT RIGHT phr.[1]).

miraculous cairn *n.* [19C] the vagina (cf. BEAUTY SPOT n.).

miraculous pitcher (that holds water with the mouth down) *n.* [late 18C–mid-19C] the vagina (cf. BAG n.[1]).

mirk *v. see* MERK v.

mirror man *n.* [1980s+] (*Aus. prison*) an officer who promises help, advice, information etc, but never manages to provide it. [he is always going to 'look into it']

mirthquake *n.* [1940s–60s] (*US*) anything amusing. [SE *mirth* + *earthquake*]

mis *n.* (*also* **miss**) [late 19C+] **1** a miscarriage. **2** (*also* **mizz**) a misery. [abbr.]

mis *adj.* (*also* **miz**) [late 19C+] miserable. [abbr.]

misbehave *n.* [20C+] (*Aus./US*) a shave. [rhy. sl.]

mischief, the *n.* [late 16C+] a euph. for 'the devil'; thus *play the mischief (with); what/how the mischief…? go to the mischief; like the mischief.*

misdeal *n.* [late 19C–1900s] (*US*) a mistake. [card imagery]

miserable *n.* [mid–late 19C] weak tea. [? play on the def. of tea as that which 'cheers but does not inebriate'; being weak, it fails to cheer the drinker]

miserable *adj.* [mid-19C+] (*Aus.*) tight-fisted, grasping, mean. [pun on SE *miserable/miser*]

miserable as a shag on a rock *phr. see* LIKE A SHAG ON A ROCK phr.

miserables, the *n.* [late 19C–1920s] a hangover.

miseries, the *n.* [1920s+] depression.

misery *n.*[1] [late 18C+] a depressing person; thus [late 19C+] *be a (right old) misery*, to be a depressing person, to act in a self-pitying manner; [late 19C+] *(long, thin) streak of misery*, a very thin, mournful and lugubrious person.

misery *n.*[2] **1** [early 19C–1930s] gin. **2** [1930s–50s] (*US*) (bad) coffee. [its effects]

misery bowl *n.* [late 19C–1900s] a bowl used for vomiting by sufferers of sea-sickness.

miseryguts *n.* [1950s+] a depressing, censorious person. [SE *misery* + -GUTS sfx]

misery-moany *n.* [1940s+] (*Irish*) a whinger, a complainer. [ext. of MISERY n.[1]]

misfortunate *n.* [early 19C] a euph. for a prostitute.

misfortune *n.* [19C] an illegitimate child; thus *have/meet with a misfortune*, to have an illegitimate child.

mish *n.*[1] [mid-17C–1910s] (*UK Und.*) a shirt, a smock; a sheet. [Ital. *camicia*, a shirt]

mish *n.*[2] **1** [late 19C–1940s] a missionary. **2** [1990s+] in sexual intercourse, missionary position. [abbr.]

mish *v.* [late 19C–1940s] to work as a missionary. [MISH n.[2] (1)]

mishegaas *n.* (*also* **meshugaas, mishegoss**) [late 19C+] nonsense, obsession, tomfoolery. [Yid.]

mish-topper *n.* [late 17C–mid-19C] (*UK Und.*) **1** an overcoat. **2** a petticoat. [MISH n.[1] + SE *topper*, lit. 'shirt topper']

mishugge *see under* MESHUGA.

mislain/misle/misli *v. see* MIZZLE v.

misplaced eyebrow *n.* [1910s–20s] (*US*) a moustache.

Miss *pfx*[1] (*also* **Mr, Mrs, Ms**) [17C+] a title used in comb. with a n. to express the subject's primary characteristic, e.g. *Miss Grind*, a very hard worker.

Miss *pfx*[2] [1920s+] (*gay*) a title prefixed to a name to imply that the subject's homosexuality is known or obvious. The pfx was a staple of pre-Gay Liberation Front camp usage, e.g. *Miss Ugly*.

miss *n.*[1] (*also* **miss of the town, town miss**) [mid-17C–19C] a prostitute, 'a Whore of Quality' (B.E.); a kept woman. [a heavily ironic use of SE]

miss *n.*[2] *see* MIS n.

miss *v.* [late 19C–1900s] (*US*) to be unlucky.

Miss Alice *n. see* ALICE BLUE (GOWN) n.

Miss Amy *n.* [1960s+] (*US Black*) a young White woman. [Folb, *Runnin' Down Some Lines* (1980), suggests source in Amy Carter, daughter of US President Jimmy Carter although generic use of proper name seems more likely given date]

Miss Ann *n.* (*also* **Miss Anne, Miss Annie**) [1920s+] (*US Black*) a White woman, esp. when considered to be hostile or patronizing to Blacks.

Miss Astor *n.* (*also* **Mrs Astor**) [1960s+] (*US*) **1** a woman who overdresses. **2** usu. mocking, an elite 'social leader' of a community. [the wealthy *Astor* family, once social arbiters of New York]

miss a trick *v.* [1920s+] (*orig. US*) to fail to see what is going on, to be ignorant of circumstances; usu. in negative as *never miss a trick*, to be highly aware. [card imagery]

Miss Big Stockings *n.* [1950s] (*US Black*) an attractive, conspicuous young woman.

Miss Brown *n.* (*also* **Madam Brown**) [late 18C–19C] the vagina. [joc./euph. use of proper name]

Miss Carrie *n.* [1960s] (*drugs*) a quantity of drugs carried on one's person. [pun on SE *carry*/proper name *Carrie*]

Miss Clean *n. see* MR CLEAN n.[2].

Miss Cubba *n. see* CUBBA n.

missee *n. see* MISSY n.[1] (1).

Miss Emma n. [1930s+] (drugs) morphine (cf. AUNTIE EMMA n.). [the initial letter M]

Miss Emma Jones n. [1950s+] an addiction to morphine. [MISS EMMA n. + JONES n.[1] (1)]

misses n. see MISSIS n.

Miss Fine n. [1950s–70s] (US) a form of address aimed at one who is considered to be overly self-opinionated. [FINE adj.[2]]

Miss Fist n. [1950s+] the hand, in the context of masturbation.

Miss Fitch n. 1 [20C+] an unpleasant woman. 2 [1970s] (US gay) a 'feminine' male homosexual (cf. ABIGAIL n.). [rhy. sl. = BITCH n.[1] (1)]

Miss Flash n. (also flash queen) [1950s–70s] (camp gay) a user of amphetamines or Benzedrine. [FLASH n.[7] (1)]

Miss Frosty Pants n. see FROSTY FACE n. (3).

Miss Horner n. [19C] the female genitals. [play on HORN n.[2] (1)]

missie n. see MISSY n.[1] (1).

missile n. [1980s+] (drugs) phencyclidine (cf. ACE n.[4]). [its 'explosive' effects]

missile basing n. [1980s+] (drugs) a mixture of liquid crack cocaine and phencyclidine. [MISSILE n. + BASING n.]

missing n. [mid-19C] courtship. [SE miss, a young woman + 'participle' sfx -ing]

missing link n. [20C+] (US) a stupid person. [the SE missing link between humans and apes]

mission n. [1980s+] (drugs) 1 a search for drugs, esp. for crack cocaine or cocaine. 2 a binge on crack cocaine. [ext. of SE mission, 'the commission, business, or function with which a messenger, envoy, or agent is charged' (OED); the specific allusion is to the introduction to episodes of the TV series Star Trek (from 1966); the overall inference is of the seriousness of such a activity]

missionary man n. [1980s+] (US campus) an uninspired lover. [SE missionary position, considered the least adventurous of all the positions of love-making]

mission squawker n. [1920s–40s] (US tramp) a mission evangelist.

mission stiff n. [20C+] (US) 1 a missionary worker. 2 a convert. 3 (also mission bum, Jesus guy) a tramp or vagrant who frequents charitable missions, looking for hand-outs, food and shelter, esp. one who pretends conversion. [SE mission/Jesus + STIFF n.[2] (4)]

missis n. (also misses, missus) [mid-19C+] one's wife; the mistress of the household. [pron. of SE Mrs]

Mississipi mud n. see MUD n.[2].

Mississippi marbles n. [1920s+] (US) dice, or the game of craps dice (cf. ABYSSINIAN POLO n.).

Mississippi mule n. [1960s] (US) illicitly distilled, 'bootleg' bourbon. [MULE n.[3] (1)]

Miss It n. [1950s+] (orig. US gay) a greeting to a fellow homosexual man (cf. ABIGAIL n.).

Miss Jane n. [1950s] (W.I.) an effeminate man.

Miss Lashey n. [1950s] (W.I.) a male gossip. [? LASHER n.[2], but while this man also chases women, it is for gossip rather than seduction, thus the effeminate Miss]

Miss Laycock n. (also Lady Laycock) [18C–19C] the vagina; thus [18C] through metonymy, as a prostitute. [pun on LAY v.[1] (1) + COCK n.[2] (1)]

Miss Lillian n. [1960s–80s] (US Black) a White girl or woman of any age, but usu. an older woman. [Folb, Runnin' Down Some Lines (1980), suggests link to Lillian Carter, mother of President Jimmy Carter]

Miss Lily n. see LILY LAW n.

Miss Lizzie Tish n. (also Miss Tizzie Lish) [1960s+] (US) 1 a woman who overdresses. 2 usu. mocking, an élite 'social leader' of a community. [? anecdotal or a joc. use of a generic proper name]

Miss Lucy n. [1970s] (US Black) a generic for a White girl or woman of any age, but usu. an older woman.

Miss Man n. [1970s+] (US Black gay) the police. [MAN, THE n. (1)]

Miss Molly n. (also molly boy/man) [mid-18C–1920s] an

effeminate or homosexual man; thus Miss Mollyism, effeminacy (cf. ABIGAIL n.). [generic use of female name; note US regional dial. cut up molly, to act in an extravagant, frolicsome manner; note ballad 'The Maid's Resolution to follow her Love' (c.1820), which uses 'Madam Molly' for a girl who poses as a soldier; MOLLY n.[1]]

Miss Morales n. [1970s+] (US gay) a Mexican homosexual (cf. ABIGAIL n.).

Miss Morph n. [1960s+] (drugs) morphine (cf. AUNTIE EMMA n.). [MORF n.]

Miss Nancy n. [early 19C–1940s] an effeminate man, presumably a homosexual; thus Miss Nancyfied, Miss Nancyish, effeminate; Miss Nancyism, effeminacy (cf. ABIGAIL n.). [generic use of female name; NANCY n.[2] (2) is a later concept]

miss of the town n. see MISS n.[1].

Miss One n. see MISS THING n.

miss one's figure v. [late 19C] to miss a chance.

miss one's guess v. [1910s+] (orig. US) to make a mistake, to err.

miss one's tip v. [mid–late 19C] (orig. circus) to fail in one's aim or objective.

Missou n. see MIZZOO n.

Missouri adj. [20C+] (US) a generic derog. term, usu. used in a variety of combs. below. [the stereotyping of the state and its natives as poor, dishonest and backward]

Missouri bankroll n. [1930s+] (US) a roll or wad of blank paper, cut to the same size as dollar bills, surrounded by a few real notes of high denomination (cf. CALIFORNIA BANKROLL n.); also in fig. use. [the term is coined by the Industrial Workers of the World (IWW or 'Wobblies'), who designed this form of 'bankroll' to foil the thieves who preyed on newly paid-off workers. A worker would create such a roll, flash it in public and inevitably face being beaten and robbed. He would, however, be rescued by sympathetic Wobblies, hitherto hidden, who would pounce on the thieves and give them the beating]

Missouri featherbed n. [late 19C–1960s] (US, mainly Western) a straw mattress.

Missouri hummingbird n. (also Missouri nightingale) [1910s–20s] (US) a mule.

Missouri toothpick n. see ARKANSAS TOOTHPICK n.

Miss Peach n. [1950s–70s] (camp gay) an informer. [MISS pfx[2] + PEACH v. (1)]

Miss Piggy n. [1990s+] a cigarette. [rhy. sl. = CIGGIE n.; ult. Miss Piggy, a character in The Muppet Show (1976–81)]

Miss Right n. see MR RIGHT n.

Miss Taylor n. [early–mid-19C] a strong Spanish liquor. [Sp. mistela]

miss the bus v. [20C+] to lose an opportunity, to forfeit a chance.

miss the cushion v. [16C–17C] to miss one's mark, to fail.

Miss Thing n. (also Miss One, Miss Thang) 1 [1960s+] (orig. US gay) a greeting to a fellow homosexual man (cf. ABIGAIL n.). 2 [1970s+] (US gay) one's innate femininity. 3 [1980s+] (UK Black/campus) any unnamed woman. 4 [1990s+] (US Black) a woman who is seen as arrogant and unpleasant.

Miss Tizzie Lish n. see MISS LIZZIE TISH n.

Missus n. [mid-19C+] (Aus.) the trad. title of the wife of the owner or manager of a sheep station. [SE missus, Mrs]

missus n. see MISSIS n.

Miss van Neck n. (also Mrs van Neck) [late 18C–early 19C] a woman with large breasts. [joc. use of supposed proper name]

Miss Xylophone n. [1950s–70s] (camp gay) a notably thin person. [MISS pfx[2] + SE xylophone (the individual's ribs protrude like the metal bars of the instrument)]

missy n.[1] 1 [late 17C+] (also missee, missie) a young girl, esp. as characterized by servants and sometimes derog. 2 [1960s–70s] (US gay) an underage boy.

missy n.[2] [1990s+] (US drugs) cocaine. [note cocaine is a 'feminine' drug, see GIRL n.[2]]

mist *n.* (*drugs*) **1** [1970s+] phencyclidine (cf. ACE n.⁴). **2** [1980s+] smoke created by a crack cocaine pipe. **3** [2000s] (*UK Und.*) a state of high excitement, drug induced or otherwise.

Mistah Big *n. see* MR BIG n.

mistake *n.* [1950s+] an unplanned pregnancy and the child that follows.

Mister/Mr the abbr. Mr has been used for all combs., unless no cits. have been found with the abbr.; all headwords are alphabetized as if spelled out.

Mr *pfx see* MISS pfx¹.

mister *n.*¹ [20C+] (*US*) a form of address to a man whose proper name one does not know.

mister *n.*² [1990s+] (*US drugs*) heroin (cf. BIG DADDY n.). [heroin is a 'masculine' drug, *see* BOY n.⁷]

Mr Anybody *n.* [1940s] a generic name for an anonymous member of the public.

Mr Arnold *n. see* ARNOLD n.

Mr Astorbilt *n. see* ASTORBILT n.

Mr Average *n.* (*also* **Mr Averageman**) [1910s+] the average member of the public.

Mr Bates *n.* (*also* **Bates, John Bates, Johnnie Bates**) [1920s–40s] (*US Und.*) a potential victim, a confidence man's dupe. [? pun on *Mr. Bates*/SE *masturbates*, thus the individual is a JERK n.¹]

Mr Big *n.* (*also* **Mistah Big, Mister Big**) [1930s+] (*orig. US*) an important, influential person, esp. a 'criminal mastermind'.

Mr Block *n.* [1930s] (*US tramp*) a gullible person.

Mr Blue *n.* [1970s] (*drugs*) hydromorphone, the basis of the synthetic opiate Dilaudid. [? a blue elixir of morphine sulphate]

Mr Boozington *n. see* BOOZINGTON n.

Mr Boss Hoss *n.* [1980s] (*US*) a slightly mocking ref. to a leader.

Mr Brown *n.* [1950s] a homosexual. [BROWN n.³]

Mr Chad *n. see* CHAD n.

Mr Charles *n. see* CHARLIE n.

Mr Charlie *n.* (*also* **Massa Charley/Charlie, Mister Charley/Charlie, Mr Charley**) **1** [1920s+] (*US Black*) any White man (cf. BOSS CHARLIE n.). **2** [1970s] the man in power. [SE *Mr* + generic 'White' name *Charlie*]

Mr Chuck *n. see* CHUCK n.

Mr Clean *n.*¹ [1960s+] (*US*) an obsessively neat and prudish man. [the character *Mr Clean* in advertisements for a brand of household cleaner of the same name, first marketed in the late 1950s]

Mr Clean *n.*² [1970s] (*orig. US*) someone who makes a point of portraying themselves (sincerely or otherwise) as free of corruption, esp. in politics, business, sport or other forms of public life in which a proclaimed moral stance is useful; ext. as *Miss Clean, Mrs Clean*. [MR CLEAN n.¹]

Mr Cool *n.*¹ [2000s] the penis (cf. ALMOND n.). [rhy. sl. = TOOL n.¹ (1)]

Mr Cool *n.*² *see* JOE COOL n.

Mr Cracker *n.* [1950s+] (*US Black*) a White person. [SE *Mr* + CRACKER n.³ (1)]

Mr Cunningham *n. see* CUNNINGHAM n.

Mr Double Tripes *n. see* DOUBLE TRIPE n.¹.

Mr Do-you-wrong *n.* [1970s–80s] (*US Black*) a man who mistreats women.

Mr Eddie *n.* [1920s–50s] (*US Black*) a White man. [generic use]

Mr Edison's rocking chair *n.* [1930s] (*US*) the electric chair. [*Thomas Edison* (1847–1931), the inventor of electricity]

Mr Fat *n. see* FAT n.².

Mr Firstnighter *n.* [1930s+] a sophisticated, upper-class person, or one who poses as such. [US radio show *Mr Firstnighter* of 1930s, featuring a white-tie-and-tails star]

Mr Fish *n.* [1930s–50s] (*US drugs*) an addict who volunteers to undergo a federal cure in prison.

Mr Five by Five *n.* [1940s] (*US*) a very short, fat man. [title of a 1942 pop song by Don Raye and Gene de Paul]

Mr Fixit *n.* **1** [1950s+] a general facilitator. **2** [1980s+] a DIY expert. [a series of short religious films in 1950s featured *Mr Fixit*, a carpenter who combined the mending of furniture with delivering pious homilies to the attendant children]

Mr Fox *n. see* FOX n.¹ (1).

Mr Franklin *n.*¹ [1950s+] a euph. for MOTHERFUCKER n. (1). [initial letters]

Mr Franklin *n.*² *see* BEN FRANKLIN n.

Mr Fuzzgug *n.* (*also* **Mrs Fuzzgug**) [1930s+] (*Aus.*) a generic term for everyman or everywoman. [ety. unknown; ? FISGIG n., i.e. humanity's propensity to laugh at each other's failings]

Mr Gotrocks *n. see* GOTROCKS n.

Mr Grim *n. see* OLD MR GRIM n. (2).

Mr Grog *n. see* GROG n.¹ (1).

Mr Gub *n. see* GUB n.¹.

Mr Happy *n.* (*also* **Mister Happy**) [1980s+] (*orig. US*) the penis.

Mr Happy Helmet *n.* [1990s+] the penis.

Mr Harding *n.* (*also* **Mister Harding**) [20C+] (*W.I.*) a hard taskmaster, a strict superior. [SE *hard*]

Mister Hawkins *n. see* HAWKINS n.³.

Mr Hickenbothom *n.* [late 18C–19C] any nameless object.

Mr Hombug *n.* [1980s] (*US Black*) a security policeman, e.g. at a school.

Mr Hopkins *n.* (*also* **Hopkins**) [late 18C–19C] a lame or limping person; thus *don't hurry, Mr Hopkins*, meaning in US 'hurry up', and in UK 'don't bother to go too fast'. [pun on SE *hop*; note *Notes and Queries*, 13 March 1858: 'It originated from the ease of one Hopkins, who, having given one of his creditors a promissory note in regular form, added to it this extraordinary memorandum: It is expressly agreed, that the said Hopkins is not to be hurried in paying the above note']

Mr Horner *n.* **1** [18C] a promiscuous man, esp. one who cuckolds others. **2** [late 19C] the penis. [HORN n.¹; (2) is the object that does the cuckolding but note also HORN n.²]

Mr Jones *n. see* JONES n.¹ (1).

Mr Ketch *n. see* JACK KETCH n.

Mr Knap is concerned *phr.*¹ [early 19C] (*UK Und.*) this is a matter involving theft (cf. MR NASH IS CONCERNED phr.; MR PALMER IS CONCERNED phr.; MR PULLEN IS CONCERNED phr.; QUODDING DUES ARE CONCERNED phr.; SLANGING DUES CONCERNED phr.; YORK STREET CONCERNED phr.). [KNAP v. (4)]

Mr Knap is concerned *phr.*² (*also* **Mr Knap has been there**) [19C] of a woman, pregnant. [KNAPPED adj.]

Mr Lo *n. see* LO n.¹.

Mr Lushington *n.* [19C] a state of drunkenness.

mister-man *n.* [1990s+] (*W.I.*) a term of respect.

Mr Mason *n. see* BENNY MASON n.

mister-me-friend *n.* (*also* **mister-me-man**) [1940s–50s] (*Irish*) a person, an acquaintance.

Mr Mention *n.* [1980s+] (*W.I./UK Black teen*) a person known as a popular figure or as a successful womanizer.

Mr Milktoast/Milquetoast *n. see* CASPAR (MILQUETOAST) n.

Mr Money *n.* **1** [1950s] a rich person. **2** [1960s+] (*US Black*) a derog. name for a Jew (cf. FAST-TALKING CHARLIE n.).

Mr Moto *n.* (*also* **Moto**) [1940s–70s] (*US*) a Japanese or Asian man (cf. BROWNIE n.²; BUDDHAHEAD n.). [the fictional Jap. detective created by novelist J.P. Marquand (1893–1960)]

Mr Mutch *n.* [20C+] (*Aus.*) the groin. [rhy. sl. = SE *crutch*]

Mr Nash is concerned *phr.* [early 19C] used of someone who is absent, having run off (cf. MR KNAP IS CONCERNED phr.¹). [NASH v.¹]

Mr Nawpost *n.* [late 17C–18C] a fool, a simpleton. [one who, if hungry enough, would 'gnaw a post']

Mr Nice Guy *n.* [1960s+] a pleasant, amenable person, although that status carries a certain conditionality; thus *no more Mr Nice Guy*; also used ironically.

Mr Palmer and his five sons *n.* [1950s+] (*orig. gay*) the hand, as used for masturbation (cf. CONVERSE WITH HARRY PALM v.; MRS PALM AND HER FIVE DAUGHTERS n.).

Mr Palmer is concerned *phr.* [early 19C] the matter involves bribery (cf. MR KNAP IS CONCERNED phr.[1]). [PALM v. (3)]

Mr Patel *n.* (*also* **Mr Patel's**) [1980s+] the local corner newspaper/sweet shop or small grocery. [*Patel*, the most common Indian surname in the UK and one borne by many of the Ugandan Asians who arrived in the early 1970s and began running such shops]

Mr Peanut *n.* [1960s–80s] (*US Black*) a White man. [? Black scientist George Washington Carver (1864–1943) who worked with *peanuts* + the image of *peanuts* as a 'typical' Black food; Folb, *Runnin' Down Some Lines* (1980), suggests a coinage during the 1976–80 presidency of Jimmy Carter, a Georgia peanut farmer]

Mr Peeler *n. see* PEELER n.[2].

Mr Plod *n. see* PLOD n.[2].

Mr Prunella *n.* [late 18C–early 19C] a parson. [SE *prunella*, a strong textile, orig. silk, commonly used for gowns worn by clergymen, barristers and graduates]

Mr Pullen is concerned *phr.* [early 19C] an arrest has been made (cf. MR KNAP IS CONCERNED phr.[1]). [PULL IN v.]

Mr Quarto *n. see* QUARTO n.

Mr Richard *n. see* RICHARD n.[2].

Mr Right *n.* (*also* **Miss Right**) [mid-19C+] the ideal lover, husband, wife, boy- or girlfriend for anyone so searching.

Mr Roper *n.* [mid-17C–mid-18C] the hangman. [his primary tool]

Mr Sin *n.* [1970s–80s] (*US Black, Los Angeles*) a member of the vice squad.

Mr Smoke-a-Bowl *n.* [2000s] (*US drugs/teen*) a regular smoker of marijuana.

Mr Speaker *n.* (*also* **Mister Speaker**) [mid–late 19C; 1940s] (*US*) a revolver, a pistol. [its noise + the political office of the *Speaker*, who 'lays down the law' in the US House of Representatives or the British Parliament; 1940s use is US Black]

Mr Stitch *n.* [early 18C] a tailor.

Mr Switch *n.* [early 18C] a coachman. [SE *switch*, a whip]

Mr T *n.* [1950s+] (*W.I. Rasta*) the boss. [ety. unknown; ? anecdotal]

Mr Ten Per Cent *n.* [1920s+] (*orig. US*) **1** an agent, usu. in show business, who takes 10% (at least) of their client's earnings. **2** a middleman, esp. between interest groups and politicians, who arranges 'favours' and directs influence for some cut of the subseq. profits.

Mr Thingstable *n.* [late 18C–early 19C] 'Mr Constable, a ludicrous affectation of delicacy in the avoiding the pronunciation of the first syllable in the title of that officer, which in sound has some similarity to an indecent monosyllable' (Grose, 1785). [i.e. to avoid saying CUNT n.[2] (1)]

Mr Thomas *n. see* UNCLE THOMAS n. (1).

Mr Three Balls *n. see* THREE BALLS n.

Mr Tom *n.*[1] [1970s] (*US Black*) the penis (cf. ABRAHAM n.[1]; UNCLE THOMAS n.). [JOHN THOMAS n. (1)]

Mr Tom *n.*[2] *see* UNCLE TOM n. (1).

Mr Twenty-six *n.* [1960s–70s] (*drugs*) a 26-gauge hypodermic syringe.

Mr Warner *n.* [1950s–70s] (*drugs*) a marijuana smoker (cf. AUNT MARY n.[2]). [var. on MARY WARNER n.]

Mr Whipple *n.* [1990s+] (*US Black/drugs*) phencyclidine mixed with formaldehyde.

Mr Whiskers *n.* [1930s–60s] (*US*) the American government or its law enforcement agencies. [the trad. portrait of a be-whiskered *Uncle Sam*]

Mr Wiggins *n.* [early 19C] a fool, a simpleton.

Mr Wigsby *n.* (*also* **wigsby, wigster**) [late 18C–early 19C] a man wearing a wig.

Mister Wind *n.* [1930s+] (*US Black*) chilly winter winds, esp. as experienced in northern cities.

Mr Wong *n. see* WONG n.[1].

Mr Wood *n.* (*also* **Charlie Wood**) [1930s+] a policeman's truncheon.

Mr Zip-Zip *n.* [1910s–40s] (*US*) a barber. [title of a 1917 pop song]

Mistress Jones *n. see* MRS JONES n.

Mistress Princum Prancum *n.* (*also* **Mrs Princum Prancum**) [late 18C–mid-19C] a woman who is preoccupied by turning herself out neatly, and thus by the mind-set that is presumed to go with such obsessions. [PRINK v.]

mit *see under* MITT and its combs.

mitch *n.* [1990s+] (*US Und.*) a fake wad of money used in a confidence trick.

mitch *v.* (*also* **mich, miche, mitche**) [late 19C+] to run off, to abandon one's duties, to play truant. [synon. UK dial.]

mite *n.*[1] (*also* **mitey**) [late 18C–19C] a cheesemonger. [SE *mite*, a tiny insect found in cheese]

mite *n.*[2] **1** [mid-19C+] a whit or jot, a bit. **2** [mid-19C+] a particle, a tiny piece. **3** [1950s] a farthing. [(1) SE 14C–mid-17C; (2) SE 17C]

mitigated afflictions *n. see* AFFLICTIONS n.

mitre *n.* [early 19C] (*US Und.*) a hat.

mitsus *n.* [1990s+] a tablet of MDMA (cf. ECSTASY n.). [*Mitsubishi*, the car manufacturer, from the common appearance of car logos on the tablets]

mitt *n.* (*also* **mit**) **1** [early 19C+] (*Aus./US*) usu. in pl., a glove; often a boxing glove. **2** [late 19C–1960s] (*US*) a hand of cards. **3** [late 19C+] (*US*) usu. in pl., the hand; thus *throw the mitts*, to pick pockets. **4** [1910s–30s] (*US tramp*) usu. in pl, a tramp who has lost 1 or both hands. **5** [1980s] (*US Und.*) a roll of money. [abbr. SE *mitten*]

mitt *v.* **1** [1900s–20s] (*US*) to punch. **2** [1900s–60s] (*also* **mit**) to shake hands, or to press something into someone's hand. **3** [1910s–50s] (*US Und.*) to handcuff, to arrest. **4** [1930s–40s] to wave to. [MITT n.]

mitt broad *n.* (*also* **mit artist**) [1920s–30s] (*US Und.*) a fortune-teller, a palm-reader. [MITT n. (3) + BROAD n.[2] (3)]

mitt camp *n.* (*also* **mitt joint**) [1920s–80s] a palmist's or fortune-teller's establishment, tent etc. [MITT n. (3) + SE *camp*/JOINT n.[4] (3)]

mitted *adj.* [1910s–40s] (*US Und.*) armed. [fig. use of MITT n.]

mitten *n.* **1** [19C+] the hand, esp. the fist. **2** [mid-19C+] (*US*) a rejection or dismissal; usu. as GET THE MITTEN v.; GIVE SOMEONE THE MITTEN v. **3** [mid-19C+] a boxing glove; usu. in pl. **4** [1920s] (*US Und.*) a knuckleduster. [SE *mitten*]

mitten *v.* **1** [mid–late 19C] (*US*) to seize or grab; usu. as *mitten onto*. **2** [late 19C] to reject, esp. as a lover. [MITTEN n.]

mitten queen *n.* [1990s+] (*US gay*) a man who masturbates other men. [MITTEN n. (1) + QUEEN n.[2] (1)/QUEEN sfx (2)]

mittens *n.* [late 19C–1930s] handcuffs.

mittflop *v.* [1930s–40s] (*orig. US milit.*) to ingratiate oneself by doing favours; thus *mittflopper*. [MITT n. (3) + SE *flop*]

mittglom *v.* [1910s–50s] (*US, orig. milit.*) to ingratiate oneself by doing favours; thus *mitt-glommer*, a sycophant. [MITT n. (3) + GLOM v. (1)]

mittimus *n.* [late 16C–mid-19C] a dismissal from an office or job; thus [mid-19C] *get one's mittimus*, to be dismissed, to be killed, to be sent to prison. [Lat. *mittimus*, we send. The word is used in legal Lat. as the first word of an arrest warrant and thus of the writ itself]

mitting *n.* [mid–late 19C] a shirt. [ety. unknown]

mitt joint *n.*[1] [1910s–30s] (*US*) a crooked gambling establishment. [MITT n. (3) + JOINT n.[4] (3)]

mitt joint *n.*[2] *see* MITT CAMP n.

mitt man *n.* **1** [late 19C–1950s] (*US Black*) a religious charlatan who uses his flock's credulity to make himself a sumptuous income. **2** [1960s] (*US Und.*) a confidence man. [? the white MITT

n. (1) often worn by such 'preachers', or the putting out of his MITT n. (3) for the suckers' money]

mitt me *phr.* [1930s–40s] (*US*) shake hands, esp. in context of congratulations.

mitt pounding *n.* [1930s–40s] (*US Black*) applause, clapping. [MITT n. (3) + SE *pound*]

mitt-pusher *n.* [1900s–20s] (*US*) a boxer. [MITT n. (3) + SE *pusher*]

mitt-reader *n.* [1920s+] (*US*) a fortune-teller, a palmist. [MITT n. (3) + SE *reader*]

mitts *n.*¹ [1910s] (*US prison*) handcuffs.

mitts *n.*² *see* MITT n.

mitt someone in *v.* [1900s–50s] (*US Und.*) to inveigle someone into a cheating card-game.

mivvy *n.*¹ [late 19C–1910s] a marble. [? pron.]

mivvy *n.*² [late 19C–1920s] **1** a contemptuous term for a woman. **2** in fig. use, a complainer, a whiner, an 'old woman'. **3** (*also* **mivey, mivy**) the landlady of a lodging-house. [? ironic abbr. SE *marvel* or Cockney pron. of 'mother' as *muvva*]

mivvy *n.*³ [1900s–50s] an expert, an adept. [? SE *marvel*]

mix *n.*¹ **1** [mid-19C+] (*US*) a fight, a brawl. **2** [late 19C–1910s] a muddle, a mess. **3** [2000s] (*US Black*) one's private life.

mix *n.*² **1** [1970s+] (*Aus. drugs*) a combination of cannabis and other herbs, usu. tobacco. **2** [1970s+] (*S.Afr.*) methylated spirits, as drunk by alcoholics. **3** [1970s+] (*US drugs*) a powder used to cut cocaine. **4** [2000s] an environment in which drugs are involved.

mix *v.*¹ [late 19C+] (*US*) to fight. [MIX n.¹ (1)]

mix *v.*² [1970s] to inject a drug, usu. heroin. [the *mix* of blood and heroin in solution that forms the injection]

mix and muddle *n.* [20C+] a cuddle. [rhy. sl.]

mixed *adj.* **1** [late 19C–1910s] confused, at a loss. **2** [late 19C–1930s] slightly drunk. [SE *mixed up* but note *mix one's drinks*, to mix 'the grape and the grain' (and to suffer the subseq. hangover)]

mixed-ale oration *n.* [late 19C–1900s] a poor political oration, typified by its illiterate use of the language; thus *mixed-aler, mixed-ale philosopher*, a drunken know-it-all. [the assumption is that the speaker is drunk or may as well be so]

mix'em *n.* *see* MIXUM n.

mixer *n.*¹ [1910s+] (*US*) a social gathering designed to introduce people to one another.

mixer *n.*² **1** [1910s+] a trouble-maker, a gossip, usu. deliberately malicious, one who 'stirs things up'. **2** [1960s] a fighter, a brawler. [MIX v.¹]

mix giblets *v.* *see* JOIN GIBLETS v.

mix in *v.* [late 19C+] to initiate or join a fight. [MIX v.¹]

mix it (up) *v.* [late 19C+] (*Aus./US*) **1** (*also* **mix matters**) to fight, to foster trouble. **2** to cause trouble for someone else. **3** to enjoy oneself. [MIX v.¹]

mix it up *v.*¹ [19C] 'to agree secretly how the parties shall make up a tale, or colour a transaction in order to cheat or deceive another party, as in case of a justice-hearing, of a law-suit, or a cross in a boxing-match for money' (Bee).

mix it up *v.*² [2000s] (*US Black*) to change a song around or play multiple songs at the same time; usu. with turntables.

Mixmaster *n.* [1950s–80s] (*US*) a helicopter. [*Mixmaster*, a brand of kitchen appliances, orig. 1940s use for a propeller-driven bomber]

mix matters *v.* *see* MIX IT (UP) v. (1).

mix-metal *n.* [late 18C–early 19C] a silversmith. [a silversmith's function]

mixologist *n.* [mid-19C+] (*orig. US*) a bartender, esp. as a mixer of cocktails; thus *mixology*, mixing cocktails. [SE *mix* + sfx *-ologist*]

mix one's peanut butter *v.* *see* PACK PEANUT BUTTER v.

mixum *n.* (*also* **mix'em**) [early 17C–early 18C] an apothecary. [the mixing of medicines]

mix-up *n.* [late 19C–1930s] a fist-fight. [now SE]

mix-up artist *n.* [1990s+] (*W.I.*) a troublemaker. [MIX IT (UP) v. + ARTIST sfx]

mixy *adj.* [1940s+] sociable, good at mixing.

miz *adj.* *see* MIS adj.

mizake the mizan *v.* [1930s–50s] (*US drugs*) to buy narcotics. [MAKE v.³ (3) + MAN, THE n. (3) + -IZ- ifx]

mizz *n.* *see* MIS n. (2).

mizzard *n.* [late 19C] the face, the mouth. [MAZARD n. (3)]

mizzle *v.* (*also* **mislain, misle, misli**) **1** [late 18C+] to leave, to go quickly, to escape; thus *do a mizzle*; thus excl. *mizzle!* go away! be off!; *on the mizzle*, leaving, en route. **2** [mid-19C] to die. [? Shelta *misli*, to go; note naut. jargon *mizzle one's dick*, to miss one's passage]

mizzled *adj.* [mid-19C–1920s] drunk (cf. ADDLED adj.). [? SE *mizmaze*, a state of confusion]

mizzler *n.*¹ [1940s] a whinger, a complainer. [SE *mizzle*, to complain, to whimper]

mizzler *n.*² *see* RUM MIZZLER n.

Mizzoo *n.* (*also* **Missou, Mizzou**) [late 19C–1950s] (*US*) the Missouri River, Missouri. [abbr./pron.]

m.j. *n.* [1960s+] (*orig. US drugs*) marijuana (cf. AUNT MARY n.²). [abbr. MARY JANE n.²]

mjieta *n.* [1960s+] (*S.Afr.*) a township playboy. [Zulu *umjita*, an urbanized man]

m.l.a. *n.* [1980s+] (*US campus*) passionate kissing. [abbr. *massive lip action*]

mlungu *n.* [1980s+] (*S.Afr. Black*) used mockingly, a White person. [Nguni *umlungu*, a White man. The term was orig. coined in early 19C, ? f. Xhosa/Zulu *lunga*, to be correct or good, to be in good order; however, the ironic/mocking use developed much more recently]

m.m.'s *n.* [1970s] (*drugs*) the hunger that follows smoking marijuana, i.e. marijuana *munchies*. [abbr. SE *marijuana* + MUNCHIE n.¹ (2)]

Mo *n.*¹ [mid-19C–1920s] the *Mogul* Music Hall, later called the Middlesex. [abbr.; the *Mogul*, near Drury Lane was established in 1850, according to Ware on the site of 'a public garden there [...] kept by some wonderful Indian']

Mo *n.*² [1990s+] (*US Black teen*) the Fillmore area of San Francisco. [abbr. Black pron. of *Fillmo'*]

Mo *n.*³ *see* IKEY-MO n. (5).

mo *n.*¹ [late 19C+] **1** (*Aus./N.Z.*) a moustache. **2** (*Aus.*) the female genital area, esp. the pubic area. [abbr.; (2) is pun on (1)]

mo *n.*² **1** [late 19C+] a *moment*, a second; often as HALF A MO n.¹. **2** [1910s–50s] (*US*) a month. [abbr.]

mo *n.*³ [1960s+] (*US campus/UK teen*) a homosexual. [abbr. HOMO n.²]

mo *n.*⁴ (*also* **m.o.**) [1970s+] (*drugs*) marijuana (cf. MARI-HA-HA n.). [initial letter; or ? abbr. MOHASKY n.]

mo *adj.* [2000s] (*US Black*) stupid. [abbr. SE *moronic*]

mo *v.* [1980s+] (*US/UK teen*) to act towards someone in a manner that is perceived as being homosexual. [MO n.³]

m.o. *n.*¹ **1** [1950s+] (*UK Und.*) the distinguishing working style of a criminal or gang. **2** [1950s+] a way of thinking. **3** [1990s+] as (1) in non-criminal contexts, a regular way of life. [abbr. Lat. *modus operandi*, the way of working]

m.o. *n.*² *see* MO n.⁴.

moab *n.* [mid–late 19C] a turban-shaped hat, worn by women. [joc. ref. to Ps. 60:8 'Moab is my washpot']

Moabite *n.* [late 17C–mid-19C] a bailiff. [SE *Moabite*, an enemy of the biblical Israelites and occas. used in 16C–17C as a pej. nickname for Roman Catholics]

moa-fugg *n.* *see* MOFUCK n.

moan *n.* [1910s+] (*orig. milit.*) a grievance, a complaint. [MOAN v.]

moan *v.* [1910s+] to complain.

moan and wail *n.* [1930s–40s] a jail. [rhy. sl.]

moaner *n.* [1920s+] (*orig. US*) a complainer, a pessimist. [MOAN v.]

moaner's bench *n.* [late 19C+] (*US Black*) a special pew reserved during a Black church revival for those who wish to be 'saved'. Under the direct eye of the preacher and other church dignitaries, they moan and groan, confess their sins and hope to be 'visited by the Spirit'; thus *moaner*, one who makes a public repentance. [Black English pron. of SE *mourner's bench*]

moat *n.* [mid-19C] (*US Und.*) a river.

moat palace *n.* [mid-19C] (*US Und.*) a river steamboat. [MOAT n.]

Mob, the *n.* **1** [1920s+] (*US*) the US Mafia. **2** [1990s+] any form of organized crime.

Mob *adj.* [1920s+] (*US*) Mafia-related. [MOB, THE n.]

mob *n.*[1] [mid-17C–early 19C] a prostitute. [var. on MAB n.[1]]

mob *n.*[2] **1** [late 17C–18C] the rabble, the city proletariat. **2** [early 19C+] a company or group of associates; thus *mobbed up (with)*, living, travelling or working alongside; occas. of non-human groups. **3** [mid-19C+] (*orig. US*) a criminal gang. **4** [mid-19C+] a gang of ruffians or thugs. [(1) SE from 1800; abbr. *mobile vulgus*, the fickle crowd; *mob* was a term cited by Swift in *Tatler* no. 230 in 1710 as one of those that should be purged from the language (cf. ety. at BAMBOOZLE v.). Surprisingly Johnson, whose *Dictionary* (1755) eschewed (*inter alia*) *dumfound*, *ignoramus* and *touchy*, allowed it]

mob *n.*[3] *see* MOBSTER n.

mob *adj.* [1940s+] (*US*) related to a criminal gang or its culture and lifestyle. [MOB n.[2] (3)]

mob *v.*[1] (*also* **mob it**) **1** [late 17C+] to move around with or act in a crowd. **2** [mid-18C+] to attack in a large group. **3** [1930s] (*US Und.*) to be murdered on the instructions of a criminal gang. **4** [1990s+] (*US Black*) to associate. [MOB n.[2]]

mob *v.*[2] [1990s+] (*US Black*) to go, to travel. [MOBILIZE v.[2]]

mobbed (out) *adj.* [1950s+] very full, crammed. [SE *mob*]

mobbed up *adj.* (*US Und.*) **1** [1920s+] connected with, usu. in a criminal context, but other than organized crime. **2** [1960s+] connected with or run by organized crime. [MOB n.[2] (3); MOB, THE n.]

mobber *n.* *see* MOBSTER n.

Mob City *n.* *see* MOB TOWN n.

mobe *n.* **1** [1900s] auto*mobile*. **2** [1990s+] a *mobile* phone. [abbr.]

mobey *n.* *see* MOBY n.

mob guy *n.* (*also* **mob gee**) (*US Und.*) **1** [1930s–40s] a member of a criminal gang. **2** [1960s+] a member of the US Mafia; thus ext. to counterparts in other countries.

mob-handed *adv.* [1930s+] accompanied by or working in a large gang. [MOB n.[2] (3) + -HANDED sfx]

mobi *n.* *see* MOBY n.

mo-bike *n.* [1920s+] a *motorbike*. [abbr.]

mobile *n.* [late 17C] the rabble. [Lat. *mobile vulgus*]

-mobile *sfx* [1990s+] (*US campus*) a vehicle, usu. a car; the sfx is added to an adj. or n. that describes the vehicle, e.g. PIMPMOBILE n.

mobile dandruff *n.* *see* GALLOPING DANDRUFF n.

mobility *n.* [late 17C–mid-19C] the populace, the masses. [backform. f. MOB n.[2] on model of NOB n.[2] (1) and SE *nobility*; Swift allowed mobility, until Johnson, *Dictionary* (1755), condemned it as 'cant', i.e. unacceptably common]

mobilize *v.*[1] (*also* **mopelize, mopolize**) [1920s–70s] (*US, esp. New York City*) of street gangs, to beat up, to vanquish. [SE *mob* but note *mopel*, to abort]

mobilize *v.*[2] [1990s+] (*US Black*) to drive a car.

mobilized dandruff *n.* *see* GALLOPING DANDRUFF n.

moboton *n.* [20C+] (*W.I.*) a great many, a large amount. [? SE *mob* + *marathon*]

mobsman *n.* **1** [mid-19C–1960s] (*UK Und.*) anyone who use manual dexterity for theft, a category that includes both pickpockets and shoplifters. **2** [1930s] (*US Und.*) a gangster. [a member of the elite ranks of pickpockets, the SWELL MOB n.]

mobs of *n.* [late 19C+] (*Aus.*) a great many, a large number, a sizeable quantity. [MOB n.[2] (4)]

mobster *n.* (*also* **mob, mobber**) **1** [1910s+] (*orig. US*) a gangster. **2** [1960s+] a member of the US Mafia. [MOB n.[2] (3)/MOB, THE n. + -STER sfx]

Mob Town *n.* (*also* **Mob City**) [19C] (*US*) Baltimore, Maryland. [MOB n.[2] (3), suggested by its 'lawless' reputation]

mob up *v.* [1920s+] (*US Und.*) **1** to join a gang. **2** to collect in a gang. **3** to ally oneself with. [SE *mob*]

moby *n.* (*also* **mobey, mobi**) [1990s+] a *mobi*le telephone. [abbr.]

moby *adj.* [1960s+] (*US campus*) enormous. [the fictional whale *Moby-Dick*, created by novelist Herman Melville (1819–91)]

moby (dick) *n.* [late 19C+] **1** prison (cf. BUCKET n.[2]). **2** the penis (cf. ALMOND n.). [rhy. sl.; (1) = NICK n.[6] (1); (2) = PRICK n. (2); ult. the novel *Moby-Dick* (1850) by Herman Melville]

moby dick *adj.* [1990s+] ill, sick. [rhy. sl.; ult. *see* prev.]

moccasined *adj.* [mid–late 19C] (*US*) drunk. [abbr. of SE phr. *bitten by the moccasin (snake)*]

moccasins *n.* [late 19C+] (*US*) any kind of footwear; also used fig. as (*walk a mile*) *in my moccasins*, to experience my life.

moccasin telegraph *n.* [20C+] (*US*) the informal way in which news moves between Native American communities. [note synon. Alaskan local use *mukluk telegraph*]

moch *n.* *see* MOCK n.[2].

mocha *n.* *see* MOCKER n.

mocha *adj.* [mid-19C+] (*US*) of people, Black, African-American. [SE *mocha*, a variety of coffee]

mocha and java *v.* [late 19C–1900s] to get on, to be friendly. [the brandnames of coffee, thus the image of chatting over a cup of coffee]

mochy *n.* *see* MOUCHEY n.

mock *n.*[1] [20C+] (*Aus.*) a halfpenny. [? MAG n.[3] (1)]

mock *n.*[2] (*also* **moch**) (*US*) **1** [1910s–30s] a newly arrived Jewish immigrant. **2** [1920s+] a Jew (cf. FAST-TALKING CHARLIE n.). [abbr. MOCKIE n.]

mock *n.*[3] [1950s+] (*mainly UK school*) usu. in pl., a mock examination (usu. preceding major state examinations, e.g. GCSE, A-levels).

mocked-up *adj.* [1970s] made-up, pretend. [SE *mock*]

mocker *n.* (*also* **mocha, mocka**) [1910s+] (*Aus./N.Z.*) clothing, esp. a woman's dress, occas. a suit or suit pattern. [link to Yid. *macha*, a big man, a 'big shot']

mockered *adj.* [mid-19C] of a face, pitted, full of holes (the result of smallpox) (cf. CRIBBAGE-FACED adj.). [Rom. *mockodo*, *mookeedo*, dirty, filthy]

mockered up *adj.* (*also* **all mockered up**) [1910s+] (*Aus.*) dressed up in one's best, poss. flashy, garments. [MOCKER n.; according to E.P., *mockered up* is 'low. late C. 19–20', but neither he nor the *OED* nor *AND* offer a possible cit.]

mockered up like a pox doctor's clerk *phr.* *see* DONE UP LIKE A POX DOCTOR'S CLERK phr.

mockie *n.* (*also* **mockey, mocky**) [1930s+] (*US*) a derog. term for a Jew (cf. ABE n.[1]; FAST-TALKING CHARLIE n.). [proper name *Moses*, but cf. SMOUS n. and MOUCHEY n.; *DARE* suggests Yid. *makeh*, a boil or sore, but why?]

mockie *adj.* (*also* **mocky**) [1930s+] (*US*) Jewish. [MOCKIE n.]

mockingbird *n.* **1** [1960s] (*UK/Aus.*, *orig. theatre*) a word. **2** [1980s+] (*Aus.*) a piece of excrement (cf. ALI OOP n.). [rhy. sl.; (2) = TURD n. (1)]

mock litany men *n.* [late 19C–1900s] (*Irish*) beggars who make their demands in a sing-song or versifying manner. [such beggars are reminiscent of the origins of the CANTING CREW n.]

mock out *v.* [1960s+] (*US campus*) to tease. [SE *mock*]

mocktail *n.* [1980s+] (*US*) a non-alcoholic drink. [SE *mock* + (*cock*)*tail*]

mocky *see under* MOCKIE.

mocs *n.* [1950s+] (*US*) slip-on shoes. [abbr. SE *moccasins*]

mod *n.*[1] [1940s+] often in pl., *mod*ification. [abbr.]

mod *n.*[2] [1960s+] **1** a member of a teenage cult orig. *c*.1961, who wore notably smart clothes, rode motor scooters and fought their main rivals, the motorcycle-riding, leather-clad 'rockers' (cf. ROCKER n.[2]). **2** (*US campus*) a well-dressed, fashionable person. [abbr. SE *modernist*]

mod *adj.* [1960s+] fashionable, up-to-date; thus (*in a*) *mod bag*, fashionable. [abbr. SE *modern*]

mod *v.* [1950s+] to *mod*ify. [abbr.]

modams *n.* [1970s+] (*drugs*) marijuana. [ety. unknown]

mod cons *n.* [1930s+] modern conveniences. [a play on estate agent advertising *all mod cons*]

moddley-coddley *v. see* MOLLYCODDLE v.

mode *adj.* [1980s+] fashionable, modern. [Fr. *à la mode* but note MOD adj.]

mode *v. see* MOULD v.

Model, the *n.* [mid-19C–1900s] Pentonville prison, Caledonian Road, north London (cf. ABBOTT'S PRIORY n.). [Pentonville was opened in 1842 and designed as a *model* prison on the 'separate system', i.e. continuous solitary confinement irrespective of one's crime. Such solitude (pioneered in the Haviland Eastern Penitentiary in Philadelphia) led to a huge increase in mental illness among inmates but no proven increase in rehabilitation]

model *n.* [late 19C–1930s] (*Scot.*) a model lodging-house.

model *v.* [1990s+] (*UK Black*) to pose, e.g. at a party or club.

modelling *n.* [1990s+] (*S.Afr.*) the parading of an offender naked through a township as a form of punishment.

models *n.* [late 19C–1900s] purpose-built 'model' housing.

Model T *adj.* [1930s–60s] (*US*) out-of-date, cheap. [the inexpensive Ford *Model T* motorcar, last manufactured in 1927]

modest quencher *n.* [mid-19C] a glass of gin and water.

modesty *n.* [1910s+] (*Aus.*) a baby's 'pilch', a triangular flannel wrapper worn over the nappy.

mo dicker *n.* [1960s+] (*US*) a synon. for MOTHERFUCKER n. (1). [*mo*, abbr. SE *mother* + DICK v.[2] (1)]

modicum *n.* **1** [early 17C] something that is eaten to make oneself thirsty. **2** [mid-17C–19C] the vagina. [as well as the comestibles, the vagina is something one can EAT v.[3] (1); (2) note Williams: 'This derives, by synechdoche, from the "woman" sense found in Dekker *Roaring Girle* I i, where a girl visiting a man is termed "a daintier bit or modicum than any lay upon his trencher at dinner"']

modie *n.* [2000s] (*US Black*) a motel. [abbr./pron.]

modigger *n. see* DOJIGGER n. (2).

modock *n.* [1930s–40s] (*US*) one who becomes an aviator for the social prestige or publicity. ['a flashy chap who goes around wearing helmet and goggles, and more than likely, leather boots and riding breeches, too, and talking about the big things he is going to do for aviation' (Allen & Lyman, *Wonder Book of the Air*, 1936). Ety. unknown; supposedly a mythical bird, which 'flies backwards to keep the sun out of its eyes', but other than an aviators' joke, this has no validity as an ety.]

modock *v.* [1940s–70s] (*US*) to rush off. [for ety. *see* MODOCK n.]

mods and rockers *n.* [1960s+] the female breasts (cf. BRACE AND BITS n.). [rhy. sl. = KNOCKERS n.[2] (2); ult. MOD n.[2] (1) + ROCKER n.[2] (1)]

mod squad *n.* [1970s–80s] plain-clothes police, usu. young and dressed in the prevailing teenage and early 20s fashions, who look for crime in colleges and local youth centres. [MOD adj. + SE *squad*]

mod to the bone *phr.* [1960s+] (*US Black*) very fashionably dressed. [MOD adj. + TO THE BONE phr.]

moe *n.* [2000s] (*US prison*) a 'married' prison homosexual.

moegie *adj.* (*also* **imoogie**) [1960s+] (*S.Afr.*) foolish, stupid. [MOEGOE n.]

moegoe *n.* [1960s+] (*S.Afr.*) a lazy lout, a country bumpkin, a gullible person. [Afk.]

moer *v.* [1960s+] (*S.Afr.*) to thrash, to beat up, to kill. [? MOER! excl. or Afk. *moor*, murder]

moer! *excl.* [1940s+] (*S.Afr.*) an abusive term of address or an obscene excl. of fury or disgust; esp. in excls. *jou moer! your moer! your mother!* [Du. *moder*, mother, thus fig. 'your mother's womb']

moey *n.* (*also* **mooe, mooey, mouee**) **1** [mid-19C+] the mouth. **2** [mid–late 19C; 1990s+] the vagina. **3** [late 19C+] (*Aus.*) a moustache. [Rom. *mooi*, the mouth]

moff *n.* (*also* **moph**) [20C+] a hermaphrodite. [abbr.; note farming jargon *moff*, a dual-purpose farm wagon]

moffie *n.* [1950s+] (*S.Afr.*) **1** a homosexual; thus *koffie-moffie*, an airline steward (lit. 'coffee-queen'). **2** a transvestite. [? Du. sl. *mofrodiet*, a hermaphrodite; note UK naut. jargon *mophy*, 'a delicate well-groomed youth' (E.P.)]

moffry *n.* [20C+] (*W.I.*) **1** a her*maph*rodite. **2** a weak, effeminate man. [abbr.; (2) is fig. use of (1)]

mofo *n.* **1** [1960s+] a synon. for MOTHERFUCKER n. (1). **2** [1980s+] a synon. for MOTHERFUCKER n. (3). [abbr.]

mofo *adj.* [1980s+] a euph. for MOTHERFUCKING adj. (1). [abbr.]

mofuck *n.* (*also* **moa-fugg**) [1960s+] a synon. for MOTHERFUCKER n. (1). [abbr.]

mog *n.*[1] (*also* **mogue**) [mid–late 19C] a lie; thus *no mogue*, no lie. [? Fr. *se moquer de*, to jeer, to deride]

mog *n.*[2] **1** [1920s–50s] a fur, a tippet, a fur coat. **2** [1920s+] a cat. **3** [1940s] a monkey. [(2) abbr. MOGGIE n.[1] (2)]

mog *v.* [late 18C–1950s] to amble, to trudge along slowly. [ety. unknown]

mogadored *adj.* [1930s+] beaten, defeated, confused. [rhy. sl. = FLOORED adj. (2); ? ult. Irish *magadh*, to mock, to jeer, to laugh at; or ? Rom. *mokardi/mokodo*, tainted]

mogg *v.*[1] *see* MOG v.

mogg *v.*[2] *see* MUG v.[1].

moggie *n.*[1] (*also* **moggy**) **1** [late 17C–19C] an untidily dressed woman, a slattern. **2** [20C+] a cat. [? proper name *Maggie* or dial. *moggie*, a calf]

moggie *n.*[2] [1980s+] (*drugs*) Mogadon, a mild sleeping pill. [abbr.]

moggie *adj.* [2000s] (*S.Afr.*) crazy. [ety. unknown]

moggy *n. see* MOGGIE n.[1].

mogue *n. see* MOG n.[1].

mogue *v.* [mid–late 19C] to trick or deceive. [MOG n.[1]]

mohair *n.* [late 18C–early 19C] a derog. name for a civilian, as named by a soldier. [a civilian's mohair-covered buttons, a soldier had the unadorned brass]

mohair knickers *n.* (*also* **mohair stockings**) [1980s+] an extremely hairy vagina.

mohasky *n.* (*also* **mohasty, mohoska, mosky**) [1930s+] (*drugs*) marijuana (cf. MARI-HA-HA n.). [ety. unknown; play on SE pron.]

mohasky *adj.* (*also* **mohasty, mohoska, mosky**) [1930s+] (*drugs*) intoxicated by marijuana. [MOHASKY n.]

mohican *n.* [mid-19C] 'A Mohican, in Cadonian phraseology, is a tremendously heavy man, who rides five or six miles [in an omnibus] for sixpence' (*Tait's Magazine*, May 1848). [*cadonian*, i.e. of a cad or bus–conductor]

mohock *n.* (*also* **mohawk**) [early 18C–19C; 1960s] a dissolute and violent young man, usu. an aristocratic rowdy, who caroused through the streets of London beating up passers–by, attacking watchmen, smashing windows etc; occas. of a woman, a prostitute. [SE *Mohawk*]

mohoska *see under* MOHASKY.

moi *pron.* [1960s+] me, used ironically or sarcastically, pointing fun at one's pretensions, 'attitude' etc, e.g. *pretentious, moi? sarcastic, moi?* (with the unspoken coda, 'damn right I am!'). [Fr. *moi*, me]

moisher *v.* [1960s] to wander. [play on the Jewish name *Moishe/Moses*, i.e. the 'wandering Jew']

moist *n.* [1900s–30s] (*US*) an alcoholic drink; thus MOIST 'UN n.; MOISTMILL n. [play on DAMP n. (1)]

moist *adj.* [1990s+] (*US campus*) second-rate, inferior.

moisten one's wick *v.* [1970s] of a man, to have sexual intercourse (cf. BURY IT v.). [SE *moisten* + WICK n.[1]]

moisten the chaffer *v.* [mid–late 19C] to take a drink. [SE *moisten* + CHAFFER n.[2] (1)]

moisten the clay *v.* (*also* **wet the clay**) [early 18C–1950s] to take a drink, to quench one's thirst. [SE *moisten* + *clay*, the human flesh]

moistmill *n.* [1900s–30s] (*US*) a bar. [MOIST n.]

moist round the edges *phr.* [1900s–20s] slightly drunk. [note MOIST n.]

moist 'un *n.* [1900s–30s] (*US*) a drunkard. [MOIST n.]

mojo *n.*[1] **1** [1920s+] (*orig. US Black*) spirituality, magic, thus power and influence. **2** [1970s] (*US Black*) a kind of dance. [? Gullah *moco*, witchcraft, magic, Fula *moco'o*, medicine man]

mojo *n.*[2] [1930s+] (*US drugs*) any narcotic drug, esp. morphine (cf. AUNTIE EMMA n.). [ext. of MOJO n.[1] (1)]

mojo *v.* (*orig. US*) **1** [1930s] to fool, to deceive. **2** [1960s+] to jinx, to charm. **3** [1990s+] to go, to leave. [MOJO n.[1] (1)]

mojo and the say-so, the *phr.* [1920s+] (*orig. US Black*) qualities giving one power and influence over others. [MOJO n.[1] (1) + SAY-SO n.]

moke *n.*[1] **1** [mid-19C–1940s] a donkey, an ass. **2** [mid-19C+] a fool (cf. AIREDALE n.). **3** [late 19C+] (*Aus.*) a horse, often a second-rate one. [? Devon/Hampshire dial. *mokus*, a donkey. E.P. suggests Rom. *moxio*, a donkey, or *Moke*, the dimin. of the proper name *Margaret*, on the pattern of MOG n.[2] (2), MOGGIE n.[1] (2); also f. *Margaret*, a cat]

moke *n.*[2] (*US*) **1** [mid-19C–1950s] a Black person, any dark-skinned foreigner. **2** [late 19C] a White person wearing 'blackface' and performing in a 'minstrel show'. **3** [late 19C–1910s] a foolish, tedious person. **4** [1960s] a Hawaiian, esp. a young, thuggish man. [? Sp. *mocha*, dark-skinned; ult. Sp. *café de Moca* (an Arabian port on the Red Sea), but note SMOKE n.[6] (1)]

mokes *n.* [1980s+] (*US*) a silly fellow. [MOKE n.[1] (1)]

mokuiner *v. see* MOSKENEER V.

mokus *n.* (*US*) **1** [1920s–50s] a depressed state, the blues. **2** [1950s–70s] a very intoxicated state. [? PUT THE MOCKERS ON v.]

mokus *adj.* [1950s–70s] (*US*) drunk but wanting another drink. [MOKUS n. (2)]

mola *n. see* MOOLA n.

molared *adj. see* MOLO adj.

mold *v. see* MOULD v.

moldy fig *n.* [1940s+] (*orig. US*) a very boring or old-fashioned person, esp. as applied by modern jazz fans to their antitheses, the fans of trad. New Orleans jazz. [the idea of stale and shrivelled beliefs]

mole *n.*[1] [late 19C–1910s] **1** the penis (cf. ANTEATER n.). **2** a male homosexual. [the animal and the penis 'burrow in'; (2) is f. (1)]

mole *n.*[2] [20C+] (*US prison*) someone who escapes by digging their way out of prison.

mole *n.*[3] [1960s+] (*Aus./N.Z.*) a woman, esp. a promiscuous one. [? MOLLY n.[1] (2) or ? MOLL n.[1] (1)]

mole *n.*[4] **1** [1970s+] a deep cover agent, who is put in place many years before they can be of use but on the assumption that they will gradually gain greater access to the centres of power and become increasingly useful and damaging as time passes. **2** [1990s+] anyone within an organization or in a position of trust who betrays confidential information. [*mole* is the perfect example of the blurring of fact and fiction. While Sir Francis Bacon uses it first in his *History of the Reign of King Henry VII* (1622) and the *OED* offers earlier uses, albeit not exactly synon., in 1925 and 1960, it has otherwise been popularized via the fictional world of John Le Carré, notably in *Tinker, Tailor, Soldier, Spy* (1974). In a BBC TV interview Le Carré claimed that *mole* was a genuine KGB term, but it was the televising of *Tinker, Tailor, Soldier, Spy*

plus the revelations of the 'Fourth Man' (Anthony Blunt) in October 1979 that took *mole* out of fiction and put it into the headlines for good]

mole-catcher *n.* [late 19C–1910s] the vagina (cf. BAG n.[1]; BITE n.[2]). [MOLE n.[1] (1) + SE *catcher*]

molehill *n.* [early 18C] a pregnant stomach. [resemblance]

moles *n.* [late 19C+] (*Aus.*) moleskin trousers. [SE *moleskin*, a strong, soft, fine-piled cotton fustian, the surface of which is 'shaved' before dyeing]

moleskin *n.* [1990s+] (*US*) a derog. term for a Black person (cf. BLACKBELLY n.).

moleskin squatter *n.* [late 19C–1940s] (*Aus./N.Z.*) 'a working man who has come to own a small sheep run' (*OED*). [his moleskin trousers]

moley *n.* [1950s] a potato, its surface jagged with the edges of safety razor blades. [it 'burrows into' the victim's flesh]

moll *n.*[1] **1** [17C+] a woman, usu. a promiscuous one. **2** [17C+] a prostitute (cf. BABY JANE n.). **3** [early 19C+] a girlfriend; esp. in *gangster's moll*, a gangster's female companion. **4** [mid-19C] (*UK Und.*) a landlady, a proprietress, the 'lady of the house'; usu. ext as *moll of the crib/drum*. **5** [1920s–70s] (*US*) an effeminate male homosexual (cf. ABIGAIL n.). [dimin. of proper name *Mary*, reinforced by the early 17C criminal *Moll Cut-purse*, immortalized in Middleton & Dekker's play *The Roaring Girl* (1611); (2) now survives only in Aus. use]

moll *n.*[2] *see* MOLLY n.[1] (1).

moll *v.* **1** [19C] to go around with women. **2** [late 19C; 1970s] of a man, to act effeminately. **3** [1950s] (*US*) to work as a prostitute. [MOLL n.[1] (1)/MOLL n.[1] (2)]

moll blood *n.* [late 18C–early 19C] the gallows. [Scot. nickname]

moll-buzzer *n.* **1** [mid-19C+] (*UK/US Und./police*) (*also* **dame-buzzer, moll-buzzard, moll-worker**) a pickpocket or a beggar who specializes in women as victims; thus *moll-buzzing*, purse- or bag-snatching. **2** [late 19C–1930s] (*US Und.*) a female thief, pickpocket or beggar. [MOLL n.[1] (1) + BUZZER n.[1]/WORKER n.[1] (1); note Goldin et al., *Dict. of American Und. Lingo* (1950): 'The theft is accomplished in the following manner: An accomplice, known as the buzzer, accosts a victim and asks to be directed to a given place in the neighborhood. The destination is so chosen that the victim must turn her back to the carriage to point. The purse-snatcher now advances from the direction which the victim is facing and deftly seizes the purse. The victim seldom discovers her loss until the thieves have disappeared. Premature discovery requires the buzzer, feigning solicitude, to block pursuit and delay any outcry until the snatcher has escaped']

moll crib *n.* [mid-19C] a brothel (cf. BADGER-CRIB n.). [MOLL n.[1] + CRIB n.[1] (2)]

molled *adj.*[1] [mid-19C] followed by a woman. [MOLL v. (1)]

molled *adj.*[2] *see* MOLO adj.

molled (up) *adj.* [mid-19C] **1** sleeping with a woman other than one's wife. **2** accompanied by a woman. [MOLL n.[1] (1)/MOLL v.]

mollesher *n. see* MOLLISHER n.

molley *n.*[1] *see* MOLL-TOOLER n.

molley *n.*[2] *see* MOLLY n.[1] (2).

moll hook *n.* [late 19C–1910s] a female pickpocket. [MOLL n.[1] (1) + HOOK n.[1] (2)]

moll house *n.* [18C] a brothel (cf. ACCOMMODATION HOUSE n.). [MOLL n.[1] (2) + SE *house*/HOUSE n.[1] (1)]

moll-hunter *n.* [late 19C–1900s] a womanizer. [MOLL n.[1] (1) + SE *hunter*]

mollie *n. see* MOLLY n.[1] (2).

mollies *n.* [1970s+] (*US drugs*) amphetamines; usu. as *blue mollies*, BLACK MOLLIES n. or even *yellow mollies* (cf. A n.[2]). [play on SE *black molly*, a species of tropical fish, which the black pills may be seen as resembling]

mollisher *n.* (*also* **mollesher**) **1** [early–mid-19C] a woman.

2 [mid-19C] a slattern. **3** [mid–late 19C] a thief's mistress. [MOLL n.¹ (1); ? link to Rom. *monishi*, a woman]

mollock *v.* [1930s+] to cavort, to have a good time, to have sexual intercourse. [? dial. *marlock*, to frolic, to gambol + *rollick*, coined by Stella Gibbons in *Cold Comfort Farm* (1932)]

moll of the crib/drum *n. see* MOLL n.¹ (4).

Moll Peatley's gig *n.* (*also* Moll Peatley's jig, Moll Pratley's gig) [late 18C–early 19C] sexual intercourse, 'a rogering bout' (Grose, 1796). [? the name of a well-known contemporary prostitute + GIG n.¹ (2)/SE *jig*]

mollsack *n.* [mid-19C] a market basket. [MOLL n.¹ (1) + SE *sack*, lit. 'woman sack']

moll shop *n.* (*also* **molly shop**) [20C+] a brothel (cf. BANGING-SHOP n.). [MOLL n.¹ (2) + SE *shop/*SHOP n.¹ (1)]

moll slavey *n. see* SLAVEY n.

Moll's three misfortunes *phr.* [late 18C] 'broke the [chamber-] pot, bes[hi]t the bed and cut her a[r]se' (Grose, 1796). [the phr., while appearing in the British Library edn, was not transferred into any of the published versions of the *Classical Dictionary of the Vulgar Tongue*]

Moll Thompson's mark *n.* [late 18C–mid-19C] a term used to describe an empty bottle. [the sign *M.T.* inscribed on empty packages]

moll-tooler *n.* (*also* **molley, moll-tool**) [mid–late 19C] a female pickpocket. [MOLL n.¹ (1) + TOOLER n.]

mollwhiz *n.* [1930s] (*US Und.*) a female pickpocket. [MOLL n.¹ (1) + WHIZ n.⁴]

moll-wire *n.* [mid-19C–1930s] **1** a pickpocket who specializes in robbing female victims. **2** a female pickpocket. [MOLL n.¹ (1) + WIRE n.³]

moll-worker *n. see* MOLL-BUZZER n. (1).

molly *n.¹* **1** [late 17C+] (*also* **moll, molly-cull, tom molly**) a male homosexual, an effeminate man (cf. ABIGAIL n.). **2** [early 18C–1940s] (*also* **molley, mollie**) a prostitute (cf. BABY JANE n.). **3** [late 19C+] (*Irish*) a girl. [the proper name; *see* ety. at MISS MOLLY n.]

molly *n.²* **see** MISS MOLLY n.

molly *n.³* **see** MOLLY (MALONE) n.

molly *v.* [early–mid-18C] to sodomize, to bugger; thus *mollying*, very keen on buggery. [MOLLY n.¹ (1)]

Molly Bán *n.* (*also* Molly Bawn) [20C+] (*Irish*) confusion, worry; thus *the times of Molly Bán*, a riotous good time. [used as (? coined by) the title of a popular ballad by Samuel Lover (1797–1868)]

molly boy *n. see* MISS MOLLY n.

mollycoddle *n.* [mid-19C+] a weakling, a mother's darling; thus *do the mollycoddle*, to toady to, to be sycophantic. [MOLLY n.¹ (1) + SE *coddle*]

mollycoddle *v.* (*also* **coddle, moddley-coddley**) [mid-19C+] to pamper, to pet, to indulge a weak person in their weaknesses. [MOLLYCODDLE n.]

mollycoddled *adj.* (*also* **mollycoddle, molly-coddlish**) [mid-19C+] spoilt. [MOLLYCODDLE v.]

molly-cull *n. see* MOLLY n.¹ (1).

molly dike *n.* [1970s–80s] (*US gay*) a lesbian.

molly-dodger *n.* [1920s–60s] (*US*) a euph. for MOTHERFUCKER n. (1).

molly-dooker *n.* (*also* **molly-hander**) [1920s+] (*Aus.*) a left-handed person; thus *molly-dook(ed)*, left-handed. [? MOLLY n.¹ (1) + DUKE n.³ (1), with derog. sense that an effeminate man, like a left-handed person, would be clumsy; or ? MAULEY n.]

mollyfock *n.* [1960s+] a euph. for MOTHERFUCK n.

mollyfocking *adj.* (*also* **mollyfogging**) [1960s+] a euph. for MOTHERFUCKING adj. (1).

mollygrubs *n. see* MULLIGRUBS n.

molly-hander *n. see* MOLLY-DOOKER n.

mollyhead *n.* [1900s] a fool, a simpleton. [MOLLY n.¹ (1) + -HEAD sfx (1)]

molly-hogan *n.* [1940s+] (*US*) anything puzzling or complicated. [logging jargon *molly-hogan*, a wire loop used as a temporary link connecting 2 cables]

mollyhouse *n.* [early 18C–19C] a male homosexual brothel (cf. ACCOMMODATION HOUSE n.). [MOLLY n.¹ (1) + SE *house/*HOUSE n.¹ (1)]

molly maguire *n.* [2000s] (*orig. Aus.*) a fire. [rhy. sl.]

molly maguired *adj.* [1990s+] tired. [rhy. sl.]

molly (malone) *n.* [20C+] the telephone. [rhy. sl.]

molly man *n. see* MISS MOLLY n.

molly-mop *n.* [early 19C] an effeminate man. [MOLLY n.¹ (1) + DOLLYMOP n.]

molly o'morgan *n.* [20C+] an organ. [rhy. sl.]

mollypuff *n.* (*also* **mullipuff, mullypuff**) [early 17C–early 18C] a weakling, used as a general term of contempt. [dial. *mullipuff*, the fungus *Lycoperdon Bovista*, a puff-ball; note F&H suggest an alternative meaning, 'a gambler's decoy' but E.P. dismisses this as an error]

molly's hole *n.* [19C] the vagina (cf. BLACK HOLE n.¹). [MOLL n.¹ (1) + HOLE n.¹ (2)]

molly shop *n. see* MOLL SHOP n.

mollyslop *adj.* [late 19C] nonsensical, weak, with overtones of effeminacy. [MOLLY n.¹ (1) + SLOP n.⁴ (2)]

molly (the monk) *adj.* [1960s–70s] (*Aus.*) drunk (cf. ADRIAN (QUIST) adj.). [rhy. sl.]

molo *adj.* (*also* **molared, molled, mowlow**) [20C+] (*Aus.*) drunk. [? SE *molly*, a meeting of ships' captains, poss. for drinking]

molocher *n.* (*also* **moloker**) [mid–late 19C] a renovated hat, ironed and greased back to something resembling its original condition. [? SE *lacquered*]

molrower *n.* [mid–late 19C] a womanizer. [MOLROWING n.]

molrowing *n.* [mid–late 19C] **1** going out on a (whoring) spree; thus *go molrowing*, of a man, to have sexual intercourse. **2** caterwauling, making a noise. [MOLL n.¹ (1)/MOLL n.¹ (2) + SE *row*, a noise (the woman's amatory groans are compared to the screeching of mating cats)]

Molson muscle *n.* [1990s+] (*Can.*) a beer belly, a paunch. [*Molson*, a popular Can. beer + SE *muscle*]

mom *n.* **1** [1950s+] the equivalent of the UK *mum*, used here as a generic term for the typical US matriarchal mother; thus *mom-bashing, mom cult, mom culture, mom-like*. **2** [1970s] (*US gay*) a passive partner in a lesbian relationship.

mome *n.* [mid-16C–early 18C] a fool, a simpleton. [? Fr. *mome*, a little child or an innocent, or *mum*, dumb]

momick *v.* (*also* **mommuck**) [1920s–30s] (*US*) to beat, to injure, to damage.

momma *n.¹* **1** [1930s+] (*US Black*) (*also* **mommy**) a woman, any woman, spec. as a term of address. **2** [1960s] a male-to-male term of friendly address. **3** [1960s+] (*US Black*) a girlfriend, a lover. **4** [1970s+] a synon. for MOTHERFUCKER n. (1). [var. on MAMA n.]

momma *n.²* **see** MAMMY n.¹.

momma-hopper *n. see* MOTHER-HOPPER n.

momma's game *n.* (*also* **momma's dozens**) [1950s+] (*US Black*) a name-calling ritual that depends heavily on mutually abusing the participants' mothers.

mommuck *v. see* MOMICK v.

mommux *n.* (*also* **momox**) [mid-19C] a mess, a muddle. [MOMMUX (UP) v.]

mommux (up) *v.* (*also* **momox (up)**) [mid-19C–1950s] (*US*) to confuse, to bewilder, to confound, to botch. [? FLUMMOX v.¹]

mommy *n. see* MOMMA n.¹ (1).

mommy up *v.* [1980s+] (*US campus*) to love, to hug, to comfort. [SAmE *mommy*, mother]

momo *n.* [1950s+] (*US*) a stupid person. [abbr. SE *moron* + redup.]

momox *see under* MOMMUX.

mompara *n.* (*S.Afr.*) **1** [late 19C+] of Black workers, a novice, a greenhorn. **2** [1940s+] a fool, an idiot, also used as a term of affection. [Fanakalo *mompara*, a fool, waste matter]

mompyns *n.* (*also* **munpins**) [mid-15C] the teeth. [lit. 'mouth-pins']

moms *n.* [1960s+] (*US Black*) **1** one's mother. **2** a term of address to one's mother.

momser/momza/momzer/momzir *n. see* MAMZER *n.*

mon *n.*[1] (*also* **mun**) [late 19C–1970s] (*US*) money. [abbr.]

mon *n.*[2] [1960s+] (*orig. US campus*) as a term of address, man. [imitation of W.I. pron.]

monacher/monack/monacker *n. see* MONNIKER *n.*

monaghan *n.* [late 17C–mid-18C] (*Irish*) a fool, a clown. [proper name, presumably of a specific individual]

monaker *n.*[1] *see* MONARCH *n.*

monaker *n.*[2] *see* MONNIKER *n.*

Mona Lisa *n.* [1980s+] **1** a freezer. **2** a pizza. [rhy. sl.]

monarch *n.* (*also* **monaker**) [mid-19C–1900s] a sovereign. [the *monarch*'s head on the coin]

monarch/monarcher *n. see* MONNIKER *n.*

Monday and Tuesday *phr.* [1950s] slow, steady, careful. [the correct order of the days of the week]

Monday comes before Sunday *phr.* (*also* **Saturday is longer than Sunday, Sunday below Monday, Tuesday is longer than Monday**) [1960s+] (*US*) a warning to a woman that her slip is showing (cf. CHARLIE'S DEAD *phr.*).

Monday morning quarterback *n.* (*also* **Saturday night quarterback, Sunday morning quarterback**) [1930s+] (*US*) a person who criticizes with the benefit of hindsight. [amateur criticism of the week's football matches played on Saturdays]

Monday morning quarterback *v.* [1930s+] (*US*) to criticize with the benefit of hindsight. [for ety. *see* MONDAY MORNING QUARTERBACK *n.*]

Monday mouse *n.* [late 19C–1900s] a black eye, resulting from a Saturday or Sunday night (drunken) fight. [SE *Monday* + MOUSE *n.*[3]]

mondo *adj.* [1980s+] considerable, substantial, huge. [MONDO *pfx*]

mondo *adv.* [1980s+] (*US teen/campus*) completely, absolutely, very, exceedingly. [MONDO *pfx*]

mondo *pfx* [1960s+] (*US*) used to describe a bizarre, surprising or anarchic view of the topic under consideration, with the implication of salaciousness or (kitschy) bad taste; usu. combined with a real or cod Italian *n.*, e.g. *mondo trasho, mondo weirdo, mondo bizarro*. [Ital. *mondo*, the world (cf. CITY *sfx*); first popularized by the Italian cult film *Mondo Cane* (1961) and, like COWABUNGA! excl., DUDE *n.* and other Californian teen/surfer sl., *mondo* gained a new lease of life with the *Teenage Mutant Ninja Turtles* craze of the late 1980s]

monekeer/monekur *n. see* MONNIKER *n.*

monet *n.* [1990s+] (*US teen*) something that (lit. and fig.) looks good from afar but appears less appealing in close-up. [a critical view of the work of the Fr. artist Claude *Monet* (1840–1926)]

money *n.*[1] **1** [late 18C+] esp. of young girls, the vagina (cf. BANK *n.*[1]). **2** [1970s+] of boys, the anus; thus used as a form of address between homosexual men. [the commercial potential of the organs]

money *n.*[2] [mid-19C] *money*'s worth. [abbr.]

money *n.*[3] [late 19C+] (*US*) in general, the critical element or aspect, used fig., e.g. *that's where the money is.*

money *n.*[4] (*also* **money dog/grip**) [1980s+] (*US Black*) **1** one's best friend. **2** a man. **3** a general form of address to any man. [the centrality and importance of cash]

money *adj.* (*orig. US*) **1** [1930s+] used prenominally to denote success, proficiency, ability to win or to fulfil high expectations; thus *money star*, a famous film star; *money jockey*, a jockey who

wins often; *money card*, the card that completes a winning hand in poker; *money shot*, a close-up shot of orgasm in a pornographic film; *money quote*, a quote of a sensational exposure in a news story. **2** [1990s+] used without a *n.* with the same meaning, e.g. *you're money; that's really money!*

moneybag *n. see* MONEYBOX *n.*

money-bag *adj.* (*also* **money-bags**) [1980s+] wealthy. [MONEYBAGS *n.*]

moneybag lord *n.* [late 19C–1900s] an ennobled millionaire or successful businessman. [MONEYBAGS *n.* + SE *lord*]

moneybags *n.* **1** [early 19C+] a lover of money. **2** [late 19C+] a wealthy person; often as *Mr Moneybags.*

money blanket *n. see* HORSE BLANKET *n.*[2].

moneybox *n.* (*also* **moneybag**) [19C] the vagina (cf. BAG *n.*[1]; BANK *n.*[1]). [its commercial potential]

money bug *n.* [late 19C–1900s] (*US*) a millionaire. [SE *money* + BUG *n.*[1] (1)]

money-cuffee *n.* [late 19C] (*W.I.*) a foolish spendthrift. [SE *money* + CUFFY *n.*]

money dog *n. see* MONEY *n.*[4].

money-dropper *n. see* GOLD-DROPPER *n.*

money for jam *n.* (*also* **money for dirt/dust**) [1910s+] (*orig. milit.*) anything, including money, that is gained through a minimal amount of effort, and is available for purely pleasurable expenditure.

money gone in Maxwell Pond *phr.* (*also* **labour gone in Maxwell Pond**) [20C+] (*W.I.*) used to describe money or effort that has been wasted or 'thrown away'. [proper name of the *Maxwell* (Sugar) Estate in Barbados; no actual pond, however, has ever been traced]

money grip *n. see* MONEY *n.*[4].

money machine *n.* [1960s–70s] (*US*) the vagina (cf. BANK *n.*[1]). [its commercial potential]

money-maker *n.* **1** [late 19C+] the vagina (cf. BANK *n.*[1]). **2** [1960s+] (*US*) the female buttocks; also used of gay men. [commercial potential]

money pocket *n.* [2000s] (*US Black*) the vagina, seen in its commercial context (cf. BANK *n.*[1]).

money-puker *n.* [1990s+] (*US*) an automatic teller machine. [SE *money* + SE *puke*, to vomit]

money shot *n. see* MEAT SHOT *n.*

money's mammy *n.* [1930s–40s] (*US Black*) a very rich person. [fig. a 'member of money's family']

money-spinner *n.* [19C] the vagina (cf. BANK *n.*[1]). [its commercial potential]

money talks, bullshit walks *phr.* [1950s+] a dismissive phr. aimed at a person.

money to burn *n.* [late 19C+] spare cash available for spontaneous excess. [TO BURN *adv.*]

mong *n.*[1] [1940s+] (*Aus.*) a dog, not necessarily of mixed breed. [SE *mongrel*]

mong *n.*[2] [1970s+] a general term of opprobrium. The overriding implication is that of stupidity. [abbr. SE *mongol*]

mong *adj. see* MONGY *adj.*

mong *v.* [1910s–50s] (*Aus.*) to cadge. [Rom. *mong*, to beg]

monged *adj.* (*also* **monged out**) [1980s+] intoxicated by a drug, usu. MDMA. [MONG *n.*[2]]

mongee *n.* [1910s–30s] (*US tramp*) food. [Fr. *manger*, to eat]

-monger *sfx* [late 16C–17C; late 19C+] an enthusiast or very knowledgeable person. [SE *monger*, a dealer, a trafficker]

mongie *adj. see* MONGY *adj.*

mong-mong *n.* [20C+] (*W.I., Gren.*) a poor White. [pron. of Carib.E. *Mount St Moritz Bajan*, a poor White one of whose ancestors moved to the Grenadan estate of St Moritz *c.*1870s, working as a market gardener]

mongo *n.*[1] [1970s+] (*US*) an idiot (cf. BOBO *n.*[1]). [MONG *n.*[2], but *Mongo* is a trad. name for a shambling idiot, often the servant of a 'mad professor' in films etc; however, that too may be rooted in SE *mongol*.

mongo n.[2] [1980s+] (*US, New York City*) **1** any discarded object that is retrieved. **2** a scrap-metal scavenger. [? MONGO n.[1]]

mongo adj. [1980s+] (*US teen/campus*) considerable, substantial, huge. [? HUMONGOUS adj.]

mongo adv. [1990s+] extremely. [MONGO adj.]

Mongolian n. (*also* **Mongol**) [mid-19C–1910s] (*Aus.*) a Chinese immigrant to Australia, or the United States (cf. AH CABBAGE n.).

mongolito n. [1980s+] (*US campus*) a term of endearment. [cod Sp. 'little mongol']

mongoloid n. [1990s+] a stupid, dumb person.

mongoose n. [1900s–50s] (*W.I.*) an albino, esp. as a term of abuse. [the animal, which has a light-brown coat and reddish eyes]

mongoose gang n. [1950s+] (*W.I., orig. Gren.*) a group of thugs working for a politician and acting as a form of private army/secret police. [1950s campaign to eradicate the mongoose in Grenada; those who claimed a bounty for killing the creatures had to produce a tail and became known as the '*mongoose gang*']

mongoree n. *see* MUNGAREE n.

mong (out) v. [2000s] to be dully comatose. [MONGED adj.]

mongrel n.[1] (*UK Und.*) **1** [16C–17C] an accomplice who helps in a confidence trickster's pose as a poor scholar. **2** [late 17C–early 19C] a hanger-on among confidence tricksters, a sponger.

mongrel n.[2] [late 16C+] (*Aus./N.Z.*) a general term of abuse, i.e. *you bloody mongrel*. [despite the synon. of *mongrel* and *half-breed*, there appears to be no racial implication]

mongrel adj. [17C+] an abusive epithet. [MONGREL n.[2]]

mongy adj. (*also* **mong, mongie**) [1970s+] stupid, dull. [MONG n.[2]]

monica/monick/monicker/moniker n. *see* MONNIKER n.

monish n. [19C–1920s] (*US*) money. [imitation of Anglo-Yid. speech]

monk n.[1] **1** [mid-19C; 1940s] a general term of contempt. **2** [late 19C–1930s] (*US*) a Chinese person (cf. AH CABBAGE n.). **3** [1930s–40s] (*US Und.*) a Supreme Court judge, often on a State level. [? abbr. SE *monkey*]

monk n.[2] **1** [mid-19C+] (*orig. US*) a *monkey*. **2** [1960s] (*US*) addiction to a drug, usu. heroin. [abbr.; (2) MONKEY n.[12] (1)]

monk n.[3] *see* MONKEY-CHASER n.[2].

monk v. (*US*) **1** [late 19C–1950s] to trifle with, to fool around. **2** [1950s–60s] to neck, to engage in sexual activity. [MONKEY v.]

monkery n. (*also* **mackry, monkry**) (*UK tramp*) **1** [late 18C–19C] the countryside. **2** [mid-19C] as *the monkery*, the world of tramps and vagrants. **3** [mid-19C] going on the tramp; thus *on the monkery*, living as a tramp. **4** [mid-19C–1930s] a specific district in which tramps or beggars work. [Shelta *munk'ri*, the country; E.P. suggests SE *monkery*, the contemplative, peaceful, monastic life]

monkey n.[1] **1** [late 16C+] a scamp, a rascal. **2** [19C+] a general insult, esp. when used derog. since mid-19C by White people of a Black or Asian person (cf. AFRICAN APE n.; BROWNIE n.[2]). **3** [19C+] a person. **4** [20C+] (*Aus./US*) (*also* **monkey man**) a Chinese person; a Mongolian (cf. AH CABBAGE n.). **5** [1900s–40s] (*US Black*) a West Indian. **6** [1910s+] (*Aus./US*) a Japanese person (cf. BUDDHAHEAD n.). **7** [1910s+] a thug, spec. one with no intelligence. **8** [1920s] (*US tramp*) a member of the public, a non-tramp. **9** [1920s+] (*US Und.*) a victim of a swindler, a dupe. **10** [1930s–40s] (*US Und.*) a prohibition agent. **11** [1940s+] (*US prison*) a correctional officer. **12** [1970s+] (*US Black*) a White person. [(1) now SE]

monkey n.[2] **1** [late 17C] a playhouse girl or prostitute (cf. ALLEY CAT n.). **2** [late 19C–1900s] as used by artisans or manual labourers, a clerk. **3** [20C+] (*US*) a person who acts as, works as, or is responsible for something, usu. a workman; used in combs., e.g. *bridge monkey*, a bridge builder. **4** [1910s–30s] (*US*) a chorus-girl or a taxi-dancer, a dancehall hostess who charges 10 cents a

dance to all-comers; thus MONKEY SHOW n. **5** [1930s–40s] (*US*) one who washes dishes in a restaurant, café etc.

monkey n.[3] [19C] a small bustle. [? the image of a baby monkey clinging to its mother's back]

monkey n.[4] [early 19C–1950s] (*UK Und.*) a padlock. [ety. unknown; but note SE *monkey*, 'applied to various machines and implements' (*OED*)]

monkey n.[5] [mid-19C] a flask, esp. as used to carry liquor on hunting expeditions. [? backform f. SUCK THE MONKEY v.]

monkey n.[6] [mid-19C–1910s] (*Aus./N.Z.*) a mortgage.

monkey n.[7] [mid-19C–1930s] ill temper, tetchiness; thus GET ONE'S MONKEY UP v.; GET SOMEONE'S MONKEY UP v. [ety. unknown; ? play on SE *monkey-wrench*/a *wrench* of pain; 20C use is US Black]

monkey n.[8] [mid-19C+] £500, A$500, $500 (cf. FOAL n.). [ety. unknown]

monkey n.[9] [late 19C–1950s] (*Aus.*) a sheep.

monkey n.[10] **1** [late 19C+] (*Aus./US*) the vagina; thus [1970s+] (*US gay*) *feed the monkey*, to have sexual intercourse with a woman. **2** [1980s+] (*US campus*) the penis (cf. ANTEATER n.). [? punning abbr. MONKEY BUSINESS n. (2)]

monkey n.[11] [1920s–40s] (*US Black*) the leader of a band or orchestra. [the on-stage cavorting or their MONKEY SUIT n. (2)]

monkey n.[12] **1** [1930s+] (*drugs*) any form of narcotics addiction, usu. of heroin or morphine; thus *kill the monkey*, to end an addiction to narcotics. **2** [1960s–70s] (*drugs*) morphine (cf. AUNTIE EMMA n.). **3** [1970s] (*US Black/drugs*) a drug addict (who is irredeemably 'hooked'). **4** [1980s+] (*drugs*) a cigarette made from cocaine paste and tobacco. [abbr. MONKEY ON ONE'S BACK n.[2]]

monkey n.[13] [1980s+] (*US campus*) 'the other woman', 'the other man', i.e. the woman or man with whom one's supposedly faithful partner is having an affair. [such a person 'climbs all over' their partner]

monkey n.[14] *see* MONKEY SUIT n. (2).

monkey, the n. [19C] fooling around, 'messing about'.

monkey adj. **1** [1920s+] (*US*) a general derog. **2** [1950s] difficult, troublesome. **3** [1970s] corrupt, illicit.

monkey v. (*also* **monkey about, ...around, ...with**) [late 19C+] (*orig. US*) to fool around, to tamper, to fiddle, usu. in a destructive clumsy manner, occas. used as a synon. for the expression 'to busy oneself' with anything, but it cannot be legitimately used of honest, useful work, except when such work is either badly done or is undertaken as a recreation rather than as a legitimate business. [supposed characteristics of the animal]

monkey and parrot time n. [late 19C–1900s] (*US*) an unhappy marriage, in which the 2 partners fight continually.

monkey-assed adj. [1980s+] (*US*) damned. [semi-euph.; SE *monkey* + ASS n. (2)]

monkeyback n. [1920s] (*US Black*) a man who dresses in formal dinner wear. [MONKEY SUIT n. (2)]

monkey bait n. [1950s+] (*drugs*) free samples of addictive drugs. [MONKEY n.[12] (1) + SE *bait*, the logical development is to MONKEY ON ONE'S BACK n.[1]]

monkey bite n. [1940s+] (*US*) a love-bite.

monkey blanket n. *see* HORSE BLANKET n.[1].

monkey board n. [mid–late 19C] the step on a bus on which the conductor stands.

monkey business n. (*also* **monkey-doodle business**) [late 19C+] (*orig. US*) **1** dubious, underhand or crooked practices. **2** foolish activities, 'messing around'.

monkey cage n. [20C+] (*Can./US Und.*) a prison cell.

monkey-catcher n. [mid-19C–1940s] (*W.I.*) a shrewd, intelligent individual. [the assumed cunningness of monkeys; those who can catch them must be doubly intelligent]

monkey-chaser n.[1] [1910s–30s] (*US*) a man who frequents taxi-dances. [MONKEY n.[2] (4)]

monkey-chaser n.[2] (*also* **monk**) [1920s+] (*US Black*) a West Indian. [racist stereotyping]

monkey-chaser n.[3] [1950s] (*US*) a cocktail composed of gin and ice, with a little sugar and a trace of water.

monkey clothes n. [1900s–30s] (*US*) men's dress or evening wear. [MONKEY SUIT n. (2)]

monkey dick n. (*US*) **1** [1960s+] a frankfurter sausage. **2** [1980s+] a contemptible person. [SE *monkey* + DICK n.[4]]

monkey-dodger n. [1900s–40s] a sheep-station hand; thus *monkey-dodging*, mustering sheep. [MONKEY n.[9] + SE *dodge*, to avoid]

monkey-doodle business n. *see* MONKEY BUSINESS n.

monkey drill n. [1950s] (*drugs*) a hypodermic syringe. [MONKEY n.[12] (1) + SE *drill*]

monkey dust n. [1970s+] (*drugs*) **1** phencyclidine (cf. ACE n.[4]). **2** opium (cf. APOSTLE n.). [SE *monkey* + DUST n.[5] (5)]

monkey-face n. [1920s–70s] **1** a grimace. **2** a stupid, ugly person.

monkey fart n. (*also* **monkey shit**) [20C+] (*W.I.*) utter rubbish, absolute nonsense. [SE *monkey* + FART n. (1)/SHIT n.[1] (4)]

monkey farting n. [1960s+] (*orig. Can.*) playing around, 'messing about', wasting time.

monkey farting adj. [1960s+] (*orig. Can.*) time-wasting, pointless.

monkey-fuck v. [1990s+] to light one cigarette from the tip of another.

monkey-hangers n. *see* APEHANGERS n.

monkey hop n. *see* MONKEY SHOW n.

monkey house n.[1] [1900s–60s] (*US*) a psychiatric institution. [MONKEY n.[1] (2) + SE *house*]

monkey house n.[2] [1950s] (*US drugs*) an opium den. [MONKEY n.[12] (1) + SE *house*]

monkey iron n. [1950s] (*W.I.*) a sweetmeat made of coconut boiled with sugar. [it is very tough to chew]

monkey jacket n. **1** [late 18C+] a short, close-fitting jacket, worn by either sex. **2** [1940s+] a dinner jacket.

monkey Jesus n. [1940s] (*W.I.*) a very ugly person.

monkey-juice n. [2000s] semen (cf. BABY FLUID n.). [JUICE n.[2] (1)]

monkey jumps n. [1950s] (*drugs*) the staggering and twitching of one who is addicted to narcotics. [MONKEY n.[12] (1) + SE *jumps*]

monkey-lip n. (*also* **monkey-shave**) [1900s] (*Aus.*) a form of beard typically worn by puritans and evangelicals. [note letter from J. Boorer: 'I've seen a pic of a 'monkey beard'. It was typical of, I gather, wowsers and puritans – and looks a little like the beards the Amish wear. Hair grows down sides of face and on and under chin – but no moustache and no hair immediately under lip. A short tuft of about 4cm grows from chin. It makes the face look round and, well, monkeyish']

monkey lotion n. [1990s+] (*W.I.*) acid that is thrown on someone resulting in burns and disfiguration.

monkey man n.[1] **1** [1920s–60s] (*US Black*) a weak man, usu. one dominated by his wife or girlfriend. **2** [1920s–60s] (*US Black*) rarely, a West Indian immigrant. **3** [1980s+] (*W.I.*) a large, unintelligent man.

monkey man n.[2] [1950s] (*N.Z.*) one who provides a mortgage. [MONKEY n.[6]; note Ware: 'Monkey on the house (*Soc.*). Expression current in Cambridgeshire. It means that the owner of the house has raised money on it. The natives also say, "A monkey on the land", the word "monkey" being exactly equivalent to "mortgage"']

monkey meat n.[1] [1910s+] (*orig US milit.*) canned corned beef.

monkey meat n.[2] [1950s–70s] (*drugs*) a heavily intoxicated drug user. [MONKEY n.[12] (1)]

monkey medicine n. [1950s] (*drugs*) morphine (cf. AUNTIE EMMA n.). [MONKEY n.[12] (2) + SE *medicine*]

monkey money n. **1** [1910s–30s] (*US*) any foreign currency. **2** [1930s] (*US tramp*) tokens issued instead of cash to be used in a specific shop. **3** [1940s] (*UK Und.*) counterfeit coins. **4** [1990s+]

(*W.I.*) a small, insignificant sum of money. [MONKEY n.[1] (2) + SE *money*]

monkey-monk n. [late 19C+] (*US*) a superior or important person, whether in fact or through pretension. [HIGH MUCK-A-MUCK n.]

monkey nuts n. [20C+] (*US prison*) prison-cooked meatballs.

monkey on a gridiron n. [late 19C–1910s] a cyclist. [SE *monkey*/MONKEY n.[1] (3) + GRIDIRON n.[3] (3)]

monkey on one's back n.[1] [mid–late 19C] anger or a bad temper. [MONKEY n.[7]; image of the clutching animal]

monkey on one's back n.[2] (*also* **monkey on one's shoulder**) **1** [1930s+] (*orig. US drugs*) drug addiction, esp. to heroin. **2** [1950s+] in fig. use, any form of addiction or long-term problem. [ety. unknown; the image is of a monkey clawing at the sufferer; note Schmidt, *Narcotics Lingo and Lore* (1959): 'in allusion to the once popular carnival and vaudeville monkey-on-the-dog act in which a monkey, riding on a performing dog, held on inseparably to the back of its mount']

monkey parade n. [late 19C–1910s] the evening promenade up and down a main thoroughfare by (Cockney) young people in search of flirtation. [SE *monkey*/MONKEY n.[1] + *parade*]

monkey piss n. [1970s] (*US*) weak beer (cf. BUFFALO PISS n.). [SE *monkey* + PISS n. (1)]

monkey root v. [1980s+] (*Aus. prison*) to light one cigarette from the tip of another. [ROOT v.[3] (1); var. on MONKEY-FUCK v.]

monkey rum n. [1940s–70s] (*US*) West Indian rum. [MONKEY n.[1] (5) + SE *rum*]

monkeys n. *see* MONKEY TRICKS n. (2).

monkey's n. [1960s+] (*orig. US*) a DAMN n.; thus *I don't care a monkey's fuck, I don't give a monkey's ass* etc. [abbr. *monkey's fuck* (*see* NOT GIVE A FUCK v.)]

monkey's allowance n. [late 18C–19C] a minimum of payment and a maximum of harsh treatment. [MONKEY n.[1] (2) + SE *allowance*]

monkey's ass n. [1970s+] (*US*) used in excls. or mild oaths, as in *I'll be a monkey's ass!* [SE *monkey* + ASS n. (2)]

monkey's cousin n. [1940s+] (*bingo*) the number 12 (cf. ALDERSHOT LADIES n.). [rhy. sl. = SE *dozen*]

monkey-shave n. *see* MONKEY-LIP n.

monkey shine n. (*also* **monkey shines**) [early 19C+] (*US*) tricks or antics. [SE *monkey* + SHINES n.]

monkey-shine v. [20C+] (*US*) to misbehave; play tricks. [MONKEY SHINE n.]

monkey shit n. *see* MONKEY FART n.

monkey show n. (*also* **monkey hop**) [1910s–30s] (*US*) a taxi-dance or burlesque show. [MONKEY n.[2] (4)]

monkey's money n. [mid-17C–18C] **1** payment in kind. **2** empty compliments and meaningless courtesies.

monkey spank n. [1990s+] an act of masturbation; lit. and fig. [rhy. sl. = WANK n.[1]; ult. SPANK THE MONKEY v.]

monkey spanker n. [1990s+] a masturbator, a general term of abuse. [rhy. sl. = WANKER n.; ult. SPANK THE MONKEY v.]

monkey spanner n. [2000s] the penis (cf. ANTEATER n.). [MONKEY n.[10] (2)]

monkey's tail n.[1] [early–mid-19C] (*orig. naut.*) a short crowbar. [resemblance]

monkey's tail n.[2] [20C+] usu. in pl., a nail. [rhy. sl.]

monkey stick n. [1940s] a malacca cane, as used by a dandy.

monkeys to junkies n. [1980s] (*US campus*) a course in anthropology. [studying mankind, from its origins as apes to JUNKIE n. (1)]

monkey suit n. [late 19C+] (*orig. US*) **1** a uniform or overalls. **2** (*also* **monkey**) a formal dress suit, evening dress, usu. as worn by a man but occas. by a woman. **3** one who is wearing a uniform, e.g. a cinema usher. [? the image of a dark-furred monkey with a light chest; or one looks like a MONKEY n.[2]]

monkey's wedding n. [1940s+] (*S.Afr.*) a situation of alternating or simultaneous sunshine and rain. [fig. use of *monkey's wedding* (*breakfast*), a presumably chaotic occasion (used as such in parts of US); ? ult. synon. Port. *casamento de rapôsa*, a vixen's wedding]

monkey swill *n.* [1920s–30s] (*US*) cheap liquor, strong liquor. [the illicit liquor manufactured during US Prohibition]

monkey tie *n.* [1940s] (*S.Afr.*) a particularly gaudy tie. [SE *monkey*/MONKEY n.¹ (2) + SE *tie*]

monkey track *n.* [1960s] the scarred veins that are the product of and indicate heroin addiction.

monkey tricks *n.* **1** [18C+] dubious activities. **2** [late 18C+] (*also* **monkeys**) (unwanted) sexual advances. **3** [20C+] any action considered irritating. [negative image of the animal + MONKEY n.¹ (2)]

monkey wagon *n.* [1960s] (*US*) an estate car, a 'family' car. [MONKEY n.¹ (1)]

monkey ward *n.* [1910s+] (*US*) the Montgomery Ward Inc. mail-order company and department store; thus *monkey ward cowboy*, a would-be cowboy, who has the clothes but is otherwise spurious. [US regional use *Monkey Ward*, the Montgomery Ward (mail-order) catalogue]

monkey with *v. see* MONKEY v.

monkey work *n.* [late 19C–1960s] (*US*) trickery, mischief. [var. on MONKEY BUSINESS n.]

monkey-wrencher/-wrenching *n. see* THROW A MONKEY WRENCH INTO THE MACHINERY v.

monkry *n. see* MONKERY n.

monniker *n.* (*also* **monacher, monack, monacker, monaker, monarch, monarcher, monekeer, monekur, monica, monick, monicker, moniker, monoger**) [mid-19C+] (*orig. tramp*) one's name, one's signature; thus [mid–late 19C] *tip someone one's monnicker*, to tell someone one's name; thus an important person. [? SE *monogram* or Ling. Fr.; E.P. suggests fig. use of SE *monarch*, a king, who like a name rules a person's life]

monniker *adj.* [1970s+] (*US*) pertaining to one's name or nickname; 'trademark'. [MONNIKER n.]

monniker *v.* [1920s+] to name. [MONNIKER n.]

mono *n.* **1** [1950s+] *mono*phonic sound. **2** [1960s+] *mono*neucleosis. **3** [1970s+] *mono*chrome colour. [abbr.]

mono *adj.* **1** [1950s+] *mono*phonic. **2** [1970s+] *mono*chrome. [abbr.]

monochrome *adj.* [1990s+] (*US teen*) boring.

monocular eyeglass *n.* [mid–late 19C] the anus.

monoger *n. see* MONNIKER n.

monolithic *adj.* [1960s–70s] highly intoxicated by a drug. [pun on STONED (OUT) adj. (2)]

monosyllable *n.* (*also* **divine monosyllable, venerable...**) [18C–19C] the vagina. [i.e. CUNT n.¹ (1)]

monotony *n.* [1970s+] (*US campus*) one's single, steady girlfriend. [pun on *monogamy*, and its tedium]

mons *n.* [1980s] a blunder. [? abbr. SE *monster*; or ? the WW1 battle of *Mons*]

mons meg *n.* [19C] the vagina. [a play on *Mons Meg*, a 15C cannon kept at Edinburgh Castle; presumably a coarse ref. to its gaping mouth + poss. play on *mons veneris*]

monster *n.¹* **1** [1920s–70s] (*US*) a large and formidable car or plane. **2** [1950s+] (*US*) an outstanding person, thing, achievement or success. **3** [1960s] (*US campus*) a difficult course or examination. **4** [1980s+] (*UK prison*) a sexual offender, a child molester etc. **5** [1990s+] an obsessive, an addict. **6** [2000s] (*US prison*) HIV/AIDS. **7** [2000s] cocaine.

monster *n.²* **1** [1970s+] (*US drugs*) amphetamine (cf. A n.²). **2** [1970s+] (*drugs*) any exceptionally powerful drug. **3** [1990s+] (*US drugs*) Methedrine.

monster *adj.* **1** [1930s+] (*US*) great in size, quantity, significance or achievement. **2** [1950s] (*US Black*) annoying, irritating. **3** [1970s+] (*US Black*) excellent, first-rate, the very best. [MONSTER n.¹]

monster *v.* [1960s+] (*orig. Aus.*) **1** to harass a woman in the hopes of seduction. **2** to attack (verbally rather than physically), to pressurize. [note 1990s+ journ. use, to subject to intense media scrutiny]

monster *sfx* [1980s+] (*US*) used with a relevant n. to denote a person's primary characteristic or passion, e.g. *party monster, munchie monster*. [MONSTER n.¹ (2)]

monstro *adj.* (*also* **monstrous**) [1960s+] (*US*) enormous, outstanding. [abbr. SE *monstrous*]

monstrous *adj.* [late 16C–19C] a general intensifier, e.g. *monstrous fatigue*.

monstrous *adv.* [17C–1940s] a general intensifier, e.g. *monstrous bad*. [20C use is US]

monte *n.¹* **1** [mid-19C+] (*US Und./gambling*) the game of 3-card trick, 'find the lady'. **2** [late 19C+] (*Aus./N.Z.*) (*also* **monty**) an absolute certainty. **3** [1900s] one who plays (1). **4** [1930s] (*Aus.*) a lie. **5** [1980s+] (*N.Z.*) an admirable person. [abbr. THREE-CARD MONTE n.]

monte *n.²* (*also* **monte-man, monty**) [late 19C–1900s] (*Aus.*) a racecourse tipster. [MONTE n.¹ (2)]

monte *n.³* [1970s+] good-quality marijuana from Mexico. [Sp. *monte*, a bush, thus a pun]

monte *n.⁴* [1990s+] a video. [the city *Montevideo*]

monte *n.⁵ see* MONTY n.¹.

Monte Cairo *n.* [2000s] a giro cheque. [rhy. sl.]

monte-man *n.¹* [1900s] (*Aus.*) a confidence trickster. [MONTE n.¹ (1) + SE *man*; however, he does not necessarily practise the 3-card monte swindle]

monte-man *n.² see* MONTE n.³.

Montezuma gold *n.* [1970s] (*US drugs*) good-quality marijuana from Mexico (cf. ACAPULCO (GOLD) n.). [for ety. *see* MONTEZUMA'S REVENGE n.]

montezumas *n.* [20C+] bloomers. [rhy. sl.]

Montezuma's revenge *n.* (*also* **Pharaoh's revenge**) [1960s+] (*orig. US*) food poisoning, esp. with diarrhoea, suffered by tourists in Mexico or Egypt (cf. AZTEC HOP n.). [named after the last Aztec emperor, *Montezuma II* (*c.*1470–1520)]

monthlies *n.* (*also* **monthly**) [late 19C+] the menstrual period.

monthly bill *n.* (*also* **monthly dues/pain**) [20C+] (*US*) menstruation.

month of Sundays, a *n.* (*also* **a passel of Sundays, a week..., a year...**) [early 19C+] a very long time, thus phr. *once in a month of Sundays*.

Monto *n.* [late 19C–1960s] (*Anglo-Irish*) the run-down, lowlife area surrounding Montgomery Street, Dublin. [abbr.]

montra *n.* [early 19C] (*UK Und.*) a watch. [Fr. *montre*, a watch]

monty *see also under* MONTE.

monty *n.* (*also* **full monte/monty, monte**) [late 19C+] everything, all that there is, 'the lot'; esp. as *the full monty*. [ety. unknown; the success of the 1997 film *The Full Monty* hugely popularized the phr. and a variety of etys. for *monty/monte* were proposed, although none has been accepted as the last word; they range from *monte*, a Sp. and US Hisp. game of chance, played with a pack of 45 cards; the tailor's *Montague* Burton, i.e. a full 3-piece suit; the 'full English breakfast' purportedly enjoyed by Field Marshall *Montgomery*, during WWII; the gambling town of *Monte* Carlo, in which the *full monte* would equate with 'breaking the bank'; and several more]

monz *n.* [1990s+] (*UK juv.*) a social reject. [? SE *monster*]

moo *n.¹* [late 19C+] a woman, esp. a foolish one; often as *silly old moo*. [SE *moo*, the noise of a cow; strengthened by abbr. MOO-COW n. (1)]

moo *n.²* (*US*) **1** [1910s–20s] a beefsteak. **2** [1940s+] milk or cream. [products of the MOO-COW n.]

moo *n.³* [1940s–50s] (*US*) money. [abbr. MOOLA n.]

moo *n.⁴ see* MOO-COW n.

mooca n. (*also* **moocah**) [1930s+] (*drugs*) marijuana. [? initial letter]

mooch n.[1] [mid-19C–1940s] **1** a street thief who specializes in snatching (drunken) men's jewellery. **2** the act of such a robbery.

mooch n.[2] (*also* **mouch**) (*orig. US*) **1** [late 19C–1900s] a departure or dismissal. **2** [late 19C+] a wander, a saunter. [MOOCH v.[1] (2); note blurb by Edison Company for the song 'Mootching Along' by Collins & Harlan (1914): 'For a long time, way back in the days before the [first world] war, negroes did a shuffling or lazy man's dance [...] They called it The Mootch. The shuffle explains the movement of the feet, and the "mootch" defines the lazy movement of the shoulders, and the sway and rhythm of the body']

mooch n.[3] [20C+] (*US*) a bad mood; thus *moochy*, tetchy.

mooch n.[4] **1** [1910s+] a sponger, a borrower, a beggar, an idler. **2** [1920s+] (*US gambling*) a gullible or naïve person. **3** [1940s–70s] (*drugs*) a drug addict. **4** [1950s+] a general term of abuse. [MOOCH v.[1]]

mooch n.[5] [1940s–50s] (*US drugs*) a drug, usu. heroin or opium; thus KICK THE MOOCH AROUND v.; ON THE MOOCH phr. (6). [MOOCH n.[4] (3)]

mooch n.[6] [1950s] a problem, a difficult situation.

mooch v.[1] (*also* **mouch**) **1** [early 19C+] (*also* **mootch**) to pilfer, to steal. **2** [mid-19C+] (*also* **moose**) to walk, to go, to amble along. **3** [mid-19C+] to beg, to sponge, to cadge. **4** [late 19C+] to loaf around. **5** [late 19C+] (*UK tramp*) to live as a tramp. **6** [20C+] (*Ulster*) to play truant; esp. as ON THE MOOCH phr. (5). **7** [1910s+] to take. [? OF *muchier*, to hide or skulk; (1) note Nares: '†*To* MOOTCH. To steal?']

mooch v.[2] [1960s+] (*US*) to kiss. [SMOOCH v.[1] (1)]

moocher n. (*also* **moucher**) **1** [mid-19C+] a beggar. **2** [mid-19C+] a loafer, a loiterer. **3** [mid-19C+] (*US*) a petty thief. **4** [1940s–50s] (*drugs*) a drug addict. **5** [1950s] a gangster. [MOOCH v.[1]]

Moocheries n. see MUCKERIES n.

moocher's mile n. [1930s–40s] the stretch of Piccadilly (in London) that runs east across the Circus and onto Leicester Square. [MOOCHER n. (2) + SE *mile*]

mooch in v. [1910s+] (*US*) to enter surreptitiously. [MOOCH v.[1] (2)]

mooching adj. [mid-19C+] idling, loafing. [MOOCH v.[1] (4)]

mooch off v. [1920s+] (*US*) to laze around. [MOOCH v.[1] (4)]

moo-cow n. (*also* **moo**, **moo-moo**) **1** [early 19C+] (*UK juv.*) a cow. **2** [1990s+] (*US campus*) an obese person.

moodies n. [1960s] depression.

moody n. **1** [1930s+] gentle persuasion, 'blarney'. **2** [1950s+] complaints, ill temper, depression. **3** [1950s+] deceit, lies, verbal trickery. **4** [1960s+] a fit of 'the sulks'; thus *pull/throw a/the moody*, to sulk. [(3) rhy. sl. *Moody & Sankey* = HANKYPANKY n. (1); ult. the US evangelists Dwight Lyman *Moody* (1837–99) and Ivo David *Sankey* (1840–1908)]

moody adj. [1950s+] illicit, untrustworthy, false. [MOODY n. (3)]

moody v. [1950s+] **1** to trick, to defraud, to play a confidence trick. **2** to complain. **3** to lie about, to act lazily. **4** to pretend. [MOODY n. (3)]

mooe/mooey n. see MOEY n.

mooer n. [19C] a cow. [SE *moo* + sfx *-er*]

mooey-mooey n. [mid-19C–1950s] romantic behaviour, flirting. [? SE *moue*, a pout]

moofky-poofky/moofty-poofty n. see MIFKY-PIFKY n.

moofty-poofty n. [1990s+] oral intercourse, whether fellatio or cunnilingus. [? MUFF n.[1] (1) + POOF n.]

mooi adj. [early 19C+] (*S.Afr.*) a general term of approval meaning pleasant, pretty good, nice. [Du. *mooi*, pretty. Note milit. jargon *mooi-moois*, full dress or 'step-out' uniform (lit. 'pretty-pretties')]

moojin n. [20C+] (*W.I.*) a fool, a simpleton. [? MOOCH n.[4]]

moo juice n. [1930s+] (*orig. US Black*) milk. [MOO-COW n. + SE *juice*]

mook n. [1930s+] (*US*) a general term of abuse, a foolish person. [? JAMOKE n.[2]]

moola n. (*also* **mola**, **moolah**, **mulla**) [1930s+] (*orig. US*) money. [ety. unknown]

mooley n. [2000s] (*US Black*) a mulatto. [abbr.]

moolie n. [1960s+] (*US*) **1** a country person. **2** a Black person. [? SE *muleskinner*]

moo-moo n.[1] [20C+] (*W.I.*) **1** an extremely shy person, too nervous to speak out. **2** a fool, a simpleton. [? Twi *e-mumu*, a person who is deaf and dumb]

moo-moo n.[2] see MOO-COW n.

moon n.[1] **1** [mid-18C; late 19C+] the buttocks, the anus, the rectum; thus FULL MOON n.[1]. **2** [1960s+] (*also* **moonie**, **moony**) the purposeful exposure of the buttocks in a provocative way.

moon n.[2] **1** [early 19C+] a month's imprisonment, or multiples thereof, e.g. *nine moon*. **2** [early 19C+] a month. **3** [late 19C–1930s] (*US tramp*) a night; thus phr. *cover with the moon*, sleep in the open air.

moon n.[3] **1** [mid–late 19C] a large, round biscuit. **2** [1910s+] a silver dollar.

moon n.[4] (*also* **moony**) [1920s+] (*US*) illicitly distilled liquor. [abbr. MOONSHINE n.]

moon n.[5] (*also* **full moon**) [1960s+] (*drugs*) a piece of peyote cactus, eaten for the mescaline it contains. [? its half-moon shape]

moon v.[1] (*also* **moon about**, **...along**, **...around**) [mid-19C+] **1** to wander around (wretchedly) lost in thought, esp. when a victim of unrequited passion. **2** to lose oneself in thought. **3** to talk nonsensically.

moon v.[2] [late 19C–1930s] (*US*) to have anal intercourse with (cf. ASK FOR THE RING v.). **2** [1960s+] (*orig. US*) to drop one's trousers and underpants and present one's bare buttocks to onlookers, often performed through a car window. [MOON n.[1]]

moon away v. [late 19C+] to lounge, to loiter, to waste time. [MOON v.[1] (1)]

moon cricket n. [20C+] (*US*) a Black person. [ety. unknown; ? a cricket that emerges at night will appear to be black]

moon-curser n. [late 17C–mid-19C] (*UK Und.*) a link-boy who either robs those for whom he provides a light, or who guides his charges towards some villainous confederates who do the job for him. [dial. *moon-curser*, a ship-wrecker. Urban *moon-cursers* specialized in working the area near Lincoln's Inn Fields in London]

moondoggle n. see BOONDOGGLE n.

mooner n. [1950s+] (*US Und.*) a pathological lawbreaker. [presumably f. the effect of the moon on the mind, or due to the effects of a full moon, during which time the crime rate supposedly increases]

mooney adj. see MOONY adj.

moon-eyed adj. [18C+] (*US*) drunk (cf. ARSEHOLED adj.). [the drunkard's seeing double, and thus 2 moons]

moon-eyed hen n. [late 18C–early 19C] 'a squinting wench' (Grose, 1785). [SE *moon-eyed*, squinting, orig. used of horses]

mooney's apron n. [20C+] (*Ulster*) in cards, the 10 of clubs.

moon-face n. [late 19C+] (*US*) an Asian person; thus *moon-faced*, having Japanese or Asian features (cf. BROWNIE n.[2]).

moonfeed n. [1980s] (*drugs*) heroin.

moon-glow n. [1950s] (*W.I.*) a light-brown complexion.

Moonie n. [1970s+] (*orig. US*) a member of the Unification Church (the Holy Spirit Association for the Unification of World Christianity). [its founder the Rev. Sun Myung *Moon* (b.1920). Founded in 1954 in Korea and now a world-wide religious/ political movement, the Church is generally seen, other than by its adherents, as a right-wing, brainwashing cult]

moonie n. see MOON n.[1] (2).

moon juice n. [1970s+] **1** (*US drugs*) cough syrup laced with amphetamine. **2** (*drugs*) heroin.

moonlight n. [19C] smuggled spirits. [var. on MOONSHINE n.]

moonlight *v.* **1** [late 19C–1940s] (*UK Und.*) to engage in criminal activity at night. **2** [1950s–60s] (*Irish*) to steal cattle. **3** [1950s+] (*orig. US*) to work at 2 jobs in order to boost one's income. The second job is usu. night work, and the other employer may not know about it. [to operate by SE *moonlight*]

moonlighter *n.* **1** [late 19C–1960s] (*UK Und.*) a thief or burglar who operates at night; (*Irish*) usu. a cattle thief. **2** [20C+] one who escapes paying the rent by leaving a house late at night. **3** [1920s–40s] a smuggler of illicitly distilled liquor. **4** [1950s+] one who takes a second job, undeclared for tax purposes. **5** [1960s] (*US teen*) one who betrays their regular partner. **6** [1970s+] (*US Black*) a prostitute (cf. DEADLY NIGHTSHADE n.). [MOONLIGHT v.]

moonlight flit *n.* (*also* **flit**) [late 19C+] the removal of one's household goods, and with them oneself, late at night in order to escape paying one's rent; usu. in phr. *do a (moonlight) flit.* [abbr. 18C MOONLIGHT FLITTING n.]

moonlight flits *n.* [1990s+] the female breasts (cf. BRACE AND BITS n.). [rhy. sl. = TIT n.³ (1); ult. MOONLIGHT FLIT n.]

moonlight flitting *n.* [early 18C–mid-19C] leaving a house late at night to avoid paying the rent. [earlier version of MOONLIGHT FLIT n.]

moonlighting *n.* [1950s+] taking a second, usu. late-night, job in addition to one's daily employment. [MOONLIGHT v. (3)]

moonlight-pon-tick *n.* [1940s+] (*W.I.*) a gas lamp. [lit. 'moonlight on a stick']

moonlights *n.* [1900s–10s] (*US*) evening dress. [one wears such clothing at night]

moonlight wanderer *n.* [early 19C] a tenant who cheats the landlord by leaving lodgings late at night, usu. with their household possessions.

moonman *n.* (*also* **moon's man**) [17C–early 19C] a gypsy. ['A moon-man signifies in English a madman [...] But these moon-men [...] are neither absolutely mad, nor yet perfectly in their wits. Their name they borrow from the moon, because, as the moon is never in one shape two nights together, but wanders up and down Heaven like an antic, so these changeable-stuff-companions never tarry one day in a place' (Dekker, *The Gull's Hornbook*, 1609); this discussion of England's gypsies is the first ever to be printed]

moon pie *n.* [1970s+] (*US*) anal intercourse. [MOON n.¹ (1) + fig. use of PIE n.¹ (1)]

moon-raker *n.* **1** [late 18C–19C] a native of Wiltshire. **2** [19C] a smuggler. ['It is said that some men of that county, seeing the reflection of the moon in a pond, endeavoured to pull it out with a rake' (Grose, 1796). However, the *OED* notes, 'in Wiltshire a more complimentary turn is given to the story: the men were caught raking a pond for kegs of smuggled brandy, and put off the revenue men by pretending folly']

moon-raking *n.* [19C] smuggling. [MOON-RAKER n. (2)]

moon rock *n.* [1980s+] (*drugs*) a mixture of crack cocaine and heroin. [ROCK n.³ (4)]

moonshi *n.* [mid-19C] (*Anglo-Ind.*) a sage, a wise man, a teacher. [Hind. *munshi*, a writer or secretary. The term was first used by the English to describe those who taught them Hindustani]

moonshine *n.* **1** [mid-17C+] nonsense, a trifle, nothing at all; often ext. as *moonshine in the mustard pot*; thus *give someone a mouthful of moonshine*, to flatter. **2** [late 18C+] illicitly distilled or contraband liquor. **3** [20C+] adulterated liquor. [the nocturnal activities of the distillers or smugglers who would explain away their boxes and barrels as 'mere moonshine'. *Moonshine* had different meanings according to the county, in Sussex and Kent it referred to white brandy, in Yorks. to gin]

moonshine *adj.* [late 18C+] usu. of liquor, illicitly distilled. [MOONSHINE n. (2)]

moonshine *v.* [mid-19C+] (*US*) to distil illicit liquor, usu. bourbon. [MOONSHINE n. (2)]

moonshine darlin' *n.* [1950s] (*W.I.*) a party to which anyone

can come as long as they contribute food or drink; it is held outdoors under the light of the moon.

moonshiner *n.* [mid-19C+] (*orig. US*) a distiller of contraband liquor, usu. whisky. [MOONSHINE v.]

moon-shooter *n. see* SHOOT THE MOON v.¹.

moon's man *n. see* MOONMAN n.

moon stick *n.* [2000s] (*US Black*) a White man's penis (cf. BAT n.⁷). [SE *moon*, i.e. the colour + STICK n.¹ (1)]

moontan *n.* [1940s+] (*US*) sexual activity at night, out-of-doors. [pun on SE *suntan*]

moontan *v.* [1940s+] (*US*) to indulge in sexual activity at night, out-of-doors. [MOONTAN n.]

moony *n.*¹ [mid-19C] a fool. [MOONY adj.]

moony *n.*² *see* MOON n.¹ (2).

moony *n.*³ *see* MOON n.⁴.

moony *adj.* (*also* **mooney**) **1** [mid-19C] melancholy. **2** [mid-19C–1930s] drunk (cf. ADDLED adj.). **3** [mid-19C+] sentimentally romantic. **4** [1930s] (*Aus.*) idiotic. **5** [1950s] (*US*) drug-crazed. [the supposed effect of the (full) moon on one's brain]

moony cove *n.* [late 19C–1900s] an eccentric person. [MOONY adj. + COVE n. (1)]

Moor, the *n.* [20C+] (*UK Und.*) Dartmoor prison in west Devon (cf. ABBOTT'S PRIORY n.). [abbr.]

Moorgate rattler *n.* [late 19C–1900s] (*East London*) a dandified person. [play on dial. *Morgan rattler*, a reckless fighter, anyone or anything exceptional or MORGAN RATTLER n. (1). Moorgate is an area in the City of London]

moose *n.*¹ (*also* **bull moose, regular moose**) (*orig. Can.*) **1** [20C+] a large, powerful, poss. clumsy man. **2** [1970s+] an object that is large and difficult to handle.

moose *n.*² (*US*) **1** [1940s+] a little sister or young girl. **2** [1940s+] a girlfriend. **3** [1950s+] a young Japanese or Korean woman, esp. a prostitute, or the wife or mistress of a serviceman stationed in Japan or Korea. [Jap. *musume*, daughter, girl]

moose *n.*³ [1990s+] an unattractive woman.

moose *v. see* MOOCH v.¹ (2).

moose-face *n.* [mid-19C–1940s] (*US*) an ugly person.

moose-fucker *n.* [1990s+] a derog. term for a resident of Canada. [SE *moose* + FUCK v.¹]

moose milk *n.* [1920s+] (*Can.*) some form of home-brewed alcohol concocted on the Yukon, e.g. milk and rum mixed.

moosey *n.* [1920s–50s] (*US*) the vagina. [? dial. *moosie/mosey*, soft, over-ripe; or covered with soft hair]

moosey-faced *adj.* [1990s+] a general term of abuse, lit. 'vagina-faced'. [MOOSEY n.]

moosh *see under* MUSH.

mooshay *n.* [20C+] (*W.I.*) a poor White, a descendant of the original Fr. settlers on St Kitts. [Fr. *monsieur*]

mooshe-man *n.* (*also* **mushe-man**) [1940s+] (*W.I.*) a confidence trickster, a hoaxer. [MUSHE n. + SE *man*; the poor image of Middle Eastern immigrants]

moota *n.* (*also* **mootah, mooter, mootie, mootos, muta, mutah**) [1930s+] (*drugs*) marijuana. [Sp. *mota*, a clod of turf, a handful of earth, thus the link to GRASS n.⁵; note also weaving jargon *mota*, an imperfection or tangle in wool or cotton, thus the link to a 'tangled' mind]

mootch *v. see* MOOCH v.¹ (1).

Mop *n.* [1920s–30s] (*US tramp*) the Missouri Pacific Railroad. [abbr.]

mop *n.*¹ **1** [early 19C+] the hair of the head. **2** [1940s] (*US*) pubic hair, of either sex. **3** [1940s] (*US Black*) a beard. **4** [1950s–70s] (*US Black*) hair that has been straightened.

mop *n.*² [mid-19C–1910s] **1** a drinking bout, a drunken spree; usu. as *on the mop*. **2** a drunkard. [SE *mop up* (liquor)]

mop *v.* **1** [late 19C+] usu. in passive, to defeat; thus *mopped out*, ruined. **2** [1950s] (*W.I./UK Black*) to beg, to ask for. **3** [1970s+] (*US gay*) to steal, esp. to shoplift. [SE *mop up*]

mop! *excl.* [1940s+] (*orig. US*) a word used to indicate a sudden occurrence, e.g. *I'm doing this, then mop! I'm doing that.* [jazz use *mop*, the last beat at the end of a jazz number with a cadence of triplets]

mop and bucket! *excl.* [20C+] an excl. of annoyance or pain. [rhy. sl.; euph. for FUCK IT! excl.]

mop and pail *n. see* BUCKET AND PAIL *n.*

mop ass *v.* [1990s+] (*US*) to win conclusively. [MOP v. (1) + ASS n. (2)]

mop down *v.* [20C+] to empty a glass.

mope *n.*[1] **1** [mid-16C+] a dim-witted, dreamy or miserable person. **2** [20C+] (*Irish*) a general term of contempt. [SE *mope* v.]

mope *n.*[2] [1910s–70s] (*US prison*) a stealthy departure; thus COP A MOPE *v.* [MOPE v. (3)]

mope *v.* **1** [mid-19C+] (*also* **mope up**) to exist. **2** [late 19C–1960s] (*orig. US*) to walk or move slowly. **3** [late 19C–1970s] to desert or escape. **4** [1930s–40s] (*US Und.*) to live as a vagrant; thus *on the mope*, living as a tramp; *moper/moping artist*, a tramp; *mopery*, tramping.

mopelize *v. see* MOBILIZE v.[1].

mopery *n.* **1** [20C+] (*US Und./police*) stupidity or ineptitude. **2** [20C+] (*US Und./police*) a trivial or minor offence, often used ironically, as in a charge of *mopery and dopery*. **3** [1970s] a second-rate figure. [SE *mope*]

mopes *n.* [early 19C–1950s] a feeling of unhappiness; thus *in the mopes*, *moped*, feeling miserable, 'down in the dumps'. [SE *mope*; subseq. use is SE]

mope up *v. see* MOPE v. (1).

mopey *n. see* DOPEY n.[3].

mopey as a wet hen *phr.* [20C+] (*Aus./N.Z.*) miserable, gloomy.

moph *n. see* MOFF n.

mopoke *n.* (*also* **morepork**) [mid-19C+] (*Aus.*) a fool. [SE *mope hawk* or *mopoke*, the tawny frogmouth, a species of owl. Its song sounds like 'more pork, more pork']

mopolize *v. see* MOBILIZE v.[1].

mopped *adj. see* MOPPY adj.[2].

mopped out *adj. see* MOP v. (1).

mopped up *adj. see* MOP UP v. (1).

mopper-up *n.* [1910s–30s] (*Aus.*) a drunkard. [they 'mop up' liquor]

moppery *n.* [early–mid-19C] the head. [MOP n.[1] (1)]

moppus *n. see* MOPUS n.

moppy *adj.*[1] [early 19C] depressed. [SE *mopey*]

moppy *adj.*[2] (*also* **mopped**) [early 19C–1940s] drunk. [MOP UP v.]

mops and brooms *phr.* (*also* **all mops and brooms**) [19C–1930s] drunk. [? the old mop fairs, annual fairs held in the UK West Country, at which servants put themselves up for hire; a young woman would carry a *mop* or *broom* to indicate the job she desired. Such fairs were accompanied by much drinking]

mopsey *n. see* MOPSY n.

mop-squeezer *n.* **1** [late 18C–early 19C] a maidservant. **2** [1940s–60s] (*US*) a queen in poker. [(2) joc. use of (1)]

mopstick *n.* **1** [late 19C] a fool (cf. DIPSTICK n.). **2** [late 19C] a thin, scrawny person. **3** [late 19C–1930s] one who loafs around a cheap saloon and cleans up the place in return for drinks. [SE *mopstick*, a mop-handle]

mopsy *n.* (*also* **mopsey**) [mid-17C–19C; 1940s] a homely woman, usu. used affectionately. [SE *mopsy*, a general term of endearment, ult. *mop*, abbr. *moppet*, an affectionate term for a baby]

mopsy *adj.* [late 19C] drunk. [MOP UP v.]

mop the floor with *v.* [late 19C+] (*orig. US*) to beat, to thrash, to surpass completely.

mop up *v.* **1** [early 19C+] to eat greedily, to drink, to empty one's glass; thus *mopped up*, drunk. **2** [mid-19C+] to absorb, to appropriate, to defeat or win. **3** [late 19C+] (*orig. milit.*) to carry out conclusively, esp. of a gangland or military shooting.

4 [1910s–20s] to believe, to acknowledge. **5** [1930s+] to make a good deal of money.

mopus *n.* (*also* **moppus**) **1** [late 17C] a farthing. **2** [late 17C–mid-19C] a halfpenny. **3** [late 18C–1900s] usu. in pl., money in general; thus *touch the mopusses*, to win money at gambling. [? surname of Sir Giles *Mompesson*, a notoriously corrupt merchant of the reign of King James I (according to B.E.)]

moragrifa *n.* (*also* **mor a grifa**) [1960s+] (*drugs*) marijuana. [? Sp.; ult. GREEFO n.]

moral *n.* [mid-19C+] (*mainly Aus.*) a certainty; usu. in phr. *it's a moral*; thus *to a moral*, perfectly. [SE *moral certainty*]

moral *adj.* [1900s] certain, definite. [MORAL n.]

moral Cremorne *n.* [late 19C] (*UK society*) the Fisheries Exhibition of 1883. [this otherwise staid exhibition was nonetheless illuminated in the evenings, bringing to mind the original *Cremorne*, the notably immoral Chelsea 'pleasure garden']

more arse than a paddock-full of cows *phr.* [1990s+] (*Aus.*) a phr. used of one who is very cheeky. [punning on ARSE n.[2] (1)/ARSE n.[1] (1)]

more arse than Jessie *phr. see* MORE HIDE THAN JESSIE phr.

more ass than a toilet seat *phr.* (*also* **more arse than a toilet seat**) [1940s+] (*orig. US*) of a man, having an active sex life or conspicuous sexual prowess; usu. as *he gets...* or *he has...*

more butt than ashtrays *phr. see* GET MORE BUTT THAN ASHTRAYS v.

more curtains! *excl.* [1910s–40s] (*Cockney*) a joc. excl. used by women to tease anyone passing by in an evening dress.

more front than Brighton (beach) *phr.* [1930s+] a phr. used of one who is very cheeky, daring or outspoken. [pun on SE (*sea-*) *front*/FRONT n.[1] (1)]

more front than Buckingham Palace *phr.* [1980s+] a phr. used of one who is very cheeky, daring or outspoken. [pun on SE *front*/FRONT n.[1] (1)]

more front than Harrods *phr.* [1970s+] a phr. used of one who is very cheeky, daring or outspoken. [pun on SE *front* (of *Harrods*, a very large London department store)/FRONT n.[1] (1)]

more front than Myers *phr.* (*also* **more front than Foy and Gibson's**) [1950s+] (*Aus.*) a phr. used of one who is very cheeky, daring or outspoken. [pun on SE *front* (of the large department stores in Melbourne and Adelaide)/FRONT n.[1] (1)]

more F than R *phr. see* MORE R THAN F phr.

more guts than a Bedford truck *phr.* [1990s+] (*Aus.*) used of a brave and admirable individual.

more guts than brains *phr.* [late 18C–early 19C] a phr. said of someone who is foolish but determined in their stupidity.

more hair on your chest *phr.* [20C+] (*Aus.*) a general phr. of approval, acclamation, good for you, well done etc. [a cliché of masculinity]

more hide than Jessie *phr.* (*also* **more arse than Jessie**) [1950s+] (*Aus.*) a phr. used of one who is very cheeky. [HIDE n.[3]/ARSE n.[2] (1) + a favourite elephant *Jessie* (1872–1939), which could be visited at the Taronga Park Zoo]

moreish *adj.* (*also* **morish**) [early 18C+] of drink or food, making one desire some more.

more kicks than ha'pence *phr.* (*also* **more kicks than coppers**) [19C] used to describe any situation that yields more trouble than it is worth. [SE in 20C+]

more like *phr.* [20C+] nearer (a specified number or quantity).

moreno *n.* [1960s+] (*US*) a Black person. [Sp. *moreno*, dark-skinned]

more or less *n.* [20C+] a dress. [rhy. sl.]

morepork *n. see* MOPOKE n.

more power to your elbow! *excl.* [mid-19C+] a generally encouraging excl. [the augmented elbow would doubtless be used for bending (cf. BEND ONE'S ELBOW v.)]

more pricks than a second-hand dartboard *phr.* (*also* **more pricks than a pin-cushion, ...a second-hand primus**)

[1940s+] used of a promiscuous woman; usu. *she's had more pricks than…*

more R than F *phr.* (*also* **more F than R**) [mid-19C–1900s] *more rogue than fool*; orig. and usu. of a servant. [abbr.]

more — than you can shake a stick at *phr.* [early 19C+] (*orig. US*) beyond number, impossible to count.

more — than you could poke a stick at *phr.* [1940s+] (*Aus.*) a very large amount.

more time *phr.* [1950s+] (*W.I. Rasta*) see you later.

Moreton (Bay) *n.* (*also* **Morton**) **1** [1950s+] (*Aus. Und.*) an informer. **2** [1970s+] (*Aus.*) a busybody. [rhy. sl.; *Moreton Bay fig* = (1) FIZGIG n.[2]; (2) GIG n.[8] (4); f. the species of fig that grows at Moreton Bay, sited at the mouth of the Brisbane River, Queensland and orig. named Morton by its discoverer Captain Cook, after James Douglas, Earl of Morton FRS (1702–68). Between 1824–39 Moreton Bay was the name of the penal settlement there, and the name of the whole area before Queensland was officially separated from New South Wales in 1859]

more war! *excl.* [late 19C–1900s] (*Cockney*) used to comment on a street fight, esp. between women. [the war in question was the contemporary Spanish-American war of 1898]

more wrinkles than inches *phr.* [20C+] (*orig. RN*) very cold. [the ref. is to the penis, which shrinks when chilly]

morf *n.* (*also* **morph, morpho**) [20C+] (*drugs*) **1** *morph*ine. **2** a *morph*ine user. [abbr.]

morganize *v.* [mid-19C] (*US*) to abduct. [one William Morgan, abducted and presumably murdered in 1826]

morgan rattler *n.* **1** [late 18C] a penis. **2** [1900s] a weighted stick used as a weapon, with a knob of lead at one or both ends, often used by garrotters. [(2) earlier use in dial. but ety. unknown; ? anecdotal. Unlike the rigid policeman's truncheon, it was made of a flexible material; ? (1) f. (2)]

morgue *n.* [late 19C–1900s] (*US*) a particularly unappealing bar or saloon. [the quality of the liquor on offer. Such drinks, often adulterated with chemicals to increase their potency, could damage the brain or even kill the drinker]

moriarty *n.* [20C+] a party. [rhy. sl.]

morish *adj. see* MOREISH adj.

mork *n.* [late 19C–1900s] a policeman. [Rom. *mooshkeroo*, a constable]

morley *n. see* MAULEY n.

Mormon *n.* [late 19C–1920s] (*US*) a promiscuous man. [the polygamy performed by 19C Mormons]

Mormon candy *n.* (*also* **Mormon currency**) [1930s–40s] (*US*) carrots. [the sect's innate Puritanism]

Mormon dinner *n.* [1930s–40s] (*US*) a meal that consists mainly of potatoes.

Mormon poison *n.* [1980s] (*US*) coffee. [the Mormon prohibition of any beverages containing caffeine]

Mormon rain *n.* (*also* **Mormon rainstorm**) [1930s+] (*US*) a dust storm. [the climate of Utah, the home of Mormonism]

morner *n.* [1970s+] (*US gay*) sexual intercourse in the morning.

morning *n.* **1** [early 19C–1930s] a morning drink. **2** [late 19C+] a *morning* newspaper. [abbr.]

morning after (the night before) *n.* (*also* **next morning feeling**) [late 19C+] the state of being hungover after an excess of alcohol.

morning drop *n.* [19C] the gallows; a hanging. [pun on SE *drop*, a popular form of medicine + *drop*, the fall through the gallows' trapdoor]

morning glory *n.* **1** [1900s–80s] (*US*) something which or someone who fails to maintain an early promise, esp. in sporting contexts. **2** [1950s] (*US drugs*) the first narcotic injection of the day. **3** [1970s+] (*Aus.*) sexual intercourse before one gets up in the morning. **4** [1990s+] an erection on waking. [puns on SE *morning glory*, the plant *Ipomoea purpurea*]

morning mick *n.* [20C+] (*Ulster Protestant*) the *Irish News*, published in Belfast with a definite Catholic/nationalist slant. [SE *morning* + MICK n.[1] (2)]

morning pride *n. see* PRIDE OF THE MORNING n.

morning shot *n.* (*US drugs*) **1** [1960s] a narcotics user's first injection of the day. **2** [2000s] any form of stimulant or amphetamine (cf. A n.[2]). [SHOT n.[6] (2)]

Morningside speed *n.* [1990s+] (*Scot. drugs*) cocaine (cf. ANDES CANDY n.). [the socially select area of Morningside, Edinburgh]

morning sneak *n.* [early 18C–mid-19C] (*UK Und.*) one who specializes in thieving early in the morning; thus the act of doing so. [SE *morning* + SNEAK n.[1] (2)]

morning wake-up *n.* [1980s+] (*drugs*) the first blast of crack cocaine from the pipe. [SE *morning* + WAKE-UP n.[3] (2)]

morning wood *n.* [1990s+] (*US*) an erection of the penis first thing in the morning (cf. BAT n.[7]). [SE *morning* + WOOD n.[4] (2)]

morocco man *n.* [late 18C–mid-19C] 'Morocco Men, who go about from house to house among their former customers, and attend in the back parlours of Public Houses, where they are met by customers who make insurances' (Patrick Colquhoun, *A Treatise on the Police of the Metropolis*, 1796).

moron *n.* [1920s+] (*orig. US*) a stupid or slow-witted person, a fool. [SE *moron* (f. Gk *moros*, stupid), defined in 1910 by the American Association for the Study of the Feeble-minded as an adult person having a mental age of between 8 and 12]

morotgara *n.* (*also* **murotugora**) [1970s+] (*drugs*) heroin. [ety. unknown]

morph/morpho *n. see* MORF n.

morphodite *n.* (*also* **morph, morphodyke, morphodyte**) **1** [18C+] a hermaphrodite. **2** [1920s+] a male homosexual. [popular mispron. of SE *hermaphrodite*]

morrice *v. see* MORRIS v.

morrie *n.*[1] [1960s] a sharp, young person, who has their eye on the main chance and is willing to take risks to achieve what they want. [ety. unknown; ? a nonce-creation by Cook, in *The Crust on its Uppers* (1962), who defines it as a 'reverse of Slag' and *slag* as 'young third-rate grafters, male or female, unwashed, useless']

morrie *n.*[2] [1970s] (*Aus.*) a male homosexual (cf. ABIGAIL n.). [? abbr. proper name *Maurice*; note E.M. Forster's eponymous book]

morris *v.* (*also* **morrice**) **1** [early 18C–early 19C] to be hanged. **2** [early 18C–mid-19C] to dance. **3** [mid-18C] (*UK Und.*) to sell or lose. **4** [mid-18C–19C] to leave; esp. as *come morris*, *morris off*, *do a morris*. **5** [19C] to move quickly. [the movements of the *Morris* dance]

morris minor *n.* [1950s+] a black eye. [rhy. sl. = SHINER n.[1] (6); ult. the car, first launched in 1948 in UK]

morry *n.* [1970s] a post mortem. [abbr.]

mort *n.* (*also* **maut**) [mid-16C–1930s] a woman, esp. a prostitute (cf. CANTING CREW n.). [ety. unknown; ? Irish *Mór te*, fiery passion, high spirits, warm affection; note SE *mort*, a salmon in its third year, i.e. the popular equation of women with FISH n.[1]; Ribton-Turner (1887) suggests Welsh *modryb*, a matron, *morwyn*, a virgin]

mortal *n.* [late 19C] (*US*) a certainty.

mortal *adj.*[1] (*also* **mortial**) **1** [early 17C–1900s] a general intensifier, e.g. *all my mortal days*. **2** [late 17C+] extreme, great. **3** [early 19C–1910s] long and tedious.

mortal *adj.*[2] [early 19C+] drunk (cf. ANNIHILATED adj.).

mortal *adv.* (*also* **mortally, mortial**) [15C+] extremely, excessively, e.g. *mortal cold*, *mortal drunk*.

mortaller *n.* [20C+] (*Irish*) a mortal sin, as set down by Roman Catholicism.

mortallious *adj.* [19C] very drunk (cf. ANNIHILATED adj.). [MORTAL adj.[2] + sfx -*ious*]

mortal lock *n.* [1950s+] (*US, orig. gambling*) a certainty, a cinch, esp. of a racehorse, a race or a winning hand in cards. [MORTAL adj.[1] (2) + LOCK n.[2] (5)]

mortally *adv. see* MORTAL adv.

mortar *n.* [18C–19C] the vagina.

mort dell *n.* [late 16C–19C] an unmarried woman or virgin girl who accompanies a mendicant villain.

mortgage alley *n.* (*also* **mortage flat**, **...heights**, **...hill**, **...hollow**, **...knob**, **...lane**, **...manor**, **...mesa**, **...row**) [1960s+] (*US*) the prosperous part of a town or city.

mortgage deed *n.* [mid-19C] a pawnbroker's ticket.

mortial *see under* MORTAL.

Morton *n. see* MORETON (BAY) *n.*

mort wap-apace *n.* [17C–early 19C] (*UK Und.*) an experienced prostitute or sexually active woman. [MORT *n.* + WAP *v.* and SE *apace* according to B.E.; but note Dekker, *O Per Se Ol* (1612), the source of much of B.E., suggests that the phr. was a one-off, noting that 'there was an abram, who called his mort Madam Wap-apace']

m.o.s. *n.* [1980s+] (*US campus*) member of the opposite sex. [abbr.]

moschineer *n. see* MOSKENEER *n.*

moschkener *see under* MOSKENEER.

Moscow *n.*[1] [1910s+] (*Aus.*) a pawnshop; thus *in Moscow*, *gone to Moscow*, in pawn; *Moscow ticket*, a pawn ticket. [MOSKENEER *v.*]

Moscow *n.*[2] [1950s] (*US*) a Communist.

mos def *phr.* [2000s] (*US Black*) most definitely. [abbr.]

mose *n.*[1] [mid–late 19C] (*US*) the generic name for a typical 'Bowery b'hoy', a proletarian New Yorker who might have worked as a fireman but whose main occupation was running with a gang, mixing street thuggery with life as a political mercenary. [the name, if not the type, was originated by Edward Judson (1823–86), a political fixer and bullyboy, who wrote a number of blood-and-thunder burlesques featuring *Mose*, *Lize* and their friend *Sykesy*. Under the pseudonym 'Ned Buntline', Judson went on to create virtually single-handedly the myths of what would become known as the 'Wild West'; note also B. A. Baker's play, *A Glance at New York* (1848), featuring 'Mose', a character based on the real-life Moses Humphreys, popularly known as 'Old Mose', a famous leader of the Bowery B'hoys and a fireman of Lady Washington Engine Co. No. 40. 'Old Mose', a huge man with a shock of flaming red hair, was a ferocious street brawler]

mose *n.*[2] [1920s–80s] (*US Black*) a Black man, esp. one who is subservient to Whites. [proper name *Moses*, a stereotypically 'Black' name]

mosekeno *v. see* MOSKENEER *v.*

Moses! *excl.* [mid-19C+] a general excl. of surprise, excitement, alarm etc.

moses *n. see* IKEY-MO *n.* (5).

mosey *n.*[1] [late 18C] a bull.

mosey *n.*[2] **1** [1960s+] a wander or walk around. **2** [2000s] a look. [MOSEY *v.*]

mosey *v.* (*also* **mosey about**, **...along**, **...around**, **...down**, **...off**, **...on**, **...on down**, **...over**) **1** [early 19C+] (*orig. US*) to leave, to wander off, to wander or hang around. **2** [mid-19C+] to go fast, to make haste. **3** [mid-19C+] to walk along, to go to. [? Sp. *vamos*, let's go, thus US *vamoose*, go away]

mosh *n.* [1980s+] violent and aggresive dancing. [MOSH *v.*[2]]

mosh *v.*[1] **1** [late 19C–1900s] to leave a restaurant without paying one's bill; thus *the mosh*, the practice of committing this fraud. **2** [1910s–30s] to pawn. [MOOCH *v.*[1]]

mosh *v.*[2] [1980s+] to dance in a violent and aggressive manner, jumping up and down, crashing into other dancers, waving one's arms etc; thus *moshing*, the dance style. [? SE *mash*; ? MOSH (ABOUT) *v.* (1)]

mosh (about) *v.* (*also* **mosh around/up**) **1** [1950s+] to hit, to fight, to mess up, to destroy. **2** [2000s] to mess about.

mosher *n.* [1980s+] a metal fan, more recently a nu metal fan; it has become as much a fashion/lifestyle description as just describing one who moshes. [MOSH *v.*[2]]

mosh game *n.* [1910s–30s] (*Aus.*) any form of illegal gambling. [ety. unknown]

moshing *n. see* MOSH *v.*[2].

mosh it up *v. see* MASH IT UP *v.*

moshkeneer *see under* MOSKENEER.

mosh pit *n.* [1980s+] the area in a club or rock arena where MOSHING *n.* takes place. [MOSH *v.*[2]]

mosh shop *n.* [1910s–30s] a pawnbroker's shop. [MOSH *v.*[1]]

mosk *v.* [1900s] to pawn, esp. to pawn at a profit. [abbr. MOSKENEER *v.*]

moskeneer *n.* (*also* **moschineer**, **moschkener**, **moshkeneer**, **moskeener**, **moskuiner**) [late 19C] a pawner, esp. one who pawns articles for more than they are worth, for a living. [MOSKENEER *v.*]

moskeneer *v.* (*also* **mokuiner**, **moschkener**, **mosekeno**, **moshkeneer**, **moskeneer**) [late 19C–1910s] to pawn, esp. to pawn for more than an article is actually worth. [Heb. *mashkon*, a pledge, whence *mishken*, to pawn]

mosker *n.* [late 19C–1940s] a swindler who specializes in defrauding pawnbrokers. [MOSKENEER *v.*]

mosking *n.* (*also* **mossing**) **1** [late 19C] placing things in pawn. **2** [1940s] (*UK Und.*) put in prison. [MOSKENEER *v.*; ? underpinned by the image of moss growing on the unredeemed article]

moskuiner *n. see* MOSKENEER *n.*

mosky *see under* MOHASKY.

mosque *n.* [late 18C] (*UK Und.*) a church.

mosquito bites *n.* [1970s+] (*US campus*) small breasts (cf. BAGS *n.*[1]).

mosquitos *n.* [1940s–50s] (*drugs*) cocaine; thus *mosquito bit*, addicted to cocaine. [? the marks left by the hypodermic rather than a ref. to the actual drug]

moss *n.*[1] **1** [18C–early 19C] (*UK Und.*) lead. **2** [mid-18C+] female pubic hair. **3** [1900s–60s] (*US*) hair, esp. of the head. **4** [1940s–60s] (*US Black*) black hair. **5** [1970s+] (*US gay*) chest hair. [(1) 'grows on the top' of buildings]

moss *n.*[2] [mid–late 19C] money. [? pvb 'a rolling stone (? a tramp) gathers no moss']

moss-back *n.*[1] (*also* **mossy-back**) **1** [mid–late 19C] (*US*) someone who hid themselves to avoid conscription during the US Civil War. **2** [1900s–20s] a recluse. [these men were willing to hide until moss grew on their backs]

moss-back *n.*[2] (*also* **mosshead**, **mossy-back**) [late 19C+] (*US*) a diehard conservative, a reactionary individual. [like some great, lumbering beast, he/she moves so slowly that moss could grow on their back]

moss-backed *adj.* (*also* **moss–back**) [20C+] of a person, extremely conservative. [MOSS-BACK *n.*[2]]

moss dog *n.* [1910s+] a miser. [image of a dog gripping hold of its MOSS *n.*[2]]

moss-grown *adj.* [late 19C–1900s] of a thing, old-fashioned or conservative.

mosshead *n. see* MOSS-BACK *n.*[2].

mossie *n.* (*also* **mozzy**) [1940s+] (*orig. Aus.*) a mosquito.

mossing *n. see* MOSKING *n.*

moss-jumper *n.* [mid-18C–early 19C] a peasant, a countryman (cf. ACORN-CRACKER *n.*). [the supposed primary preoccupation of a peasant]

mossoo *n.* [late 19C–1920s] a Frenchman. [deliberate mispron. of Fr. *monsieur*, mister, sir]

moss rose *n.* [19C] female pubic hair. [MOSS *n.*[1] (2) + SE *rose*]

moss snatcher *n.* [1950s] (*US Black*) a barber. [MOSS *n.*[1] (3) + SE *snatch*]

mossy *adj.*[1] **1** [late 16C–early 17C] stupid, dull. **2** [1900s–40s] (*US*) very conservative or reactionary; old-fashioned, old. [the image of slow growth or movement]

mossy *adj.*[2] [20C+] of a person, hirsute. [MOSS *n.*[1] (3)]

mossy-back *see under* MOSS-BACK.

mossy bank *n.* (*also* **mossy cave/vale**) [late 18C–19C] female pubic hair. [MOSS *n.*[1] (2) + SE *bank*]

mossy cell *n.* [19C+] female pubic hair. [MOSS n.¹ (2) + SE *cell*]

mossy doughnut *n.* [1940s+] (*US*) the vagina (cf. APPLE n.⁶; BEAUTY SPOT n.). [MOSSY adj.² + DOUGHNUT n.² (2)]

mossy face *n.* [late 18C–19C] the female genitals and pubic hair. [MOSS n.¹ (2) + SE *face*]

mossy vale *n. see* MOSSY BANK n.

most, the *n.* [1950s+] (*orig. US*) the best, the most exciting, the finest; often ext. as *the most on toast*.

mostest *n.* [late 19C+] (*orig. US*) the very best, a superlative; thus the popular description of Ella Maxwell (1883–1963), 'the hostess with the mostest'; also as adj.

most ricky-tick *adv.* [1970s+] (*orig. US milit.*) very quickly.

mot *n.* (*also* **mat, mott, motte**) (*orig. UK/US/Irish*) **1** [late 18C–19C] a prostitute (cf. BANGTAIL n.¹). **2** [late 18C+] a woman, a wife. **3** [early 19C] a criminal's accomplice; a female criminal. **4** [mid-19C] a public or lodging-house landlady. **5** [late 19C+] the *mons veneris*; thus the vagina. **6** [late 19C+] pubic hair, whether male or female. [most likely Du. *mot*, a woman, although a bid has been made for Fr. *amourette*, girlfriend; note *OED* classifies *mot* as alternative sp. of MORT n.]

mot *v.* [19C–1930s] to go out pursuing women, to court. [MOT n. (2)]

mota *n.* (*also* **moto**) [1950s+] (*US drugs*) marijuana. [Sp. sl. *mota*, dust; var. on MOOTA n.]

motate *v. see* MOTE v. (2).

mot-cart *n.* **1** [mid-19C] a brougham or similar vehicle owned by a kept woman or well-off prostitute. **2** [late 19C] a mattress. [MOT n. (1) + SE *cart*]

mot-case *n.* [mid-19C–1920s] a brothel (cf. BADGER-CRIB n.). [MOT n. (1) + CASA n.¹; note synon. Du *mot-kasse*]

mote *v.* **1** [late 19C–1940s] to drive or ride in a car. **2** [1920s+] (*also* **motate**) to move quickly, of a person or a vehicle. [abbr. SE *motor*]

motel hell *n.* [1970+] (*US teen*) any situation or place that is considered appalling or unacceptable – a job, a place to stay, a relationship etc.

moth *n.* **1** [mid-19C–1930s] a prostitute. **2** [1990s+] (*Irish*) a woman, a girlfriend. [common Hib.E confusion of spoken *t* and *th*]

mothball *n.* [1940s–50s] (*US Black/campus*) an irritating person. [? their mind and speech flits around like a moth]

mothbox *n.* [1930s–60s] (*orig. US Black*) a piano.

mother *n.¹* **1** [mid-16C–1930s] a madam, a bawd, a procuress; often in comb. with a proper name as *Mother —*. **2** [late 19C–1920s] a public house landlady or similar. **3** [late 19C+] one's wife. **4** [1930s+] (*US Black*) an effeminate (or homosexual) man (cf. AUNTIE n.²). **5** [1940s+] (*US gay*) a homosexual who introduces another into the gay world. **6** [1940s+] (*US gay*) a term used by an effeminate gay man to refer to himself, e.g. *Your mother...* **7** [1970s] (*US Black*) a married woman. **8** [1970s] (*US Black*) the senior member of a pimp's STABLE n. (2) of prostitutes.

mother *n.²* [late 19C; 1940s+] the ultimate example of something, the extreme version of something, something exceptional. [popularized in the 1990s as mockery of the hyperbolic use of the phr. *mother of all battles* by the Iraqi dictator Saddam Hussein (b.1937) to describe the Gulf War, 1991]

mother *n.³* [1920s+] the self-proclaimed name of a female owner of a pet, esp. a dog; thus *Come to mother, baby*.

mother *n.⁴* (*also* **motha, mothah, mutha**) **1** [1950s+] a derog. term for a person. **2** [1960s+] an unspecified object or situation. **3** [1970s+] (*US Black*) an affectionate term used between men. [abbr. MOTHERFUCKER n.]

mother *n.⁵* (*also* **mutha**) [1960s+] (*drugs*) **1** marijuana. **2** a drug seller. [? MOOTA n. or abbr. MOTHERFUCKER n. or the role of drug as a comforter, i.e. a *mother*]

mother *adj.* [1940s+] a euph. for MOTHERFUCKING adj. (1). [abbr.]

mother, be *v.* (*also* **mum, be**) [1950s+] to serve portions, usu. of food and drink and esp. to pour out cups of tea; thus the invitation *will you be mother?* will you serve/pour?

mother abbess *n. see* ABBESS n.

mother and daughter *n.* [mid-19C+] water. [rhy. sl.]

mother and father of — *phr. see* FATHER (AND MOTHER) OF — phr.

Mother Brown *n.* [20C+] town, usu. the West End of London. [rhy. sl.; ult. Cockney song 'Knees up, Mother Brown']

Mother Browns *n.* [2000s] the knees. [song 'Knees up, Mother Brown']

Mother Bunch *n.* [late 16C–early 17C] water. [joc. use of the name of a noted late 16C ale-wife]

Mother Carey's chicken *n.* [mid-18C–19C] (*orig. US*) a stormy petrel, usu. associated with misfortune. [ext. of the synon. 18C naut. *Mother Carey's goose*]

Mother Carey's chickens *n.* [early–mid-19C] **2** people who are sharing living quarters and the payment for them, or likewise sharing a cab. [? play on SE *stormy petrel* (*see* MOTHER CAREY'S CHICKEN n.), one who enjoys controversy or actively promotes it, i.e. the potential squabblings of such housemates]

Mother Cornelius' tub *n.* [late 16C–17C] the sweating tub used in the cure of venereal disease (cf. CORNELIAN TUB n.). [a presumed actual *Mother Cornelius*, whether a nurse or a procuress; but note the masc. 'Cornelius' in John Taylor, 'The Water Poet', 'Travels to Bohemia' in *Works* (1630): 'Or had Cornelius but this tub, to drench / His clients that had practis'd too much French' ('French' referrring, as ever, to sex and its unfortunate results); ? poss. ref to physician Henry *Cornelius* Agrippa (1496–1535), a leading advocate of hot baths for medicinal purposes; Henke, *Gutter Life and Language* (1988), also notes the possible use of a hard dense wood, necessary to withstand the heavy salt brine used in 'pickling' patients, known as *cornel-wood*, 'the wood of *Cornus mascula*, celebrated for its hardness and toughness, whence it was anciently in request for javelins, arrows, etc.' (*OED*); there may be one more pun on cornel and the CORNUTED adj. cuckold]

Mother Cunny *n.* [mid-17C] a generic term for a procuress or bawd. [MOTHER n.¹ (1) + CONY n.¹ (3)]

Mother Damnable *n.* [late 17C–18C] a procuress, a madam. [MOTHER n.¹ (1) + SE *damnable*]

mothereff *n.* [1960s] (*US*) a euph. for MOTHERFUCKER n. (1).

motheren *n.* (*also* **motheree**) [1940s+] (*US*) a euph. for MOTHERFUCKER n. (1). [MOTHEREN adj.]

motheren *adj.* [1950s+] (*US*) a euph. for MOTHERFUCKING adj. (1); also as adv. [MOTHERING adj.]

motherer *n.* [late 19C+] (*Aus.*) a shepherd. [SE *mother*, to look after]

motherfeeling *adj.* [1940s–60s] (*US Black*) a euph. for MOTHERFUCKING adj. (1).

motherferyer *n.* [1940s–60s] (*US*) a euph. for MOTHERFUCKER n. (1).

mother fist and her five daughters *n.* (*also* **mother five fingers**) [1960s+] the hand, in the context of masturbation (cf. CONVERSE WITH HARRY PALM v.).

mother-flicker *n.* [1960s+] (*US*) a euph. for MOTHERFUCKER n. (1).

mother-flunker *n.* [1960s+] (*US*) a euph. for MOTHERFUCKER n. (1).

mother-flunking *adj.* [1960s+] (*US*) a euph. for MOTHERFUCKING adj. (1). [MOTHER-FLUNKER n.]

mother-fouler *n.* [1940s+] (*US*) a euph. for MOTHERFUCKER n. (1).

mother-fouling *adj.* [1940s+] (*US*) a euph. for MOTHERFUCKING adj. (1). [MOTHER-FOULER n.]

motherfreying *adj.* [1940s–60s] (*US*) a euph. for MOTHERFUCKING adj. (1). [MOTHERFERYER n.]

motherfrigger *n.* [1930s+] (*US*) a euph. for MOTHERFUCKER n. (1). [FRIG v. (1)]

motherfuck n. [1960s+] (orig. US) **1** a derog. term for a person, a supreme insult. **2** a DAMN n., as in I don't give a motherfuck. **3** the hell, e.g. get the motherfuck out, what the motherfuck. [abbr. MOTHERFUCKER n.]

motherfuck v. [1940s+] (orig. US) a general curse, usu. in imper., e.g. motherfuck the pigs! [backform. f. MOTHERFUCKER n.]

motherfuck adv. [1960s+] (orig. US) used as a general intensifier, e.g. don't you motherfuck forget it! [abbr. MOTHERFUCKING adv.]

motherfuck! excl. [1960s+] (orig. US) a general excl. of surprise, rage etc. [MOTHERFUCK n.]

motherfucker n. (also **muthafucka, motherfugger**) (orig. US Black) **1** [1920s+] a supreme insult, an expletive based on the incest taboo, prob. the ultimate in obscenities. **2** [1940s+] anything one dislikes, an infuriating or surprising state of affairs. **3** [1950s+] used with a wide variety of meanings, from good to bad, often as a Black-to-Black term of affection or a compliment, e.g. Jimi Hendrix was a bad motherfucker on guitar; also simply meaning 'thing'; frequently abbr. to mother. **4** [1960s+] a thing, otherwise unnamed. **5** [1960s+] a DAMN n., e.g. I don't give a motherfucker. **6** [1960s+] an indefinite standard of comparison, e.g. crazy as a motherfucker; meaner than a motherfucker. **7** [1970s+] a large or outstanding example. **8** [1990s+] a place. [(1) dating is difficult, the earliest written cit. is in 1929 for the euph. MOTHER-PLUGGER n., although Gold, A Jazz Lexicon (1964), notes the term was in existence as early as c.1900; (3) note Folb, Runnin' Down Some Lines (1980): 'You jus' be sayin' dat [motherfucker] any way come to your mind. Like you got some o' dem sweet mothafuckas. They righteously together brothers, got they game uptight, they on dey J.O.B.! Right on! Got dem lowlife thugs. They mean mothas. Don't be messin' wid 'em. Blow you away in a minute! Johnny he my ace, now he a bad mothafucka. He together. Strong rap to d' young ladies – and he go down wi'chu right now! We tight. Gots dem little ol' punks. Think they together, be talkin' out d' side dey neck! Jive mothafucka don't hold no air! See like da's one o' dem slangs got all differn' kin'a meaning. Don't be callin' young lady dat. Dude use dat talk 'bout other dude']

motherfucker! excl. [1960s+] (orig. US) a general excl. of surprise, rage etc. [MOTHERFUCKER n.]

motherfucking adj. (also **m-fugging, motherfugging, muthafucken**) (orig. US) **1** [1930s+] a general intensifier. **2** [1960s+] used as an infix, to accentuate or denigrate the word thus altered, e.g. emanci-motherfucking-pation. [MOTHERFUCKER n. (1)]

motherfucking adv. [1960s+] (orig. US) a general intensifier, e.g. start motherfucking talking. [MOTHERFUCKING adj.]

motherfucking-A n. [1970s+] (orig. US) very little, as good as nothing, e.g. I don't know motherfucking-A about it. [ext. of FUCKING-A n.]

motherfucking-A adj. [1970s+] (orig. US) **1** excellent, superb, best. **2** a synon. of DAMNED adj. [ext. of FUCKING-A adj.]

motherfucking-A adv. [1970s+] (orig. US) generally used for emphasis, absolutely, very well, very much, utterly, completely. [ext. of FUCKING-A adv.]

motherfucking A! excl. [1970s+] (orig. US) an excl. used to denote astonishment, dismay, acceptance, praise, recognition etc. [ext. of FUCKING-A! excl.]

motherfugger n. see MOTHERFUCKER n.

motherfugging adj. see MOTHERFUCKING adj.

mother-fuyer n. [1930s+] (US) a euph. for MOTHERFUCKER n. (1).

Mother Ga-ga n. [1940s+] (gay) a fussy, gossipy, interfering older homosexual (cf. AUNTIE n.²). [MOTHER n.¹ (4) + GAGA n.¹]

mother-grabber n. (also **father-grabber**) [1960s+] (US) a euph. for MOTHERFUCKER n. (1).

mother-grabbing adj. (also **father-grabbing**) [1950s+] (US) a euph. for MOTHERFUCKING adj. (1). [MOTHER-GRABBER n.]

motherhead n. [1970s+] (US) a euph. for MOTHERFUCKER n. (1).

mother-hopper n. (also **momma-hopper**) [1970s+] (US) a euph. for MOTHERFUCKER n. (1). [HOP v.¹ (8)]

mother-hopping adj. [1960s+] (US) a euph. for MOTHERFUCKING adj. (1). [MOTHER-HOPPER n.]

mother-hubba n. (also **mother hubbard, mother hubber, mutha hubbard**) [1950s+] (orig. US) a euph. for MOTHERFUCKER n. (1).

mother hubbard n. **1** [late 19C+] a cupboard. **2** [1980s+] nonsense, fanciful talk, lies. [(1) rhy. sl.; ult. nursery rhyme Old Mother Hubbard]

mother-hugger n. [1950s+] (US) a euph. for MOTHERFUCKER n. (1).

mother-hugging adj. [1950s+] (US) a euph. for MOTHERFUCKING adj. (1). [MOTHER-HUGGER n.]

mother-humper n. [1960s+] (US) a euph. for MOTHERFUCKER n. (1). [HUMP v.¹]

mother-humping adj. [1960s+] (US) a euph. for MOTHER-FUCKING adj. (1). [MOTHER-HUMPER n.]

mothering adj. [1950s+] a euph. for MOTHERFUCKING adj. (1). [abbr.]

mother-in-law n.¹ [late 19C–1950s] a drink composed of equal proportions of old (stout) and bitter.

mother-in-law n.² (also **mother-in-law exterminator, mother-in-law's hell-fire, ...masala, ...tongue**) [1980s+] (S.Afr. Ind.) proprietary names for the hottest forms of chile-based hot sauces or curry powders (masalas).

mother-in-law's bit n. [late 18C–early 19C] a very small portion. [the stereotyped meanness of such figures; note Grose (1785): 'mothers in law being supposed not apt to overload the stomachs of their husband's children']

mother-jiver n. [1950s+] (orig. US) a euph. for MOTHERFUCKER n. (1). [JIVE v.¹ (1)]

mother-jiving adj. [1950s+] (orig. US) a euph. for MOTHER-FUCKING adj. (1). [MOTHER-JIVER n.]

Mother Jones n. [1930s+] (US) an outdoor privy (cf. AUNTIE n.¹). [the US labour leader Mary Harris (1830–1930), also known as Mother Jones]

mother-jumper n. (also **mother-jump**) [1940s+] (orig. US) a euph. for MOTHERFUCKER n. (1). [SE mother + JUMP v.¹ (1)]

mother-jumping adj. [1940s+] (orig. US) a euph. for MOTHER-FUCKING adj. (1). [MOTHER-JUMPER n.]

Mother Kelly n. [20C+] **1** jelly. **2** television. [rhy. sl.; (2) = TELLY n.]

mother knab-cony n. (also **mother nab-cony**) [late 17C–early 18C] a madam, a bawd. [MOTHER n.¹ (1) + NAB v.¹ (1) + CONY n.², lit. 'mother snatch-sucker']

motherless adj. **1** [late 19C+] (orig. Aus.) a general expletive adj. **2** [1940s+] (Irish) drunk.

motherless adv. [late 19C+] (orig. Aus.) a general intensifier; esp. as motherless broke, completely bereft of funds.

motherlove n. [1940s–60s] (US gay) **1** a homosexual man having sex with a heterosexual woman. **2** sexual intercourse between 2 homosexual men of the same 'type', i.e. passive and passive or active and active.

mother-lover n. [1950s+] a euph. for MOTHERFUCKER n. (1).

mother-loving adj. [1950s+] a euph. for MOTHERFUCKING adj. (1). [MOTHER-LOVER n.]

motherlumping adj. [1960s] (US) a euph. for MOTHERFUCKING adj. (1).

Mother Machree n. [20C+] (Aus.) tea. [rhy. sl.; ult. Irish mo chroí, my heart. Best known as the title of Rida Johnson Young's 19C ballad]

Mother Machree-ish adj. [20C+] (Irish) mawkish, lachrymose, banal. [for ety. see MOTHER MACHREE n.; the sentimentality of the song]

Mother Midnight n. [late 17C–early 19C] **1** a bawd, a madam. **2** a midwife, esp. one who delivers or aborts illegitimate children. [MOTHER n.¹ (1) + SE midnight]

mother nab-cony *n. see* MOTHER KNAB-CONY n.

mother nature *n.*[1] [20C+] (*US*) menstruation.

mother nature *n.*[2] (*also* **mother nature's own tobacco**) [1960s+] (*drugs*) marijuana.

mother of all masons *n.* [19C] the vagina; also used as a toast before drinking. [a dig at the Freemasons, for no discernible reason]

mother of all saints *n.* [late 18C–19C] the vagina. [a blasphemous joke]

mother of all souls *n.* [late 18C+] the vagina. [a blasphemous joke]

mother of pearl *n.* [late 19C+] a girl. [rhy. sl.]

mother of St Patrick *n.* (*also* **mother of St Paul**) [18C–19C] the vagina. [a blasphemous joke]

mother of shit! *excl.* [1940s] (*US*) an excl. of surprise or exasperation.

mother of that was a whisker *phr.* [mid–late 19C] a retort to an utterly implausible story. [? phr. *it has whiskers on it*]

mother of the maids *n.* [early 17C–mid-19C] a madam, a brothel-keeper.

motheroo *n.* [1950s+] a euph. for MOTHERFUCKER n. (1).

Mother Parker *n.* [1950s–70s] (*US gay*) a tough, older homosexual (cf. AUNTIE n.[2]).

mother-plugger *n.* [1920s] (*US Black*) a term of abuse, a euph. for MOTHERFUCKER n. (1). [PLUG v.[1] (1)]

motherramming *adj.* [1960s] (*US Black*) a euph. for MOTHERFUCKING adj. (1). [RAM v.[1]]

mother-rape *n.* [1960s] (*US Black*) a synon. of MOTHERFUCK n. (2). [MOTHER-RAPER n.]

mother-rape *v.* [1960s] (*US Black*) a synon. of MOTHERFUCK v. [MOTHER-RAPER n.]

mother-raper *n.* [1950s+] (*US Black*) a synon. of MOTHERFUCKER n. (1).

mother-raping *adj.* [1950s+] (*US Black*) a synon. of MOTHERFUCKING adj. (1). [MOTHER-RAPER n.]

mother-rubba *n.* (*also* **mother-rubber**) [1970s] a euph. for MOTHERFUCKER n. (1).

mother's *n. see* MOTHER'S (RUIN) n.

mothers, the *n.* [1940s–60s] (*US Black*) the ritualistic name-calling based on insulting one's rival's mother.

mother's blessing *n.* [19C] a painkiller, esp. laudanum. [a mix of brandy and tincture of opium, often used to keep children quiet]

mothers' cramp *n.* [1900s] a hernia.

mother's day *n.* [1960s+] **1** (*US Black*) the day when welfare cheques arrive from the government. **2** (*US milit.*) payday.

mother's friend *n.* [19C] a quinine pessary, an elementary form of contraceptive, whose inefficiency gave it a parallel name, the *midwife's friend*.

mother's joy *n.* [20C+] (*Aus.*) a boy. [rhy. sl.]

mother's life *n.* [1980s] imprisonment for life.

mother's little helper *n.* [1960s+] (*drugs*) the tranquillizer Miltown. [Rolling Stones' song 'Mother's Little Helper' (1966)]

mother's milk *n.* **1** [early 19C+] gin. **2** [mid-19C] brandy. **3** [1960s] Guinness stout.

mothersomething *n.* [1960s] (*US*) a euph. for MOTHERFUCKER n. (1).

mother's pride *n.* [20C+] a bride. [rhy. sl.]

mother's (ruin) *n.* [1920s+] gin (cf. BLUE RUIN n.). [the drink's supposed effects]

mother's son *n. see* SON OF YOUR MOTHER n.

mother-sucker *n.* [1950s+] a euph. for MOTHERFUCKER n. (1). [SUCK v.[1] (1)]

mother-sucking *adj.* [1950s+] a euph. for MOTHERFUCKING adj. (1). [MOTHER-SUCKER n.]

mother superior *n.*[1] [1930s–70s] (*camp gay*) **1** an older, experienced and open homosexual (cf. AUNTIE n.[2]). **2** a police sergeant.

mother superior *n.*[2] [1960s] a euph. for MOTHERFUCKER n. (1).

mother-young-girl *n.* [1990s+] (*W.I.*) an ageing woman who tries to be younger than her years.

mot-house *n.* [mid–late 19C] a brothel (cf. ACCOMMODATION HOUSE n.). [MOT n. (1) + SE *house*/HOUSE n.[1] (1); note synon. Du. *mot huys*]

motion lotion *n.* [1970s+] **1** (*US*) alcohol. **2** (*orig. US*) gasoline, petrol.

motivate *v.* **1** [1930s+] (*US Black/campus*) to move, to go, to leave. **2** [1950s–60s] (*US Black*) to force oneself to do something that one dislikes. **3** [1970s+] (*US campus*) to move around in a group, socializing. [play on SE *motivate* + MOTORVATE v.]

Moto *n. see* MR MOTO n.

moto *n.*[1] [1990s+] (*US campus*) a tedious, irritating, boring person. [abbr. *master of the obvious*]

moto *n.*[2] *see* MOTA n.

motor *n.*[1] [late 19C–1900s] a fast, hard-living man about town. [SE *motor*, to drive]

motor *n.*[2] **1** [late 19C+] a *motor*car. **2** [1940s+] (*US*) a *motor*cycle. [abbr.]

motor *n.*[3] [1970s+] (*US gay*) the buttocks.

motor *v.* **1** [1970s+] to get started, to go well. **2** [1980s+] (*orig. US campus*) to move quickly, to leave.

motor-boat *n.* [1980s] (*Aus.*) the throat. [rhy. sl.]

Motor City *n.* [1930s+] (*US*) Detroit, Michigan.

motor cop *n.* (*also* **motorcycle cop**) [1920s+] (*US*) a motorcycle policeman. [SE *motorcycle* + COP n.[1] (1)]

motorcycle *n.*[1] [1930s+] (*US*) a euph. for MOTHERFUCKER n. (1); usu. as *bad motorcycle*.

motorcycle *n.*[2] [1950s] (*US Black*) a woman (who can supposedly be 'ridden').

motorcycle bull *n.* [1930s+] (*US*) a motorcycle policeman. [SE *motorcycle* + BULL n.[10] (1)]

motorcycle cop *n. see* MOTOR COP n.

motor-flicker *n.* [1960s+] a euph. for MOTHERFUCKER n. (1).

motorhead *n.* [1970s+] (*US*) **1** an idiot. **2** a car or motorcycle enthusiast.

motorhuckle *n.* [1980s+] (*US*) a motorcycle. [joc. mispron.]

motorized dandruff *n.* [1940s] (*US milit.*) head lice.

motormouth *n.* [1960s+] (*orig. US*) **1** a chatterer, a gossip, an obsessive talker. **2** the mouth of such a person.

motormouth *v.* [1980s+] (*orig. US*) to talk ceaselessly. [MOTORMOUTH n.]

motormouthed *adj.* [1970s+] verbose, chattering. [MOTORMOUTH n.]

motor scooter *n.* [1960s+] (*US*) a euph. for MOTHERFUCKER n. (1).

motorvate *v.* [1970s+] (*US campus*) to wander about, to leave quickly. [? nonce-word *motor-vate*, coined for Chuck Berry's song 'Maybelline' (1955)]

motorway madness *n.* [1980s+] irresponsible, reckless driving on a motorway, esp. in bad and thus dangerous weather. [var. on the alliterative form of ROAD RAGE n.]

Motown *n.* [1960s+] (*US*) Detroit, Michigan. [the home of *Motown* record company, itself named after the city's original nickname MOTOR CITY n.]

motser *n.* (*also* **motsa, motza, motzer**) [1930s+] (*Aus.*) **1** money, esp. as gambling winnings or as a large sum (cf. BATTER n.[4]). **2** a 'certainty', which will guarantee such a win. [Yid. *matze*, the unleavened bread eaten at Passover. In trad. form this resembles an outsize round biscuit, and thus an enormous coin]

motshkin-shop *n. see* MASHKIN-SHOP n.

mott *n. see* MOT n.

mott *v.* [1920s+] (*Aus.*) to stare at fixedly. [ety. unknown; ? SE *mott/mete*, to ascertain the dimensions and/or quantity of]

mottab *n.* (*also* **mottob**) [mid-19C] the bottom. [backsl.]

mott-carpet *n.* (*also* **mott-fleece, motte-fleece**) [19C] female pubic hair. [MOT n. (2) + SE *carpet*]

motte *n. see* MOT n.

motter *n.* [late 19C–1900s] a name coined for the very first motorcar to be seen in the UK. It was driven through London on the day of the Lord Mayor's Show, 1896.

mott-fleece *n. see* MOTT-CARPET n.

motting *n.* [19C] pursuing women, esp. prostitutes. [MOT n. (1)]

motto *adj.* [late 19C–1950s] (*UK tramp*) drunk. [Rom.]

mottob *n. see* MOTTAB n.

motza *n. see* MOTSER n.

motzer *n.*[1] (*also* **matzo, motza, motzey, motzy**) [late 19C–1900s] (*US*) a Jew (cf. ARAB n.[2]). [Heb. *matze*, unleavened bread, trad. eaten at the Jewish festival of Passover]

motzer *n.*[2] *see* MOTSER n.

mouch *see under* MOOCH.

moucher *n. see* MOOCHER n.

mouchet *n.* [late 17C–early 19C] a synthetic beauty mark affixed to a woman's face. [Fr. *mouche*, a fly]

mouchey *n.* (*also* **mochy**) [mid-19C] a Jew (cf. FAST-TALKING CHARLIE n.). [SMOUS n. (1)]

mouee *n. see* MOEY n.

mould *v.* (*also* **mode, mold**) [1980s+] (*US campus*) to embarrass, to humiliate, to catch someone out in a contradiction or other error. [SE *mould*, the growth that appears on rotting vegetable matter]

mouldies *n.* [late 19C] old clothes.

mouldiworp *n.* [19C] the penis. [dial. *mouldiwarp*, a mole, lit. 'earth-digger'/'earth-thrower']

mouldy *adj.* **1** [late 16C+] useless, second-rate, out-of-date. **2** [mid-19C] grey-haired. **3** [late 19C–1970s] boring, gloomy, sick. **4** [1930s+] (*also* **mowldy**) very drunk.

mouldy grub *n.* [mid-19C] a travelling showman; thus *mouldy grubbing*, performing in the open air. [play on SE *mulligrubs*]

mouldy one *n.* (*also* **mouldy 'un, moulie**) [mid-19C–1950s] a copper coin. [the colour]

mouldy pate *n.* [mid–late 19C] a servant wearing a grey powdered wig. [MOULDY adj. (2) + SE *pate*]

moulenjam *n. see* MULENYAM n.

mouli *v.* [1980s+] (*Aus. drugs*) to chop cannabis in a parsley grinder. [brandname *Moulinex*, ult. Fr. *mouli-légumes*, a food processor]

moulie *n. see* MOULDY ONE n.

moulonjam/moulonjohn *n. see* MULENYAM n.

moult one's feathers *v.* [17C] to lose one's hair through syphilis.

moult the mouldies *v.* [late 19C] to change one's clothes. [SE *moult* + MOULDIES n.]

mounseer *n.* (*also* **mounsear, mounsheer, mounsier, mounsieur**) [17C–1900s] a Frenchman. [Fr. *monsieur*]

Mount, the *n.* **1** [early 18C–19C] London Bridge. **2** [20C+] (*Can.*) Montreal. [(1) one approached the Bridge up a short incline]

mount *v.* **1** [mid-19C] a wife, a mistress. **2** [mid-19C–1950s] anything one rides, esp. a dangerous and uncontrollable horse. **3** [1970s+] (*US Black*) a promiscuous woman, who is 'ridden'. [MOUNT v.[3]/SE *mount*]

mount *v.*[1] **1** [late 18C–mid-19C] to perjure oneself for money. **2** [1960s+] (*US Black*) to brag, to boast, to attack verbally. ['Derived from the borrowed clothes men used to MOUNT, or dress in when going to swear for a consideration' (Hotten, 1859)]

mount *v.*[2] [late 18C–19C] to provide for, to look after. [SE *mount*, to raise up, to exalt]

mount *v.*[3] (*also* **do a mount**) [19C+] to have sexual intercourse with, spec. to climb on, prior to sexual intercourse. [SE before 19C and when used of animals]

mount a corporal and four *v.* [late 18C–early 19C] to

masturbate. [MOUNT v.[3], 'the thumb is the corporal, the four fingers the privates' (Grose, 1785)]

mountain *n.* [1990s+] (*US campus*) an erection.

mountain canary *n.* [1920s+] (*US, mainly Western*) a donkey (cf. ARIZONA CANARY n.). [CANARY n.[10]]

mountain climber *n.* [1970s+] (*US campus*) a feeling of intoxication produced by drugs. [play on HIGH adj.[1] (2)]

mountain devil *n.* [20C+] (*Aus.*) a native of Tasmania. [the nickname for the thorn-devil (*Moloch horridus*), a Tasmanian lizard]

mountain dew *n.* [early 19C+] **1** whisky, 'advertised as from the Highlands' (Hotten, 1860). **2** illicitly distilled alcohol, contraband whisky. [coined in Scotland and exported to the US, the term is equally popular in W.I. use]

mountain goat *n.* [1940s–50s] (*US prison*) any form of prison meat.

mountain guinea *n.* [1960s+] (*US Ital.*) used by southern Italians, a northern Italian. [SE *mountain* + GUINEA n. (1)]

mountain lamb *n.* [20C+] (*US*) **1** salt pork. **2** venison.

mountain oyster *n.* [late 19C+] (*US*) a sheep's or hog's testicle as food, supposed to be a powerful aphrodisiac.

mountain passes *n.* [20C+] spectacles. [rhy. sl. = SE *glasses*]

mountain-pecker *n.* **1** [mid–late 19C] a sheep's head. **2** [late 19C] a Welshman.

mountains *n.* [1970s+] (*US Black*) large, noticeable female breasts (cf. BAGS n.[1]).

mountains of Mourne *n.* [20C+] an erection. [rhy. sl. = HORN n.[2] (3)]

mountain trout *n. see* SALMON AND TROUT n. (3).

mountain wop *n.* [1960s+] (*US*) a derog. term for an Italian (cf. DAGO n.). [SE *mountain* + WOP n.[1] (1)]

mounteer *n.* [early 18C] a hat. [Sp. *montera*, a hunter's cap having a spherical crown and a flap capable of being drawn over the ears, ult. f. *montero*, a hunter]

mounter *n.* [late 18C–19C] one who swears false oaths; a perjurer. [MOUNT v.[1] (1)]

mount-faulcon *n.* [late 16C–19C] the vagina. [lit. 'mount falcon'; coined by lexicographer John Florio (*c*.1553–*c*.1625)]

mount for *v.* [early 19C] to back up someone in their claims, to provide someone with an alibi. [ext. of MOUNT v.[1] (1)]

mount one's high horse *v.* (*also* **ride one's high horse**) [late 18C+] to act in an arrogant, superior manner.

Mount Pleasant *n.* **1** [mid-18C] as *mount pleasant of Rome*, the buttocks of a male homosexual. **2** [mid-18C–19C] the female genital area. [pun on proper name/MOUNT v.[3]]

Mount St Moritz Bajan *n.* [20C+] (*W.I., Gren.*) a poor White.

mount the ass *v.* [late 18C–19C] to become bankrupt. [old Fr. custom of exhibiting a bankrupt riding backwards on a donkey]

mount the cart *v.* [18C] to be hanged. [before the drop, prisoners stood on a cart with the rope around their neck; the cart was then driven away, leaving the victim to suffocate. This was not automatically an instant process, and friends would often haul sharply on the victim's legs to speed matters up]

mount the ladder *v.* [16C–mid-19C] to be hanged. [the ladder onto the gallows]

mourner's bench *n.* [1900s–30s] **1** (*US*) the court bench on which prisoners sit awaiting trial. **2** (*US prison*) a bench on which new inmates sit, e.g. for indoctrination talks. [SAmE *mourner's bench*, a bench set up at revival meetings for those 'in mourning for their sins']

mourning *n.* **1** [early 19C+] a black eye; usu. in phr. (*in*) *mourning*, having a black eye; thus *have one's eyes in mourning*, to have a pair of black eyes; *full (suit of) mourning*, 2 black eyes; *half-mourning*, a single black eye. **2** [late 19C+] (*UK society*) dirty fingernails, edging the hands like the black border of mourning paper; usu. as (*in*) *mourning*, having dirty fingernails; thus [20C+] *you're in mourning for the cat*, you have dirty fingernails. [the wearing of black as a sign of *mourning*; the adj. *mourning*, visibly bruised, is SE from 18C]

mourning bands *n.* [late 19C] dirty fingernails. [SE *mourning band*, a strip of black cloth or crape worn round the sleeve of a coat or round a hat as a sign of bereavement]

mourning coach horse *n.* [late 19C–1900s] (*UK middle class*) 'a tall, solemn woman, dressed in black and many inky feathers' (Ware).

mourning shirt *n.* [mid-17C] a flannel shirt. [such a shirt needs less regular washing, ref. to the custom of wearing the same clothes through the immediate period of mourning]

mouse *n.*[1] **1** [mid-16C–18C] a woman, esp. when applied to a prostitute or a woman arrested for brawling in the street (cf. ALLEY CAT n.). **2** [19C] (*US Black*) one's wife; thus *mousetrap*, marriage. **3** [late 19C+] a mistress. **4** [1900s–60s] a small, very feminine girl who invites being cuddled. **5** [1910s–60s] (*US*) a woman. **6** [1930s–80s] (*US Und.*) an effeminate male homosexual; thus a fellator. **7** [1940s+] a weakling. **8** [1970s] (*US*) a child. [there is no discernible link between (1) and (5)]

mouse *n.*[2] [19C] the penis (cf. ANTEATER n.). [its moving down dark, narrow passageways]

mouse *n.*[3] [mid-19C+] a black eye. [supposed resemblance]

mouse *n.*[4] **1** [late 19C–1900s] a barrister, a solicitor. **2** [late 19C+] (*UK Und.*) an informer. [play on RAT n.[2]]

mouse *n.*[5] [1920s+] (*Aus.*) a man who does not consummate his marriage on the wedding night. [? phr. 'are you a man or a mouse?']

mouse *n.*[6] [1940s] (*US Black*) a pocket. [ety. unknown; ? abbr. SE *mousehole*]

mouse *v.*[1] **1** [late 17C] to hit in the face. **2** [1920s+] to give a black eye. [MOUSE n.[3]; (1) earlier version or ? SE *mouse*, to handle roughly, as a cat does a mouse]

mouse *v.*[2] [1920s+] (*US campus*) to engage in sexual activity (usu. short of intercourse). [MOUSE n.[2]]

mouse *v.*[3] [1940s–50s] (*US Und.*) to inform on. [MOUSE n.[4] (2)]

mouse *v.*[4] [1970s] (*US*) to blackmail; thus *the mouse*, extortion. [? ext. of MOUSE n.[3]; ? 19C US *mouse*, to poke about]

mouse! *excl.* [19C] be quiet! [phr. *quiet as a mouse*]

mousebrain *n.* [1970s+] (*US*) a fool (cf. AIREDALE n.; BAKEBRAIN n.). [SE *mouse* + sfx *-brain*]

mousehole *n.* [19C] the vagina (cf. BAG n.[1]; BLACK HOLE n.[1]). [MOUSE n.[2]]

mouse-hunt *n.* (*also* **mouse-hunter**) [late 16C–mid-17C] a womanizer, a wencher. [MOUSE n.[1] (1) + SE *hunter*]

mouse mattress *n.* [1990s+] (*US*) a tampon.

mouse potato *n.* [2000s] (*orig. US*) one who spends what is seen as an excessive time using their computer, usu. in the context of the Internet. [SE *mouse* + var. on COUCH POTATO n.]

mouser *n.*[1] [19C–1900s] **1** the vagina. **2** a fellatrix, esp. one who nibbles rather than sucks the penis. [MOUSE n.[2]]

mouser *n.*[2] [19C+] a cat o'nine tails. [play on CAT n.[4]]

mouser *n.*[3] [mid-19C] a detective (cf. BEAGLE n.[3]). [like a cat playing with a mouse, they 'watch' criminals]

mouser *n.*[4] [mid-19C+] a black eye. [MOUSE n.[3]]

mouser *n.*[5] [1910s–60s] (*US*) a homosexual.

mouser *n.*[6] [1930s+] (*orig. US*) a moustache. [supposed resemblance]

mousetrap *n.*[1] **1** [late 17C+] the vagina (cf. BITE n.[2]). **2** [late 19C–1900s] the mouth.

mousetrap *n.*[2] [late 19C] a sovereign. [the fanciful similarity of the crown and shield (pictured on the reverse) to a set mousetrap]

mousetrap *n.*[3] *see* MOUSE n.[1] (2).

mousetrap *n.*[4] *see* PARSON'S MOUSETRAP n.

mousetrap *v.* [1960s+] (*US*) to fool or mislead by false promises, to entice, to cajole.

mousey *n.* (*also* **mousie**) [1910s–30s] (*UK tramp/Aus.*) cheese. [SE *mousetrap*]

mousse up *v.* [1980s+] (*US campus*) usu. of a man, to use a foamy hair-care preparation. [SE *mousse*, a hair styling product]

moustache *n.* (*also* **mustache**) (*US*) **1** [late 19C+] a man with a moustache. **2** [1930s–60s] oral copulation, cunnilingus (cf. BEARD RIDE n.). **3** [1940s+] pubic hair.

moustache Pete *n.* (*also* **mustache Pete**) [1930s+] **1** an original Italian immigrant to New York, typified by his heavy moustache; thus ext. to describe women (cf. DAGO n.). **2** an original member of the US Mafia.

moustache ride *n.* (*also* **mustache ride**) [1980s+] (*US*) an act of cunnilingus, from the perspective of a woman (cf. BEARD RIDE n.). [SE *moustache* + RIDE n.[1] (1)/SE *ride*]

moutagram *n.* (*also* **moutaphone**) [1940s] (*W.I.*) a source of gossip and false news. [SE *mouth* + *telegram/telephone*]

mout-a-massy *n.* [1940s–50s] (*W.I.*) a gossip, a chatterbox. [lit. 'mouth have mercy']

mouth *n.*[1] **1** [late 17C–mid-19C] a fool, a dupe; thus *you are a mouth and you will die a lip*, a general phr. of abuse/dismissal. **2** [late 17C–mid-19C; 1940s+] a noisy, talkative, boorish person; thus [early–mid-19C] *rank mouth*, an especially impudent person. **3** [late 19C+] cheek, impudence, verbosity. **4** [1940s–60s] (*US*) lawyer.

mouth *n.*[2] [late 19C+] the dry, foul-tasting mouth that follows a night's excesses; thus *have a mouth on one*, to be desperate for alcohol.

mouth *v.* **1** [mid-19C] (*US campus*) to bluff a recitation. **2** [1920s+] to insult, to criticize, to speak insolently. **3** [1990s+] (*W.I.*) to make fun of.

mout-hab-nuttin-fe-do *n.* [20C+] (*W.I.*) a chatterbox, a malicious gossip. [lit. 'mouth has nothing (better) to do']

mouth almighty *n.* [mid-19C+] a noisy, talkative, loud-mouthed person.

mouthamassy (Liza) *n.* [20C+] (*W.I.*) a chatterbox. [? Twi *mmasa-mmasa*, confused words, or f. phr. 'mouth have mercy!']

mouthar *n.* [20C+] (*W.I.*) a chatterbox, one who cannot be trusted to keep secrets. [? SE *mouth*]

mouth artist *n.* [1900s] (*US*) a braggart, an empty boaster. [SE *mouth* + ARTIST sfx]

mouth bet *n.* [late 19C] (*US gambling*) a verbal promise of a bet.

mouth-breather *n.* [1960s+] a stupid person, esp. a particularly stupid thug. [such individuals are presumed to be breathing heavily]

mouth-breathing *adj.* [1980s+] stupid, often stupid and thuggish. [MOUTH-BREATHER n.]

mouth diarrhoea *n.* [1970s] the act of informing.

mouth fuck *n.* [mid-19C] an act of fellatio (cf. COCKSUCK n.). [SE *mouth* + FUCK n.[1] (1)]

mouth fuck *v.* [1970s+] to fellate (cf. COCKSUCK n.). [MOUTH FUCK n.]

mouthful *n.* (*also* **gobful**) [20C+] a truthful, striking or confessional comment or speech.

mouth habit *n.* [1930s–50s] (*US drugs*) the consumption of narcotics orally and the subseq. addiction. [SE *mouth* + HABIT n.]

mouth half-cocked *n.* [late 17C–early 19C] a person who gapes stupidly at anything and everything. [SE *mouth* + fig. use of *half-cocked*, of a pistol that has the cock drawn back]

mouth harp *n.* [20C+] (*US*) a mouth organ. [on model of SE *jew's harp*]

mouth is sore *n.* [1960s] (*bingo*) the number 44 (cf. ALDERSHOT LADIES n.). [rhy. sl.]

mouth job *n.* [1970s+] (*US gay*) fellatio (cf. COCKSUCK n.).

mouth like a wrestler's jockstrap *phr.* [1970s+] severely hungover, suffering the effects of a heavy night's drinking.

mouth like the bottom of a cocky's cage *phr.* (*also* **mouth like the bottom of a bird's cage, ...parrot cage**) [1960s+]

(*Aus.*) having a mouth that is unpleasantly furred, the result of excessive drinking. [SE *cockatoo*]

mouth like the inside of an Arab's underpants *phr.* (*also* **mouth like a lorry-driver's crutch, ...a nun's minge, ...an Arab's sandal/arse**) [1960s+] the dry mouth, furred tongue and disgusting taste that can accompany a hangover.

mouth music *n.* [1970s+] the practice of cunnilingus.

mouth-o! *excl.* [1980s+] (*US campus*) this tastes wonderful! [SE *mouth* + orgasm]

mouth-off *n.* [1950s+] (*orig. US*) a braggart, a boaster, a chatterer. [MOUTH OFF v.]

mouth off *v.* [1950s+] (*orig. US*) **1** to speak impudently. **2** to boast, to brag. [ext. of MOUTH v. (2)]

mouth of nature *n.* [mid-18C] the vagina (cf. ADAM'S OWN (ALTAR) n.; BEAUTY SPOT n.).

mouth organ *n.* [late 19C–1920s] (*US*) **1** a spokesman. **2** the tongue. [puns]

mouth pie *n.* [late 19C–1900s] feminine scolding, nagging.

mouthpiece *n.* **1** [19C+] a spokesperson. **2** [mid-19C+] a lawyer, in the UK a solicitor, in the US an attorney. **3** [1900s–30s] (*US*) an informer. **4** [1910s–40s] (*US*) the mouth. **5** [1990s+] (*US Black*) gold caps on one's front teeth. [(1) orig. SE]

mouth queen *n. see* MOUTH-WORKER n. (1).

mouth runs like parch benny *phr.* (*also* **mouth runs like sick nigger takes salts**) [20C+] (*W.I.*) a phr. used of an incessant irritating chatterer. [Carib.E. *parch* = SE *parched* + *benny*, a form of sesame-based cooking oil, used in making sweets]

mouth thankless *n.* [19C] the vagina. [literary euph. coined by Sir Walter Scott (1771–1832)]

mouth that cannot bite *n.* [late 17C–early 18C] the vagina. [literary euph. coined by Thomas D'Urfey (1653–1723)]

mouth that says no words *n.* [18C–19C] the vagina.

mouthwash *n.*[1] [20C+] food. [rhy. sl. = NOSH n. (2) + lit. image]

mouthwash *n.*[2] **1** [1930s+] a drink of alcohol. **2** [1940s+] (*US prison*) prison coffee.

mouthwork *n.* [1950s] (*US*) bragging, boastfulness, empty words.

mouth-worker *n.* **1** [1940s+] (*gay*) (*also* **mouth queen**) a fellator. **2** [1950s+] (*drugs*) one who takes drugs orally.

mouth-wrestle *v. see* LIP-WRESTLE v.

mouthy *adj.* [1920s+] boastful, cocky.

mouti-mouti *n.* (*also* **mowti-mowti**) [1940s–50s] (*W.I.*) a gossip, a chatterbox.

mouton *n.* [19C–1900s] 'a spy quartered with an accused person with a view to obtaining incriminating evidence' (*OED*). [Fr. *mouton*, a sheep; the Fr. sl. is synon.]

move *n.* **1** [early 19C+] a trick, a scheme, a stratagem. **2** [1960s+] (*orig. US*) a sexual advance. **3** [1980s+] (*US*) the right thing, the proper way, 'what's happening'. **4** [1990s+] (*drugs*) a shipment of smuggled drugs.

move *v.*[1] **1** [mid-18C+] to leave. **2** [1950s+] (*orig. US*) to dance or play music energetically or with a strong rhythm. **3** [1950s+] (*orig. US*) to move fast, to be exciting or dynamic. **4** [1970s+] (*US drugs*) to sell off or to dispose of merchandise, including contraband, drugs and stolen property. [(1) SE from 15C–mid-18C; (4) ext. of SE *move*, of merchandise, to sell or dispose of]

move *v.*[2] [20C+] (*Irish*) to pick up a member of the opposite sex. [SE *move*, to stir, to excite]

moveables *n.* [17C–early 19C] (*UK Und.*) swords, watches, jewellery and other valuable objects that can be stolen, won at gambling or otherwise taken away from their owner.

move a cow *v. see* CHASE (UP) A COW v.

move in the blind *v.* [late 19C] to leave one's rented premises without paying the rent, to do a MOONLIGHT FLIT n. [? SE *blind spot* (of the landlord)]

movement *n.* [1920s–60s] (*US*) the provocative swaying of a woman's hips, usu. used in comparison with clocks or watches, e.g. *She's got movement like a Swiss watch*.

move off *v.* [mid–late 18C] to die.

move on *v.* [1970s+] **1** (*US Black/campus*) to hit, to assault, usu. with a weapon. **2** (*US Black*) to assault in a group.

move one's ass *v.* (*also* **move one's butt, shift one's ass**) [1970s+] (*orig. US*) to hurry up, to get a move on.

move out *v.* [1920s] (*N.Z.*) to expand, to bloom.

mover *n.* [1950s+] **1** an ambitious and successful person, both socially and with the opposite sex; ext. as *movers and shakers*, *movers and groovers*. **2** someone who moves themselves or others physically and emotionally. **3** an attractive person, usu. female. **4** the person in charge.

moves *n.* [1960s+] **1** (*orig. US*) knowledge, ability, 'smarts'; esp. in phr. *have all the moves*. **2** schemes used for seduction; esp. in phr. *put the moves on*. [MOVE n. (1)]

moves, the *n.* [1910s] (*US*) a film, a movie.

move the crowd *v.* [1990s+] (*US Black*) to leave.

move the laundry *v.* [1930s–50s] (*US Und.*) to smuggle illegal Chinese immigrants. [stereotypical image of Chinese running laundries]

move with *v.* [1950s+] to associate with, to spend time with.

movie *n.*[1] [1960s+] (*US*) a sequence of events that are unpleasant or boring; esp. in phr. *I don't like this movie*, I am not happy or comfortable.

movie *n.*[2] *see* PICTURE n.[1] (2).

movies *n.* [1970s] (*US Und.*) prison. [ironic ref. to the austerity of the prison]

moving dunghill *n.* [late 18C–early 19C] a notably filthy man or woman.

mow *n.* [mid-16C–18C] the act of copulation. [MOW v.]

mow *v.* [mid-16C–early 19C] to have sexual intercourse. [Scot./northern dial. *mow*, to copulate, and note MOULDI-WORP n.]

mow-beater *n. see* MOW-HEATER n.

mowed lawn *n. see* LAWN n.[2] (2).

mower *n.* **1** [late 17C–mid-19C] (*UK Und.*) a cow. **2** [mid-19C] in fig. use. [its *moo*-ing or its chewing of the grass]

mow-heater *n.* (*also* **mow-beater**) [late 17C–early 19C] (*UK Und.*) a drover. [the drover's habit of sleeping on hay mows + ? drover's 'heating up' of the MOWER n.'s behinds as he uses his stick to guide them through gates, down lanes etc]

mowldy *adj. see* MOULDY adj. (4).

mowlow *adj. see* MOLO adj.

mowly *adj.* [1990s+] (*W.I.*) smelly, malodorous.

mowly-aam *n.* [1990s+] (*W.I.*) body odour. [MOWLY adj. + SE *arm*]

mow on *v.*[1] [1980s+] (*US campus*) to eat heartily, to gorge oneself.

mow on *v.*[2] *see* MOW v.

mowrowsky *n. see* MARROWSKY n.

mow the brigalo suckers *v.* [1990s+] (*Aus.*) to shave one's beard. [*brigalow*, a form of acacia, found in New South Wales and Queensland; its rapid growth can render large areas of land unusable]

mow the lawn *v.* **1** [1930s–40s] (*US Black*) to cut one's hair. **2** [1930s–40s] (*US Black*) to comb one's hair. **3** [1950s+] (*US Black*) to shave with an electric razor. **4** [1970s+] to perform cunnilingus. **5** [1980s+] (*Aus./UK*) of a woman, to shave or trim one's pubic hair. [fig. use of SE *lawn*/LAWN n.[2] (2)]

mowti-mowti *n. see* MOUTI-MOUTI n.

moxie *n.*[1] [20C+] (*W.I.*) an untidy and thus unattractive young woman. [dial. *mawks*, a slattern, an unkempt woman]

moxie *n.*[2] (*also* **moxey, moxy**) **1** [1930s+] (*US*) courage, impudence, ability. **2** [1960s–70s] (*US Black*) an impudent upstart. [from the tradename of a once-popular US soft drink *Moxie*, developed *c.*1880 and patented 1924; it poss. contained *moxie*, or wintergreen; ult. Algonquin root *maski-*, medicine]

moyo *n.* [1980s+] (*US/P.R.*) a Black person. [Sp.]

moz *n. see* MOZZLE n.

moz v. (*also* **mozz**) [1940s+] (*Aus.*) to interrupt, to hinder. [SE *muzzle*]

moza-motton n. [mid-19C] a piece of luck.

Mozart and Liszt adj. *see* BRAHMS AND LISZT adj.

mozz v. *see* MOZ v.

mozzarella n. [2000s] (*US Black*) money. [CHEESE n.[1]]

mozzle n. (*also* **moz**) [mid-19C+] luck.

mozzle v. [1920s+] (*Aus.*) **1** to hinder, to interrupt. **2** to put a jinx on.

mozzy n. *see* MOSSIE n.

m.p. n. [mid–late 19C; 1960s] (*US/Aus.*) a policeman. [abbr. *member of the police*]

mpata n. [1980s+] (*S.Afr. Und.*) a new inmate, a fool, one who has not yet learned how to cope with prison conditions. [Zulu *mpatha*, a greenhorn]

Mr *see under* MISTER and its combs.

m.r.a. n. [1980s+] (*US campus*) unsociable behaviour. [REEB n.[2]; abbr. *major/massive reeb action*]

M.R.S. n. *see* M.R.S. DEGREE n.

Mrs n. [1910s+] a wife, esp. as *the Mrs*. The husband's surname is omitted, e.g. *Here is Mr Smith, Mrs is out shopping*; also in homosexual relationships. [var. on MISSIS n.]

Mrs *pfx see* MISS pfx[1].

Mrs Astor n. *see* MISS ASTOR n.

Mrs Astorbilt n. *see* ASTORBILT n.

Mrs Astor's pet horse n. (*also* **Mrs Astor's billy goat, …cow, …pet cow, …plush horse**) [1920s+] (*US*) **1** an over-made-up or overdressed person. **2** an arrogant, haughty person. [var. on ASTOR'S PET HORSE n.]

Mrs Chant n. [1930s+] an aunt. [rhy. sl.; ult. *see* next]

Mrs Chant's n. [1950s+] a lavatory; thus *visit Mrs Chant's* (cf. ANGUS ARMANASCO n.; AUNTIE n.[1]). [rhy. sl. = MY AUNT n.; Mrs Ormiston *Chant* (1848–1923) was a well-known moralist]

Mrs Clean n. *see* MR CLEAN n.[2].

M.R.S. Degree n. (*also* **M.R.S.**) [1970s+] (*US campus*) the nickname for the degree that a woman who goes to college mainly to find a husband is said to be studying for. [abbr. and pun on US 'Master of Science'/Mrs; pron. 'missus']

Mrs Doyle n. [1990s+] a boil. [rhy. sl; ult. *Mrs Doyle*, character in 1990s TV sitcom *Father Ted*]

Mrs Ducket(t) n. [1930s+] a bucket. [rhy. sl.]

Mrs Ducket(t)! excl. [1950s+] a euph. for FUCK IT! excl.

Mrs Evans n. [late 18C] a female cat. [a witch of that name, who was supposedly wont to turn herself into a cat]

Mrs Fubbs n. [early 19C] one who rents out rooms in their house to prostitutes and their clients or to (adulterous) lovers.

Mrs Fuzzgug n. *see* MR FUZZGUG n.

Mrs Gafoops n. [1930s+] (*Aus.*) any otherwise unspecified or unnamed woman. [nonsense word]

Mrs Goff n. [early–mid-19C] (*US campus*) a woman. [ety. unknown; ? anecdotal]

Mrs Greenfields phr. [20C+] (*UK tramp*) sleeping in the open air; thus *Mrs Ashpits*, sleeping near a lime-kiln. [imaginary landladies]

Mrs Hand and her five daughters n. [1980s+] the hand, as used for masturbation.

Mrs Harris and Mrs Gamp n. [mid–late 19C] the *Morning Herald* and the *Standard* newspapers. [the 2 characters, one 'real' and one imaginary, in Charles Dickens's *Martin Chuzzlewit* (1843–4). *Mrs Gamp*, a nurse, constantly quoted the fantastical *Mrs Harris* as the witness and supporter of her every opinion, 'and thus afforded a parallel to the two newspapers, which appealed to each other as independent authorities, being all the while the production of the same editorial staff' (Hotten, 1867)]

Mrs Jones n. (*also* **Mrs Jones's (counting) house, Mistress Jones**) [early–late 19C] the lavatory; thus *visit Mrs Jones*, to use the lavatory; *upset Mrs Jones*, to tip over the water closet (cf. AUNTIE n.[1]).

Mrs Lo n. *see* LO n.[1].

Mrs Lukey Props n. [19C] a brothel-keeper. [? an actual person]

Mrs Mopp n.[1] [1940s+] a cleaner. [the character *Mrs Mopp* created by Tommy Handley (1892–1949) for the radio comedy series *ITMA* (*It's That Man Again*, from 1939). Her catchphrase was 'Can I do you now, sir?']

Mrs Mopp n.[2] [1940s+] a shop. [rhy. sl.; ult. *see* prev.]

Mrs More n. [20C+] the floor. [rhy. sl.]

Mrs Murphy n. [1960s+] the lavatory (cf. AUNTIE n.[1]).

Mrs Palm and her five daughters n. (*also* **Mrs Palmer and her five daughters**) [1950s+] the hand, as used for masturbation (cf. CONVERSE WITH HARRY PALM v.; MR PALMER AND HIS FIVE SONS n.).

Mrs Philip's purse n. (*also* **Mrs Philip's ware, Mrs Phillip's…**) [late 18C] a condom. ['These machines were long prepared and sold by a matron of the name of *Phillips*, at the Green Canister, in Half-moon Street, in the Strand. That good lady, having acquired a fortune, retired from business, but learning that the town was not well served by her successors, she, out of a patriotic zeal for the public welfare, returned to her occupation; out of which she gave notice by divers hand-bills, in circulation in the year 1776' (Grose, 1796). Whether she was related to Mrs Phillips, that brothel-keeper who, in the mid-19C, ran a house at 11 Upper Belgrave Place, is alas unknown; see Williams, II 1016, for a substantial discussion]

Mrs Princum Prancum n. *see* MISTRESS PRINCUM PRANCUM n.

Mrs Suds n. [mid-18C] a washerwoman.

Mrs van Neck n. *see* MISS VAN NECK n.

Mrs White n. [1900s–50s] a drug dealer, presumably in white powders, i.e. narcotics.

Mrs White is out of jail phr. [1960s+] (*US*) a warning to a woman that her slip is showing (cf. CHARLIE'S DEAD phr.).

Ms *pfx see* MISS pfx[1].

m.s. n. [1950s+] (*drugs*) morphine (cf. AUNTIE EMMA n.). [abbr. *morphine sulphate*]

mshoza n. [1980s+] (*S.Afr.*) the female companion of a township dandy. [? SE *shows*, thus showy, well-dressed, good-looking]

M² n. [1940s] (*UK gay*) mutual masturbation.

m.t. n. [mid-19C+] an empty bottle. [pron./abbr. of *empty*]

MTF n. [1990s+] (*US gay*) a male to female transsexual, transgender or transvestite (cf. FTM n.). [abbr. *male to female*]

m.t.f. n. [1980s+] (*UK society*) an overly amorous young man. [abbr. *must touch flesh*]

MTM n. [1990s+] (*US gay*) a female to male transsexual. [abbr. *male to male*, var. on FTM n., with the idea being that although the person was biologically a woman to start with they always felt like a man]

M25 n. [1980s+] (*drugs*) MDMA (cf. ECSTASY n.). [the initial letter + the UK's *M25* motorway, an orbital route round London, which played a major part in the siting of the early ecstasy-fuelled raves]

m.u. n. [1970s+] (*drugs*) a marijuana user. [abbr.]

mu n. [1930s+] (*drugs*) marijuana. [abbr. MOOCA n.]

mubble-fubbles n. [late 16C–19C] a mental depression. [joc. uses of SE *mumble* + *fumble*]

much adj. [1950s+] (*US Black*) many, a lot of.

much v. [mid-19C; 1950s] to persuade, to fondle. [? SE *make much of*]

much adv. [1950s+] (*US Black/teen*) very, extremely, to a great extent, defined by a v. or adj. e.g. *unhappy much?* [ext. use of SE]

much! excl. [late 16C; mid-19C+] certainly not! not likely!

much clown love phr. [2000s] (*US Black*) a phr. implying great affection.

much-fake v. [2000s] (*US prison*) to make playing cards out of whatever materials are available.

much love n. [1990s+] (*US Black*) popularity, respect.

muchly adv. [late 19C+] very much; usu. in TA MUCHLY phr.

mucho adj. [1940s+] (*orig. US*) a lot of, many. [Sp.]

mucho *adv.* [1940s+] (*orig. US*) exceedingly. [MUCHO adj.]

much props *n.* [1990s+] (*US Black/teen*) respect for others. [SE *much* + PROPS n.[3]]

much-travelled highway *n.* [19C] a large and loose vagina (cf. ALLEY n.[1]).

muck *n.*[1] [14C–mid-19C] money (cf. CHAFF n.[2]). [the guilty equation of money and dirt]

muck *n.*[2] **1** [mid-19C+] a general term covering anything or anyone seen as disgusting, worthless or abhorrent; also attrib. **2** [late 19C+] rubbish, nonsense. **3** [1910s+] food or drink, not necessarily unpleasant. **4** [1940s–50s] rudeness, insults. **5** [1940s+] a euph. for SHIT n.[3] (1).

muck *n.*[3] [late 19C–1930s] a heavy fall. [abbr. MUCKER n.[1]]

muck *n.*[4] [late 19C+] semen; esp. in phr. *spill one's muck* (cf. CRUD n.[1]). [SE *muck*, anything filthy, dirty, esp. when part liquid]

muck *n.*[5] [1900s–50s] (*US*) an important or self-important person. [abbr. MUCK-A-MUCK n. (2)]

muck *n.*[6] [1920s+] a euph. for FUCK n.[1] in its various forms.

muck *v.*[1] **1** [mid–late 19C] to beat, to surpass, to ruin financially. **2** [late 19C] to dirty. **3** [late 19C] to irritate. **4** [late 19C+] to fail, to make a mess of.

muck *v.*[2] [1920s] (*US*) to work as a manual labourer, esp. a navvy.

muck *v.*[3] [1920s+] a euph. for FUCK v.[1] in its various forms.

muck about *v.* (*also* **muck around**) **1** [late 19C+] to act half-heartedly, to engage in pointless, time-wasting activity, to mess around. **2** [1910s+] to ruin, to mess up, to annoy; usu. in passive. **3** [1910s+] to fondle intimately, to seduce.

muck-a-muck *n.* (*orig. US*) **1** [mid-19C–1930s] food, drink. **2** [mid-19C+] (*also* **muckety-muck, muckti-muck, muckty-muck, mucky-muck, mucky-mucky**) an important or self-important person; esp. as *big muck-a-muck* and HIGH MUCK-A-MUCK n. [Chinook jargon *muckamuck*, food]

muck-a-muck *adj.* (*also* **muckety-muck**) [1970s] (*US*) arrogant. [MUCK-A-MUCK n. (2)]

muck and halfpenny afters *n.* [late 19C–1900s] (*UK middle class*) a pretentious, unpleasant dinner 'spotted at the corners with custard powder preparations, and half dozens of stewed prunes, etc, etc' (Ware).

muck and truck *n.* [late 19C–1900s] miscellaneous articles of trade. [SE *muck* + *truck*, worthless items for trade]

muck around *v. see* MUCK ABOUT v.

muck-arse (about) *v.* (*also* **muck-arse around**) [20C+] to 'mess about', esp. in a sexual context.

muckcook *v.* [late 19C–1900s] to laugh behind someone's back. [? fig. use *muck*, dirt; thus poss. antecedent of DISH THE DIRT v. + SE *cook*, to concoct]

mucked *adj.* [late 19C] in trouble. [MUCK v.[1] (1)]

mucked (out) *adj.* [early 19C–1910s] penniless. [stable imagery]

muckender *n.* (*also* **mucketer, muckinder**) [early 18C] a cleaning cloth, a duster. [SE *muckender*, a handkerchief or napkin, ult. Fr. *mouchoir*, Sp. *mocador*]

mucker *n.*[1] [mid-19C+] a heavy fall; thus *come/go a mucker*, to come to grief, to ruin oneself. [SE *muck*, into which one falls]

mucker *n.*[2] **1** [late 19C–1910s] (*US*) a street urchin or youth who does not go to college. **2** [late 19C–1930s] a fanatic, a hypocrite. **3** [late 19C+] a rough, coarse person. **4** [1900s–20s] (*US campus*) a mean, untrustworthy person; a 'bounder'. [SE *muck*, dirt]

mucker *n.*[3] [late 19C+] an unpleasant person. [var. on FUCKER n. (3)]

mucker *n.*[4] [20C+] (*orig. Aus.*) a companion, a friend; as a direct term of address. [MUCK IN v.]

mucker *n.*[5] [1910s–30s] (*US tramp*) a manual labourer.

mucker *v.* **1** [mid-19C+] to come to grief, to fail. **2** [mid-19C–1920s] to cause problems for someone. **3** [mid-19C+] to fall, to 'take a tumble'. **4** [late 19C] to ruin. **5** [1920s] to squander, to waste. [MUCKER n.[1]]

Muckeries *n.* (*also* **Moocheries**) [late 19C] the Inventions Exhibition, held in South Kensington in 1885. [MUCK ABOUT v. (1); a pej. ref. to the inventors]

mucker-upper *n.* [1940s–50s] a bungler. [MUCK UP v.]

mucket *n.* [1950s–60s] (*US*) a hairpiece or toupee. [? var. on SE *merkin*, a pubic wig]

mucketer *n. see* MUCKENDER n.

muckety-muck *see under* MUCK-A-MUCK.

muck-forks *n.* [mid–late 19C] the fingers.

muckheap *n.* [mid-19C–1900s] a lazy, filthy person.

muckhill *n.* [late 17C–early 18C] a pile of money; thus *have a good muckhill at one's doorstep*, to be well-off. [MUCK n.[1]]

muckhole *n.* **1** [1900s–30s] a filthy, unappetizing place or room. **2** [1930–40s] the anus (cf. A-HOLE n.; DIRT BOX n.). **3** [1960s+] (*Aus.*) the vagina (cf. BLACK HOLE n.[1]). [(1) MUCK n.[2]; (2) MUCK n.[2] (5); (3) MUCK n.[6]]

muckibus *adj.* [mid-18C–mid-19C] tipsy, slightly drunk. [SE *muck* + cod Lat. sfx *-ibus*]

muck in *n.* [1910s+] a communal activity. [MUCK IN v.]

muck in *v.* [late 19C+] to join in, to lend a hand, esp. in a dirty or unpleasant task.

muckinder *n. see* MUCKENDER n.

mucking *adj.* **1** [late 19C–1900s] repellent, filthy. **2** [1930s+] a euph. for FUCKING adj. [MUCK n.[2]/MUCK n.[6]]

mucking-togs *n.* [mid-19C–1910s] a mackintosh. [joc. mispron., but note MUCKING adj. + TOGS n.]

muck it *v.* [1920s+] (*US*) to work at a menial task, lit. 'to get one's hands dirty'.

muckle *n.* [mid–late 19C] (*US*) muscle. [joc. mispron.]

muck out *v.* [mid-19C] (*UK gambling*) to take all one's opponents' money. [SE *muck out*, to clean out]

muckrag *n.* [19C] a handkerchief. [MUCK n.[2]]

muck savage *n.* [1990s+] a peasant.

muck-shifter *n.* [late 19C] a navvy. [MUCK n.[2]]

muck-shoveller *n.* [1940s] (*Aus.*) a tin-miner. [MUCK n.[2] (1); the dirtiness of the job]

mucksnipe *n.* [mid-19C] a gambler (or anyone else) who has lost all their money. [MUCK n.[1]]

muckspout *n.* [early 19C–1910s] one who uses a good deal of obscene language, a person with a 'smutty' mentality. [MUCK n.[2] (1)]

muckstick *n.* [1920s] (*US*) a long-handled shovel; thus *muckstick artist*, a labourer. [MUCK n.[2] (1)]

mucksuck *v.* [1960s+] (*US*) to act in a disgusting manner.

mucksucker *n.* [1960s+] (*US*) one who acts in a disgusting manner. [MUCKSUCK v.]

muck-suckle *n.* [mid–late 19C] a filthy woman. [MUCK n.[2] (1)]

muck-sweat *n.* [early 19C+] perspiration, esp. induced through fear or panic; thus *be in a muck-sweat*, to be terrified, to be flustered.

muckti-muck/muckty-muck *n. see* MUCK-A-MUCK n. (2).

muckty-muck *n.* [1950s+] (*US Black*) **1** nonsense, rubbish, lies. **2** aimless, aggressive talk. [MUCK n.[2]]

muck-up *n.* [20C+] **1** a blunder, an error, a confusion. **2** a mixture. **3** of a person, a mess. [MUCK UP v.]

muck up *v.* **1** [late 19C+] to make a mess (of), to spoil or ruin. **2** [late 19C+] to fail, to go wrong. **3** [1910s+] (*Aus.*) to play the fool (cf. ACT THE ANGORA v.). **4** [1920s] to dirty. [MUCK v.[3]]

muck-worm *n.* **1** [late 16C–19C] a person of the lowest origin. **2** [late 16C–1910s] a miserly person, a 'money-grubber'. **3** [mid-17C–mid-18C] one who is mentally or morally degraded. **4** [mid–late 19C] a street urchin. [SE *muck-worm*, a worm that lives in mud; the sl. is synon. for 'money-grubber']

mucky-muck/-mucky *n. see* MUCK-A-MUCK n. (2).

mucky pup *n.* [20C+] (*orig. Aus.*) **1** a promiscuous person. **2** (*also* **mucky cow**) a dirty person, esp. a child.

mucosa de rosa *n.* [1950s–70s] (*camp gay*) one who spits. [SE mucus + fake Ital. sfx -a + assonance of *rosa*; thus an inference of 'pinkness', i.e. effeminate homosexuality]

mud n.[1] [18C–19C] a fool.

mud n.[2] (*also* **Mississippi mud**) [late 19C+] (*orig. US*) thick, strong coffee.

mud n.[3] (*drugs*) **1** [1910s+] unprocessed opium (cf. APOSTLE n.). **2** [1920s+] opium, esp. second-rate; thus *hit the mud*, to smoke opium. **3** [1950s+] methadone. **4** [1970s+] the residue of heroin or morphine processing. **5** [1980s+] heroin (cf. CACA n.). [the colour (and consistency); note abbr. *foreign mud*, trans. of Chinese name for opium]

mud n.[4] [1930s–70s] (*US*) cheap plaster figurines. [their supposed resemblance to a child's mud pies]

mud n.[5] [1970s+] excrement (cf. ADMIRAL BROWNING n.).

mud and blood n. [20C+] a drink of 'mild and bitter'. [initial letters + the colours]

mud and ooze n. [20C+] (*Aus.*) alcohol. [rhy. sl. = BOOZE n. (1)]

mud bud n. [1980s+] (*drugs*) home-grown marijuana (cf. AFRICAN BUSH n.). [SE *mud* + BUD n.[4]]

mudbutt n. [2000s] (*US campus*) diarrhoea. [MUD n.[5] + BUTT n.[1] (2)]

mudcat n. (*US*) **1** [mid-19C–1940s] a stupid or contemptible person. **2** [late 19C+] a Mississippian. [Mississippi is known as the *Mudcat* State]

mud check n. [2000s] (*US prison*) a forced confrontation to see how brave a new inmate may be. [? MUD n.[5], i.e. a check whether they will SHIT ONESELF v.]

mud-crusher n.[1] [1970s+] (*US Black*) an extreme form of bully whose aim is to crush everyone into the ground.

mud-crusher n.[2] *see* GRAVEL-CRUSHER n. (1).

mudder n. [20C+] (*Aus./US*) a horse or human runner who is at their best on a muddy course or track.

mudding-face n. [late 19C–1910s] a fool, a weakling. [MUD n.[1] + play on SE *pudding-face*]

muddle n. [1910s–30s] a state of slight drunkenness; thus *on the muddle*, on a spree. [MUDDLED adj.]

muddle v. [19C] to have sexual intercourse.

muddle-brained adj. *see* MUDDLE-HEADED adj.

muddled adj. (*also* **muddy**) [late 17C+] drunk (cf. ADDLED adj.).

muddlefug n. [1960s] (*US Black*) a euph. for MOTHERFUCK n. (1).

muddlefugging adj. [1960s] (*US Black*) a euph. for MOTHER-FUCKING adj. (1).

muddle-head n. [mid-19C+] a fool, a simpleton. [MUDDLE-HEADED adj.]

muddle-headed adj. (*also* **muddle-brained**) [mid-18C+] confused, foolish, simple (cf. AIRHEADED adj.).

muddle on v. [late 17C–18C] to carry on drinking despite one's gradually increasing drunkenness.

muddy adj.[1] [20C+] (*Aus.*) a euph. for BLOODY adj.[1].

muddy adj.[2] *see* MUDDLED adj.

muddy fuck n. [1970s] (*gay*) anal intercourse with a partner whose anus has not been properly cleaned. [MUD n.[5] + FUCK n.[1] (1)]

muddy funster n. **1** [1960s+] a euph. for MOTHERFUCKER n. (1). **2** [2000s] a homosexual. [initial letters; (2) MUD n.[5]]

muddy-headed adj. [mid-18C] drunk (cf. ADDLED adj.; ARSE-HOLED adj.).

muddy trench adj. [1910s+] French. [rhy. sl.]

muddy waters n. [1970s+] (*US Black*) the loss of a man's erection before or during sex. [ety. unknown; ? the softness of mud]

mud-fat adj. [1920s+] (*Aus.*) very fat. [the thickness and density of mud]

mud flap n.[1] [20C+] (*US*) a derog. term for a Black person (cf. BLACKBELLY n.). [the colour of mud]

mud flap n.[2] *see* MULLET n.[2].

mud flaps n. [1950s+] (*US Black*) noticeably large feet.

mud for one's turtle n. [1980s+] (*US*) from a man's point of view, sexual intercourse.

mudfuck n. [1980s+] (*US*) a synon. for MOTHERFUCK n. (1). [MUDFUCKER n.]

mudfuck v. [2000s] (*US*) a synon. for MOTHERFUCK v. [MUDFUCKER n.]

mudfucker n. [1970s+] (*US*) a euph. for MOTHERFUCKER n. (1).

mudfucking adj. [1990s+] (*US*) a euph. for MOTHERFUCKING adj. (1). [MUDFUCKER n.]

mudge n. [late 19C] a low-crowned circular hat worn by women. [ety. unknown; ? link to MUSH n.[3]]

mudger n. [early 19C] a weakling, a 'milksop'. [? dial. *nudge*, to crush or bruise]

mud-head n.[1] **1** [mid-19C+] (*US*) a native of Tennessee. **2** [20C+] (*W.I.*) a native of Guyana, the majority of whom live in the muddy coastal areas of the country. [SE *mud*]

mud-head n.[2] [late 19C–1950s] a fool. [MUD-HEADED adj.]

mud-headed adj. [late 18C] stupid (cf. AIRHEADED adj.).

mud hen n. **1** [1910s] (*US*) a derog. term for a Black woman. **2** [1970s] (*US prison*) a lazy person.

mud honey n. **1** [late 19C–1910s] street mud and slush. **2** [1910s] beer.

mud hook n. (*orig. Aus./US*) **1** [early 19C+] an anchor. **2** [mid-19C+] (*also* **mud-hopper, -masher, -splasher, -splitter, -squasher**) a foot, a heavy shoe or boot. **3** [1920s+] a finger or hand. [note *Bulletin* (Sydney), 31 January 1885, 14/4: 'To men who sailed in the good old days […] it is galling to see the manner in which the amateurs are dragging open boat sailing in the mire, by limiting such boats as the Rosetta […] to five hands, maybe to suit some old mudhooker with a ton of ballast in her']

mud in your eye n. [1940s+] a tie. [rhy. sl.; playing on the popular toast, *here's mud in your eye!*]

mud in your eye(s)! excl. *see* HERE'S MUD IN YOUR EYE! excl.

Mud Island n. [late 19C–1900s] Southend, the popular Cockney resort, which is sited at the seaward end of the Thames estuary.

mud-kicker n. [1930s+] (*orig. US Black*) **1** a prostitute who robs rather than has sex with her clients. **2** a prostitute, esp. later, a second-rate prostitute, one who fails, either through laziness or lack of appeal, to make enough money for her pimp. **3** a dedicated, very hard-working prostitute. [race-track jargon *mud-kicker*, a slow racehorse that gets stuck in the mud; but note (3) the US pimp Iceberg Slim uses the word positively]

mud-kicking adj. [1960s] (*US Black*) of a prostitute, hard-working. [MUD-KICKER n. (3)]

Mudland n. [20C+] (*W.I.*) Guyana. [MUD-HEAD n.[1] (2)]

mudlark n. **1** [late 18C–1920s] a hog. **2** [late 18C–1950s] a waterside thief, who picks up packages thrown to them by a ship's crew-member. **3** [19C; 1990s+] one who scavenges items from the Thames mud. **4** [19C–1900s] a barge boy. **5** [early 19C] a duck. **6** [early 19C] a scavenger for scrap-iron. **7** [mid-19C+] one who steals copper from the bottom of ships moored in the Thames. **8** [mid-19C] a sewerman. **9** [mid-19C–1910s] a street child, a 'gutter urchin'. **10** [20C+] (*Aus.*) a resident or native of Victoria, Australia. **11** [20C+] (*Aus./US*) a racehorse that enjoys muddy going. **12** [1910s–20s] (*UK WW1*) a soldier who sings in the trenches.

mud-masher n. *see* MUD HOOK n. (2).

mud-out n. [2000s] an act of defecation. [MUD n.[5]]

mud-packer n. [1990s+] (*US*) a homosexual man (cf. BROWN ARTIST n.). [MUD n.[5]]

mud pads n. [1910s–20s] the feet.

mud pies n. [20C+] (*Aus.*) the eyes. [rhy. sl.]

mud pipes n. [mid-19C–1930s] thick boots, gumboots.

mud-plunging n. [mid-19C–1900s] (*UK tramp*) walking through muddy streets and lanes in the hope of securing hand-outs; thus *mud-plunger*, one who does this.

mud puppy *n.* [1980s+] (*US campus*) an ugly woman. [US regional *mud puppy*, a salamander]

mud-pusher *n.* [late 19C] a street sweeper.

Mud-salad Market *n.* [late 19C] Covent Garden Market.

mud scows *n.* [early 19C–1920s] (*US*) **1** large, cheap shoes. **2** feet. [SE *mud* + *scow*, a large flat-bottomed boat]

mud shark *n.* [2000s] (*US Black*) a White girl who prefers Black men as partners.

mud show *n.* **1** [late 19C–1900s] (*UK society*) an agricultural show or any similar outdoor event. **2** [1920s–30s] (*US*) an old-fashioned circus; thus *mud-showman*, one who runs or works at such a circus.

mudsling *n.* [1950s] a slander, a malicious piece of gossip. [SLING MUD v.]

mudslinger *n.* [1910s+] one who slanders or talks maliciously about somebody. [SLING MUD v.]

mud-slinging *n.* (*also* **shit-slinging**) [late 19C+] slandering, talking maliciously behind someone's back. [SLING MUD v.]

mud snake *n.* [1990s+] (*US*) **1** the penis (cf. ANTEATER n.). **2** a turd. [(2) MUD n.⁵]

mud-splasher/-splitter/-squasher *n. see* MUD HOOK n. (2).

mud-stomper *n.* [1960s+] (*US Black*) a second-rate, impoverished prostitute. [SE *mud* + SAmE *stomp*; the image is one of a woman who has to struggle her way through deep, clinging mud (fig. as well as actually) to make ends meet]

mud student *n.* [mid-19C] an agricultural student.

mud turtle *n.* [late 19C–1930s] (*US*) a contemptible person.

mud-up *n.* [1990s+] (*W.I.*) **1** menstruation. **2** of a man, his state after sexual intercourse.

mud-up *v.* [1990s+] (*W.I.*) to be seen wearing the same outfit more than once.

muff *n.*¹ **1** [17C+] the vagina (cf. BIRD n.⁸). **2** [mid-17C+] pubic hair. **3** [mid-19C] a cat. **4** [20C+] (*US*) a woman. **5** [1910s–50s] (*US*) a prostitute (cf. BANGTAIL n.¹). **6** [1910s–50s] (*US*) a beard, a toupee. **7** [1970s] (*gay*) the anus. **8** [1970s+] (*US*) sexual intercourse. [its supposed resemblance + ext. uses]

muff *n.*² (*also* **muffer**) **1** [17C; late 19C–1910s] a fool, albeit an amiable one. **2** [early 19C–1920s] (*orig. sporting*) an incompetent, one who is awkward. **3** [early 19C–1910s] a blunder, an error; esp. in phr *make a muff of oneself*, to act in an incompetent, foolish manner. **4** [2000s] a policeman. [(1) like the SE *muff*, the fool is SOFT adj. (1) in the head, and note MUFF n.¹ (1) and the use of CUNT n.¹ (1) and other terms for the vagina as synons. for a fool; (2) MUFF v.¹; despite Vaux's use in 1812, *OED* claims that this def. 'has not been found earlier than the second quarter of the 19th c. (being unrecorded even in the slang dictionaries)'; note, however, Nares who cites Warner *Albion's England c.*1600: 'Those stiles to him weare strange, but thay / Did feofe them on the bace-borne muffe, and him as king obay' and 1648 quote for a fool in (1) above, which also suggests that (2) could come f. (1) although it is generally perceived to be the other way around]

muff *adj.* [late 19C] second-rate, 'amateur'. [MUFF n.²]

muff *v.*¹ **1** [early 19C] (*orig. sporting*) to die. **2** [mid-19C+] (*orig. sporting*) to make a blunder, to make a mess, to trip up. **3** [late 19C] to fail an examination. [ety. unknown; ? image of keeping one's hands in a SE *muff* rather than using them properly]

muff *v.*² [1940s+] (*US*) to perform cunnilingus (cf. BEARD RIDE n.). [abbr. MUFF-DIVE v.]

muff *v.*³ [1990s+] to have sexual intercourse with. [MUFF n.¹ (8)]

muff *v.*⁴ [1990s+] (*UK juv.*) to fart. [? MUFF n.¹ (7) or MUFF v.¹ (2)]

muff-dive *v.* (*also* **muff-nosh**) [1940s+] (*orig. US*) to perform cunnilingus (cf. BEARD RIDE n.; CLAMDIVING n.). [MUFF n.¹ (1) + SE *dive*/DIVE v.²/NOSH v. (2); note RMC Duntroon (Aus.) *muffdive*, the act of cunnilingus]

muff-diver *n.* (*orig. US*) **1** [1930s+] one who performs cunnilingus. **2** [1930s+] a lesbian (cf. CARPET-BITER n.). **3** [1940s+] a contemptible person. [MUFF-DIVE v.]

muff-diving *n.* (*also* **muff-noshing**) [1930s+] performing an act of cunnilingus. [MUFF-DIVE v.]

muff-diving *adj.* [1930s+] despicable, contemptible. [MUFF-DIVER n. (3)]

muffed *adj.* [late 19C+] spoilt, bungled, failed. [MUFF v.¹ (2)]

muffer *n.*¹ [1960s+] (*US*) a lesbian, i.e. a woman who performs cunnilingus (cf. CARPET-BITER n.). [MUFF v.²]

muffer *n.*² *see* MUFF n.².

muffin *n.*¹ **1** [mid-19C] (*also* **muffin-cap**) a fool (cf. BEECHAM'S PILL n.). **2** [mid-19C+] an incompetent, one who is awkward. **3** [1970s+] (*US campus*) an admirable person; usu. in combs., such as STUD-MUFFIN n. [(2) ? play on FLAT n.² (1); the muffin is a small *flat* cake; or link to MUFF n.²/MUFF v.¹ (2); (1) is rhy. sl.; ult. children's TV character *Muffin the Mule*]

muffin *n.*² **1** [mid-19C–1900s] (*Can./US*) a female companion who accompanies a bachelor on his round of social amusements. **2** [mid-19C–1930s] (*US*) a male chaperon. [ety. unknown; ? ext. of MUFFIN n.¹ (1)]

muffin *n.*³ (*also* **muffin-cap**) [late 19C–1900s] a 'pill-box' hat or cap, as worn by charity-school boys. [resemblance]

muffin *n.*⁴ **1** [1940s–50s] (*US gay*) an anal virgin. **2** [1950s–70s] (*US*) a girl, a sweetheart. **3** [1960s] (*US gay*) an attractive youth. **4** [1960s+] the vagina (cf. APPLE n.⁶). [ext. of MUFF n.¹]

muffin baker *n.* [mid-19C+] excrement when hard and retained. [rhy. sl. = QUAKER n.; n.b. orig. misunderstood by Hotten and entered in early edn. as a 'Quaker' in religious meaning]

muffin-cap *n.*¹ *see* MUFFIN n.¹ (1).

muffin-cap *n.*² *see* MUFFIN n.³.

muffin-face *n.* (*also* **muffin-countenance**) [mid-18C–19C] **1** a hairless (or expressionless) face. **2** a foolish or childish face. [supposed resemblance]

muffin-faced *adj.* [mid-18C–19C] **1** having a foolish or expressionless face. **2** having a fat face or a face with protuding muscles. [MUFFIN-FACE n.]

muffin-fight *n. see* MUFFIN-WORRY n.

muffing *n.* [mid-19C+] clumsiness, clumsy failure. [MUFF v.¹ (2)]

muffing *adj.* [mid-19C+] bungling, blundering. [MUFF v.¹ (2)]

muffin-head *n.* [late 19C; 1990s+] a fool. [SE *muffin* + -HEAD sfx (1)]

muffin-puncher *n.* [late 19C–1900s] a baker of muffins.

muffins *n.* [1960s+] (*US gay*) the buttocks. [resemblance]

muffin-struggle *n. see* BUN-STRUGGLE n.

muffin-walloper *n.* [late 19C–1900s] a gossipy woman who enjoys dissecting her friends and acquaintances over a cup of tea and a muffin. [SE *muffin* + joc. use of WALLOPER n.¹ (2)]

muffin-worrier *n.* [late 19C] (*Aus.*) one who attends a tea party (and by implication dislikes alcohol). [MUFFIN-WORRY n. (1)]

muffin-worry *n.* (*also* **muffin-fight**) **1** [mid-19C] an evening party. **2** [mid-19C–1920s] an old ladies' tea-party. [? (1) is incorrect def. by Hotten]

muffish *adj.* [mid-19C–1950s] foolish or bungling; thus *muffishness*, the state of being a bungler; *muffism*, foolishness. [MUFF n.² (1)/MUFF n.² (2)]

muff job *n.* [1970s] (*US*) cunnilingus (cf. BEARD RIDE n.). [MUFF n.¹ (2) + JOB n.⁴]

muffler *n.* [early–mid-19C] a blow to the mouth or face.

mufflers *n.* [early–mid-19C] boxing gloves.

muffling-cheat *n.* [mid-16C–early 19C] (*UK Und.*) a napkin. [SE *muffle* + CHEAT n. (1)]

muff merchant *n.* [1960s+] (*US*) **1** a prostitute (cf. ASS PEDDLER n.; BANGTAIL n.¹). **2** a pimp.

muff-muncher *n.* [2000s] one who performs cunnilingus, usu. a lesbian; thus *muff-munching*, pursuing lesbian sex (cf. CARPET-BITER n.). [MUFF n.¹ (2) + MUNCH v.¹ (2)]

muff-nosh *v. see* MUFF-DIVE v.

muff-noshing *n. see* MUFF-DIVING n.

muffy n.[1] [20C+] (Aus.) a frill-necked lizard. [the frill or 'muff' around its neck]

muffy n.[2] [1980s+] (US campus) a young woman who has the look of a typical sorority member, with bleached blonde hair, an alice band, heavy make-up and conventional clothes. [proper name Muffy, the stereotypical name of such young women]

muffy n.[3] [1990s+] (UK juv.) breaking wind. [MUFF v.[4]]

mufki-pufki n. see MIFKY-PIFKY n.

mufti n. **1** [19C] (orig. milit.) ordinary clothes worn by someone who usu. wears a uniform to work. **2** [19C] (Aus.) informal clothes. [both SE post-1900; orig. Ind. army sl., according to Y&B, f. the Mufti, a religious leader and expounder of Islamic law; thus the word 'was perhaps originally applied to the attire of dressing-gown, smoking-cap, and slippers, which was like the Oriental dress of the Mufti, who was familiar in Europe from his appearance in Molière's Bourgeois Gentilhomme'. Note the Fr. equivalent, en Pekin, Peking-style]

mufugly adj. [1980s+] (US campus) extremely ugly. [abbr. MOTHER-FUCKING adv. + SE ugly]

mug n.[1] (also **mugg**) **1** [late 18C] (US Und.) the nose. **2** [late 18C+] the human face; thus [mid-19C] (UK Und.) throw one's mug away, to let anyone see one's face, to reveal oneself; [1920s–60s] (US tramp) polish one's mug, to wash one's face. **3** [early 19C–1960s] a grimace. **4** [early 19C+] the mouth. **5** [mid-19C] a pipe. **6** [mid-19C] (UK Und.) a coin (which bears a monarch's face on one side). **7** [late 19C+] a picture of a person, esp. in police records; thus MUG BOOK n. [? 18C use of drinking mugs made in the shape of grotesque human faces]

mug n.[2] **1** [early 19C+] a fool, a dupe, orig. the victim of a corrupt card-game; thus MUG'S GAME n. **2** [late 19C+] a person, irrespective of character. **3** [20C+] used affectionately as a term of direct address. **4** [1900s–50s] (US) (also **fly mug**) a policeman or detective; a railroad policeman. **5** [1910s+] anyone not directly involved in the underworld, thus, de facto, a gullible fool, a (potential) victim. **6** [1980s] (US Black/campus) a very attractive person. **7** [1990s+] (Irish) a sulky person. [SE mug, i.e. one into whom one can 'pour' any nonsense]

mug n.[3] **1** [mid-19C] an examination. **2** [late 19C–1900s] a schoolchild or student who works hard. [MUG (UP) v.[1]]

mug n.[4] [mid-19C–1950s] (US) a chamberpot. [abbr. MEMBER MUG n.]

mug n.[5] **1** [mid-19C–1960s] (US Und.) a strong hold placed on a victim when robbing them, usu. an arm lock or a chokehold. **2** [mid-19C+] (US) (also **mugg**) a thug, a violent person, a crude loutish person. **3** [1980s+] (US Black) a euph. for MOTHERFUCKER n. (1). [MUG v.[2]; (3) is ext. of (1)]

mug n.[6] [1930s–50s] (US Black) 'the act of putting on a shadow dance' (Durst, The Jives of Dr Hepcat, 1953).

mug n.[7] [1980s] (US) a non-specific thing.

mug n.[8] see MUG SHOT n.

mug adj. [late 19C+] foolish, stupid. [MUG n.[2] (1)]

mug v.[1] (also **mogg**) **1** [early 18C–mid-19C] to refuse food. **2** [mid-18C+] to pout, to grow sullen. **3** [mid-19C+] to make a face, to make people laugh by one's antics and grimaces; thus fig. to play around. [MUG n.[1] (2)]

mug v.[2] **1** [19C–1900s] to fight, to punch, to strangle. **2** [early–late 19C] (also **mug up**) to ruin, to interfere in, to make a mess of. **3** [mid-19C] to chastise. **4** [mid-19C+] to rob, to assault, usu. in the street and often with violence; orig. to garrotte; thus MUGGER n.[2] [MUG n.[1]]

mug v.[3] (also **mug down/up**) **1** [early 19C+] (UK/Aus./US campus) to kiss, to cuddle, to neck. **2** [1950s–60s] (US Black) to have sexual intercourse with. [MUG n.[1] (2); (1) mug up and mug down are later]

mug v.[4] [mid-19C; 2000s] (UK Und.) to trick, to fool.

mug v.[5] [mid-19C–1980s] to bribe, usu. by plying with liquor. [SE mug, a container for liquids]

mug v.[6] [late 19C] to speak. [? MUG n.[1] (4)]

mug v.[7] **1** [late 19C] to take a photo, e.g. for a newspaper. **2** [late 19C+] (US police) to take identification pictures for prison/court use; thus mug room, a room in which such pictures are taken or stored. **3** [1900s–20s] (US Und.) to arrest, esp. for purposes of identification. [MUG n.[1] (7)]

mug v.[8] [late 19C–1940s] to huddle together in a confined space; to associate with. [? dial. muggle, a mess, a confusion, a disorder]

mug v.[9] [late 19C+] to act like a fool. [MUG n.[2] (1)]

mug v.[10] see MUG (UP) v.[1].

mug v.[11] see MUG (UP) v.[2].

mug aleck n. [1930s+] (Aus.) an unpleasantly conceited, smug person. [MUG n.[2] (1) + SMART ALEC(K) n.]

mug behind five v. [1930s–40s] (US Black) to speak with one's hand shielding one's lips. [MUG v.[6] or MUG v.[1] (3)]

mug book n. **1** [20C+] (US police/Und.) (also **mug file/list**) a book of pictures used to help police in keeping records of known criminals. **2** [1930s+] a reference book used for casting purposes in theatre, TV and films, containing pictures of actual and aspirant stars. **3** [1930s+] a collection of photographs of prominent people. [MUG n.[1] (7) + SE book/file]

mug-catcher n. [late 19C] (UK Und.) a confidence trickster. [MUG n.[2] (1) + SE catcher]

mug cop/copper n. see MUG JOHN n.

mug down v. see MUG v.[3].

mugfaker n. [1930s–50s] a street photographer. [MUG n.[1] (7) + FAKER n.]

mug file n. see MUG BOOK n. (1).

mugg n.[1] see MUG n.[1].

mugg n.[2] see MUG n.[5] (2).

mugger n.[1] [early–late 19C] a blow in the mouth. [MUG n.[1] (4)]

mugger n.[2] [mid-19C+] a street robber, orig. a garrotter. [MUG v.[2] (4)]

mugger n.[3] [late 19C] one who studies hard. [MUG (UP) v.[1]]

mugger n.[4] [1940s–60s] a euph. for BUGGER n.[1] (1).

muggered adj.[1] [1940s–60s] a euph. for BUGGERED adj.[2] (3). [MUGGER n.[4]]

muggered adj.[2] see MUGGY adj.[1].

mugger-fugger n. [1930s] a euph. for MOTHERFUCKER n. (1). [note FUG v.[2]]

muggie n. see MUGGLES n.[2].

muggill n. [late 16C–early 17C] (UK Und.) a beadle. [ety. unknown; ? anecdotal f. a beadle named McGill]

mugging n.[1] [mid-19C+] **1** a beating, a fight. **2** garrotting. **3** the act of street robbery and assault. [MUG v.[2] (4) has been the general use since 1960s]

mugging n.[2] [mid-19C+] learning, working hard, memorizing. [MUG (UP) v.[1]]

mugging n.[3] [late 19C+] making faces. [MUG v.[1] (3)]

mugging n.[4] [late 19C+] (US police) taking photographs of people, usu. for identification purposes. [MUG v.[7] (2)]

mugging n.[5] [1930s–40s] (US Black) standing around.

mugging adj. [1970s] annoying. [? MUG v.[4]]

mugging (up) n. [1920s+] (US) kissing, love-making. [MUG v.[3] (1)]

muggins n.[1] **1** [19C] (also **joe muggins**) a fool, a simpleton; thus [late 19C] talk muggins, to talk nonsense. **2** [mid–late 19C] a kind of card-game. **3** [late 19C–1900s] a local politician, e.g. a councillor or mayor. **4** [1950s+] oneself, a rueful self-description; the implication is of being a fool to take on a given task; often in phr. muggins here. [MUG n.[2] (1); (4) f. (1)]

muggins n.[2] **1** [mid-19C] (US) a bottle of bourbon. **2** [1930s–40s] (US prison/tramp) food. [MUG (UP) v.[2]]

muggle n. (also **miggle**) [1920s+] (orig. US drugs) a marijuana cigarette; often a real cigarette with marijuana (occas. hashish) substituted for some of the tobacco and packed back inside it. [MUGGLES n.[2]]

muggled up *adj.* [1940s] (*US drugs*) under the influence of marijuana. [MUGGLES n.²]

mugglehead *n.* (*also* **muggle-smoker**) [1920s–70s] (*US drugs*) a marijuana smoker. [MUGGLES n.² + -HEAD sfx (3)]

muggler *n.*¹ [early 19C] (*Anglo-Irish*) a drink of beer.

muggler *n.*² [1930s] (*drugs*) a smoker of marijuana. [MUGGLES n.²]

muggles *n.*¹ [mid–late 18C] restlessness. [dial. *muggle*, to move restlessly]

muggles *n.*² (*also* **miggles, muggie, muggle**) [1920s+] (*orig. US drugs*) marijuana.

muggle-smoker *n. see* MUGGLEHEAD n.

mug-grappler *n. see* GRAPPLER n.

muggsy *n.* [1930s] (*US*) a derog. term of address, i.e. stupid.

muggy *adj.*¹ (*also* **muggered**) **1** [early 19C+] drunk. **2** [1970s] (*drugs*) causing unpleasant feelings of sweatiness and stupor. [SE *muggy*, damp, close]

muggy *adj.*² [late 19C+] stupid. [MUG n.² (1)]

muggy cunt *n.* [2000s] a general term of abuse. [MUGGY adj.² + CUNT n.² (1)]

muggy-cunt *adj.* [2000s] disgusting, repellent, stupid. [MUGGY CUNT n.]

mughouse *n.* [early 18C] a cheap tavern. [SE *mug* + *house*; best known in comb. *mughouse clubs*, political clubs (of Hanoverian sympathies) which met at 'mug-houses' early in the 18C]

mug-hunter *n.* [late 19C] one who tours the streets late at night in search of drunken men who can be robbed. [MUG n.² (1) + SE *hunter*]

mug in and mug out, be *v.* [mid-19C] to dawdle, to prevaricate, to fail to make up one's mind. [dial. *muggle*, to live haphazardly, to muddle along]

mug john *n.* (*also* **mug cop/copper**) [1930s–50s] (*Aus.*) a policeman (cf. BILLY n.⁶). [MUG n.² (4) + JOHN n.⁴/COPPER n.³ (1)]

mug lair *n.* [1940s+] (*Aus.*) a contemptuous description, i.e. a stupid, gullible, flashy show-off. [MUG n.² (1) + LAIR n.]

muglet *n.* [late 19C] a young victim of a confidence trick. [MUG n.² (1) + sfx -*let*]

mug list *n. see* MUG BOOK n. (1).

mug off *v.* [2000s] to cause trouble for, to fool or deceive someone. [MUG v.⁴]

mug of gin *n. see* CUP OF TEA n. (3).

mug oneself *v.* **1** [mid-19C] to get drunk. **2** [late 19C–1900s] to make oneself comfortable. [? MUG v.² (1) or MUG v.³ (1)]

mug photo/picture *n. see* MUG SHOT n.

mug punter *n.* [mid-19C+] a sucker in any game of chance or at a racecourse. [MUG n.² (1) + PUNTER n.¹ (1)]

mugs away! *excl.* [1940s+] an excl. used in sporting matches when the winners of the previous game tell the losers to start the next contest or game. [joc. use of MUG n.² (1)]

mug's game *n.* (*also* **mug's lark, mutt's game**) [late 19C+] a foolish endeavour, a pointless effort. [MUG n.² (1) + SE *game*]

mug-shoot *v.* [1930s+] (*orig. US*) to take a picture of a prisoner for identification; thus *mug-shooter*, a police photographer. [MUG n.¹ (7) + SE *shoot*]

mug shot *n.* (*also* **mug, mug photo/picture**) **1** [1930s+] a picture taken by the police and used for criminal records. **2** [1970s+] in non-police work, a picture, e.g. a publicity photograph. [MUG n.¹ (7) + SE *shot*]

mug's lark *n. see* MUG'S GAME n.

mugster *n.* [late 19C] (*UK juv.*) a hard worker. [MUG (UP) v.¹]

mug's ticker *n.* [1970s+] (*UK Und.*) a piece of worthless jewellery or a fake Swiss watch. [MUG n.² (1) + TICKER n.¹ (1)]

mug-trap *n.* [late 19C] a con-man, one who tricks gullible victims. [MUG n.² (1) + SE *trap*]

mug-up *n.* [1910s–70s] a snack, a meal, a drink. [MUG (UP) v.²]

mug (up) *v.*¹ [mid-19C+] to study hard, to learn, to memorize, esp. a specific lesson for a specific test or examination; thus

mugging (up), studying hard. [orig. theatrical use, MUG UP v.¹, i.e. paint one's face, as part of preparing to perform a role]

mug (up) *v.*² [mid-19C+] (*US*) to eat heartily, to have a good meal. [? MUG n.¹ (4)]

mug up *v.*¹ [mid–late 19C] to apply theatrical make-up.

mug up *v.*² [late 19C] to praise, to indulge.

mug up *v.*³ [late 19C] to be trapped.

mug up *v.*⁴ [1950s+] (*US Black*) to put on one's hat, to leave. [MUG n.¹ (2)]

mug up *v.*⁵ *see* MUG v.² (2).

mug up *v.*⁶ *see* MUG v.³.

mugwump *n.* (*orig. US*) **1** [mid-19C] an impotent man. **2** [mid-19C+] a person in authority, a self-important person. **3** [late 19C+] an obnoxious, foolish person. **4** [late 19C+] in political terms, one whose vote may go either way and is thus untrustworthy. [SE *mugwump*, 'one who holds more or less aloof from party-politics, professing disinterested and superior views. In 1884, spec. applied to Republicans who refused to support the nominee of their party for president. Also, a person who withdraws his support from any group or organization' (*OED*) and, in (1), from sex]

mugwumping *adj.* [late 19C+] foolish. [MUGWUMP n. (3)]

muhfuh *n.* [1960s+] a synon. of MOTHERFUCKER n. (1). [US Black pron.]

muhfuh *adj.* [2000s] (*orig. US*) a synon. of MOTHERFUCKING adj.

muhfuhkuh *n.* [1960s+] a synon. for MOTHERFUCKER n. (1). [ext. of MUHFUH n.]

mul *n.* (*also* **muller**) [1920s+] (*Irish*) a fool, a useless object. [MULL n.¹ (2)]

mula *n.* [1970s+] a male homosexual who prefers to take the passive role in sex. [Mex. Sp. *mula*, female mule]

mulat *adj.* [1980s] (*US Black*) of a Black person, light-skinned. [abbr. SE *mulatto*]

muldoon *n.*¹ [19C; 1970s] (*US*) a policeman. [a typical Irish name; US police were stereotypically Irishmen; 20C+ use is US Black]

muldoon *n.*² [late 19C] (*US*) the truth, the real thing; something or someone dependable. [abbr. 'the solid *Muldoon*', popularized by 'Muldoon the Solid Man', a vaudeville song by Harrigan and Hart (1874)]

mule *n.*¹ [19C+] an idiot, a fool, a stubborn person (cf. AIREDALE n.). [on model of ASS n. (1)]

mule *n.*² [20C+] any small motor-powered vehicle. [now SE; the use of mules as beasts of burden]

mule *n.*³ **1** [20C+] (*US*) homemade bourbon made from grain alcohol (cf. CORN MULE n.; GRAY MULE n.; MISSISSIPPI MULE n.; WHITE MULE n.). **2** [1950s] (*US drugs*) marijuana soaked in bourbon. **3** [1960s] (*US*) vodka. [the alcohol 'kicks like a *mule*']

mule *n.*⁴ **1** [1920s+] (*drugs*) a drug runner, operating within a given city or prison. **2** [1930s+] (*drugs*) a carrier of drugs, typically across international borders, and in many cases an otherwise 'innocent' person who has no other contact with the drugs trade. **3** [1970s+] (*US prison*) a smuggler, usu. a visitor or prison warder. **4** [1990s+] any form of carrier, e.g. of weapons for a gang.

mule *n.*⁵ [1920s+] (*US*) the penis; thus LOPE ONE'S MULE v. and WATER THE MULE v. **2** [1990s+] sexual intercourse; esp. in *ride the mule*, to have sexual intercourse.

mule *n.*⁶ [1940s+] **1** an unattractive woman. **2** (*US campus*) an unattractive man. **3** an impotent man. **4** (*W.I.*) an infertile woman, who therefore suffers from *mule-belly*.

mule *v.* [1960s+] (*US Und./police/prison*) to act as a courier of contraband, esp. illicit drugs. [MULE n.²]

mule breakfast *n.* [1920s–40s] (*US*) a straw hat (cf. COW'S BREAKFAST n.).

muledick *v.* [1970s] (*US*) of a man, to copulate aggressively, violently.

mule-headed *adj.* [mid-19C+] stupid, foolish, stubborn (cf. AIRHEADED adj.).

mule-mouth *n.* [1970s+] (*US Black*) one who works regularly as a police informer.

mulenyam *n.* (*also* **moulenjam, moulonjam, moulonjohn**) [1960s+] (*US Ital.*) a Black person. [Ital. *melanzana*, an aubergine, which is a deep purple in colour]

mule shit! *excl.* [1920s+] (*US*) a mild oath, used to express disbelief or surprise. [var. on BULLSHIT! excl.]

mule-skinner *n.* 1 [late 19C–1960s] (*US*) a mule-driver. 2 [1980s+] (*drugs*) one who organizes, pays and supervises a drug courier or MULE n.[4] (1). [the lit. or fig. application of the whip]

mule-whacker *n.* [late 19C–1920s] (*US*) a mule-driver. [SE *mule* + WHACK v.[1] (1)]

muley-grubs *n. see* MULLIGRUBS n.

mulga *n.* [late 19C+] (*Aus.*) an uninhabited, sparsely populated or inhospitable region; thus used attrib. in combs.; *mulga madness*, mental decay that can overtake those spending long periods alone in such regions; *mulga scrubbers*, stock that have run wild and deteriorated in condition; *Mulga Bill*, a generic term for a bushman; thus also *go mulga*, to take to the bush, fig. to go off by oneself. [SAusE *mulga*, one of various plants of the genus *Acacia* found in the dry inland of Australia; thus the dry inland itself. The Aus. term comes from Yuwaalaraay *malga*]

mulga wire *n.* [late 19C+] 1 a 'bush telegraph', the 'grapevine'. 2 (*also* **mulga**) a rumour, a lie. [MULGA n. + SE *wire*, a telegram]

mull *n.*[1] 1 [19C] a mess; usu. in *make a mull of*, make a mess of. 2 [mid–late 19C] a simpleton, a clumsy person. [? SE *mull*, to grind, to pulverize or SE *muddle*]

mull *n.*[2] (*also* **mulligatawney**) [mid–late 19C] (*Anglo-Ind.*) a member of the Imperial Civil Service belonging to the Madras presidency. [abbr. SE *mulligatawny*, a highly seasoned soup, a speciality of Madras]

mull *v.*[1] (*orig. US*) 1 [mid-19C] to work steadily without accomplishing much. 2 [late 19C+] to think about, to cogitate upon, to work over in one's mind. [SE *mull*, to grind, to pulverize]

mull *v.*[2] [1980s+] (*Aus. drugs*) to chop and mix cannabis finely for consumption. [SE *mull*, but note MOULI v.]

mulla *n. see* MOOLA n.

mullah *v.* (*also* **muller**) 1 [1950s+] (*orig. UK prison*) to beat up severely. 2 [1990s+] to defeat resoundingly. [SE *mull*, to grind to powder, to pulverize, to crumble]

mullahed *adj.* (*also* **mullered**) 1 [1950s+] (*orig. UK prison*) beaten severely. 2 [1990s+] defeated comprehensively, broken, destroyed. 3 [1990s+] drunk, absolutely intoxicated (cf. ANNIHILATED adj.). [MULLAH v.]

mullahing *n.* (*also* **mullering**) [1990s+] a beating. [MULLAH v.]

mullarkey *n. see* MALARKEY n.

mulled (up) *adj.* [1930s–70s] drunk. [abbr. SE *mulled (ale)* or *muddled*]

muller *n.*[1] [mid-19C–1900s] 1 a hat that has had its shape altered. 2 a type of flat-topped felt hat. [Franz *Muller* (d.1864), the first person ever to commit a murder on the railway, whose attempt to flee justice was augmented by his taking his victim's hat, a topper, and cutting an inch off it. Such short hats were briefly fashionable, under the murderer's name]

muller *n.*[2] [1980s+] (*Aus. drugs*) one who chops and mixes the cannabis. [MULL v.[2]]

muller *n.*[3] *see* MUL n.

muller *v. see* MULLAH v.

mullered *adj. see* MULLAHED adj.

mullering *n. see* MULLAHING n.

mullet *n.*[1] [1950s+] (*US*) a fool (cf. AIREDALE n.). [abbr. MULLET-HEAD n.]

mullet *n.*[2] (*also* **ape drape, hockey head, mud flap**) [1970s+] a hairstyle, short on top and long at the back, popular in the 1970s.

mullethead *n.* [late 19C+] (*US*) a fool. [MULLETHEADED adj.]

mulletheaded *adj.* [mid-19C+] stupid, foolish, ignorant (cf. AIRHEADED adj.). [the freshwater fish the *mullet* has a notably large head]

mulliegrums *n. see* MULLIGRUBS n. (1).

mulligan *n.*[1] 1 [late 19C–1940s] (*US*) an Irish person (cf. DONOVAN n.[1]). 2 [1930s+] (*US prison*) a prison guard. 3 [1930s+] (*US Und.*) a policeman. 4 [1960s] a part-time, 'amateur' criminal. [*Mulligan*, a typical Irish name. Early prison guards, like early policemen, were often Irish]

mulligan *n.*[2] [1920s–50s] (*US*) a high-powered rifle.

mulligan *n.*[3] [1940s–60s] (*US Black*) a tramp. [backform. f. MULLIGAN (STEW) n., the consumers of which were mainly vagrants]

mulligan *n.*[4] [1990s+] (*US*) an unexpected second chance. [golf jargon *mulligan*, a free shot that is not counted on the score-card]

mulligan *n.*[5] *see* MULLIGAN (STEW) n.

mulligan car *n.* [20C+] (*US*) a restaurant car on a railway. [MULLIGAN (STEW) n. + SE *car*; note US army *mulligan battery*, the cook wagon]

mulligan joint *n.* [20C+] (*US*) a cheap restaurant. [MULLIGAN (STEW) n. + JOINT n.[4] (3)]

mulligan mixer *n.* [20C+] (*US, Western*) a cook. [MULLIGAN (STEW) n. + SE *mixer*]

mulligans *n.* [1940s–50s] (*Aus.*) playing cards. [ety. unknown]

mulligan (stew) *n.* [late 19C+] (*orig. US tramp*) a stew made of whatever meats and vegetables are available. [either proper name *Mulligan*, the name of an otherwise forgotten cook, or *Mulligan* as a generic for Irish and thus an Irish stew; note army jargon *mulligan battery*, the cook wagon]

mulligatawney *n. see* MULL n.[2].

mulligatawney *adj.* [1960s–70s] sexually aroused or arousing. [rhy. sl. = HORNY adj.]

mulligrubber *n.* [late 19C] (*US*) a tramp, a vagrant. [MULLIGAN (STEW) n. + GRUBBER n.[3]]

mulligrubs *n.* (*also* **mollygrubs, muley-grubs, mully-grubs**) 1 [late 16C+] (*also* **mulliegrums**) a feeling of unease, not an illness that can be diagnosed, but a general sense of not being fully well. 2 [17C–mid-19C] colic, diarrhoea. ['a grotesque arbitrary formation' (*OED*); ? SE *mull*, to grind, to pulverize + *grub*, an insect; note US regional uses: (1) stomach pains, diarrhoea; (2) menstruation]

Mullingar heifer *n.* (*also* **Munster heifer**) [19C+] (*Irish*) a woman with thick ankles; thus *beef to the heels/knees, like a Mullingar heifer*; the phr. is occas. used of men to describe them as brawny, stalwart. [the supposed characteristic of *Mullingar/Munster* women; note Ned Ward, *The London Spy* (1699): 'A Bouncing beldam, who had as much Flesh on her Bones as a Lincolnshire Heifer']

mullion *n.* [1950s–70s] (*US Black*) an unattractive woman or ugly person. [? SE *melungeon*, a member of a racially mixed group of people – half Black, half Native American – centred in the Appalachians, ult. Fr. *mélange*, mixture]

mullipuff *n. see* MOLLYPUFF n.

mullock *n.* (*Aus.*) 1 [mid-19C+] rubbish, a worthless object; thus *mullock-seller*, a con-man who sells worthless goods; *in the mullock*, in difficulties. 2 [late 19C+] an ignorant and generally useless person. [dial. *mullock*, rubbish; also SAusE *mullock*, the earth taken from a mine and piled at its mouth]

mullyfogging *adj.* [1960s+] (*US*) a euph. for MOTHERFUCKING adj. (1).

mullygrubs *n. see* MULLIGRUBS n.

mullypuff *n. see* MOLLYPUFF n.

multa *adj. see* MULTY adj.

multa bona fakement *n.* [early 19C] (*Polari*) a well-executed confidence trick. [MULTA adj. + BONA adj. + FAKEMENT n.]

multee kertever *adj.* (*also* **multicattivo**) [mid–late 19C] very bad. [Ital./Ling. Fr. *molto cattivo*, very bad]

multi *adj. see* MULTY adj.

multicoloured yawn n. [1960s+] (orig. Aus.) the act of vomiting. [the multicoloured effluvia so produced]

multi-culti adj. [1980s+] (US) multi-cultural. [abbr.]

multie adj. see MULTY adj.

multiple sadness! excl. [1980s+] (US campus) a general excl. of regret, that's really terrible! oh no! I'm so sorry!

multitask v. [1990s+] (US teen) to do more than one thing at a time. [computer jargon]

multy adj. (also **multa, multi, multie**) [late 19C–1910s] (orig. Ling. Fr./Polari) **1** of people and things, bad, unpleasant. **2** criminally obtained. [Ital. molti many; later use mainly Aus.]

mulvather v. [mid–late 19C] (Irish) to confuse. [Sp. malvader, to knock down, to stun]

mulvathered adj. [mid–late 19C] (Irish) drunk (cf. ANNIHILATED adj.). [MULVATHER v.]

mum n.[1] [mid-16C+] a refusal to speak, silence; the state of being dumb; latterly in MUM'S THE WORD phr. [late 14C SE mum, an inarticulate sound made through the closed lips. Such a sound indicates an unwillingness to speak out loud]

mum n.[2] [20C+] a chrysanthemum. [abbr.]

mum n.[3] [1930s+] (UK Und.) one's mistress of many years or one's wife, but not one's actual mother. [var. on MOTHER n.[1] (3)]

mum adj. [late 18C+] silent, quiet; often in KEEP MUM v. [MUM n.[1]]

mum! excl. [mid-16C–1900s] an excl. demanding silence. [MUM n.[1]]

mum, be v. see MOTHER, BE v.

mum and dad adj.[1] [20C+] (Aus./N.Z.) **1** mad (cf. COCK-SPARROW adj.). **2** bad. [rhy. sl.]

mum and dad adj.[2] [1990s+] (Aus.) conventional respectable and thus, by criminal standards, naïve.

mum and daddo n. [20C+] (Aus.) a shadow. [rhy. sl.]

mumble and moan n. [1930s] a telephone. [rhy. sl.]

mumble and mutter n. [20C+] butter. [rhy. sl.]

mumble-a-sparrow n. (also **mumble-sparrow**) [late 18C–early 19C] a game practised at country fairs. A cock-sparrow, with wings clipped, is placed inside an upturned hat, and a man with his arms tied behind his back attempts to bite off its head.

mumble-crust n. [mid-16C–early 17C] a toothless person. [SE mumble, to chew softly, as with toothless gums]

mumble-matins n. [mid-16C–early 17C] a priest.

mumble-peg n. [late 19C–1960s] **1** the vagina. **2** female pubic hair. [SE mumble-the-peg; mumblety-peg, a game in which each player in turn throws a knife from a series of positions, continuing until they fail to make the blade stick in the ground]

mumblers n. [1990s+] women's skintight (bicycle) shorts. [i.e. one 'can see the lips moving', but one can't understand a word they're saying]

mumble-sparrow n. see MUMBLE-A-SPARROW n.

mumble-turd n. [late 16C] a term of abuse.

mumbling cove n. [late 18C–mid-19C] (UK Und.) a shabby person. [COVE n. (1)]

mumbly pegs n. (also **mumblety-pegs**) [1920s–50s] (US) the legs. [rhy. sl.]

mumbo-jumbo n. [late 18C+] meaningless nonsense. [SE mumbo-jumbo, 'an object of unintelligent veneration' (OED); ult. Mama Dyumba, the protective spirit of the Khassonkee tribe of Senegal]

mumbojumbo v. [20C+] to talk meaningless nonsense. [MUMBO-JUMBO n.]

mum-figure n. [1950s+] a mother figure.

mum-glass n. [late 17C–early 19C] the Monument, a 95m (311ft) column erected in 1671–7 in memory of the Great Fire of London (1666) at the junction of what is now Monument Street and Fish Street Hill. [SE mum-glass, a glass used for the drinking of mum beer, a type of beer originating in Brunswick in Germany

and imported into the UK in the 17C–18C. The Monument presumably resembles such a glass]

mummer n. **1** [late 18C–mid-19C] the mouth. **2** [19C–1920s] an actor. [SE mummer, one who mutters and murmurs and thus an actor in a dumb-show]

mummery and millinery n. [20C+] religious ritualism. [the elaborate rituals and costumes of the High Church and of Roman Catholicism]

mummery-cove n. [mid–late 19C] an actor. [SE mummery, over-acting + COVE n. (1)]

mummick v. [late 19C] (US) to handle or feel an object or person. [? dial. mammock, to break into pieces, to crumble, to tear]

mummy n. [1900s–10s] (US) an incompetent.

mummy v. [1970s+] (US Black) to beat a person to death, thus making them into an Egyptian-style mummified corpse.

mummyhead n. [1990s+] (US Black gang) a fool. [SE mummy, a wrapped, embalmed corpse, orig. Egyptian + -HEAD sfx (1)]

mummy pussy n. [1970s+] (US Black) a woman who does not respond during sexual intercourse. [SE mummy, an embalmed corpse + PUSSY n. (1)]

mump n. [early 18C] a beggar, a scrounger. [MUMPER n. (2)]

mump v. **1** [late 16C+] to beg, to visit a house in the course of one's travels as a beggar. **2** [mid-17C–mid-18C] to cheat (out of); to deceive. **3** [late 17C–1910s] to obtain by begging. **4** [early–mid-18C] to disappoint. **5** [late 18C] to eat. **6** [mid-19C] to talk seriously. [? Du. mompen, to cheat; ? dial. mump, to mutter, to speak indistinctly]

mumper n. **1** [mid-17C] a prostitute. **2** [mid-17C+] (UK Und.) a genteel beggar, a scrounger, 'a Gentiler sort of Beggars, for they scorn to beg for food, but money and cloaths' (Head, The Canting Academy, 1674). **3** [mid-19C+] a half-breed gypsy, a 'second-rate' gypsy, i.e. one who has no van. **4** [20C+] a tramp. [MUMP v.]

mumper v. [20C+] (US Black) to travel around, to partner someone on their travels. [MUMP v. (1)]

mumper's brass n. [early 18C] money. [MUMPER n. (2) + BRASS n.[1] (1)]

mumper's hall n. [late 17C–early 19C] a low-class ale-house, frequented by beggars, who will be 'very Merry, Drunk and Frolicksome' (B.E.). [MUMPER n. (2) + ironic use of SE hall]

mumping n. [late 17C+] begging. [note police jargon mumping, of a policeman, accepting cheap or free goods and services from friendly tradespeople]

mumpins n. [mid-15C] alms. [predates MUMP v. (1) and MUMPER n. (2) so poss. SE although not in OED]

mumps, the n. [late 16C–19C] low spirits, 'the sulks'. [dial. mump, to complain, to speak querulously]

mumpy adj. [1990s+] impoverished. [? MUMP v.]

mums n. [late 18C–19C] the mouth, the jaws, the face, the lips. [var. on MUNS n.[1]]

mum's the word phr. [18C+] be quiet, say nothing about this. [MUM n.[1]]

mumsy adj. [1960s+] motherly, usu. with pej. implications, over-fussy, nagging, respectable. [SE mum]

mum-tip n. [early 19C] a bribe to ensure one's silence, 'hush-money'. [MUM n.[1]]

mum your dubber! excl. [late 18C–mid-19C] be quiet! shut up! [MUM! excl. + DUBBER n.[2]]

mun n.[1] (also **mund, munn, munne**) [late 17C] a member of a band of London street thugs. [northern dial.]

mun n.[2] see MON n.[1].

munch n. [1990s+] (orig. US teen) a snack. [abbr. MUNCHIE n.[1]]

munch v.[1] **1** [17C; 19C; 1980s+] to eat, esp. enthusiastically. **2** [1960s+] (also **munch the box**) to perform oral sex (cf. BASKET LUNCH n.; BOX LUNCH n.). **3** [1980s] (US campus) to kiss.

munch v.[2] [1970s+] (US) **1** to make a blunder, to perform badly. **2** to crash, as from a surfboard or a vehicle.

muncher boy *n.* [1960s+] (*US*) a fellator. [MUNCH v.¹ (2) + SE *boy*]

munchie *n.*¹ (*also* **munchy**) [1950s+] (*orig. US*) **1** a snack or small meal. **2** usu. in pl., the craving for food, often sweet or in an otherwise unlikely combination of flavours, that afflicts smokers of hashish or marijuana. **3** a snack eaten to assuage this craving.

munchie *n.*² [2000s] (*Irish*) a derog. term for a country person, a rustic.

munchied up *adj.* [1990s+] experiencing the pangs of hunger that accompany the smoking of cannabis or (occas.) heavy drinking.

Munching House *n.* [late 19C] the Mansion House, London. [SE *munch*, a pun on the aldermanic and corporation dinners that are held there]

munching house *n.* [1910s+] a cheap restaurant or café.

munching the truncheon *n.* [1990s+] fellatio (cf. BASKET LUNCH n.; MUNCH THE TRUNCH v.; PUNCHING THE TRUNCHEON n.). [MUNCH v.¹ (2) + TRUNCHEON n.]

munchkin *n.* **1** [1950s+] a child, a small person. **2** [1980s+] (*US*) a menial employee or inconsequential person. [the *Munchkins*, diminutive characters who featured in the book by L. Frank Baum, *The Wizard of Oz* (publ. 1900, filmed 1939)]

munch-out *n.* [1970s+] (*US campus*) a large meal. [MUNCH OUT v.]

munch out *v.* **1** [1970s+] (*orig. US campus*) to eat voraciously, esp. as a result of smoking cannabis. **2** [1980s+] (*US campus*) to kiss passionately.

munch-present *n.* [mid-16C–early 17C] one who takes bribes. [he fig. 'eats' the money]

munch the box *v. see* MUNCH v.¹ (2).

munch the carpet *v.* (*also* **chew the carpet, lick the carpet**) [1980s+] (*US*) to perform cunnilingus (cf. BEARD RIDE n.; BOX LUNCH n.). [MUNCH v.¹ (2) + CARPET n.⁴]

munch the trunch *v.* [1990s+] (*UK juv.*) to fellate (cf. BASKET LUNCH n.; MUNCHING THE TRUNCHEON n.). [MUNCH v.¹ (2) + TRUNCHEON n.]

munchy *n. see* MUNCHIE n.¹.

mund *n. see* MUN n.¹.

mundane *n.*¹ [late 19C] a fashionable person. [Fr. *mondaine*, a sophisticate]

mundane *n.*² [1990s+] (*US campus*) a boring, unimaginative person. [SE *mundane*, tedious, everyday]

munds *n. see* MUNS n.¹.

mung *n.* [1940s+] (*US campus*) filth or dirt of any kind, anything disgusting. [note computer jargon *mung*, to destroy maliciously, to ruin]

mung *adj.*¹ [mid–late 19C] (*US*) untrue, false, usu. in journalistic context. [SE/dial. *mong*, a mixture, a confusion]

mung *adj.*² [1960s] (*US campus*) spoiled. [MUNG n.]

mung *v.*¹ [19C] (*UK tramp/Und.*) to beg. [Rom. *mang*, to beg; note also dial. *munge*, to whine in low tones]

mung *v.*² [1960s+] (*US campus*) to spoil, to ruin. [MUNG n.]

munga *n. see* MUNGER n.

mungare *n. see* NUMGARE n.

mungaree *n.* (*also* **mongoree, mungee, mungy, munjari, munjary**) **1** [mid-19C–1940s] food. **2** [20C+] (*UK tramp*) begging. [Ital. *mangiare*, to eat; (1) 20C+ use also Aus.]

mungarly *n.* [mid–late 19C] food. [Polari, thence Ital. *mangiare*, Fr. *manger*, to eat. Note Grose, *Provincial Glossary* (1787), *mung*, food for chickens]

mungarly-casa *n.* [mid–late 19C] a baker's shop. [MUNGARLY n. + CASA n.¹]

mungas *n.* (*also* **munja**) [1910s+] (*N.Z.*) food, a meal, esp. lunch. [Ital. *mangiare*, to eat]

munge *n.* (*also* **munns, muns**) [late 17C–early 18C] (*UK Und.*) the dark. [ety. unknown]

mungee *n. see* MUNGAREE n.

munger *n.* (*also* **manga, munga**) [20C+] (*Aus./N.Z.*) **1** food. **2** a smoke taken during a rest period. [(1) MUNGARLY n.]

munging *n.* [mid-19C] begging. [MUNG v.¹]

mungo *n.*¹ [mid-18C–mid-19C] a Black person.

mungo *n.*² [late 18C] ? a person of position, a 'swell'. [def. is queried in *OED*, as also is label 'slang']

mungo *n.*³ [1990s+] (*Aus.*) a fan of Rugby League. [? SE *mungo*, a tough material, made from recycled rags, ? used for old rugby shirts]

mungous *adj.* [1990s+] (*UK juv.*) huge, enormous. [HUMONGOUS adj.]

mungy *n. see* MUNGAREE n.

mungy *adj.* [1960s] (*US*) dirty, filthy. [MUNG n.]

muni *n.* (*also* **muny**) **1** [1930s+] (*US tramp*) a municipal lodging house. **2** [1970s+] (*US*) a municipal bond. [abbr.]

munitions *n.* [1920s] (*US*) cosmetics. [play on WARPAINT n. (3)]

munja *n. see* MUNGAS n.

munjari/munjary *n. see* MUNGAREE n.

munjay *n.* [1940s] (*W.I.*) a large dumpling. [Fr. *manger*, to eat]

munn/munne *n. see* MUN n.¹.

munns *n.*¹ *see* MUNGE n.

munns *n.*² *see* MUNS n.¹.

munnu *n.* [1940s] (*W.I.*) romance. [? MUUNA n.; or ? Fr. *mon amour*, my love]

munpins *n. see* MOMPYNS n.

muns *n.*¹ (*also* **munds, munns**) **1** [mid-17C–19C] the mouth, the jaws, the face, the lips; thus as v., to kiss. **2** [mid-18C] in ext. use, the whole person. [dial. *mun*, the face; thus mid-19C street cry 'One a penny, two a penny, hot cross buns, / Butter them and sugar them and put them in your muns'; Grose (1785) traces it to Ger. *mund*, mouth]

muns *n.*² *see* MUNGE n.

munson *v.* [1990s+] to leave behind, to abandon. [coined and used in the film *Kingpin* (1996), where the character *Roy Munson*, played by Woody Harrelson, was once a ten-pin bowling champion but gets *munsoned*]

Munster heifer *n. see* MULLINGAR HEIFER n.

Munster plums *n.* [late 18C–1900s] potatoes. [proper name of the Irish county *Munster* and thus a synon. of the stereotype IRISH adj.]

munt *n.* (*also* **muntu**) [1930s+] (*orig. S.Afr.*) a derog. term for a Black person (cf. ALLIGATOR BAIT n.²). [Bantu *umuntu*, sing. of *abantu*, a person, Black person, servant]

munta *n.* [1990s+] an ugly, promiscuous woman. [? MOUNT n. (3)]

munted *adj.* [1990s+] **1** (*Aus. teen*) a general negative description, ugly, unpleasant. **2** very drunk. [? MUNTER n.]

munter *n.* [1990s+] (*UK juv.*) a very ugly woman. [? MOUNT n.]

muntu *n. see* MUNT n.

muny *n. see* MUNI n.

muppet *n.* **1** [1970s+] a child, a small person. **2** [1980s] a policeman or magistrate. **3** [1990s+] an unattractive person, a fool, poss. one who is mentally retarded; a term of abuse. [the puppets created by Jim Henson and featured on TV's *Muppet Show* during the 1970s]

mur *n.* (*also* **myrrh**) [mid-19C–1950s] rum. [backsl.]

murdelize *v.* [1960s+] (*US teen*) to trounce, to drub. [? play on fig. use of SE *murder*]

murder *n.* **1** [mid-19C+] something (or someone) unbearable, extremely difficult or infuriating. **2** [1920s+] (*orig. US Black*) an excellent or marvellous person or thing.

murder *v.* **1** [early 17C; mid-19C–1940s] (*US*) to exasperate, to infuriate, e.g. *that just murders me*. **2** [mid-19C+] (*orig. US*) to consume or desire, greedily and enthusiastically, e.g. *I could murder a roast duck noodle soup*. **3** [1910s+] (*orig. US*) to defeat totally or conclusively, esp. at a game or sport.

murder! *excl.* [late 18C–1950s] used to express annoyance, pain or surprise. [SE *murder!* 'As a cry or exclamation uttered by one who thinks or pretends to think himself or some one else in danger of murder' (*OED*)]

murderation *n.* [20C+] (*W.I.*) a severe beating, esp. of a woman or child. [ext. of SE *murder*]

murderation! *excl.* [mid-19C; 1980s+] a general excl. [ext. of MURDER! excl.; 1980s+ UK Black]

murderers' row *n.* [mid-19C–1910s] (*US police*) cells for condemned murderers.

murder house *n.* [1960s+] (*N.Z. juv.*) a school dental clinic.

murder in Irish! *excl.* [mid-18C] a general excl.

murder-mouth *v.* [1970s] (*US Black*) **1** to talk insincerely, to lie, esp. when pursuing sex. **2** to make threats that one couldn't or wouldn't ever back up with action.

murder on *phr. see* DEATH ON *phr.* (2).

murder one *n.* [1950s+] (*US drugs*) **1** heroin and cocaine. **2** a strong variety of heroin. [US legal jargon *murder one*, first degree or premeditated murder]

murder one *adj.* [1990s+] (*US*) very aggressive, murderous.

murder one dun *phr.* [1990s+] a greeting. [ety. unknown; link to US legal jargon *murder one*, first degree or premeditated murder]

murder ones *n.* [1980s+] (*US Black*) dark glasses. [for ety. *see* MURDER ONE *n.*; the wearing of dark glasses is equated with a murderous image]

murder rap *n.* [1920s+] (*orig. US*) a charge of murder. [SE *murder* + RAP *n.*[4] (3)]

murder the bishop *v. see* BANG THE BISHOP *v.*

murerk *n.* [mid-19C] (*UK tramp*) the mistress of the house. [? corruption of BURERK *n.*]

murk *n.* [1930s–80s] (*US*) coffee. [its appearance]

murkarker *n.* (*also* **murkauker**) [mid-19C] (*London*) a monkey. [proper name *Jacky Macauco*, a celebrated fighting monkey to be seen facing off against a variety of canine opponents at the Westminster Pit, *c.*1820. He beat all comers until vanquished by a pit bull. Note Port. *macaco*, a macaque monkey]

murky *n.* [20C+] (*Aus.*) an Aborigine. [the darkness of skin]

murotugora *n. see* MOROTGARA *n.*

murph *n.* [late 19C+] a potato. [abbr. MURPHY *n.*[1]]

Murphia *n.* [1990s+] the expatriate Irish people living in the UK, esp. those who have prospered. [*Murph(y)*, a common Irish surname + SE (*maf*)*ia*]

Murphy *adj.* [late 19C] (*Aus.*) pertaining to Ireland or the Irish; ext. the Catholic church.

murphy *n.*[1] [early 19C+] a potato; thus (*US short order*) *murphy with his coat on*, an unpeeled boiled potato. [the common Irish surname and the assumption that potatoes are the supreme Irish staple]

murphy *n.*[2] **1** [mid-19C–1930s] (*orig. UK*) an Irish person (cf. DONOVAN *n.*[1]). **2** [1960s] (*US*) a police officer. **3** [1960s] (*orig. US Und.*) a victim of MURPHY GAME *n.*[1]. [*Murphy*, a common Irish surname]

murphy *n.*[3] (*also* **murphy game**) [1960s+] (*US*) a swindle in general. [ext. of MURPHY GAME *n.*[1]]

murphy *n.*[4] [1980s+] (*US campus*) a condition of having one's underwear caught between the buttocks; thus *have a murphy*. [? stereotyping of an Irish person as foolish or risible]

murphy *n.*[5] *see* MURPHY GAME *n.*

murphy *v.* [1960s+] (*US Und.*) to swindle by promising some variety of illegal pleasure, usu. sex, then taking the money and failing to deliver the promised 'goods'. [MURPHY *n.*[3]]

murphy dog *n.* [1990s+] a swindler. [MURPHY *n.*[3] + DOG *n.*[3] (1)]

murphy game *n.*[1] (*also* **murphy**) [1950s+] (*orig. US Und.*) of a prostitute, luring a client either to a room or a deserted alley, hallway etc and then, instead of having sex, the client is beaten and robbed by a male accomplice, who may just strike, but may also pose as an aggrieved father, lover, brother etc. [? orig. practitioners promised the victim a meeting with 'a lovely woman

called Mrs Murphy'. The *murphy* can be ext. to drug 'deals' and other illicit commerce]

murphy game *n.*[2] *see* MURPHY *n.*[3].

murphy land *n.* [mid-19C–1940s] (*US*) Ireland. [MURPHY *n.*[2] (1)]

murphy man *n.* [1960s+] a man who specializes in the MURPHY GAME *n.*[1].

Murphy's countenance *n.* (*also* **Murphy's face**) [early–mid-19C] a pig's face. [stereotyped relationship between the Irish (*Murphy* being a typical Irish surname) and the pig]

Murphy's law *n.* [1950s+] a 'natural law' derived from human observation, stating that 'if anything can go wrong – it will'. [other laws attributed to *Murphy* include 'Nothing is ever as simple as it seems', 'Everything takes longer than you expect', 'Nature always sides with the hidden flaw'. For a comprehensive list, *see* Paul Dickson, *The Official Rules* (1978). According to the astronaut John Glenn (b.1921), *Murphy* himself 'was a fictitious character who appeared in a series of educational cartoons put out by the US Navy […] a careless, all-thumbs mechanic who was prone to make such mistakes as installing a propeller backwards' (*Into Orbit*, 1962)]

Murray whaler *n. see* MURRUMBIDGEE WHALER *n.*

Murrumbidgee jam *n.* [1900s–40s] (*Aus.*) brown sugar moistened with cold tea and spread on a damper. [proper name *Murrumbidgee*, a river in southern New South Wales]

Murrumbidgee oyster *n.* [1940s] (*Aus.*) a raw egg plus vinegar and seasoning.

Murrumbidgee whaler *n.* (*also* **Bidgee whaler, whaler**) [mid-19C–1940s] (*Aus.*) an itinerant tramp whose 'beat' focuses on the rivers of New South Wales; thus *Murrumbidgee whaling*, tramping; also as *Darling whaler; Murray whaler*. [*Murrumbidgee* + the moving about of SE *whaling*]

muscadoodle *n.* [1950s+] (*US*) cheap muscatel wine.

muscateer *n.* [1930s+] (*Aus.*) a drinker of cheap muscat wine. [pun on SE *musketeer*]

muscle *n.*[1] **1** [late 19C+] pressure, threats or coercion. **2** [20C+] (*orig. US*) strength, courage. **3** [1920s+] a thug, esp. as a group of thugs hired to intimidate by using violence. **4** [1930s+] political influence, power, usu. based on threats or intimidation. **5** [1960s+] (*US*) of an automobile, or motorcycle, speed, power. [MUSCLE *v.*]

muscle *n.*[2] (*also* **muscle missile**) [1960s+] (*US*) the penis. [abbr. LOVE MUSCLE *n.* + SE *missile*]

muscle *adj.* [1930s+] (*US*) physically violent. [MUSCLE *v.*]

muscle *v.* **1** [mid-19C+] (*orig. US*) to put pressure on, to coerce with threats of violence, poss. to beat up. **2** [1910s+] (*US*) to move something by force, to use one's strength to achieve something. **3** [1920s–30s] (*US*) to bluff.

muscle around *v.* [1930s] to search energetically. [fig. use of MUSCLE *v.* (2)]

musclebound between the ears *phr.* [1910s–40s] (*US*) very stupid.

muscle boy *n.* **1** [1930s+] (*US*) a thug. **2** [1960s+] (a homosexual) body builder. [MUSCLE *n.*[1] (3)/SE *muscle* + *boy*]

muscle car *n.* (*also* **muscle machine**) [1960s+] (*orig. US*) a motor vehicle that is specially modified to give high power and speed. [fig. use of SE *muscle* + *car*]

muscle fuck *n.* [1970s+] (*US*) **1** the rubbing of the penis between a woman's breasts. **2** sexual intercourse in which the woman uses her vaginal muscles to intensify the experience. **3** (*gay*) sexual intercourse where one man's penis is resting between the other man's buttocks while he flexes his buttock muscles. [SE *muscle* + FUCK *n.*[1] (1)]

muscle gay *n.* [1960s–70s] (*US*) a homosexual bodybuilder. [SE *muscle* + GAY *n.*[2] (1)]

musclehead *n.* [1920s+] (*US*) a stupid if brawny man. [SE *muscle* + -HEAD sfx (1)]

muscle in *v.* [1920s+] (*orig. US*) **1** to force an entrance, to use violence to gain something one desires. **2** to gain admission to, to get oneself involved. [MUSCLE v. (2)]

muscle machine *n. see* MUSCLE CAR n.

muscleman *n.* [1920s+] (*orig. US*) **1** a thug, usu. as employed by a gangster for purposes of intimidation, or any strong, aggressive man. **2** a man with an outstanding physique. [note Thomas Hughes (1863): 'I must call the persons in question "musclemen", as distinguished from muscular Christians'; his ref. is to those who celebrate physical strength but have no religious faith; note 1945 Minnesota University use *muscle moll*, a strong man]

muscle mary *n.* [1980s+] (*gay*) a gay man devoted to body-building and the resultant musculature. [SE *muscle* + MARY n.²]

muscle missile *n. see* MUSCLE n.².

muscler *n.* [1940s+] (*US*) a thug. [MUSCLE v. (2)]

muscle shirt *n.* (*also* **muscle T/tee**) [1970s+] (*US*) a T-shirt with very short sleeves or no sleeves, thus displaying the wearer's physique.

muscle-uncle *n.* [2000s] a butch homosexual. [SE *muscle* + assonance]

mush *n.¹* **1** [late 18C] (*US Und.*) a thief's girlfriend. **2** [mid-19C+] (*US*) sentimental nonsense. **3** [1910s] rubbish, nonsense. [SE *mush*, anything soft and pulpy]

mush *n.²* (*also* **moosh**) [late 18C+] (*orig. Aus./US*) the face or mouth. [orig. boxing; it rhymes with 'push' and was something that was 'pushed' by a blow]

mush *n.³* **1** [early 19C–1940s] (*UK Und.*) (*also* **mush-toper**) an umbrella. **2** [1940s] (*US Und.*) a short-con game played at a ball park where a confidence trickster poses as a bookmaker, taking bets, then raises an umbrella and disappears into the area where everybody is holding umbrellas. [abbr. MUSHROOM n.³ (1)]

mush *n.⁴* (*also* **moosh**) **1** [late 19C+] (*Aus.*) prison food, often porridge. **2** [1990s+] mushrooms. [SAmE *mush*, a porridge or pudding made of cornmeal]

mush *n.⁵* **1** [20C+] (*US*) a fool. **2** [1930s+] a man, a 'chap'; thus as a term of greeting, e.g. *Oi! Mush!* **3** [1980s] (*Liverpool*) a prostitute's client. [? Rom. *moosh*, a man]

mush *n.⁶* (*also* **moosh**) [1960s+] a moustache. [abbr.]

mush *n.⁷* [2000s] a fight. [MUSH v.³]

mush *v.¹* (*US*) **1** [1900s–30s] to go, to leave. **2** [1990s+] to urge forward. [dog sledders' *mush*, to cross snow on a dog sled; ult. Fr. *marchez! marchons!* march! let's march!]

mush *v.²* **1** [1920s–70s] (*US*) (*also* **mush it up**) to kiss and cuddle. **2** [1920s–70s] (*US*) to court a woman in a sentimental manner, to 'chat up'. **3** [1940s] (*US Black*) to kiss. [MUSH n.¹ (2)]

mush *v.³* [1980s+] (*US Black/P.R.*) to beat up, to hit.

mushbrain *n.* (*also* **mushball**) [1980s+] (*US*) **1** stupidity. **2** a dolt, a mawkishly sentimental person. [SE *mush*/MUSH n.¹ (2) + sfx *-brain*]

mush-brained *adj.* [1980s+] stupid, sentimental, nonsensical (cf. AMOEBA-BRAINED adj.). [MUSHBRAIN n.]

mushe *n.* [1940s+] (*W.I.*) a Syrian or a Chinese (cf. AH CABBAGE n.). [Fr. *monsieur*, a term of address; Syria had been under Fr. control, and thus its expatriates might speak the language, but why 'Chinese'? perhaps on basis of all foreigners being generically 'French']

mushe-man *n. see* MOOSHE-MAN n.

musher *n.¹* [1900s] (*US*) **1** one who moves from place to place. **2** an itinerant fakir. [MUSH v.¹ (1); (2) abbr. MUSH-FAKER n.¹]

musher *n.²* [1940s] (*US*) one who kisses and cuddles. [MUSH v.² (1)]

musher *n.³* [2000s] a thug, a villain. [? ext. of MUSH n.⁵ (2) or MUSH n.³]

mush-face *n.* [1920s–30s] a fool, a sentimental idiot. [MUSH-FACED adj.]

mush-faced *adj.* [1910s–30s] stupid, foolish. [MUSH n.¹ (2)]

mush-faker *n.¹* (*also* **mush-fakir, mush-rigger, mushroom-faker**) [early 19C–1940s] one who advertises themselves as a

mender of umbrellas, or peddler, but may well use this respectable job as a cover for more fraudulent pursuits; also as v., to work as above. [MUSH n.³ (1)/MUSHROOM n.³ (1) + FAKER n./SE *fakir*/RIGGER n.]

mush-faker *n.²* (*also* **mush-fakir**) [1920s] (*US tramp*) a parasite within the hobo community, a low-grade tramp. [fig. use of MUSH-FAKER n.¹]

mush, gush and lush *n.* [late 19C–1900s] favourable criticisms that are written in return for cash or food and drink. [MUSH n.¹ (2) + SE *gush* + LUSH n.¹ (1)]

mush-head *n.* [late 19C+] (*orig. US*) a fool. [SE *mush*, anything soft and pulpy + -HEAD sfx (1)]

mush-headed *adj.* [late 19C+] stupid, foolish (cf. AIRHEADED adj.). [MUSH-HEAD n.]

mushie *n.* **1** [1930s+] (*orig. Aus.*) a mushroom. **2** [1960s+] (*drugs*) usu. in pl., psilocybin, 'magic mushrooms'.

mush it up *v. see* MUSH v.² (1).

mushmouth *n.* [1930s+] (*US*) **1** indistinct speech. **2** (*also* **mush jib**) a person who mumbles. [SE *mush*]

mush-rigger *n. see* MUSH-FAKER n.¹.

mushroom *n.¹* **1** [late 16C–early 19C] a contemptible person. **2** [late 16C–mid-19C] a nouveau riche individual or an *arriviste* family. **3** [1970s+] (*orig. Irish*) a person who is lied to or kept uninformed. **4** [1980s+] (*US*) a person who is unwittingly caught in crossfire between criminals. [(2) and (4) the propensity of the fungus to 'spring up overnight'; and (3) to grow 'in the dark'; ? (1) f. (2)]

mushroom *n.²* [19C] the vagina (cf. APPLE n.⁶; CABBAGE n.⁷).

mushroom *n.³* **1** [mid-19C–1910s] a low-crowned circular hat, esp. a lady's straw hat with a down-curving brim. **2** [mid-19C–1940s] an umbrella. **3** [late 19C–1900s] a tavern clock. [the supposed resemblances]

mushroom *n.⁴* [1930s+] the head of the penis (cf. BANANA n.²). [the shape]

mushroom-faker *n. see* MUSH-FAKER n.¹.

mushrooms *n.* [1960s+] (*drugs*) psilocybin/psilocin.

mush-toper *n. see* MUSH n.³ (1).

mush worker *n.* [1920s–70s] (*US Und./police*) a woman or a prostitute who obtains money from men by playing on their sympathy, giving them a 'sob story'. [MUSH n.¹ (2) + SE *worker*/WORKER n.¹ (1)]

mushy *adj.¹* [late 19C+] romantic, sentimental. [MUSH n.¹ (2)]

mushy *adj.²* [1970s+] (*S.Afr.*) nice, pleasant. [Zulu *mu* + *hle*, good for one; orig. Zimbabwean use]

music *n.¹* [17C–early 19C] (*UK Und.*) a term used among highwaymen to signify that an individual is a friend and must not be hindered on their journey; usu. in phr. *the music's paid*. ['the Watch-word among High-way-men, to let the Company they were to Rob, alone, in return to some Courtesy' (B.E.)]

music *n.²* [late 18C–early 19C] (*Irish*) the 'tail' of a coin. [the 'tail' or reverse side of an Irish halfpenny or farthing bore the image of a harp]

music *n.³* **1** [mid-19C+] (*US*) amusement, fun, lively speech. **2** [mid-19C+] trouble; usu. in FACE THE MUSIC v. **3** [mid-19C+] (*US*) gunfire. **4** [late 19C–1970s] talking, esp. complaints or nagging.

musical *adj.* [late 19C–1900s] used of a horse that suffers from respiratory problems.

musical fruit *n.* (*also* **musicos**) [1910s+] any fruit or vegetables, esp. beans or Jerusalem artichokes, that produce flatulence.

music box *n.* **1** [mid-19C–1940s] a piano. **2** [1940s] a guitar.

Music City *n.* (*also* **Music Town**) [1970s+] (*US*) Nashville, Tennessee. [the city's association with country music]

music-duffing *n.* [1910s–20s] reconditioning musical instruments. [SE *music* + DUFF v.¹ (2)]

musicos *n. see* MUSICAL FRUIT n.

Music Town *n. see* MUSIC CITY n.

musket *n.* [mid-19C; 1930s–70s] (*US*) the penis (cf. AX n.²). [note mid-17C MUSKET AND BANDELIERS n.]

musket and bandeliers *n.* [mid-17C] the male genitals. [appearance]

muski *n.* (*also* **musky**) [1960s+] (*US*) muscatel, thus any cheap wine. [abbr. SE *muscatel*]

muskin *n.* [mid-18C; 1920s] an eccentric. ['Those who […] call a man a cabbage, […] an odd fish, and an unaccountable *muskin*, should never come into company without an interpreter' Johnson in *The Connoisseur* (1756), in a blast against sl.; James Joyce reiterated the phr. in the *OED*'s only other cit., in *Ulysses* (1922)]

muskra *n.* [late 19C–1970s] a policeman. [Rom. *mooshkeroo*, a constable]

musk-rat *n.* [mid-19C+] (*US*) a resident of the state of Delaware; or anywhere flat.

musky *n. see* MUSKI n.

muso *n.* [1960s+] a *mus*ician, usu. in a rock'n'roll band. [abbr. + -O sfx (4)]

muso *adj.* [1960s] musical. [MUSO n.]

muss *n.* [early 19C–1960s] (*US*) a fight, a dispute, a commotion. [dial.]

muss *v.* [mid-19C–1940s] (*US*) **1** to pick a fight. **2** to argue. **3** to have sexual intercourse (cf. BANG v.¹). [SE *muss*, to rumple, to untidy]

mussaulchee *n.* [mid-19C] (*Anglo-Ind.*) a domestic servant. [Hind. *mash'-alchī*, link-boy, 'the person who ran alongside of a palankin on a night journey bearing a *mussaul* (a torch) […] The word […] is however still more frequent as applied to a humble domestic, whose duty was formerly of a like kind' (Y&B)]

musser *n.* [mid-19C–1920s] (*US*) someone who picks fights. [MUSS v. (1)]

muss up *v.* **1** [1900s] to spend or waste money. **2** [1920s+] (*US*) to treat roughly, to beat up. [(1) opposite of CLEAN UP v.¹ (1); (2) SE *muss*, to rumple, to untidy (or ext. of MUSS v. (1))]

mussy *adj. see* MUZZY adj.

must *n.* [late 19C+] (*orig. US*) something that is essential, mandatory, obligatory.

must *adj.* [1910s+] (*orig. US*) essential, mandatory. [MUST n.; latterly mostly superceded by MUST-HAVE adj.]

musta *n.* (*also* **muster**) [mid-19C] (*Anglo-Ind.*) a pattern or design, whether of a coat, a palace or something in between. [Port. *mostra*, a pattern]

mustache *see under* MOUSTACHE and its combs.

mustang *n.* [1970s+] (*US Black*) an independent, dominant woman, i.e. one who is 'hard to ride'. [SE *mustang*, note US milit. jargon *mustang*, an officer who has been commissioned from the ranks]

mustard *n.*¹ **1** [early 17C; 20C+] (*US*) spirit, zest, courage, esp. in adversity. **2** [20C+] one who is keen on or excellent at a task or occupation; the best; often in phr. *proper mustard*, the genuine article. **3** [1920s+] a woman who is sexually enthusiastic; something, e.g. a play, that is sexually overt. [fig. uses of the 'hotness' of SE *mustard*; (3) note the comment, in T.R.G. Lyell, *Slang, Phrase & Idiom* (1931): 'It must never be used of the female sex']

mustard *n.*² [1930s–40s] (*US*) an Asian person, usu. Chinese (cf. AH CABBAGE n.; BROWNIE n.²). [their light brown complexion]

mustard *n.*³ *see* MUSTARD (PICKLE) n.

mustard *adj.* [1900s–50s] excellent, very good; often with *at/on* (i.e. very good at something). [MUSTARD n.¹]

mustard *phr.* [1980s] an expression of approval or agreement. [MUSTARD adj.]

mustard (and cress) *n.* [1990s+] a dress. [rhy. sl.]

mustard-and-cress *n.* [19C] pubic hair.

mustard (pickle) *n.* [1990s+] a cripple. [rhy. sl.]

mustard plaster *n.* [late 19C–1920s] a miserable and unpopular

young man. [coined in a music-hall comic song, written by E.L. Blanchard (1820–89) and premiered at Drury Lane]

mustard pot *n.*¹ **1** [late 16C–17C; late 19C+] the vagina (cf. APPLE n.⁶; BAG n.¹). **2** [1940s–50s] (*US*) the anus (cf. BOURNEVILLE BOULEVARD n.). [? resemblance; (2) has a lot to do with colour (cf. MUSTARD ROAD n.)]

mustard pot *n.*² [19C–1900s] a carriage with a light yellow body. [the stress is on the colour rather than the shape]

mustard pot *n.*³ [1930s] (*US prison*) a passive homosexual, a pedicant. [the stress is on the *pot*, but note MUSTARD POT n.¹ (2)]

mustard (pot) *adj.* [1930s+] **1** of weather, hot. **2** angry, HOT adj.¹. [rhy. sl. + the quality of mustard]

mustard road *n.* [1970s+] (*US*) the anus; thus *go up the mustard road*, to sodomize (cf. ALLEY WAY n.; BOURNEVILLE BOULEVARD n.). [colour; note MUSTARD POT n.¹ (2)]

mustard seed *n.* [1920s–30s] (*US Black*) a light-skinned Black person. [colour]

mustee *n.* (*also* **mestee**) [late 18C+] (*W.I., Bdos/Guyn.*) the offspring of a White and a mulatto parent. [Sp. *mestizo*, a half-caste]

muster *n. see* MUSTA n.

must-have *adj.* [1990s+] essential, mandatory, usu. in the context of material objects.

must-I-holler *n.* [1980s+] (*US Black*) the vagina (cf. ALL QUIET n.). [ety. unknown; lit. 'do I have to shout'; ? rhy. sl. on SE *collar*]

must job *n.* [late 19C+] a job that one must take when funds are otherwise unavailable. [SE *must*; predates MUST adj.]

mustn't-mention-'ems *n.* [mid-19C–1900s] trousers (cf. DON'T-KNOW-WHAT-TO-CALL-'EMS n.).

musty *adj.* [1980s] (*US Black*) malodorous, dirty.

mut *n. see* MUTT n.¹.

muta/mutah *n. see* MOOTA n.

mutant *n.* [1980s+] (*US campus*) a social outcast.

mutcher *n.* [mid–late 19C] a thief who steals from drunks. [var. on MOOCHER n. (3)]

mute *n.* [1960s+] (*gay*) the vagina. [it doesn't speak]

mute as mumchance (who was hanged for saying nothing) *phr.* [late 17C–19C] a phr. used to refer to an acquaintance who seems silent and miserable. [the 16C–17C game of *mumchance*, resembling hazard, was played in silence. Note dial. *mumchance*, *mumpchance*, one who is stolidly, stupidly silent]

mutha *n.*¹ *see* MOTHER n.⁴.

mutha *n.*² *see* MOTHER n.⁵.

muthafucken *adj. see* MOTHERFUCKING adj.

muthaphukka *n. see* PHUKK n.

mutile *n.* [1980s+] (*US campus*) an incapacitated, immobile person, usu. from drink or drugs. [SE *mutilated* or Fr. *mutilé*]

mutt *n.*¹ (*also* **mut**) [late 19C+] (*US*) a fool, a bungler, an ignorant person; thus used as a general term of abuse. [abbr. MUTTON-HEAD n.]

mutt *n.*² (*orig. US*) **1** [late 19C+] a dog, usu. a mongrel. **2** [late 19C+] a second-rate racehorse, i.e. a DOG n.³ (6). **3** [1970s+] an unattractive person of the opposite sex, i.e. a DOG n.³ (10). [? affectionate use of MUTT n.¹]

mutt and jeff *n.* **1** [1910s–40s] the King George V Silver medal Jubilee and the Edward VIII Coronation medals or ribbons or the 1918 Victory and Overseas medals or ribbons, which are invariably worn together. **2** [1910s+] (*orig. US*) a pair of stupid, bungling men. **3** [1930s] (*US*) foolish conversation. **4** [1960s+] (*US Und.*) a pair of (usu. police) interrogators who work as 'nice' and 'nasty', in order to elicit information. [the US cartoon characters, *Mutt and Jeff*, introduced by H.C. 'Bud' Fischer in 1907]

mutt and jeff *adj.* (*also* **mutton**) [1930s+] deaf. [rhy. sl.; ult. *see* prev.]

mutt and jeff *v.* [1980s+] (*US police/Und.*) of police interrogators, to take the parts of the 'good/sympathetic' and 'bad/potentially violent' officers when attempting to gain information from a suspect; such 'roles' are assumed only for the situation in hand. [MUTT AND JEFF n. (4)]

mutter and stutter *n.* [20C+] butter. [rhy. sl.]

mutt-eye *n.* (*also* **mutt-eyes**) [1940s+] (*Aus.*) corn (as a food). [ety. unknown; ? Aboriginal language]

mutthead *n.* [1910s+] (*US*) a stupid or contemptible person. [MUTT n.¹ + -HEAD sfx (1)]

mutton *n.*¹ **1** [early 16C–mid-19C] a promiscuous woman; a prostitute (cf. BANGTAIL n.¹). **2** [17C–early 19C] a woman. **3** [17C–19C] the vagina; thus sexual intercourse, sexual pleasure; [19C] *in her mutton*, having sexual intercourse with a woman (cf. BACON SANDWICH n.). **4** [1910s] (*Aus.*) a girlfriend. [OED suggests 'food for lust', but the image is more simple, an old sheep as opposed to a young lamb]

mutton *n.*² **1** [late 18C–1910s] (*US*) one's person, self, body or flesh. **2** [late 19C–1980s] (*orig. US*) one's preference, one's liking; usu. in pl.

mutton *n.*³ [mid-19C+] (*later use Aus./N.Z.*) the penis; thus *unbutton the mutton*, to urinate (cf. BACON n.¹).

mutton *n.*⁴ [1960s+] (*US*) cowardice. [the timorousness of sheep]

mutton *adj. see* MUTT AND JEFF adj.

mutton bayonet *n. see* MUTTON MUSKET n.

mutton-bird *n.* (*also* **muttonbird-eater, mutton-eater**) [20C+] (*Aus.*) a native of northern Tasmania; thus *muttonbirdy*, old-fashioned, unworldly. [SE *mutton-bird*, an edible species of Puffin, found on the Bass Strait (between Tasmania and the mainland)]

Muttonburg *n. see* MUTTONTOWN n.

mutton-chopper *n.* [late 19C] 'mutton-chop' whiskers.

mutton-chops *n.* [mid-19C] a sheep's head. [the similarity of fleece to mutton-chop whiskers, and pun on SE *mutton chops*. Note milit. jargon *the Mutton Chops* or *Mutton Lancers*, the Royal West Surreys, whose emblem is a lamb and flag]

mutton-cove *n.*¹ [mid-19C] the Coventry St end of Windmill St, London W1, once well-known for its prostitutes. [MUTTON n.¹ (1) + SE *cove*/abbr. Coventry]

mutton-cove *n.*² [mid-late 19C] a womanizer. [MUTTON n.¹ (2) + COVE n. (1)]

mutton dagger *n.* [1960s+] the penis (cf. AX n.²). [SE *dagger/bayonet*; they stick into MUTTON n.¹ (3)]

mutton dressed as lamb *n.* (*also* **mutton done up as lamb, mutton dressed lamb-fashion, old ewe dressed as lamb**) [late 18C+] a woman who dresses younger than her years.

mutton dummies *n.* [20C+] (*Ulster*) plimsolls, trainers. [ety. unknown; ? *mutton cloth*, a type of cloth used to wrap meat + DUMMY n.¹ (1), i.e. their relative silence, compared to the noise of leather-soled shoes]

mutton-eater *n. see* MUTTON-BIRD n.

muttoner *n.* [late 17C–early 19C] a womanizer, a promiscuous man.

mutton-eye *n.* [20C+] a nickname applied to one who has a squint. [? resemblance to a sheep's eye]

mutton-faced *adj.* [early 19C] fat-faced.

mutton-fed *adj.* [1910s–20s] large, fat and well fed.

mutton-fist *n.* [late 17C–19C] a large, coarse red hand; usu. in pl.

muttonflaps *n.* (*N.Z.*) **1** [1960s+] (*also* **muttonflap**) the stomach. **2** [1980s+] the labia majora (cf. BACON STRIPS n.; DEW-FLAPS n.).

mutton gun *n.* [1940s–50s] (*Aus.*) the penis (cf. AX n.²). [it attacks MUTTON n.¹ (3); note later MUTTON MUSKET n.]

mutton-head *n.* [19C+] a fool (cf. APPLEHEAD n.). [MUTTON-HEADED adj.]

mutton-headed *adj.* [mid-18C+] stupid, foolish (cf. AIRHEADED adj.). [SE *mutton*]

mutton in long coats *n.* [late 17C–19C] women. [MUTTON n.¹ (2)]

Muttonjerk *n. see* MUTTONTOWN n.

mutton merchant *n.* [1960s–70s] a sexual pervert, an exhibitionist. [MUTTON n.¹ (3) + MERCHANT n.]

mutton-monger *n.*¹ [mid-16C–19C] a promiscuous man; thus *go mutton-mongering*, to have sexual intercourse. [MUTTON n.¹ (3) + SE *monger*, ult. Lat. *mango*, a dealer or trafficker]

mutton-monger *n.*² **1** [late 16C–17C] a notable eater of mutton. **2** [mid-late 17C] a sheep-stealer. [SE *mutton* + *monger*, ult. Lat. *mango*, a dealer or trafficker]

mutton musket *n.* (*also* **mutton bayonet**) [1990s+] the penis (cf. AX n.²).

muttonous *adj.* [late 19C–1900s] slow, tedious, monotonous. [joc. mispron.]

mutton-pies *n.* [late 19C–1960s] the eyes. [rhy. sl.]

muttonpuncher *n.* [1930s+] (*US, mainly Western*) a sheep-herder. [play on SAmE *cowpuncher*]

mutton-shunter *n.* [late 19C] a policeman, esp. in his role of harrying street prostitutes (cf. BEAT-POUNDER n.). [MUTTON n.¹ (1) + SE *shunter*]

Muttontown *n.* (*also* **Muttonburg, Muttonjerk, Mutton-ville**) [1950s+] (*US*) a small, out-of-the-way town or settlement.

mutton-tugger *n.* [late 16C–early 17C] a degenerate; a pimp (cf. ABBOT ON THE CROSS n.). [MUTTON n.¹ (1) + SE *tug*]

mutton walk *n.* [early-mid-19C] **1** the saloon at the Drury Lane Theatre, Covent Garden; often as *the Mutton Walk*. **2** any street where one finds prostitutes, esp. the junction of Coventry Street and Windmill Street in the West End of London. [MUTTON n.¹ (1) + SE *walk*]

mutt's game *n. see* MUG'S GAME n.

mutt's nuts *n.* [1990s+] anything excellent, admirable, first-rate. [MUTT n.² (1) + NUTS n.² (1); var. on DOG'S BALLOCKS n.]

mutt up *v.* [1930s–40s] (*US Und.*) to keep a guard dog, to be guarded by a dog. [MUTT n.² (1)]

muuna *n.* [1950s] (*W.I.*) the female genitals. [? link to MOON n.¹]

muv *n.* [2000s] (*US Black*) one's personal space, spec. a 20ft radius surrounding one. [? SE *my*]

mux *n.* [mid-19C–1910s] (*US*) a muddle or a botched job. [ety. unknown; note 17C N. Eng. *mux*, a sharp, pointed tool for boring holes etc]

mux *v.* [19C–1910s] (*US*) to muddle, to botch. [*see* ety. at MUX n. although chron. suggests n. came from v.]

muz *n.* (*also* **muzz**) [late 18C–19C] one who works hard at their books. [MUZ v.²]

muz *v.*¹ (*also* **muzz**) [mid-late 18C] to loiter aimlessly, to 'hang about'. [? SE *muss*, to rumple, to untidy]

muz *v.*² (*also* **muzz**) [late 18C–1900s] to study hard. [mainly Westminster School jargon; ? MUZ v.³]

muz *v.*³ (*also* **muzz**) [late 18C–1900s; 1970s] to render 'muzzy', to bemuse; usu. through drink. [dial. *muzzle*, to drink to excess, to make drunk]

muzzed *adj.* [late 18C–19C] tipsy, befuddled by drink. [MUZ v.³]

muzzie man *n.* [2000s] a thug, a stolid, stupid person. [MUSCLE-MAN n. (1)]

muzzle *n.*¹ **1** [15C+] the face, the nose or the mouth. **2** [late 17C–early 19C] a beard, '(usually) long and nasty' (B.E.). [SE *muzzle*, the nose and mouth of an animal; (1) orig. SE]

muzzle *n.*² [1900s–30s] (*US Und.*) a trick whereby the tricksters pose as outraged citizens or police officers in order to obtain bribes from homosexuals in toilets. [MUZZLE v.¹ (5)]

muzzle *n.*³ [1950s+] (*drugs*) heroin. [ety. unknown; ? SE *muzzle*, to silence, a ref. to the immediate effects of an injection, rendering the user comatose]

muzzle *v.*¹ **1** [late 17C–early 18C; 1930s+] to kiss and fondle, esp. in a rough manner. **2** [mid-late 19C] to fight, to thrash. **3** [mid-late 19C] to hit in the face. **4** [mid-late 19C] to throttle, to garrotte. **5** [mid–late 19C] (*orig. US*) to obtain, to take, to steal. [SE *muzzle*, to put a muzzle on; to restrain (usu. speech); (1) 1930s+ US]

muzzle *v.*[2] [mid–late 19C] to drink heavily. [dial. *muzzle*, to drink to excess]

muzzle-chops *n.* [early 17C] a nickname for a man with a prominent nose and mouth. [SE *muzzle*, the front part of an animal's head + CHOPS n.[1] (1)]

muzzler *n.*[1] [early–late 19C] **1** a blow to the mouth or face. **2** [mid-19C; 1930s] (*US*) a crook, a strong-arm robber. **3** [1920s+] (*US*) a contemptible person. [(1) and (2) MUZZLE v.[1] (2)]

muzzler *n.*[2] [early–late 19C] a drink. [MUZZLE v.[2]]

muzzler *n.*[3] [1920s–60s] (*US, esp. prison*) a homosexual, spec. a fellator (cf. BONE-EATER n.). [SE *muzzle*, the mouth]

muzzle rails *n. see* HEAD RAILS n.

muzzling cheat *n.* [late 17C] a napkin. [SE *muzzle* + CHEAT n. (1)]

muzzy *n.*[1] **1** [1990s+] a moustache. **2** [2000s] a Muslim. [abbr.]

muzzy *n.*[2] [2000s] (*Irish*) a rascal, a naughty child. [ety. unknown]

muzzy *adj.* **1** [early 18C–early 19C] of places or weather, dull, gloomy. **2** [early 18C–1950s] (*also* **mussy**) of people, vague, befuddled, confused. **3** [late 18C+] (*also* **mussy**) drunk (cf. ADDLED adj.). **4** [mid–late 19C] blurred, indistinct. [SE *bemused* or dial. *mosey*, befuddled with drink]

my aching back! *excl.* [1940s+] (*US*) a general excl.; there is no actual back pain.

myall *n.* [1980s+] one who is out of their usual environment. [Aboriginal *miall/myall*, an Aborigine who has had little or no contact with Whites; a stranger]

my arse! *excl.* (*also* **my ass! …bum! …butt! …fanny! …hole!**) [late 17C+] a general excl. of disdain, dismissal or arrogant contempt, e.g. *Are you frightened? Frightened, my arse!*; latterly often implying disbelief of the previous statement.

my arse on a bandbox *phr. see* MINE ARSE ON A BANDBOX phr.

my ass is dragging *phr.* [1910s+] (*orig. US*) I am totally exhausted.

my aunt *n.* (*also* **the aunt**) [early 19C–1930s] the lavatory; thus *visit my aunt, go to see my aunt*, to visit the lavatory (cf. AUNTIE n.[1]). [euph.]

my aunt! *excl. see* MY SAINTED AUNT! excl.

my Aunt Fanny! *excl.* (*also* **my Aunt Eliza! …Jane! …Nellie!**) [20C+] a mild excl. [ext. of MY SAINTED AUNT! excl.]

my bad *phr.*[1] [1980s+] (*US, mainly teen*) my fault, sorry. [BAD n.]

my bad *phr.*[2] [2000s] (*US Black*) a term of greeting, endearment. [MY BAD phr.[1]]

my balls! *excl.* (*also* **my bollix/bollocks!**) [1950s+] (*US*) an excl. of refusal, rejection. [var. on MY ARSE! excl.]

my beads! *excl.* [1950s–60s] (*US gay*) a camp excl. [BEADS n.[2]]

my belly thinks my throat's cut *phr.* (*also* **my belly thinks my throat has been cut, my guts…, my stomach…**) [mid-18C+] I am very hungry.

my bet is *phr.* [1950s+] in my opinion, what I think is.

my blood! *excl.* [1920s+] (*Aus.*) an expression of agreement.

my body's captain *n.* [19C] the penis. [literary euph. coined by the US author Walt Whitman (1819–92)]

my bollix/bollocks! *excl. see* MY BALLS! excl.

my bum! *excl. see* MY ARSE! excl.

my bust *phr. see* BUST n.[1] (7).

my butt! *excl. see* MY ARSE! excl.

my cabbage-tree! *excl.* [mid–19C–1950s] (*Aus.*) a mild excl., synon. with MY HAT! excl. [*cabbage-tree hat*, a hat made of woven cabbage-tree or cabbage-palm leaves]

my colonial (oath)! *excl.* [mid-19C+] (*Aus./N.Z.*) a mild excl.

my dick! *excl.* [1970s+] (*US*) an excl. of disdain, disbelief. [DICK n.[4] (1)]

my dirty cousin *n.* [late 17C–mid-18C] a pej. form of address, usu. aimed at one who is judged to be affecting modesty.

my elbow! *excl.* [20C+] (*N.Z.*) an excl. of surprise or disbelief. [euph. var. on MY ARSE! excl.]

my eye! *excl.* [early 19C+] **1** (*also* **my eye(s) and a bandbox!**) a dismissive excl., nonsense! rubbish! **2** (*also* **my eyes! my eyes and limbs!**) a general excl., often of astonishment. [ALL MY EYE phr.]

my fanny! *excl. see* MY ARSE! excl.

my feet are staying *phr.* [1980s+] (*US campus*) a farewell. [a play on the Ger. *auf Wiedersehen*, goodbye]

my foot! *excl.* [20C+] an excl. used to imply one's contemptuous rejection of the previous speaker's assertion. [euph. var. on MY ARSE! excl.]

my friend *n.* (*also* **my little friend, my others**) [20C+] (*Aus./Ulster/US*) menstruation. [euph.]

my fuck! *excl.* [2000s] an excl. of amazement.

my gawd! *n.* [late 19C+] a sword. [rhy. sl.]

my goodness *n.* [1940s–50s] a drink of Guinness stout. [the advertising slogan, 'My goodness, my Guinness']

my goody! *excl.* [late 19C] my goodness!

my gosh! *excl.* [1920s+] a general excl., a euph. for *my God!* [GOSH n.]

my granny! *excl.* (*also* **my grandmother!**) **1** [late 18C+] rubbish! nonsense! **2** [mid-19C] (*also* **by granny!**) an excl. of astonishment. [note GRANNY n.[1] (2)]

my great guts are ready to eat my little ones *phr.* [late 18C–early 19C] a phr. meaning I am very hungry. [the 2 intestines]

my gun *n.* [1980s+] (*US Black*) one's best friend.

my guts chime twelve *phr.* (*also* **my guts cry cupboard, …curse my teeth**) [late 18C–19C] I am very hungry.

my guts think my throat's cut/has been cut *phr. see* MY BELLY THINKS MY THROAT'S CUT phr.

my hat! *excl.* [late 19C+] a general excl.

my hat to a halfpenny! *excl.* [late 16C] a general excl.

my hole! *excl. see* MY ARSE! excl.

my jimmy! *excl.* [1900s] (*Aus.*) a mild oath.

my joker *n.* [late 19C] a term of affectionate address.

my 'king oath! *excl.* [1910s+] (*Aus.*) a mild excl. [euph. for 'my FUCKING adj. oath!'; MY OATH! excl. + FUCKING adj.]

my knackers! *excl.* [1940s] a general term of derision. [KNACKERS n.; var. on MY BALLS! excl.]

myla *n. see* MILER n.

my land(s)! *excl.* [mid-19C+] (*Can./US*) a mild oath. [euph. for SE *my lord*]

my left foot! *excl.* (*also* **my left knacker/tit!**) [1920s+] an excl. used to imply one's contemptuous rejection of the previous speaker's assertion. [ext. of MY FOOT! excl.]

my little friend *n. see* MY FRIEND n.

my lord *n.* [early–mid-19C] a mocking nickname given to a hunchback.

my man *n.* [1950s+] an intimate; a very important person.

my man! *excl.* [1950s+] (*orig. US Black*) a term of endearment and address between 2 men. [MY MAN n.]

my mother's away *phr.* [20C+] (*Aus.*) the other day. [rhy. sl.]

my myrtle *n.* [early 19C] (*Cockney*) my friend. [SE *myrtle*, a sweet-scented plant, used in perfumery and sacred to Venus]

my nabs *n.* [late 18C–1950s] myself; also used indirectly. [as opposed to YOUR NIBS n. or HIS NABS n.]

my name is Haines *phr.* (*also* **my name is Hanes**) [mid–late 19C] (*US*) a phr. used on leaving a place or party suddenly. [an encounter between President Thomas Jefferson (1743–1826) and one *Haines* or *Hanes*, a fanatical opponent. Haines, not knowing the identity of his companion, vilified Jefferson in extreme tones as the 2 men rode side-by-side near Jefferson's home in Virginia. When they arrived at Jefferson's home, the president, affronted but still courteous, invited Haines in. Only then did Haines ask his putative host for his name: 'Thomas Jefferson'. 'Well, my name is Haines,' replied his opponent, before riding promptly away]

my name is Twyford *phr.* [late 17C–19C] I know absolutely nothing about it. [proper name of Josiah *Twyford* (1640–1729), whose secret process for glazing provided the basis for his creation of a successful firm of sanitary potters; presumably his response to those who wished to elicit his secret]

my name is Walker *phr.* [mid-19C–1950s] I'm leaving, I'm off. [pun on *Walker*/SE *walker*]

my neck! *excl.* [late 19C+] (*Irish*) an excl. of surprise or disbelief. [euph. var. on MY ARSE! excl.]

my nigger *n.* (*also* **my nigga**) [1960s+] (*US Black*) **1** a major influence, a role-model, a close friend. **2** a general term of address. [NIGGER n.¹ (1)/NIGGA n.]

mynt *n. see* MINT n.¹ (2).

my oath! *excl.* [late 19C+] (*Aus./N.Z.*) a mild excl.; often as an affirmation.

m.y.o.b. *phr.* [20C+] (*US*) *m*ind *y*our *o*wn *b*usiness; also ext. to *p.m.y.o.b.*, please... [abbr.]

my old boots! *excl.* [late 19C] an excl. of disbelief, surprise or amazement.

my old guvnor *n. see* GUVNOR n. (2).

my others *n. see* MY FRIEND n.

my patience! *excl.* [mid–late 19C] an excl. of surprise.

my people *n.* [1950s+] **1** (*US Black*) one's fellow gang members. **2** any fellow members of a group or minority, usu. used ironically. **3** (*US campus*) one's family or friends.

my pippin! *excl.* [mid–late 19C] a term of affectionate address. [PIPPIN n.]

my pleasure *phr.* [1950s+] a polite response to an offer of thanks, the equivalent of the Ital. *prego* or SAmE *you're welcome*.

my Prussian blue *phr.* [mid-19C] a term of endearment. [SE *Prussian blue*, a colour; Dickensian use as synon. for SE *true blue*]

my pudding! *excl.* [1930s] (*US*) a general excl. of dismissal, contempt, negation.

Myrmidons *n.* [late 17C–early 19C] a constable's assistants. ['Myrmidon [...] a member of a warlike people inhabiting ancient Thessaly, whom Achilles led to the siege of Troy' (*OED*)]

Myrna Loy *n.* [1930s+] a saveloy. [rhy. sl.; ult. film star *Myrna Loy* (1905–93)]

myrrh *n. see* MUR n.

myrtle *n.* [20C+] (*Aus.*) sexual intercourse. [ety. unknown; ? link to MUDDLE v.]

my sainted aunt! *excl.* (*also* **my aunt! my giddy aunt!**) [late 17C; late 19C+] a mild excl.

my sakes! *excl. see* SAKES! excl.

my shit *phr.* [2000s] (*US Black*) a phr. of apology, my mistake. [SHIT n.³ (2)]

mystall crikey! *excl.* (*also* **myst all critey!**) [20C+] (*Aus.*) a joc. reversal of CHRIST ALMIGHTY! excl.

my stars! *excl.* (*also* **ye stars!**) [late 17C+] a mild oath.

mysteries *n. see* BAGS OF MYSTERY n.

mystery *n.*¹ **1** [late 19C+] (*US short order*) a plate of corned beef hash. **2** [1930s] (*US*) a chocolate and vanilla sundae.

mystery *n.*² [1910s] (*UK Und.*) ? counterfeit money.

mystery *n.*³ [1930s+] **1** an unknown young woman, often one recently arrived in London from the provinces. **2** a young prostitute. **3** any young girl.

mystery (bags) *n. see* BAGS OF MYSTERY n.

mystery (meat) *n.* [late 19C+] (*US*) low-grade meat as used in sausages, hash, hamburgers etc, usu. as served in institutions. [note Lancaster (Ohio) Boy's Industrial School (1947) *mystery soup*, a combination of all kinds of vegetables and meats mixed together to form a soup]

mystery punter *n.* [1950s+] any man who prefers his sex and/or relationships with young, naïve women or young prostitutes; thus *mystery mad*, very keen on sex with young women. [MYSTERY n.³ + PUNTER n.¹ (4)]

Mystic Meg *n.* **1** [1990s+] the human leg; usu. in pl. **2** the penis, as in 'third leg' (cf. ALMOND n.). [rhy. sl.; ult. *Mystic Meg*, a UK astrologist, made famous in the 1990s by her appearances on the National Lottery TV show]

my stomach thinks my throat's cut/has been cut *phr. see* MY BELLY THINKS MY THROAT'S CUT phr.

myth *n.* [1950s+] an untrue or popular tale, a rumour.

my tit! *excl.* [1950s] a semi-euph. var. on MY ARSE! excl.

my troubles! *excl.* [late 19C+] (*Aus.*) a dismissive excl., don't worry about me! I don't care!; also *his troubles, her troubles* etc.

my tulip! *excl.* [mid–late 19C] my fine fellow, my good man. [? the tulip mania of 1840s]

my Uncle *n. see* UNCLE n.

my uncle('s) *n. see* UNCLE n.¹.

my unconverted friend *n.* [mid–late 19C] (*US*) a revolver, a pistol.

my very word! *excl.* [1940s+] (*Aus.*) an excl. of surprise. [an intensified version of MY WORD! excl.]

my wig! *excl.* [early 19C–1900s] a mild excl. of surprise, irritation etc; often ext., e.g. *my wig and whiskers!*

my winky! *excl.* [late 19C] a mild excl.

my word *n.* [20C+] a piece of excrement (cf. ALI OOP n.). [rhy. sl. = TURD n. (1)]

my word! *excl.* [mid-19C+] a mild excl. of surprise.

my worries! *excl.* [1940s+] (*Aus.*) a dismissive excl., don't worry about me! I don't care!

myxie *n.* (*also* **myxo, myxy**) [1950s+] the disease *myxo*matosis, introduced deliberately in the 1950s to kill off rabbits. [abbr.]

N

N *n.*[1] [1970s+] (*US*) a Black person. [abbr. NIGGER n.[1] (1)]

N *n.*[2] [1980s] (*drugs*) **1** narcotics. **2** a painkiller, Darvocet-*N*. [abbr.]

N! *excl.* [1980s+] (*US campus*) no! [abbr.]

'n' *conj.*[1] [mid-19C+] an abbr. of SE *and*, e.g. *rock 'n' roll*.

'n' *conj.*[2] [mid-19C+] an abbr. of SE *than*, e.g. *That boy's madder 'n' ever*.

naai *n.* [1990s+] (*S.Afr.*) a prostitute. [NAAI v. (1)]

naai *v.* [1990s+] (*S.Afr.*) **1** to have sexual intercourse. **2** in fig. use, a synon. with FUCK ABOUT v., FUCK WITH v.[1] etc. [Du. *naaien*, to have carnal knowledge of]

naar *adj.* (*S.Afr.*) **1** [late 19C+] unpleasant, nauseating. **2** [1960s+] sick, queasy. [synon. Afk.]

naar *v.* [1980s+] (*S.Afr.*) to stink, to smell foul. [Afk. *naar*, nauseated, nauseating]

naartjie *n.* [1970s+] (*S.Afr.*) a fool, an idiot; thus *Naartjie Republic*, a banana republic. [S.Afr.Du. *naartjie*, a variety of tangerine or mandarin orange; ? f. Tamil *narattai*, citrus]

nab *n.*[1] (*also* **nabe**) (*UK Und.*) **1** [mid-16C–17C] the head. **2** [early 17C] the head of a stick. **3** [early 17C–mid-19C] a hat. **4** [late 17C–mid-18C] a coxcomb, a fop. **5** [early 19C] an important person. **6** [1990s+] (*Irish*) the Devil. **7** [1990s+] (*Irish*) the joker in a pack of cards. [ety. unknown; ? link to dial. *nab*, a projecting lump of rock, a promontory]

nab *n.*[2] **1** [early 19C+] (*also* **the Nabs**) a policeman (cf. BEAT-POUNDER n.). **2** [1940s–50s] (*US*) an arrest, a police raid. **3** [1950s] (*US*) a railroad security man. [NAB v.[1] (2); (1) 1950s+ use mainly US]

nab *v.*[1] **1** [mid-17C+] (*also* **nib**) to snatch, to steal, to seize. **2** [late 17C+] (*UK Und.*) to catch or capture a person unawares, to apprehend and arrest; to catch, in the sense of to hit. **3** [late 18C; 1930s] to bite. **4** [late 18C+] (*also* **nib**) to catch someone out, esp. if cheating. **5** [mid-19C+] (*US*) to obtain for oneself, to grab; in sexual terms, to seduce. **6** [1920s–30s] (*US tramp*) to steal a ride on a train. [ety. unknown; but note NAP v.[2] (1)]

nab *v.*[2] [late 17C–early 18C] to cheat with dice. [var. on NAP v.[1]]

nab-all *n.* [early 17C] a fool. [? var. on SE *nab-all*, a miser, an unpleasant person; lit. 'snatch-all']

nabber *n.* **1** [19C] a thief. **2** [early 19C] a bailiff, a constable. **3** [1940s–60s] (*US*) a police officer. [NAB v.[1]]

nabbing cheat *n.* [early 19C] the gallows. [NAB v.[1] (2) + CHEAT n. (3)]

nabbing-cull *n. see* NABMAN n.

nabby *n. see* NAVVY n. (2).

nab cheat *n.* (*also* **nab chete, nabchett**) [16C–early 19C] (*UK Und.*) a hat, a cap. [NAB n.[1] (3) + CHEAT n. (1)]

nabe *n.*[1] (*US*) **1** [1930s+] a local cinema; usu. as *nabes*. **2** [1940s+] a *neigh*bourhood. **3** [1970s+] a local bar. [abbr./pron. SAmE *neigh*bourhood]

nabe *n.*[2] *see* NAB n.[1].

nab girder *n.* (*also* **nab garder, nob girder**) [late 17C–mid-19C] (*UK Und.*) a bridle. [NAB n.[1] (1) + SE *gird*]

nab in the hock *v.* [late 19C] (*US Und.*) to be caught in the act. [NAB v.[1] (2) + ? HOCK n.[1]/HOCK n.[2]]

nab it on the dial *v.* [mid–late 19C] to take a blow on the face. [NAB v.[1] (1) + DIAL n.]

nabman *n.* (*also* **nabbing-cull**) [late 18C–early 19C] a policeman (cf. BEAT-POUNDER n.). [NAB v.[1] (2) + SE *man*/CULL n.[1] (4)]

nabob *n.* [late 18C+] a capitalist. [Urdu *nawwab*; ult. Arabic *na'ib*/Port. *nababo*, deputy governor, thus transferred to a merchant who has made his fortune trading in/with India; the sl. use has no India-specific connotations]

nab one's bib *v. see* NAP ONE'S BIB v.

Nabs, the *n. see* NAB n.[2] (1).

nabs *n.* (*also* **knabs**) [late 18C–1950s] a person, usu. him or oneself as HIS NABS n. or MY NABS n. [northern dial.]

nabs on *phr.* [late 19C] (*UK Und.*) signifying the hallmark, i.e. proof of quality, on a silver or gold object. [NAB n.[1] (1)]

nab the cramp *v.* [late 18C–mid-19C] (*UK Und.*) to receive a death sentence. [NAB v.[1] + ? SE *cramp*]

nab the regulars *v.* (*also* **nap the regulars**) [mid-19C–1900s] (*UK Und.*) to take one's usual share of a robbery's proceeds. [NAB v.[1] (1) + REGULARS n.]

nab the rust *v.* [late 18C–mid-19C] **1** to be ill-tempered, sullen. **2** to be punished. **3** (*UK Und.*) to receive money. [NAB v.[1] + SE *rusty*, refractory (of horses)]

nab the snow *v.* [late 18C–early 19C] (*UK Und.*) to steal linen that has been put out to bleach or dry. [NAB v.[1] (1) + SNOW n.[1]]

nab the stifles *v.* [19C–1900s] (*UK Und.*) to be hanged. [NAB v.[1] + SE *stifle*, the condition of being choked]

nab the stoop *v. see* KNAP THE STOOP v.

nab the teize *v. see* NAP THE TEIZE v.

n.a.b.u. *n. see* S.A.B.U. n.

nace *adj. see* NASE adj.

nach *adv. see* NATCH adv.

nackers *n.* (*also* **nakers**) [mid-19C+] the testicles. [var. on KNACKERS n.]

nada *n.* [1910s+] (*US*) nothing. [synon. Sp.]

nadbag *n.* [1990s+] the scrotum (cf. BALL-BAG n.). [NADS n. (1) + BAG n.[1] (1)]

nadger *n.* [late 19C+] (*Ulster*) **1** a young boy. **2** a sulky, bad-tempered person.

nadgers *n.* [1950s+] **1** testicles. **2** a general nonsense word, much used in the 1950s on BBC Radio's *Goon Show*. [abbr. GONADS n. (1); the Goon use is technically a nonce-word, but the connection to (1) seems very likely]

nad-jam *n.* [2000s] semen (cf. BABY GRAVY n.). [NADS n. (1) + JAM n.[7] (3)]

nads *n.* **1** [1960s+] (*orig. US*) the testicles. **2** [1970s+] (*US*) courage. **3** [1980s+] (*US campus*) something great or exciting. [abbr. GONADS n.]

nael *adj. see* NALE adj.

naf *n.*[1] (*also* **naff**) [mid-19C] **1** the buttocks. **2** the vagina. [? abbr. backsl. = FANNY n.[1]; but note Scot. *nyaph*, the female genitals]

naf *n.*[2] (*also* **naff**) [1940s+] nothing. [coined in prostitute use]

naf *n.*[3] [1960s+] (*S.Afr.*) a fool, a weakling, an ineffectual person. [NAF n.[2]]

naff *adj.*[1] (*also* **naph**) **1** [1960s+] in poor taste, unappealing, unfashionable, bad. **2** [1990s+] second-rate, workaday. [? northern dial. *naffhead, naffin, naffy*, a simpleton, a blockhead, an idiot; or *niffy-naffy*, inconsequential, stupid; or Scot. *nyaff*, a term of contempt for any unpleasant or objectionable person; however, note Polari etymologist W.S. Wilcox in a letter 25 November 1999: 'I have long believed that *naff* may well derive from Romany *naflo*, a form of *nasvalo* – no good, broken, useless. Since several other Parlary words derive from Romany this is not impossible'; in this context note also 16C Ital. *gnaffa*, a despicable person]

naff *adj.*[2] [1980s+] (*gay*) heterosexual. [abbr. *not available for fucking/fun*; pun on NAFF adj.[1] (1)]

naff all *n.* [1970s+] a euph. for FUCK-ALL n. (1).

naffed off *adj.* [1990s+] fed up, annoyed. [euph. for FUCKED OFF adj.]

naffing *adj.* [1950s+] a general intensifier. [euph. for FUCKING adj. (1)]

naff off! *excl.* [1950s+] go away! [euph. for FUCK OFF! excl.]

naff omee *n.* [1960s+] (*gay*) a heterosexual. [NAFF adj.[1] (1) + OMEE n. (3); lit. an 'unappealing man']

naff up *v.* [1980s+] to make a mess, to blunder. [euph. for FUCK UP v.]

nafka *n. see* NOFFKA n.

nag *n.*[1] **1** [late 16C–early 17C] a term of abuse; spec. a promiscuous woman, a prostitute (cf. ALLEY CAT n.; BANBURY n.). **2** [mid-18C] a case of venereal disease. **3** [19C; 1970s] an ageing prostitute. **4** [mid-19C–1900s] a woman, with no pej. implication. **5** [1960s+] (*US*) of a prostitute, one who takes her time over making her daily money from her clients. **6** [1980s] (*US*) a queen in a pack of cards. [fig. uses of SE *nag*, a saddle horse; (4) note RMC Duntroon (Aus.) *nag*, a girlfriend]

nag *n.*[2] [mid-17C–mid-18C] the penis; thus TETHER ONE'S NAGS ON v.; *water one's nag*, to have intercourse or to urinate. [? KNACKERS n. or ? the image of 'riding']

nagah *n.* [1950s+] (*W.I. Rasta*) a derog. name for a Black person (cf. ALLIGATOR BAIT n.[2]). [NIGGER n.[1] (1); but note Thelwell, *The Harder They Come* (1980): 'Nagah: either a corruption of the old Nago, referring to a Yoruba person or custom, or, in the dialect, a version of 'nigger', from the plantocracy's pejorative description of the slaves dance']

nag-drag *n.* [mid-19C–1900s] (*UK Und.*) a 3-month period of imprisonment. [DRAG n.[4]]

naggie *n.* (*also* **naggy**) [19C–1900s] the vagina. [NAG n.[1] (1) + dimin. sfx *-ie*; note SE *naggie*, a pony, which can be 'ridden']

naggle *v.* [mid–late 19C] to toss one's head in a stiff and affected manner. [SE *naggle*, to quarrel]

nago *n.* [1940s+] (*W.I.*) a very stupid, ugly or notably dark-complexioned person. [*Nago*, a person born in Nago, a Yoruba-speaker; many such people were transported from Africa as slaves]

nags *n.* [19C–1900s] the testicles. [? KNACKERS n.]

nags, the *n.* [1940s+] horses, in the context of horseracing. [SE *nag*, a horse]

nah! *excl.* [1920s+] (*US*) no! [pron.]

nahpoo *adj. see* NAPOO adj.

nail *n.*[1] (*also* **dead nail, nailing rascal, nails**) [early 19C] **1** a shrewd, imposing criminal, 'a person of an over-reaching, imposing disposition' (Vaux). **2** a gambler who cheats and/or refuses to pay his losses. [NAIL v. (3)]

nail *n.*[2] [1910s–70s] (*US*) a venereal infection. [its stabbing pains]

nail *n.*[3] **1** [1910s+] a cigarette. **2** [1970s+] (*drugs*) a marijuana cigarette (cf. BONE n.[11]). [abbr. COFFIN NAIL n.[2]]

nail *n.*[4] [1930s+] (*US drugs*) a hypodermic syringe. [both a nail and a syringe are sharp and 'go in' + ext. of NAIL n.[3]]

nail *n.*[5] [1960s+] (*US Black*) a man. [the opposite of HAMMA n.]

nail *n.*[6] [1990s+] (*US campus*) a well-built male, esp. a sportsman. [abbr. *nice ass in Levi's*]

nail *v.* (*also* **nail down**) **1** [mid-18C+] (*orig. UK Und.*) to get hold of, to secure; lit. and fig. **2** [mid-18C+] to steal, to rob. **3** [mid-18C+] to catch someone out, to take advantage of, to get the better of, to cheat. **4** [late 18C+] to punch, to hit hard or squarely. **5** [late 18C+] to shoot someone, to kill someone (occas. an animal or bird). **6** [19C+] to apprehend and arrest. **7** [late 19C+] to corner or defeat, esp. an opponent. **8** [late 19C+] (*US*) to seduce, to secure someone's affections, to have sexual intercourse with (cf. BANG v.[1]). **9** [20C+] (*US*) to identify, to recognize. **10** [1910s+] to put an end to. **11** [1920s+] to approach, to address. **12** [1960s+] to charge with a debt. **13** [1960s+] (*US*) to reprimand. **14** [1970s+] to do something well, to master something, to deal with successfully. **15** [1980s+] to link someone with a person or thing. [the image for all defs. is of putting a nail through, or nailing down]

nail a goss *v.* [late 19C–1900s] (*UK Und.*) to steal a hat. [NAIL v. (2) + GOSS n.[3]]

nail a rattler *v.* [late 19C–1960s] (*US tramp*) to steal a ride on a moving train. [NAIL v. (2) + RATTLER n.[1] (3)]

nail a strike *v.* [late 19C–1900s] (*UK Und.*) to steal a watch. [NAIL v. (2) + STRIKE n.[2]]

nail bender *n.* [1920s+] (*US*) a carpenter, a blacksmith.

nail biter *n.* [1970s+] (*US*) an anxiety-provoking situation, esp. a close contest.

nail can *n.* [late 19C–1950s] (*Aus.*) a top hat. [the shape of the cylindrical hat]

nail down *v. see* NAIL v.

nailed *adj.* **1** [mid-19C+] (*orig. US drugs*) arrested. **2** [1980s+] (*US campus*) drunk (cf. NAILED UP adj.). [NAIL v. (6)/fig. use of NAIL v. (4)]

nailed up *adj.* [mid-19C] (*US*) drunk (cf. NAILED adj.) [fig. use of NAIL v. (4)]

nail 'em and jail 'em *n.* [1970s+] (*US Black*) the police. [NAIL v. (6) + SE *jail*]

nailer *n.*[1] **1** [19C] a clincher, a knockout. **2** [late 19C] a general term of excellence, applied to people, animals or objects. [lit. + fig. uses of NAIL v.]

nailer *n.*[2] **1** [mid-19C] a policeman (cf. BEAT-POUNDER n.). **2** [late 19C–1920s] an extortionist. [lit. and fig. uses of NAIL v.]

nailer, the *n.* [late 19C+] (*Anglo-Irish*) the joker in a pack of cards. [NAIL v. (7); its use as a trump or wildcard in certain games]

nailers *n.* [1960s] (*US Black*) the police. [NAIL v. (6), but note NAILER n.[2] (1)]

nail groper *n.* [mid-19C] one who scours the streets in search of old nails and similar saleable pieces of discarded metal.

nailhead *n.*[1] [1930s–40s] (*US*) a fool. [backform. f. NAILHEADED adj.]

nailhead *n.*[2] [1960s+] (*US Black*) an unattractive woman, esp. one with short, nappy hair. [her tightly curled hair supposedly resembles a collection of SE *nail heads*]

nailheaded *adj.* [early 18C; 1930s–40s] (*US*) stupid, stubborn (cf. AIRHEADED adj.). [the hardness of a SE *nail head*]

nailing *adv.* [mid-19C–1910s] exceptionally, usu. with *good*. [fig. use of NAIL v.; note NAILER n.[1] (2)]

nailing rascal *n. see* NAIL n.[1].

nail in one's coffin *n.* **1** [early 19C+] a stage in one's decline; usu. in phrs. *put another nail in one's coffin* or *that's another…* **2** [early–mid-19C] a drink of liquor. **3** [mid-19C+] anything seen as potentially harmful, however pleasurable in the short term.

nail Jell-O to a tree *v.* [1980s+] (*US campus*) to do the impossible. [SAmE jelly product, *Jell-O*]

nail keg *n.* [mid-19C–1900s] (*US*) a top hat. [the hat resembles the shape of a SAmE *nail keg*, a small barrel in which nails are shipped]

nailrod *n.* [late 19C–1920s] (*Aus./N.Z.*) **1** a stick of 'Two Seas' tobacco. **2** any dark tobacco. [resemblance to SE *nailrod*, a rod of metal from which nails are cut]

nails *n.*[1] [1980s+] (*UK juv.*) an aggressive person, a 'hard' man. [SE phr. *hard as nails*]

nails *n.*[2] *see* NAIL *n.*[1].

nails! *excl.* [late 14C–17C] an oath. [abbr. SE *God's nails!*, spec. the nails used to crucify Christ]

nails and screws *n.* [20C+] (*Aus.*) news. [rhy. sl.]

nail someone's hide to the wall *v.* (*also* **nail someone's ass to the barn door, ...ass to the wall, ...hide to the barn door**) [late 19C+] (*orig. US*) **1** to punish severely. **2** to beat up comprehensively, to kill.

nail someone to the cross *v.* (*also* **nail someone to the mast**) [late 19C+] (*orig. US*) to punish, to defeat in a decisive act, to castigate.

nail two wames together *v.* [18C–19C] to have sexual intercourse (cf. BELLY BUMP v.). [Scot. *wame*, the belly]

nair *n.* [late 19C] rain. [backsl.]

naked *adj.* [20C+] (*US Black*) without a gun, without possessions or money, generally at a disadvantage. [fig. use of SE; note 14C SE *naked*, without armour or weapons]

naked *adv.* [1970s+] (*US campus*) in an extreme manner. [note GET NAKED v.]

naked! *excl.* [1970s+] (*US campus*) a general excl. of affirmation, often as a direct response to a previous statement.

naked as a jaybird *phr.* (*also* **jaybird, jaybird-naked, jaynaked**) [1930s+] (*US*) stark naked.

naked city *n.* [1960s+] (*US*) the poor area of a town. [note film title *The Naked City* (1948)]

naked dance *n.* [1940s–50s] (*US Black*) a sexually provocative dance.

naked jazz *n.* [1940s–50s] basic, raunchy jazz music.

nakers *n. see* NACKERS *n.*

nale *adj.* (*also* **nael**) [mid-late 19C] lean. [backsl.]

nalga de angel *n.* (*also* **angelical**) [1970s+] (*US drugs*) marijuana. [Sp., lit. 'angel's ass']

nallion *n.* [20C+] (*Ulster*) a lump, a bump. [ety. unknown]

Nam *n.* [1960s+] (*US, orig. milit.*) Viet*nam*. [abbr.]

nam *n.* [mid-19C] **1** a man. **2** a policeman. [backsl.]

namas(e) *v. see* NAMMOUS *v.*

namaser *n.* [mid-19C] (*UK Und.*) **1** an absconder; one who has run away. **2** something that has vanished, e.g. one's money. [NAMMOUS v. (1)]

Nam black *n.* (*also* **Nam shit/weed**) [1960s–80s] (*drugs*) a variety of marijuana, very dark green and notably potent, grown in Vietnam (cf. ACAPULCO (GOLD) n.). [NAM n. + BLACK n.[3] (3)/ SHIT n.[5] (2)/WEED n.[1] (4)]

namby-pamby *n.* [mid-late 18C] a weakling, an affected sentimentalist. [SE after 1800; the nickname given to the versifier Ambrose Phillips (1674–1749) by his enemies Henry Carey (author himself of *Sally in Our Alley*) and Alexander Pope, who deplored such lines as 'Dimply damsel, sweetly smiling...' ('To Miss Margaret Pultney, daughter of Daniel Pultney Esq', in *The Nursery*, 27 April 1727)]

namby-pamby *adj.* (*also* **niminy-piminy, nimpy-pimpy**) [mid-18C+] of people or things, effeminate, insipid, childish. [NAMBY-PAMBY n.]

na mean? *phr. see* KNOW WHAT I MEAN? *phr.*[1].

name is Dennis *phr.* [mid-19C–1920s] (*US*) a phr. indicating failure, one has no chance, one is finished, 'done for'; as *his/my/ your name is Dennis*. [whaling jargon *dennis*, a whale that has been harpooned and is on the verge of death]

name it not, the *n.* (*also* **nameless, the**) [19C] the vagina (cf. ARTICLE n.).

name of that tune *phr.* [1980s+] (*US*) the facts, the reality, the truth; often as *that's the name of that tune*. [the TV quiz show *Name That Tune*; the 'name' is the answer and thus 'reality']

name of the game *n.* [1910s+] the most important aspect of a situation, whatever matters most, the end, the finish. [? the practice of naming the card-game when claiming a winning hand]

namesclop *n.* [mid-19C] a policeman. [backsl.]

name your poison! *excl.* [late 19C+] (*orig. US*) a joc. invitation to a fellow drinker to make a choice of drink at a party or in a bar.

name yours! *excl.* [late 19C+] choose your drink. [abbr. NAME YOUR POISON! excl.]

nammo *n.* (*also* **namo, namow, nemmo**) [mid-19C+] a woman. [backsl.]

nammous *v.* (*also* **namas, namase, nammas, nammus, namous, nommus**) (*UK Und.*) [mid-late 19C] **1** to leave, to run off, to slip away quietly. **2** to run, to hurry, to come towards. [? Sp. *vamos*, let's go, but cf. NAMUS! excl.]

namus! *excl.* (*also* **namous! nommus!**) [mid-late 19C] a warning cry on sighting a policeman, meaning 'be off!'; ext. just to mean 'go away!' [backsl. = someone (is coming)]

Nam weed *n. see* NAM BLACK n.

nan *n.*[1] [late 16C–18C] a serving maid. [the proper name or abbr. SE *nanny*]

nan *n.*[2] [1950s+] a grandmother; a term of address to one's grandmother. [childish mispron.; abbr. of SE *nana/nanna*]

nan *n.*[3] *see* NAN BOY n.

nan? *phr.* [mid-18C–mid-19C] what did you say? [SE *anan*, I beg your pardon! What did you say?]

nana *n.* **1** [1920s+] a ba*nana*. **2** [1940s+] the head (cf. NANA CUT n.). **3** [1960s] a headmaster. **4** [1960s+] (*also* **narna**) a fool, an idiot, an incompetent; esp. as *right nana*. **5** [1990s+] (*US Black*) the vagina. [abbr. SE *banana*, a soft (punning on SOFT adj. (1)) fruit; (3) f. (2)]

nana *adj.* (*also* **nana-ish**) [late 19C] as used in London's 'gentleman's clubs', outrageous, indecent. [Emile Zola's supposedly indecent novel *Nana* (1880)]

nana cut *n.* [1940s+] (*Aus.*) a haircut in which the back of the head is closely shaved. [NANA n. (2) + SE *cut*; the hair is cut close to the skull]

nan boy *n.* (*also* **nan**) [late 17C–19C] an effeminate or homosexual male (cf. NANCY BOY n.). [the girl's name *Nan*, then synon. with a serving-maid as NAN n.[1]]

nance *n.* [1910s+] an effeminate man, a homosexual (cf. ABIGAIL n.). [NANCY n.[2] (2)]

nance *adj.* [1920s+] effeminate; homosexual. [NANCE n.]

nance *v.* [1940s+] (*US*) to act or speak in an effeminate or homosexual manner. [NANCE n.]

nancified *adj.* (*also* **nancing**) [1910s+] effeminate, acting in a homosexual manner. [NANCY n.[2]]

nancifully *adv.* [1930s+] effeminately. [NANCY n.[2]]

nancy *n.*[1] [19C] the buttocks, the posterior; thus the dismissive phr. *ask my nancy*. [? joc. use of proper name]

nancy *n.*[2] [early 19C+] (*orig. US*) **1** an effeminate or weak-willed person. **2** an effeminate male homosexual (cf. ABIGAIL n.). [the female name, but note NANCY n.[1]]

nancy *adj.* [1930s+] effeminate, usu. homosexual. [NANCY n.[2]]

nancy boy *n.* [1910s+] an effeminate man, a homosexual (cf. ABIGAIL n.; NAN BOY n.). [NANCY n.[2]]

Nancy Dawson *n.* [late 19C] an effeminate youth, a homosexual (cf. ABIGAIL n.). [NANCY n.[2] + ref. to *Nancy Dawson*, a legendary 18C prostitute (d. 1767), about whom a sailor's hornpipe was written; Fraser & Gibbons, *Soldier & Sailor Words & Phrases* (1925), cite her as 'a celebrated former hornpipe dancer of Covent Garden and Drury Lane Theatres']

nancy lee *n.* [20C] **1** a flea. **2** (*also* **tancy lee**) tea. [rhy. sl.]

nancy omey *n.* [late 19C] (*Polari*) an effeminate man. [NANCY n.[2] + OMEE n. (3)]

nancy tale *n.* (*also* **nancy story**) [late 19C–1960s] humbug, nonsense. [Tshi *ananse*, spider; thus *anansesem*, spider-story; a folk- or fairy-tale found in the Gold Coast and the West Indies]

nang *n. see* NYANGA n.

nann *adj.* [2000s] (*US Black*) no, nothing. [SE *none*]

nan nan *n.* [late 19C–1940s] (*Aus.*) **1** a straw hat; thus as adj., straw hat wearing. **2** a dandy. **3** one of a gang of youths who sported straw hats as their 'colours'. [? NANCY n.²]

nanny *n.*¹ (*also* **nannie**) [late 17C–19C] a prostitute; usu. in combs., e.g. NANNY HOUSE n.; NANNY-SHOP n. (cf. BABY JANE n.). [generic use of female proper name]

nanny *n.*² [late 18C–19C] (*UK Und.*) the head; thus *lose one's nanny*, to lose one's head, i.e. temper; *off one's nanny*, mad. [ety. unknown]

nanny *n.*³ [late 19C–1900s] a banana. [abbr.]

nanny *n.*⁴ [1940s+] (*US*) an effeminate man. [NANCY n.²]

nanny *n.*⁵ [1950s+] (*S.Afr.*) a Black woman, also as a term of address. [SE *nanny*, a nursemaid]

nanny (goat) *n.* **1** [1920s+] the Totalizator. **2** [1930s+] a boat. **3** [1940s+] a coat. **4** [1960s+] the throat. [rhy. sl.; (1) = TOTE, THE n.]

nanny goat *n.*¹ [mid-19C] (*Aus.*) a drink. [ety. unknown; ? rhy. sl. = TOT n.¹ (3)]

nanny goat *n.*² [mid–late 19C] an anecdote. [mispron./semi-rhy. sl.]

nanny goat *n.*³ [1900s] (*US*) a style of side-whiskers.

nanny goating *n.* [20C+] courting. [rhy. sl., albeit imperfect rhyme]

nanny-goat sweat *n.* [1940s+] (*US*) rough or inferior liquor.

nanny house *n.* [late 17C–mid-19C] a brothel (cf. ACCOMMODATION HOUSE n.). [NANNY n.¹ + HOUSE n.¹ (1)]

nanny-shop *n.* [mid–late 19C] a brothel (cf. BANGING-SHOP n.). [NANNY n.¹ + SE *shop*/SHOP n.¹ (1)]

nantee *n.* (*also* **nante, nanti, nantois, nantoisette, nanty, nenti**) [mid-19C+] nothing, none, no; esp. as a synon. for phr. *I have none.* [Ling. Fr. *nantee*, none or not; ult. Ital. *niente*, nothing]

nantee! *excl.* (*also* **nanti! nanty!**) [mid-19C+] stop! beware! [NANTEE n.]

nantee narking *n.* (*also* **nanti narking, nanty...**) [early–mid-19C] great fun. [NANTEE n. + NARK v.¹ (4); lit. 'nothing irritating']

nantee palaver! *excl.* (*also* **nantee parlaree!**) [mid-19C+] shut up! be quiet! [NANTEE! excl. + PALAVER n. (1)]

nantes *n. see* NANTZ n.

nanti *see also under* NANTEE and its combs.

nanti pots in the cupboard *phr.* [1980s+] (*Polari*) toothless. [NANTEE n. + joc. imagery]

nantois(ette) *n. see* NANTEE n.

nants *n. see* NANTZ n.

nanty *see also under* NANTEE and its combs.

nanty crackling *n.* [late 19C–1920s] (*Polari*) the vagina. [NANTEE n. + CRACKLING n.]

nanty handbag *n.* [1990s+] (*UK gay*) no money. [NANTEE n. + metonymic use of SE *handbag*]

nanty worster *n.* [late 19C–1900s] (*Polari*) something that is 'no worse'. [NANTEE n. + SE *worst*]

nantz *n.* (*also* **nantes, nants, nantzy**) [late 17C–19C] brandy; also ext. as *cold nantz, cool nantz.* [proper name *Nantes* in France, a centre of cognac production]

Nap *n. see* NAP TOWN n.

nap *n.*¹ [late 17C–early 18C] a dose of venereal disease. [? fig. use of NAP v.²; the sufferer has been 'seized' or 'punished' by the disease]

nap *n.*² [late 17C–early 18C] an instance of cheating while playing dice. [NAP v.¹]

nap *n.*³ [late 17C–18C] a sheep (cf. NAPPER n.¹). [note KNAPPER'S POLL n.]

nap *n.*⁴ [18C] an arrest. [NAB v.¹ (1)]

nap *n.*⁵ [18C–19C] a hat. [NAB n.¹ (3)]

nap *n.*⁶ [late 18C–19C] strong ale. [Scot. *nap*, strong beer]

nap *n.*⁷ [mid–late 19C] (*orig. theatre*) a blow or hit, esp. a pretend hit.

nap *n.*⁸ [mid–late 19C] a moustache, of which the 2 points form a long line that 'cuts' the face. [abbr. proper name *Napoleon III*, whose visit to London in 1855 made the style fashionable]

nap *n.*⁹ [late 19C+] (*Aus.*) **1** a sleeping bag. **2** a blanket or some other covering used by a sleeper in the open air, a pack (as used in Northern Territory). [SE *nap*, (woollen) cloth that has a nap surface on it; or SE *knapsack*; but note SE *nap*, a short sleep]

nap *n.*¹⁰ (*also* **nap selection**) [late 19C+] **1** a tip on the winning chances of a greyhound or horse. **2** the horse or greyhound so tipped. **3** a bet on such a horse or greyhound. [GO NAP (ON) v.]

nap *n.*¹¹ [1900s–60s] (*US Black*) a Black person. [SE *nappy*, i.e. tight, curly hair]

nap *n.*¹² [1940s+] (*N.Z.*) a nappy or diaper. [abbr.]

nap *v.*¹ (*also* **nap on**) [mid-17C–early 19C] (*UK Und.*) to cheat at dice. [ext. of NAP v.²]

nap *v.*² **1** [mid-17C–19C] (*also* **nap on**) to seize, to catch, to lay hold of (a person or thing). **2** [late 17C–mid-18C] to take into custody. **3** [late 17C–18C] to consume. **4** [late 17C–19C] to suffer punishment; to receive a blow. **5** [late 17C–1950s] to steal. [NAB v.¹ or related to Sw./Norw. *nappa* or Da. *nappe*, to snatch, to snap]

nap *v.*³ **1** [mid–late 19C] to break, to hit with a hammer. **2** [1990s+] (*Irish*) to knock softly. [dial. *knap*]

nap a bellowser *v. see* BELLOWSER n.².

napalm *v.* [1990s+] to spread an idea by a serious onslaught of publicity etc.

nap and double *n.* [1930s+] trouble. [rhy. sl.]

nap a winder *v.* **1** [early–mid-19C] (*also* **nap the winding post**) to be transported for life. **2** [early–mid-19C] to be hanged. **3** [mid-19C–1930s] to receive an unpleasant shock. [NAP v.² + WINDER n.¹]

naph *adj. see* NAFF adj.¹.

naphead *n. see* NAPPY HEAD n.

nap it *v.*¹ [late 17C–early 19C] to catch venereal disease. [NAP n.¹]

nap it *v.*² [late 17C–early 19C] to receive severe punishment, esp. in a boxing-match. [ext. of NAP v.² (4)]

nap it at the nask *v.* [late 17C–early 18C] to receive a judicial flogging at Bridewell. [NAP IT v.² + NASK n.]

napkin ring *n.* [1970s+] (*US gay*) a penis ring. [the image]

napkin snatching *n.* [early 19C] stealing handkerchiefs.

Naples canker *n.* (*also* **Naples scab**) [17C–mid-18C] syphilis. [racial stereotyping]

Napoleon *n.* [1930s–50s] (*US Black*) a madman, an eccentric. [the clichéd image of the mad believing that they are Napoleon or some other world figure]

nap on *v.*¹ *see* NAP v.¹.

nap on *v.*² *see* NAP v.² (1).

nap one's bib *v.* (*also* **nab one's bib**) [late 18C–mid-19C] to weep, esp. for effect, i.e. in order to get one's way or put across one's point. [NAP v.²/NAB v.¹ + *bib*, to weep]

napoo *adj.* (*also* **nahpoo**) [1910s–50s; 2000s] finished, ended, dead, no more. [Fr. *il n'y a plus*, there is no more; orig. used by French shopkeepers as stock reply to importuning soldiers]

napoo *v.* [1910s–20s] **1** (*milit.*) to kill. **2** to die. [NAPOO adj.]

nap or nothing *n.* [mid–late 19C] (*London clubs*) a bet of 'all or nothing'. [GO NAP (ON) v. (1)]

napper *n.*¹ **1** [mid-17C–19C] (*UK Und.*) (*also* **knapper**) a thief; usu. in *napper of naps*, a sheep stealer. **2** [18C] a false witness. **3** [mid-18C–early 19C] (*UK Und.*) a cheat. [NAP v.²]

napper *n.*² **1** [late 17C–19C] a hat. **2** [early 18C+] (*also* **knapper, napper tandy, nopper**) the head; thus *go off one's napper*, to go mad. **3** [early 19C] a nose. **4** [late 19C–1920s] a face. **5** [late 19C–1920s] the mouth. [(1) ? NAB n.¹ (3)]

napper *n.*[3] [late 19C+] (*Ulster*) anything large or outstanding of its type. [Yorks. dial. *nap*, expert]

napper of naps *n. see* NAPPER *n.*[1] (1).

napper's noll/poll *n. see* KNAPPER'S POLL *n.*

napper tandy *n.*[1] [2000s] (*Aus.*) a shandy (beer and lemonade). [rhy. sl.]

napper tandy *n.*[2] *see* NAPPER *n.*[2] (2).

napping bull *n.* [mid-18C] (*UK Und.*) a bailiff. [NAP *v.*[2] (1) + ? BULL *n.*[10]]

nappy *adj.* **1** [1970s+] (*US teen*) disgusting, irritating, unpleasant, worthless. **2** [1980s+] (*US campus*) bizarre but not unattractive. **3** [1990s+] (*US Black*) proud to be Black; honest, natural, ideologically sound. [SE *nappy*, of hair, tightly curled, i.e. the natural state of many Black people's hair; (1) and (2) as a derog.; (3) with pride]

nappy (ale) *n.* (*also* **napping gear, noppy**) [early 16C–mid-19C] drink in general, esp. strong ale. [NAP *n.*[5]; it goes to one's head]

nappy-ass *adj.* (*also* **nappy-assed**) [1970s+] (*US Black teen*) referring to one who has nappy hair. [SE *nappy*, of hair, tightly curled + -ASS *sfx*]

nappy-black *adj.* [1960s] (*US Black*) very dark-skinned, with African features. [SE *nappy*, of hair, tightly curled + *black*]

nappy dugout *n.* [1990s+] (*US Black*) the female genitals. [baseball imagery; the dugout where Black players, i.e. those with nappy hair which is typically Black, wait to bat]

nappy head *n.* (*also* **naphead**) [late 19C+] (*US Black*) **1** someone with kinky hair. **2** an unsophisticated Black person. [backform. f. NAPPY-HEADED *adj.*]

nappy-headed *adj.* [1920s+] (*US Black*) **1** having kinky hair. **2** unsophisticated. [SE *nappy*, of hair, tightly curled; (2) is ext. of (1) in an era when fashionable Blacks straightened their hair]

nappy valley *n.* [1970s+] (*Aus./N.Z.*) a dormitory suburb, mainly populated by families with young babies. [SE *nappy* + play on *Happy Valley*]

naps *n.* [late 19C+] (*US Black*) kinky hair. [abbr. SE *nappy*, of hair, tightly curled]

nap selection *n. see* NAP *n.*[10].

nap the pad *v.* [mid-18C] (*UK Und.*) to go to bed. [NAP *v.*[2] (1) + PAD *n.*[2] (1)]

nap the regulars *v. see* NAB THE REGULARS *v.*

nap the stoop *v. see* KNAP THE STOOP *v.*

nap the teize *v.* (*also* **nab the tease, ...teaze, ...teize, nap the teaze**) [late 18C–19C] for a prisoner to be flogged as a punishment while in prison, rather than in public. [NAP *v.*[2] (4) + TEASE *v.*[1]; whippings were often public]

nap the winding post *v. see* NAP A WINDER *v.* (1).

nap toco for yam *v. see* GET TOCO FOR YAM *v.*

Nap Town *n.* (*also* **Nap**) [1920s+] (*US*) Indianapolis, Indiana. [abbr.]

narangy *n.* [late 19C–1900s] (*Aus.*) a dandy, a 'swell'. [Dharak *narang*, little; applied to those with authority who rank immediately lower than a station manager]

narbo *n.* [1990s+] (*US*) an insignificant, boring person. [ety. unknown]

narc *n.* (*also* **nark**) [1960s+] (*orig. US*) **1** narcotics. **2** a narcotics agent. **3** any informer. **4** in ext. use, any unpleasant person. [abbr. SE *narcotics*; but for (3) note NARK *n.*[1] (1)]

narc *v.* [1970s+] to betray someone to the police, spec. a drug dealer or user to the narcotics police. [NARC (3) + NARK *v.*[1]]

narco *n.* [1950s+] **1** (*US*) a narcotics officer. **2** (*US*) the narcotics department of a police station or hospital. **3** (*drugs*) narcotics; also attrib. **4** (*drugs*) a drug addict or drug dealer. [abbr.]

narco squad *n.* [1950s+] (*US drugs/Und.*) the narcotics squad. [abbr.]

narcotic bull *n.* [1930s+] (*US*) a federal narcotics officer. [SE *narcotics* + BULL *n.*[10] (1)]

nard *n.* [1960s] (*US*) an obnoxious person. [var. on NERD *n.*, but note NARDS *n.*]

nards *n.* (*US*) **1** [1960s+] male genitals. **2** [1990s+] the female breasts. [(1) ? GONADS *n.*]

narg *n.* [1980s+] (*N.Z.*) a derog. term for an Indian. [ety. unknown; ? Hindi]

narikin *n.* [1910s–40s] a nouveau riche. [synon. Jap.]

nark *n.*[1] **1** [mid-19C+] a police informer. **2** [mid-19C+] (*mainly Aus./N.Z.*) an irritating person, a spoilsport, a badly behaved person. **3** [late 19C+] a policeman. **4** [20C+] (*Aus.*) spite, rancour, umbrage; thus *get the nark*, to get angry; *give someone the nark*, to annoy someone. **5** [20C+] one who reports to the authorities, a telltale. **6** [1910s+] any annoying or disagreeable situation. **7** [1920s–30s] (*UK tramp*) a beggar who works part-time and lives permanently in a common lodging house, thus having a privileged relationship with the owner. **8** [1960s] an agent, a go-between. [Rom. *nak*, nose]

nark *n.*[2] *see* NARC *n.*

nark *v.*[1] **1** [mid-19C–1910s] to watch, to survey, to notice. **2** [late 19C+] to inform to the police. **3** [late 19C+] to betray someone; to inform upon. **4** [late 19C+] (*mainly Aus./N.Z.*) to annoy, to irritate. **5** [1930s+] to complain, to nag. [NARK *n.*[1]; US use of (2) is 1960s+]

nark *v.*[2] [late 19C+] to stop, to terminate, to desist, esp. to stop talking; esp. in phr. [1910s+] (*Aus.*) *I'll nark you*, I'll ruin your plan; thus NARK IT! *excl.*

narked (off) *adj.* [late 19C+] annoyed. [NARK *v.*[1] (4)]

narker *n.* **1** [1930s+] an informer. **2** [1950s] a policeman. [NARK *v.*[1] (2)]

narkey/narkie *adj. see* NARKY *adj.*

narking dues *n.* [late 19C] an arrest made on the evidence of an informer. [NARK *v.*[1] (3) + SE *dues*]

nark it! *excl.* [late 19C+] stop it! shut up! [NARK *v.*[2]]

nark the titter! *excl.* [late 19C–1900s] look at that woman! [NARK *v.*[1] (1) + TITTER *n.*]

narky *adj.* (*also* **narkey, narkie**) [late 19C+] irascible, bad-tempered, sarcastic. [NARK *v.*[1] (4)]

narly *adj. see* GNARLY *adj.* (2).

narna *n. see* NANA *n.* (4).

nar-nar *adj.* [1910s–50s] (*Aus.*) of a man, overdressed, often effeminately so. [? NANA *adj.* or NANA *n.* (4)]

nar nar goon *n.* [20C+] (*Aus.*) a generic name for any small, insignificant, out-of-the-way place. [*Nar Nar Goon*, a small town southeast of Melbourne]

narp *n.* [mid-19C] a shirt. [Scot.]

narrative *n.* [late 19C–1900s] (*UK middle class*) a dog's tail. [pun on SE *narrative*, a tale]

narrish *adj.* [late 19C] (*UK society*) thrifty, mean. [SE *narrow*]

narrow *adj.* [mid–late 18C] never a, not a, not one. [? SE *nary*, no, not (a)]

narrow-assed *adj.* (*also* **narrow-gutted**) [1910s–70s] (*US/UK*) slim, skinny; thus, in fig. use, narrow-minded. [SE *narrow* + ASS *n.* (2)/SE *gut*]

narrowback *n.* **1** [late 19C] a supporter of political reform. **2** [1950s+] (*US*) an Irish person, esp. a second-generation immigrant. **3** [1950s+] (*US*) a Protestant. **4** [1950s+] (*Irish*) an immigrant who returns from the US to live in Ireland. [? their stereotyped physique; or ? Ulster dial. *narrow*, mean, miserly]

narrow in the shoulder *phr.* [1910s–20s] lacking a sense of humour. [the hunched shoulders of a miserable person]

narrow lane *n.* [mid-16C] the throat.

narrow place in the road *n. see* BAD PLACE IN THE ROAD *n.*

narrow shave/squeak *n. see* CLOSE SHAVE *n.*

narsum *n.* [mid–late 17C] (*Irish*) the buttocks, the behind. [ARSE *n.*[1] (1)]

nasal *adv.* [1980s+] (*US campus*) no; thus *nasal on that*, forget it, no chance. [pun on *na(sal)/nay*]

nase *adj.* (*also* **nace**) [mid-16C–early 17C] (*UK Und.*) drunken, intoxicated. [ety. 'obscure' (*OED*) but B&L suggest Ger. *nass*, wet; also, given the trad. association of red noses and drunkards, there might be a link to obs. 14C SE *nase*, nose]

nase nab *n.* (*also* **nazie nab, nazy nab**) [17C–early 19C] **1** a red nose. **2** (*UK Und.*) a drunkard, drunkenness. [NASE adj./NAZIE adj. + ? NEB n.¹ (3) although this predates]

nash *n.* [1950s+] (*W.I. Rasta*) the female genitalia. [Carib.E. *nash*, soft, effeminate; ult. Eng. dial. *nesh*, juicy, succulent, tender]

nash *v.*¹ [19C; 1980s+] to leave, to rush off. [Rom. *nash, nasher*, to run]

nash *v.*² *see* NOSH v.

nash gab *n.* [19C] insolent speech. [Rom. *nash*, to run + GAB n.]

nasho *n.* [1950s–70s] (*Aus.*) **1** national service. **2** a national service-man. [abbr. *SE national (service)* + -O sfx (4); Aus. national service was discontinued in 1972; post-1970s use is historical]

Nashville *n.* [1970s+] (*US Black*) any unsophisticated, suburban, middle-American town or person. [*Nashville*, Tennessee, with its links to country music as the epitome of middle-American values]

nask *n.* (*also* **naskin**) [late 17C–mid-19C] a prison (spec. in London: the *Old Nask*, the City Bridewell; the *New Nask*, the Clerkenwell prison; and *Tuttle Nask*, in Tothill Fields).

Nassau nigger *n.* [1940s+] (*US*) a Black person from the Bahamas or Jamaica. [*Nassau*, the capital of the Bahamas + NIGGER n.¹ (1)]

nasties *n.* **1** [20C+] (*US Black*) sexual desire, lust. **2** [1930s–40s] the Nazis. **3** [1930s+] (*US*) any unpleasant, disgusting, threatening or scary things or persons. **4** [1980s] (*drugs*) drugs, of any variety.

nastiness *n.* [1950s] (*W.I.*) homosexuality or bestiality. [euph.]

nasty *n.*¹ **1** [mid-19C; 1960s] the vagina. **2** [1930s+] sexual intercourse; thus DO THE (BIG) NASTY v. (1), *have a bit of (old) nasty, nasty*, to have sexual intercourse. **3** [1960s+] the penis. [an acknowledgment, if not an agreement, with the Western ambivalence as regards sexuality; note Williams for 17C use of *nasty* as 'bedfellow']

nasty *n.*² [1930s+] anything or anyone unpleasant, varying as to context.

nasty *adj.* **1** [mid-19C+] (*orig. US*) first-class, exciting, particularly enjoyable or admirable. **2** [mid-19C+] (*orig. US*) attractive, sexy; often in negative sense, i.e. promiscuous, amoral. **3** [mid-19C+] (*orig. US*) aggressive, hostile. **4** [1980s+] (*orig. US*) difficult. **5** [1990s+] (*W.I./UK Black*) dirty. [on bad = good model or just fig. use of SE *nasty*]

nasty *adv.* **1** [1900s] (*Aus.*) fast. **2** [1970s+] (*US teen*) extremely (whether pleasant or unpleasant), e.g. *nasty cool*, very cool indeed. **3** [1990s+] (*US*) of speech, obscenely.

nasty-ass *adj.* [1960s+] (*US*) **1** of a person, unpleasant. **2** of a place, dirty, disgusting.

nasty-behind *adj.* [1960s] (*US Black*) of a woman, promiscuous.

nasty bit of work *n.* (*also* **nasty bit of goods, ...piece of work**) [1910s+] an unpleasant person.

nastygram *n.* [1960s+] (*US, orig. milit.*) an unpleasant note or letter or a communication that brings bad news. [SE *nasty* + *(tele)gram*]

nastyman *n.* **1** [mid–late 19C] the member of the garrotting team who actually does the choking. **2** [late 19C] (*UK Und.*) a thief's assistant. **3** [1950s–60s] (*US Black*) a sexual pervert.

nasty-mouthed *adj.* [20C+] (*W.I.*) foul-mouthed, given to using obscene language.

nasty-nigger *adj.* [1990s+] (*W.I.*) ill-mannered, boorish.

nasty piece of work *n. see* NASTY BIT OF WORK n.

nasty up *v.* [20C+] (*W.I.*) to make a mess of, to dirty.

nat *n.*¹ [late 19C+] (*Ulster*) a small person. [? SE *gnat*]

nat *n.*² *see* NATURAL n.⁴ (1).

Natal fever *n.* [20C+] (*S.Afr.*) a sense of laziness and resultant inactivity, attributed to the hot climate of Natal.

Natal rum *n.* [late 19C] (*S.Afr.*) rough, strong brandy, distilled in Natal.

natarnal *adj.* (*also* **netarnal**) [20C+] (*Irish*) used to express disgust. [pron. SE *eternal*, infinite, in the sense of wearisome, tedious, loathsome]

natch *n.*¹ [late 19C–1900s] one's natural life.

natch *n.*² *see* NATURAL n.⁵.

natch *adv.* (*also* **nach**) [1940s+] (*orig. US*) naturally. [abbr.]

natchie *n. see* NATURAL n.⁵.

natch trips *n.* [1960s] (*drugs*) a variety of quasi-drug experiences gained from smoking such natural substances as nutmeg, banana, mace etc. [SE *natural* + TRIP n.⁴ (3)]

nathan *n.* [1980s+] (*US Black teen*) nothing. [? pron. of SE]

nation *sfx* [20C+] (*W.I.*) a general sfx used widely to define, usu. derog., various sub-groups in the Caribbean; thus *buck nation*, the Amerindian people of Guyana; *Chinee nation*, Chinese people; *coolie nation*, East Indians; *high nation*, a high caste East Indian; *low nation*, a low caste East Indian; used alone as *nation*, a disreputable or unpleasant person. [? trans. of Hind. *jaat*, class, kind, race]

'nation *adj.* [late 18C–1930s] very much, exceedingly. [abbr. DAMNATION! excl.; Grose (1785) attributes it to 'Kent, Sussex and the adjacent counties']

national anthem *n.* [1940s] (*US*) spare-ribs and sauerkraut.

national exhibition *n.* [mid-19C] an execution at the Old Bailey. [coined by playwright and *Punch* contributor Douglas Jerrold (1803–57), punning on the Great Exhibition of 1851; public execution continued in the UK until 1868]

national front *n.* [1960s+] a general term of abuse. [rhy. sl. = CUNT n.² (1); ult. the UK Far Right movement *National Front* (established 1967)]

national hunt *n.* [20C+] audacity, cheek. [rhy. sl. = FRONT n.¹ (1)]

national indoor game *n.* (*also* **great national indoor game**) [late 19C+] (*Aus.*) sexual intercourse. [note the *great Australian game/Australia's national game* is two-up]

native *n.* [late 18C–early 19C] (*Irish*) illicitly distilled whisky, poteen. [? abbr. *native brew*]

native cavalry *n.* [early–mid-19C] unbroken horses, used by country people, as opposed to those ridden by townsmen.

Nat King Cole *n.* [1940s+] **1** unemployment benefit, the dole (cf. BLESS MY SOUL n.). **2** a mole (on the skin). **3** a bread roll. **4** (*Scot.*) sexual intercourse. [rhy. sl.; (4) = HOLE n.¹ (5); ult. US singer *Nat King Cole* (1919–65)]

natomy *n.* (*also* **nattermy**) [19C–1900s] a small, thin and/or deformed person. [abbr. SE *anatomy*]

natter *n.* [1940s+] a chat, a light conversation. [NATTER v.]

natter *v.* [1940s+] to chat, to gossip. [? dial. *gnatter*, to grumble, to 'rattle on' or *natter*, to nag; note services sl. *natter party*, a conference which leads nowhere; *natter can*, one who talks too much]

nattermy *n. see* NATOMY n.

nattum *n.* [20C+] (*Aus.*) sexual intercourse. [? *get at 'em*]

natty *n.*¹ [early 19C] a spruce, smart person; a dandy. [NATTY adj.]

natty *n.*² (*also* **knotty, natty congo/dread**) [1950s+] (*W.I. Rasta*) **1** dreadlocks. **2** a person with dreadlocks. [SE *natural* + the Congo/DREAD n.²]

natty *adj.* [late 18C+] **1** well-dressed, smart. **2** neat, spruce. **3** adept with the hands, skilful. [all SE by late 19C]

natty lad *n.* [late 18C–mid-19C] a young thief or pickpocket. [NATTY adj. (3) + SE *lad*]

natural *n.*¹ **1** [mid-16C+] an idiot, a fool because untutored, unsophisticated; often the potential victim of a confidence trick. **2** [late 17C–early 19C] a mistress; a prostitute. **3** [late 17C–early 19C] an illegitimate child. [the images are of a 'state of nature']

natural *n.*² **1** [mid-18C; late 19C–1960s] (*gambling*) a winning combination, esp. in craps dice. **2** [1900s–30s] in fig. use, good luck; often as *throw a natural*, to experience good luck. **3** [1930s–40s] (*US prison*) a 7-year sentence (suggested by a throw of 7 in craps). [abbr. SE *natural winner*]

natural *n.*³ **1** [mid-18C; 1920s+] (*orig. US*) one who is naturally suited to a job or skill; one who is naturally talented. **2** [1920s+]

(*US*) something certain to succeed, a winner; something inevitable. [now SE]

natural *n.*[4] [late 19C+] (*also* **nat**) one's life; thus *for all one's natural*, forever; *for one's natural*, as if one's life depended on it. **2** [1930s] (*US*) a life sentence. [it lasts 'all one's *natural* life']

natural *n.*[5] (*also* **natch, natchie**) [1960s+] (*US Black*) a bushy hairstyle, in which one's hair is allowed to grow naturally, rather than being subjected to straightening or similar styling.

natural *n.*[6] [1970s+] (*US Black*) one's self. [abbr. SE *natural-born self*]

natural-born *adj.* [mid-19C+] (*US Black*) by nature, as if born to, esp. used as a general intensifier.

natural-born man *n.* (*also* **natural man**) [1930s+] (*US Black*) a 'real' (i.e. heterosexual) man, a good lover, an honest, unpretentious person. [the premise is that a 'natural' person is not hidebound by social conditioning etc]

natural draft *n.* [20C+] (*Ulster*) someone or something identical, the 'living image'. [SE *natural* + *draft*, a plan or sketch]

natural pick *n.* (*also* **pick**) [1960s–80s] (*US Black*) a large comb used spec. for tidying an AFRO *n.*[2] or 'natural' hairstyle. [NATURAL *n.*[5] + SE *pick*, a pointed tool, here a comb]

natural woman *n.* [1930s+] (*US Black*) the female version of a NATURAL-BORN MAN *n.*

nature *n.* **1** [late 18C–19C] a euph. for the vagina (cf. BEAUTY SPOT *n.*). **2** [mid-19C; 1970s] the penis. **3** [1910s+] (*US Black*) one's libido, one's sex-drive. [(3) note Cleland, *Memoirs of a Woman of Pleasure* (1748–9): 'After playing repeated prizes of pleasure, nature overspent, and satisfy'd, gave us up to the arms of sleep']

nature boy *n.* [1940s+] (*US*) a naïve or unsophisticated young man.

nature calls *phr.* [20C+] a euph. excuse used when one wishes to visit the lavatory (cf. DO ONE'S BUSINESS *v.*).

nature's call *n.* [20C+] the desire to urinate.

nature's duty *n.* [18C–19C] sexual intercourse.

nature's founts *n.* [19C] the female breasts (cf. BORDENS *n.*). [literary euph.]

nature's privy seal *n.* (*also* **Dame Nature's privy seal**) [mid-17C–19C] the hymen. [pun]

nature's scythe *n.* [mid-18C–19C] the penis.

nature's treasury *n.* (*also* **nature's workshop, treasury of love**) [mid-17C–19C] the vagina (cf. ADAM'S OWN (ALTAR) *n.*; BEAUTY SPOT *n.*).

nature's tufted treasure *n.* [19C] the vagina (cf. ADAM'S OWN (ALTAR) *n.*; BEAUTY SPOT *n.*). [joc./euph. use of SE]

naughties *n.* [1980s+] sexual liaisons, sexual intercourse. [NAUGHTY *n.* (2)]

Naughton and Gold *adj.* [1930s+] cold. [rhy. sl.; ult. Charlie Naughton (1887–1976) and Jimmy Gold (1886–1967), music-hall stars and members of the Crazy Gang (1935–62)]

naughty *n.* **1** [mid-19C–1900s] the vagina. **2** [late 19C; 1950s+] (*mainly Aus./N.Z.*) sexual intercourse; also in *v.* phrs., esp. *do the naughty, go naughty*, to have sex; [late 19C] *work for one's living and do the naughty for one's clothes*, to be an amateur prostitute, who has a legitimate day-job but still goes out whoring to make extra money. **3** [1970s+] an injury; thus *do oneself a naughty*, to injure oneself.

naughty *adj.* **1** [late 17C–early 18C] of money, counterfeit. **2** [mid-19C–1900s] flashy, vulgarly overdressed. **3** [1910s+] (*UK Und.*) criminal, violent, corrupt. **4** [1950s–50s] malfunctioning, sick. **5** [1970s+] problematic, disturbing.

naughty *v.* [1950s+] to have sexual intercourse. [NAUGHTY *n.* (2)]

naughty bits *n.* [1970s+] the genitals, of either sex. [this quite deliberate euph. was coined *c.*1969 by the Monty Python's Flying Circus comedy team]

naughty dicky-bird *n.* [19C] a prostitute (cf. ALLEY CAT *n.*). [NAUGHTY *adj.* (2) + DICKY-BIRD *n.*[1] (1)]

naughty-house *n.* [late 16C–mid-19C] a brothel (cf. ACCOM-MODATION HOUSE *n.*). [SE *naughty* + *house*/HOUSE *n.*[1] (1)]

naughty pack *n.* [mid-16C–mid-18C] a person of low and worthless character, usu. a woman. [SE *naughty* + *pack* (cf. BAGGAGE *n.*[1])]

nauky *adj.* (*also* **knackety, knacky, knawky, nawky**) [late 18C+] cunning, resourceful. [Scot. *knaw*; ult. SE *know*]

naus *n.* (*also* **norz**) [1950s+] an unpleasant person. [pron. as abbr. of SE *naus*(*eating*) and commonly used with a derog. implication, but in fact rhy. sl.; *Noah's* = *Noah's Ark* = NARK *n.*[1] (2)]

nause *n.* [1950s+] the problem, the difficulty, the annoying thing. [abbr. SE *nausea*]

nause *v.* (*also* **noorse**) [1950s+] to cause problems, to annoy, to ruin a plan. [NAUSE *n.*]

naused off *adj.* [1950s+] furious, annoyed. [NAUSE *v.*]

nauseous *adj.* [mid-17C–19C; 1950s+] unpleasant, distasteful; thus *joc. nauseous toad*, an affectionate term of address. [1950s+ use is mainly US campus/teen]

nausie *n.* (*also* **naussie**) [1950s+] (*Aus.*) a recently arrived immigrant. [SE *new* + AUSSIE *n.* (2)]

nautch *n.* (*also* **nautchery, nautch house, nautch joint**) [late 19C–1940s] (*US*) a brothel. [Urdu/Hind. *nāch*, dancing, usu. as an exhibition of Indian dancing, thus a *nautch girl*, a dancing girl; the image of the 'exotic' East led inevitably to assumptions of sexual licence + HOUSE *n.*[1] (1)/JOINT *n.*[4] (3)]

nautch broad *n.* [1940s] (*US*) a prostitute working in a brothel. [NAUTCH *n.* + BROAD *n.*[2] (2)]

nautical miles *n.* (*also* **nauticals**) [20C+] haemorrhoids. [rhy. sl. = piles]

Navajo time *n.* [20C+] (*US*) unpunctuality (cf. AFRICAN (PEOPLE'S) TIME *n.*). [racist stereotyping]

naval depôt *n.* [mid-19C] the stomach. [a pun on SE *navel*]

naval engagement *n.* (*also* **engagement**) [20C+] (*orig. milit.*) sexual intercourse. [pun on SE *naval/navel*]

navel *n.* [1910s] (*Aus.*) a misfortune.

navigator of the windward passage *n.* [late 18C+] a sodomite, a male homosexual (cf. ANAL ASTRONAUT *n.*). [WINDWARD PASSAGE *n.*]

navigators *n.* (*also* **navs**) [mid-19C–1910s] potatoes; thus *navigator scot*, potatoes all hot. [rhy. sl.; the connection with the predominantly Irish *navigators* (cf. NAVVY *n.*), builders of Victorian Britain's railways and canals, whose stereotype consumed many potatoes, may or may not be coincidental]

Navvy *n.* (*also* **navvy**) [1910s+] (*US, mainly southwest*) **1** a Navaho Indian. **2** a Navaho pony. [abbr.]

navvy *n.* **1** [mid-19C–1910s] a labourer working on the railways, canals and roads of Victorian Britain. **2** [mid-19C+] (*also* **nabby**) any unskilled labourer. [both defs. virtually SE f. 1860; abbr. 18C *navigator*, a labourer excavating canals, later any earthwork]

navvy's piano *n.* [1920s+] a pneumatic drill.

navvy's prayer-book *n.* [late 19C–1900s] a shovel. [NAVVY *n.* + SE *prayer-book*; the 'prayerful' posture the shoveller has to adopt]

navy *n.* [1900s–60s] a cigar or cigarette end left burning on the pavement. [*Navy Cut*, a brand of tobacco]

Navy Office *n.* [early–mid-19C] the Fleet prison; thus *commander of the fleet*, the warden of the Fleet prison (cf. ABBOTT'S PRIORY *n.*). [pun on *fleet/Fleet*; the prison name refers to the Fleet River, itself f. OE *fléot*, a tidal inlet]

nawky *adj. see* NAUKY *adj.*

nawleed *n.* [2000s] (*US Black*) the police. [ety. unknown]

naybo! *excl.* (*also* **nayboo! neighbo!**) [1930s+] (*US Black*) used to express disagreement. [? SE *nay, no* + BO *n.*[1]]

naygah/naygar/naygur *n. see* NIGGER *n.*[1].

nay-nay *adj.* [20C+] (*W.I.*) insignificant, worthless. [Scot./Irish *nig-nay*, a trifle, a plaything; but note Igbo *neni*, to disregard, to despise]

nay nays *n.* [1950s+] the female breasts. [NINNIES *n.*]

Nazarene foretop n. [late 18C–early 19C] an ornamental wig made in imitation of Christ's head of hair, as represented by painters. [SE *Nazarene*, a synon. for Christ + *foretop*, the lock of hair (whether real or in a wig) that covers the crown of the head]

nazie adj. (*also* **nazy, nazzy**) [late 17C–mid-19C] drunk. [for ety. see NASE adj.]

nazie cove n. (*also* **nazie mort, nazy cove/mort, nazzy cove/mort**) [late 17C–early 19C] a drunken man (*cove*) or woman (*mort*). [NAZIE adj. + COVE n. (1)/MORT n.]

nazie nab n. *see* NASE NAB n.

Nazi spy n. [1940s+] (*Aus.*) a meat pie. [rhy. sl.]

nazold n. [early 17C] a silly, vain or weak-minded person. [SE *nazzard*, an insignificant or feeble person]

nazy adj. *see* NAZIE adj.

nazy cove/mort n. *see* NAZIE COVE n.

nazy nab n. *see* NASE NAB n.

nazz n. [1990s+] (*US teen*) a fool. [? 16C SE *nazzard*, an insignificant or feeble person; coined by Anthony Burgess in *A Clockwork Orange* (1962)]

nazzy adj. *see* NAZIE adj.

nazzy cove/mort n. *see* NAZIE COVE n.

n.b. adj. [1900s–10s] penniless, impoverished. [*not* a *bean* + pun on SE *N.B.*, *nota bene*, i.e. beware of such a pauper]

n.b.a. phr. [2000s] (*US Black*) cowardly. [abbr. *no balls at all*; BALLS n.¹ (4)]

n.b.d. phr. [1980s+] (*US campus*) a general expression of nonchalance. [abbr. *no big deal*]

n.b.g. phr. [20C+] *no bloody good*. [abbr.]

n.c. phr.¹ [mid-19C–1900s] (*US*) enough said, it is possible to infer all the facts from what has already been stated. [abbr. NUFF CED phr.; 'a certain theatrical manager spells the words, it is said, in this style' (Hotten, 1864)]

n.c. phr.² [1980s+] (*US campus*) said of a boorish person. [abbr. *no class*]

n.c.a.a. phr. [1980s+] (*US campus*) said of a very boorish person. [abbr. *no class at all* + a jibe at the sporting *NCAA*, National Collegiate Athletic Association; pron. 'NC double-A' based on N.C. phr.²]

n.c.d phr. *see* NO CAN DO phr.

n.d. n. [late 19C–1900s] (*UK society*) a woman who is attempting to appear younger than she is. [the bibliographical annotation *n.d.*, no date]

Neapolitan favour n. (*also* **Neapolitan bone-ache,** ...**button,** ...**court,** ...**disease,** ...**running-nag,** ...**scab,** ...**scurf, Neapolitan**...) [late 16C–early 18C] syphilis; thus *Neapolitan*, a sufferer from syphilis. [contemporary stereotyping of Italians as POX n.¹ (1)-ridden]

near adj. (*also* **nearbegone**) [late 19C–1910s] miserly, cheap; thus *nearness*, miserliness. [earlier use SE]

near and far n. 1 [late 19C+] a (public house) bar. 2 [1940s+] (*Aus.*) a motorcar. [rhy. sl.]

neardy n. [mid-19C] a boss, a master, an overseer. [northern dial. *near*, grasping, covetous]

near enough n. *see* NIGH ENOUGH n.

nearer my God to thee n. [1930s–40s] (*US Black*) straight, silky hair, seen as a badge of Whiteness. [ironic use, the *God* in question being White and the subject's aspirations disapproved of by more politically motivated Black peers]

nearer the bone the sweeter the meat, the phr. [mid-19C–1930s] a phr. used of a notably thin woman. [pvb]

near go n. (*also* **near one**) [early 19C–1930s] a near thing, a 'close shave'. [SE *near* + GO n.³ (1)]

near shave n. *see* CLOSE SHAVE n.

near-sighted adj. [1920s+] (*US gay*) uncircumcised, esp. of an uncircumcised penis with its tip protruding slightly above the foreskin (cf. BALD-HEADED HERMIT n.).

near squeak n. *see* CLOSE SHAVE n.

neat adj. 1 [early–late 19C] in ironic use, rare, fine, delightful. 2 [20C+] (*orig./mainly US*) a term of general approval, pleasant, satisfactory, attractive.

neat adv. [late 19C–1900s] (*US Und.*) skilfully.

neat as a flea phr. [1940s] (*Aus.*) small and neat.

neatnik n. [1950s+] (*US*) someone devoted to neatness and order. [SE *neat* + -NIK sfx]

neato adj. [1950s+] (*US teen*) good, excellent, a general term of approbation; often as excl. [SE *neat* + -o sfx (6)]

neb n.¹ 1 [17C–19C] the mouth. 2 [late 17C–early 19C; 1960s] (*also* **nib**) a woman's face. 3 [late 19C+] (*Ulster*) the nose; thus *longnebbed*, nosey, inquisitive. [SE *neb*, a bird's beak; the term dates back to the *Ancren Riwle*, a devotional work composed *c*.1225]

neb n.² [1920s–40s] (*US*) a nobody. [abbr. NEBBISH n.]

neb v. [late 19C+] (*Ulster*) to interfere, to 'poke one's nose in'. [NEB n.¹ (3)]

nebbie n. (*also* **neb**) [1960s+] *Nemb*utal, a barbiturate (cf. BARBIT n.). [abbr.]

nebbish n. (*also* **nebbich, nebich, nebish, neblish**) [late 19C+] a harmless eccentric, a born loser, a nobody; also attrib. [synon. Yid. *nebech*]

nebbishy adj. [1980s+] eccentric, insignificant, pitiful. [NEBBISH n.]

nebby adj.¹ [late 19C+] (*Ulster*) nosy, inquisitive. [NEB n.¹ (3)]

nebby adj.² [1990s+] (*US*) very unsophisticated. [NEBBISH n.]

nebich/nebish/neblish n. *see* NEBBISH n.

nebo n. [1960s] (*Aus.*) a drunkard. [abbr. SE *inebriated* + -o sfx (4)]

nebruary (morning) n. [20C+] (*W.I.*) never. [SE *ne(ver)* + (*Fe*)*bruary*]

nebuchadnezzar n.¹ [19C] the penis; thus *take Nebuchadnezzar out to grass*, of a man, to have sexual intercourse (cf. ABRAHAM n.¹). [*Nebuchadnezzar* II, (*c*.630–*c*.562 BC) King of Babylon; play on GREENS n.² and the king's madness, during which period he ate grass]

nebuchadnezzar n.² 1 [mid-19C–1900s] a vegetarian. 2 [mid-19C–1950s] (*Aus.*) a salad. [for ety. *see* prev.]

necessaries n. 1 [17C] the lavatory. 2 [1940s+] the genitals. 3 [1990s+] a condom. [euph.]

necessary n. 1 [early 17C–early 19C] a bedfellow, usu. a female one. 2 [early 17C–mid-19C] an outhouse, a privy. 3 [late 19C+] money (cf. ACTUAL, THE n.). 4 [1990s+] what is required, e.g. intelligence. [all plays on the supposed necessity of such items; post mid-19C use of (1) is US]

necessary house n. [early 17C–1930s] an outhouse, a privy (cf. BACKHOUSE n.).

neck n.¹ [mid-19C+] the throat. [NECK v.¹]

neck n.² 1 [late 19C+] audacity, daring, impudence. 2 [1990s+] one who speaks impudently. [orig. northern dial.; note also BRASS NECK n.; HARD NECK n.]

neck n.³ (*US*) 1 [1900s] a fool. 2 [1960s–70s] stupidity, nonsense. [TALK THROUGH (THE BACK OF) ONE'S NECK v.]

neck n.⁴ [1940s+] (*US campus*) 1 the act of kissing and cuddling. 2 one with whom one kisses and cuddles. [NECK v.⁴]

neck n.⁵ [1960s+] 1 (*US*) a poor farmer, usu. Southern and presumably racist and unsophisticated. 2 (*US campus*) a term of abuse. [abbr. REDNECK n.¹ (1)]

neck n.⁶ *see* PENCIL-NECK n.

neck v.¹ [16C; mid-19C+] to swallow, either alcohol or (latterly) drugs.

neck v.² 1 [mid-19C–1900s] (*US Und.*) to seize by the neck. 2 [mid-19C–1900s] (*US*) to apprehend and arrest. 3 [late 19C+] (*Aus./US*) to garrotte. 4 [1940s+] (*Aus.*) to kill oneself by hanging.

neck v.³ [1910s–60s] (*US*) to stare; thus *necking*, an act of scrutiny or staring. [abbr. RUBBERNECK v.¹ (3)]

neck v.⁴ [1920s+] (*orig. US*) to pursue sexual pleasure that stops short of intercourse; usu. teen use and practice; thus

NECKING n.[1]. [orig. UK dial. *neck*, to court, i.e. to put one's arm around someone's neck]

neck v.[5] [1960s] (*US campus*) to work very hard. [? from the pain in one's neck that results after reading books extensively]

neck and crop *adv.* [19C] bodily, completely, altogether. [i.e. the entire throat area; SE f. 1890]

neck and heels *adv.* **1** [18C–19C] forcefully. **2** [19C] impetuously, spontaneously. [? one commits every part of the body]

neck basting *n.* [late 19C–1900s] drinking. [SE *neck* + *baste*, to moisten, usu. in culinary context]

neck bone *n.* [2000s] (*US Black*) fellatio. [SE *neck* + BONE v.[1] (1)]

neck cloth *n.* (*also* **neck squeezer**) [late 18C–mid-19C] a hangman's rope.

necker *n.* [1920s+] (*US*) one who engages in NECKING n.[1]. [NECK v.[4]]

neckful *n.* [late 19C+] a quantity. [NECK n.[1]]

necking n.[1] [1920s+] kissing and cuddling. [NECK v.[4]]

necking n.[2] **1** [1940s] (*US Und.*) hanging. **2** [1960s] (*Aus.*) a means of pickpocketing whereby the thief puts one arm around his victim's neck and the other into his pocket. [NECK v.[2]]

necking n.[3] *see* NECK v.[3].

neckinger *n.* [mid-late 19C] a cravat. [it goes round the SE *neck*]

neck it *v.* [mid-late 19C] to stand, to exhibit moral courage. [NECK n.[2] (1)]

neck job *n.* [1990s+] strangulation. [SE *neck* + JOB n.[4]]

necklace *n.* **1** [17C] the neck. **2** [mid-17C–1960s] a hangman's noose. **3** [1940s+] (*Aus.*) a garrotter. **4** [1980s+] (*S.Afr.*) the act of placing a petrol-soaked tyre around a victim's neck and setting it on fire. [(4) NECKLACE v.]

necklace *v.* [1980s+] (*orig. S.Afr.*) to murder by placing a petrol-soaked tyre around a victim's neck and setting it alight.

necklace artist *n.* (*also* **necktie artist**) [1940s+] (*Aus.*) a garrotter. [NECKLACE n. (3)/NECKTIE n.[1] + ARTIST sfx]

necklaced *adj.* [1970s+] (*US Black*) extremely sophisticated, worldly. ['laced by the neck']

neck oil *n.* [mid-19C+] alcohol, usu. beer. [SE *neck* + *oil*; note NECK v.[1]]

neck or nothing *phr.* [early 18C–1950s] desperately, 'come what may'. [? the imagery of horseracing or of capital punishment]

neck over nozzle *phr.* [late 19C] head over heels.

neck squeezer *n. see* NECK CLOTH n.

neck stamper *n.* [late 17C–early 19C] a tavern pot-boy. [? he 'stamps' around carrying bottles by the 'neck']

necktie n.[1] [mid-19C–1950s] **1** the hangman's noose. **2** the gallows.

necktie n.[2] *see* COLOMBIAN NECKTIE n.

necktie artist *n. see* NECKLACE ARTIST n.

necktie party *n.* (*also* **necktie frolic, ...sociable, ...social**) **1** [late 19C+] (*US*) a hanging, usu. an illicit, impromptu lynching. **2** [1990s+] in fig. use, a 'lynching'. [NECKTIE n.[1]]

neck-to-knees *n.* [1910s–40s] (*Aus.*) an old-fashioned bathing costume which completely covered that area of the body. [the wearing of such costumes was actually commanded by law in a number of popular resorts, starting with those in New South Wales, under an act of 1902]

neck twister *n.* [mid-19C] (*US*) a form of cocktail. [its effect]

neck verse *n.* [mid-16C–early 19C] a Lat. verse recited as a means of escaping the gallows. [anyone claiming benefit of clergy, and thus exemption from the gallows, was obliged to read in Lat. the first verse of Psalm 51, beginning *Miserere mei* (Have mercy upon me, O God...); the aim was to weed out false clergymen]

neck warmer *n.* [1940s+] (*Aus.*) a nightdress. [its being pushed up to the neck during sexual intercourse]

neckweed *n.* [mid-16C–early 19C] **1** hemp, the basic constituent of the rope used for the gallows. **2** the hangman's rope itself.

nectar *n.* **1** [mid-18C+] alcohol; a drink. **2** [1980s+] (*US campus*)

anything exceptionally wonderful. **3** [1990s+] (*W.I.*) semen (cf. BABY GRAVY n.). [SE *nectar*, popularly, albeit incorrectly, known as the food of the gods (which is in fact *ambrosia*); note use of *amber nectar* in adverts for Foster's (Aus.) lager; note Williams for fig. use of *nectar* as vaginal secretions]

nectarine *n. see* PEACH n.[1] (1).

nectar pot *n. see* HONEYPOT n.[1] (2).

nec ultra *n.* [mid-late 19C] (*UK society*) the West End of London, thus the fashionable world. [Lat. *nec ultra*, and not beyond; the line beyond which one might not go was Temple Bar, the line between the West End and the City]

Ned *n.* [late 17C–1960s] the Devil; usu. as RAISE NED v. or *holy Ned!* [generic use of proper name]

ned n.[1] **1** [mid-18C–mid-19C] a guinea; thus HALF-NED n. **2** [mid-19C–1930s] (*US*) a $10 gold piece; thus HALF-NED n. [ety. unknown; ? joc. use of proper name on pattern of JEMMY O'GOBLIN n.]

ned n.[2] **1** [mid-late 19C] (*US*) a soldier, whose diet is mainly pork. **2** [mid-19C–1950s] (*US*) salt pork or bacon, usu. as OLD NED n.[1]. **3** [1960s] (*US Black*) a Black person who curries favour with White society. [orig. Ozark use *ned*, boar and thus generic for any pig; (1) f. (2); (3) ? the image of such a figure being effectively a PIG n.[1] (1)]

ned n.[3] [1910s+] **1** (*orig. Aus.*) the head. **2** (*Aus.*) in a game of two-up, the 'heads' side of a coin. [? rhy. sl.]

ned n.[4] [1970s+] a hooligan, a thug, a petty criminal; as adj., *neddy*. [equation with the SE *Teddy boy*, or 'Edwardian', i.e. another nickname for *Edward*]

ned n.[5] [2000s] (*Irish*) excrement.

nedash *n.* [early 19C] nothing. [Rom. *nastis*, I cannot]

neddies, the *n.* [20C+] (*Aus.*) the sport of horseracing. [NEDDY n.[1] (3)]

neddy n.[1] **1** [mid-17C–1960s] a donkey. **2** [early 19C+] a fool, a simpleton (cf. BEN n.[1]). **3** [late 19C+] (*Aus.*) a horse, esp. a racehorse.

neddy n.[2] [mid-18C–mid-19C] a guinea. [ext. NED n.[1] (1)]

neddy n.[3] [mid-late 19C] (*Irish*) a good deal, a considerable amount. [ety. unknown]

neddy n.[4] [mid-19C+] (*UK Und.*) a cosh, blackjack or life-preserver. [abbr. KENNEDY n. (1)]

neddy n.[5] [late 19C–1910s] (*Aus.*) the tucker-bag carried by an itinerant tramp. [? play on use of MATILDA n. for the swag itself, to which it is tied; it dangles 'from her apron-strings' (*AND*)]

neddy *adj. see* NED n.[4].

neddy *v.* [mid-late 19C] to hit with a cosh or blackjack. [NEDDY n.[4]]

neddyvaul *n.* [late 19C–1900s] a chief, a leader, a commander. [Cockney pron. of *ned of all*, a pun on NED n.[3] (1), i.e. the head of all]

neden *n.* [2000s] (*US Black*) the female genitals. [? SE *needing*, i.e. the woman's presumed desire for sex]

ned fool *n.* [late 16C–early 17C] a noisy fool, a simpleton (cf. BEN n.[1]). [generic use of proper name *Ned* + SE *fool*]

Ned Kelly n.[1] (*Aus.*) **1** [20C+] an unscrupulous businessman; thus *Kelly gang*, an unethical business, a tax-grabbing government. **2** [1930s+] a poker machine. [like the bushranger *Ned Kelly* (1855–80), they are all robbers]

Ned Kelly n.[2] **1** [1920s+] (*Aus.*) the stomach, the belly. **2** [1970s] television. [rhy. sl.; (2) = TELLY n.; ult. bushranger *Ned Kelly* (1855–80)]

Ned Kelly n.[3] [1920s+] (*Aus.*) a 'blood-and-thunder' romance. [the dramatic adventures of bushranger *Ned Kelly* (1855–80)]

Ned Kelly *v.* **1** [1900s] to bushrange. **2** [1950s] to kill a bird or any other game unsportingly. [for ety. *see* NED KELLY n.[1]]

ned skinner *n. see* JIMMY SKINNER n.

ned stokes *n.* [late 18C–mid-19C] the 4 of spades. [ety. unknown; ? anecdotal]

neecee princess *n.* [late 19C–1920s] (*UK society*) a nouveau riche young woman. [London postal district *East Central*, the City, as a centre of commerce, however rewarding, supposedly beyond the social pale]

needful *n.* **1** [late 18C–1940s] money; thus *do the needful*, to pay a bill (cf. ACTUAL, THE *n.*). **2** [mid–late 19C] (*US*) whisky. [the necessity of money or of money to life; thus fig. the necessity of alcohol]

Needham's shore *n.* (*also* **Needham's cross**) [late 16C] a state of great poverty. [play on SE *need 'em* and the Suffolk town of Needham Market]

needing a reef taken in *phr.* [19C] (*orig. naut.*) drunk.

needle *n.*[1] [17C+] the penis. [later usage *US*]

needle *n.*[2] (*also* **rank needle**) [late 18C–early 19C] a confidence trickster. [like a *needle*, he is very 'sharp'/play on SHARP *n.*[1] (1); SE *rank*, extreme]

needle *n.*[3] [late 19C+] resentment, bitterness, irritation; thus COP THE NEEDLE *v.*; GET THE NEEDLE *v.* [orig. tailoring jargon]

needle *n.*[4] **1** [1910s+] (*drugs*) a hypodermic, a syringe; thus ON THE NEEDLE *phr.* **2** [1930s+] (*drugs*) a narcotics addict. **3** [1950s+] (*drugs*) pertaining to narcotics and their injection. **4** [1990s+] (*US prison*) a lethal injection, as used in legal executions.

needle *n.*[5] [1910s+] a knife.

needle *n.*[6] [1930s+] (*US*) repetitious nagging and complaining; aggressive teasing. [image of a phonograph needle going round and round]

needle *v.*[1] **1** [early 19C] to haggle, esp. if one takes advantage of the other person. **2** [late 19C+] to annoy, to tease maliciously. **3** [late 19C+] to become annoyed. **4** [late 19C+] (*Irish*) to scrounge. **5** [1940s] to find one's way. [NEEDLE *n.*[3]]

needle *v.*[2] [1920s–60s] (*US*) to add alcohol or ether to a non-alcoholic beer or drink, usu. by injection through the cork. [NEEDLE *n.*[4] (1)]

needle *v.*[3] [1950s–60s] (*US*) to apply maximum power or acceleration to a vehicle or plane. [thus moving the speedometer *needle*]

needle *v.*[4] [1970s] (*US Und.*) to drill a hole, e.g. in a safe.

needle and cotton *adj.* [20C+] rotten. [rhy. sl.]

needle (and pin) *n.* [1910s+] gin. [rhy. sl.]

needle and pin *adj.* [1930s+] thin. [rhy. sl.]

needle and thread *n.* [mid-19C; 1960s+] bread. [rhy. sl.]

needle artist *n.* (*also* **needle fiend**, ...**jabber**, ...**knight**, ...**pumper**) [1920s+] (*US drugs*) **1** an intravenous drug addict. **2** one who fetishizes the needle and the mechanics of injection. [NEEDLE *n.*[4] (1) + ARTIST sfx]

needle beer *n.* (*also* **needled beer**, ...**brew**, ...**slop, shot beer**) [1920s+] (*US*) beer that has been strengthened by pure alcohol or ether. [NEEDLE *v.*[2]]

needlecase *n.* [19C] the vagina (cf. BAG *n.*[1]). [NEEDLE *n.*[1] + SE *case*]

needled *adj.* [late 19C+] upset, annoyed. [NEEDLE *v.*[1] (2)]

needled beer/brew *n. see* NEEDLE BEER *n.*

needle dick *n.* [1960s+] (*US*) **1** a particularly small penis. **2** the man who has one. [SE *needle* + DICK *n.*[4] (1); but note NEEDLE *n.*[1]]

needle dodger *n.* [mid-19C–1920s] a dressmaker; thus *needle-dodging*, dress-making.

needled slop *n. see* NEEDLE BEER *n.*

needled up *adj.* [1940s] (*US*) addicted to narcotics.

needle fiend *n. see* NEEDLE ARTIST *n.*

needle freak *n.* **1** [1960s+] (*US drugs*) an intravenous drug user who is as stimulated by the act of injection as by the action of the drug. **2** [1970s+] a prostitute's sadistic client who derives pleasure from hiring a woman with large breasts and paying her for every needle she permits him to stick into her flesh. [NEEDLE *n.*[4] (1)/SE *needle* + FREAK sfx]

needle house *n. see* NEEDLE PALACE *n.*

needle jabber *n. see* NEEDLE ARTIST *n.*

needle jerker *n.* [early 19C] a tailor.

needle knight *n. see* NEEDLE ARTIST *n.*

needle-man *n.*[1] **1** [1920s+] (*drugs*) a drug addict. **2** [1960s+] (*US*) a doctor. [NEEDLE *n.*[4] (1) + SE *man*; the use of a hypodermic syringe in both pursuits]

needle-man *n.*[2] [1930s] (*US Und.*) one who adulterates beer. [NEEDLE *v.*[2] + SE *man*]

needle neddie *n.* [1980s+] (*Aus. prison*) the spoon in which one heats the heroin/water mixture prior to making an injection. [NEEDLE *n.*[4] (1) + ? NEDDY *n.*[1] (3), with pun on HORSE *n.*[8]]

needle-nipper *n.* [1950s] (*US drugs*) an intravenous narcotic addict.

needle-nose *n.* [1930s] a lawyer.

needlenosed *adj.* [1920s–70s] (*US*) having a pointed nose; thus *needlenose*, one who has such a nose. [occas., but not invariably, used of Jews]

needle palace *n.* (*also* **needle house**) [1990s+] (*US drugs*) anywhere that narcotics drug users congregate to inject themselves.

needle park *n.* [1960s+] (*drugs*) a variety of locations in New York City, small oases of grass in the larger world of streets and buildings, frequented by heroin users. [orig. the traffic island at Broadway and 71st Street; the term was popularized by James Mills's 1966 book *The Panic In Needle Park*]

needle point *n.* (*also* **needle pointer**) **1** [late 17C–mid-19C] a card-sharp or dice cheat. **2** [early–late 19C] an aggressive person. [like a *needle*, he is 'sharp'; ? an added ref. to the pricking of cards to mark them for cheating purposes]

needle pumper *n. see* NEEDLE ARTIST *n.*

needle puncher *n.* (*also* **needle queen**) [1960s+] (*US*) a doctor or nurse. [NEEDLE *n.*[4] (1) + SE *puncher*/QUEEN *n.*[1] (3)]

needle pusher *n.* **1** [1920s–30s] (*US drugs*) an addict who injects narcotics. **2** [1920s–40s] (*US*) a tailor. **3** [1960s+] (*US*) a doctor or nurse. [NEEDLE *n.*[4] (1) + SE *pusher*]

needles *n.* **1** [1900s–50s] the shaking that accompanies withdrawal from heavy cocaine usage. **2** [1920s–30s] (*US*) the nerves, the jitters. **3** [1950s] the immediate sensation, equivalent to an electric shock, that follows an injection of a drug. [one's reactions equate with those of one who has been jabbed with a needle]

needles and pins *n.*[1] [late 19C–1900s] a warning against marriage. [the rhyme 'Pins and needles – needles and pins / When a man marries his trouble begins']

needles and pins *n.*[2] [1990s+] twins. [rhy. sl.]

needle shooter *n. see* SHOOTER *n.*[2] (1).

needle shy *adj.* [1930s–50s] (*US drugs*) of an addict, phobic of needles.

needless mark-up *n.* [1990s+] (*US*) a Neiman-Marcus department store. [pun on name and the prices of its luxury goods]

needle woman *n.* [19C] a prostitute (cf. COCKATRICE *n.*; FANCY WOMAN *n.*). [NEEDLE *n.*[1] + SE *woman*]

needlework *n.* [19C] sexual intercourse. [NEEDLE *n.*[1] + SE *work*]

needleworker *n.* [1910s] (*US*) a narcotics addict. [NEEDLE *n.*[4] (1) + SE *worker*]

need like a hole in the head *v.* (*also* **need like a third nut**) [1940s+] not to need at all. [trans. of Yid. *ich darf es vi a loch in kop*]

needmore *n.* [1960s+] (*US*) a poor, usu. Black, section of town. [the people *need more*]

need one's head read *v. see* GET ONE'S HEAD READ *v.*

need something yesterday *v. see* WANT SOMETHING YESTERDAY *v.*

needy *n.* [mid-19C–1920s] a tramp, a vagrant.

needy mizzler *n.* [early–mid-19C] **1** a shabby beggar. **2** a tramp who leaves without paying for his lodging. [NEEDY *n.* + MIZZLE *v.* (1)]

neeger *n. see* NIGGER *n.*[1].

neener *n. see* NINA *n.*

neergs *n.* [mid-19C] greens, green vegetables. [backsl.]

neetewif *n.* (*also* **netewif**) [mid-19C] 15. [backsl.]

neetewif gens *n.* (*also* **netewif gens**) [mid-19C] 15 shillings (75p). [backsl.; NEETEWIF n. + GEN n.¹]

neetexis *n.* (*also* **netexis**) [mid-19C] 16. [backsl.]

neetexis gens *n.* (*also* **netexis gens**) [mid-19C] 16 shillings (80p). [backsl.; NEETEXIS n. + GEN n.¹]

neetrith gens *n.* [mid-19C–1900s] 13 shillings (65p). [backsl.; GEN n.¹]

neetrouf *n.* (*also* **netrouf**) [mid-19C] the number 14. [backsl.]

neetrouf gens *n.* [mid-19C] 14 shillings (70p). [backsl.; NEETROUF n. + GEN n.¹]

nef *n.* [2000s] (*US Black*) a term of address to any male. [abbr. of NEPHEW n. (2)]

Nefertiti flat top *n.* [1990s+] (*US Black*) a popular hairstyle. [Egyptian Queen *Nefertiti* (*fl.*1372–50BC), subject of a celebrated limestone bust in which her hair resembles a modern FLAT TOP n. (1)]

neg *adj.* [1960s] (*Aus.*) careless, incompetent. [abbr. SE *negligent*]

neg! *excl.* (*also* **negat! negs!**) [1960s+] (*US, orig. milit.*) no! no to...! [abbr. NEGATIVE! excl.]

negaholic *n.* [1980s+] (*US*) a pessimist. [SE *nega*(*tive*) + (*alco*)*holic*]

negative! *excl.* [1940s+] no! no to...! [orig. in radio messages]

negative nancy *n.* [2000s] (*US campus*) a female pessimist.

negative perspiration *phr.* [1970s+] (*US*) no problem. [play on NO SWEAT phr.]

negatory *adv.* (*also* **negatrix, negatron**) [1950s+] (*US, orig. milit.*) no, negative. [SE *negative*]

negatory! *excl.* [1950s+] no! absolutely not! [NEGATORY adv.]

neger *n. see* NIGGER n.¹.

neggle *v. see* NIGGLE v.

nego *n.* [1960s–70s] (*US campus*) a student with a negative or objectionable attitude. [SE *negative* or Lat. *nego*, I deny]

negress *n.* [2000s] (*US Black*) a Black woman. [SE *negress* coined in late 18C but abandoned as poss. racist by 1960s for *Black* and latterly *African-/Afro-American* or *person of color*; thus 21C slang use is consciously ironic]

negro head *n. see* NIGGERHEAD n.¹.

negs! *excl. see* NEG! excl.

neighbo! *excl. see* NAYBO! excl.

neighbour *adj.* [20C+] (*Ulster*) all right, satisfactory. [? image of SE]

neighbour jones *n.* [1930s–40s] (*US*) an outdoor privy (cf. AUNTIE n.¹). [var. on MRS JONES n.]

neither one's arse nor one's elbow *phr.* [1910s+] (*Irish*) neither one thing nor another.

Nell Gwyn *n.* [20C+] gin. [rhy. sl.; ult. *Nell Gwyn* (1650–87), mistress of Charles II]

nellie *n.* (*also* **nell, nelly**) **1** [1910s+] an overtly homosexual, effeminate man (cf. ABIGAIL n.). **2** [1960s] a term of address between homosexual men. **3** [1960s+] a general term of disparagement, a fool (cf. BEN n.¹). **4** [1970s+] (*US campus*) a lesbian (cf. AMY-JOHN n.). [the female name, but note NELLIE (DUFF) n. (2); Puxley, *Cockney Rabbit: A Dick 'n' Arry of Rhyming Slang* (1992), suggests rhy. sl. *nellie dean* (a popular song) = QUEEN n.² (1)]

nellith *adj.* (*also* **nelly**) [1960s+] very effeminate. [NELLIE n. (1)]

Nellie Bligh *n. see* NELLY (BLIGH) n.

nellie (deans) *n.* (*also* **nelly (deans)**) [20C+] vegetables, i.e. greens. [rhy. sl.; ? popular song 'Nellie Dean']

nellie (duff) *n.* (*also* **nelly (duff)**) [20C+] **1** one's breath. **2** a male homosexual (cf. ABIGAIL n.). [rhy. sl.; (1) = PUFF n.¹ (1); (2) = PUFF n.³ (1)]

nelly *see also under* NELLIE *and its combs.*

nelly *n.*¹ (*also* **nellie's downfall, nelly's death**) [1940s–50s] (*Aus.*) cheap wine. [generic use of female name (+ its effects)]

nelly *n.*² [1970s] (*Aus.*) semen.

nelly *v. see* NELLY (OUT) v.

nelly-assed *adj.* [1960s–70s] (*US gay*) effeminate. [NELLIE n. (1) + -ASSED sfx]

Nelly (Bligh) *n.* (*also* **Nellie Bligh, Nelly Bly**) [1910s+] **1** a tie. **2** (*Aus.*) a meat pie. **3** an eye; usu. in pl. **4** the trousers' fly. **5** a fly; often in pl. **6** a lie. [rhy. sl.; ult. *Nellie Bly*, the pseudonym of Elizabeth Cochran Seaman (1864–1922), famous pioneering feminist newspaper reporter, who acquired her pen name from the title of a popular song at the time]

nelly kelly *n.* [20C+] (*Aus.*) the belly. [rhy. sl.]

nelly (out) *v.* [2000s] to act in an effeminate manner. [NELLIE n. (1)]

nelly's death *n. see* NELLY n.¹.

Nelson *n.*¹ *see* NELSON (MANDELA) n.

Nelson *n.*² *see* NELSON (RIDDLE) n.

Nelson Eddies *n.* [1930s+] money, cash (cf. BEES (AND HONEY) n.). [rhy. sl. = READIES n.; ult. US singer/actor *Nelson Eddy* (1901–67)]

Nelson Eddy *adv.* [1930s+] ready. [rhy. sl.; ult. *see* prev.]

Nelson (Mandela) *n.* [1990s+] Stella Artois lager. [rhy. sl. = *Stella*; ult. former S.Afr. President *Nelson Mandela* (b.1918)]

Nelson (Riddle) *n.* [1980s+] (*Aus.*) an act of urination (cf. ANGEL'S KISS n.). [rhy. sl. = PIDDLE n. (2); ult. US composer/arranger *Nelson Riddle* (1921–85)]

nembie *n.* (*also* **nemmie**) [1940s+] (*drugs*) Nembutal, a barbiturate (cf. BARBIT n.). [abbr.]

nemish *n.* [1960s–70s] (*drugs*) Nembutal, a barbiturate (cf. BARBIT n.). [abbr.]

nemmind *phr.* (*also* **nemmine**) [1910s+] (*mainly US*) popular mispron. of SE *never mind*.

nemmo *n. see* NAMMO n.

nennen *n.* [20C+] (*W.I.*) backside, buttocks. [? NAY-NAY adj. or redup. of Twi *ne*, to defecate]

nenti *n. see* NANTEE n.

neo maxi zoom dweebie *n.* [1980s+] (*US*) an inconsequential or obnoxious person. [ext. of DWEEB n.; popularized (? coined) in the film *The Breakfast Club* (1985)]

neon *n.* [1970s] (*US*) an eye. [it shines]

Neopolitan... *n. see* NEAPOLITAN FAVOUR n.

Nep *n.* (*also* **Nepalese**) [1960s+] (*drugs*) Nepalese hashish (cf. AFGHAN n.). [abbr.]

nephew *n.* **1** [1950s] (*US Und.*) a young homosexual boy (cf. AUNTIE n.²). **2** [2000s] (*US teen*) a friend, thus as a term of affectionate address. [generic use of SE *nephew* as a euph. for NIGGA n.]

nephy *n. see* NEVVY n.

Neptune's daughter *n.* [1930s–70s] (*US*) water. [rhy. sl.]

nerd *n.* (*also* **nurd**) **1** [1950s+] (*orig. US*) an unpleasant, insignificant or dull person. **2** [1960s+] (*orig. US campus/teen*) (*also* **nerdbomber**) anyone outside of a peer group and who thus fails to fit in with 'the gang', esp. a studious individual who eschews drink, drugs and similar teen pleasures. [? euph. for TURD n. (2); or ? influenced by 'Mortimer Snerd', a dummy used by US ventriloquist Edgar Bergen (1903–78); or ? f. line in *If I Ran a Zoo* (1950) by the children's author Dr Seuss (Theodore Seuss Geisel, 1904–91): 'And then, just to show them, / I'll sail to Ka-Troo / And Bring Back an It-Kutch, a Preep and a Proo, / a Nerkle, a Nerd, and a Seersucker, too!']

nerd *v.* [1980s+] (*US campus*) to study hard. [NERD n. (2)]

nerd magnet *n.* [1980s] (*US campus*) a girl who attracts boring, unattractive men. [NERD n. (1) + MAGNET sfx]

nerd pack *n.* [1980s+] (*US*) a plastic, sectioned liner for the breast pocket that keeps pens from soiling the cloth. [NERD n. (2) + SE *pack*]

nerdy *adj.* (*also* **nurdy**) [1960s+] (*orig. US*) **1** used of any form of speech or behaviour that is judged to be socially unacceptable by the speaker(s). **2** obsessive; the image is of a trainspotter. [NERD n.]

nerf *v.* [1940s+] (*US, orig. drag-racing*) to bump another vehicle slightly with one's own car. [? SE *nerve*, i.e. one has to have strong nerves to perform the manoeuvre]

nerf- *pfx* [1980s+] (*US*) used to express stupidity, e.g. *nerf-brained*, stupid. [brandname of foam-rubber toys]

nerf bar *n.* (*also* **nerfing bar**) [1940s+] (*US*) a bumper fitted to a customized car. [NERF v.]

nerk *n.* [1950s+] a fool, a yob, a generally unappetizing, unacceptable person. [? var. on BERK n.]

nerts *n.* (*US*) **1** [1930s–40s] the testicles. **2** [1980s+] nothing. [(1) var. on NUTS n.² (1)]

nerts *adj.* (*also* **nertz**) [1910s+] (*US*) crazy, foolish. [var. on NUTS adj.]

nerts! *excl.* (*also* **nertz!**) [1920s+] (*US*) nonsense! [var. on NUTS! excl.]

nerve *n.* **1** [mid-18C] a dashing man about town. **2** [late 19C+] audacity, impudence, cheek; esp. in phr. *have a nerve, have the nerve to*. [SE *nerve*, courage]

nerver *n.*¹ [late 19C–1920s] a bracing drink, a 'pick-me-up'. [it strengthens one's nerves]

nerver *n.*² [1900s–30s] (*US*) a gate-crasher. [they have a NERVE n. (2) to appear uninvited]

nervo and knox *n.* **1** [1940s+] socks. **2** [1940s+] venereal disease, esp. syphilis. **3** [1960s+] television. [rhy. sl.; (2) = POX n.¹; (3) = BOX n.⁵ (6); ult. Jimmy *Nervo* (1890–1975) and Teddy *Knox* (1896–1974), music-hall comedians and members of the Crazy Gang (1935–62)]

nervous *adj.* [1920s+] (*US, orig. jazz*) great, thrilling.

nervous finger *n.* [1940s] (*US Und.*) one given to small-time criminality. [? 'he can't keep his hands still']

nervous-jervis *adj.* [1970s] (*US campus*) extremely nervous. [assonance]

nervous nellie *n.* (*also* **nervous nelly**) [1920s+] (*US*) a fearful, foolish and timid person. [orig. used of Frank B. Kellogg, Secretary of State (1925–29)]

nervous pudding *n.* (*also* **nervous salad**) [1930s–40s] (*US*) a dish made with gelatine or aspic. [it shakes]

nervous wreck *n.*¹ [late 19C+] one who is (actually or fig.) suffering from disorder of the nerves.

nervous wreck *n.*² (*also* **I'm a wreck, total wreck**) [1940s+] a cheque. [rhy. sl.]

nervy *adj.* [late 19C+] **1** nervous, scared, cowardly, tense. **2** (*orig. US*) daring, audacious, pushing one's luck.

Nescafé *n.* [1990s+] a hand gesture used to indicate one's contempt. [the gesture, based on the shaking of a jar of coffee, imitates that of male masturbation and thus means WANKER n. (2); ? also rhy. sl. *Gareth Hunt* (the star of the Nescafé adverts who shook the coffee) = CUNT n.² (1)]

Nescaff *n.* (*also* **Nes**) [1950s+] a joc. mispron./abbr. of Nescafé, a popular brand of instant coffee.

nest *n.*¹ [late 16C+] the vagina, female pubic hair (cf. AGREEABLE RUTS OF LIFE n.). [later usage US]

nest *n.*² [1960s+] (*US*) the women who make up a pimp's collection of prostitutes.

nest *v.* [1910s–30s] (*US*) to squat, to make a homestead.

nestcock *n. see* NESTLECOCK n.

nester *n.* [late 19C–1950s] (*US, Western*) a squatter, a homesteader, a farmer, a small rancher; thus *Nestersville*, a small, out-of-the-way settlement. [SE *nest*/NEST v.]

nest in the bush *n.* [late 17C–19C] the vagina (cf. AGREEABLE RUTS OF LIFE n.; BEAUTY SPOT n.).

nestlecock *n.* (*also* **nestcock**) [mid-17C–19C] a prostitute (cf. COCKATRICE n.). [SE *nestle* + COCK n.¹ (1)]

nest of sparrows flying out of one's backside *phr. see* FLOCK OF SPARROWS FLYING OUT OF ONE'S BACKSIDE phr.

net *n.* [mid-19C] the number 10. [backsl.]

net *v.* [20C+] to use, to acquire. [SE *net*, to take, catch or capture (with a net)]

netarnal *adj. see* NATARNAL adj.

netenin *n.* [mid-19C] the number 19. [backsl.]

netenin gens *n.* [mid-19C] 19 shillings (95p). [backsl.; NETENIN n. + GEN n.¹]

netewif *see under* NEETEWIF and its combs.

netexis *see under* NEETEXIS and its combs.

net gen *n. see* GEN NET n.

netheg *n.* (*also* **net-theg**) [mid-19C] the number 18. [backsl.]

nether end *n.* [mid-18C–19C] the vagina. [SE *nether*, lower + SE *end*]

nether eye *n.* [19C] the vagina. [SE *nether*, lower + SE *eye*]

nether eyebrow *n.* (*also* **nether lashes/whiskers**) [18C–19C] pubic hair. [SE *nether*, lower + SE *eyebrow/whiskers*]

Netherlands *n.* **1** [late 16C–18C] the vagina (cf. ANTIPODES n.). **2** [late 18C–early 19C] the buttocks.

nether lips *n.* [mid-17C–19C] the vagina. [SE *nether*, lower + SE *lips*]

nether-mouth *n.* [mid-18C] the vagina. [SE *nether*, lower + SE *mouth*]

nethers *n.* [mid–late 19C] lodging-house charges. [NETHERSKEN n.]

nethersken *n.* [mid–late 19C] a cheap lodging house, frequented by beggars, criminals and the very poor. [SE *nether*, used in names of places to mean lower, low + KEN n.¹ (1)]

nether whiskers *n. see* NETHER EYEBROW n.

netnevis *n.* [mid-19C] the number 17. [backsl.]

netnevis gens *n.* [mid-19C] 17 shillings (85p). [backsl.; NETNEVIS n. + GEN n.¹]

netrouf *n. see* NEETROUF n.

netter *n.* [1930s+] (*US*) a player of lawn tennis. [the SE *net* that is an integral part of the game]

net-theg *n. see* NETHEG n.

net-theg gens *n.* [mid-19C] 18 shillings (90p). [backsl.; NETHEG n. + GEN n.¹]

nettle bed *n.* [early 18C–mid-19C] (*UK juv.*) the vagina (cf. BAG n.¹; BEAUTY SPOT n.).

netty *v.* [1940s] (*W.I.*) to be funny. [? NUTTY adj.² (2)]

net-yeneps *n.* [mid-19C] 10 pence. [backsl.; NET n. + YENNEP n.]

neuck *n. see* NYUCK n.

neuf-soixante *n. see* SIXTY-NINE n.

neuk *v.* (*S.Afr.*) **1** [1910s+] to beat up. **2** [1980s+] to interfere, to mess with. [Du. *neuken*, to knock]

neutral *adj.* [1920s] (*US*) stupid.

nevele *n.* (*also* **nevel**) [mid-19C] the number 11. [backsl.]

nevele gens *n.* [mid-19C] 11 shillings (55p). [backsl.; NEVELE n. + GEN n.¹]

nevele yeneps *n. see* LEVEN YENNEPS n.

never, the *n.* [late 19C] (*Aus. Und.*) a form of confidence trick.

never again *n.* [20C+] beer. [rhy. sl. = *Ben* (Truman), a beer brewed in East London]

never been kissed *n.* (*also* **never had it**) [1940s+] (*bingo*) the number 17 (cf. ALDERSHOT LADIES n.). [the supposed sexual innocence of a 17-year-old girl]

never better *n.* [20C+] (*Aus.*) a letter. [rhy. sl.]

never fear *n.* [mid-19C] a pint of beer. [rhy. sl.]

never hachi *phr.* (*also* **never hotchie**) [1950s+] (*US*) (it will) never happen. [play on SE *never* + mispron.; NEVER HAPPEN phr.]

never had it *n. see* NEVER BEEN KISSED n.

never happen *phr.* [1950s+] used to dismiss any idea that the speaker cannot support or wishes to deny.

never hotchie *phr. see* NEVER HACHI phr.

never mind *phr.* [early 19C+] don't worry.

never-never, the *n.* (*also* **the never-never country/land**) [mid-19C+] (*Aus./N.Z.*) the deep, deserted interior of Australia. [coined *c*.1830, the name gained wide popularity with the book *We of the Never-Never* (1908) by Mrs Aeneas Gunn; despite the logic of the English term, it may in fact come from Comderoi *nievah vahs*, unoccupied land, although this equally may be pure coincidence; on either count it precedes J.M. Barrie's coinage in *Peter Pan* (1904) by more than half a century; note Aborigine use as 'heaven' in Boldrewood, *Robbery Under Arms* (1888): 'I want to die and go up with him to the never-never country parson tell us about']

never-never (land) *n.* [late 19C+] the hire purchase system; esp. as ON THE NEVER-NEVER *phr.* [one never finishes paying for one's purchase; note *Never-never land* in J.M. Barrie's *Peter Pan* (1904)]

never-out *n.* [19C] the vagina. [it is inside the body]

never-ready morning *n.* [20C+] (*W.I.*) never. [var. on NEBRUARY (MORNING) *n.*]

never-see-come-see *n.* [20C+] (*W.I.*) **1** an unsophisticated person, seeing the sophisticated world for the first time. **2** anyone showing off their new status or possessions. [ext. of SE]

never squedge *n.* [late 19C–1900s] 'a poor, pulseless, passionless youth' (Ware). [? SE *never* + dial. *squedge*, to squeeze, thus one who never gets to 'squeeze' a woman]

never stand still *n.* (*also* **can't keep still**) [19C] a prison treadmill. [rhy. sl.; accentuated by the endless movement of the machine]

neversweat *n.* **1** [mid-19C+] a lazy person, an idler, one whose job requires little effort. **2** [1970s] (*Aus.*) a council worker. [(1) 20C+ use is US; note naut. jargon *do a never*, to shirk, to idle]

never touch it *n.* [late 19C–1900s] (*Aus.*) a teetotaller. ['it' being alcohol]

never trust me! *excl.* [late 16C+] a general excl. calling for faith from the listener, i.e. 'never trust me again if I break this promise.'

never wag (man of war) *n.* [late 18C–19C] the Fleet prison, London. [SE *never* + WAG v.¹ (1) + MAN OF WAR *n.*]

never was *n.* (*also* **never-waser, never-wozzer, never-wuzzer**) [late 19C+] (*US*) one who never rose above mediocrity, a has–been. ['he *never was* any good']

neves *see under* NEVIS and its combs.

Neville Nobody *n.* [1990s+] (*Aus.*) an insignificant individual.

nevis *n.* (*also* **neves**) **1** [mid-19C+] the number 7. **2** [late 19C+] (*UK prison*) a 7-year sentence. **3** [1950s+] £7. [backsl.]

nevis gens *n.* [mid-19C] 7 shillings (35p). [backsl.; NEVIS *n.* (1) + GEN *n.*¹]

nevis stretch *n.* [mid-19C] a 7-year sentence. [backsl.; NEVIS *n.* (2) + STRETCH *n.*¹ (3)]

nevis yeneps *n.* (*also* **neves–yenep**) [mid-19C] 7 pence. [backsl.; NEVIS *n.* (1) + YENNEP *n.*]

nevvy *n.* (*also* **nephy, nevy**) [mid-19C–1930s] a nephew. [abbr.; post mid-19C use mainly UK public school]

new *n.* [1920s] (*US tramp*) a novice within the hobo community. [note 19C RN training ship jargon *news*, the latest recruits]

new *adj.* (*US*) **1** [mid-19C–1950s] cheeky, insolent. **2** [late 19C–1900s; 1990s+] naïve and gullible.

new acid *n.* [1970s+] (*drugs*) phencyclidine (cf. ACE *n.*⁴). [SE *new* + ACID *n.*³]

newbie *n.* (*also* **newbee, newby**) **1** [1970s+] a new member, a recruit, a novice. **2** [2000s] (*US Black*) a neophyte prostitute. [? SE *new boy*]

newbie *adj.* [1970s+] (*US*) new, uninitiated, novice. [NEWBIE *n.* (1)]

new boot *n.* [2000s] (*US prison*) a new prison officer. [SE *new* + BOOT v.¹ (1)]

new booty *n.* [1990s+] (*US Black gang*) a new member of a gang. [SE *new* + BOOTY *n.* (3)]

new bran *adj.* [1990s+] (*W.I./UK Black teen*) brand new. [inversion]

newby *n. see* NEWBIE *n.*

new chum *n.* **1** [19C–1950s] (*Aus./N.Z./UK Und.*) (*also* **chummy**) a prisoner just arrived in jail, on the hulks, or in Aus. or N.Z.;

later an immigrant to Aus. or N.Z. **2** [late 19C+] a novice, an inexperienced person. [SE *new* + CHUM *n.*¹; note CHUM *n.*²]

new-chum *adj.* [mid-19C+] (*Aus./N.Z.*) inexpert, raw. [NEW CHUM *n.*]

new-chum gold *n.* [mid-19C+] (*Aus.*) iron pyrites, 'fool's gold'. [a newly arrived 'digger' might be fooled into thinking he had discovered the real metal]

new cock *n.* [late 19C–1950s] (*UK prison*) a new inmate. [SE *new* + COCK *n.*³]

New College *n.* [late 17C–early 19C] the Royal Exchange, London. [? its function as one of the sites where, trad., a new sovereign is proclaimed]

New Cut warrior *n.* [late 19C–1900s] an inhabitant of the New Cut, in south London, a tough area where fighting was an everyday and unremarked pastime.

new deal *n.* [mid-19C+] (*orig. US*) a fresh start. [poker imagery]

New Delhi *n.* [20C+] the stomach, the belly. [rhy. sl.]

New Delhi belly *n. see* DELHI BELLY *n.*

new double six *n.* (*also* **next double six**) [1940s–70s] (*US Black*) the New Year. [*double six* = 12 (months)]

Newf *n.* (*also* **Newfie**) **1** [1940s+] (*orig. Can.*) a Newfoundlander. **2** [1940s+] (*US*) Newfoundland. **3** [1980s+] (*US*) a Newfoundland dog. [abbr.; *Newfies* are the 'Irish' or 'Poles' of Canada, rural, isolated and thus considered backward and stupid]

new fish *n.* [1910s+] (*US prison*) a new inmate. [SE *new* + FISH *n.*⁶ (1)]

Newgate *n.*¹ [mid-16C–mid-19C] any prison (cf. ABBOTT'S PRIORY *n.*). [the first *Newgate* prison was built near the New Gate in the old City Wall in the 12C, poss. earlier. A jail stood on the site until the last one was demolished to make way for the Old Bailey in 1901. The original prison was rebuilt by Richard 'Dick' Whittington; this one was burned down during the Great Fire (1666) and rebuilt again in 1672 (it included a statue of Whittington plus cat in its ornamentation). This in its turn was demolished and again rebuilt in 1770–1. This version was destroyed during the Gordon Riots of 1780, and a final *Newgate* was put up in 1781. Public hangings took place in the street outside until 1868]

Newgate *n.*² [1930s] (*UK Und.*) the inside jacket pocket. [? it is the hardest to pickpocket]

Newgate bird *n.* [early 17C–19C] a prisoner, esp. a sharper (not necessarily imprisoned in Newgate). [NEWGATE *n.*¹ + BIRD *n.*³ (2)]

Newgate collar *n.* (*also* **Newgate frill/fringe**) [19C; 2000s] a collar-like beard worn under the chin. [its being fancifully reminiscent of the hangman's noose]

Newgate hornpipe *n.* [early 19C] a hanging. [hangings were conducted outside NEWGATE *n.*¹ prison; the victims would DANCE v.² as they choked to death]

Newgate knocker *n.* [mid-19C–1900s] a lock of hair shaped like the figure 6 and twisted from the temple back towards the ear. [joc. use of SE + ? implication that those who sported such a style tended to criminality]

Newgate nightingale *n.* [16C] a novice criminal. [NEWGATE *n.*¹ + SE *nightingale*, i.e. the prison in which he is destined to end up + play on BIRD *n.*³ (2)]

Newgate nob *n.* (*also* **Newgate stallion**) [18C–mid-19C] a criminal type of person. [NEWGATE *n.*¹ + NOB *n.*¹ (1)/SE *stallion*]

Newgate ring *n.* [mid–late 19C] a moustache and beard, but no side-whiskers. [for ety. *see* NEWGATE KNOCKER *n.*]

Newgate saint (canonized at the Old Bailey) *n.* [18C–19C] a prisoner under sentence of death.

Newgate solicitor *n.* [early 18C–19C] a second-rate lawyer who hangs around prisons (including but not invariably NEWGATE *n.*¹) in the hope of picking up work.

Newgate stallion *n. see* NEWGATE NOB *n.*

new hand *n.* [late 19C–1910s] **1** (*Aus.*) a newly arrived immigrant (cf. OLD HAND *n.*). **2** a first-time prisoner. [SE *new* + HAND *n.*¹]

new hat *n.* [late 19C] a guinea. [? the price of such an object]

newie *n.* **1** [mid-19C–1970s] (*US campus*) a new student, a newcomer. **2** [20C+] (*Aus.*) a new immigrant; a new arrival. **3** [1950s+] (*Aus.*) (*also* **newy**) anything new or hitherto unknown.

newington butts *n.* (*also* **newingtons**) [20C+] the stomach. [rhy. sl. = GUTS n.¹ (1); ult. *Newington Butts*, a south London thoroughfare]

new iniquity *n.* [mid–late 19C] (*Aus./N.Z.*) an immigrant. [play on OLD IDENTITY n. (2)]

new jack *n.* **1** [1980s+] (*mainly US Black*) a newcomer or novice, esp. to the fast life of the ghetto streets. **2** [2000s] (*US Black*) a sophisticate, someone who has succeeded in the ghetto culture; the female equivalent is *new jill*. [SE *new* + JACK n.⁶]

new jack *adj.* [1980s+] (*US Black*) **1** superficial, flashy, meretricious; thus *New Jack City*, Detroit, New York City or any other city with a thriving ghetto lifestyle. **2** in tune with the contemporary young Black culture. [NEW JACK n.]

New Jerusalem *n.* [mid–late 19C] the upper-class area of Belgravia in London. [the wealthy Jews who bought houses there; note Dos Passos, *Manhattan Transfer* (1925), a general comment on New York: '"I tell you the Catholics and Jews are going to run us out of our own country" [...] "It's the New Jerusalem," put in Aunt Emily']

new jill *n. see* NEW JACK n. (2).

newk *n.* [1970s+] (*US campus*) a *newc*omer, a novice. [orig. milit.]

newky (brown) *n.* [1970s+] *Newc*astle *Brown* Ale. [orig. Newcastle use only, but gradually adopted throughout the UK]

newlicks *n. see* NOOLUCKS n.

new light *n.* [mid-18C–19C] a Methodist. [16C SE *new light*, novel religious views or doctrines; the term covered a variety of 18C Protestant sects in the UK and US]

new magic *n.* [1970s+] (*drugs*) phencyclidine (cf. ACE n.⁴). [its 'magical' effects]

Newman's (college) *n.* (*also* **Newman's hotel/tea-gardens**) [19C] Newgate prison (cf. ABBOTT'S PRIORY n.; BIG SCHOOL n.). [NEWGATE n.¹ + -MANS sfx + SE *college*/HOTEL n. (2)/pun on SE *tea-gardens*]

Newman's lift *n.* [early–mid-19C] the gallows. [NEWMAN'S (COLLEGE) n. + SE *lift*]

Newmarket Heath commissioner *n.* [19C] a highwayman. [*Newmarket Heath* was a popular site for highway robbery]

new meat *n.* **1** [1930s+] (*US prison*) a new inmate. **2** [1960s+] (*US campus*) a freshman. [SE *new* + MEAT n. (5)]

new off the irons *phr. see* FRESH OFF THE IRONS phr.

new pair of boots *n.* [late 19C] (*UK middle class*) a whole new situation.

New River Head *n.* [late 18C–early 19C] tears. [the *New River Head*, a group of reservoirs in Clerkenwell, north London]

news bug *n.* [1950s] (*W.I.*) a gossip. [dial. *news-bug*, a wood-boring beetle, the appearance of which is supposed to portend coming news]

news butcher *n.* [late 19C+] (*US*) a seller of newspapers, sweets etc on a train.

new school *adj.* [1990s+] in rap music, anything recent or new, not OLD SCHOOL adj. [SCHOOL n.³]

news hawk *n.* (*also* **newshog, newshound**) **1** [1910s+] (*orig. US*) a newspaper reporter. **2** [1950s–70s] (*US*) a newspaper seller. [SE *news* + SE *hawk*/HOUND sfx]

news hen *n.* [1940s–70s] (*US*) a female journalist. [SE *news* + HEN n.¹ (1)]

newsie *n.* (*also* **newsy**) **1** [late 19C+] (*US*) a seller of newspapers in the street; orig. boys and girls only, the term spread, as did the job, to include adults. **2** [1950s+] (*US*) a news broadcaster or journalist. **3** [2000s] a newsagent's. [abbr. SE *newsboy*]

news of the day *n.* [late 19C] (*UK Und.*) a public house. [where people exchange news and gossip]

News of the Screws *n.* (*also* **the Screws**) [1990s+] a nickname for the *News of the World* (a Sunday paper in the UK). [assonance + SCREW n.¹ (2), punning on its propensity for sex stories]

new south *n.* [1990s+] (*Aus.*) the mouth. [rhy. sl.; ult. *New South Wales*]

newspaper *n.* [1920s–40s] (*US Und.*) 30 days in prison (cf. MAGAZINE n.). [the time it supposedly takes an illiterate person to read one]

Newstralian *n.* [1950s] (*Aus.*) a New Australian, i.e. any immigrant, usu. from continental Europe, whose first language is not English.

newsy *n. see* NEWSIE n.

newsy *adj.* [late 19C+] (*later use W.I.*) gossipy. [SE *news*]

newt *n.* [1920s+] (*US campus*) a stupid, unsophisticated or socially inadequate person. [SE *neuter* or *neutral*]

newted *adj.* [1970s+] drunk. [PISSED AS A NEWT phr.]

new thinger *n.* [1960s+] (*orig. US*) a devotee of the *new thing*, an experimental form of jazz, which dispensed with the normal harmonic and rhythmic framework, popular in the 1960s.

Newton and Ridley *adj.* [1990s+] tipsy, drunk (cf. ADRIAN (QUIST) adj.). [rhy. sl. = TIDDLY adj.; ult. the fictional beer/brewery of the UK ITV soap opera *Coronation Street*, which features in its pub 'Rovers Return']

Newtown pippin *n.* [late 19C–1900s] a cigar. [its fragrance; ult. *Newtown*, Long Island, US, where the *Newtown pippin* apple comes from]

newy *n. see* NEWIE n. (3).

New York *v.* [1950s] (*W.I.*) to retch, to vomit. [the supposed similarity between the sound of *york* and that of retching]

New York City silver *n.* (*also* **New York City white**) [1970s+] (*drugs*) an imaginary brand of marijuana, silver/white because its seeds have grown in darkness, after being flushed away into the sewer system (cf. ACAPULCO (GOLD) n.).

New Yorkers *n.* [1980s+] (*drugs*) MDMA (cf. ECSTASY n.).

New York minute *n.* (*also* **city minute, New York second**) [1920s+] (*US*) an instant. [the city's non-stop energy]

New York nippers *n.* [1930s+] kippers. [rhy. sl.]

New York tube steak *n.* [late 19C+] (*orig. US*) a spiced, heated sausage or frankfurter, served on a split roll and trad. garnished with 'rags and paint' (sauerkraut and mustard).

New Zealand death *n.* [mid-19C+] (*N.Z.*) drowning. [its contemporary commonness]

New Zealand mutton *n.* [late 19C] (*N.Z.*) pork. [there is no mutton in New Zealand because lamb is so popular there]

newzie *n.* [1940s] (*N.Z.*) a New Zealander. [abbr.]

next double six *n. see* NEW DOUBLE SIX n.

next morning feeling *n. see* MORNING AFTER (THE NIGHT BEFORE) n.

next parish to America *n.* [late 19C] (*Irish*) the island of Arran, the island furthest into the Atlantic from the west coast of Ireland.

next thing to the Judgement Day *n.* [19C–1900s] (*US*) an extremely shocking situation.

next time you make a pie will you give me a piece? *phr.* [late 19C–1910s] (*Can.*) a sexual *double entendre* aimed at a woman by an amorous man. [PIE n.¹ (1) + PIECE n.¹ (3)]

next (to) *phr.* [late 19C+] (*US*) **1** aware, knowledgeable, informed, sophisticated; also as a n., the state of being thus informed etc. **2** close, friendly.

next topic, please *phr.* [1990s+] (*US teen*) a phr. used to indicate that the speaker has become boring and a change of subject is requested. [? catchphrase of a TV quiz show]

nexus *n.* (*also* **bromo, spectrum, 2CB**) [1980s+] (*drugs*) 2C-B, a hallucinogen similar to LSD but without some of its more extreme side effects; most potent when used in conjunction with MDMA. [one of a large number of psychoactive substances first isolated by the American libertarian pharmacologist Dr Alexander Shulgin, including DOM, STP, DOB, DOI and MDMA]

n.f. *n.* **1** [late 19C–1900s] *no fool.* **2** [1970s] (*US campus*) *no fun.* [abbr.]

n.f.g. *phr.* [1970s+] (*US*) *no fucking good.* [abbr.]

n.f.w.! *excl.* [1970s+] (*US*) *no fucking way!* [abbr.]

n.g. *n.* [late 19C+] (*US*) a person or thing that is bad or inferior. [abbr. *no good*]

n.g. *adj.* (*orig. US*) **1** [mid–late 19C] *no go,* unsuccessful. **2** [late 19C+] *no good.* [abbr.]

n.g.b. *n.* [1980s+] (*US campus*) a pleasant person, but not one with whom one wishes to have a sexual relationship. [abbr. *nice guy but*]

Nguyen *n.* [1960s–70s] (*US*) a generic term for a Vietnamese native.

n.h. *n. see* NORFOLK HOWARD n.

Niagara Falls *n.* (*also* **niagaras**) **1** [1930s] (*US*) meatballs. **2** [1940s] rubbish, nonsense. **3** [1940s+] the testicles (cf. CHEESE AND CRACKERS n.). [rhy. sl.; (2) = BALLS n.²; (3) = BALLS n.¹ (1)]

Niagara pineapple *n. see* PINEAPPLE n.².

nias *n.* [17C–19C] a simpleton, a fool. [NIZZIE n.]

nib *n.*¹ [late 18C–19C] the mouth or face. [SE *nib,* the beak or bill of a bird]

nib *n.*² **1** [early 19C–1950s] a gentleman; thus *nibsome,* gentlemanly; *half-nibs,* one who apes a gentleman. **2** [late 19C–1920s] a smartly dressed young man. [var. on NOB n.² (1)]

nib *n.*³ [late 19C] a die. [? SE *nib,* the beak of a bird, which is bone, as is a die]

nib *n.*⁴ *see* NEB n.¹ (2).

nib *v. see* NAB v.¹.

nibbed *adj.* [early–mid-19C] arrested. [NAB v.¹ (2)]

nibble *n.* **1** [early–mid-19C] a petty thief. **2** [mid-19C] (*UK Und.*) an opportunity for gain or theft. **3** [1960s+] a non-committal enquiry. [NIBBLE v.³/SE *nibble*]

nibble *v.*¹ **1** [17C–19C] to catch, to take. **2** [late 19C+] to assess a possible purchase. **3** [1930s] to make a purchase. **4** [1980s+] (*US campus*) to have a mild argument.

nibble *v.*² (*also* **do a nibble, have a nibble**) **1** [17C–19C] to have sexual intercourse. **2** [1920s+] to perform fellatio or cunnilingus; thus NIBBLER n.² (cf. BASKET LUNCH n.; BOX LUNCH n.). [(2) plays on EAT v.³ (1)]

nibble *v.*³ [early–mid-19C] to pilfer, to work as a petty thief. [such a thief cannot take a real 'bite' at a major crime]

nibble *v.*⁴ [late 19C–1900s] (*US*) to take a drink.

nibbler *n.*¹ [early–mid-19C] a petty thief. [NIBBLE v.³]

nibbler *n.*² [1950s] (*US Und.*) a fellator. [NIBBLE v.² (2)]

nibbling *adj.* [1980s+] (*US campus*) of weather, chilly, slightly cold.

nibbling cull *n.* [18C–19C] a petty thief. [NIBBLE v.³ + CULL n.¹ (4)]

nib cove *n.* [early–mid-19C] a gentleman. [NIB n.² (1) + COVE n. (1)]

nibhead *n.* [mid-19C–1920s] a fool, a grotesque. [printers' jargon *nib,* a fool + -HEAD sfx (1)]

niblike *adj.* [mid-19C] smart, fashionable. [NIB n.² (2)]

nibs *n.* **1** [early 19C+] oneself. **2** [early 19C+] an important, esp. a self-important, person; also as HIS NIBS n. **3** [mid-19C] a shabby, genteel person, 'with no means but high pretensions' (Hotten, 1859). **4** [mid–late 19C] (*US*) as a term of address. [NIB n.² (1)]

nibshit *n.*¹ [1940s] (*US*) nil, nothing. [? Eng. dial. *nib,* a very small amount + SHIT n.³ (3)]

nibshit *n.*² [1960s+] (*US*) a nosey, inquisitive person. [SE *nib,* the beak of a bird + SHIT n.² (1)]

nibshit *v.* [1960s+] to meddle, to interfere. [NIBSHIT n.²]

nibso *n.* [late 19C–1910s] oneself. [NIBS n. (1)]

nibsome *adj. see* NIB n.² (1).

n.i.c. *n. see* H.N.I.C. n.

Nic *n.* [1930s+] (*US*) Nicaragua. [abbr.]

nic *v.* [1980s+] to crave *nicotine.* [abbr. SE *nicotine*]

nice *adj.*¹ [1940s+] (*US Black*) feeling well, happy, at one with the world, esp. as a result of taking drugs or drink (cf. ABOUT RIGHT phr.¹).

nice *adj.*² **1** [1950s+] (*W.I.*) compliant, unwilling to make a fuss or cause trouble. **2** [1980s] (*US campus*) boring. [16C SE *nice,* foolish, trifling]

nice *v.* [1980s+] to get drunk. [NICE adj.¹]

nice and *adv.* [mid-19C+] very, usu. in ironical sense.

nice and handy *n.* [1940s] brandy. [rhy. sl.]

nice as Jemima *phr. see* JEMIMA! excl.

nice as pie *phr.* **1** [late 19C+] (*orig. US*) very well-behaved, highly amenable; also as *good as pie, sweet as pie.* **2** [1920s+] attractive.

nice bit *n.* [1930s+] (*US Und.*) a long prison sentence, i.e. 10 years or more. [SE *nice* + BIT n.⁵]

nice car *n.* [1980s+] (*US campus*) a good-looking man or woman.

nice drop (of) *n.* (*also* **lovely drop (of)**) [1930s+] a fine example of, a tasty bit of.

nice egg *n. see* GOOD EGG n.

nice enough *n.* [20C+] a male homosexual. [rhy. sl. = PUFF n.³ (1)]

nice girl *n.* [1960s] (*US campus*) used ironically by men, a sexually permissive woman.

nice going *phr.* [1920s+] (*orig. US*) a phr. of approval, congratulation.

nice joint *n.* [late 19C–1900s] an attractive, if over-made-up and overdressed young woman. [SE *nice* + *joint,* a piece of MEAT n. (1)]

nicely(, thank you) *phr.* [1920s+] drunk (cf. ABOUT RIGHT phr.¹). [response to the question, 'how are you feeling/doing?']

nice name to go to bed with *n.* [late 19C] an ugly name.

nice nellie *n.* [1930s+] (*US*) a respectable or fastidious person (not necessarily a woman), also used ironically. [SE *nice* + *Nelly,* a generic term for a respectable woman]

nice-nellie *adj.* (*also* **nice-nelly**) [1950s+] (*US*) prudish, puritanical. [NICE NELLIE n.]

nice nellie *v.* [1950s] (*US*) to act in a respectable manner, often excessively and interferingly so. [NICE NELLIE n.]

nice-nellyism *n.* [1930s+] (*US*) prudishness, excessive gentility, puritanical behaviour or attitudes. [NICE NELLIE n.]

nice one *n.*¹ [mid-19C+] a fit or suitable person; usu. in a sarcastic or negative context, e.g. *he's a nice one to be telling me…*

nice one *n.*² [1930s+] a success, esp. referring to a robbery or a large payment.

nice one! *excl.* [1960s+] a general excl. of approval or admiration referring either to an action or to the report of something already carried out; also used ironically.

nice one, Cyril *n.* [1990s+] a squirrel. [rhy. sl.; ult. NICE ONE, CYRIL! excl.]

nice one, Cyril! *excl.* [1970s+] a general term of approval. [football chant created to praise *Cyril* Knowles, a Tottenham Hotspur player]

nice pair of eyes *n.* [1960s+] a euph. for attractive breasts; usu. in phr. *she's got a…*

nice thin job *phr.* [late 19C–1900s] (*orig. US*) a phr. used when accusing someone of having slipped out of keeping a promise.

nice up *v.* [20C+] (*W.I.*) to improve, to dress up, esp. to ingratiate oneself. [ext. use of SE *nice* adj.]

nicey-nice *adj.* [1930s+] (*US*) affected, prissy. [SE *nice,* fastidious, dainty, hard to please]

nic fit *n.* [1980s+] a state of withdrawal or craving for cigarettes. [abbr. SE *nicotine* + *fit*]

niche cock *n.* [late 18C–19C] the vagina (cf. BAG n.¹). [SE *niche* + COCK n.² (1)]

Nicholas *n. see* NICK n.

Nicholls *n.* [late 19C–1900s] (*UK society*) a full riding habit. [*Nicholls* of Regent Street, London, generally acknowledged as a superlative maker of such equipment]

nicht *n. see* NISHT n.

Nick *n.* (*also* **Nicholas, Nicky**) [mid-17C+] the Devil; often as OLD NICK *n.* [abbr. of proper name *Nicholas*, but no specific reason; ? link to NICK *v.*[1] (2), i.e. the Devil snatches his victims; note letter J. Boorer, 14 October 2002: 'I noticed the following in a Lord Macaulay essay written in 1827 on Machiavelli: "Out of his surname they have coined an epithet for a knave, and out of his Christian name a synonym for the Devil.*" – and the footnote quotes Hudibras, Part III, Canto I.: "Nick Machiavel had ne'er a trick, / Tho' he gave his name to our old Nick." Macaulay then says, still in footnote: "But, we believe, there is a schism on this subject among the antiquarians." Has the schism been resolved or forgotten?']

nick *n.*[1] **1** [mid-17C–early 19C] the winning throw at dice. **2** [late 18C–19C] as *the nick*, the proper thing, the fashionable thing, the best of health; thus *in the nick*, fashionable. [SE *the nick/very nick*, the critical moment]

nick *n.*[2] **1** [18C–19C] the vagina (cf. AGREEABLE RUTS OF LIFE *n.*). **2** [late 19C] the cleft of the buttocks. [SE *nick*, a notch, a groove, a slit]

nick *n.*[3] [early 19C+] a hybrid, usu. an animal. [SE *nick*, an instance of cross-breeding]

nick *n.*[4] [mid-19C] a low-class casino.

nick *n.*[5] **1** [mid-19C+] (*US*) a nickel coin. **2** [late 19C+] (*US*) a generic term for money (cf. CENT *n.*). **3** [1960s+] (*US*) $5 or $5 worth, as in a gambling chip. **4** [1990s+] (*US drugs*) a $5-bag of marijuana. [abbr. SE *nickel*, a 5-cent piece/NICKEL *n.*[1]]

nick *n.*[6] (*orig. Aus.*) **1** [late 19C+] a prison. **2** [1910s+] a police station, esp. its cells. **3** [1950s] the police. **4** [1980s] an arrest. **5** [1980s] an institutional home. [milit. use *nick*, the guardroom]

nick *n.*[7] [1900s–50s] (*US*) the proceeds of a crime, a haul. [NICK *v.*[1] (3)]

nick *n.*[8] [1980s] (*US*) a *nick*name. [abbr.]

nick *n.*[9] *see* NICKER *n.*[2].

nick *v.*[1] **1** [mid-16C–19C] to win at gambling, orig. dice or cards (esp. by cheating). **2** [17C+] to catch, to take unawares, to nab, to nail, to 'get', to understand. **3** [17C+] (*UK Und.*) to rob, to steal; thus *out on the nick*, going stealing; *nickable*, worth stealing. **4** [late 17C+] to cheat, to swindle. **5** [mid-18C+] to apprehend, to arrest. **6** [early 19C] to comprehend. **7** [late 19C–1960s] (*orig. US*) to demand, to beg. **8** [1910s] in weak use of (3) and (4), to charge, with implication of excessive price. [Rom., thus note US Hisp. sl. (CALÓ *n.*) *nicabar*, to steal; ? underpinned by SE *nick*, to catch, to seize, to take advantage of an opportunity]

nick *v.*[2] [18C–1930s] of a man, to have sexual intercourse (cf. BANG *v.*[1]). [SE *nick*, to cut a notch in; note NICK *n.*[2] (1)]

nick *v.*[3] [19C+] to slip away, to leave on the spur of the moment; often as *nick away*, *nick down (to)*, NICK OFF *v.* etc; also imper. *nick away!* go away! [ety. unknown; ? link to SE *nick of time*]

nick *v.*[4] [1910s–50s] (*US*) to shoot. [SE *nick*, to cut into or through]

nickable *adj. see* NICK *v.*[1] (3).

Nicka Lauda *n.* [1990s+] (*drugs*) cocaine (cf. BARLEY *n.*[2]). [rhy. sl. = POWDER *n.*[2]; ult. Austrian F1 racing driver *Niki Lauda* (b.1949)]

nick and froth *n.* [early 17C–mid-18C] **1** a false measure in a pot of beer; thus *nick and froth victualler*, a landlord. **2** by metonymy, a landlord. [a dent in the bottom of the pot and an excess of frothy head on top]

nick and go *n.* [20C+] (*Ulster*) a 'narrow squeak', a 'close shave'. [SE *nick*, a slit or notch + *go*]

nick away! *excl. see* NICK *v.*[3].

Nick Butts *n.* (*also* **Nicky Butts**) [1990s+] **1** nuts (edible). **2** the testicles (cf. CHEESE AND CRACKERS *n.*). [rhy. sl.; (2) = NUTS *n.*[2] (1); ult. UK footballer *Nicky Butt* (b.1975)]

nicked *adj.*[1] **1** [late 19C+] arrested. **2** [1940s+] (*UK prison*) put on report to the governor for an infringement of prison rules. [NICK *v.*[1] (5)]

nicked *adj.*[2] [1960s+] (*Aus.*) a euph. for FUCKED *adj.*[1], i.e. *go and get nicked!* [? NICK *v.*[2]]

nickel *n.*[1] **1** [1940s] a very small amount (not monetary), e.g. *not like it a nickel*. **2** [1940s+] (*US*) a $5 bill, $5 (cf. CENT *n.*). **3** [1950s+] (*US prison*) a 5-year prison sentence. **4** [1960s+] (*US drugs*) a $5 packet of marijuana, heroin or cocaine. **5** [1970s+] (*US*) the number 5. **6** [1970s+] (*US*) $500, esp. in gambling. **7** [2000s] (*US*) the general name for the SKID ROW *n.* (1) area of downtown Los Angeles that is focused on East Fifth Street. [SAmE *nickel*, a 5-cent coin]

nickel *n.*[2] [1980s+] (*US*) a dent in the bodywork of a motorcar. [ext. of SE *nick*]

nickel *adj.* [late 19C+] (*US*) second-rate, inferior. [the low value of the coin]

nickel and dime *n.* [1930s+] (*US*) time. [rhy. sl.]

nickel-and-dime *adj.* (*also* **nickel-dime**) [1920s+] (*US*) petty, small-time, insignificant. [the low value of the coin]

nickel-and-dime *v.* **1** [1940s+] (*US*) to carry on a small, cash-starved business, to manage with little money; often as *nickel-and-dime it*. **2** [1940s+] (*UK Und.*) to beg on the street. **3** [1960s+] (*US*) to treat others meanly and miserly; thus to be petty and irksome, to eat away at. [SE *nickel* + *dime*, i.e. the low value of the coins]

nickel-and-dimer *n.* [1930s+] (*US*) a mean, contemptible or insignificant person. [NICKEL-AND-DIME *adj.*]

nickel bag *n.* [1960s+] (*US drugs*) $5 worth of drugs, the quantity varies as to the drug, more marijuana, less heroin (cf. DIME BAG *n.*). [NICKEL *n.*[1] + BAG *n.*[11] (1)]

nickel-bagger *n.* [1970s] (*US Und.*) a second-rate, minor drug dealer. [NICKEL BAG *n.*]

nickel deck *n.* [1960s+] (*drugs*) $5 worth of heroin. [NICKEL *n.*[1] (2) + DECK *n.*[4] (1)]

nickel-dime *adj. see* NICKEL-AND-DIME *adj.*

nickel dump *n.* [1900s–50s] (*US*) a cheap cinema, charging only a nickel or 5 cents for admission. [SE *nickel* + DUMP *n.*[3] (2); derog. synon. of SE *nickelodeon*]

nickel grabber *n.*[1] [1950s] an insignificant person.

nickel grabber *n.*[2] *see* NICKEL SNATCHER *n.*

nickel-grinder *n.* [1930s] (*US*) a miser, a 'penny-pincher'.

nickel hop *n.* [1910s–30s] (*US*) a taxi-dance; thus *nickel-hopper*, a taxi-dancer. [SE *nickel*, 5 cents + HOP *n.*[1] (3); although the women worked for 10 cents or 'a dime a dance' they split this half and half with the management, thus leaving themselves a nickel]

nickelnose *n.* [1970s+] (*US*) a Jew (cf. FAST-TALKING CHARLIE *n.*). [? var. on NEEDLENOSED *adj.* + stereotypical ref. to money]

nickel note *n.* [20C+] (*US*) a $5 bill (cf. CENT *n.*).

nickel nurser *n.* [1910s–70s] (*US*) a miser; thus *nickel-nursing*, miserly. [lit. one who 'has a passion for seeing that his nickels don't stray' (Maines & Grant, *The Wise-Crack Dictionary*, 1926)]

nickel plate *n.* [late 19C–1900s] (*US*) a fraud, a deception. [the use of *nickel plate* to counterfeit silver]

nickel-plated *adj.* [late 19C+] (*US*) first-class, thorough. [paradoxically opposite to NICKEL PLATE *n.*; ? var. on SE *gold-plated*]

nickel rat *n.* [1950s] (*US*) a second-rate, small-time criminal.

nickel shot *n.* [1990s+] (*US Black teen*) a 5-storey public housing building in the Fillmore area of San Francisco. [SE *nickel* + SHOT *n.*[5] (2)]

nickel slick *adj.* [1970s+] (*US Black*) petty, insignificant, esp. in the context of attempting to do something beyond one's abilities (and thus failing in the effort). [NICKEL *adj.* + SLICK *adj.* (1); the low value of the coin undermines the slickness]

nickel snatcher *n.* (*also* **nickel grabber**) [1910s–50s] (*US*) a streetcar conductor.

nickel squeezer *n.* [1920s–30s] (*US*) a mean, miserly person.

nicker *n.*[1] [late 17C; late 19C–1950s] a thief, a cheat, a confidence trickster. [NICK *v.*[1]]

nicker *n.*[2] (*also* **nick**) **1** [late 19C+] £1; thus [1980s+] *nicker bit*, a pound coin. **2** [1950s+] money in general. [ety. unknown]

nicker bits *n.* [20C+] diarrhoea (cf. BANANA (SPLITS) n.). [rhy. sl. = SHITS, THE n. (1)]

nickery *n.* [late 17C–early 19C] a nickname. [abbr.]

nickie cakes! *excl.* [20C+] (*Ulster*) easy! [Scot. *nickit bake*, a small biscuit with indentations on the top]

nickin *n.* (*also* **nikey, nikin**) [late 17C–early 19C] a fool, a simpleton. [fig. use of NICK n.[2] (1); Grose (1785) suggests 'a diminutive of Isaac']

nicking *n.* [1970s+] an arrest. [NICK v.[1] (5)]

nick in the notch *n.* [19C] the vagina (cf. AGREEABLE RUTS OF LIFE n.).

nick it *v.*[1] [early 17C–19C] to win, usu. by good fortune or cheating. [NICK v.[1] (1)]

nick it *v.*[2] *see* NICK THE PIN v.

nicklette *n.* [1930s–40s] (*US Black*) an automatic record player.

nick-nack *n.*[1] [mid–late 19C] the vagina (cf. ARTICLE n.). [SE *nick-nack*, a curious or pleasing trifle]

nick-nack *n.*[2] (*also* **knick-knack, nic-nac**) **1** [1960s+] (*US*) a male homosexual, esp. a promiscuous one. **2** [1970s] (*US prison*) a man who is raped frequently in prison. **3** [2000s] (*US prison*) one who does not fit in with the group; an outsider. [? SE *nick-nack/knick-knack*, a trinket]

nick-nacks *n.* [18C–19C] the testicles (cf. GINGAMBOBS n.). [SE *nick-nack*, a trinket, a trifle]

nick-ninny *n.* [late 17C–early 19C] a fool, 'a meer Cod's head' (B.E.). [? abbr. NICKIN n. + SE *ninny*]

nick off *v.* (*also* **nick out**) [late 19C+] (*orig. Aus.*) to leave, to depart, to go from one place to another. [NICK v.[3]]

nick-pot *n.* [17C–18C] **1** a false measure in a pot of beer. **2** a publican. [the placing of a *nick* or dent in the bottom of the pot]

nicks *n.*[1] *see* KNICKS n. (3).

nicks *n.*[2] *see* NIX n. (1).

nickser *n. see* NIXER n.

nicks my doll *phr. see* NIX MY DOLL phr.

nick the pin *v.* (*also* **nick it**) [mid-17C–early 18C] to drink fairly, i.e. not taking more than one's share of the tankard (which was marked by pins).

nickum *n.* [late 17C–early 18C] **1** a card-sharp or dice fraud. **2** a cheating landlord (although the aspersion can extend to any dishonest retailer). [NICK v.[1]]

nickumpoop *n. see* NINCOMPOOP n.

Nicky *n. see* NICK n.

Nicky Butts *n. see* NICK BUTTS n.

nicky-hooky *n. see* NOOKIE n.

nic-nac *n. see* NICK-NACK n.[2]

Nicodemus *n.* **1** [late 17C–mid-18C] a religious fanatic. **2** [1940s] (*W.I.*) a late-night visitor. [the name of *Nicodemus*, the Jewish ruler who came to Jesus by night (John 3:1 etc)]

nidget *n. see* NIGIT n.

niece *n.* [mid–late 17C] (*UK Und.*) a euph. for a prostitute. [linked to AUNT n.[1] (2)]

niegor *n. see* NIGGER n.[1]

niem *n.* [2000s] (*US Black*) none, nothing.

nieve *n.* [1970s+] (*drugs*) white powdered drugs, i.e. heroin or cocaine. [Sp. *nieve*, snow, thus SNOW n.[2]]

niff *n.* [late 19C+] an unpleasant smell, a stink. [? SE *sniff*]

niff, the *n.* [1960s] bare flesh.

niff *v.* **1** [late 19C+] to smell unpleasantly, to stink. **2** [20C+] to smell something, usu. an unpleasant smell. [NIFF n.]

niffkins bridge *n.* [1990s+] the female perineum. [NIFF n. + dimin. sfx *-kins* + SE *bridge*]

niffy *adj.* [20C+] smelly, malodorous. [NIFF n.]

niffy-naffy fellow *n.* [late 18C–early 19C] a trifler, an unimportant person. [Yorks. dial. *niff-/niffy-naffy*, trifling]

niftik *n.* [1910s–30s] (*US*) an attractive girl. [NIFTIK adj.]

niftik *adj.* [1910s–30s] (*US*) stylish, neat. [NIFTY adj.[1] (1) + 'European/Slav' sfx *-ik*]

nifty *n.* **1** [1910s+] (*US*) a joke, a funny story, a clever plan. **2** [1930s] something useful, convenient. **3** [1930s+] (*also* **bit of nifty**) a pretty girl; an attractive object. **4** [1960s] (*US campus*) a well-dressed man. **5** [1980s+] (*also* **bit of nifty**) sexual intercourse. **6** [2000s] a commission. [NIFTY adj.[1] (1)]

nifty *adj.*[1] **1** [mid-19C+] neat, smart. **2** [20C+] attractive, pretty. **3** [20C+] (*orig. US*) clever, skilful, agile. **4** [20C+] (*US*) cheeky, insolent, disrespectful of authority. **5** [1910s+] amusing. [ety. unknown; according to US author Bret Harte, quoted in *OED*, abbr. *magnificat*; E.P. dismisses this as 'a joke' and suggests SE *magnificent*]

nifty *adj.*[2] [late 19C+] (*US*) of winds, unpredictable. [ext. of NIFTY adj.[1] (4)]

nifty *v.* [1930s–40s] to quip, to joke. [NIFTY n. (1)]

nifty! *excl.* [1960s+] (*US teen*) terrific! splendid! wonderful! [NIFTY adj.[1]]

nifty fifty *n.* [1980s+] (*Irish*) a 50cc scooter. [NIFTY adj.[1] (1)]

nig *n.*[1] [late 17C–mid-19C] (*UK Und.*) the clippings from doctored gold coins. [? Essex dial. *nig*, a piece or SE *nick*]

nig *n.*[2] **1** [early 19C+] a derog. term for a Black person (cf. ALLIGATOR BAIT n.[2]). **2** [mid-19C+] (*US Black*) used of a fellow Black, thus non-derog. **3** [1930s] as a term of address. **4** [1960s–70s] a derog. term for an Oriental (cf. BROWNIE n.[2]). [abbr. NIGGER n.[1] (1)]

nig *n.*[3] [mid-19C] gin. [backsl.]

nig *n.*[4] *see* NIG-NOG n.[1]

nig *v.*[1] [late 17C–early 19C] to clip money. [? Essex dial. *nig*, a piece]

nig *v.*[2] [18C–19C] to have sexual intercourse. [abbr. NIGGLE v.]

nig *v.*[3] [mid-18C] to arrest. [NICK v.[1] (5)]

nig *v.*[4] [early 19C–1950s] (*US*) to renege on one's debts. [abbr. NIGGER n.[1] (1); racist stereotyping; but also semi-abbr. of SE re*nege*]

nig *v.*[5] [1990s+] (*UK juv.*) to annoy. [abbr. SE *niggle*]

nig-bo *n.* [1990s+] a derog. term for a Black person (cf. ALLIGATOR BAIT n.[2]). [NIG n.[2] (1) + model of SAMBO n.[1] (1)]

nigel *n.* [1990s+] (*Aus.*) a friendless male. [proper name *Nigel* seen as quintessentially upper-class and vapid]

niger *n. see* NIGGER n.[1]

Nigerian *n.* [1960s+] (*gay*) a Black man. [generic use of specific nationality]

Nigerian lager *n.* [1970s+] Guinness stout. [its blackness]

nigette *n.* [1990s+] (*US*) a Black woman or girl. [NIGGA n. + SE fem. sfx *-ette*]

nigga *n.* [1970s+] (*US Black*) a Black person. [NIGGER n.[1] (1); the sp. is exclusive to the world of GANGSTA RAP n. where the SE sfx *-er* is transposed to *-a*, a foreshortening that is regularly found in Black sl. as a means of intensifying a term (cf. PLAYER n.[1] (2)/PLAYA n.)]

nigga beater *n.* [2000s] (*US Black*) any blunt instrument. [NIGGA n. + SE *beat*; adopted from White terms such as NIGGER KNOCKER n.; NIGGER STICK n. etc]

nigga chops *n.* [2000s] (*US Black*) a fellow Black person. [NIGGA n. + CHOPS n.[1] (1)]

niggah *n. see* NIGGER n.[1]

niggalicious *adj.* [2000s] (*US Black*) of a Black woman, heavily built. [NIGGA n. + *-LICIOUS* sfx]

nigga please! *excl.* [2000s] (*US Black*) an excl. of disbelief, dismissal. [NIGGA n. + SE *please*]

nigger *n.*[1] (*also* **naygah, naygar, naygur, neeger, neger, niegor, niger, niggah, niggar, niggur, nigra**) **1** [17C+] a derog. term for a Black person, a Negro slave; by ext. any non-White (cf. ALLIGATOR BAIT n.[2]; NIGGA n.). **2** [19C] of a White person, a slave. **3** [early 19C+] (*US*) a general derog. term applicable to anyone regardless of race/skin colour, used by Blacks as well as Whites; thus any foreigner. **4** [mid-19C+] used as a derog. term between Blacks, aping (1). **5** [mid-19C+] any dark-skinned foreign person. **6** [mid-19C+] (*Aus./N.Z.*) an Aborigine, a Maori.

7 [late 19C–1910s] a 'nigger minstrel', i.e. a White person performing in blackface. **8** [late 19C+] a subservient person, a servant. **9** [late 19C+] anything coloured black, e.g. the black numbers of roulette. **10** [1910s+] (*US Black*) in a reverse racism, taking pride in such epithets, used by radical Blacks of each other. **11** [1950s+] (*US Black*) a close male or female friend, companion, boyfriend or husband; usu. constructed with possessive pronoun, as in *my* (*main*) *nigger*, my (best) friend. **12** [1960s+] (*US*) a fellow human being, of any race or skin colour. **13** [1970s+] (*US Black*) a non-Black person who is considered to act in a very positive manner in relation to Black culture or who identifies strongly with it. [ult. Lat. *niger*, black in colour, thence Early Mod. Eng. (later dial.) *niger*; thus advocated by *HDAS*, although the *OED* and E.P. prefer Sp. *negro*, black. *Nigger* has been used in a variety of combs. since 19C; both *Webster III* and the *OED* list a number of these, usu. referring to birds, animals and crops, without comment – the assumption being that, for better or worse, they are an accepted (if local) usage; while they are also based on stereotypes, it is more that of colour than of racist assumptions. Those combs. listed here, usu. unlisted in the standard dictionaries, may well have been colloq. in the 19C, but by their intrinsic hostility are, *de facto*, sl. Otherwise, *nigger* implies the usual derog. stereotypes as allotted to Blacks: poverty, laziness, stupidity, lasciviousness, a propensity to mindless hedonism and violence]

nigger *n.*[2] [late 18C–mid-19C] (*UK Und.*) a clipper of gold coins. [NIG v.[1]]

nigger *n.*[3] [20C+] (*US*) anger, annoyance; usu. in phr. GET ONE'S NIGGER UP v. [fig. use of NIGGER n.[1], negative stereotyping]

nigger *adj.* [early 19C+] (*orig. US*) a derog. phr. indicating something or someone associated with Black culture; thus as derog., contemptible, odd, inferior. [NIGGER n.[1] (1)]

nigger *v.* **1** [early 19C+] (*US*) to do menial work. **2** [late 19C] (*UK Und.*) to work as a nigger minstrel. [NIGGER n.[1] (1)]

nigger and halitosis *n.* [1940s–50s] (*US*) liver and onions. [NIGGER n.[1] (1), i.e. the brown colour of liver + the effect of (raw) onions on the breath]

nigger babies *n.* [mid-19C] (*US*) cannon-balls. [coined by Confederate General Hardee (1815–73) during the siege of Charleston; the cannon from which the missiles were fired were known as *swamp angels*]

nigger baby *n.* [late 19C+] (*US*) a small liquorice or chocolate sweet or candy shaped like a baby. [NIGGER n.[1] (1) + SE *baby*]

nigger bait *n.* [1950s–60s] an excess of chrome accessories on an automobile. [NIGGER n.[1] (1) + SE *bait*]

nigger ball *n.* [1960s+] (*S.Afr.*) a large, round, black aniseed-flavoured sweet, which gradually changes as one sucks away successive layers. [NIGGER n.[1] (9) + SE *ball*, i.e. the colour and shape]

nigger bankroll *n. see* NIGGER'S BANKROLL n.

nigger box *n.* [1950s+] (*US Black*) television. [NIGGER n.[1] (1) + BOX n.[5] (6); negative stereotyping]

nigger catcher *n.* [mid-19C] (*US*) a small slotted flap on a saddle. [NIGGER n.[1] (1) + SE *catcher*; captured runaway slaves were roped to this flap and thus forced to run home alongside their master on his horse]

nigger chaser *n.* [late 19C+] (*US*) a firework that once lit leaps around along the ground. [NIGGER n.[1] (9) + SE *chaser*; in UK, a *jumping jack*]

nigger-chaser *n. see* NIGGER-SHOOTER n.

nigger day *n.* [1930s+] (*US*) Saturday. [NIGGER n.[1] (1) + SE *day*; the one day of rest permitted to slaves]

nigger daytime *n.* [19C+] (*US*) night-time. [NIGGER n.[1] (1); the darkness + the time at which Black slaves were allowed their rest]

nigger dick *n.* [2000s] (*US Black*) a large cigar. [NIGGER n.[1] (1) + DICK n.[4] (1); the alleged size]

nigger-driver *n.* [late 19C–1940s] an employer who works his men excessively hard. [fig. use of NIGGER n.[1] (1) + SE *driver*]

nigger-driving *n.* [mid-19C+] (*orig. US Black*) **1** the working of Blacks to exhaustion by White bosses. **2** any boss-employee relationship characterized by poor treatment. [NIGGER n.[1] (1) + SE *driving*]

nigger-driving *adj.* [mid-19C–1900s] highly exploitative. [NIGGER n.[1] (1) + SE *driving*]

nigger drunk *adj.* [1940s–60s] (*US*) very drunk. [NIGGER adj. + SE *drunk*]

nigger fishing *n.* [1940s–60s] (*US*) leisurely fishing for catfish or carp. [NIGGER n.[1] (1) + SE *fishing*; the implication is of the lazy Black fisherman]

nigger flicker *n.* [1950s+] (*US Black*) a weapon, usu. a small knife or a razor blade with 1 side heavily taped to preserve the user's fingers. [NIGGER n.[1] (1) + SE *flick knife*]

nigger fronts *n.* [1970s+] (*US Black*) extreme stylishness in dress. [NIGGER adj. + FRONTS n.[2]]

nigger gallery *n. see* NIGGER HEAVEN n.

nigger gin *n.* [1900s–30s] (*US*) inferior or synthetic gin. [NIGGER adj. + SE *gin*]

nigger golf *n.* [1910s] (*US*) the game of craps dice (cf. ABYSSINIAN POLO n.). [NIGGER adj. + SE *golf*]

niggergram *n.* (*also* **nigger-mouth**) [20C+] (*W.I.*) a stupid rumour, demeaning gossip. [NIGGER n.[1] (1) + (*tele*)*gram* + sfx *-mouth*]

nigger ham *n.* [1940s–60s] (*US*) a watermelon. [NIGGER adj. + SE *ham*; both are pink]

niggerhead *n.*[1] **1** [19C–1940s] (*US*) (*also* **negro head**) cheap, dark tobacco designed for smoking and chewing; thus similarly (*Aus.*) *nigger twist*, *nigger tobacco*. **2** [mid-19C+] (*US*) any outcrop of dark, rough, rounded or lumpy rock, stones or boulders. **3** [mid-19C+] any clump or hummock of thick vegetation, swamp grass, ferns, grass etc. **4** [late 19C–1960s] (*US*) a dark raincloud. **5** [20C+] (*also* **negro head**) peaks of coral that jut above the surface of the sea. **6** [1900s] an ox-eye daisy (with a large black centre). **7** [1900s] (*US campus*) hard black candy. **8** [1910s] a piece of stone, a small boulder. **9** [1930s–60s] (*US Und.*) a type of round wall safe. [all fig. uses of NIGGER n.[1] (1) + SE *head*; alleged resemblance]

niggerhead *n.*[2] [mid-late 19C] (*US*) a pro-Black civil rights agitator. [NIGGER n.[1] (1) + -HEAD sfx (1)]

niggerhead *n.*[3] [1950s+] (*W.I.*) a Black person's naturally kinky hair.

niggerhead rum *n.* [1910s–30s] (*US*) strong, dark rum. [NIGGERHEAD n.[1] + SE *rum*]

nigger heads *n.* [1940s–50s] (*US prison*) prison-cooked prunes. [NIGGER n.[1] (1) + SE *head*, alleged resemblance]

nigger heaven *n.* (*also* **nigger gallery**) **1** [mid-19C–1940s] (*US*) the top gallery of a theatre. **2** [1900s] (*US*) a state of enjoyment that is derived from vulgar activities. **3** [1920s–60s] a Black neighbourhood. [NIGGER n.[1] (1) + SE *heaven*; (1) this gallery was the only one that Black theatregoers could afford]

nigger-heel *n. see* NIGGER TOE n. (2).

nigger hill *n. see* NIGGERTOWN n.

niggerican *n.* [1970s] (*US*) a Black American (including a Puerto Rican) (cf. BATO n.). [NIGGER n.[1] (1) + SE *American*]

nigger in a blanket *n.* [1930s–40s] (*US, Western*) a pudding made with dark fruits rolled inside pastry. [NIGGER n.[1] (1) + SE *blanket*; alleged resemblance]

nigger in charge *n. see* HEAD NIGGER IN CHARGE n.

nigger in the woodpile *n.* (*also* **nigger in the fence**) **1** [mid-19C+] (*orig. US*) a hidden snag or drawback. **2** [1950s+] (*US*) a suspected or unacknowledged Black relative or ancestor. [NIGGER n.[1] (1) + SE *woodpile/fence*]

niggerish *adj.* [early 19C+] (*US*) **1** lazy, couldn't-care-less. **2** selfish. [NIGGER n.[1] (1)]

nigger it *v.* [mid-19C+] (*US*) to live in poverty. [NIGGER n.[1] (1); the social situation of many US Blacks]

niggeritis *n.* [20C+] **1** (*W.I.*) the urge to lie down and take a nap after a heavy meal. **2** (*US*) a fig. disease, based on a racist attitude to Black people. [NIGGER n.[1] + sfx *-itis*]

niggerize *v.* [1970s+] (*US*) to be politically marginalized, i.e. to be rendered 'Black' and *de facto* unimportant. [NIGGER n.[1] (1)]

nigger jigger *n. see* NIGGER STICKER n.

nigger joint *n.* [20C+] (*US*) a cheap bar, saloon or restaurant. [NIGGER adj. + JOINT n.[4] (3)]

nigger juke *n.* (*also* **nigger jook**) [1930s–40s] (*US*) a cheap bar, saloon or restaurant. [NIGGER adj. + JUKE n.[1] (1)]

nigger kickers *n.* (*also* **nigger stompers**) [1960s+] (*US*) large boots. [NIGGER n.[1] (1) + SE *kick/stomp*]

nigger killer *n.[1]* [mid-19C–1940s] (*US*) a yam. [NIGGER n.[1] (1) + SE *kill*; the supposed results of over-eating them]

nigger killer *n.[2]* **1** [1940s–70s] a slingshot. **2** [1940s–70s] a revolver. **3** [1960s] a large pocket-knife. [NIGGER n.[1] (1) + SE *kill*]

nigger knocker *n.* [1960s+] (*US*) a stick or club for use esp. against Blacks. [NIGGER n.[1] (1) + SE *knock*]

nigger knots *n.* [20C+] (*W.I.*) thick, tough Black hair. [NIGGER n.[1] (1) + SE *knots*; used as an insult between Black people]

niggerlip *v.* [1940s+] to moisten the end of a cigarette while smoking it. [NIGGER n.[1] (1) + SE *lip*]

nigger liquor *n.* [1920s+] any form of bad liquor, esp. when illicitly distilled. [such liquor is 'only good for a NIGGER n.[1] (1)']

nigger logic *n.* [20C+] (*US*) any form of reasoning considered erroneous, over-simplistic, based in fantasy, i.e. totally illogical. [NIGGER n.[1] (1) + SE *logic*; the stereotype is of the Black person as child-like and simple]

niggerlover *n.* [mid-19C+] (*orig. US*) a term of abuse, usu. aimed at a White who fails to display the supposedly necessary loathing of Blacks. [NIGGER n.[1] (1) + SE *lover*]

nigger-loving *n.* [late 19C+] (*US*) a derog. term for the refusal of Whites to take a racist attitude to Blacks. [NIGGERLOVER n.]

nigger-loving *adj.* (*US*) **1** [late 19C+] used of any White person showing favour to Black people. **2** [1960s+] used as a general derog. epithet, usu. by Southerners, irrespective of the object's actual racial opinions. [NIGGERLOVER n.]

nigger luck *n.* (*US*) **1** [mid-19C–1940s] good luck. **2** [1940s] bad luck, which one must make the best of, come what may. [NIGGER n.[1] (1) + SE *luck*]

nigger-meat *n.* [1980s] a White girl who associates with Black boys. [NIGGER n.[1] (1) + MEAT n. (1)]

nigger mess *n.* [1990s+] (*US Black*) problems within the Black community, which should be solved within that group. [NIGGER n.[1] (1) + SE *mess*]

nigger minstrel *n. see* MINSTREL n.

nigger-mouth *n. see* NIGGERGRAM n.

nigger navel *n.* [1940s–60s] (*US*) a black-eyed Susan plant (*Thunbergia alata*). [NIGGER n.[1] (1) + SE *navel*; the black centre of the yellow flower]

nigger news *n.* [mid-19C–1960s] (*US*) gossip. [NIGGER n.[1] (1) + SE *news*]

nigger night *n.* [1920s+] (*US Black*) Saturday night. [NIGGER n.[1] (1) + SE *night*]

niggerology *n.* [1950s–60s] (*US*) a derog. term for a Black studies course at college or school. [NIGGER n.[1] (1) + sfx *-ology*]

nigger out *v.* **1** [mid-19C–1940s] to exhaust land by using it constantly without fertilization. **2** [late 19C+] (*US*) to back out, to renege on. [NIGGER n.[1] (1); stereotype of Blacks as incompetent farmers or untrustworthy]

nigger pancake *n.* [1960s] (*US*) a lump of manure (cf. ADMIRAL BROWNING n.). [NIGGER n.[1] (1) + SE *pancake*; alleged resemblance]

nigger pool *n.* [1930s] (*US*) a derog. name for NUMBERS, THE n. [NIGGER n.[1] (1) + SE *pool*]

nigger pot *n.* [1900s–60s] (*US, mainly Southern*) illicitly distilled whisky. [NIGGER n.[1] (1) + SE *pot*]

nigger-rich *adj.* [1930s+] (*US*) very poor or deeply in debt but loaded down with glossy, flashy status symbols, car, jewellery etc. [NIGGER n.[1] (1) + SE *rich*]

nigger rig *n.* [1950s+] (*US*) a bodged job, a piece of do-it-yourself assembly. [NIGGER RIG v.]

nigger rig *v.* [1950s+] (*US*) to perform second-rate, sloppy work. [NIGGER n.[1] (1) + SE *rig*]

nigger rigged *adj.* [1950s+] (*US*) characterized by bad workmanship. [NIGGER RIG v.]

nigger rigger *n.* [1980s] (*US prison*) a White inmate who is seen as overly friend to Black ones. [? NIGGER RIG v.]

nigger roll *n. see* NIGGER'S BANKROLL n.

nigger row *n.* [late 19C–1900s] (*US*) the Black area of a town or city. [NIGGER n.[1] (1) + SE *row*]

nigger's bankroll *n.* (*also* **nigger bankroll/roll**) [1920s–80s] (*US*) a roll of $1 bills or a wad of small denomination notes inside one larger denomination note (cf. CALIFORNIA BANKROLL n.). [NIGGER n.[1] (1) + SE *bankroll*/ROLL n.[2]; thus negative stereotyping]

niggers' duel *n.* [late 19C–1900s] (*US*) an argument, a set-to in which no blows are actually struck. [NIGGER n.[1] (1) + SE *duel*]

nigger-shooter *n.* (*also* **nigger-chaser**) [late 19C+] (*US*) a slingshot. [NIGGER n.[1] (1) + SE *shooter/chaser*]

nigger's lips *n.* [1970s–80s] potato chips. [rhy. sl.; ult. NIGGER n.[1] (1) + SE *lips*]

nigger spit *n.* [late 19C] the lumps in Demerara sugar. [NIGGER n.[1] (1) + SE *spit*]

nigger steak *n.* [1940s–50s] (*US Black*) liver. [NIGGER n.[1] (1) + SE *steak*; it is particularly dark]

nigger stick *n.* [1970s+] (*US*) an oversized baton, used by policemen and prison officers. [NIGGER n.[1] (1) + SE *stick*]

nigger sticker *n.* (*also* **nigger jigger**) [1960s+] a large pocket-knife.

nigger stompers *n. see* NIGGER KICKERS n.

nigger talk *n.* [mid-19C–1940s] (*US*) chatter, irresponsible gossip. [NIGGER adj. + SE *talk*]

nigger tip *v.* [1940s] (*US*) to tip badly. [NIGGER n.[1] (1) + SE *tip*]

nigger toe *n.* (*US*) **1** [mid-19C–1940s] a type of potato. **2** [late 19C+] (*also* **nigger-heel**) a Brazil nut, a walnut. [NIGGER n.[1] (1) + SE *toe*; alleged resemblance]

niggertown *n.* (*also* **nigger hill, niggerville**) [mid-19C+] (*US*) a Black neighbourhood. [NIGGER n.[1] (1) + SE *town/hill/-ville*; note W.I. dial. *negro-town*, a community of runaway slaves or *maroons* who would use them as bases for raids on the plantations]

nigger up *v.* [1950s+] (*US*) to decorate in a vulgar manner. [NIGGER n.[1] (1)]

nigger war *n.* [mid–late 19C] (*US, Southern*) the US Civil War (1861–5). [NIGGER n.[1] (1) + SE *war*]

nigger work *n.* [mid-19C+] (*US Black*) menial work, illperformed work. [NIGGER n.[1] (1) + SE *work*]

nigger yard *n.* [20C+] (*W.I.*) any notably rough area in the slums. [NIGGER n.[1] (1) + Carib.E. *negro-yard*, that area on a plantation where the slaves were quartered]

nigging *n.* [late 17C–early 19C] clipping coins. [NIG v.[1]]

niggle *v.* (*also* **neggle, nigle**) [mid-16C–early 19C; 1930s] to have sexual intercourse. [ety. unknown; probable link to SE *niggle*, to trifle, to play with; the first *OED* cit. (1616) is 50 years subseq. to the sl. use *tonygle* found in Harman, which is a misprint for *to nygle*]

niggled *adj.* [1950s+] annoyed, irritated, tetchy. [SE *niggle*]

niggler *n.[1]* [17C–18C] **1** a prostitute. **2** (*also* **nigler**) a promiscuous man. [NIGGLE v.]

niggler *n.[2]* (*also* **nigler**) [late 17C–early 19C] (*UK Und.*) a clipper of coins. [NIG v.[1]]

niggling *n.* (*also* **nigling**) [17C–early 19C] sexual intercourse. [NIGGLE v.]

niggling *adj.* [mid-19C+] irritatingly petty, intrinsically unimportant but time and energy consuming. [SE *niggle*]

niggly *adj.* [1950s+] ill-tempered, obsessed with irrelevancies and petty problems. [SE *niggle*]

niggur *n. see* NIGGER n.[1].

niggy *n.* [2000s] **1** (*US Black*) a White person who acts like a Black person. **2** (*UK juv.*) a dark tan. [NIGGER n.[1] (1)]

nigh enough *n.* (*also* **near enough**) [1930s+] a homosexual male prostitute. [rhy. sl. = PUFF n.[3] (1)]

night and day *n.* [mid–late 19C] a play. [rhy. sl.]

night and day *adj.* [20C+] gray, grey. [rhy. sl.]

night and day *v.* [mid-19C] to see a play. [rhy. sl.]

nightbird *n.* (*also* **bird of the night, night fowl**) **1** [17C; mid-19C+] a prostitute (cf. ALLEY CAT n.; DEADLY NIGHTSHADE n.). **2** [early 19C] a wandering vagabond. [they 'fly at night'; note SE *night bird*, one who goes about at night, esp. a thief]

night bull *n.* [1960s] (*US prison*) a guard who works the night shift.

nightcap *n.*[1] **1** [early 17C] a bully who specializes in finding victims at night. **2** [19C–1910s] a thief who prefers to work at night. **3** [19C–1910s] a prostitute (cf. DEADLY NIGHTSHADE n.). **4** [1940s] (*US Und.*) a night watchman.

nightcap *n.*[2] **1** [early 19C+] a final drink before bed, or before the bars shut. **2** [1910s+] (*US*) the final race or contest of a day's sports, esp. the second game in a baseball 'double-header'. **3** [1950s+] the last portion of a drug prior to sleep.

nightcap *n.*[3] [1970s–80s] (*US Black*) a small skull-cap worn by many Black men. [SE *nightcap*]

night clothes *n.* [20C+] (*US Und.*) dark, close-fitting clothes used when committing a burglary at night.

night crawler *n.* **1** [1950s+] (*US*) someone who socializes or works late at night. **2** [1950s+] (*US Und.*) a prisoner who steals from other inmates. **3** [1960s] (*US gay*) a homophobic thug. **4** [1970s] (*US*) the penis.

night fighter *n.* **1** [1940s+] (*US*) a Black person. **2** [1970s] (*US campus*) a young woman who looks better by night than in daylight. [SE *night fighter* planes are painted black]

night-fossick(er) *n. see* FOSSICK n.

night fowl *n. see* NIGHTBIRD n.

night glass *n.* [1940s] (*W.I.*) a euph. for a chamberpot.

nightgown lady *n.* [late 17C] a prostitute (cf. BANKSIDE LADY n.; DEADLY NIGHTSHADE n.).

night hack *n.* [1910s–30s] (*US Und.*) a night watchman. [SE *night* + HACK n.[5] (1)]

nighthawk *n.* (*also* **night-shark**) **1** [early 19C+] anyone who likes to stay up late, usu. for a nefarious reason. **2** [mid-19C+] (*US*) a worker on a night shift. **3** [mid-19C+] (*US*) a taxi that plies for trade at night; also its driver. **4** [20C+] (*Aus./US*) a thief, esp. one who works at night. **5** [20C+] (*Aus.*) a prostitute (cf. ALLEY CAT n.; DEADLY NIGHTSHADE n.).

nighthawk *v.* [late 19C+] (*US*) **1** to work or socialize at night. **2** to drive a cab at night. [NIGHTHAWK n.]

night hunter *n.* [19C–1910s] a thief who prefers to work at night.

nightie *n.*[1] [1900s–50s] a night watchman. [abbr.]

nightie *n.*[2] [1980s+] (*US campus*) a very bad situation, esp. one over which one has no control. [abbr. SE *nightmare*]

nightingale *n.* **1** [19C] a prostitute (cf. ALLEY CAT n.; DEADLY NIGHTSHADE n.). **2** [late 19C–1910s] a singer. **3** [1930s+] (*UK Und.*) an informer. [they SE *sing*/SING v. (4)]

nightliner *n.* [late 19C–1900s] (*US*) a street robber who works at night.

night magistrate *n.* [late 17C–early 19C] a constable.

nightman *n.* **1** [late 17C–mid-19C] a collector of night-soil, i.e. the contents of cesspools, removed at night. **2** [1920s+] a thief who prefers to work at night, rather than in the daytime.

nightmare *n.* (*also* **hideous nightmare**) [1980s+] (*US campus*) an ugly, unattractive person; an unpleasant place or situation.

night on the rainbow *n.* [1940s+] (*drugs*) a night spent under the influence of drugs.

night owl *n.* **1** [mid-19C+] (*US*) a taxi that plies for trade at night. **2** [mid-19C+] anyone who is habitually out and about at night-time. **3** [late 19C+] late customers of cafés and restaurants. **4** [1920s] a night-soil worker. **5** [1980s+] one who stays up late (but does not necessarily go out).

night-owl *adj.* (*also* **owl**) [late 19C+] being open late at night, or being active late at night. [NIGHT OWL n.]

night-owl *v.* [1930s] to be active at night. [NIGHT OWL n.]

night physic *n.* [late 16C–early 18C] sexual intercourse.

night poacher *n.* [19C] **1** a prostitute (cf. DEADLY NIGHTSHADE n.). **2** a thief who works at night.

night shade *n.* [17C–19C] a prostitute (cf. DEADLY NIGHT-SHADE n.).

night-shark *n. see* NIGHTHAWK n.

night sneak *n.* [18C] robbery by night. [SE *night* + SNEAK n.[1] (4)]

night starvation *n.* [1930s+] sexual frustration. [play on SE, esp. as used in an advertisement of the period]

night stick *n.*[1] [1910s+] (*US*) the penis (cf. BAT n.[7]). [the police practice of carrying a large club on night patrol/SE *night* + STICK n.[1] (1)]

night stick *n.*[2] [1950s+] (*US Black*) anyone who lives their life in clubs and bars and generally indulges themself as a 'night person'.

night trader *n.* [17C–19C] a prostitute (cf. ASS PEDDLER n.; DEADLY NIGHTSHADE n.).

night walker *n.* **1** [mid-16C–19C] a thief or rogue. **2** [17C–1930s] a prostitute; thus *night-walk*, to work as a prostitute (cf. CURBSTONE SAILOR n.; DEADLY NIGHTSHADE n.; NYMPH OF THE PAVE n.; PAVEMENT POUNDER n.; PAVEMENT PRINCESS n.; PRINCESS OF THE PAVEMENT n.; SIDEWALK SUSIE n.; WALKER n.). **3** [late 17C–mid-18C] a bellman or town crier.

night work *n.* [late 16C–mid-19C; 1950s+] sexual intercourse. [20C+ use is W.I.]

nigit *n.* (*also* **nidget**) [17C–18C] a fool, an idiot. [play on SE *an eejit, an idiot*]

nigle *v. see* NIGGLE V.

nigler *n.*[1] *see* NIGGLER n.[1] (2).

nigler *n.*[2] *see* NIGGLER n.[2].

niglet *n.* [1990s+] (*US Black*) a Black child. [NIGGER n.[1] (1) + dimin. sfx *-let*]

nigling *n. see* NIGGLING n.

nig-mag *n.* [2000s] (*US Black*) a White woman who is popular with Black men. [NIG n.[2] (1) + SE *magnet*]

nigmenog *n.* (*also* **nimenog**) [late 17C–early 19C] a fool, an idiot. [? link to dial. *nigmanies*, a trifle]

nig-nog *n.*[1] (*also* **nig**) [1950s–70s] **1** (*orig. railway*) a novice, an unskilled person. **2** a fool, a simpleton. [NIG-NOG n.[2] but note *The Times* (30 November 1967) claims this term was used 'long before coloured immigrants appeared…'; however, the greater likelihood is that the stereotype of the incompetent Black labourer is the real origin, although note NIGMENOG n. + Scot. *nig-nag*, a worthless, useless thing]

nig-nog *n.*[2] [1950s+] any non-White, whether Black, Asian or Oriental (cf. BROWNIE n.[2]). [abbr. NIGGER n.[1] (1) + redup. + rhy. sl. on WOG n.[1] (1)]

nig-nog *v.* [mid-17C] to copulate with. [abbr. and redup. of NIGGLE v.]

nigra *n. see* NIGGER n.[1].

-nik *sfx* [1910s+] (*orig. US*) used to denote the involvement or association of a person or thing with the thing or quality described. [Rus./Yid. sfx *-nik*; the sfx had been used for some time but it was hugely popularized by contemporary fascination with the first Sputnik space craft, launched 1957; the orig. such term was *beatnik*, coined derisively by columnist Herb Caen of the *San Francisco Chronicle*]

nikey/nikin *n. see* NICKIN n.

nil *n.* [mid-19C] half; thus half-profits.

nilly-dilly adj. [1970s] (US Black) silly, foolish. [? rhy. sl.]

nim n. (also **nimmer, nym**) [17C–19C] a thief. [NIM v.]

nim v. (also **nym**) [17C–19C; 1970s+] (UK Und.) to steal; thus **nimming**, theft. [9C–16C SE nim, to take from; Grose (1785) cites 'German, nemen, to take']

nim a tatler v. (also **speak to a tatler**) [19C] to steal a watch. [NIM v. + TATLER n.]

nimbie n. (also **nimby**) [1960s+] (US drugs) Nembutal. [abbr.]

nimbles n. [early 17C] fingers. [SE nimble-fingered]

nimble-wimble n. [mid-17C] the penis. [SE nimble + wimble, a gimlet, an auger]

nimby n. see NIMBIE n.

nimby adj. [1980s+] (orig. US) used to describe an attitude to something that is unwanted, esp. new buildings or charitable services in a middle-class locality; also as a n., the person with this attitude; thus **nimbyism**, the attitude. [abbr. not in my back yard]

nimenog n. see NIGMENOG n.

nimgimmer n. [late 17C–early 19C] (UK Und.) a surgeon or physician, esp. a specialist in venereal diseases. [ety. unknown]

niminy-piminy adj. see NAMBY-PAMBY adj.

nimmer n. see NIM n.

nimpy adj. [1990s+] pert, fresh, young and budding. [? SE nymph]

nimpy-pimpy adj. see NAMBY-PAMBY adj.

nimrod n.[1] [19C] the penis (cf. BAT n.[7]). [biblical proper name Nimrod, the 'mighty hunter' of Gen., with an additional punning nod towards ROD n.[1] (1)]

nimrod n.[2] [1930s+] (orig. US campus) a socially inept person, someone not attuned to the group norms. [popularized by 1940s Warner Bros. cartoon character Elmer Fludd (a rabbit-hunter), called 'poor little Nimrod' by Bugs Bunny]

nimshi n. [mid-19C–1950s] (US) a fool. [? dial. nimshie, a flighty girl]

nimshod n. [late 19C] a cat. [? Nimrod 'a mighty hunter' or NIM n. + Rom. shosho, a rabbit]

nimwad n. [1980s+] (US) a fool. [pun on NIMROD n.[2] + -WAD sfx]

nimwit adj. [1990s+] (US) stupid (cf. BEEF-WITTED adj.). [NIMROD n.[2] + DIMWIT n.]

nina n. (also **neener**) [1980s+] (US Black) a handgun. [the 9mm barrel]

Nina with her hair down n. (also **Nina from Argentina, …Carolina, …Pasadena**) [1910s+] (US gambling) the point of 9 in craps dice (cf. ADA FROM DECATUR n.).

nincom n. (also **nincum**) [late 18C–19C] a fool. [abbr. NIN-COMPOOP n.]

nincompoop n. (also **nickumpoop, nincumpoop, ninkom-poop, ninny-cum-poop**) [late 17C+] a fool, a simpleton. ['one who never saw his wife's CUNT n.[1] (1)' (Grose, 1785); Hotten (1860) suggests 'corruption of non compos mentis']

nincum noodle n. [early 19C] a penniless fool. [NINCOMPOOP n. + NOODLE n.[1] (2); punning on a SE noodle with no income]

nine n. **1** [1920s+] (Aus.) (also **niner**) a 9-gallon (41-litre) keg of beer. **2** [1980s+] (US) (also **9, 9-millie, nines**) a 9mm pistol.

nine v. [1930s] to take advantage of. [bowling imagery, i.e. one knocks the nine pins]

nine-acre smile n. [1930s+] (Can.) a very broad grin.

nine-bob note n. [1960s+] anyone or anything fake, spurious; esp. in phrs. BENT AS A NINE-BOB NOTE phr. or QUEER AS A NINE-BOB NOTE phr. [the UK's pre-decimal currency included a '10-bob', i.e. 10-shilling note, but not a 'nine-bob' one]

nine corns n. [mid-19C] a pipeful of tobacco. [Lincolnshire/ Shropshire dial.]

nine-day blues n. [20C+] the incubation period for gonorrhoea after the initial sexual contact.

nine-dollar bill n. [1940s+] (US) **1** a fake, a second-rate imitation. **2** a homosexual; thus THREE TIMES AS QUEER AS A THREE DOLLAR BILL phr. [there is no nine-dollar bill]

nine-eight n. (also **98**) [1990s+] (US) a 98 Oldsmobile (a very limited make of Oldsmobile, usu. considered to be the company's best model of car, in any given year, and thus a real status symbol).

nine-eyed adj. [1970s] (US campus) intoxicated.

nine-inch knocker n. [17C+] the penis.

nine-mile nuts n. [late 19C–1900s] anything sustaining, whether to eat or drink. [orig. contemporary Jap. pidgin; f. the supposedly nutritive properties of chestnuts]

9-millie n. see NINE n. (2).

nine o'clock town n. [1930s] (US) a town in which all source of entertainment shuts down early.

911 n. **1** [1990s+] an emergency; the emergency services. **2** [2000s] (US prison) a warning that an officer is approaching. [US telephone code for emergencies, the equivalent of the UK 999]

ninepence n. [late 19C+] (mainly UK juv.) the vagina.

ninepence short of a shilling phr. [1980s] stupid, foolish. [var. on NOT ALL THERE phr. (1)]

ninepennyworth n. [1940s–50s] a 9-month prison sentence.

ninepins n. [late 19C] the body. [it can be easily knocked over]

niner n.[1] **1** [late 19C] a convict serving a 9-year sentence. **2** [1930s+] (Aus.) a woman in her ninth month of pregnancy. **3** [1980s+] a Tech Nine automatic gun.

niner n.[2] see NINE n. (1).

nines n. see NINE n. (2).

nine shillings n. [late 18C–mid-19C] audacity, calmness. [joc. mispron. of SE nonchalance]

nine-spot n. [late 19C–1900s] (US) a nonentity. [card imagery, the relative low ranking of 9, compared to the court cards]

nine-tail bruiser n. (also **nine-tail mouser**) [18C–19C] the cat-o'-nine-tails.

nineteen canteen adv. [1940s+] (S.Afr.) a very long time ago. [assonance]

nineteen-carat adj. see EIGHTEEN-CARAT adj.

nineteener n. [late 19C–1940s] (Aus./N.Z.) an untrustworthy, unpleasant person. [? one who talks 'nineteen to the dozen'; or ? the cribbage score of 19, an impossibility to achieve]

nineteenth hole n. [20C+] the bar at a golf club; esp. used by golfers but understood more widely. [a golf course has 18 holes]

nine-to-five n. (also **nine-till-five**) [1960s+] (orig. US) a regular, routine, uninspiring job. [the hours normally worked]

nine-to-five adj. [1960s+] working in a routine job. [NINE-TO-FIVE n.]

nine-to-five v. [1960s+] to lead a regular, routine (working) life. [NINE-TO-FIVE n.]

nine-to-fiver n. [1960s+] (orig. US) an office worker. [NINE-TO-FIVE n.]

ninety n. (also **90 dog**) [late 19C–1900s] a pug dog. [the curled tail, which resembles the number 9]

ninety days n. [1910s+] (US gambling) in craps dice, the point of 9 (cf. ADA FROM DECATUR n.). [ref. to SE 90 days, the standard sentence for petty crime]

ninety-day wonder n. [1940s+] (US) an inexperienced employee or one employed for temporary work. [orig. milit., a junior officer who has completed the 90-day officer training programme]

90 dog n. see NINETY n.

98 n. see NINE-EIGHT n.

ninety-nine n. [1940s–70s] (Aus./US gay) anal intercourse. [a play on the usu. SIXTY-NINE n. (1)]

ninety-six n. [1920s–50s] (US gay) homosexual anal intercourse. [for ety. see NINETY-NINE n.]

nine ways from breakfast adv. (also **nine ways to Sunday, three ways (and Sunday)**) [1910s+] in all sorts of ways; comprehensively.

nine winks n. [early–mid-19C] a very brief nap. [a 'shorter' var. on FORTY WINKS n.]

ning-nong *n.* (*also* **ning-nang**) [mid-19C+] (*Aus./N.Z.*) a stupid, foolish person. [note horse-coopers' jargon *ning-nang*, a worthless thoroughbred]

ninja *adj.* [1990s+] secretive. [SE *ninja*, a Japanese warrior]

ninkompoop *n. see* NINCOMPOOP *n.*

ninnies *n.* [20C+] (*orig. US*) the female breasts. [SE *ninny*, a child]

ninny *n.*[1] [late 17C–18C] (*UK Und.*) a 'canting, whining beggar' (B.E.). [SE *ninny*, a fool; ? ult. SE *innocent*]

ninny *n.*[2] [1990s+] (*US*) a Black person. [abbr. SE *pickaninny*]

ninny *n.*[3] [2000s] a penis.

ninny broth *n.* [late 17C–early 18C] coffee; thus *ninny-broth house*, a coffee house. [SE *ninny* + *broth*, i.e. 'real men' drink beer or wine]

ninny-cum-poop *n. see* NINCOMPOOP *n.*

ninny-gut *n.* [1930s] (*US*) a weakling. [SE *ninny* + *gut*]

ninnyhammer *n.* [late 16C–1910s] a fool, a simpleton; by ext. a cuckold. [? NINNY *n.*[1] or SE *ninny*, a fool + dial. *hammer*, a clumsy person or *v.* to stammer]

ninny jugs *n.* [1960s–70s] (*US*) the female breasts (cf. BORDENS *n.*). [NINNIES *n.* + SE *jug*]

ninth part of a man *n.* (*also* **tenth part of a man**) [mid-17C–19C] a tailor. [pvb 'nine tailors make a man']

Nip *n.* (*also* **Nippo**) (*orig. US*) **1** [1940s+] a Japanese person (cf. BUDDHAHEAD *n.*). **2** [1940s+] the Japanese language. **3** [1980s+] any East Asian person (cf. BROWNIE *n.*[2]). [abbr. SE *Nipponese*; ult. Jap. *ni(chi)* the sun + *pon, hon,* source]

Nip *adj.* (*orig. US*) **1** [1940s+] pertaining to Japan, the Japanese or Japanese culture. **2** [1980s+] pertaining to East Asia, East Asians or East Asian culture. [NIP *n.*]

nip *n.*[1] (*UK Und.*) **1** [late 16C–17C] a cut-purse. **2** [late 17C–mid-19C] a card-sharp, a cheat. [NIP *v.*[1] (1)]

nip *n.*[2] (*also* **nyp**) [mid-18C+] a small, usu. alcoholic, drink. [abbr. SE *nipperkin*, a small vessel, holding about half a pint (190ml), thus the amount of liquor contained in such a vessel]

nip *n.*[3] [early 19C] 'Passengers who are taken up on stage coaches by the collusion of the guard and coachman, without the knowledge of the proprietors, are called nips' (Thomas De Quincey, *King of Hayti*, 1823). [? dial. *nip*, a good bargainer, 'just honest and no more']

nip *n.*[4] [1930s–40s] (*Aus.*) one who responds favourably to cadgers, a 'soft touch'. [NIP *v.*[1] (8)]

nip *n.*[5] [1930s+] (*mainly US*) a *nip*ple; often in pl.; thus *nip tease*, a woman wearing a shirt or T-shirt without a bra. [abbr.]

nip *n.*[6] [1950s] an escape from prison. [NIP *v.*[2]]

nip *n.*[7] *see* NIPPER *n.*[3].

nip *v.*[1] **1** [mid-16C–1900s] (*UK Und.*) to cut a purse or pick a pocket. **2** [mid-16C–1960s] (*UK Und.*) to arrest. **3** [mid-16C+] to steal, to snatch, to shoplift. **4** [mid–late 19C] (*US*) to shoot someone. **5** [late 19C+] (*US*) to defeat. **6** [1900s–20s] (*US Und.*) to obtain, to get hold of. **7** [1910s–20s] of a man, to have sexual intercourse (cf. BANG *v.*[1]). **8** [1910s+] (*Aus.*) to borrow, to cadge, to wheedle (money) out of. **9** [1930s–40s] (*US*) to cheat, to take advantage of. **10** [1980s] (*US Black*) to scratch, to give a superficial wound. [SE *nip*, to cut, to snip]

nip *v.*[2] [early 19C+] to move quickly; esp. in combs. *nip along, nip away, nip in, nip off, nip out, nip up.*

nip *v.*[3] [mid-19C+] to sip a drink, to consume small measures of drink. [NIP *n.*[2]]

nip *v.*[4] [1910s] (*Aus.*) to sleep.

nip *v.*[5] [1960s+] (*S.Afr.*) to be scared, to be terrified; thus intensifier *nip straws*. [? the fig. tightening of the sphincter muscles]

nip a bung *v.* (*also* **bung-nip, nip a boung**) [mid-16C–mid-18C] (*UK Und.*) to cut a purse. [NIP *v.*[1] (1) + BUNG *n.*[1] (1)]

nipcheese *n.* [late 18C–19C] **1** a ship's purser. **2** a mean, miserly person. [NIP *v.*[1] (3) + SE *cheese*; lit. 'one who steals the cheese']

nip it *v.* [1980s+] (*US campus*) to stop something. [abbr. SE phr. *nip (it) in the bud*]

nipitate *n.* (*also* **nipitaty, nippitato, nippitatum**) [16C–17C] strong drink in general. [NIP *n.*[2]]

nip joint *n.* (*also* **shot house**) [1950s+] (*US*) an illegal drinking establishment where drink is sold in *nips* or small (orig. half-pint) measures. [NIP *n.*[2] + JOINT *n.*[4] (3)]

nip louse *n.* [mid-19C–1920s] a tailor. [SE *nip*, to pinch + *louse*; his removal of lice from the seams of clothes]

nip lug *n.* [19C] (*Scot.*) a teacher. [SE *nip*, to pinch + LUG *n.*[1]]

nippels *n.* [2000s] (*US Black*) a sophisticated Black man. [? SE *nipples*]

nipper *n.*[1] **1** [late 16C–19C] (*UK Und.*) (*also* **nypper**) a cut-purse or pickpocket. **2** [mid–late 19C] (*US*) a policeman (cf. BEAT-POUNDER *n.*). **3** [late 19C] a miser, a tight-fisted person. **4** [late 19C–1900s] (*US/Aus.*) a thief or swindler. [NIP *v.*[1]]

nipper *n.*[2] (*also* **nipperkin**) [late 18C–19C] a small drink. [ext. of NIP *n.*[2]]

nipper *n.*[3] (*also* **nip**) **1** [mid-19C–1960s] a boy who hires himself out to a costermonger or market greengrocer. **2** [mid-19C+] a baby; a small child. **3** [1950s] a small, short person. [NIP *v.*[2]; children 'nip around']

nipper *n.*[4] [late 19C+] (*Aus.*) a prawn. [SE *nip*, to pinch]

nipper *v.* [early 19C] to arrest. [NIP *v.*[1] (2)]

nipperkin *n. see* NIPPER *n.*[2].

nippers *n.*[1] **1** [early 19C–1920s] (*US*) fingers or hands. **2** [early 19C–1950s] handcuffs. **3** [1960s] (*US campus*) the female breasts. [NIP *v.*[1]; (2) 20C+ use mainly US]

nippers *n.*[2] [late 19C–1920s] (*US*) pince-nez. [their 'nipping' the bridge of the nose to gain a purchase on the face]

nipping Christian *n.* [early 17C–mid-19C] a cut-purse. [NIP *v.*[1] (1) + joc. generic use of SE *Christian*]

nipping jig *n.* [19C] (*US*) **1** a gallows. **2** a hanging. [SE *nip*, to pinch + *jig*, a dance]

nippitato/nippitatum *n. see* NIPITATE *n.*

nipple *n.*[1] [1950s] (*W.I.*) a small finger-shaped dumpling.

nipple *n.*[2] *see* TIT *n.*[3] (3).

nipply *adj.* [1990s+] cold, chilly. [pun on NIPPY *adj.*[2] + the fact that cold weather makes women's nipples erect and thus visible]

Nippo *n. see* NIP *n.*

nipps *n. see* NIPS *n.*

nippy *n.*[1] [mid-19C] the penis. [? PEE *n.*[1]]

nippy *n.*[2] [1920s–50s] a waitress. [NIP *v.*[2]; the original *nippies*, waitresses at Lyons Corner Houses, whose name was trademarked by the firm and came from their speed; later use is historical]

nippy *adj.*[1] [mid-19C+] sharp, lively, active. [NIP *v.*[2]]

nippy *adj.*[2] [late 19C+] of weather, chilly. [SE *nip*, to pinch, i.e. at one's skin]

nips *n.* (*also* **nipps**) (*UK Und.*) **1** [late 17C–early 19C] shears used to clip coins. **2** [1920s] a thief's device for unlocking locked doors. [SE *nip*, to cut, to snip]

nip shop *n.* (*also* **nyp shop**) [late 18C–early 19C] the Peacock Tavern in Gray's Inn Lane, London, where Burton ale was sold in *nips* or half-pint measures. [NIP *n.*[2] + SE *shop*]

nip shred *n.* [mid-17C–mid-18C] a tailor. [SE *nip*, to pinch + *shred*]

nire *n.* [mid-19C] rain. [backsl.]

nisey *see under* NIZZIE.

nisht *n.* (*also* **nicht, nish, nishte**) [1910s+] nothing. [synon. Yid.; *nish* is UK Black use]

nisty *adj.* [1980s+] (*US campus*) very unattractive. [? SE *nasty*]

nit *n.*[1] **1** [late 16C+] a fool; thus *nitty*, foolish. **2** [1910s] (*Aus. milit.*) a policeman (cf. ANIMAL *n.*[1]). [SE *nit*, a louse; the implication is perhaps more of its insignificance than of its verminous qualities]

nit *n.*[2] [late 17C–18C] 'Wine that is brisk [i.e. agreeable to the taste] and pour'd quick into a Glass' (B.E.). [ety. unknown; ? SE *nit*, louse]

nit *v.* [late 19C+] (*Scot./Aus.*) to escape, to decamp, to hurry away. [? NICK v.³; or ? SE *nit*, a louse]

nit! *excl.*¹ [late 19C–1940s] (*US*) used as an emphatic 'no!', also added to positive assertions to give a negative meaning, e.g. 'I should say nit!' [var. on SE *not*]

nit! *excl.*² [late 19C–1950s] (*orig. Aus.*) a term used to indicate that someone is coming and that one must stop what one is doing and run away. [NIT v.]

nite nurse *n.* [1990s+] (*W.I.*) **1** a woman who treats her boyfriend well. **2** cocaine. [the reggae song by Gregory Isaacs 'Night Nurse' (1982); note cocaine is a 'feminine' drug, *see* GIRL n.² (1)]

niterie *n.* (*also* **nitery**) [1930s+] (*orig. US*) a nightclub. [latterly SE]

nit-head *n.* [1990s+] an idiot, a fool. [NIT n.¹ (1) + -HEAD sfx (1)]

nit keeper *n.* [1930s+] (*Aus.*) one who keeps watch while a companion performs some form of illegal activity. [KEEP NIT v., i.e. NIT! excl.² + SE *keeper*]

nito *v. see* NITTO v.

nitraph *n.* [mid-19C] a farthing. [backsl.]

nitro *n.* [20C+] (*orig. US*) nitroglycerine, as used in blowing up safes. [abbr.]

nitro *adj.* [1980s+] (*US*) excellent, wonderful. [fig. use of NITRO n.]

nits and lice *n.* [20C+] a price, esp. in gambling. [rhy. sl.]

nitshit *n.* [1970s] (*US*) nonsense, trivial matters. [NIT-SHIT adj.]

nit-shit *adj.* [1960s+] (*US*) second-rate, insignificant, trivial. [SE *nit*, a louse + SHIT adj. (1)]

nit-shit *v.* [1960s–70s] (*US*) to talk in an irritating manner. [NIT-SHIT adj.]

nitski! *excl.* [1900s–20s] (*US*) an emphatic 'no!' [NIT! excl.¹ + -SKI sfx]

nit squeeger *n.* [late 18C–early 19C] a hairdresser. [SE *nit*, a louse, lit. 'nit-squeezer']

nit's tits *n.* [1900s] (*Aus.*) an excellent and admirable person or thing. [var. on BEE'S KNEES n.]

nitto *v.* (*also* **nito**) [1950s–70s] (*UK Und.*) to stop; thus *nitto!* stop it! [NIT! excl.¹]

nitty *n.* [1970s+] (*US*) the essentials, the fundamentals. [abbr. NITTY-GRITTY n.]

nitty *adj.*¹ (*also* **knitty**) [late 16C–18C] a general epithet of abuse. [lit. suffering from SE *nits*, lice]

nitty *adj.*² *see* NIT n.¹ (1).

nitty-gritty *n.* (*also* **gritty**) [1950s+] (*orig. US Black*) the basics, the essentials, the grass roots; esp. in GET DOWN TO THE NITTY-GRITTY v. [ety. unknown; redup. of SE *gritty*, composed of minute particles]

nitty-gritty *adj.* [1960s+] (*orig. US Black*) fundamental, basic. [NITTY-GRITTY n.]

nitwit *n.* [1910s+] (*orig. US*) a fool (cf. DAMWIT n.). [SE *nit*, a louse + *wit*]

nitwitted *adj.* (*also* **nitwit**) [1920s+] stupid, foolish; a term of abuse (cf. BEEF-WITTED adj.). [NITWIT n.]

nix *n.* **1** [late 18C+] (*also* **nicks**) nobody, no one, nothing; thus *for nix*, to any extent, not at all. **2** [late 19C–1900s] (*US*) nowhere. **3** [1910s] (*US*) a good-for-nothing. **4** [1980s+] (*drugs*) a stranger among the group. [colloq. Du./Ger. *nix*; ult. Ger. *nichts*, nothing]

nix *adj.* **1** [mid-19C–1950s] (*US*) worthless or damaged. **2** [20C+] (*also* **nixie**) no, none, negligible. [NIX n.]

nix *v.*¹ (*also* **nix off**) (*US*) **1** [mid-18C; 20C+] to forbid, to veto, to reject, to cancel or eliminate. **2** [1990s+] to ruin or spoil. [NIX n. (1)]

nix *v.*² [1940s] (*US Black/Harlem*) to leave, to depart (from).

nix *adv.* [mid-19C+] no, certainly not. [NIX n. (1)]

nix! *excl.* **1** [mid-19C+] a warning of someone's approach. **2** [late 19C+] (*orig. US*) an emphatic 'no!', 'stop that (at once)!' [NIX adv.]

nix deberr! *excl.* [early 19C] an excl. meaning no, my friend. [NIX! excl. (2) + *deberr*, a perversion of Rus. *tovarich*, a friend]

nixer *n.* (*also* **foxer, nickser**) [1950s+] (*Irish*) work undertaken in one's free time, as part of the 'black economy'. [NIX v.¹ (1)]

nixey *n.* (*also* **nixies**) [20C+] nothing. [NIX n. (1)]

nixey! *excl.* (*also* **nixie! nixy!**) [mid-19C–1910s] (*US*) an emphatic 'no!' [NIX! excl.]

nixie *adj. see* NIX adj. (2).

nixies *n.*¹ [1920s–30s] women's knickers. [abbr.]

nixies *n.*² *see* NIXEY n.

nixies! *excl.* [1990s+] (*UK juv.*) the hidden crossing of one's fingers that allows one to exclude oneself from a task/game/promise.

nix my doll *phr.* (*also* **nicks my doll, nix my dolly**) [late 18C–19C] nothing, never mind, it doesn't matter. [thus the sl. verse: 'In the box of a stone jug I was born, / Of a hempen widow and a kid forlorn; / And my noble father, as I have heard say, / Was a famous merchant of capers gay; / Nix my dolly, pals, fake away!'; written by William Ainsworth as 'Jenny Juniper's' chant in *Rookwood* (1834); he claimed it as the 'first flash song' but was some 300 years late. Farmer, *Vocabula Amatoria* (1896), cites Copland's *Rhymes of the Canting Crew* (*c.*1536)]

nix off *v. see* NIX v.¹.

Nixon *n.* [1960s+] (*drugs*) inferior marijuana sold fraudulently as being of high quality (cf. AUNT MARY n.²). [US President Richard M. *Nixon* (1913–94), a notably corrupt figure, latterly best known for his role in the Watergate Affair]

nix on *phr.* [20C+] (*US*) enough of, no more of. [NIX adv.]

nix on it *phr.* [1940s+] (*Aus.*) no more of that, stop it. [NIX ON phr.]

nix out (on) *v.* [1930s–50s] (*orig. US Black*) **1** to throw away, to get rid of a person or object. **2** to go; thus fig. to die. [NIX v.¹ (1)]

nixy! *excl. see* NIXEY! excl.

niyabinghi *n.* [1950s+] (*W.I. Rasta*) **1** a society of Rastafarian 'warriors', dedicated to the overthrow of White rule. **2** a large Rastafarian meeting and spiritual gathering. **3** a variety of drumming. [a supposed Ethiopian word *niyabinghi*, 'death to the White man'; orig. adopted by a group, led by Hailie Selassie, who resisted colonial domination in Ethiopia and the Congo]

niyabinghi *adj.* [1950s+] (*W.I. Rasta*) used of orthodox, trad. Rastafarians. [NIYABINGHI n.]

niyaman *n.* [1950s+] (*W.I. Rasta*) a Rastafarian. [NIYABINGHI adj. + SE *man*]

nizzie *n.* (*also* **nisey, nizy**) [late 17C–1920s] (*UK Und.*) a fool, a dunce. [? 13C SE *nice*, foolish, senseless; ? ult. Lat. *nescius*, ignorant]

nizzie *adj.* (*also* **nisey, nizy**) [early 18C] foolish, dull. [NIZZIE n.]

n.m.c. *n.* [1990s+] (*UK juv.*) a metaphorical 'club' whose members are the least popular children at school. [*no mates club*]

n.n. *n.* [late 19C–1900s] (*UK society*) a husband. [abbr. *necessary nuisance*]

N.O. *n.* [1960s] (*US*) New Orleans. [abbr.]

no-account *n.* (*also* **no-count**) [late 19C+] a worthless person. [NO-ACCOUNT adj.]

no-account *adj.* (*also* **no-count**) [mid-19C+] (*orig. US Black*) a general pej., worthless, insignificant, undependable, untrustworthy, criminal. [abbr. SE *of no account*]

no-account (nigger) *n.* [late 19C+] (*US Black*) **1** a Black who rejects the second-class role offered by the dominant White society. **2** an untrustworthy person. [NO-ACCOUNT adj. + NIGGER n.¹ (1)]

Noah *n.* **1** [mid-19C] (*US Und.*) a flatboat. **2** [1900s] (*US*) a poached egg. [their relationships with water]

Noah's (ark) *n.* **1** [19C] a lark, a game; crime. **2** [late 19C] a lark (the bird). **3** [20C+] a park. **4** [20C+] an informer. **5** [20C+] (*Aus.*) a dullard, a fool (cf. BEECHAM'S PILL n.). **6** [1940s+] (*Aus.*) a shark. **7** [1950s] a whore. **8** [1960s] (*Aus.*) a moneylender. [rhy. sl.; (4) = NARK n.¹ (1); (5) = NARK n.¹ (2); (8) = SHARK n.¹ (7); (7) is unusual in that it rhymes on the first word, *Noah's*, with the Cockney pron. of 'hoo-er']

Noah's ark *n.* [mid-19C] a long, closely buttoned overcoat, fashionable at the time. [coined by *Punch*, the term supposedly reflected the similarity of the coat to those worn by Noah and his children in toy *Noah's arks*]

Noah's ark *adj.* [20C+] dark. [rhy. sl.]

no arse! *excl.* [20C+] (*W.I.*) a general intensive excl., a synon. with LIKE HELL! excl. [SE *no* + fig. use of ARSE n.¹ (1)]

no-ass *adj.* [1980s+] (*US Black*) a general term of derision. [SE *no* + ASS n. (2)]

nob *n.*¹ 1 [late 17C+] (*orig. UK Und.*) (*also* **nobb**) the head. 2 [early 19C] a blow on the head. 3 [mid-19C] (*UK Und.*) young boy prisoners who bully weaker ones. 4 [mid-19C] a sovereign. 5 [late 19C–1910s] (*Aus.*) in two-up, a double-headed coin. 6 [1900s] to keep calm. [var. of KNOB n.¹ (1); (4) the royal head on the coin]

nob *n.*² 1 [18C+] a nobleman, a gentleman; thus *nobbish*, aristocratic; *nobbily*, aristocratically; [early–mid-19C] *nobs' houses*, the Houses of Parliament, divided into *upper nobs' house*, the Lords, *lower nobs' house*, the Commons; [mid-19C] *nob in the fur trade*, a judge. 2 [1910s] (*Aus.*) an expert. [? abbr. SE *nobility* or *nobleman*, but 18C Scot. use suggests an alternative – if unknown – ety.; according to Bee, 'the swell […] makes a show of his finery […] the nob, relying upon intrinsic worth, or bona fide property, or intellectual ability, is clad in plain-ness'; (2) f. (1)]

nob *n.*³ [mid-18C–mid-19C] the game of prick-the-garter, a form of swindling game, in which one pricked a belt with a large needle; presumably betting on the odds of hitting a given target. [ety. unknown]

nob *n.*⁴ [mid-late 19C] in cribbage, the knave of trumps. [? dial. *nob*, an interloper]

nob *n.*⁵ 1 [mid-19C+] the penis. 2 [1970s+] a socially inept person. [var. on KNOB n.¹ (3)]

nob *v.*¹ [early–mid-19C] to hit on the head. [NOB n.¹ (1)]

nob *v.*² (*also* **knob**) [mid-19C–1930s] to collect money; to make a collection after a sporting contest, a performance etc. [NOB n.¹ (4)]

nob *v.*³ [1980s+] of a man, to have sexual intercourse; thus n., *nobber* (cf. BAGAGA v.). [NOB n.⁵ (1)]

nob-a-nob *adj.* [mid-late 19C] intimate, close, friendly. [NOB n.¹ (1)]

nob artist *n. see* KNOB ARTIST n.

nobb *n. see* NOB n.¹ (1).

nobba *n.* (*also* **nobber**) [mid-19C] the number 9; thus *nobba saltee*, 9 pence. [Ital. *nove*, 9; 'introduced by the "organ-grinders" from Italy' (Hotten, 1867]

nobber *n.*¹ 1 [early–mid-19C] a blow on the head. 2 [early–late 19C] a boxer skilled at delivering such blows. 3 [1930s] (*US Und.*) a thug who knocks out his victims before robbing them. [NOB v.¹]

nobber *n.*² [late 19C–1930s] a collector of money, esp. when serving as the assistant to a street performer. [NOB v.²]

nobber *n.*³ *see* NOB v.³.

nobbies *n. see* NOBBY STILES n.

nobbily *adv.*¹ *see* NOB n.² (1).

nobbily *adv.*² *see* NOBBY adj. (2).

nobbing *n.*¹ [mid-late 19C] collecting money, 'passing the hat round'; thus *nobbings*, a collection of money, esp. money tossed into a boxing ring after an amateur or boys' fight. [NOB v.²]

nobbing *n.*² [1980s+] sexual intercourse. [NOB v.³]

nobbing *adj.* [1990s+] a euph. for FUCKING adj. [NOB v.³]

nobbish *adj.*¹ [mid-19C] showy (cf. NOBBY adj.). [NOB n.² (1)]

nobbish *adj.*² *see* NOB n.² (1).

nobble *v.*¹ 1 [mid-19C] to strike, to hit on the head. 2 [1970s+] to kill. [NOB n.¹ (1)]

nobble *v.*² 1 [mid-late 19C] to steal, to take illicitly. 2 [mid-late 19C] to cheat, to over-reach. 3 [mid-19C+] to use illicit methods to obtain a person's help, to swindle, to influence or to corrupt. 4 [mid-19C+] (*racing*) to interfere with a horse in order to spoil

its chance of victory; occas. ext. to human competitors; thus [1960s+] *jury nobbling*, the interference with the impartiality of a jury (through threats or bribes) either by defendants or their friends. 5 [mid-19C+] to get hold of, to seize, to catch. 6 [late 19C+] to ruin anything deliberately, esp. to impede a rival; to discover (a plot). 7 [1920s+] to kidnap. 8 [1930s+] to recognize. 9 [1990s+] (*US*) to obtain for oneself undeservedly. [ety. unknown; ? NAB v.¹]

nobbler *n.*¹ [mid-19C] (*orig. boxing*) 1 a knockout blow. 2 a blow on the head. [? NOBBLE v.¹ (1)]

nobbler *n.*² 1 [mid-late 19C] a man who runs a game of 'find-the-lady' or THREE-CARD MONTE n.; also his accomplice. 2 [mid-late 19C] one who lames, drugs or otherwise tampers with horses. 3 [1930s] a beggar's accomplice. [NOBBLE v.²; note northern dial. *nobbler*, a low, cunning lawyer]

nobbler *n.*³ (*also* **nobler**) [mid-19C–1950s] (*Aus.*) a small measure of spirits; thus *nobblerize*, to drink spirits, usu. as part of a group; thus the drink itself. [fig. use of NOBBLE v.² (5); it 'gets hold of you']

nobby *n.* [1950s] (*UK juv.*) a policeman. [? var. on BOBBY n. (1)]

nobby *adj.* 1 [late 18C+] (*also* **knobby**) extremely smart or elegant, aristocratic. 2 [19C+] showy, extravagant; thus *nobbily*, vulgarly, showily (cf. NOBBISH adj.¹). 3 [mid-19C–1900s] smart, canny; thus *do the nobby*, do the smart thing. 4 [late 19C] arrogant. 5 [late 19C–1900s] (*US*) (*also* **knobby**) wonderful. [NOB n.² (1)]

nobby *adv.* [late 19C] in a smart manner. [NOBBY adj. (1)]

nobby halls *n.* [20C+] the testicles (cf. CHEESE AND CRACKERS n.). [rhy. sl. = BALLS n.¹ (1); ult. *Nobby Halls*, the mono-testicled 'hero' of a music-hall song]

Nobby Stiles *n.* (*also* **nobbies**) [1990s+] haemorrhoids, piles. [rhy. sl.; ult. UK soccer star *Nobby Stiles* (b.1942)]

no beads *phr.* [1950s–60s] (*US teen*) 'no sweat', don't worry.

no beg-pardons *phr.* [20C+] (*Aus.*) no apologies. [SE apology *I beg your pardon*]

no-beyond jammer *n.* [late 19C–1900s] an extremely attractive woman. [SE *no* + *beyond* + JAM n.³ (1)]

nob girder *n. see* NAB GIRDER n.

nob hill *n.* [early 19C+] (*orig. US*) the most socially exclusive and/or richest area of a town or city. [NOB n.² (1) + SE *hill*; note New York's *Nob Hill*, a row of fine houses built *c.*1815 near Bowling Green, and *Nob's Hill*, an area of San Francisco colonized by wealthy veterans of the California Gold Rush]

no big deal *phr.* (*also* **no biggie, no big whoop**) [1980s+] (*orig. US teen*) don't worry, it's all right, it's not important etc. [SE *no* + BIG DEAL n. (2)/BIGGIE n. (1)/BIG WHOOP! excl.]

no big thing *phr.* (*also* **no thing**) [1960s+] (*orig. US teen*) don't worry, it's all right, it's not important etc. [SE *no* + BIG THING n. (2)]

nob it *v.* [early 19C] (*UK Und.*) to succeed without working in the respectable world. [NOB n.²]

no bitch! *excl.* [1980s+] (*US campus*) an excl. used when choosing seats in a car, i.e. I won't ride in the middle of the back seat. [SE *no* + RIDE BITCH v.; excl. delivered in response to a claim of SHOTGUN! excl.]

nob jockey *n. see* KNOB JOCKEY n.

noble *n.* 1 [1910s+] (*US*) a man hired as a guard to protect strike-breakers. 2 [1910s+] (*US*) the boss of a gang of such guards. 3 [1960s–70s] (*US prison*) an inmate considered to be reliable, trustworthy by the guards.

noble *adj.* [1900s–20s] (*US Black*) good, excellent.

nobler *n. see* NOBBLER n.³.

noble weed *n.* [1960s] (*drugs*) marijuana (cf. AFRICAN BUSH n.). [SE *noble* + WEED n.¹ (4)]

nobody home *phr.* [1910s+] (*orig. US*) used of someone who is dull or stupid; thus ext. to LIGHTS ARE ON BUT THERE'S NOBODY HOME phr. or *nobody home upstairs and rooms to rent*.

nobody's business *n.* [mid-19C+] something extraordinary.

nobody's fool n. [late 19C+] an intelligent, aware person.

no bon adj. [1910s–20s] no good. [pidgin Fr. no + bon, good; coined during WW1]

nob onto v. [1910s] to associate with; to accompany. [? NOB n.²]

no bottle phr.¹ [mid-19C] impossible, not allowed, out of the question. [the refusal of further drinks by a bartender]

no bottle phr.² **1** [mid-19C+] (also **not much bottle**) lacking quality or style, no good. **2** [1940s+] cowardly. [rhy. sl.; no bottle and glass = (1) no CLASS n. (1); (2) no ARSE n.² (3)]

nob pitcher n. [early 19C] (UK Und.) a sharp or confidence man who specializes in finding his victims at fairs, races and similar open-air events. [NOB n.²/NOBBLE v.² + ? PITCH n.¹]

nob rails n. see HEAD RAILS n.

no-brainer n. [1970s+] (orig. US) **1** anything that requires no intellectual effort. **2** an easy decision. **3** a foolish person or thing. [no SE brain is required]

no-brand cigarette n. (also **cigarette with no name**, **no-name brand cigarette**, **no-name cigarette**) [1970s+] (drugs) a marijuana cigarette (cf. AFRICAN WOODBINE n.). [one rolls such cigarettes oneself; there is no commercial packaging]

no bread and butter of mine phr. [late 18C–early 19C] no business of mine.

nobrow adj. [1990s+] (US) vulgar, tasteless. [pun on LOWBROW adj.]

nobs n.¹ [early–mid-16C] a term of affection, usu. used of or to a woman. [? her figure, i.e. 'knobs' or curves, or NOBS n.²]

nobs n.² [mid-19C–1950s] (US) an important person. [NOB n.² (1); var. on NIBS n. (2)]

nobscratch n. [1990s+] a general term of abuse. [NOB n.⁵ (1) + SE scratch; the implication is of pubic lice]

nobsey n. [mid-16C] a mistress. [NOBS n.¹]

nobs' houses n. see NOB n.² (1).

nobstick n. see KNOBSTICK n.

nob stilton n. see COCK CHEESE n.

nob thatch n. [mid-19C] human hair. [NOB n.¹ (1) + SE thatch]

nob-thatcher n. (also **knob-thatcher**) [late 18C–mid-19C] a wig-maker. [NOB n.¹ (1) + SE thatcher]

no-bullshit adj. [1970s] uncompromising. [SE no + BULLSHIT n. (1)]

no burner of navigable rivers phr. [late 18C–early 19C] a phr. used to describe an unexceptional person, one who will make no mark on the world. [play on SET THE THAMES ON FIRE v.]

no butter will stick on his bread phr. [late 17C+] a phr. used to describe one who has consistently bad luck in whatever they try to achieve.

no can do phr. (also **n.c.d.**) [1920s+] (orig. US) it is impossible (usu. with apologetic overtones). [SE no + CAN DO phr.]

no can tell n. [1940s] (US Und.) a silencer; a gun armed with a silencer.

no cash, no Swiss phr. (also **no money, no Swiss**) [mid-19C+] no help without payment in advance. [the trad. role of the Swiss as mercenary soldiers; note 17C prostitutes' demand: 'No money, no cony' (lit. vagina) and the pvb 'no penny, no paternoster', i.e. no payment, no prayers offered]

n.o.c.d. phr. see N.Q.O.C.D. phr.

no chance phr. [20C+] a general term of dismissal or negation, no hope or possibility whatsoever.

no cheese phr. see CHEESE n.⁴ (4).

no chicken n. [early 18C+] a name given to someone, often a woman, who is no longer young. [SE no + CHICKEN n.³ (1)]

no chop phr. (also **not much chop**) [late 19C+] (Aus.) no class, second-rate; thus not much chop, of no great value. [SE no + Hind. chhaap, a print, and thus a seal, notably that which is placed on first-rate merchandise]

nochy n. [mid-19C+] (Ling. Fr./Polari) night. [Ital. notte or Sp. noche, night]

nock n. **1** [mid-16C–19C] the anus. **2** [late 16C–17C] the vagina. [SE notch or see NOCKANDRO n.; (1) Cotgrave, Dict. French and English Tongues (1611), suggests backsl.: 'Noc. Con, Turned backward (as our Tnuc) to be the lesse offensive to chast eares']

nock v. [late 16C–18C] to have sexual intercourse. [NOCK n.]

nockandro n. (also **nockandrow**) [17C] the buttocks. [Early Mod.E nock, the cleft of the buttocks]

nocks n. [1940s–50s] (US Und.) narcotics. [abbr.]

nocktress n. [19C] a prostitute (cf. ASS PEDDLER n.). [NOCK n. (1) + fem. sfx -tress]

nocky n. [late 17C–18C] a fool, a simpleton. [Suffolk dial.; ? f. the fool's knocking on or knuckling of his forehead]

nocky boy n. [late 18C–early 19C] (UK Und.) a dullard, a simpleton. [NOCKY n. + SE boy]

no class adj. [late 19C+] styleless, socially inept, unable to fulfil the group norms. [SE no + CLASS n. (1)]

no cool n. [1980s+] (US campus) northern California. [joc. use of sl. + ref. to the status of that part of the state]

no cop phr. (also **any cop, not much cop**) [late 19C+] of little or no value or use, worthless.

no-count see under NO-ACCOUNT.

no crap! excl. see NO SHIT! excl. (2).

nocturne n. [late 19C–1910s] a prostitute (cf. DEADLY NIGHTSHADE n.). [joc. use of painting jargon nocturne, a night-piece]

nod n.¹ **1** [late 17C+] a sleep; thus knock a nod, to have a sleep. **2** [1930s+] (orig. US drugs) the drug-induced stupor or semi-sleep that follows an injection of heroin; thus cop a nod, to become comatose after injecting a narcotic. [(1) 20C+ use is US Black]

nod n.² (also **noddy**, **noddy men**) [1960s+] a policeman; thus noddy bike, a police motorcycle. [? the policeman in the Noddy books, created by author Enid Blyton (1897–1968)]

nod n.³ [1970s+] (US Black) the human hair.

nod n.⁴ see NODDLE n. (1).

nod n.⁵ see NODDY n.¹.

nod v.¹ (also **nod off/out**) [1950s+] to become temporarily comatose following the immediate effects of an injection of heroin or any other opiate drug. [NOD n.¹ (2)]

nod v.² [1980s+] (Aus. prison) to plead guilty. [the affirmative SE nod to one's crimes]

no danger phr. [1920s+] a general phr. of affirmation, no problem, absolutely, truthfully.

nod-box n. [1940s] (US Black) a bedroom. [NOD n.¹ (1) + BOX n.³ (4)]

nod cock n. (also **nodge cock**) [16C–19C] a fool, a simpleton (cf. HORSECOCK n.¹). [the foolish nodding of their head]

nodder n.¹ [1970s+] (drugs) one who becomes comatose immediately following a narcotic injection. [NOD v.¹]

nodder n.² [1950s] the head. [SE nod]

noddipol n. (also **noddy-pate**, **noddy-peake**, **noddy-pole**) [16C–early 19C] a simpleton, a fool. [NODDY n.¹ + SE poll/pate, head]

noddle n. **1** [mid-16C+] (also **nod**) the head. **2** [late 16C+] used fig. to denote the head as a seat (or not) of intelligence; thus use your noddle, use your head, act sensibly. [15C SE noddle, the back of the head]

noddle case n. [18C] a wig. [NODDLE n. (1) + SE case]

noddle-thatcher n. [18C] a wig-maker. [NODDLE n. (1) + SE thatcher]

noddy n.¹ (also **nod**) [early 16C–19C] a fool, a simpleton. [the foolish wagging of his head]

noddy n.² [late 18C+] (Irish) a one-horse conveyance; thus noddy-boy, the driver. [its 'nodding' from side-to-side]

noddy n.³ [1950s+] a weakling. [revival of NODDY n.¹ influenced by the children's character Noddy, created by author Enid Blyton (1897–1968)]

noddy n.⁴ see NOD n.².

noddy head *n.* [mid-19C–1910s] a fool. [NODDY n.[1] + SE *head/-HEAD* sfx (1)]

noddy-headed *adj.* [20C+] drunk (cf. ARSEHOLED adj.). [the nodding of the drunk person's head with ref. to NODDY n.[1]]

noddy men *n. see* NOD n.[2].

noddy-pate/-peake/-pole *n. see* NODDIPOL n.

nodge cock *n. see* NOD COCK n.

no dice *n.* [1930s+] (*orig. US*) nothing, esp. with inferences of a rejection. [NO DICE phr.]

no dice *adj.* [1930s+] insignificant, worthless, pointless. [NO DICE phr.]

no dice *phr.* [1930s+] (*orig. US*) impossible, out of the question, on no account. [the refusal of a gambling-house proprietor to allow a player to start or continue playing]

no diggety! *excl.* (*also* **no diggity!**) [1990s+] (*US teen*) a general excl. implying 'without question!' [? var. on HOT DIGGETY (DOG)! excl.]

no-do *n.* [1920s–30s] (*US*) a woman who is not interested in sex, or will not have sex with a given man.

nod off *v. see* NOD v.[1].

no doubt! *excl.* [1980s+] (*US campus*) a general expression of agreement. [emphatic var. on SE]

nod out *v. see* NOD v.[1].

no down! *excl.* [early 19C] carry on! don't stop!

nod the nut *v.* (*also* **give it the nod**) [1930s+] (*Aus./N.Z.*) to plead guilty. [SE *nod* + NUT n.[1] (2); the defendant acknowledges his guilt with a nod when asked 'How do you plead?']

no dust on *phr.* [late 19C] (*US*) up to the minute, highly fashionable. [the image of dust gathering on a conservative or old-fashioned person]

no earthly *phr.* (*also* **not an earthly**) [late 19C+] no hope whatsoever, no possible chance. [SE *no* + EARTHLY n. (1)]

no end *adv.* [mid-19C+] to a great extent, very much. [NO END (OF) adj.]

no end (of) *adj.* **1** [early 17C+] describing a vast quantity or number. **2** [late 19C+] very great, a general superlative.

no eyes *phr.* [1940s+] I'm not interested. [negative of HAVE EYES (FOR) v.]

no fear! *excl.* **1** [early 19C+] (*orig. N.Z.*) absolutely not! not a chance! **2** [late 19C+] absolutely! without any doubt!

noffka *n.* (*also* **nafka, noffgur**) [late 19C+] a prostitute. [synon. Yid.]

no flies (about)! *excl.* [mid-19C–1940s] (*Aus.*) no problem! no fuss! no doubt about it! [NO FLIES ON phr.]

no flies on *phr.* (*also* **no flies about**) [mid-19C+] as in *no flies on me/her* etc., implying the smartness and imperviousness to trickery of the speaker or subject. [? cattle that were so active that no fly could settle on them]

no fooling *phr.* [1920s+] **1** don't be silly, don't tease. **2** honest, honestly, I am not lying. [SE *no* + *fool*]

no freak *n.* [1970s] a client who wishes a prostitute to simulate the role of a rape victim, screaming 'No!' and 'struggling' before he overpowers her. [SE *no* + FREAK n.[1] (6)]

nog *n. see* NOGGY n.

noggin *n.[1]* **1** [mid-19C+] the head; thus *off one's noggin*, mad, crazy. **2** [1930s+] a hangover. [? SE *noggin*, a small drinking vessel, a mug; orig. US, but migrated to the UK in mid-19C]

noggin *n.[2]* [1940s] (*W.I.*) a farthing. [? NOGGIN n.[1] (1), i.e. the head engraved on 1 side of the coin; or ? SE *noggin*, a quarter (or less) of a pint]

noggy *n.* (*also* **nog**) [1950s+] (*Aus.*) an Asian; orig. a North Korean or North Vietnamese soldier, subseq. an Asian immigrant to Australia (cf. BROWNIE n.[2]). [abbr. NIG-NOG n.[2]]

no giggle *phr.* [1920s+] of a situation, unpleasant. [SE *no* + GIGGLE n. (1)]

no go *n.* [early 19C+] a failure, an impossibility, that which cannot be done or happen. [NO GO phr.]

no go *adj.* [1970s+] dangerous, off limits, out of bounds. [NO GO phr.]

no go *phr.* [early 19C+] impossible, out of the question.

no goat's toe *phr.* [20C+] (*Ulster*) used of one who is sensible, 'nobody's fool'.

no-good *n.* [20C+] an unappealing, unpleasant, untrustworthy person. [NO-GOOD adj.]

no-good *adj.* [late 19C+] (*orig. US*) a general term of abuse, unpleasant, untrustworthy, dishonest etc.

no-good-ass *adj.* [1970s] a general term of disparagement. [NO-GOOD adj. + -ASS sfx]

no-gooder *n.* [1930s+] (*US*) a bad person, a good-for-nothing. [NO-GOOD adj.]

no-goodnik *n.* [1930s+] (*orig. US*) a general pej., an unpleasant or unreliable person. [NO-GOOD n. + -NIK sfx]

no-goodnik *adj.* [1930s+] a general pej., unpleasant or unreliable. [NO-GOODNIK n.]

no good to gundy *phr.* [20C+] (*Aus.*) no good at all, definitely bad; thus *good enough for gundy*, reasonably good, acceptable, not too bad. [ety. unknown; ? the Welsh dial. *gundy*, to steal, thus 'not worth stealing'; ? a relic of the great flood of 1852 that devastated *Gundagai*; ? a comment by an Aborigine, one *Gundy*, when rejecting a proffered drink of whisky; ? a rebuttal of a temperance preacher, attempting to force his views on the populace of Gundagai]

no great *adv.* [mid-19C–1900s] (*US*) not very much, not particularly, e.g. *I don't care no great*.

no great guns *phr.* [1990s+] not very exceptional, not very important. [SE *no* + GREAT GUNS adv.]

no great scratch *phr.* [mid-19C] (*orig. US*) not much use, of no great importance. [i.e. it makes little impression]

no great shakes *phr. see* GREAT SHAKES adj.

no great things *phr.* [19C] of little or no importance.

no hair off one's brows *phr. see* NO SKIN OFF ONE'S NOSE phr.

no hide, no Christmas box *phr.* [1930s+] (*Aus.*) no hope of that, not a chance. [SE *no* + HIDE n.[3] + SE *Christmas box*]

no holds barred *phr.* [1940s+] (*orig. US*) anything goes. [wrestling imagery]

no-hoper *n.* [1940s+] **1** (*orig. Aus.*) (*also* **no-hope**) a useless or incompetent person, one from whom no good can be expected. **2** (*Aus.*) a recidivist. [horseracing jargon *no-hoper*, an outsider, a horse that has no hope of winning]

no-hoping *adj.* (*also* **no-hope**) [1960s+] (*Aus.*) of a person, hopeless, useless. [NO-HOPER n.]

no-horse *adj.* [1950s+] (*US*) absolutely insignificant. [ext. of ONE-HORSE adj.]

noid *adj.* [1980s+] para*noid*; thus *noiding*, being paranoid, having paranoia. [abbr.]

noise *n.[1]* **1** [mid-19C+] (*US*) chatter, gossip; empty, foolish talk. **2** [1900s–20s] (*US*) the world of the city (as opposed to the supposed quaintness of the countryside). **3** [1900s–30s] a (self-)important person. **4** [1920s+] (*US*) information, the know.

noise *n.[2]* [1920s+] (*drugs*) heroin. [? play on SE *nose*]

noise *n.[3]* [1960s+] (*W.I.*) serious trouble; usu. as *be in noise*. [the lit. or fig. SE *noise* that follows]

noise around *v.* (*also* **noise about/abroad**) [mid-19C+] to tell. [NOISE n.[1] (1)]

noise (off) *v.* [1930s+] (*US Black*) to boast, to brag, to indulge in foolish talk. [NOISE n.[1] (1)]

noise up *v.* [1990s+] to talk to. [NOISE n.[1] (1)]

noisola *n.* [1930s–40s] (*US Black*) a jukebox, a record player. [SE *noise* + -OLA sfx; on model of *pianola*, the jukebox's predecessor]

noisy *adj.* [late 19C+] (*US*) of clothes, showy, 'loud'.

noisy dog racket *n.* [early 19C] (*UK Und.*) stealing brass knockers from doors.

noisy pegs *n.* [late 19C] (*UK Und.*) boots. [SE *noisy* + ? PEG n.[4] (1)]

noisy-racket man *n.* [mid-19C] a person who steals china or glass from a china shop.

no jive *phr.* (*also* **no jibe**) [1930s+] (*US*) honestly, no fooling. [SE *no* + JIVE v.[1] (2)]

no joke *phr.* [19C+] taking all matters as seriously as possible when dealing with a certain subject, i.e. this is not a joking or laughing matter.

no Jonas tip played on me *phr.* [1950s–60s] (*US Black*) no one is going to take me for a fool. [ety. unknown; ? anecdotal]

nokes *n.* [late 17C–early 19C] a fool, a dullard. [*John-a-Nokes* was, with Tom-a-Stiles, the precursor of John Doe and Richard Roe as the legal jargon providing names for otherwise anonymous plaintiffs and defendants; also James *Nokes*, a comic actor of the Duke's Company in 1660s who was celebrated for his portrayal of solemn fools, including Sir Nicholas Cully in Etherege's *The Comical Revenge; or, Love in a Tub*]

no kidding *phr.* (*also* **no kid**) [late 19C+] (*US*) used interrog. or emphatically, i.e. Are you serious? or I'm absolutely serious. [KID (AROUND) v. (2)/KID n.[2] (3)]

no knock *n.* [1960s+] (*US police*) a clause in US drug laws that permits police to enter premises without knocking first and thus ensure surprise and probable arrests.

nol *adj.* [mid-19C] long. [backsl.]

nola *n.* [1930s+] (*US*) a (passive) homosexual male (cf. ABIGAIL n.). [the female name]

no larking (about) *phr.* (*also* **and no larks**) [1910s+] and no mistake. [SE *no* + LARK v. (2)/LARK n.[1] (2)]

noli me tangere *n.* [17C–19C] (*Scot.*) venereal disease. [Lat. *noli me tangere*, don't touch me]

noll *n.* [mid-18C–mid-19C] (*UK Und.*) a wig. [OE *noll*, the crown of the head]

nolle pros *v.* (*also* **nolle, nolle pross, nolle prosse, nol-pros**) [mid-19C+] (*orig. US*) to abandon a trial because the plaintiff or prosecutor has given up the suit, usu. because there is insufficient hard evidence, a key witness has backed down etc. [legal Lat. *nolle prosequi*, 'to be unwilling to pursue']

no load *n.* [1920s+] (*US*) a lazy, unenthusiastic or pessimistic person. [they 'carry no weight']

no-mark *n.* [1980s+] a nobody, a nonentity. [they make no mark]

no matter how you slice it *phr.* (*also* **whichever way you slice it**) [1930s+] (*US*) however you look at or assess it. [abbr. remark by US politician Al Smith in 1936: 'No matter how thin you slice it, it's still BALONEY n.[1] (1)']

no mercy *phr.* [1910s] (*Aus.*) a phr. written on the back of a pay cheque and handed to a publican when a man wanted to spend his entire season's wages in a single binge. [joc. use SE]

no messing (about) *phr.* [1950s+] without a doubt, absolutely, certainly.

nommus *v. see* NAMMOUS v.

nommus! *excl. see* NAMUS! excl.

no money, no Swiss *phr. see* NO CASH, NO SWISS phr.

no more chance than a cat in hell without claws *phr.* [late 18C–mid-19C; 1930s] absolutely no chance at all.

no more chance than a snowball in hell *phr.* (*also* **no more chance than a baldy, …than a fart in a windstorm, …than an ice-cream cornet in hell**) [late 19C+] absolutely no chance at all (cf. NOT A FART'S CHANCE IN A WHIRLWIND phr.).

no more than ninepence in the shilling *phr.* [late 19C+] referring to one considered a simpleton, a fool. [a shilling (5p) had 12 pence; var. on NOT ALL THERE phr.]

no muss, no fuss *phr.* [1940s+] (*US*) no problems, either practically or emotionally.

non *n.* [1970s+] (*US Black*) a physically uncoordinated person; a poor athlete. [? SE *non-performer*]

no-name *n.* [1990s+] (*US*) an insignificant person; one who has no public 'name'.

no-name (brand) cigarette *n. see* NO-BRAND CIGARETTE n.

no-nation *n.* [20C+] (*W.I.*) a usu. dark-skinned person of more than 2 racial mixtures. [SE *no* + NATION sfx]

no-nation *adj.* [20C+] (*W.I.*) despicable, worthless. [NO-NATION n.]

nonce *n.*[1] **1** [1970s+] a sexual offender, spec. against young children. **2** [1990s+] a general term of (usu.) abuse. [? dial. *nonce*, a good-for-nothing, thus image of a 'nothing', a 'non-person'; the *Police Review* (18 May 1984) suggests origin in NANCY BOY n.]

nonce *n.*[2] [1990s+] *nonsense*, rubbish. [abbr.]

noncey *adj.* [1990s+] stupid, ineffectual, useless. [NONCE n.[1] (2)]

non-com *n.* (*also* **non-comish**) [mid-19C+] a *non-com*missioned officer in the army. [abbr.]

non compos *adj.* **1** [early 17C+] eccentric, crazy; thus *noncompusser*, a crazy person. **2** [18C+] (*also* **non-com**) drunk; ext. as *non compos poo-poo* (cf. ADDLED adj.). **3** [1940s] (*Aus.*) unconscious. [Lat. *non compos mentis*, not of sound mind]

non-con *n.* [late 17C–mid-19C] a religious dissenter, typically a Nonconformist or Presbyterian. [abbr. SE *Nonconformist*]

nondy *adj.* (*also* **nondi**) [1990s+] inferior, second-rate. [SE *nondescript*]

no neck *n.* [1950s+] (*US Black*) a weakling, a coward. [boxing jargon *no neck*, one who cannot take a punch; note NECK n.[2] (1)]

none of your beeswax *phr. see* BEESWAX n.[2] (1).

none of your lip *phr. see* LESS (OF YOUR) LIP phr.

non est *adj.* [mid-19C–1950s] non-existent, absent. [Lat. *non est*, it is not]

nonesuch *n. see* NONSUCH n.

non-event *adj.* [1990s+] (*Aus.*) insignificant, irrelevant. [SE *non-event*, an unimportant event]

nong *n.* (*also* **nong nong**) [1940s+] (*Aus.*) an idiot, a fool, a general derog. description. [Lat. *non compos*; Seal (1999) suggests UK dial. *ning nang*, a fool]

nongy *n.* [1990s+] (*UK juv.*) a condom. [mispron./abbr. of SE *condom*]

non me *n.* [early 19C–1900s] a lie. [the trial of Queen Caroline, in 1820, when the Italian witnesses universally replied to counsel's questions with *No me ricordo*, I do not remember; the phr. became the title of a popular contemporary ballad, presumably spreading the sl.]

nonny no *n.* (*also* **nonny-nonny**) [17C] **1** the vagina; the vulva (cf. ARTICLE n.). **2** sex in general. [SE *nonny no*, the refrain of a song, thus a trifle, a nothing]

no-no *n.* [1940s+] an impossibility, something forbidden. [SE *no* + redup.]

no nothing *n.* [mid-19C+] nothing at all, nothing whatsoever. [rather than cancel itself out, the double-negative emphasizes the phr.]

non-schlock *adj.* [1980s+] (*US campus*) avant-garde. [SE *non* + SCHLOCK adj.]

nonsense *n.* **1** [late 18C–mid-19C] 'melting butter in a wig' (Grose, 1796). **2** [early–mid-19C] money. **3** [1930s+] a fiasco, a farce. [presumably (1) is Grose's own joke def.]

non-skid *n.*[1] [1920s] (*US*) a woman who can hold her drink. [she doesn't 'skid' in the 'wet']

non-skid *n.*[2] [1930s+] a Jew (cf. BILLY THE KID n.). [rhy. sl. = YID n.[1]]

nonsuch *n.* (*also* **nonesuch**) **1** [18C–19C] the vagina (cf. ARTICLE n.). **2** [mid-19C–1900s] as *Mr Nonsuch*, a conceited person. [SE *nonesuch*, an unmatched, unrivalled thing]

non-toucher *n.* [1980s+] (*drugs*) a smoker of crack cocaine who recoils from physical contact while experiencing the drug's effects. [the opposite of a TOUCHER n.[1] (3)]

noodge *n. see* NUDGE n.

noodle *n.*[1] **1** [19C+] the human head. **2** [20C+] intelligence, the mind. [ety. unknown; ? SE *nod* or *noodle*, a fool or var. of NODDLE n.; (2) is fig. use of (1)]

noodle *n.*[2] [1970s+] (*US Black*) the penis. [its resemblance, when flaccid, to a cooked noodle]

noodle *v.*[1] **1** [late 18C] to kiss and cuddle. **2** [1930s+] (*US*) to tune a musical instrument, to warm up or improvize musically. **3** [1960s+] to warm up, to excite. [? SE *doodle*]

noodle *v.*[2] [early 19C] to fool, to trick. [SE *noodle*, a fool]

noodle *v.*[3] [1940s+] (*US*) **1** to think, to brainstorm. **2** usu. constructed as *noodle out/up*, to mull something over, to work something out. [NOODLE n.[1] (2)]

noodle dick *n.* [1990s+] (*US*) a general term of abuse; the overriding image is of impotence, i.e. a penis limp as a cooked noodle (cf. PENCIL DICK n.). [SE *noodle* + DICK n.[4] (1)]

noodlehead *n.* (*also* **noodlebrain**) [1910s+] (*US*) a dull, stupid person. [SE *noodle*, a fool + -HEAD sfx (1)]

noodle juice *n.* [1920s] (*US*) tea. [SE *noodle* + JUICE n.[3] (1)]

noodle soup *n.* [1920s] (*US Und.*) nonsense.

noodle soup drinker *n.* [1900s–30s] (*US*) a Jew (cf. ARAB n.[2]). [racial stereotyping]

noodnik *n. see* NUDNIK n.

noogie *n.* (*also* **nuggie**) [1970s+] (*US*) the act of rubbing one's knuckles hard across one's victim's skull; also used on other parts of the body. [? corruption of SE *knuckle*]

noogie *v.* [1970s+] (*US*) to rub one's knuckles hard across one's victim's skull; also used on other parts of the body (cf. DRY SHAVE v.[2]). [NOOGIE n.]

noogies *n.* **1** [1970s] (*US teen*) nasal mucus. **2** [1980s] (*US*) the testicles. [ety. unknown; (1) ? var. on BOOGIE n.[1]]

no oil painting *n.* [20C+] an unattractive person; thus *oil painting*, a beautiful looking person.

nook *n.* [1910s–30s] a penny. [ety. unknown]

nook and cranny *n.* [1970s] the buttocks (cf. ALA n.). [rhy. sl. = FANNY n.[1] (2)]

nookie *n.* (*also* **nicky-hooky, nook, nookey, nooky, nucky**) **1** [1920s+] (*orig. US*) sexual intercourse. **2** [1930s+] (*orig. US*) (*also* **piece of nookie**) a woman seen as no more than an object of possible seduction. **3** [1960s+] (*orig. US*) (*also* **nooker**) the vagina. **4** [1970s+] (*US gay*) the anus. [? NUG v. or Du. sl. *neuken*, to fuck]

nookie *adj.* [1910s–30s] (*N.Z.*) tiny, little; thus a nickname for a small boy or short person. [? Maori *noke*, small]

nookie bookie *n.* [1940s+] (*US*) a pimp or a madam. [NOOKIE n. (1) + SE *book*, to reserve, to set aside]

nookie house *n.* [1980s] (*US*) a brothel (cf. ACCOMMODATION HOUSE n.). [NOOKIE n. (1) + HOUSE n.[1] (1)]

nooky *n. see* NOOKIE n.

noolucks *n.* (*also* **newlicks**) [mid-19C] an imaginary person. [a nonce-word, ety. unknown]

noom *n.* [mid-19C] the moon. [backsl.]

nooner *n.* **1** [1940s+] a midday alcoholic drink. **2** [1970s+] sexual intercourse, often adulterous, enjoyed around lunchtime. [SE *noon*]

noorse *v. see* NAUSE v.

noose *v.*[1] [early 17C–mid-19C] to marry; often as *noosed* or *noozed*. [fig. and lit. uses of NOOSE n.[2], although chronology cannot be proven; SE *noose*, to secure by a noose predates this; note synon. in James Joyce, *Dubliners* (1914): 'I'm going to have my fling first and see a bit of life and the world before I put my head in the sack']

noose *v.*[2] [late 17C–mid-19C] to hang.

nope *n.* [early 18C–early 19C] a blow to the head. [15C northern dial. *nawp, noup, nope*, a blow; ult. a supposed Scandinavian v. *nawpe*, to strike down]

nope! *excl.* [late 19C+] (*US*) no!

no picnic *n. see* PICNIC n.

no place *n.* [1930s+] (*orig. US*) nowhere.

nopper *n. see* NAPPER n.[2] (2).

noppy *n. see* NAPPY (ALE) n.

no problem *phr.* (*also* **no problemo**) [1960s+] (*orig. US*) don't worry, it's all right.

no probs *phr.* [1970s+] *no problems*. [abbr.]

no rats *n.* [late 19C–1900s] a Scotsman. ['it being supposed that a Scot is always associated with bagpipes, and that no rat can bear the neighbourhood of that musical instrument' (Ware)]

no-rep *n. see* REP n.[1] (1).

Norfolk capon *n. see* YARMOUTH CAPON n.

Norfolk dumpling *n.* **1** [early 17C] a dupe. **2** [mid-17C–19C] (*also* **Norfolk turkey**) a native of Norfolk. **3** [19C] (*Aus.*) a prisoner on Norfolk Island or the act of imprisoning someone there. [(2) the food rather than any particular rotundity of the Norfolk people, although the one can lead to the other; (3) 'Conditions on Norfolk Island [...] were appalling; Norfolk dumplings lie heavy on the stomach – fine 'settlers', as was a term on the Island' (E.P.)]

Norfolk Howard *n.* (*also* **n.h.**) [mid-19C–1900s] a bedbug. [in cruel memoriam, punning on the name of one Joseph (or Joshua) Bug who, in 1862, changed his name to *Norfolk Howard*, despite popular derision at what was seen as affectation. *The Times* came to his aid, publishing a list of other risible/unpleasant names. Among them were 'Asse, Beaste, Belly, Boots, Cripple, Cheese, Clodd, Dunce, Fatt, Frogge, Hagg, Humpe, Jelly, Kneebone, Lazy, Mudd, Honeybum, Piddle, Paswater, Pisse, Pricksmall, Quicklove, Rottengoose, Swette, Sheartlifte, Silly, Spittle, Teate and Vittels']

no risk *phr.* [1920s+] (*Aus.*) **1** no chance (of). **2** no doubt (about).

norks *n.* (*also* **norgies, norgs, norkers**) [1960s+] (*Aus.*) the breasts (cf. BORDENS n.). [the *Norco* Co-operative Ltd, butter manufacturer from New South Wales, featured a cow's udder on its labels]

Nor' Loch trout *n.* [late 18C–early 19C] (*Scot.*) a piece of mutton. [the *Nor' Loch* abattoir]

norm *n.*[1] (*also* **norma**) [1970s] (*US gay*) a heterosexual male. [SE *normal*]

norm *n.*[2] [1970s+] (*Aus.*) a generic term used to describe the average Aus. male, i.e. beer-drinking, television-watching, overweight and inactive. [the character, created by Victoria's Minister for Sport, Brian Dixon, was launched as part of a 'get fit' campaign in 1975]

norm *n.*[3] (*also* **normal**) [1980s+] (*US campus*) a dull, conventional person.

norma *n. see* NORM n.[1]

norma jean nicotine *n.* [1950s–70s] (*camp gay*) a smoker. [real name of Marilyn Monroe, *Norma Jean* Baker (1926–62) + SE *nicotine* + assonance]

normal *n.*[1] [1950s–70s] (*gay*) a heterosexual male. [usu. with ironic overtones]

normal *n.*[2] *see* NORM n.[3]

Normandy Beach *n.* [1980s+] a speech. [rhy. sl.; ult. ref. to D-Day and the Normandy landings on 6 June 1944]

normans *n.* [1960s+] tea, mainly in rock music circles. [*Norman's* café, Leicester, very popular among musicians]

Normanton cocktail *n.* [1950s–60s] (*Aus.*) an Aboriginal woman and 2 blankets. [pun on GIN n.[1] (1)/SE *gin*]

no-roast *n.* [1970s] (*Aus. Und.*) a positive or neutral statement by the police. [SE *no* + ? ROAST v.]

Norski *n.* [20C+] (*US*) a person of Norwegian origin; thus a Scandinavian. [Scandinavian *Norsk*, Norse + -SKI sfx]

Norski *adj.* (*also* **Norsky**) [20C+] Norwegian or other Scandinavian. [NORSKI n.]

north *adj.* [late 17C–19C] clever, cunning; esp. in phr. *he's too far north for me*. [stereotype of northerners, esp. Yorkshiremen, as grasping, cheating and cunning]

north *adv.* [1970s+] (*US*) increasing in value, improving. [the image of going 'upwards']

Northallerton *n.* [late 18C–19C] a spur. [the quality of spurs made in *Northallerton*, Yorks.]

north and south *n.* [mid-19C+] the mouth (cf. EAST AND SOUTH n.). [rhy. sl.]

north and south, the *n.* [1910s–20s] a quick visual inspection, a look up and down.

North Carolina *n. see* AFRICAN n.[2].

north castle *n.* [late 19C–1900s] Holloway prison (cf. HOLLOWAY CASTLE n.). [its position in north London and the 'castellated' architecture of its original gateway]

North Country compliment *n.* [late 19C] a gift that is neither desired by the recipient nor of any value to him or to the donor. [negative stereotyping of the north of England]

North Dakota beefsteak *n.* [1900s] (*US*) bacon.

North Dakota rice *n.* [1940s] (*US milit.*) warm breakfast cereals.

north end of a southbound horse *phr.* (*also* **north end of a southbound mule**) [1960s+] (*US*) a general term of abuse, used joc. as in *you look like the north end...* [play on HORSE'S ASS n.]

northern lights *n.* [1990s+] a variety of marijuana cultivated under artificial conditions for maximum strength. [SE *Northern lights*, the Aurora Borealis]

Northern Territory champagne *n.* [1970s] (*Aus.*) methylated spirits mixed with health salts, which give a fizzy head. [drunk by many Aborigines in the *Northern Territory*]

north or south? *phr.* [1970s+] (*US gay*) a question inquiring whether someone is circumcised or not.

northpaw *n.* [1960s+] (*US*) a right-handed person. [the opposite of SOUTHPAW n. (2); the term is essentially artificial and rarely used]

north pole *n.* [20C+] the anus (cf. BOTTLE AND GLASS n.). [rhy. sl. = ARSEHOLE n. (1)]

North Sea rabbit *n.* [1910s] (*N.Z.*) a herring.

north sydney *n.* [20C+] (*Aus.*) the kidney. [rhy. sl.]

Northumberland arms *n.* (*also* **Lord Northumberland's arms**) [late 17C–early 19C] a black eye. [the red and black spectacle-like badge that is the basis of the Percy, i.e. Lord Northumberland's, arms]

Norway neckcloth *n.* [late 18C–mid-19C] the pillory. [it was often made from Norway fir]

Norwegian *n.* [1950s] (*W.I.*) an albino. [their pale complexion and blond hair]

Norwegian steam *n.* [1940s+] (*US*) manpower. [image of large, muscular Norwegian immigrants]

N.O.R.W.I.C.H. *phr.* [1940s+] (k)*nickers off ready when I come home*; an amorous acronym, usu. found on the back of envelopes of love letters (orig. by soldiers) (cf. B.O.L.T.O.P. phr.). [abbr.]

norwicher *n.* [mid–late 19C] more than one's fair share; esp. one who drinks more than half of a shared tankard before passing it on. [ety. unknown; E.P. suggests stereotyping, as in the rhyme 'Essex stiles, Kentish miles, Norfolk wiles, many men beguiles']

norz *n. see* NAUS n.

no salt in a herring *phr.* [mid–late 19C] no use to anyone.

nose *n.*[1] [late 18C+] a police spy, an informer. **2** [mid-19C+] a detective. [(1) 20C+ use is US prison]

nose *n.*[2] [20C+] a win by a narrow margin, esp. in horseracing.

nose *n.*[3] [1960s+] (*drugs*) heroin or cocaine (cf. BLOW n.[6]). [one can inhale them through the *nose*]

nose *n.*[4] *see* HAVE A DIRTY NOSE v.

nose *v.*[1] [mid-17C–early 18C] to make a fool of, to fool, to dupe, to sneer at. [? SE phr. *lead by the nose*]

nose *v.*[2] (*UK Und.*) **1** [mid-17C+] to pry into someone else's proceedings. **2** [19C] to inform against; esp. in phr. *nose on* and *nose upon*.

nose *v.*[3] **1** [late 18C–early 19C] to bully. **2** [late 19C–1900s] to hit on the nose.

nose *v.*[4] [1910s+] (*US*) to curry favour. [abbr. BROWN-NOSE v.]

nose about *v. see* NOSE AROUND v.

nose and chin *n.* **1** [mid-19C] a penny. **2** [late 19C–1900s] gin. **3** [20C+] a win (on a wager). [rhy. sl.; (1) = WIN n.]

nose around *n.* [1980s+] a search. [NOSE AROUND v.]

nose around *v.* (*also* **nose about**) **1** [mid-19C+] to search, to look over, to survey. **2** [1920s+] to interfere (in). **3** [1970s] to spread rumours, to gossip about. [NOSE v.[2] (1)]

nosebag *n.* **1** [mid-19C–1910s] (*also* **nosebagger**) a day-tripper to the seaside who takes his or her own provisions and thus makes no useful contribution to the local economy; thus *the nosebag crowd* are such holiday-makers as a group. **2** [mid-19C–1910s] a veil. **3** [late 19C] a handbag. **4** [late 19C] a hospitable hotel or lodging-house. **5** [late 19C–1930s] (*Aus.*) a bag in which an itinerant or SWAGMAN n.[2] carries his provisions. **6** [20C+] food, spec. as served in a restaurant. **7** [1910s] a gasmask. **8** [1910s+] a bag of food, a lunch box, a (take-away) meal. [SE *nosebag*; ? (6) f. (8)]

nosebag *v.* [1960s+] (*US*) to eat. [NOSEBAG n. (8)]

nosebaggery *n.* [1920s] (*US*) a restaurant. [PUT ON THE NOSE-BAG v.]

nosebleed *n.* [1950s] an idiot, esp. a weakling. [play on DRIP n.[2]]

nosebleed *adj.* [1970s+] (*US*) of seating, very high up, esp. in an auditorium or sports stadium. [also used fig.; the nosebleeds that can accompany oxygen deprivation]

nose burner *n.* [1960s+] (*drugs*) the butt of a marijuana cigarette.

nose candy *n.* [1920s+] (*orig. US drugs*) **1** cocaine (cf. BLOW n.[6]). **2** heroin. [SE *nose* + *candy*/CANDY n.[4] (2)]

nosecone *n.* [1980s+] (*drugs*) a large cannabis cigarette rolled with a rosebud-shaped twist of paper on the end (cf. BONE n.[11]).

nose cough *n.* [late 19C] stertorous breathing caused by a blocked nose.

nosedive *n.* [1930s+] **1** (*US tramp*) a false show of religious belief or action to gain hand-outs from a religious mission. **2** (*US*) a loss of emotional or mental control. **3** (*orig. US*) a fainting spell or a fall. **4** (*orig. US*) in fig. use, a fall, a rejection.

nosedive *v.* [1930s–70s] (*US tramp*) to make a false show of religious belief or action to gain hand-outs from a religious mission. [NOSEDIVE n. (1)]

nosediver *n.* [1930s–70s] (*US tramp*) a vagrant who frequents charitable missions, looking for hand-outs. [NOSEDIVE v.]

nose 'em *n.* [mid-19C] tobacco. [NOSEY-MY-KNACKER n.]

nose-ender *n. see* NOSER n.[1] (2).

no-see-um *n.* [mid-19C+] (*US*) a tiny biting fly, a midge. [lit. 'no see them']

nose for *v.* [late 19C–1900s] (*US*) to pursue, to hunt down.

nosegay *n.* [1980s] (*UK prison*) tobacco.

nosegent *n.* [mid-16C–early 19C] a nun. [? Fr. *à genou*, kneeling; Ribton-Turner, *A History of Vagrants* (1887), suggests Gaelic *nuas*, 'from on high' + *gean*, a woman]

nose habit *n.* [1960s+] (*drugs*) taking narcotic drugs by sniffing them through the nose rather than by injection. [SE *nose*/NOSE n.[3] + HABIT n. (1)]

nose hit *n.* [1970s] (*drugs*) a puff of a marijuana cigarette taken through the nose rather than the lips. [SE *nose* + HIT n.[3] (5)]

nose job *n.*[1] [1960s–70s] (*US Black*) a sexual obsession with some object of desire. [HAVE ONE'S NOSE OPEN v. + JOB n.[4]]

nose job *n.*[2] [1960s+] a rhinoplasty, cosmetic plastic surgery on one's nose. [SE *nose* + JOB n.[4]]

nose-my *n. see* NOSEY-MY-KNACKER n.

nose paint *n.* [late 19C–1970s] (*US*) alcohol; thus *get one's nose painted*, to get very drunk. [it turns the nose red; note Shakespearian use of *nose-painting* (e.g. *Macbeth* III iii) refers to sexual rather than alcoholic excess]

nose picker *n.* [1940s+] (*US*) **1** a child or person with offensive habits. **2** a rustic, a peasant (cf. ACORN-CRACKER n.).

nose-pinchers *n.* [late 19C] pince-nez. [lit. translation]

nose powder *n.* (*also* **nose stuff**) [1930s+] (*drugs*) heroin, cocaine, morphine (cf. AUNTIE EMMA n.; BIRDIE POWDER n.; BLOW n.[6]). [SE *nose*/NOSE n.[3] + POWDER n.[2]]

noser *n.*[1] **1** [mid–late 19C] a bloody nose. **2** [mid–late 19C] (*also* **nose-ender**) a blow on the nose. [NOSE v.[3] (2)]

noser *n.*[2] [mid-19C+] (*US Und.*) an informer. [NOSE v.[2] (2)]

nose rag *n.* **1** [mid-19C–1950s] a handkerchief. **2** [late 19C] an unpopular person.

noser-my-knacker *n. see* NOSEY-MY-KNACKER n.

nose stuff *n. see* NOSE POWDER n.

nose trouble *n.* [1930s–80s] (*US*) a propensity for interfering. [NOSE v.[2] (1) + SE *trouble*]

nose-up *n.* [2000s] the inhalation of cocaine. [SE *nose*/NOSE n.[3]]

nose upon *v. see* NOSE v.[2] (2).

nose warmer *n.* **1** [late 19C] a short pipe. **2** [1930s] (*US*) consommé in a cup.

nose wipe *n.* [early 19C+] a handkerchief.

nose wipe *v.* [early 17C–mid-18C] to cheat, to deceive.

nose wiper *n.*[1] [mid-19C+] a handkerchief.

nose wiper *n.*[2] [1920s] a toady. [lit. image, but note ASS-WIPER n. (1)]

nosey *n. see* NOSY n.

nosey *adj.* [mid-19C+] inquisitive, esp. when used as a pej. term. [NOSE v.[2] (1)]

nosey bob *n.* [late 19C–1930s] (*Aus.*) **1** a hangman. **2** an inquisitive person, a 'nosey parker'. [(1) R.R. Howard (*c.*1836–1906), the New South Wales hangman *c.*1874–1904; he earned his nickname from a facial disfigurement; (2) + NOSEY adj.]

nosey-my-knacker *n.* (*also* **noser-my-knacker**) [mid–late 19C] tobacco; thus abbr. *nose-my* (cf. BACCA n.). [rhy. sl.]

nosey parker *n.* [20C+] an inquisitive person; thus *nosey-parkering*, inquisitive; *nosey-park*, to be inquisitive; *nosey-parkerdom*, *nosey-parkerism*, *nosey-parkery*, the display of inquisitive behaviour, the exercise of intrusive questioning; *nosey-parkerishness*, a tendency to inquisitiveness. [the *OED* suggests a blend of *nosey* + *parker*, a rabbit; E.P. prefers the peeping Toms and eavesdroppers who frequented the Great Exhibition (1851); Brewer, *Dict. of Phrase and Fable* (15th edn, 1995) suggests the earlier clergyman Matthew Parker (1504–75), archbishop of Canterbury, known for his detailed inquisitions]

nosh *n.* **1** [1910s] a delicatessen. **2** [1940s+] food, esp. a snack. **3** [1990s+] an act of fellatio (cf. BASKET LUNCH n.). [NOSH v.]

nosh *v.* (*also* **knosh, nash**) **1** [1930s+] to eat, esp. to snack, to eat between meals; occas. to drink. **2** [1970s+] to practise oral sex (cf. BASKET LUNCH n.; BOX LUNCH n.). [Yid. *nosh*, to snack and Ger. *naschen*, to nibble, to eat surreptitiously; mainly US but note *The Nosh Bar*, a long-lived delicatessen/café in Great Windmill Street, Soho, London; (2) is a pun on (1)]

nosher *n.* [1960s+] one who snacks or eats between meals. [NOSH v. (1)]

noshery *n.* [1950s+] (*orig. US*) a snack-bar. [NOSH n. (2) + sfx *-ery*, or Yid. *nasherei*, snacks]

no-shit *adj.* [1950s+] (*US*) genuine. [NO SHIT! excl. (2)]

no shit! *excl.* [1930s+] **1** an excl. of (usu.) ironic surprise; you don't say! goodness me! **2** (*also* **no crap!**) an excl. of affirmation, I mean it! this is the truth! [SE *no* + SHIT n.[3] (4)/ CRAP n.[3] (3)]

no shit, Sherlock! *excl.* (*also* **n.s.s.! NS[2]!**) [1970s+] (*orig. US*) ext. of NO SHIT! excl. [*Sherlock* is a pun on HOLMES n., which itself puns on HOMES n.; plus ironic use of the fictional detective *Sherlock* Holmes]

no-shitter *n.* [1970s+] (*US*) an emphatically true statement. [NO-SHIT adj.]

no-show *n.* **1** [1940s+] (*orig. US*) a person who unexpectedly fails to appear. **2** [1950s+] (*US*) a failure to keep an appointment. **3** [1960s+] (*US*) a person who is paid for a non-existent job; thus *no-show job*, token employment.

no show *phr.* [1960s+] (*Aus.*) no hope of success. [NO-SHOW n.]

nosh-up *n.* [1950s+] a feast; a meal. [NOSH n. (2)]

no sir! *excl.* [mid-19C+] an emphatic rejection.

no siree (bob)! [mid-19C+] (*orig. US*) an excl. of absolute denial. [NO SIR! excl. + *-ee* (+ BOB n.[2])]

no skin *phr. see* NO SKIN OFF ONE'S NOSE phr.

no skin off one's ass *phr.* (*also* **no sweat off one's arse**) [1930s+] (*orig. US*) no problem, no worries. [var. on NO SKIN OFF ONE'S NOSE phr.]

no skin off one's balls *phr.* (*also* **no skin off one's dick, no sweat off one's balls**) [1970s+] (*orig. US*) of no importance; thus *not give the sweat off one's balls*, not to care at all.

no skin off one's nose *phr.* (*also* **no hair off one's brows, no skin, no skin off one's back, ...ear, ...elbow, ...hide, ...knuckles, ...teeth**) [20C+] a phr. implying one's contemptuous lack of interest; I don't care, it doesn't bother me.

no slouch *n.* [late 18C+] something or someone good, acceptable, enterprising, energetic.

no-soap *adj.* [1920s] (*US*) hopeless. [NO SOAP phr.]

no soap *phr.* [1920s+] (*orig. US*) nothing doing, not a chance, no hope of that. [SE *no* + SOAP n.[2]; or rhy. sl. *soap* = DOPE n.[3] (1)/SE *hope*]

nosper *n.* [late 19C–1900s] **1** a person. **2** a stranger. [backsl.; (2) f. (1)]

no spiffing *phr.* [1920s] (*US juv.*) for sure, no fooling. [ety. unknown; ? link to SPIFF n.]

nosrap *n.* [mid-19C] a parson. [backsl.]

no stress *phr.* [1990s+] (*US campus*) no problems, don't worry.

no strings *phr.* [20C+] no conditions or obligations.

no stuff *phr.* [1920s–60s] (*US Black*) no fooling, no lies, absolutely honest and sincere. [SE *no* + STUFF n.[1] (3)]

no sweat *phr.* [1950s+] (*orig. US*) no problem, don't worry, it's all right. [i.e. there is no need to make an effort that might produce sweat]

no sweat off one's arse *phr. see* NO SKIN OFF ONE'S ASS phr.

no sweat off one's balls *phr. see* NO SKIN OFF ONE'S BALLS phr.

nosy *n.* (*also* **nosey**) [1930s+] an inquisitive person. [NOSEY adj.]

not! *excl.* [late 19C+] (*orig. US*) used at the end of a declaratory sentence to reverse everything that has gone before, e.g. *the Home Secretary is a liberal, tolerant and sophisticated person – not!* [coined at Princeton University in the 1890s, internationally popularized via the film *Wayne's World* (1992)]

not a bean *phr.* [20C+] nothing at all, esp. of money. [SE *not* + BEAN n.[1]]

not a bit of it! *excl.* [mid-19C+] no! you're absolutely wrong!

not able to hit the ground with his hat *phr.* [20C+] (*US*) **1** used of a complete incompetent. **2** used of one who is extremely drunk.

not about *prep.* [1950s+] (*orig. US*) not intending (to do something).

not a brass razoo *phr.* [1930s+] (*Aus./N.Z.*) nothing at all, esp. of money, i.e. absolutely penniless. [SE *not* + *brass* + RAZOO n.[1]]

not a fart's chance in a whirlwind *phr.* [2000s] no chance at all (cf. NO MORE CHANCE THAN A SNOWBALL IN HELL phr.).

not a feather to fly with *phr.* [mid-19C–1900s] ruined, penniless. [orig. university use, where to be *plucked* was to have failed one's examinations]

not a full quid *phr. see* NOT THE FULL QUID phr.

no talent *n.* [1960s+] (*US*) a useless person.

not all it's cracked up to be *phr.* [early 19C+] well below expectations. [SE *not* + CRACK UP v.[1]]

not all there *phr.* (*also* **not quite there**) **1** [mid-19C+] eccentric, insane, crazy. **2** [1930s] drunk (cf. ADDLED adj.). [the root phr. of many synons., all commenting adversely on the subject's intelligence, e.g. BUTTON SHORT, A phr.; COUPLE OF CHIPS SHORT OF A FISH DINNER, A phr.; COUPLE OF TINNIES SHORT OF A SLAB, A phr.; FEW BOB SHORT OF THE POUND, A phr.; FEW PENCE SHORT IN THE

SHILLING, A phr.; FEW SNAGS SHORT OF A BARBIE, A phr.; FULL QUID n.; LIFT DOESN'T REACH THE TOP FLOOR phr.; LOST A BUTTON phr.; NINEPENCE SHORT OF A SHILLING phr.; NO MORE THAN NINEPENCE IN THE SHILLING phr.; NOT PLAYING WITH A FULL DECK phr.; NOT THE FULL CUP OF TEA phr.; NOT THE FULL DOLLAR phr.; ONE BRICK SHORT OF A LOAD phr.; ONE SANDWICH SHORT OF THE PICNIC phr.; ONE SAUSAGE SHORT OF A B.B.Q. phr.; ONLY ONE AND NINEPENCE IN THE FLORIN phr.; ROW WITH ONE OAR (IN THE WATER) v.; SHINGLE SHORT, A phr.; TENPENCE TO THE SHILLING phr.; TWO PENCE SHORT OF A BOB phr.; TWO TACOS SHORT OF A COMBINATION PLATE phr.]

not a man jack n. see EVERY MAN JACK n.

not an earthly phr. see NO EARTHLY phr.

not a patch on phr. [mid-19C+] impossible to compare with, nowhere near.

not a pretty sight phr. [1920s+] used, ironically, of something that is actually very unpleasant to see.

not a sausage phr. [1930s+] absolutely nothing, a derisory amount. [SAUSAGE AND MASH n. (1)]

not a shit show phr. [1980s+] (N.Z.) no chance.

not a sixpence to scratch one's arse with phr. [mid-19C+] absolutely impoverished.

not a sou phr. (also **not a sous/souse**) [mid-18C–1900s] not a penny, nothing at all. [Fr. sou, a coin of very low value (1/20th of a livre, later 5 centimes), generally translated as 'a penny']

not a touch to phr. see NO TOUCH TO phr.

not a word of the pudding phr. [late 17C–early 18C] keep quiet about it, say absolutely nothing about it. [? simply the idea of not revealing the 'surprise' of the final course]

not bad phr. (also **not half bad**, **not half so bad**, **not so bad**) [late 18C+] not as bad as might have been feared, quite good.

not bad! excl. [mid-19C+] (US) good! excellent! [NOT BAD phr.]

not bat an eye(lid) v. [20C+] (orig. US) to show no emotion, to remain imperturbable.

not be able to hit a bull in the ass v. [20C+] (US) to be clumsy or inept, esp. to be a poor marksman; often ext., e.g. ...with a banjo, ...with a bass fiddle, ...with a handful of peas, ...with a handful of tapioca, ...with a shovel.

not be as stupid as one looks v. [20C+] to possess more intelligence than one has been given credit for.

not bloody likely! excl. [1910s+] an emphatic negative. [NOT LIKELY phr. + BLOODY adj.[1] (1); popularized by George Bernard Shaw's Pygmalion (1913), in which the Cockney flowergirl Eliza Doolittle shocked audiences with the then taboo excl.]

not born yesterday phr. (also **not born on Sunday**, **not born the day before yesterday**, **not come down in yesterday's rain**) [mid-19C+] aware, sophisticated, 'on the ball'.

not by a considerable/damn/darm/darned/durn sight phr. see BY A LONG SIGHT phr.

not by a long chalk phr. see BY A LONG CHALK phr.

not by a long jump phr. [late 19C–1920s] not by a very long distance.

not by a long shot phr. see BY A LONG SHOT phr.

not by a long sight phr. see BY A LONG SIGHT phr.

not by chalks phr. see BY CHALKS phr.

not care a bugger v. see NOT GIVE A BUGGER v.

not care a damn v. see NOT GIVE A DAMN v.

not care a fart v. (also **not care a fartful**, **...fart in a whirlwind**, **...good fart**, **...tuppenny fart**, **not give a fart**) [mid-17C+] to not care at all. [SE not care + FART n. (1)]

not care a fiddler's curse v. see NOT CARE A TINKER'S (CURSE) v.

not care a fiddler's fuck v. see NOT GIVE A FIDDLER'S FUCK v.

not care a fouter v. (also **not care a footer**, **not give a footer/fouter**) [early 17C–19C] to not care at all. [Fr. sl. foutre, to FUCK v.[1]]

not care a fuck v. see NOT GIVE A FUCK v.

not care a good fart v. see NOT CARE A FART v.

not care a hang v. (also **not care a twopenny hang**, **not give a hang**) [late 19C+] to not care at all. [HANG n.[1]]

not care a hoot v. see NOT GIVE A HOOT v.

not care a rap (for) v. (also **not give a rap (for)**) [mid-19C+] to not care at all. [RAP n.[1] (2)]

not care a tinker's (curse) v. (also **...cuss**, **...damn**, **...darn**, **...fart**, **...fiddler's damn**, **not give a...**) [mid-18C+] to not care at all. [the lack of importance one gives a curse thrown over the shoulder of a departing tinker who has been unable to sell anything or find work; note letter 8 February 1999 from Mr George Shaw: 'I learnt my trade as a Tinker and Plumber, and I used a tinkers cuss many, many times. When the copper kettle was heated on the open fire, the fire would burn a hole in the bend at the bottom of the spout. The tinker would take a piece of bread and ram it into the spout blocking up the hole. He would then proceed to solder a patch onto the hole. The bread would dam up the hole, hence a tinker's cuss. This was also a way the plumber would use to soak up the water in the lead pipe (if there was a small seepage of water) whilst he wiped a joint. On both occasions, once the jobs were finished, the water would wash out the bread'; the OED, however, dismisses a similar ety. for tinker's dam(n) as 'ingenious but baseless']

not care a toss v. see NOT GIVE A TOSS v.

not care a tuppenny fart v. see NOT CARE A FART v.

not care a tuppenny hang v. see NOT CARE A HANG v.

not care two shits v. see NOT GIVE A SHIT v.

notch n.[1] **1** [17C–19C] the vagina (cf. AGREEABLE RUTS OF LIFE n.). **2** [1920s+] (US) a prostitute or sexually promiscuous woman (cf. BANGTAIL n.[1]).

notch n.[2] [1990s+] (W.I./UK Black teen) a high- or top-ranking villain. [TOPNOTCH adj.]

notch house n. (also **notch joint**) [1920s–60s] (US) a brothel (cf. ACCOMMODATION HOUSE n.). [NOTCH n.[1] (2) + HOUSE n.[1] (1)/ JOINT n.[4] (3)]

notch moll n. (also **notch girl**) [1920s–40s] (US Und.) a prostitute (cf. BANGTAIL n.[1]). [NOTCH n.[1] (2) + MOLL n.[1] (2)]

not come down in yesterday's rain phr. see NOT BORN YESTERDAY phr.

note n.[1] **1** [mid-19C+] (orig. Aus.) a £1 note; usu. in pl. (cf. BANK-RAG n.). **2** [1970s+] (US) a cash payment; thus **bad notes**, a bribe.

note n.[2] [late 19C–1940s] (US) a joke. [? it 'strikes a chord' in the hearer]

no-tell hotel n. (also **no-tell motel**) [1950s+] (US) a cheap hotel which rents out its rooms by the hour to prostitutes and their clients or to illicit lovers. [the discretion of the staff]

not enough sense to pour piss out of a boot phr. [20C+] (US) a phr. used of one who is very stupid (cf. CAN'T SEE THROUGH A LADDER phr.).

notergal wash n. [late 19C] no wash at all. [? Nightingale wash, 'Miss [Florence] Nightingale [...] had the misfortune to incur the lower public satire for stating that a person could keep himself clean on a pint of washing water per day' (Ware)]

note shaver n. [early 19C–1920s] (US) a promoter of bogus financial companies, a usurer. [SHAVE A NOTE v.]

not even phr. [1980s+] (US campus) not at all, in no way.

not fit to shovel shit phr. [1940s+] of a person, absolutely worthless or incompetent.

not for all the tea in China phr. [late 19C+] (orig. Aus.) on no account, no chance whatsoever; occas. in positive use.

not for Joe phr. (also **not for Joseph**) [mid-19C–1920s] by no means, not on any account. [ety. unknown; ? anecdotal]

not fucking likely! excl. [20C+] an emphatic negative. [NOT LIKELY phr. + FUCKING adj. (4)]

not get any change out of v. (also **get no change out of**, **not get much change out of**) [mid-19C+] to get no return result or satisfaction from; to fail to get the better of (someone). [SE *not get* + CHANGE n.[1]]

not get any forrarder *v. see* GET NO FORRARDER *v.*

not get anywhere *v. see* GET NOWHERE (WITH) *v.*

not get much change out of *v. see* NOT GET ANY CHANGE OUT OF *v.*

not give a black damn *v. see* NOT GIVE A DAMN *v.*

not give a bugger *v.* (*also* **not care a bugger, not give two buggers**) [1920s+] to not care at all. [SE *not give* + BUGGER n.[3]]

not give a crap *v. see* NOT GIVE A SHIT *v.*

not give a damn *v.* (*also* **not care a damn, not give a black damn, ...a D, ...a dam, ...a darn, ...a dern, ...a domn, ...a drat, ...a durn, ...a twopenny damn**) [late 18C+] to not care at all. [DAMN n.]

not give a diddley *v. see* DIDDLEY n. (3).

not give a fart *v. see* NOT CARE A FART *v.*

not give a fiddler's fuck *v.* (*also* **not care a fiddler's fuck, not give a fiddler's screw in hell, ...a flying fiddler's mickey**) [1930s+] (*orig. US*) to not care at all. [SE *not give* + FIDDLER'S FUCK n.]

not give a footer/fouter *v. see* NOT CARE A FOUTER *v.*

not give a fuck *v.* (*also* **not care a fuck, not give a flying fuck, ...a good fuck, ...a monkey's, ...a monkey's fuck, ...a motherfuck, ...a ratfuck, ...a rat's fuck, ...a red fuck, ...a royal fuck, ...two fucks**) [1910s+] (*orig. US*) to not care at all. [note, however, one-time late 18C use in a poem 'The Discontented Student'; the word is not spelt out, but the rhyme and the context ensure that the absentee can only be 'fuck']

not give a goddam *v.* (*also* **not give a good damn, ...good doggone, ...good goddam, ...good goddurn, ...greased goddam**) [1920s+] to not care in the slightest. [SE *not give* + GOD-DAMN n.[1]]

not give a hang *v. see* NOT CARE A HANG *v.*

not give a hoot *v.* (*also* **not care a hoot, not give a hoot in hell, ...two hoots**) [late 19C+] to not care at all. [HOOT n.[3] (1)]

not give a living shit *v. see* NOT GIVE A SHIT *v.*

not give a monkey's (fuck)/motherfuck *v. see* NOT GIVE A FUCK *v.*

not give a rap (for) *v. see* NOT CARE A RAP (FOR) *v.*

not give a ratfuck *v. see* NOT GIVE A FUCK *v.*

not give a rat's arse *v.* (*also* **not give a rat's ass**) [1950s+] to not care at all.

not give a rat's fuck/red fuck/royal fuck *v. see* NOT GIVE A FUCK *v.*

not give a rotten apple *v. see* NOT GIVE ROTTEN APPLES *v.*

not give a shit *v.* (*also* **not care two shits, not give a crap, ...a living shit, ...a shite, ...a tin shit, ...two shits**) [1910s+] to not care at all. [SE *not give* + SHIT n.[3] (3)/CRAP n.[5] (1)]

not give a stuff *v.* [1960s+] to not care whatsoever. [STUFF v.[1] (2), i.e. euph. for NOT GIVE A FUCK v.]

not give a tinker's (curse) *v. see* NOT CARE A TINKER'S (CURSE) *v.*

not give a toss *v.* (*also* **not care a toss**) [late 19C+] to not care one way or another. [the random outcome of tossing a coin, although later 20C+ use often equates *toss* with TOSS n.[1] (1), i.e. masturbation]

not give a twopenny damn *v. see* NOT GIVE A DAMN *v.*

not give much away *v.* [late 19C+] to be cautious, to yield few or no advantages.

not give rotten apples *v.* (*also* **not give a rotten apple**) [1950s] (*US*) to not care at all.

not give someone the steam off one's turds *v.* [1970s+] to be very mean.

not give someone the steam on one's piss *v.* [2000s+] to hold in absolute contempt.

not give two buggers *v. see* NOT GIVE A BUGGER *v.*

not give two fucks *v. see* NOT GIVE A FUCK *v.*

not give two hoots *v. see* NOT GIVE A HOOT *v.*

not give two shits *v. see* NOT GIVE A SHIT *v.*

not go much on *v.* [20C+] to not be very keen on.

not go three rounds with a revolving door *phr.* [1960s–70s] very stupid (cf. CAN'T SEE THROUGH A LADDER phr.). [i.e. SLOW adj. (3); pun on SE boxing *round*]

not half *phr.* [early 19C+] a mild intensifier, e.g. *she hadn't half made a mess.* [i.e. a whole, a complete; earlier use is lit., i.e. not enough]

not half! *excl.* [mid-19C+] certainly! really! absolutely! [NOT HALF phr.]

not half a one *phr.* [20C+] a card, a character; usu. in phr. *you ain't half a one!* [NOT HALF phr. + ONE n.[5]]

not half (so) bad *phr. see* NOT BAD phr.

no thanks! *excl.* [late 19C–1920s] don't think you can fool or trick me!

not have a bolter's chance *phr. see* BOLTER'S CHANCE n.

not have a clue *v. see* CLUE n.[2].

not have all one's buttons *v.* [mid-19C+] to lack intelligence, to be slightly eccentric or odd.

not have a pot to piss in (or a window to throw it out of) *v.* (*also* **not have a pot to pee in, without a pot to pee in, without a pot to piss in**) (*orig. US*) **1** [1930s+] to be very poor. **2** [1980s+] to be completely destroyed. [SE *not have a pot* + PISS v.[1] (1)/PEE v.[1] (1)]

not have both oars in the water *v. see* ROW WITH ONE OAR (IN THE WATER) *v.*

not having any *phr.* (*also* **not taking any**) [20C+] wanting no part in something, rejecting a suggestion or an overture of friendship, refusing to tolerate a situation.

nothin'-ass bitch *n.* [1970s] (*US Black*) a prostitute who will not work or who will not hand over the money earned to her pimp.

nothing *adj.* [1950s+] (*orig. US*) insipid, dull, boring, insignificant.

nothing! *excl.* [late 19C+] (*orig. US*) a dismissive excl., no way! you're lying! e.g. *'It just slipped out.' 'Slipped, nothing! You couldn't resist telling...'*

nothing but *adj.* [19C+] exactly, none other than.

nothing doing *phr.* (*also* **nothing stirrin'**) [early 19C+] absolutely not, not a hope, not a chance.

nothing like leather *phr. see* LEATHER n.[2] (3).

nothing shaking *phr.* [1950s+] (*US*) used as a response to the greeting WHAT'S SHAKING? phr. and meaning things are normal.

nothing stirrin' *phr. see* NOTHING DOING phr.

nothing to the bear but his curly hair *phr.* [1930s–40s] (*US Black*) a phr. implying that a noisy, bragging aggressive person is in fact all show and cowardice.

notice box *n.* [1990s+] (*Irish*) one who is keen to attract attention; thus *Miss Notice Box*, a 'forward' woman.

notice to quit *n.* [early–mid-19C] an intimation of one's imminent death. [Egan (1821): 'A cant phrase, applied to any individual who appears to be in a state fast approaching towards dissolution']

no Tich! *excl.* [mid-19C–1900s] (*UK society*) don't be dull! that's boring! [the near-inevitability, at a certain time, of dinner-table conversations centred on the *Tichborne Claimant* case, in which Arthur Orton (1834–98) claimed in 1866 to be Roger Charles Tichborne (1829–54), the heir to an English baronetcy, who was lost at sea. Orton was finally discredited and imprisoned in 1874]

not in it *phr.* [late 19C+] (*orig. sporting*) lacking any chance, an absolute failure. [IN IT phr. (3), i.e. fig. *not in* the contest]

not in the charlie *phr. see* CHARLIE CHASE n.

not in the race *phr.* [1990s+] (*Aus.*) very stupid (cf. CAN'T SEE THROUGH A LADDER phr.).

not in the same street with *phr.* (*also* **not in the same compartment with, ...same town with**) [late 19C+] utterly unequal to, not to be compared with.

not in these boots *phr.* [late 19C] certainly not, not a chance, you must be joking.

not in these trousers *phr.* [1920s–50s] absolutely not, under no circumstances.

notion *n.* [late 19C+] (*Irish*) amorous inclinations; usu. in phr. *have a notion of*, to be sexually attracted by. [SE *notion*, an inclination, disposition or desire]

not just a pretty face *phr.* [1950s+] **1** used of a person (orig. a woman) who wishes to assert their abilities over their attractiveness. **2** used ironically of anyone who has done something worthy of praise.

not know a sparrow's shit (about) *v.* [1970s] to know nothing whatsoever.

not know if one's arsehole is bored or punched *v.* [1920s+] to be an absolute fool. [? engineering use; ARSEHOLE n. (1)]

not know if one's arse was on fire *v.* [1940s+] (*orig. N.Z.*) to be very stupid (cf. CAN'T SEE THROUGH A LADDER phr.). [ARSE n.¹ (1)]

not know one's arse from a hole in the ground *v.* (*also* **not know one's ass from a hole in the ground**) [1930s+] to be particularly stupid (cf. CAN'T SEE THROUGH A LADDER phr.). [ARSE n.¹ (1)]

not know one's arse from one's elbow *v.* (*also* **not know one's ass from one's elbow**) [late 19C+] to be ignorant, to be stupid (cf. CAN'T SEE THROUGH A LADDER phr.). [ARSE n.¹ (1)/ASS n. (2)]

not know one's butt from a gourd *v.* (*also* **not know one's butt from a bear's ass**) [1940s+] (*US*) to be very stupid (cf. CAN'T SEE THROUGH A LADDER phr.). [BUTT n.¹ (2)]

not know shit from apple butter *v.* (*also* **not know shit from beans, …clay, …salami, …tunafish**) [1940s+] **1** to have no idea about a topic. **2** to be particularly wrong in an opinion.

not know shit from Shinola *v.* [1940s+] (*US*) **1** (*also* **not know shit from shine**) to have no idea about a topic; thus *not say shit about Shinola*, to say nothing. **2** to be particularly wrong in an opinion. [SHIT n.¹ (1) + *Shinola*, a black shoe-polish; orig. 'doesn't know shit from shinola and thinks they are both fat meat']

not know someone from *v.* to proclaim one's ignorance of a person or their face, in var. combs.; thus [late 19C] *not know someone from four and sixpence*; [1940s–50s] (*US*) *not know someone from a load of coal*.

not know where one's arse hangs *v.* [20C+] to show complete indecision or bewilderment, to be a fool. [fig. use of ARSE n.¹ (1)]

not know whether to shit or go blind *v.* (*also* **not know whether to pee or go blind, …shit or buy gas**) [1950s+] (*US*) to be utterly stupid, to be totally confused (cf. CAN'T SEE THROUGH A LADDER phr.).

not likely *phr.* [late 19C+] a phr. implying absolute reluctance, 'in no way will I do that'; usu. NOT BLOODY LIKELY! excl. or NOT FUCKING LIKELY! excl.

not make head nor tail *v.* (*also* **not make head or tail**) [early 18C+] to fail to understand, to find incomprehensible.

not make it a federal case *v.* (*also* **not make a federal case out of it**) [1940s+] (*orig. US*) to not make a minor problem into a major one. [the greater importance of federal over state prosecutions]

not much *phr.* **1** [mid-19C–1900s] far from it, 'not likely'. **2** [late 19C+] in ironic use, very much, very likely.

not much bottle *phr. see* NO BOTTLE phr.² (1).

not much chop *phr. see* NO CHOP phr.

not much cop *phr. see* NO COP phr.

not much frocks *n.* [late 19C–1900s] socks. [rhy. sl.]

not my cup of tea *phr. see* CUP OF TEA n. (3).

not nominated *phr.* [1930s+] (*Aus.*) without any chance of success. [horseracing jargon]

not on *adj.* [1930s+] socially unacceptable, impossible. [billiards use, of shots that are 'not on' the table; ? also milit. use, when a proposed operation was 'not on' through unforeseen circumstances]

not one's height *phr. see* HEIGHT n.

not one's scene *phr.* [1960s+] (*orig. US*) **1** an unpleasant or unacceptable situation. **2** anything not to one's taste. [SE *not* + SCENE n. (5)]

not one's speed *phr. see* SPEED n.¹ (1).

not on your arse *phr.* (*also* **not on your ass**) [1960s+] no way at all, on no account.

not on your bird *phr. see* BIRD n.⁸ (1).

not on your crack *phr.* [1920s] (*US Black/W.I.*) in no way at all.

not on your life *phr.* (*also* **not on your life insurance, not on your's, not on your sweet life**) [late 19C+] no way at all, totally impossible.

not on your nannie *phr.* (*also* **not on your nanny**) [1950s+] (*Anglo-Irish*) no chance, not a hope. [? var. on NOT ON YOUR NELLIE phr.]

not on your natural *phr.* [20C+] absolutely not. [abbr. SE *natural life*, thus var. on NOT ON YOUR LIFE phr.]

not on your nellie *phr.* (*also* **not on your nelly**) [1940s+] not a chance, absolutely impossible. [rhy. sl.; *not on your Nellie Duff* = PUFF n.¹ (3); thus var. on NOT ON YOUR LIFE phr.]

not on your's/on your sweet life *phr. see* NOT ON YOUR LIFE phr.

not on your tintype *phr.* [late 19C+] (*orig. US*) a general term of derision and dismissal. [SE *tintype*, an old-fashioned type of photograph, i.e. a 'life portrait'; thus var. on NOT ON YOUR LIFE phr.]

no touch to *phr.* (*also* **not a touch to**) [mid-19C] (*US*) unable to approach, nowhere near.

not out *phr.* [1910s+] still alive; usu. in comb. with a person's age, e.g. *99 (and) not out*. [cricket imagery]

not pick one's teeth *v.* (*also* **unpick one's teeth**) [20C+] (*W.I.*) to make no comment, to stay absolutely silent, to say nothing.

not playing with a full deck *phr.* (*also* **only fifty cards in one's deck**) [1920s+] (*orig. US*) not very intelligent, slightly eccentric, odd; thus PLAYING WITH A FULL DECK phr. [var. on NOT ALL THERE phr.]

not plump currant *phr.* [late 18C–early 19C] out of sorts. [a plump currant would be fig. 'happy']

not put it past someone *v.* [mid-19C+] to expect or assume something (usu. negative) to be within the capabilities of someone, e.g. *I wouldn't put it past the Home Secretary to bring back hanging*.

not Pygmalion likely! *excl.* [1910s+] a euph. for NOT BLOODY LIKELY! excl. [*see* ety. there]

not quite *adj.* [1920s+] (*Aus.*) mentally deficient, i.e. 'not quite (all) there'. [abbr. NOT QUITE THERE phr.]

not quite (quite) *phr. see* QUITE (QUITE) adj.

not quite the full pound/quid/shilling *phr. see* NOT THE FULL QUID phr.

not quite there *phr. see* NOT ALL THERE phr.

not ready *adj.* [1960s+] (*US/W.I.*) naïve, unaware.

not ready for people *phr.* [1970s+] (*US Black*) used of one who acts stupidly or childishly.

not real *adj. see* UNREAL adj.

not say shit about Shinola *v. see* NOT KNOW SHIT FROM SHINOLA v. (1).

not say turkey *v.* (*also* **not say pea-turkey**) [mid-19C–1900s] (*US*) to say nothing, to stay silent.

not seem to *v.* [late 19C+] to be unable to manage, e.g. *I just can't seem to get on with my work.*

not since Julius Caesar was a pup *phr.* [late 19C–1920s] for a very long time. [proper name *Julius Caesar* + PUP n.[1] (1)]

not so bad *phr. see* NOT BAD phr.

not so cold *phr.* [late 19C] (*US*) rather good.

not so dumb *phr.* [1950s+] not as stupid as one might appear. [SE *not* + DUMB adj.]

not so dusty *phr.* [mid-19C+] surprisingly good, not as bad as expected or advertised. [SE *not* + DUSTY adj.[1] (2)]

not so hot *phr.* [1920s+] (*orig. US*) a general negative phr., not very good, unattractive, displeasing etc. [SE *not* + HOT adj.[4] (1)]

not so much (of your) lip *phr. see* LESS (OF YOUR) LIP phr.

not stand a bar of *v.* [1930s+] (*Aus.*) to detest, to reject, to be intolerant of.

not taking any *phr. see* NOT HAVING ANY phr.

not the full cup of tea *phr.* (*also* **not the full bottle**) [1980s+] not very intelligent, slightly eccentric, odd. [synon. for NOT ALL THERE phr.]

not the full dollar *phr.* [1970s+] (*Aus.*) not very intelligent, slightly eccentric, odd. [var. on NOT ALL THERE phr.]

not the full quid *phr.* (*also* **not a full quid, not quite the full pound/quid/shilling, not the full pound/shilling**) [1930s+] eccentric, insane. [FULL QUID n.]

not the full two bob *phr.* [1960s–70s] not up to standards, not as promised or advertised.

not the half of it *phr.* [1910s+] a phr. implying that there is much more to come or to be recounted.

not the l.b.w. *phr. see* LEG BEFORE WICKET n.

not the length of a street *phr.* [late 19C] by no great distance, not very far.

not the only fish in the sea *phr.* (*also* **plenty more fish in the sea**) [20C+] used of someone who, whatever they may believe, is not unique (esp. in the context of love affairs).

not the only onion in the stew *phr.* (*also* **not the only onion in the hash/soup**) [20C+] not alone, not the only person who is equally qualified. [not, as *OED* claims, only in P.G. Wodehouse]

not the only pebble on the beach *phr.* [late 19C+] used of someone who, whatever they may believe, is not unique (esp. in the context of love affairs).

not the only silver fish in the pond *phr.* [1910s] (*Aus.*) used of someone who, whatever they may believe, is not unique (esp. in the context of love affairs).

not there *phr.* [1960s] (*US Black*) boring.

not the ticket *phr.* [20C+] physically or more usu. mentally 'below par'. [SE *not* + TICKET n.[3] (2)]

nottie *n.* [1990s+] one who sees themselves as more attractive or sexier than they really are. [pun on SE *not* + HOTTIE n.[2]]

not to be sneezed at *phr.* (*also* **not to be grinned at**) [early 19C+] not to be spurned, not to be overlooked.

not today, baker *phr.* [late 19C] a phr. used to reject unwelcome advances. [the note left to tell the *baker*, in the days of daily deliveries, that one did not need bread]

not tonight, Josephine *phr.* [late 19C+] a general term of refusal, esp. of sex. [allegedly first pleaded by the Emperor Napoleon to his wife *Josephine*]

not to worry! *excl.* [1930s+] do not worry! [abbr. of 'You are not to worry']

nottub *n.* [late 19C–1900s] a button. [backsl.]

not up *adj.* [20C+] (*Aus.*) second-rate. [abbr. *not up to standard*]

not want to know *v.* [1940s+] to refuse to acknowledge some unpalatable fact or piece of information.

not while pussy's a cat *phr.* [20C+] (*Ulster*) never.

not worth a bucket of warm spit *phr.* [1930s+] (*US*) worthless.

not worth a bumper *phr.* [1940s+] (*Aus.*) worthless, useless. [SE *not worth* + BUMPER n.[3]]

not worth a button *phr.* [mid-17C–19C] worthless, useless.

not worth a cent *phr.* (*also* **not worth a red cent, ...two cents**) [19C+] (*US*) worthless, useless.

not worth a cobbler's curse *phr. see* NOT WORTH A CURSE phr.

not worth a continental damn *phr. see* NOT WORTH A DAMN phr.

not worth a crumpet *phr.* [1940s+] (*Aus.*) worthless, useless.

not worth a curse *phr.* (*also* **not worth a cobbler's curse, ...a cuss, ...a fiddler's curse, ...a tinker's curse, ...a tinker's dam, ...a tinker's damn**) [mid-14C; mid-19C+] worthless, useless. [for ety. *see* NOT CARE A TINKER'S (CURSE) v.]

not worth a damn *phr.* (*also* **not worth a continental damn, ...a D, ...a dam, ...a darn, ...a twopenny dam, ...a twopenny damn**) **1** [mid-19C+] (*orig. US*) a negative phr. used to imply uselessness or incompetence, e.g. *He can't fight worth a damn.* **2** [1980s+] as an intensifier. [DAMN n./D n.[1]/DARN n.]

not worth a fart *phr.* (*also* **not worth a fart in a breeze, ...a fart in a gale, ...a fart in a hurricane, ...a fart in a storm, ...a roasted fart, worse than a (two-bob) fart in a bottle**) [late 17C+] worthless, useless. [FART n. (1)]

not worth a fiddler's curse *phr. see* NOT WORTH A CURSE phr.

not worth a fuck *phr.* [20C+] absolutely worthless. [FUCK n.[4] (1)]

not worth a good goddam *phr.* (*also* **not worth a good damn, ...a good gosh-damn**) [1910s+] (*US*) absolutely worthless. [GOD-DAMN n.[1]]

not worth a pinch of coonshit *phr.* (*also* **not worth a pinch, ...a pinch of shit**) [20C+] (*Can.*) worthless, useless. [SHIT n.[1] (1)]

not worth a pisshole in the snow *phr.* [1960s+] worthless, useless.

not worth a plugged nickel *phr.* (*also* **not worth a plugged dime, ...a plug nickel**) [1910s+] (*US*) valueless.

not worth a pound of piss *phr.* [1960s] (*US*) utterly worthless, despicable.

not worth a rap *phr.* [19C–1900s] worthless, useless. [RAP n.[1] (2)]

not worth a red cent *phr. see* NOT WORTH A CENT phr.

not worth a roasted fart *phr. see* NOT WORTH A FART phr.

not worth a shit *phr.* (*also* **not worth two shits**) [1920s+] worthless, useless. [SHIT n.[3] (3)]

not worth a tiger tank *phr.* [1970s+] worthless, useless. [rhy. sl. = NOT WORTH A WANK phr.; ult. the advertising slogan for Esso petrol *put a tiger in your tank*, thus oblique link to PUT LEAD IN ONE'S PENCIL v.]

not worth a tinker's curse/dam/damn *phr. see* NOT WORTH A CURSE phr.

not worth a turd *phr.* [late 15C+] worthless, useless. [TURD n. (1)]

not worth a (two-bob) fart in a bottle *phr. see* NOT WORTH A FART phr.

not worth a twopenny dam/damn *n. see* NOT WORTH A DAMN phr.

not worth a wank *phr.* [1970s+] worthless, useless. [WANK n.[1] (1)]

not worth diddley-shit *phr.* (*also* **not worth diddly-shit, ...doodley-shit, ...doodly-shit**) [1960s+] (*US*) worthless, useless. [DIDDLEY-SHIT n.]

not worth dogshit *phr.* [1960s+] worthless, useless.

not worth two cents *phr. see* NOT WORTH A CENT phr.

not worth two shits *phr. see* NOT WORTH A SHIT phr.

not wrapped too tight *phr.* [1960s+] (*US*) **1** unstable, eccentric. **2** unsophisticated. [the image is of a parcel 'coming apart at the seams']

'nough said *phr. see* NUFF CED phr.

nought and carry one *n.* [20C+] (*Irish*) a lame person. [var. on DOT AND CARRY ONE n.]

noughts and crosses *n.* [1950s–60s] (*UK Und.*) criss-crossing slashes with a razor.

nouns! *excl. see* CAT'S NOUNS! excl.

nous *n.* (*also* **nouse**) [18C–19C] instinct or common sense, as opposed to actual learning. [20C+ use is SE; Gk *nous*, knowledge, perception]

nous *v.* [mid-19C] to understand or learn. [NOUS n.]

nous-box *n.* [early 19C] the head. [NOUS n. + SE *box*; on model of BRAINBOX n.¹ (1)]

nouse *n. see* NOUS n.

no-user *n.* [1980s+] (*Irish*) a failure, a 'loser'. [SE *no use* + sfx *-er*]

no van dyke *n.* [20C+] an unattractive person. [the Flemish portraitist Sir Anthony *Van Dyck* (1599–1641); note NO OIL PAINTING n.]

novel *n.* [1970s–80s] (*UK Black*) an elaborate story, a piece of information.

novelty *n.* [19C] the vagina.

Novy *n.* [late 19C+] a native of *Nova* Scotia. [abbr.]

now *adj.* [1960s+] (*US*) up-to-date, very fashionable.

— now (and) — later *phr.* [1960s+] used in various phrs. implying that someone can act (usu. pleasurably) now and take responsibility, usu. in the form of payment, in due course. [the *locus classicus* is the film *Live Now, Pay Later* (1962), satirizing the 'hire-purchase' boom of the late 1950s–early 1960s; its screenwriter Jack Trevor Storey publ. a novel of the same name in 1963]

now and never *adj.* (*also* **now or never**) [late 19C] clever. [rhy. sl.]

no way! *excl.* (*also* **no way José!**) **1** [1960s+] (*orig. US*) absolutely not! you must be joking! you can't fool me! **2** [1990s+] used in rejoinder to a story that, however bizarre, is true; surely not! really, that's amazing! The usu. affirmative reply is WAY! excl. [SE *no way*, in no way whatsoever]

no way to run a railroad *phr.* [1960s+] (*US*) used to indicate that the current situation is utterly unsatisfactory.

no way to run a whelk stall *phr.* [1970s+] used to indicate that the current situation is utterly unsatisfactory.

nowhere *adj.* **1** [mid-18C–19C] hopelessly beaten, esp. in a race. **2** [mid-19C+] (*orig. US*) utterly confused, very mixed up. **3** [mid-19C+] (*orig. US*) useless, pointless, stupid, unimpressive.

nowhere city *n.* (*also* **nowheresville**) [1960s+] a situation, place or person who/which is seen as irrelevant, pointless, of no use at all. [NOWHERE adj. (3) + CITY sfx/-VILLE sfx¹]

nowherian *n.* (*also* **nowhereian**) [1960s] (*W.I.*) anyone deemed unrespectable; a layabout, an unkempt-looking person who is characterized as a tramp. [Carib.E. *nowherian*, one who has no religious affiliation]

nowig *n.* [2000s] (*US Black*) a state of calmness, sanity. [SE *no* + WIG v.¹ (8)]

now or never *adj. see* NOW AND NEVER adj.

no worries (mate) *phr.* [1960s+] (*orig. Aus.*) a common phr. of assurance; usu. ext. by *she'll be all right*, sometimes *no worries on me*.

now you're shouting *phr.* [late 19C–1910s] (*US*) now you're saying something meaningful or relevant. [emphatic var. on NOW YOU'RE TALKING phr.]

now you're talking *phr.* [late 19C+] a phr. stating that the speaker is (finally) dealing with pertinent topics or talking to some purpose.

n.o.y.b. *phr.* [1910s+] (*US*) *none of your business*. [abbr.]

nozzle *n.* **1** [mid-18C+] the nose or a nostril. **2** [1990s+] (*US*) the penis.

nozzler *n.* [early 19C] a blow on the nose. [NOZZLE n. (1)]

n.q.o.c.d. *phr.* (*also* **n.o.c.d.**) [1980s] (*UK/US society*) used of one who is deemed socially unacceptable. [abbr. *not* (*quite*) *our class, dear*]

n.s. *phr.* [mid-19C] (*US*) enough said, it is possible to infer all the facts from what has already been stated. [abbr. NUFF adj. + SE *said*]

n.s.g. *phr.* [1950s] (*US*) *not so good*. [abbr.]

n.s.h. *phr.* [1950s] (*US*) a general negative, unattractive, unimpressive etc. [abbr. NOT SO HOT phr.]

n.s.i.t. *phr.* [1930s+] (*UK society*) a note attached to the name of a prospective male escort by a debutante or her mother. [abbr. *not safe in taxis*]

n.s.s.!/NS²! *excl. see* NO SHIT, SHERLOCK! excl.

n.t.o. *n.* [1990s+] (*US campus*) a date who does not come up to expectations. [abbr. *not the one*]

n.t.s. *n.* [1970s+] (*US campus*) an attractive man that makes a woman's heart beat so fast that her name tag shakes. [abbr. *name tag shaker*]

nub *n.¹* (*UK Und.*) **1** [late 17C–early 18C] the gallows. **2** [late 17C–early 19C] the neck. [ety unknown; ? SE *nub*, a protuberance]

nub *n.²* **1** [18C–early 19C] sexual intercourse; also *nubbing*. **2** [late 18C–mid-19C] a husband. [? dial. *nub*, to jog, to shake]

nub *n.³* [1940s+] (*US*) an ugly or repulsive person. [SE *nub*, a lump]

nub *n.⁴* [1950s] a cigarette.

nub *v.* [late 17C–mid-19C] to hang. [NUB n.¹]

nubbed *adj.* [late 17C–mid-19C] hanged. [NUB v.]

nubbies *n.* [late 19C+] (*Aus.*) the female breasts (cf. BAGS n.¹). [SE *nub*, a lump]

nubbin *n.¹* [20C+] (*US Black*) the penis. [play on SE *nubbin*, the remains of something that has been worn away, e.g. a pencil; ult. a dwarfed or imperfect ear of maize]

nubbin *n.²* see NUBBIN-HEAD n.

nubbing *n.¹* [mid-17C–19C] hanging. [NUB v.]

nubbing *n.²* see NUB n.² (1).

nubbing cheat *n.* (*also* **nubbing chit, nubbling cheat**) [late 17C–19C] the gallows. [NUB v. + CHEAT n. (1), lit. 'the hanging thing'; note also CHEAT n. (3)]

nubbing cove *n.* (*also* **nubbing cull**) [late 17C–19C] the hangman. [NUB v. + COVE n. (1)]

nubbing ken *n.* [late 17C–19C] the Sessions house. [NUB v. + KEN n.¹ (1); lit. 'the hanging house'; one's trial there might well lead to the gallows]

nubbin-head *n.* (*also* **nubbin**) [1930s+] (*US Black*) a fool, a simpleton. [NUBBIN n.¹ + -HEAD sfx (1)]

nubbling cheat *n. see* NUBBING CHEAT n.

nubian *n.* [1970s+] **1** (*US campus*) a socially unacceptable person; used of Whites and Blacks despite obvious racist base. **2** (*US gay*) a Black man. [SE *nubian*, a member of a North African people living near what is now Egypt]

nuck *n. see* KNUCK n.¹ (1).

nucker *n.* (*also* **nukka**) [1990s+] (*US Black*) a fool; also used as an affectionate term of address. [? KNUCKLEHEAD n.]

nucks *n. see* KNUCKS n. (2).

nucky *n. see* NOOKIE n.

nuclear *adj.* [1970s+] (*orig. US*) enraged.

nuclear sub *n.* [2000s] a *public* house. [rhy. sl.]

nuddikin *n.* [mid-19C] the head. [NOODLE n.¹ (1) + KEN n.¹ (1)]

nuddy *adj.* [1940s+] naked, undressed. [IN THE NUDDY phr.]

Nudes for Dudes *n.* [1980s] (*US campus*) a course in art.

nudge *n.* (*also* **noodge, nudzh**) [1960s+] (*US*) a nag, a pest. [Yid.]

nudge *v.¹* [17C–19C] of a man, to have sexual intercourse.

nudge *v.²* (*also* **nudgy**) [1960s+] to bother, to irritate. [NUDGE n.]

nudge, nudge, wink, wink, know what I mean, say no more *phr.* [1960s+] a phr. used, heavy-handedly, to make a sexual or otherwise dubious innuendo; usu. abbr. to *nudge, nudge, wink, wink* or *say no more*. [popularized by Eric Idle in *Monty Python's Flying Circus*, BBC2 TV c.1969; Idle was dressed as a SPIV n. and was making heavily sexual innuendoes]

nudger *n.* **1** [1960s+] the penis. **2** [1960s+] (*Irish*) a term of abuse (cf. BELL END n.). **3** [1990s+] (*US*) a male homosexual (cf. BONE-EATER n.). [NUDGE v.¹]

nudge (the turps) v. see GIVE IT A (BIT OF A) NUDGE v.

nudgy adj. [1960s+] (US campus) nagging, whingeing. [NUDGE n.]

nudgy v. see NUDGE v.[2].

nudie n. (orig. US) **1** [1930s+] a striptease show or burlesque. **2** [1950s+] a nude performer. **3** [1960s+] a picture featuring naked or semi-naked flesh. **4** [1960s+] in combs., e.g. nudie pic, an 'adult' cinema or film; nudie book, an 'adult' or 'men's' magazine.

nudnik n. (also **noodnik, nudnick**) [1920s+] (US) a pest, a fool, an insignificant person (cf. ALTER KACKER n.). [synon. Yid.; ? ult. Rus. nudna]

nudzh n. see NUDGE n.

Nueva York n. [1950s+] New York. [some ref. to the large Hispanic population, but on the whole, merely an affectation]

nuff adj. [mid-19C+] enough, plenty, abundant; usu. in NUFF CED phr. [mis-sp.]

nuff ced phr. (also **'nough said, nuf ced, nuff said, nuff sed, nuf sed**) [mid-19C+] (orig. US) enough said, it is possible to infer all the facts from what has already been stated. [NUFF adj. + pron. of SE said; the mis-sp. only works, of course, when printed]

nuffness n. [1980s+] (W.I.) showiness, ostentation, vulgarity, precocity. [NUFF adj. + sfx -ness]

nuff respect phr. [1980s+] (orig. W.I.) a general phr. of approval/ admiration. [NUFF adj. + SE respect]

nuff said/sed phr. see NUFF CED phr.

nug n. [late 17C–19C] a term of affection, e.g. my dear nug. [NUG v.]

nug v. [16C–19C; 1980s] to fondle, to indulge in sexual foreplay, to have sexual intercourse; thus nugging, sexual intercourse; nugging cove, a womanizer. [dial. nug, to jog with the elbow, to strike, or Lat. nugae, trifles]

nugget n. **1** [mid-19C+] (Aus.) a small, compact, stocky animal or person, a runt. **2** [1920s+] (Aus.) a very attractive woman. **3** [1980s+] (US campus) a fool, an idiot. [SE nugget, a lump; (2) it is hoped that she is not as 'good as gold'; (3) synon. with BONEHEAD n.[1] (1), LUNKHEAD n. and similar terms that equate hardness (of head) with stupidity]

nugget v. [1960s+] (N.Z.) a male 'game' in which a victim's trousers and underpants are removed and his genitals blackened with Nugget black shoe polish. [brandname, but note NUGGETS n.[2]]

nuggets n.[1] [late 19C–1900s] money (cf. CANARY n.[5]). [SE gold nugget]

nuggets n.[2] [1960s+] (US) the testicles (cf. BALLS n.[1]). [SE nugget, a lump]

nuggets n.[3] (drugs) **1** [1970s+] amphetamine pills (cf. A n.[2]). **2** [1980s+] cocaine crystals. **3** [1980s+] crack cocaine (cf. BASE n.). **4** [1980s+] high-strength, hydroponically grown cannabis. [SE nugget, a lump]

nuggety adj. [late 19C+] (Aus.) chunky, squat, thickset. [NUGGET n. (1)]

nuggie n. see NOOGIE n.

nuggies n. [1970s+] (US) a woman's breasts. [? NUBBIES n.]

nugging (cove) n. see NUG v.

nugging dress n. [late 17C–19C] **1** an old-fashioned or out-of-the-ordinary style of dress. **2** a loose dress, denoting a courtesan. [NUG v. + SE dress]

nugging house n. (also **nugging ken**) [late 17C–early 19C] a brothel (cf. ACCOMMODATION HOUSE n.). [NUG v. + HOUSE n.[1] (1)/ KEN n.[1] (1)]

nugs n.[1] [1980s+] (US drugs) high-quality, dense, small hydroponically grown marijuana. [abbr. NUGGETS n.[3] (4)]

nugs n.[2] [1990s+] (US) a woman's breasts; thus fresh nugs, a woman with large breasts. [abbr. NUGGIES n.]

nuke n.[1] **1** [1950s+] a nuclear bomb. **2** [1960s+] (US) a nuclear power station. **3** [1960s+] (US) a nuclear powered weapon or ship, or one capable of firing nuclear missiles. **4** [1980s] a nuclear family or a member of a nuclear family. [abbr.]

nuke n.[2] [1980s+] (US drugs) marijuana which has been adulterated with particularly dangerous and/or toxic substances. [fig. use of NUKE n.[1] (1)]

nuke v.[1] [1960s+] to attack with a nuclear bomb. [NUKE n.[1] (1)]

nuke v.[2] **1** [1960s+] (orig. US) to punish severely, to destroy completely, to ruin. **2** [1980s] (US campus) to end a relationship with a girl or boyfriend. **3** [1980s+] (US campus) of food, to warm up in a microwave, to cook well. **4** [1980s+] (US campus) (also **nuke oneself**) to get a tan in a tanning booth. **5** [1980s+] of hair, to blow dry or spray excessively. **6** [1990s+] (US) to electrocute. [fig./joc. uses of NUKE v.[1]]

nuke and puke n. [1990s+] (US campus) a microwave meal. [NUKE v.[2] (3) + SE puke]

nuker n. [1980s+] (US campus) a microwave oven. [NUKE v.[2] (3)]

nuking n. [1970s+] (US teen) smelling of perfume. [Rus. nyukhat, to smell]

nukka n. see NUCKER n.

null v. [late 18C–mid-19C] to beat. [? SE annul]

nulling cove n. [early 19C] a prize-fighter. [NULL v. + COVE n. (1)]

numans n. [17C] Newgate Market. [corruption of New + -MANS sfx; Newgate Market was a general market which burned down in the Great Fire (1666)]

numb n. [mid-19C] money. [? SE number, i.e. of coins]

numb adj. (US) **1** [1910s+] (also **numbs**) blind drunk; occas. intoxicated by drugs (cf. ADDLED adj.). **2** [1960s+] stupid.

number n.[1] **1** [late 19C+] (orig. US) a person, usu. a young woman, usu. in a sexual context; esp. as HOT NUMBER n. **2** [1930s+] a person, in a non-sexual context. **3** [1960s+] (US gay) a potential or actual partner for casual sex, picked up from the street, bar or baths. **4** [1970s+] (US) a romantically involved couple. [metonymy from his/her phone number]

number n.[2] [late 19C+] an item of clothing, e.g. a dainty pink number.

number n.[3] **1** [20C+] in general, a thing, place or situation, defined by context. **2** [20C+] a performance; a scene, a display of excessive emotion. **3** [1910s+] a job or task; esp. as cushy number, an easy job. **4** [1920s] belief, commitment. **5** [1930s–50s] (US Black) a jail sentence, a life sentence. **6** [1970s+] a style, a way of living, a pose, e.g. the ageing rocker number.

number n.[4] [20C+] **1** a bedroom in a hotel or boarding house. **2** one's house. [the number on its door]

number n.[5] [1960s+] (drugs) a marijuana or hashish cigarette (cf. ONE n.[4]). [ext. NUMBER n.[3] (1)]

number-chaser n. [1930s] (US) an accountant.

number comes up phr. see NUMBER IS UP phr.

number-cruncher n. [1970s+] (US) **1** an accountant or statistician. **2** a person lacking creativity or imagination. [computer jargon number-cruncher, a large, sometimes slow machine which is used for calculations that would defeat, by quantity rather than complexity, mere human efforts]

number-cruncher course n. [1970s+] (US campus) any course that involves a large amount of maths. [NUMBER-CRUNCHER n.]

number 8 n. [1950s+] (US drugs) heroin. [H is the eighth letter of the alphabet]

number eight n. [1980s+] (N.Z.) the best, the strongest, the most likely to succeed.

number eight hat n. [20C+] an intellectual. [the link of a large brain – requiring a large hat size – to a large intellect]

number fifteens n. see NUMBER TENS n.

number is up phr. (also **number comes up, ...turns up**) **1** [late 19C+] to die. **2** [20C+] to get into trouble; to reach a point from which one cannot escape.

number 9 n. [early–mid-19C] the Fleet prison, situated at 9 Fleet Market, London.

number nip n. [19C] the vagina (cf. BITE n.²). [? SE *number*, a thing + *nip*, i.e. the image of the vagina as 'biting' the male]

number one n.¹ [18C+] oneself, one's own interests; often as LOOK AFTER NUMBER ONE v.

number one n.² **1** [mid-19C+] the best, the finest quality. **2** [20C+] (*orig. US*) one's best friend or lover.

number one n.³ [20C+] (*S.Afr. Black*) refined, white mealie meal. [spec. use of NUMBER ONE n.² (1)]

number one n.⁴ (*also* **number ones**) [20C+] **1** the act of urination. **2** urine. **3** a chamberpot. [juv. euph.]

number one n.⁵ [1910s+] an extremely short 'skinhead' hairstyle. [from the setting of the hair-clippers at grade 1]

number one n.⁶ [1930s–50s] (*UK prison*) the punishment diet of bread and water.

number one n.⁷ [1950s+] (*US Und.*) first degree (i.e. premeditated) murder.

number one adj. (*also* **No. 1**) [mid-19C+] (*orig. US*) first-rate, excellent, important, influential, the best. [widely popularized after its importation by veterans of the Korean (1950–3) and Vietnam (1964–75) wars]

number ones n. *see* NUMBER ONE n.⁴.

number-one squeeze n. *see* MAIN SQUEEZE n. (2).

number one thou(sand) adj. (*also* **number ten thou(sand)**) [1970s+] (*US*) very bad, dire, the very worst. [pidgin, imported by veterans of the Vietnam War]

numbers, the n. [late 19C+] (*US gambling*) a popular form of street gambling that involves predicting a combination of the winning numbers (between 000 and 999) at a racetrack, esp. widespread in the US Black community; thus *numbers racket*, laying odds and betting on numbers; *numbers–man*, one who runs a numbers lottery; *numbers runner*, one who takes the money from individual betters to the *numbers house*, the office where the 'racket' is run, and thus the one who delivers any payouts. [the SE *numbers* upon which one bets]

numbers game n. [1960s] (*US gay*) an uninhibited and extended session of sexual activity. [comb. of SIXTY-NINE n. (1) and SIXTY-SIX n.]

number six n.¹ (*also* **number 6**) [early–mid-19C] (*US*) Thomson's Compound Tincture of Myrrh and Capsicum, a popular household remedy. [it was regularly listed as the sixth medicine in the firm's catalogue]

number six n.² [mid–late 19C] a lock of hair shaped like the figure 6 and twisted from the temple back towards the ear.

number ten adj. (*also* **number sixty-nine**) [1950s+] (*orig. US milit.*) very bad, the worst. [pidgin, imported by veterans of the wars in Korea (1950–3) and Vietnam (1964–75)]

number tens n. (*also* **number fifteens, size tens**) [late 19C+] (*US*) shoes or feet. [ref. to shoe size]

number ten thou(sand) adj. *see* NUMBER ONE THOU(SAND) adj.

number 13 n. [1950s] (*drugs*) morphine (cf. AUNTIE EMMA n.). [M is the 13th letter of the alphabet]

number 3 n. [1950s+] (*drugs*) cocaine (cf. C is the 3rd letter of the alphabet]

number three n. [20C+] masturbation, whether by oneself, a partner, or as 'executive relief', i.e. from a 'masseuse' or prostitute. [on model of NUMBER ONE n.⁴ (1), NUMBER TWO n.¹ (1), although in adult use]

number turns up phr. *see* NUMBER IS UP phr.

number two n.¹ **1** [late 19C+] (*mainly UK/US juv.*) (*also* **number twos**) defecation. **2** [1990s+] (*US Black*) anything considered bad, unpleasant, underhand or deceptive. [euph.; (2) may be fig. use of (1) but may also link to NUMBER ONE n.² (1)]

number two n.² [1950s] (*W.I.*) a large round dumpling. [it is indented around its circumference to facilitate splitting it in half, but note NUMBER TWO n.¹ (1)]

number two n.³ [1950s+] (*orig. milit.*) second-in-command, second in rank.

number twos n. *see* NUMBER TWO n.¹ (1).

numb hand n. [early–mid-19C] an inexpert or clumsy person. [SE *numb* + HAND n.¹]

numbhead n. [mid-18C+] (*US*) a fool; thus *numbheaded*, stupid. [SE *numb* + -HEAD sfx (1)]

numbnut adj. [1990s+] (*Aus.*) foolish, stupid. [NUMBNUTS n.]

numbnuts n. [1960s+] (*US*) an idiot, a fool; usu. as a term of address. [SE *numb* + NUTS n.² (1)]

numbs adj. *see* NUMB adj. (1).

numbskull n. (*also* **numcull, numscul, numscull, numskull**) [late 17C+] a fool.

numbskulled adj. [18C+] stupid, foolish (cf. CLOD-SKULLED adj.). [NUMBSKULL n.]

numbwit n. [1950s+] a fool (cf. DAMWIT n.). [SE *numb* + DIM-WIT n.]

numby n. [1940s+] (*US*) a fool, a simpleton. [abbr. NUMBHEAD n.]

numcull n. *see* NUMBSKULL n.

numero uno n.¹ **1** [1940s+] the best, whether of objects or persons. **2** [1960s+] (*US*) an important person, the boss. [Sp. *numero uno*, NUMBER ONE n.²]

numero uno n.² [1970s+] (*orig. US*) oneself. [Sp. *numero uno*, NUMBER ONE n.¹]

numerous adj. [mid–late 19C] (*US*) superior, notable.

numgare n. (*also* **mungare**) [mid-19C] food, a meal. [Ital. *mangiare*, to eat]

nummer n. [mid-19C] a vagabond.

numms n. [late 17C–early 19C] a false, detachable collar, to be worn over a dirty shirt. [ety. unknown; ? link to SE *nominal*]

nummy adj. [1980s+] (*US campus*) delicious, mouthwatering. [baby-talk pron. of SE *yummy*]

num-nums n. [1970s+] **1** (*Aus./US*) a woman's breasts. **2** (*US*) a nipple. [echoic of sucking]

numscul(l)/numskull n. *see* NUMBSKULL n.

nun n. **1** [16C–early 19C] a prostitute (cf. ABBESS n.). **2** [1980s+] a prude, a woman who is uninterested in sex.

nunga-muncher n. [1960s–70s] (*Aus.*) a fellatrix.

nungers n. [1960s+] (*Aus.*) the female breasts. [echoic of sucking]

nunky n. (*also* **nunk, nunkey, nunks**) **1** [17C–1950s] an uncle, whether lit. or as an address to/description of an older man. **2** [1920s–30s] a pawnbroker. **3** [1920s–30s] a Jew, esp. when a moneylender (cf. FAST-TALKING CHARLIE n.). [late 16C–mid-18C SE *nuncle*, an uncle; (2) UNCLE n.¹ (1); (3) f. (2)]

nunnery n. [late 16C–19C] a brothel (cf. ABBESS n.). [NUN n. (1); note synon. ref. to a *religious house* in *Coryat's Crudities* (1611)]

nunno! excl. [1900s–40s] not likely! definitely not!

nunny-bunny n. [2000s] (*Irish*) £5 (cf. BEEHIVE n.²). [the nun depicted on the note + ? rhy. sl. = *money*]

nunquam n. [mid-16C–early 17C] (*UK Und.*) a dawdling messenger. [Lat. *numquam*, never]

nun with a price on her head n. [1990s+] (*Irish*) a £5 note. [its design]

nuppence n. [late 19C] no money; also. used fig. in phr. *not worth nuppence*. [SE *no pence*]

nuprin n. [1990s+] (*US campus*) an Asian (cf. BROWNIE n.²). [the painkiller Nuprin, whose advert claimed they were 'little, yellow and different']

nupson n. [17C–18C] a fool. [ety. unknown]

nurd n. *see* NERD n.

nurdy adj. *see* NERDY adj.

nurembergs n. [1940s+] haemorrhoids. [rhy. sl.; *Nuremberg trials* = SE *piles*]

nurfing n. [1990s+] sniffing a woman's bicycle seat. [nonce-word]

nurgle n. [1990s+] (*N.Z. juv.*) a fool.

nurk n. [1990s+] (*UK juv.*) a fool. [var. on NERD n.]

nurse *n.* [early 18C] a common name for a homosexual barber.

nurse *v.* **1** [late 18C–19C] to cheat or swindle. **2** [mid-19C–1900s] for one omnibus to follow a rival closely so as to poach its passengers.

nursery *n.* **1** [mid-17C–mid-18C] a brothel, or a place frequented by prostitutes. **2** [19C] the vagina (cf. BABY CHUTE n.). [the role of both in procreation]

nursery rhyme *n.* [2000s] a crime. [rhy. sl.]

nursery rhymes *n.* [1990s+] the *Times* newspaper. [rhy. sl.]

nurse the hoe handle *v.* [late 19C–1900s] (*US*) to act lazily. [the idler leaning on his hoe, rather than wielding it]

nurse the iron baby *v.* [late 19C] (*UK Und.*) to be in prison.

nusslap *v.* [2000s] (*US Black*) to cause trouble for someone, to harm both lit. and fig. [NUTS n.² (1) + SE *slap*]

nut *n.*¹ **1** [mid-16C+] the head of the penis. **2** [mid-19C+] the head; thus *on one's own nut*, on one's own. **3** [late 19C+] brains, intelligence; thus *use one's nut*, to use one's brain, to act sensibly. **4** [1940s+] the head, as used to butt someone in a fight. **5** [1990s+] (*Aus.*) in a game of two-up, the 'heads' side of a coin. [(1) poss. SE until mid-18C]

nut *n.*² [early–mid-19C] an action that is intended to give pleasure. [the pleasant flavour of a *nut* or NUTS n.¹]

nut *n.*³ **1** [mid-19C+] a person, a fellow. **2** [late 19C+] a daredevil. [ext. use of NUT n.¹, often constrained by an unspoken 'tough']

nut *n.*⁴ **1** [mid-19C+] (*orig. US*) (*also* **nuts**) an insane person; thus NUT DOCTOR n., NUT HOUSE n., NUTCASE n. **2** [20C+] (*orig. US*) a fan, an enthusiast, an obsessive; usu. in defining combs., e.g. *cricket nut, computer nut*; thus *be a nut at*, to be an expert in. **3** [20C+] (*orig. US*) a course of action, an obsession; thus *have a nut on*, to be obsessed with. **4** [1930s] (*US Und.*) a beggar who is insane, or poses as such. [NUTS adj.]

nut *n.*⁵ **1** [late 19C] (*Aus.*) a provincial dandy. **2** [1900s–20s] a dandy, esp. a second-rate one. [? KNUT n., although this predates]

nut *n.*⁶ [late 19C–1920s] a drink. [ety. unknown; ? the pleasurable aspects of liquor and nuts]

nut *n.*⁷ [late 19C+] (*Aus.*) a horse that is hard to break in. [abbr. HARD NUT n.]

nut *n.*⁸ **1** [20C+] (*US*) orig. entertainment use, the initial outlay, overheads, expenses; the break-even sum, as in a theatre production or film, after which profit starts. **2** [1920s+] (*US*) any required sum, a pay-off. **3** [1920s+] (*US Und.*) protection money paid to corrupt policemen. **4** [1970s] (*US*) a fund used for bribery and other illegal activities, esp. by police. **5** [1970s+] the sum of money actually borrowed, as opposed to the interest that accrues on it. [SE *nut*, as being the heart of the fruit; such money is at the heart of a project, a relationship etc]

nut *n.*⁹ **1** [1930s+] (*orig. US*) an orgasm; thus BUST A NUT v.; GET A NUT v. (1). **2** [1960s+] (*orig. US*) sexual intercourse; esp. in phr. GET A NUT v. (2). **3** [1970s] (*orig. US*) the vagina. **4** [1980s+] (*orig. US*) in fig. and non-sexual use, a sense of pleasure. **5** [1990s+] (*US*) semen. [ext. use of NUTS n.² (1)]

nut *n.*¹⁰ [2000s] (*US Black*) nothing. [abbr./pron.]

nut, the *n.* (*also* **the nuts**) [1960s+] (*US*) the basic facts, the core. [abbr. NUTS AND BOLTS n.]

nut *adj.* [1910s+] crazy; pertaining to the insane (cf. NUT-CASE adj.; NUTS adj.; NUTS-AND-BOLTS adj.¹; NUTSO adj.; NUTSY adj.; NUTTY adj.²). [NUT n.⁴ (1)]

nut *v.*¹ [early–mid-19C] (*orig. UK Und.*) **1** to curry favour, to toady to. **2** to stare at. [NUT n.², i.e. one offers (1) or receives (2) something pleasant]

nut *v.*² (*also* **put in the nut, stick the nut on**) **1** [mid-19C+] to butt one's opponent in the face, usu. the bridge of his nose, using one's own forehead. **2** [2000s] to hit on the head. [NUT n.¹ (2)]

nut *v.*³ [1910s+] (*orig. Aus.*) to think; thus *nut (it) out*, to work out, to analyse. [NUT n.¹ (3)]

nut *v.*⁴ [1910s+] (*US*) to castrate, also used fig. [NUTS n.² (1)]

nut *v.*⁵ [1940s–50s] **1** (*US Und.*) to share out the profits of a confidence trick. **2** (*Aus.*) to give. [NUT n.⁸]

nut *v.*⁶ [1960s] (*US*) to renege. [NUT n.⁸]

nut *v.*⁷ **1** [1970s+] (*US*) to have sexual intercourse. **2** [1990s+] (*US Black*) to reach orgasm, to ejaculate. [NUT n.⁹]

nut alley *n.* [1930s] (*US prison*) the prison insane ward. [NUT n.⁴ (1) + SE *alley*]

nutbag *n.*¹ *see* NUTBAR n.

nutbag *n.*² *see* NUTSACK n.

nutball *n.* [1970s+] (*US*) an idiot (cf. NUTCAKE n.; NUTHEAD n.; WINGNUT n.¹). [NUT n.⁴ (1) + -BALL sfx]

nutbar *n.* (*also* **nutbag, nutbasket, nutbucket**) [1970s+] (*US*) a lunatic. [NUT n.⁴ (1) + joc. uses of SE *bar/basket/bucket*]

nutbox *n.* (*also* **nutbin**) [1950s+] (*US*) a psychiatric institution. [NUT n.⁴ (1) + SE *box/bin*/LOONY BIN n. (1)]

nutburger *n.* [1980s+] (*US*) a lunatic. [NUT n.⁴ (1) + SE *(ham)burger*]

nutbuster *n.* (*US*) **1** [1940s] a mechanic or machinist. **2** [1970s+] an insoluble difficulty, the last straw. [SE *nuts*/NUTS n.² (1) + *buster*]

nut-butter *n.* [1990s+] **1** semen (cf. BABY GRAVY n.). **2** (*US Black*) an enthuiastic and skilful fellatrix. [NUT n.⁹ + BUTTER n.¹ (1)]

nutcake *n.* [1960s+] (*US*) a fool, a lunatic, an eccentric (cf. NUTBALL n.). [NUT n.⁴ (1) + SE *cake*]

nutcase *n.* [1950s+] an eccentric, an odd person, a lunatic. [NUT n.⁴ (1) + SE *(mental) case*]

nut-case *adj.* [1990s+] crazy, insane (cf. NUT adj.). [NUTCASE n.]

nut-chokers *n.* [1960s+] male underwear. [NUTS n.² (1) + SE *choke*]

nut college *n.* [late 19C–1960s] (*US*) a lunatic asylum or psychiatric institution. [NUT n.⁴ (1) + SE *college*]

nutcracker *n.*¹ [late 17C–19C] (*UK Und.*) usu. in pl., the pillory. [despite logical links, both NUT n.¹ (2) and NUTS n.² (1) post-date this usage]

nutcracker *n.*² **1** [mid-19C–1940s] (*orig. US*) a blow to the head. **2** [late 19C–1900s] the head. **3** [1910s] (*US Und.*) a police raid. **4** [1920s] (*US*) a nightstick. [NUT n.¹ (2) + SE *cracker*]

nutcracker *n.*³ (*also* **nutcruncher, nutcrusher**) (*US*) **1** [1940s+] something difficult, impossible or dangerous. **2** [1970s+] a martinet, a disciplinarian. **3** [1990s+] a nagging woman. [NUTS n.² (1) + SE *cracker*; on model of BALL-BREAKER n.]

nutcracker *n.*⁴ [1950s+] (*US*) a psychiatrist. [NUT n.⁴ (1) + SE *cracker*]

nutcrackers *n.*¹ [late 19C–1900s] the fists. [NUT n.¹ (2) + SE *crackers*]

nutcrackers *n.*² [late 19C–1900s] the teeth. [one of their functions]

nutcrackers *n.*³ [1990s+] the testicles (cf. CHEESE AND CRACKERS n.). [rhy. sl. = KNACKERS n.]

nut croaker *n.* *see* CROAKER n.⁵ (1).

nutcut *n.* (*also* **nutcutting, nutgut**) [1960s+] (*US*) the fundamental basics, usu. of a ruthless nature, dirty work. [NUTS n.² (1); the implication is of castration]

nut-cut *adj.* [mid-19C] (*Anglo-Ind.*) roguish, mischievous. [NUT n.¹ (2)]

nutcutter *n.* [1970s+] (*US*) something difficult, impossible or dangerous. [NUTS n.² (1); var. on NUTCRACKER n.³ (1)]

nutcutting *n.* *see* NUTCUT n.

nut doctor *n.* [1930s+] (*US*) a psychiatrist. [NUT n.⁴ (1) + SE *doctor*]

nut ducker *n.* [1960s+] (*Aus.*) one who deliberately ignores a friend in the street. [NUT n.¹ (2) + SE *duck*; note Aus. cattlemen use *duck his nut*, of a horse, to (put its head down and) buck]

nut factory *n.* [late 19C+] (*Aus./US*) a psychiatric institution. [NUT n.⁴ (1) + SE *factory*]

nut farm *n.* [1930s–70s] (*US*) a psychiatric institution. [NUT n.⁴ (1) + SE *farm*]

nut foundry *n.* [1930s–40s] (*US*) a psychiatric institution. [NUT n.⁴ (1) + SE *foundry*]

nutgut n. see NUTCUT n.

nut hatch n. [1940s+] (orig. US) a psychiatric institution. [NUT n.[4] (1) + SE hatch, hutch; + ? underpinned by the well-known asylum at Colney Hatch near London, opened in 1851]

nuthead n. [1910s+] (orig. US) a fool, a simpleton (cf. NUTBALL n.). [NUT n.[4] (1) + -HEAD sfx (1)]

nut house n. (also **nut hospital**) [1920s+] **1** (orig. US) a psychiatric institution. **2** (US) a chaotic place or situation, a fig. madhouse. [NUT n.[4] (1) + SE house]

nut hut n. [1990s+] a psychiatric institution. [NUT n.[4] (1) + SE hut]

nut it out v. see NUT v.[3].

nut-job n. [1970s+] (US) a lunatic or very eccentric person. [NUT n.[4] (1) + JOB n.[6] (1)]

nutmeg (maker) n. [early–late 19C] (US) a White New Englander. [SE wooden nutmeg, anything false or fraudulent, a fraud, a cheat, a deception. New Englanders have the image of being deceitful, esp. as businessmen. Note the Nutmeg State, Connecticut, where wooden nutmegs are supposedly manufactured for export]

nutmegs n. [late 17C–early 19C; 1980s+] the testicles (cf. ACORNS n.). [predates NUTS n.[2] (1)]

nut 'n' berry n. [1990s+] (US campus) a latter-day HIPPIE n.[2] (3). [the preference for vegetarianism associated with hippies and early conservationists]

nut-nut n. [2000s] an insane, eccentric person. [redup. of NUT n.[4] (1)]

nut on v. (US) **1** [20C+] to attack physically; to abuse verbally. **2** [1960s–70s] to ignore. [NUT n.[1] (2)]

nut out v.[1] [1960s+] (US Black) to go mad, whether lit. or metaphorically. [NUT n.[4] (1)]

nut out v.[2] see NUT v.[3].

nut rock n. [1920s–30s] a bald person. [NUT n. (2), i.e. their 'nut' is as bare as a rock]

nut-rock adj. [1920s–30s] bald. [NUT ROCK n.]

nut role n. [1960s+] (US Black) a pretence of insanity or stupidity, usu. to avoid something, as in I'll play the nut role. [NUT n.[4] (1) + SE role]

nut role v. (also **nut roll**) [1960s+] (US) to act (deceptively) in an eccentric or stupid manner, to pretend to be insane. [NUT ROLE n.]

nut roll n. [1990s+] (US Black) an eccentric or mad person. [NUT n.[4] (1) + pun on the sweet]

nuts n.[1] [17C–1920s] anything agreeable, satisfactory, an acceptable situation; usu. as nuts for/to someone. ['prob. ex C.16 nuts to, an enticement to' (E.P.)]

nuts n.[2] **1** [mid-19C+] the testicles (cf. ACORNS n.). **2** [20C+] (US Black) the clitoris (cf. BABY IN THE BOAT n.). **3** [1900s–40s] (US Und.) the game of 3-card trick; lit. the shells that are used to hide the pea. **4** [1930s] female sexual desire. **5** [1970s+] (US) manly courage. [SE nut, i.e. the shape; E.P. suggests NUT n.[1] (1)]

nuts n.[3] see NUT n.[4] (1).

nuts, the n.[1] [1910s+] (US) **1** the best, the superlative. **2** something bad or objectionable.

nuts, the n.[2] [1930s+] (US) a strategic advantage, esp. in gambling, as in a winning hand in cards. [NUTS n.[1]]

nuts, the n.[3] see NUT, THE n.

nuts adj. **1** [late 18C+] fond of, fascinated by; earlier usage usu. NUTS UPON adj./NUTS ON adj., 20C+ usage usu. NUTS ABOUT adj. or nuts over and influenced by (2). **2** [mid-19C+] insane, mad, crazy; thus go nuts, to go crazy; like nuts, hysterically (cf. NUT adj.). [this predates even NUT n.[1] (2); E.P. suggests sweet as a nut, thus 'sweet on']

nuts! excl. [1920s+] (orig. US) a mild excl., nonsense! rubbish! not a chance!

nuts about adj. (also **nuts for/over**) [1910s+] obsessed with, usu. in the context of love. [NUTS adj. (1) but later chronology

means it was strongly influenced by NUTS adj. (2) and the SE phr. crazy about]

nuts about v. see NUTS AROUND v.

nutsack n. (also **nutbag**) (US) **1** [1970s+] the scrotum (cf. BALL-BAG n.). **2** [1990s+] a derog. description of a person, a term of abuse. [NUTS n.[2] (1) + SACK n.[1] (3)]

nuts and bolts n. [1960s+] the basics of a situation, the fundamental issues.

nuts-and-bolts adj.[1] (also **bolts-and-nuts**) [1920s–40s] (US) crazy, insane (cf. NUT adj.). [ext. of NUTS adj. (2)]

nuts-and-bolts adj.[2] [1960s+] basic, practical. [NUTS AND BOLTS n.]

nuts and sluts n. [1970s+] (US campus) a course in abnormal psychology. [NUT n.[4] (1) + SE slut]

nuts around v. (also **nuts about**) [1940s–60s] (US) **1** to wander around aimlessly. **2** to mess about, to fool around. [NUTS adj. (2)]

nuts for adj. see NUTS ABOUT adj.

nuts for phr. see NUTS n.[1].

nutshot n. [2000s] (US) a blow to the testicles. [NUTS n.[2] (1) + SHOT n.[9] (2)]

nutso n. [1970s+] (orig. US) a stupid, unstable or eccentric person. [NUTS adj. (2)]

nutso adj. [1970s+] (orig. US) stupid, unstable, eccentric (cf. NUT adj.). [NUTSO n.]

nuts on adj. (also **filberts on**) [early 19C+] obsessed with, in love with. [NUTS adj. (1); SE filbert, a type of nut]

nuts over adv. see NUTS ABOUT adj.

nuts to phr.[1] (also **nuts on**) [1920s+] (US) a retort to express rejection, derision etc, TO HELL WITH —!. [NUTS n.[2] (1)]

nuts to phr.[2] see NUTS n.[1].

nuts upon adj. [late 18C–19C] obsessed with, in love with; thus nuts upon oneself, extremely pleased with one's own actions. [NUTS adj. (1)]

nutsy adj. [1910s+] (orig. US) mad, insane, eccentric; occas. used as a nickname. [NUTS adj. (2)]

nutted adj. [mid-19C] fooled by the claims of one who poses as being an obsessive admirer. [NUT v.[1] (1)]

nutten-chops n. see WIND-PIES n.

nutter n.[1] [1950s+] a lunatic, an eccentric. [NUT n.[4] (1)]

nutter n.[2] [1960s] the head. [NUT n.[1] (2) or the object that can NUT v.[2] (1)]

nutter butter n. [1990s+] (US campus) someone who is unaware or inattentive. [NUTTER n.[1] + redup.; note brandname Nutter Butter, a form of peanut filled biscuit]

nuttery n. [1910s–50s] (US) a mental hospital. [NUT n.[4] (1); on model of SE nunnery]

nutting n. [1930s+] using the top of one's head to butt an opponent during a fight; such a blow can often end the fight instantly. [NUT v.[2] (1)]

nutty adj.[1] **1** [late 18C–1910s] smart, spruce, attractive. **2** [late 19C] piquant, spicy. [? SE phr. sweet as a nut]

nutty adj.[2] **1** [19C+] very fond of, obsessed with; earlier as NUTTY UPON adj., later as NUTTY ABOUT adj. **2** [late 19C+] (orig. US) crazy, eccentric; esp. in punning phrs. nutty as a fruit cake, nutty as a peach orchard boar (cf. BANANAS adj.; NUT adj.). [NUTS adj. (2)]

nutty adj.[3] [1930s+] (US Black) excellent, first-rate. [the person/object in question makes the speaker go NUTS adj. (2)]

nutty about adj. (also **nutty for**) [1910s+] (orig. US) fond of, keen on. [NUTTY adj.[2] (1); heavily influenced by NUTTY adj.[2] (2) on model of SE phr. crazy about]

nutty upon adj. (also **nutty on**) [19C] amorous, fond of, obsessed by. [NUTTY adj.[2] (1)]

nut up v. [1970s+] to lose one's temper completely, to go berserk. [NUT n.[4] (1)]

nut ward n. [20C+] (US) a psychiatric unit. [NUT n.[4] (1) + SE ward]

nut wing n. [1990s+] (US prison) the psychiatric wing. [NUT n.[4] (1) + SE wing]

nut worker *n.* [1910s+] (*Aus.*) one who works out ways of avoiding hard work; thus ext. as a white-collar worker. [NUT n.¹ (3)]

nux *n.*¹ [mid-19C] (*UK Und.*) the object in question; the 'game'. [northern dial; ? ult. Lat. *nux*, a nut]

nux *n.*² [1940s–50s] (*US prison*) prison-cooked tea. [abbr. medical Lat. *nux vomica*, the fruit from which strychnine is produced]

nyaams *n.* [1950s+] (*W.I.*) foolishness, nonsense, esp. as an excl. [fig./ext. use of NYAM v. (1), i.e. one who thinks of nothing but eating; thus cf. W.I. *coco-head*, a fool, itself the fig. use of *coco-head*, the rhizome of the coco-plant]

nyaams head *n.* [1950s] (*W.I.*) an absolute fool. [NYAAMS n. + -HEAD sfx (1)]

nyafflin' *n.* [20C+] (*Ulster*) eating noisily with an open mouth. [onomat.; note Bedfordshire dial. *nyaffle*, to eat in a hasty, gluttonous manner]

nyam *n.* [early 18C+] (*orig. W.I.*) food. [var. on YAM n.¹]

nyam *v.* **1** [early 18C+] (*orig. W.I.*) to eat. **2** [1970s+] (*UK Black*) in fig. sense, to attack, to arrest. [var. on YAM v.]

nyam dog *n.* [1940s] (*W.I.*) a Chinese person (cf. AH CABBAGE n.). [NYAM v. + SE *dog*; the Chinese predilection for cooking dog]

nyami nyami *n.* [1940s+] (*W.I.*) a greedy, omnivorous person. [NYAM v.]

nyams *n.* (*also* **nyamps**) [20C+] (*W.I.*) a weakling, a useless idiot. [? Twi *nyamma*, small or NYAM n., in context of being 'a vegetable']

nyanga *n.* (*also* **nang, yanga**) [20C+] (*W.I.*) ostentation, esp. in one's dress; ext. to stylish. [Mende *nyanga*, showing off]

nyetsi *adj.* [1990s+] (*US teen*) no good, useless, worthless. [Tswana *nyetsi*, useless]

nying'i-nying'i *adj.* [1920s+] (*W.I. Rasta*) nagging, whining. [? fig. use of NYANGA n.]

nylon *n.* [1960s+] (*S.Afr.*) a police van. [its mesh-covered sides]

nylon road *n.* [1950s+] (*W.I.*) a good, smooth road, better than the average island road.

nym *see under* NIM.

nymph *n.*¹ **1** [mid-17C+] a euph. for a prostitute. **2** [1960s] (*US campus*) an effeminate male. [SE *nymph*, a semi-divine being, imagined as a beautiful maiden inhabiting the sea, rivers, fountains, hills, woods or trees, thence a young and beautiful woman]

nymph *n.*² [1910s+] a *nymph*omaniac, an allegedly sexually insatiable woman. [abbr.]

nympha *n. see* NYMPHO n.

nymph du pavé *n. see* NYMPH OF THE PAVE n.

nymphette *n.* [1960s–80s] (*US gay*) an attractive gay male youngster. [SE *nymphette*, a sexually alluring pubescent girl]

nympho *n.* (*also* **nympha**) [1910s+] (*orig. US*) a *nympho*maniac, an allegedly sexually insatiable woman; thus NYMPHO adj. [abbr.]

nympho *adj.* (*also* **nymphy**) [1910s+] *nympho*maniacal. [abbr.]

nymph of darkness *n.* (*also* **nymph of the shade**) [18C] a prostitute (cf. DEADLY NIGHTSHADE n.). [NYMPH n.¹ (1) + SE *darkness*]

nymph of delight *n.* [early 18C] a prostitute. [NYMPH n.¹ (1) + SE *delight*]

nymph of the pave *n.* (*also* **nymph du pavé, nymph of the pavement**) [early 19C–1930s] a prostitute, a street-walker (cf. NIGHT WALKER n.). [NYMPH n.¹ (1) + SE *pave(ment)*]

nymph of the shade *n. see* NYMPH OF DARKNESS n.

nymphy *adj. see* NYMPHO adj.

nyp *see under* NIP and its combs.

nyuck *n.* (*also* **neuck**) [20C+] (*Ulster*) an unimportant person. [? fig. use of SE *nook*]

O

O *n.* (*also* **oh**) **1** [1930s+] (*US drugs*) an ounce of a narcotic. **2** [1930s+] (*drugs*) opium (cf. APOSTLE *n.*). **3** [1980s+] (*Aus. drugs*) an ounce of cannabis. [abbr.]

-o *sfx* **1** [mid-17C; late 19C+] used variously to create ext. nouns, often as terms of address, e.g. BOYO *n.*¹ (1); BUCKO *n.*¹ (2); KIDDO *n.* (3). **2** [mid-19C+] used variously to create nouns from adjs., e.g. PINKO *n.*; WEIRDO *n.*; WIDO *n.* **3** [mid-19C+] used variously to create ext. adjs., e.g. CHEAPO *adj.*, NEATO *adj.* **4** [late 19C+] (*mainly Aus.*) added to a variety of nouns (often occupational) to create sl. forms, usu. abbreviated, e.g. ARVO *n.*; BOMBO *n.*; COMMO *n.*; COMPO *n.*; DERO *n.*; ETHNO *n.*; GARBO *n.*; JOLLO *n.*; JOURNO *n.*; LESO *n.*; MADDO *n.*; METHO *n.*¹; MILKO *n.*¹; NASHO *n.*; PLONKO *n.*; RABBIT-O *n.*; REFFO *n.*; SANNO *n.*; SECKO *n.*; SHEEPO *n.*; SUSSO *n.*; SYPHO *n.* **5** [20C+] (*mainly Aus.*) less commonly added to adjs. to create shortened sl. forms, e.g. BERKO *adj.*; TROPPO *adj.* **6** [20C+] used variously to create general shortened forms, mostly of nouns, e.g. AGGRO *n.*; AMMO *n.*; COMBO *n.*¹. **7** [20C+] used as a meaningless ending, e.g. BILLY-O *n.*; CHEERIO *phr.* [(4) ? f. the *-o* sfx in street cries such as *milko!* or in the familiarization of names, e.g. *Johno*]

o.a. *n.* [1970s–80s] (*drugs*) an overdose, spec. of Methedrine. [abbr. OVERAMP *v.*]

oafo *n.* [1950s–60s] a ruffian, an oaf. [SE *oaf* + -o sfx (1)]

oafo *adj.* [1950s–60s] thuggish. [OAFO *n.*]

oagle *v. see* OGLE *v.* (2).

oak *n.*¹ (*also* **oke**) **1** [late 16C–early 17C] (*UK Und.*) in a team of confidence tricksters, the one who keeps a watch. **2** [17C–mid-19C] a rich man, a man of substance. [playing on the tree's 'oaken' qualities]

oak *n.*² [late 19C–1900s] a joke. [rhy. sl.]

oaken towel *n.* (*also* **oaken cudgel, ...plant, ...sapling, ...staff, oak towel**) [18C–mid-19C; 1920s] a cudgel; thus *rub down with an oaken towel*, to thrash, to beat.

Oakey/Oakie *n. see* OKIE *n.*

oakie *n. see* OKIE *n.*

Oakley *n.* [1920s–60s] (*US*) a free pass, orig. to a circus, but latterly to the theatre. [abbr. ANNIE OAKLEY *n.* (1)]

oak towel *n.* [late 18C–1930s] a policeman's truncheon. [note OAKEN TOWEL *n.*]

Oaktown *n.* [1990s+] (*US Black*) Oakland, California.

o.a.o. *n.* [1920s+] (*orig. US*) one's steady girlfriend. [abbr. *one and only*]

oars (and rollocks) *n.* [1990s+] nonsense, rubbish. [rhy. sl. = BALLOCKS *n.*² (2); note Williams for 17C fig. use of *oar*, penis]

oary-eyed *adj. see* ORY-EYED *adj.*

oat *n.*¹ **1** [mid–late 19C] an atom, the tiniest amount. **2** [late 19C–1900s] a penny, a halfpenny, the smallest amount of money; thus *not have an oat*, to be penniless. [? SE *iota*]

oat *n.*² [mid-19C+] the number 2. [backsl.]

oat burner *n. see* OATSMOBILE *n.*

oat consumer/destroyer *n. see* OATSMOBILE *n.*

oater *n.* [1940s+] (*orig. US*) a Western film. [abbr. OAT OPERA *n.*]

oat grinder *n. see* OATSMOBILE *n.*

oatmeal *n.* [17C] an urban rowdy, usu. in a gang. [SE phr. *sow one's wild oats*; note 'No trace of this odd appellation has yet been found except that the author of a ludicrous pamphlet has taken the name of Oliver Oat-meale' (Nares)]

oat muncher *n. see* OATSMOBILE *n.*

oat opera *n.* (*also* **oats opera**) [1930s–40s] (*orig. US*) a Western film. [the horses and the oats they eat]

oats *n.*¹ [1920s+] sexual satisfaction; thus *get one's oats*, to have sexual intercourse. [SE phr. *feel one's oats*, *sow one's wild oats*; note *double entendre* in D'Urfey, *Pills to Purge Melancholy* (1719–20): 'Sow your wild Oats, / And mind not her wild Notes']

oats *n.*² [1990s+] (*drugs*) cocaine (cf. BARLEY *n.*²). [rhy. sl.; *oats and barley* = CHARLIE *n.*⁹ (1); note OATS (AND BARLEY) *n.*]

oats *n.*³ *see* ASH BEANS AND LONG OATS *n.*

oats (and barley) *n.* **1** [mid-19C] a watchman. **2** [mid-19C+] a synon. for the proper name Charlie/Charley. [rhy. sl.; (1) = CHARLEY *n.*¹ (1)]

oats and chaff *n.* [mid-19C] a footpath. [rhy. sl.; Northern pron.]

oatsmobile *n.* (*also* **oat burner, ...consumer, ...destroyer, ...grinder, ...muncher**) [1910s+] (*Can./US*) a horse. [joc. blend of SE *oats* + (*auto*)*mobile*]

oats opera *n. see* OAT OPERA *n.*

oat-stealer *n.* [late 18C–1900s] an ostler. [pun + derog. ref. to the stereotypically corrupt ostler]

O.B. *n.*¹ [late 19C–1900s] (*UK Und.*) the Old Bailey in London, which is the Central Criminal Court of England. [abbr.]

O.B. *n.*² *see* OBIE *n.*

ob *adj.* (*US campus*) **1** [1960s] obnoxious. **2** [1980s+] obvious. [abbr.]

Obadiah *n.* [mid-17C–mid-19C] a Quaker. [the popularity of that name among the sect]

obbo *n.* [1960s+] (*UK Und./police/prison*) police observation; prison observation room. [SE *observation* + -o sfx (3)]

obbs *n. see* OBS *n.*

o-be-joyful *n.* (*also* **oh-be-cheerful, oh-be-joyful**) **1** [early 19C] brandy. **2** [early 19C+] (*US*) liquor in general. **3** [mid-19C–1900s] rum. [orig. naut. jargon]

o-be-joyful house *n.* (*also* **o-be-joyful works**) [19C] a public house. [O-BE-JOYFUL *n.* + SE *house/works*]

obelisk *n.* [19C] the penis. [SE *obelisk*, a tapering shaft of stone]

obese *adj.* [1990s+] excellent, extremely admirable. [play on SE *obese*, very fat/FAT *adj.*¹ (2)]

obey *n. see* OBIE *n.*

obfuscated *adj.* [mid-19C–1910s] drunk (cf. ADDLED *adj.*).

obfusticated *adj.* [mid-19C–1960s] (*US*) bewildered, confused, excited. [ext. of OBFUSCATED *adj.*]

obie *n.* (*also* **O.B., obey**) [1920s–80s] (*US Und.*) a post office. [ety. unknown; Irwin, *American Tramp and Und. Slang* (1931), suggests: 'Originated by the old yeggmen, who merely reversed the initials,

"P.O.," to lessen the public's understanding of their conversation, and from carelessness in speech corrupted to its present form']

obies *n.* (*also* **O.B.'s**) [1970s+] (*S.Afr. campus*) sherry. [pron. of O.B.'s, tradename *Old Brown* sherry]

obituary notice *n.* [1920s] (*US*) a letter from a creditor.

object *n.* [early 19C–1950s] a person or thing that appears ridiculous or pitiable. [SE *object of pity, object of mirth*]

oblige *v.* **1** [19C+] to have sexual intercourse. **2** [late 19C+] to perform in public, e.g. to *oblige with a song*. **3** [1930s+] a genteel euph. meaning to work as a charwoman or cleaner. [the implication of all is of offering a favour]

obliterated *adj.* [1980s+] extremely intoxicated by a drug or alcohol.

obno *n.* (*also* **obnoc, obnoxo**) [1970s+] (*US campus*) a crude, obnoxious person. [OBNO adj.]

obno *adj.* [1970s+] (*US campus*) *obno*xious. [abbr.; pron. 'obe-know']

oboe *n.* [1990s+] the penis (cf. ACCORDION n.).

O'Brien's dog *n.* [20C+] (*Irish*) one who is all things to all people. [he goes 'a little way with everyone'; presumably a lost anecdote]

O.B.'s *n. see* OBIES n.

obs *n.* (*also* **obbs**) **1** [1910s–20s] obligations. **2** [1940s+] a lookout; usu. in phr. *keep obs*, to keep a lookout. **3** [1950s+] (*Aus./US prison*) (*also* **obso**) an observation wing of a prison. [abbr.; (2) and (3) SE *observation*]

obscure *adj.* [1980s+] (*US campus*) strange, bizarre, weird.

obsocky *adj.* [20C+] (*W.I.*) **1** of objects (esp. clothes), ill-fitting, mis-shapen. **2** of people, ungainly, overweight. **3** of events, absurd, ridiculous. [? Yoruba *obo*, monkey + *so*, to break wind + *ki*, to greet; thus (3) note MONKEY FART n.]

obsquatulate *v. see* ABSQUATULATE v.

obstroculous *adj.* [1930s] (*Aus.*) obstreperous. [var. on OBSTRO-POLOUS adj.]

obstropolous *adj.* (*also* **obstriperous, obstroperous, obstro-polis**) [mid-18C–1910s] a corruption of SE *obstreperous*.

obvious *adj.* [late 19C] (*UK society*) fat, overweight. [one cannot avoid seeing the person]

obviously severe *adj.* [late 19C–1900s] (*UK society*) extremely rude. [euph.]

o.c. *n.* [1990s+] (*US Black teen*) public housing projects in the Fillmore district of San Francisco. [abbr. *out of control*]

occabot *n.* [mid–late 19C] tobacco. [backsl.]

occifer *n. see* OSSIFER n.

occupant *n.* [16C] a brothel prostitute. [she works in an OCCUPYING HOUSE n.]

occupation *n.* [17C–18C] sexual intercourse. [OCCUPY v.]

occupy *v.* [late 16C–early 19C] of a man, to have sexual intercourse. [*occupy* is one of those synons. for copulation listed in Florio's *Worlde of Wordes* (1598): 'Fottere, to iape, to sard, to fucke, to swive, to occupy.' Like many taboo terms it moved from SE (it is used 10 times in the *Authorized Version*) once it had been perceived as vulgar. Shakespeare notes this in *Henry IV Part II* (1597): 'A captaine? Gods light these villaines wil make the word as odious as the word occupy, which was an excellent good worde before it was ill sorted']

occupying house *n.* [16C] a brothel (cf. ACCOMMODATION HOUSE n.). [OCCUPY v. + HOUSE n.[1] (1)]

ocean *n. see* OCEANS n.

ocean floor *n.* [1900s] (*Aus.*) the floor. [rhy. sl.]

ocean hell *n.* [mid-19C] (*Aus.*) the penal establishment sited on Norfolk Island for particularly recalcitrant convicts.

ocean liner *n.* [20C+] (*Aus.*) a woman, a girlfriend. [rhy. sl. = CLINER n.]

ocean pearl *n.* [20C+] a woman, a girlfriend. [rhy. sl.]

oceans *n.* (*also* **ocean**) [late 16C+] a large amount, lots of. [SE *ocean*, 'an immense or boundless expanse of anything']

ocean wave *n.* [1920s–60s] a shave. [rhy. sl.]

ochive *n.* (*also* **oschive**) [early 18C–mid-19C] (*UK Und.*) a bone-handled knife. [Rom. *o chiv*, the knife; or ? Lat. *os*, a bone + CHIV n.[1] (1)]

ochorboc *n.* [late 19C–1900s] beer. [Ital. *bocca*, mouth; popularized by Italian organ-grinders]

ochre *n.* [mid–late 19C] money, gold (cf. CANARY n.[5]). [SE *ochre*, a pale brownish yellow]

ocker *n.* (*Aus.*) **1** [1910s+] a nickname for anyone called Oscar. **2** [1970s+] (*also* **ock**) a boorish, loutish, unsophisticated, ultra-nationalistic Australian, whose rise, and celebration, coincided with Gough Whitlam's Labour government (1972–5); thus *ocker*, to behave like an ocker; *ockerization*, vulgarization; *ockerized*, vulgarized; *ockerdom*, the world of the ocker. **3** [1970s+] anyone seen as boorishly nationalistic. **4** [1970s+] Australian English. [the character *Ocker* orig. portrayed by actor Ron Frazer (1924–83) in the TV series *The Mavis Bramston Show* (1965–8)]

ocker *adj.* [1970s+] (*Aus.*) boorish, loutish, ultra-nationalistic. [OCKER n. (2)]

ockerina *n.* [1970s+] (*Aus.*) a female OCKER n. (2). [OCKER n. (2) + fem. sfx *-ina*; a pun on the musical instrument, an *ocarina*]

ockerism *n.* [1970s+] (*Aus.*) boorish behaviour, oafish, self-satisfaction. [OCKER n. (2)]

ock it! *excl.* [1970s+] (*US campus*) stop it! [? mispron.]

ocky *n.* [1960s+] (*Aus.*) an *octo*pus. [abbr.]

O cricum jiminy! *excl.* [late 19C] a euph. for O CHRIST JESUS! excl.

O cry! *excl.* [late 19C–1900s] a euph. for *O Christ*!

octane *n.* [1990s+] **1** (*US*) verve, zest. **2** (*drugs*) phencyclidine laced with gasoline.

octo *n.* [1910s] (*Aus.*) an *octo*pus. [abbr.]

October *n.* [mid-19C] blood. [SE *October ale*, a strong beer brewed in October]

octopus *n.* [1930s+] (*US*) a man who proves more sexually enthusiastic, thus keen to fondle, than his girlfriend or date might wish. [his '8' hands]

O.D. *n.* (*also* **o.d.**) [1950s+] (*drugs*) **1** an *overdose*. **2** one who has taken an *overdose*. [abbr.]

O.D. *v.* (*also* **o.d., oh-dee**) **1** [1960s+] (*drugs*) to *overdose* (fatally or otherwise) on a given drug. **2** [1960s+] (*drugs*) to give someone a drug overdose. **3** [1970s+] a fig. synon. in non-drug contexts; to act excessively, without restraint, to be greedy. [O.D. n.]

o.d. *n.* (*also* **o.d.v.**) [mid-19C–1920s] brandy. [pun on pron. of Fr. *eau-de-vie*]

od *n.* (*also* **odd, ond**) [late 16C+] a euph. for *God*, used in mild oaths, e.g. OD ROT IT! excl.; also found in a variety of possessive combs. (cf. BOB n.[2]; ODS n.).

oday *n.* (*also* **O-day**) [1920s–80s] (*US*) money. [cod Lat. *oday* = DOUGH n.[1] (1)]

odd *n.*[1] [1930s–80s] **1** a policeman. **2** a police car. [ety. unknown]

odd *n.*[2] *see* OD n.

odd *adj.* [late 19C–1940s] homosexual. [euph.]

-odd *sfx* [mid-19C+] of age or number, approximately, roughly, slightly more than a stated number, e.g. *He's forty-odd*.

odd as Dick's hatband *phr. see* QUEER AS DICK'S HATBAND phr.

oddball *n.* [1940s+] (*orig. US*) an eccentric, unusual person. [SE *odd* + -BALL sfx]

oddball *adj.* [1950s+] peculiar. [ODDBALL n.]

odd bod *n.* [1940s+] (*orig. milit.*) **1** an odd man out. **2** any non-specific person. [SE *odd body*]

odd-come-shortly *phr.* (*also* **odd-come-short**) [mid-18C–1950s] a day; always in phr. *one of these odd-come shortlys*, one of these days, sooner or later.

oddcum shorts *n.* (*also* **odd-come shorts**) [early–mid-19C] small, nondescript items, 'bits and bobs'.

odd fish *n.* [mid-17C+] an eccentric person. [SE *odd* + FISH n.[3]]

oddie *n. see* ODDY n.

oddish *adj.* [late 19C–1900s] drunk (cf. ADDLED adj.).

odd kick in one's gallop *n.* [late 18C–early 19C] a whim, a fancy, an eccentricity. [equestrian imagery]

odd lot *n.* [1930s–80s] a police car. [ODD n.¹ (2) + SE *lot*]

odd-mark firm *n.* [1990s+] (*UK Und.*) a group or gang that includes various different types of minor criminals, and even a few non-criminal types. [FIRM n. (1); ? its SE *odd markings*]

odd rot it! *excl. see* OD ROT IT! excl.

odds *n.¹* [1940s] (*US Und.*) a woman, esp. one who will support her partner through prostitution. [SE *odds*, i.e. the idea of gambling on a woman being prepared to prostitute herself]

odds *n.² see* ODS n.

odds *v.* **1** [20C+] to avoid, to 'get out of'. **2** [1950s+] to risk, to take a chance. [SE *odds*, as used in betting]

odds and sods *n.* [1910s+] (*orig. milit.*) odds and ends, but used of both objects and people. [the orig. WW1 milit. use defined as '"details" attached to Battalion Headquarters for miscellaneous offices, batmen, sanitary men, professional footballers and boxers on nominal duties etc' (Brophy & Partridge, *Songs and Slang of the British Soldier*, 1930)]

odds bob(s)! *excl. see* ODSBOBS! excl.

odds, bods and sods *n.* [1950s+] (*Aus.*) people at random. [ext. of ODDS AND SODS n. + BOD n. (2)]

odds-on *n.* [20C+] (*Aus.*) the odds-on favourite, in a horserace or other sporting contest.

odds on *phr.* [20C+] very likely, in all likelihood. [gambling imagery]

oddy *n.* (*also* **oddie**) [1900s–50s] (*Aus.*) a halfpenny. [the 'odd halfpenny' in a sum of money or a price]

O'Donnell's gallon *n.* [20C+] (*Irish*) a full glass or tankard of alcohol. [generic/anecdotal use of *O'Donnell* + *gallon*, a container for liquids]

od rot it! *excl.* (*also* **add rot it! odd rot it! od rabbit! od rat it! od rut it! ord rot it!**) [mid-18C–1900s] a mild oath, lit. *God rot it!* [euph.; OD n.]

ods *n.* (*also* **odds, od's, 'ods**) [late 16C+] (*orig. US*) a mild euph. for *God's*, used in combs., e.g. *od's blood, od's body, od's bones, od's death, od's feet,* OD'S FLESH! excl., *od's foot, od's life, od's mercy, od's truth, od's vengeance, od's blessed will, od's wounds* etc. Also with dimins. and perversions of words, as ODSBOBS! excl., *od's bodikins* (little body), *od's bud* (blood), OD'S FISH! excl., *odslid* (eyelid), *odd's lifelings, odsnigs, odsnouns, odsoons* (wounds), *od's-pittikins, od's-pittkins, od's-pitlikins* (pity), *od's wucks, odzooks, od's-zookers, od's-swookers* (hooks), *od zounds* (wounds), *od's haricots, kilderkins, od's my life.* [OD n.]

odsbobs! *excl.* (*also* **odds bob! odds bobs! odsbuds!**) [late 17C–1900s] a general oath, lit. *God's babes.* [ODS n.]

od's fish! *excl.* [late 17C–1910s] a general oath, one of many ways of euphemizing God. [ODS n.; *God's flesh*, with overtones of the miracle of the loaves and fishes]

odsflesh! *excl.* [late 17C–early 19C] a mild euph. excl., lit. 'God's flesh'. [ODS n.]

odso! *excl.* (*also* **udso!**) [late 16C–early 19C] a mild euph. excl., lit. 'God's oath'. [ODS n.]

o.d.v. *n. see* O.D. n.

o.e. *n.* [1980s+] (*US Black*) Old English malt liquor. [abbr.]

oedipus rex *n.* [1970s+] sex. [rhy. sl.; ult. Gk tragedy, *Oedipus Rex* by Sophocles]

oes *adj.* [20C+] (*S.Afr.*) seedy, run-down, 'under the weather'. [Afk. *oes*, feeble]

of a certain age *phr.* [mid-18C+] a euph. description of a middle-aged or older person, usu. a woman.

of a dizzy age *phr.* [late 19C–1900s] (*UK society*) ageing. ['makes the spectator giddy to think of the victim's years' (Ware)]

ofaginzy *n.* [1940s–50s] (*US Black*) a White person. [? OFAY adj. + GINZO n.; note Cohen (ed.), *Studies in Slang* V (1997), suggests that if ofay = Fr. *au fait*, then ofaginzy = (*c'est*) *au fait ainsi*]

ofay *n.* (*also* **fay, fey, ofey, oofay**) [late 19C+] (*US*) a usu. derog. term for a White person. [ety. unknown. Links to Fr. *au fait*, aware, have been dismissed, although Cohen (ed.), *Studies in Slang* V (1997), sees this as the proper ety.; doubts are also cast on Yoruba *ofe*, 'a charm that lets one jump so high as to disappear', thus trouble (the cause of such vanishing), thus a White man (the essence of trouble); note Mezzrow & Wolfe, *Really the Blues* (1946): 'Ofay, of course, is pig Latin for *foe.*' Cohen rejects this: 'there is no indication of Blacks ever engaging in the Pig Latin type of word play']

ofay *adj.* (*also* **fay, oofay**) [late 19C+] (*orig. US Black*) White; pertaining to White culture. [OFAY n.]

ofay trash *n. see* WHITE TRASH n.

ofey *n. see* OFAY n.

off *n.¹* [1950s+] the start. [sporting jargon *off*, the start of any race, esp. one with horses or dogs]

off *n.²* [1960s+] (*S.Afr.*) free time. [abbr. SE *day/time off*]

off *n.³* [1990s+] (*UK Und.*) a fight. [the idea that things KICK OFF v.² (1)]

off *adj.¹* **1** [18C+] uninterested in, not wanting. **2** [late 19C+] unfashionable, unattractive. **3** [late 19C+] feeling or looking unwell, despondent, unenthusiastic. **4** [late 19C+] stale, in poor condition, out-of-date. **5** [20C+] of food, unavailable on a menu. **6** [1910s+] forbidden. **7** [1950s+] aloof, withdrawn. **8** [1980s] in a trance. [(7) f. (1)]

off *adj.²* (*UK Und.*) **1** [mid-19C+] of a crime, successfully achieved. **2** [1930s] of an arrest, successful.

off *adj.³* [mid–late 19C] (*US Und.*) gone, stolen.

off *adj.⁴* **1** [late 19C+] mad, very foolish (cf. OFF AT THE HEAD phr.; OFF ONE'S BASE phr.). **2** [1960s+] happy, elated, enjoying the positive effects of drugs or drink. [abbr. OFF ONE'S HEAD phr.]

off *adj.⁵* [1910s+] (*drugs*) not using an addictive drug, usu. narcotic; also of alcohol.

off *adj.⁶* [1990s+] (*Aus. Und.*) dead, dying. [SE *off*, no longer happening, cancelled]

off *v.¹* **1** [late 19C+] to leave, to go off. **2** [late 19C+] to get rid of, to reject, to dismiss. **3** [1920s–30s] to die. **4** [1960s+] (*US*) to dispose of, to sell. **5** [1970s] to humiliate. [abbr. SE *make off, send off, go off*]

off *v.²* **1** [1950s+] (*orig. US Black*) to kill or murder. **2** [1960s+] (*orig. US*) of a man, to have sexual intercourse. **3** [1960s+] (*US Und.*) to rob, usu. with violence. **4** [1960s+] (*US Black*) to beat up someone. **5** [1970s] (*US police*) to apprehend and arrest someone. [abbr. relevant uses of KNOCK OFF v.³, KNOCK OFF v.⁵]

off, be *v.* [1960s] to happen, esp. of a violent incident. [var. on GO OFF v.¹ (3) or SE *come off*]

off *prep.* [1960s+] (*orig. US*) by means of, e.g. *Sarah was grooving off Belle and Sebastian.*

off and on *adj.* [mid-19C+] indecisive, variable, vacillating.

off at the head *phr.* [mid-19C+] eccentric, mad (cf. OFF adj.⁴; OFF ONE'S BASE phr.).

off base *adj.* [1940s+] (*US*) skewed, incorrect. [OFF ONE'S BASE phr.]

off beam *phr. see* OFF (THE) BEAM phr.

off-beat *adj.* [1930s+] (*orig. US*) unconventional, out of the ordinary; later usage also as wrong or mistaken. [orig. jazz use]

off-brand *n.* [1990s+] **1** (*US*) a Black person. **2** (*US Black gang*) a rival gangster. [OFF-BRAND adj.]

off-brand *adj.* [1960s+] (*orig. US Black*) **1** of a person, odd, peculiar, inferior, outside the group norm. **2** unfashionable, esp. when wearing too many (clashing) colours. **3** of a child, illegitimate. **4** second-rate. [SE *off-brand*, not a mainstream or *brand*name product]

off-brand cigarette *n.* [1970s+] (*drugs*) a marijuana cigarette (cf. AFRICAN WOODBINE n.). [OFF-BRAND adj. (1) + SE *cigarette*]

off-breed *n.* [1960s+] (*US*) a person or animal of mixed or indeterminate ancestry, a mongrel.

off-chump *adj.* [late 19C–1900s] lacking appetite, off one's food. [SE *off* + *chump*, the thick end of a loin of mutton]

off-colour *adj.* **1** [late 19C+] in poor taste, usu. of smutty humour. **2** [1940s–70s] (*US Und.*) homosexual. [SE *off-colour*, unwell]

offee kay *n.* [1930s] coffee. [backsl.]

offer someone out *v.* [late 19C+] (*Aus.*) to challenge to a fight.

office *n.*[1] [late 17C+] the place one works; 'His Office, any Man's ordinary Haunt, or Plying-place, be it Tavern, Ale-house, Gaminghouse' (B.E.). [this use has been sustained into 20C+, found outside the SE business context in a wide range of occupations, from pimping to commercial flying, in all of which the speaker terms their place of work, whether the street or an aircraft cockpit, the *office*]

office *n.*[2] [early 18C–1960s] a toilet, a privy (cf. GINGERBREAD-OFFICE n.). [abbr. HOUSE OF OFFICE n.]

office *n.*[3] **1** [mid-18C+] a hint, a warning, a 'tip-off'; usu. in phr. GIVE SOMEONE THE OFFICE v. **2** [19C+] information (with no inference of secrecy). **3** [mid-19C+] (*UK/US prison*) a signal. [SE *office*, a duty to another, a service, i.e. the lookout's duty is to give a warning]

office *v.* [early 19C–1980s] (*esp. US Und.*) to warn, to tip off, to indicate. [OFFICE n.[3]]

office of ease *n. see* HOUSE OF EASEMENT n.

office piano *n.* [1940s+] (*US*) a typewriter.

officerette *n.* [20C+] (*US*) a policewoman (cf. COPESS n.). [SE *officer* + fem. sfx *-ette*]

officers of the 52nds *n.* [late 19C–1900s] (*Irish*) young men who attend church regularly every Sunday. [there are 52 Sundays each year]

officer-toed *adj.* [20C+] (*Ulster*) with one's toes turned out. [the stance of police officers on parade]

office sneak *n.* [mid–late 19C] one who enters and steals from an office or business, e.g. coats and/or umbrellas. [SE *office* + SNEAK n.[1] (4)]

office worker *n.* [20C+] a shirker. [rhy. sl.]

offie *n.* (*also* **offy**) [1950s+] an *off*-licence. [orig. a counter in a public house over which alcohol could be sold for consumption off the premises. The off-licence proper declined during the 1970s–80s but the term is still used for wine merchants and similar stores]

offish *adj.* [mid-19C+] reserved, distant, aloof; thus *offishness*, reserve, coolness. [abbr. SE *stand-offish* but note OFF adj.[1] (1)]

off it *phr.*[1] *see* OFF ONE'S HEAD phr.

off it *phr.*[2] *see* OFF THE WALL phr.

off-jiving *n.* [1940s] (*US Black*) distasteful behaviour.

off like a bride's nightie *phr.* (*also* **off like a prom dress**) [1950s+] (*Aus./US campus*) leaving or acting extremely fast, very speedily.

off like a bucket of prawns in the hot sun *phr.* [1960s+] (*Aus.*) **1** leaving very quickly. **2** stinking, rotten.

offmans *n.* [1990s+] (*UK Und.*) the advanced preparation of a means of escape. [SE *off*/OFF v.[1] (1) + -MANS sfx]

off one's ass *phr.* [1980s+] (*US campus*) to a very great extent, extremely.

off one's bap *phr. see* OFF ONE'S CAKE phr.

off one's base *phr.* (*US*) **1** [late 19C+] insane, crazy, confused, muddled, mistaken (cf. OFF ONE'S BEAN phr.; OFF ONE'S BLOCK phr.; OFF ONE'S CAKE phr.; OFF ONE'S CHUMP phr.; OFF ONE'S DIP phr.; OFF ONE'S DOT phr.; OFF ONE'S FACE phr.; OFF ONE'S HEAD phr.; OFF ONE'S JUMP phr.; OFF ONE'S KADOOVA phr.; OFF ONE'S KAZIP phr.; OFF ONE'S KNACKERS n.; OFF ONE'S KNOCKER phr.; OFF ONE'S LID phr.; OFF ONE'S LOOP phr.; OFF ONE'S NANA phr.; OFF ONE'S NOB phr.; OFF ONE'S NUT phr.; OFF ONE'S PANNICAN phr.; OFF ONE'S PULLEY phr.; OFF ONE'S ROCKER phr.; OFF ONE'S ROCKET phr.; OFF ONE'S SAUCER phr.[1]; OFF ONE'S TILE phr.; OFF ONE'S TOP TRAVERSE phr.; OFF ONE'S TROLLEY phr.; OUT OF ONE'S BOX phr.).

2 [1930s+] acting in an anti-social or otherwise unacceptable manner, 'out of line', 'out of order'. [baseball jargon]

off one's bean *phr.* [20C+] **1** insane, eccentric (cf. OFF ONE'S BASE phr.). **2** drunk (cf. ADDLED adj.). [SE *off* + BEAN n.[5]]

off one's beat *phr.* [1900s–10s] (*Aus.*) drifting away from the subject in hand, out of one's usual routine. [SE *off* + BEAT n.[1] (2)]

off one's bike *phr.* [1950s] (*Aus.*) very angry.

off one's block *phr.* [1910s+] (*orig. milit.*) **1** angry. **2** insane (cf. OFF ONE'S BASE phr.). [SE *off* + BLOCK n.[1] (2)]

off one's bonce *phr. see* OFF ONE'S HEAD phr.

off one's box *phr. see* OUT OF ONE'S BOX phr. (2).

off one's brain *phr. see* OUT OF ONE'S BRAIN phr.

off one's cake *phr.* (*also* **off one's bap**) [1980s+] crazy, insane (cf. BANANAS adj.; OFF ONE'S BASE phr.). [? you have to be crazy not to want to eat cake]

off one's chump *phr.* (*also* **off one's chomp/conk**) [mid-19C+] mad, eccentric (cf. OFF ONE'S BASE phr.). [SE *off* + CHUMP n.[1] (1)/CONK n.[1] (4)]

off one's dip *phr.* (*also* **off one's dipper**) [late 19C–1920s] mad, eccentric (cf. OFF ONE'S BASE phr.). [SE *off* + *dip*, a sauce]

off one's dot *phr.* (*also* **off one's dotty**) [late 19C–1920s] mad, eccentric (cf. OFF ONE'S BASE phr.). [SE *off* + DOTTY adj.]

off one's face *phr.* [1960s+] **1** under the influence of drink or drugs. **2** in fig. use, extremely enthusaistic about; thus *go off one's face*, to be extremely enthusiastic about, to collapse with laughter. **3** crazy (cf. OFF ONE'S BASE phr.).

off one's feed *phr.* **1** [mid-19C+] depressed, miserable, nervous. **2** [1900s] incompetent, unskilled. [horse stable jargon]

off one's gourd *phr. see* OUT OF ONE'S GOURD phr.

off one's head *phr.* (*also* **off it, off one's bonce, ...one's onion, ...one's thatch**) **1** [mid-19C+] insane, out of one's mind (cf. OFF ONE'S BASE phr.). **2** [1960s+] (*drugs*) intoxicated by a drug. **3** [1960s+] drunk (cf. ADDLED adj.; ARSEHOLED adj.). [SE *off* + SE *head*/BONCE n. (1)/ONION n. (2)/THATCH n. (1)]

off one's high horse *phr.* (*also* **down from one's high horse**) [late 19C+] deprived of arrogance.

off one's jump *phr.* [1950s] (*Irish*) crazy, insane (cf. OFF ONE'S BASE phr.).

off one's kadoova *phr.* [late 19C+] (*Aus.*) crazy, eccentric, mentally unstable (cf. OFF ONE'S BASE phr.). [SE *off* + ? KADI n., thus fig. *head*]

off one's kazip *phr.* (*also* **off one's kerzip**) [1900s–30s] (*US*) insane, eccentric (cf. OFF ONE'S BASE phr.). [ety. unknown]

off one's knackers *n.* [2000s] insane, stupid (cf. OFF ONE'S BASE phr.). [SE *off* + KNACKERS n.]

off one's knocker *phr.* [1900s] (*Aus.*) mad, insane, uncontrolled (cf. OFF ONE'S BASE phr.).

off one's lid *phr.* [1900s] (*US*) mad (cf. OFF ONE'S BASE phr.). [SE *off* + LID n.[1] (2)]

off one's loop *phr.* [1940s] eccentric, mad (cf. CLEAN AROUND THE BEND phr.; OFF ONE'S BASE phr.). [SE *off* + LOOPY adj. (1)]

off one's nana *phr.* [1940s+] eccentric, mad (cf. BANANAS adj.; OFF ONE'S BASE phr.). [SE *off* + NANA n. (2)]

off one's nob *phr.* [1950s+] **1** eccentric, insane (cf. OFF ONE'S BASE phr.). **2** drunk (cf. ADDLED adj.). [SE *off* + NOB n.[1] (1)]

off one's nut *phr.* [mid-19C+] **1** drunk (cf. ADDLED adj.). **2** mad (cf. OFF ONE'S BASE phr.). **3** infatuated, very enthusiastic. [SE *off* + NUT n.[1] (2)]

off one's oats *phr.* [late 19C+] feeling unwell, esp. if this diminishes one's appetite. [equine imagery]

off one's onion *phr. see* OFF ONE'S HEAD phr.

off one's pannican *phr.* (*also* **off one's pannikin**) [late 19C–1930s] (*Aus.*) eccentric, crazy; thus *go off one's pannikin*, to lose one's temper, to lose emotional control (cf. OFF ONE'S BASE phr.). [SE *off* + PANNIKIN n.]

off one's peck *phr. see* PECK n.[1] (1).

off one's pony *phr.* [1960s] (*US*) in a state of collapse from excessive drinking. [i.e. fallen over]

off one's pot *phr. see* OUT OF ONE'S BOX *phr.* (2).

off one's pulley *phr.* [1990s+] insane, eccentric (cf. OFF ONE'S BASE *phr.*). [? i.e. fallen off]

off one's rag *phr.* [1990s+] (*UK juv.*) in a furious temper. [SE *off* + RAG *n.*³ (2)]

off one's rocker *phr.* (*also* **off one's rock**) **1** [late 19C+] crazy (cf. OFF ONE'S BASE *phr.*). **2** [1950s+] in fig. use, acting excessively (although not necessarily madly). [SE *rocker*, a rocking-chair]

off one's rocket *phr.* [1910s–50s] crazy (cf. OFF ONE'S BASE *phr.*).

off one's saucer *phr.*¹ [mid-19C–1900s] (*Aus.*) disinclined, dispirited, 'out of sorts' (cf. OFF ONE'S BASE *phr.*). [the image of a pet refusing its food]

off one's saucer *phr.*² [20C+] (*Aus.*) mad, eccentric (cf. OFF ONE'S BASE *phr.*). [the image is of a spinning 'flying saucer']

off one's thatch *phr. see* OFF ONE'S HEAD *phr.*

off one's tile *phr.* [1910s] (*Aus.*) mad, angry (cf. OFF ONE'S BASE *phr.*).

off one's tits *phr. see* OUT OF ONE'S TITS *phr.*

off one's top traverse *phr.* [20C+] (*Aus.*) mad, eccentric (cf. OFF ONE'S BASE *phr.*).

off one's tree *phr. see* OUT OF ONE'S TREE *phr.*

off one's trolley *phr.* **1** [late 19C+] crazy, eccentric (cf. OFF ONE'S BASE *phr.*). **2** [1900s] physically unbalanced; thus *knock off one's trolley*, to knock down. [SE *trolley-car*, an electric-powered coach running along metal tracks set into the roadway. The Manhattan trolleys, which were not allowed overhead cables (as were those in Brooklyn) after so many came down in the hurricane of 1888, picked up their supply from an electrified third rail and so if the car became derailed, its power was lost]

off-ox *n.* [mid-19C+] (*US*) a stubborn or headstrong person. [lit. the 'offside' ox of a pair, presumably linked to such characteristics]

off-shunt *n. see* SHUNT (OFF) v. (1).

offside *adj.* [1910s+] (*Aus./N.Z.*) **1** in poor taste, socially unacceptable; thus *play offside*, to act excessively. **2** out of favour, in bad favour with. [sporting imagery]

offsider *n.* [mid-19C+] (*Aus./N.Z.*) an assistant, a helper. [SE *offsider*, an animal positioned on the off-side of a team]

off someone's titty *phr. see* ON SOMEONE'S TITTY *phr.*

off song *adj.* [late 19C+] not working well, in bad condition. [one is not 'in tune' or 'off key']

off tap *adj.*¹ [1990s+] (*US campus*) excellent.

off tap *adj.*² [1990s+] (*Aus.*) **1** acting in an unacceptable manner; thus condemned to death. **2** eccentric, mad.

off the back *phr.* [1990s+] surreptitious, on the side.

off (the) beam *phr.* [1940s+] (*orig. US*) wholly incorrect; often intensified as *way off beam*. [orig. air force use, referring to radio beams that guide aircraft]

off the boards *adv.* [late 19C–1920s] (*US*) to excess, to a great extent.

off the bus *phr. see* ON THE BUS *phr.*

off the chain *phr.* (*also* **off the string**) [20C+] (*orig. Aus.*) free, unrestrained or unrestricted. [the image of a chained convict]

off the cob *phr.* [1930s–50s] (*US*) **1** unfashionable, out of style. **2** backwards. **3** poor. [SE *corncob*, thus the implication of rustic poverty]

off the dome *phr. see* OFF THE (TOP OF THE) DOME *phr.*

off the hook *phr.*¹ [1930s–60s] (*US drugs*) ceasing to take narcotic drugs. [as opposed to ON THE HOOK *phr.*³]

off the hook *phr.*² [1950s+] out of trouble, freed from a difficult situation.

off the hook *phr.*³ [1990s+] **1** (*US Black/teen*) used of something so good as to transcend description. **2** (*US*) completely unacceptable, crazy, out of control. [telephonic imagery]

off the hooks *phr.*¹ (*also* **off the hook**) **1** [mid-17C–19C] ill-tempered, peevish; 'in a state'. **2** [mid-17C–1900s] crazy, eccentric.

off the hooks *phr.*² [late 17C] to excess. [? imagery of being unfettered; one 'flies off the hooks']

off the hooks *phr.*³ [mid-19C] at once. [synon. with SE *off the peg*, i.e. instantly available]

off the hooks *phr.*⁴ [mid-19C–1920s] dead; thus DROP OFF THE HOOK(S) v.; GO OFF THE HOOKS v.; *knock off the hooks*, to kill, to murder. [the ancient practice of exposing the head and limbs of executed traitors in public places around a city]

off the meat rack *phr.* [2000s] (*US Black*) superlative, first-rate, astonishing.

off the nail *phr.* [early 19C] tipsy, slightly drunk (cf. ADDLED *adj.*). [GO OFF AT THE NAIL v.]

off the nut *phr.* [1930s+] (*US*) free from debt. [ON THE NUT *phr.*]

off the rails *phr.* **1** [mid-19C+] emotionally unstable; thus *come off the rails*, to suffer an emotional breakdown. **2** [late 19C+] errant, mistaken; esp. in phr. *go off the rails*, to blunder, to make a mistake. [railway imagery]

off the reservation *phr.* **1** [late 19C–1900s] (*US*) absent, away; thus *off one's mental reservation*, insane, out of touch with reality (cf. OUT OF TOWN *phr.*). **2** [1930s] in fig. use, drunk (cf. ADDLED *adj.*).

off the stones *phr.* [mid-19C+] outside London. [reverse of ON THE STONES *phr.* (3)]

off the string *phr. see* OFF THE CHAIN *phr.*

off the top *phr.*¹ [20C+] taken first, esp. when sharing out money, legally or otherwise, e.g. *expenses come off the top*.

off the top *phr.*² [1990s+] (*US*) from the beginning, immediately. [musical imagery, one reads a score from the top]

off the (top of the) dome *phr.* [1980s+] (*US Black*) of rap lyrics, spontaneous, composed as one goes along; usu. as *coming off the (top of the) dome* or *going off the (top of the) dome*. [SE *off* + DOME *n.* (1)]

off (the) track *phr.* [20C+] behaving badly, making mistakes, being inconsistent.

off the wall *adv.* [1970s] (*US*) spontaneously, unconventionally. [OFF THE WALL *phr.*]

off the wall *phr.* (*also* **off it**) [1950s+] **1** (*orig. US*) difficult, obstreperous, strange. **2** (*orig. US*) bizarre, peculiar. **3** (*US Black*) unimportant, uninteresting. **4** (*US campus*) excellent, first-rate. [? the skewed bouncing of a ball thrown against a wall]

off-time *adj.* [1930s+] (*US*) **1** badly timed, at the wrong time, therefore unacceptable. **2** unfashionable.

off-time jive *n.* [1930s–40s] (*US Black*) a weak excuse. [OFF-TIME *adj.* (1) + JIVE *n.*¹ (2)]

off track *phr. see* OFF (THE) TRACK *phr.*

off-trail *adj.* [1950s] (*US*) unconventional, out of the ordinary.

off with *v.* [late 19C+] to take off at once, e.g. *off with you*, get going, go away.

offy *n. see* OFFIE *n.*

of sorts *adj.* [20C+] undistinguished, second-rate, barely adequate.

ofter *n.* [late 19C] (*sporting*) a regular attender, usu. at the races, the music hall etc. [SE *often*]

o.g. *n.*¹ [late 19C–1970s] (*US Black*) a woman, esp. one's mother or wife. [abbr. *old girl*]

o.g. *n.*² (*US Black*) **1** [1980s+] a street-smart person, a leading member of a gang. **2** [1990s+] a close male friend. **3** [1990s+] a veteran of the streets. [abbr. *original gangster*. The term allegedly appeared with the formation of the Original Gangster Crips, a breakaway group of Los Angeles' West Side Crips. Both gangs were a sub-group or SET *n.*⁴ (1) of the larger gang, the Crips. One theory suggests that only proven killers qualify as true *o.g.s*]

og *n.* (*also* **ogg**) [1930s–50s] (*Aus./N.Z.*) a shilling. [HOG *n.*¹ (1)]

o.g.b. *n.* [1980s+] (*US Black gang*) original ghetto blood, i.e. a 'real' gangster. [O.G. *n.*² (1) + BLOOD *n.*⁵ (1)]

oggins *n. see* HOGGINS *n.*

oggy *n.* [1990s+] (*UK juv.*) a supposed 'disease' contracted by boys through physical interaction with girls.

ogle *n.* **1** [late 17C+] usu. in pl., an eye. **2** [late 17C+] an amorous glance, a frankly sexual stare. **3** [mid-19C] a scarf. [OGLE v.]

ogle *v.* **1** [late 17C] to look alluring. **2** [late 17C–18C] (*also* **oagle**) to look at invitingly, amorously, to leer. **3** [18C] (*UK Und.*) to examine, to appraise, to look over. [Low Ger. *oegen*, to look at, thence Ger. *äugeln*, to ogle, to leer; (2) and (3) SE by 19C]

ogle-fakes *n.* [1980s+] (*Polari*) **1** false eyelashes. **2** spectacles. [OGLE n. (1) + SE *fake*]

ogler *n.* **1** [late 18C–early 19C] an eye. **2** [early 19C] a punch in the eye. [OGLE n. (1)]

ogles *n. see* OGLE n. (1).

ogotaspuotas *n.* [late 19C] nonsense, rubbish. [a slogan carried on a flag waved during a pro-Cretan demonstration by radicals, held in Hyde Park on 7 March 1897. The word was promptly transliterated as 'Oh go to spew!']

oh *n. see* O n.

oh-be-cheerful/oh-be-joyful *n. see* O-BE-JOYFUL n.

oh boy! *excl.* [1910s+] (*orig. US*) a general excl., usu. of surprise, excitement, amazement.

oh, by heck *n.* [1930s–40s] (*US*) the neck. [rhy. sl.]

oh-dee *v. see* O.D. v.

O-head *n.* [1960s] (*drugs*) an opium addict. [O n. (2) + -HEAD sfx (3)]

O Henry *n. see* JOHN T HENRY n.

oh mamma! *excl.* [late 19C+] (*US*) an excl. of wonder, surprise, excitement etc.

oh, my dear *n.* [20C+] beer. [rhy. sl.]

oh my leg! *excl.* [early 19C] a teasing remark, aimed at anyone recently freed from prison. [the ref. is to the leg-irons one wears there]

-oholic *sfx see* -AHOLIC sfx.

oh smack! *excl.* [1990s+] (*US teen*) a reaction to something astonishing, an excl. expressing the sudden realisation that a thing or a situation is pleasing. [fig. use of SMACK n.¹ (3)]

oh swallow yourself! *excl.* [late 19C] an excl. of dismissal, GO TO HELL! excl.

O-H-ten *n.* [20C+] (*US*) Ohio. [abbr.]

oh Winifred! *excl.* [late 19C] an excl. of disbelief. [joc. use of proper name]

oh, you —! *excl.* [20C+] (*US*) an excl. of affection; esp. as *oh, you kid!* [KID n.¹ (4)]

oh-zee *n. see* O.Z. n.

oi! *excl.* [1960s+] a general excl. of address, synon. with earlier *hoy!* come here! pay attention! etc. [note the brief 1980s *Oi music*, geared to the sensibilities of a SKINHEAD n. (3)/football fan audience and featuring such bands as Sham 69 and Cockney Rejects. Such music mutated into the racist/nationalist songs of Europe's hardcore right-wing music business]

-oid *sfx* [1940s+] (*orig. US*) used in a nominal or adjectival form to express a brainless or automatic quality, e.g. *zomboid*. [abbr. SE *android*]

oik *n.* (*also* **oick**) [1930s+] an unpleasant youth. [orig. school use, a working man, subseq. an unpopular pupil or any member of a rival school]

oikish *adj.* [1930s+] unpleasant, crude, vulgar, usu. of a youth. [OIK n.]

oil *n.*¹ **1** [17C] vaginal secretions (cf. BINDERJUICE n.). **2** [17C–1900s] semen (cf. BOLLOCK SNOT n.).

oil *n.*² **1** [mid-19C; 1910s+] (*US*) flattery, sweet talk; often in OLD OIL n. **2** [late 19C+] graft, bribery, and the money for paying it. **3** [20C+] (*Aus./N.Z.*) information, which *oils* the wheels of communication. **4** [1900s–40s] (*US Und.*) nitroglycerin; gelignite. **5** [1910s] facility, ability. **6** [1930s] lies, misinformation.

oil *n.*³ **1** [mid-19C+] (*later use US Black*) alcohol, esp. wine; thus *on the oil*, drinking alcohol. **2** [1920s–40s] (*Irish*) a drink. **3** [1940s–70s] (*US*) coffee. **4** [1960s+] (*drugs*) hashish oil or purified

hashish (cf. BLACK OIL n.). **5** [1980s+] (*drugs*) heroin. **6** [1980s+] (*drugs*) phencyclidine (cf. ACE n.⁴).

oil *n.*⁴ *see* OILER n.³.

oil *v.*¹ **1** [late 18C; 1920s–60s] (*also* **oil up**) to beat, to whip. **2** [1990s+] (*Irish*) to beat severely. [(1) 1920s–60s US Black]

oil *v.*² [late 19C+] to drink, to get drunk. [OIL n.³ (1)]

oil *v.*³ [1920s+] to move quietly, stealthily or in an underhand, surreptitious manner; also in combs. with various advs. such as *around, in, out, through*. [SE *oil*/OIL n.² (1)]

oil *v.*⁴ [1920s+] (*US*) to persuade in some deceitful manner; to bribe. [OIL n.²]

oil *v.*⁵ [1980s+] to inject oneself with a drug, usu. heroin. [OIL n.³ (5)]

oil bags *n.* [1960s] (*US Black*) the buttocks.

oil-burner *n.*¹ [1920s–40s] (*US*) a tobacco chewer. [US Navy *oil*, chewing tobacco]

oil-burner *n.*² [1930s+] (*US drugs*) **1** (*also* **oil-burner habit, oil-burning habit**) an extremely heavy level of heroin addiction. **2** an addict with a very high intake of narcotics. [predates OIL n.³ (5) so prob. more likely SE phr. *burn the midnight oil* or play on the oil lamps that were used to heat opium + HABIT n. (1)]

oil-burner *n.*³ [1930s+] a vehicle which, through a malfunctioning or dirty engine, uses up a disproportionate quantity of oil.

oil-burner *n.*⁴ [1960s+] (*US*) an exceptionally able or hard-working person. [SE phr. *burn the midnight oil*]

oil-burner/-burning habit *n. see* OIL-BURNER n.² (1).

oil-butt *n.* [early 19C] a black whale. [SE *oil* + BUTT n.¹ (2); its potential for processing for whale oil]

oil can *n.*¹ [1920s–30s] (*US*) a useless person, a good-for-nothing. [SE *oil*/OIL n.³ (1) + SE *can*]

oil can *n.*² [1940s] (*US*) a derog. term for an automobile.

oiled behind *n.* [1930s–40s] (*US Black*) the buttocks, after a beating. [OIL v.¹ (1) + BEHIND n. (1)]

oiled head *n.* [1930s–40s] (*US Black*) a head that has been beaten, usu. by the police. [OIL v.¹ (1) + SE *head*]

oiled (up) *adj.* [mid-18C+] (*orig. US*) drunk (cf. DAMP adj.). [OIL n.³ (1)]

oiler *n.*¹ **1** [late 19C–1950s] an oil well. **2** [late 19C+] (*orig. US*) an oilskin or oilcloth coat and/or trousers.

oiler *n.*² [1900s–60s] (*US*) a Mexican (cf. BATO n.). [var. on GREASER n.¹ (1)]

oiler *n.*³ (*also* **oil**) [1910s+] a heavy drinker. [OIL n.³ (1)]

oiler *n.*⁴ [1930s–40s] (*US Black*) one who is regularly involved in fights. [OIL v.¹ (1)]

oiler *n.*⁵ [1980s] (*drugs*) a cannabis cigarette mixing tobacco and hashish oil. [OIL n.³ (4)]

oil in *v.* [1920s+] to enter, to intrude. [OIL v.³]

oil it *v.* [20C+] (*US campus*) to stay up late studying. [SE phr. *burn the midnight oil*]

oil leak *n.* [1990s+] a Sikh. [rhy. sl.]

oil merchant *n.* [1930s–60s] (*US*) a flatterer or a swindler. [OIL n.² (1) + MERCHANT n.]

oil of angels *n.* (*also* **angel's oil**) [late 16C–17C] money used for bribery. [predates OIL n.² (2) so more likely fig. use of SE + SE *angel*, 'an old English gold coin, called more fully at first the angel-noble, being originally a new issue of the Noble, having as its device the archangel Michael standing upon, and piercing the dragon' (OED). Initially worth 6s 8d, it was worth 10s when last minted under Charles I]

oil of argentum *n.* [early 18C] money. [var. on OIL OF ANGELS n.; Lat. *argentum*, white money, silver]

oil of barley *n.* **1** [mid-17C–early 19C] strong ale. **2** [mid-19C] whisky. [SE *oil* + *barley*]

oil of baston *n.* [early 17C] a severe beating. [SE *oil* + *baston*, a cudgel, club or truncheon]

oil of birch *n.* [early 19C–1940s] a beating.

oil of gladness *n.* [late 18C–early 19C] a beating; often in phr. *I will anoint you with the oil of gladness*, I will beat you. [this *oil of…* usage is very common in Jamaican herbalism and religious cults; some refer to religious beliefs, others to the wishes that are invested in the oil itself. Terms include *oil of Calvary*; *oil of Virgin Mary*; *oil of power*; *oil of dead-man*; *oil of kill-him-dead*; *oil of bound-to-win*]

oil of hazel *n. see* HAZEL OIL *n.*

oil of holly *n.* [17C] a beating administered with a stick cut from a holly bush.

oil of joy *n.* [1910s–60s] (*US*) alcohol. [OIL n.³ (1) + SE *joy*]

oil of palm(s) *n. see* PALM OIL *n.*

oil of stirrup *n.* [late 18C–early 19C] a beating.

oil of strap'em/strappem *n. see* STRAP-OIL *n.*

oil of whip *n.* (*also* **oyl of rope**) [mid-17C–early 18C] a severe beating.

oil out (of) *v.* [1920s+] **1** to escape one's responsibility, to escape from an onerous duty or similar situation. **2** to slide away as if well-lubricated. [OIL v.³]

oil rigger *n.* [2000s] (*Irish*) a derog. term for a Black person. [rhy. sl. = NIGGER n.¹ (1)]

oil slick *n.* [1910s+] a Spaniard, a Greek. [rhy. sl. = SPIC n.]

oil someone's wheels *v.* [1990s+] to take care of, to be responsible for, to look after.

oil tanker *n.* [20C+] a general term of abuse. [rhy. sl. = WANKER n. (2)]

oil the hand *v.* (*also* **oil the fist/palm**) [17C; 1930s] to bribe.

oil the knocker *v.* [mid-19C–1910s] to tip or bribe a doorman or porter.

oil the machinery *v.* [late 19C] to have a drink. [euph.; OIL v.² + SE *machinery*]

oil the palm *v. see* OIL THE HAND *v.*

oil the tonsils *v.* [20C+] to have a drink. [OIL v.² + SE *tonsils*]

oil up *v.*¹ [late 19C+] (*Aus.*) to drink, to have a drink. [OIL n.³ (1)]

oil up *v.*² [late 19C+] to bribe someone. [OIL n.² (2)]

oil up *v.*³ [20C+] (*Aus.*) to impart information. [OIL n.² (3)]

oil up *v.*⁴ *see* OIL v.¹ (1).

oily (rag) *n.* [1930s+] a cigarette. [rhy. sl. = FAG n.⁴ (3)]

oily soil *n.* [2000s] human excrement. [likeness]

oingo boingo! *excl.* [1990s+] (*S.Afr./US teen*) an excl. of surprise. [nonsense words, echoic of surprise]

oink *n.* [1960s+] (*orig. US Black*) a police officer. [*oink*, onomat. for a pig's grunt, thus plays on PIG n.³ (1)]

oinker *n.* [1980s+] (*US*) **1** a glutton, a fat person. **2** an unappealing man. **3** an ugly young woman. **4** a policeman (cf. ANIMAL n.¹). [*oink*, onomat. for a pig's grunt, thus plays on PIG n.¹, PIG n.³ (1)]

oink out *v.* [1980s+] (*US*) to overeat. [*oink*, onomat. for a pig's grunt, thus plays on PIG OUT v.]

oint-jay *n.* [1930s] (*drugs*) the equipment used for injecting a narcotic. [cod Lat./backsl. = JOINT n.⁵ (1)]

ointment *n.*¹ [15C–17C] money. [its use in 'soothing' life's problems]

ointment *n.*² **1** [late 18C–19C] semen (cf. BOLLOCK SNOT n.). **2** [mid-19C] butter.

oi veh! *excl.* [late 19C+] a general excl. of dismay, goodness me! oh my! [Yid.]

oi yoi yoi *n.* [1900s–30s] (*US*) a Jew (cf. ARAB n.²). [the sounds of Yid.]

O.J. *v.* [1990s+] (*US Black*) to murder. [the former football and film star *O.J.* Simpson (b.1947), tried and acquitted of murder in 1995]

o.j. *n.*¹ [1930s+] (*orig. US*) orange juice. [abbr.]

o.j. *n.*² [1960s+] (*US drugs, orig. milit.*) marijuana laced with opium. [O n. (2) + J n. + pun on o.j. n.¹]

o.j. *n.*³ [1980s] (*US Black*) a large car, typically a Ford or Lincoln. [proper name *O.J.* Simpson (b.1947), the former football hero turned film star who advertised such cars for Hertz *c.*1980, prior to his 1995 murder trial]

OK *n.* (*also* **okay**) [mid-19C+] agreement, go-head, approval. [OK! excl.]

OK *adj.* (*also* **okay, okey**) (*orig. US*) **1** [mid-19C+] good, fine, satisfactory, acceptable, occas. splendid. **2** [mid-19C+] safe, unharmed. **3** [mid-19C+] up-to-date, fashionable, e.g. *it's the OK thing to do.* **4** [late 19C+] of a person, good, decent, e.g. *an OK guy.* **5** [1970s+] constructed with 'with' or 'about', comfortable, at ease with. **6** [1990s+] well supplied with, usu. money. [OK! excl.]

OK *v.* (*also* **okay**) **1** [late 19C+] (*orig. US*) to pass, to approve, to 'give the go-ahead'. **2** [1940s–50s] (*US*) to pay someone's bill. [OK! excl.]

OK *adv.* (*also* **okay**) [mid-19C+] well; in a satisfactory manner, all right. [OK adj. (1)]

OK! *excl.* (*also* **okay! okey!**) [early 19C+] (*orig. US*) the best-known statement of agreement, all is fine, everything is in order, I agree, go ahead etc; also used interrog. *OK?* do you agree? [corrupted abbr. of SE *all correct*, via its pron. as 'orl korrect'. It dates from 1839 in the US; Hotten (1864) has it (correctly etymologized) without ref. to US origins. The term was used in the election campaign of US president Martin Van Buren in 1840, when it conveniently suited his nickname 'Old Kinderhook', which came from the town of his birth Kinderhook, New York. It was further popularized by the *OK* Club, founded in 1840, whose members were Democrats who backed Van Buren. According to one popular story (since largely discredited) the first use of 'oll korrect' (still spelt in full) came during the campaign of the Whig Presidential candidate William Henry Harrison when a local handyman in Urbana, Ohio, was commissioned to paint a supportive banner; unfortunately he was illiterate and his slogan read 'The People is Oll Korrect'. *OK* has been the source of wide-ranging, if unproven etymological speculation; it includes: the railway freight agent who signed bills of lading *OK* – after his name Obadiah Kelley; an Indian chief known as Oled Keokuck whose friends abbreviated his name to OK and often said 'OK – he's all right'; *Aux Kayes* – a Haitian port from where the best rum came; the initials used by the multi-millionaire John Jacob Astor to sign bills presented to him for credit; an invention by US telegraphers to accompany NM meaning 'no more' and GA meaning 'go ahead'; and the British word *hoackey* or *horkey* (as *hockey* in *EDD*), meaning the last load brought from the fields and the beginning of rustic celebrations. More ideas included the Choctaw *okeh* meaning 'it is'; the French *au quai* ('on the quay') and thus either referring to goods ready for transportation, or the quays on which French soldiers met US girls in the War of Independence in 1776); the Finnish word *oikea*, meaning correct; the Orrins–Kendall company which put its initials on its boxes of high-quality crackers which were eaten widely during the US Civil War and known to soldiers as *OKs*; the House of Lords where at one time certain bills had to be signed and initialled by Lords Onslow and Kilbracken; the initials 'H.G.' – pronounced 'hah gay' – which were used by Scandinavian sailors and came from Anglo-Saxon *hofgor* meaning seaworthy; the Greek *omega chai*, a magical incantation against fleas; the signature of the Prussian General Schliesen who initialled all official documents *Oberst Kommandant* or OK; the Scottish 'och aye'; and the 18C French form of *oui* (meaning yes) which was pronounced *o qu oui*. Major, *Juba to Jive: A Dict. of Afro-American Slang* (1994), claims a root in a variety of West African languages, e.g. Djabo *o-ke*, Wolof *waw ke*, Dogno *o-kay*, Mandingo *o-key* and Fula West *eeyi-kay*. He adds that '"Oh ki" was being used by Blacks in the South by the 1770s and in Jamaica at least twenty years before the evidence of "okay" in the speech of New England.' However Cassidy & LePage, *Dict. of Jamaican English* (1967, 1992), fail to support the Jamaica ref., nor does *HDAS* offer any US cit. prior to 1839]

okapi *n.* (*also* **ou kappie**) [1960s+] (*W.I./S.Afr.*) a single-bladed knife with a pattern of 3 stars on the handle. [the tradename, itself based on the *okapi*, a rare mammal of the *Giraffidae* family]

okay see under OK.

OK coakley adj. (also **OK koakley**) [1920s] (US) fine, good, satisfactory. [OK adj. + redup./assonance]

oke n.[1] [1960s+] (S.Afr.) **1** a fellow, a chap. **2** a friend. **3** a general term of address. [abbr. Afk. outjie, little chap]

oke n.[2] see OAK n.[1].

oke adj. [1920s–50s] (orig. US) all right. [OK adj. (1)]

oke! excl. [1920s–40s] all right! [OK! excl.]

okely-dokely! excl. see OKEY-DOKE! excl.

okey see under OK.

okey-doke n. (US Black) **1** [1960s+] White values and opinions. **2** [1960s+] (also **okey-dok**) a swindle, a confidence trick. **3** [1960s+] stupidity, foolish talk. **4** [1990s+] the best, the utimate. [OK adj.; the image of going along with, i.e. saying 'OK', to whatever a listener wishes to hear]

okey-doke adj.[1] (also **hokey-dokey**) [1930s+] (US) good, fine, acceptable. [OKEY-DOKE! excl.]

okey-doke adj.[2] [1970s] (US Und.) deceitful, swindling. [OKEY-DOKE n. (2)]

okey-doke v. [1990s+] (US Black) to swindle. [OKEY-DOKE n. (2)]

okey-doke! excl. (also **hokey-dokey! okely-dokely! okey-dokey! okle-dokle!**) [1930s+] (orig. US) all vars. on OK! excl. [redup./assonance]

Okie n. (also **Oakey, Oakie**) **1** [1910s+] (US) a derog. term for a migrant worker, orig. from Oklahoma, forced off his land during the Great Depression during the 1930s. **2** [1970s+] (S.Afr.) a vagrant, a tramp. [abbr. Oklahoma; (2) is loan f. US use]

Okie adj. [1910s+] pertaining to Oklahoma or emigrants from that state. [OKIE n.]

okie n. (also **oakie, oukie**) [1970s+] (S.Afr.) **1** a form of address to a young boy. **2** an affectionate or slightly patronizing form of address to an adult. [abbr. Afk. outjie, little chap]

Okker n. see OSCAR (ASCHE) n.

OK koakley n. see OK COAKLEY adj.

Oklahoma credit card n. [1960s+] (US) a siphon tube for stealing gasoline. [the image of the poor migrant, forced to steal fuel]

Oklahoma guarantee n. [1960s] (US) no guarantee.

Oklahoma rain n. [1910s+] (US) a dust storm.

okle-dokle! excl. see OKEY-DOKE! excl.

okokay n. [1930s] cocoa. [backsl.]

okole n. [1930s+] (US) the buttocks or rear of anything. [Hawaiian okole, the buttocks]

okra n. [1920s–50s] (US) the penis (cf. BANANA n.[2]). [resemblance]

okra and prunes n. [1980s+] (US) the male genitals. [coined by Gore Vidal (b.1925) for his novel Duluth (1983) but note prev.]

OK sign n. [1940s–70s] (US) a hand sign made of a circle with thumb and forefinger, and other fingers upright, to indicate approval, good quality or excellence. [OK! excl.; orig. a visual symbol used, or popularized by 1947 Penzoil motor oil advertisement and, subseq., in used car outlets; 1980s+ SE]

-ola sfx [1910s+] (US) used in combs. with a n. as an intensifier of that n., e.g. BOFFOLA n.; CASHOLA n.; CRACKOLA n.; CREEPOLA n.; DRUGOLA n.; FAGOLA n.; GAYOLA n.; HOPOLA n.; LURKOLA n.; NOISOLA n.; PAYOLA n.; SCHNOZZOLA n.; STACKOLA n.; STUDOLA n. [the orig. use is in pianola (1901), although in that context it worked as a dimin. It was greatly popularized in the payola scandals that were unearthed in the US pop music industry during the late 1950s, although payola itself had been a recognized part of the business for 20 years]

old n. **1** [mid-19C–1900s] a master, a boss. **2** [late 19C–1960s] money (usu. owed from gambling); esp. in phr. a bit of the old.

old adj.[1] [mid-15C+] great, plentiful, excessive; usu. in comb. with good, great, high, gay etc, e.g. high old time, great old fellow.

old adj.[2] **1** [late 16C; mid-19C+] used affectionately of a person, occas. of an animal. **2** [mid-19C+] used as an expression of familiarity, e.g. the old gaff, the old boozer.

old adj.[3] [18C–early 19C] (UK Und.) ugly. [? OLD NICK n. (1), OLD BOY, THE n. (1) and similar Devil-related terms; the Devil is assumed to be ugly]

old adj.[4] [early 18C+] clever, cunning, e.g. come the old soldier.

old adj.[5] [mid-19C+] (orig. US) tiresome; usu. constructed with get, e.g. too much of a good thing gets old.

old pfx [late 17C+] used in a variety of combs. to mean the Devil; other than those listed below, vars. include old boots, ...chap, ...child, ...dad, ...Davy, ...hangie, ...hooky, ...Mahoun, ...man, ...Sanners, ...Sanny, ...Saunders, ...scooty, ...Scrat, ...Smith, ...smoke, ...soss, ...thief (see also combs. below). [for a full discussion see Partridge, 'The Devil and His Nicknames' in World of Words (1939)]

old adam n. [19C] the penis (cf. ABRAHAM n.[1]). [SE old Adam, original sin]

old-age pension n. [1940+] (bingo) the number 65 (cf. ALDERSHOT LADIES n.). [the age of male retirement]

old amber n. [1960s–70s] (Aus.) beer. [AMBER FLUID n.]

old-ass adj. [1960s+] (US) run-down, dilapidated.

old bads n. (also **old broke**) [1950s+] (W.I.) old clothes. [SE old + Shetland dial. bad, an article of clothing/SE broke or dial. brock, rubbish, refuse, remnants]

Old Bailey underwriter n. [early–mid-19C] a small-scale forger. [a pun on SE underwriter + ref. to his probable destination]

old bastard n. (also **old balls**) [late 19C+] a man, often used as a term of affection.

old bat n. [late 19C+] an unattractive or foolish old woman. [SE old + BAT n.[4]; although BAT n.[4] (2) spec. postdates this full term]

old bean n.[1] (also **old haricot**) [1910s+] a fellow, a term of address, usu. to a man. [joc. use of SE bean, but ? SE being]

old bean n.[2] [1940s] an old person, seen affectionately or kindly.

old beeswing n. [late 19C] a genial drinker. [SE old + beeswing, the crust that forms on vintage port]

old bendy n. [18C] the Devil.

old betsy n. see BETSY n.

Old Bill n. (also **Bill**) [1950s+] **1** the police; thus Bill from the Hill, officers serving at Notting Hill police station in London W11. **2** the police force as an institution. **3** a police station. [milit. old Bill, a veteran; ult. Old Bill, the character created by the WW1 cartoonist Bruce Bairnsfeather (1888–1959). There is also a poss. semantic link to BEAK n.[1] (1), but in reality it is unlikely]

old bill n.[1] [1910s] (US) corned beef.

old bill n.[2] [2000s] the penis (cf. ABRAHAM n.[1]).

old billy n. [late 19C–1900s] the Devil; usu. in the phr. like old billy, very hard, very energetically.

old bird n. **1** [mid–late 19C] (UK prison) a veteran prisoner, a recidivist. **2** [mid-19C+] a person who has become knowing through experience, esp. an experienced thief; thus wily/cunning old bird. **3** [late 19C+] (also **old birdie**) as a form of address. **4** [1910s+] a person, usu. old. [SE old + BIRD n.[2] (1)]

old black joes n. [20C+] (Aus.) the toes. [rhy. sl.]

old blazes n. [19C] the Devil.

old blind bob n. [18C] the penis (cf. ABRAHAM n.[1]).

old blue n. see LONG-TAIL BLUE n. (1).

old body n. [mid-19C+] an old woman, occas. a man.

old bogey n. [mid-19C] the Devil. [SE old + BOGIE n.[1]]

old Boney n. [18C] death.

old boy n.[1] [17C+] (also **old cove**) an old or older man, esp. as the old boy, one's father; often as a term of familiar address.

old boy n.[2] [1920s+] (US) the penis. [BOY, THE n.[1]]

old boy n.[3] see GOOD OLD BOY n.

old boy, the n. (US/Irish) **1** [late 18C+] the Devil. **2** [mid-19C] 'daylights', stuffing, e.g. I'll knock the Old Boy out of him.

old broke n. see OLD BADS n.

old brown windsor n. [1920s+] (Aus.) the anus. [play on Brown Windsor soup]

old buba n. [1950s] (W.I.) an old person who acts younger than their age. [SE *old* + dial. *buba*, a dry leaf, of cabbage, coconut or any plant]

old bubble *n. see* BUBBLE n.[3]

old buck *n.* **1** [late 18C–1920s] a general term of address. **2** [mid-19C–1910s] a man. [SE *old* + BUCK n.[1] (3)]

old bundle *n. see* DIRTY BUNDLE n.

old chap *n.* **1** [early 19C+] a man; also as a term of address. **2** [mid-19C–1930s] one's father. [SE *old* + CHAP n. (1)]

old cheese *n.* [1970s+] (*Aus.*) one's (occas. someone else's) mother. [affectionate nickname]

old china *n.* [1910s+] an old friend. [SE *old* + CHINA (PLATE) n. (1)]

old chip *n.* [late 19C] a term of endearment.

old chocker *n.* [mid-19C+] an old fellow. [? joc. use of SE *chock full*]

old chook *n.* [1910s+] (*Aus.*) a general term of intimate affection; lit. 'old chicken'.

old clo *n.* **1** [mid-19C–1900s] old clothes. **2** [mid-19C–1920s] a derog. term for a Jew. **3** [late 19C] in ext. use of (2), an intellectual. [lit. SE *old clothes*; the stereotyping of Jews and the second-hand clothes trade]

old clo *adj.* [mid–late 19C] worn-out, exhausted, out-of-date etc. [the street cry *old clo!* old clothes]

old clootie *n.* (*also* **old cloots**) [mid-18C–1900s] (*mainly Scot.*) the Devil. [dial. *cloot*, a cloven leaf]

old cock *n.* (*also* **old cocker**) [late 18C+] a man, esp. as a term of affectionate address. [SE *old* + COCK n.[3], underpinned by COCK n.[4] (1)]

old cockalorum *n.* [late 19C–1900s] a man, esp. as a term of affectionate address. [ext. of OLD COCK n.]

old cocker *n.*[1] [1940s+] (*orig. US*) an old man, usu. a disreputable one. [Yid. *alte cacka*, old man]

old cocker *n.*[2] *see* OLD COCK n.

old cole *n.* [mid-16C] (*UK Und.*) a veteran dice cheat.

old complaint *n.* [late 19C] (*Aus.*) drunkenness. [euph.]

old coon *n.* [mid–late 19C] (*US*) a shrewd individual. [SE *old* + (*ra*)*coon*]

old coot *n.* [mid-18C+] a foolish or cantankerous old person; also used affectionately. [SE *old* + COOT n.[1]]

old corpse *n.* [1930s] an affectionate term of address.

old cove *n. see* OLD BOY n.[1].

old crow *n.* [late 19C+] **1** a generally misogynistic ref. to an old woman. **2** a general term of abuse, not spec. of a woman. [predates CROW n.[6] (3) so fig. use of SE]

old curiosity *n.* [late 19C–1930s] one's wife.

old dampa *n.* [20C+] (*W.I.*) old clothes. [ety. unknown]

old darling *n. see* OLD DEAR n. (2).

Old Dart *n.* [mid-19C+] (*Aus./N.Z.*) England, or Ireland. [? SE *old dirt* (on model of OLD SOD n.)]

old Davey *n. see* DAVY JONES'S LOCKER n.

old dear *n.* **1** [late 19C+] one's wife. **2** [late 19C+] (*also* **old darling**) an old person, usu. but not invariably a woman. **3** [1900s–20s] an affectionate term of address, irrespective of sex.

old dig *n.* [1940s+] (*Aus./N.Z.*) a veteran soldier. [SE *old* + DIG n.[6]]

old ding *n.* [19C] the vagina. [? SE *ding*, to hit, to knock]

old dirt road *n. see* DIRT ROAD n.[2].

old dog *n.* **1** [late 16C+] an expert in a given field; usu. with *at*. **2** [mid-18C+] a man, usu. with overtones of admiration for his less than conventional lifestyle; also used fig. of an object. **3** [1930s+] (*orig. US Black*) a direct term of affectionate address. [affectionate use of SE *dog*]

old dog, the *n.* (*also* **the dog**) [1930s–60s] (*US*) syphilis. [? the disease 'bites' the sufferer]

old dog at common prayer *n.* [late 17C–18C] a mediocre clergyman who could read the prayers, but had no skill at the actual preaching.

old donah *n.* [19C+] one's mother. [Polari *donah*, ult. Ital. *donna*, a woman]

Old Doss, the *n.* [19C] the Bridewell prison, sited on the banks of the Fleet River (cf. ABBOTT'S PRIORY n.). [SE *old* + DOSS n.[1] (1); the prison, on the site of Henry VIII's palace of Bridewell flourished 1556–1855; there were also Bridewell prisons at Clerkenwell and Westminster and several hundreds in major towns]

old driver *n.* [late 18C–19C] the Devil.

old dutch *n.* (*also* **ancient dutch**) **1** [late 19C] a woman. **2** [late 19C+] one's wife. [*see* ety. at DUTCH n.]

old ebenezer *n.* [late 19C] (*US*) a grizzly bear. [? anecdotal]

old egg *n.* [20C+] a man, or woman, esp. as a term of affectionate address. [SE *old* + EGG n.[1] (1)]

old enough to sit at the table, old enough to eat *phr.* [1980s+] (*US*) a phr. used to suggest that an underage girl is still a feasible target for seduction. [the implication of EAT v.[3] (1) is oral sex, but the larger usage is general]

old ewe dressed as lamb *n. see* MUTTON DRESSED AS LAMB n.

old faithful *n.* [1950s+] (*US*) menstruation.

old-fashioned *adj.*[1] [mid-19C+] of sexual intercourse, performed in the conventional manner, the missionary position.

old-fashioned *adj.*[2] [late 19C–1930s] (*Irish*) precocious, forward.

old-fashioned *adj.*[3] [20C+] of a look or glance, disapproving.

old-fashioned *adj.*[4] [1930s] obscene.

old fellow *n.* **1** [early 19C] the Devil. **2** [early 19C+] a man; also used as a term of address. **3** [mid-19C–1900s] God. **4** [late 19C] an object, a thing. **5** [late 19C+] the penis. **6** [20C+] one's father; esp. Irish and often written as *oul fella*, to emphasize the Dublin pron. **7** [1980s] a husband. [(5) note synon. RMC Duntroon (Aus.) *longfellow*]

old flame *n.* [early 19C+] a former lover. [Fr. *flamme*, a sweetheart (lit. flame), much used in 17C romantic fiction]

old flint *n.* [mid-19C] a miser. [SE *old* + SKINFLINT n.]

old floorer *n.* [mid-19C–1920s] a fig. name for death. [SE *old* + FLOORER n. (1), i.e. he 'knocks you down']

old flower *n.* [20C+] (*Irish*) an affectionate term of address, esp. as *my old flower*.

old fogey *n.* [1990s+] nasal mucus. [rhy. sl. = BOGEY n.[3] (1)]

old foot *adj.* [1990s+] (*W.I.*) describing older people.

old fowl *n.* [20C+] (*Aus./W.I.*) an ageing, unattractive and prob. overdressed woman.

old fragment *n.* [1900s] an old(er) man.

old friend and shamrock *n.* [late 19C] (*US*) an order of corned beef and cabbage.

old frizzle *n.* [18C–19C] **1** in cards, the ace of spades. **2** the vagina. [SE *old* + *frizzle*, crisp, curly hair; the shape of the spade could resemble a beard; (2) is ref. to pubic hair]

old fruit *n.* (*also* **old tin of fruit**) [1920s+] a general term of affectionate address. [SE *old* + FRUIT n.[1] (2)]

old gager *n.* [18C] (*UK Und.*) a rich old man.

old gal *n.* (*also* **old girl**, **ole girl**) **1** [late 18C+] any woman, usu. old but not necessarily so; often as *the old girl*. **2** [mid-19C+] a general term of address to a woman or a female dog or horse. **3** [mid-19C+] one's wife or regular female companion. **4** [late 19C+] one's mother. **5** [1910s–20s] (*US*) used of a non-human object. **6** [1940s] a mother-in-law. **7** [1940s] (*US Black campus*) a college boy's roommate.

old gang *n.* [late 19C+] a group or clique of friends or colleagues. [GANG n.[1] (1)]

old gargoyle *n.* [1920s] an affectionate term of address.

old geezer *n.* [1910s+] one's wife, often as *the old geezer*. [joc. use of GEEZER n.[1] (1)]

old gent *n.* **1** [1900s–30s] (*US*) one's father. **2** [1940s] a husband.

old gentleman *n.* **1** [early 18C–1920s] the Devil. **2** [early 19C–1930s] (*also* **old gent**) in gambling, a card that is slightly longer than the rest of the pack and thus identifiable by cheats. [abbr. OLD GENTLEMAN IN BLACK n.]

old gentleman in black *n.* [mid–late 17C] the Devil.

old gentleman's bed-posts *n.* (*also* **old gentleman's four-poster**) [mid–late 19C] the 4 of clubs, considered an unlucky card. [OLD GENTLEMAN n. (1); var. on DEVIL'S BEDPOST n.]

old girl *n. see* OLD GAL n.

old glory *n.* [late 19C–1940s] (*US Black*) anything seen as unfashionable or out of date. [SE *Old Glory*, nickname for the US flag. The implication is of the stylelessness of trad. White values]

old gold *n.* [late 18C] human excrement.

old gooseberry *n.* [late 18C–19C] **1** the Devil. **2** anyone who puts an end to a riot or disturbance whether by threats or actual force.

old gown *n.* [mid-19C] smuggled tea. [ety. unknown; the label placed on the tea-chest for the purpose of deception]

old grabem pudden *n.* [late 19C] an old woman, whether one's wife or mother. [rhy. sl. + seen as possessing a sweet tooth, i.e. she 'grabs the pudding']

old hack *n.* [late 19C] the Devil. [var. on OLD HARRY n. (1)]

old hairy toe *n.* [1930s] the Devil. [var. on OLD HARRY n. (1); but note the Devil's depiction as half-goat]

old hand *n.* **1** [late 18C+] an expert; a veteran. **2** [mid-19C–1900s] (*Aus.*) a transported convict (cf. NEW HAND n.). [SE *old* + HAND n.[1]]

old hannah *n.* [1930s+] (*US Black*) the sun.

old haricot *n. see* OLD BEAN n.[1].

old Harry *n.* **1** [mid-17C+] (*also* **Lord Harry, old Harrington, old Henry**) the Devil; thus *play old Harry with, give old Harry*, to play the Devil with, to make mischief, to tease or scold; *like old Harry*, to a great (lit. devilish) extent. **2** [late 17C–early 19C] a form of unspecified adulterant used in wine. [*give old Harry* is still current in W.I. use; Nares defines the phr. as 'formerly applied satirically to Henry the Eighth']

old hat *n.* [late 17C–19C] the vagina. ['because frequently felt' (Grose, 1796)]

old hat *adj.* [1910s+] out-of-date, old-fashioned.

old haymaker *n. see* HAYMAKER n.[1].

old head *n.* **1** [mid-19C+] (*US*) an old-timer, an old person; a veteran, esp. a veteran convict. **2** [1950s+] (*drugs*) a long-time marijuana smoker. [fig. use of SE, boosted in (2) by HEAD n.[2] (1)]

old hen *n.* [20C+] a woman, esp. an old one. [SE *old* + HEN n.[1] (1)]

old Henry *n. see* OLD HARRY n. (1).

old hickory *n.* [1960s] (*US*) a $20 bill (cf. ABE n.[2]). [the picture of President Andrew 'Old Hickory' Jackson (1767–1845), 7th President of the US, on the notes]

old hige *n.* [1940s+] (*W.I.*) a nagging old woman. [SE *hag* + dial. *old hige*, an old witch]

old hornie *n.* (*also* **old horney/horny**) **1** [18C–19C] (*also* **old Hornington**) the penis. **2** [mid-19C+] the Devil. [SE *old* + HORNS n./the devil's trad. *horns*]

Old Horse, the *n. see* HORSE, THE n.

old horse *n.[1]* (*also* **old hoss**) (*orig. US*) **1** [mid-19C–1910s] a man. **2** [mid-19C+] a term of address by one man to another.

old horse *n.[2]* [mid-19C–1930s] salt beef.

old huddle (and twang) *n.* [mid-16C–mid-17C] a miser. [he 'huddles' around his money; the use of *twang*, usu. a prostitute (*see* TWANG n.[1] (1)), has no obvious explanation]

old identity *n.* (*also* **identity**) [mid-19C–1950s] **1** a person, usu. an eccentric, a 'character'. **2** (*Aus./N.Z.*) anyone who has lived in the same place for a long time, a regular resident.

oldie *n.* (*also* **oldy**) **1** [late 19C; 1930s+] (*mainly US/UK teen*) the old, esp. those over 40, or at least those who fail to share or appreciate the nuances and delights of the current version of

rebellious youth culture. **2** [1930s+] anything old, esp. an old joke, saying, record or song.

oldie but goodie *n.* [1950s+] (*US*) something or someone that is old or no longer fashionable or chic but still beloved by its owner/wearer/user, esp. an old song. [OLDIE n. (2) + GOODIE n.[2]]

oldies *n.* [1970s+] one's parents. [OLDIE n. (1)]

old iron and brass *n.* [20C+] grass. [rhy. sl.]

old Jack Lang *n. see* JACK LANG n.

old Jamaica rum *n.* [20C+] the sun. [rhy. sl.]

old joe *n.* [1910s+] (*US*) syphilis. [orig. US Navy]

old King Cole *n.* [1930s+] unemployment benefit, the dole (cf. BLESS MY SOUL n.). [rhy. sl.]

old kit bag *n.* [1990s+] a cigarette. [rhy. sl. = FAG n.[4] (3)]

old lad *n.* **1** [late 16C+] a man, esp. as an affectionate term of address. **2** [late 19C] (*Aus.*) the Devil. **3** [1970s] a father.

old lady *n.* **1** [early 19C] in gambling, a card that is slightly wider than the rest of the pack and thus identifiable by cheats. **2** [mid-19C+] one's mother. **3** [mid-19C+] (*orig. US*) a wife (actual or common-law). **4** [late 19C] the vagina. **5** [1910s+] (*orig. US*) a girlfriend or regular partner, heterosexual or homosexual. **6** [1920s–50s] (*US campus*) of the same sex, a roommate. **7** [1930s+] (*US prison*) a passive partner in a homosexual relationship, male or female. **8** [1930s+] of a man, a weakling, a sentimentalist. **9** [1960s+] (*US Black*) a member of a pimp's STABLE n. (2) of prostitutes; a single prostitute.

old lady five fingers *n. see* LADY FIVE FINGERS n.

old lady of Westmoreland Street *n.* [mid-19C–1940s] (*Irish*) the *Irish Times*. [its address in Dublin]

old lady white *n.* **1** [1900s–50s] a drug dealer, presumably in white powders, i.e. narcotics. **2** [1940s–50s] any powdered drug, e.g. cocaine, heroin. (cf. BLACK n.[3]; BLANCA n.). [the colour; note cocaine is a 'feminine' drug, *see* GIRL n.[2]]

old lag *n.* [19C+] a habitual prisoner, a recidivist; orig. a returnee from transportation to Australia. [SE *old* + LAG n.[2] (2). Although the original *lag* was destined for the penal colonies of Australia, the *old lag* can have served his time in any prison]

old leper *n.* [1920s] a general term of (affectionate) address.

old ling *n.* [18C–19C] the vagina (cf. BEARDED CLAM n.). [ext. of LING n. (2)]

old madge *n.[1]* [mid-17C–mid-18C] a cudgel. [note late 19C SE *madge*, a leaden hammer covered thickly with stout woollen cloth, used in solder plating]

old madge *n.[2]* [20C+] (*drugs*) cocaine (cf. AUNT NORA n.). [ety. unknown; ? woman's name, note cocaine is a 'feminine' drug, *see* GIRL n.[2]]

old maid *n.* [mid-19C+] (*US*) a kernel of popcorn that has failed to pop. [SE *old maid*, a woman 'left behind']

old man *n.[1]* **1** [late 17C+] a woman's husband. **2** [early 19C+] a father. **3** [late 19C+] the penis. **4** [1940s+] (*Can./US*) a boyfriend or lover, including a homosexual one. **5** [1950s+] (*US*) a pimp (cf. BIG DADDY n.). [(3) note MAN n.[1]]

old man *n.[2]* [early 19C+] (*Aus.*) a mature kangaroo.

old man *n.[3]* (*also* **old son/sport**) [mid-19C+] a general greeting or form of address given to a man (usu. one whom one knows), occas. to a woman.

old man, the *n.* **1** [early 19C+] (*orig. US*) any senior figure, the boss, a commanding officer; a headmaster. **2** [late 19C] in cards, the King. **3** [1900s–50s] (*US*) God.

old man *adj.* [mid-19C+] (*Aus./N.Z.*) large, important, of lengthy duration etc, e.g. an *old man kangaroo*, an *old man sand storm*.

old man has his Sunday clothes on, the *phr.* (*also* **in his Sunday best**) [late 19C] used of the penis, when erect. [OLD MAN n.[1] (3), freshly laundered Sunday clothes were stiff with starch]

old man Mose *n.* [1940s] (*US Black*) **1** time. **2** death. [abbr. *Moses*; biblical imagery, via spirituals/hymns]

old man red-eye *n. see* RED-EYE n.[1].

old man's milk *n.* **1** [early 19C] wine. **2** [mid-19C+] whisky.

old max n. see MAX n. (1).

old mick adj. see PAT AND MICK adj.

old Mr Gory n. [late 17C–early 19C] gold (cf. CANARY n.⁵). [*Fort Goree*, on the Gold Coast]

old Mr Grim n. **1** [late 18C–19C] the Devil. **2** [late 18C–19C; 1980s] (also **Mr Grim**) death.

Old Mo, the n. [late 19C–1900s] the Middlesex Music Hall. [abbr. of *The Great Mogul*, the orig. name for the place]

old moody n. [1930s+] a cunning trick, a fraud; thus *pull the old moody*; *go (all) moody (on)*, to fail, to go wrong.

old mother hubbard n. [late 19C] an unbelievable story, a fantasy. [the fairy-tale character]

old mother slipper-slopper n. [1910s–20s] a little old woman. [a nursery rhyme]

old moustache n. [late 19C] a vigorous old man with a grey moustache.

Old Muddy n. [mid-19C+] (US) **1** the Missouri River. **2** the Mississippi River.

old nag n. [20C+] a cigarette. [rhy. sl. = FAG n.⁴ (3)]

Old Nask n. [early 19C] Bridewell prison, Totillfields, London (cf. ABBOTT'S PRIORY n.).

Old Nassau n. [mid-19C+] (US campus) Princeton University. [Nassau Hall]

old Ned n. [1920s–40s] (US) the Devil.

old ned n.¹ [mid-19C–1930s] (US Black) salt pork or bacon. [orig. regional use]

old ned n.² see UNCLE NED n.¹ (3).

old net n. [1950s] (W.I.) ragged work-clothes. [both are torn and are mainly made up of holes]

Old Nick n. (also **old Nicholas, ...Nicker, ...Nickie ben**) **1** [mid-17C+] the Devil. **2** [late 19C] (Anglo-Irish) the joker in a pack of cards. **3** [1920s] in fig. use, something terrible.

old nigger n. [1950s] (W.I.) a disreputable, down-at-heel person. [SE *old* + NIGGER n.¹ (1)]

oldo n. [1950s] an old or, in context, older person.

Old Oak n. [20C+] London. [rhy. sl. = SMOKE, THE n. (1)]

old oil n. [1910s+] (US) flattery, insincere charm. [SE *old* + OIL n.² (1)]

Old One, the n. [late 18C–19C] the Devil.

old one n. (also **ould wan, oul' one**) **1** [early 19C; 1930s+] (Irish) an old woman, esp. as *the old one*, one's mother or wife. **2** [late 19C+] (Aus.) a father.

old one-two, the n.¹ **1** [late 19C] masturbation. **2** [20C+] sexual intercourse. [the rhythmic movements]

old one-two, the n.² [20C+] a knockout blow, either lit. or fig. [boxing use; ext. of ONE-TWO n. (1)]

old oyster n. [late 19C–1920s] a general term of address, esp. to a reserved, uncommunicative person.

old party n. [mid-19C–1930s] an old man or woman; also used affectionately to an animal.

old patrol n. [1940s] (US) an old prostitute.

old pie adj. see PIE adj.¹.

old pip n. [1930s] a general term of affectionate address.

old poke n. [1930s] (US) a spoilsport. [SE *old* + POKE n.³; cf. STUFFED SHIRT n.]

old poker n. (also **old poger**) [late 18C–early 19C] the Devil.

old pot n. [late 19C+] (orig. Aus.) an old man, esp. one's father. [abbr. POT AND PAN n. (1)]

Old Probabilities n. (also **Old Prob, Old Probs, proba-bilities**) [late 19C–1950s] (US) the weather bureau or its staff.

old put n. [mid-18C–19C] a pretentious old gentleman. [SE *old* + PUT n.¹ (2)]

old rale n. (also **old ral**) [late 19C–1960s] (US) syphilis. [? dial. *rail*, to stagger, to reel. The development of the disease gradually impairs mobility]

old ram n. [19C+] an old or middle-aged man who still pursues women. [SE *old* + RAM n.¹ (2)]

old raspberry n. [1910s–20s] one who has a notably red nose, presumably a drunkard.

old red socks n. [20C+] (Ulster) the pope. [the identification of Catholicism with red, e.g. 'the scarlet woman of Rome']

Old Reekie n. (also **Auld Reikie**) [late 18C+] the old town and subseq. the whole town of Edinburgh. [the smoke and smog that often covered it]

old rip n.¹ **1** [mid-19C+] (US) a person, usu. an unpleasant one; occas. applied to a horse. **2** [1900s] the Devil; thus (US) *madder than old rip*, extremely angry.

old rip n.² [1970s+] (US gay) the anus.

old robin n. [late 18C–early 19C] an experienced person. [generic use of proper name]

old Roger n. **1** [late 17C–19C; 1970s] the Devil. **2** [18C] the pirates' flag the *Jolly Roger*. [popular use of SE *roger* as nickname for a bull; (1) 1970s use is Irish]

old root n. see ROOT n.¹ (1).

old rope n. [1920s–40s] (orig. RN) very strong, rank tobacco.

old rowley n. (also **old slimey**) [mid-17C–19C] the penis. [SE *Old Rowley*, the Devil, or *rowley*, alternative sp. for SE *rolly*, thus the shape/SE *slimey*, of the semen it ejaculates]

old Ruffian/Ruffin, the n. see RUFFIN(, THE) n.

Olds n. [1930s+] (US) an *Olds*mobile car. [abbr.]

olds n. [late 19C+] old people, parents.

old salt n. [mid-19C+] a veteran sailor or US marine. [orig. naut. jargon]

old Sam n. [mid-19C–1930s] (US Black) the Devil.

old saw n. [late 19C–1940s] (US Black) one's wife. [? her nagging *saws* away at a man]

old school adj. (also **old skool**) [1980s+] (orig. US Black) **1** in rap music, used of anything pertaining to the early days of the musical style, esp. the work of such performers as Grandmaster Flash or Afrika Bambaataa. **2** used of anything typical of the fashions, music and general styles of the 1960s–70s. [SE *old school*, n. and adj. describing old-fashioned things; SCHOOL n.³]

old scone n. [1950s] a generally affectionate term of address.

old scout n. [early 19C+] a person, usu. as an affectionate term of address.

old Scratch n. (also **old Scratcher**) [mid-18C+] the Devil; thus *raise old Scratch*, to cause a disturbance. [mid-19C+ use is US only]

old scream n. [1920s] a person; usu. as a term of address.

old settler n. [1940s] (US Black) a woman in her thirties or older.

old ship n. [1910s] (Aus.) a term of affectionate address.

old shoes n. [late 19C–1900s] rum. [? joc. ref. to a strong smell]

old shot n. [late 19C] (Aus.) an old, crafty person.

old six n. [mid-19C–1910s] old ale priced at 6 pence per quart.

old skool adj. see OLD SCHOOL adj.

old slimey n. see OLD ROWLEY n.

Old Slop n. [mid-19C–1900s] *The Times* newspaper. [Fr. *salope*, a tart; applied to the newspaper when, c.1840–50, it was seen as abandoning its role as the impartial 'thunderer' and currying favour wherever it could]

old smokey n. [1920s+] (US prison) the electric chair; thus *ride old smokey*, to be electrocuted.

old socks n. (also **old sock, ...stock, ...stockings**) [mid-19C+] (Aus./US) a term of address to a man.

Old Sod n. (also **Green Sod, ould sod, sod**) [19C+] Ireland.

old sol n. [late 19C] (US) a pawnbroker. [*Sol*, abbr. of Solomon, a stereotypical Jewish name]

old soldier n.¹ **1** [early 18C+] an experienced, but somewhat cunning man. **2** [mid-19C+] a simpleton, a naïve person. [contrasting images of SE]

old soldier n.² **1** [mid–late 19C] (US) the stub of a cigar or cigarette. **2** [late 19C+] an empty bottle. **3** [1960s–70s] (US) the penis.

old son n. see OLD MAN n.³.

old sparky n. (also **old sparkey, sparkie, sparky**) [1970s+] (US prison) the electric chair.

old splendid n. [late 19C–1900s] (US) a very admirable person.

old splitfoot n. [19C] the Devil.

old sport n. see OLD MAN n.[3].

old stager n. [mid-16C+] an experienced person. [? OFr. *éstagier*, inhabitant or church Lat. *stagiarius*, an aged monk who was lodged permanently in the infirmary. Equally feasible is *stage-coach*, in this context one who is a regular traveller upon them]

Old Start, the n. **1** [late 18C–early 19C] Newgate prison (cf. ABBOTT'S PRIORY n.). **2** [20C+] the Old Bailey. [START, THE n. (2), the Old Bailey was erected on the site of Newgate prison]

oldster n. **1** [mid-19C+] (*orig. and mainly US*) an old person, or a more experienced person. **2** [1950s] a veteran. [on model of SE *youngster*]

old steve n. [1930s–50s] (*drugs*) any form of narcotic in powder form. [ety. unknown; ? a well-known dealer]

old stock/stockings n. see OLD SOCKS n.

old strike-a-light n. [late 19C] one's father. [his cry of *strike a light!* when asked for yet another 'loan']

old stripes n. (also **stripes**) [late 19C–1960s] a tiger.

old stud n. [mid–late 19C] (US) a familiar term of address. [SE *old* + STUD n.[1]]

old sweat n. (also **sweat**) **1** [1910s+] (*orig. milit.*) any veteran. **2** [1990s+] (*Irish*) an old friend. [? the *sweat* of battle and thus of one's labours. The British philologist Ernest Weekley has suggested, in *Xenophobia* (1932), that it may have originated during the Thirty Years' War as the German *alter Schweele*, old Swede, but its first appearance c.1919 militates against the theory]

old talk n. [20C+] (*W.I./UK Black*) chatter, gossip, rhetoric, empty boasting. [? SE *old people's talk*]

old-talk v. [20C+] (*W.I./UK Black*) to chatter, to gossip, to make empty promises. [OLD TALK n.]

old thing n.[1] [mid–late 19C] (*Aus.*) a meal of salt beef and damper, i.e. a form of unleavened bread, baked in the ashes of a fire.

old thing n.[2] [mid-19C+] a person, often as a term of address or as *funny old thing* etc.

old thing n.[3] **1** [mid-19C+] the vagina (cf. ARTICLE n.). **2** [1930s] (US Und.) syphilis. **3** [1960s+] the penis. [euph.]

old-time adj. (also **old-timer/-timey**) [late 19C+] veteran, old-fashioned. [OLD TIMER n.]

old timer n. [mid–late 19C] a veteran. [SE from 1900]

old tin of fruit n. see OLD FRUIT n.

old toast n.[1] **1** [late 17C–early 18C] a drunkard. **2** [late 18C–mid-19C] (UK Und.) a lively old man. [their drinking of SE *toasts*]

old toast n.[2] [late 17C–19C] the Devil. [the heat of hell, in which sinners are *toasted*]

old tom n.[1] [early 19C–1930s] gin. [according to Brewer, *Dict. of Phrase and Fable* (1894), the proper name of *Thomas Norris*, who was employed at Hodges' distillery and who opened a gin palace in Great Russell Street, Covent Garden. The drink in which he specialized was concocted by another Hodges' employee, Thomas Chamberlain, who christened his brand in honour of Mr Norris]

old tom n.[2] **1** [1960s] (US) a lesbian. **2** [1960s] (US) a prostitute catering to lesbians. **3** [1970s+] (US gay) an old lesbian (cf. AMY-JOHN n.). [SE *old* + TOM n.[3]]

old top n. [mid-19C–1950s] a general form of address to a man, or woman, one knows.

old trot n. **1** [mid-14C–1930s] an old woman. **2** [1940s+] a dubious story, esp. as *a load of old trot.*

old trout n. [late 19C+] an older person, usu. a woman and usu. pej. [SE *old* + TROUT n.[1] (1)]

old turnip n. [1920s] an affectionate term of address.

old 'un n. [mid-19C+] an old person, esp. a parent.

old whiskers n. [mid-19C–1900s] **1** a working man with long, unkempt, greying whiskers; usu. shouted out by impudent children. **2** an old man.

old wigsby n. [late 19C–1900s] (UK middle class) a crotchety, narrow-minded, elderly man, a dedicated opponent of any form of 'progress' or modernity. [such a man would still be likely to sport a wig, seen as an 18C affectation]

old wives' paternoster n. [late 16C–early 17C] grumbling, nagging. [SE *paternoster*, the Lord's Prayer]

old woman n.[1] **1** [late 18C+] a wife, a regular female partner. **2** [19C] the vagina. **3** [mid-19C] a term of address to a woman of any age. **4** [mid-19C+] one's mother. **5** [late 19C] the queen, in cards. [the reverse of OLD MAN n.[1]; (5) is equivalent to OLD MAN, THE n. (2)]

old woman n.[2] [late 19C] (UK prison) a member of the stocking knitting gang in Dartmoor prison.

oldy n. see OLDIE n.

ole girl n. see OLD GAL n.

Ole-Mas n. [20C+] (*W.I.*) a shambles, chaos, confusion; thus *turn Old-Mas*, to collapse into confusion. [Carib.E. *Ole-Mas*, the masquerade festival that opens Carnival]

olive oil n. see SOFT SOAP n. (1).

olive oil phr. [late 19C–1970s] (*orig. music hall*) goodbye. [mispron. of Fr. *au revoir*, goodbye]

oliver n.[1] [mid-18C–1920s] the moon; thus (UK Und.) *oliver is in town*, the moon is full, and thus the nights are too light for stealing safely; *oliver's up*, the moon has risen; *oliver whiddles*, the moon is shining; *oliver's nightcap*, the hour the moon goes down. [? the 'O' shape]

oliver n.[2] [late 19C] (US) the nose. [ety. unknown]

oliver n.[3] see OLIVER (TWIST) n.

Oliver (Cromwell) v. [late 19C+] to understand; usu. in phr. *do you oliver?* do you understand? [rhy. sl.; *Oliver Cromwell* (pron. 'crummle') = TUMBLE v.[2] (3)]

oliver's skull n. [late 17C–19C] a chamberpot. [originating in the Restoration's hatred of the Commonwealth's Lord Protector, *Oliver* Cromwell (1599–1658)]

oliver's summons n. [19C] (*Irish*) an idle person who is forced to work for lack of any alternative means of making money. [anecdote of one *Oliver*, a Limerick landlord, who impounded the goods of those who worked for him until the job was properly done]

oliver (twist) n. **1** [mid-19C+] a fist. **2** [late 19C+] (*Aus.*) the wrist. **3** [1930s–70s] a deliberately incorrect entry in a ledger; usu. bookmaker use. [rhy. sl.; (3) is the use of the *fist* to write]

oliver twist adj. [1990s+] drunk (cf. ADRIAN (QUIST) adj.). [rhy. sl. = PISSED adj.[1]]

ollapod n. [mid-19C] a country apothecary. [SE *ollapodrida*, a hotchpotch, a mixture, i.e. his mixing of remedies]

olli compolli n. [late 17C–mid-19C] (UK Und.) 'the name of one of the principle rogues of the canting crew' (Grose, 1785). [? Sp. *olla*, a jar, and thus a dish containing a great variety of ingredients, a hotchpotch; thus, suggests E.P., 'the Jack-of-all-trades'. He is mentioned in Dekker's *O Per Se Ol* (1612) where the name is cited as a nickname, indicating that he is the chief of a given order of rogues, rather than a designation as such]

ollie beak n. [1990s+] a Sikh. [rhy. sl.]

ollies n. [1970s] testicles.

olly n. **1** [1960s+] marijuana (cf. BOB HOPE n.). **2** [1980s] amphetamine (cf. A n.[2]). [rhy. sl. on *Oliver Reed*; (1) = WEED n.[1] (4); (2) = SPEED n.[2]; ult. UK actor *Oliver Reed* (1938–99)]

-ology n. [early 19C+] an abstract, a theory, an '-ism'.

olympic pool n. [1950s+] (*Aus.*) an outdoor cinema. [? where one does the 'breaststroke']

omadhaun n. (also **amadáin, amadan, amadaun, ohmadaun, omadawn**) [mid-19C+] (*Irish*) a fool. [Irish *amadán*, a fool, a form of *onmitán*, f. *on*, a fool]

Omahog n. [late 19C–1960s] (US) a resident of *Oma*ha, Nebraska.

O'Malley *n.* [1990s+] a policeman (cf. BILLY n.⁶). [use of Irish surname O'Malley as a generic]

Omar Sharif *n.* [2000s] unpleasantness, unhappiness. [rhy. sl. = GRIEF n.¹ (1); ult. film actor *Omar Sharif* (b.1932)]

-o-matic *sfx* [1970s+] (*US campus*) a sfx indicating intensity or repetition, e.g. CRAM-O-MATIC v. ['technological' sfx *-omatic*]

ombrey *n. see* HOMBRE n.

omee *n.* (*also* **homa, homee, homer, homey, homie, omer, omey, omi**) **1** [mid-19C] a landlord. **2** [mid-late 19C] a master, a boss. **3** [mid-19C+] a man; often (*gay*) a heterosexual man. [Polari, Ital. *uomo*, a man; (1) and (2) f. (3)]

omee-polone *n.* (*also* **homi-polone, omee-paloney, omipalone**) [1960s+] (*Ling. Fr./Polari*) a male homosexual; opposite of POLONE-OMEE n. (cf. BOY-GIRL n.¹). [OMEE n. (3) + POLONE n. (2)]

omnibus *n.* [mid-late 19C] **1** a prostitute (cf. BANBURY n.). **2** the vagina. [anyone can buy a 'ride']

omnium gatherum *n.* [late 16C–19C] a mixed gathering of people or things. [cod Lat.]

omnium gatherum *adv.* [mid-17C] chaotically, confusedly. [OMNIUM GATHERUM n.]

om-tiddly-om-pom *n.* [1910s–30s] a lavatory. [? euph.]

on *adj.*¹ **1** [19C+] tipsy, slightly drunk. **2** [1930s+] intoxicated with a drug of any kind (cf. ON prep.⁶). [(1) Hotten (1864) suggests that the intoxicated person is 'on the road', presumably to collapse]

on *adj.*² **1** [early 19C+] involved in a wager; thus *get on*, to place a bet; [1930s+] *you're on*, your bet has been taken. **2** [late 19C+] (*orig. US*) in favour of, or willing to take part in something, ready to do something, e.g. *I'm on*, I agree with that; *you're on*, I accept your challenge or bet.

on *adj.*³ **1** [mid-19C–1950s] (*US*) fully comprehending or well aware of. **2** [late 19C+] (*later use US Black*) sophisticated, informed, at an advantage, fashionable. **3** [1930s+] (*Aus.*) alert, keeping one's eye on someone.

on *adj.*⁴ [late 19C+] (*US*) good, positive. [as opposed to OFF adj.¹ (3)]

on *adj.*⁵ [1930s+] available on a menu. [as opposed to OFF adj.¹ (5)]

on *adj.*⁶ [1930s+] in love with, having a (sexual) relationship.

on *adj.*⁷ [1960s+] (*US*) being the focus of attention, performing, needing to impress. [entertainment industry, as if *on stage*]

on *adj.*⁸ [1970s+] menstruating. [ON THE RAG phr. (1)]

on *adj.*⁹ [1990s+] sexually excited. [SE *on heat*]

on *adv.* [mid-19C+] no. [backsl.]

on *prep.*¹ **1** [mid-19C–1920s] (*UK Und.*) concentrating or focused on. **2** [20C+] pitted against, attacking.

on *prep.*² [mid-19C+] to the disadvantage or detriment of someone, so as to affect or disturb, e.g. *pass out on*, have a joke on.

on *prep.*³ [mid-19C+] a synon. for SE *at*, e.g. *on weekends*.

on *prep.*⁴ **1** [late 19C+] debited to, paid for by, e.g. *lunch is on me.* **2** [1910s] due, owed.

on *prep.*⁵ [1920s+] playing a given musical instrument, e.g. *on rhythm guitar, Keith Richards.*

on *prep.*⁶ **1** [1930s+] (*orig. US drugs*) in a general sense, using or addicted to a given drug, e.g. *on acid, on smack* (cf. ON adj.¹). **2** [1960s+] consuming a given drink, e.g. *on shorts, on rum.* **3** [1960s+] (*US campus*) using the contraceptive pill.

on *prep.*⁷ [1940s+] doing, having the responsibility for, taking the job of, e.g. *Sally's on nights this week.*

on *prep.*⁸ [1940s+] destined to secure a seduction.

on *prep.*⁹ [1970s+] up to, the responsibility of, a person's choice.

on a ay yo trip *phr.* [1980s+] (*W.I./UK Black teen*) used of one who is forever demanding attention, making him or herself conspicuous. [the cry of *Ay! Yo!* + TRIP n.⁵ (1)]

on a bat *phr.* [mid-19C+] (*orig. US*) drunk, on a drinking binge. [SE *on* + BAT n.³ (2)]

on a bender *phr.* (*also* **on a bend**) **1** [mid-19C+] on a drinking spree. **2** [20C+] on any other kind of spree. **3** [1930s+] bingeing on drugs. [SE *on* + BENDER n.²]

on a blind/blinder *phr. see* BLINDER n.³ (1).

on about *phr.* [1950s+] interested in, talking about.

on a brannigan *phr.* [late 19C+] (*US*) very drunk. [SE *on* + BRANNIGAN n. (1)]

on a brave *phr.* [mid-late 19C] (*US*) suddenly and temporarily courageous. [SE *on* + *brave*]

on a bust *adv.* [mid-19C+] (*US*) enthusiastically, to a great extent.

on a bust *phr.*¹ [mid-19C+] failing, doing badly. [SE *on* + BUST n.¹]

on a bust *phr.*² (*also* **on a buster**) [mid-19C+] drinking heavily. [SE *on* + BUST n.³ (1)]

on a dead one *phr.* [late 19C–1910s] **1** betting on a horse that has no chance. **2** making any pointless effort.

on a hiding to nothing *phr.* [late 19C+] with absolutely no chance, esp. in a sporting contest.

on a jag *phr.* [1950s+] (*orig. US*) elated. [SE *on* + JAG n.¹ (1)]

on a kick *phr.* [1940s+] (*orig. US*) **1** having a good time. **2** enthusiastic about. [SE *on* + KICK n.⁵ (3)]

on a lean *phr.* [1910s] (*Aus.*) waiting, lit. leaning (e.g. on a wall).

on all fours with, be *v.* [late 19C–1920s] to square with, to conform, to agree, to fit.

on a loop *phr. see* LOOP v.¹.

on a mission *phr.* [1980s+] **1** (*US Black gang*) searching for, in pursuit of, performing any gang-related activity, esp. killing members of a rival gang or simply penetrating their territory. **2** (*drugs*) looking for and/or bingeing on drugs. **3** (*US campus*) in search of.

on and off *n.* [1990s+] a cough. [rhy. sl.]

onan's olympics *n.* [19C] masturbation. [the biblical *Onan* who 'cast his seed upon the ground' (Gen. 38:9)]

on a para *phr.* [1990s+] feeling nervous, paranoid. [SE *on* + PARA adj.]

on appro *phr.* [mid-19C+] on sale or return. [abbr. SE *on approval*]

on a roll *phr.* [1970s+] (*orig. US gambling*) on a winning streak, enjoying a period of success, whether lit. or fig. [SE *on* + *roll*, the roll of a dice]

on a skate *phr.* [20C+] drinking heavily. [orig. RN *skate*, to go in search of liquor and women; ult. fig. use of SE]

on a sneak cue *adv. see* ON THE SNEAK TIP adv.

on a spot *phr. see* ON THE SPOT phr. (3).

on a streak *phr.* [1990s+] (*US*) menstruating.

on at, be *v.* [20C+] to be critical of, to nag or tell off. [abbr. GO ON AT v.]

on a tipple *phr.* [late 18C+] very drunk. [SE *on* + TIPPLE n. (1)]

on a trip *phr.* [1960s+] (*drugs*) **1** under the influence of drugs. **2** disorientated, seemingly 'in another world'. **3** crazy, temporarily insane (cf. OUT OF TOWN phr.). [SE *on* + TRIP n.⁴/TRIP n.⁵]

on a wonk *phr. see* WONKY adj. (1).

on board *phr.* [19C+] referring to drink that has been consumed. [naut. imagery]

on bone *phr.* [2000s] (*US prison*) unpopular among fellow prisoners after committing some form of mistake in terms of inmate codes of conduct.

once *n.*¹ [late 19C] vigour, energy, cheek. [SE *on!* advance, go forward]

once *n.*² [1930s+] £1, a £1 note. [abbr. ONCER n.²]

once *n.*³ *see* ONCE-OVER n.

once a week *n.*¹ **1** [late 19C] a magistrate. **2** [20C+] impudence, audacity. [rhy. sl.; (1) = BEAK n.¹ (1); (2) = CHEEK n.² (2)]

once a week *n.*² [1920s] (*US Und.*) a regular (weekly) bribe paid to a local official or law officer.

once-a-week man *n.* [early 19C] a debtor, one who goes out only once a week. [debtors could not be arrested on a Sunday, so for the rest of the week they hid indoors]

once in a month of Sundays *phr. see* MONTH OF SUNDAYS, A n.

once-over n. (*also* once) (*orig. US*) **1** [1910s+] a quick glance of appraisal; usu. in phr. *give the once-over*, to look over, to assess. **2** [1920s+] a search, e.g. at customs. **3** [1930s+] a quick treatment or superficial job, such as a quick clean-up.

once-over v. [1920s+] to glance at, to survey. [ONCE-OVER n.]

oncer n.[1] **1** [late 19C–1910s] a person who only goes to church once on Sunday; thus *twicer*, one who goes to both matins and evensong. **2** [1920s+] (*Aus.*) anything that happens only once. **3** [1930s] (*US*) a woman who has many very brief affairs. **4** [1940s+] (*gay*) a homosexual who never repeats a sexual encounter with any one partner but continues to seek new people; thus *oncing*, refusing a second sexual act with the same partner. **5** [1960s] (*US*) a man who can only have 1 orgasm during 1 session of sexual activity.

oncer n.[2] [1930s+] (*also* one) a £1 note; a A$1 bill.

onces n. [late 19C–1900s] wages. [they come once a week]

oncing n. *see* ONCER n.[1] (4).

on clover *phr.* [late 18C+] (*Aus.*) in comfort.

oncus adj.[1] (*also* ongkus, onkiss, onkus) [20C+] (*Aus./N.Z.*) **1** of people, upset, out of sorts, disagreeable. **2** of machinery, out of order. **3** of food or drink, stale. [ety. unknown; ? link to HONK v.[2]]

oncus adj.[2] (*also* ongkus) [1910s+] (*Aus./N.Z.*) good, profitable, pleasant. [ety. unknown; Baker, *Australian Slang* (1941) sees this as 'occasional' use only; *AND* cites only ONCUS adj.[1]; *DNZE* only this]

ond n. *see* OD n.

on deck *phr.* (*US*) **1** [late 19C–1910s] on the schedule, scheduled. **2** [late 19C–1910s] alive; conscious. **3** [late 19C+] available, prepared. [naut. imagery]

on doog *adj.* [mid-19C+] no good. [backsl.; ON adv. + DOOG adj.]

on e *phr.* [1990s+] (*US Black*) lacking, usu. but not invariably money. [*on* empty]

one n.[1] (*orig. US*) **1** [mid-19C+] a blow with the fist; thus LAY ONE ON SOMEONE v. or GIVE SOMEONE ONE v., occas. ext. to *two*, *three*, *four* etc. **2** [20C+] a punishment, a beating, e.g. *I'll give you one*; also in fig. use, a bad turn. **3** [1900s] an unpleasant look. **4** [1910s+] a bullet, a gunshot.

one n.[2] **1** [mid-19C+] a joke on, an act of teasing; a hoax. **2** [late 19C] a derog. name, a word of abuse. **3** [late 19C+] an anecdote, an amusing story, a joke, e.g. *have you heard the one about…?* **4** [late 19C+] a 'line', a persuasive if mendacious story, a lie. **5** [1950s+] an excuse.

one n.[3] **1** [late 19C+] the penis. **2** [1940s+] an act of sexual intercourse. **3** [1970s] the vagina.

one n.[4] **1** [late 19C+] a drink; usu. in the phr. *come and have one*, join me for a drink. **2** [1920s] (*US*) an inhalation of cocaine. **3** [1940s+] a state of drunkenness. **4** [1960s+] a cannabis cigarette (cf. NUMBER n.[5]). **5** [1980s] a hangover. **6** [1990s+] a heroin injection. **7** [1990s+] an adventure, a time, a spree.

one n.[5] **1** [late 19C+] an eccentric or amusing person. **2** [late 19C+] one who stands out in some way, either for impudence, expertise etc, esp. as a ONE FOR n. **3** [1960s] an unpleasant person, i.e. a CUNT n.[2] (1). **4** [1980s] a fool, a dupe. **5** [1990s+] a friend.

one n.[6] [1910s+] (*UK Und.*) a crime.

one n.[7] [1930s–60s] a male homosexual. [? old US Army joke, Sergeant, counting off, 'Are you one?' Soldier, 'Yeth, are you one too?'; Trimble, *5,000 Adult Sex Words & Phrases* (1966), labels this as 'Conv.[entional]']

one n.[8] [1940s+] (*orig. US*) nothing, not a single one; usu. with qualifying negative, e.g. *He won't get dime one out of me* etc.

one n.[9] [1940s+] the female breast; usu. in pl. and qualified by an adj., e.g. *big ones*, large female breasts; *nice ones*, attractive breasts.

one n.[10] *see* ONCER n.[2].

one, the n. [1970s+] cannabis oil, THC.

one *adv.* [early 19C+] used with a n. to emphasize the adj.

describing it, e.g. *one serious boy, one angry young man*, esp. as abbr./euph. for *one hell of a*.

one *phr.* [2000s] (*US teen*) goodbye, see you later.

one a cat couldn't scratch *phr. see* CAT COULDN'T SCRATCH IT phr.

one alone n. [20C+] (*Aus.*) a moan. [rhy. sl.]

one-a-man n. [1950s] (*W.I.*) a large, round dumpling, using a pound of flour. [one of these dumplings will satisfy a man's appetite]

one-and-a-half n. [1980s] £150.

one and a peppermint-drop n. [late 19C–1900s] a person with only 1 eye.

one and eight n. [20C+] a plate. [rhy. sl.]

one and elevenpence three farden n. **1** [late 19C+] a garden. **2** [1940s] I beg your pardon. [rhy. sl.]

one and half n. [20C+] a scarf. [rhy. sl.]

one and nine n. [1980s] a line. [rhy. sl.]

one-and-one n.[1] (*also* wan and wan) [1910s+] (*Irish*) a portion of fish and chips. [? early Italian immigrant chip-shop owners, whose lack of English meant that one signalled with one finger for chips and added another for fish]

one-and-one n.[2] *see* ONE-ON-ONE n.[2].

one and one v. [1970s+] (*drugs*) to inhale cocaine or heroin. [ONE-ON-ONE n.[2] (1)]

one and other n. [2000s] (*Irish*) brother. [rhy. sl.]

one and t'other n. **1** [1910s+] a brother (cf. ONE ANOTHER n.). **2** [1930s+] a mother. [rhy. sl.]

one and two n. *see* ONES AND TWOS n.[2].

one another n. **1** [late 19C+] a brother (cf. ONE AND T'OTHER n.). **2** [20C+] a mother. [rhy. sl.]

one-arm *adj.* [1950s+] (*US*) of a shop, police post etc, run by 1 person. [backform. f. ONE-ARM (JOINT) n.]

one-armed bandit n. (*also* one-arm bandit) [1930s+] (*orig. US*) a fruit machine, a coin-operated gaming machine, orig. operated by a single lever.

one-armed trouser worm n. *see* ONE-EYED (WONDER) WORM n.

one-arm (joint) n. (*also* one-arm lunch(room), …restaurant) [late 19C–1970s] (*US*) a fast-food café. [SE *one arm* + JOINT n.[4] (3)/SE *restaurant/lunchroom*; such a café provided food one could eat with 1 hand]

one-away *adv.* [1990s+] (*W.I.*) intimately, on a one-to-one.

one-bagger n. [1980s+] (*US campus*) a very ugly person. [such an individual is so ugly one would need to put a bag over their head before having sex with them; note synon. RMC Duntroon (*Aus.*) bag job, an ugly woman – ext. as *two-bag job, three-bag job*, etc; note Urquhart, *The Complete Works of Rabelais* (1653): 'To be short, they occupied [i.e. had sex with] all like good souls; only, to those that were horribly ugly and ill-favoured, I caused their head to be put within a bag to hide their face']

one bill n. *see* BILL n.[2] (5).

one bite n. [late 19C–1900s] (*costermonger*) a sour, small apple that is good for a single bite, after which it gets thrown away.

one brick short of a load *phr.* (*also* one brick shy of a load) [1960s+] unintelligent, slightly insane, eccentric. [var. on NOT ALL THERE phr. (1)]

one-cheek squeek n. [1990s+] an instance of breaking wind.

one-drink house n. [late 19C–1900s] a public house where only one drink is allowed in a given period. The customer must then go out and come back before being eligible for another.

one-eight-seven n. (*also* one eightyseven, 187) **1** [1940s+] a homicide. **2** [1990s+] in fig. use, any form of crisis or drama. **3** [1990s+] (*US prison*) targeted for assassination. [the California penal code for homicide. Codes vary from state to state, e.g. the Oregon homicide code is 163]

one-eight-seven *adj.* [1990s+] (*US*) murdered, dead. [ONE-EIGHT-SEVEN n. (1)]

one-eight-seven v. (also **one eightyseven, 187**) [1990s+] (US Black gang) to murder; thus gang slogan used by the Crips of Los Angeles *B187*, i.e. 'we kill Bloods'. [ONE-EIGHT-SEVEN n.]

one-eighty n. [1950s+] (US, orig. milit.) a complete reversal of plans, thoughts, action. [a 180-degree turn]

one-eighty v. (also **make a one-eighty**) [1980s+] (US) to reverse, esp. of a vehicle. [a 180-degree turn]

one eightyseven see under ONE-EIGHT-SEVEN.

one-ended furrow n. [19C] the vagina.

one-er see under ONER.

one eye and a winkle n. [1950s] a blind person or a person with 1 eye.

one-eyed adj.[1] [mid-19C+] **1** (US) of a person, crooked, dishonest. **2** (orig. US) of a place or object, inferior, inadequate, unimportant, useless.

one-eyed adj.[2] [1910s+] (orig. US/Aus.) used in a variety of combs. meaning penis, e.g. *one-eyed bob, one-eyed guardsman, one-eyed rocket*. [note much earlier ONE-EYED STAG n.]

one-eyed adj.[3] [1960s+] (US) in poker, used of a king or jack, esp. as wild cards. [the face is depicted in profile on playing cards]

one-eyed boy with his shirtsleeves rolled up n. [1960s+] a circumcised penis (cf. CLIPDICK n.). [ONE-EYED adj.[2] + SE boy + visual resemblance]

one-eyed brother n. [1990s+] (US Black) the penis. [ONE-EYED adj.[2] + BROTHER n. (2)]

one-eyed cyclops n. [1990s+] the penis. [ONE-EYED adj.[2] + SE Cyclop, since all Cyclops are one-eyed (the word means 'one-eyed' in Greek) this is, of course, tautological]

one-eyed monster n. [1960s+] (US) **1** the penis; thus *slay the one-eyed monster*, to masturbate. **2** a television set. [ONE-EYED adj.[2]/SE one-eyed + monster]

one-eyed pants python n. see ONE-EYED TROUSER-SNAKE n.

one-eyed scribe n. **1** [mid–late 19C] (US) a revolver, a pistol. **2** [1970s+] (US Black) a monumental liar, an insignificant person, poss. because they cannot be trusted to tell the truth.

one-eyed stag n. [late 18C] the penis. [predates ONE-EYED adj.[2] but same image]

one-eyed trouser-snake n. (also **one-eyed pants python, …trouser mouse, tan trouser snake**) [1930s+] (orig. Aus.) the penis (cf. ANTEATER n.). [ONE-EYED adj.[2] + SE trouser + SNAKE n.[3]/SE pants + python/MOUSE n.[2]]

one-eyed (wonder) worm n. (also **one-armed trouser worm**) [1980s+] a penis (cf. ANTEATER n.). [ONE-EYED adj.[2] + WORM n.[1]]

one-eyed zipper fish n. [1990s+] the penis (cf. ANTEATER n.). [ONE-EYED adj.[2] + SE zipper + fish]

one-eye target practice n. [1990s+] masturbation. [ONE-EYED adj.[2] + SE target practice]

one fat lady n. [1950s+] (bingo) the number 8 (cf. ALDERSHOT LADIES n.). [backform. f. the more popular TWO FAT LADIES n.]

one-fifty-one n. (also **151**) [1980s+] (drugs) crack cocaine (cf. BASE n.). [ety. unknown; ? California or NY penal code number]

one-finger(ed) salute n. [1960s+] (US) an obscene gesture of contempt. [ext. of FINGER, THE n. (2)]

one-finger exercise n. [1920s+] manual stimulation of the vagina or clitoris. [pun]

one foot n. see TWELVE INCHES n.

one-foot meat n. [1950s] (W.I.) an edible fungus. [the stem of the 'meaty' fungus]

one for n. [late 19C+] a person who is interested in or proficient at a specified thing. [ext. of ONE n.[5] (2)]

one for his nob n. [20C+] a shilling (5p). [rhy. sl. = BOB n.[4] (1)]

one for the bitumen n. [1950s+] (Aus.) a last drink, before starting a journey or leaving. [the bitumen, a tarred road, esp. the road from Darwin to Alice Springs, i.e. var. on ONE FOR THE ROAD n.]

one for the book n. [1920s+] (US) anything noteworthy, remarkable or incredible, something worthy of long-term record. [the SE record book]

one for the ditch n. [1960s+] (US) a final drink, but, rather than the trad. ONE FOR THE ROAD n., this var. acknowledges the perils of drunken driving.

one for the road n. **1** [20C+] a final drink before departure; ext. to a measure of drugs, i.e. cocaine. **2** [1990s+] in fig. use. [virtually SE by 1950]

one good woman n. [1970s+] (US Black) the ideal soulmate, considerate, sympathetic and prob. sexy too.

one-hand magazine n. [1960s+] a pornographic magazine, used as an aid to masturbation.

one hell of a phr. see HELL OF A, A phr.

one-hitter n. (also **one-hit bowl**) [1970s+] (drugs) a marijuana pipe that contains just enough for a single inhalation. [SE one + HIT n.[3] (5) (+ BOWL n. (2))]

one-holer n. [20C+] a single outside lavatory or privy.

one-horse adj. (also **one-pub**) [mid-19C+] (orig. US) insignificant, petty; esp. as in *one-horse town*, a small town of no importance. [18C SE one-horse, drawn or worked by a single horse]

one hundred smackers n. [1990s+] (US prison) a prison sentence of 100 years. [ironic/fig. use of one hundred SMACKER n.[2], i.e. £100]

one in ten n. [late 17C–mid-19C] a parson. [the tithes paid over by his parishioners]

one in the bush is better than two in the hand phr. [1920s+] (Aus.) one instance of proper intercourse is always better than any amount of masturbation. [pun on trad. pvb 'a bird in the hand is better than two in the bush', punning on BUSH n.[2] (1)]

one in the dark n. [1900s–30s] (US) a cup of black coffee. [the opposite of ONE IN THE LIGHT n.]

one in the departure lounge n. [2000s] an urgent desire to defecate.

one in the eye n. [late 19C+] a sharp response, an unpleasant experience, an insult; esp. as *that's one in the eye for…* [the one is a blow, i.e. ONE n.[1] (1)]

one in the light n. [1900s] (US) a white coffee, a coffee with cream. [the opposite of ONE IN THE DARK n.]

one-legged race n. [1970s+] masturbation.

one-leg trouser n. [late 19C] a style of skirt, tight and straight, popular in the 1890s. [resemblance]

one love phr. [1950s+] (orig. W.I. Rasta) a parting phr., an expression of unity.

one-lunger n. **1** [20C+] (US) a single-cylinder vehicle, usu. a motorcycle. **2** [1930s] (US Und.) a consumptive. **3** [1940s+] (US) any small or inferior set-up or device. **4** [2000s] (US) an eccentric.

one-man band n. [1930s+] one who takes all responsibilities on him or herself, sometimes with slightly pej. undertones, i.e. they are not really capable of being successful.

onener n. [mid–late 19C] a heavy blow. [? SE one and a, i.e. ext. of ONE n.[1] (1)]

one-nighter n. (US) **1** [1910s+] of a musician, band or show, a single performance in 1 place only. **2** [1940s+] an affair or sexual relationship of 1 night's duration; the person with whom this occurs.

one-night stand n. **1** [late 19C+] (US) a small rural town. **2** [20C+] an affair that lasts only a single night, thus a person with whom one has such a relationship. [entertainment jargon *one night stand*, the giving of only 1 performance in a specific venue before moving on]

one of 'em n. [mid–late 19C] (US) a remarkable or admirable person.

one off the wrist n. [1960s+] the act of masturbation.

one of King John's men n. [late 18C–early 19C] a small person; often as *one of King John's men, eight score to the hundred*.

one of my cousins n. [late 17C–early 19C] a prostitute. [a euph.

used presumably when the man accidentally meets a friend and has to make an introduction]

one of Pharaoh's lean kine n. [late 16C–mid-18C] a very thin person, looking as if 'he'd run away from the bone-house' or 'as if he were walking about to save funeral expenses' (F&H). [SE *one* + *Pharaoh* + *lean kine*, thin cattle]

one of the blue squadron n. [late 18C–early 19C] a mulatto. [SE *one* + BLUESKIN n.[2] (1) + SE *squadron*]

one of the chaps n. [1950s+] (*UK Und.*) a member of one's own gang or group. [SE *one* + CHAP n. (1)]

one of the faithful n. 1 [17C] a drunkard. 2 [late 18C–early 19C] a tailor who gives long credit. [SE *one of the faithful*, a member of a religious sect]

one of the knights, be phr. [1940s–70s] (*gay*) to have syphilis. [the disease attacks one's SWORD n.]

one of the livery n. [late 17C] a cuckold. [*livery* companies, military or city bands distinguished by their uniforms and badges, in the cuckold's case the 'badge' he 'wears' is that of the HORNS n.]

one of them n.[1] 1 [19C+] a prostitute. 2 [1970s+] a male homosexual. [euph.]

one of them n.[2] [late 19C–1900s] a shilling (5p). [ety. unknown; ? ONE OF THEM n.[1] (1), i.e. the cost of a cheap prostitute]

one of those n. 1 [late 19C+] a male homosexual. 2 [1970s+] (*US gay*) a heterosexual woman, any woman. [euph.]

one of us n. 1 [late 18C–early 19C] a prostitute. 2 [1930s+] a male homosexual.

one on n. [late 19C] (*US*) a portion of oyster stew.

one-on-one n.[1] [1960s+] (*orig. US*) a fight between 2 individuals (as opposed to a gang fight or an unequal competition).

one-on-one n.[2] (*also* **one-and-one**) [1980s+] (*drugs*) 1 cocaine, a line of cocaine. 2 a dose of 1 tablet of Talwin (a painkiller) + 1 tablet of Pyribenzamine (an antihistamine). [(1) refers to 1 LINE n.[4] of cocaine for 1 nostril]

one-on-one adj. [1960s+] (*orig. US*) person-to-person, intimate or confrontational, e.g. of a fight.

one-on-one adv. [1970s+] in an intimate, person-to-person manner; often as GO ONE-ON-ONE v.

one or the other n. [1990s+] one's mother. [rhy. sl.]

one out adj. 1 [1940s+] (*Aus.*) alone; thus *two out*, with a single accomplice or helper; *ten out*, in a team or gang of 10 etc. 2 [1980s+] (*Aus. prison*) a prisoner who prefers his own company.

one-out fight n. [1920s+] (*Aus. teen*) a fight between the 2 champions of a pair of rival teen gangs. [1 person comes *out* of the group]

one out of the bag n. (*also* **one out of the box**) [1930s+] (*Aus.*) a surprising person; an unexpected piece of good luck or pleasant event.

one over the eight phr. [1910s+] (*orig. UK milit.*) drunk. [the *eight* being pints, a supposed 'safe' amount of beer]

one percenter n. [1950s+] (*orig. US*) an outlaw bike rider. [the supposed 1% of motorcycle users who refuse to abide by the rules and the law]

one-piece overcoat n. [1950s+] a condom.

one-pot screamer n. (*also* **middy screamer, pint...,** **schooner..., two-pot...**) [1960s+] (*Aus.*) 1 one who cannot hold their liquor without becoming obstreperously drunk; *one-* or *two-pot* refer to the need for only 1 or 2 drinks before they lose all control; *middy, pint* and *schooner* refer to glass sizes and denote the (small) amount of alcohol required for this effect. 2 one who panics easily.

one-pub adj. see ONE-HORSE adj.

oner n.[1] (*also* **one-er**) 1 [mid-19C–1910s] a remarkable or outstanding person or event. 2 [1950s+] (*Aus.*) an amusing or eccentric person. [predates ONE n.[5]; ? Cockney pron. of SE *wonder* = *wunner*; or ? ONER n.[2]]

oner n.[2] (*also* **one-er**) [mid-19C–1920s] a knockout blow. [ONE n.[1] (1)]

oner n.[3] (*also* **one-er**) 1 [late 19C–1900s] a shilling (5p). 2 [late 19C+] £1. 3 [1950s+] £100 (cf. TWOER n.).

ones and twos n.[1] [1920s+] (*Aus./US*) shoes. [rhy. sl.]

ones and twos n.[2] (*also* **one and two**) [1990s+] (*orig. US Black*) in rap music, 2 turntables, as used by a hip-hop DJ.

one sandwich short of the picnic phr. (*also* **a sandwich short of a picnic, two sandwiches...**) [1960s+] a phr. used of someone who is not very intelligent, slightly eccentric, odd. [var. on NOT ALL THERE phr.]

one's arse, be phr. (*also* **be one's ass**) [1940s+] (*orig. US*) to cause one trouble, to lead to inevitable punishment, e.g. *Do that and it's your ass*. [i.e. one's ARSE n.[1] (1)/ASS n. (2) will get 'kicked']

one's arse is grass phr. see ONE'S ASS IS GRASS phr.

one's arse makes buttons phr. (*also* **one's ass makes buttons, one's tail...**) [mid-16C–early 19C; 1980s+] one is terrified, or jittery. [SE *one* + ARSE n.[1] (1)/ASS n. (2) + SE *buttons*, dung (usu. of animals), the image of involuntarily soiling one's trousers through fear]

— one's arse off phr. (*also* **— one's ass off**) [1960s+] a general intensifier implying extreme energy, e.g. *screw one's ass off, work one's arse off* etc. [SE *one* + ARSE n.[1] (1)/ASS n. (2)]

one's ass, be phr. see ONE'S ARSE, BE phr.

one's ass is grass phr. (*also* **one's arse is grass**) [1960s+] (*orig. US*) one is in severe trouble. [SE *one* + ARSE n.[1] (1)/ASS n. (2) + onomat. redup.]

one's ass is mud phr. [1930s+] (*US*) one is in danger, one's reputation has been destroyed. [SE *one* + ARSE n.[1] (4)/ASS n. (5) + SE *mud*]

one's ass makes buttons phr. see ONE'S ARSE MAKES BUTTONS phr.

— one's ass off phr. see — ONE'S ARSE OFF phr.

one's ass sucks buttermilk phr. (*also* **one's ass sucks wind**) [1950s+] (*US*) 1 one is absolutely terrified. 2 (*also* **one's ass sucks blue mud**) one is talking (hysterical) nonsense; esp. as a threat, *your ass will suck buttermilk when/unless...* 3 to be very angry. [SE *one* + ASS n. (2) + SE *buttermilk/wind/blue mud*]

one sausage short of a B.B.Q. phr. [1990s+] (*US teen*) a phr. used of someone who is not very intelligent, slightly eccentric, odd. [var. on NOT ALL THERE phr.]

one's bread is not done phr. [20C+] (*US*) used of one who is considered mentally deficient. [play on HALF-BAKED adj.]

one's chalk is up phr. [late 19C] one's credit at a public house is exhausted. [SE *chalk up*, to put on account]

one's eggs are cooked phr. (*also* **one's potato is cooked**) [late 19C+] (*N.Z.*) one is in severe trouble, it is all over etc. [WW1 *eggs a-cook*, hard-boiled Egyptian eggs]

oneself, be v. (*also* **feel oneself**) [mid-19C+] to feel 'right'; usu. in the negative, e.g. *I'm not (feeling) myself today*.

one shingle short phr. see SHINGLE SHORT, A phr.

one's humble n. [late 19C–1900s] a person, as *your humble, his humble* etc. [SE *your humble servant*]

one-skinner n. [1970s+] (*drugs*) a marijuana cigarette using a single rolling paper (cf. AFRICAN WOODBINE n.). [SE *one* + SKIN n.[18]]

one's measure phr. [mid–late 19C] the right person for the circumstances.

one's nose is always brown phr. [1930s+] said of a dedicated sycophant. [BROWN NOSE n.]

one-spot n. 1 [late 19C+] (*US*) a $1 bill. 2 [1940s] (*US Und.*) (*also* **one-spot sleep**) a 1-year prison sentence. 3 [1990s+] (*Aus. drugs*) A$100 worth of heroin. [SE *one* + -SPOT sfx]

one's potato is cooked phr. see ONE'S EGGS ARE COOKED phr.

one's skin is cracking phr. [1950s–60s] (*Aus.*) a phr. meaning one is desperate for a drink of alcohol. [play on SE *parched*, dried out, thirsty]

— one's socks off phr. (*also* **— the socks off**) [mid-19C+] used as an intensifier, e.g. BLOW THE SOCKS OFF v.[1], KNOCK THE SOCKS

OFF v., ROT THE SOCKS OFF v.; *see also* synons. in FUCK THE ARSE OFF v.; SCREW THE ARSE OFF v.

one's tail makes buttons *phr. see* ONE'S ARSE MAKES BUTTONS phr.

one's thing *n.* [1960s+] one's personal stance, one's lifestyle, philosophy etc; esp. in the phr. DO ONE'S (OWN) THING v. [SE *one* + THING n.[5] (5)]

— one's tits off *phr.* [1990s+] a general intensifer. [SE *one* + fig. use of TIT n.[3] (1)]

one stop short of East Ham *phr.* [1990s+] mad, eccentric. [pun on London Underground stop *Barking*/BARKING adj.]

one's trumpeter is dead *phr.* [late 18C–early 19C] said of a braggart, a self-advertiser. ['he is therefore forced to sound his own trumpet' (Grose, 1796)]

one thing, the *n.* [20C+] (*Irish*) sexual intercourse. [abbr. *the one thing men desire*]

one thousand miles *n. see* THOUSAND-MILER n.

one-time *n.* [1980s+] (*US Black*) a police officer or the police as an institution. [ety. unknown; ? warning 'I'll tell you just one more time…']

one time! *excl.*[1] [1990s+] (*US Black*) exactly! you're quite right! indeed!

one time! *excl.*[2] [2000s] (*US prison*) a shout of warning that an officer has appeared. [ONE-TIME n.]

one to meet *n.* [1940s+] (*orig. Und.*) an appointment.

one-two *n.* **1** [19C+] a knockout or knockdown blow; often as OLD ONE-TWO, THE n.[2]. **2** [1900s–40s] (*US*) a speedy exit, a quick departure. **3** [1960s] an act of male masturbation. [? boxing jargon *one-two*, two quick punches or jabs]

one-two checker *n.* [1990s+] (*US Black*) a cautious person, one who assesses a given situation. [trad. *one-two, one-two* used to check a microphone or PA system; note ONES AND TWOS n.[2]]

one, two, three, be *v.* [late 19C–1910s] (*US*) to stand out, to succeed (in comparison with).

one way *n.* [1960s+] (*drugs*) LSD (cf. A n.[3]). [play on SE *one way trip*/TRIP n.[4] (1)]

one-way *adj.* **1** [1930s–40s] (*US*) honest, e.g. a *one-way guy*, an honest man; thus a *two-way guy*, a crook. **2** [1940s+] (*US*) narrow-minded, closed, obsessive. **3** [1960s] (*US gay*) heterosexual.

one-way girl *n.* [1930s] (*US Und.*) a prostitute who offers only 'straight' intercourse (cf. AWAYDAY GIRL n.). [SE *one way* + *girl*]

one-way kid *n.* [1920s] (*US*) a greedy person. [this person takes but does not give]

one-way man *n.* [1960s] (*US gay*) **1** a male prostitute. **2** a male homosexual who is passive but not active.

one-way pockets *n.* [1910s+] a miser's pockets. [money enters but never leaves]

one-way ride *n.* [1930s–50s] (*US Und.*) a gangland murder. [the victim is driven away by his killers but only they will return]

one-way ticket *n.* [1930s] (*US Und.*) a life sentence.

one with, be *v.* [mid-19C] to get even with.

one with t'other *n.* [mid-17C–19C] an act of sexual intercourse.

on fire *phr.* [1980s+] doing very well, typically of a rock band, a sportsperson or some similar achiever.

on flake *phr.* [1970s–80s] (*US Black*) passed out, unconscious, esp. as a result of drug-taking. [SE *on* + FLAKE (OUT) v. (1)]

on fly time *phr.* [1950s] (*US Black*) sophisticated. [SE *on* + FLY adj. (1) + SE *time*]

on for *phr.* [late 19C+] destined for, promised to have.

on for a tater *phr.* (*also* **on for a tatur**) [late 19C–1900s] obsessed, fascinated, usu. used of a man who is desperate to talk to a woman he is attempting to pick up. [SE *on* + Fr. *tête à tête*, an intimate conversation]

on for young and old *phr.* [1940s+] (*Aus.*) in complete disorder, in utter chaos, describing a free-for-all.

on full *phr.* [1990s+] (*US Black*) well supplied with a given commodity, usu. (but not always) money. [car fuel gauge imagery]

ongkus *see under* ONCUS.

on gur *phr. see* ON (THE) GUR phr.

on half cock *phr.* [late 19C] of the penis, semi-erect. [SE *on half cock* + COCK n.[2] (1)]

on heat *phr.* (*also* **in heat**) [late 19C+] of a woman, sexually excited; occas. of a man. [SE *on heat*, usu. applied to female animals, esp. bitches]

on hit *phr.* [1990s+] (*US campus*) fashionable, chic. [SE *on* + HIT n.[1]]

on ice *phr.*[1] **1** [mid-19C+] (*orig. US*) in reserve. **2** [late 19C+] (*orig. US*) out of the way; in storage. **3** [20C+] (*orig. US*) dead. **4** [1930s] (*US Und.*) of stolen goods, waiting to be sold. **5** [1930s+] (*orig. US*) in prison, under arrest. **6** [1930s+] (*orig. US*) in hiding, esp. from the police. **7** [1940s–50s] (*orig. US*) in secret, on the quiet. **8** [1950s] (*US Und.*) suffering confinement in a punishment cell.

on ice *phr.*[2] (*US*) **1** [late 19C–1940s] certain, definite, a foregone conclusion, esp. of a sporting contest. **2** [1920s+] to the greatest extent, to the limit. [it is 'frozen']

onicker *n.* [late 19C] a prostitute. [her price, one NICKER n.[2] (1)]

onion *n.*[1] **1** [early–mid-19C] (*UK Und.*) a watch-seal; thus *bunch of onions*, a number of seals worn on 1 ring; *onion hunter*, one who steals such seals. **2** [late 19C+] the head. **3** [1920s–40s] (*US Und.*) a watch or clock. **4** [1990s+] (*US campus*) the buttocks. [resemblance]

onion *n.*[2] **1** [1900s–40s] (*US*) an idiot (cf. APPLEHEAD n.). **2** [1930s–40s] (*US Und.*) of a crime, a failure. [? he/it 'stinks']

onion *n.*[3] **1** [1900s–50s] (*US*) $1. **2** [1980s+] (*US campus*) $100. [play on CABBAGE n.[8]; KALE (SEED) n.; POTATO n.[4] etc]

onion *n.*[4] [1930s–40s] (*US Und.*) a tear-gas bomb.

onion *n.*[5] [1960s+] (*Aus.*) **1** mass sexual intercourse with a single woman. **2** the woman who has sex with 2 or more men in such a session. [pron. 'on-i-on', i.e. 'on and on']

onion *n.*[6] [1980s+] (*US drugs*) 28g (1oz) of marijuana. [? initial letter of SE *ounce*]

onion act *n.* (*also* **onion action**) [1940s+] (*US Black*) an unacceptable, offensive act or situation. [? like an onion, it reduces one to tears + the use of onions to create fake 'tears']

onionhead *n.*[1] [1910s–50s] (*US*) a stupid person. [SE *onion* + -HEAD sfx (1)]

onionhead *n.*[2] (*US*) **1** [1930s–70s] a bald-headed person. **2** [1990s+] a close, shaved haircut. [resemblance to a smooth, peeled onion]

onion money *n.* [1970s] a fine. [? ONION n.[2] + SE *money*]

onion peeler *n.* [1940s–60s] (*orig. US Black*) a switchblade knife. [play on SE *onion peeler* but note ONION n.[1] (2)]

onions *n.* [1930s+] the testicles (cf. ACORNS n.). [resemblance]

onions! *excl. see* WEE BUNS! excl.

onion skin *n.* [1960s+] (*US gay*) a long foreskin.

on it *phr.*[1] **1** [mid-19C+] ready, prepared, capable of, skilled in, in control; thus (*US Black*) *be on it like a hornet*. **2** [1980s] (*US campus*) good, likeable. [ON adj.[2] + SE *it*]

on it *phr.*[2] **1** [late 19C+] (*Aus.*) indulging (poss. to a noticeable excess) in drugs or drink. **2** [1950s+] (*US*) addicted, whether to a drug or to a person or experience. [ON adj.[1] + SE *it*]

on jankers *phr.* [20C+] in prison or undergoing some form of punitive discipline. [orig. milit. *jankers*, punishment for defaulters; ety. unknown; thus Kersh, *They Die With Their Boots Clean* (1941): 'What is jankers, Sergeant?' 'It's a sort of general word meaning punishment']

onk *n.* [1910s] (*Aus.*) a franc.

onka *n.* (*also* **onkaparinga**) [1960s+] (*Aus.*) a finger. [rhy. sl.; ult. *Onkaparinga*, the brandname of a make of woollen blanket; note Charleston (W.Va.) *Daily Mail*, 20 January 1935: 'Onkapringa – More Chinese, or something. Means "good"']

onkiss/onkus *adj. see* ONCUS adj.[1].

onky *adj.* [1920s+] (*Aus.*) stinking, stale, 'off'. [ONCUS adj.[1] (3) or HONK v.[2] (1)]

only one and ninepence in the florin *phr.* (*also* **only one and ninepence in two bob/shillings**) [1910s–70s] of someone who is not very intelligent, slightly eccentric, odd. [var. on NOT ALL THERE phr.]

on my life! *excl.* [19C+] an affirmation of absolute truth in the face of an audience's scepticism. [esp. as a clichéd phr. forced on every stage Jew]

on my pratt *phr. see* IN MY BOLLOCKS phr.

on my sammy say-so *phr.* [18C–1910s] on my word of honour. [assonant ext. of SE *say-so*]

on my skin *phr.* [20C+] (*US Und.*) a phr. that implies absolute honesty. [the primary importance of one's skin colour in prison]

on-off *n.* [1980s] (*US*) an act of (casual) sexual intercourse (with a stranger).

on offer *phr.* [1940s+] liable to problems.

on old toes *phr.* [mid-15C] in old age.

on one *phr.* **1** [1980s+] (*US campus*) having a successful time without any problems. **2** [1990s+] behaving crazily.

on one's ace *phr.* [20C+] (*Aus./N.Z./S.Afr.*) on one's own. [SE *on one + ace*, the highest playing card, equivalent to 'one']

on one's ass *phr.* (*also* **on one's arse**) **1** [1910s+] (*orig. US*) facing serious problems, esp. financial ones; occas. ext. to *on the balls of one's ass*. **2** [1960s] (*US campus*) ill, sick. [fig. use of ASS n. (2)/ARSE n.¹ (1)]

on one's back *phr.* [late 19C+] penniless, impoverished.

on one's darby *phr. see* DARBY AND JOAN adj.

on one's ear *phr.*¹ **1** [late 19C+] (*US campus*) offended, angry. **2** [1900s–40s] (*Aus.*) drunk.

on one's ear *phr.*² [late 19C+] (*orig. US*) in disgrace. [the image of a mother grabbing her errant child by their ear and hauling them from the room, shop or street]

on one's face *phr.* [late 19C–1910s] (*US*) on credit, for free.

on one's head *phr.* [1900s–30s] (*US*) emotional, in a state.

on one's j *phr.* [1970s+] (*US Black*) alert. [abbr. ON ONE'S JOB phr.]

on one's jack (jones) *phr.* (*also* **on one's jacks/jacksee**) [20C+] on one's own. [rhy. sl.; note ON ONE'S PAT (MALONE) phr.]

on one's jildy *phr. see* JILDI adv.

on one's job *phr.* (*also* **on one's j.o.b.**) [1950s+] (*US Black*) alert, in control; successful at a given task.

on one's keeping *phr.* [late 19C+] (*Irish*) in hiding, i.e. 'keeping oneself out of sight'.

on one's lonely *phr.* (*also* **by one's lonely**) [late 19C–1930s] by oneself.

on one's nickel *phr.* [1990s+] (*US*) at one's own expense.

on one's own hands *phr.* [mid-19C] looking after oneself, taking responsibility for one's own life.

on one's own hook *phr.* (*also* **on one's own pock-nook**) [early 19C+] looking after oneself, taking responsibility for one's own life, on one's own initiative or volition.

on one's ownio *phr.* (*also* **on one's owny-o**) [20C+] by oneself. [cod Italian]

on one's own nut *phr. see* NUT n.¹ (2).

on one's own pock-nook *phr. see* ON ONE'S OWN HOOK phr.

on one's ownsome *phr.* [1920s+] by oneself.

on one's owny-o *phr. see* ON ONE'S OWNIO phr.

on one's pat (malone) *phr.* [20C+] (*Aus.*) on one's own. [rhy. sl.; note ON ONE'S JACK (JONES) phr.]

on one's pink *phr.* [late 19C] (*Aus.*) drunk.

on one's (pink) ear *phr.* [1910s–30s] (*Aus.*) down and out, homeless.

on one's puff *phr.* (*also* **in one's puff**) [20C+] on one's own. [SE *on one + ? PUFF n.¹ (3) or ? rhy. sl.]

on one's skin *phr.* [1990s+] (*US prison*) used to stress the importance/validity of a statement.

on one's sweeney *phr.* [1990s+] (*Irish*) alone. [backform. f. ON ONE'S TOD phr.; ult. *Sweeney Todd*, the musical]

on one's tibby drop *phr.* [mid–late 19C] unawares. [rhy. sl.; TIBBY DROP n. = ON THE HOP phr.² (1)]

on one's tod *phr.* [1930s+] alone. [rhy. sl.; *Tod Sloan* = alone; ult. the US jockey James Forman '*Tod*' Sloan (1874–1933)]

on one's toes *phr.* **1** [20C+] careful, alert. **2** [1910s] quickly. **3** [1950s+] on the run, fleeing justice. **4** [1970s] in the process of leaving.

on paper *phr.* [20C+] (*US prison*) on parole. [one's 'ticket-of-leave']

on pipe *phr.* [2000s] (*US prison*) living as a jail homosexual. [SE *on + PIPE n.² (1)]

on plush *phr.* [1910s–40s] in luxury. [SE *on + plush*, a type of cloth, softer than velvet, used for expensive garments]

on point *phr.* **1** [1970s+] standing guard, keeping a lookout. **2** [1990s+] alert, sharp, aware. [milit. *point*, the lead man of a patrol]

on sentry *phr.* [late 19C–1910s] drunk.

on someone's ass *phr.* (*also* **on someone's butt**) [1940s+] (*US*) in hot pursuit (of someone); persecuting or harassing someone. [fig. use of ASS n. (2)/BUTT n.¹ (2)]

on someone's back *phr.* [mid-19C+] causing problems for someone, being irritating; thus GET OFF SOMEONE'S BACK v.

on someone's case *phr.* [1960s+] (*orig. US*) **1** harassing verbally, persecuting; often as *get on someone's case*. **2** pursuing, following. [CASE n.¹]

on someone's daily *phr. see* DAILY (MAIL) n.

on someone's dick *phr.* [1980s+] (*US Black*) **1** keen on, supporting. **2** oppressing, nagging, harassing. [fig. uses of DICK n.⁴ (1)]

on someone's duster *phr.* [1970s] harassing, persecuting someone.

on someone's ginger *phr.* [1960s+] (*Aus.*) following, in pursuit of. [rhy. sl.; *ginger ale* = ON SOMEONE'S TAIL phr.]

on someone's hammer *phr.* (*Aus.*) **1** [1920s+] very close behind. **2** [1940s+] hounding, pestering. [rhy. sl.; *hammer and tack* = ON SOMEONE'S BACK phr.]

on someone's hip *phr.* [1910s] **1** of a person, acting as a burden, a dependent. **2** following someone.

on someone's jock (strap) *phr.* [1980s+] (*US*) pursuing, esp. of a woman sexually harassing a man. [JOCK n.¹]

on someone's neck *phr.* [1910s+] pressurizing or persecuting someone.

on someone's tail *phr.* (*also* **hot on someone's neck/tail**) **1** [1930s+] to be following, pursuing. **2** [1940s+] (*US*) persecuting or harassing someone. [TAIL n.² (1)/SE *neck* (+ HOT adj.¹ (2))]

on someone's tip *phr.* [1980s] (*US Black*) of a woman, to be ready for sexual activity, to be (sexually) interested in. [? the tip of the penis; note ON THE DICK phr.]

on someone's tit *phr.* [1980s] (*US campus*) pursuing, lit. or fig.; thus being annoying. [TIT n.³ (1)]

on someone's titty *phr.* (*also* **at someone's titty**) [1970s+] (*US*) dependent on someone (for money, work, protection etc); thus *off someone's titty*. [TITTY n.¹ (1), the idea is of breastfeeding]

on someone's wheel *phr.* [1920s+] (*Aus.*) close behind, in pursuit; putting pressure on someone to do something. [cycling imagery]

on song *phr.* [1960s+] working well, in prime condition. [one is 'in tune']

on speakers *phr.* (*also* **on speaks**) [1900s–20s] (*UK society*) on speaking terms.

on spec *phr.* [mid-19C+] at a risk, without making a firm decision. [SE *on + speculation*]

onswoggled *adj. see* HORNSWOGGLED adj.

on swole *phr.* [1990s+] (*US Black teen*) **1** swollen, large, usu. of a penis, erect. **2** relaxed and free of stress. [SE *swollen*; (2) f. (1)]

on T *phr.* (*also* **on time**) [1940s+] (*US Black*) at the emotionally or psychologically apposite moment (rather than the chronologically prompt one); also as phr. *get on time*, to have fun.

on the act *phr.* [late 19C] working as an actor.

on the arm *phr.* [1920s+] (*US*) for free, on credit. [? the writing of notes on one's cuff]

on the avenue *phr.* (*US Black*) **1** [1930s+] lit. in the street. **2** [1990s+] in general use, from a mass point of view.

on the backbeat *phr.* [1940s] (*US Black/Harlem*) of time, in the past, ago; before.

on the back burner *phr.* [1960s+] deferred, pending, put off. [a stove's back burners are not as hot and thus cook more slowly than the front ones]

on the back of one's arse *phr.* [late 19C+] (*Aus.*) penniless, impoverished. [ARSE n.¹ (1)]

on the ball *phr.* **1** [20C+] (*orig. US*) aware, alert, capable; thus *get on the ball*, to make an effort, to become aware. **2** [1930s+] (*US*) in an advantageous position, in good standing. [baseball jargon *put something on the ball*, to pitch with extra speed or with a deceptive motion]

on the balls of one's ass *phr.*¹ [1970s] (*US*) at the nadir of one's fortunes. [? such a thing does not exist]

on the balls of one's ass *phr.*² *see* ON ONE'S ASS phr. (1).

on the barter *phr.* [1950s] (*Aus.*) working as a prostitute.

on the bash *phr.* **1** [1910s+] (*Aus./N.Z.*) drinking, usu. to excess. **2** [1930s+] working the streets as a prostitute. **3** [1960s+] having sexual intercourse. [BASH v.²; (3) BASH v.¹ (4)]

on the bat *phr.*¹ (*also* **on the batter**) [mid-19C+] out for a drunken, sexy, brawling time, on a spree. [BAT n.³ (2); note Carew, *The History of Bampfylde Moore Carew* (1750), has *on the battu*, from *battu*, wear and tear]

on the bat *phr.*² (*also* **on the batter**) [late 19C+] working as a prostitute. [BAT n.¹]

on the bat *phr.*³ [1930s–40s] (*US Black*) in prospect, potentially.

on the batter *phr.*¹ *see* BATTER v. (2).

on the batter *phr.*² *see* ON THE BAT phr.¹.

on the batter *phr.*³ *see* ON THE BAT phr.².

on the battle *phr.* [20C+] (*Aus.*) working as a prostitute. [BATTLE v. (4)]

on the beach *phr.* [late 19C+] (*US*) out of work, impoverished. [naval jargon *on the beach*, discharged from the navy, thus unemployed]

on the beam *phr.* [1940s+] (*orig. US*) right on course, heading in the right direction; thus *on the beam in short-cut plays*. [orig. air force, referring to radio beams that guide aircraft]

on the beat *phr.* [late 19C–1960s] (*US*) working as a swindler. [BEAT n.³ (2)]

on the beer *phr.* [late 19C+] drinking.

on the bell *phr.* **1** [early 19C] on credit. **2** [1990s+] buying (a round of drinks).

on the bend *phr.*¹ [mid-19C–1940s] crooked, criminal, underhand. [predates BENT adj. (3) but presumably its derivation]

on the bend *phr.*² [1910s] at a disadvantage. [the image is one who is bending over and may thus, unaware, be kicked]

on the billiard slum *phr.* [early 19C–1910s] (*Aus., orig. UK Und.*) working as a confidence trickster; thus *give it them on the billiard slum, go on the billiard slum*, to hoax, to defraud. [SE *billiards*, with the image of a ball bouncing at various angles + SLUM n.² (3)]

on the bite *phr.* [1940s+] (*Aus.*) demanding money, either as payments, loans or bribes. [BITE v. (6)]

on the blimp *phr.* [1980s] wandering aimlessly around, looking around.

on the blind *phr.* [20C+] (*Aus.*) at risk, on chance, without any prior information.

on the blink *phr.*¹ **1** [late 19C+] (*orig. US*) malfunctioning, working badly, damaged; thus *go blink*, go wrong. **2** [1900s–40s] of a person, ill or dead. **3** [1920s–40s] (*US*) impoverished, penniless. [the blinking of electric lights that signalled a 'short' or similar malfunction]

on the blink *phr.*² [1950s] (*US Und.*) working as a fake 'blind beggar'. [the 'blind' man's surreptitious blinking]

on the blob *phr.*¹ [mid–late 19C] by word of mouth; thus *blob*, talk. [BLAB v. (1)]

on the blob *phr.*² [1990s+] (*US*) menstruating. [the *blobs* of blood]

on the block *phr.*¹ **1** [late 19C+] (*US*) in business. **2** [1940s+] (*US*) working as a street prostitute. **3** [1940s+] (*US Black campus*) hanging out in a specific meeting place.

on the block *phr.*² *see* BLOCK v.² (3).

on the bludge *phr.* [1940s+] (*Aus.*) scrounging. [BLUDGE v. (4)]

on the bo *phr.* [1920s] (*US*) living as a vagrant. [BO n.² (1)]

on the bones of one's arse *phr.* [1990s+] (*Aus./N.Z.*) very poor, impoverished. [SE *bone* + ARSE n.¹ (1), i.e. one's thinness through lack of food]

on the book *phr.* [2000s] involved.

on the books *phr.* [20C+] (*US*) good for credit.

on the boost *phr.* [1900s–60s] (*US Und.*) **1** working as a pickpocket. **2** working as a shoplifter. [BOOST v.²]

on the bot *phr. see* BOT n.¹ (2).

on the bottle *phr.* **1** [20C+] (*later use UK Black*) working as a pickpocket. **2** [1960s+] working as a male prostitute. **3** [1960s+] (*US*) working in any form of prostitution. [(1) BOTTLE n.² (1); (2) BOTTLE n.² (4)]

on the bounce *phr.* [late 19C+] on the spur of the moment, spontaneously. [the idea 'bounces' into one's brain]

on the bow *phr. see* ON THE ELBOW phr.

on the brain *phr.* [late 19C] to be thinking.

on the bricks *phr.* **1** [1930s+] (*US*) on the street after being released from prison. **2** [1960s+] (*drugs*) walking the streets searching for drugs. **3** [1980s+] working as a street prostitute.

on the bristle *phr.* [late 19C] on a spree.

on the brown side *phr.* [1940s] (*US*) older than.

on the bugle *phr.* [1930s+] (*Aus.*) smelly, both lit., i.e. no longer edible, and fig., i.e. dishonest, dubious. [BUGLE n.¹ (1)]

on the bum *phr.*¹ (*US*) **1** [mid-19C+] travelling as a tramp or beggar, scrounging, cadging. **2** [late 19C] looting. **3** [20C+] penniless. [BUM n.³ (1)]

on the bum *phr.*² **1** [late 19C+] broken, out of order, lit. and fig.; thus *put (someone/something) on the bum*, to hurt, to beat up, to cause trouble for someone. **2** [late 19C+] rubbish, second-rate, inferior, in a bad condition. **3** [1900s] (*US campus*) drunk. **4** [20C+] feeling slightly unwell. [BUM adj.]

on the burst *phr.* [mid-19C–1940s] (*also* **on the bust**) on a binge of food and drink. [BURST n.²]

on the bus *phr.* [1960s+] used of one who is part of a group, sharing the joint consciousness; thus *off the bus*, abandoning the group and its beliefs and ethos. [coined *c.*1965 by novelist and psychedelic guru Ken Kesey (b.1935), whose 'Merry Pranksters' drove across America on a bus, named Furthur (sic), from San Francisco to Millbrook, New York, where Kesey's opposite number Timothy Leary (1920–96) held court]

on the bust *phr.*¹ [1920s–30s] facing financial problems, bankruptcy. [BUST adj.]

on the bust *phr.*² *see* ON THE BURST phr.

on the bustle *phr. see* BUSTLE n.¹.

on the cannon *phr.* [20C+] working as a pickpocket. [CANNON n.²]

on the carpet *phr.*¹ [early 18C+] up for discussion, under consideration, thus fig. of something about to happen (usu. worryingly so).

on the carpet *phr.*² [mid-19C+] (*orig. US*) facing a reprimand, scolding or punishment; thus *toe the carpet, dance on the carpet*, to await and receive such a dressing down (where the image is of a fidgety, nervous person). [the carpet that stands before one's superior's desk]

on the cart *phr. see* ON THE WAGON phr.

on the castor with, be *v. see* CASTOR adj.

on the cat *phr.* (*US Black*) **1** [1940s] in hiding. **2** [1950s–60s] staying out at night. [CAT AROUND v.]

on the cheese *phr.* [late 19C–1940s] (*US*) unsatisfactory, in a bad way. [? CHEESE n.[4] (1)/CHEESE v.[1]]

on the chorie *phr.* [1990s+] (*Scot.*) engaged in thieving (as a regular occupation). [CHORE v.]

on the coat *phr.* [1940s+] (*Aus.*) out of favour; esp. in phr. *have/put on the coat*, to place someone in a position of disfavour. [the gesture of fingering someone's lapel in a vaguely minatory manner]

on the cob *phr.* [1930s] (*US*) sentimental, simplistic, banal. [play on CORNY adj.]

on the cobbles *phr.* [1950s+] looking for a fight.

on the corn *phr.* (*also* **eating corn**) [1940s–60s] (*Aus. prison*) serving time in prison. [the hominy diet therein]

on the cripple and crutch *phr.* [1950s] looking for a loan. [rhy. sl. = TOUCH n.[1] (5)]

on the cross *phr.* [early 19C–1910s] **1** obtained surreptitiously, illegally. **2** working as a professional criminal. **3** dishonest. [CROSS n.[1] (1)]

on the cross-cut *phr.* [1900s] (*N.Z.*) angry with, arguing with. [sawmill imagery]

on the cuff *phr.*[1] (*orig. US*) **1** [1910s+] on account, on credit; thus *put on the cuff*, to give credit, to ask for credit; *swing the cuff*, to obtain on credit or for free. **2** [1920s+] for free. [CUFF n.[2]]

on the cuff *phr.*[2] [1940s+] (*N.Z.*) excessive; usu. as *a bit on the cuff*. [? rhy. sl. = SE *rough*]

on the cushions *phr.* (*also* **on the cush/plush**) [20C+] (*US Und.*) travelling in a passenger coach as opposed to a freight wagon; thus symbolic of any form of luxury or comfort.

on the cutback *phr.* [1940s] (*US Black*) of time, ago.

on the dangle *phr. see* DANGLE n.

on the deck *phr.* [1920s+] bankrupt, without funds. [milit. use *on the deck*, at ground level]

on the dick *phr.* [1990s+] (*US Black*) of a woman, to be ready for sexual activity.

on the dime *phr.* [1940s] (*US Black*) by chance.

on the dink *phr.* [1900s–10s] in trouble, facing problems. [? var. on ON THE BLINK phr.[1] (1)]

on the dip *phr.* [mid-19C+] (*UK/US Und.*) working as a pickpocket; resulting from pickpocketing. [DIP v.[2] (1)]

on the d.l. *phr.* [1990s+] (*US Black*) depressed, out of sorts. [abbr. SE *down low*]

on the dodge *phr.* [20C+] **1** involved in something illegal or underhand. **2** hiding from or avoiding the authorities. [SE *dodge*, to act in a dubious, untrustworthy manner]

on the down low *phr.* (*also* **on the d.l., on the low**) [1990s+] (*orig. US Black*) **1** in the background, clandestine; as an adv., in a clandestine manner. **2** of a (married) man, having homosexual relations despite parading an ostensibly heterosexual lifestyle. **3** being a fan of hip-hop/rap music. [DOWN LOW n./D.L. n.]

on the d.q. *adv.* [late 19C] (*US*) quietly, surreptitiously, privately. [abbr. SE *dead quiet*]

on the drift *phr.* [1950s] (*Aus.*) travelling as a tramp. [SE *drift* but note DRIFT v.]

on the drip *phr.* [1950s+] bought on hire purchase.

on the earhole *phr.* [1910s+] (*UK Und.*) on the scrounge. [one is talking into a victim's *earhole*]

on the earie *phr.* **1** [1910s+] (*orig. UK Und.*) on the scrounge. **2** [1920s+] (*US Und./prison*) (*also* **on the eary, on the erie**) eavesdropping. [SE *ear*; (1) var. on ON THE EARHOLE phr.]

on the elbow *phr.* (*also* **on the bow**) [late 19C+] on the scrounge. [the scrounger nudges or tugs one's elbow]

on the erie! *excl.* (*also* **on the earie!**) [1920s+] (*US prison*) be quiet! someone is listening! [ON THE EARIE phr. (2)]

on the fence *phr.* [1940s+] (*gay*) turning to heterosexuality.

on the fiddle *phr.* [1910s+] cheating, committing fraud, swindling. [FIDDLE v.[2] (2)]

on the filch *phr.* [late 19C] working as a thief. [FILCH v. (2)]

on the floor *phr.*[1] [20C+] poor. [rhy. sl.]

on the floor *phr.*[2] [20C+] **1** drunk. **2** beaten. [where one has collapsed]

on the fly *adv.* (*orig. US*) **1** [mid-19C+] in a hurry, on the move, spontaneously. **2** [20C+] cunningly, clandestinely. [SE *fly*, to move quickly/FLY n.[2]]

on the fly *phr.* **1** [mid-19C] begging by following passers-by and asking for cash, rather than standing in one place. **2** [mid-19C–1930s] getting one's living by theft or some other form of crime. **3** [1970s] by mistake. [FLY n.[2]]

on the fritter *phr.* [1900s] (*US Und.*) not working. [SE *fritter*]

on the fritz *phr.* [20C+] **1** drunk. **2** of a person, unhealthy, out of sorts. **3** (*also* **away to the fritz**) of an object, not functioning properly. **4** of a situation, position, job, in jeopardy. **5** of machinery, broken down, not working. **6** impoverished. [? German proper name *Fritz* and thus propagandist dislike of all things German; or ? *fritz* as onomat. for the sparking of a faulty wire or connection]

on the furilla *phr.* [1980s+] (*US Black*) acting honestly, honourably. [FO' RILLA adv.]

on the G *phr.* [2000s] (*US Black*) a phr. meaning honestly, sincerely. [abbr. SE *genuine*]

on the game *phr.* **1** [mid-19C–1920s] working as a thief. **2** [late 19C+] involved in prostitution. **3** [1970s+] (*US gay*) walking the streets looking for sex.

on the gank *phr.* [1990s+] (*US Black*) looking for a violent confrontation. [GANK v. (3)]

on the go *phr.* **1** [late 17C–early 18C] on the verge of destruction. **2** [early 18C–1900s] in a state of decline. **3** [early 19C] slightly drunk, tipsy. **4** [early 19C+] active, lively. **5** [1940s] nervous. **6** [1950s+] happening, going on.

on the grass *phr.* [late 19C–1950s] (*Aus. Und.*) free (of prison).

on the grind *phr.* [late 19C+] involved in hard, demanding work. [GRIND n.[2] (1)]

on the ground *phr.* [20C+] (*US prison*) on the streets, free.

on (the) gur *phr.* [1920s–40s] (*Irish*) truanting. [? GURRIER n. or ? the *gur-cake*, a fruit pastry slice popular with poor Dublin children, consumed when truanting]

on the hammer *phr.* [1940s+] (*Aus.*) in pursuit, 'on someone's back'.

on the hard *phr. see* HARD n.[3].

on the hawks *phr.* [1960s+] (*US*) on the lookout. [a *hawk* eye]

on the head *adv.* [1940s+] exactly, precisely.

on the high fly *phr.* [mid–late 19C] working as a beggar or a cadger, working as a begging-letter writer pretending to be a gentleman fallen on hard times (cf. HIGH FLYING n.). [HIGH-FLYER n.[1] (7)]

on the hill *phr.*[1] [1950s+] (*US*) pregnant. [the shape of one's stomach]

on the hill *phr.*[2] [1980s+] (*Aus. prison*) in prison.

on the hip *phr.*[1] [late 16C+] in a position of control, near defeat. [one's *hip* would be on the ground when one was knocked down. 'This phrase seems to have originated from hunting, because, when the animal was seized upon the hip, it is finally disabled from flight' (Nares). Dr. Johnson (in *Notes on Shakespeare*, 1765) suggests a link to the cross-buttock throw in wrestling but accepted the hunting link in later edns of his Dictionary, although the *OED* still has the wrestling ety.]

on the hip *phr.*[2] [1900s–60s] (*drugs*) using narcotics, whether opium, heroin or, latterly, crack cocaine. [opium smokers rested on one *hip* as they smoked their pipe]

on the hog (train) *phr.* [late 19C+] **1** (*US*) living as a tramp. **2** (*US*) out of order, chaotic; of objects, in bad condition. **3** (*US campus*) at a disadvantage. **4** (*US*) of people, in bad condition, penniless. **5** (*US*) depressed. **6** (*US campus*) honest. [negative image of hogs in a sty]

on the hoist *phr.* [early 19C+] working as a shoplifter. [HOIST n.[1] (1)]

on the hoof *phr.* [1930s+] **1** in existence. **2** passing by, casual. [SE *on the hoof*, on the move, walking; ult. HOOF n. (1)]

on the hook *phr.*[1] [mid–19C–1940s] engaging in theft. [HOOK v.[1] (2)]

on the hook *phr.*[2] [1900s–40s] (*US*) playing truant. [PLAY HOOKY v. (1)]

on the hook *phr.*[3] [1940s+] (*drugs*) addicted to a drug. [HOOKED adj.[3]]

on the hook *phr.*[4] [1950s+] (*US*) responsible (for) something that went wrong. [as opposed to OFF THE HOOK phr.[2]]

on the hop *phr.*[1] **1** [mid–19C–1950s] busy, active, enjoying oneself. **2** [mid-19C+] spontaneously, in a rush. [HOP v.[1] in general use]

on the hop *phr.*[2] **1** [late 19C+] running away, escaping, on the run; thus *take it on the hop*, to run away, to escape. **2** [1990s+] (*Irish*) playing truant. [HOP v.[1]]

on the hot *phr.* [1930s–40s] (*US Und.*) on the run. [HOT adj.[2]]

on the hot foot *phr. see* HOT FOOT n.[1].

on the hurry-up *phr.* [1950s+] at great speed, in a hurry.

on the hustle *phr.* [1940s+] (*US*) **1** living as a confidence trickster, a swindler. **2** working as a prostitute. **3** working hard at any job. [HUSTLE n.]

on the in, be *v.* [1920s+] (*orig. US*) to be an insider, to have inside information. [IN n.]

on the inside *phr.*[1] *see* INSIDE adj.[1] (1).

on the inside *phr.*[2] *see* INSIDE adj.[2].

on the jildi *phr. see* JILDI adv.

on the job *phr.* [late 19C+] **1** a euph. for engaged in sexual activity. **2** working properly. **3** in the process of doing something. **4** aware, au fait. [SE *job*/JOB v.[1] (1)]

on the jump *adv.* [mid-19C+] promptly, immediately, very quickly.

on the jump *phr.* **1** [mid-19C+] restless, unsettled, nervous, busy. **2** [1900s–30s] (*US Und.*) on the run.

on the knocker *phr.* (*also* **on the knob**) [1930s+] (*Aus.*) at once, on demand, esp. of cash payments, exactly. [the creditor is knocking at the door]

on the lam *adv.* [1910s+] quickly, at a run, at top speed. [ON THE LAM phr.]

on the lam *phr.* [1910s+] (*US Und.*) on the run from prison or the police, thus fig. on the loose. [LAM n.[1] (1)]

on the lash *phr.* [2000s] out on a spree.

on the lay *phr.* [late 18C–1910s] involved in some form of illegal activity. [LAY n.[4] (3)]

on the lay for *phr. see* LAY FOR v.[1].

on the lee lurch *phr.* [mid-19C] (*US*) drunk.

on the level *adv.* [late 19C+] (*US*) honestly, definitely, fairly.

on the level *phr.* (*orig. US*) **1** [late 19C+] honest, straightforward. **2** [1920s] of a criminal, reformed. **3** [1930s] of a woman, sexually respectable.

on the line *phr.* **1** [20C+] of money, either put at stake or, e.g. in the case of a drug deal, advanced as a loan. **2** [20C+] honest, straightforward. **3** [1940s–50s] (*US*) prepared, in the offing. **4** [1970s] under interrogation. **5** [1980s] (*Aus.*) under police observation. **6** [2000s] (*US prison*) for sale. [gambling use]

on the link *phr.* [2000s] (*UK Black*) having sexual intercourse.

on the low *phr. see* ON THE DOWN LOW phr.

on the lug *phr.* [20C+] begging for a loan. [LUG v.[1] (2)]

on the mag *phr.* [late 19C] working as a confidence trickster. [MAG v. (3)]

on the make *phr.* **1** [mid-19C+] (*orig. US*) looking to benefit oneself, ambitious, keen to do whatever will be most useful for one's own advancement or profit. **2** [mid-19C+] (*orig. US*) engaged

in theft or swindling. **3** [late 19C+] (*orig. US*) seeking sexual activity. **4** [1900s] (*US Und.*) of a policeman, willing to be bribed. [MAKE v.[3]]

on the mallet *phr.* [mid-19C] of goods taken on trust. [they are *knocked down/out*]

on the money *phr.* [1940s+] (*orig. US*) excellent, perfect, just right. [betting imagery]

on the mooch *phr.* **1** [mid-19C+] living as a professional beggar. **2** [mid-19C+] in search of a given commodity, e.g. money or drugs. **3** [late 19C] (*also* **on the mouch**) wandering about. **4** [late 19C] on the lookout. **5** [20C+] (*Irish*) playing truant. **6** [1940s–50s] (*drugs*) addicted to drugs. [MOOCH v.[1]; (6) MOOCH n.[5]]

on the mump *phr.* [early 18C; 1910s] begging for one's living. [MUMP v. (1)]

on the Murray cod *phr.* **1** [1960s+] (*Aus.*) in gambling, betting on credit. **2** [1980s+] (*Aus. prison*) of an unspoken arrangement. [rhy. sl. = ON THE NOD phr.[1]]

on the muscle *phr.* **1** [mid-19C+] quarrelsome, ready or poised to fight. **2** [1940s] (*US*) for free, provided by someone else. **3** [1940s+] (*US*) using a threat of violence. **4** [1950s+] working as protection for a top gangster. **5** [1960s+] nervous, edgy. [MUSCLE n.[1]]

on the natch *phr.* [1960s+] (*drugs*) not using any drugs or other stimulants. [abbr. SE *natural*]

on the needle *phr.* [1940s+] (*drugs*) using narcotic drugs. [NEEDLE n.[4] (1)]

on the nest *phr.* [20C+] **1** (*US*) pregnant. **2** (*Aus.*) of a man, having sexual intercourse.

on the never-never *phr.* (*also* **on the never**) [late 19C+] bought on hire purchase. [NEVER-NEVER (LAND) n.]

on the nod *phr.*[1] **1** [late 19C+] on credit. **2** [late 19C+] without argument, typically of Parliamentary or local government business which 'goes through' or 'passes on the nod'. **3** [1910s–20s] for free. [the shop-owner *nods* his assent to one's request]

on the nod *phr.*[2] [1950s+] (*drugs*) **1** succumbing to a sleepy stupor after smoking opium or taking an injection of heroin. **2** dozing off after smoking cannabis. **3** falling asleep, exhausted from excess of any sort. [NOD n.[1] (1)]

on the nose *adv.* **1** [late 19C+] (*orig. US*) exactly, precisely, as to accuracy, later spec. factual accuracy. **2** [1930s+] (*US*) exactly, as to time.

on the nose *phr.*[1] **1** [1920s+] (*gambling*) making a wager on a particular horse to win, e.g. £5 *on the nose*. **2** [1940s] in fig. use, of a reward offered for information leading to the capture of a criminal.

on the nose *phr.*[2] [1940s+] (*Aus./N.Z.*) **1** foul-smelling. **2** in ext. fig. use, unpleasant, and thus offensive morally or aesthetically as well as to the nostrils.

on the numbers *phr.* [1990s+] (*UK prison*) voluntary solitary confinement for the sake of a prisoner's safety; child molesters, rapists etc choose this in preference to the natural justice of their peers.

on the nut *phr.* [20C+] (*US*) in debt; thus OFF THE NUT phr. [NUT n.[8]]

on the outer *phr.* [1920s+] (*Aus./N.Z.*) unpopular, out of favour, penniless or destitute. [SE *on* + *outer*, the part of a racecourse outside the enclosure]

on the outs *phr.* **1** [early 19C+] out of luck, money, favour, popularity etc. **2** [early 19C+] (*US*) (*also* **at outs**) arguing or angry with someone; estranged. **3** [1950s+] (*UK/US Und.*) (*also* **on the out**) out of prison.

on the pad *phr.* **1** [late 17C–early 19C] going out to commit a robbery, usu. on the highway. **2** [17C; mid-19C–1910s] living as a tramp. [PAD n.[1] (1)]

on the pavement *phr.* **1** [mid-19C; 1980s+] (*also* **on the pave/sidewalk**) working as a street prostitute. **2** [mid-19C+] (*UK Und.*) (*also* **on the pave**) working as a professional criminal, usu. an armed robber. **3** [1940s+] (*US Und.*) set free from imprisonment.

on the pig's back *phr.* [late 19C+] (*Irish/Aus./N.Z.*) living in luxury, living well, in good fortune; thus *home on the pig's back*, very contented, happily or successfully placed, having arrived at a successful conclusion. [translation of Erse *ar mhuin na muice*, referring to an amulet shaped like a pig, supposedly a source of good luck]

on the pipe *phr.*[1] (*drugs*) **1** [1920s–50s] using opium on a regular basis. **2** [1980s+] using crack cocaine on a regular basis. [PIPE n.[4]]

on the pipe *phr.*[2] [1990s+] (*US prison*) using the waterpipes to communicate between cells.

on the piss *phr.* [1910s+] out drinking, usu. with friends; usu. as GO ON THE PISS v. [PISS n. (4)]

on the plastic *phr.* [1970s+] (*UK Und.*) using stolen credit cards for a variety of frauds and swindles.

on the plush *phr. see* ON THE CUSHIONS phr.

on the prowl *phr.* **1** [1930s–60s] (*US Und.*) working as a house-breaker, committing or planning a robbery; living on one's wits. **2** [1980s] working as a prostitute. [PROWL n.[1]/SE *prowl*]

on the pull *phr.* [1980s+] looking for a sexual encounter. [PULL v.[2] (5)]

on the Q.T. *adv.* **1** [late 19C–1910s] living quietly, soberly; thus *do the Q.T.*, to lead a quiet life. **2** [late 19C+] surreptitiously, on the quiet; also ext. as *on the strict Q.T.* [Q.T. adj.]

on the rag *phr.* **1** [1930s+] menstruating. **2** [1960s+] irritated, testy, bad-tempered; thus *share the rag*, to be hostile, to place blame on someone else. [RAG n.[8]; (2) is f. (1) or RAG n.[3]]

on the ran-dan *phr.* (*also* **on the randy**) [mid-17C+] on a spree. [SE *ran-dan*, a spree, lit. 'random (behaviour)']

on the ran-tan *phr.* [mid-19C+] out on a spree, drunk. [RANTAN n. (2)]

on the razzle *phr.* (*also* **on the razz**, **...razzle-dazzle**) [late 19C+] indulging in a series of parties, binges and general self-indulgent excesses. [RAZZLE-DAZZLE n. (1)]

on the real *phr.* [1980s+] (*US Black teen*) a phr. meaning honestly, sincerely, truthfully.

on the ribs *phr.* [1930s+] short of money. [poverty has emptied one's stomach and one's skin thus rests *on the ribs*]

on the rocks *adv.* [1990s+] to the greatest extent. [fig. use of ON THE ROCKS phr.]

on the rocks *phr.* **1** [late 19C+] in trouble, facing problems. **2** [late 19C+] in great need of.

on the rory *phr.* [1930s+] penniless. [fig. use of RORY (O'MOORE) n. (1)]

on the scratch *phr.* [1950s] (*US Und.*) engaged in forgery.

on the scuttle *phr.* [late 19C–1920s] out drinking and/or whoring. [SCUTTLE v. (1)]

on the send *phr.* **1** [1930s–50s] (*US Und.*) working as a go-between; of the victim of a confidence trick, being sent off to get money; obtaining drugs for an addict from a dealer. **2** [1960s] (*US*) running errands.

on the sharp *adv.* [18C] fraudulently. [SHARP v.]

on the sharp *phr.* [mid-18C–19C] attempting to defraud victims; hence *go on the sharp*. [SHARP v.]

on the shelf *phr.* **1** [19C] transported. **2** [19C–1930s] dead. **3** [early–mid-19C] in pawn. **4** [early–mid-19C] past one's best, retired. **5** [mid-19C+] put on one side for unspecified future use. **6** [mid-19C+] of a woman (occas. a man), unmarried and worried about it, feeling that one has been 'put to one side'. **7** [late 19C–1920s] finished, destroyed. **8** [20C+] (*US prison*) in solitary confinement.

on the shicker *phr.* (*also* **on the shick**) [20C+] (*Aus.*) on a drinking spree, drunk. [SHICKER n. (1)]

on the short end *phr.* [20C+] lit. or fig., at the unfavourable end of the odds; thus in a 20–1 bet the 1 is the short end.

on the shoulder *phr.* [late 19C] (*US*) involved in fighting.

on the side *phr.* [late 19C+] quietly, surreptitiously, in secret; esp. in the phr. BIT ON THE SIDE n.

on the sidewalk *phr. see* ON THE PAVEMENT phr. (1).

on the skids *phr.* [1920s+] on a social and economic decline. [SE *skid*/SKID ROW n. (1)]

on the skite *phr.* (*also* **on the skyte**) [20C+] (*Scot./Irish*) engaged in serious drinking. [Scot. *scit*, a slight shower]

on the slate *phr.* [mid-19C+] on credit. [the practice of writing public house debts on a slate]

on the sleeve *phr.* [1940s+] using narcotics. [the rolling up of a sleeve before the injection]

on the snam *phr.* [late 19C] engaged in thieving. [SNAM v.]

on the sneak *adv.* [late 17C+] surreptitiously, on the sly.

on the sneak tip *adv.* (*also* **on a sneak cue**) [1980s+] (*US Black*) surreptitiously, deceitfully.

on the socket *phr.* [1930s] practising blackmail. [SOCKET-MONEY n. (4)]

on the spit *phr.* [1970s+] for a woman, to be having vaginal or anal intercourse with one man and fellating another; for a man, to be sodomized and simultaneously to be fellating another man (cf. SPIT ROAST n.). [visual resemblance]

on the spot *phr.* **1** [late 19C–1930s] alert, aware. **2** [1930s+] (*US Und.*) marked for death, facing assassination. **3** [1930s+] (*also* **on a spot**) in trouble, facing problems. [metaphorical, but note *Saturday Evening Post*, 13 April 1929: '*Spot*, the, n. A piece of carpet eight inches square on which an offending prisoner must stand for two days. In some prisons the Spot is a painted mark on the wall against which the prisoner must hold his nose']

on the spud *phr.* [1920s] (*US Und.*) practising swindling. [SPUD n.[3]]

on the square *phr.* (*also* **upon the square**) **1** [mid-17C+] in an honest manner, truthfully. **2** [late 17C–early 19C] having revenged oneself, to be 'even' with someone. **3** [late 17C+] living an honest, law-abiding (and tedious) life. **4** [early 19C] having settled all debts with someone. **5** [mid-19C+] (*US Und.*) trustworthy (to condone or perform illegal acts). **6** [mid-19C+] honest, truthful. **7** [1920s] accurate. **8** [1930s+] (*Aus.*) conducting a regular monogamous relationship. [SQUARE adj. + ? Masonic jargon]

on the stem *phr.* [20C+] (*US tramp*) walking the main street of a town, begging for subsistence. [MAIN STEM, THE n. (2)]

on the stick *phr.* [1950s+] efficient, aware, in control; thus *get on the stick*, to get down to work. [the gearstick of a car or joystick of an aircraft, both of which exert control]

on the stones *phr.* **1** [early 19C+] in the open air, usu. referring to a fight, often with sidebets and between local champions, arranged outside the normal boxing world. **2** [mid-19C] unemployed. **3** [mid-19C+] in London. **4** [20C+] homeless. **5** [20C+] selling goods laid out on the pavement rather than on a stall.

on the straight *phr.* [late 19C–1910s] behaving respectably and honestly. [abbr. SE *on the straight and narrow*]

on the straight ticket *phr.* [1920s] in a respectable manner. [STRAIGHT adj.[1] (5) + SE *ticket*, a political platform]

on the strap *phr.* [1910s+] (*Aus.*) impoverished. [STRAPPED (FOR CASH) adj. (1)]

on the strength *phr.* [1990s+] (*US Black*) used to underline the importance and seriousness of the subject under discussion. [SE *strong*, important, vital]

on the take *phr.* [1930s+] of an official, typically a politician or policeman, who accepts bribes. [TAKE n.[1] (1)]

on the tick *phr. see* TICK n.[4] (2).

on the tiger *phr.* [20C+] (*Aus.*) out on a serious drinking-bout. [TIGER n.[8] (1)]

on the tinny luck *phr. see* TINNY adj.[1] (2).

on the tommy *phr. see* TOMORROW v.

on the town *phr.* **1** [early 18C–1950s] working as a prostitute; thus *take to the town*, to work as a prostitute. **2** [early–mid-19C] living as a professional criminal. **3** [early–mid-19C] living as a sophisticate, a man of the world. [18C SE *on the town*, in the swing of fashionable life; (3) implies that those so occupied are not fashionable, although they are aiming to get their share of urban pleasures, smart or not]

on the track *phr.* [late 19C+] in the world of the outback, thus used of a person to imply a vagrant's life.

on the trot *phr.* **1** [late 19C] on holiday. **2** [late 19C+] hiding away (usu. from the police or other authorities) to avoid an arrest, usu. by leaving one's home, town etc. [TROT v.¹ (1)]

on the turf *phr.* **1** [mid-19C–1930s] working as a prostitute. **2** [1900s] (*US campus*) calling on a young woman. **3** [1900s–60s] (*US Und.*) living as a vagrant. **4** [1950s] (*US Und.*) engaged in regular criminal activity. [TURF, THE n./TURF n. (1)]

on the twirl *phr.* [1930s] working as a professional thief. [TWIRL n. (1)]

on the up and up *phr.* **1** [mid-19C+] (*orig. US*) honest, legitimate. **2** [1910s+] (*orig. US*) in an increasingly favourable, lucky, pleasant situation. **3** [1930s–50s] (*US drugs*) taking a narcotics cure.

on the verandah *phr.* [1980s+] (*N.Z.*) marginal, peripheral. [i.e. not in the house proper]

on the wagon *phr.* (*also* **on the cart, …water-cart, …water-wagon**) **1** [late 19C+] voluntarily refraining from alcohol. **2** [1970s+] in ext. use, adopting any form of self-denial, e.g. celibacy, abandoning one's use of drugs. [SE *water-wagon*]

on the wallaby *phr.* [mid-19C+] (*Aus.*) **1** on a spree. **2** on the move, tramping. **3** travelling to search for work. **4** impoverished. [WALLABY n.]

on the wax *phr. see* WAX n.¹ (1).

on the whisper *phr.* [late 19C] (*Aus.*) using influence (to gain admission) rather than paying. [WHISPER v.¹]

on the whiz *phr.* [1920s+] working as a pickpocket. [WHIZ v.¹ (1)]

on the wrong side of the hedge, be *v. see* FALL ON THE WRONG SIDE OF THE HEDGE v.

on time *phr. see* ON T phr.

onto *phr.* [late 19C+] aware of, esp. of someone's supposedly secret or underhand plans; thus *be/get onto*, to harass, to nag.

on top of one's game *phr.* [1970s+] (*orig. US Black*) in control of the situation, being successful, surviving. [SE *on top of* + GAME n.²]

on velvet *phr.* [late 18C+] secure, cheerful, enjoying a life without problems.

on wheels *phr.* [mid-19C+] (*orig. US*) used as an intensifier; *see* HELL ON WHEELS n.; SHIT ON WHEELS n.

on wires *phr.* [mid-19C–1910s] nervous.

on with *phr.* [mid-19C+] having a relationship with, e.g. *she's on with him*.

on you! *excl.* **1** [1920s+] (*Aus.*) hello! **2** [1960s+] a general term of rejection.

on your bike! *excl.* **1** [1960s+] go away! be off with you! **2** [1980s] hurry up! get moving!

o.o. *n.* [1910s–50s] (*US*) a brief glance, a visual assessment. [abbr. ONCE-OVER n. (1)]

oobtay *n.* [1990s+] (*UK juv.*) a cigarette. [backsl. = TUBE n.¹ (4)]

o.o.c. *adj.* [1980s+] (*US campus*) drunk, intoxicated with drugs, acting crazy. [abbr. *out of* control]

ooch *v. see* OOCH (OVER) v.

oochie *n.* [1980s+] (*US campus*) a charming, adorable person. [? baby-talk *coochie-coo*]

oochie-coochie *n.* [2000s] a child.

ooch (over) *v.* (*also* **ootch (over)**) [1930s+] (*US*) to slide or scoot along, to move up on a seat or bench. [Yorks. dial. *hutch*, to huddle together, to move closer]

oodle *n.* [1940s–50s] (*Aus./N.Z.*) money. [OODLES n.]

oodles *n.* (*also* **oodlins, oudles**) [mid-19C+] (*orig. US*) a large amount, a great quantity. [ety. unknown, although suggestions

include a shortening of *the whole boodle* (E.P.), a *huddle* or close-packed group (Webster), which presumes that the var. *oodlins* comes from *huddling*, pressing together in a group. Cohen (ed.), *Studies in Slang* I (1985), rejects these on the basis that *huddle/huddling* refers mainly to animals, *oodles/oddlins* to people, and suggests a simple abbr. of *scadoodles/scadoodlin'*]

oodnagalahbi *n.* [1960s+] (*Aus.*) an imaginary, out-of-the-way, 'uncivilized' place. [*Ooodna(datta)*, a small town in Western Australia + GALAH n.]

oo-er! *excl.* [20C+] (*mainly UK juv.*) an excl. of surprise, amazement, distaste etc.

oof *n.* (*also* **ooftish, uff**) [late 19C–1930s] money; thus OOFY adj.; *oofless*, poor. [Ger. *auf tische*, on the table. The term originated *c*.1850 from the fact that, according to *The Sporting Times*, 'the aristocracy of Houndsditch, being in the habit of refusing to play cards, unless the money were "on the table"'; thus Grey, *Hoods* (1952): 'Tauchess offen tisch, boyus. What's my cut?']

oofay *see under* OFAY.

oof-bird *n.* (*also* **oof-bag**) [late 19C–1910s] a source of money, one who can supply money. [OOF n. + SE *bird*/BIRD n.² (1)/SE *bag*]

oofless *adj. see* OOF n.

oofterpa *n.* [1940s+] a male homosexual. [cod Lat. form of POOFTER n. (1)]

ooftish *n. see* OOF n.

oofus *n.* [1930s+] (*US Black*) a fool, a simpleton. [? DOOFUS n. + SE *oaf*]

oofy *adj.* [late 19C–1920s] rich, wealthy. [OOF n.; note P.G. Wodehouse's wealthy character *Oofy Prosser* (lit. 'Rich Scrounger')]

ooga-booga land *n.* [1980s+] an all-purpose term for any unspecified African state. [the racist imagery of chanting Africans]

oogie *n.* [1970s+] (*US Southern campus*) a derog. ref. to Black students (cf. ALLIGATOR BAIT n.²). [abbr. BOOGIE n.² (1)]

oogle *v.* [1930s+] (*US*) to stare at, to ogle; thus *oogley*, worth staring at. [OGLE v.]

oogle eyes *n. see* GOO-GOO EYES n.

oogly *adj.* [2000s] (*US Black*) of a woman, very unattractive. [extreme pron. of SE *ugly*]

oo-gotz! *excl.* [1970s] (*US*) a general excl. of dismissal, rubbish! nonsense! TO HELL WITH —! excl. (cf. BULLSHIT! excl.). [? Ital. *ugasita*, dislike]

ooh, gravity! *excl.* [1990s+] (*US teen*) an excl. used when someone falls down.

ooh-la-la *n.* [1920s+] **1** French sexuality, which, in Anglo-Saxon eyes, is 'spicy' and 'naughty'. **2** a woman, usu. French, who possesses such 'naughty' qualities. [Fr. excl. *ooh-la-la!*]

ooh-wee *n.* [2000s] (*US Black*) very high-quality marijuana (cf. BOMB n.⁴). [the excl. made when smoking it]

oojah *n.* (*also* **oojah-capiff, oojah capivvy, ooja-ka-piv, ooja-ka-pivi, ooja-ka-pivvy, oojiboo**) [1910s+] a term used when one cannot find the correct description for an object or person. [note 1940s milit. use *oojah*, sauce, custard]

oojah-cum-spiff *adj.* [1920s–70s] all right, as required, in order. [OOJAH n. + SPIFF adj. (2)]

ook *n.* [1960s+] anything unpleasant, esp. something slimy and/or viscous. [the sound of disgust that indicates the discovery of such a thing]

ook *v.* [1990s+] (*US campus*) to vomit (cf. BARF v.). [onomat. + OOK n.]

ookey *adj.* [1950s–60s] (*US*) dangerous, difficult. [ety. unknown]

ooky *adj.* [1960s+] (*US*) disgusting, esp. sticky, slimy. [OOK n.]

oolfoo *n.* [late 19C–1900s] a fool. [backsl.]

oomph *n.* (*also* **umph**) [1930s+] (*orig. US*) enthusiasm, vitality, energy, esp. as sex appeal. [imitative]

oomphy *adj.* [1950s+] (*US*) lively, energetic or sexy. [OOMPH n.]

oompus-boompus *n.* [1940s] unacceptable or unfair behaviour.

oonchook *n.* [1920s+] (*Irish/Newfoundland*) one who acts stupidly, a simpleton. [Gael. *òinnseach*, a foolish woman, a clown. The orig. Newfoundland use refers to a man who dresses as a woman in a mummers' parade]

-ooney *sfx see* -EROONIE sfx.

oons! *excl.* (*also* **ouns! ounds!**) [late 16C–19C] a euph. oath (cf. ZOUNDS! excl.). [abbr. 'God's wounds']

oont *n.* (*Aus./Anglo-Ind.*) **1** [late 19C+] a camel. **2** [1920s+] a person, a fellow. [Hind. and Urdu *unt*, a camel]

oontz out *v.* [1940s] (*US*) to crowd out. [dial. *hootch/hutch*, to crowd, to sit huddled together]

oonu *pron.* [1980s+] (*W.I./UK Black teen*) you, you all. [abbr. SE *you now*]

oony *n.* [20C+] (*Aus.*) sea-sickness. [? cries of 'oh my stomach!']

oopizootics *n.* (*also* **ooperzootics**) [late 19C–1910s] a fit of eccentricity, craziness. [? SE the disease *epizootic*, a plague among cattle]

oops! *excl.* (*also* **ooph!**) [1920s+] an excl. used on dropping something, tripping over, bumping into someone or something, making a mistake, being surprised etc.

oops-a-daisy! *excl. see* UPSADAISY! excl.

oopsie doodles! *excl.* [1990s+] (*US teen*) a general excl., usu. on making a mistake, tripping up etc.

oorie *adj.* (*also* **oorey, oory**) [20C+] (*Ulster*) hungover. [Scot. *oorie*, sickly-looking, weakly]

007 *n.* [1980s+] **1** (*US*) a large folding knife with a wooden handle. **2** (*US*) a doctor. **3** (*Aus. prison*) a bond that ensures one's good behaviour. [the brandname; presumably a ref. to 'James Bond *007*']

oosh *v.* [1960s+] to remove, to send away, to eject. [? SE *usher* or HOOSH v.]

oot *n.* [1920s+] (*Aus.*) money. [? LOOT n.¹ (2)]

ootch *v. see* OOCH (OVER) v.

ootchimagootchi *n.* (*also* **ouchimagooga**) [1940s–70s] (*US*) love-making. [var. on HOOTCHY-KOOTCHY n.]

ootch over *v. see* OOCH (OVER) v.

ootz *v.* (*also* **ootch**) [1940s+] (*US*) to cheat or trick. [? link to CHUTZPAH n.]

oo-wop *n.* [1990s+] (*US*) a gun. [? echoic of noise of firing]

ooze *v.* **1** [20C+] (*US*) to walk or to leave, either casually or furtively. **2** [1930s–40s] (*US Black*) to walk the streets in search of sexual conquest. [SE *ooze*, to slide and slither around; (2) + CRUISE v.¹ (1)]

oozer *n. see* BOOZER n. (2).

oozing scabs *n.* [1980s+] (*US campus*) any form of venereal disease.

oozle *v.* **1** [1910s+] (*Aus./N.Z.*) to steal, to obtain illicitly. **2** [1920s] (*US*) to arrive surreptitiously. [SE *ooze*, to slide and slither around]

oozlum (bird) *n.* [late 19C+] a fantastic bird, absolutely unknown to nature. ['(It) flies round in ever-decreasing circles until it disappears up its own arsehole in a puff of blue smoke' P. Cave, *Dirtiest Picture Postcard* (1974)]

oozy *adj.* [1920s+] of a person or thing, unpleasant, 'slimy'. [SE *ooze*]

o.p. *n.* [late 19C+] (*US*) other people's things, usu. money or alcohol; also as adj. [abbr.]

o.p. *adj.* [1960s+] (*Can. prison*) restricted, off privilege. [abbr.]

op *n.*¹ [late 19C] (*UK society*) the opera. [abbr.]

op *n.*² **1** [1910s+] an *op*eration, i.e. an activity. **2** [1920s+] (*US*) a private investigator. **3** [1920s+] a surgical *op*eration. **4** [1920s+] (*US*) an *op*erator of any kind, e.g. a telephone or telegraph operator. [abbr.; (2) SE *operative*; thus Dashiell Hammett's (1894–1961) fictional detective the 'Continental Op']

op *v.* [1950s] (*US*) to manage oneself, to function or to accomplish something. [abbr. SE *operate*]

O Pollaky! *excl.* [late 19C] nonsense! rubbish! don't make such a fuss! [proper name of Ignatius 'Paddington' *Pollaky*, a celebrated contemporary private detective, with an office on Paddington Green, whose exploits and surname entered the common

language; W.S. Gilbert also found room for him in a lyric, 'the keen penetration of Paddington Pollaky' (*Patience*, 1881). That said, note the euph. for coarser excl. *oh bollocks!*]

o.p.b. *n.*¹ [late 19C–1940s] (*Aus.*) a cheap cigar. [abbr. *o*ld *p*ickled *b*umpers]

o.p.b. *n.*² [1910s–50s] (*US Black*) a hypothetical brand of cigarette; used by one who rarely purchases their own. [abbr. *o*ther *p*eople's *b*rand]

ope *n.* [1920s+] (*drugs*) *op*ium. [abbr.]

open *adj.* [1950s+] (*US Black*) **1** sexually excited, obsessed. **2** in general use, excited by something. [abbr. HAVE ONE'S NOSE OPEN v.]

open *v. see* OPEN (TO) v.

open a can of whoop-ass on *v.* [1990s+] to assault, to beat up. [SE *open* + WHIP v.³ + ASS n. (2); WHIP SOMEONE'S ASS v.]

open a keg of nails *v.* [20C+] to have a drink, to get drunk.

open and shut *n.* **1** [late 19C] an expert. **2** [late 19C–1900s] (*US*) an unarguable, inescapable situation. [SE *open and shut* adj.]

open-arse *n.*¹ [11C–19C] a medlar tree or its fruit; occas. a euph. for the anus. [the fruit's large open disk between the persistent calyx-lobes. 'A fruit [...] of which it is more truly than delicately said, that it is never ripe til it is as rotten as a t—d, and then it is not worth a f—t' (Grose, 1785)]

open-arse *n.*² [late 16C–18C] a prostitute (cf. BANGTAIL n.¹). [a coarse ref. to her stock-in-trade]

open charms *n.* (*also* **open C**) [19C] the vagina.

opener *n.* [1930s–40s] (*US*) a jemmy.

openers *n.* [1900s–30s] (*US*) aperient pills or medicines, used to cure constipation. [SE 17C–18C]

open game *n.* [1960s+] (*US*) a prostitute with no specific affiliation to a pimp. [SE *open* + GAME n.¹ (3)]

open go *n. see* FAIR GO n.

open high *n.* [1990s+] (*drugs*) the intoxication one gets from breathing in ambient cannabis or crack cocaine smoke in a room, rather than actually smoking the drug directly.

open it up *v. see* OPEN OUT v. (2).

open one's business *v.* [early 18C] of a woman, to make oneself available for sexual intercourse.

open one's face *v.* [late 19C+] (*US*) to speak, esp. to speak rudely.

open one's head *v.* [late 19C–1910s] (*US*) to open one's mouth, to speak.

open one's lunchbox *v.* (*also* **drop one's lunch**) [1980s+] to break wind.

open one's pipes *v.* [18C+] to sing. [SE *open* + PIPES n.¹ (2)]

open one's purse *v.* [1990s+] (*gay*) to break wind.

open out *v.* **1** [20C+] (*Aus.*) to act unrestrainedly; to lose one's temper. **2** [1950s] (*also* **open (it) up**) to accelerate, to drive fast. [i.e. to open out the throttle of an engine]

open packy *v.* [1940s] (*W.I.*) to reveal one's innermost thoughts. [SE *open* + PACKY n.¹]

open slather *n.* [1910s+] (*Aus.*) a situation with no restrictions or limits to one's wishes. [SE *open* + UK dial./SAmE *slather*, to squander, to use in large quantities]

open someone's nose *v.* [1960s+] (*US Black*) to provoke sexual excitement in someone. [HAVE ONE'S NOSE OPEN v. (1)]

open swinging *n.* [1970s+] a partner-swapping party in which all-comers – married or single – are welcome and all end up in the same bed; the opposite of CLOSED SWINGING n. [SE *open* + SWINGING n.²]

open the ball *v.* [early 19C–1910s] to start things off, esp. to start a fight. [orig. sporting journalists' sl.]

open the door *n.* [20C+] (*bingo*) the number 44 (cf. ALDERSHOT LADIES n.). [rhy. sl.]

open the sandwich box *v.* [1990s+] (*Aus.*) to break wind.

open (to) *v.* [mid-19C–1900s] (*UK Und.*) to confess.

open up *v.*¹ **1** [mid-19C+] of a woman, to have sexual intercourse (cf. CATCH AN OYSTER v.). **2** [late 19C+] to confess, to speak intimately. **3** [1900s–30s] to berate. **4** [1970s+] (*US gay/prison*) to sodomize a prisoner.

open up v.² *see* OPEN OUT v. (2).

open up (on) v. [20C+] (*US*) to start firing (at); also in fig. use.

open work n. [1930s–40s] (*US Und.*) safe-breaking.

opera n. [1930s] (*US dancehall*) a burlesque show.

opera cape n. [1960s+] (*US gay*) a long foreskin.

Opera envelope n. [mid-19C] a large, all-enveloping outer garment worn to the Opera.

opera queen n. [1980s] (*US gay*) a male homosexual who enjoys verbally abusing his partners. [SE *opera*, as synon. for melodrama + QUEEN n.² (1)/QUEEN sfx (2)]

operator n. **1** [early 18C+] a thief or swindler. **2** [early–mid-19C] (*UK Und.*) a pickpocket. **3** [late 19C+] (*orig. US*) a person who pursues success, often ruthlessly or manipulatively. **4** [1920s–40s] the controller of a gambling game. **5** [1920s+] a major criminal. **6** [1940s] (*US*) a private detective. **7** [1940s+] a successful seducer of women.

o per se o n. [early–mid-17C] (*UK Und.*) a crier. [Lat.; Nares suggests link to SE *a per se a*, pre-eminent excellence]

o.p.m. n. [20C+] (*orig. US Und.*) other people's money, the ideal commodity for a risky investment. [orig. used by confidence tricksters of various types, it was a staple of City or Wall Street jargon by the 1980s]

opossum n. *see* POSSUM n. (3).

opossum-trap n. [late 19C] (*Aus.*) the mouth.

o.p.p. n. [1990s+] (*US Black/campus*) **1** other people's property, usu. their wife, husband or partner, esp. in the context of their being 'off limits' to new sexual approaches. **2** other people's pussy, the wives and girlfriends of other men. [abbr.; (2) PUSSY n. (2)]

oppo n. **1** [1910s+] one's opposite number, one's best friend. **2** [1980s+] opposition. [abbr.]

opposite n. [late 19C–1930s] a public house saloon bar, which is opposite, whether actually or fig., the public bar.

Oprah v. [1990s+] (*US Black*) to question aggressively and persistently. [entertainer *Oprah* Winfrey whose TV show *Oprah* features a range of outrageously intimate human interest stories, usu. dependent on her eliciting otherwise intimate confessions from her guests]

o.p.'s n. [1920s+] (*US Black*) other people's, usu. in ref. to an unspoken commodity, e.g. cigarettes, alcohol or clothes. [abbr.]

ops v. [20C+] (*S.Afr., mainly juv.*) to swap. [? SE *opposed/opposite*, i.e. one gives the item to one's opposite number]

opsh n. [late 19C–1920s] something that is optional. [abbr./pron.]

op shop n. [1980s+] (*N.Z.*) a second-hand clothes shop. [abbr. *opportunity shop*]

o.p.t. n.¹ [20C+] other people's tobacco, always popular among poverty-stricken smokers. [abbr.]

o.p.t. n.² [2000s] (*US Black*) speed, punctualiy. [abbr. Oriental People Time]

optic n. [1910s+] (*Aus./US*) a look. [OPTICS n.]

optic (nerve) n. [1960s+] (*Aus.*) a man who ogles (usu.) women. [rhy. sl. = PERV n. (4)]

optics n. [early 17C+] the eyes; thus sing. *optic*, an eye. [SE until late 19C]

or conj. [1930s+] 'an emphatic repetition of a rhetorical question' (*OED*), e.g. *Has that dame got a swell voice or has she?*

oracle n.¹ [18C] a watch. [it 'tells', i.e. predicts, the time]

oracle n.² [late 18C–19C] the vagina. [the initial 'O' + the 'o' shape; the 'mouth piece of the deity']

-orama sfx (*also* **-arama, -erama, -rama**) [1960s+] (*orig. US teen*) used to indicate a considerable size, quality or expanse, e.g. *babe-orama*, a very attractive woman (or man) or a large number of attractive women (or men); *fun-orama*, a great deal of enjoyment. [Gk *orama*, a view and orig. used as the second syllable of *panorama, diorama, cosmorama*, and other London shows created for mass entertainment during the early 19C. This association

with large-scale entertainment has persisted in its modern sl. use]

orange n.¹ [late 17C] the vagina (cf. APPLE n.⁶). [? its suckability + ref. to Charles II's mistress the former orange-girl Nell Gwyn (*c.*1650–87)]

orange n.² [1960s+] (*drugs*) a variety of LSD, in orange-coloured capsules; usu. in combs., e.g. *orange barrels, …cubes, …haze, …micro, …Owsley, …sunshine, …wedges* (cf. A n.³). [SE *orange* + BARRELS n./CUBE n.³/HAZE n. (1)/MICRODOT n./OWSLEY ACID n./SE *sunshine*/WEDGE n.⁴]

orange banana n. [1980s+] (*US campus*) a flaring effect produced by breaking wind next to a lit match.

orange juice n. [1980s] (*Aus.*) in cards, a 2 or deuce. [rhy. sl.]

orange pip n. [1940s+] a Japanese person (cf. BUDDHAHEAD n.). [rhy. sl. = NIP n. (1)]

oranges n. [1960s+] (*drugs*) amphetamines (cf. A n.²). [the colour of the pills]

orange squash n. [2000s] money (cf. BEES (AND HONEY) n.). [rhy. sl. = DOSH n.]

orangutan n. [20C+] (*US*) a derog. term for a Black person (cf. AFRICAN APE n.).

oration-trap n. (*also* **oration-box**) [early–mid-19C] the mouth. [SE *oration* + TRAP n.³/play on SE]

orbit n. [1980s+] (*drugs*) MDMA (cf. ECSTASY n.). [ORBITAL (RAVE) n. + play on the drug's sending one IN ORBIT phr. (3)]

orbital (rave) n. [1980s+] a large party often held quasi-illegally, fuelled by MDMA and featuring house music. [a ref. to the holding of many such parties near the M25 motorway that encircles London]

orbs n. (*also* **velvet orbs**) [1970s+] (*US/Aus.*) the testicles (cf. BALLS n.¹). [the shape (and the 'feel')]

— or bust phr. [1910s+] an intensifier, suggesting that a failure to accomplish something will lead to disaster.

orch n. *see* ORK n.

orchard n. [17C; 19C; 1990s+] the vagina; the female genital area (cf. BEAUTY SPOT n.).

orchestra n. [20C+] **1** the male genitals. **2** (*also* **orchestra falls/stalls**) the testicles (cf. CHEESE AND CRACKERS n.). [rhy. sl.; *orchestra falls/stalls* = BALLS n.¹ (1) + link between Gk *orchis*, the testicles and orchestra, although SE *orchestra* is f. Gk *orchestra*, the space on which the chorus danced]

orchestration n. [1930s–40s] (*US Black*) an overcoat. [music jargon *orchestration*, which 'wraps around' the individual scores]

orchids and turnips n. [late 19C–1920s] important and commonplace people; occas. used separately.

orchids to you! excl. [1930s–50s] a general dismissive excl. [a pun on SE *orchidectomy*, castration, lit. Gk 'testicle cutting'; thus a euph. for BALLS TO —! phr.]

order of the boot n. (*also* **order of the push**) [late 19C+] dismissal, rejection, usu. from one's job. [a play on SE *Order of the Bath*/BOOT, THE n. (1)/PUSH, THE n. (1)]

order of the day n. [late 18C+] (*orig. politics*) the status quo, the current way of doing things. [SE *order of the day*, in a legislative body, that business set down for debate on a given day]

order of the hempen riband n. [mid-17C–mid-18C] a judicial hanging, esp. at Tyburn. [play on SE *hemp*, from which the rope is made]

order of the push n. *see* ORDER OF THE BOOT n.

order of the rag n. [early 18C–1900s] the military life. [SE *order* + *rag* = flag]

order of the street n. [late 19C] an act of ejection from a house.

order-racket n. [early 19C] (*UK Und.*) obtaining goods by ordering them from a shopkeeper, whose bill will never be paid. [SE *order* + RACKET n.¹ (1)]

ordinary n. **1** [late 19C–1900s] one's wife. **2** [1970s+] (*US Black*) one's regular female companion.

ordinary, the *n.* [late 19C+] what is customary or usual; often as *out of the ordinary*.

ordinary *adj.* [mid-19C+] physically plain, commonplace, unattractive.

ord rot it! *excl. see* OD ROT IT! excl.

Oregon boot *n.* [1900s–40s] (*US prison*) a heavy collar or shackle fitted around a prisoner's ankle. [its original use in Oregon prisons]

Oreo (cookie) *n.* **1** [1960s+] (*US Black*) a derog. description of a fellow Black whose opinions, attitudes and goals are taken from White society; thus *Oreolized*; *go Oreo*, to adapt oneself to White culture (cf. APPLE n.⁷). **2** [1990s+] (*orig. US gay*) (*also* **Oreo sex**) sex between 2 Black men and a White man or woman. [proper name *Oreo Cookie*, a popular US biscuit, which is black on the outside, with a white filling]

Oreo queen *n.* [1960s+] (*US gay*) a Black homosexual who engages in sexual activity with White men. [OREO (COOKIE) n. (1) + QUEEN n.² (1)/QUEEN sfx (2)]

-orexia *sfx* [1980s+] (*US campus*) a sfx based on SE *anorexia* (compulsive, excessive dieting) combined with a given n. to mean too much, excessive, e.g. TALKOREXIA n.

orey-eyed *adj. see* ORY-EYED adj.

org *n.* **1** [1910s] (*US*) an *org*an. **2** [1930s+] an *org*anization. [abbr.]

organ *n.* [late 18C–mid-19C] a pipe; thus *cock one's organ*, to smoke a pipe. [pun on SE *pipe-organ*]

organ grinder *n.*¹ [1910s+] an Italian, spec. an immigrant (cf. DAGO n.). [their common profession]

organ grinder *n.*² [1920s–60s] (*US*) the penis. [SE *organ* + GRIND v.¹ (1)]

organic *adj.* [1970s+] (*US campus*) fashionable. [acknowledgement of 'green' politics]

organize *v.* [1930s+] (*orig. milit.*) **1** to steal, to loot. **2** to arrange at short notice, to 'fix up'.

organized *adj.* [1920s+] (*orig. milit.*) **1** acquired illicitly, by underhand methods. **2** drunk.

organ-pipe *n.* [mid-19C–1920s] the windpipe, the throat, the voice.

orie-eyed *adj. see* ORY-EYED adj.

orifice *n.* [1970s+] an office. [conscious mispron.]

original *n.* [1920s+] (*US Black*) a Black person; usu. in ALL-ORIGINALS adj. [ext. use of SE]

original loser *n.* [1950s+] (*US*) a useless, talentless person; ext. as *he/she is the original Major Bowes Amateur Hour loser*.

originals *n.* [1950s+] the Levi jeans and jacket (with sleeves cut off) worn at the initiation ceremonies of outlaw bikers clubs. Liberally soiled and 'worn in', the rider wears them until they fall to pieces.

orinoko *n.*¹ (*also* **oronoko**) [late 17C–early 18C] tobacco. [? Aphra Behn's play *Oroonoko; or, The Royal Slave* (1688)]

orinoko *n.*² [mid-19C–1920s] **1** cocoa. **2** a poker. [rhy. sl.; (2) pron. 'orinoker']

orioide *adj.* [late 19C] (*US tramp*) drunk. [? SE *awry*]

o'river *phr.* [1990s+] (*US campus*) farewell. [play on Fr. *au revoir*, goodbye]

ork *n.* (*also* **orch**) [1930s+] (*orig. US*) an *orch*estra, usu. a jazz or dance band. [abbr./pron.]

orlando *n.* [1990s+] (*US Black, mainly East Coast*) a rural Black person, esp. one who does not keep up with the 'gangsta' styles of music or clothing. [? Orlando, Florida]

or my prick's a bloater *phr.* (*also* **or my uncle's a bloater**) [1930s+] a phr. used to imply the absolute impossibility or unlikeliness of what has just been said, suggested etc. [PRICK n. (2)/SE *uncle* + *bloater*, a type of fish]

ornery *adv.* [mid–late 19C] (*US*) unkindly.

ornythorhynchus *n.* [late 19C] (*Aus.*) a creditor. [SE *ornithorhynchus*, a duck-billed platypus, i.e. the punning 'beast with a bill']

oronoko *n. see* ORINOKO n.¹.

-oroonie *sfx see* -EROONIE sfx.

or out goes the gas! *excl.* [late 19C–1900s] a general threat, aimed at bringing a situation or a conversation to an abrupt end.

orphan *n.* **1** [1930s] (*US Und.*) a prostitute who works without a pimp (cf. BROTHER-IN-LAW n.). **2** [1930s–60s] (*US*) a discontinued model of a motor vehicle, a run-down, dilapidated motorcar; thus *orphaned*, discontinued.

Orphan Annie *n.* [1990s+] the vagina (cf. ALL QUIET n.). [rhy. sl. = FANNY n.¹ (1); ult. the cartoon (and later musical based upon it) 'Little Orphan Annie', created by Harold Gray in 1922]

orphan collar *n.* [late 19C–1900s] (*orig. US*) a loose collar that does not match one's shirt.

orphan paper *n.* [1940s–60s] (*US Und.*) counterfeit money.

ort *n.* [1950s+] (*Aus.*) the anus, the backside. [ety. unknown; ? dial. *orts*, odds and ends]

ory-eyed *adj.* (*also* **oary-eyed, orey-, orie-, orry-**) **1** [late 19C+] (*US*) very drunk, or looking as if one were (cf. ARSEHOLED adj.). **2** [1920s] very angry. [SE *awry* + *eyed*, but note Scot. *oorie*, of persons and things, dismal, gloomy, debauched or dissipated looking]

o.s. *adj.* [20C+] (*Aus.*) abroad, anywhere other than Australia. [abbr. *over-seas*]

Oscar *n.*¹ **1** [late 19C+] a male homosexual; thus *oscar*, to sodomize; *Oscar-Wildeing*, homosexuality; *oscarize*, to be a homosexual (cf. ABIGAIL n.). **2** [1900s–50s] (*US*) a stupid or unpleasant man, esp. when narrow-minded. **3** [1940s] (*US Black*) a man, irrespective of character. [the playwright and epigrammatist *Oscar* Wilde (1854–1901), imprisoned for his homosexuality; (2) stereotype of (1)]

Oscar *n.*² *see* OSCAR (ASCHE) n.

oscar *n.* **1** [1930s+] (*US Black*) the penis (cf. ABRAHAM n.¹; BACON n.¹). **2** [1940s+] (*US prison*) a handgun. [ety. unknown; ? play on *Oscar* Wilde + the 'wild' sex or violence; or brandname *Oscar Meyer*, a popular US weiner (thus punning on WEENIE n.¹ (4)]

oscar *v.* [1920s–30s] (*US*) to move quickly. [ety. unknown; ? corruption of SE *scurry*]

Oscar (Asche) *n.* (*also* **Okker, Oscar Nash**) [20C+] (*Aus./N.Z.*) money (cf. BEES (AND HONEY) n.). [rhy. sl. = SE *cash*; ult. actor *Oscar Asche* (1871–1936)]

oscar hock *n.* [1920s+] (*US*) usu. in pl., a sock. [rhy. sl.]

Oscar Joes *n.* [1920s–40s] (*US*) the toes. [rhy. sl.]

Oscar Nash *n. see* OSCAR (ASCHE) n.

oscars *n.* [late 19C] (*US campus*) whiskers.

oschive *n. see* OCHIVE n.

osifer *n. see* OSSIFER n.

osmosis amoebas *phr.* [1980s+] (*US campus*) farewell. [play on the more common ADIOS AMOEBAS phr.]

osnaburg *n.* [1950s] (*W.I.*) **1** rough, ill-cut clothes. **2** first-rate clothes, the product of the best tailoring. [proper name *Osnabrück* (in later Eng. corruptly *Osnaburg*), a town and district in north Germany noted for its manufacture of linen, thus a kind of coarse linen orig. made in Osnabrück. In W.I. it was orig. used for the garments issued to slaves and later prisoners]

o soldiers! *excl.* [late 19C–1900s] a general excl., presumably a euph. for something more coarse, e.g. 'oh shit!'

Ossi *n.* [1990s+] an occupant of the former East Germany; as opposed to WESSI n. [Ger. sl.; ult. *Ostdeutsche*, East German]

ossifer *n.* (*also* **occifer, osifer**) [mid-19C+] a joking, slightly offensive ref. to a police (in 19C also army) officer. [deliberate mispron.]

ossified *adj.* [20C+] highly intoxicated on alcohol or a given drug. [pun on STONED (OUT) adj. (2)]

osso *n.* [2000s] (*US Black*) one's house or home. [ety. unknown]

ostrobogulous *adj.* [1910s+] bizarre, unusual, interesting. [coined by the writer Victor B. Neuburg (1883–1940). It can be 'translated' in a variety of ways, e.g. 'mischievous but gorgeous' (of children) or 'indecent or pornographic' (words or pictures). Neuberg's own ety. mixed 'full of (Lat., *ulus*) rich (Greek, *ostro*) dirt (schoolboy, *bog*)']

otamy *n.* [18C–19C] a surgical operation. [SE *anatomy*]

otay! *excl.* [1990s+] (*US teen*) fine! good! I agree! [var. on OK! excl.]

o.t.d. *phr.* [1980s+] (*US*) gone, departed. [abbr. *out the door*]

other, the *n.* [1930s+] sexual intercourse; esp. in the phr. *a bit of the other*, usu. hetero- but sometimes homosexual intercourse. [note *Merry Drollery* (1661): 'As much as this a man may kiss / His sister or his mother; / He that will speed must give with need / A little o'th' t'on with t'other']

other half *n.*[1] [late 19C+] (*orig. naut.*) a second drink, a drink bought in return for another. [the *half* is presumed to be a half-pint]

other half *n.*[2] *see* INFERIOR HALF n.

other man *n.* [1930s–60s] (*US Black*) a White person, esp. the owner of a neighbourhood store in a Black area.

other side *n.* **1** [mid-18C–19C] (*UK Und.*) Southwark, south of the River Thames. **2** [late 18C+] either America or Britain, depending on which side of the Atlantic one is; thus *this side*; also England when used in Ireland, Britain when in Australia. **3** [late 19C–1900s] (*N.Z.*) Australia, i.e. the other side of the Tasman Sea.

other side, the *n. see* OTHER WAY, THE n.

other side of Bourke *n. see* BACK OF BOURKE n.

othersider *n. see* T'OTHER SIDER n.

other way, the *n.* (*also* **other side, the**) [1960s+] anal rather than vaginal sexual intercourse; also in adv. use.

other way, the *adj.* [2000s] homosexual.

otis *adj.* [1980s+] (*US campus*) drunk. [the town drunkard in the US TV comedy *The Andy Griffith Show* (orig. shown 1960–8)]

otium dig *n. see* DIG n.[3].

o.t.l. *phr.* [1950s+] (*US campus*) not in touch with reality, inattentive, unaware. [abbr. OUT TO LUNCH phr.]

otomy *n. see* OTTOMY n.

O-Town *n.* [2000s] (*US*) Orlando, Florida. [abbr.]

o.t.r. *phr.* [1960s+] (*US campus*) **1** menstruating. **2** in fig. use (of either sex), irritable, in a bad mood, tetchy. [abbr. ON THE RAG phr.]

o.t.t. *adj.* [1990s+] extravagant, beyond the usual bounds of taste, behaviour etc. [abbr. OVER THE TOP adj. (1)]

otter *n.*[1] [early 18C] a sailor.

otter *n.*[2] [mid–late 19C] (*Ling. Fr./Polari*) **1** (*also* **otto**) the number 8. **2** 8 pence. [Ital. *otto*, 8]

Otto *n.* [20C+] a derog. name for a German, with an implication of stolidity. [a popular Ger. name]

ottomized *adj.* [late 18C–early 19C] dissected, subjected to a post-mortem. [SE *anatomized*]

ottomy *n.* (*also* **otomy**) [mid-18C–mid-19C] a skeleton; a very thin person. [SE *anatomy*; OTAMY n.]

ou *n.* (*S.Afr. township*) **1** [mid-19C+] a form of address, often in combs., e.g. *ou china, ou maat, ou pellie*, old mate, old pal. **2** [1940s+] a fellow, a chap. **3** [1970s+] a friend. [Afk. *ou*, a fellow + Du. *ouwe*, old man]

Oubaas *n.* [1900s–50s] (*S.Afr.*) a nickname for the Roeland Street prison, Cape Town. [Afk. *ou*, old + *baas*, boss, governor]

ouchimagooga *n. see* OOTCHIMAGOOTCHI n.

ou-di-du-dat *n.* [1950s] (*W.I.*) an East Indian. [lit. 'how does he do that?'; ult. ? a question frequently asked by these individuals]

oudish *adj.* [2000s] (*UK teen*) amazing, wonderful.

oudles *n. see* OODLES n.

ought *n.* [mid-19C+] zero, nothing, esp. as the number 0. The modern *noughts and crosses* was *oughts and crosses c.*1850. [SE *nought*, i.e. 'an ought']

oui-oui *n. see* WEE-WEE n.[1].

ou kappie *n. see* OKAPI n.

---

oukie *n. see* OKIE n.

oulap *n.* [1940s] (*S.Afr.*) a penny. [Afk. *ou*, old + *lap*, rag, thus a valueless old rag]

ould sod *n. see* OLD SOD n.

ould wan *n. see* OLD ONE n.

oul fella *n. see* OLD FELLOW n. (6).

oul' one *n. see* OLD ONE n.

ouman *n.* [1970s+] (*S.Afr.*) **1** a veteran, an 'old hand'. **2** an experienced soldier. **3** a national serviceman who has completed 6 or more months of his enlistment or who has completed his entire time. [Afk. *ou*, old + SE *man*]

ounce *n.* [early 18C–early 19C] a silver coin. [the valuation of silver at 5s an ounce]

ounce-brain *n.* [1940s] (*US*) a fool (cf. BAKEBRAIN n.). [i.e. LIGHT-HEAD n.[1]; the supposedly miniscule weight of the fool's brain]

ounce-brain *adj.* [1940s] stupid, foolish. [OUNCE-BRAIN n.]

ounce man *n.* [1950s+] (*US drugs*) a small-time drug dealer. [SE *ounce* + SE *man*/MAN, THE n. (3)]

ounce of baccy *n.* (*also* **ouncer**) [1960s+] an Asian immigrant, esp. the owner of a corner shop (cf. HALF-OUNCE OF BACCY n.). [rhy. sl. = PAKI n.]

ouncer *n.* [1990s+] a bouncer at a club or bar. [abbr.]

ounds!/ouns! *excl. see* OONS! excl.

oupa juice *n.* [1990s+] (*S.Afr.*) **1** liquor. **2** opium (cf. APOSTLE n.). [Afk. *oupa*, an old Afrikaans man + JUICE n.[3] (4)]

our friend with the talking brooch *n.* [1980s+] (*gay*) a policeman (cf. BADGE n.[2]). [his walkie-talkie radio, clipped to the front of his uniform]

our Miss Brooks *n.* [1950s–70s] (*camp gay*) a teacher. [the name of a TV character]

our survey said... *n.* [1990s+] (*US teen*) a phr. used to indicate approval/disapproval or confirmation/denial. [in class, a teacher asks, 'What do you think of that?', the pupil responds, 'Our survey said... YES!!!!' (to imply approval), 'Our survey said... NO!!!' (disapproval), 'Our survey said... ding!' (a bell sound, for yes), 'Our survey said... ouourgh!' (a buzzer sound, for no); from *Family Fortunes* TV Show]

our uncle *n. see* UNCLE n.

oussie *adj.* [20C+] (*Ulster*) over-inquisitive. [ety. unknown]

out *n.*[1] [mid-18C–19C] an outing, an excursion, a holiday. [one goes *out*]

out *n.*[2] [early 19C–1930s] a dram measure of gin or a dram glass; thus *three-out*, a glass holding a third of a measure of a liquor. [three such glasses will pour *out* a full quartern measure]

out *n.*[3] [mid-19C] an outside passenger on a coach.

out *n.*[4] [late 19C–1910s] a defect, a blemish, a disadvantage.

out *n.*[5] [late 19C–1940s] a loss.

out *n.*[6] (*orig. US*) **1** [20C+] a means of escape, avoidance. **2** [1920s+] an excuse; an alibi. [one is let *out*]

out, the *n. see* OUTSIDE n. (3).

out *adj.*[1] [17C; 1930s+] unfashionable. [*out* of the current style]

out *adj.*[2] [mid-19C+] (recently) released from prison.

out *adj.*[3] **1** [late 19C] tipsy. **2** [late 19C–1940s] dead. **3** [late 19C+] (*orig. US*) knocked out, unconscious. **4** [1990s+] (*US Black*) crazy (cf. OUT OF IT phr.[2]; OUT OF ONE'S BOX phr.).

out *adj.*[4] [late 19C+] in debt, poor, penniless. [abbr. *out of pocket*]

out *adj.*[5] [1910s+] bereft of supplies.

out *adj.*[6] [1920s+] (*orig. US*) **1** banned, prohibited. **2** unfeasible, undesirable; usu. in phr. *that's out*, I won't accept that.

out *adj.*[7] [1930s+] (*gay*) openly homosexual. [no longer IN THE CLOSET phr. (1)]

out *v.*[1] [mid-19C–1920s] to go out, esp. on an excursion. [OUT n.[1]]

out *v.*[2] **1** [late 19C–1950s] to knock out, to disable. **2** [late 19C–1950s] to dismiss from a job, to discharge. **3** [late 19C–1960s] to kill. **4** [20C+] (*Aus.*) to throw out of a meeting. **5** [1900s] to outdo, to surpass. **6** [1970s] to free from a criminal charge.

out *v.*[3] [1990s+] **1** to expose someone as a homosexual against their will. **2** to reveal negative or personal information about an individual, group or organization. [OUT adj.[7]; the victim is pushed *out of the closet*. A tactic pioneered by the New York gay magazine *Outweek* and usu. in the form *outing*; thus the converse 'inning', the deliberate masking of homosexuality when a celebrity is known to be gay but the gay/lesbian community finds them (or more likely their politics) so reprehensible that it denies the fact]

out *adv.*[1] [mid-19C–1960s] (*US*) in existence, e.g. *he is the craziest person out*.

out *adv.*[2] [late 19C] on bad terms.

out *adv.*[3] **1** [1920s+] refusing to partake in or uninterested in a given plan or scheme or game, e.g. of cards. **2** [1950s+] ejected from a group.

-out *sfx* [1950s+] (*orig. US*) completely, e.g. *clapped-out, drugged-out, stressed-out*.

out and in *n.* [1920s] (*US*) the chin. [rhy. sl.]

out-and-out *n.*[1] [mid-19C] strong beer. [OUT-AND-OUT adj. (1)]

out-and-out *n.*[2] [20C+] (*US Black*) a totally unacceptable person. [OUT-AND-OUT adj. (1)]

out-and-out *n.*[3] *see* OUT-AND-OUTER n. (3).

out-and-out *adj.* **1** [early 19C] complete, thorough-going, unqualified. **2** [mid-19C+] excellent, first-rate.

out-and-out *adv.* [late 18C+] completely, absolutely, utterly.

out-and-outer *n.* **1** [early 19C+] (*also* **outer**) one who is seen as reaching extremes of behaviour, both good and bad, and defined according to context. **2** [mid-19C–1920s] a notable lie. **3** [late 19C+] (*US*) (*also* **out-and-out**) a brawl, a fist-fight. [OUT-AND-OUT adj. (1); (1) SE after 1880; (1) note def. in Egan, *Life in London* (1821): 'A phrase in the sporting world for *goodness*; a sort of climacteric – the *ne plus ultra*']

outasight/outasite *phr. see* OUT OF SIGHT phr. (2).

out back o' sunset *n. see* BACK OF BOURKE n.

out box *n.* [1990s+] (*US Black*) the start, the beginning. [OUT OF THE BOX phr.[1] or office jargon *out box*, a box into which out-going mail is placed]

outdoor library *n. see* LIBRARY n.[2].

outed *adj.*[1] [20C+] **1** (*orig. Aus.*) killed, dead. **2** attacked, knocked out. **3** (*orig. Aus.*) dismissed from employment. [OUT v.[2]]

outed *adj.*[2] [1990s+] (*orig. US*) revealed as a homosexual. [OUT v.[3] (1)]

outen sight *phr. see* OUT OF SIGHT phr. (2).

outer *n.*[1] [late 19C–1900s] a knockout punch. [OUT v.[2] (1)]

outer *n.*[2] [1950s] (*UK Und.*) a pocket.

outer *n.*[3] [1980s+] (*Aus. prison*) the 'free world' outside prison. [OUT adj.[2]]

outer *n.*[4] *see* OUT-AND-OUTER n. (1).

outer of three *n.* [mid-19C] (*UK Und.*) ? a meal (of 3 courses).

outers *n.*[1] [1970s+] (*UK Und.*) a lit. or fig. means of escape. [OUT n.[6] (1)]

outers *n.*[2] [1970s+] (*S.Afr.*) anywhere a vagrant, homeless person finds to sleep, such as a cardboard box, doorway etc. [SE *outdoors*]

outers *adj.* [1970s+] unacceptable, distasteful. [OUT OF ORDER phr. (2)]

Outfit, the *n.* [1920s+] (*US Und.*) a specific criminal organization, usu. the US Mafia or Italian gangs in US prisons. [OUTFIT n.[1] (5)]

outfit *n.*[1] **1** [mid-19C+] any object or device. **2** [mid-19C+] a travelling party or a party in charge of herds of cattle. **3** [late 19C+] any group of people. **4** [late 19C+] an organization, a business; a sports team. **5** [late 19C+] a criminal organization, a gang. **6** [20C+] a person or their possessions. ['to cross the plains, or go to the mountains, every one must get an outfit; and having outfitted, you become yourself an outfit' (J.F. Meline, *Two Thousand Miles on Horseback*, 1867)]

outfit *n.*[2] **1** [late 19C–1920s] (*UK Und.*) a burglar's or safe-breaker's equipment. **2** [1940s–50s] (*UK prison*) whatever is needed for attempting a given escape. **3** [1970s] (*US Und.*) a weapon.

outfit *n.*[3] (*US drugs*) **1** [late 19C+] equipment for the preparation

and smoking of opium. **2** [1920s+] (*also* **bang outfit**) the equipment (needle, spoon, cotton etc) used for a narcotics injection.

outfit *n.*[4] [1970s+] (*US campus*) anyone seen as odd or eccentric, one who fails to 'fit in'. [SE *out* + *fit*]

outfit *v.* [1930s] (*US drugs*) to obtain a supply of narcotics. [OUTFIT n.[3] (2)]

out for a pelter *phr.* [late 19C–1900s] in a very bad temper. [SE *out* + dial. *pelter*, a bad temper]

out for the count *phr.* [late 19C+] ruined, defeated, exhausted, asleep. [boxing imagery]

out front *see under* UP FRONT.

outhouse *n.* [20C+] (*US prison*) a 'half-way house' or hostel, in which newly released prisoners or parolees can learn to reacclimatize themselves to the 'real' world. [OUT adj.[2] + SE *house*]

outie *n.*[1] [1970s] (*S.Afr.*) a vagrant, a tramp. [SE *outdoors*]

outie *n.*[2] [1970s+] a protruding navel, as opposed to an INNIE n.

outie *phr.* (*also* **outtie**) [1990s+] (*US teen*) leaving; a phr. of farewell, usu. as *I'm outie*. [abbr./pron. of OUT OF HERE phr.[1] (1)]

outing *n.* [1990s+] the exposure of someone as a homosexual against their will. [OUT v.[3] (1)]

outing dues *n.* [late 19C–1910s] execution for murder. [OUT v.[3] (3) + SE *dues*, one's deserts]

out in the water *phr.* [20C+] (*US*) in debt.

outjie *n.* [1950s+] (*S.Afr.*) as a term of address, little fellow; used either of a child or derog. of an adult. [Afk. *ou*, a fellow + dimin. sfx *-tjie*]

outlaw *n.* **1** [late 19C–1960s] (*Aus./US*) a wild and unmanageable horse. **2** [1920s+] (*US*) a person who flouts conventional practices and regulations (whether in a respectable or criminal context). **3** [1930s+] (*US Black*) a prostitute without a regular pimp, or any independent prostitute (cf. BROTHER-IN-LAW n.).

outlaw *adj.* **1** [1900s–40s] (*Aus./US*) of a horse, wild and unmanageable. **2** [1920s+] (*W.I.*) wild, barbarous, crude. [OUTLAW n. (1)]

outlaw *v.* [1930s+] of a prostitute, to operate independently of a pimp. [OUTLAW n. (3)]

outlaw strike *n.* [1930s+] (*US*) an unofficial strike. [OUTLAW n. (2) + SE *strike*]

out-mouthed *adj.* [20C+] (*Ulster*) having protruding teeth.

out of control *adj.* [1980s+] (*US campus*) **1** of inanimate as well as animate objects, extreme, excessive, extremely good or extremely bad. **2** of people, drunk, intoxicated (cf. ADDLED adj.).

out of cooee *phr. see* WITHIN (A) COOEE OF phr.

out of flash *phr.* [early 19C] describing a show-off, 'a person who affects any particular habit, as swearing, dressing…taking snuff…, merely to be taken notice of, is said to do it "out of flash"' (Vaux). [SE *out* + FLASH n.[1]]

out of here *phr.*[1] (*also* **outta here**) **1** [1970s+] having left, esp. to leave suddenly; thus *I'm out of here*, a phr. of farewell. **2** [1990s+] not wanted, excluded.

out of here *phr.*[2] *see* OUT OF IT phr.[2].

out of hock *phr. see* IN HOCK phr.

out of it *phr.*[1] **1** [late 19C+] (*orig. US*) excluded from one's usual participation in something. **2** [1910s] dead. **3** [1940s+] (*orig. US*) out of touch, behind the times, not au fait with current affairs and interests. **4** [1950s+] (*orig. US Black*) unfashionable. **5** [1950s+] fortunately having escaped from something, as in *well out of it*.

out of it *phr.*[2] (*orig. US*) **1** [1910s; 1960s+] (*also* **out of here**) unable to function adequately because of one's intoxication by drugs or alcohol. **2** [1950s+] tired, exhausted, ill. **3** [1960s+] (*also* **out of here, outta there**) crazy, insane, in a daze (cf. OUT adj.[3]; OUT OF ONE'S BOX phr.). ['it' is one's head]

out of line *phr.* [1920s+] (*orig. US*) breaking rules, unacceptable, out of the ordinary. [SE *out* + *line*, a style of activity, a discipline]

out of one's asshole *adv.* (*also* **out the asshole**) [1960s+] (*US*) blatantly, excessively, totally no good, reprehensibly. [i.e. fig. excrement]

out of one's bag *phr. see* IN THE BAG *phr.*[3] (1).

out of one's bird *phr. see* BIRD n.[14].

out of one's books *phr.* [late 18C–early 19C] out of favour.

out of one's boots *adv.* [mid-19C–1900s] (*US*) comprehensively, convincingly, totally. [one has been 'blown' or 'knocked' out of one's boots]

out of one's box *phr.* **1** [1900s; 1990s+] (*also* **out of the box**) mad, eccentric, beyond emotional restraint (cf. OFF ONE'S BASE *phr.*; OUT *adj.*[3]; OUT OF ONE'S BRAIN *phr.*; OUT OF ONE'S GOURD *phr.*; OUT OF ONE'S HEAD *phr.*; OUT OF ONE'S NUT *phr.*; OUT OF ONE'S SKULL *phr.*; OUT OF ONE'S TREE *phr.*). **2** [1970s+] (*also* **off one's box/pot**) completely intoxicated, whether by drink or drugs.

out of one's brain *phr.* (*also* **off one's brain, out of one's cranium**) **1** [1940s+] intoxicated with drugs or alcohol; thus *go off one's brain*. **2** [1960s+] mad, crazy; thus *go off one's brain*, to go mad, to lose emotional control (cf. OUT OF ONE'S BOX *phr.*). **3** [1990s+] overwhelmed.

out of one's egg *phr. see* EGG n.[4] (1).

out of one's face *phr.* [1970s+] under the influence of drink or drugs.

out of one's gears *phr.* [late 17C–early 18C] unsettled, out of sorts. [GEAR n.[1] (1)]

out of one's gourd *phr.* (*also* **off one's gourd**) [1960s+] **1** extremely affected by a given drug, usu. cannabis or a hallucinogen. **2** extremely drunk (cf. ADDLED *adj.*). **3** crazy, insane (cf. OUT OF ONE'S BOX *phr.*). [GOURD n.[2] (1)]

out of one's head *phr.* **1** [late 19C+] eccentric, insane, obsessive, delirious; occas. in adv. use (cf. OUT OF ONE'S BOX *phr.*). **2** [1930s+] desperate, highly emotional. **3** [1940s+] (*orig. US*) (*also* **out of one's noodle**) experiencing the effects of a drug. **4** [1960s+] very drunk (cf. ADDLED *adj.*; ARSEHOLED *adj.*). **5** [1990s+] an intensifier, usu. meaning utterly bored or miserable.

out of one's nut *phr.* **1** [1930s+] crazy (cf. OUT OF ONE'S BOX *phr.*). **2** [1960s+] intoxicated, either through drink or, later, drugs. [NUT n.[1] (2); note earlier OFF ONE'S NUT *phr.*]

out of one's program *phr.* [1970s] out of one's depth, acting beyond one's actual capabilities.

out of one's skull *phr.* **1** [1950s+] crazy (cf. OUT OF ONE'S BOX *phr.*). **2** [1960s+] an intensifer, meaning extremely bored. **3** [1960s+] intoxicated, either through drink or, later, drugs.

out of one's tits *phr.* (*also* **off one's tits**) **1** [1970s+] intoxicated by drugs. **2** [1990s+] very drunk (cf. ARSEHOLED *adj.*). **3** [1990s+] an intensifier, meaning extremely bored.

out of one's tree *phr.* (*also* **off one's tree**) **1** [1960s+] crazy, insane (cf. OUT OF ONE'S BOX *phr.*). **2** [1990s+] totally intoxicated by drugs. [the sufferer has fig. fallen out of a tree]

out of order *phr.* **1** [1970s] (*US teen*) menstruating. **2** [1970s+] of events, behaviour or people, unacceptable, excessive, in bad taste.

out of pocket *phr. see* OUT OF (THE) POCKET *phr.*

out of shape *phr.* **1** [late 19C; 1970s+] out of sorts, upset. **2** [1970s+] (*US*) drunk or otherwise intoxicated.

out of sight *adv.* (*US*) **1** [mid-19C+] utterly, thoroughly. **2** [late 19C–1900s] extremely well.

out of sight *phr.* **1** [late 19C–1920s] (*US*) unattainable. **2** [late 19C+] (*orig. US*) (*also* **outasight, outasite, outen sight**) excellent, first-rate, exceptional; thus ext. as *clean out of sight*. **3** [1960s+] (*US*) extraordinary, esp. bad, insane or deranged. [note Dalzell, *From Flappers to Rappers* (1996): 'Like *far out* out-of-sight can point to serious literary roots. As Richard H. Peck of the University of Virginia noted in *American Speech* (1966, pp.78–79), *out-of-sight* was Bowery slang for astonishingly excellent in the 1890s, and was used by Stephen Crane at least four times in *Maggie: A Girl of the Streets* (1893). Visiting a museum, our heroine utters, "Dis is outa sight." She could have been speaking 70 years later. Lester V. Berrey and Melvin Van den Bark identified out-of-sight as a slang synonym for five categories – beyond comparison, very superior, excessive, completely, and expensive – in the *American Thesaurus of Slang* (1942), but I found little other evidence of the term's use until the early 1960s']

out of sorts *phr.* [early 19C+] dispirited, miserable. [SE f. early 17C–18C. Note printers' jargon *out of sorts*, run out of certain fonts of type]

out of state *phr.* [1970s+] (*US campus*) excellent, first-rate. [pun on OUT OF SIGHT *phr.* (2)]

out of the bag *phr.* [1950s+] (*Aus.*) surprising, remarkable.

out of the blue *phr.* [1910s+] surprising or surprisingly, quite unsuspected. [a 'bolt from the blue sky']

out of the box *phr.*[1] (*also* **out of the books**) [1920s+] (*Aus.*) exceptional, well above average.

out of the box *phr.*[2] *see* OUT OF ONE'S BOX *phr.* (1).

out of the car *phr.* [20C+] (*US prison*) on bad terms. [reverse of IN THE CAR *phr.*]

out of the game *phr.* [2000s] incoherent, unconscious, collapsed (through drink or drugs). [GAME n.[2] (8)]

out of the gate *phr.* [1990s+] from the very beginning. [horseracing imagery]

out of the loop *phr.* [1980s+] (*US teen*) not in on a secret, or not knowing what's going on. [orig. political jargon, the *loop* of people who have access to a given piece of information]

out of (the) pocket *phr.* [1940s+] (*US Black*) **1** acting in an unacceptable, tasteless manner. **2** referring to a bad situation, bad news. [pool jargon, an *out of pocket* shot causes a player to miss a turn]

out of there *phr.* [1970s+] (*US*) having left, esp. having left suddenly. [OUT OF HERE *phr.*[1] (1)]

out of the red *phr. see* IN THE RED *phr.* (1).

out of the spoon *phr.* [1950s+] (*drugs*) not using drugs. [SE *out* + SPOON n.[3]]

out of town *phr.* **1** [early 19C] in prison for debt. **2** [early–late 19C] hard up, penniless. **3** [mid-19C] unexcited, unstimulated. **4** [1920s–60s] (*US Und.*) in prison. **5** [1940s–60s] (*US*) crazy (cf. OFF THE RESERVATION *phr.*; ON A TRIP *phr.*; OUT TO BREAKFAST *phr.*; OUT TO LUNCH *phr.*). **6** [1960s] (*US Black*) unacceptable, unfashionable. [all have the image of not being completely present]

out of whack *phr.* [late 19C+] lit. or fig. off-centre, out of true, out of order, feeling unwell (cf. INTO WHACK *phr.*). [SE *out* + *whack*, to hit a blow, i.e. that which has been driven home askew]

out on a dike *phr. see* DIKE n.[2].

out on its own like a country shithouse *phr.* [1910s+] (*Aus./N.Z.*) unique, unrivalled. [SHITHOUSE n. (2)]

out on one's ass *phr.* (*also* **out on one's arse**) [1950s+] (*orig. US*) ejected unceremoniously, thrown out. [SE *out* + ASS n. (2)/ ARSE n.[1] (1)]

out on one's feet *phr.* [1930s+] (*orig. US*) exhausted.

out on the nick *phr. see* NICK v.[1] (3).

out on the roof *phr.* [1940s] (*US*) out on a drunken spree.

outpost *n.* [1980s+] (*US campus*) someone who is out of touch with reality, a daydreamer.

out-psych *v.* [1960s+] (*US*) to confuse, manipulate or brainwash someone by psychological means. [SE *out* + PSYCH (OUT) v. (1)]

outrageous *adj.* [1950s+] (*US*) excellent, worthy of admiration. [on bad = good model]

outrun the constable *v.* [late 17C–mid-19C] **1** (*also* **over-run the constable**) to spend more than one can afford; to live beyond one's means. **2** to go too far, whether physically or fig. **3** to change the subject.

outs, the *n.* [1960s] (*US Und.*) life outside prison.

outs and ins *n. see* IN-AND-OUT n.[1] (2).

outside *n.* **1** [late 18C–19C] a passenger who rides on top of a coach. **2** [late 19C+] (*US milit.*) the civilian world. **3** [20C+] (*US prison*) (*also* **out, the**) the world outside prison. **4** [1960s] (*US Black*) the world beyond one's home and domestic life. [(2) and (3) OUTSIDE *phr.*]

outside *adj.* [late 19C+] (*US Black*) illegitimate; thus (*W.I.*) *outside daughter/son/kid/child*, an illegitimate child; *outside man*, a woman's lover; *outside woman*, a man's lover. [i.e. *outside* the primary relationships or the (fig.) house]

outside *adv.* [mid-19C+] (*orig. US*) other than, excepting, beyond the number of.

outside *phr.* [late 19C+] out of prison, out of the services.

outside! *excl.* [20C+] a challenge. [abbr. *come outside and fight!*]

outside job *n.* [1920s+] a crime committed in a house etc by a person not connected or associated with the household or building concerned. [SE *outside* + JOB *n.*³ (1)]

outside man *n.* [mid-19C+] **1** (*UK Und.*) (*also* **outsider**) a lookout. **2** (*orig. US*) that member of a confidence trick team who locates a potential victim, lures him deeper into the hoax, and helps to fleece him; the 'steerer' for a brothel. [SE *outside*]

outsider *n.* **1** [late 19C+] a person who is considered socially inferior; esp. as *rank outsider*, a complete and utter inferior. **2** [1900s–20s] (*Irish*) a mentally deficient person. **3** [1910s] (*US Und.*) an outside pocket. **4** [1980s+] (*US*) an act of sexual intercourse performed out of doors.

outsiders *n.* [mid-19C] (*US Und.*) a device for unlocking a door by manipulating the key through the keyhole.

outside time *n.* [2000s] (*US prison/Und.*) parole. [OUTSIDE *phr.* + SE *time*/punning on TIME *n.*¹]

outslick *v.* [1940s+] (*US Black*) to outwit, to outsmart. [SE *out* + SLICK *v.*]

out someone's light *v.* (*also* **out the light for someone**) [20C+] (*W.I.*) to cripple or maim someone, to put out of action.

outs with *phr. see* OUT WITH *phr.*

outta here *phr. see* OUT OF HERE *phr.*¹

outta there *phr. see* OUT OF IT *phr.*² (3).

out the ass *adv.* [1980s+] (*US*) excessively, to a great degree.

out the asshole *adv. see* OUT OF ONE'S ASSHOLE *adv.*

out the door *phr.* [1980s+] (*US*) a general intensifier. [the situation is so bad one has to leave the room]

out the joe *phr.* [1960s] (*Aus./N.Z.*) passed out drunk. [SE *out* + JOE BLAKES *n.*]

out the light for someone *v. see* OUT SOMEONE'S LIGHT *v.*

out the monk *phr.* [1940s+] (*N.Z.*) **1** defeated, 'done for'; thus *be out the monk with*, to have fallen out with. **2** unconscious, asleep, often the result of drunkenness. **3** disabled through illness or lack of some essential. [ety. unknown; ? rhy. sl. = SE *drunk*]

out the pocket *phr.* [1990s+] (*US Black gang*) using a gun.

out there *adj.*¹ **1** [1970s+] under the influence of drugs. **2** [1980s+] bizarre, extreme.

out there *adj.*² [1990s+] **1** important, fashionable, 'in the swing'. **2** (*US Black*) involved in gang life, 'there' being the street. **3** (*US Black*) in a subservient, victimized position.

out there bad *phr.* [2000s] (*US prison*) in the wrong.

outtie *phr. see* OUTIE *phr.*

out to breakfast *phr.* [1990s+] (*orig. US*) **1** crazy, eccentric, weird. **2** intoxicated by drink or drugs. [var. on OUT TO LUNCH *phr.*]

out to buggery *phr.* [1990s+] (*Aus.*) far away or far off the mark.

out to it *phr.* [1940s+] (*Aus.*) extremely drunk, unconscious. [it being the world]

out to lunch *phr.* (*orig. US campus*) **1** [1950s+] crazy, eccentric, weird (cf. OUT OF TOWN *phr.*; OUT TO BREAKFAST *phr.*). **2** [1950s+] in a daze, stupid, naïve. **3** [1970s] absent, unavailable. **4** [2000s] intoxicated by drink or drugs. [image of not being 'all there']

out to pasture *phr.* [20C+] (*US Und.*) serving time in prison. [animals put out to pasture have 'retired' from everyday productive life]

out to the wide *phr. see* DEAD TO THE (WIDE) WORLD *phr.*

out where the bull feeds *phr.* (*also* **out where the bull gets his bleeding breakfast**) [20C+] (*Aus.*) in the outback.

out with *v.* **1** [19C+] to produce, to reveal, to bring out. **2** [mid-

19C+] to speak out, esp. to say something that has been hitherto held back or concealed. [OUT WITH IT! *excl.*]

out with *phr.* (*also* **outs with**) [mid-19C+] on bad terms with, quarrelling with, disenchanted with, opposed to. [ON THE OUTS *phr.* (2)]

out with it! *excl.* [early 17C+] speak! hand over! i.e. stop holding back, whether of speech or objects.

oven *n.* **1** [early 16C–19C; 1980s] the vagina (cf. BLACK HOLE *n.*¹). **2** [late 18C–mid-19C] a large mouth. **3** [1950s+] the womb; usu. in HAVE A BUN IN THE OVEN *v.*

oven-dodger *n.* [1980s+] a derog. term for a Jew (cf. ARAB *n.*²). [the implication that those who escaped the crematorium ovens of Auschwitz and other Nazi death camps were somehow doing it deceitfully]

over *adj.*¹ [1990s+] (*US*) out-of-date.

over *adj.*² [1990s+] (*US Black*) successful. [GET OVER *v.*¹ (3)]

over *v.* [20C+] (*Ulster*) to survive. [abbr. SE *get over*]

over, be *v.* [1970s+] (*US campus*) to dislike intensely, to be angry, to be bored with.

overamp *v.* [1960s+] (*drugs*) to overdose on cocaine or amphetamine. [SE *over* + AMP *n.* (1)/SE *amp*/abbr. SE *amphetamine*]

overamped *adj.* [1980s+] (*US*) overwrought, over-excited. [fig. use of OVERAMP *v.*]

over-and-under *n.* [1970s+] (*drugs*) a combination of a stimulant and a depressant drug. [i.e. an UPPER *n.*² (1) and a DOWNER *n.*⁵ (1)]

Overblikkiesberg *n. see* BLIKKIESDORP *n.* (1).

overboard *adj.* [1920s+] (*orig. US*) over-enthusiastic, very keen; usu. used with a prep., i.e. 'crazy for'.

over boots, over shoes *phr. see* OVER SHOES, OVER BOOTS *phr.*

overcharged *adj.* [1930s–50s] (*US*) overdosed on narcotics. [ext. of CHARGED (UP) *adj.* (2)]

overcoat *n.* **1** [late 19C+] a coffin. **2** [1910s–40s] (*US*) a pie crust. **3** [1920s–70s] (*also* **Dunlop overcoat**) a condom. **4** [1930s] (*US*) a high-value currency note around a bankroll. **5** [1930s] (*US*) a straight jacket. **6** [1940s] (*US*) a parachute.

overcoat maker *n.* [20C+] an undertaker. [rhy. sl. + OVERCOAT *n.* (1)]

over-do *n.* [1920s] (*W.I.*) showing off, ostentation.

overdraw one's badger *v.* [mid-19C] to overdraw one's bank account. [pun on SE *badger-drawing, badger-baiting*]

overdue *adj.* **1** [1960s+] of a woman, not having had a menstrual period at the expected time. **2** [1970s+] of a criminal, ripe for arrest.

over-easy *adj.* [20C+] (*US*) of fried eggs, turned over in the pan.

over-eye *v.* [late 19C–1900s] to watch, to survey. [SE *run one's eyes over*]

over goes the show! *excl.* [late 19C–1900s] an excl. of dismay when faced by a sudden disaster.

overheat one's flues *v.* [late 19C] to get drunk.

overjolt *n.* [1950s+] (*US drugs*) a drug overdose. [SE *over* + JOLT *n.*¹ (1)]

overlander *n.* [late 19C+] (*Aus.*) **1** a tramp. **2** a large mosquito. [SE *overlander*, one who herds cattle from one Aus. state to another]

overland trout *n.* (*US*) **1** [late 19C] roast pork. **2** [1900s–60s] bacon.

over-'omer *n.* [20C+] (*Can.*) an English person whose conversation centres on the better life to be found in the UK. [lit. 'over there where I have my home']

over-ripe fruit *n.* [1950s+] (*gay*) an ageing male homosexual. [SE *over-ripe* + FRUIT *n.*² (2)]

over-run the constable *v. see* OUTRUN THE CONSTABLE *v.* (1).

overs *n.* [1970s+] (*UK Und.*) proceeds of a theft that can, if not carefully disposed of, become vulnerable themselves to further theft, poss. by one of the gang. [SE *over*, an extra, a remainder; note mid-19C banking jargon *overs*, odd money remaining after the daily accounts are made up, and which is divided among the clerks]

overseas *adj.* [1930s] drunk. [modern var. on HALF SEAS OVER phr. (1)]

overseen *adj.* [17C–19C] tipsy.

overseer (of the new pavement) *n.* [late 18C–early 19C] a man standing in a pillory. [the positioning of the pillory above the passers-by]

over shoes, over boots *phr.* (*also* **over boots, over shoes**) [late 16C–18C] totally, recklessly committed. [? water pouring over the top of one's footwear]

overshot *adj.* [17C+] tipsy, drunk.

overtaken *adj.* [mid-17C–19C] drunk.

over the bay *phr.* (*also* **over the dam**) [late 18C–1920s] (*US*) drunk, tipsy.

over the bender *phr.* [mid-19C–1900s] a phr. implying that the previous statement is untrue. [SE *over* + BENDER n.[3] (2); 'it is historical in common English that a declaration made over the elbow as distinct from not over it need not be held sacred. Probably from early Christian if not pagan times. The bender is always the left elbow' (Ware). Note also the Victorian custom of 'over the left', i.e. pointing with one's right thumb over one's left shoulder, implying disbelief]

over the blue wall *phr. see* OVER THE WALL phr. (4).

over the border *phr.* [2000s] outside Greater London.

over the dam *phr. see* OVER THE BAY phr.

over the fence *phr.*[1] [1910s] (*Aus.*) out of trouble.

over the fence *phr.*[2] [1910s+] (*Aus./N.Z.*) extreme, beyond the bounds of taste.

over the hill *phr.* **1** [1910s+] free, escaped, esp. of an escaped prisoner or a soldier who has deserted etc. **2** [1930s+] worn-out, useless, too old, dead. [(1) GO OVER THE HILL v.[1]]

over the hump *phr.* **1** [1910s+] (*orig. US*) over the worst, past the midpoint of a job or experience, usu. an unpleasant one. **2** [1940s–60s] gone beyond return or reversal. **3** [1950s] (*US drugs*) enjoying the peak of a drug experience. [SE *over* + *hump/* HUMP n.[1]]

over the line *adv.* [1910s] to excess.

over the line *phr.* [1920s] drunk.

over the mark *phr.* [19C+] (*Can.*) tipsy. [a notional 'mark' that denotes a limit to 'safe' drinking]

over the moon *phr.* [1930s+] extremely cheerful, delighted, esp. as a clichéd response attributed to sportspeople, particularly professional football players, when interviewed about a successful game or competition. [E.P. adds a single mid-19C cit., in a private letter; *OED* cites earlier 19C examples of phr. *jump over the moon*]

over the odds *phr.* (*also* **above the odds**) [20C+] of people and things, extreme, beyond the normal limits.

over the plimsoll *phr.* [1920s+] (*N.Z.*) drunk. [the SE *plimsoll line*, marking the limit of loading a ship]

over the river *n.* [1910s] (*US Und.*) Blackwell's Island prison, New York.

over the road *phr.* [late 19C–1930s] in prison.

over the ropes *phr.* [1900s] (*US*) in a state of confusion, surprise. [boxing imagery]

over-the-shoulder-boulder-holder *n. see* BOULDER-HOLDER n.

over the side *phr.* [1910s+] away from one's home or place of work.

over the stile *phr.* [mid-19C–1900s] committed for trial. [rhy. sl.]

over the top *adj.* **1** [1960s+] beyond the usual bounds of taste, behaviour, credibility etc. **2** [1980s+] very drunk.

over the wall *phr.* **1** [1930s+] escaped from prison. **2** [1950s] stolen. **3** [1970s] in prison. **4** [1980s] (*US*) (*also* **over the blue wall**) in a hospital for the criminally insane.

over the water *phr. see* WATER, THE n.

ow *n.* [late 19C–1930s] (*US drugs*) the bowl of an opium pipe. [? abbr. + O n. (2); although it predates this]

o waggernery! *excl.* [late 19C] a joc. excl. meaning oh agony! [proper name Richard *Wagner* (1813–83), the ridicule of whose music provided much popular amusement during the 1890s]

Owen Nares *n.* [1910s+] chairs. [rhy. sl.; ult. UK actor *Owen Nares* (c.1888–1943)]

owie *n.* [1990s+] **1** (*US*) a bruise or minor injury. **2** (*US Black*) any jewellery that requires the piercing of one's flesh, usu. an earlobe. [the excl. *ow!* on having one's flesh pierced]

owl *n.* **1** [late 17C; late 19C+] a prostitute who works nights only (cf. ALLEY CAT n.). **2** [20C+] the late-night customers of bars, cafés and restaurants. **3** [1900s–40s] (*Aus./US*) a thief, esp. one who works at night.

owl *adj.*[1] [mid-19C+] (*orig. US*) working, operating or opening at night, e.g. *owl shift*, the night shift; *owl car*, a late-night streetcar.

owl *adj.*[2] *see* NIGHT-OWL adj.

owl *v.* [late 19C] (*US campus*) to stay late on a social visit.

owl crap/dung *n. see* OWL SHIT n.

owled *adj.* [1920s] (*US*) drunk.

owler *n.* [late 17C–mid-19C] one who smuggles wool or sheep from England to France. [in an attempt to curtail smuggling the transportation of wool by night was forbidden in 1674, therefore those who still carried on the illicit trade were known as *owlers*, because, like the bird, they worked at night]

owl-eyed *adj.* (*also* **owly**, **owly-eyed**) [mid-19C–1960s] (*US*) very drunk (cf. ARSEHOLED adj.).

owl feathers *n. see* OWL SHIT n.

owl-gal *n.* [1940s] (*W.I.*) a promiscuous woman. [like the owl she's 'out all night']

owlhead *n.*[1] (*also* **owl's head**) [1920s–60s] (*US*) a short, heavy revolver with a feature enabling it to double as a knuckleduster. [? a brandname]

owlhead *n.*[2] [1990s+] (*US*) a person.

owlhoot *n.* (*also* **owlhooter**) [1940s+] (*US*) a contemptible person, esp. a fugitive or outlaw. [? US Western *hear the owl hoot*, to travel by night]

owl milk *n. see* OWL SHIT n.

owl's bowels *n. see* CAT'S WHISKERS n.

owl's head *n. see* OWLHEAD n.[1].

owl shit *n.* (*also* **owl crap**, **...dung**, **...feathers**, **...milk**) [mid-19C+] (*US*) excrement, usu. constructed with 'sour'; also in fig. use; also in euph. forms. [SE *owl* + SHIT n.[1] (1)/CRAP n.[3] (1)/SE *dung/feathers/milk*]

Owlshit Junction *n.* [1970s] (*US*) the 'back of beyond'. [OWL SHIT n. + SE *junction*]

owly(-eyed) *adj. see* OWL-EYED adj.

own *v.* [1910s+] (*US Black*) to surpass, to overcome, to dominate. [slave-era imagery]

owner's job *n. see* CONSENT JOB n.

own the corn *v. see* ACKNOWLEDGE THE CORN v.

own up *v.* [mid-19C+] to confess.

Owsley acid *n.* (*also* **Owsley**, **Owsley's acid**, **white Owsley's**) [1960s+] (*drugs*) LSD (cf. A n.[3]). [Augustus *Owsley* Stanley III, the best known of all LSD chemists. His 'own-brand' drugs were considered the very best]

owt *n.* [mid-19C–1950s] the number 2. [backsl.]

owt gens *n.* [mid–late 19C] 2 shillings. [backsl.; OWT n. + GEN n.[1]]

owt yeneps *n.* [mid–late 19C] 2 pence. [backsl.; OWT n. + YENNEP n.]

ox *n.* [1930s+] (*US*) a large, thuggish man.

oxen-persuader *n. see* COW-PERSUADER n.

oxer *n. see* OXTER n.

Oxford *n.* [1940s] (*US Black*) a particularly dark-skinned person. [brandname of *Oxford* shoe polish]

Oxford bag *n*. [1990s+] a cigarette. [rhy. sl. = FAG n.⁴ (3)]

Oxford (scholar) *n*. **1** [late 19C+] a crown, 5 shillings (25p); thus HALF-OXFORD n. **2** [1930s] a collar. **3** [1930s+] (*Aus.*) $1 (cf. BEES (AND HONEY) n.). [rhy. sl.; (1) = DOLLAR n.¹ (1)]

oxo *n*. [late 19C–1930s] zero, nothing. [maths notation *0 × 0*]

Oxo cube *n*. [20C+] the London Underground. [rhy. sl. = TUBE n.¹ (2); ult. *Oxo cube*, the brand of stock cube]

oxter *n*. (*also* oxer) [early 18C+] (*Irish*) an armpit.

oxter *v*. [19C+] (*Irish*) to lift or move a person by holding them under the armpits. [OXTER n.]

oxy *n*. [2000s] (*US drugs*) *Oxy*contin, a painkiller based on synthetic morphine. [abbr.]

oxy *adj*. [1990s+] (*UK juv.*) impoverished looking. [the charity *Oxfam*, esp. its second-hand goods and clothes shops]

oxygen thief *n*. [1990s+] (*Aus.*) a completely worthless person. [they would even steal the air]

oyl of rope *n*. *see* OIL OF WHIP n.

oyster *n*.¹ **1** [mid-17C+] the vagina (cf. BEARDED CLAM n.). **2** [early 18C] a prostitute (cf. ALLEY CAT n.). **3** [late 18C+] a girl, a young woman. [one of many terms that equate the vagina with FISH n.¹ (1); (2) fig. use of (1); note D'Urfey, *Pills to Purge Melancholy* (1719–20): 'And now she has learnt the pleasing Game, / [...] / She daily ventures at the same, / And shuts and opens like an Oyster']

oyster *n*.² **1** [late 17C+] a lump of phlegm. **2** [late 19C; 1970s+] semen; thus *inhale the oyster*, to fellate (cf. BABY GRAVY n.). [resemblance]

oyster *n*.³ (*US*) **1** [late 19C–1950s] (*also* **sealed oyster**) a close-mouthed person; occas. as adj.; thus *dumb/close as an oyster*, silent, secretive. **2** [1930s–70s] an odd or stupid person. **3** [1960s] the mouth. [the bivalve's 'closed mouth']

oyster *n*.⁴ **1** [1910s–50s] a pearl; thus *real oysters*, genuine pearls. **2** [1970s] (*UK Und.*) a society woman who is paid to wear stolen pearls, hoping to entice an offer of purchase.

oyster *v*. *see* OYSTER (UP) v.

oyster-catcher *n*. [late 19C] the vagina (cf. BAG n.¹). [OYSTER n.² (2) + SE *catcher*]

oyster-faced *adj*. [late 19C–1910s] unshaven. [the oyster's beard]

oysterics *n*. [1900s] (*UK middle class*) hysterics. [a pun on the SE, intensified by the worries generated after bad oysters allegedly created a typhoid epidemic *c*.1900]

oyster months *n*. [late 19C] those months containing an 'r', which in Britain are trad. those in which it is safe to eat oysters.

oysters *n*. [mid-18C] the testicles (cf. ACORNS n.).

oyster's eye-tooth *n*. *see* CAT'S WHISKERS n.

oyster stew *n*. [1960s+] (*US drugs*) cocaine.

oyster (up) *v*. [1960s–70s] to shut up, to be quiet.

o.z. *n*. (*also* oh-zee, OZ) [1930s+] (*drugs*) 1oz (28g) of a drug. [1oz; pron. of the abbr. of SE *ounce*]

Oz *n*. [20C+] Australia. [pron. of *Aus*(*tralia*) + pun on *The Wonderful Wizard of Oz* (1900)]

oz *n*. [1980s+] (*drugs*) amyl nitrite (cf. AIMIES n.). [it sends you to the land of *Oz*]

ozard *adj*. [1950s] (*UK juv.*) ghastly. [a play on the book/film *The Wizard of Oz*, i.e. the opposite of *Wizard* is *Ozard*; poss. found only in Buckeridge]

ozone *n*.¹ (*orig. US*) **1** [1900s–70s] air. **2** [1920s–40s] a dismissal. [(2) is ext. of GET THE AIR v.]

ozone *n*.² **1** [1970s+] (*drugs*) phencyclidine (cf. ACE n.⁴). **2** [2000s] marijuana. [ety. unknown; ? to do with inhaling]

ozoned *adj*. *see* IN THE OZONE phr.

ozoner *n*. [1940s+] (*US*) a drive-in cinema. [SE *ozone*, fresh air]

ozone ranger *n*. [1970s+] (*US campus*) someone who is out of touch with reality. [SE *ozone* + *ranger*; their head is 'in the clouds']

Ozzie *n*. [1910s+] an Australian. [Oz n.]

Ozzie *adj*. [1910s+] Australian. [OZZIE n.]

ozzie *n*. [1980s+] (*Aus./Can. drugs*) 1oz (28g) of marijuana. [1 *oz*]

ozzy *n*. [2000s] hospital. [abbr./pron. + sfx -*y*]

P

P *n. see* PINK n.

p *n.*[1] [mid-17C] syphilis. [abbr. POX n.[1] (1)]

p *n.*[2] **1** [1920s–30s] a *ponce*, a *pimp*. **2** [1990s+] (*UK Black*) a promise (to deliver something). **3** [1990s+] (*UK Black*) the *price*. **4** [2000s] (*US Black*) a *parent*. [abbr.]

p *n.*[3] [1960s+] (*drugs*) **1** peyote. **2** heroin, lit. 'pure'. **3** phencyclidine (cf. ACE n.[4]). [abbr.]

p *n.*[4] [2000s] (*UK Black*) rejection, dismissal. [abbr. PUSH, THE n.]

p *n.*[5] *see* PEA n.[1].

p *adj.* [1970s+] *pure*, unadulterated, esp. of drugs. [abbr.]

p.a. *n.* **1** [1920s+] a press agent, a publicity agent. **2** [1930s+] a public address system. [abbr.]

pa *n.* [late 19C] the parish relieving officer, who distributed money to the poor. [abbr.]

p.a.b.a.c.a.b. *phr.* [1980s+] (*US drugs*) an exhortation to smoke cannabis. [abbr. pack *a* BOWL n. (2) and catch *a* BUZZ n.[3] (3)]

pac *n.* [mid-19C] a cap. [backsl.]

pace *v.* [1970s] (*US Black*) to live a fast, exciting and varied life.

pacer *n.* [late 19C] (*US*) anything or anyone that goes at a great pace.

pachuco *n.* (*also* **pachook**) [1940s+] (*US*) a Mexican-American, esp. a young man who joins a street gang; thus *pachuca*, his female counterpart (cf. BATO n.). [Mex. Sp. *pachuco*, flashily dressed, vulgar]

pachuco *adj.* (*also* **pachook**) [1940s+] (*US*) pertaining to Mexican-Americans (esp. street gang members) or their culture. [PACHUCO n.]

Pacific slope *n.* [late 19C] (*N.Z.*) the countries of the Pacific Rim, esp. as considered places of refuge for wanted criminals; thus *do the Pacific slope*, to flee N.Z. when accused of a crime in order to find refuge in one of the countries of the Pacific Rim. [pun on SE *Pacific slope*, the edge of the Pacific Ocean/SLOPE v.[2] (1)]

pack *n.*[1] [mid–late 19C] a night lodging for the very poor. [? PACK v.[2]]

pack *n.*[2] [1950s+] (*drugs*) **1** a packet of heroin. **2** a packet of pills. **3** a packet of marijuana. **4** a packet of cigarettes.

pack *n.*[3] [1990s+] (*US Black*) a White person. [abbr. PECKERWOOD n.]

pack *n.*[4] *see* PACKER n.[1].

pack *n.*[5] *see* PACKET n.[3].

pack *adj.* [1960s+] (*Irish*) friendly. [Scot.]

pack *v.*[1] **1** [19C+] (*orig. US*) to carry, also in fig. use. **2** [late 19C+] (*orig. US*) to carry a weapon, usu. a gun or knife. **3** [1920s+] (*US*) to carry money, to be in funds. **4** [1940s] (*US drugs*) to carry drugs for a dealer. **5** [1960s+] (*US prison*) to carry contraband in and out of a prison; to carry a concealed weapon.

pack *v.*[2] [late 19C+] to live as a tramp, travelling the country. [the SE *pack* that is carried]

pack *v.*[3] [1920s+] (*Aus.*) to surpass, to beat, to be more enjoyable than something. [? SE *send packing*]

pack *v.*[4] [1960s+] (*US campus*) of male homosexuals, to have anal sex.

pack *v.*[5] [1970s+] to reject a lover. [PACK IN v. (3)]

pack *v.*[6] [1980s+] **1** (*Aus. drugs*) to fill a cigarette with marijuana; thus *packer*, one who makes marijuana cigarettes. **2** (*US drugs*) to fill a crack cocaine pipe.

pack *v.*[7] *see* PACK (OFF) v.

package *n.*[1] **1** [late 19C–1930s] a drink. **2** [1920s+] (*US*) a man, a person; a *prize package*, a fool; (*US Und.*) a kidnap victim. **3** [1930s+] (*US drugs*) a supply of a given drug. **4** [1940s+] an attractive and usu. small, neat woman. **5** [1950s] (*US Und.*) a (long) prison term. **6** [1970s+] (*US*) the male genitals. **7** [1980s+] (*US*) the vagina. **8** [1990s+] (*US Black*) a lot, very much, a great deal.

package *n.*[2] **1** [1910s+] (*US*) a police record. **2** [1990s+] (*US prison*) a positive report on a prisoner. [the package of papers on which it is written]

package *n.*[3] *see* PACKET n.[3].

pack a punch *v.* (*also* **pack a kick, …a wallop, pack one**) [1910s+] (*orig. US*) **1** to be capable of delivering a disabling, strong punch; also in fig. use, e.g. of alcohol. **2** in fig. use, to be influential, important.

pack a rod *v.* (*also* **pack a heater**) [1920s+] (*US*) to carry a gun. [PACK v.[1] (2) + ROD n.[1] (2)/HEATER n. (3)]

pack a sad *v.* [1980s+] (*N.Z.*) to be depressed. [PACK v.[1] (1) + SE *sad*]

pack a wallop *v. see* PACK A PUNCH v.

pack chitlins *v.* [1990s+] (*US Black*) of a man, to be unable to maintain an erection during intercourse. [PACK v.[1] (1) + SE *chitlins*, pig's intestines (which are *de facto* soft)]

packed tight *adj.* [1970s] (*US*) nervous, unhappy, worried. [the image is of constipation]

packed up *adj. see* PACK UP v. (3).

pack 'em *v.* (*also* **pack one's shit, pack shit, pack them**) [1940s+] (*Aus.*) to be frightened. [image of holding back fear-induced diarrhoea]

packer *n.*[1] (*also* **pack**) [late 19C–1940s] (*Aus.*) a *pack*horse. [abbr.]

packer *n.*[2] [1990s+] (*drugs*) a thin stick, typically a chopstick, or a piece of metal coat hanger, used to pack a cocaine pipe.

packer *n.*[3] *see* FUDGE-PACKER n.

packet *n.*[1] [late 18C–mid-19C] a false report; thus *sell someone a packet*, to hoax, to deceive, to lie. [SE *packet*, a bundle of letters; thus lit. a 'packet of lies']

packet *n.*[2] [1910s+] (*orig. milit.*) **1** a bullet or missile; thus by metonymy, a wound; usu. in phr. COP A PACKET v. (1). **2** trouble; esp. in phr. COP A PACKET v. (2). [Brophy & Partridge, *Songs and Slang of the British Soldier* (1930), suggest the 'packet' of gauze and lint that comprised the First Field Dressing that would be applied to a wound]

packet *n.*[3] (*also* **pack, package**) **1** [1910s+] a large sum of money; esp. in phr. *make/win a packet*. **2** [1990s+] (*US prison*) a long sentence.

packet n.⁴ [1950s+] (*mainly gay*) the genitals, male or female.

packet, the n. [1980s+] everything, the lot.

packet from Paris n. (*also* **parcel from Paris**) [20C+] (*Aus./N.Z.*) a baby. [? clichéd identification of France with sex, though not usu. with procreative intercourse]

packets! *excl.* [late 19C] a general expression of disbelief. [PACKET n.¹]

pack fudge v. *see* FUDGE n.².

pack guts to a bear v. *see* CARRY GUTS TO A BEAR V.

pack heat v. [1920s+] (*US*) to carry a gun. [PACK v.¹ (2) + HEAT n.⁴]

packie n.¹ [1940s+] (*N.Z.*) one who transports supplies by pack animal. [abbr. SNZE *packman*]

packie n.² *see* PACKY n.².

pack in v. **1** [20C+] to stop, to cease to function, to give up, to die. **2** [1950s+] (*US Und.*) to leave. **3** [1950s+] to end a relationship.

packing n.¹ [late 19C–1910s] food, esp. of poor quality. [one *packs* it into one's stomach]

packing n.² **1** [late 19C+] (*orig. US*) carrying a gun or knife (cf. CARRYING n.). **2** [1990s+] (*US Black*) having a large penis. **3** [1990s+] (*US gay*) of a lesbian, wearing a strap-on dildo, usu. under one's clothes, or wearing other padding in the genital area to look as if one has a penis. **4** [2000s] (*US prison*) having weapons for sale. [PACK v.¹]

packing n.³ **1** [1980s+] (*US*) performing anal intercourse. **2** [1990s+] (*US Black*) of a man, having sexual intercourse. [SE *pack in*, to fill]

packing death phr. [1950s] (*Aus.*) terrified, frightened. [PACK 'EM V.]

packing-house n. (*also* **packing-ken**) [late 19C–1910s] an eating house, a café; thus *packing house quail*, spare ribs; *packing-house rules*, no rules at all. [PACKING n.¹ (+ KEN n.¹ (1))]

packing it n. [1990s+] making a large amount of money. [PACK v.¹ (3)/PACKET n.³ (1)]

pack it in v. (*also* **pack it up**) [1930s+] to stop doing something, usu. as a command. [SE *pack*, to put away]

pack mud v. [1970s+] (*gay*) to have anal intercourse (cf. ASK FOR THE RING V.). [PACK v.⁴ + MUD n.⁵]

pack (off) v. [mid-19C] to go away; often as imper.

pack of poo tickets n. [1990s+] (*Aus.*) a lavatory roll. [punning on POO n.¹ (2)/LIKE A PAKAPOO TICKET phr.]

pack of rockets n. (*also* **pack of rocks**) [1940s–50s] (*drugs*) a packet of marijuana cigarettes.

pack one v. *see* PACK A PUNCH V.

pack one's shit v. *see* PACK 'EM V.

pack peanut butter v. (*also* **mix one's peanut butter**) [1970s+] (*US*) to engage in anal intercourse (cf. ASK FOR THE RING V.). [PACK v.⁴ + the colour of the spread]

pack rat n. [20C+] (*US*) **1** an obsessive hoarder. **2** a hotel bellboy. [SE *pack rat*, the US bushy-tailed woodrat, known for its collecting of objects]

pack, shack and stack n. [1940s–60s] (*orig. US Black*) one's entire belongings, clothes, home and money. [SE *pack* + *shack* + STACK n.¹ (1)]

pack shit v. *see* PACK 'EM V.

pack the banner v. *see* CARRY THE BANNER V.

pack the game in v. [1920s+] to stop doing something. [PACK IN v. (1)]

pack the gear v. [1970s] (*US*) to achieve a given standard; lit. to 'carry the equipment'. [PACK v.¹ (1)]

pack them v. *see* PACK 'EM V.

pack the mustard v. [1930s] (*US tramp*) to work as a bricklayer or labourer. [PACK v.¹ (1) + the colour of the mortar in the hod]

pack the pillow v. [2000s] (*US*) to menstruate. [use of *pillow* = menstrual pad]

pack the trail v. [late 19C+] (*Aus.*) to journey along a trail, on foot or horseback. [SE *pack*, a rucksack]

pack up v. **1** [1910s–20s] of a person, to die. **2** [1910s+] (*orig. milit.*) to tire, to abandon one's efforts, to stop doing something. **3** [1920s+] of machinery, or of anything that works mechanically, e.g. the human heart, to stop working; usu. as *packed up*, occas. *packed*. **4** [1970s] to reject.

pack up one's alls and be gone v. (*also* **pack up one's awls and be gone**) [mid-17C–1920s] to leave for good. [SE *alls*, everything, or *awls*, tools]

pack up one's pipes v. *see* PUT UP ONE'S PIPES V.

packy n.¹ [1940s+] (*W.I.*) the skull, the head. [dial. *packy*, the calabash fruit, which resembles the human head]

packy n.² (*also* **packie**) [1970s+] (*US*) a liquor store. [the liquor is *packed up* to take away]

Pad n. **1** [late 18C+] an Irishman (cf. DONOVAN n.¹). **2** [1940s+] a nickname or intimate form of address for an Irishman. [abbr. PADDY n.]

pad n.¹ **1** [mid-16C–mid-19C] (*UK Und.*) the road. **2** [mid-17C] a villain's female companion. **3** [mid-17C–19C] (*UK Und.*) a highway robber, a footpad (but not a mounted highwayman). **4** [late 17C] a prostitute. **5** [late 17C–19C] an easy-paced horse. **6** [mid-18C–19C] (*UK Und.*) highway robbery. **7** [mid-18C–mid-19C] a tramp. **8** [mid-19C; 1950s] a walk. [Du. *pad*, and OHG *pfad*, the cant equivalent of the SE *path*]

pad n.² **1** [18C+] a bed. **2** [1930s+] a place, house or apartment, e.g. a prostitute's room. **3** [1940s+] (*US Black*) used in combs. as *pad of...* to describe a variety of shops and businesses. **4** [1940s+] (*US Und.*) a cell. **5** [1940s+] a padded cell. [SE *pad*, a mattress; best known in 20C+ in a drug context, it was orig. used for the bed or couch on which an opium smoker reclined. It was then applied to an opium den, and after that was a beatnik term for a place where one could smoke cannabis]

pad n.³ [1940s+] (*US Und.*) **1** an establishment that pays bribes to the local police. **2** the regular bribes paid to members of a US police department; thus *on the pad*, accepting bribes or paying bribes. [SE *pad* (of paper), on which the payments are listed]

pad v.¹ (*also* **pad it**) **1** [early 17C–1930s] to travel as a tramp, thief, vagrant or prostitute. **2** [mid-17C+] to walk, to wander. [PAD n.¹ (1)]

pad v.² [mid-17C–mid-18C] to work as a highway robber on foot or on horseback. [PAD n.¹ (1)]

pad v.³ [1950s] (*US Black*) to inform, to tell. [the image of padding or filling the brain with information]

pad v.⁴ (*also* **pad down**, **pad out**) [1950s–70s] (*US Black*) to live somewhere, to spend the night somewhere. [PAD n.² (1)/PAD n.² (2)]

pad (a bill) v. [1930s+] fraudulently to add items to a bill or to an expense account statement in order to obtain money that is not actually owed.

pad borrower n. [late 18C–early 19C] a horse thief. [PAD n.¹ (5) + ironic use of SE *borrow*]

padded adj. [1910s+] (*US Und.*) having concealed contraband (stolen articles, drugs etc) on one's person in order to remove it from a shop or deceive customs etc.

padden crib n. *see* PADDING CRIB n. (1).

padden ken n. *see* PADDING KEN n.

padder n. [early 17C–mid-18C] one who robs on the highway, but does not work from a horse. [PAD n.¹ (1); Rowlands, *Martin-Mark-all* (1610), differentiates between the types of highway thief: 'Such as robbe on horse-backe were called high lawyers, and those who robbed on foote ... called Padders']

padders n. [19C] **1** the feet. **2** boots or shoes. [PAD v.¹ (2)]

paddies n. (*also* **patties**) [1970s+] (*US gay*) the buttocks. [? SE *pads*]

padding n.¹ (*UK Und.*) **1** [mid-17C–mid-19C] highway robbery.

2 [late 17C] working as a highway robber; thus *go a-padding*, to rob on the highway. [PAD v.[2]]

padding n.[2] [late 17C] confidence trickery, swindling. [ety. unknown; ? PAD v.[1] (1), i.e. conversation that accompanies walking]

padding n.[3] [2000s] (*UK police*) the practice of planting extra amounts of drugs to ensure a conviction.

padding crib n. **1** [mid-19C] (*Aus./UK Und.*) (*also* **padden crib**) a lodging house. **2** [1980s] (*US Und.*) a place to hide or rest. [PAD v.[1] (1) + CRIB n.[1] (1); (2) also PAD n.[2] (1)]

padding ken n. (*also* **padden ken**) [mid-19C–1930s] (*Aus./UK Und.*) a lodging house frequented primarily by vagrants or thieves; thus *padding-ken keeper*. [PAD v.[1] (1) + KEN n.[1] (1)]

Paddington fair (day) n. [late 17C–early 19C] (*UK Und.*) the hanging day, the day of execution. [Tyburn, the site of London's main 18C gallows, was in the then village of *Paddington*. The phr. is also a grim pun on the actual Paddington Fair]

Paddington spectacles n. [early 19C] the hood that is pulled over the condemned man's head before the hanging. [see prev.]

paddist n. [late 17C–18C] (*Scot.*) a highwayman. [PAD n.[1] (3)]

paddle n. [mid-19C+] **1** the hand. **2** the fingers. **3** a foot.

paddle v.[1] [mid-19C] to run away, to leave. [SE *paddle*, to walk with short, uncertain steps, to toddle]

paddle v.[2] [late 19C] to drink strong liquor. [? SE *paddle*, to walk in shallow water]

paddlefoot n. [1940s+] (*US*) an infantryman. [he 'paddles about']

paddler n.[1] [late 19C–1930s] a paddleboat. [abbr.]

paddler n.[2] [1940s+] (*Aus.*) a policeman (cf. BEAT-POUNDER n.). [SE *paddle*, to beat, implying violence]

paddle the pickle v. [1960s+] to masturbate (cf. BEAT ONE'S MEAT v.). [SE *paddle*, to beat with a paddle]

Paddo n. [1940s+] (*Aus.*) the suburb of *Padd*ington, Sydney. [abbr. + -O sfx (4)]

pad dough n. *see* PAD MONEY n.

pad down v. *see* PAD v.[4].

Paddy n. (*also* **paddy**) **1** [mid-18C+] an Irishman (cf. DONOVAN n.[1]). **2** [19C+] a nickname or intimate form of address to an Irishman. **3** [1900s] (*Aus.*) a Chinese person (cf. AH CABBAGE n.). **4** [1940s] (*US Black*) a policeman (cf. BILLY n.[6]). **5** [1940s+] (*US Black*) (*also* **paddy boy**, **paddy girl**, **patty**) a White person, though not always Irish. **6** [1970s] (*US*) a bricklayer. **7** [1970s+] (*Irish*) Irish whisky. [common Irish name, *Patrick*; all race-related usages are derog.; the occupations are those considered to be stereotypically Irish; (3) uses *Paddy* as generic for any foreigner]

paddy n.[1] [mid-19C+] (*UK Und.*) a padlock.

paddy n.[2] [late 19C] a hobby, a fad, a pastime. [pun on PAD n.[1] (5), i.e. a hobby horse]

paddy n.[3] [late 19C+] a tantrum, a fit of temper. [PADDY n. (1), the supposed irritability of the Irish]

paddy n.[4] [1940s–50s] (*UK prison*) a padded cell for mentally disturbed prisoners. [PAD n.[2] (5)]

paddy adj. **1** [20C+] Irish. **2** [1940s+] (*US Black*) White. [PADDY n.]

paddy and mick n. a pick (axe). [rhy. sl.]

paddy and mick adj. [20C+] stupid. [rhy. sl. = THICK adj.[1] + stereotyping of Irish names]

Paddy-bashing n. [2000s] beating up Irish people, usu. used of soldiers in Northern Ireland. [PADDY n. (1) + BASHING n.[1] (1)]

paddy boy n. *see* PADDY n. (5).

paddy fever n. (*also* **white fever**) [1960s] (*US Black*) the desire for sex with White men or women. [PADDY n. (5) + SE *fever*]

paddy funeral n. (*also* **paddy's funeral**) [20C+] any boisterous occasion, not necessarily a wake. [PADDY n. (1)]

paddy girl n. *see* PADDY n. (5).

Paddyland n. (*also* **Paddy's Isle**, **Paddy's land**) [19C+] Ireland. [PADDY n. (1) + SE *land*]

Paddy O'Rourke n. [1990s+] talk, conversation. [rhy. sl.]

paddy quick n. **1** [mid–late 19C] a stick. **2** [1960s+] a kick. [rhy. sl.]

paddy quick adj. [mid-19C] stupid. [rhy. sl. = THICK adj.[1]]

paddy-row n. [early 19C–1910s] a fight that entails more verbal than physical aggression. [PADDY n. (1) + SE *row*]

Paddy's eyewater n. [late 19C+] (*Irish*) illicitly distilled whisky, poteen. [PADDY n. (1) + *eyewater*; note EYEWATER n. (3)]

paddy's funeral n. *see* PADDY FUNERAL n.

Paddy's Goose n. [mid-19C] the White Swan public house in High Street, Shadwell, the best known seaman's pub in mid-19C London. [? its Irish landlord, thus PADDY n. (1). 'During the Crimean war, the landlord, when the Government wanted sailors to man the fleet, went among the shipping in the river, and enlisted numbers of men. His system of recruiting was very successful. He went about in a small steamer with a band of music and flags, streamers and colours flying. All this rendered him popular with the Admiralty authorities, and made his house extensively known to the sailors, and those connected with them' (Mayhew, *London Labour and the London Poor*, 1861–2)]

Paddy's Isle/land n. *see* PADDYLAND n.

Paddy's lantern n. [1930s+] the moon. [PADDY n. (1) + SE *lantern*; ? a ref. to the lack of electricity in rural Ireland]

Paddy's Market n. [late 19C–1950s] (*Aus.*) **1** the weekly market for cheap or second-hand goods held in the late 19C near Haymarket Square in Melbourne. **2** any kind of cheap market. [PADDY n. (1) + SE *market*; note WW2 milit. use, the market in Cairo where Aus. troops sold illegally manufactured goods, black market commodities etc; a similarly named market, frequented by Irish immigrants, has existed in Glasgow from the late 19C]

Paddy's toothache n. *see* IRISH TOOTHACHE n.

paddy's watch n. *see* PADDYWHACK ALMANAC n.

paddy wagon n. [20C+] (*orig. US*) the vehicle in which arrested people are transported to the local police station or prison (cf. PAT WAGON n.). [PADDY n. (1), with the implication that most US police (? or criminals) would be Irish]

Paddy Ward's pig n. [mid-18C–mid-19C] a lazy person, one who is relaxing. [anecdotal]

paddywax n. [1910s–20s] a severe beating. [var. on PADDYWHACK n.[1] (4); but note PADDY n. (1) + WAX v.[2] (2)]

paddywhack n.[1] **1** [late 18C–1910s] an Irishman, esp. when large and brawny (cf. DONOVAN n.[1]). **2** [late 19C] a rage, a passionate outburst of temper. **3** [late 19C+] (*Irish*) stage or 'professional' Irishism, e.g. much use of 'Sure an' beggorah, sorr...' etc. **4** [late 19C+] a severe beating. [PADDY n. (1) + WHACK n.[1] (1) + negative stereotyping]

paddywhack n.[2] [late 19C+] (*Aus.*) a smacking, usu. of a child. [SE *paddle*]

paddywhack v. [late 19C+] to beat severely. [PADDYWHACK n.[1] (4)]

paddywhack almanac n. (*also* **paddy's watch**, **paddy-whack**) [late 19C] an unlicensed almanac. [PADDYWHACK n.[1] (1); such an almanac 'comes the PADDY n. (1) over', i.e. confuses its user]

paddywood n. [1980s] (*US Black*) a derog. term for a White person; also. ext. to Chicanos and Latinos. [PADDY n. (5) + PECKERWOOD n.]

padhouse n. [1930s–40s] (*US Black*) one's house, one's home. [PAD n.[2] (2)]

padiddle n. [2000s] (*US*) a vehicle with a burned-out headlight; thus any old or run-down vehicle. [ety. unknown; the term is used in a travelling game whereby one shouts out 'Padiddle' when seeing such a vehicle and other players suffer a forfeit]

pad it v. *see* PAD v.[1].

padlock n. [1960s–70s] the penis (cf. ALMOND n.). [rhy. sl. = COCK n.[2] (1)]

pad money n. (*also* **pad dough**) [1900s–50s] (*US*) money for a night's lodging or for admission into an opium den. [PAD n.[2] (2)]

pad monster *n. see* RACK MONSTER *n.* (1).

pad of cold cream *n.* [1940s] (*US Black/Southern*) an ice-cream parlour. [PAD n.² (3)]

pad of dry scarfs *n.* [1940s] (*US Black/Southern*) a grocery store (cf. PAD OF WET SCARF(s) n.). [PAD n.² (3) + SCARF n.]

pad of galloping snapshots *n.* [1940s] (*US Black/Southern*) a cinema. [PAD n.² (3) + GALLOPING SNAPSHOTS n.]

pad of stiffs *n.* [1940s] (*US Black*) a funeral parlour. [PAD n.² (3) + STIFF n.² (1)]

pad of stitches *n.* [1940s–70s] (*US Black*) a hospital. [PAD n.² (3) + SE (*surgical*) *stitches*]

pad of togs-in-(the-)rough *n.* [1940s] (*US Black/Southern*) a tailor's shop. [PAD n.² (3) + TOGS n. (1) + SE *in the rough*, unfinished]

pad of wet scarf(s) *n.* [1940s] (*US Black/Southern*) a restaurant (cf. PAD OF DRY SCARFS n.). [PAD n.² (3) + SCARF n.]

pad one's skull *v.* [1950s] (*US Black*) to pass on information.

pad out *v. see* PAD v.⁴.

pa-dow! *excl.* [2000s] (*US Black*) an excl. of approval, pleasure.

padre *n.* [late 18C+] a (usu. milit.) chaplain. [Sp. *padre*, father, thus a priest]

pads *n.*¹ [1930s–50s] (*US*) car licence plates. [affixed to the front and back, they 'pad' the car]

pads *n.*² [1940s–50s] (*UK prison*) a padded cell. [abbr. SE *padded cell*]

pad the hoof *v.* **1** [late 18C+] to walk, to travel on foot; thus *hoof-padder*, a pedestrian. **2** [mid-19C] to leave in a hurry. [PAD v.¹ (2) + HOOF n. (1)]

pag *n.* [20C+] (*Ulster*) a useless individual. [Ulster dial. *paughle*, a fat, lazy person]

pagan *n.*¹ [late 16C–mid-17C] a prostitute. [the idea of a paganic, i.e. Greek/Roman, worship of physical beauty, epitomized in the celebrated attractiveness of the Greek *hetaira*, mistress, concubine or courtesan]

pagan *n.*² [1980s] (*UK Black*) a White person.

pagger *n.* (*also* **pagga**) [1990s+] (*Scot.*) a fight. [Lowland Scot. *peg*, a blow or thump with the fist]

pagger *v.* [1990s+] (*Scot.*) to fight. [PAGGER n.]

pagnol *n. see* PAYOL n.

pahtner *n. see* PARTNER n.².

paid *adj.* **1** [mid-17C] drunk. **2** [2000s] (*US prison*) resulting in a favourable outcome of a parole hearing. [obs. SE *paid*, satisfied, content]

paik *v.* [20C+] (*Ulster*) to beat up, to thrash. [Scot. + northern UK dial. *paik*, to beat]

pail *n.* [1940s] **1** (*US Black*) the stomach. **2** (*US*) a car.

pail of lard *n. see* BUCKET OF LARD n.

painful *adj.* [1980s+] (*US campus*) bad.

pain in the arm *n. see* PAIN (IN THE NECK) n.¹.

pain in the arse *n.* (*also* **pain in the ass, ...asshole, ...backside, ...bum, ...butt**) [1930s+] **1** an annoying person. **2** (*also* **pain in the breakfast**) an annoying object, situation or circumstance. [someone or something that can GIVE SOMEONE A PAIN IN THE ARSE v.]

pain-in-the-ass *adj.* [1960s+] (*US*) infuriating. [PAIN IN THE ARSE n.]

pain (in the neck) *n.*¹ (*also* **pain in the arm, ...face, ...head, ...guts**) [1910s+] **1** an annoying person, a bore. **2** an annoying situation, anything considered unpleasant, typically a task one does not wish to perform. **3** (*Aus.*) a general insult. [someone or something that can GIVE SOMEONE A PAIN (IN THE NECK) v.]

pain (in the neck) *n.*² [1990s+] a cheque. [rhy. sl.]

pain in the plaster *n.* [1990s+] a bore, a nuisance, an irritation. [SE *pain* + PLASTER OF PARIS n., i.e. PAIN IN THE ARSE n.]

pain in the puku *n.* [1940s+] (*N.Z.*) a stomach-ache; lit. and fig. [Maori *puku*, the stomach]

paint *n.*¹ [17C+] make-up, cosmetics; thus as v., to use make-up.

paint *n.*² **1** [1910s–20s] (*Aus.*) jam. **2** [1930s+] (*Aus.*) cheap red wine. **3** [1940s] (*US*) ketchup/catsup.

paint *n.*³ [1920s+] (*US tramp*) playing cards, usu. the royal cards (cf. PAINTED MISCHIEF n.).

paint *adj.* [2000s] (*US Black*) stupid, rubbish, time-wasting. [phr. *as exciting as watching paint dry*]

paint *v.*¹ [mid–late 19C] to drink.

paint *v.*² [1980s+] (*US gay*) to have a bowel movement during anal intercourse.

paint-brush baronet *n.* [late 19C] (*UK society*) an ennobled artist.

painted cat *n. see* CAT n.¹ (1).

painted mischief *n.* [late 19C] playing cards (cf. PAINT n.³). [the negative image of card-playing]

painted peeper *n.* [19C–1940s] a black eye; often in pl. [SE *painted* + PEEPER n. (1)]

painter stainers *n.* [late 19C] (*UK society*) artists. [a remark made by the Lord Mayor at the Royal Academy banquet of 1883, when he referred to the ancient company of *Painter Stainers*, suggesting that it was the predecessor of the Royal Academy]

paint job *n.* [2000s] (*US*) one's skin colour.

paint remover *n.* [20C+] (*orig. US*) **1** cheap, strong whisky or another drink. **2** strong, bitter coffee.

paint someone's eye for them *v.* [late 19C–1910s] to give someone a black eye.

paint-stripper *n.* [20C+] an alcoholic drink of inordinate strength and fierceness.

paint the bucket *v. see* BUCKET n.³ (2).

paint the town pink *v.* [1900s–40s] (*orig. US*) to go on a (modest) spree. [play on PAINT THE TOWN RED v. (1)]

paint the town red *v.* **1** [late 19C+] (*orig. US*) (*also* **paint the place red**) to go on a spree. **2** [1960s+] to vomit. [? the excesses of the Marquis of Waterford and a bunch of aristocratic vandals who on the night of 5–6 April 1837 lit. painted Waterford red, daubing the buildings with paint; given the US origin, poss. linked to the image of turning an entire town into a red-light district; (2) play on (1)]

paint the walls *v.* [1990s+] to vomit forcefully.

paipsey *adj.* [20C+] (*W.I.*) insipid, weak, unattractive. [? UK dial. *papes*, a flour and water gruel, also a foolish youth; ult. SE *pap*, soft or semi-liquid food for infants or invalids]

pair *n.* **1** [late 19C+] the female breasts. **2** [1960s+] (*US*) the testicles; usu. in phr. *have a pair*, to be macho, manly.

pair of braces *n. see* AIRS AND GRACES n. (2).

pair of compasses *n.* [late 19C] the human legs, esp. when accentuated by the tight trousers fashionable *c.*1880.

pair of footprints *n.* [1930s+] (*Aus.*) a pipe-wrench. [when opened they are wide at the end and narrow in the middle, like a footprint]

pair off with *v.* [mid-19C–1910s] to marry.

pair of lawn sleeves *n.* [mid-19C] a bishop. [metonymy, i.e. a bishop's vestments]

pair of pants *n. see* PANTS n.³.

pair of tongs *n.* [late 19C–1900s] a very thin person.

pair of wheels *n.* [early 17C] a 2-wheeled vehicle.

pair of wings *n.* [18C–early 19C] (*UK Und.*) a pair of oars.

paisa *n.* (*also* **piesa, pisa**) [1940s–50s] (*W.I.*) money. [Hind. *paisa*, the lowest denomination of coin, 100 to the rupee]

paisan *n.* (*also* **paisano**) **1** [20C+] an Italian, usu. used by fellow Italians in an affectionate and congratulatory manner. **2** [1950s] a fool. [Ital. *paisan*, a peasant]

pajonk *n.* (*also* **pajawonk**) [1940s–70s] (*US*) a penis.

Pak *n.* [1950s+] **1** Pakistan. **2** a derog. term for a *Pakistani*. [abbr.]

pakalolo *n.* [1980s+] (*US drugs*) marijuana. [Hawaiian]

pakeha *n.* [early 19C+] (*N.Z.*) a White person.

Paki *n.* (*also* **Pakki**) [1960s+] a derog. term for any British Asian or Asian immigrant from East Africa (cf. BROWNIE n.[2]). [abbr. *Pakistani*]

Paki *adj.* [1970s+] used derog. with ref. to any British Asian or Asian immigrant from East Africa.

paki-basher *n.* [1970s+] a racist who beats up Asians. [PAKI n. + SE *basher*]

paki-bashing *n.* [1970s+] racially motivated attacks on the UK Asian community, usu. by White youths. [PAKI n. + BASHING n.[1] (1)]

paki pox *n.* [1960s] a derog. term for smallpox. [PAKI n.+ SE *pox*; its supposed prevalence, in racist eyes, among the era's Pakistani (in fact more likely Bangladeshi or East African Indian) immigrants]

Paki's, the *n.* (*also* **Paki, the**) [1970s+] a corner shop, a small supermarket, latterly regardless of the race of the owner. [PAKI n.]

Pakki *n. see* PAKI n.

pal *n.* **1** [mid-18C+] (*also* **pall, pell**) a friend, an accomplice. **2** [mid-19C+] a term of familiar, usu. affectionate address. [Rom. *pal*, a brother]

palace of pleasure *n.* [19C] the vagina (cf. ADAM'S OWN (ALTAR) n.).

palam-pam *v. see* PAMPER v.

palampo *n.* [mid-19C] (*Anglo-Ind.*) a quilt, a bedspread. [? proper name *Palanpore*, an Indian town renowned for its manufacture of chintz counterpanes]

Palari(e) *n. see* POLARI n.

palarie *v.* [mid-19C+] (*tramp/circus*) to talk, to speak. [Ital. *parlare*, to talk]

pal around (with) *v. see* PAL (WITH) v.

palatic *adj.* (*also* **pallatic, parlatic**) [late 19C+] drunk (cf. AFFLICTED adj.). [PARALYTIC adj.; 20C+ use is mainly Irish]

palava *n.* [1970s] (*W.I.*) an argument, a row. [PALAVER n.]

palaver *n.* (*also* **perlaver**) **1** [mid-18C+] chat, talk, conversation. **2** [mid-18C+] wearisome, idle or insincere talk. **3** [19C] (*Scot.*) a fussy, ostentatious person; usu. as *old palaver*. **4** [20C+] (*also* **palaverment**) business, concern, goings-on; thus *none of your palaver*, no business of yours. **5** [20C+] fussiness, a fuss; thus *what a palaver*, what a fuss. **6** [1980s] (*UK Black*) an argument, a fight. [Port. *palabra*, speech, talk. The term was used by Port. traders on the West Coast of Africa, where it was picked up by British sailors, incorporated into their jargon and thence to mainstream sl.]

palaver *v.* **1** [mid-18C+] (*also* **pallaber**) to talk, to converse. **2** [mid-18C+] to ask (someone) for something, to beg from, to wheedle out of; thus *palaverer*, one who wheedles and flatters. **3** [1970s–80s] (*UK Black*) to go around, to wander about. [PALAVER n.]

pale *n.* **1** [mid-19C] brandy. **2** [1900s–40s] (*US Black*) a White person.

pale about/around the gills *phr. see* GREEN ABOUT THE GILLS phr.

paled (out) *adj.* [1960s+] (*Can. teen*) intoxicated by drink or drugs. [one's complexion; ? PALEFACE n. (1)]

paleface *n.* **1** [mid-19C] (*US*) whisky. **2** [mid-19C+] (*orig. US Black*) a White person. [SE *paleface*, supposedly used by Native Americans to describe White settlers, but rarely found other than in fiction]

palefaced *adj.* [20C+] a derog. term describing a White person. [PALEFACE n. (2)]

paleface nigger *n.* [1940s+] (*US Black*) a highly unpopular White person, whose skin does not save them from the opprobrium usu. heaped on Blacks. [PALEFACE n. (2) + NIGGER n.[1] (3)]

pale in the gills *phr. see* WHITE ABOUT THE GILLS phr.[1].

Palestine in London *n.* [early–mid-19C] St Giles, Bloomsbury, mainly occupied by the poor Irish and a well-known criminal slum. [i.e. the HOLY LAND n.]

palette *n.* [late 18C–mid-19C] the hand.

palimony *n.* [1970s+] compensation claimed by a deserted partner after a couple who are not married, but have lived together for some time, split up, usu. the province only of the rich and/or famous. [PAL n. (1) + SE *alimony*]

palings *n.* [mid-19C] (*boxing*) the ribs.

pal in (with) *v.* [mid-19C–1910s] **1** to become friendly with. **2** of a man, to cohabit with a woman. **3** to live with another man. **4** (*UK Und.*) to work with, e.g. a pickpocketing gang. [PAL n. (1)/PAL (WITH) v.]

Pal Joey *n.* [1940s–60s] (*orig. US*) a kept man; a pimp. [the book *Pal Joey*, by John O'Hara (1938–40)]

pall *n. see* PAL n. (1).

pall *v.*[1] [mid-19C] to detect. [ety. unknown; ? link to SE *paw*, to handle]

pall *v.*[2] [mid-19C] to stop, to cease; thus *pall that!* stop that! *you pall me*, you confound me. [orig. naut. jargon *pawl*, a short bar that locks the windlass or capstan and stops it from unwinding]

pallaber *v. see* PALAVER v. (1).

pallatic *adj. see* PALATIC adj.

pallbearers *n.* [late 19C] (*US*) an order of crackers.

palled *adj.* [mid-19C] not daring to say any more. [SE *appalled*]

palled-in *adj.* [1900s–30s] of a man, living with a woman. [PAL n. (1)]

palliard *n.* **1** [late 15C–18C] (*UK Und.*) a professional beggar (cf. CANTING CREW n.). **2** [mid-19C] (*UK/US Und.*) a beggar woman who uses a child, either her own or one borrowed for the purpose, to excite the pity of passers-by (this pity often increased by the child's piteous cries, created by judicious pinches and prods). [Fr. *paille*, straw, upon which the beggars slept as they wandered the country, taking nightly refuge in barns or outhouses. The antithesis of the UPRIGHT MAN n., palliards adorned themselves with faked but still convincingly hideous sores and wounds. Their clothes were invariably ragged, and their patched cloaks almost a badge of office. The term emerged *c.*1484, alongside its SE definition, 'a low or dissolute knave; a lewd fellow, a lecher, a debauchee' (*OED*)]

palliasse *n.* [19C] a prostitute. [SE *palliasse*, a straw bed or mattress]

pallish *adj. see* PALLY adj.

pall mall *n.* [late 19C] a woman. [rhy. sl. = GAL n. (1)]

pall off *v.* [late 19C] to travel as friends. [PAL n. (1)]

pally *n.*[1] [late 19C+] a direct term of address; intimacy is not mandatory. [PAL n. (2)]

pally *n.*[2] [1920s+] a dancehall. [*Palais de Dance*]

pally *adj.* (*also* **pallish**) [late 19C+] friendly, affectionate. [PAL n. (1)]

palm *n.* [late 19C] (*US*) a bribe.

palm *v.* **1** [late 17C+] to pass over, or receive, anything in a surreptitious manner. **2** [18C; 19C+] to pass counterfeit money, or anything fake. **3** [19C+] to pass over money as a bribe; thus *palmed*, used of one who has been bribed.

palmer *n.* **1** [late 17C–19C] a cheat who palms cards, dice etc. **2** [mid-19C] a shoplifter. **3** [mid-19C] a beggar who visits shops and claims to be collecting halfpence engraved with a harp, offering the shopkeeper 13 pence for a shilling's worth and persuading them to empty all their coppers on the counter. While they search the pile, the palmer hides as many coins as possible. [SE *palm*, to conceal in the palm of one's hand; (2) also puns on SE *palmer*, an itinerant monk, bound by vows of eternal poverty]

palmer house *v.* [1930s–40s] (*US Black*) to walk flat-footed; thus *palmer houses*, flat feet. [the walking done by the hard-working waiters of Chicago's *Palmer House* Hotel]

palm grease *n. see* PALM OIL n.

palming *n.* [mid-19C] (*UK Und.*) the robbery of a shop by a pair of thieves, one engaging the shopkeeper in banter, the other committing the robbery. [PALMER n. (2)]

palming-racket *n.* [early 19C] (*UK Und.*) the concealing of money in one's palm. [SE *palm*, to conceal in one's palm + RACKET n.¹ (1)]

palmistry *n.* **1** [early 18C] theft. **2** [1910s–20s] bribery. [PALM v./play on SE]

palm oil *n.* (*also* oil of palm(s), palm grease, palm soap) [early 17C; 19C+] money, usu. in the form of a bribe. [used to GREASE SOMEONE'S PALM v.]

palm-oil *v.* [late 19C] to bribe; to pay off. [PALM OIL n.]

paloma *n. see* POLONE n.

palomino *n.* [1930s–60s] (*orig. US Black*) an attractive woman. [SE *palomino*, 'a light brown or cream-coloured horse with pale mane and tail, believed to have been developed from Arab stock' (*OED*)]

palone(y) *n. see* POLONE n.

pal on(to) *v. see* PAL (WITH) v.

palooka *n.* [1920s+] (*US*) **1** a boxer, occas. wrestler, usu. one who is both large and stupid. **2** (*also* **palooko**) a large and stupid person. **3** a person, irrespective of size or intelligence. [coined by Jack Conway (d.1928) of *Variety* magazine, and given wide currency by Ham Fisher's comic strip 'Joe Palooka' (launched 1930)]

pal out (with) *v. see* PAL (WITH) v.

pal squad *n.* [1980s+] (*Aus. prison*) a dog squad used for searching cells. [proprietary name *Pal*, a dog food]

palsy *n.* (*also* **palsie, palsy-walsy**) [1930s+] (*orig. US*) a friend, esp. as a form of address. [ext. of PAL n. (1)]

palsy-walsy *adj.* [1930s+] overly friendly. [PALSY n. + redup.]

pal (with) *v.* (*also* **pal around/out/up (with), pal on(to), palsy (with)**) [late 19C+] to befriend, to associate with. [PAL n. (1)]

pam *n.* **1** [late 17C–1910s] the knave of clubs. **2** [18C–early 19C] a popular card-game. [Fr. *pamphile*, a card-game in which the knave of clubs is the highest card, trumping all opposition; ult. Gk *pamphilos*, beloved of all. The Fr. game was imported to Scot., where *pamphie* and *pawnie* were popular alternatives, both meaning knave of clubs, and to England, where *pam* became the term of choice]

pam and her five sisters *n.* [1990s+] the hand as an agency of masturbation (cf. CONVERSE WITH HARRY PALM v. [pun on *Pam/palm*]

pam-pam *n.* [1940s] (*W.I.*) **1** a flogging. **2** an argument, a fuss, a noisy disorder. [echoic; but note Twi *pam*, to chase away, and *pam-pam*, to persecute, to drive away]

pamper *v.* (*also* **palam-pam**) [20C+] (*W.I., Bdos*) to feel the sting of a lashing. [? W.I. *pam-palam*, a child's term, used to register their amusement at another child's punishment]

Pamper pirate *n.* (*also* **Pamper sniffer**) [1990s+] (*US Und.*) a child molester. [*Pampers*, brandname of a line of disposable nappies or diapers + SE *pirate/sniffer*]

pampoen *n.* [1940s+] (*S.Afr.*) a fool (sometimes used affectionately). [Cape Du. *pampoen*, pumpkin]

pampootie *n.* [1900s–60s] (*Irish*) a slipper. [Irish *pamúpta*, a basic leather shoe, but note Fr. *pantouffle*, a slipper]

pan *n.*¹ **1** [late 17C+] the female genital area. **2** [mid-19C+] (*US*) the mouth. **3** [1910s+] (*orig. and mainly US*) the human face. [SE *pan*; (1) and (2) as container; (3) as something round]

pan *n.*² [mid–late 19C] the workhouse, esp. the St Pancras workhouse. [abbr. St *Pancras*]

pan *n.*³ [1920s] (*US*) talent. [SE *brainpan*]

pan *n.*⁴ [1970s+] (*US gay*) the anus.

pan, the *n.* [20C+] (*Ulster*) a frying pan of food, a fry-up.

pan *v.*¹ [late 19C] (*US*) to catch. [SE *pan*, to sieve silt for gold]

pan *v.*² **1** [20C+] (*orig. US*) to criticize severely, to denigrate; also as n.; thus *on the pan*, facing criticism, under verbal attack. **2** [1940s+] to hit in the face. [the blow is lit. or fig. given with a SE *pan*]

pan *v.*³ *see* PANHANDLE v.

Panama cut *n.* (*also* **Panama gold, ...red**) [1960s+] (*drugs*) a variety of marijuana, grown in Panama (cf. ACAPULCO (GOLD) n.).

Panamite *n. see* PENNEMITE n.

Panarly *n. see* POLARI n.

panatella *n.* [1930s–60s] (*drugs*) **1** high-grade marijuana, esp. that imported from South or Central America. **2** a large marijuana cigarette, resembling a cigar (cf. AFRICAN WOODBINE n.). [Am. Sp. *panatella*, a long slender cigar tapering at the sealed end]

pancake *n.*¹ **1** [19C+] the vagina (cf. APPLE n.⁶). **2** [1930s+] (*US*) an attractive young woman, esp. with overtones of promiscuity.

pancake *n.*² [late 19C–1940s] (*US Black*) a Black person viewed as overly friendly towards, or imitative of, Whites. [SE *pancake*, cooked brown on the outside but still white within]

pancake *n.*³ (*US gay*) **1** [1950s] a masculine lesbian who permits herself to take the passive role. **2** [1970s+] a heterosexual woman. [she is 'flipped' from being 'on top' to 'underneath' in sexual terms]

pancake *v.* **1** [1950s] to flatten. **2** [1970s] (*US*) to knock down and run over. **3** [1980s+] (*US Black/teen*) to lower the body of an automobile. [making it 'flat as a pancake']

pancakes! *excl.* [1910s–20s] used to convey one's derision for what has just been said, e.g. *She's a pretty girl. Pretty, pancakes!*

pancakes and syrup *n.* [1990s+] (*drugs*) a combination of glutetimide and codeine cough syrup.

Pancho *n.* [1960s+] (*US*) **1** a derog. form of address to an anonymous Mexican man (cf. BATO n.). **2** a Puerto Rican. [the stereotypical Mexican name]

pancho *adj.* [1940s–60s] (*US*) pertaining to Mexicans or to Mexican lifestyle, fashions etc. [the stereotypical Mexican name]

pancridge parson *n.* [early 17C–mid-19C] a general term of contempt. [corruption of St *Pancras*, London, where the clergy were presumably held in low esteem]

pancrocked *adj.* [20C+] (*Ulster*) exhausted. [ety. unknown; ? link to CROCKED adj. (2)]

panda (car) *n.* [1960s+] a type of police patrol car painted black and white and thus supposedly reminiscent of the markings of the giant panda.

p and q *n.* [1990s+] (*US prison*) solitary confinement. [abbr. *peace and q*uiet]

pane *n. see* WINDOWPANE n.¹.

panel *n.*¹ *see* PANEL THIEF n.

panel *n.*² *see* PARNEL n.

panel *v.*¹ [mid-19C–1920s] to pursue the PANEL GAME n.¹.

panel *v.*² [1990s+] to attack, to beat up. [SE *panel-beat*]

panel crib *n.* (*also* **panel den, ...house, ...joint, ...store**) [mid-19C–1950s] a brothel, esp. one which specializes in robbing the clients (cf. BADGER-CRIB n.). [PANEL GAME n.¹ + CRIB n.¹ (2)/DEN n. (2)/HOUSE n.¹ (1)/JOINT n.⁴ (3)/SAmE *store*]

panel dodger *n. see* PANEL THIEF n.

panel game *n.*¹ [mid-19C–1940s] (*US Und.*) the robbing of a prostitute's client by stealing his possessions while he is having sex. [usu. performed in a PANEL CRIB n.; such brothels were supplied with false panels that permitted access to the prostitute's room so that the client could be robbed or beaten up]

panel game *n.*² (*also* **panel trick**) [late 19C] (*US Und.*) a form of confidence trick involving the passing of counterfeit money.

panel house/joint/store *n. see* PANEL CRIB n.

panelling *n.* [2000s] a beating. [PANEL v.²]

panel thief *n.* (*also* **panel, panel dodger, panel worker**) [mid-19C–1940s] (*US*) a thief, usu. the accomplice of a prostitute, who takes advantage of her client's preoccupation to rob him, using a special panel to enter the room. [PANEL GAME n.¹ + SE *thief/dodger/*WORKER n.¹ (1)]

panel trick *n. see* PANEL GAME n.².

panem *n. see* PANNAM n.

pane of glass *n. see* WINDOW n.

pang v. [20C+] (*Ulster*) to cram full. [Scot.]

pangonadalot n. [1970s+] (*drugs*) heroin. [ety. unknown]

panhandle n.[1] [mid-19C+] (*US*) the act of begging; thus the *panhandle beat*, the world of beggary; *work the panhandle*, to beg. [SE *pan*, into which the charitable donor placed money, or the goldfields, where hopefuls panned for gold, washing earth and rocks in perforated 'pans']

panhandle n.[2] [1990s+] **1** an erect penis. **2** a fool, an unpleasant person (cf. CHOAD n.). [(1) resemblance; (2) fig. use of (1)]

panhandle v. (*also* **pan**) [late 19C+] (*US*) to beg. [PANHANDLE n.[1]]

panhandler n. [late 19C+] (*orig. US*) a professional beggar. [PANHANDLE v.]

pan-head n. [1940s] (*W.I.*) a district constable. [the resemblance of their badge to a pan-lid]

pania n. [20C+] (*W.I., Belize*) a Belizian of Spanish descent. [*Span*iard; such individuals are seen as setting themselves aside from mainstream Belize society and culture]

panic n.[1] [1910s+] (*drugs*) a period when drugs are hard to purchase; thus *panic man*, a dealer or a drug addict who is desperate for supplies.

panic n.[2] **1** [1920s–50s] (*US Black*) someone or something outstanding, exceptional. **2** [1940s+] (*Irish*) someone or something ridiculous, amusing.

panic button n. [1950s+] any form of switch or button that summons emergency aid, shuts down malfunctioning machinery etc; thus *hit the panic button*, to panic, to summon aid (lit. or fig.).

panicked out adj. [1970s+] (*US*) in a complete panic.

panicky adj. [1940s] (*US Black*) extremely elated, ecstatically happy, highly excited.

panic party n. [1940s+] (*Aus.*) any sudden move. [WW1 naut. use *panic party*, the apparent abandoning of a decoy or Q-ship by its crew with the attention of luring a submarine to the surface. If the submarine did surface, it would be attacked by those members of the crew who had remained hidden on board]

panic stations n. [1960s+] a crisis, a drama. [orig. naval use and punning on 'action stations'. Note also milit. *panic party*, a rush move (see prev.)]

pan kibba n. [1940s] (*W.I.*) a district constable. [SE *pan cover*]

pannam n. (*also* **panem, pannum, pennam, pinum**) **1** [mid-16C–19C] (*UK Und.*) bread; thus [mid-19C] *pannam-fencer*, a street pastry-seller. **2** [late 19C–1930s] (*Aus.*) any form of food. [Lat. *panis*/Fr. *pain*, bread]

pannam bound v. [mid-19C] (*UK prison*) to stop the issue of rations to a prisoner. [PANNAM n. (1) + SE *bound*]

pannam-struck adj. [mid-19C] (*UK Und.*) very hungry. [PANNAM n. (1) + SE *struck*]

panney n.[1] (*also* **panny**) [mid-18C–mid-19C] the highway. [ety. unknown; ? Rom.]

panney n.[2] (*also* **panny**) [late 18C–mid-19C] (*UK Und.*) **1** a house. **2** a burglary; thus *do a panny*, to rob a house. [? SE *butler's pantry*, the repository of the silverware and similar valuables]

panney-lay n. (*also* **panny-lay**) [early 19C–1910s] burglary, house-breaking. [PANNEY n.[2] + LAY n.[4] (1)]

pannikin n. [late 19C–1930s] (*Aus.*) the head. [SE *pannikin*, a small iron drinking vessel]

pannikin boss n. (*also* **panno**) [late 19C+] (*Aus.*) a minor official, often officious. [SE *pannikin*, a small drinking vessel + BOSS n.[2] (1); *panno* is abbr. *panni*kin + -o sfx (4); the image is of one who was allowed to serve water to a gang of convicts]

panning n. [1930s+] very harsh criticism, e.g. a very bad review. [PAN v.[2] (1)]

pannum n. see PANNAM n.

panny see also under PANNEY and its comb.

panny n. [late 19C] a fight between 2 or more women. [? link to the women who work in a PANEL CRIB n.; note PANEL v.[2]]

pannyman n. [19C] a house-breaker, a burglar. [PANNEY n.[2] + SE sfx -*man*]

panorama n.[1] [late 19C] a lover. [corruption of SE *paramour*]

panorama n.[2] [late 19C] a hammer. [rhy. sl.; pronounced with a short 'a']

pan out v. **1** [mid-19C+] (*orig. US*) to work out, to result in. **2** [late 19C] (*Aus./US*) to hand over (money). [SE *pan*, to sieve silt for gold]

pansy n. (*also* **pansie**) **1** [late 19C–1900s] (*US*) an admirable person. **2** [1910s+] an effeminate and/or homosexual man. **3** [1920s] (*US Black*) a woman, one's girlfriend.

pansy adj. [1920s+] effeminate, homosexual. [PANSY n. (2)]

pansy v. [1960s–70s] (*US*) of a homosexual man, to act in an overtly effeminate manner. [PANSY n. (2)]

pansy up v. [1930s–70s] **1** of a man, to titivate oneself in an effeminate manner. **2** of a homosexual, to flirt. [PANSY n. (2)]

panter n.[1] **1** [late 17C–mid-19C] the human heart. **2** [late 18C–early 19C] (*UK Und.*) a hart or male deer. [the line 'As pants the hart for cooling streams/When heated in the chase' (Nahum Tate and Nicholas Brady, *New Version of the Psalms*, 1696); ult. f. Ps. 42:1, 'As the hart panteth after the water brooks so panteth my soul after thee, O God'. The pun indicates, as does B.E., that (2) is the general use. However, Grose (1785) cites 'the animal' and only adds 'the human heart, which temporarily pants in times of danger' in 1796]

panter n.[2] [1940s] underwear.

panters n. [late 19C–1900s] the female breasts (cf. BOBBER n.[2]). [their motion when breathing]

panther piss n. (*also* **panther, panther milk, ...purge, ...sweat**) [1930s+] strong home-brewed or cheap liquor, usu. gin (cf. BUFFALO PISS n.). [PISS n. (4)]

panties n. **1** [mid-19C] pantaloons (cf. PANTS n.[1]). **2** [mid-19C] (*US*) trousers. **3** [1970s+] (*US prison*) the underwear worn by a prison homosexual; also in general homosexual use.

pantile n.[1] (*also* **pantiler**) [late 18C–mid-19C] a religious dissenter; thus *pantile-house/-shop*, a dissenters' meeting house. [SE *pantile*, a roofing tile; the meeting houses of rural dissenters were often roofed with pantiles]

pantile n.[2] [mid-19C] **1** a hat. **2** a hard biscuit, sometimes with jam spread on it. [SE *pantile*, a tile in an ogee shape, often used as a roofing tile]

pantile adj. [18C] dissenting. [PANTILE n.[1]]

pantile park n. [late 19C] London, as seen from a high window. [SE *pantile*, a roofing tile + SE *park*]

pantiler n. see PANTILE n.[1].

pantomime cow n. see BULL AND COW n.

pant python n. see PYJAMA PYTHON n.

pantry n. **1** [1910s–20s] (*US*) the stomach. **2** [1920s] (*US Black*) the vagina.

pantry politics n. [late 19C] (*UK society*) servants' talk.

pants n.[1] **1** [mid-19C] pantaloons (cf. PANTIES n.). **2** [mid-19C+] (*US*) trousers. **3** [1920s] by metonymy, the buttocks.

pants n.[2] [late 19C–1910s; 1990s+] nonsense, rubbish; early use in phr. *one's name is pants* (cf. KNICKERS (TO YOU)! excl.).

pants n.[3] (*also* **pair of pants**) [1930s–40s] (*US Black*) a man. [metonymy]

pants, the n. [1910s+] the essence, usu. in phrs. with a v., — *the pants off*, to do something to excess, e.g. BORE THE PANTS OFF v., KID THE PANTS OFF v., SCARE THE PANTS OFF v., TAKE THE PANTS OFF v.

pants adj. [1990s+] rubbish, second-rate, inferior. [PANTS n.[2]]

pants v. [1940s+] (*US, mainly juv.*) to remove someone's trousers whether they like it or not. [PANTS n.[1] (2)]

pants! excl. [1990s+] nonsense! rubbish! [PANTS n.[2]]

pants man n. [1960s+] (*Aus.*) a womanizer.

pants rabbit n. [1910s+] (*US*) a body louse.

pantsula n. [1970s+] (*S.Afr.*) a township dandy whose life is dedicated to the purchase of expensive, fashionable clothes.

[? S. Sotho *patsola*, to split open (referring to links with violent crime); or ? S. Sotho *pasola*, to slap, to strike sharply (with a whip) (referring to elements of typical dance styles)]

pant-worm *n.* [1990s+] (*US prison*) the penis (cf. ANTEATER n.).

panty-assed *adj.* [1970s] (*US*) effeminate, homosexual. [PANTIES n. (3) + -ASSED sfx]

pantyman *n.* [20C+] (*W.I.*) an effeminate man, a homosexual. [the image of his wearing women's *panties*; note PANTIES n. (3)]

pantywaist *n.* [1930s+] (*orig. US*) a weak, effeminate man; thus as adj., weak, effeminate. [the image of his wearing women's *panties*]

panwit *n.* [1990s+] (*UK juv.*) a fool (cf. DAMWIT n.).

panya *adj.* [1940s+] (*W.I.*) Spanish. [mispron. of *Spanish*]

panzer head *n.* [1980s] a term of abuse used of someone who is or resembles a German. [the German *Panzer*, lit. Panther, armoured units (and tanks) of WW2]

pap *n.*[1] **1** [mid-19C+] *paper* money. **2** [1900s] (*US*) a news*paper*. [abbr.; (1) orig. UK but mid-20C+ Aus. only]

pap *n.*[2] *see* PAPA n. (1).

pap *n.*[3] *see* POP n.[5].

pap *adj.* (*also* **pappy**) [1910s+] (*S.Afr.*) of persons or objects, weak, feeble. [Afk. *pap*, soft]

papa *n.* **1** [late 19C+] (*US*) (*also* **pap**) an affectionate name used by a woman to her husband, lover or pimp (cf. BIG DADDY n.). **2** [1920s+] (*US*) oneself. **3** [1930s–40s] (*US Und.*) a Lincoln automobile. **4** [1940s+] (*US*) a masculine lesbian. **5** [1950s+] (*US*) an older homosexual man. [SE *papa*, father]

papa-tree-top-tall *n.* [1930s–40s] (*US Black*) an extremely tall man.

papbroek *n.* [1930s+] (*S.Afr.*) a coward, a weakling. [Afk. *pap*, soft + *broek*, trousers, breeches]

pape *n.* [20C+] a Roman Catholic. [SE *papist*]

paper *n.*[1] (*also* **papers**) **1** [late 18C+] any form of money order, IOU, promissory note or financial document other than actual cash. **2** [late 18C+] (*orig. US Black*) money, usu. notes (cf. BANK-RAG n.). **3** [late 18C+] free passes of admission to a theatre or other entertainment. **4** [late 18C+] the people who use these passes. **5** [mid-19C] (*US*) playing cards. **6** [mid-19C] (*US*) an admission ticket, e.g. to a dance; also a forged ticket. **7** [mid-19C] (*UK Und.*) counterfeit banknotes. **8** [late 19C–1920s] (*US*) marked cards. **9** [late 19C–1940s] (*US*) posters or similar publicity material. **10** [20C+] (*US*) a forged or useless cheque or other financial instrument. **11** [1930s–60s] (*US tramp*) a railroad ticket. **12** [1930s+] (*drugs*) cigarette papers, esp. when used for rolling marijuana cigarettes. **13** [1940s+] any form of legal or similarly authoritative documentation, e.g. a marriage certificate, prison documentation. **14** [2000s] (*US prison*) proof that a prisoner is an informer.

paper *n.*[2] (*US drugs*) **1** [1920s–40s] a sheet of paper impregnated with a drug in solution or any other form of smuggling drugs into prison. **2** [1920s+] a measure of heroin, contained in a folded square of paper; the most common is the *quarter paper*, $25 worth of a narcotic. **3** [1960s–70s] a drug prescription. **4** [1990s+] crack cocaine (cf. BASE n.). **5** [2000s] a small amount of methamphetamine.

paper *v.* **1** [late 19C+] to boost an audience by giving out free passes to a show or entertainment; thus *papered/papery*, filled by means of free passes. **2** [1920s+] (*US*) to pass bad cheques or any other form of fraudulent money-related document. [PAPER n.[1]]

paper acid *n.* [1960s+] (*drugs*) LSD, esp. when dropped onto a square of blotting-paper, or when combined with another drug (cf. A n.[3]).

paper bag *v.* [20C+] to nag. [rhy. sl.]

paper boy *n.* **1** [1960s] (*drugs*) a heroin peddler. **2** [1990s+] a boy who has had sex with a lot of people in his area. [SE pun on *paper boy*; (1) + PAPER n.[2] (2); (2) they HAVE BEEN AROUND v.]

paper chaser *n.* [2000s] (*US Black*) one who is looking for money, usu. a drug dealer. [PAPER n.[1] (2)]

paper-collared swell *n.* [mid–late 19C] (*N.Z.*) a clerk, a 'white-collar worker'. [SE *paper collar*, as worn by clerks pretending to superior elegance + SWELL n. (1)]

paper doll *n.* [1970s+] a promiscuous, sexually available woman. [rhy. sl. = MOLL n.[1] (1)]

paper doll *v.* [1940s] (*US*) to play truant; thus phr. *make like a paper doll and cut*, go away. [pun on SE *cut out*/CUT OUT v.[4]]

paperer *n.* [late 19C] one who issues or receives free passes to a theatre or other entertainment. [PAPER n.[1] (3)]

paper-fake *v.* [mid-19C] to sell ballads on the street. [SE *paper* + FAKE v.[1] (2)]

paper fiend *n.* [1940s–50s] (*drugs*) one who sucks the amphetamine-impregnated strips from an amphetamine inhaler. [PAPER n.[2] (1) + FIEND n.[2] (1)]

paper-hanger *n.* (*also* **paper-layer**) [early 19C; 1910s+] (*US Und.*) one who habitually passes bad cheques; thus *paper-hanging*, passing dud cheques. [PAPER n.[1] (10) + pun; note Sutherland, *The Professional Thief* (1936), claims that this is a term used only by amateurs, never by professional thieves]

paper hat *n.* [1960s+] a fool (cf. BEECHAM'S PILL n.). [rhy. sl. = PRAT n.[1] (6)]

paper maker *n.* [mid–late 19C] **1** a gatherer of rags and other saleable rubbish from the streets and gutters. **2** a beggar who poses as an agent of a paper-mill and is thus given cast-off rags, which are then sold for profit.

paper man *n.* [mid-19C] (*Aus.*) a convict holding a ticket of leave. [SE *paper* + *man* but note later PAPER n.[1] (13)]

paper marriage *n.* [late 19C] a society wedding. [PAPER n.[1] (2); the banknotes employed in funding it; there may be an added implication of *paper*, spurious, i.e. the marriage is for social convenience rather than love]

paper mill *n.* [mid-19C] (*US*) a small, unstable bank. [PAPER n.[1] (2)]

paper minister *n.* [mid-19C] (*Scot.*) a minister who reads their sermons rather than learning them by heart.

paper mushrooms *n.* [1980s+] (*drugs*) LSD, esp. that which has been dropped onto blotting-paper (cf. A n.[3]). [the hallucinogenic qualities of certain mushrooms]

paper pusher *n.* [20C+] a bureaucrat or clerk of the lowliest rank, the implication being that they never write on, only push around, paper; thus as v., *push paper*.

paper-pushing *n.* [1970s] working in an office or as a clerk. [PAPER PUSHER n.]

papers *n.* *see* PAPER n.[1].

paper skull *n.* (*also* **paper scull**) [late 17C–early 19C] a fool; thus *paper-skulled/-sculled*, foolish, simple. [lit. 'one with a paper-thin skull']

paper stainer *n.* [mid–late 19C] a clerk. [SE *paper-stainer*, an author]

paper whip *v.* *see* PENCIL WHIP v. (2).

paperwork *n.* [1990s+] money. [PAPER n.[1] (2) + pun on SE *paperwork*, documents]

paper worker *n.* [mid-19C] a street-seller of broadsides. [SE *paper*]

paper yabber *n.* [late 19C–1930s] (*Aus.*) a letter. [SE *paper* + YABBER n.]

papes *n.* [1990s+] (*orig. US Black*) money. [PAPER n.[1] (2)]

pap feeder *n.* [mid-19C] a spoon. [SE *pap*, liquefied food given to babies and invalids]

paphian *n.* [late 16C–mid-17C; 19C–1900s] a prostitute; thus the *Paphian game*, prostitution. [*Paphos*, the city in southwestern Cyprus, where it is claimed that Aphrodite, goddess of love, was born]

papi *n.* [2000s] (*US Black*) a Black person or a Puerto Rican. [P.R. *papi*, father]

papiyot *n.* [20C+] (*W.I.*) a weakling, a frail person, a useless opponent in a game. [Fr. *papillon*, a butterfly]

paplar *n. see* POPLARS *n.*

pappy *n.* **1** [mid-18C+] (*US juv.*) father, papa. **2** [1920s–40s] (*US Black*) male lover. **3** [1940s+] an old man.

pappy *adj.*[1] [1930s–60s] (*US*) old, esp. exhibiting the signs of the old.

pappy *adj.*[2] *see* PAP *adj.*

pappy guy *n.* [1900s–20s] (*US tramp*) an old man. [PAPPY n. (1) + GUY n.[2] (1)]

pappy show *see under* POPPY SHOW.

paps *n.*[1] [16C; 1960s+] breasts (cf. BORDENS *n.*).

paps *n.*[2] [1970s–80s] (*UK Black*) a father.

paps *n.*[3] [1990s+] *paparazzi.*

par *v.* [1990s+] (*W.I.*) to relax with, to associate with. [abbr. SE *party*]

para *n.* [2000s] *paranoia.* [abbr.]

para *adj.* (*also* **parro**) [1980s+] *paranoid.* [abbr.]

parable *n.* [late 19C] (*US*) a long, dreary, egotistical statement.

parachute *n.*[1] [mid-19C] a parasol.

parachute *n.*[2] **1** [1940s] (*US Black/drugs*) a marijuana cigarette (cf. BOMB n.[4]). **2** [1980s+] (*drugs*) a mixture of crack cocaine plus heroin or phencyclidine. [it gets one HIGH adj.[1] (2); (2) + the 'slowness' of the heroin or phencyclidine reduces the 'speed' of the crack cocaine]

paracki *n.* [1950s+] (*drugs*) paraldehyde, a polymer of aldehyde used both as a narcotic and as a legitimate treatment for insomnia. [abbr.]

paradise *n.* [mid-19C] the upper gallery of a theatre, the 'gods'. [Fr. sl. *paradis*, the gods]

paradise strokes *n.* [20C+] for a man, the immediately pre-orgasmic thrusts of sexual intercourse.

paradise (white) *n.* [1980s+] (*drugs*) cocaine (cf. BLANCA n.). [its effects]

paraffin *n.*[1] [20C+] (*S.Afr.*) gin. [rhy. sl.]

paraffin *n.*[2] [1920s+] (*Scot.*) style. [rhy. sl.; *paraffin oil*, pron. 'ile' = style]

paraffin lamp *n.* **1** [20C+] a tramp. **2** [2000s] a sexually promiscuous woman. [rhy. sl.; (2) = TRAMP n. (1)]

paraic *adj.* [1980s] (*Irish*) fierce, strong. [rhy. sl.; *Padraig Pearse* = fierce; ult. Irish politician and revolutionary *Padraig Pearse* (1879–1916)]

parakeet *n.* [1960s] (*US*) a Puerto Rican (cf. BATO n.). [their stereotyped noisiness and love of bright colours; note WW1 Aus. milit. *parakeet*, 'Staff Officer [...] So called from the red gorget tabs and the red band around the hat of a Staff Officer' (*Pretty*, 1924)]

parallel parking *n.* [1980s+] (*orig. US preppie/campus*) sexual intercourse.

paralysed *adj.* (*also* **handicapped**, **paralyzed**) **1** [late 19C+] drunk; thus *paralyse*, to make drunk; also intoxicated by drugs (cf. AFFLICTED adj.). **2** [late 19C–1900s] (*US*) knocked out, incapable; also in fig. use as stunned, shocked; thus *paralyser*, that which has such effects.

paralyser *n.* [1910s] (*Aus.*) a strong drink. [PARALYSED adj. (2)]

paralytic *adj.* [mid-19C+] (*orig. Aus.*) extremely drunk, to the point of passing out cold (cf. AFFLICTED adj.).

paralytic *adv.* [1900s] (*Aus.*) completely.

paralyzed *adj. see* PARALYSED adj.

parangles *n.* [1940s] (*W.I.*) bustle and confusion, trouble and worry, any bothersome, complicated situation. [UK dial. *peramble*, a rigmarole, ult. SE *preamble*. Legal papers, wills and similar material tend to begin with a summary preamble before moving to the detailed clauses]

paranoid *adj.* [1960s] frightened, worried, disturbed. [all non-clinical uses originated in 1960s HIPPIE n.[2] (3) era, often occasioned by an excess of drug use; ult. SE *paranoia*, 'functional

psychosis characterized by delusions of grandeur and persecution, but without intellectual deterioration' (C. Rycroft, *A Critical Dictionary of Psychoanalysis*, 1968)]

parater/paratie *n. see* PRATIE *n.*

par-banging *n.* [late 19C] tramping the streets. [? Fr. *pavé*, the pavement + BANG v.[1] (1)]

parcel *n.* **1** [late 16C+] (*US*) a small group, amount or collection. **2** [late 19C] a young woman. **3** [late 19C] a British woman sold into a foreign brothel. **4** [late 19C–1920s; 1990s+] a substantial sum of money, esp. when won or lost in gambling. **5** [20C+] (*Ulster*) a difficult, troublesome person; a term of abuse. **6** [1910s] (*Aus. tramp*) a rolled blanket which contains one's possessions. **7** [2000s] a bulk consignment of drugs.

parcel from Paris *n. see* PACKET FROM PARIS *n.*

parcel post *n.* [1930s–50s] (*Aus.*) used in the Northern Territory to describe a person who is newly arrived and thus inexperienced. [? the image of an unwrapped parcel]

parched *adj.* [1920s+] very thirsty.

parchment dab *n.* [early 18C] a writ. [SE *parchment* + *dab*, a mark]

pard *n.* (*also* **pardner**, **podna**, **podner**, **potna**) [late 18C; mid-19C+] (*US*) partner, esp. as a term of address. [a classic 'Wild West' term, its 20C+ use is exclusively fictional, mainly in films]

parental units *n.* [1980s+] (*US campus*) parents (cf. RENTAL UNITS n.). [originating in the 'Coneheads' sketches on the US TV show *Saturday Night Live* (cf. CONEHEAD n.)]

parings *n.* [late 17C–mid-19C] clippings of money. [E.P. suggests it is only a spec. use of SE *paring*, a thin portion pared off the surface of anything, usu. as refuse or superfluous matter; a shaving]

Paris brothers *n.* [1950s–60s] (*gay*) homosexuals, esp. twins. [play on stereotyped views of French sexuality]

Paris bun *n.* [20C+] a Protestant. [ety. unknown; ? link to Scot. *Paris bun*, a sweet sugar-topped, sponge-like bun]

parish *n.* [late 19C+] one's own area or neighbourhood; the area in which one has influence and/or does business.

parish bull *n.* (*also* **parish prig**) [18C–mid-19C] (*UK Und.*) a parson. [SE *parish* + *bull*/PRIG n.[1] (1)]

parisheen *n.* [late 19C–1910s] (*Irish*) a child brought up by the parish. [SE *parish* + Irish dimin. sfx *-een*]

parish lantern *n.* [mid–late 19C] the moon.

parish pick-axe *n.* [late 19C] a prominent nose.

parish prig *n. see* PARISH BULL n.

parish rig *n.* [late 19C] (*orig. naut.*) a badly-rigged ship; thus an ill-dressed man. [SE *parish-rigged*, cheaply rigged]

parish soldier *n.* [late 18C–mid-19C] a militia man. [the hiring of substitutes by the parish in which the orig. chosen militia men lived]

parish stallion *n.* [late 19C] a parson.

Parisian breasts *n.* [1990s+] small female breasts.

Paris model *n.* [1980s+] (*Aus. prison*) an attractive woman.

park *n.* [early–mid-19C] a prison.

park *v.*[1] [1910s+] **1** to place, to put down. **2** to sit. **3** to place oneself.

park *v.*[2] [1920s+] (*US*) of a (usu.) teenage couple, to park in a secluded spot for petting and, perhaps, sex.

park *v.*[3] [1940s–50s] to get rid of someone or something.

park *v.*[4] [1960s–70s] (*Ling. Fr./Polari*) **1** to ask, to speak, to beg. **2** to give. [Ital. *parlare*, to speak/*partire*, to pay out]

park a custard *v.* [1930s+] (*UK society*) to vomit (cf. BLOW CHOW v.).

park a darkie *v. see* CHOKE A DARKIE v.

park a leopard *v.* (*also* **park a tiger**) [1960s+] to vomit. [the 'spotted' or 'striped' nature of the material that is vomited up]

park ape *n.* [1940s+] (*US Black*) an extremely unattractive and very dark-skinned person. [? ref. to apes in Central Park Zoo, New York City]

parker *n.*[1] [mid–late 19C] a well-dressed man, a dandy. [his strolling in the fashionable London parks]

parker *n.*[2] [1920s–40s] (*US*) one (of a couple) who uses a parked car as a venue for sexual relations, intercourse or otherwise. [PARK v.[2]]

parker *v.*[1] [late 19C] (*Ling. Fr./Polari*) to pay; thus *parker from/with dinarly*, to pay one's debts. [Ital. *partire*, to pay out]

parker *v.*[2] [late 19C+] (*Ling. Fr./Polari*) to ask, to speak, to beg. [Ital. *parlare*, to speak]

parkering ninty *n.* [mid–late 19C] wages. [PARKER v.[1] + NANTEE n.]

parkers *n.* [1960s+] (*Aus.*) parking lights.

parkie *n. see* PARKY n.

parking *n.* [1950s+] (*US*) of a teenage couple, parking a car in a discreet spot for petting and possible intercourse. [PARK v.[2]]

parking lot *n.* **1** [1960s–70s] (*US teen*) the vagina. **2** [1980s] (*US campus*) a place where men congregate. [play on SE *park*, i.e. the penis + PARK v.[2]]

parking pet *n.* [1940s–60s] (*orig. US Black*) a girlfriend. [PARK v.[2] + SE *pet*]

park in the same lot *v.* [1990s+] (*orig. US*) to agree.

park one's carcass *v.* (*also* park one's arse, …biscuit, …can, …fanny, …frame, …stern) [1940s+] (*orig. US*) to sit down, esp. as an invitation. [PARK v.[1] (2) + SE *carcass*/ARSE n.[1] (1)/BISCUIT n.[2] (2)/CAN n.[1] (2)/FANNY n.[1] (2)/FRAME n.[1] (1)/STERN n.; note US radio comedian Harry Einstein (1904–58) used the pseudonym 'Parkyakarkus']

park one's fudge *v. see* FUDGE n.[2]

park-palings *n.* (*also* park-railings) **1** [early–mid-19C] the teeth. **2** [late 19C] a neck of mutton. [SE *park* + *palings*, a fence/*railings*]

park the pink cadillac *v.* [1990s+] to have sexual intercourse (cf. BURY IT v.).

Parktown prawn *n.* [1980s+] (*S.Afr.*) the king cricket (*Libanasidus vittatus*). [*Parktown*, an upper-class Johannesburg suburb + SE *prawn*; the cricket, which grows to 7cm (2¾in), can seem to resemble an outsize prawn]

parky *n.* (*also* parkie) [1940s+] a park-keeper.

parky *adj.* [late 19C+] chilly. [Midland dial.; ? ult. SE *perky*, sharp]

park yourself in a pew *phr.* (*also* take a pew) [late 19C+] an invitation to sit down. [PARK v.[1] (2) + PEW n. (1)]

Parlare/Parlary *n. see* POLARI n.

parlatic *adj. see* PALATIC adj.

parlay *v.* **1** [early 19C+] (*orig. US*) to improve one's position, esp. by taking what one already has, material or otherwise, and using it as the basis of one's next move. **2** [1990s+] (*US Black*) to calm down, to relax. [Ital. *paroli*, a cast at dice, which was taken up by faro and other card-players to mean to leave one's winnings on the table and then to stake double the sum already staked]

parlaying *n.* [1990s+] (*US Black*) partying, enjoying oneself. [PARLAY v. (2)]

parleyvoo *n.* (*also* parlay-voo) **1** [mid-18C+] the French language. **2** [early 19C+] (*also* parly) a French person. [PARLEYVOO v. (1)]

parleyvoo *adj.* **1** [early 19C+] French. **2** [late 19C+] foreign. [PARLEYVOO n.]

parleyvoo *v.* (*also* parley-vous) **1** [mid-18C+] to speak a foreign language, esp. to speak French. **2** [20C+] to chatter meaninglessly. [Fr. *parlez-vous?* do you speak?]

parliament *n. see* PARLIAMENT (HOUSE) n.

parliamentary *adj.* [1900s–20s] (*Irish*) respectable; esp. in phr. *the parliamentary side of one's arse.*

parliamentary whisky *n.* (*also* parliament whiskey) [late 18C–19C] (*Irish*) whisky on which duty has been paid, as opposed to contraband or home-distilled whisky.

parliament (house) *n.* [late 19C] a privy (cf. BACKHOUSE n.).

[one's 'sitting' there + ? pun on Cromwell's *Rump Parliament* (1648–53)]

parlor girl *n.* (*also* parlor house girl, parlor queen) [mid-19C–1900s; 1990s+] (*US*) a prostitute who works in a sophisticated, up-market brothel (cf. AWAYDAY GIRL n.). [PARLOR HOUSE n.]

parlor house *n.* [mid-19C–1960s] (*US*) a high-class brothel, situated in what appears to be a fashionably furnished middle-class house, and run by a complaisant 'aunt' whose bevy of attractive 'nieces' gather in the front parlour to meet, and make themselves available to visitors. Cheaper brothels had little more than bedrooms in which one had sex (cf. ACCOMMODATION HOUSE n.). [HOUSE n.[1] (1)]

parlor lizard *n.* (*also* parlor/parlour snake) [1910s–30s] (*US*) **1** (*also* parlour athlete) a poor or miserly man who would rather court a woman in her own house than take her out on the town. **2** (*also* parlor pink) a womanizer. [SAmE *parlor* + LIZARD sfx/SNAKE sfx]

parlor man *n.* [1910s] (*US Und.*) the safe-breaker who lights the fuse on a charge of nitroglycerine.

parlor queen *n. see* PARLOR GIRL n.

parlor snake *n. see* PARLOR LIZARD n.

parlour *n.* [late 17C–early 19C] the vagina; thus *let out one's parlour and lie backwards*, to work as a prostitute.

parlour athlete *n. see* PARLOR LIZARD n. (1).

parlour full of razors *n.* [1930s] (*US*) a drink composed of claret and lemonade.

parlour-jumper *n.* [late 19C–1910s] (*UK Und.*) a thief who robs private rooms or houses; thus *parlour-jumping*, practising such a form of robbery.

parlour pink *n.* [1920s+] a socialist whose activism is limited by the confines of their dinner table and does not extend onto the streets, let alone the barricades; also attrib. (cf. BOLLINGER BOLSHEVIK n.). [SE *parlour* + PINK n.[4]; an earlier form was *parlour Bolshevik*]

parlour snake *n. see* PARLOR LIZARD n.

parlous *n.* [late 17C–early 18C] a notably shrewd individual. [SE *parlous*, dangerously cunning, mischievous, capable of causing harm]

parly *n. see* PARLEYVOO n. (2).

Parlyaree *n. see* POLARI n.

parm! *excl.* [1930s+] an abbr. of SE *pardon me!*

parnel *n.* (*also* panel) [17C] a prostitute who works in a brothel rather than walking the streets. [SE *parnel*, a priest's concubine or mistress, a harlot, a wanton young woman]

Parnell shout *n.* [1910s–40s] (*N.Z.*) shared payment for food or drinks. [*Parnell*, a run-down suburb of Auckland + SHOUT n.[1] (1)]

parney *n.* **1** [mid-19C+] (*Anglo-Ind.*) (*also* parny) a shower of rain. **2** [late 19C–1930s] (*also* pawnce, pawni) water. **3** [20C+] (*Ling. Fr./Polari*) tears (in the eyes). [Rom. *pani*, water, ult. Hind. *pani*, water]

paro *adj.* [2000s] extremely drunk or intoxicated by a drug (cf. AFFLICTED adj.). [abbr. PARALYTIC adj.]

parole dust *n.* [1970s+] (*US prison*) fog (which aids in escapes).

Parra *n.* [1950s+] (*Aus.*) an inhabitant of the western suburbs of Sydney. [abbr. *Parramatta*, New South Wales, one of those suburbs]

parro *adj. see* PARA adj.

parrot *n.* [1910s] (*Aus.*) a flask of whisky. [? brandname]

parrot and monkey time *n.* (*also* parrotty time) [late 19C] (*US*) an unhappy marriage, in which the 2 partners fight continually.

parsley *n.*[1] [mid-19C] female pubic hair. [? resemblance]

parsley *n.*[2] [1900s–10s] nonsense, rubbish. [? the insignificance of the herb]

parsley *n.*[3] [1970s] (*drugs*) **1** marijuana (cf. AFRICAN BUSH n.).

2 phencyclidine (cf. ACE n.[4]). [the use of parsley as a base for smoking phencyclidine]

parsley bed n. [early 17C–19C] the vagina; both in the context of copulation and as a euph. used to children (cf. BEAUTY SPOT n.). [esp. as the answer to the question 'where do babies come from'; trad. the *parsley bed* brings girls, while boys come from the less appealing nettle bed or from beneath the gooseberry bush]

parson n. [late 18C–early 19C] a signpost, esp. a finger-post. [the parson supposedly 'sets people in the right way' (Grose, 1785)]

parsoned adj. [late 19C] married.

parson palmer n. [mid-18C–early 19C] anyone who stops a communal glass circulating by talking before passing it on. [a real-life, if forgotten, clergyman]

parson's barn n. [late 18C] a place that is 'never so full but there is still room for more' (Grose, 1796).

parson's collar n. [1940s+] the froth on top of a glass of beer.

parson's face n. *see* MINISTER'S FACE n.

parson's mousetrap n. (*also* **mousetrap**) [late 17C–19C] marriage. [the role played by a clergyman in solemnizing the wedding ceremony]

parson's nose n. (*also* **bishop's nose, deacon's nose, pope's nose**) [late 18C+] the rump of a chicken, duck, goose or other poultry. [the n. varies as to one's religion, so *pope's nose* is usu. Protestant use]

parson's week n. [late 18C+] Monday to Saturday, esp. a holiday that lasts from Monday to Saturday. [irrespective of other duties, the clergyman's trad. 'working day' is Sunday]

parson's wife n. [1920s+] (*Aus.*) gin, esp. Vicker's Gin. [pun on *Vickers/vicar's* + GIN n.[1] (2)/SE *gin*]

parson trulliber n. [mid-19C] a rude, vulgar country clergyman. [SE *parson* + f. the 'pig-feeding and pig-headed' (Hotten, 1873) eponymous character in Fielding's *Joseph Andrews*]

part v. [mid-19C–1960s] to give up, to hand over, to restore (usu. of money). [SE *part with*]

partake of His Majesty's hospitality v. (*also* **partake of Her Majesty's hospitality**) [late 19C–1930s] to spend time in prison (cf. ANOTHER DAY UP THE QUEEN'S ARSE phr.). [joc. var. on SE *at His/Her Majesty's pleasure*]

part brass rags v. (*also* **part doll rags**) [20C+] to part on bad terms. [naval custom of 2 sailors, when on good terms, sharing their cleaning rags]

parter n. [mid–late 19C] a generous person, one who pays up without complaint. [PART v.]

partial adj. [late 18C] inclining more to one side than another; crooked.

Partick Thistle n. [20C+] a whistle. [rhy. sl.; ult. the Scot. football team *Partick Thistle*]

particular n. [19C–1910s] one's special choice, e.g. *a glass of my particular*.

particular adv. [mid–late 19C] especially, very much, very.

particulars n. [1970s+] (*US prison*) any member of the authorities who has an immediate effect on a prisoner's life, a warder, the sentencing judge, the parole board etc.

partner n.[1] [19C] the penis.

partner n.[2] (*also* **pahtner**) [1940s+] (*US*) a friend.

part of the furniture n. [late 18C; 1910s+] anything or anyone so familiar as to make no more impression than a familiar piece of furniture. [note SE *wallpaper*, of a person or thing, unobtrusive]

part one's head with a towel v. [late 19C] (*US*) to be bald.

partridge n. [mid-17C–18C] a prostitute (cf. ALLEY CAT n.).

parts of shame n. [19C] the vagina. [trans. of Lat. *pudendum*, lit. 'that which is shameful']

part someone's hair v. [late 19C+] (*US*) **1** to shoot at someone, to kill someone. **2** to hit someone on the head.

part that goes over the fence last n. [late 19C] (*US*) the buttocks (cf. WHERE THE SUN DOESN'T SHINE n.; YOU-KNOW n.[1]; YOU KNOW WHERE n.). [euph.]

part the red sea v. [1990s+] to masturbate a woman.

part the whiskers v. *see* SPLIT THE BEARD v.

part up v. [1900s–50s] (*Aus.*) to pay money. [ext. of PART v.]

party n.[1] **1** [19C+] a man or woman; still found in *old party*, and the basis of such legal terms as *the guilty party*, and *being a party to*. **2** [1940s] a girlfriend. [(1) SE from 15C]

party n.[2] **1** [1920s+] any form of sex act, usu. provided by a prostitute. **2** [1960s+] a sexual encounter involving 2 or more women and 1 man. **3** [1960s+] an orgy. **4** [1960s+] a sexual encounter between 2 homosexual men. **5** [1960s+] a difficult, demanding situation.

party adj. [1980s+] (*US teen*) hedonistic.

party v. **1** [1930s+] (*also* **party time, party it up**) to enjoy oneself. **2** [1940s+] to have sex, often in prostitute use. **3** [1960s+] to partake in an orgy. **4** [1960s+] to drink or take drugs. **5** [1960s+] to offer sex to another person.

party animal n. [1980s+] anyone notably devoted to going out and having a good time.

party balloon n. **1** [1970s] a breathalyser. **2** [1990s+] (*US*) a condom.

party boy n. [1960s+] (*US*) a male homosexual prostitute. [PARTY n.[2] (1)]

party down v. [1970s+] (*orig. US Black*) to enjoy oneself very much; thus as adj., hedonistic. [PARTY v. (1)]

party favors n. [1980s+] (*US campus*) drugs.

party foul v. [1980s+] (*US campus*) to behave in a socially unacceptable manner at a party, esp. to vomit or spill alcohol; also as n. or excl. *party foul!* that was a blunder! how embarrassing! (cf. PARTY HEARTY v.). [PARTY v. (1) + SE *foul*]

party girl n. [1920s–60s] a promiscuous young woman, not necessarily a prostitute, a 'good-time girl' (cf. AWAYDAY GIRL n.). [PARTY n.[2] (1)]

party hat n. **1** [1970s+] (*US*) the flashing light on top of a police car. **2** [1980s+] (*orig. US campus*) a condom.

party hearty v. [1980s+] (*US teen*) to have a good time at a party (cf. PARTY FOUL v.). [PARTY v. (1) + assonance]

party hop v. [1980s+] (*orig. US*) to move from one party to the next and so on during the course of a single evening and night. [SE *party* + HOP v.[1] (7)]

party it up v. *see* PARTY v. (1).

party on! excl. [1980s+] (*US teen*) a general excl. of approval, either 'enjoy yourself!' 'have a good time!' or, more broadly, 'good job!' [PARTY v. (1); popularized by the film *Wayne's World* (1992)]

party out v. [1990s+] (*orig. US*) to outlast one's fellow-celebrants in one's ability to consume drink and/or drugs (and to become exhausted thereby). [PARTY v. (1)]

party pooper n. (*also* **party poop**) [1950s+] (*orig. US*) a spoilsport, one who sabotages the pleasures and enjoyments of their companions, whether at a party or other amusement. [SE *party* + POOP v.[3] (3)]

party time v. *see* PARTY v. (1).

party tits n. [1990s+] artificially enlarged breasts, esp. as adopted by young and famous women, which are then displayed at social and other occasions. [SE *party* + TIT n.[3] (1)]

parve n. [1980s] (*Aus.*) a parvenu. [clipping]

pasadeno phr. [1940s+] a phr. of rejection/ignorance, 'I don't know', 'don't ask me'. [play on PASS v.[1]]

pasata grin n. *see* MEXICAN LIPSTICK n.

pas de Lafarge phr. [mid-19C] (*UK society*) don't be dull, that's boring. [lit. 'no Lafarge (talk)'; the 1840s French case of the alleged poisoner Madame *Lafarge*; the frequency of dinner-party conversations about the case led to it becoming a synon. for tedium]

pasear n. [mid-19C–1940s] (*US*) a walk or stroll, often used fig. to describe something more substantial (a trek across mountains) or portentous (a journey to prison). [Sp. *pasear*, to walk. The term is used of the trad. evening promenade in Sp. or S. American towns]

pash *n.* **1** [1910s+] an infatuation, usu. between junior and senior pupils of girls' schools or between a schoolgirl and a female teacher. **2** [1910s+] passion. **3** [1930s] a lover. **4** [1950s+] (*Aus.*) a session of sexual fondling. [abbr. SE *passion*]

pash *adj.* [1920s] passionate, obsessive. [abbr.]

pashed up *adj.* [1930s] (*US*) sexually obsessed. [PASH *n.* (1)]

pash on *v.* (*also* **pash off**) [1920s+] (*US/Aus.*) to flirt, to indulge in heavy petting or even intercourse. [PASH *n.* (2)]

pash show *n.* [1950s+] (*Aus.*) **1** a film that includes candid sex scenes. **2** enthusiastic love-making. [PASH *n.* (4)]

pas op! *excl.* [early 19C+] (*S.Afr.*) be careful! look out! [Afk. *oppassen*, to be on guard]

pass *v.*[1] (*also* **pass up, give a pass, put a pass**) [late 19C+] to ignore, to have no interest in; esp. in phr. *I'll pass*, as a response to an offer or suggestion. [card-playing imagery]

pass *v.*[2] **1** [20C+] of a light-skinned Black person, to pose as White. **2** [1930s+] of a Jew, to pretend to be a Christian. **3** [1950s] of a policeman, to masquerade as a 'citizen'. **4** [1950s+] of a homosexual, to appear heterosexual to those one encounters; similarly of a transsexual, to 'pass' as a woman or man.

pass *v.*[3] [1910s] (*Aus.*) to pawn stolen goods.

pass *v.*[4] [1980s] (*US campus*) to become unconscious (from drink or drugs). [SE *pass out*]

pass a sham saint *v.* [early 18C] to play the hypocrite.

pass-bank *n.* [late 17C–early 19C] a gaming ground.

passenger *n.*[1] **1** [mid-19C+] one who, while nominally one of a group, team, crew etc, takes no active or useful part in the general efforts. **2** [2000s] (*US prison*) a friend.

passenger *n.*[2] [late 19C–1930s] (*US*) a passenger train; thus *passenger stiff*, a tramp who rides passenger or fast freight trains.

passenger on the Cape Ann stage, be a *v.* [mid-19C] (*US campus*) to be drunk. [ety. unknown; ? anecdotal]

passer *n.* [1920s–80s] one who passes counterfeit money.

pass for grass *v.* [20C+] (*W.I., Guyn.*) to be treated disrespectfully, to be someone who does not matter. [the 'invisibility' of grass]

pass in *v.* [1900s] (*Aus.*) to die. [PASS IN ONE'S CHECKS *v.*]

pass in one's alley *v. see* THROW IN ONE'S ALLEY *v.* (1).

pass in one's checks *v.* (*also* **pass in one's counters**) **1** [mid-19C+] (*orig. US*) to die (cf. CASH (IN) ONE'S CHECKS *v.*). **2** [1900s] to come to one's limit. [gambling imagery]

pass in one's chips *v.* [late 19C+] (*orig. US*) to die (cf. CASH (IN) ONE'S CHECKS *v.*). [gambling imagery]

pass in one's dinner pail *v. see* HAND IN ONE'S DINNER PAIL *v.*

pass in one's marble(s) *v.* (*also* **roll in one's marble(s), throw...**) [1900s–50s] (*Aus.*) to die.

passion cramps *n.* [1940s] of a male, the physical signs of sexual frustration.

passion flaps *n.* [1990s+] the labia (cf. DEW-FLAPS *n.*). [FLAPS *n.* (2)]

passion fruit *n.* [1960s] (*US gay*) a masculine homosexual. [pun on SE *passion fruit*/FRUIT *n.*[2] (2)]

passion gap *n.* (*also* **love gap**) [1950s+] (*S.Afr.*) the space between the front teeth; such spaces are created by the extraction of up to 4 teeth.

passion pit *n.* **1** [19C] the vagina (cf. BLACK HOLE *n.*[1]). **2** [1930s+] (*US*) a drive-in cinema. **3** [1960s+] (*Aus.*) anywhere that sex takes place. [(2) the petting and/or sex going on]

passion stick *n.* (*also* **passion**) [1950s] (*Aus.*) the penis (cf. BAT *n.*[7]). [SE *passion* + STICK *n.*[1] (1)]

passion wagon *n.* (*also* **kiss wagon**) [1950s+] any vehicle, often a van, in which teenage boys or young men hope to seduce young women. [note 1940s+ milit. use, the truck taking men for a day's, or part of a day's, leave, into a town or place of entertainment; note synon. RMC Duntroon (Aus.) *shag wagon*]

passive bucket *n.* [1920s] a quiescent listener. [no matter what 'garbage' is poured into it, this bucket remains a willing receptacle]

pass oneself *v.* [20C+] (*Ulster*) to behave as expected. [? abbr. SE *surpass*]

pass oneself out *v. see* PASS OUT *v.* (1).

pass one's mouth on *v.* [20C+] (*W.I.*) to slander, to speak rudely about. [var. on SE *pass an opinion/a remark*]

pass out *v.* **1** [late 19C–1940s] to die; thus *pass oneself out*, to commit suicide. **2** [1900s] (*Aus.*) to disqualify. **3** [1900s–10s] (*Aus.*) to knock out. **4** [1920s+] to fall asleep, usu. as a result of drink or drugs.

pass paper *v.* [1970s] to use forged cheques, stolen credit cards etc. [SE *pass* + PAPER *n.*[1] (10)]

passremarkable *adj.* [1980s+] (*Irish*) **1** worthy of comment. **2** prone to making tactless remarks. [SE *pass a remark*, to comment]

pass someone a jolt *v. see* JOLT *v.*[1] (2).

pass someone one *v.* [1900s–10s] (*Aus.*) to hit someone.

pass the bone *v.* [1990s+] (*US campus*) to share experience, to pass on information.

pass the buck *v.* **1** [mid-19C+] (*orig. US*) (*also* **put the buck**) to shift responsibility onto another; thus *buck-passer*, one who will not take responsibility on themselves; *buck-passing*, avoiding one's responsibilities. **2** [20C+] to die. **3** [1900s–40s] (*US*) to chatter, to tell tales. [abbr. SE *buckhorn knife*; in mid-19C games of poker it was the custom to place an object, typically a knife, in front of the person who was to deal. When this person had dealt, the knife was passed onto the next player. If a player did not wish to deal, they were allowed to ante and 'pass the buck']

pass the compliment *v.* [late 19C–1900s] to give a tip.

pass the flute *v. see* FLUTE *v.*[1].

pass the pikes *v.* [mid-17C–18C] to be out of danger. [SE *turnpike*, a toll gate; villains who had passed this barrier might presume themselves free of effective pursuit]

pass through the fire *v.* [19C] to catch venereal disease, i.e. to be BURNED *adj.*[1].

pass up *v. see* PASS *v.*[1].

pasta-breath *n.* [1980s] (*US*) a derog. term for an Italian or Italian-American (cf. DAGO *n.*). [the stereotypical Ital. food]

paste *n.*[1] (*also* **population paste**) [mid-19C; 1980s+] semen (cf. BOLLOCK SNOT *n.*). [resemblance]

paste *n.*[2] [1910s–30s] a hit or blow. [PASTE *v.*]

paste *v.* [mid-19C+] to hit hard. [var. on SE *baste*, to beat, to thrash]

pasteboard *n.* **1** [mid-19C] an invitation. **2** [mid-late 19C] a visiting card; also as v., to leave one's card; thus *leave/lodge/shoot/drop one's pasteboard*, to leave one's card. **3** [mid-late 19C] a playing card. **4** [mid-19C–1900s] a railway ticket. **5** [late 19C–1910s] a betting ticket, issued by a bookmaker. **6** [late 19C–1930s] a ticket to the theatre, cinema etc. [SE *pasteboard*, a thin card made of pasting together 3 or more sheets of paper]

pasted *adj.* [1950s+] (*US*) intoxicated by drink or drugs. [fig. use of PASTE *v.*]

paste eater *n.* [1980s] (*US campus*) a socially inept person. [? one who has fig. eaten poisonous wallpaper paste; ? one who stays by the wallpaper at a social function]

paste-horn *n.* [19C] the nose. [SE *pastehorn*, a cow's horn used to hold paste]

paste in *v.* [late 19C–1900s] (*US*) to pawn. [? SE *pass in*]

pastel *n.* [1980s] (*US police*) an unmarked police car. [the usual colouring]

pasties *n.* [1980s+] (*US drugs*) dryness in the mouth after smoking cannabis. [? PASTED *adj.* or Sp. *pasto*, marijuana; lit. 'a pasture']

pasting *n.* **1** [mid-19C+] a violent assault, a beating up. **2** [1940s+] in fig. use, e.g. a critically negative review. [PASTE *v.*]

past it *adv.* **1** [mid-19C+] of animate and inanimate objects, too old or worn-out to be of use; thus of a man, impotent. **2** [1950s+] dead.

past oneself *adj.* [1990s+] (*Irish*) acting crazily, silly.

pastry *n.* [late 19C–1930s] a generic term for pretty young women. [i.e. 'good enough to eat']

pastry *v.* [1970s–80s] (*UK Black*) to roll a cannabis cigarette. [play on SE *roll*/ROLL v.² (2)]

pasty face *n.* [1940s–50s] (*US drugs*) a narcotics addict.

Pat *n.* **1** [late 18C+] a generic term for an Irishman (cf. DONOVAN n.¹). **2** [1900s] (*Aus.*) a Chinese person (cf. AH CABBAGE n.). [var. on PADDY n. (1)/PADDY n. (3)]

pat *n.* [1960s] (*drugs*) marijuana. [? mis-sp. of POT n.¹⁰]

pat *adj.* [mid-19C–1900s] (*US campus*) aristocratic, upper-class. [SE *patrician*]

patacca *n.* [1970s] worthless rubbish, esp. fake jewellery, watches etc. [Ital. *patacca*, worthless]

pata-kyat *n.* [1940s] (*W.I.*) a thief. [dial. *pata*, a kitchen shelf + *kyat*, cat]

pat and mick *n.* [20C+] the penis (cf. ALMOND n.). [rhy. sl. = DICK n.⁴ (1)/PRICK n. (2)]

pat and mick *adj.* (*also* **old mick**) [late 19C+] sick.

pat and mick *v.* [20C+] (*Aus.*) to lick; also to beat, to thrash. [rhy. sl. = SE *lick*/LICK v.¹ (1)]

pat and mike *n.*¹ (*also* **Irish mike**) [20C+] a bicycle. [rhy. sl. = SE *bike*]

pat and mike *n.*² [1970s] (*US*) the act of 2 men having sex with 1 woman. [generic Irish names, used in many jokes, 'There were 2 Paddies, Pat and Mike…']

pata-pata *n.* (*also* **phata-phata**) [1970s] (*S.Afr. township*) sexual intercourse. [Xhosa/Zulu *phatha*, to touch, to feel; thence the popular dance *pata-pata*, a highly suggestive dance characterized by the way in which pairs of dancers touch each other]

Pat Cash *v.* [1990s+] to urinate (cf. APPLE AND PIP v.). [rhy. sl. = SLASH v.¹; ult. Aus. tennis star *Pat Cash* (b.1965)]

patch *n.*¹ **1** [late 18C+] pubic hair. **2** [late 19C] the vagina.

patch *n.*² [1940s+] (*US Und.*) a go-between who 'arranges' security for criminals in a given area; a 'fixer'.

patch *n.*³ [1950s+] (*orig. US*) any form of insignia as worn by criminal or youth gangs, e.g. the Hell's Angels, US prison gangs, N.Z. street gangs etc.

patch *v.* [1960s+] (*Can. prison*) to arrange for bribes to be paid, deals to be made etc. [PATCH n.²]

patch needle and burn thread *v.* [20C+] (*W.I.*) to waste one's time in an irritating manner.

patch up *v.* [1970s+] **1** (*N.Z.*) to become a full gang member. **2** (*US gay*) to dress fashionably; to apply make-up. [one is awarded a PATCH n.³]

patent coat *n.* [mid-19C] a coat with the pockets on the inside, making it harder to pick. [? its patented design]

patent-digester *n.* [mid-19C] brandy. [its supposedly beneficial effects on the digestion; ? corruption of *Papin's digester*, a vessel designed for dissolving bones etc]

patent gentry *n.* [mid-19C] (*US*) cheating gamblers.

patent leather *n.* [late 19C] (*US short order*) a steak.

pater *n.* [early 18C; 19C+] (*school*) one's father, esp. as *the pater*. [Lat. *pater*, father; 20C+ use is ironic]

pater cove *n. see* PATRICO n.

patess *n.* [early–mid-19C] an Irishwoman. [PAT n. (1) + SE fem. sfx *-ess*]

Patland *n.* [mid-19C–1900s] Ireland. [PAT n. (1)]

Patlander *n.* [early 19C–1900s] an Irish person (cf. DONOVAN n.¹). [PATLAND n.]

pat malone *adv.* (*also* **mike malone, pat maloney**) [1930s+] (*Aus./UK*) alone. [rhy. sl.]

pato *n.* [1960s+] (*US/P.R.*) a male homosexual. [Sp. *pato*, a duck, i.e. he 'ducks' down for sex]

patootie *n.* (*US*) **1** [1910s+] an attractive young woman. **2** [1920s

the penis. **3** [1920s+] (*also* **patoot, tootie**) the buttocks; the anus. [? SE *potato*, esp. *sweet potato*]

pat out *v.* [1920s] to speak openly, honestly. [SE *pat*, appositely, directly to the point]

patriarch co *n.* (*also* **patriarke co**) [mid-16C] (*UK Und.*) a fake priest, specializing in performing illegal marriage ceremonies. [poss. punning on SE *patriarch* + *co* = COVE n. (1); *see also* PATRICO n.]

Patrick *n.* **1** [late 19C; 1940s–50s] an Irishman; thus *Patrick O'Flynn*, a beggar who imitates a stereotypical Irish man (cf. DONOVAN n.¹). **2** [2000s] (*US Black*) a red-haired man, usu. in the context of a prostitute's client. [the stereotypical Irish name; (2) plays on the stereotypical colouring of an Irishman + TRICK n.¹ (3)]

Patrick Cox *n.* [2000s] a box, a hit. [rhy. sl.; ult shoe designer *Patrick Cox* (b.1963)]

patrico *n.* (*also* **pater cove, patri-cove, patring-cove, patter-cove, pattering-cove**) (*UK Und.*) **1** [mid-16C–19C] a priest, or a wandering beggar posing as one (cf. CANTING CREW n.). **2** [late 18C–early 19C] any legitimate clergyman. [either Lat. *pater*, father, or PATTER v. (1) + *co*, abbr. COVE n. (1); 'strolling priests that Marry under a Hedge without a Gospel or Common-prayer Book, the Couple standing on each side a Dead Beast, are bid to live together till Death them do's Part, so shaking Hands, the Wedding is ended' (B.E.)]

patrico's kinchin *n.* [mid-16C] (*UK Und.*) a pig. [PATRICO n. + KINCHIN n. (1), lit. 'the (fake) priest's child']

pat someone down *v.* [20C+] to submit someone to a body search.

patsy *n.* [late 19C+] a fool, a dupe; also attrib. (cf. BEN n.¹). [the popular Irish name *Patrick* and thus an example of a racial stereotype, in this case the supposed stupidity of the Irish]

patsy *adj.* [1930s–50s] (*US*) satisfactory, all right. [ety. unknown; ? lost rhy. sl.]

Patsy Cline *n.* [1990s+] a LINE n.⁴ (4) of cocaine (cf. BARLEY n.²). [rhy. sl.; ult. US country music singer *Patsy Cline* (1932–63)]

patsy palmer and her five daughters *n.* [1990s+] (*UK juv.*) the hand, as used for masturbation (cf. CONVERSE WITH HARRY PALM v.). [in this instance, the 'person' is a real one, namely actress *Patsy Palmer* (b.1972), famous for her role as Bianca in UK BBC TV soap opera *EastEnders*]

patten-ken *n.* [1910s–20s] (*UK Und.*) a lodging house frequented primarily by vagrants or thieves. [var. on PADDING KEN n.; + ? underpinning by SE *patten*, the sort of shoe worn by the poor]

patter *n.* **1** [mid-18C–mid-19C] (*UK Und.*) a trial, verdict and sentence. **2** [mid-18C+] (*also* **patter-clatter**) any form of speech or speechifying, e.g. a street seller's sales talk, a judge's summing up; thus *tip the patter*, to flatter, to 'shoot a line'. **3** [late 18C–1900s] underworld slang, cant. **4** [19C+] talk considered as empty chatter. **5** [2000s] in fig. use, attitude, lifestyle. [PATTER v.]

patter *v.* **1** [early 15C–early 19C] to talk rapidly, fluently or glibly, to chatter, to prattle. **2** [mid–late 18C] (*UK Und.*) to sing on the streets. **3** [late 18C–early 19C] (*UK Und.*) to talk in a manner designed to confuse a potential victim of a confidence trick. **4** [late 18C–mid-19C] to put on trial. **5** [19C] to talk the cant of thieves, beggars etc, to talk slang. **6** [mid-19C] to speechify as a cheapjack does in extolling wares, or a conjurer while performing tricks. **7** [mid-19C] to sell broadsides, ballads etc in the streets. **8** [mid-19C+] (*UK Und.*) to talk, to speak. **9** [late 19C] (*Aus. Und.*) to beg. **10** [1960s] to tell tales. **11** [1960s] (*Scot.*) (*also* **patter up**) to talk so as to encourage criminality, to chat up. [SE *patter*, to mumble one's prayers at speed and without note of their meaning; ult. the *Paternoster*, 'Our Father']

patter-cove *n. see* PATRICO n.

patter-crib *n.* [mid-19C] a criminal public house or lodging house. [PATTER n. (3) + CRIB n.¹ (2)]

patterer *n.* [mid-19C] **1** a street seller, a hawker. **2** a street seller who specializes in last dying speeches, true confessions and similar melodramas. **3** a mouth, a voice. [PATTER v.; self-proclaimed, according to Mayhew, *London Labour and the London Poor* (1861–2), as 'the aristocracy of the street sellers']

patter flash v. *see* PATTER (THE) FLASH v.

pattering n. [late 17C–19C] overly 'smart' or irritatingly vague responses made by a servant. [PATTER v. (1)]

pattering-cove n. *see* PATRICO n.

pattern n. [mid-19C] a patent. [mispron.]

pattern adj. [19C] (*Irish*) excellent, first-rate, brilliant. [abbr. SE *pattern fair*, mispron. of *patron fair*, ult. *patron saint's fair*]

patter (the) flash v. [19C] to talk, usu. slang or underworld cant. [PATTER v. (5) + FLASH n.¹ (2)]

patter up v. *see* PATTER v. (11).

Pattie n. *see* PATTY HEARST n.

patties n. *see* PADDIES n.

pattin' leather phr. [1930s+] (*US Black*) **1** walking the streets. **2** in fig. use, being out of work. [one walks the streets (on shoe leather) in search of employment]

patty n. *see* PADDY n. (5).

Patty Hearst n. (*also* **Pattie**) [1990s+] a first-class degree (cf. DESMOND (TUTU) n.). [rhy. sl.; ult. US heiress-cum-urban terrorist *Pattie Hearst* (b.1954)]

patty wagon n. *see* PAT WAGON n.

patu n. [late 19C+] (*W.I.*) an ugly or foolish person. [dial. *patu*, used of an owl or a nightjar; the bird's mouth gapes hugely – out of proportion to its relatively small beak]

patu-eye n. [1950s] (*W.I.*) an albino. [PATU n. + SE *eye*]

pat wagon n. (*also* **patty wagon**) [1900s–30s] (*US*) a vehicle in which prisoners are conveyed to a police station (cf. PADDY WAGON n.). [PAT n. (1), i.e. the stereotypical Irish policeman/troublemaker + SE *wagon*]

patzer n. (*also* **potzer**) [1940s+] an inferior chess-player. [? Ger. *patzen*, to bungle, but note derog. PUTZ n. (2)]

pauca! excl. [late 16C–early 17C] quiet! be quiet! [Lat. *pauca verba*, few words]

Paul Henry n. *see* JOHN T HENRY n.

Paul Pry n. (*also* **Johnny Pry**) [early 19C+] (*orig. US*) an inquisitive person; thus *paul pry*, to be unashamedly inquisitive; *paul pryism*, the behaviour of such a person. [popular US song, composed c.1820; note WW2 USN *Paul Pry*, a searchlight]

Paul Revere phr. [1980s+] (*US campus*) goodbye. [play on Fr. *au revoir*/US revolutionary hero *Paul Revere* (1735–1818)]

paul's work n. [17C] a badly done job, a mess. [SE *poor work* or ref. to a *Paul's man*, anyone who frequented St Paul's Cathedral, London, for gossip, confidence trickery etc]

pauly n. [late 19C–1900s] during the Boer war, a derog. term for a pro-Boer. [*Paul Kruger* (1825–1904), the Boer leader + pun on SE *poor lies*]

paup along v. [late 19C–1910s] to subsist. [SE *pauper*]

paut v. [20C+] (*Ulster*) to walk around in stockinged feet. [Scot. *paut*, to move in a leisurely manner]

Pav n. (*also* **Pavvy, P.V.**) [mid-19C–1920s] the *Pavilion* Theatre, London; thus any theatre or cinema called the *Pavilion*. [abbr.]

pav n. [1960s+] (*Aus./N.Z.*) a pavlova, Australia's 'national dessert', a large, soft-centred meringue topped with whipped cream and passion fruit. [abbr.; named/created for the ballerina Anna *Pavlova* (1885–1931)]

pave v.¹ [late 19C–1930s] (*UK school*) to add marginal or interlinear translations to a classical text. [the image is of paving, i.e. smoothing the 'road' of Latin and Greek study]

pave v.² [2000s] (*Irish*) to steal. [ety. unknown]

pavee n. (*also* **pavey**) [1940s+] (*Irish*) an itinerant Jewish peddler. [? their walking the pavements]

pavement artist n. [1980s] (*UK Und.*) one who robs security vans delivering money to banks.

pavement pizza n. [1980s+] (*Aus.*) a pile of vomit.

pavement pounder n. [1940s–50s] (*orig. US*) **1** a policeman (cf. BEAT-POUNDER n.). **2** a prostitute (cf. NIGHT WALKER n.).

pavement princess n. (*also* **pavement pretty**) [20C+] (*US*) a prostitute (cf. NIGHT WALKER n.).

pavey n. *see* PAVEE n.

paviour's workshop n. (*also* **pavier's workshop, pavior's...**) [late 18C–19C] the street. [SE *paviour*, a layer of paving stones]

Pavvy n. *see* PAV n.

paw n. **1** [17C+] the human hand, usu. in pl. **2** [18C–1900s] handwriting, esp. a signature. [SE *paw*, used only of animals]

paw adj. [mid–late 17C] improper, naughty, obscene. [? excl. *pah!* nasty! horrible!]

paw v. [mid-19C+] to fondle sexually (esp. when the recipient is unwilling). [PAW n. (1)]

paw-case n. [mid-19C] a glove. [PAW n. (1) + SE *case*]

pawing-match n. [late 19C] (*Aus.*) a fist-fight. [PAW n. (1)]

pawked up adj. [late 19C] (*sporting*) poor quality, usu. of horses or dogs. [Scot. *pawk*, a trick]

pawky adj. [20C+] (*Ulster*) easy-going, lazy. [dial. *pawk*, a cheeky individual; note *pawky*, artful, sly, shrewd is SE]

pawn n. [mid-19C] a *pawn*broker. [abbr.]

pawn v.¹ [mid–late 17C] to leave an inn or tavern, forcing one's companion to pay the bill.

pawn v.² [1990s+] (*W.I.*) to take hold of someone. [? PAW v.]

pawnce n. *see* PARNEY n. (2).

pawned adj. [1940s] (*UK Und.*) imprisoned.

pawni n. *see* PARNEY n. (2).

paw-paw adj. [late 18C–early 19C] naughty, improper; thus *paw-pawness*, naughtiness, impropriety. [PAW adj.]

paw-paw tricks n. **1** [late 18C–19C] any form of naughty, childish trick. **2** [19C] masturbation. [PAW-PAW adj.; orig. used by nurses to children]

paws off! excl. [20C+] get your hands off! leave it alone! [PAW n. (1)]

pax! excl. [mid-19C+] (*UK juv.*) a cry used to call a truce in a (fighting) game; thus *pax*, a friend; *good pax*, good friends. [Lat. *pax*, peace]

pax on —! excl. [mid-17C–mid-18C] confound it! the hell with it! [Lat. *pax*, peace, i.e. enough! leave it in peace!]

pay v.¹ [late 16C–19C; 1930s+] to beat, to punish; thus *pay over face and eyes as the cat did to the monkey*, to give someone a serious beating about the head; *pay as Paul paid the Ephesians*, to beat severely.

pay v.² [mid-19C] (*Anglo-Chinese*) to deliver.

pay a bill at sight v. [early 19C] to be ready at any time to have sex.

pay a call v. [1950s+] to visit the lavatory (cf. DO ONE'S BUSINESS v.). [SE *call of nature*]

payaka adj. [1950s+] (*W.I. Rasta*) heathen. [? link to PAYOL n.]

pay and lay v. [1960s] (*US*) to use the services of a prostitute. [SE *pay* + LAY v.¹ (1)]

payaso n. (*also* **payass**) [20C+] (*W.I.*) fooling around, buffoonery. [Port. *palhaço* or Sp. *payaso*, jester, clown]

pay as Paul paid the Ephesians v. *see* PAY v.¹.

pay away v. **1** [late 17C; mid-19C] to continue, to go on with, esp. of a story that is being told. **2** [late 18C–early 19C] to fight manfully. **3** [late 18C–early 19C] to eat voraciously. [naut. jargon *pay away*, to let rope run out of a vessel]

payback n. (*also* **paybacks**) [1960s+] (*US*) revenge, retaliation. [SE *pay back*]

pay back v. [early 18C] (*UK Und.*) to return stolen goods.

paydirt n. [late 19C+] (*orig. US*) success, profit. [gold-mining imagery]

pay for one's whistle v. *see* PAY (TOO MUCH) FOR ONE'S WHISTLE v.

pay-hole n. [late 19C] (*Aus.*) a ticket-office.

pay into v. [late 19C] to attack, to lay into. [ext. of PAY v.¹]

pay me rent n. [20C+] (Aus.) a tent. [rhy. sl.]

pay no mind v. [1910s+] (US) to ignore.

pay-off n. 1 [1910s+] (US Und.) (also **pay-off game**) a confidence trick whereby the victim is encouraged to wager a large sum of money, having been lured into the trick when a smaller wager, also suggested by the trickster, seems to have paid off satisfactorily. 2 [1920s+] (UK/US Und.) the division of criminal spoils. 3 [1920s+] (US Und.) a bribe. 4 [1920s+] (orig. US) the end result, the outcome, the conclusion (whether positive or negative). 5 [1920s+] a (final) payment for services rendered. 6 [1920s+] (US prison) a prisoner's hand-out on release from prison. 7 [1920s+] (US Und.) a confidence trickster. 8 [1920s+] winnings on a wager or some form of gambling. 9 [1940s] a ransom. 10 [1940s] a gang killing. 11 [1940s] the denouement of a book, film or play. 12 [1940s+] (US Black) a generous person. 13 [1950s+] a reward, a recompense, other than financial. 14 [1960s] one's deserts.

pay off v. 1 [early 18C–1900s] to take revenge upon. 2 [1920s+] (orig. US) to bribe. 3 [1920s+] (orig. US) to recompense, to pay one's debts. 4 [1940s] (US) to get one's deserts. [PAY-OFF n.]

pay-off guy n. see PAY-OFF MAN n.

pay-off in gold v. [1930s–50s] (US drugs) for a federal agent to arrest an addict. [ext. of PAY OFF v.; he displays his gold badge as identification]

pay-off joint n. [1900s–50s] (US Und.) a fake gambling club or broker's office, in which the victim is swindled. [PAY-OFF n. (1) + JOINT n.⁴ (3)]

pay-off man n. (also **pay-off guy**) [1920s+] (US Und.) 1 a confidence trickster. 2 the cashier for a criminal gang. 3 a middleman or fellow-criminal who passes on bribes from criminals to the authorities. 4 one who pays off bets made at a bookmakers or other gambling organizations. 5 a policeman who accepts bribes. [PAY-OFF n. + SE man]

pay-off mob n. [1930s] a team of confidence tricksters. [PAY-OFF n. (1) + MOB n.² (3)]

pay-off queen n. [1940s–70s] (gay) a homosexual who prefers to pay for sex. [PAY OFF v. (3) + QUEEN n.² (1)/QUEEN sfx (2)]

pay-off Wednesday n. [mid-19C] the Wednesday before Advent. [supposedly that day on which schoolboys 'retaliate small grudges in a playful facetious way' (Hotten, 1860)]

payol n. (also **pagnol**) [20C+] 1 (W.I., Trin.) a mixed-race person who retains traces of Spanish ancestry and culture (cf. COCOA PAYOL n.). 2 (W.I., Gren.) a Spanish-speaking person, esp. a Venezuelan. [Sp. español. The word is equated with NIGGER n.¹ (1) or COOLIE n.¹ in terms of offensiveness. Payols thus call themselves 'Spanish' or, in Sp. venezolanos]

payola n. [1930s+] (orig. US) the practice (ostensibly illegal and generally denied by its practitioners) of bribing (with cash or kind) those with access to the public to tout a product. [SE pay + -OLA sfx; esp. common in the record business where disc jockeys are offered massive inducements to push a certain record or artist. Major scandals in the US c.1959 supposedly ended payola, but some believe that the practice persists]

pay one's dues v. [1940s+] (orig. US) to undergo usu. undesirable experiences before one attains a desirable goal.

pay one's last debt v. see LAST DEBT n.

pay one's shot v. (also **pay the shot**) 1 [mid–late 17C] to have sexual intercourse. 2 [mid-17C+] to pay one's share. [SE pay + SHOT n.²/SHOT n.¹]

pay one's water bill v. [1970s] (US Black) to urinate (cf. RUN SOME WATER THROUGH ONE'S PIPE v.; WATER ONE'S NAG v.; WATER THE DRAGON v.; WATER THE FLOWERS v.; WATER THE MULE v.).

pay on the stump v. (also **pay on the barrelhead**) [late 19C–1930s] to hand over, esp. of money. [the placing of the money on a stump or some equivalent]

pay out v. (also **pay up**) [mid-19C+] to take revenge upon, to give (someone) their deserts, to punch.

pay out the slack of one's gammon v. see GAMMON n.² (2).

pay over face and eyes as the cat did to the monkey v. see PAY v.¹.

pay someone's coat v. [19C] to thrash, to beat severely. [PAY v.¹]

pay someone their rent v. [14C–15C] to punish someone.

pay the bearer v. [late 19C+] to bounce a cheque. [play on the screed promising to 'pay the bearer' on a sterling note]

pay the freight v. [1950s+] (US) to pay, to bear the expense.

pay the shot v. see PAY ONE'S SHOT v.

pay through the nose v. (also **pay through one's arsehole and one's eye**) [late 17C+] to pay exorbitantly. [fig. use of SE; ? origin in the Nose tax, levied by the Danes upon the Irish during the 9C; those who refused to pay had their noses split]

pay (too much) for one's whistle v. (also **pay too dear for one's whistle**) [late 18C–1910s] to pay over the odds for something one desires. [the whistle of emphasis that acknowledges one's interest]

pay tribute v. [1990s+] (US Und.) in US Mafia, to pay a commission to one's boss.

pay up v. see PAY OUT v.

pay with a hook v. [late 19C] (Aus.) to steal. [SE pay + HOOK n.¹ (1)]

paz n. [1980s] (drugs) phencyclidine (cf. ACE n.⁴). [Sp. paz, peace]

pazazz n. see PIZZAZZ n.

p.c. n. 1 [late 19C] (UK society) the poor classes. 2 [late 19C+] (UK society) a postcard. 3 [20C+] a police constable. 4 [1950s] (US) the Police commisioner. 5 [1950s+] (US drugs/gambling) a percentage. 6 [1980s+] (UK Und.) a previous conviction. 7 [1980s+] (US teen) a private conversation. 8 [1980s+] (drugs) a piece of crack. 9 [1990s+] (US prison) protective custody. [abbr.]

p.c. adj. 1 [1980s+] politically correct, ideologically pure. 2 [1990s+] (drugs) part commission, in a drug deal. [abbr.]

PCP n. (also **PCE**, **PCPA**) [1960s+] (drugs) phencyclidine, a dangerous hallucinogen based on animal (pig) tranquillizer (cf. ACE n.⁴). [abbr. PEACE PILLS n. (1)]

P-crutch n. see CRUTCH n.³.

p.c. up v. [1990s+] (US prison) to request or be incarcerated in protective custody. [P.C. n. (9)]

p.d.a. n. [1960s+] (US) kissing and cuddling in public. [abbr. public display of affection]

p.d.k. n. [1980s+] (US campus) someone who is out of fashion. [abbr. polyester double-knit, the epitome of unfashionable tailoring]

p.d.q. phr. 1 [late 19C+] pretty damn quick(ly). 2 [1920s] fast, lively. [abbr.]

P.E. n. [late 19C+] (S.Afr.) Port Elizabeth. [abbr.]

pea n.¹ (also **p**) [late 19C+] (Aus., orig. racing) 1 the ideal, the perfect choice, the favourite. 2 someone in a favourable position; a superior person. 3 in weak use, a man. [horseracing pea, the favourite; ult. from the pea in the game of thimble-rig, played with 3 inverted thimbles and a pea]

pea n.² [1920s+] (US Und.) a bullet. [? resemblance]

pea n.³ see PEA-SOUP n.¹ (2).

pea and thimble n. [mid-19C+] (Aus.) a version of the 3-card trick; thus pea and thimble man, one who conducts the game.

peabrain n. (also **peahead**) [1950s+] (orig. US) a fool, a simpleton (cf. APPLEHEAD n.; BAKEBRAIN n.). [SE pea + sfx -brain/-HEAD sfx (1)]

peabrained adj. [1950s+] stupid, foolish (cf. AMOEBA-BRAINED adj.). [PEABRAIN n.]

peace n.¹ [1970s+] (drugs) 1 STP; 'a hallucinogenic chemical produced by the Dow Chemical Company. The initials are said to represent "serenity, tranquility, and peace," or "scientifically treated petroleum"' (Spears, Slang and Jargon of Drugs and Drink, 1986). 2 LSD (cf. A n.³). 3 phencyclidine (cf. ACE n.⁴).

peace n.² [2000s] (US Black) a place where one is happy and secure.

peace v. see PEACE (OUT) v.

peace *phr.* [1950s+] (*orig. US*) a greeting, farewell, goodbye. [much loved by hippies; post-1970s use mostly ironic or historical]

peace and quiet *n.* [20C+] a diet. [rhy. sl.]

peacemake *n. see* MATRIMONIAL PEACEMAKER n.

peacemaker *n.*[1] **1** [mid-19C+] (*US*) a pistol or revolver. **2** [1950s] (*W.I.*) a male lover. **3** [1970s] (*US Black*) the penis (cf. AX n.[2]). [? the nickname of the Wild West's legendary Colt .45 revolver, or, just poss. in (3), from the ironic nickname accorded the nuclear arsenal's MX missile]

peacemaker *n.*[2] (*also* **peaceman**) [1950s] (*W.I.*) a policeman (cf. BEAT-POUNDER n.).

peace (out) *v.* [1990s+] (*US campus*) to leave. [PEACE OUT phr.]

peace out *phr.* (*also* **peace up**) [1990s+] (*US Black/campus/teen*) goodbye. [ext. PEACE phr.]

peace person *n.* [1990s+] (*US campus*) someone who identifies with the concerns and the style of the 1960s. [the 'love and peace' era]

peace pills *n.* (*US drugs*) **1** [1960s+] phencyclidine (cf. ACE n.[4]). **2** [1970s+] a mixture of LSD and Methedrine.

peace tablets *n.* [1970s+] (*US drugs*) LSD (cf. A n.[3]). [the association of LSD with 'love and peace']

peace up *phr. see* PEACE OUT phr.

peace weed *n.* [1970s+] (*drugs*) phencyclidine (cf. ACE n.[4]). [SE *peace* + *weed*/WEED n.[1] (4)]

peach *n.*[1] **1** [mid-18C; mid-19C+] (*also* **nectarine**) a pretty young woman. **2** [mid-19C+] (*also* **peony**) someone or something of exceptional worth, quality or desirability; thus phr. *all to the peaches*, very good, very enjoyable. **3** [late 19C+] in ironic use of (2). **4** [1900s] (*US campus*) a promiscuous woman. [(1) see Williams for fig. uses of *peach* in 16C–17C]

peach *n.*[2] [mid–late 19C] a detective, esp. as employed by a stage-coach or omnibus company to check receipts. [PEACH v. (1)]

peach *adj. see* PEACHY adj.

peach *v.* **1** [late 16C+] to betray, to inform against. **2** [mid-19C] to confess, to admit. [SE *impeach*]

peacher *n.* [mid-16C+] an informer. [PEACH v. (1)]

peacherino *n.* (*also* **peacherine, peachermaroot**) [20C+] (*orig. US*) something of exceptional worth, quality or desirability, e.g. an attractive young woman. [ext. of PEACH n.[1] (1) + -ERINO sfx]

peaches *n.*[1] (*US Black*) **1** [1920s] the vagina (cf. APPLE n.[6]). **2** [1920s+] the male genitals. **3** [1960s] (*also* **peach tree**) a hermaphrodite.

peaches *n.*[2] [1960s+] (*drugs*) Dexedrine. [the colour of the capsules]

peaches *n.*[3] [1980s+] (*US gay*) the buttocks. [resemblance]

peaches *adj.* **1** [late 19C–1910s] (*US teen*) attractive, sexually alluring. **2** [1910s–60s] (*US*) fine, excellent (cf. PEACHY adj.). [PEACH n.[1] (2)]

peaches and pears *n. see* APPLES (AND PEARS) n.

peach-fuzz *n.* [1950s–70s] (*gay*) an attractive teenager.

peach tree *n. see* PEACHES n.[1] (3).

peachy *adj.* (*also* **double peachy, peach**) [20C+] wonderful, excellent, delightful (cf. PEACHES adj.). [PEACH n.[1] (2)]

peachy-keen *adj.* [1960s+] (*US*) **1** excellent, first-rate. **2** (ironically) not good enough to warrant enthusiasm but adequate. [PEACHY adj. + KEEN adj.]

peacock *v.*[1] [late 19C] (*Aus.*) **1** to buy up the best sections of land, thus making the adjoining territory worthless (cf. PICK THE EYES OUT OF v.). **2** to outwit. [the speculator 'picks out the eyes' of the land]

peacock *v.*[2] (*Anglo-Ind.*) **1** [late 19C] to pay morning calls. **2** [late 19C+] to promenade up and down in one's best clothes. [the bird's characteristic display]

peacock horse *n.* [late 19C] a horse that pulls a hearse. [such horses are bedecked in mourning black, with plumes, and step in a very ceremonial way]

pea-dodger *n.* [1930s] (*Aus.*) a bowler hat. [ety. unknown]

peahead *n. see* PEABRAIN n.

peak *n.*[1] (*also* **peake**) [mid-17C–early 19C] (*UK Und.*) lace.

peak *n.*[2] [19C] the human nose.

peak *n.*[3] [1960s+] (*drugs*) the central 2 hours or so of an LSD trip when the hallucinogen is at its most powerful.

peak *v.*[1] [1960s+] **1** (*drugs*) to reach the most extreme point of an LSD trip. **2** to reach the limit of a particular experience. [PEAK n.[3]]

peak *v.*[2] *see* PEEK v.

peake *n. see* PEAK n.[1].

peaked *adj.* (*also* **peeked**) [mid–late 19C] looking ill, tired. [SE *peak*, to look sickly]

peaked-cap *n.* [1920s] a police inspector. [the uniform]

peaking *n.* [1920s+] (*Aus.*) nagging, whingeing, making a fuss over a minor injury. [SE *peak*, to mope about]

peaky *adj.* (*also* **peeky**) [mid-19C+] feeble, weak. [SE *peak*, to look sickly]

pea-man *n. see* PEA-RIGGER n.

peamey *n.* (*also* **peamy**) [mid-19C] a pea-seller. [SE *pea-merchant*]

peanut *n.*[1] **1** [1940s] (*US Black*) a White man. **2** [1960s] (*US*) a young person, a child. **3** [1960s] (*Aus.*) a slightly foolish person. [abbr. MR PEANUT n.]

peanut *n.*[2] [1960s+] (*drugs*) a barbiturate (cf. BARBIT n.). [the shape of the pill]

peanut *n.*[3] [1990s+] (*UK juv.*) one who has an oval, peanut-shaped head; one who has recently received a haircut.

peanut *adj.* [mid-19C+] (*orig. US*) second-rate, 'small-time'.

peanut alley *n.* (*also* **peanut row**) [1950s+] (*Aus./US*) the front row of the stalls in a cinema (cf. PEANUT GALLERY n.). [the consumption of peanuts in this row]

peanut buffer *n.* [1990s+] a male homosexual (cf. BROWN ARTIST n.). [SE *buff*, to polish]

peanut butter pussy *n.* [1970s+] (*US Black*) a complimentary term for a Black or Hispanic woman's vagina and thus the person who possesses it (cf. APPLE n.[6]; BIRD n.[8]). [PUSSY n. (2); it is 'smooth, brown and easy to spread']

peanut factory *n.* [1980s+] (*Aus.*) a psychiatric institution. [PEANUT n.[1] (3)]

peanut farm *n.* [1930s] (*US tramp*) a workhouse where the inmates are made to break stones.

peanut flier *n.* [1950s–60s] (*UK Und.*) a criminal who will take on any job, however small. [PEANUT adj. + ? the idea of the ridiculous job of flying a peanut]

peanut gallery *n.* **1** [late 19C+] the top gallery, the 'gods' in a theatre. **2** [late 19C+] ignorant, vociferous spectators. **3** [1940s+] (*Aus./US*) the front row of the stalls in a cinema (cf. PEANUT ALLEY n.). **4** [1990s+] an associate who exhibits the characteristics of (2). [the consumption of peanuts by the occupants of these seats]

peanut-packer *n.* [1970s+] (*US*) a male homosexual (cf. BROWN ARTIST n.). [PACK PEANUT BUTTER v.]

peanut politics *n.* [late 19C–1920s] (*US*) underhand, clandestine politicking, aimed at the securing of minor personal gains; thus *peanut politician*, one who indulges in such tactics. [PEANUT adj. + SE *politics*]

peanut roaster *n.* [1910s+] (*US*) a small locomotive; an old or ramshackle automobile. [joc. resemblance]

peanut row *n. see* PEANUT ALLEY n.

peanuts *n.* (*also* **pretzels**) [1930s+] (*orig. US*) anyone or anything insignificant, petty, esp. money, wages. [PEANUT adj.]

peanut smuggler *n.* [1990s+] (*Aus. juv.*) a girl who is not wearing a brassiere under her clothing. [the 'peanuts' are her nipples, visible through the cloth]

peapicker *n.* [1970s] (*US*) a derog. term for a peasant (cf. ACORN-CRACKER n.).

peapicking *adj.* [1970s] (*US*) stupid, foolish, naive (cf. COTTON-PICKING adj.). [PEAPICKER n.]

pear *n.* [mid-19C] King Louis Philippe of France. [the shape of the head of Louis Philippe (1773–1850). The term was coined by the French satirist Charles Phillipon in 1831, in the magazine *La Caricature*. As well as meaning 'pear', *la poire* is Fr. sl. for 'fathead']

pear and quince *n.* [20C+] (*Aus.*) a prince. [rhy. sl.]

pea-rigger *n.* (*also* **pea-man**) [19C] a 'find-the-lady' man, betting against the likelihood of a player correctly calling which thimble a pea will be found under. [SE *pea* + RIG v.² (1)]

pearl *n.*¹ **1** [1900s] (*Aus.*) an attractive woman. **2** [1970s] (*US Black*) an attractive White woman.

pearl *n.*² *see* PEARL (DROP) n.

pearl *n.*³ *see* PURLER n. (3).

pearl *adj.* [1940s+] (*Aus.*) first-rate, excellent. [on pattern of DIAMOND adj.]

pearl dive *v.*¹ [20C+] to work as a dishwasher.

pearl dive *v.*² [1920s+] (*US*) to perform cunnilingus (cf. CLAMDIVING n.). [the clitoris is the 'pearl' + DIVE v.²]

pearl diver *n.* [20C+] (*US*) a dishwasher in a hotel or restaurant; thus *pearl-diving*, washing up.

pearl (drop) *n.* [1960s+] (*US gay*) a drop of semen. [resemblance and colour]

pearler *n. see* PURLER n.

pearl-fisher *n.* [1930s] (*US*) a cunnilinguist. [PEARL DIVE v.²]

pearl handle *n.* [1940s+] (*US prison*) a factory-made cigarette.

Pearl Harbor *n.* [2000s] cold weather. [play on NIP n. (1) (*see* next) + SE *nip*, there's a nasty 'nip' in the air]

Pearl Harbor *v.* [1970s] to make a surprise attack. [the Japanese attack on the US fleet in Pearl Harbor, 6/12/1941]

pearlies *n.* **1** [mid-19C+] pearl buttons, esp. found on a costermonger's clothes. **2** [mid-19C+] costermongers as a class. **3** [late 19C+] (*also* **pearls**) the teeth.

pearl necklace *n.* [1990s+] drops ('pearls') of semen ejaculated onto a partner's neck, usu. after fellatio. [resemblance]

pearls *n.*¹ [1960s+] (*drugs*) amyl nitrite (cf. AIMIES n.). [the resemblance of amyl nitrite capsules to pearls]

pearls *n.*² *see* PEARLIES n. (3).

pearl tongue *n.* [1980s+] (*US Black*) the vagina in the context of oral sex; one who practises cunnilingus.

pearly gate *n.* [20C+] a plate. [rhy. sl.]

pearly gates *n.*¹ [1960s–70s] the teeth.

pearly gates *n.*² [1970s+] (*drugs*) LSD (cf. A n.³). [the image of LSD giving visions of heaven]

pearly king *n.* [20C+] the anus (cf. BOTTLE AND GLASS n.). [rhy. sl. = RING n.¹ (2)]

pearly passion potion *n.* [1990s+] semen.

pearly whites *n.* [1930s–70s] (*orig. US*) teeth.

pear-making *n.* [19C] (*UK Und.*) enrolling in a regiment, taking the offered bounty and then deserting; the process can be repeated several times. [dial. *pear*, appear, i.e. one makes appearances, but does not stay]

pear-shaped *adj.* [2000s] out of order, happening incorrectly. [GO PEAR-SHAPED v.]

peasant *n.* **1** [1930s+] a general term of abuse, implying stupidity, boorishness, a lack of sophistication. **2** [1960s–70s] (*US gay*) a heterosexual male. [16C–17C SE use had derog. overtones, initially used for 'the subjects of France']

pease pudding hot *n.* [20C+] nasal mucus. [rhy. sl. = SNOT n.¹ (1)]

peashooter *n.*¹ [20C+] (*orig. US*) a small, low-powered firearm. [note WW1 Aus. milit. *pea-shooter*, a German anti-tank gun; UK WW1 *pea-shooter*, a rifle]

peashooter *n.*² [1920s] the penis (cf. AX n.²).

peas in the pot *adj.* [late 19C+] hot; lit. or fig. [rhy. sl.]

pea-soup *n.*¹ (*also* **pea-souper**) (*US*) **1** [19C+] a French-born immigrant. **2** [late 19C+] (*also* **johnny pea-soup**) a French-Canadian; thus *talk pea-soup*, to talk in French-Canadian patois. [the stereotyping of pea soup as a French-Canadian staple]

pea-soup *n.*² *see* PEA-SOUPER n.².

pea-soup *adj.* [1930s] (*US prison*) bad, of a person, untrustworthy. [ety. unknown]

pea-souper *n.*¹ [mid-19C–1900s] (*Aus.*) a newly arrived British immigrant. [PEA-SOUPER n.²]

pea-souper *n.*² (*also* **pea-soup**) [mid-19C+] a very dense fog. [orig. the pollution-based London fogs, but since the Clean Air legislation of 1950s, any exceptionally impenetrable fog]

pea-souper *n.*³ [late 19C] (*N.Z.*) a teetotaller. [? their preferred diet]

pea-souper *n.*⁴ *see* PEA-SOUP n.¹.

peat-reek *n.* [mid-19C] (*Scot.*) illicitly distilled whisky. [the flavour of peat smoke that permeates the liquor]

peazy *n.* [2000s] (*US Black*) a (mobile) telephone. [ety. unknown; ? SE *easy-peasy*]

peb *n.* [1900s–50s] (*Aus.*) a youthful gangster. [abbr. PEBBLE n.¹]

pebble *n.*¹ [early 19C+] (*orig. boxing, then Aus.*) anyone seen as hard to deal with, e.g. a youthful ruffian; thus *game as a pebble*, ready for anything, up to any challenge; thus *pebbly*, hard, challenging. [the hardness of the SE *pebble*]

pebble *n.*² [late 19C] a monocle.

pebble-beached *adj.* (*also* **pebbly-beach**) **1** [late 19C–1910s] penniless, destitute. **2** [1930s] dazed, absent-minded. [LAND ON A PEBBLY BEACH v.; but note STONE BROKE adj.]

pebble-dash *v.* [1990s+] (*Irish*) to have diarrhoea, thus splatter the lavatory with faeces.

Pebble Mill *n.* [1990s+] (*drugs*) any form of pill, i.e. an amphetamine (cf. PILL n.⁴). [rhy. sl.; ult. UK TV show *Pebble Mill at One*]

pebbles *n.*¹ [19C] the testicles (cf. AGATES n.). [play on STONE n.¹ (1)]

pebbles *n.*² [1980s+] (*drugs*) small pieces of crack cocaine (cf. BASE n.). [play on ROCKS n.⁵ (3)]

pebbles *n.*³ [1990s+] an underage, sexually active girl. [the young girl character *Pebbles* in the TV cartoon *The Flintstones*]

pebbly-beach *adj. see* PEBBLE-BEACHED adj.

pec *n.* (*also* **peck**) [1960s+] usu. in pl.; a *pec*toral muscle, the development of which is popular among body-builders. [abbr.]

peck *n.*¹ **1** [mid-16C–19C; 1940s–50s] (*orig. UK Und.*) food, often meat; thus [late 19C] *off one's peck*, having no appetite. **2** [late 19C] an apppetite. **3** [late 19C–1900s] a business, a concern. [SE *peck*, to eat (of a bird); (1) 1940s–50s use is US Black. The concepts of food and business are closely allied here]

peck *n.*² [late 19C+] a perfunctory kiss. [a 'peck on the cheek']

peck *n.*³ [1930s+] (*US Black*) a White person. [abbr. PECKERWOOD n.]

peck *v.*¹ [mid-16C+] (*orig. UK Und.*) to eat. [mid-20C+ use is US Black]

peck *v.*² [1900s] (*Aus.*) to give in, to surrender. [image of a bird 'pecking' at the pocket]

peckage *n.* (*also* **peckadge, peckeridge, peckidge**) [17C–mid-19C] (*UK Und.*) food, esp. scraps. [PECK n.¹ (1)]

peck alley *n.* [mid-19C] the throat. [PECK n.¹ (1) + SE *alley*]

peck and perch *n.* [early 19C] board and lodging. [PECK n.¹ (1) + fig. use of SE *perch*]

peck and tipple *n.* (*also* **peck and boose/booze**) [mid-18C–mid-19C] meat and drink. [PECK n.¹ (1) + TIPPLE n. (1)/BOUSE n. (1)/BOOZE n. (1)]

pecker *n.*¹ [mid–late 19C] **1** an eater. **2** an appetite. [PECK v.¹; (2) B&L suggest the 'Oxford' sfx -ER sfx]

pecker *n.*² **1** [mid-19C+] courage. **2** [late 19C+] (*orig. US*) the penis; thus as a general term of abuse (cf. BELL END n.). **3** [1980s] (*US/Can.*) a young child. [SE *pecker*, that which pecks, i.e. a beak, a bill]

pecker *n.*³ [1930s–50s] (*US Black*) a White person. [abbr. PECKERWOOD n.]

pecker cheese n. [1990s+] (US) smegma. [PECKER n.² (2) + CHEESE n.² (1)]

peckerhead n. [1940s+] (US) an objectionable, aggressive person. [PECKER n.² (2) + -HEAD sfx (1)]

peckeridge n. see PECKAGE n.

pecker palace n. [2000s] (US prison) a room set aside for conjugal visits. [PECKER n.² (2) + SE palace]

pecker snot n. [1990s+] (US) semen (cf. BOLLOCK SNOT n.). [PECKER n.² (2) + SNOT n.¹ (4)]

pecker tracks n. [1950s+] (US) semen left on a sheet or other similar object after intercourse or, usu. masturbation. [PECKER n.² (2) + SE tracks]

peckerwood n. (also **woodpecker**) [1920s+] (orig. US Black) a White person, usu. a working-class Southerner; also ext. to Chicanos and Latinos. [the red woodpecker, symbol of Whites, rather than the black crow, symbol of Blacks]

peckerwood adj. [1920s+] (US) pertaining to the rural South, esp. the working-class inhabitants thereof. [PECKERWOOD n.]

Peckham (Rye) n. [1910s–80s] a tie. [rhy. sl.; ult. Peckham Rye, south London]

peckidge n. see PECKAGE n.

peckie n. see PEKKIE n.

pecking and necking n. [1970s] (US Black) foreplay, kissing and cuddling. [SE peck, to nibble at + NECK v.⁴]

peckings n. [1940s–50s] (US Black) food. [PECK n.¹ (1)]

peckish adj. (also **pecky**) [18C–19C] hungry. [PECK n.¹ (1); 20C+ use is SE]

pecks n. [1950s] (drugs/gang) food. [PECK n.¹ (1)]

peck's bad boy n. [late 19C+] (US) a mischievous child. [the name of a fictional character created by George Wilbur Peck (1840–1916) in Peck's Bad Boy and his Pa (1883)]

pecky adj. see PECKISH adj.

pecnoster n. [late 19C] the penis. [PECKER n.² (2) + pun on SE paternoster, our father]

pecos v. [1920s–40s] to shoot someone and roll their body in the river. [the Pecos River]

pecs n. see PEC n.

peculiar n. 1 [early 17C] a wife. 2 [late 17C–19C] a mistress; occas. of a man. [SE peculiar, private]

peculiar adj. 1 [late 19C+] deranged, eccentric. 2 [20C+] homosexual. [euph.]

ped n.¹ [late 17C–early 19C] (UK Und.) a basket. [usu. dial.: 'chiefly in use in the Eastern Counties from Northants. to Essex, and in Devon and Somerset' (OED)]

ped n.² 1 [mid-19C–1900s] a competitive runner. 2 [mid-19C+] a pedestrian. [abbr.; (2) 20C+ use mainly US]

pedal n. [1900s] (US) a foot.

pedal v. [1930s–50s] (Aus.) to send a message over the radio. [the pedalling of the generator]

pedal and crank n. see CHAIN AND CRANK n.

pedal one's dogs v. [1920s+] (US) to leave, to go away; esp. as excl. pedal your dogs! [SE pedal + DOGS n.¹ (1)]

pedal-pusher n. [1910s–30s] (US) a cyclist, esp. a racing cyclist.

peddle one's arse v. (also **peddle one's ass**) 1 [1930s+] (also **peddle gash, peddle one's butt, ...hips, ...hump, ...stuff**) to work as a prostitute, of either gender. 2 [1960s] to send a prostitute out to work. 3 [1990s+] in fig. use, to prostitute oneself. [SE peddle, to sell + ARSE n.¹ (1)/ASS n. (2)/BUTT n.¹ (2)/SE hips/HUMP n.⁴ (1)/STUFF n.⁶ (1)/GASH n.¹ (1)]

peddle one's papers v. [1930s+] (US) to go about one's business.

peddle out v. [1920s–30s] (US) to sell one's possessions, esp. to a second-hand store.

peddle pussy v. (also **peddle one's pussy, sell pussy**) [1960s+] to work as a prostitute. [SE peddle, to sell + PUSSY n. (2)]

peddler n. (also **pedlar**) 1 [late 19C] (US) a seller of counterfeit money. 2 [20C+] a male prostitute (cf. ASS PEDDLER n.). 3 [1920s+] (also **dope peddler**) a drug seller. 4 [1930s] (US tramp) a freight or goods train, a stopping train. 5 [1960s] (US prison) one who provides any form of contraband within the prison.

peddler's French n. see PEDLAR'S FRENCH n.

pedestals n. [late 17C–early 18C] the feet.

pedigree n. [1910s+] (US prison) 1 a criminal record; thus pedigreed, having a criminal record; pedigree-man, a recidivist. 2 a track record, a reputation.

Pedigree Chum n. [1990s+] semen. [rhy. sl. = COME n. (2); ult. the brand of dogfood Pedigree Chum]

pedlar n. see PEDDLER n.

pedlar's French n. (also **peddler's French**) 1 [mid-16C–mid-19C] cant, criminal slang. 2 [late 19C] any incomprehensible language. [the image is of alien foreignness rather than of France itself]

pedlar's pack n. [1970s+] dismissal from one's job. [rhy. sl. = SACK, THE n. (1)]

pedlar's pony n. [late 18C] a walking stick.

pedro n.¹ [1940s+] (US) any Spanish-speaking person. [Sp. name Pedro, Peter]

pedro n.² [1990s+] cocaine; thus friend of Pedro, a cocaine user (cf. AUNT NORA n.). [the stereotyped Spanish name, thus ref. to S. American origins of cocaine]

pee n.¹ 1 [20C+] urine. 2 [1930s+] an act of urination. [PEE v.¹ (1)]

pee n.² [1970s] (drugs) pure heroin.

pee, the n. see PISS, THE n.

pee v.¹ 1 [late 18C; mid-19C+] (also **pee-pee**) to urinate. 2 [1980s+] to rain (hard). [abbr./euph. PISS v.¹ (1)]

pee v.² [1970s–80s] (US campus) to do well. [fig. use of PEE v.¹ (1) or SE perform]

pee between two heels v. (also **straddle a chamber-pot**) [1940s–60s] (US Black) a phr. used when referring to a woman, or to female qualities, e.g. the finest bitch that ever peed between two heels. [the position of a woman when urinating]

peeble v. [20C+] (Irish) to whistle out of tune. [Scot.; note Yorks. dial. peeagle, to do something badly]

peece n. see PIECE n.² (1).

peed adj. see PISSED adj.¹.

peedie n. [20C+] (Ulster) a small boy's penis. [PEE n.¹ (1)]

peed off adj. [1970s+] (US) angry, irritated. [euph. for PISSED OFF adj.]

pee-eye n. see P.I. n.

pee hard n. [1980s+] (Aus. prison) an erection on waking in the morning. [PEE n.¹ (1) + HARD-ON n. (1)]

peehole n. [1930s–60s] (US) the vagina (cf. BLACK HOLE n.¹). [PEE n.¹ (1)]

peehole pirate n. [1960s] (US) a rapist. [PEEHOLE n. + PIRATE n.¹]

pee (it) off v. [1920s] (US) to waste, to squander. [semi-euph. var. PISS AWAY v.]

peek n. [1940s] (US) a peephole, e.g. in a brothel. [SE peek]

peek v. (also **peak**) [1910s+] (Aus.) to surrender, to give in.

peek-a-boo n. 1 [late 19C+] a translucent or transparent garment, usu. a blouse. 2 [1950s+] (Aus.) a garment made of broderie anglaise (open-work embroidery). [one is able to peek at the flesh behind the garment]

peekers n. [1920s–40s] (US Black) the eyes. [SE peek]

peek freak n. [1960s+] a homosexual voyeur who watches 2 other men during sex. [SE peek + FREAK n.¹ (6)]

peekish adj. [2000s] (US Black) homosexual, effeminate. [? SE peeky, i.e. pale]

peeko n. [1910s–40s] a brief glance around. [SE peek]

peek out v. [1990s+] (US Black) to appraise someone sexually. [SE peek]

peeks, the n. see BLOCK GAME n.

peek show n. [2000s] a live sex show. [SE peek + show]

peek through one's liquor v. [1930s–40s] (US Black) to pose as sober when one is in fact drunk.

peeky adj. see PEAKY adj.

peel n. [1920s+] (Aus.) a policeman. [abbr. PEELER n.²]

peel v. (also **skin**) **1** [mid-19C+] to extract money from a wallet surreptitiously. **2** [1960s+] (US Und.) to break into a safe. **3** [1980s] (also **peel a can**) to drink.

peel a fine green banana v. [1940s] (US Black) to seduce an attractive, light-skinned woman. [BANANA n.² (2)]

peel caps v. [1990s+] (US Black/teen) to attack violently. [lit. 'to peel the flesh from someone's skull']

peeled egg n. [20C+] (Ulster) anything easy or simple.

peele garlic n. see PILGARLIC n.

peeler n.¹ [19C] (US) **1** something exceptional, usu. in terms of strength. **2** someone exceptional.

peeler n.² (also **Mr Peeler**) [mid-19C+] a policeman; orig. the Irish constabulary. [proper name Sir Robert *Peel* (1788–1850), founder of the Metropolitan Police. The term is now obs. except in Northern Ireland]

peel garlic n. see PILGARLIC n.

peel-head adj. [1920s+] (W.I.) bald, esp. as a description of certain species of chickens or vultures.

peel it v. [mid-19C] (US) to run at full speed. [var. on SE *peel off*]

peel off v. see PEEL RUBBER V.

peel off a mass v. [1990s+] (W.I./UK Black teen) to hand out money. [PEEL V. (1) + MASS n.]

peel one's (best) end v. [late 19C–1910s] to enter a woman's vagina. [the sliding back of the foreskin]

peel one's ears v. [1940s–60s] (US) to listen closely.

peel one's eye v. (also **peel one's peepers, ...peeps**) [1900s–10s] to keep a lookout; to look wide-eyed. [SE/PEEPERS n. (1)]

peel rubber v. (also **catch rubber, peel off**) [1950s+] to drive a car very fast. [the smoking tyres that accompany acceleration]

peel someone's knob v. [1930s] (US) to beat someone up. [SE *peel* + KNOB n.¹ (1)]

peel someone's potatoes v. [2000s] (US Black) to beat up, to harm badly. [lit. to 'peel' one's testicles]

peel the banana v. [1990s+] to masturbate (cf. BEAT ONE'S MEAT v.). [SE *peel* + BANANA n.² (1)]

peel the bark v. [mid-19C] (boxing) to draw blood.

peel the patch off the weak point v. [late 19C] (US) to attack a person at their most vulnerable point.

peely-wally adj. [20C+] (Ulster) sickly-looking, wan. [Scot.]

pee-man n. [1910s–30s] (UK Und.) a policeman in civilian clothes. [abbr.]

peenie n. (also **peen, peeny, penie**) [1940s+] (US juv.) the penis. [dimin. of SE *penis*]

peeny adj. [1940s] (US) tiny.

pee off v.¹ see PEE (IT) OFF v.

pee off v.² see PISS OFF v.

pee on v. [1970s+] **1** to treat harshly, to bully. **2** to ignore, to dismiss. [fig. use of PEE v.¹ (1); var. on PISS ON v.]

pee oneself v. see PISS ONESELF v.

pee one's pants v. see PISS ONE'S PANTS v.

p.e.e.p. n. [1970s] the vagina; thus ext. as a very attractive woman. [abbr. perfectly elegant eating PUSSY n. (2)]

peep n.¹ [mid-18C–1930s] an eye; thus *on the peep*, at a glance. **2** [1990s+] a look.

peep n.² [late 19C+] (orig. US) a word, esp. one of complaint; thus *not a peep*, not a sound. [SE *peep*, a shrill noise]

peep n.³ [1970s+] (drugs) phencyclidine (cf. ACE n.⁴). [pron. of the 2 'P's in PCP n.]

peep n.⁴ see PEE-PEE n.¹ (1).

peep v.¹ [late 17C–early 18C] (UK Und.) to sleep. [PEEPY adj.]

peep v.² [late 19C–1960s] (US) to talk, esp. to the authorities. [PEEP n.²]

peep v.³ **1** [1930s+] to put someone or something under surveillance; in weak use, to watch, to look at. **2** [1950s+] (US Black) to discover something that was meant to be kept secret.

3 [1990s+] to pay close attention, to listen to what somebody is saying. [PEEP n.¹ (1)]

pee-pee n.¹ **1** [1920s+] (mainly US juv.) (also **peep, pee-pee meat**) the penis; thus *pull some pee-pee*, to fellate; *pee-pee puller*, a fellator. **2** [1970s] a male homosexual prostitute (cf. BONE-EATER n.). [SE *penis*/PEE v.¹ (1)]

pee-pee n.² [1930s+] (mainly US juv.) urination; usu. in phr. *go/make pee-pee*, to urinate. [redup. PEE n.¹ (2); euph. for PISS n. (2)]

pee-pee v. see PEE v.¹ (1).

pee-pee lover n. [1940s–70s] (gay) one who prefers the youngest boys for sex. [PEE-PEE n.¹ (1) + SE *lover*]

pee-pee meat n. see PEE-PEE n.¹ (1).

peeper n. **1** [mid-17C+] an eye; usu. in pl. see PEEPERS n. (1). **2** [late 17C–19C] a looking-glass. **3** [early 18C] glass, e.g. a window. **4** [late 18C–early 19C] a telescope, a spy-glass. **5** [late 19C+] a policeman; a security man, e.g. in a hotel (cf. BEAT-POUNDER n.). **6** [1940s] a private investigator, with implications of voyeurism. **7** [1970s+] a peeping Tom, a voyeur. [SE *peep*, to look at]

peepers n. **1** [mid-17C+] the eyes; also in sing. see PEEPER n. (1). **2** [early 19C] spectacles. **3** [20C+] (US) sunglasses. [SE *peep*, to look at]

peepers in mourning n. [early–mid-19C] a pair of black eyes; also in sing. [PEEPERS n. (1) + MOURNING n. (1)]

peep freak n. [1960s+] (US) a voyeur. [SE *peep* + FREAK n.¹ (6)]

peep game n. [1990s+] (US Black) finding out something that is secret; also as excl. meaning check this out! [PEEP v.³ (2) + GAME n.² (3)]

peeping adj. see PEEPY adj.

peep in the heater v. [1930s] (US) to perform cunnilingus. [coarse use of SE]

peep-joint n. [1960s] (US) a striptease club.

pee-pot n. see PISSPOT n. (1).

peeps n. [1980s+] (US Black/campus) **1** parents. **2** friends, people in general. [SE *people*]

peeps dig the range v. [1930s–40s] (US Black) to look around one's immediate environs. [PEEP n.¹ (1) + DIG v.⁵ (5) + SE *range*]

peep someone's hole-card v. [1950s+] (US prison/Black) to work out a person's (or consider one's own) hidden attitudes and emotions. [PEEP v.³ (2) + HOLE CARD n.]

peep things out v. [1990s+] (US Black) to see what is going on. [PEEP v.³ (2)]

peepy adj. (also **peeping**) [late 17C–early 19C] (UK Und.) sleepy, drowsy. [one's eyes are opening and closing; note *Peepy*, the name of a small child in Dickens' *Bleak House*]

peer v. [late 18C–mid-19C] to act cautiously.

peer queer n. [1960s–70s] (gay) a male homosexual voyeur. [SE *peer* + QUEER n. (4) + assonance]

peery adj. **1** [mid-17C–mid-18C] shy, fearful. **2** [18C–19C] suspicious. **3** [early 18C–early 19C] (UK Und.) sly. **4** [late 18C–mid-19C] inquisitive. [SE *peer*, to look around suspiciously]

peety adj. [late 19C] cheerful. [? SE *pert*]

peeve n. [20C+] alcohol, beer; thus *peeve artist*, a regular drinker. [? BEVVY n. (1); note Rus. *peevo*, beer, Rom. whisky]

pee-warmer n. see PISS-WARMER n.

pee-wee n. **1** [late 19C] an act of urination. **2** [late 19C+] the penis, usu. of a small boy. **3** [1900s–50s] (drugs) a very thin marijuana cigarette. **4** [1910s+] (Aus.) a bowler hat. **5** [1930s+] a nickname for any noticeably small or short person. **6** [1980s+] (US drugs) crack cocaine, esp. $5 worth (i.e. very little) (cf. BASE n.). **7** [1990s+] (UK Black) a very junior member of a gang. [orig. dial. *pee-wee*, tiny; (1) and (2) also PEE-WEE v.]

pee-wee adj. (also **pewee**) [late 19C+] small, unimportant, junior.

pee-wee v. [late 19C+] (UK juv.) to urinate. [redup. of PEE v.¹ (1) but poss. predates WEE v.]

pee-willy *n.* [1920s+] (*Can.*) an effeminate man. [? PEE-WEE n. (2)/PEE-WEE adj. + WILLIE n.⁵]

peeyem *n. see* P.M. n.

Peg, the *n.* [1930s] (*Can.*) Winnipeg. [abbr.]

peg *n.*¹ [17C+] the penis.

peg *n.*² [early 18C–19C] **1** a blow, esp. a straight-armed jab; thus *peg in the daylight*, a blow in the eye; *peg in the victualling office*, a blow in the stomach; *peg in the haltering place*, a blow under the ear. **2** in fig. use, a metaphorical blow, a verbal attack.

peg *n.*³ (*also* peg stick) [late 18C–19C] (*orig. UK Und.*) a shilling (5p). [Scot. *peg*, 1 shilling; mainly Aus. use in mid–late 19C]

peg *n.*⁴ **1** [late 18C+] a leg; often in pl. **2** [19C–1940s] a wooden leg; one who wears a wooden leg. **3** [1910s–60s] (*US tramp*) a train rider who has lost a leg. [abbr. SE *pegleg*]

peg *n.*⁵ [early 19C+] (*orig. Anglo-Ind.*) a drink, esp. of brandy and soda. [? each drink was seen as 'a peg [nail] in one's coffin'; but note 17C SE *peg*, 'one of a set of pins fixed at intervals in a drinking vessel as marks to measure the quantity which each drinker was to drink' (*OED*)]

peg *n.*⁶ [20C+] (*Aus. Und.*) a look, a survey. [PEG v.⁴ (1)]

peg *n.*⁷ [1900s] (*UK tramp*) anywhere a free meal may be obtained. [? play on SPIKE n.² (1)]

peg *n.*⁸ [1940s+] (*drugs*) heroin; a capsule of heroin. [ety. unknown; ? link to opium jargon or PEG n.⁵]

peg *v.*¹ **1** [18C+] to throw (at), to pitch (at); thus [20C+] (*Aus.*) *peg a gooly*, to throw a stone; *pegger*, thrower. **2** [1950s] (*US*) to shoot at. [SE *peg*, to target or aim at with a peg]

peg *v.*² **1** [late 18C–19C; 2000s] to run, to move fast. **2** [early–mid-19C] to drive, esp. a cab. [orig. UK northern dial.; (2) ? pun on SE *peg*, to drive in a peg]

peg *v.*³ [mid–late 19C] to drink. [PEG n.⁵]

peg *v.*⁴ (*also* peg for) **1** [mid-19C+] to look at, to stare. **2** [1910s+] (*orig. US*) to recognize, to work out, to analyse. **3** [1920s–60s] to survey. **4** [1980s] (*Aus./N.Z.*) to search.

peg *v.*⁵ [mid-19C+] to have sexual intercourse; usu. as *peg up/down* (cf. BANG v.¹). [SE *peg*, to drive a peg into the ground; or *peg away*, to 'hammer away' at]

peg *v.*⁶ [late 19C+] (*Aus.*) to starve; thus *pegging for*, desperate for. [? one has *put the peg* into one's stomach, i.e. blocked it off; ? var. on SE *beg*]

peg *v.*⁷ *see* PEG OUT v.

peg a gooly *v. see* PEG v.¹ (1).

peg along *v.* [mid-19C+] to persist. [var. on PEG AWAY v.² (1)]

peg away *v.*¹ (*also* peg off) [19C] to move off quickly. [ext. of PEG v.² (1)]

peg away *v.*² **1** [19C+] (*also* peg in) to do something (usu. work, but also e.g. eating) hard and energetically for a long period; often as *peg away at*. **2** [1960s] to shoot at. [the hammering in of tent pegs]

peg-boy *n.* [1960s–70s] a male homosexual prostitute. [PEG n.¹]

peg for *v. see* PEG v.⁴.

pegged *adj.* **1** [20C+] (*Ulster*) angry. **2** [1980s] (*US campus*) disparaged. [? fig. use of PEG v.¹ (1)]

pegged out *adj.* [late 19C] notorious, infamous. [cribbage use, *pegged out*, finished]

pegger *n.*¹ [late 19C] a regular or heavy drinker, a person who 'constantly stimulates themselves by means of brandy and soda-water' (Hotten, 1873). [PEG n.⁵]

pegger *n.*² *see* PEG v.¹ (1).

peggers *n.* [2000s] (*US Black*) peg-top trousers.

pegging-crib *n.* [mid-19C] a brothel (cf. BADGER-CRIB n.). [PEG v.⁵ + CRIB n.¹ (2)]

pegging for *adj. see* PEG v.⁶.

peggy *n.*¹ **1** [mid-19C–1920s] a thin poker used to facilitate the raking out of fireplaces. **2** [late 19C–1920s] a tooth. **3** [late 19C+] a 1-legged person. **4** [20C+] a wooden leg, a peg-leg. [fig. uses of SE *peg*]

peggy *n.*² [1970s+] (*Aus.*) an unskilled worker who makes tea, sweeps up and takes on similar undemanding tasks. [naut. jargon *peggy*, a ship's mess-steward or menial; ult. *peg-leg*, a 1-legged man who was often given such duties]

peggy *n.*³ [1990s+] (*W.I.*) a woman with sexual passion for a particular group of men. [? anecdotal or ? fig. use of SE *pegleg*, i.e. she has only 1 sexual 'leg' to stand on]

Peggy Dell *n.* [2000s] (*Irish*) a smell. [rhy. sl.; ult. Irish pianist and entertainer *Peggy Dell* (*c*.1905–79)]

peggy's leg *n.* [1920s+] (*Irish juv.*) a type of boiled sweet on a stick. [dial. *peggy*, an implement for stirring washing; presumably a supposed resemblance]

peg-house *n.*¹ [1920s–30s] a public house. [PEG n.⁵ + SE *house*]

peg-house *n.*² **1** [1930s+] a male brothel (cf. ACCOMMODATION HOUSE n.). **2** [1950s] (*US Und.*) a prison with a high level of homosexuality (cf. BANDHOUSE n.). [SE *peg* + HOUSE n.¹ (1); the East Indian equivalents where the boys allegedly sat on wooden pegs to maintain a well-distended anus]

peg in *v. see* PEG AWAY v.² (1).

peg it *v. see* PEG OUT v.

peg it into *v.* [mid–late 19C] to hit. [ext. of PEG v.¹ (1)]

peg-legger *n.*¹ [1930s–40s] a 1-legged man. [SE *peg-leg*, one who has a wooden leg]

peg-legger *n.*² [1930s–40s] a beggar; thus *peg-legging*, begging. [rhy. sl.]

peglegs *n.* [1950s–60s] (*US*) tapered trousers. [PEGS n.]

pego *n.* (*also* Don Pego) [mid-17C–19C] the penis. [? Gk *pege*, spring or fountain; this 'classical' aspect made the term esp. popular in 19C pornography]

peg off *v. see* PEG AWAY v.¹.

peg out *v.* (*also* peg, peg it) [mid-19C+] **1** to die. **2** to be financially ruined. **3** to lose one's energy, esp. during a strenuous exercise or sport. [cribbage use + ? the image of taking down a tent]

peg puff *n.* [19C] an older woman dressed younger than her years. [? generic use of *Peg*, Margaret + *puffed up*]

pegs *n.* [1930s–60s] (*US Black*) trousers that taper sharply. [mid-19C *peg-top trousers*, very wide in the hips and correspondingly narrow at the ankles]

peg stick *n. see* PEG n.³.

pekkie *n.* (*also* peckie, pek) [1960s+] (*S.Afr.*) a Black person. [? Zulu *umpheki*, a cook]

pekoe *n.* [1950s] (*drugs*) top-quality opium (cf. APOSTLE n.). [SE *pekoe*, a superior variety of Chinese tea]

pelf *n.* [late 16C+] money. [SE *pelf*, stolen property]

pelfry *n.* [16C–early 17C] (*UK Und.*) stolen goods, esp. the booty gained by those who pick locks. [SE *pelf*, stolen property; *pelf* and *pelfry* are both SE in 14C–15C]

pelican *n.* [mid-19C+] (*US*) a native of Louisiana. [the pelican on the state flag]

pelile *adj.* [20C+] (*S.Afr.*) exhausted, absolutely finished. [Nguni *ukuphela*, to finish]

pell *n. see* PAL n. (1).

pellets *n.* [1960s–70s] (*drugs*) **1** capsules of LSD. **2** capsules of amphetamine.

pellicle *n.* [1950s] (*drugs*) high-quality opium (cf. APOSTLE n.). [Lat. *pellis*, the skin; the ref. is to the slashing of the skin of the poppy-heads to release opium]

pellie *n.* [1950s+] (*S.Afr., mainly Western Cape*) a friend, a pal; thus *ou pellie*, old friend; *pellie blou*, a 'real pal', a 'bosom-buddy' (the *blou* means blue, as in 'true blue'). [PAL n. (1)]

pellock *n.* [late 18C] (*US Und.*) sugar. [ety. unknown]

peloothered *adj. see* POLLUTED adj.

pelt *n.*¹ (*also* pelter) [late 16C–mid-19C] a temper, a rage. [SE *pelt*, to attack (verbally or physically)]

pelt *n.*² **1** [17C+] the human skin; thus *in one's pelt*, naked. **2** [1970s] a human being.

pelter n.[1] (*also* **pelterer**) [mid-19C–1910s] a drenching downpour. [SE *pelt*, to beat violently]

pelter n.[2] [mid-19C–1930s] a horse, esp. a slow, old one. [ironic use of SE *pelt* (*along*) or 16C *pelter*, a paltry or peddling person]

pelter n.[3] [late 19C] **1** something that goes fast, including a horse; thus *in a pelter*, in a hurry. **2** lit. or fig., anything conspicuously large. [SE *pelt*, to move rapidly]

pelter n.[4] *see* PELT n.[1]

pelterer n. *see* PELTER n.[1]

pelt for leather adv. *see* HELL FOR LEATHER adv.

pelting-irons n. [mid-17C] the testicles.

pelt your skin! excl. [20C+] (*W.I.*) be off! go away! [SE *pelt*, to move fast]

Pen n. [1900s] (*Aus.*) Pentridge Jail. [abbr.]

pen n.[1] [late 16C–1940s] the penis (cf. BLACK PENCIL n.). **2** [mid-19C–1900s] the vagina. [(1) resemblance; (2) in dial., used of a sow]

pen n.[2] [early 19C+] a *peni*tentiary. [abbr.; 20C+ use mainly US]

pen n.[3] [mid-19C+] a smell. [abbr. PEN AND INK n. (1)]

pen n.[4] [late 19C–1940s] (*Aus.*) a threepenny piece. [ety. unknown]

pen v. *see* PEN (AND INK) v.

penal n. [1910s–40s] (*UK Und./police*) penal servitude. [abbr.]

penance n. [mid-19C+] (*US*) an inhabitant of Pennsylvania. [pun on *Penn*sylvania and the religiosity of its citizens]

penance board n. (*also* **pennance-board**) [late 17C–mid-19C] the pillory.

pen and ink n. **1** [mid-19C+] a stink. **2** [1950s] a mink. **3** [1960s+] (*orig. Aus./N.Z.*) a drink. [rhy. sl.]

pen (and ink) v. [late 19C+] **1** to stink. **2** to cause problems, to complain, to 'kick up a stink'. [rhy. sl.]

pen and inker n. [1940s+] a suspicious person, esp. a possible informer. [rhy. sl. = STINKER n.[1] (1)]

Penang lawyer n. [mid-late 19C] a walking stick made from the stem of a dwarf palm (*Licuala acutifolia*) found in Malaya and Singapore. [? the use of such sticks in settling disputes at Penang; or Malay *pinang líyar*, wild areca, or *pinang láyor*, fire-dried areca]

pence n. *see* PENNIES n.

pencil n. **1** [1930s] (*US prison*) a revolver. **2** [1930s+] the penis, usu. that of a small boy; thus [1940s] *pencil and tassel*, a small boy's penis and testes (cf. BLACK PENCIL n.). [resemblance]

pencil (and chalk) v. [1910s] (*Aus.*) to walk. [rhy. sl.]

pencil dick n. **1** [1970s+] (*US gay*) a long, thin penis (cf. BLACK PENCIL n.). **2** [1980s+] (*US*) a general term of abuse, the implication being that the person in question has a small penis (cf. NOODLE DICK n.). [SE *pencil* + DICK n.[4] (1)]

pencil geek n. [1970s+] (*US campus*) anyone who works more devotedly than their peers see fit. [SE *pencil* + GEEK n.[1] (4)]

pencil head n. [1970s] an extremely diligent student.

pencil-head adj. [1990s+] academic, studious (the over-riding inference is an inability to function in the 'real' world). [PENCIL HEAD n.]

penciller n. **1** [mid-late 19C] a bookmaker's clerk. **2** [late 19C] (*US*) a journalist. **3** [late 19C+] (*Aus.*) a bookmaker or their clerk. [SE *pencil*]

pencil-neck n. (*also* **neck**) [1960s+] an intellectual, or one who is considered (negatively) to be one.

pencil-necked adj. [1960s+] intellectual. [PENCIL-NECK n.]

pencil, open, lost and found n. [late 19C] £1 (cf. CHERRY-PICKER n.[5]). [rhy. sl.]

pencil-pusher n. (*also* **pen-driver**, **pen-pusher**) **1** [late 19C+] (*orig. US*) a clerk, a white-collar worker; thus *push a pencil/pen*, to perform office work. **2** [late 19C+] a journalist; a hack writer. **3** [1920s] a letter-writer.

pencil-pushing n. (*also* **pen-pushing**) [late 19C+] writing, esp. office work. [PENCIL-PUSHER n. (1)]

pencil-pushing adj. (*also* **pen-pushing**) [20C+] pertaining to bureaucracy, clerking, paperwork. [PENCIL-PUSHING n.]

pencil-sharpener n. [1990s+] (*UK juv.*) the vagina (cf. BAG n.[1]). [PENCIL n. (2) + SE *sharpener*]

pencil-squeezer n. [1980s] a masturbator. [PENCIL n. (2) + SE *squeezer*]

pencil stiff n. [1960s] (*US*) a clerk. [SE *pencil* + STIFF n.[2] (7)]

pencil whip v. [1990s+] (*US prison*) **1** of a guard, to give a written reprimand. **2** (*also* **paper whip**) of a prisoner, to file a lawsuit or a grievance.

pencil-whipping adj. [2000s] (*US*) a general term of abuse, the implication is of masturbation. [PENCIL n. (2)]

pen-driver n. *see* PENCIL-PUSHER n.

pendulum n. [19C] the penis. [it 'swings']

penelope n. (*also* **penelopes**) [1990s+] (*US*) a policeman, the police (cf. BILLY n.[6]). [initial letters]

penguin n.[1] [20C+] (*US, mainly juv.*) a nun. [her trad. black and white habit]

penguin n.[2] [2000s] (*drugs*) a variety of LSD (cf. A n.[3]). [the black and white pill]

penguin suit n. (*also* **draught-board suit**, **penguin gear**) [1910s] a dinner jacket. [the black jacket and trousers and accompanying white shirt resemble a penguin's markings]

penie n. *see* PEENIE n.

Peninsular n. [mid-19C] a veteran of the *Peninsular* War (1808–14). [abbr.]

peninsular n. **1** [mid-19C] a female pickpocket. **2** [1950s+] a very inquisitive woman. [? play on SE *peninsular*, a projecting strip of land, i.e. she sticks in (1) a finger for thieving or (2) her nose]

penis wrinkle n. [1980s+] (*US campus*) an unpleasant, un-sophisticated man.

penitentiary agent n. [1930s+] (*US Und.*) a lawyer who seems to be working more for the courts and police than for the defence of their client.

penitentiary bait n. *see* JAILBAIT n. (2).

penitentiary dispatcher n. [1960s+] (*US Und.*) a public defender. [the supposed failing of these court-appointed lawyers, whose caseload is often said to be too heavy for them to put forward an adequate defence, and whose clients thus end up in the penitentiary]

penitentiary highball n. [1930s] (*US prison*) home-brewed prison alcohol, based on strained shellac and milk. [SE *penitentiary* + HIGHBALL n.[1]]

penitentiary punk n. *see* PUNK n.[1] (2).

penitentiary shot n. (*also* **pen shot**) [1930s–50s] (*US drugs/prison*) an injection achieved by using a rudimentary 'needle', in fact a pin and a medicine dropper. The pin is pushed into the vein and the dropper, filled with a solution of heroin and water, pushed over it. [SE *penitentiary*/PEN n.[2] + SHOT n.[6] (2)]

penitentiary turn-out n. *see* TURN-OUT n.[4] (2).

penman n. **1** [mid-19C+] (*UK Und.*) (*also* **pen**) a forger of counterfeit notes. **2** [20C+] (*US*) a student who signs their parent's name to excuse notes. **3** [1930s] (*US prison*) an inmate who writes letters to the authorities, presumably informing on his fellow prisoners. **4** [1930s+] (*US*) a forger of false signatures etc on cheques and credit cards.

pennam n. *see* PANNAM n.

pennance-board n. *see* PENANCE BOARD n.

Pennemite n. (*also* **Panamite**, **Pennamite**, **Pennite**) [late 18C+] a native or inhabitant of Pennsylvania.

pennies n. (*also* **pence**) [late 19C] money.

pennif n. [mid-late 19C] **1** a £5 note. **2** any banknote. [backsl. = FINNIP n.]

Pennite n. *see* PENNEMITE n.

penn'orth of bread n. [late 19C+] the head. [rhy. sl.]

penn'orth (of chalk) n. [20C+] a walk; also as a term of dismissal. [rhy. sl.]

penn'orth o' treacle n. [late 19C] a pretty woman.

penn'orth o' treason *n.* [late 19C] an anonymous but presumably scandalous Sunday paper, 'a notorious penny Sunday London paper which attacks every party and has no policy of its own' (Ware).

Pennsy *n.* [1920s+] *Pennsy*lvania; the *Pennsy*lvania rail route. [abbr.]

Pennsylvania salve *n.* [late 19C–1930s] (*US tramp*) apple butter. [SE *Pennsylvania* + SALVE n. (2)]

penny *n.*[1] **1** [mid-19C+] (*Can./US*) a cent; thus as adj., cheap. **2** [1940s–60s] (*US*) a dollar.

penny *n.*[2] *see* PENNY (A POUND) n.

penny *v.* [1990s+] (*W.I.*) to observe, to scrutinize. [abbr. SE *penetrate*]

penny-a-liar *n.* [late 19C] a hack journalist. [pun on PENNY-A-LINER n.]

penny-a-liner *n.* (*also* **liner**) [mid-19C+] a freelance literary or journalistic hack; thus *penny-a-lining*, freelancing. [the rate of pay offered to such writers]

penny-a-mile *n.* **1** [late 19C–1920s] a hat. **2** [late 19C–1920s] the head. **3** [20C+] a smile. [rhy. sl.; (1) = TILE n.; (2) ext. of (1)]

penny ante *adj.* [mid-19C+] (*orig. US*) insignificant, unimportant. [poker jargon; an *ante* is a deposit that entitles a player to join a round of play; thus an ante of only 1 penny is de facto insignificant]

penny (a pound) *n.* [20C+] the ground. [rhy. sl.]

penny awful *n. see* PENNY DREADFUL n.

penny banger *n.* [1950s+] a mistake, a blunder. [rhy. sl. = CLANGER n. (1)]

penny black *n.* [20C+] the back. [rhy. sl.; ult. the *penny black*, the UK's first postage stamp, issued 1840]

penny-boy *n.* **1** [late 19C–1910s] 'a boy who haunted the cattle markets on the chance of driving beasts to the slaughter-house' (F&H). **2** [late 19C–1910s] a term of mild contempt. **3** [20C+] (*Ulster*) anyone seen as being at the beck and call of someone else. [such a boy would presumably be tipped a penny]

penny brown *n.* [20C+] (*Aus.*) a town. [rhy. sl.]

penny bun *n.* [1920s+] **1** the number 1; 1 penny. **2** the sun. **3** a son. [rhy. sl.]

penny-buster *n.* [mid-19C–1900s] a small loaf. [it 'busts' one's stomach or appetite for the price of 1 penny]

penny-catcher *n.* [1940s+] (*W.I./UK Black*) one who is willing to work for derisory pay.

penny-come-quick *n.* [late 19C+] (*UK Und.*) a confidence trick. [rhy. sl.]

penny death-traps *n.* [late 19C] glass paraffin lamps. [made cheaply in Germany, they broke easily and caused a number of deaths]

penny dips *n.* [1960s–80s] (*Aus.*) the lips. [rhy. sl.]

penny dreadful *n.* (*also* **penny awful, penny horrible**) [mid-late 19C] a sensationally written 'true crime' story, sold for a penny (cf. PENNY NUMBER n.).

penny for the guy *n.* [1990s+] a pie. [rhy. sl.; ult. *penny for the guy*, the trad. demand of children making a figure to put on the bonfire on Guy Fawkes's Night, 5 November]

penny gaff *n.* [mid-late 19C] a cheap theatre or music hall. [SE *penny* + GAFF n.[1] (2)]

penny gush *n.* [late 19C] the effusive journalese found in penny newspapers, the late 19C tabloids. [SE *penny* + GUSH n.[2]]

penny hang *n.* [19C–1930s] (*orig. naut.*) a cellar or basement which features ropes strung from side to side on which drunken or exhausted clients, orig. sailors, drape themselves for a fitful sleep. In the morning one end of the rope is untied and the sleepers are dumped on the floor.

penny hop *n.* [mid-19C] a cheap, orig. country dance; thus *twopenny hop; shilling hop*. [SE *penny* + HOP n.[1] (1)]

penny horrible *n. see* PENNY DREADFUL n.

penny-hugging *adj. see* PENNY-PINCHING adj.

penny lattice-house *n.* [18C–early 19C] a poor alehouse. [RED LATTICE n.]

pennyline *n.* [1960s+] (*S.Afr. Black*) a cheap prostitute (cf. DOLLAR-WOMAN n.). [? ext. of PENNY-A-LINER n.]

penny loaf *n.* [late 19C] (*UK Und.*) a coward. [one who would rather live on a penny loaf than make a greater effort and steal beef]

penny locket *n.* [late 19C] a pocket. [rhy. sl.]

penny number *n.* **1** [mid-19C–1900s] a sensational story, serialized in weekly penny magazines; thus *by/in penny numbers*, in instalments (cf. PENNY DREADFUL n.). **2** [1950s+] in pl., very small, insignificant numbers. [the stories serialized in weekly penny magazines]

penny pick *n.* [mid-late 19C] a cheap cigar. [SE *penny* + PICK n.[1]]

penny-pinch *v.* [1920s+] to act meanly, to save money where not really necessary. [backform. f. PENNY-PINCHER n.]

penny-pincher *n.* [1910s+] a mean, miserly person.

penny-pinching *adj.* (*also* **penny-hugging**) [1910s+] **1** mean, avaricious. **2** living in a penurious manner. [PENNY-PINCHER n.]

penny pots *n.* [mid-19C–1920s] pimples found on a heavy drinker's face.

penny puzzle *n.* [late 19C] a sausage. [its dubious ingredients are 'never found out']

penny rush *n.* [1910s–20s] (*Irish*) cheap children's matinées at the cinema; thus (reflective of changing prices) [1930s–40s] *twopenny rush*; [1940s–50s] *fourpenny rush*; [1950s–60s] *sixpenny rush*.

penny starver *n.* **1** [mid-late 19C] a penny roll. **2** [late 19C] the cheapest brand of cigars, 3 for 2 pence.

penny stinker *n.* [late 19C–1930s] a cheap cigar. [STINKER n.[1] (3)]

penny swag *n.* [mid-19C] a seller of penny lots. [SE *penny* + SWAG n.[1] (6)]

penny toff *n.* [late 19C] a working-class dandy who can only imitate the richer genuine article. [SE *penny* + TOFF n. (2)]

pennyweighter *n.* [late 19C–1960s] (*US*) **1** one who steals jewellery or precious stones or metals, esp. by entering a shop, asking to inspect the stock and, using an adhesive substance on their hands, picking up certain items; thus *pennyweighting*, performing this variety of theft. **2** one who steals by substituting paste gems for the real ones. [SE *pennyweight*, a measure used to state the fineness of silver]

penny-white *adj.* [late 17C–early 18C] usu. of a woman, rich but unattractive. [lit. 'one who has been rendered *white*, i.e. beautiful, by her possession of (silver) pennies']

penocha *n.* [1960s+] (*US Black/Sp.*) the vagina. [synon. Sp. sl.]

pen-pusher *see under* PENCIL-PUSHER n.

pen shot *n. see* PENITENTIARY SHOT n.

pension *n.* [1970s] (*UK Und.*) that sum of money paid over for 'protection'.

pensionary miss *n. see* PENSIONER (TO THE PETTICOAT) n.

pensioner of the placket *n.* [mid-17C] a pimp (cf. ABBOT ON THE CROSS n.). [PENSIONER (TO THE PETTICOAT) n. + PLACKET n. (1)]

pensioner's leg *n.* **1** [1990s+] a thin, pale, knobbly, veiny penis (cf. ARM n.[1]). **2** [2000s] a thin kebab.

pensioner (to the petticoat) *n.* [late 17C–19C] a pimp; thus *pensionary miss*, a madam's or pimp's prostitute (cf. ABBOT ON THE CROSS n.). [note 1920s US theatre jargon *pensioner*, the husband of an actress]

Pent, the *n.* [mid-19C–1910s] *Pent*onville prison, London N1 (cf. ABBOTT'S PRIORY n.). [abbr.]

penthouse-nab *n.* [late 17C–early 19C] a large, high hat. [SE *penthouse*, a smaller building (often with a sloping roof) attached to the main structure + NAB n.[1] (3)]

penwiper *n.*[1] **1** [19C] the vagina. **2** [1900s–40s] a handkerchief. [(1) PEN *n.*[1] (1); (2) SE *pen*]

penwiper *n.*[2] [1900s] (*UK juv.*) a scholastic gown or coat. ['The 'pen-wiper', a small piece of folded silk which is attached to the back of the proctor's gown [at Oxford]' (*OED*)]

pen yen *n.* (*also* **ah-pen-yen, pen yan, pin yen, pin yenz, pinyon**) [late 19C+] (*drugs*) opium (cf. APOSTLE *n.*). [Chinese *nga pun-yin*, opium]

peola *n.* [1930s+] (*US Black*) a light-skinned Black woman. [Bantu *peula*, skin]

peony *n. see* PEACH *n.*[1] (2).

people *n.*[1] **1** [mid-19C–1930s] one's relatives, one's family; usu. qualified as *my people, her people* etc. **2** [late 19C+] (*US*) one's group, e.g. fellow players in a company of actors. **3** [late 19C+] (*orig. US*) an admirable person, a trustworthy individual, e.g. *Sarah is good people*; equally applicable, in context, to criminals as to the law-abiding.

people *n.*[2] (*US Black/drugs*) **1** [1950s–70s] narcotics agents; police. **2** [1960s+] as *the people*, high-level drug dealers.

people-in-law *n.* [late 19C+] one's married partner's family. [PEOPLE *n.*[1] (1) + SE sfx *-in-law*]

people's bank *n.* [1930s] (*Irish*) a pawnbroker's shop.

Peoria *n.* (*also* **Peoria water, Peory water**) [1920s–30s] (*US tramp*) a thin, meagre soup; also a 'mess' of potatoes, boiled then fried. [mispron. of Fr. *purée* + derog. ref. to the city of *Peoria*; note Irwin, *American Tramp and Und. Slang* (1931): 'perhaps so called from a similar article of food served in the Illinois State Prison at the city of the same name, perhaps from the fact that much of the State provides poor pickings for tramps who must get along as best they can on scant rations']

pep *n.*[1] [20C+] (*orig. US*) energy, enthusiasm, spirit. [? abbr. PEPPER *n.* (3)]

pep *n.*[2] *see* PEP (PILL) *n.*

pep-'em-ups *n.* [1970s+] (*drugs*) amphetamine pills (cf. A *n.*[2]). [the effects]

pepped out *adj.* [1920s] (*US*) exhausted. [PEP *n.*[1]]

pepper *n.* **1** [early–mid-19C] hard blows, e.g. in a prizefight. **2** [late 19C] serious trouble. **3** [20C+] zest, vitality. **4** [1940s–50s] (*US Black/teen*) an attractive young woman.

pepper *v.* **1** [late 16C+] to infect with venereal disease. **2** [late 16C+] to hit hard. **3** [mid-19C–1920s] to tease, to deceive. [SE *throw pepper in someone's eyes*]

pepper alley *n.* [early 19C] a state of being beaten up. [*Pepper Alley*, a landing place on the Southwark side of the Thames and thus equated with crime, violence and debauchery; + PEPPER *v.* (2)]

pepper and salt *n.*[1] [late 19C] (*US*) a severe telling-off.

pepper and salt *n.*[2] [1960s–70s] (*US Black*) Black and White people running together in the street, presumably in the civil rights, anti-Vietnam and other demonstrations of the era.

pepper and salt *n.*[3] [1980s] (*Aus.*) a Baltic immigrant. [rhy. sl. = BALT *n.*]

pepper and salts *n.* [mid-19C] (*US*) striped dress trousers.

pepper belly *n.* (*also* **hot (pepper) belly**) [1960s+] (*US*) a derog. term for a Mexican or Mexican-American (cf. BEAN *n.*[8]). [the stereotyped Mexican love of hot, peppery food]

pepper-box *n.* [mid-19C] (*US*) the head. [resemblance]

pepper-castor *n.* (*also* **pepper-caster**) **1** [late 18C] the head. **2** [late 19C] (*US*) a revolver. [? resemblance]

peppered *adj.* **1** [early 17C–18C] dead, badly hurt. **2** [mid-17C–early 19C] (*also* **peppered off**) very badly infected with venereal disease; occas. crab-lice. [PEPPER *v.* + play on HOT *adj.*[3] (1)]

pepper 'em up *v.* [1970s+] (*US Black*) **1** to prepare for something. **2** to get drunk or intoxicated on drugs. **3** to work out in a gym. **4** to fight and poss. injure one's assailant. [all imply some preparatory 'seasoning']

pepper-fly *n.* [1950s] (*W.I.*) an irascible, quick-tempered person. [dial. *pepper-fly*, a sand-fly, which can give a painful sting]

pepper gut *n.* [1920s+] (*US*) a Mexican-American (cf. BEAN *n.*[8]). [SE (*chili*) *pepper*, a main constituent of Mexican cooking]

pepper-kissing *n.* [1970s+] (*US Black*) attempting to put the best face on bad news. [euph. for ARSE-KISS *v.*]

pepper-kissing *adj.* [1970s+] (*US Black*) a negative intensifier meaning no good, useless etc. [euph. for MOTHERFUCKING *adj.*]

peppermint flavour *n.* [1960s] a favour. [rhy. sl.]

peppermint rocks *n.* (*also* **peppermints**) [20C+] socks. [rhy. sl.]

peppermint swirl *n.* [1970s–80s] LSD, esp. when combined with another drug (cf. A *n.*[3]). [? the name of a sweet]

pepper-proof *adj.* [late 17C–18C] (temporarily) free of venereal disease. [PEPPERED *adj.* (2)]

pepper-upper *n.* **1** [1930s+] alcohol. **2** [1930s+] (*also* **pepper-up**) an amphetamine. **3** [1950s] a cheerleader. [PEP UP *v.*]

pep (pill) *n.* (*also* **pep**) [1940s+] (*drugs*) an amphetamine (cf. A *n.*[2]). [PEP *n.*[1]]

peppy *adj.* [1910s+] (*orig. US*) **1** cheerful, enthusiastic; thus adv. *peppily.* **2** exciting. **3** of machines, powerful. [PEP *n.*[1]]

Pepsi *n.* [1970s–80s] (*Can.*) **1** a modern, young French-Canadian (as opposed to their older forebears). **2** an English-Canadian. [their drinking of *Pepsi-Cola*, rather than more potent 'men's drinks']

Pepsi(-Cola) habit *n.* (*also* **Pepsi-Cola kick**) [1960s+] (*drugs*) a limited or occasional use of drugs. [*Pepsi-Cola*, a soft rather than alcoholic drink + HABIT *n.* (1)]

pep squad *n.* [1950s+] a group of cheerleaders. [PEP *n.*[1]]

pepst *adj.* [late 16C] drunk. [ety. unknown]

pep talk *n.* [1920s+] any kind of talk, esp. an inspirational lecture, designed to improve the listener's morale. [PEP *n.*[1] + SE *talk*]

pep up *v.* [1920s+] **1** (*orig. US*) to cheer up, to inspire, to exhort. **2** (*orig. US*) to improve. **3** (*US*) to act in a lively manner. **4** (*drugs*) to energize. [PEP *n.*[1]]

perc *see also under* PERCOLATE.

perc *n.* (*also* **perk**) [1930s–50s] **1** (*orig. US cowboy, then tramp*) percolated coffee, as opposed to that boiled up in a pan. **2** (*US*) a coffee *percolator*. [abbr.]

percentage *n.* [mid-19C+] (*US*) advantage, use, 'point', e.g. *what's/where's the percentage?* what's the point? what's the intention?; thus *no percentage*, no point, no advantage.

perch *n.*[1] [mid-19C] a bed; thus *off to perch*, going to bed.

perch *n.*[2] [late 19C] death. [ext. of DROP OFF THE PERCH *v.* (2)]

perch *n.*[3] [1970s+] **1** (*Aus.*) a glass of beer. **2** (*US campus*) a pint of liquor. [SE *perch*, a common freshwater fish]

perch *v.*[1] [late 19C] to die. [PERCH *n.*[2]]

perch *v.*[2] [20C+] (*US*) to kiss. [the image of a pair of lovebirds perched on a branch]

percher *n.*[1] [early 18C] a dying person. [DROP OFF THE PERCH *v.* (2)]

percher *n.*[2] [1970s+] (*UK Und.*) **1** a gullible victim for a swindle or con-game. **2** a simple arrest. [the victim is 'perched' in innocent vulnerability]

percolate *v.*[1] (*also* **perc, perk**) [20C+] (*US*) to stroll, to wander around; thus *percolating*, walking around looking for sexual conquests. [misuse of SE *perambulate*]

percolate *v.*[2] (*also* **perc, perk**) [1920s+] (*US*) **1** to run smoothly, esp. of an engine. **2** to penetrate the mind. **3** to do something well. **4** to happen.

percolator *n.* [1930s–50s] **1** a party. **2** (*US Black*) a party held so that the host can collect money from their guests so as to pay the rent (cf. FISH-FRY *n.*). [? the money *percolates* through from the guests to the host]

percs *n.* (*also* **perks**) [1970s+] *Perc*odan (cf. PERRY *n.*). [abbr.]

percy *n.*[1] **1** [20C+] (*orig. US*) (*also* **percy-boy/-pants**) an effeminate man, a weakling; one who appears exhausted. **2** [1940s] a masculine girl, poss. a lesbian (cf. AMY-JOHN n.). [the 'effeminate' image of the proper name]

percy n.² [1960s+] the penis. [joc. use of proper name, based on initial letters]

percy-purse n. [1980s] the vagina. [PERCY n.¹ (1) + SE purse; PURSE n. (1) is prob. coincidental]

Percy Thrower n. [1940s+] the telephone. [rhy. sl. = BLOWER n.⁵; ult. UK gardening expert *Percy Thrower* (1913–88)]

peremptory adj. [late 16C] absolute, thorough, complete.

peremptory adv. [late 16C] absolutely, entirely.

perf! excl. [1970s] (Aus.) perfect! [abbr.]

perfect adj. **1** [early 17C+] utter, complete, total, e.g. *a perfect idiot.* **2** [1920s] wonderful, ideal, delightful.

perfect lady n. (also **real lady**) [late 19C] (US) a drunken woman; by implication a prostitute (cf. BANKSIDE LADY n.).

perfecto! excl. [1980s+] wonderful! excellent! perfect! [cod-Sp.]

perfesh n. **1** [late 19C–1930s] (Aus.) the profession, usu. that of the theatre. **2** [1930s] (US tramp) a veteran tramp. [pron. of abbr. SE (1) *profession*, (2) *professional*]

perforate v. [mid-19C+] **1** of a man, to have sexual intercourse with, esp. to take a woman's virginity (cf. BANG v.¹). **2** (US) to shoot.

perform v.¹ **1** [17C; late 19C+] to have sexual intercourse. **2** [1970s+] (US gay) to fellate.

perform v.² **1** [20C+] (Aus.) to display extreme anger or bad temper, to swear loudly, to make a great fuss. **2** [1940s–50s] (UK Und.) to commit a crime, esp. when it involves violence.

perform a bottom-wetter v. see DO A BOTTOM-WETTER v.

perform a jumble-giblets v. see DO A JUMBLE-GIBLETS v.

performer n.¹ **1** [late 19C–1900s] a philanderer, a promiscuous man. **2** [1960s+] a sexually active woman. [PERFORM v.¹ (1)]

performer n.² [1940s] an expert.

perform on v. [late 19C] **1** of a man, to have sexual intercourse. **2** to cheat, to deceive. [(1) PERFORM v.¹ (1); (2) SE *perform*, to act]

perfume v. [1940s] (US Black) to put the best possible face on otherwise unpalatable facts.

perfumed talk n. [late 19C] (US) obscenities, bad language.

perger n. see PURGER n.

perhapser n. [1910s] (Aus.) a risk.

perico n. [1970s+] (drugs) cocaine. [Sp. *perico*, parakeet]

periin n. [1940s] (W.I.) an albino. [? SE *peering*; albinos stereotypically suffer from poor eyesight]

period n. [1930s+] (orig. US) that is that, there is no more to be said. [SAmE *period* = SE *full stop*]

period hitter n. [1960s] (drugs) an occasional drug user. [SE *period* + HIT v.³ (4)]

periodical n. [late 19C–1900s] (US) a drinking bout. [? one does it *periodically*]

periphery n. [1910s–20s] a pot-belly. [play on SE *periphery*, a circumference]

perish v.¹ [late 19C] (mainly Aus.) to attack, to punish, to kill; thus *go in a perisher*, to suffer physical harm.

perish v.² [late 19C+] (Aus.) **1** to suffer a state of virtual starvation; thus DO A PERISH v. **2** to be homeless, to sleep out at night. **3** to cadge.

perisher n.¹ **1** [late 19C–1920s] a short coat. **2** [20C+] a spell or day of very cold weather; thus *do a perisher*, to feel very cold. **3** [1900s–20s] (Aus.) to feel very cold. [one 'perishes' of the cold]

perisher n.² [late 19C+] a person, often in a derog. sense, and often, as *little perisher*, applied to a child.

perishing adj. [20C+] a general intensifier, DAMNED adj.; also as infix. [PERISHING adv.]

perishing adv. [mid-19C+] a general intensifier, e.g. *perishing cold, perishing hard.*

perish me! excl. (also **perish me blind/pink!**) [mid-19C–1910s] a general excl. of surprise, shock, amazement.

periwinkle n. **1** [late 17C–early 19C] a peruke or wig. **2** [mid-

19C] a small penis. **3** [mid-19C–1900s] the vagina (cf. BEARDED CLAM n.).

perk see also under PERCOLATE.

perk n.¹ (also **perq**) [late 19C+] a bonus, esp. that which comes with a job; usu. in pl.; thus *perky*, advantageous. [SE *perquisite*]

perk n.² (also **purko**) [1910s] (Aus.) beer. [? PERK UP v. or PERKINS n.]

perk n.³ [1940s] (Aus.) an act of vomiting. [echoic; or ? PERKINS n.]

perk n.⁴ see PERC n.

perk v. [1950s+] (Aus.) to vomit, usu. after excessive drinking (cf. BARF v.). [PERK n.³]

perked adj. [late 19C–1910s] (Aus./N.Z.) drunk (cf. ABOUT RIGHT phr.¹). [? PERK UP v. or PERKINS n.]

perker n. [late 19C] one who benefits from a PERK n.¹.

perker-upper n. [20C+] (orig. US) one who cheers others up. [PERK UP v.]

perkin n. [late 18C–mid-19C] weak cider; the washings from a cider barrel. [? SE *perry*, a drink made from pears + dimin. sfx *-kin*]

perking n. [late 17C–early 18C] 'any pert, forward, silly fellow' (B.E.). [PERK UP v.]

perkins n. [mid-19C] beer. [abbr. BARCLAY (AND) PERKINS n.]

perkmeister n. [1990s+] (US) an official, typically in a company or in government, who can offers favours, jobs etc. [PERK n.¹ + -MEISTER sfx (1)]

perks n. see PERCS n.

perk up v. [mid-17C+] to cheer up, to improve one's spirits. [SE *perk*, to thrust oneself forward, to act in a brisk or jaunty manner]

perky adj. **1** [mid-19C+] jolly, cheerful. **2** [1960s] cheeky. [PERK UP v.]

perlaver n. see PALAVER n.

perma- pfx [1980s] (US campus) a pfx indicating permanence, continuity, e.g. *perma-grin.* [abbr. SE *permanent*]

permanent pug n. [late 19C] a man employed by a public house to keep order or eject troublesome customers. [orig. journ. jargon *permanent pug*, a man employed to stand at a newspaper office to head off any complainers; ult. PUG n.⁵ (2)]

pernicated dude n. [late 19C–1910s] (Can.) a swaggering dandy. [? SE *pernickety*]

perp n. [1980s+] **1** (orig. US) a *perp*etrator, an accused criminal. **2** (US Black) one who is pretending or faking. **3** (US drugs) fake crack cocaine made of candle wax and baking soda. [abbr. SE *perpetrator*, (3) is an ext. of (2)]

perp v.¹ (also **purp**) [1990s+] (US campus) to pretend. [PERPE-TRATE v.]

perp v.² [2000s] (US) to commit crime (against someone). [PERP n. (1)]

perpendicular n. **1** [mid-19C+] sexual intercourse in which the partners are standing up. **2** [late 19C] a meal taken standing up, a party at which the guests stand rather than sit in a formal 'placement'.

perpetrate v. [1980s+] (US Black teen/campus) to pretend to be something that one is not. [SE *perpetrate*, to perform (usu. a crime or other reprehensible act)]

perpetrator n. [1980s+] (US campus) one who pretends to greater attainments, social position or popularity than they actually have. [PERPETRATE v.]

perpetual staircase n. [late 19C–1900s] the prison treadmill.

perq n. see PERK n.¹.

perry n. [1960s] (US drugs) Percodan (cf. PERCS n.). [abbr.]

Perry Como n. [1950s+] a homosexual. [rhy. sl. = HOMO n.² (1); ult. singer *Perry Como* (1912–2001)]

pers adj. [1990s+] (drugs) personal, i.e. from one's own supply of drugs. [abbr. PERSONAL n. (2)]

Persian adj. see GREEK adj.² (1).

persnickety *adj.* [20C+] (*US*) over-fastidious, petty. [var. on SE *pernickety*]

personal *n.* 1 [1960s] a close friend. 2 [1990s+] (*UK drugs*) drugs kept for one's own consumption (as opposed to those which one sells).

persp *n.* [1920s+] *persp*iration. [abbr.; only used by P.G. Wodehouse (1881–1975)]

persuader *n.* 1 [late 18C–early 19C] usu. in pl., a spur. 2 [mid-19C+] (*also* **persuasive**) a weapon, usu. a pistol or revolver, which persuades victims to its wielder's point of view. 3 [late 19C] the penis.

persuasion *n.* [mid-19C+] nationality, gender, type, e.g. *of the Hebrew persuasion, of the female persuasion.*

pertish *adj.* [mid-18C–early 19C] tipsy, quite drunk (cf. ABOUT RIGHT phr.¹). [SE *pert*]

Peruvian *n.*¹ [late 19C–1900s] (*S.Afr.*) 1 a Jew, esp. an East European Jew who retains their accent, mannerisms and general culture. 2 a fellow Jew who fails to meet the community's ethical and moral standards. [? pun on initials of the *Polish and Russian Union*, an organization that facilitated the immigration of Jews from Russia and Eastern Europe]

Peruvian *n.*² (*also* **Peruvian flake/lady**) [1980s+] (*drugs*) cocaine (cf. ANDES CANDY n.). [its origin]

perv *n.* (*also* **perve**) 1 [1940s+] (*orig. Aus.*) one who is categorized as a sexual pervert, esp. a child molester. 2 [1950s+] a male homosexual. 3 [1960s] pornography, usu. featuring what is considered 'bizarre' sex. 4 [1960s+] a voyeur. 5 [1980s+] the male act of watching passing women. [abbr. SE *pervert*]

perv *adj.* (*also* **perve**) [1940s+] pornographic, e.g. *perv film, perv book, perv show,* a strip show. [PERV n.]

perv *v.* (*also* **perve**) [1940s+] (*orig. Aus./N.Z.*) 1 to behave in a sexually perverted manner, esp. used of child molesters. 2 to stare at, to watch, usu. in a prurient manner; usu. as *perv at/on.* 3 to read or watch pornography. 4 to act in an effeminate/homosexual manner. [PERV n.]

perv (about) *v.* (*also* **perve (about)**) [1940s+] (*orig. Aus.*) to search for potential sexual conquests. [the use of PERV v. (1) here is facetious rather than an actual ref. to any sexual eccentricity]

pervin' *adj.* [1990s+] (*US Black teen*) intoxicated, drunk. [? fig. use of PERV v.]

pervo *n.* [1980s+] (*Aus.*) a pervert. [PERV n. (1) + -o sfx (4)]

pervy *adj.* [1940s+] (*orig. Aus.*) 1 sexually perverted. 2 pornographic, smutty. [PERV n.]

pesh *n.* [20C+] (*W.I.*) money. [Sp. *peso*, a coin of low denomination or Fr. *pièce*, a coin]

pesky *adj.* [mid-18C+] (*US*) annoying, irritating. [? SE *pesty*, plague-ridden, or Irish *peasgach*, rough, rugged]

pesky *adv.* (*also* **peskily**) [mid-19C–1900s] (*US*) extremely, very, damnably. [PESKY adj.]

peso *n.* [19C+] (*US*) a dollar. [Mex. Sp. *peso*, a coin approx. equivalent to $1]

pest *v.* (*also* **pestify**) [1930s+] (*Aus.*) to *pester*, to annoy. [abbr.]

pester *v.* [1930s] to pay for (someone else). [apparently a nonce-word created by James Curtis]

pestilence *adv.* [early–mid-17C] a general intensifier, unpleasantly, unappealingly, e.g. *pestilence poor.* [lit. 'plaguey']

pest it (all)! *excl.* [1900s–20s] a general excl. of annoyance or irritation; thus *perstering,* a euph. for DAMNED adj. [lit. 'plague it!']

pestle *n.* 1 [late 16C–19C] the penis; thus the *burning pestle* is suffering from venereal disease. 2 [early 17C] a constable's staff. [often in *double entendres*]

pestle *v.* [late 19C–1900s] of a man, to have sexual intercourse. [PESTLE n. (1)]

pestlehead *n.* [19C] a fool. [SE *pestle* + -HEAD sfx (1)]

pestle of pork *n.* [late 19C–1900s] the leg. [SE *pestle*, the leg of certain animals used for food, esp. the ham or haunch of the pig]

petal *n.* [1970s+] a general term of address.

Pete *n.* [1920s+] used in a variety of phrs. as a euph. for Christ; e.g. *for the love of Pete, glory be to Pete, in the name of Pete.*

pete *n.*¹ *see* PETE-MAN n.

pete *n.*² *see* PETER n.⁴.

pete *n.*³ *see* PETER n.⁵.

pete *n.*⁴ 1 [1910s–50s] (*also* **pete-box**) a safe. 2 [1930s–40s] (*US*) nitroglycerine, used to open safes. [PETER n.² (2)/PETER n.⁵ (2)]

pete-busting *n.* [1950s] (*US Und.*) safe-cracking. [PETE n.⁴ (1) + BUST v.¹ (1)]

peted *adj.* [mid-19C+] (*Can.*) exhausted. [PETER OUT v. (2)]

pete-man *n.* (*also* **pete**) [1910s–50s] (*US Und.*) a safe-breaker. [PETE n.⁴ (1) + sfx *-man*]

Pete Murray *n. see* RUBY (MURRAY) n.

peter *n.*¹ [early–mid-17C] a form of Spanish wine. [abbr. PETER SEE ME n.]

peter *n.*² 1 [mid-17C–1930s] (*UK/US Und.*) (*also* **petter, pitter**) a trunk, a bundle, a bag or parcel of any kind. 2 [late 18C+] (*UK/US Und.*) (*also* **petter**) a safe or cash-box, a cash register, a till; thus *peter-work,* safe-breaking; *shoot a peter,* to blow open a safe. 3 [late 19C] (*US tramp*) a safe-breaker; thus *on the peter,* working as a safe-breaker. 4 [late 19C+] (*Aus.*) a witness box; thus *mount the peter,* enter the witness box. 5 [1930s+] (*UK/US Und.*) a cell, whether in jail, a police station or elsewhere; thus also a prison. 6 [1980s+] (*N.Z.*) a half-gallon jar. [? fig. use of proper name *Peter,* based on its ety., Gk *petros,* a stone]

peter *n.*³ [late 17C–mid-18C] (*UK Und.*) a variety of loaded dice, used for cheating. [? SE *petard,* upon which the loser is 'hoist']

peter *n.*⁴ (*also* **pete, petey**) [mid-19C+] the penis, esp. of a young boy; thus *pitch the peter,* of a man, to have sexual intercourse (cf. ABRAHAM n.¹). [joc. use of proper name + initial letters]

peter *n.*⁵ (*also* **pete, peter drop**) 1 [late 19C+] (*US tramp*) drugged or adulterated liquor, derived from nitroglycerine; a knockout drug; thus *peter-thrower,* a thief who uses knockout drops. 2 [1920s–30s] (*UK/US Und.*) nitroglycerine, as used in safe-breaking. [ety. unknown]

peter *v.*¹ 1 [mid-18C+] to stop, to cease; in fig. use, to die. 2 [mid-19C] to tire, to feel exhausted. [? PETER OUT v. but it appears to be earlier; ? Fr. *peter,* to explode weakly]

peter *v.*² [1920s–60s] (*US*) to use knockout drops on a victim. [PETER n.⁵(1)]

peter *v.*³ [1920s+] to blow open a safe with nitroglycerine. [PETER n.⁵ (2)/PETER n.² (2)]

Peter and Lee *n. see* PETERS AND LEE n.

peter-beater *n.* [1980s+] (*US*) a masturbator. [PETER n.⁴]

peter-biter *n.* [1990s+] (*UK Und.*) a safe-blower. [PETER n.² (2) + BITE v. (1)]

peter-boatman *n.* [late 18C–mid-19C] a thief who operates on the river. [PETER n.² (1)]

peter-claimer *n.* [late 19C] (*UK Und.*) one who steals unguarded parcels and bags from railway stations. [PETER n.² (1) + CLAIM v.¹ (1)]

peter-claiming *n.* [late 19C] stealing unguarded parcels and bags from railway stations. [PETER n.² (1) + CLAIM v.¹ (1)]

peter-cutter *n.* (*also* **petter-cutter**) [mid-19C] an implement used to break into safes. [PETER n.² (2)]

peter-drag *n.* [19C] the stealing of boxes, parcels, bags etc, esp. from carriages. [PETER n.² (1) + DRAG n.¹ (2)]

peter drop *n. see* PETER n.⁵.

peter-eater *n.* [1920s+] (*US*) a male homosexual fellator; a heterosexual fellatrix (cf. BONE-EATER n.). [PETER n.⁴ + EAT v.³ (1)]

peterer *n.* [late 18C–mid-19C] a thief who specializes in stealing goods from the back of vans and carts; thus fem. *peteress.* [PETER n.² (1)]

Peter Funk *n.* (*also* **Funk**) [mid–late 19C] (*US*) a fraudulent salesman, often operating in the guise of an auctioneer, who augments the appeal of their third-rate merchandise by intimating that it had in some way been acquired illegally; thus *Peter Funkism*, the practice of such swindling. [a generic proper name, orig. Ger./Du.]

peter-gee *n.* [1940s] (*US Und.*) a safe-cracker. [PETER n.[2] (2) + GEE n.[3] (1)]

peter grievous *n.* (*also* **peter grievance**) [mid-19C–1900s] a whiner, a complainer, a whingeing child.

peter gunner *n.* [17C–early 19C] a poor shot; thus [19C] *Peter Gunner who will kill all the birds that died last summer.* [a supposed name but note *peter*, saltpetre (used in bullets)]

peter-hunting *n.* [19C] (*UK Und.*) the stealing of baggage and boxes. [PETER n.[2] (1) + SE *hunting*]

Peter Jay *n.* [1980s+] (*US Black, LA*) a policeman (cf. BILLY n.[6]). [ety. unknown]

peter lay *n.* [early 18C–early 19C] (*UK Und.*) the stealing of baggage and boxes. [PETER n.[2] (1) + LAY n.[4] (1)]

peter lug *n.* [late 17C–early 19C] (*UK Und.*) a dawdling drinker, usu. as in phr. *who is peter lug?* whose glass is still undrunk? [generic use of *Peter* + SE *lug*, anything heavy or clumsy]

peterman *n.*[1] [mid-17C–early 18C] one who poaches fish from the River Thames. [SE *peterman*, a fisherman, ult. after the apostle Simon Peter, a fisherman]

peterman *n.*[2] **1** [early 19C+] a safe-cracker. **2** [mid-19C] a thief who specializes in stealing goods from the back of vans and carts. [(1) PETER n.[2] (2); (2) PETER n.[2] (1)]

peterman *n.*[3] [late 19C–1900s] one who uses knockout drops to facilitate a robbery. [PETER n.[5] (1)]

peter-meter *n.* [1960s+] (*US*) a notional means of measuring the size of a penis, or the excitement it is experiencing. [PETER n.[4] + SE *meter*. Coined by *Screw* magazine in the late 1960s, when it was used as part of reviews to assess the degree to which a pornographic film or book was arousing]

Peter O'Toole *n.* [1990s+] a (bar) stool. [rhy. sl.; ult. Irish-born actor *Peter O'Toole* (b.1932)]

peter out *v.* **1** [mid-19C+] to give out, to fade away. **2** [late 19C+] to tire, to feel exhausted. **3** [1900s–30s] to die. **4** [1910s] to reject, to scapegoat. [orig. US mining jargon, but note PETER v.[1]; note Michael Quinion, *World Wide Words* (Internet, 14 April 2001): 'There are two possibilities for where it came from. One is the *saltpetre* (US spelling *saltpeter*) that was a component of the blasting power that miners used (the second part comes from Greek "*petros*", a rock); this sounds a bit of a stretch, but you never know. The other is French "*peter*", which literally means to fart, but which I believe has been used figuratively to mean "to fizzle out" (and which famously appears in the English "*petard*" for a medieval military explosive device, from which we get "hoist by his own petard")']

peter pan *n.*[1] [20C+] **1** a van. **2** a suntan. [rhy. sl.; ult. J.M. Barrie's *Peter Pan* (1904)]

peter pan *n.*[2] [1940s] (*US*) a chamberpot. [SE *pan*; ult. J.M. Barrie's *Peter Pan* (1904)]

peter player *n.* [late 19C] (*US*) one who uses knockout drops to facilitate a robbery. [PETER n.[5] (1)]

peter puffer *n.* [1990s+] (*US*) one who performs oral sex. [PETER n.[4] + SE *puff*, to blow, i.e. BLOW v.[2] (3)]

Peters and Lee *n.* (*also* **Peter and Lee**) [1990s+] **1** a cup of tea. **2** an act of urination (cf. ANGEL'S KISS n.). [rhy. sl. = PEE n.[1] (2)/WEE n.; ult. singing duo Lennie *Peters* (1939–92) and Dianne *Lee* (b.1950)]

peter school *n.* [1900s–30s] (*Aus./N.Z.*) a gambling den. [*DNZE* claims 'unknown' but ? PETER n.[2] (2), i.e. the casino's cash-box]

peter-screwing *n.* [mid-19C+] breaking open safes. [PETER n.[2] (2) + SCREW v.[4] (1)]

peter see me *n.* [early–mid-17C] a Spanish wine, properly named *Pedro Ximenes*. [*peter* = *Pedro*, a famous grape + Cardinal *Ximenes* (1436–1517)]

peter that! *excl.* [19C] shut up! be quiet! [PETER v.[1] (1)]

peter thief *n.* [1980s+] (*Aus. prison*) one who steals from a fellow prisoner's cell. [PETER n.[2] (5)]

Pete Tong *adj.* [1980s+] wrong. [rhy. sl.; ult. UK dance DJ/mixer *Pete Tong* (b.1960s)]

petey *n. see* PETER n.[4].

peth *n.* [1980s+] (*drugs*) *peth*idine. [abbr.]

peto *phr.* [late 19C] (*UK society*) please turn over. [pron. of the abbr. *p.t.o.*]

pet one's pussycat *v.* [1980s+] of a woman, to masturbate (cf. APPLY LIP GLOSS v.; BEAT ONE'S HOG v.). [SE *pet* + PUSSY n. (2)]

Petricelli *n.* [1980s+] (*US Black*) a high fashion suit. [brandname of a popular tailors]

petrified *adj.* **1** [20C+] very drunk; thus *petrification*, a state of drunkenness. **2** [1950s] under the influence of a drug. [lit. 'turned to stone'; logically a pun on STONED (OUT) adj., but predates it by 50 years]

petro *adj.* [1980s+] (*US*) terrified, fearful, paranoid; thus *petrolyze*, to render paranoid. [P.R. Sp. *petro*, scared]

petrol *n.* [1980s+] (*Aus. prison*) heroin. [? its role as a fuel]

petrol-head *n.* [1980s+] (*Aus.*) a devotee of motor-racing or cars in general. [SE *petrol* + -HEAD sfx (4)]

petrols *n.* [1970s] (*Aus.*) trousers. [rhy. sl. on *petrol bowsers*]

petrol tank *n.* [1990s+] masturbation. [rhy. sl. = WANK n.[1] (1)]

petrolyze *v. see* PETRO adj.

petronel *n.* [late 16C–early 17C] a braggart, a blusterer, a bully. [SE *petronel*, a kind of large pistol or carbine, used in the 16C and early 17C]

petter *n.*[1] [1930s–40s] (*US*) one who enjoys indulging in sexual fondling and caresses. [SE *pet*, to fondle]

petter *n.*[2] *see* PETER n.[2].

petter-cutter *n. see* PETER-CUTTER n.

pet the poodle *v.* [1970s+] of a woman, to masturbate (cf. APPLY LIP GLOSS v.; BEAT ONE'S HOG v.).

petticoat *n.* **1** [17C–1920s] a woman; thus *Petticoat lane*, the vagina; also attrib., pertaining to women and female culture. **2** [mid-19C] in coin-tossing, the tail. **3** [1950s] (*US*) a general derog. term applied to a man. [metonymy]

petticoat government *n.* (*also* **petticoat rule**) [late 17C+] a domestic relationship in which the wife dominates her husband; or a mother her child. [PETTICOAT n. (1)]

petticoat hold *n.* [late 18C–early 19C] a husband's interest in his wife's estate, limited to his lifetime only. [PETTICOAT n. (1) + SE *hold*, freehold, tenure]

petticoat hunter *n.* [late 18C–early 19C] a womanizer. [PETTICOAT n. (1)]

Petticoat Lane *n.* [20C+] a pain. [rhy. sl.; ult. *Petticoat Lane*, the East London street market]

Petticoat lane *n. see* PETTICOAT n. (1).

petticoat merchant *n.* [19C+] a pimp (cf. ABBOT ON THE CROSS n.). [PETTICOAT n. (1) + MERCHANT n.]

petticoat peer *n. see* SQUIRE OF THE PETTICOAT n.

petticoat pension *n.* [17C–18C] the money a prostitute gives her pimp, or a woman gives her 'kept' lover. [PETTICOAT n. (1)]

petticoat pensioner *n.* (*also* **petty-coat pensioner**) [late 17C–early 19C] a kept man. [one who accepts a PETTICOAT PENSION n.]

petticoat pet *n.* [1900s] (*Aus.*) one who is beloved by women. [PETTICOAT n. (1)]

petticoat rule *n. see* PETTICOAT GOVERNMENT n.

petticoat squire *n. see* SQUIRE OF THE PETTICOAT n.

pettifogger *n.* (*also* **pettyfogger**) [mid-16C+] a second-rate lawyer, condemned by their inadequacies to dealing only in minor cases. [SE *petty* + *fogger*. The proper name *Fugger*, the great Augsburg banking family of the 15C and 16C, which appears (usu. with the 'u' changed to an 'o') in a number of European languages, meaning initially a merchant, usurer or monopolist and subseq. an avaricious rich man, a cheap huckster, and anyone who uses corrupt methods for personal gain. The term persists today. Du. *fokker*, Walloon *foukeur* etc are all contemptuous designations for a person of great wealth. Thus the *petty-* or *pettifogger* was one whose methods emulated those of the great merchants but at the lowest level]

pettifogging *adj.* (*also* **pettyfogging**) [17C+] insignificant, silly, small. [PETTIFOGGER n.]

petty *n.* [1910s+] a term of endearment. [SE *pet*]

petty-coat pensioner *n. see* PETTICOAT PENSIONER n.

pettyfogger *see under* PETTIFOGGER.

petty house *n.* [late 19C] the lavatory (cf. BACKHOUSE n.). [lit. 'small house']

pew *n.* **1** [late 19C+] a seat. **2** [1930s] (*US Und.*) the electric chair.

pewee *adj. see* PEE-WEE adj.

pewter *n.* **1** [19C–1940s] money, esp. silver (cf. BRASS n.[1]). **2** [1910s] a pewter drinking pot, esp. as given as a prize.

peysle *v.* (*also* **picell, pisel**) [20C+] (*Ulster*) to work lazily, half-heartedly. [Scot. *peist*, to work feebly]

Peyton Place *n.* [1990s+] (*US*) the human face. [rhy. sl.; ult. the bestselling novel (and later film and TV series) *Peyton Place* (1956) by Grace Metalious (1924–64)]

pez *n.* [1940s–50s] (*US Black*) facial hair, the hair on one's head. [ety. unknown]

pfat *adj.* [1990s+] (*US Black*) very wise, sophisticated. [var. on PHAT adj. (2)]

pfft *adj.* [1930s–50s] (*orig. US*) finished, terminated, over. [GO PHUT v.]

pfiz *n. see* FIZZ n.[1] (3).

pfotz *n.* [20C+] the vagina. [? euph. for FUCK n.[1] (1)]

p.g. *n.*[1] **1** [late 19C] (*US campus*) a post-graduate. **2** [1900s] (*US campus*) a pretty girl. **3** [1920s+] a paying guest. [abbr.]

p.g. *n.*[2] [1930s–60s] (*drugs*) paregoric. [abbr.; a cough medicine based on opium linctus, which heroin addicts use when no stronger drugs are available; William Burroughs, *Junkie* (1953): 'P.G....Paregoric. A weak, camphorated tincture of opium, two grains to the ounce. Two ounces will fix a sick addict. It can be bought without prescription in some states. P.G. can be injected intravenously after burning out the alcohol and straining out the camphor']

p.g. *phr.* [1950s] (*US Black*) of time, last, just happened, e.g. *four o'clock p.g.* [*past gone*]

P.G. tips *n.* [20C+] the lips. [rhy. sl.; ult. the brand of tea]

p.h. *n.* [1960s] (*drugs*) amphetamine pills (cf. A n.[2]). [abbr. PURPLE HEARTS n. (1)]

p.h.a. *n. see* PURPLE-HEADED CUSTARD CHUCKER n.

phantom *n. see* GHOST n.[1] (4).

pharaoh *n.*[1] [late 17C–18C] a particularly strong malt beer. [abbr. the brandname *Old Pharaoh*; ? ult. the power attributed to the Egyptian kings]

pharaoh *n.*[2] [19C–1920s] (*US Black*) a young woman. [Kanuri (an African lang. of N.E. Nigeria) *fero*, a girl]

Pharaoh's revenge *n. see* MONTEZUMA'S REVENGE n.

phar lap *n.* (*Aus.*) **1** [1930s+] a very slow person. **2** [1950s] a wild dog, with its hair burnt off, trussed up and cooked in the ashes. [proper name *Phar Lap*, flash of lightning, Australia's most famous racehorse, *fl.*1930s]

phar lap gallop *n.* [1930s–40s] (*Aus.*) a foxtrot. [for ety. *see* prev.]

pharmacist *n.* [1990s+] (*W.I.*) a major drug dealder.

phase out *v.* [1980s+] (*US campus*) to become unaware, as if asleep.

phat *adj.* **1** [1970s+] (*orig. US Black/campus*) used to describe an attractive woman. **2** [1990s+] a general term of approval, admiration. [deliberately skewed sp. of FAT adj.[1] (2); but also popularly linked to a variety of suggested acronyms, e.g. *p*hysically *a*ttractive or pretty *h*ips *a*nd *t*highs or pretty *h*ips, *a*ss and *t*its, or pretty *h*ot *a*nd tempting, or *p*ussy, *h*ips, *a*ss and *t*highs etc]

phata-phata *n. see* PATA-PATA n.

phat pocket *n.* [1990s+] (*US Black*) a wealthy person. [PHAT adj. + SE *pocket*]

phat tape *n. see* FAT TAPE n.

phatty *adj.* [1990s+] (*US Black*) excellent. [ext. of PHAT adj. (2)]

phaze *v.* [1990s+] (*US campus*) to ignore. [? SE *faze* or ? SE *phase* (out)]

Ph.D. *v. see* PILE IT HIGHER AND DEEPER v.

p.h.d. *n.*[1] [2000s] (*US teen/campus*) a fig. 'degree' held by a teacher who dislikes students who espouse 'gangsta' culture; thus used of anyone who undermines the activities of a 'player'. [abbr. PLAYER HATER n. + SE *degree*; pun on SE *PhD*]

p.h.d. *n.*[2] [2000s] (*US Black*) a large penis. [*p*retty *h*uge *d*ick, i.e. DICK n.[4] (1)]

p.h.d. *phr.* [1930s] (*US*) a warning to a woman that her slip is showing (cf. CHARLIE'S DEAD phr.). [*p*etticoat *h*anging *d*own]

pheasant *n.* **1** [early 17C] a term of abuse. **2** [late 17C–early 19C] a promiscuous woman. **3** [late 19C] a herring. [note naut. jargon *Spithead pheasant*, a bloater or kipper]

pheasantry *n.* [19C–1900s] a brothel (cf. BIRDCAGE n.[1]). [PHEASANT n. (2)]

pheeny *n. see* PHENNIE n.

pheeze *see under* FEEZE.

phenagle *v. see* FINAGLE v.

phennie *n.* (*also* **pheeny, phenal**) [1950s+] (*drugs*) phenobarbitol, a depressant. [abbr.]

pheno *n.* (*also* **phenobob, phenos**) [1940s–70s] phenobarbital, phenobarbitone (a soporific drug best known by the US tradename Luminol). [abbr.]

phenogler *n. see* FINAGLER n.

phenom *n.* [late 19C–1950s] (*US*) an outstanding person or thing, a prodigy. [abbr. SE *phenomenon*]

phenomenon *n.* **1** [mid-19C] an exceptional person, a prodigy. **2** [1920s] (*Irish*) a person, with no exceptional characteristics. [thus Dickens's 'infant phenomenon – Miss Ninetta Crummles' in *Nicholas Nickleby* (1838)]

phenomy *n.* (*also* **phenomony**) [early 19C] an outstanding person or thing, a prodigy. [abbr. SE *phenomenon*]

PHer *n. see* PLAYER HATER n.

phet *n.* [1990s+] (*drugs*) amphetamine (cf. A n.[2]).

Phil(a) *n. see* PHILLY n. (1).

Philadelphia (bank)roll *n. see* CALIFORNIA BANKROLL n.

Philadelphia lawyer *n.* [late 18C+] (*US*) a shrewd or unscrupulous lawyer, an expert in exploiting the minutiae of the law. [the stereotyped characteristics of the city]

philander *v.* [mid-19C–1900s] 'to ramble on incoherently, to write discursively and weakly' (Hotten, 1873). [play on SE]

philharmonic *n.* [20C+] tonic water; gin and tonic. [rhy. sl.]

phililoo *n. see* FILLALOO n.

philip! *excl.* [late 19C] (*UK Und.*) an excl. that indicates the approach of the police.

philip and cheyney *n.* (*also* **philip, hob and cheyney**) [mid-16C–early 17C] a generic term for average people, the mass. [the contemporary commonness of these names]

philiper *n.* (*also* **philliper**) [mid-19C] a thief's accomplice. [? dial. *philip*, a sparrow]

philistines *n.* **1** [late 17C–mid-19C] bailiffs. **2** [late 17C–mid-19C] a group of drunkards; thus *have been among the Philistines*, to be drunk. **3** [19C] the police. [Judg. 16:20, 'The Philistines be upon thee, Samson']

Philly *n.* **1** [late 19C+] (*US*) (*also* **Phil, Phila, Phillie**) Philadelphia. **2** [1900s] a native of Philadelphia; a player for a local sports team. **3** [1980s+] (*US Black/drugs*) (*also* **Philly blunt**) a marijuana cigarette made of buds rolled in a tobacco leaf taken from the wrapper of a *Phillies* Blunt cigar (cf. BLUNT n.[3]). [abbr.]

Philly (bank)roll *n. see* CALIFORNIA BANKROLL n.

Phil McBee *n.* [19C] a flea. [rhy. sl.]

phil the fluter *n.* [20C+] a gun. [rhy. sl. = SHOOTER n.[1] (1)]

phiz *n.*[1] (*also* **fiz, fizzog, phizog, phizz, phizzog, physiog, physog, phyz**) **1** [late 17C+] the face. **2** [1910s] a photograph. [abbr. SE *physiognomy*; (1) also US use in 20C+]

phiz *n.*[2] *see* FIZZ n.[1] (3).

phizgig *n.*[1] [late 19C] an old woman dressed younger than her years. [SE *fizgig*, a frivolous woman]

phizgig *n.*[2] *see* FIZGIG n.[2].

phizog/phizz *n. see* PHIZ n.[1].

phizzer *n. see* FIZZER n.[3].

phizzog *n. see* PHIZ n.[1].

phlegm-cutter *n.* (*also* **phlegm-disperser, -splitter**) [19C+] **1** a drink of whisky or other strong liquor. **2** the first drink of the day, usu. that taken by an alcoholic soon after waking up; thus *cut the phlegm*, to take a first drink.

phlip *n. see* FLIP n.[1].

phoby *n.* [mid-19C] a dread or horror of water; thus in general, madness. [abbr. SE *hydrophobia*]

Phoebe *n.*[1] (*also* **little Phoebe**) [20C+] (*US gambling*) the point of 5 in craps dice (cf. ADA FROM DECATUR n.). [? pron. of initial letters]

Phoebe *n.*[2] *see* FEEB n.

phoenix *n.* [1920s] the penis. [it 'rises']

phoenix men *n.* [late 17C–early 19C] firemen employed directly by the Phoenix Insurance Office.

phoenix nest *n.* (*also* **phoenix alley**) [17C–mid-19C] the vagina (cf. AGREEABLE RUTS OF LIFE n.). [? it makes the penis 'rise again']

phone *n.* [2000s] (*US prison*) a makeshift communications system created by emptying a toilet.

phone booth *n.* [1930s] (*US*) a double-bass. [supposed resemblance]

phone booth baby *n.* [1960s–70s] (*US Black*) a child whose paternity is uncertain. [the image is of the mother giving birth/having sex in a phone booth or leaving the newborn child inside one]

phone freak *n.* (*also* **phone phreak**) **1** [1970s+] (*US*) a person who uses special equipment to obtain free calls from the telephone system. **2** [1970s+] a client who arranges to phone up a prostitute and listen while she runs through a pornographic monologue and he masturbates. **3** [2000s] (*US*) one who makes obscene phonecalls for sexual arousal. [SE *phone* + FREAK sfx]

phone ho *n.* [1990s+] (*US Black*) a woman, not necessarily a working prostitute, who offers 'telephone sex' to credit-card paying clients. [SE *phone* + HO n.[1] (1)]

phones *n.* [1910s+] head*phones*. [abbr.]

phones off the hook! *excl.* [2000s] (*US prison*) a warning that a guard is listening.

phoney *n.*[1] (*also* **phony**) **1** [20C+] anything fake, counterfeit, untrustworthy. **2** [1910s+] an insincere, untrustworthy, 'fake' person. **3** [1940s+] (*gay*) a mean or cheap client for a gay prostitute. **4** [1950s] a male homosexual; a man who pursues underage girls. [PHONEY adj.; (4) implies a 'fake' male]

phoney *n.*[2] [1980s+] (*US campus*) a crank telephone call. [abbr. SE *telephone*]

phoney *adj.* (*also* **phony**) [late 19C+] (*orig. US*) fake, counterfeit, insincere; thus *phoney as a three-dollar bill*. [? FAWNEY-RIG n. and allied terms (proposed by E.P. but disputed by Simes, *A Dict. of Australian Underworld Slang* (1993); for link to *fawney* see P. Tamony in *American Speech* XII:2 p.108–10]

phoney *v.* (*also* **phoney up, phony**) [1930s+] (*US*) to counterfeit, to falsify, to make up. [PHONEY adj.]

phoney-baloney *adj.* [1910s+] (*US*) absurd, nonsensical; thus *phony-baloneyness*, insincere enthusiasm. [PHONEY adj. + BALONEY n.[1] (1)]

phoney-baloney life *n.* [1950s] (*US prison*) an ostensible life sentence which can be appreciably shortened by parole. [PHONEY-BALONEY adj. + SE *life* (sentence), i.e. a 'fake' life sentence]

phoney stiff *n.* [1910s–20s] (*US tramp*) a tramp who sells fake jewels. [PHONEY adj. + STIFF n.[2] (8)]

phoney up *v. see* PHONEY v.

phonus balonus *n.* [1930s+] (*US*) rubbish, nonsense. [PHONEY-BALONEY adj. in cod-Lat. format]

phony *see under* PHONEY.

phooey! *excl.* (*also* **fooey!**) [mid-19C+] (*orig. US*) an excl. of disdain or dismissal, rubbish! nonsense!; thus ext. as *phooey on that!* [synon. Ger. *pfui!*]

phos *n.* (*also* **foss, phoss**) **1** [early 19C] *phos*phorus, used by burglars for illumination; thus *ding the phos*, throw away the bottle of phosphorus. **2** [late 19C] *phos*phorus necrosis. [abbr.]

phossy jaw *n.* (*also* **fossy jaw**) [late 19C–1930s] *phos*phorus necrosis, the occupational disease of match-makers. [abbr.]

photie *n.* (*also* **fotie, photy**) [1960s+] a *photo*graph. [abbr. + sfx *-ie/-y*]

photo finish *n.* [1950s+] (a pint of) Guinness (stout). [rhy. sl.]

photog *n.* (*also* **fotog, photogger**) [1910s+] (*orig. US*) a *photo*grapher. [abbr.]

photy *n. see* PHOTIE n.

phreak *n.* (*also* **phreaker**) [1970s+] (*US*) a person who uses special equipment to obtain free calls from the telephone system. [abbr. of PHONE FREAK n. (1)]

phreak *v.* [1970s+] (*US*) to use a variety of special equipment ('black boxes', 'blue boxes') to obtain free calls from the telephone system. [PHREAK n.]

phrynne *n.* [19C] a prostitute. [*Phrynne*, a 4C BC courtesan]

phukk *n.* [1990s+] a euph. sp. of FUCK n.[1]; thus *muthaphukka*, MOTHERFUCKER n. (1).

phunbaba *n.* [2000s] (*US Black*) a large piece of excrement. [ety. unknown]

phungky *adj.* [1990s+] (*US*) a deliberate mis-sp. of FUNKY adj.[3] (1)/FUNKY adj.[3] (3).

phunt *n. see* FUNT n.

phutz *n. see* FUTZ n. (1).

phutz around *v. see* FUTZ v.

phuza *n.* (*also* **poosa, pusa, puza**) [20C+] (*S.Afr. township*) liquor; thus *phuza-face*, a face bearing the marks of prolonged heavy drinking; *phuza-joint*, a bar; *phuza-buddy*, a drinking companion; *phuza-cabin*, a shebeen. [Xhosa/Zulu *phuza*, a drink, a sip]

phuza *v.* (*also* **poosa, pusa, puza**) [20C+] (*S.Afr. township*) to drink. [PHUZA n.]

phy *n.* [1960s] (*drugs*) *phy*ceptone, methadone. [abbr.; both forms of synthetic heroin]

physic *n.* [late 17C–early 18C] sexual intercourse. [play on SE *physic*, medicine]

physic *v.* [early–mid-19C] to punish, either physically or through depriving of money. [SE *physic*, to give a dose of medicine]

physicals *n.* [mid-19C] physical powers.

physical torture *n.* [20C+] physical training.

physic-bottle *n.* [late 19C] a doctor. [lit. 'a medicine bottle']

physics for poets *n.* [1970s+] (*US campus*) a course in basic physics for arts specialists; thus var. for similarly 'easy' courses.

physiog/physog/phyz *n. see* PHIZ n.[1].

PI *n.* [1950s+] a Private *I*, i.e. eye.

p.i. *n.* (*also* **pee-eye**) [1920s–60s] (*US Black*) a *pi*mp. [abbr.]

pi *adj.* [late 19C+] (*orig. UK juv.*) pious, always in a derog. sense of self-righteous, unctuous, poss. hypocritical.

pianist in a brothel *n. see* PIANO-PLAYER IN A BROTHEL n.

piano *n.*[1] (*also* **piana**) [1930s+] a cash register. [abbr. JEWISH PIANO n. (2)]

piano *n.*[2] [1940s+] (*US Black*) spare ribs; thus *piano on a platter*, barbecued ribs on a plate. [supposed resemblance to piano keys]

piano *v.*[1] [late 19C] (*UK society*) to stay in the background, to act unobtrusively. [Ital. *piano*, softly, used as direction in musical scores]

piano *v.*[2] [1980s+] (*drugs*) to search on hands and knees for any small pieces of crack cocaine that may have fallen to the floor. [? one's hands are tapping at the floor in the hope of feeling a tiny piece]

pianoforte legs n. [1910s–20s] a bishop's legs when clad in gaiters. [the days when a piano's legs were covered so as to avoid offending Victorian proprieties]

piano-player n. [1970s] (US Und.) a (crooked) accountant. [he makes the accounts 'dance']

piano-player in a brothel n. (also **pianist in a brothel**) [1970s+] (Aus.) one who is involved in a situation, but adamantly refuses to take any responsibility for it.

piano wire n. [1980s+] (Aus. prison) a buyer. [rhy. sl.]

piaster n. [1900s] (US) a dollar. [SE piastre/piaster, used for a small-denomination coin in various currencies]

p.i.b. n. [1990s+] (US campus) a brooding, gloomy adolescent who wears dark clothes and listens to gloomy alternative music. [abbr. people in black]

pic n.[1] [mid-19C] (orig. US) a person or thing seen as small, mean, insignificant. [abbr. PICAYUNE n.]

pic n.[2] (also **picky**) **1** [late 19C+] a picture. **2** [1910s+] a film. [abbr.]

pic n.[3] (also **piccolo**) [1930s–40s] (orig. US Black) a jukebox, a record player. [SE piccolo pianoforte, a small piano]

pica n. [2000s] (US prison) a knife. [? Sp.]

picanniny n. see PICCANINNY n.

picaroon n. (also **picaro**, **picarre**) [early 17C–mid-19C] a rogue; thus on the picaro, looking for easy opportunities for money-making. [SE picaroon, a rogue, ult. synon. Sp. picaro]

picayune n. [early 19C+] (orig. US) a person seen as small, mean, insignificant; similarly a small thing, a low-value coin; often in phr. not care a picayune. [SAmE picayune, used in Louisiana, Florida etc for the Spanish half-real, value 6½ cents or 3 pence; later the US 5-cent piece or other coin of small value]

picayune adj. (also **picayunish**) [early 19C+] paltry, small, insignificant. [PICAYUNE n.]

piccadill n. see TYBURN PICCADILL n.

piccadilly adj. [20C+] **1** silly. **2** chilly. [rhy. sl.; ult. Piccadilly, area in central London]

Piccadilly bushman n. [1920s–40s] (Aus.) a wealthy Australian who has left their native land for London.

Piccadilly cramp n. [early 18C] venereal disease. [the prostitutes that frequented the area]

Piccadilly crawl n. [late 19C] an affected style of walking adopted by society during the 1880s.

Piccadilly daisy n. [1900s–50s] a prostitute. [before the Street Offences Act 1959, which took prostitutes off the streets; note WW2 army Piccadilly commando, a prostitute]

Piccadilly fringe n. [late 19C] a popular women's hairstyle in which the hair is cut short into a fringe and curled over the forehead. [the style allegedly orig. in Paris c.1870]

Piccadilly percy n. [1970s] mercy. [rhy. sl.]

Piccadilly weepers n. [mid–late 19C] long side whiskers, worn without a beard and temporarily fashionable.

Piccadilly window n. [late 19C–1900s] a monocle. [affected by the fashionable men promenading in Piccadilly]

piccalilli n. [1990s+] the penis (cf. ALMOND n.). [rhy. sl. = WILLIE n.[5]]

piccaninny n. (also **piccanniny**, **pickanine**, **pickaninny**) [mid-17C+] (orig. W.I.) a Black child, occas. any Black person; any child, when spoken by a Black person. [adopted in W.I. f. Sp./Port. pequeño, small or Port. pequenino, tiny. The term was seen, since used mainly of children, as neutral, but is now generally seen as patronizing and thus derog.; note vaudeville jargon pick, a Black child who danced and sang onstage with a White headliner]

piccaninny adj. [mid-19C+] (Aus.) tiny; thus piccaninny daylight, the moments just before dawn. [PICCANINNY n.]

piccaninny kaya n. (also **piccaninny kia, p.k.**) [1960s+]

(S.Afr.) an outdoor privy. [PICCANINNY adj. + Nguni kia, house]

piccie n. see PICCY n.

piccolo n.[1] [1960s+] the penis (cf. ACCORDION n.).

piccolo n.[2] see PIC n.[3].

piccolo and flute n. [20C+] a suit. [rhy. sl.]

piccolo-player n. [1960s+] a fellator or fellatrix. [PICCOLO n.[1]]

piccolo(s) and flutes n. [1930s+] boots. [rhy. sl.]

Piccy n. [1960s] the street Piccadilly in London W1. [abbr.]

piccy n. (also **piccie**, **pickie**, **pikkie**) [20C+] a picture. [abbr. + sfx -y/-ie]

picell v. see PEYSLE v.

pick n.[1] [mid–late 19C] a third-rate cigar. [abbr. SE pickwick; the type of cigar smoked by the character Mr Pickwick in Charles Dickens's Pickwick Papers (1836)]

pick n.[2] **1** [late 19C] a toothpick. **2** [late 19C+] (also **picks**) a lockpick, the tool; a person who uses it. **3** [20C+] (UK/US Und.) a pickpocket, usu. the one who removes the victim's wallet or jewellery. **4** [20C+] an ice pick or a weapon that resembles one. **5** [1980s+] (Aus. prison) a hypodermic syringe. [abbr.]

pick n.[3] **1** [20C+] (Anglo-Irish) a quick-tempered person. **2** [1900s] (US Und.) a girlfriend. [PICK ON v.]

pick n.[4] see NATURAL PICK n.

pick v.[1] **1** [late 16C–early 19C] to pilfer, to commit petty larceny. **2** [early 19C+] (US Und.) to pickpocket.

pick v.[2] [18C–19C] to eat. [SE pick, to eat daintily]

pick v.[3] [1920s+] (Aus.) to guess. [SE pick out]

pick v.[4] [1950s+] (Aus.) to victimize. [PICK ON v.]

pick a cherry v. see CRACK A CHERRY v. (1).

pick a crow with v. [mid-19C+] (US) to pick a quarrel with someone.

pick a daisy v. [mid-19C+] to defecate in the open air.

pickadilly n. [2000s] (US Black) a cigarette, usu. a cheap brand. [brandname Piccadilly]

pick a lime v. see LIME v.

pick and choose n.[1] [20C+] alcohol, liquor. [rhy. sl. = BOOZE n. (1)]

pick and choose n.[2] [1920s] (W.I.) fastidiousness, esp. if taken to irritating extremes.

pick-and-choose adj. [1950s] (W.I.) hard to satisfy, pernickety. [PICK AND CHOOSE n.[2]]

pick and cut v. [late 16C] to work as a cut-purse. [one picks up or holds the purse, then cuts it]

pick a needle without eye v. [20C+] (W.I.) of a young woman, to give oneself in marriage to a man whom one knows will be of no use as a sexual partner. [a SE needle without an eye is useless; note NEEDLE n.[1]]

pickanine/pickaninny n. see PICCANINNY n.

pickaninny adj. [1970s] (US) Black. [PICCANINNY n.]

pick at v. [1910s+] (Aus.) to irritate, to nag at, to annoy.

pick-axe n. [late 19C] (S.Afr.) a drink composed of whisky or rough brandy, Pontac (a sweet red dessert wine) and ginger beer. [its effects]

picked-hatch n. (also **pick-hatch**, **pickthatch**, **picthatch**) [late 16C–17C] a brothel, orig. one situated either in Turnmill Street, a notorious red-light district, or between Old Street and Goswell Road — both in Clerkenwell, London EC1; thus picked-hatch captain, a pimp; go to the manor of a picked/pickt hatch, go to picket-hatch grange, to go to a brothel. [SE picked, spiked + hatch, a half door, designed to prevent unauthorized entrance; commonly used as a brothel-sign. The original such address was a tavern-cum-brothel in Turnmill Street, Clerkenwell, London; later uses are historical]

pick 'em up and lay 'em down v. [20C+] (US) **1** to walk, to march. **2** to dance. ['em (them) are the feet]

picker n. (also **picker-up**) [mid-19C; 1940s] a hand, usu. in pl. [1940s use is US Black]

pickers and stealers n. [17C–mid-19C] the hands. [16C catechism, 'To keep my hands from picking and stealing']

picker-up n.[1] [late 19C] (*UK Und.*) a prostitute. [PICK UP v.[1] (1)]

picker-up n.[2] *see* PICKER n.

picker-up n.[3] *see* ROPER n.

pickethatch vestal n. (*also* **pickthatch vestal**) [17C–early 19C] a prostitute. [PICKED-HATCH n. + joc. use of SE *vestal* (*virgin*)]

pick fares v. [20C+] (*W.I., Bdos*) to work as a prostitute. [she gives her clients a 'ride']

pick-hatch n. *see* PICKED-HATCH n.

pickie n. *see* PICCY n.

picking-up moll n. [mid-late 19C] (*UK Und.*) a woman who poses as a prostitute only to rob or lure a victim into the hands of her male companion, who would then beat and rob him. [PICK UP v.[1] (1)/PICK UP v.[1] (2) + MOLL n.[1] (2)]

picking up the vibrations phr. [1940s–70s] (*gay*) watching other men perform a sex show, all-male voyeurism. [HIPPIE n.[2] (3) use, when pleasures were more cerebral]

pickle n.[1] **1** [17C+] a predicament, a difficult situation. **2** [late 18C–19C] a difficult, troublesome person, often a child but by no means invariably; 'an arch, waggish fellow' (Grose, 1785). **3** [1950s–70s] a woman of a sour, unpleasant disposition. [play on SE *pickle*, i.e. something/someone 'sharp' (cf. PICKLED adj.[1])]

pickle n.[2] [1940s+] (*orig. US*) the penis. [resemblance to a *pickled* gherkin]

pickle v. **1** [late 18C–19C] to tease, to hoax, to deceive. **2** [20C+] (*US*) to spoil, to wreck.

pickle and pork n. *see* PICKLED PORK n. (3).

pickle-chugging n. [1990s+] (*US gay*) male homosexual fellatio; thus *pickle-chugger*, a fellator (cf. BASKET LUNCH n.). [PICKLE n.[2] + CHUG v.[1](1)]

pickled adj.[1] [late 17C–18C] waggish, roguish. [play on SE *pickled*, i.e. 'sharp' (cf. PICKLE n.[1])]

pickled adj.[2] [mid-19C+] drunk (cf. DAMP adj.).

pickled onion n. [1980s+] a bunion. [rhy. sl.]

pickled pork n. [late 19C+] **1** talk, conversation. **2** chalk. **3** (*also* **pickle and pork, pickling pork**) a walk. [rhy. sl.]

pickle-herring n. **1** [17C–mid-19C] an amusing companion, a 'wag'. **2** [18C–mid-19C] (*also* **pickle-her-ring**) a professional clown, usu. one who accompanies an itinerant quack doctor. [ext. of PICKLE n.[1] (2)]

pickle it! excl. [1910s+] (*Aus./US*) a general excl. of dismissal; forget it! be quiet!

pickle-jar n. [mid-19C–1900s] a coachman with a yellow uniform. [the *yellow* colour of some pickles]

pickle kisser n. [1990s+] a male homosexual (cf. BONE-EATER n.). [PICKLE n.[2] + SE *kisser*]

pickle me...! excl. [1960s+] (*N.Z.*) in combs., a general excl. of surprise or disbelief; combs. include *pickle me bloody agates! ...me daisies! ...me nut! ...me tit!* [SE *pickle* + AGATES n./SE *daisy*/NUT n.[1] (2)/TIT n.[3] (1)]

picklepuss n. [1990s+] (*US*) a sour-faced individual. [SE *pickle*, a sour gherkin + PUSS n.[3] (1)]

pickles n.[1] (*also* **dead pickles**) [mid-late 19C] nonsense, rubbish; thus *and no pickles*, without a doubt. [PICKLE n.[1] (1)]

pickles n.[2] [late 19C] a corpse. [medical student jargon, *pickles*, a corpse used for dissection]

pickles! excl. [mid-19C–1900s] a general excl. of disbelief, nonsense! rubbish! [PICKLE n.[1] (1)]

pickling pork n. *see* PICKLED PORK n. (3).

pickling tub n. *see* POWDERING TUB n.

pickling tubs n. [mid-19C] high or Wellington boots.

picklock n. [17C–19C] the penis. [play on LOCK n.[1] (1)]

pick meat for dead goats v. [20C+] (*W.I.*) to waste one's time on fruitless tasks.

pick-me-up n. **1** [mid-19C+] any form of drink that relieves the physical and mental state of the imbiber, esp. used for those concoctions advertised as curing hangovers. **2** [late 19C+] a person, object or place that has a similar effect. **3** [1900s] (*Aus./S.Afr.*) an ambulance. **4** [1920s+] a drug having the same effect as (1). **5** [1940s+] (*S.Afr.*) a police van, a black maria.

pick-mouth n. [mid-late 19C] (*W.I.*) one who sets out to pick a quarrel.

pickney n. (*also* **picknee, picney**) [20C+] (*W.I./UK Black*) a young child. [PICCANINNY n.]

pick on v. [20C+] **1** to attack verbally, to victimize. **2** to pick a quarrel with.

pick one's hole v. [1990s+] to be at a loose end, to be idle.

pick one's teeth to v. (*also* **pick one's teeth with**) [20C+] (*W.I.*) to gossip with.

pick-penny n. [18C] a card-sharp. [SE *pick-penny*, one who greedily collects or steals money]

picks n.[1] [1910s] (*Aus.*) the cinema. [abbr. coll. SE *the pictures*]

picks n.[2] *see* PICK n.[2] (2).

pick straws v. *see* DRAW STRAWS v.

pickthank n. [16C–early 19C] a flatterer, a sycophant; a tale-bearer, a tell-tale. [lit. 'One who "picks a thank", i.e. curries favour with another, esp. by informing against some one else' (OED)]

pickthatch n. *see* PICKED-HATCH n.

pickthatch vestal n. *see* PICKETHATCH VESTAL n.

pick the bones out of that phr. [1930s+] a phr. of dismissal, retaliation, challenge, 'now see what you can do with that'.

pick the daisies v. [1920s–30s] to die.

pick the eyes out of v. [20C+] (*Aus.*) to get the best bits for oneself (cf. PEACOCK v.[1]). [orig. referring spec. to a system whereby a squatter chose the best bits of a tract of land (a 'run') so as to render the remainder useless to a rival]

pick them v. [1940s+] to choose one's partner(s) in relationships (amatory or otherwise); often in ironic form as *you can (certainly) pick them, you do (know how to) pick them*, i.e. they were a foolish choice.

pick-up n.[1] **1** [mid-19C] a confidence trick in which a prostitute lures a client to a room or deserted place, where, instead of having sex, the client is robbed by a male accomplice. **2** [mid-19C+] a casual sex partner, met and seduced without previous introduction. **3** [20C+] an arrest but no subseq. criminal charge; thus (*S.Afr.*) *pick-up van*, a police van. **4** [1920s–60s] robbery, theft; thus *at the pick-up*, working as a professional thief. **5** [1920s+] someone met in informal circumstances; sex may be involved, but not invariably. **6** [1920s+] an arrest; an order to arrest a suspect. **7** [1930s] payment for undertaking a criminal job. **8** [1930s+] the act of meeting someone in informal circumstances, usu. with a sexual relationship in mind. **9** [1940s] (*UK Und.*) a criminal who specializes in taking unguarded luggage, e.g. at railway stations. [PICK UP v.[1]]

pick-up n.[2] [1920s+] **1** (*drugs*) a dose or injection of narcotics; the feeling that follows. **2** a restorative drink.

pick-up adj. [1950s+] referring to a place or a person who is used for casual sex. [PICK UP v.[1] (1)]

pick up v.[1] **1** [mid-17C+] to accost for possible sex. **2** [18C+] (*Und.*) to accost or enter into conversation with the intention of practising a hoax or confidence trick on someone. **3** [late 18C–1920s] to rob, to steal. **4** [19C–1940s] to meet, with no sexual overtones involved. **5** [early–mid-19C] to cheat, to deceive; to rob by deception. **6** [mid-19C–1950s] to find fault with, to criticize. **7** [mid-19C+] to arrest. **8** [20C+] (*UK police*) to spot and shadow a suspect.

pick up v.[2] **1** [mid-19C+] (*US*) to tidy or clean up, to put in order. **2** [1910s–20s] to be stimulated, enlivened. **3** [1940s+] to resume where one has left off. **4** [1950s+] to stimulate, to invigorate.

pick up v.[3] (*US*) **1** [1910s–20s] to set in motion, to start. **2** [1940s+] to understand. **3** [1940s+] to do, to act, to perform. **4** [1950s+] to notice.

pick up v.[4] [1930s–40s] (*US Black*) to put together a meal from assorted left-overs and scraps.

pick up v.[5] [1930s+] (*US drugs*) **1** to use narcotics or cannabis. **2** to buy or sell drugs. **3** to resume taking narcotics after a period of abstinence. [PICK-UP n.[2]]

pick up a flat v. [19C] of a prostitute, to meet a client. [PICK UP v.[1] (1) + FLAT n.[2] (1)]

pick up a nail v. [20C+] (*W.I.*) to contract venereal disease. [the way in which venereal disease can lead to a sharp pain in the penis when urinating]

pick up fag ends v. [1910s+] to listen in to other people's conversations and attempt to comment upon them or join in, esp. as *don't pick up fag ends*. [SE *pick up* + FAG END n. (3) + pun on FAG END n. (4)]

pick-up man n. **1** [1920s] a thief, esp. of luggage. **2** [1940s–60s] (*US*) one who collects money wagered with bookmakers. [PICK UP v.[1] (3)]

pick up on v. (*orig. US*) **1** [1940s+] to notice, to understand. **2** [1950s] to get hold of, esp. drugs; to visit.

pick up one's crumbs v. [mid-19C] **1** to recover from an illness, esp. to begin eating after a period of fasting. **2** to begin enjoying improved circumstances.

pick up one's foot v. see MAKE FOOT v.

pick up pennies v. [1970s+] (*US gay*) of a male prostitute, to accept a minimal sum for one's services.

pick up sticks n. [20C+] the number 6. [rhy. sl.]

pick up the soap for v. [1940s+] (*gay*) to permit oneself to be sodomized. [the posture necessarily adopted for both activities]

pick up the tab v. [1930s+] (*orig. US*) **1** to pay a bill, usu. in a restaurant; the implication is of treating one's fellow eaters. **2** to take responsibility, to accept the consequences, esp. if financial. [TAB n.[3] (1)]

pick up yourself! excl. [20C+] (*W.I.*) get up and get out!

picky n. see PIC n.[2].

picky-picky adj. [1950s] (*W.I. Rasta*) **1** finicky or choosy, esp. in eating. **2** used of uncombed hair just starting to turn into dreadlocks. [SE *picky* + redup.]

picky-picky head n. (*also* picky head) [1960s] (*W.I.*) very short hair growing close to the scalp in small balls of fluff.

picney n. see PICKNEY n.

picnic n. [early 19C+] any simple, pleasurable experience; also in ironic use, thus (*UK/Aus.*) *no picnic*, an understated description of an unpleasant experience, a formidable task, usu. in response to another speaker, e.g. *It was no picnic, I can tell you*; also *that'll be a picnic/what a picnic*, used of a problem.

picthatch n. see PICKED-HATCH n.

picture n.[1] **1** [mid-17C–19C] a face. **2** [early 19C+] (*also* movie) anything or anyone considered very pleasing, shocking or amusing to the viewer, e.g. *you look a picture, she looks a picture, a picture of good health*.

picture n.[2] [1920s+] (*orig. milit.*) a situation.

picture n.[3] [1990s+] (*US*) a currency note, money (cf. ABE n.[2]). [the pictures of US presidents printed on the different denominations of dollar bills]

picture of Abe (Lincoln) n. [1950s+] (*US*) a $5 bill (cf. ABE n.[2]). [the face of *Abraham Lincoln* (1809–65), 16th president of the US, printed on the bills]

pictures n. [mid-19C] (*US Und.*) counterfeit notes. **2** playing cards.

pictures of the Queen n. [2000s] paper money (cf. ABE n.[2]).

piddle n. **1** [late 19C+] urine. **2** [late 19C+] an act of urination. **3** [1910s] nonsense. **4** [1980s] weak beer (cf. BUFFALO PISS n.). [PIDDLE v. (1)]

piddle v. **1** [late 18C+] to urinate. **2** [late 19C+] to rain, with an implication of drizzle rather than heavy rain. [mid-16C+ *piddle*,

to trifle, to work or act in a petty or insignificant way. The ext. to urination began as a childish expression, poss. implying the insignificant amount of urine produced. The compounds *piddle about/around* and *piddle away* thus refer back to the 16C use, even if the assumption is of the later one (cf. PISS ABOUT v.; PISS AWAY v.)]

piddle about/around v. see PISS ABOUT v.

piddle away v. see PISS AWAY v.

piddling adj. [late 16C+] small, insignificant, irrelevant. [SE *piddle*, to trifle]

piddly adj. (*also* piddly-ass) [1940s+] insignificant. [SE *piddle*, to trifle]

pie n.[1] **1** [mid-16C–17C; 1930s+] (*orig. US*) the vagina (cf. APPLE n.[6]). **2** [1960s+] (*US campus*) an attractive, sexually desirable woman; also used derog.

pie n.[2] **1** [mid-19C+] (*orig. US*) a treat, a bribe, something highly desirable. **2** [late 19C–1910s] political or other patronage or favours. **3** [20C+] money. [the image is of cutting up or distributing the 'pie' among supporters]

pie n.[3] [late 19C+] (*orig. US*) **1** anything easy or simple; often as *easy/good/sweet as pie*. **2** something to be appreciated; usu. in phr. *as pie*; thus *all pie and velvet*, total pleasure or enjoyment, usu. in neg.

pie n.[4] [2000s] (*US Black/drugs*) 1kg of cocaine.

pie n.[5] see PIE-CAN n.

pie adj.[1] (*also* old pie) [late 19C–1900s] (*Aus./US*) small-time, insignificant, second-rate.

pie adj.[2] [late 19C+] very easy. [PIE n.[3] (1)]

pie adj.[3] [1940s+] (*N.Z.*) good at, expert in. [Maori *pai*, good]

pie and liquor n. [20C+] a vicar. [rhy. sl.; SE *liquor*, the green parsley gravy that accompanies pie and mash]

pie and mash n. [1970s+] **1** money (cf. BEES (AND HONEY) n.). **2** an act of urination (cf. ANGEL'S KISS n.). [rhy. sl.; (1) = SE *cash*; (2) = SLASH n.[3] (1)]

pie and mash adj. [1970s+] showy, ostentatious. [rhy. sl. = FLASH adj.[1] (1)]

pie and one n. [20C+] **1** a son. **2** the sun. [rhy. sl.]

piebald n. [1900s–50s] (*Aus.*) a half-caste.

piebald adj. [1900s] (*Aus.*) using Blacks and Whites as fellow workers.

piebald v. [late 19C] to give a black eye; thus *piebald eye*, a black eye.

piebald mucker sheeny n. [late 19C] a dirty, old Jew. [SE *piebald* + MUCKER n.[2] (3) + SHEENY n.[1] (1)]

piebald pony n. [1920s+] (*Aus.*) a half-caste White/Aboriginal child. [PIEBALD n.]

pie-biter n. see PIE-EATER n.

pie-can n. (*also* pie) [1900s–40s] **1** a fool, a simpleton (cf. APPLEHEAD n.). **2** any second-rate object.

pie-card n. (*US*) **1** [1900s–20s] a ticket that entitles one to a meal from a *pie card mission*. **2** [1920s–60s] one who begs for a meal. **3** [1920s–60s] a union-card, esp. when used as a credential for begging. **4** [1920s–60s] the holder of a union-card.

piece n.[1] **1** [mid-16C+] a woman, esp. when appraised sexually. **2** [late 18C+] a man. **3** [1920s+] an act of sexual intercourse. **4** [1950s+] (*gay*) a man, in a sexual context. **5** [1960s+] one's body, in the context of violence. [coined 14C; SE until 18C; the primary image is that of a piece of meat]

piece n.[2] **1** [17C+] (*also* peece, pieces) a sum of money, a coin worth £1 and 2 shillings. **2** [late 19C+] a share. **3** [1920s+] a commission, a percentage.

piece n.[3] **1** [mid-19C+] a gun. **2** [mid-19C+] the penis. **3** [1910s] (*US*) a hypodermic syringe. **4** [1970s+] a knife. [(1) SE late 16C–mid-19C; (3) is play on GUN n.[1] (3)]

piece n.[4] **1** [late 19C] a tattoo. **2** [1980s+] (*orig. US*) a major work of graffiti, typically as displayed on a New York City subway train. [abbr. SE *masterpiece*]

piece n.[5] [20C+] (*Irish/Scot.*) **1** a piece of bread and butter. **2** a sandwich, a worker's packed lunch; thus *piece-plate*, a sandwich plate; *piece-time*, lunchtime.

piece n.[6] (*drugs*) **1** [1920s+] (*also* **piece of stuff**) a quantity of heroin, cocaine or morphine, approx. 28g (1oz). **2** [1960s+] (*also* **piece of stuff**) an unspecified quantity of drugs. **3** [1980s+] a container for drugs.

piece n.[7] [1960s+] something or someone undesirable. [PIECE OF SHIT n.]

piece n.[8] [1970s] (*US Black*) an automobile.

piece n.[9] [1980s+] (*US campus*) a hairdo. [abbr. SE *hairpiece*]

piece n.[10] [1990s+] (*US prison*) a jail sentence.

pieced adj. [1990s+] deflowered. [PIECE n.[3] (2); but also PIECE n.[1] (3)]

piece man n. [1970s] (*US*) a gunman, an armed bodyguard. [PIECE n.[3] (1) + SE *man*]

piece of ass n. (*also* ...**butt**, ...**cock**, ...**cunt**, ...**gash**, ...**hump**, ...**pussy**, **hunk of arse/ass**) **1** [1930s+] (*orig. US*) a woman, not used as derog. but invariably from a sexual point of view and usu. dismissive; occas. a man. **2** [1930s+] (*US*) heterosexual sexual intercourse. **3** [1940s+] (*US*) hetero- or homosexual anal intercourse. **4** [1950s] (*US Und.*) a passive male homosexual. [SE *piece*/PIECE n.[1] (1)/SE *hunk* + ASS n. (4)/ARSE n.[1] (7)/BUTT n.[1] (6)/COCK n.[3]/CUNT n.[1] (3)/GASH n.[1] (2)/HUMP n.[4] (2)/PUSSY n. (1); (3) and (4) ARSE n.[1] (1)/ASS n. (2)]

piece of cake n. (*also* **slice of cake**) [1930s+] anything seen as simple, easily achieved, no bother. [note earlier SPONGE CAKE n.]

piece of calico n. [mid–late 19C] an attractive woman. [SE *piece*/PIECE n.[1] (1) + CALICO n.]

piece of cancer n. [1980s+] (*US*) a despicable person.

piece of chickenshit n. [1980s+] (*US campus*) a coward, a weakling. [CHICKENSHIT n. (1)]

piece of entire n. [mid–late 19C] an admirable person. [they are 'entirely' excellent]

piece off v. [1920s+] (*US*) to bribe, to pay off, to give out a 'piece' of cash. [PIECE n.[2] (1)]

piece of femme n. [1930s] (*US*) sexual intercourse with a woman. [PIECE n.[1] (3) + FEMME n. (1)]

piece of fine linen n. *see* BIT OF MUSLIN n.

piece of flesh n. (*also* **piece of skin**) [20C+] (*US Black/W.I.*) an attractive woman. [note parallel use at RMC Duntroon (Aus.)]

piece of furniture n. (*also* **bedroom furniture**) [mid-19C; 1930s+] (*orig. US Black*) a woman or girl (in sexual context).

piece of goods n. **1** [late 18C+] a person. **2** [19C+] (*also* **bale of goods**) a young woman; a flighty young woman who has 'abandoned the proprieties' (Ware).

piece of iron n. *see* IRON n.[3] (2).

piece of jab n. [1930s] a talkative person. [JABBER n.[1] (1)]

piece of magnolia n. [1960s+] (*Can.*) **1** a sexually available woman. **2** sexual intercourse.

piece of meat n. **1** [late 19C+] (*also* **hunk of meat**) anyone regarded as no more than a physical object, esp. in a sexual context. **2** [1920s] (*US gay*) a penis (cf. BACON n.[1]). [MEAT n. (1)/MEAT n. (2)]

piece of muslin n. *see* BIT OF MUSLIN n.

piece of mutton n. [late 17C–early 19C] a woman, seen as a sex object. [MUTTON n.[1] (1)]

piece of nookie n. *see* NOOKIE n. (2).

piece of piss n. [1940s+] (*orig. RAF*) anything seen as supremely easy. [PISS n. (1)]

piece of pudding n. [late 19C] an example of good luck; a welcome change in circumstances.

piece of resistance n. [1930s+] (*Aus.*) constipation. [a pun on Fr. *pièce de résistance*, the supreme example, esp. the best dish in a meal]

piece of seven n. [1970s] (*US Black*) any one of the 7 days of the week.

piece of shit n. (*also* **hill of shit**, **pile of crap**, **...shit**, **...shite**) [1940s+] (*orig. US*) anything or anyone unpleasant, disgusting, of poor quality, e.g. a disliked person, a piece of gross hypocrisy etc. [fig. use of SHIT n.[1] (1)]

piece-of-shit adj. [1980s+] a general derog. term, e.g. disgusting, unattractive, unkempt. [PIECE OF SHIT n.]

piece of skin n. *see* PIECE OF FLESH n.

piece of skirt n. [1930s+] (*orig. US*) a woman, seen as a sex object. [metonymy]

piece of someone's ass n. [1950s+] (*US*) a beating, a thrashing, a punishment. [ASS n. (2)]

piece of stuff n.[1] [late 18C] a young woman.

piece of stuff n.[2] *see* PIECE n.[6].

piece of tail n. **1** [1920s+] (*orig. US*) a woman, a girl, not used derog. but invariably from a sexual point of view and usu. dismissive. **2** [1920s+] (*US*) (*also* **hunk of tail**) an act of sexual intercourse. **3** [1960s] (*US gay*) a sexual partner. [SE *piece*/PIECE n.[1] (1) + TAIL n.[2] (5); (3) TAIL n.[2] (1)]

piece of the action n. [1960s+] (*orig. US*) a share in what is going on, usu. monetary, criminal or gambling. [SE *piece*/PIECE n.[2] (2) + ACTION n. (4)]

piece of thick n. [late 19C] a cake of pressed tobacco.

piece of trade n. [1930s+] **1** a prostitute (cf. ASS PEDDLER n.). **2** (*gay*) a sexual partner. [TRADE n. (1)]

piece of work n.[1] **1** [mid-19C] a fuss, a 'to-do'. **2** [20C+] (*also* **hunk of work**) a person; usu. as *a nasty bit/piece of work*, an unpleasant person. **3** [1960s+] a formidable person. **4** [1970s+] one who is considered odd or eccentric by the speaker.

piece of work n.[2] *see* WORK n.[1] (1).

pieces n.[1] [1970s+] (*US Black*) clothes. [? SE *piece of goods*]

pieces n.[2] *see* PIECE n.[2] (1).

pieces of eight n. [20C+] weight. [rhy. sl.]

piece up v. **1** [20C+] (*US Und.*) to divide up the spoils of a robbery. **2** [1950s+] (*drugs*) to divide a large amount of a drug into smaller, saleable pieces. **3** [1990s+] to give someone a gun. [PIECE n.[2] (2); (3) PIECE n.[3] (1)]

piechopper n. [1950s] (*US Black*) the mouth.

pie-eater n. (*also* **pie-biter**) [late 19C+] (*mainly Aus.*) **1** an insignificant person. **2** one who is greedy for material possessions. **3** a fool, a simpleton (cf. APPLEHEAD n.). **4** a small-time criminal. [the negative stereotype of a greedy person who sees no further than immediate gratification]

pie-eyed adj. **1** [20C+] drunk (cf. ARSEHOLED adj.). **2** [1940s] astonished, amazed. **3** [1980s+] under the influence of drugs. [one's eyes are popping out of one's face]

pie-face n.[1] [late 19C+] a person with a round or blank face, a stupid person.

pie-face n.[2] [1980s] (*Aus.*) an Asian (cf. BROWNIE n.[2]). [the cuts in a pie-crust that supposedly resemble slanted Asian eyes]

pie-faced adj. [20C+] a general insult, stupid (and unattractive). [PIE-FACE n.[1]]

pie hole n. [1980s+] (*US teen*) the mouth. [var. on CAKEHOLE n. (1)]

pie in the sky n. [1910s+] (*orig. US*) fantasies, fond hopes and illusions. [the line 'There'll be pie in the sky when you die', in the song 'The Preacher and the Slave' (1911) penned by Joe Hill, leader of the Industrial Workers of the World, a prototype US union]

pieman n.[1] [mid-17C] a lecher. [PIE n.[1] (1)]

pieman n.[2] **1** [mid-19C+] the player who shouts out in pitch and toss. **2** [1900s] the game of pitch and toss. [the old pieman's cry 'Hot pies, toss or buy! Toss or buy!']

pie out v. [1970s] (*US campus*) to become drunk. [PIE-EYED adj. (1)]

piepiejoller n. (*also* **pippiejoller**) [1970s+] (*S.Afr.*) an adolescent. [Afk. sl. *piepie*, a penis + JOL v. (5); lit. 'one who has fun with his penis']

pie-pusher *n.* [late 19C] a street pie seller. [PUSH v.[2] (1)]

piercer *n.* **1** [mid-18C–mid-19C] a penetrating, keen glance. **2** [late 19C] the penis.

pierce the hogshead *v.* [early 17C] to have sexual intercourse, esp. to deflower a virgin.

pies *n.* [1940s] (*US Black*) the eyes. [? rhy. sl.]

piesa *n. see* PAISA n.

pie shop *n.* [mid–late 19C] a dog. [the popular belief that when in 1842 one Blauchard opened a pie shop in London, he used dead dogs as meat]

pie wagon *n.* **1** [20C+] (*US*) a police van, used to transport villains. **2** [1900s] a prison. **3** [1920s–30s] (*US*) a wagon used as sleeping quarters for chain gang workers.

piffed *adj.* (*also* **piffled**) [20C+] (*US*) drunk. [? one's drunken spluttering]

piffin bridge *n.* [1990s+] the perineum on a man. [ety. unknown; ? link to Lancashire dial. *piff*, a puff of wind]

piffle *n.* [late 19C+] nonsense, rubbish, esp. as a dismissive excl.; thus *piffler*, one who talks nonsense; *piffling*, nonsensical, insignificant. [PIFFLE v.]

piffle *v.* [mid-19C+] to talk or act in a trifling or ineffective way. [? echoic; the image is of someone talking feebly]

piffled *adj. see* PIFFED adj.

pifflicated *adj.* [1900s–30s] drunk. [PIFFLE v. + SPIFLICATE v.]

pig *n.*[1] **1** [mid-16C; 19C+] a general insult denoting unpleasantness, esp. to one who is fat, ugly and/or greedy. **2** [1920s–30s] (*US*) in horseracing, a slow or otherwise useless horse, one not to bet on. **3** [1920s+] a fat, unattractive woman. **4** [1920s+] (*US campus*) a woman considered to be drunken, promiscuous and sexually available. **5** [1950s–70s] (*Can./US*) a prostitute (cf. ALLEY CAT n.). **6** [1960s+] (*drugs*) a greedy consumer of a given drug. [stereotypically negative views of the pig]

pig *n.*[2] [early 17C–19C] a sixpence (2½p). [it is smaller than a HOG n.[1] (1); though note HOG n.[1] (2)]

pig *n.*[3] **1** [19C+] (*orig. UK Und.*) (*also* **pigman**) a policeman; thus *pigs*, the police as a group; a watchman (cf. ANIMAL n.[1]). **2** [mid-19C–1940s] an informer. **3** [1930s+] any conventional person, a member of the Establishment or authorities. **4** [1970s+] a prison warder. **5** [1980s] (*US Black*) a White person. [Egan's Grose suggests that a pig's rooting for food is the image behind the TRAP n.[2] who roots up the haunts of the PRIG n.[1] (1)]

pig *n.*[4] [late 19C] a venereal ulcer.

pig *n.*[5] **1** [20C+] (*US*) a discontinued model of motorcar, a run-down, dilapidated motorcar, a car that looks good but has a small, low-powered engine. **2** [1930s] (*US tramp*) a railroad engine. **3** [1950s+] (*US Black*) a Cadillac. **4** [1950s+] (*US*) a large motorcycle, esp. a Harley-Davidson.

pig *n.*[6] [1910s] (*US Und.*) a hardware store; the goods it sells. [joc. abbr. of SE *pig iron*]

pig *n.*[7] [1920s] (*US prison*) any form of meat.

pig *n.*[8] [1930s] (*US Und.*) a dollar.

pig *n.*[9] **1** [1930s] (*US tramp*) a hot water bottle. **2** [1980s+] (*N.Z.*) a flagon of beer.

pig *n.*[10] [1960s+] anything considered difficult or exhausting to achieve.

pig *n.*[11] *see* BLIND PIG n.

pig *adj.* [1970s+] pertaining to the police. [PIG n.[3] (1)]

pig *v.*[1] [mid-19C+] (*US Und.*) to run off.

pig *v.*[2] [1950s] to provide food.

pig *v.*[3] *see* PIG OUT v. (2).

pig- *pfx* [late 19C+] a general intensifier, usu. implying extremes of ignorance, dirt etc, e.g. PIG-IGNORANT adj.

pig and roast *n.* [1940s+] toast. [rhy. sl.]

Pig and Tinder-box *n.* [mid-19C] the Elephant and Castle tavern in south London. [a former smithy, it was converted to a tavern in 1760 and was a major 19C London coaching terminus]

pi-gas *n. see* PI-JAW n.

pig between the sheets *n.* [1940s] (*US*) a ham sandwich.

pig brother *n.* [1960s+] (*US Black*) any Black who informs against their own people to the (White) police. [PIG n.[3] (1) + BROTHER n. (2)]

pig dog *n.* **1** [late 19C–1940s] a general term of abuse. **2** [1980s+] (*US campus*) a glutton. [PIG n.[1] (1) + DOG n.[3] (2); (1) is translation of Ger. *Schweinhund*]

pig down *v.* [1980s] to eat hurriedly and greedily. [ext. PIG OUT v.]

pig-eater *n.* [19C] a general term of affection.

pigeon *n.*[1] **1** [late 16C+] (*orig. UK Und.*) a dupe, a victim; thus PIGEON DROP n. **2** [late 18C–mid-19C] (*UK Und.*) 'Pigeons – sharpers who, during the drawing of the lottery, wait ready mounted, near Guildhall, and as soon as the first two or three numbers are drawn, which they receive from a confederate, ride, i.e. "fly", with them to some distant insurance office where there is another of the gang, commonly a decent looking woman to her he secretly gives the numbers, which she insures for a considerable sum' (Grose, 1796). **3** [mid–late 19C] (*UK/US Und.*) a professional gambler.

pigeon *n.*[2] **1** [late 16C+] a young woman. **2** [1990s+] (*US Black*) a woman who trades sex for drugs. **3** [2000s] (*US teen*) a promiscuous girl. **4** [2000s] a woman's breast. **5** [2000s] (*US teen*) an unattractive girl.

pigeon *n.*[3] [mid-19C+] (*orig. US*) an informer. [abbr. STOOL-PIGEON n.[1] (1)]

pigeon *n.*[4] [20C+] concern, problem, e.g. *that's your pigeon*.

pigeon *n.*[5] *see* BLUE PIGEON n. (2).

pigeon *n.*[6] *see* YARDBIRD n.[2].

pigeon *v.*[1] [late 17C–mid-19C] to trick, to hoax, to deceive. [PIGEON n.[1] (1)]

pigeon *v.*[2] [1950s–60s] (*US*) to act as an informer. [PIGEON n.[3]]

pigeon and doves *n.* [20C+] gloves. [rhy. sl.]

pigeon artist *n.* [1960s] (*US Und.*) a confidence trickster. [PIGEON n.[1] (1) + ARTIST n. (1)/ARTIST sfx]

pigeon-cracking *n.* [mid-19C] stealing lead from the roofs of buildings. [BLUE PIGEON n. (2) + CRACK v.[3] (3)]

pigeon drop *n.* [mid-19C+] (*US Und.*) a confidence trick that involves dropping a wallet where a victim can find it or a scheme in which the con-man tells the victim that they have found a large sum of money and, if the victim will advance some money as a show of good faith, they can have a share in the 'windfall'. [PIGEON n.[1] (1)]

pigeon dropper *n.* [1940s] (*US Und.*) a confidence trickster. [PIGEON DROP n.]

pigeon dropping *n.* [1940s] (*US Und.*) playing any form of confidence trick. [PIGEON DROP n.]

pigeon-flying *n. see* FLY A BLUE PIGEON v.

pigeonhole *n.* **1** [late 16C–17C] (*UK Und.*) the stocks. **2** [late 19C–1900s] the vagina (cf. BAG n.[1]; BLACK HOLE n.[1]). [SE *pigeonhole*, a small hole or recess]

pigeon on *v.* [1940s] (*Aus.*) to drop something on (someone) from above.

pigeon pair *n.* **1** [late 19C] a family whose children are a boy (born first) and a girl. **2** [late 19C+] any male and female pair. [the pigeon's brood usu. consists of 1 male and 1 female]

pigeon's milk *n.* [mid-19C–1900s] the subject of a fool's errand which apprentices are sent on, trad. on 1 April.

pigeon-'tomach *n.* [20C+] (*W.I.*) a woman with larger than average breasts. [play on SE *pigeon-chested*]

pigface *n.* [1940s] a general term of abuse; the assumption is of ugliness.

pig-fucker *n.* [1930s+] (*US*) a worthless, very unpleasant person; thus *pig-fucking*, worthless, disgusting. [SE *pig* + FUCKER n. (1)/FUCKER n. (3)]

piggen de wiggen *n. see* PIG-WIDGEON n.

pigger *n.* (*also* **pigmouth**) [20C+] (*US Black*) a very fat woman. [PIG n.¹ (1)]

piggery *n.* **1** [mid-19C+] (*US*) a squalid drinking establishment. **2** [late 19C+] a room that is rarely cleaned or tidied but which is very much the private concern of its occupant.

pigging *adj.* [20C+] **1** an intensifier; a euph. for FUCKING adj. (1). **2** (*Irish*) filthy.

piggot *n. see* PIGOT n.

piggy *n.* [1980s+] (*Aus. prison*) one who has been jailed for bestiality.

piggy *adj.* **1** [late 19C–1950s] (*Aus.*) unpleasant. **2** [1970s+] (*US gay*) sexually abandoned.

piggyback *v.* **1** [1980s] the occupation by a dealer of several floors in a building; when one is raided others are still available. **2** [2000s] (*US drugs*) the simultaneous injection of 2 drugs.

piggy bank *n.* [1960s+] masturbation. [rhy. sl. = WANK n.¹ (1)]

pighead *n.* (*also* **pig's head**) [late 19C+] a stubborn, uncompromising person. [backform. f. PIGHEADED adj.]

pigheaded *adj.* [17C+] stubborn, uncompromising. [SE *pig* + -HEAD sfx (1)]

pig heaven *n.*¹ [1960s+] a fantasy paradise that would delight the gross rather than the fastidious. [PIG n.¹ (1)]

pig heaven *n.*² [1970s+] (*US Black*) a police station. [PIG n.³ (1) + SE *heaven*]

pig-ignorant *adj.* [1950s+] extremely stupid. [PIG- pfx + SE *ignorant*]

pig in *v.* **1** [late 17C+] to share a home; usu. as *pig in with*. **2** [20C+] to gorge oneself; often as exhortation *pig in!*

pig in the middle *n.* [20C+] an act of urination (cf. ANGEL'S KISS n.). [rhy. sl. = PIDDLE n. (2)]

pig iron *n.*¹ [late 18C] (*US*) an order of sausages.

pig iron *n.*² **1** [1920s] alcohol, often cheap and unpleasant. **2** [1980s+] (*Irish*) fun, devilment, amusement; usu. as *for the pig iron*, for the fun of it. [joc. use of SE; all refer to the low value of pig iron]

pig-iron *adj.* [1960s] terrible, useless, rubbish, a general negative. [the low value of SE *pig iron*]

pig-iron dump *n.* [1920s] (*US*) a hardware store.

Pig Island *n.* [20C+] (*Aus./N.Z.*) New Zealand; thus, *Pig Islander*, New Zealander. [the introduction of pigs to New Zealand by Captain Cook]

pig it *v.*¹ **1** [19C+] to live in squalor, albeit unworried by that squalor. **2** [1900s–30s] to renege. [PIG n.¹ (1)/SE *pig*, to live in squalor]

pig it *v.*² *see* PIG OUT v.

pig jump *v.* [late 19C–1940s] (*Aus.*) of a horse, to jump with all 4 legs in the air at once; ext. to a jumping human.

pigman *n. see* PIG n.³ (1).

pig meat *n.* **1** [1920s–30s] (*US Black*) sexual intercourse. **2** [1920s+] (*US Black*) a young woman, esp. an attractive one; a sexually attractive young man. **3** [1930s+] (*US*) a promiscuous woman; a prostitute (cf. ALLEY CAT n.). **4** [1970s+] (*US gay*) an underage boy. [PIG n.¹ (4) + MEAT n. (1)]

pig-meater *n.* [late 19C–1900s] (*Aus.*) a bullock that does not fatten; a beast only fit for pigs' food.

pig months *n.* [late 19C] the 8 months of the year that have an 'r' in their name, i.e. September to April. [prior to refrigeration, these months were considered the safest for eating pork, known to decay in the hotter summer season]

pigmouth *n. see* PIGGER n.

pig-muck *adj.* [1950s] a general derog.; a euph. for CRAPPY adj. (5) or SHITTY adj.¹ (1).

Pigopolis *n. see* PORKOPOLIS n.

pigot *n.* (*also* **piggot**) [late 19C] a flagrant lie; usu. as *piggotted*, cheated, fooled. [proper name of Richard *Pigott* (*c*.1828–89), the forger of the Parnell papers]

pig-out *n.* [1990s+] (*orig. US*) an orgy of eating. [PIG OUT v. (2)]

pig out *v.* (*also* **pig it**) **1** [mid-19C; 1930s] to die. **2** [mid-19C+] (*also* **pig**, **pork (out)**) to overeat massively; often as *pig out on* (a food or drink). **3** [1970s+] (*also* **pig up**) to overindulge in anything. **4** [1990s+] to treat someone to a (large) meal. [PIG n.¹ (1)]

pig party *n.* [1950s–80s] an orgy, a gang-rape. [PIG n.¹ (4) + SE *party*]

pigpen *n.* **1** [20C+] (*US*) any dirty, unpleasant place. **2** [1970s] a police station. [(1) SE; (2) PIG n.³ (1)]

pigpen Irish *n.* [1910s–30s] (*US*) working-class, poor Irish. [PIGPEN n. (1)]

pig-puncher *n.* [1900s] (*US*) a pig-farmer. [on pattern of COW-PUNCHER n.]

pig room *n.* [1970s+] (*US gay*) an orgy room. [PIG n.¹ (4)/PIG OUT v. (3)]

pig-root *v.* [1900s–10s] (*Aus.*) to ride. [SE *pig-root*, for a horse to buck violently with its hind legs]

p.i.g.s. *n.* [1990s+] (*US*) Poles, Italians, Greeks and Slavs. [abbr.]

pig's *n. see* PIG'S (EAR) n.

pigs! *excl.* [20C+] (*mainly Aus.*) a general expression of disgust, contempt, negation etc; often as *pigs to you!*

pig's arse *n.*¹ [20C+] (*Aus.*) a glass. [rhy. sl.]

pig's arse *n.*² [1970s+] **1** a difficult or messy situation. **2** (*Irish*) a contemptible person.

pig's arse! *excl.* (*also* **pig's ass! pig's bum!**) [1910s+] a contemptuous excl. (cf. IN A PIG'S ASS! excl.). [ARSE n.¹ (1)/ASS n. (2)/BUM n.¹ (1)]

pig's breakfast *n. see* DOG'S DINNER n.

pig's Christmas parcel! *excl.* [1940s+] (*N.Z.*) a general excl. of annoyance. [rhy. sl. = *pig's* ARSEHOLE n. (1)]

pig sconce *n.* [mid-17C–19C] a stubborn fool, a 'pig-headed' person (cf. APPLEHEAD n.). [SE *pig* + *sconce*, the head]

pig's (ear) *n.* [late 19C+] beer. [rhy. sl.]

pig's ear *n.* (*also* **pig's diddy**) [1950s+] a mess, chaos; usu. as *make a pig's ear of…* [? euph. for SE *pig's* ARSE n.¹ (1), although this predates PIG'S ARSE n.² (1)]

pig's eye *n.* **1** [mid-19C] in cards, the ace of diamonds. **2** [late 19C] (*Irish*) (*also* **pig's-eye-in-a-bottle**) a term of abuse. **3** [1930s–50s] (*Can.*) *the pig's eye*, something excellent, outstanding, first-rate.

pig's fry *n.* [1930s+] a tie. [rhy. sl.]

pig's fry *v.* [1930s+] to try. [rhy. sl.]

pig's head *n. see* PIGHEAD n.

pigshit *n.* [1960s+] **1** nonsense, rubbish; also as excl. *pigshit! rubbish!* **2** a disgusting or second-rate thing.

pig-sick *adj.* [1960s+] furious, enraged; thus *pig-sick of*, infuriated by, incapable of tolerating.

pigskin *n.* **1** [late 19C] a saddle; thus, fig., horseracing. **2** [20C+] (*US campus*) a football.

pigskin artist *n.* [1940s] (*Aus.*) a jockey. [PIGSKIN n. (1) + ARTIST sfx]

pigsnyes *n.* (*also* **pinckany**) [late 14C–early 19C] a coarse term of endearment used to a woman. [SE *pig's eyes*, small eyes; ? the implication is of a pig, greedy, in this case, for sex]

pig's scream *n. see* BEE'S KNEES n.

pigsticker *n.* **1** [late 19C–1940s] a pig-butcher. **2** [late 19C+] any form of sharpened, stabbing weapon, e.g. a lance, a bayonet, a large knife etc. **3** [1970s] a general term of abuse. [note WW1 Aus. milit. *pigstabber*, a bayonet]

pigsticking *n.* [1920s+] (*Can.*) sodomy.

pig's trotter *n.* [1990s+] a squatter. [rhy. sl.]

pigstyle *adv.* [1980s+] (*US Black*) living in filthy circumstances. [SE *pig*/PIG n.¹ (1)]

pig's vest with buttons *n.* [1930s] (*US tramp*) sow belly or any fat bacon.

pig sweat *n.* [20C+] (*US*) **1** beer. **2** inferior 'rotgut' bourbon.

pig's whiskers *n. see* CAT'S WHISKERS n.

pig's whisper *n.* **1** [mid-19C] a nearly inaudible whisper, a grunt. **2** [mid-19C+] a very short space of time; usu. as *in a pig's whisper*. [note SE *cockstride*, a very short space of time; lit. 'the length of a cock's pace']

pig's whistle *n.* [mid-19C] a very short time.

pigswill *n.* [20C+] nonsense, rubbish; thus excl. *pigswill!* rubbish!

pigtail *n.*[1] [late 17C–1930s] a roll of coarse tobacco. [resemblance]

pigtail *n.*[2] [early–mid-19C] an old man. [a ref. to the fact that some old men still wore their hair in a pigtail, an 18C affectation]

pigtail *n.*[3] [mid-19C] the penis.

pigtail *n.*[4] **1** [mid-19C–1950s] (*Aus.*) a Chinese immigrant, mainly to Australia. **2** [late 19C–1940s] (*US Und.*) (also **John Pigtail**) a Chinese man (cf. AH CABBAGE *n.*). [the wearing of pigtails by the Chinese]

pigtail *adj.* [late 19C] wearing a pigtail, thus generic for Chinese, e.g. *pigtail brigade, pigtail land, pigtail party*.

pigtail alley *n.* (*also* **pigtail town**) [late 19C] (*US*) Chinatown in New York City, centred on Mott Street. [PIGTAIL *adj.* + SE *alley/town*]

pig together *v.* [late 17C–mid-19C] to lie together. [the proximity resembles pigs in a sty]

pig tranquillizer *n. see* HORSE TRANQUILLIZER *n.*

pig up *v. see* PIG OUT *v.* (3).

pig wagon *n.* [1990s+] a police van. [PIG *n.*[3] (1) + SE *wagon*]

pig-widgeon *n.* (*also* **piggen de wiggen, pig-widgin, pig-wiggen**) [late 17C–early 19C] a fool, a simpleton (cf. APPLEHEAD *n.*). [*pig* is used as an intensifier. The word presumably comes f. SE *pigwidgen, pig-widgeon*, described in *OED* as 'of obscure origin and meaning', although it is either a proper name, as used by a constable by sl. collector Robert Greene (1558–92) or that of a 'fairy knight' as suggested by the writer Michael Drayton (1563–1631); note, however, WIDGEON *n.*]

pi-jaw *n.* (*also* **pi-gas**) [late 19C–1940s] (*orig. UK juv.*) an earnest, moralizing lecture, esp. as delivered by parents or teachers; occas. as *v.* [PI *adj.* + JAW *n.* (2)/GAS *n.*[1] (1)]

pike *n.*[1] [late 16C–19C] the penis (cf. AX *n.*[2]). [SE *pike*, a pointed weapon]

pike *n.*[2] **1** [mid-18C–19C] a toll gate. **2** [mid–late 19C] the toll paid on one; thus *pike, pike-keeper, pike-man*, one who takes the tolls; *bilk a pike*, cheat the toll gate keeper. **3** [mid-19C+] a road, a highway. [abbr. SE *turnpike*, initially a toll gate, thence the 'high road']

pike *n.*[3] [1910s–50s] a look. [PIKE *v.*[3] (2)]

pike *v.*[1] **1** [mid-17C–1920s] to leave, to run off quickly; often as *pike it/off/over*. **2** [late 17C–18C] (*UK Und.*) to die. **3** [2000s] to beg, to cadge. [fig. uses of SE *turnpike*]

pike *v.*[2] [late 19C+] (*US*) to hold back, to shirk, to act cautiously, often in gambling; thus *pike bet*, a small bet. [PIKER *n.* (2)]

pike *v.*[3] (*US*) **1** [1900s–40s] (*also* **pike around**) to ask questions. **2** [1900s–50s] (*also* **pike off**) to look at. [Nottinghamshire dial. *pike*; ult. SE *peek*]

piked off *adv.* [late 17C+] safely escaped. [PIKE *v.*[1] (1)]

pike on *v.* [1980s+] (*N.Z.*) to let down, to disappoint. [PIKE *v.*[2]]

pike on the been *v.* (*also* **pike on the bene, ...on the Leen**) [mid-17C–mid-18C] (*UK Und.*) to run away at top speed. [PIKE *v.*[1] (1) + BENE *adj.*; ? *Leen* a misprint]

pike out *v.* [1980s+] (*Aus.*) to leave a party early. [PIKE *v.*[1] (1)/ PIKE *v.*[2]]

piker *n.* **1** [mid-19C–1910s] a vagrant, a gipsy, a tramp, spec. one who walks everywhere. **2** [mid-19C+] (*US*) a small-time gambler. **3** [late 19C+] (*orig. US*) a mean, grasping person, one who will not take the least risk, esp. to help others. **4** [late 19C+] an insignificant person. **5** [1900s–20s] (*orig. US*) a lazy person. **6** [1910s–20s] a small-time burglar. **7** [1930s+] a cheat. **8** [1940s] (*Aus.*) a confidence trickster. **9** [1950s] (*Aus.*) an unpleasant, unpopular person; a bore, a 'party pooper'. [PIKE *n.*[2] (3), lit. 'one

who walks the turnpikes'. All defs. fig. uses of (1); note N.Z. agricultural *piker*, a wild bull]

piker *adj.* [1920s–60s] (*US*) in gambling, small-time, petty. [PIKER *n.* (2)]

pikestaff *n.* [late 17C–1900s] the penis (cf. BAT *n.*[7]).

pikey *n.* (*also* **piky**) [mid-19C+] a vagrant. [PIKER *n.* (1)/Kentish dial.; ult. PIKE *n.*[2] (3)]

piking *n.* [late 19C+] (*orig. US*) cheating, using sharp practices. [PIKE *v.*[2]]

pikkie *n. see* PICCY *n.*

piky *n. see* PIKEY *n.*

pil *n. see* PILLETIJIE *n.*

pilch *n.* [1930s–40s] (*US Black*) one's residence, a house, a home, an apartment. [? 11C–16C SE *pilch*, an outer garment, a wrapper]

pilcher *n.* [early–mid-17C] a general term of abuse. [? 'one who wears a pilch or leathern jerkin or doublet' or 'one who pilches, a thief' (*OED*); ult. SE *pilchard*]

pile *n.*[1] **1** [mid-18C+] a large amount of money; thus *make a/one's pile*, to become rich; *go a/one's (whole) pile*, to bet heavily, to the extent of one's purse. **2** [mid-19C+] a large amount.

pile *n.*[2] [1970s] (*US prison*) a prison. [ROCKPILE *n.* (1)]

pile *v.*[1] [late 19C] to cost, to amount to. [SE *pile up*]

pile *v.*[2] [1910s+] to move fast. [fig. use of PILE IN(TO) *v.* (1)]

pile *v.*[3] **1** [1930s+] (*US Black/campus*) to have sexual intercourse. **2** [1970s] (*US campus*) to laze about. [one 'makes a heap']

piled for French velvet *phr.* [early 17C] suffering from a venereal disease. [FRENCH *adj.* (1)]

pile drive *v.* [1960s–70s] (*gay*) to have sex with someone. [PILE-DRIVER *n.* (1)]

pile-driver *n.* **1** [19C; 2000s] the penis. **2** [1930s] (*US tramp*) strong coffee. **3** [1960s–70s] a male homosexual. [play on SE *piledriver* + in (3) SE *piles*]

pile in(to) *v.* (*also* **pile on(to)**) [late 19C+] (*orig. US*) **1** to attack physically, to crash into, to get to work on, to take part in. **2** to attack verbally.

pile it higher and deeper *v.* (*also* **Ph.D., shovel it higher and deeper**) [1970s] (*US*) to boast, to lie.

pile it on *v.*[1] **1** [mid-19C–1900s] to perform an act with greater intensity. **2** [late 19C+] to charge a high price.

pile it on *v.*[2] *see* PILE ON THE AGONY *v.*

pile of bricks *n.* (*also* **pile of stone**) [1940s–60s] (*US Black*) a building.

pile of crap/shit(e) *n. see* PIECE OF SHIT *n.*

pile on dog *v. see* PUT ON DOG *v.* (1).

pile on the agony *v.* (*also* **pile it on, pile up the agony**) [mid-19C+] to embellish an already painful or disturbing factual or fictional statement with more and more (poss. specious) details.

pile on(to) *v. see* PILE IN(TO) *v.*

pile up (at) *v.* [late 19C+] (*US*) to end up (at), esp. of an evening out.

pile up the agony *v. see* PILE ON THE AGONY *v.*

pile up the rocks *v.* [mid-19C+] to amass a great deal of money. [SE + ROCKS *n.*[1] (1)]

pilgarlic *n.* (*also* **peel(e) garlic, pilgarlick**) **1** [late 15C–mid-18C; 1990s+] an outcast; often as *poor pilgarlic*, poor me. **2** [16C; 1990s+] (*Irish*) a bald head, a bald-headed man. **3** [1990s+] (*Irish*) a shabbily dressed, sickly looking person. [SE *peel garlic*, a peeled, thus smooth, garlic clove, and thence a bald-headed man, seen presumably as an outcast]

pilgrim *n.*[1] **1** [mid-19C] (*Can./N.Z./US*) an early immigrant from Britain to New Zealand. **2** [late 19C+] a person, usu. in the context of a place or country other than one's own. **3** [1920s+] a conventional person.

pilgrim *n.*[2] (*also* **advertising pilgrim**) [1960s] (*US gay*) a well-dressed, attractive heterosexual man, unaware of the reaction he gains from gay men. [play on SE + ADVERTISE *v.* (2)]

pilgrim salve *n.* (*also* **pilgrim's salve**) [late 17C–early 19C] human excrement. [16C SE *pilgrim's salve*, an ointment, made mainly of swine's grease and isinglass]

pilgrim's staff *n.* [18C] the penis (cf. BAT n.⁷).

pill *n.*¹ **1** [early 17C+] a cannon-ball or bomb; thus [1950s] *big pill*, the atomic bomb. **2** [mid-19C] (*US Und.*) a counterfeit coin. **3** [mid-19C+] a bullet. **4** [20C+] (*orig. US*) any form of ball, esp. a basketball. [resemblance, i.e. 'roundness']

pill *n.*² **1** [mid-19C–1910s] anything unpleasant, suffering, punishment; the term is 'endless in application' (Ware). **2** [mid-19C+] an unpleasant person, a weakling, a bore. **3** [late 19C] something unfashionable. **4** [late 19C; 1950s] a man, a person. **5** [1900s] (*US campus*) a hard-working student; a teacher who makes the students work hard. [the image of a SE *pill* as something innately unpleasant]

pill *n.*³ (*also* **pills**) [mid-19C–1920s; 1990s+] (*orig. milit.*) a doctor, a surgeon; one who deals with or dispenses medicines.

pill *n.*⁴ **1** [mid-19C–1960s] (*drugs*) a 'pill' of opium; thus *pill shop*, an opium den (cf. APOSTLE n.). **2** [1930s+] a pill of heroin. **3** [1950s+] (*drugs*) a generic term for any form of barbiturate or amphetamine drug capsule (cf. ACE n.⁴; APPLE n.⁹; BEAN n.⁶; BERRY n.²; BIT n.⁹; BLUNT n.⁴; BOP n.²; BULLET n.¹; BUTTON n.⁷; CANDY n.⁴; CAP n.⁴; DAMON (HILL) n.; DOLL n.²; EGG n.⁴; EGGS n.²; GUMDROP n.²; HIT n.³; JELLY BEAN n.³; JU-JU n.; M & Ms n.; PEBBLE MILL n.; PRESCRIPTIONS n.; RAINBOWS n.; ROUNDHEAD n.³; SPLIT n.⁶; TAB n.⁷; THING n.⁷; TORPEDO n.²; VITAMINS n.; YUM-YUMS n.).

pill *n.*⁵ **1** [late 19C–1930s] a drink. **2** [1910s–60s] a cigarette or cigar; thus *pill mill*, a cigar factory. **3** [1950s+] (*orig. US drugs*) a marijuana cigarette. [? they all 'cure' one's ills]

pill *v.*¹ **1** [mid-19C–1910s] to blackball. **2** [1900s–20s] to fail a candidate in an examination. [a weakened form of PILL n.¹ (3); (2) f. (1)]

pill *v.*² [1910s] (*Aus.*) to shoot dead. [PILL n.¹ (3)]

pill and poll *v.* [16C–17C; mid-19C] (*UK Und.*) to cheat one's accomplice or partner in crime. [SE *pillage* + *poll*, to plunder, to despoil]

pillar and post *n.* [20C+] a ghost. [rhy. sl.]

pillars *n.* [1930s–40s] (*US Black*) the human legs.

pill-box *n.*¹ **1** [mid-19C] a coffin. **2** [mid–late 19C] a pulpit. **3** [late 19C–1900s] a soldier's hat. **4** [late 19C+] a small brimless hat. [joc. use of SE *pill-box* for anything small, circular and box-like]

pill-box *n.*² [mid–late 19C] (*US*) a revolver, a pistol. [PILL n.¹ (3) + SE *box*]

pill-box *n.*³ [mid–late 19C] a small carriage. [PILL n.³; such carriages were typically used by doctors]

pill-box *n.*⁴ [late 19C] a doctor. [note pre-WW2 taxidriver jargon *The Pill-box*, Harley Street, site of many private consulting rooms]

pillcock *n. see* PILLICOCK n.

pill cooker *n.* [1920s–50s] (*drugs*) an opium smoker. [PILL n.⁴ (1) + COOK v.³ (2)]

pill driver *n.* (*also* pill-monger) [mid-18C; mid-19C–1900s] a travelling apothecary.

pilled (up) *adj.* [1960s+] (*drugs*) under the influence of amphetamines or barbiturates. [PILL n.⁴ (3)]

pilletijie *n.* (*also* pil) [1960s+] (*S.Afr. drugs*) a marijuana cigarette. [lit. 'a little pill'/PILL n.⁵ (3)]

pill freak *n.* [1960s+] (*drugs*) a heavy user of pills, e.g. amphetamines, barbiturates. [PILL n.⁴ (3) + FREAK sfx]

pill-grinder *n.* **1** [late 19C] a doctor (cf. PILL-PEDDLER n.; PILL-PUSHER n.; PILL-ROLLER n.; PILL-SHOOTER n.). **2** [20C+] a pharmacist.

pill-head *n.* [1960s+] (*drugs*) a regular user of amphetamine or barbiturate drugs. [PILL n.⁴ (3) + -HEAD sfx (3)]

pillicock *n.* (*also* pillcock, pillie, pillock) **1** [early 14C–19C] the penis. **2** [late 16C–mid-17C] a term of affection for a young boy. [north. dial.; ult. Norwegian dial. *pill*, the penis + COCK n.² (1)]

pillion pussy *n.* [1950s] (*N.Z.*) a young woman who accom-

panies a motorcycle-riding young social outlaw. [SE *pillion* + PUSSY n. (1)]

pill man *n.* [1960s] (*drugs*) a pill dealer. [PILL n.⁴ (3)]

pill mill *n.* [1980s–90s] (*US*) a doctor's surgery, usu. in a ghetto area, in which the bulk of prescriptions are written for drugs which are then sold in the street. [SE *pill* + MILL n.⁴ (6)]

pill-monger *n. see* PILL DRIVER n.

pillock *n.*¹ [1960s+] **1** a fool, a simpleton (cf. CHOAD n.). **2** a general term of abuse. [PILLICOCK n. (1)]

pillock *n.*² *see* PILLICOCK n.

pillocks *n.* [1910s+] nonsense; thus *talk pillocks*, to talk nonsense; *pillocky*, stupid, nonsensical. [PILLS n.¹ (1) + BALLOCKS n.² (2)]

pillory *n.* [late 17C–18C] a baker. [? the placing of bakers who were caught giving false measure in the pillory. The baker's profession was often synon. with trickery and fraud]

pill out *v.* [1950s+] to accelerate sharply in a vehicle from a standing start and thus leave traces of rubber tyres on the tarmac. [SE *peel*, to leave]

pillow *n.* [late 19C] (*US*) a boxing glove. [its padding]

pillow-biter *n.* (*also* pillow-chewer) [1960s+] **1** (*orig. Aus.*) a homosexual, usu. the passive one (cf. KAPOK-CRUNCHER n.; MATTRESS-MUNCHER n.). **2** (*US prison*) one who has been subjected to homosexual rape. **3** a general term of abuse, irrespective of actual sexual preference. [the supposed agonies of anal intercourse; note ext. use at RMC Duntroon (Aus.) as 'a woman in the context of exceptionally aggressive or "passionate" (?) sexual intercourse when the male exclaims "Bite the pillow, bitch!"']

pillowcase *n.* [1920s] (*US*) one who talks nonsense. [play on HORSEFEATHERS n.]

pillow-mate *n.* [19C] a prostitute. [note Hindley, *The Old Book Collector's Miscellany* (1871–3): 'Serving [...] as a little Side *Pillow*, to render the Yoke of *Matrimony* more easy']

pillow pigeons *n.* [1940s] (*US Black*) bedbugs.

pillox around *n.* [1980s] to annoy, to mess around with. [PILLOCKS n.]

pill-pad *n.* [late 19C+] an opium den, a place where opium users can gather to smoke. [PILL n.⁴ (1) + PAD n.² (2)]

pill-pate *n.* [mid-16C] a friar. [14C–17C SE *pill*, to shave + *pate*, head; f. the tonsure adopted by friars]

pill-peddler *n.* [1920s–30s] a doctor (cf. PILL-GRINDER n.).

pill-popper *n.* [1960s+] (*drugs*) a regular user of any drugs in pill form. [PILL-POPPING n.]

pill-popping *n.* [1960s+] (*drugs*) taking pills regularly, esp. as an addiction; also as adj. [PILL n.⁴ (3) + POP v.⁴ (2)]

pill-pusher *n.* [1900s–30s] a doctor (cf. PILL-GRINDER n.).

pill-roller *n.* [late 19C+] **1** a pharmacist. **2** a doctor (cf. PILL-GRINDER n.).

pills *n.*¹ **1** [late 17C; late 19C+] the testicles. **2** [late 19C–1900s] billiards. [the roundness of PILL n.¹ (1) + pun on BALLS n.¹ (1)]

pills *n.*² *see* PILL n.³.

pill-shooter *n.* (*also* pill-slinger, -thrower, -twister) [1910s–60s] a doctor (cf. PILL-GRINDER n.).

pill shop *n. see* PILL n.⁴ (1).

pill up *v.* [mid-19C] (*US campus*) to get dressed up. [PILL n.² (2); thus image is of ostentation, showiness]

pilot *n.* **1** [early–mid-19C] a watchman. **2** [late 19C–1930s] (*US*) a cabdriver. **3** [20C+] (*US*) a jockey.

pilot cove *n.* (*also* pilot bloke) [1910s] (*Aus.*) a clergyman. [SKY PILOT n. + COVE n. (1)/BLOKE n. (1)]

pimgenet *n.* (*also* pimginet, pimginnit, pimpgennet) [late 17C–early 18C] a prominent, red pimple; also as adj., covered with red pimples. [? SE *pomegranate*, a fruit that might be seen as being covered in 'pimples'. Halliwell, *Dict. of Archaic and Provincial Words* (1847), cites the 'old saying': 'Nine pimgenets make a pock royal']

pimp *n.*¹ **1** [17C] a procurer. **2** [early 18C] a prostitute's customer. **3** [early 18C–early 19C] a piece of wood used for lighting a fire.

4 [1940s] a general term of abuse, esp. of a man who does not work for a living. **5** [1940s–70s] (*Aus./US Black*) a male prostitute. **6** [1960s+] (*US Black/campus*) a fashionable, stylish person. **7** [1980s+] (*US campus*) a man who sustains several relationships at the same time; a womanizer. [? Fr. *pimpreneau*, a scoundrel; *pimpant*, alluring or seducing in outward appearance or dress; or *pimpesouée*, a pretentious woman. (1) began life as sl. but entered SE 1660–1700]

pimp *n.*[2] **1** [late 19C+] (*Aus./N.Z./S.Afr.*) a police informer. **2** [20C+] (*Aus.*) a sneak, a tell-tale. [fig. use of PIMP *n.*[1] (1)]

pimp *n.*[3] [1960s+] (*US Black*) a style of walking, supposedly reminiscent of a pimp. [PIMP *n.*[1] (1); but note McCall, *Makes Me Wanna Holler* (1994): 'My Aunt Iris […] said it (i.e. the pimp) was handed down through generations from the slavery days. […] Some slaves were forced to walk with a ball and chain attached to one ankle. When they walked they took a regular step with the free leg and sort of hopped on the other to drag the heavy ball and chain'; such a reverse of a negative situation is echoed in the 1980s+ hip-hop fashion, whereby baggy jeans over revealed boxer shorts were intended to mimic prison, where no belts are permitted]

pimp *n.*[4] *see* PIMP (DUST) n.

pimp *adj.* [1960s+] (*US Black*) **1** stylish, expensive. **2** the best, the ultimate. [PIMP *n.*[1] (1); the enviable status of the pimp in Black street culture; 'this one little syllable represents a job, a mindset, a way of life, a way of walking, a way of talking, a way of dressing, a pejorative, and a high compliment' Touré, *The Portable Promised Land* (2002)]

pimp *v.*[1] **1** [17C] (*UK Und.*) to work as a procurer. **2** [1960s+] (*US Black*) to strut (in the supposed manner of a pimp). **3** [1970s+] (*US campus*) (*also* **pimp up**) to dress up, of a person and of an object. **4** [1970s+] to seduce, to flirt with. [PIMP *n.*[1]/PIMP *n.*[3]; (1) SE 18C+]

pimp *v.*[2] [mid-19C] (*US campus*) to toady, to curry favour by performing petty actions. [SE *pimping*, petty]

pimp *v.*[3] [1940s+] (*Aus./N.Z.*) to tell tales; to inform on someone. [PIMP *n.*[2] (1)]

pimp *v.*[4] [1980s+] (*US campus*) to steal.

pimpable *adj.* [2000s] (*US Black*) a woman who is a potential prostitute. [SE *pimp*, to prostitute someone]

pimp-ass *adj.* (*US Black*) **1** [1960s+] contemptible. **2** [1990s+] on bad = good model, excellent. [SE *pimp* + -ASS sfx]

pimp-boots *n.* [1970s+] (*US gay*) ankle boots, 'Beatle boots'.

pimp cane *n.* [2000s] (*US Black*) a cane used orig. by pimps to discipline their prostitutes; latterly in general use to describe a cane used as a weapon. [var. on PIMP STICK n.[2] (2)]

pimp car *n. see* PIMP RIDE n.

pimp crazy *adj.* [1950s–70s] (*US*) of a prostitute who goes from one sadistic, abusing pimp to another, apparently unable to break the habit. [SE *pimp* + -CRAZY sfx]

pimp (dust) *n.* [1970s] (*US Black/drugs*) cocaine (cf. BIRDIE POWDER n.). [SE *pimp* + SE *dust*/DUST n.[5] (2), based on the assumption that this is the pimp's drug of choice]

pimped down *adv.* (*also* **pimped out**, **...up**) [1970s+] (*US Black*) **1** of a person, fashionably or smartly dressed. **2** of an object, ostentatious, flashy. [SE *pimp* + *down/out/up*]

pimper *n.* [1990s+] (*US Black*) one who adopts the PIMP *n.*[3] walk.

pimp fronts *n.* [1950s+] (*US Black*) a particular style of dress associated with pimps. [SE *pimp* + FRONTS n.[2]]

pimpgennet *n. see* PIMGENET n.

pimp hand *n.* [2000s] (*US Black*) the skills that go to making a successful pimp.

pimpillac *n. see* PIMPMOBILE n.

pimping *n.* [1970s+] (*US campus*) doing well. [SE *pimp* v.]

pimping *adj.* (*US Black/campus*) **1** [1960s+] well-dressed. **2** [1990s+] a general term of approval. [PIMP adj.]

pimping shoes *n. see* PIMP SHOES n.

pimping stick *n. see* PIMP STICK n.[2].

pimpish *adj.* [1970s+] (*US teen*) stylishly dressed. [PIMP adj. (1)]

pimp kiss *v.* [2000s] to make a false show of affection.

pimple *n.*[1] [late 17C–early 18C] a boon companion. [ety. unknown; ? link to PIMP *n.*[1] (1)]

pimple *n.*[2] **1** [early 19C–1940s] the head. **2** [late 19C+] a baby's penis.

pimple and blotch *n.* [20C+] Scotch (whisky). [rhy. sl.]

pimple and wart *n.* [late 19C–1900s] **1** a quart. **2** port (wine). [rhy. sl.]

pimple brain *n.* (*also* **pimplehead**) [20C+] a fool (cf. BAKE-BRAIN n.).

pimple cover *n.* (*also* **pimple coverer**) [early 19C] a hat. [PIMPLE n.[2] (1)]

pimple in a bent *n.* [late 16C–mid-17C] something infinitesimally small. [SE *pimple* + *bent*, a grass-stalk]

pimply *n.* [1970s+] an acned youth. [SE *pimple*]

pimpmobile *n.* (*also* **pimpillac**) [1970s+] a flashy, ostentatious car, potentially the choice of a pimp, but not restricted to such drivers. [SE *pimp* + -MOBILE sfx/(*Cad*)*illac*]

pimpo *adj. see* PIMPY adj.

pimp oil *n.* [2000s] (*US Black*) a strong perfume or scent.

pimp on *v.* (*also* **pimp off**) [1940s+] (*orig. US Black*) to take advantage of, to scrounge off, to play on human emotions in order to obtain money. [weak form of SE *pimp*, to run prostitutes/to prostitute (someone)]

pimp playa *n.* [2000s] (*US Black*) a man who adopts the trad. pimp style, but may not actually be selling women. [SE *pimp* + PLAYER n.[1] (2)]

pimp post *n.* (*also* **pimp rest**) [1970s+] (*US Black*) the arm-rest between the driver and passenger in a car.

pimp ride *n.* (*also* **pimp car**, **...wagon**) [1970s+] (*US Black*) an expensive car, suitable for a pimp. [SE *pimp* + RIDE n.[2] (1)]

pimp roll *n.* [1980s+] (*US Und.*) a strutting style of walk affected by US Black pimps? (cf. PIMP STRIDE n.). [for ety. *see* PIMP n.[3]]

pimps *adj. see* PIMPSY adj.

pimp shades *n.* (*also* **pimp tints**) [1970s+] a style of dark glasses affected by pimps. [SE *pimp* + SHADES n.[2]/TINTS n. (1)]

pimp shoes *n.* (*also* **pimping shoes**) [1970s+] whatever fashion in shoes is currently favoured by Black pimps.

pimp slap *n.* [1970s+] (*US Black*) an open-handed slap across the face.

pimp slap *v.* (*also* **pimp smack**) [1990s+] (*US Black*) to hit in the face, either with the fist or a weapon. [PIMP SLAP n.]

pimp socks *n.* [1950s–70s] (*US Black*) ultra-thin nylon socks, usu. with a pattern of vertical stripes.

pimp steak *n.* [1940s+] (*US Black*) a frankfurter. [? its phallic dimensions]

pimp stick *n.*[1] **1** [1920s+] (*Can./US*) a cigarette. **2** [1950s+] (*Can./US drugs*) a marijuana cigarette (cf. BAT n.[8]). **3** [1960s–70s] (*US prison*) a cigarette holder. [SE *pimp* + STICK n.[8]/STICK n.[9] (3)]

pimp stick *n.*[2] (*also* **pimping stick**) [1930s+] (*US Black*) **1** 2 wire coat hangers twisted together to make an improvised and vicious whip. **2** a cane used by a pimp both as part of his 'uniform' and for beating up his prostitutes (cf. PIMP CANE n.).

pimp stride *n.* (*also* **pimp stroll**, **...strut**, **...walk**) [1970s+] (*orig. US Black*) a strutting style of walking, intended to emphasize one's pride, independence and masculinity (cf. PIMP ROLL n.). [for ety. *see* PIMP n.[3]]

pimp stride *v.* (*also* **pimp strut**, **...walk**) [1970s+] (*US*) to walk in the strutting manner associated with a Black pimp. [PIMP STRIDE n.]

pimp's turban *n.* [1920s–30s] (*US*) a derby hat.

pimpsy *adj.* (*also* **pimps**) [1980s+] far too easy, utterly simple. [dial. *pimpy*, paltry, mean, small]

pimp talk *n.* (*US Black*) **1** [1950s–70s] the 'line' used by a pimp when attempting to persuade a new young woman to join his group of prostitutes. **2** [1950s–70s] the bantering, self-aggrandizing conversations between a group of pimps. **3** [1970s+] the jargon of pimps.

pimp-talk v. [1970s] (*US Black*) to talk in a bantering, self-aggrandizing manner. [PIMP TALK n. (2)]

pimptastic adj. [2000s] (*US Black*) fantastic; self-aggrandizing. [SE *pimp* + -TASTIC sfx]

pimp tints n. see PIMP SHADES n.

pimp up v. see PIMP v.¹ (3).

pimp wagon n. see PIMP RIDE n.

pimp walk see under PIMP STRIDE.

pimp whisk n. (*also* pimp-whiskin, pimp-whisking) **1** [mid-17C–early 19C] a first-rate pimp (cf. ABBOT ON THE CROSS n.; BOSS PLAYER n.). **2** [late 17C–early 19C] a mean-spirited, bigoted man. [PIMP n.¹ (1) + WHISK n.; (1) note *whisk* is usu. derog.]

pimpy adj. (*also* pimpo) [1940s] (*US*) having the characteristics or personality of a pimp.

pin n.¹ **1** [mid-15C+] the penis; thus *take the pin*, of a woman, to have sexual intercourse. **2** [1920s+] (*drugs*) a hypodermic syringe (or a makeshift alternative), used for injecting narcotic drugs. **3** [1960s+] (*drugs*) a very thin marijuana cigarette (cf. BONE n.¹¹).

pin n.² [1980s+] a drug dealer. [? abbr. SE *kingpin*]

pin n.³ [1990s+] (*US prison*) a female inmate acting as a lookout. [PIN v.⁴ (8)]

pin v.¹ [mid-16C; 20C+] to have sexual intercourse, usu. of a man (cf. BAGAGA v.; BANG v.¹). [? SE *pin down*, but note PIN n.¹ (1)]

pin v.² **1** [mid-18C–mid-19C] to snatch, to steal. **2** [late 18C–1930s] to seize, to catch, to arrest. **3** [mid-19C] to obtain something from someone.

pin v.³ [late 19C–1930s] to pawn clothes. [? SE *pawn*]

pin v.⁴ **1** [1920s+] (*Aus.*) to target someone for one's (often amatory) attentions. **2** [1930s+] to mark down visually, to notice. **3** [1950s–70s] (*US*) to come to terms with, to work out. **4** [1950s+] (*US campus*) to state one's commitment to a person of the opposite sex by giving them one's fraternity pin. **5** [1950s+] (*US Black*) to stare at (aggressively). **6** [1970s] (*US Black*) to draw someone else's attention to, to point out. **7** [1970s–80s] (*US*) to identify. **8** [1990s+] (*US prison*) of a female prisoner, to act as a lookout.

pin v.⁵ **1** [1930s–40s] (*Aus./US*) to cause trouble for, to 'do down'. **2** [1940s–70s] (*US*) to knock out. [? wrestling imagery]

pin a can on v. see GET A CAN ON v.

pin a few on v. see PIN ONE ON v.

pin a rose v. [1930s] (*US short order*) to put a slice of onion on a hamburger.

pin artist n. [1930s–60s] (*US tramp*) an abortionist. [SE *pin* + ARTIST sfx]

pin back one's lugholes v. [1940s+] to give one's full attention (cf. PIN ONE'S EARS BACK v.). [LUGHOLE n.]

pin basket n. [late 18C–early 19C] the youngest child. [SE *pin-basket*, a large ornamented pin-cushion with pins of varying lengths arranged to resemble a basket; such a pin-cushion was trad. given to a mother after the birth of a child]

pin-box n. [late 17C] the vagina (cf. BAG n.¹). [PIN n.¹ (1) + SE *box*]

pin-case n. [mid-16C] the vagina (cf. BAG n.¹). [PIN n.¹ (1) + SE *case* + play on SE]

pinch n.¹ [late 17C–1900s] a certainty, something easily achieved. [? SE *pinch*, the critical point; or ? play on PINCH n.² (1), i.e. 'a steal']

pinch n.² **1** [mid-18C+] a theft, esp. short-changing; an act of stealing or plagiarism; also in fig. use. **2** [mid-19C+] (*orig. US*) an arrest. **3** [1900s] (*Aus.*) a prison.

pinch n.³ [1960s+] (*drugs*) **1** a small amount of marijuana, enough for perhaps 2 cigarettes. **2** a small amount of a narcotic drug.

pinch v. **1** [late 16C–19C] to rob. **2** [late 17C+] to steal. **3** [mid-19C] to pass counterfeit money in exchange for goods. **4** [mid-19C+] to arrest. **5** [1900s] to capture. **6** [1900s–50s] to raid. [orig. Und., mainstream sl. from mid-19C]

pinch a bob v. [mid-19C] to rob a till. [thus cited by Greenwood, but the *bob* may either be generic for money, or a mishearing of LOB n.¹ (2)]

pinch a loaf v. [1990s+] (*US*) to defecate.

pinch-back n. (*also* pinch-belly) [17C–early 19C] a miser. [they *pinch* someone else's *back* by refusing to pay them enough to buy new clothes]

pinch-bottom n. [19C] a pimp (cf. ABBOT ON THE CROSS n.).

pinch box n. [1900s–10s] **1** (*Aus./US*) a police station. **2** (*US*) a police call-box. [PINCH n.² (2)]

pinch-buttock n. [19C] a pimp (cf. ABBOT ON THE CROSS n.; PINCH-CUNT n.).

pinch-commons n. [late 17C–early 19C] a miser. [PINCH v. (2) + SE *commons*, provisions that are provided in common for a group/*crust*]

pinch-cunt n. [19C] a pimp (cf. ABBOT ON THE CROSS n.; PINCH-BUTTOCK n.). [SE *pinch* + CUNT n.¹ (1)]

pincher n.¹ **1** [mid-18C–early 19C] a rogue specializing in short-changing. **2** [19C] a policeman; thus *put a pincher on*, to arrest (cf. BEAT-POUNDER n.). **3** [19C+] a shoplifter, a thief. [PINCH v.]

pincher n.² [1900s] (*Aus.*) a baby.

pinchers n. [1920s–40s] (*US Black/Und.*) shoes; thus *pinchers up*, dead. [their tightness]

pinch-fart n. [late 16C–early 17C] a miser. [PINCH v. (1) + FART n. (1)]

pinch-fist n. [late 16C; late 19C–1900s] a miser. [SE *pinch* + SE *fist*]

pinch-gloak n. [19C] a petty thief who specializes in stealing small articles from jewellers. [PINCH v. (2) + GLOAK n.]

pinch-gut n. [mid–late 17C] a miser. [their constant desire to 'tighten their belt'; note naut. *pinch-gut money*: 'allow'd by the King to the Seamen, [...] on Bord the Navy [...], when their Provision falls Short' (B.E.)]

pinch-gut adj. [late 17C; 1900s] miserly, impoverished. [PINCH-GUT n.]

pinch-gut vengeance n. see WHIP-BELLY (VENGEANCE) n.

pinch hit v. [1920s+] to act as a substitute, esp. in an emergency; thus *pinch-hitter*, a temporary worker. [baseball jargon *pinch-hit*, to substitute for a batter, esp. at a crucial point in the game]

pinch-hitter n. [1980s] (*drugs*) one who is hired to inject an addict too ill to do it themselves. [for ety. see PINCH HIT v.]

pinching lay n. [late 18C–early 19C] a variety of petty crimes involving cash, passing counterfeit money, stealing from shops, giving short change etc. [PINCH v. (2) + LAY n.⁴ (1)]

pinch it off! excl. [1940s+] (*Aus.*) hurry up! [fig. use of PINCH ONE OFF v.]

pinch one off v. [1940s+] (*US*) to defecate (cf. BACK ONE OUT v.). ['one' is a piece of excrement; the phr. reflects the basic meaning of TURD n. (1), something that is 'torn off' from the body]

pinch-penny n. [15C–mid-17C; 1930s+] a miser; also attrib. [SE *pinch* + *penny*]

pinch-prick n. [late 19C] a prostitute (cf. COCKATRICE n.). [SE *pinch* + PRICK n. (2)]

pinch the cat v. [1960s–70s] of a man, to fondle one's genitals through one's trouser pocket. [joc. use of SE]

pinch-wife n. [late 19C–1900s] a mean, boorish husband, who does not trust his wife.

pinckany n. see PIGSNYES n.

pin-cushion n. [19C] the *mons veneris*; thus the vagina (cf. BAG n.¹). [PIN n.¹ (1) + SE *cushion* + play on SE]

pineapple n.¹ [1910s] the vagina (cf. APPLE n.⁶). [? male fear or fascination with the vagina as 'prickly' on the outside, sweet within]

pineapple *n.*[2] (*also* **pineapple bomb, Niagara pineapple**) [1910s+] a bomb, a grenade. [the shape]

pineapple *n.*[3] [1930s+] unemployment benefit, the dole. [the Dole *Pineapple* company]

pineapple *n.*[4] [1960s–70s] a male homosexual. [play on FRUIT n.[2] (2)]

pineapple *n.*[5] [1960s–70s] (*Scot.*) a chapel. [rhy. sl.]

pineapple *n.*[6] [1980s] (*US*) a Puerto Rican (cf. BATO n.). [the jungle associations]

pineapple *n.*[7] [2000s] (*US campus/drugs*) heroin. [ety. unknown]

pineapple bomb *n. see* PINEAPPLE n.[2].

pineapple chunk *n.* **1** [20C+] departure, escape. **2** [1990s+] semen (cf. BABY GRAVY n.). [rhy. sl.; (1) = BUNK n.[5]; (2) = SPUNK n. (4)]

pineapple cut *n.* [1940s] (*Aus.*) a rough haircut, leaving the hair shaggy and irregular.

pineapple head *n.* [1990s+] a derog. term for a Samoan American. [SE *pineapple* + -HEAD sfx (2); the jungle associations]

pineapple princess *n.* (*also* **pineapple queen**) [1960s+] (*gay*) a homosexual person from Hawaii (cf. DUCHESS n.[1]). [SE *pineapple*, Hawaii's state fruit + PRINCESS n. (3)/QUEEN n.[2] (1)]

pine-box parole *n.* (*also* **pine-box release**) [1940s+] (*US prison*) an inmate's death in prison. [the *pine box* is a coffin]

pine-box suit *n.* [1960s] a coffin.

pine drape *n.* [1940s] (*Aus./US*) a coffin. [SE *pine*, pinewood + DRAPE n. (1)]

pine-liner *n.* [late 19C] (*Aus.*) a coffin.

pin-ends *n. see* PINS n.

pine outfit *n.* (*also* **pine overcoat**) [mid-19C–1940s] (*Aus./US*) a coffin. [SE *pine*, pinewood + SE *outfit/overcoat*]

piner *n.* [late 19C] (*Aus.*) a coffin.

pine-top *n.* [mid-19C–1940s] (*US*) cheap or illicitly distilled bourbon. [? the wood used in its barrels]

Ping *n.* [1980s+] (*N.Z.*) a derog. name for an Asian person (cf. BROWNIE n.[2]). [*Ping* as a 'typical' Chinese name]

ping *n.* [1980s+] (*N.Z. drugs*) an injection of a narcotic drug. [SE *ping*, echoic of a sudden high-pitched noise]

ping *v.*[1] [early–mid-19C] (*sporting*) to speak in a quick, singing, high voice.

ping *v.*[2] [1940s+] (*Aus./N.Z.*) to hit, to shoot; also in fig. use, an attempt, a 'shot', e.g. *have a ping at*. **2** [1980s+] (*N.Z. drugs*) to inject narcotics. [(1) the pinging noise of a musket; (2) PING n.]

pinga *n.* [1970s+] (*US*) the penis. [Sp.]

ping-in-wing *n.* [1940s–50s] (*drugs*) an injection of a narcotic. [SE *ping*, echoic of the action of an injection + WING n.[1] (2)]

ping off! *excl.* [1970s–80s] (*Aus. teen*) go away!

ping-pong *n.*[1] [1940s–60s] (*drugs*) Pantopon, a synthetic opiate. [play on brandname]

ping-pong *n.*[2] [1940s+] (*W.I., Bdos*) a passport-sized photograph of one's face. [for ety. *see* PING-PONG v., i.e. not a 'real' photo]

ping-pong *adj.* [2000s] strong. [rhy. sl.]

ping-pong *v.* [1940s+] (*W.I.*) to play at something, not to take one's commitments seriously. [the image of *ping-pong* or table tennis as not a 'serious' sport]

pin-grease *n. see* AXLE GREASE n. (1).

pin gun *n.* [1950s–70s] (*US drugs*) an improvised hypodermic syringe, using a medicine dropper and a pin. [PIN n.[1] (2) + GUN n.[1] (3)]

pinhead *n.*[1] (*US drugs*) **1** [late 19C–1930s] a small pill of opium, costing 25 cents. **2** [1920s–40s] one who injects narcotics, esp. when using a rudimentary syringe based on a pin and medicine dropper. **3** [1960s] an amphetamine user. **4** [1960s+] a very thin marijuana cigarette (cf. BONE n.[11]).

pinhead *n.*[2] [late 19C+] (*orig. US*) **1** a stupid person. **2** a person with a small head. [SE *pin* + -HEAD sfx (1)/SE *head*]

pinhead *adj.* (*also* **pinheaded**) [late 19C+] stupid, with a small brain (cf. AIRHEADED adj.). [PINHEAD n.[2] (1)]

pin in the fanny *n.* [1970s] (*US*) a tedious and troublesome situation. [FANNY n.[1] (2), i.e. a PAIN IN THE ARSE n. (2)]

pin-jabber *n.* [1920s+] (*drugs*) a drug user who injects their preferred drug. [PIN n.[1] (2) + JAB v.[1]]

pin joint *n.* [1970s] (*drugs*) a very thin marijuana cigarette (cf. BONE n.[11]). [SE *pin* + JOINT n.[5] (3)]

Pink *n.* (*also* **P, Pinkerton, Pinkie**) **1** [mid-19C+] (*US*) a member of *Pinkerton's* Detective Agency; thus *the Pinks*, the Agency as a whole. **2** [1920s+] in fig. use, a detective or a sharp person (cf. EAGLE EYE n.). [abbr.]

pink *n.*[1] **1** [late 16C–mid-17C; 1950s] a prostitute. **2** [1970s+] the open vagina, esp. in pornography. **3** [2000s] sexual intercourse; esp. in phrs., e.g. GET SOME PINK v.

pink *n.*[2] **1** [late 17C–1900s] as *the pink*, something of the highest fashion, the best. **2** [19C–1920s] a fashionable, well-dressed person. [SE *in the pink*]

pink *n.*[3] [1920s+] (*US Black*) a White person; thus [1960s+] *pink boy*, a White man of any age. [the actual skin colour of a White person]

pink *n.*[4] [1920s+] (*orig. US*) one whose politics are left of centre, but who is certainly not a communist (sometimes with an implication of insincerity). [a 'paler' version of RED n.[3]]

pink *n.*[5] [1970s–80s] (*US*) the *pink* slip that confirms ownership of a vehicle. [abbr.]

pink *n.*[6] *see* DUTCH PINK n.

pink *adj.*[1] [early 19C; 1910s] (*US*) fashionable, exclusive. [SE in 16C]

pink *adj.*[2] **1** [late 19C–1940s] violent, extreme, absolute; esp. as (*not*) *a pink thing*. **2** [late 19C+] slightly indecent, violent or vulgar, mildly 'blue'.

pink *adj.*[3] [mid-19C+] left-wing, socialist (rather than communist). [pale RED adj.[2] (1)]

pink *adj.*[4] [20C+] homosexual. [use predates Gay Liberation days]

pink *adj.*[5] [1920s+] (*US Black*) racially White.

pink around the gills *phr.* [1960s] (*US campus*) drunk (cf. ARSEHOLED adj.). [SE *pink* + GILLS n. (1)]

pink cally *n.* [2000s] (*drugs*) a variety of MDMA (cf. ECSTASY n.). [the colour, but ? *cally*]

pink champagne *n.* [1990s+] (*drugs*) **1** a mixture of cocaine and heroin. **2** amphetamine sulphate (cf. A n.[2]). [(2) the colour of the powder]

pink chaser *n.* [1920s+] (*US Black*) a Black person who pursues the company and friendship of Whites. [PINK n.[3] + SE *chaser*]

pink cigar *n. see* PINK PANATELLA n.

pinked up *adj.* [late 19C–1900s] (*US*) fashionably dressed. [PINK adj.[1]]

Pinkerton *n. see* PINK n.

pinkey *n. see* PINKY n.[1].

pink-eye *n.*[1] **1** [20C+] (*Aus./Can.*) the cheapest red wine, methyl alcohol. **2** [20C+] (*Aus.*) a regular drinker of methylated spirits. **3** [1920s+] (*Aus./Can.*) a drinking bout, a party; thus *go pink-eye*, to get drunk. **4** [1950s] (*US*) cheap, 'rotgut' bourbon. [pron. of PINKIE n.[2]]

pink-eye *n.*[2] [20C+] (*US*) the vagina.

pink flamingoes *n.* [1990s+] (*drugs*) a variety of MDMA (cf. ECSTASY n.). [the pills are coloured pink]

pink hearts *n. see* PURPLE HEARTS n.

Pinkie *n. see* PINK n.

pinkie *n.*[1] (*also* **pinky**) **1** [late 19C+] a very light-skinned Black person. **2** [1960s+] (*orig. US Black*) a White person.

pinkie *n.*[2] (*also* **pinky**) (*Aus.*) **1** [late 19C+] cheap red wine; thus *pinky-shop*, a store specializing in such wine; *pinkyite*, a drinker of such wine. **2** [20C+] methylated spirits mixed with cheap red wine or Condy's crystals.

pinkie *n.*[3] [1990s+] (*US Black*) a pink automobile, esp. a Cadillac.

pinkie *n.*[4] *see* PINKO n.

pinkie *n.*[5] *see* PINKY n.[1].

pinkies *n.* [20C+] the fingers. [Scot. dial.]

pinkindindies *n.* (*also* **pinking-dindees**) [mid–late 18C] (*Irish*) a gang of dissolute, rich young men who cut off the bottom few inches of their scabbards and prod or 'pink' with their exposed sword point those whom they encounter and with whom they can start an argument. [lit. 'a turkey-cock given to pinking with a rapier']

pink ink *n.* [20C+] (*US*) a romance novel. [SE *pink*, i.e. romantic + *ink*]

pink lady *n.* [1950s+] (*drugs*) a barbiturate, usu. Seconal/Darvon (cf. BARBIT n.). [the colour of the capsules]

pinkler *n.* [late 19C+] (*UK teen*) the penis. [its colour]

pinkle-twister *n.* [1980s] a male homosexual. [? PINKLER n.; ? PINTLE n. (1)]

pink lint *adj.* [1960s+] penniless, very poor. [rhy. sl. = SKINT adj.]

pinko *n.* (*also* **pinkie**) [1930s+] (*orig. US*) a communist, socialist or even mildly liberal sympathizer (depending on the speaker's viewpoint). [PINK adj.³ + -o sfx (2); note synon. RMC Duntroon (Aus.) *pinkie*]

pinko *adj.*¹ [1920s–40s] (*Aus.*) drunk, esp. on methylated spirits. [PINKIE n.² (2)]

pinko *adj.*² [1940s+] left-wing. [PINKO n.]

pink oboe *n.* [1980s+] the penis (cf. ACCORDION n.).

pink owsley *n.* (*also* **pink panther, ...robot**) [1960s+] (*drugs*) LSD (cf. A n.³). [SE *pink* + OWSLEY ACID n./SE *panther/robot*; ? the colour of the capsules + play on *Pink Panther* films (1964–78)]

Pink Palace, the *n.* [1990s+] (*Aus. prison/Und.*) Risdon prison, Tasmania (cf. ABBOTT'S PRIORY n.).

pink panatella *n.* (*also* **pink cigar**) [1990s+] the penis. [resemblance (if White)]

pink panther/robot *n. see* PINK OWSLEY n.

pinks *n.* [1960s+] **1** (*S.Afr. drugs*) Wellconal tablets, a form of synthetic heroin. **2** (*US drugs*) Seconal, barbiturates (cf. BARBIT n.). **3** (*US drugs*) Dexytal capsules, i.e. amphetamines and barbiturates. [the colour of the tablets]

pink slip *n.* [1910s+] (*US*) **1** a notice of dismissal. **2** a brush-off, a rejection. **3** in prison, the notice that permits one's parole. [(1) the *pink* paper on which they are written/printed; (2) is fig. use of (1); also note the pink slip that, in the US, proves ownership of a car]

pink spiders *n.* [late 19C] delirium tremens. [one supposedly 'sees' them]

pink starfish *n. see* BROWN STAR n.

pink studs *n.* [1980s+] (*drugs*) MDMA (cf. ECSTASY n.). [colour of the pills]

pinktea *n.* **1** [late 19C+] (*US/Can.*) a very formal or exclusive tea party; thus also as adj., describing any similar event or place, or v., to attend such an event. **2** [1960s–70s] (*gay*) an upper-class homosexual, able to stand aloof from the pleasures and problems of their less insulated peers. [the orig. *Pink Tea* was held in 1886 by the US Women's Christian Temperance Union; men wore pink ties and women pink caps]

pinktea *adj.* [1900s–30s] (*US*) weak, effeminate. [one who frequents a PINKTEA n. (1)]

pinktoe *n.* (*also* **pink-toes**) [1940s+] (*US Black*) **1** a light-skinned Black woman. **2** a White girl, esp. a Black man's White girlfriend. **3** a generic term for the White race.

pink-tongue *n.* [1980s] (*US*) a derog. term for a Black person (cf. BRILLOHEAD n.).

pink torpedo *n.* [2000s] a penis (cf. AX n.²).

pink trumpet *n.* [2000s] the penis (cf. ACCORDION n.).

Pink 'Un, the *n.* **1** [late 19C–1930s] *The Sporting Times.* **2** [late 19C–1900s] a reporter or writer for *The Sporting Times* (esp. such 'stars' as Arthur Binstead, nicknamed 'The Pitcher', William Farn Goldberg, 'The Shifter', and Nathaniel Newnham-Davies, 'The Dwarf of Blood'). **3** [late 19C–1910s] a reader of *The Sporting Times*. **4** [1910s+] the *Financial Times*. [the colour of the newspaper, and,

in the case of *The Sporting Times*, in order to distinguish it from the *Sportsman's Guide to the Turf* which was printed on white stock (cf. BLUE 'UN, THE n.)]

pink velvet sausage wallet *n.* [1990s+] the vagina (cf. BAG n.¹).

pink wedges *n.* (*also* **pink witches**) [1960s+] (*drugs*) a variety of LSD in pink capsules (cf. A n.³).

pink whoogie *n.* [1990s+] (*US Black*) a derog. term for a White person. [PINK adj.⁵ + WHOOGIE n.]

pink widow *n.* [1990s+] (*US gay*) an HIV-negative man who forms a relationship with an HIV-positive man on the understanding that he will become his partner's sole heir. [PINK adj.⁴ + SE *widow*; such 'widows' are known to move from one such relationship to the next as funeral follows funeral]

pink wine *n.* [late 19C–1900s] (*orig. milit.*) champagne. [? the desire to pretend one were drinking something else/cheaper]

pink witches *n. see* PINK WEDGES n.

pinky *see also under* PINKIE.

pinky *n.*¹ (*also* **pinkie, pinkey**) **1** [19C+] the little finger; thus [20C+] (*US*) **pinky-crooker**, an affected person, a poseur. **2** [1970s+] (*US gay*) the erect penis. **3** [1970s+] (*US gay*) a small penis. [Scot.; (2) and (3) resemblance to (1)]

pinky *n.*² [1960s+] a passive or 'feminine' lesbian. [the image of SE *pink* as a 'feminine' colour]

pinky and perky *n.* [1950s] a turkey. [rhy. sl.; ult. *Pinky and Perky*, popular characters from children's TV]

pin money *n.* **1** [late 17C+] small sums of money allotted to a woman, occas. a man, for housekeeping. **2** [mid-19C+] any insignificant amount of money, however earned, e.g. by a woman for a part-time job. **3** [1960s+] money gained by a woman for amateur, part-time prostitution. [lit. *money* to buy *pins* or money that would do no more than buy pins]

pinna *n. see* PINNY n.

pinnace *n.* [late 16C–early 19C] a prostitute. [SE *pinnace*, a light vessel in attendance upon a larger one]

pinnacles *n.* [late 19C] spectacles, glasses. [mispron. of BARNACLES n. (1)]

pinned *adj.* **1** [1950s+] (*drugs*) used of eyes in which the pupils are reduced, irrespective of the light available, to pinpricks. **2** [1980s+] (*US campus/drugs*) under the influence of a drug, usu. cocaine. [the effect of drugs to shrink the pupils]

pinner *n.*¹ [late 18C] (*Irish*) a gaoler, a policeman (cf. BEAT-POUNDER n.). [SE *pin*, v.]

pinner *n.*² [1980s+] (*US campus*) a thin person. [SE *pin*]

pinner *n.*³ (*also* **pinroll**) [1990s+] (*drugs*) a very small marijuana cigarette (cf. BONE n.¹¹). [PIN n.¹ (3) (+ ROLL-UP n.² (1))]

pinner *n.*⁴ *see* PINNY n.

pinner *adj.* [1980s+] (*US campus*) thin. [PINNER n.²]

pinner-up *n.* [mid-late 19C] a street-seller of printed songs and ballads, which are *pinned up* at their pitch; thus *pin up*, to sell songs and ballads.

pinnie *n.* [1990s+] (*N.Z.*) a *pin*ball machine. [abbr.]

pinny *n.* (*also* **pinna, pinnie, pinner**) [early 18C+] a *pina*fore. [abbr.]

pin on *v.* [1970s+] to accuse, to lay the blame on someone. [SE *pin on*, to attach to]

pin one on *v.* (*also* **pin a few on**) [1910s–50s] (*US/Aus.*) to have a drink. [SE *pin on*, to attach to]

pin one's ears back *v.* [1950s+] to give one's full attention, esp. as *pin your ears back!* (cf. PIN BACK ONE'S LUGHOLES v.; PIN SOMEONE'S EARS BACK v.).

pin-pannierly fellow *n.* [17C] a conspicuously grasping miser. [? one who keeps all their pins in a *pannier*, a basket, or pins a pannier to their clothes]

pinroll *n. see* PINNER n.³.

pins *n.* [16C+] the legs (rarely in sing.); thus *pin-ends*, feet.

pins and needles *n.* [20C+] beetles. [rhy. sl.]

pin shot *n.* [1920s–50s] an injection of a narcotic using a rudimentary 'syringe' made of a pin or needle and an eye-dropper. [PIN n.¹ (2) + SHOT n.⁶ (2)]

pin someone's ears back *v.* **1** [1920s+] to shock, to surprise (cf. PIN ONE'S EARS BACK v.). **2** [1940s+] (*orig. US*) to defeat, to punish verbally or physically, to reprimand.

pint *n.* [1950s] (*W.I.*) a 6-month prison sentence. [i.e. half a QUART n.²]

pinta *n.* [1950s+] a pint of milk, milk in general. [SE *pint of…* From the 1958 advertising campaign called on people to 'Drinka pinta milka-day']

pinta, la *n.* [1960s+] (*US*) prison. [Sp.]

pin the basket *v.* [mid-17C–mid-18C] to bring to a conclusion, to settle. [the *pin* or peg that secured the basket-lid]

pin them *phr.* [1980s] (*US campus*) an instruction to stop talking. [SE *pin* v.]

pin the rap on *v.* [1930s+] to impute a crime (to a criminal) (whether or not they are actually implicated). [SE *pin* + RAP n.³ (1)]

pintle *n.* **1** [late 16C–19C] (*also* **pinckle, pintie**) the penis. **2** [20C+] (*Ulster*) a small, irritating person. [OE *pintel*, the penis]

pintle-bit *n.* (*also* **pintle-maid**) [19C–1900s] a mistress. [PINTLE n. (1) + BIT n.² (1)/SE *maid*]

pintle-blossom *n.* [18C–1900s] a bubo, the result of syphilis. [PINTLE n. (1) + joc. use of SE *blossom*]

pintle-case *n.* [19C] the vagina (cf. BAG n.¹). [PINTLE n. (1) + SE *case*]

pintle-de-pantledy *adj.* [mid-17C–early 19C] frightened, scared. [ety. unknown; ? echoic of nervous fidgeting]

pintle-fancier *n.* (*also* **pintle-ranger**) [early 19C–1900s] a promiscuous woman. [PINTLE n. (1) + SE *fancier*/RANGER n. (2)]

pintle-fever *n.* [19C–1900s] any form of venereal disease. [PINTLE n. (1) + SE *fever*]

pintle-keek *n.* [19C–1900s] a sexually inviting look, a leer. [PINTLE n. (1) + Scot. *keek*, a glance]

pintle-maid *n. see* PINTLE-BIT n.

pintle-merchant *n.* (*also* **pintle-monger**) [late 18C–1900s] a prostitute (cf. ASS PEDDLER n.; COCKATRICE n.). [PINTLE n. (1) + MERCHANT n./-MONGER sfx]

pintle-ranger *n. see* PINTLE-FANCIER n.

pintle-smith *n.* (*also* **pintle-tagger**) [late 18C–1900s] a surgeon. [PINTLE n. (1) + SE sfx -*smith*/SE *tag*, to stitch together]

pinto *n.* [1960s+] (*US*) a former convict. [PINTA, LA n.]

pinto bean *n.* [1960s] (*US campus*) a derog. name for a Mexican or Mexican-American (cf. BEAN n.⁸).

pint of mahogany *n.* [late 19C] a mug of coffee. [the colour]

pint-pot *n.* **1** [late 16C] a beer-seller. **2** [late 19C+] (*Aus.*) a tin can, holding a pint, which is used for boiling water. **3** [1940s] (*US*) a drunkard.

pint screamer *n. see* ONE-POT SCREAMER n.

pinum *n. see* PANNAM n.

pin up *v. see* PINNER-UP n.

pinurt pots *n.* [mid-19C] turnip tops. [backsl.]

pin work *n.* [1930s–40s] (*US Und.*) pinpricks on cards, used to aid cheating.

pin yen *n. see* PEN YEN n.

pin-yen toy *n. see* TOY n.³ (1).

pin yenz/pinyon *n. see* PEN YEN n.

pioneer (of nature) *n.* [mid-17C] the penis.

piong *n.* [20C+] (*W.I.*) an enthusiast, esp. for a food or game. [16C Fr. *pion*, excessive drinking, thus modern Fr. sl. *pion*, a hard drinker]

pious *adj.* [mid-19C] (*UK Und.*) drunk.

p.i.p. *n.* [20C+] (*W.I.*) a toady, a sycophant. [abbr. *party in power*]

pip *n.*¹ [mid-16C+] **1** ill humour or poor health; usu. as GET THE PIP v.; GIVE SOMEONE THE PIP v. **2** syphilis. [SE *pip*, 'a disease of poultry and other birds, characterized by the secretion of a thick mucus in the mouth and throat, often with the formation of a white scale on the tip of the tongue' (*OED*)]

pip *n.*² **1** [late 19C+] (*orig. US*) the very best, the finest example. **2** [1900s] (*US*) a negative, bad example. **3** [1920s–30s] (*US*) an innocent. [abbr. PIPPIN n.]

pip *n.*³ *see* PIPSQUEAK n.

pip *v.*¹ **1** [late 19C] to blackball. **2** [late 19C] (*UK campus*) to fine someone. **3** [20C+] to defeat, to beat. **4** [1900s] to fail (a candidate) in an examination. **5** [1900s–30s] to die. **6** [1910s–30s] to hit with a shot. **7** [1960s] (*W.I./US*) to have sexual intercourse (cf. BANG v.¹). [? fig. uses of SE *pip*, a spot on a die, card or domino]

pip *v.*² (*also* **pip off**) [1920s–30s] to leave. [PIP-PIP! excl. (2)]

pip! *excl.* [1960s] nonsense!

pip at the post *v.* [20C+] **1** to do something before someone else has had the chance. **2** to beat by a narrow margin at the last moment. [PIP v.¹ (3)]

pipe *n.*¹ **1** [late 16C–mid-19C] a voice (cf. PIPES n.¹). **2** [1900s] (*US*) a story. [SE *pipe*, the voice, as used in singing]

pipe *n.*² **1** [17C+] the penis. **2** [mid-19C+] the vagina. [(1) resemblance; (2) it is 'hollow'; the *double entendres* cover both tobacco pipes, bag-pipes and water pipes; (1) note D'Urfey, *Pills to Purge Melancholy* (1719–20): 'Next came a smug Physician […] He was so us'd to Glisters, she told him to his face, / He would always be bobbing his Pipe at the wrong place']

pipe *n.*³ [late 18C–1900s] 'a spell of travelling between two rest-periods at each of which a pipe is smoked; the distance covered or the time taken, in such a spell; also, the distance covered while smoking a pipeful of tobacco' (*OED*). [best-known in Sherlock Holmes' 'three-pipe' problems, although his 'travelling' was usu. in the head]

pipe *n.*⁴ (*drugs*) **1** [mid-19C] a cigar. **2** [late 19C+] an opium pipe; thus *the pipe*, the smoking of opium; PIPE-FIEND n. **3** [1930s–50s] (*also* **pipey, pipie**) an opium addict. **4** [1950s+] a marijuana or hashish pipe. **5** [1950s+] a vein into which a drug can be injected. **6** [1960s+] (*S.Afr.*) enough marijuana to fill a pipe. **7** [1970s+] a marijuana smoker. **8** [1980s+] a pipe for smoking base cocaine or crack cocaine.

pipe *n.*⁵ [mid-19C+] a glance, a look (at); usu. in *have a pipe*, to glance at; thus *on the pipe*, keeping a lookout. [PIPE v.³ (2)]

pipe *n.*⁶ [late 19C+] (*US*) anything that is easily accomplished; a certainty; thus (*campus*) *pipe course*, an easy academic course. [abbr. LEAD-PIPE CINCH n. (2)]

pipe *n.*⁷ (*US*) **1** [1930s+] a saxophone. **2** [1960s] (*also* **pipes**) a telephone.

pipe *n.*⁸ [1950s+] any form of clubbing weapon. [SE *lead pipe*]

pipe, the *n.*¹ [1950s–70s] a euph for *hell*. [? H.E. Bates nonce use]

pipe, the *n.*² [2000s] the River Thames.

pipe *v.*¹ **1** [early 17C; early 19C+] to talk; esp. as PIPE UP v.¹; thus *hit the pipe*, to inform. **2** [late 18C–19C] to weep. **3** [early–mid-19C] to breathe heavily, through exertion, e.g. in a prizefight. [SE *pipe*, to play a pipe]

pipe *v.*² **1** [mid-19C] (*US*) to smoke a pipe. **2** [1990s+] (*drugs*) (*also* **pipe up**) to smoke crack cocaine.

pipe *v.*³ **1** [mid-19C–1900s] orig. of a detective, to follow, to pursue; to spy on. **2** [mid-19C+] to look over, to inspect. **3** [1900s] to understand, to work out. [? SE *peep*]

pipe *v.*⁴ [1970s–80s] (*US*) to perform fellatio (cf. BLOW v.²). [PIPE n.² (1); note Fr. argot *une pipe*, fellatio]

pipe and drum *n.* [20C+] the buttocks (cf. ALA n.). [rhy. sl. = BUM n.¹ (1)]

piped *adj.*¹ [1900s–20s] (*US*) drunk (cf. ALED UP adj.). [SE *pipe*, a large barrel]

piped *adj.*² (*drugs*) **1** [1920s–50s] under the influence of drugs. **2** [1990s+] under the influence of crack cocaine. [PIPE n.⁴]

piped *adj.*³ [1980s+] (*US campus*) defeated, humiliated. [? misreading of PIP v.¹ (3)]

pipe down v.[1] [mid-19C] (*US Und.*) to track down and arrest a criminal. [PIPE v.[3] (1)]

pipe down v.[2] **1** [mid-19C+] to talk more quietly, to stop talking; often as imper. **2** [1930s–50s] to make someone be quiet. [naut. *pipe-down*, the call on the bosun's pipe signifying 'lights out']

pipe-fiend n. [1900s–50s] (*US*) a regular opium user. [PIPE n.[4] (2) + FIEND n.[2] (1)]

pipe-head n. [1980s+] (*drugs*) a regular user of crack cocaine; also attrib. [PIPE n.[4] (8) + -HEAD sfx (3)]

pipe-hitter n. see HIT THE PIPE v.[1] (1).

pipe in an ivy-leaf v. [14C–17C] to waste time, esp. when appearing to be busy. [? the piping god Pan, associated with nature]

pipejob n. [1970s–80s] (*US*) an act of sexual intercourse or fellatio (cf. BLOW v.[2]). [PIPE v.[4]/PIPE n.[2] (1) + JOB n.[4]]

pipe joint n. see JOINT n.[4] (1).

pipe-layer n. [mid-19C–1910s] (*US*) 'one who schemes to procure corrupt votes' (*OED*). [for extensive ety. see Bartlett, *Dict. Americanisms* (1848) pp.251–2]

pipe-man n. [1980s+] a seller of crack cocaine. [PIPE n.[4] (8) + SE sfx -*man*]

pipe off v. **1** [mid-19C] to recognize. **2** [mid-19C–1940s] to survey, to assess. **3** [late 19C] to leave, to depart. **4** [late 19C] to dismiss. **5** [1910s–30s] to make jokes. **6** [1920s–40s] to inform, to explain. **7** [1930s] to 'pump' a person for information. [ext. PIPE v.[3]]

pipe one's eye v. [late 18C–1950s] (*orig. naut.*) to cry, to weep. [PIPE v.[1] (2)]

pipe-opener n. **1** [mid–late 19C] exercise taken to clear the lungs or throat. **2** [1930s+] in fig. use, anything exploratory, e.g. a trial run, a rehearsal. [PIPES n.[1] (2)/PIPES n.[1] (3)]

pipe out v. see PIPE UP v.[1].

piper n.[1] **1** [late 18C–early 19C] a broken-down horse. **2** [early 19C] an out-of-breath human. [? PIPES n.[1] (2), the wheezing noise they make]

piper n.[2] **1** [mid-19C] (*US*) a private detective. **2** [mid-19C–1900s] a spy, esp. one employed on an omnibus. [PIPE v.[3] (1)]

piper n.[3] [1990s+] (*drugs*) a smoker of crack cocaine. [PIPE v.[2] (2)]

piper fou adj. [late 18C–19C] very drunk, lit. 'drunk as a piper'. [SE *piper* + FOU adj.[1]]

piperheidsick v. [1920s] (*US*) to look, to see. [PIPE v.[3] (2) + play on the brand of champagne]

pipero n. [1980s+] (*drugs*) a smoker of base cocaine or crack cocaine. [Sp. 'a pipe-er']

piper's cheeks n. [17C] fat or swollen cheeks.

piper's news n. [19C] (*Scot.*) stale news. [? the piper trad. receives the news last]

piper's wife n. [late 18C] (*Scot.*) a prostitute. [derog. stereotyping]

pipes n.[1] **1** [mid-16C+] the voice (cf. PIPE n.[1]). **2** [18C+] the lungs, esp. of a singer; thus OPEN ONE'S PIPES v. **3** [early 19C+] the throat.

pipes n.[2] (*also* **quill-pipes**) [late 18C–early 19C] top boots. [? the tubular shape, or cleaning with pipe-clay]

pipes n.[3] [1970s+] (*US gay*) very tight trousers. [abbr. DRAINPIPES n. (2)]

pipes n.[4] see PIPE n.[7] (2).

pipes adj. [1900s] (*US*) crazy; thus *pipe-house*, a psychiatric institution. [ety. unknown]

pipe smoker n.[1] [1900s–30s] (*drugs*) an opium user. [PIPE n.[4] (2)]

pipe smoker n.[2] [1990s+] a gay man. [PIPE n.[2] (1) + SMOKE v.[8]]

pipe talk n. [late 19C–1900s] (*US*) fantasizing; nonsense. [PIPE n.[4] (2) + SE *talk*; the image of opium-inspired fantasies]

pipe the stem v. [1920s–40s] (*US*) to beg in a city's main street. [PIPE v.[1] (1) + STEM n.[1] (1)]

pipe up v.[1] (*also* **pipe out**) [mid-19C+] to speak; to speak more audibly; to start speaking, to interrupt. [PIPE v.[1] (1)]

pipe up v.[2] see PIPE v.[2] (2).

pipey n. see PIPE n.[4] (3).

pipey adj. [1930s–50s] (*US drugs*) under the influence of opium. [PIPE n.[4] (2)]

pipie n. see PIPE n.[4] (3).

pipieri n. [mid-19C+] (*W.I.*) an aggressive person. [dial. *pipieri*, the tyrant flycatcher, a small fighting bird]

piping n.[1] [late 18C–19C] crying. [PIPE v.[1] (2)]

piping n.[2] [1980s+] smoking crack cocaine. [PIPE n.[4] (8)]

pipkin n.[1] **1** [17C–18C] the female genitals; thus *cracked pipkin*, a vagina that has been deflowered. **2** [early–mid-19C] the stomach. **3** [early–mid-19C] the head. [SE *pipkin*, a small, earthenware pot]

pipkin n.[2] see PIPPIN n. (2).

pip off v.[1] [1930s] to die. [the radio 'pips' that signal a time-check]

pip off v.[2] see PIP v.[2].

pip out v. [1910s–20s] to die. [gambling imagery; also PIP v.[1] (5)]

pipped adj. **1** [1910s–20s] wounded. **2** [1910s+] beaten. [PIP v.[1] (3)]

pipped (off) adj. [1910s+] annoyed, irritated. [GET THE PIP v. (1)]

pipper n. [1980s+] (*Aus. prison*) a senior prison officer. [the 'pips' of rank on their shoulders]

pipperoo n. [1940s+] (*orig. US*) something excellent, remarkably good. [PIP n.[2] (1) + -EROO sfx]

pippiejoller n. see PIEPIEJOLLER n.

pippin n. **1** [mid-17C–18C; 1900s–10s] a pej. term of address or description. **2** [mid-17C+] (*also* **pippins**, **pipkin**) a term of approval or congratulation, applied to a person. **3** [late 19C+] a perfect example of whatever is under discussion; usu. as *it's a pippin*. **4** [1900s] a loved one. **5** [1920s–40s] the female breast. [SE *pippin*, the name of various types of apple]

pippin-squire n. [early–mid-17C] a pimp (cf. ABBOT ON THE CROSS n.). [play on APPLE SQUIRE n. (1), i.e. SE *pippin*, used in the names of various types of apple]

pip-pip adj. [1930s] (*US*) Anglicized; in an English manner. [PIP-PIP! excl. (2)]

pip-pip! excl. **1** [late 19C] a street cry, often launched at passing cyclists (still a novelty in late 19C). **2** [20C+] goodbye! hello! **3** [1940s+] a toast when drinking. [the noise of the cyclist's horn]

pippish adj. [1910s+] irritated, out of sorts. [GET THE PIP v.]

pippy adj. [1920s+] (*Aus.*) irritated, out of sorts. [GET THE PIP v.]

pippy-poo adj. [20C+] (*US*) extremely small, tiny.

pipsqueak n. (*also* **pip**) **1** [1910s+] an insignificant person. **2** [1940s] (*Aus.*) a parasite, a toady. **3** [1980s+] (*Aus.*) a small child. [SE *pip*, a shrill, sudden noise + *squeak*; note WW1 Aus. milit. *pip-squeak*, a small shell; a high explosive high velocity shell fired from a field gun]

pipsqueak adj. [1940s+] insignificant. [PIPSQUEAK n. (1)]

pirate n.[1] **1** [20C+] (*Aus.*) a man who wanders around looking for a casual pick-up; thus *on the pirate*, looking for a casual pick-up. **2** [1940s] (*US Und.*) a pimp who steals a prostitute from a fellow pimp.

pirate n.[2] [1990s+] (*W.I.*) a general term for oppressors.

pirate v. [20C+] (*Aus.*) to pick up in the hope of seduction. [PIRATE n.[1] (1)]

pirate's dream n. [1980s+] (*US campus*) a flat-chested woman. [she has a 'sunken chest']

pisa n. see PAISA n.

pisel v. see PEYSLE v.

pish n. see PISS n.

pish v. [20C+] **1** (*Ulster*) to rain heavily. **2** to urinate. [PISS v.[1] (1)]

pisher n.[1] [1940s+] an insignificant person. [synon. Yid.]

pisher n.[2] see PISSER n.[2] (2).

pishery-pashery n. [late 16C–early 17C] nonsense, rubbish. [SE *pish!* nonsense! rubbish!]

pish on v. see PISS ON v. (1).

pish-posh n. (*also* **pish-tush**) [1910s–30s] (*US*) rubbish, nonsense.

pish-tosh *v.* [1940s] to deride, to mock. [PISH-POSH n.]

pisk *n.* [1930s] the human face. [? a Yiddishized version of PUSS n.³ (1)]

pi-squash *n.* [1910s–20s] (*mainly UK teen*) a prayer meeting. [SE *pi(ous)* + *squash(ed together)*]

piss *n.* **1** [17C+] urine. **2** [mid-19C+] an act of urination. **3** [1910s+] any sort of weak or otherwise unpalatable drink, whether alcoholic or non-alcoholic (cf. BUFFALO PISS n.). **4** [1910s+] (*also* **pish**) an alcoholic drink. **5** [1920s+] beer. **6** [1940s+] (*also* **pish, puddle of piss/shit**) rubbish, nonsense, anything or anyone unappealing, worthless. **7** [1960s] in fig. use, high spirits. [PISS v.¹ (1)]

piss, the *n.* (*also* **pee, the**) [1930s+] a general intensifier, the essence, the 'daylights'; often in *scare the piss out of*, to terrify. [fig. use of PISS n. (1)]

piss *adj.* [1950s] rubbish, second-rate. [PISS n. (6)]

piss *v.¹* **1** [17C+] to urinate. **2** [late 17C] to issue vaginal secretions. **3** [1930s+] in ext. use, to exude liquid, other than urine. **4** [1940s+] (*orig. US*) in fig. use, to complain, to whinge. **5** [1960s+] in fig. use, to deride, to attack, to disdain. [? echoic; (1) prior use is SE and medieval in origin]

piss *v.²* *see* PISS-TEST v.

piss! *excl.* [1950s+] a general excl.

piss!, a *excl.* [late 17C–early 18C] a general excl. of disgust or annoyance. [PISS n. (1)]

piss- *pfx* [1940s+] (*orig. US*) a general intensifier, usu. derog., e.g. PISS-AWFUL adj.

pissabed *n.* **1** [mid-17C+] a bed-wetter. **2** [mid-18C; 1920s] a general derisive epithet. [PISS v.¹ (1)]

piss about *v.* (*also* **piddle about/around, piss around**) **1** [20C+] to waste time, to mess about. **2** [1930s+] to wander, to go. **3** [1980s+] to irritate or tease someone. [fig. use of PISS v.¹ (1)/PIDDLE v. (1); note also ety. at PIDDLE v.]

piss all over *v.* *see* PISS ON v. (1).

piss and moan *v.* [1950s+] (*orig. US*) to complain, to whinge. [fig. use of PISS v.¹ (4)]

piss and punk *n.* [20C+] (*orig. US prison*) bread and water. [PISS n. (3) + PUNK n.³]

piss and vinegar *n.* [1920s+] (*orig. US*) energy, enthusiasm, cheekiness; usu. in phr. *full of piss and vinegar*. [fig. use of PISS n. (1) + SE *vinegar*]

piss and wind *n.* [1920s+] **1** empty talk. **2** one who is full of pompous braggadocio. [PISS n. (1)]

pissant *n.* [1930s+] an insignificant person, a 'nobody'; thus [1930s+] *drunk as a pissant*, very drunk; [1940s+] *game as a pissant*, very brave. [SE *pissant*, an ant]

pissant *adj.* [1960s+] insignificant, trifling. [PISSANT n.]

pissant (around) *v.* [1940s+] (*Aus.*) **1** to mess around. **2** to defeat, to outwit. [PISSANT n.]

piss around *v.* *see* PISS ABOUT v.

piss-arse about *v.* [1920s+] (*orig. milit.*) to mess about. [ext. PISS ABOUT v. (1)]

piss artist *n.* **1** [1940s+] a regular drunk. **2** [1970s+] a general term of abuse. [PISS n. (4) + ARTIST sfx]

piss-ass *adj.* *see* PISSY-ASS adj.

piss-ass drunk *adj.* *see* PISSY-ARSED adj.

piss away *v.* [20C+] to waste, to waste time. [fig. use of PISS v.¹ (1)/PIDDLE v. (1); note also ety. at PIDDLE v. and a single 1760 use, 'A house where she used to piddle away her leisure hours' (Charles Johnstone, *Chrysal*)]

piss-awful *adj.* [1970s+] very bad, very unpleasant. [PISS- pfx + SE *awful*]

piss backwards *v.* [late 17C–1900s] to defecate. [note 17C phr. *as easy as pissing backwards* (presumably the image is of a woman)]

piss-ball about *v.* [1920s+] to mess about, to idle.

pissballing *adj.* [2000s] mean, contemptuous. [PISS-BALL ABOUT v.]

piss blood *v.* **1** [late 19C+] to work extremely hard. **2** [1960s+] to worry excessively, to make a great fuss. **3** [1960s+] to suffer a great deal. [fig. use of PISS v.¹ (1) + SE *blood*]

piss bones *v.* (*also* **piss children, …hard**) [late 19C–1900s] to go into labour, to give birth. [PISS v.¹ (1)]

piss britches *n.* [1960s] (*US Black*) a general term of abuse. [i.e. one who 'wets their pants']

piss broken glass *v.* (*also* **piss razor blades**) [1960s+] to have venereal disease, esp. gonorrhoea. [PISS v.¹ (1); the pain experienced when urinating during a bout of VD]

piss-bucket *n.* [2000s] (*US*) a contemptible person. [PISS n. (1)]

piss bullets *v.* *see* SHIT BULLETS v.

piss-burned *adj.* [late 17C–early 19C] discoloured, esp. of a grey wig that has turned yellow. [PISS n. (1)]

pisscall *n.* [1950s+] a stop for urination, e.g. during work or on a journey etc. [PISS n. (1)]

pisscan *n.* [1940s–50s] (*US prison*) a prison. [PISS n. (1) + CAN n.³ (3)]

piss children *v.* *see* PISS BONES v.

piss-cutter *n.* [1940s+] (*US*) **1** a generally obnoxious person. **2** an admirable or exceptional person. **3** an outstanding or excellent thing. **4** a drunken spree, a binge. **5** a major confrontation. [? the sharpness, whether seen as positive or negative]

piss down *v.* [1920s+] to rain heavily. [fig. use of PISS v.¹ (1)]

piss down someone's back *v.* (*also* **piss up someone's back**) [late 18C–early 19C] to flatter someone.

piss-easy *adj.* [1980s+] (*orig. N.Z.*) very easy. [PISS- pfx]

pissed *adj.¹* (*also* **peed, pissed up**) [20C+] drunk; thus *half-pissed*, tipsy. [PISS n. (4)]

pissed *adj.²* [1950s+] (*US*) annoyed; thus *pissedness*, anger. [abbr. PISSED OFF adj.]

pissed as a… *phr.* [20C+] in combs. listed below meaning very drunk (cf. *see also* DRUNK AS (A)… phr.). [PISSED adj.¹]

pissed as a chook *phr.* [1980s+] (*N.Z.*) very drunk. [PISSED adj.¹ + CHOOK n. (1)]

pissed as a fart *phr.* [1960s+] very drunk. [PISSED adj.¹ + fig. use of FART n. (1)]

pissed as a newt *phr.* [1950s+] very drunk. [PISSED adj.¹]

pissed as a parrot *phr.* [1980s+] (*Aus.*) extremely drunk. [PISSED adj.¹]

pissed as a rat *phr.* [1980s+] very drunk. [PISSED adj.¹; note RAT-ARSED adj.]

pissed as arseholes *phr.* [1940s+] extremely drunk (cf. ARSEHOLED adj.). [PISSED adj.¹ + fig. use of ARSEHOLE n. (1)]

pissed off *adj.* [1940s+] (*orig. US*) furious, very annoyed; bored. [? US var. of BROWNED OFF adj.]

pissed out *adj.* [1960s+] (*US*) exhausted, finished. [note RMC Duntroon (Aus.) *pissed out*, 'completely drunken, totally blotto, satisfyingly boozed']

pissed to the ears *phr.* [1960s+] extremely drunk. [PISSED adj.¹]

pissed to the eyeballs *phr.* [1990s+] (*Aus.*) extremely drunk (cf. ARSEHOLED adj.). [PISSED adj.¹]

pissed to the gills *phr.* [1970s+] (*US*) very inebriated. [PISSED adj.¹ + TO THE GILLS adv.]

pissed up *adj.* *see* PISSED adj.¹.

piss-elegance *n.* (*also* **piss-elegant**) [1960s+] extreme elegance, used lit. and ironically. [PISS-ELEGANT adj.]

piss elegant *n.* [1960s] a pretentious, ostentatious, self-obsessed male homosexual. [PISS-ELEGANT adj.]

piss-elegant *adj.* [1940s+] extremely elegant (usu. used ironically or deprecatingly). [PISS- pfx + SE *elegant*]

pisser *n.¹* **1** [late 19C+] a urinal. **2** [late 19C+] the penis. **3** [late 19C+] the vagina. **4** [20C+] (*N.Z.*) a woman. **5** [1920s+] a day on which it rains heavily and continuously. **6** [1920s+] one who urinates. **7** [1930s+] an electric pylon. **8** [1950s–60s] a very unpleasant place. **9** [1970s] (*US prison*) solitary confinement. **10** [1980s] a public house. **11** [1980s] a drunkard. **12** [2000s]

(*Irish*) a heavy drinking session. [PISS n. (1)/PISS v.¹ (1); (7) f. phallic imagery]

pisser n.² [1940s+] (*US*) **1** (*also* **pisseroo**) an extraordinary person or thing. **2** (*also* **pisher**) a difficult or distasteful event or task, an unpleasant person. **3** a bloke, a chap, esp. one who is tough and purposeful. **4** something or someone considered hilariously funny. [PISS v.¹ (1), used here in the sense of 'that which makes one (fig.) *piss*']

pissface n. [1990s+] (*UK juv.*) a general term of abuse. [PISS n. (1)]

piss-factory n. [late 19C–1940s] a public house. [mix of PISS v.¹ (1)/PISS n. (3)]

piss flaps n. (*also* **piss-flappers**) [1970s+] the labia (cf. DEW-FLAPS n.). [PISS n. (1) + FLAPS n. (2)/SE *flaps/flappers*]

piss freak n. [2000s] a person who derives sexual satisfaction from being urinated on. [PISS n. (1) + FREAK n.¹ (6)]

piss hard v. *see* PISS BONES v.

piss hard-on n. (*also* **piss-horn**) [1960s+] the erection with which a man awakes, due as much to the need to urinate as to the desire for sex. [PISS n. (1) + HARD-ON n. (1)/HORN n.² (3)]

piss-head n.¹ [1950s+] a heavy drinker. [PISS n. (4) + -HEAD sfx (3)]

piss-head n.² [1980s+] an obnoxious person. [PISS n. (1) + -HEAD sfx (1)]

pisshole n. [1950s+] **1** a urinal, a lavatory. **2** any very dirty house, room or place. [PISS n. (1) + SE *hole*]

pisshole adj. [1950s+] second-rate, inferior, disgusting. [PISSHOLE n. (2)]

pisshole bandit n. **1** [1960s+] a minor criminal. **2** [1970s] a male homosexual who solicits in lavatories. [PISSHOLE n. + BANDIT sfx (2)]

pissholes in the snow n. [1960s+] of the eyes, bloodshot, shrunken and showing signs of excess.

piss-horn n. *see* PISS HARD-ON n.

pisshouse n. **1** [mid-17C; 1940s+] a lavatory (cf. BACKHOUSE n.). **2** [1930s–40s] (*US Und.*) a police station. [PISS n. (1) + SE *house*; (2) i.e. a 'vile' place]

piss in v. [1980s+] (*N.Z.*) to achieve with ease. [PISS v.¹ (1), the natural ease of urination]

piss in a quill v. [late 17C–mid-18C; 1950s] to agree on a plan. [PISS v.¹ (1); the narrowness of the quill and the need to bend the flow of urine to achieve the feat]

pissing adj. **1** [mid-16C+] urinating. **2** [1950s+] a general adj. of abuse. [PISS v.¹ (1)]

pissing contest n. [1970s+] (*mainly US*) any form of competition in which the participants are motivated more by the need to assert their superiority than by any desire to attain an accurate or positive conclusion; also attrib. [fig. use of PISS v.¹ (1) + SE *contest*; the image of 2 small boys urinating against a wall, each attempting to aim the flow of urine higher]

pissing fou adj. [19C] very drunk. [PISS v.¹ (1) + FOU adj.¹; the idea of urinating through drunkenness]

pissing place n. [mid-17C] the vagina.

pissing-tail adj. (*also* **pissy-tail**) [20C+] (*W.I.*) **1** esp. of a young person, disrespectful, bumptious. **2** officious but impoverished and socially unimportant. [PISS v.¹ (1) + TAIL n.² (1); the image is of a toddler still wetting itself]

pissing time n. [20C+] (*Irish*) a very short time. [PISS v.¹ (1), i.e. long enough to urinate]

pissing while n. [mid-16C–17C] a short time. [PISS v.¹ (1), i.e. long enough to urinate; Nares notes 'Our ancestors were not very nice; and rather chose to be exact than delicate in their allusions']

piss in one's pants v. [1920s+] **1** to be terrified. **2** to be overcome with laughter. **3** to be furious. **4** to be very keen. [PISS v.¹ (1) + supposedly to the extent that one wets oneself]

piss in someone's pocket v. (*also* **piss in the same pot**) [1920s+] (*Aus.*) to curry favour, to be extremely close to someone, to ingratiate oneself. [PISS v.¹ (1)]

piss in the hand n. [1970s+] (*N.Z.*) anything considered very easy. [PISS n. (1)]

piss in the wind n. [1960s+] a waste of time. [PISS IN(TO) THE WIND v.]

piss-in-the-wind adj. [1990s+] pointless, time-wasting. [PISS IN THE WIND n.]

piss in(to) the wind v. [1960s+] to waste one's efforts or time. [the futility thereof]

piss it v. [1970s+] to succeed with no difficulty whatsoever, to win very easily. [fig. use of PISS v.¹ (1)]

piss it on the walls/out the window/up the wall v. *see* PISS (MONEY) AGAINST THE WALL v.

piss it up v. [1960s+] to drink. [PISSED adj.¹]

piss-kitchen n. [mid-18C] a kitchen maid. [PISS v.¹ (1) + SE *kitchen*, i.e. where she (fig.) urinates]

piss-maker n. [late 18C–early 19C] a heavy drinker. [PISS n. (1); the results of alcohol consumption]

piss-making adj. [1990s+] (*US Black*) infuriating. [it makes one want to PISS v.¹ (1)]

piss (money) against the wall v. (*also* **piss it/money on the walls, ...out the window, ...up the wall**) [late 15C+] waste money on drink; thus to waste money in general. [PISS v.¹ (1); the idea of 'wasting' a drink – and therefore money – by urinating afterwards]

piss'n'tail n. [1970s] a general term of abuse. [PISSING-TAIL adj.]

pisso n. [1960s] (*Aus.*) a drunkard; a general term of abuse. [PISSED adj.¹ + -o sfx (4)]

piss-off n. [1980s+] something or someone annoying. [PISS OFF v. (2)]

piss-off adj. [1990s+] annoying, irritating. [PISS OFF v. (2)]

piss off v. (*also* **pee off**) **1** [1910s+] to leave; esp. as PISS OFF! excl. **2** [1950s+] to annoy; thus *piss-off*, a state of anger. [PISS v.¹ (1)]

piss off! excl. [1910s+] an excl. of rejection, dismissal. [PISS OFF v. (1)]

pissoir n. [1970s+] (*US campus*) the lavatory. [Fr.]

pissoliver n. [20C+] (*US*) a pistol, a revolver. [? SP. *pistolero*]

piss on v. **1** [17C+] (*also* **pish on, piss all over, piss upon**) to treat contemptuously. **2** [1930s+] to hell with; thus excl. *piss on it*, who cares! **3** [1950s+] to drench with rain; usu. as *pissed on*. [fig. use of PISS v.¹ (1)]

piss on a nettle v. [mid-16C–mid-18C] to be annoyed, uneasy, tetchy; thus *on nettles*, anxious, uneasy. [fig. use of PISS v.¹ (1)]

piss oneself v. (*also* **pee oneself**) **1** [late 18C; 1960s+] to fig. urinate on onself, in the context of being utterly terrified. **2** [1940s+] to laugh uproariously. [fig. uses of PISS v.¹ (1)]

piss one's pants v. **1** [late 18C; 1960s+] (*also* **pee one's pants, piss one's breeches**) to be terrified. **2** [1920s+] (*US*) to be very excited, in a state of suspense. [fig. use of PISS v.¹ (1)]

piss one's tallow v. **1** [late 16C–17C] of a man, to be sufficiently sexually excited as to ejaculate without actual intercourse). **2** [late 17C] to sweat. [SE *piss one's grease/tallow*, said of a deer becoming lean in rutting-time]

piss on ice v. [1920s] (*US*) to live well, esp. to visit an upmarket restaurant. [PISS v.¹ (1) + the blocks of ice placed in the urinals to keep down the smell and ensure a continual flush of water]

piss on one's shoe v. [1980s] to blunder, to fail in a task. [fig. use of PISS v.¹ (1) + SE *shoe*]

piss on someone's chips v. (*also* **piss on one's chips**) [1980s+] (*orig. Can.*) to spoil someone else's or one's own plans.

piss on someone's parade v. (*also* **rain on someone's parade, shit...**) [1970s+] (*orig. US*) to shatter illusions, to ruin an otherwise satisfactory situation. [fig. use of PISS v.¹ (1)/SE *rain*/SHIT v.¹ (1)]

piss on someone's shoe v. [1970s] (*US*) to humiliate.

piss on you! excl. [1950s+] a general abusive excl.

piss or get off the pot phr. *see* SHIT OR GET OFF THE POT phr.

piss out of a dozen holes v. [late 19C+] of a man, to

be infected with syphilis. [PISS v.[1] (1), i.e. the rotting of one's penis]

piss over teakettle *phr.* [1990s+] head-over-heels. [var. on ARSE OVER TEAKETTLE phr.]

piss-parade *v.* [1970s+] (*W.I.*) to shatter illusions, to ruin an otherwise satisfactory situation. [PISS ON SOMEONE'S PARADE v.]

piss pins and needles *v.* [late 18C–early 19C] to have venereal disease, esp. gonorrhoea. [PISS v.[1] (1); pain during urination can be one of the symptoms of venereal disease]

piss pipe *n.* [1990s+] the male urinary tract. [PISS n. (1) + SE *pipe*/PIPE n.[2] (1)]

piss-poor *adj.* **1** [1940s+] third-rate, incompetent, useless. **2** [1960s+] totally lacking in finances. [PISS- pfx + SE *poor*]

pisspot *n.* **1** [mid-16C+] (*also* pee-pot) a chamberpot; occas. a lavatory or urinal. **2** [late 16C+] an unpleasant person. **3** [1960s+] a drunkard. [PISS n. (1)/PEE n.[1] (1) + SE *pot*; (2) and (3) are fig. uses of (1)]

pisspot *adj.* [mid-17C; 1930s+] third-rate, incompetent. [PISS-POT n. (1)]

pisspot juggler *n.* [1900s–30s] (*Can.*) a chambermaid. [PISS-POT n. (1) + SE *juggler*]

piss prophet *n.* (*also* pisspot-peeper) [late 17C–early 19C] a physician who makes all their diagnoses on the basis of inspecting the patient's urine. [PISS n. (1)/PISSPOT n. (1) + SE *prophet*/*peeper*]

piss-proud *adj.* [late 18C+] of a man, having an erection on waking.

piss pure cream *v.* [late 19C] to have gonorrhoea. [PISS v.[1] (1); the discharge that accompanies the sickness]

piss-quick *n.* [early 19C] gin mixed with marmalade topped up with boiling water. [PISS v.[1] (1) + SE *quick*; its resemblance to urine or ? its micturative effect]

piss razor blades *v. see* PISS BROKEN GLASS v.

piss-rotten *adj.* [1940s+] appalling, unpleasant, distasteful. [PISS-pfx + SE *rotten*]

piss-sick *adj.* [1990s+] utterly contemptuous. [PISS- pfx + SE *sick* (and tired)]

piss-take *n.* [1970s+] a tease, a hoax, a practical joke. [PISS-TAKE v.]

piss-take *v.* [1940s+] to tease. [TAKE THE PISS (OUT OF) v.]

piss-taker *n.* [1990s+] a teaser, a joker, a mocker. [PISS-TAKE v.]

piss-taking *n.* [1940s+] teasing, mocking, fooling. [PISS-TAKE v.]

piss-tank *n.* [20C+] a drunkard. [PISS n. (4) + SE *tank*]

piss test *n.* [1990s+] (*drugs*) a urine analysis, carried out to check for drug use. [PISS n. (1) + SE *test*]

piss-test *v.* (*also* piss) [1990s+] (*drugs*) to carry out a urine analysis. [PISS TEST n.]

piss through *v.* [1910s+] to do something with no difficulty. [fig. use of PISS v.[1] (1)]

piss-ugly *adj.* [1980s+] (*orig. US*) very ugly. [PISS- pfx + SE *ugly*]

piss-up *n.* [1950s+] a drunken party; a drunken spree. [PISSED adj.[1]]

piss up *v.* [1960s–70s] (*US*) to vomit. [fig. use of PISS v.[1] (1)]

piss up a storm *v.[1]* [20C+] (*US*) to complain strongly, to make a major fuss. [fig. use of PISS v.[1] (1)]

piss up a storm *v.[2]* [1990s+] (*US*) to urinate for a relatively long time. [PISS v.[1] (1)]

piss upon *v. see* PISS ON v. (1).

piss up someone's back *v. see* PISS DOWN SOMEONE'S BACK v.

piss-walloper *n.* [1900s] (*US*) something remarkable, impressive.

piss-warm *adj.* [late 19C+] tepid, lukewarm in an unpleasant way. [the temperature of fresh PISS n. (1)]

piss-warmer *n.* (*also* pee-warmer) [20C+] (*Can.*) a general term of extreme approval. [PISS n. (1)/PEE n.[1] (1)]

piss when one cannot whistle *v.* [late 18C–early 19C] to be hanged. [PISS v.[1] (1); the loss of bowel control that results from being hanged]

piss-willie *n.* [1970s] (*US*) a coward.

pissy *adj.[1]* [1930s+] redolent of urine. [PISS n. (1)]

pissy *adj.[2]* **1** [1950s+] drunken. **2** [1950s+] weak, ineffectual, trifling. **3** [1970s+] unpleasant. [fig. uses of PISS n.]

pissy *adj.[3]* **1** [1950s+] cocky, arrogant. **2** [1970s+] angry. [(1) PISS OFF v. (2); (2) PISSED OFF adj.]

pissy-arsed *adj.* (*also* piss-ass drunk, pissy-ass drunk) [1940s+] extremely drunk (cf. ARSEHOLED adj.). [PISS n. (1) + ARSE n.[1] (4)/-ASS sfx; note PISSY adj.[2] (1)]

pissy-ass *adj.* (*also* piss-ass) [1950s+] (*US*) **1** insignificant, useless. **2** unpleasant. [PISSY adj.[2] + -ASS sfx]

pissy-drunk *adj.* [1990s+] (*US*) very drunk. [var. PISSY-ARSED adj.]

pissy-eyed *adj.* **1** [1960s+] (*US*) extremely drunk (cf. ARSEHOLED adj.). **2** [1980s+] (*N.Z.*) (mildly) drunk. [PISSY adj.[2] (1)]

pissy pal *n.* [late 19C+] an acquaintance picked up in a public house or a friend who one only sees in the pub; a close friend. [PISS n. (1)/PISS n. (4) + PAL n. (1); the pair drink and visit the urinals together]

pissy-pukey *adj.* [1960s] (*US*) very drunk. [PISSY adj.[2] (1) + SE *puke*]

pissy-tail *adj. see* PISSING-TAIL adj.

pissy weed *n.* [2000s] (*US Black/drugs*) marijuana that burns with a slightly urinous smell (cf. AFRICAN BUSH n.). [PISSY adj.[1] + WEED n.[1] (4)]

pistakle *n.* (*also* pistarckle) [20C+] (*W.I.*) **1** a foolish confusion. **2** a confused, foolish person, one who makes a fool of themselves in public. [? PISS ABOUT v. (1) + ? SE *spectacle*]

pistareen *n.* [mid-19C] (*US Und.*) a thief who claims, presumably fraudulently, to be of good family, to have never committed a crime before etc. [? Irish]

pistol *n.[1]* **1** [late 16C+] the penis (cf. AX n.[2]). **2** [1930s+] (*US*) anything or anyone seen as remarkable, exemplary etc?. **3** [1950s] a thug. **4** [1980s] a sexual athlete. [thus Shakespeare's double pun 'Pistol's cock is up' (*Henry V*, 1599); (2) underpinned by phr. 'hot as a pistol']

pistol *n.[2] see* POCKET PISTOL n.

pistol local *n.* [1950s] (*US*) a trade union local run by corrupt bosses; any rebels are suborned by physical violence. [PISTOL n.[1] (3)]

pistol pocket *n.* [1930s] the buttocks. [SE]

pistols *n.* [1940s] (*US Black*) the trousers of a ZOOT SUIT n. (1). [they 'shoot forward']

pistol-shot *n.* [mid-19C–1940s] a drink, a shot of liquor.

piston *n.* [1960s+] the penis.

pit *n.[1]* **1** [mid-17C+] (*also* sawpit) the vagina (cf. BLACK HOLE n.[1]). **2** [early 19C+] a breast pocket; thus (*UK Und.*) pit-worker, a pickpocket who specializes in robbing inside pockets. **3** [late 19C+] (*UK Und.*) a wallet. **4** [1960s] (*drugs*) the place on the inside of the elbow that is often used for injections. **5** [1960s+] usu. in pl., the armpit, with an implication of body odour.

pit *n.[2]* [late 17C–early 19C] (*UK Und.*) the common grave, beneath the gallows, in which those who fail to pay a burial fee of 6s 8d are buried after their remains have been cut down.

pit *n.[3]* [1940s+] **1** a bed. **2** a real mess, esp. a room that is untidy. **3** an unattractive, unpleasant place.

pit *n.[4]* [1960s+] (*orig. US*) a pit bull terrier. [abbr.]

pit *n.[5] see* PITS n.

pitch *n.[1]* **1** [mid-19C; 1910s+] (*orig. US*) any plan that should benefit its maker, a scheme, esp. a piece of trickery or deceit. **2** [mid-19C+] sales talk, esp. when inflated; also in fig. use. **3** [late 19C–1910s] a conversation, a chat. **4** [1930s+] the line of talk used by a swindler. **5** [1940s+] an area conducive to crime. **6** [1940s+] (*US*) a situation. [fig. uses of SE *pitch*, to throw]

pitch *n.[2]* [20C+] (*Aus.*) a camp. [SE *pitch camp*; although Mayhew, *London Labour and the London Poor* (1861–2), apostrophizes it; *pitch*, 'a spot in a street or other public place at which a stall for the sale or display of something is pitched or set up, or at which a street performer, a bookmaker, etc stations himself' (*OED*) has been SE since late 17C]

pitch *n.*³ [1970s] (*US campus*) an unattractive, unpleasant, promiscuous woman. [PIG n.¹ (3) + BITCH n.¹ (1)]

pitch *v.*¹ **1** [mid-19C–1910s] (*UK Und.*) to pass counterfeit coins; thus *pitcher*, one who passes coins. **2** [mid-19C+] to tell a tale, to speak persuasively. **3** [1930s+] (*drugs*) to sell drugs. [fig. use of SE *pitch*, to throw]

pitch *v.*² **1** [1960s+] (*gay*) to be the active partner in anal sex or in sado-masochism. **2** [1980s+] (*Aus. prison*) to act in an ostentatiously homosexual manner. **3** [1990s+] (*US campus*) to ejaculate. [baseball imagery; ult. fig. use of SE *pitch*, to throw]

pitch a ball *v.* (*also* **pitch a party**) [1930s] (*US Black*) to enjoy oneself at or host a party. [SE *pitch* + BALL n.⁷ (1)/play on SE]

pitch a bitch *v.* (*US Black*) **1** [1940s+] to complain, to fight, to cause a disturbance. **2** [1990s+] to reject, to leave. [SE *pitch*, to throw + BITCH n.³]

pitch a boogie-woogie *v.* [1920s+] (*US Black*) to make a fuss. [SE *pitch*, to throw + fig. use SE *boogie-woogie*, a form of jazz-based dance]

pitch a fork *v.* (*also* **pitch the fork**) [mid-19C–1930s] to tell a story, esp. a sad or romantic one. [PITCH v.¹ (2) + ? play on SE *pitch*, throw/*pitchfork*]

pitch and fill *n.* [mid-19C] the proper name Bill, ult. William. [rhy. sl.]

pitch and pay *v.* [mid-16C–mid-19C] to pay promptly.

pitch and toss *n.* **1** [1940s+] the boss. **2** [1980s] (*Aus.*) King's Cross, the 'bohmeian' area of Sydney. [rhy. sl.]

pitch a party *v. see* PITCH A BALL v.

pitch a tale *v.* (*also* **pitch a yarn, pitch the tale**) [mid-19C+] to recount a story, to tell exaggerated stories, esp. as a confidence trickster; thus TALE-PITCHER n. [PITCH v.¹ (2) + SE *tale*]

pitch a tent (in one's shorts) *v.* [1990s+] (*orig. US*) to get an erection.

pitch boogie *v.* [1950s] (*US*) of a man, to seduce a woman. [BOOGIE n.³ (3)]

pitcher *n.*¹ [late 16C–1900s] the vagina (cf. BAG n.¹). [SE *pitcher*, a jug]

pitcher *n.*² [early 19C] a prison, esp. Newgate in London. [SE *pitcher*, a jug, thus play on JUG n.² (1)]

pitcher *n.*³ **1** [mid–late 19C] (*UK Und.*) a person who passes counterfeit coins. **2** [mid-19C+] a member of a 3-card monte team. **3** [mid-19C+] a street vendor. **4** [1980s+] (*drugs*) a drug dealer, esp. when working on the street and actually handing over the drugs to the buyer. [SE *pitch*, the place in the street where such an individual works]

pitcher *n.*⁴ [20C+] (*Aus.*) a chatterbox. [PITCH A TALE v.]

pitcher *n.*⁵ **1** [1960s+] (*gay*) the dominant partner in male homosexual intercourse. **2** [1980s] (*US*) the male partner in heterosexual intercourse. [PITCH v.² (1)]

pitcher-bawd *n.* [late 17C–early 18C] a worn-out or semi-retired prostitute who runs errands in a tavern, either bringing drinks or providing customers with her more alluring peers. [SE *pitcher*, a jug + *bawd*]

pitch-fingers *n.* [19C] a thief. [SE *pitch*, a sticky substance used, *inter alia*, for sealing ships' timbers + *fingers*]

pitch fly *n.* [1970s] someone who takes over another's street-selling position without permission. [SE *pitch*, a street seller's site + fig. use of *fly*, an insect which has settled on one's spot]

pitch-in *n.* [late 19C] (*Scot.*) a railway collision.

pitching and catching *n.* [1960s+] the 2 opposed and complementary sides of any form of physical sex, esp. sado-masochism, bondage and discipline or coprophilia. [baseball imagery]

pitch into *v.* **1** [early 19C+] to fight, esp. to commence a fight. **2** [early 19C+] to attack verbally, to reprimand. **3** [mid-19C+] (*also* **pitch in**) to set to work, to join in. **4** [mid-19C+] (*also* **pitch**

in) to commence eating or drinking (voraciously); often as imper. *pitch in!*

pitch it strong *v.* (*also* **pitch it high, ...hot, ...into, ...warm**) [mid-19C+] to speak forcefully, to state a case with feeling or enthusiasm, to exaggerate. [PITCH v.¹ (2) + STRONG adv. (1)/HIGH adv./HOT adv. (1)/WARM adv.]

pitch-kettled *adj.* [mid-18C–mid-19C] utterly puzzled, nonplussed. [? the image of black pitch being poured over a person, obscuring their vision]

pitchman *n.* [1920s+] a street-seller of cheap articles. [SE *pitch*, a street-seller's site + sfx *-man*]

pitch on *v.* **1** [late 17C–19C] to target. **2** [1930s+] (*Aus.*) to nag, to attack verbally, to tell off. [PITCH v.¹ (2)]

pitch the crack *v.* [mid-19C] (*UK Und.*) to stop doing something.

pitch the cuffer *v.* [late 19C–1900s] to tell exaggerated stories, esp. as a confidence trickster. [PITCH v.¹ (2) + SE *cuffer*, a yarn or story; ult. *cuff*, to discuss, to tell a story]

pitch the dirt *v.* [1950s] (*US*) to gossip (maliciously), to slander. [PITCH v.¹ (2) + DIRT n.²]

pitch the fork *v. see* PITCH A FORK v.

pitch the nob *n. see* PRICK THE GARTER n.

pitch the peter *v. see* PETER n.⁴.

pitch the tale *v. see* PITCH A TALE v.

pitch (the) woo *v.* [1930s+] (*Aus./US*) to utter affectionate pleasantries. [PITCH v.¹ (2) + SE *woo*]

pitchy-man *n. see* DOLLY-MAN n.

pitchy-patchy *n.* [1940s] (*W.I.*) **1** ragged old work-clothes. **2** one who is wearing them. [SE *patch* + redup.]

pit hole *n.* **1** [17C] a grave. **2** [19C] (*also* **pit mouth, pit of darkness**) the vagina (cf. BLACK HOLE n.¹). [(1) SE; (2) negative characterization + ext. PIT n.¹ (1)]

pit job *n.* [1960s] intercourse *in axilla*, i.e. beneath the armpit. [PIT n.¹ (5) + JOB n.⁴]

pit-man *n.* [early–late 19C] a small pocketbook, worn in the inside pocket of a jacket. [PIT n.¹ (2)]

pit mouth/pit of darkness *n. see* PIT HOLE n. (2).

pit-pat's the way! *excl.* [late 19C] carry on! don't stop! [SE *pit-pat*, patteringly, making a repeated sound]

pits *n.* (*also* **pit**) [1960s–80s] (*US campus*) body odour. [PIT n.¹ (5)]

pits, the *n.* [1950s+] (*orig. US*) **1** a situation, object or person who is totally undesirable. **2** the depths of despair; thus *in the pits*, very depressed.

pit stop *n.* **1** [1960s+] (*orig. US*) a visit to the lavatory; a stop on a car journey, usu. for passengers to relieve themselves; usu. as *make a pit stop*. **2** [1980s+] a stop on a journey or a rest from an activity to have a drink. [joc. use of motor-racing jargon]

pitter *n. see* PETER n.² (1).

Pittsburgh feathers *n.* [1910s–30s] (*US tramp*) coal, as slept on in a freight train. [coal that is being transported to the steel mills of Pittsburgh]

Pitt's picture *n.* [late 18C–early 19C] a bricked-up window. [in order to help finance the war against the American colonists, Prime Minister William *Pitt* the Younger (1759–1806) increased the tax on windows, charging householders for each one they owned. This was generally disliked and the poor and mean preferred to brick up windows rather than pay the tax]

Pitt Street bushman *n.* (*also* **Pitt Street drover, ...stockman**) [1920s–60s] (*Aus.*) a business person who owns or shares a farm from which they take annual profits but which they rarely visit. [*Pitt Street*, the financial centre of Sydney]

Pitt Street farmer *n.* [1970s+] (*Aus.*) a business person who owns or shares a farm from which they take annual profits but which they rarely visit. [later var. on prev.]

pitty *adj.* [1970s+] (*US campus*) messy, untidy, disgusting. [PIT n.³ (3)]

pity fuck *n. see* CHARITY FUCK n.

pitzu n. [1980s+] (drugs) impure morphine base. [? Sp.]

pivot v. [1910s–60s] (US Und.) of a beggar, to solicit for alms; of a street prostitute, to attract customers.

pix n. [1920s+] (orig. US) pictures, whether still or motion. [abbr./pron.]

pixie n.[1] (also **pix**) [1930s–70s] a homosexual man. [var. on FAIRY n.[3]]

pixie n.[2] [1950s+] (US Black) **1** of women, a short hairstyle. **2** of men, straightened hair. [SE pixie, a sprite; the haircut supposedly resembles illustrations of such figures]

pixie stick n. [1960s–70s] (US gay) any phallic object carried by a cruising gay man, e.g. a cigarette holder, a rolled umbrella (on a dry day), a long-stemmed rose. [PIXIE n.[1]+ SE stick; play on FAIRY'S WAND n.]

pixillated adj. (also **pixielated, pixilated, pixolated**) **1** [mid-19C+] confused. **2** [1930s+] drunk (cf. ADDLED adj.). [SE pixie, a sprite, thus lit. 'one who has been taken over by pixies']

piz n. (also **pizz**) [late 18C] a fashionable man about town. [var. on PUZ n.]

pizaro n. [1900s] (US) a fad, a discovery. [? the explorer Pizarro]

pizazz n. see PIZZAZZ n.

pizz n. see PIZ n.

pizz adj. (also **pizzicato**) [1930s] tipsy. [euph. for PISSED adj.[1]]

pizza face n. [1960s+] (US/UK teen) one who suffers from a severe case of acne; thus adj. pizza-faced.

pizza-head n. [1990s+] (Aus. teen) a general insult.

pizza toppings n. [1980s+] (drugs) psilocybin/psilocin 'magic' mushrooms.

pizzazz n. (also **pazazz, pizazz**) **1** [1910s+] (US) an expert, an exemplar. **2** [1930s+] (orig. US) style, glamour, ostentation. **3** [1930s+] energy, zest. [ety. unknown but note RAZZLE n. (1); RAZZMATAZZ n. (1)]

pizzicato adj. see PIZZ adj.

pizzle n. [mid-17C; mid-19C+] the penis. [SE pizzle, a bull's penis; thus pizzle guard, a fictitious object in search of which young drovers are sent, only to be told 'I've only got a left-handed one']

pizzle v. [mid-17C; 18C–19C] of a man, to have sexual intercourse. [SE pizzle, a bull's penis]

p.j. n. [2000s] (US) a housing project. [abbr.]

p.j.'s n. **1** [1920s–30s] physical jerks. **2** [1960s+] (also **p.j.**) pyjamas. [abbr.]

p.k. n. see PICCANINNY KAYA n.

plaasjapie n. [1950s+] (S.Afr.) a country bumpkin. [Afk. plaas, farm + JAAP n. (2)]

plaba n. (also **ploba**) [1950s] (W.I.) an argument. [Carib.E. plaba, a stew, but note PALAVER n. (6)]

plabbery adj. [1920s] (Irish) foolish. [Irish plab, a person who is easily taken in]

placcy adj. see PLACKY adj.

place n. [late 19C–1950s] a lavatory. [euph.]

place, the n. **1** [late 17C–19C] the vagina (cf. ARTICLE n.). **2** [early 19C] the life of prostitution. [euph.]

placebo n. [mid-14C–17C] a toady or sycophant; thus dance/hunt/make/play with/sing (a) placebo, to be a toady or sycophant. [Lat. placebo, I shall please; popularized as the name commonly given to Vespers in the Office for the Dead, f. the first word of the first antiphon (Placebo Domino in regione vivorum, Ps. cxiv. 9)]

place of convenience/resort n. see CONVENIENCE n.

place of sixpenny sinfulness n. [early 17C] a suburban brothel. [costing less than its equivalent in the London's West End]

placer n. [1960s+] a middle-man who places stolen goods with a purchaser.

place where one coughs n. [1920s+] a euph. for the lavatory. [the shy person's coughing, hoping to disguise the sound of urination/defecation]

placido n. [2000s] £10. [ult. Placido Dominguez, one of the '3 tenors', i.e. TENNER n. (1)]

plack n. **1** [mid-16C–early 19C] (Irish) anything of small value. **2** [19C+] (Ulster) a mouthful. [SE plack, either a small 15C–16C Flemish coin or contemporary Scot. coin, worth 4d]

placket n. [late 16C–18C] **1** (also **placket-box, -hole**) the vagina; thus tear one's placket, of a woman, to lose one's virginity (cf. AGREEABLE RUTS OF LIFE n.). **2** (also **placket-lady**) a woman considered only as a sex object, a prostitute. [SE placket, the slit at the top of an apron or petticoat, facilitating dressing and undressing; note Shakespearian uses of placket as a double entendre, e.g. in Love's Labours Lost, The Winter's Tale and Troilus and Cressida]

placket-racket n. [17C] the penis. [PLACKET n. (1) + SE racket, an implement for hitting balls]

placket-stung adj. [mid-17C–mid-18C] suffering from a venereal disease. [PLACKET n. (1) + SE stung]

placky adj. (also **placcy, plakky**) [1970s+] plastic; esp. in placky bag, a polythene carrier bag. [abbr.]

plague n.[1] [mid-16C+] any object or person considered a nuisance, an irritation.

plague n.[2] [late 16C+] a euph. for hell or the devil, used in a variety of mild oaths.

plague, the n. [1990s+] AIDS. [note Williams for 17C use of plague as a synon. for venereal disease]

plagued adj. [1990s+] (US) suffering from AIDS. [PLAGUE, THE n.]

plaguer n. [1990s+] (US) a person with AIDS. [PLAGUE, THE n.]

plaguey adj. (also **plagued, plaguing, plaguy**) [late 16C–1940s] 'confounded', excessive, exceeding, very great; also as adv. [SE plague; a euph. for DAMNED adj. (1)]

plaguily adv. (also **plaguely, plaguyly**) [late 16C–mid-19C] irritatingly, annoyingly, to a great extent. [PLAGUEY adj.]

plain n. [1930s+] (Irish) Guinness stout, seen as the basic Irish drink.

plain and jam n. [1900s–20s] a tram. [rhy. sl.]

plain people n. [mid-19C] (US Black) White people. [a deliberate play on the SE White term, coloured people]

plain-turkey n. (also **plains-turkey, turkey**) [1930s–50s] (Aus.) a tramp, a vagrant living in the Great Plains of Western Queensland. [SE plains-turkey, the Aus. bustard, Ardeotis australis]

plain vanilla adj. see VANILLA adj.

plaister of warm guts n. (also **plaister of hot guts, plaster of warm guts**) [late 17C–early 19C] sexual intercourse. ['one warm belly clapped to another: a receipt frequently prescribed for different disorders' (Grose, 1785)]

plak v. [1960s+] (S.Afr.) **1** to stick on, to slap on, to glue on. **2** to plaster, to paint. [Du. plakken, to glue]

plakkies n. [1960s+] (S.Afr.) thongs, flip-flops. [PLAK v. (1); they 'stick' to one's feet]

plakky adj. see PLACKY adj.

planes hit the towers, the phr. [2000s] a phr. meaning 'the difficulties really start to happen', unexpected trouble begins. [var. on SHIT HITS THE FAN, THE phr., based on terrorist attacks of 11 September 2001]

plank n.[1] [1950s+] (Irish) a cache of money. [? PLANK v. (1) or the SE planks beneath which it is hidden, or the wooden box in which it is kept]

plank n.[2] [1960s+] (Aus.) a surf board; thus ride the planks, to surf.

plank n.[3] [1990s+] the penis, implied in PLANKSPANKER n.; YANK THE PLANK v.

plank n.[4] [2000s] a fool. [THICK AS TWO SHORT PLANKS phr.]

plank n.[5] see STICK n.[6] (2).

plank v. **1** [19C+] (also **plink**) to place, to put, to deposit, to plant. **2** [19C+] to pay money down, to lay out money, esp. when done without quibbling. **3** [1950s] to bury. **4** [1950s+] to have sexual intercourse (cf. BANG v.[1]). [fig. uses of SE *plank*, to lay a floor, thus in (4) added pun on *lay*/LAY v.[1] (1)]

plank down v. (*also* **plank out, …up**) [mid-19C+] to pay money down, to lay out money, esp. when done without quibbling. [ext. PLANK v. (2)]

plank it v. [2000s] (*Irish*) to be anxious. [ety. unknown]

plankspanker n. [2000s] a masturbator. [PLANK n.[3] + SPANK… v.]

plank up v. *see* PLANK DOWN v.

plant v.[1] **1** [17C+] to hide an object, usu. stolen. **2** [late 18C+] to bury a body. **3** [19C+] (*UK Und.*) (*also* **plant upon**) usu. of the police, to hide evidence in the clothes, home or car of a suspected person in order to ensure they have something with which to charge their victim. **4** [19C+] (*also* **plant upon, take a plant**) to post a spy, a detective or any individual, or listening device, for the purposes of surreptitious surveillance. **5** [mid-19C] to mark out a potential victim for robbery. **6** [mid–late 19C] (*UK Und.*) to pass counterfeit coins or notes; thus *planter*, one who undertakes this. **7** [late 19C] to 'salt' a gold-field in the hope of attracting investors. **8** [late 19C+] to abandon, to leave. **9** [1920s–40s] to hide oneself. **10** [1930s] to swindle, to deceive; to play a trick. [(1) is mainly Aus. from mid-19C+]

plant v.[2] **1** [17C+] of a man, to have sexual intercourse. **2** [early 19C+] (*Irish*) to hit; to kill; to shoot dead; also as n., a blow.

plantain leaf n. [1940s+] (*W.I.*) a £1 note (cf. ALFALFA n.). [like the note, it is green]

plant a man v. [18C–19C] usu. of a man, to have sexual intercourse. [the ejaculation of 'seed']

planter n.[1] [mid–late 19C] (*Anglo-Ind.*) a bad-tempered horse. [? it *plants* its feet and refuses to obey the rider]

planter n.[2] [late 19C+] (*Aus.*) one who steals and then hides cattle. [PLANT v.[1] (1)]

planter n.[3] [late 19C+] (*Ulster*) an outsider. [the 'plantation' of Ulster in 17C–18C by English and Scot. settlers]

planter n.[4] *see* PLANT v.[1] (6).

planter's medicine n. [mid-19C] (*W.I.*) a flogging. [administered every Monday to slaves who complained of ulcers and went to the plantation hospital. The punishment was meted out until the ulcers healed]

plant home v. [late 19C–1900s] in an argument, to make a telling point. [fig. use of PLANT v.[2] (2), i.e. 'hit home']

planting n. **1** [late 18C+] (*Aus.*) the hiding of stolen items, esp. horses, and then 'discovering' them as soon as a reward is offered. **2** [20C+] (*Aus./US*) a funeral. [PLANT v.[1]]

planting beets n. [1980s] (*Aus.*) the act of vomiting.

plants n. [17C–18C] the feet.

plant the books v. *see* BOOKS n.[1].

plant the whids and stow them v. [17C–mid-18C] (*UK Und.*) to talk carefully, to guard one's tongue. [SE *plant*, lay down + WHID n. (1) + STOW v. (1)]

plant upon v. *see* PLANT v.[1].

plant you now, dig you later phr. [1940s–50s] (*US Black*) goodbye for now, see you later. [pun on SE *dig*/DIG v.[5] (1)]

plaque n.[1] [1940s] (*Irish*) the human face.

plaque n.[2] [1990s+] (*US campus*) the accumulation of dirt, food particles etc beneath the keys of a computer keyboard. [SE *plaque*, a similar accumlation on the teeth]

plarry n. [20C+] (*Ulster*) an unappealing mess of food. [Scot. *plorie*, a piece of ground that has been trodden into mud; ult. SE *plough*]

plasma n. [1980s] (*US campus*) coffee. [its importance in maintaining life]

plaster n.[1] **1** [mid-19C+] (*US*) a banknote (cf. BANK-RAG n.). **2** [1910s] (*US*) a fine. **3** [1920s+] (*Can.*) a mortgage; thus as v., to pay money towards a mortgage. **4** [1930s+] (*Aus.*) a bill, an account. [the rectangular shape + its efficacy in 'curing' financial ills]

plaster n.[2] [late 19C] an outsize collar. [resemblance, though E.P. suggests Fr. *plastron*, a stiff shirt-front. The style was popularized by the Duke of Clarence (1864–92)]

plaster n.[3] **1** [late 19C–1930s] (*US tramp*) butter; usu. in PUNCH AND PLASTER n. **2** [20C+] (*US*) a follower, a 'tail'. **3** [20C+] (*Irish*) an encumbrance, a burden. **4** [20C+] (*Irish*) (*also* **sticking plaster**) one's wife. **5** [1930s+] (*Irish*) an unpleasant person or creature. [they all 'stick' to you like a plaster]

plaster v. **1** [late 19C–1930s] to bet (heavily) on. **2** [1910s+] to hit. **3** [1960s+] (*Irish*) to persuade. **4** [1970s+] (*US Black*) to flatter. **5** [1970s+] (*US Black*) to shoot someone.

plastered adj.[1] [1900s] a euph. for DAMNED adj. (1).

plastered adj.[2] [1910s+] (*orig. milit.*) drunk (cf. ANNIHILATED adj.). [joc. use of PLASTER v. (2)]

plasterer's trowel and seringapatam n. (*also* **seringapatam**) [late 19C] a fowl and ham. [rhy. sl.; *Seringapatam*, apparently used purely for assonance, was the former capital of the Indian state of Mysore]

plaster of Paris n. [1990s+] the buttocks (cf. ALA n.). [rhy. sl. = ARRIS n. (2)]

plaster of warm guts n. *see* PLAISTER OF WARM GUTS n.

plastic n. [1970s+] **1** any form of credit card; thus (*US*) **work plastic**, to obtain goods using a stolen credit card. **2** (*UK Und.*) plastic explosive, used for safe-breaking. [the *plastic* construction of such cards]

plastic adj. [1960s+] synthetic, false, insincere.

plastic cow n. [1980s] (*US campus*) non-dairy creamer. [SE *plastic*/PLASTIC adj. + COW n.[5] (1)]

plastic hippie n. [1960s] a part-time or uncommitted HIPPIE n.[2] (3), more interested in the hedonistic and clothes-wearing side of the movement than in its philosophies. [PLASTIC adj. + HIPPIE n.[2] (3)]

plastic job n. [1940s+] (*orig. US*) **1** plastic surgery. **2** one who has had plastic surgery. [SE *plastic (surgery)* + JOB n.[4]]

plastic out v. [1970s+] (*US campus*) to assume temporarily an artificial mode of behaviour or personality. [PLASTIC adj.]

plastic paddies n. [1980s+] the children of first-generation Irish immigrants to the UK. [PLASTIC adj. + PADDY n. (1)]

plastic people n. [1960s] conventional people, characterized by their rejection (and fear) of alternative modes of thought or action.

plastic screw n. [1990s+] (*UK Und.*) a security guard employed by the courts and prison services. [PLASTIC adj. + SCREW n.[2] (3)]

plat n. [1920s+] (*Aus.*) a fool, an 'easy mark'. [Fr. *plat*, flat; ? thus play on FLAT n.[2] (1)]

plate n.[1] (*orig. US*) **1** [1930s+] a gramophone record. **2** [1960s] a record deck. [resemblance]

plate n.[2] [1960s+] an act of oral sex, usu. fellatio; thus *plater*, a hetero- or homosexual fellator. [PLATE v.[1]]

plate v.[1] [1960s+] to fellate (cf. BLOOD RED n.). [rhy. sl.; *plate of ham* = GAM v.[2] (1) (cf. PLATE OF HAM n.[1]) or *plate of meat* = EAT v.[3] (1)]

plate v.[2] [1990s+] (*UK Und.*) to change the number plates of a stolen car.

plate and dish n. [1990s+] a wish. [rhy. sl.]

plate-face n. [1980s+] (*Aus.*) a derog. term for an Asian, orig. Vietnamese (cf. BROWNIE n.[2]). [the perceived 'flatness' of some Asian faces]

plate it v. [late 19C–1900s] to walk. [PLATES (OF MEAT) n.]

plate of ham n.[1] [1950s+] fellatio (cf. BLOOD RED n.). [rhy. sl. = GAM n.[3](cf. PLATE v.[1])]

plate of ham n.[2] *see* BEEF AND HAM n. (1).

plate of meat n.[1] [mid-19C] the street. [rhy. sl.]

plate of meat n.[2] *see* CUP OF TEA n. (3).

plate of straight n. [1950s] (*W.I.*) a dish of boiled bananas. [? SE *straight*, no trimmings]

plate-rack *n.* [late 19C+] a horse. [rhy. sl. = SE *hack*, a horse for everyday riding]

plates and dishes *n.* **1** [1930s+] kisses. **2** [1950s+] the wife, 'missus'. [rhy. sl.]

plates (of meat) *n.* (*also* **blades of meat**) [mid-19C+] the feet. [rhy. sl.]

platforms *n.* [1970s+] (*orig. US*) platform-heeled shoes, i.e. shoes with high heels and extra layers added to increase the height of the sole.

plating *n.* (*also* **tongue-plating**) [1960s+] oral sex, fellatio, cunnilingus. [PLATE v.¹]

platinum *adj.* **1** [1950s–60s] having a big heart, generous. **2** [1980s+] (*US*) excellent. [on pattern of DIAMOND adj.]

plato *n.* [1960s+] (*US*) a fight, a problem, an argument. [Mex. Sp.]

Plato to NATO *n.* [1980s] (*US campus*) a course in European civilization.

plats *n.* [2000s] (*US Black*) platform-heeled shoes. [PLATFORMS n.]

platsak *adj.* [1950s+] (*S.Afr.*) out of funds, impoverished. [Du. *plat*, flat + *sak*, pocket]

platter *n.*¹ [late 19C] broken crockery. [? SE *plates* + *clatter*]

platter *n.*² [1930s+] (*orig. US Black*) a gramophone record. [resemblance]

platter-faced *adj.* [late 17C–1940s] plain, broad-faced. [20C use appears to be Irish]

platters (of meat) *n.* [1920s+] the feet. [rhy. sl.; var. on PLATES (OF MEAT) n.]

plausy *adj.* (*also* **plausey, plazy, plossey**) [mid-19C] (*Anglo-Irish*) smooth-tongued, overly polite, apparently weak. [SE *plausible*]

play *n.*¹ **1** [late 17C+] sexual activity. **2** [late 18C+] (*US*) any form of action, plan or scheme. **3** [late 19C+] the situation, the state of affairs. **4** [20C+] (*US Und.*) the performance of a single confidence trick, esp. one which requires substantial preparation, props etc.

play *n.*² (*orig. US*) **1** [late 19C+] a show of interest, patronage, publicity; thus *to give* (*it/one*) *a play*, to try out, to give a chance. **2** [1930s+] way of life, well-being.

play *n.*³ [1970s] (*US Black*) a form of greeting that involves the slapping of palms. [note 9C–14C SE *play*, to clap the hands]

play *v.*¹ **1** [16C+] to trick, to deceive. **2** [16C+] (*US*) (*also* **play turnabout**) to pursue sexually; to seduce. **3** [mid-19C+] to be involved in an affair outside one's primary relationship. **4** [late 19C+] to conduct oneself; to approach a situation. **5** [late 19C+] to manipulate, to exploit, to 'use' someone. **6** [late 19C+] to mock, to make fun of, to tease. **7** [1930s+] (*orig. US*) to cooperate, to comply, to accept, to tolerate, to make sense; usu. in negative, e.g. *I don't play that, that doesn't play.* **8** [1980s] (*US drugs*) to adulterate.

play *v.*² *see* PLAY OFF v.

playa *n.* [1990s+] (*US Black*) **1** anyone who uses wit, charm, intelligence to gain objectives, whether honestly or (more usu.) dishonestly. **2** a womanizer. [PLAYER n.¹ (2); part of the general sp. changes used by GANGSTA n. (2) rappers]

play a-cross *v.* (*also* **play across**) [early 19C] (*UK Und.*) to lose deliberately, so as to lure one's victim deeper into the game.

play a flute solo (on one's meat whistle) *v.* [19C+] to masturbate (cf. PLAY A MOUTH ORGAN v.; PLAY AN ORGAN SOLO v.; PLAY THE MALE ORGAN v.; PLAY THE SKIN FLUTE v.).

playa from the Himalaya *n.* [2000s] (*US Black*) one who is popular with the opposite sex. [PLAYA n. (2) + assonance + the importance/size of the mountain range]

play a full hand *v.* [1900s] (*US*) to act from a position of strength. [poker imagery]

play a game at loll-tongue *v.* [late 18C–early 19C] to have one's saliva checked for traces of syphilis.

play a good knife and fork *v.* [early 19C] to eat and drink well.

play a good stick *v.* [mid-18C–mid-19C] of a fiddler, to perform competently.

play a harp *v. see* PLAY THE HARP v.¹.

playa hata/hater *n. see* PLAYER HATER n.

play a little five-on-one *v.* [20C+] to masturbate (cf. AUDITION THE FINGER PUPPETS v.; LARK v.). [5 fingers, 1 penis or vagina]

play a lone hand *v.* [20C+] (*orig. US*) to act independently. [poker imagery]

play along *v.* (*orig. US*) **1** [1920s+] to agree, to cooperate. **2** [1930s+] to deceive gradually, to 'take for a ride'.

play a lute solo *v. see* LUTE n.¹ (2).

play a mouth organ *v.* (*also* **play a piccolo**) [1960s+] (*US*) to perform oral sex (cf. PLAY A FLUTE SOLO (ON ONE'S MEAT WHISTLE) v.).

play an organ solo *v.* [1990s+] to masturbate (cf. PLAY A FLUTE SOLO (ON ONE'S MEAT WHISTLE) v.). [pun]

play a record *v.* [1950s] to boast, to brag.

play-around *n.* [1980s] (*Liverpool*) an act of masturbation, as provided by a prostitute. [PLAY AROUND v. (4)]

play around *v.* [1910s+] (*orig. US*) **1** to have a number of affairs, lovers, entanglements. **2** to seduce. **3** to play mental or emotional 'games' with someone. **4** to indulge in sexual play.

play a safe card *v. see* PLAY ONE'S CARDS RIGHT v.

play a store *v.* [1950s] (*US*) to go shoplifting.

play (at)... [16C+] a phr. used in various combs. as synons. for having sexual intercourse, e.g. *play at bouncy-bouncy, ...brangle, ...buttock, ...cock in cover, ...mumble-peg, ...prick the garter, ...pully-hauly, ...put in all, ...stable my naggie, ...thread the needle, ...tops and bottoms, ...top sawyer, ...where the Jack takes Ace, ...pyrdewy; see also* below or at individual nouns.

play at Adam and Eve *v.* [18C–19C] to have sexual intercourse.

play at all fours *v.* [late 17C–19C] to have sexual intercourse. [note Cotton's description in *The Compleat Gamester* (1674): 'This game [...] is called All-Fours from *Highest, Lowest, Jack* and *Game*', all of which terms can be taken as *doubles entendres*]

play at belly-to-belly *v.* (*also* **turn belly to belly**) [late 16C–1960s] to have sexual intercourse (cf. BELLY BUMP v.).

play at blindman's buff *v.* [17C] to have sexual intercourse.

play at bo-peep *v.* **1** [late 16C–early 18C] to have sexual intercourse. **2** [mid-17C–early 19C] to keep watch, to lie hidden. **3** [late 18C] to live alternately hidden and then appearing in public. [SE *bo-peep*, a nursery game in which one amuses a child by hiding (usu. the face), revealing, then repeating the process]

play at buttock and leave her *v.* [late 17C–mid-18C] to have sexual intercourse.

play at chaneys *v. see* PLAY CHANEYS v.

play at cherry pit *v.* [17C–19C] to have sexual intercourse. [SE *cherry pit*, the chewy stone]

play at doctors and nurses *v. see* PLAY (AT) MOTHERS AND FATHERS v.

play at grapple-my-belly *v.* [late 19C–1900s] to have sexual intercourse.

play at handie dandie *v.* [16C] (*Scot.*) to have sexual intercourse. [Scot./SE *handie-dandy*, a children's game based on the rapid moving of an object from one hand to another, then back]

play (at) handies *v.* [1910s+] (*Aus.*) of a pair of lovers, to hold hands.

play at hide-and-seek *v.* [late 18C–early 19C] to go into hiding in order to avoid arrest, one's creditors etc.

play at hooper's hide *v.* (*also* **play at hoop and hide**) [late 17C] to have sexual intercourse. [SE *hooper's hide*, hide-and-seek]

play at hot cockles *v.* [17C–18C] to caress and stimulate the female genitals. [SE *hot cockles*, 'A rustic game in which one player lay face downwards, or knelt down with his eyes covered, and being struck on the back by the others in turn, guessed who struck him' (*OED*); note later COCKLES n.]

play at houghmagandie *v.* [late 18C+] to have sexual intercourse. [SE/Scot. *hough* = hock = back of the knee + Scot. *canty*, cheerful, active]

play (at) in and in *v.* (*also* **throw in and in**) [late 16C–19C] to have sexual intercourse. [Nares: 'IN-AND-IN. A gambling game, played by three persons with four dice, each person having a box. It was the common diversion at ordinaries, and places of inferior resort [...] it appears that *in* was, when there was a doublet, or two dice alike out of the four; *in and in* when there were either two doublets, or all four dice alike, which swept the stake']

play (at) in and out *v.* [17C] to have sexual intercourse.

play at Irish whist (where Jack takes the ace) *v. see* IRISH WHIST n.

play (at) itch-buttocks *v.* [late 16C–19C] to have sexual intercourse.

play (at) level-coil *v.* [late 16C–17C] to have sexual intercourse. [SE *level-coil*, any form of rough game, spec. that once played at Christmas (an embryonic form of musical chairs) in which each player is in turn driven from their seat and replaced by another; Fr. (*faire*) *lever la cul* (*à quelqu'un*), to make someone raise their buttocks, properly 'arse'; also found in Ital. as *levaculo*]

play at lift-leg *v.* [early 18C–mid-19C] to have sexual intercourse.

play (at) mothers and fathers *v.* (*also* **play (at) doctors and nurses, ...mummies and daddies**) [late 19C+] to have sexual intercourse. [the adult versions of children's sex games]

play at potfinger *v.* [late 16C] to stimulate the vagina with the fingers.

play at pully-hawly *v. see* HAVE A GAME AT PULLY-HAWLY v.

play at push-pin *v.* (*also* **play at push-pike, ...put-pin**) [early 17C–mid-19C] to have sexual intercourse. [PUSH v.¹ + PIN n.¹ (1) + pun on children's game *push-pin* or *put-pin*, in which each player pushes or fillips their pin with the object of crossing that of another player]

play at rantum-scantum *v.* (*also* **play rantum**) [late 17C–early 19C] to have sexual intercourse. [SE *rantum-scantum*, chaos, a disorderly situation]

play (at) stink-finger *v.* [late 19C+] of a man, to manipulate the vagina.

play at the close-buttock game *v.* [mid-17C–19C] to have sexual intercourse.

play at top sawyer *v.* [late 19C–1900s] to have sexual intercourse.

play at two-handed put *v.* [18C–early 19C] to have sexual intercourse. [pun on *put* = Fr. *putain*, prostitute]

play a tune (on the one-holed flute) *v.* [1970s+] (*US gay*) to fellate (cf. BLOW v.²). [SE *play a tune* + FLUTE n.² (1)]

play at up and down *v.* [mid-19C] (*UK Und.*) to serve time on the treadmill.

play at up-tails all *v.* [17C–mid-18C] of a man, to have sexual intercourse. [SE *uptails-all*, the name of a song; ult. SE *up* + TAIL n.² (2)/TAIL n.² (3)/TAIL n.² (1) (which are all 'up' during sexual intercourse)]

play away *v.* [1970s+] **1** to philander, to commit adultery. **2** to do something outside one's experience. [sporting imagery]

play baby *v.* [late 19C+] (*US*) to act in a childish, infantile manner.

play bad *v.* [20C+] (*W.I.*) **1** of a child, to behave badly, rudely. **2** of an adult, to put on a show of defiance.

play bad-mind *v.* [20C+] (*W.I.*) to act in a spiteful, malicious way. [SE *play* + BAD-MIND n.]

play ball (with) *v.* **1** [20C+] to cooperate. **2** [1940s] to behave in an honourable manner. [one 'plays a game' with]

play bedwarmer *v.* [1940s–60s] (*orig. US Black*) to have sexual intercourse.

play big *v.* [20C+] (*W.I.*) to pretend to be more worthy, powerful, important, wealthy etc than one is.

play billy with *v.* [late 19C–1930s] to tease, to mess someone about. [? BILLY BARLOW n.¹ or fig. use of Scot. *billy-blind*, blind man's buff]

play boldface *v.* [1950s] (*W.I./UK Black*) to pretend to be braver or more confident than one is; to put on a bold face to mask one's guilt. [SE *play* + BOLDFACE adj.]

play booty *v.* [mid-16C–19C] to cheat in cards or dice (occas. bowls), usu. in conspiracy with a confederate. The result of such play is either to gang up on a third party, and share the resulting profits or 'booty', or deliberately to play to lose; also in fig. use.

play both sides of the fence/game/street *v. see* WORK BOTH SIDES OF THE STREET v.

playboy *n.* [late 19C+] (*Irish*) a fun-loving rascal.

play brother *n.* [1960s+] (*US Black*) an extremely close friend, one who resembles a brother; thus also *play cousin/mother/sister*.

play buggery with *v.* [1980s+] to play havoc with. [BUGGERY n.]

play cagey-cannon *v.* [1940s] (*Irish*) to act cautiously. [SE *cagey*; ety. of *cannon* unknown]

play camels *v.* [late 19C] (*Anglo-Ind.*) to drink excessively, to get drunk. [the animal's large capacity for liquid]

play carnival *v.* [1940s+] for a woman, to position her vagina directly above her partner's mouth, either sitting or squatting above their face, in order to facilitate cunnilingus. [guessing the weight competitions that are a fairground attraction]

play catch-up *v.* [1940s+] (*US*) to recover from a setback, to make good a disadvantage.

play chaneys *v.* [late 19C] (*Aus.*) to exert influence; thus *play at chaneys*, to bribe. [? SE *Chinese*, so far as the racial stereotype is concerned, the Chinese person is 'not straight']

play checkers *v.* [1940s+] (*US gay*) to move from seat to seat in a cinema in search of a receptive sexual partner. [the movements in checkers (UK draughts)]

play chick *v.* (*also* **play chicken, ...chickie, ...chicky**) [1940s+] (*US*) to maintain a lookout during the carrying out of a crime. [SE *play* + CHICK! excl.]

play chicken *v.*¹ [1950s+] **1** to indulge in dangerous games. **2** to challenge another person by attempting to see who 'cracks' first in a given situation. [the loser is a CHICKEN n.¹ (1) but note CHICKEN n.¹ (5)]

play chicken *v.*² [1970s+] (*US Black*) to intrude on another (man's) sexual advances. [fig. use of CHICKEN n.¹ (5), i.e. the intruder 'dares' his rival]

play chicken/chickie/chicky *v. see* PLAY CHICK v.

play chopsticks *v.* [1940s+] (*orig. gay*) to indulge in mutual masturbation. [joc. use of *Chopsticks*, a basic piano piece learnt by a novice requiring 2 players, one at either end of the piano keys]

play close *v.* [1980s+] (*US Black*) to become intimate with, esp. with the aim of using one's supposed friend for one's own purposes.

play cock in cover *v.* [late 19C] to have sexual intercourse. [pun on SE *play cock*, to display oneself/COCK n.² (1)]

play cocum *v.* (*also* **cokum, fight cocum, play cokum**) [mid–late 19C] to act in an artful, cunning manner, to deceive, usu. in illegal contexts. [COCUM n. (1)]

play comrade wobbly hides his helmet *v.* (*also* **play Mr Wobbly hides his helmet**) [1990s+] to have sexual intercourse (cf. BURY IT v.).

play con *v.* [1960s–70s] to trick, to hoax, to practise confidence trickery. [CON n.¹ (7)]

play consumption *v.* [late 19C] (*US*) to malinger, to fake an illness. [SE *consumption*, tuberculosis]

play cool v. see PLAY IT COOL v.

play couple your navels v. [18C] to have sexual intercourse.

play cousin n. see PLAY BROTHER n.

play crimp v. (also **crimp**) [late 17C–1920s] to cheat, to act criminally, esp. to bet openly on one side and then to cheat in favour of the other, on which one has bet surreptitiously. [SE *crimp*, one who entraps seamen into service, often by violence. Such activities were banned after the Merchant Shipping Act (1854)]

play cuddle my cuddie v. [mid-17C–early 18C] to have sexual intercourse. [SE *cuddle* + dial. *cuddy*, a woman]

play dead! excl. [1950s] (*US teen*) be quiet!

play diddle-diddle v. [16C] to play tricks, to importune. [pun on SE *diddle-diddle*, a fiddle/SE *to fiddle*]

play dirt v. [late 17C–1930s] (*US*) to deceive.

play dirty v. (also **get dirty**) [1910s+] (*orig. US*) to behave reprehensibly, to cheat. [DIRTY adj.[1] (2)]

play doctors and nurses v. see PLAY (AT) MOTHERS AND FATHERS v.

play dog v. see PLAY (THE) DOG v.

play doggo v. see LIE DOGGO v.

play dolly up, dolly down, dolly sick v. [20C+] to masturbate (cf. LARK v.). [coarse use of a children's game]

play down on v. [mid-19C] to take a mean or unfair advantage of someone.

play drag v. [1960s] (*US Black*) for a female prostitute to dress as a man in order to attract clients. [DRAG n.[8] (2)]

play drop the soap v. [1950s–70s] (*US*) to indulge in homosexual activity. [DROP THE SOAP v.]

play ducks and drakes with v. (also **make ducks and drakes of**) [17C–mid-19C] to squander one's fortune, to spend money unwisely. [SE *ducks and drakes*, a game based on the tossing of flat stones across a pond; thus in a financial context one is idly tossing away one's money]

played adj. [1990s+] (*US Black*) **1** insulted. **2** cheated on by one's girlfriend or boyfriend. [PLAY v.[1]]

played (out) adj. [mid-19C+] (*US*) exhausted, worn-out, finished. [PLAY OUT v. (1)]

player n.[1] **1** [late 19C+] a participant. **2** [1950s+] (*orig. US Black*) anyone who uses intelligence, wit, brains to gain objectives, whether a businessman, politician, womanizer, or criminal. **3** [1950s+] (*orig. US Black*) a pimp (cf. CANDYMAN n.). **4** [1950s+] (*orig. US Black*) a man who is a gambler by nature, who makes friends easily, and never gives up trying. **5** [1960s+] (*US campus*) a promiscuous person; a sexual cheat. **6** [1970s+] (*US drugs*) a drug user.

player n.[2] [1960s+] (*N.Z.*) a woman, occas. a man, who is seen as enthusiastic about sex. [SE *play*/PLAY AROUND v.]

player-hate v. [1990s+] **1** to resent the achievements and extravagant lifestyle of a ghetto success, whether gained legally or otherwise. **2** (*US campus*) to interfere in someone else's life or business. [backform. f. PLAYER HATER n.]

player hater n. (also **hata, hater, PHer, playa hata/hater**) [1990s+] (*US Black*) **1** one who resents the achievements and extravagant lifestyle of a ghetto success, whether gained legally or otherwise; thus ext. into non-ghetto environments. **2** spec. someone who hates a PLAYER n.[1] (2). [PLAYER n.[1] (2)/PLAYA n. (1) + SE *hater* or 'gangsta' sp. *hata*]

play fast and loose with a woman's apron-strings v. [17C] to have sexual intercourse.

play favourites v. [20C+] (*orig. US*) to show favouritism.

play footsie v. (also **play footie-footie, ...footies, ...footy-footy**) [1930s+] **1** to nudge someone's foot with one's own – out of sight of companions, usu. beneath a table – as a possible prelude to further intimacy. **2** to indulge in the cautious sounding out of any relationship, economic, political etc; to curry favour. **3** to waste time, to prevaricate.

play for v. [20C+] (*US Und.*) to treat with contempt or as a fool; to subject to a confidence trick. [ext. PLAY v.[1] (1)]

play for a chump v. (also **play for a clown, ...duffer, ...mug**) [late 19C+] (*orig. US Black*) to treat like a fool.

play for a sucker v. [late 19C+] (*US*) to deceive a gullible victim. [SUCKER n.[3] (2)]

play for blood v. [1990s+] (*US Black*) to play seriously, whether the game is lit. (sporting or electronic etc) or fig.

play for keeps v. [mid-19C+] to commit oneself permanently; to commit oneself in absolute earnest. [FOR KEEPS phr.]

play for the other team v. [2000s] to be a male homosexual.

play Fourteenth Street v. [1940s] (*US Black*) to disparage, to treat in a condescending manner. [the cheap shops of New York's 14th St]

play funny buggers v. see PLAY SILLY BUGGERS v.

play games v. [20C+] to manipulate, to manoeuvre, to act in a deceptive, dishonest manner; thus adj., *game-playing*.

play gooseberry v. [mid-19C+] (*mainly UK teen*) for an unwanted third party to hang around a couple who would prefer to be left alone. [GOOSEBERRY n.[3]]

play grab-ass v. [1950s+] (*US*) to make physical advances towards someone. [SE *grab* + ASS n. (2)]

playground n. (also **chippy's playground**) [1940s+] (*US Black*) the stomach.

play handies v. see PLAY (AT) HANDIES v.

play hardball v. [1970s+] (*orig. US*) to act ruthlessly and single-mindedly in pursuit of a goal. [HARDBALL n.[1]]

play hard to get v. [1920s+] **1** usu. of a woman, to resist sexual advances, although not necessarily to reject them altogether. **2** in fig. non-sexual use, to act reluctantly.

play hell v. see GIVE SOMEONE HELL v.

play hell with v. see PLAY (MERRY) HELL WITH v.

play hide the salami v. (also **play hide the wienie**) [1980s+] (*US*) to have sexual intercourse (cf. BURY IT v.; HIDE THE SALAMI v.). [SALAMI n./WEENIE n.[1] (4)]

play hide the sausage v. [1930s+] (*US*) to have sexual intercourse (cf. BURY IT v.). [SAUSAGE n.[1] (1)]

play hob v. [mid-19C+] (*orig. US*) to cause as much trouble as one can. [SE *Hob*, a mischievous sprite]

play holy hell v. see PLAY (MERRY) HELL WITH v.

play Hookey Walker v. see HOOKEY WALKER! excl. (2).

play hooky v. (also **play hookey**) [mid-19C+] (*US*) **1** to play truant from school. **2** to be absent or missing. **3** to be adulterous. [SE *play* + ? Du. *hoekje* (*spelen*), to play hide-and-seek]

play hoop-snake with v. [1940s–70s] (*gay*) for 2 homosexual men to indulge in mutual fellatio.

play horse with v. **1** [late 19C–1910s] (*US*) to indulge in horseplay. **2** [late 19C–1950s] (*US campus*) to ridicule, to tease. **3** [1900s] (*US campus*) to overcome easily; to confuse. [HORSE n.[5]]

playhouse n. **1** [late 17C] a brothel (cf. ACCOMMODATION HOUSE n.). **2** [1920s] (*US Und.*) a prison known for its liberal regime (cf. BANDHOUSE n.). **3** [1940s] (*US Und.*) ext. use of (2), in non-prison contexts, e.g. a town with little law and order. **4** [1970s+] (*US gay*) a room filled with implements to augment sado-masochistic sex.

play house v. **1** [20C+] (*US*) to cohabit. **2** [1930s+] (*US campus*) to have sexual intercourse. **3** [1960s] of 2 male homosexuals, to play around in a sexual manner.

play huggy-bear v. [1960s+] (*US*) to kiss and cuddle.

play ice for v. [1930s] to criticize, to look down on. [ICE n.[2] (1)]

play in and in v. see PLAY (AT) IN AND IN v.

play in and out v. see PLAY (AT) IN AND OUT v.

play Indian v. [1920s] (*US*) to ambush. [negative stereotyping]

playing out of the pocket phr. [1980s] (*US Black*) **1** cheating or tricking. **2** letting something happen without noticing it. [OUT OF (THE) POCKET phr. (1)]

playing too close *phr.* [1960s+] (*US prison*) becoming over-familiar and invading the privacy of a fellow inmate.

playing with a full deck *phr.* [1960s+] to be aware, intelligent, 'all there'. [i.e. opposite of NOT PLAYING WITH A FULL DECK phr.]

play in Peoria *v.* [20C+] to succeed in rural, provincial areas. [*Peoria*, Illinois, as a emblematic stop on theatrical/vaudeville tours]

play in someone else's yard *v.* [1950s+] (*US Black*) to have an adulterous affair.

play in the family *v.* (*also* **play in someone's family**) [1920s–30s] (*US Black*) to indulge in a bout of ritualized name-calling, based on insulting each other's mother.

play Irish whist *v. see* IRISH WHIST n.

play it — *v.* [1920s+] to act in a given manner, defined by an adj., e.g. PLAY IT COOL v.

play it by ear *v.* (*also* **play it by skyhook**) [1960s+] to act in an ad hoc manner, to behave spontaneously. [a musician who has no score as a guide]

play itch-buttocks *v. see* PLAY (AT) ITCH-BUTTOCKS v.

play it chilly *v. see* CHILLY adj.[2] (1).

play it close to one's chest *v.* (*also* **play it close to one's vest**) 1 [late 19C] to conserve one's funds. 2 [1940s+] to act in a reserved, secretive manner. [card-playing imagery, the player holds their cards close to their body in order to stop people seeing them]

play it cool *v.* (*also* **play cool, pluck it cool**) [1940s+] (*orig. US Black*) to act in an uninterested or disinterested manner, to control every emotion, to be relaxed. [PLAY IT — v. + COOL adj.[1]]

play it cool *phr.* [1950s–70s] (*US*) a phr. of farewell. [PLAY IT COOL v.]

play it off *v.* 1 [late 16C–mid-17C] to bring something to an end. 2 [1980s+] (*US campus*) to dismiss something, to not care.

play it (off) on (someone) *v.* [late 19C–1900s] (*Aus./UK*) to deceive, to trick. [PLAY v.[1] (1)]

play it straight *v.* [1920s+] (*orig. theatre*) to behave in an honest manner, to resist embellishing one's actions with artifice?. [PLAY IT — v.; ult. the warning used to actors not to overact]

play (it) strong *v.* [1950s–70s] (*US Black*) to act in an aggressive, determined manner. [PLAY IT — v.]

play jip *v.* [1940s] (*Aus.*) to irritate. [dial. *jip*, to trick, to cheat]

play john *v.* 1 [mid-19C] of a man, to flirt. 2 [1980s] (*US*) (*also* **play jim**) to fool about. [? JOHN n.[1] (1), i.e. behave like a 'typical' man]

play john henry *v. see* JOHN HENRY n.[1].

play least in sight *v.* [late 18C–early 19C] to hide, to keep out of the way.

play level-coil *v. see* PLAY (AT) LEVEL-COIL v.

play low (down) *v.* [late 19C–1910s] (*US*) to act meanly. [LOWDOWN adv.]

play (merry) hell with *v.* (*also* **play holy hell**) 1 [1910s+] to give someone a hard time. 2 [1940s+] to damage (an object, a plan etc).

play Mr Wobbly hides his helmet *v. see* PLAY COMRADE WOBBLY HIDES HIS HELMET v.

play mother *n. see* PLAY BROTHER n.

play mothers and fathers/mummies and daddies *v. see* PLAY (AT) MOTHERS AND FATHERS v.

play musical beds *v.* [1960s+] 1 to swap partners for sexual experimentation. 2 for a number of people sharing the same living quarters (a house, a hotel etc), to commit adultery. [SE *musical chairs*, a children's party game]

play night baseball *v.* [1960s+] to have sexual intercourse.

play nug a nug *v.* [early 17C] to caress, to fondle; to have sexual intercourse. [NUG v.]

play off *v.* (*also* **play, play off one's dust**) [late 16C–early 17C; late 19C–1910s] to finish a drink, to toss off a glass.

play off on *v. see* PLAY ON v. (1).

play offside *v. see* OFFSIDE adj. (1).

play old gooseberry *v.* [late 18C–19C] to 'play the devil'. [OLD GOOSEBERRY n. (1)]

play on *v.* 1 [19C+] (*also* **play off on**) to trick, to fool. 2 [1950s] to cheat on sexually, to cuckold. [PLAY v.[1]]

play on ass *v.* [2000s] (*US prison*) gambling without money, but in the knowledge that the loser will earn a beating. [ASS n. (2)]

play one's ace *v.* [late 19C+] of a woman, to have sex with a man. [SE *play* + ACE OF SPADES n.[2]]

play one's cards right *v.* (*also* **play a safe card, play one's cards well**) [mid-17C+] to behave sensibly, to act in one's best interests. [note Egan, *Book of Sports* (1832): 'If you will play your cards with as much judgement as the swell dragsman does, you are sure to *vin* the game, and no mistake']

play oneself *v.* [1950s+] (*US Black*) to delude oneself as to one's success, sexuality, character etc, to aggrandize oneself. [PLAY v.[1] (1)]

play oneself off *v.* [18C–19C] to masturbate (cf. BALL OFF v.[2]; LARK v.).

play on velvet *v.* [mid-19C+] to gamble with one's winnings. [SE *play* + ON VELVET phr.]

play out *v.* 1 [mid-19C+] (*orig. US Black*) to wear out, to lose usefulness, interest or value. 2 [1930s] (*US campus*) to use so much that it will eventually be worn out, usu. fig. rather than lit. 3 [1950s+] to go along with something for the sake of appearance, until it loses its interest or value.

play owings *v.* [late 19C] (*sporting*) to live on credit.

play past *v.* [1960s] (*US Black*) 1 to circumvent obstacles, mental as well as physical. 2 to lose an opportunity.

play patty-fingers *v.* [1920s+] (*Irish*) to touch hands in the holy water font. [SE *pat* + *finger*]

play pickle-me-tickle-me *v.* [mid-17C–early 18C] to have sexual intercourse (cf. PLAY TICKLE THE PICKLE v.).

play-play *n.* [1940s+] (*S.Afr.*) a pretence, insincerity.

play-play *adj.* [1940s+] (*S.Afr.*) fake, make-believe. [PLAY-PLAY n.]

play-play *v.* [1940s+] (*S.Afr.*) to pretend. [PLAY-PLAY n.]

play pocket pool *v.* (*also* **play pocket billiards, ...pinball**) [1940s+] 1 to play with one's genitals through a trouser pocket. 2 to masturbate (cf. LARK v.). [POCKET POOL n.]

play possum *v.* [early 19C+] (*orig. US/Aus*) 1 to pretend to be ill or even dead (cf. POSSUM v.). 2 to dissemble. 3 to run away in a cowardly manner. [SE *play* + SE *possum*/POSSUM n. (2), i.e. the habits of the animal]

play pussy and get fucked *v.* [1990s+] (*US Black*) to act weakly and to suffer as a result. [play on PUSSY n. (2)/PUSSY n. (10) + FUCK v.[1]/FUCK v.[2] (1)]

play rabbit *v. see* RABBIT v.[3].

play rantum *v. see* PLAY AT RANTUM-SCANTUM v.

play ring a rosie *v.* [20C+] (*US*) to fool about, to make great effort with no result. [*ring a ring o'roses*, a children's game]

play rough *v.* [1950s+] (*orig. US*) to be tough or ruthless, to act unfairly. [ROUGH adv., the idea of not playing by the rules in sport]

play second fiddle *v. see* SECOND FIDDLE n.

play shut-eye *v.* [1940s] to stop working or shut down. [SHUT-EYE n. (1)]

play silly buggers *v.* (*also* **play funny buggers, ...silly fannies, ...silly fuckers**) 1 [1960s+] to act uncooperatively, to mess around, to cause a deliberate nuisance. 2 [1990s+] to indulge in sexual relations. [var. on BUGGER ABOUT v.; (2) f. (1)]

play sister *n. see* PLAY BROTHER n.

play smash *v.* [mid-19C–1910s] (*US*) 1 to come to grief. 2 to cause trouble for, to 'play hell with'. [SE *smash*, to break]

play solitaire *v.* [1930s–70s] to masturbate (cf. LARK v.).

play someone against the wall *v.* [1960s] (*US Und.*) to practise a confidence trick. [PLAY v.[1] (1) + UP AGAINST THE WALL phr. (1)]

play someone any of one's parts v. [late 19C] to play a mean or unpleasant trick on. [theatrical imagery]

play someone cheap v. [1940s–60s] (*US Black*) to take seriously; often as *don't play someone cheap*, make sure someone is not underrated.

play someone for a Chinaman v. [late 19C] (*US*) to treat someone like a fool. [racial stereotyping of the Chinese]

play someone off v. [mid-19C+] (*US*) to avoid someone's attentions through guile.

play someone too close v. [1980s+] (*US prison/Black*) **1** to invade someone's privacy. **2** to tease or intimidate someone.

play square (with) v. [1900s–50s] to behave in a decent manner, to treat someone honestly. [SQUARE adv. (2)]

play staff v. *see* RIDE STAFF v.

play stickers (with) v. [1930s] (*UK Und.*) to steal money which one is supposedly passing on to a confederate.

play sticky fingers v. [1940s+] to steal, usu. money; thus *sticky fingers*, a thief.

play stink-finger v. *see* PLAY (AT) STINK-FINGER v.

play stinky pinky v. [1990s+] of a woman, to masturbate (cf. APPLY LIP GLOSS v.; LARK v.). [SE *stinky* + *pinky*, the little finger]

play strippers (on) v. [late 19C+] (*US gambling*) to cheat at cards by using a deck in which the sides of certain cards have been microscopically shaved or 'stripped'.

play strong v. *see* PLAY (IT) STRONG v.

play stuff v. [1960s+] (*US Black*) to deceive or defraud by a smart line of verbal patter. [PLAY v.¹ (1) + STUFF n.¹ (3)]

play that shit v. [1960s+] (*US Black*) to act in a particular way; usu. in negative as *I don't play that shit*, I don't do that. [SHIT n.⁶]

play the — act v. *see* DO THE — v.

play the angles v. [1930s+] (*US*) to scheme, to plot. [ANGLE n.]

play the arse v. [1960s+] (*W.I.*) to play the fool, to trick (cf. ACT THE ANGORA v.). [ARSE n.¹ (5)]

play the bear v. [16C–17C] to act roughly or coarsely, to act rudely; thus [19C] *play the bear with*, to inflict great damage upon.

play the charley wag v. [mid–late 19C] to play truant. [var. on HOP THE WAG v.]

play the chill v. [1920s+] (*US*) to ignore, to avoid, to act coldly towards. [CHILL n.¹ (1)]

play the con v. [1940s+] (*orig. US Und.*) to pretend, to attempt to swindle or deceive. [CON n.¹ (7)]

play the cows v. [1920s] (*US Und.*) of a man, to have a steady relationship. [? COW n.¹ (1)]

play (the) dog v. [1960s] (*US*) to display oneself sexually, to act in an ostentiously promiscuous manner. [DOG n.³ (8)]

play the dozens v. (*also* **shoot the dozens, slip in the dozens**) [1910s+] (*US Black*) **1** to compete in ritualized mutual insults, often about one's family. **2** to take advantage of, to deceive. [SE *play/shoot* + DOZENS n.]

play the dozens with one's uncle's cousin v. [1940s] (*US Black*) to go about things in quite the wrong way, to make a mess of things. [DOZENS n., i.e. by insulting their family one is also insulting oneself]

play the duck v. **1** [mid-17C] to behave in a cowardly manner. **2** [1920s+] to avoid. [SE *duck*, to lower one's head/DUCK v.¹ (2)]

play the fag role v. [2000s] (*US prison*) pretending sexual interest in another inmate; the aim is to annoy a third party. [FAG n.⁵ (1)]

play the field v. [1930s+] to enjoy a variety of lovers. [betting imagery; one bets on several horses instead of concentrating on a particular one]

play the first game ever played v. [19C] to have sexual intercourse.

play the flute v.¹ [late 19C+] (*US*) to perform fellatio (cf. BLOW v.²). [FLUTE n.² (1)]

play the flute v.² (*drugs*) **1** [1940s+] to smoke opium. **2** [1980s+] to smoke crack cocaine. [the visual equation of the pipe with a flute]

play the fox v.¹ [late 19C–1920s] to cheat, to sham, to dissemble. [FOX n.¹ (1)]

play the fox v.² [1930s] to vomit. [var. FLAY THE FOX v.]

play the gallery v. [late 19C] to applaud. [theatrical imagery]

play the game v. **1** [mid-19C+] to act in an honourable, 'sporting' manner. **2** [1940s+] to acquiesce. [the mid-19C cult of 'good sportsmanship'; modern use of (1) is often ironic]

play the giddy goat v. [late 19C–1960s] to act foolishly, impetuously (cf. ACT THE ANGORA v.). [var. on PLAY THE GOAT v. (3)]

play the goat v. **1** [18C] to copulate energetically. **2** [late 19C–1920s] to lead a degenerate, dissipated life. **3** [late 19C+] to mess around, to act ineffectually. [goatish characteristics; (3) var. on ACT THE GOAT v.]

play the harp v.¹ (*also* **play a harp**) [late 19C+] to die. [the harp-playing angels of heaven]

play the harp v.² [20C+] (*Anglo-Irish*) to wander drunkenly, tapping the railings as one passes. [the supposed similarity of the railings to harp-strings]

play the heel v. [1910s+] (*US*) to act unpleasantly, to be mean or cruel. [HEEL n. (2)]

play the hop v. (*also* **go on the hop**) [1930s–60s] to play truant from school. [HOP THE WAG v.]

play the horse(s) v. *see* PLAY THE PONIES v.

play the iggie v. [1960s–70s] (*US*) to ignore. [abbr.]

play the jack v. **1** [17C] to act the villain. **2** [19C] to play the fool (cf. ACT THE ANGORA v.). [(1) SE *jack*, a 'knave'; (2) JACK n.¹]

play the male organ v. [19C+] to masturbate (cf. PLAY A FLUTE SOLO (ON ONE'S MEAT WHISTLE) v.).

play the monkey v. *see* ACT THE HOG v.

play the mouth organ v. [1960s+] (*drugs*) to smoke heroin with a rolled-up matchbook cover substituted for the usual roll of tinfoil, which is used to suck up the heated, smoking heroin.

play the nanny goat v. [20C+] to play the fool (cf. ACT THE ANGORA v.). [var. on PLAY THE GIDDY GOAT v.]

play the nod v. [1930s–50s] (*drugs*) to doze off as a result of injecting a narcotic drug. [NOD n.¹ (2)]

play the nut role v. [1960s+] (*US Black*) **1** to pose as a shambling incompetent in order to swindle or otherwise trick a possible victim. **2** to pretend to madness. [NUT ROLE n.]

play the organ v. [20C+] (*Aus.*) to have sexual intercourse. [pun on SE]

play the part of the strong man v. [late 18C–early 19C] to be whipped at the cart's tail. [one is 'pushing' the cart]

play the percentages v. [1940s+] to act in a cautious manner, the opposite of GO FOR BROKE v. [gambling use]

play the piano v. [1970s] (*US*) to rob the till, e.g. as a barmaid or waiter. [the keys of the till resemble a piano]

play the pink oboe v. [1990s+] to fellate (cf. BLOW v.²). [PINK OBOE n.]

play the ponies v. (*also* **play the horse(s)**) [20C+] to bet on horseracing. [PONY n.⁵]

play the Scotch fiddle v. [19C–1910s] 'to work the index finger of the right hand like a fiddlestick between the index and middle finger of the left. This provokes a Scotchman in the highest degree, it implying that he is afflicted with the itch' (Hotten, 1864). [SCOTCH FIDDLE n.]

play the skin flute v. [1980s+] **1** to masturbate (cf. PLAY A FLUTE SOLO (ON ONE'S MEAT WHISTLE) v.). **2** to fellate (cf. BLOW v.²). [SKIN FLUTE n.]

play the sober Indian v. [mid-19C] (*US*) to resist joining in a drinking session. [racist stereotyping]

play the streets v. [1940s] (*US*) to work as a street prostitute.

play the tom v. [late 19C+] (*US Black*) to pretend to a fawning stupidity, in order to fool a gullible or self-important White person. [UNCLE TOM n. (1)]

play the violin v. *see* VIOLIN n.

play the wag v. **1** [late 17C] to be amusing or mischievous, to play the fool (cf. ACT THE ANGORA v.). **2** [mid-19C+] to play truant. [SE *wag*, a mischievous boy; ult. ? SE *waghalter*, one likely to end up 'wagging a halter', i.e. being hanged]

play the warm for v. [1930s] (*US*) to make advances towards, to ingratiate with.

play the whale v. [1960s–70s] (*Aus.*) to vomit. [? the biblical story of Jonah, who was vomited up by a whale]

play the whole game v. [late 18C–early 19C] to play at cards or dice with the intention of losing. [? one has to play to one's utmost – the whole extent of one's game – to ensure defeat; presumably the context is of a cheat aiming to ensnare a victim, for whom this will be their only success]

play-three n. [1990s+] (*W.I.*) death; dying. [ety. unknown]

play three to one (and sure to lose) v. [late 18C–19C] of a man, to have sexual intercourse. [*three*, the penis and testes, and *one*, the vagina; what the man is *sure to lose* is semen]

play tickle the pickle v. [20C+] (*US*) to have sexual intercourse (cf. PLAY PICKLE-ME-TICKLE-ME v.).

play tiddlywinks v. **1** [20C+] to have sexual intercourse. **2** [1990s+] of a woman, to masturbate (cf. APPLY LIP GLOSS v.; LARK v.).

play tonsil hockey v. (*also* play tonsil tennis) [1980s+] (*US campus*) to kiss deeply.

play touchy-touchy v. [1980s] (*US*) to indulge in sexual fondling.

play tricks v. [late 19C–1900s] to become pregnant.

play turnabout v. *see* PLAY v.[1] (2).

play up v.[1] **1** [mid-19C+] of people or animals, to irritate, to 'mess around'. **2** [mid-19C+] to break the rules, esp. sexually. **3** [late 19C+] of a wound or disease, to cause discomfort, e.g. *my bad arm's playing me up today*. **4** [1920s+] of machinery or an object, to malfunction.

play up v.[2] [1900s] (*Aus.*) to bet, to gamble (at a horserace).

play up a drip v. [1900s] (*Aus.*) to buy a round of drinks.

play up old gooseberry with v. [mid-19C] to deal with in a peremptory manner, to shut (someone) up. [OLD GOOSEBERRY n. (2)]

play upon the prick v. [mid-16C] (*UK Und.*) to mark cards with pinpricks. [play on SE]

play up to v. [early 19C+] to indulge, to humour. [SE *play*, to act]

play-White n. [1950s+] (*S.Afr.*) one who attempts to 'pass' as White.

play whupass v. [2000s] (*US*) to play or fight roughly. [WHIP SOMEONE'S ASS v. (1)]

play with oneself v. [late 19C+] to masturbate (cf. LARK v.).

play with one's stuff out the window v. [1900s–40s] (*US Black*) to act with caution, e.g. when playing cards; esp. to act carefully when conducting a love affair. [? image of one who, planning an escape, has already placed their possessions outside the house]

play yankee with v. *see* YANKEE v.

plazazus n. *see* BEJAZUS, THE n.

plazy adj. *see* PLAUSY adj.

plazzy adj. [1960s+] **1** plastic. **2** in fig. use, false, second-rate. [abbr. SE *plastic*]

plea at the bar n. [mid-19C] (*US*) a drink in a tavern.

plea-cop v. *see* COP A PLEA v.

pleader n. [1910s–20s] a person, a fellow, a 'bloke'. [? euph. for BLEEDER n.[4] (1)]

pleading adj. [1900s] a euph. for BLEEDING adj. (1).

plead the baby act v. [mid-19C+] (*US*) to attempt to mitigate unpleasant circumstances by pleading one's innocence or inexperience.

plead the fifth v. (*also* take the fifth) [1950s+] (*US*) to avoid committing oneself, to refuse to take an action or make a statement. [the Fifth Amendment (1791) to the US Constitution states that no person 'shall be compelled in any criminal case to be a witness against himself']

plea out v. [1980s+] (*US Und.*) to plead guilty in the hope of getting a lighter sentence.

pleasant adj. [mid-19C] drunk, tipsy (cf. ABOUT RIGHT phr.[1]). [euph.]

please v. [mid-16C–18C] to have sexual intercourse with; lit. to gratify sexually.

pleased as a dog with two cocks phr. (*also* pleased as a dog/pup with two tails) [1910s+] very pleased, delighted. [COCK n.[2] (1)/CHOPPER n.[1] (3)/SE *tail*]

please one's pisser v. [2000s] to masturbate. [PISSER n.[1] (2)]

pleaser n. [1960s] (*US campus*) an indiscriminately promiscuous young woman.

please the pope v. (*also* fax the pope) [1990s+] to masturbate (cf. DISOBEY THE POPE v.). [the Catholic rejection of contraception]

pleasure n. [late 17C; late 19C] an orgasm.

pleasure v. [early 18C; 19C] to have sexual intercourse with.

pleasure and pain n. [20C+] rain. [rhy. sl.]

pleasure boat n. (*also* pleasure conduit, …girth, …ground, …pit, …place) [late 16C–19C] the vagina (cf. ADAM'S OWN (ALTAR) n.).

pleasure garden padlock n. [17C–early 19C] a menstrual cloth or towel.

pleasure-lady n. [mid-17C] a prostitute (cf. BANKSIDE LADY n.).

pleasure pit n. *see* PLEASURE BOAT n.

pleasure-pivot n. [mid-18C] the penis.

pleasure place n. *see* PLEASURE BOAT n.

pleb n. (*also* plebbie, plebby, plebe) [19C+] a *pleb*ian, i.e. a member of the (unintelligent, unsophisticated) working classes; also as adj. [abbr.]

pledge n. [20C+] (*US*) a student who has promised to join or has been promised membership of a fraternity or sorority.

plenish v. [20C+] to furnish a house. [SE *replenish*; ult. Fr. *plenir*, to fill]

plenty adj. [1930s+] (*US*) excellent.

plenty adv. [mid-19C+] (*US*) abundantly, very much.

plenty more fish in the sea phr. *see* NOT THE ONLY FISH IN THE SEA phr.

plenty of guts, but no bowels phr. [late 18C–early 19C] a phr. used of one who is tough and ruthless but lacks compassion. [GUTS n.[2] (1) + SE *bowels*, 'pity, compassion, feeling, "heart"' (*OED*)]

pleuro n. (*also* pleura, ploorer) [late 19C–1910s] (*Aus.*) contagious bovine *pleuro*-pneumonia, a disease of cattle. [abbr.]

plex v. **1** [1960s+] (*US prison*) to get psychologically prepared to start a (gang) fight. **2** [1990s+] (*US*) to show disrespect, to slander. **3** [2000s] (*US prison*) to be anxious or nervous. [ety. unknown; (1) ? SE *flex*; (3) ? SE *perplex*]

plier n. (*also* plyer) **1** [late 17C–early 18C] a prostitute (cf. ASS PEDDLER n.). **2** [late 17C–early 19C] (*UK Und.*) a crutch. **3** [late 18C–early 19C] a tradesman. **4** [mid–late 19C] a hand. [SE *ply one's way*; *ply one's trade*]

pliers n. [1950s] (*W.I.*) a small, finger-shaped dumpling. [because of its toughness, it would need a pair of pliers to break it]

pling v. [1910s–50s] (*US tramp*) to beg. [? abbr. SE *pleading*]

plinger n. [1910s–50s] (*US Und.*) a street beggar. [PLING v.]

plink n. [1910s+] (*Aus.*) cheap or second-rate wine. [PLONK n.[1] + PINK-EYE n.[1] (1)]

plink v. *see* PLANK v. (1).

plinker n. [1980s+] (*US*) **1** an airgun. **2** a cheap, low-calibre weapon. **3** one who owns and uses such weapons. [the 'plinking' noise it makes]

plinkity plonk n. (*also* plink plonk) [1910s+] (*Aus.*) white wine; cheap or second-rate wine (cf. PLONK n.[1]). [rhy. sl. = *vin blanc*, white wine; orig. WW1 milit.]

plizzow v. [2000s] (*US Black*) of a man, to perform sexual intercourse in an aggressive manner. [PLOUGH v.¹ (1) + -IZ- ifx]

ploba *n. see* PLABA n.

plocker *n.* (*also* **plugher**) [20C+] (*Ulster*) **1** a clearing of the throat. **2** a smoky atmosphere. [Irish *plúch*, to choke; *plúchadh*, asthma]

plod *n.*¹ (*Aus.*) **1** [1920s+] a story, a piece of information. **2** [1940s+] a work sheet giving information about the ground worked by a miner; thus *pitch the plod*, for miners to gossip as they come off and on shift. **3** [1940s+] a specific piece of ground worked by a miner. [Cornish dial. *plod*, a short story, a lying tale; (3) is what is accounted for in (2)]

plod *n.*² (*also* **Mr Plod**) [1970s+] a policeman. [children's story character *Mr Plod*, created by Enid Blyton (1897–1968) in her *Noddy* books; ult. SE *plod*, to walk slowly]

ploll-cat *n.* [17C] a prostitute. [corruption of SE *pole-cat*, poss. a mis-sp.]

plongkas *n.* (*also* **pluncas**) [1940s] (*W.I.*) **1** a heavy cake or dumpling. **2** a heavy shoe. [echoic *plonk*, the noise it makes hitting a plate or the floor]

plonk *n.*¹ [1910s+] cheap or second-rate wine; thus (*Aus.*) *plonk bar*, a wine bar; *plonk-dot*, a heavy drinker of wine; *plonk-up*, a cheap wine party; *plonked-up*, drunk; *on the plonk*, to get drunk (cf. PLINKITY PLONK n.). [? mispron. of Fr. *vin blanc*, white wine, picked up by Anglophone soldiers during WW1; the brandname 'Plonque' was merchandised in the early 1970s]

plonk *n.*² *see* PLONKER n. (3).

plonk *n.*³ *see* PLONKO n.

plonk *v.* **1** [1930s+] to put down (cf. PLUNK (DOWN) v.). **2** [1940s+] to have sexual intercourse (cf. BANG v.¹).

plonk! *excl.* (*also* **plonkety-plonk!**) [1920s+] echoic of the sound of an object hitting the ground.

plonker *n.* **1** [mid-19C+] anything large or substantial. **2** [1910s+] the penis. **3** [1980s+] (*also* **plonk**) a general term of abuse (cf. BELL END n.). [fig. use of SE *plonk*, to hit or strike with a plonking noise; (2) note PLONK v. (2); (3) widely popularized by the 1980s BBC TV series *Only Fools and Horses*]

plonkie *n.* [1980s+] a wine-drinking alcoholic. [PLONK n.¹]

plonko *n.* (*also* **plonk**) [1960s+] (*Aus.*) one who is addicted to cheap wine, an alcoholic. [PLONK n.¹ + -O sfx (4)]

plonk oneself down *v.* [1940s+] to sit down, often as an invitation, e.g. *please plonk yourself down*, please sit down. [PLONK v. (1)]

plook *n. see* PLUKE n.

ploorer *n. see* PLEURO n.

plootered *adj.* [1920s+] (*Scot.*) drunk. [Scot. *plouter*, to wade through water or mud]

plop *v.* [1920s] (*US*) to hit.

plossey *adj. see* PLAUSY adj.

plot *n.* [1970s+] (*UK Und.*) the place where street-sellers or confidence tricksters operate, e.g. the street, an alley or a doorway.

plot up *v.*¹ [1960s+] (*UK Und.*) **1** of a gang or group, to seek out and establish territory, e.g. in a soccer stadium, club, crowded place etc. **2** of an individual or group, to make a base. [SE *plot* (of land)]

plot up *v.*² (*also* **plot on**) [1970s+] (*UK Und.*) to make a plan, e.g. for an escape from prison, a robbery. [SE *plot*, to plan, to scheme]

plotz *v.* [1920s+] (*orig. US*) **1** to lose emotional control. **2** to collapse physically. [Yid. *plotzen*/Ger. *platzen*, burst, split]

plotzed *adj.* [1990s+] drunk. [PLOTZ v.]

plough *n.* [late 16C–18C] the penis. [PLOUGH v.¹ (1)]

plough *v.*¹ (*also* **plow**) **1** [mid-16C+] to have sexual intercourse. **2** [1940s+] to beat up.

plough *v.*² [mid–late 19C] to reject a candidate as not reaching the pass standard in an examination. [SE *plough under*]

ploughed *adj.* (*also* **plowed**) [mid-19C; 1960s+] drunk (cf. ANNIHILATED adj.). [? PLOUGH v.²]

plough into *v.* [1900s–20s] to begin eating enthusiastically.

ploughshare *n.* [mid–late 19C] the penis. [PLOUGH v.¹ (1)]

plough the back forty *v.* (*also* **plow the back forty**) [1950s+] (*US*) **1** to waste time. **2** to have sexual intercourse. [SE *plough*/PLOUGH v.¹ (1) + BACK FORTY n.]

plough the deep *v.* (*also* **plow the deep**) [late 18C+] to (go to) sleep; also as a euph. for to have sexual intercourse. [fig. use of SE; ? 20C+ reinforced by rhy. sl.; note PLOUGH v.¹ (1)]

plouter *v. see* PLOWTER v.

plover *n.* [17C] **1** a victim, a dupe. **2** a promiscuous woman, a prostitute (cf. ALLEY CAT n.). [fig. uses of the bird's name]

plow *v. see also under* PLOUGH and its combs.

plowhandle *n.* [1930s] (*US*) a peasant, a farmer. [metonymy]

plow jockey *n.* (*also* **plow-jogger**) [mid-19C+] (*US*) a farmer, a rustic (cf. ACORN-CRACKER n.). [SAmE *plow* = SE *plough* + JOCKEY n.³ (2)]

plowter *v.* (*also* **plouter**) [19C] to have sexual intercourse. [northern dial. *plowter*, to splash about in mire or water]

p.l.u. *n.* [1980s+] (*UK society*) people like *us*. [abbr.]

pluck *n.*¹ **1** [late 18C–1900s] courage. **2** [late 19C] (*US*) an order of beef stew. [SE *pluck*, the intestines of an animal that are plucked out during its cleaning. The term began as early boxing jargon, then moved into sl. Despite its apparent neutrality, the term was not used by women before the 1860s; 20C+ use is SE]

pluck *n.*² [1950s] (*Aus.*) a stone. [? one *plucks* it from the ground]

pluck *n.*³ [1960s+] (*US Black*) wine, esp. cheap wine. [? SE *pluck*, to harvest grapes]

pluck *n.*⁴ [1960s+] (*US Black*) an attractive woman. [she is 'plucked' from the bunch; or ? ref. to fig. use of SE *pluck*, offal, i.e. the vagina]

pluck *v.* **1** [mid-17C–mid-18C; 1960s+] to have sexual intercourse. **2** [late 17C+] to rob. **3** [mid-19C+] (*US campus*) to find lacking, deficient. **4** [20C+] (*US*) to arrest. **5** [1900s] (*US campus*) to expel. **6** [1900s] (*US campus*) to reprimand. **7** [1940s] (*US*) to cashier or retire a military officer. **8** [1980s+] (*US Black*) to choose one's woman.

pluck a pigeon *v.* **1** [late 18C+] to fleece a victim. **2** [1910s+] in weak use, to conclude a business deal. [PIGEON n.¹ (1) + pun]

pluck a rose *v.* (*also* **pull a rose**) **1** [17C–early 19C] to visit the lavatory (cf. DO ONE'S BUSINESS v.). **2** [mid-17C] to have sexual intercourse (cf. ARRIVE AT THE END OF THE SENTIMENTAL JOURNEY v.). [euph.]

pluck'd 'un *n.* [mid-19C–1920s] a brave person, a 'stout fellow'; usu. with preceding adj., such as *rare, bad, good, real, hard* etc. [PLUCKED adj.¹]

plucked *adj.*¹ [mid-19C–1900s] brave; courageous. [PLUCK n.¹ (1)]

plucked *adj.*² [1960s+] (*US Black*) enjoying a feeling of mental and physical contentment following sexual intercourse. [PLUCK v. (1) or euph. for FUCK v.¹]

plucker *n.* [early–mid-19C] (*US*) a robber; a confidence trickster. [PLUCK v. (2)]

pluckey *adj. see* PLUCKY adj.¹.

pluck it cool *v. see* PLAY IT COOL v.

pluck Sir Onion *v.* [late 17C–early 18C] to knock on the tavern door. [? the round 'onion-shape' of a tavern knocker]

pluck that! *excl.* [1990s+] (*US campus*) an excl. of rejection. [euph. for FUCK THAT! excl.]

pluck up *v.* [early 19C] to be brave, also as imper. [PLUCK n.¹ (1)]

pluck-up fair *n.* [late 16C–mid-17C] 'a general scramble for booty or spoil' (*OED*). [SE *pluck up*, to gather, to grab]

pluck up stakes *v. see* PULL UP v.¹.

plucky *adj.*¹ (*also* **pluckey**) [mid-19C+] brave, courageous; thus adv. *pluckily*; n. *pluckiness*. [PLUCK n.¹ (1)]

plucky *adj.*² [late 19C–1900s] a negative intensifier; usu. in phr. *a plucky lot...*

plug *n.*¹ [late 18C–1900s] a blow, a punch.

plug *n.*[2] [early 19C] **1** a draught of beer. **2** wine, esp. cheap wine. [? play on SE *plug*, i.e. it 'fills a gap']

plug *n.*[3] [mid–late 19C] a translation of a text, classical or otherwise, for the illegitimate use of students (cf. ANIMAL *n.*[3]). [? it 'plugs up' the gaps in one's knowledge]

plug *n.*[4] [mid-19C–1920s] a top hat. [abbr. PLUG HAT *n.* (1)]

plug *n.*[5] **1** [mid-19C–1940s] (*US*) an incompetent or undistinguished person. **2** [mid-19C+] (*US*) a worn-out old horse. **3** [mid-19C+] (*US*) a damaged or malfunctioning object. **4** [mid-19C+] (*US*) a fellow, a person, a chap. **5** [late 19C] (*Aus./N.Z.*) a sturdy horse, standing about 15 hands high, that does the work required. **6** [1900s] (*Can.*) an unpleasant person. **7** [1930s] a worn-out racing greyhound. [Du. *plug*, a worn-out horse; (1) and all other defs. f. (2)]

plug *n.*[6] [late 19C] (*US*) **1** a silver dollar. **2** a counterfeit coin. [ext. use of SE *plug*, a small piece of solid material used to stop up a hole]

plug *n.*[7] [20C+] (*orig. US*) **1** an advertisement, a puff, esp. when filtered through a TV or radio programme. **2** a self-aggrandizing or promoting statement. [PLUG *v.*[5]]

plug *n.*[8] [1900s] (*US campus*) a hard-working student. [PLUG *v.*[2]]

plug *n.*[9] [2000s] (*US Black*) a woman with whom one is having an affair (in addition to one's primary relationship). [? PLUG *v.*[1] (1) or SE *plug a hole* (in one's life)]

plug *v.*[1] **1** [late 18C+] to have sexual intercourse (cf. BANG *v.*[1]). **2** [mid-19C+] to strike, either with the fist or with a missile, usu. a bullet. **3** [1920s] (*US Black*) to damage oneself. **4** [1940s+] (*gay*) to perform anal intercourse (cf. ASK FOR THE RING *v.*). **5** [2000s] (*drugs*) to hide sealed packets of illegal drugs in the rectum.

plug *v.*[2] (*also plug along/at/away/on*) [mid-19C+] to persist, to struggle hard against whatever odds.

plug *v.*[3] [late 19C] (*US*) to experience problems, to get into trouble. [SAmE *plug*, to hinder another person's plans]

plug *v.*[4] [late 19C] (*US*) to wager, to lay a bet.

plug *v.*[5] [late 19C+] to advertise, to promote something, esp. when filtered through a TV or radio programme.

plug *adv.* [1900s] (*Aus.*) directly. [var. on PLUM *adv.*]

plug along/at/away *v. see* PLUG *v.*[2].

plug for *v.* [20C+] to act in support of, to make favourable statements about. [PLUG *v.*[5]]

plugged in *adj.* [1960s+] **1** abreast of the times, fashionable. **2** involved. [electrical imagery]

plugger *n.*[1] [mid-19C+] a person who shoots, a killer. [PLUG *v.*[1] (2)]

plugger *n.*[2] [20C+] (*US/Aus.*) one who does not give up; a hard worker. [PLUG *v.*[2]]

plugger *n.*[3] [1900s] (*US*) a promoter. [PLUG *v.*[5]]

plugging *n.* [late 19C–1920s] persistence; effort. [PLUG *v.*[2]]

plug hat *n.* **1** [mid–19C–1950s] a top hat, a silk hat. **2** [1940s] (*Aus.*) a bowler hat. [the head supposedly fits the hat like a plug]

plugher *n. see* PLOCKER *n.*

plug in both ways *v.* [1970s+] of a man, to be bisexual. [electrical imagery]

plug in the neon *v.* [1970s] (*US gay*) to inhale amyl nitrite at the moment of orgasm. [the drug 'brightens up' one's senses]

plug money *n.* [1940s] an illicit payment for promoting a record or song. [PLUG *v.*[5]]

plugola *n.* [1950s+] (*orig. US*) an illicit payment or favour given for mentioning a commercial product in a non-commercial context. [PLUG *v.*[5] + -OLA sfx]

plug on *v. see* PLUG *v.*[2].

plug-tail *n.* [late 18C–mid-19C] the penis (cf. BUTT-PLUNGER *n.*). [SE *plug* + TAIL *n.*[2] (3)]

plug the mug *v.* [1940s] (*US Black*) to be quiet, to stop talking. [SE *plug* + MUG *n.*[1] (4)]

plug-ugly *n.* [mid-19C+] (*orig. US*) **1** (*also pug-ugly*) a thug, a violent person. **2** a professional boxer. **3** an extremely unattractive person. [proper name *Plug-Uglies*, a New York (and Baltimore)

street gang of the period. The origin of the name is debatable. One suggestion is that they were named after the large PLUG HAT *n.* (1), stuffed with paper, that each member wore for protection from the clubs of such opponents as the Dead Rabbits or the Bowery Boys. Alternatively f. UGLY PLUG *n.*, or, as a correspondent of *The Times* (4 November 1876), writing of the Baltimore variety, suggested, 'it was derived from a short spike fastened in the toe of their boots, with which they kicked their opponents in a dense crowd, or, as they elegantly expressed it, "plugged them ugly"', i.e. PLUG *v.*[1] (2)]

plug-ugly *adj.* [20C+] (*orig. US*) extremely unattractive. [PLUG-UGLY *n.* (3)]

plug up *v.* [2000s] to hide something.

pluke *n.* (*also* **plook**) [1960s+] **1** a spot, a pimple, a boil. **2** a general term of abuse. [Scot. dial. *plook*, *pluke*, a pimple, a spot; (2) is fig. use of (1)]

plukey-faced *adj.* [1990s+] a general term of abuse, lit. 'spotty, acne-faced'. [PLUKE *n.*]

plum *n.*[1] (*also* **plumb**) **1** [late 17C–19C] a fortune of £100,000, usu. as a legacy or as the possession of an heiress. **2** [mid-19C] a rich man. **3** [mid-19C] a member of the upper classes. **4** [late 19C–1950s] a fortune or something that will yield one. **5** [late 19C–1950s] a political office that is lucrative, esp. when it has been obtained by bribery or influence of some kind. [SE *plumb*, a lump of lead; (2) note Egan, *Book of Sports* (1832) def. '*City Slang.* — A man worth 100,000']

plum *n.*[2] (*Aus.*) **1** [late 19C] a good horse. **2** [1900s] an attractive (young) woman. [SE *plum*, excellent]

plum *n.*[3] [1990s+] a repressive puritan. [? var. PRUNE *n.*[2] (1)]

plum *adv.* (*also* **plumb, plump**) [17C+] a general intensifier, completely, entirely, absolutely, quite. [SE *plum-ripe*; primarily US since mid-19C, esp. in such clichés as *plumb loco*, utterly crazy]

plumb *n. see* PLUM *n.*[1].

plumb *v.*[1] [mid-19C–1900s] to fool, to deceive. [? SE *plumb someone's depths* + prior gambling jargon]

plumb *v.*[2] [1920s+] to have sexual intercourse.

plumb *adv. see* PLUM *adv.*

plumb a track *v.* [mid–late 19C] (*US*) to trace or follow a road or path. [SE *plumb*, to sound out]

plumber *n.*[1] [1950s] (*US Und.*) a hired killer. [note the political 'plumbers' of the 1972–4 US Watergate Scandal, similarly deputed to 'plug leaks']

plumber *n.*[2] [1970s+] (*US Black*) a man with a frequent and varied sex life. [PLUMBING *n.* (1)/PLUMB *v.*[2]]

plumber *v.* [1930s] (*US*) to blunder, to make a mistake. [? negative stereotype of the occupation]

plumbing *n.* **1** [1920s+] (*orig. US*) the excretory tract, the urinary system; the genitals. **2** [1930s–50s] (*US*) a trumpet, trombone or similar wind instrument. **3** [1950s] fillings in the teeth.

plum-in-the-mouth *adj. see* HAVE A PLUM IN THE MOUTH *v.*

plum jam *n.* [1980s+] (*N.Z.*) a lamb. [rhy. sl.]

plummy *adj.* **1** [late 18C–19C] good, excellent. **2** [mid-19C–1900s] round, sleek, fat, jolly. **3** [late 19C+] (*also* **plummy-voiced**) of a voice, affected or upper-class. **4** [1920s–30s] (*Scot.*) dull. [SE *plum*; (3) HAVE A PLUM IN THE MOUTH *v.*]

plummy *adv.* [19C] **1** nicely, satisfactorily, pleasantly. **2** excellently. [PLUMMY *adj.* (1)]

plump *n.* [mid-18C–early 19C] a blow; thus *plump in the breadbasket*, a blow to the stomach; *plump in the peepers*, a blow to the eyes.

plump *v.* [late 18C–1900s] to hit, to shoot. [PLUMP *n.*]

plump *adv. see* PLUM *adv.*

plump currant *n.* [late 18C–early 19C] a description of someone in good health; usu. in negative, e.g. *Charles is not the plump currant*.

plumper *n.*[1] [mid-17C–mid-18C] a prostitute. [? PLUMP *v.*/ SE *plump*]

plumper n.[2] **1** [late 18C] a (large) female breast. **2** [late 18C–19C] a heavy blow; also fig. use. **3** [early–mid-19C] a major lie. **4** [late 19C] an unusually large version of its type. [lit. and fig. uses of PLUMP n.]

plumper n.[3] **1** [late 18C–1910s] a single vote at an election. **2** [late 19C+] a heavy bet. [SE *plump for*, to commit whole-heartedly]

plumpies n. [1990s+] large female breasts. [SE *plump*/PLUMPER n.[2] (1)]

plump in the pocket adj. [late 17C–early 19C] satisfactorily well-off.

plump-pate n. [19C] a fool (cf. CLODPATE n.). [var. on FAT-HEAD n.]

plump someone up to v. [1910s–20s] to tell someone something secretly. [they are 'plumped up' with the information]

plum pud adj. [20C+] (*Aus.*) good. [rhy. sl.]

plum-pudding (dog) n. [mid-19C] a variety of the dog Dalmatian, with notable dark spots. [the spots resemble the plums]

plumpy n. [2000s] (*US*) the (erect) penis. [var. FAT n.[4]]

plums n. [17C; 20C+] the testicles; thus *long plum*, the penis (cf. ACORNS n.). [resemblance]

plum tree n.[1] **1** [mid-16C–17C] the vagina; thus *plum tree shaker*, the penis (cf. APPLE n.[6]; BEAUTY SPOT n.). **2** [early 17C] the penis (cf. BANANA n.[2]). [? PLUMS n.]

plum tree n.[2] [20C+] (*US*) the spoils of political office; thus *shake the plum tree*, to extract graft from one's office. [one shakes the fig. 'tree' to gain the PLUM n.[1] (5)]

pluncas n. see PLONGKAS n.

plunge n.[1] (*also* **plunger**) [late 19C–1920s] a (heavy) bet. [PLUNGE v.[1] (1)]

plunge n.[2] (*US tramp*) **1** [1910s] the act of street begging, esp. with a specific sum in mind. **2** [1920s] money obtained by begging.

plunge n.[3] **1** [1950s] (*US drugs*) a narcotics injection. **2** [1990s+] an act of sexual intercourse.

plunge v.[1] **1** [mid-19C+] to spend money or bet recklessly, to speculate heavily, to run into debt. **2** [2000s] to perform anything intensely.

plunge v.[2] [1990s+] **1** to kill, to murder. **2** to stab. [the plunging of a knife]

plunger n.[1] **1** [late 19C+] a reckless gambler; also used fig. in non-gambling use. **2** [1990s+] (*US campus*) a spendthrift. [PLUNGE v.[1] (1); they 'plunge' deep into the game; but note milit. jargon *plunger*, a cavalryman; (1) post-WW2 use is historical]

plunger n.[2] **1** [1930s+] the penis; thus *plunger-pumping*, to have sex. **2** [1970s+] (*US gay*) an energetic, speedy copulator.

plunger n.[3] [1940s] (*US Black/Harlem*) a bathtub.

plunger n.[4] [1950s] (*US drugs*) a hypodermic syringe.

plunger n.[5] see PLUNGE n.[1].

plunk n. **1** [mid-18C–mid-19C] a large sum, a fortune. **2** [early 19C–1930s] (*US*) (*also* **plunker**) a dollar; also in pl., money in general. **3** [1900s–10s] a blow, a hit. [ety. unknown; ? PLUNK (DOWN) v. (2) this is much earlier]

plunk v.[1] [late 19C+] (*orig. Aus.*) to hit someone; also in fig. use. [echoic of the sound of a blow]

plunk v.[2] [20C+] (*Ulster*) to fail an examination.

plunk v.[3] see PLUNK (DOWN) v.

plunk adv. [late 19C] (*US*) directly. [fig. use PLUNK v.[1]]

plunk a baby v. [1930s+] (*Aus./N.Z.*) to have a baby; thus *get plunked*, to be pregnant. [the Royal New Zealand *Plunket* Society, founded 1907, the N.Z. version of the UK Royal Society for the Protection of Women and Children; ult. Lady *Plunket*, wife of the then governor of N.Z.]

plunk (down) v. [late 19C+] (*orig. US*) **1** to wager. **2** to lay money down forcibly (cf. PLONK v.). **3** to sit down, to put down. [money is 'plunked' on the table]

plunker n. see PLUNK n. (2).

plunk for v. [1940s] (*US*) to opt for, to give one's support to. [fig. use of PLUNK (DOWN) v. (1)]

plurry adj. [late 19C+] (*Aus./N.Z.*) a synon. for BLOODY adj.[1]. [Maori mispron.; but note McGill, *Dict. of Kiwi Slang* (1988): 'Partridge says it is from Aboriginal's natural use of the word, OEDS says NZA slang, Turner thinks it is a convention of journalists rather than Maori, in support of which was the slanguage of the character Hori in the bestselling book *The Half-Gallon Jar*']

plus adj. [1920s+] used with a n. to indicate a better-than-average version.

plush n. [19C] female pubic hair. [the texture; note Ital. *peluccio*, *peluzzo*, a little hair, soft down, fine hair]

plush adj. (*also* **plushy**) [20C+] luxurious, expensive, stylish, thus also snobbish. [SE *plush*, a type of soft material]

plushery n. [20C+] (*orig. US*) a luxurious hotel, expensive restaurant, smart nightclub etc. [PLUSH adj.]

plush horse n. [1910s–20s] (*US*) a socially conservative, rigid person; usu. upper-class and overdressed.

plush-horse adj. [1920s] (*US*) wealthy, privileged. [PLUSH HORSE n.]

plushite n. [1900s] a servant. [James Yellowplush, the fictional servant of Thackeray's *Yellowplush Papers*]

plushy adj. see PLUSH adj.

plute n. (*also* **plut**) [20C+] (*US/Aus.*) the very rich, the social elite; thus *plutish*, elitist, *pluty*, wealthy and consciously elitist. [abbr. SE *plutocrat*]

plyer n. see PLIER n.

Plymouth Argyll n. [20C+] a file. [rhy. sl.; name of a soccer team]

Plymouth blade n. (*also* **Plymouth cloak**) [17C] a cudgel. [the violence of the naval town]

ply the toby v. see TOBY v. (1).

p.m. n. (*also* **peeyem**) [mid-19C+] the afternoon. [SE *p.m.*, *post meridiem*, used in chronological notation]

p-maker n. [mid-19C–1900s] the vagina. [abbr. PISS n. (1)-*maker*]

p.m.s. v. [1990s+] (*US campus*) of a woman, to feel irritable, anxious. [abbr. pre-menstrual syndrome, or *putting up with men's shit*]

p.m.s. monster n. [1980s+] (*US campus*) a menstruating woman. [abbr. pre-menstrual syndrome + MONSTER sfx]

p-nut n. [2000s] (*US Black*) the outline of the male genitals visible through very tight trousers. [PRICK n. (2)]

p.o. n. **1** [late 19C+] a postal order. **2** [1910s+] (*US*) a post office. **3** [1950s+] (*US*) a parole officer. [abbr.]

p.o. adj. see P.O.'ED adj.

p.o. v.[1] [1910s] (*Aus.*) to go away; also as imper. [abbr. PISS OFF v. (1)]

p.o. v.[2] [1940s+] (*US*) to annoy. [PISS OFF v. (2)]

po n. (*also* **poe**) **1** [late 19C+] a chamberpot; a commode. **2** [1920s+] the lavatory. [abbr. SE *chamberpot* + Fr. pron. of *pot de chambre*]

poach v. see POOCH v.

poached egg n. [1930s–40s] (*Aus.*) a yellow 'sleeping policeman' placed in the centre of intersections.

po'chaise n. (*also* **po'chay**, **pochay**, **post-chay/-shay**) [18C–19C] a travelling carriage seating 2 or 4 people, with the coachman or postilion riding one of the horses. [abbr. SE *post-chaise*]

pocket billiards n. see POCKET POOL n.

pocket-book n. **1** [1950s] (*W.I.*) a large, flat, fried dumpling. **2** [1970s] (*US Black*) the vagina (cf. BANK n.[1]). [(1) resemblance; (2) var. PURSE n. (1)]

pocketful of rocks n. see ROCKS n.[1] (1).

pocket pistol n. (*also* **pistol**) [mid-18C–1900s] a dram flask, a hip-flask. [it gives one a 'shot in the arm']

pocket pool *n.* (*also* **pocket billiards, ...pinball**) [1940s+] playing with one's genitals through a trouser pocket; usu. as PLAY POCKET POOL *v.*

pocket rocket *n.*[1] [1980s+] (*drugs*) marijuana (cf. BOMB n.[4]). [it gets one HIGH adj.[1] (2)]

pocket rocket *n.*[2] [1990s+] (*UK juv.*) the erect penis (cf. AX n.[2]).

pocket roll *n.* [1960s+] (*US Black*) a roll of paper money kept in the pocket (cf. CALIFORNIA BANKROLL n.). [ROLL n.[2]]

pocket-thunder *n.* [19C] the breaking of wind.

pock-pudding *n.* (*also* **poke-pudding, pock-pud**) [early 18C–19C] (*Scot.*) an Englishman. [Scot. *poke-pudding*, a bag-pudding, thus a glutton]

pocky *adj.* (*also* **pockey**) [16C–mid-19C] a general term of abuse, lit. 'syphilitic'. [SE *pocky*, covered in syphilitic sores]

p.o.d. *adj.* [1990s+] (*US Black/drugs*) extremely intoxicated by a given drug, usu. marijuana. [*passed overdose*]

pod *n.*[1] [late 19C–1910s] a large stomach. [orig. dial.]

pod *n.*[2] [1940s+] (*US drugs*) marijuana. [POT n.[10]]

p.o.'d *adj. see* P.O.'ED *adj.*

poddy *n.* [late 19C–1950s] (*Aus.*) a bottle of alcohol. [? dial. *poddinger*, an earthenware pot, orig. used for porridge]

poddy *adj.*[1] [mid-19C–1900s] corpulent, obese. [POD n.[1]]

poddy *adj.*[2] [1900s–10s] drunk. [PODDY n.]

poddy calf *n.* [20C+] (*Aus.*) half-a-crown, 2s 6d (12½p). [rhy. sl.]

poddy dodger *n.* [1910s–50s] (*Aus.*) one who steals unbranded cattle, a cattle rustler. [SAusE *poddy*, an unbranded calf + *dodge*, to steal (cattle)]

podge *n.* [late 19C+] **1** a short, fat person, esp. a chubby child. **2** a short, stout, thick-set animal. **3** excess weight, fat. [dial. *pudge*, anything or anyone short and thick; also used as a nickname]

podger *n.* **1** [early–mid-19C] a hard blow. **2** [late 19C] (*Irish*) a cudgel. [dial. *podge*, to hit]

podgy *adj.* [mid-19C] drunk (cf. AFFLICTED adj.). [? Ital. *poco acqua*, a little water; or ? Rom. *pogado*, crooked, thus the way one walks; or ? POGY adj.]

podna/podner *n. see* PARD n.

pod people *n.* [1980s+] stupid or robotic people; fundamentalist Christians; thus *podspeak*, meaningless talk. [film *Invasion of the Body-Snatchers* (1956, 1978), in which aliens spawn in pods]

podunk *n.* [mid-19C+] (*US*) a generic term for a small town. [Algonquin *podunk*, a marshy meadow, used esp. by a small tribe of Indians formerly inhabiting an area around the Podunk river in Hartford County, Connecticut. When the word was used (on the grounds of its amusing sound) in a series of letters featuring the supposed small town of Podunk, publ. in the US in 1846, it gained a greater currency and took on the meaning it has retained ever since. A secondary ety. notes the 'po-dunk' croak of a bullfrog, *podunker* in dial.; thus such towns are out where the bullfrogs can croak undisturbed]

podunk *adj.* [1960s+] (*US campus*) worthless, insignificant; lost. [PODUNK n.]

poe *n. see* PO n.

p.o.'ed *adj.* (*also* **p.o., p.o.'d**) [1940s+] (*orig. US*) very annoyed, angry. [abbr. PISSED OFF adj.]

poegaai *adj.* (*also* **poeg-eyed**) [1940s+] (*S.Afr.*) **1** drunk (cf. ADDLED adj.). **2** exhausted. [Du. *pooien*, to tipple + sfx *-eyed*]

poep *n.* [1960s+] (*S.Afr.*) **1** an act of breaking wind. **2** faeces. **3** a fool. [Afk. *poep*, a FART n. (1)]

poep *adj.* [1960s+] (*S.Afr.*) bad, unpleasant. [POEP n.]

poephol *n.* [1940s+] (*S.Afr.*) a general term of abuse, fool, idiot. [POEP n. (2), lit. SHITHOLE n.]

poep-scared *adj.* [1960s+] (*S.Afr.*) terrified, lit. 'shit-scared'. [POEP n. (2); note Afk. *poepbang*, dead scared]

poes *n.* [1960s+] (*S.Afr.*) **1** the vagina. **2** a general term of abuse (cf. BAMBA n.[1]). [synon. Afk. sl.]

poet's day *n.* [1970s+] Friday. [abbr. *piss off early, tomorrow's Saturday*]

po-faced *adj.* [1930s+] arrogant, stand-offish, humourless. [? PO n. (1) or SE *poh*! + sfx *-faced*]

p. off! *excl.* [1960s+] go away! [abbr. PISS OFF! excl.]

poge *see under* POGUE.

pogee *n.* [1970s] (*US/P.R.*) a passive male homosexual. [POGUE n.[3] (2)]

poge-hunter *n.* [late 19C–1900s] a purse-snatcher or pickpocket who specializes in taking purses. [POGUE n.[2]]

poger *n.* (*also* **pogey**) [1950s–70s] (*orig. US tramp*) an active male homosexual. [? POKE v. (1)]

pogey *n.* (*also* **pogie, poggie**) **1** [late 19C–1960s] (*US Und.*) (*also* **pogy**) a workhouse; a relief centre. **2** [1920s–70s] a prison hospital. **3** [1930s] a prison cell. **4** [1930s–60s] a house of correction, a prison. [? POKE n.[2] (2), i.e. something in which one is 'put away'; ? dial. *poghole*, a boggy hole or Fr. *poche*, a pocket]

pogey *adj.* [20C+] (*Ling. Fr./Polari*) small. [Ital. *poco*, little]

pogey bait *n. see* POGY BAIT n.

poggie *n. see* POGEY n.

poggle *n.* (*also* **puggle, puggly**) [late 19C–1930s] a fool, an eccentric. [Hind. *pagal*, a madman]

poggled *adj.* (*also* **poggle, puggle(d)**) [20C+] mad, drunk, crazy; thus *poggle-khana*, a picnic, lit. a 'fool's dinner' (cf. ADDLED adj.). [POGGLE n.]

poggler *n.*[1] [1970s] **1** a pocket. **2** a wallet or purse. [? POGUE n.[2]]

poggler *n.*[2] [1970s+] a male homosexual. [POGUE n.[3] (2)]

poggy *adj. see* POGY adj.

pogie *n. see* POGEY n.

pogo *v.* [1970s+] to perform a rough form of dance, orig. by fans of PUNK n.[4] rock and involving much jumping up and down, flailing of the arms etc. [SE *pogo* stick]

pogo stick *n.* [1960s+] (*Aus./US*) the penis (cf. ALMOND n.; BAT n.[7]). [rhy. sl. = PRICK n. (2)]

pogram *n.* [mid-19C] a dissenter. [proper name *Pogram*, a well-known dissenting preacher of the time]

pogue *n.*[1] **1** [early 18C] an act of copulation. **2** [mid-19C+] (*Irish*) a kiss. [POKE n.[1] (1)]

pogue *n.*[2] (*also* **poge**) [early 19C+] (*UK Und.*) a purse, a wallet, a pocket. [? POKE n.[2] (2) or 9C SE *pough*, a bag, a sack]

pogue *n.*[3] (*also* **poge**) **1** [1930s+] a young boy; in ext., an inexperienced person. **2** [1970s+] (*US gay*) the passive partner in anal intercourse. [Ital. *poco*, small; (2) note POGUE v.]

pogue *v.* [1940s–70s] to have anal intercourse, also in fig. use (cf. ASK FOR THE RING v.). [POKE v. (1); note POGUE n.[3] (2)]

pogue the hone *v.* [early 18C] (*Irish*) to copulate. [? POKE v. (1)]

pogy *see also under* POGEY and its combs.

pogy *adj.* (*also* **poggy**) [late 18C–19C] drunk (cf. AFFLICTED adj.). [? Rom. *pogado*, crooked]

pogy bait *n.* (*also* **pogey bait**) [1930s+] (*orig. US milit.*) snack foods, occas. cigarettes, money; underlying image of the use of such snacks as a lure by child molesters. [POGUE n.[3] (1)]

poh-poh *n. see* PO-PO n.

poindexter *n.* [1980s] (*US teen*) a derog. term for an intellectual, bookish person. [play on POINTY-HEAD n. (2)]

Point, the *n.*[1] **1** [early 19C+] (*US*) West Point, properly the United States Military Academy at West Point, New York. **2** [1930s] San Quentin prison (cf. ABBOTT'S PRIORY n.). [(1) abbr.; (2) ? misreading]

Point, the *n.*[2] [1990s+] (*US Black teen*) Hunter's Point, San Francisco. [abbr.]

point *n.*[1] [late 19C–1940s] the chin, the face, the nose.

point *n.*[2] **1** [1930s+] (*drugs*) a hypodermic syringe. **2** [1960s–70s] (*gay*) any form of writing implement.

point *n.*[3] [1940s+] (*US*) anyone standing guard or leading the way; thus *keep point*, to keep a lookout. [milit. jargon *point*, the man walking at the head of a patrol; ult. ranching jargon *point*, the front of a herd]

point v. (*Aus.*) **1** [mid-19C–1910s] to take unfair advantage of. **2** [1950s+] to waste time, to malinger. [SE *score points*]

point blank n. [1910s] (*milit.*) white wine. [play on Fr. *vin blanc*]

pointed-head n. *see* POINTY-HEAD n.

pointer n.[1] **1** [mid-18C–19C] the penis. **2** [1930s] (*W.I.*) a knife.

pointer n.[2] (*Aus./N.Z.*) **1** [mid–late 19C] a confidence trickster, a card-sharp. **2** [mid-19C+] an idler, a loafer, a malingerer. **3** [late 19C+] one who takes an unfair advantage, esp. by trickery; an informer. [POINT v. (1)]

pointer n.[3] [late 19C+] (*orig. US*) a hint, a suggestion.

pointers n. **1** [1930s] crooked dice. **2** [1950s] the female breasts (cf. BOBBER n.[2]).

pointhead n. *see* POINTY-HEAD n.

point percy at the porcelain v. [1960s+] to urinate; thus *point percy at the pavement*, to urinate on the street (cf. AIM ARCHIE AT THE ARMITAGE v.). [PERCY n.[2] + SE *porcelain*, i.e. the lavatory bowl]

point-shave v. [1990s+] (*US Black*) to lie.

point shot n. [1930s–50s] (*US drugs*) an injection using a makeshift 'needle' made of a pin and a medicine dropper. [SHOT n.[6] (2)]

point the bone v. [1940s+] (*Aus.*) to betray a friend and leave them in the lurch; thus *bone-pointer*, *bone-pointing*. [Aborigine practice of pointing a bone (the 'death bone') at one whose death is desired]

pointy-head n. (*also* pointed-head, pointhead) [1960s+] (*orig. US*) **1** a fool. **2** an intellectual. [both terms are derog. and suggest that an excess or an absence of brain lead to a 'pointed' head]

pointy-headed adj. (*also* pointy-head) [1960s+] (*orig. US*) intellectual, cultured. [POINTY-HEAD n. (2)]

poison n.[1] [mid-17C; 19C+] an ironic term for drink in general.

poison n.[2] **1** [mid-19C+] an unpleasant person, best to be avoided; also used semi-affectionately. **2** [1910s–30s] something that one should avoid, i.e. something suspicious. **3** [1930s–50s] (*US drugs*) a doctor who refuses to prescribe narcotics.

poison n.[3] **1** [1950s+] (*drugs*) heroin, esp. in its pure state (cf. CACA n.). **2** [2000s] fentanyl.

poison adj. [1960s+] (*S.Afr.*) excellent, admirable, first-rate. [on bad = good model]

poison dwarf n. [1970s+] a very unpleasant person.

poisoned adj. [17C+] pregnant. [the swelling that often follows actual poisoning; 20C+ use is US Black]

poisoner n. [1900s–40s] (*Aus./N.Z.*) a cook, esp. one serving a team of sheep shearers; thus *poison*, to cook.

poison joint n. [1930s–40s] (*US Und.*) a pharmacy; a drug store. [SE *poison* + JOINT n.[4] (3)]

poison oneself v. [late 19C] to take a drink.

poisonous adj. [late 19C+] very unpleasant.

poison-pate n. [late 17C–early 19C] a red-headed person; thus *poison-pated*, red-haired. [SE *red* being a symbolically 'dangerous' colour + *pate*]

poison people n. [1960s–70s] (*US Black*) heroin addicts, taken as a group. [POISON n.[3] (1)]

poison shop n. (*Aus.*) **1** [1910s+] a public house. **2** [1950s] a brothel (cf. BANGING-SHOP n.). [SE *poison*/POISON n.[1] + SE *shop*/SHOP n.[1] (1)/SHOP n.[1] (3)]

poitín n. *see* POTEEN n.

poke n.[1] **1** [18C; mid-19C+] sexual intercourse. **2** [late 18C+] a blow; thus [20C+] *take a poke at*, to attack, to aim a blow at; also used fig. **3** [late 19C+] a man or woman seen as a partner in sexual intercourse; often as *good poke*, *lousy poke*. **4** [1950s+] usu. of cars or motorcycles, speed, horsepower.

poke n.[2] **1** [mid-19C–1900s] stolen property. **2** [mid-19C+] (*US*) a wallet, a purse; thus *poke-getter/-lifter*, a pickpocket. **3** [mid-19C+] a bag of food handed out to a beggar. **4** [20C+] (*Irish*) a cone-

shaped bag, esp. for sweets or chips, or an ice-cream cornet; thus *poke man*, an ice-cream seller; *poke van*, an ice-cream van. **5** [1920s+] a roll of banknotes, money in general. **6** [1940s] (*US Und.*) a variety of confidence trick. [SE *poke*, a bag; ult. Fr. *poche*, pocket]

poke n.[3] [1900s–20s] (*US*) a shirt collar. [abbr. ? SE *poke bonnet*, which had a projecting rim]

poke n.[4] (*drugs*) **1** [1940s+] a puff on a marijuana cigarette. **2** [2000s] a puff on a crack cocaine pipe. [play on POKE n.[1] (2)/ HIT n.[3] (5)]

poke n.[5] *see* POKEY n.[2] (1).

poke v. **1** [17C+] of a man, occas. woman, to have hetero- or homosexual intercourse (cf. BANG v.[1]). **2** [20C+] (*orig. US*) to hit, to strike.

poke along v. (*also* poke about) [mid-19C+] to walk slowly.

poke a smipe v. [mid-19C] to smoke a pipe. [joc. reversal]

poke bogey (at) v. [late 19C–1900s] to trick, to fool, to deceive. [SE *poke* + *bogus*]

poke borak/borax v. *see* POKE (THE) BORAK v.

poked adj. [1970s+] (*N.Z.*) exhausted. [POKE v. (1); thus euph. for FUCKED adj.[1] (2)]

poked up adj. [late 19C] (*US*) embarrassed. [SE *poke*; the image is of a poked fire, in which the flames, i.e. blushes, roar up]

poke-hole n. (*also* poking-hole) [late 19C+] the vagina (cf. BLACK HOLE n.[1]). [POKE v. (1) + SE *hole*]

poke it v. *see* POKE (THE) BORAK v.

poke mullock v. [20C+] (*Aus.*) to mock, to tease, to deride. [SE *poke* + *mullock*, nonsense, rubbish (orig. mining refuse)]

poke-nose n. [1910s] an interfering person.

poke one's bib in v. *see* STICK ONE'S BIB IN v.

poke one's mouth off v. [1970s+] (*US Black*) to lose one's temper.

poke one's pussy v. [1960s+] of a woman, to masturbate (cf. APPLY LIP GLOSS v.; BEAT ONE'S HOG v.). [POKE v. (1) + PUSSY n. (2)]

poke-out n. **1** [late 19C–1930s] food given to a tramp who begs at the door. **2** [1950s–60s] (*US*) food cooked outdoors; a gathering to eat such food; a long trek that involves eating outdoors. [POKE n.[2] (3)]

poke-pudding n. *see* POCK-PUDDING n.

poker n.[1] **1** [late 17C–mid-19C] a sword. **2** [early 19C+] the penis. **3** [1980s] (*US Und.*) a single-barrelled shotgun. **4** [1990s+] (*US*) a knife.

poker n.[2] [mid-19C] (*UK Und.*) an idler, a casual labourer. [POKE ALONG v.]

poker-breaker n. [late 19C–1900s] one's wife. [POKER n.[1] (2)/SE *poker* + SE *breaker*]

poker talk n. [late 19C] **1** exaggerated talk, boasting, bragging. **2** a fireside chat. [CHANT THE POKER v.]

poke-shakings n. [20C+] (*Irish*) **1** the last pig in a litter. **2** the last child of a family. [POKE n.[2] (2) + SE *shaking*; the image of turning out one's wallet]

poke someone under the fifth rib v. [late 19C] **1** to hit, to punch. **2** to amaze, to dumbfound. [POKE v. (1)]

poke (the) borak v. (*also* borrak, poke borax, poke it) [late 19C+] (*Aus./N.Z.*) to make or poke fun. [SE *poke* + BORAK n.]

poke up one's pipes v. *see* PUT UP ONE'S PIPES v.

pokey n.[1] [20C+] (*orig. W.I. teen*) the vagina. [POKE v. (1)]

pokey n.[2] **1** [1910s+] (*also* poke) a prison, usu. small and local. **2** [1940s] a turnkey, a jailer. **3** [1990s+] a prison cell. [? POGEY n. (1) or the 'poky' conditions]

pokey n.[3] *see* POKIE n.[1].

pokey adj. (*also* poky) [mid-19C–1940s] (*US*) slow, boring. [POKE ALONG v.]

pokey stiff n. [1910s–30s] (*US tramp*) a tramp who subsists on nothing but hand-outs. [POKE-OUT n. (1) + STIFF n.[2] (4)]

pokie n.[1] (*also* pokey, pokie bandit) [1960s+] (*Aus.*) an electronic *poker* machine, used in casinos. [abbr.]

pokie n.[2] [1980s] a person or vehicle that travels slowly. [POKE ALONG v.]

poking n. [mid-19C+] sexual intercourse. [POKE v. (1)]

poking-hole n. see POKE-HOLE n.

poking-stick n. [early 17C] the penis (cf. BAT n.[7]). [POKE v. (1)]

poky adj. see POKEY adj.

pol n. [1930s+] (US) a politician. [abbr.]

pol! excl. [late 16C–early 17C] a general excl. [abbr. by Pollux, one of the twins of the Gemini constellation]

Polack n. (also **Polacki, Polak, Pollacky, Pollock**) [late 19C+] **1** a Pole. **2** (mainly Jewish) a Jew whose family come from Poland.

Polack adj. [early 17C; mid-19C+] pertaining to Poles or Polish culture. [POLACK n. (1)]

Polack town n. [20C+] (US) the Polish community within an urban area. [POLACK n. (1) + SE town]

Polak n. see POLACK n.

Polari n. (also **Palari, Palarie, Panarly, Parlare, Parlary, Parlyaree**) [late 18C+] theatrical or camp gay slang. [Ital. parlare, to speak, Ling. Fr. parlare, patter. It was evolved, according to E.P. (Slang Yesterday and Today, 1933), because 'until about the end of the eighteenth century, actors were so despised that, in self-protection, they had certain words that, properly, should be described as cant and were actually known as Parlyaree'. He also notes that rather than a whole language, it was a 'glossary, a vocabulary'. Relatively few terms remain, and their last great showcase was BBC Radio's 1960s comedy series 'Round the Horne', in which the camp duo Julian and Sandy, ostensibly a pair of actors, still conversed in a variety of Polari terms. It is still, however, extant in gay use]

polboron n. (also **pulboron**) [1970s] (drugs) heroin. [Sp. polboron, 'big powder'; a dry powdered candy]

polcat n. see POLECAT n.

pole n. [17C+] the penis (cf. BAT n.[7]).

pole v.[1] [mid-19C–1910s] (US campus) to work hard.

pole v.[2] [1900s] (Aus.) to arrive, to appear. [SE pole, the shaft fitted to a vehicle to permit the harnessing of draft animals; thus the image of movement]

pole v.[3] [1960s+] **1** usu. of a man, to perform sexual intercourse. **2** (Irish) to rape. **3** to make pregnant. [POLE n.]

pole v.[4] see POLE (ON) v.

pole-axe n. [mid-19C] a policeman. [mispron. + ? allusion to police violence]

polecat n. (also **polcat**) **1** [late 16C–18C] a woman. **2** [late 19C–1960s] an untrustworthy, violent, dangerous man. **3** [1950s+] (US Black) a dirty, untrustworthy woman. [SE polecat, a notoriously aggressive animal]

pole hole n. [1970s+] the vagina (cf. BLACK HOLE n.[1]). [POLE n. + SE hole]

pole (on) v. **1** [20C+] (Aus./N.Z.) to take advantage of someone, to impose or sponge off. **2** [1930s+] (Aus.) to steal; thus poled, stolen. [bullock-driving use; polers, the pair of bullocks nearest the wagon's pole, seen as most likely to 'take things easy']

pole pleaser n. [1990s+] (US) a (passive) homosexual man (cf. BONE-EATER n.). [POLE n. + SE pleaser]

poler n.[1] [mid-19C–1910s] (campus) a very diligent student. [POLE v.[1]]

poler n.[2] [1900s–50s] (Aus.) a cadger, a sponger, one who shirks work; thus poling, doing less than a fair share of work. [POLE (ON) v. (1)]

poles apart adj. [1910s+] extremely different, irreconcilable. [the global SE poles]

pole sitter n. [2000s] (US Black) a homosexual man (cf. BONE-EATER n.). [POLE n.]

pole-work n. [mid-19C+] sexual intercourse. [POLE n. + SE work]

police n. **1** [mid-19C+] (Scot./US) a policeman. **2** [1990s+] (US prison) a prison guard. [abbr.]

police v. [2000s] (US prison) to maintain prison discipline and rules. [POLICE n. (2)]

police clothes n. [1930s] (Irish) free second-hand clothes distributed to the poor by the police.

policed adj. [1950s] (US Black) aware, knowledgeable.

police dog n. [1920s] (US) one's fiancé. [? he follows you around and offers protection]

policeman n. **1** [mid-19C] a bluebottle fly. **2** [mid-19C] 'among the dangerous classes, a man who is unworthy of confidence, a sneak or mean fellow' (Hotten, 1873). **3** [1920s] (US prison) a term of abuse. **4** [1920s+] an informer. [(1) play on BLUEBOTTLE n. (2); negative views of the police]

policeman's helmet n. [1930s+] the glans penis. [resemblance to UK police helmets]

policy n. [mid-19C+] (US) a popular form of street gambling that involves predicting a combination of the winning numbers at a racetrack; thus policy runner, one who acts as a go-between between bettors and the policy 'banker'; policy king, one who controlled a network of policy shops. [SE policy certificate; the original game may date to the lotteries of early 18C UK, although it is now US and esp. widespread in the Black community; although policy is usu. synon. with NUMBERS, THE n., Carlson, in 'Argot of Number Gambling' (1947), defines it: 'A number game in which players wager on numbers within a range of 1–78. Winning wagers are determined by a drawing. Capsules or balls numbered from 1 to 78 are placed in a container. From these twelve, twenty-four, or thirty-six numbers are drawn, depending on the type of house'; for details and history see Asbury. Sucker's Progress (1938), pp.88–106]

polish n. **1** [1900s] (US) a fool, a synon. for SHINE n.[2] (2); a failure. **2** [1900s] affrontery, arrogance. **3** [1980s+] (N.Z.) fellatio (cf. CLEAN SOMEONE'S PIPE v.). **4** [1990s+] an act of masturbation.

polish v.[1] **1** [early 19C–1900s] to beat, to thrash. **2** [mid-19C] to hoodwink, to exploit.

polish v.[2] see POLISH (SOMEONE'S GUN) v.

polish... v. [1970s+] used in combs. to mean to masturbate, e.g. polish Charlie Brown, ...one's antlers, ...one's bayonet, ...one's knob, ...one's sword, ...percy, ...the lighthouse, ...the penguin, ...the pole, ...the rocket, ...the sword, ...the viper (cf. BUFF THE BANANA v.; POLISH (SOMEONE'S GUN) v.; POLISH THE KNOB v.; POLISH THE OLD GERMAN HELMET v.).

polish a bone v. [late 18C–early 19C] to eat a meal.

Polish airlines n. [1960s] (gay) walking. [racial stereotyping]

polish and gloss v. [20C+] to masturbate (cf. COTTON WOOL v.). [rhy. sl. = TOSS (OFF) v.[1]]

polish and shine n. [1990s+] (W.I.) fellatio (cf. CLEAN SOMEONE'S PIPE v.).

polish apples v. see POLISH THE APPLE v.

polisher n. see POLISH THE KING'S IRON WITH ONE'S EYEBROWS v.

Polish handball n. [1970s] (gay) dried nasal mucus. [racial stereotyping; the image of the peasant picking their nose]

polish it up v. [1960s] (US campus) to toady, to act sycophantically. ['it' is the pvb 'apple for teacher', i.e. POLISH THE APPLE v.]

polish off v. [mid-19C+] **1** to attack. **2** to complete or finish, esp. of a meal or a job of work. **3** to defeat. **4** to kill (clandestinely).

polish one's arse on the top sheet v. [late 19C] of a man, to have sexual intercourse. [ARSE n.[1] (1); presumably in the missionary position]

Polish pop n. [1940s] (US) vodka. [POP n.[2] (1)]

Polish shower n. (also **English shower**) [2000s] (US) a cursory wash or the application of deodorant to unwashed armpits.

polish (someone's gun) v. [1990s+] (Aus.) to fellate (cf. CLEAN SOMEONE'S PIPE v.; POLISH... v.). [GUN n.[1] (2)]

polish someone's knob v. see POLISH THE KNOB v.

polish the apple v. (also **polish apples**) [1920s–60s] to curry favour, to act the sycophant. [APPLE-POLISHER n.]

polish the bishop v. see BUFF THE BISHOP v.

polish the king's iron with one's eyebrows *v.* [late 18C–mid-19C] to look through one's prison bars; thus [20C+] (*Aus.*) *polisher*, a gaolbird.

polish the knob *v.* (*also* polish someone's knob) [1960s+] (*US*) to perform oral sex (cf. CLEAN SOMEONE'S PIPE v.; POLISH... v.). [SE *polish* + KNOB n.[1] (3)]

polish the old German helmet *v.* [1990s+] (*US*) to perform oral sex (cf. CLEAN SOMEONE'S PIPE v.; POLISH... v.). [SE *polish* + GERMAN HELMET n.]

politic *v.* [2000s] (*US Black*) to talk rather than act. [the empty verbosity of politicians]

political *adj.* [1990s+] (*US Und.*) concerning prison gang life and activities. [the racial politics that underpin US prison gangs]

political tats *n.* [1990s+] (*US Und.*) specialized tattoos that refer to one's membership of a gang. [POLITICAL adj. + TAT n.[4]]

politician *n.* **1** [20C+] a flatterer, a clever talker. **2** [1920s–70s] (*US prison*) one who gains good jobs and maximum privileges. [both uses take a dim view of the SE use]

politico *n.* [20C+] one involved in *politics*, both conventional and 'alternative' activists. [abbr.]

poll *n.*[1] **1** [mid-17C+] the hair. **2** [18C–early 19C] a wig. [SE *poll*, the head]

poll *n.*[2] [late 18C–1900s] a prostitute, a loose woman (cf. BABY JANE n.). [the proper name *Polly*]

poll *v.* **1** [16C–17C; late 19C] (*UK Und.*) to rob, by trickery rather than violence. **2** [mid-19C] (*UK Und.*) to cheat one's accomplice in crime. **3** [late 19C–1900s] to ignore, to snub. **4** [1910s] (*Aus.*) to take advantage of someone's good nature. [fig. uses of SE *poll*, to plunder, to fleece; ult. to cut hair]

Pollacky *n. see* POLACK n.

poll axe *n.* [late 16C; 19C] the penis (cf. AX n.[2]). [pun on SE *poleaxe*/POLL n.[2]]

polled off *adj.* [late 19C–1930s] drunk. [GET ON THE POLE v.]

polled up *adj.* [mid-19C] living 'in sin' with a woman. [POLL n.[2]]

poller *n.* [late 17C] a pistol. [SE *poller*, plunderer, extortionist]

pollie *n. see* POLLY n.[2] (2).

polling *n.* **1** [17C; late 19C] robbery. **2** [mid-19C] one thief robbing another. [POLL v. + SE *pillage*]

polling and pilling *n.* [16C–early 17C] robbery. [POLL v. (1) + SE *pillage*]

pollo *n.* **1** [1970s] (*US/P.R.*) a girl, usu. pretty and young; thus phr. *tremendos pollos*, good-looking (lit. 'tremendous') girls. **2** [1980s] (*US*) an illegal Mexican immigrant. [Sp. *pollo*, a chicken]

Pollock *n. see* POLACK n.

pollock *v.* [mid–late 18C] (*Irish*) to trick, to hoax, to defraud. [? racist allusion to a Pole, i.e. POLACK n./POLACK adj.]

pollone *n. see* POLONE n.

poll parrot *n.* [mid-19C+] a talkative, gossipy woman.

poll talk *n.* [mid–late 17C; 20C+] (*Irish*) slander, tale-telling. [ME *poll*, the nape of the neck, i.e. one is 'talking through the back of one's neck']

poll up *v.* [mid–late 19C] to court, to live with without being married. [? POLL n.[2]]

polluted *adj.* (*also* peloothered) **1** [20C+] extremely drunk. **2** [1930s+] (*drugs*) intoxicated by a drug. **3** [1940s–60s] (*Aus.*) a term of abuse. [joc. use of SE; ? the state of one's bloodstream]

polly *n.*[1] [19C–1900s] **1** a mistress, a prostitute who lives with a man (cf. BABY JANE n.). **2** a woman. [? POLL n.[2] or ? *Polly*, nickname for *Mary* = MOLL n.[1] (1)]

polly *n.*[2] **1** [1910s] an *apology*. **2** [1930s+] (*Aus./US*) (*also* pollie) a *politician*, esp. when corrupt. [abbr.]

polly *n.*[3] [1950s] a bathroom. [ety. unknown]

polly *n.*[4] (*also* pretty polly) [1970s+] money (cf. BEES (AND HONEY) n.). [rhy. sl. = LOLLY n.[4]]

polly flinder *n.* [late 19C+] **1** a window. **2** a cinder. [rhy. sl.; (1) note Cockney pron. 'winder'; ult. the nursery rhyme, 'Little Polly Flinders sat among the cinders']

polly parrot *n.* [20C+] a carrot. [rhy. sl.]

polly waffle *n.* [1980s] (*Aus.*) a brothel. [rhy. sl.]

pollywogger *n.* [2000s] a penis. [SE *pollywog*, tadpole]

P.O.L.O. *phr.* [1990s+] a lover's acronym used in letters or or envelopes: 'pants off, legs open'.

polo mint *n.* [2000s] a woman. [rhy. sl. = BINT n. (1); ult. brand-name of mint]

polo mint *adj.* [1990s+] penniless, impoverished. [rhy. sl. = SKINT adj.]

polone *n.* (*also* paloma, palone(y), pollone, polony) [late 19C+] (*Ling. Fr./Polari*) **1** a young woman. **2** an effeminate man. [Ital. *pollone*, chick; however, note Polari etymologist W.S. Wilcox in a letter 25/11/99: 'On the origins of *polone* I venture to suggest an alternative to previous ideas: Mayhew, *London Labour and the London Poor* (1861–2), gives the cant term *hay-bag* (a hay or straw mattress) for woman, very insulting, but *paglione* is an almost exact Italian translation of this. One of the possible suggested sources, *pollone* – plant-shoot, I feel unlikely, since in Italy it also has the slang meaning of penis']

polone-omee *n.* (*also* polone-homi) [1960s+] a lesbian, opposite of OMEE-POLONE n. [POLONE n. (1) + OMEE n. (3)]

polony *n.*[1] **1** [mid-19C+] a sausage, a salami. **2** [1910s] a silly person. [Ital. *Bologna* sausage]

polony *n.*[2] *see* POLONE n.

polter *v.* (*also* poulter, powter) [late 19C+] (*orig. Ulster*) **1** to work carelessly. **2** to potter about. [synon. Scot. *pouter/powter*]

polvo *n.* [1970s+] (*drugs*) **1** heroin. **2** (*also* polvo de angel) phencyclidine (cf. ACE n.[4]). [Sp. *polvo*, powder, dust, *polvo de angel*, angel powder, i.e. ANGEL DUST n. (4)]

poly *n.* (*also* polynesian) [1990s+] (*UK drugs*) marijuana of no particular origin or quality. [abbr. SE *Polynesian*, generic for a far-away place]

poly *adj.*[1] [1970s+] *polythene*; esp. in *poly bag*, a polythene bag, usu. the carrier bags available in shops and supermarkets. [abbr.]

poly *adj.*[2] [1990s+] (*gay*) *polygamous*, open to or preferring 2 or more partners at once. [abbr.]

polyester *n.* [1990s+] (*US campus*) something out of style or fashion; thus *polyester princess*, a woman who dresses in out-of-date fashions.

polynesian *n. see* POLY n.

polyphemus *n.* [19C] the penis. [from Homer's *Odyssey*, where *Polyphemus* is a Cyclops, distinguished by his single eye]

pom *n.*[1] [20C+] a *Pom*eranian dog. [abbr.]

pom *n.*[2] *see* POMMIE n.

pom *adj. see* POMMIE adj.

pomegranate *n.* (*also* pommygranate, pommygrant) [1910s–20s] (*Aus.*) an immigrant from Britain. [play on the similarity of the sound of *pomegranate* and *immigrant*]

Pomgolia *n.* (*also* Pongolia) [1970s+] (*N.Z.*) Britain. [POMMIE n. + play on *Mongolia*]

Pomland *n. see* POMMYLAND n.

pommie *n.* (*also* pom, pommy) [1910s+] (*Aus.*) an English or British person, usu. an immigrant; thus POMMYLAND n. [abbr. POMEGRANATE n.; but note Lawson (1921): 'An' the Pommy he says "Pom-me-word" [i.e 'pon my word] — and that's how *I* think Pommies got their name']

pommie *adj.* (*also* pom, pommy) [1910s+] (*Aus.*) British, English. [POMMIE n.]

pommie-bashing *n.* (*also* pommy-bashing) [1970s+] (*N.Z.*) verbal abuse of British immigrants (occas. affectionate). [POMMIE n. +BASHING n.[1] (2)]

pommygranate/pommygrant *n. see* POMEGRANATE n.

Pommyland *n.* (*also* Pomland) [1910s+] (*Aus.*) Britain. [POMMIE n.]

pommy's breakfast *n.* [1990s+] (*Aus.*) a cup of tea and a cigarette (cf. BARBER'S BREAKFAST n.). [POMMIE n. + SE *breakfast*]

Pomp *n. see* POMPEY n.[1].

pomp n.[1] [1910s+] (US) a *pomp*adour hairstyle, esp. beloved of 'rockers', Teddy Boys etc. [abbr.]

pomp n.[2] [1940s+] (US campus) someone who acts as if they are better than others; thus *pomp up*, to give someone false praise. [abbr. SE *pompous*]

pomp v. [20C+] (S.Afr.) to have sexual intercourse. [Afk. *pomp*, to pump]

Pompey n.[1] (also **Pomp**) [mid-19C] (US) a generic name for a Black slave. [the use of classical names for slaves, e.g. Cassius]

Pompey n.[2] [late 19C+] (orig. naut.) Portsmouth; also used in expressions such as *Pompey Royal*, a Hampshire-brewed beer. [abbr.]

Pompey's pillar to a stick of sealing-wax phr. [early–mid-19C] the longest possible odds, an absolute certainty (cf. ALL THE WORLD TO A CHINA ORANGE phr.).

Pompey whore n. [1910s+] (bingo) the number 4 (cf. ALDERSHOT LADIES n.). [rhy. sl.]

pompkin see also under PUMPKIN and its combs.

pom-pom n.[1] [1950s] sexual intercourse. [? imitative of the rhythm of intercourse]

pom-pom n.[2] [1970s+] (US Und.) a pump-action shotgun. [milit. *pom-pom*, a quick-firing gun]

poms n. [1930s–40s] (Irish) dancing shoes. [ety. unknown; ? their shine resembled hair greased with pomade]

ponce n. **1** [mid-19C+] one who lives off the earnings of one or more prostitutes. **2** [1930s+] a derog. epithet for any man or woman, including the police. **3** [1970s+] (Aus.) a male homosexual. **4** [2000s] one who lives off beggars' collections. [ety. unknown; OED suggests SE *pounce*; Hancock, 'Shelta and Polari' (1984), notes Fr. argot *pont* (*d'Avignon*) or *pontonnière*, a prostitute (who works from the arches of a bridge); E.P. offers Fr. *pensionnaire*, a lodger and thus poss. link to earlier PENSIONER (TO THE PETTICOAT) n.; note that many 'ponce' usages show the very different status of such a man in the UK compared with the US pimp]

ponce adj. [1970s+] second-rate, unpleasant. [PONCE n. (2)]

ponce v. [1930s+] **1** to work as a pimp or ponce. **2** to sponge (although with no implication of 'immoral earnings'). **3** to act in an affected, effeminate manner. [PONCE n.]

ponce about v. (also **ponce around/in**) **1** [1950s+] to act in a pretentious, affected manner. **2** [1970s+] to wander aimlessly, to live as a good-for-nothing. **3** [1970s+] to waste time. **4** [1970s+] to tease, to be impudent. [PONCE n.]

ponce off v. (also **ponce on**) [1930s+] **1** to live off immoral earnings (cf. PIMP ON v.). **2** to scrounge (money) from someone. [PONCE v.]

ponce-shicer n. see POUNCE-SHICER n.

ponce up v. [1920s+] (orig. milit.) to decorate (an object), to dress up (a person). [fig. use of PONCE n.; the term implies some ostentation and flashiness]

poncey adj. see PONCY adj.

ponch n. [1980s+] (US campus) a term of address for a man. [? the character nicknamed *Ponch* in the 1980s TV police show *C.H.I.P.S.*; Eble's suggestion of *Poncho* refers in fact to the character *Pancho* and is thus less feasible]

poncing adj. [1960s+] a general term of abuse. [PONCE v.]

poncy adj. (also **poncey**) [1960s+] affected, ostentatiously 'artistic', poss. homosexual. [PONCE n., although there is no actual link to a pimp or procurer]

pond n. see BIG POND n.

pond, the n. **1** [late 18C+] the Atlantic Ocean (cf. BIG DITCH n.). **2** [1910s–20s] the English Channel. **3** [1960s] (US) the Pacific Ocean.

pondlife n. [1990s+] a term used to describe someone seen as unintelligent, simple.

pond scum n. see SHOWER SCUM n.

pong n.[1] [20C+] (orig. Aus.) a smell. [ety. unknown; ? negative stereotyping of PONG n.[2] (1), i.e. a Chinese person; or ext. of SE *pong*, the sound of a blow; usu. reserved for use in mass-market children's comics or by society speakers who retain much juvenile vocabulary from school]

pong n.[2] **1** [1910s–40s] (Aus.) a Chinese person (cf. AH CABBAGE n.). **2** [1950s] a Japanese person (cf. BUDDHAHEAD n.). [the *ong* sound in Chinese speech]

pong n.[3] see PONGELO n.

pong v.[1] [mid-19C–1900s] to drink. [PONGELO n.]

pong v.[2] [1920s+] to stink, to smell bad. [PONG n.[1]]

pongelo n. (also **pong, ponge, pongellorum, pongelow, ponjello**) [mid-19C–1930s] beer, esp. pale ale or half-and-half. [ety. unknown; given origins of the word in the Indian Army there may be a link to the Tamil festival of Pongol, the festival of the new rice and which if so may pun on BOILED adj. (1), since *pongal* means 'boiled', albeit of rice]

pongo n. **1** [1900s] (US) a Black person, esp. an African. **2** [1910s+] (Aus./N.Z.) a marine, a soldier. **3** [1940s+] (Aus./N.Z.) a British person. [Angola or Loango *mpongo*, a large anthropoid ape, the chimpanzee or gorilla; this 17C use was in late 18C transferred to the orang-utan of Borneo and Sumatra]

Pongolia n. see POMGOLIA n.

pongy adj. [1930s+] smelly. [PONG n.[1]]

ponjello n. see PONGELO n.

ponk n. [20C+] (mainly N.Z.) a stench. [Baker, *Australian Slang* (1941) suggests that the word in N.Z. context is a mix of PONG n.[1] + Maori *puhonga*, stinking]

ponk v. [1910s–40s] (Aus./N.Z.) to stink; to give off a bad odour. [PONK n.]

'pon my life n. [late 19C] a wife. [rhy. sl.]

ponte n. [mid-19C] (Ling. Fr./Polari) £1 sterling. [Ital. *pondo*, a weight]

Pontius Pilate n. [late 18C–early 19C] a pawnbroker. [his supposed venality]

pontoon n. [1950s+] (UK prison/Und.) a 21-month sentence. [card use, the game of *pontoon* or '21']

ponum n. [late 19C] (Aus.) the face or head. [Yid. *punim*, the face]

pony n.[1] **1** [late 18C–mid-19C] money in general. **2** [late 18C+] £25, orig. 25 guineas (cf. FOAL n.). **3** [late 19C+] a double-headed coin. **4** [1910s] (N.Z.) a £5 note; £5. **5** [1960s+] (Aus.) A\$25; A\$50. [(1) f. (2); ? relatively small sums, as a pony is a small horse; Bee claims 'the one [i.e. the bet] being derived from the other [i.e. the horse]']

pony n.[2] [19C] a bailiff, esp. one who accompanies a debtor on a day out from prison. [? he carries people off]

pony n.[3] (also **automobile**) [early 19C+] (US campus) a translation of a text, classical or otherwise, for the illegitimate use of students (cf. ANIMAL n.[3]). ['so called, it may be, from the fleetness and ease with which a skilful rider is enabled to pass over places which to a common plodder present many obstacles' (Hall, *College Words and Customs*, 1856)]

pony n.[4] **1** [mid-19C+] (orig. US) a small glass of beer or other liquor; thus *pony-glass*, a small glass, with a capacity of approx. 6ml (2fl oz). **2** [1900s–50s] (US) a (small) dancer or chorus girl. **3** [1940s–50s] (US drugs) a weak measure of heroin. [fig. use of SE *pony* in its sense of a small horse]

pony n.[5] [late 19C+] (US) a racehorse; thus *the ponies*, horseracing.

pony n.[6] **1** [1940s] (US Black) a young woman, a lover. **2** [1960s+] a prostitute (cf. ALLEY CAT n.; BANBURY n.). [she is 'ridden']

pony n.[7] [1980s+] (drugs) crack cocaine (cf. BASE n.). [ety. unknown; ? one 'rides' the drug]

pony n.[8] [1990s+] a *pony*tail in one's hair.

pony v.[1] **1** [mid-19C–1900s] (US campus) to use any form of translation as an aid to work (cf. CRIB v.[2]). **2** [1990s+] (US teen) to understand. [PONY n.[3]]

pony v.[2] [1900s] (US campus) to pressurize, to urge.

pony v.[3] [1930s+] to defecate. [PONY (AND TRAP) n. (1)]

pony (and trap) *n.* [1930s+] **1** an act of defecation; a piece of excrement (cf. ALI OOP *n.*; ANDY CAPP *n.*). **2** in fig. use, nonsense, rubbish. **3** difficulties, problems. **4** silver items. **5** imitation jewels. **6** loaded dice. [rhy. sl. = CRAP *n.*³ (1); (4) the inference is the relative worthlessness of such items as compared with gold]

pony boy *n.* [2000s] (*US*) a young male homosexual. [PONY *n.*⁶ (2)]

pony up *v.* [early 19C+] (*orig. US*) to pay one's debts or one's dues. [PONY *n.*¹ (1)]

poo *n.*¹ [1940s+] **1** the vagina. **2** (*mainly US/UK juv.*) (*also* **pooh**) excrement. **3** in fig. use of (2), rubbish, nonsense. [SE *poo!* excl. announcing an unpleasant smell or expressing disbelief]

poo *n.*² [1980s+] champagne. [abbr. SHAMPOO *n.*]

poo *v.* (*also* **pooh**) [1950s+] to defecate (cf. CACA *v.*). [POO *n.*¹ (2)]

poo-bah *n. see* POOH-BAH *n.*

poo-butt *n. see* POOH-BUTT *n.*

pooch *n.* [20C+] a (small) dog; thus *pooch-flop*, dog excrement. [? Ger. *Putzi*, a popular name for a lap-dog]

pooch, the *n.* [1990s+] (*US teen*) a Greyhound bus. [POOCH *n.*, i.e. DOG, THE *n.*¹]

pooch *v.* (*also* **poach, pouch**) [1920s+] (*Irish*) to poke around, to laze about. [SE *poke*]

pood *n.*¹ [1910s+] (*Aus.*) an effeminate young man. [abbr. SE *poodle*, seen as an 'effeminate' species of dog]

pood *n.*² (*also* **poodle, poodle-dink**) [1920s–50s] (*US*) the penis. [? abbr. PUDDING *n.*¹ (1)]

poodle *n.*¹ **1** [late 19C–1900s] any breed of dog. **2** [1900s–10s] a sausage.

poodle *n.*² [1940s] the female genitalia; the vagina.

poodle *n.*³ **1** [1970s+] (*US Black*) a sexy or sophisticated woman. **2** [2000s] an unattractive woman. [positive and negative images of the over-groomed pedigree French poodle; (2) also plays on DOG *n.*³ (10)]

poodle *n.*⁴ *see* POOD *n.*².

poodle *v.* [1930s+] to move or travel in a leisurely manner; often as *poodle around/down/off*. [the image of the strolling dog; note WW2 N.Z. milit. *on poodle*, relaxing]

poodle-dink *n. see* POOD *n.*².

poodle-faker *n.* [1900s–40s] (*orig. milit.*) **1** one who cultivates women's society, esp. for social advancement. **2** one who interferes. **3** a womanizer, a 'ladies' man'. [the role of a *poodle* as a fashionable pet]

pooey *adj.* **1** [1930s+] (*orig. Aus.*) used of anything unpleasant, smelly; thus excl. *pooey!* that's rubbish! that's disgusting! **2** [1980s] of a person, hostile, snobbish. [SE *poo(h)!* an excl. of disgust]

poof *n.* (*also* **poove, pouf, pouffe**) **1** [mid-19C; 1910s+] a homosexual. **2** [1960s+] an effeminate man. [? PUFF *n.*³ (1)]

poof *adj.* [1950s+] homosexual. [POOF *n.* (1)]

poof *v.*¹ [1970s] (*US campus*) to kiss. [SE *puff*]

poof *v.*² [1990s+] (*US campus*) to leave. [? to vanish in a 'puff of smoke']

poofdah *n. see* POOFTER *n.*

poof out *v.* [1930s] to vanish, to fade away, to evaporate. [SE *puff* (of air)]

poof-rorting *n.* (*also* **poof-wroughting**) [1930s–40s] beating and robbing male prostitutes. [POOF *n.* (1) + RORT *v.* (1)]

poofter *n.* (*also* **poofdah, poofta, pooftah, poufter**) [1910s+] (*orig. Aus.*) **1** (*also* **boofter**) a homosexual man. **2** an effeminate-looking but not necessarily gay man, often a derog. term of address. **3** anyone considered to have 'unmanly' interests, e.g. art, reading. [POOF *n.*; note WW2 RN jargon *poofter*, a flashy civilian suit, supposedly indicative of homosexual tastes]

poofter-bashing *n.* [1970s+] (*Aus.*) the homophobic beating up of male homosexuals; thus *poofter-basher*. [POOFTER *n.* (1) + BASHING *n.*¹ (1)]

poofterish *adj.* [1980s+] (*Aus.*) effeminate, weak; the subject may or may not be actually homosexual; thus *poufterism,* homosexuality. [POOFTER *n.*]

poofter-rorter *n.* (*Aus.*) **1** [1940s] a procurer for male homosexuals. **2** [1960s+] one who beats up homosexuals. [POOFTER *n.* (1) + RORT *v.* (1)]

poof-wroughting *n. see* POOF-RORTING *n.*

poofy *adj.*¹ [1940s+] (*UK juv.*) smelly. [SE excl. *poof!* what an unpleasant smell!]

poofy *adj.*² (*also* **poovy, poovey, poufy**) [1950s+] effeminate, pertaining to homosexuality. [POOF *n.*]

poogie *n.* [1920s+] (*US Und.*) prison. [POKEY *n.*² (1)]

pooh *see also under* POO.

poo-hammer *n.* [2000s] (*US Black*) a male homosexual. [POO *n.*¹ (2)]

pooh-bah *n.* (*also* **poo-bah, pooh-ba**) [late 19C+] an important person. [Gilbert and Sullivan's Savoy Opera, *The Mikado* (1885) in which 'Ko-Ko' is 'Lord High Executioner of Titipu' and 'Poo-Bah' is 'Lord High Everything Else']

pooh-butt *n.* (*also* **poo-butt**) [1990s+] a general derog. term (cf. POOPBUTT *n.*). [POO *n.*¹ (2) + BUTT *n.*¹ (2)]

pooh chute *n.* [1990s+] the anus (cf. ALLEY WAY *n.*; DIRT BOX *n.*). [POO *n.*¹ (2) + SE *chute*]

poo-head *n.* [1980s+] (*US campus*) an irritating person. [POO *n.*¹ (2) + -HEAD *sfx* (1); euph. for SHITHEAD *n.* (1)]

poohed (out) *adj.* [1930s+] (*US*) exhausted, tired out. [var. on POOPED (OUT) *adj.*]

poo-hole *n.* [1980s+] (*Aus.*) **1** the anus (cf. A-HOLE *n.*; DIRT BOX *n.*). **2** an unpleasant place. [POO *n.*¹ (2) + SE *hole*]

pooh-pooh *see also under* POO-POO.

poohpooh *n.* [1910s+] (*N.Z.*) a rifle; a large gun. [echoic]

poo-jabber/-jammer *n. see* POO-STABBER *n.*

pookie *n.* [2000s] (*US Black*) an obsessive drug user. [ety. unknown]

Pool, the *n.* [1960s+] Liver*pool*. [abbr.]

pool *v.* [1910s+] (*Aus.*) to involve someone in, to implicate, to inform against; thus *in the pool*, in trouble. [? the image of tossing someone into a swimming pool; SAmE *pool*, to place resources in a common stock or fund]

poole *n.* [late 19C] (*UK society*) perfectly cut and tailored clothing. [proper name *Poole*, a leading Savile Row tailor]

pooley *n.* (*also* **poolie**) (*Irish*) **1** [1920s+] urination; usu. as *do pooley*, to urinate. **2** [1990s+] sexual intercourse. [SE *pool* (of liquid)]

pool shark *n.* [20C+] (*US*) an expert pool-player, esp. one who makes money by winning at pool. [SE *pool* + SHARK *n.*¹ (1)]

poon *n.*¹ **1** [1920s+] (*also* **pooney, poonie, poononny, pune**) the vagina; occas. the male genitals. **2** [1950s+] (*also* **poonie**) a woman or women in general when seen purely in a sexual context. **3** [1970s+] (*US gay*) the anus. **4** [1980s+] sexual intercourse. **5** [2000s] a general term of abuse (cf. ARSE *n.*¹; BAMBA *n.*¹). [abbr. POONTANG *n.*]

poon *n.*² [1940s+] (*Aus.*) **1** one who lives alone in the outback. **2** a simpleton, a fool, a useless person. [ety. unknown; note Northamptonshire dial. *pun*, a slow, dreamy, inactive person]

poon *v.* [1940s+] (*Aus.*) to dress up in a showy manner; thus *pooned up*, dressed up. [ety. unknown; ? link to POONTANG *n.*]

poona *n.* [mid-19C] (*Ling. Fr./Polari*) a sovereign, £1 sterling. [SE *pound*]

poonce *n.* (*also* **punce**) **1** [late 19C+] the vagina. **2** [1930s+] (*Aus.*) a procurer; thus a general insult. **3** [1970s+] (*Aus.*) a catamite; a male homosexual prostitute. [Yid. *punse*, the vagina]

pooner *n.* [1960s] (*US campus*) a male sexual athlete, a womanizer. [POONTANG *n.*]

pooney *n. see* POON *n.*¹ (1).

poon hound *n.* [1980s+] (*US*) a dedicated womanizer. [POON *n.*¹ (1) + HOUND *sfx*]

poonie *n. see* POON *n.*¹.

poonj *v.* [1990s+] to have sexual intercourse. [allegedly Ojibwe *poonjegay*, to dip meat in grease]

poononny *n. see* POON n.¹ (1).

poontang *n.* **1** [1920s+] sexual intercourse; thus *on a poontang trip*, obsessed with seducing women; also occas. in homosexual use. **2** [1920s+] (*also* **puntang**) the vagina. **3** [1920s+] a woman or women in general, when seen purely in a sexual context. **4** [1990s+] in a homosexual context, the penis. **5** [1990s+] semen. [? Fr. *putain*, a prostitute]

poontang *v.* [1990s+] to perform cunnilingus. [POONTANG n. (2)]

poontanger *n.* [1960s+] (*US*) the penis. [POONTANG n. (2)]

poontang juice *n.* [2000s] (*US*) vaginal secretions (cf. BINDER-JUICE n.). [POONTANG n. (2)]

poontang magnet *n. see* BABE MAGNET n.

poonts *n.* [late 19C] the female breasts. [? SE *font* or *fountain*]

poop *n.*¹ **1** [late 16C–17C] the vagina. **2** [17C–early 18C] the 'dickey' or rear seat of a coach. **3** [mid-17C+] the buttocks. [SE *poop*, the stern or highest stern deck of a boat]

poop *n.*² **1** [mid-18C; 1930s+] the act of breaking wind. **2** [1930s+] (*also* **poopee, poopy**) excrement; thus *take a poop*, to defecate. **3** [1940s+] (*orig. US*) rubbish, nonsense. [SE *poop*, echoic of the report of a gun and thus the sound of defecation/breaking wind; (3) is fig. use of (1)]

poop *n.*³ [1910s+] a fool. [? abbr. NINCOMPOOP n.]

poop *n.*⁴ [1940s+] (*orig. US*) **1** news, information, gossip. **2** (*also* **straight poop**) the facts, the situation. [OED suggests ety. unknown, but ? fig. use of POOP n.² (2) (cf. SHIT n.⁴)]

poop *adj.* [2000s] out of date, dead. [? POOP n.² (2)]

poop *v.*¹ [18C] of a man, to have sexual intercourse. [? SE *poop*, to deceive, to cheat]

poop *v.*² **1** [early 18C+] to break wind. **2** [1910s–40s] to shoot a weapon. **3** [1920s+] to shoot someone. **4** [1920s+] to defecate; also fig. use (cf. CACA v.). **5** [1940s] (*US*) to give, to hand out. [SE *poop*, onomat. for the report of a gun/POOP n.²]

poop *v.*³ [1900s–30s] **1** to malfunction, to destroy. **2** [1920s+] (*orig. US*) to tire, to exhaust, to waste. **3** [1950s+] to ruin someone's enjoyment. **4** [1960s] (*US campus*) to fill in, to explain. [ety. unknown]

poo-packer *n.* [1990s+] a male homosexual (cf. BROWN ARTIST n.). [POO n.¹ (2) +SE *packer*]

poopants *adj.* [2000s] stupid. [POO n.¹ (2)]

poop around *v.* [1960s] (*US*) to socialize.

poopbutt *n.* (*also* **pootbutt**) [1960s+] (*US Black*) **1** a lazy person. **2** an uninformed, unsophisticated, immature person. **3** a general term of abuse (cf. POOH-BUTT n.). [POOP n.² (2)/POOT n.² (2) + BUTT n.¹ (2)]

poopbutt *adj.* [1970s] lazy, inefficient. [POOPBUTT n. (1)]

poop-catchers *n. see* SHIT-CATCHERS n.

poop-chute *n.* (*also* **poop-hole, poop-shoot**) [1970s+] the anus (cf. ALLEY WAY n.; DIRT BOX n.). [POOP n.² (2) + SE *chute*]

pooped (out) *adj.* [1920s+] (*orig. US*) exhausted, tired out. [POOP v.³ (2)]

poopee *n. see* POOP n.² (2).

pooper *n.* **1** [late 19C; 1940s+] the posterior, the buttocks; the anus (cf. DIRT BOX n.). **2** [20C+] the penis. [(1) POOP v.² (1); (2) POOP n.¹ (1)]

poo percolator *n.* [1990s+] a male homosexual (cf. BROWN ARTIST n.). [POO n.¹ (2) + SE *percolator*]

pooper-scooper *n.* [1970s+] (*orig. US*) a small scoop used by dog owners to remove traces of a dog's excreta from urban pavements or parks. [POOP n.² (2) + SE *scoop*]

poophead *n.* [1970s+] (*US campus*) a fool, a dullard. [POOP n.² (2) + -HEAD sfx (1)]

poop-hole *n. see* POOP-CHUTE n.

poopie *n.* [1980s] (*US juv.*) an act of defecation. [POOP n.² (2)]

poopie-plops *n.* [1950s+] (*UK juv.*) excrement. [ext. of POOP n.² (2)]

poo-pipe pirate *n.* [1990s+] a male homosexual (cf. BROWN ARTIST n.). [POO n.¹ (2)]

poo pirate *n.* [1990s+] (*Aus.*) a male homosexual (cf. BROWN ARTIST n.). [POO n.¹ (2)]

poop noddy *n.* (*also* **pup noddy**) [17C] sexual intercourse. [POOP n.¹ (1) + SE *nod*, to bob up and down]

poop off *v.* **1** [1920s] to leave. **2** [1960s] (*US*) to spend.

poop one's pants *v.* [2000s] to be terrified. [POOP v.² (4) + SE *pants*]

poo-poo *n.*¹ (*also* **pooh-pooh**) [late 19C] an act of dismissal, derision. [POO-POO v.¹]

poo-poo *n.*² (*also* **pooh-pooh**) **1** [1930s+] excrement. **2** [1970s+] (*US gay*) the anus (cf. DIRT BOX n.). [POO n.¹ (2) + redup.]

poo-poo *v.*¹ (*also* **pooh-pooh**) [mid-19C+] to deride, to dismiss. [SE *poo!* + redup.]

poo-poo *v.*² (*also* **pooh-pooh**) [1960s+] to defecate (cf. CACA v.). [POO-POO n.² (1)]

poo-poo head *n.* [1980s] (*US juv.*) a general term of abuse. [POO-POO n.² (1) + -HEAD sfx (1)]

poop-out *n.* [1950s] a mechanical failure. [POOP OUT v. (2)]

poop out *v.* [1920s+] (*US*) **1** to fail. **2** to have a breakdown, whether mental or physical; also of a machine, to go wrong. **3** to die. **4** to faint; to collapse; to be excessively drunk. [POOP v.³ (2)]

poop sheet *n.* [1940s+] (*US campus*) any form of information posted on a noticeboard or distributed to students. [POOP n.⁴ + SE *sheet*]

poop-shoot *n. see* POOP-CHUTE n.

poop stick *n.* [1930s] an unpleasant person. [POOP n.² (2) + STICK n.²]

poo-puncher/-pusher *n. see* POO-STABBER n.

poopy *n. see* POOP n.² (2).

poor as Friday *phr.* [early 19C] penniless. [Friday is payday]

poor as Job's turkey *phr.* (*also* **poor as Job's ass, …cat, …mouse**) [mid-19C+] (*orig. US*) extremely poor, thin. [the biblical *Job*, regarded as the personification of poverty]

poor as mud *phr. see* POOR AS WOOD phr.

poor-ass *adj.* (*also* **poor-assed**) [1960s+] (*US*) wretched, lousy, unpleasant. [SE *poor* + -ASS sfx/-ASSED sfx]

poor as wee-wee *phr.* [1960s] (*N.Z.*) unacceptable, second-rate. [WEE n.; var. on PISS-POOR adj. (1)]

poor as wood *phr.* (*also* **poor as mud**) [20C+] (*Aus.*) second-rate.

poor boy it *v.* [1990s+] (*US*) to be extremely poor, to be severely deprived.

poor circumstance *n. see* MERE CIRCUMSTANCE n.

poor creatures *n.* [early 19C] potatoes. [mispron. + ref. to their role as poverty food]

poor-great *adj.* [20C+] (*W.I.*) proud but impoverished, unwilling to take charity however much it might be needed.

poor john *n.* [17C–early 19C] dried, salted hake.

poorly *adj.* [late 19C] menstruating. [SE *poorly*, unwell]

poor man's alcohol *n.* [2000s] (*US Black*) cough syrup.

poor man's blessing *n.* [19C] the vagina. [sex, if nothing else, is free]

poor man's cocaine *n.* **1** [1980s+] isobutyl nitrite (cf. AIMIES n.). **2** [1990s+] (*drugs*) methamphetamine (cf. BOMBITA n.). [similar effects for less expenditure]

poor man's diggings *n.* [late 19C–1940s] (*Aus.*) alluvial gold deposits, which can be mined far more easily than reef-gold that requires capital to develop.

poor man's goose *n.* [19C] baked liver with sage and onions.

poor man's oyster *n.* [late 19C] a mussel.

poor man's piano *n.* [mid-19C] (*Can.*) a meal of dried beans. [the wind-inducing, 'musical' effect it has on one's stomach]

poor man's sugar *n.* [2000s] (*US Black*) heroin. [play on BROWN SUGAR n. (2)/SE *brown sugar*, i.e. seen as 'poorer' than white sugar]

poor man's treacle *n.* **1** [17C] garlic. **2** [19C] onions. [not so sweet, but flavoursome]

poor-me-one *n.* [20C+] (*W.I.*) a miserable looking person, desperate for sympathy.

poor-me-one *adj.* [20C+] (*W.I.*) miserable-looking. [POOR-ME-ONE n.]

poormouth *adj.* [1940s+] (*US*) weary, depressed, 'down in the mouth', whether or not genuinely so.

poor mouth *v.* [early 19C+] to belittle oneself or others; to pose as impoverished; thus (*Irish*) *make/play the poor mouth*, to complain, to slander.

poor relation *n.* [20C+] a railway station. [rhy. sl.]

poor robin *n.* [early–mid-18C] an almanac; an astrologer. [the title *Poor Robin's Almanac* (1661), sometimes attributed to the poet Robert Herrick (1591–1674)]

poosa *see under* PHUZA.

pooshey/pooshie/pooshy *n. see* PUSHIE n.

poo-stabber *n.* (*also* poo-jabber, -jammer, -puncher, -pusher, -shooter) [1990s+] a male homosexual; the active partner in homosexual anal intercourse (cf. BROWN ARTIST n.). [POO n.[1] (2) + SE *stabber*]

poot *n.*[1] [late 19C] a shilling (5p). [Hind. *poot*, a shilling, coined by East London's many Indian beggars]

poot *n.*[2] [1950s+] (*US*) **1** a fart. **2** soft excrement. **3** an unpleasant person. [POOT v. (1)]

poot *v.* [1950s+] (*US*) **1** to break wind. **2** to defecate (cf. CACA v.). [a US Southernism, from the Fr. *péter*, to fart]

poot about *v.* (*also* poot around, pootle about/around) [1950s+] to dawdle, to mess around. [fig. use of POOT v. (1); var on FART ABOUT v. (1)]

pootbutt *n. see* POOPBUTT n.

pootenanny *n.* (*also* pootie-tootie) [1970s+] (*US Black*) the vagina. [PUNAANY n. (1) + HOOTENANNY n.]

pootle about/around *v. see* POOT ABOUT v.

poove *n. see* POOF n.

poove *v.* (*also* poove about/around) [1960s] to act in an ostentatiously homosexual manner. [POOVE n.]

poovey/poovy *adj. see* POOFY adj.[2].

poozle *n.* [late 19C+] the vagina (cf. BIRD n.[8]). [? PUSSY n. (2)]

poozle *v.* [1970s+] (*N.Z.*) to scavenge for collectable objects. [ety. unknown]

pop *n.*[1] **1** [18C+] (*also* popp) a pistol, usu. in pl. **2** [mid-19C] a bullet. [onomat.]

pop *n.*[2] **1** [early 19C+] (*mainly US juv.*) a fizzy drink. **2** [mid-19C–1930s] champagne. **3** [late 19C] in fig. use of (1), something insubstantial, meaningless. **4** [1970s–80s] (*US*) any form of alcoholic drink. [the pop of a cork; note WW1 milit. *pop wallah*, a teetotaller]

pop *n.*[3] **1** [early 19C+] a try, an attempt, a 'go'; thus *first pop*, the first try, the first time; FAIR POP n. **2** [mid-19C+] as *a pop*, a go, an item, each. **3** [late 19C+] a hit at, also in fig. use. [SE *pop*, the sound of an explosion, thus fig. an instant]

pop *n.*[4] [mid-19C+] **1** the act of pawning; thus *in pop*, in pawn. **2** the pawnbroker's. [POP v.[2]]

pop *n.*[5] (*also* pap) **1** [mid-19C+] one's father. **2** [mid-19C+] an older, respected man. **3** [late 19C+] a term of address to or nickname of an old(er) man.

pop *n.*[6] **1** [mid-19C+] an orgasm, usu. male. **2** [1960s+] a single instance of sexual intercourse. [SE *pop*, the firing of a gun]

pop *n.*[7] **1** [1930s+] (*drugs*) an injection of a narcotic drug. **2** [1960s+] a sip or swig of a drink.

pop *n.*[8] [1960s–70s] an arrest, a criminal charge. [POP v.[1] (11)]

pop *n.*[9] *see* LOLLIPOP n.[2] (2).

pop, a *n. see* POP n.[3] (2).

pop *v.*[1] (*also* pop off) **1** [17C; mid-19C; 1950s+] (*US*) (*also* pop in) to seduce, to have sexual intercourse (cf. BANG v.[1]). **2** [18C+] to fire a gun; to shoot at. **3** [late 18C; late 19C+] (*orig. US*) to hit, to punch. **4** [mid-19C+] to shoot dead, to murder someone, to kill someone. **5** [mid-19C+] to set off, to set in motion. **6** [1920s] (*US*) to execute by a firing squad. **7** [1920s+] (*US*) to hit with a bullet. **8** [1930s+] to give birth; to be born. **9** [1950s+] to ejaculate, to reach orgasm (cf. FIRE v.[1]). **10** [1960s] to identify. **11** [1960s+] to arrest, to catch. **12** [1960s+] to bring someone to orgasm. **13** [1980s+] (*US campus*) to initiate someone into drug use. **14** [1980s+] (*US*) to make pregnant.

pop *v.*[2] [late 18C+] to pawn. [SE *pop something in*]

pop *v.*[3] **1** [mid-19C+] of things, to come to a head, to suddenly start happening?, to be energized. **2** [1950s+] (*orig. US Black*) to live well. **3** [1960s] (*US Black*) to live a full social life. **4** [1970s+] to feel elated, extremely pleased, enthusiastic. [one/the thing is 'exploding']

pop *v.*[4] (*drugs*) **1** [1930s+] to inject a drug; thus SKINPOP v. **2** [1960s+] to swallow a pill. **3** [1960s+] (*US campus*) to take amphetamine spec. for staying up and working all night. **4** [1960s+] to take a drink. **5** [1980s] to smoke a drug. **6** [1990s+] to inhale cocaine.

pop *v.*[5] **1** [1940s+] (*US Black/W.I.*) to tell, to reveal, to gossip. **2** [1950s+] (*US Black*) to lie, to cheat, to manipulate.

pop *v.*[6] [1950s+] (*orig. US Black*) **1** to steal; thus *pop a car*, to steal an automobile. **2** to take, to extract from. [? the SE *popping* open that prefaces theft]

pop *v.*[7] [1950s+] to break.

pop *v.*[8] *see* BODY-POP v.

pop *v.*[9] *see* POP (FOR) v.

pop *v.*[10] *see* POP THE QUESTION v.

pop a cap *v.* [1900s; 1950s+] to fire a weapon; to shoot someone. [POP v.[1] (2) + CAP n.[2]]

pop a cherry *v.* (*also* pop someone's cherry) [1950s+] **1** to deflower a girl or woman, occas. a young man. **2** in fig. use. [POP v.[1] (1) + CHERRY n.[1] (1)/CHERRY n.[1] (4)]

pop a gut *v.* **1** [late 17C+] to work very hard. **2** [late 19C+] to laugh uproariously. **3** [1940s+] to be furious. [SE *pop*, to explode + SE *gut*]

pop a nut *v.* [1950s+] **1** to masturbate. **2** to reach orgasm; thus by ext. to feel happy, satisfied (cf. FIRE v.[1]). **3** to bring someone to orgasm. [SE *pop*/POP v.[1] (9) + NUT n.[9] (1)]

pop a roll *v.* [1970s+] (*drugs*) to swallow a number of pills in one go. [POP v.[4] (2) + ROLL n.[6] (2)]

pop around (with) *v.* [1950s] (*US*) to associate (with).

pop a wad (by hand) *v.* [1990s+] to masturbate. [POP v.[1] (9) + WAD n.[6]; i.e. var. om POP ONE'S WAD v.]

popcorn *n.*[1] [20C+] an erection. [rhy. sl. = HORN n.[2] (3)]

popcorn *n.*[2] **1** [1940s–50s] (*US prison*) a fool, a dullard (cf. APPLEHEAD n.). **2** [1950s] one with a legitimate job, rather than a criminal or a confidence man. [POPCORN adj.]

popcorn *adj.* **1** [late 19C+] (*orig. US Und.*) foolish, slow-witted, lightweight. **2** [1950s] (*US*) respectable, law-abiding. [the banality of the foodstuff]

popcorn pimp *n.* (*also* popcorn) **1** [1960s+] (*US Black*) a small-time, ineffectual pimp; thus anyone of little or no importance (cf. CHILE CHUMP n.). **2** [1980s] a man who claims to be, but is not, a pimp. [POPCORN adj. (1) + SE *pimp*]

pope *v.* [20C+] (*W.I.*) to get in without paying, to 'crash' a party. [? obs. SE *poop*, to deceive, to cheat; ? ult. Du. *poep*, a clown]

popehead *n.* [1990s+] (*Ulster*) a Roman Catholic. [SE *pope* + -HEAD sfx (2)]

Pope (of Rome) *n.* [mid-19C+] home. [rhy. sl.]

poperin pear *n.* (*also* poperine pear) [late 16C–mid-17C] the penis (cf. BANANA n.[2]). [*Poperinghe*, in west Flanders. The word comes in Shakespeare's *Romeo and Juliet* (1594), that repository of so much innuendo. 'O Romeo, that she were / An open et-caetera / Thou a poperin pear!' says Mercutio. The term may even, as E.P. suggests in *Shakespeare's Bawdy* (1947), pun on 'pop her in'; Nares complains that 'it seems that there is much attempt at wit on this pear, in some old dramas; but such as it is not worthwhile to repeat, or attempt explaining']

pope's eye *n.* [mid-19C] the lymphatic gland surrounded with fat, found in a leg of mutton. [earlier use is SE]

pope's nose *n. see* PARSON'S NOSE n.

pope's telephone number *n.* [1900s–60s] Vat 69 whisky. [pun on *Vatican*; from an era that mixed letters and numbers in big city telephone numbering]

popeyed *adj.* [1930s+] **1** drunk (cf. ARSEHOLED adj.). **2** regrettable, bad. [SE *pop-eyed*, with bulging eyes; (2) is fig. use of (1)]

pop (for) *v.* **1** [1950s–60s] (*US Black*) (*also* **pop to**) to pay (for), to treat. **2** [1970s] to provide without payment.

pop goes the weasel *n.* [20C+] diesel. [rhy. sl.]

pop in *v. see* POP v.¹ (1).

pop it *v. see* POP THE QUESTION v.

pop it in *v.* [mid-19C+] to enter a woman or in gay use a man, to have sexual intercourse (cf. BURY IT v.). [SE]

pop it in the toaster *v.* [1980s+] (*US gay*) to have anal intercourse (cf. ASK FOR THE RING v.). [the toaster makes white bread 'brown']

pop it on *v.* **1** [late 19C+] to ask for more, esp. when raising a commodity's price. **2** [1900s] to make a bet. [SE *pop on*, to place on]

pop junk *v.* [1940s+] (*US*) to gossip (cf. TALK SMACK v.). [POP v.⁵ (1) + JUNK n.³ (4)]

popla *n.* (*also* **poplar**) [1970s+] (*S.Afr. township*) beer. [ety. unknown]

poplars *n.* (*also* **paplar, poplar, poplers, poppelars**) [mid-16C–mid-19C] (*UK Und.*) porridge. [SE *pap*, infant food]

poplars of yarrum *n. see* YARRUM n.

pop nine *n.* [1990s+] a 9mm pistol. [POP n.¹ (1)]

po-po *n.* (*also* **poh-poh**) [1980s+] **1** (*US Black*) the police. **2** (*US prison*) a prison officer. [abbr. + redup.]

popo *n.* [1950s+] (*US*) the buttocks; thus *pound someone's popo*, to sodomize. [abbr./redup. of SE *posterior*]

pop-off *n.*¹ [1930s+] (*US*) **1** a brash or boastful statement. **2** a brash or boastful person. **3** an informer. **4** any form of comment. [POP OFF v.²]

pop-off *n.*² **1** [1950s] (*US*) a death, a killing. **2** [1990s+] (*W.I.*) the act of reaching for a firearm. [POP v.¹ (4)]

pop-off *n.*³ [1940s+] (*W.I.*) the proceeds of some form of illegal deal or racket, a reduction in price, e.g. on stolen goods.

pop off *v.*¹ **1** [mid-18C+] to die. **2** [19C+] to depart. **3** [1990s+] to happen, to start. [SE *pop*, to move]

pop off *v.*² (*also* **pop off at (the mouth)**) **1** [19C+] to make a fuss about. **2** [1920s] to confess, to tell the truth. **3** [1930s–50s] to joke. **4** [1930s+] to talk in an aggressive, threatening manner. **5** [1960s+] to brag, to boast. **6** [1980s] to criticize. [SE *pop*, to explode sharply]

pop off *v.*³ *see* POP v.¹.

pop off *v.*⁴ *see* POP ONE'S NUTS v.

pop off the handle *v.* [mid-19C] (*US*) to reject, to dismiss.

pop off the hooks *v.* **1** [19C+] to die. **2** [1930s+] (*US*) to exit, to vanish. [SE *pop*, to move]

pop one's buttons *v. see* BUST ONE'S BUTTONS v.

pop one's cake *v. see* POP ONE'S COOKIES v. (1).

pop one's cap *v.* [1950s] (*US Black*) to feel depressed, to suffer pain. [SE *pop* + CAP n.⁶ (1)]

pop one's clogs *v.* [1970s+] to die. [POP v.²/SE *pop*, to explode + SE *clogs*]

pop one's collar *v.* [2000s] (*US Black*) to have a conversation.

pop one's cookies *v.* **1** [1920s+] (*US*) (*also* **pop one's cake, snap one's cookies**) to vomit (cf. BLOW CHOW v.). **2** [2000s] to reach orgasm (cf. FIRE v.¹). [SE *pop*, to explode/POP v.¹ (9) + lit./fig. use of COOKIES n.¹]

pop one's cork *v.* **1** [1950s+] to lose one's temper, to lose

patience. **2** [1960s+] to surrender sexually, to come to orgasm (cf. FIRE v.¹). **3** [1960s+] to masturbate. [SE *pop*, to explode/POP v.¹ (9)]

pop one's drawers *v.* [1970s] to have an orgasm; also in fig. use, to get very excited (cf. FIRE v.¹). [SE *pop*, to explode/POP v.¹ (9)]

pop one's nuts *v.* (*also* **pop off, pop one's nut**) [1950s+] (*orig. US*) to achieve male orgasm; thus in fig. use, to feel exhilarated (cf. FIRE v.¹). [SE *pop*, to explode/POP v.¹ (9) + NUTS n.² (1)]

pop one's rocks *v.* [1960s] (*US*) to become excited; to lose emotional control; lit. to ejaculate (cf. FIRE v.¹). [SE *pop*, to explode/POP v.¹ (9) + ROCKS n.⁴ (1)]

pop one's wad *v.* [1970s] (*US*) to achieve male orgasm (cf. FIRE v.¹). [SE *pop*, to explode/POP v.¹ (9) + WAD n.⁶]

pop-out *n.* [1920s] a jeer, a ridicule.

popp *n. see* POP n.¹ (1).

poppa *n.* (*also* **popper**) **1** [late 19C+] (*orig. US*) (*also* **poppy**) a father. **2** [1920s] a boyfriend. **3** [1940s+] a term of address betwen men. **4** [1970s+] (*US gay*) a fellow lesbian. [SE *papa*]

poppa large *n.* [1990s+] (*US Black teen*) an important, influential figure. [POPPA n. (1) + LARGE adj. (2)]

poppa-stoppa *n.* (*also* **poppa-loppa**) [1930s–40s] (*US Black*) **1** a man; also as an intimate term of address. **2** an older man who still possesses his faculties and strength. **3** a euph. reverse of MOTHERFUCKER n. (1). [POPPA n. (1) + SE *stop*, i.e. (1) and (2) his ability to 'stop' an opponent; (3) used like 'plug']

popped *adj.* **1** [20C+] shot. **2** [1960s+] arrested. **3** [1980s] (*US campus*) in a difficult situation. [POP v.¹]

popped out *adj.* [1940s–50s] intoxicated with a drug. [POP v.⁴ (1)]

popped up *adj.* [1960s] drunk. [POP v.⁴ (4)]

poppelars *n. see* POPLARS n.

popper *n.*¹ **1** [mid-18C+] a pistol, a gun. **2** [2000s] a gunman. [POP v.¹ (2); (1) 20C+ use is US Black]

popper *n.*² (*drugs*) **1** [1930s+] an intravenous drug user. **2** [1930s+] an injection. **3** [1960s+] a pill-taker. [POP v.⁴]

popper *n.*³ [1960s+] (*drugs*) amyl or (iso)butyl nitrite; usu. in pl. (cf. AIMIES n.). [SE *pop*, to explode, i.e. the necessity of breaking open the ampoule that contains the drug]

popper *n.*⁴ *see* POPPA n.

poppers *n.* [1940s] (*US Black*) the fingers. [? one 'pops' them in time to music]

popping *n.* [1940s] (*US Black*) spending money recklessly and enthusiastically.

pop-pop *n.* [1990s+] (*US Black teen*) the noise of a gun being fired. [echoic]

poppy *n.*¹ **1** [mid-19C+] (*drugs*) opium; thus *picking the poppies*, addicted to opium (cf. APOSTLE n.). **2** [1990s+] heroin. [prior 17C–19C use was literary SE, e.g. Shakespeare's 'Not Poppy, nor Mandragora' in *Othello* (1604)]

poppy *n.*² (*Irish*) **1** [1940s+] (*also* **pop-pop**) a hole in one's sock or stocking. **2** [1990s+] a potato. [? the flesh 'pops out', in (2) when baked (cf. POTATO n.²)]

poppy *n.*³ [1970s+] money. [? SE *popular*]

poppy *n.*⁴ *see* POPPA n. (1).

poppycock *n.* (*also* **poppycocks**) [mid-19C+] nonsense, rubbish. [Du. *pappekak*, soft faeces; thus orig. euph. for excreta]

poppyhead *n.* [1950s] (*US drugs*) an opium addict. [POPPY n.¹ (1) + -HEAD sfx (3)]

poppy love *n.* [1980s+] (*US Black*) an elderly Jewish man. [? POPPA n. (1)]

poppy show *n.*¹ [late 19C–1900s; 1950s+] an inadvertent display of one's underclothes, orig. those made of red or brown flannel. [SE *poppy* + *show*; 1950s+ use is N.Z.]

poppy show *n.*² (*also* **pappy show, puppy show**) [20C+] (*W.I.*) **1** foolishness, showing off. **2** one who makes a stupid exhibition of themselves. [dial. *poppy-show*, a puppet show]

poppy-show *adj.* (*also* **pappy-show, puppy-show**) [20C+] (*W.I.*) foolish, ridiculous. [POPPY SHOW n.²]

poppy show *v.* (*also* **pappy show, puppy show**) [20C+] (*W.I.*) to make a fool of someone. [POPPY SHOW n.²]

pop quiz *n.* (*also* **pop test, shotgun quiz**) [1960s+] (*US campus*) a surprise test. [it 'pops up' or 'explodes']

pops *n.* [1920s+] **1** one's father; thus *grandpops*, grandfather. **2** (*orig. US Black*) a term of address, usu. from a younger man to an older one. **3** (*US*) an old man. [POP n.⁵]

popsee *n. see* POPSIE n.¹.

pop shit *v.* [1960s+] to boast, to talk nonsense. [POP OFF v.² (5) + SHIT n.³ (4)]

pop shop *n.* [late 18C+] a pawnbroker's shop. [POP v.² + SE *shop*]

pop shot *n.* [1990s+] in a pornographic film, the shot in which a male actor ejaculates. [POP v.¹ (9)]

popsicle *n.* [1980s+] (*US gay*) the penis. [SAmE *popsicle* = SE *lollipop*]

popsicle stand *n.* [1970s+] (*US campus*) wherever one is currently situated.

popsie *n.¹* (*also* **popsee, popsy**) [mid-19C+] a woman, usu. one who is young and attractive. [SE *pop/poppet*, a term of endearment for a woman + sfx *-sy*, as in Betsy, Topsy etc]

popsie *n.²* [1910s] (*US*) a SUGAR DADDY n. [POP n.⁵ (1)]

popskull *n.* **1** [mid-19C+] (*US*) illicitly distilled whisky (cf. BUSTSKULL n.). **2** [1940s] any form of strong drink. [SE *pop*, to explode + *skull*]

pop someone's cherry *v. see* POP A CHERRY v.

pop someone's cork *v.* [1970s+] (*US gay*) to deflower anally.

pop-squirt *n. see* SQUIRT n.² (2).

pop style *v.* [1950s+] (*W.I.*) of a woman, to walk in a provocative manner or to act stylishly.

popsy *n. see* POPSIE n.¹.

popsy-wopsy *n.* [late 19C–1920s] 'a smiling, doll-like attractive girl' (Ware). [POPSIE n.¹+ redup.]

pop test *n. see* POP QUIZ n.

pop the question *v.* (*also* **pop, pop it**) [mid-18C+] to propose marriage. [SE *pop the question*, to question abruptly]

pop to *v. see* POP (FOR) v. (1).

pop tops *v.* [1980s+] (*US campus*) to drink beer. [SE *pop open* + *top* (of a beer can)]

popular *adj.* (*US*) **1** [mid–late 19C] conceited. **2** [late 19C] good, e.g. *a popular pie*.

population paste *n. see* PASTE n.¹.

pop up *v.* [1930s] to create, to make happen, to cause.

pop visit *n.* [early 17C] (*UK society*) a brief visit. [one 'just pops in' for a moment]

pop wallah *n. see* CHAR WALLAH n.

pop wine *n.* [20C+] (*US*) sweet wine with a low alcohol content. [SE *wine* that is no stronger than POP n.² (1)]

p.o.(q.)! *excl.* [1910s+] (*Aus.*) go away! [PISS OFF! excl. + SE *quick/quickly*)]

porangi *adj.* [mid-19C+] (*N.Z.*) mad; eccentric; stupid. [Maori *porangi*, beside oneself, out of one's mind, mad]

porch *n.* [1980s+] (*US gay*) the buttocks.

porch climber *n.* (*also* **window climber**) [20C+] (*US*) a burglar.

porch monkey *n.* [1980s+] (*US*) a derog. term for a Black person (cf. AFRICAN APE n.). [SE *porch* + MONKEY n.¹ (2); the stereotyped image of Black laziness, i.e. sitting on the porch]

porcupine *n.* [1980s] a lie. [corruption of PORKY n.³ (1)]

pork *n.¹* **1** [18C+] a generic term for a woman or women viewed as sex objects. **2** [1920s+] (*US tramp*) (*also* **dead pork**) a corpse. **3** [1980s] (*UK Black*) a White person.

pork *n.²* (*also* **purple pork, spicy pork roll**) **1** [mid-19C; 1960s+] the penis (cf. BACON n.¹). **2** [1970s] a fool (cf. APPLEHEAD n.; CHOAD n.).

pork *n.³* **1** [late 19C+] (*US*) federal funds obtained for particular areas or individuals on the basis of political patronage. **2** [1970s] (*US Black*) money. [fig. use of SE]

pork *n.⁴ see* PORKY n.¹ (2).

pork *v.¹* **1** [1940s+] of a man, to have sexual intercourse; thus *pork time*, the act of intercourse; *porker*, a male sexual partner; *porkee*, a female sexual partner; *pork pit*, a place used for intercourse. **2** [1960s] (*US*) to shoot dead, to kill. [(1) he uses his PORK SWORD n.; (2) fig. use of (1)]

pork *v.² see* PIG OUT v. (2).

pork and bean *n.* [1960s+] (*Aus.*) a male homosexual. [rhy. sl. = QUEEN n.² (1)]

pork-and-beaner *n.¹* [1910s] (*US*) a second-rate person. [PORK-AND-BEANS adj.]

pork-and-beaner *n.²* [1920s] (*US*) a cowboy. [the stereotypical ingredients of cowboy food]

pork and beans *n.* [1920s–40s] a Portuguese person. [joc. pron.]

pork-and-beans *adj.* (*also* **pork-and-bean**) [1910s–30s] (*US*) basic, unenterprising, second-rate. [the banality of the dish]

pork barrel *n.* [late 19C+] (*US*) a political 'slush' fund; thus as *adj.*, corrupt. [PORK n.³ (1)]

pork chop *n.¹* [20C+] a policeman (cf. BOTTLE (AND STOPPER) n.). [rhy. sl. = COP n.¹ (1)]

pork chop *n.²* [1920s+] (*US*) an attractive young woman. [? PORK CHOPS n.; or she is 'good enough to eat']

pork chop *n.³* [1940s] (*US*) a dollar. [image of money as a staple of life]

pork chop *n.⁴* [1970s+] (*US*) a Black person who, despite supposed advances in equality, is willing to accept an inferior position to that of Whites. [the stereotypical linkage of pork chops and Black people]

pork-chopper *n.* [1960s] (*US*) the penis. [it *chops* PORK n.¹ (1)]

pork chops *n.* [1920s–60s] (*US*) material or sensual gratification, often referring to sex. [SE + PORK n.¹ (1)]

porker *n.¹* [late 17C–mid-18C] (*UK Und.*) a sword. [? POKER n.¹ (1), but note later PIGSTICKER n.]

porker *n.²* [late 18C+] a Jew (cf. ARAB n.²). [SE *porker*, a pig; the Jewish laws of *kashrut*, which forbid the consumption of pig flesh]

porker *n.³* [late 19C+] a fat person?. [SE *porker*, a pig, when raised for its meat]

porker *n.⁴* [1980s+] a policeman (cf. ANIMAL n.¹). [var. on PIG n.³ (1)]

pork fritz *n. see* FRITZ n.

porkhead *n.* [1980s+] a stupid, thuggish person. [SE *pork* + -HEAD sfx (1)]

porking *n.* [1980s+] (*US Black*) sexual intercourse. [PORK v.¹ (1)]

pork leg *n.* [1970s] (*US*) the penis (cf. BACON n.¹; ARM n.¹).

Porkopolis *n.* (*also* **Hogopolis, Pigopolis**) (*US*) **1** [mid–late 19C] Cincinnati; thus *Porkopolitan*, a resident of Cincinnati; also *adj.* **2** [mid-19C–1900s] Chicago. [both centres of the meat trade]

pork out *v. see* PIG OUT v. (2).

pork pie *n. see* PORKY n.³ (1).

pork-pie (hat) *n.* **1** [mid-19C] a style of fashionable women's hat. **2** [mid-19C] a fashionable 'toreador'-style hat. **3** [late 19C+] a style of men's hat. [resemblance]

pork puller *n.* [1970s] one who masturbates. [PORK n.² (1) + PULL v.⁷]

pork sword *n.* [1940s+] the penis; thus *do the pork sword jiggle*, to masturbate (cf. AX n.²; BACON n.¹).

porky *n.¹* **1** [late 19C] a pork-butcher. **2** [1900s–40s] (*also* **pork**) a Jew (cf. ARAB n.²). [their respective relations with pork]

porky *n.²* [1920s+] an obese person.

porky *n.³* **1** [1940s+] (*also* **pork pie, porky pie**) a lie. **2** [1990s+] an eye. [rhy. sl. on *porky pie*]

porky *adj.¹* **1** [mid-19C+] fat, even obese. **2** [1920s] (*US*) dissatisfied.

porky *adj.²* [1900s] (*US*) second-rate, inferior.

porky pie *n. see* PORKY n.³ (1).

porky pig *adj.* [1990s+] big, esp. in sense of generous, i.e. BIG adj.[2] (3). [rhy. sl.]

porn *n.* [1960s+] *porn*ography. [abbr.]

porn *adj.* [1970s+] *porn*ographic; thus *porn flicks/movies*,'blue' films; *porn shop*, an 'adult' bookshop specializing in pornography. [abbr.]

porno *n.* [1960s+] **1** a writer of *porn*ography. **2** *porn*ography in general. **3** a *porn*ographic film or video. [abbr.]

porno *adj.* [1950s+] *porn*ographic; pertaining to the world of pornography. [abbr.]

porny *adj.* [1960s+] *porn*ographic, though usu. only mildly so. [abbr.]

pornzine *n.* [1970s+] a *porn*ographic magazine. [abbr.]

porpus *n.* [mid-18C] (*UK Und.*) a stupid, pompous fellow. [? joc. use of SE *porpoise*, i.e. an ODD FISH n.]

Porra *n.* [1970s+] (*S.Afr.*) a derog. term for a person of Portuguese descent. [? mispron. of SE *Portuguese* or Port. *porra!* a coarse excl.]

porridge *n.*[1] [20C+] imprisonment. [the staple morning diet of such establishments in the UK + pun on STIR n.[1] /SE *stir*]

porridge *n.*[2] [1920s+] (*Irish*) **1** a confusion, e.g. a traffic jam. **2** nonsense; as in phr. *you have your porridge*. [SE *porridge*, a hotch potch]

porridge gun *n.* [1990s+] the penis (cf. AX n.[2]). [the supposed similarity of semen to porridge]

porridge hole *n.* [late 19C] (*Scot.*) the mouth.

porridge stuffer *n.* [late 19C] (*Aus.*) a Scottish person. [stereotypical Scot. food]

porridge wog *n.* [1990s+] a derog. term for a Scottish person. [stereotypical Scot. food + WOG n.[1] (3)]

Porsche *n.* [1970s+] (*US Black*) a woman whose body is small, rounded, compact and stylish. [resemblance to *Porsche* cars]

port *n.* [20C+] (*Aus.*) *port*manteau; a school satchel. [abbr.]

portable pocket rocket *n.* [1990s+] the penis (cf. AX n.[2]).

Portagee colonial *n.* (*also* **immigrant chic, Portagee chic, Portugee colonial/chic**) [1980s] (*US*) cheap furniture, touted as ultra fashionable and peddled mainly to gullible recent immigrants. [racial stereotyping]

Portagee lawnmower *n.* (*also* **Portugee lawnmower**) [1980s] a goat used to keep the grass down. [racial stereotyping]

Portagee lift *n.* (*also* **Portugee lift**) [late 19C+] one who carries less than their share of a load. [racial stereotyping; orig. used on US docks]

Portagee overdrive *n. see* JEWISH OVERDRIVE n.

port and brandy *adj.* [20C+] sexually aroused. [rhy. sl. = RANDY adj. (2)]

port and sherry *adj.* [1930s] fine, well. [rhy. sl. = JERRY adj. (2)]

portcullis *n.* [late 16C–17C] a halfpenny. [the SE *portcullis* engraved on 1 side of the silver coin]

porter-without-froth *n.* [1950s] (*W.I.*) a layabout, a ne'er-do-well. [SE *porter*, a dark beer, so called from its being preferred by market porters. Porter, e.g. Guinness, should have a head or 'froth' if poured properly]

porthole *n.* [17C] **1** the anus (cf. A-HOLE n.). **2** the vagina (cf. BLACK HOLE n.[1]).

portie *adj.* [2000s] a mobile phone. [abbr. *portable*]

portion *n.* [late 17C; 1990s+] an act of sexual intercourse.

Port Melbourne Pier *n.* [1940s+] (*Aus.*) an ear. [rhy. sl.]

porto *adj.* [1960s–70s] (*US*) Puerto Rican. [pron. of *Puerto*]

portrait *n.*[1] [mid-19C] a sovereign (cf. ABE n.[2]). [the monarch's face on the coin]

portrait *n.*[2] [1940s] (*US Black*) one's face.

portrait of Madison *n.* [1940s+] (*US*) a $5000 bill (cf. ABE n.[2]). [the portrait of James *Madison* (1751–1836), 4th President of the US, printed on the bills]

portsammy *n.* (*also* **sammy**) [20C+] (*N.Z.*) a portmanteau, a travelling bag. [joc. mispron.]

port-sider *n.* [20C+] (*US*) a left-hander. [naut. imagery; *port*, the left-hand side of the boat]

Portugee *n.* **1** [mid-19C+] a Portuguese person. **2** [1900s–10s] the Portuguese language.

Portugee... *see under* PORTAGEE combs.

Portuguese parliament *n.* [late 19C+] a meeting at which everyone gathers but no one listens to anyone else. [negative stereotyping; orig. naval jargon]

Portuguese pump *n.* [late 19C–1900s] masturbation.

Portuguese time *n.* [1980s] any time later than that set up for an appointment (cf. AFRICAN (PEOPLE'S) TIME n.). [negative stereotyping]

port wine *n.* [mid-19C] (*boxing*) blood (cf. BADMINTON n.).

p.o.s. *n.* [2000s] (*US Black*) something bad, useless or undesirable. [abbr. PIECE OF SHIT n.]

pos *adj.*[1] (*also* **poz**) **1** [early 18C–1900s] *pos*itive. **2** [late 19C] inflexible. [abbr.; (2) SE *positive*, in a dogmatic way]

pos *adj.*[2] *see* POSS adj.

posa *n.* [mid-19C] (*Anglo-Chinese*) a treasurer, as employed by Anglo-Chinese merchants. [mispron. of SE *purser*]

pose off *v.* [1950s] (*W.I./UK Black*) to strike an exaggerated pose.

poser *n.* (*also* **poseur**) [1970s+] someone who pretends to be other than what they actually are. [SE *pose*]

posey *adj.* [1990s+] (*orig. US*) pretentious. [SE *pose*]

posh *n.*[1] [mid-19C–1900s] a dandy. [despite the links in sense, this n. predates POSH adj. and apparently comes from a different root; E.P. suggests link to POSH n.[2], i.e. one who is rich, while *OED* prefers a completely discrete word]

posh *n.*[2] (*also* **posher, poshery**) [mid-19C–1910s] a coin or money, usu. a halfpenny. [Rom. *posh*, a half]

posh *n.*[3] [1950s] nonsense, rubbish. [SE *piffle* + *tosh*]

posh *n.*[4] [1990s+] (*drugs*) cocaine. [POSH adj., i.e. the drug's image]

posh *adj.* [1910s+] (*orig. milit.*) smart, pertaining to the upper classes; thus [1940s–50s] (*Aus.*) *do the posh*, to spend to excess, to do something in style. [ety. unknown. The *OED*, like most modern authorities, rejects the trad. 'port out, starboard home' derivation. E.P. and J.P. Mayer (in Cohen (ed.), *Studies in Slang* I, 1985) opt for a contraction of *polished*, well turned out, smart, sophisticated. The novelist P.G. Wodehouse uses *push* in 1903, which *OED* sees as a synon., but this may be linked to PUSH n.[2] (1), a clique]

posh *v. see* POSH (UP) v.

posh *adv.* [1950s+] in an aristocratic, upper-class manner. [POSH adj.]

posher *n. see* POSH n.[2].

poshery *n.*[1] [1960s] upper-class airs. [POSH adj.]

poshery *n.*[2] *see* POSH n.[2].

posh horri *n.* (*also* **poshero**) [mid-19C] a halfpenny. [Rom. *posh*, half + *horri*, penny]

posh korona *n.* (*also* **posh-korauna**) [mid–late 19C] half-a-crown, 2s 6d (12½p). [Rom. *posh*, half + *korona*, crown]

posho *see under* POSHY.

posh (up) *v.* [1910s+] of a person, to smarten one's clothes, house etc; thus *all poshed up*, dressed up. [POSH adj.]

posh wank *n.* [1990s+] an act of masturbation while wearing a condom. [POSH adj. + WANK n.[1] (1)]

poshy *n.* (*also* **posho**) [1950s+] an upper-class person. [POSH adj.]

poshy *adj.* (*also* **posho**) [2000s] smart, upper-class. [POSHY n.]

posie *n.* [20C+] (*W.I.*) a chamberpot. [ext. of PO n. (1)]

posilutely *adv.* [1920s+] (*US*) without a doubt, irrefutably. [comb. of SE *absolutely* + *positively*; inverse of ABSOTIVELY adv.]

posish *n.* [mid-19C+] (*orig. US*) a *posi*tion, a situation. [abbr.]

positively *adv.* [mid-19C] yes indeed, absolutely.

poss *n.*[1] [1940s] a *poss*ibility. [abbr.]

poss *n.*[2] [1940s+] (*Aus.*) a fool, esp. a trickster's victim. [abbr. POSSUM n. (6)]

poss *adj.* (*also* **pos**) [early 18C+] *poss*ible. [abbr.]

poss *v. see* POSS (OUT) v.

posse *n.* [1980s+] **1** (*orig. US Black*) a gang, usu. teenage. **2** (*orig. US campus*) one's own circle of friends. **3** (*orig. US Black*) oneself, as described in the third person, e.g. *the posse can't dig this*, I am unhappy. **4** an in-group. **5** a band. [SE *posse*, an armed band recruited to pursue law-breakers]

posse (down) *v.* [1980s+] (*orig. US Black*) to move in a gang or group. [POSSE n. (1)]

posse mobilitatis *n.* [late 17C–early 19C] the mob. [play on Lat. *posse comitatus*, force of the county, a band of citizens summoned by the sheriff to deal with outbreaks of rioting and similar disorder]

possesh *n.* **1** [1910s] possession; usu. as *in one's possesh*, in one's possession, on one's person. **2** [1920s–40s] a homosexual boy who is used for sex by the tramp he accompanies. [abbr. SE *possession*]

posse up *v.* [1980s+] (*US Black/teen*) of a gang, to move together as a group. [POSSE n. (1)]

possible *n.* [early 19C–1900s] a coin; thus *not have a possible*, not have a chance. [i.e. it makes things possible]

possibles *n.* **1** [early 19C] money (cf. ACTUAL, THE n.). **2** [mid-19C–1940s] necessities, supplies.

possible sack *n.* [late 19C+] (*orig. US*) **1** a bag for personal belongings. **2** a bag containing items that can be taken to the pawnbroker. [POSSIBLES n. (2)]

possie *n.* (*also* **possy, pozzie, pozzy**) [1910s+] (*Aus.*) **1** a position, usu. an advantageous one. **2** a seat. [abbr.]

possle *n.* [late 19C] an earnest advocate of a course or opinion; used ironically. [abbr. SE *apostle*]

posso-de-luxe *n.* [1930s+] (*Aus.*) an extremely rich fool, esp. when used as a confidence trickster's victim. [POSSUM n. (6)]

poss (out) *v.* [1920s+] (*Irish*) to wash; thus *possing*, very wet; *posser*, one who gets wet.

possum *n.* **1** [mid-19C] (*US*) a friend. **2** [late 19C] (*US*) a coward. **3** [late 19C+] (*Aus.*) (*also* **opossum**) a person (used either affectionately or derog.). **4** [20C+] (*Aus.*) a fraudulent substitution. **5** [1900s] (*US*) a Black person. **6** [1930s+] (*Aus.*) a fool, esp. a trickster's victim; sometimes intensified as POSSO-DE-LUXE n. **7** [1940s+] (*Aus.*) a thief. [one of the animal's characteristics is feigning death when threatened]

possum *v.* [early 19C+] to dissemble; to feign sickness; thus *possum trick*, a feigning of injury to lure an intended robbery victim (cf. PLAY POSSUM v.). [SE *possum*/POSSUM n. (2), i.e. the habits of the animal]

possum belly *n.* [19C–1940s] 'a baggy, dried cowhide fastened horizontally beneath the wagon box and used for carrying a reserve of fuel' (P.A. Rollins, *Gone Haywire*, 1939). [thus used for similar arrangements on livestock and circus wagons]

possum belly *v.* [1920s–40s] (*US tramp*) to ride under a railroad car.

possum-eater *n.* [1900s–60s] (*Aus.*) a peasant, a country bumpkin; thus *possum-eating*, countrified (cf. ACORN-CRACKER n.). [their supposed diet]

possum-guts *n.* **1** [mid-late 19C] (*Aus.*) a general term of abuse. **2** [1950s–60s] (*Aus.*) a coward; thus *possum-gutted*, cowardly. [SE *possum*/POSSUM n. (2) + -GUTS sfx; reflecting low opinion of the animal]

possum-scoffer *n.* [late 19C] a Native Australian. [their supposed diet]

possy *n. see* POSSIE n.

post *n.* [1900s–30s] (*US*) a *post*-graduate. [abbr.]

post *v.*[1] [late 18C+] to lay down or stake money, esp. to put up bail; thus [late 18C] *post the cole*; [late 18C] *post the neddies*; [early 19C] *post the pony*; [mid-19C] *post the tin*. **2** [early 19C] (*UK Und.*) to swear on oath. [SE *post*, a trading station, or Ital. *posta*, a stake (+ COLE n. (1)/NEDDY n.[2]/PONY n.[1] (1)/TIN n.[1] (1))]

post *v.*[2] [mid-19C+] (*orig. US*) to inform; thus *keep someone posted*, keep someone up to date. [? *posting* accounts in a ledger or nailing announcements to a post]

post *v.*[3] [1950s+] (*Aus.*) to abandon, to 'leave in the lurch'. [SE *post*, to hurry]

post *v.*[4] [1990s+] **1** (*US*) to appear, to make oneself available. **2** (*W.I.*) to miss an appointment. [SE to take up a *post*]

post a flyer *v.* [1970s+] (*gay*) to advertise one's sexual availability.

postage stamp *n.*[1] [mid-late 19C] any tavern or hotel named the 'Queen's Head'. [the head of Queen Victoria (1819–1901) also adorned contemporary stamps]

postage stamp *n.*[2] [1930s+] a bar. [rhy. sl. = RAMP n.[3]]

postal *n.* [late 19C–1920s] (*US*) a postcard. [abbr. SAmE *postal card*]

postal *adj.* [1990s+] (*US*) crazy, psychotic; usu. as GO POSTAL v. [reflecting a spate of mass killings (of fellow workers) by disgruntled US postal workers]

post a letter *v.* [late 19C+] **1** to have sexual intercourse. **2** to defecate.

post-and-rail *n.*[1] [late 19C–1940s] (*Aus.*) a wooden match. [the resemblance to a *post-and-rail* fence]

post-and-rail *n.*[2] [1940s+] (*Aus.*) a lie, a (fairy) tale. [rhy. sl. = *fairy tale* (see FAIRY STORY n.)]

post-and-rail (tea) *n.* (*also* **post-and-rails**) [mid-19C–1940s] (*Aus.*) poor-quality tea, with particles of stalk and other impurities floating on its surface; such impurities may have been deliberately added to bulk out a grocer's measure. [the idea of chunks of wood floating in it]

post bills *v.* [1940s] (*US Und.*) to pass counterfeit money.

post-chay *n. see* PO'CHAISE n.

posted *adj.*[1] [mid-19C+] (*orig. US*) aware, in the know, shrewd. [POST v.[2]]

posted *adj.*[2] [1960s+] (*Aus.*) abandoned. [? image of a horse or dog left tied to a post]

postern gate *n.* (*also* **postern passage**) [18C] that part of a pair of trousers, or other clothing, that fits over the buttocks. [SE *postern*, a backdoor or gate]

postgrad *n.* [1950s+] a *postgrad*uate; also as adj. [abbr.]

post-horn *n.* [19C] the nose. [one blows it]

postie *n.* **1** [1910s+] (*orig. Aus.*) a *post*man. **2** [1990s+] a *post* office clerk. **3** [2000s] a *post* office. [abbr.]

postilion *v.* [19C+] to insert and manipulate a finger in the anus of a partner as a means of sexual excitement. [SE *postilion*, a swift messenger; thus the practice makes one 'COME v.[1] faster']

postilion of the gospel *n.* [late 18C–early 19C] a parson who rushes through the service.

post-knight *n. see* KNIGHT OF THE POST n.

postman's knock *n.* (*also* **knock**) [20C+] a clock. [rhy. sl.]

postman's sister *n.* [late 19C] a secret informant. [the implication is that her brother can somehow read the mail – perhaps the postcards – and gossips about its contents]

postmaster-general *n.* [late 18C–early 19C] the prime minister. [their patronage of official *posts*]

post nointer *n.* [late 18C–early 19C] a house painter. [he 'anoints' the door posts]

post office *n.* [1930s] (*US Und.*) one who receives or delivers letters to criminals.

post-op *n.* [1990s+] a *post-op*erative transsexual (cf. PRE-OP n.). [abbr.]

post-op *adj.* [1970s+] *post-op*erative, having recently undergone an operation. [abbr.]

post-shay *n. see* PO'CHAISE n.

post toasties *n.* [1970s] (*US camp gay*) the mailman. [brandname of a US breakfast cereal]

post up *v.* **1** [mid-late 19C] (*US*) to supply with the latest information, to learn the latest news; usu. as *posted up*, informed. **2** [1990s+] (*US Black*) to frequent a popular meeting-place with one's friends. [POST v.[2]]

posture moll *n.* [early 18C] a prostitute who specializes in stripping and adopting sexually arousing positions before her customer. [MOLL n.[1] (2)]

posy *n.*[1] [late 19C] (*US campus*) an attractive person. [SE *posy*, a small bunch of flowers]

posy *n.*[2] [late 19C] (*US campus*) a term of abuse. [SE *poser*, something that poses problems]

pot *n.*[1] [mid-16C–mid-19C; 1930s] (*US*) a woman.

pot *n.*[2] **1** [mid-16C+] a generic term for alcohol; thus *potter*, a drink. **2** [18C; 1910s+] a glass of beer, irrespective of measure. **3** [1980s] (*Aus.*) in Queensland, a 10oz (285ml) beer glass.

pot *n.*[3] [17C–18C; 1960s] the vagina (cf. BAG n.[1]). [1960s use is US Black]

pot *n.*[4] **1** [early 19C+] a large sum of money; often in pl.; thus *put on the pot*, to bet heavily. **2** [late 19C–1900s] the favourite in a horserace, upon whom 'pots of money' have been wagered.

pot *n.*[5] [mid-19C] a sixpence. [the contemporary price of a quart pot of HALF-AND-HALF n.[1] (1)]

pot *n.*[6] [mid-19C] the top. [backsl.]

pot *n.*[7] **1** [late 19C–1910s] an important person. **2** [1910s] (*Aus.*) a person, irrespective of status. **3** [1930s] (*US*) an obnoxious person. [abbr. BIG POT n.; (1) later use is SE]

pot *n.*[8] [late 19C+] **1** a prize, esp. a cup given to a sporting victor. **2** (*UK Und.*) the rewards of a crime or a bet. [SE *pot*]

pot *n.*[9] (*also* **pot gut**) [1920s+] an enlarged stomach, usu. developed through excessive drinking. [abbr. SE *pot belly*; ult. a *pot* of ale]

pot *n.*[10] [1930s+] (*drugs*) marijuana, occas. hashish; thus *pot party*, a gathering of people to smoke marijuana. [Mexican Sp. *potiguaya*, marijuana leaves]

pot *n.*[11] *see* POT HAT n.

pot *n.*[12] *see* POTTIE n.

pot *v.*[1] **1** [mid–late 19C] to outdo, to outwit, to deceive. **2** [late 19C] to punish. [16C–17C SE]

pot *v.*[2] **1** [mid-19C+] to shoot, esp. food for eating; thus SE *pot-shot*. **2** [late 19C–1910s] to take from, to extort. **3** [20C+] (*Aus.*) to throw a stone. **4** [20C+] (*US*) to hit, to strike. **5** [1940s] to render drunk. **6** [1990s+] of a man, to seduce, to have sexual intercourse with. [the food goes in the SE *pot*; subseq. defs. are fig. uses of (1)]

pot *v.*[3] (*Aus./N.Z.*) **1** [1900s–10s] to arrest, to charge. **2** [1900s–50s] to inform against, to hand over for trial. [to put in the fig. SE *pot*]

-pot *sfx* [late 19C+] a person; usu. found in combs. (cf. BARMPOT n.; CHARM-POT n.; COME-POT n.; CRACKPOT n.; CRANKPOT n.; FUSSPOT n.; GLUM-POT n.; RUMPOT n.; SEXPOT n.; SOUSEPOT n.; SWANKPOT n.; TOSSPOT n.; WAX-POT n.). [SE *pot*, container. In such combs. the person is seen as a container for a characteristic]

pot and pan *n.* **1** [late 19C+] a man; esp. as *old pot and pan*, often abbr. to OLD POT n. **2** [20C+] one's husband or father; often as *old pot and pan*. [rhy. sl.]

potash *n.* [1940s] (*Irish*) a stew. [Fr. *potage*, soup]

potash and perlmutter *n.* [1910s–50s] butter. [rhy. sl.; ult. a play by Montague Glass, first performed in 1914]

potato *n.*[1] [mid-18C; late 19C+] a person, often as an insult in comb. with a negative adj.

potato *n.*[2] [mid-19C+] a large hole in a sock or stocking through which the flesh shows (cf. SPUD n.[2]). [? the shape + the dirt that accrues to the bare flesh]

potato *n.*[3] (*US*) **1** [1920s] the head. **2** [1930s] a bump, a swelling. [the shape]

potato *n.*[4] (*also* **potato chip**) [1920s+] a dollar; money; usu. in pl. (cf. BANANAS n.[3]).

potato *n.*[5] [1950s] (*Can.*) a native of New Brunswick. [the province grows many potatoes; the implication is one of rural stolidness and stupidity]

potato *n.*[6] *see* POTATO (PEELER) n.

potato, the *n.* [mid-19C] the right thing, the apposite thing; usu. as *quite the potato*; thus negative, *not quite the potato*.

potato *v.* [1980s+] (*US campus*) to lie around doing nothing. [? COUCH POTATO n.]

potato-box *n.* [late 19C] the mouth.

potato chip *n. see* POTATO n.[4].

potato-eater *n.* (*also* **potato-consumer, -head, tater-eater**) [19C+] (*mainly US*) an Irishman (cf. BOG ARAB n.). [racial stereotyping]

potatoes in the mould *adj.* [1910s+] cold. [rhy. sl.]

potato-face *n.* [mid-19C; 1980s] (*US*) a mild term of abuse.

potato-finger *n.* [17C] **1** a long, thick finger. **2** the penis. **3** a dildo. [the shape + the supposed aphrodisiac quality of the sweet potato]

potato-fingered Irishman *n.* [20C+] a clumsy person. [the alleged predilection of the Irish for potatoes]

potato-grabler *n.* [mid-19C] (*US*) the hand.

potato-head *n.* [mid-19C+] (*US*) a fool, a simpleton; thus *tatur-headed*, stupid (cf. APPLEHEAD n.). [SE *potato* + -HEAD sfx (1)]

potato jack *n.* [1970s+] (*US prison*) illicit liquor distilled from potatoes. [SE *potato* + JACK n.[16] (1)]

potato jaw *n.* [late 18C] the mouth. [its use in consuming the vegetable]

potato (peeler) *n.* [1950s+] (*Aus.*) a woman, a girlfriend. [rhy. sl. = SHEILA n. (1)]

potato-pillin' *n.* [1930s] a shilling. [rhy. sl.; pron. of SE *peeling*]

potato queen *n.* [1980s+] (*US gay*) an Oriental gay man who prefers Western partners. [? the *potato* as a quintessential Western food + QUEEN n.[2] (1)/QUEEN sfx (2)]

potato-stealer *n.* [mid-19C] (*US*) a hand.

potato-trap *n.* [late 18C–1900s] the mouth. [SE *potato* + SE *trap*/TRAP n.[3]]

pot-boiler *n.* [mid-19C+] a literary or similar work created purely for the money; also a successful activity. [it keeps the creator's 'pot boiling']

pot burst *phr.* [20C+] (*W.I.*) a phr. used of a friendship to indicate that it has come to an end. [the pot breaks under the relationship's stress]

potch *n.* [20C+] a slap, a smack, usu. given to a child. [Yid./Ger. *Patsch*, a smack, a splash]

potch *v.* [20C+] to slap, to smack, usu. a child. [POTCH n.]

potcharooney *n. see* HOT POCKAROO n.

potchky *v.* (*also* **potchkie, potskie**) [20C+] (*US*) to mess about. [fig. use of POTCH v.]

pot convert *n.* [late 18C–early 19C] a convert to Roman Catholicism who is won over by the free provision of food and drink. [SE *pot*, a container for food or drink]

pot-cover love *n.* [1990s+] (*W.I.*) lesbianism. [? Jam. *pot-cover*, a species of flat-fish, thus play on FISH n.[1] (1)]

poted *adj. see* POTTED (OUT) adj.[2].

poteen *n.* (*also* **poitín, potheen**) [19C+] (*Irish*) illicitly distilled whisky, 'moonshine'. [Irish *poitín*, little pot]

pot-eyed *adj.* [1900s] drunk (cf. ARSEHOLED adj.). [POT n.[2] (1)]

pot-faker *n.* [mid-19C] a hawker of crockery, a cheap-jack. [SE *pot* + FAKER n. (4)]

pot gut *n. see* POT n.[9].

pot-guts *n.* (*also* **pot-gut**) [18C+] a fat person. [SE *pot*/POT n.[9] + -GUTS sfx]

pot-gutted *adj.* [late 18C+] (*US/Aus.*) pot-bellied. [POT-GUTS n.]

pot hat *n.* (*also* **pot**) **1** [late 18C–19C] a bowler hat. **2** [late 19C] a low-crowned hat, as opposed to the more common top hat of the period.

pothead *n.*[1] [mid-19C] a fool; thus *potheaded*, stupid. [SE *pot* + -HEAD sfx (1)]

pothead *n.*[2] [1960s+] (*drugs*) a smoker of marijuana or hashish. [POT n.[10] + -HEAD sfx (3)]

potheen *n. see* POTEEN n.

pothooks and hangers n. [19C] shorthand. [SE *pothooks and hangers*, the curved strokes used in writing, which supposedly resemble the hooks and hangers found in a kitchen]

pothouse n.[1] [mid-17C–1920s] a small, unpretentious tavern or public house. [SE *pot + house*]

pothouse n.[2] [2000s] a madman, one who goes to excessive lengths, esp. criminal. [POTTY adj. (4)]

pothouse adj. [19C] of politicians, contemptible, cheap. [POTHOUSE n.[1]]

pot-hunter n.[1] [late 16C–early 17C] a confidence trickster, one of a team but posing as an independent person, often drunk, who befriends a potential victim and lures them into a swindle. [SE *pot*, a tankard, i.e. the pose as a drunkard + *hunter*]

pot-hunter n.[2] **1** [late 18C–1910s] one who goes hunting for food rather than pleasure. **2** [mid-19C] an unwelcome guest who carefully arrives just in time for dinner. **3** [late 19C–1920s] in punning use of (1), one who pursues medals and/or prizes; thus *pot-hunting*, such a pursuit. **4** [20C+] (*US*) a scavenger. [SE *pot*/POT n.[8] (1) + SE *hunter*]

potion n. [1990s+] (*W.I.*) a large quantity.

pot-jostler n. [1910s] (*Aus.*) a barman.

pot-jostling adj. [late 19C] (*Aus.*) drunken.

potless adj. [2000s] impoverished. [NOT HAVE A POT TO PISS IN (OR A WINDOW TO THROW IT OUT OF) v. (1)]

pot-lick v. [1920s–60s] to toady to, to curry favour, thus POT-LICKER n.[1]. [backform. f. POT-LICKER n.[1]]

pot-licker n.[1] [mid-19C+] a sycophant, a contemptible person; thus *pot-licking*, toadying. [POT-LICK v.]

pot-licker n.[2] [1930s–50s] (*US/W.I.*) a mongrel, kept as a watch-dog and allowed to forage for its food.

pot liquor n. (*also* potlikker) [1960s+] (*drugs*) a drink derived from brewing marijuana leaves and stalks. [POT n.[10] + play on SE *pot liquor*, the liquid derived from boiling greens]

potna n. see PARD n.

pot o' bliss n. see POT OF BLISS n.

pot of all n. [late 19C] a supreme hero. [POT n.[7] (1)]

pot of beer n. [late 19C] amongst teetotallers, a bottle of ginger beer.

pot of bliss n. (*also* pot o' bliss) [late 19C] a handsome, good-looking woman.

pot of glue n. [20C+] **1** a Jew (cf. BILLY THE KID n.). **2** a queue. [rhy. sl.]

pot of honey n. [late 19C+] money (cf. BEES (AND HONEY) n.). [rhy. sl.]

pot of jelly n. [1940s+] the belly. [rhy. sl.]

pot out v. [1960s+] (*drugs*) to smoke marijuana. [POT n.[10]]

potpig n. [2000s] one who smokes more than their share of a cannabis cigarette. [POT n.[10] + PIG n.[1] (1)]

pot pork for v. [20C+] (*W.I.*) **1** of a young woman, to cook special meals for the object of one's affections. **2** to get a husband through deliberate scheming.

pots n. [1980s+] (*Polari*) the teeth.

pots adj. [1920s–30s] insane, eccentric. [POTTY adj. (4)]

pots and dishes n. [1970s] wishes. [rhy. sl.]

pot-shaken adj. [17C] drunk (cf. ALED UP adj.).

pot-shot adj. [mid-17C] drunk (cf. ALED UP adj.). [one has been fig. *shot* by drinking a *pot* of beer]

potsick adj. [early 17C] drunk (cf. AFFLICTED adj.).

potskie v. see POTCHKY v.

pot-slinger n. [20C+] (*US*) a cook.

potsy n. [1930s+] (*US*) a police badge, an identification card. [the tin (used for *pots*) that is allegedly made into badges]

potted see under POTTED (OUT).

potted bush n. [1950s+] (*drugs*) hashish (cf. AFGHAN n.). [SE *potted*, confined in a small space + BUSH n.[5] (1)]

potted head adj. [1990s+] dead. [rhy. sl.]

potted (out) adj.[1] **1** [mid–late 19C] confined. **2** [mid–late 19C]

dead and buried. **3** [late 19C] snubbed, suppressed. [gardening imagery]

potted (out) adj.[2] (*also* poted, potted off) [20C+] (*US*) drunk (cf. ALED UP adj.). [SE *pot*, a container for drink]

potted (out) adj.[3] [1960s+] (*drugs*) intoxicated by marijuana. [POT OUT v.]

potter n. see POT n.[2] (1).

potter-carrier n. [mid-18C] an apothecary. [mispron.]

pot the white v. [1930s+] of a man, to have sexual intercourse. [billiards/snooker use, in which potting the white is a 'foul stroke']

pottie n. (*also* pot, potty) **1** [1940s+] a chamberpot. **2** [1960s] (*US campus*) a washroom, a lavatory; thus *go potty*, to defecate. [abbr.]

potting n. [mid-19C] drinking. [SE *pot*]

potty n.[1] [late 19C] a tinker. [SE *pot*, which they mend]

potty n.[2] [1950s] a fool. [POTTY adj. (4)]

potty n.[3] see POTTIE n.

potty adj. **1** [mid-19C+] usu. of a plan or scheme, dubious, indifferent. **2** [mid-19C+] insignificant, feeble. **3** [late 19C+] easy to manage, simple. **4** [20C+] crazy, eccentric; thus *potty about*, madly in love with, obsessed by. **5** [1900s] (*Aus.*) drunk (cf. ADDLED adj.). [SE *pot*, a tankard, thus lit. 'drunken']

potty house n. [1900s–30s] a lunatic asylum. [POTTY adj. (4) + SE *house*]

potty mouth n. [1960s+] (*US*) one who uses a great deal of obscenities. [POTTIE n. (1)]

potty watch n. [2000s] (*US prison*) the checking of a prisoner's body waste for contraband. [POTTIE n. (1)]

pot-valiant n. [early 17C] a drunkard. [POT-VALIANT adj.]

pot-valiant adj. [17C–1910s] exhibiting the bravado that comes from imbibing alcoholic drink (cf. IN ONE'S ARMOUR phr.[1]). [play on SE]

pot-wallop v.[1] [mid-19C] to drink heavily. [fig. use of WALLOP v. (2)]

pot-wallop v.[2] [1920s–50s] to wash dishes. [WALLOP v. (2)]

pot-walloper n. **1** [mid-19C+] a scullion, a kitchen servant. **2** [late 19C] (*US*) a slovenly person. **3** [late 19C] a heavy drinker. [a pun on SE *pot-walloper*, lit. 'the boiler of a pot'. 'The term applied in some English boroughs, before the Reform Act of 1832, to a man qualified for a parliamentary vote as a householder (i.e. tenant of a house or distinct part of one) as distinguished from one who was merely a member or inmate of a householder's family; the test of which was his having a separate fire-place, on which his own pot was boiled or food cooked for himself and his family' (*OED*)]

pot-wrestler n. [1900s–40s] a scullion, a kitchen-hand. [SE *pot + wrestler*]

potz n. see PUTZ n.

potzer n. see PATZER n.

pouch n. [mid-19C; 1940s+] **1** the vagina (cf. BAG n.[1]). **2** women considered purely as sex objects. [(2) is fig. use of (1)]

pouch v.[1] **1** [early 19C–1920s] to steal, to grab. **2** [mid-19C] to give a gift of money. **3** [late 19C] to eat. **4** [1910s] (*Aus.*) to drink. [SE *pouch*, to place in a bag]

pouch v.[2] see POOCH v.

pouf/pouffe n. see POOF n.

poufter n. see POOFTER n.

poufy adj. see POOFY adj.[2].

poulain n. [mid-17C–early 19C] a venereal bubo. [synon. Fr., which also means the penis]

poule n. [1920s+] a prostitute; thus *poule-de-luxe*, a high-class prostitute, a courtesan (cf. JAMETTE n.). [adoption of Fr. sl. *poule*, a prostitute (lit. 'a chicken')]

poulter v. see POLTER v.

poulterer n. [early 19C] a thief who specializes in removing the contents of letters. [the image is of a poulterer gutting chickens]

poultice n. **1** [late 19C] (*UK society*) a high stiff collar, which resembles a medical poultice. **2** [late 19C] (*UK society*) a fat woman. **3** [late 19C] a Bohemian. **4** [20C+] (*Ulster*) an unpleasantly persistent person. **5** [1900s] (*UK Und.*) a heavy blow. **6** [1920s–60s] (*US tramp*) a dish of bread and gravy. **7** [1930s–50s] a mortgage. **8** [1940s] (*US Und.*) a money belt. **9** [1940s–70s] (*Aus.*) a large sum of money; a bribe. **10** [1980s+] (*N.Z.*) a very large sandwich with multiple ingredients.

poultice over the peeper *n.* [late 19C] a blow on the eye. [SE *poultice* + PEEPER *n.* (1)]

poultry *n.* [17C] **1** women in general. **2** prostitutes; thus *poulterer*, a pimp. [play on CHICKEN *n.*³ (1)]

poultry dealer *n.* [1950s+] (*US gay*) a pimp who trades in young homosexuals. [play on CHICKEN *n.*⁴ (4)]

pounce *n.* [2000s] a pimp; thus a general term of abuse. [POUNCEY *n.*]

pounceable *adj.* [1990s+] (*US teen*) sexually alluring. [SE *pounce*, to jump on]

pounce-shicer *n.* (*also* ponce-shicer) [late 19C] a pimp (cf. ABBOT ON THE CROSS *n.*). [PONCE *n.* (1) + SHICER *n.* (3)]

pouncey *n.* [mid-19C] a pimp (cf. ABBOT ON THE CROSS *n.*). [PONCE *n.* (1)]

pound *n.*¹ [late 19C–1910s] the human head. [rhy. sl.; *pound of lead*]

pound *n.*² **1** [1920s+] (*US*) money, esp. $1 or $5. **2** [1950s+] (*US Und.*) a 5-year sentence. [an era when the *pound* sterling equalled $5]

pound *n.*³ [1960s+] (*Aus. Und.*) the punishment cells. [SE *pound*, an enclosure]

pound *n.*⁴ [1990s+] **1** (*US Black*) a slap on the back used as a greeting. **2** (*US*) a .357 handgun. [SE *pound*, to hit]

pound *n.*⁵ [1990s+] an act of sexual intercourse. [POUND *v.*² (1)]

pound *v.*¹ (*also* pound it) [early–mid-19C] to place a bet that one is sure one will win. [the cockfighting practice of offering £10 to 5s, a very extravagant bet which was known as *pounding a cock*. If no one took it the match was automatically off]

pound *v.*² [1920s+] **1** (*US*) of a man, to perform sex vigorously (cf. BANG *v.*¹). **2** [1970s+] (*US Black/campus*) to drink beer quickly.

poundable *adj.* [early 19C] certain, definite, inevitable, esp. as regards the result of a wager. [POUND *v.*¹]

pound a cotton *v.* [1990s+] (*US drugs*) to soak a used COTTON *n.*¹ (1) in order to strain out the water/heroin residue.

poundage cove *n.* [mid-19C] (*UK Und.*) 'a fellow who receives poundage for procuring customers for damaged goods'. [SE *poundage*, 'an impost, duty, or tax of so much per pound sterling on merchandise' (*OED*) + COVE *n.* (1)]

pound brass *v.* [1910s] (*US*) to work as a telegraph operator.

poundcake *n.* **1** [1930s+] (*US*) an attractive woman. **2** [1970s+] (*US gay*) the buttocks; thus *make poundcake*, to have anal intercourse (cf. BAKERY GOODS *n.*). **3** [1990s+] (*US*) pornographic writing or magazines.

pounded *adj.* [early–mid-19C] caught out in some form of (? homosexual) impropriety. [SE *pound*, an enclosure where animals are kept]

pounder *n.* [1930s–60s] (*US Black*) a policeman. [abbr. BEAT-POUNDER *n.*]

pounders *n.* [17C] the testicles (cf. BANGERS *n.*). [? their knocking together]

pounding match *n.* [mid-19C] a boxing match, a fight.

pound it *v. see* POUND *v.*¹.

pound note *n.*¹ [20C+] a coat. [rhy. sl.]

pound note *n.*² [1920s–50s] an upper-class person. [i.e. rich]

pound note *n.*³ [1930s–40s] (*US*) $5. [the then contemporary exchange rate of $5 = £1]

pound-note *adj.* [1920s–70s] affected, pretentious; upper-class. [POUND NOTE *n.*²]

pound-note geezer *n.* [1950s+] (*orig. Aus.*) a rich man. [SE *pound note* + GEEZER *n.*¹ (1)]

pound-noteish *adj.* [1930s–60s] pompous, affected, affecting superiority, arrogant. [POUND NOTE *n.*²]

pound of butter *n.* [1980s+] an eccentric, a mad person (cf. BREAD AND BUTTER *n.*²). [rhy. sl. = NUTTER *n.*¹]

pound off *v.* [1970s+] (*orig. US*) to masturbate (cf. BALL OFF *v.*²; BANG THE BISHOP *v.*).

pound of lead *n.* (*also* pound o'lead) [late 19C–1900s] the head. [rhy. sl.]

pound one's ear *v.* (*also* pound one's pillow) [late 19C–1960s] (*US*) to sleep. [tramps attempting to sleep in the boxcars of US railroads as they bumped over the rails]

pound one's meat *v.* [1950s+] (*US*) **1** to masturbate (cf. BANG THE BISHOP *v.*; BEAT ONE'S MEAT *v.*). **2** to have sexual intercourse (cf. BURY IT *v.*). [MEAT *n.* (2)]

pound one's pork *v.* (*also* flog one's pork) [1970s+] to masturbate (cf. BANG THE BISHOP *v.*; BEAT ONE'S MEAT *v.*). [PORK SWORD *n.*]

pound one's pud *v.* [1950s+] to masturbate (cf. BANG THE BISHOP *v.*; BEAT ONE'S MEAT *v.*). [PUD *n.*³ (1)]

poundrel *n.* [17C] the head. [SE *poundrel*, scales]

pound salt up your ass! *excl.* [20C+] (*US*) a euph. for GO TO HELL! excl.

pound sand in a rat hole *v.* [late 19C+] (*US*) to be reasonably intelligent; usu. in phr. *not enough sense to pound sand in a rat hole*.

pounds and pence *n.* [20C+] sense. [rhy. sl.]

pound someone's name *v.* [20C+] (*W.I.*) to denigrate someone, to criticize someone behind their back.

pounds to peanuts *adv.* [20C+] (*Aus./UK*) for sure, certainly.

pound-text *n.* [late 18C–19C] a parson. [his thumping of the Bible]

pound the air *v.* [1920s] (*US Und.*) to sleep.

pound the beat *v.* [1960s+] (*Aus.*) to walk the streets as a prostitute. [on the model of the police use]

pound the books *v.* [1920s+] (*US campus*) to study hard.

pound the headboard *v.* [1980s] (*US campus*) to have sexual intercourse.

pound the pavement *v.* **1** [19C+] (*US Und.*) to work as a street prostitute. **2** [20C+] (*US*) to walk the streets, esp. in search of a job. **3** [1900s–30s] (*US*) of a policeman, to walk the streets. **4** [1990s+] (*US drugs*) to search for drugs, which can often require hours of walking.

pound the rails *v.* [1910s] (*US*) to travel by train, esp. as a hobo.

pound the stuffing out of *v. see* KNOCK THE STUFFING OUT OF *v.*

pour it on *v.* **1** [1930s+] (*orig. US*) to make a great effort; to intensify one's efforts. **2** [1950s+] (*also* pour it to) to punish harshly. **3** [1960s] (*US*) to seek a verbal or physical confrontation. **4** [1960s] to have sexual intercourse. **5** [1980s] to flatter outrageously.

pour-man *n.* [1940s] (*US Black*) a bartender. [pun]

pour (on) the coal *v.* **1** [1940s+] (*US*) of a person or a vehicle, to accelerate. **2** [1950s] to punish severely. [railroad use]

pour the pork *v.* [1950s+] (*orig. US*) to have sexual intercourse, hetero- or male homosexual. [PORK SWORD *n.*]

pout *n.* [mid-18C] a mistress. [SE *pullet*, a young hen]

pouter *n.* **1** [late 18C–19C] the vagina; in pl., the labia (cf. CUNT-LIPS *n.*). **2** [1910s] (*Aus.*) the male chest. [i.e. 'that which pouts']

pov *n.* (*also* povvo) [1990s+] (*UK juv.*) an impoverished person. [SE *poverty-stricken/impoverished*]

poverty *n.* [early–mid-18C] gin. [its effect and/or its drinkers]

poverty-basket *n.* [early 19C] a wicker cradle.

Poverty Row *n.* [late 19C] (*US*) a metaphorical 'street' denominating a state of impoverishment.

poverty-truck *n.* [1920s] (*W.I.*) ? a small hand-cart. [no absolute def. is available (see Cassidy & LePage, *Dict. of Jamaican English*, 1967, 1992)]

povvo *n. see* POV *n.*

pow *n.* [20C+] (*Ulster*) a bald head. [SE *poll*]

powder *n.*[1] [1910s–60s] (*US*) a drink of liquor. [joc. use of SE *powder*, a medicine or a dose of medicine]

powder *n.*[2] [1920s+] (*drugs*) any form of powdered drug, e.g. heroin, cocaine, amphetamine (cf. A n.[2]; BIRDIE POWDER n.).

powder *v.*[1] [mid-17C–mid-19C; 1920s+] to run off. [the explosive qualities of powder; 1920s+ ety. more likely abbr. TAKE A POWDER v. (1)]

powder *v.*[2] (*Aus./US*) **1** [1900s] to hit very hard. **2** [1930s–80s] to kill, to murder. [fig. to reduce to powder]

powder away *v.* [1920s] to do morally admirable but ultimately pointless activities. [the sprinkling of powder]

powder car *n.* [1940s] (*US Und.*) a car used by criminals to flee from the scene of the crime. [POWDER v.[1]]

powdered chalk *n.* [late 19C+] a walk; thus *take a powdered chalk*, to take a walk. [rhy. sl.]

powdered diamonds *n.* (*also* **powder diamonds**) [1950s–70s] (*US drugs*) cocaine (cf. BIRDIE POWDER n.). [its cost and the sparkle of high-quality cocaine]

powdering tub *n.* (*also* **pickling tub**) **1** [late 16C–early 19C] the sweating tub used for the cure of venereal disease. **2** [late 17C–early 19C] the hospital for sexual diseases, near Kingsland, London. **3** [mid-19C] (*UK Und.*) shoes or boots. [SE *powdering/pickling tub*, the tub in which the flesh of dead animals was pickled or 'powdered']

powder one's hair *v.* [18C] to get drunk. [euph.]

powder one's nose *v.* (*also* **powder one's schnoz**) [1970s+] (*drugs*) to take cocaine. [pun on SE euph. for visiting the lavatory]

powder puff *n.* **1** [1920s+] an effeminate male homosexual. **2** [1950s] a cautious fighter. **3** [1990s+] (*W.I.*) a special woman. [the term was notoriously used to attack the silent film god Rudolph Valentino (1895–1926)]

powderpuff *adj.* (*US*) **1** [1930s–60s] of a man, weak. **2** [1960s] of a woman, pampered. [POWDER PUFF n. (1)/SE *powder puff*]

powder up *v.* [1930s–60s] (*US*) to drink alcohol; to become drunk. [POWDER n.[1]]

powder wagon *n.* [1920s] (*US Und.*) a sawn-off shotgun. [like a SE *powder-wagon* it carries an explosive charge]

power *n.* **1** [late 17C+] a good deal, a large number. **2** [mid-19C+] the penis. **3** [late 19C–1930s] (*US Black*) money (cf. ACTUAL, THE n.). **4** [1920s] (*US Und.*) nitroglycerin.

power, the *n.* [1990s+] (*US prison*) the authorities.

power *adj.* [1960s+] (*US campus*) extreme. [POWER n. (1)]

power *v.*[1] [1980s] (*US*) to persuade through threats and/or violence.

power *v.*[2] [1980s+] (*US campus*) to drink beer quickly. [SE *power*, to move with speed or force]

power *adv.* [1980s+] (*US campus*) extremely. [POWER adj.]

power dance *n. see* BLACK POWER DANCE n.

powerful *adj.* [mid-19C+] **1** great in quantity or number. **2** of objects and people, attractive, beautiful.

powerful *adv.* [early 19C+] (*orig. US*) in a great degree, very, exceedingly. [POWERFUL adj. (1)]

powerhouse *n.* [1910s+] a strong, important, energetic and influential person.

power on *v.* (*also* **power through**) [1980s+] (*US campus*) to do well, to succeed. [SE *power*, to move with speed or force]

power point *n.* [1990s+] (*Aus.*) a derog. term for an Asian (cf. BROWNIE n.[2]). [play on SLANT n.[4]; ety. offered by a respondent to Moore, *Lexicon of Cadet Language* (1993): 'So called because in a power point, that is the socket in the wall, the two top holes for the plug are on a slant and look like slanting eyes, and the bottom hole is vertical and looks like a nose, so the whole power point is said to resemble an Asian face']

power sludge *n.* [1980s] (*US campus*) coffee.

power someone's cheeks *v.* [1970s+] (*US gay*) to have anal intercourse. [SE *power* + CHEEKS n.[1]]

power through *v. see* POWER ON v.

power tool *n.*[1] [1960s+] (*US campus*) a very annoying person. [SE *power*, supreme, outstanding + TOOL n.[1] (3)]

power tool *n.*[2] *see* TOOL n.[2] (7).

power tool *v. see* TOOL v.[4].

power trip *n.* [1970s+] (*orig. US*) a show of personal power, esp. if blatant; also attrib. [SE *power* + TRIP n.[5] (1)]

power-trip *v.* [1970s+] (*orig. US*) to exercise one's personal power, esp. at the expense of others, to flaunt one's ego and importance. [POWER TRIP n.]

powo *adj.* [2000s] (*Aus.*) impoverished. [exaggerated pron. of SE *poor*]

powter *v. see* POLTER v.

pow-wow *n.* (*orig. US*) **1** [early 19C+] a meeting. **2** [early–late 19C] a noise, a commotion. **3** [late 19C] a fight. **4** [late 19C+] a chat, a conversation. [Algonkin (Narragansett) *pow'waw* or *po'wah*, a priest, a medicine man; thus the ceremonies over which such figures officiated and thus any gathering or conference]

pow-wow *v.* [mid-19C+] (*orig. US*) to chat, to converse with, to talk to. [POW-WOW n.]

pox *n.*[1] **1** [16C+] syphilis. **2** [17C+] any venereal disease. [the SE *pocks* or eruptive pustules on the skin that are a sign of syphilis; SE *pox* is smallpox; syphilis was also called the *great* or *grand pox*, to distinguish it from 'lesser' venereal diseases]

pox *n.*[2] [1930s–50s] (*drugs*) opium (cf. APOSTLE n.). [? abbr. YEN POK n.]

pox, the *n.* [17C–18C] a synon. for *hell* etc in interrog. phr. *who the…, how the…* etc. [POX!, A excl.]

pox *v.* [late 16C–mid-19C] to infect with syphilis. [POX n.[1] (1)]

pox!, a *excl.* (*also* **pox!**) [mid-16C+] a general excl. of annoyance, irritation; usu. as *(a) pox on/upon*; also in phr. *(a) pox take…* [POX n.[1] (1)]

pox bottle *n. see* POXHEAD n.

pox doctor *n.* [mid-18C; 1930s+] a doctor specializing in venereal diseases. [POX n.[1]]

pox-eaten *adj.* (*also* **pox-rotten**) [1930s–50s] a general negative. [POX n.[1] (1) + SE *eaten/rotten*]

poxed(-up) *adj.* [17C+] venereally diseased, esp. suffering from syphilis; also in fig. use. [POX n.[1] (1)]

poxhead *n.* (*also* **pox bottle**) [1980s+] (*Aus./Irish*) a general term of abuse. [POX n.[1] (1) + -HEAD sfx (1)/SE *bottle*]

pox-hospital *n.* [1930s–40s] a hospital or clinic specializing in sexually transmitted diseases. [POX n.[1] (2) + SE *hospital*]

pox-rotten *adj. see* POX-EATEN adj.

poxy *adj.* **1** [1920s+] unpleasant, dirty, disgusting. **2** [1950s+] piffling. [POX n.[1] (1)]

poxy-faced *adj.* (*also* **poxy-puss**) [1930s–60s] a general term of abuse, lit. 'syphilitic-faced'. [POXY adj. (1)]

poz *adj. see* POS adj.[1].

pozzie/pozzy *n. see* POSSIE n.

p.p. *n.* **1** [late 19C; 1930s] a pickpocket. **2** [1920s+] (*Irish*) a parish priest. [abbr.]

p.p.c. *n.* [late 19C] (*UK society*) a curt, barely polite farewell; thus as v., to fall out, to quarrel, to 'cut'. [abbr. Fr. *pour prendre congé*, to take leave, written on a visiting card]

p.p.d. *n.* [1980s+] (*US campus*) an attractive person of the opposite sex. [abbr. *possible/potential prom date*]

p.p.m. *phr.* [late 19C] (*UK society*) goodbye, as inscribed on visiting cards. [abbr. Fr. *pour p'tit moment*, for a little while]

PP9-ing *n.* [2000s] (*UK prison*) an act of coshing another prisoner with a sock or similar loaded with PP9 batteries.

p.q. *n.* [1980s+] (*US campus*) someone who is out-of-date, unfashionable. [abbr. *polyester queen* (cf. POLYESTER n.)]

P.R. *n.* [1950s+] (*US*) **1** a Puerto Rican. **2** Puerto Rico. [abbr.]

p.r. *n.*[1] [19C] the prize ring, a generic term for the world of prize-fighting and pugilism. [abbr.]

p.r. *n.*[2] [1960s+] (*drugs*) marijuana. [abbr. *Panama Red*]

practitioner *n.* [mid-19C] a thief. [euph.]

prad n. (also **praddle, pred**) [18C–1930s] a horse; thus *pradback*, horseback; *prad-cove*, a horse-dealer; *prad-holder*, a bridle; *prad-napper*, a horse-thief. [Du. *paard*, a horse; ult. Lat. *paraveredus*, which gives the SE *palfrey*, a riding horse as opposed to a war-horse; 20C use is Aus./N.Z. only]

prad borrower n. [late 18C] (*UK Und.*) one who steals a horse, but (sometimes) returns him. [PRAD n.]

prad lay n. [18C–mid-19C] the stealing of bags from horses. [PRAD n. + LAY n.⁴ (1)]

prad-napping n. (also **pred-napping**) [mid-19C] horse-stealing. [PRAD n. + NAP v.² (5)]

prad prigger n. see PRIGGER (OF PRANCERS) n.

prag n. [late 16C] (*UK Und.*) a thief. [var. on PRIG n.¹ (1)]

prairie nigger n. [2000s] (*US Black*) a derog. term for a Native American. [SE *prairie* + NIGGER n.¹ (1)]

prairie oyster n. (also **prairie cocktail**) [late 19C+] (*orig. US*) 'an egg broken into a cup without smashing the yolk, the toast [a shot of liquor] poured in on the top of it, and the whole taken at a swallow' (J.T. Keane, *On Blue-Water*, 1883); generally, but not invariably taken as a hangover cure.

pram-face n. [2000s] a derog. term for a working class, council-estate dwelling young woman and single mother.

pram! pram! excl. [1980s+] (*W.I./UK Black teen*) a sound made by the mouth, simulating gun shots fired, used in appreciation of something, such as a dancehall song etc. [echoic]

prams n. [1920s–30s] (*Scot.*) the legs.

prancer n. [mid-16C–mid-19C] (*UK Und.*) **1** a horse. **2** a highway-man. **3** a horse thief. **4** a cavalry officer. [SE *prancer*, a mettlesome, spirited horse]

prancers n. [mid-18C] (*UK Und.*) stairs. [one *prances* up them]

prancer's nab n. (also **prancer's nob, …poll**) [late 17C–early 19C] (*UK Und.*) a horse's head seal, when used for counterfeiting documents. [PRANCER n. (1) + NAB n.¹ (1)/NOB n.¹ (1)/SE *poll*, head]

prang n. **1** [1940s+] a crash. **2** [1950s] a joke or prank. [? echoic; ? mispron. of SE *prank*]

prang adj. [1990s+] (*Black*) extremely intoxicated, esp. by crack cocaine. [? PRANG n. (1)]

prang v. [1940s+] **1** (also **prang in**) to attack, to crash one's car or plane. **2** to break, e.g. an arm, a leg. **3** to have sexual intercourse (cf. BANG v.¹). [PRANG n. (1); orig. WW2 RAF use; note 1960s US Air Force Academy *prang in*, to make a very serious mistake]

pranker n. [late 16C] (*UK Und.*) a horse. [PRANCER n. (1)]

prannet n. [1970s] a fool, an idiot. [PRANNIE n.]

prannie n. (also **pranny**) **1** [late 19C+] the vagina. **2** [1980s+] a general term of contempt. [? Scot. *pran/prann*, to squeeze, to crush; (2) is fig. use of (1)]

pra-pra adj. [20C+] (*W.I.*) cheating, mixed up. [PRA-PRA v.]

pra-pra v. [20C+] (*W.I.*) to snatch, to steal. [Twi *pra*, to carry away]

prat n.¹ (also **pratt**) **1** [16C+] (*orig. UK Und.*) (also **praty**) a buttock, the buttocks. **2** [late 17C–early 19C] a tinder-box. **3** [19C+] the vagina. **4** [20C+] a young woman. **5** [1910s+] (*US*) a hip pocket; thus *prat-digger*, a pickpocket; *prat frisk*, the theft of a wallet from a hip pocket; *prat leather*, a wallet kept in the hip pocket; *prat poke*, a wallet stolen from the hip pocket. **6** [1960s+] a general term of abuse; mainly a fool, an idiot (cf. ARSE n.¹; BAMBA n.¹). **7** [1970s] (*US*) a young homosexual man. [? echoic of the buttocks hitting a hard surface; subseq. defs. are fig. uses of (1)]

prat n.² [1960s] (*US Black*) a hoax, a deception, a confidence trick.

prat v.¹ **1** [16C+] to beat. **2** [late 19C–1910s] to go. [Rom. *praster*, to run]

prat v.² [1910s+] (*Aus.*) to talk to someone. [abbr. SE *prattle*]

prat v.³ **1** [1930s–50s] (*US Black*) of a woman, to play sexually hard to get, to tease physically. **2** [1940s–60s] of a confidence trickster, to play with the potential victim. [PRAT n.¹ (1)]

prat about v. (also **prat around**) [1960s+] to act foolishly, to act in an irritating manner. [PRAT n.¹ (6)]

prat-boy n. (*US*) **1** [1940s–50s] a catamite. **2** [2000s] one who takes the punishment for another's crime, a FALL GUY n. [PRAT n.¹ (1) + SE *boy* + fig. use]

prate(e) n. see PRATIE n.

prater n. **1** [mid-16C–18C] a boaster. **2** [late 17C–19C] an itinerant, bogus preacher. **3** [19C] the mouth. [SE *prater*, an obnoxious or idle talker]

prate-roast n. [late 17C–mid-19C] a talkative boy. [SE *prate*, chatter]

pratfall n. [1950s+] (*orig. US*) **1** a humiliating defeat, a sudden failure. **2** a danger, a pitfall. [PRAT n.¹ (1) + SE *fall*; orig. theatre jargon *pratfall*, a fall onto the buttocks, usu. as part of a slapstick routine]

prat for v. (also **pratt for**) **1** [1940s–50s] (*US drugs*) in weak use of (2), to work for in an subordinate role. **2** [1940s+] (*gay*) to indulge, actively or passively, in anal intercourse (cf. ASK FOR THE RING v.). [PRAT n.¹ (1)]

pratie n. (also **parater, paratie, prate, pratee, praty**) [late 18C+] (*Anglo-Irish*) a potato. [pron.]

prat in v. [20C+] **1** (*US Und.*) for a pickpocket's assistant to push the victim so as to place them in the correct position for the theft. **2** (*Aus.*) to push oneself forward, to barge in; thus *prat one's frame in*. [PRAT n.¹ (1) (+ FRAME n.¹ (1))]

prating-cheat n. [mid-16C–mid-19C] (*UK Und.*) the tongue (cf. PRATTLING-CHEAT n.). [SE *prate*, to talk, to chatter + CHEAT n. (1)]

prat-kick n. [1910s–40s] (*US Und.*) the back pocket of one's trousers. [PRAT n.¹ (1) + KICK n.⁴]

pratt n. see PRAT n.¹.

pratt for v. see PRAT FOR v.

pratting-ken n. [mid–late 19C] a cheap lodging house. [PRAT n.¹ (1) + KEN n.¹ (1), i.e. a place one can rest one's buttocks]

prattish adj. [1990s+] stupid. [PRAT n.¹ (6)]

prattle-box n. [mid-17C–mid-18C] a chatterer, a gossip.

prattle-broth n. [late 18C–mid-19C] tea (cf. SCANDAL-BROTH n.). [the stereotypical chattering women supposed to gather around a tea-table]

prattling-box n. [mid-18C–early 19C] a pulpit.

prattling-cheat n. [mid–late 16C] (*UK Und.*) a tongue (cf. PRATING-CHEAT n.). [SE *prattle* + CHEAT n. (1)]

prattling parlour n. [mid-19C] a private apartment.

prat whids v. [17C] to break wind. [SE *prate* + WHID n. (1), lit. 'speak words']

praty n.¹ see PRAT n.¹ (1).

praty n.² see PRATIE n.

prawn n. [late 19C+] (*Aus.*) a fool (cf. AIREDALE n.). [the image of the SE *prawn* as a 'humorous' or 'stupid' fish]

prawn cocktail offensive n. [1960s+] the after-dinner-speaking circuit; esp. as followed by political hopefuls. [the poor quality of the food (almost always including the prawn cocktail, a perennial middle English favourite) on offer]

prawnhead n. [1960s+] (*Aus.*) a fool, a simpleton (cf. AIREDALE n.). [PRAWN n. + -HEAD sfx (1)]

prawn-headed mullet n. [1960s+] (*Aus.*) a fool (cf. AIREDALE n.). [ext. of PRAWN n./PRAWNHEAD n.]

prawnie n. (also **prawny**) [1940s+] (*Aus.*) a fisher or seller of prawns.

prayer-bones n. (also **prayer-handles**) [late 19C–1940s] (*US Black*) the knees. [one's genuflection]

prayer book n. **1** [late 18C] (*UK Und.*) a small piece of stolen lead, which can be carried in a pocket. **2** [mid-19C+] (*US*) a pack of rolling papers. **3** [late 19C] *Ruff's Guide to the Turf*, the racing man's 'Bible'.

prayer-dukes n. (also **prayer-handles**) [1920s–40s] (*US Black*) the hands. [SE *prayer* + DUKE n.³ (1)/SE *handle*; they are clasped in prayer]

prayer-factory n. [1930s–50s] (*Irish*) a convent.

prayer meeting *n.* [1940s] (*US gang*) a game of dice, a crap game. [? use of one's hands]

pray to the enamel god/porcelain god(dess) *v. see* KISS THE PORCELAIN GOD(DESS) *v.*

pray TV *n.* [1980s+] (*orig. US*) religious broadcasting, esp. TV evangelism, which uses its broadcasts to gather donations from the faithful. [SE *pray* + *TV* + pun on 'pay TV']

pray with one's knees upwards *v.* [late 18C–early 19C] of a woman, to have sexual intercourse (cf. CATCH AN OYSTER *v.*). [the 'missionary position']

pre *n.* [2000s] a young (underage) sex object, male or female, seen as suitable for exploitation. [SE *pre-*, before, i.e. the age of consent]

preach *n.* **1** [late 16C–mid-19C] an act of preaching, a sermon, esp. a tediously moralizing one. **2** [mid-19C] a preacher. [abbr. SE *preacher*]

preach at Tyburn cross *v.* [late 16C–18C] to be hanged. [TYBURN n., the site of the main Middlesex gallows]

preachify *v.* [late 18C+] to preach a dull, moralizing sermon; thus *preachification*, preaching in this way; *preachifying*, moralizing.

preaching-shop *n.* [mid-late 19C] a church, a chapel.

preach on Tower Hill *v.* [16C] to be hanged. [ironic use of SE *preach*, referring, perhaps, to the criminal's last words on the scaffold + *Tower Hill*, the site of many London executions]

preachy *adj.* [early 19C+] tediously moralizing.

preachy-preachy *adj.* [late 19C] tediously moralizing. [PREACHY adj. + redup.; 20C+ use is W.I.]

precheck *n.* [1970s+] an inspection of a client's penis made by a prostitute before intercourse.

precious *adj.* **1** [late 16C+] arrogant. **2** [mid-17C+] awful, terrible, disastrous, e.g. *a precious mess.* **3** [early 18C+] over-fastidious, over-refined. [(3) note orig. use of SE *nice*]

precious *adv.* [mid-19C+] very, exceedingly, e.g. *precious few, precious little.*

precious juice *n.* [1980s+] (*US campus*) any alcoholic drink.

preciously *adv.* [mid-late 19C] very greatly, exceedingly, extremely.

pred *n. see under* PRAD and its combs.

pre-dawn vertical insertion *n.* [1980s] (*US campus*) sexual intercourse that takes place in the early morning. [a satirical ref. to the description of the invasion of Grenada given by the government of President Ronald Reagan (1983)]

preem *n.* [1930s+] (*orig. US*) a theatrical or cinematic *prem*ière; thus *preem*, to have a première, a first night. [abbr.]

preemie *n.* (*also* **preemy, premie**) [1920s+] (*US*) a *prem*ature baby. [abbr./pron.]

preesh! *excl.* [1980s+] (*US campus*) an expression of approval; thanks! [abbr. SE *appreciation*]

prefab *n.* [1940s+] a *prefab*ricated house. [abbr.]

preg *adj.* [1950s+] (*US*) *preg*nant. [abbr.]

preggers *adj.* (*also* **preggars**) [1940s+] *preg*nant. [abbr. + -ER sfx]

preggo *adj.* (*also* **prego**) [1950s+] (*Aus.*) *preg*nant. [abbr. + -o sfx (5)]

preggy *adj.* [1930s+] *preg*nant. [abbr. + sfx -*y*]

pregnant *adj.* [1980s+] (*US drugs*) referring to a marijuana cigarette that is rolled incorrectly, usu. with a bulge in the middle.

prego *n.* [1950s+] (*US*) a pregnant teenager. [PREGGO adj.]

prego *adj. see* PREGGO adj.

preke *n.* (*also* **preky**) [1940s+] (*W.I.*) **1** a fool, a gullible person. **2** a low-class prostitute. **3** a good-for-nothing, an ill-kempt, dirty, slovenly man. [Sp. *pereque*, an intolerable person]

prekkah *v.* [1990s+] (*W.I.*) to be exploited, to be 'put upon'. [PREKE n. (1)]

premie *n. see* PREEMIE n.

premises *n.* **1** [late 17C–1900s] the vagina. **2** [19C] a brothel. [euph.]

premiums *n.* [1990s+] (*US prison*) commercially produced branded cigarettes.

premmie *n.* [1990s+] a *prem*ature ejaculator. [abbr. + sfx -*ie*]

premo *adj.* [1990s+] amazing, excellent, attractive. [? abbr. SE *premium* + -o sfx (5)]

prems *n.* [1900s] *prem*ises, buildings. [abbr.]

prenup *n.* [1990s+] (*US*) a *pre-nup*tial agreement. [abbr.]

pre-op *n.* [1990s+] a *pre-op*erative transsexual (cf. POST-OP n.).

prep *n.* [20C+] *prep*aration.

prep *v.* (*also* **prep up**) **1** [20C+] (*US*) to *prep*are, to get ready. **2** [1980s] (*US campus*) (*also* **prep out**) to get dressed up, esp. overdressed, or elaborately made up. [abbr.]

preppie *n.* (*also* **prep, prepette, preppy, prepster**) [1950s+] (*US campus*) one who attends one of the major US 'prep' schools (St Paul's, Choate, Groton, Miss Porter's, Dana Hall etc), the equivalent of UK public (i.e. fee-paying, private) schools. The graduates of such schools are the children of the US establishment and share similar mainstream styles, language and society.

preppie *adj.* (*also* **preppy**) **1** [1900s] silly, immature. **2** [1950s+] (*US*) mainstream in style and thought, as a result of having been to a major US prep school. [(1) SAmE *prep* school; (2) PREPPIE n.]

preppie *adv.* (*also* **preppy**) [1970s+] (*US/Can.*) in a manner pertaining to PREPPIE n.

pre-pre *v.* [1960s] (*W.I.*) to suffer from diarrhoea. [dial. *pre-pre*, to lose control, to become hysterical]

prepster *n. see* PREPPIE n.

pres *n.*[1] (*also* **prez**) [1920s+] a *pres*ent, a gift. [abbr.]

pres *n.*[2] *see* PREZ n.[1]

presbo *n.* [1950s+] (*Aus.*) a *Presb*yterian. [abbr. SE + -o sfx (4)]

prescott *n. see* CHARLIE PRESCOTT n.

prescriptions *n.* [1970s+] (*drugs*) any drug that comes primarily in pill form, barbiturates, amphetamines etc; thus *prescription reds*, Seconal (cf. PILL n.[4]). [the SE *prescription* that is issued for it]

presenterer *n.* [mid-19C] a prostitute (cf. ASS PEDDLER n.). [she presents herself for trade]

presents *n.* [late 19C+] white spots on one's fingernails, supposedly auguring good luck. [play on synon. SE *gift*]

presh *adj.* [1980s+] (*US campus*) favourable, enjoyable. [abbr. SE *precious*]

preshun *n. see* PRUSHUN n.

president *n. see* DEAD PRESIDENT n.

press and scratch *n.* [19C] a safety match. [rhy. sl.]

pressed *adj.*[1] [1950s+] (*US Black*) very well-dressed. [the state of one's clothes]

pressed *adj.*[2] [1980s] (*US Black*) used of hair that has been chemically straightened. [PRESS ONE'S HAIR v.]

pressed to the max *phr.* [1980s+] very well-dressed, very smart. [PRESSED adj.[1] + TO THE MAX phr.]

press ham *v.* [1960s+] (*US campus*) to press a bare buttock against a window in order to shock passers-by; also to press the genitals against glass where they can be seen. [SE *ham*/HAM n.[5]]

pressie *n.*[1] [1950s+] (*Aus.*) a *Presb*yterian. [abbr.]

pressie *n.*[2] [1960s+] a gift, a *pres*ent. [abbr.]

press one's hair *v.* [1960s–80s] (*US Black*) to straighten one's hair (cf. CONK v.[2]).

press someone's button *v.* [1960s+] to annoy someone, to irritate someone.

press the bricks *v.* [20C+] (*US*) **1** to stand around in the street, loafing and gossiping. **2** to walk the streets in search of work. [SE *press* + BRICKS n. (1)]

press the button *v.* [1910s+] to set an event or a chain of circumstances in motion.

press the ether *v.* [1950s] (*US Black*) to play music.

press the flesh *v.* [1920s+] (*orig. US*) to shake hands; usu. of a politician on a campaign tour, thus to meet the electors; thus *press-the-flesh*, ingratiating, insincere, oleaginous; FLESH-PRESSER n. (1).

press the sheets v. see BEAT THE SHEETS v.

pretender to the throne n. [1950s–60s] (US gay) **1** a heterosexual who poses as gay for the purposes of avoiding the draft. **2** a vice squad policeman who poses as gay to entrap genuine homosexuals. [pun on SE + THRONE n.]

preterite n. [late 19C] (UK society) an old person, but esp. a woman. [SE preterite, pertaining to former times]

pretties n. **1** [1900s–50s] (US) attractive objects, e.g. jewellery. **2** [1980s+] innocent, hitherto untouched young sex objects, either male or female. [SE pretty]

prettify v. [mid-19C+] to make pretty, esp. in a 'cheap and cheerful' manner; thus prettification, the act of prettifying.

pretty adj. [mid-16C+] (US campus) a general negative, ridiculous, unpleasant, problematical.

pretty adv.[1] [late 16C+] rather, considerable, e.g. pretty awful, pretty much.

pretty adv.[2] [mid-19C+] a synon. with SE prettily.

pretty-boy n. [late 19C+] an effeminate-looking young man, although not necessarily a homosexual.

pretty-boy clip n. [late 19C] a hairstyle for men in which the hair is brushed straight forward over the forehead and cut in a straight line from ear to ear. [PRETTY-BOY n.]

pretty horse breaker n. (also horsebreaker) [mid-19C] a high-class prostitute; orig. a woman hired to ride in Hyde Park. [the way such women showed themselves off in a horse and trap, mixing with society as it too paraded in Hyde Park in London and similar places. Their riding costume was often known as ABANDONED HABITS n.]

pretty please (with sugar on it) phr. [1950s+] an intensified form of 'please'; thus an exaggerated, even self-abasing, form of request.

pretty police n. [1990s+] a policeman or police squad specializing in the entrapment of gay men.

pretty polly n. see POLLY n.[4].

pretty steep adj. **1** [mid-19C+] (orig. US) rather expensive. **2** [late 19C] (US) threatening. [PRETTY adv.[1] + STEEP adj.]

pretty up v. [1950s+] (Aus.) to disfigure. [ironic reverse of SE]

pretzel n.[1] [1930s–40s] (US jazz) a French horn; thus pretzel bender, a French horn-player. [the shape]

pretzel n.[2] [1940s] a German. [the stereotypically Ger. foodstuff]

prevert n. [1970s+] a pervert. [deliberate mispron. of SE]

previous n. **1** [1930s+] (UK Und./police) previous convictions. **2** [2000s] (Aus.) a previous appointment.

previous adj. **1** [late 19C+] (orig. US) arriving or occurring too soon, hasty, premature; often as a bit previous. **2** [20C+] (US) usu. of clothing, tight, snug. **3** [1920s+] forward, cheeky, unacceptable or in poor taste; often as a bit previous; get previous.

previous adv. [late 19C–1900s] hastily, quickly. [PREVIOUS adj. (1)]

previousness n. [late 19C] (US) anything seen as coming too soon, too hastily or prematurely; the state of being too hasty or premature. [PREVIOUS adj. (1)]

prexy n. (also prex) [early 19C+] (orig. US campus) a president (of a college, a corporation or firm) or the President of America. [mispron.]

prey n. [late 17C–18C] (UK Und.) money. [i.e. what one 'preys upon']

prez n.[1] (also pres) **1** [late 19C+] (US) a president (of a college, a corporation or firm) or the President of America. **2** [1950s+] (US Black) an important, influential individual. **3** [1950s+] (US) a term of address, genuinely respectful or ironic. [tenor saxophonist Lester Young (1909–59) was so nicknamed by Billie Holiday]

prez n.[2] see PRES n.[1].

prezzie n. (also prezzo) [1930s+] (orig. Aus.) a present. [abbr. + sfx -ie/-o sfx (4)]

priceless adj. [20C+] very amusing, witty, droll.

price of... phr. [20C+] (Irish) all one is worth, one's due deserts, one's fate; esp. as the price of me.

price of a pint n. [late 19C] any sum less than 6 pence. [contemporary values]

price of greens n. [mid–late 19C] the cost of hiring a prostitute. [GREENS n.[2]]

price of meat n. [19C+] the cost of hiring a prostitute. [MEAT n. (1)]

price of one's hat isn't the measure of one's brain, the [19C–1940s] (US Black) one's material possessions have no bearing on one's intelligence and wisdom.

pricey adj. see PRICY adj.

prick n. **1** [mid-16C–17C] a woman's term of endearment for a man. **2** [mid-16C+] the penis. **3** [1920s+] (orig. US) (also pricker) a general derog. term, an idiot, a fool, an incompetent (cf. CHOAD n.; PRICKFACE n.; PRICKHEAD n.). **4** [1950s] (US drugs) a hypodermic syringe. **5** [1970s] anything phallic, e.g. a flagpole. **6** [1970s] aggression, attacks. [SE prick, a pointed weapon or implement. Although the OED, with its first cit. in 1592, labels (2) unequivocally 'coarse slang', E.P. suggests that prick was SE before becoming taboo c.1700. The OED's cit. – 'The pissing Boye lift up his pricke' ('R.D.', Hypnerotomachia) – may appear coarse to modern ears, but it should be noted that piss, certainly, was still SE at the time. In 1540, prick denoted 'a pert, forward, saucy boy or youth; a conceited young fellow', thus (1). The term is defined as 'humorous or contemptuous', but not indecent; it might have referred simply to the lad's 'sharpness'. That said, given that the synon. alongside which it appears is princock (lit. 'prime cock'), a sexual interpretation is possible]

prick adj. [1960s+] (US) a general term of abuse, wretched, damnable. [PRICK n. (3)]

prick v. [17C–mid-19C] to enter a woman. [PRICK n. (2)]

prick a louse v. see PRICK-(THE-)LOUSE n.

prick around v. [1980s] to mess about. [PRICK v., i.e. synon. FUCK ABOUT v. (1)]

prick-arsed adj. [1980s] a term of abuse. [PRICK n. (2) + -ASSED sfx]

prick cheese n. see COCK CHEESE n.

prick-chinking n. [18C] having sexual intercourse. [PRICK n. (2) + CHINK n.[2]]

prick-ear n. (also prick-ears) [mid-17C] a Roundhead, a Parliamentarian, 'a Crop, whose Ears are longer than his Hair' (B.E.). [PRICK-EARED adj. (1); the Roundheads and Puritans were typified by their tight-fitting black skullcaps, which sat above the ears]

prick-eared adj. **1** [mid-16C–18C] crop-headed, thus a generic term for a Puritan. **2** [16C; 1980s] a term of abuse. [PRICK-EAR n./PRICK n. (2) + SE ear]

pricker n. see PRICK n. (3).

prickface n. [1960s+] a general term of abuse, lit. 'penis face'. [PRICK n. (2) + SE face]

prickhead n. **1** [1980s+] a fool, a simpleton; used both derog. and affectionately. **2** [1990s+] a bald-headed man. [PRICK n. (2) + -HEAD sfx (1)]

prick-holder n. (also prick-purse, -scourer, -skinner) [19C] the vagina (cf. BAG n.[1]). [PRICK n. (2) + SE]

prick hole n. [late 19C] the vagina (cf. BAG n.[1]; BLACK HOLE n.[1]). [PRICK n. (2) + SE hole]

prickish adj. see PRICKY adj.

prick-lick v. [1970s+] (US) to perform fellatio; thus prick-lick(er), a fellator (cf. COCKSUCK n.). [PRICK n. (2) + SE lick]

prick-louse n. see PRICK-(THE-)LOUSE n.

pricknic n. [1980s+] (US gay) fellatio. [PRICK n. (2) + pun on SE picnic + EAT v.[3] (1)]

prick office n. [mid-17C] either a brothel staffed by heterosexual male prostitutes or a group of regular brothel patrons. [PRICK n. (2); note OFFICE n.[1]]

prick peddler *n. see* DICK PEDDLER n.

prick-pride *n.* [late 19C] an erect penis. [PRICK n. (2) + SE *pride*]

prick-purse/-scourer/-skinner *n. see* PRICK-HOLDER n.

prick sucker *n.* [late 19C+] one who sucks the penis, whether male or female. [PRICK n. (2) + SE *sucker*]

pricksucking *adj.* [1960s] of a woman, performing oral sex on a man. [PRICK n. (2)]

pricktease *n.* [1950s+] a woman (or man in a homosexual context) who appears to be offering unrestrained sexual favours but stops short of intercourse, leaving the male partner frustrated; also in fig. use. [PRICKTEASE v.]

pricktease *v.* [1940s+] to lead on sexually but to stop short of intercourse. [PRICK n. (2) + SE *tease*]

prickteaser *n.* [1940s+] a woman who allows some physical intimacies but who always stops short of intercourse. [PRICK-TEASE v.]

prick the belt *n.* [late 16C–early 19C] a gambling and cheating game, in which a belt is folded and held out to the punter, who bets that by pricking with a pin they can hit the place where the material is folded (cf. FAST AND LOOSE n.).

prick the garter *n.* (*also* **pitch the nob**) [mid-18C–1930s] (*UK Und.*) a gambling and cheating game, in which a garter is folded and held out to the punter, who bets that by pricking with a pin they can hit the place where the material is folded; almost inevitably they fail and lose their money. [note earlier versions PRICK THE BELT n. and FAST AND LOOSE n.]

prick-(the-)louse *n.* [early 16C–early 19C] a tailor; thus *prick a louse*, to work as a tailor. [SE *prick*, i.e. the needlework + the lice that accrued to clothing]

prick the master vein *v.* [late 17C] of a man, to have sexual intercourse (cf. HIT ON THE MASTER VEIN v.). [SE *master-vein*, a major vein, usu. the carotid artery or jugular vein]

pricky *adj.* (*also* **prickish**) [1960s+] (*US*) obnoxious. [PRICK n. (3)]

pricy *adj.* (*also* **pricey**) [1930s+] (*orig. Aus./N.Z.*) expensive.

pride (and joy) *n.* [1930s–40s] (*Aus./US*) the penis.

pride and joy *n.* [1930s–70s] (*Aus./US*) a boy. [rhy. sl.]

pride-and-pockets *n.* [late 19C–1910s] a half-pay officer. [lots of pride, empty pockets]

pride of the morning *n.* (*also* **morning pride**) [late 19C] an early morning erection, more due to the need to urinate than actual sexual desire.

priest-linked *adj.* [late 17C–early 19C] married.

priest of the blue bag *n.* [mid-19C] a barrister. [the trad. colour of the bag in which they carry their gown and wig]

priest's share *n.* [late 19C–1910s] (*Irish*) one's soul.

prig *n.*[1] (*UK Und.*) **1** [mid-16C–19C] (*also* **prigg, prigman**) a thief, esp. a mendicant villain who specializes in stealing clothes from hedgerows where they are left to dry, or poultry from the farmyard. **2** [mid-16C–19C] a ne'er-do-well who, accompanied by his woman, wanders the country, mixing villainy and legitimate work, pursuing neither, it appears, with particular enthusiasm (sometimes known as the DRUNKEN TINKER n.). **3** [late 17C–mid-19C] a dandy, a fop. **4** [18C–mid-19C] a cheat. [either Lat. *pregare*, to pray, or SE *prig* = prick = sting = rob or cheat. SE *prig*, meaning a carping know-all, may have similar roots, but may be based on the divine Richard Baxter (1615–91), who in 1684 associated it with the initial letters of *proud ignorance*]

prig *n.*[2] [late 16C–mid-19C] a horse. [? it is 'pricked' with spurs]

prig *v.*[1] [mid-16C–early 19C] to ride; thus *priger*, a rider. [SE *prick*, to urge a horse forward]

prig *v.*[2] (*UK/US Und.*) **1** [mid-16C–1910s] to steal; thus *priggism, priggery*, theft. **2** [mid-18C–mid-19C] to cheat, to swindle, to haggle. [? SE *prick*, to skewer]

prig *v.*[3] [17C–early 19C] to have sexual intercourse. [PRIG v.[1], i.e. RIDE v.[1] (1); or ? PRICK v.]

prig and buzz *n.* [late 18C] pick-pocketing; thus *work upon the prig and buzz*. [PRIG v.[2] (1) + BUZZ n.[2] (3)]

prig-beard *n.* [late 16C–early 17C] a degenerate, a seducer. [PRIG v.[3] + BEARD n.[1] (1)]

prigg *n.*[1] [1950s] (*Aus.*) a busybody. [rhy. sl.; *Wally Prigg* = GIG n.[12] (3)]

prigg *n.*[2] *see* PRIG n.[1] (1).

prigger *n.*[1] **1** [mid-16C–mid-19C] a thief. **2** [late 17C] a highwayman. [PRIG v.[2] (1)]

prigger *n.*[2] [early 19C] a fornicator, a womanizer. [PRIG v.[3]]

prigger (of prancers) *n.* (*also* **prad prigger, prigger of prainers, …paulfreys**) [mid-16C–early 19C] (*UK Und.*) a horse-thief (cf. CANTING CREW n.). [PRIGGER n.[1] (1) + PRANCER n. (1)]

prigger of (the) cacklers *n.* [late 17C–mid-19C] (*UK Und.*) a chicken stealer. [PRIGGER n.[1] (1) + CACKLING-CHEAT n.]

priggery *n. see* PRIG v.[2] (1).

prigging *n.*[1] [mid-16C–18C] (*UK Und.*) riding. [PRIG v.[1]]

prigging *n.*[2] **1** [mid-16C–early 18C] horse-stealing; thus *prigging law/lay*, horse-stealing as a criminal profession. **2** [18C–19C] pilfering, small-time thieving. [PRIG v.[2] (1) + LAW n.[1]/LAY n.[4] (1)]

prigging *n.*[3] [17C–18C] having sexual intercourse. [PRIG v.[3]]

priggish *adj.* [late 17C–mid-19C] (*UK Und.*) having the characteristics of a thief. [PRIG n.[1] (1)]

priggism *n. see* PRIG v.[2] (1).

prigman *n. see* PRIG n.[1] (1).

prig-napper *n.*[1] [late 17C–18C] (*UK Und.*) a horse-thief. [PRIG n.[2] + NAP v.[2] (5)]

prig-napper *n.*[2] [late 17C–early 19C] (*UK Und.*) a thief-taker. [PRIG n.[1] (1) + NAP v.[2] (5)]

prigster *n.* (*also* **prigstar**) **1** [17C–19C] (*UK Und.*) a thief. **2** [late 17C–18C] a general pej. **3** [late 17C–early 18C] a rival in love. [ext. of PRIG n.[1]]

prim *n.* [16C–17C] 'a silly, empty, starcht fellow' (B.E.). [SE *prim*, 'consciously or affectedly strict or precise; formal, stiff, demure' (*OED*)]

prima donna *n.* **1** [mid-19C] the second rank of superior prostitutes, immediately below that of kept mistresses. **2** [1930s+] one who behaves in a self-important or temperamental manner. [Ital. *prima donna*, the first or principal female singer in an opera]

prime *adj.*[1] [17C] sexually excited. [SE *primed*, prepared, orig. of a gun]

prime *adj.*[2] [mid-17C+] excellent, first-rate.

prime *adv.* (*also* **primely**) [mid-18C–1900s] excellently. [PRIME adj.[2]]

prime cut *n.* [1970s+] the vagina (cf. BACON SANDWICH n.). [SE *prime cut*, a superior cut of meat]

primed *adj.* **1** [19C+] stimulated rather than intoxicated by drink. **2** [late 19C+] prepared, ready. **3** [1940s–50s] intoxicated by drugs. [SE *prime*, to prepare a gun for firing; all imply a readiness to 'explode into action']

prime flat *n.* [early 19C] (*UK Und.*) an extremely susceptible person, the ideal victim for a confidence trickster. [PRIME adj.[2] + FLAT n.[2] (1)]

primely *adv. see* PRIME adv.

prime one's pump *v.* [1990s+] to masturbate. [PRIME SOMEONE'S PUMP v.]

prime plant *n.* [mid-19C] (*UK Und.*) a potential victim, as assessed by a villain. [PRIME adj.[2] + PLANT v.[1] (5)]

prime someone's pump *v.* **1** [1940s+] to fellate (cf. PRIME ONE'S PUMP v.). **2** [1950s+] to excite sexually.

primo *n.* (*drugs*) **1** [1970s+] any top-quality drug. **2** [1980s+] (*also* **primo square**) a marijuana cigarette laced with cocaine and/or heroin. [the intensified effects]

primo *adj.* [1960s+] first-rate, excellent; usu. referring to the quality of a drug. [Sp. *primo*, first]

primp *v.* [mid-19C+] to preen, to show off.

primpy *adj.* [1910s] (*US*) affected, 'precious'. [PRIMP v.]

prinado *n.* [mid-17C] a card-sharp. [ety. unknown; Sp. *prenada*, pregnant (as cited in the *OED*) is hard to justify. E.P. opts for *primada*, first and thus most skilful, but the fem. '-a' ending makes this link unlikely]

prince *n.* **1** [early 19C; 1910s+] a general term of approval, an admirable or generous person. **2** [1970s–80s] (*US Black*) a charismatic man.

Prince Albert *n.* [1990s+] a body piercing performed on the penis, usu. a small bolt through the glans. [? Victoria's consort, *Prince Albert* (1819–61) was pierced]

Prince Alberts/Alfreds *n. see* ALBERTS *n.*

prince prig *n.* [17C–early 19C] (*UK Und.*) **1** a leading thief, esp. one who acts as a receiver for the robberies of colleagues. **2** the King of the Gypsies. [SE *prince* + PRIG *n.*[1] (1)]

prince's points *n.* [late 19C] (*UK society*) whist played for a shilling a point. [Edward, Prince of Wales (1841–1910), a whist devotee, suggested that the best players were not invariably the richest, and suggested a limit of a shilling per point, thus making it possible for poorer, if more talented players, to join him. The habit became highly fashionable for a while]

princess *n.* **1** [1950s+] a general form of (affectionate) address to a woman. **2** [1960s] a prostitute. **3** [1960s+] (*gay*) an effeminate and relatively youthful male homosexual (cf. DUCHESS *n.*[1]).

Princess Di *n.* [1990s+] a pie. [rhy. sl.; ult. *Diana, Princess of Wales* (1961–97)]

princess of the Nile *n.* [1970s] (*gay*) a Black homosexual male. [PRINCESS *n.* (3)]

princess of the pavement *n.* [1940s+] a prostitute (cf. NIGHT WALKER *n.*).

Princeton rub *n.* (*also* **college fuck, Princeton first-year**) [1950s+] (*US gay*) body-to-body rubbing; intercrural intercourse; also adv. as *Princeton/college style*. [a practice attributed to freshmen at Princeton University; note Rodgers, *The Queen's Vernacular* (1972): 'It was alleged that college men, wanting to explore homosexuality, would refuse to actually penetrate one another for fear of turning queer; so, they turned to a position which most resembled heterosexual coitus']

princock *n.* (*also* **princocks, princox, prinkockes, prinkox**) **1** [mid-16C–early 19C] a dandified, conceited young man. **2** [19C] the vagina. [? SE *prime cock* (as suggested by John Florio in *World of Wordes*, 1598) or Lat. *praecox*, early, precocious]

princod *n.* [late 18C–early 19C] a plump man or woman. [Scot. *preencod*, a pincushion]

princum-prancum *n. see* PRINKUM-PRANKUM *n.*

prink *v.* [mid-16C+] to dress up, to spruce oneself up; thus *prinked* (*up*), spruced up, dressed in one's best clothes; *prinking*, sprucing oneself up. [SE *prank*, to dress oneself up in a bright or showy manner; ult. Du. *pronk*, show, finery, ornament]

prinkockes/prinkox *n. see* PRINCOCK *n.*

prinkum-prankum *n.* (*also* **princum-prancum**) [late 16C–mid-17C] **1** a trick, a game, a prank. **2** sexual intercourse. [redup. of SE *princome*, a prank, ult. SE *prank*; note also *prinkum-prankum*, 'a round dance, formerly danced at weddings, in which the women and men alternately knelt on a cushion to be kissed' (*OED*)]

print *n.* [1920s+] finger*print*, usu. in pl. [abbr.]

print *v.* [1930s+] to take someone's fingerprints. [PRINT *n.*]

prints *n.* [late 19C] (*UK Und.*) boots. [abbr. SE *footprints*]

prior *n.* [1930s+] a prior conviction, a criminal record; often in pl.

prison-bird *n. see* GAOLBIRD *n.*

prison wolf *n.* [1960s+] (*Can. prison*) a prisoner who prefers women when free, but turns to men when imprisoned. [SE *prison* + WOLF *n.*[1] (4)]

prison-yard queen *n.* [1980s+] (*US Und.*) a prison homosexual. [SE *prison-yard* + QUEEN *n.*[2] (1)]

priss *n.* **1** [1920s+] a weakling; a killjoy. **2** [1960s] (*US campus*) an effeminate male. [PRISSY *adj.*]

prissy *n.* [1940s–60s] (*camp gay*) a Black homosexual. [*Prissy*, the Black maid in the book/film *Gone With The Wind* (1936/1939)]

prissy *adj.* (*also* **priss, prissy-pants**) [mid-19C+] over-particular, prim, prudish, esp. in a supposedly effeminate way. [? SE *prim* + *sissy*]

prissy-pants *n.* (*also* **prissy, prisspants**) [1920s–70s] a person who is prim, prudish, often also effeminate, esp. when old. [PRISSY *adj.*]

prittle-prattle *n.* [mid-16C–early 19C] idle chatter, gossip. [redup. of SE *prattle*]

private *n.* [1970s] (*US Black*) the penis. [abbr. SE *private parts*]

private dick *n.* (*also* **private D**) [1910s+] (*orig. US*) a private detective. [SE *private* + DICK *n.*[6] (1)/D *n.*[3]]

privateer *n.* [late 17C; late 19C–1910s] an amateur, part-time prostitute. [SE *privateer*, a volunteer soldier, a guerrilla]

privateer *v.* [mid-19C] (*US*) to cause trouble, to act as a rowdy. [SE *privateer*, 'a volunteer soldier, a free-lance, a guerilla' (*OED*)]

private eye *n.* [1930s+] (*orig. US*) a private detective (cf. EAGLE EYE *n.*). [the orig. *eye* was that displayed as a badge of the Pinkerton's National Detective Agency (founded 1852)]

private Idaho *n.* [1980s+] (*US campus*) one's own little world. [? the perceived peace of the US state; note the title of the film *My Own Private Idaho* (1991) comes later]

privates *n.*[1] (*also* **privities**) [late 18C+] the male or female genitals. [abbr. of euph. SE *private parts*]

privates *n.*[2] [1900s–20s] (*US tramp*) a private house.

private star *n.* [1950s] (*US*) a private detective (cf. BADGE *n.*[2]). [the star-shaped badge of identification]

private ticket *n.* [1980s] (*US*) a private detective. [SE *private* + TICKET *n.*[2] (12)]

privities *n. see* PRIVATES *n.*[1].

privy *n. see* PRIVY PARADISE *n.*

privy council *n.* [1950s] (*US*) a privy, an outhouse (cf. ALTAR *n.*).

privy-counsel *n.* [mid-17C; mid-19C] the vagina.

privy paradise *n.* (*also* **privy, privy hole**) [18C] the vagina (cf. ADAM'S OWN (ALTAR) *n.*).

privy-queen *n.* [1940s+] (*gay*) a homosexual who seeks sex in or around public lavatories. [SE *privy* + QUEEN *n.*[2] (1)/QUEEN sfx (2)]

prize *adj.* [20C+] absolute, complete, utter, e.g. *prize idiot*. [i.e. worthy of a SE *prize*]

prize faggots *n.* [late 19C] large female breasts. [in culinary terms a 'prize' faggot implies a larger than average specimen]

prize of the poor *n.* [2000s] (*US prison*) capital punishment.

Pro *n. see* PROHI *n.*

pro *n.*[1] **1** [mid-19C+] a *pro*fessional, an expert in a field; esp. as *the pro*, the professional employed by a golf club. **2** [1930s+] a prostitute. [(2) abbr. is of *professional* woman, not *prostitute*]

pro *n.*[2] [1940s–50s] (*US*) a condom. [abbr. SE *prophylactic*]

pro *adj.* [1920s+] *professional*. [abbr.]

pro *v.* [1940s–60s] (*N.Z.*) to take out a *pro*hibition order against a heavy drinker. [abbr.]

pro *adv.* [1950s+] *pro*fessionally. [abbr.]

prob *n.* [1930s+] a *prob*lem; often in pl. [abbr.]

probabilities *n. see* OLD PROBABILITIES *n.*

probably *adv.* [1980s+] (*US campus*) *prob*ably not.

probie *n.* [1970s–80s] (*N.Z. prison*) a *prob*ation officer. [abbr.]

proboscis *n.* (*also* **'boscis**) [mid-17C+] a joc. term for the human nose. [joc. use of SE, coined to describe an elephant's trunk]

process *n.* [1960s+] (*US Black*) straightened hair. [the *process* of straightening]

process *v.* [1960s+] (*US Black*) to straighten one's hair (cf. CONK *v.*[2]).

processed mind *n.* [1960s] (*US Black*) a Black mind that appears to prefer seeing things from a White perspective. [fig. use of PROCESS *v.* + SE *mind*]

process-pusher *n.* [late 19C] a lawyer's clerk. [SE *process*, a legal writ or summons; note artists' jargon *process-server*, a photogravure printer]

Prod *n.* [late 19C; 1940s+] a *Protestant*, esp. in Northern Ireland. [abbr./pron.]

Prod *adj.* [1940s+] pertaining to a Northern Ireland Protestant or to their culture. [PROD n.]

prod *n.* **1** [late 19C+] the act of sexual intercourse. **2** [1930s–50s] (*US drugs*) an injection. **3** [1950s+] the penis. [SE *prod*, a pointed implement]

prod *v.* **1** [late 19C+] usu. of a man, to engage in sexual intercourse. **2** [1920s–50s] (*US drugs*) to inject a narcotic; thus *prodder*, one who injects. [SE *prod*, to push at]

Proddie *adj. see* PRODDY *adj.*

Proddo *n.* [1910s+] (*Aus.*) a Protestant. [PROD n. + -o sfx (4)]

Proddy *n.* [1950s+] (*mainly Anglo-Irish*) a Protestant, as used by Roman Catholics; ext. as *Proddywoddy/Proddywhoddy*; *Proddy dog*. [PROD n.]

Proddy *adj.* (*also* **Proddie**) [1940s+] pertaining to a (Northern Ireland) Protestant or to their culture.

proddyhopper *n.* [1960s+] (*N.Z., mainly juv.*) a derog. term for a Protestant.

prod someone's kidneys *v. see* KIDNEY-PRODDER n.

produce *v.* [20C+] to produce good results or money.

product *n.* **1** [1930s+] (*drugs*) a quantity of a drug, usu. as described by a dealer. **2** [1940s+] (*Irish*) a bottle of Guinness stout. **3** [2000s] crack cocaine (cf. BASE n.).

prof *n.* [mid-19C+] (*orig. US*) a professor. [abbr.]

profesh *n.* **1** [late 19C–1930s] (*US tramp*) a *professional*, full-time vagrant. **2** [late 19C+] (*US*) a *profession*, esp. the criminal or theatrical profession. [abbr.]

professor *n.* (*also* **prof**) **1** [late 18C+] anyone considered particularly clever or even educated; also in ironic use. **2** [mid-19C–1940s] (*US*) a pianist in a bar, cabaret or brothel; by ext. any musician. **3** [late 19C] (*UK Und.*) a sophisticated criminal, preferring confidence trickery to violence. **4** [1920s] a bartender. [(2) stereotyped identification of piano-playing with intellectual types; (4) f. (2)]

profile *v.* [1960s+] (*US Black/teen*) to show off, to act in an exhibitionistic manner; thus *profiling for the fans*, showing off for an audience.

Prog *n.* [1960s+] (*S.Afr.*) a member of the *Progressive Party* (1959–75) and its successors the Progressive Reform Party (1975–7), Progressive Federal Party (1977–89) and the Democratic Party (from 1989). [abbr.]

prog *n.*[1] [mid-17C–19C] (*orig. UK Und.*) food, esp. supplies that have been secreted away for later use, e.g. on a journey; thus *rum prog*, high-quality food. [PROG v. (1); note Carib.E. *prag*, to beg for, to forage]

prog *n.*[2] **1** [1920s; 1970s] a *programme*, a plan. **2** [1950s+] a radio or TV *programme*, e.g. *the J.Y. prog*, the Jimmy Young programme. [abbr.]

prog *v.* **1** [mid-17C–1900s] to poke about for food, to scavenge; thus *on the prog*, scavenging. **2** [1900s] to poke. [OED cits. suggest non-food uses and OED states 'it is not certain whether all the senses belong to one word'; Nares has poss. link to *progue*, to steal, although OED only has this as alternative sp. of *prog*]

progger *n.* [1900s] (*Irish*) a scavenger. [PROG v. (1)]

progging *n.* **1** [17C] foraging. **2** [mid-18C] begging. [PROG v. (1)]

progging day *n.* [late 19C] (*W.I.*) market day. [PROG n.[1]]

program *n.* (*US*) **1** [1900s; 1960s+] the established routine of an institution. **2** [1960s+] any form of verbal plan or stratagem whereby one can deal with circumstances, one's preferred way of conducting one's life; thus *jump on someone's program*, to harass, to castigate, to cause trouble for.

program *v.* **1** [1960s+] (*US*) to look after one's own interests.

2 [1980s+] (*US prison*) to follow the prison rules in the hope of gaining time off for good behaviour. [(2) PROGRAM n. (1)]

progressive rope *n.* [1990s+] (*W.I.*) a tie. [the tie is seen as a sign of upward mobility, i.e. progress]

Prohi *n.* (*also* **Pro, Prohy**) [1920s–30s] (*US Und.*) a *Prohibition* agent. [abbr.]

prole *n.* (*also* **prolet**) [late 19C+] a member of the working class or underclass. [abbr. SE *proletarian*]

prole *adj.* [1930s+] pertaining to the working class or underclass, in lifestyle, taste etc. [PROLE n.]

prole *v. see* PROWL v. (1).

prom *n.* [late 19C+] (*US*) a dance, usu. at a school or college; thus *prom queen*, the most outstanding young woman at the dance; *prom date*, one's partner for the prom. [abbr. SE *promenade*]

prom date *n.* [1980s+] (*US campus*) an unattractive person of the opposite sex. [PROM n. + DATE n.[1] (1); the implication being that no one fashionable or sophisticated would attend such a dance]

prominence *n.* [late 19C] an important or prominent person.

promiscuous *adj.* **1** [mid-late 19C] casual, carelessly irregular. **2** [late 19C] a general descriptive term denoting derision and contempt. [SE *promiscuous*, part of a mixed company]

promise land *n.* [1950s] a promise.

promo *n.* [1960s+] **1** *promotion*, publicity, public relations etc. **2** *promotion* in rank. **3** *promotional* copy, esp. of records. [abbr.]

promote *v.* **1** [1920s–50s] (*Aus./US*) to borrow, to exploit someone else for one's own advantage. **2** [1920s+] (*US Und./tramp*) to obtain; to survive by theft, begging or persuasion. **3** [1930s–70s] (*US*) to seduce; to flatter.

promoted *adj.* [late 19C] dead. [coined at the funeral of Mrs Booth, wife of General William Booth (1829–1912), the founder of the Salvation Army]

promoted pimp *n.* [1970s+] (*US Black*) **1** a pimp who gives advice to other pimps or to their prostitutes (cf. BOSS PLAYER n.). **2** a method of getting money, i.e. the way a pimp would set about using his brains/mouth to get funds.

promoter *n.* [early 17C; late 19C–1910s] a confidence trickster. [from the fraudulent schemes he promotes; note Holyoake, *Dictionary* (1617): 'A *promotour*, which, having part of the forfeit, bringeth men into trouble'; Nares defines *promoter* as 'an informer']

prong *n.* (*also* **pronger**) **1** [mid-19C; 1940s+] the penis, esp. when erect. **2** [1930s] (*drugs*) a hypodermic syringe.

prong *v.* [1940s+] **1** to seduce. **2** to have sexual intercourse (cf. BAGAGA v.). **3** (*US Black*) to enjoy oneself. [PRONG n. (1); (3) poss. euph. for (2)]

pronk *n.* [1940s+] a fool, an idiot. [? PRAT n.[1] (6) + PONCE n. (2) + WANK n.[1] (1)]

pronto *adv.* [mid-19C+] immediately, at once. [Sp.]

prop *n.*[1] **1** [18C; 1920s] a proprietor. **2** [20C+] *property*. **3** [1910s+] a *propellor*. [abbr.]

prop *n.*[2] **1** [late 18C–19C] the arm, esp. when extended to strike a blow (cf. PROPS n.[1]). **2** [mid-19C] a blow, esp. an upper-cut.

prop *n.*[3] [mid-19C] the gallows. [it 'holds one up']

prop *n.*[4] **1** [mid-late 19C] a scarf- or tie-pin. **2** [late 19C] a woman's brooch. **3** [20C+] a diamond or other valuable piece of jewellery. [Du. *proppe*, a brooch, a skewer]

prop *n.*[5] [1950s–60s] (*US Und.*) **1** a suggestion, made by the police, that one turns informer in return for a lighter sentence or reduction in charges; thus *shoot someone a prop*, to make such a suggestion. **2** a suggestion, a plan. [abbr. SE *proposition/proposal*]

prop *v.*[1] [mid-late 19C] to hit, to knock down. [PROP n.[2] (2)]

prop *v.*[2] **1** [late 19C–1950s] (*Aus./N.Z.*) to stop, i.e. to come to a halt. **2** [1960s+] (*Aus./N.Z.*) to stop, i.e. remain. **3** [1980s] (*N.Z. prison*) to hold a sit-down strike or similar protest. [PROP n.[1] + SE *prop oneself up*]

prop *v.*[3] [1950s–70s] to *propose*, to suggest. [abbr.]

propel v. [mid-19C] (US) to drink (heavily).

propeller n. [mid-19C] a leg. [SE *propel*]

propeller head n. [1990s+] a fool. [the SAmE *propeller beanie*, a small hat, like a skullcap, with a propeller fixed to the top, worn by children]

proper adj. **1** [17C+] a general intensifier, e.g. a *proper idiot*. **2** [mid-19C+] correct, first-rate, often used ironically. [SE 14C–16C]

proper adv. **1** [mid-19C+] a general intensifier. **2** [late 19C+] properly, correctly.

proper charlie n. *see* RIGHT CHARLIE n.

proper crowd n. (*also* **proper bunch, ...mob**) [1920s+] (*Aus.*) one's intimates, one's best friends. [PROPER adj. (2) + SE *crowd*]

properly adv. [mid-19C+] thoroughly, perfectly, completely, very.

propers n.[1] [late 19C] ? sexual intercourse. ['Meaning refused – but thoroughly comprehended by the costermonger classes. Erotic' (Ware); ? abbr. of a *proper seeing-to*]

propers n.[2] *see* PROPS n.[3].

proper stiff n. [1910s–20s] (*US tramp*) a tramp who refuses to perform manual labour. [PROPER adj. (2) + STIFF n.[2] (4)]

prop-getter n. (*also* **stone-getter**) [1900s–30s] a pickpocket, a thief, spec. one who steals diamonds and other jewellery. [PROP n.[4] (3)/STONE n.[1] (2)]

prophet n. [mid–late 19C] a racing tipster.

propho n. [1910s] (*US milit.*) the regimental *prophy*laxis clinic, issuing contraceptives and dealing with venereal disease. [abbr.]

prop-man n. [1930s–40s] (*US*) a thief specializing in small pieces of personal jewellery. [PROP n.[4] + sfx *-man*]

prop-nailer n. [mid–late 19C] a thief who steals scarf- or tie-pins, brooches and similar small pieces of jewellery. [PROP n.[4] + NAIL v. (2)]

proposition cheat n. [20C+] a ruthless card-sharp who never gives victims even the slightest chance of winning, but takes 100% of the pots.

props n.[1] **1** [late 18C–19C] the arms (cf. PROP n.[2]). **2** [late 18C–1910s] the hands, esp. as fists. **3** [late 18C–1940s] crutches. **4** [mid-19C–1970s] the legs, esp. a woman's legs if attractive. **5** [1930s] (*UK tramp*) trousers. [(4) 1940s–70s use is US Black]

props n.[2] [1920s+] (*US*) any form of support, e.g. weapons, friends, influence.

props n.[3] (*also* **propers**) [1970s+] (*US Black/campus*) respect, admiration; usu. in GET PROPS v.; GIVE PROPS v. [abbr. SE *proper respect*]

prop up v. [1970s] (*UK Und.*) **1** to make a proposition. **2** to arrange, to suggest, to fabricate a story. [ext. PROP v.[3]]

propvol adv. [1970s+] (*S.Afr.*) full to bursting. [Afk. *propvol*, stuffed]

prop worker n. [1940s] (*UK Und.*) a thief specializing in tie-pins or other pieces of small jewellery. [PROP n.[4] + WORKER n.[1] (1)]

pros n.[1] (*also* **pross**) [20C+] a prostitute; prostitution. [abbr.]

pros n.[2] *see* PROSS n.[1] (2).

prose n. **1** [19C] a chat, a gossip, a talk. **2** [mid-19C] (*also* **prosy**) a dull, boring person.

prose v. [19C] **1** to write or talk in a long-winded, tedious manner. **2** to gossip, to chat. [PROSE n.]

proslang n. [2000s] (*US Black*) an articulate person. [PROSLANG adj.]

proslang adj. [2000s] (*US Black*) first-rate, esp. in the context of lyrics or speech. [PRO adj. + SE *slang*]

prospect n. **1** [1940s] (*gay*) a potential client for a street prostitute. **2** [1950s+] (*orig. US*) a recruit to an outlaw motorcycle gang before any initiation rites. **3** [1960s–70s] (*gay*) one who may prove to be a fellow homosexual. **4** [1970s] a suspect.

pross n.[1] **1** [mid-19C] one who can be sponged on or is good for a loan. **2** [mid–late 19C] (*also* **pros**) a sponger, a cadger; thus *on the pross*, sponging. [PROSS v.[1]; (2) abbr. PROSSER n.]

pross n.[2] [1930s] (*UK Und.*) a person with previous convictions. [PROSS v.[2]]

pross n.[3] *see* PROS n.[1].

pross v.[1] [mid-19C–1910s] to sponge on one's acquaintances, to cadge, usu. drinks or money. [ety. unknown; ? SE *prose*]

pross v.[2] [1930s] (*UK Und.*) to prosecute. [abbr.]

pross about v. [late 19C–1900s] to hang around, to mooch about. [PROSS v.[1]]

prosser n. [mid-19C–1930s] an idler or sponger. [PROSS v.[1]; note the celebrated *Prossers' Avenue* in London's Gaiety Theatre, the theatre bar where the more raffish elements of society were wont to promenade; also note the P.G. Wodehouse (1881–1975) character *Oofy Prosser*, lit. 'rich sponger']

prossie n. (*also* **prosso, prossy, prozzy**) [1910s+] (*orig. Aus.*) a prostitute. [abbr.]

prostie n. (*also* **prost, prosty**) **1** [1940s+] (*orig. US*) a prostitute. **2** [1980s] (*US juv.*) a term of abuse. [abbr.]

prostie adj. (*also* **prosty**) [1930s+] (*US*) pertaining to prostitution. [PROSTIE n. (1)]

prosy n. *see* PROSE n. (2).

protected adj. [1910s+] (*Aus./N.Z.*) lucky, fortunate. [? the protection is that of the gods]

protection n. [1950s+] (*US Black*) a condom.

Protestant herring n. [mid-19C+] (*Irish*) **1** a bad, stale herring. **2** any form of stale or unpleasant food. **3** anything second-rate, inferior.

proud adj. [late 16C–early 19C] sexually aroused, 'desirous of Copulation' (B.E.). [a man's penis, which 'stands erect'; ? underpinned in 19C by SE *proud*, slightly raised or projecting. See *Dialect Notes* III v. 360, *proud*, of a female dog, to be in heat]

prough n. (*also* **pruck, prugh**) [20C+] (*Ulster*) anything gained for free, a perquisite, esp. when illicitly come by. [Scot. *pruch*, a perquisite; ult. PROG v. (1)]

provender n. (*UK Und.*) **1** [17C–mid-19C] the victim of highway robbery. **2** [early 18C] the money that is stolen in such a robbery. [SE *provender*, provisions, food]

proverbial, the adj. (*also* **a proverbial**) [1910s+] archetypal, typical, e.g. *the proverbial lovelorn lad*.

provide one's chump v. *see* GET ONE'S CHUMP v.

Provie n. (*also* **Provvie**) [1970s+] a member of the *Provi*sional IRA. [abbr.]

provincial n. [mid-17C] a procuress, a brothel-keeper (cf. ABBESS n.). [SE *provincial*, the chief of a religious order in a district or province]

Provo n. [1970s+] a member of the *Provi*sional IRA. [abbr.]

provo n. [late 18C–mid-19C] a temporary prison of the military police. [abbr. SAmE *provost*]

Provvie n. *see* PROVIE n.

prowl n.[1] [1910s–60s] (*US Und.*) **1** a survey of somewhere that is to be robbed; a search of a place or individual. **2** a burglary.

prowl n.[2] *see* PROWL CAR n.

prowl n.[3] *see* PROWLER n. (2).

prowl v. **1** [late 17C–18C] (*also* **prole**) to wander around in search of seducible women. **2** [1900s–60s] (*US Und.*) to rob a place. **3** [1910s+] to inspect either a potential victim or the site of a possible robbery before carrying out the robbery. **4** [1930s–40s] (*US*) to search a person, to frisk someone.

prowl car n. (*also* **prowl, prowler, prowl heap**) [1930s+] (*US*) a police car that patrols the streets, thus *prowl cop/prowly*, the police driver.

prowler n. **1** [mid-19C+] a petty thief; a sneak-thief. **2** [1910s+] (*US*) (*also* **prowl**) a house-breaker.

prozzie n. [1990s+] Prozac. [abbr.]

prozzy n. *see* PROSSIE n.

Pru, the n. [1920s+] the *Pru*dential Assurance Company; esp. in phr. *the man from the Pru*, a representative of the company who calls at private houses to collect insurance premiums. [abbr.]

pruck *n. see* PROUGH n.

prude *v.* [1900s] (*Aus.*) to act as a chaperon(e). [SE *prude*]

prugge *n.* [17C] a street-walker. [PRIG v.³]

prugh *n. see* PROUGH n.

prune *n.*¹ **1** [late 19C] the face. **2** [1920s–50s] (*US*) a Black person's head. **3** [1960s–70s] (*US prison*) the anus. [supposed resemblance]

prune *n.*² **1** [late 19C+] a disagreeable, odd or irritable person. **2** [20C+] a simpleton, a fool (cf. APPLEHEAD n.). **3** [1900s] (*US campus*) a mistake, a blunder. **4** [1920s+] a person. **5** [1970s+] an unattractive, prudish woman. [note WW2 RAF jargon *P.O.* (Pilot Officer) *Prune*, the personification of stupidity and incompetence. The character was created by Squadron Leader Anthony Armstrong and the artist 'Raff' (L.A.C. W. Hooper) to teach pupils and other flying personnel how things should not be done]

prune and plum *n.* [1990s+] the buttocks, the behind (cf. ALA n.). [rhy. sl. = BUM n.¹ (1)]

pruneface *n.* [1960s+] (*US*) a plain or miserable-looking person.

prunehead *n.* [1980s] (*Aus.*) a general term of abuse. [SE *prune* + -HEAD sfx (1)]

prune-juice *n.*¹ [1920s–60s] (*US*) nonsense. [? SE *prune-juice*, i.e. its laxative effects on the stomach; thus euph. for BULLSHIT n. (1)]

prune-juice *n.*² [1930s+] hard liquor.

prune-picker *n.* [1910s–50s] (*US*) a native-born Californian. [the prevalence of the crop]

prune-pusher *n.* [1950s–60s] (*gay*) a male homosexual (cf. BROWN ARTIST n.). [his predilection for anal intercourse]

prunes *n.* [1990s+] (*US prison*) a Black person. [the colour]

pruney *n.* [2000s] (*US Black*) a prostitute working for the narcotics squad.

pruning *n.* [1990s+] (*Irish*) the act of grabbing someone by the testicles to inflict pain and humiliation.

pruno *n.* [1940s+] (*US prison*) illegally distilled liquor. [The Other Side of the Wall A Prisoner's Dictionary (2000): 'Pruno: Homemade alcohol, fermented juice, the classic prison drink. It is made by putting fruit juice, fruit, fruit peelings in a plastic bag with bread and/or sugar. The yeast in the bread along with the sugar helps ferment the fruit juice, fruit, or peelings. The plastic bag is usually placed down the toilet and secured so that it is not detected']

prushun *n.* (*also* **preshun, prushon, Prussian**) [late 19C+] a tramp's young companion; 'PRUSHUN.–A boy enslaved by an older tramp or "jocker." The boy is forced to beg and at times to steal for the jocker, and is often forced into unnatural practices. Those "prushuns" who stay with their "jockers" for any length of time find themselves absolutely at a loss when the older tramp dies, unable to think or act for themselves. On the other hand, if the "jocker" fears that the "prushun" may betray him to the law, or if the boy grows so large that he is a danger to the older man, the "jocker" has little compunction about "losing" [i.e. murdering] the luckless "prushun"' (Irwin, *American Tramp and Und. Slang*, 1931) (cf. JOCKER n.¹).

prussian guard *n.* **1** [1910s] (*milit.*) a flea. **2** [1940s+] a card, esp. a bingo card. [(2) rhy. sl.]

p.'s *n.* [1980s+] (*US campus*) parents. [abbr.]

p.s. *n.*¹ [20C+] (*US prison*) protective segregation; thus those who seek protective segregation: *punks* and *snivellers*.

p.s. *n.*² [1910s–20s] penal *servitude*. [abbr.]

psalm-singer *n.* **1** [mid-19C] a soft-hearted, pious person. **2** [1910s] (*US prison*) an informer, a prison trusty.

psalm-smiter *n.* [mid-19C–1910s] a Nonconformist, a street preacher. [their thumping of their text]

psalm-snuffling *n.* [late 19C] (*Aus.*) religiosity.

p's and q's *n.* [1910s–60s] shoes. [rhy. sl.]

pseud *n.* (*also* **pseudo**) [1960s+] a *pseudo*-intellectual; a derog. description, often of quite genuine, if pretentious, intellectuals, who offend their perhaps less academic critics. [abbr.]

pseudie tudie *adj.* (*also* **pseudo-tudo**) [1950s+] an architectural style popular in the UK Home Counties, featuring fake beams and the other appurtenances of (Hollywood-style) Elizabethan and Tudor England. [SE *pseudo* + *Tudor*]

pseudo- *pfx* [1980s+] (*US campus*) phoney, imitation, e.g. *pseudo-rebel*.

psych *n.* (*also* **psyc**) **1** [late 19C+] (*US campus*) *psych*ology or *psych*iatry, as a course. **2** [1940s] (*Aus.*) superstition. **3** [1960s+] (*orig. US*) a *psych*iatrist. **4** [1970s+] *psych*ology. **5** [1990s+] (*US*) a *psych*iatric patient. [abbr.]

psych *adj.* [1960s+] **1** *psych*iatric. **2** *psych*ological. [abbr.]

psych *v.*¹ **1** [1920s] (*also* **psyche**) to *psych*oanalyse, to undergo *psych*ological testing. **2** [1930s+] to work out. **3** [1980s+] (*US campus*) to fool, to trick, to tease. [abbr.]

psych *v.*² *see* PSYCH (OUT) v.

psych *v.*³ *see* PSYCH (UP) v.

psych! *excl.* (*also* **sike!**) [1980s+] (*US campus/teen*) fooled you! just kidding! [abbr. PSYCH (OUT) v. (1)]

psychedelic to the bone *phr.* [1970s+] **1** (*US Black drugs*) extremely intoxicated by a drug, but not necessarily a hallucinogen. **2** (*US Black*) of clothes, very colourful. [fig. use of SE *psychedelic* + TO THE BONE phr.]

psyched (up) *adj.* (*also* **psyched out**) [1960s+] (*orig. US*) **1** extremely excited; a more extreme version is *psyched to death*. **2** emotionally ready. **3** very happy. **4** insane. [SE *psychology*, i.e. psychologically prepared; PSYCH (UP) v.]

psychey *n. see* PSYCHO n. (2).

psychey *adj.* [1960s] (*Scot. gang*) crazy, mad (cf. PSYCHO adj.). [PSYCH adj. (1)]

psych-jockey *n.* [1950s+] (*US*) one who hosts a radio/TV programme or phone-in on emotional and sexual problems. [PSYCH n. (1) + JOCKEY n.³ (2)]

psycho *n.* (*orig. US*) **1** [1920s+] *psycho*analysis or *psycho*logy. **2** [1940s+] (*also* **psychey**) a *psycho*path, or the act of mad person. **3** [1940s+] an insane, strange or eccentric person. **4** [1940s+] a *psych*iatrist, *psych*ologist or *psycho*-analyst. **5** [1990s+] a *psych*iatric ward. [abbr.]

psycho *adj.* [1920s+] (*orig. US*) **1** *psycho*logical, *psych*iatric; thus *psycho doc*, *psycho ward* etc. **2** *psycho*tic, violent, threatening. **3** weird, eccentric, bizarre, mad (cf. PSYCHEY adj.). [abbr.]

psycho *v.* [1930s–40s] (*Aus.*) to work out a person's intentions. [SE *psychoanalyse*]

psychobabble *n.* [1970s+] (*orig. US*) the jargon of the New Age and the New Therapy, esp. when used by lay people to aggrandize (discussions of) their own condition. [coined by R.D. Rosen in his book *Psychobabble* (1977)]

psycho hosebeast *n.* [1990s+] (*US campus/teen*) a very attractive, sexy, hopefully promiscuous girl. [PSYCHO adj. (2) + HOSEBEAST n.]

psycho (off) *v.* [1990s+] (*UK prison*) to be sent to a psychiatric prison. [PSYCHO n. (5)]

psychopathic *n.* [1990s+] traffic. [rhy. sl.; Cockney pron. 'psychopaffic']

psych (out) *v.* **1** [1930s+] to frighten or at least perturb someone else by playing on their inner fear; to break someone down psychologically. **2** [1960s–70s] to lose emotional control, to break down. **3** [1970s] in weak use, to astonish, to amaze. [SE *psychologize*]

psych-up *n.* [1990s+] (*US*) an act of emotional self-energizing prior to undertaking something challenging. [PSYCH (UP) v. (2)]

psych (up) *v.* **1** [1960s] to feel tense, nervous. **2** [1960s+] to put oneself or another person into a confident, aggressive etc frame of mind as preparation for dealing with a situation; to energize or persuade. [SE *psychologize*]

psyl *n.* [1970s] (*drugs*) *psil*ocybin, *psil*ocin. [abbr.]

p.t. *n.* [1940s+] (*orig. US*) **1** a woman (or man in a homosexual context) who appears to be offering unrestrained sexual favours but stops short of intercourse, leaving the male partner frustrated. **2** an attractive, desirable woman. [abbr. PRICKTEASER n.]

p.t.a. n. [1970s+] (*US Black*) the washing by a woman of only the genital area, the breasts and armpits, all of which are most likely to smell. [*pussy, tits and armpits*]

P-town n. [1970s+] (*US*) **1** Philadelphia. **2** Portland. [abbr.]

pub n. **1** [mid-19C+] a *pub*lic house; thus *block a quiet pub*, to loiter in a pubic house. **2** [1900s] the *pub*lic. [abbr.]

pub v. (*also* **pub it**) [late 19C+] to visit a public house. [PUB n. (1)]

pubby n. [1900s] (*Aus.*) a *pub*lican. [abbr. + sfx -*y*]

pub-crawl n. [late 19C+] a gradual progress from public house to public house, with the participants becoming gradually more drunk as they go along. [PUB n. (1) + CRAWL n. (2)]

pub-crawl v. [late 19C+] to visit a succession of public houses, getting gradually more drunk as one goes. [PUB-CRAWL n.]

pube n.[1] [1960s+] (*US*) a *pube*scent. [abbr.]

pube n.[2] *see* PUBES n.

pube adj. [1990s+] *pube*scent. [abbr.]

pubehead n. [1980s+] (*US teen*) a person with short, curly hair. [PUBES n. + SE *head*]

pubes n. (*also* **pube, pubies**) [1950s+] pubic hair. [abbr.]

pubickers n. [1990s+] (*Irish*) pubic hair.

pub it v. *see* PUB v.

public n. [18C+] a *public* house. [abbr.]

Publican, the n. [late 19C] General William Booth, founder of the Salvation Army. [in 1883 Booth (1829–1912) purchased 2 former public houses, the Grecian Theatre and the Tavern in the City Road]

public convenience n. [20C+] a prostitute (cf. CONVENIENT n.). [pun]

public ledger n. [late 18C–early 19C] a prostitute (cf. BANBURY n.). ['Like that paper, she is open to all parties' (Grose, 1796). The newspaper *The Public Ledger* was founded in 1760]

public man n. [early 19C] a bankrupt. [? the publication of his name in the newspapers]

public patterer n. [mid-19C] a confidence trickster who poses as a dissenting preacher, thus attracting a crowd who can be robbed by the 'preacher's' confederates. [SE *public* + PATTERER n.]

published adj. [1990s+] (*US campus*) very ugly. [play on BOOKED adj.[2]]

pub pet n. [1980s+] (*N.Z.*) a 2-litre plastic beer flagon or the beer it contains. [PUB n. (1)]

pub-stiff n. [1940s] (*N.Z.*) a lookout or sentinel acting on behalf of a licensee selling alcoholic drinks after the legal closing time. [PUB n. (1) + STIFF n.[2] (5)]

puce n. [1980s+] (*Aus. prison*) a gun. [ety. unknown]

puck n.[1] [1950s–60s] (*Irish*) a large quantity. [Irish *poc*, bag]

puck n.[2] [1970s+] (*US campus*) anyone deemed socially unacceptable. [? PUCKEY n. or ? euph. for FUCK n.[6]]

puck n.[3] [2000s] a lump of hashish (cf. AFGHAN n.). [resemblance/ colour]

puck-chaser n. (*also* **puck-pusher**) [late 19C+] (*orig. US*) an ice-hockey player. [also Can. 1920s+]

pucker n. [mid-18C+] a state of fear or excitement, a fuss, a panic; usu. as *in a pucker*. [one's face puckers up when expressing excitement; 19C+ use is mainly Irish/US]

pucker adj. *see* PUKKA adj.

pucker v. **1** [mid 19C] to speak incomprehensibly. **2** [mid-19C; 1930s] to talk privately. [SE *pucker*, to draw the lips tightly together]

pucker-assed adj. [1960s+] (*US*) timid, fearful. [SE *pucker* + -ASSED sfx]

puckering string n. *see* FARTING STRINGS n.

puckeroo adj. (*also* **pukaroo**) [1910s+] (*N.Z.*) useless, broken; thus as v., to ruin. [Maori *pakaru*, broken]

puckerow v. (*also* **pukkaroo**) [mid–late 19C] (*Anglo-Ind.*) to seize. [imper. of Hind. *pakro*, to seize]

pucker up v. [mid-19C+] to get into a bad temper, to become tense. [the facial expression]

pucker-water n. [late 18C–early 19C] water mixed with alum or a similar astringent, used to tighten the vaginal muscles by those who wish to counterfeit virginity.

puckey n. (*also* **pucky**) [1950s+] excrement. [? similarity to SE *puck*, a disk of hard rubber, used in hockey; or ? POO n.[1] (2)]

puckfist n. (*also* **puckfoist**) [late 16C–mid-17C] a braggart. [SE *puckfist*, the Puff-ball, *Lycoperdon Bovista*]

puck-pusher n. *see* PUCK-CHASER n.

pucky n. *see* PUCKEY n.

pud n.[1] **1** [1910s+] a *pud*ding. **2** [1940s] (*US*) a young girl. [abbr.]

pud n.[2] [1930s+] (*US teen/campus*) an easy job, an easy course at college; thus *pud course*, an easy course. [abbr. PUDDING n.[2] (1)]

pud n.[3] [1940s+] (*US teen/campus*) **1** the penis. **2** the vagina. **3** a fool, an idiot (cf. APPLEHEAD n.; BAMBA n.[1]; CHOAD n.). [abbr. PUDDING n.[1]]

pud n.[4] *see* PUDSEY n.

pud v. [mid–late 19C] to greet affectionately. [SE *pud*, a child's hand; ult. SE *pad*]

pudden v. [mid-19C] to drug a dog in order to silence it during the carrying out of a burglary. [PUDDING n.[1] (6)]

pudding n.[1] **1** [mid-16C–19C] (*also* **white pudding**) the penis; thus *pudding-bag*, the vagina; *pudding prick*, the penis; thus *have hot pudding for supper*, of a woman, to have sexual intercourse. **2** [late 17C–19C] sexual intercourse. **3** [late 17C–early 19C] (*also* **puddings**) the stomach. **4** [mid-18C] an unborn child, a foetus. **5** [late 18C–mid-19C] the vagina. **6** [mid-19C] (*UK Und.*) meat, usu. liver, that has been impregnated with drugs or poison, used by a thief to silence a house dog. **7** [1970s] semen (cf. BABY GRAVY n.). [SE *pudding*, guts, entrails]

pudding n.[2] **1** [late 19C+] (*US*) anything easily accomplished. **2** [1940s+] of a person, a weakling, a 'pushover'. [var. PIE n.[3] (1)]

pudding n.[3] [1960s+] (*US*) an affectionate term of address.

pudding and gravy n. [1940s+] the Royal Navy. [rhy. sl.]

pudding chef adj. [1990s+] deaf. [rhy. sl.]

pudding club n. [late 19C+] the state of pregnancy; usu. in phrs. e.g. *in the pudding club*, pregnant; *put in the pudding club*, to make pregnant; *join the pudding club*, to become pregnant. [PUDDING n.[1] (4)]

pudding-head n. [mid-19C+] a fool, a simpleton (cf. APPLEHEAD n.). [backform. f. PUDDING-HEADED adj.]

pudding-headed adj. (*also* **pudding-faced**) [mid-18C–1920s] stolid, stupid (cf. AIRHEADED adj.).

pudding-house n. **1** [late 16C–18C] the stomach. **2** [mid-19C] (*UK Und.*) the workhouse.

pudding-ken n. [19C] a cook-shop. [SE *pudding* + KEN n.[1] (1)]

pudding-pie n. [17C] the vagina (cf. APPLE n.[6]). [euph.]

puddings n. *see* PUDDING n.[1] (3).

puddings and pies n. [mid-19C; 1930s+] the eyes. [rhy. sl.]

pudding-sleeves n. [late 18C–early 19C] a parson. [the voluminous sleeves of his vestments]

pudding-snammer n. (*also* **pudding-snapper**) [mid-19C] one who robs a cook-shop. [SE *pudding* + SNAM v.]

puddle n. (*also* **big puddle**) [late 19C+] the sea, esp. the Atlantic Ocean; thus *this/the other side of the puddle*, the UK or the US (cf. BIG DITCH n.).

puddle v. [late 18C–early 19C] to have sexual intercourse. [SE *puddle*, to poke about in mud or shallow water]

puddled adj. [1930s–70s] eccentric, insane. [? Scot. *puddle*, to drink]

puddlejumper n. (*US*) **1** [1920s+] any form of small, speedy transport, e.g. a small fast car, a light aeroplane or lightweight truck. **2** [1950s] a farmer, an unsophisticated rustic (cf. ACORN-CRACKER n.).

puddle of piss/shit *n. see* PISS n. (6).

puddy *n.* [1990s+] (*US campus*) **1** a pudding. **2** the vagina. [abbr. SE *pudding*/PUDDING n.[1] (5)]

pudenany *n. see* PUNAANY n.

puderhead *n.* [1980s+] (*US campus*) a disappointment, a person who fails to come up to one's expectations. [? PUD n.[3] (3) + SE *head*]

pudge *n.* (*also* **pudgy**) [late 19C+] a short squat person, occas. a thing. [orig. dial.]

pudgy *adj.* [mid-19C+] fat, often squat; also as a nickname.

pud juice *n. see* PUD WATER n.

pudpuller *n.* [1970s+] (*US*) a masturbator. [PUD n.[3] (1) + PULL v.[7]]

pudsey *n.* (*also* **pud, pudsy**) **1** [17C] the hand. **2** [late 18C+] a foot. **3** [late 18C+] a term of affection for a child. [? Du. *poot*, a paw]

pud water *n.* (*also* **pud juice**) [2000s] semen (cf. BABY FLUID n.; BABY GRAVY n.). [PUD n.[3] (1) + SE *water*]

pudwhacker *n.* [1980s] (*US teen*) a masturbator; thus a general term of abuse. [PUD n.[3] (1) + WHACKER n.[4]]

puella *n.* [1940s] (*US*) a lesbian prostitute. [Lat. *puella*, a girl]

Puerto Rican Pendleton *n.* [1960s] (*US*) an old work shirt. [derog. ref. to the poverty of Puerto Rican labourers, for whom an expensive Pendleton shirt would be an impossible dream]

puff *n.*[1] **1** [18C+] breath, a breaking of wind. **2** [mid-18C] (*UK Und.*) an informer. **3** [late 19C+] (*also* **puff-puff**) life; esp. as *in my puff, on my puff,* ALL ONE'S PUFF *phr.* [SE *puff*, breath, thus breath of life]

puff *n.*[2] [mid-18C; 1950s] a house player in a gambling house, one who decoys victims into a crooked game. [SE *puff*, to praise to excess and for one's own interest; Grose 1785 notes auction jargon *puff* or *puffer*, one who bids at auctions, not with an intent to buy, but only to raise the price of the lot; for which purpose many are hired by the proprietor of the goods on sale]

puff *n.*[3] **1** [early 19C+] a male homosexual. **2** [1970s+] a general term of abuse; the object's actual sexuality is irrelevant. [SE *puff of air*, i.e. the perceived 'insubstantiality' of an effeminate man]

puff *n.*[4] **1** [1900s–60s] (*US Und.*) dynamite. **2** [1910s] the explosion caused by 'blowing' a safe. [the 'puff' that accompanies the explosion]

puff *n.*[5] (*drugs*) **1** [1940s–50s] an opium user. **2** [1970s] tobacco. **3** [1980s+] cannabis; thus *puff-head*, a smoker of cannabis. [SE *puff*, an emission of smoke]

puff *v.*[1] [mid-17C+] to break wind. [SE *puff*, to discharge a puff of air]

puff *v.*[2] [mid-18C] (*UK Und.*) to impeach.

puff *v.*[3] (*drugs*) **1** [1920s+] to smoke opium. **2** [1950s+] to smoke cannabis. [PUFF n.[5]]

puff *v.*[4] [1930s] (*US Und.*) to open a safe with an explosive charge. [PUFF n.[4] (1)]

puff *v.*[5] [1950s] (*US Black*) to ride, walk or fly.

puff and dart *n.* [late 19C–1930s] a start; thus *make a puff and dart*, to begin, to make a start. [rhy. sl.]

puff and drag *n.* [20C+] a cigarette. [rhy. sl. = FAG n.[4] (3) + the action of smoking]

puff artist *n.* [20C+] (*US*) one who flatters or praises insincerely, esp. in the commercial world. [SE *puff*, to praise excessively + ARTIST sfx]

puff daddy *n.* [2000s] (*US Black*) a pimp whose girls specialize in oral sex (cf. BIG DADDY n.; CANDYMAN n.). [SE *puff* + DADDY n. (11)]

puffed air *n.* [1940s] (*US Black*) no food; thus *I'm eating puffed air*, I'm hungry. [play on the cereal *Puffed Wheat*]

puffer *n.* **1** [late 19C] (*US*) a cigar. **2** [1970s+] (*drugs*) an opium smoker. **3** [1980s+] (*drugs*) a smoker of crack cocaine. **4** [1980s+] (*drugs*) a smoker of cannabis or hashish. [SE *puff*, to smoke tobacco]

puff guts *n.* [mid-17C–early 19C] a fat man. [SE *puff*, a swelling + GUTS n.[1] (1)/-GUTS sfx]

puff lye *v.* [1990s+] (*US Black drugs*) to smoke marijuana. [SE *puff* + ? LAH n.]

puffoon *n. see* BAFOON n.

puff-puff *n.*[1] [late 19C+] (*UK juv.*) a steam engine.

puff-puff *n.*[2] *see* PUFF n.[1] (3).

puffwad *n.* [2000s] (*US*) a weakling; an effeminate man. [PUFF n.[3] (2) + -WAD sfx]

puffy *n.*[1] [1980s] (*drugs*) phencyclidine (cf. ACE n.[4]). [one 'puffs' it]

puffy *n.*[2] [2000s] (*US Black*) fellatio.

puffy *adj.* [2000s] (*US*) adulatory. [SE *puff*, to extol]

pug *n.*[1] **1** [mid-16C–19C] a pet name for an animal, usu. a dog or monkey; and also for a person, usu. a woman or child. **2** [19C] a fox. [? SE *pug*, a demon, an imp]

pug *n.*[2] [late 16C–early 17C] a bargee; thus *western pugs*, those who navigate barges down the Thames to London. [? SE *pug*, to pull, to tug]

pug *n.*[3] [17C–early 18C] **1** a prostitute or courtesan. **2** an unpleasant woman, esp. one who is regarded as sexually immoral. [PUNK n.[1] (1); but note PUG n.[1] (1)]

pug *n.*[4] [mid–19C] an upper servant in a great house; thus *pug's hole/parlour*, the housekeeper's room in such a house. [fig. use of PUG n.[1] (1), i.e. their role as the master's 'pet']

pug *n.*[5] **1** [mid-19C+] a prize-fighter, a boxer, esp. one who relies more on savagery than skill. **2** [late 19C+] a thug, a hoodlum. [abbr. SE *pugilist*]

pug *n.*[6] [late 19C] (*Anglo-Ind.*) a footprint. [synon. Hindī *pag*]

pug *n.*[7] [1930s] (*Aus.*) a lift on a horse. [ety. unknown]

pug *n.*[8] [1940s–50s] (*US drugs*) a narcotics addict, esp. one who is attempting to give up their addiction.

pug *n.*[9] [1980s] the penis. [? var. PUD n.[3] (1)]

pug *n.*[10] [1990s+] (*US Black*) a homosexual. [? PUNK n.[1] (10)]

pug *v.*[1] [20C+] to hide, to secrete. [? Northamptonshire dial. *pug*, to crush]

pug *v.*[2] [1930s–40s] (*US*) to fight as a professional boxer. [PUG n.[5] (1)]

pug drink *n.* [late 18C–early 19C] watered-down cider. [dial. *pug*, the pulp of apples that have been pressed for cider, presumably used in its making]

puggard *n.* [early 17C] (*UK Und.*) a thief. [SE *pug*, to pull, to tug, thus to steal from + sfx *-ard*]

puggle *n. see* POGGLE n.

puggle(d) *adj. see* POGGLED adj.

puggly *n. see* POGGLE n.

puggy *n.* **1** [17C–early 18C] a term of affection used to women or children. **2** [19C] (*Scot.*) a monkey. [PUG n.[1] (1)]

pug-nancy *n.* [early 18C] a bawd. [var. on PUGNASTY n.]

pugnasty *n.* [late 17C–early 18C] an unpleasant woman, esp. one who is cast as sexually immoral. [PUG n.[3] (2) + SE *nasty*]

pug-ugly *n. see* PLUG-UGLY n. (1).

pukacker *n.* [1900s] (*Aus.*) a lazy, shiftless person. [ety. unknown]

pukaroo *adj. see* PUCKEROO adj.

puke *n.*[1] **1** [mid-19C+] (*US*) (*also* **pukeface**) an obnoxious person or thing, a pest; also attrib. **2** [mid-19C+] a person from Missouri. **3** [20C+] a college freshman. **4** [1970s+] an insignificant person. **5** [1980s+] (*Scot.*) nonsense, rubbbish. [apparently but not definitely linked to late 17C+ SE *puke*, vomit (ety. unknown), although it may be an abbr. of unrecorded *spuke*. This would lead logically to the Indo-European root *spu-, speu-*, which certainly lies behind OE and OHG *spiwan*, to spew, spit, and Lat. *spuere*. An alternative ety. is at PUKE n.[2]]

puke *n.*[2] [20C+] (*Ulster*) a supercilious person, a picky eater, an unhealthy-looking, poor person. [Irish *pioc*, to pick at food]

puke *n.*[3] [2000s] any form of disgusting drink. [SE *puke*, to vomit]

pukeface *n. see* PUKE n.[1] (1).

puke-in *n.* [2000s] a meeting or public occasion at which participants express their strong, usu. antagonistic, feelings about a topic. [fig. use of SE *puke* on model of BE-IN n.]

puke (it) out *v.* (*also* **puke one's guts, puke up**) [1920s+] to speak unrestrainedly. [SE *puke*, to vomit]

puke someone off *v.* [1960s] to attack, to cause trouble for.

pukey/puking/pukish *adj. see* PUKY adj.

pukka *adj.* (*also* **pucker**) **1** [late 18C+] genuine, correct, honest. **2** [20C+] of the highest class, best, excellent. [Hind. *pakka*, substantial, initially used of buildings in the Raj]

pukka *adv.* [1920s] correctly, properly. [PUKKA adj. (1)]

pukkaroo *v. see* PUCKEROW v.

puky *adj.* (*also* **pukey, puking, pukish**) [20C+] disgusting, 'sick-making'. [SE *puke*, to vomit]

pulboron *n. see* POLBORON n.

pull *n.*[1] **1** [16C; late 18C+] influence, advantage. **2** [early 17C–19C] a trick, a fraud, a knack. **3** [mid-19C] a physical advantage. **4** [late 19C] an ulterior motive, a hidden agenda. **5** [1900s–50s] an anxious or worrying moment that 'tugs at one's heartstrings'.

pull *n.*[2] **1** [mid-19C] (*UK Und.*) a successful theft or the profits that it brings. **2** [1960s] (*Aus.*) that which has been earned.

pull *n.*[3] **1** [late 19C–1900s] (*US*) a police raid. **2** [late 19C+] (*also* **pulley**) an arrest. **3** [20C+] an object of sexual conquest; one who can be seduced. **4** [1950s] a talking-to; often in GIVE SOMEONE A PULL v. [PULL v.[2]]

pull *n.*[4] [1920s] (*US Und.*) the act of drawing a gun. [PULL v.[5]]

pull *n.*[5] [1940s+] a (puff on a) cigarette.

pull *v.*[1] [mid-18C–mid-19C] to drink.

pull *v.*[2] **1** [19C+] to arrest, to stop and search on the street; thus *in pull*, under arrest. **2** [early–mid-19C] (*also* **pull a/the bag (away/off), pull away**) to pilfer, to steal. **3** [late 19C+] to accuse, to have someone arrested. **4** [1910s+] (*US Black*) of a pimp, to enlist a new prostitute. **5** [1920s+] to pick up for sexual purposes, to seduce. **6** [1920s+] of a prostitute, to attract a client. **7** [1950s+] of a club doorman, a 'steerer', to attract clients. **8** [1960s+] to lure a woman away from another man; esp. of a pimp.

pull *v.*[3] **1** [mid-19C+] to act in a way that is calculated to shock, amuse or deceive, e.g. *pull a gag, pull some dirty stuff, pull a stunt* (see also combs. below). **2** [1940s+] (*orig. US*) used with a proper name to mean to imitate, to act in the manner of, esp. when the proper name is almost synon. with a certain type of extreme or easily identifiable behaviour, e.g. *pull a Daniel Boone*, to act drunkenly; *pull a Lindbergh*, to act in a heroic manner.

pull *v.*[4] **1** [late 19C+] (*Aus.*) to obtain money. **2** [20C+] (*US campus*) to obtain, to achieve. **3** [1920s] to earn a wage. **4** [1920s+] (*US campus*) to earn a grade in an examination. **5** [1930s+] to be allotted. **6** [1940s+] (*US Und.*) to receive a jail sentence; to serve a jail sentence.

pull *v.*[5] [late 19C+] (*orig. US Und.*) to draw a gun or other weapon.

pull *v.*[6] **1** [1910s+] to leave, to go away. **2** [1950s+] to remove, to censor. [SE *pull out*, to leave]

pull *v.*[7] [1910s+] to masturbate (cf. BOFF v.).

pull *v.*[8] *see* PULL DOWN v. (3).

pull *v.*[9] *see* PULL OFF v.[2].

pull *v.*[10] *see* PULL (OUT) v.

pull a bag (away/off) *v. see* PULL v.[2] (2).

pull a bit *v.* [1960s] (*US prison*) to survive one's sentence. [SE *pull through* + BIT n.[5]]

pull a blank *v.* [1920s] (*US*) to be rejected.

pull about *v.* [19C] **1** to masturbate. **2** to handle roughly or unceremoniously, esp. of a man abusing or harassing a woman.

pull a brodie *v.* **1** [1920s] to jump. **2** [1940s] (*US*) to fail. [BRODIE n. (1)/BRODIE n. (4)]

pull a chirper *v. see* CHIRP OUT v.

pull a cross on *v.* [1950s] to double-cross. [PULL v.[3] (1) + CROSS n.[1] (1)]

pull a disappearing act *v.* [1950s+] (*US*) of a spouse or lover,

to run off without warning and without leaving any message. [PULL v.[3] (1)]

pull a double train *v.* (*also* **run a double train**) [1980s+] (*US Black*) for 2 men to penetrate a woman simultaneously by the vagina and the anus. [var. on PULL A TRAIN v.]

pull a fade-out *v.* (*also* **do a fade-out**) [1910s–60s] (*US*) to vanish, to escape, to depart. [PULL v.[3] (1) + FADE-OUT n. (1)]

pull a fast one *v.* (*also* **get/put over a fast one, pull a fast shuffle, …switch**) **1** [1920s+] to get away with something, usu. a slightly nefarious scheme. **2** [1930s] to stage a crime, e.g. a hold-up. [PULL v.[3] (1) + FAST ONE n.; orig. milit. use, to malinger]

pull a Ferris Bueller *v.* [1980s+] (*US campus*) to cut class, to take time away from studies. [PULL v.[3] (2) + film *Ferris Bueller's Day Off* (1986)]

pull a fooley *v.* [2000s] (*US Black*) to act very stupidly; to act in an exceptional manner. [PULL v.[3] + SE *fool*]

pull a gag *v.* [20C+] (*US*) to play a trick. [PULL v.[3] (1) + GAG n. (1)]

pull a Hank Snow *v.* (*also* **do a Hank Snow**) [1960s+] (*US*) to leave, to move on. [PULL v.[3] (2)/SE *do* + song 'I'm Moving On' by Country and Western star *Hank Snow* (b.1914)]

pull a head *v.* (*also* **slew (a head)**) [1970s] (*Aus. Und.*) to divert a bystander's attention from a crime. [SE]

pull a heist *v.* [1950s+] (*US Und.*) to commit a robbery. [PULL v.[3] (1) + HEIST n.[1] (1)]

pull a horse *v. see* PULL A RACE v.

pull a Houdini *v.* (*also* **do a Houdini, Houdini**) [1920s+] (*US*) to escape, to vanish suddenly, to leave stealthily (cf. HOUDINI n.[1]). [PULL v.[3] (2)/SE *do* + escapologist Harry *Houdini* (1874–1926)]

pull a hypo *v.* [1940s] (*drugs*) to sell poor-quality drugs. [PULL v.[3] (1) + ? HYPO n.[2]]

pull a jap *v.* [1950s+] (*US*) to take by surprise, to ambush. [PULL v.[3] (1) + JAP n. (3)]

pull a job *v.* [1910s+] (*orig. US*) to carry out a robbery or other criminal act. [PULL v.[3] (1) + JOB n.[3] (1)]

pull a johnson *v.* [1990s+] (*US teen*) to execute a U-turn in the middle of the street, usu. as a last-minute decision; this is illegal in most states. [PULL v.[3] (1) + the shape of the 'J' in Johnson]

pull a jones *v.* [1990s+] (*US teen*) constantly to scrounge from one's friends; thus *Mr/Mrs Jones*, one who scrounges constantly. [PULL v.[3] (1) + generic *Jones*]

pull a kite *v.* [late 19C] to make a face, to grimace. [PULL v.[3] (1) + ? dial. *kite-nipped*, suffering from stomach cramps]

pull a long face *v.* (*also* **pull a long phiz**) [early 19C+] to look miserable, serious or worried. [SE/PHIZ n.[1] (1)]

pull a MacGyver *v.* [1990s+] (*US campus*) to do something mechanically very clever. [PULL v.[3] (2) + 1980s TV detective show *MacGyver*]

pull an act *v.* [1930s+] to put on a show with the intention of deceiving or defrauding someone. [PULL v.[3] (1) + SE *act*]

pull an all-nighter *v.* [1960s+] (*US campus*) to stay up all night working. [PULL v.[3] (1) + ALL-NIGHTER n. (4)]

pull an el-foldo *v.* [1950s+] (*US*) to collapse, to give in. [PULL v.[3] (1) + EL FOLDO n.]

pull a number *v.* [1970s+] (*orig. US*) **1** to trick, to deceive. **2** in comb. with a n., to act in a given manner, usu. in order to deceive, e.g. *pull a cop number*, to pretend to be a policeman. [PULL v.[3] (1) + NUMBER n.[3] (2)]

pull a pee-wee *v.* [1990s+] (*US teen*) to make a fool of oneself or say something stupid. [PULL v.[3] (2) + the entertainer *Pee-Wee* Herman (b.1952), who poses as a foolish, child-like figure]

pull a quick park *v.* [1970s+] (*US Black*) to make a quick pick-up of a sexual partner. [PULL v.[3] (1) + PARK v.[2]]

pull a rabbit *v.* [1950s] (*US prison*) to make an escape. [PULL v.[3] (1) + RABBIT n.[8]]

pull a race *v.* (*also* **pull a horse**) [1940s+] (*US Und.*) for a jockey to lose deliberately. [he 'pulls up' his horse]

pull a Rommel v. [1940s; 2000s] (*US Black*) to turn back, to reverse direction (lit. or fig.). [PULL v.³ (2) + the about-turn made by Nazi General Erwin *Rommel* (1891–1944) as he began to face defeat in the North African desert]

pull a Ronnie v. [1980s+] (*US campus*) to do something stupid. [PULL v.³ (2) + a negative view of the intelligence of former US president *Ronald* Reagan (1911–2004)]

pull a rose v. *see* PLUCK A ROSE v.

pull a shrewdie v. [1960s] (*N.Z.*) to trick, to deceive. [PULL v.³ (1) + SHREWDY n. (2)]

pull a smartie v. [1930s] (*US*) to trick, to deceive, to PULL A FAST ONE v. [PULL v.³ (1) + SE *smart*]

pull a stroke v. [1910s+] to attempt and/or get away with anything outrageous or daring. [PULL v.³ (1) + SE *stroke*. *Stroke* may be used here in the sense of 'a vigorous attempt to gain or do something'. A suggested link with rowing strokes seems implausible]

pull a switch v. [1950s] (*US*) to change sides. [PULL v.³ (1) + SE *switch*]

pull a train v. 1 [1940s+] (*also* **run a train**) to participate in a gang-rape. 2 [1960s+] to be the victim of a gang-rape. 3 [1960s+] of a woman, to have sex voluntarily with a number of partners in quick succession. [the woman is the 'engine', her assailants/partners are the 'rolling-stock' or the 'passengers']

pull a trick v.¹ [1930s+] to play a trick. [PULL v.³ (1) + SE *trick*]

pull a trick v.² [1950s] (*US Und.*) to perform male homosexual fellatio. [SE *pull* + TRICK n.¹ (1)]

pull away v. *see* PULL v.² (2).

pull a will v. [1980s+] (*drugs*) to vomit after excessive drug consumption. [PULL v.³ (1) + ? SAmE *pull a will*, to shoot a basket in basketball; ? proper name *William*, thus orig. anecdotal]

pull bacon v. (*also* **make (long) bacon, pull long bacon, show bacon**) [late 19C+] to thumb one's nose. [SE *pull* + BACON n.¹ (1)]

pull bull v. [20C+] (*W.I.*) to run an illegal, unlicensed taxi service, to use one's own car as an unlicensed taxi. [PULL v.³ (1) + fig. use of BULL n.¹¹ (1), i.e. their illicit service is 'nonsense']

pull caps v. [mid-18C–early 19C] of women, to fight, to squabble, esp. over a man. [they tear at each other's headgear]

pull chocks! *excl. see* CHOCKS AWAY! *excl.*

pull-down n. [mid–late 19C] a style of moustache with long extensions to the sides that became fashionable c.1870–90. [one pulls on its ends]

pull down v. 1 [mid–late 19C] (*Aus./UK Und.*) to steal. 2 [mid-19C+] to provide (with). 3 [late 19C+] (*also* **pull**) to earn, usu. money, e.g. *I pulled down £500*. 4 [late 19C+] to win money.

pull down on v. [1980s+] (*US Und.*) to threaten with a gun or weapon. [ext. PULL v.⁵]

pull down someone's ear v. [late 19C–1920s] to extract money from someone.

pull down the blind! *excl.* [late 19C] an excl. used to an overly amorous couple whose activities are embarrassing those around them.

pull down the shutter n. [20C+] butter. [rhy. sl.]

pull down your basque! *excl.* [late 19C] (*US*) an excl. used to a young woman seen as acting with less than proper decorum, behave yourself! [SE *basque*, a corset-like garment]

pull down your vest! *excl.* [late 19C] (*US*) an excl. used to a young man, behave yourself! [SAmE *vest*, waistcoat]

pull dude n. [1990s+] (*US Black*) an informer. [PULL n.³ (2) + DUDE n. (1)]

pulled (in) *phr.* (*also* **pulled up, pullied**) 1 [early 19C+] arrested (and taken before a magistrate) or caught and taken before any authority figure. 2 [1980s] (*US campus*) stopped by the police for a driving offence. [PULL IN v.]

pullemaside n. [1960s+] (*Aus.*) a racecourse tout. [SE *pull them aside*]

puller n.¹ [1930s] (*US*) a smuggler (of liquor). [they 'pull in' contraband]

puller n.² [1940s] 1 (*UK Und.*) that member of a smash-and-grab team who pulls the merchandise from a shop window. 2 (*US Und.*) a pickpocket.

puller n.³ (*US drugs*) 1 [1950s] a marijuana smoker. 2 [1990s+] a crack cocaine user who pulls at parts of their body when intoxicated. [SE *pull*, to puff on a pipe or cigarette]

puller n.⁴ [1960s] (*US drugs*) one who lures addicts to buy and non-addicts to try heroin, a PUSHER n.³.

puller-in n. (*also* **puller-inner**) [mid-19C–1950s] (*US*) an employee of a shop or saloon or other place of recreation and entertainment whose task is to lure passers-by in from the street; also used of a specific feature of the place which serves as an attraction.

pullers n. *see* COME-ALONG n.

pullet n. 1 [mid-16C+] an adolescent girl; thus *pullet-party*, a party for teenage girls (and boys). 2 [17C] (*UK Und.*) a young woman who accompanies a RUFFLER n., i.e. a vagrant posing as a discharged soldier as a disguise for robbery. [SE *pullet*, a young fowl, thus precursor of CHICKEN n.³ (1)]

pullet-squeezer n. [mid–late 19C] a womanizer who prefers younger partners. [PULLET n. (1)]

pulley n.¹ [mid-19C] a thief's accomplice, usu. a female one. [Fr. *poulet*, chicken]

pulley n.² *see* PULL n.³ (2).

pulleys n. [1940s] (*US Black*) suspenders, braces.

pull finger v. *see* PULL ONE'S FINGER OUT v.

pull foot v. [19C+] (*US/W.I.*) to run away. [20C+ use mainly W.I.]

pull for v. [late 19C+] to support, to back up.

pull for tall timber v. *see* TAKE TO THE (TALL) TIMBER v.

pull freight v. *see* PULL (ONE'S) FREIGHT v.

pull-guts n. [late 17C–early 18C] a fishmonger. [his 'evisceration' of the fish]

pull hemp v. *see* STRETCH (THE) HEMP v.

pullied *phr. see* PULLED (IN) *phr.*

pull in v. (*also* **pull up**) [early 19C+] (*orig. Und.*) to arrest. [PULL v.² (1)]

pulling party n. [1970s] (*US*) group masturbation. [PULL v.⁷ + SE *party*]

pull in one's ear v. [1910s–30s] (*US*) to mind one's own business.

pull in one's neck v. [1920s+] (*US*) to mind one's own business. [the image of a tortoise]

pull in one's shingle v. [mid-19C+] to close down a business (cf. HANG OUT ONE'S SHINGLE v.). [SAmE *shingle*, a small signboard]

pull in the pieces v. [mid-19C–1920s] to make a good wage. [SE *pieces* of money]

pull it v. 1 [early 19C] to run off as fast as one can. 2 [1960s] (*US*) to leave.

pull it out v. *see* PULL ONE'S FINGER OUT v.

pull leather v. *see* LEATHER n.³ (7).

pull long bacon v. *see* PULL BACON v.

pull no punches v. [1930s+] to speak or act openly, candidly (cf. PULL ONE'S PUNCHES v.). [boxing imagery]

pull off v.¹ [mid-19C–1900s] (*UK/US Und.*) to steal. [PULL v.³ (1)]

pull off v.² (*also* **pull**) [late 19C+] to achieve in, to succeed in. [sporting imagery]

pull off v.³ (*also* **pull oneself off**) [20C+] to masturbate, oneself or another person (cf. BALL OFF v.²). [SE *pull* but note later PULL v.⁷]

pull off v.⁴ [1900s] (*Aus.*) to stop doing something. [? SE *pull up*]

pull on v.¹ [20C+] (*Aus.*) to marry a woman.

pull on v.² 1 [20C+] (*Can./US*) to adopt something as an excuse. 2 [1920s+] (*Aus.*) to deal with, to test, to tackle. 3 [1930s] (*US Black*) to flirt. [the image of trying on a garment]

pull one off (on) v. (*also* **pull one on, pull one over**) [1920s+] (*US*) to hoax, to trick, to PULL A FAST ONE v. (on someone).

pull one's dick v. [1980s] (Aus./US) **1** to masturbate. **2** in fig. use, to talk nonsense. [PULL v.⁷ + DICK n.⁴ (1)]

pull oneself off v. see PULL OFF v.³.

pull oneself over v. [late 19C] to eat.

pull one's finger out v. (also pull finger, pull it out, remove one's digit, take one's finger out) [1910s+] (orig. Aus.) to get on with something, to stop malingering and commit oneself to positive action; esp. as command pull your finger out (cf. GET ONE'S FINGER OUT (OF ONE'S ASS) v.). [it is withdrawn, presumably, from the anus]

pull (one's) freight v. [mid-19C–1960s] (US) to rush off, to leave in a hurry.

pull one's handkerchief v. [late 19C] (US teen) to make (sexual) advances.

pull one's joint v. (also pull one's meat) [1970s+] **1** to masturbate. **2** in fig. use, to whine, to complain. [PULL v.⁷ + JOINT n.¹/MEAT n. (2)]

pull one's lay v. [1950s] (US Black) to do something, e.g. perform music.

pull one's load v. [late 19C+] (Can.) to make one's best effort.

pull one's meat v. see PULL ONE'S JOINT v.

pull one's pegs v. [1930s–40s] (Aus) to die. [gold-mining imagery]

pull one's plonker v. [1910s+] to masturbate. [SE pull/PULL v.⁷ + PLONKER n. (2)]

pull one's plum v. [2000s] (Irish) to be idle. [? nursery rhyme 'Jack Horner': Little Jack Horner sat in a corner [...] He put in his thumb, and pulled out a plum, And said, 'What a good boy am I!']

pull one's pocket v. [20C+] (W.I.) to pay with difficulty. [one must pull out the pocket's lining to find the necessary coins]

pull one's pod v. [1960s] to masturbate. [var. on PULL ONE'S PUD v.]

pull one's prick v. **1** [1960s–70s] to masturbate. **2** [1980s] (US) to promote oneself. [PULL v.⁷ + PRICK n. (2)]

pull one's pud v. (also pull one's pudding) [1910s+] (orig. US) **1** to masturbate (cf. BEAT ONE'S MEAT v.). **2** to masturbate someone else. [PULL v.⁷ + PUD n.³ (1)]

pull one's punches v. [1920s+] to restrain oneself, esp. in conversation or speech (cf. PULL NO PUNCHES v.). [boxing imagery]

pull one's string v. [1990s+] (US) to amuse, to excite, to stimulate.

pull one's taffy v. see TUG ONE'S TAFFY v.

pull one's weight v. [late 19C+] to take one's fair share of a job of work, manual or otherwise. [rowing imagery]

pull one's wire v. (also pull one's wood) [1940s+] to masturbate. [PULL v.⁷ + WIRE n.⁵ (1)/WOOD n.⁴ (1)]

pull on peter v. [late 19C+] to masturbate. [SE pull + PETER n.⁴]

pullout n. [1990s+] (Black) any item that can be stolen and carried away, e.g. car stereos, jewellery, computer games etc. [one pulls it out of the car, house etc]

pull out v. [mid-19C] **1** to extend oneself, to make a great effort. **2** to exaggerate.

pull (out) v. [late 19C+] to leave; of a person or an object, to withdraw.

pull out (all) the stops v. (also pull the stops out) [late 19C+] to make an intense effort. [the stops are those of an organ]

pull out, the dogs are pissing on your swag phr. [1960s] (Aus.) a phr. used to advise someone who finds themselves in a no-win position that the only sensible course of action is retreat.

pull rank v.¹ (also pull stripes) [1920s+] (orig. US) to use one's status within a hierarchy to impose one's will on one's inferiors, irrespective of the justice of one's position. [milit. rank or the stripes that go with rank]

pull rank v.² [1950s+] to masturbate (cf. COTTON WOOL v.). [rhy. sl. = WANK v. (1)]

pull shit v. [1960s+] (US Black) to do something devious, underhand, treacherous. [PULL v.³ (1) + SHIT n.³ (4)]

pull shoe strings v. [1930s–40s] (US Black) to exert influence, esp. surreptitiously. [ext. of PULL (THE) STRINGS v.]

pull someone's bitch card v. [2000s] (US Black) to correct someone by using excessive force. [BITCH n.¹ (5)]

pull someone's card v.¹ [1980s+] to attack, to beat up, to kill.

pull someone's card v.² [2000s] (US prison) to find out information about another inmate. [the image is of file cards, although the records are now computerized]

pull someone's chain v. [1940s+] **1** to annoy someone, to agitate. **2** to lie, to deceive.

pull someone's coat v. **1** [late 19C+] (orig. US Black) (also pull someone's coat-tails, tug someone's coat) to draw attention, to point out, to nag, to give information on. **2** [1940s+] to arrest. [Mezzrow & Wolfe, Really the Blues (1946): 'The phrase pulling my coat [...] refers to what a man does when he grabs your coat-tail and tugs it two or three times, as a warning or hint or cue when he can't speak up directly; the sort of thing someone might do when you're in a group of people and he wants to call your attention to something; a variation on the nudge']

pull someone's cock v. (also pull someone's prick) [1970s] (US) to tease, to deceive, to hoax. [SE pull + COCK n.² (1)/PRICK n. (2); fig. use of PULL ONE'S PRICK v. (1)]

pull someone's cover(s) v. (also blow someone's cover) [1960s+] (US Black) to reveal some hidden characteristic or activities, usu. in another but occas. in oneself. [the image of pulling back the bedclothes]

pull someone's head v. [1990s+] (Aus.) to gain or divert someone's attention.

pull someone's leg v. **1** [early 19C+] to tease, to hoax. **2** [late 19C] (US campus) to curry favour with, to act the toady. **3** [late 19C] to default in payment of a bill. **4** [late 19C+] (US) to ask for a loan of money. **5** [1920s] (Aus.) to subject to a confidence trick.

pull someone's pisser v. (also pull someone's plonker) [1920s+] to tease, to deceive. [SE pull + PISSER n.¹ (2)/PLONKER n. (2)]

pull someone's prick v. see PULL SOMEONE'S COCK v.

pull someone's pud v. [1920s+] (US) to tease, to hoax. [fig. use of PULL ONE'S PUD v.]

pull someone's tit v. [1910s+] (Aus./N.Z.) to tease. [SE pull + TIT n.³ (1)]

pull someone's wire v. [1950s+] (Irish) to provoke, to fool someone. [fig. use of PULL ONE'S WIRE v.]

pull someone's wool v. **1** [late 19C] (US) to get angry with. **2** [1920s] (Aus.) to annoy, to drive into a temper.

pull some slack v. [1970s] (US) to idle, to be lazy. [SLACK n.¹ (2)]

pull something out of one's ass v. [1970s+] (US) to invent or produce something, apparently 'by magic'. [ASS n. (2)]

pull something out of the bag v. (also pull something out of the hat) [1920s+] to come up with something special or surprising, something held in reserve.

pull strings v. see PULL (THE) STRINGS v.

pull stripes v. see PULL RANK v.¹.

pull the — act v. see DO THE — ACT v.

pull the bag (away/off) v. see PULL v.² (2).

pull the bung out v. [1950s] (US) to deflate someone's ego, to wreck an object.

pull the chain v. **1** [1930s+] (orig. US) to bring to a conclusion, to make a decisive move to end a period of uncertainty. **2** [1990s+] (US) to masturbate. [lavatory imagery]

pull the chain! excl. [1920s] (US) shut up! stop talking (rubbish).

pull the chain on v. [20C+] (US) **1** to murder, to kill. **2** to dismiss, to abandon, e.g. an idea.

pull the coat v. [1970s] (Aus.) to make little effort. [the image is of being held back by a hand pulling one's coat]

pull the come-along v. see COME-ALONGS n.

pull the covers off v. [1970s] (US prison) to expose a fellow prisoner's sexual preferences.

pull the other one (it's got bells on)! excl. [1960s+] a derisive rebuttal of an improbable statement.

pull the pin v.¹ **1** [1920s+] (US) to resign, to retire, to quit, to be fired from a job. **2** [1930s–60s] (US Und.) to leave, to go (away). [the pulling of the connecting pin between 2 railroad wagons]

pull the pin v.² [2000s] (US prison) to call for help.

pull the plug v. **1** [20C+] to commit suicide. **2** [1930s–40s] (US Und.) to set things going. [electrical imagery]

pull the plug (on) v. **1** [1970s+] to terminate, to bring to an end, usu. abruptly. **2** [1990s+] to treat very harshly. [electrical imagery]

pull the rug (out) from under v. [1940s+] (orig. US) to discomfit by a sudden withdrawal of presumed support.

pull the stops out v. see PULL OUT (ALL) THE STOPS v.

pull the string (of the shower-bath) v. **1** [mid-19C–1930s] to cause something to be released or made common knowledge, to reveal something previously hidden. **2** [late 19C] to die.

pull (the) strings v. [late 19C+] to exert influence, esp. behind the scenes. [puppet imagery; later var. on PULL (THE) WIRES v.]

pull the weight v. [1910s+] (Aus.) to deal with a sudden financial problem.

pull (the) wires v. [19C+] to exert influence, esp. behind the scenes. [puppet imagery]

pull-through n. **1** [1910s–20s] a tall thin person. **2** [1970s+] a Jew (cf. BILLY THE KID n.). [(1) SE pull-through, a piece of cloth attached to a string used to clean rifle barrels; (2) rhy. sl.]

pull time v. **1** [1940s+] (US prison) to be sentenced or to serve a term of imprisonment. **2** [1980s] (US) to spend time in a place. [TIME n.¹/SE time]

pull to a set v. [1970s+] (US Black) to attend a party. [SET n.¹ (3)]

pull up v.¹ (also **haul up stakes, pluck up stakes, pull up stakes**) **1** [mid-17C+] (US) to leave; to get ready to leave. **2** [1970s] (US prison) to abandon the world of crime.

pull up v.² [early–mid-19C] to work as a highwayman; thus pull up a jack, to stop a coach in order to rob it.

pull up v.³ [1990s+] (Aus. Und.) **1** to restrain someone, usu. from a violent or homicidal act. **2** to stop something happening.

pull up v.⁴ see PULL IN v.

pull up one's boot v. [late 19C] (costermonger) to prosper, to make money. [the adoption of smart boots as a sign of affluence]

pull up stakes v. see PULL UP v.¹.

pull wires v. see PULL (THE) WIRES v.

pull your head in (your hole)! excl. (also **pull your lid/scone in!**) [1940s+] (US/Aus.) an excl. of annoyance, mind your own business! don't interfere! [the action of the tortoise; LID n.¹ (2)/SCONE n.²]

pull your head out! excl. [1960s+] (US) stop being so stupid! [HAVE ONE'S HEAD UP ONE'S ARSE v. (1)]

pulpit n. [17C] the vagina.

pulpit-banger n. (also **pulpit-cackler, ...comedian, -cuffer, -drubber, -drummer, ...hector, -plugger, -pounder, -smiter, -thumper**) [late 17C+] a ranting parson, a clergyman. [his thumping of the Bible]

pulver n. [1980s+] (drugs) amphetamine (cf. A n.²). [Sp. polvo, powder]

pulverized adj. [mid-19C] (US) drunk (cf. ANNIHILATED adj.).

puma n. [1990s+] (US) in show business, a comeback, a revival of one's career.

puma phr. [1990s+] a ref. to having one's underwear caught between the buttocks. [panties up my arse]

pummeled adj. [mid-18C; 1990s+] (US campus) drunk (cf. ANNIHILATED adj.).

pump n.¹ **1** [18C; 1920s+] the penis. **2** [mid-18C] an indirect question. **3** [1940s+] a promiscuous woman. **4** [1960s] (Aus.) an act of sexual intercourse. **5** [1990s+] a nose.

pump n.² **1** [19C] a pompous fool. **2** [late 19C+] (Scot.) a breaking of wind.

pump n.³ [late 19C–1900s] (Scot.) a public house. [its beer pumps]

pump n.⁴ [1910s+] the heart.

pump n.⁵ [1970s+] a gun, esp. a pump-action shotgun. [abbr.]

pump v.¹ [mid-17C+] to ask questions, to cross-examine, esp. [20C+] to interrogate in a police station; thus your pump is good but your sucker is dry, your questions are good, but I have nothing to offer.

pump v.² [late 17C–19C] to duck someone under the pump, as a punishment.

pump v.³ **1** [mid-18C+] to have sexual intercourse. **2** [1980s+] (US teen) to excite sexually. [SE pump, to move vigorously up and down]

pump v.⁴ [19C; 1980s+] to break wind.

pump v.⁵ [mid-19C] to weep. [SE pump, to raise up water]

pump v.⁶ [mid-19C] to exploit, to extort from.

pump v.⁷ [1950s+] (US teen) to ride pillion on a motorcycle or scooter. [ety. unknown]

pump v.⁸ [1990s+] (US Black) to play music loudly. [one 'pumps up the volume']

pumpage n. [1960s–70s] sexual intercourse. [PUMP v.³ (1) + -AGE sfx; but poss. a nonce-word coined for the novel King's Road (1971) by Mariella Novotny]

pump dale n. [17C] the vagina (cf. BEAUTY SPOT n.; DAMP n.). [SE pump, one of several equations of water production and the vagina + SE dale]

pumped adj.¹ **1** [mid-19C–1900s] out of breath, exhausted. **2** [1950s] exhausted from a surfeit of sexual intercourse. [one's heart is pumping fast]

pumped adj.² [1990s+] (orig. US) having well-developed muscles. [PUMP IRON v.]

pumped nuts n. [1990s+] (US) temporary courage. [PUMPED adj.² + NUTS n.² (5)]

pumped (up) adj. **1** [1970s+] (US) excited, full of something, usu. oneself. **2** [2000s] (US campus) drunk.

pumper n. **1** [late 19C] anything exhausting, e.g. a running race. **2** [1930s–40s] (Aus) the heart. [(1) one's pounding heart; (2) PUMP n.⁴]

pumpernickel n. [1920s] a Black prostitute, esp. a mulatto. [SE pumpernickel, dark wholemeal rye bread]

pump-handle n. **1** [18C; 1970s] the penis. **2** [1910s] (Aus.) an arm.

pump-handle v. [late 19C–1900s] to shake hands vigorously, as if wielding a pump-handle; thus pump-handler, a handshake of this nature.

pumping adj. [2000s] usu of music, excellent, first-rate.

pump iron v. (also **push iron, throw iron**) [1960s+] (orig. US) to work out with weights, to practise bodybuilding. [IRON n.³ (8)]

pump jockey n. [1940s+] (US) a petrol pump attendant. [SE pump + JOCKEY n.³ (2)]

pumpkin n.¹ (also **punkin**) **1** [mid-18C+] a fool (cf. APPLEHEAD n.). **2** [mid-19C+] (US) an important person or object; usu. as SOME PUMPKINS n. **3** [20C+] a term of affectionate address, usu. by a man to a woman.

pumpkin n.² (also **pompkin**) [late 18C–early 19C] a native of Boston, Massachusetts. [the popularity of the pumpkin as a crop and a foodstuff; an alternative ety. suggests the use of a hollowed-out pumpkin as a form of template for Puritan haircuts]

pumpkin n.³ **1** [mid-19C+] (also **punkin(-piece)**) the head. **2** [1940s] (US Black) the sun, the moon. **3** [1950s] a breast, usu. in pl. (cf. APPLES n.¹). [the shape]

pumpkin-face n. [late 19C] (US) a round, expressionless face.

pumpkin head n. **1** [19C+] a fool (cf. APPLEHEAD n.). **2** [mid-19C; 1970s+] (also **pumpkin pate**) a person with an abnormally large head. **3** [1970s+] a term of address. [SE pumpkin + SE head/-HEAD sfx (1)/SE pate]

pumpkin head v. [2000s] (*US prison*) to beat up a victim using a pillowcase containing some form of hard object.

pumpkin-headed adj. [mid-19C; 1950s] (*US*) stupid (cf. AIRHEADED adj.). [PUMPKIN HEAD n. (1)]

pumpkin-husker n. see PUMPKIN-ROLLER n.

pumpkin pate n. see PUMPKIN HEAD n. (2).

pumpkin pie n. [1960s] (*US gay*) an underage boy; thus *pumpkin-eater*, an older man who prefers sex with such boys.

pumpkin-roller n. (*also* pumpkin-husker, punkin-roller) [20C+] (*US*) a rustic, a farmer (cf. ACORN-CRACKER n.).

pumpkin-seed n. (*also* pumpkin-skin) [19C–1920s] (*US Black*) a light-skinned person.

Pumpkinshire n. (*also* **Pompkinshire**) [late 18C] Boston, Massachusetts. [PUMPKIN n.² + sfx -*shire*]

pump lead v. [late 19C+] (*US*) to fire a gun. [LEAD n.¹ (1)]

pump off v. [1950s+] to masturbate (cf. BALL OFF v.²). [SE *pump*]

pump oneself up v. [20C+] (*orig. US*) to exert or arouse oneself, to prepare oneself mentally for a challenge.

pump one's pickle v. (*also* **pump one's meat**) [1970s–80] to masturbate (cf. BEAT ONE'S MEAT v.). [PICKLE n.²/MEAT n. (2)]

pump out v. [1930s] (*US Und.*) to kill by shooting.

pump-pump n. [1990s+] (*US Black teen*) an imitation of the sound of gunfire. [echoic]

pumps n. [19C] the eyes. [they *pump* out tears]

pump ship v. **1** [late 18C–early 19C] to vomit. **2** [late 18C+] to urinate; thus as n., an act of urination. [naut. jargon *pump ship*, to pump the ship dry of water]

pump-sucker n. [late 19C–1920s] a teetotaller. [they fig. 'suck' the water-*pump*]

pump the stump v. [1940s] (*US Black*) to shake hands.

pump-thunder n. [19C] a braggart, a boaster. [PUMP n.² (1) + SE *thunder*]

pump-thunder v. [late 19C–1900s] to bluster. [PUMP-THUNDER n.]

pum-pum n.¹ [18C–mid-19C] a fiddler. [the 'pum-pum, pum-pum' of the tunes]

pum-pum n.² [1980s+] (*W.I./UK Black*) the vagina; thus *pum-pum-pum*, a fool (cf. BAMBA n.¹). [? Krio *pumbe*, the female vulva]

pump up v. **1** [1970s+] to exaggerate. **2** [1980s+] (*US Black/campus*) to make livelier, to fill with energy.

punaany n. (*also* pudenany, punani, punny) [1980s+] (*US/W.I./UK Black teen*) **1** the female genitals. **2** women in general in a sexual way. **3** sexual intercourse. **4** something good. [ety. unknown; ? link to PUM-PUM n.²; also note PUNDU n. (2)]

punce n. see POONCE n.

punch n.¹ (*also* **punch date**) [1960s+] (*orig. US campus*) a promiscuous woman. [PUNCH v. (1)]

punch n.² see MAKE A PUNCH v.

punch v. **1** [mid-17C; 1940s+] (*US campus*) to engage in sexual intercourse (cf. BANG v.¹). **2** [late 17C–early 19C] to deflower. **3** [1930s] (*US campus*) to give a failing grade. **4** [1940s+] (*US Und.*) to break open a safe using a steel punch and a hammer to knock out the combination. **5** [1990s+] (*US*) to accelerate a car.

punchable adj. [late 17C–early 19C] a woman considered ripe for seduction; thus *punchable nun*, a prostitute. [PUNCH v. (2)]

punch and judy n.¹ [late 19C–1910s] lemonade. [ety. unknown; ? a brandname]

punch and judy n.² [1930s] a school inspector. [? rhy. sl.]

punch and judy adj. [20C+] sulky, depressed. [rhy. sl. = SE *moody*]

punchboard n. (*also* **punchcard**) [1940s+] (*US*) a promiscuous woman, a cheap prostitute. [pun on SE *punchboard*/PUNCH v. (1)]

punch clod n. [late 19C–1900s] a peasant, a farm labourer (cf. BOGHOPPER n.). [SE *punch* + CLOD n.¹ (1)]

punch cows v. (*also* **punch bulls, …cattle**) [late 19C+] to be a cowboy. [backform. f. COW-PUNCHER n.]

punch date n. see PUNCH n.¹.

puncher n. **1** see BULL-PUNCHER n. **2** see COW-PUNCHER n.

punch gun v. [1910s] (*US Und.*) to use criminal sl. or cant. [ety. unknown]

punch house n. **1** [late 17C–mid-19C] a brothel, or a tavern that doubles as such (cf. ACCOMMODATION HOUSE n.). **2** [1920s–40s] (*US Black*) a spontaneous get-together, a party. **3** [1970s] (*US Black*) a party frequented by pimps and their women, usu. an orgy. [HOUSE n.¹ (1); orig. the provision of alcoholic *punch* at such establishments but underpinned by PUNCH v. (1)]

punchie n. [1950s] a boxer.

punch in v. [1940s+] (*US*) to arrive at work (cf. PUNCH OUT v.¹). [the *punching* of a time clock]

punching bag n. [late 19C+] one who is constantly beaten up, e.g. an abused woman. [boxing jargon *punching bag*, a fighter who has no real abilities and is useful only as the recipient of a fortunate opponent's punches]

punching the truncheon n. [1990s+] male masturbation (cf. MUNCHING THE TRUNCHEON n.). [SE *punch* + TRUNCHEON n.]

punch in the mouth n. [1960s] cunnilingus. [pun on SE *punch*/PUNCH v. (1)]

punch it v.¹ **1** [late 18C–early 19C; 1970s] (*UK/US Und.*) to run away, to escape. **2** [early 19C] to walk; thus *punch outsides*, to go outside. **3** [1980s] (*US campus*) to hurry. [one's feet 'punch' the street]

punch it v.² [1970s+] (*US gay*) to take the passive role in anal intercourse (cf. ASK FOR THE RING v.).

punch-on n. [1960s+] (*Aus.*) a fight, esp. in a street or public house.

punch-out n. [1940s+] (*US*) a fight. [PUNCH OUT v.²]

punch out v.¹ **1** [1940s+] (*US*) to leave work, i.e. to punch the timeclock (cf. PUNCH IN v.). **2** [1960s–70s] (*US campus*) to fail in one's studies. **3** [1970s] (*US*) in fig. use, to reject, to turn against. [note USAF *punch out*, to eject from an aircraft]

punch out v.² [1940s+] (*US*) to beat up, to assault with the fists.

punch-out artist n. [1960s+] (*US*) anyone who enjoys and is expert in beating up their opponents with their fists. [PUNCH OUT v.² + ARTIST sfx]

punch out someone's lights v. see PUT OUT SOMEONE'S LIGHT(S) v.

punch someone's ticket v. [1930s+] (*US*) **1** to murder, to kill. **2** to beat comprehensively. [the image of 'cancelling' the victim's life]

punch the apple v. see PUNCH THE CLOWN v.

punch the bag v. [1900s–20s] (*US*) to gossip, to chatter, to complain; thus *bag-puncher*, a gossip, a whinger; *bag-punching*, gossiping, complaining. [boxing imagery]

punch the breeze v. [1900s–40s] (*US*) to leave.

punch the bundy v. [1930s+] (*Aus.*) to work hard, less from choice but from the desire to make more money. [ety. unknown]

punch the clock v. **1** [1920s+] to 'clock on' or 'clock off' for work. **2** [1930s+] to be employed, to go to work. **3** [1990s+] in fig. use, to die. [SE *punch* + (*time*)*clock*; (3) implies 'clocking off' at the end of the day]

punch the clown v. (*also* **punch the apple**) [1960s+] to masturbate.

punch the gas v. [1970s+] (*US*) to accelerate an automobile, to drive fast.

punch the wind v. [1920s–30s] (*US tramp*) to ride on the outside of a train.

punch-up n. [1950s+] **1** a fight, usu. in the street, a pub etc. **2** a beating.

punchy adj. [1930s+] **1** disorientated, eccentric, out of control. **2** looking like a boxer, e.g. broken nose, 'cauliflower' ears etc. **3** aggressive. [boxing jargon *punchy*, abbr. *punch drunk*, a boxer who has taken too many punches and is becoming eccentric]

punda n. (also **pundah**) [1980s+] (S.Afr.) women, seen collectively as sex objects. [PUNDU n. (2)]

pundu n. [1970s+] (S.Afr.) 1 the buttocks, the posterior. 2 the vagina. [Xhosa *impundu*, buttocks]

pune n. see POON n.¹ (1).

punga n. [1980s+] (N.Z.) the penis; thus *how's your punga?* a phr. of greeting. [Maori *ponga*, a tree fern]

pungle (down) v. [mid-19C+] (US) to hand over money. [Sp. *póngale*, put it down; ult. *poner*, to put, to give]

punish v. 1 [early 19C] to hurt badly in a boxing match or a fight. 2 [early 19C] to make inroads into, esp. a stock of food or wine. 3 [mid-19C+] to attack, esp. in sports. 4 [1940s+] to use something vigorously. 5 [1960s+] to play a musical instrument badly, thus 'abusing' it.

punisher n. 1 [19C] a heavy hitter; thus *punishing*, hard-hitting. 2 [early 19C] a demanding, laborious task; thus *punishing*, difficult, laborious. 3 [late 19C] a heavy user. 4 [1950s+] a long-winded bore.

punishment n. 1 [early 19C+] physical or emotional pain, damage or loss. 2 [1940s+] (gay) taking an extra-large penis either in the mouth or the anus.

punish one's teeth v. [1920s] (US tramp) to eat.

punish percy in the palm v. [1960s+] to masturbate. [PERCY n.]

punish the pope v. see DISOBEY THE POPE v.

punk n.¹ 1 [late 16C–1920s] (also **punque, punquetto**) a young female prostitute. 2 [20C+] (also **penitentiary punk, punkie**) (US prison) a young inmate used for sex by older, stronger peers; an inmate's 'boyfriend' or 'wife'; thus *punkfucker*, the active partner in such a relationship; *punk tank*, a segregation zone for punks in a prison. 3 [20C+] (US) a tramp's younger companion, usu. a catamite. 4 [20C+] a general term of disparagement. 5 [1900s] (US) a person, irrespective of character. 6 [1910s+] (US) (also **punkie**) a young criminal or street gang member. 7 [1910s+] an adolescent boy. 8 [1930s–40s] a youngster, a child. 9 [1930s+] (US/W.I.) a coward, a weakling. 10 [1940s+] (US) a male homosexual. 11 [1960s–70s] (US) a male prostitute. [? SE *punch*, to pierce and linked to PUNCH v. (1); note Sp. *punto, puto*, a male prostitute]

punk n.² [mid-19C+] nonsense, rubbish. [? US *punk*, rotten wood or a fungus growing on it]

punk n.³ [late 19C+] (US) bread. [ety. unknown]

punk n.⁴ [1970s+] 1 a mid-1970s youth cult, starting in the UK but spreading to the US by such apostles as the Sex Pistols (*fl.*1975–8) and Malcolm McLaren (b.1946). While the hippies had been bourgeois, *punks* were proletarian, complaining not against a consumer society but against their exclusion from its delights; they specialized in bizarre hair styles (mohican, multicoloured), ripped clothes and safety pins, through flesh as well as fabric; thus *punk rock*, the music; *punk rocker*, a fan of punk; *punky, punkish, punkoid*, characteristic of a punk fan. 2 a member of this youth cult, a devotee of punk music; thus PUNKETTE n. [PUNK n.¹ (6); as with similar movements, *punk*, while technically sl., has become effectively SE]

punk adj. 1 [late 19C+] (US) (also **punko**) of people and things, second-rate, inferior, distasteful, worthless, unimportant. 2 [late 19C+] weak, effeminate. 3 [1920s+] unwell, out of sorts. 4 [1930s+] young. [PUNK n.¹]

punk v.¹ [early 18C] (US) to work as a prostitute. [PUNK n.¹ (1)]

punk v.² 1 [1940s+] to engage in anal intercourse; to sodomize (cf. ASK FOR THE RING v.; PUNK (OUT) v.). 2 [1960s+] to beat up severely. [PUNK n.¹ (2)]

punk v.³ 1 [1980s+] (US Black) to criticize, to insult. 2 [2000s] (US campus) to trick, to tease. [PUNK n.¹ (4)]

punk v.⁴ [2000s] (US teen) to steal. [? PUNK n.¹ (4)]

punk v.⁵ see PUNK (OUT) v.

punk! excl. [1920s] (US juv.) an excl. of annoyance, disappointment. [PUNK n.²]

punkah one's face v. [late 19C] (Anglo-Ind.) to fan one's face. [Hind. *panka*, a fan, esp. the large fixed fans, essentially a sheet stretched across a hinged frame and operated by a servant, designed to keep whole rooms cool]

punk and gut n. [1920s–60s] (US tramp) a bread and bologna/cheese sausage sandwich. [PUNK n.³ + GUT n.¹ (2)]

punk and plaster n. [late 19C–1930s] (US) bread and butter. [PUNK n.³ + PLASTER n.³ (1)]

punk-ass n. [1970s+] (US) a general term of abuse. [PUNK-ASS adj.]

punk-ass adj. [1970s+] (US) 1 of a person, object or situation, useless, second-rate, worthless. 2 young, immature. [PUNK n.¹ (4) + -ASS sfx]

punkawn n. [mid-19C+] (Irish) a talkative, self-assertive person. [Irish *poncán*, an American, esp. a Yankee]

punked-out adj. [1980s] (US campus) furious. [PUNK v.³ (1)]

punker n.¹ 1 [late 17C–18C] one who pursues prostitutes. 2 [1960s] (US prison) a male homosexual who takes the active role in anal intercourse. [(1) PUNK n.¹ (1); (2) PUNK n.¹ (2)]

punker n.² [1970s+] (US) a fan of punk rock music. [PUNK n.⁴ (1)]

punkette n. [1970s+] a female PUNK n.⁴ (2). [PUNK n.⁴ + SE fem. sfx -*ette*]

punkie n. see PUNK n.¹.

punkin see under PUMPKIN and its combs.

punkish adj.¹ [17C–18C] showy, flashy. [PUNK n.¹ (1)]

punkish adj.² [1960s+] (US) weak, effeminate. [PUNK n.¹ (2)]

punk jacket n. [1990s+] (US prison) a reputation for cowardice. [PUNK n.¹ + JACKET n.³ (1)]

punk-master n. [early 17C] a pimp (cf. ABBOT ON THE CROSS n.). [PUNK n.¹ (1)+ SE *master*]

punko adj. see PUNK adj. (1).

punk-out n. [1950s–60s] (US) a coward. [PUNK (OUT) v. (1)]

punk (out) v. 1 [1920s+] (US) to display cowardice. 2 [1960s+] (US prison) (also **ride**) to force or persuade someone to have homosexual anal intercourse (cf. ASK FOR THE RING v.; PUNK v.²). 3 [1960s+] (US campus) to cause trouble for someone, to intimidate. 4 [1980s] to dance to PUNK n.⁴ music, to adopt the lifestyle. 5 [1990s+] to make someone into an acquiescent weakling. [PUNK n.¹ (2)/PUNK n.¹ (9); (4) PUNK n.⁴ (1)] [PUNK v.²]

punk pills n. [1960s–70s] (drugs) any form of tranquillizer. [PUNK n.¹ (9) + SE *pills*; their creation of artificial courage]

punk-simple adj. [1950s] (US prison) obsessed with young homosexual boys. [PUNK n.¹ (2) + -SIMPLE sfx (1)]

punk's run n. [1980s+] (US prison) the protective custody unit for those whose lives would be at risk if they were kept with the prison population as a whole. [PUNK n.¹ (2) + pun on SE *chicken run*]

punky adj. (US) 1 [20C+] cowardly, weak; second-rate. 2 [1980s] strong and unpleasant. [(1) PUNK n.¹ (2); (2) PUNK n.¹ (6)]

punny n. see PUNAANY n.

punque/punquetto n. see PUNK n.¹ (1).

punse n. [late 19C] the vagina. [Yid.]

punt n.¹ 1 [early 18C] one who bets in a gambling game. 2 [late 19C+] a bet; thus TAKE A PUNT v. [PUNT v.¹]

punt n.² [1970s] (US gay) a heterosexual male. [? SE *peasant*]

punt v.¹ 1 [18C+] to gamble, to wager; lit. and fig. 2 [1930s+] to pay up. 3 [1980s+] to sell, to promote. 4 [2000s] to make an investment in. [ety. unknown; orig. SE use in certain card-games, to bet against the bank; note also Sp. *ponto*, a point, faro jargon *punt*, a point]

punt v.² [1960s+] (US campus) to give up, esp. one's work. [US football imagery; the team that fails to score within 4 downs is forced to punt the ball to the opposition]

punta n.¹ [mid-19C] (Ling. Fr.) a sovereign, £1 sterling. [? cod-Ital.]

punta *n.*[2] [2000s] (*US Black*) the odour of vaginal secretions. [POONTANG n. (2)]

puntang *n. see* POONTANG n. (2).

punt around *n.* [1970s] an attempt to find someone or something. [PUNT AROUND v.]

punt around *v.* [1970s+] to try one's luck, esp. when looking for a person. [fig. use of PUNT v.[1] (1)]

punter *n.*[1] **1** [early 18C+] a gambler, on cards, dice, horses, dogs etc. **2** [1930s–40s] (*N.Z.*) a pickpocket's assistant. **3** [1930s+] the victim of a confidence trickster's schemes. **4** [1930s+] a generic term for a member of the general public, particularly when in the role of customer, esp. of a prostitute, a casino and other slightly 'shady' enterprises. **5** [1960s–70s] (*Scot. gang*) a gang member. [PUNT v.[1] (1)]

punter *n.*[2] [1930s+] a large beer mug. [pun on SE *mug*/MUG n.[2] (1)/MUG PUNTER n.]

punting-shop *n.* [mid-19C] a casino, a gambling house. [PUNT v.[1] (1) + SHOP n.[1] (1)]

punt off *v.* [1970s+] (*US campus*) to forget, to put to the back of one's mind. [PUNT v.[2]]

pup *n.*[1] **1** [mid-19C+] a youthful, inexperienced person; esp. as *young pup.* **2** [1930s+] a child. **3** [1950s+] (*US*) a 4-wheeled trailer drawn by a tractor, lorry or other road vehicle. [PUPPY n.[1] (1)]

pup *n.*[2] (*US*) **1** [1920s–40s] (*also* **hot pup**) a spiced, heated sausage, served on a split roll. **2** [1970s] penis. [play on HOT DOG n.[1]]

pup *v.* [mid-19C+] to experience childbirth; thus *pupped,* born; also in fig. use. [reverse anthropomorphism]

pupa-lick *n.* (*also* **pupperlick**) [late 19C+] (*W.I.*) a somersault. [Carib.E. *pupa,* father + LICK v.[1] (1); the image is of being turned over the father's knees, buttocks in the air, for a spanking]

pup noddy *n. see* POOP NODDY n.

puppet-head *n.* [1960s+] (*US teen*) a gullible, conventional person, esp. one who permits hearsay to 'pull their strings' in matters of current taste. [SE *puppet* + -HEAD sfx (1)]

puppies *n.*[1] (*also* **pups**) **1** [1920s+] the feet. **2** [1980s] shoes. [play on DOGS n.[1]; thus the brandname *Hush Puppies,* supposed to comfort one's feet]

puppies *n.*[2] **1** [1970s] nipples. **2** [1990s+] the female breasts (cf. BAGS n.[1]). [their 'snuggling' together]

puppies, the *n.* [1940s+] (*Aus.*) greyhound racing. [var. on DOGS, THE n.]

puppy *n.*[1] (*also* **puppy dog**) **1** [late 16C+] a socially or sexually inexperienced man. **2** [1930s] cowardice. **3** [1960s+] a love-sick young man. [reverse anthropomorphism; (2) predates synon. DOG n.[3] (16)]

puppy *n.*[2] **1** [18C] the penis (cf. ANTEATER n.). **2** [1930s+] (*US Black*) a half-pint bottle of fortified wine. **3** [1980s+] (*US Black*) a small penis. **4** [1980s+] (*US campus*) an otherwise unspecified and nameless object. **5** [1990s+] (*US*) a handgun. [SE *puppy*; i.e. implying smallness]

puppy *n.*[3] [mid-19C–1900s] a blind man. [the blindness of newborn puppies]

puppy *n.*[4] [1980s+] an idea, a suggestion. [used as a generic]

puppy boy *n.* [1990s+] (*US teen*) a young man who is deeply in love. [PUPPY n.[1] (3)]

puppy dog *n. see* PUPPY n.[1]

puppy-foot *n.* (*also* **puppy-dog foot**) [20C+] in cards, any of the club suit, esp. the ace. [the similarity to a small paw-print]

puppy-match *n.* (*also* **puppy-snatch**) [late 17C–mid-18C] a trap, a snare.

puppy paws *n.* [2000s] (*US*) a throw of double 5 in craps dice (cf. ADA FROM DECATUR n.). [the similarity of the 5 on a die to a small paw-print]

puppy-prick *n.* [1940s] (*US*) a lipstick so made that once uncapped the stick slowly 'erected' itself and protruded from the container.

puppy show *see under* POPPY SHOW.

puppy's mamma *n.* [late 18C] a euph. for BITCH n.[1] (1).

puppy-snatch *n. see* PUPPY-MATCH n.

pups *n. see* PUPPIES n.[1]

purchase *n.* [late 16C–18C] (*UK Und.*) money procured by a confidence trickster team.

pure *n.*[1] [17C–early 19C; 1990s+] a mistress, a prostitute. [ironic use of SE]

pure *n.*[2] **1** [1910s+] top-quality drugs, unadulterated. **2** [1960s+] (*drugs*) the best heroin.

pure *adj.* [late 17C–19C] fine, jolly, splendid, esp. when ironic.

pure *adv.* [mid-18C+] a general intensifier, purely, absolutely, completely.

pure-d *adj.* (*also* **pure dee, pure idee**) [1950s+] (*US*) complete, absolute, utter. [PURE adv. + ? D adj.]

pure grit *n. see* REAL GRIT n. (1).

pure love *n.* [1970s] (*drugs*) LSD (cf. A n.[3]). [LSD's image as a creator of 'love and peace']

purely *adv.* [late 17C–mid-19C] excellently, nicely, satisfactorily.

pure merino *n.* [early 19C+] 'an early immigrant to Australia with no convict origins; a member of a leading family in Australian society; a person of fine breeding or good character' (*OED*); a person with good manners. [*Merino sheep,* a variety of sheep with especially fine wool, introduced from Spain to England in the late 18C and used for the improvement of the fleece-bearing sheep of Britain and the colonies. *AND* notes 'one who finds in this a basis for social pretension']

pure merino *adj.* (*also* **pure wool**) [mid-19C+] first-class, well-bred, excellent. [PURE MERINO n.]

pure nast! *phr.* [1990s+] (*US teen*) really disgusting. [PURE adv. + SE *nast(y)*]

pure quill *n.* (*also* **clear quill, the quill**) [late 19C+] (*US*) something that is excellent or flawless. [? a perfect SE *quill* or feather]

pure silk *n.* [1970s] (*US Black*) a male homosexual. [an image of softness and smoothness]

purest pure *n.* [late 17C–18C] the highest class of prostitute, a courtesan. [ext. of PURE n.[1]]

pure wool *adj. see* PURE MERINO adj.

purge *n.* [late 19C+] any form of alcoholic liquor. [SE *purge,* an aperient; 20C+ use is only N.Z.]

purger *n.* (*also* **perger**) [mid-19C–1930s] **1** a teetotaller. **2** a general pej. [negative image of teetotallers]

puritan *n.* [17C] an ironic term for a prostitute. [? the hypocrisy of Puritans or play on PURE n.[1]]

purko *n. see* PERK n.[2]

purl *n.*[1] [mid-17C–mid-19C] beer warmed nearly to boiling, mixed with gin or wormwood (the basis of absinthe), sugar and ginger; a later version substituted gin for the wormwood. Both were considered suitable for a morning pick-me-up; thus *purl-royal,* a glass of Canary wine with a dash of wormwood. [? link to SE *purl,* a rill or whirl of water]

purl *n.*[2] [mid-19C] **1** a heavy fall. **2** whirling or pitching head-first or head-over-heels. [PURL v.]

purl *v.* [mid-19C] to turn upside down, to overturn, to upset, to turn a somersault. [SE *purl,* often of a top, to spin round and round]

purler *n.* **1** [mid-19C+] (*also* **pearler**) a crash, an accidental fall; thus COME A PURLER v. **2** [mid-19C+] a knockout blow. **3** [20C+] (*Aus./N.Z.*) (*also* **pearl, pearler, purl**) something of outstanding excellence or perfection. [PURL v.; (3) is fig. use of (2)]

purp *v. see* PERP v.[1]

purple *n.* (*drugs*) **1** [1960s+] amphetamine (cf. A n.[2]). **2** [1960s+] LSD (cf. A n.[3]). **3** [1980s+] ketamine. [the colour of the pills]

purple *adj.* **1** [late 19C–1920s] splendid, regal. **2** [1940s–50s] homosexual (cf. LAVENDER adj.; LILAC adj.). [the image of purple as a 'royal' colour, thus of a 'queen']

purple and mauve *n.* [2000s] (*Aus.*) the stove. [rhy. sl.]

purple barrels n. (also **purple dragons, ...flats, ...hearts, ...microdots, ...owsley, ...wedges**) [1970s+] (drugs) LSD (cf. A n.³; PURPLE HAZE n.; PURPLE OHM n.). [SE purple, i.e. the colour of the pill + BARRELS n./SE dragons/hearts, i.e. the stamp on the pill/FLAT BLUES n./MICRODOT n./Owsley ACID n./WEDGE n.⁴]

purple death n. [1940s+] (mainly N.Z.) cheap Italian wine. [its colour and possible effect]

purple down v. [1990s+] (US drugs) to calm down, with the help of tranquillizers. [the purple colour of the Xanax tranquillizer]

purple dragons n. see PURPLE BARRELS n.

purple dromedary n. see DROMEDARY n.

purple flats n. see PURPLE BARRELS n.

purple haze n. (drugs) 1 [1960s+] LSD (cf. A n.³; PURPLE BARRELS n.). 2 [1990s+] a strong variety of cannabis (cf. BLACK DOMINA n.; BOMB n.⁴). [the Jimi Hendrix song title (1967)]

purple-headed custard chucker n. (also **p.h.a., purple-headed avenger, ...love truncheon, ...monster, ...warrior, ...womb broom, ...yoghurt-slinger**) [1970s+] the penis. [SE + CUSTARD n.; note synon. RMC Duntroon (Aus.) purple-headed darth vader]

purple hearts n. (also **pink hearts**) [1960s+] (drugs) 1 amphetamines (cf. A n.²). 2 (rarely) barbiturates (cf. BARBIT n.). 3 see PURPLE BARRELS n. [the colour of the pills]

purple-helmeted junket gun n. see BLUE-VEINED JUNKET PUMP n.

purple microdots n. see PURPLE BARRELS n.

purple ohm n. [2000s] (drugs) a variety of LSD (cf. A n.³; PURPLE BARRELS n.). [the colour of and the stamp on the pill]

purple owsley n. see PURPLE BARRELS n.

purple para n. [1960s+] (Aus.) cheap, unpleasant port wine. [SE purple + abbr. paraffin]

purple pork n. see PORK n.².

purple wedges n. see PURPLE BARRELS n.

purse n. 1 [mid-16C+] the vagina (cf. BANK n.¹). 2 [18C+] the scrotum (cf. BALL-BAG n.). [BAG n.¹ (1); (1) is underpinned by the commercial potential of the vagina]

purse v. [late 16C–early 17C] to steal purses.

purse-bouncer n. [1900s] a swindler.

purse-catcher n. [early 17C] a pickpocket.

pursed-up adj. see PURSIE adj.

purse-emptier n. 1 [early 17C] a swindler. 2 [late 19C] a highwayman.

purse-fakir n. see PURSE-TRICK MAN n.

purse-finder n. [19C] a prostitute (cf. ASS PEDDLER n.). [the 'purse' is both the SE money-bag and PURSE n. (1)]

purse-lifter n. [1900s] a pickpocket.

purse-milking n. [early 17C] swindling, robbery; also as adj. [SE purse + MILK v.¹ (1)]

purse-net n. [late 16C–early 19C] a small purse. [for. ety. see next]

purse-nets n. [late 16C–mid-19C] goods sold to a gullible young person at vastly inflated prices and on credit. [SE purse-net, a bag-shaped net, the mouth of which can be drawn together with cords; used esp. for catching rabbits, also used as a fishing net]

purse-proud adj. 1 [late 17C–18C] lecherous, amorous. 2 [late 17C+] snobbish on account of one's wealth. [(1) PURSE n. (1); (2) SE purse]

purse-snatcher n. [1900s] a pickpocket.

purse-trick man n. (also **purse-fakir**) [1900s–30s] (UK/Aus.) a confidence trickster, a swindler. [presumably involving the selling of supposedly money-bearing purses]

pursie adj. (also **pursed-up**) [1940s–60s] (Aus.) well-off, 'in funds'. [SE pursy]

purting glumpot n. [late 19C] a sulky, miserable person. [dial. purt, to sulk, to pout + GLUM-POT n.]

pusa see under PHUZA.

pus-bag n. (also **pus brain, pushole, pus pocket, puss-bag, pussbucket**) [1960s+] (orig. US) a general derog. term, a contemptible person. [SE pus + -BAG sfx; the use of pus may offer a link to earlier derog. terms relating to venereal diseases]

pus-gut n. (also **pustle-gut**) [mid-19C+] a fat stomach; one who has a fat stomach; thus adj., **pus-gutted/pusley-gutted**. [pron. SE purse, i.e. a full purse]

push n.¹ [mid-17C+] sexual intercourse; thus DO A PUSH v. (2). [the thrusting movements of the man]

push n.² 1 [late 17C–early 19C] a crowd, a 'press' of people. 2 [late 18C] a robbery, a swindle. 3 [mid-19C] (UK Und.) a small gang who mask the activities of a pickpocket by surrounding the victim. 4 [late 19C+] (Aus.) a criminal gang, a gang of tramps, a prison work gang; thus pushism, the world of such gangs; pushite, a gang member. 5 [late 19C+] (US/Aus.) a crowd, thence a clique, a set, among the most celebrated of which was the Sydney Push, or Sydney University Libertarian Society of the early 1960s; thus pushite, a member of a gang or 'crowd'; in the push, moving in fashionable circles. 6 [1930s] (US) a family.

push n.³ [mid-19C; 1980s] influence. [var. on PULL n.¹ (1)]

push n.⁴ [late 19C] money. [? fig. use of SE, i.e. it lets one 'push forward' in life]

push n.⁵ [20C+] (Irish) 1 help, encouragement. 2 a problem, a difficult situation. [SE push; (1) used positively, (2) negatively]

push n.⁶ see PUSHOVER n. (2).

push, the n. [late 19C+] 1 dismissal from a job, rejection; usu. as get/give the push, to be dismissed, to dismiss, esp. a lover. 2 ejection from a place, e.g. a public house.

push v.¹ [mid-17C+] to have sexual intercourse. [PUSH n.¹]

push v.² 1 [late 19C+] (orig. US) to sell, to promote, to advertise. 2 [1920s+] (drugs) to sell drugs. 3 [1930s–50s] to distribute counterfeit money. 4 [1940s] to smuggle. 5 [1940s+] to sell any item. [SE push, 'to advance or try to advance or promote' (OED)]

push v.³ [1910s+] 1 to leave. 2 to go. [abbr. PUSH OFF v.¹]

push v.⁴ [1920s+] to approach, e.g. a certain age; usu. as pushing, e.g. pushing 50, nearly 50 years old.

push v.⁵ [1960s+] (US Black) to drive a car. [one pushes the accelerator]

push a face v. see PUSH ONE'S FACE v.

push along v. [1910s+] to leave.

push a pen(cil) v. see PENCIL-PUSHER n. (1).

push a pike n. [early 18C] sexual intercourse. [SE push of pike, close combat, fighting at close quarters]

push a turd uphill with a toothpick v. see PUSH SHIT UPHILL v.

push-bike n. [1910s+] a pedal cycle, as opposed to a motorcycle; thus as v., to ride a bicycle.

push clouds v. [late 19C–1930s] (US) to die; to be dead. [one's ascent to heaven]

pushed adj.¹ [early 19C+] lacking, bereft, in need of, e.g. pushed for cash, pushed for time.

pushed adj.² [mid-19C–1930s] drunk (cf. ANNIHILATED adj.). [one of many words associating physical violence with drunkenness]

pushed out of shape adj. (US) 1 [1960s+] upset, angry. 2 [1970s] (also **pushed out**) drunk.

pusher n.¹ 1 [late 19C] (US) a salesman. 2 [1900s] (US Und.) a bank teller, a cashier. 3 [1920s+] (US tramp) the foreman on a construction site.

pusher n.² [1910s–40s] a young woman, esp. a prostitute; thus SQUARE PUSHER n. (1). [PUSH v.¹]

pusher n.³ 1 [1920s+] (drugs) (also **pusherman**) one who sells drugs; usu. in his 'small-time' or 'retail' role as opposed to the wholesale DEALER n. (2). 2 [1930s+] (US Und.) a distributor of counterfeit money. 3 [1950s] (US gay) a man who runs a string of homosexual male prostitutes. [PUSH v.²]

pusher n.⁴ [1950s+] (Aus.) a pushchair.

pusher n.⁵ [1980s+] (drugs) 1 a thin stick, typically a chopstick, used to pack a cocaine pipe. 2 a metal hanger or umbrella rod used to scrape residue in crack stems.

pusherman *n. see* PUSHER n.[3] (1).

push fire *v.* [20C+] (*W.I.*) to urge others into a fight, with no intention of participating oneself. [one 'fans the flames']

push-foot *n.* [1920s–40s] (*W.I.*) a Ford Model T automobile. [on this car low gear was engaged by pressing a foot-pedal]

pushie *n.* (*also* **pooshey, pooshie, pooshy**) [1960s+] (*Ulster*) **1** an over-sensitive person. **2** a coward; also as adj., cowardly, effeminate. [(1) SE *push*; (2) PUSSY n. (10)]

pushing school *n.* [late 17C–early 19C] a brothel (cf. ACADEMY n.). [PUSH v.[1] + SE *school*. Note SE *pushing school*, a fencing school, linking to the various sl. uses of DAGGER n.[1] and other synons. meaning the penis; despite date, B.E. has only the fencing school use, thus categorized by him as sl.]

pushing tout *n.* [early 18C] (*UK Und.*) a thief's watchman or scout.

push-in job *n.* [1970s+] a mugging that takes place on the victim's doorstep. [SE *push-in* + JOB n.[3] (1)]

push in one's cut-off *v.* [1910s] (*Aus.*) to stop talking.

push in the bush *n.* [1920s+] sexual intercourse. [PUSH n.[1] + BUSH n.[2] (1)]

push in the truck *n.* [1930s+] sexual intercourse. [rhy. sl. = FUCK n.[1] (1); but note PUSH n.[1]]

push iron *v. see* PUMP IRON v.

push it *v.* [1950s+] to approach a limit, often in one's conduct; esp. as *don't push it*, don't go too far (or you will face the consequences).

push money *n.* [1930s+] (*US*) commission paid to a salesperson on each item sold. [PUSH v.[2] (1) + SE *money*]

push off *v.*[1] (*also* **push on**) **1** [mid-18C+] to leave; esp. as imper. *push off!* go away. **2** [1910s+] to go somewhere. **3** [1920s–30s] to kill.

push off *v.*[2] [20C+] to start, esp. to start a game. [SE *push off*, to push a boat off from its mooring]

pushhole *n. see* PUS-BAG n.

push on *v. see* PUSH OFF v.[1].

push one's face *v.* (*also* **push a face**) [mid-18C] to obtain credit through deceit or bravado. [ext. use of SE *push one's face forward*]

push one's luck *v.* [1960s+] to take (dangerous) chances.

push one's own barrow *v.* [1910s+] (*Aus.*) **1** to brag. **2** to look out for one's own interests first.

pushover *n.* **1** [late 19C+] (*orig. US*) a situation that presents no difficulties or problems. **2** [1910s+] (*orig. US*) (*also* **push**) one who is easily overcome, convinced or imposed upon. **3** [1920s+] one, esp. a woman, who is easily seduced. **4** [1930s] (*US*) a trick, a hoax.

push ponies *v.* [1960s+] of a pimp, to promote prostitutes. [PUSH v.[2] (1) + PONY n.[6] (2)]

push-push *n.* [20C+] (*US*) sexual intercourse. [PUSH n.[1] + redup.; Trimble, *5,000 Adult Sex Words & Phrases* (1966), suggests orig. pidgin use by 'Americans in foreign countries']

push shit uphill *v.* [1980s+] (*mainly N.Z.*) (*also* **push a turd uphill with a toothpick**) **1** to work, talk etc unsuccessfully, against the odds. **2** (*US gay*) to have anal intercourse (cf. ASK FOR THE RING v.).

push shorts *v.* (*also* **shove shorts**) [1930s–50s] (*drugs*) to sell in small amounts; to sell short measure. [PUSH v.[2] (2) + SHORT n.[3] (2)]

push someone's buttons *v.* (*also* **push the right buttons**) [1970s+] **1** to manipulate someone emotionally. **2** to make someone feel special, turned on, loved etc.

push someone's face in *v.* [20C+] to hit someone in the face.

push someone's key *v.* [1990s+] (*US prison*) to irritate someone, to tease someone.

push the boat out *v.* **1** [1910s+] to spend heavily, usu. on pleasure, eating, drinking etc, often treating others. **2** [1910s+] to do something to excess. **3** [1960s] to exaggerate.

push the cart up Holborn Hill *v. see* WALK BACKWARDS UP HOLBORN HILL v.

push the glass about *v.* [early 19C] to drink.

push the queer *v.* [1930s–50s] (*US Und.*) to pass counterfeit money. [PUSH v.[2] (3) + QUEER n. (2)]

push the right buttons *v. see* PUSH SOMEONE'S BUTTONS v.

push-up *adj.* [1990s+] (*W.I.*) presumptuous, arrogant.

push up daisies *v. see* PUSH UP (THE) DAISIES v.

push-up man *n.* [1910s–30s] (*Aus.*) a pickpocket's accomplice who *pushes up* the arm of the victim to facilitate access to their wallet; thus *push-up mob*, a gang of pickpockets specializing in this; *at the push-up*, working as a pickpocket.

push up on *v.* [1990s+] (*US Black*) **1** to make romantic moves towards someone, usu. in the hope of seduction. **2** to frighten, to intimidate.

push up (the) daisies *v.* [1910s+] to die; thus *pushing up (the) daisies*, dead.

pushy *adj.* [1930s+] (*orig. US*) unpleasantly forward, self-assertive or aggressive.

pus pocket *n. see* PUS-BAG n.

puss *n.*[1] **1** [17C+] a (young) woman. **2** [mid–late 17C] a prostitute, a madame (cf. ALLEY CAT n.). **3** [mid-17C+] the vagina (cf. BIRD n.[8]). **4** [1970s+] the 'female' of a lesbian couple. **5** [1970s+] (*US gay*) the buttocks. **6** [1970s+] (*US gay*) an underage boy. [SE *puss*; the association of women and cats (cf. PUSSY n.)]

puss *n.*[2] [mid-17C+] a hare. [dial.]

puss *n.*[3] **1** [late 19C+] the face. **2** [1910s+] the mouth. **3** [1910s+] (*Irish*) a sulky look; also as v., to pout or sulk. [Irish *pus*, the mouth, a sulky expression]

puss *n.*[4] (*W.I.*) **1** [1940s] rubber-soled canvas shoes. **2** [1950s] a thief. [SE *puss*, a cat, i.e. one walks as quietly as a cat]

puss *n.*[5] [1950s] (*W.I.*) an albino. [abbr. PUSS-EYE n.]

puss *n.*[6] *see* PUSSY n.

puss-bag *n. see* PUS-BAG n.

puss-boots *n.* [1940s] (*W.I.*) rubber-soled canvas shoes. [the quietness of one's steps in such shoes + ? ref. to the folktale 'Puss-in-Boots']

pussbucket *n. see* PUS-BAG n.

pussery *n.* [1950s] (*W.I.*) **1** trickery. **2** theft. [PUSS n.[4] (2)]

puss-eye *n.* [1950s] (*W.I.*) an albino. [? SE *pus* + *eye*; the stereotype of short-sighted albinos]

puss gentleman *n.* [1960s+] (*US Black*) a weak man. [PUSSY n. (10)]

puss-in *n.* [20C+] (*W.I.*) a young woman. [var. on PUSSY n. (1)]

pussing *n.* [1990s+] (*Irish*) crying, whingeing. [PUSS n.[3] (3)]

puss out *v. see* PUSSY OUT v.

puss-pelmet *n. see* PUSSY-PELMET n.

pussy *n.* **1** [late 16C; mid-19C+] women in general, with an implication of their being sexually available. **2** [18C+] the vagina; thus metonymic for sexual intercourse (cf. BIRD n.[8]). **3** [late 19C+] female pubic hair. **4** [1900s–40s] (*also* **puss**) the *cat*-o'-nine-tails. **5** [1920s] in fig use of (1), one who is gentle, kind. **6** [1920s+] an old woman, usu. a spinster, who is inquisitive and meddling. **7** [1930s+] (*Aus.*) a rabbit. **8** [1930s+] a fur garment; thus *pussy-hoisting*, stealing furs; *pussy mob*, a gang of fur thieves. **9** [1940s+] a male homosexual; or a man judged to be or teased as being so. **10** [1950s+] (*also* **puss**) a coward, a weakling, with an implication of homosexuality. **11** [1960s–70s] (*gay*) the anus, i.e. a play on (2). **12** [1970s] cowardice. [SE *pussy*, an affectionate name for a cat (cf. PUSS n.[1])]

pussy *adj.* **1** [mid-19C–1910s] fat, corpulent. **2** [20C+] easy, undemanding (the inference being not worthy of a 'real man'). **3** [1950s+] (*orig. US*) scared, cowardly. **4** [1960s+] effeminate, implying homosexuality. **5** [1970s+] female. **6** [1970s+] (*US*) pertaining to sex; pornographic. **7** [1980s+] useless, insignificant. [PUSSY n.]

pussy v. [1910s+] (Aus.) to move (in) quietly or unobtrusively. [SE pussy, i.e. like a cat]

pussy (around) v. [1960s+] (Scot./US) of a man, to play sexual games, to have sexual intercourse. [PUSSY n. (2)]

pussy-ass adj. [1970s+] (US) cowardly, weak. [PUSSY adj. (3) + -ASS sfx]

pussy bandit n. [1990s+] (US) a man who is obsessed with sex and seduction. [PUSSY n. (2) + BANDIT sfx (3)]

pussyboy n. 1 [1950s+] a passive male homosexual, a catamite. 2 [1980s+] a general insult, implying cowardice or homosexuality. [PUSSY n. (9) + SE boy]

pussy-bully n. [1990s+] (W.I.) a male sexual athlete. [PUSSY n. (2)]

pussy bumper n. [1940s–70s] 1 (US Und.) a male homosexual. 2 an effeminate whipping boy. 3 a lesbian (cf. BEAN FLICKER n.). [(1) PUSSY n. (9); (2) PUSSY n. (10); (3) PUSSY n. (2) + SE bumper/ BUMPER n.[5]]

pussycat n. 1 [19C+] (orig. US Black) the vagina (cf. BIRD n.[8]). 2 [1950s+] a weak or at least amiable and passive person. [ext. of (1) PUSSY n. (2), (2) PUSSY n. (10)]

pussycat adj. (also **pussy-kitten**) [1900s–20s] (US) weak, effeminate. [ext. of PUSSY adj. (3)]

pussy claat n. (also **pussyclaht, pussyclot**) [1960s+] (W.I./UK Black) a general pej., a coward, an informer; also as adj. [PUSSY n. (2) + SE cloth, i.e. a sanitary towel]

pussy-eating n. [1980s] (orig. US) cunnilingus (cf. BOX LUNCH n.). [PUSSY n. (2) + EAT v.[3] (1)]

pussyfoot n. 1 [1910s] (US Und.) a detective (cf. BEAT-POUNDER n.). 2 [1930s] (also **pussyfooter**) a coward, a weakling; someone sly or underhand; a general derog. term of address. [PUSSYFOOT (AROUND) v.]

pussyfoot adj. 1 [1910s+] cowardly, weak; a general derog. epithet. 2 [1920s] teetotal. [PUSSYFOOT (AROUND) v.]

pussyfoot (around) v. [20C+] to compromise, to act in a cowardly or weak manner. [the animal's cautious movements]

pussyfooter n. see PUSSYFOOT n. (2).

pussyfooting adj. [1920s+] weak, dithering, ineffectual. [PUSSYFOOT (AROUND) v.]

pussy game n. [1950s+] (US) the world of prostitution. [PUSSY n. (2) + GAME n.[2] (3)]

pussy glommer n. [1920s] (Can. tramp) a hand. [PUSSY n. (2) + GLOM v. (1)]

pussy-gutted adj. (also **pussle-gutted**) [1900s] (US) fat, with a large stomach; thus pussy guts, a fat person. [PUS-GUT n.]

pussy hair n.[1] [1970s+] female pubic hair. [PUSSY n. (2) + SE hair]

pussy hair n.[2] see CUNT HAIR n.

pussy hole n. [1980s+] (UK/US Black/W.I.) the vagina; also as insulting adj., a synon. with CUNT adj. (cf. BIRD n.[8]; BLACK HOLE n.[1]). [PUSSY n. (2) + SE hole]

pussy-hound n. [1970s+] a man who is obsessed with the pursuit of sex. [PUSSY n. (2) + HOUND sfx]

pussy in a can n. [1960s+] (US prison) sardines sold in a can at a prison commissary. [PUSSY n. (2) + SE can; the association of the smell of the vagina with the smell of fish]

pussy juice n. [1960s+] vaginal secretions (cf. BINDERJUICE n.). [PUSSY n. (2) + JUICE n.[2] (1)]

pussy-kisser n. [1960s] (US) a general insult, lit. a cunnilinguist (cf. COCKMUNCH n.). [PUSSY n. (2)]

pussylicker n. (also **pussy-lapper**) [1960s] (US) a general term of abuse, lit. a cunnilinguist (cf. COCKMUNCH n.). [PUSSY n. (2)]

pussy magnet n. [2000s] (US) a sporty automobile, supposedly appealing to young women. [PUSSY n. (1) + MAGNET sfx]

pussy out v. (also **puss out**) [1960s+] (orig. US) to act in a cowardly manner, to give up under pressure. [PUSSY n. (10)]

pussy-parlor n. [1980s] (US) a striptease club. [PUSSY n. (2)]

pussy patrol n. see PUSSY POSSE n.

pussy-pelmet n. (also **puss-pelmet**) [1960s+] a very short miniskirt. [PUSSY n. (2)/PUSS n.[1] (3) + SE pelmet]

pussy picture n. [1940s] (US) a pornographic photograph of a woman. [PUSSY n. (2) + SE picture]

pussy posse n. (also **pussy patrol**) [1970s+] (US police/Und.) the Vice Squad, esp. those members who deal with prostitutes. [PUSSY n. (2) + fig. use of SE posse]

pussy-printer n. [1990s+] (W.I.) shorts so tight they outline the genital area. [PUSSY n. (2)]

pussy prober n. [1980s] (US) a gynaecologist. [PUSSY n. (2)]

pussy pusher n. [1970s] (US gay) a heterosexual. [PUSSY n. (2) + PUSH v.[1]]

pussy queer n. (also **pussy queen**) [1960s–80s] (US) a lesbian (cf. BEAN FLICKER n.). [PUSSY n. (2) + QUEER n. (4)/QUEEN n.[2] (1)]

pussy-struck adj. [1920s+] obsessed by sex. [PUSSY n. (2) + SE struck, fascinated]

pussy tickler n. [1940s+] (orig. US Black) a moustache. [PUSSY n. (2) + SE tickler]

pussy whip v. [1990s+] (orig. US) of a woman, to dominate her husband or partner. [backform. f. PUSSY-WHIPPED adj.]

pussy-whipped adj. 1 [1960s+] (orig. US) (also **hen-whipped, p.w.'d**) of a man, dominated by a woman, esp. one's wife or girlfriend. 2 [1980s] (US Black/campus) besotted with, infatuated by. [PUSSY n. (2) + fig. use of SE whip]

pussy willow n. [1960s] a pillow. [rhy. sl.]

pustle-gut n. see PUS-GUT n.

put n.[1] 1 [late 17C–mid-19C] a peasant, a countryman. 2 [mid-18C–1910s] a general term of derision; usu. as OLD PUT n. [ety. unknown; ? one who is easily 'put upon' (cf. ety. at BAMBOOZLE v.)]

put n.[2] [19C] a prostitute (cf. JAMETTE n.). [Fr. putain, a prostitute]

put v. 1 [mid–late 19C] (US) to make off, to be off, to 'clear out'. 2 [1900s] (US campus) to vomit (cf. BLOW v.[3]).

puta n. (US Hisp.) 1 [1930s+] a prostitute; a very promiscuous woman; also attrib. 2 [1960s+] a general term of abuse. [synon. in Sp.]

put a baby on v. [1990s+] (US Black) 1 of a woman, to have a child without the father's knowledge and/or agreement. 2 to claim a man as one's child's father, even though he is not.

put a beating on v. see PUT A HURTING ON v.

put a blossom on it for v. [1950s] (Aus.) to commit pederasty. [ety. unknown; ? ref. to the freshness of a SE blossom + IT n.[1] (2)]

put a blue on v. see BUNG ON A BLUE v.

put a bone in someone's hood v. [mid–late 16C] to cuckold someone. [BONE n.[1] (1); ext. of SE phr. put a bone in someone's hood, to break or cut off someone's head]

put a bug in someone's ear v. see BUG n.[5] (5).

put a bung in it! excl. 1 [late 19C] to stop talking, also as imper. 2 [1910s] shut the door!

put a bun on v. see HAVE A BUN ON v.

put a churl upon a gentleman v. 1 [late 17C–early 19C] to drink malt liquor after drinking wine. 2 [18C] to drink ale immediately after drinking wine. [the supposed links of social class and drinking habits]

put a cork in it! excl. [1930s+] (US) shut up! be quiet!

put a crimp into v. (also **apply a crimp, crimp**) [late 19C+] (US) to thwart, to block, to impair, to interfere with. [SE crimp, to compress]

put a curl in someone's hair v. see PUT SOMEONE'S HAIR IN(TO) A CURL v.

put a dent in one's hip v. [1970s+] (US Black) to cost an appreciable amount of cash. [one's wallet is carried on one's hip]

put a down on v. (also **put a down upon**) [early–late 19C] to inform against someone. [DOWN n.[2] (1)]

put a few back v. (also **put a few down**) [20C+] to have a few drinks. [FEW, A n. (2)]

put a finger in one's eye v. [18C–early 19C] to weep. [the implication is of forced, and thus insincere, tears]

put a finger on *v.* [1930s+] **1** (*US*) to betray, esp. to the police. **2** to work out, to identify. **3** to identify someone, esp. as someone about to die. [note FINGER v.[2]]

put a foot in someone's ass *v. see* PUT ONE'S FOOT IN SOMEONE'S ASS v.

put a freeze on *v. see* PUT THE FREEZE ON v. (1).

put a hat on someone *v.* (*also* **hang a hat on someone**) **1** [mid-19C–1900s] (*UK Und.*) to beat someone, to put them in their place. **2** [1970s+] (*US Black*) to dislike someone intensely. **3** [1970s+] (*US Black*) to single someone out for revenge.

put a head on someone *v. see* PUT A (NEW) HEAD ON SOMEONE v.

put a hole in *v.* [1910s+] to kill someone. [with a bullet]

put a hole in one's manners *v. see* MAKE A HOLE IN ONE'S MANNERS v.

put a hurting on *v.* (*also* **give someone a hurting, put a beating on, put a hurt on**) [1970s+] (*orig. US Black*) to cause deliberate harm to someone.

put a jerk in it *v.* [1910s–30s] to act vigorously, smartly or quickly.

put a lid on *v. see* PUT THE LID ON v.[1] (1).

put a man in one's belly *v.* [late 16C–early 17C] for a woman to permit sexual intercourse.

put a name up *v.* [1950s+] (*UK Und.*) to inform against someone, often to save one's own skin.

put and take *n.*[1] [1920s+] **1** sexual intercourse. **2** homosexual intercourse. [the 'backwards-and-forwards' movement of intercourse]

put and take *n.*[2] [1920s+] a cake. [rhy. sl.]

put an egg in your shoe and beat it! *excl.* [1950s] (*US*) go away! [a pun on BEAT IT v.]

put a (new) head on someone *v.* **1** [mid-19C–1920s] (*US*) to punch or assault someone, to disfigure in a fight. **2** [late 19C] to defeat, to overcome. **3** [late 19C] to silence, to make someone be quiet.

put an iron on one's shoulder *v.* [1980s+] (*N.Z.*) to become indebted, lit. or fig.

put another nail in one's coffin *v.* [19C] to get drunk. [pun on the sealing of a coffin + the pegs that once marked off alcoholic measures in a tankard]

put another record on! *excl.* (*also* **change the record!**) [1920s+] an excl. used in the hope of silencing a nagging or critical person.

put a pass *v. see* PASS v.[1].

put a pincher on *v. see* PINCHER n.[1] (2).

put a poor mouth on *v.* [late 19C] (*Irish*) to complain, to whinge. [POOR MOUTH v.]

put a ring around *v.* [1950s+] (*N.Z.*) to be sure of, to be certain of; esp. in phr, *you can put a ring around that one.* [image of *ringing* important dates on a calendar]

put a set on *v.* [1910s] (*Aus.*) to terminate, to bring to an end. [fig. use SE *set*, to place in a sitting posture, i.e. no longer moving forward]

put a sham upon *v.* [late 17C–early 18C] to trick, to hoax, to defraud. [SHAM n.[1] (1)]

put a slap down *v.* [2000s] (*US Black*) to hit someone when they are behaving in a cowardly manner.

put a sock in it *v.* (*also* **shove/stuff a sock in it**) [1910s+] to stop talking, to be quiet; esp. as imper. [the sock gags the mouth]

put a steam on the table *v.* [late 19C] to make enough money to buy a piece of meat for Sunday lunch. [the meat would be boiled rather than roasted]

put a streak into it *v.* [20C+] (*Anglo-Irish*) to hurry up, to 'get a move on'; esp. as imper. [STREAK n.[1] (1)]

put a tin ear on *v.* [1920s+] (*US*) to batter someone's head and ears, giving the victim a 'cauliflower' ear.

put a tooth in it *v.* [1930s+] to come straight to the point;

also in negative *not put a tooth in it.* [one starts 'chewing' immediately]

put a tooth on it *v.* [1940s] (*Aus.*) to refrain from criticism.

put-away *n.* **1** [late 19C–1900s] imprisonment. **2** [1930s] (*Aus.*) an object or piece of information that gives something away. **3** [1950s] (*Aus.*) an informer. [PUT AWAY v.[2]]

put away *v.*[1] **1** [late 16C+] to kill, to murder. **2** [late 19C+] to bury. **3** [late 19C+] to knock out.

put away *v.*[2] **1** [mid-19C+] to imprison. **2** [mid-19C+] (*orig. UK Und.*) to inform against and thus be instrumental in having imprisoned. **3** [late 19C–1920s] to pawn. **4** [1930s+] to put someone in a lunatic asylum or old people's home.

put away *v.*[3] [mid-19C+] to eat or drink, esp. a large amount.

put away *v.*[4] **1** [late 19C+] (*orig. US*) to defeat an opponent; lit. and fig. **2** [1930s–40s] (*US*) to pose as someone important. **3** [1940s] to praise. **4** [1960s+] of an entertainer, to score a resounding success with one's audience, to impress greatly.

put away *v.*[5] [1940s] (*orig. US Black*) to perform.

put back *v.* [1970s+] to eat or drink, esp. a large amount.

put beans up one's nose *v.* [20C+] (*US*) to do something stupid despite having been warned not to.

put-down *n.* [1950s+] a verbal attack, criticism, condemnation. [PUT DOWN v.[3] (1)]

put down *v.*[1] [early 19C; 1970s] (*UK/US Und.*) to make (someone) aware. [DOWN adj.[1] (1)]

put down *v.*[2] [mid-19C+] to eat or drink.

put down *v.*[3] **1** [late 19C+] to deride, to slander, to attack verbally, to tease. **2** [1960s+] to attack physically, to kill.

put down *v.*[4] **1** [20C+] of an activity, to abandon. **2** [1910s] (*UK Und.*) to successfully cash a forged cheque at a bank; to pass counterfeit money. **3** [1950s+] (*US*) of a person, to reject, to give up. **4** [1970s] (*US*) of a place, to leave. [SE *put down*, to set down]

put down *v.*[5] [1940s+] to act, to do, to say.

put down *v.*[6] [2000s] (*US Black*) to enlist a candidate in a gang or similar group.

put down a routine *v.* [1950s+] (*US*) to hoax or otherwise persuade someone with a clever story. [SE *put down* + show business *routine*, a regularly performed sketch, song, dance etc]

put down shoe leather *v.* [1960s] to run fast.

put down some hair *v. see* HAIR n.[1] (2).

put down south *v. see* SOUTH v.

put-em-up *n.* [1910s] (*US Und.*) a violent, potentially homicidal criminal. [the hold-up man's command of 'Put 'em up!']

put flash (to) *v.* [19C] (*UK Und.*) to inform, to put on guard, to pass on information. [FLASH adj.[1] (2)]

put fly *v.* [19C] (*Aus./UK Und.*) to make (someone) aware. [FLY adj. (1)]

put foot *v.* [1980s+] (*S.Afr.*) to drive fast. [abbr. of 'put one's foot on the accelerator']

put for tall timber *v. see* TAKE TO THE (TALL) TIMBER v.

put four quarters on the spit *v.* [18C] to have sexual intercourse. [cooking imagery; the *quarters* are the couple's legs]

put fowl to mind corn *v.* [20C+] (*W.I.*) to make a very foolish decision, to trust someone unwisely. [a chicken, of course, would eat the corn]

put France on *v.* [1920s+] (*W.I.*) to scold severely, to give a tongue-lashing to. [FRANCE n.]

put game on someone *v.* [1970s+] (*US Black*) to confuse, to play tricks on, to deceive. [GAME n.[2] (3)]

put hair on one's chest *v.* **1** [1920s+] to embolden. **2** [1940s+] to cheer up, to strengthen, esp. in context of offering a drink, e.g. *that'll put hair on your chest.* [the perceived masculinity of body hair + drinking]

pu the elop *adj.* [20C+] pregnant. [backsl. = UP THE POLE phr.[2]]

put her there! *excl. see* PUT IT THERE! excl.

put-in *n.* **1** [mid-19C] of a man, an act of sexual intercourse. **2** [mid-19C+] (*US*) one's turn to speak, one's affair. [poker imagery]

put in *v.*[1] [mid-19C+] of time, to expend, to serve, usu. referring to a job.

put in *v.*[2] **1** [late 19C] (*US*) to introduce. **2** [1920s+] (*Aus./US*) to get someone into trouble, esp. to inform on (to the police). **3** [1930s+] to give information. **4** [1980s+] to put someone forward for a job. [abbr. *put in trouble/put in a word*]

put in chancery *v.* [19C+] to have absolute control over an opponent, to dominate completely. [boxing jargon *put in chancery*, to pin one's opponent's head beneath the crook of one arm, thus immobilizing them and making it easy for one to hit their face at will; ult. f. the supposed inflexibility of the Court of Chancery, and the financial 'damage' incurred there by plaintiffs]

put in lay-away *v.* [1960s] (*US Black*) to postpone, to put 'on hold'.

put in one's motto *v.* [late 19C] to interfere in a conversation, esp. to thrust forward one's own point of view.

put in one's oar *v.* (*also* **put in one's shovel, put one's oar in, ...spoon in**) [early 18C+] to meddle, to interfere in another's concerns. [the last and surviving var. on 16C *have an oar in every man's boat/barge* and *put one's oar in another man's boat*]

put in one's papers *v.* [20C+] **1** (*US campus*) to apply for admission. **2** (*US*) to resign.

put in one's spoke *v.* [late 16C+] to interfere.

put in one's two cents (worth) *v.* (*also* **...three cent's worth, ...twopennorth**) [1910s+] (*orig. US*) to make a contribution, usu. gratuitous and/or malicious, to an argument or conversation.

put in the boot *v. see* PUT THE BOOT IN *v.*

put in the bucket *v.* (*also* **put in the garden, ...hole, ...well**) [early 19C+] (*UK Und.*) to deceive, to cheat, to swindle, to ruin, esp. to rob an accomplice of their share of a robbery. [BUCKET *v.* (1)/SE *garden/hole/well*; the image is of hiding away the partner's share; only *hole* is 20C+]

put in the frame *v.* [1960s+] (*UK Und./police*) to concoct evidence against a criminal, whether or not guilty of the crime under investigation. [FRAME(-UP) n. (2)]

put in the gee *v.* [1920s+] to deceive, to 'tell the tale'. [GEE n.[2] (2)]

put in the hole *v. see* PUT IN THE BUCKET *v.*

put in the knock *v.* [1910s] (*US*) to reject, to refuse. [KNOCK BACK *v.*[3]]

put in the leather *v.* [1940s+] to kick. [i.e. the use of leather shoes]

put in the nut *v. see* NUT *v.*[2].

put in the peg *v.* [late 19C–1920s] (*Aus.*) **1** to stop doing something, esp. to stop drinking. **2** to cut off someone's credit. [the pins or pegs that once divided a large tankard]

put in the pin *v.* [mid-19C] to stop drinking during a session, or to give up drinking completely. [PUT IN THE PEG *v.*]

put in the poison *v.* [1920s] to slander, to malign a person's character, esp. in court.

put in the slipper *v.* [1940s+] (*Aus., orig. prison*) to give a kicking.

put in the stings *v.* [1910s+] (*Aus.*) to demand a loan or a gift. [STING *v.* (4)]

put in the well *v. see* PUT IN THE BUCKET *v.*

put into mothball *v.* [1920s] to be quiet, usu. as imper.

put into soak *v. see* SOAK *v.*[2] (1).

put in work *v.* [1990s+] (*US Black gang*) to get busy, esp. in the performance of any dangerous and/or illegal act, e.g. theft or murder. [WORK n.[1] (1)/an ironic allusion to SE]

put in wrong with *v.* [1930s+] (*orig. US*) to denigrate, to ruin someone's reputation.

put it about *v.* (*also* **put it around**) [1960s+] to indulge in a wide-ranging sex life; to wlork as a prostitute.

put it across *v.* [20C+] **1** (*also* **put one across**) to beat, to get the better of. **2** to hoax, to trick, to defraud. **3** to punish.

put it all on one's back *v. see* HANG IT ALL ON ONE'S BACK *v.*

put it all over *v. see* PUT ONE OVER (ON) *v.*

put it all together *v.* [1960s+] to consolidate one's position, to work out one's life satisfactorily.

put it around *v.*[1] [1970s] to circulate information.

put it around *v.*[2] *see* PUT IT ABOUT *v.*

put it down one's neck *v. see* WASH ONE'S NECK *v.*

put it in and break it *v.* [late 19C+] of a man, to have sexual intercourse (cf. BREAK A BIT OFF *v.*; BURY IT *v.*). [the erect penis 'breaks' after orgasm]

put it in cruise mode *v.* (*also* **put it in overdrive**) [1990s+] (*US campus*) to seek a partner for romance or sex. [automobile imagery]

put it in the wind *v.* [1970s+] (*US Black*) to leave.

put it in the woods *v.* [1970s] (*US prison*) to escape.

put it into gear *v. see* GET INTO GEAR *v.*

put it on a bullet (and put it in your brain) *phr.* [1990s+] (*US Black teen*) remember that, don't forget.

put it on (someone) *v.* **1** [mid-19C–1900s] to extort money, with or without menaces; to charge to someone else's account. **2** [late 19C+] to assault, to beat someone up, to murder. **3** [20C+] to show off. **4** [20C+] to overcharge. **5** [1910s+] (*Aus.*) to make a suggestion, to propose. **6** [1950s] to demand, to extort, to persuade. **7** [1950s] (*US gang*) to declare war.

put it on the street *v.* [1950s+] (*orig. US*) to make gossip, information etc available for general consumption.

put it over (someone) *v.* [late 19C+] (*orig. US*) **1** to cheat or confuse someone. **2** to defeat, to surpass.

put it over the plate *v.* [late 19C] (*US*) to achieve a success, a coup. [baseball imagery]

put it there! *excl.* (*also* **put her there!**) [mid-19C+] shake hands!; esp. in the context of sealing a deal or affirming a friendship. ['there' being the speaker's outstretched hand and 'it'/'her' being the hand of the person spoken to]

put it to *v.* (*US*) **1** [1920s+] to beat up, to put under pressure, e.g. of the police. **2** [1930s+] to have sexual intercourse with. [note Shakespeare's *Love's Labour's Lost* (1594–5): 'If their daughter be capable, I will put it to them']

put it to the wood *v.* [1970s] (*US campus*) to accelerate an automobile. [i.e. press the accelerator to the floor of the car]

put it up *v.* [mid-19C; 1990s+] of a man, to have sexual intercourse (cf. BURY IT *v.*). ['it' being the penis]

put it up! *excl.* [mid-19C] stop it! be quiet!

put it up to *v.* **1** [1910s+] (*US*) to attack verbally, to criticize. **2** [1990s+] (*Irish*) to attack physically. ['it' being a fist or boot]

put it where the monkeys put their nuts! *excl.* [late 19C+] an excl. of coarse dismissal, i.e. SHOVE IT UP YOUR ARSE! *excl.*

put lead in one's pencil *v.* [1920s+] (*orig. Aus.*) to cheer one up, to strengthen, esp. in a sexual context; thus *this will put lead in your pencil/here's lead in your pencil*, a toast used to accompany the offer of a drink, food or even drug – any of which is cited as a presumed adjunct to potency.

put legs on someone *v.* [late 19C–1930s] to make someone hurry up.

put manners on *v.* [1980s+] (*Irish*) to discipline, to force into line.

put milk in the coffee *v.* [1940s+] (*W.I.*) to have sexual intercourse.

put Mr Kleenex's kids through college *v. see* CLOBBER THE KLEENEX *v.*

put next (to) *v.* [late 19C+] (*US*) **1** to introduce, to direct towards. **2** to warn, to inform.

puto *n.* [1950s+] **1** a male homosexual. **2** a male prostitute (cf. JAMETTE n.). **3** the penis. **4** a general derog. term. [masc. version of Sp. *puta*, a prostitute]

put off *v.*[1] [mid-18C–1900s] (*Aus./US Und.*) to distribute counterfeit money.

put off *v.*[2] [20C+] to disconcert.

put off *v.*[3] (*Aus.*) **1** [1930s] to lay off from work, to dismiss. **2** [1990s+] to kill, to murder.

put-on *n.* **1** [mid-19C+] a joke, a hoax. **2** [late 19C] an old female beggar who specializes in *putting on* a look that makes her look as pitiful as possible. [PUT ON *v.*[2] (2)]

put-on *adj.* [late 19C+] (*US*) affected, pretentious. [PUT ON *v.*[1]]

put on *v.*[1] (*also* **put up**) [early 18C; late 19C+] to affect airs; thus *put-on*, one who puts on airs.

put on *v.*[2] **1** [mid-19C–1910s] (*UK/US Und.*) to inform, to let someone know. **2** [mid-19C+] to tease, to joke with, to deceive for one's own gain. **3** [1910s+] (*Aus. Und.*) to arrest and/or charge on the basis of concocted evidence, to 'frame up'. **4** [1960s] to annoy, to irritate. [the image is of adding things in excess of the actual facts]

put on *v.*[3] [20C+] (*Ulster*) to get dressed. [abbr. *put on one's clothes*]

put on *v.*[4] [1930s+] to eat, e.g. *put on the chicken pie.* [abbr. PUT ON THE FEEDBAG *v.*]

put on *v.*[5] [1960s] **1** (*orig. US Black*) to do to, to make happen to. **2** to request.

put on a blue *v. see* BUNG ON A BLUE *v.*

put on a boss *v.* [late 19C] to affect a squint in order to make oneself look more threatening. [BOSS-EYED *adj.* (1)]

put on a bridge *v. see* CHUCK A BRIDGE *v.*

put on a cigar *v.* [late 19C] to smoke a cigar in order to make oneself seem smarter than one is. [PUT ON *v.*[1]; a cigar was seen as more genteel than the working-class pipe]

put on a crumb act *v.* [1950s] (*Aus.*) to impose on another person. [CRUM *n.* (2)]

put on a face *v.* [late 19C+] lit. or fig., to change one's expression.

put on an act *v.* [1930s+] to show off, to talk for display, to behave insincerely.

put-on artist *n.* [1930s+] (*US*) a hoaxer, a tease. [PUT-ON *n.* (1) + ARTIST *n.* (1)/ARTIST sfx]

put on a slab *v.* [20C+] (*US prison*) to fight in private to settle a score.

put on a smoke *v.* [late 19C–1900s] to light a pipe or cigarette.

put on beef *v.* [mid-19C+] to put on weight. [BEEF *n.*[1] (3)]

put on dog *v.* (*orig. US*) **1** [mid-19C+] (*also* **pile on dog**, **put on the dog**) to show off, to put on airs; to do something energetically, noisily. **2** [1970s] to have sexual intercourse. [DOG *n.*[5] (1); (2) ext. of (1)]

put one across *v. see* PUT IT ACROSS *v.* (1).

put one back *v.* [20C+] to cost; often as *how much did that put you back?* [var. SET SOMEONE BACK *v.*]

put one in *v.* [1980s] (*US*) to shoot dead. [the *one* is a bullet]

put one on *v.* (*also* **put one in/over**) [1910s+] (*orig. Aus.*) to hit. [the *one* is a blow]

put one over (on) *v.* (*also* **get one over (on)**, **slip...**, **sneak...**, **put it all over**, **put something over on**) [late 19C+] (*orig. US*) to cheat, to deceive. [ext. of PUT ON *v.*[2] (2); the 'one' is a trick, a hoax]

put one's ass on the line *v.* (*also* **put one's balls...**) [1980s+] (*US*) to put oneself into a position of responsibility, to take risks; to face punishment. [ASS *n.* (5)/BALLS *n.*[1] (4)]

put one's best side towards London *v.* [late 19C] to make the best of things. [the practice of country people putting on their best clothes for their visits to the capital]

put one's bones up *v.* (*also* **put up one's forks**) [late 19C] to get ready to fight. [abbr. SE *knuckle-bones*/FORKS *n.* (2)]

put one's checks in the rack *v.* [1930s+] (*US*) to die. [gambling imagery]

put one's cue in the rack *v.* [1980s+] **1** to retire. **2** to die. [billiards/snooker imagery]

put one's ears out *v.* [1990s+] to listen for news, to gather information.

put oneself about *v.* [1970s+] **1** to lead an active social or sexual life. **2** to go into action.

put oneself away *v.* [1930s] to pretend, to hoax.

put oneself in someone's face *v. see* GET IN SOMEONE'S ASS *v.*

put oneself outside *v. see* GET OUTSIDE *v.* (1).

put one's eye on *v.* [20C+] (*W.I.*) to become obsessed with at first sight and thus to desire to possess immediately.

put one's face on *v.* (*also* **put on one's face**) [1950s+] usu. of women, to put on make-up. [the term has also gained male currency among gay men and male teenagers who enjoy make-up]

put one's fist to *v.* [mid-19C] to sign. [FIST *n.*[1] (3)]

put one's foot down *v.* **1** [mid-19C+] to insist, to be adamant. **2** [1910s+] to curtail, to restrict. **3** [1930s+] to accelerate and drive a vehicle fast. [a pettish stamp of the foot]

put one's foot in it *v.* (*also* **put one's hoof in it**, **get one's foot in**, **stick one's foot in it**) [late 18C+] to make an error. ['it' = the dirt, 'the shit']

put one's foot in one's hand *v. see* MAKE FOOT *v.*

put one's foot in one's mouth *v.* [1940s+] to make an embarrassing verbal mistake, discomfiting oneself as well as the hearer.

put one's foot in someone's ass *v.* (*also* **put a foot in someone's ass**) [1940s+] (*US Black*) to attack someone physically; to treat someone unkindly. [ASS *n.* (2)]

put one's foot on the floor *v.* [1920s+] to accelerate a motorcar. [the pressing down of one's foot on the accelerator pedal]

put one's hand down *v.* [20C+] to pay, to stand one's turn. [i.e. down into one's trouser pocket]

put one's hand in an empty corn-jar *v.* [20C+] (*W.I.*) to marry a poor woman.

put one's hand up *v.* [1970s+] to confess. [classroom practice]

put one's hat up *v. see* PUT UP ONE'S HAT *v.*

put one's head on the block *v.* (*also* **put one's head under the knife**) [1950s+] to declare oneself openly, to take a risk or a stand that may be dangerous.

put one's head out *v.* [2000s] (*US Black gang*) to murder.

put one's hoof in it *v. see* PUT ONE'S FOOT IN IT *v.*

put one's money where one's mouth is *v.* [1940s+] (*orig. US*) fig., to back one's boasting with suitable action; lit., to back one's opinions with wagered money.

put one's mouth in one's pocket *v.* [20C+] (*W.I.*) to be forced to make a heavy payment after losing a libel suit.

put one's mouth on *v.* [20C+] (*W.I.*) to denigrate, to slander.

put one's oar in *v. see* PUT IN ONE'S OAR *v.*

put one's pen to the wind *v.* [2000s] (*US prison*) of a prisoner, to tell an officer to file disciplinary report; of officers, to tell a prisoner to file a grievance.

put one's shirt on *v.* (*also* **have one's shirt on**, **put one's socks on**) [late 19C+] (*gambling*) to bet heavily.

put one's skates on *v. see* GET ONE'S SKATES ON *v.*

put one's snout in the trough *v. see* HAVE ONE'S SNOUT IN THE TROUGH *v.*

put one's spoon in *v. see* PUT IN ONE'S OAR *v.*

put one's time in *v.* [late 19C+] to spend time, to occupy one's time.

put one's weight on it *v.* [2000s] (*US Black*) to dance energetically.

put one's weights up *v.* [1920s] (*N.Z.*) to cause trouble deliberately.

put one together *v.* [1970s+] (*UK Und.*) to plan a crime. [ONE *n.*[6]]

put on hold v. [1970s+] to delay, to postpone, to defer. [telephone etiquette]

put on ice v. **1** [late 19C+] (orig. US) of a person, to hide away, to keep out of the limelight until required, e.g. a witness, the 'star' of a newspaper exclusive etc. **2** [1910s+] of a project, idea etc, to put aside for later development or use. **3** [1930s+] (orig. US) to maintain a distant, minimally emotional relationship. **4** [1930s] (US campus) to forget deliberately. **5** [1930s] (also **pack on ice**) to kill, to murder. **6** [1930s+] (US) to imprison. [ON ICE phr.[1]]

put on jam v. (also **lay on jam**) (Aus.) **1** [late 19C–1900s] to put on airs. **2** [1900s] to flatter.

put on one's face v. see PUT ONE'S FACE ON v.

put on one's frills v. [late 19C] (orig. US) **1** to swagger. **2** to become very amorous.

put on one's own pot v. [20C+] (W.I.) to take care of oneself; thus **not put on the pot for**, **not make one's pot bubble**, to refuse to help someone.

put on roll v. **1** [1910s] (UK juv.) to put on airs, to swagger. **2** [1930s] (US Black) to fight.

put on show v. [1980s+] (Aus. prison) to humiliate in public.

put on someone's ear v. [late 19C–1900s] to set on, to attack. [the victim is knocked down, 'on their ear']

put on starch v. [1900s] (Aus.) to act in an arrogant manner.

put on the ... v. [1980s+] (Aus. prison) phr. used with pertinent n. to indicate that an individual is being labelled, e.g. put on the dog: he is an informer.

put on the agony v. see AGONY n.[1] (1).

put on the bag v. see PUT ON THE FEEDBAG v.

put on the black v. see PUT THE BLACK ON v.

put on the bounce v. [1930s+] (Aus.) to accost, esp. in pursuit of a loan. [BOUNCE n.[1] (3)]

put on the clampers v. [20C+] to restrain, to hold back. [SE clamp or ? CLAMPERS n.]

put on the dog v. see PUT ON DOG v. (1).

put on the Fair Persian v. [late 19C] (Aus.) of a woman, to act lazily. [? stereotyped image of Persian women lying around in the harem]

put on the feedbag v. (also **put on the bag**) [1910s+] to eat.

put on the fie-fie v. see FIE-FIE v.

put on the front burner v. [1970s+] to make into a priority.

put on the gee v. [1920s+] to boast, to brag, to 'swank about'. [GEE n.[2] (2)]

put on the griller v. [1970s] (Aus. Und.) for police to give negative testimony against a criminal with the aim of ensuring a lengthy sentence.

put on the guiver v. [late 19C+] (UK Und.) to affect an upper-class accent. [GUIVER n.[1] (1)]

put on the jump v. [1900s] (US) to alert, to get someone moving, to 'ginger up'.

put on the kitz v. [1930s] to put on one's best clothes. [ety. unknown; KIT n.[4] or link to Yid. or Ger.]

put on the long finger v. [1950s+] (Irish) to postpone indefinitely. [one pushes it as far away as one can]

put on the moan v. [1930s] (US) to complain.

put on the nosebag v. (also **put the nosebag on**) [mid-19C+] to eat.

put on the pot v. [late 19C–1900s] to put on airs. [BIG POT n.]

put on the ritz v. **1** [1920s+] (orig. US) to make a display of wealth or luxury, to dress stylishly. **2** [1930s] (US) to snub. [César Ritz (1850–1918), Swiss hotelier and the hotels he founded. Popularized by Irving Berlin's song 'Putting on the Ritz' (1929): 'If you're blue and you don't know what to do/Why don't you go where Harlem sits/Puttin' on the Ritz']

put on the screw v. [mid-19C] to set a limit on someone's credit. [SE screw, that which tightens]

put on the screws v. [1950s] to pressurize.

put on the send v. [1900s–1970s] (US Und.) **1** for a confidence trickster to persuade the victim to fetch (more) money. **2** thus send store; any kind of trick that involves the sending of a victim home to get his money.

put on the skid v. [late 19C] to speak or act cautiously. [SE skid, a block used to retard a wheel]

put on the spot v. (orig. US) **1** [1920s+] (also **put in a spot, put the spot on**) to place in a difficult or disadvantageous position. **2** [1920s–50s] to arrange to have someone killed; to put someone in the position of being killed. **3** [1920s] (US tramp) to leave waiting at an appointed meeting place.

put on the steam v. [1950s] (US) to whistle. [railroad or factory whistle imagery]

put out adj. [late 19C+] murdered, killed. [PUT OUT v.[1] (2)]

put out v.[1] **1** [mid-19C+] to knock out, to assault. **2** [late 19C+] (also **put out of the way**) to murder, to kill. [abbr. SE put out, to extinguish; (1) poss. also SE put out of one's misery]

put out v.[2] **1** [late 19C+] to pay money. **2** [1930s+] (US) to offer oneself for sex. **3** [1930s] to make an effort. [SE put out, to display]

put out of sight v. **1** [mid-19C] to drink. **2** [late 19C] to eat.

put out one's hand v. [1950s+] to go through a drunk's pockets looking for cash and/or valuables.

put out one's shingle v. see HANG OUT ONE'S SHINGLE v.

put out someone's light(s) v. (also **blow out —, punch —, shoot —, turn out someone's lights, put someone's light(s) out**) **1** [early 17C; mid-19C+] to kill, to murder. **2** [late 19C+] to knock unconscious. [fig. use of SE daylights. The orig. use may have referred to one's eyes and/or one's intestines, i.e. 'liver and lights', but the 'electrical' imagery has long since superseded this]

put out the miller's thumb v. see DROWN THE MILLER v. (1).

put out to grass v.[1] [late 16C–early 17C] to send out to work as a prostitute.

put out to grass v.[2] (also **put out to pasture**) [1940s+] to send into retirement. [animal imagery]

put over v. [mid-19C–1910s] to knock over with a gunshot.

put over a fast one v. see PULL A FAST ONE v.

put paid to v. [1910s+] to bring (someone's hopes, aspirations, efforts) to an end, to dispose of, to terminate. [SE pay off]

putrid adj. [late 19C+] a general neg. intensifier. [SE putrid, rotten, stinking]

put roach on one's bread v. [20C+] (W.I.) to be sexually unfaithful, to cuckold. [SE cockroach]

put sand in someone's Vaseline v. [1970s+] to ruin someone else's pleasure or endeavours. [SE sand is gritty; cosmetic product Vaseline is a smooth cream]

put shit in the game v. (US Black) **1** [1960s] to take advantage. **2** [1960s+] to trick, to deceive. [SHIT n.[1] (2) + GAME n.[2] (3)]

put shit on v. [1960s] **1** (also **put the shit on**) (Aus./US) to deride, to attack verbally. **2** (US Black) to take advantage; to trick, to deceive. [SHIT n.[1] (2)]

put snow in one's game v. [1960s+] (US Black) to ensnare a White person for financial gain. [SNOW n.[3] (4) + GAME n.[2] (3)]

put some beef into it v. [20C+] to make a physical effort; often as excl. put some beef into it! [BEEF n.[1] (4)]

put someone crook with v. [1930s+] (Aus./N.Z.) to lower someone's standing, to get someone into trouble. [CROOK adj.]

put someone down v. [early 19C] to convey information to someone, to explain, to make someone aware; thus (UK Und.) put a swell down, to alert one's target (typically the target of a pickpocket) that one is about to rob them. [DOWN adj.[1] (1)]

put someone down the track v. see SEND DOWN THE ROAD v.

put someone in v. (also **put someone in it, put someone in with**) **1** [1920s+] (orig. Aus.) to inform against. **2** to ruin someone's reputation, to talk maliciously behind someone's back.

3 to incriminate. ['one' is the report or the person thus 'put in' prison]

put someone in a bag *v.* [17C] to gain an advantage over someone.

put someone in the dozens *v.* [1920s+] (*US*) to put somone in a negative situation. [fig. use of DOZENS n.]

put someone in the picture *v. see* IN THE PICTURE phr. (2).

put someone in with *v. see* PUT SOMEONE IN v.

put someone off their stroke *v.* [1910s+] to disconcert someone, to disturb someone. [fig. use of golfing imagery]

put someone on *v.*[1] (*also* **put someone upon**) [19C–1900s] (*US*) to inform, to explain.

put someone on *v.*[2] **1** [1940s–60s] (*drugs*) to give or sell drugs. **2** [2000s] (*US Black*) to recruit someone into a criminal organization, thus allowing them to start enjoying the financial and social benefits of membership. [(1) ON prep.[6] (1)]

put someone on blast *v. see* PUT THE BLAST ON v. (1).

put someone on front street *v.* (*also* **put someone on front street, put someone's business on the street**) **1** [1960s+] (*US Black*) to make indiscreet disclosures about oneself or another person. **2** [1970s] (*US Black*) to trick, to deceive. **3** [1990s+] (*US prison*) to confront, to defy. [FRONT STREET n. (2)]

put someone on shine *v. see* SHINE SOMEONE ON v.

put someone on the arse *v.* [1970s] (*Aus. Und.*) to attack someone verbally. [ARSE n.[1] (1)]

put someone on the block *v.* (*also* **put someone on the corner**) **1** [1950s+] (*US*) of a pimp, to launch a woman into a career as a prostitute. **2** [1970s+] (*N.Z.*) to subject a woman (or a homosexual man) to gang-rape.

put someone on the heavy jacket *v.* [1980s+] (*N.Z.*) to ostracize.

put someone on the hood *v.* [1990s+] (*US Black gang*) to enrol in a gang. [HOOD n.[3] (1)]

put someone on the line *v.* [1990s+] to place someone in a difficult or challenging position. [ON THE LINE phr.]

put someone on the linger *v.* [1940s] (*US Black*) to abandon someone.

put (someone) on the pan *v.* [1900s–10s] (*US*) to subject someone to criticism.

put someone on the shine *v. see* SHINE SOMEONE ON v.

put someone onto *v.* [late 19C+] (*orig. US*) to introduce a topic, to point out, esp. to point out a chance of possible social or financial gain etc. [ONTO phr.]

put someone onto someone *v.* [20C+] to introduce someone, to give access to someone.

put someone out of business *v.* (*also* **put someone out of commission**) [20C+] to halt someone's activity and/or efforts, usu. through injury, destruction of their premises etc.

put someone over a barrel *v. see* HAVE SOMEONE OVER A BARREL v.

put someone over the jumps *v. see* PUT SOMEONE THROUGH THE HOOP(S) v.

put someone's ass in a sling *v.* (*also* **have someone's ass in a sling**) [1940s+] (*US*) to cause trouble for. [ASS n. (2)]

put someone's ass out *abbr.* [1960s] to eject, to throw out, to send away. [ASS n. (2)]

put someone's back up *v.* [mid-18C+] to annoy someone, to irritate someone. [the risen hairs on a cat's back that denote, *inter alia*, aggression]

put someone's balls in a knot *v.* [1930s+] (*Aus.*) to discomfit, to embarrass, to irritate. [BALLS n.[1] (1)]

put someone's balls in the fire *v.* [1960s] (*US*) to agitate or excite someone. [BALLS n.[1] (1)]

put someone's business on the street *v. see* PUT SOMEONE ON FRONT STREET v.

put someone's hair in(to) a curl *v.* (*also* **make someone's hair curl, put a curl in someone's hair**) **1** [mid-19C–1920s] to

make someone extremely healthy or fit. **2** [late 19C+] to shock.

put someone's head in a loop *v. see* THROW FOR A LOOP v.

put someone's light(s) out *v. see* PUT OUT SOMEONE'S LIGHT(S) v.

put someone's monkey up *v. see* GET SOMEONE'S MONKEY UP v.

put someone's pipe out *v.* [mid-19C] **1** to ruin someone's plans. **2** to shock, to disgust.

put someone's pot on *v.* [20C+] (*Aus./N.Z.*) **1** (*also* **put someone's pot away**) to tell tales, to inform against, to destroy the hopes of. **2** to catch someone out in wrong-doing. [POT v.[3] (2)]

put someone's stuff down *v.* [1970s+] (*US Black*) to disparage, to ridicule. [PUT DOWN v.[3] (1) + STUFF n.[1] (1)]

put someone's tail in a crack *v.* [1980s] (*US*) to cause trouble for someone. [TAIL n.[2] (1)]

put someone's tits in a tangle *v.* [1930s+] (*Aus.*) to discomfit, to embarrass, to irritate someone (cf. GET ONE'S TITS IN A TWIST v.).

put someone through *v.* [mid-19C–1900s] (*US/Aus.*) to play a trick on someone, to overcome. [? PUT SOMEONE THROUGH THE MILL v.]

put someone through the hoop(s) *v.* (*also* **put someone over the jumps, take someone through the hoop(s)**) [20C+] (*orig. milit.*) to make suffer, to punish, to reprimand, to interrogate.

put someone through the mill *v.* (*also* **run someone through the mill**) [early 19C+] to subject to an arduous or harsh situation or experience.

put someone to bye-bye *v.* [1930s] (*UK Und.*) to knock unconscious; to kill.

put (someone) to the curb *v.* [1990s+] (*US*) to dismiss from employment.

put someone up to *v.* [19C+] to make someone aware of, to inform someone of, to persuade or incite someone, esp. to do something underhand or nefarious.

put someone up to his arm-pits *v.* [mid-19C] (*UK Und.*) to cheat an accomplice out of his share of the proceeds.

put some slobber on the knobber *v.* [1990s+] (*US*) to fellate. [SE *slobber* + KNOB n.[1] (3)]

put something down *v.* [1950s+] (*US Black*) to stop what one is doing.

put something on *v.* [1920s+] to accuse, to find evidence against (cf. HANG SOMETHING ON v.).

put something on someone *v.* [1960s] (*US Black*) to present (something or someone) to someone.

put something on the radio *v.* [1960s] to publicize. [i.e. to 'broadcast']

put something over on *v. see* PUT ONE OVER (ON) v.

put squeezers on *v.* [1960s] (*US*) to pressurize. [SQUEEZE n.[8] (2)]

put stuffing into *v.* [1930s+] to strengthen someone's morale or resolution.

putsy *n. see* PUTZ n. (2).

putter-up *n.* [early 19C–1940s] (*UK Und.*) one who plans a robbery or tips off thieves as to where a robbery might profitably be committed, e.g. a servant in a great house, a bank clerk etc. [SE *put up* (*a plan*)]

put that in your pipe and smoke it! *excl.* [early 19C+] an excl. meaning deal with that, whether you like it or not.

put that on *phr.* [2000s] (*US teen*) used to intensify a statement.

put the acid in *v.* [1900s–50s] to inform on, to tell tales about, to poison another's mind against. [var. on COME THE (OLD) ACID v.]

put the acid on *v.* **1** [20C+] (*Aus.*) to exert pressure on a person for a loan, a favour, sexual compliance etc. **2** [1900s] to render impoverished. **3** [1910s] to put a stop to. **4** [1910s–20s] to test out a person or a statement. [supposedly orig. used by gold assayers who tested 'real' gold with acid]

put the arm on v. [1930s+] (US/UK Und.) **1** (also **arm, give the arm, put the strong arm on**) to attack from behind by choking the victim with one's forearm before robbing them. **2** (also **lay the arm on**) to pressurize with threats of violence, to extort 'protection' payments, to beg for money, to blackmail. **3** to reveal scandalous facts about someone, to inform on. **4** to make an arrest. [lit. or threatened violence; note STRONG-ARM v.]

put the bag on v.[1] [20C+] (orig. US) to halt, to interfere with, to bring to a standstill. [SE bag, the image of covering something up]

put the bag on v.[2] [20C+] (Ulster) to start out as a beggar. [a beggar's bag]

put the bag on v.[3] [1970s+] (Aus./N.Z.) to breathalyse. [the polythene bag that is part of the breathalysing kit]

put the bash in v. [1940s] (UK Und.) to commit a smash-and-grab raid. [BASH n.[2] (1)]

put the beat down v. see PUT THE SMACK DOWN v.

put the bee on v.[1] (also **put the B on**) (US) **1** [1900s–70s] to extort, to blackmail, to pressurize, esp. for a loan. **2** [1920s–50s] to swindle, to hoax, to victimize. [play on STING v. (1) but note initial letter of BITE n.[1] (3)]

put the bee on v.[2] [1900s–40s] (US) to quash, to bring to an end, to ruin. [initial letter of 'bag' in PUT THE BAG ON v.[1]]

put the beggar on the gentleman v. [mid–late 19C] to drink beer after spirits.

put the bite on v. (also **put the bite (in)to**) **1** [1930s+] (orig. Aus.) to extort, to blackmail, to force someone to do something they would rather avoid. **2** [1930s+] to ask for a loan or for the repayment of a debt. **3** [1940s–70s] (US) to beg. **4** [1960s] (US) to put the blame on. [BITE n.[1]]

put the bit on v. [1950s] (Aus.) to extort, to blackmail, to force someone to do something they would rather avoid. [SE bit, the mouthpiece of a horse's bridle, used to restrain the animal]

put the black on v. (also **put on the black**) [1920s+] to blackmail. [BLACK n.[2] (3)]

put the blast on v. (US) **1** [1920s+] (also **put someone on blast**) to attack verbally, to criticize severely. **2** [1940s] to betray, to inform on. **3** [1940s–50s] to shoot dead. [BLAST n.[1] (1); (3) BLAST v.[2] (2)]

put the blind on v. [20C+] (Irish) to curse someone. [BLIND v.[2]]

put the block on v. (also **put the blocks on/to, put the blockers on**) [1930s+] to interfere with, to stop someone's actions or plans. [SE block, to impede]

put the blocks to v. [1920s+] (US) of a man, to have sexual intercourse. [SE block, a lump of wood, i.e. the penis]

put the B on v. see PUT THE BEE ON v.[1].

put the bone to v. see BONE n.[1] (1).

put the boogaloo on v. [1970s] to annoy, to cause trouble (for). [fig. use of BOOGALOO v. (2)]

put the boot in v. (also **put in the boot, sock/stick the boot in**) [1910s+] (orig. Aus.) **1** to kick someone during a fight; thus in with the boot, no holds barred. **2** in fig. use, to victimize, to attack.

put the boot(s) on v. [1920s–40s] (Irish) to bring to a close. [one puts on one's boots before leaving the house]

put the boots to v. (also **throw the boots to**) (US) **1** [late 19C+] to give a kicking; thus get the boots, to receive a kicking. **2** [late 19C+] to victimize, to treat harshly. **3** [1920s+] to have sexual intercourse with; to rape. [var. on GIVE SOMEONE THE BOOT v. (2)]

put the bounce into v. [1950s] (Aus.) to threaten, to intimidate. [BOUNCE v.[1] (3)]

put the breeze up v. see GET THE BREEZE UP v.

put the bubble in v. [1920s+] (UK Und.) to inform. [BUBBLE v.[1]]

put the buck v. see PASS THE BUCK v. (1).

put the bug on v. **1** [mid-19C–1920s] (US) to tease, to play tricks on. **2** [1930s] (US Und.) to burn a young tramp's flesh to improve his appeal when begging. [(1) BUG n.[5] (1); (2) ? BUG n.[4] (13)]

put the bum on someone v. **1** [1920s+] (US) to beg from someone. **2** [1970s] (US gay) to offer oneself for homosexual sex. **3** [1970s] to interfere, to harass. [(1) and (3) BUM v.[4] (2); (2) BUM n.[1] (1)]

put the bump on v. [1970s] to deceive someone, to trick someone out of something. [BUMP v.[3] (1)]

put the bung in v. [1950s] to bribe, to hand over a bribe. [BUNG n.[1] (4)]

put the burn on v. [1940s] (US) to pressurize. [BURN v.[2] (3)]

put the buzz on v. [1920s] (US) to pressurize, to bribe. [BUZZ v.[4] (1)]

put the change on v. [mid-17C–19C] to mislead. [one has 'changed' the truth for lies]

put the chill on v. **1** [20C+] (US prison) (also **put the shake on**) to intimidate, to threaten with blackmail; occas. just to ignore, to snub. **2** [1930s+] (US) to snub, to ignore. [fig. use of SE chill/CHILL n.[1] (1)]

put the cinch on v. [1910s–60s] (US) to ensure, to make something certain. [CINCH n.[1] (1)]

put the clamps on v. [20C+] **1** (US) to steal. **2** (US Und.) of the police, to clamp down on crime. **3** (US) to make somebody one's spouse. [i.e. one SE clamps hold of the item, villains or person]

put the claws on v. [20C+] (US Und.) **1** to arrest. **2** to inform on.

put the clip on v. [1920s+] (US) to overcharge, to defraud; to extort from. [CLIP v.[1] (4)]

put the comether on v. (also **put the come-hither on**) [mid-19C+] (Aus./Irish) to coax, to wheedle, to impress. [SE come hither]

put the cool on v. see COOL v.[3] (2).

put the crab on v. see CRAB v.[1] (7).

put the cross on v. **1** [1900s–50s] to double-cross, to cheat. **2** [1930s–50s] to mark for death. [(1) CROSS n.[1] (1); (2) a cross placed, lit. or fig., against the victim's name]

put the crusher on v. [1900s–40s] (US) **1** to attack physically. **2** to eject, to throw out. **3** to mount a police raid. **4** to treat harshly. [CRUSHER n.[1]/CRUSHER n.[2]]

put the devil into hell v. (also **put the pope into Rome**) [17C+] to have sexual intercourse (cf. ARRIVE AT THE END OF THE SENTIMENTAL JOURNEY v.). [a euph. coined by Boccaccio in a ribald story in the Decameron (1358), in which a hermit seduces a virgin by persuading her of the necessity of letting him 'put the devil into hell']

put the double on v. [late 19C] to double-cross. [abbr.]

put the drags on v. [1910s+] (Aus.) to ask someone for a loan. [SE drag, in the sense of dragging on someone's sleeve; + poss. link to DRAG n.[6] (2)/DRAG n.[12]]

put the eye on v. [1930s+] (orig. US) **1** to look at seductively. **2** to examine, to stare at. **3** to place under surveillance.

put the fangs into v. [1910s+] (Aus.) **1** to pressurize, to blackmail. **2** to demand a loan or favour. [var. on PUT THE BITE ON v.]

put the feedbag on v. [1950s+] to eat, to have a meal.

put the feel on v. [1930s] (US) to sound out, to assess.

put the finger on v. [1920s+] (orig. US) **1** to betray, to inform against. **2** to identify a target or possible victim. [FINGER v.[2] (3)]

put the flimp on v. [mid-19C–1900s] to rob on the highway, to rob and garrotte. [FLIMP v. (1)]

put the fluence on v. **1** [late 19C] to influence through mental, rather than physical, pressure. **2** [1910s+] (orig. Aus./N.Z.) to persuade. **3** [1910s+] (orig. Aus./N.Z.) to hypnotize. [FLUENCE n.]

put the freeze on v. **1** [1950s+] (also **put a freeze on**) to reject, to snub. **2** [1970s+] (US) to stop. [(1) FREEZE n.[2] (2); (2) FREEZE v.[1] (2)]

put the frighteners on v. (also **stick the frighteners on**) [1950s+] (UK Und.) **1** to menace, to blackmail, to threaten with violence. **2** to terrify (with no criminal overtones). [FRIGHTENER n. (1)]

put the gas on v. [1900s] (*Aus.*) **1** to test out a person or a statement. **2** to put a stop to. **3** to exert pressure on a person for a loan, a favour, sexual compliance etc.

put the gloves on someone v. [late 19C] (*Scot. Und.*) to improve someone's standing and circumstances. [wearing gloves is a sign of gentility]

put the hammer down v. [1970s+] to drive fast, esp. used by truck-drivers. [HAMMER n.⁴ (1)]

put the hammer on v. (*US*) **1** [1940s+] to take decisive action. **2** [1960s+] to demand money. **3** [1980s+] to attack verbally, to slander.

put the hammers to v. [1940s] (*US*) to beat up.

put the hard word on v. [1910s+] **1** (*orig. Aus./N.Z.*) to make demands (esp. financial or sexual) of someone. **2** (*Aus.*) to interrogate, to question. [HARD WORD n. (2)]

put the heat on v. [1920s+] to pressurize, to threaten. [HEAT n.³ (2)]

put the heist on v. [1960s] (*US Und.*) to steal. [HEIST n.¹ (1)]

put the hooks in v. [1940s] (*US*) to take advantage of.

put the horns on v. [1940s+] (*US*) **1** to jinx. **2** to cuckold. [fig./lit. use of HORNS n.; its usual use as adultery can also be said to jinx the victim]

put the hurt on v. [1960s+] (*orig. US*) to hurt deliberately, to assault physically and/or emotionally.

put the Indian sign on v. (*also* **get the Indian sign on**) [20C+] (*US*) to place a curse on someone, to jinx or 'hex'. [the belief that Native Americans have the power of cursing. Note also SE *Indian sign*, a smoke-signal]

put the josh on someone phr. see JOSH v.

put the kibosh on v. (*also* **put the kybosh on**) [mid-19C+] to spoil, to ruin. [KIBOSH n. (1)]

put the knock on v. [late 19C+] to disparage, to criticize. [KNOCK v.¹ (2)]

put the latch on v. [1950s] to beg from. [SE *latch onto*]

put the leak into v. [mid-19C] (*US*) to trick, to deceive.

put the leather in v. (*also* **put the leather to**) [1910s+] to kick someone, esp. during a fight. [one's leather footwear]

put the leg-rope on v. [20C+] (*Aus.*) to curb a person who is acting in an hysterical or very bad-tempered manner. [SE *leg-rope*, a rope used to tether or control an animal]

put the lid on v.¹ **1** [late 19C+] (*orig. US*) (*also* **put a lid on**) to cover up, to hide, esp. news that is offensive or embarrassing to an establishment; thus imper. *put a lid on it!* be quiet! stop talking! **2** [20C+] to clamp down on activities such as corruption, esp. that of an urban administration. **3** [20C+] to be the ultimate, the 'last straw'. **4** [1920s+] to stop something from happening.

put the lid on v.² [1920s+] (*Aus.*) to shut a bar at the legal closing time.

put the loop on v. [1920s] (*US*) to capture.

put the lug on v. (*also* **drop the lug on**) **1** [1920s+] to beg; to demand money with menaces, to extort, to blackmail. **2** [1930s–40s] (*US*) to beat up, to use violence against. **3** [1960s+] (*US Black*) to confront someone either as to their character or actions, to criticize, both seriously and in fun. [(1) LUG v.¹ (2); (2) LUG v.³; (3) ? LUG n.¹, i.e. an 'earful']

put the mack down v. [1990s+] (*US Black*) to act in a smooth, sophisticated manner, reminiscent of the idealized pimp. [MACK n.¹ (1)]

put the maginnis on v. (*also* **put the macginnis/mcginnis on**) [1900s–40s] (*Aus.*) to put in a position from which there is no escape, to pressurize; thus *crooked maginnis*, an unfair form of control, e.g. (moral) blackmail. [SE *mcginnis*, a wrestling hold]

put the make on v.¹ [1920s] (*US*) to assess. [MAKE FOR v.]

put the make on v.² [1950s+] (*US*) to make sexual advances. [MAKE n.³ (1)]

put the make to v. see MAKE n.⁴.

put the meat to v. [1970s] of a man, to have sexual intercourse (cf. BURY IT v.). [MEAT n. (2)]

put the mix in v. [1950s–60s] to cause trouble deliberately, to interfere in a malicious manner. [SE *mix things up*]

put the mockers on v. (*also* **put the mocks on**) [1910s+] to jinx, to put a curse on, to frustrate someone's plans. [? Yid. *makkes*, ult. Heb. *makot*, plagues, blows, (evil) visitations. The phr. was poss. orig. used in Aus. but, given the ety., there may be a link to 19C London market traders]

put the moves on v. **1** [1960s+] (*orig. US*) usu. of a man, to make advances towards the opposite sex. **2** [1980s] (*US Black*) to harass. [MOVE n.]

put the moz on v. (*also* **put the mozz on**) [1920s+] (*Aus.*) to inconvenience, to jinx. [PUT THE MOCKERS ON v.]

put the mug on v. [mid-19C–1940s] to throttle. [MUG n.² (4)]

put them up! excl. [mid-19C+] get ready to fight. ['them' are the fists or arms]

put the muscle on v. [1940s+] (*US Und.*) to coerce, to threaten with violence. [MUSCLE n.¹ (1)]

put the muzzle on v. [20C+] (*US*) to silence, e.g. an informer.

put the muzzle on! excl. [1900s–10s] shut up! stop talking! [PUT THE MUZZLE ON v.]

put the nadgers on v. [1950s+] to jinx, to cause trouble for, to 'hex'. [NADGERS n.]

put the nark on v. [20C+] to put off, to ruin (a plan), to discourage. [NARK v.²]

put the nips in(to) v. [1910s+] (*Aus./N.Z.*) to cadge from. [NIP v.¹ (8)]

put the nosebag on v. see PUT ON THE NOSEBAG v.

put the nut in v. (*also* **put the nut on**) [1960s] (*Irish*) to headbutt. [NUT n.¹ (2)]

put the nuts on v. [1940s–50s] (*US prison*) to threaten or intimidate, physically and/or verbally. [ie. one 'turns a screw']

put the old soldier on v. see COME THE OLD SOLDIER V.

put the oliver on v. [1920s+] to do something illegally. [play on *Oliver Twist*/SE *twist*, to cheat]

put the pedal to the metal v. [1960s+] (*orig. US*) to accelerate an automobile.

put the pinch on v. **1** [1940s+] (*US*) to reduce to poverty. **2** [1970s] to put pressure on. [in both one 'feels the pinch']

put the pope into Rome v. see PUT THE DEVIL INTO HELL v.

put the pot on v. **1** [mid-19C] to exaggerate. **2** [mid-19C] to bet (too) heavily on a horse. **3** [mid-late 19C] to overcharge. [ext. use of BIG POT n.]

put the quilt on v. see QUILT v.

put the screws on v. (*also* **get one's screws into**, **put the screws to**) [early 19C+] to pressurize. [SE *thumbscrew*]

put the shake on v. see PUT THE CHILL ON v. (1).

put the shit up v. (*also* **put the shits up**) [1940s+] to terrify. [SHIT n.¹ (1)]

put the shoe on the left foot v. [1970s+] (*US Black*) to put blame where it does not belong. [opposite of next]

put the shoe on the right foot v. [late 19C+] to place blame where it duly belongs.

put the shuck on v. [1970s+] (*US*) to trick, to deceive, to fool verbally. [SHUCK n. (1)]

put the siphon on v. [1930s] (*US*) to interrogate. [play on PUMP v.¹]

put the skibunk on v. [1900s] (*US*) to impose upon, to defraud. [var. on PUT THE KIBOSH ON v.]

put the skids to v. (*also* **put the skids under**) [1910s+] (*orig. US*) **1** to dismiss someone from a job. **2** to make someone hurry up, usu. in doing their work. **3** (*also* **have the skids put under**, **throw the skids under**) to hasten someone's downfall. **4** to bring to a conclusion.

put the sleeve on v. [1930s] **1** (*US*) to arrest. **2** (*US*) to borrow money (from); to request favours (from). **3** (*US Und.*) to manhandle a victim for mugging. [the police officer or mugger grabs the target's sleeve]

put the slug on v. (US) **1** [1920s+] to beat up. **2** [1930s] to criticize harshly. **3** [1940s] to deliver an official punishment. [SLUG n.⁴ (1)]

put the smack down v. (also **put the beat down**) [1990s+] to hit, to assault. [SMACK n.¹ (3)]

put the smother on v. [1960s] (Aus.) to censor, to suppress. [SE smother]

put the snatch on v. [1920s+] (US) **1** to kidnap, to seize, to take over. **2** to arrest. [SNATCH n.²]

put the squeal on v. (also **put the squeaks in**) [1930s+] to betray, to inform against. [SQUEAL n.¹]

put the steam on v. [late 19C] to go fast, to accelerate. [railway imagery]

put the stick about v. [1960s+] to use violence, usu. in a criminal context.

put the strong arm on v. see PUT THE ARM ON v. (1).

put the stunners on v. [mid-19C] to astonish, to amaze, to surprise. [SE stun]

put the stuns on v. [late 19C] (Aus.) to amaze, to astound.

put the swerve on v. [1930s] (US Und.) to deceive (with a confidence trick).

put the tin hat on v. [1910s+] to finish off for good. [WW1 milit. tin hat, a steel helmet]

put the touch on v. [late 19C+] to (attempt to) borrow or extort money. [TOUCH n.¹ (5)]

put the whammy on v. [1930s–50s] **1** to cause problems for; to condemn. **2** (US) to influence, to 'hex'. **3** (US Black) to hit hard. [WHAMMY n. (1)]

put the windows in v. [late 19C+] to smash windows.

put the wind up v. [1910s+] to worry, to frighten.

put the winkers on v. [mid-19C] to deceive, to hoodwink. [SE winker, a horse's blinker]

put the wood to v. [1970s+] (US) **1** to punish, to coerce by threats. **2** to cause serious trouble for. **3** of a man, to have sexual intercourse (cf. BURY IT v.). [? image of hitting with a wooden club]

put the works on v. **1** [1900s–40s] (US Und.) to beat up. **2** [1920s] (US) to direct one's energies towards, e.g. in order to deceive or seduce. [lit. and fig. use of WORKS, THE n. (5)]

put the Yorkshire on v. see COME YORKSHIRE OVER v.

put the zing on v. [1930s–40s] **1** to subject to one's emotions, either positive or negative. **2** to ask for money. [ZING n. (1)]

put this reckoning up to the Dover wagoner v. [early–mid-19C] put this (usu. tavern bill) on credit. [a pun on the contemporary Dover wagoner, one Owen, i.e. 'owing']

put through adj. [1900s] (Aus.) suffering, abused.

put through v. [1960s] (Aus.) to cheat someone.

put through the wringer v. (also **put through the wringer, run...**) [1940s+] (orig. US) to pressurize, to subject to severe interrogation, to enforce harsh treatment.

put to bed v. [1900s–50s] (US) to trail a subject until they return home and stay there.

put to bed with a mattock (and tucked up with a spade) v. [18C–early 19C] dead and buried. [SE mattock and spade, tools for digging graves]

put to bed with a shovel v. (also **...with a pickaxe and shovel, ...with a spade**) [late 18C–1930s] dead and buried.

puttock n. [17C] **1** an unpleasant person. **2** a prostitute. [SE puttock, a kite or buzzard, hence the human version of a 'bird of prey']

put to find v. [late 19C–1900s] to imprison. [i.e. where one can always be found]

put to one's trumps v. [mid-17C–19C] to be an extreme situation, to be in great difficulties. [SE put to one's trumps, of a

card-player, to be forced to play one's trumps, since no alternative cards are available]

put to the pin of the collar v. [late 19C+] to put in very great difficulties, to be stretched to the limit. [saddlery imagery; 20C+ use is Irish]

putt-putt n. **1** [20C+] (orig. US) a small vehicle or motor-boat. **2** [1920s] (UK Und.) a machinegun. [the sound of its mechanism]

putty n.¹ [mid-late 19C; 1970s] (mainly US) money (cf. ACTUAL, THE n.). [i.e. it 'fills in the cracks']

putty n.² [1980s+] (Aus. prison) second-rate hashish (cf. AFGHAN n.).

putty adj. [1910s–20s] stupid, foolish. [play on putty's flexible consistency and on SOFT adj. (1); note dial. putty-brain, a fool]

putty-brained adj. (also **putty-faced, -nosed**) [late 19C+] stupid (cf. AMOEBA-BRAINED adj.).

putty-head n. (also **putty-brain**) [mid-19C+] (US) a fool. [SE putty + -HEAD sfx (1)]

putty in one's hands, be v. [1940s+] to be ineffectually malleable to another's whims or wishes.

putty medal n. [late 19C–1900s] a fig. award given to someone who has botched a job or in some other way failed to do what is required. [a proper medal would be made of metal]

putty-nosed adj. see PUTTY-BRAINED adj.

putty pusher n. [1990s+] a male homosexual (cf. BROWN ARTIST n.). [image of anal intercourse]

put under v.¹ see PUT UNDER (THE SOD) v.

put under v.² see UNDER adj.

put under the jail v. [1970s+] (US Black) to imprison in the severest conditions. [the punishment cells are often under the main prison]

put under the screw v. [early–mid-19C] to coerce, to compel, to force. [PUT THE SCREWS ON v.]

put under (the sod) v. [late 19C+] to kill, to murder. [SE sod, a lump of earth]

put-up n. [mid-19C–1920s] (UK Und.) a planned act of robbery/ burglary (cf. PUT-UP JOB n.). [PUT UP v.¹ (1)]

put up v.¹ **1** [early 19C–1920s] to plan in advance, esp. a crime or some form of deception. **2** [early 19C+] to propose, to put forward. **3** [late 19C+] to pay out money in advance, esp. on a bet or for the purchase of drugs. **4** [20C+] (US Black) to explain, to 'put in the picture'. **5** [1900s] (Aus.) to set aside. **6** [1960s] (N.Z.) to report a crime to the authorities.

put up v.² see PUT ON v.¹.

put up a beef v. see PUT UP A SQUAWK v.

put up a black v. [1940s+] (orig. RN) to make a mistake. [? the 2 black balls hauled to the mast of Royal Navy ships when a ship was out of control; but note the general negative imagery of SE black]

put up a fight v. [20C+] to make an effort, whether in a lit. or fig. fight.

put up a job (on) v. [late 19C+] (US) **1** to trick, to deceive (someone). **2** to concoct an injurious story. [JOB n.³ (2)]

put up a squawk v. (also **put up a beef, ...holler, ...howl**) [1900s–50s] to make a fuss. [SQUAWK n. (1)/HOLLER n. (1)/SE howl]

put up a stall v. [1910s] to act in a deceptive, misleading manner. [STALL v.² (5)]

put up a stunt v. [1910s] (Aus.) to make something happen. [STUNT n.]

put-up job n. (also **put-up go, ...thing**) [19C+] a pre-arranged, and usu. criminal or at least deceptive, plan (cf. PUT-UP n.). [PUT UP v.¹ (1) + JOB n.³ (1)]

put-up man n. [1900s–50s] (US Und.) one who points out or sets up a victim for the thief. [PUT UP v.¹ (1)]

put up one's forks v. see PUT ONE'S BONES UP v.

put up one's hat v. (also **put one's hat up**) [late 19C] to pay court to; thus put your hat up there, make yourself at home. [the image is of the lover looking forward to joining the family]

put up one's pipes *v.* (*also* **pack up one's pipes, poke...**) [mid-16C–mid-18C] to cease from an action; to stop talking. [PIPES n.[1] (1)]

put up or shut up! *excl.* [late 19C+] (*orig. US*) a challenge meaning back your big talk with genuine commitment. [gambling imagery]

put up paper for oneself *v.* [1940s–60s] (*US*) to brag, to aggrandize oneself. [the image is of putting up posters in praise of oneself]

put up the dooks *v.*[1] *see* DOOK n.[1] (2).

put up the dooks *v.*[2] *see* DOOKS n.

put up the flag *n.* [1900s] (*US*) a plate of macaroni. [ety. unknown]

put up the ropes *v.* [late 19C] to acquaint with correct information, to 'put in the picture'. [var. on KNOW THE ROPES v.]

put up the shutters *v.* [1900s–10s] to give up, to abandon one's efforts.

put-up thing *n. see* PUT-UP JOB n.

put wise *v.* [20C+] (*orig. US*) **1** to explain, to tell about. **2** to pass on information. [WISE adj. (1)]

put work in *v.* [1980s+] (*US gang*) to take part in an attack on a rival gang.

put work on *v.* [1960s–70s] (*Aus.*) to attempt the verbal stages of seduction, to 'chat up'.

put years on someone *v.* [20C+] to make someone wretched, worried, tired etc. [it makes one feel old]

put your head in a bag! *excl.* [1900s] be quiet! shut up!

put your money where your mouth is! *excl.* [1940s+] a challenge meaning back your big talk with a genuine commitment. [gambling imagery]

putz *n.* (*also* **potz, putzo**) [1930s+] **1** the penis. **2** (*also* **putsy**) an idiot, a fool, a simpleton; also attrib. (cf. ALTER KACKER n.; CHOAD n.). [Yid. *putz*, the penis]

putz (around) *v.* [1930s+] to act like a fool, to mess around. [PUTZ n. (2) + SE *around*]

puz *n.* (*also* **puzz**) [mid–late 18C] a young man about town. [ety. unknown]

puza *see under* PHUZA.

puzz *n. see* PUZ n.

puzzle *n.* [late 16C–17C] a prostitute. [Fr. *pucelle*, a virgin; the tricks played by young girls, esp. when fresh from the country, of presenting themselves as virgins (and thus demanding higher prices)]

puzzle-cause *n.* [late 18C–early 19C] an ignorant, incompetent lawyer. [SE *puzzle* + *cause*, a legal suit]

puzzle-cove *n.* [mid–late 19C] a lawyer. [SE *puzzle* + COVE n. (1)]

puzzlegut *n.* [1900s–40s] (*US Black*) an exceptionally large stomach. [var. on PUS-GUT n.]

puzzle-palace *n.* [1950s+] (*US*) a place where decisions are made, e.g. the White House; thus *five-sided puzzle-palace*, the Pentagon, HQ of the US armed forces.

puzzle-text *n.* [late 18C–early 19C] an uneducated clergyman. [SE *puzzle* + *text*]

puzzling stick *n.* [early 19C] a triangle to which a criminal is tied to receive a judicial whipping. [the criminal fig. 'puzzles' the crimes while being punished]

P.V. *n. see* PAV n.

p.v. *n.* [1960s+] (*US prison*) **1** parole violator. **2** parole violation. [abbr.]

p.w. abney *n.* [late 19C] a style of hat fashionable 1896–1900, featuring 3 black, upright ostrich feathers, reminiscent of the 3 feathers of the Prince of Wales' crest. [*Prince of Wales Abney Cemetery*; Abney Park Cemetery, Stoke Newington, was founded in 1840 as London's main Nonconformist burying ground]

p.w.'d *adj. see* PUSSY-WHIPPED adj. (1).

p.w.t. *n.* [1990s+] (*US*) the poor White population of the Southern states of the US. [abbr. SE *poor* + WHITE TRASH n.]

pyah *adj.* (*also* **pyaa-pyaa**) [mid-19C+] weak, inadequate, useless. [20C+ use W.I.; SE *pariah* or Fante *piapia*, to constrain]

pyaka *adj.* [1950s+] (*W.I. Rasta*) tricky or dishonest. [Carib.E. *pyaka-pyaka*, messy, dirty; ult. unknown Afr. language's *poto-poto*, muddy]

p.y.c. *phr.* [1930s+] (*Aus.*) pay your cash. [abbr.]

pye *v.* [mid-17C] to have sexual intercourse, of a man only; thus *pyeman*, a womanizer, a lecher.

pygostole *n.* [mid–late 19C] a short coat worn by Tractarians. [Greek lit. 'rump-stole']

pyjama python *n.* (*also* **pant python**) [1960s–80s] the penis (cf. ANTEATER n.).

pyjams *n.* (*also* **pyjies, pywags**) [1950s+] *pyjamas*. [abbr.]

py korry! *excl.* [late 19C+] (*N.Z.*) by golly!; thus in fig. use as a n., a Maori. [mispron.]

Pyrmont Yank *n.* [1950s+] (*Aus.*) a relatively unsophisticated person who attempts to emulate the supposed greater sophistication of an American. [proper name *Pyrmont*, a suburb + YANK n. (1)]

pyu *v.* [1950s+] (*W.I. Rasta*) of a running sore etc, to drip or ooze. [SE *spew*, to vomit]

pywags *n. see* PYJAMS n.

py-woman *n.* [mid-17C] (*UK Und.*) a prostitute (cf. FANCY WOMAN n.). [PYE v.]

Q

Q *n.*[1] [late 19C+] **1** (*US Und.*) San Quentin prison, in California (cf. ABBOTT'S PRIORY n.). **2** the Chicago, Burlington and Quincey Railroad. [abbr.]

Q *n.*[2] [1940s–50s] (*US Black*) barbecued ribs. [abbr.]

Q *n.*[3] [1970s] (*drugs*) methaqualone. [the brandname Quaalude]

q *n.*[1] [1960s–70s] (*US*) a male homosexual. [abbr. QUEER n. (4)]

q *n.*[2] [1990s+] (*UK drugs*) ¼oz (7g) of hashish. [abbr. SE *quarter*]

q *adj.* (*also* **queue**) [1940s+] homosexual. [abbr. QUEER adj.[1] (3)]

Q.E. *v.* [1950s+] (*UK prison*) to turn Queen's Evidence, thus to inform. [abbr.]

Q.H.B. *n. see* HIS MAJESTY'S BAD BARGAIN n.

q.p. *n.* (*also* **QP**) [1980s+] (*US drugs*) a quarter pound of cannabis. [abbr.]

q.q. *n.* [1950s] (*W.I.*) a quarter-quart (of rum). [abbr.]

q.s. *n.* [late 19C–1900s] any difficult situation. [abbr. QUEER STREET n.]

Q.T. *adj.* [late 19C+] surreptitious; thus ON THE Q.T. adv. [first and last letters of *quiet*]

q.t. *n.* [1990s+] (*US*) proper care and attention. [abbr. *quality time*]

quack *n.*[1] **1** [late 16C+] an incompetent medical charlatan; thus adj. *quacky*. **2** [late 17C+] (*orig. Aus./N.Z.*) a doctor, irrespective of their abilities. **3** [mid-18C+] a charlatan (other than in a medical context). [abbr. of SE *quacksalver*, one who 'quacks' mendaciously about the quality of their medicines and salves]

quack *n.*[2] (*also* **quacker**) [late 19C–1910s] a duck.

quack *n.*[3] [1960s+] (*US Black*) a homosexual. [? he 'ducks down' for sex]

quack *n.*[4] [1990s+] an act of breaking wind. [echoic]

quack *adj.* [late 18C+] pertaining to a charlatan doctor or his medicines; occas. ext. to other professions. [QUACK n.[1] (1)]

quack *v.*[1] **1** [late 17C–mid-19C] to be an incompetent doctor, to work as an itinerant doctor. **2** [mid-19C] to promote one's business through fraudulent claims. [QUACK n.[1] (1)]

quack *v.*[2] **1** [1940s+] to complain. **2** [1990s+] to break wind noisily.

quacker *n.*[1] [2000s] (*Aus.*) the female genital area. [? noise during sexual intercourse]

quacker *n.*[2] *see* QUACK n.[2].

quacking cheat *n.* [mid-16C–early 19C] (*UK Und.*) a drake or duck (cf. QUAKING CHEAT n.). [SE *quack* + CHEAT n. (1)]

quacks *n.* [1980s] (*US drugs*) quaaludes.

quacktail *n.* [1960s–70s] (*S.Afr.*) the girlfriend of a township gangster. [her hairstyle, either a ponytail or a DUCK'S ARSE n. (1)]

quaco *n.* [1940s+] (*W.I.*) an unsophisticated, ignorant person, a countrified person. [Twi *kwacu*, a boy who is born on a Wednesday]

quad *n.*[1] [late 18C–mid-19C] a prison. [abbr. SE *quadrangle*]

quad *n.*[2] **1** [mid-19C] a horse. **2** [late 19C] a quadricycle. [pfx *quad-*, 4, i.e. legs, wheels]

quad *n.*[3] [1970s+] (*US drugs*) methaqualone. [abbr. *Quaalude*, a brandname]

quad *n.*[4] **1** [1970s+] (*US campus*) a very clumsy person. **2** [1990s+] a *quad*riplegic. [abbr.; ? (2) f. (1)]

quad cull *n. see* QUOD CULL n.

quaecall *n.* [late 18C] (*US Und.*) a turnkey. [var. on QUOD CULL n.]

quaedam *n.* [late 17C] a prostitute. [Lat. *quaedam*, one of those, thus a euph.]

quaegemes *n.* [early 18C–early 19C] an illegitimate child. [Lat. *quaegemes*, of what marriage?]

quaggot *n.* (*also* **quag**) [1930s+] (*US gay*) a male homosexual. [QUEER adj.[1] (3) + FAGGOT n.[2] (3)]

quail *n.* **1** [17C+] a prostitute (cf. ALLEY CAT n.). **2** [mid-19C; 1920s–30s] (*US tramp*) an 'old maid'. **3** [mid-19C+] a young woman, poss. under the age of consent. **4** [late 19C] (*US*) an order of chicken stew. **5** [1960s–70s] (*US gay*) an attractive young man. [SE *quail*, a supposedly amorous bird]

quailer *n.* [20C+] (*Aus.*) a stone. [ety. unknown; ? link to dial. *quail*, to frighten]

quail pipe *n.* **1** [17C–mid-19C] a woman's tongue, esp. as the seducer of foolish men. **2** [late 17C–18C] the throat. [SE *quail pipe*, a pipe or whistle that imitates the notes of the female quail and lures birds into a net]

quaint *n.* [late 14C–19C] the vagina. [CUNT n.[1] (1)]

'quake *n.* [late 19C+] an earthquake. [abbr.]

quake breach *n.* (*also* **quake buttock**) [late 16C–early 17C] a coward. [lit. 'fear-anus', 'fear-buttock']

quaker *n.* [mid–19C] a hard, and poss. lengthy, piece of excreta. [it is long and thin, hard and 'wears brown']

Quaker oat(s) *n.* [1930s+] a coat. [rhy. sl.]

Quaker's bargain *n.* [late 17C–early 18C] a 'take it or leave it' bargain. [for ety. *see* YEA AND NAY MAN n.]

Quaker's burying ground *n.* [18C–19C] a lavatory. [QUAKER n.]

quaking cheat *n.* [mid-16C–mid-19C] **1** a sheep (cf. QUACKING CHEAT n.). **2** a calf. [SE *quake*, to tremble + CHEAT n. (1)]

Quaky Isles *n.* [20C+] (*Aus.*) New Zealand. ['QUAKE n., i.e. the islands' earthquakes]

qualified *adj.*[1] [late 19C+] a euph. for DAMNED adj. [play on SE *qualified*, modified, i.e. the word is modified by the expletive]

qualified *adj.*[2] [1960s+] (*US Black*) of a prostitute, experienced.

qualify *v.* [1970s] (*US Und.*) for a confidence trickster to assess the potential of a possible victim.

quality, the *n.* [18C+] the upper classes; 'society'.

quality Joe *n.* (*also* **quality folks**) [1950s] (*US drugs*) a non-addict. [joc. use of QUALITY, THE n. + JOE PUBLIC n./SE *folks*]

quality toss *n.* [1910s–20s] (*Irish*) the attributes and style of the upper classes. [QUALITY, THE n. + SE *toss*, a heap]

qually *n.* [late 17C–early 18C] cloudy, sour wine. [? SE *cloudy* or *squally*]

quamin *n.* (*also* **quarmin**) [1940s+] (*W.I.*) an unsophisticated, ignorant person, a countrified person. [Twi *kwamé*, a boy who is born on a Saturday]

quams *n.* [2000s] (*US Black*) problems, worries. [SE *qualms*]

quandary *n.* [mid-16C–18C] a dilemma, a state of extreme uncertainty; also as v. [SE f. 1800; ? Fr. *qu'en dirai-je*, what shall I say of it?, but the pron. militates against this; 'possibly a corruption of some term of scholastic Latin' (*OED*)]

quandong *n.* (*Aus.*) **1** [1910s+] a country bumpkin; thus *have the quandongs*, to behave stupidly, to be stupid (cf. BUCKWHEAT n.). **2** [1930s+] a disreputable figure, living on their wits. **3** [1960s+] a young woman who accepts any amount of gifts but still refuses to cede her sexual favours. [SE *quandong*, a fruit which is soft on the outside but hard inside]

quanger *n.* [1960s+] (*Aus. teen*) a quince. [initial letters]

quantum *n.* [late 18C–mid-19C] a drink. [Lat. *quantum*, enough]

quare *adj.* [mid-19C+] (*Irish*) **1** good, excellent; also as a general intensifier, occas. adv. use. **2** odd, eccentric, 'queer'; thus *quare fella/fellow*, an eccentric, an unusual person. [Irish pron. of SE *queer*]

quare harp/hawk *n. see* QUEER HAWK n.

quare man m'da! *excl.* [20C+] (*Ulster*) a general excl. of disbelief. [QUARE adj. (2); lit. 'odd man, my father']

quare place *n.* [1960s+] (*Irish*) **1** hell. **2** somewhere unpleasant. [fig. use of QUARE adj. (2) + SE *place*]

quare stuff, the *n.* [1960s+] (*Irish*) illicitly distilled whisky. [QUARE adj. (1) + SE *stuff*]

quare thing, the *n.* [1970s] (*Irish*) an act of sexual intercourse. [QUARE adj. (1)]

quarm *n.* (*also* **quarmburger**) [1990s+] (*UK juv.*) a male homosexual. [? QUEER n. (4)]

quarmin *n. see* QUAMIN n.

quarrel picker *n.* [late 17C–early 19C] a glazier. [pun on SE *quarrel*, a small, usu. diamond-shaped pane of glass, used for lattice-windows, ult. Fr. *carreau*, pane + SE *picker*]

quarrom *n.* (*also* **quarren, quarrome, quarromes, quarroms, quarron, quarrons**) [mid-16C–mid-19C] (*UK Und.*) a body. [Ital. *carogna* or Fr. *charogne*, flesh]

quarry *n.* [18C] the vagina (cf. AGREEABLE RUTS OF LIFE n.). [SE *quarry*, a pit + ? SE *quarry*, that which is hunted]

quarry cure *n.* (*also* **rockpile cure**) [1930s–60s] (*US drugs*) a 'cure' for drug addiction that involves being imprisoned and working in the rock quarry. [Maurer, 'Lang. of the Underworld Narcotic Addict' Pt.2 (1938) notes 'Restricted to the Chicago Bridewell and to addicts who have done time there']

quart *n.*[1] [late 19C–1900s] (*Aus.*) a quart pot, used for drinking; thus *quart-pot tea*, tea, made in the open air and in a quart.

quart *n.*[2] [1950s] (*W.I.*) a 1-year prison sentence (cf. PINT n.).

quart *n.*[3] [1990s+] (*drugs*) **1** ¼oz (7g) of cannabis. **2** ¼oz (7g) or ¼g of a given drug. [abbr. SE *quarter*]

quarter *n.*[1] **1** [mid-18C–mid-19C] 5 shillings (25p), 5 dollars. **2** [late 19C–1900s] (*UK Und.*) a 3-month prison sentence, i.e. a quarter of a year. **3** [20C+] (*US Und.*) a 25-year prison sentence. **4** [20C+] £25. **5** [1970s] (*US*) $25.

quarter *n.*[2] **1** [mid-19C–1900s] (*UK prison*) a quarter inch of tobacco. **2** [1960s+] (*drugs*) ¼oz (7g) of a narcotic drug. **3** [1980s+] (*drugs*) $25 of a given drug.

quarter bag *n.* (*also* **quarter sack**) [1960s+] (*drugs*) $25 of a given drug. [QUARTER n.[2] (3) + BAG n.[11] (1)]

quarter clift *n. see* CLIFT n.

quartereen *n.* [mid-19C] a farthing. [? Ital. *quattrino*; a farthing was ¼ of a penny]

quarter flash and three parts stupid *phr.* (*also* **quarter flash and three parts foolish**) [early 19C] a phr. describing a fool who claims to have a small degree of fashionable worldliness. [FLASH adj.[1] (2)]

quarter house *n.* [1970s] (*US drugs*) a place where drug users can obtain a ¼oz (7g) of narcotics. [QUARTER n.[2] (2) + SE *house*]

quartern o'Bry *n.* [mid-19C] a ¼ pint of gin. [BRIAN (O'LINN) n.]

quartern of bliss *n.* [late 19C] a short, attractive woman.

quartern o'finger *n.* [mid-19C] a measure of rum. [SE *quartern* + FINGER AND THUMB n. (1)]

quarter piece *n.* [1930s–50s] (*US drugs*) ¼oz (7g) of drugs. [SE *quarter* + PIECE n.[6] (1)]

quarter-pint *adj. see* HALF-PINT adj. (2).

quarter-pound of bird's eye *n.* [late 19C] a ¼oz (7g) of tobacco. [SE *bird's-eye*, a variety of tobacco in which the ribs of the leaves are cut together with the fibre]

quarter sack *n. see* QUARTER BAG n.

quarter to two *n.* [20C+] a Jew (cf. BILLY THE KID n.). [rhy. sl.]

quart mania *n.* [19C] a hangover, delirium tremens.

Quarto *n.* (*also* **Mr Quarto**) [18C] a bookseller. [SE *quarto*, a paper size]

quartz *n.* [late 19C–1900s] (*US*) money (cf. BRASS n.[1]).

quas *n.* [1970s] (*drugs*) methaqualone. [abbr. *Quaalude*, brand-name]

quashee *n. see* QUASHIE n. (2).

quashiba *n.* [1940s+] (*W.I.*) a foolish, uncultivated woman. [Twi *akwasiba*, a girl born on a Sunday]

quashie *n.* **1** [late 18C–mid-19C] a generic term for a Black person. **2** [mid-19C+] (*also* **quashee**) a country bumpkin, a peasant, a stupid person; thus generic for the working or lower classes *en masse*. [Twi *kwasi*, a boy born on a Sunday; modern use is W.I.]

quasimodo *n.* [20C+] soda. [rhy. sl.; Cockney pron.]

quat *n.* [early 17C] a derog. term used for a young man. [SE *quat*, a pimple]

quat *v. see* GO TO QUAT V.

quattie *n.* (*also* **quatty**) [20C+] (*W.I.*) 1½ (old) pence. [? a *quarter* of 6d]

quaver *n.* [mid-19C–1950s] a musician. [SE *quaver*, a note, equal in length to half a crotchet or an eighth of a semibreve]

quaw *n.* (*also* **quawy**) [mid-19C+] (*W.I.*) **1** a stupid, ugly person, a peasant or bumpkin. **2** an albino. [Twi *kwaw*, a boy who is born on a Thursday]

quay *n.* (*also* **quee**) [mid-18C–mid-19C] (*US Und.*) prison. [? QUOD n. (1)]

quean *n.*[1] [mid-16C–19C] a strumpet, a prostitute. [11C SE *quean*, woman (with no pej. aspect); Nares suggests AS *cwean*, a barren cow]

quean *n.*[2] *see* QUEEN n.[2] (1).

queanie *n.* [1930s+] (*Aus.*) a homosexual (cf. QUEENIE n.[1]). [ext. of QUEEN n.[2] (1)]

queanie *adj.* (*also* **queany**) [1930s+] (*Aus.*) effeminate. [QUEANIE n.]

quean up *v.* (*also* **queen up**) [1930s+] (*Aus.*) to dress carefully, although not necessarily effeminately; usu. in phr. *all queaned up*. [QUEEN n.[2] (1)]

quee *n. see* QUAY n.

queeb *n.* [1960s] (*US teen*) any small problem, esp. mechanical. [ety. unknown; ? SE *quibble* n.]

queef *n.* [1990s+] a vaginal fart. [QUEEF v.]

queef *v.* [1990s+] (*US*) of a woman, to make a vaginal fart (usu. noisy rather than smelly). [QUIFF n.[1] (1) + ? SE *whiff*]

queen *n.*[1] **1** [18C+] (*US*) a pretty young woman, a beauty. **2** [late 19C+] a woman. **3** [1920s+] a woman, usu. categorized by her job. **4** [1940s+] (*S.Afr.*) a woman who runs an illicit township bar or shebeen.

queen *n.*[2] **1** [late 19C+] (*also* **quean**) an effeminate (older) homosexual male. Popular culture offers a number of var. based on words and phrs. including *queen*, e.g. *Queen for a day; Queen Mother; Queen of All the Fairies; see also* QUEEN sfx (cf. DUCHESS n.[1]). **2** [1960s] (*gay*) used ironically by a homosexual of a heterosexual. **3** [1970s+] (*US prison*) an attractive, effeminate young prison homosexual; as such much sought after and fought over. **4** [1980s+] (*Aus. prison*) a transsexual. [SE *quean*/QUEAN n.[1]; this sp. is still occas. used to distinguish it f. SE sign]

queen *v.* [1970s+] to act in an effeminate manner; to pose ostentatiously. [QUEEN n.[2] (1)]

queen *sfx* **1** [late 19C+] (*US*) a combining form used with a suitable n. or v. to denote the best woman of that type; the female equivalent of KING n.[1] (1), e.g. DERB QUEEN n.; HOSE QUEEN n. **2** [1940s+] (*orig. US gay*) a combining form used with a suitable n. to indicate a male homosexual with a specific enthusiasm or taste (cf. AFRICAN QUEEN n.; AMYL QUEEN n.; ASS QUEEN n.; BEAN QUEEN n.; BELLY QUEEN n.; BODY QUEEN n.; BOG QUEEN n.; BONE QUEEN n.; BROWNIE QUEEN n.; CATALOGUE QUEEN n.; CHICKEN QUEEN n.; CLEAN QUEEN n.; COTTAGE QUEEN n.; CURRY QUEEN n.; DANGLE QUEEN n.; DINGE QUEEN n.; DISH QUEEN n.; DRAG QUEEN n.; FELCH QUEEN n.; FISH QUEEN n.[1]; FLADGE QUEEN n.; GAS QUEEN n.; GOLDEN SHOWER QUEEN n.; GUCCI QUEEN n.; HAND QUEEN n.; HEAD QUEEN n.; KAKA QUEEN n.; LACE QUEEN n.; LEATHER QUEEN n.; MACARONI QUEEN n.; MIDNIGHT QUEEN n.; MITTEN QUEEN n.; OPERA QUEEN n.; OREO QUEEN n.; PAY-OFF QUEEN n.; POTATO QUEEN n.; PRIVY-QUEEN n.; RAINBOW QUEEN n.; RICE QUEEN n.; RIM QUEEN n.; ROAD QUEEN n.; RUBBER QUEEN n.; SCENE QUEEN n.; SIZE QUEEN n.; SNOW QUEEN n.; TACO QUEEN n.; TALCUM QUEEN n.; TEAROOM QUEEN n.; TOE-JAM QUEEN n.; TOE QUEEN n.; VANILLA QUEEN n.; VIKING QUEEN n.; WALL QUEEN n.; WATCH QUEEN n.; XEROX QUEEN n.). [SE *queen*/QUEEN n.[2] (1)]

Queen Anne's fan *n.* (*also* **Anne's fan**) [early 18C–mid-19C] the act of thumbing one's nose. [the spread fingers resemble a fan]

queen bee *n.*[1] [1950s–70s] (*camp gay*) **1** a woman who likes to surround herself with young men, who may or may not be homosexual. **2** as (1) but of a man, usu. homosexual himself. [play on SE; QUEEN n.[2] (1) + SE *bee* or ? abbr. *bitch*]

queen bee *n.*[2] [2000s] (*US Black*) the woman with the largest breasts in a group.

Queen Bess *n.* [late 18C–mid-19C] in cards, the queen of clubs. ['perhaps because that queen (Elizabeth I), history says, was of a swarthy complexion' (Hotten, 1867)]

queen drag *n. see* DRAG QUEEN n.

queenie *n.*[1] **1** [late 19C] an affectionate nickname used of 'a fat woman trying to walk young' (Ware). **2** [1920s+] (*US*) (*also* **queeny**) a derog. name for an effeminate male homosexual (cf. DUCHESS n.[1]; QUEANIE n.). [(1) the line 'Queenie, come back, sweet', from the 1884 Drury Lane pantomime in which it was addressed to 'Mr H. Campbell, one of the heaviest men on the stage, and then playing "Eliza" a cook' (Ware); (2) QUEEN n.[2] (1)]

queenie *n.*[2] [1950s] (*Aus.*) a prostitute. [QUEAN n.[1]]

queen mama *n.* [1990s+] (*US teen*) the very best of a person, place or thing; the female counterpart of KING DADDY n.

Queen Mary *n.* [1980s+] (*US gay*) an obese gay man. [QUEEN n.[2] (1) + MARY n.[2] (1); ult. the size of the transatlantic liner *Queen Mary*]

Queen Mum *n.* [2000s] the buttocks (cf. ALA n.). [rhy. sl. = BUM n.[1] (1)]

queen of holes *n.* [late 17C] the vagina (cf. BLACK HOLE n.[1]).

queen of Scotch *n.* [1970s] (*US gay*) an alcoholic gay man. [pun on *Mary Queen of Scots*/QUEEN n.[2] (1) + *Scotch* whisky]

queen of the south *n.* [20C+] the mouth. [rhy. sl.; a Scot. soccer team]

queen pin *n.* [1960s+] the female equivalent of KINGPIN n., i.e. a woman who heads an institution or arranges an event.

queen's bad bargain/shilling *n. see* HIS MAJESTY'S BAD BARGAIN n.

queen's gold medal *n.* [late 19C–1900s] a shilling (5p). [the monarch's head on the coin]

queen's hard bargain *n. see* HIS MAJESTY'S BAD BARGAIN n.

queen's head *n.* [mid-19C] a postage stamp. [the monarch's head on the stamp]

Queensland salute *n. see* BARCOO SALUTE n.

Queen's Park Ranger *n.* [1960s+] a stranger; often in pl. [rhy. sl.; ult. the West London football club]

queen's pictures *n.* (*also* **queen's portrait**) [early 18C; mid-late 19C] money (cf. ABE n.[2]). [the pictures of the reigning monarch, in this case of Queen Anne and Queen Victoria, on one side of the coin]

Queen's Row *n.* **1** [1950s+] (*US gay*) the Public Gardens, Boston, Massachusetts. **2** [1960s+] (*US prison*) a section of the prison where homosexual inmates have their cells. [QUEEN n.[2] (1) + ? ref. to 1941 film *King's Row*, starring Ronald Reagan]

queen's tears *n.* [1940s+] (*S.Afr.*) alcohol, usu. gin. [? ref. to the tears Queen Victoria supposedly shed after the defeat at Isandhlwana]

Queen Street cocky *n.* (*also* **Queen Street bushie/farmer**) [1950s+] (*N.Z.*) a businessman who owns a farm as an investment. [*Queen Street*, the business/financial centre of Auckland + COCKY n.[2] (1)]

Queen Street yank *n.* [1950s] (*N.Z.*) a New Zealander who apes American styles etc. [*Queen Street*, the business/financial centre of Auckland + YANK n. (1)]

queen's weather *n.* [mid-19C–1900s] excellent, sunny weather. [Queen Victoria (r.1837–1901), so it was claimed, always enjoyed good weather to accompany her public appearances]

queen's woman *n.* [mid-19C] 'a prostitute who received medical attention under the terms of the Contagious Diseases Acts of the 1860s' (*OED*).

queen up *v. see* QUEAN UP v.

queen ween *n.* [1990s+] (*US campus*) someone who backs out of a commitment. [SE *queen*/QUEEN n.[2] (1) + WEENIE n.[1] (5)]

queeny *n. see* QUEENIE n.[1] (2).

queeny *adj.* [1930s+] (*gay*) flamboyant and effeminate; also as adv. [QUEEN n.[2] (1)]

queer *n.* **1** [mid-18C; 1910s] a hoax, a confidence trick; thus phr. *play the queer*, to hoodwink. **2** [mid-18C+] (*also* **queer stuff**) counterfeit money; thus *queersman*, one who makes or distributes counterfeit money. **3** [late 19C] a look (on one's face); a look (at something). **4** [1910s+] (*also* **queerie, queervert, queery**) a homosexual, usu. male, occas. female. **5** [1940s] an eccentric. **6** [1950s] (*Aus.*) a fool, a simpleton. **7** [1960s] (*US campus*) one who works (overly) hard. [SE *queer*, odd/QUEER adj.[1]]

queer *adj.*[1] **1** [mid-16C+] (*UK Und.*) (*also* **quer, quire**) an all-purpose negative adj.; the antonym of RUM adj. (1). **2** [late 17C+] (*UK Und.*) fake, counterfeit, esp. of money, jewellery, official papers, etc, e.g. *queer peg*, a 'bad' shilling. **3** [1910s+] homosexual; thus *queerness*, homosexuality; of a female, lesbian. **4** [1930s] (*US Und.*) of a heterosexual male, sexually unorthodox. [Ger. *quer*, oblique, skewed; the line between SE *queer*, strange, odd or peculiar, and the Und. use is both semantically and chrono-logically slim; the SE slightly predates (at least in printed cits.) the cant, but as the *OED* remarks, some examples of the one may in fact equally well serve for the other. Only the context gives any real clue, the most obvious of which occur in such undeniably Und. combs. as QUEER CUFFIN n.; QUEER COLE n. etc. Ribton-Turner, *A History of Vagrants* (1887), suggests Welsh *chwired*, craft, deceit or cunning. The use as a pej. description of homosexuals does not emerge until *c*.1915; like NIGGER n.[1], it has been repossessed by some homosexuals as an affirmative]

queer *adj.*[2] **1** [late 18C+] ill, out of sorts; esp. in phr. *feel queer, look queer*. **2** [late 19C] of machinery etc, out of order. **3** [1920s] in difficulties. [the potential for *double entendre* has rendered the term, and its combs., almost obs., at least in 'PC' circles]

queer *v.* **1** [late 18C–mid-19C] to quiz or ridicule, to puzzle. **2** [late 18C–1930s] to impose on, to swindle, to cheat; thus *queer a flat*, to hoodwink a gullible victim. **3** [late 18C+] to spoil, to put out of order. **4** [early 19C; 1970s] to act in an odd manner. **5** [mid-19C+] of a person, to spoil the reputation of, to spoil someone's efforts or opportunities. **6** [1910s] (*US*) to cause trouble for. **7** [1970s+] to abuse sexually. [SE *queer*, odd]

queeralities *n.* [20C+] (*Ulster*) eccentricities, peculiarities. [SE *queer*]

queer as a clockwork orange *phr.* **1** [1950s+] extremely odd. **2** [1970s] ostentatiously homosexual. [SE *queer*/QUEER adj.¹ (3)]

queer as a coot *phr.* [1940s+] undeniably homosexual. [QUEER adj.¹ (3)]

queer as a nine-bob note *phr.* (*also* **queer as a two-quid note**) [1960s+] unusual, particularly suspicious; the phr. survives the demise of the currency. [SE *queer* + NINE-BOB NOTE n.]

queer as a three-dollar bill *phr.* [1950s+] (*orig. US*) **1** (*also* **queer as a three-pound note**) extremely odd. **2** (*also* **queer as a four-dollar bill, ...nine-dollar bill**) ostentatiously homosexual. [SE *queer*/QUEER adj.¹ (3); such a bill does not exist]

queer as beer *phr.* [1990s+] (*Aus.*) extremely odd; outrageously homosexual. [SE *queer*/QUEER adj.¹ (3)]

queer as Chloe *adj.* [1980s+] (*N.Z.*) homosexual. [QUEER adj.¹ (3) + var. on CAMP AS CHLOE phr.]

queer as Dick's hatband *phr.* (*also* **odd as Dick's hatband**) **1** [18C+] odd, eccentric. **2** [18C+] referring to something comical. **3** [18C+] referring to something one cannot recognize or identify; thus *I wouldn't know him from Dick's hatband*. **4** [late 18C] out of sorts, dispirited, 'under the weather'. [SE *queer* + DICK'S HATBAND n.; the dial. phr. is *as queer as Dick's hatband that went nine times round and wouldn't meet*]

queer as duck soup *phr.* [1940s] (*US*) ostentatiously homosexual or effeminate. [QUEER adj.¹ (3)]

queer bail *n.* [late 18C–mid-19C] fraudulent bail. [QUEER adj.¹ (1) + SE *bail*]

queerbait *n.* [1950s+] an effeminate young boy who attracts, or is supposed to attract older male homosexuals; thus as v., to seek out a homosexual encounter for money. [QUEER n. (4) + SE *bait*]

queer-basher *n.* [1960s+] one who specializes in beating up (and usu. robbing) male homosexuals. [QUEER-BASHING n.]

queer-bashing *n.* [1960s+] the homophobic beating up (and usu. robbing) of male homosexuals. [QUEER n. (4) + BASHING n.¹ (1)]

queer beak *n.* [19C] (*UK Und.*) an incorruptible magistrate. [QUEER adj.¹ (1) + BEAK n.¹ (1)]

queer beer *n.* [1970s] (*US*) 'near bear', beer with a low alcohol content. [QUEER adj.¹ (3) + SE *beer*]

queer belch *n.* [mid-19C] sour beer. [QUEER adj.¹ (1) + BELCH n.¹ (1)]

queer bird *n.* **1** [mid-16C–mid-19C] (*UK Und.*) (*also* **choir bird, quire bird**) a mendicant villain who, recently released from prison, returns to robbery, specializing in stealing horses. **2** [late 18C–early 19C] (*also* **choir bird, quire bird**) a recidivist. **3** [mid-19C+] an odd, eccentric person. **4** [1960s] (*US gay*) a heterosexual who dabbles in homosexuality. [(1) QUEER adj.¹ (1); (2) SE *queer*; (3) QUEER adj.¹ (3) + BIRD n.² (1); by 18C the term referred to any unreformed villain]

queer bit *n.* [late 18C–mid-19C] counterfeit money. [QUEER adj.¹ (2) + BIT n.¹ (1)]

queer bitch *n.* [late 18C–early 19C] 'an odd out of the way fellow' (Grose, 1785). [QUEER adj.¹ (1) + BITCH n.¹ (5); despite appearances, there is no hint of homosexuality]

queer bit-maker *n.* [late 18C–19C] (*UK Und.*) a coiner, a counterfeiter. [QUEER BIT n. + SE *maker*]

queer blowing *n.* [early–mid-19C] (*UK Und.*) an ugly woman. [QUEER adj.¹ (1) + BLOWING n.¹]

queer bluffer *n.* (*also* **queer buffer**) [late 17C–mid-19C] a 'sneaking, sharping, Cut-throat Ale-house or Inn-keeper' (B.E.). [QUEER adj.¹ (1) + BLUFFER n.¹ (1)]

queer booze *n.* [mid-16C–19C] sour or inferior beer, 'small and naughtye drynke' (Harman). [QUEER adj.¹ (1) + BOUSE n. (1)/BOOZE n. (1)]

queer bub *n.* [mid-17C–mid-19C] second-rate or sour beer. [QUEER adj.¹ (1) + BUB n.¹]

queer buffer *n. see* QUEER BLUFFER n.

queer bung *n.* [late 17C–early 19C] (*UK Und.*) an empty purse (viewed as an object of robbery). [QUEER adj.¹ (1) + BUNG n.¹ (1)]

queer card *n.* [mid-19C–1940s] an odd, eccentric person. [QUEER adj.¹ (1) + CARD n.² (2)]

queer chum *n.* [early–mid-19C] a suspicious companion. [QUEER adj.¹ (1) + CHUM n.¹ (1)]

queer clout *n.* [late 17C–18C] (*UK Und.*) a cheap, prob. cotton handkerchief that as such is not worth stealing. [QUEER adj.¹ (1) + CLOUT n.¹ (1)]

queer cole *n.* (*also* **quer cole**) [late 17C–19C] (*UK Und.*) counterfeit money; thus *queer cole fencer*, the distributor of counterfeit money; *queer cole maker*, a counterfeiter. [QUEER adj.¹ (2) + COLE n. (1) (+ -FENCER sfx)]

queer cove *n.* (*also* **choir cove, quire cove**) **1** [late 16C–mid-19C] (*UK Und.*) a villain. **2** [mid-18C] (*also* **quer cove**) a poor man. **3** [mid-19C] a turnkey. [QUEER adj.¹ (1) + COVE n. (1)]

queer cramp-ring *n. see* CRAMP-RINGS n.

queer cuffin *n.* (*also* **queer cuffen, quire cuffin**) **1** [mid-16C–mid-19C] (*UK Und.*) a Justice of the Peace. **2** [late 17C–early 19C] a peasant. [QUEER adj.¹ (1) + CUFFIN n.]

queer cull *n.* [late 17C–mid-18C] **1** a foolish dandy, a fop. **2** a poor, ill-dressed person. **3** (*UK Und.*) a passer of counterfeit money. [QUEER adj.¹ (1)/QUEER adj.¹ (2) + CULL n.¹ (4)]

queer customer *n.* (*also* **queer merchant**) [mid-19C+] an odd or eccentric person. [QUEER adj.¹ (1) + CUSTOMER n. (1)/MERCHANT n.]

queer degen *n.* [late 17C–mid-19C] (*UK Und.*) a brass, iron or steel-hilted sword, with no special ornamentation. [QUEER adj.¹ (1) + DEGEN n. (1)]

queer diver *n.* [late 17C–early 19C] (*UK Und.*) a bungling, incompetent pickpocket. [QUEER adj.¹ (1) + DIVER n. (2)]

queer doxy *n.* [late 17C–mid-19C] (*UK Und.*) a slatternly woman. [QUEER adj.¹ (1) + DOXY n. (2)]

queer drawers *n.* [late 17C–18C] (*UK Und.*) yarn, coarse worsted, ordinary or old stockings. [QUEER adj.¹ (1) + SE *drawers*]

queer duke *n.* [late 17C–18C] (*UK Und.*) **1** an impoverished gentleman. **2** a lean, half-starved person. [QUEER adj.¹ (1) + DUKE n.¹]

queered *adj.* [early–mid-19C] tipsy. [QUEER adj.² (1)]

queer 'em *n.* (*also* **queer'm, queerum**) [early 19C] the gallows. [QUEER v. (3)]

queer-faced *adj.* [1980s+] a general pej.; lit. 'looking like a homosexual'. [QUEER n. (4) + sfx -*faced*]

queer fellow *n.* **1** [early 18C+] an odd, eccentric person. **2** [1980s] a prisoner condemned to hang. [QUEER adj.¹ (1) + SE *fellow*; (2) ref. to Brendan Behan (1923–64) play *The Quare Fellow* (1954)]

queer fish *n.* [late 18C+] an odd or eccentric person. [QUEER adj.¹ (1) + FISH n.³]

queer for *adj.* [1940s+] obsessed with, sexually or otherwise. [the origin is QUEER adj.¹ (3), but there need be no actual homosexuality involved]

queer fun *n.* [late 17C–18C] (*UK Und.*) a cheat or trick that does not work out as intended. [QUEER adj.¹ (1) + FUN n.²]

queer-gammed *adj.* **1** [late 18C] lame, crippled. **2** [early 19C] bandy-legged. [QUEER adj.¹ (1) + GAM n.¹ (1)]

queer gill *n.* [19C] **1** a shabby fellow. **2** an untrusting, suspicious person. [QUEER adj.¹ (1) + GILL n.¹ (2)]

queer gum *n.* [mid-19C] (*UK Und.*) strange talk. [QUEER adj.[1] (1) + GUM n.[1] (1)]

queer hawk *n.* (*also* quare harp/hawk, queer harp) [20C+] (*Irish*) an odd person. [SE *queer*/QUARE adj. (2) + HAWK n.[5] (3)/ ? HARP n.[1] (2) or fig. use of the *harp* as a symbolic Irish artefact, thus person]

queerie *n. see* QUEER n. (4).

queer in the attic *phr.* [early–mid-19C] mad and/or drunk. [SE *queer* + ATTIC n. (1)]

queer in the garret *phr.* (*also* queer in the upper storey) [late 18C–19C] eccentric, mad. [SE *queer* + GARRET n. (1)/UPPER STOREY n. (1)]

queer in the nut *adj.* [1950s] mad, eccentric. [SE *queer* + NUT n.[1] (2)]

queer ken *n.* (*UK Und.*) **1** [mid-16C–17C] a prison. **2** [late 17C– mid-19C] (*also* quer ken) a house not worth robbing. [QUEER adj.[1] (1) + KEN n.[1] (1)]

queer kicks *n.* [late 17C–early 19C] (*UK Und.*) old, worn-out trousers. [QUEER adj.[1] (1) + KICKS n.[1]]

queer lamp *n. see* LAMP n. (1).

queer lap *n.* [late 18C–mid-19C] (*UK Und.*) bad liquor. [QUEER adj.[1] (1) + LAP n.[2] (2)]

queerly *adv.* **1** [late 17C–mid-19C] in a criminal manner. **2** [late 18C] (*UK Und.*) badly. [QUEER adj.[1] (1)]

queer'm *n. see* QUEER 'EM n.

queer merchant *n. see* QUEER CUSTOMER n.

queer money *n.* [19C+] (*UK Und.*) counterfeit money. [QUEER adj.[1] (2) + SE *money*]

queer mort *n.* **1** [mid-17C–19C] (*UK Und.*) a woman suffering from venereal disease; 'a dirty Drab, a jilting Wench, a Pockey jade' (B.E.). **2** [mid-18C] (*also* quer mort) a poor woman. [QUEER adj.[1] (1) + MORT n.]

queer nab *n.* [late 17C–early 19C] (*UK Und.*) a cheap, shabby hat, thus one that is not worth stealing; 'a felt, Carolina, Cloth or ord'nary Hat, not worth whipping off a man's head' (B.E.). [QUEER adj.[1] (1) + NAB n.[1] (3)]

queer nicks *n.* [early–mid-19C] (*UK Und.*) worn-out breeches. [QUEER adj.[1] (1) + ? misreading of KICKS n.[1]]

queer ogles *n.* [early–mid-19C] (*UK Und.*) cross eyes; thus *queer-ogled*, squinting. [QUEER adj.[1] (1) + OGLE n. (1)]

queer on *adj.* [1940s+] (*orig. Aus.*) homosexually attracted towards. [QUEER adj.[1] (3)]

queer paper *n.* [mid–late 19C] **1** counterfeit paper money. **2** in fig. use, something dubious, unreliable. [QUEER adj.[1] (2) + SE *paper*]

queer patter *n.* [early–mid-19C] (*UK Und.*) a foreign language. [QUEER adj.[1] (1) + PATTER n. (2)]

queer peeper *n.* [late 17C–early 18C] a badly made, thus distorting mirror. [QUEER adj.[1] (1) + PEEPER n. (2)]

queer peepers *n.* [18C–19C] (*UK Und.*) squinting or short-sighted eyes. [QUEER adj.[1] (1) + PEEPERS n. (1)]

queer people *n.* [1940s] (*UK Und.*) criminals. [QUEER adj.[1] (1)]

queer place *n.* **1** [1920s–30s] a prison. **2** [1940s–50s] a lavatory. [QUEER adj.[1] (1), with poss. implication of QUEER adj.[1] (3) + SE *place*]

queer plunger *n.* [late 18C–mid-19C] a confidence trickster who plunges into water and is saved from 'drowning'. Conveniently pre-assembled 'rescuers' then claim money for saving the person. [QUEER adj.[1] (1) + SE *plunger*, a diver]

queer prancer *n.* (*UK Und.*) **1** [late 17C] an ageing prostitute. **2** [late 17C–mid-19C] a second-rate horse. **3** [18C–early 19C] a cowardly horse stealer. [QUEER adj.[1] (1) + (1) SE *prancer*; (2) and (3) PRANCER n. (1)]

queer put *n.* [early–mid-19C] an odd, simple person. [QUEER adj.[1] (1) + PUT n.[1] (2)]

queer rag *n.* [early–mid-19C] (*UK Und.*) counterfeit money. [QUEER adj.[1] (2) + RAG n.[1] (1)]

queer ridge *n.* [mid-19C] (*US Und.*) counterfeited gold coins. [QUEER adj.[1] (1) + RIDGE n. (1)]

queer rolling *n.* [1960s+] the beating up (and robbery) of homosexual men; thus *queer-roller*. [QUEER n. (4) + ROLL v.[4] (1)/ROLLING n.[1]]

queer rooster *n.* [late 18C–19C] a police spy who frequents thieves' haunts, often feigning sleep in order to listen to their conversations. [QUEER adj.[1] (1) + SE *rooster*]

queer rotan *n.* [early–mid-19C] (*UK Und.*) a run-down coach. [QUEER adj.[1] (1) + ROTAN n.]

queer rums *n.* [early 19C] confusing talk. [QUEER adj.[1] (1) + RUM adj. (1), lit. 'bad good things']

queers, the *n.* [late 19C] sea-sickness. [QUEER adj.[2] (1)]

queer screens *n.* [19C] (*UK Und.*) forged banknotes. [QUEER adj.[1] (2) + SCREEN n.[1] (1)]

queer shover *n.* [late 19C–1950s] (*UK Und.*) a passer of counterfeit money. [SHOVE THE QUEER v.]

queer soft *n.* [mid-19C] counterfeit money. [QUEER adj.[1] (2) + SOFT MONEY n. (1)]

queer someone's ogle(s) *v.* [late 18C–mid-19C] to get or give a black eye. [QUEER v. (3) + OGLE n. (1)]

queer start *n.* [mid-19C] a strange affair, an odd situation. [SE *queer* + START n.[1]]

queer stick *n.* [late 19C+] an odd person, an eccentric. [QUEER adj.[1] (1) + STICK n.[2]]

Queer Street *n.* [early 19C+] any difficult situation; usu. as *in Queer Street*, in (financial) difficulties. [QUEER adj.[1] (1) + SE *street*; *Queer Street* begins as a fig. 'place' where the only 'dwellers' are problems and difficulties; the financial aspect, now dominant, was added in mid-19C]

queer street *n.* [1960s] (*US*) the world of homosexuality. [QUEER adj.[1] (3) + generic SE *street*]

queer stuff *n. see* QUEER n. (2).

queer tats *n.* [late 18C–mid-19C] (*UK Und.*) false dice. [QUEER adj.[1] (1) + TATS n. (1)]

queer the game *v.* [late 19C–1910s] to cause trouble for someone. [QUEER v. (3) + GAME n.[2] (3)]

queer the quod *v.* [late 18C] (*US Und.*) to break out of jail. [QUEER v. (3) + QUOD n. (1)]

queer the stifler *v.* (*also* queer the noose) [early 19C] to escape the gallows. [QUEER v. (3) + STIFLER n. (1)/SE *noose*]

queer thimble *n.* [early–mid-19C] (*UK Und.*) a watch of no value. [QUEER adj.[1] (1) + THIMBLE n.]

queer topping *n.* [late 17C–18C] (*UK Und.*) a second-rate or worn-out wig. [QUEER adj.[1] (1) + SE *topping*]

queerum *n. see* QUEER 'EM n.

queer up *n.* [1950s+] male homosexual intercourse. [QUEER n. (4)]

queervert *n. see* QUEER n. (4).

queer vinegar *n.* [early–mid-19C] (*UK Und.*) a worn-out woman's cloak. [QUEER adj.[1] (1) + VINEGAR n.[1]]

queer wedge *n.* **1** [late 18C–early 19C] a large belt or shoe buckle. **2** [early 19C] pointed shoes. **3** [19C] adulterated gold or silver. [QUEER adj.[1] (1) + WEDGE n.[1] (1)/WEDGE n.[1] (2)]

queery *n. see* QUEER n. (4).

queery *adj.* [mid-19C] shaky. [SE *queer*]

quegg *n.* [2000s] a male homosexual. [? QUEER n. (4)]

Quego *n.* [1980s+] (*N.Z.*) a Pacific Islander. [? Fijian greeting *ko iko*]

quencher *n.* [mid-19C–1900s] a drink; when quenching one's thirst. [SE *quench*]

Quentin *n.* [1920s+] (*US Und./prison*) San Quentin prison, California (cf. ABBOTT'S PRIORY n.). [abbr.]

que pasa? *phr.* [1980s+] (*US campus*) a greeting. [Mexican Sp., lit. WHAT'S HAPPENING? phr.]

quer *see under* QUEER and its combs.

querier *n.* [mid-19C] a chimney sweep who goes from house to house offering their services. [they *query* householders]

question lay *n.* [18C] (*UK Und.*) 'To knock at a Door early in the Morning and ask for the Master of the House, and if he's a Bed, to desire the Servant not to disturb him, for you'll wait till he rises, and so you take an Opportunity of stealing something' (*Tyburn Chron.*, 1768). [SE *question* + LAY n.⁴ (1)]

queue *adj. see* Q *adj.*

queynte *n.* [14C–16C] the vagina. [CUNT n.¹ (1)]

quick *n.* [1950s+] (*US Black*) instantly available money.

quick *adj.* [late 19C] (*UK society*) well-dressed and clever.

quick *adv.* [20C+] quickly.

quick and dirty *n.* [1960s–70s] (*orig. US*) a cheap café. [the standard of the service, the hygiene and the food]

quick-and-dirty *adj.* [1970s+] used of any kind of instant remedy, poss. not the best one for long-term dependence.

quick as bunny fucks *phr.* [1990s+] (*US*) very fast.

quick buck *n. see* FAST BUCK n.

quick fix *n.* [1960s+] any kind of instant remedy, poss. not the best one for long-term dependence.

quick-fix *adj.* [1970s+] of a solution, instant, if not wholly dependable. [QUICK FIX n.]

quickie *n.* (*also* **quicky**) **1** [1930s+] anything performed in a speedy, perfunctory manner. **2** [1940s+] a spontaneous and brief act of sexual intercourse; thus the person with whom one has that intercourse. **3** [1940s+] a quick drink. **4** [1940s+] a quick, 'dirty' story, related at the end of a party or drinking session. **5** [1970s+] (*US gay*) fellatio. **6** [1990s+] beer. [SE *quick*]

quick one *n.* **1** [20C+] a spontaneous and brief act of sexual intercourse. **2** [20C+] a quick drink, usu. of alcohol. **3** [1910s+] an act of urination. **4** [1940s] a brief act of masturbation.

quick on the draw *phr.* (*also* **quick on the buzzer/trigger**) **1** [19C+] bright, intelligent, quick to act. **2** [late 19C+] impetuous. **3** [1930s+] suffering from premature ejaculation. [gunfighting imagery]

quick quid *n.* [1920s+] (*Aus.*) money that is earned quickly and, poss., illicitly. [SE *quick* + QUID n. (2)]

quickshit *n.* [2000s] (*Aus.*) absolute nonsense. [SE *quick* + SHIT n.³ (4)]

quicksilver *n.* [1970s+] (*drugs*) **1** LSD when combined with another drug (cf. A n.³). **2** isobutyl nitrite (cf. AIMIES n.).

quick starts *n.* [1970s+] (*US campus*) rubber-soled sneakers; popular with those who need to make a speedy exit.

quick step *n.* [1900s] (*US*) diarrhoea (cf. APPLE-BLOSSOM TWO-STEP n.). [pun on the dance and the haste in finding a lavatory]

quick sticks *adv. see* IN QUICK STICKS *adv.*

quicksville *adv.* [1960s+] (*US*) fast, quickly. [SE *quick* + -VILLE sfx¹]

quicktime *adv.* [mid-19C; 1990s+] (*UK Black*) quickly, immediately.

quick worker *n. see* FAST WORKER n.

quicky *n. see* QUICKIE n.

quicumque vult *n.* (*also* **quicunque vult**) [late 18C] a prostitute. [Lat. *quicumque vult*, whomsoever wants; ? ref. in *quicunque* to CUNT n.¹ (1)]

quid *n.* **1** [late 17C–mid-19C] a guinea. **2** [19C+] a pound sterling. **3** [late 19C] the vagina. [? Lat. *quid*, what (one needs)]

quid box *n.* [late 18C–mid-19C] a snuff box. [SE *quid*, something, usu. tobacco, that can be held in the mouth and chewed + *box*]

quiddish *adj.* [mid-18C] good-natured.

quid fishing *n.* [late 19C] (*UK Und.*) first-class, expert thieving. [QUID n. (2) + SE *fish*]

quidlet *n.* [1900s–10s] a pound sterling. [QUID n. (2) + dimin. -*let*]

quids *n.* [late 17C+] money; thus phr., *not for quids*, not for anything. [QUID n.]

quids in *phr.* (*also* **quids, quids up**) **1** [1910s+] doing well. **2** [1950s] (*UK Und./prison*) first-class, excellent; of a person, reliable.

[QUID n. (2)/QUIDS n.; the image of making a successful bet and the money thus gained]

quid to a bloater *n.* [late 19C–1900s] a certain bet; esp. in phr. *it's a quid to a bloater.* [QUID n. (2); lit. 'a sovereign to a herring']

quien *n.* [mid-19C–1900s] a dog. [Fr. *chien*, or a Fr. dial.]

quiet-clothes boy *n.* [1930s] (*US Und.*) a plain-clothes policeman.

quiet down *v.* [1970s] (*US*) to kill, to murder. [euph.]

quiet is kept *phr.* [2000s] (*US Black*) a phr. used to request secrecy after making a revelation.

quiet mouse *n. see* LONE DUCK n.

Quiet Village *n.* [1980s+] (*US Black, Los Angeles*) Venice, California.

quiff *n.¹* (*also* **quoiff**) **1** [18C+] the vagina. **2** [1930s+] a generic term for women, esp. sexually available ones. **3** [1950s–70s] (*US*) a homosexual. [on pattern of QUEYNTE n. etc, thus ult. CUNT n.¹ (1)]

quiff *n.²* [late 19C–1910s] a smart trick or clever dodge, esp. one that makes a task easier. [ety. unknown]

quiff *adj.* [1960s] (*US*) second-rate, lightweight. [fig. use of QUIFF n.¹ (3)]

quiff *v.¹* [late 17C–19C] to have sexual intercourse (cf. BAGAGA v.). [QUIFF n.¹ (1)]

quiff *v.²* [late 19C] to come up with a cunning dodge or trick; to go or do well, to get along pleasantly. [QUIFF n.²]

qui-hi *n.* (*also* **qui-hai, qui-hy**) (*Anglo-Ind.*) **1** [19C+] a former colonial administrator or Ind. Army soldier; often as *old qui-hi.* **2** [mid–late 19C] an English resident of Calcutta. [Urdu *koi hai*, is anyone there?, the usual summons to a servant; note E.F. Benson's ex-Indian Army Major Flint, in the *Lucia* stories, whose catchphrase this is]

quill *n.¹* [17C–early 18C] a penis (cf. BLACK PENCIL n.).

quill *n.²* (*drugs*) **1** [1910s+] a folded over matchbook cover that hides a narcotic drug. **2** [1960s+] anything, e.g. a dollar bill, rolled up to make a 'straw' through which to sniff a powdered narcotic. **3** [1980s+] methamphetamine (cf. BOMBITA n.). **4** [1980s+] heroin. **5** [1980s+] cocaine. [(1) and (2) are ext. of SE; subseq. defs. ety. unknown other than in their relationship to (1) and (2)]

quill *n.³* [1920s–30s] (*US*) **1** first-rate whisky, the genuine thing as opposed to the 'bathtub' or 'rotgut' versions producing during Prohibition. **2** first-rate opium (cf. APOSTLE n.). [PURE QUILL n.]

quill, the *n. see* PURE QUILL n.

quill-driver *n.* (*also* **quill-walloper**) **1** [late 18C–19C; 2000s] (*US*) a clerk. **2** [late 18C–1910s] (*Aus.*) a journalist; thus *quill-driving*, working as a journalist.

quiller *n.* [mid-19C] a toady, a parasite. [one who 'sucks up' (through a *quill*, the precursor of the modern straw)]

quill-pipes *n. see* PIPES n.².

quills *n.* [mid-19C] (*US*) money. [? 16C *quill*, synon. with SE *coil*]

quill-walloper *n. see* QUILL-DRIVER n.

quilt *n.* **1** [mid–19C] (*US*) a wife. **2** [20C+] (*Irish*) a petulant, pedantic, pernickety man. **3** [20C+] a timid, effeminate man. **4** [20C+] (*Irish*) a fool, someone who acts against their own interests. [the making of quilts is a quintessentially female occupation]

quilt *v.* (*also* **put the quilt on**) [early 19C+] (*Aus./Irish/US*) to thrash, to beat, to flog. [Scot./Cumberland dial.]

quilting *n.* [19C–1940s] a thrashing, a beating. [QUILT v.]

quilty *adj.* [1960s] (*US Black*) of clothes, luxurious.

quim *n.* (*also* **quin**) **1** [early 18C+] the vagina. **2** [20C+] a woman, women collectively, viewed in a sexual context. **3** [20C+] (*US gay*) the anus. **4** [1970s+] (*US gay/prison*) a heterosexual inmate, subjected to homosexual rape. [? play on Celtic *cwm*, a valley; ult. CUNT n.¹ (1); Williams notes *queme*, 'which not only means pleasure, but in the sense of joining or fitting closely, or slipping in']

quim *adj.* [20C+] (*Ulster*) **1** prim, affectedly 'nice'. **2** moving easily, precisely. [Scot. *queem*, pleasant]

quim *v.* [early 18C+] to have sexual intercourse; usu. as *quimming* (cf. BAGAGA v.). [QUIM n. (1)]

quim bush *n.* [late 18C+] female pubic hair. [QUIM n. (1) + BUSH n.² (1)/SE *bush*]

quim chin *n.* [1990s+] a bearded person. [QUIM n. (1) + SE *chin*]

quimfill *adj.* [1990s+] having one's penis fully embedded in the vagina. [QUIM n. (1) + SE *fill*]

quimling *n.* [1990s+] manipulation of a woman's body in an attempt to produce orgasm, generally regarded as cunnilingus, but not limited to such. [QUIM n. (1)]

quim nuts *n.* [1990s+] (*US*) notably large and pendant labia. [QUIM n. (1) + NUTS n.² (1)]

quimp *n.* [1970s] (*US campus*) a socially inept person. [? QUEER n. (4) + WIMP n.²; note WW1 milit. *quimp*, slack, unsoldierly]

quimsby *n.* [early 18C+] the vagina. [ext. of QUIM n. (1)]

quimstake *n.* (*also* **quim-stick, quimwedge**) [19C] the penis. [QUIM n. (1) + SE *stake/stick/wedge*]

quim-sticker *n.* [19C] a womanizer (cf. GO QUIM-STICKING v.). [QUIM n. (1) + SE *sticker*]

quimwedge *v.* [late 19C+] to have sexual intercourse (cf. GO QUIM-STICKING v.).

quim whiskers *n.* (*also* **quim wig**) [19C] female pubic hair. [QUIM n. (1) + SE *whiskers/wig*]

quin *n. see* QUIM n.

quince *n.* **1** [20C+] (*Aus./US*) a weakling, a fool (cf. APPLEHEAD n.). **2** [1900s–20s] (*US*) of a situation/object, a failure. **3** [1960s+] (*Aus./US*) a homosexual, esp. one who can be both active and passive. **4** [1990s+] (*Aus.*) the buttocks. [puns on SE *quince*, a SOFT adj. (5) FRUIT n.¹ (1)/FRUIT n.² (2)]

quinine *n.* (*also* **strychnine**) [20C+] (*US gambling*) the point of 9 in craps dice (cf. ADA FROM DECATUR n.). [play on SE *nine*]

quinkydink *n.* [1990s+] (*US teen*) a coincidence. [deliberate mispron.]

quips *n.* [1950s+] (*W.I. Rasta*) a tiny piece or amount. [? SE *quip*, an odd or whimsical trifle]

quire *see under* QUEER and its combs.

quirk *n.* [20C+] (*Ulster*) an untrustworthy individual. [synon. Scot. *quirk*]

quirley *n.* (*also* **quirly**) [1930s+] (*Aus./US*) a hand-rolled cigarette. [SE *quirl*, to twist, to twirl]

quisby *n.* [early–mid-19C+] an idler; thus *doing quisby*, not working, idling. [ext. of QUIZ n.¹]

quisby *adj.* [mid–late 19C] **1** (*also* **quisby snitch**) of people, unwell; out of sorts. **2** of events, objects or people, unpleasant or malfunctioning. **3** bankrupt, poverty-stricken. [QUISBY n.]

quitam *n.* [late 18C–mid-19C] a solicitor who takes an informer's fee for their prosecution of the case. [Lat. *qui tam*, to whom so much]

quite! *excl.* [mid-19C+] an expression of agreement, absolutely, indeed; sometimes expanded as *quite so!*

quite (quite) *adj.* [20C+] (*UK society*) socially acceptable, *comme il faut*, usu. in negative. [abbr. SE *quite the thing* or *quite the lady/gentleman*]

quite too *adv.* [late 19C–1900s] (*UK society*) a general intensifier, e.g. *quite too amusing*.

quitsest *n.* [late 16C–17C] a release, a discharge. [Lat. *quietus est*, it is discharged, thus modern SE *quits*]

quitter *n.* [1950s+] (*drugs*) one who has abandoned drug use. [SE *quit*]

quit the scene *v.* [1950s] (*US Black*) to die. [SE *quit* + SCENE n. (3)]

quit the sphere *v.* [mid-19C] to die.

quiver *n.* [mid-16C–mid-18C] the vagina. [the lit. translation of Lat. *vagina*]

quiver and shake *n.* [20C+] (*Aus.*) a steak. [rhy. sl.]

quiz *n.*¹ [late 18C–mid-19C] an eccentric person, thus an odd-looking thing. [? Lat. *quis*? who?]

quiz *n.*² [mid-19C] a monocle. [abbr. SE *quizzing-glass*]

quiz *n.*³ [1920s–40s] (*US Und.*) a question.

quiz *v.* [19C–1900s] to watch, to spy on; as n., a look. [SE *quiz*, to interrogate, to find out]

quizzy *adj.* [1950s+] (*Aus./N.Z.*) inquisitive. [abbr.]

quockerwodger *n.* [mid-19C] a politician acting in accordance with the instructions of an influential third party, rather than properly representing their constituents. [SE *quockerwodger*, a wooden puppet which can be made to 'dance' by pulling its strings]

quod *n.* **1** [late 17C+] prison; also attrib. **2** [early 19C] a prisoner. **3** [mid-19C–1900s] a police station. [abbr. SE *quadrangle*; the original was Newgate, but the term became general]

quod *v.* **1** [19C+] to imprison. **2** [late 19C] to serve a prison sentence. [QUOD n. (1)]

quod cove *n.* [early 19C] (*UK Und.*) the governor of a prison. [QUOD n. (1) + COVE n. (1)]

quod cull *n.* (*also* **quad cull**) [mid-18C–mid-19C] a prison warder, a turnkey. [QUOD n. (1) + CULL n.¹ (4)]

quodded *adj.* [late 17C+] imprisoned. [QUOD v. (1)]

quodding dues are concerned *phr.* [early 19C] (*UK Und.*) it is a matter that will involve imprisonment (cf. MR KNAP IS CONCERNED phr.¹). [QUOD v. (1) + SE *concerned*]

quoiff *n. see* QUIFF n.¹.

quoit *n.* [1940s+] (*Aus.*) the anus, the buttocks; thus GO FOR ONE'S QUOITS v. [it is 'round with a hole in it']

quoniam *n.* [late 14C–early 18C] the vagina. [Lat. *quoniam*, whereas, or one of the CUNT n.¹ (1)/QUEYNTE n. group]

quot *n. see* COT n.

quota *n.* [late 17C–early 19C] (*UK Und.*) a share of plunder.

quotquean *n. see* COTQUEAN n.

quoz *n.*¹ [late 18C–early 19C] an absurd person. [var. on QUIZ n.¹]

quoz *n.*² (*also* **quozzie**) [1990s+] (*UK juv.*) a handicapped person. [*Quasi*modo, the hunchback in the novel *The Hunchback of Notre Dame* (1831) by Victor Hugo (1802–85)]

quoz! *excl.* [late 18C–mid-19C] an all-purpose excl. in which the speaker, according to context, makes fun of the subject of the excl.

quozzie *n. see* QUOZ n.².

quter *n. see* CUTER n.².

qwasha *n.* [1980s+] (*S.Afr. township*) a homemade gun, made from piping, springs and rubber tubing. [Zulu ideophone for a crunching noise; in this context echoic of the sound of the explosive click that is made when the gun is fired]

R

r *adv.* [1900s] right, correct. [abbr.]

r.a. *n. see* RED ARSE n.

ra, the *n.* [1980s+] (*orig. Ulster*) the provisional IRA. [abbr.]

raany *n.* (*also* **ranny**) [20C+] (*Ulster*) an emaciated, stunted or delicate looking person. [Irish *ranaí*, thin]

raas *n.* (*also* **raashole, rarse, rass, rasshole**) [1950s+] (*W.I./UK Black*) **1** the buttocks, thus fig. the whole person, esp. as a target for violence. **2** nonsense, rubbish. **3** a derog. description of a person, an idiot (cf. ARSE n.¹). **4** a euph. for FUCK, THE n. (1) or FUCK n.⁴ (1). **5** a Rastafarian. [ARSE n.¹ (1) or elision of *your arse* or Du. *raas*, to rage, to rave; one of the most taboo words in the W.I., it has been banned from public use in the majority of the islands]

raas *adj.* [1950s+] (*W.I./UK Black*) **1** (*also* **raashole, raass, rarse, rasshole**) a general negative epithet, the equivalent of DAMNED adj. **2** as an infix. [RAAS n. (1)]

raas *v.* [1950s+] (*W.I.*) **1** to thrash. **2** to rush about. **3** (*also* **rass up**) to stir up, to excite.

raas! *excl.* (*also* **rass!**) [1950s+] (*W.I./UK Black*) an all-purpose abusive excl. [RAAS n.]

raasclat *n.* (*also* **rassclat, rass-cloth**) [1940s+] (*orig. W.I./Jam.*) **1** an extreme derog. term. **2** as an infix. [lit. *arse/ass cloth*, i.e. a sanitary towel]

raasclat *adj.* [1950s+] (*W.I./UK Black*) a general negative epithet. [RAASCLAT n. (1)]

raasclat *adv.* [1950s+] (*W.I./UK Black*) used as an intensifier. [RAASCLAT adj.]

raasclat! *excl.* [1950s+] (*W.I./UK Black*) a general excl. [RAASCLAT n. (1)]

raashole *n. see* RAAS n.

raashole *adj. see* RAAS adj. (1).

raass *adj. see* RAAS adj. (1).

raatid *n.* (*also* **rhatid**) [1950s+] (*W.I.*) used as a synon. for DAMN n. [RAATID! excl.]

raatid *adj.* (*also* **rarted, rawted**) [1940s+] (*W.I./UK Black*) **1** furious, very angry; stupid. **2** used as a general intensifier, a synon. for DAMNED adj.; thus *to rarted*, for the hell of it. [? SE *wrath/wrathed*; used as euph. for RAAS adj. (1)]

raatid! *excl.* (*also* **rahtid! rawtid!**) [1940s+] an excl. implying great anger, surprise, amazement, envy etc. [RAATID adj. (2)]

rab *n.*¹ [20C+] (*W.I./UK Black*) a lawless, rowdy person. [SE *rabble*]

rab *n.*² [1930s+] (*UK Und.*) a cash register. [ety. unknown]

rabbi *n.* (*also* **angel**) [1930s+] (*US, orig. police*) an influential sponsor or patron. [a person 'looking out for you']

rabbit *n.*¹ **1** [late 16C] a prostitute (cf. ALLEY CAT n.). **2** [late 16C] a term of abuse. **3** [1950s] (*Aus.*) a girl.

rabbit *n.*² [late 17C–early 19C] a wooden drinking vessel.

rabbit *n.*³ [late 18C–early 19C] a newborn baby. [an affectionate nickname, but ? ref. to one Mary Tofts (*c.*1701–63) who, in 1726, allegedly (but fraudulently) 'gave birth' to a litter of rabbits]

rabbit *n.*⁴ [mid-19C] (*US*) a rowdy person. [Irish *ráibéad*, a big, hulking person]

rabbit *n.*⁵ [late 19C+] a coat made of, or lined with, rabbit fur.

rabbit *n.*⁶ **1** [late 19C+] a coward. **2** [20C+] (*Aus.*) a simpleton, a victim. **3** [1920s+] a poor player, esp. in golf or tennis; thus *rabbitry*, a state of being such a player. **4** [1940s+] (*S.Afr.*) a male homosexual. **5** [1960s+] a client who ejaculates quickly and thus leaves the prostitute free to carry on her trade. **6** [1960s+] (*US Black*) a White person. **7** [1970s] (*US*) a runaway. [the animal's perceived characteristics]

rabbit *n.*⁷ (*also* **bunny**) [1910s–50s] (*US/Aus.*) a bottle of beer; thus RUN THE RABBIT v. [? late 17C *rabbit*, a wooden drinking vessel]

rabbit *n.*⁸ [1920s+] **1** (*US*) the desire to run away. **2** (*also* **rabbit blood**) one who makes or wishes to make an escape. [stereotypes of the SE *rabbit*]

rabbit *n.*⁹ [1940s–50s] (*Aus.*) a native-born Australian.

rabbit *n.*¹⁰ [1940s+] **1** a talk, a conversation. **2** audacity, cheek. [RABBIT (AND PORK) v.]

rabbit *n.*¹¹ [1970s+] (*US gay*) a fellator. [ety. unknown]

rabbit *v.*¹ [mid-18C] a euph. for DAMN v., used in mild oaths, e.g. *rabbit it!* [cf. DOD RABBIT IT! excl.]

rabbit *v.*² [20C+] to scrounge. [naut. jargon *rabbit*, a smuggled or stolen article; note N.Z. use (post-1950) which comes from the image of a *rabbit* attacking the tops of root crops]

rabbit *v.*³ (*also* **play/turn rabbit**) [1930s+] to leave quickly, to run away. [RABBIT n.⁸ (1)/stereotype of the SE *rabbit*]

rabbit (and pork) *v.* [1940s+] to talk; thus *rabbit on*, to chatter, to grumble, to complain. [rhy. sl.]

rabbit blood *n. see* RABBIT n.⁸ (2).

rabbit catcher *n.* [late 18C–early 19C] a midwife. [RABBIT n.³ + SE *catcher*]

rabbitchoker *n.* [1950s] (*US*) a farmer, an unsophisticated peasant (cf. ACORN-CRACKER n.).

rabbit-chop *n. see* RABBIT-KILLER n.

rabbit ears *n.* [1950s+] (*orig. US*) a V-shaped television antenna.

rabbit fever *n.* [1920s+] (*US Und.*) **1** the compelling desire to run off whenever things get difficult. **2** the compulsion to attempt escapes from any form of imprisonment. [RABBIT n.⁸ (1)]

rabbit food *n.* (*also* **rabbit's food**) [20C+] vegetables or salad greens considered unfit for consumption, esp. by a carnivore.

rabbit foot *n.*¹ [late 19C–1930s] (*US Black*) **1** attention. **2** good luck. [the trad. wearing of a rabbit's foot as a good-luck charm]

rabbit foot *n.*² **1** [1920s] (*US Black*) a coward, a timid person. **2** [1920s–40s] (*US*) an escaped convict. [RABBIT n.⁸]

rabbit foot! *excl.* [1920s] (*US Black*) an excl. of annoyance.

rabbit hutch *n.* [20C+] **1** the crotch. **2** a crutch. [rhy. sl.]

rabbit in the thicket *n.* [1980s] (*Aus.*) **1** a ticket. **2** cricket. **3** a wicket. [rhy. sl.]

rabbit-killer *n.* (*also* **rabbit-chop/-punch**) [1940s+] (*Aus.*) a chopping blow to the back of the neck. [the blow used by farmers etc to dispatch rabbits]

rabbit-o *n.* (*also* **rabbit-oh**) [20C+] (*Aus.*) an itinerant seller of rabbits as food. [the cry, but note Aus. -o sfx (4); thus rugby jargon *The Rabbit-Os*, the South Sydney Rugby Club, whose fortunes suffered so much in the 1930s Depression that its officials were reduced to raffling and selling rabbits]

rabbit on *v.* *see* RABBIT (AND PORK) v.

rabbit pie *n.* [19C] a prostitute (cf. ALLEY CAT n.). [LIVE RABBIT n.]

rabbit-pie shifter *n.* [19C] a policeman (cf. BEAT-POUNDER n.). [RABBIT PIE n.]

rabbit-punch *n.* *see* RABBIT-KILLER n.

rabbitry *n.* [1930s] **1** in a sport, poor players considered collectively. **2** poor play. [RABBIT n.[6] (3)]

rabbit's food *n.* *see* RABBIT FOOD n.

rabbit-snatcher *n.* [1950s] (*US Und.*) an abortionist. [RABBIT n.[3]]

rabbit's paw *n.* [1990s+] talk, conversation. [rhy. sl.; var. on RABBIT n.[10]]

rabbit sucker *n.* **1** [late 16C–early 19C] (*UK Und.*) a rich young man who is gulled into running up large bills by confidence tricksters who later dun him for their debts. **2** [early 18C] a pawnbroker.

rabbit trap *n.* [1910s] (*Aus.*) the mouth. [SE *rabbit* + SE *trap/*TRAP n.[3]]

rabbo *n.* [1900s–40s] **1** a *rabb*it; *rabb*its as a group; thus *rabbo!* the street-cry of a seller of rabbits. **2** a street-seller of rabbits. [abbr.]

rabshackle *n.* (*also* **rabshakle**) [18C] a ne'er-do-well, a wastrel. [? SE *ramshackle*]

racan *n.* [20C+] (*Irish*) a lanky, raw-boned person. [Irish *racán*, a rake]

race *n.*[1] [late 19C] a bet on a horserace.

race *n.*[2] [20C+] (*Ulster*) a short visit or journey. [16C SE *race*, a journey]

racehorse *n.*[1] [1950s+] (*Aus./N.Z.*) **1** a very thin roll-up cigarette. **2** a thin pack. [SE *racehorse*, used to mean sleek and lean]

racehorse *n.*[2] [1960s+] (*US*) an up-market prostitute (cf. ALLEY CAT n.; BANBURY n.). [on pattern of THOROUGHBRED n. (6)]

racehorse charlie *n.* [1930s–70s] (*drugs*) **1** any narcotic drug. **2** a morphine user. [var. on HORSE n.[8]; although note CHARLIE n.[9]]

race man *n.* (*also* **race woman**) [1920s–60s] (*US*) a culturally conscious Black person, esp. one who advocates Black civil rights. [i.e. one who is conscious of their SE *race*]

race off *v.* (*also* **whiz(z) off**) [1940s+] (*Aus.*) to seduce, to go off with a woman in the hope of achieving seduction.

race one's motor *v.* (*also* **rev one's motor**) [1940s+] (*US*) to become over-excited.

race woman *n.* *see* RACE MAN n.

racial *adj.* [1940s] (*W.I.*) generous, open-handed. [i.e. characteristic of the Black race]

rack *n.*[1] [mid-19C+] (*Irish*) **1** coarse hair. **2** a comb. [Irish *raca*, a comb]

rack *n.*[2] [late 19C] (*US*) an omnibus.

rack *n.*[3] [1930s+] (*US*) the female breasts, esp. when large and firm. [note RACKS (OF MEAT) n.]

rack *n.*[4] [1940s+] (*orig. US milit.*) a bed; thus *hit the rack*, to go to bed; *rack time*, sleep, a nap.

rack *n.*[5] [1970s+] (*US Black*) a card holding bubble-packed birth control pills.

rack *n.*[6] **1** [1970s+] (*US drugs*) a quantity of drugs, e.g. pills, vials of crack etc. **2** [2000s] (*US Black*) of money, a large quantity.

rack *v.*[1] [mid-19C+] (*Irish*) to comb. [RACK n.[1]]

rack *v.*[2] **1** [1940s–60s] (*orig. US Black*) to go to sleep. **2** [1950s+] (*US*) to sleep; thus *racked out*, asleep. **3** [1950s+] (*also* **rack with**) to seduce a woman, to make love; thus *rack-date*, a seducible woman. [RACK n.[4]]

rack *v.*[3] [1980s+] (*UK juv.*) **1** to admonish. **2** to kick in the testicles.

rackaback *n.* [late 18C–early 19C] a man on horseback with a woman behind him riding side-saddle. [for Grose's explanation, *see* GORMAGON n.]

rackabone *n.* *see* RACK OF BONES n.

rack attack *n.* [1970s+] (*US campus*) a sudden onset of sleepiness. [RACK n.[4] + SE *attack*]

rack back *v.* *see* RACK UP v.[3] (1).

racked *adj.* [1960s+] tired out, exhausted. [RACK n.[4]]

racked up *adj.* [1950s] neat, smartly turned out. [pool/snooker jargon *rack up*, to place the balls in order preparatory to a game]

racker(bone) *n.* *see* RACK OF BONES n.

racket *n.*[1] **1** [early 19C+] any form of deception, criminal trickery, hoaxing. **2** [late 19C] a theory, an idea. **3** [late 19C+] a job, an occupation, not necessarily illegal. **4** [late 19C+] a story, a 'line'. **5** [1900s–20s] (*US*) a plan, a scheme. **6** [1920s] in weak use, any form of activity. **7** [1920s] (*US*) an easy job or situation, esp. a sinecure. **8** [1920s+] (*US*) as *the rackets*, organized crime. **9** [1960s] (*US*) as *the racket*, prostitution.

racket *n.*[2] (*US*) **1** [late 19C+] an organized social event, designed to make money for the sponsor. **2** [20C+] a large party; thus (*Aus.*) *on the racket*, on a spree. **3** [1910s–60s] an organized dance, held in a dancehall and frequented by working-class young people. [SE *racket*, a noise, a disturbance; SAmE *racket*, a type of waltz]

racket *sfx* [late 19C+] a combining form, used with a defining n. to indicate a particular job or occupation, often but not necessarily illegal. [RACKET n.[1] (3)]

racketeer *n.* [1920s+] (*US*) a member of an organized crime syndicate, a criminal. [RACKET n.[1] (8)]

racketeer *v.* [1920s+] to practise any form of criminal deception, trickery, extortion etc; thus *racketeering*. [RACKETEER n.]

racket jacket *n.* [1930s–40s] (*US Black*) a ZOOT SUIT n. [SE *racket*, a noise + *jacket*; in visual terms it 'makes a noise']

racket man *n.* **1** [mid-19C] a thief. **2** [1930s+] (*US*) (*also* **racket ghee/guy**) a member of an organized crime syndicate. [RACKET n.[1] + SE *man*]

rackety *adj.* [mid-late 19C] insalubrious. [RACKET n.[1] (1) + ? pun on SE *racket*, noise]

rack (it) *v.* [1940s] (*US campus*) to work hard. [SE *book rack*]

rack man *n.* [1930s+] an official in a crap game who deals with making change, paying winners etc. [he deals with the *racks* of coins]

rack monster *n.* (*US campus*) **1** [1960s+] (*also* **pad monster**) sleepiness, the result either of boredom or exhaustion. **2** [1980s+] a bed. [RACK n.[4]/PAD n.[2] (1) + SE *monster*; note RMC Duntroon (*Aus.*) *rack monster*, 'a cadet with a reputation for sleeping excessively']

rack of bones *n.* (*also* **rackabone, racker, rackerbone, rack-o'-bones**) [early 19C–1940s] (*US*) a skeleton, an emaciated person or animal.

rack off *v.* [19C] to urinate. [wine trade jargon *rack off*, to draw off liquor from the lees]

rack off! *excl.* [1970s+] (*Aus.*) go away! be off! [SE *rack*, to move, to travel]

rack one's soul-case *v.* *see* BURST ONE'S SOUL-CASE v.

rack out *v.* [1960s+] (*US*) to fall asleep, to go to bed. [RACK n.[4]]

rack pick *n.* [1960s+] (*US Black*) a comb designed spec. for use on a NATURAL n.[5] or an AFRO n.[2] hairstyle. [SE *rack*, i.e. the widely spaced teeth resemble objects hanging from a rack + *pick*, a pronged instrument]

racks (of meat) *n.* [20C+] the female breasts (cf. BRACE AND BITS n.). [rhy. sl. = *teat*/TIT n.[3] (1) but note RACK n.[3]]

rack up *v.*[1] **1** [mid-19C; 1960s+] to go to bed. **2** [1940s–70s] to retire, to abandon an occupation or action. [(2) pool imagery, one puts one's cue in the *rack*; (1) presumably similar, the idea of putting oneself 'on the rack'; the link to RACK n.[4] is coincidental]

rack up v.[2] [1950s+] (US) to damage, to wreck, to harm. [SE *rack*, to strain, to stretch]

rack up v.[3] 1 [1960s+] (US) (also **rack back**) to accumulate, to register, to achieve. 2 [1990s+] (*drugs*) to cut up lines of a narcotic, usu. cocaine. [the *racking up* of pool balls before a game]

rack with v. see RACK v.[2] (3).

raclan n. [mid-19C] (*UK tramp*) a married woman. [Rom. *rakli*, a girl]

rad n.[1] [mid–19C+] a radical. [abbr.]

rad n.[2] [1980s+] (*UK Black*) a policeman, usu. in pl. [abbr. RADICATION n.]

rad adj. (also **rad-o**) [1980s+] (*orig. US teen*) a general intensifier, extreme, excessive, very much, excellent, best. [abbr. RADICAL adj.]

Rada n. see RADO n.

radar! excl. [1990s+] (*US drugs/teen*) a cry of warning at the arrival of the police.

raddie n. 1 [20C+] an Italian living in London, orig. spec. in Clerkenwell EC1 (cf. DAGO n.). 2 [1930s+] a radical. [(1) ? image of Italians as anarchistic, i.e. SE *radical*]

raddled adj. [late 17C+] drunk. [play on SE]

radge n. [1990s+] 1 (also **radgehead, radgy**) a psychotic person. 2 a temper tantrum. [orig. northern dial.; ult. SE *rage*]

radge adj. (also **radgy**) [1990s+] 1 of a person or situation, mad, furious, insane. 2 of an idea or situation, foolish, absurd. 3 in fig. use, 'crazy', i.e. wonderful. [RADGE n. (1)]

radge v. [1990s+] to lose one's temper. [RADGE n. (1)]

radical n. [mid-19C] roasted corn. [so called from its being the favourite breakfast of the *radical* Henry 'Orator' Hunt (1773–1835)]

radical adj. [1970s+] (*US campus*) a term of utmost approval. [SE use of *radical* as basic, essential, from the roots and eschewing political overtones; like a number of other terms, the word moved from surfer jargon to 'Valley Girls' use and thence, via the *Teenage Mutant Ninja Turtles* craze, to general use]

radication n. (also **radics, radix**) [1970s–80s] (*UK Black*) the police. [SE *eradication*; the Metropolitan Police's violent and racist attitude towards Black youth]

radio! excl. [1960s+] (*US prison*) be quiet! stop that! [the 2-way radios carried by guards; the term initially used to warn of an approaching *radio* or guard, widened into a general imper.; ? also the imper. 'Shut up and listen to the radio!']

radio ham n. see HAM n.[4].

radio (rental) adj. [1960s+] insane, mad (cf. COCK-SPARROW adj.). [rhy. sl. = MENTAL adj. (1)]

radish n. [late 19C–1900s] the penis (cf. BANANA n.[2]).

radishes! excl. [1970s+] (*US campus*) a general excl. of disgust and annoyance.

radix n. see RADICATION n.

radjy adj. [1930s] delightful. [? Scot.]

Rado n. (also **Rada**) [1970s+] (*US Black*) a Cadillac Eldorado. [abbr.]

rad-o adj. see RAD adj.

rael adv. see REAL adv.

r.a.f. adj. [1990s+] used of a very unattractive woman. [abbr. *rough as fuck*]

rafe n. (also **ralph**) [mid-19C] a pawnbroker's ticket. [? Suffolk dial. *rafe/ralph*, a fool]

raff n. [early–mid-19C] (*UK campus*) a vulgar, worthless person. [SE *riff-raff*]

Rafferty's rules n. (also **Rafferty rules**) [1920s+] (*Aus./N.Z.*) no rules whatsoever, anything goes. [despite use of capital 'R', which implies a proper name, the term comes f. mispron. of SE *refractory*; note Seal, *The Lingo* (1999): 'RAFFERTY'S RULES, meaning no rules at all, seems to be an Australianisation of a British dialect term for confusion or mess, RAFF or RAFFETY']

raffle coffin n. [19C] a ruffian, a villain. [SE *rifle-coffin*, a resurrectionist or grave-robber]

raffle ticket n. [1950s+] a mistake. [rhy. sl. = RICKET n.]

raff off v. [1980s] to leave, to go. [? var. NAFF OFF! excl.]

raft n.[1] [early 19C+] (US) a large number; a large amount.

raft n.[2] [20C+] (*Ulster*) a tall, thin person. [synon. Norw. dial. *raft*]

raft n.[3] [late 19C+] (US) a piece of toast.

rafter n. [1990s+] (US) a Cuban refugee who arrives in Florida after a journey on a raft.

rag n.[1] 1 [late 16C–1920s] money in general. 2 [late 17C–early 19C] a farthing. 3 [early 19C–1940s] a banknote, paper money; usu. in pl. (cf. BANK-RAG n.). 4 [mid-19C–1900s] (*US Und.*) in pl., counterfeit notes. 5 [1940s–50s] (*US Und.*) a confidence game based on stocks and shares. [SE *rag*, a small amount, ext. to a small and then any amount of money; thus (2) the minimally valuable farthing; (3) the early 19C introduction of banknotes adds secondary ref. to *rag*, a piece of cloth + note the use of rags in paper-making; (5) ext. of (3) to any paper monetary document]

rag n.[2] 1 [19C+] an article of clothing, esp. a dress; thus *raggery*, clothes; thus RAGS n. 2 [mid-19C–1910s] a theatre curtain. 3 [mid-19C+] a pocket handkerchief. 4 [1900s] (US) a flag. 5 [1900s] a towel. 6 [1910s] (US) a necktie. 7 [1920s] a wig. 8 [1950s] a baby's nappy. 9 [1960s+] a bandanna. 10 [1990s+] (*W.I./UK Black*) the semi-uniform clothes worn by a RAGAMUFFIN n. (3). 11 [1990s+] (*US Black*) a gang member.

rag n.[3] 1 [early 19C+] the tongue. 2 [mid-19C+] abuse, teasing, talk; usu. as *ragging*. [RED RAG n.[1]]

rag n.[4] 1 [late 19C+] a newspaper. 2 [1940s+] (*US Black*) a magazine. [derog. ref. to its worthlessness, but note the use of *rags* in paper-making]

rag n.[5] 1 [late 19C+] (US) a girlfriend, a female companion. 2 [1960s] (*US campus*) an unattractive woman. 3 [1970s] (*Aus.*) a promiscuous woman. [ety. unknown; ? derog. use of SE]

rag n.[6] 1 [20C+] (US) a playing card. 2 [1930s–40s] (*N.Z.*) a low playing card in a suit.

rag n.[7] [1910s] anything physically energetic, a party, a fight, a battle.

rag n.[8] 1 [1920s+] a sanitary towel; thus *ride the rag*, to be menstruating. 2 [1990s+] a menstrual period. [RED RAG n.[2]]

rag n.[9] 1 [1960s] (*N.Z.*) a general derog. term for a man. 2 [1960s+] a fool. 3 [1970s+] (*US campus/teen*) an unpleasant person. [abbr. WET RAG n., but ? ult. 16C–19C SE *rag*, a derog. description of a person, a 'rag of a man']

rag n.[10] [1980s+] (US) a second-rate, run-down car.

rag n.[11] see DO-RAG n.

rag n.[12] see RAG TOP n. (3).

rag v.[1] 1 [mid-18C+] to scold, to talk severely to. 2 [19C+] to annoy, to tease (esp. in context of school or university). 3 [20C+] to attack, to cause trouble; in context, to rob. 4 [1900s] (*US campus*) to talk nonsense. 5 [1910s] to fight, to beat up. 6 [1910s] (*UK juv.*) to create disorder. 7 [1910s] to argue over a topic, to wrangle. 8 [1970s] (US) to gossip. 9 [1970s+] to complain. 10 [2000s] to question closely, to interrogate. [despite chronology, presumably RAG n.[3] (2) or ? abbr. BULLYRAG v.]

rag v.[2] [mid-19C] to share, esp. to divide up the proceeds of a crime; thus *go rags*, to share out. [? SE *rag*, to tear in pieces]

rag v.[3] [1900s–20s] (US) to play or dance to ragtime music. [abbr. SE *ragtime*]

rag v.[4] [1960s+] to menstruate. [RAG n.[8]]

rag v.[5] [1990s+] (*US Black*) to dress (fashionably). [RAG n.[2] (1)]

rag alley n. see RAG TRADE n. (2).

ragamofi n. (also **ragamorfi**) [1950s] (*W.I.*) ragged clothes. [SE *ragamuffin*]

ragamuffin n. (also **raga, ragga(muffin)**) [1990s+] 1 (*UK Black*) a hooligan, a lout. 2 (*US Black*) an unaffected, down-to-earth person. 3 (*W.I./UK Black*) a lover of modern dancehall reggae. [SE *ragamuffin*, orig. the name of a demon, latterly a ragged, dirty, disreputable man or boy; like a number of teen terms, this pej. is used as a term of approval]

ragamuffin tip *n.* [1990s+] (*US Black*) a down-to-earth situation. [RAGAMUFFIN n. (2) + TIP n.⁷]

rag and bone *n.* [1920s+] the lavatory (cf. ANGUS ARMANASCO n.). [rhy. sl. = THRONE n.]

rag-and-bone shop *n.* **1** [late 19C] a filthy, untidy room. **2** [1910s–20s] a decrepit old woman. [SE *rag-and-bone-shop*, a junk shop]

raga-raga *adj.* (*also* **ragga-ragga**) [1940s+] (*W.I.*) ragged, worn-out, usu. of clothes. [SE *rags, ragged*]

rag-ass *n.* [1990s+] (*US Black*) an impoverished person. [SE *rag* + -ASS sfx]

rag baby *n.*¹ [mid-19C] a dollar bill; a silver dollar. [? RAG n.¹ (1)]

rag baby *n.*² [20C+] (*US Black*) a poor, ill-clothed woman, who is nonetheless attractive.

rag bag *n.*¹ **1** [mid-19C+] a miscellaneous collection of anything. **2** [1940s] the lowest category of touring carnival.

rag bag *n.*² (*also* **rag doll**) **1** [late 19C+] a sloppily dressed woman, a slattern. **2** [1920s+] (*Aus./US*) a messy, unkempt person. **3** [1920s+] a general derog., the implication is of unkempt slovenliness. **4** [1990s+] a person who can be easily persuaded to give up sex or money. [play on SE; note also BAG n.⁴ (2)/DOLL n.¹ (2)]

rag box *n.* (*also* **rag shop**) **1** [late 19C] the mouth. **2** [1970s+] (*US Black*) in ext. use, the vagina. [RAG n.³ (1) + SE *box/shop*; (2) ? also RAG n.⁸ (1)]

rag carrier *n.* [late 18C–early 19C] an ensign, charged with carrying the flag. [RAG n.² (4) + SE *carrier*]

rag chewer *n.* [1900s] a story. [CHEW THE RAG v.]

rag chewing *n.* [late 19C+] (*US*) talking, esp. chatting or arguing. [CHEW THE RAG v.]

rag doll *n. see* RAG BAG n.².

rage *n.*¹ [late 18C+] the current fashion; esp. in phr. *all the rage*. [people 'go mad for' the item in question]

rage *n.*² [1970s+] (*Aus./N.Z.*) a noisy, exciting party; a good time.

rage *v.* [1970s+] (*Aus./N.Z./US campus*) **1** to have a great time. **2** to look fashionable. **3** to have sexual intercourse. [RAGE n.¹/RAGE n.²]

rager *n.* [1970s+] (*Aus./N.Z./US campus*) **1** a particularly good party. **2** (*also* **rage**) a person, or animal, known for wild behaviour. [RAGE v. (1)]

rag fair *n. see* RAG TRADE n. (2).

ragga(muffin) *n. see* RAGAMUFFIN n.

ragga-ragga *adj. see* RAGA-RAGA adj.

ragged *adj.* **1** [mid-18C] drunk (cf. ADDLED adj.). **2** [late 18C+] of person or object, second-rate, inferior. **3** [late 19C] of an era, unfortunate, ill-fated. **4** [1930s+] (*orig. Aus.*) nervy, out of sorts, 'under the weather', tired.

ragged-arse *n.* (*also* **ragg-arse, raggedy-arse/-pants**) [1930s] a disreputable, seedy, run-down person. [RAGGED-ARSED adj. (2)]

ragged-arsed *adj.* (*also* **ragg-arsed/-assed, raggedy-arsed/ -ass/-assed**) **1** [late 19C+] of clothes, tattered. **2** [late 19C+] of people, disreputable, seedy, run-down. **3** [1940s+] of things, worthless. [SE *ragged* + -ARSED sfx¹/-ASS sfx/-ASSED sfx]

ragged down (heavy) *adj.* (*also* **ragged out**) [1950s+] (*US Black*) exceptionally well-dressed. [RAG OUT v.¹ + HEAVY adv. (1)]

ragged out *adj.* **1** [1970s+] (*US campus*) tired out. **2** [2000s] (*US teen*) appalling, unattractive etc. [SE *ragged*/RAGGED adj. (4); (2) note RAG n.⁵ (2)]

ragged to the bone *phr. see* CLEAN TO THE BONE phr.

raggedy *adj.* (*also* **raggety, ragidy**) [1930s+] (*US Black*) run-down, second-rate, dilapidated; of emotions and objects.

raggedy android *n.* [1950s–60s] (*camp gay*) an unsuccessful and thus impoverished male prostitute. [play on *Raggedy Ann*, a children's doll + SE *android*]

raggedy Ann *n.* [1980s] (*US Black*) an untidy, unkempt woman. [*see* prev.]

raggedy-arse *n. see* RAGGED-ARSE n.

raggedy-arsed/-ass/-assed *adj. see* RAGGED-ARSED adj.

raggedy-ass ride *n.* [1950s+] (*US Black*) an old car, any form of motor vehicle that has become run-down and dilapidated. [RAGGED-ARSED adj. (3) + RIDE n.² (1)]

raggedy-pants *n. see* RAGGED-ARSE n.

ragger *n. see* RAG TOP n.

raggety *adj. see* RAGGEDY adj.

ragging *n.* [20C+] teasing, an act of teasing. [RAG v.¹ (2)]

rag gorger *n.* (*also* **rag gorgy**) [early 19C] a wealthy man. [RAG n.¹ (1) + Rom. *gorgio*, a (non-gypsy) man]

raggy *adj.* [late 19C–1900s; 1960s] irritated. [RAG v.¹ (2)]

raggy-arsed *adj.* [1990s+] (*Aus.*) very poor. [var. RAGGED-ARSED adj. (2)]

rag-head *n.*¹ **1** [20C+] (*US*) a gypsy. **2** [1920s] (*US*) a Hindu. **3** [1920s+] (*Aus./US*) an Arab native of the Middle East (cf. ABDUL n.). **4** [1920s+] (*UK/US*) a Sikh. [the cloth that each wears as a head-covering]

rag-head *n.*² (*US Black*) **1** [1960s+] one who wears a scarf or bandanna tied round their head. **2** [1980s+] anyone who is not absolutely up to date with current information, gossip, style etc. [the bandanna or DO-RAG n. worn by old ladies and latterly gang members]

rag house *n.* (*also* **cot house, rag shanty**) (*US*) **1** [mid-19C–1920s] a cheap rooming house or 'hotel', esp. in a town based on an oil-drilling camp. **2** [late 19C–1930s] a tent. [the canvas sides or roofs that such buildings often had]

ragidy *adj. see* RAGGEDY adj.

raging *adj.* **1** [late 19C+] a general intensifier; esp. in phr. *raging favourite*, a 'hot' favourite in racing. **2** [1980s+] (*US campus/teen*) of a party, of a drug, wild, fantastic, very enjoyable. [RAGE n.¹/SE *rage*; (2) RAGE v. (1)]

rag-mannered *adj.* [late 17C] aggressively uncouth, very badly mannered. [SE *rag* adj., a general derog. term]

ragman's coat *n.* [1990s+] the vagina, esp. with pronounced labia and substantial pubic hair.

rag mob *n.* [1960s] (*US Und.*) a team of confidence men working 'the rag', a trick based on persuading the victim that they can profit from a fixed stock swindle. [RAG n.¹ (5) + MOB n.² (3)]

rag on *v.* [1980s+] (*US*) to nag, to criticize. [RAG v.¹ (2)]

rag out *n.* [1970s] (*US campus*) a person who plays tricks; something unpleasant. [RAG OUT v.³ (2)]

rag out *v.*¹ [mid-19C; 1950s–70s] (*US*) to dress up, to wear one's best clothes. [RAGS n. (1); 20C use is mainly Black]

rag out *v.*² [1970s] (*US campus*) to become tired. [? RACK OUT v.]

rag out *v.*³ [1980s+] (*US/Can.*) **1** to be in a bad mood. **2** to abuse verbally. [ON THE RAG phr. (2)/RAG v.¹ (2)]

rags *n.* **1** [mid-19C+] (*orig. US*) clothes. **2** [1960s+] (*US Black*) stylish, fashionable clothes. **3** [1990s+] (*US Und.*) clothing and insignia that indicate one's membership of a prison gang. [RAG n.² (1)]

rags and bones *n.* [1970s] (*US Black*) the corpse of a poor person.

rags and jags *n.* [mid-19C–1900s] tattered clothing. [SE *rag* + *jag*, a shred of cloth, a rag]

rag shanty *n. see* RAG HOUSE n.

rag shop *n.*¹ [early–mid-19C] a bank; thus *rag-shop boss*, a banker; *rag-shop cove*, a banker, a cashier. [RAG n.¹ (1) + SHOP n.¹ (1)]

rag shop *n.*² *see* RAG BOX n.

rag splawdger *n.* (*also* **rag splawger**) [mid–late 19C] a wealthy man. [RAG n.¹ (1) + SPLODGER n.²]

rag stick *n.* [late 19C] an umbrella, esp. one that is not rolled up. [SE *rag*, a piece of cloth + *stick*]

rag top *n.* (*also* **ragger**) (*US*) **1** [1950s+] a car with a 'convertible' soft top. **2** [1970s] a truck that has an open back, which, when loaded, is covered with a tarpaulin. **3** [1970s+] (*also* **rag**) the car or truck's soft top.

rag trade *n.* **1** [mid-19C] the purchasing of counterfeit banknotes and the subseq. passing them off to innocent victims. **2** [mid-19C+] (*also* **rag alley/fair**) the garment industry. [RAG n.¹ (4)/SE *rag + trade*]

rag up *v.* [1900s] (*US Und.*) to dress oneself up. [RAG n.² (1)]

rag water *n.* [late 17C–early 19C] spirits, esp. gin. [the effect of over-indulgence, 'these liquors seldom failing to reduce those that drink them to rags' (Grose, 1796)]

ragweed *n.* (*drugs*) **1** [1960s+] inferior-quality marijuana (cf. AFRICAN BUSH n.). **2** [1980s+] heroin. [SE *rag + weed* n.¹ (4)/SE *ragweed*, a form of hardy weed, of the genus *Ambrosia*]

rag week *n.* [1980s+] the menstrual period. [RAG n.⁸ (1) + punning link to university *rag weeks*]

rah! *excl.* [2000s] (*UK Black*) a general excl., used for anger, surprise, amazement, approval, envy etc. [abbr. RAATID! excl.]

rah-rah *n.*¹ **1** [1940s–60s] (*US Black*) clothes fashionable among students in Black colleges. **2** [1990s+] (*US*) enthusiastic speech, a pep talk. [*rah! rah!* the stereotypical college yell]

rah-rah *n.*² **1** [1970s] (*US campus*) a sports enthusiast. **2** [1980s+] (*Aus.*) a fan of Rugby Union; thus the game itself. [(1) the encouraging cries of *rah! rah!*; (2) implying the educated, middle-class image of rugby union, i.e. the *rah-rah* accents of the fans]

rah-rah *n.*³ [1990s+] (*US prison*) a female inmate who fraternizes with the authorities. [RAH-RAH adj.]

rah-rah *adj.* [1910s+] **1** (*mainly US*) enthusiastic, excited, esp. in the context of college students cheering a team; thus *rah-rah boy/girl*, over-excited students; *rah-material*, a freshman. **2** upper-class, esp. British; thus *give someone the rah-rah*, to mock (on the grounds of supposed snobbishness). [(1) *rah! rah!* the stereotypical college yell; (2) a ref. to their accent; (1) used slightly disparagingly]

rahtid! *excl. see* RAATID! excl.

rahzoo *n. see* RAZOO n.¹.

raid the ice box *v.* [1970s+] to have intercourse with a corpse.

raifield *v.* (*also* **rayfield**) [1950s–70s] (*US Black*) to steal without concealment or regard for the consequence, to break the law in a contemptuous manner. [? dial. *raffle*, an idle vagabond]

rail *n.*¹ [1920s] (*US tramp*) an employee of a railroad.

rail *n.*² [1980s+] (*US drugs*) a thin line of a powdered narcotic. [such lines tend to be cut in a parallel pair, 1 per nostril]

railbird *n.* (*gambling*) **1** [late 19C+] a racetrack fan who stands next to the rails to get as near as possible to the racing. **2** [1940s+] a fan or spectator who crowds round the rails that surround a big game in a casino.

railings *n.* **1** [mid-19C–1910s] the ribs. **2** [1910s+] the teeth. [resemblance]

railroad *n.*¹ [mid-19C] (*US*) rough whisky. [? as drunk by railroad workers and tramps]

railroad *n.*² [late 19C+] (*US*) any arrest and allied criminal proceeding that ignores the facts, evidence, truth etc and concentrates on a speedy conviction, the guilt or innocence of the person notwithstanding. [RAILROAD v. (3) + image of the direct line from arrest to conviction, i.e. that of railroad tracks]

railroad *v.* **1** [mid-19C] (*US*) to enforce a mild punishment by dragging the victim up and down along the floor until the seat of their trousers is worn through. **2** [late 19C–1930s] to hurry or rush somewhere. **3** [late 19C+] (*US*) to arrest, try and convict without allowing the person concerned due process of law; to imprison on trumped up charges and faked evidence; to accelerate the legal process in order to ensure – through inadequate defence, legal knowledge etc – that a person will be found guilty and sentenced, even though their trial is ostensibly 'fair'. **4** [late 19C+] in general use of (3), to force somebody to do something, to rush something. **5** [1920s] (*US*) to throw someone out of a city or town (on the railroad). **6** [1970s] (*US campus*) to use influence in the pursuit of personal interests.

railroad bible *n.* [late 19C] (*US*) a pack of cards. [note Wink Martindale's country/pop hit 'Deck of Cards' (1959) in which the cards are reinterpreted along religious lines]

railroad dick *n. see* YARD BULL n. (1).

railroad Irish *n.* [1910s] (*US*) a generic for the Irish working class. [they live on 'the wrong side of the tracks']

railroad tracks *n.* [1970s+] (*drugs*) the scars that accompany repeated injections of narcotics into one's veins. [SE *railroad + tracks* n.²]

railroad weed *n.* [1970s] (*drugs*) marijuana (cf. AFRICAN BUSH n.). [SE *railroad + weed* n.¹ (4); ? it grows at the side of the tracks]

railroad whisky *n.* [1970s+] (*US Black*) cheap wine, esp. Santa Fe Tokay. [Santa Fe wine, based on the name of a US railroad]

railsplitter *n.* [mid-19C–1950s] (*US*) a farmer, an unsophisticated rustic (cf. ACORN-CRACKER n.).

rail up *adj.* [1970s–80s] (*UK Black*) angry. [SE *riled up*]

rain *n.* [mid-19C] (*UK Und.*) gin.

rain and pour *v.* [20C+] to snore. [rhy. sl.]

rainbow *n.*¹ [18C] a golden guinea (cf. BRASS n.¹). [it sparkles in the sun; E.P. suggests link to RHINO n.¹]

rainbow *n.*² **1** [early 19C] a large, discoloured bruise, gained through boxing. **2** [early 19C] a pattern book. **3** [early–mid-19C] a footman. **4** [early–mid-19C] a mistress. **5** [mid-19C] a young man about town. **6** [1950s] (*W.I.*) a tall, thin person. **7** [1970s+] (*US Black*) one who dresses in gaudy bad taste. [the colourfulness, usu. in context of clothes; (3) abbr. KNIGHT OF THE RAINBOW n.]

rainbow *n.*³ [1960s+] (*US drugs*) **1** Tuinal, a barbiturate (cf. BARBIT n.). **2** LSD (cf. A n.³). [(1) the colours that are one of its effects; (2) the colours of the capsule]

rainbow kiss *n.* [1990s+] (*US*) a passionate kiss, which follows an orgasm reached through reciprocal oral sex between a man and a menstruating woman, and thus involves mixing the semen and vaginal secretions/blood in the mouth. [SE *rainbow + kiss*]

rainbow necker *n.* [1990s+] a person who has oral sex with a women while she is menstruating. [SE *rainbow + NECK* v.¹]

rainbow queen *n.* [1970s+] **1** (*US Black/gay*) anyone who is involved in a Black/White sexual relationship. **2** (*US gay*) a homosexual man who prefers inter-racial sex and/or relationships. [SE *rainbow* (*coalition*), a campaign involving a variety of races + QUEEN n.² (1)/QUEEN sfx (2)]

rainbows *n.* [1960s+] (*drugs*) any form of pill (usu. the barbiturates Amytal and Seconal which have red-and-blue capsules) in a coloured jacket (cf. PILL n.⁴).

rain bullock sterks *v.* [20C+] to rain very hard. [Scot. *stirk*, a steer]

raincoat *n.* **1** [1930s+] a contraceptive sheath. **2** [1990s+] (*UK Und.*) an Ingram Mac-10 machine pistol. [(2) pun on SE *macintosh*]

rain curtain-rods *v. see* COME DOWN STAIR-RODS v.

rain Duke Georges *v.* (*also* **rain like a dunken dog**) [1930s+] (*N.Z.*) to rain heavily.

rainjuice *n.* [1950s] (*US*) water.

rain like a cow pissing on a flat rock *v.* (*also* **...a bull...**) [1950s+] (*US*) to rain heavily.

rainmaker *n.* [20C+] (*US*) an extremely successful member of a firm, often a lawyer, who commands high fees and is thus a lucrative asset to their employer; thus *rainmaking*, promoting trade.

rain napper *n.* [mid–late 19C] an umbrella. [SE *rain + NAP* v.² (1)]

rain on *v.* [1920s+] (*US*) **1** to kill. **2** to make suffer, to beat up, to lose one's temper with.

rain on someone's parade *v. see* PISS ON SOMEONE'S PARADE v.

rain stair-rods *v. see* COME DOWN STAIR-RODS v.

rainwater *n.* [1930s] (*US prison*) coffee.

rainy day woman *n.* [1960s] (*drugs*) marijuana. [ety. unknown; popularized and poss. coined by Bob Dylan in the song 'Rainy Day Women Nos. 12 and 35' (1966)]

raise *n.*[1] **1** [early 19C; 1990s+] an opportunity to pick up some money, legal or otherwise; usu. as *make a raise*. **2** [mid-19C] (*UK Und.*) a substantial amount of (stolen) money. **3** [mid-19C+] a tip or monetary contribution, whether given voluntarily or extorted. **4** [late 19C+] an increase in salary or wages. **5** [1950s] (*UK Black*) robbery.

raise *n.*[2] [1940s+] (*US Black*) **1** an arm; thus *on your left raise*, on your left-hand side. **2** a pocket.

raise *n.*[3] [1970s+] (*US Black/campus*) one's parents. [SE *raise*, to rear]

raise *v.*[1] **1** [20C+] to obtain, to get hold of. **2** [1940s] (*US Und.*) to steal. **3** [1940s+] (*W.I.*) to get hold of some money (legally or otherwise). **4** [1960s] to put up bail for. [RAISE n.[1]/SE *raise money*]

raise *v.*[2] **1** [1940s–50s] (*US Und.*) to make a signal by raising one's hat. **2** [1950s] (*UK Und.*) to forge cheques. **3** [1960s] (*US Black*) to stop, to pause. **4** [1980s] (*US campus*) to have a good time.

raise *v.*[3] [1960s+] (*US*) **1** to go, to leave. **2** to escape, to get out of, to be released from prison. [SE *raise up/rise up*, to get up]

raise a breeze *v. see* KICK UP A BREEZE v.

raise a cloud *v.* [late 17C–mid-18C] to smoke a pipe of tobacco.

raise a kite *v.* [1940s] (*W.I.*) to grumble, to make a fuss.

raise an ants' nest *v.* [20C+] (*W.I.*) to make trouble, to foster an argument. [the effect on ants when one breaks open their nest]

raise blazes *v. see* RAISE HELL v.

raise Cain *v.* [mid-19C+] (*orig. US*) to cause as much trouble as one can. [Adam's wicked son, *Cain*, here used as synon. for *hell*, as in RAISE HELL v. (1)]

raise dust *v.* [1910s] (*US*) to hurry, to go quickly.

raise hair *v. see* HAIR n.[2].

raise hell *v.* (*also* **raise blazes**, ...**Hades**, ...**heck**) **1** [mid-19C+] (*orig. US*) to cause a good deal of trouble deliberately; to make a fuss. **2** [1920s+] to celebrate rowdily. **3** [1920s+] to castigate; sometimes intensified as *raise merry hell and put a shingle under it*; *raise hell and stick a prop under it*. [ext. of SE; earlier cits. invalidate the popular ety. crediting the phr. to a slogan, *Kansas should raise less corn and more hell*, attributed *c*.1896 to Mrs Mary Ellen Lease (1853–1933)]

raise her petticoats *v. see* GO UP HER PETTICOATS v.

raise Hob *v.* [1910s–40s] (*US*) to cause as much trouble as one can. [SE *raise* + SE *Hob*, the Devil]

raise jack *v. see* CUT UP JACK v.

raise-my-thoughts *n.* [1900s] (*W.I.*) a drink of rum. [its effects]

raise Ned *v.* (*also* **raise merry Ned**, ...**old Harry**, ...**old Ned**, ...**promiscuous Ned**) [mid-19C+] to cause a disturbance, to make trouble. [SE *raise* + NED n.]

raise old Scratch *v. see* OLD SCRATCH n.

raise sand *v.* **1** [late 19C+] (*US*) to cause a stir, a commotion. **2** [1920s] (*US Black*) to have a good time. **3** [1930s+] to complain. **4** [1980s] (*US Und.*) to fight. [image of kicking sand in someone's face or blowing up a sand storm]

raise shit *v.* [1990s+] (*US*) to cause trouble, to make a fuss.

raise the ante *v. see* UP THE ANTE v.

raise the breezes *v. see* RAISE THE WIND v. (1).

raise the colour *v.* [mid-late 19C] (*Aus.*) to discover gold. [the *colour* being gold; 20C+ use is historical]

raise the down *v.* [early 19C] (*Scot. Und.*) to give the alarm.

raise the flag *v. see* FLY THE FLAG v.[2] (1).

raise the roof *v.* (*also* **take/tear the roof off**) [mid-19C+] to cause an uproar, to make a great noise.

raise the wind *v.* **1** [late 18C+] (*also* **raise the breezes**, **whistle up a breeze**) to obtain money, to obtain a loan; thus *wind-raising*, obtaining a loan. **2** [late 19C–1920s] to create a rumour, to make up stories.

raise-up *n.* [1940s] (*US Und.*) an armed robbery or hold-up.

raise up *v.* **1** [1970s+] (*US Black*) to leave a place. **2** [1970s+] (*US prison*) to be given leave or parole to leave a prison. **3** [1990s+]

(*US Black teen*) to get out of the way. **4** [1990s+] (*US Black*) to prepare oneself, e.g. for a fight.

raisin *n.* [1970s–80s] (*US*) a derog. term for a Black person (cf. BLACKBELLY n.).

raisin bag *n.* [1990s+] (*Can.*) the scrotum (cf. BALL-BAG n.). [BAG n.[1] (1); play on NUTSACK n. (1)]

raisin-brain *n.* [1990s+] (*US Black*) a fool, a term of abuse (cf. APPLEHEAD n.; BAKEBRAIN n.).

raj *n.* [1940s+] (*W.I.*) a villain, a trickster. [? SE *rogue*]

Rajah, the *n.* [mid-late 19C] the Mogul, a well-known centre of entertainment on Drury Lane, London WC2.

rajah *n.* [1940s+] (*N.Z.*) an erection. [ety. unknown]

raj-ma-taj *n. see* RAZZMATAZZ n. (1).

rake *n.*[1] [mid-19C+] a comb.

rake *n.*[2] [1950s] (*W.I.*) **1** a hunch. **2** any form of trickiness, e.g. a duplicitous answer that hides the true situation. [SE *rake*, an implement used for smoothing over soil]

rake *n.*[3] [1950s] (*W.I.*) a piece of gossip. [SE *rake up*, a fabrication, a concoction]

rake *n.*[4] [1960s+] (*Irish*) a large number. [Irish *reic*, lavish spending]

rake *n.*[5] *see* RAKE-OFF n. (1).

rake *v.*[1] **1** [late 17C–18C] of a man, to have sexual intercourse. **2** [18C–19C] (*also* **come upon the rake**) to live in a rakish manner. [SE *rake*, 'a man of loose habits and immoral character; an idle dissipated man of fashion' (*OED*)]

rake *v.*[2] **1** [mid-19C] (*UK Und.*) to divide (loot). **2** [1960s] (*Scot.*) to search.

rake *v.*[3] [1910s] (*Irish*) to comb. [RAKE n.[1]]

rake *v.*[4] *see* RAKE (IT) IN v.

raked *adj.* [1980s+] (*US campus*) **1** humiliated. **2** emotionally or intellectually exhausted. **3** having suffered an horrific experience. **4** having lost in a competition. **5** drunk (cf. ANNIHILATED adj.). [all SE phr. *raked over the coals*]

rake down *v.* [mid-19C+] (*orig. US*) to win money at gambling, esp. cards. [? the croupier's *rake* at a casino]

rake-in *n. see* RAKE-OFF n. (1).

rake (it) in *v.* (*also* **rake**, **rake together**, **rake up**) [mid-19C+] to make a great deal of money.

rake jakes *n.* [18C] a villain. [SE *rake* + JAKES n.; lit. 'clean out the privy'; play on SE *rake-kennel*, a scavenger]

rake-off *n.* **1** [late 19C+] (*orig. US*) (*also* **rake**, **rake-in**) a commission, esp. on some form of illegal deal. **2** [20C+] a profit. [the croupier's *rake* in a casino]

rake on *v.* [1980s+] (*US campus*) to humiliate, to criticize.

rake-out *n.* [late 19C–1900s] a pipeful of tobacco. [SE *rake out*, to clean out, e.g. a boiler, a grate]

rake out *v.* [late 19C] of a man, to have sexual intercourse. [ext. of RAKE v.[1] (1)]

raker *n.*[1] [mid-19C] a comb.

raker *n.*[2] [mid-late 19C] **1** a heavy bet. **2** a very fast pace. [SE *rake*, a 'fast' man about town]

rake together *v. see* RAKE (IT) IN v.

rake-up *n.* [1940s] a hand-rolled cigarette. [one 'rakes up' the tobacco]

rake up *v. see* RAKE (IT) IN v.

rake up the persimmons *v.* (*also* **knock persimmons**) [mid-19C–1900s] to succeed, to win, to make a profit.

raleigh bike *n.* (*also* **village bike**) [1950s+] a lesbian. [rhy. sl. = DYKE n.; ult. the popular UK bicycle maker *Raleigh*]

rally *v.* [1960s+] (*US campus*) to have a good time; to act utterly madly, drunkenly, obstreperously. [? SAmE *pep rally*; but note 18C SE *rally*, to banter with, to tease with pleasantry]

rally up *n.* [1960s] (*Aus. prison*) a prison riot.

ralph *n.*[1] **1** [mid-late 17C; 1920s] a country bumpkin, a simpleton (cf. ALVIN n.). **2** [1950s–60s] (*camp gay*) an effeminate, timid or plain and undistinguished man. [stereotyping of *Ralph* as a (1) peasant, (2) 'sissy' name]

ralph n.² see RAFE n.

ralph n.³ [1980s] (US campus) the penis. [so-called in Judy Blume's teenage novel *Forever* (1975)]

ralph v. (also **bob, rolf**) [1960s+] (US campus) to vomit (cf. BARF v.; CALL CHARLES v.). [echoic; note RMC Duntroon (Aus.) *ralf*, a drink that causes one to vomit]

ralphie n. see REGGIE n.².

Ralph Lynn n. [1920s–40s] gin. [rhy. sl.; ult. UK actor *Ralph Lynn* (1882–1964), best known in the Ben Travers farces of the 1920s]

ralph spooner n. [late 17C–early 19C] a fool (cf. BEN n.¹). [Suffolk dial.]

ram n.¹ **1** [early 17C–1900s] a penis. **2** [mid-17C+] a virile and/or promiscuous man; often as OLD RAM n. **3** [1980s+] an act of sexual intercourse. [animal imagery]

ram n.² **1** [mid-19C] (US campus) a practical joke. **2** [1950s] (US) something unpleasant.

ram n.³ [1940s+] (Aus.) a trickster's confederate who encourages the public to lose their money in a con-game. [RAMP v.² (2) + image of the animal's horns, pushing at the victim]

ram n.⁴ [1980s+] (drugs) alkyl nitrites. [ety. unknown]

ram adj. (also **rammed, ram up**) [1980s+] (UK Black) full. [SE *ram*, to force]

ram v.¹ [17C; mid-19C+] to have sexual intercourse. [RAM n.¹ (1)]

ram v.² [1950s+] (Aus.) to work as a confidence trickster's accomplice. [RAM n.³]

ram! excl. [mid-19C; 1930s+] a euph. for DAMN! excl.; thus **rammed, DAMNED** adj. [orig. Irish/Kent dial.]

rama n. [1970s] (drugs) marijuana. [Sp. *rama*, a branch]

-rama sfx see -ORAMA sfx.

ram and dam n. (also **ram and damn**) [mid–late 19C] a muzzle-loading gun. [one *rams* in the charge and *damns* the target]

ramasammy n. see RAMSAMMY n.

ramatracks n. [20C+] (Ulster) purposeless wandering. [? SE *ramble + track*; Share suggests 'nonce-wd.' but note Shetlands Islands dial. *rammattrack*, a rabble]

ram, bam, thank you ma'am phr. see WHAM BAM, THANK YOU MA'AM phr.

ramble v. [early 17C–mid-19C] to go out looking for sex.

rambler n.¹ [early 17C–early 19C] a person who goes out looking for sex. [RAMBLE v.]

rambler n.² (also **rambler wolf**) [1910s–60s] (US tramp) a tramp who travels on passenger trains.

rambling adj. [1920s+] (US tramp) fast, e.g. a *rambling freight*.

rambustious adj. see RUMBUSTIOUS adj.

ram cat n. (also **ram-cat cove**) [mid–late 19C] a man wearing furs. [SE *ram–cat*, a tomcat + COVE n. (1)]

Ram Chundur n. (also **Chunder**) [1900s–10s] (Aus.) a generic for any Indian (Hindu) immigrant. [stereotypical Hindu name]

ramfeezled adj. [late 19C] exhausted. [Scot.]

ram it! excl.¹ [1930s+] (orig. US) an excl. of dismissal, GO TO HELL! excl.; occas. ext. by ...*up your arse/ass*.

ram it! excl.² [1980s+] (UK Black) an expression of praise, encouragement.

ramjam n. [1970s–80s] (UK Black) a crowd.

ram jam v. **1** [late 19C+] to stuff with food. **2** [1970s–80s] (UK Black) to fill up, to cram.

ram-jam full adj. [late 19C] completely full. [RAM JAM v.]

rammaged adj. [18C] drunk. [SE *ramage*, wildness, high spirits]

rammed adj. see RAM adj.

rammer n. **1** [late 17C+] (also **cunt-rammer**) the penis. **2** [late 18C–19C] (UK Und.) the arm. **3** [mid-19C] the leg. **4** [1970s+] (US gay) an enthusiastic, energetic copulator.

rammies n. **1** [1910s–60s] (Aus./S.Afr.) trousers. **2** [1950s] knickers. [Malay *rami*, a Chinese and East Indian plant of the nettle family (*Boehmeria nivea*); thus the fine fibre of this plant, extensively employed in weaving]

ramming adj. [early 19C] forcible, 'go-ahead'.

rammish adj. (also **rammy**) [mid-17C–early 19C] of either gender, sexually enthusiastic. [RAM n.¹ (2)]

rammy n. [1920s+] (Scot. juv.) a fight. [SE *rampant*/Scot. *rammish*, violent, untamed]

rammy adj.¹ **1** [1950s–70s] (US prison) suffering from delirium tremens. **2** [1960s] (US) drunk (cf. ADDLED adj.). **3** [1970s] (US) eccentric.

rammy adj.² see RAMMISH adj.

rammy rousers n. (also **ripsy rousers**) [20C+] (Aus.) trousers. [rhy. sl. + link to RAMMIES n. (1)]

ramp n.¹ [mid-15C–19C] a high-spirited, independent woman, usu. synon. with a prostitute; thus *ramping*, high-spirited, promiscuous. [SE *rampant*, exhibiting fierceness or high spirits]

ramp n.² **1** [mid–late 19C] robbery with violence; thus *done for a ramp*, convicted of a violent crime. **2** [mid-19C+] any form of swindle or fraud. **3** [late 19C] a spree, a boisterous good time. **4** [late 19C–1910s] a racecourse swindler; thus ext. to any type of swindler. **5** [1980s+] (Aus.) a search. [RAMP v.²]

ramp n.³ [1930s+] a public house or its bar. [the long wooden bar]

ramp v.¹ [mid-16C–17C] of a woman, to act in a promiscuous manner; to work as a prostitute. [RAMP n.¹]

ramp v.² **1** [early–mid-19C] to rob with violence. **2** [early 19C–1900s] to swindle. **3** [late 19C] to force someone to pay their debts. **4** [1910s+] (Aus.) to search a prisoner and/or their cell. **5** [1930s+] (Aus./W.I.) to play around, lit. or fig. **6** [1980s] (UK Black) to tease, to banter, to trick. [20C+ use is UK Black; SE *ramp*, to act in a threatening manner]

rampacious adj. [mid-19C–1920s] crazy, eccentric. [SE *rampageous*, violent, unruly, boisterous]

rampallian n. [late 16C–early 19C] a ruffian, a scoundrel, a villain. [SE *ramp*, to act in a threatening manner]

ramped adj. [1990s+] (US campus) drunk. [SE *ramage*, high spirits or *rampage*, a state of boisterous excitement]

ramper n. **1** [early 19C] (UK prison) one who initiates a new prisoner by robbing them of their possessions. **2** [late 19C] a racehorse swindler. **3** [late 19C–1900s] a street thug, a hooligan. [RAMP v.²]

ramping adv. [early 19C–1910s] extremely, very much; esp. in phr. *ramping mad*, very drunk. [SE *rampant*]

ramps n. [1910s–20s] a faked-up argument or similar commotion intended to disguise a swindle or confidence trick. [RAMP n.² (2)]

rampsman n. [mid-19C] a robber with violence. [RAMP v.² (1)]

ramraid n. [1990s+] a method of stealing from shops whereby the thief steals a car, then drives at high speed into the shop-front, smashing its way through any defences; the car is filled with loot, then driven away. [RAMRAID v.]

ramraid v. [1990s+] to perform a RAMRAID n. [SE *ram + raid*]

ramraider n.¹ (also **ramrodder**) [1990s+] one who carries out a RAMRAID n. [RAMRAID v.]

ramraider n.² [1990s+] (UK drugs) amphetamine sulphate (cf. A n.²). [its harsh, immediate effect]

ramrod n. **1** [mid-18C+] the penis (cf. AX n.²; BAT n.⁷). **2** [mid-19C–1900s] a landlord. **3** [late 19C+] (also **rod**) a manager or leader, usu. a tough person or harsh disciplinarian. [fig. use SE *ramrod*, 'a rod used for ramming down the charge of a muzzle-loading fire-arm' (OED); (1) + ROD n.¹ (1)]

ramrod v. [1940s+] to be the boss, to run or lead, esp. in a tough or disciplinarian way; to act aggressively in pursuit of a project. [RAMROD n. (3)]

ramrodder n. see RAMRAIDER n.¹.

rams n. [20C+] delirium tremens. [ety. unknown]

ramsammy n. (also **ramasammy**) **1** [late 19C+] (orig. Indian Army) a generic name for any Hindu, esp. Indian coolies. **2** [1900s] a commotion, a riotous party. **3** [1900s] a fight, a family quarrel. [Hind. *Ramaswami*, Lord Rama]

ramscootrify v. [20C+] (*Ulster*) **1** to defeat verbally. **2** to beat up. [Scot. *ramscooter*, to induce panic]

ramsgate sands n. [20C+] the hands. [rhy. sl.; ult. *Ramsgate* (coastal town) Kent, UK]

ram-shackled adj. [1990s+] subjected to anal intercourse, usu. by a person with a large penis. [pun on SE *ramshackled*/RAM n.¹ (1) + SE *shackle*]

ram's horn n. [1910s–20s] someone who speaks very loudly; thus as adj., noisy.

ram skin n. [early 19C] (*Anglo-Irish*) a bailiff. [their willingness to take any and all possessions, even a *ram skin* mat]

ramsquaddle v. [mid-19C] (*US*) **1** to overcome, to 'use up'. **2** to drink heavily; thus as adj., drunk.

ram up adj. see RAM adj.

ram (up) v. [1970s–80s] (*UK Black*) to fill up, to crowd.

ranch v. [1990s+] (*US*) **1** to ejaculate. **2** to bring to orgasm, to make ejaculate. [? RAUNCH v.]

ranchy adj. [early 19C+] (*US*) dirty, disgusting, indecent. [? OED suggests var. on RAUNCHY adj., but impossible given cited chronology; ref. to a SE *ranch* and the conditions associated with it]

rancid adj.¹ [1900s] infatuated.

rancid adj.² [1980s+] (*US teen*) ugly, unattractive.

rancy-tancy adj. [1950s] (*Aus.*) fancy, refined. [rhy. sl.]

randal's man n. [mid-19C] a silk handkerchief with a green base and white spots. [its being favoured by the contemporary boxer Jack *Randal*]

randem tandem n. (*also* **random tandem**) [mid–late 19C] 3 horses driven in tandem.

r. & i. phr. [1980s+] (*US campus*) extremely exciting or enjoyable. [abbr. radical (i.e. RADICAL adj.) and intense]

randle n. [late 18C–19C] a set of nonsense verses that a schoolchild was forced to recite, to the accompaniment of pinching, hair-pulling and similar juv. tortures, if they were caught breaking wind in public; thus also as v. and *randling*, punishing a child in this way. [the verses varied as to the area. In Cumberland: 'The offender is seized by the ear or by the back hair, whilst the following is repeated "Rannel me! Rannel me! Grey goose egg / Let every man lift up a leg. / By the hee (high) by the low, by the buttocks of a crow; Fish, cock or hen." If "cock" was the reply then the other said, "Hit him a good knock" and did so. If "fish" was the answer, the other said, "Spit in his face".' (*EDD*)]

Randolph Scott n. [20C+] a spot. [rhy. sl.; ult. film star *Randolph Scott* (1903–87)]

random n. [1960s+] (*US campus*) a stranger; someone who does not fit in.

random adj. [1980s+] (*US campus/teen*) **1** ordinary, run-of-the-mill. **2** eccentric, bizarre, odd. **3** spontaneous, unexpected.

random joe n. [1980s+] (*US campus*) an unspecified person. [RANDOM adj. (1) + JOE n.¹ (2)]

random tandem n. see RANDEM TANDEM n.

r and r n. [1990s+] rape and robbery. [abbr. + play on US milit. *r and r*, rest and recreation]

randy adj. **1** [18C–mid-19C] violent, emotional. **2** [mid-19C+] sexually aroused, eager; also occas. in non-sexual use. [Scot. *randy*, wanton, lustful]

randy v. [late 19C] to make sexually excited. [RANDY adj. (2)]

randy-arsed adj. (*also* **randy-assed**) [late 19C+] sexually voracious. [RANDY adj. (2) + ARSE n.¹ (2)]

randyvoo n. **1** [late 19C] noise, arguments. **2** [1910s] (*Aus.*) a tavern. **3** [1940s] a sexual encounter. [(1) and (2) milit. jargon *randyvoo*, a tavern frequented by recruiting sergeants; (3) RANDY adj. (2); all ult. Fr. *rendezvous*, meeting (place)]

ranfla n. [1990s+] (*US*) a car that has been lowered and otherwise customized for teen use. [Sp.]

rangatang n. (*also* **ranggatan, rango**) [20C+] (*W.I.*) a belligerent, aggressive, coarse person. [SE *orang-utang*]

Range n. [2000s] a *Range* Rover. [abbr. brandname]

range n. [1910s+] (*Can./US prison*) the open area outside a row of cells.

range v. **1** [late 16C–early 18C] (*UK Und.*) (of either sex) to live promiscuously. **2** [late 17C] to live or work as a prostitute. [SE *range*, to wander around or RANGER n.]

ranger n. **1** [17C] the penis. **2** [17C] a prostitute. **3** [late 19C–1900s] (*Aus.*) a bushranger. [SE *ranger*, a wanderer; (1) and (2) + RANGE v.]

ranggatan n. see RANGATANG n.

ranging adj. [mid-17C–early 19C] of a man, pursuing women, philandering. [RANGE v. (1)]

Rangitoto yank(ee) n. [1980s+] (*N.Z.*) a derog. term for an Aucklander. [*Rangitoto*, an island in Auckland harbour + YANK n., i.e. the supposedly Americanized city]

rango n. see RANGATANG n.

rangoon n.¹ (*also* **rangood**) [1960s] (*drugs*) marijuana grown wild. [ety. unknown; ? wild marijuana is common in *Rangoon*]

rangoon n.² [1960s+] a prune. [rhy. sl.]

Rangoon runs n. [1940s+] diarrhoea, esp. contracted on foreign holidays (cf. AZTEC HOP n.). [proper name *Rangoon* + RUNS, THE n.]

ranikaboo n. see RANNYGAZOO n.

rank n.¹ [1920s–60s] (*US Und.*) a failed crime, esp. when foiled by the authorities; thus *in the rank*, arrested, captured while committing a crime. [RANK v.² (1)]

rank n.² [1990s+] (*W.I./UK Black*) a criminal, a gangster.

rank adj.¹ **1** [mid-18C+] (*also* **rank-ass**) second-rate, inferior, disgusting. **2** [20C+] (*W.I.*) impertinent, extremely cheeky. [ext. uses of SE *rank*, (1) rancid, strong-smelling, rotten (usu. of meat); (2) grossly coarse or indecent]

rank adj.² [1970s+] (*UK Black*) excellent, first-rate, admirable. [SE *rank*, stout, strong]

rank v.¹ **1** [mid-19C] to cheat. **2** [1920s–60s] (*US*) to catch in the act of committing a crime. **3** [1920s+] (*US*) to betray, to let down. [SE *rankle* or dial. *rank*, to lead a dissipated life]

rank v.² **1** [1920s–40s] (*US Und.*) to fail, esp. in the commission of a crime. **2** [1930s+] (*US*) to disdain, to disparage. **3** [1930s+] to lower; to lose status or job seniority. **4** [1930s+] (*orig. US Black*) to cause problems for another person's plans or actions. **5** [1950s+] (*also* **rank on/out**) to insult, often by ritual insults directed at the other person's mother. [RANK adj.¹ + SE *rank*, to assign a rank, in this case low and thus to put someone 'in their place']

rank and ritches n. (*also* **rank and riches**) [late 19C] trousers, breeches. [rhy. sl.]

rank and smell n. [late 19C] a common person. [a pun on SE *rank*, (high) class and *swell*]

rank-ass adj. see RANK adj.¹ (1).

ranked adj. [1990s+] (*US campus*) drunk. [? RANK adj.¹ (1), thus play on STINKING adj.² (1)]

ranker n. [mid-19C] an absolute idiot. [abbr. SE *rank* + DUFFER n.² (1)]

ranking n. [1960s+] (*US Black*) the act of insulting, usu. one's family and esp. one's mother. [RANK v.² (5)]

rank mouth n. see MOUTH n.¹ (2).

rank needle n. see NEEDLE n.².

rank on v. see RANK v.² (5).

rank out v.¹ [1980s+] (*US Black*) to beg for help, to surrender to pressure, to behave badly or weakly. [RANK v.² (4) + *out*, i.e. to abandon one's aggressive posture (on model of COP OUT v.³ (2) etc)]

rank out v.² see RANK v.² (5).

rank outsider n. see OUTSIDER n. (1).

rank rider n. **1** [17C–early 19C] (*UK Und.*) a highwayman. **2** [late 17C] a jockey. [SE *rank rider*, a reckless rider; ult. Danish *rank*, upright, erect and thence proud, headstrong]

rank someone's game v. (*also* **rank someone's action, ...play, ...style**) [1930s+] (*US Black*) to obstruct deliberately another's sexual advances. [RANK v.² (4) + GAME n.² (3)/ACTION n. (4)/PLAY n.¹ (1)/SE *style*]

ranky dank *n.* [1960s–70s] (*US Black*) an unsophisticated, unworldly person. [? RINKY-DINK adj.² (2) + RANK adj.¹]

ranny *n. see* RAANY n.

rannygazoo *n.* (*also* **ranikaboo**) [late 19C+] nonsense; irrelevant, irritating activity. [ety. unknown; links to ? dial. *ranny*, rash, giddy + ? Fr. sl. *gazouiller*, to sing, to speak]

rant *n.* [mid-17C] a spree. [Scot./dial. *rant*, boisterous merry-making]

rant *v.* [late 19C] to take by violence. [RAMP v.² (1)]

rantallion *n.* [late 18C–early 19C] 'one whose scrotum is relaxed as to be longer than his penis' (Grose, 1785). [ety. unknown]

rantan *n.* **1** [mid-17C–mid-19C] a loud, banging noise. **2** [mid-19C+] a drinking bout, a spree, a riot. [echoic, but note SE *randan*, riotous behaviour; thus mid-19C SAmE *rantankerous*, 'a row, a drunken frolic, means given to quarrelling' (Schele de Vere, *Americanisms*, 1872)]

rantipole *n.* (*also* **rantipoll**) **1** [mid-17C–early 19C] sexual intercourse with the woman taking the superior position; thus *ride a rantipole*, to have intercourse in this position; also as adj., sexually ardent. **2** [late 17C–mid-19C] a 'rude, romping boy or girl' (Grose, 1785). **3** [18C–early 19C] a prostitute. [SE *rantipole*, a wild, abandoned woman]

rantum scantum *n.* **1** [mid-18C–early 19C] (*also* **rantie-tantie**) sexual intercourse; thus *play at rantum scantum*, to have sexual intercourse. **2** [late 18C–early 19C] a noisy argument. [redup. of SE *rant*, to lead a dissolute life, to be merry]

rap *n.¹* **1** [18C–early 19C] (*orig. Irish*) a counterfeit halfpenny, seen in 1700–50. **2** [mid-18C–1900s] a halfpenny; thus in US a cent; thus *not matter a rap*, not to matter whatsoever; NOT CARE A RAP (FOR) v.; NOT WORTH A RAP phr. **3** [late 19C] money in general. [Ger. penny engraved with an eagle that had been drawn so crudely that it was known as a *Rabe*, a raven. The coin was presumably introduced to Ireland by Ger. mercenaries]

rap *n.²* [mid-18C] the theft of a purse. [fig. use of SE *rap*, a blow, stroke]

rap *n.³* **1** [late 18C+] (*orig. US*) a rebuke, the blame; esp. in phr. TAKE THE RAP v. **2** [20C+] (*US*) an official complaint or reprimand; thus *rapper*, one who makes a complaint. **3** [1920s+] a lecture, a reprimand. **4** [1920s+] speech or conversation, esp. the spontaneous wise-cracking repartee of street life. **5** [1940s+] (*orig. US Black*) a 'line' used for seduction or picking up members of the opposite sex. **6** [1970s] the received opinion. **7** [1980s+] a set speech, e.g. that used by a street salesman. [fig. uses of SE *rap*, a blow; (4) adopted in 1960s by HIPPIE n.² (3)]

rap *n.⁴* **1** [mid-19C+] (*mainly US*) an arrest. **2** [late 19C–1900s] (*US*) confinement to an institution, other than a prison. **3** [20C+] a criminal charge. **4** [1910s] the identification of somebody as a murder target. **5** [1910s–60s] (*US*) an identification by the police. **6** [1920s+] (*US*) a jail sentence. **7** [1930s] (*US prison*) a 1-year sentence. **8** [1930s+] (*Aus.*) congratulations, a commendation, praise. **9** [1930s+] a situation. **10** [1990s+] (*US Und.*) a criminal speciality. [SE *rap*, a blow, a tap (on the shoulder)]

rap *n.⁵* [1970s+] a style of music with singing or chanting of the lyrics against a heavy bass line, usu. produced by a drum machine or synthesizer. [RAP v.⁵ (2); while the terms are often used interchangeably, *rap* gives more emphasis to the words, while HIP-HOP n. often features a more elaborate, even dominant backing track]

rap *v.¹* **1** [late 16C+] to curse. **2** [mid-18C–mid-19C] to swear (evidence) against someone or for someone. **3** [mid-18C–mid-19C] to swear a false oath, to perjure oneself. **4** [mid-19C] (*UK Und.*) to stand accused, to appear guilty. **5** [late 19C+] to attack verbally, to criticize, to say sharply. **6** [20C+] (*US*) to charge; to prosecute, to arrest with a view to prosecution. [SE *rap*, to hit]

rap *v.²* [late 17C–early 19C] to swap, to exchange, to barter. [? SE *rap*, to seize or snatch]

rap *v.³* **1** [mid-19C+] to inform, esp. to the police. **2** [late 19C+] to talk, to converse. **3** [1920s] (*US Und.*) to recognize. **4** [1940s] (*US*) to persuade, to trick out of. **5** [1950s+] (*Aus.*) (*also* **rap up, wrap (up)**) to praise, esp. to praise to excess. **6** [1960s+] to indulge in repartee or street-talk, to have a rapport with. **7** [1960s+] to have any form of impromptu dialogue. **8** [1970s+] (*US Black*) to talk with the aim of seduction. [SE *rap*, to hit; note synon. Yorks. dial.]

rap *v.⁴* [late 19C+] (*orig. Aus.*) to knock out, to kill. [SE *rap*, to knock]

rap *v.⁵* **1** [1960s+] (*US Black*) to speak lines in the DOZENS n. **2** [1970s+] (*orig. US Black*) to sing or chant a RAP n.⁵ song. [RAP v.³ (2)]

rap attack *n.* [1980s+] (*US Black*) extended, emotional, aggressive talk. [RAP v.⁵ (2) + SE *attack*]

rap buddy *n.* [1990s+] (*US Black*) a close friend. [RAP n.⁴ (1) + BUDDY n. (1), lit. a friend with whom one suffers an arrest]

rape *n.* [mid-19C] a pear. [backsl.]

rape *v.* (*US campus*) **1** [1970s] to abuse. **2** [1980s+] to diminish the effects of; to reduce someone's pleasure. **3** [1990s+] to misuse, to steal. **4** [1990s+] to defeat. [weak uses of SE]

rape artist *n.* (*also* **rape hound**) [1960s] a rapist. [SE *rape* + ARTIST sfx/HOUND sfx]

rape-o *n.* (*also* **rapo**) [1940s+] (*US Und.*) a rapist.

rape someone's buzz *v.* (*also* **step on someone's buzz**) [1980s+] (*US campus*) of a person or thing, to put a damper on someone's pleasure (cf. BUZZ CRUNCHER n.). [RAPE v. (2) + BUZZ n.³ (2)]

rape wagon *n.* [1960s] (*US*) a flashy car belonging to a pimp.

rap game *n.* [1990s+] (*US Black*) the ability to talk persuasively in pursuit of sexual conquests. [RAP n.³ (5) + GAME n.² (3)]

rap group *n.* [1960s–70s] (*US*) a discussion or encounter group. [RAP v.³ (2) + SE *group*]

rapid! *adj.* [1980s+] (*Irish*) a general term of approval, excellent! wonderful!

rapless *adj.* [late 19C–1900s] penniless. [RAP n.¹ (3)]

rap on the real *v.* [1980s+] (*US Black*) to speak sincerely, honestly. [RAP v.³ (2) + ON THE REAL phr.]

rap over the knuckles *n.* (*also* **rap on…**) [19C+] a scolding or reprimand.

rap parlor *n.* [1970s+] (*US*) a euph. for a massage parlour, itself a cover for a store-front organization behind which, while legitimate massage may be available, men pay for a variety of sexual services from 'relief' or 'executive' massage (masturbation) to full intercourse. [SAmE *rap parlor*, 'any establishment advertising, offering or selling the service of engaging in or listening to conversation, talk or discussion between an employee of the establishment and a customer, regardless of whether those other goods or services are also required to be licensed']

rap partner *n.* [1960s+] (*US Und.*) someone who is on the same charge sheet as oneself; someone who is jailed for the same crime. [RAP n.⁴ (3)]

rapper *n.¹* [late 17C–early 19C] a major lie. [SE *rap*, a blow]

rapper *n.²* **1** [late 18C–1900s] a professional perjurer. **2** [1900s–60s] (*US*) a plaintiff, a prosecutor. **3** [1920s–30s] (*US Und.*) an informer. **4** [1920s–40s] (*US Und.*) a judge. [RAP v.¹ (3)/RAP v.³]

rapper *n.³* [1940s] (*US*) one who takes or is given the blame for a crime, even if they are not actually guilty. [TAKE THE RAP v. (1)]

rapper *n.⁴* [1960s+] **1** (*US*) a chatterer, a talker. **2** (*US*) the voice. **3** (*US Black*) one who talks articulately and persuasively. [RAP v.³ (2)]

rapper *n.⁵* [1970s+] (*orig. US Black*) a practitioner or devotee of RAP n.⁵ music. [RAP n.⁵/RAP v.⁵ (2)]

rappie n. [1920s+] (*US prison*) a confederate. [both men have faced or would face the same charge or RAP n.⁴ (3); they would also talk or RAP v.³ (2) together when plotting]

rapping n.¹ [mid-18C–mid-19C] perjury. [RAP v.¹ (3)]

rapping n.² [1960s+] (*orig. US Black*) talking. [RAP v.³ (2)]

rapping n.³ [1980s+] (*orig. US Black*) performing RAP n.⁵ music. [RAP v.⁵]

rapping adj. [mid-19C] enormous, huge. [SE *rap*, a blow]

rap session n. [1970s+] an intense conversation; by ext., in new therapy use, an encounter group. [RAP v.³ (2)]

rap sheet n. [1950s+] (*US*) a criminal record. [RAP n.⁴ (1)]

rapt adj. [1960s+] (*Aus.*) **1** overjoyed with, carried away, delighted. **2** emotionally and/or sexually excited by. [SE *enraptured*]

raptavist n. (*also* **raptivist**) [1980s+] (*US Black*) a politically active rap artist. [RAP n.⁵ + SE *activist*]

rap to v. (*US*) **1** [late 19C] to own up to, to declare. **2** [1920s] to work out, to discover. [RAP v.³ (2)/RAP v.³ (3)]

rap up v. see RAP v.³ (5).

Raquel Welch n. [1960s+] a belch. [rhy. sl.; ult. film star *Raquel Welch* (b.1940)]

rare adj. **1** [late 16C–19C] a general term of approval, splendid, excellent, fine; also in ironic negative use. **2** [mid-18C+] an intensifier of a n., often as *rare and*, e.g. *a rare passion, rare and hungry*.

rare v. [1940s–70s] to inhale narcotics. [the injected drug must first be 'cooked']

rare as rocking horse manure phr. (*also* **rare as a pregnant nun, rare as fairies**) [1940s+] (*Aus.*) a phr. used of anything extremely rare.

rare-lapper n. see LAPPER n.¹.

rarse see under RAAS.

rarted adj. see RAATID adj.

rarzer/rarzo n. see RASPBERRY TART n. (2).

rascal n. [late 18C–early 19C] a man without genitals. [SE *rascal*, a young or inferior deer, whose antlers have yet to grow properly; Grose (1785) also suggests Ital. *rascaglione*, a eunuch]

rash v. [1990s+] (*US teen*) to go to a party.

rash act n. [1910s] (*Aus.*) suicide. [SE *rash*, foolhardy, precipitous]

rasher n. [1990s+] (*Irish*) the vagina, sexual intercourse; thus ext. as *rub of a rasher*. [ety. unknown; ? SE *rash* which results from rubbing or BACON SANDWICH n.]

rasher and a doorstep n. [late 19C] a rasher of bacon and a thick slice of bread. [SE *rasher* + DOORSTEP n.]

rasher and bubble n. [1970s] in darts, a 'double'. [rhy. sl.]

rasher and fingers n. [1930s] a rasher of bacon and chips. [the shape of the chips resembling fingers]

Rasherhouse n. [1990s+] (*Irish*) the Mountjoy women's prison (cf. ABBOTT'S PRIORY n.; BANDHOUSE n.). [RASHER n. + SE *house*]

rasher of bacon n. [mid-18C] a fiery drink. [ety. unknown]

rasher of wind n. [mid-19C–1940s] **1** a very thin person. **2** a weak, spineless person. **3** anything of little or no account.

rasher wagon n. [mid–late 19C] a frying pan. [it cooks SE *rashers* of bacon]

rashing n. [1970s] (*US Black*) an assault, violence. [SE *thrashing* + *harassing*]

rasp n. **1** [late 19C–1900s] the vagina. **2** [1940s–50s] a shave. [SE *rasp*, a file, that which rubs]

rasp v. [late 19C+] to have sexual intercourse. [SE *rasp*, to rub against; 20C+ use mainly Aus.]

raspberries! excl. [1910s–20s] (*US*) an excl. used to express disbelief or defiance. [RASPBERRY n.¹ (1)]

raspberry n.¹ (*also* **razzberry**) **1** [late 19C+] a coarse, dismissive, jeering noise; thus *blow a raspberry*, to make an obscene noise with one's lips, usu. intended to imply derision. **2** [1910s+] a rejection, dismissal; thus *give someone the raspberry*, to deride or dismiss, to escape from. [rhy. sl.; *raspberry tart* = FART n. (1), the noise of which this resembles]

raspberry n.² [1910s] the nose. [? one that is reddened from drink]

raspberry n.³ **1** [1960s–70s] (*drugs*) an abscessed injection site. **2** [1980s] (*US campus*) a bloody wound. [the resemblance to the fruit]

raspberry n.⁴ [1980s+] (*drugs*) a woman who trades sex for crack cocaine or money to buy the drug. [? var. on STRAWBERRY n.² (2) or pun on abbr. *raspberry tart*, i.e. TART n.¹ (2)]

raspberry n.⁵ see RASPBERRY (RIPPLE) n.

raspberry v. [1910s–40s] to deride, to dismiss. [RASPBERRY n.¹ (2)]

Raspberry-land n. [20C+] (*Aus.*) Tasmania; thus *Raspberry-landers*, Tasmanians. [? the raspberry is a common plant there]

raspberry (ripple) n. [1970s+] **1** a nipple. **2** a disabled person. [rhy. sl.; (2) = *cripple*; ult. a type of ice-cream]

raspberry tart n. (*also* **cherry tart, gooseberry…, strawberry…**) **1** [late 19C+] the heart. **2** [1950s+] (*also* **rarzer, rarzo, razzo**) an act of breaking wind; thus *let go a razzo*. [rhy. sl.; (2) = FART n. (1)]

rasper n. **1** [mid-19C+] a person or thing of an unpleasant character. **2** [mid-19C+] anything remarkable or extraordinary. **3** [20C+] a very noisy breaking of wind. [SE *rasp*, to rub roughly]

raspin n. [early 19C] a prison. [? Scot. *rasp-house*, ult. Du. *rasphuis*, house of correction in which prisoners were employed in rasping wood]

rasping gang n. [mid-19C] toughs and thieves who attend prize fights. [SE *rasp* or RASPIN n. + SE *gang*]

raspy adj. (*also* **rasty**) **1** [late 19C+] (*US Black*) unattractive, unkempt. **2** [2000s] (*US teen*) excellent, wonderful (by bad = good model). [SE *rasp*, to grate upon, to irritate]

rass see under RAAS and its combs.

rasta n. [2000s] (*US Black*) one who takes drugs obsessively. [the *Rasta*farian use of marijuana as a sacrament]

Rastus n. [late 19C+] **1** a derog. term for a Black man (cf. AFRICAN APE n.). **2** as a term of address. [popular mid-19C slave name *Erastus*; depending on context, as much patronizing as actively derog.]

rasty adj. see RASPY adj.

rat n.¹ [17C–mid-19C] a clergyman. ['Rats. Of these there are the following kinds, a black rat and a grey rat, a py-rat and a cu-rat' (Grose, 1788)]

rat n.² **1** [17C+] an unpleasant person. **2** [19C+] a person who changes allegiance out of self-interest. **3** [19C+] an informer. **4** [late 19C] (*US*) a worker who undercuts standards established by unionized labour. **5** [late 19C+] (*orig. Aus.*) a street urchin. **6** [20C+] a person, esp. an enthusiast. **7** [1900s] (*US Und.*) a thieving prisoner. **8** [1900s] (*Aus.*) a bus inspector. **9** [1940s] (*US*) the quality of being an informer. **10** [1970s] (*Aus. Und.*) an incompetent. [negative stereotyping]

rat n.³ [mid-17C–mid-19C] a drunken person who has been arrested and taken to the cells (cf. RAT CASTLE n.). [? phr. DRUNK AS A RAT phr.]

rat n.⁴ **1** [late 19C+] (*US*) a hair-pad with tapering ends used as the base of the elaborate pompadour hairstyles affected by women in the late 19C. **2** [1930s] (*US Black*) a wig. **3** [1990s+] pubic hair. **4** [1990s+] the vagina. [? the rat's fur and, in (1), its tail]

rat n.⁵ **1** [1910s] (*UK juv.*) a bad temper. **2** [1920s] (*Aus.*) a bout of madness. **3** [1920s] an obsession, an eccentricity. [RATTY adj.²]

rat n.⁶ **1** [1910s–50s] (*US Und.*) a train; thus *rat stand*, a railway station; *on the rats*, breaking into and stealing from freight cars. **2** [1940s+] (*US*) a near-derelict but just driveable second-hand car. [abbr. RATTLER n.¹ (3)]

rat n.⁷ **1** [1920s+] (*US/W.I.*) the lowest rank of prostitute. **2** [1990s+] (*US campus*) a promiscuous, attractive woman. [SE but note Fr. *rat*, a young woman, esp. a young ballet dancer between ages of 7–14, cited as a young prostitute in Balzac *A Harlot High and Low* (1839–47)]

rat *adj.* [1910s+] (*orig. US*) unpleasant, untrustworthy, generally despicable. [RAT n.² (1)]

rat *v.*¹ **1** [early 19C+] to betray one's own party or cause. **2** [early 19C+] (*also* **do a rat**) to change sides. **3** [1910s+] (*orig. US*) to inform on, to betray. [RAT n.² (2)/RAT n.² (3)]

rat *v.*² [1910s+] (*Aus./N.Z.*) to steal, to ransack; esp. as *ratted*, of people, robbed, or of objects, stolen. [note mining jargon *ratter*, one who steals one's finds]

rat *v.*³ [2000s] (*US Black*) to go out in pursuit of women. [RAT n.⁷ (2)]

rat *sfx* [1930s+] (*US*) constructed with a n. to indicate someone's habit or particular preference e.g. BAND RAT n., MALL RAT n., REEFER RAT n.

rat-and-fowl *n.* [1910s] (*Aus.*) an Aus. shilling. [? the images engraved upon it]

rat and mouse *n.* **1** [1910s+] a house. **2** [1970s+] an unpleasant person. [rhy. sl.; (2) = LOUSE n.]

rat around *v.* [20C+] (*US*) to loaf about, to idle.

rat-arse *n.* [1990s+] a drunkard. [backform. f. RAT-ARSED adj.]

rat-arsed *adj.* [1980s+] drunk (cf. ARSEHOLED adj.). [SE *rat* + -ASSED sfx; note PISSED AS A RAT phr.]

rat-ass *n.* [1950s+] (*US*) a general term of abuse; also as adj. [SE *rat* + -ASS sfx]

rat back clip *n.* [mid-19C] a short haircut. [the supposed similarity to a rat's fur]

ratbag *n.* **1** [late 19C; 1930s+] (*orig. Aus./N.Z.*) a general term of abuse, a rogue, an eccentric; thus *ratbaggery*, acting in such a manner. **2** [1960s] (*US*) an unpleasant situation or job. [SE *rat* + -BAG sfx]

ratbag *adj.* [1950s+] (*Aus.*) a general negative adj. [RATBAG n. (1)]

rat bastard *n.* [1920s+] (*orig. US*) a general term of abuse. [RAT n.² (1) + BASTARD n. (1)]

ratboy *n.* **1** [1980s] (*US drugs*) a street chemist, testing illicit drugs for purity. **2** [1990s+] a young boy exploited by a paedophile.

rat castle *n.* (*also* **rat's castle**) [early 18C] a prison, esp. the Poultry Counter, a prison in London (cf. HOLLOWAY CASTLE n.). [its population of vermin but note RAT n.³]

ratcatcher's daughter *n.* [20C+] water, as drunk rather than sailed or swum in. [rhy. sl.]

ratchet mouth *n.* (*also* **rachet jaw**) [1970s] a chatterer. [SE *ratchet*, a notched wheel used in a machine + *mouth/jaw*]

ratchet mouth *v.* (*also* **ratchet jaw**) [1970s+] to talk nonsense, to talk for the sake of hearing oneself talk. [RATCHET MOUTH n.]

rat crusher *n.* [1910–60s] (*US Und.*) a thief who specializes in robbing railroad boxcars. [RAT n.⁶ (1) + CRUSH v.¹ (2)]

rat-drawn *adj.* [1960s] (*US Black*) of shoes, pointed; such shoes were part of the pimp's 'uniform'. [? a rat's pointed nose]

rate *v.* [1910s+] **1** to assess positively, optimistically. **2** to deserve or merit, to be highly regarded.

ratepayers' hotel *n.* [1920s–30s] (*UK tramp*) a workhouse. [paid for by the ratepayers]

rat face *n.* [1910s+] (*orig. US*) a contemptible person, esp. if treacherous or cunning; also as a derog. term of address.

rat-faced *adj.* (*also* **rat-face**) [1910s+] a general term of abuse. [RAT FACE n.]

rat-factory *n. see* RATHOUSE n. (1).

rat fink *n.* [1960s+] an unpleasant person, with overtones of working as an informer. [RAT n.² (1) + FINK n. (4)]

rat fink *v.* [1980s+] (*US campus*) to play a practical joke on. [RAT FINK n.]

rat fuck *n.*¹ **1** [1920s+] (*US*) a general term of personal abuse. **2** [1970s+] (*US*) a synon. for DAMN n., e.g. *who gives a rat fuck*. **3** [1970s+] (*US campus*) a term of approval (on bad = good model). [SE *rat* + FUCK n.¹ (1); the rat is stereotyped as a 'bad' animal]

rat fuck *n.*² [1950s+] (*orig. US campus*) **1** a prank, a practical joke. **2** a difficult examination. [SE *rat* + FUCK n.¹ (1)/-FUCK sfx; note political jargon *rat fuck*, to sabotage an opponent's campaign by whatever means (usu. illegal) necessary; the orig. *rat fuckers* learned their trade in college politics and were later recruited to Richard Nixon's national campaign team; it was their techniques that would lead to Watergate]

rat fuck *v.* [1960s+] (*US, mainly campus*) **1** to blunder, to make a (stupid) mistake. **2** (*also* **r.f.**) to play a practical joke on someone, to outwit, to trick. **3** to break off a relationship. [RAT FUCK n.² (1)]

rat fucker *n.*¹ [1950s–60s] (*US campus*) a homemade tool, which approximates a car's starting-handle. [RAT n.⁶ (2) + FUCKER n. (7)]

rat fucker *n.*² [1960s+] a general term of dislike.

rat fucking *n.* (*also* **rat kissing**) [1920s+] (*US*) any form of destructive, negative activity, esp. on campus or in the forces. [RAT FUCK v. (2); SE *kiss* is euph.]

rather! *excl.* [mid-19C+] a general term of agreement, indeed! I agree! very much so! [later uses are historical or satirical]

rathers *n. see* DRUTHERS n.

rathole *n.* **1** [mid-19C+] (*orig. US*) a dirty or unpleasant place or room; occas. attrib. **2** [1940s] (*US Black*) a pocket.

rathole *v.* (*US*) **1** [1930s] to palm money during a gambling game. **2** [1970s] to hide away, to save up money, to hoard. [RATHOLE n.]

rathouse *n.* **1** [1920s+] (*Aus.*) (*also* **rat-factory**) a psychiatric institution. **2** [1980s+] (*Aus. prison*) a prison (cf. BANDHOUSE n.). [RATTY adj.²]

rat in *v. see* MAKE RAT v.

rations *n.* **1** [1930s] a cache of drugs. **2** [1930s–50s] (*drugs*) a dose or injection of drugs.

rat it! *excl. see* RAT ME! excl.

rat jacket *n.* [1970s+] (*US prison*) a reputation as an informer. [RAT n.² (3) + JACKET n.³ (2)]

rat-joint *n.*¹ [1910s] (*Aus.*) a psychiatric institution. [RATTY adj.² + JOINT n.⁴ (8)]

rat-joint *n.*² [1970s] (*US*) a second-rate, unpleasant establishment. [RATTY adj.¹ (1) + JOINT n.⁴ (3)]

rat kissing *n. see* RAT FUCKING n.

rat me! *excl.* (*also* **rat it!**) [late 17C–19C] a general excl. [SE *rot*]

rat muncher *n.* [1980s+] a general term of abuse. [lit. one who eats rats]

rat-off *n.* [1950s] a betrayal, an act of informing. [RAT OFF (ON) v.]

rat off (on) *v.* [1950s+] (*US*) to betray, to inform against. [RAT v.¹ (3)]

rat on *v.* [1910s+] to betray, whether as an informer, or morally and ethically. [RAT v.¹ (3)]

rat one's hair *v.* [1950s] to backcomb one's hair in order to create the once popular 'beehive' style. [the resulting style resembles a 'rat's nest']

rat out *v.*¹ [1910s+] to abandon one's responsibilities or friends, to betray someone or something. [RAT v.¹ (1)]

rat out *v.*² [1920s+] (*W.I.*) of a woman, to work as a prostitute. [RAT n.⁷ (1)]

rat pack *n.* [1950s+] (*US*) **1** a juvenile or prison gang (cf. WOLF PACK n.). **2** a group of sycophants, hangers-on. [best known of such gangs are Hollywood's *Holmby Hills Rat Pack*, whose members included not juveniles but such stars as Humphrey Bogart; and its successor, the *Rat Pack*, led by Frank Sinatra, Dean Martin et al. (which group had formerly been known as *The Clan*)]

rat pack *v.* [1960s+] (*orig. US prison*) to attack in a group. [RAT PACK n. (1)]

rat prick *n.* [1940s+] a general term of abuse. [SE *rat*/RAT n.² (1) + PRICK n. (3)]

rat-prick *adj.* [1970s] a general term of abuse. [RAT PRICK n.]

rat run *n.* (*also* **rat race**) [1920s+] any narrow passageway, back alley or relatively unknown short cut.

rats, the *n.* (*Aus.*) **1** [mid-19C–1920s] tetchiness, bad temper. **2** [1910s+] a hangover, delirium tremens; usu. as *in the rats*. **3** [1950s] mad. [GET RATS v.]

rats! *excl.* [late 19C+] (*orig. US*) a general excl. of disgust or disbelief.

rats and mice *n.* **1** [20C+] a dice game. **2** [1960s+] rice. [rhy. sl.]

rat's arse *n.* (*also* **rat's, rat's ass**) [1950s+] a general pej. implying anything bad or insignificant, small or trivial, e.g. *not worth a rat's ass.* [SE *rat* + ARSE n.¹]

rat's castle *n. see* RAT CASTLE n.

rat shagger *n.* [1980s+] a general term of abuse. [SE *rat* + SHAGGER n.¹ (1)]

ratshit *n.* (*also* **r.s.**) [1970s+] (*orig. US*) **1** a very unpleasant person. **2** rubbish, something annoying. [RATSHIT adj. (1)]

ratshit *adj.* (*also* **r.s.**) [1970s+] (*orig. Aus.*) **1** unpleasant, disgusting, annoying. **2** malfunctioning, useless. [SE *rat* + SHIT n.¹ (1)]

ratshit! *excl.* [1960s+] a general excl. of annoyance or distaste. [RATSHIT adj. (1)]

rats in the attic *phr.* (*also* **rats in the garret, …loft, …upper storey**) [mid-19C+] insane, mad (cf. APEY adj.; RATTY adj.²). [var. on HAVE BATS IN THE BELFRY v.]

rat's piss *n.* [2000s] weak beer (cf. BUFFALO PISS n.).

rat's tail *n.* **1** [early 18C; 1980s+] a pig-tail, as fashionable as a man's hairstyle. **2** [1920s–60s] (*US Black*) a straight-haired wig. [(1) the fashion – as part of the MULLET n.² – and thus the word, re-emerged in the 1980s]

rat stand *n. see* RAT n.⁶ (1).

ratta *n.* [1940s–50s] (*W.I.*) a bulging bicep. [dial. *ratta*, a rat, thus the supposed resemblance to a large rat]

ratta castle *n.* [1940s–50s] (*W.I.*) a run-down old house filled with idling inhabitants. [dial. *ratta*, a rat; ? link to the Anancy folktale in which Rat lives in a castle]

rat-tail *adj.* [19C+] a general term of disapproval, disdain.

rattat *n. see* RUTTAT n.

ratted *adj.* [1980s+] (*UK society*) drunk. [RAT-ARSED adj.]

ratter *n.* [1930s+] (*US*) an informer. [RAT v.¹ (3)]

rattle *n.¹* **1** [mid-17C+] the tongue, the voice; thus noise. **2** [early 18C] a dispute, a quarrel. **3** [late 19C] a person who talks a lot. **4** [late 19C] spirit, ebullience. **5** [1970s] (*US prison*) petty grievances.

rattle *n.²* [late 18C–early 19C] a dicebox.

rattle *n.³* **1** [late 18C–early 19C] a coach. **2** [mid-19C–1910s] money, cash; thus phr. *have a bit of rattle,* to be well-off (cf. CHING n.²). **3** [1960s+] an act of sexual intercourse.

rattle *n.⁴* [1930s–40s] an opportunity, a chance. [play on shake of the dice]

rattle *n.⁵* [2000s] (*UK drugs*) withdrawal from narcotics addiction. [the aches and pains that *rattle* the body]

rattle *v.¹* **1** [mid-17C+] to unnerve, to frighten. **2** [mid-17C+] to have sexual intercourse. **3** [20C+] (*Ulster*) to work energetically. **4** [1910s–20s] to hit someone; thus *rattle the ivories,* to hit someone in the teeth. **5** [1940s] (*US Und.*) to blackmail. **6** [1990s+] (*drugs*) to tremble, from heroin addiction.

rattle *v.²* **1** [late 17C+] (*also* **rattle along/away/off**) to leave, to move off, usu. quickly and noisily. **2** [mid-19C+] to move about, to act with energy.

rattle and clank *n.* [20C+] a bank. [rhy. sl.]

rattle and hiss *n.* [20C+] an act of urination (cf. ANGEL'S KISS n.). [rhy. sl. = PISS n. (2)]

rattle and jar *n.* [1920s+] (*US*) a car. [rhy. sl.]

rattle and pad *n.* [late 18C–early 19C] a coach and horses. [RATTLE n.³ (1) + PAD n.¹ (5)]

rattle away *v. see* RATTLE v.² (1).

rattle-belly-pop *n.* [late 19C] (*US*) whisky and lemonade. [the effect on the stomach + POP n.² (1); 'changed, when speaking to the more elegant sex, to "rattle-blank-pop"' (Ware)]

rattle bollocks *n.* [18C] the vagina. [SE *rattle* + BALLOCKS n.¹ (1)]

rattle-box *n.* **1** [1940s] a machinegun. **2** [1960s] (*Irish*) the male genitals.

rattle-brained *adj.* [18C+] mentally unstable, untrustworthy.

rattle-brain(s) *n. see* RATTLE-HEAD n.

rattle can *n.* [20C+] (*Ulster*) a noisy child.

rattle cap *n.* [mid-19C] a volatile, unsteady person. [SE *rattle* + *cap*, head]

rattled *adj.* [mid-19C+] **1** anxious, unnerved. **2** drunk (cf. ADDLED adj.).

rattle-head *n.* (*also* **rattle-brain(s), -pate, -skull**) [late 17C+] an excitable, foolish person, a fool. [RATTLE-HEADED adj.]

rattle-headed *adj.* [mid-17C+] foolish, chattering.

rattle off *v. see* RATTLE v.² (1).

rattle one's beads *v.* [1960s+] **1** (*mainly gay*) to complain. **2** (*US gay*) to gossip, to chatter. [BEADS n.²]

rattle one's dags *v.* [1960s+] (*Aus./N.Z.*) to hurry up, to get a move on. [SE *rattle* + DAGS n.²]

rattle-pate *n. see* RATTLE-HEAD n.

rattler *n.¹* **1** [early 17C–19C] (*UK Und.*) a coach. **2** [19C] a cab. **3** [mid-19C+] a passenger train or carriage of the train; esp. in phr. *the rattlers.* **4** [mid-19C+] (*Aus./US*) a freight train or carriage of a train. **5** [1900s–60s] (*US*) the Manhattan elevated railway, cable cars or streetcars. **6** [1910s–20s] (*US Und.*) a tramp who rides on freight cars. **7** [1910s–20s] any tram. **8** [1920s] (*US*) an automobile. **9** [1920s] a bicycle. **10** [1920s+] the New York or London underground railway.

rattler *n.²* **1** [19C] a blow. **2** [late 19C] something serious or impressive. **3** [late 19C] an admirable person. [it rattles the teeth, jaw etc]

rattler *n.³* [mid-19C; 1920s] an amorous man; a promiscuous woman. [RATTLE v.¹ (2)]

rattlers *n.* [19C] the teeth.

rattles, the *n.* **1** [late 18C–19C] the croup. **2** [19C] the death-rattle. **3** [mid-19C–1900s] nerves, anxiety; esp. as *case of (the) rattles.* [abbr. SE *death-rattle*]

rattle-skull *n. see* RATTLE-HEAD n.

rattlesnake canyon *n.* [20C+] the vagina (cf. AGREEABLE RUTS OF LIFE n.).

rattlesnakes *n.* [20C+] delirium tremens. [rhy. sl. = SHAKES, THE n. (1)]

rattle someone off *v.* (*also* **rattle someone up**) [late 17C–early 19C] to scold, to tell off.

rattle someone's cage *v.* [1960s+] to annoy, to irritate.

rattle someone's chain *v.* [1960s+] (*orig. US*) to annoy, to distract forcefully, to taunt. [var. on JERK SOMEONE'S CHAIN v.]

rattle someone up *v. see* RATTLE SOMEONE OFF v.

rattle the can *v.* [1940s] (*US*) to beg in the street.

rattle the cup (on) *v.* [1930s–50s] (*US*) to betray, to inform against.

rattle the ivories *v. see* IVORY n. (2).

rattletrap *n.* **1** [early 19C] the mouth. **2** [late 19C+] a gossip, a chatterer. **3** [1910s–50s] a run-down vehicle or other form of transport. [SE *rattle* + TRAP n.³]

rattletrap *adj.* **1** [late 19C] insubstantial, untrustworthy. **2** [1920s+] (*US*) run-down, seedy. [RATTLETRAP n.]

rattling-cove *n.* [late 17C–mid-19C] (*UK Und.*) a coachman. [RATTLER n.¹ (1) + COVE n. (1)]

rattling gloak *n.* (*also* **rattling gloke**) [mid-18C–mid-19C] (*UK Und.*) a coachman. [RATTLER n.¹ (1) + GLOAK n.]

rattling lay *n.* [early–mid-18C] (*UK Und.*) stealing goods from a moving coach. [RATTLER n.¹ (1) + LAY n.⁴ (1)]

rattling mumper *n.* [late 17C–mid-19C] (*UK Und.*) a beggar who specializes in approaching those who ride in coaches. [RATTLER n.¹ (1) + MUMPER n. (2)]

rat trap *n.¹* **1** [mid-19C+] a shabby or ramshackle building or dwelling. **2** [1920s–50s] a vehicle; esp. as *rolling rat trap.*

rat trap *n.²* [late 19C+] the mouth. [SE *rat* + SE *trap*/TRAP n.³]

rat trap *n.³* [1940s+] a Japanese person (cf. BUDDHAHEAD n.). [rhy. sl. = JAP n.]

ratty *adj.¹* **1** [mid-19C+] (*orig. US*) run-down, ramshackle, unkempt. **2** [late 19C+] irritated, annoyed, obstreperous. **3** [20C+]

(*US*) drunk (cf. ADDLED adj.). **4** [1960s] (*US*) of a person, run-down, exhausted. [negative imagery of the animal]

ratty *adj.*[2] [late 19C+] (*Aus./N.Z.*) mad, eccentric; thus *ratty on/over*, infatuated with. [RATS IN THE ATTIC phr.]

raughty *adj. see* RORTY adj.

raunch *n.* [1960s+] (*orig. US*) **1** vulgarity, grubbiness, shabbiness. **2** obscenity, pornography. [backform. f. RAUNCHY adj. (1)/RAUNCHY adj. (3)]

raunch *v.* [1940s+] (*US*) to have sexual intercourse. [backform. f. RAUNCHY adj. (1)]

raunch out *v.* [1970s+] (*US campus*) to offend by making sexual remarks or using offensive language. [backform. f. RAUNCHY adj. (3)]

raunchy *adj.* (*also* **ronchie**) **1** [1930s+] (*orig. US*) sordid, sloppy, contemptible, excessive, seedy. **2** [1940s+] (*US teen*) inferior, cheap. **3** [1960s+] (*orig. US*) suggestive, sexually provocative, smutty, salacious. **4** [1970s] (*US campus*) ill, unwell. **5** [1970s] (*US*) drunk. **6** [1990s+] (*US*) violent. [ety. unknown; E.P. suggests SE *rancid* or fig. use of dial. *raunch*, of vegetables, uncooked, i.e. 'raw']

raus mit 'em! *excl.* [20C+] (*US*) get out! away with you! [Ger. *heraus mit ihm!* out with him!]

rave *n.*[1] **1** [20C+] a sudden display of enthusiasm, a 'craze'. **2** [1900s] (*US*) talk, conversation. **3** [1930s–40s] an obsession with someone or something. **4** [1920s+] (*orig. US*) an extremely favourable review of a show, film, book etc. **5** [1920s+] (*orig. US*) any strong, negative or positive, opinion. [RAVE v.[1] (1)]

rave *n.*[2] [1950s+] **1** (*also* **rave-up**) a party; initially in the late 1950s/early 1960s, the term was popularized again in the 1980s, with much the same meaning, although the parties concerned were often held in clubs or, in the case of the much-vilified ACID HOUSE PARTY n., in disused warehouses, hangars etc. **2** in ext. use, anything pleasurable, amusing, exciting. **3** an admirable individual.

rave *adj.* **1** [1950s+] usu. of a critical review, ecstatic, hugely positive. **2** [2000s] fashionable. [RAVE n.[1]]

rave *v.*[1] **1** [mid-19C+] to praise enthusiastically. **2** [1970s] (*Aus. Und.*) for a shoplifter to make a fuss so as to cause a distraction while his accomplices work.

rave *v.*[2] **1** [1950s+] to have or go out in search of a good time. **2** [1980s+] to attend a club or larger gathering to listen to music and, almost invariably, to take MDMA. [RAVE n.[2]]

ravel up one's ball of yarn *v. see* WIND ONE'S BALL OF YARN v.

raven *n.*[1] [early 19C] an undertaker. [SE *raven*, a carrion-eating bird]

raven *n.*[2] [late 19C] a small portion of bread and cheese. [the biblical story of ravens taking small portions of food to the prophet Elisha]

raver *n.* **1** [1950s+] anyone devoted to having an energetically good time with variations of 'dope, sex and rock 'n' roll' as to individual taste and situation. **2** [1950s+] a hedonistic woman who is also presumed to be sexually available, esp. in *right little raver*. **3** [1960s] a fan of dixieland jazz. **4** [1990s+] a devotee of rave parties. [RAVE v.[2] (1)]

rave-up *n. see* RAVE n.[2] (1).

ravey *adj.* [1950s] party-going, pleasure-seeking. [RAVE n.[2] (1)]

raving *adj.* [mid-19C+] complete, utter, extreme; also as adv. [SE *raving*, insane, crazed]

raw *n.*[1] **1** [mid-19C] (*UK Und.*) neat gin. **2** [mid-19C] whisky. **3** [1980s+] (*drugs*) crack cocaine that has not been adulterated or 'cut' (cf. BASE n.). [SE *raw*, a natural, unadorned and undiluted state]

raw *n.*[2] *see* JOHNNY RAW n.

raw *adj.* **1** [mid-18C+] inexperienced, unsophisticated. **2** [late 19C+] angry, upset. **3** [20C+] unfair. **4** [20C+] (*US*) honest, candid, unadorned. **5** [1900s–60s] (*US*) harsh, inhospitable. **6** [1910s+] (*US*) uncouth, bold, brazen. **7** [1940s+] naked. **8** [1960s+] (*US Black*) excellent, powerful, impressive. **9** [1990s+] (*US*) used of

sexual intercourse without a condom. **10** [1990s+] (*W.I.*) hungry. [SE *raw*, in a natural, unadorned and undiluted state]

raw *v.* [1990s+] (*US*) to treat badly, unfairly. [RAW DEAL n.]

rawalpindi *adj.* [1940s+] of the weather, windy. [rhy. sl.; ult. the city in Pakistan]

raw and ripe *n.* [20C+] a tobacco pipe. [rhy. sl.]

raw chaw *n.* [1940s+] (*W.I.*) **1** an uncouth, ill-mannered person. **2** the unvarnished truth. [SE *raw* + *chaw* (*chew*), to chew coarsely]

raw-chaw *adj.* [1950s+] (*W.I.*) coarse, vulgar; unadorned. [RAW CHAW n.]

raw deal *n.* (*also* **rough deal**) [1910s+] (*orig. US*) unfair, harsh treatment, particularly poor luck; usu. from the point of view of the victim. [RAW adj. (3) + DEAL n.[1] (3)]

rawdog *adj.* [2000s] (*US campus*) outrageous, exciting. [RAW adj. (6) + play on HOT DOG n.[2] (4)]

raw dogg *n.* (*also* **rawdog**) [1990s+] (*US Black teen*) sexual intercourse (without a condom); also as v., to have sexual intercourse. [RAW adj. (7) + DOG OUT v. (3)]

rawhide *n.* (*also* **rawhider**) [1900s–60s] (*US*) **1** a cowboy. **2** a hard worker; a hard taskmaster. [metonymy, i.e. his *rawhide* whip]

rawhide *v.* **1** [1910s] (*US*) to beat. **2** [1930s–60s] (*US tramp*) to work hard; to make others work hard. [see prev.]

raw-jaw *adj.* (*also* **raw-jawed**) [1930s+] (*US*) tough, 'strong-arm'.

raw jaw *v.* [20C+] (*US Und.*) to ignore, to refuse to speak to. [SE *raw* + JAW v.[1] (1)]

raw jaws *n.* [1970s+] (*US gay*) someone who is still a novice as a fellator; thus an inexperienced street prostitute. [RAW adj. (1) + SE *jaws*]

raw lobster *n.* [mid–late 19C] a policeman (cf. ANIMAL n.[1]; BABY-BLUES n.[2]). [SE *raw* + LOBSTER n.[1] (2), i.e. the blue uniform, which resembles an unboiled or raw lobster]

raw meat *n.* **1** [18C; 1970s] (*also* **raw sausage**) the penis (cf. BACON n.[1]). **2** [late 19C–1900s] a woman who partakes, naked, in sex shows. **3** [1900s] a prostitute caught *in flagrante*; thus *raw-meat business*, prostitution. [SE *raw* + MEAT n. (2)/MEAT n. (1); (1) SAUSAGE n.[1] (1)]

raw meat man *n.* [late 19C] (*Aus.*) a bare-knuckle boxer.

raw ones *n. see* RAWS n.

raw prawn *n.* [1940s+] (*Aus.*) **1** an unfair action or circumstance, anything far-fetched; thus COME THE RAW PRAWN v. **2** someone who is easy to deceive, a dupe. [the foodstuff and the concept are both 'hard to swallow']

raw recruit *n.* [late 19C] a shot of undiluted spirits.

raws *n.* (*also* **raw ones**, **raw 'uns**) [mid-19C–1930s] the bare fists, as used in street-fighting. [one's bare skin]

raw sausage *n. see* RAW MEAT n. (1).

rawser *n. see* ROZZER n.[1].

rawskin *n.* [1940s+] (*Aus.*) an inexperienced criminal. [RAW adj. (1) + SKIN n.[7] (1)]

raw sole *n.* [1950s+] (*US Black*) a virgin Black woman. [SE *raw* + pun on *sole*/SOUL n.[2]]

rawted *adj. see* RAATID adj.

rawtid! *excl. see* RAATID! excl.

raw 'uns *n. see* RAWS n.

rax (up) *v.* [1940s+] (*W.I.*) to abuse. [? RAZZ v.[1]]

ray *n.* [mid-19C] 1 shilling and 6 pence. [? obs. SE *ray*, a small piece of gold or gold-leaf]

rayfield *v. see* RAIFIELD v.

Ray Milland *n.* [1980s] (*Aus.*) the hand. [rhy. sl.; ult. US film star *Ray Milland* (1907–86)]

rays *n.* [1960s+] (*US*) sunshine; usu. in phr. CATCH SOME RAYS v.

razmataz *see under* RAZZMATAZZ.

razoo *n.*[1] (*also* **rahzoo**) [1930s+] (*orig. N.Z., then Aus./N.Z.*) a small amount of money; usu. in phr. NOT A BRASS RAZOO phr.; thus *not worth a brass razoo*, utterly worthless. [AND says 'unknown origin'; E.P. suggests Maori *rahu*; but note *Ozwords*,

April 2000, in which for *not worth a brass razoo* a correspondent suggests a bowdlerization of *arse razoo*, a FART n. (1) (i.e. abbr. of an *arse raspberry*); this seems feasible, although *brass razoo* is not noted till 1960s while *razoo* by itself is cited 1910s+ (*see* RAZZ n.[1] (2))]

razoo *n.[2] see* RAZZ n.[1].

razor *n.* 1 [mid-19C] (*US campus*) a pun. 2 [1980s+] a notably 'sharp' person.

razor *v.* [1980s+] (*Irish*) to be spoiling for a fight. [one is feeling 'sharp'; note Westminster School jargon *razor*, 'a defiant, quarrelsome or bad-tempered person' (Ware)]

razorback *n.* [late 19C–1960s] (*US*) 1 a manual labourer; thus *razorbacked*, uncouth. 2 a circus roustabout. [SAmE *razorback*, a breed of hog found in the Southern states]

razor (blade) *n.* [1960s+] a Black person. [rhy. sl. = SPADE n.]

razorridge *n.* [early 18C] shaving. [SE *razor* + sfx -*age*]

razz *n.*[1] (*also* **razoo, razzoo**) 1 [20C+] a scolding, a telling-off. 2 [1910s+] (*US*) as *the razz*, mocking insults, rude noises; thus *give someone the razz*, to tease. 3 [1930s] (*US Und.*) the sales pitch used by a financial swindler. [abbr. RASPBERRY n.[1] (1)]

razz *n.*[2] see RAZZLE n.

razz *v.*[1] [1910s+] (*orig. US*) to tease, to heckle, to barrack, to scold. [RAZZ n.[1] (1)]

razz *v.*[2] see RAZZLE v.[1].

razzberry *n.* see RASPBERRY n.[1].

razzer *n.* see ROZZER n.[1].

razzing *n.* [1920s+] (*orig. US*) 1 a scolding, a telling off. 2 a teasing. [RAZZ v.[1]]

razzle *n.* (*also* **razz**) 1 [20C+] a spree, a good time. 2 [1900s] (*Aus.*) a problem, a contretemps. [abbr. RAZZLE-DAZZLE n. (1)]

razzle *v.*[1] (*also* **razz**) [20C+] (*Aus.*) to steal. [? SE *rustle*]

razzle *v.*[2] [1900s] (*US*) to harass. [? ext. RAZZ v.[1] although predates]

razzle-dazzle *n.* (*US*) 1 [late 19C+] enjoyment, pleasure, celebration. 2 [20C+] confusion, chaos, often deliberately engineered to 'blind' the onlooker. 3 [20C+] showy nonsense, boasting. 4 [1920s–40s] a form of confidence trick. 5 [1930s] in carnival use, a merry-go-round. 6 [1970s+] extravagant publicity. [ety. unknown; redup. of SE *dazzle* + ? link to fig. use of Yorks. dial. *razzle*, to scorch, to burn]

razzle-dazzle *adj.* [late 19C+] 1 (*US*) spectacular, dazzling. 2 (*Aus./US*) showing off, ostentatious. [RAZZLE-DAZZLE n.]

razzle-dazzle *v.* 1 [late 19C+] (*US*) to dazzle, to deceive. 2 [1920s] to harass, to pressurize. 3 [1980s] (*US Black*) to hang around, to loiter. 4 [1980s] (*US Black*) to pretend something has happened or is happening when in fact nothing is. [RAZZLE-DAZZLE n.]

razzle-dazzled *adj.* [late 19C] (*US campus*) confused. [RAZZLE-DAZZLE v. (1)]

razzle-dazzler *n.* [late 19C] a very brightly patterned sock. [RAZZLE-DAZZLE v. (1)]

razzle mag *n.* [1990s+] a pornographic magazine. [note actual magazine title *Razzle* (1973–) + colloq. SE *mag*, a magazine]

razzler *n.* [2000s] a loud fart. [RASPBERRY n.[1] (1)]

razzmatazz *n.* (*also* **razmataz**) 1 [late 19C+] (*orig. US*) (*also* **raj-ma-taj**) a garish, meretricious display, an event or occasion surrounded by such excesses. 2 [1930s–40s] (*orig. US*) anything old-fashioned, corny, out-of-date. 3 [2000s] (*US*) a slick deception. [jazz use *razzmatazz*, a variety of old-fashioned, trad. jazz; ult. echoic of the brassy, syncopated music]

razzmatazz *adj.* (*also* **razmataz**) [late 19C] (*US*) showy, highclass. [RAZZMATAZZ n. (1)]

razzmatazz! *excl.* (*also* **razmataz!**) [1930s–40s] (*US*) an excl. of delight or pleasure. [RAZZMATAZZ n. (1)]

razzo *n.* see RASPBERRY TART n. (2).

razzoo *n.* see RAZZ n.[1].

r.b. *n.*[1] [2000s] (*US prison*) a rich inmate. [*rich bitch*]

r.b. *n.*[2] see RUGGER BUGGER n.

RDs *n.* see RED DEVILS n.

rea *n.* (*also* **ree**) [mid-17C] the female genitals. [SE *rea, ree*, female bird of the ruff family]

reach *n.* [1980s+] (*US campus*) someone who is out of touch with reality. [? they are *reaching* for the stars]

reach *v.* 1 [20C+] (*US*) to bribe or otherwise suborn. 2 [1970s] (*US Black*) to help. 3 [1970s+] (*UK/US Black*) to go somewhere.

reach for a cloud/the moon/the roof/the sky/the stars *v. see* GRAB SKY v.

reach-me-down *adj.* 1 [20C+] (*US*) inferior, shoddy. 2 [1910s–20s] thrown together, improvised. [SE *reach-me-down*, a readymade new or second-hand garment, often trousers; ult. any garment that is hung up on display and must be 'reached down']

reach-round *n.* [1990s+] during inter-male anal intercourse, the reaching round by the passive partner to masturbate the active partner's penis.

read *v.*[1] 1 [1910s+] to understand. 2 [1980s] (*US campus*) to appraise, to look over. [fig. uses of SE]

read *v.*[2] (*also* **read off/out**) 1 [1930s+] (*Irish*) of a priest, to censure. 2 [1950s+] (*US Black/campus*) to reprimand. [READ THE RIOT ACT v.; (1) the practice of Catholic priests to read out names of alleged sinners from the altar]

read and write *n.* 1 [mid-19C] a flight, an escape. 2 [1930s+] a fight. [rhy. sl.]

read and write *v.* [mid-19C+] to fight; thus [20C+] *reader and writer*, a fighter. [rhy. sl.]

read braille *v.* [1970s] (*US gay*) to grope someone's genitals through their clothing. [SE *braille*, the written language of the blind which is accessed by touch]

read 'em and weep *phr.* (*also* **read them and weep**) [1910s+] (*US*) a phr. describing some unwelcome or distressing news or information, the truth; often as an imper., either delivered on retelling bad news or as a confirmation of the speaker's superiority. [gambling jargon, to acknowledge/announce a winning hand]

reader *n.* 1 [18C–1900s] (*UK Und.*) a wallet or pocketbook. 2 [mid-19C+] (*also* **luminous reader**) a marked card; thus (*gambling*) *readers*, a crooked deck of cards that a cheat can read from the backs. 3 [1910s–40s] (*US Und.*) a permit, e.g. to beg, to street-sell. 4 [1930s] a newspaper. 5 [1930s] (*US Und.*) a smalltime thief who follows postmen or delivery men to their destination, having sneaked a look at the label, then claims to be the official recipient. 6 [1930s–40s] (*UK Und.*) a 'wanted' poster. 7 [1930s+] (*US Und.*) a warrant for arrest. 8 [1930s+] (*drugs*) a drug prescription; thus *reader with a tail*, an illegally issued prescription which had been traced by narcotics agents. 9 [1940s+] (*UK prison*) any form of reading matter, books, magazines, comics etc. 10 [1960s] a pornographic novel, without pictures.

reader hunter *n.* [early 19C] (*UK Und.*) a pickpocket specializing in stealing wallets and pocketbooks. [READER n. (1) + SE *hunter*]

reader merchant *n.* [late 18C–early 19C] a pickpocket specializing in the theft of wallets and pocketbooks. [READER n. (1) + MERCHANT n.]

readers *n.*[1] [1920s+] spectacles.

readers *n.*[2] see READER n. (2).

readies *n.* [1930s+] cash, rather than cheques etc. [READY n.[1]]

reading room *n.* see LIBRARY n.[2].

read off *v.* see READ v.[2].

read of tripe *n.* [mid-19C] transportation for life. [rhy. sl.; SE *read*, the stomach of an animal (from which comes *tripe*) + the '*tripe*' that is *read* out in court]

read out *v.* see READ v.[2].

read someone's beads *v.* [1960s+] (*orig. gay*) to chastise, to berate, to attack someone verbally. [ref. to SE *rosary beads/* BEADS n.[2]]

read someone's shirt *v.* [1910s–30s] (*orig. milit.*) to check the seams of someone's shirt for lice.

read the maker's name *v. see* LOOK AT THE MAKER'S NAME v.

read them and weep *phr. see* READ 'EM AND WEEP *phr.*

read the music *v.* [1940s] (*US gay/prison*) to know what is going on.

read the riot act *v.* [late 19C+] to tell off severely and threateningly. [the practice, before its repeal in 1973 but effectively abandoned in 19C, of reading the Riot Act (1715) to unruly crowds before attacking with police or troops if they refused to calm or disperse]

read the tea leaves *v.* [1970s] (*drugs*) to smoke marijuana. [TEA n.² (1)]

ready *n.*¹ (*also* **reddy**) [mid-17C+] (*orig. UK Und.*) cash in hand; usu. as *the ready* or READIES *n.* [abbr. *ready money*]

ready *n.*² [1910s+] (*Aus.*) a swindle; a lie. [SE *ready*, to prepare, in this case the victim]

ready *n.*³ *see* READY (ROCK) *n.*

ready *adj.* **1** [1930s+] (*US Black*) aware, sophisticated, prepared to deal with the real world. **2** [1930s+] (*US Black*) esp. of musicians, excellent, first-rate, mature, fully competent. **3** [1930s+] (*W.I./UK Black teen*) sexually attractive. **4** [1940s] (*US*) drunk. **5** [1980s] (*US Black*) well-dressed.

ready *v.* **1** [late 19C–1900s] to bribe. **2** [late 19C+] to contrive, to manipulate, to 'wangle'. **3** [1910s+] to drug someone so as to knock them out. [SE *ready*, to prepare]

ready as Freddie *phr. see* READY FOR FREDDIE *phr.*

ready-come-at *n.* [20C+] (*Irish*) any form of skimpy woman's garment.

ready-eye *n.* [2000s] a policeman or other offical conducting a surveillance. [READY EYE *v.* (2)]

ready eye *v.* [20C+] (*UK Und.*) **1** to plan, to scheme; to know something in advance. **2** to conduct a surveillance.

ready-eyed *adj.* [20C+] fully aware of a situation in all its ramifications, both obvious and hidden. [READY EYE *v.* (1)]

ready for Freddie *phr.* (*also* **ready as Freddie**) [1940s+] (*US*) ready and eager. [redup.]

ready gelt *n.* (*also* **ready gilt**) [mid–late 19C] cash in hand. [var. on READY *n.*¹ + GELT *n.*/GILT *n.*¹]

ready Hedy *n.* [1940s] (*US teen*) an attractive young girl (cf. ABLE GRABLE *n.*). [SE *ready* + Austrian-born Hollywood film star *Hedy* Lamarr (1913–2000)]

ready john *n.* [mid-17C; late 19C–1900s] (*orig. US*) money. [SE *ready*/READY *n.*¹ + JOHN *n.*⁵ (ety. for 17C use may be different)]

ready-made *n.* **1** [1900s–10s] (*US*) shop clothing. **2** [1940s–50s] (*N.Z.*) a factory-made cigarette. **3** [1990s+] (*US prison*) a handmade, pre-rolled cigarette.

ready rhino *n.* [late 18C–early 19C+] (*UK Und.*) money. [SE *ready*/READY *n.*¹ + RHINO *n.*¹]

ready (rock) *n.* [1990s+] (*drugs*) crack cocaine; ext. to cocaine and heroin (cf. BASE *n.*). [READYWASH *n.* + ROCK *n.*³ (4)]

ready to spit *phr.* [20C+] on the verge of ejaculation. [SE *ready* + SPIT *v.*¹ (2)]

ready-up *n.* [1920s–60s] (*Aus.*) a conspiracy or swindle; a fake. [READY UP *v.* (1)]

ready up *v.* (*Aus.*) **1** [late 19C–1930s] to manipulate events or a person so as to achieve an improper or illegal end, usu. a fraud or swindle. **2** [1910s+] to find or hand over some money. **3** [1910s+] to hand on information, to 'put someone in the picture'.

readywash *n.* [1990s+] (*drugs*) crack cocaine (cf. BASE *n.*). [the process of chemical purification that is used when making the drug]

real, the *n.* [late 19C+] the genuine article, esp. in phr. *what's the real?* what's going on? what's the meaning? [abbr. REAL THING, THE *n.* (1)]

real *adj.* [1940s+] (*orig. US*) used by a succession of teen generations as an all-embracing term of approbation.

real *adv.* (*also* **rael**) [mid-19C+] (*orig. US*) very, really, e.g. *real bad, real soon.*

real Ally Daly, the *n.* (*also* **the real Alie Daley**, **...Ally Dooley**, **...Annie Daly**) [late 19C–1960s] (*Irish*) the real thing, the ultimate example. [*Alice Daley* (*fl.* early 19C), a noted producer of butter]

real article, the *n. see* REAL THING, THE *n.*

real A.V. *n.* [1920s–30s] (*US*) pre-Prohibition liquor, thus 'pure' liquor. [ante-Volstead Act]

real babe *n.* [1990s+] (*US teen*) an admirable, attractive person of the opposite (or preferred) sex. [SE *real* + BABE *n.* (1)]

real cheese, the *n. see* CHEESE, THE *n.*

real deal *n.* [1970s+] (*orig. US Black*) the end result, the final assessment, the absolute truth. [SE *real* + DEAL *n.*¹ (4)]

real deal *adj.* [1970s+] (*orig. US Black*) genuine, trustworthy. [REAL DEAL *n.*]

real folks *n.* [1920s] (*US Und.*) people who have been in prison or live by crime. [SE *real* + FOLKS *n.* (1)]

real George, the *n.* [1940s–50s] (*US teen*) the best, the ideal. [GEORGE *adj.* (2)]

real grit *n.* **1** [mid-19C] (*also* **pure grit**) the genuine item, the 'real thing'. **2** [mid–late 19C] (*US*) (*also* **true grit**) an admirable person. **3** [1970s] (*US Black*) the absolute truth, the essential facts. [GRIT *n.*¹; ? strengthened by NITTY-GRITTY *n.*]

real jam *n.* (*also* **real Peruvian doughnuts**) [mid-19C–1910s] of objects or people, the best, the superlative. [sporting jargon]

real Kate *n.* [late 19C] a kindly older woman. [one *Kate*, a well-known and well-loved stall holder at Clare Market; whence the phr. spread]

real kittens *n.* [1900s] (*US*) something or someone exceptional.

real lady *n. see* PERFECT LADY *n.*

real McCoy, the *n.* (*also* **the McCoy**, **the real McKay**, **...McKie**, **...McKoy**) **1** [mid-19C+] (*orig. US*) the genuine article, the 'real thing'. **2** [1900s] (*US*) money. [a variety of popular etys. have focused on the fighting name of Norman Selby 'Kid' *McCoy* (1873–1940), welterweight champion (1898–1900) and sometime strike-breaker or 'scab-herder' for the Ford Motor Co. Ironically, Selby was not in fact the *real McCoy*, this was another, slightly older welterweight, Peter *McCoy*, who toured with John L. Sullivan *c.*1885 and who killed himself after a bad loss. However the *Scot. National Dict.* (1870) notes that the saying, albeit spelt 'McKay' was adopted (? or coined) in 1856 by Messrs G. Mackay and Co, whisky distillers of Edinburgh, as their advertising slogan. A further cit., as the 'real Sandy McKay' is found in 1871; and both these are substantially earlier than the boxing attribution, although this may well have broadened the usage]

real Maginnis *n.* [late 19C] (*Aus.*) the genuine article, the 'real thing'. [*Maginnis* whisky]

real man *n.* [1960s+] **1** (*US prison*) a prisoner well respected by his peers. **2** (*US campus*) a macho male.

real noise *n.* [1900s] (*US*) the height of fashion.

real papa, the *n.* [late 19C] the best, the ultimate. [cognate with DADDY *n.* (6)]

real people *n.* [1910s–70s] (*US*) one's peers; trustworthy people; also as adj.; equally applicable to criminals as to the law-abiding. [PEOPLE *n.*¹ (3)]

real Peruvian doughnuts *n. see* REAL JAM *n.*

real pietro *n.* [1900s] (*US*) an absolute certainty. [? play on STONE *adv.*, i.e. *Pietro* as the name of a sculptor]

real puddle, the *n.* [late 19C–1900s] (*US*) New York City. [play on 'a big fish in a small pond' and its antithesis]

real raspberry jam *n.* [late 19C–1900s] an extremely attractive woman. [var. on BIT OF RASPBERRY *n.*]

reals *n.* [2000s] (*US prison*) commercially branded cigarettes (rather than cheap, generic substitutes usu. distributed to inmates).

real scorcher *n.* [late 19C] a very attractive young woman, but also a chaste one. [the non-sexual aspect of SCORCHER *n.* (4)]

real stuff, the *n. see* REAL THING, THE *n.*

real tabasco n. [1920s–30s] a clever, intelligent person. [play on HOT STUFF n.[2] (1); ? a P.G. Wodehouse nonce-word]

real thing, the n. (also **the real article/stuff**) **1** [19C+] of people, circumstances or objects, the genuine article. **2** [mid-19C+] (Irish) the finest whisky, often with a suggestion that it has been obtained illicitly. **3** [1940s–50s] (US drugs) heroin. **4** [1970s] marijuana.

real-thing adj. [1900s] of people, circumstances or objects, genuine. [REAL THING, THE n. (1)]

real-time adj. [1990s+] (US Black) honest, candid. [SE real time, the actual time during which a process or event occurs, i.e. nothing has been faked or otherwise altered]

real woman n. [1970s+] (US Black) a heterosexual woman.

ream adj. [mid-19C] good; thus ream bloak, a good man. [var. on RUM adj. (1)]

ream v. **1** [1910s+] (US) to cheat, to swindle. **2** [1940s+] (US) to scold, to reprimand. **3** [1970s+] (US campus) (also **reem**) to treat unfairly. [SE ream, to stretch, to tear in pieces]

reamer n.[1] [1930s] (US Und.) a cheat, a swindler. [REAM v. (1)]

reamer n.[2] **1** [1930s–40s; 1980s] (also **reemer**) a sodomite. **2** [1940s+] the penis. [SE ream, to enlarge a hole/REAM (OUT) v.]

reaming n. [1970s+] a telling-off, a scolding. [REAM v. (2)]

ream job n. [1960s–70s] **1** (US, orig. gay) anilingus (cf. AUSTRALIAN n.; RIM JOB n.). **2** (US) in fig. use, something difficult. [REAM (OUT) v. + JOB n.[4]]

ream (out) v. [1930s+] (orig. US gay) to penetrate the anus, either in anilingus or intercourse; also used fig., to cause harm to or trouble for. [SE ream, to enlarge or widen a hole; usu. gay use but note heterosexual synon. at RMC Duntroon (Aus.)]

ream out v. [1940s+] to scold, to reprimand. [ext. of REAM v. (2)]

reaper n. [1960s] (US drugs) a marijuana cigarette. [REEFER n.[2] (2)]

rear n.[1] [mid-18C+] the buttocks (cf. ARSE-END n.).

rear n.[2] (also **rears**) [20C+] (orig. campus) a lavatory. [the position in the rear of a college or REAR n.[1]]

rear v. (also **do/have a rear**) [late 19C+] to defecate. [REAR n.[2]]

rear-admiral n. [1990s+] a male homosexual (cf. ANAL ASTRO-NAUT n.). [REAR n.[1]]

rear end n. [1920s+] (orig. US) the backside or buttocks (cf. ARSE-END n.).

rear end v. **1** [1970s+] of a vehicle, to run into the back of another. **2** [1990s+] to have sexual intercourse in the rear entry position.

rear-ender n. [1970s+] a crash in which a vehicle hits the back of the one in front. [REAR END v. (1)]

rearend loader n. [1980s+] (N.Z.) a male homosexual (cf. ANAL ASTRONAUT n.). [pun on SE rear end/REAR END n.]

rearrange someone's face v. see BREAK SOMEONE'S FACE v.[1].

rear rank n. [1940s] a bank. [rhy. sl.]

rears n. see REAR n.[2].

rear (seat) gunner n. [1990s+] a male homosexual (cf. ANAL ASTRONAUT n.). [the image of sodomy]

rear up v. [1910s+] to become very angry; thus rear-up, an argument.

reat adj. see REET adj.

Reb n. [mid-19C+] (US) a White Southerner, orig. spec. a fighter for the Confederacy. [the Confederate, i.e. Southern 'Rebels' that triggered the US Civil War (1861–5)]

Rebecca n. (also **Rebekah**) [1900s] (Aus.) a generic name for a Jewish girl or woman.

rebel n. [20C+] (US) a derog. term for a native of the Southern states. [the role of the South during the US Civil War]

rebop n. [1940s–60s] (US) nonsense. [SE rebop, an echoic nonsense syllable used by jazz musicians, coined c.1945 as a description for the music of Dizzy Gillespie and Charlie Parker and ult. derived from Sp. Arriba! (up!) as used by rhumba bands to accompany a sudden shift in tempo]

rebore n. [1980s+] (Aus. prison) used of a woman who is sexually active and is thought to have an enlarged vagina. [SE rebore, the re-boring of one or more cylinders of an internal combustion engine when it is worn out from use]

rec n. [1950s+] recreation; usu. in combs., e.g. rec room, rec hall or as the rec, a recreation ground. [abbr.]

recce n. (also **recco, recon**) [1940s+] reconnaissance; orig. milit. use, now a general term for making a preliminary exploration, assessment etc. [abbr.]

recce v. [1940s+] to look around, to explore. [RECCE n.]

receipt of custom n. [late 18C] the vagina (cf. BANK n.[1]). [for ety. see CUSTOM HOUSE n.]

receive a notice to quit v. [early–mid-19C] to be informed of one's imminent death.

receive one's marching orders v. see GET ONE'S MARCHING ORDERS v.

receiver n. [1960s] a passive male homosexual. [baseball terminology]

receiver general n. [early 19C] a prostitute (cf. ASS PEDDLER n.). [pun, i.e. she 'receives' such lovers as pay their money]

receive the canvas v. [17C] to be dismissed from a job. [play on GET THE SACK v. (1), which was often made of canvas]

Recent Incision, the n. [mid-19C] the New Cut, London SE1. [pun; running from Waterloo Road to Great Charlotte Street, the New Cut was one of the busiest and most notorious Victorian street markets, as well known for its pickpockets and con-men as for the wide range of goods on sale]

recently struck it n. [late 19C] (US) a nouveau riche. [he has 'recently struck gold']

receptacle n. [1900s] vagina (cf. BAG n.[1]).

reck n. [1980s+] (N.Z.) something second-rate, useless.

reckless eyeballing n. [20C+] (US) shameless ogling of the opposite sex.

reckon v. **1** [17C+] to consider, to think, to suppose, to be of the opinion. **2** [mid-19C+] to esteem, to value; usu. as a negative, e.g. I don't reckon that lot. **3** [1990s+] to know, to be aware of. [ext. use of SE reckon, to count, to ascertain; (1) mainly US since mid-19C]

reckon! excl. [1940s+] **1** a general excl. of affirmation, you bet! absolutely! **2** a challenging excl. of disbelief, do you really think so? [RECKON v. (1)]

reckon oneself v. [1940s+] to think a great deal of oneself, to be arrogant. [RECKON v. (2)]

recluse n. [1980s+] (US prison) someone who has been inside a prison for 5 years or more without hearing from anyone in the free world.

recognize v. [2000s] (US teen) to give respect.

recompress v. (also **reconstitute**) [1980s] (US drugs) to press together cocaine flakes so they resemble a ROCK n.[3] (3).

recon n. see RECCE n.

recorder's nose n. [early 19C+] the rump of a chicken, duck, goose or other poultry. [unlike the usual refs. to clergyman, this phr. depends on the Recorder, a legal official appointed by the Mayor and aldermen of London as the guardian of the City's customs and of their own legal proceedings; thus ? an underlying ref. to ALDERMAN n.[1] (1)]

record jockey n. [1940s] (US) the predecessor of the disc jockey. [SE record + JOCKEY n.[3] (2)]

recoup v. [1970s+] (US Und./Black) to start off fresh and determined on one's release from prison, undeterred by a few years' absence from the world. [SE recoup (one's losses)]

recroots n. see DAISY (ROOTS) n.

recruit v. [late 18C–early 19C] to obtain a new supply of money. [RECRUITS n.]

recruiting service n. [early 19C] highway robbery. [RECRUITS n.[1] + play on SE]

recruits n.[1] [late 17C] (UK Und.) money, esp. when expected; thus the punning phr. raise the recruits, to obtain money.

recruits *n.*[2] *see* DAISY (ROOTS) n.

rectal ranger *n.* (*also* **rectum ranger**) [1990s+] a male homosexual (cf. ANAL ASTRONAUT n.).

rectify *v.* [1970s+] (*US gay*) to have anal intercourse (cf. ASK FOR THE RING v.). [pun on SE *rectify/rectum*]

rector *n.* [late 19C–1920s] **1** the bottom half of a sliced teacake, which received the most butter. **2** a poker kept only for show. [(1) the *rector* was given (and expected) the best part of the cake; (2) such a poker was brought out when the rector was visiting]

rector of the females *n.* [17C] the penis. [SE *rector*, ruler + ? pun on *erection*]

rectum ranger *n. see* RECTAL RANGER n.

Red *n.* [late 19C+] a red-headed person, esp. as a nickname or as a direct address.

red *n.*[1] [18C–19C] a soldier. [abbr. SE *redcoat*]

red *n.*[2] **1** [19C] a smoked herring. **2** [mid-19C–1930s] (*UK Und.*) gold, thus money, i.e. sovereigns (cf. CANARY n.[5]). **3** [mid-19C+] (*US*) a cent, a penny. **4** [20C+] (*US/Texas*) chilli. [the colour; note RED CENT n.]

red *n.*[3] [20C+] a Bolshevik, a communist, a socialist or anyone considered to have left-wing leanings; often generically as *the reds*. [RED adj.[2] (1)]

red *n.*[4] (*also* **red-skin**) [1920s+] (*W.I.*) a person with a lighter skin colour, from brown to near-White, but not pure Black. [RED adj.[3]]

red *n.*[5] [1990s+] (*W.I.*) a difficult or problematic situation. [? RED ARSE n. (2)]

red *n.*[6] *see* REDNECK n.[1] (1).

red *adj.*[1] **1** [17C+] golden, made of gold. **2** [late 19C–1900s] in cash (rather than paper) money. **3** [1930s+] (*Aus.*) having red or ginger hair. [(1) and (2) RED n.[2] (2); (3) RED n.]

red *adj.*[2] **1** [mid-19C+] communist, socialist, left-wing. **2** [1970s] (*US campus*) conservative, strait-laced. [*red* has been synon. with communism since its birth in 1848 and has been thus used as a synon. adj.; its mass and thus slangier use came after the Russian Revolution of 1917; a handy right-wing insult, it is often used of anything that frightens a conservative speaker]

red *adj.*[3] (*also* **red-ass, red-skinned**) [1920s+] (*US Black*) light-skinned. [SE *red* (+ -ASS sfx/SE *skin*)]

red *adj.*[4] [1960s–70s] (*US*) used of an impoverished, bigoted White Southerner. [abbr. REDNECK adj. (1)]

red *adj.*[5] [1990s+] (*W.I.*) intoxicated by drugs. [? one's red eyes]

redaa *adj.* [1950s+] (*W.I. Rasta*) extremely intoxicated by marijuana. [pron. of *red eye*]

red ace *n.* (*also* **red c**) [late 19C] **1** the vagina. **2** female pubic hair. [SE *red* + ACE OF SPADES n.[2]/abbr. CUNT n.[1] (1)]

red and blue *n.* [1960s–70s] (*drugs*) Tuinal, a barbiturate (cf. BARBIT n.). [the colour of the pills]

red 'Arry *n.* [1930s–60s] (*Aus.*) a £10 note (cf. ABE n.[2]). [the colour + ? the signature on the note]

red arse *n.* (*also* **red ass, r.a.**) **1** [1940s] (*N.Z.*) an incompetent person. **2** [1940s+] bad temper, irritation; thus *red-arsed/-assed*, furious. **3** [1970s] a scolding.

red ass *v.* [1970s] (*US*) to tell off, to scold. [RED ARSE n. (3)]

red-ass *adj. see* RED adj.[3].

redball *n.* [1920s] (*US*) a fast freight train. [on early railroads such trains mounted a red ball on the engine as a signal calling for priority; note US police jargon *redball*, a high priority high-pressure case]

red band *n.* [1950s+] (*US prison*) a trusty, i.e. a prisoner given special privileges. [the *red band* around the arm that denotes privileged status]

red beard *n.* [early 17C] a watchman, a constable, poss. a young man. [the implied youthfulness, thus energy of a *red beard*, as opposed to the 'white hair' of an older man]

red biddy *n.* (*also* **biddy**) [1920s+] **1** methylated spirits, as a drink, often mixed with red wine. **2** the cheapest red wine,

beloved of down-and-outs. [SE *red* + fig. use of *Biddy*, nickname for Bridget]

red birds *n.* [1950s+] (*US drugs*) barbiturates, esp. Seconal (cf. BARBIT n.). [the colour of the pills]

red bit *n.* [1980s+] (*Aus. prison*) a A$20 note.

red blanket *n.* [1920s] (*Aus.*) tinned meat. [the otherwise unmarked red-painted tins in which it was sold]

red bob *n.* [1940s+] (*Aus.*) a pimp, thus the money he extorts. [play on proper name *Bob*/BOB n.[4] (1)/RED SHILLING n.]

redbone *n.* [1930s+] (*US Black*) a pale-skinned Black person, esp. one who has native American blood. [Fr. *os rouge* (lit. 'red bone'), one who has native American blood]

redbone *adj.* [2000s] (*US Black*) of a light-skinned woman, attractive. [REDBONE n.]

red boots *n.* (*also* **red tennis shoes**) [1980s] (*drugs*) Seconal. [the colour of the pill]

red bread *n.* [1960s] (*drugs*) money obtained by blood donation. [SE *red*, the blood + BREAD n.[1] (2)]

redbreast *n. see* ROBIN REDBREAST n.

red bud *n.* [2000s] (*US drugs*) a variety of potent marijuana, containing red hairs from the flower buds (cf. AFRICAN BUSH n.; BLACK DOMINA n.). [SE *red* + BUD n.[4]]

red bullets *n.* [1970s+] (*drugs*) Seconal, a barbiturate (cf. BARBIT n.). [the colour of the pills]

red c *n. see* RED ACE n.

redcap *n.* (*also* **red one**) [1900s–60s] the penis. [the colour]

red caps *n.* [1980s+] (*drugs*) crack cocaine (cf. BASE n.). [the *red-capped* vial in which the drug is sold]

red carpet *n.* [1970s+] (*US gay/prison*) the tongue.

red cent *n.* (*also* **blue cent, red copper, red penny, white quarter**) [mid-19C+] (*US*) a trivial amount of money; usu. in phr. *not a/one red cent*, absolutely nothing (cf. CENT n.). [the copper colour of a cent; the blue cent may refer to the blue cardboard ration tokens issued in US during WW2 as payment for processed foods (meat tokens were red)]

red centre *n.* [20C+] (*Aus.*) the central areas of Australia. [the predominantly *red* soil]

red chenke *n. see* RED LEG n.[2].

red chicken *n.* [1960s+] (*drugs*) Chinese heroin (cf. BLACK n.[3]). [SE *red*, i.e. the brown colour and/or packaging]

red clock *n.* [late 19C] a gold watch. [RED adj.[1] (1) + SE *clock*]

redcoat *n.* [20C+] a member of the Royal Canadian Mounted police. [their uniform]

red-collar *adj.* [late 19C] (*UK Und.*) of a prisoner, privileged.

red copper *n. see* RED CENT n.

red cross *n.* **1** [1920s–60s] (*drugs*) morphine (cf. AUNTIE EMMA n.). **2** [1980s+] marijuana (cf. BLACK DOMINA n.). [? the packaging]

red death *n.* [1970s+] (*US prison*) **1** prison-cooked barbecue beef or pork. **2** jam (jelly in US).

red deener *n. see* RED SHILLING n.

reddener *n.* [2000s] a blush.

red devils *n.* (*also* **RDs**) **1** [1950s+] (*drugs*) any form of barbiturate available in a red capsule, e.g. Seconal (cf. BARBIT n.). **2** [1980s+] (*Aus. prison*) amphetamines (cf. A n.[2]). [the colour of the capsules]

redding *n.* [mid–late 19C] a gold watch. [var. pron. of RED 'UN n.[1] (1)]

red dirt *n.* [1950s+] (*US drugs*) marijuana that is or has been growing in the wild (cf. BLACK DOMINA n.). [SE *red* + SAmE *dirt*, earth]

red disturbance *n.* [mid–late 19C] (*US*) whisky. [the colour and the effects]

red dog *n.*[1] [mid–late 18C] (*Anglo-Ind.*) prickly heat, or *Lichen tropicus*, an inflammatory disorder of the sweat glands. [SE *red*, the colour of the inflammation + fig. use of SE *dog* to mean a feeling of being 'out of sorts', i.e. 'dogged' by illness]

red dog *n.*[2] [mid–late 19C] (*US*) a short-lived, unstable bank; thus the money it issues. [the stamping of certain New York State banknotes, which proved worthless, with a large red stamp]

red dog *adj.* [mid-19C–1910s] (*US*) of a bank, its money or financial affairs generally, unstable, dubious etc. [RED DOG n.[2]]

red dog on a white horse *n.* (*also* **red knight on a white horse**) [1970s+] (*US Black*) a woman having her menstrual period.

reddy *n.*[1] [20C+] an Italian living in London (cf. DAGO n.). [var. on RADDIE n. (1) but note Ital. *red* wine]

reddy *n.*[2] [1930s] (*US*) a person with red hair.

reddy *n.*[3] *see* READY n.[1].

red eel *n.* [late 19C] a general term of derision.

red-eye *n.*[1] (*also* **old man red-eye**) [early 19C+] (*US*) strong, poor-quality whisky. [the after-effects on the hungover drinker]

red-eye *n.*[2] 1 [1920s–60s] (*US*) tomato ketchup. 2 [1970s+] (*Can.*) a drink made from mixing beer and tomato juice. [the colour + play on RED-EYE n.[1]]

red-eye *n.*[3] [1960s+] the anus. [SE *red* + EYE sfx]

red-eye *n.*[4] [1960s+] (*orig. US*) 1 any air flight that deprives the traveller of proper sleep, due to take-off times, arrival times or differences in time zones. 2 of other forms of transport, e.g. an overnight long-distance bus. [abbr. SE *red-eye special*]

red-eye *n.*[5] [1970s–80s] (*UK Black*) jealousy. [one's *eyes* supposedly *redden*, although the usu. colour of envy is green]

red-eye *adj.* [1980s+] (*W.I./UK Black teen*) jealous, envious. [RED-EYE n.[5]]

red-eye *v.* [1990s+] (*US campus*) to stay up all night (working). [RED-EYE n.[4]]

red-eye after *v. see* HAVE RED-EYE FOR v.

red fed *n.* [1910s+] (*N.Z.*) a left-winger, an agitator, a militant. [RED adj.[2] (1) + abbr. SNZE *Federation of Labour*]

red fed *adj.* [1910s+] (*N.Z.*) left-wing, socialist. [RED FED n.]

redfern *n.* [late 19C] (*UK society*) a perfectly cut lady's coat or jacket. [the makers, *Redfern* of Maddox Street, London, renowned for their tailoring]

red-flag day *n. see* RED-LETTER DAY n.

red flannel *n.* [19C] the tongue. [resemblance]

red fustian *n.* 1 [late 17C–early 19C] port or claret. 2 [late 19C] porter. [SE *red* + FUSTIAN n.]

redge *n.* [late 17C–19C] gold, thus money (cf. CANARY n.[5]). [var. on RIDGE n. (1)]

red grate *n. see* RED LATTICE n.

red gravy *n.* [1940s] (*US Black*) blood (cf. BADMINTON n.).

redgut *n. see* GUT n.[1] (2).

red head *n.* [1950s+] (*US prison*) a match, presumably one with a red tip (cf. RED 'UN n.[2]).

red herring *n.* [mid-19C] a soldier. [play on LOBSTER n.[1] (1)]

red horse *n.*[1] [mid-19C] (*US*) an inhabitant of Kentucky.

red horse *n.*[2] [mid-19C+] (*US*) corned beef.

red hot *n.*[1] 1 [late 19C+] (*US*) a frankfurter, a hot dog. 2 [1930s+] a small, cinnamon-flavoured sweet. [its flavour and temperature]

red hot *n.*[2] 1 [1920s–40s] (*US*) a gangster. 2 [1930s+] (*US Black*) a highly aggressive, volatile person.

red hot *n.*[3] *see* HOT MAMA n.

red-hot *adj.*[1] 1 [late 18C+] very keen on. 2 [mid-19C+] obsessive; utterly dedicated. 3 [mid-19C+] (*US campus*) excellent, perfect. 4 [late 19C] (*US*) furious, enraged. 5 [late 19C+] of a bet, very likely, certain. 6 [late 19C+] (*US*) erotic, sexy, provocative. 7 [1930s] in a relationship, intense, devoted. 8 [1930s–50s] (*US prison*) tense, nervous, on edge. 9 [1950s–70s] (*US Und.*) extremely suspect; intensely pursued by the law. [ext. of HOT adj.[1]]

red-hot *adj.*[2] [late 19C+] (*Aus.*) unfair, unreasonable.

red-hot! *excl.* [1900s] (*Aus.*) excellent! wonderful! [RED-HOT adj.[1] (3)]

red hot cinder *n. see* BURNT (CINDER) n.

red-hot mama *n. see* HOT MAMA n.

red-hot poker *n.* [late 19C+] the penis (cf. AX n.[2]). [HOT adj.[1] (1) + POKER n.[1] (2)]

red hots *n.* [1950s+] (*Aus.*) 1 trotting races. 2 dysentery. [rhy. sl.; (1) = TROTS, THE n.[1]; (2) = TROTS, THE n.[2]]

red-hot treat *n.* [late 19C] a very dangerous person.

red house *n.* [1900s] (*US milit.*) a psychiatric institution. [? a particular institution]

red ink *n.*[1] 1 [mid-19C–1920s] blood (cf. BADMINTON n.). 2 [mid-19C–1940s] (*US*) cheap red wine. 3 [20C+] tomato ketchup.

red ink *n.*[2] [1920s+] 1 (*orig. US*) the debit side of an account. 2 (*US*) a financial loss. [in pre-computing days debts were written in *red*, credits in black]

red-ink joint *n.* [1940s] (*US*) a cheap Italian restaurant. [RED INK n.[1] (2) + JOINT n.[4] (3)]

red jackets *n.* [1960s–70s] (*drugs*) Seconal, a barbiturate (cf. BARBIT n.). [packaging]

red jerry *n.* [late 19C] (*UK Und.*) a golden watch chain. [RED adj.[1] (1) + JERRY n.[7]]

red kettle *n. see* RED TOY n.

red knight on a white horse *n. see* RED DOG ON A WHITE HORSE n.

red lady *n. see* RED MAN n.

red lamp *n.* [1910s] a brothel. [such a lamp hung outside]

red lane *n.* 1 [18C+] the throat. 2 [20C+] the vagina (cf. ALLEY n.[1]).

red lattice *n.* (*also* **red grate**) [late 16C–mid-17C] an inn; often doubling as a brothel. [a *red lattice* or *grate* was a popular tavern sign and thence, if the tavern was thus inclined, could also indicate a brothel; at one time an actual *Red Lattice* inn stood at Butcher's Row, off the Strand]

red lead *n.* 1 [1920s+] (*US*) jam (jelly in US). 2 [1920s+] (*US*) tomato ketchup. 3 [1990s+] (*Irish*) luncheon meat.

Red Leb *n. see* LEB n.[1].

red leg *n.*[1] [late 19C–1940s] (*US milit.*) an infantryman.

red leg *n.*[2] (*also* **red chenke, red shanks**) [20C+] (*W.I., Bdos*) a poor White. [SE *red* + *leg/chenke/shank*; i.e. their skin tone; *chenke* is pron. of *shank*]

red-letter day *n.* (*also* **red-flag day**) [1960s+] (*US*) menstruation.

red-letter man *n.* [late 17C–early 19C] a Roman Catholic. [SE *red-letter day*, a saint's day or church festival indicated in the calendar by *red letters*]

red light *n.*[1] [late 19C–1930s] a supervisor, a manager. [the use of a *red light* as a warning signal]

red light *n.*[2] (*also* **red-light house**) [late 19C+] a brothel.

red light *n.*[3] [20C+] a negative response, a refusal (cf. GREEN LIGHT n.).

red light *v.* [1930s+] (*US*) 1 to kill someone by pushing them from a moving train. 2 to throw someone out of a car or other vehicle and force them to walk home, often over a great distance. 3 to ambush and rob couples in parked cars by flashing a red light and pretending to be a police officer. [the red rear-lights of the train or car recede into the distance]

red-lighter *n.* (*also* **red-light girl/sister**) [1910s+] (*US*) a prostitute. [RED LIGHT n.[2]]

red-light house *n. see* RED LIGHT n.[2].

redline *v.* [1970s+] (*US*) to drive a vehicle at top speed; also in fig. use.

red liner *n.* (*also* **red lioner**) [mid-19C] an officer of the Mendicity Society, a mid-Victorian society devoted to the suppression of street beggars. [when a boy was caught begging his name was noted down, with a *red line* drawn beneath it]

red lizzie *n.* (*also* **red liz**) [1930s–50s] cheap red wine. [var. on RED BIDDY n.]

red lobsters *n.* [mid-19C] the Metropolitan Police. [SE *red* + LOBSTER n.[1] (2); many were ex-soldiers]

red lot *n.* [late 19C] a gold watch and chain. [RED adj.[1] (1) + SE *lot*]

red man n. (also **red lady**) [1980s] (drugs) Seconal. [the colour of the capsules]

red mare n. (also **red steer**) [late 19C+] (Aus.) a bush fire.

red mary n. [1970s+] (US Black) a menstrual period.

red mike n. **1** [1900s] (US milit.) canned salmon. **2** [1920s–30s] corned beef.

red mike and (a bunch of) violets n. [1920s] (US) corned beef and cabbage.

redneck n.[1] **1** [late 19C+] (orig. US) (also **red**) a derog. term for a country dweller, a peasant, esp. a Southern US poor farmer who is stupid and racist; strictly rednecks came from swampy areas whereas hillbillies, their peers, came from the mountains. **2** [20C+] (Irish) a yokel. **3** [1950s] (US) an Irish immigrant. [their sunburn; orig. a Presbyterian, then transferred to all poor Whites; (2) borrows f. (1); note 19C Lancashire dial. redneck, a Roman Catholic]

redneck n.[2] [20C+] (S.Afr.) an English immigrant. [Boer War era redneck, a British soldier, f. his uniform and the sunburn]

redneck adj. (also **red-necked**) **1** [1920s+] pertaining to a country dweller, a peasant, esp. a Southern US poor farmer who is stupid and racist. **2** [1950s] Irish. [REDNECK n.[1]]

redneck cocaine n. [2000s] (US drugs) methamphetamine (cf. BOMBITA n.). [REDNECK n.[1] (1), i.e. 'poor man's cocaine']

red-necked adj.[1] [late 19C+] (US) angry. [one's neck blushes with emotion]

red-necked adj.[2] see REDNECK adj.

redneck foreplay n. [1960s+] the complete absence of any preliminary physical contact. [REDNECK n.[1] (1) + SE foreplay]

red ned n. [1940s+] (Aus./N.Z.) cheap red wine. ['male' var. on RED BIDDY n. (2)]

red nigger n. **1** [mid-19C] (US) a native American, a red Indian. **2** [1920s+] (US/W.I.) a person both of whose parents are of mixed-African/White descent. [SE red/RED adj.[3] + NIGGER n.[1] (1)]

rednose n. **1** [mid-17C; 20C+] a drunkard. **2** [1910s] (US) cheap whisky.

red nugget n. [1930s] (US) an illicit saloon. [ety. unknown; ? the name of a specific saloon]

red oil n. [1970s–80s] (US drugs) hashish oil (cf. BLACK OIL n.).

red one n. see REDCAP n.

red one's eye v. see HAVE RED-EYE FOR v.

red paint n. [1900s–30s] (US) tomato ketchup.

red pants n. [1970s+] irritation, bad temper. [euph. RED ARSE n. (2)]

red penny n.[1] see RED CENT n.

red penny n.[2] see RED SHILLING n.

red peppers! excl. [late 19C] (US) a euph. oath. [one feels so HOT adj.[1] (4)]

red quid n. see RED SHILLING n.

red rag n.[1] [late 17C–19C] the tongue; thus too much red rag, speaking too long and too loud; give the red rag a holiday, be quiet, stop talking. [its colour and its 'flapping']

red rag n.[2] [late 19C+] a menstrual cloth or sanitary towel; thus flash the red rag, to menstruate. [SE red + rag]

red-ragger n. [1910s+] (Aus.) a left-winger, a socialist; thus adj. red-rag. [the red flag/RAG n.[2] (4), the symbol of the revolutionary left]

redraw n. [late 19C] a warder. [backsl.]

red ribbon n. [early 19C–1900s] brandy. [SE red + RIBBON n.[1]]

red rock n. [1960s+] (drugs) **1** heroin (cf. BLACK n.[3]). **2** methadone. [the brown grains of the cheap Chinese heroin]

red rogue n. [early 17C] a gold coin (cf. CANARY n.[5]). [RED adj.[1] (1) + SE rogue]

red rum adj. [1970s+] dumb. [rhy. sl.; ult. the triple Grand National winning horse Red Rum]

reds n.[1] [late 19C] **1** the menstrual period. **2** blushes. [the colour]

reds n.[2] [late 19C] (US short order) chops.

reds n.[3] [1960s+] (drugs) barbiturates, usu. Seconal (cf. BARBIT n.). [the colour of the capsules]

red sail-yard docker n. [late 18C–early 19C] a criminal dealer who specialized in goods and stores stolen from the Royal Navy's dockyards. [? the identification of such goods with a red mark]

red sea n. [late 18C+] the throat.

red seal n. [1980s+] (drugs) a variety of hashish (cf. AFGHAN n.). [a brand of cannabis stamped with a red seal]

red seam n. [1910s+] (W.I.) a police officer. [the red seam that runs up the uniform trousers]

Red Sea pedestrian n. [late 19C+] (Aus.) a Jew (cf. ARAB n.[2]). [the exploits of the Hebrews during their Exodus from Egypt, among them the crossing of the Red Sea, temporarily dried up with divine assistance]

redshank n.[1] **1** [mid-16C–early 19C] a duck. **2** [early 18C] a turkey. [dial., usu. as redshank gull (Totanus calidris) of the snipe family (Scolopacidae)]

redshank n.[2] **1** [18C] a derog. term for a Scottish Highlander. **2** [mid-19C–1910s] (Irish) a woman wearing no stockings. [the kilted Highlander's or the woman's bare legs, thus coloured through exposure to the elements]

red shanks n. see RED LEG n.[2].

red shilling n. (also **red deener, red penny, red penny man, red quid**) [1940s+] (Aus.) a pimp; also the money he takes from his prostitute. [ety. unknown; ? fig. use of SE red, i.e. scarlet meaning sinful + SE shilling/DEENER n./PENNY n.[1]/QUID n.]

red shirt n.[1] [mid-19C] a back that has been scarred by a judicial flogging. [the colour of the blood and subseq. the scars]

red shirt n.[2] [1930s–60s] (US) a troublemaker; latterly mainly prison use, a recalcitrant, tough prisoner. [in mid-20C US prisons known troublemakers were issued red shirts; they thus became an easy target during a riot]

red shirt v. [1960s] (US campus) to miss a class or examination. [for ety. see next]

redshirted adj. [1990s+] (US campus) jilted. [college sports jargon redshirt, an athlete taking a year off from playing sport to extend their eligibility as a 'student']

red-skin n. see RED n.[4].

red-skinned adj. see RED adj.[3].

red slang n. [mid-19C–1910s] (UK/US Und.) a gold watch chain. [RED adj.[1] (1) + SLANG n.[2] (2)]

red snapper n. [1990s+] (US) the vagina (cf. BEARDED CLAM n.; BITE n.[2]). [play on the fish name (i.e. FISH n.[1] (1)) + ref. to the mythical vagina dentata]

red steer n.[1] [1940s+] (US) beer. [rhy. sl.]

red steer n.[2] see RED MARE n.

red stuff n.[1] **1** [late 19C–1920s] (US) red wine. **2** [1900s] blood (cf. BADMINTON n.).

red stuff n.[2] **1** [1900s–20s] money, presumably golden sovereigns (cf. CANARY n.[5]). **2** [1920s+] (UK Und.) gold, esp. jewellery. [RED adj.[1] (1) + SE stuff]

red super n. [mid-19C–1950s] (US Und.) a gold watch. [RED adj.[1] (1) + SUPER n.[2] (1)]

red tackle n. [late 19C–1930s] (UK Und.) a gold chain. [RED adj.[1] (1) + TACKLE n.[2]]

red tag v. [2000s] (US prison) to confine an inmate to their cell.

red tape n. **1** [late 18C–mid-19C] brandy. **2** [mid-19C] red wine. [SE red + TAPE n.]

red tennis shoes n. see RED BOOTS n.

red tide n. [1990s+] (US) the menstrual flow, menstruation.

red top n.[1] [1950s–60s] (US gay) a lesbian who prefers blondes. [RED adj.[1] (3)]

red top n.[2] [1990s+] a tabloid newspaper. [the masthead is often printed in red]

red toy n. (also **red kettle**) [late 19C–1930s] a gold watch. [RED adj.[1] (1) + TOY n.[2]/KETTLE n.[2] (2)]

red 'un n.[1] **1** [mid-19C–1930s] (also **red thing**) a gold watch. **2** [late 19C–1900s] a gold coin, a sovereign (cf. CANARY n.[5]). [RED adj.[1] (1) + SE one/'un/thing]

red 'un *n.*² [1930s] a match with a red tip. [SE *red* + *one*/'*un*]

red-up *adj.* [1990s+] (*W.I.*) intoxicated by marijuana. [one's *red* eyes]

red, white and blue *n.*¹ (*US*) **1** [late 19C] corned beef hash. **2** [1900s] a plate of mixed-flavour ice-cream.

red, white and blue *n.*² [1970s] a shoe. [rhy. sl.]

red wings *n.* [1960s+] cunnilingus with a menstruating woman. [orig. Hell's Angels, where those who achieved this were awarded a patch in the shape of a pair of red wings]

ree *n.*¹ [1980s] (*US prison*) respect. [abbr.]

ree *n.*² *see* REA n.

reeb *n.*¹ [mid-19C+] beer. [backsl.]

reeb *n.*² [1980s+] (*US campus*) a socially inept person, an outsider. [? var. on DWEEB n.]

Reebs *n.* [1990s+] a pair of *Reebok* trainers. [abbr.]

reebs *n.* [1980s] (*US campus/drugs*) marijuana. [? play on HERB n.² (3)]

reed horn *n.* [1940s] (*US*) a saxophone.

reed-roof'd cot *n. see* THATCHED HOUSE (UNDER THE HILL) n.

reef *n. see* REEFER n.².

reef *v.* **1** [mid-19C–1950s] (*US/UK/Aus. Und.*) to steal money; thus *reef a leather*, to steal a wallet by pulling out the lining of the pocket that contains it. **2** [20C+] (*Irish*) to gouge out, to attack, to remove forcibly. **3** [1940s] (*Irish*) to criticize, to tell off. **4** [1940s–70s] (*gay*) to fondle someone's genitals. [SE *reef*, to roll up and secure all or part of a sail]

reefer *n.*¹ [1910s+] (*orig. US*) a refrigerated wagon or ship. [abbr.]

reefer *n.*² (*also* reef) [1920s+] (*drugs*) **1** marijuana. **2** a marijuana cigarette, esp. [1980s] a large and slender version. **3** someone who smokes marijuana. [abbr. GREEFO n.]

reefer *n.*³ [1930s–40s] (*Aus./UK/US Und.*) **1** a pickpocket. **2** a pickpocket's accomplice. [REEF v. (1)]

reefer den/flat *n. see* REEFER PAD n.

reefer-head *n.* [1930s] (*US drugs*) a smoker of marijuana. [REEFER n.² (1) + -HEAD sfx (3)]

reefer man *n.* [1920s+] (*drugs*) a marijuana seller. [REEFER n.² (1) + SE *man*]

reefer pad *n.* (*also* reefer den, ...flat, ...joint) [1930s–60s] (*US drugs*) a house, apartment or room where cannabis users can gather to smoke. [REEFER n.² (1) + PAD n.² (2)/DEN n. (2)/SE *flat*/JOINT n.⁴ (3)]

reefer rat *n.* [1930s] (*US Black/drugs*) a marijuana smoker. [REEFER n.² (1) + RAT sfx]

reefer weed *n.* [1940s] marijuana (cf. AFRICAN BUSH n.). [REEFER n.² (1) + WEED n.¹ (4)]

reefing man *n.* [1930s–50s] (*US drugs*) a marijuana smoker. [REEFER n.² (1)]

reef it off in lumps *v.* [1920s+] (*Aus.*) to obtain large sums of money. [REEF v. (1) + LUMP n.¹ (1)]

reeking *adj.* [20C+] drunk. [var. on STINKING adj.² (1)]

reeler *n.*¹ [late 19C] a policeman (cf. BEAT-POUNDER n.). [they *reel* in the criminal; ? var. PEELER n.²]

reeler *n.*² [1930s–50s] (*US*) a spree, a drunken carouse. [SE *reel*]

reeling *n.* [late 19C] a feeling. [rhy. sl.]

reeling and rocking *n.* [1950s–60s] a stocking. [rhy. sl.]

reel in the biscuit *v.* [1970s+] (*US campus*) to seduce a woman successfully. [SE *reel in* + BISCUIT n.¹]

reels of cotton *adj.* [1960s+] rotten. [rhy. sl.]

reem *v. see* REAM v. (3).

reemer *n. see* REAMER n.² (1).

re-entry *n.* [1970s+] returning to the 'normal' world after a period spent taking drugs, esp. a hallucinogen. [spaceflight jargon *re-entry*, a space vehicle returning to the pull of Earth gravity]

reesbin *n.* [mid–late 19C] (*UK tramp*) a prison. [Shelta]

reesch *adj.* [1980s+] (*US campus*) disgusting, unpleasant. [SE *retch*, or echoic]

reestie *n.* [1990s+] (*US*) an unpleasant odour, object or person. [? Scot. *reest*, to smoke (fish)]

reet *adj.* (*also* reat, root) [1930s+] (*orig. US Black*) ideal, perfect, excellent, quintessential. [mispron. SE *right*]

reet? *phr.* [1960s] right? [mispron. SE *right*]

reet pleat *n.* [1930s–40s] (*US Black*) a sharply pleated ZOOT SUIT n. [REET adj. + the large *pleats* that distinguish the suit trouser]

ref *n.* **1** [late 19C+] a *ref*eree. **2** [1900s–50s] (*US*) *ref*orm school. **3** [1910s+] a *ref*erence (for a job etc.). **4** [1950s+] with *ref*erence to. [abbr.]

ref *v.* [1920s+] to *ref*eree. [REF n. (1)]

reffo *n.* (*also* refo) [1930s+] (*Aus.*) a derog. term for any European (esp. Italian, Greek, Yugoslav) immigrant to Australia (cf. DAGO n.). [abbr. SE *refugee* + -O sfx (4)]

reformer *n.* [2000s] (*US Black*) one who attempts to inculcate the ghetto with suburban values.

refresh *n.* [late 19C] an alcoholic drink. [abbr. SE *refreshment*]

refresh *v.* [1910s–20s] to drink alcohol. [REFRESH n.]

refreshed *adj.* [early 19C] drunk (cf. ABOUT RIGHT phr.¹). [euph.]

refresher *n.* [mid-19C+] an alcoholic drink. [it *refreshes* the consumer]

refujew *n.* [1930s–40s] (*US*) a Jewish refugee from Germany or Central Europe. [abbr./elision of SE *refugee* + *Jew*]

reg *n.* **1** [1900s] (*US milit.*) a regular soldier. **2** [1970s] (*drugs*) regular strength marijuana. **3** [2000s] a *reg*ular, e.g. regular customer. [abbr.]

regent *n.* [mid-19C] half a sovereign. [pun]

rege-rege *n.* [1950s+] (*W.I.*) **1** rags, ragged old clothes. **2** a quarrel. [Yoruba *rege-rege*, rough, in a rough manner or Hausa *rega*, to shake]

reggie *n.*¹ [1970s] the buttocks.

reggie *n.*² (*also* ralphie) [1990s+] in driving, a right turn (cf. LOUIE n.²). [initial letter *r* of the name]

reggie and ronnie *n.* [1960s+] a condom. [rhy. sl. = JOHNNIE n.¹¹; ult. UK gangsters *Reggie* Kray (1933–2000) and his brother *Ronnie* (1933–95), who offered 'protection']

reggin *n.* [1950s+] (*US prison*) a Black person. [despite origin in backsl. = NIGGER n.¹ (1), there are no racist overtones]

reggo *n.* (*also* rego) [1960s+] (*Aus.*) registration, usu. of a motor vehicle; thus as v., to register. [abbr. + -O sfx (4)]

Reg Grundys *n.* (*also* reggys, reginalds) [1980s+] (*Aus.*) underwear (cf. GRUNDIES n.). [rhy. sl. = UNDIES n.; ult. Aus. media executive *Reg Grundy* (b.1923)]

regimentals *n.* **1** [mid-19C+] (*UK prison*) prison uniform. **2** [1900s] (*US police*) police uniform. **3** [1940s] any uniform. [SE *regimentals*, a uniform]

Reginald Denny *n.* [1940s–50s] a penny. [rhy. sl.; ult. the British film actor *Reginald Denny* (1891–1967)]

reginalds *n. see* REG GRUNDYS n.

register *n.* [late 19C] the human face. [it *registers* the emotion]

register *v.* [1930s+] (*drugs*) to draw up blood into an eyedropper or syringe while injecting a vein; thus as n., the mix of heroin/water/blood drawn up into the syringe.

regjegs *n.* [1940s] (*W.I.*) rags, old clothes. [? SE *rags* + *jags*, rags, tatters]

regmaker *n.* [1950s+] (*S.Afr.*) a drink taken in the hope of curing a hangover, the 'hair of the dog'. [Du. *recht*, right + SE *maker*; the word is also used as the title of the house magazine of the S.Afr. Alcoholics Anonymous and for a brand of caffeine tablets, supposed to cure hangovers]

rego *n. see* REGGO n.

regroup *v.* [1960s–70s] (*US Black/campus*) to recover from an unpleasant surprise.

regs *n.*¹ [1920s+] *reg*ulations. [abbr.]

regs *n.*² *see* REGULARS n.

regular *n.* **1** [mid-19C+] one's usual or habitual drink or order in a pub, bar etc. **2** [late 19C+] (*US*) a close friend, a boy- or girlfriend, a lover. **3** [20C+] one who frequents the same public house or bar on a regular basis. **4** [1930s+] (*US Und.*) an admirable person (in criminal sense); a career criminal.

regular *adj.* **1** [early 19C+] thorough, complete, absolute, total. **2** [20C+] (*US*) dependable, trustworthy, honest. **3** [1920s+] ordinary, unpretentious.

regular *adv.* [mid-19C+] completely, utterly.

regular crow *n.* [mid-19C–1920s] a big success. [SE *regular* + CROW n.[5]]

regular flat fish *n. see* FLAT FISH n.

regular guy *n.* (*also* **regular fellow/folks**) [1910s+] (*US*) a thoroughly good person; in the speaker's opinion their peer, intellectually, in sense of humour, opinions, politics etc, also used adj.; occas. of a woman. [REGULAR adj.]

regular Indian *n.* [20C+] (*Can.*) a habitual drunkard. [racist stereotyping]

regular joe *n.* (*also* **right Joe**) [1940s+] a conventional, conservative person; as such seen as honest and dependable. [REGULAR adj./RIGHT adj.[1] (6) + JOE n.[1] (2)]

regularly *adv.* [late 18C–19C] thoroughly, completely.

regular moose *n. see* MOOSE n.[1].

regular oner *n.* [late 19C] an incorrigible rogue, 'one who is past praying for' (Ware); by no means invariably derog. but often implying a sneaking admiration.

regulars *n.* (*also* **regs**) [19C–1900s] a share of criminal booty; thus *go regulars*, to share profits.

regulate *v.* [mid-19C; 2000s] (*US teen*) to take an action of enforcement; to punish or hurt.

regulator *n.* [19C] the vagina. [? it stops men getting 'overheated']

rehab *n.* [1940s+] **1** *rehab*ilitation, from drug or alcohol abuse; thus ext. to emotional or non-drug-related physical problems. **2** the ward or hospital in which *rehab*ilitation takes place. **3** the state of being *rehab*ilitated. [abbr.]

rehab *v.* [1970s+] **1** to *rehab*ilitate, e.g. a broken-down house. **2** to undergo *rehab*ilitation. [abbr.]

rehabilitative conversation *n.* [1980s+] (*Aus. prison*) a beating from prison officers. [ironic ref. to the prison system's claim to *rehabilitate* criminals]

rehitch *v. see* HITCH (UP) v. (1).

rehoboam *n.* [mid-19C] a shovel hat. [the name of *Rehoboam*, son of Solomon, King of Judah (1 Kgs 12–14)]

Reilly *n. see* LIFE OF RILEY n.

reimburse *v.* [1970s] (*US Black*) to lose one's life for the refusal or inability to pay off a debt or favour. [play on SE *reimburse*, to pay back a debt]

reindeer dust *n.* [1930s–50s] (*drugs*) any powdered narcotic. [play on SNOW n.[2] (1)]

relation *n.* [mid-19C] a pawnbroker. [play on UNCLE n.[1] (1)]

release a chocolate hostage *v.* [1990s+] to defecate.

release the hounds *v.* [1990s+] (*UK juv.*) to defecate.

relic *n.* [mid-19C+] an old person; thus *relics*, parents.

relief *n.* [1990s+] (*US prison*) anything sent in to a prisoner from the outside world.

reliefer *n.* [1930s–40s] (*US Black*) someone who exists on welfare *relief*.

reliever *n.* **1** [mid-19C] a coat that is kept in a variety of public places, that can be lent to anyone who does not possess one. **2** [20C+] (*Irish*) slippers. **3** [1920s–60s] (*US tramp*) in pl., shoes. [the garments or footwear *relieve* suffering]

relieving officer *n.* [mid-late 19C] one's father. [SE *relieving officer*, an officer appointed by a parish or union to administer relief to the poor]

religious *adj.* [late 18C–early 19C] of a horse, one that is always on its knees. [pun]

religo *n.* [1940s] (*N.Z.*) one who objects to war on *relig*ious grounds. [abbr.]

Relish, the *n.* [late 18C–early 19C] the Cheshire Cheese tavern, in Wine Office Court, off Fleet Street; frequented by such figures as Johnson, Garrick and later Dickens. [also known as *The House*, according to Weinreb and Hibbert]

relish *n.* [early 19C] sexual intercourse.

rellie *n.* (*also* **rello, relo**) [1990s+] (*orig. Aus.*) a family *rela*tive. [abbr.]

reload *v.* [1940s+] **1** (*US Und.*) to trick a person for a second time. **2** (*UK Und.*) to ensnare a victim in a confidence game, e.g. the 3-card trick, by allowing them small victories, thus increasing their confidence (and bets) prior to taking their money.

reltney *n.* [20C+] (*US*) the (erect) penis. [ety. unknown]

rem *n.* (*also* **remhead**) [1990s+] (*UK juv.*) a stupid, poss. mentally deficient person. [their need for *rem*edial classes]

remedy *n.* [18C] a sovereign. [pun on SE phr. *sovereign remedy*]

remedy critch *n.* [late 18C–early 19C] a chamberpot. [SE *remedy*, ease + *critch*, an earthenware vessel; ult. *cratch*, a stable hayrack and thus a *crèche*; the term is used as such in early descriptions of Christ's birth]

remember Parson Malham! *excl.* [late 17C–early 19C] drink up! finish your glass! [? the proper name of a once celebrated drunken cleric; presumably, since B.E. adds 'Norfolk', from that county]

r.e.m.f. *n.* [1960s+] (*orig. US milit.*) rear echelon mother*f*uckers; used by combat troops and brought into civilian life by veterans; also as a term of address and attrib. [abbr.]

remhead *n. see* REM n.

remish *n.* [1950s] of a prison sentence, *remis*sion. [abbr.]

remo *n.* [1980s+] (*US campus*) a fool, an incompetent (cf. BOBO n.[1]). [? SE *remo*dial + -O sfx (2)]

remote circumstance *n. see* MERE CIRCUMSTANCE n.

remove one's digit *v. see* PULL ONE'S FINGER OUT v.

renee *n.* [1980s] a girlfriend. [the popular working-class name]

renk *adj.* [1950s+] (*W.I. Rasta*) out of order, impudent, as in a rank-imposter; thus *yu too renk*, your behaviour is unacceptable. [RANK adj.[1] (2)]

renk *v.* [1970s–80s] (*UK Black*) to stink; to render stinking. [SE *rank*, foul]

renking meat *n.* [1990s+] (*W.I.*) the vagina (cf. BACON SANDWICH n.). [lit. 'stinking meat']

rent *n.*[1] **1** [late 18C–mid-19C] loot, booty. **2** [early 19C–1930s] money. **3** [20C+] protection money; thus *rent-collector*, a thug who gathers in such payments. **4** [1920s–50s] blackmail. **5** [1990s+] (*Aus. Und./police*) bribes paid to policemen, and the division thereof.

rent *n.*[2] [1960s+] a male homosexual prostitute (cf. ASS PEDDLER n.). [abbr. RENTER n./RENT BOY n.; note that the website Gaymart.com 'Queer Slang in the Gay 90s' claims use throughout 19C]

rent *v.* [late 19C+] to obtain money either by criminal means or by offering homosexual favours.

rent-a- *pfx* [1960s+] (*orig. US*) a general pfx used to demean whatever n. it is attached to by implying a monetary rather than emotional basis for its existence, e.g. *rent-a-crowd*, *rent-a-mob*, a group of demonstrators who, it is inferred, will turn up purely to demonstrate, irrespective of the actual event; thence in general use e.g. *rent-a-nigger*, a Black private security guard, seen as protecting White interests against Black individuals; *rent-a pig*, *rent-a-cop*, a security guard. [a play on the car-hire firm *Rentacar*, a US proprietary name, dating from 1921]

rental units *n.* (*also* **rentals, units**) [1980s+] (*US campus*) parents (cf. RENTS n.). [abbr. PARENTAL UNITS n.]

rent boy *n.* (*also* **rent queen**) [1960s+] a young male homosexual prostitute; also attrib. (cf. ASS PEDDLER n.). [RENTER n.]

rent collector *n.* [late 18C–19C] a highwayman, esp. one who prefers cash to jewels etc; thus *collect rent* (cf. COLLECTOR (OF THE HIGHWAYS) n.). [RENT n.[1] (1) + SE *collector*]

renter *n.* [late 19C+] a young male homosexual prostitute (cf. ASS PEDDLER n.). [he is for hire; note that the website Gaymart.com 'Queer Slang in the Gay 90s' claims use throughout 19C]

rent party *n.* (*also* **rent rag**) [late 19C+] (*orig. US Black*) a party where the guests buy their refreshments to help pay the rent (cf. FISH-FRY n.). [note Allen, *The City in Slang* (1993): 'Rent party seems to be a short form of the Southernism *house-rent party*, denoting the custom among rural and small-town blacks to raise money to pay rents, or just to supplement incomes. The transplanted institution of the Harlem rent party grew in the 1920s']

rent queen *n. see* RENT BOY n.

rents *n.* [1960s+] (*US campus*) parents (cf. RENTAL UNITS n.). [abbr.]

rep *n.*[1] **1** [18C+] *rep*utation; thus *no-rep*, one who has no reputation. **2** [1950s+] (*orig. US teen*) a member's standing and status in a street gang; thus *make one's rep*, to establish oneself as a successful, respected criminal. [abbr. SE *reputation*]

rep *n.*[2] **1** [late 18C] something worthless. **2** [late 18C–mid-19C] a man or woman who has a (usu. bad) reputation. [abbr. SE *reprobate*, underpinned by *reputation*]

rep *n.*[3] **1** [mid-19C+] a *rep*resentative, e.g. of a trade union. **2** [1910s+] (*US*) a member of a state or national House of *Rep*resentatives. **3** [1930s+] a commercial traveller, a sales *rep*resentative. [abbr.]

rep *n.*[4] [1920s+] *rep*ertory theatre. [abbr.]

rep *adj.* [1910s] (*Aus.*) well-respected. [abbr. SE *reputed, reputable*]

rep *v.* **1** [1970s+] to *rep*resent. **2** [1990s+] (*US Black*) to maintain a reputation as. [(1) abbr.; (2) REP n.[1] (2)]

repap *n.* [mid-19C+] paper. [backsl.]

repeater *n.* **1** [mid-19C] a second (third, fourth etc) drink after one's first. **2** [late 19C–1920s] (*US tramp*) a veteran tramp. **3** [late 19C+] (*Can./US*) a recidivist. **4** [1920s] a college student who is retaking a whole year.

repeaters *n.* [20C+] **1** (*Aus.*) belching after rich or 'windy' food. **2** (*US*) beans. [the food 'repeats']

repentance curl *n.* [mid–late 19C] (*UK society*) a woman's hairstyle, pioneered by the Princess of Wales (later Queen Alexandra; 1844–1925), in which a single lock of the back hair was brought forward over the left shoulder and allowed to hang over the left breast. [? the lock of hair hanging over the heart signified *repentance*]

repent pad *n.* [1940s–70s] (*US Black*) a bachelor's apartment. [SE *repent* + PAD n.[2] (2); a woman who visits may 'repent of her sins' later]

repo *n.* [1970s+] **1** (*Aus./US*) the *repo*ssession of items bought on hire purchase, but not paid for. **2** (*US*) a car which is *repo*ssessed for non-payment of instalments. [abbr.]

repo *v.* [1950s+] to *repo*ssess. [abbr.]

repo man *n.* [1970s+] (*US*) a *repo*ssession man, one who is employed by finance companies to repossess goods on which the owner is defaulting on their payments. [abbr. + SE *man*]

reposer *n.* [late 19C] a nightcap, a final drink of the night. [SE *repose*, rest, sleep]

repository *n.* [late 18C–early 19C] a lock-up, a prison.

reppock *n.* [mid-19C+] a policeman. [backsl. = COPPER n.[3] (1)]

represent *v.* [1990s+] (*orig. US Black*) to act positively, to perform as required, to do (something) well, to behave authentically.

reptiles *n.* [1970s] (*US Black*) shoes. [the skins used for many popular styles]

republic of letters *n.* [early 19C] the post office. [pun on SE *republic of letters*, the world of literature]

res *n.*[1] [1980s+] (*drugs*) an oily deposit left in a pipe after smoking crack cocaine. [abbr. SE *residue*]

res *n.*[2] [2000s] house, home. [abbr. SE *residence*]

rescue station *n.* [1970s+] (*US Black*) a liquor store. [ironic var. on SE *rescue mission*, a centre for alcoholics and other down-and-outs]

residenter *n.* [20C+] (*Irish*) **1** an old inhabitant, an old creature. **2** a fixture. [SE *resident*]

resin scraping *n.* [1980s+] (*US drugs*) scraping out and then smoking the resin that has accumulated in a cannabis pipe.

reso *n.* [1950s+] (*Aus.*) a residential boarding house. [abbr. SE *residential* + -O sfx (4)]

respeck/respect *see under* RISPECK and its combs.

rest *n.*[1] [late 19C–1950s] (*Aus.*) a year's imprisonment; thus *resting*, in prison. [note theatre euph. *resting*, out of work]

rest *n.*[2] [1910s–20s] a *rest*aurant. [abbr.]

rest *n.*[3] [1990s+] (*US campus*) one's home.

rest and be thankful *n.* [19C] for a man, the vagina.

resthouse *n.* **1** [1900s] (*UK Und.*) a prison or police station (cf. BANDHOUSE n.). **2** [1930s] (*US Und.*) any prison where the discipline is lax and the work undemanding.

rest of it *n.* [1950s] life imprisonment.

rest one's jaw *v.* [20C+] (*US*) to cease talking, to be quiet.

rest one's neck *v.* [2000s] (*US prison*) to be quiet, esp. as an imper.

rests *n. see* CABMAN'S RESTS n.

rest stop *n.* [1960s–70s] (*US*) the navel, in the context of oral sex.

result *n.* [1950s+] (*orig. UK Und.*) **1** a successful outcome to an endeavour, a sporting victory, an arrest for policemen, a lucrative robbery for villains etc. **2** a verdict of not guilty.

resurrection cove *n.* (*also* **resurrection man/woman, resurrectionist**) [late 18C–19C] a body snatcher, who robbed (usu. fresh) graves to sell the corpses to a surgeon for dissection. [SE *resurrection* + COVE n. (1)]

resurrection jarvey *n.* [mid-19C] a driver of a night hackney carriage. [SE *resurrection* + JARVEY n. (1); a play on RESURRECTION COVE n.]

resurrection pie *n.* [mid-19C+] any dish made from yesterday's left-overs which have thus 'risen from the dead'; thus *resurrection bolly*, a beefsteak pudding.

resurrection rig *n.* [late 18C–early 19C] (*UK Und.*) body-snatching; the corpse is then sold to a surgeon. [SE *resurrection* + RIG n.[2] (2); the dissection of human corpses was then illegal]

resurrection woman *n. see* RESURRECTION COVE n.

reswort *n.* [mid-19C] trousers. [backsl.]

ret *n. see* RETTE n.

retard *n.* (*also* **retardo**) [1960s+] (*orig. US*) a derog. term for a mentally retarded person, whether actually or fig.

retarded *adj.* [1990s+] **1** (*US*) a general negative; stupid, bad, inferior. **2** (*US Black*) intoxicated by a drug or drunk (cf. ADDLED adj.).

retired *adj.* [2000s] (*US prison*) serving a life sentence.

retread *n.* [1940s+] **1** (*orig. Aus.*) any object or anyone old that has been given a new lease of life, esp. someone who has been retrained for a new job. **2** (*Aus.*) someone who has recently been divorced. **3** (*Aus.*) a retired schoolteacher who is still teaching. [SE *retread*, a tyre that has been reprocessed, with a new tread, to extend its practical life; orig. 1940s Aus. milit. jargon *retread*, a WW1 soldier who re-enlisted for WW2]

retriever *n. see* VERSER n.

retsio *n.* [mid-19C] an oyster. [backsl.]

rette *n.* (*also* **ret**) [1960s–70s] (*US campus*) cigarette (cf. GRETTE n.). [abbr.]

reub *see under* RUBE.

reuben *n.* **1** [19C+] (*US*) a country bumpkin, a farmer; also generically (cf. ALVIN n.). **2** [1900s] a fool, a gullible person, irrespective of geography. [the 'rustic' proper name]

re-up *v.* **1** [20C+] (*orig. US milit.*) to re-enlist, to join up again. **2** [1980s+] (*US drugs*) to replenish one's stocks of a drug. **3** [1990s+] (*US drugs*) to take another dose of a drug. **4** [1990s+] to replenish one's energy.

rev *n.* **1** [20C+] a clergyman; also as a term of address. **2** [2000s] (*US prison*) a religious inmate. [abbr. SE *Reverend*]

rev *adj.* [1990s+] disgusting, *rev*olting. [abbr.]

revelation *n.* [mid–late 19C] (*US*) a drink of liquor. [pun on 'outpouring of the spirit']

Reverend Ronald Knox *n.* [1950s] syphilis. [rhy. sl. = POX n.[1] (1); ult. the Catholic clergyman *Ronald Knox* (1888–1957)]

reverse *v.* [late 17C–early 19C] (*UK Und.*) to turn someone upside down and shake them until the money falls out of their pockets.

reverse cowboy *n.* (*also* **reverse western**) [1970s+] a position of heterosexual intercourse whereby the woman straddles the man; also as *v.*

reverse English *n.* [1900s–10s] (*US*) the opposite; thus as *adj.* negative, oppositional. [billiards/pool imagery]

reverse game *v.* [1970s] (*US Black*) of a pimp, to manipulate the relationships of his prostitutes to his best advantage. [GAME v. (2)]

reverse gears *v.* [1980s+] (*US teen*) to vomit.

reverse western *n. see* REVERSE COWBOY *n.*

rev-head *n.* [1970s+] (*Aus.*) a young man dedicated to driving fast as well as drinking heavily and getting sex whenever possible. [SE *rev up* + -HEAD sfx (4)]

review of the black cuirassiers *n.* [late 18C–early 19C] a gathering of black-garbed clergymen.

reviver *n.* [mid-19C+] a stimulating drink.

revlis *n.* [mid-19C] silver. [backsl.]

revolver *n.* **1** [mid-19C–1930s] (*US*) a recidivist. **2** [late 19C–1920s] (*US tramp*) a veteran tramp or criminal.

revolving-door *adj.* [1980s+] (*US*) rapid or of short duration e.g. *revolving-door policies, presidents* etc.

rev one's motor *v. see* RACE ONE'S MOTOR *v.*

rev-out *adj.* [1990s+] (*W.I.*) prematurely past one's sexual prime.

revved (up) *adj.* [1960s+] excited, tensed up, emotionally intense. [SE *rev up*]

revving *adj.* [1910s] (*Aus.*) very busy. [from the 'revolutions' of an aeroplane engine]

rewired *adj.* [1970s] (*drugs*) of an addict, returning to drug use after abstention. [electrical imagery + WIRED adj.[1] (3)]

rez *n.* [1980s+] (*US drugs*) cannabis *res*in. [abbr.]

r.f. *n.*[1] [1960s] a general term of personal abuse. [abbr. RAT FUCK n.[1] (1)/RAT FUCKER n.[2]]

r.f. *n.*[2] *see* ROYAL FUCKING *n.*

r.f. *v. see* RAT FUCK v. (2).

r.f.d. boob *n.* [1920s] a country bumpkin, simpleton. [abbr. *Rural Free Delivery* + BOOB n.[2] (1)]

r.f.d. dopehead *n.* (*also* **r.f.d. gowster/junker**) [1930s–50s] (*US drugs*) a drug addict who travels between small towns, hoping to persuade sympathetic or naïve doctors to write narcotics prescriptions. [abbr. *Rural Free Delivery* + DOPEHEAD n.[1]/GOWSTER n.[1]/JUNKER n.[1] (1)]

r.f.d. queen *n.* [1940s–70s] (*US*) a homosexual living in a rural area, outside the main gay world. [abbr. *Rural Free Delivery* + QUEEN n.[2] (1)]

r.g. *n. see* ARGEE *n.*

rhatid *n. see* RAATID *n.*

rheumatiz *n.* (*also* **rheumatis, rheumatize, rumatiz**) [mid-18C–1950s] *rheumatism*. [abbr.]

rhine *n.* [1980s+] (*drugs*) heroin. [abbr./pron.]

rhino *n.*[1] (*also* **rhine, rhyno, rino, ryno**) [late 17C+] (*orig. UK Und.*) money; thus [19C] *rhino-fat*, wealthy. [ety. unknown; one suggestion, that it refers to the rhinoceros, then a fabulous creature 'worth its weight in gold', implies a certain lexicographical desperation; the term moved f. Und. to general sl. in mid-19C]

rhino *n.*[2] [1980s] a *rhino*plasty. [abbr.]

rhinocerical *adj.* (*also* **rhinoceral**) [late 17C–mid-19C] well-off, wealthy. [RHINO n.[1]]

rhode *n.* [1940s] (*US Black*) one's best friend. [ety. unknown; too early for ROAD DOG n.]

Rhodes scholar *n.* [1950s] (*Aus. Und.*) **1** a derog. description of someone who the speaker feels is trying to set themselves above the masses. **2** a non-derisive phr. of thanks for a favour done, *you're a Rhodes scholar, mate*. [the *scholarships* established by Cecil *Rhodes* (1853–1902), sending students born and educated in the then British colonies (including the US) to Oxford University]

Rhodie *n.* [1980s+] (*S.Afr.*) a White southern Rhodesian who emigrated to South Africa (and Australia) when the country became Zimbabwe in 1980 and Black rule was instituted. [abbr. *Rhodesia*]

rhodo *n.* (*also* **rhodie, rhody**) [1920s+] a *rhodo*dendron. [abbr.]

rhoid *n.* [1970s] (*US Black*) anyone or anything that makes one's life less easily manageable. [abbr. SE *haemor*rhoid]

rhoids *n.* [1990s+] (*US*) haemor*rhoids*. [abbr.]

rhubarb *n.*[1] **1** [mid-19C+] nonsense, rubbish. **2** [1940s+] (*orig. US*) an argument, a noisy dispute, esp. one that takes place on the field of play at a sporting event. [a mix of origins, e.g. theatrical, the actors' trad. muttering of *rhubarb* to provide background in crowd scenes; and sporting, baseball fans' term to describe a disturbance. The term was popularized *c.*1943 by the US baseball commentator 'Red' Barber, whose memoirs were entitled *Rhubarb in the Catbird Seat* (1968); for detail see Cohen (ed.), *Studies in Slang* IV, pp.52–55]

rhubarb *n.*[2] [late 19C+] the genitals, of either sex; thus the coarse query, *How's your rhubarb, Missus?* [20C+ use is US]

rhubarb *n.*[3] [20C+] an advance on one's wages. [rhy. sl. = SUB n.[1] (4), with Cockney pron. 'roobub']

rhubarb and custards *n.* [1990s+] (*drugs*) capsules of MDMA (cf. ECSTASY n.). [the colour of the pills; note cricket jargon *rhubarb and custard*, the MCC tie, again f. the colour]

rhubarb pill *n.* [late 19C] **1** a bill. **2** a hill. [rhy. sl.; (1) also puns on requiring a 'giving out']

rhubarbs, the *n.* [20C+] (*US*) the suburbs, the provinces. [play on SE *rhubarbs/suburbs* + pun on STICKS n.[3]/SE *sticks* of rhubarb]

rhygin *adj. see* RYGIN adj.

rhyme *v.* [1950s+] **1** (*W.I.*) to tell funny stories, to joke; thus *rhymer*, a teller of jokes or amusing tales. **2** (*US Black/teen*) to compete with ritualized insults.

rhyme slinger *n.* (*also* **rhyme thumper**) [late 19C–1910s] a poet.

rhynie *n.* [1940s] (*US Black*) a term of ridicule. [ety. unknown]

rhyno *n. see* RHINO n.[1].

rhythm *n.* [1960s–70s] (*drugs*) amphetamine (cf. A n.[2]). [play on BLUE n.[9] (1)/SE *rhythm* and blues]

rhythm and blues *n.* [1980s+] shoes. [rhy. sl.]

'ria *n.* [mid-19C–1950s] a generic name for a costermonger's woman, often a coster herself. [abbr. proper name *Maria*]

riah *n.* (*also* **riha**) [mid-19C+] (*orig. Ling. Fr./Polari*) hair; thus *riah-zshumpah*, a hairdresser. [backsl. but note Sp. *raya*, a parting in the hair]

rial *n.* [1940s+] (*W.I.*) a half-caste, the offspring of an East Indian woman and a Black man; usu. in combs. e.g. *Chiney-rial, Indian-rial*. [SE *rial*, a coin of low value]

Rialto *n.* [mid-19C–1920s] (*US*) the centre of New York's theatrical life; spec. the south side of Union Square, on 14th Street; thus ext. to local equivalents. [proper name *Rialto*, that quarter of Venice in which the Exchange was situated, thus the centre of commercial life; actors presumably picked up the ref. from Shakespeare's use of the name in *The Merchant of Venice* (1596); like the STROLL n. (1), the *Rialto* moved, as did the activities it denoted. In 1890 it meant the stretch of Broadway between Union and Madison Squares, in 1905 it centred on Herald Square, by 1910, during theatrical Broadway's heyday it meant the stretch between 34th and 47th Streets, centring on Times Square; its last gasp was the blocks along West 42nd Street]

rib *n.*[1] **1** [17C–19C] a wife. **2** [1910s–60s] (*US Black*) a woman. [the biblical story of the first woman, Eve, being created from Adam's *rib*]

rib *n.*[2] [1910s+] (*US*) a joke, a trick, an act of teasing. [RIB v. (2)]

rib *n.*[3] [1950s] (*US Black*) a shoe. [ety. unknown]

rib *v.* **1** [late 17C–early 19C] to hit someone in the ribs. **2** [1910s+] (*US*) (*also* **give the rib**) to tease, to make fun of; thus *n.* *ribber*. **3** [1910s+] (*Aus./US Und.*) (*also* **rib up**) to prepare a victim for being swindled; to cheat. **4** [1920s–30s] (*US*) (*also* **rib up**) to discredit, to incriminate. **5** [1920s–30s] (*US*) to annoy or threaten, to pressurize (someone). [one lit. or fig. 'tickles' or pokes the *ribs*]

ribband *n. see* RIBBIN n.

rib baste *v.* [late 16C–mid-17C] to thrash, to beat up.

ribbed-up *adj.* [late 19C–1900s] (*Aus./US*) (financially) secure. [one's full wallet, sitting next to one's ribs]

ribben *n.* [late 18C] (*UK Und.*) a whip. [SE *ribbon*]

rib-bender *n.* (*also* **rib-winder**) [late 19C] a blow to the ribs. [boxing jargon]

ribber *n.* [early 19C] a blow, esp. one to the body.

ribbin *n.* (*also* **ribband, ribbon**) [late 17C–mid-19C] (*UK Und.*) money; thus *the ribbin runs thick/thin*, implying the availability or lack of cash. [? SE *ribbon*, the image being of the richness of ribbon-bedecked packages]

ribbing *n.* (*also* **ribbing-up**) [1910s+] the act of teasing. [RIB v. (2)]

ribbon *n.*[1] [early–mid-19C] gin; spirits in general. [var. on SATIN n.[1] (1) and like it implying the smoothness of good gin]

ribbon *n.*[2] *see* RIBBIN n.

ribbon *v.* [1900s] (*Aus.*) to whip.

ribbon and curl *n.* [20C+] a little girl. [rhy. sl.]

ribbon clerk *n.* **1** [1950s] (*US*) a small-time trader, esp. in the stock market. **2** [1950s+] (*US gay*) a gay man who has a desk job. **3** [1990s+] (*US gay*) a heterosexual woman who prefers the company of gay men.

ribbons *n.* [19C–1910s] reins.

ribby *adj.*[1] [1930s+] short of money. [ON THE RIBS phr.]

ribby *adj.*[2] [1930s+] second-rate, poor-quality, dirty, run-down. [fig. the 'ribs are showing']

rib joint *n.*[1] [1940s+] (*US*) **1** a brothel (cf. BADGER-CRIB n.). **2** any form of sex show which permits the customers to watch, but definitely not to touch. [SE *rib* + JOINT n.[4] (3)]

rib joint *n.*[2] [1940s+] (*US*) a restaurant featuring spare ribs. [SE (*spare*) *rib* + JOINT n.[4] (3)]

rib oneself up *v.* [1930s] to convince oneself, to pluck up one's courage. [RIB v. (2)]

rib roast *n.*[1] (*also* **rib-roasting**) [late 16C–17C; mid-19C] a beating. [pun]

rib roast *n.*[2] [1930s–40s] (*US Und.*) an infant, a young child.

rib-roast *v.* [17C–mid-19C] to thrash, to beat up. [RIB ROAST n.[1]]

rib-roaster *n.* [mid–late 19C] a body-blow, esp. one to the ribs. [RIB-ROAST v.]

rib-roasting *n. see* RIB ROAST n.[1].

ribs *n.* [late 19C–1900s] a fat person. [ironic use of SE; the *ribs* are unlikely to be visible]

rib shirt *n.* [late 19C] a false shirt-front, covering only the ribs and chest, worn over an otherwise dirty garment.

rib stickers *n.* [1940s] (*US Und.*) beans.

ribston(e) *n.* [late 19C] a general term of affection, admiration. [the *Ribston pippin*, a dessert apple orig. introduced from Normandy *c.*1707]

rib tickle *v.* (*also* **tickle someone's ribs**) [mid-19C+] to thrash, to beat.

ribuck *see under* RYEBUCK.

rib up *n.* [1930s–60s] (*US Und.*) a pre-arranged deal; the concoction of criminal guilt or charges. [RIB v. (4)]

rib up *v.*[1] [1910s] (*US*) **1** to dress, to provide an outfit of clothes. **2** to create, to flesh out, to embellish.

rib up *v.*[2] *see* RIB v.

rib-winder *n. see* RIB-BENDER n.

Rican *n.* [1960s+] (*US*) a Puerto *Rican* (cf. BATO n.). [abbr.]

rice *v.* [20C+] (*W.I.*) to maintain financially, to look after, to feed; thus *rice at* (*one*), to be supported as a servant, a kept woman etc. [the role of SE *rice* as a staple]

rice-and-bean *n.* [1970s–80s] (*US*) **1** Puerto Rican. **2** Mexican (cf. BEAN n.[8]). [the stereotyped P.R. diet]

rice and beaner *n.* [1990s+] (*US campus*) someone who identifies with the styles and concerns of the 1960s. [the popular staple macrobiotic diet of the era]

rice-and-beans *adj.* [1970s] second-rate, impoverished, unimpressive. [SE/RICE-AND-BEAN n.; the poverty of the foodstuff and/or racist stereotyping]

rice and sago *n.* [1980s] (*Aus.*) a Greek or Italian immigrant (cf. DAGO n.). [rhy. sl. = DAGO n. (1)]

rice bags *n.* [late 19C–1900s] trousers.

rice-belly *n.*[1] [20C+] (*W.I.*) **1** a stomach swollen from malnutrition and eating only rice. **2** a child who has such a stomach.

rice-belly *n.*[2] [20C+] (*US*) a derog. term for a Chinese person (cf. AH CABBAGE n.). [racist stereotyping]

rice-burner *n.* [1980s] (*US campus*) a Japanese manufactured motorcycle. [racist stereotyping]

rice Christian *n.* [late 19C–1910s] (*Aus./UK society*) an inhabitant of a rice-growing country who volunteered for conversion less through religious fervour and more through a desire to gain food from gullible missionaries. [the use continued in the Far East to 1960s]

rice crispies *n.* (*also* **rice krispies**) [1970s] (*drugs*) amyl nitrite (cf. AIMIES n.). [the cereal's slogan, 'Snap, crackle and pop' and the snapping open of the vial]

rice dog *n.* [20C+] (*W.I.*) a mongrel, fed on scraps (mainly rice) and useless as a watchdog.

rice-eater *n.* [1990s+] (*Aus.*) a derog. term for a Chinese or Asian person (cf. AH CABBAGE n.; BROWNIE n.[2]). [racist stereotyping]

rice krispies *n. see* RICE CRISPIES n.

rice man *n.* [1940s] (*US Black*) an Oriental (cf. BROWNIE n.[2]). [racist stereotyping]

rice paddy Hattie *n.* **1** [1940s] rural Chinese prostitutes. **2** [1980s+] (*US gay*) one who has a penchant for Oriental men. [stereotyped link between *rice* and the East + joc./assonant use of the female name, a nickname for Harriet]

rice-picker *n.* [2000s] (*US Black*) a Chinese person (cf. AH CABBAGE n.).

rice queen *n.* [1970s+] (*gay*) a male homosexual who favours Asian partners. [SE *rice* + QUEEN n.[2] (1)/QUEEN sfx (2)]

ricer *n.* [1980s+] a derog. term for an Asian person (cf. BROWNIE n.[2]). [SE *rice*, the predominant Oriental staple]

rice rocket *n.* [1990s+] **1** (*orig. US Black*) a Japanese-made car (usu. a 4-wheel drive Jeep clone, e.g. a Shogun) or motorcycle. **2** a cheap or old automobile, usu. owned by someone of Hispanic descent. [racist stereotyping]

rich *adj.* **1** [early 19C+] surprising, highly unlikely; usu. *that's rich.* **2** [mid–19C+] very funny.

Richard *n.*[1] [mid-19C] (*US Und.*) a hunchback. [the infamous characteristic of Richard III]

Richard *n.*[2] (*also* **Mr Richard**) [1910s–30s] (*US Und.*) a detective. [play on DICK n.[6] (1)]

Richard Burton *n.* [20C+] a curtain. [rhy. sl.; ult. actor *Richard Burton* (1925–84)]

richard snary *n.* (*also* **richard, richardanary**) [late 18C–19C] a dictionary. [play on abbr. *dick*; 'A country lad, having been reproved for calling persons by their christian names, being sent by his master to borrow a dictionary, thought to show his breeding by asking for a *Richard Snary*' (Grose, 1796)]

Richard (the Third) n. 1 [late 19C+] a piece of excrement; thus fig. an unpleasant person (cf. ALI OOP n.). 2 [late 19C+] a word. 3 [late 19C+] booing, barracking. 4 [1940s+] a young woman, a girlfriend. 5 [1960s+] a bird. 6 [1980s+] a third-class degree (cf. DESMOND (TUTU) n.). [rhy. sl.; (1) = TURD n.; (3) = BIRD n.⁵ (1); (4) = BIRD n.¹ (2)]

rich as mud phr. (also **rich as cream/custard**) [mid–19C+] (US) very rich.

rich face n. (also **rich nose**) [late 17C–early 19C] a heavily acned face or nose. [seen as the product of a diet of rich food]

rich friend n. [early 19C] a prostitute's keeper, i.e. a wealthy man rather than a pimp. [euph.]

rich one n. [late 19C] a wealthy but unloved wife. [the term was used by up-market prostitutes with ref. to the wives that their clients dared not leave altogether]

rick n. [1950s+] an error, a mistake. [? RICKET n. or ? bookmakers' jargon rick, a spurious bet]

rickaticks n. [20C+] (W.I.) a very bad temper; thus get in one's rickaticks, to lose one's temper and stay furious for some time. [UK dial. rickmatick, a (rowdy) affair]

ricket n. [1950s+] a mistake, a blunder. [ety. unknown; link to the disease SE rickets]

rickets n. [2000s] (US Black) an infestation of pubic lice. [ety. unknown]

rickety kate n. [20C+] (Aus.) a gate. [rhy. sl.]

ricky-tick adj. (also **ricky-tick-tock, ricky-ticky**) [1930s+] 1 (orig. US) old-fashioned, predictable, monotonous. 2 (US) cheap and shabby. [jazz use ricky-tick, old-fashioned jazz]

ricockulous adj. [1990s+] (US Black) ludicrous, absurd, worthy of verbal denigration. [SE ridiculous ? + COCK n.⁵ (2)]

riddle-me-ree n. [1980s+] 1 an act of urination (cf. ANGEL'S KISS n.). 2 the number 3. [rhy. sl.; (1) = PEE n.¹ (2)]

ride n.¹ 1 [late 15C; mid–19C+] sexual intercourse. 2 [late 19C+] (orig. Irish) a woman when regarded as a (potential) sexual partner. 3 [1960s+] (Scot.) a term of abuse, synon. with FUCKER n. (3). 4 [1990s+] (Irish) an attractive man. [RIDE v.¹ (1)]

ride n.² 1 [1920s+] (US) an automobile. 2 [1980s+] (US campus) a bicycle or motorcycle. 3 [1990s+] (US Black) a skateboard.

ride n.³ [1940s–60s] (US prison) a jail sentence.

ride n.⁴ [1970s+] (US prison) a companion, esp. a fellow gang-member. [a member of the same group or CAR n. (1)]

ride v.¹ 1 [16C+] of a man, to have sexual intercourse; occas. of a woman. 2 [1930s–50s] (US) to play an instrument with rhythm and competence. 3 [1990s+] (US prison) to trade sexual favours for immunity from physical attack by fellow inmates. [prior use SE]

ride v.² [late 19C–1930s] (US campus) to use a translation in an examination or when preparing classwork (cf. CRIB v.²). [pun on PONY n.³/HORSE n.⁶]

ride v.³ [20C+] 1 to annoy, to irritate. 2 to tease, to taunt. 3 to pressurize. 4 (US campus) to reprimand, to scold. 5 to pursue closely. [one is 'on one's back']

ride v.⁴ [20C+] (US Und.) to move from a local jail to prison proper.

ride v.⁵ [1930s+] (US) to endure, to suffer, to experience.

ride v.⁶ see PUNK (OUT) v. (2).

ride v.⁷ see TAKE FOR A RIDE v.¹ (2).

ride a blind piece v. [1940s–60s] (gay) to fellate an uncircumcised penis. [play on SE ride + BLIND adj.³ + PIECE n.³ (2)]

ride a desk v. [2000s] (US) to work as a clerk or in any otherwise deskbound occupation. [play on DESK JOCKEY n.]

ride a jock v. [1980s+] (US campus) of a woman, to attempt to get to know a man of her own peer group with the intentions of ultimately having a relationship with that person because of his personality, not his material possessions. [SE ride + JOCK n.¹ (5)]

ride a St George v. [mid-18C–19C] to have sexual intercourse with the woman on top of the man. [illustrations of a mounted St George slaying the Dragon; note Lat. use, translated as 'mounting the Hectorean horse']

ride backwards up Holborn Hill v. see WALK BACKWARDS UP HOLBORN HILL v.

ride bareback v. [1950s+] to have sexual intercourse without a condom. [RIDE v.¹ (1) + BAREBACK adv.]

ride Bayard of ten toes v. [late 16C–18C] to walk. [proper name Bayard, a horse that featured in various medieval romances; the name itself comes from Fr. bayard, bay-coloured; Henke, Gutter Life and Language (1988), notes a one-off use in A Hundred Merry Tales (1526) in which Bayard is synon. with a young woman's buttocks, the cleft of which is 'Bayard's mouth', a play between the brown horse and the brown anus]

ride below the crupper v. [mid-17C–18C] of a man, to have sexual intercourse. [SE crupper, the hind-quarters or rump of a horse; also the human buttocks]

ride bitch v. (also **ride punk/pussy, sit bitch**) [1970s+] (US Black/teen) to ride in the middle of the back seat or on the pillion of a motorcycle (cf. RIDE SHOTGUN v.). [SE ride + BITCH n.¹ (1)/PUNK n.¹ (10)/PUSSY n. (1), i.e. the supposed 'woman's seat']

ride blind baggage v. see RIDE THE BLINDS v.

ride down v. [1990s+] (US prison) to attack in a group. [image of a 'Wild West' posse]

ride down to the ground v. [1970s+] (US Black) to attack verbally, to criticize heavily. [image of a 'Wild West' posse]

ride grub v. [late 18C] to be bad-tempered or sulky. [SE grub, an unpleasant person]

ride herd on v. [late 19C+] (US) to control or manage someone or something, to admonish, to beat. [cowboy imagery]

ride in a cart up Holborn Hill v. see WALK BACKWARDS UP HOLBORN HILL v.

ride in another man's boots v. (also **ride in another's/anyone's old boots, ride in old shoes**) [mid-17C–early 19C] to marry another man's ex-wife or widow, or to start keeping his former mistress.

ride like a/the town bike v. see TOWN BIKE n.

rideman n. [1920s–40s] (US jazz) a soloist.

ride old smokey v. see OLD SMOKEY n.

ride one's cock horse to Banbury Cross v. [1970s] of a woman, to have sexual intercourse. [COCK n.² (1); plus the nursery rhyme, itself allegedly containing sexual imagery]

ride one's high horse v. see MOUNT ONE'S HIGH HORSE v.

ride one's low horse v. [1930s+] to act as a drunken fool.

ride one's thumb v. [1960s] to hitchhike.

ride on your back! excl. [1910s] (Aus.) a general term of abuse; the implication is that the subject is 'a goat'.

ride out v. 1 [early 17C–18C] to be a highwayman. 2 [1950s+] (US Black/teen) to leave; also as imper. 3 [2000s] (US prison) to move to another prison. [(2) and (3) are cowboy imagery]

ride out! excl. [2000s] (US Black) an excl. of dismissal, disbelief. [RIDE OUT v. (2)]

ride plush v. [20C+] (US tramp) to pay for one's seat (and thus travel in comfort). [SE ride + PLUSH adj. + the lit. plush-covered seats]

ride punk/pussy v. see RIDE BITCH v.

rider n.¹ 1 [17C+] a womanizer; thus, a male copulator. 2 [1970s] (US gay) a male homosexual who takes the active role in anal intercourse. [RIDE v.¹ (1)]

rider n.² 1 [late 18C–early 19C] someone who receives part of the salary for a job through an agreement with the job's actual appointee or with their patron; the rider is said to be 'quartered' on the job's possessor and a single possessor may have several riders in tow. 2 [2000s] (US drugs) free heroin provided to a purchaser of bulk cocaine, e.g. 5kg of heroin for every 100kg of cocaine. [SE rider, one who rides + legal jargon, an additional clause tacked onto a document after its first drafting]

rider n.³ [1920s] (US prison/Und.) a prosecutor.

riders n. [1970s+] (US gay) very tight trousers. [i.e. they ride up one's anus]

ride rusty v. [late 18C–mid-19C] to be ill-tempered or sullen. [SE *ride* + *rusty*, refractory (of horses)]

ride shotgun v. (*also* **ride shottie, sit shotgun**) [1950s+] **1** (*orig. US*) to sit in the seat next to the driver in a car, also in fig. use (cf. RIDE BITCH v.). **2** (*US*) to act as a security guard, esp. on a vehicle. [SHOTGUN n.²]

ride someone's leg v. [2000s] (*US prison*) to befriend officers in the hope of gaining favours. [the image of a dog rubbing itself amorously against one's leg]

ride staff v. (*also* **play staff**) [1960s+] (*S.Afr.*) to cling to the outside, or stand on the roof, of a moving train, having boarded it while in motion. [Zulu sl. *ukubamb' istuff*, to board a moving train; ? ult. *staff*, the pole in the doorway of railway carriage, which is grasped by those jumping aboard when the train is already moving]

ride tantivy v. [18C] a euph. for to have sexual intercourse, i.e. to gallop. [SE *tantivy*, a gallop at full tilt]

ride the baloney pony v. *see* RIDE THE PONY v.

ride the beams v. *see* RIDE THE ROD(S) v.

ride the beef v. [1950s+] (*US Und.*) to take the blame. [SE *ride* (*out*) + BEEF n.² (5)]

ride the bitch's seat v. *see* RIDE BITCH v.

ride the black donkey v. [mid-19C] to be in a bad temper.

ride the blinds v. (*also* **ride blind baggage**) [late 19C+] (*US tramp*) to ride for free in the closed baggage compartment of a train. [BLIND n.³ (2)]

ride the broom v. [1970s+] (*US prison*) to threaten or intimidate another inmate; to prophesy. [the trad. witch on her broomstick]

ride the buick v. (*also* **go to Europe with Ralph and Earl in a Buick**) [1970s+] (*US*) to vomit. [ext. of BUICK v. (+ RALPH v. + EARL v.)]

ride the bumpers v. *see* RIDE THE ROD(S) v.

ride the cotton pony v. (*also* **ride the white horse, ...the cotton horse**) [1960s+] to be menstruating (cf. RIDE THE RED HORSE v.). [cotton sanitary towels]

ride the cushions v. [1910s+] (*US tramp*) **1** to ride in a passenger car rather than a boxcar. **2** in fig. use, to prosper, to be comfortable. [the upholstered seats]

ride the deck v. [1940s+] (*US prison*) to perform anal intercourse (cf. ASK FOR THE RING v.). [RIDE v.¹ (1) + fig. use of DECK n.¹ (1)]

ride the Erie v. (*also* **ride the earie**) [1940s] (*US*) to eavesdrop. [ON THE EARIE phr. (2) + play on the *Erie* railroad]

ride the E-train v. [1990s+] (*US campus/drugs*) to feel the effects of the drug MDMA. [play on the New York subway *E-train*/E n.]

ride the goat v. [1900s–20s] (*US*) to be initiated into a secret society. [the fantasy that initiate Masons have to ride a live goat]

ride the gravy train v. (*also* **ride the gravy boat**) [20C+] (*US*) to enjoy a comfortable life. [GRAVY TRAIN n.]

ride the grub line v. [1900s–40s] (*US*) of an out-of-work cowboy, to travel around seeking work while subsisting on handouts. [GRUB-LINER n.]

ride the gun v. [1970s+] (*US teen*) to ride in the front passenger seat of a car. [var. on RIDE SHOTGUN v. (1)]

ride the handcar v. [1940s+] (*US*) to masturbate (cf. AUDITION THE FINGER PUPPETS v.). [from the up-and-down movement of a handle with which one drives the vehicle]

ride the hobby horse v. [1980s+] (*US campus*) to have sexual intercourse. [it is unlikely that the ref. to HOBBY HORSE n.² is more than coincidental]

ride the horse v. [1940s–70s] (*drugs*) to take heroin; thus *horse-riding, on horseback,* using heroin. [SE *ride* + HORSE n.⁸]

ride the horse foaled by an acorn v. (*also* **...of an acorn**) [mid-17C–mid-19C] to be hanged. [i.e. the oak tree gallows]

ride the lightning v. [1930s+] (*US*) to be executed in the electric chair. [note LIGHTNING n.² (1)]

ride the mainline v. (*also* **rock the mainline**) [1950s] (*drugs*) to inject narcotics; to be a narcotics addict. [SE *ride*/ROCK v.⁵ (1) + MAINLINE n.² (1)]

ride the mule v. *see* MULE n.⁵ (2).

ride the odno v. [late 19C] to travel by train without paying a fare. [backsl.; *odno* = nod, thus ON THE NOD phr.¹ (1)]

ride the pilot v. [1930s] (*US tramp*) to ride on the cowcatcher of the locomotive.

ride the pine v. [1980s] (*US campus*) to sit on the bench during an athletic event, esp. when one desperately wants to play. [the *pine* bench]

ride the planks v. *see* PLANK n.².

ride the plush v. [1920s–40s] (*US tramp/Und.*) **1** to ride inside a passenger train. **2** in fig. use, to be well provided with material comforts.

ride the pony v. (*also* **ride the baloney pony, ...white pony**) [1980s+] (*US*) of a woman, to have sexual intercourse astride the man (cf. CATCH AN OYSTER v.). [SE *ride* + *pony*/ BALONEY n.²]

ride the poppy train v. [1950s–60s] (*drugs*) to smoke opium.

ride the porcelain bus v. (*also* **ride the porcelain Honda/pony**) [1960s+] (*orig. US campus*) **1** to vomit (cf. DRIVE THE (PORCELAIN) BUS v.). **2** to have diarrhoea. [i.e. the porcelain lavatory bowl]

ride the rag v. [1960s+] (*US Black/campus*) to have a menstrual period. [RAG n.⁸ (1)]

ride the rap v. [1980s+] (*US*) to accept the consequences of one's crimes, such as arrest and imprisonment, and deal with them as well as possible. [SE *ride* (*out*) + RAP n.⁴ (3)]

ride the red horse v. [1990s+] (*US*) to be menstruating (cf. RIDE THE COTTON PONY v.).

ride the rod(s) v. (*also* **ride the beams/bumpers**) [late 19C+] (*US tramp*) to ride on the steel bars beneath a freight car; fig. to be a tramp. [ROD n.² (1)]

ride the rumble v. [1950s] (*US Und.*) to take responsibility for a crime. [RUMBLE n.² (2)]

ride the tan track v. [1990s+] to have homosexual anal intercourse (cf. ASK FOR THE RING v.). [TAN TRACK n.]

ride the toby v. [early–mid-19C] to practise highway robbery. [SE *ride* + TOBY n.² (1)]

ride the wagon v. [1970s] (*US Black*) to enjoy a pleasant experience on a drug. [the image of lying on a hay-laden wagon as it moves through the fields]

ride the white horse v.¹ [1950s+] (*US Black*) to be intoxicated with drugs. [WHITE HORSE n.³]

ride the white horse v.² *see* RIDE THE COTTON PONY v.

ride the white pony v. *see* RIDE THE PONY v.

ride the wild mare v. [late 16C–early 17C] to ride on a seesaw; thus fig. to live a riotous, wild life.

ride to Romford v. (*also* **ride to Rumford**) **1** [mid–18C] to be blunt; usu. as *you may ride to Romford on this knife.* **2** [late 18C–early 19C] to get a new pair of breeches or to get a new bottom put in an old pair. [proper name *Romford,* Essex, esteemed for the quality of its leather breeches]

ride tough v. [1970s+] (*US Black*) **1** to be intoxicated by a drug. **2** to be riding in a noteworthy car. [TOUGH adv.]

ride up a gumtree v. [1910s+] (*Aus.*) to fall off one's horse. [? lit. + UP A GUM TREE phr. (1)]

ride with v. [1970s+] (*US prison*) **1** to side with (in a fight). **2** to be friends with. [fig. use of SE, but note CAR n. (1)]

ridge n. **1** [mid-17C–mid-19C; 1920s+] (*also* **rige**) gold, thus money, a guinea (cf. CANARY n.⁵). **2** [mid-19C+] (*UK/US Und.*) coins, rather than notes. [the term vanished in the UK during the 19C but reappeared in Aus. in the mid-20C+]

ridge adj. **1** [19C] (*UK Und.*) gold, golden. **2** [1930s+] (*Aus.*) valuable, good. [RIDGE n. (1)]

ridge cove n. [late 18C–mid-19C] (*UK Und.*) a goldsmith. [RIDGE n. (1) + COVE n. (1)]

ridge cully *n.* [mid-17C–early 19C] (*UK Und.*) a goldsmith. [RIDGE n. (1) + CULLY n. (3)]

ridge montra *n.* [early 19C] (*UK Und.*) a gold watch. [RIDGE adj. (1) + MONTRA n.]

ridgerunner *n.* [1930s+] (*US*) a Southern mountain farmer, a hillbilly. [orig. f. Arkansas only]

ridge-super *n.* [mid-19C] (*UK Und.*) a gold watch. [RIDGE adj. (1) + SUPER n.² (1)]

ridgey-didge *n.* [1980s] (*Aus.*) a refrigerator. [rhy. sl. = SE *fridge*]

ridgie-didgie *adj.* (*also* **ridgey-the-didge, ridgie-didge, ridgy-dite**) [1950s+] (*Aus.*) genuine, honest. [RIDGE adj. (2) + redup.]

ridic *adj.* [1910s+] (*US campus*) ridiculous. [abbr.]

ridiculous *adj.* [1950s–60s] (*orig. US Black*) outstanding, excellent.

riding *n.* [1920s–30s] (*orig. US*) annoying, irritating, teasing. [RIDE v.³]

riding academy *n.* [1930s–60s] (*orig. US Black*) a brothel; a hotel where one can go with a prostitute (cf. ACADEMY n.). [RIDE v.¹ (1)]

riding a thorn *phr.* [1950s–70s] (*drugs*) injecting narcotics. [i.e. the needle]

riding the wave *phr.* (*also* **riding a wave**) [1920s–50s] (*drugs*) under the influence of drugs. [surfing imagery]

riding the witch's broom *phr.* [1950s] (*drugs*) using heroin. [it gets one HIGH n.¹ (2)]

riff *n.* **1** [1940s+] (*orig. US Black*) one's personal style. **2** [1960s+] (*US*) information. **3** [1970s] (*US campus*) exaggeration, boastful talk. **4** [1970s] (*US*) a joke, a line. **5** [1970s] (*US*) an argument. **6** [1970s+] (*orig. US Black*) familiar or habitual words. **7** [1980s+] (*US campus*) one who takes advantage of another person. **8** [2000s] a rumour. [jazz use *riff*, a simple musical phrase repeated over and over]

riff *v.* **1** [1940s+] (*orig. US Black*) to chatter, to talk. **2** [1970s] (*US campus*) to boast, to exaggerate. **3** [1980s+] (*US*) to complain. **4** [1980s+] (*US campus*) (*also* **riff on**) to take advantage of someone. **5** [1990s+] to inform on; to reveal facts about. **6** [1990s+] to offend. [RIFF n.]

riffle *n.* [mid–late 19C] (*US Und.*) a large amount of money acquired by deceit or trickery. [SE *riffle* the notes]

riff-raff *n.* [20C+] **1** a Welsh person. **2** a café, i.e. 'caff'. [rhy. sl.; (1) = TAFF n.]

rifle *v.* (*also* **riffle**) [mid-16C–mid-19C] to have sexual intercourse; thus *rifler*, a prostitute's customer. [SE *rifle*, of a hawk, to tread the hen; + overtones of SE *rifle*, to despoil, to plunder]

rifler *n. see* TOLLER n.

rifle range *n.¹* [1960s–70s] (*drugs*) **1** a house, apartment or room in which addicts gather to inject drugs. **2** a detoxification ward. [play on SHOOTING GALLERY n.]

rifle range *n.²* [2000s] **1** change (monetary). **2** a change. [rhy. sl.]

rift *n.* [1960s+] (*Irish*) a belch. [echoic]

rig *n.¹* **1** [late 16C–mid-19C] a wanton, promiscuous woman. **2** [mid-19C] a smart, 'sharp' young man. [? SE *rig*, to play the wanton, to romp about; ult. ety. unknown]

rig *n.²* **1** [early 18C–mid-19C] ridicule, mockery. **2** [mid-18C+] (*also* **rigging**) a dodge, a confidence trick; thus *run the rig on*, to deceive, to trick. **3** [late 18C–1900s] a prank or game. [? dial.]

rig *n.³* **1** [late 18C+] one's clothing, one's style of dress. **2** [early 19C] in fig. use, one's personal style. [RIG v.¹ (1)]

rig *n.⁴* [1930s] (*Irish*) a man with 1 testicle. [SE *rig*, half-castrated animal]

rig *n.⁵* **1** [1930s+] (*drugs*) the equipment needed to inject narcotics. **2** [1940s+] the male genitals. **3** [2000s] (*US*) a gun. [SE *rig*, equipment/EQUIPMENT n. (1); note RIG n.⁴]

rig *n.⁶* [1930s+] (*orig. US*) **1** a truck. **2** a vehicle in general. [early 19C SE *rig*, a horse and its vehicle; ult. the 'rigging' or harness]

rig *v.¹* (*also* **rig out/up**) [17C+] **1** to clothe; thus *rigged out/up*, dressed (up). **2** in fig. use, to 'patch up'. [naut. imagery]

rig *v.²* **1** [late 17C–mid-19C] to play tricks on, to fool. **2** [mid-19C+] to manipulate illegally. [? link to RIG n.¹ (2)]

rig a jig *v.* [1970s] (*US Black*) **1** of a pimp, to set up a potential customer with a woman. **2** of a confidence man, to set up a victim for deception. [SE *rig (up)* + (1) JIG n.⁵; (2) JIG n.² (1)]

rige *n. see* RIDGE n. (1).

rigged *adj.* [20C+] of a contest, manipulated or set up. [RIG v.² (2)]

rigger *n.* [1940s] (*Aus./N.Z.*) a quart bottle of beer, esp. a quart of draught beer in a square-faced gin bottle. [? SE *square-rigger*]

rigging *n.¹* [17C–19C] (*UK Und.*) clothes; thus *rum rigging*, fashionable, expensive clothes; *under-rigging*, underclothes. [RIG v.¹ (1) + naut. *rigging*, the various ropes that are used on a sailing ship]

rigging *n.²* [1980s] (*US*) the male genitalia.

rigging *n.³ see* RIG n.² (2).

riggish *adj.* [late 16C–19C] lecherous, amorous, lascivious. [RIG n.¹ (1)]

right *adj.¹* **1** [mid-19C+] (*Und.*) reliable, trustworthy (from the criminal's point of view); thus corrupt (i.e. of a policeman). **2** [late 19C+] (*Aus./N.Z.*) safe, secure; lit. and fig. **3** [20C+] (*US Und.*) justifiable, e.g. an arrest that follows a crime that one did commit. **4** [1900s] sober. **5** [1910s+] sane, mentally balanced; usu. in negative phrs. to mean insane, e.g. *not right*, and usu. in combs. e.g. *right in the wits, right in the head*. **6** [1910s+] (*US*) respectable, honest, dependable. **7** [1970s] (*US*) good, in good spirits. [note Williams refs. to the 17C use of *right* to mean whorish, immoral]

right *adj.²* [1930s+] (*US*) drunk or intoxicated (cf. ABOUT RIGHT phr.¹). [the inference is that the sober/drugless state is 'wrong']

right *v.* (*also* **right up**) [1940s] (*US Und.*) to corrupt, to make someone, e.g. a policeman, a politician, amenable to bribery and thus the permitting of criminal activity. [RIGHT adj.¹ (1)]

right *adv.* **1** [mid-19C+] (*also* **rite**) used for emphasizing how good or bad someone or something is, e.g. *a right bastard, a right good 'un.* **2** [mid-19C+] (*also* **rightly, right smart**) totally, completely. **3** [1900s–20s] (*US Und.*) of a criminal, under protection from corrupt authorities. **4** [1910s+] (*US*) properly; thus *get (one) right*, to capture 'dead to rights'.

right *phr.* (*also* **yeah, right**) [1980s+] a dismissive, sarcastic phr. 'sure, I (don't) believe you'.

right arm! *excl.* [1970s] (*US campus*) a parody of the 1960s slogan RIGHT ON! excl.

right as a bank *phr.* [1900s–50s] (*N.Z.*) perfectly satisfactory, perfectly happy.

right bower *n.* **1** [late 19C] (*US*) a deputy or second in command. **2** [late 19C–1920s] in cards, the knave of trumps; also in fig. use. **3** [1900s] a preferred suitor. [Ger. *bauer*, peasant, which can be seen as a 'knave'; orig. used in the card-game euchre for the 2 highest cards – the knave of trumps, and the knave of the same colour, called *right* and *left bower* respectively]

right charlie *n.* (*also* **proper charlie**) [1950s+] a fool, a simpleton (cf. BEN n.¹). [RIGHT adv. (1)/PROPER adj. (1) + CHARLIE n.⁶]

right copper *n.* (*also* **right cop**) [1930s+] a corrupt policeman. [RIGHT adj.¹ (1) + COPPER n.³ (1)]

right croaker *n.* [1920s–50s] (*US*) a doctor who is willing to write prescriptions for narcotic drugs, patch up wounded villains and perform other illegal services. [RIGHT adj.¹ (1) + CROAKER n.⁵ (1)]

right down *adv.* [early 19C–1920s] a general intensifier, completely, utterly, absolutely.

right enough! *excl.* [late 19C+] indeed! certainly!

righteo! *adj. see* RIGHTO! excl.

righteous *n.* [1900s–10s] (*Aus.*) riotous behaviour; also as adj. [joc. mispron.]

righteous *adj.* **1** [late 19C] (*UK Und.*) legitimate. **2** [late 19C] honest, truthful. **3** [1930s+] (*orig. US Black*) honest, trustworthy, honourable. **4** [1930s+] of things, esp. drugs, excellent, first-rate.

5 [1940s+] attractive, beautiful. **6** [1960s+] ideologically pure. **7** [1970s] (*UK Black*) respectable. **8** [1970s] extreme, very great. **9** [1980s] as a general intensifier. [SE, with undertones of the biblical sense of 'God on one's side']

righteous *adv.* [1960s+] (*US Black*) absolutely, completely. [RIGHTEOUS adj.]

righteous! *excl.* [1990s+] an affirmative excl., absolutely! sure! [RIGHTEOUS adj.]

righteous bush *n.* [1940s+] (*drugs*) marijuana (cf. AFRICAN BUSH n.). [RIGHTEOUS adj. (4) + BUSH n.5 (1)]

righteous grass *n. see* RIGHTEOUS MOSS n.

righteous jones *n.* [1950s+] (*drugs*) a severe drug addiction. [RIGHTEOUS adj. (4) + JONES n.1 (1)]

righteously *adv.* **1** [1940s+] openly, undisguisedly, intensely. **2** [1970s+] honestly, dependably, with integrity. [RIGHTEOUS adj.]

righteous man *n.* [mid-19C] (*UK Und.*) a house-breaker. [? RIGHTEOUS adj.]

righteous moss *n.* (*also* **righteous grass**) [1940s+] (*US Black*) White people's hair. [RIGHTEOUS adj. (5) + MOSS n.1 (3)/GRASS n.1 (2)]

righteous nod *n.* [1940s] (*US Black*) a good night's sleep. [RIGHTEOUS adj. (4) + NOD n.1 (1)]

righteous rags *n.* [1940s] (*US Black*) expensive, well-cut, fashionable clothes. [RIGHTEOUS adj. (4) + RAGS n. (1)]

righteous riff *n.* [1940s] (*US Black*) good conversation, inspiring, intelligent talk. [RIGHTEOUS adj. (4) + RIFF n. (1)]

righteous yellow *n.* [1940s] (*US Black*) an attractive, light-skinned young woman. [RIGHTEOUS adj. (5) + YELLOW n.3]

right grift *n.* [1900s–20s] (*US Und.*) working confidence tricks after bribing the police and thus without fear of arrest. [RIGHT adj.1 (1) + GRIFT n. (1)]

right guy *n.* **1** [20C+] (*US, mainly Und.*) a trustworthy person. **2** [1950s+] (*US prison*) a popular prisoner, respected by his peers. [RIGHT adj.1 (1) + GUY n.2 (1)]

right-hander *n. see* LEFT-FOOTER n.1.

right-ho! *excl. see* RIGHTO! excl.

right-ho *v.* [1940s] to agree. [RIGHTO! excl.]

rightid *adj.* [1990s+] sensible.

rightie *n.* (*also* **righty**) (*US*) **1** [1910s+] a person who has lost their limbs on their right side (arm and leg). **2** [1940s] right-handedness. **3** [1940s+] a right-hander.

right into (one's barrel) *phr. see* RIGHT UP ONE'S BARREL phr.

right Joe *n. see* REGULAR JOE n.

rightly *adv. see* RIGHT adv. (2).

rightness *n.* [1950s] (*US Und.*) defiance of authority. [RIGHT adj.1 (1)]

righto *adj.* [1910s] (*Aus.*) excellent, admirable. [RIGHTO! excl.]

righto! *excl.* (*also* **righteo! right-ho! righty-ho!**) [late 19C+] an excl. of affirmation, certainly! yes!

right oil *n.* [1920s+] (*Aus.*) the honest truth, true facts. [RIGHT adj.1 (6) + OIL n.2 (3)]

right on *adj.* [1960s+] **1** absolutely correct. **2** politically correct, ideologically pure. [RIGHT ON! excl.]

right on *adv.* [1950s] absolutely, completely, unreservedly. [RIGHT ON adj.]

right on! *excl.* [1920s; 1960s+] an excl. of encouragement, approval: excellent, perfect, exactly right; orig. Black use but taken up by White hippies, radicals etc. [abbr. earlier *right on T/right on time*; the later use implied movement/progress rather than chronology]

right one *n.1* **1** [early 19C; 1930s+] something that is an exceptional example of its type, usu. humorous or bizarre. **2** [late 19C–1920s] an admirable person (or animal). [SE *right*/RIGHT adj.1]

right one *n.2* [20C+] (*Ulster*) an unpredictable person. [RIGHT adv. (1)]

rights and wrongs *n.* [1980s] (*Aus.*) a pair of thongs, i.e. footwear. [rhy. sl.]

right screw *n.* [late 19C+] a corrupt prison warder. [RIGHT adj.1 (1) + SCREW n.2 (3)]

right smart *adv. see* RIGHT adv. (2).

right sort *n.* [early–mid-19C] an alcoholic drink, esp. gin. [play on SE]

right stuff *n.* **1** [late 19C+] any alcoholic drink; esp. in phr. *a drop of the right stuff.* **2** [1920s–30s] money. **3** [1930s] attractive women.

right town *n.* [1910s–40s] (*US Und.*) any town or small city where the authorities – police, local politicians – have been bribed into allowing criminal activity to flourish. [RIGHT adj.1 (1) + SE *town*]

right twirl *n.* [late 19C] a corrupt prison warder. [RIGHT adj.1 (1) + TWIRL n. (2)]

right up *v. see* RIGHT v.

right up one's barrel *phr.* (*also* **right into (one's barrel)**, **…barrow**) [20C+] (*Aus.*) absolutely perfect, completely to one's taste. [fitting snugly into a gun barrel/barrow]

right up there *phr.* [20C+] (*US*) in the running, in a winning position, at the forefront of things.

righty *n. see* RIGHTIE n.

righty-ho! *excl. see* RIGHTO! excl.

right you are! *excl.* [mid-19C+] a general excl. of agreement.

rigid *adj.* [1960s+] drunk and passed out.

rig mutton *n.* [late 16C] a wanton, promiscuous woman. [RIG n.1 (1) + MUTTON n.1 (1)]

rig-out *n.* (*also* **rig-up**) [early 19C+] a suit of clothes, an outfit. [RIG v.1 (1)]

rig out *v. see* RIG v.1.

rig sale *n.* [19C] a false sale, a mock auction. [RIG n.2 (2) + SE *sale*]

rigsby *n.* [mid-16C–early 17C] a wanton, promiscuous woman. [RIG n.1 (1)]

rig-up *n.1* [1990s+] (*US Black*) an unpleasant, intolerable situation. [RIG n.2 (2)]

rig-up *n.2 see* RIG-OUT n.

rig up *v. see* RIG v.1.

riha *n. see* RIAH n.

Rikki Lake *adj.* [2000s] counterfeit, fake. [rhy. sl.; ult. US TV personality *Ricki Lake*]

rile *v.* (*also* **ryle**) [mid-19C+] (*orig. US*) to annoy, to irritate; thus *riled*, irritated; *riling*, annoying. [SE *roil*, to stir up, thus to annoy, to vex]

rile up *v.* [late 19C–1950s] to get angry, tense or worried. [RILE v.]

Riley *n. see* LIFE OF RILEY n.

riley *adj.* [mid-19C] (*US*) angry. [RILE v.]

rileyed *adj.* [late 19C–1930s] (*US*) drunk. [typical Irish surname *Riley* (plus *Reilly* and *O'Reilly*) and thus the stereotyping of the Irish as drunkards; the spec. source is the stage production of *The Mulligan's Silver Wedding* 'a low life comedy' in Feb. 1881, in which was featured a song 'John Riley's Always Dry' which listed the eponymous Riley's prodigious drinking]

rily *phr.* [1940s] (*US*) affectionate acronym used in telegrams: remember *I love you*.

rim *n.* [2000s] (*US*) an automobile tyre.

rim *v.1* [1940s+] (*US*) **1** to cheat, to swindle. **2** to cause failure, to ruin someone's chances, esp. by deception. [var. on REAM v. (1)]

rim *v.2* [1940s+] (*mainly gay*) to stimulate the anus with the lips and tongue; thus *rimming*, anilingus (cf. AUSTRALIAN n.). [var. REAM (OUT) v.]

rimadona *n.* [1960s] (*gay*) a male homosexual. [puns on SE *primadonna*/RIM v.2]

rimble-ramble *n.* [late 17C; 1910s] nonsense, thus as adj., nonsensical, absurd.

rim job *n.* [1970s+] an act of anilingus (cf. AUSTRALIAN n.; REAM JOB n.). [RIM v.2 + JOB n.4]

rimmer *n.* [1970s+] someone who stimulates another's anus with their tongue, an anilinguist. [RIM v.²]

rimming *n. see* RIM v.².

rim queen *n.* [1950s+] a homosexual who enjoys anilingus. [RIM v.² + QUEEN n.² (1)/QUEEN sfx (2)]

rim slide *n.* [1960s+] (*US prison*) a silent but foul-smelling breaking of wind. [the FART n. (1) *slides* from the *rim* of the anus]

rince *n.* (*also* rinse) [19C] a drink.

rince *v.* (*also* rinse) [19C] to drink. [RINCE n.]

rinctum *n.* (*also* rinktum) [1970s+] (*US Black*) the rectum, the anus. [US regional *rinctum*, a gadget, something that has no name or which one prefers not to name]

rind *n.*¹ [late 19C+] cheek, impudence, effrontery (cf. CRUST n.³). [SE *rind*, an outer covering or shell that is difficult to penetrate]

rind *n.*² [1920s–40s] (*US Black*) the human skin.

ring *n.*¹ **1** [late 16C–18C] the vagina. **2** [late 19C+] the anus, the buttocks; thus *ring-snatcher*, a sodomite; *ring-snatching*, sodomy. **3** [1940s] anal intercourse, sodomy. [the shapes]

ring *n.*² (*UK Und.*) **1** [17C] the money that is stolen by a highwayman. **2** [late 17C–early 19C] money that is procured by begging. [? SE *ring*, thus an object worth money, or the ringing noise the cash makes as it is thrown from the coach/into the begging bowl]

ring *n.*³ [1940s+] (*Aus.*) the site of a two-up game. [boxing imagery]

ring *n.*⁴ *see* RINGER n.¹.

ring *v.*¹ **1** [mid–18C] (*UK Und.*) to change a good coin for a counterfeit one. **2** [mid-18C+] to change, to alter; thus *ringing castors*, changing hats, typically by going to some public place, stealing an expensive hat from where it has been deposited and leaving a cheap one; *ring togs*, to change clothes. **3** [mid-19C] to desert, i.e. a lover. **4** [mid-19C] (*UK Und.*) of individuals or groups, to substitute, to swap. **5** [mid-19C] to substitute cards. **6** [mid–late 19C] (*UK Und.*) to be disturbed in the act of a robbery, and thus having to flee without the goods. **7** [late 19C+] to cheat. **8** [late 19C+] (*US*) illegally to substitute a horse for another in a horserace. **9** [1900s] to substitute crooked dice. **10** [1910s] (*US Und.*) as *ring up*, to assume a disguise. **11** [1940s+] to alter a car for the purposes of using it as a getaway vehicle, hold-up van etc, or for reselling it to an unsuspecting customer. [fig. use of abbr. SE phr. *ring the changes*]

ring *v.*² [late 19C+] (*Aus.*) to be the most successful shearer in a shed. [SE *ring the bell*, to win a victory]

ring *v.*³ [1960s] to open and then steal the contents of a cash register. [the ring of the 'no change' key on an old-fashioned till]

ring a bell *v.* [1930s+] to remind one of something, to jog one's memory.

ring-a-dang-doo *n. see* RING-DANG-DO n. (1).

ring-a-ding *n.* [1980s] Bell's whisky. [pun]

ring-a-ding *adj.* (*also* ring-a-ding-ding) **1** [1950s–60s] a term of approval for a beautiful woman. **2** [1990s+] perfect, ideal. [the image of celebratory bell-ringing]

ring a peal (in a man's ears) *v.* [late 18C–early 19C] to scold, usu. of a wife scolding her husband.

ring-a-rang-roo *n. see* RING-DANG-DO n. (1).

ring around the rosy *n.* **1** [1920s–60s] (*US*) a waste of time, a lightweight matter. **2** [1960s+] (*US gay*) an orgy. [the children's game]

ring a tat into *v. see* TAT n.³.

ringbarked *adj.* [1980s+] (*N.Z.*) circumcised. [SE *ringbark*, to kill a tree by removing a ring of bark from the trunk]

ringbolt *v.* [1960s+] (*N.Z.*) to obtain a free ship voyage by posing as a crew member. [the use of SE *ringbolts* on ships]

ringburner *n.* [1960s+] (*UK society*) diarrhoea, or very painful defecation. [RING n.¹ (2) + SE *burner*]

ring chopper *n.* [mid-16C] (*UK Und.*) a swindler who sells counterfeit gold rings.

ring-dang-do *n.* **1** [1930s+] (*also* ring-a-dang-doo, ring-a-rang-roo) the vagina. **2** [1950s+] (*Aus.*) a spree, a party. **3** [1950s+] (*US*) a complicated affair, a rigmarole. [RING n.¹ (1)]

ring-ding *n.*¹ (*W.I.*) **1** [1900s] hilarity, lively entertainment. **2** [1940s] a quarrel.

ring-ding *n.*² [1950s+] (*US*) a fool, a second-rate person, a no-hoper. [? a punch-drunk boxer who has 'bells ringing' in his head]

ringdinger *n.* [1910s] (*US*) a person or object of excellence.

ring dropper *n.* [late 18C–mid-19C] a con-man who plays a trick of dropping a fake valuable object in the road and offering to let their victim buy it so they can have all the supposed profit (cf. RING FALLER n.). [RING DROPPING n. (1)]

ring dropping *n.* **1** [late 18C–19C] a swindle whereby some valuable object is dropped in the road, where it is found by a potential victim. This leads to an encounter, after which the victim is either lured into a fixed game or, in the case of the (fake) valuable, persuaded by the trickster to buy it, claiming that while they should share the profits, he, the con-man, will sell his share and let the victim have the whole benefit. **2** [late 19C] a term of scorn, 'equivalent to "tell your grandmother to suck eggs"' (Ware); so common had (1) become that anyone could spot a ring-dropper.

ringer *n.*¹ (*also* ring, ringer-in, wringer) (*orig. US*) **1** [mid-19C+] a fake; someone posing as a person they are not; esp. a pool or bowling hustler who pretends not to be an expert. **2** [late 19C+] a simulacrum, someone who looks exactly like another; also of an object. **3** [late 19C+] a horse or dog illegally substituted either for a better or a worse animal for the purposes of those betting either for or against it. **4** [late 19C+] someone who illegally substitutes a horse or animal in a race. **5** [1910s] (*Aus.*) a coward. **6** [1940s] one who uses a number of disguises (of themselves and their cars) during the committing of a crime. **7** [1960s+] a second-hand car made up to look better than it is. **8** [1960s+] someone who specializes in stealing then improving second-hand cars for sale in the UK or Europe. **9** [1960s+] a false registration plate attached to a stolen motor vehicle; thus the thief who uses one, and the car itself. [RING v.¹]

ringer *n.*² [late 19C+] (*Aus.*) **1** the fastest and best shearer in a shed. **2** an expert; anything or anyone outstanding or superlative of its/their kind. [RING v.²]

ringer *n.*³ [1920s–40s] (*US tramp*) a doorbell.

ringerangeroo *n.* [1930s+] (*US*) the vagina. [nonce-word but ? ref. to RING n.¹ (1)]

ringer-in *n. see* RINGER n.¹.

ring faller *n.* [mid-16C] a con-man who plays a trick of dropping a fake valuable object in the road and offering to let their victim buy it so they can have all the supposed profit. [early var. on RING DROPPER n.]

ring her bell *v.* **1** [1910s+] to produce (female) orgasm during intercourse. **2** [1930s+] to make pregnant.

ringie *n.* [1940s+] (*Aus./N.Z.*) the keeper of the RING n.³ in a game of two-up.

ring-in *n.* [1920s+] (*Aus./N.Z. Und.*) **1** anything that has been fraudulently substituted for something else, typically a racehorse or dog. **2** a stacked deck of cards. [RING IN v.¹]

ring in *v.*¹ **1** [early 19C+] to substitute fraudulently, e.g. one racehorse for another. **2** [mid-19C+] (*US*) to gain admission, to force one's way in. **3** [late 19C–1920s] to tell lies, to deceive. **4** [20C+] (*US*) to involve someone in something fraudulent; to subject someone to fraudulent acts. [ext. RING v.¹ (2)]

ring in *v.*² **1** [late 19C] (*US Und.*) to attract, to ensnare. **2** [late 19C–1920s] (*US Und.*) to join, to associate with. **3** [1900s] (*US*) to obtain. **4** [1910s] (*US*) to use.

ring it *v.* [1910s+] (*Aus.*) to act in a cowardly way. [RINGTAIL n.² (1)]

ring it on *v.* [1910s+] (*orig. Aus./N.Z.*) to outwit, to fool. [ext. RING v.¹ (2)]

ring jerk *n. see* CIRCLE JERK *n.*

ring job *n.* [1990s+] (*UK Und.*) a car that has been 'ringed', i.e. has had its identification changed for illicit resale. [RING v.¹ (11) + JOB n.⁴]

ring master *n.* [1990s+] a male homosexual (cf. ANAL ASTRONAUT n.). [RING n.¹ (2) + SE *master*]

ring neck *n.* (*also* **wring neck**) [20C+] (*W.I., Guyn.*) a tough, brawling person, esp. a woman. [SE *wring a neck*]

ring off *v.* **1** [late 19C] (*US*) to tell someone to be quiet. **2** [1910s–20s] to stop talking (other than on a telephone).

ring off! *excl.* [late 19C–1920s] be quiet! shut up! stop doing that! [telephone imagery]

ring one's tail *v.* [20C+] (*Aus.*) to surrender, to give in, in a game. [RINGTAIL n.²]

ringpiece *n.* **1** [1930s+] the anus; thus [1990s+] *ringpiece licker*, an anilinguist. **2** [2000s] a general term of abuse (cf. ARSE n.¹). [RING n.¹ (2)]

ring pigger *n.* [mid–late 16C] a drunkard. [ety. unknown]

ring raider *n.* [1990s+] a male homosexual, a sodomite (cf. ANAL ASTRONAUT n.). [RING n.¹ (2) + SE *raider*]

rings *n.* [1990s+] (*W.I.*) firearms. [? the circular barrels]

Ringsend handshake *n.* (*also* **Ringsend uppercut**) [1920s+] (*Irish*) a kick in the testicles. [*Ring's End*, a rough area of Dublin]

ringside *n.* [1920s+] (*orig. US*) the tables nearest to the stage in a nightclub or similar establishment. [boxing imagery]

ring snatcher *n.* [1960s–70s] a sodomite; thus *ring-snatching*, sodomy. [RING n.¹ (2) + SE *snatcher*; note synon. RMC Duntroon (*Aus.*) *ring stinger*]

ring someone's bell *v.* **1** [1930s+] to appeal to, to impress, to carry any weight with, usu. in negative. **2** [1940s+] (*US*) to attract sexually, e.g. *she really rings my bell.* **3** [1960s+] (*orig. US*) (*also* **ring someone's hat**) to concuss, esp. in US football use when this may well follow a clash of helmets.

ring-stiff *n.* [1920s] (*US tramp*) an itinerant seller of worthless jewellery at fraudulently inflated prices. [SE *ring* + STIFF n.² (4)]

ring-sting *n.* (*also* **ring-stinger**) [1990s+] a painful act of defecation, attributed to a meal with an excess of hot spices. [RING n.¹ (2) + SE *sting*]

ringtail *n.*¹ **1** [20C+] the anus. **2** [1920s+] (*also* **ringtail wife**) a tramp's young homosexual companion. [RING n.¹ (2) + TAIL n.² (1)]

ringtail *n.*² [1910s+] **1** (*Aus.*) a coward. **2** (*US*) an irritable, unpleasant person. **3** (*US*) a tramp (who is seen as inevitably ill-tempered). **4** (*US tramp*) a tramp who is a poor beggar and sponges off his peers or takes temporary employment. [SAusE *ringtail*, a possum, known for 'playing dead' when threatened]

ringtailed *adj.* [19C+] describing a person or thing that is superlative, unique, extraordinary, usu. positive but occas. negative.

ringtailed snorter *n.* (*also* **ringtailed peeler, ...roarer, ...squealer, ...tooter, ringtail snorter**) [early 19C+] (*US*) an impressive person, usu. physically aggressive. [RINGTAILED adj. + SE *snorter*, perhaps of dragon-like fire; a fantasy creature]

ringtail wife *n. see* RINGTAIL n.¹ (2).

ring the bell *v.* [20C+] to carry off the prize; to be the best of a lot; to be acquitted. [the 'try-your-strength' machine found at a trad. fairground]

ring the bell on *v.* (*also* **ring the tinkler on**) [1900s–40s] (*US*) to dismiss, to declare useless. [boxing imagery]

ring the changes *v.* **1** [19C+] (*UK Und.*) to defraud, to deceive, esp. by passing counterfeit money or substituting a worse article for a better one; thus *change-ringer*, one who practises this form of fraud. **2** [early 19C] in fig. use, to manipulate facts and figures. **3** [early 19C] to use deceptive language (in a non-criminal context). **4** [late 19C] (*UK prison*) of a prisoner, to move surreptitiously from one companion to another in the exercise yard. **5** [late

19C–1920s] to adopt a series of variant disguises with the intention of confusing; thus *ringer*, one who practises this form of deception.

ring-ting *n.* [1940s] (*W.I.*) the genuine article, the real thing. [? the *ring* of a glass that indicates it is pure crystal]

ringy *adj.* [1920s+] (*US*) ill-tempered, tetchy. [RINGTAIL n.² (2)]

rinktum *n. see* RINCTUM n.

rinky-dink *n.*¹ [20C+] (*US*) a swindle, a deception; often as GIVE SOMEONE THE RINKY-DINK v. [ety. unknown]

rinky-dink *n.*¹ **1** [20C+] (*US*) an insignificant person. **2** [1960s] (*US campus*) an easy course.

rinky-dink *n.*³ *see* DINK n.² (4).

rinky-dink *adj.*¹ [20C+] pink. [rhy. sl.]

rinky-dink *adj.*² (*also* **rinky-dinky**) (*US*) **1** [1910s+] cheap, second-rate. **2** [1940s+] outdated, unfashionable. [ety. unknown; OED suggests link to jazz use *ricky-tick*, old-fashioned, monotonous rhythms]

rinky-dink joint *n.* [1930s+] (*US Black*) a cheap tavern or inn. [RINKY-DINK adj.² (1) + JOINT n.⁴ (3)]

rino *n. see* RHINO n.¹.

rinse *n.*¹ [1980s] (*Aus.*) an ejaculation of semen (cf. BABY FLUID n.). [RINSE v.¹ (1)]

rinse *n.*² *see* RINCE n.

rinse *v.* **1** [1980s+] (*Aus. prison*) to fellate; occas. to masturbate (cf. BOFF v.; CLEAN SOMEONE'S PIPE v.). **2** [2000s] (*W.I.*) to exploit.

rinse *v.*² *see* RINCE v.

rinse pitcher *n.* [mid-16C] a drunkard. [lit. one who drinks even the rinsings of a barrel or tankard]

rinsings *n.* [1930s–50s] (*US drugs*) the residue of the narcotic/water solution that remains after it has been strained through a cotton filter.

Rin Tin Tin *n.* [1980s] (*Aus.*) gin. [rhy. sl.]

riot *n.* [20C+] **1** a great success. **2** an extremely enjoyable and amusing, if somewhat rowdy, occasion or performance. **3** a very funny person or thing. **4** noise, excitement. **5** (*US*) a 'riot' sale, i.e. one in which the prices are even lower than normal.

rip *n.*¹ **1** [late 18C–1910s] an exhausted, worn-out horse. **2** [late 18C+] a worthless person, a rake; usu. used of a (young) man but occas. (*Irish*) of a woman. [? SE *rebrobate*]

rip *n.*² [1910s+] (*Aus. Und.*) a blow, a punch.

rip *n.*³ [1970s] (*US Und.*) a scar. [SE *rip*, a tear]

rip *n.*⁴ [1990s+] a pound sterling; usu. in pl., e.g. *twenty rips.*

rip *n.*⁵ [2000s] **1** (*US prison*) a hand-rolled cigarette. **2** (*US drugs*) marijuana. [? one rips a cigarette paper from the packet; ? it is more likely to rip]

rip *n.*⁶ *see* RIP-OFF n.¹.

rip *adj. see* RIPPED adj.¹ (1).

rip *v.*¹ **1** [20C+] (*US*) to steal, to rob. **2** [1970s] to kill, to murder. [SE *rip*, to tear (off)]

rip *v.*² **1** [1920s+] to do without restraint. **2** [1980s] (*US campus*) to fail. **3** [1980s+] to do very well, to be successful. [SE *rip*, to move fast; (2) ? SE *rip*, to tear]

rip *v.*³ [1940s+] (*orig. Aus.*) to annoy intensely; thus *wouldn't it rip you*, wouldn't it drive you mad? [fig. use of SE *rip*, to tear]

rip and run *v.* [1900s–70s] (*US Black*) to move restlessly, to act in an aimless but frenzied manner. [SE *rip*, to move fast + *run*]

rip and tear *n.* [1940s] (*US Und.*) robbery without forethought or planning. [RIP v.¹ (1) + SE *tear*]

rip and tear *adj.* [1900s–30s] (*US Und.*) unplanned, unsophisticated. [RIP AND TEAR n.]

rip and tear *v.*¹ [mid-19C; 1970s+] to swear. [rhy. sl.]

rip and tear *v.*² [1940s] (*US Und.*) of a confidence man, to operate at will, without fear of interference from the authorities; also as adj. [RIP v.¹ (1) + SE *tear*]

ripcord *n.* [1960s+] the small loop attached to the back of some men's shirts.

ripe *adj.*¹ [early 17C; 19C–1950s] drunk (cf. ABOUT RIGHT phr.¹).

ripe *adj.*[2] [mid-19C+] **1** excessive, in poor taste, beyond the bounds of acceptability, e.g. *a bit ripe, ripe old time.* **2** thoroughgoing, complete; esp. in phr. *(you) ripe bastard.* **3** appealing, sensible.

ripe *adj.*[3] [20C+] **1** (*W.I.*) old, esp. too old to work. **2** of food, overcooked, stale, poss. smelling bad.

ripe *adj.*[4] [1960s] angry, irritated.

ripe banana *n.* [1950s] (*W.I.*) a derog. term for an albino. [BANANA n.[2] (2); their colour]

ripe fruit *n.* [1970s+] (*US gay*) someone who is just discovering their homosexuality. [pun on SE *fruit*/FRUIT n.[2] (2)]

rip hell out of *v.* [20C+] (*orig. Aus.*) **1** to defeat comprehensively. **2** to tell off, to reprimand. **3** to tease unmercifully.

rip her guts down *v.* [1970s+] (*US Black*) to copulate aggressively, sadistically, but with the implication that both partners achieve mutual satisfaction.

rip into *v.* (*also* **rip it into**) **1** [late 19C+] to start a fight, to attack physically. **2** [1910s+] (*also* **rip it off**) to criticize harshly. **3** [1960s+] to do something energetically, enthusiastically. **4** [1970s] (*Aus.*) of a man, to have sexual intercourse (cf. BANG v.[1]).

rip it up *v.* [1950s+] to have a good time.

rip job *n.* [1990s+] (*US*) a negative attack, e.g. a piece of critical journalism. [RIP INTO v. (2) + JOB n.[4]]

rip joint *n.* [1970s+] (*US campus*) any store that charges exorbitant prices to students. [RIP-OFF n.[1] (2) + JOINT n.[4] (3)]

rip me! *excl.* [mid-19C–1900s] a general excl. of anger, surprise.

rip-off *n.*[1] (*also* **rip**) [1970s+] **1** (*orig. US*) a fraud, a cheat, a disappointment. **2** an act of theft or robbery. **3** something stolen or plagiarized. **4** (*US prison*) a physical attack. [RIP OFF v.]

rip-off *n.*[2] *see* RIP-OFF ARTIST n.

rip off *v.* **1** [1910s] (*US*) to create, to make. **2** [1960s] to take, to secure (with no implication of theft). **3** [1960s+] (*US Black*) to have sexual intercourse. **4** [1960s+] (*US Black/prison*) to rape. **5** [1960s+] to steal (from). **6** [1960s+] (*orig. US*) to cheat, to defraud, esp. in drug deals. **7** [1970s] to raid. **8** [1970s+] to kill, to assassinate. **9** [1970s+] to beat up, to attack physically. **10** [1970s+] to satirize. **11** [1970s+] to copy, to plagiarize. **12** [1970s+] to exploit financially. **13** [1980s+] (*US Black*) usu. of Whites, to exploit, socially or economically, to place at a disadvantage. [SE *rip off*, to tear off]

rip off a piece *v.* (*also* **rip off a hunk**) [1930s+] (*US*) to seduce, to have sexual intercourse (cf. BREAK A BIT OFF v.). [SE *rip off*/RIP OFF v. (3) + PIECE n.[1] (3)/HUNK n.[1] (3)]

rip-off artist *n.* (*also* **rip-off, rip-off merchant**) [1970s+] **1** a thief. **2** a prostitute who specializes in robbing her clients and as such is more thief than purveyor of commercial sex. **3** any form of cheat, emotional as well as material. [RIP OFF v. (5)/RIP OFF v. (6) + ARTIST n. (1)/ARTIST sfx/MERCHANT n.]

rip on *v.* [1980s+] **1** (*US campus*) to criticize (behind someone's back), to nag. **2** (*US Black*) to harass, to insult. [RIP INTO v. (2)]

rip out *v.* [mid-19C] (*US*) to talk without restraint, to swear. [? LET RIP v.]

ripped *adj.*[1] [1960s+] **1** (*orig. US*) (*also* **rip, ripped off/up**) extremely intoxicated by drink, drugs or a mixture. **2** unhappy. **3** very unattractive. [SE *ripped*, torn]

ripped *adj.*[2] [1980s+] (*orig. US campus*) well-built, muscled. [var. on CUT adj.[5]]

ripped off *adj.*[1] [1970s+] of people, exploited, stolen from. [RIP OFF v. (6)]

ripped off *adj.*[2] *see* RIPPED adj.[1] (1).

ripped out of one's gourd *adj.* [1970s+] (*US campus*) drunk. [RIPPED adj.[1] (1) + GOURD n.[2] (1)]

ripped to the tits *phr.* (*also* **ripped off one's ass**) [1970s+] (*orig. US*) very intoxicated by drink, drugs or a combination. [RIPPED adj.[1] (1) + TO THE TITS adv./OFF ONE'S ASS phr.]

ripped up *adj. see* RIPPED adj.[1] (1).

ripper *n.*[1] [mid–late 19C] a very great lie. **2** [mid-19C+] a first-rate man or woman, an excellent article or thing. **3** [mid-19C+] an attractive young woman. [SE *rip*, to tear open, i.e. all uses 'tear open' the usual standards]

ripper *n.*[2] [late 19C] a person who behaves recklessly. [RIP n.[1] (2)]

ripper *n.*[3] **1** [late 19C+] a murderer who specializes in mutilation, often for sexual purposes. **2** [2000s] (*US prison*) a rapist. [late 19C criminal Jack the *Ripper*, thus christened by the contemporary press]

ripper *n.*[4] [late 19C+] (*US Und.*) a tool used in the opening of a safe, thus the safe-breaker who uses such a tool. [SE *rip*]

ripper *adj.* [20C+] (*Aus.*) excellent, wonderful, perfect, first-class; also as excl. *ripper!* [RIPPER n.[1] (2)]

rippers *n.* [1960s–70s] (*drugs*) amphetamines (cf. A n.[2]). [RIPPED adj.[1] (1)]

ripperty man *n.* [1930s+] (*Aus.*) a confidence trickster. [? RIP OFF v. but predates so ? RIP v.[1] (1)]

ripping *adj.* [mid-19C+] excellent, first-rate, wonderful.

ripping *adv.* (*also* **rippingly**) [mid-19C] wonderfully, in an excellent manner. [RIPPING adj.]

ripping! *excl.* [late 19C+] excellent! wonderful! [RIPPING adj.]

ripping slum *n.* [late 19C] a successful trick or hoax. [RIPPING adj. + SLUM n.[2] (3)]

rippish *adj.* [late 18C] of a person, worthless. [RIP n.[1] (2)]

ripple *n.* [1960s] (*US*) a try, an attempt. [? one fig. 'ripples' the surface]

rippling *n.* [1970s] (*US Black*) enjoying oneself.

rip rap *v.* [1930s+] to borrow money; thus *the rip-rap*, the act of obtaining such a loan. [rhy. sl. = TAP v.[3] (2)]

rip-shit *adj.* [1990s+] angry. [RIP SHIT OUT OF v.]

rip shit *v.* (*also* **rip shit up**) [1980s+] **1** to have a party, to act energetically, to make a disturbance. **2** to excel, to do something really well or intensely; thus *rip shit and bust*, to make a big effort. [SE *rip* + SHIT n.[6]]

rip, shit or bust *phr.* [1940s+] (*N.Z.*) used of a situation in which one forges on, irrespective of the consequences. [ext. of SHIT OR BUST v.]

rip shit out of *v.* [1980s+] (*orig. US*) to assault physically. [ext. of RIP SHIT v.]

rip shit up *v. see* RIP SHIT v.

ripskated *adj.* [1990s+] (*US campus*) drunk. [ety. unknown]

rip-snorter *n.* **1** [mid-19C+] (*orig. US*) (*also* **rip-staver**) a remarkable or wonderful person or thing of which the speaker approves. **2** [1940s+] a very loud breaking of wind. [SE *rip* + SNORTER n.[2] (3)]

rip-snorting *adj.* (*also* **rip-sneezing, rip-staving**) [mid-19C+] wonderful, very enjoyable. [RIP-SNORTER n. (1)]

rip someone a new ass(hole) *v. see* TEAR SOMEONE A NEW ASS(HOLE) v.

rip someone's ass(hole) *v. see* TEAR SOMEONE'S ASS(HOLE) v.

rip-staver *n. see* RIP-SNORTER n. (1).

rip-staving *adj. see* RIP-SNORTING adj.

ripsy rousers *n. see* RAMMY ROUSERS n.

rip the rug *v.* [1970s] (*US campus*) to dance. [var. on CUT THE RUG v.]

rip up *v.* [20C+] (*US Und.*) to rob on a large scale. [ext. of RIP v.[1] (1)]

rip van winkle *v.* [1960s+] to urinate (cf. APPLE AND PIP v.). [rhy. sl. = TINKLE v.]

rise *n.*[1] **1** [mid-19C] a commotion, a noise. **2** [mid-19C+] a response, esp. a fit of anger; thus *get or take a rise out of*, to cause to respond, to spur to anger. **3** [1950s] a moment of pleasure.

rise *n.*[2] **1** [late 19C+] an erection; thus *get/have a rise*, to get an erection; *give a rise*, of a woman, to give a man an erection. **2** [1940s+] in fig. use, a stimulus, excitement.

rise *v.* [mid-19C+] **1** to listen credulously. **2** to become foolishly annoyed (by what one hears). **3** to make someone annoyed. [angling imagery, the fish *rising* to the bait]

rise a barney v. [mid–late 19C] (*UK Und.*) to gather a group of criminals to assist in confidence trickery. [BARNEY n.³ (3)]

rise and shine n. [20C+] wine. [rhy. sl.]

rise and shine! excl. [20C+] a joc. wake-up call; sometimes preceded by *wakey-wakey!*

riser n.¹ [1910s–60s] (*US Und.*) a surprise, a scare, an 'eye-opener'.

riser n.² [1940s] (*US tramp*) an artificial sore.

rise to the occasion v. [1920s+] to have an erection when required.

rise up v. [2000s] (*US teen*) to go away, to leave alone.

rising n. [1900s] (*Aus.*) a sentence of 1 night in jail. [one stays in jail until the next *rising* of the sun]

rising blowback n. [1980s+] (*US drugs*) exhaling cannabis smoke into someone else's mouth, then moving from a crouching position and slowly standing up for an increased sensation. [SE *rising* + BLOWBACK n.¹]

rising damp n. [20C+] cramp. [rhy. sl.]

risk it for a biscuit v. [1980s+] (*Irish*) to take a chance, esp. in a sexual context.

risky adj. **1** [late 19C] (*UK society*) clandestinely adulterous. **2** [1910s] (*W.I.*) flirtatious, bold, cheeky.

rispeck v. (*also* **respeck, respect**) [1980s+] (*W.I./UK Black teen*) to hold someone or something in high esteem.

rispeck due phr. (*also* **respeck (due), respect (due)**) [1970s+] (*W.I./UK/US Black teen*) a phr. used to accord the subject the respect they have earned on the basis of earlier positive or praiseworthy actions.

rissole v. [1970s+] (*Aus.*) to defeat (comprehensively), to overcome. [joc. mispron. and euph. for ARSEHOLE v.; usu. in context of Aus. cricket]

risto adj. [1990s+] (*W.I.*) upper-class. [abbr. SE *aristocratic*]

rit n.¹ [late 19C–1900s] a ritualistic clergyman. [abbr.]

rit n.² [1980s+] (*drugs*) a tablet of *Ritalin*. [abbr.]

rita n. [1940s–70s] (*S.Afr. camp gay*) a male prostitute (cf. BABY JANE n.). [gay icon Hollywood star *Rita* Hayworth (1918–87)]

rite adv. see RIGHT adv. (1).

rith n. [1910s–20s] the number 3. [backsl.]

rities n. [1980s+] (*drugs*) *Ritalin* (methylphenidate hydrochloride, a central nervous system stimulant related to amphetamine). [abbr.]

ritz n. [1920s+] glamour, elegance, wealth, sophistication; thus phr. *in the ritz*, living well; *this ain't the Ritz*, don't expect anything special; *ritz it*, to live luxuriously. [the chain of hotels established by César *Ritz* (1850–1918), esp. the *Ritz-Carlton* in New York City]

ritz adj. see RITZY adj.

ritz v. [1920s–30s] (*US Und.*) to snub. [RITZ n.]

ritzy n. [1950s] a smart, fashionable person. [RITZ n.]

ritzy adj. (*also* **ritz**) [1920s+] **1** smart, chic, fashionable; wealthy, affluent. **2** pretentious, posturing; esp. in phr. *don't get ritzy with me*. [RITZ n. + sfx -*y*]

Riv n. (*also* **Rivie, Rivie hog**) [1970s+] (*US Black*) a Buick *Riviera*. [abbr. (+ HOG n.⁴ (2))]

river n. see RIVER OOZE n.

riverina n. [1940s+] (*Aus.*) a shilling. [rhy. sl. = DEANER n. (1)]

River Lea n. **1** [mid-19C] tea. **2** [late 19C–1900s] the sea. [rhy. sl.]

River Murray n. [20C+] (*Aus.*) a curry. [rhy. sl.]

River Murrays phr. [1990s+] (*Aus.*) a phr. of affirmation, assurance, encouragement. [rhy. sl. = NO WORRIES (MATE) phr.]

River Nile n. [20C+] a smile. [rhy. sl.]

River Ooze n. (*also* **river, River Ouse**) [20C+] alcohol, liquor; thus *on the ooze*, drinking or drunk. [rhy. sl. =BOOZE n. (1); ? Derek Raymond nonce-word]

river rat n. **1** [19C] a thief who specializes in stripping the corpses of those who have drowned in London's River Thames. **2** [1930s] (*US*) a dock labourer. **3** [1940s] (*US Und.*) a thief who steals on the river front.

River Tyne n. [20C+] wine. [rhy. sl.]

riveted adj. **1** [early–mid-18C; 1930s] married. **2** [1970s+] (*UK society*) fascinated by; thus *riveting*, absolutely fascinating.

rivets n. (*also* **rivits**) [mid-19C–1930s] money (cf. ACTUAL, THE n.). [fig. use of SE on pattern of BRAD n.¹ (2)/HORSE-NAILS n.]

Rivie (hog) n. see RIV n.

riz adj. [mid-19C+] (*Irish/US*) annoyed. [SE *rise*]

rizolin phr. [1930s–50s] (*US drugs*) a term meaning 'the drugs are on their way'. [ROLL v.³ (2) + -IZ- ifx]

roach n.¹ **1** [1900s] (*US*) an inferior racehorse. **2** [1930s+] (*US*) a pej. term for a policeman; a prison guard (cf. ANIMAL n.¹). **3** [1950s+] (*US campus*) an unattractive man or woman. [joc. uses of SE *cockroach*]

roach n.² [1930s+] (*drugs*) **1** marijuana. **2** a marijuana cigarette. **3** the unsmoked portion of a cannabis cigarette. **4** the cardboard 'filter' of a cannabis cigarette, often made of a rolled up piece of a Rizla packet. **5** a marijuana smoker. **6** the unsmoked portion of a cigarette. [SE *cockroach*]

roach v. [1900s] (*US*) to cut one's hair very short. [SAmE *roach*, to cut (a horse's mane) short, so that it stands up like the bristles of a hog]

roach and dace n. [20C+] the face. [rhy. sl.]

roach bender n. [1940s] (*drugs*) a marijuana smoker. [ROACH n.² (3) + SE *bend*, i.e. the grasping of the very last portion of the cigarette]

roach clip n. (*also* **roach holder/pick**) [1950s+] (*drugs*) a small spring clip or pair of tweezers used to hold the last fragments of a marijuana cigarette, which is otherwise too hot to hold in one's fingers. [ROACH n.² (3) + SE *clip/holder*]

roach coach n. (*US*) **1** [1970s–80s] the 'coach' or economy section of a passenger aircraft. **2** [1980s+] a food service wagon. [abbr. SE *cockroach* + *coach*]

roaches n. see ROCHE n.

roach holder n. see ROACH CLIP n.

roach hotel n.¹ [1980s+] (*US drugs*) a collection of cannabis cigarette stubs that can be recycled. [ROACH n.² (3) + pun on US *Roach Motel*, a patented cockroach trap]

roach hotel n.² (*also* **roach palace/trap**) [1980s+] (*US*) a cheap, dilapidated, dirty hotel. [it is full of *cockroaches*]

roachies n. see ROCHE n.

roach killers n. [1960s] highly pointed shoes. [abbr. COCKROACH KILLERS n.]

roach palace n. see ROACH HOTEL n.².

roach-palace adj. [2000s] (*US*) infested with cockroaches.

roach pick n. see ROACH CLIP n.

roach stompers n. [2000s] (*US*) heavy, unfashionable shoes.

roach trap n. see ROACH HOTEL n.².

road n.¹ **1** [late 16C] a prostitute. **2** [17C] the vagina (cf. ALLEY n.¹).

road n.² [2000s] (*UK Black*) the 'real world', which exists on the streets, rather than in the protected environments of home, office, family etc. [var. on STREET, THE n. (1)]

road apple n. [20C+] horse manure (cf. ALLEY APPLE n.²). [SE *road* + APPLE n.¹]

road brew n. (*also* **roadies, road sauce**) [1970s+] (*US campus*) beer. [SE *road* + BREW n.¹ (3)/dimin. sfx -*ies*/SAUCE n.² (6)]

road bull n. [1970s] (*US*) a highway patrolman. [SE *road* + BULL n.¹⁰ (1)]

road-bums' Coronas n. [1930s] tobacco that is extracted from discarded 'fag-ends' and recycled in a pipe or 'roll-up'. [a *Corona* is an expensive Cuban cigar]

road dog n. (*also* **roadie**) [1980s+] (*US Black/prison*) an extremely intimate friend. [SE *road* + DOG n.² (3)]

road dope n. [1980s+] (*drugs*) amphetamine (cf. A n.²). [DOPE n.¹ (6); the drug's use during long-distance driving]

roader n. [late 19C] (*London, East End*) a young man who disports himself on the Mile End Road, London, in his finest clothes, usu. with his woman, on a Sunday. [abbr. Mile End *Road*]

roadhog *n.* 1 [1920s–30s] (*US tramp*) a tramp who is perpetually riding the trains. 2 [2000s] a young woman who follows rock bands and offers herself for sex. [*roadhog*, a careless, selfish driver, is SE]

roadie *n.*[1] 1 [1960s+] a member of a rock band's support unit who sets up and dismantles the stage, the equipment etc. 2 [1980s+] (*N.Z.*) one employed in road maintenance. [(1) they go 'on the road' with the band or (2) they lit. work on it]

roadie *n.*[2] *see* ROAD DOG *n.*

roadie *v.* [1970s+] to be a ROADIE *n.*[1] (1).

roadies *n. see* ROAD BREW *n.*

road kid *n.* [late 19C–1940s] (*US*) a young tramp; the (catamitic) companion of an older JOCKER *n.*[1] (2).

roadkill *n.*[1] (*also* road pizza) [1970s+] (*orig. US*) 1 any form of creature (usu. small animals or birds) killed by a vehicle on the roads (whether accidentally or on purpose) and used for food. 2 a person or object that is considered absolutely useless, i.e. 'dead meat'; also attrib.

roadkill *n.*[2] [1990s+] a recently shaved vagina. [resemblance to ROADKILL *n.*[1] (1); + ? ROAD *n.*[1] (2)]

road less travelled *n.* [1990s+] the female anus as a hosting place for a penis (cf. ALLEY WAY *n.*). [play on new age book title *The Road Less Traveled: A New Psychology of Love, Traditional Values and Spiritual Growth* by M. Scott Peck (1979)]

road-louse *n.* [1910s] (*US*) a Ford motor car.

road maggot *n.* [1980s] (*US campus*) a camper van or recreational vehicle.

road making *phr.* (*also* road up for repairs) [mid–late 19C] used of a woman who is menstruating.

road man *n.* [1920s–50s] (*US*) an itinerant thief.

road pizza *n. see* STREET PIZZA *n.*

road queen *n.* [1970s+] (*US gay*) a gay hitch-hiker, looking for sex with those who pick him up. [SE *road* + QUEEN *n.*[2] (1)/QUEEN sfx (2)]

road rage *n.* [1980s+] the blind fury that overtakes a driver, who in other circumstances may well be a reasonable individual, when trapped in a traffic jam or similar hindrance to driving. [the convenience of the phr. for media use made it SE almost immediately]

road rash *n.* [1970s+] (*orig. US*) cuts, scratches and grazes that come with falling off a motorcycle or skateboard.

road roller *n.* [1900s–30s] (*N.Z.*) an unsophisticated country person, a bushman.

road sauce *n. see* ROAD BREW *n.*

road smart *adj.* [1990s+] (*US tramp*) used of an experienced tramp (cf. ROADWISE adj.). [SE phr. *on the road* + var. on STREET SMART adj.]

road stake *n.* [1920s–60s] (*US tramp*) money. [SE *road* + *stake*, a bet, a wager]

road starver *n.* [late 19C] (*UK tramp*) a long coat made without pockets. [the pockets would be used to hold food for a journey]

roadster *n.* [late 19C+] (*Aus.*) a tramp, someone who has no fixed abode.

road to a christening *n.* (*also* road to heaven, way to heaven) [19C] the vagina (cf. ALLEY *n.*[1]). [ext. of ROAD *n.*[1] (2) and its role as baby-making/pleasure-giving]

road up for repairs *phr. see* ROAD MAKING *phr.*

Roadwatch accent *n. see* DART ACCENT *n.*

road whore *n.* [1980s+] (*US campus*) a promiscuous woman.

roadwise *adj.* [1930s–40s] (*US*) of a tramp, 'wise' in the ways of travelling (cf. ROAD SMART adj.). [SE *road* + -WISE sfx (1); note STREETWISE adj.]

road work *n.* [1920s–50s] (*US*) crimes committed by an itinerant thief. [SE *road* + WORK *n.*[1] (1)]

roaf *n. see* ROUF *n.* (3).

roak *v.* [1970s] (*US Black*) to beat savagely about the head. [? abbr. CROAK *v.*[2] (2)]

roapies *n. see* ROCHE *n.*

roar *n.* [late 19C–1960s] (*US*) 1 an uproarious joke. 2 a complaint.

roar *v.* 1 [17C–mid-19C; 1950s] to riot; to act in a riotous manner. 2 [1900s–40s] to complain; to inform.

roaration *n. see* RORATION *n.*

roaratorios and uproars *n.* [late 18C–early 19C] oratorios and operas. [joc. mispron.]

roaratorious *adj. see* RORTORIOUS *adj.*

roarer *n.*[1] 1 [late 16C–19C] a riotous hooligan, a roisterer; an outstanding performer. 2 [1940s] (*US*) a noisy argument. 3 [1950s] a riotous good time. [SE *roar*, to riot, to behave in a boisterous manner]

roarer *n.*[2] [19C–1940s] a broken-down horse. [the sound of its breathing]

roarer *n.*[3] [mid-19C] 1 (*US*) something superlatively good. 2 something notably large.

roaring *adj.* 1 [17C+] boisterous, exuberant. 2 [mid-19C+] a general intensifier, extreme, uncompromising. [SE *roar*, to riot, to behave in a boisterous manner]

roaring *adv.* [late 17C; mid-19C+] extremely, very, often in comb. *roaring drunk*. [ROARING adj.]

roaring boy *n.* (*also* roaring blade/girl) [late 16C–19C] a riotous hooligan, a roisterer; of a girl, promiscuous, tom-boyish. [ROARING adj. (1) + SE *boy*/BLADE *n.*[2] (1)/SE *girl*]

Roaring Forties *n.* (*also* Forties) [1920s–40s] (*US*) Broadway, New York City, in the area immediately around Times Square, spec. 40th Street to 49th Street. [joc. use of ROARING adj. (1) + naut. jargon *Roaring Forties*, exceptionally rough seas that occur between latitudes 40° and 50° south, where strong westerly winds blow; formerly also applied to the part of the Atlantic Ocean between latitudes 40° and 50° north]

roaring fou *n.* [late 17C–18C] a drinking spree. [ROARING adj. (1) + state of being FOU adj.[1]]

roaring fou *adj.* [19C] extremely drunk, lit. roaring drunk. [ROARING adj. (1) + FOU adj.[1]]

roaring girl *n. see* ROARING BOY *n.*

roaring horn *n.* (*also* roaring jack) [late 19C] (*Aus.*) an erection, esp. one that feels very demanding. [ROARING adj. (1) + HORN *n.*[2] (3)/JACK *n.*[3] (2)]

roaring horsetails *n.* [20C+] (*Aus.*) Aurora Australis. [rhy. sl.]

roaring rain *n.* [20C+] (*Aus.*) a train. [rhy. sl.]

roar like a town bull *v.* [late 18C–early 19C] to make a good deal of noise. [SE *roar* + *town bull* or ROAR *v.* (1) + TOWN BULL *n.* (1)]

roart *n. see* RORT *n.*

roar up *v.* 1 [1910s] to talk loudly, to abuse. 2 [1910s+] (*Aus.*) to scold, to tell off, to reprimand. [SE *roar*/ROAR *v.* (2)]

roast *n.*[1] 1 [late 18C–1920s] a criticism. 2 [1900s] (*US campus*) a joke. 3 [1900s] (*US campus*) something that can be easily accomplished. 4 [1900s] (*US*) a disappointing entertainment. 5 [1950s+] (*Aus.*) a piece of information, usu. accusatory. 6 [1960s] (*US campus*) a difficult examination.

roast *n.*[2] [1950s+] (*W.I.*) a second job, kept secret and thus part of the 'black economy'. [ROAST COCO *v.*]

roast *v.* 1 [late 17C–early 19C; 1990s+] to arrest. 2 [mid-18C+] to jeer, to ridicule or banter. 3 [mid-18C+] to criticize aggressively. 4 [late 18C; 1900s] to put at a disadvantage. 5 [mid-19C+] to give someone a tough questioning, a 'grilling'. 6 [late 19C] (*US*) to renege on one's debts or bills. 7 [1930s] to beat up. 8 [1940s] (*US Und.*) to die in the electric chair. [? play on SE *roast*, i.e. to give the subject 'a hot time']

roast a time *v.* [20C+] (*W.I.*) to enjoy oneself thoroughly.

roast beef *n.* [20C+] teeth. [rhy. sl.; Cockney pron. 'teef']

roast beef curtains *n. see* BEEF CURTAINS *n.*

roast coco *v.* [1950s] (*W.I.*) to plot, to scheme, to bide one's time. [the habit of roasting coco-yams as the conclusion of the meal; thus fig. waiting for something desirable]

roasted *adj.* [1990s+] intoxicated, usu. with drugs, sometimes drink. [var. on BAKED adj.]

roasted duck *n.* [1930s] sexual intercourse. [rhy. sl. = FUCK n.[1] (1); unmentioned by E.P. or Franklyn, *Dict. of Rhyming Slang* (1960), this may be a nonce-word, invented by Isherwood and Auden in their play *The Dog beneath the Skin* (1935): 'O how I cried when Alice died / The day we were to have wed! / We never had our Roasted Duck / And now she's a Loaf of Bread']

roastie *n. see* ROAST POTATO n.

roasting *n.*[1] **1** [mid-19C+] a thorough criticism; verbal hostility. **2** [late 19C] (*US Und.*) police surveillance. **3** [1940s] (*US Und.*) the 'third degree'. **4** [2000s] a state of being held in suspense. [ROAST v.]

roasting *n.*[2] [2000s] group sex, spec. the simultaneous penetration of a woman by 2 men, one in the mouth, the other in the vagina; she is thus ON THE SPIT phr. (cf. SPIT ROAST n.).

roasting jack *n.* [19C] the vagina. [pun on SE/JACK n.[3] (1)]

roast joint *n.* [20C+] a pint of beer. [rhy. sl.; Cockney pron.]

roast me! *excl.* [late 19C] (*Aus.*) a general excl.

roast-meat clothes *n.* [late 17C–early 19C] one's best clothes. [the meat in question being the 'Sunday roast' and the clothes one's 'Sunday best' outfit; note naval jargon *roast-beef dress*, full uniform]

roast plantain for someone *v.* [1920s+] (*W.I.*) **1** to get ready to benefit from someone else's misfortune. **2** to plot actively to bring about this downfall.

roast pork *n.*[1] **1** [1910s+] a talk. **2** [1940s+] a table fork. [rhy. sl.]

roast pork *n.*[2] [1940s] (*W.I.*) a variety of cactus whose leaves resemble chunks of meat; such leaves can be roasted for medicinal use.

roast potato *n.* (*also* **roastie**) [20C+] a waiter. [rhy. sl.; note Cockney pron. 'pertater']

rob *n.* [1990s+] (*Aus. Und.*) a robbery. [abbr.]

rob *v.* [1980s+] (*US campus*) to silence with a witty remark or rejoinder. [one's victim is 'robbed' of speech]

robardsmen *n. see* ROBERDSMEN n.

robberdy *n. see* RUBBEDY n.

robbing the dago in Rome *v.* [1900s] (*US Und.*) to steal from the collection plate.

rob blind *v.* [1930s+] to rob without restraint. [SE rob + BLIND adv.]

robbo *n.* [late 19C–1900s] (*Aus.*) a cab; thus *robbo man*, a cab-driver. [the late 19C Sydney cabbie Four Bob *Robbo* who specialized in undercutting his rivals]

rob-davy *n.* (*also* **roberdavy, rob-o'-davy**) [17C] metheglin or spiced mead. [*Davy*, the Welsh name *Dafyyd*, anglicized as *Taffy*; + ? SE *rob*]

roberdsmen *n.* (*also* **robardsmen, roberts men**) [late 17C–early 19C] (*UK Und.*) 'the third (old) rank of the CANTING CREW n.', outlaw thieves who act, according to B.E., like real-life Robin Hoods. [early 14C SE *Roberdsmen*, a type of marauding vagabond, who were outlawed under an act of 1331; Ribton-Turner, *A History of Vagrants* (1887), notes the coincident 15C *Roberts men* who followed one Hugh Roberts, a former soldier and one of the leaders, with the better known Jack Cade (a.k.a. Jack Mendall) of the Peasants' Revolt; Roberts fled after the revolt and lived as an outlaw with 100 other 'rakehells and vagabonds' until he was killed, as a follower of Edward IV, during the Wars of the Roses]

robert *n.*[1] (*also* **roberto**) [late 19C–1910s] (*Aus.*) a shilling. [play on BOB n.[4] (1)]

robert *n.*[2] (*also* **roberto**) [late 19C–1950s] a policeman (cf. BILLY n.[6]). [play on BOBBY n. (1)]

Roberta (Flack) *n.* [1970s] (*Aus.*) **1** the bed; thus *hit the Roberta*, to go to bed. **2** dismissal from one's job. [rhy. sl.; (1) = SACK n.[3] (1); (2) = SACK, THE n. (1); ult. disco diva *Roberta Flack* (b.1937)]

robert dinero *n.* [1990s+] (*US teen*) money. [pun on DINERO n./US film star *Robert de Niro* (b.1943)]

robert e. *n.* [1950s+] **1** a knee. **2** an act of urination (cf. ANGEL'S KISS n.). [rhy. sl.; (2) = PEE n.[1] (2); ult. Confederate general *Robert E.* Lee (1807–70)]

roberto *n.*[1] *see* ROBERT n.[1].

roberto *n.*[2] *see* ROBERT n.[2].

roberts men *n. see* ROBERDSMEN n.

Robertson and Moffatt *n.* [1940s+] (*Aus.*) a profit. [rhy. sl.; ult. the eponymous Melbourne firm]

Robert Young *n.* [1960s–80s] (*Aus.*) the tongue. [rhy. sl.; ? ult. US film/TV actor *Robert Young* (1907–98)]

robin *n.*[1] [mid-17C–19C; 1950s+] the penis (cf. ANTEATER n.). [1950s+ use is US]

robin *n.*[2] [late 19C] a child beggar, 'standing about like a starving robin' (Ware). [a philanthropic clergyman, the Rev. Charles Bullock, organized a series of 'Robin dinners', at which he fed thousands of such unfortunate children]

robin *n.*[3] [late 19C–1910s] a penny. [ety. unknown; perhaps misreading: the robin was engraved on a *farthing* rather than a penny]

robin hog *n.* [early 18C] a constable. [ety. unknown; ? simply derog. since the PIG n.[3] (1) is not coined until 19C]

Robin Hood *n.* [late 19C] an audacious lie. [the 'tale' of *Robin Hood*]

Robin Hood *adj.* [1910s–70s] good; usu. in negative. [rhy. sl.]

Robin Hoods *n.* [20C+] **1** (material) goods. **2** the woods. [rhy. sl.]

Robin Hood's pennyworth *n.* (*also* **Robin Hood's bargain**) [17C] a very good bargain. ['it takes from the rich and gives to the poor']

robin redbreast *n.* (*also* **redbreast**) [early 19C] a Bow Street Runner. [Charles Dickens, letter (18 April 1862): 'The Bow Street runners […] had no other uniform than a blue dress–coat, brass buttons […] and a bright red cloth waistcoat. The waistcoat was indispensable and the slang name for them was "red-breasts" in consequence'; founded in 1750 the Runners, London's first organized constables, were replaced by the Metropolitan Police in 1829]

robin ruddock *n. see* RUDDOCK n.

Robinson and Cleaver *n.* [20C+] a fever. [rhy. sl.; ult. the defunct London department store]

Robinson Crusoe *v.* [late 19C–1950s] to do so; often as imper. [rhy. sl.]

rob my pal *n.* [1950s+] a woman. [rhy. sl. = GAL n. (1)]

robocop *n.* [1980s] (*US*) a policeman, esp. one who is known to be brutal or racist. [film *Robocop* (1987), in which the hero is a half-man/half-robot policeman]

rob-o'davy *n. see* ROB-DAVY n.

robot *n.* [1940s+] (*W.I.*) a privately owned vehicle, used to provide public transport when the usual drivers of such transport are on strike.

Rob Roy *n.* [mid-19C–1920s] a boy. [rhy. sl.; ult. Scot. hero *Rob Roy* McGregor (d.1734)]

rob the barber *v.* [late 19C] to wear one's hair long and uncut.

rob the cradle *v.* [1920s+] (*orig. US*) to have a relationship with someone much younger than oneself; thus CRADLE-ROBBER n.

rob the mail *v.* [1930s] (*US tramp*) to steal the best bits of a food parcel or handout; also to steal milk and food from someone's doorstep.

rob the ruffian *n.* [19C] the vagina. [SE rob + BELLY RUFFIAN n.]

robustious *adj.* [mid-18C–19C] violent, boisterous, noisy, strongly self-assertive, pompous. [SE mid-16C–mid-18C, thereafter condemned by Dr Johnson as 'low']

roby douglas *n.* [late 18C–early 19C] the posterior, the buttocks. ['with one eye and a stinking breath' (Grose, 1785); presumably f. a real person]

roche *n.* (*also* **roaches, roachies, roapies, rochas dos**) [1990s+] (*drugs*) Rohypnol, better known as the 'date rape drug', as it is allegedly given to people to knock them out and facilitate their rape. [the manufacturer, *Roche*]

Rochester portion *n.* [late 17C–early 19C] the vagina, lit. 'two torn smocks and what Nature gave' (B.E.). [orig. use is in a Kentish pvb]

Rock, the *n.* **1** [mid-19C] (*UK Und.*) the prison at Gibraltar, used for transported UK felons (cf. ABBOTT'S PRIORY n.). **2** [1930s–70s] (*also* **Big Rock**) Alcatraz Federal prison on Alcatraz Island, California. **3** [1950s] (*US Und.*) Florida State Penitentiary, Raiford. **4** [1960s+] Rikers Island prison, New York City. [the rocky islets on which they are built]

rock *n.*[1] **1** [mid-19C+] (*US*) a dollar; thus *half a rock*, 50 cents. **2** [1990s+] (*US prison*) 1 carton of prison cigarettes, the equivalent of $1 in a barter economy.

rock *n.*[2] **1** [20C+] a diamond. **2** [20C+] a man who is sturdy and solid both emotionally, physically and in his character. **3** [1990s+] (*US*) in fig. use, the essence, the 'bottom line'.

rock *n.*[3] (*drugs*) **1** [1920s] opium (cf. APOSTLE n.). **2** [1940s–50s] a piece of hashish (cf. AFGHAN n.). **3** [1960s+] (*also* **rock cocaine**) cocaine, when in uncrushed form. **4** [1980s+] crack cocaine; a piece of crack cocaine (cf. BASE n.). **5** [1990s+] heroin, prior to being crushed to powder. **6** [2000s] methamphetamine, when in uncrushed form (cf. BOMBITA n.).

rock *n.*[4] [1970s+] (*S.Afr.*) an Afrikaner. [abbr. ROCK SPIDER n.[2]]

rock *n.*[5] [1980s+] (*US Black*) a basketball.

rock *n.*[6] [1960s+] (*US prison*) a cellblock. [the stone walls]

rock *adj.*[1] [1940s+] excellent, outstanding. [i.e. it knocks one off balance]

rock *adj.*[2] [2000s] very firm, adamant, uncompromising. [SE *rock-hard*]

rock *v.*[1] **1** [mid-19C–1940s] (*mainly US*) to throw rocks or stones at. **2** [1930s+] (*US Black*) to trouble emotionally. **3** [1980s+] (*US campus*) to fight with, to beat up. **4** [1980s+] (*US campus*) to suffer badly.

rock *v.*[2] [late 19C+] to talk. [Rom. *roker*, to talk]

rock *v.*[3] [20C+] to get drunk. [one's unsteadiness]

rock *v.*[4] (*orig. US Black*) **1** [1920s+] to have sexual intercourse. **2** [1930s+] of music, to make one move in a rhythmical manner. [cognate with the sexual v. JAZZ v.[1] (1) the word *rock* works both as a style of music and a term for intercourse, e.g. in the 1922 song title 'My man rocks me (with one steady roll)'; for further details on sexual imagery of rock/blues see Cohen (ed.), *Studies in Slang* V (1997), pp.127 ff.]

rock *v.*[5] **1** [1930s+] to delight, to bring excitement to. **2** [1940s+] of a place, to be carried away with emotion, usu. through a performance. **3** [1940s+] to be active. **4** [1980s+] to perform, to offer up. **5** [1980s+] to do well in something. **6** [1990s+] to display, to indulge oneself in, esp. of clothes.

rock *v.*[6] [2000s] (*drugs*) to make pure cocaine into crack cocaine. [ROCK n.[3] (4)]

rock a beat *v.* [1990s+] (*US*) to play music. [ROCK v.[5] (4) + SE *beat*]

rock along *v.* [20C+] (*orig. US*) to proceed, to go on with life in one's usual manner.

rockalow *n.* [mid-19C] an overcoat. [Fr. *roquelaure*, an overcoat]

rock and lurch *n.* [20C+] (*Aus.*) a church. [rhy. sl.]

rock and roll *n.* (*also* **rock 'n' roll**) [1980s+] unemployment benefit (cf. BLESS MY SOUL n.). [rhy. sl. = SE *dole*]

rock and roll *v.* [1930s+] to have sexual intercourse; also as *n.*, sexual intercourse. [fig. use of SE]

rock ape *n.* [1970s+] (*Aus.*) **1** a derog. term for a Black person (cf. AFRICAN APE n.). **2** anyone viewed with disfavour, e.g. a teenager.

rock candy *n.* [1920s–40s] (*US Black*) diamonds. [resemblance]

rockchopper *n.* (*also* **R.C.**) [1940s+] (*Aus.*) a derog. term for a Roman Catholic. [used by Protestants as a derog. ref. to the original Irish immigrants, who were mainly convicts and, as such, condemned to hard labour; although this term is also abbreviated to *R.C.*, the use of the common initials for a Roman Catholic only strengthen this term rather give it its origin; note synon. RMC Duntroon (Aus.) *rock crunchie, rock crusher*]

rock cocaine *n. see* ROCK n.[3] (3).

rock college *n.* [1980s+] (*N.Z.*) a prison (cf. BIG SCHOOL n.). [SE *rock* + COLLEGE n. (3)]

rock crank *n.* [1980s+] (*drugs*) methamphetamine (cf. BOMBITA n.). [SE *rock* + CRANK n.[4] (1)]

rock crusher *n.*[1] [20C+] (*US*) **1** a convict. **2** a prison. [hard labour in the rock quarry]

rock crusher *n.*[2] **1** [1920s] (*US*) an automobile. **2** [1930s] (*orig. US Black*) an accordian.

rocked *adj.* **1** [early 19C] forgetful, esp. used of an ex-prisoner whose mental state has been affected by their punishment, whether prison or transportation. **2** [1980s+] (*US campus*) drunk or drugged. [i.e. they have 'rocks in the head']

rocked in a stone kitchen *phr.* [late 18C–early 19C] foolish, stupid. [someone who has been thus rocked will have had their brain injured]

Rockefeller bid *n.* [1980s+] (*US Und./prison*) a sentence of 10 years to life. [the sentence instituted by Nelson *Rockefeller*, as governor of New York state + BID n.[2]]

rocker *n.*[1] [1900s] a stone-thrower. [ROCK v.[1] (1)]

rocker *n.*[2] [1960s+] **1** a member of a youth cult whose members wear leather, ride powerful motorcycles and fight their ritual rivals, the mods; latterly the hardcore rockers developed into a UK version of the US Hell's Angels (cf. MOD n.[2]). **2** a fan of rock music.

rocker *v.* (*also* **roker, rokker**) **1** [mid-19C–1950s] to speak, esp. to speak tramps' jargon. **2** [1900s–10s] to understand. [Rom. *roker*, to talk]

rockers *n.* [1970s+] (*W.I. Rasta*) reggae music, esp. the latest sound.

rocket *n.*[1] [1940s+] (*orig. milit.*) a severe reprimand or telling off; thus *get/give a rocket*.

rocket *n.*[2] [1940s+] (*drugs*) a marijuana cigarette (cf. BOMB n.[4]). [one 'blasts' off, i.e. HIGH adj.[1] (2)]

rocket *v.*[1] [1940s+] (*orig. milit.*) to scold severely, to reprimand. [ROCKET n.[1]]

rocket *v.*[2] [1990s+] (*drugs*) suddenly to become extremely intoxicated when smoking cannabis. [ROCKET n.[2]]

rocket fuel *n.* **1** [1970s+] (*drugs*) phencyclidine (cf. ACE n.[4]). **2** [1990s+] cocaine.

rocket rattling *n.* [1960s] using one's force of nuclear weapons to threaten other countries. [SE *sabre rattling*]

rockets *n.* **1** [1960s+] (*US Black*) bullets. **2** [1990s+] the female breasts (cf. BAGS n.[1]). [the shape]

rocket scientist *n.* [1980s+] (*orig. US campus*) someone who is stupid or someone who is saying the very obvious. [ironic use of SE]

rock fiend *n.* [2000s] (*US drugs*) a habitual user of crack cocaine. [ROCK n.[3] (4) + FIEND n.[2] (1)]

rock-head *n.*[1] [1950s+] (*US*) a stupid person; thus *rock-headed*, very stupid. [SE *rock* + -HEAD sfx (1)]

rock-head *n.*[2] [1990s+] (*drugs*) a consumer of crack cocaine. [ROCK n.[3] (4) + -HEAD sfx (3)]

rock ho *n.* [2000s] (*US Black*) a woman who takes crack cocaine; thus a general derog. [ROCK n.[3] (4) + HO n.[1] (1)]

rock hound *n.* (*also* **rock sharp**) [late 19C+] (*orig. US*) **1** a geologist. **2** an amateur mineralogist. [SE *rock* + HOUND sfx/SHARP n.[1] (2)]

rock house *n.* [1980s+] (*drugs*) a place where crack cocaine is sold and smoked. [ROCK n.[3] (4) + SE *house*]

rockin' *n.* [20C+] (*US prison*) a prison riot. [SE *rock*, to shake]

rock in *v.*[1] [20C+] (*Aus.*) **1** to eat heartily. **2** to intensify, to accelerate; esp. in phr. *rock it in!* hurry up! make it snappy!

rock in *v.*[2] (*also* **rock over/up**) [1970s+] (*S.Afr.*) to arrive without prior announcement or appointment, to 'roll up'. [SE *rock*, to stagger]

rockiness *n.* [late 19C] **1** drunkenness. **2** insanity, madness. [SE *rock*, to shake; thus the images are of instability]

rocking *adj.* [1980s+] (*US campus/teen*) a general term of approval. [fig. use of ROCK *v.*[4] (2)]

rocking chair *n.* [1930s–40s] (*US Black*) sexual intercourse, esp. as used metaphorically in blues lyrics.

rocking horse *n.* [1960s+] **1** a sauce, a condiment. **2** cheek, impudence. [rhy. sl.; (2) = SAUCE *n.*[1]]

rocking-horse manure *n.* [1950s+] (*orig. Aus.*) something extremely hard, if not impossible to find.

rock it *v.* **1** [1930s–50s] to fight. **2** [1950s] (*Aus.*) to hurry up.

rock it in *v.* [1940s] (*Aus./N.Z.*) **1** to boast. **2** to tease. **3** to upset, to hurt. [one is throwing verbal 'rocks']

rock monster *n.* [1980s] (*US campus*) a drug addict who steals to support their habit. [ROCK *n.*[3] (4) + MONSTER *n.*[1] (5)/SE *monster*]

rock 'n' roll *n. see* ROCK AND ROLL *n.*

rock of ages *n.*[1] [1920s] (*US*) an older woman.

rock of ages *n.*[2] (*also* **rocks**) [1930s+] wages. [rhy. sl.]

rock on *v.* [1960s+] (*US*) to enjoy oneself, esp. by playing or dancing to rock music.

rock one's world *v.* [1980s+] (*US campus*) to have sexual intercourse. [ROCK *v.*[4] (1)/ROCK *v.*[5] (1); note the now clichéd description of love-making – 'make the earth move' – from Ernest Hemingway's *For Whom the Bell Tolls* (1940)]

rock out *v.*[1] **1** [1960s+] (*US*) to enjoy oneself, esp. by playing or dancing to rock music. **2** [1980s] (*US Black*) to collapse, to be exhausted.

rock out *v.*[2] [1980s+] (*drugs*) to collapse through an excessive consumption of crack cocaine. [ROCK *n.*[3] (4)]

rock out! *excl.* [1980s] keep enjoying yourself! have a great time!

rock over *v. see* ROCK IN *v.*[2].

rockpile *n.* **1** [late 19C+] (*US prison*) (*also* **pile**) the prison quarry, in allusion to the convict's task of breaking stones; thus fig. the prison. **2** [1940s] (*US Black*) any tall building; thus *topside of the rockpile*, the top flat, the penthouse. **3** [1950s] (*US*) one's home. [note naut. use *rockpile*, a ship on which the work is especially demanding]

rockpile cure *n. see* QUARRY CURE *n.*

rocks *n.*[1] **1** [mid-19C+] (*US*) money; usu. in phr. *pocketful of rocks*. **2** [20C+] the teeth. **3** [20C+] precious stones, jewels, esp. diamonds. **4** [1940s] (*US Und.*) a particular confidence trick based on fake diamonds. **5** [1940s+] (*orig. US*) ice-cubes. [resemblance]

rocks *n.*[2] (*also* **rocksy**) [late 19C] (*US*) as a term of address.

rocks *n.*[3] [1940s–50s] (*US drugs*) withdrawal symptoms.

rocks *n.*[4] [1940s+] **1** the testicles (cf. AGATES *n.*). **2** in fig. use, courage, bravery. [play on STONE *n.*[1] (1)]

rocks *n.*[5] (*drugs*) **1** [1960s+] a form of crystallized, smokeable heroin. **2** [1970s+] cocaine. **3** [1980s+] crack cocaine (cf. BASE *n.*). [resemblance]

rocks *n.*[6] *see* ROCK OF AGES *n.*[2].

rocks *n.*[7] *see* ROCKS (FOR JOCKS) *n.*

rocks! *excl.* [1920s] nonsense! rubbish! [ROCKS *n.*[4] (1), i.e. BALLOCKS! *excl.* (1)]

rocks and boulders *n.* [1910s–70s] the shoulders. [rhy. sl.]

rocks (for jocks) *n.* [1960s+] (*US campus*) an undergraduate course in 'introductory geology'. [SE *rock* + JOCK *n.*[1] (3)]

rock sharp *n. see* ROCK HOUND *n.*

rocks of Gibraltar *n.* [1950s] (*mainly UK juv.*) roast potatoes.

rock someone's frame *v. see* CLIMB SOMEONE'S FRAME *v.* (2).

rock someone's mic *v.* [2000s] (*US Black*) of a woman, to fellate (cf. BLOW *v.*[2]).

rock someone's world *v.* [1990s+] **1** (*US*) to render unconscious. **2** to amaze; to move emotionally.

rock spider *n.*[1] (*also* **spider**) **1** [1930s+] (*Aus.*) a thief who robs courting couples in parks or at the seaside when their attention is elsewhere. **2** [1990s+] (*Aus.*) (*also* **rocky**) a child molester. [in nursery rhyme 'Little Miss Muffet': 'There came a big spider / And sat down beside her']

rock spider *n.*[2] [1950s+] (*S.Afr.*) an Afrikaner. [? literary ref.]

rock star *n.* [1980s+] (*drugs*) a smoker of crack cocaine, esp. a woman who trades sex for crack cocaine or money to buy crack cocaine. [ROCK *n.*[3] (4) + play on SE]

rocksy *n. see* ROCKS *n.*[2].

rock the boat *v.* [1930s+] (*orig. US*) to cause (unnecessary) trouble, to disturb the status quo; often in negative imper. *don't rock the boat*.

rock the mainline *v. see* RIDE THE MAINLINE *v.*

rock up *v. see* ROCK IN *v.*[2].

rock worker *n.* [1940s] (*US Und.*) a seller of cheap jewellery. [ROCK *n.*[2] (1) + WORKER *n.*[1] (1)]

Rocky *n.* (*also* **Rocky III**) [1990s+] (*drugs*) crack cocaine (cf. BASE *n.*). [ROCK *n.*[3] (4) + play on the *Rocky* films of 1980s]

rocky *n.*[1] [1990s+] (*UK drugs*) a variety of hashish (cf. AFGHAN *n.*).

rocky *n.*[2] [1990s+] (*UK juv.*) the erect penis. [it is 'rock-hard']

rocky *n.*[3] [1990s+] (*UK juv.*) a scavenger.

rocky *n.*[4] *see* ROCK SPIDER *n.*[1] (2).

rocky *adj.* **1** [mid-18C+] drunk. **2** [mid-19C+] (*orig. US*) difficult, problematical. **3** [late 19C] unfair, cruel. **4** [late 19C+] (*orig. US*) unwell, 'off-colour'. **5** [1920s] (*orig. US*) penniless, impoverished. [SE *rock*, to sway]

Rocky Mountain canary *n.* [20C+] a donkey, an ass (cf. ARIZONA CANARY *n.*). [CANARY *n.*[10]]

rocky road *n.* [1990s+] (*US*) the anus (cf. ALLEY WAY *n.*; BOURNE-VILLE BOULEVARD *n.*). [? an ice-cream variety, which features *chocolate*, punning on CHOCOLATE *adj.* (2)]

Rocky III *n. see* ROCKY *n.*

rod *n.*[1] **1** [17C+] the penis, esp. the erect penis; thus GET A ROD ON *v.* (cf. AX *n.*[2]; BAT *n.*[7]). **2** [20C+] (*US*) a gun, a pistol. **3** [1930s–50s] (*US*) a gunman. [the shape]

rod *n.*[2] (*US*) **1** [late 19C+] the draw-rod of a railway carriage or truck; usu. in pl.; thus RIDE THE ROD(S) *v.* **2** [1900s–60s] a freight train. [abbr.]

rod *n.*[3] [1930s+] an overcoat. [? play on SE phr. *a rod for one's back*]

rod *n.*[4] *see* HOT-ROD *n.* (1).

rod *n.*[5] *see* RAMROD *n.* (3).

rod *v.* **1** [late 19C+] of a man, to have sexual intercourse (cf. BAGAGA *v.*). **2** [1910s] (*US Und.*) to hold up with a gun. **3** [1920s+] to arm oneself with a gun. [ROD *n.*[1]]

rodda *n.* [1960s] (*US Black*) a Cadillac. [? HOT-ROD *n.* (1)]

rodded (up) *adj.* [1920s+] carrying a gun. [ROD *n.*[1] (2)]

rodder *n.* [1950s+] (*US*) one who drives a customized HOT-ROD *n.* (1).

roddy *n.* [mid-19C] a *rhodo*dendron. [abbr.]

rodeo *n.*[1] [1920s] (*US tramp*) a vagrant, a traveller. [? play on SE *road*]

rodeo *n.*[2] [1990s+] (*US Black teen*) a style of sexual intercourse, where the man 'rides' the woman; usu. anal intercourse, while pulling her hair and slapping her buttocks. [the image of a rodeo bronco-rider]

rodge *n.* [1970s] (*US campus*) a fact, anything that's true. [airforce jargon *roger* = message received and understood]

rod in pickle *n.* (*also* **rod in lye/piss**) **1** [late 16C–1910s] a punishment in prospect. **2** [early 19C] any agent of revenge or aggression that has been put aside for use at the right time. **3** [1940s] (*Aus.*) in horseracing, a certainty. [from the toughening of rods by marinating them in lye]

rodman *n.*[1] [1920s+] (*US*) a gunman. [ROD *n.*[1] (2) + sfx *-man*]

rodman *n.*² (*also* **rod rider, rodsman**) [1930s–40s] (*US tramp*) a tramp who travels by clinging onto the metalwork beneath a coach or wagon. [RODS n. + SE *man*]

rodney *n.*¹ [late 19C+] (*Irish*) a fool. [dial. *rodney*, an idler, a loafer, a fool]

rodney *n.*² [1960s–70s] the penis (cf. ABRAHAM n.¹). [ROD n.¹ (1)]

Rodney King *n.* [1990s+] (*US Black*) an arrest, esp. one involving brutality; thus *pull a Rodney King*, to initiate police brutality. [*Rodney King*, a Black man, was severely beaten by the police during his arrest. A videotape of the beating led to the trial of the officers involved and, after their controversial acquittal, the Los Angeles riots of 1992]

rod rider *n. see* RODMAN n.².

Rod's *n.* [1970s+] (*UK society*) Harrods. [abbr.]

rods *n.* [1900s–40s] (*US tramp*) the metalwork – struts, supports etc – found underneath a railroad coach or wagon.

rodsman *n. see* RODMAN n.².

rod up *v.*¹ [1920s+] (*US Und.*) to arm oneself with a gun. [ROD n.¹ (2)]

rod up *v.*² [1970s+] (*US*) to convert a car by giving it a very powerful engine to make it go fast. [HOT-ROD n. (1)]

rod walloper *n.* [1960s+] (*orig. Aus.*) a masturbator; lit. or fig. [ROD n.¹ (1) + SE *walloper*]

roe *n.* [mid-19C–1900s] semen (cf. BABY GRAVY n.). [SE *roe*, fish eggs]

rofe *n.* [1940s–50s] (*UK prison*) a 4-year sentence. [backsl.]

rofefil *n.* (*also* **rouf-efil**) [mid-19C] a life sentence. [backsl.; lit. 'for life']

rogan gosh *n.* [2000s] money (cf. BEES (AND HONEY) n.). [rhy. sl. = DOSH n.; ult. an Indian dish]

roger *n.*¹ [mid-16C] a wandering beggar who pretended to be a poor scholar from Oxford or Cambridge. [despite the 'e' the 'g' was pronounced hard, thus ? corruption of SE *rogue*; Ribton-Turner, *A History of Vagrants* (1887), notes Gaelic *ruaigair*, a pursuer, a hunter, Erse *ruaigaur* and Lowland Scot. *rugger*, an outlaw]

roger *n.*² **1** [mid-16C–early 19C] a goose. **2** [late 17C+] the penis, an erect penis. **3** [mid–late 19C] an act of sexual intercourse. [SE *roger*, a bull]

roger *n.*³ [mid-17C–mid-19C] (*UK Und.*) a suitcase. [? dial. *roger*, the paunch of a pig]

roger *n.*⁴ [late 17C–18C] a country simpleton (cf. ALVIN n.).

roger *v.*¹ [early 18C+] to have sexual intercourse, to seduce; also as *do a roger*. [ROGER n.² (2)/SE *roger*, a bull]

roger *v.*² [1940s–50s] (*Aus.*) of a man, to be betrayed sexually by one's wife or partner during one's absence. [ROGER THE LODGER n.]

roger gough *n.* [late 19C+] (*Aus.*) scrub, brushwood. [? General *Roger Gough*, victor of Sobraon and Ferozeshah or f. long-lost Native Aus. word]

Roger Hunt *n.* [1990s+] the vagina (cf. ALL QUIET n.). [rhy. sl. = CUNT n.¹ (1); ult. the former Liverpool and England footballer *Roger Hunt* (b.1938)]

rogering *n.* [19C+] sexual intercourse. [ROGER v.¹]

rogering iron *n.* [early 18C–19C] the penis (cf. AX n.²). [ROGER v.¹ + SE *iron*]

Roger Moore *n.* [1990s+] **1** a prostitute, a whore. **2** a door. [rhy. sl.; ult. UK film actor *Roger Moore* (b.1927), most famous for his role as James Bond]

roger ramjet *n.* [1990s+] a homosexual. [the children's TV cartoon character, but note ROGER v.¹ + SE *ram*, to force]

rogers *n.* [late 19C] (*UK society*) a ghastly face. [? the pirate 'skull-and-crossbones', the Jolly *Roger* or Samuel *Rogers* (1763–1865), who combined banking with poetry and apparently, while not chronologically old, had a notably aged face]

roger the lodger *n.* [1920s+] a lodger who seduces his landlady, or the wife of his landlord; thus used of anyone who seduces a woman while her partner is absent. [rhyme, but also pun on ROGER n.² (2)]

roglan *n.* [late 19C] a 4-wheeled vehicle. [Shelta]

rogue *n.*¹ [mid-16C–18C] (*UK Und.*) a professional villain, 'neither as stout or hardy as the upright-man' (Harman) (cf. CANTING CREW n.). [the term is an orig. cant coinage and refers to a specific order of villain, the Fourth Order of Canters; its absorption into SE, meaning a general-purpose rascal, ran in parallel, albeit slightly later by some 20 years]

rogue *n.*² [late 18C–early 19C] a corn chandler. [his trad. negative image]

rogue *n.*³ [1960s+] (*US Black*) a ladies' man, a sexually active man. [SE *rogue male*; note Urquhart, *The Complete Works of Rabelais* (1653), in list of names for the penis: 'my lusty live sausage, my crimson chitterlin, rump-splitter, shove-devil, down right to it, stiff and stout, in and to, at her again, my coney-borrow-ferret, wily-beguiley, my pretty rogue']

rogue *v.* **1** [mid-16C–mid-17C] (*UK Und.*) to live as a professional beggar; thus *roguing*, living in this way; *roguishness*, being a rogue. **2** [1980s+] (*US campus*) to steal. [ROGUE n.¹]

rogue and pullet *n.* [mid-19C] (*UK Und.*) a man and woman working together as a criminal team. [ROGUE n.¹ + PULLET n. (1)]

rogue and villain *n.* (*also* **rogue and dillion**) [mid–late 19C; 1960s] a shilling. [rhy. sl.; 1960s use is Aus., as *rogue and dillion*]

rogue in grain *n.* [late 17C–early 19C] a very great rogue. [stereotyping]

rogue in spirit *n.* [late 18C–mid-19C] a distiller or brandy merchant. [pun]

rogue's walk *n.* [late 19C] (*UK society*) a stroll along Piccadilly from the Circus to Bond Street. [ROGUE n.¹ + SE *walk*; a ref. to the deviousness that created the fortunes of many of the strollers]

rogue with one ear *n.* [late 17C–early 18C] a chamberpot. [the 'ear' is the handle]

roguing Joe *n.* (*also* **roguing Tom**) [1950s] (*W.I.*) **1** a wandering scrounger or pilferer. **2** the bag into which such a person places their finds. [mid-16C–mid-17C SE *rogue*, to wander as a rogue or vagrant]

Rohie *n.* (*also* **Rohy**) [1990s+] (*drugs*) the sedative *Rohy*pnol. [abbr.]

roid-head *n.* [2000s] a stupid thug. [abbr. SE *steroid* + -HEAD sfx (1)]

roid rage *n.* [1980s+] (*drugs*) aggressive behaviour caused by excessive steroid use. [abbr. SE *steroid* + play on ROAD RAGE n.]

roids *n.* [1980s+] (*US*) steroids. [abbr.]

roister *n.* (*also* **roisterer, royster, roysterer**) [mid-16C+] (*UK Und.*) a swaggering, blustering bully, a noisy reveller; also as adj., *roistering*. [Fr. *rustre*, a ruffian, a swaggerer; ult. Lat. *rusticus*, a peasant]

roker *n.* (*also* **rooker**) [late 19C+] (*S.Afr.*) a marijuana smoker. [Du. *roken*, to smoke]

roker/rokker *v. see* ROCKER v.

Roland Young *n.* [1990s+] the tongue. [rhy. sl.; ult. the UK character actor *Roland Young* (1887–1953)]

rolf *v. see* RALPH v.

rolie *n.* [1980s+] (*N.Z. drugs*) a *Roly*pnol. [abbr.]

roll *n.*¹ [mid-19C; 1940s] the penis.

roll *n.*² [mid-19C+] a bankroll. [abbr.]

roll *n.*³ [1930s–40s] (*US*) the vagina. [abbr. JELLY ROLL n.¹ (3)]

roll *n.*⁴ [1940s+] (*orig. US*) sexual intercourse; thus *roll ass*, to have sexual intercourse. [abbr. ROLL IN THE HAY n. (1)]

roll *n.*⁵ [1950s–60s] (*US Black*) a double-breasted suit.

roll *n.*⁶ **1** [1960s] (*US drugs*) a small package of heroin. **2** [1960s+] (*US drugs*) a roll of Benzedrine tablets. **3** [1970s+] (*US Black*) a month's supply of contraceptive pills. **4** [1970s+] (*US drugs*) 3 barbiturate pills, as sold by a dealer. **5** [2000s] (*US drugs/campus*) a tablet of MDMA (cf. ECSTASY n.).

roll n.[7] [1970s–80s] (*UK Black*) a fight.

roll n.[8] *see* ROLL-UP n.[2] (1).

roll v.[1] [mid-19C; 1920s+] (*US Black*) to have sexual intercourse. [orig. meaning work, it was ext. in blues songs to mean intercourse, i.e. the physical effort involved]

roll v.[2] **1** [mid-19C+] to make a cigarette. **2** [late 19C; 1960s+] (*drugs*) to roll a marijuana cigarette.

roll v.[3] **1** [late 19C–1920s; 1990s+] (*US Black*) to walk. **2** [1910s+] (*US*) (*also* **roll off**) to start moving, lit. or fig.; thus phr. *let's roll*, let's go, let's leave. **3** [1940s+] (*US*) to drive a car. **4** [1980s+] (*US campus*) to leave, to avoid a class. **5** [1990s+] (*US*) to leave home. **6** [2000s] (*US Black*) to perform, e.g. as a rapper.

roll v.[4] **1** [late 19C+] to rob, usu. a drunk or any helpless person; thus *roll a stiff/lush*. **2** [20C+] to attack. [one *rolls* the victim over]

roll v.[5] **1** [1950s+] (*US*) to prosper, to do well, to succeed. **2** [1980s+] (*US Black*) to survive, to live, to conduct oneself. [fig. use of SE]

roll v.[6] [1990s+] (*drugs*) for a vein to move away from the syringe when one is attempting to inject oneself with narcotics.

roll v.[7] [1990s+] (*US drugs/campus*) to take MDMA. [ROLL n.[6] (5)]

roll v.[8] *see* ROLL IN v.

roll a kangaroo couldn't jump over, a n. *see* ROLL JACK RICE COULDN'T JUMP OVER, A n.

roll and lurch n. [1900s] (*Aus.*) a church. [rhy. sl.]

roll a number v. [1960s+] (*drugs*) to prepare a marijuana cigarette. [ROLL v.[2] (2) + NUMBER n.[5]]

roll big enough to choke a bullock/the tunnel, a n. *see* ROLL JACK RICE COULDN'T JUMP OVER, A n.

roll dog n. [1990s+] (*US Black*) someone with whom one drives around. [ROLL v.[3] (3) + DOG n.[2] (3)]

rolled adj. *see* ROLLING adj.[2].

Roller n.[1] [1950s+] a *Rolls* Royce car. [abbr. + -ER sfx]

Roller n.[2] *see* HOLY ROLLER n. (1).

roller n.[1] (*drugs*) **1** [late 19C–1940s] someone who rolls opium into smokeable pellets. **2** [1920s–40s] a drug user or addict. **3** [1930s] a tobacco cigarette. **4** [1970s+] a vein that rolls as one attempts to insert a needle. **5** [1990s+] a drug seller; thus *rolling*; dealing drugs.

roller n.[2] **1** [20C+] (*US Black*) someone who keeps moving continuously. **2** [1900s] (*US*) a hansom cab. **3** [1950s+] (*US*) (*also* **rollo**) a police car. [ROLL v.[3]]

roller n.[3] **1** [1910s+] (*US*) a robber, esp. one who robs drunks and other defenceless people. **2** [1960s+] (*US prison*) a prison guard. [ROLL v.[4]]

rollers n. **1** [early 19C] a nightly patrol, on both horse and foot, that covered London in the hope of preventing robberies. **2** [1950s+] (*US Black*) the police; occas. in sing. [? SE *patrol*]

rollerskate n. [1960s+] (*US*) a small foreign-made car. [note 1940s UK hauliers' jargon *roller skate*, a small, light wagon]

roll hard v. [2000s] (*US Black*) to be very aggressive, fearless. [ROLL v.[5] (2) + HARD adv. (4)]

rollick v. (*also* **rollux**) [1930s+] to tell off, to reprimand. [euph. for BALLOCK v.[3]; ult. TOMMY ROLLOCKS n.]

rollicking n. [1930s+] a telling off, a reprimand; esp. in phr. *a good rollicking*. [ROLLICK v.]

rollicking adj. [1990s+] nonsensical. [ROLLICK v./euph. for BOLLICKING adv.]

rollie n. [1940s+] (*orig. US prison*) a hand-*rolled* cigarette. [abbr.]

rollies n. [1930s+] the testicles. [abbr. ROLLOCKS! excl.]

roll-in n. [1990s+] (*US gang*) a female recruit to a gang rolls dice to ascertain how many members will have sex with her.

roll in v. (*also* **roll**) **1** [late 18C+] of people, to arrive, to come home. **2** [late 19C–1920s] (*US*) to go to bed. **3** [20C+] of objects, to appear, to arrive.

rolling n.[1] [late 19C+] robbery. [ROLL v.[4]]

rolling n.[2] [1980s+] (*US Black teen*) **1** driving around very slowly. **2** being associated either with an individual or a larger group. [(1) ROLL v.[3] (3); (2) ROLL WITH v. (2)]

rolling n.[3] [1990s+] (*drugs*) under the influence of MDMA (cf. ECSTASY n.). [ROLL v.[7]]

rolling n.[4] *see* ROLLER n.[1] (5).

rolling adj.[1] [late 18C–mid-19C] clever, sophisticated.

rolling adj.[2] (*also* **rolled**) [mid-19C+] very well-off, or abundantly supplied with anything. [abbr. SE phr. *rolling in money*]

rolling adj.[3] [20C+] very drunk. [SE *roll*, to tumble]

rolling billow n. [late 19C–1950s] a pillow. [rhy. sl.; later joc. use in Borough market, SE London, for sacks of potatoes]

rolling deep n. [20C+] (*Aus.*) sleep. [rhy. sl.]

rolling kiddy n. [early–mid-19C] (*UK Und.*) a dandified thief. [ROLLING adj.[1] + KIDDY n.[1] (1)]

rolling-pin n. [late 17C+] the penis (cf. BAT n.[7]).

rolling rat trap n. *see* RAT TRAP n.[1] (2).

rolling refinery n. [1970s] (*US*) a truck that hauls petrol/gasoline or oil.

rollin' ome n. [1940s] a comb. [rhy. sl.]

roll in one's alley v. *see* THROW IN ONE'S ALLEY v. (1).

roll in one's ivory v. (*also* **roll in one's ivories**) [late 18C–19C] to kiss. [IVORY n. (1)]

roll in one's marble(s) v. *see* PASS IN ONE'S MARBLE(S) v.

roll in the hay n. [1940s+] (*orig. US*) **1** sexual intercourse, with the implication of spontaneity, adultery or the open air. **2** a person viewed as a possible sexual partner. [SE *roll* + SE *hay*]

roll in the hay v. [1940s+] to have sexual intercourse. [ROLL IN THE HAY n.]

roll into v. **1** [19C+] to arrive. **2** [late 19C–1900s] (*Aus.*) to attack.

roll Jack Rice couldn't jump over, a n. (*also* **a roll a kangaroo couldn't jump over, a roll big enough to choke a bullock/the tunnel**) [1910s–70s] (*Aus.*) a large quantity of money (cf. ROLL THAT WOULD CHOKE A MULE, A n.; WAD THAT WOULD CHOKE A WOMBAT, A n.). [ROLL n.[7] + proper name of the racehorse *Jack Rice*, Aus. champion hurdler]

roll me (in the dirt) n. [late 19C] a shirt. [rhy. sl.]

roll (me) in the gutter n. [20C+] (*Aus.*) butter. [rhy. sl.]

roll me in the kennel n. [early–mid-18C] gin. [the drunkard will sleep anywhere]

rollo n. *see* ROLLER n.[2] (3).

rollocking n. [1930s+] a scolding, a reprimand; thus as a v., to reprimand. [ROLLICK v.; euph. for BALLOCKING n.[2]]

rollocks n. *see* TOMMY ROLLOCKS n.

rollocks! excl. [1960s+] nonsense, rubbish. [euph. for BALLOCKS! excl. (1); ult. TOMMY ROLLOCKS n.]

roll off v. *see* ROLL v.[3] (2).

roll of tar-paper n. [1950s–70s] (*US*) a Black man's penis.

roll on v.[1] [late 19C+] used to introduce a variety of wishes, usu. referring to escaping the environment that one is in, e.g. *roll on payday/Friday* etc.

roll on v.[2] (*US*) **1** [1970s] to address, to talk to. **2** [2000s] to betray; to inform on.

roll on! excl. [1950s+] a general excl. of dismissal, resignation, amazement, surprise etc; often intensified as *fucking roll on!*

roll one's bones v. (*also* **roll one's trail**) [20C+] (*US*) to get into action, to move oneself.

roll one's dice v. [2000s] (*US Black*) to masturbate.

roll one's hoop v. **1** [late 19C–1920s] to do well, to succeed. **2** [1900s–30s] (*US*) (*also* **roll one's tail**) to leave.

roll one's trail v. *see* ROLL ONE'S BONES v.

roll one up v. *see* ROLL UP v.[3].

roll out v. **1** [mid-19C+] (*US Black/campus*) to leave, to depart. **2** [late 19C+] to get out of bed, to get up. **3** [1990s+] (*US prison*) to release from jail. **4** [2000s] (*US prison*) to move to a new cell. [the image of a wagon 'rolling' off on a journey]

roll out the red carpet v. [1920s+] to give someone a grand welcome. [the *red carpet* ceremonially laid for visiting dignitaries]

rollover *n.*[1] [1920s–50s] (*US prison*) the last night of a prison sentence. [one wakes up, rolls out of bed, and the sentence is over]

rollover *n.*[2] [1980s] (*US Und.*) a confession; a plea of guilty. [ROLL OVER v.]

roll over *v.* [1970s+] **1** to give up, to acquiesce, to surrender. **2** as *roll over on*, to betray, to inform against. [the way in which a dog *rolls over* on its back to indicate surrender]

roll right *n.* [2000s] (*US prison*) a generically branded cigarette.

rolls *n.* [1970s+] (*US gay*) the buttocks.

Rolls Canardly *n.* (*also* **Rolls Can-hardly**) [1950s+] (*orig. Aus.*) a run-down old car. [it *rolls* down the hills but *can hardly* get up them + ref. to the antithetical *Rolls* Royce; note the letter once sent to the manufacturers of Rolls Royce by Sir W.S. Gilbert (1836–1911): 'your car rolls but it will not royce']

roll sets on *v. see* RUN SETS ON v.

Rolls Royce *n.*[1] [20C+] the voice. [rhy. sl.]

Rolls Royce *n.*[2] [1910s+] the best of its kind; also adj.

roll stuff *v.* [1930s] (*US drugs*) to move around wholesale quantities of narcotics. [SE *roll* + STUFF n.[3] (2)]

roll that would choke a mule, a *n.* (*also* **a roll that would choke a cow/an anteater**) [1910s+] (*US Black*) a very large bankroll; occas. of things other than money (cf. ROLL JACK RICE COULDN'T JUMP OVER, A n.).

roll the bars *v.* [1990s+] (*US prison*) to open a row of cell doors using a remote mechanism that opens every door simultaneously.

roll the bones *v.* (*also* **shake the bones, trundle the bones**) [19C+] (*US*) to play at dice. [BONES n.[1] (1)]

roll the log *v.* (*also* **roll the boy**) [1930s–40s] (*drugs*) to smoke opium.

roll them in the aisles *v. see* LAY THEM IN THE AISLES v.

roll-up *n.*[1] [late 19C–1910s] (*Aus.*) **1** an assembly, a 'get-together'. **2** in spec. use, an unofficial trial, held in the goldfields. [ROLL UP v.[1] (1)]

roll-up *n.*[2] **1** [1940s+] (*orig. UK prison*) (*also* **roll**) a hand-rolled cigarette. **2** [1980s+] (*N.Z.*) an illicit smoke. **3** [1990s+] a hand-rolled marijuana/tobacco cigarette (cf. AFRICAN WOODBINE n.).

roll-up *n.*[3] [1990s+] (*US prison*) of an inmate, the act of leaving the prison, whether temporarily (for a court appearance) or permanently (after completing a sentence or moving to a new prison). [ROLL UP v.[2] (2)]

roll up *v.*[1] **1** [late 19C+] (*orig. US*) to congregate, to assemble. **2** [late 19C+] (*orig. US*) to arrive, to appear. **3** [1940s+] to die.

roll up *v.*[2] **1** [late 19C+] (*Aus.*) to pack one's belongings before leaving. **2** [1970s+] (*US prison*) of an inmate, to leave the prison, whether temporarily (for a court appearance) or permanently (after completing a sentence or moving to a new prison). **3** [2000s] (*US Black*) to prepare to fight. [(1) the rolling up of one's pack; (2) the old practice of rolling up one's mattress on every occasion of leaving one's cell; (3) to roll up one's sleeves]

roll up *v.*[3] (*also* **roll one up**) [1960s+] to prepare a marijuana cigarette. [ROLL v.[2] (2) (+ ONE n.[4] (4))]

roll up on *v.* [1990s+] (*US Black*) **1** to approach sexually. **2** to attack.

roll up the sidewalk *v.* [mid-19C] (*US*) of shops and entertainment in towns or cities, to close down at nightfall.

rollux *v. see* ROLLICK v.

roll with *v.* [1960s+] (*US Black*) **1** to agree with, to accept. **2** to associate with. [ROLL v.[3] (2)]

roll with the punches *v.* [1950s+] (*orig. US*) to take events as they come and not to be unbalanced by problems. [boxing imagery]

roll your own *v.* **1** [1970s] (*US Black*) an invitation to make yourself at home, do whatever you fancy. **2** [1990s+] to masturbate. [image of rolling one's own cigarettes]

roly-poly *n.*[1] (*also* **rowly-powly**) [19C] a game known as 'un-deux-cinq'. [? the same game as that noted by Johnson, *Dictionary*

(1755): 'a sort of game, in which, when a ball rolls into a certain place, it wins']

roly-poly *n.*[2] [mid-19C+] the penis. [play on PUDDING n.[1] (1) + ? SE *roly-poly*, stout, podgy]

Roman *adj.* [1950s+] in the world of gay sex, used to describe group sex. [Rome is identified with orgies, thanks to popular fantasies of the 'decline and fall' of Rome]

Roman candle *n.*[1] **1** [mid-19C; 1970s+] (*UK/US gay*) a penis. **2** [1940s+] a Roman Catholic. **3** [1970s+] an Italian (cf. DAGO n.).

Roman candle *n.*[2] [20C+] a sandal. [rhy. sl.]

romance boy *n.* [1950s] (*W.I.*) a young man who chases women.

Roman collar *n.* [1960s+] (*Irish*) a generous head on a glass of stout. [SE *Roman collar*, a priest's white collar]

Roman culture *n.* (*also* **Roman history**) [1960s+] orgies, group sex. [ROMAN adj.]

Roman engagement *n.* [1960s+] (*gay*) anal intercourse with a virgin woman. [? runs contrary to usu. sexual use of ROMAN adj.]

Roman fall *n.* [mid-19C] a way of walking in which the shoulders are thrust back, thus creating a droop backwards. [masc. play on fem. GRECIAN BEND n.[1] (1); officers of the Fr. Empire were forced to adopt this unnatural posture because of the tightness of their uniforms]

Roman fountains *n.* [1960s+] (*gay*) urinals. [ROMAN adj.]

Roman historian *n.* [1960s+] (*gay*) an enthusiast of orgies. [ROMAN adj.]

Roman history *n. see* ROMAN CULTURE n.

Roman night *n.* [1960s+] (*gay*) an orgy. [ROMAN adj.]

Roman roulette *n.* [1960s] contraception using no other system than the notoriously hit-and-miss 'rhythm method' as ordained by conservative popes.

romantic ballad *n.* [1990s+] salad. [rhy. sl.]

Romany rye *n.* [mid-19C] a non-gypsy gentleman who associates with gypsies. [Rom. *rai*, a gentleman; best-known through George Borrow's book *Romany Rye* (1857)]

romboyle *n.* (*also* **rumboyle**) [late 17C–early 19C] the watch (an early form of policing). [ety. unknown]

romboyle *v.* (*also* **rumboyle**) [17C–early 19C] (*UK Und.*) **1** to seek out by hue and cry. **2** to arrest on a warrant; thus *romboyled*, wanted by the watch. [ety. unknown]

rombustical *adj. see* RUMBUSTIOUS adj.

rome *see also under* RUM *and its combs.*

rome cove *n.* [17C] (*UK Und.*) a leading beggar, whether through strength or intelligence. [RUM adj. (1) + COVE n. (1); lit. a 'good man']

Rome-ville *n. see* RUMVILE n.

Romford lion *n.* (*also* **Rumford lion**) [late 17C–early 19C] a calf. [joc. ref. to *Romford*, Essex, then a market town]

romp *v.* (*US*) **1** [1930s+] to have sexual intercourse. **2** [1950s–60s] of street gangs, to fight, to beat up. [note the coincidental UK tabloid press use of *romp*, a sexual entanglement, e.g. 'three-in-a-bed romp']

romper room *n.* [1980s+] (*US campus*) a place where one can enjoy oneself in an uninhibited manner.

romp home *v.* (*also* **romp in**) [late 19C+] (*orig. racing*) to win easily.

romp it *v.* [1970s+] (*US campus*) to accelerate in a car.

rompworthy *adj.* [1930s+] of a woman, ripe for sexual conquest. [ROMP v. (1) + sfx *-worthy*]

ronald rich *n.* [1990s+] an extremely unpleasant woman. [rhy. sl. = BITCH n.[1] (1)]

ronchie *adj. see* RAUNCHY adj.

roni *n.* [1990s+] (*US Black teen*) a sweet woman. [cod Ital. *tenderoni*]

Ronnie Biggs *n.* [1960s+] lodgings. [rhy. sl. = DIGS n.[1]; ult. notorious UK criminal *Ronald Biggs* (b.1929), one of the Great Train Robbers of 1963]

ronnies *n.* [early 19C] (*Scot.*) potatoes. [? SE *round*, i.e. their shape]

ron randell *n. see* JACK RANDALL *n.*

ronson *n.*[1] [1950s] a pimp (cf. ALPHONSE *n.*[2]). [rhy. sl.; *rons(on)* = PONCE *n.* (1)]

ronson *n.*[2] [1990s+] the anus; thus dismissive excl. *up your ronson!* (cf. BOTTLE AND GLASS *n.*). [rhy. sl.; *Ronson lighter = shiter (see under* SHITTER *n.*[1])]

roo *n.* [late 19C+] (*Aus.*) a kangaroo. [abbr.]

roody-poo *adj. see* ROOTIE-POOT *adj.*

roof *n.* **1** [mid-19C] (*US campus*) a hat; thus *drop one's roof,* to lose one's hat. **2** [mid-19C–1940s] the human head.

roof *v.*[1] (*US Und.*) **1** [1910s] to travel on the roof of a railway passenger carriage. **2** [1960s] to break into a building via the roof.

roof *v.*[2] [1940s+] (*Aus.*) to kick or punch. [? SE *rough* or phr. *knock him through the roof*]

roofer *n.*[1] **1** [mid-19C+] (*orig. US*) a hat. **2** [1910s–20s] a third-rate, run-down theatre. [SE *roof*; (1) 20C+ use Aus.]

roofer *n.*[2] [1900s] (*US Und.*) a country gentleman. [they have 'a roof over their head']

roofer *n.*[3] [1910s–40s] (*US Und.*) a tramp who travels on the roofs of passenger carriages. [ROOF *v.*[1] (1)]

roofie *n.*[1] [1970s+] (*S.Afr.*) a junior National Serviceman, part of the latest intake. [? Afk. *roof,* scab]

roofie *n.*[2] (*also* **roofies, rophies, rophy, ruffies, ruffles, wolfies**) [1990s+] (*drugs*) *Roh*ypnol; a strong sedative. [abbr.; the drug, which causes users to appear drunk, is allegedly popular as a new form of knockout drop, prob. used to facilitate a number of 'date rapes']

roogodoo *n.* [20C+] (*W.I.*) a commotion, a noisy uproar. [? SE *ruckus*]

roogodung *adj.* (*also* **rukadung**) [20C+] (*W.I.*) tumble-down, dilapidated. [? ROOGODOO *n.* + SE *down*]

rooibaard *n.* [1990s+] (*S.Afr. drugs*) very strong marijuana, with tiny red hairs. [Afk. *rooibaard,* red beard]

rooinek *n.* [late 19C+] (*S.Afr.*) an Englishman. [Afk. *rooinek,* redneck; the effect of the sun]

rook *n.*[1] **1** [late 16C+] (*UK Und.*) a cheat or swindler. **2** [1930s+] a swindle. [the allegedly larcenous character of the bird]

rook *n.*[2] [late 18C–early 19C] (*UK Und.*) a small crowbar. [pun; a reverse of nature, where the rook is larger than the crow]

rook *n.*[3] [mid-19C+] a clergyman. [the black clothes or, according to Hotten (1864) f. the nursery rhyme *Who Killed Cock Robin?,* 'I, says the Rook, / With my little book, / I'll be the parson']

rook *n.*[4] *see* ROOKIE *n.*

rook *v.* [late 16C+] to cheat, to swindle, to steal. [ROOK *n.*[1] (1)]

rooked *adj.* [1920s] (*US*) impoverished. [? ext. of ROOK *v.*]

rooker *n. see* ROKER *n.*

rookery *n.* **1** [mid-18C–mid-19C] a gambling den. **2** [19C+] a criminal slum 'inhabited by dirty Irish and thieves' (Hotten, 1860); the best known was the *St Giles Rookery* (now occupied by the Centre Point tower) in central London. **3** [early 19C] a brothel (cf. BIRDCAGE *n.*[1]). **4** [early 19C–1940s] a row, a disturbance. **5** [1960s] in ext. use, any centre of the like-minded but marginal. [note milit. jargon *rookery,* that part of the barracks occupied by the subalterns]

rookery nook *n.* **1** [1920s+] a book. **2** [1960s] a cook. [rhy. sl.; ult. the farce *Rookery Nook* (1926) by Ben Travers]

rookie *n.* (*also* **rook, rooky**) **1** [late 19C+] (*mainly US*) a novice, a beginner, a new recruit, esp. in milit., police and sports use. **2** [1960s] (*US Black*) an outsider, one who is outside the group norms. [? SE *recruit* or children's use *rookie,* a lookout, if one considers that a lookout would have the least active and thus newest/youngest member of a gang; note *crow-boy,* a lookout, used in Southwark in the late 19C and derived f. the rural term for the boy who scared birds away from growing crops]

rookie *adj.* [1910s+] (*mainly US*) newly recruited, unfledged, unsophisticated. [ROOKIE *n.* (1)]

rookus juice *n. see* RUCKUS JUICE *n.*

rooky *n. see* ROOKIE *n.*

rooky *adj.* [mid–late 19C] rascally, roguish. [ROOK *n.*[1] (1)]

rooled up *adj.* [mid-19C] (*UK Und.*) placed in the watchman's lock-up. [SE *ruled up*]

roombelow *n.* [early 17C] (*UK Und.*) a prostitute. [coarse pun on what she offers]

roomer *n.* [late 19C+] (*orig. US*) a lodger.

roomie *n.* (*also* **roomy**) [1910s+] (*US*) **1** a *room*-mate, one who shares an apartment or other dwelling. **2** a prison cell mate. [abbr.]

rooms *n.* [1990s+] (*US campus*) a *room*-mate. [on pattern of HOMES *n.*]

room to rent *n.* [1980s] (*US teen*) a stupid person. [their brain is 'vacant']

roomy *n. see* ROOMIE *n.*

roosevelt *n. see* F.D.R. *n.*

roosher *n.* [late 19C–1900s] a policeman. [ROZZER *n.*[1]]

Rooshian/Roosian *n. see* RUSSIAN *n.*[1].

Rooskie *n. see* RUSSKI *n.*

roost *n.* **1** [mid-19C+] a bed. **2** [1900s–50s] one's home, one's house. **3** [1910s] (*US*) the upper gallery or 'gods' in a theatre. [post-1940s use of (2) is US Black]

roost *v.* **1** [17C–1900s] to sleep. **2** [19C+] to sit down. [SE *perch*]

rooster *n.*[1] [early 19C+] (*US*) a person.

rooster *n.*[2] **1** [mid-19C–1900s] the vagina. **2** [late 19C+] the penis. **3** [late 19C+] (*US*) a sexually active man. **4** [1910s] (*Aus.*) a man, with derog. implications. [the farmyard bird; note RMC Duntroon (*Aus.*) *rooster* [...] 'a nickname for a cadet who is reputed to be "continuously [sic] sexually active"']

rooster *n.*[3] [1940s] (*US*) a chair, a seat. [ROOST *v.* (2)]

rooster *n.*[4] [1950s–60s] (*UK Und.*) a lookout. [ext. use of ROOST *v.* (2)]

rooster brand *n.* [late 19C–1940s] (*US drugs*) ashes from smoked opium, sold for recycling by poor but desperate users. [ety. unknown; ? packaging]

roostered *adj.* [mid-19C–1900s] (*US*) drunk. [fig. use of SE *rooster*]

rooster time *n.* [1960s+] (*US teen*) the early morning, cock's crow.

roosting ken *n.* [19C] a lodging house. [ROOST *v.* (1) + KEN *n.*[1] (1)]

roost lay *n.* [early 19C] poultry-stealing. [SE *roost* + LAY *n.*[4] (1)]

root *n.*[1] **1** [mid-16C+] (*also* **old root**) the penis. **2** [mid-18C] the female genitals. **3** [late 19C+] an erection; thus phr. *get/have the root,* to get an erection. **4** [1910s] (*US*) a nose. **5** [1950s+] (*Aus.*) the act of sexual intercourse. **6** [1970s+] (*orig. Aus.*) the person with whom one has intercourse, usu. the woman; thus *weekend root,* a casual sexual partner. **7** [1990s+] (*Aus. teen*) a good-looking (and thus sexually attractive) male.

root *n.*[2] [mid-19C] a person, a man.

root *n.*[3] [late 19C–1900s] money. [the '*root* of all evil']

root *n.*[4] [20C+] a kick. [ROOT *v.*[2] (1)]

root *n.*[5] **1** [1900s–30s] a cigarette. **2** [1950s+] (*drugs*) marijuana. [? SE *cheroot*]

root *adj. see* REET *adj.*

root *v.*[1] **1** [mid-19C] (*US campus*) to act as a sycophant in the hope of favours and career advancement. **2** [mid-19C–1920s] (*US campus*) to work hard. **3** [1920s+] (*US Und.*) to steal. [? ROOT ABOUT *v.*]

root *v.*[2] **1** [late 19C–1950s] to kick a ball or a person. **2** [1910s] (*US*) to attack. **3** [1930s] (*Aus.*) to throw off. [? SE *uproot*]

root *v.*[3] **1** [1930s+] to have sexual intercourse; also used as euph. for FUCK *v.*[1] in a variety of similarly negative uses, e.g. to outwit, to baffle, to exhaust, to utterly confound (someone); thus excl. *get rooted!* go to hell!; *wouldn't it root you,* would you believe it? (cf. FRIG *v.*). **2** [1970s+] (*US gay/prison*) to fellate.

root *v.*[4] *see* ROOT (FOR) *v.*

root about *v.* (*also* **root around, root into**) [mid-19C+] to rummage, to search through.

rooted *adj.* [1940s+] (*Aus.*) exhausted, crippled, out of action. [ROOT v.³ (1)]

rooter *n.*¹ [mid-19C] a form of pony-tail, worn by men. [the hair appears to be throwing out a root]

rooter *n.*² [mid-19C–1910s] **1** anything considered excellent, first-class. **2** anything extreme, violent, highly aggressive. [SE *root*, the basis, the ultimate]

rooter *n.*³ [late 19C+] (*US*) **1** a sports fan, esp. a baseball fan. **2** an enthusiast, a supporter, in non-sports contexts. [ROOT (FOR) v.]

rooter *n.*⁴ [1930s] (*US Und.*) an armed robber. [ROOT v.¹ (3)]

rooter *n.*⁵ [1940s+] a sexually active person. [ROOT v.³ (1)]

root-faced *adj.* [20C+] humourless, sanctimonious, censorious. [a face carved into the hard twists of a tree root]

root (for) *v.* [late 19C+] (*US*) **1** to cheer and urge on. **2** to support a cause. [ety. unknown; Cohen (ed.), *Studies in Slang* II (1989), pp.67–8, suggests *root* = SE *dig*, and thus an image of cheering and stamping so hard that one 'digs a hole' in the grandstand]

root, hog or die *n.* [1920s–40s] (*US*) a euph. for ROOT n.¹ (1), the penis.

root, hog or die *v.* (*US*) **1** [early 19C+] to work extremely hard, or face inevitable failure. **2** [1920s+] a euph. for ROOT v.³ (1), to have sexual intercourse (cf. FRIG v.).

rootiepoot *n.* (*also* **rootypoot**) [1960s+] (*US Black*) an uninformed, unsophisticated person. [var. on POOPBUTT n. (2)]

rootie-poot *adj.* (*also* **roody-poo**) [1960s+] (*US Black*) inferior, superficial. [ROOTIEPOOT n.]

rooting *n.*¹ [late 19C+] (*US*) cheering, encouraging, supporting one's sports team. [ROOT (FOR) v. (1)]

rooting *n.*² [1920s+] (*mainly Aus.*) the act of copulation. [ROOT v.³ (1)]

rooting and tooting *n.* (*also* **rooting-tooting**) [1940s–50s] (*US Black*) violent behaviour. [ROOTING-TOOTING adj.]

rooting-tooting *adj.* (*also* **rootin'-tootin'**) [mid-19C+] noisy, boisterous, rip-roaring. [? orig. Lancashire dial.; SE *root around* + *toot*]

root into *v. see* ROOT ABOUT v.

rootle *v.* (*also* **do a rootle**) [mid-19C–1920s] to have sexual intercourse. [SE *rootle*, to rummage about]

root like a rattlesnake *v. see* FUCK LIKE A RATTLESNAKE v.

root my boot! *excl.* [1960s+] (*Aus.*) a general expression of exasperation, amazement. [ROOT v.³ (1)]

root-on *n.* [1990s+] an erection. [ext. of ROOT n.¹ (3); on the pattern of HARD-ON n. (1)]

rootrat *n.* [1980s+] (*N.Z.*) an active heterosexual. [ROOT v.³ (1) + RAT sfx]

roots *n.* [20C+] (*Aus.*) boots. [abbr. DAISY (ROOTS) n.]

roots *adj.* (*also* **rootsy**) [1960s+] (*orig. W.I. then US/UK Black*) authentic, culturally sound (by Rastafarian standards); thus *roots people*, those who feel they belong in Africa, rather than in the W.I. or the Black diaspora; *rootsheads*, fans of roots music.

roots! *excl.* [1960s+] (*W.I./Rasta*) used as a greeting to a fellow Rastafarian.

rooty *adj.*¹ [late 19C] (*US*) of a sporting context, well- and fervently supported. [ROOT (FOR) v. (1)]

rooty *adj.*² [1910s+] (*US*) sexually aroused. [ROOT v.³ (1)]

rootypoot *n. see* ROOTIEPOOT n.

ropable *adj.* (*also* **ropeable**) [mid-19C+] (*Aus./N.Z.*) in a very bad temper, infuriated. [the image of an enraged horse or bull]

rope *n.*¹ [1900s–40s] (*US*) **1** a cigar, esp. a foul-smelling one. **2** tobacco. [the similarity of some cigars to a piece of tarry rope]

rope *n.*² [1930s–60s] (*US*) money. [? an image of that which 'holds one together']

rope *n.*³ [1940s+] (*drugs*) **1** marijuana (cf. BOB HOPE n.). **2** a marijuana cigarette. [? the use of hemp in rope-making or rhy. sl. = DOPE n.¹ (6)]

rope *n.*⁴ [1940s+] (*drugs*) a vein. [resemblance]

rope *n.*⁵ [1960s] (*US Und.*) a form of confidence game. [ROPE v.]

rope, the *n.* [late 16C–1950s] execution by hanging.

rope *adj.* [2000s] (*US Black*) good, remarkable.

rope *v.* [mid-19C–1960s] (*US Und.*) for a confidence man to gain a victim's trust and thus lure him deeper into the 'game'.

ropeable *adj. see* ROPABLE adj.

rope in *v.* [mid-19C+] (*orig. US*) **1** to swindle or cheat; to ensnare a victim into a (crooked) gambling game. **2** to involve, to include, to force someone to be involved. **3** as *rope in the pieces*, to make money. **4** to arrest. [all images of roping cattle; (2) post-1920s use is SE]

roper *n.* (*also* **picker-up, roper in**) **1** [late 18C+] that member of a confidence trick team who first meets and lures the victim into the plot. **2** [early 19C+] (*US Und.*) an employee of a dancehall or gambling house whose task was to entice passers-by into the establishment; some ropers worked from hotel lobbies, where they paid the clerk a fee to introduce them to wealthy or gullible tourists. **3** [mid-19C] (*US*) a detective (cf. BEAT-POUNDER n.). [ROPE IN v.; see Williams for 17C use of *runner* as a brothel errand-boy]

roper, the *n.* [mid-17C–mid-18C] the hangman. [his primary tool]

rope walk *n.* [mid–late 19C] the Old Bailey. [London's major court; one might *walk* thence to the gallows, i.e. ROPE, THE n.]

ropey *adj.* (*also* **ropy, roupy**) **1** [late 18C+] second-rate, inadequate, mediocre, run-down etc. **2** [1940s–50s] (*Aus.*) of a person, unpopular. [? SE *roup*, a form of catarrh, orig. a disease of poultry, thence Scot. *roupy*, husky, hoarse]

rophies/rophy *n. see* ROOFIE n.².

ropper *n.* [19C] a scarf. [Scot. *roppin*, to wrap + SE *wropper*]

ropy *adj. see* ROPEY adj.

roration *n.* (*also* **roaration**) [late 18C] a speech given in a 'loud, unmusical voice' (Grose, 1785). [SE *roar* + *oration*]

rorf *v.* [1950s+] (*S.Afr.*) to indulge in horseplay. [ety. unknown]

roritorious *adj. see* RORTORIOUS adj.

roro *n.* [20C+] (*W.I.*) slander, malicious gossip; thus *put one in roro*, to slander, to cause trouble for. [? Fr. *ronron*, whirring, buzzing]

rort *n.* (*also* **roart, wrought**) (*Aus./N.Z.*) **1** [1920s+] any form of trick or deception, usu. qualified by a relevant n., e.g. 'New Labour election rort'. **2** [1920s+] anything exceptionally good. **3** [1940s+] a crowd, a wild, noisy party. **4** [1970s+] an act of sexual intercourse. **5** [1970s+] a woman seen as a sex object. [RORT v.]

rort *v.* (*also* **wrought**) (*Aus./N.Z.*) **1** [1910s+] to deceive, to defraud, to hoax. **2** [1930s+] as *rort at*, to shout, to complain loudly, to shout abuse. **3** [1940s+] to have sexual intercourse. **4** [1950s+] to go out on a spree. **5** [1980s+] to manipulate ballots or any form of record; thus *rorted*, rigged. [? RORTY adj. (3)]

rorter *n.*¹ **1** [1910s] (*UK Und.*) that member of a confidence trickery team who jostles the victim and thus attracts their attention. **2** [1920s+] (*Aus.*) a professional fraudster or confidence trickster. **3** [1980s+] (*Aus.*) someone who engages in a form of fraudulent manipulation. [RORT v. (1)]

rorter *n.*² [1920s+] something exceptionally good. [RORT n. (2)]

rorting *n.* [1910s+] confidence trickery; in weak sense, any form of 'sharp practice'. [RORT v. (1)]

rortorious *adj.* (*also* **roaratorious, roritorious, rorytorious**) [early 19C; 1910s] happily, triumphantly noisy. [RORATION n.]

rorty *adj.* (*also* **raughty**) **1** [mid-19C–1900s] fine, splendid, jolly; thus *do the rorty*, to enjoy oneself. **2** [late 19C] of drinks, intoxicating. **3** [late 19C] boisterous, rowdy, noisy; also as a nickname. **4** [late 19C+] of behaviour, speech etc, coarse, earthy, crudely comic. [? Yid., *rorität*, anything choice or rhy. sl. = SE *naughty*]

rorty bloke *n.* (*also* **rorty dasher/toff**) [late 19C] a good fellow, an engaging companion, a fashionable upper-class gentleman. [RORTY adj. (1) + BLOKE n. (1)/DASHER n. (3)/TOFF n. (2); the *bloke* is seen (according to Ware) as a superior being to the *toff* (? because the *toff* had pretensions, while the *bloke* was down to earth)]

rortyness *n.* [late 19C] energy, vitality. [RORTY adj. (3)]

Rory (O'Moore) *n.* **1** [mid-19C+] (*also* **Georgie Moore**) the floor; also in fig. use, *on the Rory O'Moore*, in a bad way. **2** [late 19C+] a prostitute (cf. BOAT AND OAR n.). **3** [late 19C+] a door. **4** [1980s+] (*Aus.*) the number 4. [rhy. sl.; note St Vincent Troubridge (1946): 'Probably derived from the tremendously popular song of that name, sung by Madame Vestris in the 1830's and 1840's']

rorytorious *adj. see* RORTORIOUS adj.

rosa *n.* [1980s+] (*drugs*) amphetamine (cf. A n.²). [Sp. *rosa*, red]

rosa maria *n.* [1930s] (*US drugs*) marijuana (cf. AUNT MARY n.²). [play on MARY JANE n.² (1)]

rosary *n.* **1** [1930s] (*US prison/Und.*) a 30-day sentence. **2** [1950s+] (*US prison*) a sentence to be served for the remainder of one's natural life; thus *do the rosary*. [the SE *rosary* is made of *decades* of prayers]

rosary man *n.* [1940s] (*UK Und.*) a confidence man who ensnares a victim by the fortuitous 'dropping' of a wallet.

roscoe *n.* (*also* **john roscoe, rosca**) [1910s+] (*US*) a handgun. [? anecdotal]

roscoe *v.* [1970s] (*US*) to hold up with a gun. [ROSCOE n.]

rose *n.*¹ [late 16C–17C; late 19C] the vagina, esp. of a virgin; thus *pluck a rose*, to deflower (cf. BEAUTY SPOT n.). [literary euph.]

rose *n.*² [mid-19C] an orange. [? the pleasant smell]

rose among the thorns *n.* [1960s–70s] (*US*) a good-looking prostitute in a group of less attractive women.

Roseanne (Barr) *n.* [1990s+] a *brassiere*. [rhy. sl.; ult. US comedienne and TV star *Roseanne Barr* (b.1953)]

rosebowl *n.* [1940s–50s] (*Aus. milit.*) a latrine. [ironic comment on the smell]

rosebud *n.*¹ [1910s+] a potato. [rhy. sl. = SPUD n.² (1)]

rosebud *n.*² **1** [1910s] the mouth. **2** [1960s–70s] (*drugs*) a distended, inflamed rectum after passing a painful stool, the result of extended opium or heroin use. **3** [1960s+] (*US gay*) the anus. [resemblance]

rose-coloured *adj.* [1920s] a euph. synon. for BLOODY adj.¹ (1).

roseleaf *v.* [mid-19C+] to perform anilingus (cf. AUSTRALIAN n.). [? synon Fr. *faire feuille de rose*, 'to do the rose-leaf'; note ROSEBUD n.² (3)]

roses *n.*¹ [mid-19C–1920s] the menstrual period. [pun on REDS n.¹]

roses *n.*² [1960s+] (*drugs*) amphetamines (cf. A n.²). [play on REDS n.³]

roses (are) red *n.* [1910s+] (*Aus./US*) a bed. [rhy. sl.]

rosey *n.* [1970s+] (*US gay*) the buttocks, the rectum. [ROSEBUD n.² (3)]

rosie *n.* [1920s] (*US*) a garbage can. [ironic comment on the smell]

rosie (lea) *n.* (*also* **rosey lee, rosy, rosy lea/lee**) [1910s+] **1** (*orig. milit.*) tea. **2** a flea. [rhy. sl.]

rosie loader *n.* (*also* **rosie loder, rosy loader/loder**) [20C+] a whisky and soda. [rhy. sl.]

Rosie O'Grady's *n.* [1990s+] the ladies (lavatory) (cf. ANGUS ARMANASCO n.). [rhy. sl.]

rosin *n.* **1** [mid-18C] liquor. **2** [early–mid-19C] beer or other drink given to the musicians who entertain at a dance or party; thus *rosin*, to supply the musicians with drink. **3** [mid–late 19C] a fiddler, a violinist, also *rosin-the-bow*. [? SE *rosin*, a sticky material that is smeared on a violin string or bow, to facilitate its playing; fiddlers were assumed to be drinkers; or ? Irish *raisín*, a snack]

rosin chewer *n. see* ROSIN HEEL n.

rosin-drunk *adj.* (*also* **rosinned**) [20C+] drunk. [? ROSIN n. (1) or the rosy pinkness of the drunkard's cheeks and nose]

rosiner *n.* (*also* **rosner, rossiner, rozener, rozner, rozziner**) [20C+] (*Aus./Irish*) any form of stiff drink, a pick-me-up. [ROSIN n. (1)]

rosin heel *n.* (*also* **rosin chewer**) **1** [19C] (*US*) a native of Florida. **2** [1980s] (*US Black*) a derog. term for a White peasant. [ety. unknown; ? play on TARHEEL n.]

rosinned *adj. see* ROSIN-DRUNK adj.

rosner/rossiner *n. see* ROSINER n.

rosy *n. see* ROSIE (LEA) n.

rosy, the *n.*¹ **1** [mid-19C–1900s] (red) wine. **2** [late 19C] blood (cf. BADMINTON n.). [colour + ? (1) Fr. *rosé*]

rosy, the *n.*² [late 19C] the good life.

rosy *adj.* [1900s–40s] drunk, tipsy. [one's pink face]

rosy god *n.* [late 19C] (*Aus.*) red wine.

rosy lea/lee *n. see* ROSIE (LEA) n.

rosy loader/loder *n. see* ROSIE LOADER n.

rosy palm (and her five sisters) *n.* (*also* **rosy palm (and her five daughters)**) [1950s+] the hand, as used in masturbation; used in phrs. e.g. *date rosy palm...; entertain...; go on a date with...; have a big date with...; hit on...; visit...* (cf. CONVERSE WITH HARRY PALM v.). [pun on SE *palm* (+ DATE v.¹ (1)/DATE n.¹ (2))]

rosy-red *n.* [1900s] (*Aus.*) the head. [rhy. sl.]

rot *n.*¹ **1** [mid-19C+] rubbish, nonsense; esp. in *talk rot*, to talk nonsense. **2** [1910s] an unfortunate situation.

rot *n.*² *see* ROTGUT n. (3).

rot *v.*¹ [late 19C–1930s] to spoil, to interfere with, to ruin. [SE *rotten*]

rot *v.*² **1** [late 19C+] to talk nonsense. **2** [late 19C+] to tease heavily, to abuse, to denigrate. [ROT n.¹]

rot! *excl.*¹ [late 16C–19C] a general excl. of irritation, disbelief, dismissal; usu. in phr. *rot it! rot 'em! rot on!* [abbr. SE *God rot...!*]

rot! *excl.*² [mid-19C+] nonsense! rubbish! [ROT n.¹ (1)]

rot about *v.* (*also* **rot along**) [late 19C–1920s] (*UK society*) to laze around, to idle, to fool around. [? ROT v.²]

rotan *n.* [18C–mid-19C] (*UK Und.*) a wheeled vehicle, esp. a cart. [? Lat. *rota*, a wheel]

rotgut *n.* **1** [late 16C+] cheap or inferior beer. **2** [18C+] cheap wine. **3** [early 19C+] (*US*) (*also* **rot**) cheap whisky. **4** [mid-19C+] cheap alcohol in general. **5** [1950s+] illicitly distilled alcohol. [its effects]

rotic *adj.* [1990s+] (*US campus*) romantic, without the 'man' and thus used in a non-sexual context. [abbr. SE *romantic*, lit. without the 'man']

roti ou *n.* [1970s+] (*S.Afr.*) a Hindi speaker. [Hind. *roti*, bread (in the form of a chapatti) + OU n. (2)]

ro' tow *v.* [2000s] (*US Black*) to drive under the influence of drink or drugs. [ROLL v.³ (3) + TORE UP adj. (2)]

rots *adj.* [1980s] (*US campus*) bad.

rotten *adj.* **1** [late 16C+] in a very poor state, of a very bad quality, quite worthless. **2** [mid-19C+] a general intensifier, e.g. *rotten luck, rotten bastard* etc. **3** [1940s+] (*Aus.*) very drunk; thus *get rotten*, to become very drunk.

rotten *adv.* [mid-19C+] a general intensifier, e.g. appallingly, disgustingly, extremely.

rotten apple *v.* [late 19C] (*US*) of an audience, to boo, hiss and generally give the actors a hard time. [the throwing of rotten fruit]

rotten egg *n. see* BAD EGG n. (1).

rotten guts *n.* [1910s–20s] a person who has bad breath. [SE *rotten* + GUTS n.¹ (1)]

rotten orange *n.* [late 17C] a pej. term for a follower of King William III (r.1688–1702). [pun on SE *rotten*, stale/rotten, unpleasant; William had been Prince of *Orange* before ascending the English throne]

rotten row *n.* **1** [late 19C+] a bow. **2** [20C+] a blow. [rhy. sl.; *Rotten Row* is a riding track, used by 19C fashionable society, around Hyde Park; promenading on horseback 'in the Row' was a daily necessity for the smart]

rotten sheep *n.* [late 19C] an unpleasant person, esp. (*Irish*) a traitor to the Fenian cause.

rotten with *adj.* [1920s+] usu. of money, well supplied with (cf. FILTHY WITH adj.).

rotter *n.*[1] **1** [late 19C+] a 'bad lot', a socially unacceptable person. **2** [1910s] (*Aus.*) a half-trained horse. [ROT v.[2]]

rotter *n.*[2] [1930s+] (*Aus.*) an expert. [in sceptical eyes a talker of ROT n.[1] (1)]

rot the socks off *v.* [1950s+] to defeat comprehensively. [ROT v.[2] (1)]

rotto *adj.* [late 19C–1950s] (*Irish*) drunk. [ROTTEN adj. (1)]

rot you! *excl.* [late 17C; mid-19C–1900s] a general excl. of derision, dismissal, synon with 'to hell with you!'

rouf *n.* **1** [mid-19C+] the number 4. **2** [1940s–70s] 4 pence; 4 shillings. **3** [1940s+] (*also* **roaf**) £4, £40, £400. **4** [1950s+] a 4-year prison term etc. [backsl.]

rouf-efil *n. see* ROFEFIL n.

rouf gens *n.* [mid-19C] 4 shillings. [backsl.; ROUF n. (1) + GEN n.[1]]

rouf yeneps *n.* [mid-19C] 4 pence. [backsl.; ROUF n. (1) + YENNEP n.]

rough *n.* [1960s+] rough cider. [abbr.]

rough *adj.*[1] [mid-late 19C] of foodstuffs, coarse, stale, decaying.

rough *adj.*[2] **1** [mid-19C+] unfair, unreasonable; thus *on the rough*, in difficulties. **2** [mid-19C+] a general pej.; the inference is physically or mentally run-down or depressed. **3** [20C+] exhausting, demanding. **4** [1930s+] (*US Black/campus*) excellent, admirable, very good. **5** [1940s+] (*Aus.*) promiscuous. [(4) on bad = good model]

rough *adv.* [mid-19C+] badly, unpleasantly. [ROUGH adj.[2] (1)]

rough and ready *n.* (*also* **rough and tumble**) [mid-19C+] the vagina.

rough around *v. see* ROUGH UP v. (1).

rough as a badger's arse *phr.* (*also* **rough as a badger**, ...**badger's behind/bottom**, ...**rat's back**) [early 18C+] bristly, straggly, coarse; also in fig. use.

rough as a bag *phr.* (*also* **rough as bags**) [1910s+] (*Aus./N.Z.*) uncouth, ill-mannered. [abbr. SE *sandbag*]

rough as a pig's breakfast *phr.* (*also* **rough as a dog's breakfast**) [1940s+] (*Aus./N.Z.*) uncouth, ill-mannered.

rough as guts *phr.* (*also* **rough as old guts**) [1960s+] (*Aus./N.Z.*) **1** lacking in refinement (usu. fig. but also lit.). **2** a phr. of admiration, praising the 'rough diamond' who may be vulgar but remains tough and ingenious and ultimately successful.

rough-ass *adj.* [20C+] (*US*) crude, coarse. [SE *rough* + -ASS sfx]

rough as sacks *phr.* [1940s+] (*N.Z.*) very rough.

rough as sandbags *phr.* [1910s] (*Aus.*) performing an offensive action; telling exaggerated stories.

rough deal *n. see* RAW DEAL n.

rough-dried hair *n.* [1930s–40s] (*US Black*) very kinky hair. [as opposed to blow-dried hair and thus neatened or even straightened]

rough end of the pineapple *n.* (*also* **rough end of the stick**) [1960s+] (*Aus.*) hostile or unfair treatment; also something unattractive (cf. FUZZY END OF THE LOLLIPOP n.).

roughey *n. see* ROUGHIE n.[1]

rough fam *n.* (*also* **rough-fammy**) [early 19C] (*UK Und.*) a waistcoat pocket. [SE *rough* + FAM n.[1] (1); ? f. one's putting one's thumbs into the waistcoat pockets and the rubbing this entails]

rough-guts *n.* [1940s+] (*N.Z.*) a hooligan, an uncouth person. [SE *rough* + -GUTS sfx]

roughhouse *n.* [late 19C+] (*orig. US*) **1** boisterous behaviour, usu. harmless. **2** physical violence, a fight. **3** unpleasant behaviour.

roughhouse *adj.* [20C+] **1** of a person, violent, emotionally unrestrained. **2** usu. of a fight, violent. **3** of a place, tough, rough.

roughhouse *v.* **1** [late 19C+] (*orig. US*) to fight, to beat up; thus *rough-houser*, a fighter. **2** [20C+] (*orig. US*) to behave in a rowdy, boisterous manner. **3** [1990s+] (*US*) to enjoy the sleazier aspects of sex; to be a devotee of sado-masochism.

roughie *n.*[1] (*also* **roughey**, **roughy**) (*orig. Aus./N.Z.*) **1** [20C+] any person or animal considered tough and intractable. **2** [1910s] an unpleasant place or situation. **3** [1910s] an unqualified or incompetent worker. **4** [1910s+] an implausible story. **5** [1930s+] a fraud, a deception; esp. in phr. *put a roughie over*, to cheat. **6** [1930s+] in horse and dog racing, an outsider. **7** [1980s] (*US Black*) a person who is looking for trouble, wanting to start a fight. [SE *rough*/ROUGH adj.[2]]

roughie *n.*[2] *see* ROUGHNECK n. (3).

rough it *v.* **1** [late 18C+] to live deprived of life's material comforts; not simply to be poor, but to volunteer oneself, as in camping, the forces etc, for such hardy existence; thus *rough-un*, a good spot for sleeping out of doors. **2** [1910s] (*US*) to treat roughly. **3** [1920s] to fight.

rough malkin *n.* [mid-16C] the vagina (cf. BIRD n.[8]). [SE *rough* + MALKIN n. (2)]

roughneck *n.* **1** [mid-19C+] (*orig. US*) a thug, a hoodlum, a fighter. **2** [20C+] (*US*) an unmannered, informal person. **3** [1910s+] (*US*) (*also* **roughie**) a labourer, usu. on an oil rig. **4** [1990s+] (*W.I.*) a dancehall enthusiast.

roughneck *adj.* (*also* **roughnecked**) **1** [1910s–20s] (*US*) aggressive, tough. **2** [1910s+] (*orig. US*) a general pej. term. **3** [2000s] (*US/UK Black*) excellent, admirable, very good. [(3) on bad = good model]

rough nut *n. see* TOUGH NUT n.

rough-o *n.* [19C] the vagina.

rough on rats *n.* [late 19C] (*Aus.*) bad luck. [proper name *Rough on Rats*, a proprietary rat and vermin poison]

rough riding *n.* [1940s] having unprotected sex.

rough shake *n. see* UNFAIR SHAKE n.

rough spin *n.* [1910s+] (*Aus*) **1** bad luck; a (period of) ill fortune. **2** unfair treatment. [ROUGH adj.[2] (1) + SPIN n.[3] (2); two-up imagery]

rough stuff *n.* **1** [20C+] (*also* **rough work**) physical violence. **2** [1900s–30s] severe criticism; intense teasing. **3** [1910s–20s] (*Aus./US*) a disrespectful, reckless, indecent or disorderly person; disrespect, recklessness, indecency. **4** [1970s+] (*orig. US*) sadomasochistic sex. **5** [1970s+] (*drugs*) marijuana that contains a lot of unsmokeable debris. [SE *rough*; (5) STUFF n.[3] (2)]

rough trade *n.* **1** [1910s+] (*gay*) a violent sexual partner; often a man who is, or poses as, a construction worker, serviceman, truck driver, motorcyclist etc, with appropriate costumes, often of leather. **2** [1960s] a male heterosexual who has interourse with a male homosexual.

rough-trade *adj.* [1920s+] pertaining to sex with a violent, aggressive partner. [ROUGH TRADE n. (1)]

rough trot *n.* (*also* **stiff trot**) [1910s+] (*Aus.*) a period of bad luck. [ROUGH adj.[2] (1) + TROT n.[2] (4)]

rough-up *n.* **1** [late 19C–1940s] a street fight, a violent fracas. **2** [1910s] a violent or aggressive person. [ROUGH UP v. (1)]

rough up *v.* (*mainly US*) **1** [late 19C+] (*also* **rough around**) to beat up, to injure, esp. to intimidate. **2** [late 19C] to act aggressively; to cause a fuss.

rough up the suspect *v.* [1990s+] to masturbate. [pun on ROUGH UP v. (1)]

rough work *n. see* ROUGH STUFF n. (1).

roughy *n. see* ROUGHIE n.[1]

round *n.*[1] [17C+] a walk; a spree.

round *n.*[2] *see* ROUNDS n.[1]

round *v.*[1] **1** [mid-19C] to elicit information from someone by trickery. **2** [1900s] (*UK Und.*) to confess, to tell the truth. **3** [1900s–40s] to obtain information about someone by questioning a third party. [abbr. GET ROUND v.]

round *v.*[2] *see* ROUND (ON) v.

round *adv.*[1] [1920s+] (of time) approximately, nearly, e.g. *round 9.45 p.m.*

round *adv.*[2] [1990s+] at/to the house of someone.

roundabout *n.*[1] [early 19C] (*UK prison*) the treadmill.

roundabout n.[2] [mid-19C] (US) a prize-ring.

roundakin n. see ROUNDYKEN n.

round and square adv. [late 19C–1900s] everywhere. [rhy. sl.]

roundball n. [1970s+] (US Black) basketball (as opposed to American football, played with an oval ball).

round brown n. see BROWN n.[3] (1).

roundem n. **1** [mid-19C–1900s] a button. **2** [1910s–20s] the head. [ext. of SE round]

rounder n.[1] (US) [mid-19C–1900s] a rich, fashionable man about town, a playboy. **2** [1920s] a pimp, a procurer. [SE do the rounds/know one's way around]

rounder n.[2] [late 19C] a tight, short jacket.

rounder n.[3] **1** [late 19C–1930s] (US) a vagrant. **2** [late 19C+] (Can. prison) anyone familiar with the underworld. **3** [1900s] (US Und.) a recidivist. **4** [1990s+] (US prison) a member of a prison gang, esp. of an Italian gang. [one who has 'been around']

rounder n.[4] [late 19C+] (US Und.) an informer. [SE round on, to turn against]

rounders n. [20C+] (W.I.) confusion, trouble. [events have fig. 'turned around' on the sufferer + the image of the running in a game of SE rounders]

roundeye n. [1950s+] (US) **1** the anus. **2** a male homosexual. **3** a White person, as opposed to an East Asian person; usu. of women. [(1) SE round + EYE sfx; (2) metonymy; (3) as opposed to SLANT n.[4]]

round-eyed adj. (also **roundeye**) [1960s+] (US) Caucasian. [ROUNDEYE n. (3)]

round file n. (also **round filing cabinet**) [1970s+] (orig. US) a wastepaper basket (cf. CIRCULAR FILE n.).

roundhead n.[1] [late 19C+] (US) an immigrant from northern Europe, esp. a Swede. [? physiognomy]

roundhead n.[2] [20C+] (mainly UK teen) a circumcised penis; thus the boy or man who has one (cf. CLIPDICK n.). [the antonym of CAVALIER n.]

roundhead n.[3] [1970s+] (drugs) any drug contained in a capsule with curved ends (cf. PILL n.[4]).

roundheel n. (also **roundheels, roundheeler**) **1** [1920s+] (US) an inferior prize-fighter; also in fig. use. **2** [1920s+] a promiscuous woman. **3** [1970s+] (US gay/prison) a victimized young inmate, forced into homosexuality. [both of them fall over easily; the image is of pivoting on the rounded heel]

roundheeled adj. [1920s+] (US) **1** easily defeated. **2** of a woman or gay man, promiscuous. [ROUNDHEEL n.]

roundhouse n. [1910s+] a blow delivered with a wide sweep of the arm.

roundhouse v.[1] [1920s+] to hit someone with a wide sweep of the arm. [ROUNDHOUSE n.]

roundhouse v.[2] [1960s+] (US) of a prostitute, to lick, suck and otherwise stimulate every orifice and erogenous zone her client has to offer.

roundie n. [1940s+] (N.Z.) a factory-made cigarette.

roundman n. [1920s] (US) a dollar. [the round coin]

round-me-houses n. (also **round-my-houses, round-mys, round-the-houses**) [mid-19C+] trousers. [rhy. sl.]

round mouth n. [early 19C] the anus. [abbr. BROTHER ROUND MOUTH n.]

round o n. [early 17C] a great lie. [the oh! of disbelief it elicits]

round (on) v. [mid-19C–1900s] to inform against, to betray; to become an informer. [SE round on, to turn against, to attack]

round pussy n. [1990s+] (US) the anus. [SE round + PUSSY n. (2)]

round robin n. **1** [mid 16C–mid-17C] the host (in communion). **2** [mid-16C+] a complainant, a petitioner. **3** [late 19C] a swindle. [SE round robin, a document, typically a complaint or petition, in which the signatories place their names in a circle, thus hiding any form of hierarchy]

round-robin v. [1960s+] to have sex on a single occasion with a succession of partners. [SE round robin, a sports tournament, e.g. tennis, in which each competitor plays all the rest]

rounds n.[1] [mid-19C+] shirt collars; occas. in sing. [abbr. all rounds, all rounders, trade names of fashionable collars]

rounds n.[2] [late 19C] trousers. [abbr. ROUND-ME-HOUSES n.]

rounds of the kitchen n. [20C+] (Ulster) a thrashing. [the victim is beaten up and down the room]

round steak n. **1** [1970s] (US prison) bologna sausage. **2** [2000s] (US Black) the penis (cf. BACON n.[1]).

roundtable n. [1910s; 1970s] (US Und.) a meeting.

round the bend phr. (also **around the bend**) [1920s+] (orig. naut.) eccentric, crazy, insane; ext. as [1950s+] round the bend and back again; round the bend and half-way down the straight (cf. CLEAN AROUND THE BEND phr.). [the image is of one who is 'not straight']

round the clock phr. [1940s] (Aus. Und.) a sentence of 12 months.

round-the-houses n. see ROUND-ME-HOUSES n.

round the johnny (horner) phr. [1900s] round the corner, i.e. at a public house. [JOHNNIE n.[7]/JOHNNY HORNER n.]

round the twist phr. (also **around the twist**) [1960s+] mad, eccentric, insane (cf. CLEAN AROUND THE BEND phr.). [var. on ROUND THE BEND phr.]

round the world for a dollar phr. [1960s] (Aus) inferior, as of wine, usu. laced with methylated spirits.

round the world for threepence phr. (also **round the world for fourpence, …ninepence**) [1980s+] (N.Z.) drinking methylated spirits. [the effects and cheap price]

round-up n.[1] [1900s] (US Und.) dismissing the victim after a confidence trick has been concluded successfully. [SE round up, to conclude]

round-up n.[2] [1920s+] a get-together, an assembly. [ROUND UP v.]

round up v. [1920s+] (orig. US) to assemble, to get together. [Western imagery]

roundyken n. (also **roundakin**) [early–mid 19C] a lock-up, an early police station. [SE + KEN n.[1] (1); lit. 'round-house']

roupy adj. see ROPEY adj.

rouse n. [mid-16C–mid-19C] a large glass; a full glass. [? SE carouse, or Ger. rausch, intoxication, drunken fit]

rouse v. (also **rouse on, roust**) [mid-18C; 20C+] (Aus.) to scold, to berate; thus get roused on, to be scolded. [Scot. roust, to roar, bellow]

rouser n.[1] [mid-19C] (US) an outstanding individual; an exceptional creature; a startling event.

rouser n.[2] **1** [late 19C–1930s] the first drink of the day, used as a 'pick-me-up'. **2** [1970s+] (drugs) any type of amphetamine or stimulant drug which 'gets one up' (cf. A n.[2]).

rouser n.[3] [1940s] a womanizer. [? SE arouse]

rouse the possum v. see STIR THE POSSUM v.

rousie n. (also **rouser**) [late 19C+] (Aus.) a general hand on a rural property. [SE rouseabout]

roust n.[1] [late 16C–early 17C] sexual intercourse. [ROUST v.[1]]

roust n.[2] **1** [1930s] a kick. **2** [1960s+] (orig. US Und.) an arrest. [(1) SE roust; (2) ROUST v.[2] (7)]

roust v.[1] [late 16C–early 17C] to have sexual intercourse. [SE roust, to roar, to bellow]

roust v.[2] **1** [early 19C; 1940s+] (US Black) to steal; to rob. **2** [1900s–60s] (UK Und.) to jostle, as in picking a pocket. **3** [1910s+] (US) to harass, esp. of the police. **4** [1920s+] to awaken. **5** [1930s+] to raid an establishment. **6** [1950s] (US) to beat up. **7** [1960s+] to arrest. **8** [1980s+] (US campus) to tease, to harass. [SE roust, to stir, to wake up, to arouse]

roust v.[3] see ROUSE v.

rout v. [1970s] (US campus) to engage in sexual intercourse. [SE rout, to poke about]

routine n. [1930s+] (US) **1** an evasive or contrived response. **2** a fraudulent scheme, esp. as practised by confidence tricksters. [show business jargon routine, a carefully rehearsed act]

Rover n. [late 19C+] (*US*) an inhabitant of Colorado. [ety. unknown]

Row, the n. **1** [early 17C] Goldsmith's Row, London E2. **2** [late 17C; mid-19C] Paternoster Row, London EC4, the contemporary centre of London publishing. **3** [late 18C] (*Irish*) New Row, Dublin, site of a prison (cf. ABBOTT'S PRIORY n.). **4** [19C] Rotten Row, Hyde Park, London. **5** [mid-19C] BOOKSELLERS' ROW n., a euph. for Holywell St, London WC2, the contemporary centre of pornographic publishing. **6** [late 19C] Club Row, London E1. **7** [1930s+] (*US prison*) the condemned cells, i.e. DEATH ROW n. **8** [1980s+] (*US campus*) a fraternity or sorority row, i.e. the line of adjacent fraternity or sorority houses on a campus.

row n.[1] [mid-18C+] a disturbance, a noisy quarrel; thus *what's the row?* what's all the noise about?; *hold your row*, be quiet. [virtually SE today, *row* began as sl. and is cited as 'a very low expression' in Todd's revision of Johnson's *Dictionary* (1818)]

row n.[2] [1970s+] (*US drugs*) a small quantity of a narcotic, esp. cocaine. [var. on LINE n.[4] (4)]

row v. **1** [late 18C] to rouse up by making a noise. **2** [late 18C–mid-19C] to attack or assail a person in a rough manner. **3** [late 18C+] to make a row or disturbance, to quarrel noisily or heatedly. **4** [late 18C+] to scold or criticize a person angrily or severely, to take sharply to task. [ROW n.[1]]

row-de-dow n. (*also* **row-dow**) [mid–late 19C] (*Irish*) an argument, a set-to; thus *row-de-dow*, to argue, to make a disturbance. [ext. of ROW n.[1]]

row-de-dow adj. [late 19C] boisterous, noisy. [ROW-DE-DOW n.]

rowdy n. (*also* **rowdie**) [mid–late 19C] money; the term implies the efforts involved in obtaining money. [note Thackeray's fictitious bankers, *Rowdy and Stump*, a firm who can also be found in Cuthbert Bede's *Adventures of Mr Verdant Green* (1853)]

rowdy-dow n. [late 19C–1900s] a socially unacceptable person, one who is vulgar, noisy or reprobate. [ROW-DE-DOW n.]

rowdy-dow adj. [mid-19C+] socially unacceptable, vulgar, noisy, rough. [redup. of SE *rowdy*, rough, disorderly]

rowdy-dowdy adj. [mid-19C–1920s; 2000s] aggressive, antagonistic; also as n. [redup. of SE *rowdy*, but note ROWDY-DOW adj.]

rowdy-dows n. [1900s] (*US*) trousers. [? rhy. sl.]

row in v. (*UK Und.*) **1** [late 19C+] to allow someone to join a scheme, a conspiracy. **2** [1910s+] to implicate a suspect in a crime; thus *row out*, to exonerate a suspect from a crime. **3** [1910s+] to include.

row in the (same) boat v. [late 18C+] to join, to take shares with.

rowl n. [19C] money. [? SE *royal*, i.e. the portraits of monarchs found on coins and notes]

rowly-powly n. *see* ROLY-POLY n.[1].

row of beans/pins, a n. *see* HILL OF BEANS, A n.

row oneself onto v. [1940s+] to associate oneself with a group. [ROW IN v. (1)]

row out v. [1960s+] to exclude someone from a deal or organization. [antonym of ROW IN v. (1)]

Rowton Houses n. (*also* **Rowtons**) [1900s–50s] trousers. [rhy. sl.; ult. *Rowton Houses*, working men's lodges established by Lord *Rowton* (Montagu Lowry), the first opened in Vauxhall in 1982]

row up v. [mid–late 19C] **1** to wake up someone roughly and noisily. **2** to scold, to criticize. [ROW n.[1]]

row up Salt River v. [early 19C–1940s] (*US*) **1** (*also* **soak one's head in Salt River**) to become drunk, i.e. to send oneself 'to oblivion'. **2** (*also* **go to Salt River**, **row up Salt Creek**) to suffer a political defeat. **3** as *row someone up Salt River*, to defeat (a political opponent); to overcome, to send to oblivion. [? *Salt River roarer*, a backwards, unsophisticated country dweller (poss. from Kentucky, where there is an actual Salt River); note J. Inman in Bartlett, *Dict. Americanisms* (1848): 'To row up Salt river has its origin in the fact that there is a small stream of that name in

Kentucky, the passage of which is made difficult and laborious as well by its tortuous course as by the abundance of shallows and bars. The real application of the phrase is to the unhappy wight who has the task of propelling the boat up the stream; but in political or slang usage it is to those who are *rowed up*—the passengers, not the oarsman']

row with one oar (in the water) v. (*also* **not have both oars in the water**) [1980s+] (*US*) to be irrational or stupid. [var. on NOT ALL THERE phr.]

rox n. (*also* **roxanne**) [1980s+] (*drugs*) **1** cocaine. **2** freebase, later crack cocaine (cf. BASE n.). [ROCKS n.[5]]

roy n.[1] **1** [1960s–70s] (*Aus.*) a chic, sophisticated, 'trendy' Australian. **2** [1990s+] (*US Black*) a stupid White boy. [a stereotypically (1) 'smart' and (2) 'White' name]

roy n.[2] [1980s] a gentleman. [Rom.]

royal n.[1] [20C+] **1** (*W.I., Jam.*) any Black person from a race other than West Indian; thus in combs. *coolie royal* (East Indian) and joc./derog. *jackass–royal*, *monkey-royal*. **2** (*W.I.*) (*also* **chiney-royal**) a mixed Black/Chinese person. **3** (*US Black*) a West Indian. [? fig. use of Sp. *real*, a coin of very low value and considered inferior to UK sterling; such individuals have low social status; the US use is prob. ignorant of such overtones]

royal n.[2] [20C+] (*W.I., Trin.*) the buttocks. [fig. use of ROYAL n.[1] (1); in this case the physical 'lowness' of the buttocks]

royal n.[3] (*also* **boss's royal**) [1930s–60s] (*N.Z.*) a management stooge. [SE *royal*, i.e their privileged position in the working hierarchy]

royal adj. [mid-19C+] (*orig. US*) a general intensifier, often used before so-called taboo terms, e.g. *a royal screwing*, *a royal shafting*. [SE *royal*, pertaining to a royal family]

royal adv. [1920s+] completely, comprehensively. [ROYAL adj.]

royal alberts n. *see* ALBERTS n.

royal blues n. **1** [mid-19C] the police force. **2** [1970s] (*drugs*) LSD (cf. A n.[3]). [the uniform/pills are blue]

royal bob n. [18C] gin. [SE *royal* + BOB n.[3]]

royal boozer n. [mid-19C–1930s] a heavy drinker. [ROYAL adj. + BOOZER n. (1)]

royal docks n. [20C+] venereal disease. [rhy. sl. = POX n.[1] (2)]

royal fucking n. (*also* **r.f.**) [1950s+] (*US*) harsh or very bad treatment. [ROYAL adj. + FUCKING n.[2]]

royalie n. (*also* **royaly**) [1900s–20s] (*Aus.*) an effeminate young man, a homosexual. [play on QUEEN n.[2] (1)]

royally adv. **1** [18C+] well. **2** [mid-19C+] extremely, very, e.g. *royally drunk*.

royal mail n. [20C+] (*mainly UK Und.*) bail. [rhy. sl.]

royal navy n. [20C+] gravy. [rhy. sl.]

royal order, the n. [1920s+] (*Aus.*) dismissal from one's job. [abbr. ORDER OF THE BOOT n.]

royal palace of Holloway n. *see* HOLLOWAY CASTLE n.

royal poverty n. [mid–late 18C] gin. [gin may be drunk when one is 'feeling right royal' but it will lead to poverty]

royal repose n. [mid-19C] the Queen's Bench prison.

royal scamp n. [late 18C–mid-19C] a highwayman who specializes in robbing rich victims and in causing them no physical harm. [the highwayman more of romantic fiction than record]

royal screw n. [1950s–60s] (*US*) an act of extreme harshness or unfairness, as meted out on oneself or to another person. [ROYAL adj. + SCREWING n.[2] (2)]

royal shaft(ing) n. (*also* **king's elevator**) [1950s+] an act of extreme harshness or unfairness, as meted out on oneself or to another person. [ROYAL adj. + SHAFT n.[2]/SHAFTING n. (2); *king's elevator* is a pun on SE *elevator shaft*]

royalty n. [1980s+] (*drugs*) cocaine. [its superior ranking in the hierarchy of drugs]

royaly n. *see* ROYALIE n.

Roy Castle n. [1990s+] the anus (cf. BOTTLE AND GLASS n.). [rhy. sl. = ARSEHOLE n. (1); ult. UK comedian *Roy Castle* (1932–94)]

roy rodgers *n.* [20C+] second-rate builders. [rhy. sl. = SE *bodgers*; ult. film cowboy *Roy Rogers* (1912–98)]

royster/roysterer *n. see* ROISTER *n.*

rozener/rozner *n. see* ROSINER *n.*

rozzer *n.*[1] (*also* **rawser, razzer, roz**) [late 19C+] a policeman. [? Rom. *roozlo*, strong or *roast*, a villain]

rozzer *n.*[2] [1970s] (*US Black*) a rubber contraceptive with small protrusions for extra stimulation of the vagina. [? SE *arouser/rouser*]

rozziner *n. see* ROSINER *n.*

r.s. *n. see* RATSHIT *n.*

r/s *phr.* [1970s+] used in sex contact advertisements, rough stuff, i.e. sadomasochism, urolagnia, piercing and rubberwear. [abbr.]

rub *n.*[1] [late 16C+] an impediment. [bowls jargon *rub*, an obstacle hindering the ball's smooth progress across the green]

rub *n.*[2] [late 18C–19C] a round or rubber of a card-game, usu. whist. [abbr. SE *rubber*]

rub *n.*[3] **1** [1900s–10s] (*US*) a dance, typified by the overt sexuality and physical proximity of the partners. **2** [1950s] (*W.I.*) (*also* **rub-up**) a dance or dancing party.

rub *n.*[4] [1960s] (*US Black*) a successful confidence trick.

rub *n.*[5] *see* RUB(-OUT) *n.*

rub *v.*[1] [late 17C–early 19C] (*UK Und.*) to run away.

rub *v.*[2] **1** [1920s+] (*US*) to steal, to burglarize. **2** [1970s+] (*US Black*) to criticize.

rub *v.*[3] *see* RUB OUT *v.*

rub *v.*[4] *see* RUB (TO) *v.*

rubacrock *n.* (*also* **rubbacrock**) [mid-18C–19C] a dirty, lazy woman. [dial.]

rub-a-dub *n.* **1** [late 19C+] (*also* **rub-a-dub-dub, rubbity dub, rubbledub, ruddity dub**) a pub or public house. **2** [1930s] a 'sub' or advance on wages. **3** [1930s+] a drinking club, a social club. [rhy. sl.]

rub-a-dub(-dub) *n.* [1950s+] (*orig. US*) sexual intercourse, esp. quick and spontaneous. [SE *rub-a-dub*, the beat of a drum]

rub-a-dub soldier *n.* [1990s+] (*W.I.*) a dancehall music enthusiast. [Carib.E. *rub-a-dub*, heavy instrumental music, also a type of dance]

rub and tug shop *n. see* RUB-A-TUG SHOP *n.*

rub a sentence *v.* [1990s+] (*W.I.*) to serve a prison sentence.

rub-a-tug shop *n.* (*also* **rub and tug shop**) [1980s+] a cheap brothel, an 'escort agency' (cf. BANGING-SHOP *n.*). [RUB-A-DUB (-DUB) *n.* + TUG *v.* (1) + SE *shop*/SHOP *n.*[1] (1)]

rub bacons *v.* [late 19C–1900s] to have sexual intercourse. [SE *rub* + BACON *n.*[1] (3)]

rubbacrock *n. see* RUBACROCK *n.*

rubbed *adj.* [20C+] murdered, killed. [RUB OUT *v.*[1] (1)]

rubbed down with the Book, be *v.* [late 19C] to take an oath on the Bible.

rubbed off *adj.* [late 17C–mid-19C] (*UK Und.*) bankrupt and thus run away. [RUB *v.*[1]]

rubbed out *adj.* **1** [mid-19C+] dead. **2** [20C+] murdered. [SE *rub*/RUB OUT *v.*; (1) has no implication of foul play, one has simply been erased from the 'Book of Life']

rubbedy *n.* (*also* **robberdy, rubberdy, rubbidy, rubbity, rubby, rupperty**) [late 19C+] (*Aus.*) a public house. [RUB-A-DUB *n.* (1)]

rub bellies *v.* **1** [1930s–60s] to have sexual intercourse (cf. BELLY BUMP *v.*). **2** [1970s+] (*US gay*) to indulge in an act of frottage.

rub belly *n.* [18C–19C] sexual intercourse.

rubber *n.*[1] **1** [mid-16C] (*UK Und.*) that member of a team of confidence tricksters who works as a back-up to those running the fraud; if the victim realizes they are being tricked, the *rubber* swiftly causes a disturbance, usu. by picking a fight with the earnest bystander, thus allowing their confederates to grab the stakes and run. **2** [early 17C; 1900s–50s] any form of deception or trick. [? SE *rub* (*up against*); ? link to the sporting use, coined in the 16C, meaning a match, adopted in the 17C as a quarrel or fight]

rubber *n.*[2] [1930s] (*US*) a cosh.

rubber *n.*[3] [1930s–40s] (*US Und.*) a professional killer. [RUB OUT *v.* (1)]

rubber *n.*[4] **1** [1930s–40s] (*US Black*) a car; thus *on rubber*, to be driving a car. **2** [1970s] (*US*) a set of tyres. [its tyres; cf. WHEELS *n.*[1] (3)]

rubber *n.*[5] [1940s+] (*orig. US*) a contraceptive sheath. [the thin rubber from which such sheaths are made]

rubber *n.*[6] [2000s] a spastic. [rhy. sl. on *rubber and plastic*]

rubber *n.*[7] *see* RUBBERNECK *n.*[1].

rubber *v.* [1900s] (*US campus*) to annoy; to deceive or trick; to put at a disadvantage, to question.

rubber (around) *v. see* RUBBERNECK *v.*[1].

rubber boot *n.* [1970s+] a contraceptive sheath. [ext. of RUBBER *n.*[5]]

rubber cheque *n.* (*also* **inner tube, rubber, rubber check/ kite**) [1920s+] a cheque that is not honoured by the writer's bank; thus *rubber chequebook* (cf. DUNLOP CHEQUE *n.*). [SE *rubber* + *cheque*/SAE *check*/KITE *n.*[2] (6); it 'bounces']

rubber-chicken circuit *n.* (*also* **mashed potato circuit**) [1930s+] (*US*) the after-dinner-speaking circuit, esp. as followed by political hopefuls. [the poor quality of the food (almost invariably chicken) on offer]

Rubber City *n.* [1970s+] (*US*) Akron, Ohio. [tyre-making, its primary industry]

rubber cunt *n. see* RUBBER GASH *n.* (2).

rubber dick *v.* [1970s+] to fool, to con, to hoax. [SE *rubber* + DICK *n.*[4] (1) = a dildo, i.e. a fake penis]

rubber dollies *n.* [1970s+] (*Irish*) plimsolls, gymshoes, trainers. [dial. *dollies*, rags]

rubber drink *n.* [1920s] (*US*) a drink that causes vomiting. [it 'bounces back']

rubber duck *n.*[1] [1980s+] **1** sexual intercourse. **2** (*Aus. prison*) fellatio (cf. BLOOD RED *n.*). [rhy. sl. = FUCK *n.*[1] (1)]

rubber duck *n.*[2] (*also* **rubber duckie**) [1980s+] (*Aus./S.Afr./US*) a small, inflatable rubber boat. [Aus./US prefer the sfx *-ie*]

rubberdy *n. see* RUBBEDY *n.*

rubberer *n.* [1900s] (*US*) an inquisitive person. [RUBBERNECK *v.*[1] (3)]

rubber gash *n.* [1980s+] **1** a fake 'vagina' sold as a masturbation aid. **2** (*also* **rubber cunt**) a term of abuse. [SE *rubber* + GASH *n.*[1] (1)/CUNT *n.*[1] (1)]

rubber glove *v.* [2000s] to love, i.e. to enjoy. [rhy. sl.]

rubber guts *n.* [1910s] (*Aus.*) a clumsy or pompous person. [? the image of a pompous individual with a large stomach that appears to have been blown up]

rubber heel *n.* [1920s+] **1** (*US*) (*also* **rubberglue, soft heel**) a private detective; a store detective (cf. FLATFOOT *n.*[1]). **2** someone who spies on their fellow employees; thus *rubber heel boy, rubber heel inquiry, rubber heel mob*. [note police jargon *rubber heels*, Special Branch, the internal investigations department of Scotland Yard, policing the police]

rubber heels *n.* [1940s] (*US prison*) meatloaf. [negative comment on the dish's consistency/flavour]

rubber in *v. see* RUBBERNECK *v.*[1] (1).

rubber johnny *n.* [1960s+] a contraceptive sheath. [SE *rubber*/ RUBBER *n.*[5] + JOHNNIE *n.*[11]]

rubber kite *n. see* RUBBER CHEQUE *n.*

rubber knackers *n.* [20C+] a cheeky fellow. [SE *rubber* + KNACKERS *n.*; ? they keep 'bouncing back']

rubberneck *n.*[1] (*also* **rubber, rubbernecker**) [late 19C+] (*orig. US*) **1** a tourist, esp. to New York City. **2** a very inquisitive, curious person, usu. naïve. [RUBBERNECK *v.*[1]]

rubberneck *n.*[2] *see* RUBBERNECK WAGON *n.*

rubberneck *v.*[1] (*also* **rubber, rubber around**) **1** [late 19C– 1950s] (*also* **rubber in**) to eavesdrop on someone else's conversation (feasible in the era of party line telephones). **2** [late 19C+]

to act as an obvious tourist. **3** [late 19C+] to stare at, to peer, to gaze around. **4** [1900s–20s] to investigate, e.g. as a reporter. **5** [1910s] to search for. [visitors to New York City craning their necks to view the high buildings]

rubberneck v.² [1970s] (*US Black*) to masturbate, to self-fellate (if one is acrobatically capable). [joc. use of RUBBERNECK v.¹ + SE *rub*]

rubbernecker n. *see* RUBBERNECK n.¹.

rubberneck wagon n. (*also* **rubberneck, rubberneck auto**, **...bus, ...car, ...coach**) [late 19C–1940s] (*US*) a sightseeing bus or similar vehicle; thus *rubberneck ride/tour.* [RUBBERNECK n.¹ (1) + SE *wagon*]

rubber out v. [1900s] (*US*) to work out, to elucidate. [RUBBERNECK v.¹ (4)]

rubber pill n. [1950s–70s] (*drugs*) a condom or the finger of a rubber glove used to store or transport narcotics.

rubber queen n. [1970s+] (*orig. gay*) a male homosexual rubber fetishist. [SE *rubber* + QUEEN n.² (1)/QUEEN sfx (2)]

rubber room n. [1930s+] a padded cell.

rubbers n. [late 19C+] rubber overshoes; galoshes.

rubber shop n. [1930s–50s] a sex shop. [RUBBER n.⁵; in a puritan era, such shops were a primary source of contraceptives]

rubber sock n. [1930s–40s] (*US tramp*) a timid person. [? the limpness of such a supposed garment]

rubber tramp v. [1920s] (*US*) to live as a vagrant. [? image of bouncing from place to place + pun on SE *rubber-stamp*]

rubberwrist n. [1970s+] an effeminate male homosexual. [his stereotypically limp wrist]

rubbidy n. *see* RUBBEDY n.

rubbish n. **1** [late 18C–early 19C] money (cf. CHAFF n.²). **2** [late 19C+] (*orig. S.Afr.*) an unpleasant person.

rubbish adj. [1960s+] inferior, second-rate.

rubbish v. [1950s+] (*orig. Aus.*) **1** to attack verbally, to slander. **2** to treat badly, with disrespect. **3** to beat up. **4** to wipe out, to destroy. [i.e. to talk *rubbish* about, to treat like *rubbish*]

rubbity n. *see* RUBBEDY n.

rubbity dub/rubbledub n. *see* RUB-A-DUB n. (1).

rubblehead n. [1990s+] a fool, an idiot, an incompetent. [SE *rubble* + -HEAD sfx (1)]

rubby n. *see* RUBBEDY n.

rubby-dub n. (*also* **rubby, rubby-dubby**) [1920s+] (*Can./US*) a drinker of cheap alcohol or some substance, e.g. paint-thinner, bay-rum, that can substitute; the liquids themselves. [joc. ref. to SE *rubbing alcohol*]

rubby-dubby n. [1910s] (*Aus.*) a small, underpowered car. [? echoic of its underpowered engine]

rubdown n. **1** [1930s+] a search of a person's clothes and body, either for security reasons or as a preliminary to picking their pocket; thus *rub-down dippy*, a prison guard who searches new prisoners. **2** [1940s–60s] (*orig. US Black*) a beating. [RUB DOWN v. (2)]

rub down v. **1** [early 19C–1920s] to scold, to reprimand. **2** [early 19C+] to search a person's clothes and body, either for security reasons or as a preliminary to picking their pocket. **3** [1970s+] (*UK Black*) to dance very close, rubbing one's body against one's partner.

rub down with an oaken towel v. *see* OAKEN TOWEL n.

rube n.¹ (*also* **hay rube, reub**) [late 19C+] (*US*) **1** a rustic, a farmer (cf. ALVIN n.). **2** a fool, an unsophisticated person. **3** a general term of abuse or disdain. [abbr. REUBEN n.; for *hay rube* note ety. at HEY RUBE! excl.]

rube n.² [1920s+] (*Aus.*) something seen as exceptional, first-rate etc. [? SE *ruby*]

rube adj. (*also* **reub**) [late 19C–1970s] (*US*) pertaining to a small town or the country and the supposedly unsophisticated inhabitants thereof.

Rube Goldberg n. [1950s+] a very complicated thing, machine or arrangement. [the intricate machine drawings of cartoonist *Rube Goldberg* (1888–1970)]

rub elbows (with) v. (*also* **brush elbows (with)**) [mid-19C+] (*US*) to mix and mingle with people in a social or public context. [var. on SE *rub shoulders (with)*]

rubia (de la costa) n. [1980s+] (*US drugs*) light-coloured Colombian marijuana. [Sp. *rubia*, blonde]

rubies n. [1940s–70s] (*US Black*) the lips, esp. large or full lips. [? film star *Ruby* Keeler (1909–93)]

rubigo n. [late 16C] (*Scot.*) the penis. [? Lat. *ruber*, red]

rubik's (cubes) n. [1990s+] pubic hair. [rhy. sl. = PUBES n.]

rub in v. **1** [mid-19C+] to emphasize, often with malicious pleasure; thus [late 19C] (*UK Und.*) *rub it in well*, to give (true or false) evidence that will certainly lead to a conviction. **2** [1910s] (*US*) to treat harshly.

rub joint n. [1910s–40s] a low dancehall, which features dances such as the *lovers' two-step*, the *bunny hug* and the *turkey trot*, all of which permit much more physical intimacy than those on offer at more staid establishments. [RUB n.³ (1) + JOINT n.⁴ (3)]

rub-off n. **1** [late 17C] sexual intercourse. **2** [19C+] masturbation. [RUB OFF v.]

rub off v. **1** [late 17C] to have sexual intercourse. **2** [19C+] to masturbate (cf. BALL OFF v.²).

rub offal v. [1990s+] to have sexual intercourse.

rub of the relic n. (*also* **rub of the rasher**) [1970s+] (*Irish*) sexual intercourse.

rub(-out) n. [1930s–60s] (*orig. US Und.*) a murder, esp. an assassination. [RUB OUT v. (1)]

rub-out n. [1970s] a failure, a disappointment. [SE *rub out*, to erase]

rub out v. (*also* **rub, rub off**) **1** [early 19C+] (*orig. US*) to murder, to assassinate, to kill. **2** [late 19C+] (*Aus.*) to reject an idea or a suggestion. **3** [20C+] (*Aus.*) to debar, to ban (a person). **4** [1900s–30s] (*Aus.*) to destroy something. **5** [1910s] (*US*) to leave.

rub-out guy n. [1960s] (*US*) an assassin, a murderer. [RUB OUT v. (1) + GUY n.² (1)]

rub parlor n. [1960s+] (*US*) a massage parlour. [SE *rub*/RUB OFF v. (2)]

rub the grub v. [1990s+] (*Aus.*) to masturbate. [SE *rub*/RUB OFF v. (2) + assonance/resemblance]

rub the rod v. [20C+] to masturbate. [SE *rub*/RUB OFF v. (2) + ROD n.¹ (1)]

rub (to) v. [late 17C–mid-19C] (*UK Und.*) to carry off to jail, to imprison. [RUB v.¹]

rub to the whit v. [late 17C–mid-19C] (*UK Und.*) to send to prison. [ext. RUB (TO) v. + WHIT, THE n.]

rub-up n.¹ **1** [mid-17C; 19C+] an act of sexual intercourse. **2** [19C+] stimulating another's genitals. **3** [19C+] masturbation. [RUB UP v.¹]

rub-up n.² *see* RUB n.³ (2).

rub up v.¹ **1** [mid-17C+] to stimulate the penis to erection using the hands. **2** [late 18C+] to stimulate the vagina. **3** [19C+] to masturbate. **4** [1970s] to have sexual intercourse.

rub up v.² [late 17C+] to revise, to refresh one's memory. [the image of cleaning something tarnished]

rub up the wrong way v. [mid-19C+] to annoy, to infuriate. [stroking a cat against the 'grain' of its fur]

Ruby n. *see* RUBY (MURRAY) n.

ruby n.¹ [mid-19C–1900s] blood; also as adj. (cf. BADMINTON n.).

ruby n.² [1950s–70s] (*camp gay*) a man with large, prominent lips. [? film star *Ruby* Keeler (1909–93)]

ruby-dazzler n. [1940s+] (*Aus./N.Z.*) something exceptional. [var. on BOBBY-DAZZLER n.]

rubyfruit n. [1960s+] the female genitals. [the colour and supposed appearance; best known as title of novel *Rubyfruit Jungle* (1973) by Rita Mae Brown (b.1944)]

Ruby (Murray) n. (*also* **Arthur Murray, Pete Murray**) [1980s+] a curry. [rhy. sl.; ult. the popular singer *Ruby Murray* (1935–96)/the ballroom dancing instructor and businessman

Arthur Murray (1895–1991)/BBC radio disc jockey Peter Murray (b.1928)]

ruby red *n.* [1910s] the head. [rhy. sl.]

ruby rose *n.* [20C+] the nose. [rhy. sl.; note 17C–18C *ruby*, a carbuncle on the nose]

ruca *n.* **1** [1950s–60s] (*US gang*) a female gang member. **2** [1990s+] (*US prison*) an inmate's wife or girlfriend. [Sp. *ruca*, old lady]

ruck *n.*[1] **1** [late 19C] (*US*) nonsense, rubbish. **2** [1920s] a cigarette end. [SE *ruck*, the general run of things, the undistinguished crowd]

ruck *n.*[2] [1950s+] an argument, a fight, esp. a gang fight; also in fig. use. [? SE *ruckus*]

ruck *v.* **1** [late 19C–1960s] to get angry with; in fig. use, to pain. **2** [late 19C+] to lay information against, to inform on. **3** [1950s+] to scold, to tell off. **4** [1950s+] to involve oneself in a fight, esp. a gang fight. **5** [1960s–70s] to masturbate (cf. BOFF v.). [? SE *ruck*, to disturb, orig. clothes and thence tempers]

ruck and row *n.* [20C+] an unpleasant woman. [rhy. sl. = COW n.[1] (1)]

rucker *n.* **1** [1950s+] an arguer, a combative person. **2** [1970s+] a fighter. [RUCK n.[2]]

ruckerky *adj.* [late 19C] (*UK society*) choice, rare. [deliberate mispron. of synon. Fr. *recherché*]

ruck in *v.* [late 19C] to join in a group.

rucking *n.* **1** [1920s+] (*Irish*) (*also* **rucky-up, ruggy-up**) a fight. **2** [1950s+] a severe reprimand. [RUCK v. (1)]

ruck on *v.* **1** [late 19C] to betray, to abandon one's loyalty to, to go back on. **2** [1930s] to quarrel with. [RUCK v.]

ruckus juice *n.* (*also* **rookus juice**) [1920s–60s] (*US*) alcohol; prob. cheap and potent and thus liable to inflame one's passions. [SE *ruckus*, a commotion + JUICE n.[3] (1)]

rucky-up *n. see* RUCKING n. (1).

ruction(s) *n.* [mid-19C+] disturbances, riots; disorderly disputes or quarrels; with implications of unpleasant consequences. [? SE *insurrection*; note the Irish Insurrection of 1798, known locally as the *ruction*]

ructious *adj.* [mid-19C] (*US*) turbulent, harrowing. [RUCTION(S) n.]

rudder *n.* **1** [mid-16C–mid-19C] the penis. **2** [20C+] an animal's, usu. a dog's, tail.

ruddity dub *n. see* RUB-A-DUB n. (1).

ruddling *n.* [late 19C] sexual intercourse. [? dial. *ruddle*, to smear]

ruddock *n.* (*also* **robin ruddock**) [mid-16C–early 17C] a gold coin; in pl. money; often ext. as *red/golden ruddock*. [SE *ruddock*, a robin redbreast, i.e. the 'red' colour of the golden money]

ruddy *adj.* **1** [late 19C+] a general intensifier, a euph. synon. for BLOODY adj.[1] (1). **2** [1930s] of a person, unpleasant, unacceptable, crooked. [play on SE *ruddy*, red in colour]

rude *adj.*[1] **1** [20C+] (*W.I.*) sexually aggressive. **2** [1930s] wild, uncontrolled, openly hostile to authority. **3** [1950s+] sexual. [ext. of SE]

rude *adj.*[2] (*orig. US campus*) **1** [1960s+] unfair, distasteful, offensive, generally poor, flagrantly bad. **2** [1980s+] excellent, admirable; on bad = good model.

rude boy *n.* (*also* **rude bwai/bwoy**) **1** [1960s+] (*orig. W.I.*) (*also* **rudey, rudie**) 'a young, Black Jamaican male who is an aggressive social drop-out; he may be a ghetto type, a gang type or one who adopts some Rastafarian cultist habits' (Allsopp); also a term of address. **2** [1960s+] someone who poses as such a 'drop-out' but is in fact more middle-class. **3** [1970s+] young people of any colour, who like W.I. music, typically blue-beat, rock-steady and ska; the term was revived in the early 1980s for fans of two-tone music (itself reviving the old blue-beat etc). [ext. use + W.I. pron. of SE *rude boy*]

rude girl *n.* (*also* **rude gal**) [1960s+] (*W.I./UK Black teen*) the female equivalent of the RUDE BOY n. (1).

rudeness *n.* [1960s] (*W.I.*) sexual intercourse; thus *do rudeness*, to have sex.

rude parts *n.* [1970s+] the genitals, both male or female (in the latter case ext. to breasts also). [euph.]

rudesby *n.* [late 16C–early 17C] an unpleasant, boorish person. [SE *rude* + sfx *-by*]

rudey *n. see* RUDE BOY n. (1).

rudie *n.*[1] [1970s] (*Aus.*) a coarse comment, an obscenity.

rudie *n.*[2] *see* RUDE BOY n. (1).

rudipoop *n.* [2000s] (*US prison*) one who does not fit in with the group; an outsider.

rudolph *n.* [1950s] a red nose, gained through drinking. [the Christmas song 'Rudolph, the red-nosed reindeer']

Rudolph (Hess) *n.* [1990s+] a mess. [rhy. sl.; ult. Nazi leader *Rudolph Hess* (1894–87); note ephemeral 1940s US Black sl. *Rudolph Hess*, to leave, to disappear, echoing the Nazi's flight to Scotland during WW2]

ruff *n.* [1930s–40s] (*US Black*) 25 cents, a quarter. [ety. unknown]

ruffelar/ruffeler *n. see* RUFFLER n.

ruffer *n.*[1] [18C; late 19C] a rough person, a thug.

ruffer *n.*[2] [1930s] (*UK tramp*) a bed in a bush, thus with no overhead protection. [? modern adoption of RUFFMANS n. or SE *rough sleeping*]

ruffian *see also under* RUFFIN and its combs.

ruffian *n.*[1] [17C–early 19C] an assassin, a (murderous) thug; a bouncer for a brothel.

ruffian *n.*[2] (*also* **ruffin**) [mid-17C–early 18C] a justice of the peace.

ruffian *n.*[3] *see* BELLY RUFFIAN n.

ruffian cly thee!, the *excl.* (*also* **ruffin...**) [mid-16C–mid-19C] (*UK Und.*) an excl. meaning 'the Devil take thee'. [RUFFIN (, THE) n.+ CLY v.]

ruffies *n. see* ROOFIE n.[2].

ruffin *see also under* RUFFIAN and its combs.

Ruffin(, the) *n.* (*also* **the old Ruffian/Ruffin, Ruffian**) [mid-16C–early 19C] the Devil. [SE *ruffian*, rogue + 13C SE *Ruffin*, the name of a specific demon]

Ruffin's Hall *n.* (*also* **Ruffian's Hall**) [late 16C–17C] that area of London, now Smithfields, where trials of skill were held amongst 'ordinary, Ruffianly people, with Sword and Buckler' (T. Blount, *Glossographia*, 1674), thus phr. *he is only fit for Ruffian's Hall*, used of an overdressed apprentice.

rufflar *n. see* RUFFLER n.

ruffle *n.*[1] **1** [1900s] (*US*) a girl, a woman. **2** [1960s+] (*gay*) the passive partner in a lesbian relationship. [(1) SE *ruffle*, as adjoining a dress; (2) ? RUFUS n.[1] (1)]

ruffle *n.*[2] [1970s] (*US Black*) a fight.

ruffle *v.* [mid-19C] (*UK Und.*) to place in handcuffs. [RUFFLES n.[1]]

ruffler *n.* (*also* **ruffelar, ruffeler, rufflar, ruffleer, rufler**) [mid-16C–mid-19C] (*UK Und.*) a villain, of the 'first rank of canters', who posed as a discharged soldier (and might indeed have been one, although equally likely might have been a former servant), but actually worked as an itinerant (cf. CANTING CREW n.). [SE *ruffle it*, to swagger; it is linked to the idea of a bird ruffling up its feathers]

ruffles *n.*[1] (*also* **ruffs**) [late 18C–1930s] (*UK Und.*) handcuffs. [? ironic use of SE *ruff*, which is worn round the neck]

ruffles *n.*[2] [1940s+] (*US Black*) chitterlings. [? their appearance]

ruffles *n.*[3] *see* ROOFIE n.[2].

ruffmans *n.* [mid-16C–early 19C] (*UK Und.*) the woods or bushes. [SE *rough* (as in ground) + -MANS sfx]

ruff neck *n.* [1980s+] (*W.I./US Black teen*) a rebellious person; a bohemian; a person with a couldn't-care-less attitude. [deliberate mis-sp. of ROUGHNECK n. (2)]

ruff peck *n.* [mid-16C–mid-18C] (*UK Und.*) bacon. [SE *rough* + PECK n.[1] (1); lit. 'rough food']

ruffs *n. see* RUFFLES n.[1].

rufler *n. see* RUFFLER n.

rufus *n.*[1] **1** [19C] the female genitals. **2** [1950s] a person with red hair. [Lat. *rufus*, red]

rufus *n.*[2] [1900s–50s] (*US*) a country person, a peasant (cf. ALVIN n.). [the 'rustic' name]

rug *n.*[1] **1** [20C+] (*orig. US*) a wig, a toupee, a hairpiece, esp. in show business. **2** [1930s+] pubic hair, usu. female. **3** [1940s+] the hair. [it lies on/covers one's head/bald patch]

rug *n.*[2] [1940s–80s] (*Aus.*) a £1 note. [? RAG n.[1] (3)]

rug *n.*[3] [1970s+] (*US prison*) a Black prisoner. [? abbr. SE *rugged*]

rug *n.*[4] *see* RUGHEAD n.

rug ape *n.* [1960s+] (*US*) a small child.

rug beat *n.* [1920s–50s] (*US Black*) a noisy, festive party where the dancing 'beats the rug'.

rugby team *n.* [1940s+] (*bingo*) the number 15 (cf. ALDERSHOT LADIES n.). [the 15 members of a rugby team]

rug cut *v. see* CUT THE RUG v.

rug cutter *n.* (*also* **rug shaker**) [1920s–50s] (*US Black*) a good and energetic dancer. [CUT THE RUG v.]

rugged *adj.* **1** [mid-18C+] of people, tough. **2** [1940s+] of an activity, tough, difficult.

rugged up *adj.* [1990s+] (*Aus.*) wearing warm clothes. [SE *rug*]

rugger *n.* [late 19C+] rugby football, usu. Rugby Union. [SE *rugby* + -ER sfx]

rugger bugger *n.* (*also* **r.b.**) [1950s+] a dedicatedly masculine man, whose lack of sensitivity/intelligence is more than compensated for by his enthusiasm for all forms of sport. [RUGGER n. + BUGGER n.[1] (1)]

ruggins *n.* (*also* **ruggins's**) [early 19C] in bed; thus *go to ruggins*, to go to bed. [one is under the SE *rug*]

ruggy *adj.* [mid-19C] fusty, frowsy. [the warmth and cosiness of being wrapped in a *rug*]

ruggy-up *n. see* RUCKING n. (1).

rughead *n.* (*also* **rug**) [1960s+] a derog. term for a Black person (cf. BRILLOHEAD n.). [the texture of Black hair]

rug joint *n.* (*US*) **1** [late 19C+] an elegant, expensive restaurant, patronized by the wealthy. **2** [1960s+] an upmarket, luxury casino. [SE *rug*, a carpet + JOINT n.[4] (3); such restaurants were as distinguished by the splendours of their interior decoration as by their menus]

rug-muncher *n. see* CARPET-MUNCHER n.

rug peddler *n.* [1920s] (*US*) an Arab (cf. ABDUL n.). [negative stereotyping]

rug rat *n.* [1960s+] a small child who is still crawling on the carpet.

rug's the word *phr.* [early 18C] everything is fine, all is safe; thus [late 19C–1900s] *ruggy*, safe. [? the security of a *rug*]

rug up *v.* [1990s+] (*Aus.*) to dress warmly.

rugy *adj.* [1970s+] (*US Black*) unattractive; ill-tempered. [? elision of *rude guy*]

ruin *n.*[1] [19C] cheap, inferior gin. [its effects]

ruin *n.*[2] [1910s] (*UK juv.*) a despised schoolboy.

ruin *v.* [1960s+] (*gay*) to deliberately exaggerate one's effeminacy as a shock tactic.

ruin and spoil *n.* [20C+] oil. [rhy. sl.]

ruined *adj.* [1960s+] (*orig. US Black*) **1** beaten, injured. **2** (*also* **ruint**) drunk, under the influence of drugs (cf. ANNIHILATED adj.).

ruin't *adj.* (*US Black*) **1** [1940s] pregnant. **2** [1960s–80s] of a person, unattractive.

rukadung *adj. see* ROOGODUNG adj.

rulable *adj.* [late 19C] (*US*) permissible. [it 'falls within the rules']

rule *v.* **1** [1980s+] (*US campus*) to do well or be something admirable or good. **2** [1990s+] (*US Black*) to be in control.

rule 43 *n.* [1970s+] (*UK prison*) voluntary solitary confinement for the sake of a prisoner's safety; child molesters, rapists etc

choose this in preference to the natural justice of their peers; thus phr. *on the rule*, segregated in this manner.

rule of three *n.* **1** [18C] the male genitals. **2** [19C] sexual intercourse. [SE *rule* + *three*, i.e. the penis and testicles; note Williams: 'This alludes to the golden rule whereby a fourth number is deduced from a given three numbers']

Rules *n.* [1940s+] (*Aus.*) Australian *Rules* Football. [abbr.]

— rules (OK) *phr.* [1960s+] the text of a graffito proclaiming the excellence of a star, a local gang etc, e.g. *Eric rules OK*. [SE *rule*]

rum *n.* **1** [1900s] (*US*) an eccentric. **2** [1900s–70s] (*US Black*) a fool, a dupe, a victim. **3** [1950s–60s] a drunkard. [abbr. RUMMY n.[1] (2)/RUM adj. (2)]

rum *adj.* (*orig. UK Und.*) **1** [mid-16C–1920s] (*also* **rome**) excellent, first-rate; the antonym of QUEER adj.[1] (1). **2** [mid-18C+] (*also* **rummish**) odd, peculiar, strange, thus *rummily*, oddly. **3** [19C] illicit, illegal, criminal. **4** [mid-19C] drunk, tipsy. [most prob. from SE *Rome* (and indeed could be spelled 'rome' until the 18C), which, as a city, meant glory and grandeur. Other origins include the Rom. *rom*, a male gypsy, or the Turkish *Röm*, a gypsy, many of whom passed through the Ottoman Empire. Reversing the process, the Lat. *Roma* (Rome) is cognate with the Teutonic root *hruod* (fame) (as found in the names Roger and Roderick) which appears in the German *Ruhm* (fame)]

rum *adv.* [mid-19C] **1** (*UK Und.*) smartly. **2** strangely, eccentrically. [RUM adj.]

rumatiz *n. see* RHEUMATIZ n.

rumba *n.* (*US*) **1** [1930s] a spree, a celebration, a party. **2** [1950s] a fight, esp. a gang fight.

rumba *v.* [1950s] (*US*) to fight with. [RUMBA n. (2)]

rum beak *n.* [late 18C–mid-19C] (*UK Und.*) a corruptible magistrate. [RUM adj. (1) + BEAK n.[1] (1)]

rum beck *n.* [early 17C–mid-19C] (*UK Und.*) **1** a justice of the peace. **2** a magistrate who is susceptible to corruption. [RUM adj. (1) + BECK n.[1]]

rum bite *n.* **1** [late 17C–early 19C] (*UK Und.*) a clever trick, a cunning ploy. **2** [late 18C–early 19C] a clever fraud or confidence trickster. [RUM adj. (1) + BITE n.[1]]

rumble *n.*[1] **1** [1900s–60s] the act of discovery, usu. in the context of a crime. **2** [1910s–50s] an alarm (during the course of a crime). **3** [1910s+] a tip-off. **4** [1920s] (*US Und.*) an accident, a problem. **5** [1960s+] (*US*) a rumour. [RUMBLE v.[2] (1)]

rumble *n.*[2] **1** [1920s–60s] sexual intercourse. **2** [1940s+] (*US*) a street gang fight. **3** [1940s+] a fight; an argument. **4** [1950s+] (*US drugs*) a police drug raid. **5** [1960s] (*US campus*) a wild party. [RUMBLE v.[1]; but note 14C–18C SE *rumble*, a commotion, an uproar]

rumble *n.*[3] [1930s–40s] (*US*) a car. [the sound of the engine]

rumble *v.*[1] **1** [early 19C] (*UK Und.*) to pickpocket, to steal. **2** [early–mid-19C] to handle roughly, to rule out without any discussion. **3** [1910s] (*Aus.*) to obtain through deception; to deceive. **4** [1910s–20s] (*UK milit./US Und.*) to spoil, to upset. **5** [1940s+] to hit, to fight, esp. of teen gangs; thus *rumbling*, ready to fight. **6** [1950s+] (*US*) to steal, esp. from an aeroplane. **7** [1950s+] (*drugs*) to be searched by the police.

rumble *v.*[2] **1** [late 19C+] to discover, to find out, to unmask. **2** [1940s] (*US Und.*) to reveal one's plans, to make a potential victim aware of one's criminal intentions. [? modern ext. of ROMBOYLE v.]

rum-bleating cheat *n.* [late 17C–early 19C] (*UK Und.*) a very fat wether or castrated ram. [RUM adj. (1) + BLEATING CHEAT n.]

rumbler *n.* **1** [late 18C–early 19C] a cart (e.g. as used in a hanging). **2** [early 19C] a hackney carriage. **3** [mid-19C] a 4-wheeled cab; thus *rumbler's flunkey*, a footman who runs for cabs in return for tips.

rumble-tumble *n.* [early–mid-19C] a stage-coach. [note Anglo-Ind. use *rumble-tumble*, scrambled eggs]

rum blowen *n.* (*also* **rum blower/blowing**) [late 17C–18C] (*UK Und.*) a good-looking woman, esp. an attractive mistress or kept woman. [RUM adj. (1) + BLOWEN n. (1)/BLOWER n.[1]/ BLOWING n.[1]]

rum bluffer *n.* [late 17C–early 19C] (*UK Und.*) an honest, jovial, accommodating alehouse-keeper or publican. [RUM adj. (1) + BLUFFER n.[1] (1)]

rumbo *n.*[1] (*also* **rumbo-ken**) [18C–early 19C] Newgate, thus any prison. [? ironic use of RUM adj. (1) + KEN n.[1] (1)]

rumbo *n.*[2] [mid-18C–19C] a mixture of rum, water and sugar. [SE *rum*]

rumbo *n.*[3] [late 19C] a sufficiency, a plenitude. [Sp. *rumbo*, liberality, generosity]

rumbo *adj.* [mid–late 19C] **1** plentiful, sufficient. **2** elegant, fashionable. [RUMBO n.[3]]

rumbo! *excl.* [mid-19C] (*UK middle class*) an excl. of congratulation, i.e. *splendid! excellent!* used (exclusively) between men. [Sp. *carambo* and ? adopted f. gypsy use]

rum bob *n.* [late 17C–early 19C] (*UK Und.*) **1** a smart young apprentice. **2** a sharp, fly trick. **3** (*also* **bob**) a neat, short wig. [RUM adj. (1) + (1) BOB n.[2]; (2) BOB v.[1] (1); (3) SE *bobbed hair*]

rumbo-ken *n.*[1] [early 18C] a pawnshop. [ety. unknown + KEN n.[1] (1)]

rumbo-ken *n.*[2] *see* RUMBO n.[1].

rum booze *n.* (*also* **rome bowse, rum bouse, ...bouze, ...bues, ...buse, ...buze**) [mid-16C–19C] good drink, esp. good wine. [RUM adj. (1) + BOOZE n. (1)/BOUSE n. (1)]

rum-boozing welts *n.* [late 17C–early 19C] (*UK Und.*) bunches of grapes. [RUM BOOZE n. + SE *welt*, a ridge or raised portion]

rum bow *n.* [late 18C–mid-19C] (*UK Und.*) rope stolen from a royal dockyard. [RUM adj. (2) + SE *bowline*]

rumboyle *see under* ROMBOYLE.

rum bub *n.* [late 17C–mid-19C] excellent liquor. [RUM adj. (1) + BUB n.[1]]

rum bubber *n.* [late 17C–18C] a thief who specializes in stealing silver tankards from taverns. [RUM adj. (1) + BUBBER n.[1] (3)]

rum bues *n. see* RUM BOOZE n.

rum buffer *n.* [late 18C–mid-19C] (*UK Und.*) a valuable and attractive dog. [RUM adj. (1) + BUFE n.]

rum bug *n.* [late 19C] (*Aus.*) an important (or self-important) person. [RUM adj. (2) + BUG n.[1] (1)]

rum bughar *n.* (*also* **rum bugher**) [late 17C–early 19C] (*UK Und.*) a valuable and attractive dog. [RUM adj. (1) + BUGHER n.]

rum-bump *n.* [1950s] (*W.I.*) **1** an adam's apple. **2** a swelling in the throat supposedly caused by excessive rum drinking.

rum-bumper *n.* [1950s] (*W.I.*) a rum drunkard. [SE/RUM-BUMP n. (2)]

rumbumtious *adj.* (*also* **rumbumptious**) **1** [late 18C–early 19C] obstreperous. **2** [mid-19C] haughty. [vars. on SE *rambunctious*]

rum bung *n.* [late 17C–mid-19C] (*UK Und.*) a full purse. [RUM adj. (1) + BUNG n.[1] (1)]

rum buse *n. see* RUM BOOZE n.

rumbusticate *v.* **1** [mid-19C] (*US*) to be (fig.) knocked down, to be confused. **2** [late 19C–1900s] in euph. use of (1), of a man, to have sexual intercourse. [RUMBUSTIOUS adj. + sfx *-ate*, e.g. in SPIFLICATE v.]

rumbustious *adj.* (*also* **rambustious, rombustical, rum-bustical**) [late 18C–19C] boisterous, noisy, unruly, turbulent.

rum buze *n. see* RUM BOOZE n.

rum chant *n.* [late 18C–mid-19C] (*UK Und.*) a song; thus *throw off a rum chant*, to sing a good song. [RUM adj. (1) + CHANT n. (2)]

rum clank *n.* [18C–early 19C] (*UK Und.*) a gold or silver cup or tankard. [RUM adj. (1) + CLANK n. (1)]

rum clout *n.* [late 17C–mid-19C] (*UK Und.*) a handkerchief made of silk or other high-quality material. [RUM adj. (1) + CLOUT n.[1] (1)]

rum cly *n.* [late 18C–mid-19C] (*UK Und.*) a full pocket, i.e. of money. [RUM adj. (1) + CLY n. (2)]

rum cod *n. see* LUSTY COD n.

rum coe *n.* (*also* **rum co**) [late 17C–early 19C] a smart lad. [RUM adj. (1) + COVE n. (1)]

rum cole *n.* (*also* **rum gelt, ...ghelt, ...gilt**) [late 17C–mid-19C] (*UK Und.*) **1** new money. **2** 'Medals, curiously Coyn'd' (B.E.), presumably counterfeit. [RUM adj. (1) + COLE n. (1)/GELT n./GILT n.[1]]

rum coll *n. see* RUM CULLY n. (3).

rum-cove *n.* **1** [17C–mid-18C] a rich man. **2** [17C–early 19C] a successful villain. **3** [late 17C–mid-18C] (*UK Und.*) the hangman. **4** [late 18C–mid-19C] (*UK Und.*) a good-natured landlord. **5** [mid-19C+] an odd or eccentric character. [RUM adj. + COVE n. (1)]

rum covey *n.* [mid-19C] **1** an attractive man. **2** a sharp fellow. [RUM adj. (1) + COVEY n. (1)]

rum cully *n.* (*also* **rum cull**) (*UK Und.*) **1** [mid-17C–early 19C] a gullible, rich fool, open to fraud. **2** [late 17C] a man who is very generous to his mistress. **3** [18C–19C] (*also* **rum coll**) an intimate friend; a good man. [RUM adj. (1) + CULLY n. (3)/CULL n.[1] (4); note mid-19C theatrical jargon *rum cull*, the manager]

rum cuttle *n.* [early 17C] a sword. [RUM adj. (1) + CUTTLE n.]

rum dab *n.* [late 17C–early 18C] (*UK Und.*) a very successful sharper, pickpocket and thief. [RUM adj. (1) + DAB n.[1]]

rumdadum *n.* [1910s–20s] the buttocks (cf. ALA n.). [? rhy. sl. = BUM n.[1] (1)]

rum degen *n.* (*also* **ram dagen, ...job, ...tilter, ...tol**) [late 17C–mid-19C] (*UK Und.*) a sword with a silver hilt or a hilt or blade inlaid with silver. [RUM adj. (1) + DEGEN n. (1)/SE *jab*/TILTER n./TOL n.[1]]

rum diver *n.* [late 17C–early 19C] (*UK Und.*) an accomplished pickpocket. [RUM adj. (1) + DIVER n. (2)]

rum doxy *n.* (*also* **rum dell**) [late 17C–early 19C] (*UK Und.*) a beautiful woman or attractive prostitute. [RUM adj. (1) + DOXY n. (2)/DELL n. (1)]

rum drag *n.* [late 18C] (*UK Und.*) a confidence trick where someone pretends to be drunk and offers to pay a wagonner to let him sleep it off in the wagon, where, instead of sleeping, he re-addresses the labels on the packages so they are sent to his confederates; thus *rum dragger*. [SE *rum* + DRAG v.[1] (1)]

rum drawers *n.* [late 17C–18C] (*UK Und.*) stockings made of silk or some similar quality material. [RUM adj. (1) + DRAWERS n.]

rum dropper *n.* (*UK Und.*) **1** [late 17C–mid-19C] (*also* **dropper**) a vintner. **2** [early 18C] a landlord. [SE *rum* + *drops* of liquor]

rum dubber *n.* [late 17C–early 19C] (*UK Und.*) an expert picklock. [RUM adj. (1) + DUBBER n.[1]]

rum duchess *n.* [late 17C–mid-18C] (*UK Und.*) a jolly, buxom woman. [RUM adj. (1) + DUCHESS n.[1] (1)]

rum duke *n.* (*UK Und.*) **1** [late 17C–early 19C] a tough villain who is sent by a bankrupted individual to guard their possessions, while they leave home and take refuge from arrest in a criminal rookery. **2** [late 17C–early 19C] a notably handsome man. **3** [late 18C–early 19C] an odd, eccentric, showy man. [RUM adj. + generic use of SE *duke* but note DUKE n.[1]]

rum-dum *n.* (*also* **rum-dumb, rumdummy, rundum**) (*US*) **1** [late 19C+] a heavy drinker. **2** [1930s] a stupid, mad person. [SE *rum* + *dumb* + assonance]

rum-dum *adj.* (*also* **rum-dumb**) (*US*) **1** [late 19C–1960s] drunk. **2** [1930s–70s] stupid. [RUM-DUM n.]

rum factory *n. see* BOOZE FACTORY n.

rum fam *n.* (*also* **rum fem**) (*UK Und.*) **1** [early 18C] a gold ring. **2** [late 19C] a diamond ring. [RUM adj. (1) + FAMBLE n. (2)]

rum feeder *n.* [late 18C–mid-19C] (*UK Und.*) a large silver spoon. [RUM adj. (1) + FEEDER n.[1]]

rum file *n.* [late 17C–early 19C] (*UK Und.*) an expert pickpocket. [RUM adj. (1) + FILE n. (2)]

rumfoozeled *adj.* [mid-19C] untidy, disarrayed (cf. BAMBOOZLE v.). [RUMFOOZLE n.]

rumfoozle *n.* [early 19C] a muddle, a surprising occurrence. [nonsense word]

Rumford lion *n. see* ROMFORD LION *n.*

rum fun *n.* [late 17C–mid-19C] (*UK Und.*) a clever trick, a cunning fraud. [RUM adj. (1) + FUN n.²]

rum gagger *n.* [late 18C–mid-19C] (*UK Und.*) a confidence trickster who raises money on the basis of telling fraudulent tales of supposed suffering at sea, at the hands of the pirates of the Barbary Coast and so on. [RUM adj. (1) + GAGGER n.¹ (1)]

rum gelt/ghelt *n. see* RUM COLE *n.*

rum gill *n.* [late 18C–mid-19C] (*UK Und.*) a well-off man who thus presents a target for robbery. [RUM adj. (1) + GILL n.¹ (1)]

rum gilt *n. see* RUM COLE *n.*

rum glimmer *n.* (*also* **rum glymmar**) [late 17C–mid-19C] (*UK Und.*) the head of the link-boys, who were employed to carry a link to light passengers along the street. [RUM adj. (1) + GLIMMER n. (1)]

rum gloak *n.* [late 18C–mid-19C] (*UK Und.*) a well-dressed man. [RUM adj. (1) + GLOAK n.]

rumgumption *n.* (*also* **rummelgumption**) [mid-18C–mid-19C] knowledge, ability; thus *rumgumptious*, knowing, positive, blunt, pert. [? abbr. Scot. *rumblegumption*, common sense]

rum gutlers *n.* **1** [late 17C–mid-19C] (*UK Und.*) Canary wine. **2** [18C] good eating. [RUM adj. (1) + SE *guzzle*]

rumhead *n.* [late 19C+] a drunkard, esp. a rum-drinker. [SE *rum* + -HEAD sfx (3)]

rum-hole *n.* (*also* **rum-joint**) [early 19C–1920s] (*US*) orig. a cheap tavern, specializing in rum; a bar. [SE *rum* + HOLE n.² (2)/JOINT n.⁴ (3)]

rum hopper *n.* [late 17C–mid-19C] (*UK Und.*) someone who draws ale or wine at a tavern. [RUM adj. (1) + SE *hopper*, one who moves quickly and efficiently, who 'hops to it']

rum hound *n.* [1910s–50s] a heavy drinker. [SE *rum* + HOUND sfx]

rum-jar *n.* [late 19C] (*Aus.*) a heavy drinker; a drunkard.

rum-jem *n. see* JEM n.¹.

rum-joint *n. see* RUM-HOLE n.

rum ken *n.* (*UK Und.*) **1** [mid–late 18C] a large, substantial house. **2** [mid–late 19C] a well-known criminal public house or brothel (cf. BADGER-CRIB n.). [RUM adj. (1) + KEN n.¹ (1)]

rum kicks *n.* [late 17C–mid-19C] (*UK Und.*) breeches that have been adorned with silver or gold embroidery. [RUM adj. (1) + KICKS n.¹]

rum kiddy *n.* [late 18C–early 19C] (*UK Und.*) a popular, successful young thief. [RUM adj. (1) + KIDDY n.¹ (1)]

rumkin *n.* [2000s] (*US prison*) one who does not fit in with the group; an outsider. [RUM adj. (2)]

rumly *adv.* **1** [early 17C] nimbly. **2** [mid-17C–early 19C] (*also* **rumley**) excellently. **3** [late 17C] honestly. **4** [late 17C–18C] bravely. [RUM adj. (1)]

rummage *v.* [late 17C–19C] of a man, to have sexual intercourse.

rummarian *n. see* RUMMER n.

rum maund *n.* (*also* **rum maunder/mawnd**) [late 17C–mid-19C] (*UK Und.*) a beggar who poses as more stupid than they really are to encourage donations. [RUM adj. (2) + MAUND n.]

rummed up *adj.* (*also* **rummied**) [1920s–40s] tipsy, drunk. [SE *rum*]

rummelgumption *n. see* RUMGUMPTION n.

rummer *n.* (*also* **rummarian**) [1940s] (*W.I.*) a rum drunkard. [SE *rum*]

rummery *n.* [mid-19C–1910s] a saloon.

rummied *adj. see* RUMMED UP adj.

rum-mill *n.* [mid–late 19C] (*US*) a cheap tavern or saloon, selling primarily rum. [SE *rum* + *mill*]

rumminess *n.* [19C–1920s] something difficult, problematic, odd. [RUM adj. (2)]

rummish *adj. see* RUM adj. (2).

rum mizzler *n.* (*also* **mizzler**) **1** [late 18C–mid-19C] (*UK Und.*) someone who is clever at escaping difficult situations, whether physically or through words. **2** [mid-19C] a general derog. term. [RUM adj. (1) + MIZZLE v. (1)]

rum mort *n.* (*also* **rome mort, rum mot**) **1** [mid-16C–early 19C] (*UK Und.*) a queen. **2** [early 17C–mid-19C] a great lady; an attractive woman. **3** [mid-17C–mid-19C] a prostitute. **4** [mid-18C] a rich woman. [RUM adj. (1) + MORT n.; (1) was orig. coined for Elizabeth I]

rum-muns *n.* [mid-18C] (*UK Und.*) a good-looking man. [RUM adj. (1) + MUNS n.¹ (1)]

rummy *n.¹* (*US*) **1** [mid-19C] a rum seller. **2** [mid-19C+] a drunkard; also attrib. **3** [1910s] a fool. [SE *rum*]

rummy *n.²* [1900s–30s] a fool, an eccentric, a dupe. [RUM adj. (2)]

rummy *adj.* **1** [18C+] odd, peculiar, bizarre; thus adv. *rummily*. **2** [mid–late 19C] first-rate, excellent. [RUM adj.]

rummy stiff *n.* [1910s] (*US tramp*) an alcoholic tramp. [RUMMY n.¹ (2) + STIFF n.² (4)]

rum nab *n.* [late 17C–early 19C] (*UK Und.*) a well-made, fashionable hat, a beaver hat. [RUM adj. (1) + NAB n.¹ (3)]

rum nantz *n.* [late 17C–mid-19C] (*UK Und.*) the best-quality French brandy. [RUM adj. (1) + NANTZ n.]

rum ned *n.* [late 17C–early 19C] (*UK Und.*) a very foolish rich man. [RUM adj. (1) + NEDDY n.¹ (2)]

rumness *n.* [mid-19C] oddness, eccentricity. [RUM adj. (2)]

rum ogles *n.* [late 17C–early 19C] (*UK Und.*) bright, clear eyes. [RUM adj. (1) + OGLE n. (1)]

rum one *n.* (*also* **rum 'un**) **1** [late 18C–mid-19C] an admirable fellow or object. **2** [late 18C–1920s] anything considered odd or eccentric, whether animate, inanimate or theoretical. [RUM adj.]

rump *n.* **1** [17C] a prostitute (cf. BANGTAIL n.¹). **2** [1990s+] sexual intercourse. [SE *rump*, the buttocks]

rump *v.* **1** [late 18C–mid-19C] to turn one's back on. **2** [late 18C+] to copulate. **3** [early 19C] to flog. **4** [20C+] (*US*) to have anal intercourse (cf. ASK FOR THE RING v.). **5** [1990s+] in fig. use, a synon. for FUCK v.² (1). [SE *rump*, the buttocks]

rum pad *n.* [mid-17C–mid-19C] (*UK Und.*) (*also* **rom(e) pad**) the highway. **2** a highwayman. [RUM adj. (1) + PAD n.¹]

rum-padder *n.* (*also* **rom-padder**) [late 17C–mid-19C] (*UK Und.*) a highwayman. [RUM adj. (1) + PADDER n.]

rump and a dozen *n.* (*also* **rump and dozen**) **1** [late 18C–19C] an orig. Irish wager, a rump of beef and a dozen of claret. **2** [1920s] a whipping, 12 lashes.

rump-and-kidney men *n.* [late 17C–early 19C] fiddlers who play for weddings, feasts, fairs and similar festivities. [their payment in kind, they were given the left-overs]

rum patter *n.* [late 18C] (*UK Und.*) criminal sl., cant. [RUM adj. (1) + PATTER n. (3)]

rum peck *n.* [late 17C–early 19C] (*UK Und.*) good food. [RUM adj. (1) + PECK n.¹ (1)]

rum peeper *n.* [late 17C–mid-19C] (*UK Und.*) a silver mounted looking-glass. [RUM adj. (1) + PEEPER n. (2)]

rumper *n.* **1** [mid-17C] (*also* **cully-rumper**) a pimp, a prostitute's customer (cf. ABBOT ON THE CROSS n.). **2** [19C] a prostitute (cf. BANGTAIL n.¹). [SE *rump* (+ CULLY n. (2))]

rum phiz *n.* (*also* **rum phyz**) [late 18C–early 19C] an odd-looking face. [RUM adj. (1) + PHIZ n.¹ (1)]

rumping *n.* [1970s] sexual intercourse. [RUMP v. (2)]

rumpkin *n.* (*also* **rumpskin**) [1960s+] (*US Black*) a fool. [RUM adj. (2) + SE *bumpkin*]

rumplety-thump *adj.* [20C+] (*Ulster*) muddled, untidy. [echoic of the noise of objects being tossed to the floor]

rumpo *n.* [1950s+] sexual intercourse. [RUMP v. (2)]

rumpot *n.* [1930s+] a drunkard. [SE *rum* + -POT sfx]

rum prad *n.* [late 19C–mid-19C] (*UK Und.*) a highwayman's horse. [RUM adj. (1) + PRAD n.]

rum prancer *n.* [late 17C–early 19C] (*UK Und.*) a beautiful, well-made horse. [RUM adj. (1) + PRANCER n. (1)]

rump ranger *n.* (*also* **rump wrangler**) [1980s+] a male homosexual (cf. ANAL ASTRONAUT n.).

rump shaker *n.* [1990s+] (*US*) an act of sexual intercourse.

rumpskin *n. see* RUMPKIN n.

rump-splitter *n.* (*also* **split-rump**) **1** [mid-17C] the penis (cf. ARSE-OPENER n.). **2** [19C–1900s] a lecher, a womanizer.

rump-tee-vump *n. see* RUMPTYVUMP n.

rumpty *adj.* [1910s+] (*Aus.*) excellent, first-rate. [ety. unknown]

rumpty (dooler) *n.* [1940s+] (*Aus./N.Z.*) **1** anything excellent, first-rate. **2** something broken down, unattractive, disreputable. **3** a fuss, an uproar. [ext. of RUMPTY adj.]

rumpty-foo *adj.* [mid-19C] thrown together, amateurish. [echoic]

rumptyvump *n.* (*also* **rump-tee-vump**) [1980s+] (*US campus*) a course in radio-television-motion pictures. [initial letters of radio *motion* pictures and *TV*]

rumpus *n.* **1** [mid-18C–19C] an uproar, a disturbance. **2** [early–mid-19C] a masquerade. [? Gk *rombos*, a spinning top, thus a commotion or disturbance; E.P. suggests SE *rumble*, the noise of an upset stomach; (1) SE 20C+]

rump work *n.* [late 19C–1900s] sexual intercourse.

rump wrangler *n. see* RUMP RANGER n.

rumpy-pumpy *n.* (*also* **humpy-pumpy, rumty-tumty**) [1970s+] sexual intercourse. [SE *rump* + PUMP v.³ (1)/HUMP v.¹/ assonance]

rum quids *n.* (*also* **rum quidds**) (*UK Und.*) **1** [late 17C–early 19C] a large amount of stolen money, or a share thereof. **2** [late 18C–mid-19C] a 'good', i.e. not counterfeit, guinea. [RUM adj. (1) + QUIDS n.]

rum repository *n.* [late 19C–1900s] (*US*) a bar.

rum row *n.* [1920s] (*US Und.*) a bootlegger's fleet, held in international waters and thus beyond US jurisdiction. [SE, on the lines of agglomerations of similar enterprises, e.g. *Publishers' Row, Restaurant Row* etc]

rum ruff peck *n.* [late 17C–mid-19C] (*UK Und.*) Westphalia ham. [RUM adj. (1) + RUFF PECK n.; Westphalia ham was considered to be of the best quality]

rum screen *n.* [late 18C] (*UK Und.*) a banknote (cf. BANK-RAG n.). [RUM adj. (1) + SCREEN n.¹ (1)]

rum slim *n.* [late 18C–mid-19C] rum punch. [SE *rum* + var. on SAmE *sling*, a form of cocktail; ? ult. SLING n.¹]

rum snitch *n.* [late 17C–early 19C] (*UK Und.*) a hard blow on one's nose. [RUM adj. (1) + SNITCH n.¹ (1)]

rum snooze *n.* [late 18C] (*UK Und.*) a sleep induced by alcohol. [RUM adj. (1) + SNOOZE n. (1)]

rum snoozer *n.* [late 18C] (*UK Und.*) one who falls asleep in a tavern and is robbed. [RUM SNOOZE n.]

rum squeeze *n.* (*UK Und.*) **1** [late 17C–mid-19C] a good measure of drink distributed among the fiddlers at a wedding or similar event. **2** [late 18C] a crush at the theatre; its members are susceptible to pickpockets. [RUM adj. (1) + SE *squeeze*; (1) a few drops squeezed out; (2) a crush]

rum strum *n.*¹ [late 17C–early 19C] a long wig. [RUM adj. (1) + STRUM n.¹]

rum strum *n.*² [late 17C–early 19C] a pretty young strumpet. [RUM adj. (1) + STRUM n.²]

rum-sucker *n.* [mid-19C] (*US*) a heavy, habitual drinker.

rum swag *n.* [late 17C–early 19C] (*UK Und.*) a shop full of expensive goods. [RUM adj. (1) + SWAG n.¹ (1)]

rum talking *phr.* [20C+] (*W.I.*) used of one's state of drunkenness, as an excuse for talking nonsense or being rude (cf. IT'S THE BEER TALKING phr.).

rum tilter *n. see* RUM DEGEN n.

rumtitum *n.* [1900s] enthusiastic, if ultimately empty talk. [echoic of the chatter]

rumtitum *adj.* (*also* **rum-ti-tum**) [mid–late 19C] in excellent condition, usu. of a bull or a pimp; intensified as *rum ti tum with the chill off.*

rum tol *n. see* RUM DEGEN n.

rum tom pat *n.* [late 18C–mid-19C] (*UK Und.*) a clergyman. [RUM adj. (1) + TOM PAT n.¹]

rum topping *n.* [late 17C–early 19C] (*UK Und.*) a first-rate or brand-new wig. [RUM adj. (1) + SE *topping*]

rum touch *n.* [early 19C] an odd, eccentric person; a strange affair. [RUM adj. (2) + SE *touch*, with the implication of someone against whom one brushes up]

rumtowzle *n.* [late 19C] boisterousness. [? SE *tousle*]

rum twang *n.* [late 18C] (*UK Und.*) a silver stock buckle.

rumty *n.* [1980s+] (*N.Z.*) an admirable person or object. [RUMTITUM adj.]

rumty-tumty *n. see* RUMPY-PUMPY n.

rum 'un *n. see* RUM ONE n.

Rumvile *n.* (*also* **Rome-vile, Rome-ville, Rumvil, Rumvill, Rumville**) [mid-16C–mid-19C] (*UK Und.*) London. [RUM adj. (1) + -VILE sfx]

rum wiper *n.* (*also* **rum wipe**) [late 17C–19C] (*UK Und.*) a handkerchief made of silk or other high-quality material. [RUM adj. (1) + WIPER n.¹/WIPE n.³ (1)]

rumy *n.* [mid-19C] a good woman. [Rom. *romeni*, a wife, a bride]

run *n.*¹ **1** [1920s] (*UK Und.*) time spent out of prison. **2** [1990s+] (*US Und.*) the walkway that runs the length of a line of cells.

run *n.*² **1** [1950s+] amongst outlaw motorcyclists, a full-scale club outing involving all the members of a given chapter or gang and devoted to maximum excess in all possible areas of activity. **2** [1950s+] (*drugs*) the immediate and intense feeling that follows the injection of heroin into a vein; or that follows the ingestion of any drug. **3** [1960s+] (*drugs*) an extended period of drug use. **4** [1990s+] (*drugs*) a search for drugs. [fig. use of SE *run*; (2) the drug is doing the 'running']

run, the *n. see* RUNAROUND, THE n.

run *v.*¹ [mid-19C] to understand, to comprehend.

run *v.*² [mid-19C–1920s] (*Aus./US*) to harass verbally, to tease; thus *running*, teasing, scolding.

run *v.*³ [1900s–40s] (*Aus.*) to cover the expenses of. [SE *run to*, to cover, to extend sufficiently, usu. of money]

run *v.*⁴ **1** [1910s] to go out with someone, usu. a boyfriend or girlfriend, on a regular basis. **2** [1910s+] of a partner, usu. a man, to dominate and control the other partner's life. **3** [1980s+] to go around together, to play together.

run *v.*⁵ (*drugs*) **1** [1930s+] to sell drugs. **2** [1970s+] to be an habitual drug user; to inject narcotics. **3** [1990s+] to work as a drug dealer's assistant. **4** [2000s] to steal drugs.

run *v.*⁶ [1970s+] (*US Und.*) to use stolen credit cards; to pass any form of false document, e.g. a traveller's cheque. [one 'runs up' debts]

run *v.*⁷ *see* RUN IN v. (1).

run a banker *v.* [late 19C–1940s] (*Aus.*) to be intense, usu. of emotions or feelings. [SE *banker*, a river with its water level with or over-running its banks]

run a boat *v.* [1990s+] (*W.I.*) to pool resources in order to buy a meal. [the multi-person crew required to sail a boat]

runabout *n.* [1970s] (*US Black*) the facts of a situation. [var. on RUNDOWN n.]

run a buck *v.* [late 18C–early 19C] (*Anglo-Irish*) to register an invalid vote. [ety. unknown]

run a crimp *v.* [early–mid-18C] to set up a crooked horserace. [CRIMP n. (1)]

run a double train *v. see* PULL A DOUBLE TRAIN v.

run a drag on v. [1980s+] (*US Black*) to deceive, to trick, to hoax. [DRAG v.[8] (2)]

run (a) game on v. [1960s+] (*US Black*) to bamboozle, to deceive, to seduce, to confuse, to obtain money by trickery. [GAME n.[2] (3)]

run a hooligan on v. [1920s] (*US*) to play tricks on, to defraud.

run a line v. see SHOOT A LINE v.

run a make v. [1970s+] (*US police*) to identify a suspect. [MAKE n.[4]]

run a railroad v. [1970s] (*drugs*) to be addicted to narcotics. [RAILROAD TRACKS n.]

runaround n.[1] (*also* **run-round**) [mid-19C–1910s] (*US*) a suppurative inflammatory sore or swelling in a finger or thumb.

runaround n.[2] [1900s–40s] (*US prison*) an area of confinement that is outside the cells proper.

runaround n.[3] [1950s+] (*orig. US*) a short trip, an excursion.

runaround, the n. (*also* **the run**) [1910s+] (*orig. US*) to deceive, to delay, to put off, to avoid – all such efforts usu. in order to give oneself some form of advantage, breathing space etc; usu. as *give someone the runaround*.

run around v. (*orig. US*) **1** [late 19C–1970s] to have a relationship; also a friendship. **2** [1920s+] to carry on sexual affairs, deceiving one's primary partner.

run around in circles v. see GO AROUND IN CIRCLES v.

run around like a blue-arsed fly v. see BUZZ AROUND LIKE A BLUE-ARSED FLY v.

run around like a cut cat v. [1950s+] (*Aus.*) to be very angry; thus comparative *meaner than a cut cat*. [SE *cut*, castrated]

run a saw on v. [mid–late 19C] (*US/Aus.*) to deceive, to hoax. [obs. SE *saw*, a tale]

run a skirt v. [20C+] to keep a mistress. [SKIRT n. (1)]

run a temperature v. [1990s+] (*US*) to be wanted, usu. by the police. [i.e. one is HOT adj.[2] (3)]

run a tight ship v. [1960s+] to keep full control of a situation, to be an efficient organizer or leader; thus antithetical *run a loose ship*. [naut. imagery]

run a train v. see PULL A TRAIN v. (1).

run at the jaw v. see RUN OFF AT THE MOUTH v.

run bag v. [1950s] to work as a go-between, esp. to collect or administer money obtained by various criminal activities. [BAG n.[2] (3)]

run belly v. [1990s+] (*W.I.*) to cause diarrhoea.

runcible adj. [1920s–30s] of women, sexually attractive. [play on Edward Lear's nonsense word, coined in 1871 to describe a spoon with 3 broad prongs, thus ? pun on SPOON v.[1]]

run circles (a)round v. see RUN RINGS (A)ROUND v.

rundown n. [1910s+] (*orig. US*) an explanation, a summary, a brief list of the most important facts or points on which to act. [ety. unknown]

run down v.[1] **1** [mid-18C+] to denigrate someone, to slander someone. **2** [1940s+] to rehearse, to practise, to explain.

run down v.[2] [1940s] (*W.I.*) to seduce someone, to persuade them to become one's lover.

run down game v. [1960s+] (*US Black*) of a pimp, to explain the principles of the pimping business, both from experienced pimps to novices and from the pimp to his prostitutes, telling them the tricks of their trade. [RUN DOWN v.[1] (2) + GAME n.[2] (3)]

run down some lines v. [1980s+] (*US Black*) **1** to make conversation. **2** to attempt seduction by smooth talking. [RUN DOWN v.[1] (2) + LINE n.[1] (3)]

rundum n. see RUM-DUM n.

rung adj. [1950s+] of cars, supplied with false plates, documents etc for use in a robbery. [RING v.[1] (11)]

run game on v. see RUN (A) GAME ON v.

run goods n. [late 18C–early 19C] a woman's virginity. [SE *run*, to smuggle; smuggled goods 'have never been entered' (in the customs' ledger)]

run home on one's ear phr. [late 19C] (*US*) utterly crushed, comprehensively defeated.

run hot v. **1** [1980s+] (*Aus. prison*) to do something illegally with a chance of being found out. **2** [1980s+] (*Aus. prison*) to have a run of good luck, e.g. in gambling. **3** [1990s+] (*W.I.*) to be wanted, whether by fans or the police. **4** [1990s+] (*W.I.*) to have prolonged intercourse. [SE *hot*/HOT adj.[2]]

run-in n.[1] [late 19C+] an argument, a controversy, a fight.

run-in n.[2] [1920s] (*US tramp*) of a beggar, obtaining a free meal from someone whom one solicits for a donation.

run-in n.[3] [1950s–60s] a place to which stolen goods are delivered and where they are subseq. hidden.

run in v. **1** [mid-19C+] (*also* **run**) to arrest, to run in to prison, to report to the police, to set aside for punishment; also in fig., non-criminal use. **2** [1910s] to report on, to inform against, to betray.

run into money v. [late 19C+] (*orig. US*) to amount to a considerable sum, to cost a considerable amount.

run into the ground v. [mid-19C+] to persist in an action or in speech to the extent that all meaning and importance is lost. [orig. cowboy use; the image of riding a horse (or driving a car) until it collapses]

run it down v. (*also* **run it to**) [1950s+] (*mainly US Black*) to explain, to point out facts. [ext. of RUN DOWN v.[1] (2)]

run it out v. [1920s] (*US campus*) to behave in a socially unacceptable manner, esp. when acting 'above one's station' as stated by the larger group.

run it to v. see RUN IT DOWN v.

run like a hairy goat v. (*Aus./N.Z.*) **1** [1940s+] of a racehorse, to run very badly; occas. to run fast. **2** [1960s+] of a motor vehicle, to run badly.

run mouth n. [20C+] (*W.I., Gren.*) a gossip, a rumour-monger.

runner n.[1] **1** [late 17C–18C] (*UK Und.*) a sneak-thief, esp. one who specializes in entering houses and taking furs, cloaks and coats. **2** [mid-18C] an employee of a casino who keeps track of police activity. **3** [mid-18C; 1920s+] (*US Und.*) someone engaged in conveying prohibited goods (such as drugs, liquor), or illegal immigrants, secretly; spec. a drug dealer's assistant, who ferries drugs from seller to buyer. **4** [early 19C+] (*US Und.*) an employee of a dancehall or gambling house whose task was to entice passers-by into the establishment; some worked from hotel lobbies, where they paid the clerk a fee to introduce them to wealthy or gullible tourists. **5** [late 19C] (*UK Und.*) a dog-stealer. **6** [1910s] (*US*) a commercial traveller. **7** [1930s+] a bookmaker's clerk or assistant. **8** [1940s+] (*US*) in numbers gambling, one who picks up bets and takes the money to the central operator(s). **9** [1950s] (*US drugs*) one who recruits new customers for a narcotics dealer.

runner n.[2] **1** [1930s] (*US*) a soda to take away. **2** [1970s+] an escape from the police whether before or after capture; always as DO A RUNNER v. **3** [1970s+] someone who is on the run from the police. **4** [1980s+] (*Aus. prison*) an escapee.

runner and rider n. [20C+] cider. [rhy. sl.]

runners n. **1** [1920s] (*US Und.*) a foot. **2** [1930s+] (*Aus./Can./Irish*) track shoes, training shoes.

running at the ring n. [late 16C–17C] (adulterous) sexual intercourse. [SE *run at the ring*, to compete for a circlet of metal suspended from a post which each of a number of riders endeavoured to carry off on the point of his lance]

running bawd n. [mid-17C] a prostitute (or one who sets up a client with a prostitute) who uses an establishment, such as a tavern, which provides rooms to be used on a freelance basis for prostitution.

running belly n. [1990s+] (*W.I.*) diarrhoea.

running buddy n. see RUNNING PARTNER n.

running for Sweeney phr. [1900s] (*US*) running away from something threatening or dangerous. [? the idea of running for help from a stereotypically Irish policeman, i.e. 'Sweeney']

running glazier *n.* [late 18C] (*UK Und.*) a criminal who poses as a window cleaner/mender so as to find empty houses that can be robbed.

running horse *n.* (*also* **running nag**) [mid-17C–early 19C] a venereal discharge. [SE *running*, oozing + HORSE-POX n./NAG n.[1] (2); note HORSE n.[12]]

running partner *n.* (*also* **running buddy/mate**) [20C+] (*US*) a close friend with whom one pursues most of one's daily activities.

running patterer *n.* (*also* **running stationer**) [late 17C–19C] a street-hawker of books, pamphlets, ballads and similar printed material. [SE *running* + PATTERER n. (2)/SE *stationer*]

running range *n.* [1920s–50s] (*US Black*) the discharge from the penis or vagina that accompanies gonorrhoea. [? SE *running* + Fr. *reins*, kidneys]

running rumbler *n.* [late 18C] (*UK Und.*) one of a team of pickpockets who rolls a large grindstone down the street; when pedestrians move out of his way, the attendant pickpockets rob them.

runnings *n.* [1980s+] (*UK Black*) **1** what is going on, the situation, 'the score', a plan. **2** business.

running smoble *n.* (*also* **running smabble/smobble**) [18C–early 19C] (*UK Und.*) a shop-thief. [SNABBLE v. (1)]

running snavel *n.* [late 18C] (*UK Und.*) one who robs children on their way to school. [SNAFFLE v. (2)]

running stationer *n. see* RUNNING PATTERER n.

running with *adj.* [1930s+] (*orig. US Black*) allied to, in partnership with, on the same side as.

run-off *n.* **1** [1910s] (*US*) diarrhoea. **2** [1930s+] urination. [SE *run off*, of liquid, to let flow away]

run off *v.*[1] [mid-19C+] (*US*) to talk excessively, to talk rubbish. [SE *run off*, of water, to flow away]

run off *v.*[2] [1970s] to masturbate (cf. BALL OFF v.[2]). [SE *run off*, of liquid, to let flow away]

run off at the mouth *v.* (*also* **run off at the chin, ...jaw, ...jibs, ...head, run at the jaws**) [20C+] (*orig. US*) to talk to excess and to the irritation of one's audience. [RUN OFF v.[1] + SE *mouth/chin/jaw*/JIB n.[1] (4)/*head*]

run off of *v.* [1970s+] (*US Black*) to be sustained by something, esp. a drug. [SE *run*, to function]

run off one's mouth *v.* [1940s+] (*US*) to be annoyed, to talk angrily.

run off the straight *v.* [late 19C] to abandon a respectable life for criminality. [i.e. the 'straight and narrow']

run of one's Dover *phr.* [late 19C] (*Aus.*) board and lodging. [DOVER n.; development of orig. mid-19C phr. *run of one's knife*]

run on *adj.* [1960s] (*US Und.*) arrested.

run on dim lights *v.* [1960s] (*US*) to be unintelligent.

run one's ass off *v.* [1960s] to move at high speed, esp. in the context of searching.

run one's chops out *v.* [1960s+] (*US Black*) to talk, to complain. [CHOPS n.[1] (1)]

run one's face (for) *v.* (*also* **go on one's face, run one's shape for**) [mid-19C+] (*orig. US*) to obtain credit. [SE *run*, to enter into a race, i.e. to bet one's *face* or *shape*, i.e. body, as the agent of obtaining credit]

run one's gibs *v. see* RUN ONE'S JIBS v.

run one's gums *v. see* BUMP (ONE'S) GUMS v.

run one's hand up the flagpole *v.* [1990s+] to masturbate (cf. AUDITION THE FINGER PUPPETS v.). [ironic use of SE]

run one's head *v.* [1970s+] (*US*) to talk at length or out of turn; thus *head-running*, talking to excess. [HEAD n.[4] + var. on RUN ONE'S MOUTH v.]

run one's jibs *v.* (*also* **jaw at the jibs, run one's gibs/jaws**) [1960s+] to chatter aimlessly. [RUN OFF v.[1]/JAW v.[1] (1) + JIB n.[1] (4)]

run one's mouth *v.* (*also* **fly one's mouth**) [1930s+] (*orig. US/W.I.*) **1** to gossip, to tell tales. **2** to give advice. **3** to talk without

restraint. **4** as *run up one's mouth*, to brag, to boast, to fantasize. [one's *mouth runs* like an engine]

run one's rig upon *v.* [late 18C–mid-19C] to ridicule. [RIG n.[2] (1)]

run one's shape for *v. see* RUN ONE'S FACE (FOR) v.

run one way and look another *v.* [1970s+] (*US Black*) to act in a duplicitous manner, to cheat deliberately.

run on pattens *v.* [mid-16C–early 17C] to talk very fast and volubly. [the click-clack noise of wooden pattens]

run on tick *v.* [mid-17C–early 18C] to set up a line of credit, to get into debt. [TICK n.[3] (1)]

run-out *n.*[1] **1** [mid-19C] (*UK Und.*) a pickpocketing expedition. **2** [1950s] an escape, an evasion.

run-out *n.*[2] [1910s–30s] (*UK Und.*) a mock auction of cheap goods.

run out of gas *v.* [1920s+] (*US*) to lose impetus, to weary, to fail.

run out of road *v.* [1960s+] of a motorcar or its driver, to fail to negotiate a curve properly and to skid off the road rather than turn the corner; thus also in fig. use.

run out of steam *v.* [1920s+] to lose energy and impetus, to tire.

run out on *v.* **1** [late 19C–1910s] to embellish a story. **2** [20C+] to leave suddenly. **3** [1910s] in fig. use of (4), to negate, to set aside. **4** [1910s+] to desert, to abandon. **5** [1950s] to betray.

run over *v.* [mid-19C+] to treat contemptuously, to victimize; to defeat.

run over shoes, be *v.* [late 16C–early 17C] to be in serious debt, to get oneself into serious debt. [i.e. the poor state of repair of one's shoes]

run rings (a)round *v.* (*also* **make rings (a)round, run circles (a)round**) [late 19C+] (*orig. Aus.*) to defeat comprehensively, to make someone look foolish.

run-round *n. see* RUNAROUND n.[1].

run rusty *v.* [mid-19C] to misbehave, to act counter to discipline.

runs, the *n.* [1930s+] diarrhoea. [the diarrhoea runs from one's body; or one runs to the lavatory]

run scared *v.* [20C+] (*orig. US*) to show signs of fear and panic, to flee.

run sets on *v.* (*also* **roll/throw sets on**) [1970s+] (*US Black*) to hit with combination left and right punches. [a *set* of punches]

run sly *v.* [late 18C] to escape or evade.

run someone ragged *v.* [1920s+] (*orig. US*) **1** to exhaust or wear out someone or something. **2** to beat.

run someone's tags *v.* [2000s] (*US prison*) to discover information about a fellow inmate. [one reads their notional *dogtags*]

run someone through the mill *v. see* PUT SOMEONE THROUGH THE MILL v.

run some water through one's pipe *v.* [1970s] (*US*) to urinate (cf. PAY ONE'S WATER BILL v.).

run straight *v.* **1** [late 19C] (*UK society*) of a woman, to remain faithful to one's husband. **2** [1900s] (*UK Und.*) of a criminal, to lead a law-abiding life. [horseracing imagery + STRAIGHT adj.[1] (3)/STRAIGHT adj.[1] (5)]

runt *n.* [early 17C+] a short person, thus a contemptible person. [weak use of SE *runt*, the smallest of a litter]

run taper *v.* [mid–late 19C] of money, to run short. [SE *run* + *taper*, to grow thinner]

run the block *v. see* DO THE BLOCK v. (1).

run the cutter *v.* [late 19C–1940s] (*Aus./N.Z.*) to buy beer in bulk, to be brought home and drunk there. [Scot. *cutter*, a small whisky bottle, but note phr. *run the cutter*, to smuggle liquor ashore, avoiding the customs' cutter]

run the gears *v.* [1990s+] (*US prison*) to eviscerate.

run the rabbit *v.* [1910s–50s] (*Aus.*) **1** to bring home liquor from a public house; thus *rabbit-runner*, one who carries out this errand. **2** to obtain liquor illegally. [RABBIT n.[7]]

run the rig on *v. see* RIG n.[2] (2).

run the rule over v. 1 [mid-19C–1900s] of a pickpocket, to check all a person's pockets. 2 [late 19C–1910s] to search. 3 [1900s–10s] to give someone a medical examination; thus in fig. use, to subject to any form of examination. 4 [1940s+] of police, to interrogate a suspect.

run the show v. [20C+] to take charge, to direct operations or activities.

run the street(s) v. [1930s+] (US Black) to spend one's time in self-indulgence, partying, drinking and enjoying the freedoms of a non-domestic life.

run through v. [late 19C–1920s] to rob someone, to defraud. [one 'runs through' their pockets]

run to v. 1 [mid-19C] to understand. 2 [late 19C] to be able to afford, usu. in negative. [(2) is SE 20C+]

run up a score v. [mid-17C; mid-19C] to buy on credit, esp. at a public house. [? the old scoring of one's debts on some form of tally]

run up on v. 1 [1940s+] (US) to meet (a person). 2 [1970s] (US) in fig. use, to encounter (an idea, a situation). 3 [1990s+] (US Black) to challenge, to attack physically.

run up side o' one's head v. [1950s+] (US Black) to beat up.

run up the walls v. see CLIMB UP THE WALLS v.

run with v. [mid-19C+] (orig. US Black) to associate with, to be friends with.

run with the big dogs v. [1980s+] (US campus) to do anything anyone else can.

rupert n.[1] [1910s+] (orig. milit.) a generic name for any young male aristocrat. [the stereotypical 'classiness' of the name]

rupert n.[2] [1960s–70s] the penis.

Rupert Bears n. [1980s+] (business) shares. [rhy. sl.; ult. the children's cartoon strip Rupert Bear (launched in the Daily Express in 1920)]

rupperty n. see RUBBEDY n.

ruption n. [1990s+] (W.I.) a disturbance. [SE eruption]

rupture a gut v. see BUST A GUT v.

ruptured duck n. [1940s+] (US milit.) the lapel pin or pocket insignia worn by an honourably discharged US serviceman; thus the honourable discharge itself. [orig. USAF jargon for a damaged aircraft; the 'ruptured' presumably indicates the fact that one wing of the eagle is underneath and extends beyond the circular design of the button]

rush n.[1] 1 [late 18C–early 19C] (UK Und.) robbery with violence; as the rush, usu. of a single item, e.g. a cloak hanging outside a shop; as a rush, an assault by a number of men on a house with the intent of robbing the owners of their money and valuables. 2 [mid-19C–1900s] (US campus) a perfect recitation. 3 [mid-19C–1910s] (US campus) a mass confrontation, groups of students massed against each other. 4 [mid-19C–1920s] a swindle. 5 [mid-19C+] (Aus./US) a stampede. 6 [1930s] a winning streak. [RUSH v.[1]]

rush n.[2] [20C+] the lavishing of attention on someone, usu. a woman, in the hope of gaining their affections; thus put on the rush, to attempt to impress.

rush n.[3] (drugs) 1 [1950s+] the immediate effect of any drug. 2 [1960s+] the immediate and intense feeling that follows the injection of heroin into a vein. 3 [1960s+] a rush of adrenaline. 4 [1970s+] amyl or isobutyl nitrite, which produces an instant effect (cf. AIMIES n.).

rush n.[4] see BUM'S RUSH n.

rush adj. [late 19C+] (US campus) describing objects, people or activities that are to do with paying court to a student with the hope of having them join a fraternity, e.g. rush party. [RUSH v.[1] (6)]

rush v.[1] 1 [late 18C–early 19C] (UK Und.) to rob; 'A number of villains assemble at the door of a house, and as soon as opened rush in, bind the family, and plunder the house' (Gentleman's Magazine LV 1785). 2 [mid-19C+] (Aus./US) to

stampede. 3 [late 19C] to court, to make advances towards. 4 [late 19C+] (US campus/W.I.) to make a pass at, to court, to make sexual advances towards. 5 [late 19C+] to cheat, to overcharge, the victim is not given time to think. 6 [late 19C+] (US campus) to pay court to a student with the hope of having them join a fraternity; also in fig. use. 7 [late 19C+] (US campus) to confront, esp. groups of students against each other. 8 [late 19C+] (US Black) to jump on someone, to beat someone up. 9 [20C+] to show intense interest in something or someone. 10 [1900s–30s] to charge, to obtain from someone. 11 [1910s] (Aus.) to eat. 12 [1980s+] (US campus) to gang up on a particular person.

rush v.[2] [mid–late 19C] (US campus) to make a perfect recitation.

rush v.[3] [1960s+] 1 (drugs) of a drug, to take effect, to work on the user. 2 of a person, to experience the immediate effects of a drug, esp. heroin or cocaine. [RUSH n.[3] (1)]

rush a beat v. [1950s] (US Black) to get very excited.

rush act, the n. 1 [20C+] (US) the seduction of a woman. 2 [1920s] an attempt to befriend somebody. 3 [1940s] (US Und.) fast working by a pickpocket in a crowd. 4 [1980s] (UK Und.) impersonating the police in order to extort bribes from fellow criminals. [RUSH v.[1]]

rush around in circles v. see GO AROUND IN CIRCLES v.

rush buckler n. [mid-16C] a thug, a bully. [SE rush, to force violently + buckler, a shield]

rusher n.[1] [late 18C–early 19C] 1 a thief, as in 'Thieves who knock at the doors of great houses in London, in summer time, when the families are gone out of town, and on the door being opened by a woman, rush in and rob the house' (Grose, 1785). 2 a housebreaker who specializes in breaking into secluded houses. [RUSH v.[1] (1)]

rusher n.[2] [mid-19C–1900s] (US) a 'go-ahead', fashionable person. [ext. use of SE]

rushing business n. [late 19C] (UK Und.) robbery through confidence tricks and hoaxes. [RUSH v.[1] (5)]

rushlight n.[1] [mid-18C] a fiery drink. [SE rushlight which 'blazes up']

rushlight n.[2] [late 19C] a very thin person. [SE rushlight, something insignificant or of little account; a glimmer]

rush the growler v. (also **rush the can/duck, work the growler**) [late 19C+] (US) to buy beer from a tavern and bring it home to drink. [16C SE rush, to carry rapidly + GROWLER n.[3] (2)/SE can/DUCK n.[6]]

rush the kip v. [1900s–10s] (N.Z.) to make a precipitate, over-hasty decision. [SE rush + kip, the small flat piece of wood used to toss the pennies into the air, in the game of two-up]

Rusky n. see RUSSKI n.

Russell Harty n. [2000s+] a party. [rhy. sl.; ult. TV personality Russell Harty (1934–88)]

russia n. [late 19C] (UK Und.) a pocketbook. [made of Russia leather, a durable leather often used in bookbinding]

Russian n.[1] (also **Rooshian, Roosian**) [early 19C+] (Aus.) a wild horse, wild cattle. [? pun on rush around]

Russian n.[2] [1930s–50s] (US Black) a newly arrived Southern Black who has moved to the North. [pun on rush-in; many Blacks moved north during WW2 to work in war-related manufacturing industries]

Russian n.[3] [1940s+] (S.Afr.) 1 any of the gangs from the south townships in South Soto known for their violence and terror from 1940s. 2 any south Sotans. [negative image of Russia during the Cold War]

Russian n.[4] [1980s] (US) intercrural intercourse whereby the man rubs his penis between his partner's thighs but does not enter the vagina.

Russian coffeehouse n. [late 18C–early 19C] the Brown Bear public house in Bow Street, Covent Garden, a popular haunt for both thieves and thief-takers. [the bear is a 'Russian' animal]

Russian duck *n*. **1** [1910s–20s] dirt. **2** [1970s] sexual intercourse. [rhy. sl.; (1) = SE *muck*; (2) = FUCK *n*.¹ (1)]

Russian high *n*. [1950s–60s] (*gay*) simultaneous fellatio and anal intercourse. [? assumptions of Russian sexual preferences]

Russian law *n*. [mid-17C] a punishment of 100 blows on the shins. [a trad. Russian punishment]

Russian salad party *n*. [1950s–70s] (*gay*) an orgy in which all participants are covered in baby oil. [SE *Russian salad*, a mix of chopped or shredded vegetables and mayonnaise]

Russian Turk *n*. [late 19C] work. [rhy. sl.]

Russki *n*. (*also* **Rooskie, Rusky**) [1910s+] a derog. term for a Russian. [abbr. + -SKI sfx; orig. WW1 milit.]

rust *n*. **1** [mid-19C] money. **2** [late 19C] old metal.

rust *v*. [late 19C–1920s] to collect and sell old metal.

rust bowl *n*. (*also* **rust belt**) [1980s+] (*US*) the declining industrial areas, esp. of the Midwest.

rust bucket *n*. **1** [1940s+] (*US*) a rusty old ship. **2** [1960s+] (*Aus./N.Z./US*) a car that is noticeably and dangerously rusty. **3** [1990s+] an old plane.

rust eater *n*. [1920s–30s] (*US tramp*) a construction worker.

rusted in *adj*. [late 19C] (*US*) settled down.

rustiness *n*. [mid-19C–1900s] irritability, bad temper.

rustle *n*.¹ [late 19C–1920s] (*US*) bustle, hustle; thus *get a rustle on*, to hurry up. [RUSTLE *v*.]

rustle *n*.² [1940s] (*US Black*) an orphan, esp. one whose parents are unknown. [SE *rustle*, to act quickly, to hurry about; such a child is the product of a quick, brief relationship]

rustle *n*.³ [2000s] (*US prison*) a riot or lesser disturbance.

rustle *v*. [mid-19C+] (*US*) to rush around, to bustle about; thus ext. as *rustle one's bustle*.

rustler *n*. **1** [mid-19C–1900s] (*US*) a busy, active person. **2** [late 19C] (*Aus./US*) one who enjoys a good time. **3** [2000s] (*US prison*) a sexual predator. [RUSTLE *v*.; a *rustler* of cattle is SAmE]

rustle up *v*. (*also* **rustle, rustle out**) [mid-19C+] (*orig. US*) to obtain or (of food) put together very quickly and without prior preparation. [RUSTLE *v*.]

rustling *n*. [late 19C–1900s] (*US*) energetic, bustling activity. [RUSTLE *v*.]

rustling *adj*. [late 19C–1900s] (*US*) bustling, energetic, active. [RUSTLE *v*.]

rusty *n*.¹ [mid-19C] **1** an informer. **2** a fight, a skirmish. [? CUT UP RUSTY *v*.]

rusty *n*.² [20C+] a nickname for anyone with red or auburn hair. [the colour]

rusty *adj*.¹ [17C; 20C+] (*Aus.*) lecherous, amorous. [? Somerset dial. *rusty*, gross, obscene]

rusty *adj*.² **1** [17C–1920s] ill-tempered. **2** [1960s+] anti-social. [one who lacks the 'polish' to make a successful path in the world]

rusty bullet wound *n*. (*also* **rusty sheriff's badge**) [1990s+] the anus. [supposed resemblance]

rusty-dusty *n*. [1930s+] (*US*) the buttocks, esp. with the implica-tion that someone has been sitting around doing nothing; thus they are *rusty* and *dusty* from lack of movement.

rusty gun *n*. **1** [1960s+] (*US*) a veteran policeman (cf. BADGE *n*.²). **2** [2000s] (*UK Und.*) an armed robber who has retired from his profession. [his weapon has rusted in its holster]

rustyguts *n*. [late 17C–early 19C; 1930s–50s] a surly, unpleasant old man. [SE *rustic*, countrified, rough, boorish + -GUTS sfx]

rusty sheriff's badge *n*. *see* RUSTY BULLET WOUND *n*.

rusty water *n*. [1990s+] diarrhoea.

rutabaga *n*. **1** [1920s] a poor (Southern) peasant. **2** [1930s+] an ugly woman. **3** [1950s] (*US*) a dollar. [SAmE *rutabaga* = SE *swede*]

rutat *n*. *see* RUTTAT *n*.

Ruth Buzzy *n*. [1960s–70s] (*US Black*) a plain-looking woman. [proper name *Ruth Buzzi* (b.1936), the actress best known for her work on *Rowan & Martin's Laugh-In* (1967–73)]

ruthers *n*. *see* DRUTHERS *n*.

ruttat *n*. (*also* **rattat, rutat**) [mid–late 19C] a potato. [backsl. = TATER *n*. (1)]

ruttat pusher *n*. [late 19C] the owner of a potato-cart. [RUTTAT *n*. + SE *pusher*]

rutter *n*. [late 16C–early 17C] (*UK Und.*) one of a team of 4 swindlers operating the BARNARD'S LAW *n*.; the *rutter's* task was to stand at the door and keep watch. [? SE *router*, a lawless person, a robber, a ruffian]

Ruud Gullit *n*. [2000s] a bullet. [rhy. sl.; ult. the Dutch football player and manager *Ruud Gullit* (b.1962)]

r.w.v. *n*. [1940s+] (*UK Und.*) robbery with violence. [abbr.]

RX *n*. [1950s+] (*US drugs*) a prescription. [the ? notation placed on prescriptions, meaning *recipe*, i.e. of the medical preparation]

ryache *n*. [mid-19C+] a chair. [backsl.]

Ryan Giggs *n*. [1990s+] lodgings. [rhy. sl. = DIGS *n*.¹; ult. Manchester United and Wales footballer *Ryan Giggs* (b.1973)]

rybeck *n*. [mid-19C] a share. [? Yid.]

rybuck *see under* RYEBUCK.

ryder *n*. [late 18C–mid-19C] a cloak. [? Rom. *ruder*, to clothe]

rydim *n*. [1940s] (*W.I.*) the buttocks. [SE *rhythm*, i.e. that of the moving buttocks]

ryebuck *n*. (*also* **ribuck, rybuck**) [mid-19C+] (*Aus.*) something good, worthwhile, the 'real thing'. [RYEBUCK *adj*.]

ryebuck *adj*. (*also* **ribuck, rybuck**) [mid-19C–1960s] (*orig. UK Und.*) good, excellent, first-rate. [ety. unknown; ? Ger. *Reibach*, var. of *rebbach*, profit, ult. synon. Yid./Heb. *revach*]

ryebuck! *excl*. (*also* **ribuck! rybuck!**) [mid-19C–1960s] (*Aus.*) a general expression of agreement or approval. [RYEBUCK *adj*.]

rye mush *n*. [1930s] a gentleman; thus *rye mort*, a lady. [Rom. *rei*, a gentleman + MUSH *n*.⁵ (2)/MORT *n*.]

rygin *adj*. (*also* **rhygin**) [1940s+] (*W.I.*) **1** angry. **2** vigorous, lively, spirited. **3** first-class, extremely able. [SE *rage* + RAG *v*.¹; the *locus classicus* is the eponymous *Rygin*, the name adopted by the hero of the film *The Harder They Come* (1972)]

ryno *n*. *see* RHINO *n*.¹.

S

's *abbr.*[1] (*also* **'z**) [16C–18C] an abbr. of 'God's', as found in a number of oaths.

's *abbr.*[2] [1930s+] an abbr. of 'does', e.g. *what's he know?* [abbr.]

s.a. *n.* [1920s–50s] sex appeal. [abbr.]

saali *adj.* [1940s+] (*W.I.*) attractive, well-dressed. [SE *salty*]

s.a.b. *n.* [1980s+] (*US campus*) a social airhead *bitch.* [abbr.]

sab *n.* [1950s] (*W.I.*) a haircut in which the back of the hair is rounded rather than tapered. [the film star *Sabu* (Dastagir) (1924–63), 'the Elephant Boy', whose hair was thus cut]

sabana *n.* [1990s+] (*US prison/Hisp.*) a White person. [Sp.]

Sabba-day *n.* (*also* **Sabber-day**) [late 18C–mid-19C] (*US*) Sunday. [abbr. SE *Sabbath*-day]

sabbe/sabby *n. see* SAVVY *n.*

Sabé *n.* [late 19C–1900s] (*US*) an immigrant of French origin. [SAVVY *v.*]

sabe *see under* SAVVY.

sable maria *n.* [late 19C–1910s] a police or prison van. [SE *sable*, black, i.e. var. on BLACK MARIA *n.*[1] (1)]

s.a.b.u. *n.* (*also* **n.a.b.u.**, **t.a.b.u.**) [1940s] (*orig. US milit.*) a complete disaster (cf. S.N.A.F.U. *n.*). [abbr. self-*adjusting balls–up* or *non-adjusting balls–up* or *typical army balls–up*; ult. BALLS-UP *n.*]

Sac *n.* [1930s–60s] (*US tramp/Und.*) *Sac*ramento, California. [abbr.]

sac *n. see* ZAC *n.*

sach *n.*[1] *see* SATCH *n.*[2].

sach *n.*[2] *see* STASH *n.*[2] (4).

sachem *n.* [19C+] (*US*) a political leader, spec. one of the leaders of New York's Tammany Society. [Algonquian *sachem*, a supreme chief]

sacherea *n.* [2000s] (*US Black*) the state of being outrageously homosexual. [SASHAY *v.* (3)]

sacht *n. see* SATCH *n.*[2].

sack *n.*[1] **1** [late 17C–early 18C] the vagina (cf. BAG *n.*[1]). **2** [late 17C–mid-19C] a pocket; thus *sack-diver*, a pickpocket. **3** [late 19C+] scrotum; often in combs., e.g. NUTSACK *n.* **4** [2000s] (*US Black*) attractive female buttocks.

sack *n.*[2] **1** [1910s+] (*US prison*) a sack of tobacco, used as prison 'currency'. **2** [1980s+] (*drugs*) heroin. **3** [1990s+] a bag of drugs, usu. marijuana or crack cocaine. [the packet in which it is sold]

sack *n.*[3] **1** [1920s+] a bed; thus *sack time*, the time one spends in bed. **2** [1980s] (*US Black*) one's home. [naut. use *sack*, a hammock]

sack *n.*[4] **1** [1950s] (*US*) a pitiable, downtrodden person. **2** [1960s] (*US campus*) an unattractive woman. **3** [1980s+] (*US Black/campus*) a second-rate athlete. [? SAD SACK OF SHIT *n.*]

sack *n.*[5] [1960s+] (*US Black*) an overcoat, a jacket. [mid-19C SE *sack*, a loose-fitting coat]

sack, the *n.* **1** [early 19C+] (*also* **the bag**) dismissal from one's job; usu. as GET THE SACK *v.* or GIVE SOMEONE THE SACK *v.* **2** [mid-19C] expulsion from school. [one is given one's possessions, lit.or fig., in a *sack*; current in Fr. f. 17C: '*On luy a donné son sac*, hee hath his pasport giuen him (said of a seruant whom his master

hath put away)' (Cotgrave, *Dict. French and English Tongues*, 1611). Note Du. *iemand den zak geven*, to give someone the sack (already in MDu.), *den zak krijgen*, to get the sack]

sack *v.*[1] **1** [late 18C+] to rob, to steal, to take possession of, to pocket. **2** [19C] to put in one's pocket. **3** [1940s] (*US Und.*) to sort out, to arrange; thus *sacked*, 'in the bag'. [SACK *n.*[1] (2)]

sack *v.*[2] **1** [mid-19C+] to dismiss someone from a job. **2** [mid-19C+] to reject or dismiss something or someone. **3** [mid-19C+] to expel from school or university. **4** [1970s+] to end a relationship, esp. in an abrupt, brutal manner. **5** [1980s] (*US campus*) to humiliate someone. **6** [1980s+] (*Aus. prison*) to ostracize. [SACK, THE *n.*]

sack *v.*[3] [1930s–50s] (*US Und.*) to tie someone up with the cord round their limbs and throat; they are then placed in a sack and when they struggle to get free they will asphyxiate themselves.

sack artist *n.* [1940s+] (*US*) a chronic idler. [SACK *n.*[3] (1) + ARTIST sfx; note RMC Duntroon (Aus.) *rack artist*, 'a cadet with a reputation for sleeping excessively']

sack-chaser *n.* [1990s+] (*US Black*) a woman (but not a prostitute) who pursues men, bartering her sexual favours for his financial status. [SACK *n.*[1] (2), as a wallet + SE *chaser*]

sack down *v.* [1940s+] to go to bed, to sleep. [SACK *n.*[3] (1)]

sack drill *n.* [1940s–50s] (*orig. US milit.*) sleep, time spent in bed. [SACK *n.*[3] (1) + SE *drill*]

sack duty *n.* [1940s+] (*orig. US milit.*) sleep, time spent in bed. [SACK *n.*[3] (1) + SE *duty*]

sacked out *adj.* [1940s+] fast asleep. [SACK OUT *v.*]

sack 'em up man *n.* [mid-19C] a resurrectionist or grave-robber. [the corpse is placed in a *sack* before its delivery to a hospital]

sack in *v.* [1940s+] (*US*) to go to bed, to sleep. [SACK *n.*[3] (1)]

sacking *n.*[1] [late 16C–early 17C] working as a prostitute. [SACKING LAW *n.*]

sacking *n.*[2] [1930s] a method of killing a person using a sack. [SACK *v.*[3]]

sacking law *n.* [16C–early 17C] (*UK Und.*) the occupation of a prostitute. [SE *sack*, to plunder, to lay waste + LAW *n.*[1]; the object of such 'sacking' is the client; or OE *sæccing*, a bed]

sack it up *v.* [1970s–80s] (*US Black*) to terminate, to bring to a conclusion. [SE *sack*]

sack lunch *n.* [1960s+] cunnilingus (cf. BOX LUNCH *n.*). [SACK *n.*[1] (1) + LUNCH *n.*[3] (1)]

sack mouth *n.* [1980s+] (*US Black*) a chatterer, a gossip. [joc. resemblance to an open, spilling *sack*]

sack mouth *v.* [1980s] (*US Black*) to talk nonsense, to talk for the sake of it. [SACK MOUTH *n.*]

sack of shit *n. see* BAG OF SHIT *n.*

sack o' nuts *n.* [1970s+] (*US Black*) the scrotum (cf. BALL-BAG *n.*). [SE *sack*/SACK *n.*[1] (3) + NUTS *n.*[2] (1)]

sack out *v.* [1940s+] to fall asleep, to go to bed. [SACK *n.*[3] (1)]

sack rat *n.* [1940s+] (*US*) a chronic idler. [SACK *n.*[3] (1) + RAT sfx]

sacks of rice *n.* [1990s+] mice. [rhy. sl.]

sack time *n.* [1940s+] (*orig. US milit.*) time spent in bed, time to go to bed. [SACK n.³ (1) + SE *time*]

sack up *v.*¹ [1920s+] (*US*) to go to bed. [SACK n.³ (1)]

sack up *v.*² [2000s] (*drugs*) to divide up and place bulk drugs into separate bags prior to sale.

sack up *v.*³ [1990s+] (*US campus*) to survive a challenging situation. [? one puts one's head in a *sack*]

sackwah *n.* [1970s] (*UK Black*) anywhere that drinking, generally illicit, takes place. [ety. unknown; ? Fr. *ce quoi*, that which, thus a euph.]

sacrament *n.* [1960s–70s] (*drugs*) LSD (cf. A n.³). [the placing of the pill or the blotter on the tongue, reminiscent of a Communion wafer]

sacred mushroom *n.* [1960s+] (*drugs*) a psilocybe mushroom, usu. in pl. (cf. MAGIC MUSHROOM n.).

sad *n.* **1** [1920s] (*US*) one who leads a supposedly 'degenerate' sex life. **2** [1990s+] a general term of abuse.

sad *adj.* **1** [17C–mid-18C] usu. of a place, mischievous, troublesome, corrupt. **2** [late 17C+] a general term of abuse, esp. for someone who is unfashionable by current teen standards. **3** [late 19C+] very bad (of quality). [note paradoxically that the earliest use of *sad*, *c.*1000, is wholly positive, meaning satisfied or sated and thence settled, firmly established in purpose or condition, steadfast, valiant, orderly, trustworthy etc. The negative connotation emerges only in the mid-14C; the positive use is found in the 1920s–50s in the W.I. where *sad* = excellent, first-class]

sad and sorry *n.* [20C+] a lorry. [rhy. sl.]

sad apple *n.* [1910s–40s] **1** (*US*) (*also* **sad bird**) a contemptible person. **2** a pessimist.

sad-ass *n.* [1960s+] (*US gay*) a sadist. [deliberate mispron. with ref. to ASS n. (2)]

sad-ass *adj.* (*also* **sad-assed**) [1960s+] (*US*) depressing. [SE *sad* + -ASS sfx]

sad bird *n. see* SAD APPLE n. (1).

sadcase *n.* [2000s] (*Aus.*) one who tells unamusing jokes.

sad cattle *n.* [late 17C–early 19C] (*UK Und.*) prostitutes, viewed as a group.

Saddam Hussein *n.* [1990s+] a pain. [rhy. sl.; ult. the former Iraqi dictator *Saddam Hussein* (b.1937)]

sadder than a map *phr.* [1930s–40s] (*US Black*) very bad, terrible, disgusting.

saddity *n.* (*also* **sadit, seddity, sidity, siditty**) [1960s+] (*US Black*) a stuck-up, conceited, snobbish person. [SADDITY adj. (1)]

saddity *adj.* (*also* **seddity, sidity, siditty**) [1960s+] (*US Black*) **1** arrogant, haughty, snobbish, conceited. **2** elegant, high-class, sophisticated. [SIDE n.¹]

saddle *n.*¹ [mid-16C–mid-18C; 2000s] the vagina. [play on RIDE v.¹ (1)]

saddle *n.*² **1** [mid–late 19C] a loaf. **2** [late 19C] (*UK tramp*) an overcoat. [? resemblance]

saddle and bridle *n.* [1930s–50s] (*US drugs*) an opium smoker; the equipment used for smoking opium.

saddleback *n.* [mid–late 19C] a louse. [its shape]

saddlebag *n.* [1990s+] (*UK juv.*) a promiscuous woman (cf. BANBURY n.). [play on RIDE v.¹ (1)]

saddle bags *n.* **1** [1960s+] excess flesh around the upper thighs, or occas. a portly stomach. **2** [1990s+] the labia majora; the scrotum.

saddle blanket *n.*¹ [1990s+] (*US*) a sanitary towel. [? SADDLE n.¹]

saddle blanket *n.*² *see* HORSE BLANKET n.².

saddle one's nose *v.* [late 18C–mid-19C] to wear spectacles.

saddler *n.* [late 19C–1940s] (*US*) a saddle-horse.

saddle-sick *adj.* [late 18C–early 19C] tired or injured through excessive riding.

saddle the spit *v.* [late 18C–early 19C] to host a dinner or supper. [SE *saddle a spit*, to put meat upon a spit]

saddle-tramp *n.* [20C+] (*US*) a cowboy who moves from ranch to ranch, dependent for survival on local hospitality.

saddle up *v.* **1** [1970s+] to engage in mutual fellatio and cunnilingus. **2** [1970s+] to have sexual intercourse. **3** [1980s+] (*US gay*) to have anal intercourse (cf. ASK FOR THE RING v.). [play on RIDE v.¹ (1); note SADDLE n.¹]

saddling paddock *n.* (*Aus.*) **1** [mid–late 19C] the bar of the Theatre Royal, Melbourne, generally accepted as a place to pick up prostitutes. **2** [late 19C–1950s] any place of assignation.

saddo *n.* [1990s+] a pathetic individual. [SE *sad* + -O sfx (2)]

sad dog *n.* [18C–19C] a wicked, debauched fellow. [SAD adj. (1) + SE *dog*, a general term of abuse]

sadfuck *adj.* [1990s+] a general term of abuse. [SAD adj. (2) + FUCK n.⁶]

sadie (and) maisie *n.* [1960s+] sado-*masochism. [euph. based on initial letters]

sadistics *n.* [1980s] (*US campus*) a statistics course. [joc. mispron.]

sadit *n. see* SADDITY n.

sado-maso *n.* [1970s] (*US*) a sado-*maso*chist. [abbr.]

sado-maso *adj.* [1970s] (*US*) sado-*maso*chistic. [abbr.]

sad sack *n.* [1940s+] (*orig. US milit.*) a miserable, depressed (and depressing) person, usu. thus singled out in an institution, such as prison or the army; also attrib. [abbr. SAD SACK OF SHIT n., and thus the eponymous cartoon, created by George Baker (1915–75) in the US Army's *Yank* magazine]

sad sack *v.* [1970s] (*US*) to act or move in a miserable, depressed manner. [SAD SACK n.]

sad sack of shit *n.* (*also* **lazy-ass sack of shit, sorry…**) [1940s+] (*orig. US*) a miserable, pessimistic, morale-lowering person. [SE *sad* + *sack* + SHIT n.¹ (1)]

sad vulgar *n.* [late 19C] (*UK society*) a common, vulgar person.

safe *n.*¹ [late 19C+] (*US*) a condom. [SE *safety*]

safe *n.*² [1990s+] (*US prison*) **1** the anus. **2** the vagina, when used for hiding contraband. [the image of the SE *safe*, into which things can be placed for security]

safe *adj.*¹ [mid-19C] relevant to membership of the sporting fraternity.

safe *adj.*² **1** [late 19C+] a general term of approval, the overall implication is of social acceptability to a given peer group. **2** [1950s+] satisfactory, pleasant.

safe *adj.*³ [1980s+] used in sex contact advertisements, the man advertising has had a vasectomy.

safe! *excl.* [1960s+] (*US/UK teen*) all-purpose term of approval. [SAFE adj.² (1)]

safe and sound *n.* [20C+] the ground. [rhy. sl.]

safe as Kelsey *phr.* [1910s+] extremely conservative. [for ety. *see* KELSEY'S NUTS n.]

safe card *n.* [mid-19C–1920s] a trustworthy person. [SE *safe* + CARD n.² (2)]

safety *n.*¹ (*US Black*) **1** [1930s+] a condom. **2** [1940s–50s] a bed.

safety *n.*² [1950s] (*US drugs*) a safety pin used as a hypodermic needle.

safety pin mechanic *n.* [1950s] (*US drugs*) a narcotics user who is forced to resort to an improvised syringe.

sag *n.* [1930s] (*US tramp*) a policeman's truncheon. [? SAG v.¹]

sag *v.*¹ [1930s] (*US tramp*) to beat with a truncheon. [? fig. use of SE *sag*]

sag *v.*² [1990s+] (*US Black*) to wear one's trousers hanging low, exposing the top of one's underwear.

sag *v.*³ *see* SAG (OFF) v.

saga *adj.* (*also* **sagger**) [1950s] (*W.I.*) fashionable, showy, garish, overdressed; thus *saga-boy/-girl*, a young person who adopts a particular style of dressing, e.g. tight-waisted jackets and peg-top trousers. [SE *swagger*]

sagaciate v. [mid-19C–1940s] (US) to get along; to endure; to work out. [? SE *sagacious*]

sagebrusher n. [1920s] (US) a Western cowboy film.

sage hen n. [late 19C+] (US) an inhabitant of Nevada. [? the state's abundance of prairie fowl]

sagger adj. *see* SAGA adj.

sagging deuce n. [1990s+] (US Black) a lowered Cadillac automobile. [SE *sagging* + DEUCE 25 n.]

sago n. [1950s+] (Aus.) a Pacific Islander. [their stereotyped diet]

sag (off) v. [1990s+] (UK juv.) to truant from school. [? fig. use of SE *sag*]

Sahara n. [1940s] (S.Afr.) a very tall, thin person. [? they look as if they have walked across the *Sahara* desert]

sail v. [1930s–50s] (US drugs) of a doctor or dentist, to write prescriptions for narcotics. [SAIL CLOSE TO THE WIND v.]

sail (about) v. [late 17C–early 18C; 1910s] to saunter.

sail close to the wind v. [mid-19C+] to take risks, esp. with a set of rules and regulations. [naut. imagery]

sail in(to) v. [mid-19C+] **1** (orig. US) to attack, physically or verbally. **2** to launch oneself headlong on a course of action. **3** to arrive, to enter, esp. in a slow and measured manner.

sail on another board v. [16C] to alter one's behaviour.

sailor's champagne n. [late 19C] beer.

sailor's farewell n. [late 19C+] any form of goodbye that is essentially a curse.

sailors on the sea n. [20C+] tea. [rhy. sl.]

sails n. [1940s] (US Black) the human ears. [resemblance]

saint n. [early–mid-19C] (US campus) a notably religious student.

St Alban's clean shave n. [late 19C] a clergyman's beardless face, typical of the High Church.

saint and sinner n. [20C+] dinner. [rhy. sl.]

St George (a-horseback) n. **1** [17C–19C] sexual intercourse in which the woman takes the superior position. **2** [1990s+] sexual intercourse from the rear-entry position. [for ety. *see* RIDE A ST GEORGE v.]

St Giles's breed n. (also **Giles's breed**) [18C–early 19C] criminals. [for ety. *see* ST GILES'S GREEK n.]

St Giles's carpet n. [late 19C] (London) a sprinkling of sand on the street. [coined in the parish of *St Giles*, which included the criminal slums of Seven Dials]

St Giles's Greek n. [late 18C–mid-19C] slang, cant. [proper name *St Giles*, the central London criminal 'rookery', destroyed when New Oxford Street was cut through the slums in 1847 + GREEK n.[2]]

St Grotlesex n. [1980s+] (US) a portmanteau description of the East Coast preparatory schools *St Marks*, *St Paul's*, *Groton* and *Middlesex*.

St Hugh's bones n. **1** [17C] shoemaker's tools. **2** [mid-19C] dice. [given that the trad. patron saints of shoemakers are St Crispin and St Crispinian, the link to (1) is not obvious; whether the Hugh in question was St Hugh (c.1140–1200) or Hugh of Lincoln (d.1255), supposedly murdered in a race libel against the city's Jews, is unknown]

St Joe n. (also **St Jo**) [mid-19C+] (US tramp) Saint Joseph, Missouri. [abbr.]

St Johnstone's tippet n. (also **tippet**) [early 19C] the noose. [? a hanging judge or prison governor]

St John's Wood dona n. [late 19C] an up-market prostitute or kept woman. [*St John's Wood*, the home of many courtesans + DONA n. (1)]

St Looie n. (also **St Loo**) [late 19C+] (US) Saint Louis, Missouri. [abbr.]

St Louis blues n. [1960s+] (Aus.) shoes. [rhy. sl.]

St Louis flats n. [1900s–30s] (US Black) flat, moccasin-like shoes with a design on the toe – often a club, diamond or other playing-card suit – a style of shoe popular among jazz musicians and gamblers.

St Lubbock n. [late 19C] a drunken riot; thus *feast of St Lubbock*, *St Lubbock's day*, a bank holiday. [the invention of the August and other bank holidays by Sir John *Lubbock*, 1st Baron Avebury (1834–1913), in 1871]

St Luke's bird n. [late 18C–early 19C] an ox. [pictures of St Luke always feature him with an ox]

St Margret's ale n. (also **St Marget's ale**) [early 17C] water. [ety. unknown; ? anecdotal]

St Martin's n. (also **Martin-le-Grand**, **Martin's**, **St Martin's le Grand**) [mid-19C–1960s] a hand. [rhy. sl.; *St Martin-le-Grand* was a monastery and college founded c.1050; its bells rang the nightly curfew, and prisoners on their way from Newgate to Tyburn regularly passed it; those who managed to escape were able to claim sanctuary within its walls – thieves and coiners were accepted, Jews and traitors were barred. It was suppressed in 1540, and its only memory is a street name]

St Martin's lace n. (also **St Martin's rings/stuff/ware**) [early 17C] respectively, fake gold lace, imitation gold rings and counterfeit goods of any sort; thus *Martin chain*, an imitation gold chain. [16C SE *St Martin's*, 'the parish of St Martin-le-Grand, London, formerly celebrated as the resort of dealers in imitation jewellery' (OED)]

St Mary n. [1980s] (Aus.) a homosexual male (cf. ABIGAIL n.). [rhy. sl. = FAIRY n.[3] + joc. ref. to MARY n.[2] (1)]

Saint Moritz n. [1990s+] diarrhoea (cf. BANANA (SPLITS) n.). [rhy. sl. = SHITS, THE n. (1)]

St Nicholas's clergyman n. (also **St Nicholas's clerk**) [late 16C] a highwayman. [? misreading of OLD NICK n. (1), i.e. the Devil]

St Peter n. [19C] the penis (cf. ABRAHAM n.[1]). [he 'keeps the keys of Paradise']

St Peter's sons n. (also **St Peter's children**) [18C–early 19C] petty thieves, who take anything they can lay their hands on. [proper name *St Peter*, 'the greatest fisherman' and disciple of Christ; such thieves 'having every finger a fish-hook' (Grose, 1785)]

St Tibb's eve n. (also **St Tib's eve**) [late 18C–1940s] never. [defined as 'the evening of the last day, or day of judgment' (Grose, 1785)]

St Vitus's dance n. [20C+] **1** nerves, jitters, shakes. **2** (Aus.) pants. [(1) SE *St Vitus's dance*, chorea (Lat. a dance), which promotes spasmodic convulsions of the limbs; (2) rhy. sl.]

sakes! excl. (also **my sakes! sakes alive!**) [mid-19C+] (US) a mild oath. [i.e. for *Lord's/God's sake!*]

sakes alive n. [1990s+] the number 5. [rhy. sl.]

Sal n.[1] *see* AUNT SALLY n. (1).

Sal n.[2] *see* SALLY n.[1] (2).

sal n.[1] [mid-18C–early 19C] a form of treatment for syphilis; thus *in a high sal*, undergoing such a treatment. [abbr. SE *salivation*]

sal n.[2] *see* SALTING n.

salad n. [1980s+] (US drugs) a mixture of different varieties of cannabis (cf. AFRICAN BUSH n.).

Salada crackers n. [1980s+] (Aus. prison) the testicles (cf. CHEESE AND CRACKERS n.). [rhy. sl. = KNACKERS n.]

salad basket n. [1950s] a police van. [trans. of Fr. sl. *panier à salade*, lit. 'salad basket'. So called from the iron grating or trellis that covered the rear of the orig. 'baskets', horse-drawn carts in which prisoners were transported]

salad dodger n. [1990s+] a fat person.

salad oil n. [1910s–20s] hair oil.

Salamanca wedding n. [late 19C] the marriage of an old man to a (rich) young woman. [? anecdotal]

salamander n. [mid–late 19C] a fire-eating juggler. [SE *salamander*, a mythical lizard-like animal, once thought to be capable of living in fire; Williams notes used in the 17C to invoke sexual coldness (i.e. the cold-blooded lizard)]

salami *n.* [1970s+] a penis (cf. BACON n.[1]).

salami slapper *n.* [1990s+] **1** a masturbator. **2** a general term of abuse. [SALAMI n.]

salamon *n. see* SOLOMON n.[1].

sales lady *n.* [1920s–70s] (*US*) a prostitute (cf. ASS PEDDLER n.; BANKSIDE LADY n.).

salesman *n.* (*US Und.*) **1** [1920s] a confidence trickster. **2** [1940s–60s] a pimp.

salesman's dog *n.* [late 17C–mid-18C] a shop tout. [pun on BARKER n.[1] (2)]

sal hatch *n.* [late 19C] an umbrella. ['origin quite obscure – but probably salacious' (Ware). However, ? SE *sal hatch*, a dirty wench, via the fictional embodiment of umbrella users, Charles Dickens's Mrs Sarah Gamp in *Martin Chuzzlewit* (1843–4)]

salisbury *n.* [late 19C] a polite evasion, a 'white lie'. [the alleged characteristic of British Prime Minister, Lord *Salisbury* (1830–1903)]

Salisbury Crag *n.* [1990s+] (*drugs*) heroin (cf. HAMMER (AND TACK) n.). [rhy. sl. = SCAG n.[2] (2); ult. Edinburgh's famous geological landmark *Salisbury Crags*]

Sally *n.*[1] **1** [late 19C] (*Aus.*) a Salvation Army girl; usu. as *Salvation Sally*. **2** [1910s+] (*Aus./US/UK*) (*also* **Sal, Sallie, Sallies**) the *Salvation Army*; a Salvation Army hostel. [abbr.]

Sally *n.*[2] *see* AUNT SALLY n. (1).

Sally *adj.* [1950s+] (*US*) pertaining to the Salvation Army. [SALLY n.[1] (2)]

sally *n.* [1980s+] (*US campus*) **1** a person who is punctilious to an absurd, near-certifiable degree. **2** a likeable person. [film *When Harry Met Sally* (1989)]

Sally Ann *n.* (*also* **Sally Army**) [1920s+] **1** the *Salvation Army*. **2** (*Aus.*) a female Salvationist. [abbr.]

Sally B. *n.* [late 19C] (*US*) a tall, thin woman. [abbr.; a ref. to the actress *Sarah Bernhardt* (1844–1923)]

Sally bash *n.* [1970s+] the *Salvation Army*. [abbr. + SE *bash*]

sally fairy ann *phr. see* SAN FAIRY ANN phr.

Sally Gunnell *n.* [1990s+] the Blackwall Tunnel. [rhy. sl.; ult. UK athlete *Sally Gunnell* (b.1966)]

Sally Lunn *n.* [19C+] a round, flat bun made with sweet yeast dough, usu. served hot. [proper name of the bun's inventor. 'The bun [...] called the Sally Lunn, originated with a young woman of that name in Bath, about thirty years ago. She first cried them [...] Dalmer, a respectable baker and musician, noticed her, bought her business, and made a song [...] in behalf of Sally Lunn' (William Home, *Every-day Book*, 1827)]

salmon *n.*[1] [late 19C] (*UK Und.*) the drowned corpse of a wealthy person.

salmon *n.*[2] [1980s] (*Aus.*) the anus. [rhy. sl.]

salmon *n.*[3] *see* SOLOMON n.[1].

salmon and trout *n.* (*also* **salmon trout**) **1** [mid-19C+] the mouth. **2** [1910s+] the nose. **3** [1930s–60s] (*also* **mountain trout**) a bookmaker's tout. **4** [1930s–80s] gout. **5** [1950s+] stout beer. **6** [1970s+] (*also* **salmon**) tobacco, esp. prison use. [rhy. sl.; (2) = SE *snout*; (6) = SNOUT n.[2] (1)]

Salmon Arm salute *n.* [1970s+] (*Can.*) a derisive gesture based on clenching the fist and raising the middle finger. [the giving of such a gesture by then Prime Minister Pierre Trudeau to protesters in Salmon Arm B.C.]

salmon belly *n.* [1920s] (*US Und.*) a high-denomination bill. [the colour]

salmon canyon *n.* [1990s+] the female genitals. [equation of the female genitals with SE *fish*]

salmon-tot retriever *n.* [20C+] (*W.I.*) a mongrel, kept as a watch-dog and allowed to forage for its food. [Carib.E. *salmon-tot*, a salmon-tin + mockery of the pedigree *retriever* breed]

salmon trout *n. see* SALMON AND TROUT n.

salomon *n. see* SOLOMON n.[1].

saloon smasher *n.* [1900s] (*US*) one who wrecks saloons as a

protest against the supposed 'evils of alcohol'. [the best known was the US temperance campaigner Carrie Nation (1846–1911)]

salop *n.* [20C+] (*W.I.*) a dirty, grubby person, esp. a woman or child. [Fr. *salope*, a slut, a prostitute]

sal slappers *n.* [late 19C] (*costermonger*) a prostitute or promiscuous woman. [*Sal*, abbr. proper name *Sally* + the *slapping* of her feet on the pavement; ? SLAPPER n.[2] although this significantly predates]

salt *n.*[1] [mid-17C–early 18C] sexual intercourse. [SE *salt*, lecherous]

salt *n.*[2] **1** [mid-19C] in non-naval contexts, a fine example. **2** [mid-19C+] a veteran sailor; also attrib. **3** [1960s+] a veteran of any experience or discipline. [abbr. OLD SALT n.]

salt *n.*[3] [late 19C–1900s] (*US*) money. [generic use of *salt* as a necessity of life, like money]

salt *n.*[4] [1950s+] (*US Black/W.I.*) trouble, annoyance, difficulties; thus *get salt*, to be thwarted, to encounter misfortune. [the image of oversalting one's food]

salt *n.*[5] [1970s] (*drugs*) heroin. [resemblance]

salt *adj.*[1] [early 18C–19C] costly, expensive, esp. over-expensive. [the 'salting' of mines, thus the padding of bills]

salt *adj.*[2] [late 19C+] very drunk (cf. ADRIAN (QUIST) adj.). [later use W.I.; ? rhy. sl. SALT JUNK adj. = drunk. Allsopp prefers pun on PICKLED adj.[2]]

salt *adj.*[3] [1950s+] (*W.I. Rasta*) unlucky, in a bad state; impoverished, empty-handed, low on food. [SALT n.[4]]

salt *v.*[1] **1** [late 16C–early 17C] (*UK campus*) to initiate new students by a variety of rituals, esp. making them drink salt water or swallow dry salt. **2** [1940s] (*UK prison*) to initiate a new prisoner. [(2) f. (1)]

salt *v.*[2] **1** [mid-19C–1900s] (*US*) to shoot (dead). **2** [late 19C–1900s] to ignore, to not bother. [SE *salt away*]

salt *v.*[3] [mid-19C+] (*orig. US*) to 'improve' the apparent quality of a mine by planting specimens of the ore it supposedly yields; also in fig. use.

salt *v.*[4] *see* SALT (AWAY) v.

salt and pepper *n.*[1] [1940s–50s] (*drugs*) marijuana, esp. of poor quality. [ety. unknown]

salt and pepper *n.*[2] [1950s+] (*orig. US Black*) **1** an inter-racial couple. **2** friends or colleagues of different races. **3** a police team, usu. operating from a squad car, that consists of one Black and one White policeman. **4** a black and white squad car.

salt and pepper *n.*[3] [1960s] (*US Black*) courage, cheek, 'guts'.

salt-and-pepper *adj.* [1950s+] (*US*) **1** of a person, mixed-race. **2** segregated. **3** of a place, frequented by both Blacks and Whites, e.g. *salt-and-pepper neighbourhood*. **4** anything, e.g. a pair of TV anchors, involving both Blacks and Whites. **5** of hair, black and grey/white. **6** of 2 men having sex with 1 woman. [SALT AND PEPPER n.[2]]

salt-and-pepper queens *n.* [1970s+] (*gay*) a mixed-race gay couple. [SALT-AND-PEPPER adj. (4) + QUEEN n.[2] (1)]

salt (away) *v.* [20C+] to store, to put away.

salt-bitch *n.* [late 17C] a homosexual. [SE *salt bitch*, a bitch in heat]

salt bomb *n.* [2000s] (*US Black*) personal vilification.

salt-box *n.* [19C] the condemned cell at Newgate prison. [? its dimension; the salt tears shed within it]

salt-box cly *n.* [early 19C] (*UK Und.*) the outside coat pocket, with a flap. [supposed resemblance to a SE *salt-box*, which has a flap + CLY n. (2)]

salt-cellar *n.* **1** [19C] the vagina. **2** [late 19C] the cavity above a woman's collar-bone. **3** [1950s+] (*UK juv.*) the navel. [(1) plays on SE *salt*, lecherous]

salt creek *n.* [1910s–20s] (*US Und.*) execution in the electric chair. [var. on UP SHIT('S) CREEK (WITHOUT A PADDLE) phr.]

salt-cunted *adj.* [late 19C] sexually voracious. [SE *salt*, lecherous + CUNT n.[1] (1)]

salt down *v.*[1] [mid-19C+] to put by, to store away.

salt down v.[2] [1900s–10s] (US) to tell off, to reprimand. [one speaks in a SE *salt*, i.e. sharp manner]

salted adj. [mid–late 19C] experienced, esp. after overcoming some form of problem. [SE *salted*, of a horse, having survived a disease]

salted (down) adj. [mid-19C] drunk. [? play on PICKLED adj.[2]]

saltee n. (also **soldi**) [mid-19C] (*Ling. Fr./Polari*) a penny; usu. in combs. [Ital. *soldi*, pl. of *soldo*, 1/20th of a lira]

salt eel n. [early 17C–early 19C] a rope's end, used for flogging; thus *have (a) salt eel for supper*, to be flogged.

salt horse n. [mid-19C–1940s] salt beef.

saltie n. [1950s+] (*Aus.*) a *salt*-water crocodile. [abbr.]

salting n. (also **sal**) [1950s+] (*W.I. Rasta*) the vagina. [fig. use of Carib.E. *salting*, i.e. 'salt thing', or *salt food*, dishes cooked with salt fish or meat]

salt it for someone v. [1910s–20s] to make problems for someone.

salt junk n. *see* JUNK n.[1] (1).

salt junk adj. [late 19C–1900s] drunk (cf. ADRIAN (QUIST) adj.). [rhy. sl.]

salt the books v. [late 19C+] to improve the state of a firm's accounts by judicious, if illicit, alterations to the figures. [SALT v.[3]]

salt up v. [1980s+] (*US campus*) to cause trouble for, to place in a difficult or embarrassing situation. [? the image of 'adding flavour' to the situation]

salt water n. **1** [late 17C–early 18C] urine. **2** [mid-19C] tears. **3** [mid-19C] a sailor. **4** [1920s] (*US Black*) alcohol.

salt-water negro n. [early 19C] (*W.I.*) an African-born Black person, so called by the Creoles, who were born in the West Indies. [note *salt-water Creole*, a Black person born during the voyage from Africa; to be a full Creole it is necessary to be born on the islands]

salt-water taffy n. [1970s] (*US gay*) a sailor's penis as an object for fellatio. [play on SAmE *salt-water taffy*, which one licks and sucks]

salt-water vegetable n. [mid-19C] an oyster or clam.

salty adj. (also **saltyback**) **1** [1920s+] (*US*) irritated, annoyed, feeling sour. **2** [1920s+] (*US*) tough, aggressive, used of a veteran of a particular environment, e.g. a prison. **3** [1920s+] (*US teen*) a general pej., unpleasant, uncouth, crude; of language, obscene. **4** [1980s+] of a garment, well-worn, 'lived-in'. [? US navy jargon *salty*, tough, aggressive; Dillard, *Lexicon of Black English* (1977), suggests link to UK dial. *salty*, 'of a bitch, *maris appetens* [desirous of a male]']

salty bananas n. [20C+] (*Aus.*) sultanas. [rhy. sl./mispron.]

salty dog n. (*US Black*) **1** [late 19C–1930s] something or someone very exceptional. **2** [1970s] one who uses an excess of obscene language. [fig. use of SE *salty*/SALTY adj. (3)]

salty yogurt slinger n. (also **yoghurt truck**) [1990s+] the penis.

salubrious adj. [19C] drunk (cf. ABOUT RIGHT phr.[1]). [SE *salubrious*, conducive to good health]

Salv' n. *see* SALVO n.

Salvador Dali n. [2000s] cocaine (cf. BARLEY n.[2]). [rhy. sl. = CHARLIE n.[9] (1); ult. Spanish surrealist artist *Salvador Dalí* (1904–89)]

salvage v. [1910s+] (*Aus./US*) to steal, to pilfer.

salvarmy n. *see* SALVO n.

salvation n. [late 19C–1910s] a station. [rhy. sl.]

Salvation Army adj. [late 19C] **1** crazy, eccentric (cf. COCK-SPARROW adj.). **2** drunk (cf. ADRIAN (QUIST) adj.). [rhy. sl. = BARMY adj./BALMY adj.]

salvation juggins n. [late 19C] a member of the Salvation Army; also *salvation rotter*, *salvation soul-sneaker*. [SE *salvation* + JUGGINS n./ROTTER n.[1] (1)/SE *soul-sneaker*; all these nega-

tive nicknames came from many people's dislike of the Army's heavy-handed religiosity, esp. its attacks on drinking and similar pleasures, which undermined its charitable reputation]

salve n. **1** [mid-19C–1940s] (*US*) praise, flattery; any form of 'line' that facilitates a confidence trick; thus *spread/give/shoot the salve*, to talk in a conciliatory, soothing manner; *salve over*, to persuade by smooth talking. **2** [late 19C+] (*US tramp*) butter. **3** [20C+] (*US*) money, esp. as a reward for something difficult (cf. ACTUAL, THE n.). **4** [1910s] (*US campus*) exaggeration. **5** [1910s–20s] (*US/US tramp*) a bribe. **6** [1920s] (*US tramp*) a complaint.

salve v. [20C+] (*US*) to pay, usu. a reward; also to bribe. [SALVE n. (3)]

salve-eater n. [late 19C–1930s] (*US*) an immigrant from northern Europe, esp. a Swede. [derog. ref. to national habits; ? anecdotal]

Salvo n. (also **Salv'**, **salvarmy**) [late 19C+] (*Aus.*) the *Salvation* Army or one of its members. [abbr. + -o sfx (4)]

SAM n. [1990s+] (*US gay*) a masochist who is rude in order to receive punishment. [smart-*assed* *m*asochist]

Sam n. *see* UNCLE SAM n.[1].

sam n.[1] [mid-19C] a fool, a simpleton (cf. BEN n.[1]). [abbr. SAMMY (SOFT) n.]

sam n.[2] **1** [mid-19C–1930s] a familiar nickname or generic term used to address a Black man. **2** [1930s–70s] (*US Black*) a Black man who willingly conforms to White stereotyping. [*Old Black Sam* or SAMBO n.[1] (1)]

sam n.[3] [1950s–60s] a generic name used when someone's proper name has been forgotten, esp. of women.

sam n.[4] [1950s–60s] (*camp gay*) the embodiment of the male side of one's personality.

sam v.[1] [late 19C] to pay for a drink. [abbr. STAND SAM v.]

sam v.[2] [1960s–70s] to cheat, to deceive. [? SAM n.[1]]

Sam and Dave n. [1980s+] (*US Black*) the police, when working in a team of 2. [the eponymous soul duo, *Sam* Moore (b.1935) and *Dave* Prater (1937–88)]

sambo n.[1] **1** [late 17C+] a derog. term for a Black man (cf. AFRICAN APE n.). **2** [early 19C; 1950s+] (*W.I.*) the colour between mulatto (brown) and Black; a person of this colour. **3** [1960s+] (1) as a direct term of address. **4** [1980s] (*US Black*) an obsequious Black person. [Sp. *zambo*, used to describe those of mixed Negro and Indian or European blood. The word also describes a breed of yellow monkey. US use of (1), which emerged during the era of slavery, may have a different root; the Foulah *sambo*, uncle or Hausa *sambo*, second son, or name of the spirit. The suggestion by F&H of a third root, an African tribe, the Samboses (for whom they claim an appearance in a text of 1558) has no validity. *Sambo* began as a neutral term, but as slavery fell into increasing disrepute, so did its terminology. The word was widely popularized by Helen Bannerman's best-selling children's book *The Story of Little Black Sambo* (1923), but the term, and that book, have long since been considered unacceptable]

sambo n.[2] (also **sambie**) [1970s+] (*Aus./Irish*) a sandwich (cf. SAMMO n.). [abbr.]

sambo adj. [1950s] a derog. term pertaining to Black people or culture. [SAMBO n.[1] (1)]

sambo backra n. [1950s] (*W.I.*) a person of mixed race, usu. three-quarters Black. [SAMBO n.[1] (1) + BACKRA n. (2)]

sambolio n. *see* SIMOLEON n.

same again n. **1** [1930s] the third drink of a session. **2** [1930s+] a general response to an offer of another drink, usu. in a public house setting; as a query *same again?* it can be the offer.

same difference n. (also **same diff**) [1940s+] exactly the same thing, no difference at all.

same o.b. n. [late 19C] a shilling (5p), esp. in the context of the charge for most contemporary places of entertainment. [abbr. SE *same old* + BOB n.[4] (1)]

same old same old phr. (also **same ol' same ol'**, **same-o**

same-o) [1970s+] (*orig. US Black*) a general expression to imply that nothing has changed in one's life, used in response to a question as to one's current health or feelings. [SE *same old thing*]

same old three and four *n.* [late 19C] a weekly wage, 6 days at 3 shillings and 4 pence a day gives £1 for a 6-day week.

same shit, different day *phr.* [1980s+] (*orig. US Black*) life goes on as normal, with no surprises, good or bad. [SHIT n.³ (1)]

samey *adj.* [1920s+] boring, tedious, undistinguished. [SE *same*]

samfie *n.* [20C+] (*W.I.*) a confidence trick. [dial. *samfai*, an obeah-man, one who has magical powers, ult. ? Twi *asumanfo*, a magician, a sorcerer]

samfie *v.* (*also* **samfai, samfi**) [20C+] (*W.I./UK Black teen*) to trick, to 'lead down the garden path'. [SAMFIE n.]

samfie (man) *n.* [20C+] (*W.I.*) a confidence trickster; thus *samfieism*, deceit, trickery. [SAMFIE n.]

s.a.m.f.u. *n.* [1940s+] (*orig. milit.*) a self-adjusting military *fuck-up* (cf. S.N.A.F.U. n.). [abbr.; comb. of S.A.B.U. n. and S.N.A.F.U. n.]

Sam Henry *n. see* JOHN T HENRY n.

Sam Hill! *excl.* [early 19C+] (*orig. US*) a euph. for *hell* and as such often found as WHAT THE SAM HILL! excl.

Sami *n.* [1980s+] (*N.Z.*) a *Samo*an. [abbr.]

sammo *n.* [1930s+] (*Aus./US*) a sandwich (cf. SAMBO n.²). [abbr.]

sammy *n.*¹ **1** [late 19C–1940s] (*S.Afr.*) a generic name for any Hindu, esp. Indian people living in South Africa. **2** [1910s] an Indian fruit peddler. [abbr. RAMSAMMY n. (1)]

sammy *n.*² [1910s] (*US*) a US soldier during WW1. [UNCLE SAM n.¹]

sammy *n.*³ (*also* **skinny**) [1990s+] (*US milit.*) a derog. name for a *Somal*i. [abbr./appearance]

sammy *n.*⁴ *see* PORTSAMMY n.

sammy *n.*⁵ *see* SAMMY (SOFT) n.

sammy *adj.* [early 19C–1930s] foolish, dull. [SAMMY (SOFT) n.]

Sammy Lee *n.* [1990s+] an act of urination (cf. ANGEL'S KISS n.). [rhy. sl. = PEE n.¹ (2)/WEE n.; poss. ult. the US diver *Sammy Lee* (b.1920)]

sammy (soft) *n.* [early 19C–1930s] a fool (cf. BEN n.¹). [orig. dial. *sammy*, a simpleton, compounded by SOFT adj. (1)]

samoleon *n. see* SIMOLEON n.

sample *v.* **1** [mid-19C–1900s] to drink. **2** [late 19C–1910s] to caress or fondle a woman sexually.

sampler *n.* [19C] the vagina. [SE *sampler*, a piece of embroidery, which is worked with a NEEDLE n.¹]

sample room *n.* [mid–19C–1930s] (*US*) a bar, often as attached to a grocery, in which one can purchase liquor by the glass. ['Sometimes the bar is at the side, screened off, and genteelly disguised under the name of "sample room". You enter ostensibly to purchase cherries, and immediately "put yourself outside" a "tot" of Bourbon' (G.A. Sala, *My Diary in America*, 1865)]

sampson *n. see* SAMSON n.

samshoo *n.* [mid-19C] (*Anglo-Chinese*) a fiery liquor, distilled from rice or sorghum. [Chinese pidgin *samshoo, sam shu*; ult. ? *san shao*, thrice distilled, but this is a popular rather than scholarly ety.]

samson *n.* (*also* **sampson**) [mid-19C–1900s] a drink combining brandy, cider, sugar and water. [the biblical strongman *Samson*; ? either the strength of the drink or the strength it imparts to the drinker]

Samuel Pepys *n.* [1980s+] a sense of uneasiness or distaste, a nervous feeling. [rhy. sl. pron. *Samuel Peeps* = CREEPS, THE n.; ult. British diarist and civil servant *Samuel Pepys* (1633–1703)]

samurai sword *n.* [1980s+] (*US gay*) the penis of a Japanese gay man.

san *n.* [20C+] a *san*itarium, esp. at a boarding school. [abbr.]

-san *sfx* [1990s+] (*US campus*) a sfx that conveys familiarity. [Jap. honorific; abbr. of formal *sana*, Mr/Mrs etc]

San Bardoo/Berdoo *n. see* BERDOO n.

Sancho *n.* [1980s+] (*US prison*) used by Hisp. inmates for the new boyfriend/lover who takes one's place while one is incarcerated. [generic use of Hisp. proper name]

sancocho *v.* [1980s+] (*drugs*) to steal. [Sp.'to cut up into little pieces and stew']

sanctification *n.* [1970s+] blackmail, esp. by secret services or foreign diplomats. [SANCTIFY v.]

sanctify *v.* [1970s+] to blackmail someone, esp. for the purposes of extracting political favours. [SE *sanctify*, to render holy, to set apart as sacred]

sancy *n. see* SONSY adj.

sand *n.* **1** [early 19C+] (*mainly US prison/short order*) sugar; thus *Joe with cow and sand*, a cup of coffee with milk and sugar. **2** [mid-19C] (*US*) courage, firmness of purpose, determination; thus *have sand in one's craw/on one's gizzard*, to act courageously. **3** [late 19C–1900s] (*orig. US*) money (cf. CHAFF n.²). [fig. uses of SE; (3) refers to money not as a 'staff of life' but as dirt; (1) Vaux glosses 'moist sugar']

sand and canvas *v.* [1910s–30s] (*orig. naut.*) to clean thoroughly. [the use of such materials for cleaning the decks]

s and b *n. see* B AND S n.

sandbag *n.* [1900s] (*US*) a confidence trick. [SANDBAG v.¹ (1)]

sandbag *v.*¹ (*US*) **1** [late 19C–1920s] to cheat. **2** [20C+] to feign weakness in order to mislead an opponent. **3** [1940s+] in poker, to resist raising the bet immediately in the hope of making a larger raise later on. [the use in war of SE *sandbags* as a protective wall from which one can then emerge]

sandbag *v.*² **1** [late 19C+] (*orig. US*) to ambush, to take by surprise. **2** [1910s+] to get rid of. **3** [1920s+] (*US*) to intimidate. **4** [1930s] to extort. [i.e. to hit with a SE *sandbag*]

sandbag and jemmy *adv.* [1900s] (*Aus.*) completely. [a villain's tools]

sandbagger *n.* [late 19C–1920s] (*US*) a street robber, a 'mugger'. [SANDBAG v.² (1)]

sandbeef *n.* [late 19C–1920s] a sandwich. [mispron. by Italian snack-bar owners]

sand-coon *n.* [2000s] a derog. term for an Arab from the Middle East (cf. ABDUL n.). [SE *sand* + COON n. (5)]

sand-duster *n.* [1950s] (*US*) a short person.

sandfly's garters *n. see* CAT'S WHISKERS n.

sand-grope *v.* [late 19C] (*Aus.*) to bungle. [SE *sand-grope*, to walk in soft sand]

sand-groper *n.* [late 19C+] (*Aus.*) an inhabitant of Western Australia; thus *sand-groper land*, Western Australia. [SE *sand-grope*, to walk through soft sand. Western Australia encompasses a large area of sandy desert]

sand-hog *n.* [late 19C+] a caisson worker, working under compressed air, digging and laying the foundations of bridges etc.

sand-hopper *n.* [1970s] a derog. term for an Arab (cf. ABDUL n.).

sandies *n.* [1980s] (*Aus.*) sand flies.

sandiness *n.* [late 19C] (*US*) the quality of having courage or 'guts'. [SAND n. (2)]

sand-jockey *n.* [2000s] a derog. term for an Arab from the Middle East (cf. ABDUL n.). [SE *sand* + JOCKEY n.³ (2)]

S and M *n.* (*also* **S&M, S/M, S-M**) [1960s+] **1** *sado-masochism*. **2** a *sado-masochist*. [abbr.]

S and M *adj.* (*also* **S&M, S/M, S-M**) [1960s+] pertaining to *sado-masochism*. [abbr.]

sandman *n.* [1910s+] (*Aus.*) a footpad, a mugger. [they 'sandbag' their victim]

sand nigger *n.* [1980s+] (*US*) a derog. term for an Arab or any other native of the Middle East (except Israelis) (cf. ABDUL n.). [SE *sand* + NIGGER n.¹ (1)]

sandoz *n.* [1960s+] (*drugs*) LSD (cf. A n.³). [the discovery of the drug by Dr Albert Hofmann of *Sandoz* Pharmaceuticals, Switzerland]

sandpaper suit n. [1930s–40s] (N.Z.) a school cadet uniform. [the roughness of the material]

Sandra Bullocks n. [1990s+] itching, uncomfortable testicles. [play on *sweaty bollocks*; ult. the film star *Sandra Bullock* (b.1966)]

sand scratcher n. [2000s] (US) a derog. term for a Syrian, an Indian (from India). [note 19C Aus. *sandscratcher*, a gold miner]

sand toad n. [1990s+] (US) an Arab, a Middle Easterner (cf. ABDUL n.).

sandwich n.[1] [mid–late 19C] a sandwich man, carrying a pair of advertising boards around the streets. ['the doleful broken-down men employed at one shilling a day to carry pairs of advertisement boards, tabard-fashion, one on the unambitious chest, the other on the broken back' (Ware)]

sandwich n.[2] (also **triple-decker sandwich**) [1970s+] a sexual threesome, involving any permutation of the sexes (cf. CHOCOLATE SANDWICH n.).

sandwich v. [1950s] (W.I.) to kiss.

sandwich lane n. [1970s+] (US) the middle lane of a 3-lane highway. [one is sandwiched between the fast and slow lanes]

sandwich man n. [1970s+] (US Black) a man having sex with 2 women at the same time. [SANDWICH n.[2] + SE *man*]

sandwich short of a picnic, a phr. see ONE SANDWICH SHORT OF THE PICNIC phr.

sand wog n. [1990s+] a derog. term for an Arab or Middle Eastern person (cf. ABDUL n.). [SE *sand* + WOG n.[1] (1)]

Sandy n. [late 18C+] a generic name for any Scotsman (cf. SAWNEY n.). [abbr. common Scot. name *Alexander*]

sandy n. (US) **1** [late 19C] a drunken spree of which one has no memory. **2** [1930s] a trick, trickery. [SE phr. *throw sand in someone's eyes*; (1) may be gambling jargon]

Sandy Bay peach n. [20C+] (S.Afr.) a nectarine, as termed by street vendors. [the name of a popular nudist beach; the nectarine lacks the peach's furry 'coat']

Sandy Macnab n. (also **Sandy McNab**) **1** [1910s] (Aus.) the stomach. **2** [1910s+] a crab, a body louse; usu. in pl. **3** [1920s+] (Aus.) a scab. **4** [1940s+] a taxi-cab. [rhy. sl.; (1) = SE *flab*]

Sandy Powell n. [1940s–50s] **1** a trowel. **2** a towel. [rhy. sl.; the northern radio/music-hall comedian Albert 'Sandy' Powell (1898–1982)]

sane n. (also **sein**) [1930s+] (Aus.) 10, in a variety of contexts, e.g. a 10-shilling note, a 10-year prison sentence, 10oz (280g) of tobacco. [Ger. *zehn*, 10]

san fairy ann phr. (also **sally fairy ann, san ferry ann, send for mary ann**) [1910s+] (orig. milit.) no matter, forget it. [synon. Fr. *ça ne fait rien*]

San Fran n. [20C+] (US) San Francisco. [abbr.]

San Francisco Bay, one small boat half sunk n. [late 19C] (US) a cocktail.

sang n. [mid-19C+] (US) ginseng. [abbr.]

sang v. [mid–late 19C] (US) to gather ginseng. [SANG n.]

sangaree n. [early–mid-19C] a drinking bout. [SE *sangaree*, spiced wine, diluted with water; ult. Sp. *sangria*]

sanger n. (also **sanga, sango**) [1940s+] (Aus./Irish) a sandwich. [abbr.]

sangster n. [late 19C] an umbrella. [one *Sangster*, who patented a lightweight umbrella]

sanguinary adj. (also **sanguineous**) [late 19C–1940s] a euph. for BLOODY adj.[1] (1).

sanguinary doubles n. [mid-19C] the Piccadilly Saloon, at 222 Piccadilly, London W1. [play on BLOODY adj.[1] (1); ? the site of much bloodshed]

sanguinary james n. [mid-19C] an uncooked sheep's head. [play on BLOODY JEMMY n.]

sanguineous adj. see SANGUINARY adj.

sanitize v. [1960s–70s] (US) to shoot dead, to kill.

San Juan Hill n. [1900s–10s] (US) an area of New York City with a predominantly Black population, covering those blocks between 10th and 11th Avenues, between 59th Street and the low 60s. [the Battle of San Juan Hill (1898) in which many Black troops were involved]

sankey n. [1920s–50s] (W.I.) a hymn; a hymn book. [Ira David Sankey (1840–1908), who, with his partner Dwight Lyman Moody (1837–99), was the best known evangelist of the mid-19C]

sank work n. [late 18C–19C] the making of soldiers' clothes; thus *sank*, a tailor employed in this way. [? Fr. *sang* (thus Norman *sanc*), blood, referring either to the scarlet uniform or the blood-letting that comes with soldiering]

san lo n. (also **son lo**) [1930s–50s] (US drugs) cheap, refined opium residue. [Chinese or fake Chinese]

sanno n. [1930s+] (Aus.) a sanitary carter or inspector. [abbr. + -o sfx (4)]

sanny n. **1** [late 19C+] (Aus.) (also **sano man**) a sanitary man, who removes sewage. **2** [1940s+] a sanitary towel. [abbr.]

sanpaku adj. [1960s+] out of touch, out of balance, physically and spiritually. [Zen use *sanpaku*, visibility of the white of the eye above and below the iris as well as (as usual) on either side; ult. Jap. *san*, three + *haku*, white]

San Q n. [1930s–60s] (US Und.) San Quentin prison, California (cf. ABBOTT'S PRIORY n.). [abbr.]

San Quentin briefcase n. [1990s+] (US) a large, portable tape-recorder-cum-radio. [*San Quentin* prison, California; the suggestion that those who carry such pieces of equipment are, *de facto*, criminals; accentuated by the racist stereotyping of the original users, young Black men]

San Quentin cross n. [1970s] (US prison) blackmail of one inmate by another, who desires homosexual favours. [*San Quentin* prison + CROSS n.[1] (1)]

San Quentin quail n. [1930s+] (US) a girl still under the age of consent who sleeps with an older man. [*San Quentin* prison + QUAIL n. (3); having sex with such a girl is likely to result in being imprisoned for statutory rape]

Santa Claus n. **1** [20C+] (US) a generous benefactor. **2** [1960s+] an older man who is willing to provide the various material wants of a younger mistress or, if gay, a younger male lover. **3** [1980s] (US Black) a vulgar, gaudy and tasteless dresser. [the popular image of the Christmas figure as both generous and gaudy]

Santa Marta (gold) n. (also **Santa Marta red**) [1970s+] (drugs) a potent brand of marijuana from Colombia (cf. ACAPULCO (GOLD) n.).

santar n. (also **senter**) [late 16C–early 17C] (UK Und.) that member of a team of parcel thieves who actually removes the stolen goods and takes them to a hideout. [SE *sanctuary*/SE *sent*]

san toys n. [1900s–30s] villains, criminals. [rhy. sl. = BOYS, THE n. (4); ult. *San Toy*, brandname of a small cigar]

sap n.[1] **1** [late 18C+] (UK school) (also **sapper**) a hard worker. **2** [mid–late 19C] a derog. term for an intellectual. [Lat. *sapiens*, wise]

sap n.[2] (also **john sap, sapolio, sapper, sappo**) [19C+] a fool, a dupe. [SE *sap*, the vital juice of a plant; the image is of one who is thus 'green'; note SAP-HEAD n./SAP-HEADED adj.]

sap n.[3] **1** [late 19C–1930s] (US tramp) an act of clubbing with (2). **2** [late 19C+] (US) a small club, orig. of wood, latterly a small leather 'bag' filled with sand, lead shot or similar material. [SE *sapling*, from which the weapons were orig. made]

sap v.[1] [late 18C–19C] (UK school) to work overly hard. [SAP n.[1] (1)]

sap v.[2] (also **sap down/up**) **1** [late 19C+] to attack using a blackjack. **2** [1920s] (US Und.) to hit with any implement, e.g. a whip. [SAP n.[3] (2)]

s.a.p.f.u. phr. [1940s+] (US milit.) surpassing all previous fuck-ups (cf. S.N.A.F.U. n.). [abbr.]

sap-happy adj. [1930s+] (US) drunk (cf. ALED UP adj.). [SE *sap*, juice/JUICE n.[3] (1) + sfx -*happy* + pun on SLAP-HAPPY adj.]

sap-head *n.* [late 18C+] a fool; thus *sapheadism*, foolishness. [SAP-HEADED adj.]

sap-headed *adj.* (*also* **sap-head**) [mid-late 17C; mid-19C–1920s] foolish (cf. AIRHEADED adj.). [fig. use of SE *sap*, liquid, juice]

sapient *n.* [mid-16C] (*UK Und.*) a travelling quack. [SE *sapient*; ult. Lat. *sapiens*, wise man]

sapolio *n. see* SAP n.[2].

sap-pate *n.* [late 17C–early 18C] a fool (cf. CLODPATE n.). [SE *sap*/SAP n.[2] + SE *pate*]

sapper *see also under* SAP.

sapper *n.* [mid-late 19C] a man about town, a 'gay dog'. [a line sung by the Parisian music-hall star Theresa, who visited London *c.*1866, 'Rien est sacré pour un s–s–sapeur!', although note Fr. cant *sapeur*, a judge]

sapphire *n.* [1940s–70s] (*US Black*) an unpopular woman. [? she makes one BLUE adj.[1] (like the jewel); or f. the character Sapphire in the radio (later TV) show *Amos 'n' Andy* (late 1920s–50s), a portrait, as stereotyped as the rest of the cast, of a complaining, emasculating, unpleasant Black woman. Note the use of the name as the pseudonymous author of the 1996 novel *Push*, a story of poverty and abuse in the ghetto]

sappho *n.* [mid-18C; late 19C+] a lesbian; thus *sapphic*, codeword for female homosexuality. [proper name *Sappho* (*c.*600 BC), the poetess of the island of Lesbos]

sappho daddy-o *n.* [1990s+] (*US gay*) a heterosexual man who socializes extensively with lesbians. [SAPPHO n. + DADDY-O n. (2)]

sappiness *n.* [mid-19C+] (*US*) stupidity. [SAPPY adj. (1)]

sappo *n. see* SAP n.[2].

sappy *adj.* **1** [mid-17C+] foolish, stupid. **2** [late 19C+] (*US*) sentimental and mawkish. [SAP n.[2] /SE *sap*, which is SOFT adj. (1)/SOFT adj. (3)]

sappyhead *n.* [mid-19C–1920s] a fool; thus *sappy-headed*, foolish. [SAPPY adj. (1) + -HEAD sfx (1)]

sapscull *n.* (*also* **scapskull**) [mid-18C–1910s] a fool. [SE *sap*, juice, liquid + *skull*; thus one who is 'soft in the head']

sap up *v. see* SAP v.[2].

sarah soo *n.* [1920s+] a Jew (cf. BILLY THE KID n.). [rhy. sl.]

sarajevo *phr.* [1980s+] (*US campus*) goodbye. ['see you later']

sarc *n.* (*also* **sark**) [1900s–10s] *sarc*asm. [abbr.]

sarcy *adj. see* SARKY adj.

sard *v.* [16C–17C] to copulate. [10C when the *Lindisfarne Gospel* used it in its translation of Matt. 5:27, 'Ye have heard that it was said by them of old time, Thou shalt not commit adultery'. By the 17C it was the basis of a Nottingham pvb 'Go teach your Grandma to sard', but vanished soon afterwards. It is one of Florio's synon. for Ital. *fottere* in *World of Wordes* (1598)]

sardine *n.* **1** [mid-19C–1910s] (*US*) a general term of abuse. **2** [mid-19C–1930s] (*US*) a person. **3** [1910s–20s] (*US campus*) a girl. **4** [1940s] a run-down prostitute (cf. ALLEY CAT n.).

sardine box *n.* **1** [late 19C–1940s] a prison or police van. **2** [late 19C+] (*Aus.*) (*also* **sardine tin**) any extremely small dwelling. [the close-packing of the prisoners]

sarey gamp *n.* [mid-19C] an outsize umbrella used by stall-holders; thus *gamp(ish)*, of an umbrella, bulging. [Charles Dickens's character *Sarah Gamp* in *Martin Chuzzlewit* (1843–4)]

sarge *n.* (*also* **sarg, sarj, serg**) [mid-19C+] a *serge*ant, esp. as a familiar term of address. [abbr.]

sargentlemanly *adv.* [late 19C] a sarcastic allusion to one who is acting 'so gentlemanly'.

sark *n.*[1] [1980s+] (*N.Z.*) a sanitary towel. [? Scot. *sark*, a woman's undergarment]

sark *n.*[2] *see* SARC n.

sarky *adj.* (*also* **sarcy**) [20C+] (*mainly UK teen*) *sarc*astic, ill-tempered. [abbr.]

sarmie *n.* (*also* **sarmy**) [1960s+] (*S.Afr.*) a *s*andwich. [abbr.]

sarnie *n.* (*also* **sarney, sarny**) [1960s+] a *s*andwich. [abbr.]

sarse *n.* (*also* **sarpidilly**) [1920s+] (*Aus.*) *sars*parilla, the dried root of *Smilax officinalis*, at one time used as a tonic. [abbr.]

sarve out *v. see* SERVE OUT v.

sarvo *n.* [1940s+] (*Aus./N.Z.*) this afternoon. [abbr. SE *this* + ARVO n. (1)]

sasfras *n. see* SASSAFRAS n.[2].

sashay *n.* [1900s–30s] a walk that is casual and yet confident. [SASHAY v.]

sashay *v.* (*also* **sasshay**) (*orig. US*) **1** [mid-19C+] to walk or travel in a casual manner; to saunter. **2** [20C+] to hurry, to move briskly. **3** [1900s] to strut, to parade, to walk in an ostentatious or provocative manner. [Fr. *chassé*, a gliding step in dancing]

sass *n.* [mid-19C+] (*orig. US*) cheek, impertinence, rudeness. [SAUCE n.[1]]

sass *v. see* SASS (OUT) v.

sassafras *n.*[1] [1930s] (*US*) a beard. [the facial hair supposedly resembles *sassafras* leaves; cognate with SPINACH n.[1] (1)]

sassafras *n.*[2] (*also* **sasfras, sassfras**) [1960s+] (*drugs*) marijuana (cf. AFRICAN BUSH n.). [SE *sassafras* tree, the leaves of which are also used for *sassafras* tea, thus linked to TEA n.[2] (1)]

sass-box *n. see* SASSY BOX n. (1).

sasshay *v. see* SASHAY v.

sassiger *n.* (*also* **sassenger, sassinger, saussinger, sossinger**) [19C] a *saus*age. [mispron.]

sass (out) *v.* [mid-19C+] (*US*) to answer back, to cheek; to tease. [SASS n.]

sass-talking *n.* [2000s] (*US*) talking in a cheeky manner. [SASS n. + SE *talking*]

sassy *adj.* **1** [mid-19C+] (*US*) cheeky, spirited, back-talking; also as adv. **2** [late 19C+] smart, fashionable. [SE *saucy*/SASS n.]

sassy-ass *adj.* [1960s] (*US Black*) a general derog. term. [SASSY adj. (1) + -ASS sfx]

sassy box *n.* **1** [late 19C+] (*US*) (*also* **sass-box**) a saucy young woman. **2** [1980s] the vagina (cf. BAG n.[1]). [SASSY adj. (1)/SASS n. + SE *box*/BOX n.[1] (1)]

sata *v.* (*also* **satta**) [1950s+] (*W.I. Rasta*) to rejoice, to meditate, to give thanks and praise; thus *go satta*, to claim how spiritual one is.

Satan *n.* [late 19C] a euph. for HELL, THE phr.[1] (2), e.g. *belt Satan out of*.

Satan's bones *n.* [early 18C] dice.

Satan's own —, the *phr. see* DEVIL'S OWN —, THE phr.

satan's scent *n.* (*also* **satan's secret**) [1980s] (*drugs*) any inhalant.

satch *n.*[1] [1900s–40s] **1** (*US Black*) a notably large mouth; thus a person with a large mouth. **2** (*US*) a talkative person. [abbr. SE *satchel*]

satch *n.*[2] (*also* **sach, sacht**) [1930s–60s] (*drugs*) paper or clothing that is saturated with a drug solution (usu. used to smuggle drugs into prisons or hospitals). [SE *saturate*]

satch *n.*[3] [1940s–50s] (*US Black*) a jacket. [? SACK n.[5]]

satch cotton *n.* [1960s] (*drugs*) fabric used to filter a solution of narcotics before injection; the cotton may be boiled later and the drug residue used. [SATCH n.[2] + COTTON n.[1] (1)]

satchel *n.* **1** [1930s] (*US Und.*) a prison. **2** [1930s–50s] (*US*) the vagina (cf. BAG n.[1]). **3** [1940s+] (*US*) the anus or buttocks. **4** [2000s] the scrotum. **5** [2000s] a term of abuse (cf. BALLOCKS n.[2]).

satchel *v.* [20C+] (*US*) to pre-arrange the outcome of a contest, race or fight. [it is thus IN THE BAG phr.[1] (1)]

satchel-arsed *adj.* (*also* **satchel-arse**) [18C+] a general term of abuse; often ext. to *satchel-arsed son of a whore*. [SE *satchel* + -ARSED sfx[1]]

satchel-mouth *n.* [1930s–40s] (*US Black*) anyone with a large mouth. [note the jazz musician Louis 'Satchmo' (*Satchel-Mouth*) Armstrong (1900–72)]

satchel-mouthed *adj.* [1930s–60s] (*orig. US Black*) **1** used of someone who has a large mouth. **2** in fig. use, used of someone who talks a great deal, e.g. an informer. [SATCHEL-MOUTH n.]

sate-poll *n.* [late 19C] a fool. [SE *sate*, to fill + *poll*, head; ? a head that is filled with nonsense]

satin *n.*[1] **1** [mid-19C–1930s] gin (cf. FUSTIAN n.; RIBBON n.[1]). **2** [1970s+] (*US Black*) Italian Swiss Colony Silver *Satin* wine mixed with lemon juice. [its supposed smoothness]

satin *n.*[2] [2000s] (*US Black*) death. [the SE *satin* that lines a coffin]

satin and lace *n.* **1** [late 19C–1930s] His Grace, i.e. a Duke. **2** [1990s+] the human face. [rhy. sl.]

satin and silk *n.* [20C+] milk. [rhy. sl.]

sativa *n.* [1970s+] (*drugs*) cannabis. [abbr. botanical name *Cannabis sativa*]

satta *v. see* SATA v.

sat-upon *adj.* [late 19C] depressed, miserable.

saturated *adj.* [late 19C+] very drunk (cf. DAMP adj.). [metaphorical, but also a lit. description of the bloodstream; its 1980s resurgence emerged in US campus use]

Saturday gangster *n.* [1990s+] (*Aus. Und.*) a 'wannabe' gangster.

Saturday is longer than Sunday *phr. see* MONDAY COMES BEFORE SUNDAY phr.

Saturday night butch *n.* [1950s–60s] (*US gay*) a lesbian who dressed up as a BUTCH n.[4] (3) at the weekend, i.e. not a real 'full-time' butch. [BUTCH n.[4] (3)]

Saturday night habit *n.* [1930s–50s] (*US drugs*) an occasional (perhaps lit. weekly) use of narcotics. [HABIT n. (1)]

Saturday night palsy *n.* (*also* **Saturday night itis, …paralysis**) [1920s+] (*US*) the temporary paralysis of the arm, esp. a weakness in the wrist, after it has rested on a hard edge for a long time, as during sleep following a bout of drinking. [one has passed out drunk on Saturday night]

Saturday night pistol *n.* [1920s–30s] (*US*) a small handgun.

Saturday night security *n.* [1940s+] (*Aus.*) a regular boyfriend.

Saturday night smile *n.* [1940s] (*US*) an enthusiastic smile.

Saturday night special *n.* [1960s+] (*US*) a small handgun, often used in the many fracas that occur over Saturday night in big US cities.

Saturday pie *n.* [late 19C] pastry, esp. when covering the week's collected left-overs.

Saturday soldier *n.* [late 19C] a milit. volunteer.

Saturday-to-Monday *n.* [1900s–10s] a mistress whom one sees only at weekends.

satyr *n.* [mid-18C] (*UK Und.*) a professional horse thief. [SE *satyr*, a mythological Greek woodland demon, usu. pictured with the ears and tail of a horse. 'Men living wild in the Fields, that keep their Holds and Dwellings in the Country and forsaken Places, stealing Horses, Kine, Sheep, and all other sort of Cattle' (A. Smith, *Lives of the Highwaymen*, 1714)]

sauce *n.*[1] [late 16C+] cheek, impudence. [? SE *saucy*, impudent + *sauce*, something that adds piquancy to a word, thought or action]

sauce *n.*[2] **1** [late 17C; 1930s] vaginal fluids (cf. BINDERJUICE n.). **2** [late 17C–early 19C] a venereal disease. **3** [mid-18C] money. **4** [1910s] (*US*) petrol, gasoline. **5** [1930s+] (*orig. US*) alcohol, (rarely) drugs. **6** [1970s] (*US campus*) beer. **7** [1970s+] (*US gay*) semen (cf. BABY GRAVY n.).

sauce *n.*[3] [1990s+] (*US campus*) something bad or inferior.

sauce *v.*[1] [mid-19C+] to cheek, to tease. [SAUCE n.[1]]

sauce *v.*[2] [1990s+] (*US campus*) to ruin. [SAUCE n.[3]]

saucebox *n.*[1] [late 16C–19C] an impudent person. [SE *sauce*, impudence + *box*]

saucebox *n.*[2] [mid-late 19C] the mouth. [SE *sauce*]

sauced (up) *adj.* [1940s+] (*US*) drunk, tipsy (cf. ALED UP adj.). [SAUCE n.[2] (5)]

sauce-hound *n.* [1940s+] (*US*) a drunkard, an alcoholic. [SAUCE n.[2] (5) + HOUND sfx]

saucepan handle *n.* [2000s] the penis.

saucepan lid *n.* **1** [late 19C] money, esp. in pl. (cf. BEES (AND HONEY) n.). **2** [late 19C+] a tease, a 'leg-pull'. **3** [1950s+] a Jew (cf. BILLY THE KID n.). **4** [1960s+] a child (cf. BILLY LID n.). [rhy. sl.; (1) = QUID n. (2); (2) = KID n.[2] (2); (3) =YID n.[1]; (4) = KID n.[1] (1)]

saucer *n.* [mid-19C–1910s] an eye. [SE phr. *eyes like/as big as saucers*, coined 14C]

saucy *adj.* [1990s+] (*US campus*) a general negative. [SAUCE n.[3]]

saucy box *n.* [early 18C] an impudent person. [SE *saucy* + *box*]

saucy jack *n.* [mid-16C–early 19C] a cheeky, impudent man. [SE *saucy* + JACK n.[2]]

sauerkraut *n.* (*also* **sauerkrauter, sourcrout, sourkraut**) (*mainly Aus./US*) **1** [mid-18C+] a derog. term for a German. **2** [mid-19C] a cantankerous person, a term of abuse. [the popular German dish]

sauncy *n. see* SONSY adj.

sausage *n.*[1] **1** [mid-19C+] the penis (cf. BACON n.[1]). **2** [1990s+] (*US campus*) as a generic term for a man; esp. in phrs. e.g. *sausage fest/party*, a mostly male gathering.

sausage *n.*[2] [late 19C+] a German. [the stereotypical German partiality to sausages]

sausage *n.*[3] [late 19C+] an ineffectual, easily imposed-upon person; esp. in teasing phr. *silly (old) sausage*.

sausage *n.*[4] [1930s] (*US*) a prize-fighter, esp. one with a swollen bruised face. [? resemblance]

sausage *n.*[5] [1970s–80s] (*UK prison*) a cannabis or cannabis/tobacco cigarette (cf. BONE n.[11]). [shape]

sausage *v.* [1920s+] to cash (a cheque). [rhy. sl. based on *sausage and mash*]

sausage a goose's *v.* [1920s–60s] to cash a cheque. [SAUSAGE v. + GOOSE'S NECK n.[2]]

sausage and mash *n.* **1** [late 19C+] cash. **2** [1950s+] a smash, a car crash. [rhy. sl.]

sausage-eater *n.* [1910s+] a German; thus *adj.* *sausage-eating*. [ext. SAUSAGE n.[2]]

sausage jockey *n.* [1980s+] (*US*) a male homosexual (cf. BONE-EATER n.). [SAUSAGE n.[1] (1) + JOCKEY n.[3] (2)]

sausage roll *n.* **1** [1920s+] unemployment benefit, the dole (cf. BLESS MY SOUL n.). **2** [1940s+] a Pole. **3** [1960s+] (*Aus.*) a goal. [rhy. sl.]

sausages *n.* **1** [mid-19C] fetters; thus *string of sausages*, a chain. **2** [mid-late 19C] side-whiskers. [resemblance]

sausage sandwich *n.* [1990s+] **1** intercourse between the breasts. **2** sex between 2 men and 1 woman (cf. CHOCOLATE SANDWICH n.). [SAUSAGE n.[1] (1) + SE *sandwich*/SANDWICH n.[2]]

sausage smuggler *n.* [1990s+] a male homosexual (cf. BONE-EATER n.). [SAUSAGE n.[1] (1) + SE *smuggler*]

sausage wrapper *n.* [late 19C–1910s] (*Aus.*) a newspaper.

sausie *n.* (*also* **sossie**) [1990s+] (*N.Z.*) a *sausage*. [abbr.]

saussinger *n. see* SASSIGER n.

sav *n.* [1940s+] (*Aus.*) a *saveloy*; thus *battered sav*, a saveloy covered in a flour and water paste, impaled on a lollipop stick and then deep fried. [abbr.]

savage *n.* [1930s–40s] (*US*) a keen young police officer eager to make arrests.

savage *adj.* **1** [late 18C+] extremely annoyed, furious. **2** [1940s+] strong, intense. [weak use of SE]

savage as a meat axe *phr. see* MAD AS A MEAT AXE phr. (1).

save a life *v.* [late 19C] to take a drink, to give a timely drink.

save-alls *n.* [late 18C–early 19C] (*Anglo-Irish*) 'boys running about gentlemen's houses in Ireland, who are fed on broken meats that would otherwise be wasted' (Grose, 1785). [SE *save-all*, 'a kind of candlestick used by our frugal forefathers to burn snuffs and ends of candles' (Grose, 1785)]

save it! *excl.* [1930s+] (*US*) be quiet! shut up!

save it for Sweeney! *excl. see* TELL IT TO SWEENEY! excl.

saveloy *n.* [20C+] a boy. [rhy. sl.]

Saveloy Square *n.* [late 19C] Duke Place, Aldgate. [as a centre of the East End Jewish community, no pork sausages, only beef *saveloys* were to be found there]

save one's ass *v.* (*also* **save one's arse**) [1960s+] (*orig. US*) to take care of oneself, to save oneself; esp. in phr. *couldn't — to save one's ass*. [SE *save* + ASS *n.* (5)/ARSE *n.*[1] (4)]

save one's bacon *v.* (*also* **save one's beef**) [late 17C+] to escape safely from a place or situation (cf. SAVE SOMEONE'S BACON *v.*). [SE *save* + BACON *n.*[1] (1)]

save one's groats *v.* [late 18C–19C] to succeed, to do well. [university custom, those taking their finals deposit 9 groats (= 32 old pennies) with an academic officer; if they pass with honours the groats are returned]

saver *n.* [late 19C–1900s] a hedging bet. [the gambler hopes to 'save' their money, which may be lost on the other, main bet]

save someone's bacon *v.* [late 17C+] to rescue someone from difficulties (cf. SAVE ONE'S BACON *v.*). [SE *save* + BACON *n.*[1] (1)]

save them all for Lisa *n.* [late 19C] used of a young man who will neither swear nor fight. [the assumption is that this public probity is overturned when in private; there he berates and even beats his girlfriend]

savey *n. see* SAVVY *n.*

savey/savez *v. see* SAVVY *v.*

saving chin *n.* [late 18C] a protruding chin. [it supposedly catches the food that drops from the mouth when its owner is eating badly]

savoury rissole *n.* [20C+] **1** a lavatory (cf. ANGUS ARMANASCO *n.*). **2** anywhere dirty or unpleasant. [rhy. sl. = PISSHOLE *n.*]

savvy *n.* (*also* **sabbe, sabby, sabe, savey, savv, savvey, scavey**) [late 18C+] understanding, intelligence, awareness. [SAVVY *v.* (1)]

savvy *adj.* [late 19C+] bright, knowledgeable, aware. [SAVVY *n.*]

savvy *v.* (*also* **sabe, savey, savez, savvey, scavey**) **1** [late 18C+] to understand, to be aware of. **2** [20C+] as interrog.; often as *do you savvy?* [Fr. *savoir*, to know, to understand]

saw *n.*[1] [mid-19C+] (*US*) $10. [abbr. SAWBUCK *n.* (1)]

saw *n.*[2] [1940s] (*US Black*) **1** a woman, esp. when a nag. **2** the landlady of a cheap rooming house. [? their 'rough/sharp edges']

saw *n.*[3] *see* SAW-HANDLE *n.*

saw away *v.* [early 19C] to talk incessantly, to chatter on.

sawbones *n.* [mid-19C+] a doctor, a surgeon (cf. BONE-BENDER *n.*[1]).

sawbox *n.* [1930s–60s] (*orig. US Black*) a cello.

sawbuck *n.* (*also* **sawski, sawsky, sawzie**) (*US*) **1** [mid-19C+] $10. **2** [1920s+] a 10-year prison sentence. [SE *sawbuck*, an X-shaped sawhorse; the X of the sawhorse is equated with the Roman numeral *X*, 10 + BUCK *n.*[3] (1)/joc. use of -SKI sfx]

sawder *see under* SOFT SAWDER.

sawdust *n.*[1] [late 19C] flattery, insincerity. [? SOFT SAWDER *n.*]

sawdust *n.*[2] **1** [20C+] (*US Und.*) dynamite. **2** [1900s] (*US campus*) sugar. **3** [1940s] (*US*) cheap tobacco, used for rolling cigarettes.

sawdust game *n.* [late 19C–1930s] (*US*) a confidence trick based on the passing of bad banknotes; thus *sawdust swindler/man*. [? SAWDUST *n.*[1]]

sawdust joint *n.* (*also* **sawdust parlor, ...place, ...saloon**) [20C+] a down-market restaurant or bar, or gambling saloon. [SE *sawdust* + JOINT *n.*[4] (3)/SE *parlour/place/saloon*; such places lacked smart interiors and their plank floorboards were covered only by sawdust]

sawed *adj.* [mid-19C] (*US*) drunk.

sawed-off *n.* **1** [1900s–10s] a short person. **2** [1920s+] (*US*) (*also* **sawn-off**) a sawn-off shotgun.

sawed-off *adj.* (*also* **sawn-off, sawny**) [late 19C+] of a person or occas. object, short; or legless. [the presumption being that a short person was once taller than they are now]

saweer *v.* [mid-18C] (*UK Und.*) of a gang member, to keep watch. [SE *see-er*, one who sees]

saw gourds *v.* [mid-19C+] (*orig. US*) to snore loudly.

saw-handle *n.* (*also* **saw**) [mid-19C] (*US*) a saw-handled pistol. [abbr.]

saw logs *v. see* SAW WOOD *v.*[2].

sawn *n.* [1950s+] (*Aus.*) a simpleton. [abbr. SAWNEY *n.*[1] (1)]

Sawney *n.* [late 17C–19C] a generic term for a Scotsman (cf. SANDY *n.*). [proper name *Sawney*, abbr. common Scot. name Alexander]

sawney *n.*[1] (*also* **sawny**) [late 17C+] **1** a fool. **2** a clumsy person, a thug. [SE *zany*, a fool, a laughing-stock]

sawney *n.*[2] [early 19C–1900s] bacon. [? SE *sawn*, i.e. the 'sawing off' of bacon into rashers, or the cannibalistic *Sawney* Beane (*fl.*15C), who killed people, smoked their corpses and ate them]

sawney *adj.* [late 17C–19C; 1940s] foolish. [SAWNEY *n.*[1] (1)]

sawney-hunter *n.* [mid-19C] one who steals bacon or cheese from grocers' shops. [SAWNEY *n.*[2]]

sawn-off *see under* SAWED-OFF.

sawny *n. see* SAWNEY *n.*[1].

sawny *adj. see* SAWED-OFF *adj.*

saw off *v.* **1** [1900s–40s] (*US*) to stop talking, usu. as imper. **2** [1940s–60s] to berate, to reprimand.

saw off a chunk *v.* (*also* **saw off a length/piece**) [1920s+] to have sexual intercourse (cf. BREAK A BIT OFF *v.*).

sawpit *n. see* PIT *n.*[1] (1).

sawski/sawsky *n. see* SAWBUCK *n.*

saw them off *v.* [1930s–40s] to snore.

saw wood *v.*[1] [late 19C–1930s] (*US*) to carry on as normal, to get on with one's work, to keep to oneself. [the mundane act of sawing wood]

saw wood *v.*[2] (*also* **saw logs**) [20C+] (*US*) to snore. [the noise produced]

sawyer *n.* [1940s] (*US Und.*) a sawn-off shotgun.

saw your timber! *excl.* [mid-19C] go away! be off!

sawzie *n. see* SAWBUCK *n.*

sax *n.* **1** [1920s+] a saxophone. **2** [1920s–70s] (*Aus./N.Z.*) a sixpence. **3** [1960s] a saxophone-player. [abbr.; (2) is mispron.]

saxa *n.* [1930s] (*Aus.*) a saxophone. [abbr.]

saxophone *n.* (*also* **Chinese saxophone**) [1930s–50s] (*US drugs*) an opium pipe; thus *saxophone-player*, a smoker of opium.

say *n.* (*also* **sei, sey**) [mid-19C+] (*Ling. Fr./Polari*) the number 6. [Ital. *sei*, 6]

say *v.* [1900s] (*US Und.*) to rob; to break into.

say *adv.* [mid-19C] yes. [backsl.]

say! *excl.* [mid-19C+] (*mainly US*) listen! wait a minute! excuse me!

say a mouthful *v.* (*also* **say an armful, speak a mouthful/ an armful**) **1** [1910s+] (*orig. US*) to say something important and true. **2** [1920s+] (*US*) to talk at length, esp. critically. **3** [1940s–70s] (*US gay*) to reprove a fellow homosexual in detail and at great length.

say calf-rope *v. see* HOLLER CALF-ROPE *v.*

say-cordi box *n.* [1940s+] (*Polari*) a guitar. [lit. '6-cord box']

say-dooe *n.* (*also* **sey-dooe**) [mid-19C+] (*Ling. Fr./Polari*) the number 8. [SAY *n.*+ DOOE *n.*]

say it like it is *phr. see* TELL IT LIKE IT IS *phr.*

say my name! *excl.* [1990s+] (*US teen*) an excl. used to intimidate or used for celebration.

say no more *phr. see* NUDGE, NUDGE, WINK, WINK, KNOW WHAT I MEAN, SAY NO MORE *phr.*

say nothing *v.* [1950s–60s] (*US Black*) to talk trivially.

say one's piece *v.* [1910s+] to make oneself heard, to say what one has decided to say, esp. for moral reasons.

say-oney *n.* (*also* **sey-oney**) [mid-19C+] (*Ling. Fr./Polari*) the number 7. [SAY *n.* + SE *one* + sfx -y]

say-so *n.* [mid-18C+] the power of decision, permission.

say something *v.* [1910s+] (*US*) to make an important statement, to say something profound; lit. or fig.

says which? *phr. see* SAY WHAT? *phr.*

says you! *excl.* (*also* **sez you!**) [mid-19C+] a general excl. of contempt and disbelief, dismissing as beneath argument the previous speaker's words.

say-tray *n.* (*also* **sey-tray**) [mid-19C+] (*Ling. Fr./Polari*) the number 9. [SAY n.+ TRAY n. (1)]

say uncle *v. see* CRY UNCLE *v.*

say what? *phr.* (*also* **says which? say which?**) [20C+] (*US*) an expression of mock disbelief, e.g. what did you say? are you telling the truth?

say when *phr.* [late 19C+] a phr. used when pouring someone else a drink, i.e. say when you want me to stop pouring.

sazeech *n.* [1960s] (*US*) the penis. [pron. of SAUSAGE n.¹ (1)]

s.b. *n.*¹ [late 19C+] (*US*) a euph. abbr. for SONOFABITCH n. (cf. S.O.B. n.).

s.b. *n.*² [1910s] (*US*) bacon. [abbr. sour *bosom/belly*]

s.b.d. *n.* [1960s+] the breaking of wind silently and with a foul smell. [abbr. silent *but deadly*]

'sblood! *excl.* (*also* **'sbud! 'slud!**) [late 16C–mid-19C] a euph. oath, lit. 'God's blood'.

'sbody! *excl.* (*also* **'sbobs**) [mid-17C–mid-19C] a euph. oath, lit 'God's body'.

s.c. *n.* [1990s+] (*US Black teen*) South-Central Los Angeles. [abbr.]

scab *n.* **1** [late 16C] a sheriff's officer, a constable. **2** [late 16C+] (*also* **scab neck**) an unpleasant person. **3** [17C] a prostitute. **4** [late 18C+] (*also* **scalie**) a strike-breaker or anyone who stands out against a mass action. **5** [1950] as ext. of (4), an amateur. **6** [1960s+] (*US Black/campus*) an unattractive man or woman. **7** [1970s–80s] (*N.Z. prison*) an inmate who curries favour with the authorities. **8** [1990s+] (*UK juv.*) one who attempts to beg money or food.

scab *adj.* **1** [late 19C+] pertaining to strike-breakers or strike-breaking. **2** [1960s] in fig. use, illegal, e.g. of an after-hours drinking club. [SCAB n. (4)]

scab *v.* (*also* **scab it**) **1** [19C–1920s] to brand a company or fellow worker as a strike-breaker. **2** [19C+] to break a strike, refuse to join a union or any form of mass action; ext. to 'letting down the side' in non-work contexts. **3** [1920s+] to take a job without belonging to the relevant union. **4** [1970s–80s] (*N.Z. prison*) of an inmate, to curry favour with the authorities. [SCAB n. (4)]

scabbado *n.* [mid-17C–early 18C] syphilis. [a 'Spanish' version of SE *scab*, syphilis]

scabbard *n.* [17C–19C] the vagina (cf. BAG n.¹). [a trans. of Lat. and euph. for SE *vagina*]

scabbed *adj.* [1960s–70s] (*drugs*) cheated in a deal. [weak use of SCAB v.]

scabbery *n.* [20C+] (*Aus./US*) the betrayal of one's fellow workers, the breaking of a strike. [SCAB v. (2)]

scabby *n.* [1910s+] (*Aus.*) a non-union worker. [SCAB n. (4)]

scabby *adj.*¹ [mid-17C+] of a person or thing, unpleasant, contemptible, generally distasteful. [SE *scab*, a variety of skin diseases, including syphilis, which is the most likely ref. in a sl. context]

scabby *adj.*² [late 19C+] (*Aus.*) non-union. [SCAB n. (4)]

scabby-neck *n.* [mid-19C] a native of Denmark. [orig. naut. use]

scabby sheep *n.* [mid-19C] 'a person who has been in question-able society, or under unholy influence, and become tainted' (Hotten, 1864). [SE *scabby sheep*, a sheep that has a diseased mouth; thus a moral leper, a corrupt person; *sheep* also puns on the popular religious use of the word]

scab it *v. see* SCAB *v.*

scab neck *n. see* SCAB n. (2).

scad *n.*¹ [early 17C] semen. [? Cornwall/Devon dial, *scad*, a brief shower of rain]

scad *n.*² [19C–1940s] (*US*) $1. [ety. unknown]

scadger *n.* [mid–late 19C] a general term of abuse, a mean, contemptible person, someone who always wants a loan. [SE *cadger* + ? Cornish *scadgan*, a tramp]

scadoodle *v.* [mid-19C] to run off, to leave in a hurry. [SKEDADDLE v. + SCOOT v. (2)]

scads *n.* (*also* **scadoodles, skadoodles, skads**) [mid-19C+] large quantities. [ety. unknown]

scaffe *n.* [1970s] (*Aus. drugs*) a smoke of marijuana. [ety. unknown]

scaffold pole *n.* [late 19C] a chipped potato. [joc. resemblance]

scag *n.*¹ (*also* **skag**) [1910s–40s] (*US*) a cigarette, a cigar, a cigarette butt. [? elision of SE *cigar(ette)*]

scag *n.*² (*also* **skag**) **1** [1940s] bad liquor. **2** [1960s+] (*drugs*) heroin. [ety. unknown; note Smitherman, *Black Talk* (1994): 'low-grade heroin that has been diluted']

scag *n.*³ [1960s+] (*US campus/Black*) an unattractive woman. [var. on SCAG n. (1)]

scagged (out) *adj.* (*also* **skagged**) [1970s+] (*drugs*) addicted to heroin. [SCAG n.² (2)]

scag hag *n.* (*also* **skag hag**) [1990s+] **1** one who enjoys associating with heroin addicts. **2** a female heroin addict. [SCAG n.² (2) + SE *hag*]

scaghead *n.* [1990s+] a heroin addict. [SCAG n.² (2) + -HEAD sfx (3)]

scag jones *n.* (*also* **skag jones**) [1960s+] (*US drugs*) a heroin addiction. [SCAG n.² (2) + JONES n.¹ (1)]

scag-nasty *n.* (*also* **skag-nasty**) [1990s+] (*UK juv.*) an unpleasant person. [? var. on SHAG-NASTY n.]

scal *n. see* SCALLY n.

scalawag *n. see* SCALLYWAG n.¹.

scald *n.* [20C+] (*Irish*) tea; also as v., to make tea. [Irish *scal*, hot tea]

scald *adj.* [late 16C–mid-17C] suffering from venereal disease. [obs. 16C dial. *scald*, scabbed, afflicted with the 'scall' (any scaly or scabby disease of the skin, esp. of the scalp; *dry scall* was psoriasis, *humid* or *moist scall* was eczema)]

scald *v.*¹ [late 16C–17C] to infect with venereal disease; thus *scalding-house*, a brothel. [SCALD adj.]

scald *v.*² [late 19C+] (*Irish*) **1** to be mortified. **2** to reprimand, to scold. [Irish *scall*, to scald; thus fig. to grieve bitterly]

scalded *adj.* **1** [17C] suffering from venereal disease. **2** [1980s] (*US campus*) rejected. [ext. of SCALD adj. + (2) fig. use of SE *scald*]

scalder *n.*¹ [early 19C] venereal disease. [SCALD v.¹]

scalder *n.*² [late 19C] tea. [SE *scald*, to burn]

scalding *n.* [mid-19C] (*US*) a beating.

scaldrum dodge *n.* [mid-19C–1900s] (*UK Und.*) the practice of deliberately burning the body with a mixture of acids and gunpowder in order to simulate scars and wounds that should soften the hearts of those from whom one begs; thus *scaldrum/scoldrum*, the beggar who adopts this pose. [SE *scald*, burn + DODGE n. (1)]

scaldy *n.* [20C+] (*Irish*) **1** a bald-headed or very short-haired person, thus a baby. **2** a mean, cadging person; also as adj., stingy. [ON *scalle*, a bald head; Irish *scalltán*, a fledgling]

scale *n.*¹ (*also* **shadscale**) [late 19C–1920s] (*US*) money. [SE *scale*, a thin piece of metal, used in scale-armour]

scale *n.*² [1960s+] (*US prison*) a louse. [SE *scale*, a form of skin disease]

scale *v.*¹ [early 16C; 1960s] of a man, to enter a woman and commence intercourse. [SE *scale*, to climb; thus synon. with MOUNT v.³]

scale *v.*² [late 19C] to impress, to astonish. [? SE phr. *scale the heights*]

scale *v.*³ [1910s+] (*Aus./N.Z./S.Afr.*) **1** to steal, to defraud; thus *scale a train/tram*, to board and ride without paying. **2** to leave surreptitiously or speedily; esp. as *scale off*. [SE *scale*, to strip the scales from]

scale *v.*⁴ [1990s+] (*drugs*) to weigh a measure of a drug; thus *scale boy*, one who weighs and measures out portions of the drug.

scale-backed 'un *n.* [1910s–20s] a louse. [lit. 'scale-backed one']

scaler *n.* [1910s+] (*Aus./N.Z.*) **1** a fraud, anyone who betrays a financial trust. **2** one who rides illegally for free on public transport; thus *scaling*, riding for free on buses etc. [SCALE *v.*³ (1)]

scalie *n. see* SCAB *n.* (4).

scallawag *see under* SCALLYWAG.

scalloped potatoes *n.* [1970s] (*US gay*) sunburned testicles (cf. ACORNS *n.*).

scallowag *n. see* SCALLYWAG *n.*¹.

scally *n.* (*also* scal) [1960s+] a hooligan youth. [abbr. SCALLYWAG *n.*¹ (2); coined in Liverpool, where it is tinged with a degree of admiration]

scally *adj.* [1990s+] pertaining to a hooligan. [SCALLY *n.*]

scallybip *v. see* BIPE *v.*

scallywag *n.*¹ (*also* scalawag, scallawag, scallowag, skalawag) **1** [mid–late 19C] (*US*) a White Southerner who was willing to accept the terms of Reconstruction after the US Civil War (1861–5). **2** [mid-19C+] (*orig. US*) a ne'er-do-well, a disreputable person. **3** [late 19C–1930s] (*orig. US*) a political intriguer, a corrupt politician; thus *scallywaggery/scallywagism*, roguery, political opportunism; *scallywagging*, acting in a corrupt manner. **4** [1990s+] (*US*) the penis. [? link to Scot. *scurryvaig*, a vagabond or *scalrag*, a raggedly dressed person, ? ult. Lat. *scurra vagas*, a wandering fool]

scallywag *n.*² (*also* scallawag) [mid-19C–1900s] undersized or ill-conditioned cattle. [ext. use of SCALLYWAG *n.*¹ (2)]

scalp *v.*¹ **1** [mid-19C+] to tout tickets (orig. for railroads) at above face value price. **2** [1930s] (*gambling*) to take a commission on a bet. **3** [1940s+] to re-sell any item for a profit. [orig. Stock Exchange use, to buy shares very cheap, then sell below the prevailing price; *theatre scalpers* look for greater profits]

scalp *v.*² [1970s] (*US Black*) to perform cunnilingus. [play on HEAD *n.*¹⁰]

scalp *v.*³ [1990s+] (*N.Z.*) to capture the insignia or PATCH *n.*³ of a rival gang member. [SE *scalp*, to remove the enemy's scalp as a trophy]

scalper *n.* **1** [mid-19C+] (*orig. US*) a ticket tout. **2** [late 19C] one who buys the unused portions of long-distance railroad tickets in order to sell them at a profit. **3** [late 19C+] 'any human being of merciless tendencies, especially in his financial dealings' (Ware). **4** [1950s+] (*gambling*) a person who bets in such a way that he never loses. [SCALP *v.*¹]

scalp hunter *n.* [1960s–70s] (*US gay*) a homosexual who likes to seduce otherwise heterosexual males.

scalping *n.* [late 19C+] (*orig. US*) working as a ticket tout. [SCALP *v.*¹ (1)]

scalp ticket *n.* [1940s] (*Aus.*) the unused half of a return ticket. [SCALP *v.*¹ (1)]

scaly *n.* [1930s+] (*Aus.*) a crocodile.

scaly *adj.* **1** [late 18C–mid-19C] sick, run-down. **2** [late 18C–1910s] mean, miserly. **3** [late 18C–1950s] despicable. **4** [mid-19C–1920s] shabby. **5** [mid-19C+] unpleasant. [SE *scaly*, suffering from a skin disease, typically ringworm]

scaly bloke *n.* [1930s] (*N.Z.*) a thin man. [SCALY *adj.* (1) + BLOKE *n.*]

scaly fish *n.* [late 18C–early 19C] 'an honest, rough, blunt sailor' (Grose, 1796). [FISH *n.*⁴]

scalyleg *v.* [1960s+] (*US*) to work as the cheapest level of prostitute; thus as *n.*, a promiscuous woman; as *adj.*, promiscuous.

scam *n.*¹ **1** [1940s+] (*also* scamus) a plan, a scheme. **2** [1960s–70s]

(*US*) information. **3** [1970s+] a large-scale plan to smuggle and distribute illegal drugs. **4** [1970s+] a confidence trick; thus *scamster*, a confidence trickster. [? SE *scheme*]

scam *n.*² [2000s] (*US prison*) heroin. [abbr. SCAMMISH *n.*]

scam *v.* **1** [1950s+] (*also* scam out) to defraud, to trick. **2** [1960s+] to carry out any form of scheme, usu. dubious or illegal; thus *scam in*, to gain entry to a concert, performance etc. without paying for a ticket. **3** [1980s] (*US Und.*) to escape. **4** [1980s+] (*US campus*) to go in search of and look over the opposite sex for casual sex; thus *scam on*, to flirt; also used of desirable objects. [SCAM *n.*¹]

scamander *v.* [mid-19C] of persons, to wander about, to take a devious or winding course. [the classical river *Scamander*, ult. SE *meander*; note Yorks. dial. *skimaundering*, hanging or hovering about]

scammed *adj.* [1990s+] subjected to a confidence trick. [SCAM *v.* (1)]

scammer *n.* **1** [1970s+] a confidence trickster. **2** [1980s+] (*US campus*) a flirt. [SCAM *v.*]

scammer *v. see* SCUMMER *v.*

scammered *adj.*¹ [mid–late 19C] drunk. [? dial. *scammed*, injured or Somerset dial. *scammish*, rough, untidy]

scammered *adj.*² [1930s+] (*US prison*) homosexual. [? fig. use of SCAM *v.* (1), the image of deception]

scamming *n.* [1970s+] practising confidence tricks and similar schemes. [SCAM *v.* (1)]

scammish *n.* [1910s] (*US drugs*) the acquiring and preparation of unadulterated opium.

scam out *v. see* SCAM *v.* (1).

scamp *n.* **1** [mid-18C–early 19C] highway robbery; thus *on the scamp*, working as a highwayman. **2** [mid-18C–mid-19C] a highwayman. **3** [early 19C–1910s] a cheat, a swindler. **4** [mid–late 19C] (*UK Und.*) a thief. [Scot. *scamp*, to wander, to shirk; note late 16C *scampant*, a burlesque 'coat-of-arms', modelled on SE *rampant* and illustrating 'a roge in his ragges' (OED)]

scamp *v.*¹ [mid-18C–mid-19C] (*UK Und.*) to work as a highwayman. [SCAMP *n.* (2)]

scamp *v.*² [mid-19C–1930s] to give short measure, to cheat generally. [SCAMP *n.* (3)]

scamper *v.* [late 17C–18C] to run, to run off. [SE since early 19C]

scamperer *n.* [early 18C–mid-19C] a street thug. [SCAMP *n.* (2)]

scamper juice *n.* [1970s] (*US*) whisky.

scamp-foot *n. see* FOOT-SCAMP *n.*

scampi belt *n.* [1960s+] the middle-class commuter villages around London and other large cities where, in the late 1950s–early 1960s, it was considered fashionable to eat scampi. [by the 1980s scampi was reserved for the 'basket meal' trade, and such areas should perhaps be renamed the 'fresh pasta belt' or 'sun-dried tomato belt']

scamping *adj.* [early–mid-19C] dishonest. [SCAMP *v.*¹]

scampsman *n.* (*also* scamping blade) [late 18C–mid-19C] a highwayman. [ext. SCAMP *n.* (2)]

scamus *n. see* SCAM *n.*¹ (1).

Scan *n.* (*also* Scand) [1930s+] a *Scand*inavian. [abbr.]

scan *v.* [mid-19C–1900s] to see, to notice.

Scandahoovian *n.* [late 19C+] (*US*) a Scandinavian person. [joc. mispron.]

Scandahoovian *adj.* (*also* Scandahoofian, Scandihoovian) [late 19C+] (*US*) Scandinavian. [SCANDAHOOVIAN *n.*]

scandal-broth *n.* (*also* scandal-soup, scandal-water) [late 18C+] tea (cf. PRATTLE-BROTH *n.*).

scandalous *n.* [late 17C–18C] (*UK Und.*) a wig. [? joc. use of SE]

scandalous *adj.* [1980s+] (*orig. US Black*) **1** extremely bad. **2** excellent, first-rate. [17C–18C SE *scandalous*, 'guilty of grossly disgraceful conduct, infamous' (OED); (2) on bad = good model]

scandalously *adv.* [1990s+] (*US teen*) in a totally unacceptable manner (on the basis of a group's standards).

scandal-proof *adj.* [late 17C–18C] applied to a professional thief 'harden'd or past Shame' (B.E.).

scandal-soup/-water *n. see* SCANDAL-BROTH n.

Scandihoovian *adj. see* SCANDAHOOVIAN adj.

Scandy *n.* [late 19C+] (*orig. N.Z.*) a *Scandi*navian. [abbr.]

Scandy *adj.* [late 19C+] (*orig. N.Z.*) *Scandi*navian. [abbr.]

scanger *n.* (*also* **skanger**) [2000s] (*Irish*) **1** a silly woman. **2** a lout. [ety. unknown]

scank *see under* SKANK.

scanmag *n.* [early 18C; 19C–1910s] chatter, gossip, scandal; thus *scanmag*, to chatter, to gossip. [legal jargon *scandalum magnum*, the 'scandal of magnates', coined in a statute of King Richard II (*2 Ric. II* stat. 1 c. 5), which forbade anyone from publishing a malicious report against any person holding a position of dignity]

scan on *v.* [1960s–70s] (*US Black*) to watch closely, to look closely, esp. at something one intends stealing. [SE *scan*]

scanties *n.* [1920s+] (*orig. US*) women's (brief) lingerie. [SE *scant* + *panties*]

scanting *n.* [1990s+] (*UK juv.*) tugging the victim's underwear upwards, in order to give them a painful shock. [SCANTS n.]

scants *n.* [1970s+] (*UK juv.*) underwear.

scapa (flow) *v.* [1910s+] to go, esp. to run off. [rhy. sl., ult. British naval anchorage in the Orkney Islands used in both WW1 and WW2]

scapali *v. see* SCARPER v.

scapegallows *n.* [late 18C–mid-19C] a dedicated villain who has (so far) escaped the gallows.

scapper *v.* [1960s+] (*Irish*) to go, to run off. [SCAPA (FLOW) v.]

Scarborough Fair *n.* [1990s+] hair. [rhy. sl.]

scarce-o-fat *n.* [1950s] (*W.I.*) a nickname for a thin person. [SCARCE-O-FAT adj.]

scarce-o-fat *adj.* [1950s] (*W.I.*) thin.

scare, the *n.* [1930s] (*US Und.*) extortion using menaces.

scarecat *n. see* SCAREDY-CAT n.

scarecrow *n.* [mid-19C] (*UK Und.*) a pickpocket's young assistant, who is disposable and can be turned over to the police. [? his visibility resembles that of a scarecrow standing in a field]

scared-cat *n. see* SCAREDY-CAT n.

scared fartless *adj.* [1930s+] (*Can.*) extremely frightened. [semi-euph. for SCARED SHITLESS adj.]

scared shitless *adj.* (*also* **scared crapless, …pissless, …titless, scared shit, shitless**) [1910s+] extremely frightened; occas. as n., a state of terror. [SHIT n.[1] (1)]

scared spitless *adj.* (*also* **scared witless**) [1920s+] absolutely terrified. [euph. for SCARED SHITLESS adj.]

scared stiff *adj.* (*also* **scared rigid**) [20C+] utterly terrified; thus *scare someone stiff/rigid*, to terrify. [one is unable to move through terror]

scaredy-cat *n.* (*also* **scarecat, scared-cat, scaredy, scaredy-shite**) [20C+] (*mainly UK/US juv.*) anyone who is, or appears to be, frightened.

scarehead *n.* **1** [1900s] (*UK Und.*) a puritanical religious preacher. **2** [1910s] (*US*) a sensational newspaper headline, thus any sensational writing.

scare party *n.* [1940s–50s] (*US Black*) a Halloween party. [the ghost motif]

scare seven bells out of *v. see* KNOCK SEVEN BELLS OUT OF v.

scare someone shitless *v.* [1970s+] to terrify. [backform. f. SCARED SHITLESS adj.]

scare the bejazus out of *v.* (*also* **scare the bejab(b)ers out of**) [1920s+] to terrify completely and utterly. [BEJAZUS! excl.]

scare the crap out of *v. see* SCARE THE SHIT OUT OF v.

scare the daylights out of *v. see* SCARE THE (LIVING) DAYLIGHTS OUT OF v.

scare the dookey out of *v.* [1960s+] (*US*) to terrify. [DOOKEY n. (2)]

scare the fuck out of *v.* [1990s+] to terrify. [FUCK n.[2] (2)]

scare the (liver and) lights out of *v.* (*also* **scare the guts out of, scare the stuffing out of**) [mid-19C+] to terrify.

scare the (living) daylights out of *v.* (*also* **scare the living hell out of**) [1930s+] to terrify. [SE *scare* + DAYLIGHTS n. (2)/HELL, THE phr.[1] (2)]

scare the pants off *v.* (*also* **scare the nuts/slacks off**) [1930s+] to terrify. [SE *scare* + PANTS, THE n./NUTS n.[2] (1)/SE *slacks*]

scare the shit out of *v.* (*also* **scare the crap/piss out of**) [1920s+] (*orig. US*) to terrify?; often intensified by *living* or *holy*. [SHIT, THE n.[2]/CRAP n.[3] (6)/PISS, THE n.; the image of defecating or urinating with fright]

scare the stuffing out of *v. see* SCARE THE (LIVER AND) LIGHTS OUT OF v.

scare the whosis out of *v.* [1950s] (*US*) to terrify. [WHOOZIS n. (1), as a euph. for SCARE THE SHIT OUT OF v.]

scare up *v.* (*also* **scare together**) [mid-19C+] (*US*) to obtain, usu. with some difficulty and poss. by threatening the supplier. [SE *scare up*, to frighten game out of cover]

scarf *n.* [1930s+] (*US*) food. [SCOFF n.]

scarf *v.* (*also* **scarf up, skarf**) **1** [1940s+] (*orig. US*) to eat, esp. to gobble up, to eat aggressively. **2** [1960s+] (*US campus*) to pilfer; to steal. **3** [1970s] (*US campus*) to throw away, to abandon. **4** [1970s+] to consume, esp. in an aggressive manner. **5** [1970s+] (*US gay*) to fellate (cf. BASKET LUNCH n.). **6** [1980s] (*US campus*) to borrow. **7** [1990s+] to obtain, to get hold of. [SCOFF v.]

scarfer *n.* [1980s+] a football supporter. [the SE *scarf* that is worn]

scarlet *n.* [mid-19C] an upper-class ruffian. [a synon. for BLOOD n.[1]]

scarlet *adj.* [1980s+] (*Irish, Dublin*) highly embarrassed. [red with embarrassment]

scarlet fever *n.* [mid-late 19C] a partiality for soldiers or soldiering. [the scarlet uniform]

scarlet horse *n.* [late 18C–early 19C] a hired or hack horse. [pun on SE *hired/high-red*]

scarlet runner *n.* **1** [mid-19C] a Bow Street Runner. **2** [mid-late 19C] a footman. **3** [late 19C–1900s] a soldier. **4** [1940s+] (*Aus.*) cheap red wine. [the colour of their uniforms or of the wine]

Scarlet-town *n.* [mid-19C] Reading. [pun on pron. of Reading as 'red-ing']

scarp *v.* [1910s+] (*Aus.*) to escape, to run off. [abbr. SCARPER v. (1)]

scarper *n.* [late 19C–1970s] an escape, an act of running way. [SCARPER v. (1); note WW1 Aus. milit. *scarperer*, a runner, a front-line messenger]

scarper *v.* (*also* **scapali, scarpa, scarpy**) **1** [mid-19C+] (*orig. Ling. Fr./Polari*) to escape, to run off. **2** [1920s] to run. [Ital. *scappare*, to escape, to get away]

scars *n.* (*also* **whore scars**) [1940s–60s] (*US Black*) the scars left from continuous injections of narcotics.

scarve *n.* [late 19C–1900s] (*Polari*) a ring. [although Polari lacks the usual Ital. root; E.P. suggests adaptation of SE *scarf-ring*]

scary *adj.* [1980s+] (*US campus*) horrible, unattractive.

scat *n.*[1] [1910s–40s] (*US Und.*) whisky, esp. of poor quality. [the *-sky* ending of SE]

scat *n.*[2] (*also* **scate**) [1940s+] (*drugs*) heroin. [var. on SCAG n.[2] (2)]

scat *n.*[3] [1970s+] (*US Black*) the vagina. [ety. unknown]

scat *n.*[4] [1980s+] *scatology*, defecation for sexual purposes. [abbr.; SE is properly 'filthy writing']

scat *n.*[5] [1980s+] an itinerant, a tramp. [? abbr. obs. SE *scatterling*, a vagrant; or ? Billingsgate fish market jargon *scat*, a man employed to push barrows]

scat *v.* (*also* **scat up, skat**) [mid-19C+] to leave, to go away, esp. as a command; thus *get scat of*, to get rid of; *like scat*, quickly. [echoic of hissing at a cat: 'Ssss! cat!]

scate *n.*[1] [17C] **1** the vagina. **2** a prostitute (cf. ALLEY CAT n.). [SE *scat*, a skate; thus ref. to equation of the vagina with fish (FISH n.[1] (1))]

scate *n.*[2] *see* SCAT *n.*[2].

scatman *n.* [1990s+] a male homosexual. [? SCAT *n.*[3] + sfx *-man*]

scats *adj. see* SCATTY adj.

scatter *n.*[1] [mid-19C] (*US Und.*) a musket. [? the shot *scatters* once it leaves the weapon]

scatter *n.*[2] (*also* **scatter joint**) **1** [1910s–50s] anywhere that addicts frequent in order to buy drugs and socialize. **2** [1920s–40s] (*US*) a bar, saloon, nightclub or speakeasy where one can purchase alcoholic drinks. **3** [1930s–40s] a place; a room. [? SE *scatter* one's money + JOINT *n.*[4] (3)]

scatter *v.*[1] [20C+] to leave, to go away.

scatter *v.*[2] [2000s] (*US Black*) to shoot dead.

scatter! *excl.* [20C+] go away! leave! [SCATTER *v.*[1]]

scattered *adj.*[1] [1940s] (*Irish*) drunk (cf. ADDLED adj.).

scattered *adj.*[2] *see* SCATTY adj.

scatter-eye *n.* [1950s] (*US*) a derog. nickname for a cross-eyed or squinting person. [SCATTER-EYED adj.]

scatter-eyed *adj.* [1950s] (*US*) cross-eyed.

scatter joint *n. see* SCATTER *n.*[2].

scatters *n.* [1910s] diarrhoea.

scatting *n.* [1980s+] the sexual practice of defecating on one's partner's face. [SCAT *n.*[4]]

scatty *adj.* (*also* **scats**, **scattered**, **scatty-arsed**) [20C+] incapable of logical thought or speech, feather-brained, eccentric. [SE *scatter-brained*]

scat up *v. see* SCAT v.

scav *n.* (*also* **scavvy**) [1990s+] (*UK juv.*) a *scav*enger, used as a general insult. [abbr.]

scavenge *v.* [1940s+] (*Aus.*) to pilfer.

scavenger's daughter *n. see* SKEFFINGTON'S DAUGHTER n.

scavey *see under* SAVVY.

scavvy *n. see* SCAV n.

scavvy *adj.* [1990s+] (*UK juv.*) second-rate. [i.e. only of interest to a SCAV n. or scavenger]

scene *n.* **1** [late 19C+] any situation. **2** [20C+] a place, esp. a party. **3** [1920s+] the fashionable world, usu. of the young, as defined by the current trends. **4** [1940s+] (*drugs*) the drug-taking environment. **5** [1960s+] (*orig. US Black*) choice, preference; usu. as NOT ONE'S SCENE phr. **6** [1960s+] (*mainly gay*) a lengthy sexual encounter; often paid-for. **7** [1970s+] a sexual relationship. **8** [1990s+] (*US gay*) a situation created as a backdrop to a given sexual fantasy.

scene! *excl.* [1990s+] (*US campus*) do you understand? or I understand! [SCENE n. (5)]

scene on *v.* [1970s+] (*US Black*) **1** to belittle. **2** to attempt to gain an advantage over someone by out-talking them. **3** to show off, to attempt to impress. [SCENE n. (3)]

scene queen *n.* [1980s+] (*gay*) one who frequents the world of bars, restaurants and streets equated with the gay lifestyle. [SCENE n. (3) + QUEEN *n.*[2] (1)/QUEEN sfx (2)]

sceneries *n.* [1910s] (*US Und.*) spectacles or pince-nez.

scenery *n.*[1] **1** [late 19C–1930s] (*US*) clothing or uniform. **2** [1930s] (*US Und.*) an impressive board of directors, used to bolster the credibility of a financial fraudster. **3** [1930s] (*US Und.*) fake dividend cheques, used to reassure the potential victim of a financial swindler.

scenery *n.*[2] [1970s+] (*US gay*) **1** sexually attractive individuals in a particular environment, e.g. the baths or a club; thus *have lots of scenery*, to be filled with sexually available men. **2** anyone in whom one is interested but who does not share one's sexual orientation. [play on SE + SCENE n. (3)]

scenery skirt *n.* [1940s] (*UK Und.*) a girl used as a decoy for a brothel, nightclub etc. [SE *scenery* + SKIRT n. (1)]

scenery stiff *n.* [1920s–30s] (*US tramp*) a tramp who loves nature. [SE *scenery* +STIFF *n.*[2] (4)]

scenic route *n.* [1950s+] (*orig. US*) the long way around; also in fig. use, to do something to excess.

scent-bottle *n.* [late 19C] a lavatory.

scent-box *n.* [early–mid-19C] the nose.

sceptre *n.* (*also* **scepter**) [mid-17C+] the penis; thus *sceptre and jewels*, the male genitals. [joc. resemblance]

sces *n.* [1980s+] (*US drugs*) cannabis. [pron. 'sess', i.e. SESS n.]

scew *n. see* SKEW *n.*[1].

scharn *n.* [1910s] excrement. [dial. *scharn*, cowdung]

sched *n.* [1950s+] a *sched*ule. [abbr.]

scheisty *adj. see* SHYSTY adj.

scheitl *n.* (*also* **shyckle**) [1960s–80s] a wig. [Yid. *sheitl*, the wig trad. worn by orthodox Jewish women after their marriage]

scheme *v.* **1** [1930s+] (*Irish*) to play truant. **2** [1970s+] (*S.Afr.*) to think, to 'reckon'.

scheme (on) *v.* [1960s+] (*orig. US Black*) **1** to make sexual designs on. **2** to make plans (for someone/something).

scheme out *v.* [1930s] (*US*) **1** to deceive, to trick. **2** to plan.

schemie *n.* [20C+] a person who lives on a Scot. *scheme* or council estate.

schemish *adj.* [1980s+] (*US Black/P.R.*) cunning. [SE *scheme*, to plot, to plan]

schemozzle *n. see* SHEMOZZLE n.

schfatzer *n.* [1930s+] an old or elderly man; often as a pej. term. [Ger. *Schwatzer*, a chatterbox, a bore]

schicer *n. see* SHICER n.

schickery *adj.* [mid-19C] shabby, bad. [SHICER n.]

schickery *adv.* [mid-19C] shabbily, badly. [SCHICKERY adj.]

schicksie/schikse(h) *n. see* SHIKSA n.

schiest *v.* [2000s] (*US*) to rob.

Schindler's List *adj.* [1990s+] drunk (cf. ADRIAN (QUIST) adj.). [rhy. sl. = PISSED *adj.*[1]; ult. the film *Schindler's List* (1993), based on the novel *Schindler's Ark* (1982) by Thomas Keneally (b.1935)]

schism-shop *n.* [late 18C–mid-19C] a nonconformist meeting house. [the theological *schisms* debated there]

schitz *see under* SCHIZ.

schitzy *adj. see* SCHIZZY adj.

schiz *n.* (*also* **schitz**, **skitz**, **skiz**) [1950s+] (*orig. US*) an eccentric, a mad person; one who has a split personality. [abbr. SE *schizophrenic*]

schiz *adj. see* SCHIZZY adj.

schiz *v. see* SCHIZ (OUT) v.

schizo *n.* (*also* **shizo**) [1940s+] (*orig. US*) an eccentric, a mad person. [abbr. SE *schizophrenic*]

schizo *adj.* (*also* **shizoid**) [1950s+] **1** of a person, eccentric, insane, disorientated; esp. when demonstrating 2 extreme forms of behaviour (cf. SCHIZZY adj.). **2** of an event, bizarre. [SCHIZO n.]

schiz (out) *v.* (*also* **schitz (out)**, **schizz (out)**, **skiz (out)**) [1960s+] **1** (*orig. US*) to go mad, to exhibit the signs of insanity. **2** (*US drugs*) to hallucinate from crack cocaine use. **3** (*orig. US*) to become emotional, tense. [SCHIZ n.]

schizzed *adj.* [2000s] drunk (cf. ADDLED adj.). [SE *schizophrenic*]

schizzy *adj.* (*also* **schitzy**, **schiz**, **schizy**) [1940s+] **1** of a person, eccentric, insane, disorientated; esp. when demonstrating 2 extreme forms of behaviour (cf. SCHIZO adj.). **2** of an event, bizarre. [SE *schizophrenic*, having schizophrenia, 'a mental disorder [...] characterized by a breakdown in the relation between thoughts, feelings and actions, usu. with a withdrawal from social activity and the occurrence of delusions and hallucinations' (*OED*)]

schlacky *adj. see* SCHLOCKY adj.

schlag *adj. see* SCHLOCK adj.

schlamming *n. see* SLAMMING *n.*[1] (1).

schlang *n. see* SCHLONG n.

schlanter *n. see* SLANTER *n.*[1].

schlap *n. see* SLAP *n.*[2].

schlap *v. see* SCHLEP(P) v.

schlapper *n. see* SCHLEPPER n.

schlemazel *n.* (*also* **schlemasel, shlemozzle**) [late 19C+] a fool, esp. an unfortunate, an incompetent (cf. ALTER KACKER *n.*). [west Yid. *schlimm Masel*, bad luck]

schlembo *n.* [2000s] a fool (cf. ALTER KACKER *n.*; BOBO *n.*[1]). [cod-Yid.]

schlemiel *n.* (*also* **schlemihl, shlemiel**) [mid-19C+] a fool, a clumsy person, a misfit, a gullible person etc (cf. ALTER KACKER *n.*). [Yid. *schlemiel*, a bungler, a simpleton; ? the proper name *Shelumiel*, cited in Num. 25:8, as meeting an unfortunate end. He is generally equated with Zimri, whose fornication with a pagan, as recounted in the Talmud, led to his being killed *in flagrante delicto* by Phinehas. The details of the execution were suppressed by pious Jewish historians, but when *schlemiel* entered Yid. it meant anyone in 'an unfortunate (if unspecified) predicament' and thence, by phonetic confusion with Western Yid. *schlimm Masel*, a luckless fellow (cf. SCHLEMAZEL *n.*) it took on the 20C+ popular meaning]

schlemozzle *n.* *see* SHEMOZZLE *n.*

schlent *n.* [1920s+] an imposter. [abbr. SCHLENTER *n.*]

schlent *v.* [1920s+] to double-cross, to hoax, to be evasive. [SCHLENT *n.*]

schlenter *n.* *see* SLANTER *n.*[1].

schlenter *adj.* (*also* **slenter, slinter**) [late 19C+] (*Aus./S.Afr.*) counterfeit, spurious, fake; thus (mining jargon) *schlenter*, a fake diamond sold as the real thing. [Du. *slenter*, a trick/SLANTER *n.*[1]]

schlenter *v.* **1** [late 19C] to pretend (for criminal purposes), to defraud. **2** [1970s+] (*S.Afr.*) to obtain by underhand means; thus *schlenterer*, a devious, untrustworthy person. [SCHLENTER *adj.*]

schlep *n.*[1] [1930s+] (*orig. US*) **1** a general term of abuse. **2** an ordinary working person. [Yid. *schlep*]

schlep *n.*[2] (*also* **shlap, shlep**) [1960s+] a long and unappealing distance. [SCHLEP(P) *v.*]

schlep(p) *v.* (*also* **schlap, shlap, shlep(p)**) [1920s+] **1** to carry an inconvenient weight for an equally inconvenient distance. **2** to travel further than one might prefer. **3** to take someone somewhere; to drag physically; thus *schlepalong*, one who is dragged along. **4** to drag off something for one's own benefit. **5** to travel, to walk wearily or slowly. [Yid. *schlep*, Ger. *shleppen*, to drag]

schlepper *n.* (*also* **schlapper, shlepper**) [1940s+] (*orig. US*) **1** an insignificant person, a second-rater. **2** a miserly person who wants something for nothing. **3** a tout. [Yid. *schlep*]

schleppy *adj.* [1970s] (*US*) awkward, clumsy, stupid. [SCHLEP *n.*[1] (1)]

schliver *n.* [19C] a clasp-knife. [CHIV *n.*[1] (1)]

schlock *n.* (*also* **schlocker, shlock**) **1** [1910s+] cheap, inferior merchandise; anything, concrete or abstract, e.g. a piece of popular culture, defective or in poor taste. **2** [1930s] a large amount. **3** [1930s–50s] (*drugs*) narcotics, usu. heroin. [Ger. *Schlag*, a blow; thus merchandise that has been 'knocked about']

schlock *adj.* (*also* **schlag, shlock**) [1910s+] cheap, inferior; in poor taste, e.g. a *schlock movie*. [SCHLOCK *n.* (1)]

schlockmeister *n.* [1960s+] (*US*) a successful seller of cheap, meretricious goods. [SCHLOCK *n.* (1) + -MEISTER sfx]

schlock shop *n.* (*also* **schlock house/joint/store**) [1910s+] a store selling flashy but cheap clothes. [SCHLOCK *n.* (1) + SE *shop*/JOINT *n.*[4] (3)/*store*]

schlocky *adj.* (*also* **schlacky, shlocky**) [1960s+] in poor taste, vulgar, second-rate. [SCHLOCK *n.* (1)]

schloep *n.* (*also* **schloop, shloep, shloop**) [1960s+] (*S.Afr.*) a sycophant, a toady; thus *schloep*, to ingratiate oneself; *schloepy*, ingratiating. [? SCHLUB *n.* or onomat. for sucking 'slurping' noise]

schlog it on *v.* (*also* **slog it on**) [1930s+] (*Aus.*) to raise a price extortionately; thus *get schlogged/slogged*, to be charged an

excessive price. [? Ger. *auf den Preis schlagen*, 'clap the price on', or SCHLOCK *n.* (1)]

schlong *n.* (*also* **schlang, schlontz, shlang, shlong, shlontz**) **1** [1950s+] the penis. **2** [1970s] an idiot (cf. ALTER KACKER *n.*; CHOAD *n.*). [Yid. *schlang*, snake; note RMC Duntroon (Aus.) *schlong holder*, a girlfriend]

schloomp *n.* (*also* **schlump, shloomp, shlump**) [1940s+] (*US*) a stupid person. [Ger. *Schlumpe*, a slovenly woman]

schloop *n.* *see* SCHLOEP *n.*

schlub *n.* (*also* **shlub, shlubbo, zhlob, zhlub**) [1950s+] **1** a fool, a moron (cf. ALTER KACKER *n.*). **2** a coarse bumpkin (cf. BLOOTER *n.*). **3** in non-judgemental use, a person. [Yid. *schlub*, ult. Slavic *zhlob*, a coarse fellow]

schlub *v.* [1980s+] (*US campus*) to fight. [SCHLUB *n.*]

schlubette *n.* [1990s+] a stupid young woman. [SCHLUB *n.* + SE fem. sfx -*ette*]

schlump *n.* *see* SCHLOOMP *n.*

schlunk *n.* [1970s] (*US*) a passive, inactive person. [var. on Yid *schlump*, a slattern]

schm- *pfx see* SHM- pfx.

schmack *n.* *see* SCHMECK *n.*

schmaltz *n.* (*also* **schmalz, schmultz, shmaltz**) [1930s+] **1** anything mawkish, over-emotional, esp. in show business use. **2** sentimental nonsense. **3** (*US*) any viscid substance. [fig. + lit. uses of Yid. *schmaltz*, (animal) fat]

schmaltzy *adj.* (*also* **schmalzy, shmaltzy, smaltzy**) [1930s+] sentimental, mawkish. [SCHMALTZ *n.* (1)]

schmatte *n.* (*also* **schmattah, schmatteh, shmatte, shmotte**) **1** [1960s+] (*US*) a shabby or unfashionable garment. **2** [1970s+] (*US gay*) a sanitary napkin. [Pol. *szmata*, a rag]

schmear *see under* SCHMEER.

schmeck *n.* (*also* **schmack, schmeek, shmeck, smeck**) (*drugs*) **1** [1930s+] heroin; also as v., to take heroin. **2** [1960s+] cocaine. [Yid./Ger. *schmecken*, a taste; Yid. *schmeck*, to sniff]

schmecker *n.* (*also* **shmecker, smecker**) [1930s+] (*drugs*) a heroin user. [SCHMECK *n.* (1)]

schmeen *n.* *see* SCHMO *n.*

schmeer *n.*[1] (*also* **schmear, shmear**) (*US*) **1** [1950s+] a daub or spread of butter, cream cheese etc; thus fig. **2** [1950s+] a bribe. **3** [1960s+] political or other influence. [SCHMEER *v.*]

schmeer *n.*[2] (*also* **schmear, shmear**) **1** [1940s] (*US police*) something of little consequence. **2** [1950s] (*US Und.*) flattery. **3** [1950s+] (*US*) a slander, a slur. [mispron. of SE *smear*]

schmeer *v.* (*also* **schmear, shmear, smear**) **1** [1930s+] to bribe; to flatter and cajole someone. **2** [1940s] to spend money. [Yid. *schmir*, to apply ointment, to lubricate]

schmegegge *n.* (*also* **schmegeggy, shmegeggy**) [1930s+] (*US*) **1** an unpleasant, petty person. **2** an inept, incompetent person. **3** a sycophant, a toady. **4** nonsense. [US Yid.]

schmegma *n.* [1990s+] (*US campus*) any slimy substance. [a 'Yiddishizing' of SE *smegma*]

schmendrick *n.* (*also* **shmendrick, shmendrik**) [1940s+] a contemptible, foolish or immature person, an upstart, a 'sucker'. [the name of a character in an operetta by Abraham Goldfaden (1840–1908); cited as Yid. by Rosten, *The Joys of Yiddish* (1968), but no further/previous ety. given]

schmiel *n.* (*also* **schmele, schmielage**) [1980s+] (*US campus*) a woman. [cod-Yid.]

schmiel on *v.* [1980s+] (*US campus*) to act pleasantly in order to pick up a woman. [SCHMIEL *n.*]

schmo *n.* (*also* **schmeen, schmoe, schmoo, schmooh, shmo, shmoe**) [1930s+] (*orig. US*) a fool (cf. ALTER KACKER *n.*). [*schmo* is not a Yid. word *per se*, but was invented as a deliberate euph. for the taboo SCHMUCK *n.* (2)]

schmock *n.* *see* SCHMUCK *n.*

schmooge *n.* *see* SCHMOOZE *n.*

schmooh *n.* *see* SCHMO *n.*

schmoos *see under* SCHMOOZE.

schmoose *n. see* SMOUS n. (2).

schmooze *n.* (*also* **schmooge, schmoos, shmooze**) [1930s+] **1** a chat, a long and intimate conversation. **2** inconsequential words. **3** flattering talk. [SCHMOOZE v.]

schmooze *v.* (*also* **schmoos, shmooze**) [late 19C+] **1** to flatter, to butter up. **2** to act in a romantic, seductive manner. **3** to chatter inconsequentially. **4** to gossip about. **5** to pretend, to pose. [Heb. *schmuos*, rumours, idle talk, lit. 'things heard']

schmoozefest *n.* [1980s+] any gathering devoted to mutual (if momentary and insincere) congratulation. [SCHMOOZE v. (1) + -FEST sfx]

schmoozer *n.* (*also* **schmooser, shmoozer**) [late 19C+] a liar, a braggart; a flatterer. [SCHMOOZE v. (1)]

schmozzle *n. see* SHEMOZZLE n.

schmuck *n.* (*also* **schmock, schmuch, schmucko, shmuck**) [1930s+] **1** the penis. **2** (*also* **schmuckette**) a fool, an unpleasant person (cf. ALTER KACKER n.; CHOAD n.). [Yid. *schmuck*, the penis; ult. Ger. *Schmuck*, an ornament]

schmucky *adj.* (*also* **schmuck**) [1950s+] stupid. [SCHMUCK n. (2)]

schmultz *n. see* SCHMALTZ n.

schmutter *n.* (*also* **schmuter**) [1930s+] clothes, usu. cheap. [Yid. *shmatte*, rags, ult. Polish *szmata*, a piece of cloth, a rag]

schmutz *n.* **1** [1960s+] filth, dirt. **2** [1990s+] heroin (cf. CACA n.). [synon. Ger.; (2) on the pattern of DIRT n.[4] (2)]

schmutzig *adj.* [1960s+] dirty. [SCHMUTZ n. (1)]

schnack *n.* [1990s+] (*US campus*) affection. [cod. Yid. sp. of SE *snack*, i.e. 'I like you so much I could eat you']

schneider *n.* **1** [19C] a tailor. **2** [1980s] a Jew (cf. FAST-TALKING CHARLIE n.). [Ger. *Schneider*, a butcher, a cutter]

schnicky-schnacky *n.* [1990s+] (*US campus*) physical affection in public. [redup. of SCHNACK n.]

schnide *n.* (*also* **shnide**) [1940s+] an unpleasant, despicable person. ['Yiddishized' var. on SNIDE n. (2)]

schnip *n.* [1960s] an insignificant person. [Yid.]

schnitz *n.* [1960s–70s] (*US*) an act of destruction. [SCHNITZEL n. (1), i.e. the destoyed object has been FUCKED adj.[1] (3) or given the SHAFT n.[2]]

schnitzel *n.* [1950s+] **1** the penis (cf. BACON n.[1]). **2** a term of abuse (cf. BELL END n.). [Ger. *Schnitzel*, a veal cutlet]

schnob *n.* [1930s] the nose. [var. on SCHNOZZLE n.]

schnoink *n.* [1970s] used by a non-Jew, a derog. term for a Jew (cf. ARAB n.[2]). [a deliberately faked 'Yiddish' word]

schnook *n.* (*also* **schnoorp, shnook**) [1930s+] a fool, a naïve or ineffectual person, esp. as a victim (cf. ALTER KACKER n.). [US Yid.; there is no orig., i.e. European Yid., equivalent]

schnookered *adj. see* SNOOKERED adj.

schnorrer *n.* (*also* **shnurrer**) [late 19C+] **1** a beggar, esp. one who lives by his wits. **2** a person, i.e. a BEGGAR n. **3** a cheat, a mean person. **4** a tramp, a drifter. **5** a compulsive bargain-hunter, a haggler. [Yid. *schnorrer*, a beggar, itself Ger. sl. *schnurren*, to go out begging, and poss. related to *schnarchen*, to snore, a ref. to the beggar's supposed 'whining']

schnozzed *adj.* [1980s] (*US campus*) drunk. [ety. unknown]

schnozzle *n.* (*also* **schnoz, schnozz, schnozzer, shnoz, shnozzle**) [1920s+] the nose. [Ger. *Schnauze*, a snout]

schnozzola *n.* (*also* **shnozolla**) [1930s+] the nose. [ext. of SCHNOZZLE n. + -OLA sfx]

schoful *see under* SHOFUL and its combs.

schonk(y) *n. see* SHONK n.

school *n.*[1] **1** [early 19C+] a group of gamblers gathered for a game. **2** [mid-19C–1910s] a gang of beggars or thieves (usu. pickpockets) working as a team.

school *n.*[2] [early 19C+] prison (cf. BIG SCHOOL n.). [SE *school* of crime]

school *n.*[3] [1990s+] any specific era in the history of HIP-HOP n./

RAP n.[5] music (cf. NEW SCHOOL adj.; OLD SCHOOL adj.). [the exact division between the 2 remains a source of much debate among fans]

school *v.*[1] [1930s+] to gamble in a group. [SCHOOL n.[1] (1)]

school *v.*[2] (*also* **take to school**) **1** [1940s+] (*orig. US Black*) to explain a situation or a plan to someone else, to teach; thus *come to school*, to be educated (in 'street' terms). **2** [1980s+] (*US campus*) to defeat (in a game).

school bike *n.* [1990s+] (*UK juv.*) a promiscuous schoolgirl (cf. BANBURY n.). [BIKE n. (1)]

schoolbook chump *n.* [1970s+] (*US Black*) one who is academic, but not very sophisticated or worldly wise.

schoolboy *n.* **1** [1960s–80s] (*drugs*) codeine, cough syrup, even cocaine, anything seen (by heroin users) as a drug for 'beginners'. **2** [1970s+] (*US Black*) a neophyte in the street life, an apprentice criminal.

schoolboy scotch *n.* [1970s+] (*US Black*) cheap wine.

school-butter *n.* [late 17C–early 19C] a whipping.

schooled *adj.* [1960s+] (*US Black*) intelligent, sophisticated. [SCHOOL v.[2] (1)]

schoolie *n.* **1** [late 19C+] (*Aus.*) a *school*teacher. **2** [1970s+] a *school*girl. [abbr.]

schooling *n.*[1] [mid-19C] a criminal gambling party. [SCHOOL n.[1] (1)]

schooling *n.*[2] [late 19C] a term of confinement in a reformatory. [SCHOOL n.[2]]

schoolman *n.* [mid–late 19C] a fellow member of a gang. [SCHOOL n.[1] (2) + SE *man*]

school of hard knocks *n.* (*also* **school of hard fact, university of hard knocks**) [1910s+] (*orig. US*) a hard life, seen as a means of education.

school of Venus *n.* **1** [mid-17C–early 19C] (*UK Und.*) a brothel (cf. ACADEMY n.). **2** [early 18C] a synon. for a BUTTOCK-BALL n. (1).

schooly *n.* [1980s+] (*US Black*) **1** anyone who wishes to go to school and further their education. **2** a naïve, unsophisticated person, a conformist.

schooner screamer *n. see* ONE-POT SCREAMER n.

schpritz *n.* [1950s+] (*US*) **1** a small bit, a dose. **2** a 'take', a version. [Yid. *schpritz*, a squirt]

schpritz *v.* (*also* **shpritz**) [1950s+] (*US*) **1** to attack, to slander. **2** to deliver a stand-up monologue, usu. composed of fast one-liners. [Yid. *schpritz*, to spray]

schroff *n.* (*also* **shroff**) [mid-19C] (*Anglo-Ind.*) **1** a banker, a treasurer. **2** an official who specializes in sorting good coin from counterfeit; thus as v., to check the validity of coins; *shroffing-school*, the office in which one is taught the skill. **3** a confidential clerk. [Anglo-Ind. *saraf*, a banker or money-changer; ult. Arab. *saraf*, to exchange]

schronch *n. see* SCRONCH n.

schtarka *n.* (*also* **shtarka, shtarker, shtorikue**) [1950s–70s] **1** a strong, brave man, an important person (esp. used ironically). **2** a thug, a hoodlum. [Yid.]

schtick *n.* (*also* **schtuck, shtick, shtik, stick**) [1950s+] (*orig. US*) **1** an act, a performance. **2** a personal habit or trait; a speciality. **3** a device or gadget. [show business jargon *shtick*, one's stage speciality, one's act, esp. of a comedian's monologue; ult. Ger. *Stück*, a piece]

schtick *v.* [1960s] (*US*) to perform, to 'put on an act'; to act in an extreme way. [SCHTICK n. (1)]

schtoonk *n.* (*also* **schtunk, shtonk, shtoonk, shtunk**) [1930s+] (*US*) a detestable person. [Ger. *Stunk*, a scandal, a 'stink']

schtum *adj. see* SHTUM adj.

schtup *n.* (*also* **shtup**) [1950s+] (*US*) sexual intercourse. [SCHTUP v.]

schtup *adj.* [1960s] (*US*) pertaining to sexual intercourse. [SCHTUP n.]

schtup v. (also **shtup, stupp**) [1930s+] (orig. US) **1** to have sexual intercourse; to have anal intercourse. **2** to destroy, to humiliate, to defeat. [Yid.; ult. Ger. *stupsen*, to push; (2) is fig. use of (1)]

schtupper n. (also **shtupper**) [1960s+] (US) one who has sexual intercourse. [SCHTUP v. (1)]

schtupping n. [1960s] (US) sexual intercourse. [SCHTUP v.]

schv… see also under SCHW…

schvug n. (also **schvoog, shvoogie**) [1960s+] (US) a Black person. [SCHWARTZE n. (1) + BOOGIE n.² (1)]

schwacked adj. see SCHWAGGED adj.

schwag n. [1980s+] (US drugs) inferior-quality cannabis. [ety. unknown; ? SE *shag* tobacco]

schwag adj. [1990s+] (US campus) second-rate, inferior, bad. [SCHWAG n.]

schwagged adj. (also **schwacked**) [1990s+] (US Black/drugs) intoxicated by marijuana. [SCHWAG n., although there is no inference of poor quality]

schwantz n. (also **schvantz, schvonce, schvontz, schwanz, shvantz**) **1** [1930s+] (US) the penis. **2** [1930s+] a general derog. description. **3** [1960s] (US gay) a sexually successful male, assumed to have a large penis. [Yid. *schwantz*, the tail]

schwartze n. (also **schvartza, schvartze, schvartzeh, schvartzer, schwartza, schwartzer, shva, shvartz, shvartze, shvartzer, swartzer**) **1** [1950s+] a Black person. **2** [1960s+] (US gay) one who prefers Black partners. [Ger. *schwartz*, black]

schwartze adj. (also **shvartze**) [1960s+] Black, African-American. [SCHWARTZE n. (1)]

schwassle-box n. see SWATCHEL-BOX n.

schwoz n. [1990s+] (UK juv.) an act of urination. [? WAZ n. (1)]

science n. **1** [1950s+] (W.I. Rasta) obeah, witchcraft. **2** [1980s+] (US Black) wisdom, skill. **3** [1990s+] information, knowledge.

science, the n. **1** [early 18C] (UK Und.) stealing, pickpocketing. **2** [early–mid-19C+] boxing or fencing, esp. the former; also known as *the sweet science*; thus *scientific*, pertaining to boxing.

scientist n. [1950s+] (W.I. Rasta) an occult practitioner. [SCIENCE n. (1)]

sci-fi n. (also **s.f.**) [1950s+] (orig. US) science fiction. [abbr.]

scillion n. see SKILLION n.

scissorbill n. **1** [mid-19C–1940s] (US) a foolish, incompetent, gossipy or objectionable person. **2** [1910s–40s] a wealthy or privileged person. **3** [1920s] (US tramp) a railroad detective or police officer (cf. BEAGLE n.³). **4** [1920s] (US tramp) an itinerant knife-sharpener. **5** [1920s–30s] (US tramp) a farmer, a peasant. **6** [1920s+] (US tramp) anyone unwilling to join a union or otherwise improve their lot.

scissors n. [1960s–70s] (drugs) marijuana. [ety. unknown; ? link to late 19C *scizzors*, a type of firecracker that had to be bent double and stamped on to make it explode; note also HAIR-CUT n.⁴]

scissors! excl. [mid–19C+] a mild excl.

scivvie n. see SKIVVY n.².

scode n. [1980s+] (N.Z. drugs) the butt end of a marijuana cigarette that is unwrapped and recycled.

scoff n. (also **skoff**) [mid-19C+] food; thus *cop/knock a scoff*, to eat. [SCOFF v.]

scoff v. **1** [mid-19C+] (also **scorf, skoff**) to eat, to gobble up (cf. SCARF v.). **2** [late 19C] to give food, to feed. **3** [late 19C+] to grab. **4** [20C+] in fig. use of (1), to defeat, to attack. **5** [1930s–50s] (US drugs) to take narcotics orally. **6** [1950s+] (US teen) to steal, to pilfer. **7** [1960s] (US campus) to fellate (cf. BASKET LUNCH n.). [Scot. *scaff*, to beg or ask for (food etc) in a mean or contemptible manner, but note S.Afr. *scoff*, food, a meal, f. Du. *schoft*, a quarter of a day, thus each of the day's 4 meals]

scoff fishheads (and scramble the gills) v. [1940s–50s] (US Black) to have a difficult time, to encounter problems. [fig. use of SCOFF v. (1)]

scoffings n. [1900s–40s] (US tramp) food. [SCOFF n.]

scoff jack n. [1930s] (US tramp) money for food collected amongst a group of tramps when they have been unable to beg successfully. [SCOFF n. + JACK n.⁴ (2)]

scoldrum n. see SCALDRUM DODGE n.

scold's cure n. [late 18C–early 19C] a funeral, a coffin; thus *nap the scold's cure*, to be placed in one's coffin. [the misogynistic concept that only death would silence a nagging woman]

scollogue v. [mid–late 19C] to live in a debauched, degenerate manner. [? link to SCALLYWAG n.¹ (2)]

scolopendra n. [mid-17C] a prostitute. [SE *scolopendra*, a centipede or millipede, orig. 'a fabulous sea-fish which feeling himselfe taken with a hooke casteth out his bowels vntill hee hath vnloosed the hooke and then swalloweth them vp againe' (Bullokar, *English Expositour*, 1616)]

sconce n. (also **skonce**) **1** [mid-16C–1950s] the head, the brain. **2** [mid-16C–19C] judgement, sense. **3** [late 16C] a person (whose head it is). **4** [late 18C] the penis. [either SE *sconce*, a lantern or *sconce*, a fort or earthwork]

sconce off v. (also **sconce the reckoning**) [mid-17C–19C] to run off without paying a bill. [orig. univ. jargon *sconce*, to mulct, to fine, usu. a tankard of ale or similar forfeit]

sconce one's diet v. [19C] to eat less, to diet. [for ety. see SCONCE OFF v.]

scone n.¹ [1940s–50s] (Aus.) a policeman, a detective (cf. BOTTLE (AND STOPPER) n.). [rhy. sl.; SE *hot scone* = JOHN n.⁴]

scone n.² [1940s+] (Aus./N.Z.) the head; thus DO ONE'S SCONE v.; *scone-doer*, an over-emotional person; *scone-doing*, a loss of control; *off one's scone*, mad, eccentric; *use one's scone*, to act sensibly. [joc. resemblance]

scone v. [1940s+] (Aus./N.Z.) to hit someone on the head. [SCONE n.²]

scone-hot adv. [1930s+] (Aus.) a general intensifier, either positive or negative; thus GO SCONE-HOT AT v.

scoob n. [1990s+] (Aus./Can. drugs) cannabis. [abbr. SCOOBY-DOO n.² (1)]

scoob v. [1980s+] (US campus) to eat, esp. snacks. [TV cartoon character *Scooby-Doo* and his *Scooby Snacks*]

scoobied adj. (also **skoobied**) [1990s+] **1** beaten up, defeated. **2** under the influence of drink or drugs. **3** confused. [SCOOBY v.]

scoobie snax n. (also **scooby snacks**) [1980s+] (US drugs) food eaten when suffering the hunger-pangs promoted by smoking cannabis. [SCOOBY-DOO n.² (1) + SE *snacks* but note TV cartoon character *Scooby-Doo* and his *Scooby Snacks*]

scooby v. (also **skooby**) [1990s+] **1** to defeat, to trounce, to outwit. **2** to confuse. [? rhy. sl.; *scooby-doo* = SCREW v.² (2); ult. cartoon character *Scooby-Doo*]

scooby-doo n.¹ **1** [1960s+] (UK prison) a warder. **2** [2000s] a clue. [rhy. sl.; (1) = SCREW n.² (3)]

scooby-doo n.² [1990s+] **1** (US Black/teen) a large cannabis cigarette. **2** (US campus) someone who eats a lot and never gains weight. **3** (US Black) a firearm. [the cartoon character *Scooby-Doo*]

scooby snacks n. see SCOOBIE SNAX n.

scooch n. [1990s+] (Irish) a lift in a car. [? nonce-word *scootch up*, move over]

scood! excl. [1990s+] (US campus) an elision of the SE *it's good*; thus *scoodnuff*, it's good enough.

scoop n.¹ **1** [late 19C–1950s] (US) a glass of beer. **2** [late 19C+] (Irish/Scot.) a drink; thus *on the scoop*, on a spree. **3** [1960s] (drugs) a folded matchbox cover used to sniff narcotics. **4** [2000s] (drugs) gamma hydroxybutyrate (GHB).

scoop n.² **1** [late 19C+] an advantage, a lucky result in one's business or similar dealings. **2** [1930s+] information, knowledge, 'the low-down'. [journalist jargon *scoop*, an exclusive or (as yet) unrivalled story]

scoop v.¹ **1** [late 19C–1900s] (US) to beat, to defeat. **2** [1950s+] (US) to arrest. **3** [1960s] (drugs) to sniff cocaine through a SCOOP n.¹ (3). **4** [1970s] to pick up, to seduce. **5** [1970s+] (US campus) to obtain, to acquire. **6** [1990s+] (*US*) to watch, usu. people in the street.

scoop *v.*² *see* SCOOP IN *v.*

scooper *n.*¹ [late 19C] (*UK Und.*) a hasty escape.

scooper *n.*² [2000s] (*US prison*) one who eats with a spoon.

scoop in *v.* (*also* **scoop**, **scoop up**) **1** [mid-19C–1910s] to take someone in, to dupe or defeat someone. **2** [mid-19C+] (*orig. US*) to have a stroke of luck, a 'lucky break', usu. in business. **3** [mid-19C+] to gather or gain something, often in large quantities (esp. to the exclusion of others).

scoop on *v.* [1980s+] (*US campus*) to pick up, to make advances to.

scoop up *v.*¹ [1990s+] (*US campus*) to give someone a lift in a car.

scoop up *v.*² *see* SCOOP IN *v.*

scoot *n.*¹ **1** [late 19C] a run. **2** [late 19C+] an escape. **3** [1920s] (*US*) an elevator boy. **4** [1990s+] speedy movement. [SCOOT *v.* (2)]

scoot *n.*² [late 19C+] diarrhoea; thus a general term of abuse. [euph. for SHIT *n.*¹ (1)/SHIT *n.*² (1)]

scoot *n.*³ [1960s+] a motorcycle or motorcar.

scoot *v.* **1** [mid-19C; 1920s+] (*US*) of a person or object, to slide. **2** [mid-19C+] (*also* **scoot off**) to run off, to escape; to move suddenly or swiftly. **3** [late 19C] to travel. [mid-18C–early 19C naut. jargon *scout*, to run off swiftly]

scooter *n.*¹ [19C] one who leaves quickly, an escapee. [SCOOT *v.* (2)]

scooter *n.*² [1930s–40s] (*US Und.*) **1** an automobile, esp. a car used for the smuggling of rum. **2** a legless tramp who travels on a wheeled platform.

scooter *n.*³ [1970s+] (*UK juv.*) an individual with freckles and glasses. [the character *Scooter*, in the *Muppet Show*, who had such characteristics]

scooter tracks *n. see* SKID MARKS *n.*

scoot off *v. see* SCOOT *v.* (2).

scoots *n.*¹ [20C+] (*US campus*) diarrhoea. [ext. of SCOOT *n.*²]

scoots *n.*² [1940s+] dollars. [ety. unknown]

scope *n.*¹ (*also* **telescope**) [1950s–60s] the erect penis. [joc. use of/abbr. SE *telescope*]

scope *n.*² [1970s+] (*US Black/campus*) a look, a stare, a looking-out point. [abbr. SE *telescope*]

scope *v.* (*also* **scope down/on/out**) **1** [1950s+] (*orig. US*) to look over, to stare at, to investigate. **2** [1970s] (*US campus*) to cheat by copying in an exam. **3** [1970s+] to stare at someone intently, usu. with sexual interest. **4** [1970s+] to look in various public places for a partner for romance or sex. **5** [2000s] (*US*) to ascertain, to work out. [abbr. SE *telescope*]

scoped in *adj.* [1970s+] (*US*) focused on. [SCOPE *v.* (1)]

scorch *n.* [1980s] (*UK Und.*) arson.

scorch *v.* **1** [20C+] (*Aus./US*) to go or move very fast. **2** [1930s] (*US Black*) to find, to provide. **3** [1940s] (*US Black*) to escort.

scorcher *n.* **1** [mid–late 19C] a severe reprimand, a telling-off; thus an unpleasant situation. **2** [mid-19C+] a very hot day. **3** [late 19C–1910s] an outspoken or domineering person. **4** [late 19C–1930s] an attractive and/or sexually voracious woman. **5** [late 19C–1940s] one who cycles or motors with above average speed or energy. **6** [late 19C+] anything or anyone exceptional of its type. **7** [1940s+] anything sensational, esp. when seen as risqué or 'naughty'.

scorching *adj.* [late 19C+] astounding, sensational, licentious, risqué. [SCORCHER *n.* (6)]

score *n.*¹ [early 19C+] 20, in a variety of contexts, e.g. 20 years' prison, a 20oz (56g) packet of tobacco, $20, £20 etc. [SE *score*, a group of 20s; ult. the counting of sheep in 20s, each of which was 'scored' on some form of tally, e.g. by cutting notches in a stick]

score *n.*² **1** [mid-19C+] the situation, the facts, what is going on; usu. as in *know the score*, to be aware; *what's the score?* what's going on? **2** [1900s] a successfully made point in an argument. [sporting imagery]

score *n.*³ **1** [1910s+] (*UK Und.*) the profits from a robbery, fraud or similar criminal act. **2** [1930s–70s] (*Can./US Und.*) the site of a robbery or similar crime. **3** [1930s+] (*US Und.*) a planned killing. **4** [1930s+] (*orig. US Und.*) a success or coup; usu. in criminal activity or gambling. **5** [1940s+] (*Can./US Und.*) a robbery. **6** [1960s+] any form of material gain. **7** [1990s+] (*US Und.*) anything sent in to a prisoner from the outside world. **8** [2000s] (*US Black*) a cache of illicit goods. [SCORE *v.*²]

score *n.*⁴ [1940s+] (*drugs*) a purchase of drugs. [SCORE *v.*¹ (4)]

score *n.*⁵ [1960s+] (*orig. US*) **1** a male or female prostitute's client. **2** a potential partner for sex. **3** a sexual conquest. **4** money gained from commercial sex. [SCORE *v.*² (2)]

score *v.*¹ **1** [early 18C; 1910s+] to obtain, to get. **2** [late 19C] to consume. **3** [1910s+] to commit a robbery, to make a dishonest gain, to filch something from a counter or stall. **4** [1930s+] (*drugs*) (*also* **score (for) a connection**) to buy drugs. [SE *score*, to win, to gain a victory]

score *v.*² **1** [late 19C+] to succeed, to do well. **2** [late 19C+] (*orig. US*) (*also* **score on**) to seduce, to have sexual intercourse. **3** [1910s+] to obtain money. **4** [1960s+] (*orig. US*) to obtain something desirable, usu. sex. **5** [1960s+] to procure sex for a third party. **6** [1960s+] (*US gay*) for a male prostitute to secure a client.

score! *excl.* [1990s+] an excl. of satisfaction, pleasure. [SCORE *v.*²]

score a connection *v. see* SCORE *v.*¹ (4).

score a home run *v. see* HIT A HOME RUN *v.*

score between the posts *v.* [1960s+] (*Aus.*) to have sexual intercourse, to seduce a woman. [SCORE *v.*² (2) + football imagery]

score-card *n.* **1** [1930s] (*US*) a menu. **2** [1970s+] (*US gay*) an address book.

score for a connection *v. see* SCORE *v.*¹ (4).

score money *n.* (*also* **score dough**) [1930s–50s] (*drugs*) money set aside or offered for a purchase of drugs. [SCORE *v.*¹ (4) + SE *money*/DOUGH *n.*¹ (1)]

score off *v.* [late 19C+] to make a point at another's expense.

score on *v.*¹ [1910s+] (*Aus. Und.*) to inform against.

score on *v.*² *see* SCORE *v.*² (2).

scorf *v. see* SCOFF *v.* (1).

scot *n.* **1** [early–mid-19C] (*also* **fine Scot**) an ill-tempered person, esp. one who is susceptible to teasing. **2** [mid-19C–1910s] a bad temper, a fit of irritation. [stereotyping; but ? note Grose 1796 *scot*, a young bull + Bee: 'the small Scots oxen coming to their doom with little resignation to fate']

Scotch *adj.* [20C+] mean. [racial stereotyping]

Scotch bait *n.* (*also* **Welsh bait**) [late 18C–mid-19C] a rest taken as one walks along. [SE *Scotch/Welsh + bait*, a snack]

Scotch bum *n.* [early 17C] a form of dress-bustle. [SE *Scotch* + BUM *n.*¹ (1)]

Scotch by absorption *phr.* [1930s+] describing one who likes Scotch whisky.

Scotch casement *n.* [late 18C–mid-19C] the pillory. [negative stereotyping; SE *casement*, a window frame]

Scotch chocolate *n.* [late 18C–mid-19C] brimstone (sulphur) and milk.

Scotch coffee *n.* [mid-19C] hot water flavoured with burned biscuit. [orig. naut. jargon]

Scotch convoy *n.* [20C+] (*Ulster*) a walk home with a visitor, who then comes back with you.

scotched up *adj.* [1930s] (*US*) drunk (cf. ALED UP *adj.*). [*Scotch* whisky]

Scotch eggs *n.* [1950s+] legs. [rhy. sl.]

scotches *n.* [mid-19C+] the legs. [abbr. SCOTCH PEGS *n.* (1)]

Scotch fiddle *n.* (*also* **Welsh fiddle**) [late 17C–19C] venereal disease. [note that a fiddle or violin also symbolizes the vagina, thus the 17C riddle commencing 'I've two holes in my Belly and none in my Bum / Yet me, with much pleasure, Italians do thrum']

Scotch greys n. (also **grays, greys, Scotch grays, Scots grays/greys**) **1** [early 19C–1900s] lice; thus *headquarters of the Scots greys*, a lousy head; *the Scots greys are in full march by the crown office*, lice are crawling on one's head. **2** [late 19C] (*Aus.*) large mosquitoes. [Hotten (1860), partly eschewing Johnson's prejudice, notes that 'our northern neighbours are calumniously reported, from their living on oatmeal, to be particularly liable to cutaneous eruptions and parasites']

Scotch hobby n. [late 17C–18C] a small, stunted Scot. horse. [SE *Scotch* + *hobby*, a small or middle-sized horse]

Scotchie n. (also **Scotchy, Scottie, Scotty**) [mid-19C+] a Scot; a nickname for a Scotsman.

scotchie n. (also **scotty**) [late 19C–1930s] a leg; a false leg. [abbr. SCOTCH PEGS n. (1)]

Scotch lick n. [20C+] (*Irish*) a poorly done cleaning job. [stereotyping; SE *Scotch* + *lick*, a hit, a dab]

Scotch louse-trap n. see LOUSELAND n.

Scotchman n.[1] [mid–late 19C] (*S.Afr.*) a florin (a 2-shilling/10p piece). [the story that a Scottish immigrant to S.Afr. fooled his Black employees by giving them florins (worth 2s) but calling the coins half-crowns (worth 2s 6d/12½p)]

Scotchman n.[2] [1980s+] (*Aus. prison*) a rapist. [SCOTCH TAPE n.]

Scotchman's shout n. see YANKEE SHOUT n.

Scotchmen n. [late 19C] lice. [SCOTCH GREYS n. (1)]

Scotch mist n. [1940s+] anything insubstantial, mythical, esp. used sarcastically when one wants to imply that the other speaker has failed to grasp the point or, lit., perceive something that is clear and obvious. [note B.E. (c.1698): '*Scotch-mist*, a sober, soaking Rain']

Scotch ordinary n. [late 18C–early 19C] a lavatory. [SE *Scotch* + *ordinary*, an eating house]

Scotch pegs n. **1** [mid-19C+] the legs. **2** [20C+] eggs. [rhy. sl.]

Scotch pint n. [early 19C] a bottle holding 2 quarts (4 pints/3 litres).

Scotch polo n. [20C+] (*US*) golf.

Scotch screw n. [20C+] a nocturnal emission. [SE *Scotch* + SCREW n.[1] (2); the stereotypical Scot is too mean to offer sexual pleasure to anyone but themself]

Scotch shout n. see YANKEE SHOUT n.

Scotch tape n. [1980s+] (*Aus.*) rape. [rhy. sl.]

Scotch warming-pan n. (also **Scottish warming-pan**) **1** [mid-17C–18C] a complaisant young woman. **2** [19C] (*also* Scots warming-pan) the breaking of wind.

Scotch wine n. [1900s–60s] whisky.

Scotchy n. see SCOTCHIE n.

scotia! excl. [1970s] (*US Black*) all right!

Scotland (the Brave) v. [1990s+] to shave. [rhy. sl.]

Scotland Yard n. [1970s] (*US Black*) a plain-clothes police officer. [? New *Scotland Yard*, the headquarters of the Metropolitan Police in London]

Scots grays/greys n. see SCOTCH GREYS n.

Scotsman's grandstand n. (also **Scotsman's stand/zoo**) [1970s+] **1** a grandstand erected on private property overlooking a sports arena in which seats are available cheaply. **2** a vantage point that allows people to watch an event, usu. sporting, for free. [negative stereotyping]

Scotsman's half-crown n. [1940s–70s] (*N.Z.*) a 2-shilling (10p) coin. [negative stereotyping; a proper SE *half-crown* was worth 2s 6d (12½p)]

Scotsman's shout n. [1940s+] (*N.Z.*) a round of drinks in which everyone pays for their own. [negative stereotyping + SHOUT n.[1] (2)]

Scotsman's stand/zoo n. see SCOTSMAN'S GRANDSTAND n.

Scots warming-pan n. see SCOTCH WARMING-PAN n. (2).

scott n.[1] [1970s] (*drugs*) heroin. [? SCAT n.[2]]

scott n.[2] [1990s+] (*Aus. teen*) a socially inept male. [the stereotypical middle-class name *Scott*, and the perceived social inadequacies of such public-school educated young men]

Scottie n. see SCOTCHIE n.

scottie n. see SCOTTY n.[1].

Scottish adj. [early–mid-19C] irritable, easily annoyed. [negative stereotyping]

Scottish fleas n. [early 17C] syphilis.

Scottish Football Association n. [1990s+] absolutely nothing. [play on initial letters of SWEET FUCK-ALL n.]

Scottish warming-pan n. see SCOTCH WARMING-PAN n.

Scotty n. see SCOTCHIE n.

scotty n.[1] (also **scottie**) [1980s+] (*drugs*) cocaine; crack cocaine (cf. AUNT NORA n.; BASE n.). [the character *Scotty*, in the TV series *Star Trek* (from 1966), 'makes one's engines run' + BEAM ME UP, SCOTTY! excl. (2)]

scotty n.[2] see SCOTCHIE n.

scotty adj. [mid-19C+] (*Aus.*) tetchy, irritable. [racial stereotyping; note Vaux: '*Scot*, a person of irritable temper, who is easily put in a passion']

scour v.[1] (also **scoure**) [mid-15C–early 19C] to wear (fetters), thus to sit in the stocks. [SE *scour*, to rub]

scour v.[2] (also **scowre**) **1** [late 16C–early 19C] to travel at speed, to run away. **2** [mid-17C–mid-18C] to roam about at night uproariously, breaking windows, beating the watch and molesting wayfarers. **3** [mid-17C–1940s] of a man, to have sexual intercourse; occas. of a woman. [SE *scour*, to move around hastily and energetically]

scourer n. (also **scowrer**) [mid-17C–18C] (*UK Und.*) a dissolute young man who roams the streets, usu. as one of a gang, beating up passers-by, breaking windows, attacking the watch and generally acting in a hooligan manner. [SCOUR v.[2] (2); the term was used as the title of the play by Thomas Shadwell, *The Scowrers* (1691) 'an excellent but coarse comedy, which gives an interesting picture of the times' (*DNB*)]

scouring n. [early 18C] imprisonment. [SCOUR v.[1]]

scours n. [1910s–20s] a purge. [SE *scours*, diarrhoea]

scour the cramp-rings v. [mid-16C–early 19C] to wear chains or fetters. [SCOUR v.[1] + CRAMP-RINGS n.]

scour the darbies v. [late 17C–early 19C] to wear chains or handcuffs. [SCOUR v.[1] + DARBIES n. (1)]

Scouse n. **1** [1940s+] a Liverpudlian; a nickname for a Liverpudlian. **2** [1960s+] the dialect spoken in Liverpool. **3** [1990s+] used a term of direct address. [LOBSCOUSE n.]

Scouse adj. [1940s+] Liverpudlian; esp. as *Scouse accent*. [SCOUSE n. (1)]

scouse n. [mid-19C+] cheap, tasteless food, esp. a thin stew. [abbr. LOBSCOUSE n.]

scouse v. [1960s] to speak with a Liverpudlian accent or in a Liverpudlian dialect. [SCOUSE n. (2)]

Scouser n. [1950s+] a Liverpudlian; thus *Scousers*, a collective name for Liverpudlians. [SCOUSE n. (1)]

scout n.[1] **1** [late 16C–17C] a bawd, a pimp; one who obtains clients for a prostitute (cf. ABBOT ON THE CROSS n.). **2** [early 18C+] (*Anglo-Irish*) a bold, forward young woman. **3** [mid–19C] a mean person. **4** [mid-19C] (*Irish*) a disreputable person. **5** [1950s+] (*W.I. Rasta*) a person of inferior status. [? late 14C–19C SE *scout*, a term of contempt]

scout n.[2] **1** [late 17C–early 19C] a pocket watch. **2** [late 17C–mid-19C] a member of the watch. [(2) orig. milit. use; (1) puns on (2)]

scout n.[3] [1910s+] a person; esp. as *good scout*, an admirable person. [the popular image of the Boy Scouts]

scout-cull n. [early 18C] (*UK Und.*) a watchman. [SCOUT n.[2] (2) + CULL n.[1] (4)]

scout ken n. [early 19C] a watch-house. [SCOUT n.[2] (2) + KEN n.[1] (1)]

scout off v. [early 19C] to put off, to ignore.

scowbanker n. (also **skowbanker, skullbanker**) [mid-late 19C] (orig. Aus.) a rogue, a rascal, one who loiters around in the hope of hand-outs, which will save him from earning a living; thus *scowbanking*, loafing, idling. [dial., lit. one who scours or wanders the banks; E.P. and OED offer alternative etys. but the EDD ety., cited here, seems obvious]

Scowegian n. [1910s+] (Aus./Can./US) a Scandinavian. [SE *Scandinavian + Norwegian*]

scowre see under SCOUR.

scrag n.[1] **1** [mid-18C] the hangman's noose. **2** [mid-18C–19C] the neck. **3** [late 19C] the gallows.

scrag n.[2] **1** [1960s] (Aus.) an ill-kempt person. **2** [1980s+] (US campus) an unattractive woman. [? backform. f. SCRAGGY adj./SE *scrag-end*, the worst part of anything]

scrag v. **1** [mid-18C–mid-19C] to hang (on the gallows). **2** [mid-19C+] (also **skrag**) to do harm, to beat up, to kill. **3** [1900s] to throttle, to choke, to garrotte. **4** [1930s] to commit suicide. **5** [1950s] (US drugs/gang) (also **skrag**) to steal. **6** [1990s+] (Aus./US) to have sexual intercourse (cf. BANG v.[1]). [SCRAG n.[1] (2)]

scrag a lay v. [late 18C–early 19C] to steal clothes that have been laid out on a hedge to dry. [SCRAG v. (5) is too late; thus fig. use of SCRAG v. (1), i.e. to grasp tightly + SE *lay*, to place upon]

scrag-boy n. [late 18C–mid-19C] a hangman. [SCRAG v. (1)]

scrag 'em fair n. [late 18C–early 19C] an execution by hanging. [SCRAG v. (1)]

scrag fair n. [early 19C] a judicial hanging day, plus the procession to Tyburn, last words etc. [SCRAG v. (1)]

scragged adj. **1** [early 18C–19C] hanged. **2** [20C+] killed; dead. [SCRAG v.]

scragger n. [late 19C] a hangman. [SCRAG v. (1)]

scragging n. **1** [19C] a hanging. **2** [mid-19C+] a beating. **3** [1930s] a shooting. [SCRAG v.]

scragging match n. [mid-19C] (UK Und.) a judicial hanging. [SCRAGGING n. (1) + SE *match*]

scragging post n. [19C] the gallows. [SCRAGGING n. (1) + SE *post*]

scragg's hotel n. [late 19C] (UK tramp) a workhouse. [? a lost proper name or SE *scrag-end*, the worst part of anything]

scraggy adj. (also **scraggly**) [late 18C+] (Aus./US) unkempt, scrawny; usu. of a person, occas. of a place or thing. [SE *scrag-end*]

scrag squeezer n. [early-late 19C] (UK Und.) the gallows. [SCRAG n.[1] (2) + SE *squeezer*]

scram n. [1920s+] (US Und.) money, clothing; thus *scram money*, cash reserved for a sudden departure; *scram-bag*, a suitcase packed ready for leaving in a hurry. [SCRAM v.]

scram, the n. [1940s] (US) an act of rejection or ejection. [SCRAM v.]

scram v. (also **scram out**) [1920s+] (orig. US) to escape, to run off; often as imper. *scram!* [SE *scramble* or Ger. *schrammen*, to run away]

scramble n.[1] [early 19C+] (US) money. [i.e. that which one *scrambles* to obtain]

scramble n.[2] [1950s+] (Aus./N.Z.) pedestrians rushing across a 'buzz crossing'.

scramble v. [1960s+] (US Black) to make one's money by a variety of schemes, not always legal ones.

scrambled eggs n.[1] [1940s+] **1** the gold braid that adorns a senior officer's cap. **2** a senior officer. [(1) colour; (2) f. (1)]

scrambled eggs n.[2] [1990s+] the legs. [rhy. sl.]

scrambler n. [1990s+] (US drugs) a low-level runner for a drug dealer.

scramboose v. (also **scrambooch**) [1940s-60s] (US) to leave. [SCRAM v. + VAMOOSE v.]

scrammy n. [mid-late 19C] (Aus.) one who has a withered or defective hand or arm; thus *chuck a scrammy*, to pretend to have a withered arm (so as to shirk work). [dial. *scram*, withered]

scram out v. see SCRAM v.

scramsville n. [1950s-60s] desertion, running off. [SCRAM v. + -VILLE sfx[1]]

scran n. **1** [18C–19C] payment for food at an inn. **2** [early 18C+] (also **scranny, scrand**) food, esp. various bits of food, left-overs, 'broken victuals' etc, thrown together for an impromptu meal or a meal taken onto their job by a labourer; thus *scran-time*, a mealtime. [ety. unknown; note RN jargon *scran*, rations]

scran v. **1** [mid-18C–mid-19C] to provide with food. **2** [mid-18C–mid-19C] to collect scraps of food to make up a meal; thus *out on the scran*, begging for scraps of food. **3** [1990s+] to eat. [SCRAN n. (2)]

scran-bag n. (also **scran-pocket**) [mid-late 19C] **1** a beggar's receptacle for the scraps of food they solicit. **2** any form of bag into which bits of food can be placed. [SCRAN n. (2) + SE *bag*; note milit. jargon *scran-bag*, a haversack]

scrand n. see SCRAN n. (2).

scranning n. [mid-19C] (Scot.) begging for scraps of food. [SCRAN v. (2)]

scranny n. see SCRAN n. (2).

scran-pocket n. see SCRAN-BAG n.

scrap n.[1] (also **scrapp**) [late 17C–mid-19C] a plot, a villainous scheme. [SE *scrape*]

scrap n.[2] (orig. boxing) **1** [mid-19C+] (also **scrape, scrap-up**) a fight. **2** [20C+] a heated argument, a quarrel. [? SE *scrape*]

scrap n.[3] (also **scrappet**) [late 19C+] a small person; usu. as *a scrap of a...*

scrap v. **1** [mid-19C+] to fight, to box. **2** [late 19C+] to argue heatedly. **3** [1950s] (UK juv.) to remove someone's trousers against their will. [SCRAP n.[2] (1)]

scrap a lick v. [1990s+] to have a poor fighting ability. [SCRAP v. (1) + LICK n.[1] (3)]

scrape n.[1] **1** [mid-19C–1900s] short shrift. **2** [mid-19C–1920s] a shave. **3** [mid-19C–1940s] butter; thus *bread and scrape*, bread and butter, esp. as offered in institutions. **4** [20C+] (Irish) a sexually complaisant woman. **5** [1960s+] (also **scrape job**) an abortion; thus *scrape clinic*, an abortion clinic; *scrape doctor*, an abortionist.

scrape n.[2] see SCRAP n.[2] (1).

scrape v.[1] **1** [mid-19C–1960s] (also **scrape the mug, scrape the pavement**) to shave. **2** [late 19C] (US) to vaccinate. **3** [1980s+] (US) to perform an abortion.

scrape v.[2] [1950s+] (Aus.) to have sexual intercourse. [the early 19C use of SCRAPER n.[1] (2) suggests this might have been in use much earlier]

scrape v.[3] [1970s+] (US Black/teen) to have one's car lowered to such an extent that it scrapes the road and shoots up showers of sparks.

scrape-all n. **1** [mid-late 17C] an unpleasant person. **2** [late 17C] a miser. [they *scrape* everything into their own hands/pocket]

scrape Dixie v. [1940s] (US Black) to walk the streets of a Southern city or town in search of work. [SE *scrape* + DIXIE n.]

scrape job n. see SCRAPE n.[1] (5).

scrape one's horns v. (also **cut one's horns**) [1960s+] (US) **1** of a man, to engage in sexual activity, esp. after a period of abstinence. **2** to masturbate. [SE *scrape/cut* +HORN n.[2] (1)]

scraper n.[1] **1** [late 18C; 1920s–40s] (also **chin-scraper**) a barber. **2** [early 19C] the penis. **3** [mid-19C–1930s] a razor.

scraper n.[2] (also **three-cornered scraper**) [late 18C–19C] a cocked hat. [its shape]

scraper n.[3] [late 18C+] (Irish/US) a foot; a shoe.

scraper n.[4] [late 19C] (UK society) of a man's beard or moustache, a short (2.5–5cm/1–2in) whisker, slightly curved. [? resemblance to some form of SE *scraper*]

scraper *n.*[5] [late 19C] a cheating beggar, one who shams suffering.

scrape the mug/pavement *v. see* SCRAPE *v.*[1] (1).

scraping castle *n.* [mid-19C] a water closet, a lavatory (cf. ALTAR n.). [one 'scrapes' oneself clean; but note CRAPPING CASTLE n.]

scrap iron *n.*[1] **1** [1940s+] (*US*) homemade whisky, bad liquor. **2** [1990s+] (*UK prison*) a drink made of rubbing alcohol, mothballs and chlorine solution.

scrap iron *n.*[2] [1960s+] (*US prison*) weights, used for exercising and body-building.

scrapp *n. see* SCRAP *n.*[1].

scrapper *n.* **1** [mid-19C+] a fighter, a boxer, a brawler. **2** [late 19C] (*US tramp*) a victim of either tramps or criminals who 'puts up a fight'. [SCRAP v. (1)]

scrappet *n. see* SCRAP *n.*[3].

scrappy *adj.* [late 19C+] pugnacious, aggressive. [SCRAP v. (1)]

scrap-up *n. see* SCRAP *n.*[2] (1).

scratch *n.*[1] [mid-18C] (*UK Und.*) a mile.

scratch *n.*[2] [late 18C–mid-19C] a wig, designed to resemble the wearer's own hair.

scratch *n.*[3] [mid-19C] any competitor who has no advantage given to him in a handicapped contest; thus also in fig. use. [SE *scratch*, the starting line; such competitors must run the full race, play the full distance of the holes etc]

scratch *n.*[4] **1** [mid-19C+] (*also* **scratch spread**) a letter. **2** [late 19C–1900s] the struggle to 'make ends meet'. **3** [1910s–50s] (*US Und.*) a bad cheque. **4** [1910s+] money; sometimes a small amount. **5** [1910s+] (*US*) a loan. **6** [1930s+] (*US*) publicity, a favourable mention in the media. **7** [1940s] an I.O.U. **8** [1940s] (*UK Und.*) silver in quantity. **9** [2000s] (*Irish*) unemployment benefit, social security. [the image of scratching in the dirt for funds, scratching words on a page etc]

scratch *n.*[5] *see* SCRATCH SHEET n.

scratch *v.*[1] (*also* **scratch off**) [mid-19C+] (*Aus./US*) to leave or move at speed. [one's tracks are scratched in the ground, but note Aus. cattlemen use *scratch*, to rowel a horse with one's spurs]

scratch *v.*[2] [mid-19C+] (*US*) to forge banknotes or other documents.

scratch *v.*[3] **1** [mid-19C+] to get rid of, to wipe out, e.g. a police record, a debt. **2** [late 19C+] (*US*) to kill, to murder. **3** [1960s] (*US prison*) to catch in the commission of a disciplinary offence. [SE *scratch*, to remove a horse (or dog) from those running in a given race]

scratch *v.*[4] **1** [1920s+] (*US Black*) to work. **2** [1940s] (*US Black campus*) to hand over. [abbr. SE *scratch for* (money)]

scratch *v.*[5] [1960s] of a man, to seduce, to have sexual intercourse. [note Williams for 17C *scratch one's itch*, to satisfy a sexual urge]

scratch *v.*[6] *see* SCRATCH (OFF) v.

scratch (around) *v.* [20C+] (*orig. US*) to search for something, esp. when hard to find.

scratch-ass *adj.* [2000s] (*US*) impoverished. [SE *scratch*, i.e. for a living + -ASS sfx]

scratch-cat *n.* [1910s] (*N.Z.*) a bad-tempered woman.

scratch-crib *n.* (*also* **scratch-pad**) [1940s] (*US Black*) a cheap hotel or rooming house. [SE *scratch* + CRIB n.[1] (1); one scratches at the bites inflicted by bedbugs]

scratch down *v.* [late 19C] for a woman to tell her husband off in public.

scratched *adj.* [early 17C; mid-19C] drunk.

scratcher *n.*[1] [early–mid-19C] (*Anglo-Irish*) **1** a toe. **2** a hand; often in in pl., fingers.

scratcher *n.*[2] [mid-19C–1940s] (*US*) a forger, a counterfeiter. [SCRATCH v.[2]]

scratcher *n.*[3] **1** [late 19C+] a match. **2** [1970s+] (*Irish*) a lottery scratch-card. [SE *scratch*; (1) prison use only by 1950s]

scratcher *n.*[4] [1940s+] (*Irish/Scot.*) a bed. [the scratching caused by the bedbugs]

scratcher *n.*[5] [1960s] (*US*) a writer, a journalist.

scratch gravel *v.* [mid-19C+] (*Aus./US*) **1** to work hard. **2** (*also* **chuck up gravel, throw dust/gravel**) to leave hurriedly, to move very fast. [the image of wheels spinning in gravel]

scratch house *n.* **1** [late 19C+] a cheap hotel or lodging house; anywhere suffering an infestation of insects. **2** [1950s] a third-rate musical show, verging on burlesque. [the scratching caused by bedbugs + HOUSE n.[1] (1)]

scratching *n.*[1] [1930s+] (*Aus.*) **1** worried, bemused, in a quandary. **2** struggling for a living. [the image is of a hen]

scratching *n.*[2] [1950s–70s] (*US Black*) writing.

scratching rake *n.* [late 19C] a comb. [the image is of removing lice]

scratch it *v.* [1910s–20s] to rush off. [SCRATCH v.[1]]

Scratchland *n.* [late 18C–early 19C] Scotland. [derog. image of Scotland as louse-ridden]

scratchman *n.* [1910s–60s] (*US Und.*) a forger. [SCRATCH v.[2]]

scratch me *n.* [late 19C] a match. [var. on SCRATCHER n.[3] (1)]

scratch (off) *v.* [1910s+] (*Aus.*) to accept a resignation from a job. [SE *scratch*, to erase the name of (a person) from a list]

scratch off *v. see* SCRATCH v.[1].

scratch one's ass *v.* (*also* **scratch oneself**) [mid-19C+] to waste time, to daydream.

scratch-pad *n. see* SCRATCH-CRIB n.

scratch platter *n.* [late 18C–early 19C] bread soaked in the dressing in which cucumbers have stood. [SE *scratch*, impromptu + *platter*]

scratch-rash *n.* [late 19C] scratches on one's face, presumed to be caused by an angry woman.

scratch sheet *n.* (*also* **scratch**) [1930s+] (*US*) a betting sheet.

scratch spread *n. see* SCRATCH n.[4] (1).

scratch the gravel *v. see* SCRATCH GRAVEL v. (2).

scratch the monkey *v. see* FEED THE MONKEY v.[1].

scraunched *adj.* (*also* **scronched**) [20C+] (*US*) drunk. [? dial. *scranched*, crushed or SE *scrunch*]

scrav *v.* [1990s+] (*UK juv.*) to borrow or steal (usu. money); thus *scrav*, the borrower or thief. [? SE *scavenge* + *scrape up*; note dial. *scravvle*, to grope with the hands]

scream *n.* (*orig. US*) **1** [late 19C+] someone or something considered uproariously funny. **2** [1900s–20s] an urgent message. **3** [1900s–50s] someone considered excellent, attractive. **4** [1910s–20s] a success. **5** [1920s] a fuss. **6** [1920s+] a good time. **7** [1920s+] the act of informing on or betraying a criminal accomplice. **8** [1930s+] a complaint, esp. against criminal activities or to the police. **9** [1930s+] an alarm, a hue and cry. **10** [1980s+] an appeal against conviction or sentence.

scream *v.* **1** [1920s+] to inform, usu. to the police but occas. against them. **2** [1950s+] to complain. **3** [1960s+] (*US Black*) to engage in verbal confrontation. **4** [1970s+] (*US gay*) to be obviously homosexual.

scream and hollar *n.* (*also* **scream and holler**) [1930s+] (*US Und.*) a dollar (cf. BEES (AND HONEY) n.). [rhy. sl.]

scream blue murder *v.* (*also* **scream bloody murder**) [mid-19C+] to be in a state of hysteria, utterly and completely over-wrought or terrified. [SE *scream* + BLUE MURDER n.]

scream cold *v.* (*also* **scream foul/hard**) [1980s] (*US Black*) to use language that is likely to cause a fight.

scream copper *v. see* CALL COPPER v.

scream down some heavy lines *v.* (*also* **scream some heavy lines down**) [1970s+] (*US Black*) **1** to impress with one's smart talk. **2** to debate or argue intensely and emotionally. [SE *scream* + HEAVY adj.[1] (9) + LINE n.[1] (3)]

screamer *n.*[1] **1** [early 19C+] (*orig. US*) anything or anyone exceptional, in size, attractiveness, wit etc. **2** [mid-19C] a ballad singer. **3** [mid-19C] a serious and unpleasant situation. **4** [mid-late 19C] (*orig. US*) a teller of exaggerated or very funny stories. **5** [mid-19C–1930s] (*orig. US*) a thrilling or funny story, a 'screaming' farce. **6** [late 19C+] an exclamation mark. **7** [late 19C+] a powerful shot in a game, e.g. of cricket, golf, hockey. **8** [20C+] (*US*) a sensational newspaper headline or story. **9** [20C+] (*US*) a conspicuous advertisement. **10** [1900s] a sensational or propagandist piece of writing. **11** [1930s–60s] (*US Und.*) an arrest warrant. **12** [1960s+] (*orig. gay*) a flagrant homosexual. **13** [1970s+] (*US campus*) anything exceptionally challenging, difficult, esp. work. **14** [1980s+] something horrifying.

screamer *n.*² [1920s+] an informer. [SCREAM v. (1)]

screamer *n.*³ (*also* **screamer and creamer**) [1940s+] a woman who screams or otherwise makes a good deal of noise during intercourse. [SE *scream* + CREAM v.¹ (3)]

screamer *n.*⁴ [1960s+] (*US Black*) a siren, esp. on a police car.

scream foul/hard *v. see* SCREAM COLD v.

screaming *adj.* **1** [mid-19C–1940s] first-rate, splendid. **2** [mid-19C+] very funny. **3** [mid-19C+] a general intensifier. **4** [1910s+] (*US Black*) fantastic, amazing, extreme. **5** [1920s] (*US*) of clothing, loudly patterned or coloured. **6** [1930s+] (*gay*) blatantly homosexual. [SE *scream*; note 19C Adelphi Theatre playbills, which advertised a 'screaming farce']

screaming abdabs *n.* [1950s+] **1** the horrors, utter disgust, abhorrence; usu. as in *give someone the screaming abdabs*. **2** delirium tremens. [SE *screaming* + ABDABS n.]

screaming eagle *n.* [1940s+] (*US*) a GI discharge button, issued after WW2. [the image engraved on it]

screaming fairy *n.* (*also* **screaming faggot/queen**) [1940s+] an ostentatiously effeminate homosexual man. [SE *screaming*/ SCREAMING adj. (3) + FAGGOT n.² (3)/FAIRY n.³/QUEEN n.² (1)]

screaming for it *phr.* [1960s+] desperate for sex, usu. but not invariably of a woman.

screaming gasser *n.* [1940s] (*US Black*) a police car moving at speed and sounding its siren.

screamingly *adv.* [late 19C] a general intensifier, incredibly, remarkably. [SCREAMING adj. (3)]

screaming meemies *n.* (*also* **screaming meamies/mimis**) [1940s+] (*US*) **1** nerves, paranoia. **2** delirium tremens. [SE *screaming* + MEEMIES n.]

screaming queen *n. see* SCREAMING FAIRY n.

scream on *v.* **1** [1960s–70s] (*US Black*) to betray a confidence, to inform against, to gossip about. **2** [1960s+] (*US Black*) to attack verbally. **3** [1970s] to embarrass. **4** [1970s+] (*US gay*) to pick a fight; to be very keen on (something). [SCREAM v.]

scream sheet *n.* [1940s+] (*US*) a tabloid newspaper. [SCREAMER n.¹ (8) + SHEET n. (1)]

scream some heavy lines down *v. see* SCREAM DOWN SOME HEAVY LINES v.

scream someone out *v.* [1990s+] to criticize, to tell off, to reprimand.

screamy *adj.* **1** [late 19C] extreme, exaggerated, undignified; of colour, glaring, violent. **2** [1970s] (*gay*) pertaining to a flamboyant, effeminate homosexual man. [used of something that fig. SE *screams*]

screave *n. see* SCREEVE n.

screech *n.*¹ [20C+] (*US*) cheap, rotgut whisky; thus *screechers*, drunk. [its effect on women]

screech *n.*² [1900s] a hit, a success.

screech *n.*³ [1970s+] (*gay*) the throat, the mouth.

screecher *n.* [mid-19C] (*Irish*) a jorum of hot punch.

screechie *v.* (*also* **screechy**) [1950s+] (*W.I. Rasta*) to sneak by, to move stealthily. [var. on SE *squeak by*]

screeching *adj.*¹ [1900s] (*Aus.*) extreme, complete. [play on HOWLING adj.]

screeching *adj.*² [1920s] (*US*) drunk.

screechy *v. see* SCREECHIE v.

screen *n.*¹ **1** [late 18C–19C] a banknote (cf. BANK-RAG n.). **2** [early 19C] a counterfeit note. [? SCREEVE n. (2)]

screen *n.*² [1960s+] (*US Black*) a television.

screens *n.* [1930s] (*US prison*) an isolation cell for psychotic prisoners with a mesh screen.

screeve *n.* (*also* **screave, scrieve, scrive**) **1** [late 18C–1940s] a letter, a note. **2** [early–mid-19C] (*UK Und.*) a banknote, a guinea or a pound sterling (cf. BANK-RAG n.). **3** [mid-19C] a chalk drawing on the pavement. **4** [mid-late 19C] a counterfeit banknote. **5** [mid-late 19C] a begging letter. [? Scot. *scrieve*, to read or write quickly or continuously; or SCREEVE v. (2)]

screeve *v.* **1** [mid-19C] to draw on the pavement with chalk. **2** [mid-19C–1930s] to write, esp. to write fraudulent documents or letters; thus *screeve a fakement*, to concoct or write a begging letter or any other document aimed to extract money by trickery. [Ital. *scrivere*; ult. Lat. *scribere*, to write]

screever *n.* (*also* **screeve, scriever, scrivener**) **1** [mid-19C–1940s] a pavement artist, who draws in coloured chalks on the paving stones. **2** [mid-late 19C] a writer of begging letters. **3** [mid-19C] a begging letter. [SCREEVE v.]

screigh *n.* [19C] (*Scot.*) whisky. [ety. unknown; ? Scot. *screigh*, screech, thus cf. SCREECH n.¹]

screw *n.*¹ **1** [early 18C–early 19C] a prostitute. **2** [mid-19C+] an act of sexual intercourse; also in fig. use. **3** [mid-19C+] one's partner in intercourse; usu. applied to a woman; esp. as a *good/bad screw*. **4** [1960s] (*US*) as a synon. for FUCK n.² (2). **5** [1960s+] a dismissive and pej. ref. to a woman, relegating her to the status of a pure sex object. [SCREW v.² (1)]

screw *n.*² **1** [late 18C+] (*UK Und.*) a skeleton key. **2** [early 19C] a robbery achieved with a skeleton key. **3** [early 19C+] (*also* **bull-screw, screwsman**) a turnkey; a prison warder. **4** [1900s] (*Aus.*) a station overseer.

screw *n.*³ (*US campus*) **1** [19C] a particularly demanding instructor. **2** [19C; 1970s] the essays and examinations they set. [SCREW v.³]

screw *n.*⁴ [mid-late 19C] a miser. [? they *screw down* their money or *screw* it out of creditors]

screw *n.*⁵ **1** [mid-19C–1910s] an old and/or broken-down horse. **2** [1900s] (*Aus.*) an unpleasant old woman. [? racing jargon *screw*, to force a horse to the front; thus a horse can be made to gain a better than expected place; note late 19C local New Orleans *screw*, a fool]

screw *n.*⁶ **1** [mid-19C+] wages, salary. **2** [1900s] pocket money. [? the money one can *screw* out of one's employer]

screw *n.*⁷ [late 19C] a pick-me-up, a tonic. [it 'pulls one together']

screw *n.*⁸ [20C+] (*orig. Aus.*) a look, a stare, a gaze, esp. a challenging one; thus *have/give/take a screw at*, to survey, to stare, esp. in an aggressive manner.

screw *n.*⁹ [1950s] a mad person. [SCREWY adj.¹ (3)]

screw *n.*¹⁰ [1960s–70s] a swindle. [SCREW v.² (2)]

screw *v.*¹ [mid-17C; late 19C] to render drunk. [SCREWED adj.¹]

screw *v.*² **1** [early 18C+] to have sexual intercourse; poss. the most common example of the equation sex = violence (cf. BANG v.¹; FRIG v.). **2** [mid-18C+] (*orig. US*) (*also* **screw out of, screw with**) to cheat, to swindle, to take advantage of, to treat badly or unfairly; esp. as *get screwed*, to be swindled, cheated. **3** [mid-19C] to act like a miser. **4** [1940s+] (*orig. US*) to ruin, to pervert, to upset. **5** [1940s+] used as a synon./euph. for FUCK v.² in a variety of senses, e.g. *screw the government! screw you!* **6** [1960s+] to hurt. **7** [1960s+] (*US*) to sodomize. **8** [1980s+] to drive, to travel about.

screw *v.*³ (*US campus*) **1** [19C] to subject a student to an extremely searching examination. **2** [1960s] to fail a test or examination. [SE *screw*, to pressurize]

screw *v.*⁴ **1** [early 19C+] to break into, to rob, orig. with a skeleton key; thus *screwable*, suitable for a robbery. **2** [mid-19C] to lock, e.g. a door, a moneybox. **3** [1920s] to escape by unlocking a door. [SCREW n.²]

screw *v.*⁵ [late 19C+] (*US*) to run off, to leave; also as imper. *screw*, go away.

screw *v.*⁶ [20C+] (*orig. Aus.*) **1** to survey, to look at an object.

2 to stare intently at someone; thus WHO YOU SCREWIN'? phr. [SCREW n.[8]]

screw v.[7] **1** [1980s+] (*W.I./UK Black teen*) to crumple up one's face in annoyance, tightly puckering the lips and features into a vexed look. **2** [1990s+] (*UK Black*) to complain, to make a fuss. **3** [2000s] (*UK Black*) to vilify, to humiliate.

screw! *excl.* [1950s+] a euph. for FUCK! excl.

screw a chat v. [late 19C] (*UK Und.*) to break into a house. [SCREW v.[4] (1) + CHEAT n. (1)]

screw-and-spew movie n. [1980s] a pornographic film depicting extreme violence. [SCREW v.[2] (1) + SE spew]

screw around v. [1930s+] (*orig. US*) **1** to act in a promiscuous manner. **2** to fiddle with, to mess around with; to waste time. **3** to annoy, to irritate. [lit./fig. uses of SCREW v.[2]]

screwbado n. *see* SCRUBBADO n. (2).

screwball n. [1930s+] (*orig. US*) an eccentric, an out-of-the-ordinary person. [baseball use *screwball*, a ball pitched with reverse spin against the natural curve; also playing on SCREWY adj.[1] (3) + -BALL sfx]

screwball adj. [1930s+] (*orig. US*) **1** (*also* **screwballed**) of a person, eccentric, mad, crazy (cf. SCREWY adj.[1]). **2** of a thing or procedure, bizarre, eccentric. [SCREWBALL n.]

screw-belly n. (*also* **scribley**) [late 19C] sour, weak beer (cf. BELLY VENGEANCE n.). [SE screw + belly]

screwdriver n.[1] [1970s+] (*Aus./UK prison*) a principal officer who 'drives' his subordinates. [SCREW n.[2] (3) + pun]

screwdriver n.[2] [1970s+] the penis. [SCREW n.[1] (2) + pun]

screwed adj.[1] (*also* **screwed up**) [mid-19C+] drunk; thus *half-screwed*, tipsy.

screwed adj.[2] **1** [late 19C+] in trouble, in great difficulties. **2** [1940s+] (*also* **scrod**) cheated, deceived. [SCREW v.[2] (2)]

screwed adj.[3] [late 19C+] (*Aus.*) worn-out with hard work.

screwed, blued and tattooed phr. (*also* **screwed, jewed and tattooed; stewed, screwed and tattooed**) [1950s–70s] (*US*) comprehensively defeated; suffering very great harm. [SCREWED adj.[2] (1) + ? *blewed*, robbed + SE *tattooed*, to be repeatedly struck (+ JEW (DOWN) v./? STEWED adj.[1]]

screwed up adj.[1] **1** [late 19C] in serious financial difficulties. **2** [20C+] in a mess, out of order, malfunctioning. **3** [1930s+] neurotic, very miserable, anxious. **4** [1960s] absurd, improbable, unlikely. [abbr. phr. *screwed up in a corner*]

screwed up adj.[2] *see* SCREWED adj.[1].

screwee n. [2000s] (*US*) one's sexual partner. [SCREW v.[2] (1)]

screwer n. [1930s–50s] (*UK Und.*) **1** a thief, a burglar. **2** burglary. [SCREW v.[4] (1)]

screwess n. [1980s+] (*Aus. prison*) a female prison officer. [SCREW n.[2] (3) + fem. sfx *-ess*]

screw face n. [1980s+] (*W.I./UK Black teen*) one whose face is crumpled up in annoyance. [SCREW v.[7] (1)]

screw factory n. [1970s] a psychiatric hospital. [SCREW n.[9]]

screwing n.[1] [mid-19C+] **1** house-breaking. **2** (*also* **screwing job**) an act of burglary. [SCREW v.[4] (1)]

screwing n.[2] **1** [late 19C+] sexual intercourse. **2** [late 19C+] punishment; harsh or unfair treatment. **3** [1940s+] cheating, fooling, deceiving. [SCREW v.[2]]

screwing adj. [1960s] a synon. for FUCKING adj.

screwing job n. *see* SCREWING n.[1] (2).

screw it! *excl.* [1940s+] the hell with it! forget it! [SCREW v.[2] (5), i.e. euph. for FUCK IT! excl.]

screw it on v. [1960s+] to drive one's car or motorcycle very fast. [SE screw, to tighten]

screwman n. [1930s–50s] a thief, a burglar. [var. on SCREWS-MAN n.[1]]

screwnoodleous adj. [late 19C] drunk (cf. ADDLED adj.). [ext. of SCREWED adj.[1]; note NOODLE n.[1]]

screwnut n. [1990s+] (*UK juv.*) a failure, a blunderer. [SCREW UP v.[3] (2) + NUT n.[4] (1)]

screw-off n. [1960s+] (*US*) an idler, a loafer. [SCREW OFF v. (2)]

screw off v. [1960s+] (*mainly US*) **1** to masturbate (cf. BALL OFF v.[2]). **2** to take time off work or duty. [SCREW AROUND v. (2)]

screw off out v. *see* SCREW OUT v.

screw one's nut v. **1** [late 19C] to dodge a blow aimed at one's head. **2** [1900s–20s] (*US*) to turn around, to leave, to go. **3** [1930s–70s] to think hard. [SE *screw* + NUT n.[1] (2)]

screw on wheels n. [1980s+] (*Aus. prison*) a parole officer. [SCREW n.[2] (3)]

screw out v. (*also* **screw off out**) [late 19C+] (*orig. US*) to leave, to depart. [mid-20C+ uses seem to be euph. for FUCK OFF v. (1), but early ones may be autonomous]

screw over v. [1970s+] to cheat, to swindle, to treat badly or harshly. [ext. of SCREW v.[2] (2)]

Screws, the n. *see* NEWS OF THE SCREWS n.

screws, the n. [late 19C+] rheumatism, sciatica, fibrositis. [SE *screw*; the pains it causes]

screwsman n.[1] [19C+] a skilled house-breaker. [SCREW v.[4] (1) + sfx *-man*]

screwsman n.[2] *see* SCREW n.[2] (3).

screws me phr. [1970s+] (*US campus*) excuse me. [joc. mispron.]

screw someone out of v. [1970s+] (*orig. US*) to defraud, to cheat, to deceive. [SCREW v.[2] (2)]

screw someone up v. **1** [late 18C–early 19C] to cheat, to defraud. **2** [1940s+] (*orig. US*) to make trouble, to cause difficulties for. [SCREW v.[2] (2)]

screw the arse off v. (*also* **screw the ass/socks off**) [1940s+] to indulge in aggressive, vigorous copulation (cf. FUCK THE ARSE OFF v.). [SCREW v.[2] (1) + ARSE, THE n./— ONE'S SOCKS OFF phr.]

screw the dog/pooch v. *see* FUCK THE DOG (AND SELL THE PUPS) v.

screw-up n. **1** [1920s+] of an object, a plan or a scheme, a disaster. **2** [1960s+] (*orig. US*) of a person, a failure, an incompetent. [SCREW UP v.[3] (2)]

screw up v.[1] [early 19C] to imprison. [SCREW n.[2]]

screw up v.[2] [mid–late 19C] to garrotte. [SE *screw up*, to tighten]

screw up v.[3] **1** [mid-19C; 1940s+] to cause trouble for. **2** [1930s+] (*orig. US*) to make a mess, to blunder badly. **3** [1950s+] to hurt, to put out of order. [SCREW v.[2] (4)]

screw up (with) v. [1960s] (*US*) to get involved with, associated with.

screwy adj.[1] **1** [mid-19C] drunk (cf. ADDLED adj.). **2** [mid-19C] worn out. **3** [late 19C+] (*orig. US*) foolish, stupid, insane (cf. SCREW-BALL adj.). **4** [1920s+] odd, strange. **5** [1930s] suspicious, alarmed. **6** [1930s+] illegal; counterfeit. [HAVE A SCREW LOOSE v.; note Tok Pisin (Papua New Guinea pidgin) *waialus*, an unstable, crazy person (f. 'wire loose')]

screwy adj.[2] [mid–late 19C] mean. [SCREW n.[4]]

screwy adj.[3] [1940s+] weak, malfunctioning. [SCREWED adj.[2] (1)]

screw you! *excl.* [1950s+] (*US*) an excl. of dismissal, contempt. [SCREW v.[2] (5)]

screw your buddy week phr. *see* FUCK YOUR BUDDY WEEK phr.

scribble one's teeth v. [2000s] (*US Black*) to talk; to preach.

scribe n. **1** [mid-19C+] a writer. **2** [late 19C+] (*US*) a newspaper-man. **3** [1930s–40s] (*UK Und.*) a forger. **4** [1930s–60s] (*US Black*) a letter. **5** [1940s] (*US Black*) a girl.

scribe v. [1960s+] to write.

scribley n. *see* SCREW-BELLY n.

scrieve *see under* SCREEVE.

scrilla n. (*also* **scrill, skrill, skrilla**) [1990s+] (*US Black teen*) money; thus *gotta get me scrill on*, I must find some cash. [? Sp.]

scrilla monger n. [2000s] (*US Black*) someone who does whatever they can to get money. [SCRILLA n. + SE *monger*]

scrilling n. (*also* **skrilling**) [1990s+] (*US Black*) **1** wasting time, lounging around with friends. **2** making money. [SCRILLA n.]

scrimmage n. (*also* **skrimmage, skrummage**) [late 18C+] a disturbance, a confused, noisy struggle. [? SE *skirmish*]

scrimy *adj.* [1920s–40s] (*US*) unpleasant, dirty, run-down. [? SE *scratchy* (i.e. from fleas/bed-bugs) + *grimy*]

scrip *n.*[1] [1900s–40s] (*US*) $1. [SE *scrip*, a scrap of paper or a certificate of indebtedness, as issued to workers in lieu of actual cash]

scrip *n.*[2] [1920s+] (*drugs*) a pre*scrip*tion. [abbr.]

scripper *n.* (*also* **scrippet**) [late 16C–early 17C] (*UK Und.*) the member of a team of highway robbers who keeps a watch. [? Lat. *scripsit*, he wrote, and poss. referring to written instructions given to this member of the gang]

script *n.* **1** [1920s+] (*drugs*) a pre*script*ion for narcotics. **2** [1980s] pre*script*ion drugs. [abbr.]

script mill *n.* [1990s+] (*US drugs*) a doctor's surgery where, for a price, one can obtain prescriptions for narcotics, painkillers etc. [SCRIPT n. (1) + MILL n.[4] (4)]

scripture-tickler *n.* [late 19C] (*Aus.*) a preacher, a clergyman.

scrive *n. see* SCREEVE n.

scrivener *n. see* SCREEVER n.

scroat *n. see* SCROTE n.

scrob *v.* [1910s] to thrash, to beat hard. [SCROBY n.]

scroby *n.* [late 18C–19C] (*UK Und.*) a judicial flogging. [? dial. *scrobble*, a quarrel, a problem, a scratching]

scrod *adj. see* SCREWED adj.[2] (2).

scrog *v.* [1980s+] (*US campus*) to have sexual intercourse. [var. on SCREW v.[2] (1)]

scronch *n.* (*also* **schronch**) [1920s–30s] a dance. [SCRONCH v. (1)]

scronch *v.* **1** [1920s–30s] to dance. **2** [1940s] in fig. use, any activity. [SE *scrunch*, the proximity of the dancers]

scronched *adj. see* SCRAUNCHED adj.

scrooch *v. see* SCRUNCH v.

scrooched *adj.* [1920s] (*US*) drunk. [Yorks. dial. *scrooch*, to crouch]

scroodge *v. see* SCROUGE v.

scroof *n.* (*Irish*) **1** [1910s] a crust of bread. **2** [1990s+] dandruff. **3** [1990s+] unpleasant people, scum. [(1) 16C *scruff*, a thin crust; (2) SE *scurf*; (3) SE *scruff*, someone worthless]

scroof *v.* [19C–1920s] to sponge off. [? SE *scrounge* + *off*]

scrooge *n.* [1930s+] a miser; thus **scroogey**, miserly. [the miserly Ebenezer *Scrooge*, created by Charles Dickens in *A Christmas Carol* (1843); ult. SCROUGE v. (1)]

scrooge *v. see* SCROUGE v.

scroogie *n.* [1990s+] (*US Und.*) a *screw*driver. [abbr.]

scrooly *adj.* [1940s] (*US*) mad. [? var. on SCREWY adj.[1] (3)]

scroop *v.* [1910s–20s] to rub up against, to pass very closely. [SE *scroop*, to make a scraping noise]

scrope *n.* [18C–early 19C] (*UK Und.*) a farthing. [proper name of Sir John *Scrope*, secretary of the Treasury from 1724–52]

scrote *n.* (*also* **scroat**, **scrot**, **scrotum**) [1970s+] a general term of abuse (cf. BALLOCKS n.[2]). [abbr. SE *scrotum*]

scrot rot *n.* [1990s+] (*UK juv.*) unpleasant itchiness/sweating around the testicles. [abbr. SE *scrotum*]

scrotum-face *n.* [1940s–50s] a term of abuse, a promiscuous man.

scroucher *n.* (*also* **scrouger**, **scrousher**, **scrowcher**) [20C+] (*Aus.*) a general derog. term for a person. [? SE *scrounger*; dial. *scringer*, one who pries around looking for trifles or dial. *skreenger*, one who is (negatively) energetic]

scrouge *n.* (*also* **scrowge**) [mid-19C] **1** a crowd, a crush. **2** (*US campus*) anything considered unpleasant, e.g. a tedious lesson. [SCROUGE v.]

scrouge *v.* (*also* **scroodge**, **scrooge**, **scrowge**, **skrowdge**) **1** [mid-18C+] to encroach on a person's space, to crowd, to push forward in a crowd; occas. as *scrouge up*. **2** [early 19C+] to push something out of the way, to squeeze a thing. **3** [mid-19C] (*US campus*) of a teacher, to impose unpleasant tasks. [? 16C SE *scruze*, to squeeze]

scrouger *n.*[1] (*also* **scrouge**) [mid-19C] (*orig. US*) something or someone large or forceful. [SCROUGE n.]

scrouger *n.*[2] *see* SCROUCHER n.

scrounge *n.* **1** [1910s] a search, a hunt. **2** [1930s+] (*US*) a general derog. term; lit. one who scrounges.

scrounge *v.* **1** [mid-19C+] to cadge; thus *scrounger*, one who cadges from others; *on the scrounge*, begging, cadging. **2** [1910s+] (*Aus.*) to steal. **3** [1960s–70s] to hunt about, to rummage.

scroungy *adj.* [20C+] (*US*) inferior, second-rate, grubby. [SCROUNGE v. (1), i.e. something that has been cadged]

scrouperize *v.* [mid-17C–early 18C] to have sexual intercourse. [SE *scroop*, to rub against]

scrousher *n.* (*Aus./N.Z.*) **1** [mid–late 19C] a worn-out prospector. **2** [20C+] a prostitute. [? SCROUNGE v. (1)]

scrousher/scrowcher *n. see* SCROUCHER n.

scrowge *see under* SCROUGE.

scrub *n.* **1** [late 17C+] a general pej. term, a lout, a failure, a dirty or unpleasant person or thing. **2** [early 18C] (*UK Und.*) a low-class thief. **3** [early 18C+] a low-class prostitute. **4** [mid-18C–early 19C] one who does not pay their share of the tavern bill. **5** [mid-19C+] (*US*) a derog. term for a Black person (cf. ALLIGATOR BAIT n.[2]). **6** [late 19C] (*US*) a beggar who is willing to perform occasional paid work, usu. as a 'shabbos goy', performing work that orthodox Jews may not do on the Sabbath. **7** [1910s+] (*US Black*) a fool. **8** [1990s+] (*US teen*) a sponger, a parasite. **9** [2000s] (*US teen*) an exploitative womanizer. [SE *scrub*, an insignificant, unattractive person]

scrub *v.* **1** [early 19C; 1940s+] (*orig. US*) to cancel, to wipe out, to forget. **2** [1940s–50s] of a lover, to abandon. **3** [1980s] to kill. **4** [1980s+] (*US campus*) to fail. **5** [2000s] (*US teen*) to trip or fall down. [SE *scrub out*; (2) *OED* has a single early 19C cit., but then nothing until WW2]

scrub along *v.* [mid-19C+] to survive with difficulty.

scrubbado *n.* (*also* **scrubado**) **1** [mid-17C–early 19C] 'the itch', venereal disease. **2** [late 18C–mid-19C] (*UK Und.*) (*also* **screwbado**) a general term of abuse. [SE *scrub*, 'the itch' + Sp./Port. sfx *-ado*, thus giving an underpinning of racist stereotyping]

scrubber *n.*[1] (*Aus./N.Z.*) **1** [mid-19C–1910s] a rough, unkempt person. **2** [mid-19C–1930s] one who lives in the scrub or wooded countryside. **3** [mid-19C+] a cow or horse that has run wild in the scrub and has deteriorated in condition. **4** [1940s+] an unpleasant weakling. [SE *scrub*, heavily wooded country, whether growing small or large bushes and trees]

scrubber *n.*[2] **1** [1940s+] a promiscuous woman, usu. young. **2** [1960s+] (*Irish*) a common working-class woman, with no sexual implications. [? SE *scrubber*, a charwoman, one who scrubs; orig. sl. use was in jazz community, where it described 'a girl who slept with a jazzman but for her own satisfaction as much as his' (George Melly, *Owning Up*, 1965); ? link to Aus. term, defined as 'a mare that runs wild in the scrub country, copulating indiscriminately with stray stallions' (quote cited in *OED*)]

scrubbing brush *n.* **1** [mid-19C+] pubic hair. **2** [late 19C–1920s] (*Aus.*) a loaf of bread made from inferior materials.

scrub bull *n.* [1950s+] (*Aus.*) a solo prospector, living out in the desert and characterized by surliness, taciturnity and general misanthropy. [SAusE *scrub bull*, a bull that was bred in, or escaped into, the wild]

scrubby *adj.* **1** [19C] (*US campus*) vulgar, ill-bred, mean. **2** [1960s] promiscuous. [SCRUB n. (1)]

scrub cockie *n.* (*also* **scrub cocky**) [20C+] (*Aus.*) a small farmer working tree-covered or otherwise rough land. [SE *scrub* + COCKY n.[2] (1)]

scrub-dangler *n.* [late 19C–1910s] (*Aus.*) a wild bullock.

scrub-dashing *n.* [1940s–50s] (*Aus.*) riding through bush or scrub in pursuit of strayed cattle or horses.

scrub it! *excl.* [1940s+] forget it! ignore it! cancel it! [SCRUB v. (1)]

Scrubs, the *n.* [20C+] (*UK police/Und.*) Wormwood *Scrubs* prison, London (cf. ABBOTT'S PRIORY n.). [abbr.]

scrub the kitchen *v. see* CLEAN UP THE KITCHEN v.

scrub the slate clean *v.* [late 19C+] (*US*) to cancel or ignore the past and start again.

scrub-turkey *n.* (*Aus.*) **1** [1950s–70s] an itinerant who moves around the Australian bush; his long absence from urban life may have rendered him slightly eccentric. **2** [1950s+] a contemptible woman.

scrub up well *v.* [1980s+] (*Aus.*) of a man, to look presentable despite being in the aftermath of a drunken night out; of a woman, to show good dress sense.

scrud *n.[1]* [1930s+] (*US, orig. milit.*) a painful disease, esp. a venereal disease. [ext. of CRUD n.[1] (3)]

scrud *n.[2]* [1990s+] (*UK juv.*) the junior members of a school. [ext. of CRUD n.[1] (3)]

scrudge *n.* [18C] a prostitute. [SCROUGE v. (1), from her approaching people in a crowd]

scruff *n.[1]* [1950s+] an unkempt, messy person; also a term of abuse. [dial. *scruff*, refuse, thus human refuse in dial. use since mid-19C; ult. SE *scurf*, a skin disease; note RMC Duntroon (Aus.) *scruff*, a woman (without any particular derog. implication)]

scruff *n.[2]* [1990s+] pornographic literature. [SE *scruff*, rubbish, that which is worthless]

scruff *adj.* [1950s] messy, unkempt. [SCRUFF n.[1]]

scruff *v.* **1** [19C] to hang. **2** [mid-19C–1940s] (*Aus.*) to grab by the scruff of the neck. **3** [mid-19C–1940s] (*Aus.*) to attack, to manhandle. [dial. *scruff*, the nape of the neck]

scruff-bag *n.* [1920s+] **1** a down-and-out. **2** a messy, unkempt creature. [SCRUFF n.[1] + -BAG sfx]

scruff-hound *n.* [1940s] a rough, tough individual. [SCRUFF n.[1] + HOUND sfx]

scrum *n.* (*also* **scrummy**) [late 19C–1900s] (*Aus./N.Z.*) a threepenny piece. [rhy. sl. = THRUMS n. (1)]

scrumdolious *adj.* (*also* **scrumbotious**) [1910s–30s] wonderful, excellent, often but not always of food.

scrummy *adj.[1]* (*also* **scrum, skrum**) **1** [late 19C+] of food, enjoyable, delicious. **2** [20C+] excellent, fine. [abbr. SCRUMPTIOUS adj.]

scrummy *adj.[2]* [1910s] (*N.Z.*) lice-ridden. [? misreading of CRUMMY adj.[2] (1)]

scrump *n.* [1990s+] (*US Black/campus*) sexual intercourse. [SCRUMP v.[2]]

scrump *v.[1]* [mid-19C+] to steal fruit, usu. apples, from orchards. [dial. *scrump*, anything withered or dried up, esp. a withered or stunted apple]

scrump *v.[2]* [1980s+] (*US campus*) **1** to have sexual intercourse; to neck. **2** to engage in an adulterous sexual relationship; thus *scrumper*, an adulterer. [? SCRUMPTIOUS adj.]

scrumplicate *v.* [late 19C] to beat up, to thrash, to defeat. [? var. SPIFLICATE v. (2)]

scrumptious *adj.* [mid-19C+] (*orig. US*) **1** fastidious, hard to please. **2** (*also* **scronchous**) first-rate, excellent. **3** stylish, handsome. **4** delicious, extra-tasty, nearly always of food but occas. of an attractive person. [dial. *scrumptious*, mean, stingy, close-fisted; although the senses seem totally opposed, cf. SE *nice* for a similar shift in meaning from overly fastidious to attractive and appealing]

scrunch *n.* [1920s+] (*Aus.*) food, esp. sweets. [SE *scrunch*, the noise of crunching]

scrunch *v.* (*also* **scrooch**) **1** [late 19C+] to squeeze. **2** [1920s+] (*US Black*) to dance extremely close to someone; to snuggle up; thus *have a scrunch on*, to be infatuated.

scruncher *n.* [late 19C+] a glutton. [SE *scrunch*, to bite with a crunching noise]

scrunge *n.* **1** [1970s+] (*orig. US campus*) filth, mess, dirt. **2** [2000s] (*US*) a filthy, unpleasant person, a 'lowlife'. [? GRUNGE n.]

scrungy *adj.* (*also* **skrungy**) [1970s+] (*orig. US campus*) filthy, messy, dirty, disgusting. [SCRUNGE n. (1); var. on GRUNGY adj.]

scrunt *v.* [20C+] (*W.I.*) to eke out a living, to suffer great poverty, to be forced into begging. [dial. *scrunt*, to scratch + SE *scrounge*]

scuba *v.* [2000s] (*US Black*) to perform cunnilingus. [play on SE *scuba-dive* + DIVE v.[2]]

scuba (diver) *n.* [1990s+] a £5 note (cf. BEEHIVE n.[2]). [rhy. sl. = FIVER n. (1)]

scud *n.* **1** [mid-19C] (*school*) a fast runner. **2** [1960s+] (*Ulster*) a jinx. **3** [1960s+] a general term of abuse. [Scot. *scud*, a blow]

scud *v.* [1990s+] to partake in an act of copulation. [SE *scud*, to move fast; ? reinforced by the *Scud* missiles used in the Gulf War (1991)]

scuddick *n.* (*also* **scuddock**) [early–mid-19C] a tiny sum of money. [dial. *scud*, a wisp of straw]

scuddy *adj. see* SCUZZY adj. (1).

scudi *n.* [late 19C–1900s] money; also in pl., with an amount, e.g. *ten skudi*, £10. [Ital. *scudo*, 'A silver coin and money of account formerly current in various Italian states, usually worth about 4 shillings' (*OED*)]

scud mag *n.* [1990s+] a pornographic magazine; thus *scuddy*, pornographic. [SCUD v. + colloq. SE *mag*, a magazine]

scuff *n.[1]* [late 19C] a crowd of people.

scuff *n.[2]* **1** [1930s+] (*US Und.*) a shoe; thus as v., to walk. **2** [1970s+] (*Aus./US*) a slipper.

scuffer *n.* (*also* **scufter, skuffter**) [mid-19C+] (*UK, mainly northern*) a policeman; thus *judy scuffer*, a policewoman (cf. BEAT-POUNDER n.). [? dial. *scuff*, to strike; Yorks. dial. *scuff*, 'mean, sordid fellow, the scum of the people' (*EDD*); or *scurf*, the back of the neck, and thus one who grabs you by it]

scuffle *n.[1]* [1920s+] (*US Black*) **1** difficult circumstances, poverty. **2** a job. [SCUFFLE v.[2] (1)]

scuffle *n.[2]* (*also* **skuffle**) [1970s+] (*drugs*) phencyclidine (cf. ACE n.[4]). [ety. unknown]

scuffle *v.[1]* [late 19C+] (*US, orig. jazz*) to dance. [SE *scuffle*, shuffle]

scuffle *v.[2]* **1** [1920s+] (*US, orig. jazz*) to survive with difficulty, to eke out a bare living, often through unpleasant, degrading methods. **2** [1940s+] (*US Black*) to collect, raise or obtain money.

scuffle-hunter *n.* [18C] a dockside pilferer. [they *scuffle around*, hunting for items to steal]

scuffler *n.* [1940s+] **1** anyone who ekes out a living, esp. a petty criminal; thus *skuffling*, a derog. epithet. **2** (*US Black*) one who works hard and honestly for their living. [SCUFFLE v.[2] (1)]

scuff up *v.* [1990s+] (*US prison*) to fight, usu. with the fists. [abbr. SE *scuffle*, to struggle confusedly together]

scufter *n. see* SCUFFER n.

scug *n.* [1910s+] a despicable person. [public school use *scug*, 'a boy of untidy, dirty, or ill-mannered habits; one whose sense of propriety is not fully developed' (*Everyday Life in Public Schools*, 1881)]

scull *n.[1]* (*also* **skull**) [early 18C–mid-19C] the head, principal or master of a university college.

scull *n.[2]* (*also* **sculler**) [late 18C–early 19C] a 1-horse chaise or buggy. [SE *scull*, a light boat rowed by a single oarsman]

scull around *v.* [1920s+] to wander aimlessly.

scullery-science *n.* [mid-19C] phrenology. [pun on SE *skull*]

scully *n.* [1980s+] (*US campus*) an unspecified person. [? SE *scullion*]

scully *v.* [1990s+] (*US*) to doubt. [the perennially sceptical character *Scully* in the TV series *The X-Files*]

scum *n.* [1940s+] (*US*) semen (cf. CRUD n.[1]).

scum *v.* [1990s+] (*US*) to ejaculate. [SCUM n.]

scumbag *n.* [1950s+] (*orig. US*) **1** a contraceptive sheath. **2** (*also* **scum**) a general term of abuse. [SCUM n. + SE *bag*/BAG n.[7]/ -BAG sfx]

scumbag *adj.* [1970s+] (*orig. US*) repellent, disgusting, despicable. [SCUMBAG n. (2)]

scumball *n.* [1980s+] (*US*) an unpleasant person. [SCUM n. + -BALL sfx]

scumber *n.* (*also* **scummer**) [mid-17C] excrement. [dial. *scumber*, animal dung or sticky, viscous mud]

scumber *v.* [mid-17C] to defecate (cf. CACA v.). [SCUMBER n.]

scumbucket *n.* [1980s+] (*US*) **1** an unpleasant person. **2** an unpleasant, dirty place. [SCUM n. + SE *bucket*]

scum fuck *n.* (*also* **scumfucker**) [1980s+] a general term of abuse.

scumhead *n.* [1940s+] a general term of abuse. [SCUM n. + -HEAD sfx (1)]

scummer *n.*[1] [1980s+] (*US*) an outlaw biker. [SE *scum*]

scummer *n.*[2] *see* SCUMBER n.

scummer *v.* (*also* **scammer**) [late 16C–mid-17C] to defecate (cf. CACA v.). [SCUMBER n.]

scummy *adj.* [1920s+] unpleasant, disgusting. [SE *scum*]

scumpig *n.* [1990s+] a general term of derision or abuse; sometimes used affectionately.

scumpteen *n.* [1940s] an undetermined but substantial number. [ext. UMPTEEN n.]

scumsucker *n.* [1960s+] (*orig. US*) **1** a person who performs fellatio. **2** a derog. term of general abuse; thus adj. *scumsucking* (cf. COCKMUNCH n.). [SCUM n. + SE *sucker*]

scunge *n.* **1** [20C+] (*Ulster*) one who is always 'on the make'. **2** [1960s+] (*Aus./N.Z./US*) (*also* **scungeel**) an unpleasant, objectionable person. **3** [1960s+] (*Aus./N.Z.*) dirt, filth, often associated with the body. [Scot. *scunge*, slink around; note RMC Duntroon (Aus.) *scunge*: 'a stingy miserly person, a penny-pinching niggard']

scungies *n.* **1** [1970s] (*Aus.*) men's bikini-style swimming trunks, often worn under surf shorts or 'baggies'. **2** [1990s+] old clothes. [joc. use of SCUNGY adj.; such trunks are seen as too sordid for public display]

scungy *adj.* [1960s+] (*Aus./N.Z.*) filthy, dirty. [SCUNGE n. (3) or var. on SCRUNGY adj.; note RMC Duntroon (Aus.) *scungy*, mean miserly, parsimonious]

scunner *n.* [20C+] (*US*) extreme dislike, hostility; thus *scunnered*, to arouse hostility. [Scot. *scunner*, an abomination]

scunted *adj.* [1990s+] (*Aus. teen*) caught out doing something. [? Yorks. dial *scunted*, having lost all one's marbles]

scupper *n.* [1930s–70s] a prostitute. [? SE *scupper*, a boat's drain through which dirty water can run]

scupper *v.* [late 19C+] (*orig. milit.*) to defeat, to ruin, to put an end to; to kill. [i.e to pour down the SE *scupper*; a drain]

scurf *n.* [mid-19C–1900s] **1** an unpleasant person, esp. a miser or skinflint; also as collective n. **2** an employer who pays less than average wages. **3** a worker who accepts less than the average rate. [SE *scurf*, a general term referring to a variety of skin diseases]

scurf *adj.* [mid–late 19C] of labour, cheap. [SCURF n. (3)]

scurf *v.* [early 19C] to arrest; thus *scurfed*, arrested. [? SE *scruff*, to seize by the nape of the neck]

scurrick *n. see* SKERRICK n. (1).

scurryfunging *n.* [late 19C] wandering like a tramp. [Scot. *scurryvaig*, a vagabond]

scurve *n.* [20C+] **1** (*US*) a contemptible person. **2** (*US Black*) any form of ugliness or shabbiness. [SCURF n. (1) or ? SE *scurvy*]

scurvy *adj.* [1980s] (*US Black*) of a woman, unattractive. [SE *scurvy*]

scut *n.*[1] **1** [late 16C–early 19C] the female genitals and pubic hair. **2** [late 17C; 1900s–20s] the buttocks, the posterior. **3** [1990s+] (*UK juv.*) a promiscuous girl, beneath or just at the age of consent. [SE *scut*, a rabbit or hare's tail]

scut *n.*[2] **1** [late 19C+] a contemptible person. **2** [20C+] (*US*) a novice or new recruit. [? dial. *scutter*, diarrhoea or SCOUT n.[1]]

scut *v.* [1930s+] (*Irish, esp. juv.*) to grab a free ride by hanging onto the rear of a vehicle, unbeknown to the driver; thus phr. *scut the whip*, a warning to a driver that riders are on his vehicle.

scutcher *n.* [1910s+] (*Aus.*) anything notably large or esp. outstanding. [? SE *scotch*, to kill; thus a 'killer']

scutter *n.*[1] [20C+] an unpleasant person; thus adj., *scuttering*. [Scot. *scutter*, a slovenly, untidy worker]

scutter *n.*[2] [1960s+] (*Irish*) excrement; thus as v., to defecate; *the scutters*, diarrhoea; *tail-skutter*, a fart. [Irish *sciodar*, diarrhoea]

scuttered *adj.* [1960s+] (*Irish*) tipsy, drunkenly loquacious. [dial. *scutter*, to expend a great deal of energy in doing nothing constructive + Irish *sciotarálaí*, idle chatter]

scuttle *n.* [1900s] (*US*) a derog. term for a Black person (cf. BLACKBELLY n.). [abbr. SE *coalscuttle*]

scuttle *v.* **1** [19C] to deflower a woman. **2** [mid-19C–1900s] to stab; thus *scuttler*, a knife-carrying villain; one using a leather belt as a weapon. [SE *scuttle*, to make a hole in a ship's bottom in order to sink her]

scuttle a ship *v.* [19C] to deflower a woman. [ext. of SCUTTLE v. (1)]

scuttlebutt *n.* **1** [20C+] gossip, rumour. **2** [1960s] a gossip. [US Navy *scuttlebutt*, a ship's water barrel, around which sailors gathered and gossiped; the term, however, was orig. RN]

scuttler *n.* [mid–late 19C] (*Manchester*) a young street thug. [Lancashire dial. *scuttle*, a street brawl; ? SE *scuttle*, to run off]

scuttle someone's nob *v.* (*also* **scuttle someone's hull**) [early–mid-19C] to break someone's head. [SE *scuttle* + NOB n.[1] (1)/SE *hull*]

scut work *n.* [1950s+] (*US*) menial or routine work. [? SCUT n.[2] (1)]

scuzbag *n. see* SCUZZBAG n.

scuzz *n.* (*also* **scuz, skuz**) (*orig. US*) **1** [1960s+] any unpleasant person. **2** [1980s+] dirt, mess, any horrible substance. **3** [2000s] a sexually active, thus by sexist definition, promiscuous, woman. [? SE *disgusting* or SCUMMY adj. + SE *fuzzy*]

scuzz *v.* [1980s+] **1** to filthy, to make a mess of. **2** in fig use, to act in a sordid manner. [SCUZZ n. (2)]

scuzzbag *n.* (*also* **scuzbag**) [1980s+] **1** (*US campus*) a sexually promiscuous woman. **2** (*US*) a contemptible person. [SCUZZ n. (1) + -BAG sfx]

scuzzball *n.* [1980s+] a contemptible person. [SCUZZ n. (1) + -BALL sfx]

scuzzbucket *n.* [1980s+] an unpleasant person. [SCUZZ n. (1)]

scuzzbucket *adj.* [1980s] unpleasant, distasteful, repellent. [SCUZZBUCKET n.]

scuzzed out *adj.* [1980s+] (*US teen*) disgusted, nauseated. [SCUZZ v.]

scuzzhead *n.* [1990s+] a general term of abuse. [SCUZZ n. (1) + -HEAD sfx (1)]

scuzzy *n.* [1970s] (*US*) an old person, on the verge of death. [SCUZZ n. (1)]

scuzzy *adj.* (*also* **skuzzy**) **1** [1960s+] (*US teen*) (*also* **scuddy**) filthy, repellent. **2** [1970s+] unkempt, down-at-heel, ragged. [SCUZZ n. (1)]

'sdeath! *excl.* [17C+] a euph. oath, lit. 'God's death'.

sea-coal *n.* **1** [mid-18C–mid-19C] smuggled spirits. **2** [19C] money. [SE *sea-coal*, coal that is exposed at low tide or washed up on the coastline]

sea-crab *n.* [late 18C–mid-19C] a sailor.

sea dust *n.* [1930s–40s] (*US milit.*) salt.

seafood *n.*[1] [1920s] (*US Und.*) whisky. [? the smuggling of whisky by sea during the Prohibition era, 1920–33]

seafood *n.*[2] [1930s+] (*gay*) sailors as sex objects. [i.e. something to EAT v.[3] (1)]

seafood plate *phr.* [1980s] (*US campus*) please. [joc. pron. of Fr. *s'il vous plaît*, please]

seagull *n.* [1950s+] (*Aus./N.Z.*) a casual wharf labourer. [like the seagull, they hope to pick up 'scraps', in this case, of work]

seal *n.*[1] [late 16C–mid-17C] **1** the penis. **2** the vagina. [coined by John Donne (1572–1631)]

seal *n.*[2] (*also* **sealskin**) [20C+] (*US*) a Black woman; also attrib. [the smoothness of her skin]

seal *v.* [late 16C–early 18C] to have sexual intercourse, esp. to impregnate a woman. [SEAL *n.*[1]]

seal-a-meal *n.* [1980s+] (*drugs*) small plastic bags used for the selling of crack cocaine. [brandname]

sealed oyster *n. see* OYSTER *n.*[3] (1).

sealer *n.* [late 17C–early 19C] (*UK Und.*) 'one ready to give bond and judgement for goods or money' (Grose, 1785). [SE *sealer*, one who affixes a seal to a document]

sealing wax *n.* [20C+] (*Aus.*) tax. [rhy. sl.]

seals *n.* [mid-19C] the testicles. [which 'seal' a sexual 'bargain']

sealskin *n. see* SEAL *n.*[2].

seam squirrel *n.* [1910s+] (*US*) a body louse.

Seamus *n.* [2000s] a generic name for an Irishman (cf. DONOVAN *n.*[1]). [the common Irish name]

sea pie *n.* [mid-19C–1950s] a stew. ['A dish of meat and vegetables, etc, boiled together, with a crust of paste, or in layers between crusts, the number of which denominate it a two or three decker' (Smyth, *Sailor's Word-book*, 1867); Brendan Behan, *Borstal Boy* (1958): 'a kind of Irish stew with suet instead of potatoes in it']

sea pussy *n.* [1960s+] (*US gay*) a homosexual sailor. [SE *sea* + PUSSY *n.* (9); note Dos Passos, *The Big Money* (1936): '"Not too far out, on account of the seapussies." "What?" "Currents, she shouted"']

sear *n.* (*also* **sere**) [16C] the female genitals. [SE *sear*, the touchhole at which the match sets off the charge in a pistol, but note *tickle/light of the sear*, 'easily made to "go off", readily yielding to any impulse' (OED)]

searcher *n.* [1920s–50s] a penetrating or embarrassing question.

searchlights *n. see* HEADLIGHTS *n.* (3).

search me! *excl.* [late 19C+] (*orig. US*) a general assertion of ignorance, I don't know! don't ask me!

search-my-heart *n.* [1900s] (*W.I.*) a drink of rum. [its effects]

search the placket *v.* [early 18C] to have sexual intercourse, esp. with a prostitute or mistress. [SE *search* + PLACKET *n.* (1)]

sea-rover *n.* [late 19C–1910s] a herring.

Sears Roebuck library *n. see* LIBRARY *n.*[2].

seaside moths *n.* [late 19C] (*UK middle class*) bedbugs. [euph.]

season breast *n.* [1990s+] (*W.I.*) a female breast which has been smeared with vaginal secretions.

seasoner *n.* [1910s–20s] a fashionably dressed person. [SE *the* (social) *season*]

seat *n. see* HOT SEAT *n.*

seat *v.* (*Aus./N.Z., orig. prison*) **1** [1950s+] to sodomize; thus *seatman*, a sodomite. **2** [1980s] to knock down. [SE *seat*, the buttocks]

seat of honour *n.* (*also* **seat of shame/vengeance**) [late 18C–mid-19C] the posterior, the buttocks.

seat of pleasure *n.* (*also* **seat of love**) [18C] the vagina (cf. ADAM'S OWN (ALTAR) *n.*).

seaweed *n.* [1930s–40s] (*US milit.*) spinach. [? its consumption by cartoon hero Popeye the Sailorman]

sec *n.* **1** [late 19C+] a *sec*ond. **2** [20C+] (*also* **seck**) a *sec*retary. [abbr.]

seccy *n.* (*also* **seggs, seggy**) [1960s+] (*drugs*) *Sec*onal. [abbr.]

secko *n.* (*also* **secco, sekko**) [1940s+] (*Aus.*) a sexual pervert, usu. prison use. [SE *sex* + -o sfx (4)]

seco *n.* [1960s] (*drugs*) a *Sec*onal pill. [abbr.]

second *n.* [late 19C] (*Aus.*) a girlfriend.

second banana *n.* [1940s+] the second most important person, the second-in-command. [show business use *second banana*, a supporting comedian to the star, a 'straight man']

second base *n.* [1930s+] (*US Black/teen*) sexual exploration above the waist (cf. FIRST BASE *n.*). [baseball imagery]

second closet *n.* [1960s+] (*gay*) the hiding of one's specific sexual preferences and practices, even if the basic fact of homosexuality can be admitted. [SE *second* + CLOSET *n.*[2]]

second fiddle *n.* (*also* **third fiddle**) [19C+] someone or something that is considered less than the best or is not in the top position; thus *play second fiddle*, to take a secondary, subsidiary role; (less common) *play first fiddle*, to play a leading role. [orchestra imagery]

second-hand glove *n.* [late 17C] the vagina of a widow (cf. BAG *n.*[1]). [VENUS'S GLOVE *n.*]

second-hand sue *n.* [1940s–50s] (*Aus.*) **1** a worn-out prostitute. **2** an ageing passive homosexual. [SE *second-hand* + assonant use of proper name *Sue*]

second-hand sun *n.* [late 19C] reflected sunlight, as found in many poor homes, deprived in the narrow streets of direct sunlight.

second-hand woman *n.* [late 19C] (*Anglo-Ind.*) a widow; thus *second-hand gentleman*, one who marries a widow.

second hole from the back of the neck *n.* [2000s] the vagina (cf. BLACK HOLE *n.*[1]).

second liker *n.* [late 19C] a second drink, of the same sort as the first. ['I'll have a second one like that']

second line *v.* [1910s+] (*US*) to follow a leader or someone firstrate, with the hope of advancement or promotion.

seconds *n.* **1** [late 18C; 1910s+] a second helping of food or similar. **2** [late 19C–1900s] opium residue. **3** [20C+] (*US*) coffee brewed from used grounds. **4** [1950s+] taking second (or later) place in an act of group sex (usu. forced).

second-storey job *n.* (*also* **second-storey trade/work**) [late 19C+] (*US*) a break-in, spec. one that involves climbing above ground level. [SE + JOB *n.*[3] (1)]

second-storey man *n.* (*also* **second-storey worker**) [late 19C+] (*US*) a thief who climbs into buildings above the ground floor. [SE *second-storey* + *man*/WORKER *n.*[1] (1)]

secrets of the alcove *n.* [late 19C] (*UK society*) a wife's influence over her husband, which was not, in late 19C, generally paraded in public.

sectioned *adj.* [1980s+] **1** mandatorily detained in a mental institution under section 3 of the Mental Health Act; also as v. **2** used of any one seen as eccentric, though not actually mad.

section eight *n.* [1940s+] (*US*) **1** a section 8 discharge, discharge from the US army on grounds of mental instability; thus in fig. use. **2** insanity, instability. **3** a crazy, neurotic or eccentric person.

seddity *see under* SADDITY.

seduce my ancient footwear! *excl. see* FUCK MY OLD BOOTS! *excl.*

seducer *n.* [1970s+] (*US Black*) one who supplies the means of making fast, poss. illegal, money.

see *v.*[1] [mid-18C–early 19C] to take care, to do something, usu. combined with another v., e.g. *see that you get*.

see *v.*[2] **1** [19C] to have sexual intercourse. **2** [2000s] to have a sexual relationship with.

see *v.*[3] [mid-19C+] (*orig. US*) **1** to understand, to appreciate the veracity of an idea or statement; often as interrog., do you understand? **2** to consider, to think of doing something.

see *v.*[4] [mid-19C+] **1** (*orig. US*) to visit a person, esp. a politician, in order to influence them, either legally or, more likely, illegally. **2** to take care of. **3** (*UK Und.*) to pay protection money.

see *adv.* [mid-19C] yes. [backsl.]

see a dog about a man *v.* [1920s+] **1** to go out for a drink. **2** to urinate. [joc. var. on SEE A MAN ABOUT A DOG *v.*]

see a man about a dog *v.* (*also* **see a man about a horse/ rose, see a cat about a horse**) **1** [late 17C; mid-19C+] a euph. used to disguise one's need or desire to visit the lavatory (cf. DO ONE'S BUSINESS *v.*). **2** [mid-19C–1940s] (*orig. US*) (*also* **go see a man**) to go for a drink; usu. in the form of an excuse before going out for a drink; also when absenting oneself from home in order to visit one's mistress. **3** [1910s+] (*also* **write a letter to a man about a dog**) used as an excuse to leave.

see a sick friend *v.* (*also* **sit up with a sick friend**) [late 19C+] used as an excuse by a married man slipping out to consummate an illicit affair.

see a thing or two *v. see* KNOW A THING OR TWO *v.*

see a wolf *v.* [19C] of a woman, to be seduced.

see candles *v. see* SEE STARS *v.*

see company *v.* **1** [mid–late 18C] to visit a brothel. **2** [mid-18C–early 19C] to live as a prostitute. [euph.]

seed *n.*[1] **1** [mid-19C–1940s] (*US*) a dollar; money. **2** [1900s] a poker chip.

seed *n.*[2] [mid-19C+] (*US campus*) a person, esp. when unpopular or notably rowdy.

seed *n.*[3] [1960s+] (*drugs*) **1** marijuana; usu. in pl. **2** the butt end of a marijuana cigarette.

seed *n.*[4] [1970s+] (*US Black*) a child, children. [SE *seed* of one's loins]

seedbags *n.* [1970s–80s] (*UK Black*) the testicles.

seed corn *n. see* CORN *n.*[1].

seedy *n.* [1980s] (*US Black*) a dealer in pills.

seedy *adj.* [mid-19C] (*US campus*) rowdy, noisy. [SEED *n.*[2]]

seedy (boy) *n.* [mid–late 19C] a derog. term for a Black person (cf. ALLIGATOR BAIT *n.*[2]). [ironic use of Urdu *sidi*, my lord]

see foot *v.* [20C+] (*W.I.*) to see how fast a person runs away.

see France *v.* (*also* **see one's days, …one's nennen, …one's skin, …one's tail**) [1920s+] (*W.I.*) to endure hardships, esp. in the hope of ultimate success. [SE *see* + FRANCE *n.*/SE *days*/NENNEN *n.*/SE *skin*/TAIL *n.*[2] (1)]

see hell *v.* (*also* **smell hell**) [1950s] (*UK/W.I.*) to suffer, to have a hard time, to find it hard to make enough money to live.

see how the land lies *v.* [late 17C–early 19C] to check the state of one's tavern bill.

see if I care *phr.* [1920s+] a dismissive phr. indicating one's lack of concern.

see if it fucks *v.* [20C+] to see if something works or runs. [fig. use of FUCK *v.*[1]]

seeing double *phr.* [late 18C] drunk.

seeing Steve *phr.* [1940s] (*US drugs*) taking cocaine to the extent that one hallucinates. [? anecdotal]

seeing-to *n.* [1970s+] **1** referring to a woman, sexual intercourse (cf. SEE TO *v.*). **2** referring to a man, a beating up, violence.

seek a clove *v.* [late 19C] (*US*) to take a drink. [? the use of *cloves* to disguise the smell of drink on the breath]

seek and search *n.* [1990s+] a church. [rhy. sl.]

seek others and lose oneself *v.* [late 16C] to play the fool (cf. ACT THE ANGORA *v.*).

seek-sorrow *n.* [late 16C; 1900s] a general term of abuse, esp. a whining malcontent.

see Mrs Murray *v.* (*also* **see Mrs Murphy**) [1930s–50s] (*Aus.*) to visit the lavatory (cf. AUNTIE *n.*[1]). [ult. ref. is to the *Murray* River, Australia's longest river]

seen! *excl.* [1950s+] (*orig. W.I.*) **1** a general excl. of affirmation. **2** a general excl., 'do you understand?' [although the term is used as a synon. for SE *yes*, the implication is one of bearing witness and thus of a more profound agreement with the speaker]

see ning-ning *v.* [20C+] (*W.I.*) to reel from shock, to suffer a spell of dizziness. [Carib.E. *ning-ning*, dizziness]

see-o *n.* [mid-19C] shoes. [backsl.]

see off *v.* **1** [1930s+] to deal with, to dismiss, to send away, to defeat. **2** [1980s+] (*Aus. prison*) to murder.

see one's days/nennen/skin/tail *v. see* SEE FRANCE *v.*

seer *n.* [19C] the eye. [lit. 'see-er']

see rats *v. see* GET RATS *v.*

see red *v.* [20C+] to become very angry. [a bull's trad. reaction to a red rag]

see royal *v.* [20C+] (*W.I.*) to find it hard to make enough money to live, to subsist, to suffer great hardship. [SE *see* + fig. use of ROYAL *n.*[1]]

sees *n.* [late 18C–early 19C] (*UK Und.*) the eyes.

see sailor *n.* [late 19C] a beggar who poses as a discharged seaman. [? one *sees* him as a *sailor*]

see-saw *n.* [1970s] (*US Black*) an up-and-down, uncertain relationship.

see snakes *v.* **1** [late 19C+] (*US*) to have delirium tremens. **2** [1900s] to be in a state of shock.

see someone coming *v.* [late 19C+] to take advantage of someone. [the implication is that the swindler saw a 'soft touch' coming before putting the price up or setting up the swindle]

see stars *v.* (*also* **see candles/spots, shoot stars**) [mid-18C+] 'to have a sensation as of flashes of light, produced by a sudden jarring of the head, as by a direct blow' (*Century Dict.*, 1889). [*candles*, mid-18C–mid-19C; *spots*, mid–late 19C]

see the breeze *v.* [late 19C] to enjoy the fresh air, usu. on a trip out of the city.

see the elephant *v.* (*orig. US*) **1** [mid-19C+] to see the world and to become bored and jaded by doing so; to be disappointed in one's optimistic expectations. **2** [mid-19C+] to seek out excitement, esp. in the context of going slumming in poor and/or dangerous urban areas. **3** [late 19C] to be seduced, to be fooled. [despite US origin, poss. popularized in the UK by the appearance in London in 1867 of the original Jumbo, a major attraction at first but then palling in the face of greater novelties. After many years at London Zoo, Jumbo was sold to Barnum and Bailey's Circus in 1882]

see the light at the end of the tunnel *v.* [1920s+] to glimpse the end of a long or difficult process or situation, to feel some optimism.

see the lions *v.* **1** [late 16C] to have some experience of life. **2** [mid-17C] to be drunk. **3** [early–late 19C] to see the fashionable 'sights'.

see them *v.* (*also* **have them**) [late 19C–1900s] (*US*) to suffer delirium tremens. ['them' = snakes, pink elephants etc]

see the nose-cheese first *v.* [mid-18C–1900s] to make a refusal rudely or contemptuously. [ety. unknown]

see the stars lying upon one's back *v.* [19C] of a woman, to have sexual intercourse (cf. CATCH AN OYSTER *v.*).

see through a brick wall *v.* (*also* **see through a stone wall**) [mid-19C+] to be particularly perceptive, to be intelligent, to be aware; sometimes ext. as *see further through a brick wall than most*.

see through a mill-stone *v.* [late 16C; 18C] to be aware, to understand what is going on.

see to *v.* [1980s+] of a man, to have sexual intercourse, to give a woman sex. [backform. f. SEEING-TO *n.*]

see two moons *v.* [mid-18C; 1920s] (*US*) to be drunk.

see which way the cat jumps *v.* [early 19C+] to wait to see how events turn out before making one's own decision or move.

see with half an eye *v.* [mid-16C–18C] to possess shrewdness or native wisdom, to be well aware. [later use is SE]

see ya! *excl.* (*orig. US campus*) **1** [1970s+] an excl. of farewell, goodbye! **2** [1980s] a general excl. of dismissal, shut up! leave me alone!

seeyabye! *excl.* [1980s] (*US teen*) an excl. of farewell, goodbye! [SEE YA! excl. (1) + SE *goodbye*]

see you *phr.* [1940s+] goodbye.

see you anonski *phr.* [1930s–50s] (*orig. Aus.*) a general phr. of farewell. [SE phr. *see you anon* + -SKI sfx]

see you in court *phr.* [1960s+] a joc. synon. for goodbye.

see you in the funny papers *phr.* [1920s+] (*US*) goodbye, see you later.

see you later alligator *phr.* [1950s–60s] an all-purpose synon. for goodbye; often ext. or replied to with *in a while crocodile*; popularized by the 1956 Bill Haley and the Comets pop hit of the same name, and by the widely publicized use of the phr. by Princess Margaret (1930–2002). [according to *DARE* f. ALLIGATOR n.³ (2); given that alligator is essentially (if not invariably) derog., the phr. certainly began as a dismissal, even if its popular use among those who had no idea of its origin rendered it neutral; an alternative response is 'on the Nile, crocodile']

see you some more *phr.* [1940s] (N.Z.) goodbye.

seg *n.*¹ (*also* **seggie**) [1960s+] **1** (*orig. US*) a *seg*regationist. **2** (*orig. Can./US prison*) a *seg*regation unit or cell. [abbr.]

seg *n.*² [1960s+] (*US campus*) a toadying or hypocritical smile. [abbr. SHIT-EATING GRIN n.]

seg *v.* [1960s–70s] (*orig. US*) to *seg*regate, to have a *seg*regationist policy. [SEG n.¹ (1)]

seggie *n. see* SEG n.¹.

seggs/seggy *n. see* SECCY n.

seh one *v.* [1990s+] (*W.I.*) of a woman, to be attractive. [ety. unknown]

seh-seh seh-seh *n.* [1990s+] (*W.I.*) gossip.

sei *n. see* SAY n.

sein *n. see* SANE n.

sekko *n. see* SECKO n.

seldom see *n.* [1920s] (*US*) underwear, BVDs. [rhy. sl.]

seldom seen *n.* [20C+] the queen. [rhy. sl.]

self-starter *n.* **1** [1930s] (*US drugs*) an addict who volunteers themself for a cure, taken in prison or a similar institution. **2** [1960s+] one who acts, esp. when employed, on their own initiative rather than await instructions or orders.

Selina Scott *n.* [1980s+] a spot. [rhy. sl.; TV personality *Selina Scott*]

sell *n.*¹ **1** [mid-19C] betrayal to the police. **2** [mid-19C–1900s] a lying joke. **3** [mid-19C–1910s] a disappointment. **4** [mid-19C–1920s] a hoax, a trick, a deception. **5** [late 19C] (*Aus.*) a show-off; an unreliable person. **6** [late 19C–1900s] (*US*) a swindler. [SELL v.]

$ell *n.* [1990s+] (*US Black teen*) an act of betrayal. [the $ sign is used to emphasize the lit. or fig. payment involved]

sell *n.*² [1970s] (*US*) an opportunity to sell something.

sell *v.* **1** [17C+] to deceive, to swindle, to take someone in by promoting something. **2** [19C+] (*UK Und.*) to betray, to inform against. **3** [mid-19C] in sports, to take a bribe to influence the outcome of a contest, usu. by losing deliberately.

sell a bargain *v.* [late 16C–early 19C] to fool, to hoax. [Shakespeare used the term in late 16C. Grose (1796) mentions a specific 'bargain', quoted by Swift, as being popular among Queen Anne's courtiers: 'A lady would come into a room full of company, apparently in a fright, crying out, "It is white, and follows me!" On any of the company asking, "What?", she sold him the bargain, by saying, "Mine a--e"']

sell a boy *v.* [1940s+] (*gay*) for one man to obtain the services of a boy prostitute at a price and then to offer him to a second man for the actual sex.

sell a hog *v. see* HOG v.¹ (2).

sell a pup *v.* [20C+] to deceive, esp. in business or financial transactions; thus the person deceived *buys a pup*. [stock market jargon *pup*, a worthless investment]

sellary *n.* [early 17C] a male homosexual prostitute. [Lat. *sellarius*, one who sits upon a *sella*, a couch, i.e. in a brothel]

sell a woof ticket *v.* (*also* **sell a wolf ticket**) [1960s+] (*US Black*) **1** to boast, to brag. **2** to talk nonsense, to lie. **3** to threaten, to intimidate. [ext. WOOF v.¹]

sell body *v.* [1960s] (*US Black*) to work as a prostitute.

sell down the river *v.* [late 19C+] (*orig. US Black*) to betray. [the practice of selling an errant slave to a Mississippi sugar-cane plantation. The journey to the plantation, where work was especially hard, meant a trip 'down the river']

sell honey for a halfpenny *v.* [late 16C–early 17C] to think very badly of someone. [? pvb]

selling a horse *n.* [1910s–30s] (*N.Z.*) a bar game played to determine who buys a round of drinks; occas. used in non-bar contexts. [play on SELL THE PONY v.; one person thinks of, or writes down, a number under 10; the group starts counting down, and the one who gets the chosen number pays]

sell one's cabbage twice *v. see* BOIL ONE'S CABBAGE TWICE v.

sell one's crack *v.* [1980s+] (*Aus. prison*) to prostitute oneself. [CRACK n.⁶ (1)/CRACK n.⁶ (5)]

sell oneself *v.* [1920s+] (*orig. US*) to attempt to make oneself appealing in the eyes of others.

sell one's pigs in a bad market *v. see* BRING ONE'S HOGS TO A FAIR MARKET v.

sell-out *n.* **1** [mid-19C+] an act of betrayal or sacrificing of beliefs and principles for money or position. **2** [1950s+] a person who betrays someone, or who sacrifices their principles for money. [SELL OUT v.¹]

sell out *v.*¹ [mid-19C+] (*orig. US*) **1** to betray someone or some external cause, for money or a similar reason. **2** to sacrifice one's own beliefs and principles for money or position.

sell out *v.*² [1930s–40s] (*US Und.*) to die in a gunfight rather than surrender to the police.

sell out *v.*³ [1930s–40s] (*US Black*) to leave, to run away (in terror).

sell out *v.*⁴ [1940s–50s] (*Aus.*) to vomit.

sell pussy *v. see* PEDDLE PUSSY v.

sell someone blind *v.* [late 19C] to deceive, to defraud.

sell someone on *v.* [1920s+] to convince, to persuade, to convey enthusiasm. [SELL v. (1)]

sell the pony *v.* (*also* **sell the lady**) [late 19C–1900s] to toss a coin to determine who pays for a round of drinks; thus *buy the pony/lady*, to pay for that round.

selopas *n.* [mid-19C] apples. [backsl.]

s'elp me (bob)! *excl.* (*also* **s'help me...! so help me...! swelp me...! swop me...!**) [early 19C+] a general excl. of intensification and affirmation; other combs. include *s'elp me baub!* ...*cat!* ...*Dash!* ...*davy!* ...*greens!* ...*Hannah!* ...*Jemima!* ...*lucky!* ...*never!* ...*tater!* ...*ten men!* [SE *so help me* + BOB n.²]

semen demon *n.* [1990s+] (*US*) a (passive) male homosexual, the inference is of a fellator (cf. BONE-EATER n.).

semi *n.* **1** [1910s+] a *semi*-detached house. **2** [1940s+] (*Aus./US*) a *semi*-trailer or articulated truck. **3** [1960s] (*US gay*) of a place, e.g. a club, half-homo- and half-heterosexual in clientele. **4** [1980s+] (*also* **semi-on**) a *semi*-erection of the penis. [abbr.]

semi *adv.* [1970s+] partly, to some extent.

seminary *n.* **1** [mid-17C] a brothel (cf. ABBESS n.; ACADEMY n.). **2** [19C] the vagina. [pun on SE *semen*]

semi-on *n. see* SEMI n. (4).

semolia *n.* [late 19C–1930s] (*US Black*) a fool. [? name of a lunatic asylum]

semolina *n.* [20C+] a cleaner, a charwoman. [rhy. sl.]

sempstress *n.* [17C–early 18C] a prostitute.

senal pervitude *n.* [late 19C] penal servitude. [a weak joke based on reversing the initial letters + a possible pun on 'senile perversity']

send *v.* **1** [1930s–40s] (*US drugs*) to smoke marijuana. **2** [1930s+] (*orig. US*) to excite emotionally, i.e. the effect equates with (1). [(2) orig. beatnik use, esp. as used of music; near obs. for a while, but revived in late 1990s]

send across *v.* [1920s–40s] (*US*) to send to prison.

send a line *v. see* DROP A LINE v. (1).

send along *v.* [late 19C–1910s] **1** (*Aus.*) to have someone arrested, to send to prison. **2** (*Aus.*) to criticize severely. **3** (*US*) to cost, to charge.

send away *v.* [1910s+] to imprison, to have someone imprisoned.

send by John Long the carrier *v.* (*also* **send by Tom Long the carrier**) [16C–19C] to postpone, to put off for a long time. [TOM LONG n.]

send down(stairs) *v.* [mid-19C+] to imprison. [walking down the steps from the dock (orig. at the Old Bailey) back to the cells; but note SEND UP THE RIVER *v.*]

send down the road *v.* (*also* **send down the track, put someone down the track**) **1** [1950s+] (*N.Z.*) to dismiss from employment; thus *go/get/be sent down the road/track*, to be dismissed. **2** [1970s] (*US Und.*) to send to prison.

sender *n.* [1930s–40s] (*US Black*) a person (usu. a musician) or thing (usu. a record) who or which is emotionally arousing. [SEND *v.* (2)]

send for mary ann *phr. see* SAN FAIRY ANN *phr.*

send her down Hughie! *excl.* (*also* **send it down Hughie! send her/it down Davey!, ...Steve!**) [20C+] (*Aus./N.Z.*) a general appeal to the gods for rain. [*Hughie*, the mythical deity of surfing and as such invoked by surfers who want suitable waves (also used as synon. for God by US loggers of Pacific Northwest)/ *Davey*, ? St David, the patron saint of Wales, the land of 'leeks'/ generic use of proper name *Steve*]

send-in *n.* (*US Und.*) **1** [1910s] an endorsement, a recommendation; as *v.*, to praise or recommend for one's own purposes. **2** [1930s] information about a possible crime.

send in by the servant's entrance *v.* [1960s+] of a man, to have sexual intercourse from the rear position. [SE *servant's entrance*, usu. in the rear or bottom storey of the house]

send in one's checks *v.* [mid-19C+] (*US*) to die (cf. CASH (IN) ONE'S CHECKS *v.*). [gambling imagery]

send it down Davey!/Hughie!/Steve! *excl. see* SEND HER DOWN HUGHIE! *excl.*

send it in *v.* **1** [early–mid-19C] to push in, to drive something home. **2** [1960s] (*US gambling*) to make big bets.

send-off *n.* **1** [19C+] (*Aus./US*) a funeral. **2** [late 19C+] some form of celebratory memorial at the time of someone's death, not spec. a funeral. **3** [late 19C+] some form of celebration to mark a person's departure. [the imagery of starting a race]

send off *v.* [1950s+] (*Aus.*) to steal.

send off the blue *v. see* BLUE *n.*[8] (2).

send on a hombug *v.* (*also* **send on a humbug, ...merry-go-round, ...trip**) [1950s+] (*US Black*) to send on a wild goose chase, a fool's errand.

send over *v.*[1] [1990s+] (*US Und.*) to betray to the authorities.

send over *v.*[2] *see* SEND UP *v.*[1].

send someone into Cornwall without a boat *v.* [mid-16C–early 19C] to cuckold.

send someone south *v.* [1960s] (*US*) to get rid of a person; to terminate a relationship.

send someone to the cleaners *v. see* TAKE SOMEONE TO THE CLEANERS *v.*

send the daylights out of *v.* [20C+] (*W.I.*) to beat severely, to hit an animal hard enough to kill it. [DAYLIGHTS *n.* (2)]

send to Birching Lane *v.* (*also* **send to Birchen/Birchin Lane**) [18C] to administer a flogging. [SE *birch* + *Birchin Lane*, London EC3, once known for its ready-made clothes shops, although the name ? f. OE meaning 'lane of the barbers']

send to Georgia *v. see* GEORGIA *v.* (3).

send to grass *v. see* GRASS *v.*[1] (1).

send to Long Beach *v.* [1960s–70s] (*US/Los Angeles drugs*) to flush drugs down the lavatory before or during a drugs raid. [? the sewer outlets at Long Beach]

send to the dogs *v.* [1930s] to bring down in the world. [GO TO THE DOGS *v.* (1)]

send to the pack *v.* [1910s–20s] (*Aus./N.Z.*) to discard, to dismiss.

send to the showers *v.* [1960s+] (*US*) to dismiss, to reject. [sporting imagery]

send to uncle's *v.* [19C] to pawn. [UNCLE *n.*[1] (1)]

send-up *n.* [1950s+] an instance of teasing, a joke at someone's expense. [SEND UP *v.*[2] (2)]

send up *v.*[1] (*also* **send over**) [mid-19C+] (*US Und.*) to imprison. [abbr. SE *send up* for punishment, or SE *send* UP THE RIVER *phr.*]

send up *v.*[2] **1** [1910s] (*Aus.*) to cheat, to defraud. **2** [1930s+] to mock, to tease, esp. to parody or imitate.

send up Green River *v. see* GO UP GREEN RIVER *v.*

send up the river *v.* (*also* **send up the hill**) [20C+] (*US Und.*) to imprison. [ext. of SEND UP *v.*[1] + UP THE RIVER *phr.*]

Senegambian *n.* [late 19C–1940s] (*US*) a derog. term for an African-American. [SE *Senegambian*, a native or inhabitant of Senegambia, former name of the region surrounding the Senegal and Gambia rivers in West Africa]

seni *n.* [1970s] (*drugs*) peyote; mescaline. [ety. unknown]

senor-eater *n.* [1970s+] (*US gay*) **1** a gay man who prefers Latin or Hispanic partners. **2** a Hispanic homosexual (cf. BONE-EATER *n.*). [puns on Sp. *señorita*, miss + *señor*, mister + SE *eater*; i.e. one who indulges in oral sex]

sensation *n.* (*also* **slight sensation**) **1** [mid-19C] 143ml (¼ pint) of gin. **2** [mid–late 19C] a taste, a small quantity. **3** [mid-19C+] (*Aus.*) a half glass of sherry. [ironic understatement]

sensimillia *n.* (*also* **sensamilia, sense, senseed, sensi, sinsemilla**) [1970s+] (*W.I./UK Black teen*) a variety of extremely potent marijuana; it has no seeds because it is isolated from male pollen during the blooming process; instead, the marijuana plant makes more tetrahydrocannabinol (THC), thus intensifying the effects (cf. AFRICAN BUSH *n.*). [lit. 'seedless']

sensitive plant *n.* **1** [mid-18C+] the penis. **2** [early–mid-19C] (*orig. boxing*) the nose.

sensitive truncheon *n.* [19C] **1** the nose. **2** the penis (cf. AX *n.*[2]).

sent *adj.*[1] [late 19C] imprisoned. [abbr. of *sent to prison*]

sent *adj.*[2] **1** [1930s–50s] (*drugs*) experiencing the effects of alcohol or marijuana. **2** [1930s–60s] emotionally overcome, esp. by a jazz solo. [SEND *v.*]

senter *n. see* SANTAR *n.*

sentimental *n.* [1920s–70s] (*Aus.*) a cigar or cigarette. [rhy. sl.; *sentimental bloke* = SMOKE *n.*[3] (1)]

sentimental hairpin *n.* [late 19C] (*UK society*) an affected, insignificant woman.

sent up *adj.* [late 19C+] (*orig. US*) imprisoned. [SEND UP *v.*[1]]

separate(s) *n.* [mid-19C–1920s] (*Aus./UK Und.*) solitary confinement in prison.

September morn *n.* [1970s+] an erection. [rhy. sl. = HORN *n.*[2] (3); note *September Morn*, a painting by Paul Chabas of a young woman bathing nude, which was first exhibited at the 1912 Salon in Paris. Censors attempted to ban a reproduction of the picture from public exhibition in the US, a farcical effort, which led to the sale of more than 7 million reproductions – appearing on dolls, statues, umbrella handles, tattoos and many other places – and the assurance that Chabas need never work again]

septic *n.* (*also* **seppo**) [1960s+] (*orig. Aus.*) **1** an American. **2** a bank. **3** a septic tank. [rhy. sl./abbr. (1) *septic tank* = YANK *n.* (1)]

septic *adj.* **1** [1910s+] unpleasant, rotten, mean. **2** [1970s+] (*Irish*) affected. **3** [1980s] (*N.Z.*) foolish, self-deluded, incompetent. [(1) and (2) SE; (3) rhy. sl.; *septic tank* = WANK *adj.*]

sepulchre *n.* [late 19C] (*UK middle class*) a flat cravat that covers the shirt-front, effectively hiding that portion that would otherwise appear between the coat and the throat. [SE *sepulchre*, a tomb; it 'buries' a shirt that is no longer clean]

sere *n. see* SEAR *n.*

serg *n. see* SARGE *n.*

sergeant *n.* [1950s] a 'masculine' lesbian. [abbr. TOP SERGEANT *n.*]

Sergeant Kite *n.* (*also* **Sergeant Snap**) [mid–late 19C] a recruiting sergeant. [? SE *kite*, a bird of prey/*snap*, the click of a fig. lock or the order, 'Snap to it!']

sergeant-major *n.*[1] [late 19C] (*UK Und.*) a burglar's chisel.

sergeant-major *n.*[2] [1910s–20s] the crown in the gambling game of 'Crown and Anchor'. [the NCO's badge of office]

sergeant-major n.[3] **1** [1910s+] strong sweet tea or tea with rum. **2** [1920s+] (US) coffee with cream or milk and sugar. [the NCO's preferred beverage]

Sergeant Snap n. see SERGEANT KITE n.

sergeant space n. [1980s+] (US campus) someone who is out of touch with reality. [SPACED (OUT) adj.]

seringapatam n. see PLASTERER'S TROWEL AND SERINGAPATAM n.

serious adj. **1** [1910s+] an all-purpose intensifier, e.g. serious drinking. **2** [1940s+] (US Black) excellent, first-rate.

serious joint, the n. see JOINT n.[7] (1).

seriously adv. [1980s+] an all-purpose intensifier, e.g. seriously rich.

serpent n. (also **silver serpent**) [1960s–70s] a hypodermic syringe and needle.

Serps n. (also **Turpentine, Turps**) [1930s+] the Serpentine lake, Hyde Park, London. [abbr./rhy. sl./pun]

servant n. [late 16C–mid-17C] a womanizer, a promiscuous man. [SE service, usu. of an animal, to copulate]

servant's meat n. see BOY'S MEAT n.

serve n. [1960s+] (Aus.) **1** negative criticism, a reprimand; verbal abuse, usu. as phr. give (someone) a serve; thus give something a serve, to deal with or consume enthusiastically, e.g. of food or drink, to 'punish'. **2** a beating. [SERVE v.[2] (1)]

serve v.[1] **1** [mid-16C+] (also **serve one's turn**) to have sexual intercourse. **2** [1980s+] (US Black/prison) to assault sexually, to rape. [SE service, usu. of an animal, to copulate; (+ TURN n.[2])]

serve v.[2] **1** [late 16C+] (UK Und.) to injure, to wound; thus serve out and out, to murder; also in fig. use, to treat badly. **2** [early 19C] (UK Und.) to convict and sentence. **3** [early–mid-19C] (UK Und.) to rob. **4** [1970s+] (N.Z.) to abuse. **5** [1970s+] (N.Z.) to tell lies. **6** [1980s+] (US Black teen) to give someone their due deserts. **7** [1990s+] (US) to dominate. **8** [1990s+] (US Black) to kill.

serve v.[3] [late 19C+] to serve a term of imprisonment.

serve v.[4] [1950s+] (drugs) to sell narcotics. [SE serve, to sell goods in a shop]

serve one's turn v. see SERVE v.[1] (1).

serve out v. (also **sarve out**) [19C–1900s] **1** to revenge oneself upon, to retaliate. **2** to punish. [boxing jargon]

serve someone a ticket v. [early 19C] (Anglo-Irish) to hit someone. [SERVE v.[2] (1)]

serve someone glad v. [late 19C–1930s] to give someone their deserts, to 'serve them right'. [orig. northern dial.]

service lay n. [18C] (UK Und.) a method of thieving whereby someone enters a house posing as a servant later to decamp with whatever they can steal. [SE service + LAY n.[4] (1)]

service of beef n. [1990s+] sexual intercourse. [SERVE v.[1] (1) + BEEF n.[1] (1)]

service station n. **1** [1940s] a brothel. **2** [1980s+] (US gay) a public lavatory used for sexual assignations. [play on SE/SERVE v.[1] (1)]

servo n. [1990s+] (Aus.) a service station. [abbr. + -o sfx (4)]

sese n. [1980s+] (W.I./UK Black teen) whisperings, rumours, gossip. [SESE v.]

sese v. [1980s+] (W.I./UK Black teen) to whisper. [echoic + Twi sise, to talk a lot]

sesh n. [1980s+] a session of drinking or taking drugs. [abbr. SESSION n. (4)]

sesh adj. [1990s+] (UK juv.) very good, excellent. [the implied excellence of a SESH n.]

sess n. (also **cess**) [1980s+] (US Black) top grade marijuana. [? SENSIMILLIA n.]

session n. **1** [1910s+] (Aus./US) a disturbance, an argument. **2** [1930s] a conversation. **3** [1930s+] (US teen) a dance, a party. **4** [1940s+] (orig. Aus.) a period of time devoted to drinking. **5** [1950s+] (drugs) a period of time devoted to drug taking. **6** [1950s+] a period of time devoted to sex.

sessions n. [late 19C] noise, chaos, disturbance, quarrelling.

[SE legal sessions, events that were rarely known for their quietness]

sessions v. [mid-19C] to commit a person to the sessions for trial. [SE sessions]

Sessions Pie n. [1940s] (UK prison) a type of pasty based on bully beef, served to prisoners who had to attend the Sessions court.

set n.[1] **1** [late 19C+] (US, esp. US Black) a group of friends. **2** [1950s+] (US Black) wherever the hedonistic, criminal or night life takes place. **3** [1950s+] (US Black) a party, a gathering. **4** [1960s+] (drugs) a place where drugs are sold. **5** [1970s+] (US Black) a discussion. **6** [1980s+] (US Black) the neighbourhood. **7** [1990s+] (W.I.) the outsized speakers used in a dancehall sound system. [(1) SE set, a matching selection, a group; subseq. defs. theatre/film jargon set, the backdrop to the action]

set n.[2] **1** [1960s+] (Aus.) the female breasts. **2** [1970s] the male genitals. [SE set]

set n.[3] (US drugs) **1** [1960s+] a dose of 2 Seconals and 1 amphetamine. **2** [1980s] 3 to 10 pills of similar or varying strength or type. **3** [2000s] an injection of combined Talwin and Ritalin, the effect of which mimics a mix of heroin and cocaine. [jazz use set, 2 pieces of music played consecutively before a break]

set n.[4] **1** [1980s+] (US Black/gang) a local gang, part of the larger gang but working autonomously in its own neighbourhood or area of influence, e.g. the Crips are the larger gang, but sets include Eight Trey Gangsters or ETGs, West Side Crips, Compton Santana Block Crips etc. **2** [1990s+] a prison gang. [SE set, 'a number, company, or group (of persons) associated by community of status, habits, occupations, or interests' (OED)]

set adj. [late 19C–1930s] conquered, defeated. [? SE set back]

set v. **1** [late 17C–19C] to target a potential victim, to survey before robbing. **2** [late 19C] (Aus.) of a (young) woman, to target a man as a potential husband/lover. **3** [1910s+] (Aus.) to attack verbally, to think little of. [? SE set upon]

set about v. [late 19C+] to attack, often in phrs. that specify the weapon, e.g. set about him with a stick.

set-down n. [early 19C–1940s] (US) a sit-down meal, thus a square meal; spec. when a tramp is invited into a house and offered a meal indoors. [regional pron. of SE sit]

set fire v. [1900s–50s] to cause suspicion.

set going v. see GET GOING v.

set horses v. [1930s+] (US Black) to get along in a friendly manner. [i.e. fig. hitching one's horses to the same pole]

set in a crack v. [late 19C+] (N.Z.) to settle something quickly. [? the speedy crack of a whip]

set it alight! excl. [1940s+] (N.Z.) get a move on! hurry up!; also as v., set (something) alight, to get (something) started.

set-me-up n. (also **young set-me-up**) [late 19C–1930s] a person/young person who poses as someone more important than they are, usu. pej.

set mouth (on) v. [1970s+] (US Black) to gossip, to malign.

set off v. [1980s+] (US prison) to deny a prisoner parole.

set of seven brights n. [1930s–40s] (US Black) a week, 7 days.

set of tits n. [1970s] a sexually attractive woman. [TIT n.[3] (3)]

set of wheels n. [1950s+] (orig. US) a car. [metonymy]

set one's back up v. see GET ONE'S BACK UP v.

set one's cap at v. (also **set one's cap for, throw one's cap at**) [mid-18C+] to determine to gain the affections of the object of one's desires. [the cocking of one's headgear at an appealing angle. Orig. used of women but subseq. applicable to either sex]

set one's child a-crying v. [early–mid-19C] for a watchman, to 'spring his rattle', i.e. to sound an alarm. [the watchman's rattle was the predecessor of the policeman's whistle]

set oneself back v. [1930s] to spend money. [SET SOMEONE BACK v.]

set on one's ass v. [1970s+] (drugs) to be made unconscious from excessive drug consumption. [SE set + ASS n. (2)]

set o' sun n. [1900s] (Aus.) any rural nowhere. [WAYBACK n.]

set-out n. **1** [19C] a person's horse or horses and carriage. **2** [19C] a display of china and plate. **3** [19C] a table full of dishes of food. **4** [mid-19C] a group of people. **5** [mid–late 19C] a person's clothes or way of dressing. **6** [late 19C–1930s] a disturbance, a fuss. **7** [1940s] (US tramp) a meal given to a tramp.

set over v. [1920s–40s] (US Und.) to kill, to murder.

set someone back v. [late 19C+] (orig. US) to cost, e.g. her coat must have set him back a few quid.

set someone on fire v. [18C] to give someone a venereal disease. [FIRE n.¹]

set (something) on v. [1930s+] (US Black) **1** to give, esp. of drugs. **2** to tell, to impose facts upon.

setter n.¹ **1** [mid-16C–18C] the member of a criminal gang who keeps watch or entices a victim into a crooked gambling game. **2** [mid-17C] a pimp (cf. ABBOT ON THE CROSS n.). **3** [mid-17C–mid-19C] a police spy or informer. **4** [late 17C–18C] one of a number of officials – 'a Sergeant Yeoman, or Bailiffs' Follower, or Second, and an Excise Officer' (B.E.) – whose job is to ensure that brewers do not defraud the Excise. **5** [mid-19C] 'A person employed by the vendor at an auction to run the biddings up' (Hotten, 1860). [SE setter, a species of hunting dog]

setter n.² (also **setta**) [mid-19C] (orig. Ling. Fr./Polari) **1** the number 7. **2** 7 pence. [Ital. sette, 7]

set the hare's head to the goose's giblets v. [early 17C] to give as good as one gets, to pay like with like. [the perceived 'equivalence' of the 2 foodstuffs]

set the Hudson on fire v. (also **set the North River on fire**) [19C+] (US) to accomplish something remarkable. [the Hudson River/North River, New York City]

set the Thames on fire v. (also **set the river on fire**) [late 18C+] to accomplish a noteworthy feat. [London's River Thames; a similar phr. was used in 1638 of the River Rhine]

settle v. **1** [late 18C+] to knock down, to stun; also in fig. use. **2** [19C+] to deal with, to get even with. **3** [mid-19C] to sentence to penal transportation. **4** [mid-19C+] to kill, to murder. **5** [late 19C–1950s] to sentence to a term of imprisonment, usu. life. [semi-euph.]

settled adj. **1** [mid-19C] (also **winded-settled**) sentenced to transportation. **2** [late 19C–1960s] imprisoned; thus settled right, convicted and imprisoned after a fair trial; settled wrong, convicted and imprisoned unfairly. **3** [1900s–10s] (Aus.) finished, 'done for'. [SETTLE v.]

settlement n. [20C+] (Aus.) a cemetery. [pun]

settler n. **1** [mid-18C–mid-19C] a parting drink, 'one for the road'. **2** [early 19C+] a knockout blow, esp. in fig. use, i.e. something that brings things to a conclusion. [(1) such a final drink supposedly 'settles' the stomach after an evening's indulgence]

settler's clock n. [late 19C+] (Aus.) a kookaburra. [i.e. it wakes one up]

settler's matches n. [late 19C] (Aus.) easily lit strips of bark, used to light fires.

settle someone's coffee v. [mid-19C] (US) to deal with someone who has wronged you, to take revenge.

settle someone's hash v. (also **cook someone's gruel/hash, fix someone's hash, settle someone's gruel**) [19C+] to deal with someone who has wronged you, to take revenge. [SETTLE v. (2) + SE hash, a mess, a jumble]

settle someone's tater v. [late 19C+] to beat someone up. [SE settle + fig. use of TATER n. (1)]

settle the hash v. **1** [early–mid-19C] to deal with a situation. **2** [mid-19C+] (also **settle someone's hash**) to resolve one's difficulties or someone else's. [SETTLE SOMEONE'S HASH v.]

set to one's pumps v. see TAKE TO ONE'S SCRAPERS v.

set trip v. [1990s+] (US gang) to attack another gang. [SET n.⁴ (1) + TRIP v.² (3)]

set tripping n. [1990s+] (US gang) the attacking of another gang. [SET TRIP v.]

set-up n.¹ **1** [late 19C–1930s] a person's carriage, deportment or body. **2** [20C+] (US) a place, esp. one's home, office etc.

set-up n.² **1** [20C+] any situation, experience, e.g. what's the set-up over there? **2** [1910s+] a situation planned to put a third party in a position of weakness, poss. to be murdered. **3** [1920s+] in sport, a 'fixed' match. **4** [1930s+] a criminal scheme. **5** [1930s+] an organization, often criminal. **6** [1960s+] (US Und.) a scheme whereby a criminal is caught red-handed. **7** [1980s] (US) a person who is easily duped, a 'sucker'. [SE set up, put in place]

set-up n.³ **1** [1910s+] (US) a place setting in a restaurant. **2** [1930s+] (US) the ice, mixer and other ingredients provided in unlicensed premises, to which patrons must bring their own alcohol, but in which they can then drink. **3** [1940s–50s] the preparation of an injection of a drug. **4** [1990s+] (US prison) the uniform, bedding, washing equipment etc issued to a new prisoner. **5** [2000s] (US) the makings of a drink, e.g. whisky, ice and a chaser, served in a bar.

set-up n.⁴ [1920s–40s] (US Und.) a 1-day prison sentence. [one 'sets' or sits it out]

set-up adj. **1** [mid-19C+] successful or comfortable; usu. as well set-up. **2** [20C+] (orig. US) pleased, happy. **3** [1900s] (US campus) drunk. **4** [1900s] (US campus) conceited, snobbish. **5** [1930s] physically 'built'. [SET UP (FOR) v.]

set up v. **1** [late 19C+] to place a potential victim in a position of weakness, esp. a target for murder. **2** [1950s+] of police, to concoct evidence or create a situation whereby an innocent person is charged with a crime.

set up (for) v. **1** [mid-19C+] to be well provided with. **2** [late 19C+] (US) to treat.

set-up man n. [1950s+] (US Und.) **1** someone who organizes and plans major robberies, recruits those who carry them out, disposes of the loot etc. **2** a criminal who works for the police. [(1) SE set up, i.e. a robbery; (2) SET UP v.]

set up one's ebenezer v. [mid-19C–1900s] (US) to make up one's mind. [Heb. eben ha-ezer, the stone of help, the memorial stone set up by Samuel (1 Sam. 7:12), i.e. the enduring solidity of such a memorial]

seven n. **1** [late 19C+] (Und.) a 7-year jail sentence. **2** [1970s+] (Aus.) a 7fl oz (200ml) glass of beer.

seven and a three n. see FIVE AND TWO n.

seven and six n. see WAS SHE WORTH IT? n.

Seven Dials n. [1970s+] haemorrhoids. [rhy. sl. = SE piles]

Seven Dials raker n. [late 19C–1920s] a prostitute whose home is in Seven Dials and who pursues her trade elsewhere; thus she 'never smiles out of the Dials' (Ware). [SE Seven Dials + RAKE v.¹ (2)]

sevendible adj. [mid-19C+] (Ulster) severe, harsh, esp. of a beating; thus adv. sevendably. [SE seven double, 7-fold; thus the severity is fig. multiplied 7-fold]

seven digits n. [1980s+] (US Black) a telephone number (in the multiple exchanges of the major cities).

sevener n. **1** [late 19C] (Aus.) a convict sentenced to a 7-year prison sentence. **2** [1920s] (Irish) a fainting fit. [such convicts were lower in the prison hierarchy than those serving longer terms or life sentences]

seven kinds of hell phr. (also **seven kinds of shit**) [20C+] intense unpleasantness; usu. as knock/kick/beat/thump…

seven out v. [1950s] (US Black) to lose, to be defeated. [the losing throw of 7 in craps]

sevenpence n. [early–mid-19C] (UK Und.) a sentence of 7 years' transportation.

seven pennorth n. [mid-19C] **1** a sentence of 7 years' transportation. **2** 7 months in prison. **3** 7 years in prison.

seven-sided animal n. [late 18C–mid-19C] 'A one-eyed man or woman, each having a right side and a left side, a fore side and a backside, an outside, an inside and a blind side' (Grose, 1796).

seven-sided son of a bitch *n.* (*also* **seven-sided son of a so-and-so**) [19C–1940s] (*US*) a man or a woman with one eye; thus as a term of abuse. [this US term was presumably taken direct from Grose (*see* prev.); 20C uses are only general derog.]

seventeen-carat *adj. see* EIGHTEEN-CARAT *adj.*

seventeener *n.* [20C+] (*Aus. Und.*) a corpse. [ety. unknown]

seven-times-seven man *n.* [late 19C] a hypocritical evangelist. [? rhy. sl. *seven-times-seven* = heaven]

seventy-five cent word *n.* [late 19C] (*US*) a polysyllabic word. [one 'pays' for all the syllables]

seventy-'leven *n.* [20C+] (*US*) an indefinite number of anything.

seventy-one *n.* [1960s] (*Aus./US gay*) anal intercourse. [a play on SIXTY-NINE *n.* (1)]

seventy-three *phr.* (*also* **73**) [1940s] (*US*) goodbye, best wishes. [ety. unknown; ? telegraphese]

seven up *n.* [1940s] (*US Und.*) a general store; the robbery of a general store; thus *seven-up hustler*, a robber of a general store; *seven-up hustling* robbing general stores. [ety. unknown]

severe *adj.* **1** [19C–1900s] (*US*) very big or powerful, hard to overcome. **2** [1980s] excellent, first-rate.

severely *adv.* [mid-19C+] to a great or excessive degree, esp. unwisely. [SEVERE *adj.* (1)]

se voet! *excl.* [1970s+] (*S.Afr.*) an excl. of dismissal or disbelief; a synon. for MY FOOT! excl. [Afk. *se voet*, my foot]

sew *v.* **1** [late 19C+] to have sexual intercourse. **2** [1940s+] (*US Black/gay*) to masturbate (cf. BOFF *v.*). [the movements of the needle and of the body or hand]

sewed up *adj.* (*also* **sewn up**) **1** [mid-19C] cheated, swindled. **2** [mid–late 19C] ill, sick. **3** [mid-19C–1900s] orig. of horses only, exhausted. **4** [mid-19C–1940s] drunk. **5** [late 19C] pregnant. **6** [1920s+] confirmed, unsusceptible to error, esp. of a sporting contest in which the result has already been assured. [SEW UP *v.*]

sewer *n.*[1] [late 19C–1900s] the Metropolitan and Metropolitan District Railway. [like a *sewer* it runs beneath the London streets]

sewer *n.*[2] [1930s–60s] (*drugs*) the median cephalic vein in the arm; thus *go into/hit the sewer*, to inject a narcotic, usu. heroin, into that vein (cf. CACA *n.*). [play on SHIT *n.*[5] (1)]

sewer *v.* [2000s] to ruin.

sewermouth *n.* [1970s+] (*US campus*) anyone who regularly uses obscenities or profanities. [the image of such language as 'dirty']

sewermouth *adj.* [1970s] (*US*) obscene, profane. [SEWER-MOUTH *n.*]

sewer trout *n.* [1940s+] (*US milit./prison*) any species of fish served at mealtimes.

sewing machine *n.* **1** [1950s] the vagina. **2** [1970s] the penis. [SEW *v.* (1)]

sewn up *adj. see* SEWED UP *adj.*

sew someone's sees *v.* [late 18C–mid-19C] to give someone a black eye. [SEES *n.*]

sew up *v.* **1** [early 19C+] to make hopelessly drunk. **2** [early 19C+] of a person, to tire out, to put at a disadvantage, to nonplus, to bring to a standstill. **3** [mid-19C; 1940s] to surround, to seal off; in lit. and fig. uses. **4** [mid-19C–1950s] to outwit, to cheat, to swindle. **5** [late 19C+] to impregnate. **6** [late 19C+] (*orig. US*) (*also* **sew**) to conclude, to possess completely, to finalize, to place under complete control; thus *(all) sewed/sewn up*, brought to a satisfactory conclusion. **7** [1920s–30s] to bring about the conviction of someone. **8** [1940s] (*US Und.*) to ensure that a victim causes no trouble once they have been defrauded in a confidence trick.

sew up someone's stocking *v.* [mid-19C] to put to silence, to strike dumb.

sex *n.* **1** [mid-18C+] the vagina. **2** [late 19C+] the penis.

sex *v.* (*also* **sex down/up**) [1950s+] to have sexual intercourse.

sexboat *n.* [1960s] a very attractive woman or occas. man.

sex-bomb *n.* [1960s+] a very attractive woman or occas. man.

sex bunny *n. see* SEX KITTEN *n.*

sex down *v. see* SEX *v.*

sexed up *adj.* [20C+] sexually excited.

sex fight *n.* [1990s+] (*US*) a sexual game played between 2 people (of the same or opposite sex) in which each partner tries to make the other reach orgasm first; thus *sex fighter*, a participant in such a game.

sex goddess *n.* [1930s+] (*US*) a woman, esp. a film star (and latterly rock star), who is viewed as sexually provocative.

sex house *n.* [1990s+] (*US*) anywhere where sex is on sale.

sexile *n.* [1980s+] (*US campus*) exclusion from a dorm room overnight or temporarily so that a roommate may use the room for sex.

sex in *v.* [1990s+] (*US Black/teen*) to gang-rape.

sexing-piece *n.* [1920s+] the penis. [SEX *v.*]

sex job *n.* [1930s+] (*US*) a sexually provocative or available person. [SE *sex* + JOB *n.*[4]]

sex kitten *n.* (*also* **sex bunny**) [1950s+] a young woman with overt sex appeal. [coined in the late 1950s for the charms of the young Brigitte Bardot (b.1933); note RMC Duntroon (Aus.) *cum kitten*, a girlfriend]

sex machine *n.* **1** [1950s–60s] a promiscuous, sexually eager woman. **2** [1960s+] a sexually virile man, a womanizer.

sexo *n.* (*also* **sexoh**) (*N.Z./Aus.*) **1** [1940s+] a sexual offender. **2** [1950s+] someone seen as over-sexed or obsessed with sex. [SE *sex* + -O sfx (4)]

sex on *v.* [1950s+] (*Aus.*) to indulge in 'heavy petting' or even intercourse.

sex on a stick *n.* [2000s] one who is exceptionally sexually attractive, usu. of a woman.

sexpert *n.* [1960s+] (*US*) a sex expert, typically a sex therapist.

sexploitation *n.* [1960s+] (*US*) the commercial exploitation of sex.

sexpot *n.* [1950s+] **1** a very attractive woman or occas. man. **2** one who is obsessed with sex. [SE *sex* + -POT sfx]

sex tank *n.* [1960s] (*US*) a holding cell used to confine prostitutes or homosexuals.

sexton blake *n.* **1** [20C+] a cake. **2** [1970s+] a fake. [rhy. sl.; ult. the name of a fictional detective created by 'Hal Meredith' (Harry Blyth) in *The Halfpenny Marvel* magazine (1893)]

sex up *v.*[1] **1** [1940s+] to increase the sexual content of, e.g. a film script. **2** [2000s] to make the content of something more attractive or exciting.

sex up *v.*[2] *see* SEX *v.*

sex with Jesus *phr.* [1980s+] (*orig. US*) a general phr. of satisfaction, praise, delight, e.g. *that movie was sex with Jesus.*

sexy *adj.* [1960s+] **1** (*orig. media*) used of anything that pulls in audiences, readers etc, thus usu. violence, disaster, scandal etc. **2** (*US*) used of anything very appealing. **3** used of anything 'clever' or 'smart'.

sey *see under* SAY *n.* and its combs.

sez you! *excl. see* SAYS YOU! excl.

s.f. *n. see* SCI-FI *n.*

s.f.a. *n.* [1940s+] absolutely nothing at all. [abbr. *sweet fuck all*]

s.f. & t. *phr.* [1990s+] sucked, fucked and tattooed. [abbr.]

S.F.C. *n.* (*also* **s.f.c.**) [1990s+] (*US Black teen*) San Francisco City or sucka-/sucker-free city. [abbr.; capitals and lower case letters are interchangeable]

'sfoot! *excl.* [17C; early 19C] a mild oath, lit. 'God's foot!'

shab *n.* [early 17C–19C] an unpleasant, sneaky person. [? SCAB *n.* (2)/SE *scab*, a rascal, a scoundrel or *shabby*]

shab *v.* [mid-18C–mid-19C] to cheat, to deceive, to act in an underhand manner. [SHAB *n.*]

shabba v. [1990s+] to masturbate (cf. BOFF v.; COTTON WOOL v.). [rhy. sl.; *shabba rank* = WANK v.; ult. reggae star *Shabba* Ranks (Rextion Gordon; b.1965)]

shabberoon n. (*also* **shabaroon, shabroon**) [late 17C–early 19C] **1** a shabby, down-at-heel person. **2** a mean person. [SE *shabby*]

shabby adj. [mid-19C+] of weather, unpleasant. [SE *shabby*; ult. SE *scab*, a disease of sheep]

shabeen n. see CHABEN n.

shabers n. [1940s] (*W.I.*) a disreputable person. [? SHAB n.]

shab off v. [late 17C–mid-18C] **1** to cheat someone, then to dismiss them without apology or explanation. **2** to sneak away. [? SHAB v./SHAB n.]

shaboney n. see JIBONE n.

shab-rag adj. [mid-late 18C] shabby, damaged, worn. [dial. *shab-rag*, a mean beggarly person, a ragamuffin]

shabroon n. see SHABBEROON n.

shabster n. [mid-late 19C] an unpleasant, sneaky person. [SHAB n. + -STER sfx]

shabu n. [1980s+] (*drugs*) methamphetamine (cf. BOMBITA n.). [Jap. sl.; ult. ? Jap. *shaberu*, to talk animatedly, i.e. one of the drug's effects]

shack n.[1] **1** [mid-18C–1910s] (*US tramp*) a tramp, a vagrant. **2** [late 19C–1940s] (*US tramp*) a railroad brakeman. **3** [1920s] (*US tramp*) any place where tramps congregate. **4** [1920s] (*US Und.*) a policeman. [SE *shake-rag*, a beggar + dial. *shackle-bag*, a lazy loiterer, a vagabond]

shack n.[2] [20C+] (*US*) one's home, one's house.

shack v. (*US*) **1** [mid-late 19C] to idle, to loaf. **2** [late 19C+] (*also* **shuck out**) to live alone, to live as a bachelor or single woman. **3** [1940s+] (*also* **shack out**) to have sexual intercourse; thus n., an act of sexual intercourse. **4** [1940s+] to live with a partner. **5** [1960s+] to stay the night at someone's house, whether sexually or not. [SE *shack*/SHACK n.[2]; cf. SHACK UP v.]

shack baby n. see SHACK JOB n. (3).

shack bully n. [1940s–50s] (*US Black/teen*) the outstanding person, the 'boss'.

shack fever n. [mid-19C] (*US tramp*) weariness, fatigue. [SHACK n.[1] (1) + SE *fever*]

shackie n. [1950s] a White woman living with a Black man. [SHACK v. (4)]

shack job n. [1940s+] **1** the person with whom one lives. **2** a couple or the state of being a couple. **3** (*also* **shack baby**) a casual sex partner. [SHACK v. (4) + JOB n.[4]]

shackles n. [1900s–40s] **1** the off-cuts from a butcher's preparing of meat for sale. **2** (*UK/US tramp*) soup. **3** (*US*) cheese. [? dial. *shacklebone*, the hind leg of a pig's carcass; (2) note Irwin, *American Tramp and Und. Slang* (1931): 'No doubt the word was coined in some prison where the dish was of such a nature as to keep the prisoners near a toilet, or "shackled" to one place. It is generally used on the road to indicate any article of food that exercises a definite effect upon the elimination'; (3) cheese is trad. 'binding']

shackle-up n. [1930s–50s] (*UK tramp*) a midday meal cooked at the roadside. [SHACKLE UP v.]

shackle up v. [1930s–50s] (*UK tramp*) to cook a midday meal. [? SHACKLES n.]

shack man n. (*also* **shack rat**) [1940s] (*US*) an adulterous man. [SHACK v. (3) + SE *man/rat* n.[2] (1)]

shack out v. see SHACK v. (3).

shacks! excl. [1980s+] (*US campus*) a mild excl. of surprise, regret, annoyance etc. [var. on SHUCKS! excl. (1)]

shack-stoner n. [late 19C–1900s] (*Aus./N.Z.*) a sixpence. [ety. unknown]

shack-up n. **1** [1920s+] (*US*) a person with whom one has a sexual relationship. **2** [1950s–70s] an act of sexual intercourse. **3** [1970s] a sexual relationship. [SHACK UP v.]

shack up v. **1** [1920s+] (*orig. US*) to live or reside, usu. temporarily. **2** [1930s+] (*orig. US*) to live with a sexual partner. **3** [1940s+] (*orig. US*) to have sex with someone. **4** [1950s] (*Aus.*) to pick up, for sexual purposes. [SHACK v.]

shaddup! excl. [1950s+] a mispron. of SE *shut up!*

shade n.[1] [mid-19C] (*US Und.*) an umbrella or sunshade.

shade n.[2] **1** [mid-19C–1960s] (*US*) a derog. term for a Black person (cf. BLACKBELLY n.). **2** [1920s+] (*US Und.*) a receiver of stolen goods. **3** [1930s+] (*Irish*) a policeman. **4** [1960s+] (*US Black*) a derog. term for a White person. [SE *shade*, partial darkness]

shade n.[3] **1** [mid-19C+] a minute quantity. **2** [1900s–20s] (*US*) a (marginal) advantage.

shade v.[1] [1920s+] (*orig. Aus.*) to be superior to, albeit by a small margin. [SHADE n.[3]]

shade v.[2] **1** [1930s–40s] (*US Und.*) to protect a pickpocket while he/she works; thus as n., the accomplice who shields the working pickpocket. **2** [1950s+] (*US Black*) to hide, to conceal. [SE *shade*, to protect from the light]

shade v.[3] see THROW SHADE v.

shade-glim n. see GLIM n.[1] (6).

shades n.[1] [mid-late 19C] a variety of late-night music-halls and bars on or near the Strand, London; used generically in US. [their opening during the 'shady' hours]

shades n.[2] (*also* **sunshades**) [1950s+] dark glasses, sunglasses. [note 19C *shades*, goggles, e.g. for use during stone-breaking]

shad mouth n. [1930s–40s] (*US*) **1** a person with a large upper lip. **2** a derog. term for a Black person (cf. BRILLOHEAD n.). [the fish; note 19C US regional *shad-eaters*, members of the legislature of the State of Connecticut]

shadow n. **1** [mid-19C–1960s] (*US*) a plain-clothes detective (cf. BEAT-POUNDER n.). **2** [late 19C] (*UK Und.*) a pimp, male or female (cf. ABBOT ON THE CROSS n.). **3** [late 19C+] (*US*) a derog. term for a Black person (cf. BLACKBELLY n.).

shadow v. [mid-19C+] (*orig. US*) usu. of a detective, to follow someone. [SHADOW n. (1)]

shadscale n. see SCALE n.[1].

shady adj. **1** [mid-19C; 1960s] stupid. **2** [mid-19C+] (*orig. UK campus*) uncertain, unreliable. **3** [mid-19C+] illicit, criminal.

shady spring n. [late 18C] the vagina (cf. BEAUTY SPOT n.; DAMP n.).

shaft n.[1] [17C+] the penis. [20C+ use mainly US Black; note blaxploitation films of the 1970s starring private eye 'John Shaft']

shaft n.[2] [1910s+] (*orig. US*) unfair treatment, often as *the shaft*; thus *shaft job*, an example of unfair treatment. [SE *shaft*]

shaft n.[3] [1930s+] a woman's body, considered simply as a sexual object. [SE *shaft*, a slender column]

shaft v. **1** [1950s+] to have sexual intercourse (usu. of a man with a woman); thus *shaftable*, of a woman, suitable for and hopefully susceptible to seduction (cf. BANG v.[1]). **2** [1950s+] (*orig. US*) to defeat, to defraud, to harm, to treat unfairly. **3** [1990s+] (*US campus*) to steal. [SE *shaft*, to shoot with an arrow]

shaft artist n. (*also* **shaftsman**) [1970s] (*US*) a cheat. [SHAFT v. (2) + ARTIST sfx]

shafted adj. [1950s+] **1** treated unfairly, in serious trouble; usu. as *get shafted*. **2** stood up by one's date. **3** suffering a broken relationship. [SHAFT v.]

shaftesbury n. [late 17C–early 19C] a gallon pot full of wine, with a cock (i.e. tap). [? proper name of the Dorset town]

shafting n. [1960s+] **1** an act of sexual intercourse. **2** unfair treatment. [SHAFT v.]

shaft of delight n. [mid-18C] the penis. [ext. of SHAFT n.[1]]

shafts n. [1920s–40s] (*US*) the human legs.

shaftsman n. see SHAFT ARTIST n.

shag n.[1] **1** [late 18C+] an act of sexual intercourse. **2** [1930s] (*US teen*) a party where teenagers experiment sexually. **3** [1940s–60s] a person in general use. **4** [1960s+] a person, usu. a woman but in

1990s+ also a man, seen simply as a sexual object; thus *good shag, lousy shag* (cf. BAD SHAG n.). [SHAG v.¹ (1)]

shag n.² [1930s–60s] (*US tramp*) a chase, a hue and cry. [SHAG v.² (2)]

shag n.³ [1950s+] (*W.I. Rasta*) home-cured tobacco, straight from the field. [SE *shag*, strong tobacco, cut into shreds]

shag n.⁴ [1990s+] (*drugs*) heroin. [var. on SCAG n.² (2)]

shag n.⁵ [2000s] (*US Und.*) the patter used to lure victims into a confidence game. [ety. unknown]

shag adj.¹ [1930s–50s] (*US prison*) worthless. [? SE *shag*, a rascal, a rogue]

shag adj.² [1940s+] (*US teen*) excellent, wonderful. [? fig. use SHAG n.¹ (1)]

shag v.¹ **1** [late 17C+] (*also* **shog**) to have sexual intercourse; thus *shag around*, to lead a promiscuous sex life (cf. BANG v.¹; FRIG v.). **2** [late 19C+] used as a semi-euph. for FUCK v.¹ in var. non-copulatory uses. **3** [1980s+] to masturbate (cf. BOFF v.). **4** [2000s] to cheat. [? SE *shake*/SHAKE v.¹]

shag v.² **1** [1910s] (*US Und.*) to discover, to identify. **2** [1910s] (*US*) to chase, lit. and fig. **3** [1920s+] (*US*) to wander around; to walk, esp. slowly, whether through laziness or exhaustion. **4** [1930s–40s] to give someone a false impression. **5** [1940s+] to move fast. **6** [1950s] (*US gang*) to deliver. **7** [1960s+] to deal with. **8** [1960s+] to throw. **9** [1960s+] to obtain. **10** [1980s] (*US teen*) to tease, to harass. [Gloucester dial. *shag*, to make off, to traipse around]

shag v.³ [1940s–50s] (*drugs*) to inject a narcotic.

shag! *excl. see* SHAG (OFF)! excl.

shagability n. [1990s+] one's sex appeal. [SHAG v.¹ (1)]

shag-all n. *see* FUCK-ALL n.

shag artist n. [1960s+] a womanizer, a sexual athlete. [SHAG n.¹ (1) + ARTIST sfx]

shag ass v. [1950s+] (*US*) **1** to work hard, to move fast, to expend effort and energy. **2** to depart or leave hurriedly. [SE *shake*/SHAG v.² (5) + ASS n. (5)]

shag-bag n. **1** [late 17C+] (*also* **shake-bag**) a worthless, shabby person. **2** [1970s] (*orig. milit.*) a prostitute (cf. BAG n.⁴). **3** [1990s+] (*orig. Aus.*) a general pej. term for a woman; sexual availability is presumed, but not automatic. **4** [2000s] (*US*) the vagina (cf. BAG n.¹). [(1) 17C SE *shag*, a rascal; subseq. defs. SHAG v.¹ (1) + SE *bag*/-BAG sfx; note synon. RMC Duntroon (Aus.) *root bag*]

shaggable adj. [1990s+] sexy, lit. (potentially) available for seduction. [SHAG v.¹ (1)]

shagged (out) adj. **1** [1930s+] exhausted. **2** [1940s+] a euph. for FUCKED adj.¹. [fig. use of SHAG v.¹ (1)/SHAG v.¹ (2)]

shagged to a thin whisker adj. [1940s–50s] absolutely exhausted. [ext. of SHAGGED (OUT) adj. (1)]

shagger n.¹ **1** [20C+] one who copulates; a sexual enthusiast. **2** [1970s] any thing or person. **3** [1990s+] a nuisance, a disobedient person. [SHAG v.¹ (1)]

shagger n.² [1930s] (*US*) a policeman; a person who shadows or follows someone (cf. BEAT-POUNDER n.). [SHAG v.² (2)]

shagger's back n. [1980s+] (*orig. Aus.*) a particularly painful backache, supposedly the result of over-enthusiastic copulation. [SHAGGER n.¹ (1) + SE *back*]

shagging n. [mid-19C+] an act of sexual intercourse. [SHAG v.¹ (1)]

shagging adj. **1** [1940s+] a semi-euph. for FUCKING adj. **2** [1980s] as an infix. [SHAG v.¹ (1)]

shagging hell! *excl. see* FUCKING HELL! excl.

shagging machine n. [late 19C] (*US*) the vagina. [SHAG v.¹ (1)]

shagging-station/-wagon n. *see* SHAG-WAGON n.

shag-happy adj. [2000s] keen on sexual intercourse. [SHAG v.¹ (1) + -HAPPY sfx]

shag-leg n. [1930s] (*US Black*) a person. [anyone who can SE *shake (a) leg*]

shag like a rattlesnake v. *see* FUCK LIKE A RATTLESNAKE v.

shag magnet n. *see* BABE MAGNET n.

shag me! *excl.* [1980s+] (*N.Z.*) an excl. of astonishment and/or resignation; semi-euph. for FUCK ME! excl. [SHAG v.¹ (1)]

shag-nasty n. [20C+] **1** a general pej. name for any unpopular man. **2** (*N.Z.*) used affectionately. [SHAG v.¹ (1)]

shag (off)! *excl.* [1960s+] (*US*) go away! [semi-euph. for FUCK OFF! excl. (1)]

shag out v. [1950s] to exhaust. [backform. f. SHAGGED (OUT) adj. (1)]

shag pad n. [1990s+] an apartment or room where one can bring a casual sex partner; a nickname for a bachelor's apartment. [SHAG v.¹ (1) + PAD n.² (2)]

shagpit n. [2000s] a bed. [SHAG v.¹ (1) + PIT n.³ (1)]

shag-rag n. [late 16C–early 19C] a ragged, disreputable person; a low rascally fellow. [synon. SE *shake-rag*]

shagroon n. [mid–late 19C] (*N.Z.*) an early settler in Canterbury, New Zealand, from anywhere except Britain, esp. one from Australia. [? Irish *seachrán*, wandering]

shagtastic adj. [2000s] extremely sexually alluring. [SHAG v.¹ (1) + -TASTIC sfx]

shag that for a lark! *excl. see* FUCK THAT FOR A LARK! excl.

shag-wagon n. (*also* **shagging-station/-wagon**) [1960s+] a van or car used primarily for sex. [SHAG v.¹ (1) + SE *wagon*]

shah n. [late 19C] (*Cockney*) one whose superiority, real or imagined, suggests an Oriental potentate. [Pers. *shah*, a king]

shaka n. [1990s+] (*W.I.*) an unattractive person. [? SE *shaker*]

shake n.¹ **1** [16C–1900s] an act of sexual intercourse. **2** [mid-19C] a disreputable man. **3** [mid–late 19C] a prostitute or kept woman.

shake n.² **1** [mid-19C+] (*US*) a dance. **2** [mid-19C+] a moment, a second. **3** [1930s+] (*US Black*) a party at which the guests pay an admission fee to help to pay the rent and pay for the refreshments (cf. FISH-FRY n.). **4** [1970s] a party.

shake n.³ (*also* **shaker**) [1900s] (*US*) a derog. term for a Black person (cf. ALLIGATOR BAIT n.²). [? SHADE n.² (1) or play on chocolate milk*shake*]

shake n.⁴ [1910s+] (*US Und.*) **1** blackmail, extortion, often from homosexuals; thus *square the shake*, to pay the bribe required to escape conviction. **2** an arrest; a search by the police or prison guards. [abbr. SHAKEDOWN n.²]

shake n.⁵ [1970s+] (*drugs*) marijuana, esp. the residue of a bag of cannabis after the smokeable buds are removed. **2** [1980s] diluted cocaine. [note dial. *shake*, the residue of grain after harvesting]

shake n.⁶ *see* FAIR SHAKE n.

shake, the n.¹ [mid-19C] (*US*) malaria.

shake, the n.² [1980s+] (*US campus*) an undesirable person.

shake v.¹ [17C–1960s] to have sexual intercourse; thus *shake oneself*, to masturbate (cf. BANG v.¹; BOFF v.).

shake v.² **1** [early 19C+] (*Aus./UK Und.*) to steal, to run off with. **2** [1950s+] (*Can. Und.*) to serve a prison sentence. [(1) use after mid-19C mainly Aus.]

shake v.³ (*orig. UK Und.*) **1** [mid–late 19C] to abandon. **2** [mid-19C–1910s] to leave. **3** [mid-19C+] to get rid of a person. **4** [20C+] to evade a pursuer. [abbr. SE *shake off*]

shake v.⁴ [mid-19C+] to disturb, to shock.

shake v.⁵ [late 19C] (*US Und.*) to divide criminal spoils.

shake v.⁶ **1** [1910s] (*US*) to hurry up; usu. as imper., get going, hurry up. **2** [1950s+] to happen, to start to happen. **3** [1990s+] (*W.I.*) to move on.

shake v.⁷ [late 19C] (*US*) to win when gambling.

shake v.⁸ *see* SHAKE DOWN v.¹ (1).

shake a cloth in the wind v. **1** [late 18C–early 19C] to be hanged in chains. **2** [1930s] to be slightly drunk. [(1) refers to one's flapping clothes; (2) orig. naut. jargon]

shake a free leg v. *see* SHAKE A LOOSE LEG v.

shake a leg v. **1** [early 19C+] (*also* **shake a foot/hoof/toe**) to dance. **2** [late 19C] to go out on a spree. **3** [20C+] to hurry up, to get a move on; often as imper.

shake a leg! *excl.* (*also* **shake a hoof!**) [20C+] get on with it! wake up! (both lit. and fig.). [SHAKE A LEG v. (3)]

shake along *v.* [1910s] to move on.

shake a loose leg *v.* (*also* **shake a free leg**) [mid-19C] (*UK tramp*) to live wandering as a tramp.

shake and shiver *n.* (*also* **stand and shiver**) [20C+] (*Aus.*) a river. [rhy. sl.]

shake apart *v.* [1900s–50s] (*US Black*) to lose emotional control, whether through an excess of happiness or sorrow.

shake artist *n.* [1940s] (*US Und.*) a blackmailer. [SHAKE n.⁴ (1) + ARTIST sfx]

shake a sock *v.* [20C+] to urinate.

shake a tail-feather *v.* [1960s+] (*orig. US*) to dance energetically. [note Ward, *A Compleat and Humorous Account of all the Remarkable Clubs and Societies* (1709): 'A Set of Dancers were wantonly engaged in their Shake-Tail Exercise']

shake a tart *v.* [late 19C+] of a man, to have sexual intercourse. [SHAKE v.¹ + TART n.¹ (1)]

shake a toe *v. see* SHAKE A LEG v. (1).

shake baby *n.* [1920s–30s] (*US Black*) a dress that is tight across the hips and has a short, full skirt. [BABY n.³ (1) is encouraged to 'shake that thing']

shake-bag *n.*¹ **1** [18C] a prostitute (cf. BAG n.⁴). **2** [late 19C] the vagina (cf. BAG n.¹).

shake-bag *n.*² [2000s] (*US drugs*) a bag of second-rate marijuana. [SHAKE n.⁵ (1)]

shake-bag *n.*³ *see* SHAG-BAG n. (1).

shake-buckler *n.* [mid-16C–mid-17C] a bully, a thug. [SE *shake* + *buckler*, a sword]

shakedown *n.*¹ [early 19C+] (*Aus./US*) an impromptu bed, somewhere to sleep, not necessarily a proper bed.

shakedown *n.*² **1** [late 19C] (*US*) a rough dance. **2** [late 19C+] blackmail, extortion; thus *shakedowner, shakedown artist/man*, an extortionist. **3** [1910s+] a search, either of a person, a place or one's belongings. **4** [1910s+] (*US prison*) a search, whether of a cell or of an individual prisoner. [the image of shaking one's clothes (or cell) until money falls out]

shake down *v.*¹ **1** [mid-19C+] (*also* **shake**) to blackmail, to extort money (from). **2** [late 19C–1910s] to obtain a financial contribution, e.g. to a political campaign. **3** [20C+] of (usu.) police, to search, to raid; also (*prison*) to search a cell. **4** [1910s] to pay protection to the police involuntarily. **5** [1930s+] to interrogate; to elicit information. **6** [1930s+] (*W.I.*) to rob. **7** [1950s] to empty out. **8** [1980s+] (*US Black*) to rape. **9** [1990s+] (*US Black*) to have sex with. **10** [1990s+] to beat at cards.

shake down *v.*² **1** [mid-19C+] to sleep in an impromptu bed. **2** [late 19C] to settle into living quarters. [SHAKEDOWN n.¹]

shake-em-up *n.* [1970s+] (*US Black*) white port and lemon juice. [its effects]

shake five! *excl.* [1950s+] (*W.I.*) a greeting between 2 men, lit. 'shake my five fingers'.

shakefoot *n.* (*also* **shake-up**) [1940s+] (*W.I.*) a party or dance, esp. one to which an invitation is not required; thus *shakefoot*, to dance. [SHAKE A LEG v. (1)]

shake-glim *n.* [mid–late 19C] a begging letter, based on the fantasy that the writer has lost all their possessions through fire. [SE *shake*, to wave + GLIM n.¹ (5)]

shake hands with an old friend *v.* (*also* **shake hands with him, ...Mr Right, ...the baby, ...the fellow who stood up with me at my wedding**) [1960s+] to urinate.

shake hands with the governor *v.* [1990s+] to masturbate (cf. AUDITION THE FINGER PUPPETS v.).

shake hands with the unemployed *v.* [1960s+] **1** to urinate. **2** (*also* **shake hands with the bloke who enlisted with me**) to masturbate (cf. AUDITION THE FINGER PUPPETS v.).

shake hands with the wife's best friend *v.* [1960s+] (*orig. Aus.*) **1** to masturbate (cf. AUDITION THE FINGER PUPPETS v.). **2** to urinate. [SE *shake hands* + WIFE'S BEST FRIEND n.]

shake it like a polaroid *v. see* SHAKE ONE'S ARSE v. (2).

shake it rough *v.* [1940s+] (*Can.*) to serve a prison sentence 'the hard way', i.e. rebelling, refusing to cooperate with authority, fighting with fellow prisoners etc.

shake it (up) *v.* **1** [mid-19C+] (*Aus./US*) (*also* **shake her up, shake oneself up**) to hurry up. **2** [1930s] (*US*) to walk in a provocative manner.

shake-lurk *n.* [mid-19C] a piece of paper, carried by a beggar, which purports (falsely) to give an account of a terrible disaster, usu. a shipwreck, in which the beggar has suffered. [SE *shake*, to wave + LURK n. (1)]

shake man *n.* [1900s–50s] (*US Und.*) an extortionist. [SHAKE DOWN v.¹ (1)]

shake mob *n.* [1900s–30s] (*US Und.*) a gang of extortionists. [SHAKE DOWN v.¹ (1)]

shake 'n' bake *n.* [1970s+] (*US Black*) any form of trickery that ensures that one eludes work and/or responsibilities. [brandname of popular US instant food. Note US milit. jargon *Shake 'n' Bake*, a sergeant who attended NCO school and gained rank after only a short time in uniform. This, in turn, has similar synon., *Ready Whip, Nestlé's Quick*]

shake-off *n.* [1910s–30s] (*US*) the act of dismissing or abandoning someone.

shake off *v. see* SHUFFLE (OFF) v.

shake of the bag *n.* (*also* **shakings of the bag, shake-poke**) [mid-19C+] (*Irish*) **1** the runt of the litter. **2** an unappealing person. [the image of shaking the very last crumbs from a bag]

shake one's arse *v.* (*also* **shake one's ass/ankle/rusty-dusty**) [1920s+] **1** (*orig. US*) to hurry up. **2** (*US*) (*also* **shake it like a polaroid**) to move vigorously as in sexual intercourse or dancing. [SE *shake* + ARSE n.¹ (4)/ASS n. (5)/SE *ankle*/RUSTY-DUSTY n.]

shake one's ashes *v. see* HAUL ONE'S ASHES v.

shake one's elbow *v.* **1** [17C–19C] to play dice, to gamble. **2** [mid–late 19C] to play cards. [the shaking of the dice-box]

shake oneself up *v. see* SHAKE IT (UP) v. (1).

shake one's fleas *v.* [late 19C] to beat, to thrash.

shake one's heels *v.* [late 16C] to be hanged.

shake one's rusty-dusty *v. see* SHAKE ONE'S ARSE v.

shake one's shambles *v.* [late 17C–early 18C] to hurry up, to get started.

shake one's shirt *v.* [1930s+] (*N.Z./US*) to make an effort, to 'get stuck in'.

shake one's skirt *v.* [1980s+] (*US campus*) of a woman, to go out dancing. [note Ned Ward, 'The Dancing School' (1700): 'Away they moved in couples [...] and shook their Breeches with so much seeming satisfaction to both Sexes concer'd']

shake one's tail *v.* [1910s] (*US*) to leave. [TAIL n.² (1)]

shake one's teeva *v.* [2000s] (*US Black*) to dance in an exuberant manner. [SE *shake* + var. on BATI n.]

shake one's toe-rag *v.* [late 19C] (*UK tramp*) to run away. [SE *shake* + *toe-rag*]

shake one's trotters at Beilby's ball *v.* (*also* **shake/shiver one's trotters at Bilby's ball**) [mid-18C–early 19C] to be hanged. [for ety. *see* DANCE AT BEILBY'S BALL v.]

shake out *v.* [1950s+] (*W.I. Rasta*) to leave without haste, casually.

shake-poke *n. see* SHAKE OF THE BAG n.

shaker *n.*¹ [mid-19C] a shirt. [? dial. *shaker*, a worn-out, shabby garment]

shaker *n.*² **1** [mid-19C] a beggar who pretends to have fits. **2** [mid-19C] a hand. **3** [late 19C] (*Aus.*) a rickety motor vehicle. **4** [1930s] (*US Und.*) in pl. (loaded) dice.

shaker *n.*³ [1980s+] (*drugs*) a small glass bottle used for heating and 'cooking' crack cocaine.

shaker *n.*⁴ *see* SHAKE n.³.

shakes, the *n.* (*also* **the shivery-shakes**) **1** [mid-19C+] delirium tremens, the shaking associated with an alcoholic who has been deprived of sufficient drink to achieve normality; thus the similar experience of a withdrawing narcotics addict. **2** [1910s+] extreme terror, nervousness. **3** [1940s] a similar effect to (1), caused by excess coffee. **4** [1940s] palsy. **5** [1950s+] great excitement.

shake someone's back v. [late 16C] of a woman, to copulate enthusiastically. [horseriding imagery]

shake someone's jolt v. [1950s] (*US prison*) to interfere with the way another person is dealing with their sentence. [SE *shake* + JOLT n.² (1)]

shake someone's tree v. [1970s+] to pressurize someone emotionally.

Shakespeare navel n. [mid-late 19C] a long-pointed and turned-down collar. [? reminiscent of the classic portrait of the playwright]

shakester n. [mid-late 19C] **1** a gentile woman. **2** a non-Jewish servant-girl. **3** (*also* **shickster**) a woman. [mispron. of Yid. *shikse*, a gentile female; according to Hotten (1867), a term used by the costermongers to refer to the women of the class immediately above, i.e. tradesmen's wives/daughters]

shake the bones v. see ROLL THE BONES v.

shake the bullet (at) v. [mid-19C] to threaten with dismissal, but not actually to dismiss. [BULLET n.² (1)]

shake the cross v. [late 19C] to give up thieving. [CROSS n.¹ (3)]

shake the dew off the lily v. (*also* **shake the dew off one's weenie**) [1940s+] to urinate. [LILY n.⁴ (1)/WEENIE n.¹ (4)]

shake the fleas out v. [1940s] (*US*) to make an effort, to 'get a move on', to stop being lazy.

shake the ghost into v. [mid-19C–1900s] to terrify.

shake the hoof v. see SLING THE HOOF v.

shake the lettuce v. [1990s+] to urinate.

shake the money tree v. [20C+] (*US*) to make a large financial profit. [the fantasy of money 'growing on trees']

shake the pagoda-tree v. [mid-19C–1900s] (*Anglo-Ind.*) to become rich quickly. [SE *pagoda*, a gold (occas. silver) coin, formerly current in southern India, worth about 7 shillings; it had a pagoda engraved on it]

shake the tree v. [early 17C] to have sexual intercourse.

shake-up n.¹ [late 19C] an unnerving experience.

shake-up n.² [1900s–50s] the process of 'cleaning up' a city/establishment.

shake-up n.³ (*US Black*) **1** [1920s–40s] a form of cocktail, made from a variety of liquors, plus wine. **2** [1940s] cheap corn whisky.

shake-up n.⁴ see SHAKEFOOT n.

shake up v. [1960s] (*US*) of police, to raid and search an individual and/or their premises.

shaking n. [1950s+] (*US Black*) news, events, what is going on. [SHAKE v.⁶ (2)]

shakings of the bag n. see SHAKE OF THE BAG n.

shaky adj. [1940s–60s] (*US Und.*) of a town or city, unsafe for criminal operations.

Shaky City n. [1960s+] (*US*) **1** Los Angeles, California. **2** San Francisco, California. [frequency of earthquakes on the San Andreas Fault]

Shaky Isles n. [1930s+] (*Aus.*) New Zealand. [the frequency of earthquakes]

shaler n. [mid-late 19C] (*Aus.*) a woman. [proper name *Sheila*, ult. Irish *caille*, a young girl]

shall-I n. [1940s] (*W.I.*) cheap material. [abbr. dial. *shalligonaked*, 'a thin flimsy garment, cloth of an inferior kind' (*EDD*)]

shall I put a bit of hair on it? phr. [20C+] directed at a workman who is failing to put something into something else. [the hair in question would be female and pubic]

shallow n. **1** [late 18C–early 19C] a hat. **2** [mid-19C] a basket, used by a costermonger. **3** [1900s] a fool. [its shape]

shallow adj. [mid-late 19C] naked; thus *do/go on the shallows*,

run shallow, to go around half-naked (for the purpose of begging); very poorly dressed.

shallow cove n. (*also* **shallow, shallow bloke, ...chap, ...covey, ...fellow, ...runner**) [mid-late 19C] a wandering beggar, adopting tattered clothing and posing as a madman, or shipwreck survivor; thus the *shallow brigade*, a party or group of beggars; *go on the shallows*, to beg half naked. [SHALLOW adj. + COVE n. (1)]

shallow dodge n. [mid-late 19C] the practice of dressing in minimal rags for the purpose of begging; also as phr. *on the shallow(s)*. [SHALLOW adj. + DODGE n. (1)]

shallow mot n. [mid-19C] the female companion of a wandering beggar. [SHALLOW adj. + MOT n. (2)]

shallow pate n. [mid-17C–1900s] a fool, a simpleton (cf. CLODPATE n.). [SE *shallow*, lacking depth of mind + *pate*, head]

shallow runner n. see SHALLOW COVE n.

shallow screever n. [mid-late 19C] a pavement artist. [ext. of SCREEVER n. (1)]

sham n.¹ (*UK Und.*) **1** [mid-17C–19C] a trick, a hoax, a fraud. **2** [late 18C–19C] something intended to impose upon, delude or disappoint. [subseq. use is SE. SE *shame* or *shamed*; thus this anecdote: 'The word Sham is true Cant of the Newmarket Breed. It is contracted from ashamed. The native Signification is a Town Lady of Diversion, in Country Maid's Cloaths, who to make good her Disguise, pretends to be so sham'd! Thence it became proverbial, when a maimed Lover was laid up, or looked meager, to say he had met with a Sham' (R. North, *Examen*, 1740); cf. ety. at BAMBOOZLE v.]

sham n.² (*also* **shammy**) [mid-19C] *cham*pagne. [abbr.]

sham n.³ see SHAMUS n.

sham v.¹ [late 17C+] to deceive, to hoax, to fool. [SHAM n.¹ (1)]

sham v.² [1900s] to ply with, or treat oneself to, champagne. [SHAM n.²]

sham abram v. (*also* **sham abraham**) **1** [mid-18C–19C] to fake illness. **2** [mid-19C] of a beggar, to travel the country posing as a madman. [SHAM v.¹ + ABRAM n.]

shame (down) v. [1980s+] to humiliate; thus *shame*, a state of disgrace.

sham-legger n. [late 18C–early 19C] a seller of second-rate goods at very low prices. [SHAM n.¹ (2) + LEGGER n.¹ (1)]

shammus n. see SHAMUS n.

shammy n. see SHAM n.².

sham on v. [1980s+] **1** (*US Black*) to cheat, to deceive. **2** (*US campus*) to tease, to make fun of someone. [SHAM n.¹ (1)]

shamos n. see SHAMUS n.

shampata n. [20C+] (*W.I. Rasta*) a sandal of wood or tyre rubber. [Sp. *zapato*]

shampers n. see CHAMPERS n.

shampoo n. [1950s+] *cham*pagne. [elaboration on CHAMPERS n.]

shampoo the rug v. **1** [1970s+] (*US gay*) to dribble saliva onto the pubic hair during fellatio. **2** [1990s+] to ejaculate onto a pubic mound.

shamrock n. **1** [17C; 1940s] (*US Und.*) an Irishman (cf. BOG ARAB n.). **2** [19C+] (*US*) a policeman. **3** [19C+] a mixed drink, esp. whisky and stout. **4** [2000s] (*drugs*) MDMA (cf. ECSTASY n.). **5** [2000s] (*US Und.*) an Irish gang. [the stereotyped link between the Irish and the police and drinking; (4) is the logo on the pills]

Shamrockshire n. [early 18C] Ireland. [SE *shamrock*, an emblem of Ireland + sfx -*shire*]

shamrock tea n. [20C+] (*UK tramp*) weak tea. [it has only 3 leaves in it]

shams n. [early 19C] 'false sleeves to put on over a dirty shirt, or false sleeves with ruffles to put over a plain one' (*Lex. Bal.*). [SHAM n.¹ (2)]

sham saint n. [early 18C] a hypocrite.

shamus n. (*also* **sham, shammus, shamos, shommus**) **1** [1920s+] (*US*) a policeman (cf. BILLY n.⁶). **2** [1930s+] a detective, esp. a private operative. **3** [1930s+] a police informer. **4** [1940s+] any person, esp. as affectionate term of address. [*Seamus*, the common Irish name of many policemen; but note Heb./Yid. *shames*, a synagogue official]

shan *n.* **1** [early 19C; 1900s] (*UK Und.*) (*also* **shand**) counterfeit money. **2** [early 19C] in fig. use, an untrustworthy person. [Scot. *shan*, pitiful, paltry, poor]

shan *adj.* [1990s+] unsteady. [see prev.]

shananigan *n. see* SHENANIGAN *n.*

shandah *n.* [1960s] (*US*) a nuisance, an annoyance. [ety. unknown]

shandy *n.* [20C+] a male homosexual. [rhy. sl. *shandy = chandelier* = QUEER *n.* (4) but note also the perceived effeminacy of the drink shandy]

shandygaff *n.* [late 19C–1930s] (*Aus./N.Z.*) an uneasy compromise, anything that fails to please either party in a dispute; thus *shandygaffy*, prone to compromise; *shandygaff*, to mix things up. [SE *shandygaff*, a drink composed of beer and ginger-beer, both mixed and alcoholically weak]

shanghai *n.*[1] (*also* **shang, shangie, shong**) [mid-19C+] (*Aus./N.Z.*) a catapult. [? SHANGHAI *v.*; or ? Scot. *shangie*, a cleft stick; note McGill, *Dict. of Kiwi Slang* (1988): 'Macquarie suggests a derivation from British dialect word "shangan", a cleft stick for putting on a dog's tail; the act of shanghai-ing or press–ganging by stupefying the victim, although clearly related to the East China seaport of Shanghai, has related merit for the impact of a child's shanghai']

shanghai *n.*[2] [20C+] a broken-down old vehicle. [? dial. *shandry-dan*, a rickety, old-fashioned vehicle]

shanghai *v.* **1** [mid-19C+] to kidnap, to abduct; thus *shanghai game*, kidnapping; also in fig. use. **2** [late 19C] in ext. use, to destroy, to remove. **3** [20C+] (*US*) to trick, to cheat. **4** [1960s+] (*Aus. prison*) to transfer to a new prison without prior warning. **5** [2000s] (*US Black*) to cut someone. **6** [2000s] (*US Black*) to have sexual intercourse very energetically (cf. BANG *v.*[1]). [naut. use *shanghai*, to press a man into service at the port of *Shanghai*; see Asbury, *The Barbary Coast* (1933), p.199, for discussion of the ety.]

shanghai ballast *n.* [1910s–50s] (*N.Z.*) rice. [the Chinese city of *Shanghai* + SE *ballast*]

shanghaied *adj.* [20C+] (*Aus.*) thrown from one's horse. [SHANGHAI *v.* (2)]

shanghaier *n.* [1920s] a kidnapper, an abuctor. [SHANGHAI *v.* (1)]

shangie *n. see* SHANGHAI *n.*[1].

shank *n.*[1] [late 19C+] (*US*) the end or last part of a period of time, e.g. *the shank of the evening*. [SE *shank*, a shaft or stem]

shank *n.*[2] (*US prison/Und.*) **1** [1940s+] a stiletto-like weapon, similar to a screwdriver, used by street gangs, prisoners etc; thus *shanked*, carrying a knife. **2** [1960s+] any form of knife. [17C SE *shank*, the tang of a knife or chisel, i.e. the part that is inserted into the handle]

shank *n.*[3] *see* SKANK *n.*[1] (1).

shank *v.*[1] **1** [1950s+] (*US*) to stab with a knife; also in fig. use; thus *shanking*, a stabbing. **2** [1980s] (*US campus*) to try one's hardest. **3** [1990s+] (*US campus*) to harm. [SHANK *n.*[2]]

shank *v.*[2] [1990s+] to walk. [abbr. SHANKS'S PONY *n.*]

shank *v.*[3] [2000s] to masturbate (cf. BOFF *v.*; COTTON WOOL *v.*). [rhy. sl.; *ham shank* = WANK *v.* (1)]

Shank End, the *n.* [late 19C+] (*S.Afr.*) the Cape Peninsula; thus *Shankender*, an inhabitant of Cape Peninsula. [SE *shank*, a shaft or stem]

shanker *n.* **1** [mid-17C–early 19C; 1930s–50s] a venereal wart. **2** [mid-19C] a button, as worn by a costermonger to decorate his clothing. [SE *chancre*, an ulcer arising from venereal disease; (1) 20C+ use is Aus.]

shanker mechanic *n.* [1950s] (*US*) a doctor. [SHANKER *n.*, but the disease is not necessarily an STD]

shank-painter *n.* [early 19C] a leg. [SE *shank*, a leg + naut. *painter*, a boat's rope]

shanks's pony *n.* (*also* **shank's, shanks's mare/nag/naggie, shank's...**) [late 18C+] walking, on foot; usu. as *ride/take...* [SE *shank*, a leg + *pony/mare/nag/naggie*; note synon. US regional *ride one's mother's colt/granny's colt/mother's pony* etc]

shanky *adj. see* SKANKY *adj.*

shanny *adj.* (*also* **shanny-pated**) [19C] crazy, insane. [Suffolk dial. *shanny*, half-witted, crack-brained]

shant *n.* (*also* **shanty**) **1** [mid-18C–19C] a quart pot or a quart of liquor. **2** [mid-19C+] a drink, esp. beer. **3** [late 19C] beer money. [? Aus./N.Z. *shanty*, a public house, esp. when unlicensed; ult. SE *shanty*, a makeshift dwelling]

shant *v.* [1980s] to have a drink. [SHANT *n.* (2)]

shants *n.* [1990s+] (*US teen*) extremely baggy, long shorts. [SE *shorts* + *pants*, i.e. trousers]

shanty *n.*[1] [late 19C–1940s] (*US*) a black eye.

shanty *n.*[2] *see* SHANT *n.*

shanty Irish *n.* (*also* **shanty mick**) [20C+] (*US*) working-class Irish. [SE *shanty*, a rough cabin, a hut; ? Fr. *chantier*, a woodcutters' hut]

shap *n. see* SHAPO *n.*

shape *n.* [late 17C] a fop, a dandy. [his figure]

shape *v.*[1] (*also* **throw shapes**) [late 19C+] (*Irish*) to show off, to display oneself; thus *shaper*, one who poses.

shape *v.*[2] *see* SHAPE UP *v.*

shapes *n.*[1] **1** [late 17C–mid-18C] an ugly, ill-proportioned man. **2** [mid-18C] 'a nice finikin Lass that goes extream tightly laced' (Dyche & Pardon, *A New General English Dictionary*, 1735).

shapes *n.*[2] [1920s–60s] (*US*) crooked dice with bevelled faces on some sides of the cube, thus causing an irregular roll.

shape to *v.* (*also* **shape up (to)**) [20C+] to prepare to fight someone.

shape up *v.* **1** [mid-19C+] (*also* **shape**) for a boxer to ready himself; ext. to general use. **2** [mid-19C+] (*also* **shape**) of a situation or person, to develop or turn out. **3** [late 19C+] of a person, to improve one's behaviour, activities, attitude etc. **4** [1930s–50s] to prepare oneself to commit a crime. **5** [1930s–50s] to achieve a successful outcome. **6** [1940s+] to seem, to appear.

shapo *n.* (*also* **shap, shappeau, shappo**) [late 17C–mid-19C] a hat. [Fr. *chapeau*, a hat]

share *n.* [1920s+] a sexually available woman; ext. as *a bit of share*. [? her favours have been shared around]

share certificate *n.* [1960s+] (*US*) a pimp's favourite woman. [she is his 'investment']

share lashes *v.* (*also* **share licks**) [20C+] (*W.I.*) **1** to flog a number of people, usu. schoolchildren, at the same time. **2** orig. political use, to trounce the opposition. [SE *share (out)* + SE *lashes/licks*]

share the rag *v. see* ON THE RAG *phr.* (2).

sharge *v.* [19C] to have sexual intercourse. [? dial. *sharge*, to grind]

shark *n.*[1] **1** [late 16C+] a confidence trickster, a crooked gambler. **2** [17C] a parasite, a hanger-on. **3** [17C+] a sharp operator, a crooked businessman. **4** [late 18C–mid-19C] a pickpocket. **5** [late 18C–1910s] a custom house officer. **6** [mid-19C+] (*orig. US Und.*) a lawyer. **7** [1910s+] a supplier of private loans at maximum interest; a LOAN SHARK *n.* **8** [1920s] (*US*) a pawnbroker. **9** [1920s–40s] a womanizer. **10** [1920s+] (*US*) an employment agent. **11** [1930s] (*US*) a private detective (cf. BEAGLE *n.*[3]). **12** [1940s+] (*Aus.*) a second-hand car salesman. **13** [1940s+] a pool shark. **14** [1990s+] (*US prison*) a dangerous, violent person.

shark *n.*[2] **1** [mid-19C] (*US campus*) one who deliberately misses a lesson or similar compulsory attendance; the act of choosing to miss such an attendance. **2** [late 19C–1920s] (*US campus*) a very intelligent or hard-working student. **3** [1910s+] (*US*) an expert, an authority.

shark *v.* **1** [late 16C+] (*also* **go on the shark**) to cheat, to defraud, to steal. **2** [1960s] to treat unfairly, to victimize. [(1) SHARK n.[1] (1); (2) SE *shark*]

shark and taties *n.* [1980s+] (*N.Z.*) fish and chips.

shark-bait *n.* (*also* **shark-baiter**) [1910s+] (*Aus.*) a solitary swimmer swimming too far out at sea.

shark biscuit *n.* [1920s+] (*Aus.*) **1** a novice surfer. **2** the victim of a shark attack. **3** a bodyboard. [on model of SE *dog biscuit*]

shark-hunter *n.* [1920s] (*US Und.*) a thief who robs a drunk.

sharking *n.* [1960s+] the practice of a private credit company taking high interest on loans. [SHARK v. (1)]

sharking *adj.* **1** [17C] underhand, cheating. **2** [20C+] (*W.I., Nevis*) greedy, gluttonous. [SHARK v. (1)]

shark out *v.* [19C] to run off, to decamp.

sharks *n.* [1970s+] (*US Black/teen*) a sharkskin suit. [abbr.]

sharks, the *n.* [early–mid-19C] the press gang. [ext. of SHARK n.[1] (3)]

shark's piss *n.* [1900s] weak beer or other alcohol (cf. BUFFALO PISS n.).

sharma *n.* [2000s] (*US Black*) a person of Indian descent who tries to act Black. [stereotyped Indian surname]

Sharon *n.* (*also* **Shaz, Tracey**) [1980s+] (*UK middle class*) a pej. description of a working-class young woman regarded as overly flashy and socially unacceptable; a female KEVIN n. [archetypal working-class name]

Sharon Stone *n.* [1990s+] a (usu. mobile) telephone. [rhy. sl., ult. US film actress *Sharon Stone* (b.1957)]

sharp *n.*[1] **1** [late 18C+] a confidence trickster. **2** [19C–1920s] an expert or connoisseur, a clever person or one who poses as such; also, in comb. with n., a job title, e.g. *doctor sharp, revenue sharp*. **3** [1960s] (*US campus*) an attractive and/or socially adept person. [SHARP v.; note shop assistants' jargon *Mr Sharp*, a known shoplifter or fraud]

sharp *n.*[2] [mid-19C] (*US Und.*) a rifle.

sharp *n.*[3] **1** [1950s] (*US Black*) fashionable clothing. **2** [1960s+] (*US*) a second-hand car in excellent condition. [SHARP adj. (4)]

sharp *adj.* **1** [late 17C+] cunning, on the lookout for oneself. **2** [18C+] intelligent, perceptive. **3** [1910s+] of a woman, attractive. **4** [1920s+] (*also* **sharpy**) fashionable, good, admirable. **5** [1940s–60s] good (of quality). **6** [1940s+] used of a person who dresses well and with style, e.g. a *sharp dresser, sharp threads*. **7** [1940s+] (*S.Afr.*) good (of health). **8** [1950s] (*US drugs*) intoxicated by a given drug.

sharp *v.* **1** [late 17C–early 18C] to obtain through trickery. **2** [late 17C–19C] to trick, to defraud.

sharp *adv.* **1** [19C+] quickly, speedily. **2** [19C+] intelligently, smartly. **3** [1990s+] fashionably. [SHARP adj.]

sharp and blunt *n.* [late 19C+] the vagina; thus HAVE A BIT OF SHARP AND BLUNT v. (cf. ALL QUIET n.). [rhy. sl. = CUNT n.[1] (1)]

sharp as a mosquito's peter *phr.* (*also* **sharp as a rat turd**) [1970s+] (*US Black*) very smartly and fashionably dressed. [pun on SE *sharp*/SHARP adj. (4) + *mosquito* pron. 'moskeeter' for assonance + PETER n.[4]]

sharp end *n.* [1980s+] the challenging, demanding and sometimes unpleasant aspect of an experience.

sharpener *n.* [2000s] an alcoholic drink. [it supposedly makes the drinker SHARP adj. (2)]

sharpen one's pencil *v.* [1990s+] (*UK juv.*) to have sexual intercourse (cf. BURY IT v.). [SE *sharpen* + PENCIL n. (2)]

sharper *n.* **1** [late 17C+] a confidence trickster; a cheating gambler. **2** [late 18C] in a non-criminal context, a trickster. **3** [1940s] someone who sees themselves as 'clever'. [SHARP v. (2)]

sharpie *n.*[1] (*also* **sharpy**) (*mainly US*) **1** [1920s–30s] a devotee of swing music. **2** [1940s+] a slick operator, one who lives and hopes to prosper by their wits. **3** [1940s+] a cheat, a liar, a confidence trickster. **4** [1940s+] a stylish dresser. **5** [1960s+] anything in conspicuously good condition, esp. a motorcar. [SHARP adj.]

sharpie *n.*[2] [1960s–70s] (*Aus.*) a member of a crop-haired teen cult. [the equivalent of the SKINHEAD n. (3)]

sharping *n.* [late 17C–mid-18C] swindling and cheating in its various forms. [SHARP v. (2)]

sharping-omee *n.* (*also* **sharpy**) [mid-19C] a policeman. [SHARP adj. (2) + OMEE n. (3)]

sharpish *adj.* [mid-19C+] sharply, quickly.

sharps *n.* **1** [1900s–30s] household needles. **2** [1980s+] (*drugs*) needles. [orig. medical jargon *sharps*, needles, scalpels etc]

Sharp's Alley blood worms *n.* [mid–late 19C] beef sausages or black puddings. [proper name *Sharp's Alley*, an abattoir near the Smithfield meat market in London]

sharps and flats *n.* [late 17C] the penis and vagina, in the context of intercourse. [the erect penis is 'sharp', the vagina 'flat']

sharpshoot *v.* [1950s] (*US*) to defraud, to cheat out of one's money. [backform. f. SHARPSHOOTER n.[1]]

sharpshooter *n.*[1] [19C+] a cheater, a fraudster. [play on SE]

sharpshooter *n.*[2] (*also* **sharpy**) **1** [1910s–40s] a professional gambler. **2** [1920s+] a womanizer. **3** [1930s–40s] (*US Und.*) a successful criminal. **4** [1930s–50s] (*US*) an expert. **5** [1950s] (*US drugs*) a narcotics addict. [puns]

sharpster *n.* [1950s] a confidence trickster, a gambler. [SHARP n.[1] (1) + -STER sfx]

sharp stick *n. see* STICK n.[14].

sharp up *v.* [1930s] (*US*) to dress oneself up smartly. [SHARP adj. (4)]

sharpy *n.*[1] *see* SHARPIE n.[1].

sharpy *n.*[2] *see* SHARPING-OMEE n.

sharpy *adj. see* SHARP adj. (4).

sharrer/sharry *n. see* CHARA n.

shat *n.* [early 18C] a chatterbox, a gossip, a 'tattler'. [? SE *chat*]

shat *adj.* (*also* **shat-off**) [1940s+] (*Aus.*) very angry, furious. [past participle of SHIT v.[1] (1); thus cognate with PISSED OFF adj.]

shat on *adj.* (*also* **shat upon**) [1940s+] abused, humiliated; ext. as *shat on from a great height*. [past participle of SHIT ON v. (1)]

shattered *adj.* [1930s+] **1** drunk. **2** utterly exhausted (physically or emotionally).

shatting on one's uppers *phr.* [late 19C–1930s] (*US*) (to be) completely out of money. [var. on SHIT v.[1] (1) + SE *uppers*]

shat up *adj.* [1990s+] utterly emotionally destroyed. [fig. use of SHIT v.[1] (1)]

shat upon *adj. see* SHAT ON adj.

shaun spadah *n.* [1920s] a motorcar. [rhy. sl.; ult. the horse *Shaun Spadah*, winner of the 1921 Grand National]

shave *n.*[1] [19C] (*US*) an excessive discount on a note. [SHAVE A NOTE v.]

shave *n.*[2] **1** [mid-19C] a trick, a hoax. **2** [mid-19C+] a narrow escape; esp. as *close shave*. [SE *shave*, a glancing touch]

shave *n.*[3] [mid–late 19C] a drink. [? excuse given as 'I'm just off out for a shave']

shave *v.* **1** [late 16C–early 18C] to steal. **2** [late 16C–1900s] to defraud, to rob, to overcharge; thus intensified as [mid-16C] *shave to the quick*. **3** [1930s–50s] (*US drugs*) to reduce the size of a supposed 1oz (28g) cube of morphine. **4** [1950s–60s] (*UK Und.*) to attack with a razor. [SE *shave*; (2) used in this sense as SE in late 14C–early 16C]

shave-and-a-haircut *n.* [20C+] (*orig. US*) a sequence of knocks, tum-ti-ti-tum-tum, often as *shave-and-a-haircut – two/six bits*, which has a final tum-tum. [the echoic rhythm of the phr.]

shave a note *v.* [19C–1900s] (*US*) to discount a promissory note at a very high rate of interest. [SHAVE v. (2)]

shaved *adj.* [19C] drunk; esp. as *half-shaved*. [? SHAVE n.[3]]

shaver *n.* **1** [late 16C+] a man; occas. a woman. **2** [17C+] a young or adolescent boy; esp. as *young shaver*; occas. a young girl. **3** [mid-19C] (*US*) an errand boy. [lit. one who shaves and has thus reached manhood; now used ironically; but note Rom. *chavo*, a boy]

shaver n.² 1 [early 17C] a thief. 2 [mid-17C–mid-18C] a roisterer. 3 [19C] someone who discounts a promissory note at a very high rate of interest. 4 [early 19C] a merchant or shopkeeper who charges high prices. 5 [mid-19C] a bank that issues such discounted notes. [SHAVE v./SHAVE A NOTE v.]

shaver n.³ [1920s] a shave-coat, a man's casual garment resembling a housecoat and worn when shaving.

shavetail n. 1 [late 19C–1930s] (US tramp) a young mule. 2 [late 19C+] (US) an inexperienced person; a new lieutenant. [milit. use shavetail, an untrained pack animal, identified by a shaven tail; thus a newly commissioned second lieutenant]

shavetail adj. [1950s+] (US) inexperienced. [SHAVETAIL n. (2)]

shaving n. 1 [early 17C–mid-19C] the act of swindling or defrauding. 2 [early–mid-19C] (US) discounting bills or promissory notes at a very high rate of interest. [SHAVE v. (2)/SHAVE A NOTE v.]

shaving brush n. [late 19C] pubic hair.

shavings n. 1 [late 17C–early 19C] (UK Und.) the clippings from shaved coins. 2 [1950s] (US Und.) alcohol.

shavoo n. see SHIVOO n.

shawl n.¹ [19C] (UK middle class) an announcement of one's engagement. [? the putative groom being now allowed the intimacy of placing a shawl around his beloved's shoulders]

shawl n.² [1900s–20s] a prostitute. [SHAWLIE n. (2)]

shawlie n. (also **shawly**) [late 19C–1930s] (Irish) 1 an Irish, usu. Dublin, fisherwoman. 2 any working-class woman wearing a shawl.

shay n. see CHAY n.

shaygets n. (also **sheygets**) [late 19C+] 1 (Jewish) a young male gentile. 2 a mischievous rascal, a 'charming devil', whether Jewish or gentile. 3 an arrogant person. 4 an illiterate, one who lacks education, which in trad. learning-focused Jewish eyes is equated with (1). [Heb. sheygets, a rascal]

Shaz n. see SHARON n.

She n. [late 19C] (UK society) Queen Victoria. [Ayesha, 'she who must be obeyed' the heroine of H. Rider Haggard's novel She (1887), coincidentally the year of the queen's golden jubilee]

she n.¹ 1 [late 16C+] a girl, a woman; thus she-inmate, a prostitute of a brothel. 2 [1930s+] a term used by homosexuals of other homosexuals. 3 [1990s+] (US) one's wife.

she n.² 1 [late 19C+] the vagina. 2 [1920s+] the penis; esp. in phr. up she rises.

shear v. [late 16C+] to fool, to trick; thus shorn, swindled. [SE shear a sheep]

shearer n. [1900s] (Aus.) a bookmaker. [play on SHEAR v. + SE sheep, a gullible fool]

shearer's joy n. (also **shearer's delight**) [late 19C+] (Aus./N.Z.) beer.

'sheart! excl. [late 16C–early 18C] a mild, if blasphemous, oath, lit. 'God's heart.'

sheave-o n. see SHIVOO n.

sheba n. 1 [1920s–30s] (US) an attractive, fashionable woman. 2 [1970s+] (US gay) a homosexual Black man. [the Queen/QUEEN n.² (1) of Sheba]

shebang n. 1 [mid-19C+] (US) a house, a home, a dwelling place, a shop. 2 [late 19C–1900s] a vehicle. 3 [late 19C] (US) a saloon bar. 4 [late 19C–1900s] (US) a thing, an object. 5 [20C+] an event. 6 [1940s–50s] (US Und.) a criminal rendezvous. 7 [1940s–50s] (UK/US Und.) a prison cell. [SE shebang, a hut, a dwelling, one's quarters]

shebeen n. (also **shebean-house, sheebeen shop**) [late 18C+] an unlicensed drinking place, an illegal, late-night drinking club; thus shebeener, one who drinks illegal liquor and frequents shebeens. [Irish síbín, illicit whisky; 20C+ use usu. linked to S.Afr. townships or to UK W.I. community]

she boss n. [mid-19C] a madam.

she-bro n. [2000s] (US Black) a very attractive female. [SE she + BRO n.¹ (1)]

she can sit on my face anyday phr. [1960s+] (orig. US) said by a man of a woman by whom he is very sexually aroused.

she-centaur n. [late 17C] a lesbian. [SE centaur, 'a fabulous creature, with the head, trunk, and arms of a man, joined to the body and legs of a horse' (OED); the play is on horseriding and RIDE v.¹ (1)]

sheckles n. see SHEKELS n.

sheckles! excl. [1900s–10s] a general excl. [? euph. for SHIT! excl.]

shed n.¹ [1920s+] (Aus./N.Z.) a term of general abuse. [elision of SHITHEAD n. (1)]

shed n.² 1 [1930s–40s] a solid-top car. 2 [1940s] (US Und.) any form of depot or terminus, esp. of trains. 3 [1990s+] (UK juv.) a run-down car.

shed n.³ [1990s+] an unattractive, promiscuous young woman. ['something you put your tools/TOOL n.¹ (1) in']

shed v. [1980s] (US campus) to work very hard, esp. when 'cramming' for an examination or test.

shed a tear v. [mid-19C+] 1 to take a drink, esp. a quick one. 2 to urinate.

shed a tear for Nelson v. [mid-19C+] (orig. RN) to urinate. [presumably the UK naval hero Horatio, Lord Nelson (1758–1805)]

shedder n. [mid-19C] (US) a counterfeit note.

she'd fuck anything in trousers phr. see ANYTHING IN TROUSERS n.

shed ink v. [late 19C] to write, usu. in a more general way than SLING INK v. as a journalist.

shed one's skin v. [1950s] (Aus.) to become hysterical with rage.

sheeba n. [1990s+] (US drugs) marijuana. [var. on CHIBA n.² (1)]

shee-it! excl. [20C+] (US) a joc. imitation of a Southern pron. of SHIT! excl.

sheela n. [late 19C–1910s] (Irish) a man who takes excessive interest in stereotyped 'women's affairs', i.e. housework, gossip, child-rearing. [Irish proper name Síle, but note SHEILA n. (1)]

sheen n.¹ 1 [mid-late 19C] a counterfeit coin. 2 [late 19C+] (Aus.) money (cf. BRASS n.¹). [the SE sheen of the coins or Ger. Schein, a banknote]

sheen n.² [1960s–70s] (US Black) a machine, either a car or a motorcycle. [abbr./pron.]

sheena n. [1950s–60s] (camp gay) a Black homosexual man (cf. ABIGAIL n.). [the cartoon character, Sheena, Queen of the Jungle/QUEEN n.² (1)]

sheeney's fear n. [late 19C] (UK Und.) bacon. [SHEENY n.¹ (1), i.e. the Jewish practice of not eating pork]

sheeny n.¹ (also **sheeney, sheenie, sheney**) 1 [19C+] a derog. term for a Jew (cf. ARAB n.²). 2 [1930s–40s] a derog. term for a person with dark skin, often of Mediterranean origin. [as laid out by Nathan Süsskind (in Cohen (ed.), Studies in Slang II, 1989), Yid. shayner Yid, a pious (lit. 'beautiful-faced') Jew. According to the Talmud such a Jew has a full beard – beauty in this case being spiritual rather than physical. The phr. was used by assimilated German Jews, who had emigrated to England, as a derog. term, meaning 'an old-fashioned Jew', i.e. in habits, clothing and religion, which mocked their less sophisticated successors, who followed them from Germany and clung on (at least initially) to their old-fashioned ways. The first half of the phr., which the 'uncultured' Jews pronounced sheena rather than the more Germanic schön, was taken up by gentile Jew-baiters to create sheeny; note WW1 milit. sheeny, a careful, extra-economical man]

sheeny n.² 1 [mid-19C+] a pawnbroker. 2 [1900s] a mean, grasping person. [occupational/racial stereotyping of SHEENY n.¹ (1)]

sheeny adj. (also **sheeney, sheenie**) 1 [mid-19C+] Jewish; also as a nickname for someone Jewish or having a Jewish appearance. 2 [late 19C] of people, deceitful, dubious, fraudulent. 3 [late 19C] of money, counterfeit. [SHEENY n.[1] (1) + reinforced in (3) by SE *sheeny*, shiny]

sheeny wagon *n.* [1950s] (*US*) a peddler's cart. [SHEENY n.[1] (1)]

sheep-biter *n.* **1** [late 16C–18C] a wretched, miserable person; thus *sheep-biting*. **2** [17C–early 18C] a womanizer. **3** [late 17C–18C] a butcher. **4** [mid-18C] a sheep-stealer. [(2) plays on MUTTON n.[1] (2)]

sheep cocky *n.* [late 19C+] (*Aus./N.Z.*) a small-scale sheep farmer. [SE *sheep* + COCKY n.[2] (1)]

sheep dip *n.* **1** [1910s] (*Aus./US*) inferior whisky. **2** [1940s] (*US*) nonsense. **3** [1960s] (*Aus.*) coarse tobacco, issued in prisons.

sheep-dodger *n.* [20C+] (*Aus.*) a sheep hand.

sheep-guts *n.* [19C] a general term of contempt. [SE *sheep* + -GUTS sfx]

sheepie *n.* [1990s+] a *sheep*skin coat or jacket. [abbr. + sfx *-ie*]

sheepish *adj.* [1970s] (*US campus*) of men, long-haired.

sheepo *n.* (*also* **sheep-ho**) **1** [late 19C–1900s] (*Aus./N.Z.*) a sheep-shearer, spec. one who works in the catching sheds, filling the catching pens. **2** [1980s] (*N.Z.*) a shepherd. [SE *sheep* + -O sfx (4)]

sheep's arse *n.* [2000s] nonsense, deception.

sheep's back *n.* [late 19C+] (*Aus.*) luxury, indolence, security; usu. in phr. *on the sheep's back*, living very comfortably, securely. [the wealth of sheep farmers]

sheep-shagger *n.* **1** [1970s] a Scot. **2** [1970s+] a peasant. **3** [1990s+] a Welshman; also attrib. [SHAGGER n.[1] (1); neg. racial stereotyping; note RMC Duntroon (Aus.) *sheep shagger*, a derog. term for a New Zealander]

sheep-shagging *n.* [1940s+] committing bestiality with a sheep. [SE *sheep* + SHAG v.[1]; the act is often used attrib. to mock the Welsh]

sheep's head *n.* [late 16C–1910s] a fool, esp. a talkative one (cf. AIREDALE n.). [the perceived stupidity of sheep, reinforced by later saying, 'like a sheep's head, all jaw']

sheep-shearer *n.* [late 16C–mid-18C] a swindler, a confidence trickster, esp. one who works the JACK IN A BOX n. confidence trick. [pun on SE *fleece*, to rob + SHEAR v.]

sheepskin *n.*[1] **1** [19C+] a college diploma, received on graduation. **2** [mid-19C–1900s] a document. **3** [1930s–60s] (*US prison*) a pardon or discharge certificate. [the use of sheepskin for parchment; (1) such diplomas are trad. made of *sheepskin*-based parchment]

sheepskin *n.*[2] [1990s+] (*US campus*) a condom. [an allegedly superior material for contraceptives]

sheepskin fiddle *n.* [early 19C] a drum; thus *sheepskin fiddler*, a drummer.

sheep's piss *n.* [2000s] weak alcohol, usu. beer (cf. BUFFALO PISS n.).

sheep-tail *n.* [1970s] (*W.I.*) **1** a bit of shirt-tail that protrudes through a hole in torn trousers. **2** the person (usu. a boy) who has such a costume.

sheep-wash *n.* [20C+] (*Aus./N.Z.*) **1** poor liquor. **2** poor tobacco.

sheesh! *excl.* [1950s+] (*US*) a mild oath; a euph. for JESUS! excl. or SHIT! excl. [? popularized through the *Yogi Bear/Huckleberry Hound* TV cartoons]

shee-shee *adj.* *see* CHEE-CHEE adj.

sheet *n.* **1** [mid-18C+] a newspaper, a magazine. **2** [1920s+] paper money, e.g. a £1 note, a $1 bill; often in pl. (cf. BANK-RAG n.). **3** [1930s–40s] (*US Und.*) a cigarette paper; often in pl. **4** [1950s+] (*US Und.*) an official police record. [abbr. SE *sheet of paper*. (1) mainly US in 20C+; note WW1 milit. *on the sheet*, charged with an offence]

sheet *v.* [1980s+] (*Aus. prison*) to charge with a prison misconduct.

sheet alley *n.* (*also* **sheet lane**) [mid-18C–1900s] bed; thus *go down sheet alley into Bedfordshire*, to go to bed.

sheet-boy *n.* [1930s] (*Aus.*) a bookmaker.

sheet it home to *v.* [late 19C–1960s] to prove something against

someone in criminal terms; occas. in non-criminal contexts. [? putting a criminal on a charge sheet]

sheet lane *n.* *see* SHEET ALLEY n.

sheet passer *n.* [1930s–40s] (*US Und.*) one who passes counterfeit notes. [SHEET n. (2)]

sheets *n.* **1** [1960s+] perforated sheets of LSD-impregnated blotting-paper, which can be torn into 100 separate doses of LSD. **2** [1970s+] phencyclidine (cf. ACE n.[4]).

Sheffield handicap *n.* [20C+] an act of defecation (cf. ANDY CAPP n.). [rhy. sl. = CRAP n.[3] (1)]

she-flunkey *n.* [late 19C–1910s] a lady's maid. [SE pfx *she-*, female + SE *flunkey*]

sheg *v.* (*W.I./UK Black*) **1** [1940s+] to annoy, to provoke. **2** [1950s+] to seduce. **3** [1970s] to do badly. [SE *shag*, to shake about]

shegarry *n.* [1980s] (*UK Black*) annoyance, irritation. [SHEG v. (1) + ? CARRY-ON n. (1)]

sheg round *v.* [1940s] (*W.I.*) to work as a petty criminal. [ext. of SHEG v. (1)]

sheg-up *n.* (*W.I.*) **1** [1940s] a confidence trickster whose role is to appear as gullible as the potential victim. **2** [1970s+] an unpleasant attitude. [SHEG ROUND v.]

sheg up *v.* [1950s+] (*W.I. Rasta*) **1** to be messed up, to be ruined. **2** to bother; thus *all sheg up*, all hot and bothered, or all spoiled, as of work that has been ruined. [SE *shake(n)*]

she has to cross her legs to keep her guts from falling out *phr.* [1960s] (*US*) used of a promiscuous or allegedly promiscuous woman.

she-he *n.* [1940s+] (*US*) **1** a lesbian (cf. BOY-GIRL n.[1]). **2** a transvestite or transsexual. [note Hindley, *The Old Book Collector's Miscellany* (1871–3): 'The She He Barman of Southwark' who 'engaged herself as a barman, / And said her name was Tom'; how much this cross-dressing should be seen as implying lesbianism or transsexuality is debatable]

she house *n.* [late 18C–early 19C] a house in which a wife rules her husband.

sheik *n.*[1] (*also* **sheikh**) (*orig. US*) **1** [1920s–30s] a fashionably dressed young man. **2** [1920s+] a man who considers himself irresistible to women, a romantic lover. [*The Sheik*, a novel by E.M. Hull, publ. 1919 + its film adaptation, released 1921, starring Rudolph Valentino; ult. Arabic *sheikh*, a tribal chieftain, a leader]

sheik *n.*[2] [1940s+] (*Can.*) a condom. [proprietary name *Sheik*]

sheik *v.* [1920s] (*orig. US*) to go out looking for female conquests. [SHEIK n.[1] (2)]

sheiked out *adj.* [1920s–30s] (*orig. US*) dressed in a rakish style. [SHEIK n.[1] (1)]

sheikh *n.* *see* SHEIK n.[1].

sheikha *n.* [1920s] the female consort of a SHEIK n.[1] (1). [*Sheikha*, an Arab lady or matron of good family; the chief wife of a *sheikh*]

sheik up *v.* [1920s] (*US*) to smarten/dress (oneself) up. [SHEIK n.[1] (1)]

sheiky *adj.* (*also* **sheikhy**) [1920s–30s] with the character of or pertaining to a 'lady-killer'. [SHEIK n.[1] (2)]

sheila *n.* (*also* **sheilah**) **1** [20C+] (*Aus.*) a woman; for 19C uses *see* SHALER n. **2** [1960s–70s] (*S.Afr.*) the girlfriend of an urban gangster. [proper name *Sheila*; ult. Irish *caille*, a young girl]

sheila-day *n.* (*also* **sheila's day**) [1970s+] (*S.Afr. Black*) Thursday, the day that most nannies and maids are allowed off work. [*Sheila*, generic name for Black domestic servants]

sheila rorter *n.* [1980s+] (*Aus. prison*) a prisoner obsessed with women. [SHEILA n. (1) + RORTER n.[1] (2)]

sheila-trap *n.* [1960s–70s] (*Aus.*) a man's flat or house, in which he attempts seductions. [SHEILA n. (1)]

she is so innocent she thinks fucking is a town in China *phr.* (*also* **she was so innocent...**) [1940s+] a phr. used of an especially naïve young woman. [pun on *Fukien*, an area in southeast China]

sheisty adj. (also **shiesty, shisty**) [1990s+] (US Black/campus) underhand, unethical, untrustworthy, criminal. [SHIT adj. (1)/ SHICER n. (3) + FEISTY adj. (1)]

sheive n. see SHIV n.

shekel v. [1990s+] (US campus) to give, to hand out. [SHEKELS n.]

shekels n. (also **sheckles, sheks**) 1 [mid-19C+] money; thus *rake in the shekels*, to prosper. 2 [2000s] (US) dollars. [Heb. *shekel*, a Babylonian, hence Heb. monetary unit; ult. Heb. *shāqāl*, to weigh]

shelf n.[1] [1920s+] (Aus./N.Z.) a police informer. [SHELF v.]

shelf n.[2] [1940s+] (Aus.) the dress circle in a cinema.

shelf, the n. [1930s–60s] (US prison) a holding cell, a punishment unit. [ON THE SHELF phr. (8)]

shelf v. [1910s+] (Aus./N.Z.) to inform to the police, or any authority. [SE *shelf*, to put aside]

shelfer n. [1960s+] (Aus.) a police informer. [SHELF v.]

she-lion n. [late 18C–mid-19C] a shilling (5p). [a pun on the pron.]

shell n. 1 [mid-18C–19C] the vagina (cf. BAG n.[1]; BEARDED CLAM n.). 2 [19C] (US Und.) a safe. 3 [late 19C–1910s] (US) a portion of opium. 4 [late 19C–1910s] (Aus.) a coffin. 5 [1900s] (Aus.) a corpse. 6 [1910s–20s] a hearse.

shell adj. (US campus) 1 [1980s] crazy. 2 [2000s] second-rate. [ety. unknown]

shell v. 1 [mid-19C] to remove some or all of one's clothes, e.g. preparatory to a fight. 2 [1980s+] (N.Z. drugs) to remove pain-killing drugs from their capsule before making home-produced narcotics.

shellac v. (also **shellack**) [1920s+] to beat, to thrash, to punish. [SE *shellac*, to coat or varnish with shellac; note Dennis Wilson on *American Dialect Society-List* (Internet, 14 November 2002): 'Here are my guesses; I find any of them plausible, or a combination. (1) Derivative of German "schlagen" (= "strike") or equivalent. Cf. supposed etymology of "schlock" (from Yiddish). Cf. "Our team really got clobbered", "I really got hammered on schnapps last night", "They really gave him a pounding". (2) Onomatopoeic (cf. "smack", "whack", etc.). (3) [The books seem to favor this one] Shellacking being the last step in finishing something; thus something shellacked is something completed, something which has been "finished off"']

shellacked adj. [1920s+] (US) drunk (cf. ANNIHILATED adj.). [for ety. see SHELLAC v.]

shellacking n. [1920s+] a severe beating or defeat; also a scolding. [SHELLAC v.]

shell-back n. [late 19C+] an ultra-conservative, slow-witted person. [the image of a slow-moving turtle]

she'll be right phr. see SHE'S RIGHT phr.

shelled adj. [2000s] (US Black) drunk; acting stupidly (cf. ANNI-HILATED adj.). [? SHELL n. (3) or SHELLACKED adj.]

she'll fuck anything in trousers phr. see ANYTHING IN TROUSERS n.

shell game n. [late 19C+] 1 a swindling game in which a small object is concealed under a walnut shell or the like; the manipulator then moves the shells round at speed; bets are made on the shell under which the object is found. 2 a generic for any form of confidence trick.

shell man n. see SHELL WORKER n.

shellmex n. [20C+] sex. [rhy. sl.; ult. *Shell-Mex* brand from the *Shell* oil company]

shell out v.[1] 1 [early 19C+] (also **shell off/over**) to hand over, usu. money. 2 [1920s] to take an opponent's money when playing cards or dice. 3 [1940s] to do what is required or demanded. [the removal of a seed from a shell]

shell out v.[2] [1900s–30s] (US) to leave, to depart.

shell road v. [1900s–30s] (US) to throw a person, often a woman who refuses to have sex, out of a vehicle and thus force them to walk home an inconvenient and poss. embarrassing distance. [SAmE *shell road*, a back road having a bed or layer of shells]

shells n. [late 16C–early 17C; 1990s+] (UK Und.) money, esp. as taken from a victim by cut-purses or pickpockets.

shell-shock n.[1] 1 [1910s–50s] cocoa. 2 [1920s–30s] (UK tramp) tea served in a casual ward or hostel. 3 [1930s–50s] (Aus./N.Z.) a mixed alcoholic drink, usu. very potent, e.g. port and stout.

shell-shock n.[2] [1920s] (US) a joc. term of address; the implication is that the subject has an 'explosive' personality.

shell worker n. (also **shell man**) [late 19C–1940s] (US Und.) one who operates a SHELL GAME n. [SHELL GAME n. + WORKER n.[1] (1)]

s'help me...! excl. see S'ELP ME (BOB)! excl.

she-male n. 1 [mid-19C–1920s] a woman, usu. a feminist or an intellectual. 2 [20C+] a male homosexual or transvestite (cf. BOY-GIRL n.[1]). 3 [1970s] (US gay) a lesbian.

shemale adj. [1900s–10s] (Aus.) pertaining to female or feminist concerns. [SHE-MALE n. (1)]

she-man n. [20C+] a homosexual man (cf. BOY-GIRL n.[1]). [play on SE *he-man*]

she-medico n. see MEDICO n. (1).

she-mi-a-play-wid n. [1950s] (W.I.) one's female sweetheart. [lit. 'she plays with me']

shemmy n. see SHIMMY n.[1].

shemozzle n. (also **chemozzle, chermozzle, chimozzle, schemozzle, schlemozzle, schmozzle, shimozzle, shlemozzle**) [late 19C+] 1 a fuss, a disturbance. 2 a state of difficulty. [coined in UK and not 'real' Yid.; similar sp. to SCHLEMAZEL n., but with no other links]

shemozzle v. [1910s+] to run off, to decamp. [SHEMOZZLE n.]

shenanigan n. (also **shananigan, shenanagan, shenannigan, shenannigin, shinanigan, shinan(n)ickin**) [mid-19C+] trickery, skulduggery, machination, intrigue, teasing, 'kidding', nonsense; (usu. pl.) a plot, a trick, a prank, an exhibition of high spirits, a carry-on. [? Erse *sionnach* (pron. 'shinnuck'), hiding, malingering; East Anglian dial. *nannicking*, playing the fool, messing about]

she-napper n. [late 17C–mid-19C] 1 a madam. 2 a female pimp or procuress. 3 a female thief-taker. [SE *she* + NAP v.[2] (1)]

sheney n. see SHEENY n.[1].

shent-per-shent/-shenter n. see CENT-PER-CENT n.

she-oak n. [late 19C–1950s] (Aus.) beer. [SE *she-oak*, a tree of the genus *Casuarina*; note Aus. use of *she* for wood to indicate inferior texture, colour etc]

Sheol n. [late 19C–1970s] a joc. euph. for SE *hell*, e.g. *sheol to pay*, *this side of sheol*, *sheol for hides*, hell for leather. [Heb. *she'ol*, the underworld, the abode of the dead or departed spirits, translated as 'the pit' or 'hell']

shepherd v. 1 [late 19C] (Und., mainly Aus.) to follow someone who is a potential target for robbery or fraud. 2 [late 19C+] to watch over carefully, to shadow.

shepherd's bush n. [20C+] dismissal. [rhy. sl. = PUSH, THE n. (1)]

shepherd's clock n. [late 19C+] (Aus.) a kookaburra or laughing jackass. [its sounds punctuate the day]

shepherd's pie n. [20C+] the sky. [rhy. sl.]

shepherd's (plaid) adj. [1930s–50s] bad. [rhy. sl.]

sherbet n. (also **sherbert**) 1 [late 19C] grog or any warm, alcoholic drink; also as *old sherbert*. 2 [20C+] (Aus.) any form of alcoholic drink. 3 [1970s+] beer. 4 [2000s] cocaine (cf. BIRDIE POWDER n.). [Turk. *sherbet* (ult. Arab. *sharbah*, a drink), a cooling drink made of fruit juice and water sweetened, often cooled with snow; (4) resemblance to a popular UK sweet, a *sherbet dab*, a bag of sherbet powder with a liquorice 'straw' through which it is sucked up]

sherbet (dab) n. [1990s+] a taxi-cab. [rhy. sl.]

sherbet dip n. [20C+] a tip. [rhy. sl.]

sherbet(t)y *adj.* [late 19C] drunk (cf. ALED UP *adj.*). [SHERBET n. (1)]

sheriff *n.* [1980s+] (*Aus. prison*) an informer.

sheriff's ball *n.* [late 18C–mid-19C] a hanging.

sheriff's basket *n.* (*also* sheriff's tub) [early–mid-17C] a basket or tub placed outside a prison to receive charitable gifts for the prisoners.

sheriff's bracelets *n.* [late 18C–early 19C] handcuffs. [SE *bracelets*/BRACELETS n.]

sheriff's hotel *n.* [late 18C–early 19C] a prison (cf. BOARDING HOUSE n.). [SE *sheriff* + *hotel*/HOTEL n. (2)]

sheriff's journeyman *n.* [early 19C] the hangman.

sheriff's picture frame *n.* [late 18C–mid-19C] the gallows or pillory.

sheriff's posts *n.* [late 16C] 2 painted posts, set up at the sheriff's door, to which proclamations are affixed.

sheriff's tub *n. see* SHERIFF'S BASKET n.

sherk *n. see* SHIRK n.

sherlock *n.*[1] [1940s] (*US Und.*) (*also* sherlocko) a policeman or detective (cf. DICK n.[6]). 2 [1980s+] (*US campus*) a friend. [for ety. *see* SHERLOCK HOLMES n.]

sherlock *n.*[2] *see* SHYLOCK n. (2).

Sherlock Holmes *n.* [1950s+] (*US Black*) the police. [proper name *Sherlock Holmes*, the private consulting detective invented by Sir Arthur Conan Doyle (1859–1930)]

sherm *n.* (*also* shermans, sherms) [1980s+] (*US Black/ drugs*) 1 phencyclidine; thus *shermed*, intoxicated (cf. ACE n.[4]). 2 embalming fluid, formaldehyde. [the smoking of *Sherman* cigarettes laced with phencyclidine; (2) note William Shaw, *Westsiders* (2000): 'It probably acquired the name sherm when users started dipping Sherman cigarettes in the fluid, choosing the brand because its cigarettes are more robustly constructed than most and don't fall apart when steeped in fluid']

sherman (tank) *n.* 1 [1940s+] an American. 2 [1990s+] masturbation. [rhy. sl.; (1) = YANK n. (1); (2) = WANK n.[1] (1)]

shermhead *n.* [1990s+] (*US drugs*) one who is addicted to marijuana cigarettes dipped in phencyclidine. [SHERM n. (1) + -HEAD sfx (3)]

sherms *n. see* SHERM n.

sherm stick *n.* [1980s+] (*US Black/drugs*) a cigarette composed of marijuana laced with phencyclidine. [SHERM n. (1) + STICK n.[9] (3)]

sherry *n.*[1] [mid-19C] a *sheriff*. [abbr.]

sherry *n.*[2] [late 19C] cheap beer, sold at 4 pence a quart (2 pints/ 1 litre).

sherry (off) *v.* [late 18C–1900s] to run away, to leave. [? SE *sheer off*, to change one's course, to turn]

sherry one's ribs *v.* [late 19C–1900s] (*US*) to leave in a hurry. [ext. of SHERRY (OFF) v.]

she-she *n.* [1950s+] (*US*) a young woman. [Oriental Pidgin English, but note date of SHE-SHE TALK n.]

she-she talk *n.* [mid-19C–1920s] (*US Black*) women's talk.

she-spanker *n.* [late 19C] an exceptional woman. [SE *she* + SPANKER n.[2] (1)]

she's right *phr.* (*also* she'll be right) [1940s+] (*Aus.*) a phr. used to reject offers of assistance, don't worry, don't fuss, everything will be fine in the end.

she's sweet *phr.* [1940s+] (*Aus.*) everything is satisfactory. [SWEET adj.[1] (1)]

shevvle *n.* [late 19C] cat's meat. [Fr. *cheval*, horse]

she-wolf *n.* [1940s] a woman who actively pursues men (or women) for sex. [SE *she* + WOLF n.[1] (1)]

she wouldn't know if someone was up her *phr.* [1910s+] (*Aus.*) a phr. used of a very stupid young woman (cf. CAN'T SEE THROUGH A LADDER *phr.*). [SE *up*/UP v.[3] (1)]

sheygets *n. see* SHAYGETS n.

shice *n.*[1] (*also* shise) 1 [mid–late 19C] counterfeit coins. 2 [mid-19C–1930s] anything worthless; a wash-out. [SHICE adj.]

shice *n.*[2] *see* SHYSTER n.[1] (1).

shice *adj.* (*also* shise) 1 [mid-19C] out of funds, impoverished. 2 [mid–late 19C] of money, counterfeit. 3 [mid-19C+] (*also* shyse) useless, worthless. [SHICER n.]

shice *v.* [mid-19C+] to defraud, to cheat, to betray, to abandon. [SHICER n.]

shicer *n.* (*also* schicer, shiser, shyster) 1 [mid-19C] one who has no money, i.e. lit. 'worthless'. 2 [mid-19C] (*UK Und.*) a prostitute. 3 [mid-19C+] a worthless, idle person, a general term of abuse. 4 [mid-19C+] nothing, something worthless. 5 [mid-19C+] counterfeit money. 6 [mid-19C+] (*Aus.*) a worthless or worked-out mine. 7 [late 19C+] a cheat, one who does not pay their debts. 8 [20C+] (*Aus.*) a criminal. 9 [1900s–20s] (*UK Und.*) a dishonest racecourse bookmaker. [? fig. use of Ger. *Scheisse*, shit or SHYSTER n.[1]]

shicery *adj. see* SHICKERY adj.[2].

shicker *n.* (*also* shick, shicka) [20C+] (*mainly Aus./N.Z.*) 1 alcohol; a drink; thus ON THE SHICKER *phr.*; *shicker saloon*, a public house. 2 (*also* shikker) a drunkard. 3 a drunken spree. [SHICKER adj.]

shicker *adj.* (*also* shick, shicked, shiker, shikka, shikker, shikkor, shikkur) [late 19C+] (*mainly Aus./N.Z.*) drunk; thus *on the shicker*, drinking heavily (cf. SHICKERED (UP) adj.). [synon. Yid.; ult. Heb. *shikor*, drunk]

shicker *v.* [20C+] (*Aus./N.Z.*) to drink, usu. to drunkenness; thus *shickering*, drinking; *shicker-up*, a drinking bout. [synon. Yid.; ult. Heb. *shikor*, drunk]

shicker! *excl.* [1910s–40s] (*Aus./N.Z.*) a mild oath, e.g. *shicker me grandmother!* [? euph. for SHIT! excl.]

shickered (up) *adj.* (*also* shikkered (up)) 1 [late 19C+] (*mainly Aus./N.Z.*) drunk. 2 [1960s] out of funds, impoverished. [SHICKER n. (1); (2) is prob. a nonce-use]

shickerhood *n.* [1920s] (*Aus./N.Z.*) drunkenness. [SHICKER n. (1)]

shickery *adj.*[1] [mid-19C–1900s] drunk. [SHICKER n. (1)]

shickery *adj.*[2] (*also* shicery) [mid–late 19C] 1 bad, fake. 2 shabby, useless. [SHICE adj.; but note dial. *shiggyry*, shaky]

shickseh *n. see* SHIKSA n.

shickster *n.*[1] [mid-19C] a promiscuous woman, 'a "gay" lady' (Hotten, 1864). [? SHIKSA n. (1)]

shickster *n.*[2] *see* SHAKESTER n. (3).

shickster-crabs *n.* [mid-19C] (*UK tramp*) women's shoes. [SHAKESTER n. (3) + CRABS n.[2] (1)]

shield *n.* [1910s+] (*US*) 1 the badge as a symbol of being a policeman. 2 by metonymy, a policeman or prison guard (cf. BADGE n.[2]). [the wearer's shield-shaped badge of office]

shiesty *adj. see* SHEISTY adj.

shieve *n. see* SHIV n.

shiever *n.* [1920s] (*US Und.*) a traitor. [? CHIV n.[1] (1); thus 'backstabber']

shif *n.*[1] [mid-19C] fish. [backsl.]

shif *n.*[2] *see* CHIV n.[3].

shife *adj.* [1990s+] pretending to be more experienced than one actually is. [? SHIF-MAN n.]

shif-man *n.* [1950s] (*W.I.*) 1 an effeminate man. 2 a ne'er-do-well, a lazy idler. [? (1) SE *shift*, the woman's undergarment; ? (2) SE *shiftless*, lazy]

shift *v.*[1] 1 [mid-17C+] to have sexual intercourse. 2 [1970s] to deep kiss. 3 [1980s+] (*Irish*) to pursue women. [SE *shift*, i.e. the element of movement basic to many terms for intercourse]

shift *v.*[2] 1 [late 19C] to kill, to murder. 2 [late 19C+] to consume, esp. to eat or drink a large amount. 3 [20C+] (*orig. Aus.*) to move fast, to run. 4 [1900s] (*Aus.*) in fig. use, to die. [fig. or ext. uses of SE *shift*, to move; (1)/(2) note similar relation in PUT AWAY v.[1] (1) and PUT AWAY v.[3]]

shifted _adj._ [1990s+] (_UK Black_) arrested. [SE _shift_ but note SHAFTED adj.]

shifter _n._[1] **1** [mid-16C–17C; 1920s] (_UK Und._) a trickster, a confidence man. **2** [early 19C] (_UK Und._) a warning from one thief to another. **3** [1920s+] (_US Und._) a receiver of stolen goods. [SE _shift_, to employ underhand methods, to deceive, also to live by one's wits; note the nickname of the resourceful but impoverished _Sporting Times_ journalist William Farn Goldberg, 'The Shifter']

shifter _n._[2] [late 19C] (_SHIFT_ v.[2] (2))

shifting cove _n._ [early 19C] (_UK Und._) a confidence trickster. [SHIFTER n.[1] (1) + COVE n. (1)]

shift-monger _n._ [late 19C] a young man about town. [SE _shift_, a large, highly starched shirt-front, sported as part of such a person's evening dress + sfx -_monger_]

shift one's ass _v._ _see_ MOVE ONE'S ASS v.

shift one's bob _v._ [mid-18C–early 19C] to leave, to run off. [? naut. _bobstay_, a rope that keeps the bowsprit steady]

shift-round _n._ [1940s+] movement, a changing of one's place.

shift service _n._ _see_ SHIFT WORK n.

shift someone's ears _v._ [late 19C] (_Aus._) to knock someone down.

shift someone's jaw _v._ [late 19C] to assault.

shift the weight _v._ [20C+] to place the blame on someone else.

shift work _n._ (_also_ **shift service**) [19C] sexual intercourse. [play on SE _shift_, a female undergarment]

shifty _adj._ [2000s] (_US Black_) calm, cool, unruffled. [SE _shifty_, 'full of shifts or expedients; well able to shift for oneself'; this 16C–19C def. has been superseded in SE by the negative 'fond of indirect or dishonest methods; addicted to evasion or artifice; not straightforward, not to be depended on' (_OED_)]

shigs _n._ [mid-19C] money, esp. shillings. [? abbr.]

shik... _see also under_ SHICK...

shiksa _n._ (_also_ **schicksie, schikse(h), shickseh, shiksa, shikse(l)**) **1** [mid-19C+] (_Jewish_) a gentile woman. **2** [late 19C+] a non-Jewish servant-girl. [Yid. _shikse_, a gentile female; ult. Heb. _sheques_, a blemish; while _goy_, a gentile man, or gentiles in general, is a relatively neutral term, _shicksa_, strictly the fem. of SHAYGETS n. (1), always carries pej. overtones]

shill _n._[1] **1** [mid-19C] (_also_ **shillaluh**) the penis. **2** [late 19C+] (_US_) a police officer's truncheon. [abbr. Irish _shillelagh_, cudgel + links of the Irish and the police]

shill _n._[2] **1** [late 19C+] (_also_ **shillaber, shiller, shilliber, shilliver**) any form of criminal who poses as a member of the public to lure victims, usu. into confidence tricks. **2** [1910s] (_US Und._) an apprentice criminal. **3** [1930s+] (_gambling_) a house player in a casino. **4** [1930s+] used fig. for anyone who advocates something enthusiastically. **5** [1940s+] a member of a 3-card trick team who appears to be another innocent gambler and who lures players into the game. **6** [1980s] a confidence trick. **7** [1990s+] a spokesperson – the implication is of mendacity – for an institution. [abbr. _shillaber_, one who publicizes a circus, carnival etc]

shill _v._ [1910s+] (_orig. US_) to act as a frontman, either in a confidence trick, a casino, where one is a house player, or in ext. senses. [SHILL n.[2] (1)]

shilling dreadful _n._ _see_ SHILLING SHOCKER n.

shilling in (and the winner shouts) _n._ [late 19C–1900s] (_Aus./N.Z._) a bar-room dice gambling game in which everyone put a shilling (5p) in a kitty and the winner paid for the round (and poss. made a small profit). [var. on BOB IN n. (2)]

shillings _n._ [2000s] money.

shillings and pence _n._ [20C+] sense. [rhy. sl.]

shilling shocker _n._ (_also_ **shilling dreadful, shocker**) [late 19C–1920s] a short sensational novel, published at a shilling (5p).

shilling tabernacle _n._ [late 19C] a Baptist or Methodist tea-meeting, where refreshment was available at a shilling (5p) a head.

shilliver _n._ _see_ SHILL n.[2] (1).

shilly-shally _n._ [late 18C–mid-19C] **1** hesitation, vacillation. **2** one who hesitates, an irresolute, undecided person. [SE after 1850; orig. _stand shill I, shall I_; f. _shall I this? shall I that?_]

shilly-shally _v._ (_also_ **shilly-shamble**) [late 18C–mid-19C] to vacillate. [SHILLY-SHALLY n. (1); SE after 1850]

shim _n._[1] [1950s] (_US_) a person who does not appreciate rock and roll. [ety. unknown ? SE _shimmy_]

shim _n._[2] [1960s+] a piece of plastic used to open a door. [SE _shim_, a sliver of metal, used to fill the space between parts of machinery that are subject to wear]

shim _n._[3] **1** [1970s+] a male homosexual (cf. BOY-GIRL n.[1]). **2** [1970s+] (_US Black_) a lesbian; a masculine-looking female. **3** [1990s+] a transsexual. [SE _she_ + _him_]

shim _v._ [1970s] (_US_) to open a door or lock with a piece of plastic. [SHIM n.[2]]

shimmy _n._[1] (_also_ **shemmy**) **1** [mid-19C+] a woman's undergarment, essentially synon. with a petticoat. **2** [1950s–70s] a man's shirt. [abbr. SE _chemise_, a shift or smock; the _OED_ suggests that this 'vulgar corruption' was the result of people assuming _chemise_ was a pl.]

shimmy _n._[2] (_also_ **chimmy**) [1920s+] the gambling game of _chemin de fer_. [abbr.]

shimmy _n._[3] [1940s] (_US_) jello. [it 'shimmies' or wobbles]

shimozzle _n._ _see_ SHEMOZZLE n.

shim-sham _n._ [1970s+] (_US campus_) feelings of unease or nervousness. [? JIM-JAMS n.[1] (3)]

shim sham _adj._ [18C] (_UK Und._) second-rate, fake. [redup. SE _sham_]

shin _n._[1] [late 19C] (_US campus_) velocity. [SHIN v.[2] (1)]

shin _n._[2] [1930s+] (_US prison_) any contraband gun or knife. [? SHIV n. (1)]

shin _v._[1] [mid–late 19C] (_US_) to borrow money. [for ety. _see_ BREAK SHINS v.]

shin _v._[2] [mid–late 19C] (_US_) **1** to pay a social visit. **2** to walk off.

shinanigan/shinan(n)ickin _n._ _see_ SHENANIGAN n.

shin battle _n._ [1950s–60s] (_gang_) a fake, practice battle. [? one kicks only shins; weapons are not used]

shindig _n._ [mid-19C+] an altercation, a violent quarrel, a tremendous fuss. [SE _shindig_, a noisy party or festivity + SHINDY n.]

shindy _n._ (_also_ **shinty**) [mid-19C] a noise, a disturbance, a commotion; thus _cut shindies, kick up a shindy_, to create a disturbance; _shindying_, acting boisterously. [naut. jargon _shindy_, a form of dance among sailors; ? ult. SE _shinty_, a game, mainly played in Ireland, that resembles a rougher form of hockey]

shindykit _n._ (_also_ **swindlecat**) [1900s–10s] (_Aus._) a business consortium. [SE _syndicate_ + SHINDY n./SE _swindle_]

shine _n._[1] [mid–late 19C] money (cf. BRASS n.[1]). [? SHINERS n.[1] (1)]

shine _n._[2] **1** [mid–late 19C] a noise, a commotion. **2** [late 19C–1910s] (_US_) a fool. **3** [1900s] a noisy person; a show-off.

shine _n._[3] [late 19C] (_US_) a smile. [? one's glinting teeth]

shine _n._[4] (_US_) **1** [late 19C+] (_also_ **chinee, shiner**) a derog. term for a Black person (cf. BRILLOHEAD n.). **2** [1920s+] as used by a Black person, thus not derog. [the reflection of a blue-Black skin. As used in W.I. the term refers to someone with a very dark, smooth complexion and has no derog. connotations; note synon. RMC Duntroon (Aus.) _shoeshine_]

shine _n._[5] [1900s] (_US_) a fake diamond.

shine _n._[6] **1** [1920s+] (_US_) illicitly distilled whisky. **2** [2000s] (_US prison_) homemade prison alcohol. [abbr. MOONSHINE n. (2)]

shine _n._[7] _see_ SHINER n.[4].

shine _adj._[1] [20C+] (_W.I./US_) Black or pertaining to Black culture. [SHINE n.[4] (1)]

shine _adj._[2] (_also_ **shyin'**) (_Aus./N.Z./US_) **1** [late 19C+] of objects, excellent, first-rate. **2** [1940s+] of people, likeable.

shine _adj._[3] [1900s] second-rate, crafty.

shine _v._[1] [mid-19C] to raise money, to display money. [SHINE n.[1]]

shine v.[2] (US campus) **1** [late 19C+] to play truant, to skip classes. **2** [1970s] to get rid of. **3** [1970s] to abandon, to fail. [ety. unknown]

shine v.[3] [1960s+] (US Black) to fool, to delude.

shine v.[4] see SHINE UP TO v.

shine! excl. [1980s+] (US campus) impossible! absolutely not! on no account! [euph. SHIT! excl.]

shine box n. [1940s–50s] (US) a nightclub featuring entertainment by Black jazz musicians; it may also be patronized by a primarily Black clientele. [SHINE adj.[1] + BOX n.[3] (3)]

shined adj. [1920s] (US) drunk. [SHINE n.[6] (1)]

shine-eye gal n. [1970s+] (W.I./UK Black) a materialistic young woman.

shine it on v. see SHINE SOMEONE ON v.

shine joint n. [1940s–50s] (US) **1** an establishment selling illicit liquor. **2** a nightclub patronized by a primarily Black clientele. [(1) SHINE n.[6] (1); (2) SHINE adj.[1] + JOINT n.[4] (3)]

shine like a diamond in a goat's ass v. (also **shine like a dime in a goat's ass**) [1980s+] (US) to shine brightly.

shine like a shitten barn door v. [mid-18C–early 19C] to shine brightly. [SE shitten, filthied with excrement; the image of wet ordure glistening on a barn door]

shine-on adj. [1960s+] (US Black) dismissive?. [SHINE SOMEONE ON v.]

shine one's pole v. [1990s+] to masturbate (cf. BUFF THE BANANA v.). [POLE n.]

shiner n.[1] **1** [mid-17C–19C] a gold coin. **2** [19C+] (Und.) a mirror, esp. as used by card-sharps to spy on otherwise hidden hands. **3** [mid-19C–1920s] a silver dollar. **4** [late 19C–1900s] a silk hat. **5** [late 19C–1930s] a diamond, or other jewel; also in pl. **6** [20C+] a black eye. **7** [1910s] (Aus.) an attractive person. **8** [1930s] (US tramp) a 10-cent piece.

shiner n.[2] **1** [19C+] a clever person. **2** [1930s+] (Aus.) one who wants the limelight, but is unwilling to work towards gaining it.

shiner n.[3] [1950s+] a window-cleaner. [their job]

shiner n.[4] (also **shine, shiners**) [1990s+] (W.I./UK Black) fellatio (cf. CLEAN SOMEONE'S PIPE v.). [spittle 'shines' the head of the penis; note SHINE UP v.]

shiner n.[5] see SHINE n.[4] (1).

shiners n.[1] (also **shinery**) **1** [early 18C–19C] money, esp. sovereigns, guineas (cf. BRASS n.[1]). **2** [1990s+] (W.I.) sparkly fabrics. [the shininess of coins and the cloth]

shiners n.[2] see SHINER n.[4].

shines n. **1** [mid-19C] (orig. US) tricks. **2** [late 19C] sexual intercourse. [SE shine, a brilliant display]

shine someone on v. (also **put someone on (the) shine, shine it on**) [1960s+] (US Black) to ignore. [euph. SHIT v.[1] (1)]

Shinetown n. [1940s] (US) a derog. name for any predominantly Black area of a town or city. [SHINE n.[4] + SE town]

shine up v. [2000s] (US Black) to fellate (cf. CLEAN SOMEONE'S PIPE v.).

shine up to v. (also **shine**) [mid-19C+] (US) to flatter someone, to curry favour, to court. [? to shine a fig. light on the object of one's admiration]

shiney see under SHINY.

shingle n. [1950s] (US) a lawyer. [metonymy]

shingle short, a phr. (also **one shingle short**) **1** [mid-19C+] (Aus.) eccentric, crazy; thus shingle short, an eccentric. **2** [1910s] in fig. use, deficient, lacking in something physical. [var. on NOT ALL THERE phr.]

shingle-splitting n. [mid-late 19C] (Aus.) escaping one's creditors by vanishing into the countryside. [SAusE shingle-splitter, a builder of houses, esp. in the outback]

Shinkin (ap Morgan) n. (also **Shon Ap Morgan, Shone...**) [17C–early 18C] a generic nickname for any Welshman. [a stereotypical Welsh name, lit. 'Jenkins/Jones son of Morgan']

Shinner n. [1920s+] a member of the Irish nationalist movement Sinn Féin. [pron. of Sinn as 'shin']

shinner n. [mid-19C] (US) a merchant who borrows money from his peers in order to meet a note drawn on a bank. [? SHINPLASTER n. (1)]

shinnies n. [late 19C] (US) money (cf. BRASS n.[1]). [var. SHINERS n.[1] (1)]

shinny n. [1920s+] (US Black) illegally distilled alcohol. [SHINE n.[6] (1)]

shino n. [late 18C] a guinea (cf. BRASS n.[1]). [SE shine/SHINE n.[1] + RHINO n.[1]]

shin off v. [late 19C+] (Aus./US) to run away, to abscond. [SHIN v.[2] (2)]

shinola n. [1980s] (US) nothing. [NOT KNOW SHIT FROM SHINOLA v.]

shin out v. [mid-late 19C] to pay up (one's share, one's debts). [ext. of SHIN v.[1]]

shinplaster n. **1** [early 19C+] (US) a banknote of low denomination and poss. lacking proper security; thus as adj., worthless (cf. BANK-RAG n.). **2** [20C+] (Aus.) a promissory note. [SE shinplaster, a square piece of paper saturated with vinegar etc, used as a plaster for sore legs. The implication is that the 'folk remedy' has no real, or certainly long-term efficacy]

shinrapper n. [19C] (UK prison/Und.) the prison treadmill. [its knocking against the shins of the 'walker'; note SE shin-rapper, one who disables horses by striking the splint-bone]

shinscraper n. [mid-late 19C] (UK prison/Und.) the treadmill. [for ety. see prev.]

shin stage n. [18C] walking, travelling on foot. [SE shin + stage-coach]

shinty n. see SHINDY n.

shiny n. (also **shiney**) [late 19C–1930s] (US) a Black person. [SHINE n.[4] (1)]

shiny, the n. (also **the shiney**) [mid-late 19C] money (cf. BRASS n.[1]). [glittering coins]

shiny adj. **1** [late 19C] (also **shiney**) smart, successful. **2** [late 19C–1900s] (US) tipsy. **3** [1990s+] happy.

shiny and bright phr. [20C+] all right. [rhy. sl.]

shiny Bob n. [1920s+] one who has a very high opinion of themselves. [SE shiny + BOB n.[1]]

shiny-bum n. (also **shiny-arse/-seat**) [1940s+] (orig. Aus.) one who has a desk job; an office worker; thus adj. shiny-arsed. [SE shiny + BUM n.[1] (1)/ARSE n.[1] (1)/SE seat; one's bottom polishes the seat]

shiny-bum v. [1940s] (Aus.) to hold down a desk job. [SHINY-BUM n.]

shiny button n. see BUTTON n.[3] (3).

shiny-seat n. see SHINY-BUM n.

shiny ten n. [20C+] (bingo) the number 10 (cf. ALDERSHOT LADIES n.). [? late 19C, 'The Shiny Tenth': the 10th Royal Hussars]

ship n.[1] [1910s–60s] (US) an aeroplane.

ship n.[2] [1950s] (US) a scholarship. [abbr.]

ship v. [1930s+] (US Und.) to move or be moved from one prison to another.

ship in full sail n. [mid-19C; 1930s+] a pot of ale. [rhy. sl.]

ship-moll n. (also **shippie**) [1970s+] (N.Z.) a prostitute who works on docked ships; a descendant of the 19C Maori ship-girl. [SE ship + MOLL n.[1] (2)]

ship out v. [1930s+] (orig. milit.) **1** to leave, to depart; to release from prison. **2** in fig. use, to die.

shippy n. [mid-19C] (US) a shipmate; also as a term of address. [abbr. + sfx -y]

ship under sail n. [1930s] a story used for begging or for a confidence trick. [rhy. sl. = TALE n.[1] (1)]

shipwreck n.[1] [mid-19C] (US campus) an absolute failure.

shipwreck n.[2] [late 19C–1950s] (US) scrambled eggs; also as v., to scramble eggs.

ship-wrecked adj. [late 19C–1900s] drunk.

shiralee n. [late 19C+] (Aus.) a bundle of blankets or personal belongings. [ety. unknown]

shirk *n.* (*also* **sherk**) **1** [mid-17C–18C] a cheating gamester. **2** [mid-17C–19C] a sponger, a parasite. [SHARK n.¹ (1)/SHARK n.¹ (2); but note 17C SE *shirk*, to practise fraud or trickery, esp. instead of working, to sponge upon others]

shirk the roundbottom *v.* [early 19C] (*UK Und.*) to avoid a criminal charge, through bribery.

shirl *n.* [1970s] (*Aus.*) the female counterpart of the OCKER n. (2). [the proper name *Shirley*]

shirley *n.* [1980s] (*US*) a gay man. [*Shirley Temple* (*see* next)]

shirley temple *n.* [1980s] a young girl, poss. below the age of consent. [the US film actress *Shirley Temple* (b.1928) whose early career was as a child star]

shirt (and) collar *n.* [1930s] 5 shillings (25p) (cf. BEES (AND HONEY) n.). [rhy. sl. = DOLLAR n.¹ (1)]

shirt-fly *n.* [1990s+] a toady. [they are 'always up the gaffer's arse']

shirtlifter *n.* [1960s+] (*orig. Aus.*) a male homosexual; thus *shirt-lifterish*, pertaining to homosexuality (cf. CHEMISE-LIFTER n.). [i.e. prior to sodomy]

shirt rat *n.* (*also* **shirt-rabbit**) [1910s–20s] (*US*) a body louse, a bedbug.

shirt-stretcher *n.* [1990s+] the female breast; thus a woman with large breasts (cf. BOBBER n.²).

shirt-tail *adj.* [1920s+] (*US*) impoverished, deprived, mean. [one's shirt-tail is (fig.) hanging out]

shirt-tail relation *n.* [20C+] (*Aus./US*) a distant relation, a family friend.

shirty *adj.* [mid-19C+] irritable, angry, tetchy. [GET ONE'S SHIRT OUT v.]

shise *see also under* SHICE.

shise *n. see* SHYSTER n.¹ (1).

shishi *adj. see* CHI-CHI adj.

shista *n.* [1990s+] (*US Black*) a crooked lawyer. [SHYSTER n.¹]

shisty *adj. see* SHEISTY adj.

shit *n.*¹ **1** [mid-17C+] excrement. **2** [late 19C+] in fig. use, anything seen as unpleasant and disgusting. **3** [1920s+] an act of defecation. **4** [2000s] (*US prison*) HIV or AIDS. [OE *scite*/MLG *Schite*, dung + OE *scitte*, diarrhoea; (1) SE 14C–17C, henceforth sl.]

shit *n.*² **1** [late 19C+] a contemptible person; often in combs., e.g. *little shit, dumb shit.* **2** [1980s+] a person. **3** [1980s+] (*US*) a criminal. **4** [1990s+] a boastful, pretentious person, a 'bullshitter'. [fig. uses of SHIT n.¹ (1); (1) prior use SE since early 16C; Florio, *World of Wordes* (1598) includes a *shitten fellow*, which he defines as synon. with *goodman turd*]

shit *n.*³ **1** [1910s+] an unpleasant situation; usu. as phr. IN (THE) SHIT phr. **2** [1910s+] problems, difficulties; thus *hit the shit*, get into difficulties, or HIT SOME SHIT v. **3** [1910s+] (*also* donkeyshit) nothing; thus AIN'T SHIT phr.; *not mean shit*, not matter, not mean anything; *not worth shit*, not worth anything. **4** [1920s+] nonsense, rubbish, lies, prevarications; often in TALK SHIT v.². **5** [1920s+] any inferior, rubbishy, shoddy or pretentious thing. **6** [1930s+] any thing (material or otherwise), irrespective of its actual quality. **7** [1930s+] anything, something. **8** [1950s+] abuse, offensive and contemptuous treatment, e.g. *don't take any shit* (*see* TAKE SHIT v.); thus *put the shit on*, to criticize harshly. **9** [1960s+] as a general negative intensifier, e.g. *would I shit! did she shit!* **10** [1970s] influence. **11** [1980s+] (*Aus. prison*) prison food. **12** [1990s+] negative information. **13** [1990s+] (*US prison*) violence; a prison riot.

shit *n.*⁴ [1930s+] (*orig. US Black*) a general abstract term, a thing, a situation, an opinion or idea, the precise meaning varies as to the context, e.g. *I don't like this shit*, I don't like what's happening; *woofing some crazy shit*, talking nonsense etc.

shit *n.*⁵ (*drugs*) **1** [1940s+] heroin, occas. morphine (cf. AUNTIE EMMA n.; CACA n.). **2** [1950s+] cannabis. **3** [1950s+] (*also* shite) any form of drug. **4** [1970s+] cocaine; crack cocaine (cf. BASE n.). **5** [1980s+] (*Aus. prison*) tobacco. [the 'guilty' image of drug use]

shit *n.*⁶ [1960s+] in abstract use, one's possessions, one's actions, one's life; thus GET ONE'S SHIT TOGETHER v.

shit *n.*⁷ [1960s] (*US*) money (cf. CHAFF n.²).

shit *n.*⁸ [1980s+] (*US Und.*) any form of weapon.

shit, the *n.*¹ **1** [1920s] (*US*) something bad. **2** [1960s+] (*orig. US Black*) of things or people, the best, the ideal, the ultimate; on bad = good model.

shit, the *n.*² [1920s+] the essence, the 'daylights'; thus BEAT THE SHIT(E) OUT OF v.

shit, the *n.*³ [1960s+] (*orig. US*) a general intensifier, e.g. *who the shit are you? let's get the shit out of here.* [note synon. uses of the stronger FUCK n.¹ (1) and the milder HELL, THE phr.²]

shit, the *n.*⁴ [1980s+] (*orig. US campus*) an important person (in their own opinion).

shit *adj.* **1** [1920s+] (*orig. US*) applied to any thing or person considered bad, obnoxious, unpleasant, inferior, worthless, e.g. a *shit teacher.* **2** [1960s] untidy, unkempt. **3** [1980s+] on the bad = good model, excellent, first-rate. [SHIT n.¹ (1)]

shit *v.*¹ (*also* **shite**) **1** [mid-16C+] to defecate; also used fig. (cf. CACA v.). **2** [1960s+] (*Aus.*) to annoy. **3** [1970s] to stop. **4** [1990s+] (*also* shite out) to act in a cowardly manner. **5** [2000s] to frighten. [SHIT n.¹ (1)]

shit *v.*² [late 19C] to vomit. [abbr. SHIT THROUGH ONE'S TEETH v. (1)]

shit *v.*³ **1** [1930s+] (*also* shit around) to deceive, to bamboozle, to tell lies, to exaggerate. **2** [1940s] (*US*) (*also* shit around) to waste time. **3** [1960s+] to respond dramatically, with alarm, fear, anger, e.g. *he'll shit himself when he hears this!* **4** [1980s+] to do something badly, to fail, to make a mess. [abbr. BULLSHIT v.]

shit *v.*⁴ *see* SHIT OFF v. (2).

shit *adv.* [1910s+] extremely, very, completely.

shit! *excl.* [1920s+] **1** an excl. of fury, irritation, disappointment. **2** nonsense! rubbish! **3** a general excl. of emphasis, usu. implying approval. **4** an excl. of amazement, disbelief. [SHIT n.¹ (1)]

shit a brick *v.* (*also* **shit bricks/pickles**) **1** [late 19C+] to defecate after a lengthy period of constipation. **2** [1930s+] (*also* **sweat bricks**) to tremble with extreme fear. **3** [1960s+] to be furious. **4** [1960s+] to be absolutely delighted. [SHIT v.¹ (1) + fig. use of SE *brick/pickles*]

shit a brick! *excl.* [1950s+] (*orig. Aus.*) an excl. of extreme surprise, annoyance. [SHIT v.¹ (1)]

shit-all *n. see* FUCK-ALL n.

shit and wish *phr.* [20C+] (*US Black*) a general retort to anyone who says 'I wish…' [SHIT v.¹ (1); 18C phr. 'shit in one hand and wish in the other; see which fills up first'; Bridges in *Homer Travestie* (4 edn 1797) offers euph. 'spit' for shit]

shit around *v. see* SHIT v.³.

shit-ass *n.* (*also* **shit-arse, shite-arse**) [20C+] (*orig. US*) a contemptible person; also attrib. [SHIT n.¹ (1) + ARSE n.¹ (1)/ASS n. (2)]

shit-ass *adj.* (*also* **shit-arse, shit-assed**) [1960s+] (*orig. US*) very bad. [SHIT-ASS n.]

shitbag *n.* **1** [late 19C–1910s] the stomach. **2** [1920s+] (*orig. Aus.*) (*also* **shite-bag**) a general pej. term, whether of people or things?. **3** [1990s+] (*US Black/teen*) a colostomy bag. [SHIT n.¹ (1) + SE *bag*/-BAG sfx]

shitball *n.* [1960s+] (*US*) a general term of abuse. [SHIT n.¹ (1) + -BALL sfx]

shitbird *n.*¹ [1950s+] a narcotic drug abuser, a heroin addict. [SHIT n.⁵ (1) + BIRD n.² (1)]

shitbird *n.*² [1950s+] a general term of abuse. [SHIT n.¹ (1) + BIRD n.² (1)]

shitbird *adj.* [1990s+] (*US*) a general term of abuse. [SHITBIRD n.²]

shit-box *n.* [1980s+] (*US*) **1** the anus (cf. DIRT BOX n.). **2** a run-down vehicle. **3** anything bad or inferior. [SHIT n.¹ (1) + SE *box*/BOX n.¹ (4)]

shit-brained *adj.* [1970s] stupid, brainless (cf. AMOEBA-BRAINED adj.). [SHIT n.¹ (1)]

shit-breeched *adj.* [mid–17C] a general term of abuse. [SHIT n.¹ (1)]

shit bricks *v. see* SHIT A BRICK v.

shit bullets *v.* (*also* **piss bullets**) [1940s+] (*US*) to be terrified. [SHIT v.¹ (1)/PISS v.¹ (1) + SE *bullets*]

shitbum *n.* [1960s+] a general term of abuse. [SHIT n.¹ (1) + BUM n.¹ (1)]

shitbum *adj.* [2000s] (*US*) contemptible, unpleasant, worthless. [SHITBUM n.]

shitcan *n.*¹ [1970s] (*US prison*) the punishment cells. [SHIT n.¹ (1) + SE *can*]

shitcan *n.*² [1970s] (*US*) a near-derelict but just drivable second-hand car, or motorcycle, one step from the junkyard. [fig. use of SHIT n.¹ (1)]

shitcan *v.* [1950s+] (*Aus./US*) **1** to do someone a wrong. **2** to stop, to abandon a course of action, to toss away. [SHIT n.¹ (1) + SE *can*/as intensifier of CAN v.²; (1) note RMC Duntroon (Aus.) *shitcan*, to give a cadet a bad assessment]

shit-catchers *n.* (*also* **poop-catchers**) [1930s] (*Aus.*) knickerbockers. [SHIT n.¹ (1)/POOP n.² (2) + SE *catchers*]

shit-chute *n.* **1** [1960s+] the anus (cf. ALLEY WAY n.; DIRT BOX n.). **2** [2000s] a disgusting, filthy place. [SHIT n.¹ (1) + SE *chute*]

shit comes in piles *phr.* [1990s+] (*US Black*) problems always come at the same time, rather than one by one. [SHIT n.³ (2)]

shit creek *n.* [1950s+] an unpleasant, problematic situation. [fig use of SHIT n.¹ (1) + SE *creek*]

shit detail *n.* [1940s+] (*orig. milit.*) any unpleasant or dirty task. [SHIT adj. (1) + SE *detail*, a job]

shit dimes and quarters *v.* [2000s] (*US Black/drugs*) to excrete bags of drugs after swallowing them when facing a police search. [SHIT v.¹ (1) + DIME n.² (1) + QUARTER n.² (3)]

shit-disturber *n.* [20C+] a malicious gossip. [SHIT n.³ (1)]

shite *see also under* SHIT and its combs.

shite *n.* **1** [mid–17C+] excrement. **2** [late 18C+] an act of defecation. **3** [1920s+] rubbish, nonsense. **4** [1920s+] an unpleasant person. **5** [1920s+] the essence, 'the daylights'. **6** [1970s+] a derog. form of address. **7** [1990s+] something useless, second-rate, inferior etc. [var. on SHIT n.¹/SHIT n.²/SHIT n.³; before 1990s usu. found in dial. and often put into the mouths of those a writer is attempting to portray as Irish. For no discernible reason it is now often found in place of the more usu. *shit*]

shite *adj.* [1940s+] a general negative epithet, second-rate, unpleasant, distasteful etc. [var. on SHIT adj. (1)]

shite *v.* [early 17C+] to defecate (cf. CACA v.). [var. on SHIT v.¹ (1)]

shite! *excl.* [1920s+] a general excl. of annoyance. [SHITE n. (1)]

shit-eater *n.* [1940s+] a general term of abuse. [SHIT n.¹ (1)]

shit-eating *adj.* [1940s+] **1** a general term of disparagement. **2** sly, duplicitous. **3** toadying, subservient. [SHIT-EATER n.]

shit-eating grin *n.* (*also* **cat-eating-shit grin**, **shit-eating smile**) [1950s+] (*orig. US*) a smug, self-satisfied smile. [SHIT-EATING adj.]

shitehawk *n.* (*also* **shitehound**) [1940s+] a person of little worth. [SHITE n. (1) +SE *hawk*/HOUND sfx]

shite-poke *n.* **1** [late 18C+] (*Can.*) the bittern. **2** [1930s] a general term of abuse. [SHITE n. (1) + SE *poke*, a bag; (1) its habit of defecating when frightened; (2) synon. with SHITBAG n. (2)]

shite-poke *adj.* [1950s] (*US*) a general term of abuse. [SHITE-POKE n. (2)]

shite-rags *n.* [late 16C] 'an idle lazie fellow'. [SHITE v.]

shite shifter *n.* [1970s] (*Irish*) a term of abuse. [SHITE n. (1) + SE *shift*, to move, i.e. lit. 'a defecator']

shitface *n.*¹ [1950s+] an unpleasant, distasteful person; also directly as term of abuse?. [SHIT n.¹ (1) + SE *face*]

shitface *n.*² [1960s+] a drunken party. [backform. f. SHITFACED adj.² (1)]

shitface *adv.* (*also* **shitfaced**) [1960s+] extremely, very, completely, totally; usu. *shitface drunk*. [SHITFACED adj.² (1)]

shitfaced *adj.*¹ **1** [1930s+] (*orig. US*) stupid, ignorant. **2** [1970s+] a general intensifier, total, complete. [SHIT n.¹ (1) + SE *face*]

shitfaced *adj.*² (*also* **shitface**) (*orig. US*) **1** [1960s+] (*also* **shitty**) very drunk (cf. ARSEHOLED adj.). **2** [1970s+] under the influence of cannabis. [SHIT n.¹ (1) + SE *faced*]

shit-fight *n.* [1990s+] a bitterly contested struggle, e.g. a sporting encounter. [fig. use of SHIT n.¹ (1)]

shitfire *n.* [early 18C] a term of abuse applied to a hot-headed person. [SHIT v.¹ (1) + SE *fire*; lit. trans. of CACAFUEGO n.]

shitfire *adv.* [1960s] enthusiastically, energetically. [SHITFIRE! excl.]

shitfire! *excl.* [1940s+] a general excl. [SHITFIRE n.]

shitfit *n.* [1950s+] (*US*) an emotional outburst. [SHIT n.¹ (1) + SE *fit*]

shit-for-brains *n.* (*also* **dick-for-brains**, **shite-for-brains**) [1970s+] an all-purpose insult (cf. CRAPBRAIN n.). [SHIT n.¹ (1) + SE *brains*]

shit-for-brains *adj.* [1970s+] an all-purpose insult, the implication being of stupidity. [SHIT-FOR-BRAINS n.]

shit-for-nothing *adj.* (*also* **shit for the catfish**) [1980s] (*US*) third-rate, of very poor quality. [SHIT n.¹ (1)]

shit-fuck *v.* [1980s+] (*US gay*) to have anal intercourse (cf. ASK FOR THE RING v.). [SHIT n.¹ (1) + FUCK v.¹]

shitfuck! *excl.* [1970s+] a general excl. [SHIT-FUCK v.]

shit green *v.* [1960s+] (*US*) **1** to be extremely shocked. **2** to be enraged. **3** to be afraid. [SHIT v.¹ (1) + SE *green* as the image of disturbed stomach, thus emotions]

shit happens *phr.* [1980s+] an all-purpose statement of resignation in the face of life's vicissitudes, i.e. these things happen. [SHIT n.⁴]

shithead *n.* (*also* **shathead**, **shitehead**) **1** [1940s+] a derog. term of general abuse; thus adj., *shitheaded*. **2** [1990s+] (*US prison*) a prison guard. [SHIT n.¹ (1) + -HEAD sfx (1); note synon. RMC Duntroon (Aus.) *turdhead*]

shitheap *n.* [1960s+] **1** a dirty, unpleasant, disgusting place or object. **2** a contemptible person. [SHIT n.¹ (1) + SE *heap*]

shit-heel *n.* (*also* **shit-healer**, **shit-heeler**) **1** [1940s+] (*US*) a generally derog. term of abuse; also as adj. **2** [1990s+] (*UK/US Und.*) an informer. [SHIT n.¹ (1) + HEEL n. (2)]

shit hits the fan, the *phr.* [1940s+] the difficulties start to happen, esp. when such problems have been expected to occur sooner or later; usu. with *when*. Euph. alternatives include *the ca-ca hits the fan, the doo-doo..., the egg..., the omelette..., the excrement/solids hit(s) the air conditioning.* [SHIT n.³ (2)]

shithole *n.* (*also* **shitehole**) **1** [19C+] a lavatory. **2** [19C+] the anus (cf. A-HOLE n.; DIRT BOX n.). **3** [1960s+] a general term of hostility or abuse (cf. ARSE n.¹). **4** [1960s+] a disgusting place, an absolutely worthless place, esp. of a bar or venue. [SHIT n.¹ (1) + SE *hole*/HOLE n.¹ (1); (4) intensifier of HOLE n.² (2)]

shithole *adj.* [1970s+] usu. of places, terrible, very disgusting. [SHITHOLE n. (4)]

shithook *n.* [1960s+] (*orig. US campus*) **1** a foolish, clumsy person. **2** an unpleasant, aggressive individual. [SHIT n.¹ (1) + SE *hook*; note US milit. use *shithook*, CH-47 'Chinook' helicopter]

shit-hooks *n.* [1970s] (*US campus*) the hands. [SHIT n.¹ (1) + SE *hook*/HOOK n.¹ (1)]

shit-hot *adj.* [1910s+] **1** excellent, fashionable. **2** first-rate. [SHIT adv. + HOT adj.¹ (9)]

shit-hot *adv.* [1910s+] extremely, superlatively, especially. [SHIT-HOT adj. (2)]

shit hot! *excl.* [1980s] an excl. of approval. [SHIT-HOT adj.]

shithouse *n.* (*also* **shitehouse**) **1** [mid–17C; 1940s+] an unpleasant person. **2** [late 18C+] a lavatory (cf. BACKHOUSE n.). **3** [1940s+] any dirty, messy, disgusting place. **4** [1960s] a jail.

5 [1970s+] (*orig. Aus.*) a bad situation. **6** [1990s+] a coward. [SHIT n.[1] (1) + SE *house*]

shithouse *adj.* **1** [1930s+] unpleasant, disgusting, filthy, messy, second-rate. **2** [1990s+] of a person, ill, exhausted, run-down, highly nervous. [SHITHOUSE n. (3)]

shithouse full *n.* [20C+] (*US*) a very large number or amount. [SHITHOUSE n. (2) + SE *full*]

shit howdy! *excl.* [1970s] (*US*) a mild excl.

shit-hunter *n.* [late 19C–1900s] a sodomite. [SHIT n.[1] (1) + SE *hunter*]

shitily *adv. see* SHITTY *adv.*

shit in *v.* [1980s+] (*N.Z.*) to win easily.

shit in high cotton *v.* (*also* **shit in tall cotton**) [1930s+] (*US*) to live prosperously, to feel happy, to be important; euph. alternatives include *fly/live/travel in high cotton.* [SHIT v.[1] (1) + HIGH COTTON n.;]

shit in high grass *v.* [20C+] (*W.I.*) to aim for or reach a higher social class than that to which one was born. [SHIT v.[1] (1)]

shit in one's britches *v. see* SHIT ONE'S PANTS *v.*

shit in one's own backyard *v.* (*also* **shit in one's nest**) [1950s+] (*orig. US*) to do anything that jeopardizes one's life by its proximity to one's personal, social or professional life, e.g. to steal from one's own workplace, to conduct an affair with an in-law etc (cf. SHIT ON ONE'S OWN DOORSTEP v.). [SHIT v.[1] (1)]

shit in your teeth! *excl.* [18C–mid-19C] a general excl. of dismissal. [SHIT v.[1] (1)]

shit it *v.* (*also* **shite it**) [1950s+] to be terrified, to act in a cowardly manner. [abbr. SHIT A BRICK v.]

shit jacket *n.* [1970s] (*US Black*) an outside lavatory. [SHIT n.[1] (1) + SE *jacket*]

shitkick *v.* [1990s+] (*US*) to beat up, to kill. [KICK THE SHIT OUT OF v.]

shitkicker *n.* **1** [1940s+] a shoe or boot, esp. one used for everyday wear or work. **2** [1940s+] (*Aus.*) one who performs menial tasks; an unskilled labourer. **3** [1950s+] (*US*) (*also* **kicker**) a farmer or other country person (cf. BOGHOPPER n.). **4** [1960s] (*US*) a Western film. **5** [1960s] (*US*) a depressive person. **6** [1960s+] (*US*) (*also* **crap-kicker, shitkick**) a fool, a person of meagre intelligence. **7** [1960s+] something exceptional and powerful, i.e. that 'kicks shit'. **8** [2000s] (*US*) a thug. [SHIT n.[1] (1) + SE *kicker*; either f. kicking one's way through animal dung or f. KICK THE SHIT OUT OF v.]

shitkicker *adj.* (*also* **S.K.**) [1960s+] (*US*) pertaining to rural or stereotypically Western life. [SHITKICKER n. (3)]

shitkicking *adj.* [1960s+] (*US*) rough, crude, rural. [SHITKICKER n. (3)]

shitkicking music *n.* [1950s+] (*orig. US*) music that makes the hearer want to get up and dance, shout, sing, generally have a good, boisterous time. [SHITKICKING adj. + SE *music*]

shitlaw! *excl.* [1980s+] (*US campus*) a general excl. of annoyance. [? SHIT! excl. (1) + *Lord!*]

shitless *adj. see* SCARED SHITLESS *adj.*

shitless *adv.* [1910s+] to an extreme extent; usu. as SCARED SHITLESS adj.

shit list *n.* (*also* **s-list**) [1940s+] a list of people one considers distasteful, untrustworthy and otherwise unacceptable; thus *on my shit list*, very unpopular in my eye; similarly ext. to places. [SHIT n.[2] (1) + SE *list*]

shitload *n.* (*also* **shitloads, shitpot**) [1960s+] a great many, a large amount; usu as *a shitload of*; thus *by the shitload*, in large amounts. [SHIT n.[1] (1) + SE *load*]

shitlover *n.* [1960s] (*US*) a term of abuse. [SHIT n.[1] (1), i.e. a coprophile]

shitman *n.* **1** [1980s] (*Aus.*) one who gossips maliciously. **2** [1980s+] (*Aus. prison*) an unimportant person. **3** [1980s+] (*Aus. prison*) an assistant, one who is low(er) in the hierarchy. [SHIT n.[1] (1)/SHIT n.[2] (1)]

shit me! *excl.* [1990s+] an excl. of surprise, astonishment, resignation.

shit off *v.* **1** [20C+] to annoy, to irritate. **2** [1950s+] (*also* **shit**) to run away. [SHIT v.[1] (1)]

shit on *adj.* [1960s+] humiliated. [SHIT ON v. (1)]

shit on *v.* **1** [late 19C+] to abuse, to humiliate. **2** [1970s+] to deal with comprehensively. [fig. uses of SHIT v.[1] (1)]

shit on *phr.* [early 17C; 1930s+] a synon. with *the hell with.*

shit on a shingle *n.* (*also* **SOS**) [1930s+] (*mainly US milit.*) minced beef on toast; thus *shingles*, toast. [SHIT n.[1] (1) + SE *shingle*]

shit on a stick *n.* **1** [1950s+] (*US*) someone important. **2** [1980s] (*US Black*) a self-appointed tough guy, more words than action. [SHIT n.[1] (1) + SE *stick*; note RMC Duntroon (Aus.) *shit on a stick*, '(highly derogatory) an unpleasant, offensive person']

shit one's brains out *v.* [1940s] to be absolutely terrified. [SHIT v.[1] (1), i.e. fear-induced defecation]

shit oneself *v.* (*also* **crap oneself**) **1** [mid-19C+] to defecate in one's underclothes; thus *shit yourself!* a dismissive insult. **2** [1920s+] in fig. use, to be terrified. [SHIT v.[1] (1), i.e. the effect of terror on the sphincter muscle]

shit one's load *v.* [1990s+] to be absolutely terrified. [SHIT v.[1] (1) + LOAD n.[5] (1)]

shit one's pants *v.* (*also* **cack one's pants, shit in one's britches**) [1930s+] to be terrified or extremely excited. [SHIT v.[1] (1), i.e. the effect of terror on the sphincter muscle]

shit on from a great height *v.* [1920s+] (*orig. RAF*) to be extremely unpleasant, to make a great deal of trouble for someone else. [fig. use of SHIT v.[1] (1)]

shit on one's own doorstep *v.* (*also* **shit on one's own backdoor**) [late 19C+] used of one who foolishly has adulterous affairs within their circle of friends and acquaintances (cf. SHIT IN ONE'S OWN BACKYARD v.). [fig. use of SHIT v.[1] (1)]

shit on someone's parade *v. see* PISS ON SOMEONE'S PARADE v.

shit on the dining room table *v.* [2000s] (*US*) to become involved in a sexual relationship with a friend or employee. [var. on SHIT ON ONE'S OWN DOORSTEP v.]

shit on wheels *n.* **1** [1950s+] (*orig. US*) an important person or one who thinks that they are. **2** [1970s] an old run-down vehicle. [SHIT n.[2] (1)/SHIT n.[1] (1) + ON WHEELS phr.]

shit on you! *excl.* [1930s+] (*orig. US*) a general term of abuse. [SHIT v.[1] (1)]

shit or bust *v.* (*also* **shit or go blind**) [late 19C+] to make a last, desperate gamble; also as an excl. of exasperation. [SHIT v.[1] (1) + SE *burst/bust*]

shit or get off the pot *phr.* (*also* **crap or get off the hole, get off the pot (or shit), piss or get off the pot**) [1930s+] a phr. meaning either make a decision or let someone else do it; esp. as excl. [SHIT v.[1] (1)/CRAP v.[1]/PISS v.[1] + SE (chamber) *pot*]

shit out *v.* (*also* **shite out**) [1960s+] to behave as a coward, to run away from danger or confrontation. [SHIT v.[1] (1)]

shit out (of luck) *phr.* [1930s+] (*US*) at the end of one's good fortune, in serious trouble with no escape. [SHIT adv.]

shit-packer *n. see* TURD-PACKER n.

shit-pan *n.* [1940s] a general term of abuse. [SHIT n.[1] (1)]

shitpaper *n.* [1990s+] (*US*) lavatory paper. [SHIT n.[1] (1)]

shit pickles *v. see* SHIT A BRICK V.

shit pie *n.* [1990s+] nothing. [SHIT n.[3] (3)]

shit-pit *n.* [1990s+] **1** a lavatory. **2** any dirty and/or disgusting place. [SHIT n.[1] (1) + SE *pit*]

shitpot *n.[1]* [mid-19C+] **1** an unpleasant person. **2** an unpleasant place. **3** a chamberpot, a lavatory. [SHIT n.[1] (1) + SE *pot*]

shitpot *n.[2] see* SHITLOAD n.

shitpot *adj.* [1970s+] (*Aus.*) second-rate, inferior. [SHITPOT n.[1]]

shit-ringer *n.* [1940s+] (*Aus.*) a stockman. [SHIT n.[1] (1) + SAusE *ringer*, a stockman]

shits, the *n.* **1** [1930s+] (*also* **shits**) diarrhoea. **2** [1940s+] terror, fear. **3** [1960s+] (*Aus.*) a bad temper; thus GET THE SHITS (WITH) v.; GIVE SOMEONE THE SHITS v. **4** [1970s+] anything objectionable or unpleasant. [SHIT n.[1] (1)]

shitsack *n.* **1** [late 18C–early 19C] a Nonconformist. **2** [late 18C+] a general pej., an unpleasant person. [fig. use of SHIT n.[1] (1) + SE *sack*; (2) the term was euphemized in 19C as *shick-shack* (also *shig-shag*; *sic-sac*; *shuck-shack*; *shiff-shack* etc). Orig. a term of abuse for people who were found not wearing the customary oak-apple or sprig of oak before noon on Royal Oak Day (29 May, commemorating Charles II's hiding in an oak tree). Such people would most likely be Nonconformists or Puritans. That day became known in dial. as *Shick-shack Day* and the oak-apple or sprig of oak became known as *shick-shack*. Anyone wearing their oak sprig after noon became a *shick-shack*, a fool]

shit sandwich *n.* **1** [1960s+] a humbling experience; 'humble pie'. **2** [1980s] (*N.Z.*) homosexual anal intercourse. [SHIT n.[1] (1)]

shit-scared *adj.* [1950s+] terrified. [SCARE THE SHIT OUT OF v.]

shit-shark *n.* [mid–late 19C] a night-soil collector. [SHIT n.[1] (1) + SE *shark*]

shit-shoe *n.* (*also* **shit-shod**) [late 19C] one who has trodden in excrement. [SHIT n.[1] (1) + SE *shoe/shod*]

shit-skin *n.* [20C+] a derog. term for a Black person (cf. BLACKBELLY n.). [SHIT n.[1] (1) + SE *skin*, i.e. a derog. ref. to colour]

shitskin *adj.* [1960s] (*US Black*) a derog. meaning pertaining to Black people. [SHIT-SKIN n.]

shit-slinging *n. see* MUD-SLINGING n.

shit (someone) up *v.* [2000s] to disturb, to terrify. [terror makes one SHIT v.[1] (1)]

shit-stab *v.* [1990s+] to have anal intercourse, usu. in a male homosexual context (cf. ASK FOR THE RING v.). [backform. f. SHIT-STABBER n.]

shit-stabber *n.* [1960s+] (*orig. gay*) **1** the penis (cf. ARSE-OPENER n.). **2** a male homosexual (cf. BROWN ARTIST n.). [SHIT n.[1] (1) + SE *stabber*]

shitstain *n.* [1990s+] (*orig. US*) a fool (cf. DIPSHIT n.). [SHIT n.[1] (1) + SE *stain*]

shit-stick *n.* (*also* **shite-sticks**) **1** [late 16C] a contemptible person. **2** [1980s] (*US*) the penis, esp. when used for anal intercourse (cf. BAT n.[7]). **3** [1990s+] (*UK prison*) a billy-club. [SHIT n.[1] (1) + SE *stick*/STICK n.[1] (1)]

shit-stir *v.* [late 19C+] to gossip maliciously in the hope of causing trouble. [SHIT n.[1] (1)/SHIT n.[3] (1)]

shit-stirrer *n.* **1** [late 19C+] a malicious gossip. **2** [1930s+] a trouble-maker; a political activist. [SHIT-STIR v.]

shit stompers *n.* [1970s+] (*US campus*) **1** cowboy boots. **2** cowboys. [SHIT n.[1] (1) + STOMPERS n. (1)]

shit-stopper *n.* [1960s+] a prank, a funny scene, an escapade. [SHIT n.[1] (1) + SE *stopper*; the image of an event so dramatic or surprising that it suspends one's normal bodily processes]

shitstorm *n.* [1940s+] (*US*) a very confused or frightening situation. [SHIT n.[1] (1) + SE *storm*]

shit street *n.* [1960s+] a fig. bad place; esp. as *in shit street*, in disgrace; *up shit street*, in difficulties. [SHIT n.[3] (1)]

shit-sucking *adj.* [1990s+] (*US*) an abusive intensifier. [SHIT n.[1] (1)]

shitsure *adv.* [1950s+] (*US*) certainly, definitely. [SHIT adv. + SE *sure*]

shit-talker *n.* [1990s+] (*US Black*) one who talks nonsense. [TALK SHIT v.[2] (1)]

shitted *adj.* [1990s+] terrified. [SHIT A BRICK v.]

shitten *adj. see* SHITTY adj.[1].

shitten! *excl.* [17C; 1930s] a general excl. of derision. [SE *shitten*, fouled with excrement; thus disgusting]

shitten end of a brick *n. see* SHORT END (OF THE STICK) n.

shitten Saturday *n.* [mid-19C] (*mainly school/provincial*) Easter Saturday. [mispron. of SE *shut-in Saturday*, referring to the day on which Christ's body was enclosed in his tomb]

shitter *n.*[1] (*also* **shiter**) **1** [20C+] the anus (cf. DIRT BOX n.). **2** [1960s] in fig. use of (4), a disgusting place or situation. **3** [1960s–70s] (*US prison*) a punishment cell. **4** [1960s+] (*US*) a lavatory, a commode. **5** [1960s+] one who defecates in a public place. **6** [1970s] (*US gay*) in coprophiliac sex, one who defecates on their partner. **7** [1970s+] (*UK Und.*) a thief who likes to excrete inside the places he robs. [SHIT v.[1] (1)]

shitter *n.*[2] (*also* **shiter**) [1970s+] (*orig. US*) **1** a braggart, a boaster. **2** a term of abuse. [abbr. BULLSHITTER n. (1)]

shitters *n.* [1940s] (*Aus.*) cattle. [SHIT v.[1] (1), i.e. the state of the average cowyard]

shitters, the *n.* [late 19C+] diarrhoea. [SHIT v.[1] (1)]

shitters *adj.* (*also* **shiters**) [1990s+] terrified. [one wishes to SHIT v.[1] (1)/SHITE v. with terror]

shit through one's teeth *v.* **1** [late 18C+] to vomit. **2** [1970s+] (*also* **shit through one's mouth**) to lie blatantly. **3** [1980s] (*W.I.*) (*also* **shit through one's nose**) to suffer, to be humiliated. [SHIT v.[1] (1) + SE *teeth/mouth/nose*]

shit ticket *n.* [1990s+] (*US juv.*) a sheet of lavatory paper. [SHIT n.[1] (1)]

shitting *adj.* (*also* **shiteing**) [1930s+] **1** cowardly. **2** a general term of abuse.

shitty *n.* [1970s+] (*Aus./N.Z.*) a fit of temper. [SHITTY adj.[1] (7)]

shitty *adj.*[1] (*also* **shitey**) **1** [mid-16C–mid-18C; 1920s+] (*also* **shitten**) unpleasant, disgusting; mediocre, second-rate; thus *shittiness*, unpleasantness. **2** [mid-17C–mid-18C; 1920s+] (*also* **shitten**) covered in excrement; generally filthy. **3** [1920s+] (*US*) mean, malicious, nasty. **4** [1920s+] (*US*) tedious, futile. **5** [1920s+] (*US*) unwell, ill. **6** [1960s+] depressed, guilty. **7** [1960s+] (*Aus.*) bad-tempered. **8** [1970s] (*US*) dangerous. **9** [1970s] incompetent. [SHIT n.[1] (1)]

shitty *adj.*[2] *see* SHITFACED adj.[2] (1).

shitty *adv.* (*also* **shitily**) [1920s+] badly, unsatisfactorily. [SHITTY adj.[1] (1)]

shitty end of the stick *n. see* SHORT END (OF THE STICK) n.

shitty-livered *adj.* [1980s+] (*N.Z.*) bad-tempered. [SHITTY n.]

shit up *v.* [1990s+] to terrify. [i.e. to make someone SHIT v.[1] (1)]

Shitville *n.* [1970s] (*US*) a very out of the way, rural place. [fig. use of SHIT n.[1] (1) + -VILLE sfx[1]]

shitwagon *n.* [1970s+] (*US*) a second-rate, run-down automobile. [SHIT adj. (1)]

shitweasel *n.* [1990s+] a term of abuse, used of a person or an unpleasant thing.

shit where one eats *v.* [1980s+] (*orig. US*) to commit a crime in one's own neighbourhood; lit. and fig. (cf. SHIT ON THE DINING ROOM TABLE v.). [SHIT v.[1] (1)]

shitwork *n.* [1960s+] unpleasant, unwanted, prob. dirty occupations. [SHIT adj. (1) + SE *work*]

shiv *n.* (*also* **sheive, shieve, shive**) **1** [late 19C+] a knife; thus *shiv man*, one who uses a knife in crimes of violence. **2** [1910s+] (*US tramp*) a razor. **3** [1940s] (*US Und.*) a form of confidence trick that employs a knife. [CHIV n.[1] (1)]

shiv *v.* (*also* **shive (up)**, **shiv up**) [1930s+] (*US Und.*) to stab; also in fig. use. [SHIV n. (1)]

shivaree *see also under* SHIVOO.

shivaree *n.* **1** [1920s+] verbose official talk. **2** [1960s+] abuse. [SHIVOO n.; but more likely euph. for SHIT n.[3] (4)/SHIT n.[3] (8)]

shivaroo *see under* SHIVOO.

shive *see also under* SHIV.

shive *n.* [late 17C–19C] (*UK Und.*) a slice.

shive *v. see* SHUCK AND JIVE v. (1).

shiver and shake *n.* [1940s] a (slice of) cake. [rhy. sl.]

shivering James *n.* (*also* **shivering Jemmy/Jimmy**) [mid–late 19C] a beggar who parades in rags and tatters in the hope of attracting greater sympathy. [SE *shivering* + generic *James/Jemmy*]

shiver one's trotters at Bilby's ball *v. see* SHAKE ONE'S TROTTERS AT BEILBY'S BALL v.

shivers, the *n.* [late 19C] (*US Und.*) terror, induced by a fear of arrest.

shivers! *excl.* [1980s] (*N.Z.*) a euph. excl. for SHIT! excl.

Shivery Isles *n.* [1930s–50s] (*Aus.*) New Zealand. [var. on SHAKY ISLES n.; the frequency of earthquakes; ? a *Bulletin*-ism]

shivery-shakes, the *n. see* SHAKES, THE n.

shiving *n.* [1970s] a stabbing. [SHIV v.]

shivoo *n.* (*also* **cheveaux, chivoo, shavoo, sheave-o, shivaree, shivaroo, shivvoo**) [early 19C+] a party, a celebration; thus *ginger-beer shivoo*, a teetotal party. [Fr. *chez vous*, at your house]

shivoo *v.* (*also* **shivaree, shivaroo**) [mid-19C+] (*Aus.*) to entertain. [SHIVOO n.]

shiv up *v. see* SHIV v.

shivver *n.* [1950s] a knife-wielder, one who stabs. [SHIV v.]

shivvoo *n. see* SHIVOO n.

shiznit *n.* (*also* **shiz, shiznet, shiznits**) [1990s+] (*US Black/campus*) **1** a euph. for SHIT n.[1] (1). **2** a euph. for SHIT, THE n.[1] (2); the ultimate, the best. [ext. of SHIT n.[1] (1) + -IZ- ifx]

shizo *n. see* SCHIZO n.

shizoid *adj. see* SCHIZO adj.

shl... *see also under* SCHL...

shlap *n. see* SLAP n.[2].

shlemozzle *n. see* SHEMOZZLE n.

shlenter *n. see* SLANTER n.[1].

shm... *see also under* SCHM...

shm- *pfx* (*also* **schm-**) [1940s+] a facetious pfx, used to nullify the word (and thus the statement) to which it is appended. [cod-Yid.]

shmeez *v.* [1980s+] (*US drugs*) to smoke good cannabis. [Yid. *schmeiss*, to hit, thus cognate with HIT v.[3] (7)]

shmyes *v.* [2000s] to leave. [? Yid. *schmeis*, a bang, a wallop; thus fig. 'hit the road']

shn... *see also under* SCHN...

shnide *adj. see* SNIDE adj.

shock *n.* [late 19C–1930s] (*US*) a measure of cheap liquor. [phr. 'You get a shock, walk a block and fall in the gutter']

shock a broe *phr.* (*also* **shock a brew**) [1980s+] (*US campus*) an invitation to have a beer. [Hawaiian pidgin *shaka brah*, right on, brother; but note BREW n.[1] (3)]

shock-absorbers *n.* [1950s+] the female breasts.

shock and sting *adj.* [1990s+] (*W.I.*) excellent.

shocker *n.[1]* [late 19C+] an appalling person, thing or situation.

shocker *n.[2] see* SHILLING SHOCKER n.

shocker! *excl.* [1990s+] (*US campus*) an ironic excl. referring to something that is not remotely surprising.

shock house *n.* (*also* **shock joint**) [late 19C–1930s] (*US*) a tavern, catering mainly to Black people, in which customers would most likely be given some form of knockout drop in one's drink and then robbed. [SHOCK n. + SE *house*]

shocking *adj.* [mid-18C+] a general intensifier, terrible, utter.

shocking *adv.* (*also* **shockingly**) [mid-18C+] a general intensifier, usu. as *shocking bad*; thus *shocking bad hat*, a very unpleasant person.

shock joint *n. see* SHOCK HOUSE n.

shock-out *adj.* [1990s+] (*W.I.*) anything exceptionally eye-catching.

shocks for jocks *n.* [1960s+] (*US campus*) a course in introductory engineering. [SE *shocks* + JOCK n.[1] (3)]

shod all round *phr.* **1** [18C–19C] *au fait* with the niceties of married life. **2** [late 18C–1900s] a phr. used of a parson at a funeral who receives a hat-band, gloves and scarf. [SE *shod*, wearing shoes]

shoddy *adj.* [mid-late 19C] (*US*) used of those who either claim a degree of importance to which they have no actual right or of *nouveaux riches*, whose importance is not backed up by breeding or manners; thus *shoddydom*, the world of social climbers;

as a n., *shoddies, shoddyites, shoddy aristocracy, shoddy society, shoddy(o)cracy*. [SE *shoddy*, woollen yarn obtained by tearing to shreds refuse woollen rags, which, with the addition of some new wool, is made into a kind of cloth; thus, worthless material that is made to appear as if it boasts a higher quality. The sl. use was underlined after the US Civil War (1861–5), when fortunes were made by the sellers of shoddy, who then attempted to use their money to enter society]

shoddy-doo *n.* [1960s–70s] (*US Black*) any form of ritual hand-slapping that serves as a greeting or farewell. [? corruption of SE *how do you do*]

shoddy-dropper *n.* [1940s+] (*mainly Aus./N.Z.*) a hawker, a peddler. [SE *shoddy* (for ety. *see* SHODDY adj.) + DROPPER n.[3] (2)]

shoe *n.[1]* [late 19C] the debtors' ward in Newgate prison. [those incarcerated begged by letting down a shoe from the window]

shoe *n.[2]* [20C+] (*US Und.*) a private detective (cf. FLATFOOT n.[1]). [abbr. GUMSHOE n. (1)]

shoe *n.[3]* **1** [1910s–30s] a tyre. **2** [1940s+] (*Aus.*) a sanitary towel.

shoe *n.[4]* **1** [1950s+] (*orig. US Black*) a smartly dressed person, by ext. one who is smart, sophisticated. **2** [1960s] (*US Black*) a Black person. [orig. jazz use; the quality of the subject's footwear]

shoe *adj.* **1** [1950s] smart, fashionable. **2** [1960s] (*US Black*) racially Black. [SHOE n.[4]]

shoebox *n.* [1940s] a prison cell.

shoe-horn *v.* [17C] to cuckold. [? play on HORN n.[1] (1)]

shoe it *v.* [1970s] to walk.

shoelaces *n.* [20C+] (*S.Afr. Black*) chicken intestines, as used in cooking. [resemblance]

shoe-leather! *excl.* [mid-19C] (*UK Und.*) a warning cry uttered by a thief to his confederate on sighting the police. [i.e. get one's *shoe-leather* (shoes) moving]

shoemaker's pride *n.* [19C–1900s] creaking shoes or boots. [new leather shoes often creak, thus drawing attention to the maker's handiwork]

shoemaker's stocks *n.* [late 17C–early 19C] tight shoes; thus *in the shoemaker's stocks*, wearing tight shoes.

shoe one's mule *v.* [mid-17C–early 18C] to embezzle.

shoe-polish *n.* (*also* **floor-polish, furniture-polish**) [1900s] (*US*) whisky; thus *shoe-polish shop*, a saloon.

shoes and sox *n.* [20C+] venereal disease. [rhy. sl. = POX n.[1] (2)]

shoe the goose *v.* [early 17C] to be drunk. [? the impossibility of such a task, other than to a drink-sodden mind]

shoe the horse *v.* [1910s–20s] to cheat one's employer.

shoe thief *n. see* HEEL-THIEF n.

shoe with a hole in it *n.* [late 16C–early 17C] the vagina.

shoful *n.* (*also* **schoful, shofell, shofle, showful(l)**) **1** [mid-19C] a low tavern. **2** [mid–late 19C] counterfeit coins, sham jewellery. **3** [mid–late 19C] a humbug, an impostor. **4** [mid-19C–1910s] a cab other than that patented by Hansom. [Gk thence Yid. *schofel*, worthless stuff, rubbish; ult. Ger.-Jewish pron. of Heb. *shāphāl*, low; (4) may be a separate word; Hotten (1864) and Ware, however, define *showfull/shofel* as a 'Hansom cab']

shoful *adj.* (*also* **showful(l)**) [mid–late 19C] (*UK Und.*) low, inferior, second-rate. [SHOFUL n. (2)]

shofulman *n.* [mid–late 19C] one who passes counterfeit money. [SHOFUL n. (2) + sfx *-man*]

shoful-pitcher *n.* (*also* **schofel-pitcher, showful(l)-pitcher**) [mid–late 19C] a distributor of counterfeit money; thus *shoful-pitching*, passing counterfeit money. [SHOFUL n. (2) + PITCHER n.[3] (1)]

shoful-pullet *n.* [mid-19C] a spurious 'virgin' prostitute, whose maidenhead is miraculously renewed for each new client. [SHOFUL adj.+ PULLET n. (1)]

shog *v. see* SHAG v.[1] (1).

shoke *n.* [1930s] (*US*) a derog. term for a Black person (cf. ALLIGATOR BAIT n.[2]). [ety. unknown]

sholl v. [mid-19C–1900s] to crush someone's hat over their ears. [ety. unknown; link to SE *shell*, i.e. to turn the hat into a shell for the head]

sho-lo n. [2000s] (*US*) a MULLET n.² hairstyle. [*short* on top, *long* in the back]

shommus n. *see* SHAMUS n.

Shon Ap Morgan n. *see* SHINKIN (AP MORGAN) n.

Shone n. [late 17C–early 18C] a generic term for a Welshman. [supposedly 'Welsh' pron. of stereotypical name *Jones*]

shoneen n. [1910s+] (*orig. Irish*) a would-be gentleman who puts on superior airs; orig. an Irish person aping the English gentry. [Irish *seonin*, a person of foreign ways, a poor Protestant]

shong n. *see* SHANGHAI n.¹.

shonk n. (*also* **schonk, schonky**) **1** [1910s+] a derog. term for a Jew or foreigner (cf. BIGNOSE n.). **2** [1960s+] the nose. [? SHONNICKER n.; note RN *shonky*, a miser whose meanness is typified by their like of drinking but unwillingness to stand a round]

shonky adj. [1970s+] (*Aus./N.Z.*) unreliable, dishonest, 'crooked'; thus one who is engaged in irregular or illegal business activities. [SHONK n. (1)/SHONNICKER n. (2); note WW1 milit. *shanky*, thrifty, close-fisted]

shonnicker n. (*also* **shonnacker**) **1** [1910s] (*US Und.*) a novice criminal. **2** [1910s+] a derog. term for a Jew (cf. FAST-TALKING CHARLIE n.). [Yid. *shonnicker*, a small trader or peddler]

shont n. [late 19C–1910s] a foreigner. [? SHONK n. (1)]

sho' 'nuff adj. (*also* **sure 'nuff**) [20C+] (*US*) a general term of approval, genuine, qualified, responsible, trustworthy. [SHO' 'NUFF phr.]

sho' 'nuff v. [1970s] (*US Black*) to be in earnest, to do something seriously. [SHO' 'NUFF adj.]

sho' 'nuff adv. (*also* **sure 'nuff**) [late 19C+] (*US*) definitely, certainly, completely. [SHO' 'NUFF phr.]

sho' 'nuff phr. [late 19C+] (*orig. US Black*) yes indeed. [SE *sure enough*]

shoo! excl. *see* SHOOT! excl.² (1).

shoob v. [1950s+] (*W.I. Rasta*) to shove.

shoobie n. [1970s+] (*US*) a passenger on a day-trip excursion. [the *shoebox* in which they carry their lunch]

shoo-fly n. **1** [late 19C+] (*US Und.*) a plain-clothes police officer on observation duty. **2** [20C+] an undercover police officer who spies on his colleagues. **3** [1920s–50s] a drug used to deal with troublesome drinking club customers. [song lyric 'Shoo fly! Don't bother me']

shoo-fly! excl. [late 19C] an excl. of denial, disdain, get away! get out of here!

shoofti n. *see* SHUFTIE n.

shoo-in n. [1930s+] a dead certainty, usu. in political use. [SE *shoo-in*, of a racehorse, an easy winner]

shook adj. **1** [19C] robbed, lost by robbery. **2** [early 19C+] forgetful, esp. used of an ex-prisoner whose mental state has been affected by prison or transportation. **3** [mid-19C+] (*Irish*) drunk (cf. ADDLED adj.). **4** [late 19C+] (*US*) (*also* **shooked**) highly excited, disturbed, frightened, upset.

shook on adj. (*also* **shook, shook after**) [late 19C+] (*Aus./N.Z.*) infatuated with, obsessed with. [SE *shake*, quiver, tremble (in this case with passion)]

shook one n. [1990s+] a person who is scared, upset, emotionally unstable etc. [SHOOK adj. (4) + SE *one*]

shook up adj. [mid-16C; 20C+] upset, disturbed. [ext. of SHOOK adj. (4)]

shool n. [late 19C] a place of worship. [adapted by Londoners from Yid. *shool*, a synagogue]

shool v. (*also* **shoole, shule**) **1** [mid-18C] to impose upon someone. **2** [mid-18C–mid-19C] to go begging, to find what one can by chance. **3** [late 18C–early 19C] to skulk around. **4** [early 19C] to carry something as a 'front'. [SE *shoal*, to move as a shoal; thus

the meanderings of a shoal of fish or dial. *shool*, to go about begging]

shooler n. (*also* **shoolman, shuler**) [mid-19C–1930s] a beggar and scrounger, a tramp. [SHOOL v. (2)]

shoomer n. [1980s] a fan of acid house music. [London's *Shoom* club, which was at its most popular *c.*1988]

shoon n. [late 19C–1900s] a fool. [ety. unknown]

shoop v. [1990s+] (*US Black*) to have sexual intercourse. [? echoic]

shooper n. *see* SHUPER n.

shoosh n. [1940s] (*Aus.*) quiet, silence.

shoosh v. [1920s] to dismiss someone, to send away. [echoic]

shoo-shoo v. [1930s–40s] (*US Black*) to whisper; thus *shoo!* be quiet! [SE *ssh*, quiet, be quiet]

Shoot, the n. [late 19C–1900s] **1** Walworth Road station, London. **2** Walthamstow, London. [SE *rubbish-chute*, both areas were associated with the poor or with menial workers]

shoot n.¹ *see* SHOT n.³.

shoot n.² *see* SHOUT n.¹ (2).

shoot v.¹ **1** [17C+] to ejaculate; thus as n., an ejaculation (cf. FIRE v.¹). **2** [mid-17C+] of a man, to have sexual intercourse (cf. BANG v.¹). **3** [late 19C] to have a wet dream. **4** [late 19C+] to speak, to sing. **5** [2000s] (*US prison*) to have sex with an effeminate, younger male prisoner. [the equation of sex and violence]

shoot v.² [19C+] to move, to travel, to leave; usu. as *shoot along/down/for/over* etc (cf. SHOOT OFF v.¹).

shoot v.³ **1** [mid-19C–1910s] to (make a) bet. **2** [late 19C–1950s] to get rid of, to expend. **3** [1900s–70s] to consume. **4** [1920s+] to throw dice.

shoot v.⁴ [late 19C] (*Aus.*) to dismiss from a job. [pun on FIRE v.² (1)]

shoot v.⁵ **1** [late 19C+] (*also* **shoot to**) to send; to convey. **2** [1900s–20s] (*Aus./US*) to give, to pay for.

shoot v.⁶ **1** [20C+] to hurry someone along, to send someone quickly to a place. **2** [1900s–60s] to perform, to do. **3** [1910s–50s] to fetch, to bring, to send; as an imper. **4** [1990s+] to promote, to propel.

shoot v.⁷ [20C+] (*drugs*) **1** to inject a narcotic, usu. in comb. with the drug, e.g. *shoot smack/coke*, to inject heroin/cocaine. **2** to inject someone else with a narcotic.

shoot v.⁸ [1950s] to cheat someone.

shoot v.⁹ [1990s+] (*W.I.*) to be infected with an STD.

shoot v.¹⁰ *see* SHOOT (IT) v.

shoot! excl.¹ [20C+] (*orig. US*) go on! go ahead! get on with it! esp. as regards telling a story, delivering a piece of gossip etc. [SHOOT v.¹ (4)]

shoot! excl.² (*also* **shoots!**) [1910s+] **1** (*also* **shoo! shoot it!**) an excl. of annoyance or surprise. **2** (*also* **shoot me!**) a general excl. of intensification, affirmation. [euph. for SHIT! excl.]

shoot a bishop v. (*also* **shoot the bishop**) [late 19C+] to have a nocturnal emission, a 'wet dream'. [BISHOP n.³ (4)]

shoot a blank v. **1** [1950s–70s] (*US*) to fail, to have no luck. **2** [1970s+] (*US Black*) (*also* **shoot a dud, shoot blanks**) to attempt sophisticated conversation but to fail in so doing.

shoot a bug v. [1900s] (*US prison*) to feign insanity. [SHOOT v.⁶ (2) + BUG n.⁵ (4)]

shoot a butt v. [1910s–30s] (*US*) to extinguish a cigarette. [BUTT n.² (1)]

shoot a card v. [1900s–20s] to leave a visiting card.

shoot a cat v. (*also* **shoot the cat**) [late 18C–mid-19C] to vomit. [var. on WHIP THE CAT v.² (2)]

shoot a dog v. [1900s] (*US*) to defecate.

shoot a dud v. *see* SHOOT A BLANK v. (2).

shoot a good shot v. [1970s+] (*US Black*) to have a sophisticated verbal wit; to defeat someone in a verbal contest, e.g. DOZENS n.

shoot a line v. (*also* **run a line**) [late 19C+] to concoct a smooth verbal patter, esp. with the aim of seduction. [SHOOT v.¹ (4) + LINE n.¹ (3)]

shoot a lion v. [late 19C] to urinate (cf. FLOG THE LIZARD v.).

shoot a paper-bolt v. [1910s–20s] to circulate a false or dubious rumour.

shoot a pete v. [1920s] (US Und.) to beak into a safe using explosives. [SHOOT (IT) v. + PETE n.⁴ (1)]

shoot at v. [1950s–60s] to make (sexual) advances towards.

shoot balls v. [20C+] (W.I.) to talk nonsense. [BALLS n.² + pun]

shoot between wind and water v. (also **shoot betwixt wind and water**) 1 [late 17C] to infect with venereal disease. 2 [late 17C–1900s] of a man, to have sexual intercourse. [for ety. see SHOT BETWEEN WIND AND WATER phr.]

shoot blanks v.¹ 1 [1950s+] to ejaculate infertile semen; thus *blank shooter* (cf. FIRE v.¹). 2 [1960s+] of a man, to fail to achieve an erection, to be impotent. [SHOOT v.¹ (1)]

shoot blanks v.² see SHOOT A BLANK v. (2).

shoot con v. see SHOOT (THE) CON v.

shoot crap v. see SHOOT (THE) CRAP v.

shoot cuffs v. [1990s+] (US Black) to grab someone's legs and bring them down, as part of a fight. [SAmE *cuffs*, trouser turn-ups]

shoot down (in flames) v. 1 [1940s+] to reject an invitation to dance or go for a date. 2 [1940s+] to humiliate, to ridicule. 3 [1950s+] to reject a line of argument, to overrule an opinion. 4 [1960s+] to place at a disadvantage. 5 [1960s+] (US prison) to reject a parole application.

shoot-'em-up n. 1 [1930s+] (orig. US) a Hollywood Western film. 2 [1960s] (US) a Western book or short story. [the predominant activity]

shooter n.¹ 1 [mid-19C+] (UK/US Und.) a gun, a revolver. 2 [1920s+] (gambling) the player currently throwing the dice in a game of craps (cf. GUNNER n.⁵). 3 [1940s+] one who fires a weapon, an assassin.

shooter n.² 1 [1930s+] (US drugs) (also **needle shooter**) a heroin or other narcotics addict. 2 [1990s+] a hypodermic syringe. [SHOOT v.⁷ (1)]

shooter n.³ 1 [1960s] a martini and pernod cocktail. 2 [1970s+] (US) a measure of spirits, esp. whisky, tequila. [SHOT n.⁶ (1)]

shooter's hill n. [19C] the vagina (cf. ANTIPODES n.). [play on the proper name, but note SHOOT v.¹ (1)]

shoot eyes v. [1970s+] (US gay) to flirt; to stare; to glower.

shoot-flier n. [late 19C–1930s] (UK Und.) a thief who specializes in snatching wallets, watches and similar small items. [SHOOT-FLY n.]

shoot-fly n. [late 19C–1930s] (UK Und.) the robbery of watches, wallets and similar small personal items; thus *shoot-flying*. [? SHOOT OFF v.¹ + SE *fly*]

shoot for v. [1910s+] to aim for, to target; often as *shooting for*, e.g. *he's got 50 runs and now he's shooting for a century*.

shoot for two v. [2000s] (US campus) to defecate. [NUMBER TWO n.¹ (1)]

shoot from the hip v. [1930s+] (orig. US) to attack a problem head-on, to be a tough, purposeful performer. [Western film imagery]

shoot gravy v. [1960s+] (drugs) for a narcotics addict to reinject the blood that has been drawn into the syringe and there mixed with the heroin solution. [SHOOT v.⁷ (1) + GRAVY n.³ (1)]

shooting n. [1920s–70s] (US Black) aggressive, provocative talk, often leading to a fight.

shooting adj. [late 19C–1950s] (Aus.) verbally aggressive. [SHOOT ONE'S MOUTH OFF v. (1)]

shooting beaver phr. see SHOOTING MOON phr.

shooting gallery n. (also **gallery**) 1 [1950s–60s] (UK Und.) a venue for burglary, robbery or other crimes. 2 [1950s+] (drugs) a place, often an apartment or an abandoned building, used by a number of heroin addicts to take the drug. 3 [1960s] (US drugs) as ext. of (2), the hospital ward for drug addicts undergoing withdrawal. 4 [2000s] (drugs) as (1) but used for smoking

crack cocaine. [pun on SE, the fairground sideshow; note SHOOT v.⁷ (1)]

shooting iron n. 1 [late 18C+] (also **talking iron**) a pistol or gun. 2 [19C] (US) the penis (cf. AX n.²). [note WW1 Aus. milit. *shooting iron*, 18-pounder field gun]

shooting moon phr. [1960s] (US) the act of dropping one's trousers and underpants and presenting one's bare buttocks to onlookers; the female version is *shooting beaver*.

shooting stick n. 1 [19C] the penis (cf. BAT n.⁷). 2 [mid–late 19C] a gun. [play on SE + (1) SHOOT v.¹ (1) + STICK n.¹ (1); (2) STICK n.⁴]

shoot in the eye v. [late 19C] to do someone a bad turn.

shoot in the stubble v. [19C] to have sexual intercourse; thus *shoot over the stubble*, to ejaculate prematurely, outside the vagina. [SHOOT v.¹ (1) + STUBBLE n.]

shoot in the tail v. [mid-19C+] 1 to have anal intercourse (cf. ASK FOR THE RING v.). 2 to copulate. [SHOOT v.¹ (1) + TAIL n.² (1)/TAIL n.² (3)]

shoot into the brown v. [late 19C–1910s] (orig. milit.) to fail. [in rifle practice the outermost part of the target, denoting a 'miss', is brown; but note shooting jargon *into the brown*, an indiscriminate blast into the heart of a covey of passing birds. By ext. this was used by sporting officers of firing into a large group of advancing (brown-uniformed) troops]

shoot (it) v. [1920s] (US Und.) to use explosives to open a safe.

shoot it! excl. see SHOOT! excl.² (1).

shoot it into v. see THROW IT INTO v. (2).

shoot jokes (on) v. [1970s+] (US Black) to belittle, to tease aggressively. [SHOOT v.¹ (4) + SE *jokes*]

shoot London Bridge v. [early 18C] to have sexual intercourse. [? a nonce usage in Ned Ward, *The London Spy* (1699), punningly describing a 'buttocking brimstone' who could 'show you how the Watermen shoot London Bridge or how the lawyers go to Westminster']

shoot me! excl. see SHOOT! excl.² (2).

shoot off v.¹ [mid-19C+] to leave quickly. [ext. of SHOOT v.²]

shoot off v.² [1920s+] to ejaculate (cf. FIRE v.¹). [ext. of SHOOT v.¹ (1)]

shoot off one's face v. (also **shoot off one's head/pan**) [late 19C–1950s] (US) to talk effusively.

shoot off one's mouth v. see SHOOT ONE'S MOUTH OFF v.

shoot off one's trap v. [1930s–40s] to talk injudiciously, to boast. [TRAP n.³]

shoot off the fat v. [mid-19C] (Can.) to ask for credit. [ety. unknown]

shoot on v. [1960s+] (US Black) 1 to mock, to tease, to discredit. 2 to talk seductively.

shoot one's best mack v. [1970s+] (US Black) to make an all-out effort at seduction by one's persuasive conversation. [SHOOT v.¹ (4) + MACK(, THE) n.]

shoot one's best shot v. see TAKE ONE'S BEST SHOT v.

shoot one's cookies v. (also **drop one's cookies**) [1970s+] (US campus) to vomit (cf. BLOW CHOW v.). [SE *shoot* + COOKIES n.¹]

shoot one's cuff v. [late 19C] to dress up as smartly as one can, generally to present oneself in the most positive way possible. [the 'shooting' of the cuffs – making them project fashionably beyond the jacket sleeves]

shoot oneself in the foot v. [20C+] (orig. US) to blunder so that one harms oneself or exposes oneself to further hardship.

shoot one's gab v. [1910s–20s] to talk excitedly. [SHOOT v.¹ (4) + GAB n. (2)]

shoot one's head off v. [1910s–30s] 1 to complain, to make a fuss, to argue. 2 to talk, esp. boastfully. [HEAD n.⁴]

shoot one's jib off v. [1950s–60s] to talk, esp. arrogantly or boastfully. [JIB n.¹ (1)]

shoot one's linen v. [late 19C] to shoot one's cuffs, by making them project fashionably beyond the jacket sleeves.

shoot one's load v. **1** [1920s+] to ejaculate, to orgasm, usu. of a man (cf. FIRE v.¹). **2** [1950s+] to expend one's best effort. **3** [1960s] to blame, to pass on a responsibility. [SHOOT v.¹ (1)/SE *shoot* + LOAD n.⁵ (2); (2) and (3) are fig. uses]

shoot one's milt v. [mid-19C–1910s] to ejaculate (cf. FIRE v.¹). [SHOOT v.¹ (1) + SE *milt*, seed]

shoot one's mouth off v. (*also* **shoot off one's mouth**) (*orig. US*) **1** [mid-19C+] to talk, esp. in a loud or boastful way. **2** [1930s+] to betray secrets. **3** [1960s] to reprimand, to threaten. **4** [1960s+] to vomit. **5** [1960s+] to lose one's temper. [ext. of SHOOT v.¹ (4)]

shoot one's rocks v. [1970s] of a man, to reach orgasm, to ejaculate (cf. FIRE v.¹). [SHOOT v.¹ (1) + ROCKS n.⁴ (1)]

shoot one's roe v. [mid-19C–1900s] to ejaculate (cf. FIRE v.¹). [SHOOT v.¹ (1) + SE *roe*, seed]

shoot one's star v. [late 19C–1900s] to die.

shoot one's wad v. **1** [late 19C+] (*orig. US*) to exhaust oneself or one's possibilities. **2** [1920s+] (*orig. US*) to ejaculate (cf. FIRE v.¹). **3** [1950s+] (*US*) to commit or bet everything one has, to say all one has to say. **4** [1960s+] (*US*) to break down emotionally. [SHOOT v.¹ (1) + SE *wad*, a plug that holds in the powder in a cartridge/WAD n.¹ (1); (2) WAD n.⁶]

shoot-out n. **1** [1930s+] a gun battle. **2** [1970s] a decisive confrontation.

shoots! excl. *see* SHOOT! excl.².

shoot shit v. *see* SHOOT (THE) SHIT v.

shoot skin v. (*also* **go in the skin**) [1930s+] (*drugs*) to inject narcotics into the skin rather than into a vein; thus SKIN SHOT n. [SHOOT v.⁷ (1) + SE *skin*]

shoot someone out v. [1960s] (*US Und.*) to prepare someone for a given occupation.

shoot someone's star v. [1970s+] (*US Black*) **1** to perform anal intercourse (cf. ASK FOR THE RING v.). **2** to arrest a homosexual. [SE *star*, a shape supposedly resembling the anus]

shoot stars v. *see* SEE STARS v.

shoot that hat! excl. [mid–late 19C] (*US*) a mild oath. [SHOOT! excl.² (1) + SE *hat*]

shoot the agate v. [1900s–10s] (*US Black*) to walk jauntily with one's thumbs extended. [the extension of the thumb when playing marbles; note nonce def. by Trimble, *5,000 Adult Sex Words & Phrases* (1966): 'SHOOTING THE AGATE [...] Looking for a chance love partner by walking along with hands at the sides and thumbs extended. In hipster code, this means that a man is asking for sexual companionship, and if a hip female is interested, she may respond without a word being spoken']

shoot the baloney v. [1930s] (*US*) to talk nonsense. [SHOOT v.¹ (4) + BALONEY n.¹ (1)]

shoot the beaver v. [1960s+] **1** for a man to look under a woman's skirt in the hope of seeing pubic hair or her vagina. **2** for a woman to display her genitals, usu. while otherwise dressed. [SE *shoot* + BEAVER n.⁵ (1)]

shoot the bird v. [1970s+] (*orig. US*) to make a mocking, derisory gesture by clenching the fist and raising the middle finger. [SE *shoot* + BIRD n.¹³]

shoot the bishop v. *see* SHOOT A BISHOP v.

shoot the boots off v. [20C+] (*Ulster*) to wipe out, lit. or fig.

shoot the breeze v. [1930s+] (*orig. US*) to gossip, to talk idly.

shoot the bull v. [20C+] to gossip, to chat; to talk deliberately deceptive nonsense. [SHOOT v.¹ (4) + BULL n.¹¹ (1)]

shoot the cat v.¹ [late 19C+] to have sexual intercourse.

shoot the cat v.² *see* SHOOT A CAT v.

shoot the chimney v. [late 19C] (*US*) to be quiet, to stop talking. [SE *shoot*, to discard, to get rid of + ? SE *chimney* to mean throat]

shoot the chutes v. *see* GO DOWN THE CHUTE(S) v.

shoot (the) con v. [1930s+] (*US tramp*) to talk nonsense. [SHOOT v.¹ (4) + CON n.¹ (9)]

shoot (the) crap v. (*also* **sling the crap**) [1930s–60s] to talk nonsense. [SHOOT v.¹ (4)/SLING v.¹ (3) + CRAP n.³ (3)]

shoot the crow v. **1** [19C–1920s] to leave without paying. **2** [1960s+] (*Scot.*) to leave. [ety. unknown]

shoot the curve v. **1** [1930s] (*US prison*) to negotiate privileges, esp. a drug supply. **2** [1930s–50s] (*US drugs*) to buy narcotics.

shoot the dozens v. *see* PLAY THE DOZENS v.

shoot the gift v. [1990s+] (*US Black*) **1** to gossip, to talk idly. **2** to rap well. [SHOOT v.¹ (4) + GIFT OF THE GAB n.]

shoot the gulf v. [mid-17C–mid-18C] to succeed in a very hard task, to achieve the impossible. [? according to Daniel Defoe, *A Voyage Round the World* (1725): 'Such a mighty and valuable thing also was the passing this strait [the Straits of Magellan] that Sir Francis Drake's going through it gave birth to that famous old wives' saying viz., that Sir Francis Drake shot the gulf; [...] as if there had been but one gulf in the world']

shoot the gut v. (*also* **drag the gut**) [1960s+] (*US teen*) to drive up and down the main street. [SE *shoot*/DRAG v.¹⁰ (1) + GUT n.³]

shoot the lights out v. [20C+] (*US*) to excel, to perform outstandingly. [fig. marksmanship]

shoot the marbles from all sides of the ring v. [1930s–40s] (*US Black*) to be in a position to take action.

shoot the moon v.¹ (*also* **bolt the moon**) [early 19C–1950s] to abscond from a house or flat, taking one's furniture and possessions but avoiding payment of any outstanding rent, utility bills etc; thus *moon-shooter*, one who absconds with their possessions but without paying the rent.

shoot the moon v.² [1920s–30s] (*US*) to take a major gamble.

shoot the pill v. (*also* **shoot the peel**) [1980s+] (*US Black/campus*) to shoot baskets, to play a pick-up game of basketball. [SE *shoot* + PILL n.¹ (4)]

shoot the regular v. [1970s+] (*US Black*) to chatter on in the usual, predictable manner. [SHIT n.³ (4) is unspoken]

shoot the roll v. *see* SHOOT THE WORKS v. (2).

shoot (the) shit v. [1930s+] to gossip, to chat. [SHOOT v.¹ (4) + SHIT n.³ (4)]

shoot the squirrel v. [1970s] (*US campus*) to catch a glimpse of a woman's panties or pubic hair. [SE *shoot* + SQUIRREL n.² (3)]

shoot the thrill v. [1970s] (*US Black*) to lead a promiscuous and varied sex life.

shoot the willie v. [1960s] (*US campus*) to make a derisory, insulting gesture by raising the middle finger. [? the single finger represents a WILLIE n.⁵]

shoot the works v. (*US*) **1** [1920s] to vomit. **2** [1920s+] (*also* **shoot the roll**) to commit oneself absolutely, to make every effort no matter what the cost. **3** [1930s] to die. **4** [1930s] to have an orgasm (cf. FIRE v.¹). **5** [1930s] to make a full confession. [WORKS, THE n. (1)]

shoot through v. [1940s+] (*Aus./N.Z.*) to leave, to exit quickly; in milit. use, to go absent without leave.

shoot through like a Bondi tram v. (*also* **go Bondi**) [1940s+] (*Aus.*) to leave very quickly, to run off. [SHOOT THROUGH v. + *Bondi tram*, a tram running through a suburb in Sydney]

shoot through the grease v. [1950s–60s] (*US Black/campus*) to let down, to betray, to deceive, to victimize.

shoot to v. *see* SHOOT v.⁵ (1).

shoot to kill v. [20C+] to aim ruthlessly for a goal without reservation or compromise.

shoot-up n.¹ [1930s–40s] a gun rampage, firing weapons indiscriminately to destroy a place. [SHOOT UP v.¹]

shoot-up n.² [1960s] the act of injecting a drug. [SHOOT UP v.²]

shoot up v.¹ [late 19C+] (*orig. US*) to rampage around firing weapons, to destroy a place with gunfire; also in fig. use.

shoot up v.² [1920s+] (*drugs*) **1** to take narcotic drugs by injection. **2** to inject someone with a narcotic. [ext. of SHOOT v.⁷ (1)]

shoot up the straight v. (*also* **do a rush up the straight**) [mid–late 19C] of a man, to have sexual intercourse. [SHOOT v.¹ (1) + SE *straight*]

shoot white *v.* [late 19C] to ejaculate (cf. FIRE v.[1]). [SHOOT v.[1] (1) + the colour of semen]

shoot with the long bow *v. see* DRAW A LONG BOW v.

Shop, the *n.* **1** [late 19C+] the Royal Military Academy, Woolwich. **2** [1960s+] (*Aus.*) Melbourne University. [ironic use of SE]

shop *n.*[1] **1** [16C+] a place, a place of business, any place where one pursues one's occupation, e.g. a brothel (cf. BANGING-SHOP n.). **2** [late 17C–1900s] (*UK Und.*) a prison. **3** [early 19C–1910s] a public house.

shop *n.*[2] [19C+] conversation about one's personal occupation or profession; thus TALK SHOP v.

shop *n.*[3] [mid–late 19C] the mouth.

shop *n.*[4] [1960s+] an act of shopping.

shop *v.*[1] [late 16C+] (*UK Und.*) to imprison; thus *shopping*, a jail sentence. [SHOP n.[1] (1)]

shop *v.*[2] [mid-19C] to dismiss, esp. to dismiss a shop assistant.

shop *v.*[3] [mid-19C+] to inform on and thus cause to be imprisoned, or in trouble; to denounce. [ext. of SHOP v.[1]]

shop *v.*[4] [1960s–70s] (*US gay*) to look for a sexual partner, whether in the street or in bars, clubs etc.

shop around *v.* [1940s+] to have a number of sexual relationships before choosing one that will serve for marriage or the longer term. [SE *shop around*, to search out the best bargain]

shop-bouncer *n.* [mid–late 19C] **1** a thief who steals from shops while distracting the merchant's attention with his argumentative bargaining; thus *shop-bouncing*, shoplifting. **2** a thief who poses as a respectable customer and, while buying a cheap item, steals a more valuable one. [SE *shop* + BOUNCER n.[2] (4)]

shop cookie *n. see* COOKIE n.[1] (2).

shop-cop *n.* [2000s] a security man working in a shop. [SE *shop* + COP n.[1] (1)]

shop-door *n.* [late 19C+] the fly buttons; thus warning *your shop-door is open*, your flies are undone.

shop-dropper *n.* [1950s–60s] (*Aus.*) one who delivers goods, liquor etc from a market or store to retailers.

shop in *v.* [1940s–60s] (*Irish prison*) for a non-prisoner, usu. a warder, to smuggle contraband goods or letters into/out of the prison.

shoplift *n.* [mid–late 17C] a shoplifter, one who steals goods from shops while pretending to be a legitimate customer. [SE f. 1700]

shop-lobber *n.* [late 18C–mid-19C] a dandified shop assistant. [SE *shop* + LOB v.[1], i.e. his langorous pose]

shop-masher *n.* [late 19C–1900s] a dandified shop assistant. [SE *shop* + MASHER n.[1] (2)]

shop-pad *n.* [18C] a shoplifter. [SE *shop* + PAD n.[1] (3)]

shopped *adj.* **1** [late 16C+] imprisoned. **2** [19C] in work. **3** [mid-19C+] betrayed, informed on. [(1) SHOP v.[1]; (2) SHOP v.[3]; (3) SE]

shopper *n.* [1920s–50s] an informer. [SHOP v.[3]]

shoppie *n.* (*also* **shoppy**) **1** [1900s–30s] a female *shop* assistant. **2** [1970s+] (*Aus.*) (*also* **shopper**) a *shop*lifter. [abbr.]

shopping *n.*[1] [1930s+] an act of betrayal, of informing. [SHOP v.[3]]

shopping *n.*[2] [1990s+] **1** (*US Und.*) shoplifting. **2** (*US prison*) looking for something to steal. [ironic use of SE]

shopping and fucking *adj.* [1980s+] used of a type of blockbusting novel, developed during the materialist 1980s, in which the normal ingredient of a certain type of bestseller – 'procrastinated rape' (V.S. Pritchett) – is boosted by regular excursions into the world's up-market shopping malls in search of lovingly delineated designer-labelled garments and other consumables. When bowdlerized the term is found as *sex and shopping*.

shoppy *n. see* SHOPPIE n.

shoppy *adj.* [mid–late 19C] wholly engrossed in one's occupation. [talking SHOP n.[2]]

shoppying blue *n.* [1970s] (*Aus. Und.*) a signed confession. [SHOP v.[3] + BLUE n.[7]]

shop teeth *n.* [20C+] (*Irish*) false teeth, dentures.

shore dinner *n.* [1970s+] (*US gay*) a homosexual sailor who only takes the passive role in fellatio (cf. BONE-EATER n.). [play on SE *dinner*/EAT v.[3] (1); SAmE *shore dinner*, a dinner of seafood]

Shoreditch fury *n.* [late 16C] an aggressive woman; a harlot. [*Shoreditch*, a notably tough area of East London]

short *n.*[1] [early 19C+] **1** neat gin. **2** any form of undiluted spirits. [? the shortness of the measure compared with that of beer]

short *n.*[2] **1** [1910s+] (*US*) a street car. **2** [1930s+] (*US*) (*also* **shot**) an automobile. [the comparatively short distance a street car or automobile would travel compared to a railway train; note *Current Slang* III:2 (1968): 'This seems to be derived from the idea that most cars, especially compacts, are short in comparison with the old favorites, especially the Cadillac']

short *n.*[3] **1** [1930s–40s] (*US*) a *short*-barrelled or sawn-off revolver. **2** [1930s–50s] a *short* measure of drugs (cf. SHORT PIECE n.). **3** [1940s+] (*US Black/prison*) a cigarette butt; a half-smoked cigarette. **4** [1980s+] a measure of drugs, esp. crack cocaine, that is sold at a reduced price. **5** [1980s+] a child. [abbr./length/height]

short *adj.*[1] **1** [17C+] impoverished, out of cash. **2** [mid-18C+] insufficient, esp. of money; thus *short bread*, not enough cash. **3** [1950s] (*drugs*) of an injection, weak. **4** [1990s+] (*drugs*) in insufficient quantity for the money paid.

short *adj.*[2] [early 19C+] of spirits, undiluted; often as *something short*. [SHORT n.[1] (2)]

short *adj.*[3] [mid–late 19C] of banknotes, in large denominations. [orig. cashiers' jargon; large denominations mean fewer notes, which take a *shorter* time to count]

short *adj.*[4] [1930s+] (*Aus.*) eccentric, insane. [abbr. SHINGLE SHORT, A phr. (1)]

short *adj.*[5] **1** [1930s+] (*US prison*) of a prisoner, with only a few weeks or days of a sentence left to serve. **2** [1960s+] (*US milit.*) near the end of a term of duty, spec. the 12-month tours of Vietnam.

short *v.*[1] **1** [1920s+] to cheat in any form of share-out or distribution, e.g. of food or attention. **2** [1970s+] (*US*) to cheat when dividing the spoils of a robbery or of drug dealing; to underpay. [SHORT adj.[1] (2)]

short *v.*[2] [2000s] (*US Black*) to share a cigarette.

short and curlies *n.* (*also* **curlies, curly fellas/hairs, short hairs**) **1** [1910s+] in fig. use of (2); usu. in phr. *have by the short and curlies*, to have at a severe disadvantage. **2** [1960s+] pubic hair.

short arm *n. see* SHORT-ARM INSPECTION n.

short-arm bandit *n.* [1960s–70s] (*gay*) a male homosexual. [SHORT ARM n. + BANDIT sfx (2)]

short-arm heister *n.* (*also* **short-arm bandit**) [1950s+] (*US Und.*) a rapist; thus *short-arm heist*, rape. [SHORT ARM n. + HEISTER n. (1)/BANDIT sfx (1)]

short-arm inspection *n.* (*also* **short arm**) [1910s+] (*orig. milit.*) a medical inspection of the genitals; *short arm* as the penis is always implied, but rarely found alone (cf. ARM n.[1]). [similar to THIRD LEG n. but note Williams who makes a link to 17C milit. metaphor *arms*, the genitals]

short-arse *n.* (*also* **short-ass**) [early 18C; 1920s+] a small person, an insignificant person.

short-arsed *adj.* (*also* **short-assed**) [1920s+] a non-specific insult, usu. aimed at a short person. [SHORT-ARSE n.]

short bit *n.*[1] [mid-19C–1950s] (*US*) 10 cents, in contrast to 12½ or 15 cents, a LONG BIT n.[1]. [SE *short* + BIT n.[1] (4)]

short bit *n.*[2] [1910s+] a short prison sentence. [SE *short* + BIT n.[5]]

short boy *n.* [mid–late 19C] (*US Und.*) a thug. [the *Short Boys* gang, *fl.*c.1850 in New York City]

short-brim *n. see* STINGY-BRIM n.

short-coat *v.* [1900s] to circumcise.

short con *n.* (*also* **short coin, short money racket**) [1930s+] (*US Und.*) any variety of confidence trick that can be performed spontaneously and on the spot, with no elaborate props, preparation etc. [abbr. SE *short* (*time*) + CON n.¹ (7)]

short con *adj.* [1960s] (*US Und.*) prone to petty dishonesty. [SHORT CON n.]

short con *v.* [1930s–50s] (*US Und.*) to perform such confidence tricks as are known as the SHORT CON n. [SHORT CON n.]

short con artist *n.* (*also* **short con worker**) [1920s–50s] (*US Und.*) a confidence trickster who specializes in spontaneous or short-term trickery. [SHORT CON n. + ARTIST sfx]

short count *n.* [1950s+] (*drugs*) a short measure.

short digs *n. see* SHORT STROKES n.

short dog *n.* [1960s+] (*orig. US Black*) a small bottle of cheap wine. [SE *short* + DOG n.¹¹]

short-end money *n.* [20C+] (*gambling*) money bet on the possibility of a team or individual (esp. in boxing) losing a contest. [in a bet of 20–1 or 9–4 the smaller digit is the 'short' end]

short end (of the stick) *n.* (*also* **dirty end of the stick, shitty…, shitten end of a brick, short end of the funnel/ shitstick**) [mid-19C+] (*orig. US*) unfair treatment, deliberately engineered bad luck, the bad side of a deal or situation; by ext. the unfavoured option in a bet on sport; thus *short-ender*, a contestant who is expected to lose (cf. FUZZY END OF THE LOLLIPOP n.). [the *funnel* is that which feeds meat into a mincing machine]

shorter *n.* [mid-19C] a clipper of coins.

short eyes *n.* [1970s+] (*US prison*) a child molester. [corruption of SHUT EYES n.]

short fuse *n.* [1960s+] (*orig. US*) a short temper.

short go *n.* (*US drugs*) **1** [1930s–60s] short measure on a drug deal; a weak injection. **2** [1960s] a shortage of drugs.

short hair *n.* [1970s] a convict, esp. a new one. [their shaved heads]

short hairs *n. see* SHORT AND CURLIES n.

short-heeled wench *n.* (*also* **short heels**) [mid-16C–early 19C] a promiscuous woman. [her 'short heels' mean that she is constantly falling on her back]

short heist *n.* [1950s+] (*US Und.*) petty theft. [SE *short* (*time*) + HEIST n.¹ (1)]

shorthorn *n.* [late 19C–1940s] (*US, mainly Western*) **1** a Northerner (cf. LONGHORN n.). **2** a newcomer, an innocent. [agricultural imagery]

short-house *n.* [1970s+] a short person. [euph. for SHORT-ARSE n.]

short john *n. see* CHEAP JOHN n.².

short-length *n.* [mid-19C] (*Scot.*) a glass of brandy.

short-limbered *adj.* [late 19C–1900s] short-tempered. [SE *short* + *limber*. 'The detachable fore part of a gun-carriage, consisting of two wheels and an axle, a pole for the horses, and a frame which holds one or two ammunition-chests. It is attached to the trail of the gun-carriage proper by a hook' (*OED*)]

short money *n.* [1950s–70s] of a prostitute, insufficient money to satisfy her pimp; for a drug dealer or user, insufficient money to make a desired purchase. [SHORT adj.¹ (2)]

short money *v.* [1950s–60s] (*US Black pimp*) to exploit an unsatisfactory prostitute for as much money as possible.

short-money game *n.* [1960s] (*US Und.*) the money that a pimp can make from a prostitute who works for him for only a short period. [SHORT MONEY v.]

short-mouthed *adj.* [1900s] (*W.I.*) verbally agile, good at snappy repartee.

short nail *n.* [1960s–70s] (*US Black*) an unkempt, unattractive woman, esp. with messy hair. [SE *short* + NAILHEAD n.²]

short-nose *n.* [1960s–70s] (*US*) a .38 revolver, which has a short barrel.

short of a sheet of bark *phr. see* HAVE A SHEET SHORT v.

short on *adj.* [1940s+] badly supplied, wanting. [SHORT adj.¹ (2)]

short-order shrimp *n.* [1970s] (*US gay*) 'a drunk sailor leaned up against an alley wall and quickly sucked off' (Rodgers, *The Queen's Vernacular*, 1972).

short pants court *n.* [1950s] (*US juv.*) a juvenile court.

short piece *n.* [1930s–50s] (*US drugs*) a purported measure, usu. 1oz (28g), of a narcotic that has in fact been shaved or otherwise reduced (cf. SHORT n.³). [SHORT adj.¹ (2) + PIECE n.⁶ (1)]

shorts *n.* [1970s+] the last few puffs of a discarded cigarette.

shorts, the *n.*¹ [1910s+] (*US*) an urgent need to visit the lavatory; the inability to control one's bowels and/or bladder. [TAKEN SHORT adj.]

shorts, the *n.*² [1930s+] (*US*) lack of money. [SHORT adj.¹ (2)]

short sheet *v.* [20C+] (*US*) to mistreat, to trick someone. [SAmE *shortsheet*, the UK 'apple-pie bed']

short short *n.* [2000s] (*US Black*) a very short time, very soon.

short shoves *n. see* SHORT STROKES n.

short skate *n. see* CHEAPSKATE n. (2).

short stop *n.* **1** [1950s–60s] (*US Black*) a temporary arrangement, a short period of time. **2** [1950s–70s] a fool, a dupe, a coward. **3** [1960s–70s] of money, a small amount, just enough to carry one over for a short time; thus a gambler with little money. **4** [1980s] a short person. [baseball imagery]

short stop *v.* [1970s] **1** (*US Black*) to abruptly stop someone from moving or carrying on with what they are doing. **2** (*US*) to take food as it is being passed to someone else at a meal. [SE *stop short*]

short story *n.* [1930s–50s] (*US Und.*) a forged cheque; thus *write short stories*, to pass bad cheques.

short story writer *n.* [1930s–50s] (*US Und.*) one who passes bad cheques. [SHORT STORY n. + SE *writer*]

short strokes *n.* (*also* **short digs/shoves**) [late 19C+] the final stage of sexual intercourse, immediately preceding male orgasm; thus *be on the short strokes*, of a man, to be approaching orgasm; also in fig. use, to be running out of time.

short stuff *n.* [1980s+] (*US Und.*) a quick and spontaneous con trick, thought up on the spur of the moment and workable only while the target is on hand.

short time *n.* **1** [20C+] (*UK prison*) a short sentence, a short part of one's sentence left to run; thus *short-time pains*, pre-release nerves. **2** [20C+] (*milit.*) a short-service commission, a short period of enlistment. **3** [1910s+] of a prostitute, the time spent with one client before taking on a new one, rather than spending a whole night with the same man; the *short time* allows a single copulation. [(1) TIME n.¹]

short-time *v.* [1960s–70s] **1** (*US prison*) to reach the end of one's sentence. **2** in fig. use of (1), to take the short view as regards one's lifestyle. **3** to have sex with a prostitute for a short time (rather than a whole night). [SHORT TIME n.]

short-time girl *n.* [1900s] a basic, cheap prostitute who satisfies her client's immediate need and then looks for her next customer (cf. AWAYDAY GIRL n.). [SHORT TIME n. (3) + SE *girl*]

short-timer *n.* **1** [20C+] (*US prison*) one who is serving a short prison sentence. **2** [1920s+] one who frequents a prostitute for a brief visit, involving a single act of intercourse. **3** [1930s–40s] (*US prison*) one who has only a short time left of their sentence. **4** [1940s+] (*US*) one who has only a short period left of his service in the military. **5** [1960s+] one who has only a short time in a given occupation or institution. [SHORT TIME n.]

short-timers *n.* [1920s] a couple who rent a room for an hour in order to have adulterous sex. [SHORT TIME n. (3)]

short trill *n.* [1940s] (*US Black*) a short walk. [? obs. SE *trill*, to trundle, to whirl]

short 'un *n.* [late 19C] 285ml (½ pint) of coffee. [SE *short one*]

short-weight *n.* [1920s] a fool. [SHORT-WEIGHT n.]

short-weight *adj.* [1920s+] mentally defective, stupid.

shorty *n.* **1** [late 19C+] a short person, often as a term of address. **2** [1930s+] (*US Black*) a young person. **3** [1970s+] (*US Black*) a child. **4** [1990s+] (*orig. US Black*) a woman, a girlfriend; occas. a boyfriend. **5** [2000s] (*US Black*) a small penis.

sho-sho gun *n.* [1910s–40s] (*US Und.*) a machine gun. [? echoic]

shot *n.*[1] [mid-16C+] money, esp. an amount that is due to be paid or one's share of it, e.g. at a tavern.

shot *n.*[2] [mid-17C+] (*US*) an ejaculation, an act of sexual intercourse. [SHOOT v.[1] (1)]

shot *n.*[3] (*also* **shoot**) **1** [early 19C+] (*orig. US*) a sneering remark, aimed at another person with the express purpose of wounding them. **2** [mid-19C] (*US*) any form of remark. **3** [2000s] (*US prison*) a disciplinary report.

shot *n.*[4] [mid-19C] a corpse that has been disinterred by body-snatchers for the purpose of selling it to a medical school.

shot *n.*[5] **1** [mid-19C+] an opportunity, a chance, an attempt, a guess; thus HAVE A SHOT AT v.[2]. **2** [late 19C+] anything that has a reasonable chance of success, usu. preceded by a qualifying figure indicating the odds against, e.g. *ten to one shot*. **3** [1940s+] (*Aus./US*) one's preference, style or choice; thus *just the shot*, exactly what one requires. **4** [1960s] (*US campus*) attendance at a party, movie, sporting match etc. [SE *shoot* (at a target)]

shot *n.*[6] **1** [late 19C+] a measure of liquor; usu. with the drink specified, e.g. a *shot of rum*. **2** [20C+] (*drugs*) an injection, or dose, of a narcotic drug. **3** [20C+] (*drugs*) the amount of a drug required to get a user intoxicated. **4** [1910s+] any form of injection. **5** [1960s+] in fig. use, an 'injection', a dose.

shot *n.*[7] [1910s–20s] a very hard cake. [SE *shot*, a cannonball]

shot *n.*[8] [1920s] anything very hard to understand or believe.

shot *n.*[9] **1** [1920s–50s] (*US Und.*) the detonation of an explosive during safe-breaking. **2** [1940s+] a blow, a hit; also in fig. use.

shot *n.*[10] [1930s–50s] (*Aus.*) an abortion.

shot *n.*[11] [1960s–70s] (*US Black*) a professional pickpocket; thus *shot broad*, a female pickpocket.

shot *n.*[12] [1990s+] (*US prison*) a friend.

shot *n.*[13] *see* BIG SHOT n.

shot *n.*[14] *see* SHORT n.[2] (2).

shot *adj.* **1** [mid-19C+] (*US/Aus./N.Z.*) drunk. **2** [1920s–30s] (*US*) nervous, on edge. **3** [1920s+] (*US*) of a thing, lost, useless, worn-out or beyond repair. **4** [1920s+] (*orig. Aus.*) of a person, exhausted or in bad shape.

shot *v.* [2000s] (*UK Black*) to deal drugs. [? SE *shoot*; ? SHOOT v.[7] (1)]

shot beer *n. see* NEEDLE BEER n.

shot between wind and water *phr.* (*also* **shot betwixt wind and water**) [late 17C–19C] infected with venereal disease. [naut. jargon *betwixt wind and water*, that part of a ship's side that is sometimes above water and sometimes submerged, in which part a shot is particularly dangerous]

shot-caller *n.* [1960s+] a person who has authority or takes the lead in saying what should happen. [CALL THE SHOTS v.]

shot-clog *n.* [mid–late 19C] a fool who is tolerated only because of their willingness to pay their share for drinks. [SHOT n.[6] (1) + SE *clog*]

shot down *adj.* [1950s+] **1** (*drugs*) under the influence of drugs. **2** (*US campus*) miserable, useless, distasteful. [SE + (1) play on SHOT n.[6] (2); (2) DOWN adj.[2] (1)]

shot full of holes *phr.* **1** [1910s+] (*Aus./N.Z.*) drunk. **2** [1940s] (*US*) suffering a nervous breakdown. [ext. of SHOT adj.]

shot-ging *n.* [1920s+] (*Aus.*) a catapult. [ext. GING n.]

shotgun *n.*[1] [20C+] (*US*) a matchmaker, a marriage broker. [play on SHOTGUN WEDDING n.]

shotgun *n.*[2] (*also* **shotgun seat**) [1950s+] (*orig. US*) the seat next the driver in a vehicle; usu. as RIDE SHOTGUN v. [stage-coach era use of a shotgun-wielding assistant who sat next to the coachman and protected him against marauding Indians, bandits etc]

shotgun *n.*[3] **1** [1960s+] (*US drugs*) a type of pipe used for smoking marijuana. **2** [1970s+] (*drugs*) a means of intensifying the effect of cannabis smoke; the cigarette is reversed, the lit end in the mouth,

sealed there by the lips; its holder then blows into the cigarette and the resultant powerful stream of smoke passes into a receiver's mouth (cf. BLOWBACK n.[1]).

shotgun *n.*[4] [1980s+] **1** (*drugs*) a guard who accompanies a drug courier to ensure that all goes well on their trip (and that they do not attempt to abscond with the consignment). **2** any form of guard. [RIDE SHOTGUN v.]

shotgun *v.* **1** [1960s+] to drink a full can of beer in a single swallow, esp. when a hole has been poked through the bottom. **2** [1970s+] (*drugs*) to blow cannabis smoke into someone else's mouth by reversing the cigarette inside one's own mouth and blowing; the other person places their open lips near the stream of smoke and inhales for as long as they can; thus *shotgun*, *shotgunning*, the act of doing this. [(2) SHOTGUN n.[3] (2)]

shotgun! *excl.* [1980s+] (*US teen*) an excl. shouted just before getting into a car meaning 'I want to ride in the front seat next to the driver!'; whoever shouts first usu. gets the seat. [RIDE SHOTGUN v. (1)]

shotgun marriage/shotgunner *n. see* SHOTGUN WEDDING n.

shotgun quiz *n. see* POP QUIZ n.

shotgun seat *n. see* SHOTGUN n.[2].

shotgun wedding *n.* (*also* **shotgun marriage**, **shotgunner**) [20C+] (*orig. US*) a wedding that is forced on the man due to his girlfriend being pregnant. [the image of the aggrieved father holding a shotgun to the reluctant groom's back]

shot house *n. see* NIP JOINT n.

shot in *v.* [1910s+] (*Aus.*) to be imprisoned. [SE *shoot in*, to throw in]

shot in the arm *n.* **1** [1910s+] (*orig. US*) anything (verbal, physical, stimulant) that cheers one up, energizes one etc. **2** [1920s+] a narcotics injection. [SHOT n.[6] (2)]

shot in the ass *adj.* [1950s–60s] (*US*) obsessed with, excessively dedicated to. [image of narcotic addiction]

shot in the dark *n.* [late 19C+] a wild guess, a random try.

shot in the neck *n.* [mid-19C] a drink. [SHOT n.[6] (1)]

shot in the neck *phr.* [19C] (*US*) drunk. [SHOT adj. (1)]

shot in the tail *phr.* [late 19C–1900s] pregnant. [SHOOT v.[1] (1)/SE *shot* + TAIL n.[2] (3)]

shot-locker *n.* [20C+] (*US*) **1** the vagina (cf. BAG n.[1]). **2** the penis. [into which goes or from where comes a SHOT n.[2]]

shot on the swings *n.* [1940s+] (*Scot.*) sexual intercourse. [ety. unknown; ? the movements of the 2 bodies]

shot-out *adj.* [1990s+] (*drugs*) of a narcotics addict, worn-out from an excess of drug use. [SHOT n.[6] (2)]

shot pocket *n.* [1970s] (*US Und.*) a special pocket adapted for secreting items that have been shoplifted.

shot-rodder *n.* [1950s] (*US Black*) one who is emotionally unstable.

shotten herring *n.* [late 16C–early 19C] an emaciated, worthless and generally good-for-nothing person. [Du. *schoten haringh*, a fish, esp. a herring that has spawned. Such herrings are 'empty' of their spawn. In a human context, therefore, it also means fig. 'empty']

shotten soul *n.* [early 17C] an emaciated, worthless and generally good-for-nothing person; thus *shotten-souled*, worthless. [lit. an 'empty soul']

shotter *n.* [2000s] (*UK Black*) a drug dealer. [SHOT v.]

shottie *n. see* SHOTTY n.

shottie *v.* [1980s+] (*N.Z. drugs*) to inhale a puff of a marijuana cigarette through a large funnel and then drop from a standing position to a crouch when the lungs are filled to capacity, to force more smoke into the lungs. [abbr. SE *shotgun*]

shotting (game) *n.* [2000s] (*UK Black*) drug-dealing, being a drug dealer.

shot to hell *phr.* (*also* **shot to pieces**) [20C+] in a state of complete and utter collapse.

shot (to the curb) *phr.* [2000s] (*US prison*) exhausted, worn-out, esp. as a result of using crack cocaine.

shotty *n.* (*also* **shottie**) [1990s+] (*orig. US Black*) a *shot*gun. [abbr.]

shot-up *adj.*[1] [1930s+] (*drugs*) experiencing the effect of narcotic drugs. [SHOOT UP v.[2] (1)]

shot-up *adj.*[2] **1** [1930s+] (*US*) of a person, severely wounded. **2** [1940s+] of the body, not well. **3** [1950s+] of an object, e.g. a car, damaged by shooting. [SE *shot*]

shot up the back *phr.* [1910s] (*Aus.*) disconcerted; confused.

shoulder *v.* **1** [early 19C] of a stage-coachman, to take on (and charge) extra passengers, without informing the coach company; thus *shoulder-stick*, a passenger who takes advantage of such corruption. **2** [mid-19C] of a servant, to cheat or embezzle from their master. [ety. unknown]

shoulder boulders *n.* [1990s+] large female breasts (cf. BOULDER-HOLDER n.).

shoulder-clapper *n.* [late 16C–early 19C] a bailiff. [the physical action that accompanies an arrest for debt]

shoulder-dab *n.* [early 19C] a bailiff. [their 'dabbing' or tapping their target on the shoulder]

shoulder-hitter *n.* (*also* **shoulder-striker**) [mid-19C–1930s] (*US*) a bully, a ruffian. [lit. 'one who hits from the shoulder']

shoulder-knot *n.* [mid-19C] a bailiff. [they take their victim by the shoulder]

shoulder-sham *n.* [late 17C–early 19C] (*UK Und.*) a partner to a pickpocket. [SE *shoulder* + SHAM n.[1] (1)]

shoulder-striker *n. see* SHOULDER-HITTER n.

shoulder-surfing *n.* [1990s+] a general term for a variety of 'distraction crimes', i.e. street robberies performed where one member of a team distracts the target by starting an argument, pouring liquid on their clothes etc; while the argument is being resolved or the clothes cleaned, the actual robber has the opportunity to steal.

shoulder-tapper *n.* **1** [late 18C–mid-19C] a bailiff. **2** [1940s] (*US Und.*) a policeman (cf. BEAT-POUNDER n.).

shouse *n.* (*also* **shoush, sh'touse**) [1940s+] (*Aus.*) a lavatory (cf. BACKHOUSE n.). [elision of SHITHOUSE n. (2)]

shouse *adj.* [1980s+] (*N.Z.*) a general negative, unpleasant, disgusting etc. [SHOUSE n.]

shout *n.*[1] [mid-19C+] (*orig. Aus./N.Z.*) **1** a round of drinks. **2** (*also* **call, shoot**) one's turn to order a round of drinks; thus *your shout, my shout, go on the shout, stand the shout*; thus *shout-dodger*, one who avoids his turn; also in ext. use. [SHOUT v.[1] (1)]

shout *n.*[2] [1920s] (*US Black*) **1** a party, esp. a RENT PARTY n. (cf. FISH-FRY n.). **2** a dance. [its noisiness]

shout *n.*[3] [1970s] a piece of information, a 'tip-off'.

shout *n.*[4] *see* SHOUT(-OUT) n.

shout *v.*[1] (*Aus./N.Z.*) **1** [mid-19C+] to buy a round of drinks. **2** [20C+] to treat (other than to liquor). [one shouts to the publican for drink]

shout *v.*[2] [late 19C–1940s] (*US*) of things, to be undeniably important.

shout and holler *n.* [20C+] a collar. [rhy. sl.]

shouted *adj.* [1940s] (*Aus./N.Z.*) used of a drink that is paid for by someone other than the drinker. [SHOUT v.[1] (1)]

shouter *n.*[1] [mid–late 19C] (*Aus./N.Z.*) one who stands a round of drinks. [SHOUT v.[1] (1)]

shouter *n.*[2] **1** [late 19C–1920s] (*US*) a gospel or blues/gospel singer. **2** [late 19C–1920s] (*US*) a Black church. **3** [20C+] (*US*) a soapbox or street-corner orator. **4** [1920s] (*US Und.*) a criminal's girlfriend. [SE *shouter*, a loud or voluble speaker]

shout for murder *v. see* HOLLER (BLOODY) MURDER v.

shout for Ruth *v.* [1980s] (*Aus.*) to vomit (cf. CALL CHARLES v.). [*Ruth* = echoic]

shout oneself hoarse *v.* **1** [late 19C–1900s] to get drunk. **2** [late 19C+] to buy a round of drinks for the whole bar. [SHOUT

v.[1] (1) ? + pun on the actual shouting – to attract attention to one's generosity and as a result of one's drunkenness]

shout(-out) *n.* [1990s+] as used on (pirate) radio stations, esp. those playing jungle music, a greeting, an acknowledgement to a named listener or group of listeners.

shout the odds *v.* [1910s+] to talk loudly, to boast.

shout-up *n.* [1960s+] a noisy argument.

shout up *v.* [1930s] to shout at by way of warning.

shov *n.* [late 19C] (*UK Und.*) a knife. [CHIV n.[1] (1) + SE *shove*, one 'shoves it in' to the victim]

shove *n.* **1** [early 18C+] sexual intercourse; thus *give her a shove*, to have sexual intercourse with a woman. **2** [mid-19C] (*UK Und.*) a crowd. **3** [late 19C] energy, high spirits, self-glorification, hollow talk. **4** [late 19C–1940s] (*US tramp*) a gang of tramps. [(1) SHOVE v.[1] (1); subseq. defs. play on PUSH n.[2] (1)]

shove, the *n.* [late 19C] dismissal from one's employment; usu. AS GET THE SHOVE v.; GIVE SOMEONE THE SHOVE v.

shove *v.*[1] **1** [mid-17C+] to have sexual intercourse (cf. BANG v.[1]). **2** [early 19C+] (*US*) to pass counterfeit money. **3** [mid-19C] (*UK Und.*) to deceive, to cheat, to take advantage of. **4** [1920s] (*US Und.*) to sell stolen goods. **5** [1920s–60s] (*US Und.*) (*also* **shove across**) to kill. **6** [1930s–50s] (*US drugs*) to sell narcotics. **7** [1940s+] a synon. with FUCK v.[3]; usu. in phr. *you can shove that* or imper. *shove it!*

shove *v.*[2] [mid-19C+] to put, to place.

shove *v.*[3] *see* SHOVE OFF v.

shove along *v.* **1** [mid-19C+] (*also* **shove**) to leave. **2** [late 19C–1920s] to move (quietly). **3** [1910s–10s] to go along with, to support. **4** [1940s] to survive.

shove-and–let-go *n.* [1920s–40s] (*W.I.*) a Model T Ford. [on this car low gear was engaged by pressing a foot pedal]

shove a sock in it *v. see* PUT A SOCK IN IT v.

shove a trunk *v.* [late 18C–19C] to interfere where one has been neither asked nor invited. [SE *shove* + TRUNK n.[2]]

shove-devil *n.* [mid-17C] the penis. [? the trad. joke whereby a monk seduces a virgin by explaining the necessity of 'shoving the devil back into hell']

shove for *v.* [late 19C] to move towards, to go to.

shove in *v.* [late 19C] to pawn. [one 'shoves' the pawned item across the pawnbroker's counter]

shove in the eye *n.* [late 19C+] a punch in the face.

shove in the mouth *n.* [19C] a glass of spirits.

shove it! *excl.* [1940s+] (*orig. Aus.*) a general excl. of dismissal and rudeness. [abbr. SHOVE IT UP YOUR ARSE! excl.]

shove it in and break it *v.* (*also* **shove it up someone's ass and break it**) [1960s+] to defeat an opponent, to cause a good deal of trouble.

shove it up your arse! *excl.* (*also* **shove it up your ass! …butt! …hole!** **stick it…! stuff it…!**) [20C+] an excl. of contempt, dismissal. [SE *shove* + ARSE n.[1] (1)/ASS n. (2)/BUTT n.[1] (2)/HOLE n.[1] (1)]

shovel *n.* **1** [1930s] (*US*) a banjo. **2** [1970s+] (*US gay/prison*) the penis.

shovel *v.* [1920s–50s] (*orig. S.Afr.*) to hand over, to pass.

shovel (and broom) *n.* [1920s–50s] (*Aus./US*) a room. [rhy. sl.]

shovel (and pick) *n.* [1940s+] **1** a prison (cf. BUCKET n.[2]). **2** an Irishman (cf. GOODIE AND BADDIE n.). [rhy. sl.; (1) = NICK n.[6] (1); (2) = MICK n.[1] (1)]

shovel and spade *n.* [20C+] a blade, a knife. [rhy. sl.]

shovel and tank *n.* [20C+] a bank. [rhy. sl.]

shovel guts *v.* [20C+] (*US*) to perform menial, distasteful tasks.

shovelhead *n.* [1980s+] (*Aus./US*) an idiot. [SE *shovel* + -HEAD sfx (1)]

shovel it! *excl.* [1980s+] (*N.Z.*) an excl. of dismissal, disbelief.

shovel it higher and deeper *v. see* PILE IT HIGHER AND DEEPER v.

shovel of malt *n.* [early 19C] a pot of porter. [SE *malt*, the main constituent of the drink]

shovels and spades *n.* [1990s+] AIDS. [rhy. sl.]

shovel shit *v. see* SHOVEL (THE) SHIT *v.*

shovel shit against the tide *v.* [1930s+] to make one's best efforts, despite overwhelming odds. [SHIT *n.*[1] (1)]

shovel stiff *n.* [1900s–30s] (*US tramp*) a tramp who would beg but does it poorly and will therefore work (at a labouring job) when necessary. [SE *shovel* + STIFF *n.*[2] (4)]

shovel (the) shit *v.* [1930s+] **1** to gossip, esp. maliciously; to talk nonsense. **2** to do an unpleasant job of work. [SE *shovel* + SHIT *n.*[3] (1)/SHIT *n.*[3] (4)/SHIT *n.*[1] (1)]

shove off *v.* (*also* **shove, shove on/out**) [mid-19C+] to leave, to go away, usu. as imper. [naut. jargon, to push a boat away from the side of another one or off the harbour wall before setting out]

shove one's oar in *v.* (*also* **stick one's oar in**) [19C+] to interfere where one is not wanted.

shove one's trunk *v.* [late 18C] to move.

shove out *v. see* SHOVE OFF *v.*

shover *n.*[1] (*also* **shuffer**) [1900s–20s] **1** a chauffeur. **2** a driver. [mispron.]

shover *n.*[2] [1930s–50s] (*US drugs*) a drug dealer. [synon. with PUSHER *n.*[3] (1)]

shover (of the queer) *n.* [mid-19C–1940s] a passer of counterfeit money. [SHOVE THE QUEER *v.*]

shove shit uphill *v.* [1960s+] to sodomize. [SE *shove* + SHIT *n.*[1] (1)]

shove shorts *v. see* PUSH SHORTS *v.*

shove-straight *n.* [18C] the penis.

shove the moon *v.* [early–mid-19C] to abscond from a house or flat, taking one's furniture and possessions, but paying no bills. [such exits are usu. nocturnal]

shove the queer *v.* [early 19C–1950s] to pass counterfeit money. [SHOVE *v.*[1] (2) + QUEER *n.* (2)]

shove the tumbler *v.* [late 17C–mid-19C] (*UK Und.*) to be whipped at the cart's tail. [SE *shove* + TUMBLER *n.*[2]; the image is of pushing the cart forward as one strains beneath the blows]

shove under *v.* [20C+] (*Aus.*) to kill, usu. in passive, i.e. *to be shoved under*, to be killed. [i.e. to push under the ground]

shove-up *n.* [early 19C] (*UK Und.*) nothing.

shovin' and pushin' *adj.* [1970s] (*US Black*) trying as hard as possible to succeed.

shoving *adj.* [1940s] a general intensifier, synon. with FUCKING *adj.* (1).

show *n.*[1] **1** [late 18C+] (*orig. US*) a matter, an event, an affair; thus *good show, bad show, poor show, the whole show.* **2** [mid-19C+] (*Aus./US*) a chance, an opportunity; thus *give him a show,* give him a chance; *no show,* no chance. **3** [late 19C+] (*orig. milit.*) a battle, a military engagement, a war; thus *big show,* a major campaign, a war. **4** [1900s–10s] a home. **5** [1910s] (*Aus.*) a business. **6** [1920s–30s] (*UK Und.*) any form of crime. [SE *show,* a display]

show *n.*[2] [1920s+] (*N.Z.*) a house.

show *n.*[3] *see* HOLY SHOW *n.*

show, the *n.* [1960s+] (*US Black*) a state of prominence, 'the spotlight'.

show *v.* [1930s+] of a woman, to be obviously pregnant; thus *showing,* pregnant.

show a leg *v.* (*also* **show leg**) [19C] to run off, to escape; to move at speed.

show a leg! *excl.* [mid-19C+] an excl. used as a wake-up call. [orig. used in institutions to ensure that the leg was male and not, illicitly, female; note Fraser & Gibbons, *Soldier & Sailor Words & Phrases* (1925): 'In the Navy, it dates from long ago, when women, ostensibly as sailors' wives, were allowed to live on board ship. The usual call was, 'Show a leg or a purser's

stocking!' Everybody had to put a leg outside the hammock, a stockinged leg denoting that its occupant was a woman, who was then allowed to remain until the men had cleared out']

show an Abyssinian medal *v.* [late 19C] of a man, to have a fly-button undone, to have one's penis sticking inadvertently through one's flies. [the *Abyssinian* War 1893–6]

show and prove *v.* [1990s+] (*US Black*) to demonstrate.

show and tell *n.* [1950s+] (*US*) an elaborate exhibit intended to impress, persuade or inform. [play on elementary school use]

show a point to *v.* [late 19C–1910s] (*Aus./N.Z.*) to swindle, to act dishonourably towards.

show bacon *v. see* PULL BACON *v.*

showbiz *n.* [1940s+] (*orig. US*) **1** show business, the entertainment industry; thus *that's showbiz,* that's how things are (and there's nothing you can do about it). **2** in fig. use, ostentation, melodrama, showing off.

showbiz *adj.* [1940s+] pertaining to show business, entertainment. [SHOWBIZ *n.* (1)]

showbiz sherbet *n.* [2000s] (*drugs*) cocaine (cf. BIRDIE POWDER *n.*). [SHOWBIZ *n.* (1) + SHERBET *n.* (4); the image of cocaine as an expensive drug]

showboat *n.* [1970s] a flashy car. [*see* next]

showboat *v.* [1960s+] (*orig. US*) **1** to show off, esp. by parading oneself in front of an audience. **2** to show someone off, to display, to parade. [SE *showboat,* a river steamer on which entertainments are given]

showboating *n.* [1960s+] (*US*) ostentatious self-promotion. [SHOWBOAT *v.* (1)]

showcase nigger *n.* [1960s+] (*US Black*) a token Black employee, hired to parade the liberal racial attitudes of a White-owned organization. [SE *showcase,* a display cabinet + NIGGER *n.*[1] (1)]

showdown *n.* **1** [late 19C+] (*orig. US*) a confrontation. **2** [1970s] (*US prison*) an opportunity to break the prison rules without discovery. [SE *showdown,* the moment in poker when all the cards are revealed to see who wins the pot]

show drink *v.* [late 19C] (*US*) to be tipsy, to be drunk.

shower *n.*[1] [late 19C+] (*Aus.*) a dust-storm, usu. prefaced by a local name, e.g. *Cobar shower, Darling shower.*

shower *n.*[2] *see* SHOWER (OF SHIT) *n.*

shower bath *n.* [20C+] (*orig. sporting*) 10 shillings (50p); thus *showers to a shilling,* odds of 10–1 (cf. BEES (AND HONEY) *n.*). [rhy. sl.; Cockney pron. of *shower bath,* 'shahr barf' = half (a pound)]

shower of rain *n.* [20C+] (*Aus.*) a train. [rhy. sl.]

shower (of shit) *n.* [1940s+] **1** (*also* **shower of cunts, ...savages, ...shites, ...whore's bastards**) an unimpressive group of people. **2** a pile of second-rate things. **3** a term of abuse aimed at a single person. [SE *shower of* + SHIT *n.*[1] (1)/CUNT *n.*[2] (1)/SHITE *n.* (4)]

shower scum *n.* (*also* **pond scum**) [1980s+] (*US campus*) a highly unpleasant person; also attrib.

shower spank *v.* [1980s+] (*US teen*) to masturbate in the shower. [SPANK *v.*[2] (4)]

showful(l) *see under* SHOFUL and its combs.

showhouse *n.* [1940s+] (*gay*) a brothel, a place where homosexuals can meet openly (sex is usu. performed off the premises) (cf. ACCOMMODATION HOUSE *n.*).

showie *n.* (*also* **showy**) [1950s+] (*Aus.*) a display handkerchief, worn in one's top jacket pocket. [abbr.; it is worn for 'show']

showing up *n.* **1** [mid-19C] (*UK Und.*) that which reveals one's presence to the authorities. **2** [1910s–20s] a shameful predicament.

show leg *v. see* SHOW A LEG *v.*

show-leg day *n.* (*also* **shulleg-day**) **1** [late 19C] a very windy day. **2** [late 19C–1920s] a very muddy day. [on such days women accidentally/are forced to raise their long skirts and thus 'show a leg', or at least an ankle]

show more roots than Kunta Kinte v. [1970s] (*US Black*) of a woman with dyed hair, to be showing the original colour at the roots, to need to have it re-dyed. [a pun on the hero of *Roots* (1976), the best-selling novel by Alex Haley]

show one's ass v. [1950s+] (*US Black*) to appear foolish, to show off, to make an exhibition of oneself.

show one's cards v. (*also* **show one's hand**) [late 19C+] (*orig. US*) to reveal oneself, usu. to a greater extent than desired. [poker imagery]

show one's color v. [1950s–80s] (*US Black*) to act in a stereotyped way, to behave in the way Whites expect Blacks to behave. [ironic reversal of SE *show one's colours*, to declare one's own standpoint, to act proudly despite any opposition]

show one's paces v. [late 19C+] to display one's abilities. [horse-riding imagery]

show one's shape v. [18C–19C] to make an appearance, to come into view. [SE *shape*, one's figure]

show one's shapes v. **1** [late 17C–early 18C] to turn around, to march off. **2** [late 18C–early 19C] to take off one's clothes, esp. preparatory to a judicial flogging. [SE *shape*, one's figure]

show out v.[1] [late 19C] (*Aus.*) to try, to attempt.

show out v.[2] [late 19C+] (*US Black*) **1** to show off, to flaunt oneself. **2** to lead on, to deceive.

show pony n. [1940s+] (*Aus.*) one who cares more for appearance than performance. [SE *show pony*, one that looks good in shows but may be less useful in practical life]

show shapes v. **1** [mid-19C] to play pranks, to act in a flighty manner. **2** [1960s+] to dance, esp. at a discotheque.

show someone the ropes v. (*also* **show the ropes to**) [20C+] to show someone how to do a task. [naut. imagery]

show someone what time it is v. (*also* **tell someone what time it is**) [1990s+] (*orig. US Black*) to explain, to 'put someone in the picture', to 'teach someone a lesson'. [KNOW WHAT TIME (OF DAY) IT IS v.]

showstopper n. **1** [1950s+] (*camp gay*) a particularly attractive young man. **2** [1980s+] a very attractive woman.

show the elephant v. [mid–late 19C] (*US*) to show someone the sights, esp. of the town-dweller thus regaling their 'country cousins'. [var. on SEE THE ELEPHANT v.]

show the lions and tombs v. [late 18C–early 19C] to point out the sights. [in the original context of London, the *lions* refer to the Tower of London, the *tombs* to Westminster Abbey]

show the ropes to v. see SHOW SOMEONE THE ROPES v.

show the white feather v. (*also* **show the white rag**) [early 19C+] to surrender or act in a cowardly manner (cf. HAVE A WHITE FEATHER v.). [a white feather in a game-bird's tail is a mark of inferior breeding; note earlier *find a white feather in one's tail*, *mount the white feather*]

showtime n. [1990s+] (*US Black*) a show-off. [SHOWTIME v.]

showtime adj. [1990s+] (*US Black*) ostentatious. [SHOWTIME v.]

showtime v. [1990s+] (*US Black*) to show off, to flaunt oneself.

show tunes n. [1970s] (*US gay*) noises made during intercourse or fellatio. [SE *show tunes*, the songs performed in a musical]

show-up n. **1** [mid-19C+] an identification parade. **2** [2000s] an embarrassment. [SHOW UP v.]

show (up) v. [late 19C+] (*US*) to appear, to arrive.

show up v. [mid–late 19C] (*UK Und.*) **1** to identify (and arrest). **2** to make a complaint against.

show-up man n. [1930s] (*US Und.*) the member of a hijack team who holds up the truck driver.

showy n. see SHOWIE n.

shpeiler/shpieler n. see SPIELER n. (7).

shpilkes n. [20C+] (*US*) anxiety, nervousness. [Yid.]

shpritz v. see SCHPRITZ v.

shrap n. (*also* **shrape**) [late 16C] (*UK Und.*) wine used to weaken the will of a confidence trickster's victim. [SE *shrape*, bait of chaff or seed laid for birds; hence a snare]

shrapnel n. (*also* **shrap**) [1910s+] (*orig. N.Z.*) copper coins, small change. [SE *shrapnel*, shell or bomb fragments]

shred n. [late 17C–early 19C] a tailor. [the shreds of cloth he discards]

shred v. [1980s+] **1** (*US campus*) to overcome, to conquer. **2** (*US Black*) to travel fast.

shredded adj. **1** [1980s+] (*US teen*) drunk. **2** [2000s] very upset.

shreddie n. [1990s+] (*UK juv.*) one who has badly thinning hair but still combs it in an attempt to disguise the situation. [the breakfast cereal *Shreddies*, made of spaced strands of wheat]

shreddies n. [1990s+] **1** underpants. **2** (*UK juv.*) a 'game' whereby the victim's underpants are tugged upwards so hard that they tear.

shred the tube v. [1980s] (*US teen*) to go surfing. [SE *shred* + surf jargon *tube*, the top part of the wave, where it starts to curl over, forming a tube]

shrewd-head n. [20C+] (*Aus./N.Z.*) a cunning person. [SE *shrewd* + -HEAD sfx (1)]

shrewdy n. (*also* **shrewdie**) [1910s+] (*Aus./N.Z.*) **1** a shrewd person, one who lives on their wits. **2** a shrewd, cunning trick; esp. in phr. PULL A SHREWDIE v.

shriek n. [1900s–30s] **1** something or someone seen as very funny. **2** something ostentatiously fashionable.

shriek! excl. [1900s–30s] an excl. of alarm, annoyance or similar emotion.

shrimp n.[1] **1** [15C+] a small, weak, insignificant person. **2** [late 19C+] a term of address, used affectionately or derisively. **3** [1960s+] a midget. **4** [1970s+] (*US gay*) a small penis (cf. ANTEATER n.). **5** [1990s+] a baby.

shrimp n.[2] [mid-17C] a prostitute (cf. ALLEY CAT n.). [the association of prostitution/women with FISH n.[1]]

shrimper n. [1970s+] a foot fetishist. [toes are supposed to resemble pink shrimps]

shrimping n. [1970s+] toe-sucking. [for ety. see SHRIMPER n.]

shrimps and rice n. [1940s] (*US Black*) a metaphor for whatever it is one wants.

shrimpy adj. [mid-19C; 1950s+] (*US*) small, insignificant, physically slight. [SHRIMP n.[1] (1)]

shrine of Venus n. see VENUS'S HIGHWAY n.

shrink n.[1] [1960s+] (*orig. US*) a psychoanalyst, a psychiatrist. [HEAD-SHRINKER n.]

shrink n.[2] [1970s] (*US campus*) a young woman's tight-fitting sweater.

shrinkette n. [1970s] a female psychoanalyst or psychiatrist. [SHRINK n.[1] + SE fem. sfx *-ette*]

shrink klink n. [1980s] (*Aus.*) a psychiatric institution. [SHRINK n.[1] + CLINK n.[1] (1)]

shrink someone's head v. [1950s+] (*orig. US*) to psychoanalyse. [HEAD-SHRINKER n.]

shrinksville n. [1950s+] (*orig. US*) madness; spec. a state of mind that makes it advisable for a person so afflicted to consult a psychoanalyst. [SHRINK n.[1] + -VILLE sfx[1]]

shritter n. [2000s] (*US Black*) the victim of a beating. [ety. unknown]

shroff n. see SCHROFF n.

shroom v. **1** [1980s] (*US campus*) to act wild, to be madly excited. **2** [1990s+] (*US*) to ambush. [? SHROOMS n.]

shroom dog n. [1980s+] (*US campus*) someone who uses hallucinogens. [SHROOMS n. + DOG n.[2] (3)]

shrooms n. [1980s+] psilocybin mushrooms, used as a recreational hallucinogenic drug. [abbr. SE *mushrooms*]

shroud and boiler n. [1900s–40s] (*US*) a formal dress suit and starched dress shirt.

shrubbery n. **1** [19C] pubic hair. **2** [1920s–40s] (*US prison*) sauerkraut. **3** [1940s] whiskers.

sht... see also under SCHT...

sh'touse n. see SHOUSE n.

shtum *adj.* (*also* **schtum, shtoom, stumm, stumpf**) [late 19C+] quiet, silent, dumb. [synon. Yid.]

shtum up *v.* (*also* **shtoom up, stumm up**) [1950s+] to be quiet. [SHTUM *adj.*]

shubalafa *n.* [2000s] (*US Black*) a Black woman who assumes the dominant role in a relationship. [ety. unknown]

shuck *n.* **1** [mid-19C+] (*US, esp. Black*) a hoax, a lie, a deceit. **2** [1940s] (*US Black*) a theft, a fraud. **3** [1960s] an easy job. [SE *shuck*, a husk; thus fig. nonsense, deception]

shuck *v.*[1] [mid-19C+] (*US*) to strip off one's clothes, to undress; usu. with preps. e.g. *shuck out of/off*. [SE *shuck*, to pod, to strip husks]

shuck *v.*[2] **1** [mid-19C+] (*US, esp. Black*) to defraud, to tease, to lie. **2** [1960s] (*US Black*) to have sexual intercourse with. **3** [1960s+] to do something half-heartedly or deceptively. [(1) and (3) SHUCK n. (1); (2) ? SHAKE v.[1]]

shuck and jive *n.* [1960s+] (*US, esp. Black*) deception, play-acting, obfuscation; also attrib. [SHUCK n. (1) + JIVE n.[1] (2)]

shuck and jive *v.* [1960s+] (*US, esp. Black*) **1** (*also* **shive**) to act deceptively, to confuse. **2** to make a promise one has no intention of keeping. [SHUCK AND JIVE n.]

shuck drop *v.* [1940s] (*US Black*) to take advantage of a victim or fool. [SHUCK n. + DROP v.[2] (4)]

shucking and jiving *n.* (*also* **shucking and sliding**) [1950s+] (*US Black*) fooling, playing around. [SHUCK AND JIVE v. (1)]

shuckman *n.* [1960s] a swindler. [SHUCK n. (1)]

shuck out *v. see* SHACK v. (2).

shucks *n.* [mid-19C] (*US*) **1** the paper money issued by the Confederate States during the US Civil War (cf. CHAFF n.[2]). **2** in fig. use, nothing. [SE *shuck*, shells of peas, husks of corn and similar refuse; thus implying the worthlessness of the Confederate currency]

shucks! *excl.* **1** [mid-19C+] (*orig. US*) a mild excl. of surprise, regret, annoyance etc. **2** [1970s] (*US campus*) a synon. for SUCKS (TO YOU)! excl. [SE *not worth shucks*, worthless, useless]

shuck the corn *v.* [20C+] to masturbate (cf. BEAT ONE'S MEAT v.).

shuffer *n. see* SHOVER n.[1].

shuffle *n.* [1900s–60s] (*US Black*) a Black man deliberately playing dumb and acting out the White man's stereotyped view of their race; thus as v., to play this part. [the shuffling walk, along with shiny smiles and 'natural rhythm', are major parts of this image]

shuffle *v.*[1] [mid-18C–1960s] to practise a confidence trick, a hoax or a deception; thus *shuffle-sharper*, a confidence trickster.

shuffle *v.*[2] **1** [1950s] (*US street gang*) to have a fist-fight. **2** [1980s] (*US prison*) to play the passive role in a homosexual couple.

shuffle (off) *v.* (*also* **shake off**) [early 17C; 19C+] to die. [orig. in *Hamlet* (1602) III.i.67: 'When we have shuffel'd [*sic*] off this mortall coile']

shuffler *n.*[1] [mid-17C] one who cadges drinks. [their shuffling, hesitant demeanour]

shuffler *n.*[2] [mid-19C+] (*US Und.*) a confidence trickster. [their ability, lit. or fig., to 'shuffle one's deck', i.e. either to perform as a card-sharp or to render the victim confused]

shufflers *n.* [mid-19C] the feet.

shuffle the deck *v.* [1990s+] to masturbate (cf. LARK v.).

shufti *v.* (*also* **shufty**) [1940s+] to watch, look at. [SHUFTIE n.]

shuftie *n.* (*also* **shufti, shufty, shoofti**) [1940s+] a brief glance, a quick look. [Arabic *sufti*, have you seen?; note Aus milit. *shooftie room*, the viewing room of an Egyptian brothel]

shufty *v.* [1950s] to tell, to assure. [SHUFTIE n.]

shug *n.* (*also* **sug**) **1** [mid-19C+] (*US Black*) an affectionate name, usu. for a woman or homosexual man. **2** [late 19C+] (*Aus.*) money. [abbr. (1) SE *sugar*; (2) SUGAR n.[1] (1)]

shuks *v.* [1950s] (*W.I.*) to hurt someone's feelings. [SHAKE v.[3] (3) or SE *shuck (off)*, but note excl. of disappointment, SHUCKS! excl. (1)]

shule *see under* SHOOL.

shulleg-day *n. see* SHOW-LEG DAY n.

shundicknick *n.* [late 19C–1930s] a pimp, a ponce. [Yid.]

shunt *n.*[1] [1950s] the vagina; also attrib.

shunt *n.*[2] **1** [1970s+] a car crash. **2** [1980s] sexual intercourse. [orig. racing driver jargon]

shunt *v.* **1** [late 19C–1910s] to leave, to run off quickly. **2** [late 19C+] to dismiss from a job; thus as n., dismissal; thus *give someone the shunt*, to get rid of.

shunter *n.*[1] [1990s+] a male homosexual. [? play on his 'coupling up' but note PULL A TRAIN v.]

shunter *n.*[2] [2000s] a member of the public, one who is outside the criminal world. [rhy. sl. = PUNTER n.[1] (4)]

shunter's pole *n.* [1980s+] the penis. [railway jargon *shunter's pole*, a rod used to facilitate the coupling and uncoupling of goods wagons and engines/POLE n.]

shunt (off) *v.* (*Aus.*) **1** [late 19C] to get rid of a thing; thus *off-shunt*, an act of dismissal. **2** [1910s+] (*also* **shunt out**) to dismiss a person.

shuper *n.* (*also* **shooper**) [1900s–20s] (*US*) a large beer glass. [ety. unknown; ? link to SE *super*]

shurk *n.* [late 17C–18C] (*UK Und.*) **1** a pickpocket. **2** a card-sharp. [SE *shirk*]

shut *n.* [late 18C] a *shutter*. [abbr.]

shut *v. see* SHUT UP v. (3).

shut ass *v.* [1960s] (*US Black*) to keep quiet. [SE *shut* + ASS n. (5)]

shut-door *n.* [2000s] a private conversation.

shut down *v.* **1** [1960s+] (*US Black*) to leave someone bereft of repartee. **2** [1970s] (*US Black*) to prove someone wrong. **3** [1980s] (*US campus*) to go to sleep.

shut-eye *n.* **1** [late 19C+] sleep, rest; thus *go shut-eye*, to go to sleep. **2** [1920s] (*US tramp*) a victim, a dupe.

shut eyes *n.* [1960s+] (*US police*) a sexual offender. [their suggestion, 'Now just shut your eyes…']

shut-in *n.* **1** [20C+] one who stays in a lot, esp. due to illness. **2** [1950s] (*US prison*) a prisoner.

shut it! *excl.* [late 19C+] be quiet! shut up! ['it' is the mouth]

shut off! *excl.* [1910s] be quiet!

shut one's arse *v.* (*also* **shut one's ass**) [1980s+] to be quiet; esp. in imper. [SE *shut* + ARSE n.[1] (4)/ASS n. (5)]

shut one's face (up) *v.* (*also* **close one's face**) [late 19C+] to be quiet; esp. as imper. *shut your face!*

shut one's gob *v.* [mid-19C+] to be quiet; esp. in imper. [SE *shut* + GOB n.[1] (1)]

shut one's head *v.* (*also* **shut one's neck, shut up one's head**) [mid-19C+] (*US*) to be quiet; usu. as imper.; thus *open one's head*, to speak. [HEAD n.[4]]

shut one's hole *v.* [1940s+] to be quiet; esp. in imper. [HOLE n.[1] (3)]

shut one's knickers *v.* [1960s] to be quiet, to stop talking; esp. as imper.

shut one's neck *v. see* SHUT ONE'S HEAD v.

shut one's noise *v. see* HOLD ONE'S NOISE v.

shut (one's) pan *v.* [late 18C–1920s] to be quiet; esp. as imper. [SE *shut* + PAN n.[1] (2)]

shut one's puss *v.* [1950s] (*US*) to be quiet, to stop talking; also as imper.

shut one's row *v.* [1930s+] to be quiet; esp. as imper. [ROW n.[1]]

shut one's trap *v.* (*also* **close one's trap**) [late 18C+] to be quiet; usu. as imper. [SE *shut* + TRAP n.[3]]

shut pan *v. see* SHUT (ONE'S) PAN v.

shut someone down *v.* [1950s+] (*US*) **1** to beat a rival in a drag race. **2** to gain victory in any competition.

shutter-bug *n.* [1930s+] (*orig. US*) a photographer; both a professional and an enthusiastic amateur. [SE *shutter* + BUG n.[5] (2)]

shutter clicker *n.* [1940s] (*US Black*) a cinema projectionist.

shuttered *adj.*[1] [late 19C] taken away on a shutter, esp. of drunkards.

shuttered *adj.*[2] [late 19C] in a state of total ignominy. [SE *shutter*, which one pulls down over one's shame]

shutter-girl *n.* [1930s] (*US*) a prostitute working from a room with shutters, attracting customers from the street (cf. AWAYDAY GIRL n.).

shutter-racket *n.* [early 19C] a robbery committed by boring through a shutter, removing a pane of glass and reaching through for anything to steal; thus *shutter-racket worker*, one who specializes in such robberies. [SE *shutter* + RACKET n.[1] (1) (+ WORKER n.[1] (1))]

shutters *n.* **1** [late 19C+] (*US Black*) the eyes. **2** [1990s+] the eyelids.

shuttle *n.* [late 17C] the penis. [euph.; the weaver's *shuttle* goes backwards and forwards/in and out]

shuttlebutt *n.* [1970s+] (*US campus*) a fat woman, esp. referring to the buttocks. [SE *shuttle*, i.e. its movement backwards and forwards + BUTT n.[1] (2); play on SCUTTLEBUTT n.]

shut up *v.* **1** [mid-17C+] to stop talking. **2** [early 19C+] to bring to an end, to reduce to a state of incapacity, to kill. **3** [mid-19C+] (*also* **shut**) to stop someone else talking, or making a noise.

shut up! *excl.* **1** [mid-19C+] be quiet! stop talking! **2** [1980s+] a general excl. of disbelief, you can't fool me! forget it! don't make me laugh!

shut up in the parson's pound *phr.* [late 18C–early 19C] married.

shut up one's garret *v.* [late 19C] to be quiet, to stop talking. [GARRET n. (3)]

shut up one's head *v. see under* SHUT ONE'S HEAD v.

shut up shop *v.* **1** [mid-16C+] to stop, usu. talking. **2** [late 17C] (*also* **shut up shop-windows**) to go bankrupt.

shut up someone's shop *v.* [late 19C–1900s] to kill someone, to murder someone.

shut your...! *see also under* SHUT ONE'S...

shut your beak! *excl.* [20C+] (*W.I.*) shut up! be quiet! [BEAK n.[2] (2)]

shut your rag-box! *excl.* [late 19C] shut up! be quiet! [RAG BOX n. (1)]

shv... *see also under* SCHW...

shvitz *v.* [20C+] to sweat. [synon. Yid.]

shvoogie *n. see* SCHVUG n.

shy *see also under* SHYLOCK.

shy *n.* **1** [late 18C–19C] a quick, jerking or careless throw, as of a stone etc. **2** [mid-19C] an attempt to damage by sarcasm or verbal attack. **3** [mid-19C–1920s] an attempt, a 'go'. [ety. unknown; OED suggests link to SE *shy-cock*, a cowardly cock and thus person, but the logic is hard to comprehend – unless one had to throw the cock at its opponent]

shy *adj.*[1] [mid-19C+] doubtful in amount or quality. [orig. gambling]

shy *adj.*[2] [late 19C+] (*orig. US*) short of, esp. short of money.

shyckle *n. see* SCHEITL n.

shy-cock *n.* **1** [mid-18C–mid-19C] one who hides from the bailiff. **2** [late 18C–early 19C] fig. a coward. [SE *shy-cock*, a fighting cock that will not fight; but ? pun on *Shylock*, one who does not wish to let go of their money]

shyin' *adj. see* SHINE adj.[2].

shylock *n.* (*also* **shy**) **1** [mid-19C+] one who supplies private loans. **2** [1900s–10s] (*also* **sherlock**) a crooked businessman. [the moneylender in Shakespeare's *The Merchant of Venice* (1600)]

shylock *v.* (*also* **shy**) **1** [20C+] to lend money at extortionate rates of interest. **2** [1950s–70s] to offer 'protection'. [SHYLOCK n.]

shypoo *n.* [20C+] (*Aus./N.Z*) **1** second-rate liquor. **2** (*also* **shypoo house, ...joint, ...shanty, ...shop**) the place that sells such liquor. [SHYPOO adj.]

shypoo *adj.* [20C+] (*Aus./N.Z.*) second-rate, inferior. [ety. unknown; ? 'bastard Chinese' (cit. in *AND*) for 'soft drink'; ? Cantonese *sai po*, a small shop]

shyse *adj. see* SHICE adj. (3).

shyst *adj.* [2000s] (*UK Black/teen*) aggressive, promiscuous. [backform. f. SHYSTY adj. (2)]

shyster *n.*[1] **1** [mid-19C+] (*orig. US*) (*also* **shice, shise**) a lawyer, usu. a crooked one, or with the implication that any lawyer is innately untrustworthy. **2** [1920s–30s] a crooked businessman. [? Ger. *Scheisser*, shitter or Du. *scheidsman* or *schiedsreichter*, an arbitrator, an umpire. Alternatively, f. a New York lawyer named *Scheuster* (pron. *shyster*), whose courtroom antics so infuriated Justice Osborne of the city's Essex Market Court that he began talking of 'scheuster' practices; for full discussion see Michael Quinion, *World Wide Words* (Internet)]

shyster *n.*[2] *see* SHICER n.

shyster *adj.* [mid-19C+] (*US*) crooked, corrupt; fraudulent; often as *shyster lawyer*. [SHYSTER n.[1] (1)]

shyster *v.* [mid-19C+] to trick money out of someone; usu. as adj. *shystering*. [SHYSTER n.[1] (1)]

shysty *adj.* (*also* **scheisty**) **1** [mid-19C+] (*US*) tight-fisted. **2** [1990s+] (*orig. US*) a general negative, used of situations, objects and primarily people, in which case a degree of arrogance/cockiness is implied. [SHYSTER n.[1] (1)]

Siamese twins *n.* [mid-19C] (*US*) fish balls.

Siberia *n.* [1930s+] (*US prison*) **1** the solitary confinement cells. **2** Sing Sing Pentitentiary, NY (cf. ABBOTT'S PRIORY n.). **3** Clinton prison, Dannemora, NY. **4** a fig. place of abandonment or being ignored or sent to Coventry. [*Siberia*, centre of the Russian *gulag*]

sice *n.* [mid-17C–mid-19C] a sixpence. [14C SE *sice*, the 6 on a die]

sices *n.* [mid-19C] in dice-playing, a throw of six. [14C SE *sice*]

Sicilian necktie *n. see* COLOMBIAN NECKTIE n.

sick *n.* (*also* **sickness**) **1** [late 19C] illness. **2** [1930s+] (*drugs*) (*also* **kick-sick**) the illness that accompanies withdrawal from drug addiction.

sick *adj.*[1] **1** [mid-19C; 1980s+] (*US campus*) a general pej., of poor quality, unfashionable, unappealing, stupid, weak, bizarre. **2** [mid-19C+] annoyed, worried, disgusted, often with undertones of jealousy. **3** [1950s+] (*US*) mentally disturbed, psychopathic, esp. in a sadistic way. **4** [1950s+] (*orig. US*) morbid, depraved, e.g. *sick sense of humour*. **5** [1980s+] (*Aus./US campus*) excellent, first-rate. [(5) on the bad = good model]

sick *adj.*[2] [1930s+] (*drugs*) suffering from withdrawal symptoms when addicted to narcotics, esp. heroin; thus *go sick*, to suffer withdrawal symptons.

sick and wrong *phr.* [1980s+] (*US campus*) a general pej., absolutely impossible, unthinkable, totally disgusting; also used ironically. [ext. of SICK adj.[1] (1)]

sick as a cat *phr.* [late 17C; mid-19C+] very sick.

sick as a cushion *phr.* [late 17C–18C] very hungry, thus not sick at all.

sick as a dog *phr.* [late 16C+] very sick; also in fig. use; thus ext. (*Aus*). *sick as a blackfellow's dog*.

sick as a horse *phr.* (*also* **sick as a mule**) [mid-18C–1930s] extremely ill. [a horse cannot vomit, so such sickness has no immediate relief]

sick as a parrot *phr.* [1970s+] extremely depressed, usu. mentally rather than physically distressed. [the term became widespread as the clichéd response attributed to many sportsmen, esp. soccer players and managers, after a loss or defeat. Note 17C *melancholy as a parrot*, quoted by E.P.]

sick as a rat *phr.* [late 17C] very sick.

sick as mud *phr.* [1930s] very depressed or upset.

sick-ass *adj.* [1990s+] (*US*) unpleasant, crazy. [SICK adj.[1] (3) + -ASS sfx]

sickener *n.* (*also* **sickner**) [19C+] anything depressing, disappointing, frustrating.

sickie *n.*[1] [1950s+] (*Aus.*) a day's sick leave; thus THROW A SICKIE v. [SE *sick leave*]

sickie *n.*[2] **1** [1960s] a heroin addict. **2** [1960s] (*US campus*) a homosexual. **3** [1960s+] (*orig. US*) (*also* **sicky**) anyone considered to be 'sick in the head', insane, crazy. [SICK adj.[2]/SICK adj.[1] (3)]

sick in fourteen languages *phr.* [late 19C] (*US*) very sick.

sickner *n. see* SICKENER *n.*

sickness *n. see* SICK *n.*

sicko *n.* [1970s+] a mentally unstable person, with overtones of sexual perversion. [SICK adj.[1] (3)]

sicko *adj.* [1970s+] perverted, insane. [SICKO *n.*]

sick on *v. see* SIC ON *v.*

sickrel *n.* [late 17C–early 18C] a puny, weak, sickly person. [SE *sick* + sfx *-rel*]

sicky *n. see* SICKIE *n.*[2] (3).

sic on *v.* (*also* **sick on**) [mid-19C+] to set on, to have someone attack a third party, to set someone on another person. [SE *sick on*, to set a dog on]

side *n.*[1] [late 19C+] pretentiousness, swagger, conceit; thus *put on side*, to give oneself airs; *more side than a billiard ball*, very arrogant, snobbish. [? play on billiards jargon *side*, spin; or ? dial. *side*, proud; post-1940s use tends to be consciously archaic]

side *n.*[2] **1** [1930s] (*US*) America, as opposed to England. **2** [1960s] (*US Black*) the Black area of town; the original was Chicago's *South Side*. **3** [1970s+] an area of a town or city; used (in London) as *West Side*, Shepherd's Bush, *South Side*, Brixton, in somewhat romanticized analogies with areas of US cities.

side *n.*[3] [1930s–80s] (*US Black*) a gramophone record.

side *n.*[4] [1960s+] (*US Black*) a woman. [ideally she is on or at one's *side* in all circumstances]

side *adj.* [20C+] surreptitious, clandestine. [ON THE SIDE *phr.*]

side *v.* [1910s] to act in a pretentious manner, to put on airs. [SIDE *n.*[1]]

sidearms *n.* [1940s] (*US milit.*) cream and sugar; salt and pepper.

sideboard *n.* **1** [mid-late 19C] a stand-up collar. **2** [mid-19C+] side-whiskers, sideburns.

side boys *n.* [1900s] (*US*) a style of side-whiskers.

sidebust *v.* [1990s+] (*US Black*) to gossip, to tell tales.

side chick *n.* (*also* **side-gal**) [1920s+] (*US*) a woman who is an alternative to a man's wife or regular girlfriend. [BIT ON THE SIDE *n.* (1)]

side dish *n.* [1940s] (*US Und.*) a mistress.

side-door Pullman *n.* [late 19C–1920s] (*US tramp*) a freight car. [the side-opening doors of the freight wagon. The real Pullman is a luxury passenger coach]

sidedywry *adj.* [late 18C–early 19C] crooked. [SE *side* + *awry*]

side-flaps *n. see* FLAPS *n.* (1).

side-gal *n. see* SIDE CHICK *n.*

side-hill salmon *n.* [1950s] (*US*) bacon.

sidekick *n.*[1] [20C+] (*Aus./US*) **1** an assistant, a partner, an accomplice. **2** in fig. use, something on which one depends; a regular pleasure. [backform. f. SIDEKICKER *n.*]

sidekick *n.*[2] [1910s–50s] (*US Und.*) a side pocket. [SE *side* + KICK *n.*[4]]

sidekicker *n.* [1900s–30s] (*Aus./US*) an assistant, a partner, an accomplice.

side-levers *n.* [1920s+] sideburns, side-whiskers.

side-money *n.* [1920s–60s] (*US*) money earned in addition to one's regular job.

side of a funeral *n.* [late 19C] (*US*) a pork chop.

side-partner *n.* [late 19C–1920s] (*US*) an accomplice, an assistant.

side-pocket *n.* **1** [late 18C–early 19C] used in a variety of phrs. implying a lack of need, e.g. *as much need of a wife as a dog of a side-pocket*, of a worn-out old man; *want as much as a toad/dog wants a side-pocket*, does not want at all. **2** [late 19C] (*US*) an out-of-the-way drinking saloon.

side-pork *n.* [1950s] (*W.I.*) an albino. [the similarity in colour of the meat and the human skin-tone]

sides *n.* [1920s–40s] (*US Black*) padding used by women to enlarge the appearance of the hips.

side-scrapers *n.* [late 19C] (*UK middle class*) short sideburns, fashionable 1879–8.

side-sim *n.* [early 17C] a fool, a simpleton. [SE *side* + abbr. *simpleton* or abbr. *Simon* as in late 16C *Sim subtle*, a cunning fellow]

side-splitter *n.* [mid-19C+] something exceedingly funny.

side-splitting *adj.* [mid-19C+] extremely funny.

sidetrack *v.* [1920s–60s] (*US Und.*) to arrest.

side valve *v.* [1980s+] (*Aus. prison*) to act the gangster.

sidewalk snail *n.* [1930s–50s] (*US*) a policeman (cf. ANIMAL *n.*[1]). [his slow and steady pace]

sidewalk surfing *n.* [1970s+] (*US*) skate-boarding; thus *sidewalk surfer*, a skate-boarder.

sidewalk susie *n.* [mid-19C] (*US*) a prostitute (cf. NIGHT WALKER *n.*).

sideways *n.* [1960s+] (*N.Z. prison/US campus*) suicide. [euph.; weak rhy. sl.]

sideways *adj.* [1990s+] (*US prison*) eccentric.

sideways! *excl.* [1990s+] (*US Black*) a general excl. of departure, I'm off! goodbye! see you later!

side-wheeler *n.* [20C+] (*US, orig. baseball*) a left-handed person.

sidewinder *n.* **1** [mid-late 19C] a powerful blow. **2** [1940s+] a thug, esp. a gangster's bodyguard.

side-wings *n.* [late 19C–1900s] sideburns, side-whiskers.

sidey *adj.* (*also* **sidy**) [late 19C–1940s] conceited. [SIDE *n.*[1] + sfx *-y*]

sidge *n.* [1970s] (*US Und.*) Sicilian. [abbr.]

sidies *n.* [1960s] *side*burns. [abbr.]

siding *n.* [1980s+] (*US Black, Los Angeles*) leaning to the side in an exaggerated relaxed manner while driving.

sidity/siditty *see under* SADDITY.

sidney rocks *n.* (*also* **charlie rocks**) [1920s–30s] (*US*) socks. [rhy. sl.]

sidy *adj. see* SIDEY *adj.*

siege *n.* [mid-16C–mid-17C] excrement. [Lat. *sedem*, a seat + 16C *siege*, a privy]

sieg heils *n.* [2000s] haemorrhoids. [rhy. sl. *seig heils* = piles]

Sif *n.* [1970s] (*US*) San Francisco. [abbr.]

sif(f) *n. see* SYPH *n.*

sift *v.*[1] [mid-late 19C] to steal small coins; thus *sifter*, a housebreaker, a burglar. [such that would pass through a sieve]

sift *v.*[2] [20C+] (*US/UK Black*) to move, to start moving; thus *sift in*, to arrive. [SE *shift*]

sig *v. see* SIGNIFY *v.*

sigging *n.* [1940s] (*US Black*) competing in rounds of ritualized mockery. [SIGNIFY *v.* (3)]

sighs and tears *n.* [1930s+] (*US Und.*) ears. [rhy. sl.]

sight *n.*[1] [early 18C–mid-19C] a gesture of derision, made by placing the thumb on the tip of one's nose and spreading out the fingers like a fan; thus *double sight*, the same gesture, intensified by joining the tip of the little finger to the thumb of the other hand, which in turn has its fingers extended fanwise.

sight *n.*[2] [early 19C+] a good deal, a large amount; usu. in phr. *a sight more*; usu. prefixed by *darned*, *bloody*, *dashed* etc; thus BY A LONG SIGHT *phr.*

sight *n.*[3] **1** [mid-19C+] anything that gives rise to horrified, amused or disgusted glances. **2** [late 19C+] a shocking, repulsive or ridiculous spectacle, esp. used of people who see themselves or others improperly or inelegantly dressed.

sight *v.* **1** [1910s+] (*Aus.*) to tolerate, to put up with. **2** [1930s; 1970s+] (*UK Und./Black*) to observe, to see.

sight? *excl.* [1950s+] (*W.I. Rasta*) do you understand?

sight a pebbly beach *v. see* LAND ON A PEBBLY BEACH v.

sight delight *n.* [1980s+] (*US campus*) a good-looking man.

sight for sore eyes *n.* [mid-19C+] a welcome appearance, often used as an affectionate greeting, *you're a sight for sore eyes*.

sightseers *n.* [1970s+] (*UK Und.*) the crowd that gathers round illicit street traders or gamblers.

sigmunds *n.* [1990s+] haemorrhoids. [rhy. sl. on *sigmund freuds*; ult. *Sigmund Freud (1856–1939)*]

signboard *n.* [late 19C–1900s] the human face.

signification *n.* [20C+] (*US Black*) negative or hostile talk, criticism, ritualized abuse. [SIGNIFY v.]

signifier *n.* [1930s+] (*US Black*) one who boasts or makes insulting remarks. [SIGNIFY v.]

signify *v.* (*also* sig) (*US Black*) **1** [1920s+] to boast or to pretend to a greater sophistication than one actually possesses. **2** [1930s+] to cause trouble, to stir things up, often purely for fun, whatever the actual results. **3** [1930s+] to recite one of a variety of purpose-written 'tales', usu. recounting the exploits of some mythical gangster-cum-sexual athlete.

signifying *n.* [1940s+] (*US Black*) boasting, insinuating; esp in the form of a ritual game of testing a rival's emotional strength by insulting their relatives. [SIGNIFY v. (3)]

sign of a house to let *n.* (*also* sign of tenements to let) [late 18C–early 19C] a widow's weeds. [ext. of APARTMENT TO LET n.]

sign of the five shillings *n.* [late 18C–early 19C] any public house called the Crown; thus the *sign of the 10 shillings*, the Two Crowns; ...*15 shillings*, the Three Crowns. [SE *5 shillings* (25p), the value of the obs. crown piece]

sign on *v.* [1980s+] (*Aus. prison*) to enter into a stable homosexual relationship.

signs on you! *excl.* (*also* signs on it!) [1920s+] (*orig. Irish*) bad luck to you! consequences will follow!

sign up *v.* [1970s+] (*Aus. Und.*) to make a written confession.

sigoggling *adj. see* SKYGODLIN adj.

Sigourney Weaver *n.* [1990s+] the female genitals, esp. the pubic hair. [rhy. sl. = BEAVER n.⁵ (1); ult. film star Sigourney Weaver (b.1949)]

sigster *n.* [mid-19C] a nap, a short sleep. [ety. unknown]

sike! *excl. see* PSYCH! excl.

sil *adj.* (*also* sill) [1930s+] foolish; also infatuated; thus of a lesbian, involved in an affair. [abbr. SE *silly about*]

silence *v.* **1** [early 18C+] to stun, to knock down. **2** [19C+] to kill.

silencer *n.* [19C+] a stunning blow. [SILENCE v. (1)]

silence-yelper *n.* [late 19C] (*UK Und.*) a courtroom usher. [their main task, the frequent orders of 'Silence in court!']

silent *adj.* [early 18C] murdered.

silent beard *n.* [18C] pubic hair; the vagina. [development of 18C BEARD n.¹ (1)]

silent beef *n.* [1960s+] (*US Und.*) a note attached to an individual's police record stating that they have been suspected (but not charged due to lack of proof) of committing a crime; the note requests that they be punished to the maximum extent for such lesser charges as can be brought; also as v. [SE *silent* + BEEF n.² (5)]

silent but deadly *phr.* (*also* silent but violent) [1950s+] a silent, but very smelly, breaking of wind.

silent city *n.* [1970s] (*US Black*) a graveyard.

silent cop *n.* [1930s+] (*Aus.*) a yellow 'sleeping policeman' placed in the centre of road intersections. [SE *silent* + COP n.¹ (1)]

silent flute *n.* [early 18C–early 19C] the penis (cf. ACCORDION n.). [SE *silent* + FLUTE n.² (1)]

silent night *n.* [20C+] light (ale). [rhy. sl.]

silk *n.*¹ [early 19C+] a King's or Queen's Counsel. [the material of their gowns, rather than the cotton of a junior barrister's]

silk *n.*² **1** [mid-19C; 1960s+] (*UK/US Black*) a White person. **2** [1980s] (*US*) an authority figure. [the supposed wearing of silk clothes by (rich) Whites]

silk *n.*³ *see* SILK BROAD n.

silk *adj.* [1920s+] (*US*) admirable, excellent, acceptable.

silk and satin *n.*¹ [1970s+] (*drugs*) any combination of amphetamines and barbiturates or tranquillizers.

silk and satin *n.*² [1970s+] (*US Black*) an attractive White or light-skinned woman. [ext. of SILK BROAD n.]

silk and top *n. see* STRING AND TOP n.

silk and twine *n.* (*also* string and twine) [1920s–50s] (*US*) wine. [rhy. sl.]

silk broad *n.* [1960s] (*US Black*) a White woman. [SILK n.² (1) + BROAD n.² (3)]

silked (to the bone) *adj.* [1940s+] (*US Black*) dressed in the height of fashion. [SILKS n. + TO THE BONE phr.]

silker *n.* [late 19C–1900s] (*US*) a silk top hat.

silk hat *n. see* SILK STOCKING n.

silkies *n.* [1980s] (*US*) silk female underwear.

silko *n.* [2000s] (*Irish*) a thug, a thief. [ety. unknown]

silks *n.* [1940s+] (*US Black*) expensive clothing, poss. actually made of silk. [SE early 16C–19C]

silk-snatcher *n.* **1** [early 18C–early 19C] a thief who grabs the bonnets and hats from pedestrians. **2** [mid-18C] (*UK Und.*) a thief who specialized in stealing cloaks by twitching them from the wearer's back.

silk stocking *n.* (*also* silk hat) [late 19C+] (*US, later US Black*) a rich person; in pl., the social élite. [SILK STOCKING adj.]

silk stocking *adj.* [late 18C+] designating the social élite, pertaining to the wealthy; thus *Silk Stocking District*, the Upper East Side of Manhattan. [metonymy; such stockings, as opposed to the more usual cotton stockings, were a luxury item until the invention of nylon *c.*1935]

silkworm *n.* **1** [early–mid-18C] a woman who tours clothes shops and examines the goods but never buys. **2** [late 19C–1970s] (*US/UK Und.*) a shoplifter who specializes in silk items or jewellery.

sill *adj. see* SIL adj.

sillikin *n.* (*also* silliken) [mid-19C–1910s] a fool, a simpleton. [SE *silly* + dimin. sfx -*kin*]

silly *n.*¹ [mid-19C+] a foolish person.

silly *n.*² [1970s] (*N.Z. juv.*) an erection. [? it makes one 'feel silly']

silly *v.* [mid-late 19C] to stun, i.e. to render silly or 'insensible'.

silly-arse *n.* [1990s+] (*Aus.*) a fool (cf. FART-ARSE n.). [SILLY-ARSE adj.]

silly-arse *adj. see* SILLY-ASS adj.

silly as a bag *phr.* [1930s+] (*Aus./N.Z.*) extremely silly.

silly as a chook (with its head cut off) *phr.* (*also* silly as a curlew) [1940s+] (*Aus./N.Z.*) **1** extremely silly. **2** tipsy, drunk.

silly as a cut snake *phr.* [1930s+] (*Aus./N.Z.*) extremely silly.

silly as a hatful of arseholes *phr.* [1940s–50s] (*Aus.*) extremely silly. [ARSEHOLE n. (1)]

silly as a hatful of worms *phr.* [1950s+] (*orig. Aus.*) very silly. [a euph. for prev.]

silly as a two-bob watch *phr.* (*also* crazy/mad as a two-bob watch, silly as a Woolworth's watch) [1940s+] (*Aus.*) extremely silly or crazy.

silly as a wet hen *phr.* [1980s+] (*N.Z.*) extremely foolish.

silly as a wheel *phr.* [1950s+] (*Aus.*) extremely foolish.

silly as a Woolworth's watch *phr. see* SILLY AS A TWO-BOB WATCH phr.

silly-ass *adj.* (*also* silly-arse, silly-assed) [1910s+] (*mainly US*) a general term of disparagement, stupid, foolish (cf. CLAY-ASSED adj.). [SE *silly* + -ASS sfx]

silly billy *n.* [mid-19C+] a fool, a simpleton (cf. BEN n.¹). [SE *silly billy*, a clown's stooge]

silly-born *adj.* [1940s–50s] stupid, foolish.

silly cow *n.* [late 19C+] a derog. ref. to a woman, irrespective of her actual character. [SE *silly* + COW n.¹ (1)]

silly-grin! *excl.* [1910s] (*Aus.*) 'an ironical ejaculation importing pain or misfortune' (Downing, *Digger Dialects*, 1919).

silly house *n.* [1960s] a psychiatric institution.

silly moo *n.* [late 19C+] a stupid woman. [softened version of SILLY COW *n.*; it enjoyed a nationwide revival in the UK in the late 1960s with the success of the TV sitcom *Till Death Us Do Part*, in which it was used by Alf Garnett (played by Warren Mitchell) as a knee-jerk description of his put-upon wife]

sillypop *n.* [late 19C] a fool, esp. a foolish, flighty woman.

silly putty *n.* [1960s] (*drugs*) psilocybin/psilocin. [joc. use of proprietary name of the children's toy]

silly season *n.* [20C+] (*Aus.*) the Christmas holidays. [note journ. jargon *silly season*, the summer holiday period, esp. August, when no real news is supposed to happen]

silly willy *n.* [mid-17C–18C; 1960s] a fool, a simpleton (cf. BEN N.[1]).

silo *n.* [1910s] (*US*) alcohol made of fermented vegetables.

silver *n.* [1980s+] (*N.Z. drugs*) aluminium foil, used for smoking heroin.

silver and gold *n.* [1990s+] a cold. [rhy. sl.]

silver (and gold) *adj.* [1990s+] old. [rhy. sl.; the image is of ageing hair]

silverback riding *n.* [2000s] (*US Black*) male homosexual intercourse.

silver bangle *n.* [1990s+] (*W.I.*) handcuffs.

silver beggar *n.*[1] [mid-19C] a counterfeit banknote or forged document.

silver beggar *n.*[2] (*also* **silver lurker**) [mid-late 19C] a beggar who claims to have suffered in some disaster or other, e.g. a fire or shipwreck, and asks for money in order to rebuild their life; such pleas are accompanied by a variety of documents, supposedly 'proving' the legitimacy of their claims.

silver cooper *n.* [19C] a kidnapper. [naut. jargon, the press gang, who 'cooped up' men for a payment of silver coins]

silver hell *n.* [mid-19C] a low-class casino. [SE *silver*, fig. inferior to gold + HELL N.[2] (3)]

silver jeff *n.* [1950s] (*US*) a quarter or a nickel coin. [the image of Thomas *Jefferson* on the nickel, ? presumably confused with that of George Washington on the quarter]

silver-laced *adj.* [19C] suffering from an infestation of lice. [SE *silver-laced*, silver-threaded]

silver lurker *n. see* SILVER BEGGAR N.[2].

silver pearl *n.* [1990s+] (*drugs*) a type of marijuana (cf. BLACK DOMINA N.). [? the silveriness of this particular strain]

silver pheasant *n.* [1920s] a beautiful upper-class woman.

silver plate *phr.* [1910s–20s; 1990s+] please. [pron. of Fr. *s'il vous plait*; 1990s+ use is US campus]

silver serpent *n. see* SERPENT n.

silver spoon *n.* **1** [20C+] (*Aus.*) the moon. **2** [1990s+] a pimp (cf. ALPHONSE N.[2]). [rhy. sl.; (2) = HOON n. (1)]

silvertail *n.* **1** [late 19C+] (*orig. Aus.*) a wealthy or upper-class person. **2** [1940s–50s] one who puts on 'airs and graces', a social climber. **3** [1940s–50s] (*UK prison*) a better-class prisoner. **4** [1980s+] (*Aus. prison*) a prisoner who colludes with the authorities. [SE *silver* + TAIL N.[2] (1)]

silver-wig *n.* [1920s] a grey-haired man. [SE *silver* + *wig*/WIG N.[3] (1)]

silver wing *n.* [1950s] (*US*) a 50-cent piece. [the engraving of eagle's wings on the coin]

silvery moon *n.* (*also* **silvery**) **1** [1950s+] a derog. term for a Black person (cf. DAPTO DOG n.). **2** [1990s+] (*Aus.*) a pimp (cf. ALPHONSE N.[2]). [rhy. sl.; (1) = COON n. (5); (2) = HOON n. (1)]

sim *n.* [1990s+] (*Aus. Und.*) a fool, a dupe. [abbr. SE *simpleton*]

simkin *n.*[1] (*also* **simpkin**) [late 17C+] a fool, a simpleton. [proper name *Simon*, presumably as in the nursery rhyme *Simple Simon*; note 19C theatrical jargon *Simkin* or *Simpkin*, the fool in (usu. comic) ballets]

simkin *n.*[2] (*also* **simpkin**) [mid-late 19C] (*Anglo-Ind.*) champagne. [Ind. pron.]

simloons *n. see* SIMOLEONS n.

simmer (down) *v.* [mid-19C+] to calm down.

simmon *n.* [late 18C+] per*simmon*, esp. in *simmon beer*. [abbr.]

simoleon *n.* (*also* **sambolio, samoleon, simoleum, simolion**) [late 19C+] (*US*) $1 (cf. ABE N.[2]). [? SIMON n. (2) + SE *Napoleon*, a Fr. coin worth 20 francs]

simoleons *n.* (*also* **simloons**) [late 19C+] (*US*) money. [SIMOLEON n.]

simon *n.* **1** [late 17C–19C] a sixpence. **2** [late 19C+] (*US*) $1. [for ety. *see* TANNER n.]

simon! *excl.* [1960s+] (*US*) yes indeed! [Sp.]

simon legree *n.* [20C+] (*US Black*) a cruel overseer or employer. [the character *Simon Legree*, the stereotypically evil slavemaster, in the novel *Uncle Tom's Cabin* (1852) by Harriet Beecher Stowe]

simon (pure) *n.* **1** [early 19C+] the genuine article, the real thing. **2** [1900s] poteen. [proper name of a Quaker character in *A Bold Stroke for a Wife* (1718) by Susannah Centlivre; he is impersonated by another character during Act V]

simon-pure *adj.* [mid-19C+] genuine, real. [SIMON (PURE) n.]

simon soon gone *n.* [mid-late 16C] a lazy servant; 'he, that when his Mayster hath any thing to do, he will hide him out of the way' (Awdeley, *Fraternitie of Vagabondes*, *c.*1561).

simp *n.* [20C+] (*orig. US*) a fool, a simpleton. [abbr.]

simp *adj.* [1970s] (*US campus*) easy. [abbr. SE *simple*]

simp *v.* **1** [1900s] (*Aus.*) to do things in a simplistic manner. **2** [1960s–70s] (*US Black*) to act like a fool. [SIMP n.]

simper like a frumety-kettle *v.* (*also* **simper like a furmity-kettle**) [late 17C–19C] to smile, to look cheerful. [SE *frumenty*, a dish made of hulled wheat boiled in milk and seasoned with cinnamon, sugar etc]

simpkin *see under* SIMKIN.

-simple *sfx* **1** [1920s+] (*US*) used with a variety of nouns to imply obsessiveness. **2** [1990s+] as a sfx implying ignorant.

simple animal *n. see* ANIMAL N.[1] (5).

simple as falling off a log *phr. see* EASY AS FALLING OFF A LOG phr.

simple pimp *n.* [1950s–70s] (*US Black*) one who barely manages as a pimp and has no hope of transcending that level of employment within the criminal hierarchy (cf. CHILE CHUMP n.).

simpler *n.* [late 16C–early 17C] (*UK Und.*) the dupe or victim of a confidence trickster or a prostitute. [SE *simple*]

simple simon *n.*[1] **1** [late 18C+] a fool, a simpleton. **2** [1950s] (*drugs*) a non-addict. [the nursery rhyme]

simple simon *n.*[2] **1** [1910s–40s] a diamond, usu. a diamond ring. **2** [1970s] (*drugs*) psilocybin/psilocin. [rhy. sl.]

simpson *n.* [late 19C] **1** water used in adulterating milk. **2** adulterated milk. **3** a milkman. [one *Simpson*, a dairyman who *c.*1868 was prosecuted for watering down his milk supply]

simp togs *n.* [1960s] best clothes, smart clothes. [SE *simply* the best + TOGS n. (1)]

simpy *adj.* [1940s+] foolish, gullible. [SIMP n.]

sin *n.* [2000s] (*US Black*) a tough, aggressive Black man. [? his sinfulness]

sin bin *n.*[1] [1950s+] (*orig. US*) **1** (*sporting*) an enclosure where errant players, e.g. in ice hockey, have to sit for a pre-determined period of time. **2** a school to which otherwise uneducable pupils, whose activities have disrupted their original school, are sent as a last resort.

sin bin *n.*[2] [1980s+] (*Aus.*) a van or car used primarily for sex.

sin-buster *n.* [1930s–40s] (*US*) a clergyman.

sincanter *n.* [late 16C] a contemptuous or depreciatory term applied to men, usu. as *old…* [Fr. *cinquante*, fifty, which in 16C was considered old]

sinch *n. see* CINCH N.[1] (1).

Sin City *n.* [1970s+] (*orig. US*) any city seen as a centre of vice and corruption, esp. Las Vegas, Nevada.

sinful *adj.* [1920s+] excessive, far too much.

sing *v.* **1** [early 19C+] to speak. **2** [late 19C] to speak insincerely, hypocritically. **3** [1920s+] to make a confession, usu. to the authorities. **4** [1930s+] to inform against, to betray. [pvb 'he that sings once, weeps all his life after'; note Shakespearian *sing*, of a woman, to make advances to; of a man, to have sexual intercourse]

Singapore tummy *n.* [20C+] the diarrhoea that often afflicts travellers in foreign countries (cf. AZTEC HOP n.).

sing dumb *v.* (*also* **sing dummy**) [mid-19C] (*UK/US Und.*) to say nothing (esp. under interrogation). [SING v. (1) + SE *dumb/* DUMMY n.[1] (1)]

singer *n.* [1930s–60s] (*US Und.*) an informer. [SING v. (4)]

singe someone's eyebrows *v.* [1990s+] (*US gay*) to attack verbally.

singing *n.* **1** [1930s+] the act of informing. **2** [1970s] (*US gay*) a sustained verbal attack. [SING v. (4)]

single *n.* [1930s+] (*US*) **1** a $1 bill. **2** a person, esp. a criminal, who works or lives alone.

single *v.* [1930s–40s] (*US*) to work as a criminal by oneself. [SINGLE n. (2)]

single broth *n.* [17C] small beer.

single-jack *n.* [1920s–30s] (*US tramp*) a 1-legged, 1-armed or 1-eyed beggar. [SE *single* + JACK n.[2]]

single-o *n.* **1** [1930s] (*US*) an unmarried person. **2** [1930s–40s] (*US tramp*) a tramp who travels alone. **3** [1930s+] (*US Und.*) a criminal who works alone and the crimes they commit; thus as adj., solo, working alone. [SE *single/*SINGLE n. (2) + -o sfx (2)]

single peeper *n.* [late 18C–early 19C] a 1-eyed person. [SE *single* + PEEPER n. (1)]

single-pennif *n.* **1** [mid–late 19C] a £5 note. **2** [20C+] £1. [backsl.; PENNIF n.]

singleten *n.* (*also* **singleton**) [late 17C–early 19C] a very foolish person. [? SE *single*, simple or as an elision of a *single ten*; the 10 in cards ranks 1 below the knave, 'he' must therefore be a fool]

singleton *n.*[1] [late 18C–early 19C] a corkscrew. [*Singleton*, a Dublin corkscrew maker, who lived 'in a place called Hell […] his screws are famous for their excellent temper' (Grose, 1785)]

singleton *n.*[2] [1990s+] an unmarried person. [popularized by Helen Fielding in *Bridget Jones's Diary* (1996)]

sing like a canary *v.* (*also* **sing like a bird/lark, trill like a canary**) [1930s+] (*UK Und.*) to make a full confession to the police. [SING v. (4)]

sing o-be-joyful *v.* (*also* **sing oh-be-easy**) [late 18C–early 19C] to pretend to satisfaction when one wants, in fact, to complain but dare not.

sing on *v.* [20C+] (*W.I.*) to gossip about. [Carib.E. *sing on*, to sing a song or hymn with the intention of using its lyrics to mock a third party]

sing out *v.* [early–mid-19C] for a villain, on being arrested, to betray their accomplices. [SING v. (1), since it predates SING v. (3), + naut. jargon *sing out*, to call out]

sing out beef *v.* [19C] to cry 'stop thief!' [SE *sing out* + HOT BEEF! excl.]

sing small *v.* [mid-18C–1950s] to modify one's speech, esp. when it had previously been arrogant and boastful.

sings more like a whore's bird than a canary bird *phr.* [late 18C–early 19C] a phr. said of one who has a strong, manly voice. [WHORE'S BIRD n.]

sing someone a kyrie eleison *v. see* GIVE SOMEONE A KYRIE ELEISON v.

sing the black psalm *v.* [late 18C–early 19C] usu. of children, to weep.

sing the blues *v.* [1910s+] to complain, to whinge. [BLUES n.[1]]

sing the hallelujah chorus *v.* [1990s+] (*US prison*) to be released from prison; to die in prison.

sin-hiders *n.* [late 19C] (*UK Und.*) trousers. [? they cover the male genitals]

sin hound *n.* [1920s–40s] (*orig. US Black*) a priest. [SE *sin* + HOUND sfx]

Sinjin's Wood *n.* [late 19C] St John's Wood. [the affectedly smart pron. of *St John's* + deliberate puns on the 'sin' and 'gin' available in St John's Wood, then an area of London notorious for its kept women and prostitutes]

sink *n.* [mid-19C–1910s] a drunkard. [SINK v.[2]]

sink *v.*[1] **1** [early 18C–19C] (*US Und.*) to embezzle the takings of an illegal card-game, confidence trick etc. **2** [1900s] to betray, to inform on.

sink *v.*[2] [late 18C+] to drink alcohol, e.g. *sink the amber*, to drink beer; thus *sinker*, a drunk. [note *Antidote against Melancholy* (1661): 'In a pint there's small heart, Sirah, bring a quart / […] / Wee'l sink him before sunset']

sink *v.*[3] [late 19C–1900s] (*US*) to bury; also in fig. use.

sink a darkie *v. see* CHOKE A DARKIE v.

sinker *n.*[1] **1** [mid–late 19C] a counterfeit coin. **2** [late 19C–1900s] (*US*) $1. **3** [1930s] (*UK tramp*) a shilling (5p). [SE *sinker*, a small circular lead weight]

sinker *n.*[2]

sinker *n.*[3] [late 19C+] (*US*) any form of doughy cake, esp. a doughnut; thus *sinkers and suds*, doughnuts and coffee (cf. COFFEE-AND n.). [the habit of dunking a doughnut into one's coffee]

sinkers *n.* [late 18C–mid-19C] (*UK Und.*) 'old stockings that have sunk the small parts into the heel' (*Sinks of London*, 1848).

sink her *v.* [20C+] of a man, to have sexual intercourse (cf. DO HER JOB FOR HER v.).

sink-hole *n.* [mid–late 19C] the throat.

sink me! *excl.* (*also* **sink you!**) [mid-17C–1940s] a general oath.

sink-pocket *n.* [1910s] (*Aus.*) a winner at cards who leaves the game without offering a chance for his opponents to redeem their losses. [the winnings *sink* into his *pocket* and are lost there forever]

sinks *n.* [mid-19C] in dice-playing, a throw of 5. [Fr. *cinq*, 5]

sink the black *v.* [1990s+] to drink stout. [snooker imagery + ref. to the colour of stout]

sink the little man in the boat *v.* [1990s+] of a man, to have sexual intercourse (cf. BURY IT v.). [LITTLE MAN (IN THE BOAT) n. (2)]

sink the sausage *v.* (*also* **sink the log/shaft/weenie**) [1960s+] to have sexual intercourse; also anal intercourse (cf. BURY IT v.). [SE *sink* + SAUSAGE n.[1] (1)/LOG n.[4]/SHAFT n.[1]/WEENIE n.[1] (4)]

sink the soldier *v.* (*also* **sink the sailor**) [1960s+] of a man, to have sexual intercourse (cf. BURY IT v.).

sink you! *excl. see* SINK ME! excl.

sinner *n.*[1] [mid-19C–1920s] a publican. [Luke 18:13: 'And the publican, standing afar off, would not lift up so much as his eyes unto heaven, but smote upon his breast, saying, God be merciful to me a sinner']

sinner *n.*[2] [late 19C+] an affectionate term for an otherwise unnamed man; usu. prefaced by *old…*

sinse *n.* [1980s+] (*drugs*) marijuana. [abbr. SENSIMILLIA n.]

sinsemilla *n. see* SENSIMILLIA n.

sin-shifter *n.* [1910s] (*Aus.*) any form of clergyman. [? pun on SE *scene-shifter*]

sip *n.* [mid-19C–1900s] a kiss. [a bee 'sipping' nectar from a flower]

sip *v.*[1] [late 19C+] to urinate. [backsl. = PISS v.[1] (1)]

sip *v.*[2] [1940s–70s] (*US drugs*) to smoke cannabis; thus n., a puff of a marijuana cigarette.

sip at the fuzzy cup *v.* (*also* **drink at the fuzzy cup**) [1970s+] (*US Black*) to perform cunnilingus (cf. BEARD RIDE n.; BOX LUNCH n.). [FUZZY CUP n.]

sip from the hairy teacup *v.* [2000s] to perform cunnilingus (cf. BEARD RIDE n.; BOX LUNCH n.). [var. on prev.]

siph *n. see* SYPH n.

siphon the python *v.* (*also* **syphon the python**) **1** [1960s+] (*Aus.*) to urinate (cf. BLEED ONE'S TURKEY *v.*). **2** [2000s] (*US*) to have sexual intercourse (cf. BURY IT *v.*). **3** [2000s] (*US*) to masturbate (cf. BEAT ONE'S HOG *v.*).

sipper *n.* [late 19C] gravy. [SE *sibber-sauce*; ? ult. Lat. *cibarius*, pertaining to food]

sip the syrup *v.* [1990s+] (*US teen*) to drink (beer or liquor).

si quis *n.* [mid-19C] a candidate for holy orders. [the notification of the candidacy begins *si quis...*, if anyone...]

Sir Andrew's knot *n.* (*also* **Sir Tristram's knot**) [16C] the hangman's noose. [? notorious hanging judges]

Sir Anthony Blunt *n.* [1980s+] a highly objectionable person. [rhy. sl. = CUNT *n.*² (1); ult. UK art historian and traitor *Anthony Blunt* (1907–83)]

Sir Berkeley *n.* [1930s] the vagina; thus by metonymy, sexual intercourse (cf. ALL QUIET *n.*). [rhy. sl.; *Sir Berkeley Hunt* = CUNT *n.*¹ (1)]

Sir Cloudesley *n.* [late 17C–18C] a hot drink of small beer mixed with brandy, plus lemon juice, spices and sugar. [orig. a naval speciality, proper name *Sir Cloudesley* Shovel (1650–1707), a notable British admiral who was knighted for his suppression of piracy]

Sir Courtly Nice *n.* [late 17C–18C] a foolish, foppish dandy. [the play *Sir Courtly Nice* (1685) by John Crowne (c.1640–c.1700)]

siretch *n.* (*also* **sirretch**) [mid-19C] cherries. [backsl.]

Sir Harry *n.* **1** [mid-19C] a close-stool, a commode. **2** [1920s] constipation. [euph.]

Sir James Cotterell's salad *n. see* COTTERELL'S SALAD n.

Sir John *n.* **1** [14C–18C] a country parson. **2** [19C] a close-stool, an enclosed chamberpot. **3** [late 19C] the penis (cf. ABRAHAM *n.*¹).

Sir Martin Wagstaffe *n.* [mid-17C] the penis (cf. ABRAHAM *n.*¹). [play on SE *wag* + STAFF OF LOVE n.]

Sir Oliver *n.* (*also* **Sir Olive**) [early–mid-19C] the moon. [ext. of OLIVER *n.*¹]

Sir Posthumous Hobby *n.* [late 17C–early 19C] an obsessive dandy. [a pun on SE *hobby*: 'one that Draws on his Breeches with a Shoeing-horn; also a Fellow that is Nice and Whimsical in the set of his Cloaths' (B.E.)]

Sir Quibble-Queer *n.* [late 17C–early 18C] a trifling fool.

sirretch *n. see* SIRETCH n.

sir-reverence *n.* (*also* **surreverence**) [mid-17C–mid-19C] faeces, excrement; also used as excl. [14C formal phr. (Nares suggests orig. *save reverence*) meaning 'begging your pardon' and used as 'a kind of apologetical apostrophe, when anything was said that might be thought filthy, or indecent'. By the late 16C it had taken on this euph. secondary meaning and is the basis of the 20C+ euph. to 'excuse oneself' and the schoolchild's cry of 'Can I be excused?' Thus: '*reverence*, an ancient custom which obliges any person easing himself near the highway or foot-path, on the word *reverence* being given to him by a passenger, to take off his hat with his teeth, and without moving from his station to throw it over his head, by which it frequently falls into the excrement' (Grose, 1796)]

sirrocco-sifters *n.* [late 19C] (*US campus*) whiskers. [? rhy. sl.]

Sir Sydney *n.* [early–mid-19C] a clasp-knife. [ety. unknown]

Sir Thomas *n. see* JOHN THOMAS n. (1).

Sir Timothy (Treat-all) *n.* [late 17C–18C] a very generous man. [from the play *The City-Heiress, or, Sir Timothy Treat-all* (1682) by Aphra Behn (1640–89)]

Sir Tristram's knot *n. see* SIR ANDREW'S KNOT n.

Sir Walter Scott *n.* [mid–late 19C] a pot, usu. of beer. [rhy. sl.; ult. Scot. novelist *Sir Walter Scott* (1771–1832)]

sis *n.*¹ (*also* **cis, siss, sissy, suz**) **1** [mid-17C+] a sister. **2** [mid-19C+] used as a term of direct address whether or not to one's actual sister. **3** [late 19C+] (*US*) a young woman. [abbr. SE]

sis *n.*² *see* SISSY n.

siserary *n.* (*also* **siserara**) **1** [late 18C–mid-19C] a severe reprimand. **2** [mid-19C] a hard blow. [popular corruption of a writ of *certiorari*: 'A writ, issuing from a superior court, upon the complaint of a party that he has not received justice in an inferior court, or cannot have an impartial trial, by which the records of the cause are called up for trial in the superior court' (*OED*)]

siss *n.*¹ **1** [early 17C] a large, fat woman. **2** [early 18C] a prostitute.

siss *n.*² *see* SIS *n.*¹.

sissy *n.* (*also* **ciss, cissie, cissy, sis, siss**) **1** [late 19C+] a weakling, an effeminate man or boy. **2** [1920s+] an effeminate homosexual man. [SE *sissy*, a coward; ult. SIS *n.*¹ (1)]

sissy *adj.* (*also* **cissy, sissified, sissyish**) **1** [late 19C+] (*orig. US*) weak or effeminate. **2** [1920s+] homosexual; pertaining to the world of male homosexuality. [SISSY n.]

sissy-bar *n.* [1960s+] a metal loop fixed behind the seat of a cycle or motorcycle. [SISSY n. (1), i.e. the perceived cowardice of one who holds onto the loop]

sissy-boy *n.* [20C+] (*US*) a weakling; a male homosexual. [SISSY n. (1)]

sissy cure *n.* [1950s] (*US drugs*) tapering off a narcotics addiction rather than stopping immediately (with the concomitant withdrawal pains). [SISSY n. (1); the implication being that 'real men' simply stop and suffer]

sissy pants *n.* (*also* **sissy britches**) [1940s+] a weakling; thus an effeminate homosexual man. [ext. of SISSY n. (1); on model of SMARTY-BOOTS n.]

sissy soft sucker *n.* (*also* **soft sucker**) [1980s+] (*US Black*) a weak, effeminate man (though not necessarily a homosexual). [SISSY adj. (1) + SE *soft* + SUCKER *n.*³ (1)]

sister *n.*¹ **1** [1910s+] (*US*) a term of address to any woman whose proper name one does or does not know. **2** [1920s+] a term of address between effeminate male homosexuals; thus self-referential as *your sister*. **3** [1940s] (*gay*) the platonic gay friend of another gay man; similarly used by lesbians. **4** [1960s+] (*orig. US*) a feminist or fellow woman.

sister *n.*² [1920s+] (*US Black*) a Black woman; esp. as *the sisters*.

sister-act *n.* [1940s–70s] **1** a homosexual couple. **2** a homosexual man having sex with a heterosexual woman.

sister girl *n.* [1980s+] (*US campus*) a term of address among female friends.

Sister Hicks *n. see* JIMMY HIX n.

sister in black *n. see* BROTHER IN BLACK n.

sister-in-law *n.* [1940s+] (*US Black*) any woman working for a pimp other than his favourite; also used by homosexual prostitutes (cf. BROTHER-IN-LAW n.).

sisters *n.* [1950s–60s] (*camp gay*) the police, when working in pairs.

sisters (of the scabbard) *n.* [17C] prostitutes, as a group. [play on BROTHER (OF THE) BLADE n.]

sit a woman *v.* [mid-19C+] (*US Black*) to entertain a woman. [trans. use of SE *sit*, to sit someone down]

sit beside her *n.* [20C+] **1** cider. **2** a spider. [rhy. sl.; ult. f. the nursery rhyme 'Little Miss Muffet']

sit bitch *v. see* RIDE BITCH v.

sitch *n.* [1960s+] (*US campus*) a difficult situation.

sit chilly *v. see* LAY CHILLY v.

sit-down *n.*¹ [1910s–30s] (*US tramp*) a free sit-down meal.

sit-down *n.*² [1970s+] a conference.

sit down *v.* [20C+] (*Aus.*) to settle in a place, to take up a piece of land.

sit down like Miss Priss *v.* (*also* **sit down like Miss Queensie**) [20C+] (*W.I.*) to sit around while others are working. [the names of fig. lazy women]

sit-down money *n.* [1970s+] (*Aus.*) unemployment benefit. [SE *sit-down*, a rest + *money*]

sit-down-upons *n.* [mid-19C] trousers.

sit eggs v. [late 19C+] to overstay one's welcome. [the image of a hen awaiting her chicks]

sit fat v. [1990s+] (*US*) to be successful and powerful. [FAT adj.² (1)]

sith-nom n. [mid-19C] a month. [backsl.]

sit-in-'ems n. [late 19C] trousers.

sit in the catbird seat v. [1940s+] (*US*) to be in an advantageous position. [CATBIRD SEAT n.]

sit in the garden with the gate unlocked v. [late 19C–1900s] **1** to conceive an illegitimate child. **2** to catch a cold.

sit in the plush v. [1910s] to live in luxury. [ON PLUSH phr.]

sit like a toad on a chopping-block v. [late 18C–19C] to sit badly on a horse.

sit-me-down n. [1920s+] the buttocks.

sit off v. [1990s+] (*Aus. Und.*) to place under surveillance, to stake out.

sit on v. (*also* **sit upon**) [mid-19C+] to squash, to snub.

sit (on) a beast v. (*also* **sit (on) a dago**) [1970s+] (*US Black teen, Los Angeles*) to ride in a car that has been mechanically lifted and appears higher off the ground than normal models. [SE *beast*, a monster, i.e. the height of the car/fig. use of DAGO n. (1); i.e. a style preferred by Hispanics]

sit on chrome v. [2000s] (*US Black*) to possess an automobile that is fitted with chrome rims on the wheels.

sit on it (and rotate)! excl. (*also* **sit on it and swivel!**) [1950s+] (*US*) a general excl. of abuse suggesting that a hard and painful object be thrust into the subject's anus.

sit on it, Potsie phr. [1990s+] (*US Black teen*) a general phr. of dismissal or mockery. [*Potsie* Weber, a character in the 1970s *Happy Days* TV show; the names of other characters can be substituted]

sit on one's ass v. (*also* **sit on one's butt/tail**) [20C+] (*US*) to be idle when one has responsibilities to carry out. [ASS n. (2)/BUTT n.¹ (2)/TAIL n.² (1)]

sit on oneself v. [late 19C] (*US*) to calm down, to quieten down.

sit (on) one's stuff v. [1970s] (*US Black*) to work as a prostitute. [STUFF n.⁶ (1)]

sit on someone's face v. **1** [1960s+] for a woman, to position her vagina directly above her partner's mouth, either lit. sitting or squatting above their face, in order to facilitate cunnilingus; also used by males as a synon. for enjoying fellatio (cf. FACE n.²). **2** [1980s] (*US campus*) as a dismissive retort.

sit on the penniless bench v. [late 16C–mid 17C] to be impoverished. [SE *penniless bench*, a small bench provided for passing poor travellers; the first was at Carfax, Oxford]

sit on the throne v. [1920s+] to use a lavatory. [THRONE n.]

sit on tight v. [1990s+] (*US Black*) to stay where one is, esp. to stand firm and unruffled in the face of adversity.

sit on top of the world v. [1930s+] (*orig. US*) to be absolutely secure, satisfied, happy etc; often as *sitting*…

sit pad v. *see* STAND PAD v.

sit pat v. *see* STAND PAT v.

sit shotgun v. *see* RIDE SHOTGUN v.

sitter n.¹ **1** [mid-19C–1900s] a drunk, who sits around in a bar sleeping off the drink or generally wasting time. **2** [late 19C] (*US*) a part-time prostitute. **3** [late 19C] (*US*) a tramp who, lacking any alternative accomodation, sits in a tenement hallway. **4** [late 19C–1940s] (*US*) a homeless person, employed by a tavern to sit near the fire and shiver in an obvious way so that kind-hearted patrons would buy them drinks (thus profiting the tavern). **5** [1940s+] a woman who frequents certain taverns or nightclubs and who receives a percentage on the drinks they induce male patrons to buy. [they are all sitting indoors rather than walking the streets]

sitter n.² **1** [late 19C+] an easy target, both in shooting and in metaphor. **2** [1910s] a certainty. **3** [1920s] a racehorse that is bound to win. [in shooting, a bird that is *sitting* rather than flying, and thus presents an easy target]

sitter n.³ [1940s] (*UK Und.*) one who takes part in confidence tricks.

sitter n.⁴ [1940s+] (*Aus., mainly Sydney*) a regular and heavy drinker in a bar or public house. [they do nothing but sit and drink]

sit there with one's finger up one's ass v. (*also* **sit there with one's thumb up one's ass, stand around with one's finger/thumb up one's ass**) [20C+] (*US*) to be passive, unresponsive, idle and useless. [ASS n. (2)]

sit tight v. [late 19C+] to stay where one is, esp. to stand firm and unruffled in the face of adversity.

sitting duck n. [1940s+] (*orig. milit.*) an easy target, someone or something vulnerable and defenceless, both lit. and fig. [hunting imagery]

sitting-pad n. [mid-19C] (*UK Und.*) the cross-legged position adopted by beggars on the pavement. [SE *sit* + PAD n.¹ (1)]

sitting pretty adj. **1** [1920s] (*US*) drunk. **2** [1920s+] secure, safe, enjoying an easy life, esp. as to material things.

situ n. [1970s+] situation. [abbr.]

situation n. [1960s+] (*S.Afr. Black*) a member of the Black middle class, a Black 'white-collar' worker regarded as a social climber. [SE *situation*, a job]

sit under Dr Greenfields v. [1930s] (*UK tramp*) to sleep in the open air. [one is listening to an imaginary sermon or lecture]

sit up and beg v. [late 19C+] of the penis, to become erect.

sit up (and take notice) v. [late 19C+] (*orig. US*) to take an interest in something.

sit up like jacky v. [1940s+] (*Aus./N.Z.*) to sit up straight and confident. [SE *sit up* + JACKY JACKY n. (1) or *Jacky*, the trad. name for the organ grinder's monkey]

sit upon v. *see* SIT ON v.

sit-upons n. [mid-19C] trousers. [abbr. SIT-DOWN-UPONS n.]

sit up with a sick friend v. *see* SEE A SICK FRIEND v.

siwash n. **1** [late 19C–1930s] (*US tramp*) a dirty or ill-mannered person. **2** [1930s+] (*US*) any small, archetypal college. [cowboy jargon *siwash outfit*, a second-rate ranch (*see* SIWASHED adj.)]

siwash v. [1910s+] (*US*) to ban someone from buying alcohol. [ext. of SIWASHED adj.; drunkenness was stereotyped as one of many endemic Native American vices]

siwashed adj. [19C] (*US, Western*) 'blackballed', i.e. used of a ranch that was barred from sending cowboys to the general round-up or to work on other ranches. [*Siwash*, a Native American of the northwest Pacific Coast. The term, ult. f. Fr. *sauvage*, savage, became a generic pej.; such exclusions were often made when ranchers were seen as being over-friendly to known cattle-rustlers]

siwash side n. [late 19C+] (*US*) **1** anything done ineptly or clumsily. **2** the right-hand side of a horse. **3** the left-hand side of a cow. [*Siwash*, pej. for a Native American, who mounted horses from the right-hand side, and wrestled down cows from the left; Whites preferred the left and right sides respectively]

six n.¹ **1** [mid-18C] (*UK Und.*) a 36-shilling piece. **2** [mid-late 19C] 6-pennyworth of a given drink, as sold in a public house. **3** [mid-19C+] a 6-month prison sentence. **4** [1920s] a 6-year prison sentence. **5** [1980s+] a 6-pack of beer. [abbr.]

six n.² [1940s] (*US Black*) a grave. [SIX FEET UNDER adj.]

six! excl. [1970s+] (*Can. Und./US prison*) a shout of warning. [? link to 6-5 n.]

six and eight n. [1960s+] an emotional 'state'. [rhy. sl.]

six-and-eight adj. [1930s+] honest. [rhy. sl. = STRAIGHT adj.¹ (3)]

six and eightpence n. **1** [late 17C–18C] the accepted fee demanded for the removal of a felon from the gallows and for their burial in sacred ground. **2** [mid-18C–1910s] (*also* **six and eight**) a solicitor, whose basic fee usu. came to this amount.

six-and-eightpenny *adj.* [mid-19C–1900s] legal, pertaining to a solicitor. [SIX AND EIGHTPENCE n. (2)]

six and four *n.* **1** [1950s] (*UK Und.*) a prostitute (cf. BOAT AND OAR n.). **2** [1960s+] (*drugs*) heroin that has been adulterated and weakened by mixing 1 part pure heroin to 6 or 4 parts sugar. [(1) rhy. sl. = SE *whore*]

six and tips *n.* [late 18C–early 19C] whisky and small beer. [SIXES n.]

six-bit *adj.* [mid-19C+] (*US*) cheap, worth 75 cents, e.g. *a six-bit sandwich*. [SIX BITS n. (1)]

six bits *n.* **1** [mid-19C+] (*US*) 75 cents. **2** [1940s] (*US Und.*) $75. [BIT n.¹ (4)]

six-cornered oath *n.* [late 19C] (*US*) a complex and many-worded oath.

sixer *n.* **1** [mid-19C] a sixth term of imprisonment of whatever length. **2** [mid-19C+] a 6-month prison sentence, 6 months' hard labour. **3** [late 19C] a 6oz (170g) loaf. **4** [1980s+] (*US Black/campus*) a 6-pack of beer. **5** [1990s+] (*drugs*) 6 pills.

sixes *n.* [mid-17C–early 19C] small beer. [its trad. price of 6 shillings (30p) per barrel]

six feet by two *n.* (*also* **six times three**) [1920s–40s] a grave.

six feet under *adj.* [1930s+] (*orig. US*) dead and buried.

6-5 *n.* [2000s] (*US prison*) code for a correctional officer; thus a warning when one approaches.

six-foot bungalow *n.* [1930s] (*US*) a coffin.

six foot of tripe *n.* [late 19C] a large policeman. [pun on SE *tripe*, intestines/TRIPE n.²]

six-foot subway *n.* [1940s] (*US Black*) a grave.

six-four *n. see* SIXTY-FOUR n.¹.

six man *n.* [1960s+] (*Can. prison*) a lookout. [ety. unknown]

six-monthser *n.* [late 19C] a severe magistrate, who, whenever they can, gives the longest sentence that the law allows, 6 months.

six months' hard *n.* [20C+] (*bingo*) a card. [rhy. sl.]

six months in front and nine behind *phr.* [1930s–40s] (*US Black*) obese. [the resemblance of one's stomach and buttocks to the swelling stomach of a pregnant woman]

six-nine *n. see* SIXTY-NINE n.

six o'clock swill *n.* [1940s+] (*Aus./N.Z.*) the rushed orders of drinks that took place in pubs in New South Wales and parts of New Zealand before 'last orders', until a change in the law in 1955 (1967 in New Zealand). [SE *six o'clock* + SWILL n.]

six of everything *adj.* [late 19C] respectable. [used by working families to describe a woman about to be married; her trousseau has 6 sets of everything necessary]

six-pack *n.¹* (*also* **eight-pack**) [1990s+] (*orig. US Black*) a tight, flat stomach. [the ripples resemble beer cans]

six-pack *n.²* [1990s+] (*Ulster*) a paramilitary punishment involving shots to the knees, ankles and hands. [the 6 parts of the body]

six-pack girl *n.* [1980s] a very ugly girl whom no boy would consider seducing unless he were drunk.

sixpenny *n.* [mid-19C] a pint of beer costing 6 pence (2½p).

sixpenny *adj.* [late 16C–mid-17C] second-rate, cheap, worthless.

sixpenny rush *n.* [1950s–60s] (*Irish*) cheap admission to children's matinées at the cinema.

sixpenny suburb-sinnet *n.* (*also* **sixpenny damnation**) [early 17C] a prostitute (cf. DOLLAR-WOMAN n.). [SE *sixpenny*, the prostitute's usual fee + play on SE *sinnet*, a trumpet-blast that introduced actors on the stage/SE *sinner*]

sixpennyworth *n.* [1940s–50s] a 6-month prison sentence.

six pennyworth of God help us *n. see* THREE PENNORTH OF GOD HELP US n.

six-pounder *n.* [late 18C] a maid. [her annual wages were for many years set at £6]

sixteener *n. see* EIGHT-PAGER n.

sixteenth *n.* [1950s+] (*drugs*) ¹⁄₁₆th of an ounce of a given drug.

sixteen-year-old after shave *n.* (*also* **sixteen-year-old shaving lotion**) [1970s] (*US Black*) very cheap and unpleasant wine.

sixth finger *n.* [1950s] a knife.

six times three *n. see* SIX FEET BY TWO n.

six to four *n. see* TWO BY FOUR n.

sixty-eight *n.* [1970s+] fellatio. [play on SIXTY-NINE n. (1), i.e. 'you suck me and I'll owe you one']

sixty-four *n.¹* (*also* **six-four, 64**) [1990s+] **1** (*US*) a 64oz (9-litre) bottle of malt liquor. **2** a 1964 Chevrolet Impala. [abbr.]

sixty-four *n.² see* TWO BY FOUR n.

sixty-minute man *n.* (*also* **sixty-minute boy**) [1950s+] a sexual athlete, one who can postpone his orgasm for sixty minutes.

sixty-nine *n.* (*also* **neuf-soixante, soixante-neuf, six-nine, 69, sixty-niner**) **1** [late 19C+] mutual oral-genital stimulation. **2** [1910s; 1960s] (*US campus*) a homosexual. **3** [2000s] in fig use, something pleasing. [synon. Fr. *soixante-neuf*; the numerals 69 supposedly mimic the head-to-tail bodily positions]

sixty-nine *v.* [1960s+] to perform mutual oral-genital stimulation. [SIXTY-NINE n. (1)]

sixty-per-cent *n.* [mid–late 19C] a moneylender, a usurer, a bill-discounter. [the exorbitant rate of interest]

sixty-second man *n.* [1970s] (*US Black*) a premature ejaculator. [play on SIXTY-MINUTE MAN n.]

sixty-six *n.* [1940s–70s] (*Aus.*) anal intercourse. [play on SIXTY-NINE n. (1)]

six up! *excl.* [1980s+] a warning shout to alert drug users or illicit street vendors to the presence of the police or security guards; the drugs or merchandise should be hidden or even thrown away to prevent problems in a search. [DEEP SIX v. (1)]

six ways from Sunday *phr.* (*also* **six ways for/to Sunday**) [late 19C+] askew, at an angle. [ety. unknown]

size *n.¹* [late 18C–early 19C] a half-pint (285ml). [16C *size*, the portion of bread and beer allowed to undergraduates in Cambridge colleges]

size *n.²* [mid-19C] a jelly. [? play on SE *shape*, a jelly mould]

size *v. see* SIZE (UP) v.

size freak *n.* [1990s+] of either sex, one who is obsessed by the size of a man's penis (which obsession determines their willingness to have sex). [SE *size* + FREAK sfx]

sizendizup *n.* [1930s–50s] (*US drugs*) used between a dealer and addict to indicate that the drugs are on their way.

size queen *n.* [1960s+] (*mainly gay*) one who is obsessed by the size of the penis of a potential partner. [SE *size* + QUEEN n.² (1)/QUEEN sfx (2)]

size tens *n. see* NUMBER TENS n.

size (up) *v.* (*orig. US*) **1** [mid-19C+] to estimate, to assess, to get to know about. **2** [late 19C–1920s] to amount to. **3** [1930s] to appear, to seem to be.

sizzle *n.* [1960s] (*US Black*) narcotics, when carried on the person. [SIZZLE v. (2)]

sizzle *v.* **1** [1930s–40s] (*US Und.*) to die or execute in the electric chair. **2** [1930s+] (*US drugs*) to be exceptionally prone to arrest, esp. when holding drugs or acting in an outrageous manner. [(1) SE *hot*; (2) HOT adj.² (3)]

sizzled *adj. see* SOZZLED adj.

sizzler *n.* **1** [mid-19C+] (*US*) any exciting thing or person; thus *adj. sizzling*. **2** [1900s–50s] (*US*) (*also* **frizzler**) a very hot day. **3** [1940s] a shot, e.g. from a sling shot. **4** [1940s–60s] (*US*) the electric chair. **5** [1950s–70s] something salacious, risqué, e.g. a book.

sizzle seat *n.* [1930s+] (*US prison*) the electric chair. [SIZZLE v. (1)]

S.K. *adj. see* SHITKICKER adj.

skaam *n.* [1970s+] (*S.Afr.*) shame. [synon. Afk.]

skaam *adj.* [1970s+] (*S.Afr.*) shy, embarrassed. [SKAAM n.]

skaap *n.* [1920s+] (*S.Afr.*) a country bumpkin, a fool. [Afk. *skaap*, a sheep]

skadoodles/skads *n. see* SCADS n.

skag *see also under* SCAG and its combs.

skag *n.* **1** [1920s+] (*orig. US Black*) an unattractive, slutty-looking woman. **2** [1980s] a promiscuous woman. **3** [1980s+] a tease. [? dial. *scag*, a putrid herring]

skaggy *adj.* [1980s] (*US Black/campus*) ugly, sluttish. [SKAG n. (1)]

skaggy-bawed *adj.* [1990s+] (*Scot.*) comatose or impotent as a result of taking heroin. [SCAG n.² (2) + Scot. *baw*, to sleep]

skaintch *n. see* SKANCH adj.

skalawag *n. see* SCALLYWAG n.¹.

skamas *n.* [1930s–50s] (*US drugs*) opium (cf. APOSTLE n.). [ety. unknown; ? Yid.]

skamp *n.* [2000s] (*US Black*) an unattractive, dirty and promiscuous woman. [SKANK n.¹ (1) + TRAMP n. (1)]

skanch *adj.* (*also* **skaintch**) [1990s+] (*US campus/teen*) anything, or anybody, seen as repulsive, disgusting etc. [SKANK n.¹]

skanger *n. see* SCANGER n.

skank *n.*¹ **1** [1960s+] (*orig. US Black*) (*also* **scank, shank**) an unattractive, easily available young woman. **2** [1970s+] (*US Black*) a woman who smells badly. **3** [1970s+] (*US*) a prostitute. **4** [1980s+] (*US campus*) a repulsive person of either sex. **5** [1980s+] (*US*) filth, malevolence, dirtiness. **6** [2000s] an unsatisfactory situation. **7** [2000s] a mean, mercenary person. **8** [2000s] (*also* **skankface**) on bad = good model, an affectionate term of address.

skank *n.*² [1980s+] (*W.I./UK Black teen*) a confidence trick, a fraudulent scheme. [SKANK v. (8)]

skank *n.*³ [2000s] (*drugs*) marijuana. [? SKANK n.¹ (8); ? SKANK v. (1)]

skank *v.* [1980s+] **1** (*orig. W.I.*) to dance in a style associated with ska, dub or reggae music; thus *skanker*, one who dances in this manner. **2** (*UK Black*) to move rhythmically. **3** (*orig. W.I.*) to steal and run away. **4** to loaf around. **5** (*US campus*) to use deception to get one's way. **6** (*US campus*) to observe members of the opposite sex. **7** (*UK Black*) to play truant. **8** to cheat, to 'stab in the back'. [Allsopp suggests the dance style is 'derived from the kind of hip-swinging dancing which is both typical of people of generally low social status and reminiscent of the waist movements of a motorcyclist speeding in and out of other traffic']

skank-ass *adj. see* SKANKY adj.

skanked out *adj.* [1990s+] (*US drugs*) intoxicated by a drug. [SKANK n.³]

skanker *n.* **1** [1970s+] (*W.I.*) an untrustworthy, dissolute person. **2** [1990s+] an alcoholic tramp. [SKANK v.]

skankface *n. see* SKANK n.¹ (8).

skanky *adj.* (*also* **scanky**) [1970s+] (*orig. US Black*) **1** (*also* **shanky, skank-ass**) dirty, second-rate, unattractive, cheap-looking, ugly, promiscuous. **2** of a woman, attractive, sexy. [SKANK n.¹; (2) on bad = good model]

skanky box *n.* [1980s+] (*US*) an unpleasant, dirty (physically and ethically) woman. [SKANKY adj. (1) + BOX n.¹ (1)]

skarf *v. see* SCARF v.

skat *v. see* SCAT v.

skate *n.* **1** [late 19C] (*US*) a second-rate sportman. **2** [late 19C–1920s] (*US*) a person, irrespective of qualities. **3** [late 19C+] (*US*) an inferior horse. **4** [late 19C+] (*US*) (*also* **skater**) a mean or contemptible person; thus CHEAPSKATE n. **5** [1900s] (*US campus*) a reckless person. **6** [1900s–30s] (*US*) an old person. **7** [1960s] (*US*) a lazy person, a shirker. **8** [1970s] (*US teen*) a motorcycle. **9** [1970s] (*US campus*) an easy course. **10** [1970s+] (*S.Afr.*) 'a disreputable White male (from a working-class background) whose behaviour is uncouth, hedonistic, and irresponsible' (*DSAE*). [fig. uses of (3), but for (10) note Afk. *skuit*, excreta]

skate *adj.* [1970s+] (*US campus*) easy, simple, esp. of work or a course. [SKATE n. (9), i.e. one can SE *skate* it]

skate *v.*¹ **1** [mid-19C+] (*also* **do a skate, skate off, skeete, skite**) to rush off, to leave at speed, to go quickly; thus *get a skate on*, to go fast, to hurry up; note GET ONE'S SKATES ON v. **2** [1940s+]

(*orig. US Black*) to get away with anything, to shirk one's responsibilities, esp. to avoid paying one's debts. **3** [1960s+] to perform or do something, e.g. an essay, quickly. **4** [2000s] (*US prison*) to be in a forbidden area of the prison.

skate *v.*² [1920s–50s] (*US drugs*) to use morphine or cocaine. [skating should be on *ice* but this predates ICE n.⁶ (1); thus ? ref. to SNOW n.² (1)]

skater *n.*¹ [1930s–40s] (*US Und.*) a legless person who uses a wheeled board for transportation.

skater *n.*² *see* SKATE n. (4).

skate rat *n.* [1980s+] (*US teen*) a fanatical skate-boarder. [SE *skate* + RAT sfx]

skates *n.* [late 19C–1900s] (*US*) shoes.

skates-lurk *n.* [mid-19C] (*UK Und.*) the practice of posing as a sailor for the purpose of begging. [? SE *skate*, the fish + LURK n. (1). Paul Beale in *DSUE* (1984) suggests that this might 'just poss[ibly]' be the origin of SKATE n. (4)]

skating *adj.* [1950s+] intoxicated with drugs or drink.

skating rink *n.* (*also* **flies' skating rink, fly rink**) [late 19C–1910s] a bald head. [the image of ice-skating flies]

skedaddle *n.* **1** [mid-19C+] a rush, a hurry; an act of running away or escaping. **2** [1990s+] a fuss, an excitement, a disturbance. [SKEDADDLE v.]

skedaddle *v.* (*also* **skedoo, skidaddle, skidoodle**) [mid-19C+] (*orig. US*) of people, to rush off, to scamper, to escape. [orig. US milit. jargon *skedaddle*, to flee the battlefield, to retreat quickly; thence 'civilian' uses. Webster (1867) suggests Scand. roots, but *OED* and other authorities reject this. The term may have existed in Eng. dial./Scot. (meaning to scatter, to spill, as of a pail of milk, a bucket of potatoes) slightly earlier than its US use, but that seems merely coincident. Hotten (1864) adds a ref. to 'very fair Greek, the root being that of "skedannumi" to disperse, to "retire tumultuously" [...] it was probably set afloat by some professor at Harvard'. A number of other commentators – including Cohen in *Studies in Slang* I (1985), Flexner and Bartlett – agree. Other theories include a link to the Irish *scegadol*, scattered, which has been disproved, but there may still be a link to a variety of other Gaelic words, e.g. *scead*, fright, *sgadarlach*, anything scattered or dispersed, *scaoll*, fright, panic. Cohen, in an extensive analysis (Cohen, 1985, pp.29–63), suggests Scot. *skiddle*, to scatter + ? comb. *jabble*, to scatter. Thus the earlier use must be accepted and the Scot./northern 'spill/scatter' transfers to the US 'flee' through the image of blood and corpses being thus 'spilled and scattered' on the battlefield before the flight of a demoralized army]

skedaddler *n.* [mid-19C] (*US*) a fugitive. [SKEDADDLE v.]

skee *n.*¹ [1900s–60s] (*US, then Aus./N.Z.*) whisky. [abbr./pron.]

skee *n.*² [1930s–50s] (*drugs*) opium (cf. APOSTLE n.). [? SKEE n.¹ or SKAMAS n.]

skeed-up *adj.* [1990s+] (*US drugs*) intoxicated by drugs. [SKEE n.²]

skeef *adj.* [1960s+] (*S.Afr.*) crooked, off-beat. [Afk. *scheef*, askew]

skeek *n.* [2000s] (*US*) an unpleasant person. [? var. on SKANK n.¹ (4)]

skeesicks *n. see* SKEEZICKS n.

skeet *n.*¹ [20C+] a general term of abuse. [var. on SKATE n. (4)]

skeet *n.*² [2000s] (*US prison*) a single injection of heroin. [? SCAG n.² (2) + HIT n.³ (7) or SKEET v.¹]

skeet *v.*¹ [1970s+] (*drugs*) to flush out a hypodermic syringe by using the plunger. [dial. *skeet*, to squirt, to eject fluid]

skeet *v.*² [1980s+] (*US Black*) **1** to have sexual intercourse. **2** to ejaculate (cf. BLOSH v.). [dial. *skeet*, to squirt, to eject fluid]

skeete *v. see* SKATE v.¹ (1).

skeeter *n.* (*also* **skeet**) [mid-19C+] (*Aus./US*) a mosquito. [abbr. + Aus./N.Z. pron.]

skeeve *n.* [1990s+] (*US*) a disgusting person. [SKEEVE (OUT) v.]

skeeve (out) *v.* [1990s+] (*US*) to disgust, to repel. [? Ital. *schifoso*, disgusting]

skeevy *adj.* [1990s+] disgusting. [SKEEVE (OUT) v.]

skeeza/skeeze *n. see* SKEEZER n.

skeeze *n.* [1900s] (*US*) something easily achieved. [ety. unknown; ? link to SE *easy*]

skeeze *v.*[1] [1920s+] to ogle. [ety. unknown]

skeeze *v.*[2] [1980s+] (*orig. US Black*) **1** to have sexual intercourse. **2** to seek members of the opposite sex. **3** to have an orgy. [? SAmE *skeezicks*, a 'mean, contemptible fellow' (Bartlett, *Dict. Americanisms*, 1877); ? ult. Cornish *skeese*, to frisk about + *skicer*, a lamb that kills itself through excess activity]

skeezer *n.* (*also* **skeeza, skeeze**) [1980s+] (*orig. US Black*) **1** a woman who trades sex for status or for free drugs; her chosen partners are often drug dealers or performers. **2** a person, usu. female, who attempts to have a relationship with a member of the opposite sex only for their material possessions, in order to make an impression on other people. **3** a man. **4** a term of abuse for any disliked person. [SKEEZE v.[2]]

skeezicks *n.* (*also* **skeesicks, skeezix, skeezucks**) [mid-19C–1970s] (*US*) a person, usu. a troublemaker.

skeffington's daughter *n.* (*also* **scavenger's daughter**) [mid-16C–early 17C] an instrument of torture, consisting of a broad iron hoop, which was locked around the prisoner's body, compressing it unnaturally to such an extent that the victim was effectively squeezed to death. [its inventor, Sir William *Skeffington*, Lieutenant of the Tower of London *c*.1530–40]

skeg *n.*[1] (*also* **skeghead**) [1980s+] (*Aus.*) a surfer. [SE *skeg*, the fin beneath a surfboard]

skeg *n.*[2] (*also* **skeggy**) [2000s] a smelly vagrant or one who resembles such a person. [dial. *scag*, putrid fish]

skeggy *adj.* [1990s+] unpleasant, disgusting, the implication is of rotting or faecal matter. [echoic; the sense is of a cry of disgust]

skein of thread *n.* [1920s+] a bed. [rhy. sl.]

skelder *v.* **1** [late 16C–early 17C] to work as a professional beggar, esp. to pose as a wounded or discharged soldier. **2** [late 16C–18C] to swindle, to defraud; thus *skeldering*, begging, swindling. [Du. *skellum*, a rogue, a villain, a pestilence]

skeleton army *n.* [late 19C] street-fighters. [the *Skeleton Army* flourished briefly as an opposition force to the Salvation Army, a more physically militant organization *c*.1880s than subseq.]

skell *n.* [1960s+] (*US*) a villain, a rogue, esp. a vagrant who lives on the streets. [SKELDER v.]

skelly *n.*[1] [20C+] (*Irish*) a glance, a look; thus *skellying*, looking. [Scot. *skelly*, a squint; ult. OE *sceolh*, a squint]

skelly *n.*[2] [2000s] *skele*ton. [abbr.]

skelm *adj.* [20C+] (*S.Afr. Und.*) fake, counterfeit. [SKELM v.]

skelm *v.* [20C+] (*S.Afr. Und.*) to do something in an underhand way. [Afk. *skelm*, a villain, a rascal; note obs. SE *skelm*, a rascal, itself f. Du. *schelm*, a rascal]

skeng *n.* [1970s+] (*W.I./UK Black*) a ghetto weapon, e.g. a gun, a ratchet-knife. [? Carib.E. *skengay*, a form of music in which the guitar sounds are seen as mimicking those of gunfire]

skepper *n. see* SKIPPER n.[1] (2).

skerrick *n.* [early 19C+] (*mainly Aus./N.Z.*) **1** (*also* **scurrick, skirrach**) a halfpenny. **2** a small amount, a small fragment, the slightest bit. [dial. *skewick*, an atom, a fragment]

sket *n.* [2000s] (*UK Black teen*) a derog. term for a promiscuous girl. [? abbr. SKETEL n.]

sketch *n.*[1] [late 19C] a very small quantity, a single drop. [SE *sketch*, an outline]

sketch *n.*[2] [20C+] a ridiculous or amusing person or sight.

sketch *n.*[3] [1980s+] (*US campus*) (*also* **sketchball, sketcher**) one who looks or feels confused, unstable, odd. **2** (*US drugs*) methamphetamine (cf. BOMBITA n.).

sketch *n.*[4] [2000s] (*Scot.*) a look at, a view of.

sketch *n.*[5] [2000s] the rules, the situation.

sketch *n.*[6] *see* HOT SKETCH n.

sketch *adj.* [1970s+] (*US campus*) risky, dangerous. [? SKETCHY adj.]

sketch *v.*[1] [1980s] (*UK Black*) to slash with a knife or other edged weapon. [SE *sketch*, to draw, i.e. on someone's flesh]

sketch *v.*[2] *see* SKETCH (OUT) v.

sketchball *n. see* SKETCH n.[3] (1).

sketched (out) *adj.* [1980s+] **1** (*US campus*) bad, bizarre, weird. **2** (*US drugs*) suffering paranoia due to the effects of hallucinogenic or other drugs, e.g. cocaine; thus *sketching*, coming down from a drug-induced high. [SKETCH (OUT) v.]

sketcher *n. see* SKETCH n.[3] (1).

sketch (out) *v.* [1980s+] **1** (*US campus*) to feel unstable or confused. **2** (*US drugs*) to experience the after-effects of amphetamines. [SKETCH n.[3]]

sketchy *adj.* **1** [late 19C+] flimsy, insubstantial, vague. **2** [1980s+] (*US campus*) confused, unstable, strange, unsettling. **3** [1990s+] (*US campus*) untrustworthy, suspicious. **4** [1990s+] (*US campus*) second-rate. [a *sketch*, rather than an oil painting]

sketel *n.* (*also* **sketell, skets, skittle**) [1990s+] a promiscuous woman or one who is judged as such. [? she falls over like a *skittle*; note Catherine 'Skittles' Walters, mistress of Edward VII, Napoleon III et al.]

skew *n.*[1] (*also* **scew**) [mid-16C–early 19C] a cup or dish. [Lat. *scutula*, a dish; Harman has *askew*, a cup, and E.P. offers an ety. of Fr. *escuelle*, a cup; however a simple misprint of *a skew* or mishearing is more likely]

skew *n.*[2] [mid-19C] weeks. [backsl.]

skewer *n.* **1** [mid-19C–1910s] a sword. **2** [late 19C–1920s] a pen.

skew-fisted *adj.* [late 17C–early 18C] awkward, ungainly. [SE *askew*]

skewgee *n.* [late 19C–1900s] a squint. [SKEWGEE adj.]

skewgee *adj.* [late 19C+] **1** squinting, crooked. **2** mixed up, confused. [SE *askew*]

skewings *n.* [mid-19C] extras, bonuses; any form of money, esp. when gained for nothing. [SE *skew*, to escape; i.e. money that has 'escaped' from the regular accounts]

skew-jawed *adj.* [mid-19C] (*US*) awkward, ungainly. [SE *askew*]

skewvow *adj.* [late 18C–early 19C] askew, out of true, crooked. [var. on SKEW-WHIFF adj.]

skew-whiff *adj.* **1** [mid-18C+] crooked, out of true, aslant. **2** [1900s] (*also* **skew-whiffy**) drunk (cf. AFFLICTED adj.). [dial.; ult. SE *askew*]

skezag *n.* [1970s+] (*drugs*) heroin. [SCAG n.[2] (2) + -IZ- ifx]

ski *n.*[1] [1950s+] (*Aus.*) a taxi. [? weak rhy. sl.]

ski *n.*[2] [1980s+] (*US drugs*) cocaine. [play on SNOW n.[2] (1)]

ski *n.*[3] *see* SKY n.[4].

-ski *sfx* (*also* **-sky**) [20C+] (*orig. US campus*) a sfx added to names in humorous imitation of Russian; a general intensifier.

skibby *n.* (*also* **skippy**) (*US*) **1** [1910s+] an Oriental prostitute, thus, when addressing a Japanese speaker, any prostitute. **2** [1920s+] a derog. term for a Japanese person (cf. BUDDHAHEAD n.). [Jap. *sukebei*, randy or lecherous. The word had also meant a courtesan, and the sense was ext. to mean 'loose' or 'unchaste'. In US mouths it tended to refer to a female domestic servant, but the seeming synon. of the term SKIVVY n.[2] may in fact be coincidental]

ski-bunk *n.* [1900s] (*US*) a rejection; an act of dismissal. [SKIDOO! excl. (2) + DO A BUNK v. (1)]

ski bunny *n.* [1960s+] (*US*) a woman who frequents ski resorts to solicit rather than to ski. [SE *ski* + BUNNY n.[1] (2)]

skid *n.*[1] [1990s+] one who likes to go out at night; an ill-dressed, dirty, dishevelled person. [? SKID ROW n.]

skid *n.*[2] *see* SKIV n.[1].

skid *adj.* [1990s+] unattractive, dirty, dishevelled. [SKID n.[1]]

skid *v.* (*also* **skids**) **1** [1910s–20s] to leave, to go. **2** [1920s+] (*US*) to blunder, to make a mistake, to decline. **3** [1950s] (*US Und.*) to get rid of.

skidaddle v. see SKEDADDLE v.

skid artist n. [1970s] (UK Und.) an expert driver of a getaway car, used on robberies. [the speedily driven car *skids* around corners + ARTIST sfx]

skid-bid n. [1990s+] (US prison) a term in prison or in juvenile detention. [SE *skid*, i.e. off the 'straight and narrow' + BID n.²]

skiddies n. see SKID MARKS n.

skiddoo see under SKIDOO.

skiddy n. [1990s+] (N.Z.) something repulsive. [? SKID MARKS n. (1)]

skid grease n. [1920s–40s] (US) butter.

skidlid n. [1950s+] a crash helmet. [SE *skid* + LID n.¹ (1)]

skid-mark v. [1990s+] to stain. [SKID MARKS n.]

skid marks n. (also **scooter tracks, skiddies**) 1 [1930s+] faecal stains on one's underwear. 2 [1990s+] any form of bodily stain. 3 [1990s+] a general term of abuse.

skidoo n. [1900s–10s] 1 bad luck. 2 an exit. [(1) SE *skid*; (2) SKIDOO v.]

skidoo v. (also **skiddoo**) [1900s–50s] (US) to leave quickly, to run off. [? SKEDADDLE v. or SCADOODLE v. or SE *skid*]

skidoo! excl. (also **skiddoo!**) 1 [1900s–10s] an excl. of pleasure or surprise. 2 [1900s–50s] a general dismissive excl., go away! get out! [SKIDOO v.; see also TWENTY-THREE SKIDOO! excl.]

skidoodle v. see SKEDADDLE v.

skid-pipe plumber n. [1990s+] a male homosexual.

skid row n. 1 [1920s+] (also **skid road**) the centre, in any town or city, for down-and-outs, alcoholics, tramps and other poor or homeless individuals. 2 [1940s] a dead end for one's career. 3 [1980s] a down-and-out alcoholic. [late 19C logging jargon *skid road*, a grassed track over which logs were hauled towards the river that would float them down to the sawmill; c.1915 the term was extended into sl. to mean that part of a town where loggers spent their free time or lived when they were out of work. It was the latter meaning, with its added implication of a man, rather than a log, who was 'skidding downhill' economically that dominated usage by the 1930s, when *skid road* became *skid row*, once more with an overtone, the use of *row* to denote the concentration of certain businesses or occupations in certain urban streets, e.g. Hollywood's *Poverty Row*, the area where the cheaper studios congregated]

skid-row adj. [1940s+] (US) down-and-out, alcoholic, tramp-like. [SKID ROW n. (1)]

skids v. see SKID v.

skidsville n. [1950s+] (US) a state of poverty. [ON THE SKIDS phr. + -VILLE sfx¹]

skid the rig v. [1940s] (US) to cuckold. [fig. use of oil rig jargon *skid the rig*, to move a derrick]

skied adj.¹ [1960s+] (US campus) ready for anything. [play on PSYCHED (UP) adj. (2)]

skied adj.² [1980s+] (drugs) extremely intoxicated by a drug. [pun on SE *sky*/HIGH adj.¹ (2)]

skiets n. [20C+] (S.Afr.) diarrhoea. [Afk. *skyt*, to defecate.]

skiet und donder n. [1960s+] (S.Afr.) a melodrama, an action film or book; also ext. as *skop, skiet and donder*, lit. 'kick, shoot and thunder'. [Afk. *skiet und donder*, shoot and thunder; thus blood and thunder]

skiff n. [late 19C–1900s] a leg. [? Dorset dial. *skife*, to kick up one's heels]

skiffle n. [1930s–40s] (US Black) a party at which the guests pay a subscription to cover refreshments and to help the host out with the rent (cf. FISH-FRY n.). [SE *scuffle* via dial. *skiffle*; music at such parties was provided by non-professional musicians; thus the *skiffle groups* (who were paid but performed on essentially homemade instruments) of the 1950s]

skiffling and skuffling n. [1940s–60s] (US Black) any form of frenetic activity. [SKIFFLE n. and SE *shuffle*]

skilamalink adj. [late 19C] secret, under cover. [ety. unknown;

Ware traces its popularity (if not its origin) to a burlesque performed at the Olympia Theatre]

skill adj. [1990s+] (UK teen) first-rate, very good.

skillagalee n. (also **skilligolee, skillogalee, skillygolee**) [19C] 1 (prison/workhouse) thin, un-nourishing broth, gruel. 2 (Aus.) any broth or stew. 3 a small coin of minimal value, usu. in phr. *not worth a skilagolee*; thus *skilagolee*, worthless. [ety. unknown; 'prob. a purely fanciful formation' (OED)]

skillet n. 1 [1930s] an old car. 2 [1930s–70s] (US Black) a Black person. [SE *skillet*, a cast-iron (black) frying pan]

skillet blonde n. [1930s] (US Black) 1 a Black woman wearing a blonde wig. 2 a very dark-skinned Black person. [SKILLET n. (2) + SE *blonde*]

skilligareen n. [1910s–20s] a very thin person. [SKILLAGALEE n. (1), the link being the thinness]

skilligolee n. see SKILLAGALEE n.

skillion n. (also **scillion**) [2000s] (US) a very large and indefinite number. [pattern of SE *trillion* etc]

skillogalee n. see SKILLAGALEE n.

skilly n. (also **skiley**) 1 [mid-19C–1950s] (UK prison/workhouse) gruel, broth. 2 [1920s–40s] (US prison) gravy. 3 [1920s–50s] any weak beverage, e.g. tea or coffee. [abbr. SKILLAGALEE n.; note London (1903): '"Skilly" is a fluid concoction of three quarts of oatmeal stirred into three buckets and a half of hot water']

skilly and toke phr. [mid–late 19C] anything mild or insipid. [fig. use of SKILLY n. (1) + TOKE n.¹ (2)]

skillygolee n. see SKILLAGALEE n.

skillz n. [1990s+] (orig. US Black) skills, capabilities. [deliberate 'hip-hop' mis-sp.]

skim v. (orig. US) 1 [1910s+] of an employee, to hold back a proportion of the profits from their job (usu. in some form of gambling), thus stealing from one's employer. 2 [1940s+] to conceal some part of one's earnings in order to avoid paying tax on it. 3 [1980s+] to steal from a store of money, drugs etc. 4 [1980s+] to forge a credit card.

skimish n. (also **skimmish**) [1900s–70s] (mainly tramp) beer, alcohol; thus *skimisher/skimmisher*, a heavy drinker. [Shelta *skimis*, to drink, *skimisk*, drunk]

skimished adj. (also **skimmished**) [1900s] drunk. [SKIMISH n.]

skimmer n.¹ [mid-19C+] (US) a broad-brimmed boater with a very low crown, esp. when made of straw. [SE *skimmer hat*, so called from the potential of skimming it like a frisbee]

skimmer n.² [1930s+] (US) a financial criminal who withholds money from their firm's profits. [SKIM v. (1)]

skimming n. [1960s+] stealing from the till, taking money 'off the top', esp. as found in casinos, strip clubs and other places where a degree of criminality is already endemic. [SKIM v. (1)]

skimmish see under SKIMISH.

skimmy n. [1990s+] (US Black) an attractive woman. [? she is the 'cream', which has been *skimmed*]

skin n.¹ [late 18C–1940s] a purse, a pocketbook, a wallet; thus *queer skin*, an empty wallet. [the leather of which it is made]

skin n.² [mid-19C] a sovereign. [? SKIN n.⁸ (1)]

skin n.³ (US campus) 1 [mid-19C–1900s] a lesson one has not learned properly; a lesson learned by any form of cheating aid. 2 [1900s] a cheat; a liar.

skin n.⁴ [mid-19C–1910s] (US Und.) a shirt.

skin n.⁵ [late 19C–1900s] (US) a mean, avaricious person. [abbr. SKINFLINT n.]

skin n.⁶ [late 19C–1920s] a cheater. [SKIN v.¹ (5)]

skin n.⁷ 1 [late 19C+] a person, e.g. *decent old skin*. 2 [1910s–20s] (US) oneself, one's life. 3 [1980s] a term of address to an unknown person. [metonymy]

skin n.⁸ (US) 1 [late 19C+] $1 (cf. BAT HIDE n.). 2 [1940s–70s] in pl., banknotes. [abbr. FROGSKIN n.²]

skin n.⁹ (also **skins**) 1 [20C+] (orig. naut.) a derog. generic term for women. 2 [1950s] (US Und.) a male homosexual.

skin *n.*[10] [1910s–40s] (*US/Aus.*) a horse, a mule.

skin *n.*[11] [1920s+] (*US Black*) a drum. [abbr. SE *drumskin*]

skin *n.*[12] [1930s–40s] (*US*) sexual intercourse.

skin *n.*[13] [1940s–50s] a painter.

skin *n.*[14] [1940s+] (*US Black*) the hand, as in a handshake or a palm-slapping greeting.

skin *n.*[15] [1950s–70s] a tyre.

skin *n.*[16] [1950s+] (*US*) a condom.

skin *n.*[17] [1960s] (*US*) a rasher of bacon.

skin *n.*[18] [1960s+] a cigarette paper, esp. those used for rolling cannabis joints; usu. in pl. [it provides a *skin* for the tobacco (and cannabis)]

skin *n.*[19] [1970s+] a *skin*head. [abbr.]

skin *n.*[20] *see* GEORGIA SKIN n.

skin *n.*[21] *see* SKIN GAME n. (1).

skin *n.*[22] *see* SKINPOP n.

skin *adj.*[1] [1900s] (*US campus*) unfair. [SKIN v.[1] (5)]

skin *adj.*[2] [1950s+] (*orig. US*) featuring nudity; usu. in the context of pornography.

skin *v.*[1] **1** [mid-18C–1960s] to steal from. **2** [late 18C+] (*US*) to beat, to overcome completely. **3** [early 19C+] to take all a person's money, esp. in a gambling game. **4** [mid-late 19C] to drop in price or value. **5** [mid-19C+] (*also* **skin out of**) to cheat or defraud someone of their money or other possessions; thus in fig. use, to exploit. **6** [late 19C] (*US*) to renege on one's bills or debts. **7** [1910s] to pass off surreptitiously.

skin *v.*[2] [mid-late 19C] (*US campus*) to copy, to cheat in an examination. [? ext. of SKIN v.[1] (5)]

skin *v.*[3] (*also* **skin out**) [mid-19C–1920s] (*US*) to abscond, to run off.

skin *v.*[4] [late 19C] (*US*) to glance at, to examine. [one fig. 'removes their skin']

skin *v.*[5] [1910s] to survive.

skin *v.*[6] [1920s] (*US prison*) to shave a prisoner's head.

skin *v.*[7] [1920s] (*US*) to remove and put down one's guns, to disarm oneself.

skin *v.*[8] *see* PEEL v.

skin *v.*[9] *see* SKINPOP v.

skin-a-guts *n.* [1910s–20s] a very thin person. [SE *skin-and-bones*]

skin alive *v.* [late 19C+] (*orig. US*) to thrash.

skin a louse *v.* (*also* **skin a fart/flea/fly**) [mid-19C+] (*Aus./Irish*) to be extremely mean and covetous.

skin-and-blister *n.* (*also* **blister**) [1910s+] a sister. [rhy. sl.]

skin-and-grief *n.* [late 19C–1950s] a very thin person.

skin and grin *v.* **1** [1950s+] (*W.I.*) to laugh foolishly or ingratiatingly, to pretend to be friendly; thus *skinning and grinning*, laughing foolishly, pretending to be friendly. **2** [1990s+] (*US Black*) to act in an openly friendly, happy manner. [GIVE SOME SKIN v. + SE *grin*]

skin a razor *v.* [late 19C–1900s] to drive a very hard bargain.

skin artist *n.* [mid-late 19C] (*US Und.*) a cheating gambler, a card-sharp. [SKIN v.[1] (3) + ARTIST sfx]

skin-beater *n.* [1930s–50s] a drummer. [SKIN n.[11] + SE *beater*]

skin book *n. see* SKIN MAG n.

skin boy *n.* [1980s] (*N.Z.*) an uncircumcised male. [abbr. SE *foreskin*]

skin catch fire (for) *v.* [20C+] (*W.I.*) to become obsessed with someone at first sight and thus to desire to possess them immediately.

skinch *n. see* CINCH n.[1] (1).

skincoat *n.* [mid-16C] the vagina.

skinder *n.* (*also* **skinner**) [1970s+] (*S.Afr.*) gossip, slander; thus *skinderbek*, a scandalmonger (lit. 'scandal-mouth'). [Afk. *skinder*, to slander, to gossip, to tattle]

skin-disease *n.* [late 19C–1910s] fourpenny ale. [? its deleterious effects or its (relatively) high cost, which will SKIN v.[1] (5) the purchaser]

skin-dive *v.* [1980s+] (*Aus. prison*) to inject narcotics.

skin-diver *n.* [1960s–70s] **1** a male homosexual (cf. BONE-EATER n.). **2** a fellatrix. [(1) his supposed appetite for fellatio]

skin flick *n.* [1960s+] a pornographic film. [SKIN adj.[2] + FLICK n.[3] (1)]

skinflint *n.* [late 17C+] a mean person. [obs. SE phr. *skin a flint*, to be very mean or greedy]

skin flute *n.* [1940s+] the penis (cf. ACCORDION n.).

skin frisk *n.* [1930s+] (*US prison*) a skin search. [SE *skin* + FRISK n.[2]]

skinful *n.* **1** [early 17C] a large amount. **2** [late 18C+] a very large amount of alcohol; esp. in phr. **have/get a skinful**, to get very drunk. **3** [1920s] the state of being drugged. [lit. one's skin is full of alcohol]

skin gambler *n.* [1900s–50s] (*US Und.*) a cheating gambler. [SKIN v.[1] (3)]

skin game *n.* **1** [mid-19C+] (*US*) (*also* **skin**) any form of gambling that is designed to fleece the uninitiated. **2** [1930s+] (*US Black*) a card-game, spec. tonk or coon can. [SKIN v.[1] (3) + SE *game*]

skinhead *n.* **1** [1950s+] (*orig. US*) a bald person; thus as a nickname. **2** [1960s+] a shaven head. **3** [1960s+] a member of a teen youth cult whose main identifying features are shaven heads, BOVVER BOOTS n., turned-up jeans and braces and who provide much of the 'heavy' element of the modern neo-Nazi movements. **4** [1970s] one who resembles (3).

skin house *n.*[1] [mid-19C–1900s] (*US*) a corrupt gambling establishment. [SKIN v.[1] (3) + SE *house*]

skin house *n.*[2] [1970s+] (*US*) an establishment providing pornographic entertainment. [SKIN adj.[2] + SE *house*]

skin hustling *n.* [1930s] (*US Und.*) selling fake fur.

skin joint *n.* **1** [1930s] (*US Und.*) a crooked casino or gambling house. **2** [1990s+] a nightclub or bar with young women employed to entertain customers. [SKIN v.[1] (3)/SKIN adj.[2] + JOINT n.[4] (3)]

skink *n.* [1990s+] (*UK Black*) a term of abuse for a White person. [ety. unknown]

skin mag *n.* (*also* **skin book/magazine/rag**) [1960s+] a pornographic magazine. [SKIN adj.[2] + colloq. SE *mag*, a magazine/RAG n.[4] (2)]

skin me! *excl.* [1950s+] (*US Black*) a form of greeting involving ritual palm slapping. [imper. form of GIVE SOME SKIN v.]

skin-merchant *n.* [late 18C–mid-19C] a milit. recruiting officer. [ironic use of SE]

skinned *adj.* **1** [mid-19C] empty of, lacking in. **2** [late 19C–1930s] comprehensively beaten, utterly defeated. **3** [late 19C–1940s] (*also* **skinned out**) deprived of one's money, esp. after gambling unsuccessfully. **4** [1950s–60s] (*orig. Aus.*) totally bereft. [SE *skin*/SKIN v.[1]]

skinned rabbit *n.* [late 19C–1910s] a very thin person. [resemblance]

skinner *n.*[1] **1** [late 18C–1950s] one who defrauds another of their money. **2** [mid-19C; 1940s] (*orig. UK Und.*) one who has no money. **3** [late 19C+] a bet that brings large profits to the bookmakers. **4** [late 19C+] (*Aus.*) a horse that wins despite very long odds; by ext. any form of racing or otherwise coup. **5** [1940s+] (*N.Z.*) an object that is useless or used up. [SKIN v.[1]; (3) 20C+ use is mainly Aus./N.Z.]

skinner *n.*[2] [mid-late 19C] a thief, usu. a woman, who waylays young children and strips them of their clothes, which she then sells. [SE *skin*]

skinner *n.*[3] [1910s–60s] (*Can./US*) a horse-driver. [abbr. SE *mule-skinner*]

skinner *n.*[4] [1920s+] (*Aus.*) an appointment that one has deliberately avoided. [? phr. 'by the skin of one's teeth']

skinner *n.*[5] [1950s+] (*US prison/Und.*) a rapist; a sex offender. [SE *skin*]

skinner *n.*[6] *see* SKINDER n.

skinners *n.* [late 19C] mental torture. [one's mind, rather than one's body, is 'flayed alive']

skinning *n.*[1] [mid-19C] (*US Und.*) the theft of cargo from ships by harbour thieves. [SKIN v.[1] (1)]

skinning *n.*[2] **1** [mid-19C+] the fleecing of a victim, e.g. by a confidence trickster. **2** [1920s+] (*US*) a beating, whether physical or verbal. [SKIN v.[1] (3)/SE *skin*]

skinning game *n.* [mid–late 19C] (*US*) any form of corrupt, crooked gambling, e.g. poker, faro, and the establishment where it takes place. [SKIN v.[1] (3)]

skinning house *n.* (*also* **brace house, skinning den/joint**) [late 19C–1940s] (*US*) a casino or any place of entertainment where confidence trickster or crooked gamblers operate. [SKIN v.[1] (3)/BRACE n.[2] + SE *house/den/*JOINT n.[4] (3)]

skinny *n.*[1] [1940s] (*Aus.*) a woman; a girl. [SKIN n.[9] (1)]

skinny *n.*[2] [1940s] (*US Und.*) a 10-cent piece, a dime. [? a thin coin]

skinny *n.*[3] **1** [1950s+] information; often as *inside skinny, hot skinny*. **2** [1970s+] the truth. [? play on SE *skin*, i.e. 'the naked truth', 'the bare facts']

skinny *n.*[4] *see* SAMMY n.[3].

skinny as a broom *n.* [20C+] a bridegroom. [rhy. sl.]

skinny-ass *adj.* (*also* **skinny-assed**) [1950s+] (*orig. US*) of a person, thin. [SE *skinny* + -ASS sfx]

skinny-dip *n.* [1960s+] a swim in the nude. [SKINNY-DIP v.]

skinny-dip *v.* [1950+] (*orig. US*) to swim in the nude.

skinny-dipper *n.* [1970s+] a person who swims in the nude. [SKINNY-DIP v.]

skinny-dipping *n.* [2000s] picking pockets on the London Underground; the idea being that the pickpocket has to be thin to work in the crowds. [SE *skinny* + DIP v.[2] (1)]

skinny down *v.* [2000s] (*US*) to reduce something to a minimum. [SE *skinny down*, to lose weight]

skinny Lizzie *n.* [1950s+] a thin woman.

skinny worker *n.* [1940s] (*US Und.*) a sneak-thief. [SE *skinny* + WORKER n.[1] (1)]

skin off your nose! *excl.* [1900s–60s] (*orig. naut.*) a popular toast when drinking; often ext. as *here's to the skin off your nose!*

skin of the creature *n.* [mid-19C+] (*Anglo-Irish*) a bottle of whisky. [SE *skin* + CREATURE, THE n. (3)]

skin one's eels *v.* [mid–late 19C] to mind one's own business.

skin (one's) teeth *v.* (*also* **'kin teet'**) [1970s+] (*W.I./UK Black teen*) **1** to have a laugh or a joke with someone or at something, to mess around. **2** to bare one's teeth, to smile broadly, esp. falsely. [the amount of gum revealed by such a broad, empty smile]

skin one's thing *v.* [1970s] (*US*) to masturbate. [THING n.[2] (3)]

skin one's weather eye *v. see* KEEP ONE'S EYE PEELED v.

skin-out *n.* [1990s+] (*W.I.*) sexual abandonment. [SKIN OUT v.[1]]

skin out *v.*[1] [1990s+] (*W.I.*) to enjoy oneself.

skin out *v.*[2] *see* SKIN v.[3].

skin out of *v. see* SKIN v.[1] (5).

skinpop *n.* (*also* **skin**) [1940s+] (*drugs*) an injection into the flesh rather than directly into a vein. [SKINPOP v.]

skinpop *v.* (*also* **skin**) [1940s+] (*drugs*) to inject a narcotic beneath the skin rather than directly into a vein; the effect of such an injection is less immediate and somewhat weaker. [SE *skin* + POP v.[4] (1)]

skinpopper *n.* [1950s+] (*drugs*) a narcotics user who injects into the skin rather than into a vein; the assumption is that such a user is less wholly habituated. [SKINPOP v.]

skin queen *n.* [1960s+] (*US gay*) a male homosexual who views his partners as no more than sex objects, a gay sexist. [SE *skin* + QUEEN n.[2] (1)]

skin rag *n. see* SKIN MAG n.

skin-roll *n.* [1990s+] (*UK juv.*) a totally inadequate, inept person. [the resemblance of a penis to a roll of skin; thus cognate with DORK n. (2), PRICK n. (3) etc]

skins *n.*[1] [late 18C] a tanner. [his job]

skins *n.*[2] [1920s+] a set of drums. [SKIN n.[11]]

skins *n.*[3] [1970s+] (*US gay*) very tight trousers.

skins *n.*[4] *see* SKIN n.[9].

skin-search *n.* [1930s+] a search in which the subject is stripped naked and searched, usu. for narcotics or, in prison, concealed weapons; thus the person subjected to such a search.

skin-search *v.* [1970s] to search somebody for narcotics or, in prison, concealed weapons after stripping them naked.

skin shake *n.* [1960s] (*US prison*) a body search.

skin shot *n.* [1930s+] (*drugs*) an injection of a narcotic that is made into the skin, rather than a specific vein; thus *skin-shooter*, one who injects. [SE *skin* + SHOT n.[6] (2)/SHOOT SKIN v.]

skint *adj.* [1910s+] without money, out of funds, sometimes intensified as *skint stony*; also *skun(t)*, to be made penniless. [SKINNED adj. (3)]

skin teeth *n.* [1970s+] (*W.I.*) a false smile. [SKIN (ONE'S) TEETH v. (2)]

skin teeth *v. see* SKIN (ONE'S) TEETH v.

skin the cat *v.* [19C+] to have sexual intercourse. [SE *skin* + CAT n.[3] (1)]

skin-the-lamb *n.* [mid-19C] the card-game *lansquenet*, sometimes as *lamb skin-it*. [pun on pron.]

skin the lamb *v.* **1** [mid–late 19C] to swindle, to hoax, to blackmail. **2** [mid-19C–1900s] of a bookmaker, to take bets on every horse in a race other than the winner; thus to make a substantial profit. **3** [1900s] to 'fix' a horserace. [SKIN v.[1] (3); a play on SE *fleece*]

skin the live rabbit *v.* **1** [19C] to have sexual intercourse (cf. BURY IT v.). **2** [late 19C–1900s] of a man, to peel back one's foreskin. [SE *skin* + LIVE RABBIT n.]

skin-the-pizzle *n.* [mid-19C–1900s] the vagina. [PIZZLE n.]

skin through *v.* [1900s–20s] to slip through, to pass through narrowly, to get through something with a narrow margin.

skintight *adj.* [1960s] really friendly. [pun on SE *skintight* + TIGHT adj.[6]]

skintights *n.* [1900s] sausages.

skintop *n.* [1990s+] (*US*) a bald head.

skin up *v.*[1] [20C+] (*W.I.*) **1** to overturn. **2** of a woman, to expose oneself, esp. one's buttocks, in an indecent manner; also as *skin up one's clothes/dress*. [SE *skin*]

skin up *v.*[2] **1** [1960s+] (*drugs*) to roll a cannabis-filled cigarette. **2** [1990s+] in fig. use, to involve oneself with. [SKIN n.[18]]

skin up *v.*[3] [1990s+] (*W.I.*) to be on friendly terms. [the proximity of human *skin*]

skin up one's face *v.* (*also* **skin up one's lip/mouth/nose**) [1950s+] (*W.I.*) to make a grimace of displeasure, scorn or disapproval. [the movement of the skin that is part of the grimace]

skin up (with) *v.* [1950s+] (*W.I.*) to laugh foolishly and ingratiatingly. [the movement of the lips]

skin worker *n.* [20C+] (*US Und.*) a shoplifter, usu. of furs; thus *on the skin*, stealing furs. [SE *skin*, a fur + WORKER n.[1] (1)]

skip *n.*[1] **1** [mid-19C+] the captain. **2** [1920s] (*US prison*) a jailer. **3** [1930s+] a term of address, esp. to a boss, a manager, barman etc. [abbr. SKIPPER n.[2] (2)]

skip *n.*[2] [late 19C–1900s] (*Anglo-Irish*) a dance.

skip *n.*[3] **1** [late 19C–1930s] (*US*) the act of absconding, running away; thus *on the skip*, running away. **2** [20C+] an act of ignoring, passing by. **3** [1910s+] (*US*) an absconder, esp. one who leaves without paying their debts. [SKIP v. (1)]

skip *n.*[4] [2000s] (*Aus.*) an Anglo-Australian. [? SE *skip*, to dance]

skip *n.*[5] *see* SKIP-KENNEL n.

skip *n.*[6] *see* SKIPPY n.[2].

skip *v.* **1** [early 19C+] to leave, to escape, to run off. **2** [late 19C–1900s] to die. **3** [20C+] to avoid, to run away from, e.g. a school lesson. **4** [20C+] to overlook, to forget. **5** [1980s] to expel from school. [SE 15C–early 19C]

skip and jump *n.* [1950s+] **1** a pump. **2** the heart. [rhy. sl.; (2) = PUMP n.[4]]

skip it! *excl.* **1** [20C+] (*orig. US*) forget it! don't bother! etc. **2** [1950s+] (*orig. US*) go away! leave! [SKIP v. (4)/SKIP v. (1)]

skip-jack *n.* **1** [mid-16C–1920s] a conceited fop or dandy. **2** [17C] a jockey. **3** [17C–early 19C] (*UK Und.*) a horse-trader's boy, who puts the horses through their paces. [SE *skip* + SE *jack*, generic for a man]

skip-kennel *n.* (*also* **skip**) [mid-17C–mid-19C] a footman. [he *skips* or jumps over the *kennel* or gutter]

skip on *v.* [1980s+] (*US campus*) to go away, to leave. [ext. of SKIP v. (1)]

skip-out *n.* [1950s] (*US*) an absconder, e.g. from a hotel bill. [SKIP OUT (ON) v.]

skip out (on) *v.* [mid-19C+] (*orig. US*) to desert, to abandon, to run off. [ext. of SKIP v. (1)]

skipper *n.[1]* **1** [mid-16C+] a shelter for tramps and other homeless people. **2** [late 16C–1930s] (*also* **skepper**) a barn. **3** [1920s+] one who sleeps in hedges and outhouses. [Welsh *ysgubor*, a barn]

skipper *n.[2]* **1** [19C] the Devil. **2** [mid-19C+] a boss, a manager, a police sergeant or captain etc. **3** [1910s+] a general mode of address. [SE *skipper*, a ship's captain]

skipper *n.[3]* [late 19C; 1930s] one who is retreating or leaving; an absconder. [SKIP v. (1)]

skipper *n.[4]* [1990s+] a young woman, esp. promiscuous and under the age of consent. [SE *skip*, i.e. from bed to bed, from partner to partner]

skipper *n.[5]* [1990s+] the clitoris (cf. BABY IN THE BOAT n.). [play on LITTLE MAN (IN THE BOAT) n.]

skipper *n.[6] see* CAPTAIN n.[4] (2).

skipper-bird *n.* [mid-19C] one who sleeps in a barn, a tramp, a vagrant. [SKIPPER n.[1] (2) + BIRD n.[2] (1)]

skippering *n.* [mid-19C+] sleeping in derelict, empty houses or barns, sleeping rough. [SKIPPER (IT) v.]

skipper (it) *v.* (*also* **do a skipper**) [mid-19C+] to sleep rough. [SKIPPER n.[1]]

skippies *n.* [1990s+] (*US*) cheap trainers, rather than those manufactured by major labels.

skippy *n.[1]* [1930s–40s] (*US Black*) an effeminate homosexual man. [SE *skip*, to jump around]

skippy *n.[2]* (*also* **skip**) [1980s] (*Aus.*) a derog./racist term for a White child; a White youth. [the TV series *Skippy, the Bush Kangaroo*]

skippy *n.[3] see* SKIBBY n.

skippy *adj.* [1970s+] (*US Black*) right, correct. [ety. unknown]

skips *n.* [1980s–90s] (*US campus/teen*) tennis shoes.

skip tracer *n.* [1950s+] (*US*) an investigator who tracks down those who default on hotel and other bills; thus *skip-tracing*, the investigation. [SKIP n.[3] (3) + SE *tracer*]

ski-ride *n.* [1940s–60s] (*orig. US Black*) a cocaine binge. [play on SNOW n.[2] (1)]

skirmish *v.* [mid-19C–1910s] (*US*) to look around in search of something.

skirrach *n. see* SKERRICK n. (1).

skirt *n.* [late 19C+] **1** a woman, usu. an attractive woman; thus BIT OF SKIRT n. **2** a generic term for women as a group. [metonymy]

skirt-chaser *n.* [1920s+] (*orig. W.I./US*) a Don Juan, a habitual and dedicated ladies' man. [SKIRT n. + SE *chaser*]

skirt duty *n.* [1920s] of a woman, the practice of acting in a way designed to attract men; of a man, associating with women. [SKIRT n. (2)]

skirt-foist *n.* [mid–late 17C] a female cheat. [SE *skirt* + FOIST n.[2] (2)]

skirt-lifter *n.* [1980s] a lesbian (cf. CHEMISE-LIFTER n.). [play on SHIRTLIFTER n.]

skirtman *n.* [1970s] (*US Black*) a man who is dominated by his female partner.

skis *n.* [1940s–60s] (*US Black*) very large shoes.

skish *n.* [1900s] (*US*) a state of drunkenness. [? echoic of his slurred tones]

skit *n.* [late 18C+] (*Irish*) a joke, a game.

skit *v.[1]* [late 18C–early 19C] to wheedle. [SE *skit*, to caper or leap around]

skit *v.[2]* [1950s+] (*S.Afr.*) to steal. [Afk. *skut*, to impound]

skite *n.* **1** [mid-19C+] (*Aus./N.Z.*) boasting, bragging. **2** [20C+] (*Aus./N.Z.*) a braggart, a boaster. **3** [1910s] (*Irish*) a silly, frivolous person. **4** [1910s] (*Aus./N.Z.*) a complaint. **5** [1910s] nonsense. [SKITE v.[1]]

skite *v.[1]* [mid-19C+] (*Aus./N.Z.*) to boast or brag; thus *skite up*, to extol, to praise; *nothing to skite about*, nothing to make a fuss about. [BLATHERSKITE n.]

skite *v.[2] see* SKATE v.[1] (1).

skiter *n.* [late 19C+] (*Aus./N.Z.*) an incessant talker; a braggart. [SKITE v.[1]]

skite-the-gutter *n.* [20C+] (*Ulster*) an unimportant person. [OE *skite*, to defecate]

skitey *adj.* [1940s+] (*Aus./N.Z.*) boastful. [SKITE v.[1]]

skiting *n.* [1910s+] (*Aus./N.Z.*) boasting, bragging. [SKITE v.[1]]

skits *n.* [1960s] (*US Black*) clothes. [? link to Scot. *skit*, a piece of ostentation]

skitter *n.* **1** [1900s–20s] a person. **2** [1940s+] (*Irish*) an unruly child, a disreputable young person. [? SE *skit*, to act skittishly]

skitters, the *n.* [mid-19C+] diarrhoea. [dial. *skitter*; ult. OE *scitte*, diarrhoea]

skittle *n. see* SKETEL n.

skittle *v.* (*also* **skittle out/over**) [1910s+] (*orig. Aus.*) to knock down, to kill.

skittles *n.[1]* [mid-19C–1940s] nonsense, rubbish; also used as excl. *skittles!* rubbish! [i.e. one can 'knock it down' easily; note chess jargon *skittles*, chess played without serious application]

skittles *n.[2]* [1950s] food or drink.

skitz *n. see* SCHIZ n.

skitzing *n.* [1990s+] (*US Black teen*) acting in a bizarre or eccentric manner. [SCHIZ (OUT) v. (1)/SE *schizophrenia*]

skiv *n.[1]* (*also* **skid**) [mid–late 19C] a sovereign. [ety. unknown; 'fashionable slang' (Hotten, 1859)]

skiv *n.[2] see* SKIVVY n.[2].

skive *n.* [1910s+] an evasion, a way of getting out of one's responsibilities. [SKIVE (OFF) v.]

skive (off) *v.* [1910s+] (*orig. milit.*) to neglect one's duties or work. [? dial. *skive*, to move quickly or Fr. *esquiver*, to dodge, to slink away]

skiver *n.* [1940s+] a 'lazybones', a shirker. [SKIVE (OFF) v.]

skivver *v.* [1940s] (*US Black*) to wander around. [? dial. *skive*, to move quickly]

skivvies *n.* **1** [1910s+] (*US*) men's underwear, esp. underpants. **2** [1950s] a vest, esp. in the form of a *skivvy shirt*. [ety. unknown]

skivvy *n.[1]* [late 19C+] a derog. term for a Japanese person (cf. BUDDHAHEAD n.). [presumably a var. on SKIBBY n. (2), although cits. put dates at variance]

skivvy *n.[2]* (*also* **scivvie**, **skiv**, **skivy**) [late 19C+] a maid of all work. [? SLAVEY n.; *see also* ety. for SKIBBY n.]

skivvy *v.* [1910s+] to perform menial tasks. [SKIVVY n.[2]]

skiz *see under* SCHIZ.

skizzah *n.* [2000s] (*US Black*) an unpopular person. [? ext. of SKEEZER n. + -IZ- ifx]

skizzle *v.* [1930s+] (*US*) to have sexual intercourse; thus *skizzel*, a promiscuous woman.

skizzy *adj.* **1** [1960s] a general term of approval, admiration. **2** [1970s] disgusting, dirty, repellent, a general term of disapproval. [(1) var. on SCHIZZY adj. (1) on bad = good model; (2) var. on SCUZZY adj. (1)]

sko *n.* [1990s+] (*US Black/campus*) a disgusting, promiscuous woman (cf. SKOOCHIE n.). [abbr. SKANKY adj. (1) + HO n.[1] (4)]

skoff see under SCOFF.

skoll v. see SKULL v.[3].

skolly n. (also **skollie**) [1930s+] (S.Afr.) a street thug, a hoodlum, usu. a member of a gang. [? Du. schoelje, a scavenger, but note skorriemorrie, a rascal, riffraff; ult. Yid. soyrerumoyre, a rogue, a hoodlum; DSAE suggests SE scullery boy, 'a very low form of humanity']

skonce n. see SCONCE n.

skoobied adj. see SCOOBIED adj.

skooby v. see SCOOBY v.

skoochie n. [1990s+] (US Black/campus) a disgusting, promiscuous woman; also (derog.) a lesbian (cf. SKO n.). [abbr. SKANKY adj. (1) + HOOCHIE n.[1] (1)]

skoofer n. (also **skoofus, skroofus, skrufer**) [1970s+] (US Black/drugs) a marijuana cigarette. [ety. unknown; ? link to SKUIF n.]

skookum adj. [late 19C+] (Can., mainly West Coast) satisfactory, fine. [Chinook jargon skookum, strong]

skookum house n. (also **skookum**) [late 19C–1920s] (Can., mainly West Coast/US) a prison; often preceded by strong (cf. BANDHOUSE n.). [Chinook jargon skookum, strong + SE house]

skop n. (S.Afr.) **1** [1920s+] a kick. **2** [1960s+] a good time, a dance, a party; thus skop, skiet en donder, lit. 'kick, shoot and thunder', any rough and tough activity, an action film. **3** [1980s+] a thrill, a kick (from a drink or drug). [Afk. skop, a kick]

skop v. [1960s+] (S.Afr.) **1** to enjoy oneself, to 'party'; thus skop lawaai, to have a rowdy, noisy good time. **2** to kick something or someone; thus skop it, to die. [SKOP n. (2)/Afk. skop, to kick]

skorking n. [2000s] (US) sexual intercourse. [ety. unknown]

skosh n. [1940s+] (orig. US milit.) a little bit. [Jap. sukoshi]

skowbanker n. see SCOWBANKER n.

skr... see also under SCR...

skrik n. [late 19C+] (S.Afr.) a fright, a tremor of fear. [Du. schrik, a fright]

skrik v. [late 19C+] (S.Afr.) to be terrified. [SKRIK n.]

skroofus/skrufer n. see SKOOFER n.

skrunty adj. [1970s] (US) unpleasant, mean. [? SE runt]

skuffle n. see SCUFFLE n.[2].

skuffter n. see SCUFFER n.

skuif n. (also **skuifie, skyf, skyfie**) [1970s+] (S.Afr.) **1** a cigarette. **2** a marijuana cigarette. [Afk. skuif, a draw, a puff]

skulk v. [1970s] (US campus) to steal.

skulker n. [late 18C–early 19C] one who hides themselves to avoid labour. [Scand. skulka, to lurk, skolka to play truant; orig. milit. jargon skulker, a soldier who shirks his duties by hiding away; SE from mid-19C]

skull n.[1] [20C+] (W.I., Trin.) a trick, an act of deception; thus pull a skull on, to deceive. [? SE skulk]

skull n.[2] **1** [1910s] (US) a fellow soldier, with derog. implication. **2** [1940s] (Aus.) a person in authority, e.g. in the armed forces.

skull n.[3] [1910s–40s] (US) a free ticket.

skull n.[4] [1920s] a share, a portion, a 'go'; in phr. denoting price, so much a skull.

skull n.[5] [1940s] (US Black) a star, an outstanding performer. [i.e. what is within the skull: brains, talent, ability]

skull n.[6] [1940s+] (Aus.) in the game of two-up, the 'heads' side of a coin.

skull n.[7] [1970s+] (orig. US Black) **1** fellatio (cf. BRAIN n.[2]). **2** cunnilingus. [var. on HEAD n.[10]]

skull n.[8] see SCULL n.[1].

skull v.[1] [1940s+] (US/Aus.) to hit someone on the head.

skull v.[2] [1970s+] (orig. US Black) to perform oral sex (cf. BRAIN n.[2]). [SKULL n.[7]]

skull v.[3] (also **skoll**) [1980s+] (Aus./N.Z.) to drink down a large container of beer in one go. [SE skull, into which it is poured + skol! a toast]

skull v.[4] [1990s+] (W.I.) to play truant. [? SE skulk]

skull and crossbones n. **1** [1930s] (US) blackmail. **2** [1980s] (US Black) poison. **3** [1980s] (US prison) anyone who is 'poison', esp. one who disrupts one's plans. [the acknowledged sign for 'poison']

skullbanker n. see SCOWBANKER n.

skull book n. [1960s] (US Black) anything committed to memory; oral tradition.

skull-buggery n. [1990s+] fellatio (cf. BRAIN n.[2]). [SE skull + buggery; note SKULL n.[7] (1)]

skull-buster n. **1** [1920s+] (US) anything seen as particularly intellectually challenging, esp. a hard college course. **2** [1930s+] (US Black) a policeman (cf. BEAT-POUNDER n.). [SE skull + BUST v.[1] (4)]

skullbusting adj. [1940s] (US) intellectualy challenging. [SKULL-BUSTER n. (1)]

skull-cracker n. (US) **1** [late 19C–1930s] very strong alcohol. **2** [1910s–50s] a large thuggish person.

skull-cracking n. [1920s] (US) hard physical work.

skulldrag n. [1940s–60s] (US Black) any activity that taxes the mind or emotions. [SE skull + drag, a bore]

skull drag v. **1** [mid-19C+] (Aus.) to haul along, to drag by force. **2** [1920s–40s] (US Und.) to demand a free drink in a bar. [note late 19C N.Z. gang, the Skulldraggers; Lincoln U. (Oxford, Penn.) use c.1934: 'SKULL-DRAG. To play hard']

skull-drive v. [late 19C–1920s] (Aus.) to work as a schoolteacher. [i.e. to drive knowledge into reluctant skulls]

skulled adj. [1960s+] **1** (also **skulled out**) intoxicated by a drug or by an excess of alcohol. **2** insane, crazy. [OUT OF ONE'S SKULL phr.]

skull file n. [1960s] (US Black) one's mind, esp. in context of thoughts/memories that are stored there.

skull-filler n. [1900s] (Aus.) a schoolteacher.

skull fry n. see FRY n.

skull fuck n. [1990s+] (US) heterosexual male–female intercourse whereby the male substitutes the mouth for the vagina; this differs from fellatio in that the man is active rather than passive (cf. BRAIN n.[2]). [SE skull + FUCK n.[1] (1); note SKULL n.[7] (1)]

skull fuck v. [1990s+] for a man to have intercourse with a woman, using her mouth rather than her vagina. [SKULL FUCK n.]

skull game n. [1970s] an intellectual pursuit.

skull job n. [1950s+] oral sex, whether fellatio or cunnilingus (cf. BRAIN n.[2]). [SE skull/SKULL n.[7] (1) + JOB n.[4]]

skullneck v. [20C+] to decapitate. [one removes the skull from the neck]

skull note n. [1960s] (US Black) a mental note.

skull note v. [1960s] (US Black) to memorize. [SKULL NOTE n.]

skull orchard n. [1930s–50s] (US Black) a cemetery.

skull pussy n. [1970s+] (US gay) a fellator. [SE skull/SKULL n.[7] (1) + PUSSY n. (2)]

skull session n. [1950s+] (US) a discussion, a conference.

skull-thatcher n. **1** [late 18C–19C] a wig-maker. **2** [mid-19C] a maker of straw bonnets. **3** [mid-19C] a hat.

skull trouble n. [1900s–30s] (US) a blow on the head. [SE skull]

skunk n.[1] **1** [mid-19C+] a very unpleasant, contemptible person, although sometimes in joc. use. **2** [1950s] (US) (also **skunkie**) a bedwetter. **3** [1960s–80s] a woman, esp. one who smells badly. [the animal's poor image; the humans lit. or fig. smell]

skunk n.[2] **1** [1980s+] (drugs) (also **skunkweed**) an exceptionally strong variety of marijuana (often grown in the user's home) with up to 30% tetrahydrocannibonol (THC) content, thus intensifying the effects from the merely stimulating to those of such hallucinogens as LSD; thus SUPERSKUNK n. **2** [2000s] (US Black) poor-quality marijuana. **3** [2000s] heroin. [play on SE skunk, an animal with a particularly strong smell]

skunk adj. [1940s+] (US Black) second-rate, inferior.

skunk v. 1 [mid-19C] (US campus) to renege on a bill. 2 [mid-19C+] (US/W.I. sporting) to beat decisively. 3 [late 19C–1960s] (US tramp) to cheat. 4 [1900s–30s] to finish off, to consume.

skunked adj.[1] [1920s+] deceived, tricked. [SKUNK v. (3)]

skunked adj.[2] [1920s+] very drunk. [phr. drunk as a skunk]

skunked adj.[3] [1990s+] intoxicated by very strong marijuana. [SKUNK n.[2] (1)]

skunkie n. see SKUNK n.[1] (2).

skunkweed n. see SKUNK n.[2] (1).

skunky adj. [1920s–60s] disgusting, contemptible. [SKUNK n.[1] (1)]

skunky adv. [1950s] of being drunk, very, extremely. [phr. drunk as a skunk]

skutcher n. [1930s+] (Aus./N.Z.) anything or anyone considered excellent, attractive etc. [ety. unknown]

skuz see under SCUZZ.

sky n.[1] [1920s+] (Aus.) an Italian (cf. DAGO n.). [rhy. sl. = EYETIE n. (1)]

sky n.[2] [1930s–40s] (US Black) a policeman; a prison warder (cf. BABY-BLUES n.[2]). [the blue uniform]

sky n.[3] [1930s+] (US Black) a hat. [abbr. SKY-PIECE n. (2)]

sky n.[4] (also **ski**) [1940s+] (Aus.) whisky. [clipping]

sky n.[5] see BLUE SKY n.[2].

sky v.[1] 1 [19C+] to toss into the air. 2 [late 19C–1900s] to spend all one's funds, esp. in a carefree, spendthrift manner. 3 [late 19C–1920s] of a picture, to hang high on the gallery wall. 4 [1970s+] (US campus) to jump high. [SE sky]

sky v.[2] (also **sky out**) 1 [1930s+] (orig. US milit.) to leave. 2 [1970s] (US prison) to escape.

-sky sfx see -SKI sfx.

sky a copper v. 1 [19C] to toss a coin. 2 [mid–late 19C] to make a noise, to make a nuisance of oneself. [SKY v.[1] (1) + COPPER n.[2] (1)]

sky-artist n. [1940s] a psychiatrist. [mispron.]

skybird n. [1940s] (US Black) a hallucination.

sky blue n.[1] 1 [mid-18C–mid-19C] gin, esp. second-rate gin. 2 [late 18C–19C] 'London milk, much diluted with water, or from which the cream has been too closely skimmed' (Hotten, 1860). 3 [mid-19C] (N.Z.) a milkman or a nickname for a milkman. 4 [1900s–10s] vegetable soup. 5 [1970s] (drugs) LSD (cf. A n.[3]).

sky blue n.[2] 1 [19C] (Can.) an officer of the Hudson's Bay Company; usu. in pl. 2 [20C+] (S.Afr.) a long-term prisoner. [their blue uniforms]

sky-diver n. [20C+] £5 (cf. BEEHIVE n.[2]). [rhy. sl. = FIVER n. (1)]

sky-drummer n. [1900s] (Aus.) a missionary. [SE sky + DRUMMER n.[2]]

skyf n. see SKUIF n.

skyfarmer n. 1 [mid-18C–early 19C] (UK Und.) a criminal beggar who tours the country posing as a gentleman farmer fallen on hard times, backed by suitably impressive, if counterfeit, papers. 2 [19C–1910s] (Anglo-Irish) a farmer with very little, if any, land. ['the isle of Sky(e), or some other remote place [...] or else from their farms being in nubibus, "in the clouds"' (Grose, 1785)]

skyfie n. see SKUIF n.

skyfoozle v. [late 19C] to disconcert. [var. on BAMBOOZLE v. (1)]

skygodlin adj. (also **sigoggling**, **skygoggling**) [mid-19C+] (US) askew, slanted. [? SE sky + GOGGLE (AT) v., i.e. one who, instead of looking straight ahead, looks upwards]

skyhacking n. [1920s+] (Aus.) slandering, talking behind someone's back. [CHI-IKE n. (2)]

sky-high v. see BLOW SKY HIGH v. (1).

sky-hoot v.[1] [late 19C–1920s] (US) to rise, to increase. [SE sky + hoot, i.e. blow (sky high)]

sky-hoot v.[2] [late 19C–1920s] to run off, to move fast; to act irresponsibly. [elaborate pron. of SCOOT v. (2)]

sky in one's alley v. see THROW IN ONE'S ALLEY v. (1).

sky-juice n. [1920s–40s] (US) rainwater.

sky kick n. [1940s] (US Und.) the inside pocket of a jacket or coat. [fig. use of SE sky, i.e. an upper garment + KICK n.[4]]

sky-lantern n. [mid-19C] the moon.

skylark n. [20C+] a park. [rhy. sl.]

skylark v. see LARK v. (2).

skylarker n. [late 18C] a thief who doubles as a journeyman bricklayer. [using the legitimate job to facilitate the villainy, he gets up early – 'with the lark' – to spy out vulnerable houses]

skylight n. [early–mid-19C] a small space between the top of one's glass and the level of the drink within it.

skylights n. 1 [early 19C–1910s] eyes. 2 [1900s] spectacles.

sky-lodging n. [late 19C] a garret.

sky off v. [1970s+] (US Black) to depart, to exit. [ext. of SKY v.[2] (1)]

sky out v. see SKY v.[2] (1).

sky-parlour n. [late 18C–19C] a garret.

sky-piece n. (US) 1 [1900s] the head. 2 [1900s–70s] any form of headgear.

sky pilot n. (also **kirk pilot**, **sky pi**, **sky scout**, **sky sharp**, **soul aviator**) [late 19C+] a priest, a prison chaplain, a preacher, a missionary; also attrib. [he guides one to heaven]

sky-pocket n. [1940s] (US Black) an inside pocket. [? var. on SKY KICK n.]

sky (rocket) n. [late 19C+] a pocket; thus [1950s+] (Aus.) touch one's sky, to pay for a round of drinks. [rhy. sl.]

sky rocket n.[1] [mid-19C–1940s] (US) a form of college cheer, rounded off with a cry of sis-boom-bah!, supposedly that of an ascending and exploding rocket.

sky rocket n.[2] [1980s+] (Aus. prison) a homosexual.

sky rug n. [1940s+] (US) a wig or toupee. [SKY-PIECE n. (2) + RUG n.[1] (1)]

sky scout n. see SKY PILOT n.

sky-scraper n.[1] 1 [19C] a tall hat or bonnet. 2 [mid-19C–1900s] a notably tall person. 3 [late 19C] a rider on a 'penny-farthing' cycle. 4 [late 19C] the penis. [18C naut. jargon sky-scraper, a triangular sky-sail, the highest sail on a boat. Such sails were also known as moon-rakers. The orig. US use of the term to mean a tall building began life as sl. (c.1888; cited as such in Maitland's American Slang Dictionary, 1891), but had entered the mainstream by 1920; note NY Times 18 Aug. 1837 2/7: '[Balloon flights are] so common a business that the people call it nothing more than "skylarking", or "sky scraping"'; also 1880s baseball jargon skyscraper, a 'towering fly ball']

sky-scraper n.[2] [19C] a tall horse. [the horse Skyscraper, sired by Highflyer, which won the Epsom Derby in 1789]

skyscraper n. [1960s+] a newspaper. [rhy. sl.]

sky sharp n. see SKY PILOT n.

sky the wipe v. (also **sky the rag/towel**) [1900s–50s] (Aus.) to surrender. [orig. boxing jargon; SKY v.[1] (1) + WIPE n.[3] (1)/RAG n.[2] (3)/SE towel]

sky-topper n. [late 19C–1920s] someone or something very high.

slaat n. [20C+] (S.Afr.) a blow. [synon. Du.]

slaat v. [20C+] (S.Afr.) to hit, to beat up. [SLAAT n.]

slab n.[1] 1 [early 19C–1900s] a milestone. 2 [late 19C+] a sandwich or bread. 3 [1900s] (US Und.) a display tray. 4 [1920s+] (US) a stretcher, an undertaker's table. 5 [1930s+] (US Black) a bed. 6 [1970s+] (US Black) $1. 7 [1990s+] (Aus.) a case of 24 bottles or tins of beer.

slab n.[2] [late 19C–1920s] (Aus.) a tough(-looking) person. [SAusE slab, 'a coarse, axe-hewn plank, two or three inches in thickness' (OED)]

slab n.[3] [1980s+] (drugs) 1 weak or impure crack cocaine (cf. BASE n.). 2 a large piece of crack cocaine, the approx. dimensions of a piece of chewing gum. [? SE (mortuary) slab, i.e. it is 'dead']

slab v. [1980s+] (Aus. prison) to murder. [i.e. to send to the mortuary/undertaker's slab]

slabba-slabba *adj.* [20C+] (*W.I. Rasta*) big and fat, slobby, droopy. [dial. *slabby*, sloppy + redup.]

slabbed and slid *adj.* [1940s–80s] (*UK prison*) dead and gone, or certainly long since departed from the prison and thus the immediate knowledge or interest of those left behind. [SE (mortuary) *slab* + *slid*]

slabber *see also under* SLOBBER and its combs.

slabber *n.* **1** [late 18C–early 19C] a filthy, slobbering person. **2** [1990s+] (*Irish*) talkativeness; thus as v., to talk nonsense. [Du. *slabberen*, muddy ground + SE *slobber*, to dribble saliva]

slabberdegullion *n.* (*also* **slubberdegullion**) [early 17C–19C] a filthy, slobbering fellow. [Du. *overslubberen*, to wade through mud + SE *slabber*, to drool]

slabbering bib *n.* [late 18C–mid-19C] a neckband as worn by a lawyer or parson. [SE *slobber*, to dribble + *bib*]

slabbing *n.* [1970s+] sexual intercourse with a corpse; thus *slab boy*, a necrophiliac. [the corpse is laid out on a mortuary *slab*]

slab boy *n.* [1980s] a necrophiliac.

slabdab *n.* [late 17C–early 18C] a glover. [? SE *slap* + *dab*, i.e. actions involved in making gloves]

slab-dabber *n.* [late 19C] a left-wing hack journalist. [journ. jargon *slab*, a lengthy paragraph + SE *dab* (down)]

slabs *n.* [20C+] the testicles. [backsl. = BALLS n.¹ (1)]

slab-sides *n.* [mid-19C] (*US*) a stupid person.

slack *n.*¹ **1** [19C] impertinence, cheek. **2** [mid-19C+] a spell of inactivity, idleness. **3** [1940s+] (*W.I.*) a promiscuous woman. **4** [1950s] a prostitute. **5** [1950s+] (*W.I.*) a slovenly person. **6** [1950s+] freedom, leeway, relief of pressure; thus *give some slack*, to let someone relax, to stop pressurizing. [SE *slack*, that which hangs loose]

slack *n.*² [1970s] (*US Black*) a form of ritualized handshake, intended to imply absolute agreement between the 2 participants.

slack *adj.* **1** [late 19C+] (*US teen*) or a person, either unmotivated or just plain lazy; often as *slack daddy*. **2** [1950s+] of work or performance, below standard. **3** [1970s+] (*Aus./W.I./UK Black*) sexually available. **4** [1980s] (*US campus*) easy.

slackarse *n.* [1970s+] (*Aus.*) a general term of abuse, usu. aimed at women it implies promiscuity, or laziness. [SE *slack*/SLACK adj. (1) + ARSE n.¹ (2)/ARSE n.¹ (4)]

slack-arsed *adj.* (*also* **slack-assed**) **1** [1970s] (*Aus.*) of a woman, promiscuous. **2** [1980s] (*US*) lazy, undisciplined. [SE *slack*/SLACK adj. (1) + -ARSED sfx¹/-ASSED sfx]

slacked out *adj.* [1970s] (*US*) inefficient, second-rate, below par.

slacken your glib! *excl.* [late 19C] shut up! be quiet! [SE *slacken* + GLIB n. (2)]

slacker *n.* **1** [late 19C+] one who shirks work or avoids exertion etc. **2** [1990s+] (*orig. US*) a member of the generation in their 20s (*c*.1995) who sees no point in joining the social mainstream, for whatever reason, perhaps cynicism or indolence. [SE *slack*]

slackie *n.* [1980s] (*Aus.*) an ageing woman. [a negative ref. to her flesh]

slack-jaw *n.* [mid-19C–1910s] cheek or impudence; thus adj. *slack-jawed*. [ext. of SLACK n.¹ (1) + SE *jaw*/JAW n. (1)]

slack jeff *n. see* JEFF v. (3).

slackness *n.* **1** [1950s+] (*W.I.*) sloppiness, incompetenece. **2** [1950s+] vulgarity; overt sexiness. **3** [1980s] (*W.I.*) lewd, vulgar lyrics used in popular songs. [(1) SLACK n.¹ (5); (2) and (3) SLACK n.¹ (3)]

slack off *v.* [late 19C+] to urinate. [the relaxation of one's bladder]

slackum yackum *v.* [2000s] (*US Black*) to have sexual intercourse. [ety. unknown]

slag *n.*¹ **1** [18C–early 19C; 1950s+] a worthless or insignificant person, frequently used as a term of contempt, e.g. *you slag!* **2** [1930s–60s] a rough or brutal person. **3** [1940s–60s] rubbish, nonsense. **4** [1940s+] any objectionable or contemptible person. **5** [1950s+] a prostitute, a promiscuous woman, a slattern.

6 [1950s+] a vagrant, a petty criminal; thus [1950s–60s] *the slag*, such persons collectively. [18C *slag*, a coward, f. *slack-mettled*]

slag *n.*² [mid-19C; 1920s–40s] (*UK Und.*) a gold or silver chain; thus *nip the slag*, to cut a watch chain. [SLANG n.² (2)]

slag *adj.* **1** [1960s+] second-rate, worthless. **2** [1970s+] promiscuous. [SLAG n.¹]

slag *v.*¹ [1960s+] (*Aus.*) to spit. [dial. *slag*, to smear]

slag *v.*² *see* SLOG v. (1).

slag about *v.* [1970s] to wander about aimlessly. [SLAG n.¹ (6)]

slagbag *n.* [2000s] a promiscuous woman. [SLAG n.¹ (5) + -BAG sfx]

slagger *n.* [late 19C] one who keeps a brothel or ACCOMMODATION HOUSE n. (2). [? SE *slacker* or spec. use of SLAG n.¹ (1)]

slaggery *n.* [1960s] the world of villains, layabouts etc. [SLAG n.¹ (6)]

slagging (off) *n.* [1960s+] criticism, verbal attack. [SLAG (OFF) v.]

slaggy *adj.* **1** [1940s+] dirty, unpleasant, offensive. **2** [1970s+] promiscuous, immoral. [SLAG n.¹]

slag (off) *v.* (*also* **slag off at**) [1960s+] to criticize, to slander, to attack verbally. [i.e. to call a SLAG n.¹ (5) or whatever kind]

slam *n.*¹ **1** [late 19C+] (*US*) an insult. **2** [1900s–20s] (*US*) a try, an attempt. **3** [1900s–60s] (*US*) a violent blow (given to a ball); also in fig. use. **4** [1920s] (*US*) a disappointment. **5** [1980s] (*US campus*) of a man, an act of sexual intercourse. **6** [2000s] (*US prison*) the use of force by an officer.

slam *n.*² [1930s] (*US*) a drink of alcohol. [one 'slams' the glass on the bar counter]

slam *n.*³ [1960s+] (*orig. US*) a prison. [abbr. SLAMMER n.² (1)]

slam *n.*⁴ *see* SLAM DANCE n.

slam *v.*¹ **1** [18C–19C] to talk, to boast. **2** [late 19C+] (*US*) to insult, to criticize harshly; thus *slamming contest*, a fight in which the contestants criticize each other verbally. **3** [late 19C+] (*orig. US*) to beat up, to hurt badly, to hit; also fig. use. **4** [1940s+] (*US Black/campus/W.I./UK Black teen*) of a man, to have sexual intercourse (cf. BANG v.¹). **5** [1970s] (*US Black*) to imprison. **6** [1980s] (*US campus*) to do well. **7** [1980s+] (*US Black/campus*) to drink fast, usu. beer; thus *slam a forty*, to drink a 40oz (1-litre) bottle of beer. **8** [1990s+] to shut down, to close.

slam *v.*² **1** [20C+] (*US*) to hurry off. **2** [1980s] (*US campus*) to reject someone. [? the *slamming* of a door behind one or the *slamming* of one's feet on the ground]

slam *v.*³ [1980s+] (*US*) to imprison. [SLAM n.³]

slam *v.*⁴ [1990s+] (*drugs*) **1** to use heroin regularly. **2** to inject a narcotic, usu. heroin.

slam *v.*⁵ *see* SLAM DANCE v.

slambam *adv.* [1940s+] (*W.I.*) at once, immediately. [echoic]

slam bam, thank you ma'am *phr. see* WHAM BAM, THANK YOU MA'AM phr.

slam-bang *n.* [1920s] (*US*) a vicious prize-fight. [SE *slam-bang*, rough, aggressive]

slam-bang *adj.* (*also* **slam-bam**) **1** [1930s+] vigorous, energetic. **2** [1960s+] (*orig. US*) exciting, first-rate, excellent. [SLAM-BANG adv.]

slam-bang *adv.* [mid-19C+] **1** vigorously, energetically. **2** (*US*) exactly, precisely, directly. [echoic]

slam-bang shop *n. see* SLAP-BANG(-SHOP) n.

slam dance *n.* (*also* **slam, slam-dancing, slamming**) [1970s+] a particular energetic style of dance that involves physical collision with other dancers. [SE *slam* + *dance*; usu. associated with the audiences of PUNK n.⁴ (1) or THRASH n. (3) music]

slam dance *v.* (*also* **slam**) [1970s+] (*US*) to perform a SLAM DANCE n.; thus *slam dancer*, one who dances in this way. [SLAM DANCE n.]

slam down *v.* [1970s+] (*US prison*) to lock into one's cell as a punishment – no association is permitted. [SE *slam* the door/ SLAM v.¹ (5)]

slam-dunk *n.* [1980s+] a certainty. [*see* next]

slam-dunk *v.* **1** [1980s+] (*US Black*) to make an aggressive, powerful move. **2** [1990s+] to reject a request. [basketball jargon *slam-dunk*, to slam the ball down through the basket, jumping high and using both hands]

slamkin *n.* (*also* **slammerkin, slammocks, slommack**) **1** [late 18C–mid-19C] a slovenly woman; also as adj., slovenly. **2** [mid-19C] a servant. **3** [late 19C] a run-down animal. [note the slovenly Mrs Slammekin in John Gay's *Beggar's Opera* (1727); however, this name may have reflected the *slammerkin*, a loose gown or dress, rather than the later sl.]

slammack *v.* [late 19C] to act in a slovenly manner. [SLAMKIN *n.* (1)]

slam me! *excl.* [mid-late 18C] a euph. for *damn me!* [DAMN *v.*]

slammed *adj.*[1] [1970s] (*US prison*) locked into one's cell during a crisis, e.g. a prison strike. [SE *slam* the door/SLAM *v.*[1] (5)]

slammed *adj.*[2] [1980s+] (*US campus*) **1** drunk (cf. ANNIHILATED adj.). **2** intoxicated by drugs. [SLAM *v.*[1] (3)]

slammer *n.*[1] [late 19C+] anything or anyone exceptional. [SE *slam*, to hit with a bang]

slammer *n.*[2] **1** [1930s+] (*also* **slammers**) prison. **2** [1940s–60s] (*US Black*) a door. **3** [1960s] (*US*) a psychiatric hospital. [the *slamming* shut of (cell) doors]

slammerkin *n. see* SLAMKIN *n.*

slamming *n.*[1] **1** [1950s+] (*US Und.*) (*also* **schlamming**) very violent assault, stopping short of murder. **2** [1980s+] (*US Black*) fighting, either with fists or knives; thus *slamming and jamming*, of the Guardian Angels group, raiding a crack house or similar establishment to smash it up, rough up the patrons and take away the drugs. [SLAM *v.*[1] (3)]

slamming *n.*[2] *see* SLAM DANCE *n.*

slamming *adj.* [late 19C–1900s; 1960s+] a general intensifier, overwhelming, extraordinary, the best, the most fashionable, attractive etc; thus superlative *slamminest*. [SLAM *v.*[1] (3)]

slamming and jamming *n.*[1] [1980s+] (*US Black*) of a disk jockey, playing exciting music.

slamming and jamming *n.*[2] *see* SLAMMING *n.*[1] (2).

slammocks *n. see* SLAMKIN *n.*

slam off *v.* **1** [1930s+] to die. **2** [1990s+] (*UK juv.*) to play truant. [ext. SLAM *v.*[2] (1)]

slam-piece *n.* [1990s+] (*US campus*) a sexual partner. [SLAM *v.*[1] (4) + PIECE *n.*[1] (1)]

slam pit *n.* [1980s+] that part of a nightclub dedicated to slam dancers. [SLAM DANCE *n.*]

slams *n.* [1930s+] (*US prison*) **1** cell doors. **2** the cells. [the sound they make when shut]

slam-slam *v.* [mid-19C–1900s] (*Anglo-Ind.*) to salute. [Urdu *salaam*, to salute, to compliment]

slam the clam *v.* [1960s+] of a woman, to masturbate (cf. APPLY LIP GLOSS *v.*; BEAT ONE'S HOG *v.*). [SE *slam* + BEARDED CLAM *n.*]

slam the gate *v.* [late 19C–1930s] (*US tramp*) to beg from private houses.

slam the ham *v.* (*also* **slam the salami/salmon/spam**) [1950s+] of a man, to masturbate (cf. BANG THE BISHOP *v.*; BEAT ONE'S MEAT *v.*). [SE *slam* + *ham/salami/salmon/spam*]

slam the hammer *v.* (*also* **slam the wapper**) [1990s+] of a man, to masturbate (cf. BANG THE BISHOP *v.*). [SE *slam* + HAMMER *n.*[1] (1)/WAP *v.*]

slam the slats *v.* [1990s+] (*US Und.*) to close a row of cell doors using a remote mechanism that closes every door simultaneously. [SE *slam* + *slat*, a bar]

slam-up *see also under* SLAP-UP.

slam up *v.* [1970s+] (*US Und.*) to imprison. [ext. of SLAM *v.*[1] (5)]

slang *n.*[1] **1** [mid-18C] nonsense, rubbish. **2** [mid-18C] (*UK Und.*) things acquired by trickery or pickpocketing. **3** [mid-late 18C] (*also* **slango**) a line of work, an occupation; thus *on/upon the slang*, involved in one's own profession or job. **4** [mid-18C–

mid-19C] cant, i.e. the jargon of criminals. **5** [mid-18C–mid-19C] illiterate, 'low' language. **6** [early 19C] the criminal fraternity. **7** [mid-19C] a travelling show. **8** [mid-19C] a set of counterfeit scales, as used by cheating costermongers; counterfeit measures; thus *slang quart*, a measure with a false bottom that actually holds only 1½ pints (855ml) as opposed to a full quart (2 pints/1 litre); *slang pint*, ¾ pint (428ml) etc; *work slang*, to use such weights and measures. **9** [mid-19C] a legal warrant. **10** [mid-late 19C] a single performance or 'house' in a travelling show. **11** [mid-19C–1930s] a hawker's licence; thus *out on the slang*, working as an itinerant hawker. **12** [late 19C] a salesman's or showman's speech to attract customers; also as *bad slang*, an exaggerated but successful speech and performance to attract the public. [ety. debatable. Of the various theories the most likely is SE *sling*, to throw; thus fig. 'thrown' language, underpinned by cognates in Norw. *slenjaketen*, sling the jaw etc]

slang *n.*[2] **1** [late 18C–1910s] any form of chains or fetters used to secure a prisoner; usu. in pl. **2** [19C–1940s] a watch chain. **3** [1930s] (*US Und.*) a necklace. [Ger. *Schlange*, a chain, watchchain or Du. *slang*, a snake]

slang *adj.* **1** [early–mid-19C] (*UK Und.*) defective or crooked, usu. of weights and measures. **2** [mid-19C] nouveaux riche, raffish. [SLANG *n.*[1] (8)]

slang *v.*[1] **1** [mid-18C–mid-19C] to cheat, to swindle, to defraud. **2** [mid-18C+] to abuse, to banter with. **3** [late 18C] to exhibit at a fair. **4** [19C+] to use slang. **5** [2000s] (*US Black*) to pose, to assume a role that one cannot sustain. [SLANG *n.*[1]]

slang *v.*[2] [early 19C] to place in chains or fetters. [SLANG *n.*[2] (1)]

slang *v.*[3] [1980s+] (*orig. US Black*) to sell drugs. [SE *sling*/SLING *v.*[6]]

slang and pitcher shop *n.* [late 19C–1900s] a cheapjack's stall; thus the stock it holds. [SLANG *n.*[1] (8) + PITCHER *n.*[3] (3)]

slang-boy *n.* (*also* **boy of the slang**) [late 18C] one who can speak underworld cant. [SLANG *n.*[1] (4)]

slang cove *n.* (*also* **slang cull**) [mid-late 19C] a showman. [SLANG *n.*[1] (7) + COVE *n.* (1)/CULL *n.*[1] (4)]

slang-dipper *n.* [20C+] one who gilds ordinary metal chains and attempts to pass them off as 'gold'; thus *slang-dropper*, the person who actually does the 'trade', usu. by dropping a chain in the street, picking it up as the victim is passing, then asking them to suggest how much it might be worth; they then get the dupe to buy it, assuring them that they themselves are losing by the deal. [SLANG *n.*[2] (2) + SE *dip*]

slanged *adj.* [early 19C] chained up, fettered. [SLANG *v.*[2]]

slanger *n.* [mid-18C] (*UK Und.*) a thief or pickpocket who uses an assistant to carry the stolen goods. [SLANG *v.*[1] (1) or SE *sling*, to throw]

slanging dues concerned *phr.* [early 19C] (*UK Und.*) a phr. used to claim that cheating has gone on(cf. MR KNAP IS CONCERNED phr.[1]). [SLANG *v.*[1] (1)]

slanging match *n.* [late 19C+] a vituperative argument. [SLANG *v.*[1] (2)]

slango *n. see* SLANG *n.*[1] (3).

slang the mauleys *v.* **1** [late 18C–19C] to shake hands. **2** [early 19C] to fight with one's hands or fists. [SE *sling* + MAULEY *n.* (1)]

slangy *adj.* [mid-19C+] flashy, vulgar, whether in speech or appearance. [SLANG *adj.* (2)]

slant *n.*[1] **1** [mid-19C–1900s] an opportunity to push forward a plan or stratagem. **2** [late 19C–1940s] (*Aus.*) a plan or scheme spec. designed to ensure a favourable result. [naut. jargon *slant*, a favourable wind]

slant *n.*[2] [1910s–40s] (*US*) a glance, a brief look; usu. as *get/have/take a slant*, to glance (at). [i.e. 'out of the corner of one's eye']

slant *n.*[3] [1920s] (*US*) any plan that should benefit its maker, an exploitable gimmick, an ulterior motive. [var. on ANGLE *n.*]

slant *n.*[4] (*also* **slant-eye, slanty-eye**) [1920s+] a derog. term for an Oriental person (cf. BROWNIE *n.*[2]). [the shape of Oriental eyes]

slant *adj.* [1960s+] Asian, esp. Vietnamese. [SLANT *n.*[4]]

slant *v.* **1** [late 19C–1900s] to run away. **2** [late 19C–1900s] to exaggerate. **3** [1900s–30s] to glance at.

slantendicular *adj. see* SLANTINDICULAR adj.

slanter *n.*[1] (*also* **schlanter, schlenter, shlenter, slinter**) (*mainly Aus./S.Afr.*) **1** [late 19C] a counterfeit coin. **2** [late 19C] a counterfeit object. **3** [late 19C+] a fraudulent trick; thus *work a slanter*, to defraud, to hoax, to play a confidence trick on; *run a slanter*, to make no effort to win. **4** [1900s] a third-rate performance, e.g. in a boxing match. [Du. *slenter*, knavery, a trick]

slanter *n.*[2] [1910s] (*US*) the nose. [the angle at which it projects from the face]

slanters *n.* [1940s] (*US Black*) the eyes. [SLANT v. (3)]

slant-eye *n. see* SLANT n.[4].

slant-eyed *adj.* (*also* **slant-eye**) [mid-19C+] a derog. term pertaining to Asians, esp. Japanese. [SLANT n.[4]]

slanthead *n.* [1920s–40s] (*US*) a general pej. [SE *slant* + -HEAD sfx (1)]

slantindicular *adj.* (*also* **slantendicular, slantingdicular**) [mid-19C] (*orig. US*) oblique, awry. [a play on SE *perpendicular*]

slanty-eye *n. see* SLANT n.[4].

slaoc *n.* [mid-19C] coals. [backsl.]

slap *n.*[1] **1** [late 18C–early 19C] (*mainly Anglo-Irish*) booty, the proceeds of a robbery, 'swag'. **2** [mid–late 19C] a go, an attempt; thus *a bet*. **3** [20C+] (*Irish*) a large amount, a quantity. [SE *slap*, a blow]

slap *n.*[2] (*also* **schlap, shlap, slop**) [mid-19C+] make-up, esp. in theatre use; thus *slap up*, to apply make-up. [one SE *slaps* it on]

slap *n.*[3] [late 19C+] an attack on someone.

slap *adj.* [mid-19C] first-rate, excellent. [SLAP-UP adj. (1)]

slap *v. see* SLAP SKINS v. (2).

slap *adv.* **1** [late 17C+] quickly, unexpectedly, suddenly. **2** [mid-18C+] (*also* **slap off**) exactly, perfectly, e.g. *slap in the middle*. **3** [mid-19C+] directly; completely. [SE *slap*, the sound of a sharp blow]

slap (along) *v.* [mid-19C; 1990s+] to move or walk quickly. [one's shoes SE *slap* the ground; 1990s+ use is UK Black]

slap and tickle *n.*[1] [20C+] a pickle. [rhy. sl.]

slap and tickle *n.*[2] **1** [1920s+] playful kissing and cuddling. **2** [1980s] empty verbosity. **3** [1980s] physical violence.

slap-bang *n.*[1] [mid-19C] a form of alcoholic drink. [used by Benjamin Disraeli in *Sybil* (1863) as 'the Mowbray slap-bang', but otherwise unspecified. Presumably it was tossed off in a single gulp, guaranteed to 'hit the spot' or, like the *tequila slammers* of the 1990s, the glass was knocked against the table before taking a drink]

slap-bang *n.*[2] [mid-19C] the food available at a SLAP-BANG(-SHOP) n.

slap-bang *adv.* (*also* **bang-slap, smack-bang**) [late 18C+] energetically, vigorously, directly. [ext. SLAP adv. (1)/SMACK adv. (1)]

slap-bang(-shop) *n.* (*also* **slam-bang shop, slap-dash**) [late 18C–mid-19C] a small eating-house or restaurant where one pays on receipt of the food, rather than eating then receiving a bill. [SLAP-BANG adv.; 'a petty cook's shop where there is no credit given, but what is had must be paid down with the ready slap-bang, i.e. immediately. This is a common appellation for a night cellar frequented by thieves, and sometimes for a stage coach or caravan' (Grose, 1796)]

slap cuckoo *v. see* KNOCK CUCKOO v.

slapdab *n.* [late 19C] anything put together quickly but not well. [SLAP-DAB adv.]

slap-dab *adv.* [mid-19C–1930s] directly, straight at, immediately. [echoic]

slap-dash *n. see* SLAP-BANG(-SHOP) n.

slap-dash *adv.* [late 17C+] suddenly, immediately, violently. [UK usage became SE in 18C, and the term was taken up by Aus. speakers; the adj. meaning careless, undisciplined is SE]

slap five *v.* (*also* **five-slap, lay five, slip five**) [1910s+] (*US*) to indulge in a mutual hand-slapping ritual used by Blacks (and some Whites) for greeting, emphasis, congratulation etc.

slap ham *v.* [1980s] (*US campus*) to have sexual intercourse.

slap-happy *n.* [1940s] (*US Black*) a devotee of swing music. [the use of the jazz jargon *slap bass*]

slap-happy *adj.* [1930s+] cheery, slightly eccentric. [SE *slap* + -HAPPY sfx; orig. boxing use, someone whose brain has suffered from an excess of fighting]

slap-head *n.* [1980s+] a bald person. [note RMC Duntroon (Aus.) *slaphead*, an Asian]

slaphead *adj.* [mid-19C; 1990s+] bald, hairless. [SLAP-HEAD n.]

slap into *adv.* [mid-19C+] used with verbs of collision or impact, directly, straight at, e.g. *ran slap into the wall*. [SLAP adv. (3)]

slap it *v.* [1990s+] to masturbate (cf. BANG THE BISHOP v.).

slapman *n.* [1920s–30s] (*US Und.*) a policeman (cf. BEAT-POUNDER n.). [SE *slap*, i.e. his violent treatment of suspects]

slap off *adv. see* SLAP adv. (2).

slap on *v. see* SLAP SKINS v. (2).

slapped with an ugly stick *phr.* [1960s–80s] (*US*) unattractive.

slapper *n.*[1] [early 19C] a hard blow; a fatal wound.

slapper *n.*[2] [1980s+] **1** a promiscuous woman. **2** a prostitute. [? Yid. *schlepper*, an unkempt, untidy person or the 'slapping on' of make-up (cf. SLAP n.[2])]

slapping *n.* [1990s+] a beating.

slapping *adj.* [mid-19C+] first-rate, excellent; also as an adv. intensifier.

slapping (the plank) *n.* [1930s+] (*US Black*) exchanging ritualized slaps of greeting, congratulation etc. [var. on SLAP FIVE v.]

slapsie maxie *n.* [1960s+] (*Aus./N.Z.*) a taxi. [rhy. sl.; ult. US boxer *Slapsie Maxie* Rosenbloom (1904–76)]

slap skins *v.* (*orig. US Black*) **1** [1960s+] to exchange a greeting by slapping each other's hands. **2** [1990s+] (*also* **slap, slap on**) to have sexual intercourse.

slap someone's shit away *v.* [1980s] (*US Black*) to attack, physically or verbally.

slap tar *v. see* BEAT TAR v.

slap the monkey *v.* [1990s+] to masturbate (cf. BANG THE BISHOP v.; BEAT ONE'S HOG v.).

slap the pavement *v.* [1920s+] (*orig. US Black*) to walk around.

slap the salami *v.* (*also* **slap the sausage**) [1990s+] to masturbate (cf. BANG THE BISHOP v.; BEAT ONE'S MEAT v.).

slap-up *adj.* **1** [early 19C+] (*also* **slam-up**) fashionable, first-rate, of superior quality; thus *slap-uppish*, smartly, fashionably. **2** [mid-19C] in good spirits, comfortable. **3** [mid-19C] drunk. **4** [late 19C] of a person, honest, honourable.

slap up *v.* [mid-19C+] to assemble or put together in a haphazard, bodged manner.

slap-up *adv.* (*also* **slam-up**) [mid-19C; 1930s] excellently, pleasantly, very well. [SLAP-UP adj. (1)]

slash *n.*[1] [mid-19C] an outside pocket. [SE *slash*, a slit in a garment that is designed to reveal the colour of the lining]

slash *n.*[2] [1930s–80s] an alcoholic drink. [E.P. suggests ext. of SLASH n.[3], on model of PISSED adj.[1]/SLASHED adj.]

slash *n.*[3] [1930s+] **1** an act of urination. **2** urine. [? SE *slash*, a thin, sloping line, i.e. that of urine; or echoic of the urine hitting the lavatory water]

slash *n.*[4] [1960s+] (*Aus./US*) the vagina (cf. AGREEABLE RUTS OF LIFE n.). [note Cleland, *Memoirs of a Woman of Pleasure* (1748–9): 'The agreeable interior red of the sides of the orifice came into view, and with respect to the white that dazzl'd round it, give somewhat the idea of a pink-slash in the glossiest of white sattin']

slash *v.*[1] [1960s+] to urinate. [SLASH n.[3]]

slash *v.*[2] [1960s+] (*US Black/campus*) to demolish someone verbally, with a rapier-like wit.

slashed *adj.* [1990s+] very drunk. [*see* ety. at SLASH n.[2]]

slasher *n.* **1** [mid-16C–19C] a violent thug, a bully. **2** [19C] anyone or anything seen as exceptional, whether positively or otherwise. **3** [early 19C+] a sword; a knife. **4** [late 19C–1940s] (*Aus.*) a general term of praise, an excellent fellow; thus [1940s+] *slasheroo*, an intensified form. **5** [1920s–30s] (*UK Und.*) a criminal accomplice who cheats on his partners. **6** [1980s+] (*Aus. prison*) a self-mutilator. [note the comedian Sid Field's 1940s SPIV *n.* character *Slasher* Green, whose name may have equally referred to the contemporary 'razor gangs' of Soho and the racetrack]

slasher-gaff *n.* [mid-19C] (*US*) very harsh criticism. [SLASHER *n.* (1) + GAFF *n.*² (3)]

slashers *n.* [1960s] **1** the testicles. **2** the penis. [SLASH *v.*¹]

slashing *adj.* [19C+] excellent, wonderful, the best. [SLASHER *n.* (2); 20C+ use is mainly Aus.]

slashing *adv.* [late 19C] excellently, wonderfully, exceptionally. [SLASHING adj.]

slash job *n.* [1990s+] (*US prison*) slashing one's own wrists in a suicide attempt. [SE *slash* + JOB *n.*⁴]

slat *n.*¹ [late 17C–18C] (*UK Und.*) a sheet. [SLATE *n.*¹]

slat *n.*² **1** [18C–early 19C] (*UK Und.*) half-a-crown, 2s 6d (12½p). **2** [mid-18C] (*UK Und.*) a guinea, 21 shillings. **3** [1950s–60s] (*US Black*) $1. [SLATE *n.*²; the term was used by market traders in the 20C until decimalization made the half-crown obs.]

slat *n.*³ (*US*) **1** [20C+] a ski. **2** [1900s] a thin person. [SE *slat*]

slat *n.*⁴ [1920s] (*US*) a kick, a punch. [UK dial. *slat*, a (slapping) blow]

slat *n.*⁵ [1920s; 1970s] (*US*) a young man.

slat *n.*⁶ [1940s–70s] (*US Black*) used as a term of quantity, esp. in the context of the length of a prison sentence; thus a prison sentence. [? Irish *slat*, a rod or measuring stick]

slate *n.*¹ [mid-16C–mid-19C] a bedsheet. [SE *slate*]

slate *n.*² [late 17C–early 19C] (*UK Und.*) half-a-crown, 2s 6d (12½p). [ety. unknown]

slate *n.*³ [mid-19C+] one's bill, the credit one has run up; usu. in a public house or bar. [ON THE SLATE phr.]

slate *n.*⁴ [late 19C] an argument, a quarrel; a reprimand, a scolding. [SLATE *v.*¹ (2)]

slate *v.*¹ **1** [17C; mid-19C] (*orig. Irish*) to thrash or beat up. **2** [mid-19C+] to criticize severely. **3** [late 19C] to punish. **4** [1900s] to abuse. **5** [1990s+] to rain hard. [Scot. *slate*, to attack with a dog, to drive away with abuse; ? Irish *slat mara*, ult. *slad-mhara*, murder and robbery]

slate *v.*² [mid-19C] to knock a man's hat over his eyes. [SE *slate*, a roof-covering]

slate *v.*³ **1** [late 19C–1900s] to bet heavily against a boxer, a racehorse etc. **2** [20C+] (*orig. milit.*) to assign to a job or other situation. [SE *slate*, to set down in writing]

slated *adj.* [late 19C] dead. [hospital practice of writing the names of those currently likely to die on a *slate*]

slater *n.* [late 19C] (*Aus.*) a critic. [SLATE *v.*¹ (2)]

slater's pan *n.* [late 18C–early 19C] the prison at Kingston, Jamaica. [proper name *Slater*, the deputy provost-marshal in Grose's era; given the heat of the West Indies, prisoners were presumably 'cooked' in the 'pan']

slather *n.* (*also* **slathers**) [mid-19C+] (*US*) a large amount, e.g. *a whole slather of pretty women*; *slathers of fresh fruit*. [SE *slather*, to squander]

slather *v.* [1910s+] to defeat utterly, to thrash, to criticize harshly. [SE *slather*, to spread, or smear liberally]

slathered *adj.* [1920s+] (*Aus.*) tipsy, slightly drunk. [? SLATHER *v.* or ? dial. *slather*, to spill, to slobber]

slathers *n. see* SLATHER *n.*

slather-up *n.* [1910s] (*N.Z.*) a fight, a brawl. [SLATHER *v.*]

slat mara *n.* [1920s] (*Irish*) a contemptible person. [Ir. *slad-mhara*, murder and robbery; *slad-mharoir*, freebooter]

slats *n.* **1** [late 17C+] (*orig. US*) the ribs; thus a skinny person; thus *slatty*, skinny; thus *wouldn't that rattle your slats?* isn't that

amazing? wouldn't that give you a shock? **2** [1920s+] (*US prison*) the steel mesh that covers the front of a prison cell. [SE *slat*, a long, thin piece of wood]

slaughter *n.* [1950s+] (*UK Und.*) an immediate dumping ground for recently stolen property before it is shared out, also tools and equipment used in a robbery, before being hidden more permanently, e.g. in a hired lock-up. [abbr. SLAUGHTERHOUSE *n.*¹ (2)]

slaughter *v.* **1** [mid-19C+] to defeat completely, lit. and fig. **2** [1990s+] to criticize harshly.

slaughtered *adj.* **1** [late 19C] heavily overworked, 'sweated'. **2** [1980s+] (*US campus*) drunk (cf. ANNIHILATED adj.).

slaughterer *n.* [mid-19C] a dealer who buys from small makers at extremely low prices. [such one-sided deals *slaughter* the sellers]

slaughter floor *n. see* SLAUGHTERHOUSE *n.*³.

slaughterhouse *n.*¹ **1** [early 19C] a crooked gambling house or casino. **2** [mid-late 19C] a shop where goods are bought from small makers at very low prices. **3** [late 19C] a factory paying very low wages. **4** [1920s+] a cheap brothel (cf. ACCOMMODATION HOUSE *n.*). [in all cases, the buyer or customer is fig. *slaughtered*]

slaughterhouse *n.*² [late 19C] (*UK Und.*) the Surrey Sessions House.

slaughterhouse *n.*³ (*also* **slaughter(ing) floor**) [1960s+] (*US Black*) anywhere a couple can indulge in sexual intercourse. [play on KILLING FLOOR *n.*]

slaughtering-knife *n.* [late 17C–early 18C] the penis (cf. AX *n.*²).

slaughter in the pan *n.* [late 19C–1950s] (*US short order*) steak.

slave *n.* **1** [1900s] (*US campus*) a college servant. **2** [1930s+] (*Black/campus*) work, any form of job.

slave *v.* [late 19C+] to work.

slave and Turk *n. see* TERRIBLE TURK *n.*

slave market *n.* (*US*) **1** [mid-19C+] an office, a café or any other meeting place where unemployed actors seek work. **2** [1910s+] cheap employment agencies, offering menial jobs for poor wages.

slaves and masters *n.* [1960s+] (*US*) sadists and masochists.

slave tip *n.* [1940s] (*US Black*) work. [SLAVE *n.* (2) + TIP *n.*⁷]

slavey *n.* (*also* **moll slavey**) [late 18C+] a servant, whether male or female; thus [1920s] *slavey market*, an employment agency for servants. [note Egan, *Life in London* (1821): 'A *slang* term for servant maids; being servants of all work; and also in allusion to their laborious employment and hard work']

slaving gloak *n.* [late 19C] a servant. [SE *slaving* + GLOAK *n.*]

slavver *n.* [1990s+] (*UK juv.*) nonsense, a lie. [lit. *saliva*]

slawminyeux *n.* [mid-19C] a Dutchman. [? Du. *ja mynheer*, yes sir]

slay *v.* **1** [20C+] to reduce to complete hysterical laughter, to amaze, to impress, to shock. **2** [1950s+] (*gay*) to gossip maliciously behind a third party's back.

slay the one-eyed monster *v. see* ONE-EYED MONSTER *n.* (1).

sleaze *n.* (*also* **sleeze**) **1** [1950s+] (*US*) anything considered disgusting, shabby or offensive. **2** [1970s+] (*also* **sleazter**) an unappealing, seedy person. **3** [1970s+] (*US*) (*also* **sleazebitchlet**) a sexually promiscuous woman. [backform. f. SLEAZY adj.]

sleaze *v.* [1960s+] to move in a repellent or seedy manner. [note RMC Duntroon (Aus.) *sleaze*, to go on the prowl for sex; to approach a woman in the hope of sex; to 'chat up' a woman]

sleazebag *n.* (*also* **sleazeball, sleazyball, sleezebag**) [1980s+] a distasteful person, with overtones of dirtiness, criminality and sexual excess. [SLEAZE *n.* (2) + -BAG sfx/-BALL sfx]

sleazebitchlet *n. see* SLEAZE *n.* (3).

sleazebucket *n.* **1** [1980s+] (*US campus*) (*also* **sleeze bucket**) a sexually promiscuous woman. **2** [1990s+] a revolting, repellent individual. [SLEAZE *n.*]

sleazebucket *adj.* [1990s+] (*US*) revolting, disgusting. [SLEAZE-BUCKET *n.* (2)]

sleazehole *n.* [1990s+] a seedy, run-down place, a down-market bar or club. [SLEAZE *n.* (1) + HOLE *n.*² (2)]

sleazemonger *n.* [1960s+] (*US*) a producer or seller of inferior, trashy or pornographic entertainment. [SLEAZE n. (1) + sfx -MONGER sfx]

sleazo *n.* (*also* **el sleazo, sleazoid**) [1970s+] (*US*) **1** a disgusting, obnoxious person. **2** a sexually promiscuous woman. [SLEAZY adj. + -O sfx (2)]

sleazter *n. see* SLEAZE n. (2).

sleazy *adj.* (*also* **sleazo, sleazoid, sleazy**) **1** [1930s+] of a person, unpleasant, poss. criminal, generally distasteful, often with sexual overtones. **2** [1930s+] of a thing, dirty, run-down, decayed. **3** [1980s] (*US juv.*) lucky. [SE *sleazy*, of textile fabrics or materials, thin or flimsy; ult. *sleazy*, of ropes or yarn, rough from projecting fibres]

sleazyball *n. see* SLEAZEBAG n.

sleazycheesin' *n.* [2000s] (*US Black*) taking drugs then wandering in pursuit of women willing to have sex. [SLEAZY adj. (1) + CHEESE v.[1] (2)]

sled *n.* [1950s+] (*US*) **1** an automobile. **2** a motorcycle.

sledge *v.* [2000s] to become bored.

sleek and slum (shop) *n.* [early 19C] a public house frequented by 'single men and their wives' (Bee), i.e. prostitutes and their male clients. [SE *sleek*, i.e. a well-dressed, 'smooth' man + SLUM n.[2] (3), i.e. the tricks the woman might play or SLUM n.[1] (1)]

sleek lady *n.* [1960s–80s] (*US Black*) an extremely attractive woman.

sleek wipe *n.* [19C] a handkerchief.

sleep *n.* [1910s+] (*UK/US/Aus.*) a short term in prison. [one could sleep it away; the UK/US versions are somewhat longer, about 12 months, than the Aus., which is 3 months]

sleep, the *n.* [1940s] (*US Black campus*) a college lecture.

sleep *v.* [2000s] (*US prison*) to knock someone down. [SE *put to sleep*]

sleep around *v.* [1950s+] (*orig. US*) to be sexually promiscuous.

sleep at Mrs Green's *v.* (*also* **sleep with Mrs Green**) [1930s–50s] (*Aus./N.Z.*) to sleep in the open air.

sleeper *n.*[1] **1** [late 19C–1910s] (*US sporting*) a potentially successful racehorse that has eluded the eye of the betting public. **2** [late 19C+] (*orig. US sporting*) any product that gains acceptance and success only slowly. **3** [1900s] (*US*) a financial collapse. **4** [1950s] a surprise.

sleeper *n.*[2] **1** [late 19C–1930s] (*gambling*) (*also* **snoozer**) a stake that has been left on the table, when neither the croupier/banker nor a winning bettor has realized it is to be picked up. **2** [1910s–20s] (*US*) a bar customer who was too drunk to pick up their change when they left, so the bartender kept it.

sleeper *n.*[3] (*drugs*) **1** [1960s+] any form of barbiturate sleeping pill (cf. BARBIT n.). **2** [2000s] heroin.

sleeper *n.*[4] [1970s] (*US campus*) a lazy, useless person.

sleeper *n.*[5] [1970s] (*Can. prison*) a means of subduing violent prisoners (and patients in mental hospitals) by strangling them unconscious with a towel.

sleep in chapters *v.* [1960s] (*drugs*) to experience broken, fragmentary sleep during withdrawal from heroin.

sleeping beauty *n.* [1970s] (*US gay*) an impotent penis, incapable of erection.

sleeping dictionary *n.* [1920s+] a foreign woman with whom a man has a sexual relationship and from whom he learns her language.

sleeping Jesus *n.* (*US Black*) **1** [1920s+] a dull, tedious person. **2** [1980s] a person who is comatose due to the influence of heroin. [pun on CREEPING JESUS n.]

sleeping time *n.* [1950s–60s] (*US Und.*) a short prison sentence. [SE *sleeping* + TIME n.[1]; var. on SLEEP n.; one could sleep it away]

sleepless hat *n.* [mid-19C–1900s] a hat on which the nap has worn off. [pun on SE *nap, sleep*]

sleep like a cow *v.* [late 18C–early 19C] to sleep like a married

man, i.e. with one's back to one's wife. [Grose (1785) defines it as 'i.e. with a ****' [i.e. CUNT n.[1] (1)] at one's a--se' and quotes a contemporary rhyme: 'All you that in your beds do lie / Turn to your wives, and occupy [have sex],/ And when that you have done your best, / Turn a--se to a--se, and take your rest']

sleep on *v.* [1980s+] (*US Black*) **1** to ignore. **2** to be unaware or unprepared but otherwise awake. **3** to attack, to criticize negatively.

sleep on bones *v.* [19C–1910s] of a child, to fall asleep on one's nurse's lap.

sleeps, the *n.* [late 19C] (*US*) sleep.

sleep upon the queer roost *v.* (*also* **dorse upon the queer roost**) [late 18C] to live together as man and wife. [SE *sleep*/DORSE v. + QUEER adj.[1] (1) + SE *roost*; the arrangement is 'queer' because it is fraudulent]

sleepville *n.* [late 19C+] (*US*) sleep. [SE *sleep* + -VILLE sfx[1]]

sleepwalker *n.* [1940s] (*Aus.*) a sneak-thief.

sleep with *v.* (*also* **snooze with**) [late 17C; mid-19C+] to have sexual intercourse with (cf. ARRIVE AT THE END OF THE SENTIMENTAL JOURNEY v.). [euph.; SNOOZE v. (2)]

sleep with Mrs Green *v. see* SLEEP AT MRS GREEN'S v.

sleep with one's glasses on *v.* [1940s] (*US Black*) to act in an arrogant manner.

sleep with the fishes *v.* [1950s+] **1** to have been drowned, whether accidentally or as a form of homicide. **2** to die. **3** in fig. use, to be over, to be defeated. [invariably associated with the US Mafia thanks to Mario Puzo's book *The Godfather* (1969)]

sleepy *adj.*[1] [late 18C–early 19C] old, worn-out. [punning remark 'the cloth of your coat must be extremely sleepy, for it has not had a nap this long time' (Grose, 1796)]

sleepy *adj.*[2] [mid-19C] (*US*) a euph. for drunk (cf. ADDLED adj.).

sleepy dust *n.* [early 19C] some form of sleeping draught, used to help in robberies.

sleepytime girl *n.* [1950s+] (*US*) a promiscuous woman, a man's mistress. [SAmE *sleepytime*, bedtime]

sleestak *n.* [1980s+] (*US campus*) an unappealing, sexually promiscuous woman. [creature in the 1980s TV series *Land of the Lost*]

sleeve button *n.*[1] [late 19C–1900s] (*US short order*) **1** a dropped egg. **2** codfish balls; fishcakes.

sleeve button *n.*[2] [20C+] a long drink. [? SLEEVER n.]

sleever *n.* **1** [late 19C+] (*mainly Aus./N.Z.*) a beer glass holding 369ml (13fl oz). **2** [20C+] (*N.Z.*) a drinking straw. [abbr. LONG-SLEEVER n.]

sleeves *n.* [1990s+] (*US prison*) tattoos running the full length of one's arms, a sign of one's prison experience.

sleeze *see under* SLEAZE and its combs.

sleighride *n.*[1] [1910s–60s] (*US drugs*) **1** the taking of cocaine (rarely heroin or morphine); thus *sleighrider*, one who sells or takes cocaine; *on a sleighride*, on a cocaine binge. **2** rarely, the taking of morphine (which is also white) or heroin. [pun on SE *snow*/SNOW n.[2] (1)]

sleighride *n.*[2] [1920s–30s] (*US Und.*) a deception, a trick. [fig. use of SE, the hoax is fast-moving and beyond control]

sleighride *v.*[1] (*US drugs*) **1** [1910s–60s] to inhale cocaine. **2** [1920s–40s] to take morphine (which is also white). [SLEIGHRIDE n.[1]]

sleighride *v.*[2] [1940s–60s] (*US Und.*) to deceive, to trick. [SLEIGHRIDE n.[2]]

sleng teng *n.* [2000s] (*W.I./Rasta*) marijuana. [ety. unknown]

slenter *adj. see* SCHLENTER adj.

slept on *adj.* [1990s+] (*US Black*) attacked, criticized negatively.

slew *v.* (*also* **slue**) **1** [19C+] (*Aus.*) to defeat, to 'do for', to 'settle'. **2** [late 19C+] (*Aus.*) to deliver a tale. **3** [2000s] (*UK teen*) to abuse one's rivals. [dial. *slew*, to twist around]

slew (a head) *v. see* PULL A HEAD v.

slewed *adj.* (*also* **slued**) **1** [19C+] drunk, off balance (cf. AFFLICTED adj.). **2** [mid-19C+] confused, baffled. **3** [late 19C+] (*Aus.*) lost, esp. in the bush. [dial. *slew*, to twist around, then naut. jargon; note also SLEW v.]

slewfoot *n.* (*also* **sluefoot**) **1** [20C+] (*US*) a shambling or clumsy person. **2** [1930s–50s] a police officer.

slice *n.*[1] **1** [mid-18C+] the vagina (cf. AGREEABLE RUTS OF LIFE n.). **2** [1960s+] a generic for women; thus *take a slice*, to have an affair with a married woman. **3** [1980s] an attractive woman. [the equation of women with food, reinforced in (2) by pvb 'a slice off a cut loaf is never missed']

slice *n.*[2] [1940s–70s] (*Aus.*) a £1 note; latterly A$2. [? a single 'slice' of a wad of notes]

slice *n.*[3] [1980s+] (*US campus*) a friend, an intimate. [abbr. HOME SLICE n. (1)]

slice *v.* [1940s+] to attack, usu. with a knife.

slice and dice *n.* [1950s+] (*US*) a horror film. [the fate of the victims]

Slice City *n.* [1940s] (*orig. US Black*) an assault with a razor or a knife.

sliced *adj.* [1980s+] (*US gay*) circumcised.

slice of cake *n. see* PIECE OF CAKE n.

slice off the legs *n.* [1960s+] (*Irish*) sexual intercourse.

slice of ham *n.* [20C+] fellatio (cf. BLOOD RED n.). [rhy. sl. = GAM n.[3]]

slice of knuckle pie *n.* [1960s] a punch in the face.

slice of life *n.* (*also* **spice of life**) [20C+] the vagina (cf. AGREEABLE RUTS OF LIFE n.).

slice of toast *n.* [20C+] a ghost. [rhy. sl.]

slice one's chops *v.* [1940s] (*US Black*) to talk. [SE *slice* + CHOPS n.[1] (1) + pun]

slicer *n.* [1940s–80s] (*US Black/Und.*) a knife.

slicing *n.* [1970s] (*US prison*) a knifing. [SLICE v.]

slick *n.*[1] **1** [mid-19C+] (*orig. US Black*) a smart, charming, fashionable, sophisticated person. **2** [late 19C] (*US campus*) an unpopular, unpleasant person. **3** [1940s+] a swindler, a hoaxer. **4** [1990s+] as a term of address. [SE *slick*, smooth, plausible, glib]

slick *n.*[2] [1940s] (*US Und.*) silk.

slick *n.*[3] [1980s+] (*drugs*) methcathinone. [ety. unknown; ? its effects]

slick *n.*[4] [1990s+] (*US prison*) a criminal speciality.

slick *adj.* **1** [mid-19C+] (*US, mainly teen*) a general term of approval, clever, sharp. **2** [1970s] (*US campus*) attractive (of either gender).

slick *v.* [mid-19C+] to swindle, to hoax, to cheat. [SE *slick*]

slick *adv.* [mid-19C+] (*US Black*) smartly. [SLICK adj. (1)]

slick ace *n.* [1920s] (*US Und.*) a card in a crooked deck.

slick-a-dee *n.* (*also* **slick-a-die**) [mid-19C] a pocketbook. [SE *slick* + DEE n.[1]]

slick as owl shit *phr.* (*also* **slick as a biscuit, …a button, …a greased pig/rope, …an eel, …a piece of chalk (o)iled at both ends, …a ribbon, …a whistle**) (*US*) **1** [mid-19C+] very smooth, very smart or clever. **2** [1910s] attractive, good. [SLICK adj. (1) + SHIT n.[1] (1)]

slick-ass *adj.* [1970s] smooth, sophisticated, smart. [SLICK adj. (1) + -ASS sfx]

slick-boy *n.* [1990s+] (*US Black*) a confidence trickster, a cheat, a liar. [SLICK adj. (1) + SE *boy*]

slick chick *n.* [1930s+] (*US Black*) a smart, attractive young woman. [SLICK adj. (1) + CHICK n.[4] (2)]

slick citizen *n.* [1900s–10s] (*US*) an unprincipled individual. [SLICK adj. (1)]

slickdick *adj.* [1990s+] cunning, self-promoting, 'smooth'. [SLICK adj. (1) + proper name]

slick duck *n.* (*also* **slick coot**) [1900s–10s] (*US*) a cunning, sly person. [SLICK adj. (1) + DUCK n.[1] (4)/COOT n.[1] (1)]

slick-'em-plenty *n.* [1970s] (*US Black*) **1** a derog. term for a Jew (cf. FAST-TALKING CHARLIE n.). **2** a pawnbroker. **3** a smooth-talking

confidence trickster. [racial stereotyping both as to ethics and occupation]

slicker *n.* **1** [20C+] (*US*) a cunning or dishonest person, usu. of a businessman, a shrewd and predatory lawyer, a confidence trickster. **2** [1910s+] (*orig. US*) a dandy, a smart dresser. **3** [1920s+] (*US*) ext. of (2), a socially sophisticated, wordly individual. **4** [1950s] (*US*) a smooth, plausible person, esp. in the context of seduction. [SLICK adj. (1)]

slicker *v.* **1** [1920s] (*US*) to act in a sophisticated, wordly manner; to be cunning. **2** [1950s] to trick. [SLICKER n.]

slickies *n.* [1990s+] (*US campus*) members of a sorority. [their 'slick' appearance]

slicking *adj.* [1970s] smooth, plausible, cunning. [SLICK v.]

slick-leg *adj.* [1990s+] (*US prison*) innocent of a crime; too clever to get caught, even though guilty. [SLICK adj. (1) + SE *leg*]

slick-leg *v.* [1960s+] (*gay*) to rub one's penis against the thigh of one's sexual partner.

slicks, the *n.* [1930s+] (*US*) glossy, expensive, middle-class magazines. [SE *slick*, i.e. high-quality, glossy paper]

slick shit *n.* [1950s+] (*orig. US Black*) any clever stratagem that gets one what is desired. [SLICK adj. (1) + SHIT n.[4]]

slickster *n.* [1950s+] (*orig. US Black*) a cheat, a smooth talker, a hustler. [SLICK v.]

slickum *n.* [20C+] (*US*) hair oil. [SE *slick*, to polish]

slick up *v.* [mid-19C+] (*US*) to tidy, to make neat. [SLICK adj. (1)]

'slid! *excl.* [late 16C–early 18C; mid-19C] a euph. oath, lit. 'God's eyelid!'

slide *n.*[1] (*UK Und.*) **1** [mid-19C] a money box as used in a shop. **2** [late 19C] a purse. [it *slides* off and on a shelf/in and out of a pocket]

slide *n.*[2] [1930s–70s] (*UK Und.*) an establishment where transvestites can solicit conventionally dressed men.

slide *n.*[3] [1930s+] (*US Und.*) that member of the 3-card trick team who keeps an eye out for police and warns the rest so that all can *slide off* in time.

slide *n.*[4] [1930s+] (*US Black*) a trouser pocket. [? SE *side*; or one 'slides' things into it]

slide *n.*[5] [1970s+] (*US campus*) an easy course. [one *slides* through it]

slide *n.*[6] [1990s+] (*drugs*) a syringe, used for injecting narcotic drugs. [the sliding plunger that is part of the syringe]

slide *v.*[1] (*also* **do the slide, slide out/off**) [mid-19C+] to move, to travel; to run away; thus *slide someone off*, to take someone away.

slide *v.*[2] **1** [1920s+] to forgive, to pardon, to let someone off. **2** [1970s+] to ignore. **3** [1990s+] (*US Black*) to give credit, esp. in a drug deal. **4** [2000s] (*US*) to escape a criminal charge. [LET IT SLIDE v.]

slide *v.*[3] [1930s–40s; 1990s+] (*orig. US Black*) to dance. [the use of smooth parquet dance-floors]

slide and sluther *n.* [1990s+] a brother. [rhy. sl.]

slide by *v.* [1950s–60s] (*US Black*) **1** to drop in uninvited, without previous notice. **2** to fool, to deceive.

slide down the middle aisle *v.* [1920s–30s] to get married.

slide off *v. see* SLIDE v.[1]

slide off a log *v.* [late 19C] (*Aus.*) to blunder, to make a mistake.

slide one's jib *v.* [1930s–40s] (*US Black*) to talk unrestrainedly. [SE *slide* + JIB n.[1] (4)/JIB n.[1] (3)]

slide out *v. see* SLIDE v.[1]

slider *n.*[1] [1910s+] an ice-cream placed between 2 wafers. [Irish *sliodarnach* slithering, sliding – its potential for sliding out]

slider *n.*[2] [1940s–60s] (*US*) a small, greasy hamburger.

slider *n.*[3] [1950s] (*UK prison*) a hacksaw.

slides *n.* [1920s–60s] (*US Black*) shoes.

slidewalk *n.* [1940s+] (*US Black*) a specific style of walking, one foot takes normal paces, the other drags; one hand is tucked into the side, the other is positioned with the wrist pressed to the waist and the elbow sticking out.

'slife! *excl.* [17C–1920s] a mild oath, lit. 'God's life!'

'slight! *excl.* [late 16C–mid-17C] a mild oath, lit. 'God's light!'

slightly tightly *adj.* [late 19C] tipsy but not actually drunk. [SE *slightly* + TIGHT adj.[5]]

slight sensation *n. see* SENSATION n.

slim *n.*[1] [late 18C–mid-19C] rum. [ety. unknown]

slim *n.*[2] **1** [1920s–30s] an informer. **2** [1930s–40s] (*US prison*) a police spy. [? their attempts to be unobtrusive; but note SLIM adj.]

slim *n.*[3] [1940s–60s] (*US Black*) a plain hand-rolled tobacco cigarette, as opposed to a marijuana-filled one. [its dimensions, which tend to be leaner than those of a marijuana cigarette]

slim *n.*[4] [1960s+] (*US Black*) a term of address, a friend.

slim *adj.* [early 19C+] (*S.Afr./US*) clever, crafty, wily. [Du. *slim*, crafty]

slim-dilly *n.* [1930s+] (*Aus.*) a young woman. [ety. unknown; ? link to DILLY n.[3]]

slime *n.*[1] [late 17C; 1910s+] semen (cf. BOLLOCK SNOT n.). [its consistency + implication of distaste]

slime *n.*[2] **1** [late 19C; 1940s+] (*Aus.*) flattery, ingratiation. **2** [1960s+] an extremely unpleasant person. [note the character Chevy *Slime* in Charles Dickens's *Martin Chuzzlewit* (1843–4)]

slime *v.*[1] [late 19C+] (*Aus.*) to flatter; thus *slimer*, a sycophant. [SLIME n.[2] (1)]

slime *v.*[2] [1990s+] (*Aus.*) to ejaculate (cf. BLOSH v.). [SLIME n.[1]]

slimebag *n.* (*also* **slimeball, slime-mouth**) [1970s+] (*US*) a highly objectionable or offensive person. [SLIME n.[2] (2)/SE *slime* + -BAG sfx/-BALL sfx; note RMC Duntroon (Aus.) *slime bag*, a (usu.) disreputable woman; a girlfriend]

slimebucket *n.* [1980s+] (*US campus*) a highly objectionable or offensive person. [SLIME n.[2] (2)/SE *slime* + *bucket*]

Slim Jim *n.* **1** [late 19C–1900s] (*orig. US*) a thin person. **2** [1950s] (*US*) long trousers. **3** [1950s+] (*orig. US*) a narrow tie, fashionable in 1950s. **4** [2000s] (*US Und.*) a small, narrow crowbar used for break-ins.

slims *n.* [1960s] (*US gay*) very tight trousers. [abbr. SLIM JIM n. (2)]

slimy *adj.* [1980s+] (*US Black/campus*) very unattractive. [SE *slime*]

sling *n.*[1] [late 18C] a draught, a 'pull' at a bottle or glass. [SE *sling*, to throw (back)]

sling *n.*[2] (*also* **slingback**) [1940s+] (*Aus.*) **1** a bribe, a gift. **2** a tip. [lit. 'a throwback']

sling *n.*[3] [1990s+] (*US prison*) a belt with a sharpened buckle, used as an offensive weapon.

sling *v.*[1] **1** [19C+] to give. **2** [mid–late 19C] to pass from one person to another. **3** [mid-19C+] to speak. **4** [mid-19C+] (*Aus.*) to bribe, to pass over a bribe. **5** [mid-19C+] to write, to perform etc. **6** [late 19C] to do easily. **7** [late 19C+] to tell; esp. as SLING A YARN v. **8** [late 19C+] (*orig. Aus.*) to abandon, to give up, to get rid of; to end a relationship. **9** [1910s] to criticize, to abuse. [SE *sling*, to throw]

sling *v.*[2] [late 19C] to blow one's nose with one's fingers. [abbr. SLING A SNOT v.]

sling *v.*[3] [mid-19C+] (*US*) to work as a waiter or waitress; esp. as *sling hash*, to wait at tables; *sling beer*, to work as a bartender. [SE *sling*, to throw]

sling *v.*[4] [late 19C] to steal; thus *sling the smash*, to steal tobacco. [SE *sling* or SLANG v.[1] (1)]

sling *v.*[5] **1** [20C+] to throw, to cast, to hurl, to fling; also in fig. use. **2** [1960s+] (*US*) to fight with the fists. [(1) SE until late 19C]

sling *v.*[6] [1980s+] (*drugs*) to sell drugs. [SE *sling*, to throw, to pass]

sling about *v.* (*also* **sling along**) [mid–late 19C] to loiter, to hang around with particular intent.

sling a cat *v.* (*also* **throw the cat**) [19C] to vomit. [SE *sling/throw* + var. on WHIP THE CAT v.[2] (2)]

sling (a daddle) *v.* [mid–late 19C] to shake hands. [SE *sling* + DADDLE n.]

sling a deaf 'un *v. see* COP A DEAF 'UN v.

sling a foot *v.* [mid–late 19C] to dance.

sling along *v. see* SLING ABOUT v.

sling a pot *v.* [late 19C] to drink heavily.

sling a poultice *v.* [1950s+] (*Aus.*) to offer a bribe. [SLING v.[1] (4) + POULTICE n. (9)]

sling a slobber *v.* [late 19C] to throw a kiss, to kiss. [SE *sling* + SLOBBER n.[2]]

sling a snot *v.* [late 19C] to blow one's nose with one's fingers. [SE *sling* + SNOT n.[1] (1)]

sling a tinkler *v.* [late 19C–1920s] to ring a bell. [SE *sling* + TINKLER n.[2]]

sling a yarn *v.* **1** [late 19C+] to tell a story. **2** [1900s] to tell a lie. [SLING v.[1] (3) + SE *yarn*]

slingback *n. see* SLING n.[2].

sling colonial *v.* [late 19C] (*Aus.*) to talk idiomatic/vernacular Australian (rather than 'English') English. [SLING v.[1] (3)]

slinge *n.* [early 19C] (*UK Und.*) stolen cloth. [ety. unknown]

slinger *n.*[1] **1** [mid-19C+] (*US*) a waiter or waitress. **2** [20C+] any form of worker, with a comb. n. [SLING v.[3]]

slinger *n.*[2] [1980s+] (*US Und.*) a drug dealer. [SLING v.[6]]

slingers *n.* **1** [late 19C–1910s] (*orig. milit.*) bread or ship's biscuits soaked in tea or coffee. **2** [1930s–40s] sausages. [? elision of SE *sailing* or SE *sling*, i.e. one 'throws' the food into the liquid]

slingers, the *n.* [1940s+] rejection, dismissal. [SE *sling out*]

sling hash *v. see* SLING v.[3].

sling in *v.* [late 19C] to arrive.

sling ink *v.* **1** [mid-19C+] (*orig. US*) (*also* **spill ink**) to write, esp. professionally, to work as a journalist. **2** [1930s] (*US*) to compose or arrange music. **3** [1990s+] (*US prison*) to apply a tattoo.

sling in one's alley *v. see* THROW IN ONE's ALLEY v. (1).

sling it *v.* **1** [20C+] (*Aus.*) to abandon or give up something; thus as imper., forget it! **2** [1930s+] (*Aus.*) (*also* **sling it in**) to leave one's job or one's work. [ext. SLING v.[1] (8)]

sling joints *v.* [late 19C] (*US*) to make one's living by physical rather than mental effort.

sling lead *v.* (*also* **squeeze lead**) [1920s+] (*US*) to fire a gun; to shoot. [SE *sling/squeeze* + LEAD n.[1] (1)]

sling mud *v.* (*also* **fling mud**) [late 19C+] (*orig. US*) to defame, to malign.

sling off *v.* [1920s+] (*Aus.*) to leave. [SLING ONE's HOOK v.[2] (1)]

sling off (at) *v.* [20C+] (*orig. Aus./N.Z.*) to mock, to tease, to cheek; to berate, to scold. [SLING v.[1] (3)]

sling one's body *v.* [late 19C] to dance vigorously.

sling one's bunk *v.* [mid-19C–1900s] to leave, to depart. [naut. imagery]

sling one's daniel *v.* (*also* **take one's daniel**) [mid-19C] (*US*) to leave. [ety. unknown; ? lost rhy. sl. referring to some form of pack; given occas. synon. *sling one's dannet* thus ? link to dial. *donnot/dannet*, a good-for-nothing]

sling oneself *v.* [late 19C] (*US campus*) to show off.

sling one's hook *v.*[1] [mid–late 19C] to pick pockets. [SE *sling* + HOOK n.[1] (1)]

sling one's hook *v.*[2] **1** [mid-19C+] to leave (cf. HOOK v.[4]). **2** [late 19C–1900s] to die. [? the raising of the anchor (*hook*) before departure or the SE *hook* on which a working miner left his day clothes. When he finished his shift he removed his possessions from the hook and left for home]

sling one's jelly *v.* [19C] of a woman, to masturbate (cf. APPLY LIP GLOSS v.; BEAT ONE's MEAT v.). [SE *sling* + JELLY n.[1] (2)]

sling one's juice *v.* [19C] of a man, to masturbate. [SE *sling* + JUICE n.[2] (1)]

sling one's mauley *v.* [late 18C–19C] to shake hands. [SE *sling* + MAULEY n. (1)]

sling out *v.* [1920s+] to eject, to throw out. [SE *sling*]

sling pussy *v.* [1960s+] to work as a prostitute. [SE *sling* + PUSSY n. (2)]

sling round on the loose *v.* [late 19C] to act in a reckless manner. [SE *slink*]

sling-shot *n.*[1] [1960s] (*US*) a flick-knife.

sling-shot *n.*[2] [1980s] (*US Black*) a Cadillac Eldorado. [ety. unknown]

sling-shot *n.*[3] **1** [1980s] (*US Black*) a sanitary towel. **2** [1990s+] (*W.I.*) skimpy underwear; a thong. **3** [1990s+] (*US prison*) male underwear, briefs. [the shape]

sling someone one in the eye *v.* [late 19C] to punch someone in the eye.

sling (someone) the whisper *v.* **1** [mid-19C+] (*UK Und.*) (*also* **give (someone) the whisper**) to ask for a loan. **2** [20C+] (*Aus./US*) (*also* **chuck (someone) the whisper, whisper**) to inform, to impart information. [WHISPER n.[1]/WHISPER n.[2] (2)]

sling the bat *v.* [late 19C–1920s] (*orig. milit.*) to speak the local (foreign) language. [SLING v.[1] (3) + Hind. *bat*, speech]

sling the billy *v.* (*also* **swing the billy**) [mid-19C+] (*Aus.*) to make a cup of tea, esp. as an act of hospitality.

sling the booze *v.* [late 19C] to treat one's companions. [SE *sling* + BOOZE n. (1)]

sling the bull *v.* [late 19C+] (*US*) to talk nonsense, to chatter about trivialities; thus *n.* *bullslinging*. [SE *sling*/SLING v.[1] (3) + BULL n.[11] (1)]

sling the crap *v. see* SHOOT (THE) CRAP v.

sling the dirt at *v.* [1930s] (*Aus./N.Z.*) to malign, to slander. [SE *sling*/SLING v.[1] (3) + DIRT n.[2] (1)]

sling the gab *v. see* SLING THE LINGO v.

sling the hatchet *v.* **1** [mid-19C] to skulk about. **2** [1920s] to run away, to abscond.

sling the hoof *v.* (*also* **fling the hoof, shake the hoof**) [mid-19C–1920s] (*US*) to dance.

sling the lingo *v.* (*also* **sling the gab**) [1900s–30s] to speak fluently and creatively. [SE *sling* + LINGO n. (1)/GAB n. (3)]

sling the tip *v.* [mid–late 19C] to warn, to 'tip off'. [SE *sling* + TIP n.[5] (1)]

sling to *v.* [1920s+] (*Aus./N.Z.*) to pay a bribe or a commission, esp. on one's winnings at gambling. [SE *sling*/SLING v.[1] (4)]

sling trout *v.* [1990s+] (*US prison*) to throw excrement or urine over another prisoner. [BROWN TROUT n.]

sling up *v.* [1980s+] (*US campus*) to have sexual intercourse.

sling yourself! *excl.* (*also* **let her sling!**) [late 19C] an excl. urging immediate action, hurry up! get on with it!

sling your tross! *excl.* [late 19C] go away! be off! [SE *sling* + DABTROS n.]

slink *n.* [19C–1910s] a general pej. term, a sneak, a skulker, a cheat; also as *adj.* [SE *slink*, a premature calf or lamb (thus a human illegitimate child) or *slink*, to creep around]

slink *v.* [1920s+] to abort. [SE *slink*, of animals, to abort]

slinter *n. see* SLANTER n.[1].

slinter *adj. see* SCHLENTER adj.

slip *n.*[1] [late 16C–mid-17C] a counterfeit coin. [ety. unknown]

slip *n.*[2] [early 19C] the back pocket of a tail-coat. [for *slipping* things into]

slip *n.*[3] [1960s] (*Aus.*) a loan (from a friend). [SLIP v. (1)]

slip *v.* **1** [late 19C+] to give, to hand over. **2** [20C+] to pass on information, to tell tales. **3** [1910s+] (*US*) to lose one's competence, to decline. **4** [1990s+] (*US Black*) to let one's attention waver, to become too casual, to abandon one's vigilance. **5** [1990s+] (*drugs*) to become somnolent after taking heroin.

slip a cog *v.* [1910s–20s] to make a mistake, to blunder. [engineering imagery]

slip a fast one (over) *v.* (*also* **slip over a fast one**) [1910s+] to take advantage of someone by trickery, to hoodwink.

slip a gear *v.* [2000s] to lose emotional control.

slip a joey *v.* [20C+] (*Aus.*) **1** to have a miscarriage. **2** to give birth. [SE *slip*, of animals, to miscarry, to give birth prematurely + *joey*, a young kangaroo]

slip a length into *v.* (*also* **slip her a length**) [1950s+] (*Aus.*) of a man, to have intercourse with a woman; occas. in homosexual use (cf. DO HER JOB FOR HER v.). [LENGTH n.[2]]

slip a mickey *v.* [late 19C+] (*US*) to add a sedative, esp. choral hydrate, secretly to a drink. [SE *slip* + MICKEY FINN n. (1)]

slip five *v. see* SLAP FIVE v.

slip-gibbet *n.* (*also* **slip-halter**) [mid-17C–early 19C] a thief or pickpocket or one who associates with them. [SE *slip*, to escape + *gibbet*, the gallows]

slip her a length *v. see* SLIP A LENGTH INTO v.

slip her a (quick) crippler *v.* [1950s+] of a man, to have sexual intercourse with a woman (cf. DO HER JOB FOR HER v.).

slip in Daintie Davie *v.* (*also* **slip in Willie Wallace**) [late 18C] (*Scot.*) of a man, to have sexual intercourse (cf. BURY IT v.).

slip in the dozens *v. see* PLAY THE DOZENS v.

slip in the gutter *n.* [20C+] butter. [rhy. sl.]

slip into *v.* **1** [mid-19C+] to beat; thus *let slip at*, to attack violently. **2** [late 19C] to set about a task enthusiastically. **3** [late 19C+] of a man, to have sexual intercourse (cf. BURY IT v.).

slip in Willie Wallace *v. see* SLIP IN DAINTIE DAVIE v.

slip it about *v.* [20C+] of a woman, to have sexual intercourse (cf. CATCH AN OYSTER v.).

slip it across *v.* [1920s] **1** to fool, to 'do down', to upset. **2** to hit, to punch.

slip it into *v.* [1920s] to attack verbally.

slip it to *v.* (*also* **slip it over**) [1940s+] of a man, to have sexual intercourse with a woman (cf. BURY IT v.).

slip me five! *excl. see* GIVE ME FIVE! excl.

slip of the shoulder *n.* [19C] by a woman, seduction. [her body language]

slip one over on *v. see* PUT ONE OVER (ON) v.

slip one's anchor *v.* [1900s] (*Aus.*) to leave (surreptitiously).

slip one's breath *v.* [early 19C] to die. [naut. imagery]

slip one's cable *v.* [mid-18C–1910s] to die; to abscond. [naut. imagery]

slip one's elbow *v.* [1990s+] to have an illegitimate child.

slip one's lip *v.* [1950s] (*US Black*) to talk rudely, aggressively.

slip one's top *v.* [1960s] (*US*) to go mad. [SE *top*, i.e. the head/brain]

slip one's trolley *v.* [late 19C+] to lose emotional control, to go mad. [? trolley-bus or tram imagery; i.e. the vehicle 'comes off the rails'; note OFF ONE'S TROLLEY phr. (1)]

slip one's wig *v.* [1940s] (*US*) to go mad. [WIG n.[3] (1)]

slip one's wind *v.* [late 18C–1910s] to die. [naut. imagery]

slip on one's guava *v. see* COME ON ONE'S GUAVA v.

slip over a fast one *v. see* SLIP A FAST ONE (OVER) v.

slipped *adj.* [1960s] (*US teen*) insane, eccentric. [one has 'slipped over the edge of the world']

slipper *n.*[1] [1980s] (*Aus.*) a kicking.

slipper *n.*[2] [1990s+] (*UK juv.*) one who looks much older/younger than they actually are. ['Derived from the "poorer estates" in towns where there are always 3 shops – a chip shop, a video shop and an offie. People from the estate would shop, rent a video but mostly play the bandit in the chip shop wearing their slippers – never shoes, they'd walk to the shops in their slippers. Slippertown – the part of town would be then named' (*OnLine Dict. of Playground Slang*, 2001)]

slipper *v.* [1920s+] (*US Und.*) to reform and renounce the criminal life. [the SE *slippers* that symbolize a peaceful life]

slippery *n.* [mid-19C] soap. [its essential quality]

slippery *adj. see* SLIPPY adj.

slippery-dip *n.*[1] **1** [20C+] (*Aus.*) cheekiness. **2** [1980s+] (*Aus. prison*) LSD (cf. A n.[3]). [rhy. sl.; (1) = LIP n.[1] (1); (2) = TRIP n.[4] (2)]

slippery-dip *n.*[2] [1990s+] (*Aus.*) a children's slide.

slippery sam *n.* [late 18C; 1970s] an unreliable, evasive, untrustworthy person.

slippery (Sid) *n.* [1980s+] a Jew (cf. BILLY THE KID *n.*). [rhy. sl. = YID *n.*[1]]

slippery tit *n.* [1940s] (*US Und.*) a cheap restaurant.

slippin' *adj.* [1990s+] (*US teen*) a general adj. of approval. [SE *slipping along nicely*]

slipping *n.* [1990s+] (*US Black*) not paying attention. [SLIP *v.* (4)]

slipping and sliding *n.* [1960s+] (*US Black*) sneaking around, acting in a clandestine manner.

slippy *adj.* (*also* **slippery**) **1** [late 19C] confident. **2** [late 19C+] agile, nimble, speedy; also as adv., quickly. **3** [1940s] as a general intensifier. **4** [1980s+] cunning.

slippy-sloppy *n. see* SLIP-SLOPS *n.* (3).

slippy tit *n.* [1980s+] (*Ulster*) a sly, untrustworthy person. [SLIPPY *adj.* (4) + TIT *n.*[4]]

slip-slapping *n.* [1970s] a mutual hand-slapping ritual used by Blacks (and some Whites) for greeting, emphasis, congratulation etc. [SLAP FIVE *v.*]

slip-slop *n.*[1] [early 18C] kissing. [echoic of the exchange of spittle]

slip-slop *n.*[2] [1960s+] (*S.Afr.*) a thong sandal. [the noise it makes as one walks]

slip-sloppy *adj. see* SLOPPY *adj.* (4).

slip-slops *n.* **1** [early 18C] (*also* **slops**) a non-alcoholic drink taken for medicinal purposes. **2** [late 18C–early 19C] any form of soft drink, esp. tea. **3** [mid-19C] (*also* **slippy-sloppy**) any drink. [SE *slip-slop*, any form of sloppy mixture, whether food or drink]

slip someone some ham *v.* [1950s] to press one's bare buttocks against a car window.

slip someone the fish *v.* [1990s+] of a man, to have sexual intercourse (cf. BURY IT *v.*). [? ONE-EYED ZIPPER FISH *n.*]

slip some skin *v. see* GIVE SOME SKIN *v.*

slip something over (on) *v.* (*also* **slip something to**) [1910s+] to deceive, to take advantage of in a surreptitious manner.

slipstick *n.* [1930s–50s] (*US campus*) a slide rule.

slip the calf *v. see* CAST THE CALF *v.*

slip to glory *v. see* GO TO GLORY *v.* (2).

slip up *v.* (*Aus.*) **1** [late 19C–1900s] to defraud, to swindle. **2** [1910s] in weakened use, to let down, to disappoint.

s-list *n. see* SHIT LIST *n.*

slit *n.*[1] **1** [early 17C+] the vagina (cf. AGREEABLE RUTS OF LIFE *n.*). **2** [1940s+] a derog. term for a woman.

slit *n.*[2] (*also* **sliteye**) [1940s+] a derog. term for an Asian or Oriental person (cf. BROWNIE *n.*[2]). [the shape of the Oriental eye]

slit groat *n. see* CRACKED GROAT *n.*

slither *n.*[1] [late 19C+] a lodge (e.g. of Freemasonry). [rhy. sl.; *slither and dodge* = lodge]

slither *n.*[2] (*also* **slitherum**) [1910s–40s] counterfeit money. [it slithers through one's fingers]

slither *v.* (*also* **do a slither**) [mid-19C+] to hurry away. [SE *slither*, a rush, a hurry; later use is Aus.]

slithery *n.* [1930s+] **1** the vagina. **2** women in general (viewed as sex objects). **3** sexual intercourse.

sliver-brain *n.* [1930s] a fool (cf. BAKEBRAIN *n.*). [one has but a 'sliver' of the normal brain]

sliz *n.* [2000s] (*US Black*) a promiscuous woman. [SE *slut* + -IZ- ifx]

sloan *v.* (*also* **Tod Sloan**) **1** [late 19C] to balk, to hinder, to get in the way of, to 'cut up'. **2** [1910s] (*Aus.*) a pun on (1), to cut up, as with a knife and fork. [(1) coined and abandoned in 1899; f. the US jockey Tod *Sloan* (1874–1933), who cut his horse Holocaust across those of his rivals in an attempt to win that year's Derby; Sloan had picked up the trick from the British champion Archer, but the sl. gave him the tribute]

Sloane (Ranger) *n.* [1970s+] a stereotypical British upper-middle-class young person (usu. female), resolutely trad., invariably Conservative-voting and happier with dogs or horses than humans; they may live in London, but their spiritual home remains the country; thus adj. *Sloaney*. [coined by Peter York and Ann Barr in *Harpers & Queen*, October 1975. It puns on *Sloane Square*, London SW3, home of such people + the TV lawman the Lone *Ranger*; note RMC Duntroon (Aus.) *sloane* (*ranger*), a cadet who attempts to display themselves as trendy in manners and dress and is duly teased for it]

slob *n.* **1** [mid-19C+] (*orig. US*) a lazy, dirty, unkempt, good-for-nothing person, usu. a man; thus *slobhood*, the world of slobs. **2** [late 19C+] (*US*) an average person. **3** [20C+] (*orig. US*) a harmless simpleton, a 'soft', fat fellow. **4** [1990s+] (*US gang*) a derog. term used by Crip gangs for their rivals the Bloods. [Slavic *zhlub*, a coarse fellow, note also Irish *slaba*, mud; thus a slovenly person]

slob *v.* [1900s–70s] (*US Black*) to kiss. [abbr. SE *slobber*/SLOBBER *n.*[2]]

slob a knob *v.* [1940s+] (*US*) to perform fellatio. [SE *slob(ber)*/SLOBBER *n.*[2] + KNOB *n.*[1] (3)]

slob (around) *v.* (*also* **slob out**) [1990s+] to act lazily, to act in a slovenly manner. [SLOB *n.* (1)]

slobber *n.*[1] [late 19C–1910s] nonsensical, sentimental chatter. [SLOBBER *v.* (2)]

slobber *n.*[2] [late 19C–1950s] a kiss. [the swapping of spittle]

slobber *v.* **1** [late 16C+] (*also* **slabber**) to kiss. **2** [mid-19C+] to talk sentimental, mawkish nonsense. **3** [20C+] (*US*) to cry. **4** [1970s] to masturbate. [orig. UK dial.]

slobberation *n.* [1910s–20s] sloppy kissing. [SLOBBER *n.*[2]]

slobber-chops *n.* (*also* **slabber-chops**) [late 18C–19C] a large-joweled person, a term of ridicule. [SE *slobber*, spittle + CHOPS *n.*[1] (1); modern use seems primarily for naming a pet]

slobberer *n.* [late 18C] a general insult, spec. a bad farmer. [dial. *slobber*, to work in a slovenly manner]

slobber-slobber *n.* [1950s] (*W.I.*) a slovenly, unkempt, lazy person. [see prev.]

slob out *v. see* SLOB (AROUND) *v.*

slock *n.* [1990s+] (*US prison*) any form of bludgeon-like weapon, e.g. batteries or a padlock in a sock. [SLOCK *v.*]

slock *v.* [1990s+] (*US prison*) to hit someone with a heavy padlock concealed in a sock. [SE *sock* + SLUG *v.*[2] (3)]

slockdolager/slockdologer *n. see* SOCKDOLAGER *n.*

slog *n.* **1** [late 19C+] work that is definitely hard and poss. unrewarding. **2** [1990s+] an exhausting journey, usu. on foot. [SLOG *v.* (3)]

slog *v.* **1** [early 19C+] (*also* **slag**) to hit, to punch. **2** [mid-19C+] to thrash, to beat; also in fig. use. **3** [late 19C+] to work hard. **4** [20C+] to persist; often as *slog on*. [? Yorks. dial./SE *slug*, to hit hard]

slogger *n.* **1** [early 19C+] one who delivers heavy blows, esp. in boxing or cricket. **2** [mid-19C–1950s] a hard, ponderous worker. **3** [late 19C–1900s] a weight attached to a string and used as a weapon. **4** [1980s] a heavy, hard-wearing shoe. [SLOG *v.*]

slogging *n.* **1** [mid–late 19C] a beating, a thrashing. **2** [mid-19C–1900s] hitting, fighting. **3** [1950s+] working hard; esp. as *slogging away (at)*. [SLOG *v.*]

slog it on *v. see* SCHLOG IT ON *v.*

slog it out *v.* (*also* **slog it through**) **1** [late 19C+] to engage in a (hard and lengthy) fight. **2** [1980s] to work hard. [SLOG *v.*]

slog one's guts out *v. see* SWEAT ONE'S GUTS OUT *v.*

slommack *n. see* SLAMKIN *n.*

sloop of war *n.* [mid-19C; 1930s] a prostitute (cf. BOAT AND OAR *n.*). [rhy. sl. = SE *whore*]

sloosh *n.* (*also* **sluish**) [late 19C–1910s] a quick wash. [echoic]

sloosh *v.* **1** [1910s] to have a quick wash. **2** [2000s] ext. in fig. use. [SLOOSH *n.*]

slop *n.*[1] **1** [mid-18C–mid-19C] tea. **2** [late 19C+] (*US*) food in general, usu. second-rate. **3** [1900s–60s] (*Aus./N.Z./US*) beer. **4** [1960s] (*US prison*) coffee. [SE *slop*, watered-down food]

slop *n.*[2] [mid-19C–1930s] (*UK prison*) a form of smock, in easily distinguishable colours, worn by prisoners on work parties. [SE *slop*, a loose outer garment]

slop *n.*[3] [mid-19C–1950s] a policeman (cf. BOTTLE (AND STOPPER) n.). [backsl.; or rhy. sl. *esclop/slop* = COP n.[1] (1)]

slop *n.*[4] **1** [mid-19C+] sentimentality, mawkish emotion. **2** [late 19C+] nonsensical talk. [SE *slop*, liquid or semi-liquid food, esp. as served to invalids]

slop *n.*[5] [1940s] (*US Black campus*) a sophomore.

slop *n.*[6] *see* SLAP n.[2].

slop *v.* [1900s] (*Aus.*) in fig. use, to feed, to give, to apportion. [SE *slop*, to feed an animal with slops]

slop about *v.* (*also* **slop around**) [20C+] **1** to wander around aimlessly. **2** to move in a slovenly manner. [SE *slope*, to move obliquely, underpinned by SLOPPY adj. (1)]

slop and flop *n.* [1920s–30s] (*US tramp*) food and accommodation, esp. in transient camps, typically those set up by an oil-drilling company. [SLOP n.[1] (2) + FLOP n.[5] (1)]

slopchute *n.* [1960s] (*US gay*) the anus (cf. ALLEY WAY n.).

slope *n.*[1] [mid-19C] (*US*) a trick, a hoax. [York dial. *slope*, deception]

slope *n.*[2] (*also* **slopehead, slopie, slopy**) **1** [1940s+] a derog. term for an Oriental person, esp. Vietnamese, Korean; also attrib. (cf. BROWNIE n.[2]). **2** [1980s] any foreigner, not necessarily Asian. [the supposed 'slope' of Oriental eyes; note synon. RMC Duntroon (Aus.) *slop head*]

slope *adj.* [1940s+] (*US*) Oriental, esp. Vietnamese. [SLOPE n.[2] (1)]

slope *v.*[1] [17C] to sleep. [synon. Du.; Rowlands, *Martin-Mark-all* (1610), notes that this replaces Harman's and Dekker's synon. COUCH A HOGSHEAD v., which is 'like an Almanac that is out of date']

slope *v.*[2] **1** [mid-19C+] (*orig. US*) to leave, to move off. **2** [1900s–20s] (*US Und.*) to escape from prison. **3** [1900s–50s] to cheat, e.g. a publican, a shopkeeper; to avoid payment. **4** [1950s] to leave one's lodgings without paying. [SE *let's lope* or *slope*, to move obliquely; note Schele de Vere, *Americanisms* (1872): 'The term came first into use here, when the new State of Texas offered a ready asylum to unfortunate speculators, dishonest creditors, and even escaped criminals, so that the words Gone To Texas (G. T. T.) meant to be gone to the American Alsatia, and the act of going so far "down South" became known as *sloping*. It implied, virtually, that the *sloper* had cheated his creditors, plundered a bank, or robbed his employers. The precise meaning of the word has been elucidated in the statement that "a mean fellow does not slope, he sneaks or slinks away; but the scoundrel, bold and unabashed, when defeated, slopes to parts unknown"']

slopehead *n. see* SLOPE n.[2].

slope in a cup with the light out *n.* [late 19C] (*US short order*) black coffee.

slope off *v.* [mid-19C+] (*orig. US*) to leave, esp. surreptitiously. [ext. SLOPE v.[2] (1)]

slopeout *n.* [1960s] (*US*) anything seen as easy to perform.

sloper *n.*[1] [late 19C] an act of sexual intercourse in which the couple are leaning against something, e.g. a table or the edge of a bed.

sloper *n.*[2] [late 19C+] (*Aus.*) one who leaves without paying their debts or bills. [dial. *sloper*, a trickster + SLOPE v.[2] (1)]

sloper's island *n.* [late 19C–1900s] a neighbourhood of weekly tenements (i.e. flats that are rented by the week). [F&H cite 'the artisans' village near Loughborough Junction, originally in the midst of fields; now in the centre of a densely populated neighbourhood'. The possibility that impoverished tenants would SLOPE OFF v. without paying]

slop-feeder *n.* [early 19C] a teaspoon. [SLOP n.[1] (1) + SE *feeder*]

slophouse *n.* [1940s] (*US Und.*) a cheap restaurant. [SLOP n.[1] (2) + play on FLOPHOUSE n. (1)]

slopie *n. see* SLOPE n.[2].

slopie *adj.* [1980s] (*Aus.*) Oriental, Asian. [SLOPE n.[2] (1)]

slop (it) back *v.* [1920s+] (*N.Z.*) to drink.

slop-jaw *n.* [1950s] a garrulous, self-opinionated talker. [SLOP n.[4] (2)]

slop joint *n.* [20C+] a cheap, unappetizing restaurant. [SLOP n.[1] (2) + JOINT n.[4] (3); note US milit. *slop chute*, the barracks/base canteen]

slop-made *adj.* [late 19C–1900s] (*Aus.*) disjointed; of clothes, badly tailored; also in fig. use; thus *slop-suit*, a badly tailored suit; *slop-tailor*, a second-rate tailor. [synon. with SE *slop-built*]

slop out *v.* **1** [1950s+] (*UK prison*) to empty a chamberpot. **2** [1990s+] to masturbate. [SE *slop*, to spill, to pour]

slop over *v.* [mid-19C–1920s] to treat with exaggerated, mawkish sentiment. [late 17C SE *slop*, to slobber (over)]

slop-pail *n.* [1920s] a man who does housework.

slopped *adj.* [20C+] drunk. [SLOP n.[1] (3); underpinned by SE *sloppy*, weak, feeble, waterlogged]

sloppiness *n.* [1910s] some form of liquid-based food, e.g. a stew. [SLOPS n.[2] (2)]

slopping up *n.* [late 19C–1920s] (*US tramp*) a session of heavy drinking.

sloppy *adj.* **1** [early 19C+] lazy, inefficient, imprecise. **2** [late 19C+] mawkishly sentimental. **3** [1910s+] (*US*) messy. **4** [1920s+] (*US*) (*also* **slip-sloppy**) drunk. [SE; ult. *slop*, an act of spilling, the liquid thus spilt]

sloppy Joe *n.* (*US*) **1** [1940s+] a loose, floppy sweater. **2** [1940s+] a multi-decked sandwich (the fillings ooze out when eating). **3** [1940s+] a slovenly, inefficient person. **4** [1960s+] a type of hamburger in which the meat filling is diluted to a form of sauce.

sloppy joe's *n.* [1930s+] (*US*) a cheap restaurant or snack bar. [generic use of a supposed cook + SLOPPY JOE n. (2); the orig. Sloppy Joe's was a bar in Havana, Cuba, run by Jose (Joe) Abeal Otero (d.1942), allegedly thus nicknamed for its low standards of hygiene]

sloppy seconds *n.* **1** [1960s+] (*also* **slops**) sexual intercourse with a woman who has had another partners/partners immediately previously, whether forced or voluntary. **2** [1960s+] the woman who is participating in this sequential sex. **3** [1970s+] (*US gay/prison*) the man who participates second or later in such sequential sex. [note RMC Duntroon (Aus.) *go slops*, to have sex with a woman immediately after one or more people have already ejaculated into her]

slops *n.*[1] [mid-16C–1910s] wide, baggy breeches or hose; thus *slop-shop*, a clothier's. [SE *slop*, an outer garment; dial. the leg(s) of a pair of breeches; ult. ety. unknown]

slops *n.*[2] **1** [18C–mid-19C] tea, esp. when still in a chest. **2** [late 19C+] any form of badly cooked or ill-tasting food. **3** [1910s–60s] (*Aus./US tramp*) beer. **4** [1950s] (*Aus.*) tea. [SE *slop*, watered-down food]

slops *n.*[3] *see* SLOPPY SECONDS n. (1).

slops *n.*[4] *see* SLIP-SLOPS n. (1).

slops and slugs *n.* [1940s] (*US Black*) coffee and doughnuts. [SE *slops* + SE *slug*, i.e. the hardness of the doughnut]

slop-tubs *n.* [early 19C] a tea-service. [SLOP n.[1] (1) + SE *tub*]

slop up *v.* [late 19C+] to drink heavily, to become drunk. [SE *slop up*, to absorb]

slopy *n. see* SLOPE n.[2].

slorch *n.* [1990s+] (*US campus*) a promiscuous woman. [? SE *slut* + *whore* + BITCH n.[1] (1)]

slosh *n.*[1] **1** [mid–late 19C] a drink, alcoholic or otherwise. **2** [late 19C+] mawkish emotionalism; thus *slush-bucket*, a highly sentimental person. **3** [1920s+] (*Aus.*) coffee. [SE *slosh*, weak, watery, unappetizing; ult. *slush*, liquid mud]

slosh *n.*[2] **1** [20C+] a hit, a blow. **2** [1950s] an attempt at hitting. [SLOSH v.[1]]

slosh *v.*[1] (*also* **sloush**) [mid-19C+] to hit; thus *slosh the burick*, *slosh the old gooseberry*, to hit one's wife.

slosh v.[2] [late 19C+] **1** to swallow carelessly, to eat heartily. **2** to pour out liquid in an abrupt manner. [the consumption of SLOSH n.[1] (1)]

slosh and mud n. [20C+] a (collar or ear) stud. [rhy. sl.]

slosh around v. **1** [mid–late 19C] (US) to go out drinking. **2** [late 19C] (US) to hit out at random; physically and verbally. **3** [late 19C–1920s] to strut about, to swank. [(1) SLOSH v.[2] (1); (2) (3) SLOSH v.[1]]

sloshed adj. (also **soshed**) [20C+] drunk. [SLOSH n.[1] (1) + SLOSH v.[2]]

slosh sex n. [1990s+] sexual intercourse at a time when one is very drunk. [SLOSHED adj.]

slot n.[1] **1** [late 19C–1950s] (US) an Automat. **2** [1950s+] (orig. US) a slot-machine. [the slot into which one places money. (1) the coin-operated self-service Automats, popularized in New York (although in no other city) by the Horn & Hardart Baking Co.]

slot n.[2] **1** [late 19C+] the vagina (cf. AGREEABLE RUTS OF LIFE n.). **2** [1970s] (US gay) the anus. **3** [1970s+] (Aus./N.Z.) a prison cell. [(3) into which one is put]

slot n.[3] [1940s] (orig. US Black) a general term of address. [Mezzrow & Wolfe, *Really the Blues* (1946): 'A private inner-racial joke, suggesting a mouth as big and as avaricious as the coin slot in a vending machine, always looking for something to put in it']

slot n.[4] [1960s+] (Aus./N.Z. prison) a cell.

slot v. **1** [1950s] to hit, to beat up. **2** [1980s+] (Aus. prison) to lock into a cell. **3** [1990s+] to kill. **4** [1990s+] to obtain.

sloth n. [1980s+] a very lazy person.

slouch n. **1** [late 19C+] an indifferent, second-rate or inefficient thing, place, person etc. **2** [1970s] (US Black) an eccentric, lazy, unprofessional prostitute. [SE slouch, 'an awkward, slovenly, or ungainly man; a lubber, lout, clown; also, a lazy, idle fellow' (OED)]

slough n.[1] **1** [1900s–50s] (US Und.) (also **cold slough**) a temporarily empty house, thus a target for a robbery; thus *cold slough prowler*, a thief who robs empty houses. **2** [1910s] (Aus.) a prison; a state of imprisonment. [(1) SLOUGH v. (1)]

slough n.[2] [1920s–50s] the vagina (cf. AGREEABLE RUTS OF LIFE n.). [SE slough, a piece of muddy ground]

slough v. (also **slough in/up**) **1** [mid-19C–1950s] to lock up, to put in prison; thus *unslough*, to release, to unlock. **2** [1900s–60s] (US Und.) to throw away, to abandon, to dispose of; to conceal quickly. **3** [1920s–60s] (US tramp) to assault. **4** [1960s] (US Und.) to steal, to shoplift. [SE slough, to be swallowed up; ult. slough, a piece of soft, muddy ground]

sloughed (up) adj. [mid-19C+] (UK/US Und.) imprisoned, locked up. [SLOUGH v. (1)]

slougher n. [1910s] (US Und.) one who helps a thief dispose of stolen goods. [SLOUGH v. (2)]

slough in/up v. see SLOUGH v.

slough worker n. [1900s–40s] (US Und.) one who robs a house or apartment in the absence of its owners. [SLOUGH n.[1] (1) + WORKER n.[1] (1)]

slour (up) v. **1** [early–mid-19C] to button up a garment; thus *sloured hoxter*, a buttoned inside pocket. **2** [early–mid-19C; 1990s+] (UK Und.) to lock up, to fasten. [ety. unknown]

sloush v. see SLOSH v.[1].

slousher n. [1900s] (N.Z.) a lazy person; usu. in phr. *be no slousher (at)*. [SE slouch]

slow adj. **1** [early–mid-19C] unfashionable. **2** [mid–19C+] of places or events, dull, boring. **3** [mid-19C+] of people, dull, lifeless, insipid. **4** [mid-19C+] sexually timid. **5** [1960s+] (US Black) unsophisticated, lacking in knowledge.

slow as a wet week phr. [late 19C+] very backward, dull, esp. in sexual matters.

slow as a wet wick phr. [1990s+] (Aus.) very backward or dull. [? mis-reading of prev.]

slow-ass adj. [1970s+] (US Black) slow. [SE slow + -ASS sfx]

Slowbart n. [late 19C–1900s] (Aus.) Hobart, the capital city of Tasmania. [the slow pace of its life]

slow boat n. [1970s+] (S.Afr. drugs) a marijuana cigarette. [? the song 'On a Slow Boat to China'; the emphasis is on the supposed exoticism of marijuana, although, given China, the link should be to opium]

slow burn n. [1930s+] (orig. US) the gradual development of an intense fury, slowly brought to a peak, rather than simply exploding with rage.

slowcoach n. [mid-19C] an unfashionable person. [SE slowcoach, one who acts, works or moves slowly]

slow con n. [20C+] a fraudulent scheme or confidence trick in which the victim is nurtured slowly and carefully towards their downfall. [SE slow + CON n.[1] (7)]

slow connecter n. [1930s] (US Und.) a second-rate criminal (by criminal standards).

slowed adj. [mid-19C] (UK prison) locked up. [pron. of SLOUGHED (UP) adj.]

slow-em-ups n. (also **slow-me-down juice**) [1970s+] (drugs) any form of barbiturate, tranquillizer or sleeping pill (cf. BARBIT n.). [the effects]

slowie n. [1980s+] a slow dance or song.

slow-mo adj. [1970s+] slow-*mo*tion. [abbr.; orig. film use]

slow one's roll v. [1990s+] (US Black) to slow down whatever one is doing. [SE slow + ROLL v.[5] (2)]

slow one's row v. **1** [1940s+] (US Black campus) to relax. **2** [1980s+] (US Black) to lower one's profile, to keep off the streets, perhaps through fear of police or rival criminal interest. [ploughing imagery or Black pron. of *roll*, thus predating SLOW ONE'S ROLL v.]

slow on the draw phr. [20C+] **1** not very intelligent. **2** (Irish) reluctant to stand one's round of drinks. [gun-fighting imagery]

slow on the trigger phr. [20C+] stupid, dull. [gun-fighting imagery]

slow-play v. (also **slow-walk**) [1990s+] (US prison) to waste time deliberately; to stall someone, e.g. in the payment of a debt.

slowpoke n. [mid-19C+] (US) a sluggard, a lethargic, lazy person. [SE slow + POKE ALONG v.]

Slow Town n. [1900s] (US tramp) Detroit.

slow track n. [1940s] (US Black) **1** the whoring and high-life centre in a small town or city. **2** the West Coast (cf. FAST TRACK n.). [TRACK n.[2] (4); the image of the small town or the West Coast being 'slower' than New York]

slow up v. [1980s+] (Aus. prison) to place in isolation.

slow walk v. see SLOW-PLAY v.

slubberdegullion n. see SLABBERDEGULLION n.

'slud! excl. see 'SBLOOD! excl.

sludge n. [1960s+] (US Black) the anus.

sludgeball n. [1960s+] (US) a slovenly person. [SE sludge + -BALL sfx]

slue see under SLEW and its combs.

sluff v. [1920s–50s] (US) to avoid or shirk one's responsibilities or work; thus *sluff course*, a course that requires little work. [SE slough off]

slug n.[1] [late 16C+] a very lazy person. [the slow progress of a SE slug]

slug n.[2] **1** [18C+] a bullet. **2** [mid-19C+] (US) $1; thus *half a slug*, 50 cents; thus money, irrespective of amount. **3** [1910s+] a token. [SE slug, a piece of lead; note SAmE slug, the name of various large gold coins issued privately in California c.1850, usu. worth $50]

slug n.[3] **1** [mid-18C] a fiery drink. **2** [mid-18C+] a portion or measure of liquor. **3** [1940s+] a portion of a non-alcoholic drink, e.g. coffee. **4** [1950s] in general use, a portion, a share. **5** [1960s] a portion or measure of a drug. [SLUG n.[2] (1); thus that which is 'shot']

slug *n.*[4] **1** [early 19C+] (*US*) a blow; lit. and fig. **2** [1920s] (*US Und.*) a blackjack. **3** [1950s+] (*US*) a thug. [*OED* suggests the n. comes from v. (SLUG *v.*[2]) but the cits. here predate those of the v.; thus ? SLOG v. (1)]

slug *n.*[5] **1** [1910s] (*US*) a piece of nasal mucus. **2** [1940s+] (*orig. Aus. navy*) the penis; thus *slug slewer*, one who watches men in the shower; thus TUG ONE'S SLUG v. [resemblance to the gastropod]

slug *v.*[1] (*also* **slug down, slug up**) [mid-19C+] to drink. [SLUG *n.*[3] (2)]

slug *v.*[2] **1** [late 19C] to criticize harshly. **2** [late 19C–1900s] in fig. use, to overcome. **3** [late 19C+] (*orig. Und.*) to hit hard; often as *slug it out*, to fight. **4** [1920s–40s] to shoot. **5** [1930s] to kill, to murder. **6** [1940s+] in fig. use, to dispute aggressively; often as *slug it out*. **7** [1940s+] (*Aus.*) to overcharge. **8** [1940s+] (*US*) to trudge, to move with an effort, to make effort. [SLUG *n.*[4] (1)]

slug *v.*[3] [1980s] (*US campus*) to sleep.

slug and snail *n.* [20C+] a fingernail; a nail. [rhy. sl.]

slugbug *n.* [1990s+] (*US campus*) a Volkswagen 'Beetle'. [a supposed resemblance to the SE *slug* + *bug*, the car's popular nickname]

slug down *v. see* SLUG *v.*[1].

slugfest *n.* [1910s+] (*US*) a rough battle, a hard-hitting contest. [SLUG *v.*[2] (3) + -FEST sfx]

slugged *adj.* [1950s] (*US*) drunk (cf. ANNIHILATED adj.). [SLUG *n.*[3] (2)]

slugger *n.* **1** [late 19C+] a fighter, professional or otherwise, esp. one who relies on brute force rather than skill for their conquests. **2** [1950s+] used as an affectionate term of address. **3** [1970s] (*US campus*) a sexual success, a seducer. [SLUG *v.*[2] (3)]

sluggers *n.* [late 19C+] (*US*) whiskers that extend from the ear to the chin, typically worn by a stage Irishman. [SLUG *v.*[2] (3); such whiskers were orig. a sign of a pugnacious fighter, stereotypically Irish]

slugging *n.* **1** [mid-19C+] (*US*) a beating, fatal or otherwise. **2** [1930s] in fig. use, strenuous efforts. [SLUG *v.*[2] (3)]

slug it out *v. see* SLUG *v.*[2].

slug-nutty *adj.* [1930s–50s] (*US*) lit. or fig., punch-drunk. [SLUG *n.*[4] (1) + NUTTY adj.[2] (2)]

slug up *v. see* SLUG *v.*[1].

sluice *n.* **1** [late 17C–early 18C] the vagina (cf. AGREEABLE RUTS OF LIFE n.; DAMP n.). **2** [late 17C–mid-18C] the penis. **3** [mid-19C–1920s] the mouth. **4** [1950s–70s] sexual intercourse. [SE *sluice*]

sluice *v.* [late 16C–early 17C] to have sexual intercourse.

sluice-cunted *adj.* [mid-19C+] having a large vagina. [SE *sluice* + CUNT n.[1] (1)]

sluice-house *n.* [mid-19C] **1** a public house, a tavern. **2** the mouth. [SE *sluice*, to wash down + *house*]

sluice one's gob *v.* (*also* **sluice one's bolt, …neck, …whistle**) [mid-18C–1940s] to take a hearty drink. [SE *sluice* + GOB n.[1] (1)/BOLT n.[2]/SE *neck*/WHISTLE n.[1] (1)]

sluice one's ivories *v. see* SLUICE THE IVORIES v.

sluicery *n.* [early–mid-19C] a gin-shop or public house. [SE *sluice*, to wash down; note Egan, *Life in London* (1821): '[…] from the lower orders of society, and women of the town, *sluicing* their throats as it were with gin']

sluice the dominoes *v.* [19C] to drink heartily. [SE *sluice* + DOMINO n.[1] (1)]

sluice the ivories *v.* (*also* **sluice one's ivories, wash one's/the ivories**) **1** [late 18C–19C] to drink heartily. **2** [early 19C] to ply with drink. [SE *sluice* + IVORY n. (1)]

sluish *n. see* SLOOSH n.

sluk *v.* [1970s+] (*S.Afr.*) to gulp down, to drink. [Afk. *sluk*, to swallow]

sluker *n.* [late 19C–1900s] a prostitute who works in the City Road, London, itself part of the parish of *St Luke's*. [such women were considered socially inferior to those who worked in Islington]

slum *n.*[1] **1** [late 18C–mid-19C] (*UK Und.*) a room, usu. defined by a descriptive n. **2** [mid-19C] a chest or box. **3** [mid-19C] a shop, usu. defined by a n. **4** [late 19C] a back alley. [? SE *slumber*]

slum *n.*[2] **1** [early–mid-19C] nonsensical talk or writing, 'gammon', 'blarney'. **2** [early–mid-19C] the jargon of gypsies. **3** [early–late 19C] a trick, a hoax. **4** [mid-19C] a professionally written begging letter; thus *slum-scribbler*, a writer of such documents, letters. **5** [mid-19C] an insinuation, an innuendo. **6** [mid-19C] (*UK Und.*) a letter written from prison. [SE *slum*, a run-down, poverty-stricken area; thus a generic negative]

slum *n.*[3] **1** [mid-19C–1940s] (*US prison/tramp*) stew; thus *slum-slinger*, *slum-burner*, a cook. **2** [1910s] (*US*) soup. **3** [1930s] (*UK tramp*) anything edible. [SLUMGUDGEON n. (1)]

slum *n.*[4] [1910s–40s] (*US*) a disparaging name for a person; thus adj., *slummy*.

slum *n.*[5] **1** [1910s+] cheap or counterfeit jewellery, typically that sold illegally by street vendors. **2** [1930s] stolen jewellery. **3** [1940s+] the virtually worthless prizes offered at fairs, carnivals etc. [ety. unknown]

slum *n.*[6] [1920s] (*US drugs*) narcotics.

slum *v.*[1] [early–mid-18C] (*UK Und.*) to break into.

slum *v.*[2] **1** [mid-19C] to boast; to talk nonsense; to speak criminal cant. **2** [mid-19C] (*UK Und.*) to fake illness. **3** [mid-late 19C] to trick or cheat. **4** [1920s] (*US Und.*) to drink. **5** [1990s+] (*US drugs*) to be sold inferior or fake drugs. [SLUM *n.*[2]]

slum *v.*[3] **1** [mid-19C+] (*also* **do the slums**) to saunter about, esp. in poor or 'red–light' areas, poss. with an eye on 'immoral pursuits'. **2** [late 19C+] to visit impoverished areas, looking for 'atmosphere' and 'characters', but secure in the knowledge that one's real life is elsewhere, either as a tourist, or for personal reasons, e.g. political support; thus n. *slumming*. **3** [1920s+] in fig. use of (2), to do something ostensibly demeaning, while telling oneself that one is really above it. [SE *slum*]

slumber party *n.* [1930s–40s] (*US drugs*) morphine (cf. AUNTIE EMMA n.).

slum-box *n.* [1920s] a typical example of slum housing. [SE *slum* + *box*]

slum-dragger *n.* [1900s] a member of the London working classes.

slum dump *n.* [1950s] (*US drugs*) anywhere that users take narcotics. [SLUM *n.*[6] + DUMP n.[3] (2)]

slumgudgeon *n.* (*also* **slumgullion**) **1** [mid-19C–1950s] (*also* **gullion**) 'any cheap, nasty, washy beverage' or foodstuff (Hotten, 1874). **2** [late 19C] a representative or servant. [ety. unknown; ? SE *slum* + Lancashire dial. *gullion*, a worthless wretch]

slumgullion *adj.* [1940s] (*US*) second-rate, run-down. [fig. use of SLUMGUDGEON n. (1)]

slumguzzle *v.* [mid-19C–1910s] (*orig. US*) to trick, to cheat. [SLUM *n.*[2] (3) + GUZZLE *v.*[2] (2)]

slum hustler *n.* [1920s+] (*UK Und.*) one who sells cheap jewellery or clothing, pretending to the gullible buyer that it is stolen property; thus *slum hustle/hustling*. [SLUM *n.*[5] (1) + HUSTLER n. (4)]

slum joint *n.* [1930s–40s] (*US Und.*) a jewellery store. [SLUM *n.*[5] (1) + JOINT n.[4] (3)]

slummer *n.* [late 19C+] one who plays the tourist in impoverished areas, looking for 'atmosphere' and 'characters', but secure in the knowledge that one's real life is elsewhere. [SLUM *v.*[3] (2)]

slumming *n.* [mid-19C] the practice of passing counterfeit money. [? SLUM *v.*[2] (3)]

slummock *v.* (*also* **slummuck**) **1** [late 19C] to become run-down, slovenly. **2** [late 19C+] to move in a slovenly manner. **3** [1910s–40s] to clean carelessly or half-heartedly. [SE *slummocky*, slovenly]

slummy *n.*[1] **1** [late 19C–1930s] a servant girl. **2** [1920s–60s] a slum-dweller. **3** [1980s] an ill-dressed, unattractive woman. [SE *slum*]

slummy *n.*[2] [2000s] small change, coppers. [SLUM n.[5]]

slummy *adj.* [1940s] (*US*) socially inferior. [SE *slum*]

slums and bums *n.* [1970s+] (*US campus*) a course in urban local government. [SE *slum* + BUM n.[3] (1)]

slum-scribbler *n.* [mid-19C] (*UK Und.*) a writer of begging letters, posing as an honest labourer fallen on hard times. [SLUM n.[2] (4)]

slum the gorger *v.* [mid-19C] **1** to cheat on the sly, to be an *eye servant*, i.e. a servant who works hard only when the master's or mistress's eye is on them. **2** to hide, to pass to a confederate. [SLUM v.[2] (3) + GORGER n.[1] (1)]

slum worker *n.* [1950s] (*US Und.*) one who sells cheap or imitation jewellery as its expensive equivalent. [SLUM n.[5] (1) + WORKER n.[1] (1)]

slung *adj.* **1** [1930s+] (*Aus.*) thrown from one's horse. **2** [1980s] acquitted. [SE *get slung off*, to be thrown]

slur *v.* [mid-17C–early 19C] (*UK Und.*) to cheat at dice, spec. to slide a dice out of the dice-box without actually letting it roll. [? Low Ger. *slurrn*, to drag the feet]

slurb *n.* [1970s] (*US*) the dormitory suburbs of a big city, mass-produced, featureless, sprawling and aesthetically null. [SE *slum* + su*burb*]

slurp *n.* [1960s] (*Aus.*) a drink.

slurp *v.* [1990s+] to consume, to eat.

slush *n.*[1] **1** [mid-19C+] (*orig. US*) (*also* **slushiness**) blatant sentimentality. **2** [late 19C] worthless information. [SE *slush*, watery, melted snow]

slush *n.*[2] **1** [mid-19C+] (*UK tramp*) the tea or coffee available in lodging houses. **2** [late 19C] (*US*) beer. **3** [20C+] any form of sloppy food, e.g. a thin stew. **4** [1980s] (*US campus*) a heavy drinker. [RN jargon *slush*, the refuse fat from boiled meat, the selling of which was a perk accorded the SLUSHY n. (1) or ship's cook; (4) SLUSH UP v.]

slush *n.*[3] [1920s+] (*UK Und.*) forged, counterfeit money. [for ety. *see* SLUSH n.[2]]

slush *n.*[4] *see* SLUSHY n.

slush-bucket *n.* (*also* **slush-tub**) [late 18C–mid-19C] an ill-mannered eater; one who eats much greasy food. [RN jargon *slush*, refuse fat + SE *bucket*]

slushed *adj.* [1940s] (*US Und.*) drunk. [? var. on SLOSHED adj.]

slusher *n.*[1] [late 19C] a period of (very) wet weather.

slusher *n.*[2] [1920s] a printer and distributor of counterfeit notes. [SLUSH n.[3]]

slusher *n.*[3] *see* SLUSHY n.

slush fund *n.* [late 19C+] an emergency fund for unforeseen expenditure, esp. that which may be illegal or extra-legal; such funds came into prominence during the Watergate affair of 1972. [fig. use of RN jargon *slush*, refuse fat, the sale of which was a cook's perk (*see* SLUSH n.[2])]

slushie *n. see* SLUSHY n.

slushiness *n. see* SLUSH n.[1] (1).

slush lamp *n. see* SLUSHY n. (2).

slush pile *n.* [1960s] average or run-of-the-mill people, objects or situations. [orig. publishing jargon *slush pile*, unsolicited manuscripts, or those unmediated by an agent]

slush pump *n.* [1930s–50s] (*US*) a trombone. [the spittle that collects while playing it]

slush-tub *n. see* SLUSH-BUCKET n.

slush up *v.* [1900s–40s] (*US Und.*) to drink.

slushy *n.* (*also* **slush, slusher, slushie**) **1** [early 19C+] a cook. **2** [mid-19C–1900s] (*Aus.*) (*also* **slush lamp**) a fat lamp, a wick placed in a dish of fat. **3** [late 19C+] (*Aus./N.Z.*) a cook's assistant, esp. for a shearing gang. **4** [20C+] any unskilled assistant; a servant, thus a derog. label. [orig. naut. jargon *slushy*, a ship's cook, who collected and sold refuse fat or *slush*]

slushy *adj.* [1910s+] sentimental. [SLUSH n.[1] (1)]

slushy *v.* [1900s] (*Aus.*) to cook; to work as a cook. [SLUSHY n. (1)]

slut *n.* **1** [1900s] (*US*) in cards, the queen. **2** [1980s+] (*US campus*) an affectionate term of address among women. **3** [1980s+] an habitué; usu. in combs, e.g. *media slut*. [SE *slut*, a promiscuous woman]

slut hut *n.* [1980s+] (*US gay*) **1** a gay brothel. **2** anywhere that gay men congregate for sex. ['homosexualizing' of SE *slut*, usu. applied to women + *hut*]

slut lamp *n.* [late 19C–1930s] (*US, Western*) an improvised lamp made of a twist of rag in a container of grease (cf. BITCH n.[2]). [ety. unknown]

slut-puppy *n.* [1980s+] **1** (*US*) a derog. term for a lesbian. **2** (*orig. US campus*) a promiscuous woman. **3** (*US gay*) a promiscuous or available man. [SE *slut* + play on DOG n.[3] (8)]

slut's wool *n.* [mid-19C] particles of lint and similar household dirt that gather behind or beneath sofas, tables or beds (often following the shaking of an eiderdown).

sly *n. see* SLY-GROG n.

sly *adj.* **1** [mid-19C+] (*orig. Aus.*) illicit, illegal. **2** [1950s] (*US teen*) excellent. [SE *sly*, secretive, underhand]

sly-bag *n.* [1940s+] (*Aus.*) a cunning person. [SE *sly* + -BAG sfx]

slyboots *n.* [late 17C+] a cunning, deceptive person, usu. with overtones of affection rather than an expression of outright disapproval.

sly-grog *n.* (*also* **sly**) [late 19C+] (*Aus./N.Z.*) liquor sold without a license, often through a *sly-grog shop*; thus *sly-groggery, sly-grog shanty/house*, an illicit saloon or liquor store; *sly-grogger/-groggist/-grogster, sly-grog man*, an illicit liquor seller; *sly-grogging*, selling liquor illegally. [SLY adj. (1) + GROG n.[1] (1)]

sly, slick and wicked *n.* [1920s+] (*US Black*) an individual who plans to be caught out in a small act of deceit, which exposé will facilitate plans for a larger confidence trick.

S/M *see under* S AND M.

smaak *v.* [1960s+] (*S.Afr*) to like, to enjoy, to 'fancy' someone. [synon. Afk.]

smabble *see under* SNABBLE.

smack *n.*[1] (*orig. US*) **1** [late 17C; mid-19C+] a try, a 'go'; thus *have a smack at*, to have a go at. **2** [late 19C] a telling-off, a punishment. **3** [20C+] a blow, a slap.

smack *n.*[2] (*US Black*) **1** [19C–1940s] a kiss. **2** [1950s–60s] sexual intercourse. [SE 17C–early 19C]

smack *n.*[3] [mid-19C+] a liking for. [SE *smack*, enjoyment, appreciation]

smack *n.*[4] **1** [1900s] a pound sterling. **2** [1910s+] (*US tramp*) a dollar. [? the noise of smacking it down on the table]

smack *n.*[5] (*US Und.*) **1** [1900s–40s] a form of confidence trick based on matching pennies. **2** [1930s+] the use of a specially doctored coin for heads-or-tails gambling. [the trickster smacking his hand on the coin as he catches it]

smack *n.*[6] (*also* **smock**) **1** [1930s+] (*drugs*) heroin. **2** [1990s+] adulterated cocaine. [Yid. *schmeck*, to hit, to sniff (cf. SCHMECK n.)]

smack *n.*[7] (*US Black/teen*) **1** [1960s] flirtatious talk. **2** [1980s+] nonsense, esp. malicious rumours. **3** [1990s+] aggressive talk. [SMACK v.[1] (2)]

smack *n.*[8] [1980s+] (*US campus*) an overly hard-working student. [? they are constantly smacking their head in concentration]

smack *v.*[1] **1** [late 16C–1960s] to kiss. **2** [late 17C+] to hit, to beat. **3** [1930s–50s] to throw (into). **4** [1990s+] (*US Black gang*) to act sycophantically, to toady.

smack *v.*[2] (*also* **smack ass**) [1990s+] to be very good, to excel.

smack *adv.* (*also* **smacko**) [late 18C+] **1** directly. **2** immediately. [echoic/SMACK v.[1] (2)]

smack a blue *v.* [1930s+] (*Aus.*) to get into trouble. [SMACK v.[1] (2) + BLUE n.[7]]

smackarola *n. see* SMACKEROO n.

smack around *v.* [1920s] (*US*) to travel in an ostentatious manner, to parade.

smack ass v. see SMACK v.[2].

smack-bang adv. see SLAP-BANG adv.

smack calf-skin v. [late 18C–19C] (UK Und.) to kiss the Bible when taking an oath. [SMACK v.[1] (1) + the SE calfskin cover]

smack-dab adv. [late 19C+] (US) exactly, precisely, entirely. [echoic + SMACK adv.]

smackdown n. [1990s+] (US campus) a (punishment) beating. [SMACK DOWN v.]

smack down v. [late 19C+] (US) **1** to hit hard, esp. to hit in the face. **2** to tell off, to reprimand, to put in one's place. [SMACK v.[1] (1)]

smacked out adj. (also smacked back, smacked up) [1980s+] (drugs) under the influence of heroin. [SMACK n.[6] (1)]

smacker n.[1] **1** [early 19C] a blow, a slap. **2** [mid-19C+] a kiss. **3** [1980s+] (N.Z.) the mouth. [the sound/SMACK v.[1]]

smacker n.[2] [1920s+] (orig. US) a dollar or a pound sterling; usu. in pl. [ext. of SMACK n.[4]]

smacker n.[3] [1930s] a perfect example. [SMACK adv. (1)]

smacker n.[4] [1930s+] (Aus.) a boy, a young man. [on pattern of CRACKER n.[12] (1)]

smackeroo n. (also smackarola, smackola) [1940s+] a dollar or a pound sterling; usu. in pl. [ext. SMACKER n.[2] + -EROO sfx/ -OLA sfx]

smackeroo gun n. [1980s+] (Aus. prison) a hypodermic syringe. [SMACK n.[6] (1) + GUN n.[1] (3)]

smack freak n. [1970s+] (drugs) a heroin addict. [SMACK n.[6] (1) + FREAK sfx]

smack-head n. [1960s+] (drugs) a heroin addict. [SMACK n.[6] (1) + -HEAD sfx (3)]

smacking adj. [19C+] good, excellent. [orig. dial.]

smacking-cove n. [late 17C–early 19C] a coachman. [SMACK v.[1] (2), i.e. his whipping of the horses + COVE n. (1)]

smack in the eye n.[1] [20C+] a pie. [rhy. sl.]

smack in the eye n.[2] [1940s+] a rebuff, a rejection, a severe and surprising disappointment.

smacko n.[1] [1930s] (US Und.) a car that has been rebuilt following a serious crash. [it has been smacked]

smacko n.[2] [1940s] (US Black) a street person; a thug. [SMACK v.[1] (2), i.e. one who either hits or, lit. or fig., is likely to be hit]

smacko adv. see SMACK adv.

smackola n. see SMACKEROO n.

smack on adj. [1950s] good, wonderful. [SMACK ON adv.]

smack on adv. [late 19C+] accurately, right in the middle of. [ext. SMACK adv. (1)]

smack pack n. [1990s+] (Aus. drugs) a 'starter kit' of heroin, containing a portion of the drug and the equipment for injection. [SMACK n.[6] (1) + SE pack; assonance]

smack-smooth adj. [late 18C–mid-19C] absolutely level, perfectly smooth. [SMACK adv.]

smackster n. [1990s+] (US drugs) a heroin addict. [SMACK n.[6] (1) + -STER sfx]

smacktastic adj. [2000s] (US Black) physically violent. [SMACK n.[1] (3) + -TASTIC sfx]

smack the bit v. [mid-19C] (UK Und.) to share out booty. [SE smack down + BIT n.[1] (1)]

smack-up n. (Aus./N.Z.) **1** [1900s–10s] a fight. **2** [1950s] a caning at school. **3** [1950s+] a crash, an accident. [SMACK v.[1] (2)]

smack up v. **1** [1910s+] to attack physically; thus smacked up, bested in a fight. **2** [1930s] to lay a criminal charge on someone. [SMACK-UP n.]

small and early n. [mid-19C–1910s] (UK society) an informal dance (as opposed to a full-scale ball), to which few guests are invited and which starts early and ends before midnight.

small beans n. [20C+] an insignificant thing; usu. in negative.

small beer n. [17C+] inferior things, worthless or second-rate matters; thus THINK SMALL BEER OF v.; chronicle small beer, to record insignificant events. [SE small beer, weak, inferior-quality beer]

small beer adj. [17C–19C] inferior, insignificant, worthless. [SMALL BEER n.]

small bones n. [late 19C] (Aus.) insignificant; thus make small bones (of), to deal with easily.

small-bore adj. [1900s] (US) trivial, insignificant. [SE small bore, a small-calibre gun barrel]

small bread n. [1940s–50s] (US Black) anything insignificant, esp. a small amount of money. [SE small + BREAD n.[1] (2)]

small change n. [1940s+] (US) **1** an insignificant, weak person. **2** as a term of address to a smaller person. [monetary imagery]

small-change adj. [1970s+] (US) insignificant. [SMALL CHANGE n. (1)]

small cheque n. [late 19C] a dram; thus to knock down a cheque, to spend all one's money on alcohol.

small coals n. [mid-19C] that which is inferior, worthless, second-rate.

smaller n. [mid-19C] (US) a glass of undiluted spirits.

smallest room n. [1930s+] a euph. for the lavatory in a private house.

small fortune n. [20C+] (orig. US) a very large sum of money, esp. when paid out for some commodity. [understatement]

small gang v. [mid–late 19C] to rob in the street. [? the 'gang' requires only 1 or 2 people]

small meat n. [1960s+] (US gay) a small penis (cf. BACON n.[1]). [SE small + MEAT n. (2)]

small nickel n. [20C+] (US gambling) a bet of $50. [SE small + NICKEL n.[1] (6)]

small pipe n. [1940s–50s] (US) an alto saxophone.

small-potato adj. **1** [mid–late 19C] (orig. US) insignificant, irrelevant. **2** [1900s] (also small potatoes) selfish, mean. [SMALL POTATOES n.]

small potatoes n. (also mean potatoes, small potato) (orig. US) **1** [mid-19C+] something, or someone, seen as insignificant, of little worth, irrelevant; ext. as small potatoes and few in a/the hill. **2** [1920s+] in fig. use, a hanger-on, one who acts as a parasite on the powerful or influential.

small shit n. [1970s+] (US) someone or something insignificant, unimportant. [SHIT n.[2] (1)]

small timber n. see TIMBER n. (2).

small time n. [1960s] (US) a term of insulting address. [SMALL-TIME adj.]

small-time adj. [1920s+] second-rate, inferior. [theatre jargon small time, a vaudeville circuit for second-rate acts]

small-time v. [1970s+] (orig. US) to occupy oneself with minor business, usu. in a criminal context. [SMALL-TIME adj.]

small-time joint n. [1970s+] (S.Afr.) the lowest class of shebeen; thus big-time joint, a superior shebeen. [SMALL-TIME adj. + JOINT n.[4] (3)]

small-timer n. [1920s+] a mediocrity, a failure. [SMALL-TIME adj.]

smaltzy adj. see SCHMALTZY adj.

smarm n. [1930s+] flattering or toadying behaviour, an unctuous bearing. [backform. f. SMARMY adj. (1)]

smarm v. [1930s+] to toady, to ingratiate. [backform. f. SMARMY adj. (1)]

smarmy adj. **1** [1920s+] unctuous, ingratiating. **2** [1950s+] smug and self-righteous. **3** [1990s+] of a voice, sonorous, rich. **4** [2000s] unpleasant. [SE smarm, to smooth down with some form of greasy substance]

smart n. [1900s–60s] used insultingly, a 'clever' person.

smart alec(k) n. (also smart Elick, wise alec(k)) [mid-19C+] (orig. US) an unpleasantly conceited, smug person; as v., to act in this way. [proper name Alec Hoag, a celebrated New York City thief of 1840s, who, with his wife Melinda and his accomplice French Jack, specialized in the PANEL GAME n.[1]; for a detailed account of Hoag and his career, see Cohen (ed.), Studies in Slang I (1985)]

smart-alec(k) *adj.* (*also* **smart-alecky, smart-alexist**) [20C+] cocky, conceited, smug; occas. in fig. use of inanimate objects. [SMART ALEC(K) n.]

smart apple *n.* [20C+] (*US*) a bright, intelligent person.

smart-arse *n.* (*also* **smart-ass**) [1960s+] **1** (*orig. Aus.*) one who sees themselves as cleverer than they really are. **2** (*US campus*) a hard-working, academically successful student; any offensive male. **3** self-confidence; cockiness. [SMART-ARSED adj.]

smart-arse *v.* (*also* **smart-ass**) [1960s+] to cheek someone, to be impudent to. [SMART-ARSE n. (1)]

smart-arsed *adj.* (*also* **smart-arse, smart-ass, smart-assed**) [1950s+] self-opinionatedly clever, smug, complacent. [SE *smart* + ARSE n.¹ (4)/ASS n. (5)/-ASS sfx/-ASSED sfx]

smart as a carrot new scraped *phr.* [late 18C–19C] smartly dressed.

smart as a rat with a gold tooth *phr.* [1970s] (*Aus.*) very smartly dressed.

smart-ass *see under* SMART-ARSE.

smart blunt *n.* [mid-19C] (*UK Und.*) forfeit money. [SE *smart*, to feel pain + BLUNT n.¹]

smart bucks *n.* (*also* **smart dollar**) [1950s] (*US Und.*) money gained through crime. [BUCK n.³ (3)]

smart cookie *n.* [1940s+] (*orig. US*) a bright, opportunistic person; also ironically. [SE *smart* + COOKIE n.²]

smart Elick *n. see* SMART ALEC(K) n.

smarten someone (up) *v. see* SMART SOMEONE UP v.

smart-eye *v.* [2000s] (*US*) to stare in a challenging manner.

smart guy *see under* WISE GUY.

smarti(e)pants *n. see* SMARTY-BOOTS n.

smart money *n.* **1** [1920s+] (*orig. US gambling*) (*also* **wise money**) the way in which experienced or knowledgeable gamblers bet, the opinion of the experienced bettor. **2** [1920s+] (*orig. US*) in fig. use, general good sense. **3** [1950s] (*US Und.*) a clever and successful criminal. [note milit. jargon *smart money*, compensation for injuries received in service]

smart-mouth *n.* [1960s+] (*US*) **1** (*also* **smarty-mouth**) an insolent person. **2** cheek, insolence.

smart-mouth *adj.* (*also* **smart-mouthed**) [1980s+] (*US*) cheeky, disrespectful. [SMART-MOUTH n.]

smart mouth *v.* [1970s+] (*orig. US Black*) to attack verbally, to slander; to be cheeky, to tease. [SMART-MOUTH n.]

smartpants *n. see* SMARTY-BOOTS n.

smarts *n.* [1960s+] (*orig. US*) wit, intelligence.

smart someone up *v.* (*also* **smarten someone (up)**) [1920s–60s] (*US*) to pass on information, to explain.

smarty *n.* **1** [mid-19C+] (*orig. US*) an unpleasantly conceited, 'clever' person; also one who is 'too smart to work' and lives by his wits (prob. illegally). **2** [late 19C; 1950s] a fashionable person. **3** [20C+] a general, usu. negative, form of address. **4** [1950s] an aristocrat. **5** [1960s] (*US campus*) a hard worker; an intellectual success.

smarty *adj.* [late 19C–1960s] (*US*) clever, esp. in ironic use. [SMARTY n. (1)]

smarty-boots *n.* (*also* **smarti(e)pants, smartpants, smarty-drawers, smarty-pants**) **1** [1930s+] (*orig. US*) a general term of usu. light-hearted abuse, implying someone is smug or 'clever'; also attrib. **2** [1940s–50s] (*US Black*) a young man at the outset of his sexual career. [note the nickname *Smartyboots* given to essayist and critic Cyril Connolly (1903–74)]

smarty-mouth *n. see* SMART-MOUTH n. (1).

smash *n.*¹ **1** [late 18C–mid-19C] mashed turnips. **2** [mid-19C] mashed potatoes. [note 1960s+ *Smash*, brandname for instant mashed potatoes]

smash *n.*² [late 18C–1900s] counterfeit money. [? it smashes the hopes of those who use it]

smash *n.*³ **1** [early 19C+] bankruptcy, financial collapse. **2** [mid-19C+] (*US*) a failure, a disaster; thus GO TO SMASH v. [late 19C]

an argument. **4** [1900s] a glamorous social event. **5** [1920s+] a great success, a 'smash hit'.

smash *n.*⁴ [mid-19C–1950s] (*UK Und.*) a smash-and-grab raid.

smash *n.*⁵ **1** [mid-19C+] iced brandy and water. **2** [1950s+] (*US Black*) wine. [abbr. SE *brandy-smash*]

smash *n.*⁶ [mid-19C+] cash, usu. change. [rhy. sl.]

smash *n.*⁷ [late 19C] (*UK prison*) tobacco. [ext. of SMASH n.⁶, i.e. its role as prison currency]

smash *n.*⁸ **1** [late 19C+] a heavy blow. **2** [1910s+] (*Aus.*) a violent, frightening man, usu. one who is drunk.

smash *n.*⁹ [1910s–20s] (*US*) a time, a 'go', each.

smash *v.*¹ **1** [late 17C–early 19C] (*UK Und.*) to kick downstairs. **2** [late 18C+] (*also* **go smash, smash up**) to fail financially, to be ruined, to become bankrupt. **3** [mid–late 19C] to beat. **4** [1900s] (*Aus.*) to spend recklessly. **5** [1900s] (*US campus*) to fail in recitation. **6** [1920s] (*US*) to dismiss from a job. **7** [1960s] to be a smash hit.

smash *v.*² [late 18C–19C] to pass counterfeit money. [SMASH n.²]

smash *v.*³ [mid-19C+] to give or obtain change for a note. [SMASH n.⁶]

smash *v.*⁴ [1990s+] to paint a piece of graffito on a wall or similar surface. [cognate with BOMB v.¹ (4)]

smash *adv.* [2000s] a general intensifier.

smash and grab *n.* [20C+] a cab. [rhy. sl.]

smashed *adj.* **1** [mid-19C; 1940s+] very drunk (cf. ANNIHILATED adj.). **2** [late 19C] infatuated with; usu. with *on*. **3** [mid–late 19C] (*also* **smashed-up**) impoverished. **4** [1960s+] intoxicated with a drug, esp. cannabis or LSD. **5** [1980s] very tired. [SE *smash*/SMASH v.¹]

smashed out *adj.* [2000s] overwhelmed.

smasher *n.*¹ (*UK Und.*) **1** [late 18C–1910s] one who makes or passes counterfeit money. **2** [mid-19C] in fig. use, one who commits a libel. **3** [1920s] a receiver of stolen goods. **4** [1940s] a receiver who specializes in buying and recycling stolen money. [SMASH v.²]

smasher *n.*² **1** [late 18C+] anything exceptionally large or excellent. **2** [19C] a hard blow, lit. or fig. **3** [mid-19C] a crushing remark, a highly negative review. **4** [1930s+] a pretty woman, an attractive person of either sex. **5** [1940s+] an admirable, likeable person.

smash-feeder *n.* (*UK Und.*) **1** [mid-19C] a silver spoon. **2** [mid-19C–1900s] a Britannia-metal spoon, made from a metal resembling silver but in fact an alloy of tin and regulus of antimony. [SMASH n.² + SE *feeder*; the best counterfeit coins were made from such spoons]

smashing *adj.* (*also* **smasho**) [mid-19C+] wonderful, delightful, excellent. [i.e. it *smashes* all rivals]

smash it *v.* [1960s] (*US campus*) to do well in an examination.

smash me! *excl.* [mid-19C] (*US*) an excl. of surprise, disbelief.

smash my glim! *excl.* (*also* **smash my apple-cart!**) [mid-19C] a general excl., synon. with *blast my eyes!*

smasho *adj. see* SMASHING adj.

smash-on *adj.* [1950s] a general intenisifier.

smash one's teapot *v.* [late 19C] (*UK prison*) for a prisoner to forfeit the privilege – gained for good behaviour – of substituting tea for the usual gruel.

smash the teapot *v.* [late 19C] to abandon one's pledge of abstinence (taken earlier at the urging of the Salvation Army or a similar teetotalist body). [the symbolic rejection of tea as one's sole liquid stimulant]

smash up *v. see* SMASH v.¹ (2).

smashy! *excl.* [mid-19C] (*US*) an excl. of surprise and delight.

smatter-hauling *n.* [mid–late 19C] (*UK Und.*) the stealing of handkerchiefs. [SCHMATTE n. + SE *haul*]

smear *n.*¹ **1** [early 18C] (*also* **smeer**) a house-painter. **2** [early 18C–early 19C] a plasterer. **3** [1940s–50s] (*Aus.*) the corpse of a murdered person. [metonymy]

smear *n.*[2] [mid-19C] (*US campus*) food, esp. in the context of a formal dinner.

smear *n.*[3] **1** [1920s] something showy, ostentatious. **2** [1920s+] (*orig. US*) a slanderous or defamatory remark; an attempt to defame by slander.

smear *v.* **1** [late 19C+] (*orig. US*) to knock unconscious, to beat up, to hit. **2** [1910s–30s] (*US*) to defeat, to trounce. **3** [1930s–50s] to kill, to murder. **4** [1930s+] (*US*) to bribe. **5** [1930s+] to slander, esp. to cause trouble for someone by discrediting their reputation.

smear and smudge *n.* [2000s] a judge. [rhy. sl.]

smear-gelt *n.* [late 18C–mid-19C] a bribe. [Yid. *smiergelt*, a bribe, lit. 'money for greasing' (the palm)]

smears *n.* [1970s] (*drugs*) LSD (cf. A n.[3]). [it has been smeared onto paper or tablets]

smeb *v.* [2000s] (*US Black*) to adopt the strutting, rolling walk trad. associated with a pimp. [ety. unknown]

smeck *see under* SCHMECK.

smeer *n. see* SMEAR n.[1] (1).

smeerlap *n.* [mid-19C+] (*S.Afr.*) a general term of abuse, a 'bastard', a 'swine'. [Du. *smeerlap*, 'grease cloth'; i.e. a cloth used for wiping spillage, stains etc]

smeg *n.* [1980s+] **1** *smeg*ma. **2** a dirty, unkempt person. [abbr.; (2) f. (1)]

smeg! *excl.* [1980s+] a general excl. of annoyance, surprise; thus *smegging*. [SMEG n. (1); coined as a deliberate euph. for FUCK! excl. by Grant Naylor, co-scriptwriter of the BBC's *Red Dwarf* science fantasy series, from 1988]

smeggy *adj.* [1980s+] dirty, unkempt. [SMEG n.]

smeghead *n.* [1980s+] a general term of abuse. [SMEG n. (1) + -HEAD sfx (1)]

smell *v.*[1] [1930s+] to appear, to seem, usu. with negative overtones.

smell *v.*[2] [1960s] (*US drugs*) to inhale a narcotic drug.

smell *v.*[3] [1990s+] (*US Black*) to understand.

Smellbourne *n.* (*also* **Smellbun, Smellburn**) [late 19C–1910s] (*Aus.*) Melbourne, capital city of Victoria. [coined by *The Bulletin* magazine. The name reflects the city's poor sewage, which was simply dumped into the Yarra River]

smeller *n.*[1] **1** [early 17C] (*UK Und.*) a garden. **2** [late 19C+] (*N.Z.*) an unpleasant person. **3** [1910s] (*Aus.*) a camel. [positive and negative uses of SE *smell* v.]

smeller *n.*[2] **1** [late 17C–1940s] the nose (cf. SMELLERS n.). **2** [early–mid-19C] a blow on the nose. **3** [late 19C] (*US*) a spy, a prying person. **4** [late 19C–1920s] anything exceptional, esp. very strong, very aggressive etc. [SE *smell* v.; (4) the 'smell' is fig.]

smeller *n.*[3] [late 19C–1930s] a heavy fall; thus *come a smeller*, to tumble down heavily. [one *smells* the ground on hitting it]

smellers *n.* **1** [late 17C–early 19C] the nostrils (cf. SMELLER n.[2]). **2** [late 18C–early 19C] a cat's whiskers. [SE *smell* v.]

smell garlic *v.* [late 19C–1920s] to be suspicious of people or situations. [? underpinned by xenophobia, i.e. the image of garlic as 'funny foreign food']

smell hell *v.*[1] [mid-19C+] (*US*) to face danger.

smell hell *v.*[2] *see* SEE HELL v.

smelling-cheat *n.* (*also* **smelling-chete**) **1** [mid-16C–17C] the nose. **2** [mid-16C–early 19C] a garden, an orchard. **3** [late 17C–early 19C] a nosegay. [SE *smell* + CHEAT n. (1)]

smell like a ram-goat *v.* [20C+] (*W.I.*) to smell disgusting, esp. after one has passed out drunk and urinated down one's legs.

smell like a rose *v.* [20C+] (*US*) to appear pure and innocent.

smell one's hat *v.* [late 19C] to pray into one's hat on reaching one's pew in church.

smell-powder *n.* [early 19C] a duellist. [the *powder*-powered pistols that are used in duelling]

smell-smock *n.* **1** [16C] a derog. term for a priest. **2** [late 16C–mid-18C] a pimp; thus *smock-smelling*, pimping (cf. ABBOT ON THE CROSS n.). **3** [mid-17C] the penis. [SE *smell* + *smock*/ SMOCK n.[1]]

smelly belly *n.* [1990s+] (*UK juv.*) a person who is playing the fool.

smell you (later) *phr.* [1990s+] (*US campus*) goodbye.

smell your mother! *excl.* [1990s+] an insult, usu. accompanied by waving one's middle finger under the insultee's nose; the implication is of recent sexual foreplay with the victim's mother.

smelly welly *n.* [1990s+] (*UK juv.*) a poor person who looks like a tramp.

smelt *n.* [late 17C–mid-19C] (*UK Und.*) a half-guinea or 10 shillings (50p). [ety. unknown, but E.P. suggests SE *melt*, to melt down; thus a half-guinea is a 'melted down' guinea]

smicket *n.* [late 17C–mid-19C] the vagina. [*double entendre* for SE *smicket*, a woman's smock or chemise]

smiddys *n.* [1990s+] the female breasts. [var. on TITTY n.[1] (1)]

smidge *n.* [20C+] a very small amount. [SE *smidegon*]

smiggins *n.* (*also* **smiggen**) [19C] (*UK Und.*) a poor-quality soup served up to convicts, esp. those imprisoned on the hulks. [ety. unknown; ? SE *smidgen*, i.e. the small amount of appetizing meat or vegetables present in the broth]

smile *n.*[1] (*also* **fancy smile**) [mid-19C–1940s] (*orig. US*) a drink, usu. of whisky. [i.e. it promotes a smile or one's lips open in a 'smile' as one drinks]

smile *n.*[2] **1** [1910s–40s] the gap of bare flesh between a stocking and a suspender belt. **2** [1950s+] bare flesh appearing between the top of a skirt or pair of trousers and the shirt, blouse etc.

smile *v.* **1** [mid-19C–1930s] (*orig. US*) to drink, esp. whisky. **2** [late 19C] to buy a (round of) drinks. [SMILE n.[1]]

smile and smirk *n.* [20C+] work. [rhy. sl.]

smile and titter *n. see* GIGGLE AND TITTER n.

smile like a basket of chips *v. see* GRIN LIKE A BASKET OF CHIPS v.

smiler *n.* **1** [mid-19C] (*US*) a drinker. **2** [late 19C] a form of shandygaff, a mixture of beer and ginger beer. [? SMILE v.]

smiley *n.*[1] [1980s+] (*US*) a man who is showing a slice of flesh above the top of his trousers. [SMILE n.[2] (2)]

smiley *n.*[2] [1990s+] (*S.Afr.*) a sheep's or goat's head (sometimes split in half), cleaned and grilled or stewed with or without the tongue and brain. [the 'grinning' aspect of the cooked head]

smiling faces *n.* [1970s] (*US Black*) hypocrites, false friends.

smim *n.* [1990s+] (*UK juv.*) one who is both highly conformist and physically uncoordinated. [? SE *spastic* + *mimic*]

smirk *n.* [late 17C–18C] 'A finical [finicky], spruce Fellow' (B.E.). [SE *smirk*, an affected, simpering smile]

smish *n.* (*also* **smisk**) [mid-18C–19C] a shirt. [abbr. COMMISSION n.]

smitchy *adj.* [late 19C] tiny, insignifcant.

smiter *n.* [late 17C–mid-19C] the arm. [SE *smite*, to hit]

smithereen *v.* [1920s+] to break, to smash into pieces. [SMITHEREENS n.]

smithereens *n.* [mid-19C+] tiny fragments, atoms; esp. in phrs. *smashed to smithereens*, *blow/break/knock/split to/into smithereens*, to shatter into fragments, *all to smithereens*, smashed to pieces; often in fig. rather than lit. use. [SMITHERS n. + Irish dimin. *-een*. Share suggests Irish *smiodar*, a fragment]

smithers *n.* [mid-19C+] tiny fragments, atoms. [Lincolnshire dial. *smithers*, fragments, shivers; ult. ? SE *smite*, to smash]

Smithfield bargain *n.* **1** [late 17C–mid-19C] a bargain in which the buyer is cheated. **2** [early 18C–mid-19C] a marriage of convenience, based on financial interest. [proper name *Smithfield* market, London's horse and cattle, and later meat market, flourishing on the same site since the 12C]

Smithfield jade *n.* [late 17C] an inferior horse which has been smartened up to deceive a prospective buyer; in ext. use, a prostitute. [proper name *Smithfield* market, London's horse and cattle, and later meat market, flourishing on the same site since the 12C]

Smithy *n.* [1990s+] (*US Und.*) a firearm manufactured by Smith & Wesson.

smit smoke *n.* [1940s] (*US Black*) a highly intelligent Black person. [? SE *smart* + SMOKE n.⁶ (1)]

smoaky *adj. see* SMOKY adj.¹.

smock *n.*¹ [late 16C–early 18C] an immoral woman, esp. when used as a pfx in combs. below. [SE *smock*, a chemise or shift; thus generically 'womankind']

smock *n.*² *see* SMACK n.⁶.

smock *v.* [late 16C–mid-18C] to have sexual intercourse. [SE *smock*/SMOCK n.¹]

smock agent/attorney *n. see* SMOCK MERCHANT n.

smock alley *n.* 1 [17C–early 18C] those streets occupied by brothels. 2 [late 17C–19C] (*also* **smock castle**) the vagina (cf. ALLEY n.¹). [SMOCK n.¹ + SE *alley*; the actual Smock Alley, running off Petticoat Lane in London's East End, was well known in 17C for its brothels]

smockface *n.* [19C] a male homosexual; thus *smockfaced*, homosexual. [SE *smockface*, a pale, smooth or effeminate face; thus one who is so endowed]

smock-faced *adj.* [mid-17C–mid-19C] attractive. [SE *smock*, a chemise; thus the smooth whiteness of the garment]

smock fair *n.* [17C] a gathering place of prostitutes. [SMOCK n.¹ + SE *fair*]

smock hunter *n.* (*also* **hunt-smock, smock hero/soldier**) [17C–early 18C] a womanizer. [SMOCK n.¹ + SE *hunter/hero/soldier*]

smock merchant *n.* (*also* **smock agent, …attorney, …tearer, …tenant, smockster**) [late 16C–early 17C] a pimp (cf. ABBOT ON THE CROSS n.). [SMOCK n.¹ + MERCHANT n./SE *agent/attorney/ tearer/tenant*]

smock pensioner *n.* [18C] a pimp, a kept man (cf. ABBOT ON THE CROSS n.). [SMOCK n.¹ + SE *pensioner*]

smock piece *n.* (*also* **smock servant**) [19C] a prostitute. [SMOCK n.¹ + PIECE n.¹ (1)/SE *servant*]

smock rampant *n.* [17C] a promiscuous woman, lit. one who raises her smock. [SMOCK n.¹ + SE *rampant*]

smock shop *n.* [17C] a brothel (cf. BANGING-SHOP n.). [SMOCK n.¹ + SE *shop*/SHOP n.¹ (1)]

smock soldier *n. see* SMOCK HUNTER n.

smockster/smock tearer/smock tenant *n. see* SMOCK MERCHANT n.

smock toy *n.* [late 16C–early 17C] 1 a mistress. 2 a woman's male lover. [SMOCK n.¹ + SE *toy*]

smock vermin *n.* [17C] prostitutes. [SMOCK n.¹ + SE *vermin*]

smogged *adj.* [20C+] (*US prison*) executed in the gas chamber. [SE *smog*, a dense, toxic fog]

Smoke, the *n.* 1 [mid-19C+] London, as regarded from the provinces, occas. as *Smokes*. 2 [mid-19C+] (*Aus./US*) any big city. 3 [1940s+] (*Aus.*) Sydney, Melbourne. [the pall of pollution that, before the clean air legislation of the 1950s, hung over the industrialized city]

smoke *n.*¹ [mid-16C] suspicion.

smoke *n.*² 1 [mid-16C+] myth, illusion, fantasy, esp. when actively promoted as disinformation or lies; thus *all smoke*, nonsense. 2 [late 19C] (*US*) a fuss.

smoke *n.*³ 1 [17C+] anything smokeable, a cigar, a pipe, a cigarette, tobacco. 2 [mid-19C+] the action of smoking a cigarette, cigar or pipe; thus *do a smoke*. 3 [20C+] (*drugs*) any form of smokeable drug, e.g. marijuana, opium, heroin and, latterly, crack cocaine. 4 [1900s–50s] the action of smoking opium. 5 [1930s+] a marijuana cigarette (cf. AFRICAN WOODBINE n.). 6 [1960s+] the action of smoking cannabis. 7 [1970s] nonsense. 8 [1980s+] crack cocaine (cf. BASE n.).

smoke *n.*⁴ [late 19C] (*Aus.*) a party. [SE *smoker*]

smoke *n.*⁵ [late 19C] (*US*) a portion or share taken from a can or pail of beer. [the putting of one's lips to the can and sucking down the beer resembles puffing on a pipe]

smoke *n.*⁶ 1 [late 19C+] a derog. term for a Black person (cf. BLACKBELLY n.). 2 [1920s–40s] as used by a Black person, thus not derog. 3 [1930s] (*US*) a Mexican (cf. BATO n.). 4 [2000s] (*US campus*) an attractive woman.

smoke *n.*⁷ [20C+] any cheap, rotgut alcohol, esp. denatured alcohol shaken up with water and drunk by down-and-out alcoholic tramps; thus *smoke bum*, a regular drinker of such alcohol. [the liquid turns cloudy when shaken]

smoke *n.*⁸ [1900s] (*US*) the ideal, the best.

smoke *n.*⁹ [1970s] (*US campus*) $1. [so small a sum 'goes up in smoke']

smoke *v.*¹ 1 [mid-16C–mid-19C] to suspect. 2 [late 16C] (*UK Und.*) for a member of a pickpocket team to elect a potential victim. 3 [late 16C–mid-17C] to be discovered. 4 [late 16C–1930s] (*also* **smoke out**) to discover, to unmask. 5 [18C–mid-19C] as imper., take notice of. 6 [mid-19C] (*US*) to understand. [SE *smoked out/ smoke out*]

smoke *v.*² 1 [17C] to have sexual intercourse (cf. BANG v.¹). 2 [18C] to beat, to kill. [SE *smoke*, to move or ride at a rapid pace]

smoke *v.*³ [late 17C–mid-19C] to ridicule or attack a stranger verbally as soon as they enter the room. [the image of blowing smoke deliberately in another's face]

smoke *v.*⁴ 1 [late 17C–mid-19C] to cheat, to deceive; thus *smoker*, one who deceives. 2 [20C+] (*US*) to fool, to give the wrong idea; thus *smoke up*, to confess, to tell the truth. [one blows *smoke* in the victim's eyes]

smoke *v.*⁵ 1 [mid–late 19C] (*UK teen*) to blush; thus *smoking*, blushing. 2 [20C+] (*US*) to get angry. 3 [1970s] (*US*) to be dangerous (for criminal activity), i.e. to be HOT adj.² (1).

smoke *v.*⁶ [late 19C+] (*Aus./N.Z.*) to make a hasty departure. [SE late 17C–19C; the fig. smoke exuded by one's rapid departure]

smoke *v.*⁷ 1 [1910s+] to throw very fast, usu. of a ball. 2 [1920s+] to kill, to murder, to shoot at (with a firearm). 3 [1970s+] to beat comprehensively (at sport). 4 [1970s+] (*US campus*) to perform well. 5 [1980s+] to beat up. [all depend on the imagery of smoke being created by the energy involved in the action; (2) has the added image of smoke coming from the gun]

smoke *v.*⁸ [1960s+] to perform fellatio; thus *smoke it!*, an excl. of dismissal or derision. [note Fr. *faire une pipe*, to fellate]

smoke a bowl *v.* [1970s+] (*US*) to smoke marijuana, usu. from a pipe. [SE *smoke* + BOWL n. (2); ? imported by veterans of the Vietnam War (1964–75), where pipes, rather than cigarettes were the preferred means of smoking]

smoke a horn *v.* [2000s] to fellate. [SMOKE v.⁸ +HORN n.² (1)]

smoke a toke *v.* [1980s+] (*US*) to smoke marijuana. [SE *smoke* + TOKE n.² (2); lit. 'smoke a smoke', thus as much f. assonance as accuracy]

smoke bacon *v.* [2000s] to work well and enthusiastically.

Smokeburg *n.* [late 19C–1900s] (*US*) Pittsburgh. [its polluting heavy industry]

smoked *adj.* 1 [mid-19C+] (*US*) drunk. 2 [1920s–30s] emotional. 3 [1970s+] intoxicated by cannabis. [fig. uses of SE *smoke*/ SMOKE v.⁷]

smoked Irishman *n. see* SUNBURNED IRISHMAN n.

smoked out *adj.* (*also* **smoke-out**) [1990s+] (*US Black gang*) heavily intoxicated by a drug, usu. marijuana or crack cocaine. [SMOKE n.³ (3)]

smoked (up) *adj.* [1900s] (*Aus./US*) Black.

smoked up *adj.* (*US drugs*) 1 [1970s+] intoxicated with cannabis. 2 [1990s+] intoxicated with crack cocaine. [SMOKE n.³ (3)]

smoked Yankee *n.* (*also* **smoked Yank**) [mid-19C; 1940s–50s] a derog. term for a Black person, usu. a freed slave (cf. BLACKBELLY n.). [SMOKY adj.² + SAmE *Yankee*/YANK n. (1)]

smoke-eater *n.* (*US*) 1 [late 19C–1930s] a firefighter. 2 [1920s] a heavy smoker. [SMOKE n.³ (1)/SE *smoke*]

smoke factory *n.* (*also* **smoke joint**) [1900s–20s] (*US*) an opium den. [SMOKE n.³ (4) + SE *factory*/JOINT n.⁴ (3)]

smokehead n. [1980s+] a crack cocaine addict. [SMOKE n.³ (8) + -HEAD sfx (3)]

smoke-ho n. see SMOKO n.

smoke-hole n. [early 18C] the mouth.

smoke-hound n. [1930s+] (US) an alcoholic who drinks rotgut alcohol. [SMOKE n.⁷ + HOUND sfx]

smoke house n.¹ see SMOKER n.¹ (2).

smoke house n.² see SMOKER n.² (2).

smoke it white v. [1960s+] (S.Afr. drugs) to smoke a mixture of marijuana and powdered Mandrax (methaqualone). [Mandrax capsules are white]

smoke joint n.¹ [1930s] (US) a bar that specializes in selling cheap, second-rate liquor. [SMOKE n.⁷ + JOINT n.⁴ (3)]

smoke joint n.² see SMOKE FACTORY n.

smoke like that phr. [2000s] (US Black) in phr. I can/can't smoke like that, I can/cannot do something.

smoke-o(h) n. see SMOKO n.

smoke one v. [20C+] (drugs) to smoke marijuana.

smoke-out adj. see SMOKED OUT adj.

smoke out v.¹ **1** [1920s+] to get information from someone. **2** [1970s+] (US Black) to impress, to outdo.

smoke out v.² [2000s] (US) to collapse, to break down. [automobile imagery]

smoke out v.³ see SMOKE v.¹ (4).

smoke over v. [1930s–50s] **1** (US Black) to stare at, to look at closely; usu. as smoke someone over. **2** (Aus.) to think over. [SMOKE v.¹ (4)/SMOKE v.¹ (5)]

smoke pad n. [1940s–50s] (drugs) anywhere that people can gather to smoke opium, later marijuana. [SMOKE n.³ (3) + PAD n.² (2)]

smoke-pole n. [1930s–40s] a firearm.

smokepole v. [1980s] (US campus) usu. of a man, to have sexual intercourse. [play on SMOKE-POLE n./SMOKE v.² (1) + POLE n.]

smoker n.¹ **1** [late 17C–early 19C] (UK Und.) a tobacconist. **2** [late 19C–1950s] (US) (also **smoke house**) the smoking carriage on a train.

smoker n.² **1** [19C] a chamberpot. **2** [1940s] (also **smoke house**) a privy. [the steam that rises from hot urine in cold weather]

smoker n.³ **1** [mid-19C] (US) a steamship. **2** [1960s+] a motor vehicle that emits stronger than average exhaust fumes.

smoker n.⁴ [mid-19C] (UK teen) one who blushes. [SMOKE v.⁵ (1)]

smoker n.⁵ [late 19C] a hot day.

smoker n.⁶ **1** [late 19C–1930s] (drugs) a smoker of opium. **2** [1960s+] a smoker of marijuana. **3** [1990s+] a smoker of crack cocaine.

smoker n.⁷ [1970s+] (US campus) something difficult. [it fig. makes the brain smoke with effort]

smoker n.⁸ [1970s+] a woman or homosexual man who performs fellatio. [SMOKE v.⁸]

smoker n.⁹ [1990s+] a pornographic film. [? SE smoker, a social gathering of men, sometimes with organized entertainment; such men-only gatherings might well run a pornographic movie]

smoker n.¹⁰ [1990s+] (US campus) a fool. [the negative effects of smoking, presumably used by non-smokers]

smoker's tickers n. [20C+] (Aus.) any variety of dark tobacco.

smoke rubber v. see BURN RUBBER v.

smoke screen n. [1940s] (US Black) underarm deodorant. [its masking of body odour]

smoke shop n. [1930s+] (US drugs) a place or shop where marijuana is sold, esp. somewhat openly. [SMOKE n.³ (3) + SE shop]

smokestack n. [late 19C+] (US Black) a Black person, esp. when very dark.

smokestack v. [1970s] (US) to talk boastfully. [one 'blows off steam']

smoke-stick n. [1900s–40s] a firearm.

smoke the habit off v. [1930s–50s] (US drugs) for an opium user to smoke heavily after a period of abstinence. [HABIT n. (3)]

smoke the White House cigar v. [2000s] of a woman, to fellate. [the Bill Clinton/Monica Lewinsky liaison + SMOKE v.⁸]

smoke-up n. [1960s] a break for smoking.

smoke up v. (US drugs) **1** [1900s] to smoke opium. **2** [1960s+] to smoke cannabis.

smoke wagon n.¹ [1900s–60s] **1** (US Und.) a revolver, a pistol. **2** (US) a taxi-cab.

smoke wagon n.² [2000s] (US Black) a large and smoky marijuana cigarette (cf. AFRICAN WOODBINE n.).

smokey see also under SMOKY.

smokey n.¹ [1930s] (US Und.) an opium addict. [SMOKE n.³ (3)]

smokey n.² [1980s+] (Aus. prison) a mysterious or private person; a 'closeted' homosexual.

smoking adj. **1** [1960s+] first-rate, excellent. **2** [1970s+] (US Black) very urgent, very excited, esp. in a sexual context. **3** [1970s+] (US campus) difficult, intense. **4** [1980s+] (US Black) attractive, well-dressed, elegant. **5** [2000s] of a place, tense, expectant. [orig. jazz use smoking, technically skilled]

smoking gun n. [1990s+] (drugs) a mixture of heroin and cocaine. [its powerful effects]

smokkel v. [1940s+] (S.Afr.) to deal in drugs or in illicit liquor; thus smokkelhuis, smokkie, an illicit bar or shebeen. [Du. smokkeln, to smuggle]

smoko n. (also **smoke-ho, smoke-o(h)**) **1** [mid-19C+] (Aus./N.Z.) a break for smoking. **2** [1950s] the cup of tea that often accompanies such a break. **3** [1980s+] (Aus. prison) marijuana. [SE smoke + -o sfx (4); (3) SMOKE n.³ (3)]

Smoky n. see SMOKY (BEAR) n.

smoky n. (also **smokey**) **1** [1930s–60s] (US Black) a Black person; esp. as a generic term for Blackness or a number of Black people gathered together (cf. BLACKBELLY n.). **2** [1970s+] (US Black) (also **smokey the fire bear**) a derog. term for a dark-complexioned Black person. **3** [1970s+] (US campus) a policeman. **4** [1980s+] (N.Z.) a derog. term for a Maori.

smoky adj.¹ (also **smoaky**) **1** [late 17C] jealous. **2** [mid-18C–1910s] suspicious, inquisitive, suspect. [SMOKE v.¹ (1)]

smoky adj.² (also **smokey**) [1940s–70s] (US) Black; pertaining to Black people or culture.

Smoky (Bear) n. [1970s+] a traffic policeman, a Highway Patrolman. [Smoky the Bear, a character used in US fire prevention campaigns]

smoky beaver n. [1970s] (US) a female motorcycle police officer. [SMOKY (BEAR) n. + BEAVER n.⁵ (2)]

smoky seat n. [1930s–60s] (US prison) the electric chair. [the smoke that rises from the electrocuted victim]

smooch n. [1930s+] a bout of kissing and cuddling; thus adj., smoochy. [SMOOCH v.¹ (1)]

smooch v.¹ **1** [1910s+] (Aus./US) to caress amorously, to kiss. **2** [1980s+] to sing in a mawkish, sentimental way. [late 16C SE smouch, to kiss]

smooch v.² (also **smootch**) [1900s–40s] (US) to steal, to pilfer. [? MOOCH v.¹ (1)]

smooching n. [1940s+] (orig. US) kissing and cuddling. [SMOOCH v.¹ (1)]

smoodge v. (also **smooge, smooze**) [20C+] (Aus.) to ingratiate oneself, to cuddle up; thus come the smoodge, do a smoodge; smoodging, ingratiation. [SCHMOOZE v. (1) or SMOOCH v.¹ (1) or SE smudge, to caress]

smoodger n. (also **smooger**) [20C+] (Aus.) **1** a toady, a sycophant, a flatterer. **2** an informer. [SMOODGE v.]

smooey n. [1940s–80s] (Aus.) the vagina; thus by metonymy, sexual intercourse; thus have a bit of smooey, to have sexual intercourse. [SMOODGE v.]

smooge v. see SMOODGE v.

smoogy n. [1910s] (Aus.) a collective term for people who kiss and cuddle. [SMOODGE v.]

smoogy *adj.* [1900s–50s] (*Aus.*) affectionate, ingratiating. [SMOODGE v.]

smootch *v. see* SMOOCH v.[2].

smooth *adj.* **1** [late 19C+] (*orig. US*) (*also* **smoothe**) clever, skilful, superior. **2** [late 19C+] of manners or dress, elegant, fashionable, suave. **3** [late 19C+] (*US campus*) performed well. **4** [20C+] of a situation, pleasant. **5** [1920s+] (*US Black*) (*also* **smoothe**) good, admirable. **6** [2000s] of an individual, affable, courteous.

smooth article *n.* (*also* **smoothie, smooth operator**) [20C+] a sophisticated, smart person, both mentally and physically.

smoothie *n.*[1] (*also* **smoother, smoothy**) [1920s+] one who is suave or stylish in conduct or appearance, usu. a man; often with unfavourable sense, a slick but shallow or insinuating person.

smoothie *n.*[2] [2000s] (*US Black*) an iron. [it smooths clothes]

smoothiechops *n.* [1980s+] **1** a lightweight, affable but pretentious person. **2** (*N.Z.*) (*also* **smoothieboots**) a womanizer. [SMOOTH adj. (2) + CHOPS n.[1] (1)/on model of SMARTY-BOOTS n.]

smoothiepuss *n.* [1980s+] (*N.Z.*) an attractive woman. [SMOOTH adj. (2) +PUSS n.[1] (1)/PUSS n.[3] (1)]

smooth operator *n. see* SMOOTH ARTICLE n.

smooth up *v.* [1920s] (*US campus*) of a man, to attempt seduction. [SMOOTH adj. (2)]

smoothy *n. see* SMOOTHIE n.[1].

smooze *v. see* SMOODGE v.

smother *n.*[1] [20C+] a coat, a wrap; thus (*UK Und.*) *smother game*, pickpocketing with the aid of an overcoat for cover. [SE *smother*, to hide, to cover up; it 'smothers' the wearer]

smother *n.*[2] [1900s] (*Aus.*) a plan, an undercover stratagem. [SE *smother*, to hide]

smother *v.* **1** [1910s] (*UK Und.*) to stand guard and cover for an accomplice breaking into a premises. **2** [1970s] (*Aus. Und.*) to use some form of object to obscure the shopkeeper's view while a shoplifter abstracts a targeted object; also of a pickpocket. [SE *smother*, to hide]

smother a parrot *v.* (*also* **strangle a parrot**) [1900s–10s] to drink off a glass of absinthe in a single gulp. [trans. of Fr. argot *asphyxier un perroquet*, to drink a glass of absinthe]

smouge *v.* (*also* **smouch**) [mid-19C–1900s] (*US*) to steal. [? derog. generic use of SMOUS n. (1)]

smous *n.* (*also* **smouch, smouse, smouser, smoutch**) **1** [early 18C–19C] a German Jew (cf. FAST-TALKING CHARLIE n.). **2** [mid-19C+] (*UK/S.Afr.*) (*also* **schmoose**) an itinerant Jewish peddler. [Du. *smous*/Yid. *schmus*, patter or profit; ult. Heb. *schmuoss*, news or tales]

smous *v.* (*also* **smouch, smouse**) (*S.Afr.*) **1** [mid-19C+] to work as an itinerant Jewish peddler. **2** [mid-19C+] to solicit business, esp. in a demeaning manner. **3** [1970s+] to obtain in an underhand way. **4** [1990s+] to search out bargains. [SMOUS n.]

smoush *n.* [1960s+] (*Aus.*) a kiss. [SMOOCH n.]

smoutch *n. see* SMOUS n.

smuckered *adj.* [1970s+] (*US campus*) drunk (cf. ANNIHILATED adj.). [SMACK v.[1] (2)]

smudge *n.*[1] [1930s+] **1** a photograph. **2** a (gay) pornographic magazine.

smudge *n.*[2] [1940s+] (*US*) a derog. term for a Black person (cf. BLACKBELLY n.). [SE *smudge*, a dirty mark]

smudge *n.*[3] *see* SNUDGE n.

smudge (up) *v.* [2000s] to photograph. [SMUDGE n.[1] (1)]

smug *n.*[1] [early 17C–early 19C] a blacksmith. [? SE *smuggy*, dirty, grimy. The late 20C+ use of *Smugs* for W.H. Smith, the chain of stationers and booksellers, is prob. coincidental – the term refers more to the company's reputation as self-appointed guardian of its customers' morals than for any back-ref. to the name *Smith*]

smug *n.*[2] [mid-19C] (*Anglo-Chinese*) *smuggling*. [abbr.]

smug *n.*[3] [late 19C–1910s] **1** (*UK teen*) a hard worker. **2** an intellectual. [SE *smug*, i.e. their self-satisfaction]

smug *adj.* [late 16C–early 18C; mid-19C] extremely neat and tidy; thus *smug*, a person who is excessively neat. [*OED* accepts *smug* as SE, but its early cits. – Greene, Dekker, Middleton, Wycherley – are all colloq. if not sl.]

smug *v.* **1** [early 18C; 19C] to snatch another's property and run off with it. **2** [early–mid-19C] to silence, to 'hush up'. **3** [mid-late 19C] to copy, to cheat. **4** [late 19C–1920s] to arrest. **5** [20C+] (*Irish*) to engage in homosexual practices. [? SE *smuggle* or dial. *smug*, to hide, to move stealthily]

smugger *n.* [late 19C] a thug, specializing in snatch-and-grab thefts; also in fig. use, anyone who steals, e.g. ideas. [SMUG v. (1)]

smuggings! *excl.* [mid-19C] (*UK teen*) mine! [SMUG v. (1); the excl. used at the end of a game of marbles or spinning tops when the child who shouted thus first was allowed to keep the toy in question]

smuggle the coal *v.* (*also* **smuggle the cole**) [late 17C] to pretend that one has no money when it is time to pay a bill at an inn or tavern. [SE *smuggle* + COLE n. (1)]

smuggling-ken *n.* [early 18C–early 19C] a brothel (cf. BADGER-CRIB n.). [dial. *smuggle*, to smother with hugs and kisses + KEN n.[1] (1)]

smug-lay *n.* [early–mid-19C] the selling of virtually worthless goods on the pretext that they are actually smuggled contraband. [SE *smuggle* + LAY n.[4] (1)]

smug up *v.*[1] [17C] to smarten oneself up. [SMUG adj.]

smug up *v.*[2] [late 19C] to hide oneself away; to lead an uneventful life. [SMUG v. (2)]

smurf *n.* **1** [1980s+] (*Aus. prison*) an inexperienced or short prison officer. **2** [1990s+] (*US gay*) a blond young homosexual man. [from the *Smurfs*, the animated children's TV characters]

smush *n.* [1910s–30s] (*Irish/US*) the mouth. [? MUSH n.[2]]

smush *v.* [late 18C–early 19C] to snatch, to seize. [obs. SE]

smut *n.*[1] [late 17C+] pornography, obscenity; thus *smut-peddler*, a seller of pornography. [SE *smut*, a black stain, i.e. the identification of sexuality and 'dirt']

smut *n.*[2] [early–mid-19C] a copper boiler, a furnace. [its smokiness]

smut *n.*[3] **1** [1920s+] (*US Black*) a derog. term for a woman. **2** [1970s] (*US campus*) a prostitute.

smut-butt *n.* [1970s] (*US campus*) a derog. term for a Black student (cf. BLACKBELLY n.). [SE *smut* + BUTT n.[1] (2)]

smut-hound *n.* [1920s+] one who is obsessed by the tiniest trace of obscenity, esp. in the arts or media, a censor. [SMUT n.[1] + HOUND sfx; coined by H.L. Mencken (1880–1956) and one of the coinages (along with *bible belter* + *booboisie*), of which he was 'vainest' (letter, 2 December 1927)]

smutter *n.* [1980s] (*US*) a maker of or dealer in pornography. [SMUT n.[1]]

snaaks *adj.* [1910s+] (*S.Afr.*) strange, peculiar, bizarre. [Du. *snaaks*, droll, comical]

snabble *v.* (*also* **smabble**) **1** [18C] to arrest, to seize. **2** [mid-18C–early 19C] to knock down, to plunder. **3** [late 18C–early 19C] to kill in battle. **4** [late 19C] to have sexual intercourse with (cf. BANG v.[1]). [? dial. *snabble*, to eat greedily]

snabbled *adj.* (*also* **smabbled**) [late 18C–mid-19C] killed in battle. [SNABBLE v. (3)]

snabby *adj.* (*also* **snab**) [mid-19C] (*US campus*) stylish, fashionable; perfect, excellent.

snack *n.*[1] **1** [mid-17C–mid-19C] (*UK Und.*) a share of booty. **2** [late 19C] (*US Und.*) a confederate. **3** [late 19C+] a snide remark. [SE *snack*, a portion; itself linked to root for (3) SE *snack*, a snap or bite, esp. of a dog]

snack *n.*[2] [1940s+] (*Aus.*) anything simple. ['a piece of cake']

snack *n.*[3] [1950s–60s] (*US Black*) the penis, often when small.

snack *v.*[1] **1** [mid-17C–19C] (*UK Und.*) to divide up, to hand over a share of the loot. **2** [late 19C] to nag, to criticize. [SNACK n.[1] (1)/SNACK n.[1] (3)]

snack v.[2] [1980s+] (US campus) to kiss passionately; thus *snackbar*, one's boyfriend or girlfriend. [the couple nibble on each other]

snackpack n. (US gay) **1** [1970s+] an athletic supporter, a jock-strap. **2** [1980s+] the male genitalia, when seen in a jockstrap or bikini briefs. [SNACK n.[3] + SE *pack*; also a proprietary food name]

snaffle n.[1] [17C–18C] (UK Und.) a successful highwayman. [SE *snaffle*, a light bridle + SNAFFLE v. (2)]

snaffle n.[2] **1** [mid-19C] talk that no one but the speaker either understands or cares about. **2** [1910s–20s] secret talk. [SE *snaffle*, a horse's bridle-bit; a speaker is similarly restrained]

snaffle v. (also **snavvle**) **1** [late 16C; mid-19C–1910s] to arrest. **2** [17C+] to steal. **3** [20C+] to grab, to take hold of; to pilfer (and as such seen as less immoral than stealing); thus *snaffler*, one who is miserly. [SE *snaffle*, to place a bridle-bit on a horse]

snaffle-biter n. [early 18C] a horse-thief. [SE *snaffle* + BITE v. (1)]

snaffler n.[1] [18C–early 19C; 1940s–50s] a highwayman. [SNAFFLE v. (2)]

snaffler n.[2] [early 19C] a blow, a punch.

snaffling lay n. [mid-18C–early 19C] the profession of highway robbery. [SNAFFLE v. (2) + LAY n.[4] (1)]

s.n.a.f.u. n. (also **g.a.f.u**) [1940s+] (orig. US milit.) a mistake, an error, a situation, often within an institution/organization, that has gone awry. [abbr. situation *normal*, *all fucked up*; fouled-up can provide a euph. substitute; orig. a WW2 milit. catchphrase, *s.n.a.f.u.* quickly entered mainstream sl. and generated a number of vars., although none has had the same impact (cf. F.I.G.M.O. phr.; F.U.B.A.R. phr.; F.U.B.B. phr.; F.U.M.T.U. phr.; F.U.B.I.S. phr.; G.F.O. n.; G.M.B.U. n.; M.F.U.T.U. phr.; S.A.B.U. n.; S.A.M.F.U. n.; S.A.P.F.U. phr.; S.N.A.F.U. n.; S.N.A.F.U. phr.; S.U.S.F.U. phr.; T.A.R.F.U. phr.; T.U.I.F.U. n.)]

s.n.a.f.u. v. [1940s+] (orig. US milit.) to mess up, to go wrong, esp. in a complex, elaborate manner. [S.N.A.F.U. n.]

s.n.a.f.u. phr. (also **snafu**) [1940s+] (orig. US milit.) messed up, gone wrong. [S.N.A.F.U. n.]

snag n.[1] [mid-19C; 20C+] (Aus./N.Z.) an adversary worthy of consideration. [SE *snag*, an impediment or obstacle]

snag n.[2] [late 19C] (N.Z.) a tramp's backpack.

snag n.[3] [1940s+] (Aus./US) a jagged tooth. [SE *snag*, a jagged or angular projection, a short stump projecting from a tree trunk]

snag n.[4] [1950s–60s] (US Black) an unattractive or unpleasant woman. [? dial. *snag*, to carp, to nag]

snag n.[5] [1980s+] (US campus) a sensitive *new-age guy*. [acronym]

snag n.[6] see SNAGGER n.

snag v. **1** [late 19C+] to grab, to steal. **2** [20C+] to catch or arrest. **3** [1920s] (N.Z.) to hunt for bargains, as a means for poor people to survive. **4** [1920s–70s] (US tramp) to sodomize. **5** [1940s–80s] (US Black) to have sexual intercourse. **6** [1950s] (gang) to attack an individual without warning. **7** [1960s+] to woo, to wed, to seduce. **8** [1980s] (US campus) to ridicule. **9** [1990s+] to win. [SE *snag*, to be caught or pierced by a snag or rough projection]

snagg n. [late 18C–early 19C] (UK Und.) a snail. [Sussex dial. *snag*, a snail]

snagger n. (also **snag**) (Aus./N.Z.) **1** [late 19C–1900s] an itinerant worker or tramp, esp. one who is lazy or work-shy. **2** [late 19C–1900s] in ext./fig. use, a parasite. **3** [1930s+] a poor person who seeks cheap bargains.

snaggers n. see SNAGS n.

snagging n. see DOZENS n.

snaggles n. see SNAGS n.

snaggle-tooth n. [20C+] a person with poor, uneven teeth. [SE *snaggle-tooth*, irregular or projecting teeth]

snaggling n. [mid-19C] the practice of angling for geese with a hook and line, the bait being a worm or snail. [? dial. *snaggler*, an eel-fisher]

snaggs n. (also **snags**) [late 17C–mid-19C] large teeth. [SE *snag*, a broken or unsightly tooth]

snags n. (also **snaggers**, **snaggles**) [1940s+] (Aus./N.Z.) sausages; rarely used in sing. [dial. *snag*, a morsel, a snack]

snail n.[1] [late 19C] (Aus.) a shepherd, a musterer, one who mends boundary fences.

snail n.[2] [late 19C] (US) a freight train. [its slow pace]

snail n.[3] [1920s–60s] (US tramp) a cinnamon roll or bun. [? the shape]

snailer n. [1990s+] (Irish) a trail of mucus running down the face. [resemblance to a snail track]

'snails! excl. [16C–early 17C] a mild, if blasphemous, oath. [SE *God's nails* (the nails in question are those suffered by Christ rather than God the Father)]

snail trail n.[1] [1990s+] vaginal secretions marking the underwear.

snail trail n.[2] see HAPPY TRAIL n.

snake n.[1] **1** [mid-19C+] (US) an unreliable, deceptive person. **2** [1950s+] (US gang) a spy. **3** [1960s] (US campus) a promiscuous or ugly girl. **4** [1970s] (US Black) a homosexual, whether male or female. **5** [1970s+] (US campus) someone who steals something, particularly someone else's date. [(1) note Urquhart (1653): 'Cursed snakes, dissembling varlets, seeming sancts / Slipshod caffards, beggars pretending wants'; Nares defines it as 'a term of reproach, equivalent to a wretch, a poor creature']

snake n.[2] **1** [1910s–30s] (US Und.) a railroad switchman. **2** [1940s] (Aus.) a non-commissioned officer. **3** [1940s] (US) a policeman (cf. ANIMAL n.[1]).

snake n.[3] [1930s+] the penis (cf. ANTEATER n.). [abbr. ONE-EYED TROUSER-SNAKE n.]

snake n.[4] [1950s] (US drugs) a regular smoker of marijuana. [play on VIPER n. (1)]

snake v.[1] [mid-19C] (US) to beat, to thrash. [the snake-like whip]

snake v.[2] **1** [late 19C+] to take in a surreptitious manner, to pilfer, to sneak. **2** [1950s+] to steal. **3** [1960s+] to steal someone else's date. **4** [1960s+] to cheat. [SNAKE n.[1] (1)]

snake v.[3] [1980s+] **1** to masturbate (cf. BEAT ONE'S HOG v.; BOFF v.). **2** (US campus) to flirt, esp. with someone else's date. **3** to have sexual intercourse (cf. BAGAGA v.). [SNAKE n.[3]]

snake sfx [1910s–30s] (US) used in combs. to describe a person with a particular habit or type of behaviour.

Snake and Kidney n. [1900s] (Aus.) Sydney. [rhy. sl.]

snakebit adj. [1970s] (US) defeated.

snakebite n. **1** [1920s+] (US) a strong alcoholic drink, usu. cheap but strong whisky. **2** [1950s–60s] an injection of heroin and morphine. **3** [1980s+] a 'cocktail' of cider mixed with lager. [its effects]

snakebite remedy n. [1950s+] (US) potassium permanganate, washing with which after sexual intercourse is used as a pro-phylactic against venereal disease.

snake-bitten adj. [1920s+] (US) incapacitated. [SE]

snake charmer n.[1] [1930s] (Aus.) a railway plate-layer (in Western Australia); also *hairy leg* (New South Wales); *woolly nose* (South Australia). [the prevalence of snakes along the track]

snake charmer n.[2] **1** [1930s] (US) an oboe. **2** [1970s+] (US gay) a fellator. [(1) the image of a snake-charmer luring a snake by playing a flute-like instrument; (2) SNAKE n.[3]]

snake eyes n.[1] [1910s–30s] (US) tapioca (cf. FISHEYES n.). [resemblance]

snake eyes n.[2] **1** [1930s+] (gambling) the (losing) point of 2 in craps dice (cf. ADA FROM DECATUR n.). **2** [1930s+] thus in ext. use, bad luck. **3** [1960s] (bingo) the number 11 (cf. ALDERSHOT LADIES n.). [i.e. a pair of ones; such a throw loses one's bet]

snake gully n. [1940s+] (Aus.) **1** an imaginary place that is a byword for backwardness and remoteness. **2** the vagina (cf. BAG n.[1]). [(1) *Snake Gully* was the location of the long-running radio serial *Dad and Dave*; (2) SNAKE n.[3]]

snake-headed adj. **1** [early 19C] (UK Und.) quickwitted, cunning. **2** [1900s–40s] (Aus.) testy, irritated. [the negative image of the reptile]

snake in the grass *n.* [mid-19C+] **1** a looking-glass, a mirror. **2** a drinking glass. [rhy. sl., either of which might prove a 'treacherous friend']

snake juice *n.* [late 19C+] (*orig. Aus.*) any form of liquor, esp. when cheap and potent; thus *snake-juicer*, a drinker of such liquor.

snake medicine *n. see* SNAKE POISON n.

snake off *v.* (*also* **snake out**) [1910s+] (*orig. Aus.*) to slip along, to move stealthily. [the reptile's characteristic]

snake out *v.* [early–mid-19C] (*US*) to hunt down, to pursue. [the hunting of deadly snakes]

snakepit *n.* **1** [1950s–70s] (*US gay*) a bar frequented by homosexuals. **2** [1960s] (*US*) the vagina (cf. BAG n.¹; BLACK HOLE n.¹). **3** [1960s] a red-light area. **4** [1960s+] (*also* **snake ranch**) a brothel (cf. BIRDCAGE n.¹). [SNAKE n.³]

snake poison *n.* (*also* **snake medicine**) [late 19C–1940s] (*Aus./US*) whisky. [var. on SNAKE JUICE n.]

snake room *n.* [1920s–30s] (*US*) a bar, esp. when full of drunkards.

snake's *n. see* SNAKE'S (HISS) n.

snakes *n. see* SNAKES (IN ONE'S BOOTS) n.

snakes (alive)! *excl.* [mid-19C+] (*US*) a mild excl.

snakes and sawdust! *excl.* [late 19C] (*Aus.*) a mild excl.

snake's eyebrows/hips *n. see* CAT'S WHISKERS n.

snake's (hiss) *n.* [1960s+] (*Aus.*) **1** an act of urination (cf. ANGEL'S KISS n.). **2** urine. **3** a lavatory (cf. ANGUS ARMANASCO n.). [rhy. sl. = PISS n.]

snake's house *n.* [1960s+] (*orig. Aus.*) a lavatory (cf. BACKHOUSE n.). [var. on SNAKE'S (HISS) n. (3); or SNAKE n.³ + SE *house*]

snakes (in one's boots) *n.* [mid-19C+] alcoholic hallucinations, delirium tremens. [from the *snakes*, pink elephants and other wonders one supposedly sees]

snakesman *n.* [late 18C–19C] a member of a gang of thieves who is sufficiently small and lithe to enter buildings through any narrow entrance that would otherwise be impassable; once within they unlock a main door through which all can pass.

snake's piss *n.* [1960s–70s] (*Aus.*) beer.

snake's toenail *n. see* CAT'S WHISKERS n.

snake-tart *n.* [mid-19C–1900s] eel pie. [joc. resemblance]

snakey *see under* SNAKY.

snake yarn *n.* [20C+] (*Aus.*) a fantastical tale, a 'tall story'. [lit. or fig. involving snakes]

snakies *n.* [2000s] snakeskin shoes or boots.

snaky *adj.*¹ **1** [late 19C+] (*orig. US*) devious, underhand, cunning. **2** [1920s+] unpleasant, sinister. [the biblical story of Eden]

snaky *adj.*² (*also* **snakey**) (*Aus.*) **1** [1910s+] irritable, tetchy. **2** [1930s+] jealous. [SNAKE n.¹ (1)]

snaky *adj.*³ (*also* **snakey**) [1920s–70s] (*US*) **1** drunk. **2** suffering from alcoholic hallucinations. [SNAKES (IN ONE'S BOOTS) n.]

snaky-bony *n.* [1950s] (*W.I.*) a very thin person.

snaky-bony *adj.* [1950s] (*W.I.*) very thin. [SNAKY-BONY n.]

snam *v.* [mid-19C–1900s] to steal, to pilfer. [Scot. *snam*, to snap at greedily. 'That kind of theft which consists in picking up anything lying about, and making off with it rapidly' (Hotten, 1874)]

snammer *n. see* PUDDING-SNAMMER n.

snap *n.*¹ **1** [mid-16C–mid-19C] a share, a portion; thus *snap/go snap*, to share half-and-half. **2** [late 16C–early 17C] (*UK Und.*) a cut-purse's assistant. **3** [late 16C–19C] a pickpocket, cut-purse or card-sharp, spec. an experienced one who demanded a share of his younger peers' profits. [SE *snack*, a share or part; synon. with *snatch*, the image is of a grabbed or snatched handful or mouthful]

snap *n.*² **1** [late 19C–1900s] (*US campus*) a lenient instructor. **2** [late 19C–1900s] (*US*) an event, a circumstance; a trick. **3** [late 19C+] (*orig. US*) anything easy, a simple task or achievement. **4** [late 19C+] (*US campus*) an easy course. **5** [1900s] (*US campus*) an advantage; a foregone conclusion. [? a *snap* of the fingers]

snap *n.*³ (*drugs*) **1** [1960s] amyl nitrite (cf. AIMIES n.). **2** [2000s] amphetamine (cf. A n.²). [the snapping of the ampoules in which the drug is packaged; and the intense energy]

snap *n.*⁴ [1980s+] (*US Black*) a wisecrack, a witty retort. [SNAP v.⁴ (1)]

snap *adj.*¹ [1900s–60s] (*US campus*) relatively easy. [SNAP n.² (3)]

snap *adj.*² *see* SNAPPY adj.¹ (3).

snap *v.*¹ **1** [early 18C; mid-19C; 1980s] (*UK Und.*) to arrest. **2** [late 18C–1920s] to grab. [? the *snapping* on of handcuffs]

snap *v.*² [1900s] (*US campus*) to skip a recitation. [ety. unknown]

snap *v.*³ [1910s+] to alter one's behaviour quickly; usu. in combs, e.g. SNAP OUT OF v.

snap *v.*⁴ [1960s+] (*US Black*) **1** to tease. **2** to laugh along with.

snap *v.*⁵ [1960s+] **1** (*US prison*) to understand, to work out. **2** (*US*) to act more carefully, to stop doing something.

snap *v.*⁶ [1970s+] (*US Black*) to convey displeasure by directing a loud fingersnap towards the offending party.

snap! *excl.* [1970s+] (*US Black/teen*) **1** an excl. of surprise or apology, esp. after making a mistake or blunder. **2** an excl. of displeasure. [SNAP v.⁶]

snap a cap *v.* [mid-19C–1920s] (*US*) to fire a shot. [SE *snap* + CAP n.²]

snap a snapper *v.* [1940s] (*US Black*) to light a match. [SE *snap* + SNAPPER n.⁶]

snap assholes *v.* [1950s+] (*US*) to fight. [ASSHOLE n.¹ (1)]

snap back *v.* [1940s+] to make a quick recovery from a setback. [SNAP v.³]

snapcase *n.* [1960s] (*US*) a mentally unstable person.

snap house *n.* [mid-19C] (*US*) a cheap, poss. crooked casino.

snap into *v.* [1910s+] to involve oneself enthusiastically. [SNAP v.³]

snap it up *v.* [1910s+] to speed up, to hurry up; often as imper. [SE *snap*/SNAPPY adj.¹ (2)]

snap one off *v.* **1** [1980s+] (*Aus. prison*) to defecate (cf. BACK ONE OUT v.). **2** [1990s+] to masturbate (cf. BALL OFF v.²).

snap one's cap *v.* [1940s+] (*US*) to lose control, to become insane. [SE *snap* + CAP n.⁶ (1)]

snap one's cookies *v. see* POP ONE'S COOKIES v. (1).

snap one's twig *v.* [1980s] (*Aus.*) to lose emotional control. [SE; pun on next]

snap one's wig *v.* [1950s–70s] to lose emotional control. [SE *snap* + WIG n.³ (1)]

snap out *v.* [1910s–60s] (*US*) to lose emotional control.

snap out of *v.* [1920s+] to make an abrupt and self-willed change in one's attitude, emotions, behaviour etc (usu. from negative to positive); often as imper. *snap out of it!* cheer up! pull yourself together!; occas. as *snap someone out of*. [SNAP v.³]

snappage *n.* [early 17C] (*UK Und.*) a share in the booty. [SNAP n.¹ (1)]

snapped *adj.*¹ [late 17C–18C; 20C+] arrested, caught. [SNAP v.¹ (1)/abbr. SE *snapped up*]

snapped *adj.*² [mid-19C] (*US, Southern*) drunk.

snapped *adj.*³ [late 19C] abrupt, sudden, surprising.

snapped up *adj.* [1960s] (*drugs*) under the influence of amyl nitrite. [SNAP n.³ (1)]

snapper *n.*¹ [mid-16C] an assistant or lookout man for a criminal gang or team of fraudsters. [ext. of SNAP n.¹ (2)]

snapper *n.*² **1** [mid-19C+] (*US*) a caustic remark. **2** [mid-19C+] (*US*) the point of a story or joke. **3** [late 19C] (*US*) a braggart. **4** [1930s+] (*US gay*) the foreskin. [SAmE *snapper*, the cracker on the end of a whip]

snapper *n.*³ [late 19C–1900s] the penis.

snapper *n.*⁴ [1910s+] (*orig. US*) a photographer. [SE *snap*, a photograph]

snapper *n.*⁵ [1920s–50s] a ticket inspector. [the clipping of tickets]

snapper *n.*⁶ [1940s] (*US Black*) a match. [one 'snaps' it alight]

snapper *n.*⁷ [1950s+] **1** (*US*) the vagina (cf. BEARDED CLAM n.; BITE n.²). **2** (*US Black*) excellent sex. **3** (*US campus*) a very attractive young woman. [the image of the vagina as both a fish (FISH n.[1] (1)) and a predator]

snapper n.[8] [1950s+] (*Irish*) a baby, a small child. [abbr. BREAD-SNAPPER n.]

snappers n.[1] **1** [late 16C–19C] pistols. **2** [1920s–70s] teeth, usu. false. [their noise]

snappers n.[2] [1960s+] (*drugs*) amyl nitrite, isobutyl nitrite (cf. AIMIES n.). [SNAP n.[3] (1)]

snapping adj. [1990s+] (*US Black teen*) excellent, wonderful. [the finger-snapping that demonstrates one's approval]

snapping new adj. [late 19C] (*US*) of notes, absolutely fresh. [the snapping of the notes to emphasize their crisp freshness]

snappings n. [late 16C–early 17C] (*UK Und.*) goods that are pilfered from stalls or shop windows. [SE *snap up*]

snapping turtle (puss) n. [1950s+] (*US*) the vagina (cf. BEARDED CLAM n.; BIRD n.[8]; BITE n.[2]). [PUSS n.[1] (3)]

snappish adj. see SNAPPY adj.[2].

snapps n.[1] [mid-19C] (*UK Und.*) **1** a share, a portion. **2** anything that will serve as a means of making money; thus *looking out for snapps*, waiting for a lucky break or a windfall. [var. on SNAP n.[1] (1)]

snapps n.[2] [mid-19C] Dutch gin, genever.

snappy adj.[1] [late 19C+] (*orig. US*) **1** smart, clever, esp. of language. **2** energetic. **3** (*also* **snap**) neat, elegant. **4** sharply flavoursome. **5** sexy, titillating.

snappy adj.[2] (*also* **snappish**) [late 19C+] (*orig. US*) irritable, irascible. [SE *snap one's head off*]

snaps n.[1] [late 19C+] (*US*) handcuffs. [they *snap* onto the wrist]

snaps n.[2] **1** [1970s] (*US Black*) someone or something amusing. **2** [1980s] (*US campus*) snack foods. [SNAPPY adj.[1]/SE *snap up*]

snaps n.[3] [1980s+] (*orig. US Black teen*) money. [the 'snapping' of a dollar bill]

snap the glaze v. [late 18C–early 19C] (*UK Und.*) to smash shop windows. [SE *snap* + GLAZE n. (1)]

snap the rubber v. [1940s–50s] to masturbate.

snap the whip v. [1950s–60s] to masturbate, to masturbate another person.

snap to v. [1980s] to work something out.

snap to (it) v. (*also* **snap up**) [1930s+] (*US*) to get going, to get busy, to hurry up, esp. as imper. *snap to it!* [SE *snap*/SNAPPY adj.[1] (2)]

snap up v. [1970s] (*US*) to become insane (or pose as such).

snare n. [1900s] (*US*) a house, an apartment, a room.

snare v. **1** [late 19C; 1940s] (*US tramp*) to arrest. **2** [late 19C–1920s] (*US tramp*) to entice a boy into tramping. **3** [late 19C+] (*Aus.*) to obtain, to grab, to win.

snarf n. [1950s] something edible. [SNARF v. (1)]

snarf v. **1** [1950s+] to eat, to drink; to consume, e.g. a drug. **2** [1960s+] (*US campus*) in fig. use, to pick someone up. **3** [1960s+] to grab, to take possession of. **4** [1990s+] to expel liquid (or, more rarely, food) out of one's nose by laughing in the middle of a swallow. [? var. on SCARF v. (1)]

snark n.[1] [1960s] an informer. [dial. *snark*, to fret, to grumble]

snark n.[2] [2000s] a sense of anger, irritation, tetchiness. [SNARKY adj.]

snark v. [2000s] (*US gay*) to gossip, usu. maliciously. [SNARKY adj. (2)]

snarky adj. [1910s+] **1** (*orig. US*) irritable, touchy. **2** (*US gay*) maliciously gossipy, bitchy. [dial. *snark*, to fret, to grumble]

snarler n. [1980s+] (*N.Z.*) a sausage.

snarl(-up) n. **1** [mid-19C+] any form of difficulty. **2** [1930s+] (*orig. US*) a traffic jam. [SNARL UP v.]

snarl up v. [1910s+] to confuse, to entangle, to impede.

snash n. [1950s+] (*Ulster*) nonsense, cheek.

snatch n.[1] **1** [late 16C+] sexual intercourse, esp. quick or illicit or with a prostitute. **2** [mid-19C+] the vagina (cf. BITE n.[2]). **3** [1940s+] a generic term for women, esp. when viewed in a

sexual context. **4** [1940s+] (*US gay*) the anus. **5** [1950s] (*US prison*) a male homosexual. **6** [1970s] (*US campus*) a notably ugly woman. **7** [2000s] (*US Black*) a fight. [Yorks. dial.; ult. SE *snatch*, to grab; thus negative image of the vagina]

snatch n.[2] **1** [late 18C–mid-19C; 1940s–50s] an arrest. **2** [late 19C+] (*UK/US Und.*) a robbery, a victim ripe for robbing. **3** [1920s+] (*orig. US*) a kidnapping.

snatch v. **1** [early 18C; late 19C+] (*US*) to steal, esp. to shoplift. **2** [1930s+] (*mainly US*) to kidnap. **3** [1940s+] (*US Black*) to threaten someone by grabbing their lapels and talking menacingly into their face; also in fig. use, to butt in critically.

snatch-and-grab booster n. (*also* **boot-and-shoe booster**) [1900s–30s] (*US Und.*) an amateur shoplifter, rather than one who works with a professional team.

snatch-back n. [1980s] repossession, e.g. of a car when the buyer defaults on credit payments.

snatch bald(-headed) v. see JERK BALD-HEADED v.

snatch-blatch n. [late 19C–1910s] the vagina. [SNATCH n.[1] (2) + ? dial. *blatch*, dirt]

snatch-box n. [mid-late 19C] the vagina (cf. BAG n.[1]). [SNATCH n.[1] (2) + SE *box*/BOX n.[1] (1)]

snatch cly n. [late 18C–early 19C] (*UK Und.*) a thief who specializes in stealing from women's pockets. [SE *snatch* + CLY n. (2)]

snatcher n. **1** [mid-late 19C] (*UK Und.*) a body-snatcher or resurrectionist. **2** [late 19C] a young and inexperienced pickpocket. **3** [late 19C–1960s] a thief, esp. a pickpocket. **4** [1900s–40s] a policeman, esp. a detective (cf. BEAT-POUNDER n.). **5** [1910s] one who arrests a specific type of person, used with the qualifying n., e.g. *hobo-snatcher*. **6** [1930s–40s] (*US*) a kidnapper. [SE *snatch*/SNATCH v.]

snatch game n. (*also* **snatch racket**) [1920s+] kidnapping. [SNATCH n.[2] (3) + GAME n.[2] (3)/RACKET n.[1] (1)]

snatch one's time phr. (*also* **snatch it**, **snatch one's bit/rent**) [1910s+] (*Aus.*) to resign. [i.e. to snatch one's time back for oneself]

snatchpad n. [1940s] (*US Black*) a house, a home.

snatch racket n. see SNATCH GAME n.

snatch salami n. [2000s] the penis (cf. BACON n.[1]). [SNATCH n.[1] (2) + SALAMI n.]

snatch-thatch n. [18C] female pubic hair. [SNATCH n.[1] (2) + THATCH n. (2)]

snatch-up n. [1950s+] (*US Black*) an arrest.

snavel v. (*also* **snawel**) **1** [late 18C–1920s] to steal, to pilfer; thus *snaveller*, a thief, esp. one who thieves from children. **2** [1910s] to catch, to grab hold of. [dial. *snavel*, to remove slyly; post-19C use mainly Aus.]

snavvle v. see SNAFFLE v.

snazz n. [1930s+] (*US*) style, elegance. [backform. f. SNAZZY adj.]

snazz up v. [1930s+] (*US*) to enliven by making something smarter and more attractive. [SNAZZ n.]

snazzy adj. (*also* **snazz**) [1930s+] (*orig. Aus.*) smart, fashionable, brightly coloured; thus *snazzy chassis*, an attractive (female) figure. [? SNAPPY adj.[1] (3) + JAZZY adj.[1] (1)]

sneak n.[1] **1** [late 17C–1900s] an act of theft. **2** [mid-18C+] a thief. **3** [mid-19C–1930s] an escape; thus *do/make/take a sneak*, to leave, to escape. **4** [mid-19C–1950s] (*US Und.*) a sneak-thief. **5** [late 19C–1950s] (*US Und.*) a bank robber (using guile rather than force).

sneak n.[2] **1** [mid-late 19C] an unpleasant person, irrespective of tale-telling. **2** [mid-19C+] (*UK teen*) one who tells tales on their fellows, usu. in the context of school.

sneak n.[3] [late 19C+] a soft-soled, canvas-topped shoe; often in pl. [abbr. SNEAKER n.[4] (1)]

sneak n.[4] [1940s+] (*orig. US*) a sneak preview (usu. of a film) to an unsuspecting audience to assess its appeal.

sneak adj. **1** [mid-19C] (*UK Und.*) working as a sneak-thief. **2** [1960s] (*US*) secret. [SNEAK n.[1] (4)]

sneak *v.*[1] **1** [early 17C+] to rob, to steal. **2** [mid-18C+] to act in a surreptitious manner, esp. when looking for something to steal. **3** [early 19C] (*UK Und.*) of a prisoner, to escape surreptitiously. **4** [mid-19C] (*UK Und.*) to seduce someone's wife or lover. **5** [late 19C+] (*US*) to slip away quietly. **6** [1990s+] to make a surprise attack. **7** [2000s] (*US Black*) to hit someone hard in the face.

sneak *v.*[2] [mid-18C+] (*mainly UK teen*) to tell tales on one's fellows. [SNEAK n.[2] (2)]

sneak-a-toke *n.* [1980s+] (*US drugs*) a hand-held smokeless pipe. [SE *sneak* + TOKE n.[2] (1)]

sneaker *n.*[1] [late 17C–mid-19C] a small bowl of punch. [SE *sneaker*, a small bowl with a lid or cover]

sneaker *n.*[2] [early 18C] (*UK Und.*) a house-breaker. [SNEAK v.[1] (1)]

sneaker *n.*[3] [early–mid-19C] a coward. [they *sneak* about]

sneaker *n.*[4] **1** [late 19C+] (*orig. US*) a soft-soled, noiseless slipper or shoe, a gym shoe; usu. in pl. **2** [1930s] (*US Und.*) a motorboat. **3** [1980s+] (*US*) quiet or silent breaking of wind. [SE *sneak*, to move quietly; (2) presumably in the context of smuggling liquor]

sneaking budge *n.* [late 17C–18C] a sneak-thief, esp. one who specializes in entering houses and taking furs, cloaks and coats, or shoplifting; thus the act of performing this crime. [SNEAK v.[1] (1) + BUDGE n.[1] (1)]

sneak job *n.* [1920s–30s] (*US Und.*) house-breaking. [SNEAK v.[1] (1) + JOB n.[3] (1)]

sneak one over (on) *v. see* PUT ONE OVER (ON) *v.*

sneak play *n.* [20C+] a surreptitious entrance and exit from a brothel. [baseball imagery or SE *sneak* + PLAY n.[1] (2)]

sneaksby *n.* [late 18C–early 19C] a term of general disparagement. [SNEAK v.[1] (2)]

sneaksman *n.* **1** [mid-18C–mid-19C] the lowest order and more contemptible species of thieves who lurk around and grab whatever they can regardless of value. **2** [mid-19C] a shoplifter. [SNEAK v.[1] (2)]

sneaky joe *n.* [1950s] cheap brandy. [play on SNEAKY PETE n. (1)]

sneaky pete *n.* **1** [1940s+] cheap, rotgut wine. **2** [1950s+] (*US drugs*) marijuana mixed with wine. [the effects 'sneak up' on the consumer]

sneaky pete *adj.* [1960s] (*US*) confidential, top secret.

sneaky pete *v.* [1940s+] (*US*) to creep quietly, to move stealthily.

sneck drawer *n.* [early–mid-19C] a sly, cunning, flattering person. [Scot *sneck*, a latch + SE *drawer*, one who pulls; lit. one who opens a latch (in order to enter surreptitiously)]

sneck up! *excl.* (*also* **snick up!**) [late 16C–mid-17C] an excl. of dismissal, the hell with you! [SE *sneck*, a latch, i.e. 'draw the latch and go to the other side of the door!']

sned *v.* [20C+] (*Ulster*) of a man, to have sexual intercourse. [dial. *sned*, to prune, to cut off]

sneerg *n.* [mid-19C] greens, green vegetables. [backsl.]

sneeze *n.* **1** [19C–1910s] the nose. **2** [1910s] (*US drugs*) a portion of a powdered narcotic, e.g. cocaine (cf. BLOW n.[6]). **3** [1960s+] (*US prison*) pepper, esp. red pepper.

sneeze *v.* **1** [1910s–40s] (*US Und.*) to arrest; also as n. **2** [1930s] (*US prison*) to kidnap. **3** [1930s–40s] to steal.

sneeze (at) *v.* [early 19C+] to disdain, to regard as of low worth.

sneeze-box *n.* [mid-19C] a snuffbox. [the immediate effects of snuff]

sneeze in the cabbage *v.* (*also* **sneeze in the canyon**) [1940s+] to perform cunnilingus. [SE *sneeze* + CABBAGE n.[7] (1)/ CANYON n. (1)]

sneeze it out *v.*[1] [1930s–70s] (*US drugs*) to withdraw from narcotic addiction. [the sneezing that accompanies withdrawal]

sneeze it out *v.*[2] [1970s+] to confess.

sneeze-lurker *n.* (*also* **snuff-luker**) [mid-19C] (*UK Und.*) a thief who temporarily blinds a victim by throwing snuff in their face and then robs them as they stagger around blindly; thus *give it on the sneeze-/snuff-racket*, to attack and rob someone in this way. [SE *sneeze/snuff* + LURK n. (3)]

sneeze machine *n.* [1970s+] (*S.Afr.*) an appliance for the dispersal of tear gas and other crowd-breaking irritants carried by army and police vehicles.

sneezer *n.*[1] **1** [early 18C–19C] a snuff-box. **2** [late 18C–mid-19C; 1940s] a pocket handkerchief. **3** [early 19C] a measure of alcohol, a dram. **4** [early–mid-19C] the nose. **5** [mid–late 19C] a blow on the nose. **6** [late 19C] (*UK Und.*) a gag. **7** [1930s–50s] (*US*) prison.

sneezer *n.*[2] **1** [mid-19C] (*US*) a very hot day. **2** [mid-19C–1940s] something or someone exceptionally good, strong, violent etc. [dial. *sneezer*, a severe blow]

sneezer *n.*[3] [1940s–50s] (*US Und.*) a local jail; a police station house.

sneezer *adj.* [1940s] (*Aus.*) excellent, wonderful. [SNEEZER n.[2] (2)]

sneezer to breezer *phr. see* BREEZER TO SNEEZER *phr.*

sneeze wagon *n.* [1900s–40s] (*US Und.*) an automobile. [the sounds of the engine]

sneezing coffer *n.* [early 19C] a snuff-box. [SE *sneeze* + *coffer*]

sneezing powder *n.* [1950s] (*US teen*) heroin.

snells *n.* [mid–late 19C] needles and buttons and other small wares carried by a street-hawker; thus *snell-fencer*, a hawker of such items. [Scot. *snell*, sharp + ? Somerset dial. *snell*, a short stick pointed at both ends]

snelt *n.* [20C+] (*Aus./N.Z.*) a sneak-thief. [? link to SNAVEL v. (1)]

snib *n.* [early 17C–mid-19C] (*Scot. Und.*) a petty thief. [Scot. *snib*, to cut into]

snib *v.* [19C] **1** (*Scot.*) to have sexual intercourse with a woman. **2** (*Scot Und.*) to snatch, to pickpocket. [Scot. *snib*, to cut into, to snuff a candle]

snibbet *n.* [20C+] sexual intercourse. [SNIB v. (1)]

snibley *n.* [20C+] sexual intercourse; often as a *bit of snibley*. [SNIB v. (1)]

snich *n. see* SNITCH n.[1].

snicker *n.*[1] [late 18C–early 19C] a horse suffering from glanders, a contagious disease typified by swellings beneath the jaw and discharge of mucus from the nostrils. [ety. unknown]

snicker *n.*[2] [mid-19C] a drinking glass. [ety. unknown]

snicket *n.* **1** [1940s] a woman as a sexual object; thus sexual intercourse, esp. as *a bit of snicket*. **2** [1990s+] the vagina. **3** [1990s+] (*Irish*) a penis. [? Yorks. dial. *snicket*, a narrow passage; or Lancashire dial. *snicket*, a forward woman]

snick fadger *n.* [mid–late 19C] a petty thief. [SE *snick*, to cut, snip, clip, nick + FADGE v.]

snick up! *excl. see* SNECK UP! *excl.*

snid *n.* (*also* **snide**) [mid-19C] a sixpence. [? SNIDE n. (1)]

snide *n.* **1** [mid-19C+] (*orig. US*) (*also* **snyde**) counterfeit money; thus *snide lurk*, the passing of counterfeit money; *snide shop*, an agency that organizes the passing of counterfeit money; *snide tickler*, a passer of counterfeit money. **2** [late 19C+] a deceptive, fake person; a confidence trickster. **3** [1910s] worthless goods, touted as valuable. **4** [1940s+] (*UK Und.*) anything counterfeit. **5** [1970s+] (*orig. S.Afr.*) imitation diamonds, fake gold, platinum and silver jewellery. [? Ger. *aufschneiden*, to boast, to brag, to show off, or Ger. *schneiden*, to cut, i.e. the cutting of fake coins]

snide *adj.* (*also* **shnide, snyde(y)**) **1** [mid-19C+] fake, counterfeit. **2** [mid-19C+] second-rate, useless. **3** [mid-19C+] unpleasant, mean, sneering. **4** [late 19C] smart, aware. **5** [late 19C+] corrupt. **6** [1900s] deemed to have contravened rules. [SNIDE n.]

snide *v.* [late 19C] to deceive, to trick. [SNIDE n. (2)]

snide and shine *n.* [late 19C] an East End Jew. [SNIDE adj. + SHEENY n.[1] (1)]

snideness *n.* [late 19C] astuteness, awareness, mental acuity. [SNIDE adj. (4)]

snide pitcher *n.* (*also* **snide pusher, snyde-pitcher**) [mid–late 19C] one who passes bad money; thus *snide pitching*, passing counterfeit money. [SNIDE n. (1) + PITCH v.[1] (1)/PUSH v.[2] (1)]

snider *n. see* SNYDER n.

snidesman n. (also **snider**) [late 19C–1910s] a counterfeiter. [SNIDE n. (1) + sfx -*man*]

snide sparkler n. [late 19C] a counterfeit diamond. [SNIDE adj. (1) + SPARKLER n.¹ (2)]

snide 'un n. [late 19C] one who is smart, aware, 'fly'. [SNIDE adj. (4)]

snidey adj. **1** [late 19C] counterfeit. **2** [late 19C+] bad, unfavourable. **3** [1950s+] sneering, supercilious. [SNIDE adj.]

snidger adj. see SNODGER adj.

snidget adj. [1930s+] (*Aus. teen*) excellent, first-rate. [? SNODGER n.]

snidy adj. [2000s] unpleasant, menacing. [SNIDE adj. (3)]

sniff n. **1** [1900s] (*Aus.*) perfume. **2** [1910s+] (*drugs*) narcotics, esp. cocaine (cf. BLOW n.⁶). **3** [1970s+] (*drugs*) amyl nitrite, butyl nitrite; thus (*US gay*) sniff queen, a homosexual devotee of such drugs (cf. AIMIES n.). **4** [1990s+] (*drugs*) glue, paint-thinner and other chemicals used for intoxication. [SE *sniff*, i.e. the methods of consumption]

sniff v. **1** [1910s+] (*drugs*) to inhale heroin, cocaine, glue or any other intoxicating substance. **2** [1920s+] to drink alcohol.

sniff a powder v. [1940s] (*US Black*) to leave fast, to run away. [var. on TAKE A RUN-OUT POWDER v.]

sniffed up adj. [1980s–90s] (*US drugs*) intoxicated by a narcotic. [SNIFF v. (1)]

sniffer n. **1** [mid-19C+] the nose. **2** [late 19C] a snob, one with their 'nose in the air'. **3** [20C+] (*drugs*) a cocaine, morphine or heroin user. **4** [1930s] (*US Black*) a nervous, excitable mood. **5** [1940s+] any device used to sense gas, radiation etc; thus *sniffer dog*, a dog trained to sniff out drugs or explosives. **6** [1950s] (*US*) an (unpleasant) odour. **7** [1960s+] (*drugs*) one who sniffs glue. **8** [1970s] an investigator from the DHSS/Benefits Agency who checks on the validity of unemployment benefit claims. **9** [1970s+] a prostitute's client who enjoys sniffing her used underwear. [SE *sniff*]

sniffer (and snorter) n. [1980s] a newspaper reporter. [rhy. sl.]

sniffler n. [late 19C–1930s] (*Anglo-Irish*) an alcoholic drink; usu. in phr. *will you have a sniffler?*

sniffles, the n. [1900s] (*US*) a fit of depression. [SE *sniffles*, weeping, tearfulness]

sniffs n. see SNIPS n. (2).

sniffy adj. [late 19C+] disdainful, arrogant, ill-tempered. [the *sniffs* of contempt]

snifter n.¹ **1** [19C] the nose. **2** [1920s–50s] (*US drugs*) a cocaine user. **3** [1930s] (*US drugs*) a morphine user. **4** [1930s+] (*US drugs*) a measure of cocaine, enough for a single inhalation. [SE *sniff*/SNIFF v. (1) + play on SNIFTER n.²]

snifter n.² **1** [mid-19C+] an alcoholic drink. **2** [1920s] in fig. use, a (small) portion. [SE *snifter*, a brandy glass, shaped to be warmed by the hands and for the fumes, so intensified, to be sniffed]

snifter n.³ [late 19C–1910s] **1** anyone or anything seen as especially important, large or powerful. **2** an attractive woman. [? fig. use of dial. *snifter*, a strong breeze]

snifter adj. [1910s] first-rate, the best. [SNIFTER n.³ (1)]

snifty adj. **1** [late 19C] having a pleasant smell. **2** [late 19C–1940s] (*US*) haughty, arrogant, disdainful. [(1) var. on SNIFFY adj.]

snig v. [late 19C; 1960s] to steal, to pilfer. [Yorks. dial. *snig*, to chop off, to steal]

sniggle n. [1930s+] (*Aus.*) a woman seen as a sex object; thus through metonymy, sexual intercourse. [? SNIGGLE v. or SE *snuggle*]

sniggle v. [19C] to wriggle, to creep stealthily. [? dial.]

snilch v. [late 17C–early 19C] (*UK Und.*) to look at closely; to spy on. [ext. of SE *sneck*]

sninny n. [1940s] (*Aus.*) a young woman. [var. on SKINNY n.¹]

snip n.¹ [late 16C–1940s] a tailor; also used as a generic proper name, e.g. *Master Snip, Snip the Tailor*. [SE *snip*, to cut]

snip n.² **1** [early 18C; 1920s] (*UK Und.*) a cheat. **2** [early 18C–early 19C] a swindle, a deception. **3** [late 19C+] a certainty. **4** [1920s+] anything simple, an easy task. **5** [1920s+] a bargain. [SE *snip*, a single slice of the scissors]

snip v. **1** [early 18C; 1960s+] to swindle, to deceive. **2** [1960s] (*Aus.*) to borrow money. [SE *snip*, to slice, to cut; (1) 1960s+ use Aus.]

snip a dolly v. [1940s] (*US Black*) to leave, to go away. [ety. unknown]

snip-cabbage n. (also **snip-louse**) [18C; 19C] a tailor. [SE *snip* + CABBAGE n.¹ (1)/SE *louse*]

snipe n.¹ [mid-18C–19C] a lawyer, esp. one who has presented a large bill; thus the inflated bill itself. [SE *snipe*; a pun on the bird's long bill]

snipe n.² **1** [late 19C–1900s] a defaulter on Stock Exchange. **2** [late 19C+] a derog. term of abuse. **3** [1950s] (*US*) a male prostitute or one who befriends homosexuals to acquire money, esp. by robbing.

snipe n.³ [late 19C+] (*orig. US tramp*) a cigarette or cigar butt; thus *snipe-shooting/-hunting*, picking up cigar or cigarette ends from the gutter. [SE *snipe*, the long-beaked bird or SE *snip*, to cut off; note dial. *snipe*, a mean person]

snipe n.⁴ **1** [late 19C+] (*Ulster*) one who has a long nose. **2** [2000s] the human nose. [the bird's long beak]

snipe n.⁵ **1** [20C+] (*Aus./US*) a small wall poster, a flyer, usu. political. **2** [1920s–30s] (*US prison*) a newspaper. [SE *snipe*, to shoot at]

snipe v.¹ **1** [late 19C+] (*mainly US*) to pick up, to pilfer, to filch. **2** [1900s] to prospect for gold in old diggings. **3** [1980s+] (*Aus. prison*) to request a loan. [? image of the bird foraging with its beak]

snipe v.² [1970s+] (*US Black*) to kill. [orig. milit. use]

snipe (on) v. [1930s+] (*US Black*) to malign, to criticize, to gossip about someone. [var. on synon. SE *snipe at*]

sniper n.¹ [1920s–50s] (*US*) one who picks up cigar or cigarette ends from the gutter or sidewalk. [SNIPE n.³/SNIPE v.¹ (1)]

sniper n.² [1930s+] (*Aus.*) a non-union wharf worker. [SE *sniper*, i.e. he 'shoots down' available work]

sniper n.³ [2000s] (*US Black*) one who places illicit fly-posters. [SNIPING n.²]

sniper n.⁴ [2000s] (*US Black*) an act of ejaculating in a woman's eye as a climax to fellatio.

snipes n. [early–mid-19C] a pair of scissors. [SE *snip*]

snipe shooter n. [late 19C–1970s] (*US*) one who picks up cigarette ends from the gutter; thus v. *shoot snipes*. [SNIPE n.³ + SE *shooter*]

sniping n.¹ [late 19C] (*US*) prospecting for gold in old, abandoned diggings. [SNIPE v.¹ (2)]

sniping n.² [2000s] (*US Black*) the illegal flyposting of advertisements on available surfaces, e.g. lamp-posts etc. [SNIPE n.⁵ (1)]

snip-louse n. see SNIP-CABBAGE n.

snippety n. [late 19C] any form of publication, e.g. the former *Tit-Bits*, made of material cut (or *snipped*) from others.

snippy adj. (also **snippety, snippish**) [mid-19C+] (*orig. US*) hypercritical, having a tendency to complain over petty problems or cut other people; thus *snipster*, a petty complainer; *snippishness*, tetchiness, ill temper. [categorized as a 'woman's word' in its orig. cit. in Bartlett, *Dict. Americanisms* (1848)]

snips n. **1** [late 19C] handcuffs. **2** [1900s–60s] (also **sniffs**) a pair of scissors.

sniptious adj. [early 19C–1930s] (*US*) neat and elegant. [anything unnecessary has been *snipped* away]

snit n. **1** [1930s; 1960s] (*orig. US*) an outbreak of temper, generally a children's term; thus *snittiness*, ill temper, verbal unpleasantness; also as adj., *snitty*. **2** [1960s] an aloof individual. [? echoic; coined by US writer/diplomat Clare Booth Luce (1903–87)]

snitch *n.*[1] (*also* **snich**) **1** [late 17C–mid-18C] a blow on the nose. **2** [late 17C+] (*UK Und.*) the nose. **3** [late 18C+] an informer, initially in phr. TURN SNITCH *v.*; also attrib. **4** [late 19C] in pl., handcuffs. **5** [1910s] a contemptible person. [(3) SNITCH *v.* (1)]

snitch *n.*[2] (*also* **snitcher**) [1940s+] (*N.Z.*) a grudge; hostility, bad feeling; thus *get/have/take a snitch/snitcher on*. [ety. unknown; ? link to SNIT *n.* (1)]

snitch *n.*[3] *see* SNITCHER *n.*[3].

snitch *v.* **1** [18C+] (*also* **snitch off/out**) to inform, to turn King's/Queen's evidence, to betray. **2** [20C+] to steal, to take; lit. and fig. **3** [1990s+] (*Aus.*) to arrest. [SNITCH *n.*[1] (2), i.e. one sticks one's nose in]

snitch-ass *adj.* [1980s+] (*US Black*) untrustworthy, tale-telling. [SNITCH *n.*[1] (3) + -ASS sfx]

snitchball *n.* [1990s+] (*US prison*) any game played by those inmates, among them informers, who live in protective segregation. [SNITCH *n.*[1] (3) + sfx. *-ball*]

snitch box *n.* (*also* **kite box**) [1990s+] (*US prison*) a box used both for institutional correspondence and for passing on messages that accuse fellow inmates of illegal activity. [SNITCH *n.*[1] (3)/KITE *n.*[2] (5)]

snitchel *n.* [late 17C–early 18C] a blow on the nose. [SNITCH *n.*[1] (1)]

snitchel *v.* [late 17C–early 19C] to hit on the nose. [SNITCHEL *n.*]

snitcher *n.*[1] [mid-18C] a member of a set of fashionable young men or 'bloods'. [? SNITCH *n.*[1] (1), i.e. their devotion to tweaking or punching people on the nose]

snitcher *n.*[2] **1** [late 18C+] an informant, a tell-tale. **2** [mid-19C–1930s] (*Scot.*) in pl., handcuffs, esp. strings used in place of handcuffs. **3** [1900s–20s] a detective. **4** [1940s] (*US Black*) a newspaper reporter or columnist. [SNITCH *n.*[1] (3)]

snitcher *n.*[3] (*also* **snitch**) [1930s+] (*Aus./N.Z.*) any person or thing considered notably excellent, attractive, strong etc. [? SNEEZER *n.*[2] (2)]

snitcher *n.*[4] [1930s] (*US*) a petty thief. [SNITCH *v.* (2)]

snitcher *n.*[5] *see* SNITCH *n.*[2].

snitcher *adj.* [1930s+] (*Aus./N.Z.*) first-rate, excellent, attractive. [SNITCHER *n.*[3]]

snitch game *n.* [1990s+] (*US prison*) obtaining information from inmates by threatening to falsely expose them as informers. [SNITCH *n.*[1] (3)]

snitching *n.* **1** [early 19C+] informing. **2** [1930s+] (*US*) stealing. [SNITCH *v.*]

snitching-rascal *n.* [early 19C] an informer. [SNITCH *v.* (1) + SE *rascal*]

snitch jacket *n.* [1960s+] (*US Und.*) a reputation as an informer. [SNITCH *n.*[1] (3) + JACKET *n.*[3] (2)]

snitch-off *n.* [1950s] (*US Und.*) an act of betrayal. [SNITCH *v.* (1)]

snitch off/out *v. see* SNITCH *v.* (1).

snitch-pad *n.* [1930s–40s] (*US Black*) **1** a notebook. **2** a newspaper. [weak uses of SNITCH *v.* (1) + SE *pad*]

snitch-rag *n.* [1940s] a handkerchief. [SNITCH *n.*[1] (2)]

snitch-sheet *n.* [1930s–40s] (*US Black*) a newspaper. [weak use of SNITCH *v.* (1) + SHEET *n.* (1)]

snitchy *adj.* **1** [1910s] (*US*) petty, mean or stingy. **2** [1970s+] (*N.Z.*) tetchy, ill-tempered. [(1) SNITCH *n.*[1] (3); (2) SNITCH *n.*[2]]

snite someone's snitch *v.* [late 17C–early 19C] to hit someone's nose. [SE *snite*, to wipe + SNITCH *n.*[1] (2)]

snitzy *adj.* [1930s–40s] (*US*) elegant, smart. [? SE *snobbish* + RITZY *adj.* (1)]

sniv *v.* [early–mid-19C] (*UK Und.*) to hold one's tongue. [SE *snib*, to reprove, to reprimand]

sniv! *excl.* [early 19C] nonsense! humbug! rubbish! [SNIV *v.*]

sniveller *n.* [mid-19C] an onion. [the propensity of raw onions for causing tears]

snizzle *v.* [1910s–20s] to have sexual intercourse. [? dial. *sniggle*, to wriggle]

snoach *v.* [late 18C–early 19C] to snuffle. [echoic]

snob *n.* **1** [late 18C+] (*also* **snobber**) a cobbler, a shoemaker; thus *snobbing*, shoemaking or repairing. **2** [mid-19C] a strike-breaker. **3** [20C+] (*Aus./N.Z.*) the last, most recalcitrant sheep to be sheared. [the class-conscious, modern use of SE *snob*, one who despises their inferiors and/or toadies to those seen as superior, began as Cambridge University jargon *c*.1793 as a description of a townsman, as opposed to a university member. This may have been based on (1), the orig. sl. use, implying the desire of tradesmen to flatter custom out of the undergraduates. It was widely popularized through the success of William Thackeray's *Book of Snobs* (1848). Ironically, a parallel use (early–mid-19C) means simply an ordinary person, with no pretensions to superiority, and in mid-19C Aus. *snobs* were tradesmen, while *nobs* were the 'gentlemen'. Similarly, in university use *snobocracy*, in SE the world of the influential upper classes, meant the world of townspeople, as opposed to undergraduates – again the use returns to the orig. sl. meaning]

snob *v.* **1** [late 19C+] (*US Black*) to snub, to ignore, to treat disdainfully. **2** [1960s] (*US*) to associate with upper-class people. [SE *snob*]

snob-nob *n.* [1900s] (*N.Z.*) the self-appointed rural 'aristocracy'. [SE *snob* + NOB *n.*[2] (1)]

snob's duck *n.* [19C] a leg of mutton stuffed with sage and onions. [SNOB *n.* (1) + SE *duck*]

snobstick *n.* [mid-19C] a strike-breaker. [ext. of SNOB *n.* (2); var. on or misreading of SE *knobstick*, a strike-breaker; ult. *knobstick*, a knobbed stick or cane]

snob zoning *n.* [1960s+] (*US*) a method of placing restrictions on specific city areas in a deliberate attempt to make it impossible for low-income families, e.g. non-White, non-middle-class families, to purchase homes there. [SE *snob* + *zoning*]

snockered *adj.* (*also* **schnookered, snookered**) [1950s+] drunk or intoxicated by a drug (cf. ANNIHILATED *adj.*). [? dial. *snock*, a blow]

sno-cone *n.* [1990s+] (*US*) a frigid woman.

snoddy *n.* [late 19C–1910s] a soldier. [var. on SWADDY *n.*]

snodger *n.* [1910s+] (*Aus./N.Z.*) an excellent example of something. [ety. unknown; *OED* suggests link to Scot./dial. *snod*, smart, neat, comfortable and/or Scot. *snog*, smooth, neat]

snodger *adj.* (*also* **snidger**) [1910s+] (*Aus./N.Z.*) excellent, first-rate, very good. [SNODGER *n.*]

snoek-town *n.* [late 19C] (*S.Afr.*) Cape Town. [Du. *snoek*, the European pike (*Esox lucius*), in S.Afr. use usu. the snake mackerel (*Thyrsites atun*) + SE *town*; Cape Town was once the home of the *snoek* fishing and processing industry]

snoep *adj.* [1960s+] (*S.Afr.*) mean, greedy, selfish, stingy. [Afk. *snoep*, greedy]

snog *n.* [1940s+] kissing, cuddling; caresses short of intercourse. [SNOG *v.*]

snog *v.* [1940s+] to enjoy sexual preliminaries, stopping short of intercourse, usu. of teenage experimentation; [1980s+] use usu. implies kissing with tongues; thus *n. snogging*. [? SE *snug*; orig. RAF usage]

snollygoster *n.* [mid-19C+] (*US*) a shrewd, unprincipled person, esp. a politician. [? Ger. *schnelle Geister*, lit. 'wild host', and thus a bird of prey that terrorizes man, or *schnelle Geeschte*, lit. 'quick spirits', also defined as a monster. According to Safire, *Political Dict.* (1978), it was coined during or near the time of the US Civil War (1861–5). There may be a link to the Maryland *snallygaster*, a mythical monster supposedly part reptile and part bird, designed to terrify ex-slaves out of voting]

snoodge *v. see* SNOOZE *v.*

snook *n. see* SNOOKS *n.* (2).

snook *v.* **1** [1930s] (*Irish*) to sniff out news and gossip. **2** [1950s] (*UK prison*) to look through; thus *snook the Judas*, to look through the observation window or 'Judas hole' in a cell.

snooker *n.* [1970s–80s] (*N.Z. prison*) a hiding place. [SNOOKER v. (1)]

snooker *v.* **1** [20C+] (*Aus.*) to hide. **2** [1980s+] to trick, to cheat. [SE *snooker*, to impede]

snookered *adj.*[1] [1910s+] **1** cheated, hoaxed. **2** trapped in a difficult position. [SE *snooker*]

snookered *adj.*[2] *see* SNOCKERED *adj.*

snooks *n.* **1** [mid-19C–1920s] 'an imaginary personage often brought forward as the answer to an idle question, or as the perpetrator of a senseless joke' (Hotten, 1860). **2** [1920s+] (*also* **snook**) a term of endearment, either to a child or lover. [seen as a foolish name]

snookums *n.* [1920s+] a term of endearment. [ext. of SNOOKS *n.* (2); orig. addressed esp. to lap-dogs]

snookums! *excl.* [1950s] (*US*) an excl. of surprise.

snooky *adj.* [1910s–50s] (*Aus.*) critical, fault-finding. [? SE phr. *cock a snook*, to disdain]

snoop *n.*[1] **1** [late 19C+] an inquisitive person, a 'nosey parker'. **2** [1940s+] (*orig. US*) a detective (cf. BEAT-POUNDER *n.*). **3** [1970s] a spy. [SNOOP v. (1)]

snoop *n.*[2] [1990s+] (*US Black gang*) a derog. name for a member of the Bloods gang, as used by a Crip.

snoop *v.* (*orig. US*) **1** [mid-19C+] to pry, to interfere, to listen in. **2** [20C+] to survey (surreptitiously). **3** [1920s–60s] to steal. [Du. *snoepen*, 'to appropriate and consume dainties in a clandestine manner' (*OED*)]

snoop and pry *n.* [20C+] a cry, an act of weeping. [rhy. sl.]

snoop and pry *v.* [20C+] to cry. [rhy. sl.]

snooper *n.* **1** [late 19C+] one who pries, one who is inquisitive; often applied to local government officials. **2** [1920s] a thief. **3** [1930s+] (*also* **snooper hound**) a private detective (cf. BEAT-POUNDER *n.*).

snoop out *v.* [1950s] (*US*) to investigate, to uncover. [ext. of SNOOP v. (2)]

snoopy *adj.* [1920s] (*US*) inquisitive. [SNOOP v. (1)]

snoos(e) *n. see* SNOOZE *n.* (1).

snoot *n.* **1** [mid-19C+] the nose. **2** [late 19C+] arrogance, superciliousness. **3** [1920s+] a snob, an arrogant person who 'sticks their nose in the air'. [SE *snout*]

snoot *v.* [1920s+] (*US/Aus.*) to snub. [backform. f. SNOOTY *adj.*]

snoot-cloot *n. see* CLOUT *n.*[1] (1).

snooted *adj. see* SNOOTERED *adj.* (1).

snooter *n.* [1960s+] (*drugs*) anyone who inhales a narcotic rather than injecting it. [SNOOT *n.* (1)]

snooter *v.* [1920s] to cause trouble for someone. [SNOOT *n.* (1), i.e. 'shove one's nose in'; ? nonce-coinage by P.G. Wodehouse; all cites are his; however, note SNOTTER v.]

snootered *adj.* **1** [1910s+] (*also* **snooted**) drunk (cf. ALED UP *adj.*). **2** [1920s+] troubled. [(1) backform. f. SNOOTFUL *n.*[1]; (2) SNOOTER v. see prev. note]

snootful *n.*[1] [20C+] (*US*) an alcoholic drink; thus by metonymy, a state of drunkenness; thus *have/get/pack a snootful*, to be drunk or to get drunk. [SNOOT *n.* (1)]

snootful *n.*[2] [1910s] (*US*) an experience, a 'flavour'. [fig. use of SNOOT *n.* (1)]

snootily *adv.* [1920s+] conceitedly, snobbishly. [SNOOTY *adj.*]

snootiness *n.* [1910s+] conceitedness, superciliousness. [SNOOTY *adj.*]

snooty *adj.* (*also* **snooty-nosed**) [1910s+] snobbish, stand-offish, used of one who 'looks down their nose'. [SNOOT *n.* (2)]

snooze *n.* **1** [mid-18C+] (*also* **snoos(e)**) a nap, a brief or light sleep. **2** [early–mid-19C] a lodging, a bed. **3** [1940s+] (*Aus.*) a 3-month prison sentence. **4** [1960s+] (*also* **snooze job**) something or someone considered boring. [? SE *snore* + *doze*]

snooze *v.* **1** [late 18C–mid-19C] (*UK Und.*) to have sexual intercourse. **2** [late 18C+] (*also* **snoodge**) to doze, to sleep for a short time; thus *snooze-case*, a pillow-slip. [SNOOZE *n.* (1)]

snoozem *n.* [mid-19C] a nap, a sleep. [ext. of SNOOZE *n.* (1)]

snoozer *n.*[1] **1** [early 19C+] a person, a 'chap', a woman. **2** [1910s] as a term of address. **3** [1910s–50s] (*US*) a sheep-herder. **4** [1940s+] (*Aus.*) a baby. [SNOOZE v. (2)]

snoozer *n.*[2] **1** [mid-late 19C] a thief who steals from the hotel or house in which they are staying. **2** [mid-19C–1930s] (*US Und.*) one who is asleep and thus a potential victim of crime. **3** [1910s] a bedroom. [SNOOZE *n.*]

snoozer *n.*[3] *see* SLEEPER *n.*[2] (1).

snooze with *v. see* SLEEP WITH v.

snoozing and snoring *adj.* [20C+] boring. [rhy. sl.]

snoozing ken *n.* **1** [late 18C–mid-19C] a brothel (cf. BADGER-CRIB *n.*). **2** [19C] (*also* **snoozing-crib**) a lodging house. **3** [early–mid-19C] (*also* **snuskin**) a bedroom, a bed. [SNOOZE v. (2) + KEN *n.*[1] (1)/CRIB *n.*[1] (1)]

snoozy *n.* [early 19C] a night constable. [SNOOZE v. (2)]

Snor City *n.* [1980s+] (*S.Afr.*) Pretoria. [Afk. *snor*, a moustache + SE *city*; many male Pretorians supposedly wear moustaches]

snore *n.* **1** [20C+] a sleep or sleep in general. **2** [1950s–80s] (*Aus.*) a sleeping place, esp. a hostel for tramps and vagrants. **3** [1950s+] a boring person or thing.

snore-off *n.* [1940s–60s] (*Aus./N.Z.*) a sleep or nap, esp. after a drinking session. [SNORE OFF v.]

snore off *v.* [1920s–60s] (*Aus.*) to go to sleep. [ext. of SE *snore*]

snorer *n.*[1] [mid-19C–1950s] the nose. [SE *snore*]

snorer *n.*[2] *see* SNORRER *n.*

snore through (it) *v.* [early 19C] to glide along, to move easily.

snoreville *n.* (*also* **snoresville**) [2000s+] (*orig. US*) anything or anywhere considered tedious, boring; also as adj. [SE *snore(s)* + -VILLE sfx[1]]

snoring kennel *n.* [late 17C–early 18C] a bedroom.

snork *n.* (*Aus./N.Z.*) **1** [1940s+] a baby. **2** [1970s+] a young man, a boy. [SE *snork*, a piglet]

snorker *n.* (*Aus.*) **1** [1940s+] (*also* **snorks**) a sausage. **2** [1960s–70s] the penis.

snorrer *n.* (*also* **snorer**) [20C+] **1** a scrounger, a beggar. **2** a difficult customer. [SCHNORRER *n.*]

snort *n.* **1** [mid-19C+] a gulp or single shot of alcohol. **2** [late 19C+] (*Aus.*) a pot of tea. **3** [1920s] a large glass of beer. **4** [1940s+] (*drugs*) a dose or measure of a powdered narcotic. **5** [1970s+] (*drugs*) cocaine (cf. BLOW *n.*[6]).

snort *v. see* SNORT (UP) v.

snorter *n.*[1] **1** [early 19C] a blow on the nose. **2** [early 19C+] the nose. **3** [1940s+] (*drugs*) one who inhales (rather than injects) narcotics. [(3) SNORT (UP) v. (1)]

snorter *n.*[2] **1** [mid-19C] (*US*) 'a dashing, riotous fellow' (Bartlett, *Dict. Americanisms*). **2** [mid-late 19C] a gale, a stiff breeze. **3** [mid-19C+] anything or anyone exceptionally large, strong, violent etc. **4** [late 19C] a difficulty. **5** [1910s] a severe reprimand. **6** [1920s] (*N.Z.*) an ill-tempered, tetchy person. **7** [1950s] a sausage.

snorter *n.*[3] **1** [late 19C+] a drink of alcohol. **2** [1910s] a drunkard. [SNORT *n.* (1)]

snorting *adj.* [mid-19C+] a general intensifier, excellent, first-rate, very large, very unpleasant etc. [SNORTER *n.*[2] (3)]

snort out *v.* [1980s+] (*US campus*) to overeat, to eat voraciously. [SE *snort*, i.e. the noise one makes while eating]

snorts *n.* [1970s] (*drugs*) phencyclidine (cf. ACE *n.*[4]). [? play on HOG *n.*[9]]

snort (up) *v.* (*drugs*) **1** [1930s+] to inhale narcotics, usu. cocaine or heroin, through the nostrils; thus *snorted*, under the influence of the drug. **2** [1960s+] to inhale glue etc. **3** [1970s+] to drink alcohol. [SE *snort*; (3) SNORT *n.* (1)]

snorty *adj.* [late 19C] bad-tempered, disagreeable. [SE *snort*]

snossidge *n.* [late 19C] a sausage. [joc. mispron.]

snot *n.*[1] **1** [18C+] nasal mucus. **2** [mid-19C+] a pej. term for a person, the usual implication being of their arrogance or, in the case of women, their promiscuity. **3** [late 19C+] the nose. **4** [1930s+] semen (cf. BOLLOCK SNOT n.). **5** [1980s+] (*drugs*) residue produced from smoking amphetamine. [MDu. *snotte*; SE in 15C–17C but was generally seen as sl. by 18C; cognate with 14C SE *snite*, to wipe mucus from the nose and thus ult. to SE *snout*]

snot *n.*[2] *see* SNOTNOSE n. (3).

snot *v.* **1** [early 19C+] (*US*) to treat disdainfully. **2** [1990s+] to hit in the nose. [(1) SNOT n.[1] (2); (2) SNOT n.[1] (3)]

snotbag *n.* [2000s] (*US*) an arrogant, pompous individual. [SNOT n.[1] (2) + -BAG sfx]

snot ball *n.* [1980s+] (*drugs*) rubber cement rolled into a ball and burned so that the fumes can be inhaled; usu. in pl. [SNOT n.[1] (1) + SE *balls*]

snot-box *n.* [early 19C; 20C+] (*US*) the nose. [SNOT n.[1] (1) + SE *box*]

snotgobbler *n.* [1990s+] a general term of derision. [SNOT n.[1] (1)/SNOT n.[1] (4) + SE *gobbler*]

snot-locker *n.* [1970s+] (*US*) **1** the nose. **2** the vagina (cf. BAG n.[1]). [SNOT n.[1] (1)/SNOT n.[1] (4) + SE *locker*]

snotnose *n.* [1920s+] (*orig. US*) **1** an arrogant, snobbish person. **2** a small child with a running nose, a grubby child; also in fig. use. **3** (*also* **snot, snothole**) a young person. [SNOT n.[1] (1) + SE *nose*]

snot-nosed *adj.* (*also* **snotnose**) **1** [1940s+] young or immature. **2** [1940s+] arrogant, snobbish. [SNOTNOSE n.]

snot-poor *adj.* [1960s] (*US*) impoverished. [SNOT n.[1] (1)]

snotrag *n.* [late 19C+] a handkerchief. [SNOT n.[1] (1) + SE *rag*]

snotter *n.* **1** [mid-19C] the nose. **2** [mid-19C] a pickpocket who specializes in stealing handkerchiefs. **3** [mid-19C+] a (dirty, ragged) handkerchief; thus *snotter-hauling*, stealing handkerchiefs; a paper handkerchief. **4** [20C+] (*Ulster*) a dirty, unpleasant person. [SNOT n.[1] (1)]

snotter *v.* [1910s] (*Aus.*) to kill. [ext. of Scot. *snotter*, to hit on the nose]

snottery *adj.* [20C+] unpleasant, arrogantly annoyed. [? var. on SNOTTY adj. (2)]

snottinger *n.* [mid-19C] a pocket handkerchief. [SNOT n.[1] (1)]

snottle-box *n.* [19C] the nose. [SNOT n.[1] (1) + SE *box*]

snotty *adj.* **1** [mid-19C+] superior, snobbish, stuck-up. **2** [1910s+] (*Aus./US*) angry, irritated; thus *snottiness*, ill-temper, irritation. **3** [1950s+] dirty, paltry, contemptible. [orig. late 17C SE]

snotty *adv.* [1930s+] arrogantly, in a domineering manner. [SNOTTY adj. (1)]

snotty-nose *n.* [19C+] **1** a dirty, contemptible, grubby person. **2** an arrogant, snobbish person. [SNOTTY adj. (1); SE until 19C]

snotty-nosed *adj.* **1** [1940s–70s] young, immature, childish. **2** [1950s+] arrogant, snobbish. [SE *snotty-nosed*, having a runny nose]

snout *n.*[1] [late 18C–early 19C] (*UK Und.*) a hogshead. [play on SE *hogshead*, i.e. a 'pig's nose']

snout *n.*[2] **1** [late 19C+] tobacco; thus (*UK prison*) *snout baron*, one who controls the clandestine sale of tobacco, the prison 'currency'; *snout day*, the weekly issue of tobacco. **2** [1950s+] a cigarette. [SE *snout*; when tobacco was barred from prisons, a prisoner would mask his smoking by pretending to rub his nose]

snout *n.*[3] [1930s+] an informer; thus *snouting*, passing on information to the police. [SNOUT v.[2]]

snout *v.*[1] [1910s–50s] (*Aus./N.Z.*) to bear ill-will towards, to treat with disfavour, to rebuff. [SE *snout*; to 'stick one's nose in the air']

snout *v.*[2] [1920s+] to act as a police informer. [SE *snout*, i.e. one who 'pokes their nose in']

snout china *n.* [1940s–50s] (*UK prison*) an intimate friend, lit. a person with whom one shares tobacco, as opposed to a GRAFT CHINA n. [SNOUT n.[2] (1) + CHINA (PLATE) n. (1)]

snouted *adj.* [1910s–50s] (*Aus.*) in trouble, out of favour, rebuffed. [SNOUT v.[1]]

snouter *n.* [1940s–70s] a tobacconist; thus *snoutery*, a tobacco wholesaler. [SNOUT n.[2] (1)]

snout-piece *n.* [17C–19C] the nose, the face. [SE *snout*]

snouty *n.* [1930s] (*UK Und.*) tobacco. [var. on SNOUT n.[2] (1)]

snouty *adj.* [mid-19C] overbearing, insolent. [having one's 'snout' or nose in the air]

snow *n.*[1] [early–late 19C] (*UK Und.*) (wet) linen. [the colour + it 'falls' on the hedges where it is left to dry]

snow *n.*[2] (*also* **snowball**) (*orig. US drugs*) **1** [1910s+] cocaine (cf. BLANCA n.). **2** [1920s+] heroin (cf. BLACK n.[3]). **3** [1930s–80s] morphine (cf. AUNTIE EMMA n.). **4** [1990s+] crack cocaine (cf. BASE n.). **5** [2000s] amphetamine (cf. A n.[2]). [the colour and consistency; the usu. ref. is to cocaine]

snow *n.*[3] **1** [1910s+] money, silver coins, small silver change. **2** [1940s+] (*Aus.*) (*also* **snowy**) a blond-haired person. **3** [1950s–60s] (*US Black*) a White woman. **4** [1950s+] any White person. **5** [1960s+] (*Aus. school*) a blond-haired weakling. [the colour of the money, hair or skin]

snow *n.*[4] [1950s+] (*orig. US*) smooth talk, bluff, bluster, lies. [abbr. SNOW JOB n.[1]]

snow *adj.* [1970s] (*US Black*) White. [SNOW n.[3] (3)]

snow *v.* (*also* **snow under/up**) [late 19C+] (*US*) to confuse with a deluge of smooth, if insincere, talk. [fig. use of SE *snow*]

snow and ice *n.* [20C+] the price. [rhy. sl.]

snow and slushed *adj.* [2000s] flushed. [rhy. sl.]

snowball *n.*[1] **1** [late 17C] an ejaculation. **2** [1990s+] semen that has been ejaculated in a partner's mouth and that is then returned via a passionate kiss. [? SE *snowball*, a cocktail orig. based on crème de menthe, now on advocaat; (2) SNOWBALL v.[2]]

snowball *n.*[2] **1** [late 18C–early 19C] a Black person. **2** [1940s+] (*US Black/W.I.*) a White person. **3** [1980s] (*US gay*) a Black homosexual. [(1) a humourless 'joke']

snowball *n.*[3] [1940s] (*US drugs*) a narcotic drug addict. [SNOW n.[2]]

snowball *n.*[4] [1990s+] (*drugs*) MDMA (cf. ECSTASY n.). [the white pill]

snowball *n.*[5] *see* SNOW n.[2].

snowball *v.*[1] [1910s] (*US*) to predict. [? weather forecasting]

snowball *v.*[2] [1970s+] to fellate and then spit the ejaculated semen back into one's partner's mouth.

snowball in hell, a *n.* (*also* **a snowflake in hell**) [1910s] nothing at all, a general intensifier, e.g. *amount to a snowball in hell*. [SNOWBALL'S CHANCE (IN HELL), A n.]

snowball's chance (in hell), a *n.* [1910s+] no possibility at all.

snowbank *n.* [1930s–50s] (*US drugs*) a place where cocaine users gather to take their drug. [SNOW n.[2] (1)]

snow bird *n.*[1] **1** [1900s–30s] (*US*) an impoverished tramp who enlists in the forces as the winter arrives in order to get food and shelter for the next few months, then deserts when the warmer weather returns. **2** [1920s–40s] (*US tramp*) a tramp who goes to the South for the winter. **3** [1920s+] (*US, Southern*) a winter tourist who travels to the South to avoid the chilly weather. **4** [1920s+] a fan of winter weather and/or winter sports. **5** [1990s+] (*US gay*) a wealthy gay man who moves to Miami, Florida, one of the US's gay capitals, to enjoy sun and sex. [SE *snow* + BIRD n.[2] (1)]

snow bird *n.*[2] (*US drugs/Und.*) **1** [1910s+] a cocaine user. **2** [1920s+] a heroin or morphine addict. **3** [1930s] a woman involved in the cocaine trade. [SNOW n.[2] + BIRD n.[2] (1)/BIRD n.[1] (2)]

snow-birding *n.* [1970s+] (*Aus./N.Z.*) stealing washing, usu. women's underwear, from clothes-lines. [SNOW n.[1]]

snowbound *adj. see* SNOWED adj.

snow-broth *n.* [late 19C–1910s] cold tea. [SE *snow-broth*, water produced or obtained by the melting of snow, esp. from natural causes]

snow bunny *n.* **1** [1950s+] (*orig. US*) a woman who frequents the ski slopes as much for the sex as for the sport. **2** [2000s] (*US Black*) a White woman. [SE *snow* + BUNNY n.[1] (2)]

snow cap *n.* [1980s] (*drugs*) cocaine sprinkled onto a pipe of marijuana and smoked. [SNOW n.² (1) + SE *cap*]

snowdrop *n.* [1940s+] a military policeman. [the distinctive white caps]

snow-drop *v.* [late 19C+] to steal clothes from a washing line; thus *snow-dropper*, one who does this. [SNOW-DROPPING n.]

snow-dropping *n.* (*also* **snow-hunting**) [mid-19C+] (*Aus./UK Und.*) the stealing of washing, usu. women's underwear, from unguarded clothes-lines; thus *snow-dropper/-gatherer*, one who steals from clothes-lines. [SNOW n.¹]

snowed *adj.* (*also* **snowbound**) [1920s+] (*drugs*) under the influence of heroin or cocaine; thus punningly ext. to *snowed in/up*. [SNOW n.² (1)]

snowed over *adj.* [1970s+] (*US campus*) obsessively in love, infatuated. [play on SE *snowed under*, overburdened]

snowfall *n.¹* [1950s] (*US drugs*) the using of cocaine or morphine. [SNOW n.²]

snowfall *n.²* *see* SNOW JOB n.¹.

snowflake *n.¹* **1** [1950s] cocaine (cf. BLANCA n.). **2** [1980s+] (*drugs*) crack cocaine (cf. BASE n.). [SNOW n.² (1) + FLAKE n.¹]

snowflake *n.²* [1970s+] (*US Black*) White; or of a Black person who apes Whites. [SNOW n.³ (4) + SE *flake*/FLAKE n.² (1)]

snowflake in hell, a *n.* *see* SNOWBALL IN HELL, A n.

snow-flower *n.* [1920s–50s] (*US drugs*) a female cocaine addict. [SNOW n.² (1) + literary synon. for woman]

snow gatherer *n.* [mid-19C] (*UK Und.*) one who who steals clean clothes off the hedges. [SNOW n.¹]

snowing *n.* [mid–late 19C] the stealing of linen from the drying grounds. [abbr. SNOW-DROPPING n.]

snowing down below! *excl.* [1930s–40s] (*N.Z.*) an excl. to a woman that her petticoat is showing.

snow job *n.¹* (*also* **snowfall**) [1940s+] (*US*) an untrue but totally convincing story, a con-man's patter; also as *v.* [SNOW v. + JOB n.⁴/JOB n.³ (2)]

snow job *n.²* [1960s] (*US gay*) fellatio. [the whiteness of semen]

snowjob *v.* [1950s] (*US*) to flatter, to confuse. [SNOW JOB n.¹]

snowman *n.* [1960s+] (*US*) anyone who has a smooth, seductive line of talk. [SNOW v.]

snow powder and rocks *n.* [1980s+] (*Aus. prison*) a specific grade of heroin (cf. BLACK n.³).

snow queen *n.* (*also* **snow shoveller**) [1970s+] (*US Black/gay*) a homosexual, whether Black or White, who prefers blond, 'Nordic' partners. [SNOW n.³ (2) + QUEEN n.² (1)/QUEEN sfx (2)]

snow rig *n.* [late 18C] (*US Und.*) stealing clothes hanging in the open air. [SNOW n.¹ + RIG n.² (2)]

snow seals *n.* **1** [1980s] a kind of waterproof packet used to package cocaine. **2** [2000s+] (*drugs*) a mix of cocaine and amphetamine. [SNOW n.² (1)]

snow shoveller *n.* *see* SNOW QUEEN n.

snow storm *n.* [1970s+] (*US gay*) a heavy ejaculation of semen. [the whiteness of semen]

snow toke *n.* [1990s+] (*drugs*) crack cocaine (cf. BASE n.). [SNOW n.² (4) + TOKE n.² (1)]

snow-top *n.* [1950s] (*US*) a white-haired person.

snow under/up *v.* *see* SNOW v.

snow white *n.* [1950s+] (*drugs*) cocaine (cf. BLANCA n.). [SNOW n.² (1); ult. fairy tale *Snow White*]

snow whites *n.* [1970s+] tights. [rhy. sl.]

snowy *n.¹* [late 19C] linen. [SNOW n.¹]

snowy *n.²* *see* SNOW n.³ (2).

snozzle *n.* (*also* **snoz**) [1930s+] the nose. [var. on SCHNOZZLE n.]

snozzle *v.* **1** [1920s] (*US*) to drink. **2** [1930s] (*US drugs*) to inhale cocaine or heroin. [SNOZZLE n.]

snozzled *adj.* [1920s+] (*US*) drunk. [SNOZZLE v. (1)]

snozzler *n.* [1930s+] (*Aus./N.Z.*) anything or anyone considered excellent or attractive.

snubbed *adj.* [mid-19C] (*US*) drunk.

snubby *n.* (*also* **snubbie**) [1960s+] (*US*) a cheap, short-barrelled revolver. [SE *snub-nosed*]

snub devil *n.* [late 18C–19C] a parson. [SE *snub*, to reject, i.e. he 'renounces the Devil and all his works']

snubs! *excl.* [1930s–40s] (*mainly UK teen*) used to indicate one's complete contempt for the subject of the excl.; usu. as *snubs to him/her*. [SE *snub*; ult. Scand. *snubba*, to cut short]

snudge *n.* (*also* **smudge**) [mid-17C–early 18C] (*UK Und.*) a thief who first enters a house, then hides, and emerges when the coast is clear to effect the robbery. [? SNEAK n.¹ (2) + BUDGE n.¹ (1); Nares defines it as 'a miser, or curmudgeon; a sneaking fellow']

snuff *n.* [1960s+] a murder. [SNUFF v.² (2)]

snuff *adj.* [1980s+] (*orig. US*) describing a film, usu. pornographic, that climaxes in the death (allegedly real) of one of the participants, usu. an actress or, if paedophiliac, a child; usu. as *snuff film/movie*; thus *snuff*, a collective term for the genre. [SNUFF v.² (2)]

snuff *v.¹* [19C] (*UK Und.*) to throw snuff into a victim's face, rendering them temporarily blind and thus easier to rob.

snuff *v.²* **1** [late 19C] to stop doing something. **2** [1960s+] to murder, to kill. **3** [1970s+] (*US Black*) to knock someone down. [SNUFF (IT) v.]

snuff *v.³* [1910s–50s] (*US drugs*) to sniff cocaine or similar drug. [SE *snuff*, to sniff]

snuff *v.⁴* [1930s] to eat.

snuff-box *n.* **1** [early–mid-19C] the nose. **2** [mid-19C] a coffin. **3** [1940s] a gas mask. **4** [1980s] a short person.

snuffer *n.* **1** [1910s] (*US drugs*) a cocaine user. **2** [1910s–40s] (*US Black*) the nose (cf. SNUFFERS n.). [SE *snuff*, to sniff/SNUFF v.³]

snuffers *n.* [mid-17C–early 18C] the nostrils. [SE *snuff*, to sniffle or *snuffer*, a cone-shaped implement for extinguishing candles]

snuffers! *excl.* [late 19C] a mild excl. [? the insubstantiality of SE *snuff*]

snuffer-tray *n.* [mid-19C–1900s] (*boxing*) the nose. [it 'carries' the SNUFFERS n.]

snuff (it) *v.* [mid-19C+] to die. [SE *snuff out*/SNUFF OUT v.]

snuffle *n.¹* [early–mid-19C] the nose. [SE *snuff*, to sniffle or *snuffer*, a cone-shaped implement for extinguishing candles]

snuffle *n.²* [mid-19C+] (*Aus./N.Z.*) pious cant, humbug; thus phr. *on the snuffle*, canting, uttering sanctimonious pieties; thus a nickname for a puritan. [the SE *snuffling* tones of the self-appointed moralist]

snuffle-buster *n.* (*also* **snufflebody**) [late 19C–1900s] (*Aus./N.Z.*) a puritan; thus *snuffle-busting/snufflebustious*, puritanical. [ext. SNUFFLE n.²]

snuffling community *n.* [early 18C] prostitutes, seen collectively. [ety. unknown; SE *snuffle*, to sniff; ? to talk through the nose was a characteristic of contemporary prostitutes]

snuff-lurker *n.* *see* SNEEZE-LURKER n.

snuff out *v.* [mid-19C–1940s] **1** to die. **2** to kill. [SE *snuff out*]

snuff powder *n.* [1960s] (*US drugs*) a poisoned injection, a 'hot shot'. [SNUFF v.² (2) + POWDER n.²]

snuff racket *n.* [early 19C] (*UK Und.*) temporarily blinding shopkeeper with a handfull of snuff, then seizing his money or stock. [SE *snuff*/SNUFF v.¹ + RACKET n.¹ (1)]

snuff stick *n.* [1970s] (*N.Z.*) a cigarette. [SE *snuff-stick*, an implement for dipping snuff]

snuffy *n.¹* [1950s] (*US drugs*) one who inhales (rather than injects) a narcotic. [SNUFF v.³]

snuffy *n.²* [1960s–70s] (*US*) a combat infantryman; a marine. [ety. unknown]

snuffy *adj.* [mid-18C–mid-19C] tipsy, drunk. [*OED* links this to SE *snuff*, but no real relevance]

snug *n.* **1** [mid-19C+] the parlour-bar of a public house or inn. **2** [20C+] (*US Und.*) a small revolver that can be concealed easily. [SE *snug*, comfortable, cosy]

snug *adj.* [19C] drunk (cf. ABOUT RIGHT phr.¹). [SE *snug*, comfortable, cosy]

snug v.[1] [19C] to have sexual intercourse with. [SE *snug*, to snuggle]

snug v.[2] [mid-19C] (*US*) to steal, to conceal from the proper owner. [SE *snug*, to place neatly]

snuggies n. [1970s] (*US campus*) women's underwear. [despite the root in SE *snug*, i.e. cosy, not necessarily of winter thickness]

snuggle-pup n. [1920s–30s] (*US teen*) a young man or woman who enjoys partying; one's boyfriend or girlfriend.

snuggy n.[1] **1** [1940s–50s] a woman's muff. **2** [1990s+] (*US*) a sexually attractive woman who is looking for sexual liaisons. [SE *snug/snuggle*]

snuggy n.[2] *see* WEDGIE n.

snug's the word! excl. [18C–mid-19C] say nothing about this! [SE *snug*, i.e. covered up]

snurge n. **1** [1920s–40s] a Poor Law Institution. **2** [1930s–50s] a tattle-tale, a sycophant. **3** [1930s+] a generally contemptible person (reputed to sniff women's bicycle seats). [ety. unknown]

snurge v. [1930s+] to sneak off to avoid work or responsibilities. [ety. unknown; ? link to SNEAK n.[2]]

snuskin n. *see* SNOOZING KEN n. (3).

snyde *see under* SNIDE.

snyder n. (*also* **snider**) [17C–mid-19C] a tailor. [Ger. *schneider*, a tailor]

so adj. **1** [19C] drunk. **2** [mid-19C] flustered, overcome emotionally. **3** [mid-19C+] menstruating. **4** [late 19C] pregnant. **5** [late 19C–1950s] homosexual. [euph.]

so adv. [1970s+] (*US campus/teen*) completely, utterly.

so! excl. [1910s+] used to add emphasis to a statement contradicting a negative assertion made by the previous speaker, e.g. '*No you didn't.' 'I did so!*'

soak n.[1] **1** [late 17C+] (*also* **soaker**) a drunkard, usu. with *old*. **2** [mid-19C] (*US*) a drink. **3** [mid-19C+] a heavy drinking session; thus *get a soak on*, to drink heavily; [late 19C] *come out of soak*, to get over one's hangover. **4** [1900s–50s] a despised person. [SOAK v.[1] (1)]

soak n.[2] [1900s] (*US*) a blow. [SOAK v.[3]]

soak v.[1] **1** [17C+] to drink heavily; thus *soaky*, drunk. **2** [19C] to ply with liquor. **3** [1900s] to spend money on drink.

soak v.[2] **1** [mid-19C–1920s] (*also* **put into soak**) to pawn. **2** [1910s–40s] (*US campus*) to borrow. [one leaves one's possession 'to soak']

soak v.[3] (*also* **soak it to**) [late 19C+] **1** (*US*) to hit. **2** in fig. use, to give, to punish, to criticize. **3** (*US campus*) to overcharge, to cheat, to treat unfairly. **4** (*US*) to win money from; thus in passive, to lose. [var. on SOCK v.[1] (1)]

soak v.[4] [late 19C+] (*orig. US*) to charge a high price, to tax heavily, to extort money from.

soakapee n. [1940s] (*W.I.*) a habitual drunkard, an alcoholic. [SE *soak* + PEE n.[1]; such drunkards may well foul their clothes]

soak away v. *see* SOCK v.[2].

soaked adj. **1** [late 16C; mid-19C+] (*also* **soakful**) drunk (cf. DAMP adj.). **2** [1910s+] (*US*) intoxicated by a drug. [SOAK v.[1] (1)]

soaked bum n. [1900s] (*US short order*) a portion of beets.

soaker n.[1] **1** [late 16C+] a drunkard, a drinker. **2** [1910s] a drunken spree. [SOAK v.[1] (1)]

soaker n.[2] **1** [mid-19C–1910s] very wet weather, a very wet day. **2** [late 19C] (*US tramp*) a sickening experience.

soaker n.[3] [1940s–50s] (*US prison*) a warder.

soaker n.[4] *see* SOAK n.[1] (1).

soakful adj. *see* SOAKED adj. (1).

soak it v. (*also* **let it soak**) [late 19C+] of a man, to linger before withdrawing the penis after intercourse.

soak it to v. *see* SOAK v.[3].

soak one's clay v. [mid-19C] to drink, to quench one's thirst. [SE *soak* + *clay*, one's body or 'mortal clay']

soak one's head in Salt River v. *see* ROW UP SALT RIVER v. (1).

soak the mill v. [late 19C] (*US*) to drink away one's possessions. [SE *mill*, used as a generic for one's property]

so-and-so n. **1** [mid-19C+] an unspecified object, person or place. **2** [late 19C+] a euph. for any derog. name, esp. SONOFABITCH n.

so-and-so adj. **1** [mid-18C; 1920s+] a euph. for any obscenity. **2** [1910s–20s] in a given manner.

soap n.[1] **1** [19C] a thick soup. **2** [late 19C+] (*Aus.*) processed cheese.

soap n.[2] [mid-19C–1930s] (*US*) money, esp. corruption money.

soap n.[3] [mid-19C+] flattery; the act of flattering someone. [abbr. SOFT SOAP n.]

soap n.[4] (*also* **bit of soap**) [late 19C–1900s] women, esp. promiscuous ones or prostitutes. [? their smell or household chores]

soap n.[5] [1950s+] (*Aus.*) a fool, a simpleton. [? JOE SOAP n.]

soap n.[6] [1980s+] (*Aus. prison*) a prisoner who does not wash.

soap n.[7] [2000s] (*drugs*) cannabis (cf. BOB HOPE n.). [rhy. sl. = DOPE n.[1] (6)]

soap n.[8] *see* SOAP OPERA n.

soap v. [mid-19C+] to flatter. [SOAP n.[3]]

soap and flannel n. [1910s–40s] the drawing of sickness benefit. [rhy. sl. = *the panel*, those doctors who accepted patients under the National Health Insurance Act (1913)]

soap and lather n. [late 19C+] a father. [rhy. sl.]

soap and water n. [20C+] a daughter. [rhy. sl.]

soapbox artist n. [1930s] (*N.Z.*) a public orator, esp. an extremist or rabble-rouser. [SE *soapbox* + ARTIST sfx]

soap-crawler n. [mid-19C–1900s] a toady, a sycophant. [SOAP n.[3] + CRAWLER n.[2]]

soapdodger n. [1990s+] **1** a Protestant, as used in Scotland and Northern Ireland. **2** (*UK prison*) a prisoner who chooses to avoid showering. **3** anyone seen as dirty, e.g. a 'New Age' traveller. **4** (*Aus.*) a newly arived British immigrant. [the supposed dirtiness of those concerned]

soaper n.[1] *see* SOAP OPERA n.

soaper n.[2] *see* SOPOR n.

soap-freak n. [2000s+] (*US*) a fan or devotee of daily television or radio drama series. [SOAP OPERA n. + FREAK sfx]

soap game n. [1930s–40s] (*US Und.*) a form of confidence trick that inolves the apparent wrapping of bars of soap in $20 bills; the bars are then sold to victims.

soapie n. [1980s+] (*Aus./N.Z.*) a radio or TV soap opera.

soap-locked adj. [mid-19C] wearing SOAP LOCKS n. [SOAP LOCKS n.]

soap locks n. [mid-19C] (*US*) **1** a hairstyle favoured by the New York gangs of the period, a lock of hair was carefully curled then covered with soap to make it lie flat. **2** in sing., one who wears this hairstyle, usu. a rowdy young man, thus a gang member, a thug.

soap opera n. (*also* **soap, soaper**) [1930s+] (*orig. US*) **1** a radio or TV drama series, e.g. *The Archers, Coronation Street*, which tells the interminable tale of supposedly 'ordinary life'. **2** in fig. use, of anything endlessly repetitive, albeit melodramatic. [the original 1920s radio show, *The Goldbergs*, was sponsored by US soap manufacturer Proctor & Gamble]

soap opera adj. [1930s+] (*US*) typical of family and social life as it is portrayed in the television and radio drama series, e.g. *soap opera mentality*. [SOAP OPERA n.]

soaps, the n. [1940s+] (*orig. US*) a generic term for radio and television series.

soap someone over v. [mid-19C] to humbug. [SOAP v.]

soap suds n. [early 19C] hot gin and water, with lemon and lump sugar.

soap the geyser v. [1940s+] (*N.Z.*) to get started, to set off. [the addition of special *soap* to a geyser to improve its spouting]

soap up v. [1950s] (*US*) to act kindly, to ingratiate oneself. [SOAP v.]

soapy *adj.* **1** [mid-19C+] ingratiating, unctuous, smoothly insincere. **2** [1930s+] (*Aus.*) foolish, silly, effeminate. **3** [1990s+] typical of family and social life as portrayed in radio drama or television series. [? originated in the nickname 'Soapy Sam', used of Bishop Wilberforce (1805–73); (3) SOAP OPERA n.]

soapy bubble *n.* [1990s+] trouble. [rhy. sl.]

soapy fits *n.* [late 19C] (*UK Und.*) a fake fit used to obtain sympathetically donated alms, created by chewing a small piece of soap, thus creating 'foam' at the mouth.

soapy Isaac *n. see* SUETY ISAAC n.

soar *v.* [late 19C] (*Aus.*) to die. [i.e. up to heaven]

s.o.b. *n.* **1** [1910s+] a general term of abuse, i.e. son of a bitch (cf. S.B. n.[1]). **2** [1910s+] silly old bugger/bastard. **3** [1920s+] shit or bust. **4** [1940s+] an unspecified object or person, without pej. overtones. [abbr.]

sob *n.*[1] **1** [20C+] a pitiful, if dubious tale, a 'sob-story'. **2** [1900s] (*Aus.*) talk; conversation.

sob *n.*[2] *see* SOV n.

sob act *n.* [1950s+] (*US*) a pretence of emotion, an appeal to someone's sympathies.

sob brother *n.* [1910s] (*US*) a sentimental man. [play on SOB SISTER n.]

SoBe *n.* [1990s+] (*US gay*) South Beach Miami, Florida, popular among gay men. [abbr.]

sober-water *n.* [mid-19C] soda water. [the pun reflects its use as a partial cure for hangovers]

sob-raiser *n.* (*also* **sob specialist**) [1910s–30s] (*US*) one who plays on the public's emotion to elicit sympathy for a cause.

sob-reporter *n.* [1920s] (*US*) a journalist specializing in 'human interest' stories.

sob sister *n.* **1** [1910s+] (*US*) an advice columnist, usu. a woman; a woman journalist. **2** [1920s+] (*US*) in ext. use of (1), a liberal, a 'do-gooder'. **3** [1920s+] (*US*) a woman, occas. a man, given to tearfulness. **4** [1940s] (*US Und.*) a beggar (of either sex) who attempts to play on people's emotions to elicit money.

sob specialist *n. see* SOB-RAISER n.

sob squad *n.* [1910s] (*US*) a generic term for journalists specializing in 'human interest' stories.

sob story *n.* [1910s+] a pitiful tale, which may reduce the listener to tears whether it has any basis in truth or is designed merely for felonious purposes.

sob stuff *n.* [1910s+] distressing facts, stories etc, often used to obtain sympathy and poss. money too; also attrib.

sob the blues *v.* [1920s–30s] to be very unhappy. [BLUES n.[1]]

so busy I've had to put a man on to help *phr. see* CLIMBING TREES TO GET AWAY FROM IT phr.

soc *n.* (*also* **soch, sosh**) **1** [1900s–70s] one who behaves in a socially acceptable manner, usu. in a negative sense, i.e. lacking in anything other than polish. **2** [1960s+] (*US teen*) a social climber. [abbr. SE *social*]

socdol(l)ager *n. see* SOCKDOLAGER n.

Social, the *n.* [1970s+] the local office of the Department of Health and Social Security, from where one gets unemployment and other benefits.

social dandruff *n.* [1970s+] (*US gay*) a pubic louse. [they spread through physical proximity]

social donut (hole) *n.* [1980s+] (*US campus*) a socially inept person. [i.e. an 'empty space']

social E *n.* [late 19C] (*UK middle class*) a euph. for *social evil*, itself coined in 1857 as a euph. for prostitution.

social worker *n.* [1960s–70s] (*US gay*) a homosexual who find partners among homeless and destitute men.

society *n.* [late 19C] the workhouse.

society-maddist *n.* [late 19C] a social climber.

socio *n.* [1970s] (*US/P.R.*) a social worker. [abbr.]

sock *n.*[1] **1** [late 17C–18C] a pocket. **2** [late 17C; mid–late 19C] credit; esp. as *on sock*, on credit. **3** [1920s–50s] a sock used as a

receptacle for money. **4** [1930s–50s] the store of money itself, as in a bag, safe etc. **5** [1970s] a filthy, messy room, i.e. as used by a student, young man etc. [(5) was coined by UK novelist Martin Amis (b.1949) and enjoyed brief popularity]

sock *n.*[2] [late 17C; 1900s–50s] a farthing or any small coin.

sock *n.*[3] **1** [late 17C+] a blow. **2** [1900s–10s] a shock. **3** [1930s] (*US*) a thrill, excitement, a 'kick'. **4** [1930s+] in show business, a success. [SOCK v.[1] (1)]

sock *adj.* [20C+] excellent, first-rate. [fig. use of SOCK n.[3] (1)]

sock *v.*[1] **1** [late 17C+] to hit, to punch; thus *sock into*, to assault, to beat; *give someone sock*, to give someone a thrashing. **2** [mid-19C] (*US*) to knock someone's hat over their head. **3** [late 19C] (*US*) to throw. **4** [late 19C–1900s] (*US*) to pay. **5** [20C+] in fig. use, to 'hit'. **6** [1900s] (*US*) to give. [ety. unknown]

sock *v.*[2] (*also* **soak away, sock away/in**) **1** [mid–late 19C] to obtain credit. **2** [late 19C–1950s] (*orig. US*) to set aside money for savings. **3** [1900s] (*Aus.*) to pocket. [SOCK n.[1]]

sock *v.*[3] (*also* **sock away/down**) [1910s–60s] (*Aus.*) to drink (alcohol). [fig. use of SOCK v.[1] (1)]

sockdolager *n.* (*also* **slockdolager, slockdologer, socdol(l)ager, sockdoliger, sogdoliger, stockdolager**) **1** [early 19C+] (*orig. US*) a knock-down blow, a heavy blow; thus fig., something conclusive. **2** [mid-19C+] an exceptional person or thing, esp. if large. [SOCK v.[1] (1) + ? Irish *dallacher*, the act of blinding or dazing or UK dial. *dallack*, to dress gaudily. The adj. form, *sockdolagizing*, was among the last words that President Abraham Lincoln heard: it is used in the play *Our American Cousin* in a line that was spoken by the cousin himself (Asa Trenchard) at the very moment when Lincoln's assassin fired the fatal shot]

socked *adj.* [2000s] intoxicated by drink or drugs. [fig. use of SOCK v.[1] (1)]

socked in *adv.* [1950s] (*Irish*) joined up with, as in having a sexual relationship.

socker *n.* **1** [late 18C] a thug, a lout. **2** [late 18C] a simpleton, a fool. **3** [late 19C+] a heavy blow. **4** [1920s+] one who hits powerfully. [SOCK v.[1] (1)]

sockeroo *n.* [20C+] (*orig. US*) something very successful, a hit. [SOCK n.[3] (4) + -EROO sfx]

socket *n.* [mid-15C–19C] the vagina (cf. BLACK HOLE n.[1]). [note SOCKET-MONEY n.]

socketer *n.* [mid-19C] a blackmailer. [SOCKET-MONEY n.]

socket-money *n.* **1** [late 17C–mid-19C] a dowry. **2** [18C–19C] money paid by a man to his wife to placate her after he has been caught in an adulterous affair. **3** [early 19C] the payment given to a prostitute. **4** [mid-19C] hush-money. [SOCKET n. + SE *money*]

sock frock *n.* [1940s] (*US Black*) one's best suit. [SOCK adj. + joc./assonant use of SE *frock*]

sockful *n.* [1940s] (*US*) a large amount of money.

sock in *v. see* SOCK v.[2]

socking *n.* [20C+] a beating. [SOCK v.[1] (1)]

socking *adj.* [late 19C+] very great, enormous.

sock it on *v.* [20C+] to wager money. [SOCK v.[1] (4)]

sock it to *v.* **1** [mid-19C+] to hit hard, lit. or fig., e.g. to charge someone a high price; thus excl. of exhortation, *sock it to me!* **2** [late 19C–1900s] to reprimand. **3** [late 19C–1900s] in fig. use, to 'hit', e.g. in playing an instrument. **4** [1950s+] to shock, to surprise; thus excl. *sock it to me!* amaze me! surprise me! **5** [1960s] (*orig. US Black*) to have sexual intercourse (cf. BANG v.[1]; BURY IT v.). **6** [1960s] to explain. [fig. use of SOCK v.[1] (1); *sock it to me!* was popularized on TV's *Rowan & Martin's Laugh-In* (1967–73)]

socko *n.* [1930s+] a major success, a show business 'hit'. [SOCKO adj.]

socko *adj.* [1930s+] wonderful, excellent, esp. in show business use. [SOCK n.[3] (4)]

sock someone for *v.* [1920s+] to demand money from, to extort. [SOCK v.[1] (5)]

sock the boot in *v. see* PUT THE BOOT IN *v.*

so cool *n.* [1980s+] (*US campus*) southern *Cal*ifornia. [abbr. + COOL adj.[1] (2); a play on the area's self-image]

sod *n.*[1] **1** [early 19C+] an unpleasant person. **2** [late 19C+] a sodomite, a male homosexual. **3** [1910s+] a person, either pej., neutral or affectionate. **4** [1930s+] an animal, an object. **5** [1940s+] anything categorized as difficult or annoying to perform. **6** [1950s+] a general term of address, not necessarily pej. [abbr. SE *sodomite*, but, except in (2), the sexual ref. is coincidental]

sod *n.*[2] [20C+] (*Aus.*) a wet damper, i.e. a flour and water pancake. [abbr. SE *sodden*]

sod *n.*[3] [1920s+] (*US campus*) a drunkard. [SE *sot*]

sod *n.*[4] [1960s] (*Scot.*) a mod, i.e. a member of a teenage cult *c.*1961, who wore specific, distinguishing clothes, rode motor scooters and fought their main rivals, the motorcycle-riding, leather-clad 'rockers'. [rhy. sl. = MOD n.[2] (1)]

sod *n.*[5] *see* OLD SOD n.

sod *v.* [late 19C; 1930s+] lit. to *sodomize*; thus in fig. use, synon. with TO HELL WITH —! excl.; also in a variety of semi-euph. combs., e.g. SOD (IT)! excl.; SOD OFF! excl.; SOD YOU! excl. [abbr.]

sod! *excl. see* SOD (IT)! excl.

soda *n.*[1] [1930s+] (*Aus.*) something easy to accomplish, a simple task, an easy victim. [? faro jargon *soda*, the top card that is exposed before the start of the game; this card is not counted for betting]

soda *n.*[2] [1980s+] (*US drugs*) a form of injectable cocaine used in Hispanic communities.

soda and B *n.* [late 19C] a drink of brandy and soda.

sod about *v.* (*also* **sod around**) [1950s+] to mess around, to waste time. [SOD n.[1] (1)]

soda cracker *n.* (*also* **soda biscuit**) [1960s+] (*US campus*) a White person. [such *crackers* or (UK) water biscuits are light in colour]

soda-jerker/-juggler *n. see* JERKER n.[1] (1).

sod-all *n.* [1940s+] absolutely nothing.

sod around *v. see* SOD ABOUT v.

sod-buster *n.* **1** [1910s+] a peasant, a farmer, an unsophisticated rural person (cf. BOGHOPPER n.). **2** [1920s] (*US*) an undertaker. [SE *sod*, a lump of earth + BUST v.[1] (4)]

sodden *adj.* [late 19C+] drunk (cf. DAMP adj.). [note Shakespearian use of *sodden*, heavy, dull, stupified]

sodding *adj.* [late 19C+] a derog. intensifier. [SOD v.[1]]

sodgeries *n.* [late 19C] a military exhibition, held in 1890 at the Chelsea Barracks. [mispron. of SE *soldier*]

sod (it)! *excl.* [1940s+] a general excl. of exasperation, resignation, annoyance etc. [SOD v.]

sod off! *excl.* [1940s+] go away!; thus as v., to go away, to leave. [SOD v.; semi-euph. for FUCK OFF v.]

Sodom and Gomorrah *v.* [1990s+] to borrow. [rhy. sl.]

sod's law *n.* [1970s+] a metaphorical 'law' of human experience, in this case the belief that 'if anything can go wrong in any situation, it will'. [SOD n.[1] (5)]

so dumb she thinks her bottom is just to sit on *phr.* [late 19C+] used of a very stupid (and naïve) woman (cf. DUMB AS A BOX OF ROCKS phr.). [DUMB adj.]

sod widow *n.* [1900s–30s] an actual widow, whose husband has died. [the corpse is 'under the sod']

sod you! *excl.* [late 19C+] a general excl. of hostility, dismissal. [SOD v.; semi-euph. for FUCK YOU! excl.]

sofa-pounder *n.* [1900s] (*US*) an observer, a non-participant.

sofa spud *n.* (*also* **sofa yam**) [1980s+] (*US campus*) someone who lies around doing nothing. [var. on COUCH POTATO n.; SE *sofa* + SPUD n.[2] (1)/*yam*]

soft *n.*[1] **1** [mid-19C–1900s] a weakling. **2** [20C+] a male homosexual. **3** [1930s] (*US Black*) a woman, a girlfriend.

soft *n.*[2] *see* SOFT MONEY n.

soft *adj.* **1** [late 17C; 19C+] stupid, dull, foolish; thus phr. *soft*

as shite. **2** [mid-18C; 1920s] (*US campus*) partially or totally intoxicated by drink or drugs. **3** [19C+] overly kind, easily imposed upon, insufficiently ruthless, vulnerable. **4** [mid-19C+] easy, comfortable, requiring no effort. **5** [20C+] (*US campus*) weak, timid, not able to defend oneself. **6** [1940s] (*US Und.*) of a place, vulnerable. **7** [1980s+] (*W.I. Rasta*) (*also* **soff**) unable to cope, impoverished. **8** [1980s+] (*W.I. Rasta*) not well done, amateurish.

soft *adv.* [mid-19C+] foolishly, stupidly.

soft-arsed *adj.* [1990s+] foolish (cf. CLAY-ASSED adj.).

soft ass *n.* [1960s] a weak, ineffectual man, a coward. [SOFT adj. (3) + -ASS sfx]

soft-ass *adj.* [1970s+] (*US*) weak, ineffectual. [SE *soft* + -ASS sfx]

soft as shit and twice as nasty *phr.* [late 19C+] a general pej. phr. used of anyone the speaker dislikes.

soft as silk *n.* [20C+] (*Aus.*) milk. [rhy. sl.]

softball *adj.* [1970s+] (*US*) trivial, not worthy of consideration, easy. [SAmE *softball* rather than baseball]

softballs *n.* [1970s] (*drugs*) barbiturates (cf. BARBIT n.).

soft bit *n.* (*also* **soft time**) [20C+] (*US Und.*) a system of imprisonment whereby an inmate must serve 50% of the sentence before becoming eligible for parole. [SOFT adj. (4) + BIT n.[5]/TIME n.[1]]

soft butch *n.* [1990s+] (*gay*) a 'masculine' lesbian with a soft side and gentle character. [SE *soft* + BUTCH n.[4] (3)]

soft clothes *n.* [1940s+] (*US*) civilian clothes, plain clothes.

soft collar *n.* [1900s–20s] (*Aus.*) an easy job. [SE *soft*, easy + COLLAR n.[3]]

soft con *n.* [1970s] flattery, persuasion, any form of deceit based on soft words. [SE *soft* + CON n.[1] (7)]

soft cop *n.*[1] [1920s+] (*Aus.*) anything seen as easy; esp. as *be on a soft cop*, to have it easy. [SOFT adj. (4) + COP n.[2] (2)]

soft cop *n.*[2] [1980s+] a gullible, well-meaning person, e.g. a community/social worker whose sympathies can be exploited. [SOFT adj. (3) + COP n.[1] (1); the trad. *soft cop/hard cop* interrogation routine]

softcore *adj.* [1970s+] (*orig. US*) mild, not extreme. [on model of SE *softcore* pornography, titillating but not legally 'obscene']

soft corn *n. see* SOFT SAWDER n.

soft dough *n. see* SOFT MONEY n. (3).

soften the cough *v.* [1990s+] (*Irish*) to reduce, to 'take down a peg'.

soften up *v.* [1930s+] to break down someone's resistance. [orig. in milit. use]

soft gut *n.* [1910s] (*US*) something unexceptional.

soft ha'porth *n.* (*also* **daft ha'porth**) [20C+] a weakling, a simpleton. [SOFT adj. (1) + SE *ha'porth*]

soft heel *n. see* RUBBER HEEL n. (1).

softhorn *n.* **1** [19C] a donkey, an ass. **2** [mid-19C] a simpleton, a fool. [a donkey has soft ears rather than horns]

soft-horned *adj.* [mid-19C] stupid. [SOFTHORN n. (2)]

softie *n. see* SOFTY n.[1].

softing loose *n.* [1990s+] taking things easy and not doing anything. [one is living a *soft*, *loose* life]

soft-leg *n.* (*also* **soft legs**) [1950s–70s] (*US Black*) a woman, esp. an attractive woman.

soft mark *n.* [late 19C+] a gullible victim. [SOFT adj. (3) + MARK n.[1] (1)]

soft-mash *n.* (*also* **soft-shoes**) [20C+] (*W.I.*) a pair of rubber-soled, canvas sneakers. [SE *soft* + *mash*, to crush/*shoes*]

soft money *n.* (*also* **soft**) **1** [mid-19C+] notes, bills, paper money (cf. BANK-RAG n.). **2** [mid-19C+] (*US*) currency that is likely to lose its value. **3** [1910s+] (*also* **soft dough**) money that is easily earned or otherwise gained.

soft nothings *n. see* SWEET NOTHINGS n.

soft number *n.* [1910s+] (*orig. milit.*) an easy job. [SOFT adj. (4) + NUMBER n.[3] (3)]

soft one *n.* **1** [early 19C+] (*UK Und.*) a gullible, easily fooled victim. **2** [1900s] in betting, a certainty. [SOFT adj.]

soft pedal v. [1910s+] to play down, to diminish, to keep a low profile, to act in a restrained manner. [piano imagery]

soft-roed adj. [late 19C–1900s] kind-hearted; weak. [SE soft roe, the sperm of a male fish]

soft roll n. [1940s–50s] a woman who is easy to seduce. [SOFT adj. (3) + ROLL IN THE HAY n. + play on SE]

soft salve n. see SOFT SOAP n. (1).

soft sawder n. (also **sawder, sawder to order, soft corn**) [mid-19C+] flattery. [SE (soft) solder, a pliable form of solder, made of tin and lead]

soft sawder v. (also **sawder**) [mid-19C–1900s] to flatter. [SOFT SAWDER n.]

soft-sawderer n. [mid–late 19C] a flatterer. [SOFT SAWDER v.]

softshell n. see HARD-SHELL n. (1).

soft-shoe adj. [20C+] of talk, restrained, as in give the soft-shoe, to be unforthcoming.

soft-shoes n. see SOFT-MASH n.

soft snap n. [mid-19C+] (Aus./US) an easy, pleasant job, a profitable business or undertaking. [SOFT adj. (4) + SNAP n.[1] (1)]

soft soap n. [mid-19C+] (orig. US) **1** (also **soft salve, olive oil**) flattery. **2** an act of flattering someone. **3** kindness.

soft soap v. [mid-19C+] (orig. US) to flatter, to charm. [SOFT SOAP n.]

soft-soft adj. [1950s] (W.I.) gullible, easily taken in. [SOFT adj. (3) + redup.]

soft spot n. **1** [mid-19C+] a feeling of kindness, sympathy. **2** [late 19C+] anything, esp. a job, considered easy and enjoyable, undemanding. **3** [1900s–50s] a weakness. [SE soft/SOFT adj.]

soft stuff n. **1** [late 19C+] (Aus.) 'soft', i.e. non-alcoholic, drinks. **2** [1920s] (US Und.) (also **soft sugar**) paper money, notes (cf. BANK-RAG n.). **3** [1960s] (drugs) 'soft' drugs, e.g. cannabis, amphetamines rather than narcotics. [(1) SE soft + STUFF n.[3] (1); (2) var. on SOFT MONEY n. (1); (3) SE soft + STUFF n.[3] (2)]

soft sucker n. see SISSY SOFT SUCKER n.

soft swinging n. [1970s+] a partner-swapping party where the only intercourse is performed by couples who arrived together; non-penetrative sex, however, is enjoyed at random. [SE soft + SWINGING n.[2]]

soft tack n. **1** [mid–late 19C] (orig. naut.) bread as opposed to biscuits or hard tack. **2** [1900s] (Aus.) a soft drink, as opposed to hard liquor. [SE soft + TACK n.[2] (1)]

soft thing n. **1** [mid-19C+] an easily duped simpleton. **2** [late 19C+] an easy job, an easy win etc; thus have a soft thing on, to be in an advantageous position. [SOFT adj.]

soft time n. see SOFT BIT n.

soft tommy n. [late 18C–19C] white bread. [SE soft + TOMMY n.[1] (1)]

soft-top n. [1940s] (US Black) a padded stool, esp. as found in a bar.

soft touch n. [1930s+] **1** one who can easily be solicited for money, or goods or favours. **2** an easy job or sinecure; thus an easily achieved robbery or similar crime. **3** one who is easily beaten. **4** a sympathetic person, one who is easily persuaded. [SOFT adj. + TOUCH n.[1]]

softy n.[1] (also **softie**) **1** [mid-19C+] a foolish weakling; the image is of unneccesary kindliness. **2** [1970s] an impotent man, i.e. one whose penis is soft. [SOFT adj./SE soft]

softy n.[2] [1940s] (US Black) a bed.

sogdologer n. see SOCKDOLAGER n.

soggy adj. [late 19C–1920s] (US) drunken; initiated by drunkenness; thus **sogged**, drunk; **sog**, drunkenness (cf. DAMP adj.).

soggy biscuit n. (also **soggy Saos**) [1960s+] (orig. Aus.) a game, popular among schoolboys, whereby the participants all masturbate together and then ejaculate onto a biscuit; the last to reach orgasm must eat the semen-covered biscuit. [SE, plus Aus. brandname Sao]

sogs n. [1960s] (Aus.) sausages. [abbr.]

so help me...! excl. see S'ELP ME (BOB)! excl.

s.o.h.f. n. [1970s+] (UK society) a sense of humour failure. [abbr.; often discerned in someone who fails to appreciate such hilarious practices as the throwing of bread rolls, baiting of minorities etc]

soil n. [1980s+] (Aus. prison) hashish oil (cf. BLACK OIL n.). [rhy. sl.]

soiled dove n. (also **dove of the roost**) [late 19C–1920s] (Aus./US) a prostitute; thus dovecotery, prostitution (cf. ALLEY CAT n.). [literary euph.]

soixante-neuf n. see SIXTY-NINE n.

s.o.l. n. [1930s+] (Aus.) a bad temper. [abbr. shit on one's liver]

s.o.l. adj. [1910s+] (US) unfortunate, unlucky, in a difficult situation. [abbr. shit out of luck]

sol adj. [20C+] (US Und.) in solitary confinement. [abbr.]

sold adj. **1** [early 19C+] tricked, fooled. **2** [late 19C+] convinced, successfully persuaded. [SELL v. (1); E.P. notes phr. sold again and got the money as 'a costermonger's catch-phrase on having successfully "done" someone in a bargain']

soldi n. see SALTEE n.

soldier n.[1] [early–mid-19C] **1** a red herring. **2** a boiled lobster. **3** (W.I.) a crayfish. [they both have a 'red coat']

soldier n.[2] [1930s] (US) a term of address to one whose name one does not know.

soldier n.[3] [1940s] (US) a dollar.

soldier n.[4] **1** [1960s+] (US Mafia) a lower echelon member of a Mafia family, the run-of-the-mill gangsters who fight the gang wars. **2** [1970s+] (UK Black) a member of a (teen) gang. **3** [1990s+] (Aus./US prison/Und.) a member of a prison gang.

soldier ants n. [20C+] pants. [rhy. sl.]

soldier bold n. [20C+] (Aus.) a (head) cold. [rhy. sl.]

soldiers bold adj. [20C+] cold. [rhy. sl.]

soldier's bottle n. [late 17C–early 19C] a very large bottle. [orig. naut. jargon; the presumption being that soldiers either drink excessively or need alcohol to fortify their courage]

soldier's farewell n. **1** [late 19C+] (also **lag's farewell**) any kind of less than friendly farewell; 'goodbye, good luck and fuck you!' **2** [1930s+] the weekly maintenance paid by the father of an illegitimate child.

soldier's joy n. [mid-19C–1900s; 2000s] masturbation. [note naut. jargon soldier's joy, pease pudding]

soldier's maund n. (also **soldier's mawnd**) [late 17C–18C] (UK Und.) a fake wound, assumed by beggars who wish to pose as soldiers returned from the wars; thus the beggar who uses this ruse. [SE soldier + MAUND n.]

soldiers on horseback n. [late 19C] (US short order) fishballs and dropped eggs.

soldier's pomatum n. [late 18C–mid-19C] a piece of tallow or animal-fat candle. [SE soldier + pomatum, pomade; thus a sneer at soldiers who cannot afford to dress their hair with anything better than tallow]

soldier's supper n. [late 19C] nothing; a drink of water and a cigarette or pipe. [the soldier's last meal of the day was tea; there was no supper]

soldier's thigh n. [mid–late 19C] an empty pocket. [milit. poverty]

soldier's wash n. [20C+] the washing of one's face with a scoop of water in cupped hands rather than using a flannel. [the privations of the battlefield]

sold on adj. [1920s+] convinced, fascinated by. [ext. SOLD adj. (2)]

sold out adj.[1] (also **sold up**) **1** [mid-19C] bankrupt. **2** [mid-19C–1930s] defeated, beaten.

sold out adj.[2] [1930s+] (US) corrupted, susceptible to bribery. [SELL OUT v.[1] (2)]

soles n. [1970s] (drugs) hashish (cf. AFGHAN n.). [the piece of hashish is approx. shaped like a sole; or the smuggling of hashish in the soles of purpose-built shoes]

sole-slogger *n.* [late 19C] a bootmaker. [SE *sole* + SLOGGER n. (2)]

sol-fa *n.* [late 18C–early 19C] a parish clerk. [SE *sol-fa man*, a music teacher; thus f. the clerk's leading of the sung responses in church]

solicitor general *n.* [19C] the penis. [SAmE *solicitor general*; a pun on SE *solicit*]

solid *n.*[1] [20C+] (*UK tramp*) the road.

solid *n.*[2] [1920s] (*US Und.*) a trustworthy fellow criminal or prison inmate. [SOLID adj. (3)]

solid *n.*[3] [1950s+] (*US Black*) a favour. [SE *solid*, something that has substance, thus something dependable]

solid *adj.* **1** [mid-19C+] full, complete, entire, esp. of time, e.g. *a solid month*. **2** [late 19C] as *solid on*, devoted to. **3** [late 19C+] (*orig. jazz*) trustworthy, dependable, exciting, outstanding. **4** [late 19C+] trusted; usu. as *solid with*. **5** [late 19C+] definite. **6** [1910s–60s] (*Aus./N.Z.*) severe, difficult, unfair, unreasonable. [SE *solid*, thorough, downright, vigorous; note Mezzrow & Wolfe, *Really the Blues* (1946): 'Solid, which is short for *solid as the Rock of Gibraltar* and describes a man who isn't going to be washed away so easy']

solid *adv.*[1] **1** [late 19C] (*orig. US Black*) trustworthily, dependably, excitingly, outstandingly. **2** [1920s–50s] (*US*) secure, free of problems. [SOLID adj.]

solid *adv.*[2] [late 19C+] completely, unreservedly.

solid! *excl.* [1910s+] (*orig. US*) a general excl. of approbation, implying a firm bond, honesty, excellence etc. [SOLID adj.]

solid con *n.* [20C+] (*US Und.*) a trustworthy fellow criminal or prison inmate. [SOLID adj. (3) + CON n.[1] (8)]

solid ivory *adj. see* IVORY DOME n.

solid man *n.* [late 19C] (*US Und.*) a woman's long-term male lover (as opposed to any transient entanglements). [SOLID adj. (3)]

solidment! *excl.* [1990s+] (*US campus*) an affirmative response. [Fr. *solidement*, solidly]

solid sender *n.* [1930s+] (*US Black*) **1** an admirable person, esp. a jazz or swing musician. **2** a real, genuine, amazing thing. [SOLID adj. (3) + SENDER n.]

solid shot *n.* [late 19C] (*US short order*) an apple dumpling.

solitaire *n.* **1** [1900s] (*US prison*) a solitary confinement cell. **2** [1940s] (*US Black*) suicide. [SE *solitaire*, a game played alone by oneself]

solitary *n.* [mid-19C+] *solitary* confinement in prison, also in fig. use. [abbr.]

solitary as a bastard on Father's Day *phr. see* LONELY AS A BASTARD ON FATHER'S DAY phr.

sollicker *n.* (*Aus.*) **1** [late 19C+] something notably large, 'a whopper'. **2** [1940s–50s] a large penis. [? SOCKDOLAGER n.; or ? dial. *sollock*, impetus, force]

Solly *n.* [late 19C–1950s] a generic term for any Jew (cf. ABE n.[1]). [the once-popular Jewish given name *Solomon*]

solly *n.* [1910s] (*Aus.*) the sun. [Lat. *sol*, the sun]

Solly Isaacs *n. see* SOLOMON ISAAC n.

solo *n.* [1940s] (*US Black*) the number 1.

solomon *n.*[1] (*also* **salmon, salamon, salomon**) [mid-16C–mid-19C] (*UK Und.*) an altar or mass; thus *by the solomon! by the salomon!* by the Mass! [the biblical king, *Solomon*; or ? Fr. *serment*, an oath or a sermon (*OED*) or a cant term for an altar (Harman). Rowlands, *Martin-Mark-all* (1610), notes that while *solomon/salomon* duly means Mass, 'Many men I have heard take this word Solomon to be the chief commander among the beggars. But to put them out of doubt, this is not he. Marry, there was one Solomon in King Henry the Eighth's time that was a jolly fellow among them, who kept his court most an end at Foxhall (Vauxhall) [...] who was successor to Cock Lorel']

solomon *n.*[2] [late 19C] a job.

Solomon Isaac *n.* (*also* **Solly Isaacs**) [late 19C–1910s] a Jew (cf. ABE n.[1]).

so long *phr.* [mid-19C+] (*orig. mainly US*) goodbye. [? Heb. *shalom*, peace, and used as a basic word of greeting and farewell; or ? Heb. *selah*, God be with you]

solo player *n.* [late 18C–early 19C] a poor player of any instrument, whose musicianship immediately empties a room of listeners and leaves them playing without an audience. [pun on SE use, in this case the soloist performs alone whether they wish it or not]

soma *n.* [1970s] (*drugs*) phencyclidine (cf. ACE n.[4]). [Skrt *soma*, a drug used in Vedic rituals. Note *Soma*, Aldous Huxley's name for the 'happiness' drug used in his novel *Brave New World* (1932) + SOMA, the Society of Mental Awareness, formed in 1967 to campaign for the legalization of cannabis in the UK]

sombitch *n. see* SONOFABITCH n. (1).

some *n.* **1** [mid-19C+] (*US*) violence, physical hurt. **2** [20C+] sexual intercourse; esp. in phrs. *give me some*; GET SOME v.; thus antonym *none*. **3** [1960s] (*US campus*) sexual caresses short of intercourse. **4** [1970s] (*US campus*) an attractive, alluring person. **5** [2000s] energy, spirit, commitment. [euph.]

some *adj.* [mid-19C+] (*orig. US*) **1** of an object or situation, great, splendid; also used ironically. **2** of a person, exceptional, also used ironically.

some *adv.* (*also* **any**) [mid-18C+] to a great extent, very well or much.

so mean... *phr.* [20C+] (*Aus.*) a phr. denoting an individual's meanness, and prefaced by *he/she's so mean he/she wouldn't...*; combs. include *...give you a light for your pipe at a bushfire, ...give a dog a drink at his mirage, ...give a shout if a shark bit him, ...give a wave if he owned the ocean, ...give you a fright if he was a ghost, ...give you a shock if he owned the powerhouse, ...give a rat a railway pie, ...spit in your mouth if your throat was on fire, ...give you their cold* and *so mean they still have their lunch money from school*.

some kind of — *phr.* [20C+] (*US*) very good, special.

someone blew out their pilot light *phr.* [1970s+] (*US campus*) referring to anyone considered somewhat odd, or who is intoxicated on drugs etc.

someone's ass, be *v.* [1980s+] (*US campus*) to cause someone's downfall, to destroy someone. [ASS n. (2)]

some people! *excl.* [20C+] a derisory or critical comment by the speaker on the opinions or more likely the activities of others; the details are unspoken but will be a condemnation of what *some people* are doing.

some pig *n.* [1940s–50s] (*US Black*) talk, conversation.

some pumpkins *n.* (*also* **some punkins**) [mid-19C+] (*US*) anything or anyone of importance. [SOME adj. (1) + PUMPKIN n.[1]]

somersault *v.* [1980s+] (*Aus. prison/Und.*) **1** to reverse one's plea in court. **2** to take either the passive or active role in a homosexual relationship.

Somerset (Maugham) *adj.* [1920s+] warm. [rhy. sl.; ult. UK writer *Somerset Maugham* (1874–1965)]

some shakes *adj. see* GREAT SHAKES adj.

some stuff *adj.* [late 19C+] (*US*) impressive, outstanding. [SOME adj. (1) + STUFF n.[1] (1)]

something *n.*[1] [mid-19C+] a euph. for the obscenity or oath of the speaker's choice, e.g. *I don't give a something*. [i.e. a FUCK n.[4] or DAMN n.]

something *n.*[2] [1920s+] (*orig. US*) a remarkable person or thing, e.g. *she's really something!*

something *adv.*[1] [mid-19C+] a euph. for DAMN adv., a general intensifier, usu. negative, e.g. *something cruel, something dreadful*.

something *adv.*[2] [late 19C] a euph. for *damn well* or *bloody well*, e.g. *I'll do as I something well please*.

-something *sfx* [1980s+] of age, a little more than, in a specified decade, e.g. *thirty-something*; thus used in pl. to categorize a generation, *thirty-somethings, twenty-somethings*. [the popular 1980s TV show *Thirty-something*]

something damp *n.* [mid-19C–1900s] a drink.

something else! *excl.* [20C+] an excl. or description of approval or wonder.

something in socks *n.* [1910s+] a bachelor, a single man, supposedly what 'every woman wants'.

something in the City *n.* [late 19C] a dubious figure, prob. a fraudster or even a burglar. [ironic play on SE]

something short *n.* [mid-19C–1900s] a glass of spirits. [SHORT n.¹ (2)]

something's rotten in Denmark *phr.* [1950s+] (*gay*) referring to someone who is presumed to have had a sex change (cf. COPENHAGEN CAPON n.). [*Hamlet* I:iv: 'Something is rotten in the state of Denmark' + ref. to the pioneering operation undergone in Denmark in 1952 by Christine (formerly George) Jorgensen]

something the cat brought in *n.* (*also* **something the cat dragged in**) [20C+] a distasteful, prob. dirty or unkempt, object or person; usu. as *look/feel like...*

something to shout about *phr.* (*also* **something to write home about**) [20C+] anything worthy of note, surprising, exciting etc.

sometime *n.* [1960s+] (*US prison*) one who cannot be depended upon. [? the excuse, 'I'll do it sometime, I'll get round to it sometime'; cf. Sp. *mañana*, lit. 'tomorrow']

sometimey *adj.* [mid-19C+] (*US Black*) moody, changeable, inconsistent. [i.e. *sometimes* they are this, *sometimes* that]

sommer *adv.* [20C+] (*S.Afr.*) just, merely, simply, without further fuss, used of an action of which the speaker may have had a few doubts but has decided to go ahead and do it. [Afk.]

somnambulance *n.* [1980s+] (*US campus*) someone who is amusing, likeable, eccentric. [play on SE *somnambulance*, sleepwalking]

son *n.*¹ (*also* **sonnie, sonny**) [mid-19C+] a general term of address to a man or boy.

son *n.*² [2000s] (*US prison*) the passive partner in a homosexual couple.

son *n.*³ *see* SONOFABITCH n. (1).

sonabitch *n. see* SONOFABITCH n.

son and daughter *n.* [1940s] water. [rhy. sl.]

son and daughter *v.* [2000s] to murder. [rhy. sl. = SE *slaughter*]

sonbitch *n. see* SONOFABITCH n.

song *n.* 1 [late 16C; 18C+] a small amount of money. 2 [1990s+] usu. of money, a large amount.

song and dance *n.*¹ [late 19C+] 1 an elaborate excuse or account of a situation aimed at persuading or manipulating the listener; often in GIVE SOMEONE A SONG AND DANCE v. 2 (*also* **song**) anything (over-)elaborate.

song and dance *n.*² [1910s–30s] a male homosexual. [rhy. sl. = NANCE n.]

songbird *n.* [1970s] (*US Und.*) an informer. [SING v. (4)]

song-factory *n.* [1910s] (*US Und.*) a prison. [play on BIRD n.³ (2) + SE *factory*]

songs and sighs *n.* [1920s] (*US*) thighs. [rhy. sl.]

sonk *n.* [1950s–60s] (*Aus.*) an ungainly, clownish figure. [backform. f. SONKEY n.]

sonk *v.* [1950s] (*N.Z.*) to hit, to thump. [SOCK v.¹ (1) or backform. f. SONKEY n. (1)]

sonkey *n.* (*also* **sonky**) 1 [mid-19C+] a thug. 2 [mid-19C+] a foolish, clumsy person. 3 [1910s] (*Aus.*) an upper-class weakling. [dial. *sonkie*, a man like a sackful of straw]

sonkey *adj.* (*also* **sonky**) [20C+] (*Aus.*) foolish. [SONKEY n. (2)]

son lo *n. see* SAN LO n.

sonnie *n. see* SON n.¹.

sonno *n.* [1910s+] (*Aus.*) a general form of address to a man or boy. [SE *son*/SON n.¹ + -o sfx (4)]

sonny *n. see* SON n.¹.

sonofa *n.* (*also* **sonova**) [1950s+] abbr. of SONOFABITCH n.

son of a biscuit-eater *n. see* BISCUIT-EATER n. (1).

sonofabitch *n.* (*also* **sombitch, sonabitch, sonbitch, sonofabastard, son of a big-shoe, sonofawhore, sonovabitch, sonumbitch, sonuvabitch, sumbitch**) 1 [17C+] a derog. general term of abuse. 2 [late 19C] (*Aus.*) a moustache, as worn by cattle-buyers and wool inspectors. 3 [1910s] (*US*) a stew. 4 [1920s+] an affectionate term of address. 5 [1930s+] something or someone exceptional. 6 [1950s+] a thing, 'it', e.g. *pass the sonofabitch over here*. [coined *c*.1330 in the form *Biche-sone* and in its current form in Shakespeare's *King Lear* (1605). Like a number of otherwise derog. terms (cf. BASTARD n.; MOTHERFUCKER n.), it can be used affectionately and, albeit rarely, of a woman as much as of a man.

sonofabitch *adj. see* SONOFABITCHING adj.

sonofabitch! *excl.* [1940s+] a general excl. of frustration, surprise, annoyance, affirmation.

sonofabitchbastard! *excl.* [1950s+] a general excl. of surprise, annoyance etc.

sonofabitching *adj.* (*also* **sonofabitch, sonofabitchy, sonsabitching**) [mid-18C; 20C+] a general term of abuse.

sonofagun *n.* (*also* **son of a wooden gun, sonsagun**) [19C+] a euph. for SONOFABITCH n. (1). [SE *son* + *gun*/GONNOF n.]

sonofagun! *excl.* [20C+] a general excl. [SONOFAGUN n.]

son of a horned cow *n. see* SON OF A SOW(-GELDER) n.

son of a sea-cook *n.* (*also* **son of a hickory, ...sand turtle, ...sawbuck, ...sea-calf, ...sheep-stealer, ...shite-breeks, ...shotten herring, ...tinker**) [mid-18C; mid-19C+] a general pej., a euph. for SONOFABITCH n. (1).

son of a sheep *n.* (*also* **son of an ape, ...a mule, ...a shedawg, ...a skunk, ...a woodlouse**) [1910s–30s] a euph. for SONOFABITCH n. (1).

son of a son *n.* [1940s] a euph. for SONOFABITCH n. (1).

son of a sow(-gelder) *n.* (*also* **son of a horned cow**) [17C+] a general pej., a euph. for SONOFABITCH n. (1).

son of a tinker *n. see* SON OF A SEA-COOK n.

sonofawhore *n. see* SONOFABITCH n.

son of a wooden gun *n. see* SONOFAGUN n.

son of a woodlouse *n. see* SON OF A SHEEP n.

son of ebony *n. see* EBONY n.

son of nobody out of nothing *n.* [mid-19C] a general pej., a euph. for SONOFABITCH n. (1).

son of prattlement *n.* [early 18C–early 19C] a lawyer.

son of the brush *n. see* BROTHER OF THE BRUSH n.

son of wax *n. see* COCK-A-WAX n. (2).

son of your mother *n.* (*also* **mother's son**) [1930s–60s] (*US*) a euph. for SONOFABITCH n. (1).

sonova *n. see* SONOFA n.

sonovabitch *n. see* SONOFABITCH n.

sonsabitching *adj. see* SONOFABITCHING adj.

sonsagun *n. see* SONOFAGUN n.

sonsy *adj.* (*also* **sancy, saucy, sunsey**) [mid-19C+] (*Irish*) lively, fun, of a woman, buxom.

sonumbitch/sonuvabitch *n. see* SONOFABITCH n.

soogan *n. see* SUGAN n.

sook *n.* (*also* **sookey, sookie, sooky**) [1930s+] (*Aus./N.Z.*) a coward, a crybaby. [dial. *suck*, a stupid fellow]

sook *v.* [1990s+] (*Aus./N.Z.*) to make a fuss, to whinge. [SOOK n.]

sooky *adj.* [1950s] (*mainly Aus./N.Z.*) cowardly, weak. [SOOK n.]

sool *v.* (*Aus./N.Z.*) 1 [late 19C+] to set a dog on. 2 [late 19C+] to persuade someone to attack a third party. 3 [late 19C+] of a dog, to worry a person or animal. 4 [20C+] to confuse, to fool; thus *soolin' sod*, a hypocrite. 5 [1900s–10s] lit. and fig., to chase. 6 [1930s] to dismiss. 7 [1940s–50s] to run. [? dial. *sowl*, to handle roughly or *sowl into*, to attack fiercely]

sool after *v.* [1940s+] (*Aus./N.Z.*) to pursue for sexual purposes. [SOOL v. (5)]

Sooner *n.* [late 19C+] (*US*) an Oklahoman. [SE *sooner than*; used of those who attempted to take over a territory before official permission, the main example was in Oklahoma]

sooner *n.*[1] **1** [late 19C+] (*Aus.*) a lazy person, one who would 'sooner' loaf around than work or, in context, fight. **2** [20C+] a dog or cat that would 'rather feed than fight'. **3** [1920s+] (*Aus.*) a confidence trickster. **4** [1930s–40s] (*US Black*) a dirty, unkempt person. **5** [1930s–40s] (*US Black*) dirty, ragged clothes. **6** [1950s] (*US*) a choice. **7** [1980s] (*N.Z.*) an ill-behaved, lazy horse. [all refer to something or someone that would 'soon as be/sooner do one thing as another']

sooner *n.*[2] [20C+] (*US*) an illegitimate child. [too *soon* for the wedding]

sooner *n.*[3] [1900s] (*US Und.*) one who takes things for granted; a mistaken optimist. [they feel optimistic too *soon*]

soon-man *n.* (*also* **soon-woman**) [late 19C–1930s] (*US Black*) a smart, alert, intelligent man or woman.

sooper-dooper *adj. see* SUPER-DUPER *adj.*

soor *n.*[1] [mid-19C–1930s] a general pej. term. [Hind. *soor*, a pig; pron. 'sewer' and used famously as such by Nancy Mitford's fictional Uncle Matthew (in *The Pursuit of Love*, 1945 *et al.*), although he confuses matters by spelling it 'sewer']

soor *n.*[2] [20C+] (*W.I., Guyn.*) a useful piece of confidential information, esp. when passed on to ingratiate or flatter. [? SE *swear*, i.e. 'I swear this is true…']

soot-bag *n.* [mid–late 19C] a reticule or small basket.

soother *n.* [late 19C] a drink. [its positive effects]

sooty *n.* [mid-19C+] a derog. term for a Black person (cf. BLACK-BELLY *n.*). [SOOTY *adj.* (1)]

sooty *adj.* **1** [18C–19C] (*US*) Black, in the context of a person. **2** [1900s] black in mood, despondent, depressed.

sooty jimmy *n.* [1980s+] (*US Black*) a Black penis. [SE *sooty* + JIMMY *n.*[5] (1)]

sop *n.* **1** [mid-19C+] a fool, a simpleton. **2** [1900s] a drunkard. [abbr. SE *milksop*, a weakling, a spiritless person, lit. a piece of bread soaked in milk]

sop-can *n.* [1950s+] a simpleton, a weakling. [ext. of SOP *n.* (1)]

soper *n. see* SOPOR *n.*

soph *n.* **1** [late 17C–mid-19C] (*UK campus*) a *soph*ister, a student in their second or third year. **2** [late 18C+] (*US*) a *soph*omore. [abbr.]

sophisticated lady *n.* [1970s+] (*US Black*) cocaine. [play on GIRL *n.*[2] (1) + the 'smart' image of the drug]

sop joint *n.* [1960s] (*US Black*) the bath-house and masseur's salon. [SE *sop*, liquid + JOINT *n.*[4] (3)]

sopor *n.* (*also* **soaper, soper**) [1970s+] (*drugs*) any form of barbiturate drug, usu. methaqualone (cf. BARBIT *n.*). [brandname of *Sopor*, a form of methaqualone, but note SE *soporific*]

soppie *n.* (*also* **soppies**) [1960s–70s] (*S.Afr.*) a cinema tea-room or bio-café, a form of cinema at which one can eat snacks while watching a film. [ety. unknown; ? one can SE *sop up* food or drink]

soppings *n.* [1920s] (*US tramp*) gravy.

soppy *adj.* **1** [late 19C+] (*UK teen*) vapid, naïve, esp. romantic; thus *soppy date*, a sentimentalist, a romantic. **2** [1940s] drunk (cf. DAMP *adj.*). [? joc. use of SE *sopping wet*]

soppy *adv.* [1940s] vapidly, sentimentally, stupidly. [SOPPY *adj.*]

soppyballs *n.* [1980s] a general derog.; the implication is of stupidity. [ext. SOPPY *adj.* (1)]

soppy ha'porth *n.* [1930s+] a fool, often used affectionately. [SOPPY *adj.* (1)]

sordid *n.* [1950s] an unpleasant person.

sore *adj.* [mid-19C+] (*mainly US*) angry, irritated.

sore *adv.* [mid-19C+] (*Irish*) an intensifier, absolutely, utterly.

sore as a boil *phr.* (*also* **sore as a boiled owl, …a gum boil, sorer than a mashed thumb**) [20C+] (*orig. Aus.*) very angry, annoyed. [ext. of SORE *adj.*]

sore as a snouted sheila *phr.* [1940s+] (*Aus.*) extremely angry, as angry as a woman who has been 'stood up'. [SORE *adj.* + SNOUT *v.*[1] + SHEILA *n.* (1)]

soreback *n.* [20C+] (*US*) a native of Virginia. [the supposed hospitality of Virginians, an attitude that is underlined by their constantly slapping one another's backs in camaraderie]

sored up *adj.* [1930s–40s] (*US*) angry. [SORE *adj.*]

sorefoot *n.* [20C+] (*W.I.*) any unsightly, continually bandaged sore, irrespective of its position on the body.

sore hand *n.* [1980s+] (*Ulster*) a very thick sandwich of bread and jam. [resemblance to a cut hand]

sorehead *n.* [mid-19C+] (*US*) a grumpy, irritable person.

soreheaded *adj.* [mid-19C+] (*US*) bad-tempered, grumpy. [SORE-HEAD *n.*]

sore leg *n.* [late 19C] **1** a sausage. **2** plum pudding. [the supposed resemblance]

sore piece *n.* [20C+] (*Ulster*) a troublesome person. [SE *sore* + *piece*, a person]

sorer than a mashed thumb *phr. see* SORE AS A BOIL *phr.*

sorghum *n.* [1970s] (*S.Afr.*) a derog. term for a Black person (cf. AFRICAN APE *n.*). [the racist response to the replacement of such offensive terms as 'kaffir beer' or 'kaffir corn' by 'sorghum beer' and 'sorghum corn']

sorority house *n.* [1940s] (*US Und.*) a women's prison (cf. BANDHOUSE *n.*).

sorrel-pate *n.* [late 17C–early 19C] a red-headed person.

sorrel-top *n.* [mid-19C–1930s] (*US*) a red-headed person. [the reddish colour of SE *sorrel*]

sorrel-topped *adj.* [1930s] having red hair. [SORREL-TOP *n.*]

sorrowful tale *n.* **1** [mid-19C] a prison (cf. BUCKET *n.*[2]). **2** [mid-19C–1940s] 3 months in prison. [rhy. sl. = SE *jail*]

sorry *n.* [late 19C] (*US*) the remorse that can accompany a serious hangover.

sorry and sad *n.* [20C+] a father, i.e. 'dad'. [rhy. sl.]

sorry and sad *adj.* [1950s+] bad. [rhy. sl.]

sorry-ass *adj.* (*also* **sorry-assed**) [1960s+] (*orig. US Black*) unfortunate, despicable. [SE *sorry*, worthless + -ASS sfx]

sorry-looking *adj.* [1970s+] (*US*) unattractive.

sorry sack of shit *n. see* SAD SACK OF SHIT *n.*

sort *n.* **1** [mid-19C+] a person, a type; usu. as *bad sort*, GOOD SORT *n.* (1). **2** [1910s+] (*orig. Aus.*) a woman; very occas. applied also to men.

sort *v. see* SORT (OUT) *v.*

sorted *adj.* [1980s+] an all-purpose term of approval, worked out, content, satisfactory, supplied with drugs etc.

sort of *phr.* (*also* **sorta, sorter**) [mid-19C+] to an extent, in a way.

sort (out) *v.* **1** [20C+] to tease, to 'pull someone's leg'. **2** [1940s+] (*orig. Aus.*) to deal with, esp. violently. **3** [1950s] (*UK prison*) of a warder, to harass an inmate. **4** [1970s+] to arrange, to organize. **5** [1990s+] to provide someone with drugs. **6** [1990s+] to pay one's debts. **7** [2000s] to provide with sexual pleasure or satisfaction.

S.O.S. *n.*[1] [1920s+] (*US*) the same thing as usual. [abbr. same old shit]

S.O.S. *n.*[2] [1990s+] (*US gang*) a contract to murder. [abbr.; smash on sight or shoot on sight]

S.O.S. *n.*[3] *see* SHIT ON A SHINGLE *n.*

sosh *n.*[1] [late 19C] (*US*) a state of drunkenness.

sosh *n.*[2] *see* SOC *n.*

soshed *adj. see* SLOSHED *adj.*

so-so *adj.*[1] **1** [mid-18C–early 19C] drunk. **2** [mid–late 19C] menstruating. [euph.]

so-so *adj.*[2] [1910s+] (*US Black*) important, special, superior, usu. in derog. contexts.

so-so *adv.* [1940s+] (*W.I. Rasta*) only, solely, unaccompanied. [? SE *solo* + redup.]

so-so *phr.* [1900s] (*US Und.*) goodbye.

soss-brangle *n.* [late 18C–mid-19C] a slatternly woman. [SE *soss*, a sloppy mess of food + *brangle*, a muddle]

sosselled *adj. see* SOZZLED *adj.*

sossie *n. see* SAUSIE n.

sossinger *n. see* SASSIGER n.

sossled *adj. see* SOZZLED *adj.*

so's your old man! *excl.* [1910s+] (*orig. US*) an excl. used as a retort to an insult or slur.

sot *adj.* [20C+] stupid, silly, foolish. [Fr. *sotte*, foolish + UK dial. *sot*, a fool]

sothead *n.* [20C+] a fool. [dial. *sot*, a fool + -HEAD sfx (1)]

so thin you can smell shit through them *phr.* [late 19C+] a phr. used of a very slim person. [SHIT n.[1] (1)]

sot-weed *n.* [late 17C–early 19C] tobacco. [SE *sot*, a fool or a drunkard + *weed*; the implication being that only such figures smoked]

sou *n.* (*also* **sou-markee, sous, souse**) [late 17C+] an extremely small amount of money. [for ety. *see* NOT A SOU phr.]

soul *n.*[1] **1** [late 17C–mid-18C] a drunkard, esp. on brandy. **2** [1950s] (*US Black/drugs*) marijuana.

soul *n.*[2] [1940s+] (*orig. US Black*) the essential quality of Blackness which is unavailable to anyone who is not Black (and American), despite much aping and pirating.

soul *n.*[3] *see* SOUL FOOD n.

soul *adj.* [1940s+] (*orig. US Black*) Black, used in a variety of combs. for which *see* below. [SOUL n.[2]]

soul aviator *n. see* SKY PILOT n.

soul-bolt *n.* [mid-19C–1900s] (*Aus./US*) a metaphorical 'bolt' that holds the soul, and thus the person, together; esp. in *knock/shake the soul-bolts out of*, to disturb or worry to a substantial degree; *start my soul-bolts!* an excl. of alarm.

soul brother *n.* [1930s+] (*orig. US Black*) a (fellow) Black man; thus SOUL SISTER n. [SOUL adj. + SE *brother*]

soul brother number one *n.* (*also* **soul sister number one**) (*US Black*) a Black person who epitomizes everything positive in the Black experience; thus *soul brother/sister number two*, a lesser version, or a sympathetic White person. [SOUL BROTHER n./SOUL SISTER n. + NUMBER ONE adj.]

soul-butter *n.* [mid–late 19C] (*US*) moralizing drivel. [SE *soul* + BUTTER n.[2]]

soul-case *n.* **1** [late 18C–early 19C] the body; thus *make a hole in one's soul-case*, to wound. **2** [late 19C+] (*US/Aus.*) one's spirit, usu. in the context of worry, suffering or oppression; thus *worry/belt/sweat the soul-case out of*, to annoy, to drive, to punish.

soul child *n.* [1970s] (*US campus*) any Black student with conspicuous Black pride and identity. [SOUL adj. + SE *child*]

Soul City *n.* [1960s+] (*US*) Harlem, New York, the centre of Black America. [SOUL adj. + CITY sfx]

soul dancing *n.* [1950s+] (*US Black*) dancing in accordance with the current dance style favoured in the Black community. [SOUL adj. + SE *dancing*]

soul-doctor *n.* **1** [late 18C–19C] a clergyman. **2** [1950s] a psychiatrist.

soul-driver *n.* [late 17C–mid-19C] a clergyman, or one who acts as such.

soul-faker *n.* [late 19C] a member of the Salvation Army. [SE *soul* + FAKER n.]

soul folks *n.* [1960s] (*US Black*) Black people. [SOUL adj.]

soul food *n.* (*also* **soul**) **1** [1960s+] (*US Black*) food prepared and preferred by the Black community. **2** in ext. use, any nationally preferred food. [SOUL adj. + SE *food*]

souling *n.* [1960s] (*US Black*) doing anything well, esp. when playing jazz. [SOUL adj.]

soul kiss *n.* [1900s; 1950s+] a deep kiss, involving putting one's tongue into one's partner's mouth; thus *soul-kiss*, to kiss in this way.

soul language *n.* [1940s+] (*US Black*) Black American sl. [SOUL adj. + SE *language*]

soul minority *n.* [1960s–70s] (*US Black*) African Americans considered collectively. [SOUL adj. + SE *minority*]

soul patch *n.* [1990s+] (*orig. US Black*) a single tuft of hair worn beneath the lower lip. [SOUL adj. + SE *patch*]

soul power *n.* [1960s–70s] (*US Black*) the political and cultural influence wielded by the Black community. [SOUL adj. + SE *power*]

soul sauce *n.* [1970s+] (*US gay*) a Black man's semen, or, by metonymy, the man himself (cf. BABY GRAVY n.). [SOUL adj. + SE *sauce*/SAUCE n.[2] (7); *see also* SAUCE v.[1]]

soul-searcher *n.* [1900s–10s] a drink. [one of the effects of drunkenness]

soul session *n.* [1960s–70s] (*US Black*) a gathering of Black people. [SOUL adj. + SE *session*]

soul shake *n.* [1960s+] (*orig. US Black*) the ritualized shaking and slapping of hands. [SOUL adj. + SE *shake*]

soul sister *n.* **1** [1900s] (*US*) a girlfriend. **2** [1960s+] (*orig. US Black*) a Black woman. [SE *soul*/SOUL adj. + SE *sister*; var. on SOUL BROTHER n.]

soul sister number one *n. see* SOUL BROTHER NUMBER ONE n.

soul-snatcher *n.* (*also* **soul-snaveller**) [late 19C–1900s] a preacher, a missionary.

soul sounds *n.* [1950s–70s] (*US Black*) music. [SOUL adj. + SOUNDS n.]

soul talk *n.* [1950s–70s] (*US Black*) a conversation between 2 or more Black people. [SOUL adj. + SE *talk*]

Soulville *n.* [1950s+] (*US Black*) **1** the Black area of a city or town. **2** in fig. use, any Black place or situation. **3** Africa. [SOUL adj. + -VILLE sfx[1]]

sou-markee *n. see* SOU n.

sound *n.*[1] **1** [1940s–50s] (*US Black*) one's point of view. **2** [1950s] (*US gang*) conversation, talk.

sound *n.*[2] [1980s+] (*UK/US Black/W.I.*) a group of reggae or rap artists.

sound *adj.* **1** [mid-17C–early 18C] healthy, esp. free of venereal disease. **2** [19C+] excellent, first-rate, totally satisfactory, admirable, dependable. **3** [mid-19C+] (*orig. US*) knowledgeable about, expert in. **4** [mid-19C+] dependable, trustworthy, of sober judgement (in the view of the speaker). **5** [2000s] safe.

sound *v.*[1] (*UK Und.*) **1** [early 19C+] to elicit information from a person. **2** [early 19C+] to check out, to check over. **3** [1920s+] in fig. use, to work something out, to ascertain. **4** [1930s] to knock on a door to see if the occupants are at home.

sound *v.*[2] **1** [1940s–50s] (*US Black/teen*) to inform, to tell. **2** [1950s] (*US gang*) to tease, to taunt, to joke with. **3** [1950s] to listen. [SOUND n.[1] (2)]

sound *v.*[3] *see* SOUND ON v. (3).

sound! *excl.* [1960s+] a general excl. of approval, excellent! fine! no problems!

sound boy *n.* (*also* **sound man**) [1970s+] (*W.I./UK Black teen*) a sound system operator.

sound egg *n.* [1920s–30s] a 'good chap', a 'decent fellow'. [SOUND adj. + EGG n.[1] (1)]

sounder *n.* [1910s] a person who checks a place out in advance, esp. in preparation for a burglary. [SOUND v.[1] (2)]

sound man *n. see* SOUND BOY n.

sound off (about) *v.* **1** [1910s+] (*orig. US*) to boast, to brag. **2** [1910s+] (*US Black*) to initiate a conversation. **3** [1920s+] to make a noisy fuss, to become angry about a topic or situation.

sound on *v.* [1950s–80s] **1** (*US*) to flirt. **2** (*US*) to criticize. **3** (*US*) (*also* **sound**) to compete in ritualized mutual insults. **4** (*US prison*) to speak to, to make a request to.

sounds *n.* [1950s+] (*orig. US*) music, spec. records; occas. sing.

sounds and tunes *n.* [1970s] (*US campus*) songs.

sound system *n.* [1970s+] (*orig. W.I./UK Black teen*) a huge, high-wattage, mobile disco.

sound the bugle! *excl.* [1940s] (*US Black*) start playing! start the music!

soup n.[1] (also **white soup**) [late 18C–19C] (Aus./UK Und.) melted silver plate; thus *soup-shop*, a place where such plate is melted down and disposed of.

soup n.[2] **1** [20C+] (orig. US Und.) gelignite, nitroglycerine, as used in the blowing open of a safe; thus *cook soup*, to dissolve a stick of dynamite in hot water to extract crude nitroglycerine. **2** [1940s] (US) insecticide. **3** [1940s+] (US) gasoline, petrol, esp. high-performance fuel used in customized cars. **4** [1990s+] (Aus.) electricity.

soup n.[3] [1970s] (US gay) sweat; anal oil; fecal matter.

soup n.[4] see SUPER n.[2].

soup v. **1** [late 19C+] to cause someone to fail. **2** [1920s] to fail, to get into trouble. [IN THE SOUP phr.]

soup and fish (clothes) n. [1910s+] a dinner jacket. [the food one eats when wearing it]

soup and gravy n. [20C+] the Royal Navy. [rhy. sl.]

soup and peter man n. [1940s] (US Und.) a safe-breaker. [SOUP n.[2] (1) + PETER n.[2] (2)]

soup and peter work n. [1940s] (US Und.) safe-breaking with nitroglycerine. [SOUP n.[2] (1) + PETER n.[2] (2)]

soupbone n. (also **super**) [1900s–10s] (US) an arm.

soup-bone bitch n. [2000s] (US Black) a regular, long-term female partner. [her role as a cook]

souped adj. [late 19C+] (Anglo-Irish) in trouble.

souped (up) adj. **1** [1940s+] intensified, accelerated, usu. of a car that has been modified by its owner to exceed the basic factory-created performance. **2** [1980s+] in fig. use, of a person. [SOUP n.[2] (3), or racing use *soup*, anything injected into a horse to alter its speed or temperament]

souped up adj. [late 19C] (Aus.) drunk (cf. ALED UP adj.). [ety. unknown]

souper n.[1] **1** [mid-19C+] (orig. Irish) a convert from Roman Catholicism to Protestantism; thus any Protestant. **2** [late 19C] one who scrounges free soup tickets. [such conversions, however nominal, were often achieved by the appeal of Protestant missionaries handing out free soup, orig. at the time of the great famine of 1845–7]

souper n.[2] see PEA-SOUP n.[1] (2).

souper n.[3] see SUPER n.[2].

soup house n. [1920s–30s] (US tramp) a cheap restaurant.

soup job n. [1940s+] (US) anything (orig. a car) that is increased, heightened in value, competence or attractiveness. [SOUPED (UP) adj. + JOB n.[4]]

soup jockey n. [1930s] (US) a waiter or waitress. [SE *soup* + JOCKEY n.[3] (2)]

soup man n. **1** [1910s+] a professional villain who specializes in handling nitroglycerine to blow open safes. **2** [1950s] a person who mixes their own high-performance petrol for customized cars. [SOUP n.[2] + SE *man*]

soup-plate track n. [1930s–50s] (Aus.) a small racecourse. [it is fig. no bigger than the circumference of a *soup-plate*]

soup-strainer n. [1910s+] a large moustache.

soup up v.[1] [1940s+] to make something (orig. an engine) more powerful, more impressive etc. [SOUP n.[2] (3)]

soup up v.[2] [1950s+] (US) to stimulate a woman's vagina. [the moisture thus produced]

soupy adj.[1] [late 19C] extremely drunk, usu. to the point of vomiting. [SE *soup*, i.e. the vomit]

soupy adj.[2] [1910s–20s] vapid, naïve, esp. romantic. [var. on SOPPY adj.]

sour n. (also **sour dough/paper**) **1** [late 19C–1930s] counterfeit money, apparently silver but made from pewter; or forged cheques. **2** [1920s–40s] (US Und.) a bad cheque. [fig. use of SE *sour* + DOUGH n.[1] (1)/PAPER n.[1]]

sour v. see CURDLE v.

sour-apple quickstep n. [1990s+] diarrhoea (cf. APPLE-BLOSSOM TWO-STEP n.). [the result of eating sour fruit + pun on SE *trot/ TROTS, THE* n.[2]]

sourball n. (also **sourbelly**) [1900s–50s] (US) **1** a grumpy person. **2** ill temper. [SE *sour* + -BALL sfx]

sour-balled adj. [1900s–30s] grumpy. [SOURBALL n. (1)]

sour belly n. see SOW-BELLY n.

sourcrout n. see SAUERKRAUT n.

sour cudgel n. [early 17C] a severe thrashing.

sour dough n. see SOUR n.

sourdough n. [late 19C+] (orig. Can.) an experienced prospector in Alaska, the Yukon or the Northwest Territories. [the use of sourdough (fermenting dough, esp. that left over from a previous baking, used as leaven) in the making of bread in mining camps. Allegedly, the need to keep this warm meant that, on cold nights, the miners would sleep with a lump]

soured on adj. see SOUR ON adj.

sour grape n. [1980s+] (Aus./N.Z. Und.) a rape. [rhy. sl.]

sourkraut n. see SAUERKRAUT n.

sour on adj. (also **soured on**) [20C+] (orig. Aus./US) hostile towards. [SOUR ON v.]

sour on v. [mid-19C+] (orig. US) to become hostile towards.

sour paper n. see SOUR n.

sourplanter n. [19C] a distributor of counterfeit money; thus *plant the sour*, to spread around such 'money'. [SOUR n. (1) + PLANT v.[1] (6)]

sourpuss n. [1930s+] (orig. US) **1** a sour-faced person, a grumbler, a killjoy. **2** a grumpy expression. [SE *sour* + PUSS n.[3] (1)]

sourpussed adj. [1950s+] (orig. US) **1** mean, puritanical. **2** sour-featured. [SOURPUSS n. (1)]

souse n. **1** [20C+] a drunkard. **2** [1900s] a state of drunkenness. **3** [1900s–20s] a drinking bout. [? backform. f. SOUSED (UP) adj.]

souse v. **1** [19C] (US) to eat. **2** [20C+] to drink heavily, to become drunk. [? backform f. SOUSED (UP) adj.]

souse-crown n. [late 17C–18C] a fool. [SOUSE n. + SE *crown*, lit. a 'drunken head']

soused (up) adj. [17C+] drunk (cf. DAMP adj.).

souse me! excl. [late 18C] an excl. of denial or refusal.

sousepot n. [1920s–60] (US Black) a drunkard. [SOUSE n. (1) + -POT sfx]

soush n. [mid-19C] a house. [backsl.]

sous/souse n. see SOU n.

sousy adj. [1950s] drunken. [SOUSE v. (2)]

south adj. [19C+] used in various phrs. to mean 'downwards', e.g. DIP SOUTH v.; GO SOUTH v.[1]; SOUTH POLE n. **2** [1930s] morally 'down', i.e. racy, sexy, pornographic. **3** [1990s+] less than.

south v. (also **put something down south**) [1940s+] to pocket. [SOUTH adj. (1)]

South County Indian n. [20C+] a Portuguese immigrant to the US. [South County, Rhode Island, where such immigrants have congregated]

south end n. [mid-19C+] (US) the buttocks (cf. ARSE-END n.). [SOUTH adj. (1)]

Southend-on-Sea n. [20C+] urination (cf. ANGEL'S KISS n.). [rhy. sl. = PEE n.[1] (2)]

Southend pier n. [20C+] an ear. [rhy. sl.]

southerly buster n. (also **southerly burster**) **1** [mid-19C+] (Aus.) the cool, gusty wind that springs up at the end of a hot day, sometimes accompanied by a shower. **2** [1940s] a cocktail.

southern can n. [1930s+] (US Black) the buttocks. [SE *southern*, thus SOUTH adj. (1) + CAN n.[1] (2)]

south gate discharge n. see BACK-GATE PAROLE n.

southie n. [1970s] (US) a left-hander. [SOUTHPAW n.]

south of France n. [20C+] a dance. [rhy. sl.]

south of the border phr. [1970s+] (US) below the waist, usu. referring to the vagina. [SOUTH adj. (1)]

southpaw n. (orig. US baseball) **1** [mid-19C+] the left hand. **2** [late 19C+] a left-hander, esp. in boxing. **3** [1920s] a blow with the left hand. [SOUTH adj. (1), i.e. the image of the left hand as being 'beneath' the right + PAW n. (1)]

southpaw *adj.* [late 19C+] **1** left-handed. **2** in fig. use, eccentric, odd. [SOUTHPAW n. (2)]

south pole *n.* **1** [19C] the vagina (cf. ALL QUIET n.; ANTIPODES n.). **2** [20C+] the anus (cf. BOTTLE AND GLASS n.). [rhy. sl. = HOLE n.[1] but note SOUTH adj. (1)]

South Sea (Mountain) *n.* [early 18C–mid-19C] gin, or any other strong liquor. [? the *South Sea Bubble*, a financial scandal of 1727; the effects of gin, like that of the Bubble, are to promote deleterious fantasies]

south Sydney *n.* [20C+] (*Aus.*) a kidney. [rhy. sl.]

soutie *n.* [1940s+] (*S.Afr.*) an Englishman who retains his colonialist mentality. [abbr. SOUTPIEL n.]

soutpiel *n.* [1970s+] (*S.Afr.*) an Englishman who has a notably colonialist mentality. [Afk. *sout*, salt + *piel*, penis; thus lit. 'salt-dick', because he has one foot in South Africa, one in England and his penis dangling in the ocean in between. Despite the date, as cited in *DSAE*, it must be assumed that the term is much older, but left unprinted through taboo; thus Namibian synon. *sandpiele*, in this case the penis rests on the burning sands of the Kalahari desert]

souvenir *n.* (*also* **souvy**) [1910s] a trophy, something that has been found, thus euph. for something stolen.

souvenir *v.* **1** [1910s+] to steal. **2** [1970s+] (*US*) to give, to hand over; usu. as phr. *souvenir me.* [SOUVENIR n.; orig. WW1 milit. use]

souvenir egg *n.* [late 19C–1930s] (*US*) an old, rotten egg.

souvy *n. see* SOUVENIR n.

sov *n.* (*also* **sob**) **1** [early 19C+] a *sovereign*, £1 sterling; thus *half-sov*, half a sovereign, 10 shillings (50p.). **2** a ring made out of an old gold sovereign. [abbr.; *sob* is mispron.]

sovvy *n.* [1960s] (*Aus.*) £1, A$2. [SOV n. (1)]

sow *n.*[1] **1** [mid-16C; early 18C+] a derog. term for a (fat) woman. **2** [1910s+] a general term of abuse, irrespective of gender.

sow *n.*[2] [1930s–40s] (*US Black*) any coin, esp. a nickel (5 cents). [on pattern of UK GRUNTER n.[2] (1), HOG n.[1] (1) and SOW'S BABY n. (2), but no apparent connection]

sow-belly *n.* (*also* **sour belly, sow bosom**) [mid-19C+] (*US*) a side of salted pork; bacon.

sower *n.* [mid-18C] (*UK Und.*) a purse.

sowface *n.* [1950s] a derog. term applied to an ugly woman. [SOW n.[1] + SE *face*]

so what? *phr.* [1930s+] a widely used term of disinterest or defiance, a rejoinder to the previous speaker's announcement or revelation etc.

sow-pen *n.* [1960s] (*Aus.*) any area of a hotel (i.e. public house) reserved for women only. [SOW n.[1] (1)]

sow's baby *n.* **1** [late 17C–18C] a suckling pig. **2** [mid-19C] a sixpence (2½p), occas. a shilling (5p). [(1) euph; (2) a sixpence is smaller than a HOG n.[1] (1)]

soy pucks *n.* [20C+] (*US prison*) prison-cooked hamburgers. [their constituent and their resemblance to an ice-hockey *puck*]

sozzle *n.* [late 19C–1900s] (*US*) the act of drinking; thus *sozzle session*, a drunken spree. [backform. f. SOZZLED adj.]

sozzle *v.* [1930s–50s] **1** to drink heavily. **2** (*US*) to walk unsteadily, as if drunk. [backform. f. SOZZLED adj.]

sozzled *adj.* (*also* **sizzled, sosselled, sossled**) [mid-19C+] drunk (cf. DAMP adj.). [? US *sozzle*, to splash; ult. dial. *sozzle*, to mix or mingle in a sloppy manner]

s.p. *n.* [1970s+] basic information, facts. [orig. racing jargon *starting price*]

spa *n.* [1980s+] (*Irish*) a general derog. term, an incompetent. [abbr. SPASTIC n.]

spa *adj.* [1980s+] (*Irish*) crazy, inept, socially unacceptable. [SPA n.]

spa bar *v.* [1980s+] (*Aus. prison*) to beat up. [rhy. sl. = IRON BAR v.]

space *n.* [1900s–40s] (*US Und.*) a jail sentence. [SE *space and time/* TIME n.[1]]

space *v. see under* SPACE (OUT).

space base *n.* (*also* **space ball/dust**) [1990s+] (*drugs*) a cigar stuffed with a mixture of phencyclidine and crack cocaine. [SPACED (OUT) adj. (1) + BASE n. (4)/SE *ball/dust* + play on the 1980s confectionery Space Dust]

space biscuit *n. see* SPACE PILL n.

space cadet *n.* [1970s+] **1** (*drugs*) any heavy user of drugs, esp. cannabis or hallucinogens, who is continually 'flying'. **2** (*US*) (*also* **space cowboy/queen**) a mad or eccentric person. **3** (*US campus*) (*also* **cadet**) a misfit, an unappealing person. [SPACED (OUT) adj. + SE *cadet*]

space cake *n.* [1990s+] (*drugs*) cake which is baked with cannabis as an extra ingredient. [SPACED (OUT) adj. (1)]

space case *n.* (*also* **space cookie**) [1980s+] a crazy person. [SPACED (OUT) adj. (2) + CASE n.[4] (4)/COOKIE n.[2]]

space cowboy *n. see* SPACE CADET n. (2).

spaced (out) *adj.* [1960s+] (*orig. drugs*) **1** intoxicated by a drug, esp. a hallucinogen. **2** generally disorientated, with or without drugs. [the image of 'flying']

space dust *n. see* SPACE BASE n.

spaceman *n.* [1940s+] (*Aus. prison/US*) one who is intoxicated on drugs; a madman. [SPACED (OUT) adj.]

space opera *n.* [1940s+] (*US*) an SF or outer space drama film. [on model of HORSE OPERA n. (2); SOAP OPERA n. (1)]

space (out) *v.*[1] [1960s+] (*US*) to daydream, to drift off, esp. when under the influence of drugs. [one 'flies' into space]

space (out) *v.*[2] [1970s] (*US Black*) to leave. [SE *make a space*]

space pill *n.* (*also* **space biscuit**) [2000s] (*drugs*) MDMA (cf. ECSTASY n.). [SPACED (OUT) adj. (1)]

space queen *n. see* SPACE CADET n. (2).

spacer *n.*[1] [1920s] (*US Und.*) a convicted criminal. [SPACE n.]

spacer *n.*[2] [1980s+] (*Irish*) **1** a streetwise young person. **2** a crazy person. [SPACED (OUT) adj.; the underlying implication is of their probable drug-taking]

spacey *n.* [1970s+] (*drugs*) anything that simulates the intoxication of LSD or other hallucinogens. [SPACEY adj. (1)]

spacey *adj.* (*also* **spacy**) [1960s+] (*orig. drugs*) **1** of a person, disorientated, whether through drug use or not. **2** exhibiting characteristics actually or fig. reminiscent of those experienced when taking a hallucinogen. **3** of an experience or event, generally disorientating, with or without drugs. **4** edgy, nervous. [SPACED (OUT) adj.]

spacies *n.* [1980s+] (*N.Z.*) the video/computer game *Space Invaders*; thus generically for other electronic games. [abbr.]

spacka *n.* (*also* **spack, spacker**) [1990s+] a general term of abuse. [abbr. SPASTIC n.]

spackahead *n.* [1990s+] a fool, an eccentric. [SPACKA n. + -HEAD sfx (1)]

spackle-filler *n.* [1980s] (*Aus.*) foundation make-up. [proprietary name *Spackle*, a compound used to fill cracks in plaster and produce a smooth surface before decoration]

spacy *adj. see* SPACEY adj.

spade *n.* [20C+] (*orig. US*) a Black person, esp. West Indian or African; thus *spadelet*, a Black child; *Spadesville*, the Black area of a city. [SE phr. *black as the ace of spades*; *spadelet* is a nonce-word, found only in Colin MacInnes, *Absolute Beginners* (1959); poss. derog. in the US, it is seen as a neutral/affectionate term in the UK; Kuethe (1934) defines as 'a very dark Negro']

spade *adj.* [20C+] referring or pertaining to the Black community or Black culture. [SPADE n.]

spadet *n.* [1980s+] (*US campus*) a student who is preoccupied with studies. [? SPACE CADET n. (3)]

spadge *n.* [1990s+] (*UK juv.*) a general term of abuse. [SPASTIC n.]

spadger *n.* **1** [late 19C] a boy. **2** [1990s+] (*Aus.*) the vagina. [dial. *spadger*, a sparrow; (1) thereafter historical use]

spaff *v.* [1990s+] to ejaculate (cf. BLOSH v.). [echoic]

spag *n.*[1] [1950s+] (*Aus.*) a sparrow. [dial. *spadger*]

spag *n.*[2] [1960s+] **1** (*Aus.*) (*also* **spaggie**) an Italian (cf. DAGO n.). **2** spaghetti; thus *spag bol*, spaghetti bolognese (usu. an adulterated British version). [abbr. SE *spaghetti*, a staple Italian food]

spag *n.*[3] (*also* **spagga**) [1980s+] (*US campus/UK juv.*) an unpleasant, stupid person; can be used affectionately. [SPASTIC n.]

spag *n.*[4] *see* SPAGHETTI WESTERN n.

spa-gag-me *n.* [1990s+] (*US prison*) prison-cooked spaghetti. [abbr./joc. pron. SE *spaghetti* + *gag*, to choke]

spag fag *n.* [1990s+] (*gay*) one who prefers Italian partners. [SPAG n.[2] (1) + FAG n.[5] (1); play on FAG-HAG n.[2]]

spagga *n. see* SPAG n.[3].

spaggie *n. see* SPAG n.[2] (1).

spaghetti *n.* (*also* **spaghetti-eater**) [1910s+] (*orig. US*) an Italian (cf. DAGO n.). [stereotyping]

spaghetti bender *n.* [1960s+] (*US*) an Italian (cf. DAGO n.).

spaghetti corner *n.* [1950s+] (*US*) an Italian community within an urban area.

spaghetti-eater *n. see* SPAGHETTI n.

spaghetti head *n.* (*US*) **1** [20C+] an Italian (cf. DAGO n.). **2** [1980s+] a stupid person. [SE *spaghetti* + -HEAD sfx (2)/-HEAD sfx (1)]

spaghetti junction *n.* [1960s+] a complex of motorways forming a multi-levelled interchange, esp. the Gravelly Hill interchange between the M1 and M6 outside Birmingham, UK.

spaghetti western *n.* (*also* **spag**) [1970s+] (*orig. US*) a cowboy film, usu. made in Europe by Italian directors.

spagingy-spagade *n.* (*also* **spaginzy**) [1920s+] (*US Black*) a Black person; thus *spaggot*, a Black homosexual. [cod Lat. for SPADE n.]

spalpeen *n.* [mid-18C+] a rogue, a rascal. [Irish *spailpín*, a low or mean fellow, orig. a casual farm labourer]

spam *n.* [1990s+] the penis (cf. BACON n.[1]). [*Spam*, proprietary name for a brand of pork luncheon meat]

spam *adv.* [1940s] (*US*) echoic of the sound of a suden blow.

spam alley *n.* [1990s+] the vagina (cf. ALLEY n.[1]). [SPAM n.]

spam chasm *n.* [1990s+] the vagina (cf. AGREEABLE RUTS OF LIFE n.). [SPAM n.]

spam fritter *n.* [2000s] the anus (cf. BOTTLE AND GLASS n.). [rhy. sl. = SHITTER n.[1] (1)]

spamhead *n.* [1990s+] (*UK juv.*) one who has a notably large forehead. [*Spam* (*see* SPAM n.)]

spamjagger *n.* [2000s] the penis (cf. BACON n.[1]). [ext. of SPAM n.]

spam javelin *n.* (*also* **spam lance**) [1990s+] the penis (cf. AX n.[2]; BACON n.[1]). [ext. of SPAM n.]

spam juice *n.* [2000s] semen (cf. BABY FLUID n.). [SPAM n. + JUICE n.[2] (1)]

spam sceptre *n.* [1990s+] the penis (cf. BACON n.[1]). [SPAM n. + SCEPTRE n.]

spam supper *n.* [2000s] fellatio (cf. BASKET LUNCH n.). [SPAM n.]

span *adj.* [mid-19C; 1980s+] (*UK/Irish*) brand-new. [abbr. SE *spic and span*; ult. ON *spán-nýr*, chip-new]

span *adv.* [1960s+] (*S.Afr., mainly teen*) a lot, very much. [fig. use of S.Afr.E *span*, a team of oxen]

spang *adv.* [late 18C+] (*orig. US*) absolutely, entirely, e.g. *right spang in the middle*. [? SPANK v.[2] (2)]

spangle *n.* **1** [19C] a 7-shilling piece; thus used fig. for a pound. **2** [late 19C] a generic term for money (cf. BRASS n.[1]). [SE *spangle*, i.e. its glitter and shininess]

spangles *n.* [late 17C–mid-18C] (*UK Und.*) off-cuts of gold or silver.

spaniard *n.* [1940s–50s] (*Can.*) a louse, a flea. [? negative stereotyping]

Spanish *n.*[1] [late 18C–early 19C] sack, a type of white wine produced in Spain and the Canary Islands.

Spanish *n.*[2] [1900s] (*US campus*) nonsense. [the language being supposedly incomprehensible]

Spanish *n.*[3] [1980s] (*US*) intercourse whereby the man reaches orgasm by rubbing his penis between a woman's breasts.

Spanish, the *n.* [late 18C–mid-19C] cash, ready money. [? the association of Spain with bullion fleets]

Spanish *adj.* [16C+] used in combs. below to denote arrogance, duplicity, treachery, sexual corruption etc. [the role of Spain as England's primary national enemy during 16C–17C; these stereotypes, presumably encouraged by the late 19C Spanish–American War, persist in 20C+ US use]

Spanish archer *n.* (*also* **Spanish fiddle**) [1980s+] dismissal, rejection. [pun on cod Spanish *El Bow* i.e. ELBOW n.[3]]

Spanish athlete *n.* [1930s] (*US campus*) a braggart, a boaster. [play on THROW THE BULL v.]

Spanish buttons *n.* [late 16C] syphilitic sores.

Spanish coin *n.* [late 18C–mid-19C] empty compliments and meaningless courtesies. [stereotyping of the Spanish as impeccably courteous but deeply untrustworthy]

Spanish cure *n.* [20C+] treatment of drug addiction by forced, total abstinence. [? as used in Spain]

Spanish faggot *n.* [late 18C–mid-19C] the sun. [SE *faggot*, a piece of kindling wood; the stereotype of the Spanish Inquisition; the sun burns, as did the Inquisition]

Spanish fiddle *n. see* SPANISH ARCHER n.

Spanish gout *n.* (*also* **Spanish needle**) [late 17C–early 19C] venereal disease, syphilis. [reflecting the contemporary role of Spain as the national enemy. This was soon replaced by France (cf. FRENCH CROWN n. etc), although the old term lingered into 19C]

Spanish guitar *n.* [20C+] (*US*) a cigar. [rhy. sl.]

Spanish machete *n.* [late 19C+] (*W.I.*) a hypocrite. [the Spanish machete has a 2-edged blade and thus 'cuts both ways']

Spanish main *n.* [20C+] a drain. [rhy. sl.]

Spanish money *n.* [late 17C–18C] empty compliments and meaningless courtesies. [stereotyping of the Spanish as impeccably courteous but deeply untrustworthy]

Spanish needle *n. see* SPANISH GOUT n.

Spanish onion *n.* [20C+] a bunion. [rhy. sl.]

Spanish padlock *n.* (*also* **Italian lock/padlock**) [16C–early 19C] a chastity belt. [negative racial stereotyping]

Spanish pip *n.* [late 16C–early 17C] venereal disease. [PIP n.[1] (2)]

Spanish pox *n.* [mid-16C–early 18C] venereal disease, syphilis. [POX n.[1] (1)]

Spanish rice *n.* [1970s] (*gay*) lumpy semen (cf. BABY GRAVY n.).

Spanish supper *n.* [1940s–50s] (*US*) no supper at all or very little supper.

Spanish time *n.* [1990s+] (*Aus.*) unpunctuality (cf. AFRICAN (PEOPLE'S) TIME n.). [the Spanish, stereotypically, are reputed to maintain a flexible attitude to appointments]

Spanish trick *n.* [early 17C–early 18C] sexual intercourse. [SPANISH adj.; Williams suggests additional ety. of conventional or 'missionary position' intercourse]

Spanish trumpeter *n.* [late 18C–mid-19C] a donkey. [pun on SE *Don Key/donkey* + the sound of braying]

Spanish tummy *n.* [1960s+] diarrhoea or any form of stomach upset experienced by tourists to Spain (cf. AZTEC HOP n.).

Spanish waiter *n.* [20C+] a potato. [rhy. sl. (Cockney pron. 'potater')]

Spanish walk *n.* [mid-19C–1940s] (*US*) a constrained style of walking assumed, willy-nilly, by those who are being ejected from a bar or saloon; thus v. *walk Spanish*. [? the way Spanish pirates supposedly forced their prisoners to walk on tiptoes while they were held by the scruff of the neck; or ? the tip-toeing gait of flamenco dancers]

Spanish worm *n.* [late 18C–early 19C] a nail found embedded in a piece of wood that one is sawing. [contemporary dislike of Spain]

spank *n.*[1] [early 18C–mid-19C] a coin. [SPANKER n.[1] (1)]

spank *n.*[2] **1** [late 18C] a slap with an open hand. **2** [early 19C] the breaking of a shop window before grabbing whatever can be reached. [(1) later use of is SE]

spank *v.*[1] **1** [early 18C] to slap. **2** [early 19C] (*UK Und.*) to rob a shop by breaking its window and grabbing whatever is within reach. **3** [late 19C] to play at. **4** [late 19C–1940s] (*N.Z.*) to milk a cow. **5** [1930s+] to beat comprehensively in a sport or game. **6** [1960s+] to beat up. **7** [2000s] (*US Black*) to buy an item of clothing. [(1) later use is SE]

spank *v.*[2] **1** [late 18C–1900s] to move smartly, briskly and stylishly, esp. when seated on horseback; thus *full spank*, quickly. **2** [mid-19C] to crack a whip. **3** [mid-19C] to drive a horse stylishly and fast. **4** [1980s+] (*US teen*) to masturbate (cf. BANG THE BISHOP v.; BOFF v.).

spank *adv.* [mid-19C–1940s] a general intensifier, completely, entirely, absolutely, quite.

spank... *v.* [20C+] in various combs. meaning, of a man, to masturbate; thus *spank frank, ...one's little boy, ...one's turkey, ...the bishop, ...the carrot, ...the donkey, ...the plank, ...the salami, ...the tank, ...wank* (cf. BANG THE BISHOP v.; SPANK THE MONKEY v.).

spank a glaze *v.* (*also* **spank the glaze**) [early–mid-19C] (*UK Und.*) to break a shop window, reach in and grab whatever one can, having previously tied up the shop door so the shopkeeper cannot pursue. [SPANK v.[1] (2) + GLAZE n. (1)]

spanked *adj.* [1920s+] intoxicated. [fig. use of SE *spank*]

spanker *n.*[1] **1** [mid-17C–mid-18C] a gold coin. **2** [late 18C–early 19C] money in general. [dial. *spank*, to sparkle]

spanker *n.*[2] **1** [mid-18C–1920s] anything exceptional or particularly admirable of its type. **2** [late 18C–1900s] a fast horse or ship, any creature.

spanker *n.*[3] [late 18C–19C] a hard, resounding slap or blow.

spanker *adj.* [mid-17C] large, first-class, showy.

spanking *n.* [mid-19C+] a beating. [SPANK v.[1] (1); modern use is of adults, usu. as ironic euph. for serious harm, thus in a criminal context]

spanking *adj.* **1** [late 17C+] large, first-class, showy. **2** [mid-18C–19C] of horse or vehicular movement, fast or vigorously. **3** [early 19C] of people, dashing, lively.

spanking *adv.* [late 19C+] very, exceedingly; thus *brand spanking new*.

spank the glaze *v. see* SPANK A GLAZE v.

spank the monkey *v.* (*also* **spank one's monkey**) [1980s+] to masturbate (cf. BANG THE BISHOP v.; BEAT ONE'S HOG v.). [SPANK... v. + MONKEY n.[10] (2)]

spanky *adj.* [late 19C–1930s] smart, esp. when overly so. [SPANKING adj. (1)]

spanner *n.* [1980s+] **1** a fool; an unpleasant person. **2** a physically handicapped person.

spanners *n.* [1950s+] (*Aus.*) a sexually provocative woman. [she 'tightens one's NUTS n.[2] (1)']

spar *n.* (*also* **sparring partner**) [1970s+] (*orig. W.I.*) a friend. [SE *sparring partner*]

spar *v.*[1] [late 19C] (*US*) to ask for credit.

spar *v.*[2] [1970s+] (*W.I./UK Black*) to befriend, to associate with. [SPAR n.]

sparagrass *n. see* SPARROW-GRASS n.

spare *n.*[1] [1900s–60s] the buttoned fly of a man's trousers. [dial. *spare*, a slit in the front of a garment]

spare *n.*[2] **1** [1930s] a married man's mistress, a wife's lover; esp. as *bit of spare*. **2** [1940s] (*US Black*) a friend. **3** [1960s+] an unattached woman, usu. at a party or club and considered to be open to male sexual advances; esp. as *bit of spare*; thus *have a bit of spare*, to

commit adultery. **4** [1990s+] an idiot, a boring person. **5** [2000s] an unattached person.

spare, the *n.* [1980s] cash, money to spend.

spare *adj.* **1** [20C+] idle, useless, superfluous. **2** [1940s+] (*orig. milit.*) overwrought, distraught; thus GO SPARE v.

spare boy *n.* [1920s+] (*Aus. rural*) treacle, golden syrup. [ety. unknown; ? the sugar gives one extra energy, i.e. the equivalent of an assistant]

spare my days! *excl.* [late 19C+] (*mainly Aus./N.Z.*) a mild excl.

spare my grief! *excl. see* GOOD GRIEF! excl.

spare rib *n.* [1990s+] a lie. [rhy. sl. = FIB n.[1] (2)]

spare tyre *n.* (*also* **spare tire**) **1** [1920s+] the roll of flesh that surrounds an overweight stomach. **2** [1940s+] (*US*) an unwelcome or irrelevant person, a boring person.

spark *n.*[1] **1** [mid-19C–1950s] (*orig. UK Und.*) (*also* **sparker**) a diamond; a diamond pin. **2** [1940s] (*US Black*) a light.

spark *n.*[2] [1940s] (*US Black*) a marijuana cigarette (cf. AFRICAN WOODBINE n.).

spark *adj.* [mid-late 19C] (*UK Und.*) diamond. [SPARK n.[1] (1)]

spark *v.*[1] (*also* **spark it**) [late 18C+] (*US*) to pay court to, to make love to, to play the suitor. [SE *spark*, a beau, lover or suitor]

spark *v.*[2] [1900s–50s] (*Aus. Und.*) to watch carefully. [? SE *spark*, a beau, i.e. a womanizer, who watches women intently]

spark *v.*[3] **1** [1990s+] to hit. **2** [2000s] (*US Black*) (*also* **spark up**) to shoot dead. [(2) ? the flash of the gun]

spark *v.*[4] *see* SPARK (UP) v.

sparker *n. see* SPARK n.[1] (1).

sparkers *adj.* [1930s+] asleep, exhausted. [SPARK OUT adj. (1) + -ER sfx]

spark fawney *n.* [mid-19C–1910s] (*UK/US Und.*) a diamond ring. [SPARK adj. + FAWNEY n. (1)]

spark grafter *n.* [1900s] (*US Und.*) a jewel-thief. [SPARK n.[1] (1) + GRAFTER n.[1] (1)]

sparkie *n. see* OLD SPARKY n.

spark it *v. see* SPARK v.[1].

spark jiver *n.* [1950s] (*US Black*) an electric organ. [SE *spark*, i.e. electricity + SE *jive*]

sparkle *n.* [1930s+] (*UK Und.*) **1** a diamond. **2** jewels. [appearances notwithstanding, this use has no link other than homonymic with the mid-15C–17C SE *sparkle*, a small ruby or diamond]

sparkle plenty *n.* [1960s–70s] (*drugs*) amphetamine (cf. A n.[2]). [*Sparkle Plenty*, a character in the *Dick Tracy* comic strip by Chester Gould (1900–85)]

sparkler *n.*[1] **1** [mid-18C–1900s] usu. in pl., a bright or sparkling eye. **2** [late 18C+] usu. in pl., jewellery, spec. diamonds. **3** [late 19C] (*UK Und.*) a match. **4** [late 19C] an admirable person.

sparkler *n.*[2] **1** [early–mid-19C] a drink of liquor. **2** [1970s] (*drugs*) amphetamine (cf. A n.[2]). [they both help the consumer 'sparkle']

sparkler *n.*[3] [1960s] a lie. [? it shines out of the rest of one's conversation, but note dial. *spark*, a spot of dirt]

sparkle up *v.* [mid–late 19C] to hurry up, to 'get on with' things.

sparkly *n.* [2000s] champagne.

sparko *adj.* [1970s+] asleep, exhausted; unconscious. [var. on SPARKERS adj.]

spark out *adj.* **1** [1920s+] asleep, unconscious, exhausted. **2** [2000s] rendered incapable by drug use. [electrical imagery]

spark out *v.* **1** [1930s+] to fall fast asleep. **2** [1970s+] to be knocked unconscious. [SPARK OUT adj. (1)]

spark-plug *n.* [1920s+] (*US*) one who sets events or plans in motion, a facilitator; thus *spark-plug*, to initiate, to spur on.

spark-prop *n.* [mid-19C–1920s] (*UK Und.*) a diamond pin or tie-pin. [SPARK adj. + PROP n.[4] (1)]

sparks *n.*[1] **1** [mid-19C–1930s] diamonds, precious stones in general. **2** [1970s] (*US gay*) imitation jewels. [SPARK n.[1] (1)]

sparks *n.*[2] (*also* **sparky**) [1910s+] **1** (*US milit.*) a radio operator. **2** an electrician, usu. theatrical and film use.

spark (up) *v.* [1980s+] (*orig. UK/US Black*) to light a tobacco or cannabis cigarette. [the *spark* of one's lighter flint]

spark up *v. see* SPARK *v.*[3] (2).

spark-waggon *n.* [1900s] a motor-car.

sparky *n.*[1] *see* OLD SPARKY *n.*

sparky *n.*[2] *see* SPARKS *n.*[2].

sparring bloke *n.* [mid–late 19C] a boxer, usu. a sparring partner. [SE *spar* + BLOKE *n.* (1)]

sparring partner *n. see* SPAR *n.*

sparrow *n.*[1] **1** [early 18C] a prostitute (cf. ALLEY CAT *n.*). **2** [1940s] (*US Und.*) a young girl who moves from one lover to the next. [classical and later writers believed that sparrows had sex up to 7 times every hour, thus symbolizing lust (and shortening their lives); the orig. 17C use of the Cockney cliché 'cock-sparrow' as a term of address, was invariably a ref. to the addressee's sexlife]

sparrow *n.*[2] **1** [late 19C] a tip, as given to a dustman or milkman or any regular provider of services to one's door. **2** [1960s] money, a dollar bill. [note dustman's jargon *sparrow*, anything saleable, e.g. a silver spoon or thimble, found in a dustbin]

sparrow *n.*[3] [late 19C–1940s] (*Aus./US*) a physically weak individual. [the image of the small bird]

sparrow-brain *n.* [1930s+] a person of little or no intelligence.

sparrow-cheater *n.* [late 19C–1900s] a boy who cleans horse-dung from the streets with a brush and dustpan. [the bird's appetite for horse-dung]

sparrow cop *n.* [late 19C–1960s] (*US*) a park policeman (cf. ANIMAL *n.*[1]). [SE *sparrow* + COP *n.*[1] (1); a duty often allotted officers currently out of favour with their superiors]

sparrow-fart *n.*[1] (*also* **sparrow chirp, sparrow's fart**) [20C+] dawn.

sparrow-fart *n.*[2] [1920s+] (*Irish*) **1** an unimportant person. **2** an irritable child. [its insignificance]

sparrow-grass *n.* (*also* **sparagrass**) [late 19C+] asparagus. [the word, based on the 16C–18C *sparagus*, was SE mid-17C–mid-19C, but dropped into sl. thereafter]

sparrowhawk *v.* [1990s+] to pick up homeless youngsters of either sex for sexual exploitation, esp. runaways who have just arrived at rail or bus stations. [var. on CHICKEN-HAWK *n.*]

sparrow-mouth *n.* [early 17C–1920s] a very large mouth; thus *sparrow-mouthed*, wide-mouthed. [the bird's anatomy]

sparrow's chirp *n. see* BEE'S KNEES *n.*

sparrow's fart *n. see* SPARROW-FART *n.*[1].

sparrow's knees *n.* [1940s] the number 3. [rhy. sl.]

sparrow-starver *n.* [1900s–20s] (*Aus./UK*) a street-cleaner. [*sparrows* peck at garbage]

sparsie *n. see* SPRARSER *n.*

spar up *v.* [1930s] (*Aus.*) to hand over. [? SPAR *v.*[1]]

spas *see under* SPAZ and its combs.

spasm band *n.* [1900s–20s] (*US Black*) a spontaneously assembled musical group, playing on homemade instruments (washboards etc); the precursors of the skiffle groups of the 1950s. [the jerky, arrhythmical sounds of the makeshift instruments; orig. by Emile 'Stale Bread' Lacoume, a white racetrack tout]

spasm chasm *n.* [1990s+] the vagina (cf. AGREEABLE RUTS OF LIFE *n.*). [the SE *spasm* is that of orgasm]

spaso *n.* [1980s+] (*Aus.*) a spastic, either actual or as a general derog. term. [SPAZ *n.* (1) + -O sfx (4)]

spastic *n.* [1960s+] a general derog. term, an incompetent. [for ety. *see* SPAZ *n.*]

spastic *adj.* [1960s+] **1** convulsed with laughter and thus incapable of coherent mental or physical activity. **2** uncoordinated, socially unacceptable. **3** dull, foolish. [SE *spastic*, afflicted by spastic paralysis, characterized by sudden muscle spasm; this term is generally considered unacceptable since it is, in effect, a derog. attack on those who suffer this paralysis; note RMC Duntroon (Aus.) *spastic*, drunk]

spastically *adv.* [1960s] (*US*) helplessly. [SPASTIC *adj.*]

spasticated *adj.* [1990s+] a general term of derision, implying physical inadequacy. [SPASTIC *adj.*]

spat *n.* (*orig. US*) **1** [19C+] a tiff, a dispute, a quarrel. **2** [1900s] a smart blow, smack or slap; also the sound thereof. [echoic]

spat *v.* [19C+] to fight, esp. in the context of a lover's tiff. [SPAT *n.*]

spatter *v.* [1940s+] to beat up severely.

spawny *adj.* [1990s+] lucky. [ety. unknown; ? link to Scot. game *spawnie*, played with buttons, in which one player throws a button, the others attempt to throw theirs nearest to it, and the button that comes within a *spawn* (SE *span*) is the winner]

spaz *n.* (*also* **spas**) **1** [1960s+] (*US/UK campus/school*) one who is useless, clumsy, incompetent and is thus socially unacceptable; thus *spaz attack*, a state of excitement. **2** [2000s] (*US campus*) a general pej.; no physical incompetence is implied. [SE *spastic*, one who suffers from spastic paralysis, i.e. 'a condition in which some muscles undergo tonic spasm (sometimes resulting in abnormal posture) [...] so that voluntary movement of the part affected is difficult and poorly co-ordinated' (*OED*); this term is generally considered unacceptable since it is, in effect, a derog. attack on those who suffer this paralysis]

spaz *adj.* [1980s+] uncoordinated. [SPAZ *n.* (1)]

spaz *v.*[1] [1980s+] to make twitch. [SPAZ *n.* (1)]

spaz *v.*[2] *see* SPAZ (OUT) *v.*

spaza (shop) *n.* (*also* **sphaza (shop)**) [1980s+] (*S.Afr. township*) an illicit (thus 'camouflaged') or latterly informal grocery or general store. [Ngwenya *spaza*, camouflaged]

spaz cut *n.* [1990s+] (*UK juv.*) an unflattering haircut. [SPAZ *n.* (2)]

spazmo *n.* [1970s+] a general term of abuse; an incompetent, an inadequate. [SPASTIC *n.*+ SE *spasmodic*]

spaz (out) *v.* (*also* **spas (out)**) [1960s+] to act foolishly, to lose control, to act in an uncoordinated manner – whether mentally or physically. [SPAZ *n.* (1)]

spaz pads *n.* [1970s+] orthopaedic shoes. [SPAZ *n.* (1) + SE *pads*]

spazwheels *n.* [1990s+] a wheelchair. [SPAZ *n.* (1) + WHEELS *n.*[1] (3)]

spaz-wit *n.* [1980s+] a fool, an idiot (cf. DAMWIT *n.*). [SPAZ *n.* (2) + sfx *-wit*]

spazzed *adj. see* SPAZZY *adj.*[2] (1).

spazzled *adj.* [1920s] bizarre, intense. [ety. unknown]

spazzy *adj.*[1] [1950s] good, wonderful. [ety. unknown]

spazzy *adj.*[2] **1** [1980s+] (*also* **spazzed**) stupid, unusual, a general negative. **2** [1990s+] physically uncoordinated, spastic. [SPAZ *n.*]

speak *n.*[1] [early 19C] (*UK Und.*) a stolen item. [SPEAK *v.*]

speak *n.*[2] [1920s–30s] (*US*) an illicit drinking establishment. [abbr. SPEAKEASY *n.*]

speak *v.* (*also* **make a speak**) [early 18C–mid-19C] (*UK Und.*) to hold up; to rob; thus *rum speak*, a particularly lucrative robbery. [ironic euph.]

speak a mouthful/an armful *n. see* SAY A MOUTHFUL *v.*

speak a piece *v.* (*also* **speak one's piece**) [late 19C+] (*orig. US*) to make oneself heard, to say what one has decided to say, esp. for moral reasons.

speak bandog and Bedlam *v.* [late 16C–early 17C] to fall into a rage, to act like a madman. [BANDOG *n.* (1) + SE *Bedlam*, Hospital of St Mary of Bethlehem, London, celebrated as the capital's main lunatic asylum]

speak big *v. see* TALK BIG *v.*

speak brown tomorrow *v.* [late 19C] to get sunburned.

speakeasy *n.* (*also* **speakie**) [late 19C+] (*US*) an illicit drinking establishment. [SE *speak* + *easy*, speak softly, e.g. the tone of voice in which one addressed the lookout or in which the patrons were urged to talk in case the police were at the door; the *speakeasy* appeared *c.*1890, when it meant an illicit liquor shop or an unlicensed bar. The advent of Prohibition (1920–33) elevated the once-marginal institution into the mainstream of US life]

speak French v. [20C+] to indulge in unconventional sexual play. [FRENCH adj. (2)]

speako n. [1920s–30s] (US) an illicit drinking establishment. [abbr. SPEAKEASY n. + -O sfx (4)]

speak one's piece v. see SPEAK A PIECE v.

speak pound notes v. [1980s] (Irish) to speak Standard English. [the assumed correspondence of wealth and 'good' English]

speak pretty v. (also **talk pretty**) [late 19C–1910s] (mainly Aus.) to speak in an affectionate, friendly manner.

speak to v. [early 19C] (UK Und.) to rob. [ext. of SPEAK v.]

speak to a tatler v. see NIM A TATLER v.

speak Welsh v. [1990s+] to vomit (cf. CALL CHARLES v.). [echoic]

speak white v. [1960s+] (Can.) used by English speakers, to speak English (as opposed to French, which is the first language of many Canadians, esp. the Québecois).

speak with v. [late 18C–early 19C] to rob. [ext. of SPEAK v.]

speaky n.[1] [late 19C] the proceeds of a robbery. [SPEAK v.]

speaky n.[2] [1930s] (US Und.) a speakeasy. [abbr.]

spear n.[1] [late 19C+] (Aus.) dismissal from a job; thus GET THE SPEAR v.

spear n.[2] (US drugs) 1 [1930s+] a hypodermic syringe. 2 [1980s+] a branch of marijuana, 15–35cm (6–14in) long, weighing several ounces.

spear v. 1 [20C+] (Aus.) to dismiss from a job. 2 [20C+] (Aus.) to throw out of a pub, dancehall etc. 3 [1910s–60s] (US) to beg, to obtain through begging. 4 [1930s–40s] (US prison) to arrest. 5 [1980s+] (Aus. prison) to put something somebody's way.

spear a job v. [1940s+] (Aus.) to get a job.

spear-carrier n. [1960s+] 1 a proponent, an advocate. 2 an insignificant person. [theatrical jargon spear-carrier, an actor with a walk-on and thus minor (non-speaking) role]

spearchucker n. [1950s+] 1 (US) a derog. term for a Black person (cf. AFRICAN APE n.). 2 (US campus) a college student, a young adult. [the image of the African tribesman as (1) a 'primitive', (2) a young warrior]

spearo n. [1960s–70s] (Aus.) a spear-fisherman. [SE spear + -O sfx (4)]

spear the bearded clam v. [1960s+] (Aus.) to have sexual intercourse with a woman (cf. BANG v.[1]). [SE spear + BEARDED CLAM n.]

spear the hairy doughnut v. [1990s+] to have sexual intercourse with a woman (cf. BANG v.[1]). [SE spear + HAIRY DOUGHNUT n.]

spec n. 1 [late 18C–1900s] (also **speck**) a business, a commercial enterprise. 2 [mid-19C] a lottery. 3 [1930s–60s] a speculator. [SE speculation]

spec adj. [1990s+] speculative. [abbr.]

spechie n. [1980s+] (W.I./UK Black teen) a gun, particularly a .38 special. [SE special]

special n. 1 [1970s+] a prostitute's client who has any particular tastes, costumes, bondage, fetishes etc. 2 [1990s+] (UK juv.) a pupil requiring special needs.

special adj. 1 [early–mid-19C] particularly interested or informed. 2 [1980s] (US campus) unpleasant.

Special K n. (also **vitamin K**) (drugs) 1 [1970s+] ketamine. 2 [1980s+] a synthetic, heroin-based hallucinogen, allegedly 5000 times stronger than LSD. [the breakfast cereal Special K, supposedly an adjunct to better health]

Special K pinches n. [1980s+] (US campus) bulges of fat around the waist. [the 1980s+ advertisements for Special K cereal, which feature such bulges or their lack]

specimen n. [mid-19C+] a human being, esp. in pej. use, e.g. queer specimen, odd specimen.

Speck, the n. [1910s+] (Aus.) Tasmania. [its relatively small size compared to mainland Aus.]

speck n.[1] [mid-19C–1910s; 1950s] (costermonger/Aus.) a decaying

orange; any spotted or damaged fruit or vegetable; thus specky/specked, rotten. [it has specks of mould]

speck n.[2] [1970s] (US Black) a Black person. [? abbr. SE speck of dirt; if so then used ironically]

speck n.[3] see SPEC n. (1).

speck bum n. [1920s–40s] (US tramp) a very decrepit, alcoholic tramp. [SE speck, a contemptible person + BUM n.[3] (1)]

specked wiper n. (also **speckled wipe**) [late 17C–early 19C] a coloured handkerchief, presumably with spots. [SE speckled + WIPER n.[1]]

specker n. [1910s] (Aus.) a financial speculator. [abbr.]

speckle n. [1950s] (W.I.) an albino. [their complexion]

speckle-belly n. [late 19C] (US) a dissenter, a Nonconformist. [? a distinctive style of garment, presumably a waistcoat, sported by such figures, but note also northeastern US dial. speckle-belly, a grey duck. Nonconformist clergymen were more likely to dress in muted than colourful tones]

speckled birds n. [1970s–80s] (US drugs) amphetamines (cf. A n.[2]).

speckled wipe n. see SPECKED WIPER n.

specky adj. 1 [1910s+] wearing spectacles. 2 [1990s+] in fig. use, weak, inadequate. [SPECS n. (1)]

specs n. (also **specks**) 1 [early 19C+] glasses, spectacles. 2 [1930s+] a nickname for one who wears glasses. [abbr.]

spectacles-seat n. (also **spectacle-beam**) [late 19C–1900s] the nose.

spectrum n. see NEXUS n.

sped n. [1980s+] (UK/US campus/teen/Black) a slow or stupid person. [abbr. special education]

spee n. [1990s+] (UK Black) a friend. [var. on SPAR n.]

speech n. [mid–late 19C] a horseracing tip; esp. in get the speech, to receive a tip; give the speech, to pass on information.

speech v. [1980s+] (UK Black) 1 to argue. 2 to persuade.

speeching n. [1980s+] (US Black) 1 talking seductively to a woman. 2 talking fluently and well. 3 defeating in an argument. [SE speech]

speechless adj. [late 19C+] a euph. for drunk.

speed n.[1] 1 [1910s+] a metaphorical term for style, way of life or action; thus about/just one's speed, suitable, suited to one's own taste; not one's speed, not suited to one's taste. 2 [1910s+] energy. 3 [1920s–30s] (US) a fast liver, a hedonist. 4 [1930s] of a man, an affectionate term of address. 5 [1930s] a good time.

speed n.[2] [1960s+] (drugs) any amphetamine-based stimulant drug (cf. A n.[2]). [its effect on the heart and brain]

speed v. 1 [1960s+] (drugs) to use amphetamine. 2 [1980s] (US campus) to work very hard, esp. when preparing for a test or examination. [(1) SPEED n.[2]; (2) SE speed]

speedball n.[1] 1 [20C+] (drugs) a mixture of cocaine and heroin and/or morphine, either injected or sniffed by the user. 2 [1920s–30s] (US) a glass of wine, strengthened by a shot of spirits. 3 [1930s] (drugs) a dose of a narcotic. 4 [1950s–60s] (drugs) a mixture of valium and marijuana. 5 [1970s] (drugs) amphetamine (cf. A n.[2]).

speedball n.[2] [1960s+] (Aus.) a rissole, esp. as cooked for shearers. [? the speed with which it is cooked or passes through the eater's stomach]

speedball v.[1] [1950s] to run off fast.

speedball v.[2] [1960s+] (drugs) to inject or sniff a mixture of heroin and cocaine or morphine and cocaine. [SPEEDBALL n.[1] (1)]

speedballer n. [1990s+] (drugs) one who injects or sniffs a mixture of heroin and cocaine. [SPEEDBALL n.[1] (1)]

speed bug n. [1910s–20s] (US) a fan of travelling at high speed. [SE speed + BUG n.[5] (2)]

speed bugs n. see BUG n.[6] (2).

speed bump n. [1990s+] (US) an act of casual sex. [SE speed + BUMP n.[1] (2)]

speedcoke n. [1990s+] (drugs) a mixture of amphetamine and heroin, seen and experienced as a potent rival/replacement for crack cocaine. [SPEED n.² + COKE n.¹ (1)]

speed cop n. [1920s+] (orig. US) a motorcycle-mounted policeman, charged with enforcing speed limits. [SE speed + COP n.¹ (1)]

speed for lovers n. (also **lover's speed**) [1980s+] (drugs) MDMA (cf. ECSTASY n.). [SPEED n.²; its aphrodisiac or at least affection-enhancing effects]

speed freak n. 1 [1960s+] (drugs) a regular user of amphetamine. 2 [1990s+] (US Black) one who enjoys driving or being driven at high speed. [SPEED n.²/SE speed + FREAK sfx]

speed hog n. [1910s+] one who consistently ignores speed limits when driving. [SE speed + HOG n.² (2)]

speeding n. 1 [1960s+] (drugs) the taking of or experiencing amphetamine or a similar 'go-faster' drug. 2 [1990s+] in fig. use, an energized experience similar to above, but without the use of drugs. [SPEED v. (1)]

speeding ticket n. [2000s] (US prison) a rules violation notice for inappropriate behaviour in the visiting room.

speed limit n. [1940s+] (bingo) the number 30 (cf. ALDERSHOT LADIES n.). [the UK urban speed limit, 30mph (48kph)]

speedo n. [1930s+] a speedometer. [abbr.]

speedos n. [1990s+] (Aus.) tight-fitting male swimming briefs. [the brandname Speedo]

speedrap v. [1970s] to talk fast, usu. under the influence of amphetamine. [SPEED n.² + RAP v.³ (2)]

speed shop n. [1950s+] (US) an automobile supplier specializing in the parts for (and sometimes building) modified cars.

speed the wombats! excl. [1920s+] (Aus.) a general excl. of surprise, alarm, fascination etc.

speed trap n. [1930s+] (S.Afr.) methylated spirits, as drunk by alcoholics and tramps. [ety. unknown]

speed wagon n. [1940s] (US Und.) a police patrol car. [SE speed + WAGON n.¹ (1)]

speedy n. [2000s] (Irish) a police motorcycle.

speedy adj. [1910s–20s] living a pleasure-seeking, hedonistic life. [play on FAST adj.¹ (1)]

speedy Gonzales n. [20C+] (US) a person who moves, works or operates very fast. [the old joke about Speedy Gonzales, a quick and eager fornicator]

speel see also under SPIEL.

speel v. [mid–late 19C] to run away, to decamp. [Scot. speel, to clamber]

speelken n. see SPELLKEN n.

speel the drum v. [mid–late 19C] to go off with stolen property. [SPEEL v. + DRUM n.³ (6)]

speewa n. see SPEWAH n.

speil see under SPIEL.

spell n.¹ [mid-18C–mid-19C] a theatre. [Ger. spiel, to play]

spell n.² [late 19C–1910s] a sentence of 3 months' imprisonment. [SE spell, a short time]

spell v. [mid-19C] to advertise, to put into print. [SE spell out]

spell baker v. [mid-19C] (US) to perform a difficult or challenging task, to be up to the mark. [ety. unknown; ? ironic since baker is easily spelled; ? baker was the first word of 2 syllables in Webster's 'Blue-back Speller']

spell for v. 1 [mid–late 19C] to long for. 2 [20C+] (W.I.) to wait for, with the intention of attacking verbally or physically. [SE spell, to engage in study or contemplation of something]

spell job n. [1980s+] (Ulster) a job of uncertain or indefinite duration. [SE spell, a period of time]

spellken n. (also **speelken**) 1 [late 18C–mid-19C] a theatre. 2 [early–mid-19C] (UK Und.) a cockpit. [Ger. spiel, to play + KEN n.¹ (1)]

spell-o n. [late 19C+] (Aus.) a rest. [SAusE spell, to relieve any interval of rest; to rest + -O sfx (4)]

spence n. [20C+] (W.I.) ejaculated semen. [obs. SE spendings/SPEND n. (1), semen]

spencer n. [early–mid-19C] a small glass of gin. [ety. unknown; ? a local landlord or well-known drinker]

spend n. [late 19C] 1 semen. 2 an orgasm. [SPEND v.]

spend v. [mid-17C–19C] to have an orgasm, to ejaculate.

spend a penny v. [1930s+] to urinate. [the 1d (pre-decimalization) charge in public lavatories]

spends n. [1990s+] spending money.

speng n. [1980s+] (W.I./UK Black teen) 1 a gun. 2 a form of strutting walk. 3 an urban gangster. 4 a fool. [? Carib.E. spengle, a fighting cock]

sperm-bucket n. [1980s] an ageing prostitute (cf. COCKATRICE n.).

sperm burper n. [1990s+] 1 a person who performs fellatio. 2 spec. a male homosexual (cf. BONE-EATER n.). 3 an insult.

sperm spouter n. see SPOUTER n.².

sperm sucker n. [late 19C] the vagina (cf. BITE n.²).

sperm the worm v. [1990s+] to masturbate (cf. BEAT ONE'S HOG v.). [WORM n.¹]

sperrib n. [late 19C] (UK middle class) a wife. [SE spare rib, the bone from which the Bible claimed Eve was created]

spesh n. 1 [1900s] a specialist. 2 [1990s+] Carlsberg Special Brew, a strong beer popular with alcoholic tramps. [abbr.]

spew n. [1980s+] (orig. US campus) semen (cf. BOLLOCK SNOT n.). [SE spew, vomit]

spew v. 1 [late 17C; late 19C; 1980s] (US campus) to ejaculate (cf. BLOSH v.). 2 [late 18C; mid-19C+] to speak, esp. to confess. 3 [1970s–80s] (N.Z. prison) to inform on, to betray. 4 [1980s+] (Aus./N.Z./US Black) to argue angrily, to let loose a diatribe. [SE spew, to vomit]

spewah n. (also **speewa**) [late 19C+] (Aus.) a fantasy outback station, used as a site for a variety of far-fetched tales; thus the tale itself. ['The stories of Speewah and Crooked Mick first came to notice in the Australian Worker in the early 1920s, when a writer named Julian Stuart started writing some articles. Stuart was an ex-shearer who had been at the 1891 Shearers' Strike and he reckoned that these stories had been very popular in the shearing sheds throughout the 1880's' (David Mulhallen, 'A Swag of Yarns', Internet, 2002)]

spew alley n. 1 [19C] the vagina (cf. ALLEY n.¹). 2 [mid-19C–1900s] the throat. [SPEW v. (1)/SE spew + alley]

spew chunks v. see BLOW CHUNKS v.

spewing adj. [1980s+] (Aus. teen) in a furious temper. [fig. use of SE spew]

spew one's goo v. [1990s+] to ejaculate (cf. BLOSH v.). [SPEW v. (1) + GOO n.¹ (1)]

spew one's guts v. [1930s+] 1 to vomit violently (cf. BLOW CHOW v.). 2 to make a full confession of crimes. [SE spew/SPEW v. (2)]

spew one's ring v. [1960s+] 1 (also **throw up one's ring**) to be violently sick. 2 in fig. use, to talk openly, candidly. [SE spew/ SPEW v. (2) + RING n.¹ (2), despite anatomical impossibility]

spewsome adj. [late 19C; 1990s+] of food, drink, objects, events or people, disgusting, repellent. [SE spew + AWESOME adj.; lit. 'enough to make one vomit']

spewy adj. [1980s] (Aus.) angry. [SPEW v. (4)]

sphaza (shop) n. see SPAZA (SHOP) n.

sphinc n. [2000s] the anal sphincter. [abbr.]

sphukupuk(u) n. [20C+] (S.Afr.) a fool, a dunce, a blockhead. [used in Fanagalo, a Zulu/English/Nguni pidgin spoken in the mines; this pidgin, created by Whites, is generally disliked by Black miners]

spic n. (also **spick**, **spik**) 1 [1910s+] (mainly US) a derog. name for an Italian (cf. DAGO n.). 2 [1910s+] (US) a derog. term for a Puerto Rican, a Mexican (cf. BATO n.). 3 [1940s] (US) any Spanish language. 4 [1970s] (US campus) a course in Spanish. 5 [1980s+] Spanish; Spanish-American. [abbr. SPIGGOTY n.; orig. an Italian, when seen as a mispron. of spaghetti or 'no spicka da

English'; note RMC Duntroon (Aus.) *spick*, a person from Victoria (they are 'south of the border']

spic *adj.* (*also* **spick, spicky**) **1** [1930s+] (*orig. US*) pertaining to Latin American or Puerto Rican people or culture. **2** [1980s] Spanish. [SPIC n.]

spic and span *n.* [1950s+] (*US Black*) a mixed Puerto Rican and Black couple. [play on SE phr. + SPIC n. (2) + Span(*ish*), although both refer only to the Hispanic partner]

spice *n.*[1] [early 19C] (*UK Und.*) mugging, robbery. [SPICE v.[3]]

spice *n.*[2] [late 19C+] sexual provocativeness; in anecdotes, jokes etc, smuttiness. [SPICY adj. (3)]

spice *v.*[1] [mid–late 17C] to infect with venereal disease.

spice *v.*[2] [late 18C] to adulterate. [ext. of SE]

spice *v.*[3] [late 18C–mid-19C] (*UK Und.*) to rob; thus *spice the swell*, to rob the gentleman. [? Ger. *speissen*, to eat; or ? SPEAK v.]

spice gloak *n.* [early–mid-19C] a footpad, a highway robber, a mugger. [SPICE n.[1] + GLOAK n.]

spice island *n.* [early 19C] **1** the anus. **2** a privy. **3** any dirty, stinking place. [pun]

spice of life *n. see* SLICE OF LIFE n.

spicer *n.* [late 18C–mid-19C] (*UK Und.*) a highway robber, a footpad. [SPICE v.[3]]

spick *see under* SPIC and its combs.

spicket *n.* [late 17C–early 18C] the penis. [SE *spicket*, a spigot, a tap]

spicky *adj. see* SPIC adj.

spic town *n.* (*also* **spicktown**) [1950s–60s] (*US*) a derog. term for the Puerto Rican or Mexican area of a town. [SPIC n. (2) + SE *town*]

spicy *adj.* **1** [19C+] smart, spirited. **2** [mid–late 19C] smart-looking, neat. **3** [mid-19C+] sexually provocative. [(3) may have started out as a genuine euph. but invariably carries slightly ludicrous 'dirty old man' overtones]

spicy pork roll *n. see* PORK n.[2].

spider *n.*[1] **1** [mid-19C+] (*Aus.*) a drink composed of brandy and lemonade, brandy and beer or sherry and lemonade. **2** [late 19C] claret and lemonade. **3** [1940s] (*US*) the dregs of a bottle. [? it 'creeps up' on the drinker]

spider *n.*[2] [late 19C–1930s] (*US*) a wire picklock, a skeleton key.

spider *n.*[3] **1** [1900s] a bicycle. **2** [1900s–40s] (*Aus.*) a light gig or 2-wheeled, 1-horse carriage. **3** [1930s] (*US tramp*) a Ford automobile. **4** [1940s] (*US Und.*) a stripped-down automobile.

spider *n.*[4] [1920s] (*US*) a term of abuse.

spider *n.*[5] [1970s] (*US campus*) a hard worker. [the industrious arachnid]

spider *n.*[6] *see* ROCK SPIDER n.[1].

spider-brusher *n.* [mid-19C] a domestic servant. [their housework]

spider-catcher *n.* **1** [late 16C; mid-19C] a monkey. **2** [late 17C–early 18C] an extremely thin man. [(2) note SE *spider-catcher*, a general, if vague, term of abuse, referring not to anatomy but propensity]

spider claw *v.* [late 19C] of a man, to play with one's testicles. [the clawing movements of one's hand, reminiscent of a spider's scrabbling legs]

spider monkey *n.* [2000s] (*US prison*) a prisoner who is finding it hard to do their sentence. [they are 'climbing the walls']

spider-shanked *adj.* [late 18C–early 19C] used to describe a man with very thin legs.

spider's legs *n.* [1990s+] (*UK teen*) pubic hairs that protrude beyond a girl's knickers or bikini.

spiel *n.* (*also* **speil**) **1** [late 19C] (*US tramp*) the commodity that a peddler is selling. **2** [late 19C–1900s] (*US*) a drinking spree. **3** [late 19C–1930s] (*US*) a dance, as found in New York dancehalls; thus as v., to dance. **4** [late 19C+] patter, speech, esp. of a salesman or market stall-holder, fairground stall-holder or confidence trickster. **5** [late 19C+] a verbose, 'wordy' explanation. **6** [late

19C+] a conversation, a chat. **7** [20C+] a situation. **8** [1900s] (*US campus*) an eloquent passage in an oration or essay. **9** [1930s+] (*orig. Aus.*) formal advice, a set of instructions. **10** [1940s] a letter. **11** [1990s+] a drinking club. [SPIEL v.[1]; (1) f. (4)]

spiel *v.*[1] (*also* **speil**) **1** [mid-19C+] (*also* **speel**) to gamble. **2** [late 19C] to pose. **3** [late 19C–1900s] (*US campus*) to play, to dance. **4** [late 19C+] to talk. **5** [late 19C+] to patter, to talk glibly. **6** [late 19C+] to 'shoot a line', to tell a tale; to perform a confidence trick. [Ger. *spielen*, to play]

spiel *v.*[2] [late 19C–1910s] (*Aus.*) to gallop; thus *spieler*, a good horseman. [dial. *speel*, to move fast]

spieler *n.* (*also* **speeler, speiler**) **1** [mid-19C+] a swindler, a fraud, a card-sharp, a crooked gambler. **2** [late 19C] (*Aus.*) a bookmaker. **3** [late 19C–1950s] a shop tout or fairground stall-holder. **4** [late 19C+] (*Aus./US prison*) a fluent talker; a plausible, 'sharp' individual. **5** [20C+] a persuasive talker, e.g. an evangelical preacher. **6** [1900s–40s] (*US*) a young, working-class single woman, esp. as found frequenting dancehalls; also applied to male dancers. **7** [1920s+] (*also* **shpeiler, shpieler**) an illegal gambling club. **8** [1930s] (*US Und.*) a corrupt lawyer. **9** [1930s+] a street seller, e.g. of perfumes. **10** [1940s–50s] (*Aus.*) a fast horse. [SPIEL v.[1]; (1) briefly US, Matsell includes it in *Vocabulum* (1859); the underlying implication of (1) is a sense of humour behind the cheating; thus Lawson (1895): 'He was [...] good-natured in his way; he was a "spieler" pure and simple, and did things in humorous style']

spieling *n.* **1** [mid–late 19C] (*UK Und.*) gambling. **2** [late 19C+] (*Aus./N.Z./UK*) card-sharping, swindling. [SPIEL v.[1] (1)]

spieling club *n.* [late 19C–1920s] a gambling club where the innocent patrons are swindled. [SPIELING n. (1) + SE *club*]

spiel the nuts *v.* [1910s–40s] (*US Und.*) to play the 'shell game', using a good deal of talk to disguise the cheating. [SPIEL v.[1] (6) + NUTS n.[2] (3)]

spiff *n.* **1** [mid-19C+] a dandy. **2** [late 19C] something first-rate, exciting, stimulating. [SPIFF adj. (1); note drapery jargon *spiff*, a percentage allowed to salesmen when they sell off old or unfashionable stock, thus 'Mr. Spiffs, the linendraper' in Greenwood, *Dick Temple* (1877)]

spiff *adj.* **1** [mid-19C+] smartly dressed, dandified. **2** [late 19C+] first-rate, excellent. [? echoic of a sharp sound and thus fig. exciting, important, astonishing]

spiffed *adj.* [mid-19C–1960s] (*orig. Scot.*) tipsy, slightly drunk (cf. ABOUT RIGHT phr.[1]).

spiffing *adj.* [mid-19C+] excellent, first-rate. [? Derby dial. *spiffyn*, work well done or *spiffer*, anything exceptional in quality or size]

spiffingly *adv.* (*also* **spiffing, spifflingly**) [late 19C+] extremely well. [SPIFFING adj.]

spifflicate *see under* SPIFLICATE.

spiffs *n.* [1930s–40s] (*US Und.*) bonus money. [note drapery jargon *spiff*, a percentage allowed to salesmen when they sell off old or unfashionable stock]

spiff up *v.* (*also* **spiff out**) [1970s+] to smarten up. [SPIFF adj. (1)]

spiffy *adj.* (*also* **spifly**) [mid-19C+] excellent, wonderful, neatly dressed; occas. as adv. [SPIFF adj. (1)]

spiflicate *v.* (*also* **spifflicate**) 1 [late 18C–19C] to confound, to silence, to dumbfound. **2** [late 18C+] to thrash, to beat, to overcome completely. **3** [early 19C] to betray to the authorities. **4** [1900s] to cause pain or unhappiness, in some unspecified manner. **5** [1900s] to be killed. [ety. unknown; ? 'fanciful' (*OED*); SE *stifle* + *suffocate* (Hotten, 1864); SE *suffocate* or dial. *smothercate* (Ware); SE *spill* + *stifle*/dial. *stiffle* (E.P.)]

spiflicated *adj.* (*also* **spifflicated**) **1** [mid-19C] unkempt, messy. **2** [20C+] (*orig. US*) drunk. [SPIFLICATE v.]

spiflicating *adj.* (*also* **spifflicating**) [mid-19C] aggressive, crushing. [SPIFLICATE v.]

spiflication *n.* (*also* **spifflication**) [mid–late 19C] absolute destruction. [SPIFLICATE v.]

spifly *adj. see* SPIFFY *adj.*

spig *adj.* [1910s–40s] (*US*) pertaining to Central or South America. [SPIGGOTY n.]

spiggoty *n.* (*also* **spig**) (*US*) **1** [1900s–50s] a Spanish-speaking native of Central or South America. **2** [1910s] the Spanish language. **3** [1940s] an Italian (cf. DAGO n.). [? broken English 'spikka da English'; (3) SE *spaghetti*]

spigot *n.* [mid-17C–19C] the penis; thus *spiggot-hole*, the vagina; *spigot-sucker*, a fellator or fellatrix. [SE *spigot*, a tap]

spij *n.* [1990s+] (*UK juv.*) chewing gum. [? SE *spit*]

spik *n. see* SPIC n.

spike *n.*[1] **1** [mid–late 19C] the erect penis. **2** [1920s] a needle. **3** [1920s] (*US Und.*) a lock. **4** [1930s+] a hypodermic syringe; thus *on the spike*, using or addicted to narcotics. **5** [1940s+] the act of injecting a narcotic drug.

spike *n.*[2] **1** [mid-19C+] a lodging house, orig. local authority workhouse or lodging house; thus *spike-ranger*, a tramp who wanders from one such place to another. **2** [1960s+] (*Irish*) a maternity hospital. [the lack of comfort]

spike *n.*[3] [1900s] (*US*) a shot of alcohol (when added to an otherwise non-alcoholic drink). [SPIKE v.[2] (1)]

spike *v.*[1] **1** [late 19C–1900s] (*US campus*) to get possession of, thus to convict. **2** [late 19C+] to harm, to undermine. **3** [20C+] (*US*) to reject, to quash, to delete. [? SE *spike a gun*, to immobilize a cannon by driving a spike into the touchhole, or *spike*, a pointed stick for holding papers, bills etc]

spike *v.*[2] **1** [late 19C+] to add alcohol (clandestinely) to an ostensibly non-alcoholic drink. **2** [1920s–40s] to adulterate 'near-beer' (brewed during Prohibition) with a mixture of ginger beer and pure alcohol. **3** [1920s+] to adulterate a drink, alcoholic or otherwise, or food, with a knockout drug. **4** [1960s] to add a stronger drug to another less potent one. **5** [1960s+] to dose someone with a hallucinogenic drug (usu. LSD) without their knowing (usu. by putting it into a drink or, occas., food). **6** [2000s] to adulterate food or drink with a foreign substance other than a drug, e.g. glass. [such adulteration adds 'sharpness']

spike *v.*[3] **1** [late 19C+] to have sexual intercourse (cf. BANG v.[1]). **2** [1930s+] (*Aus.*) to hit someone hard, to knock someone down. [(1) SPIKE n.[1] (1); (2) SE *spike*, to pierce]

spike *v.*[4] (*also* **spike up**) [1930s+] (*drugs*) to inject a drug with a hypodermic syringe. [SPIKE n.[1] (4)]

spiked *adj.* **1** [late 19C–1920s] upset. **2** [1930s+] of an ostensibly non-alcoholic drink, having had alcohol added to it. [(2) SPIKE v.[2] (1)]

spike hotel *n.* [early–mid-19C] a prison (cf. BOARDING HOUSE n.). [the metal *spikes* on the walls]

Spike Park *n.* [mid-19C] the Queen's Bench prison; thus *spike park*, the grounds of a prison (cf. ABBOTT'S PRIORY n.).

Spikes, the *n.* [early 19C] the King's Bench prison (cf. ABBOTT'S PRIORY n.).

spikes *n.* [1980s+] **1** stilettos or 'spike'-heeled shoes. **2** (*US campus*) shoes, for either sex and of any kind. [the spike of the heel and/or the spikes used on running and other sports shoes]

spike team *n.* [mid–late 19C] (*US*) a coach drawn by 3 horses, with 2 side by side and 1 in the lead. [the lead horse represents the *spike*]

spike up *v. see* SPIKE v.[4].

spiky *n.* **1** [late 19C+] in religious terms, extremely ritualistic or High Church Anglican. **2** [1950s+] aggressive, harsh, unsympathetic, uncompromising. [(1) the SE *spike* or spire of a trad. church]

spill *n.*[1] **1** [late 17C–early 19C; 1940s] a small gift of money or reward. **2** [late 19C–1910s] a drink. [? SE *spill*, to pour out a small amount; (2) SPILL v.[1]]

spill *n.*[2] [1940s] (*US Und.*) a betrayal, a confession. [SPILL v.[3] (2)]

spill *n.*[3] [1940s–50s] (*US Black*) a person of mixed US Black and Puerto Rican blood; a Puerto Rican; a Black person. [ety. unknown; ? SE *spill*, either of blood or semen]

spill *v.*[1] [late 18C–1910s] to drink.

spill *v.*[2] **1** [late 18C+] to cause to fall. **2** [mid-19C–1920s] to knock down in a fight. **3** [1920s] (*US Und.*) to release from prison. **4** [1980s+] (*US campus*) to fall.

spill *v.*[3] (*also* **spill it**) **1** [early 19C] (*UK Und.*) to betray a confederate. **2** [20C+] (*orig. US*) (*also* **spill out**) to confess. **3** [20C+] (*also* **spill off**) to tell, to recount.

spill a line *v.* (*also* **spill a bibful, spill some gab**) [1920s+] to concoct a smooth patter with the specific aim of seduction; also in ironic use. [SPILL v.[3] (3) + LINE n.[1] (3)]

spillin' *n.* [1980s+] (*US Black*) a gunfight in which quantities of bullets are fired and wounds inflicted. [SE *spill blood*]

spill ink *v. see* SLING INK v. (1).

spill it *v. see* SPILL v.[3].

spill lead *v. see* THROW LEAD v.

spill off *v. see* SPILL v.[3] (3).

spill one's breakfast *v.* [1990s+] to vomit (cf. BLOW CHOW v.).

spill one's guts *v.* (*also* **spill one's insides**) **1** [1910s+] (*orig. US*) to confess one's crimes in full; to tell all. **2** [1940s] to vomit (cf. BLOW CHOW v.). **3** [1950s+] to speak out forcefully; to lose one's temper. **4** [1950s+] to divulge intimacies of one's personal life. [SPILL v.[3] + GUTS n.[1] (2)]

spill out *v. see* SPILL v.[3] (2).

spill some gab *v. see* SPILL A LINE v.

spill the beans *v.* **1** [1900s–10s] to cause a disaster. **2** [1910s+] (*orig. US*) (*also* **spill the dirt/works**) to confess, to let out a secret, to talk unguardedly. [SPILL v.[3]]

spin *n.*[1] [late 19C] (*Aus. Und.*) a jail sentence.

spin *n.*[2] [late 19C–1910s] a poor, unmarried young woman who travels to India in the hope of finding a husband. [abbr. SE *spinster*]

spin *n.*[3] **1** [late 19C+] a try, a chance; thus *give it a spin*, to have a go. **2** [1910s+] (*Aus./N.Z.*) an experience, a piece of luck, whether good or bad; thus FAIR SPIN n. [? a spin of the dice or coin]

spin *n.*[4] [1940s+] (*Aus.*) 5 in various contexts, e.g. £5 sterling, 5oz (144g) in weight, a 5-year prison sentence. [SPINNAKER n.]

spin *n.*[5] [1970s+] the playing of a gramophone record, esp. on a radio station.

spin *n.*[6] [1970s+] **1** (*UK Und./police*) any form of search or interrogation. **2** (*UK prison*) a search of a cell. [SPIN v.[3]]

spin *v.*[1] [mid-19C–1920s] to fail a candidate for a military or university examination, esp. in passive.

spin *v.*[2] [late 19C–1900s] (*US*) to wager.

spin *v.*[3] [1970s+] (*UK Und.*) to search; usu. as *spin a drum*, to search a house, also a prison cell.

spin *v.*[4] [2000s] (*UK Und.*) of money, to take illegally earned money and pass it through a legitimate business to render it free of criminal taint; to 'launder'. [? the illegal money is made to 'turn around' + play on the idea of money-laundering/the *spin*-dryer in a launderette]

spinach *n.*[1] (*US*) **1** [20C+] a beard. **2** [1910s–40s] a moustache. **3** [1920s–40s] pubic hair.

spinach *n.*[2] [1900s–40s] (*US*) rubbish, nonsense. [note GAMMON AND PICKLES n.]

spinach *n.*[3] [1920s–60s] money; dollar bills (cf. ALFALFA n.). [like the vegetable, it is green]

spinach *n.*[4] *see* CABBAGE n.[5].

spin a dit *v.* [1940s] (*Aus.*) to tell a story. [SE *spin* + *ditty*]

spin a hen *v.* [1940s] (*US Black*) to dance with an older woman. [SE *spin* (around) + HEN n.[1] (1)]

spin at the track with a fool's dim *v.* [1940s] (*US Black*) to go out dancing with a maid-servant on her night off.

spin a wren *v.* [1940s] (*US Black*) to dance with a (pretty) woman. [WREN n. (2)]

spin crooked spindles *v. see* MAKE CROOKED SPINDLES v.

spindle *n.*[1] **1** [mid-16C–19C] the penis. **2** [1900s] a leg.

spindle *n.*[2] [1920s–40s] (*US prison*) a guard.

spindleshanks *n.* [mid-16C+] a long, thin person; lit. 'thin legs'; thus adj., *spindle-shanked.*

spinebasher *n.* [1940s+] (*Aus.*) an idler, a loafer; thus *spine-bashing*, loafing; *spinebash*, a rest, time off from work, also sleeping. [SE *spine* + BASH v.¹ (1), i.e. hitting one's back against a chair]

spiney biff *n.* [1990s+] (*UK juv.*) a physically uncoordinated person. [SE *spina bifida*, 'a congenital malformation of widely varying severity in which there is a failure of one or more vertebræ to surround completely the meninges and spinal cord, usu. with effects on spinal cord function' (*OED*); this term is generally considered unacceptable since it is, in effect, a derog. attack on those who suffer this malformation]

spin for *v.* [1940s+] (*Aus.*) to court a woman. [the game of two-up or fishing imagery]

spin-house *n. see* SPINNING HOUSE n.

spinifex wire *n.* [1930s+] (*Aus.*) the outback version of the 'bush telegraph'; thus a rumour. [SE *Spinifex*, 'One or other of a number of coarse grasses […] which grow in dense masses on the sand-hills of the Australian deserts, and are characterized by their sharp-pointed, spiny leaves' (*OED*) + *wire*, a telegraph]

spiniken/spinikin *n. see* SPINNING HOUSE n.

spin it out of one's ass *v.* [1970s] (*US*) to lie, to brag. [ASS n. (2)]

spinnaker *n.* [late 19C–1950s] (*Aus.*) a £5 note, a $5 bill. [SE *spinnaker*, a large 3-cornered sail carried by racing-yachts]

spinner *n.¹* [late 19C] (*Aus.*) a fast horse.

spinner *n.²* [1910s+] (*Aus.*) in a game of two-up, the man who is tossing, i.e. *spinning* the coins.

spinner *n.³* [1940s–60s] (*Aus.*) £5. [SPINNAKER n.]

spinner *n.⁴* [1970s] a coarse ref. to a fantasized female. [the image of the woman spinning like the propellor on a *propeller-beanie* hat]

spinner *n.⁵* [1980s+] (*Aus. prison*) an eccentric. [their brain is *spinning*]

spinning *adj.* [late 19C] speedy, quick.

spinning house *n.* (*also* **spin-house, spiniken, spinikin, spinning ken**) [mid-17C; mid-18C; 19C] a workhouse, esp. the St Giles's workhouse. [Du. *spinnhuis*, a women's house of correction; presumably the inmates were forced to spin thread + KEN n.¹ (1)]

spinning jenny *n.* [19C] the vagina. [SE *spinning jenny*, a prototype spinning machine]

spinning jinny *n.* (*also* **spinning jenny**) [mid-19C–1930s] a roulette table. [resemblance to naut. *spinning jenny*, a prismatic compass]

spinning ken *n. see* SPINNING HOUSE n.

spinning top *n.* [1930s+] a policeman (cf. BOTTLE (AND STOPPER) n.). [rhy. sl. = COP n.¹ (1)]

spinny *adj.* [1970s] (*Can.*) insane, eccentric. [their head is 'in a spin']

spin off *v.* [late 16C–early 17C] for a woman to bring a man to orgasm.

spin one's wheels *v.* [1970s+] (*US*) to waste time or work fruitlessly.

spin out *v.* **1** [1950s+] (*orig. US*) of a vehicle, to go out of control. **2** [1980s+] (*Aus. prison*) to suffer the effects of prison life.

spin someone's wheels *v.* [1980s+] (*US campus*) to excite, esp. sexually.

spinsrap *n.* [mid-19C] parsnips. [backsl.]

spinster *n.* [early 17C–early 18C] a prostitute. [SE *spinster*, an unmarried woman, irrespective of age]

spin the bat *v.* [late 19C–1900s] (*Anglo-Ind.*) to speak in sl. [SE *spin* + Hind. *bat*, speech, a word]

spin the dope *v.* [1920s+] (*Aus.*) to tell a good story; to 'read the cards' as a fortune-teller. [SE *spin* + DOPE n.³ (1)]

spin top in mud *v.* [20C+] (*W.I.*) to waste one's time attempting a frustrating task.

spintry *n.* [late 16C–mid-17C] a male homosexual prostitute; thus adj., *spintrian*. [? Lat. *spinter*, a bracelet; thus those men who wear them and the image of male homosexual sex as having bodies linked togther like the links of a bracelet]

spire and steeple *n.* [20C+] (*Aus.*) people. [rhy. sl.]

spirit *n.* [1970s+] (*US Black*) jazz or blues music.

spiritual flesh-broker *n.* [late 17C–18C] a parson.

spiry *adj.* [early 19C] highly distinguished. [fig. resembling a tall spire]

spit *n.¹* [17C–early 19C] a sword. [SE *spit*, a sharpened rod used to roast meat]

spit *n.²* [18C+] identity, similarity, esp. in familial resemblance; thus in phrs. *the (dead/very) spit of*. [earlier phr. 'as like his father as if he had been spit out of his mouth']

spit *n.³* [1940s–50s] a cigarette, a puff of a cigarette. [? SPIT AND A DRAG n.]

spit *v.¹* **1** [late 18C–19C] of a man, to have sexual intercourse (cf. BANG v.¹). **2** [1970s] to ejaculate (cf. BLOSH v.). [SE *spit*, to pierce]

spit *v.²* [1990s+] (*US Black*) to write and perform HIP-HOP n. or RAP n.⁵ lyrics; unlike these, however, there is no necessity to produce rhyming lines.

Spitalfields' breakfast *n.* [mid-19C] a tight necktie and a short pipe, i.e. no breakfast (cf. BARBER'S BREAKFAST n.). [*Spitalfields*, in the East End of London and, as such, an impoverished area]

Spitalfields crawl *n.* [1900s–10s] (*UK tramp*) the squirming action of someone who is covered in lice. [the insanitary condition of housing in Spitalfields, East London]

Spital whore *n.* (*also* **Spital lady, spittle whore**) [mid-16C–early 17C] a prostitute. [*Spitalfields*, a tough East End area of London + SE *spital*, a hospital (and origin of the district's name), thus underlining the physical perils of being a prostitute]

spit amber *v.* [late 19C] (*US*) to spit while chewing tobacco. [the colour of the spittle]

spit and a drag *n.* (*also* **spit and a draw**) **1** [late 19C+] (*orig. RN*) a surreptitious smoke. **2** [1930s–70s] a cigarette. [? rhy. sl. = FAG n.⁴ (3), or the result of a badly rolled cigarette, from which one spits out the odd strand of tobacco, while dragging or drawing down the smoke]

spit-and-scratch game *n.* [1910s–20s] a fight, usu. between women. [woman supposedly do not use their fists]

spit beef *v.* [1970s] (*US campus*) to vomit (cf. BLOW CHOW v.).

spit-bit *n.* [1970s] (*US Black*) smooth, persuasive talk. [SE *spit* + BIT n.⁸ (2)]

spit blood *v.* [1960s+] to be in a furious temper.

spit cards *v.* [late 18C–1920s] to leave visiting cards on one's social round.

spit-cat *n.* (*also* **spit-kitten**) [late 19C–1910s] a termagant, one who has a very short temper. [cf. SE *spitfire*]

spit chips *v.* (*orig. Aus.*) **1** [late 19C+] to feel extreme thirst. **2** [1960s+] to manifest acute anger or vexation. [SE *spit* + *chips* of wood]

spit cotton *v.* **1** [mid-19C–1940s] (*US*) to be very thirsty, to have a dry mouth. **2** [1940s] to be very angry. **3** [1950s] (*drugs*) to spit white balls of spittle while under the influence of amphetamine.

spitfire *n.* [mid-17C] the vagina (cf. BLACK HOLE n.¹).

spit-fire machine *n. see* MACHINE n.¹ (2).

spit-fuck *n.* [1990s+] (*gay*) anal intercourse or penetration of the anus by the fingers or fist where the only lubricant is spit. [SE *spit* + FUCK n.¹ (1); thus the saying 'if spit doesn't work, it isn't love']

spit game *v. see* TALK GAME v.

spithead *n.* [1940s] (*US*) a general term of abuse. [SE *spit* + -HEAD sfx (1)]

spit it out! *excl.* [mid-19C+] speak up! confess! explain yourself!

spit-kitten *n. see* SPIT-CAT *n.*

spit me death! *excl.* [1940s–50s] (*Aus.*) a defensive retort, meaning that one's last statement is absolutely true. [SPIT ONE'S DEATH V.]

spit meth *n.* [1990s+] regurgitated *meth*adone.

spit o' my hand! *excl.* [late 19C–1920s] used to emphasize whatever it is one has said, e.g. *spit o' my hand, you know it's the truth.* [the spitting on one's hand that seals a bargain]

spit one's death *v.* [1900s–10s] to swear one's honesty. [the practice of spitting to confirm the sincerity of one's oath]

spit one's guts *v.* [1930s] (*US*) to confess one's crimes in full.

spit or get off the cuspidor *phr.* [1940s+] (*Can.*) a euph. for SHIT OR GET OFF THE POT *phr.*

spit out of the window *v.* [1930s+] (*gay*) to spit out one's partner's semen after fellatio.

spit (out) the dummy *v.* [1980s+] (*Aus.*) to lose one's temper badly. [the image of a furious baby]

spit roast *n.* [1990s+] a woman or homosexual man who is simultaneously fellating one man while having intercourse, from the rear, with another (cf. ROASTING *n.*[2]).

spit sixpences *v.* (*also* **spit white (broth)**) [late 16C–18C] to spit out small gobbets of white spittle.

spit tacks *v.* [1950s+] (*Aus./US*) to be irate, furious. [note synon. UK milit. *spit button-sticks*]

spitter *n.*[1] [1970s] (*US Und.*) a hoodlum, a thug, a gangster.

spitter *n.*[2] [1980s] (*Aus.*) a derog. term for a woman. [she spits out the semen after performing fellatio]

spit the dummy *v. see* SPIT (OUT) THE DUMMY *v.*

spitting at the tongs *phr.* [20C+] (*Ulster*) pregnant. [ety. unknown; ? a folk saying]

Spittleonian *n.* [mid-19C] (*UK Und.*) a yellow (silk) handkerchief. [its manufacture in Spitalfields, east London]

spittle whore *n. see* SPITAL WHORE *n.*

spit up *v.* **1** [1940s] (*Aus.*) to vomit (cf. BARF v.). **2** [1940s–60s] to confess.

spit white (broth) *v. see* SPIT SIXPENCES *v.*

spitz poodle *n.* [late 19C] (*US*) a mild degree of drunkenness. [ety. unknown; the variety of dog seems to have no relevance]

spiv *n.* (*also* **spive**) [1920s+] a flashy, sharp individual who exists on the fringes of real criminality, living by their wits rather than a regular job. [? Rom. *spiv*, sparrow, used by gypsies as a derog. ref. to those who existed by picking up the leavings of their betters, criminal or legitimate; alternative theories include the reverse of *V.I.P.s* or police abbr. *suspected persons* and *itinerant vagrants*]

spiv *v.* [1940s+] to work as a street trader, esp. with overtones of illegality. [SPIV *n.*]

spivish *adj.* [1940s+] exhibiting the characteristics and/or lifestyle of a SPIV *n.*

spivmobile *n.* [1980s+] an exceptionally ostentatious and flashy car, such as might be driven by a SPIV *n.* or their successors. [SPIV *n.* + -MOBILE sfx]

spivvy *adj.* (*also* **spivy**) [1940s+] exhibiting the characteristics and/or lifestyle of a SPIV *n.*

spizz *n.* [1960s] (*US drugs*) a hypodermic syringe. [? var. on SPIKE *n.*[1] (4)]

spizzerinktum *n.* (*US*) **1** [mid-19C] a dollar; money in general. **2** [1940s] vigour, zest. [(1) SE *specie*; (2) nonce-word, reminiscent of *fizz, pizzazz* etc]

S.P. joint *n.* (*also* **S.P. shop**) [1920s–50s] (*Aus.*) a betting shop, offering only starting prices. [SE starting price + JOINT *n.*[4] (3)]

splang *n.* [1970s] (*US Black*) sharp words; thus as v., to curse. [? echoic]

splash *n.*[1] [late 18C] style, dash; a striking or ostentatious display, appearance or effect; usu. in phr. CUT A SPLASH v.

splash *n.*[2] [mid-19C] make-up, cosmetics; esp. *poudre de riz* used to whiten the complexion.

splash *n.*[3] **1** [1920s] an alcoholic drink. **2** [1920s+] any form of water, e.g. a river, a lake, the sea, a bath, or water as added to a drink of spirits.

splash *n.*[4] (*drugs*) **1** [1960s+] liquid amphetamine (cf. A *n.*[2]). **2** [1980s] an injection of methamphetamine and the quasi-orgasmic sensation this brings.

splash *n.*[5] [1980s+] a woman, or in gay use a man, who is the object of gang-rape or a voluntary participant in multiple intercourse. [the bodily fluids thus discharged]

splash *n.*[6] [1990s+] an act of urination.

splash *adj.* [mid-19C–1930s] elegant, fashionable, distinguished. [SPLASH *n.*[1]]

splash *v.*[1] **1** [late 19C+] to spend money extravagantly. **2** [1930s+] to masturbate.

splash *v.*[2] [1940s] (*US*) for a boxer to lose a fight voluntarily, usu. in return for payment. [play on TAKE A DIVE v. (1)]

splashing *n.* [late 19C–1900s] garrulous or foolish chatter.

splashing *adj.* (*also* **splashy**) [late 19C–1910s] fine, excellent, first-rate; also as adv. [SPLASH *n.*[1]]

splash on *v.* [1990s+] (*US Black gang*) to shoot. [the *splash* of blood]

splash out (on) *v.* [1970s+] to spend money unrestrainedly; thus *splash*, a spending spree.

splash the boots *v.* [1960s+] to urinate (cf. BURN THE GRASS v.).

splash the salties *v.* [1940s] (*US Black*) to weep. [i.e. *salt* tears]

splash-up *adj.* [late 19C+] first-rate, excellent.

splashy *adj. see* SPLASHING *adj.*

splat *v.* [1920s+] to hit a hard surface, with a slapping or splashing noise. [SPLAT! *excl.*]

splat *adv.* [mid-19C+] evocative of a solid but soft body hitting a hard surface. [echoic]

splat! *excl.* [20C+] the slapping or splashing noise of something that hits a hard surface. [echoic]

splat movie *n. see* SPLATTER MOVIE *n.*

splatter dabs *n.* [1940s] (*US*) pancakes.

splatterdash *n.* [late 19C] an uproar. [synon. Yorks. dial.]

splatter face *n.* [mid-19C] a broad face. [Northumberland/ Oxfordshire dial. *splatter-faced*, broad-faced, 'platter-faced']

splatter movie *n.* (*also* **splat movie**) [1970s+] a genre of ultra-violent films, coined as a name by director George Romero (b.1939), e.g. *The Texas Chainsaw Massacre* (1974), *The Driller Killer* (1979); thus *splatterpunk*, a similarly violent genre of fiction.

splatter one's batter *v.* [1990s+] to ejaculate (cf. BLOSH v.). [SE *splatter* + BATTER *n.*[1] (2)]

splay head *n.* [1980s] (*US campus*) a fool.

spleef *n.* [1980s] (*US campus*) a particle of food lodged between the teeth. [SE *teeth* + ? SE *split*]

spleefer *n.* (*also* **spleef**) [1980s+] (*US drugs*) a cannabis cigarette. [SPLIFF *n.* (1) + REEFER *n.*[2] (2)]

splendacious *adj.* (*also* **splendidious, splendidous**) [17C; late 19C–1910s] splendid, excellent, first-rate. [intensifier of SE *splendid*]

splendiferous *adj.* [mid-19C+] wonderful, perfect. [intensifier of SE *splendid*]

spleuchan *n.* [late 18C] the vagina. [Gael. *spliùchan*, a tobacco pouch, a purse]

splib *n.* **1** [1960s+] (*US Black*) a fellow Black person. **2** [1970s] 'a liberal Black who looks angry but will not upset the status quo' (*American Speech*, XLIX, 1976); i.e. a derog. term for a Black person. **3** [1970s] a drunkard. [ety. unknown]

splice *n.* **1** [early 19C–1920s] one's wife. **2** [mid–late 19C] the act or institution of marriage; thus *do a splice*, to get married. [SPLICE v.(1)]

splice *v.* **1** [mid-18C+] (*also* **splice up**) to marry; thus *spliced*, married. **2** [late 19C] to have sexual intercourse. **3** [1900s] to perform the marriage ceremony. [SE *splice*, to join, orig. of ropes]

splice the mainbrace *v.* [19C+] (*orig. naut.*) to drink. [SE *splice* + *mainbrace*, the brace attached to the main-yard of a sailing ship]

splice-toby *n.* [mid–late 19C] the highway, the main road. [SE *splice*, to join + TOBY n.[2] (2)]

splice up *v. see* SPLICE v. (1).

spliff *n.* (*also* **splif**) **1** [1930s+] (*orig. W.I., esp. Rasta*) a cannabis cigarette. **2** [1980s] (*UK prison*) a hand-rolled cigarette. **3** [2000s] cannabis. **4** [2000s] (*US Black*) a male companion or friend. [SPIFLICATE v., i.e. the effects]

spliff *v.* [2000s] to smoke a cannabis cigarette. [SPLIFF n. (1)]

spliffhead *n.* [1990s+] (*drugs*) a smoker of cannabis. [SPLIFF n. (1) + -HEAD sfx (3)]

splinter *n.* [1910s–50s] (*US*) a notably thin person.

splinter belly *n.* [1920s–40s] (*US tramp*) a tramp who works as a part-time carpenter.

splinter one's toupée *v.* [1940s] (*US*) to lose emotional control, to 'blow one's mind'.

splish and splash *v.* [1970s+] (*US Black*) to debate a topic, to ponder without coming to a decision.

split *n.*[1] **1** [mid-19C] (*UK Und.*) the parting of a group of criminals. **2** [late 19C+] the division of criminal spoils or of any sum of money.

split *n.*[2] (*also* **splitter**) **1** [mid-19C+] (*UK Und.*) an informer. **2** [late 19C+] a detective or policeman. **3** [1950s] (*US Und.*) an act of betrayal. [SPLIT v.[3] (1)]

split *n.*[3] **1** [mid-19C+] the vagina (cf. AGREEABLE RUTS OF LIFE n.). **2** [1930s+] (*also* **split end/stuff**) a woman; women in general, esp. as viewed as sex objects. [physiology]

split *n.*[4] **1** [late 19C] small change. **2** [1920s–30s] a 10-shilling note (50p), i.e. a *split* pound note.

split *n.*[5] [late 19C] a pimp, a procurer (cf. ABBOT ON THE CROSS n.). [he *splits* the woman's earnings with her]

split *n.*[6] **1** [late 19C–1900s] a drink composed of 2 different alcoholic liquors. **2** [late 19C–1900s] a half-glass of spirits. **3** [late 19C–1910s] (*US*) a drink composed of half water/half alcohol. **4** [late 19C] a half-bottle of champagne. **5** [late 19C] a small bottle of mineral water. **6** [1960s–70s] (*US drugs*) any pill – an amphetamine or barbiturate – that has a groove embedded in its surface (cf. PILL n.[4]).

split *n.*[7] [1930s–50s] (*Aus./US*) a safety match.

split *v.*[1] [mid-17C; 19C+] to have sexual intercourse (cf. BANG v.[1]).

split *v.*[2] **1** [late 18C–mid-19C] to walk or run at great speed. **2** [mid-19C+] to leave, to depart. **3** [1960s] (*US Black*) to die. [the fig. *split* or 'tear' in a group that such a departure makes]

split *v.*[3] **1** [late 18C+] to betray, to inform against; usu. *split on*. **2** [early 19C] to believe. **3** [mid-19C+] to disclose, to reveal secrets. [to *split* or break a confidence]

split *v.*[4] **1** [mid-19C+] to quarrel with someone, to break off relations. **2** [1940s+] (*orig. US*) (*also* **split the blanket/sheets**) to divorce.

split *v.*[5] [20C+] to share out profits or proceeds. [SPLIT n.[1] (2)]

split a gut *v.* **1** [late 17C; 1950s] to vomit. **2** [mid-19C+] (*also* **split**) to laugh hysterically. **3** [1940s+] to be overcome with emotion, e.g. rage, delight etc. **4** [1950s+] (*US*) to exert maximum effort. [var. on BUST A GUT v.]

split a kipper *v.* [1990s+] to have sexual intercourse. [KIPPER n.[4]]

split apricot *n.* [late 17C–19C] the vagina (cf. AGREEABLE RUTS OF LIFE n.; APPLE n.[6]).

split arse *n.* (*also* **split tail**) **1** [1970s+] a woman. **2** [2000s] (*US*) a male homosexual. [SE *split* + ARSE n.[1] (1)/TAIL n.[2] (1)]

split-arse *adj.* [1920s–40s] daring.

split-arse *adv.* [1910s–20s] very quickly; thus as v., to move quickly. [SE *split* + ARSE n.[1] (1); the movement of one's legs and buttocks]

split-arsed *adj.* [1980s] of a man, cowardly, effeminate. [SPLIT ARSE n. (1)]

split-arsed one *n.* [late 19C] a woman, esp. a baby girl. [SE *split* + ARSE n.[1] (2)]

split-arse mechanic *n.* [late 19C] a prostitute; thus *take on a split-arse mechanic*, to have sexual intercourse (cf. BANGTAIL n.[1]). [SE *split* + ARSE n.[1] (2) + SE *mechanic*; note RAF jargon *split-arse merchant*, a reckless, showy or daring airman; *split-arse cap*, the Royal Flying Corps cap, similar to a Glengarry]

split-ass *adj.* [1910s] (*Aus.*) unusual.

split asunder *n.* [mid–late 19C] a costermonger. [rhy. sl.]

split beaver *n.* (*also* **spread beaver**) [1970s+] the wide-open vagina, esp. as found in hardcore pornography (cf. AGREEABLE RUTS OF LIFE n.). [SE *split*/*spread* + BEAVER n.[5] (1)]

split bit *n.* [1950s+] (*US Und.*) an indeterminate sentence, subject to the decisions of the parole board. [SE *split* + BIT n.[5]]

split-cause *n.* (*also* **splitter (of causes)**) [late 17C–early 19C] a lawyer. [the profession's reputation as splitters of legal hairs]

split crow *n.* [late 18C–early 19C] the sign of the spreadeagle. [supposed resemblance]

split end *n. see* SPLIT n.[3] (2).

split fair *v.* [mid–late 19C] to tell the truth. [SPLIT v.[3] (3) + SE *fair*]

split fig *n.* **1** [late 17C–early 19C] a grocer. **2** [late 19C–1940s] the vagina (cf. AGREEABLE RUTS OF LIFE n.; APPLE n.[6]). [(2) note synon. Ital. *fica*, a fig]

split finger *n.* [1930s–40s] (*US prison/Und.*) a (prison) clerk.

split kipper *n. see* SPLIT KIPPER n.[4].

split me! *excl.* [late 17C–mid-19C] an oath used by contemporary upper-class dandies.

split mutton *n.* **1** [17C–19C] the penis (cf. ARSE-OPENER n.). **2** [18C–1900s] the vagina (cf. AGREEABLE RUTS OF LIFE n.; BACON SANDWICH n.). **3** [18C–1900s] a derog. generic term for womankind. [SE *split* + MUTTON n. (3)]

split one's wig *v.* [1950s–60s] (*US*) to suffer pain, to feel depressed, to be at the end of one's tether. [SE *split* + WIG n.[3] (1)]

split out *v.* **1** [late 19C+] to separate. **2** [1930s+] (*US*) to part company, to take one's leave. **3** [1970s] (*US prison*) to escape. [(1) SPLIT v.[4] (1); (2) ext. of SPLIT v.[2] (2)]

split pea *n.* [mid-19C] tea. [rhy. sl.]

split-rump *n. see* RUMP-SPLITTER n.

split someone's wig *v.* [2000s] (*US prison/Black*) to hit someone quickly and hard, esp. in the head; thus to kill. [SE *split* + WIG n.[3] (1)]

split stuff *n. see* SPLIT n.[3] (2).

splitsville *n.* [1960s+] (*orig. US*) **1** the end of a relationship, a divorce etc. **2** the state of departure. [SPLIT v.[4] (2)/SPLIT v.[2] (2) + -VILLE sfx[1]]

split tail *n. see* SPLIT ARSE n.

splitter *n. see* SPLIT n.[2].

splitter (of causes) *n. see* SPLIT-CAUSE n.

split the beard *v.* (*also* **part the whiskers**) [1970s+] of a man, to have sexual intercourse. [BEARD n.[1] (1)/WHISKERS n.[2] (2)]

split the blanket *v. see* SPLIT v.[4] (2).

split the breeze *v.* [1950s+] to depart, to travel, to run fast.

split the cup *v.* [1970s] (*US Black*) to deflower a virgin. [SE *split*/SPLIT v.[1] + FUZZY CUP n.; plus the image of running blood]

split the difference *v.* [1970s] of a man, to have sexual intercourse. [pun]

split the peach *v.* [1990s+] to sodomize. [PEACHES n.[3]]

split the scene *v.* [1950s+] (*orig. US*) to leave, to depart. [SPLIT v.[2] (2) + SCENE n. (1)]

split the sheets *v. see* SPLIT v.[4] (2).

split the wind *v. see* HIT THE WIND v.

split 'un *n.* [1930s+] (*Aus.*) a banknote that has been divided in halves.

split up *v.* [1940s+] (*orig. US*) to become divorced. [ext. of SPLIT v.[4] (2)]

split-whisker *n.* [1940s+] (*Aus.*) a collective term for women, viewed sexually. [SE + SPLIT n.[3] (1) + WHISKERS n.[2] (2)]

split wig *n.* [1960s] (*US*) a lunatic. [SPLIT ONE'S WIG v.]

spliv *n.* [1960s–70s] (*US Black*) a fellow Black person. [var. on SPLIB n. (1)]

splivins *n.* [1960s–70s] (*drugs*) amphetamine (cf. A n.²). [ety. unknown]

splodger *n.*¹ [mid-19C] **1** a lout, a rough countryman. **2** a grave-robber. [dial. *splodge*, to wade through mud]

splodger *n.*² (*also* **sploger, splojer**) [mid-19C] an old man. [rhy. sl. = CODGER n. (1)]

splooge *n.* (*also* **sploodge**) [1980s+] (*US campus*) semen (cf. BOLLOCK SNOT n.). [SPLOOGE v.]

splooge *v.* [1980s+] (*US campus*) to ejaculate (cf. BLOSH v.). [var. on SE *splurge*]

splosh *n.*¹ (*also* **sploosh**) [late 19C+] money. [? SPLASH v.¹ (1)]

splosh *n.*² [1940s–70s] tea. [SE *splosh*, the sound of a liquid falling or having something dropped into it]

splosher *n.* [2000s] a woman. [? var. on SLAPPER n.² (1)]

splosh it on *v.* [1920s+] to bet heavily, esp. at racetracks. [ext./var. SPLASH v.¹ (1)]

splow *n.* [1960s] (*US Black*) ritual hand-slapping that signifies a greeting or farewell. [? echoic]

splurge *n.* [mid-19C] a rush, a sudden movement. [SE *splurge*, an ostentatious display or effort]

splush! *excl.* [1920s] (*US*) nonsense! rubbish!

splutter *n.* [1910s–20s] a scandal. [dial. *splutter*, a fuss, a disturbance]

spod *n.* [1990s+] (*UK teen*) an unpopular schoolchild. [? Scot. *spodlin*, a child who is just learning to walk]

spod *v.* [1990s+] **1** to engage in meaningless activities whether or not there is work to do. **2** to spend time on newsgroups on the Internet. [SPOD n.]

spoda *n.* [2000s] (*US Black*) a White person who attempts (unsuccessfully) to adopt Black culture and style.

spodiodi *n.* [1940s+] (*orig. US*) a mixture of cheap port and generic bar whisky, much loved by jazz musicians and beatniks. [ety. unknown, the port is seen as a 'jacket' for the rough whisky; noted as a song lyric, 'Drink wine spodiodi', in Jack Kerouac, *On the Road* (1957); ? the rhythmic sound of the word is echoic of the mixing of the drinks; Décharné, *Straight from the Fridge* (2000), suggests McGhee's lyrics were a bowdlerised version of 'an obscene US army drinking song which ran 'Drinking wine, motherfucker, drinking wine']

spoffish *adj.* [mid-19C] interfering, meddlesome, acting like a busybody. [? SE *officious*]

spoffskins *n.* [late 19C–1900s] a prostitute, esp. one who poses as her regular client's 'wife'. [ety. unknown]

spog *v.* (*also* **spogh**) [mid-19C+] (*S.Afr.*) to boast, to brag. [Du. *spochen*, to boast]

spoil *v.* **1** [early 19C] to stop someone else achieving their object. **2** [mid-19C] (*US*) to kill. **3** [mid-19C] in fig. use of (2), to finish (a drink).

spoil (a woman's shape) *v.* [late 17C–early 18C] to make pregnant.

spoilers *n.* [1940s+] (*S.Afr.*) a township thug or criminal. [proper name *Spoilers*, a leading gang in the 1940s, then applied to all such young men, gang members or not; ult. title of a popular film]

spoil-iron *n.* [late 18C–early 19C] a blacksmith.

spoil-pudding *n.* [late 18C–early 19C] a parson. [a long-winded parson keeps his congregation in church so long that their cooking spoils]

spoke-box *n.* [19C] the mouth. [the 'spokes' are the teeth]

spoken to *phr.* [mid-19C] deceived, tricked. [SPEAK TO v.]

spoke to *phr.* **1** [late 18C–early 19C] suffering a great misfortune, beyond help. **2** [early 19C] (*UK Und.*) robbed; the type of robbery can be added; thus *spoke to upon the screw/crack/sneak/hoist/buz.* [? SPEAK TO v. or ? (1) a message from the deity]

spon *n.* (*also* **spondos, sponds, spons**) [late 19C+] money. [abbr. SPONDULICKS n.]

sponditious *adj.* [1980s] excellent. [coined by UK comedian Lenny Henry (b.1958); ? SE *spon*taneous + deli*cious*]

spondulicks *n.* (*also* **spondooli, spondooli(c)ks, spondulics, spondulix**) [mid-19C+] money. [? Gk *spondulikos*, the adj. form of *spondulox*, a type of shell used as early 'money'; or ? corruption of GREENBACK n.² (1); note Michael Quinion, *World Wide Words* (Internet, 29 September 2001): 'Doug Wilson pointed out that the Greek stem suggested as the origin of this term in last week's Weird Words piece is also the source of various English words beginning in 'spondylo-' that refer to the spine or vertebrae. He suggested that a stack of coins may have been likened to the spine, with each coin a vertebra. He found a supporting reference in an 1867 book, 'A Manual of the Art of Prose Composition: for the Use of Colleges and Schools', by John Mitchell Bonnell. A list of provincialisms included: "Spondulics – coin piled for counting"]

sponge *n.*¹ (*also* **spunge**) **1** [late 16C+] a heavy drinker; thus adj. *spongy*. **2** [17C] a dedicated scholar. **3** [17C+] someone who lives by cadging off others. **4** [1920s–30s] (*US Und.*) a prohibition officer. [their absorption, whether of alcohol, knowledge or another's favours]

sponge *n.*² [1960s] a hollow sponge that is placed inside the mouth of the vagina by a prostitute as protection against disease and accidental pregnancy; thus as v., to use such a sponge; *sponge tricks*, to deceive clients by using a sponge.

sponge cake *n.* [late 19C–1940s] (*US*) anything simple, ridiculously easy. [earlier var. on PIECE OF CAKE n., i.e. it is SOFT adj. (4)]

sponge hair *n.* [1930s–50s] (*US Black*) hair that resists combing.

sponge it out *v.* [late 19C] (*US*) to forget something, to wipe something from one's memory.

sponging-house *n.* (*also* **sponge house, spunging-house**) [late 17C–1960s] a bailiff's lock-up. ['to which persons arrested are taken, till they find bail, or have spent all their money; a house where every species of fraud and extortion is practised, under the protection of the law' (Grose, 1785). The corrupt bailiff's officers 'sponge up' their victims' money]

spons *n. see* SPON n.

sponsor *n.* **1** [1950s] (*US Black*) a man who is conned into paying in general. **2** [1970s] (*US Black*) a man who 'keeps' a woman, in return for sexual favours. **3** [1970s+] (*US gay*) an older homosexual man who supports his young lover. **4** [1990s+] (*US prison*) (*also* **financier**) a man who sends money and gifts into a female inmate.

sponsor *v.* [1970s–80s] (*UK Black*) to lend or give money.

spoo *n.* [1980s+] (*US campus*) semen; thus as v., to ejaculate (cf. BOLLOCK SNOT n.). [SPEW n.]

spooch *n.* [1980s+] (*US campus*) semen; thus as v., to ejaculate (cf. BOLLOCK SNOT n.). [ext. of SPOO n./SPEW n.]

spoof *n.*¹ [late 19C+] a hoax, a confidence trick. [SE *spoof*, a game, involving hoaxing one's rival players, invented by the comedian Arthur Roberts (1852–1933)]

spoof *n.*² [1910s+] (*Aus.*) semen; thus as v., to ejaculate. [? *spit* + *poof!* onomat. noise of a small explosion]

spoof *adj.* [late 19C+] fake, spurious, sham. [SPOOF n.¹]

spoof *v.* **1** [late 19C+] to hoax, to fool, to trick. **2** [1940s] (*UK prison*) of an informer, to be looking for information; usu. as *on the spoof.* **3** [1940s] (*US*) to make fun of. **4** [1980s] (*US campus*) to engage in sexual activity short of intercourse. [SPOOF n.¹; (3) ? link to SPOOF n.²]

spoofer *n.* [1910s+] a trickster. [SPOOF v. (1)]

spooferies *n.* [late 19C–1900s] a second-rate sporting club. [SPOOFERY n.; the orig. *Spooferies* seems to have been the Trafalgar Club in Maiden Lane near the Strand, but the term was generic and the card-game *spoof* (in which the appearance of certain cards at the same time is called a 'spoof') was invented at the

Adelphi Club; for details see Binstead, *Pitcher in Paradise* (1903), pp.227 ff. and Binstead & Wells, *A Pink 'Un and a Pelican* (1898), p.56]

spoofery *n.* [late 19C] trickery, hoaxing. [SPOOF v. (1)]

spoofie *n.* [1970s] (*Aus.*) an attractive young woman. [? SPOOF v. (4)]

spoof tube *n.* [2000s] (*US drugs*) an empty toilet paper roll stuffed with sheets of fabric softener; thus works as a 'filter' for tell-tale smoke when smoking marijuana surreptitiously. [SPOOF n.[1]/ SE *puff*]

spooge *n.* **1** [1980s+] (*US*) semen (cf. BOLLOCK SNOT n.). **2** [2000s] (*US Black*) a verbal explosion. [? ext. of SPOO n.]

spooge *v.* [1990s+] **1** to explode or splurge out; thus adj., *spooged*. **2** to ejaculate (cf. BLOSH v.). [SPOOGE n.]

spook *n.*[1] **1** [1930s–70s] (*US Black*) a White person. **2** [1940s] (*US*) a derog. term for an Italian (cf. DAGO n.). **3** [1940s+] (*US*) a derog. term for a Black person (cf. ALLIGATOR BAIT n.[2]). **4** [1960s–80s] (*US Black*) a fellow Black person. **5** [1960s–70s] (*US*) a derog. term for a Vietnamese. **6** [1970s] (*US drugs*) a heroin addict. **7** [1970s] (*Aus.*) a derog. term for a native Australian. **8** [1980s+] (*S.Afr.*) a fright, a scare. [SE *spook*, a ghost]

spook *n.*[2] [1940s+] (*orig. US*) an intelligence agent, esp. CIA; thus *spookic, spookical, spookish, spookism, spookological, spookology*. [Yale University secret society Skull & Bones, from among whose members were recruited the personnel of the OSS, the WW2 predecessor of the CIA; note RMC Duntroon (Aus.) *spook*, a member of the Australian Intelligence Corps; also WW1 Aus. milit. *spook*, an army signaller, esp. a wireless operator]

spook *adj.*[1] [1950s+] (*US*) relevant to Black people or Black culture or lifestyle. [SPOOK n.[1] (3)]

spook *adj.*[2] [1960s+] (*US*) pertaining to undercover/intelligence operations. [SPOOK n.[2]]

spook *v.* (*orig. US*) **1** [mid-19C+] to scare, to unnerve. **2** [1930s+] to take fright, to become scared. [SE *spook*]

spooked *adj.* **1** [1920s+] under the influence of a malign spirit. **2** [1950s+] frightened, alarmed. **3** [1950s+] annoyed, disgusted. [SE *spook*/SPOOK v. (2)]

spook juke *n.* [1980s] (*US prison*) a White inmate who is seen as overly friendly to Black ones. [SPOOK n.[1] (3) + ? JUKE v.[2] (3), i.e. one who has sex with Blacks]

spooks, the *n.* [1980s+] (*Aus.*) a sense of terror or emotional uneasiness.

spooky *adj.*[1] **1** [mid-19C+] (*orig. US*) frightening, eerie, pertaining to the 'spirit world'. **2** [1920s+] (*US*) nervous, easily frightened, superstitious. **3** [1950s+] of a person, frightening, menacing.

spooky *adj.*[2] [1950s] (*US*) pertaining to Black people or culture. [SPOOK n.[1] (3)]

spoon *n.*[1] **1** [late 18C–19C; 1980s+] a fool, a simpleton. **2** [mid-late 19C; 2000s] a flirt; thus COME THE SPOON v.; *do spoons*, to offer sentimental and ridiculous protestations of love. **3** [mid-19C–1910s] a foolishly infatuated lover. **4** [late 19C] a foolish, sentimental affection. **5** [1910s] an act of flirtation. [SE *spoon*, which is 'open' and 'shallow'. A spoon has been defined to be "a thing that touches a lady's lips without kissing them"' (Hotten, 1860); note *Online Dict. of Playground Slang* (2001) defines (1) as 'a person so dense they were not allowed to use a sharp object, they could only have a spoon']

spoon *n.*[2] [1920s] (*US*) a shovel.

spoon *n.*[3] (*drugs*) **1** [1950s+] 2g ([1]/16th oz) of heroin or cocaine. **2** [1970s+] enough heroin to provide a single injection. [(1) approx. 1 teaspoonful; (2) the contents of the spoon that is used to heat the drug]

spoon *v.*[1] [mid-19C+] to flirt with, esp. in a foolish or sentimental manner; thus *spooning*, flirtation. [SPOON n.[1]]

spoon *v.*[2] [1960s] (*US campus*) to eat together. [SE *spoon*]

spoon and gravy *n.* [20C+] a dinner jacket.

spooner *n.* [mid-19C–1930s] a flirt. [SPOON v.[1]]

spooney *n.* (*also* **spoony**) **1** [late 18C–1900s] a fool, a simpleton; thus used as a derog. term of address. **2** [early–mid-19C] one who is sentimentally in love. **3** [early–mid-19C] a coward. **4** [1900s–60s] an effeminate young man, poss. homosexual. [SPOON n.[1]]

spooney *adj.* (*also* **spoony**) **1** [early 19C] greedy, avaricious. **2** [early–late 19C] very drunk. **3** [early 19C–1900s] weak-minded, simple. **4** [mid-19C] effeminate. **5** [mid–19C–1960s] besotted with a member of the opposite sex. [SPOON n.[1]]

spoonified *adj.* **1** [mid-19C] tricked, deceived. **2** [1910s] sentimental. [SPOON n.[1]]

spooniness *n.* [mid-19C] sentimentality. [SPOONEY adj. (5)]

spoons on *adj.* [mid-late 19C] **1** sentimentally in love with. **2** (*also* **spoons about/with**) courting. [SPOON n.[1] (2)]

spoon the burick *v.* [late 19C] to pay attentions to one's best friend's wife or girlfriend. [SPOON v.[1] + BURICK n. (2)]

spoony *see under* SPOONEY.

spoops *n.* (*also* **spoopsey**) [mid-19C] (*US campus*) an insignificant person, a weakling.

spoopsy *adj.* [mid-19C] (*US campus*) foolish. [SPOOPS n.]

spoorie *n.* [20C+] (*S.Afr.*) a Black artisan. [Afk. *spoor(weg)*, railway + sfx -*ie*; lit. 'a railway worker', the term is used as a generic for all artisans]

spoot *n.* [2000s] (*US Black*) semen. [var. on SPOOGE n. (1)]

spoot-canned *adj.* [2000s] (*US*) dismissed from a job. [var. on SHITCAN v. (2)]

spores *n.* (*drugs*) **1** [1960s] a psilocybe or 'magic' mushroom. **2** [1970s+] phencyclidine (cf. ACE n.[4]).

sporran *n.* [19C] pubic hair. [Gael. *sporan*, a purse, worn in front of the kilt by Scottish Highlanders]

sport *n.*[1] [16C+] sexual intercourse. [SPORT v.[1]]

sport *n.*[2] **1** [mid-19C+] a playboy, a man about town, with the accent on gambling, womanizing and other areas of the 'fast' life. **2** [late 19C] an eccentric. **3** [late 19C+] (*esp. Aus.*) a man, esp. as a general term of address. **4** [late 19C+] in weaker form of (3), a general term of approbation, 'a good chap'; esp. in phr. *be a sport*. **5** [1970s+] (*US gay*) a male prostitute.

sport *v.*[1] [16C+] to have sexual intercourse (cf. ARRIVE AT THE END OF THE SENTIMENTAL JOURNEY v.). [euph.]

sport *v.*[2] **1** [mid-17C–1940s] to behave showily or ostentatiously in public. **2** [late 17C–early 18C; mid-19C] to read an author for amusement (rather than instruction). **3** [early 18C–mid-19C] to make a speculative investment in sport or business, to wager, to make a bet. **4** [early–mid-19C] to treat, usu. to food and/or drink. **5** [early–late 19C] to spend money freely or extravagantly. **6** [mid-19C; 1920s+] (*US Black/campus*) to wear stylish clothes. **7** [1930s–40s] to live the 'fast' life of a gambler, a pimp and other underworld figures. **8** [1980s+] (*US campus*) to give. **9** [1980s+] (*US Black*) to spend money, usu. on a woman.

sport a toe *v.* [early–mid-19C] to dance.

sport a woody *v.* [1980s+] (*US teen*) to have an erection. [SE *sport*, to show off + WOODIE n.[2]]

sport blubber *v.* [late 18C–early 19C] to expose one's bosom, esp. of a large, coarse woman. [SE *sport* + BLUBBER n.[2] (1)]

sportfuck *v.* [1960s+] to have spontaneous, casual sexual intercourse. [SE *sport* + FUCK v.[1]]

sport-house *n.* [20C+] (*W.I.*) a brothel (cf. ACCOMMODATION HOUSE n.). [SPORT n.[1] + HOUSE n.[1] (1)]

sportify *v.* [1950s] (*W.I.*) to make people laugh, to amuse.

sporting *adj.* [1980s+] (*US Black/campus*) well-dressed, looking good. [SPORT v.[2] (6)]

sporting chance *n.* [late 19C+] a fair chance, although one that cannot be predicted.

sporting equipment *n.* [1990s+] (*Aus.*) a contraceptive sheath, a condom. [SPORT v.[1]]

sporting gent *n. see* SPORTING MAN n. (2).

sporting girl *n. see* SPORTING LADY n.

sporting goods *n.* [1970s+] (*US*) a male homosexual prostitute. [ext. of SPORT n.[2] (5)]

sporting house *n.* [mid-19C–1970s] (*US*) a brothel or a gambling den (cf. ACCOMMODATION HOUSE n.). [SPORT v.[1] + SE *house*/HOUSE n.[1] (1)]

sporting lady *n.* (*also* **sporting girl/woman, sportswoman**) [18C–1950s] (*US*) a prostitute, esp. when employed in a brothel (cf. BANKSIDE LADY n.). [SPORT v.[1] + SPORTING HOUSE n.]

sporting life *n.*[1] **1** [20C+] the 'good' life, i.e. money, liquor, women, all the desired pleasures of the flesh; the term is particularly popular as a description of the lifestyle of a US pimp. **2** [1950s] a term of address, usu. ironic, to one who sets themselves up as a pimp, gambler etc. [SPORT v.[2]; (2) may be specific ref. to the 1951 musical *Porgy & Bess* and its eponymous 'city slicker' character]

sporting life *n.*[2] [20C+] a wife. [rhy. sl.]

sporting life *n.*[3] [1970s] (*drugs*) cocaine. [its prominence in the SPORTING LIFE n.[1] (1)]

sporting man *n.* **1** [19C+] one who lives a hedonistic, enjoyable life. **2** [mid-19C–1920s] (*also* **sporting gent**) a genteel term for a gambler. [SPORT v.[2]]

sporting woman *n. see* SPORTING LADY n.

sport one's ivory *v.* [late 18C–early 19C] to grin. [SE *sport* + IVORY n. (1)]

sport one's wood *v.* [2000s] to display an erection. [SE *sport* + WOOD n.[4] (2)]

sport out *v.* [1980s] (*W.I.*) to go out spending money, enjoying oneself, usu. in pursuit of/accompanied by a woman. [SPORT v.[2] (5)]

sports king *n.* [1930s] (*Irish*) a noisy, drunken, hedonistic individual. [SPORT v.[2] (5)]

sportsman *n.* **1** [mid-16C–19C] (*also* **sportster**) a womanizer, a promiscuous man. **2** [mid-18C–19C] a genteel term for a gambler. **3** [late 19C–1910s] a person; no sporting prowess is suggested. **4** [1900s] a general term of familiar address. **5** [1900s–30s] an admirable human being. [SPORT v.[1]/SPORT v.[2]; note Ned Ward, *The London Spy* (1699), referring to the prostitutes available at the Bedlam Hospital: "Tis a new *Whetstone's Park* [...] where a *Sports–man*, at any Hour in the Day, may meet with *Game* for his purpose'; (3) and (5) the English fantasy of 'good sportsmanship']

sportsman for liquor *n.* [late 19C–1900s] a dedicated drinker (but not, in this context, a drunkard).

sportsman's gap *n.* (*also* **sportsman's hole**) [19C] the vagina (cf. AGREEABLE RUTS OF LIFE n.). [SPORTSMAN n. (1)]

sportster *n. see* SPORTSMAN n. (1).

sportswoman *n. see* SPORTING LADY n.

sport the dairy *v.* (*also* **sport the dairies**) [late 18C–early 19C] of a woman, to reveal one's breasts. [SE *sport* + DAIRY n.[1]]

sporty *adj.* **1** [late 19C–1940s] sexy, provocative, 'fast'. **2** [1910s+] (*US Black/campus*) attractive, good-looking. [SPORT n.[2]]

spot *n.*[1] **1** [18C+] a small amount, a little bit, a portion; esp. in combs., e.g. *a spot of bother/trouble*. **2** [late 19C+] a small drink.

spot *n.*[2] [mid-19C–1910s] a detective; thus *get a spot on*, to make a surveillance of. [omnibus jargon *spot*, a plain-clothes official, employed by the company to oversee drivers and conductors; ult. SE *spot*, to notice]

spot *n.*[3] **1** [mid-19C+] (*orig. US*) a term of imprisonment, usu. 1 year; usu. with a preceeding number as -SPOT sfx (1). **2** [mid-19C+] a dollar or pound sterling; here often with a number pfx but not a specific denomination of a note, for which *see* -SPOT sfx (2). **3** [1940s–50s] (*Aus./N.Z.*) a £10 note. **4** [1960s] (*US Black*) a $10 note. **5** [1960s+] (*Aus./N.Z.*) £100; latterly A$100 or NZ$100. [-SPOT sfx]

spot *n.*[4] [late 19C] a cake; thus *spot and scalder*, cake and tea.

spot *n.*[5] [1920s+] difficulties, trouble; usu. in phr. *in a spot*. [abbr. phr. *spot of bother*]

spot *n.*[6] [1920s+] (*US Und.*) anywhere seen as a potential site for a robbery, e.g. a jewellery store, wealthy apartment etc. [SPOT v.[1] (4)]

spot *n.*[7] [1930s–40s] a guess, a gamble. [SPOT v.[2]]

spot *n.*[8] **1** [1930s+] (*orig. US Black*) a nightclub. **2** [1930s+] a restaurant. **3** [1930s+] (*orig. US Black*) an after-hours club. **4** [1970s+] (*S.Afr.*) an illicit bar, a shebeen. **5** [1970s+] (*US gay*) any homosexual gathering place other than a gay bar. **6** [1990s+] (*US*) an apartment used spec. for the sale of drugs. **7** [1990s+] (*US Black/drugs*) anywhere in the street that drug dealers congregate. [abbr. SE *night spot*]

spot *n.*[9] [1950s] (*US*) a job. [orig. northern UK dial.]

spot *v.*[1] **1** [early 18C; mid-19C] to mark or note as a criminal or suspected person. **2** [mid-19C] to inform against. **3** [mid-19C–1960s] to place a watch, to observe, to spy on. **4** [mid-19C+] (*UK Und.*) (*also* **spot off/out**) to reconnoitre possible sites for future burglary or look over victims for pickpocketing. **5** [late 19C–1930s] (*US*) to kill, to murder.

spot *v.*[2] [late 19C] to gamble. [*spotting* winners]

spot *v.*[3] [20C+] **1** to advance on credit. **2** [1920s+] to offer an advantage to. [? to place a mark or 'spot' on a ledger]

spot *v.*[4] [1920s+] (*N.Z.*) to treat (others or oneself) to a drink; thus *spotting*, occasional drinking. [SPOT n.[1] (2)]

-spot *sfx* **1** [mid-19C; 20C+] (*orig. US*) used in combs. with a number to describe a term of imprisonment (cf. SPOT n.[3]). **2** [mid-19C+] used in combs. with a number to describe a denomination of a dollar or pound note, e.g. FIVE-SPOT n., TEN-SPOT n., TWENTY-SPOT n. [orig. used to describe the number of pips on a playing card]

spot in the road *n. see* BAD PLACE IN THE ROAD n.

spotlight *n.* [1960s–70s] (*US Black*) a light-skinned Black woman.

spot off *v. see* SPOT v.[1] (4).

spot-on *adj.* [1950s+] perfect, exactly right, accurate.

spot on burnt *n.* [1920s] a poached egg on toast; often in pl. with pfx *two*, *three* etc.

spot one's pants *v. see* WET ONE'S PANTS v.

spot out *v. see* SPOT v.[1] (4).

spot someone out *v.* [1970s] (*US Black*) to ascertain the characteristics, hidden or otherwise, of a person. [SPOT v.[1] (3)]

spotted *adj.* [mid-19C–1930s] known by the police, under surveillance. [SPOT v.[1] (1)]

spotted dick *adj.* [20C+] sick. [rhy. sl.]

spotted dog *n.* **1** [mid-late 19C] (*also* **spotted duff**) a plum pudding. **2** [20C+] a currant loaf. [joc. pron. of SE *spotted dough*, the 'spots' are plums]

spotted leopard *n.* (*also* **spotted donkey**) [late 19C] a plum pudding. [var. on prev.]

spotter *n.*[1] **1** [mid-19C–1950s] a detective (cf. BEAT-POUNDER n.). **2** [mid-19C+] (*US Und.*) one who searches for suitable places or victims to rob. **3** [20C+] (*drugs*) a lookout. **4** [1910s–60s] an informer. [SPOT v.[1]/SE *spot*]

spotter *n.*[2] [1990s+] an insignificant weakling. [the stereotype of the SE *trainspotter*]

spotters *n.* [1940s] (*US Black*) the eyes. [SPOT v.[1]]

spotty dog *n.* [1970s] a derog. term for any foreigner, irrespective of colour or race. [rhy. sl. = WOG n.[1] (3)]

spot your dot! *excl.* [1990s+] (*Aus.*) an invitation to sit down. [billiards jargon *spot*, to place a ball + DOT n.[2] (4)]

spounce *n.* (*also* **spunks**) [20C+] (*W.I.*) brashness, sauciness, courage, esp. of a young woman. [SPUNK n. (1) + SE *bounce*]

spouse *n.* [1980s+] (*US campus*) one's regular boy- or girlfriend.

spout *n.*[1] [19C] a lift formerly in use in pawnbrokers' shops, up which the articles pawned were taken for storage; thus the pawnbroker's shop. [note Egan, *Life in London* (1821): 'It was a *long narrow spout*, which reached from the top of the house of the *Money-Lender* down to his counter, and through which articles of property when *redeemed*, were conveyed, in order to facilitate business']

spout *n.*[2] [early 19C] a police cell, a prison.

spout *n.*[3] [mid-19C; 1940s+] the penis.

spout *n.*[4] [late 19C] **1** a large and ever-open mouth. **2** a political orator.

spout *v.*[1] [early 17C+] to talk effusively.

spout *v.*[2] [early 19C–1910s] to pawn. [SPOUT *n.*[1]]

spout Billy *v.* [19C] to make one's living by reciting portions of Shakespeare in public houses. [SPOUT *v.*[1] + proper name *Billy*, i.e. William Shakespeare]

spouter *n.*[1] **1** [mid-18C–1920s] a verbose, effusive speaker; a preacher or lecturer. **2** [mid-19C–1900s] (*Aus.*) spec. a 'soap-box' orator. [SPOUT *v.*[1]]

spouter *n.*[2] (*also* **sperm spouter**) [late 19C] the penis.

spouting *n.* [mid-18C–19C] oratory, speechifying. [SPOUT *v.*[1]]

spout ink *v.* [late 16C; late 19C–1920s] to write for a living. [SPOUT *v.*[1] + SE *ink*]

spout off *v.* (*also* **spout on**) [mid-19C+] to gabble on. [ext. of SPOUT *v.*[1]]

spow *n.* [1940s–50s] (*US prison*) prison-made coffee. [? SE *spew*, *vomit*]

spraff *v.* [20C+] to talk, to chat. [ety. unknown]

sprag *n.* [early 18C] a fop, a dandy. [SE *sprag*, a sprightly young fellow; ? ult. SE *sprig*]

sprag *v.* **1** [1910s] to accost truculently. **2** [1910s] to persuade. **3** [1910s–30s] (*Aus.*) to meddle in someone's plans, to thwart. **4** [1990s+] (*UK juv.*) (*also* **spragg**) to inform on another pupil. [SE *sprag*, a piece of wood used to check the revolution of a wheel or roller, usu. by inserting it between 2 of the spokes; a rod or bar used to prevent a vehicle from running backwards; thus fig. to arrest a person's progress]

sprain one's ankle *v. see* BREAK ONE'S ANKLE *v.*

sprang *adj.* [1990s+] (*US Black*) extremely intoxicated, esp. by crack cocaine. [var. on PRANG *adj.*]

sprarser *n.* (*also* **sparsie**, **sprarzy**, **sprasy**, **sprazzy**, **sprowsie**) [1900s–70s] a sixpence. [? SPRAT *n.*[1]]

sprat *n.*[1] [mid-19C–1950s] a sixpence. [its small size, like that of the fish]

sprat *n.*[2] [late 19C+] an affectionate name used between lovers. [like many such names, it is based on a dimin., i.e. the small fish]

sprat day *n.* [mid–late 19C] the Lord Mayor's Day in London. [the arrival of *sprats* in the market at approx. the same time, i.e. early September]

sprats *n.* [late 19C] one's possessions. [ety. unknown; ? fig. use of SPRAT *n.*[1]]

sprauncy *adj.* [1950s+] smart or showy in appearance or sound of voice. [? dial. *sprouncey*, cheerful]

spray and pray *n.* [1990s+] an Ingram MAC 10 sub-machine gun.

sprayhead *n.* [1990s+] (*US teen*) one who recreationally inhales the fumes of spray paint. [SE *spray* + -HEAD sfx (3)]

spray someone's tonsils *v.* [1940s+] (*gay*) to ejaculate in a fellator's mouth.

spray starch *n.* [1960s+] (*US gay*) a fig. substance that keeps heterosexual wrists from drooping. [the theory that every man would be gay given the opportunity]

sprazzy *n. see* SPRARSER *n.*

spread *n.*[1] [late 18C–mid-19C] a saddle. [SE *spread*, a coverlet; the saddle also *spreads* the rider's legs]

spread *n.*[2] [late 18C–mid-19C] (*UK/US Und.*) butter. **2** [early–mid-19C] jam, marmalade or any similar addition to bread and butter. **3** [mid-19C] an umbrella. **4** [mid-19C] a lady's shawl. **5** [mid-19C+] (*US*) a newspaper; thus a page, as in coverage of a news article or advertisement in a paper or magazine, e.g. a *two-page spread*; thus *spread-crib*, a printer's or newspaper office. **6** [1930s+] the thickening of one's waistline; esp. in *middle-aged spread*, the onset of fat in middle age. [lit. + fig. uses of SE]

spread *n.*[3] [early 19C+] a meal, esp. a sumptuous one; sometimes further defined as *morning spread*, breakfast, etc; also as v. [by 20C the term was mainly facetious/archaic, classically found in the children's stories of Enid Blyton (1897–1968); note RMC Duntroon (*Aus.*) *bread and spreads*, food]

spread *v.*[1] [1900s] (*Aus.*) to hit.

spread *v.*[2] *see* SPREAD (FOR) *v.*

spread beaver *n. see* SPLIT BEAVER *n.*

spread city *n.* [1960s+] (*US*) the dormitory suburbs of a big city. [the SE *spread* of such real estate developments + CITY sfx]

spread eagle *n.* [20C+] a position of heterosexual intercourse.

spreadeagle *adj.* [mid-19C–1920s] (*US*) pompous, verbose; also as v.

spreader *n.* (*also* **spreadum**) [17C–mid-18C] (*UK Und.*) butter. [its properties]

spread (for) *v.* **1** [mid-19C+] to have sexual intercourse. **2** [1970s+] (*US gay*) to sodomize or be sodomized. [(1) the man *spreads* and the woman *spreads for*]

spread it thick *v.* **1** [mid-19C+] (*orig. US*) to exaggerate or elaborate. **2** [1920s] to live well; thus *spread it thin*, to live in poverty. [the spreading of butter and/or jam on bread]

spread one's jenk *v.* [1920s–30s] (*US Black*) to have a good time, to celebrate, to have sex. [ety. unknown but note SE (*high*) *jinks* or dial. *jannock*, liberal, hospitable, one who pays their share]

spread one's shots *v.* [2000s] (*US prison*) to borrow from a number of people.

spread out *v.* [1990s+] (*W.I.*) to relax, to 'let off steam'.

spread the broads *v.* [mid-19C+] to play cards, esp. to cheat or to play a swindling game such as find the lady. [SE *spread* + BROADS *n.* (1), from the fanning out of the cards across the table for the punters to make their choice]

spread the bull *v.* [1910s+] to talk boastfully, if inaccurately, of one's prowess. [SE *spread* + BULL *n.*[11] (1)]

spread the joint *v.* [1930s–50s] (*US drugs*) to prepare the equipment for smoking opium. [SE *spread* + JOINT *n.*[5] (1)]

spread trick *n.* [1920s] a way of dealing cards that guarantees a confederate a good hand.

spreadum *n. see* SPREADER *n.*

spreck up *v.* [1990s+] to ejaculate (cf. BLOSH *v.*). [SE *spray*]

spree *n.*[1] [early 19C+] **1** a hearty, boisterous good time. **2** a prolonged bout of drinking; thus [mid-19C+] *on a/the spree*, out on a party. [? SE *spray*, a drinking bout, but ? dial. *spreagh/spreath*, a cattle raid, ult. Gaelic *spréidh*, cattle (E.P.); Hotten (1860) suggests Fr. *ésprit*, spirit or Du. root, as do B&L]

spree *n.*[2] [1940s] (*W.I.*) a girlfriend. [? fig. ext. of SPREE *n.*[1]]

spree *v.* **1** [early 19C+] to go out on a party, to take it easy; ext. to any form of spree, i.e. serial robberies. **2** [1900s] (*Aus.*) to treat someone else to a party. [SPREE *n.*[1]]

spree-boy *n.* [1950s] (*W.I.*) **1** a very well-dressed man, a dandy. **2** one who prefers pursuing pleasure to working hard; thus *spree-girl/-man/-master/-woman*. [SPREE *n.*[1] + SE *boy*]

spree-child *n.* [1950s] (*W.I.*) a very well-dressed, stylish woman. [SPREE *n.*[1] + SE *child*]

spreeish *adj.* [early–late 19C] tipsy, drunk. [SPREE *n.*[1] (2)]

sprig *n.* [late 18C+] a show-off. [? SE *sprig*, a young descendant]

spring *n.* [1900s–50s] an escape or release from prison; thus *make a spring*, to escape, to cause to be released; also attrib. [SPRING *v.*[4]]

spring *v.*[1] **1** [17C+] to make something appear or happen suddenly. **2** [mid-19C+] to appear suddenly, e.g. *where did you spring from?* **3** [1980s+] (*Aus. prison*) to catch someone engaged in an illicit activity.

spring *v.*[2] **1** [19C+] (*orig. UK Und.*) of both persons and objects, to discover, to come upon. **2** [1940s] to alter. **3** [1940s+] to see. [(1) late 19C+ use is Aus.]

spring *v.*[3] **1** [mid-19C] to offer a higher price. **2** [mid-19C+] (*also* **spring for**) to pay over a sum of money, to buy a certain amount; to produce; to pay for, to treat. **3** [late 19C–1910s] to afford. [SE *spring*, to cause to appear]

spring v.⁴ **1** [20C+] (*orig. US*) (*also* **spring out**) to escape from prison. **2** [20C+] (*orig. US*) to get a person out of prison, to have someone released, to release. **3** [1900s] (*US Und.*) to open (a lock). **4** [1940s] as (2) in a non-prison context. **5** [1970s] (*US prison*) to leave prison after completing one's sentence.

spring a leak v. see TAKE A LEAK V.

spring ankle warehouse n. **1** [late 18C–early 19C] a prison (cf. BANDHOUSE n.). **2** [19C] the workhouse. [SE *spring*, i.e. sprain an *ankle + warehouse*, once confined in such a place, the inmates are unable to run off]

spring a partridge v. [17C–18C] of a confidence trickster, to entrap a victim and then rob or otherwise defraud them. [sporting jargon *spring a partridge*, for a beater to cause a partridge to rise from cover]

springbutt n. [1960s+] (*US*) a keen, eager person. [SE *spring* + BUTT n.¹ (2)]

spring cleaning n. [1990s+] (*US Und.*) cleaning up, hiding or getting rid of evidence.

springer n. [1940s–50s] (*US Und.*) a bail bondsman. [SPRING v.⁴ (2)]

springer-up n. [mid-19C] **1** a cheap tailor, selling off-the-peg clothing. **2** a tailor who pays his employees the lowest possible wages. [the clothes 'spring up' without much art]

spring for v. see SPRING v.³ (2).

spring in v. [1920s] (*US tramp*) to break into a loaded boxcar.

spring it v. (*also* **spring on**) **1** [late 19C+] to reveal a plan or idea, with some element of surprise. **2** [1920s] to pull a joke. [SPRING v.¹ (1)]

spring out v. see SPRING v.⁴ (1).

springs n.¹ [1910s–50s] (*US Und.*) a small, solitary cell; thus phr. *at the springs*, confined in a strait-jacket.

springs n.² [1990s+] (*US Black*) the ability to jump high during a game of basketball.

spring-sides n. [20C+] (*Aus.*) elastic-sided boots.

spring to v. **1** [late 19C–1900s] to afford, to come up with sufficient money for. **2** [late 19C–1900s] to achieve, to manage. **3** [20C+] to treat, e.g. to a free meal. [ext. of SPRING v.³ (2)]

sprinkle v.¹ [mid-19C+] to christen. [the application of holy water]

sprinkle v.² [1990s+] (*US Black teen*) to tell a story, to lay out a situation.

spritz n. [1910s+] (*US*) **1** carbonated water as a mixer for drinks. **2** a light shower of rain. **3** any form of spray, e.g. of blood. [Yid. *spritz*, spray]

spritz v. [1950s+] (*US*) **1** to perform a stage monologue with much impromptu ad libbing, free-associating etc. **2** to air one's feelings, to emote. **3** of an object, e.g. a gun, to spray. [Yid. *spritz*, to spray]

sprog n. (*also* **sproglet, sprogster**) [1940s+] a child; thus as v., to have a child. [18C *sprag*, a lively young fellow; note milit. *sprog*, a recruit]

sprout n. [early 18C+] a child, a youngster. [SE *sprout*, an offshoot]

sproutsy adj. [1970s+] (*US*) unconventional, HIPPIE adj. [? the HIPPIE n.² (3) diet of bean *sprouts* etc]

sprowsie n. see SPRARSER n.

spruce v. [20C+] to tell lies, 'stories'; thus *sprucer*, a liar or one who exaggerates. [SE *spruce up*, i.e. the facts, or SPRUIK v.]

spruik n. **1** [1910s] (*Aus./N.Z.*) a rant; an oration; a showman's or other salesman's patter. **2** [1950s] (*Aus.*) a chat, a visit. [SPRUIK v.]

spruik v. [1910s+] (*Aus./N.Z.*) **1** to speak in a way that resembles a showman, thus to speak in an insincere manner. **2** to chatter. [? Yid. *shpruch*, saying, charm, incantation; or ? Du. *spreken*, to talk]

spruiker n. [1910s+] (*Aus.*) **1** a barker for a fairground or carnival sideshow or a cinema, theatre or similar entertainment, who stands on the street to promote the show and attract an audience. **2** a loud and continual talker. **3** a platform speaker, an orator. **4** a barrister. [SPRUIK v.]

sprung adj. (*also* **cup-sprung**) [early 19C–1920s] drunk. [? one bounces along]

sprung on adj. [2000s] (*US Black teen*) having an erection. [one's penis *springs up*]

sprung on the cat phr. [2000s] (*US Black*) of a man, addicted to sex. [SPRUNG ON adj. + CAT n.³ (1)]

S.P. shop n. see S.P. JOINT n.

spud n.¹ [mid–late 19C] a baby's hand. [SE *pudgy* or dial. *spud*, a short, stumpy person]

spud n.² **1** [mid-19C+] a potato. **2** [late 19C+] a hole in a sock (cf. POTATO n.²). **3** [20C+] (*W.I.*) a ripe banana. **4** [1910s–30s] a nickname for an Irishman (cf. BOG ARAB n.). **5** [1930s] any person. **6** [1940s] (*US Und.*) a revolver, a pistol. **7** [1980s+] (*N.Z. teen/US*) a general term of abuse. **8** [1990s+] (*US*) a child, a young person. [? SE *spud*, a digging fork with 3 broad prongs; or ? dial. *spud*, a stumpy thing; (4) note 19C US *little potato skin*, an Irish child]

spud n.³ [1910s–40s] (*US Und.*) a swindle in which the con-men convince the victim that he can buy real money from a man who has stolen plates from the government but it is, in fact, counterfeit money. [ety. unknown; ? the low value of the SPUD n.² (1)]

spud v. [1920s–30s] (*US Black*) to play cards for low stakes. [? dial. *spud*, to muddle, to be uselessly busy]

spud barber n. [1930s–40s] one who peels potatoes. [SPUD n.² (1) + SE *barber*]

spud-bashing n. [1940s+] peeling potatoes. [SPUD n.² (1) + BASH v.¹ (1); orig. milit. use, when the job was compulsory and part of kitchen fatigues]

spuddy n. [mid-19C] **1** a seller of bad potatoes. **2** a seller of hot baked potatoes. [SPUD n.² (1)]

spud-grinder n. [1970s] the throat. [SPUD n.² (1) + SE *grinder*]

spud islander n. [1950s+] a native or inhabitant of Prince Edward Island, Canada. [SPUD n.² (1); the high quality of its potatoes]

spud juice n.¹ [1960s] (*US prison*) illegally distilled alcohol, based on potatoes. [SPUD n.² (1) + SE *juice*]

spud juice n.² [1990s+] semen (cf. BABY FLUID n.; BABY GRAVY n.). [LOVE SPUDS n. + JUICE n.² (1)]

spud-miner n. [late 19C] (*Aus.*) a peasant. [SPUD n.² (1) + SE *miner*]

spuds and swimmers n. [1900s] fish and chips. [SPUD n.² (1) + SE *swimmer*]

spudwater n. [1990s+] thin, watery semen (cf. BABY FLUID n.; BABY GRAVY n.). [SPUD n.² (1) + SE *water*]

spuff n. [1990s+] semen. [SPUFF v.]

spuff v. [1990s+] to ejaculate (cf. BLOSH v.). ['echoic' of the ejaculation]

spug n. [1920s+] (*Aus./N.Z.*) a sparrow. [dial. *spadger*, a sparrow]

spum v. [2000s] (*US Black*) to ejaculate. [SE *sperm* + CUM v.]

spume n. [1990s+] semen (cf. BOLLOCK SNOT n.). [SE *spume*, foam]

spumoni adj. [1990s+] (*US campus*) excellent, first-rate. [SAmE *spumoni*, a variety of ice-cream; ult. synon. Ital. *spumone*]

spun adj. **1** [20C+] defeated, lost for ideas. **2** [1920s] exhausted, drained of energy. **3** [1990s+] drunk. **4** [1990s+] intoxicated by drugs. **5** [1990s+] confused, stressed.

spunge see under SPONGE and its combs.

spunk n. **1** [late 18C+] courage, bravery. **2** [late 18C+] spirit. **3** [early 19C] (*Scot Und.*) life. **4** [mid-19C+] semen. **5** [1960s+] (*Aus.*) (*also* **spunky**) someone seen as sexually attractive. [? fig. use of Scot./dial. *spunk*, a spark]

spunk v. **1** [late 19C+] (*also* **spunk off**) to ejaculate. **2** [1990s+] to consume, to use up. [lit./fig. uses of SPUNK n. (4)]

spunk-bag n. [1990s+] **1** a condom. **2** a general term of abuse. [SPUNK n. (4) + SE *bag*/BAG n.⁷/-BAG sfx]

spunkbone n. [2000s] the penis. [SPUNK n. (4) + SE *bone*/BONE n.¹ (1)]

spunkbone jockey n. [2000s] a male homosexual (cf. BONE-EATER n.). [SPUNKBONE n. + JOCKEY n.³ (2)]

spunk-bound *adj.* [late 19C+] of a man, lethargic, lacking energy. [SPUNK n. (4); ? the belief that sexual inactivity leads to indolence]

spunk bubble *n.* [1990s+] (*UK juv.*) a mild insult or a 'capper' in an argument.

spunk-bucket *n.* (*also* **spunk-dustbin**) [1990s+] a promiscuous woman or one who is branded as such. [SPUNK n. (4) + SE *bucket/dustbin*]

spunker *n.*[1] [1990s+] **1** a general term of abuse, usu. aimed at a male. **2** a sexually provocative person. **3** an affectionate man-to-man term of address. **4** one who ejaculates. [SPUNK n. (4)]

spunker *n.*[2] [2000s] a spendthrift. [SPUNK v. (2)]

spunk-fencer *n.* [mid–late 19C] (*Aus./UK Und.*) a match-seller. [dial. *spunk*, spark, tinder; note dial. *spunks*, lucifer matches + -FENCER sfx]

spunk-gobbed *adj.* [1990s+] a general term of abuse; lit. 'semen-mouthed'. [SPUNK n. (4) + GOB n.[1] (1); the image is of a man fellating another]

spunk-gullet *n.* [2000s] a general term of abuse, lit. 'a fellator' (cf. COCKMUNCH n.). [SPUNK n. (4) + SE *gullet*]

spunkhammer *n.* [2000s] the penis (cf. AX n.[2]). [SPUNK n. (4) + HAMMER n.[1] (1)]

spunk-head *n.* [1990s+] a general term of abuse. [SPUNK n. (4) + -HEAD sfx (1)]

spunkie *n.* [19C–1900s] (*Irish*) a lively young man. [SPUNK n. (2)]

spunk off *v. see* SPOUNCE n.

spunk-pot *n.* [1990s+] the vagina (cf. BAG n.[1]). [SPUNK n. (4) + SE *pot*; note Rochester *c*.1673: 'To be a Whore, understanding, / A Passive *Pot* for *Fools* to spend in']

spunk rat *n.* [1980s+] (*Aus.*) a sexually attractive person. [SPUNK n. (5) + SE *rat*]

spunks *n. see* SPOUNCE n.

spunk trumpet *n.* [1990s+] the penis (cf. ACCORDION n.). [SPUNK n. (4)]

spunk up *v.* **1** [mid-19C+] (*US*) to act aggressively, courageously. **2** [mid-19C+] (*US*) to encourage someone to be courageous. **3** [1940s] (*US Black*) to speak out. [SPUNK n. (1)]

spunky *n. see* SPUNK n. (5).

spunky *adj.* **1** [late 18C+] courageous, brave, plucky. **2** [mid-19C–1910s] (*US*) angry. **3** [late 19C+] pertaining to semen. **4** [1980s+] (*Aus.*) sexy. [SPUNK n.]

spun out *adj.* [1990s+] of a person, out of control, crazy. [motor-racing imagery]

spur *v.* (*also* **give someone the spur**) [late 19C–1900s] to irritate, to annoy.

spurge *n.* [1920s+] (*Aus.*) an effeminate young man. [SE *spurge*, one or other of several species of the genus *Euphorbia*, some of which are considered near weeds; thus a pun on WEEDY adj. (2)]

spurt *n.* [mid-19C] a small amount, a small quantity, esp. of alcohol.

sputnik *n.* [1980s+] (*drugs*) a mixture of Pakistani cannabis and opium (cf. BOMB n.[4]). [SE *sputnik*, the Russian spacecraft (lit., 'travelling companion', 'fellow traveller') launched in 1957; it puts you 'into orbit', i.e. HIGH adj.[1] (2)]

sputterbudget *n.* [1910s] (*US*) one who chatters on to excess. [SE *sputter* + *budget*, one who has certain characteristics]

sputterer *n.* [1930s] (*US drugs*) a novice opium smoker, still assured that they will never become addicted. [? the *sputtering* pipe]

spuzz *n.* [1990s+] semen. [SE *sperm* + JIZZ n.]

spy *n.* [late 16C–early 17C] the eye.

spy-smashers *n.* [1970s+] (*US gay*) wrap-around sunglasses.

spy the cloven foot *v.* [late 18C–early 19C] to see the worst side of a situation, to suspect criminality or fraud. [the pvb belief that no matter how hard the Devil tries to disguise his true personality, he can never hide his cloven foot]

squab *n.*[1] **1** [late 17C–early 19C; 1920s] a very fat person. **2** [mid-19C] a short person. [? SE *squab*, a fat cushion or a well-upholstered sofa]

squab *n.*[2] (*US*) **1** [19C+] a fool, an unsophisticated person, a peasant. **2** [1910s–60s] a young woman. [SE *squab*, a raw, inexperienced person + later uses as a young, unfledged bird or animal; ult. play on CHICKEN n.[3] (1)]

squab *n.*[3] [1990s+] (*US gang*) an argument or fight.

squab *v.* [1990s+] (*US Black*) to confront. [? abbr. SE *squabble*]

squabby *adj.* (*also* **squab**, **squobby**) [mid-17C–1950s] squat, short and thick. [SQUAB n.[1] (1)]

squab-job *n.* [1910s] a job that suits a young woman. [SQUAB n.[2] (2) + SE *job*]

Squad, the *n.* [1920s+] (*UK Und.*) the Flying *Squad*. [abbr.]

squad *n.*[1] [late 18C] a group of prostitutes.

squad *n.*[2] [1990s+] (*US Black*) a gang or group of friends.

squaddie *n.* (*also* **squaddy**, **squatti**, **swaddie**) [1920s+] a regular private soldier. [SE *squad*]

squadrol *n.* [1940s–70s] (*US*) a small police van. [SE *squad* + *patrol*]

squalino *v.* [early 19C] to squeal or squall. [SE *squall*, to scream loudly or discordantly]

squall *n.*[1] [late 16C–mid-17C] an up-market prostitute, kept by a rich gallant; also used as an endearment. [SE *squall*, an insignificant person]

squall *n.*[2] (*also* **squawl**) [early 18C–mid-19C] (*UK Und.*) a voice. [weak use of SE]

square *n.*[1] **1** [mid-19C] (*UK Und.*) a respectable pose; an excuse; thus a shield from arrest. **2** [late 19C+] (*Aus.*) a respectable woman; thus ext. as *square Jane and no nonsense*. **3** [20C+] (*orig. US*) a regular working man or woman; usu. pej., implying a tedious conventional person. **4** [1930s+] (*orig. US Black*) a naïve person, one who believes in White America's promises, one who has little sexual sophistication; the use has similar pej. implications to (3). **5** [1940s–60s] (*US drugs*) one who eschews drugs. **6** [1940s+] (*US Black*) a man who pursues women and is thus tricked out of his money. **7** [1950s+] (*gay*) a heterosexual, or a gay man who is not used to the gay scene. **8** [1970s] (*US Black*) a sexual deviant. [fig. rectilinearity; the American Dialect Society (November 1958) suggests the steady 1-2-3-4 rhythm played without variation]

square *n.*[2] (*also* **square cut**) [mid-19C–1960s] (*Aus.*) gin, a bottle of gin. [the shape of the bottle]

square *n.*[3] [mid-19C+] (*US*) a proper or *square* meal. [abbr.]

square *n.*[4] [late 19C] (*UK society*) a quadrille or the lancers (a dance that developed from the quadrille in the mid-19C). [such dances involve the forming of squares]

square *n.*[5] [1920s+] (*US, mainly prison*) a factory-made cigarette, whether prison-issue or commercially produced. [SQUARE adj. (1)]

square, the *n.* **1** [mid-19C] (*UK Und.*) the laws and customs of the underworld, by which all criminals should abide. **2** [mid-19C+] a respectable way of life. **3** [1930s] (*US Black*) a trustworthy individual. [SQUARE adj.]

square *adj.* **1** [mid-17C+] of a thing, honest, truthful, fair. **2** [19C+] of a person, honest, respectable, upright. **3** [mid-19C] (*US*) substantial. **4** [mid-19C–1910s] (*Aus.*) safe. **5** [mid-19C+] (*UK/US Und.*) dependable; as (1) but from a criminal standpoint. **6** [mid-19C+] sorted out, dealt with, even. **7** [1930s+] correct, real. **8** [1930s+] (*orig. US Black*) conventional, conservative, naïve, dull; thus *squareness*, conventionality. **9** [1940s] (*US Black campus*) cheap. **10** [1940s–60s] (*US Black/teen*) sober. [(1) prior use SE from 16C]

square *v.*[1] **1** [early 19C+] (*also* **square up**) to settle, to put right, spec. to deal with problems, often by using influence, bribes, threats etc; thus *square his nibs*, to pay off a policeman. **2** [mid-19C–1930s] to pay one's debts; to pay a bill. **3** [mid-19C+] (*UK*

Und.) to sort things out with another person. **4** [late 19C] to murder, to kill. **5** [late 19C–1920s] to give or lend money. **6** [late 19C+] to make things equal. **7** [1920s] (*US Und.*) to gain a pardon. **8** [1920s–40s] to take up a respectable, honest life. **9** [1970s+] (*US gay*) to have heterosexual intercourse. [SQUARE adj.]

square *v.*[2] *see* SQUARE (OFF) *v.*[1].

square *adv.* [mid-19C+] (*US*) **1** completely, unreservedly. **2** fairly, honestly, straightforwardly. **3** precisely, exactly. **4** properly, correctly. [SQUARE adj.]

square affair *n.* (*also* **square bit/piece**) [late 19C–1910s] one's regular girlfriend. [SQUARE adj. (1) + SE *affair*/BIT n.[2] (1)/PIECE n.[1] (1)]

square an' all *phr.* [20C+] (*Aus.*) absolutely, honestly, truly. [SQUARE adj. (1)]

square apple *n.* [1930s–50s] (*US Und.*) an innocent, a naïve, gullible individual. [SQUARE adj. (8) + APPLE n.[3]]

square a rap *v.* [1940s+] to have a criminal charge dropped. [SQUARE *v.*[1] (1) + RAP n.[4] (3)]

square article *n.* [early 19C] (*UK Und.*) anything one has purchased or otherwise acquired honestly. [SQUARE adj. (1) + SE *article*]

square as a billiard ball *phr.* (*also* **square as a golf ball,** **...a tennis ball**) [1940s–50s] (*Aus.*) anything but honest or 'square', whether morally, sexually or otherwise. [SQUARE adj. (1) + SE *billiard ball/golf ball/tennis ball*]

square-ass *adj.* (*also* **square-assed**) [1940s+] (*US Black*) unsophisticated, naïve, 'straight'. [SQUARE adj. (8) + -ASS sfx]

square at *v. see* SQUARE UP *v.*[1].

square away *v.* **1** [20C+] to deal with, to settle. **2** [20C+] to sort out, to put away; also in fig. use. **3** [1920s] to explain, to put in the picture. **4** [1980s] (*Aus.*) to bribe. [milit. jargon *square away*, to put in proper order]

square-ball *adj.* [1950s] (*US*) conventional.

square-bashing *n.* [1950s+] military drill; thus *square-basher*, a private soldier. [SE *square*, the parade ground + BASH *v.*[1] (1)]

square bit *n. see* SQUARE AFFAIR n.

squarebrain *n.* **1** [20C+] a fool (cf. BAKEBRAIN n.). **2** [1940s–50s] (*US Black*) a conventional person, a fool, a dullard, with overtones of conservatism. [SQUARE n.[1] (3) + sfx *-brain*]

square broad *n.* [1940s–70s] (*US Black*) any woman who is not a prostitute. [SQUARE adj. (2) + BROAD n.[2] (3)]

square business *n.* [1970s+] (*US Black/prison*) honesty, truth; often affixed to a declaratory sentence as a means of emphasizing the speaker's sincerity. [SQUARE adj. (1) + SE *business*]

square concern *n.* [early 19C] (*UK Und.*) anything one has purchased or otherwise acquired honestly. [SQUARE adj. (1) + SE *concern*]

square cove *n.* [19C] an honest man. [SQUARE adj. (1) + COVE n. (1)]

square-crib *n.* [early 19C] a respectable house. [SQUARE adj. (1) + CRIB n.[1] (1)]

square cut *n. see* SQUARE n.[2].

squared away *adj.* [1940s+] sorted out, in order, whether emotionally or physically. [naut. imagery]

square deal *n.* [mid-19C+] (*orig. US*) honest treatment, a proper business deal, a good bargain etc. [SQUARE adj. (1) + SE *deal*]

squaredom *n.* [1950s+] (*orig. US*) the world of the unsophisticated, the unworldly. [SQUARE n.[1] (3)]

square-eyes *n.* [1960s+] one who watches an excess of TV and who, supposedly, develops eyes the same shape as the screen; thus *square-eyed*, obsessed with watching television.

squareface *n.* [late 19C–1920s] gin. [the shape of the bottle]

square-go *n.* [20C+] a fair fight, a fight without weapons. [SQUARE adj. (1) + GO n.[3] (9)]

squarehead *n.*[1] **1** [mid-19C+] an honest person, a respectable person. **2** [1910s+] a stupid person. **3** [1920s+] (*Aus.*) a timid or conscience-ridden thief. **4** [1930s+] (*Aus.*) one who has no

previous criminal convictions. [SQUARE adj. (1) + -HEAD sfx (1); (2) SE *square*]

squarehead *n.*[2] **1** [20C+] a German or one of German origins. **2** [20C+] (*Aus./US*) a Scandinavian. **3** [1930s] (*US*) a Pole. **4** [1970s] (*Can.*) an Anglophone Canadian. [SE *square + head*; (1) and (3) ? the severe 'Prussian' haircuts]

squarehead *adj.* [1930s+] (*US*) stupid (cf. AIRHEADED adj.). [SQUAREHEAD n.[1] (2)]

squareheaded *adj.* [1910s+] **1** stupid (cf. AIRHEADED adj.). **2** Swedish. **3** German. [SQUAREHEAD n.[1]]

square his nibs *v. see* SQUARE *v.*[1] (1).

square in a social circle *n.* [1930s–40s] (*US Black*) a misfit. [var. on SE *square peg in a round hole*]

square it *v.* **1** [mid-19C+] to live or act honestly. **2** [mid-19C+] to explain, to make excuses. **3** [late 19C] to render acceptable, appealing; to make things right. [ext. SQUARE *v.*[1]]

square john *n.* **1** [1920s+] a respectable member of society. **2** [1920s+] (*US Und.*) a prisoner who is not a professional criminal. **3** [1930s–50s] (*drugs*) one who eschews drugs. **4** [1940s–60s] (*US Und.*) in criminal terms, a dependable, reliable person. **5** [1970s+] (*US gay*) a heterosexual man who enjoys the company of lesbians. [SQUARE adj. (1) + JOHN n.[1] (1)]

square-john *adj.* [1940s+] (*US*) respectable, upright, esp. when pertaining to a non-criminal world or sensibility. [SQUARE JOHN n.]

square moll *n.* [mid-19C] an honest woman. [SQUARE adj. (1) + MOLL n.[1] (1)]

square-off *n.* [1920s+] (*Aus.*) an excuse. [SQUARE OFF *v.* (1)]

square (off) *v.* [mid-19C+] (*US*) to prepare for a fight, to adopt an aggressive posture. [SE *square*]

square off *v.* [1920s+] (*Aus./N.Z.*) **1** to placate or conciliate someone, to apologize. **2** to pay; can be used quite legitimately, but often carries a sense of corruption, bribery etc. **3** to pay off, e.g. a debt. [SQUARE *v.*[1] (1)]

square one *n.* [1960s+] (*orig. US*) the starting point, the beginning. [the image of children's board-games, e.g. snakes and ladders]

square one's circle *v.* [1980s+] (*US campus*) to have sexual intercourse with someone.

square out *v.* [1960s+] (*US Black*) **1** to ridicule, to tease. **2** for 2 people, to indulge in a series of ritual insults. [SQUARE (OFF) *v.*/ SQUARE UP *v.*[1]]

square pair *n.* (*also* **windows**) [2000s] (*US*) the throw of double 4 (8) in craps dice (cf. ADA FROM DECATUR n.).

square paper *n.* [1940s] (*US Und.*) an honest, respectable person. [SQUARE adj. (1) + fig. use of PAPER n.[1]]

square party *n.* [1920s] 2 pairs of married people indulging in a wipe-swapping party. [the 4 sides of the 'square']

square piece *n. see* SQUARE AFFAIR n.

square plug *n.* (*US Und.*) **1** [1910s–40s] a 'civilian' who admires and mingles with criminals but lacks the courage or desire actually to commit a crime. **2** [1920s+] a prisoner who is not a professional criminal. [SQUARE adj. (1) + SE *plug*, which does not 'fit in the round hole' of criminality]

square pusher *n.* **1** [1910s–30s] a young woman, usu. respectable; thus *square-pushing*, courting. **2** [1920s] a boyfriend. [SQUARE adj. (1) + PUSHER n.[2]]

squarer *n.* **1** [late 19C–1900s] (*Aus.*) one who 'fixes' a situation, usu. through bribery (however well disguised). **2** [1900s] something that helps sort out a problem. [SQUARE *v.*[1] (1)]

square-rigged *adj.* [mid-19C–1920s] well-dressed, smart, respectable. [naut. jargon]

square rigger *n.*[1] (*N.Z.*) **1** [20C+] a square gin bottle, often used to hold beer. **2** [1980s] a half-gallon (3-litre) flagon of beer.

square rigger *n.*[2] [20C+] a derog., euph. term for a Black person (cf. DAPTO DOG n.). [rhy. sl. = NIGGER n.[1] (1)]

square setting *n.* [1950s–60s] (*US Black*) a respectable party, without drugs, loud music etc. [SQUARE adj. (2) + SET n.[1] (3)]

square shake n. [1930s+] (US) a fair deal, honest treatment. [SQUARE adj. (1) + SE *shake* (of the dice)]

square shooter n. [1910s+] (US) **1** an honest, trustworthy person. **2** one who espouses a respectable (as opposed to criminal) life. [SQUARE adj. (1) + SE *shooter*]

square-shooting adj. [1920s–30s] (US) honest. [SQUARE SHOOTER n. (1)]

squaresville n. (also **squareville**) [1960s+] (US Black/teen) a conventional and thus boring place, person or event. [SQUARE n.[1] (4) + -VILLE sfx[1]]

square the beef v. [20C+] (orig. US Und.) to repair a difficult or grievous situation. [SQUARE v.[1] (1) + BEEF n.[2]]

square-toes n. [mid-18C–mid-19C] an old man. [his chosen, old-fashioned style of footwear]

square to the wood phr. [1940s+] (US Black) extremely respectable, conservative, naïve. [intensifier of SQUARE adj. (8)]

square up v.[1] (also **square at, …up to**) [late 18C+] to challenge, usu. preparatory to a fight; often in fig. use. [the head-on postures of the opponents]

square up v.[2] [mid-19C+] to pay off one's debts, whether financial or otherwise; thus *squaring-up*, the settlement of debts. [SQUARE v.[1] (1)]

square up v.[3] (orig. US Black) **1** [1940s+] to leave the underworld, whether of pimping, drug sales and use or general criminality, and devote oneself to a conventional lifestyle. **2** [1960s] to persuade someone to take up a respectable lifestyle. **3** [1960s] to betray. **4** [1990s+] to calm down. [SQUARE adj. (2)]

square up v.[4] see SQUARE v.[1] (1).

square up to v. see SQUARE UP v.[1].

squareville n. see SQUARESVILLE n.

square with adv. [mid-19C+] **1** in an honest, honourable manner. **2** having made amends with, made up with, even with. [(1) SQUARE adj. (1); (2) SQUARE v.[1] (1)]

squarie n.[1] (also **squarey**) [1910s+] (Aus. navy) a young woman, a girlfriend. [SQUARE n.[1] (2)]

squarie n.[2] (also **squarey**) (Aus.) **1** [1920s+] a timid or conscience-ridden thief. **2** [1930s+] one who has no previous criminal convictions. [abbr. SQUAREHEAD n.[1]]

squash n. **1** [late 19C–1960s] (US campus) a fool (cf. APPLEHEAD n.). **2** [1930s+] (US) the head, the face.

squash v. [20C+] **1** to crush verbally. **2** to argue, to fight. **3** (US) to sort out a problem.

squashed adj. [1970s+] very drunk (cf. ANNIHILATED adj.).

squashed flies n. (also **dead-fly cake, fly pies, squashed fly**) [late 19C+] biscuits containing currants, Garibaldi biscuits.

squasho n. [late 19C+] (US) a derog. term for a Black person (cf. ALLIGATOR BAIT n.[2]). ['the negro's love of melons, pumpkins, squashes etc' (Ware) but more likely QUASHIE n.]

squat n.[1] **1** [late 19C–1910s] a seat, a chair. **2** [1970s] (US) an act of defecation. **3** [1970s+] (US) excrement. **4** [1990s+] (US prison) the electric chair; electrocution.

squat n.[2] [1950s+] (US) nothing, zero. [abbr. DIDDLY-SQUAT n.[1]]

squat v. **1** [mid-19C+] (US) to sit down, usu. to do nothing is implied. **2** [1930s–40s] (US prison) to be executed in the electric chair; to execute. **3** [1960s] (US) to defecate.

squat hot v. [1940s] (US) to be executed in the electric chair. [HOT SQUAT n.]

squativoo n. [1930s] (US) the electric chair. [cod-French *squattez-vous*, sit down + HOT SQUAT n.]

squat on v. [late 19C] (US) to oppose.

squat-pad n. [1940s] (US Black) **1** a lobby, a lounge. **2** a stool; a chair. [SQUAT v. (1) + PAD n.[2] (2)]

squattage n. [1930s+] (Aus.) a farmer's home and the land they own. [SE *squatter* + -AGE sfx, implying a sphere of action]

squatter n. **1** [20C+] the buttocks. **2** [1930s+] (Ulster) a voyeur. **3** [1940s] (US Black) a stool, a chair.

squatter's daughter n. [1960s+] (Aus.) water. [rhy. sl.]

squattez-vous! excl. [late 19C–1930s] sit down! [cod Fr.]

squatti n. see SQUADDIE n.

squattocracy n. [mid-19C+] (Aus.) the élite of the country's farming magnates, viewed as an Australian aristocracy; thus *squattocrat*, a member of the group; adj. *squattocratic*. [SE *squatter* + sfx *-ocracy*]

squatty adj. [mid-19C–1960s] of a person, squat, thickset; thus as a nickname for such a person.

squaver v. [20C+] (Ulster) to wave one's arms, to direct vehicles (as in parking), to square up to. [SE *quaver*]

squaw n. **1** [mid-19C+] (US) a woman. **2** [late 19C–1950s] a subservient woman, occas. man. **3** [20C+] a wife. **4** [1990s+] (US prison) a passive homosexual.

squawk n. **1** [20C+] (US) a complaint. **2** [1930s–40s] (US) a complainer. **3** [1930s+] a verbal betrayal. **4** [1940s–50s] (UK prison) any form of petition, to the governor or to the Home Secretary. **5** [1950s+] (US Black) a comment. [SQUAWK v. (1)]

squawk v. **1** [late 19C+] (US) to complain, to make a fuss. **2** [1920s+] to inform, to betray.

squawk-box n. [1940s+] (orig. US) an internal communication system; usu. in the context of an office or similar business.

squawker n. **1** [1920s] (US) one who makes a complaint, esp. a victim of crime. **2** [1920s–40s] an informer. **3** [1950s] (US teen) a parent. [SQUAWK v.]

squawl n. see SQUALL n.[2].

squawman n. [1900s–30s] (US) a White man living with a native woman.

squeak n. **1** [late 18C–mid-19C; 1950s+] an informer, esp. one who turns informer to save themselves after being arrested. **2** [20C+] a piece of information passed over to the police. **3** [1940s] (US police) a complaint. [SQUEAK v.]

squeak v. **1** [late 17C+] (UK Und.) to inform, to confess; thus [20C+] *squeak on*, to betray, to inform against; [1930s+] *put the squeak in*, to turn informer, to inform. **2** [1910s] to complain.

squeak beef v. see CRY (HOT) BEEF v.

squeak box n. [1940s–50s] (US Black) a violin.

squeaker n.[1] **1** [late 17C–18C] a child, esp. an illegitimate child. **2** [late 17C–mid-19C] a pot-boy. **3** [late 18C–early 19C] an organ pipe. **4** [early 19C] a foxhound. **5** [mid–late 19C] a young pig. **6** [1930s–40s] a violinist. [(2) note Hay, *The Lighter Side of School Life* (1914): 'Lastly, comes the little boy – the Squeaker, the Tadpole, the Nipper, what you will']

squeaker n.[2] [late 19C] a heavy blow. [it makes the recipient 'squeak']

squeaker n.[3] **1** [late 19C–1900s] a general insult; the image is of one who complains. **2** [late 19C+] an informer. [SQUEAK v.]

squeakers n. [20C+] (Aus.) boots, shoes. [SE *squeak*]

squeaky adj. [2000s] nervous, cowardly.

squeaky shoe n. [1940s] a plain-clothes police officer.

squeal n.[1] **1** [early 19C] an informer. **2** [mid-19C–1950s] a complaint; a fuss. **3** [mid-19C+] (US Und.) the report of a crime by a member of the public, or an informer. **4** [1940s] (US Black campus) talk. **5** [1950s+] (US) the investigation by police of a crime, using an informer. [SQUEAL (ON) v.]

squeal n.[2] **1** [1900s] (US) boiled meal served with molasses. **2** [1930s–40s] bacon; ham. [esp. in short order use]

squeal v. see SQUEAL (ON) v.

squeal copper v. see HOLLER COPPER v.

squealer n.[1] (also **squeeler**) **1** [mid-19C+] an informer. **2** [late 19C–1910s] a complainer. **3** [1930s] (US Und.) a pack of *Jack Rose* cigars. [SQUEAL (ON) v.]

squealer n.[2] **1** [mid-19C+] (US) a child. **2** [1980s] (Aus.) a promiscuous young girl.

squealer n.[3] [1930s] (UK tramp) a pork sausage. [SE *squeal*]

squeal (on) v. **1** [mid-19C–1920s] to complain. **2** [mid-19C–1940s] to own up. **3** [mid-19C+] to inform against one's partners, esp. partners in crime. **4** [20C+] to report a crime to the police or any other authority. [late 19C+ use mainly US, but note Edgar Wallace title, *The Squealer* (1927)]

squeal rule *n.* (*also* **squeal law**) [1960s+] (*US*) the law requiring parental notification when an underage girl applies for a prescription for contraceptives. [SQUEAL (ON) v. + SE *rule*]

squeeg *n. see* SQUEEZE n.¹ (1).

squeegee *n.*¹ [1920s] (*UK Und.*) a homemade cosh.

squeegee *n.*² *see* SQUEEZE n.⁵.

squeek *v.* [1980s] (*US campus*) to have sexual intercourse. [? play on SE *squeak*]

squeeler *n. see* SQUEALER n.¹.

squeezable *adj.* [1910s–20s] used of one whom it is easy to make speak (and reveal information). [SQUEEZE v.¹ (2)]

squeeze *n.*¹ **1** [late 18C–19C] (*also* **squeeg**) the neck. **2** [mid-19C] the rope used for a hanging. **3** [1940s] (*Aus.*) the female waist. **4** [1940s] (*US Und.*) a dishonest device for controlling a mechanical gambling game. [i.e. that which squeezes or is squeezed]

squeeze *n.*² **1** [late 18C–mid-19C] a crowded social gathering. **2** [19C–1900s] a hard bargain. **3** [19C+] an escape; thus *narrow squeeze*, a lucky escape. **4** [20C+] a difficult situation. **5** [1990s+] (*UK Und.*) a short prison sentence.

squeeze *n.*³ [mid-19C] (*UK Und.*) a break-in for the purpose of robbery.

squeeze *n.*⁴ [mid-19C–1900s] a plan, an occupation. [? one 'squeezes' the brain]

squeeze *n.*⁵ (*also* **squeegee**) [mid-19C+] silk, and any garment made of it, e.g. a silk tie, a silk handkerchief. [the quality of the fabric that will squeeze into a minuscule space]

squeeze *n.*⁶ [late 19C–1940s] (*orig. Aus.*) an impression of a key made for criminal purposes.

squeeze *n.*⁷ **1** [1910s] (*US Und.*) the head of an institution or an undertaking. **2** [1970s+] (*orig. US Black*) a close friend. **3** [1970s+] a girl- or boyfriend. **4** [2000s] something very special. [SE *squeeze*, i.e. the physical affection involved]

squeeze *n.*⁸ [1920s+] **1** (*US*) an act of blackmail or extortion; thus *give someone the squeeze, put the squeeze on/to*, to blackmail, to extort. **2** pressure, emotional stress; thus *put the squeeze on*, to pressurize. **3** (*US Und.*) extortion money. [SQUEEZE v.¹; but note 18C use of SE *squeeze* to mean the same thing]

squeeze *n.*⁹ **1** [1970s] (*US Black*) liquor. **2** [1990s+] (*drugs*) phencyclidine (cf. ACE n.⁴). [ety. unknown; (1) ? the *squeezing* of grapes]

squeeze *n.*¹⁰ [1970s–80s] (*UK Black*) a discount; something free or cut-price.

squeeze *adj.* [1980s+] (*US campus*) **1** accidental, fortunate. **2** of poor quality, second-rate. [events, objects that *squeeze through*]

squeeze *v.*¹ **1** [mid-19C–1910s] to bring in trouble, to cause difficulties for. **2** [late 19C+] (*orig. US*) to pressurize, to blackmail. **3** [1940s+] (*orig. US*) to inform, to pass on information.

squeeze *v.*² *see* SQUEEZE (ONE'S HEAD) v.

squeeze and a squirt *n. see* SQUIRT AND A SQUEEZE n.

squeeze-box *n.* **1** [late 19C–1900s] a harmonium. **2** [1930s+] an accordion or concertina. [(1) the pressing of feet on the pedals; (2) the pressing together of the 2 sides of the instrument]

squeeze clout *n.* [late 18C] a neck-cloth. [SQUEEZE n.¹ (1) + SE *clout*]

squeeze crab *n.* [late 18C–19C] a morose man, a short man. [SE *squeeze* + CRAB n.¹ (1)]

squeeze-'em-close *n.* [late 19C] sexual intercourse.

squeeze-eye *n.* [1940s–60s] (*W.I.*) a derog. term for a Chinese person (cf. AH CABBAGE n.). [the 'squeezed' shape of Oriental eyes]

squeeze lead *v. see* SLING LEAD v.

squeeze off (on) *v.* [1950s+] to fire a gun, to fire a gun at someone. [SE *squeeze* the trigger]

squeeze (one's head) *v.* [20C+] to defecate (cf. DESPATCH ONE'S CARGO v.).

squeeze one's lemon *v.* (*also* **squeeze the lemon**) **1** [1930s+] (*orig. US Black*) of a man, to have sexual intercourse (cf. BURY IT v.). **2** [1950s+] of a man, to urinate. [note blues use, as a sexual euph.: 'Squeeze my lemon, till the juice runs down my leg']

squeeze-pidgin *n.* [late 19C] a bribe. [SE *squeeze* + *pidgin*, language (here of corruption); but note PIGEON n.¹ (1)]

squeeze play *n.* [1910s+] (*US*) the application of force or pressure to get what one wants. [SQUEEZE v.¹ (2) + PLAY n.¹ (2) + pun on baseball jargon *squeeze play*, 'a tactic whereby the batter bunts so that a runner at third base can attempt to reach home safely and score' (*OED*)]

squeezer *n.*¹ **1** [late 18C–19C] the gallows. **2** [mid-19C] the neck. **3** [20C+] (*W.I.*) a pair of pince-nez spectacles. **4** [1940s] (*US Black*) a belt.

squeezer *n.*² **1** [1970s] (*UK Und.*) a blackmailer. **2** [1990s+] (*US campus*) an untrustworthy person. [SQUEEZE v.¹ (2)]

squeeze the lemon *v. see* SQUEEZE ONE'S LEMON v.

squeeze up *v.* [20C+] for a man, to enter his female partner to begin intercourse.

squeeze-wax *n.* [late 17C–early 19C] a surety for a loan; 'a good-natured foolish fellow, ready to become security for another, under hand and seal' (Grose, 1785).

squelch *v.* [early 17C+] to deal a crushing blow; also in fig. use.

squelcher *n.* [mid–late 19C] a crushing blow. [SE *squelch*]

squelch-gutted *adj.* [late 18C–early 19C] fat-bellied.

squelching *n.* [1950s–80s] (*gay*) sex without any pretence at affection. [note former punk star Johnny Rotten (John Lydon; b.1957): 'Love is two minutes fifty-two seconds of squishing noises. It shows your mind isn't clicking right']

squelchy monkey *n.* [1990s+] a very wet vagina. [SE *squelchy* + MONKEY n.¹⁰ (1)]

squib *n.*¹ [mid-18C] a casino employee who checked on the activities of the house players.

squib *n.*² [mid-19C] a gun; thus DOUBLE-TONGUED SQUIB n. [SE *squib*, a small firework]

squib *n.*³ [mid-19C] **1** a paintbrush. **2** (*costermonger*) a head of asparagus. **3** a form of sweet made from treacle. [resemblance]

squib *n.*⁴ (*Aus.*) [20C+] a coward, one who backs down. **2** [1910s+] a weakling, a small person. **3** [1930s+] a plan that fails to work. [SE *damp squib*]

squib *v.* [early–mid-19C] to fire a gun; also in fig. use.

squibbed off *adj.* [1930s] (*US*) shot, murdered.

squib (it) *v.* [1910s+] (*Aus.*) **1** to behave in a cowardly manner, to back down, to squirm. **2** to evade a responsibility, to shirk a duty, to betray, to let down. [SQUIB n.⁴, but note UK dial. *squib*, to run away]

squib off *v.* [mid-19C] (*Aus.*) to explode. [SE *squib*, a small firework]

squib on *v.* [1930s+] (*Aus.*) to betray; to back down; to surrender. [SQUIB n.⁴ (1)]

squid *n.*¹ [1900s; 1990s+] £1 sterling. [ext. of QUID n.]

squid *n.*² (*also* **squidjigger**) [20C+] (*Can.*) any resident of the Maritime provinces. [fishing jargon *squidjigging*, fishing for squid with a baited hook that one 'jigs' in the hope of luring one's target]

squid *n.*³ **1** [1970s+] (*US campus*) a fool, an incompetent. **2** [1980s+] (*Aus. teen/US campus*) a particularly hard worker. **3** [1990s+] a fast, dangerous driver.

squiff *n.* **1** [1900s] (*Aus.*) a drunkard. **2** [1930s] a contemptible person. **3** [1950s] menstruation. [SQUIFFY adj.]

squiff *v.* **1** [19C] to drink. **2** [1950s] to menstruate. [(1) ? SE *quaff*]

squiffed *adj.* [late 19C+] drunk. [SQUIFF v. (1)]

squiffer *n.* [late 19C–1910s] a concertina. [? SE *squeezer*]

squiff it *v.* [1940s+] (*Aus.*) to die. [ext. of SQUIFF OUT v. or var. on SNUFF (IT) v.]

squiff out *v.* [1950s] to collapse through drunkenness. [SQUIFF v. (1)]

squiffy *adj.* **1** [mid-19C+] drunk (cf. AFFLICTED adj.). **2** [1930s+] (*UK teen*) menstruating. **3** [1940s+] (*Aus.*) foolish, silly. **4** [1940s+] askew, unbalanced. **5** [1950s] malfunctioning, broken. [SQUIFF v.; ? underpinned by SKEW-WHIFF adj.; note dial. *squiffy*, left-handed]

squiffy eyed *n.* [late 19C+] drunk (cf. ARSEHOLED adj.). [ext. of SQUIFFY adj. (1)]

squigger *n.* [2000s] (*US Black*) an Asian who attempts to adopt Black style and culture (cf. CHIGGER n.¹). [the script of Asian languages, e.g. Hindi or Urdu, seen as 'squiggles' + WIGGA n.]

squillion *n.* [1940s+] a hypothetical and enormous number, a multiple of many millions.

squills *n.* [mid-19C] (*US Und.*) boots.

squinny eyes *n.* [17C; mid–late 19C] squinting eyes; thus *squinny-eyed*, squinting.

squint *n.* **1** [late 18C+] a glance, a look. **2** [1900s–20s] (*Aus.*) an eye.

squint-a-pipes *n.* [late 18C–mid-19C] a squinting man or woman. ['said to be born in the middle of the week, and looking both ways for Sunday' (Grose, 1796)]

squinter *n.* [mid-19C] a squinting eye.

squint-eye *n.* [1960s–70s] (*US*) a derog. term for an Asian, esp. a Vietnamese (cf. BROWNIE n.²). [derog. physiological stereotyping]

squint like a bag of nails *v.* [late 18C–early 19C] to squint in a noticeable manner. [the squinter's eyes point in as many directions as nails dropped into a bag]

squire *n.¹* **1** [late 16C–1900s] a general title used ironically in a number of contexts, e.g. APPLE SQUIRE n.; SQUIRE OF ALSATIA n.; SQUIRE OF THE BODY n.; SQUIRE OF THE COMPANY n.; SQUIRE OF THE GIMLET n.; SQUIRE OF THE PAD n.; SQUIRE OF THE PETTICOAT n.; SQUIRE OF THE PLACKET n. **2** [17C] a fool. **3** [mid-19C] (*UK Und.*) a successful criminal. **4** [mid-19C] (*US*) a magistrate. [SE *squire*, a title orig. used to denote an esquire, a young man of good birth, attendant upon a knight, but by 17C referring mainly to a country gentleman; (2) a squire is one who is foolish enough to serve another; cf. KNIGHT n. (1) and its combs.]

squire *n.²* [early 19C+] a general term of address, no particular rank or intimacy indicated.

squire of Alsatia *n.* **1** [late 17C] a gentleman who has been drawn to the criminal world and there found himself fleeced, robbed and generally rendered destitute by its denizens. **2** [late 17C] an overly generous man. **3** [late 17C–early 19C] a rich fool. [SE *squire* + ALSATIA n.; best known as the title of Thomas Shadwell's play, first staged in 1688]

squire of the body *n.* [17C–early 18C] a pimp, or a term of abuse (cf. ABBOT ON THE CROSS n.). [SQUIRE n.¹ (1), mocking the SE *esquire* or the 'country squire' + SE *body*]

squire of the company *n.* [late 18C] one who treats the rest of the company. [SQUIRE n.¹ (1) + SE *company*]

squire of the cross *n.* [mid-19C] (*UK Und.*) a thief. [SQUIRE n.¹ (1) + CROSS, THE n. (1)]

squire of the gimlet *n.* [late 17C–18C] a publican, a tapster. [SQUIRE n.¹ (1) + SE *gimlet*, used as a corkscrew]

squire of the gusset *n. see* BROTHER OF THE GUSSET n.

squire of the pad *n.* [early 18C] a highwayman. [SQUIRE n.¹ (1) + PAD n.¹ (1)]

squire of the petticoat *n.* (*also* petticoat peer/squire) [late 17C] a pimp; as a term of abuse (cf. ABBOT ON THE CROSS n.). [SQUIRE n.¹ (1) + PETTICOAT n. (1)]

squire of the placket *n.* [17C] a pimp (cf. ABBOT ON THE CROSS n.). [SQUIRE n.¹ (1), mocking the SE *esquire* or the 'country squire' + PLACKET n.]

squirish *adj.¹* [late 17C–early 18C] used of 'one that pretends to Pay all Reckonings, and is not strong enough in the Pocket' (B.E.). [? he poses as a SE *squire*]

squirish *adj.²* [late 18C–early 19C] foolish. [SQUIRE n.¹ (2)]

squirly *adj.* (*US campus*) **1** [1960s] sexually frustrated. **2** [1990s+] emotionally unrestrained.

squirm, the *n.* [1900s–10s] the art nouveau style. [the curves and curlicues that typified it]

squirrel *n.¹* [early 17C–early 19C] a prostitute (cf. ALLEY CAT n.). ['like that animal she covers her back with her tail' (Grose, 1796)]

squirrel *n.²* **1** [early 18C] the vagina (cf. BIRD n.⁸). **2** [1910s+] a woman, usu. as a sex object. **3** [1970s] (*US campus*) female pubic hair. [? coined independently of SQUIRREL n.¹]

squirrel *n.³* [mid-19C–1930s] (*US*) illicitly distilled liquor. [? it is 'squirrelled away']

squirrel *n.⁴* **1** [1910s+] (*US*) an eccentric person. **2** [1930s] a psychoanalyst. **3** [1940s] (*US*) a stupid, shortsighted person. **4** [1970s] (*US campus*) one who is slow on the uptake. **5** [1970s+] a mentally ill person, a psychopath; thus *squirrelly*, unstable, neurotic. **6** [2000s] (*US prison*) a mentally ill prisoner. [pun on NUTS adj. (2)]

squirrel *n.⁵* [1950s] (*US drugs*) a careful heroin user, who always hides away some drugs for an emergency.

squirrel *n.⁶* [1970s+] (*drugs*) a mixture of LSD and some other drug, or of cocaine, marijuana and phencyclidine. [the effects are to make one SQUIRRELY adj.]

squirrel cage *n. see* SQUIRREL RANCH n.

squirrel-food *n.¹* [1910s–60s] (*US*) one who appeals to women. [SQUIRREL n.² (2) + SE *food*]

squirrel-food *n.²* (*also* squirrel-feed) [1920s] (*US*) one who is crazy or eccentric. [pun on NUTS adj. (2)]

squirrel-hunter *n. see* SQUIRREL-SHOOTER n.

squirrel hunting *n. see* HUNTING n.

squirrel-kisser *n.* [1990s+] (*US campus*) an environmentalist.

squirrelly *adj. see* SQUIRRELY adj.

squirrel ranch *n.* (*also* squirrel cage) [1930s–40s] (*US prison*) the prison mental ward. [SQUIRREL n.⁴ (5) + SE *ranch*]

squirrel-shooter *n.* (*also* squirrel-hunter, squirrel-popper) [1900s–40s] (*US*) a farmer, a rustic; thus a novice or inexperienced person (cf. ACORN-CRACKER n.).

squirrely *adj.* (*also* squirrelly) **1** [1930s+] (*orig. US campus*) (*also* squirrel-shit) eccentric, odd, insane (cf. APEY adj.). **2** [1960s] (*US campus*) reckless. **3** [1980s+] nervous. [pun on NUTS adj. (2)]

squirt *n.¹* **1** [late 16C–mid-18C] as *the squirt*, *squirts*, diarrhoea. **2** [mid-19C] (*US campus*) a showy recitation. **3** [1940s+] (*orig. US*) ejaculation. **4** [1960s+] an act of urination. **5** [1980s+] (*US campus*) a faecal stain on one's underwear due to liquid emitted when breaking wind or through a badly cleaned anus.

squirt *n.²* **1** [early 18C; mid-19C+] (*orig. US*) a dandy, a fop. **2** [mid-19C+] (*also* pop-squirt) a small, insignificant person or, occas., place or thing. **3** [1920s] a general insult, irrespective of size.

squirt *n.³* **1** [mid-19C] champagne. **2** [1920s+] very cheap but still effective beer. **3** [1960s] (*N.Z.*) petrol. [it *squirt*s from the bottle, beer-tap or pump]

squirt *n.⁴* [mid–late 19C] a doctor, a chemist. [their use of syringes]

squirt *n.⁵* **1** [late 19C–1950s] (*mainly Aus.*) a revolver. **2** [1910s] (*Aus.*) a bayonet. [it *squirt*s bullets]

squirt *v. see* SQUIRT (OFF) v.

squirt and a squeeze *n.* (*also* squeeze and a squirt) [late 19C] sexual intercourse; thus *do a squirt and a squeeze*, to have intercourse. [note RMC Duntroon (Aus.) *quick squirt*, a brief act of sexual intercourse; note Williams for 17C/18C use of *squirt* to mean ejaculate]

squirter *n.* [1900s–30s] a pistol. [ext. of SQUIRT n.⁵ (1)]

squirtish *adj.* (*also* squirty) [mid-19C] (*US campus*) ostentatious. [SQUIRT n.² (1)]

squirt 'n' spurt *n.* [1990s+] (*US*) masturbation; thus *play squirt 'n' spurt*, to masturbate.

squirt (off) *v.* **1** [late 17C; 1930s+] to ejaculate (cf. BLOSH v.). **2** [mid-19C] (*US campus*) to make a showy recitation. **3** [1970s] to confess, to give away secrets.

squirt one's juice *v.* [late 19C] of a man, to ejaculate (cf. BLOSH v.). [SE *squirt* + JUICE n.² (1)]

squirts *n. see* SQUIRT n.¹ (1).

squirty *adj. see* SQUIRTISH adj.

squish *adj.* [2000s] (*US Black*) a general term of approval, attractive, sophisticated. [? var. on SWISH adj.¹]

squish *v.* **1** [mid-19C; 1950s+] to squash, to squeeze. **2** [1990s+] to destroy, to spoil. [echoic]

squishy *adj.* [1950s+] (*US*) sentimental, mawkish. [fig. use of SE *squish*, to move through soft substances with a 'squishy' sound]

squit *n.¹* **1** [mid-19C+] a worthless, contemptible person. **2** [1950s+] (*UK juv.*) a short person. [SQUIRT n.² (2)]

squit *n.²* [1950s] sentimental nonsense. [fig. use of SQUITTERS, THE n.]

squitters, the *n.* (*also* **squits, squitter**) [late 19C+] diarrhoea. [SHIT n.¹ (1)/ME *scite*; prior use f. 17C is SE; also as SE v., thus D'Urfey, *Pills to Purge Melancholy* (1719–20): 'And here be de Mob make 'em squitter and tremble']

squivalens *n.* [late 19C–1900s] (*Aus.*) extras, 'perks'. [? SE *equivalents*]

squiz *n.* (*also* **squizz**) [1910s+] (*Aus./N.Z.*) a look, a glance; thus *squiz, take a squiz* to inspect, to peep at surreptitiously. [SE *quiz,* to look at + ? *squint* or ? Devon dial. *squiz,* to examine critically]

squizz *v.* [1930s+] (*Aus.*) to look at.

squobby *adj. see* SQUABBY adj.

squooshy *adj.* (*also* **squoo, squoodgy, squshy**) [late 19C+] (*US*) soft and insubstantial. [SE *squashy/squishy*]

sres-wort *n.* [mid-19C] trousers. [backsl.]

sret-sio *n.* (*also* **swret-sio**) [mid-19C] oysters. [backsl.]

Sri Lanka *n.* [1990s+] a general term of abuse. [rhy. sl. = WANKER n. (2)]

Sri Lankan brown *n.* [1990s+] (*Aus. drugs*) a variety of heroin refined in Sri Lanka (cf. CHINA WHITE n.).

s.r.o. *n.¹* [20C+] (*orig. entertainment*) **1** a full house. **2** anything that sells out or is very popular. [abbr. *standing room only*]

s.r.o. *n.²* [1990s+] (*US*) a hotel offering single rooms only. [abbr.]

s.s. *n.¹* [early 19C–1930s] a fool. [abbr. SAMMY (SOFT) n.]

s.s. *n.²* [1930s] (*drugs*) a skin shot, i.e. one that does not hit a vein. [abbr.]

s.s. *n.³* [1940s–70s] (*US Und.*) a suspended sentence. [abbr.]

s/s *phr.* [1980s+] used in contact advertisements, safe sex; either condoms are used or the sex is non-penetrative. [abbr.]

St all combs. with St are alphabetized under SAINT.

stab *n.¹* [late 19C+] (*orig. US*) a try, an attempt; thus *have/make a stab at,* to try.

stab *n.²* **1** [1910s+] a woman, esp. in the context of sexual intercourse. **2** [1950s+] (*Aus./US*) sexual intercourse. [STAB v.]

stab *v.* (*also* **stob**) [late 16C–early 17C] to have sexual intercourse (cf. BANG v.¹). [the image of the penis as a weapon]

stabbed with a Bridport dagger, be *phr.* [mid-17C–early 19C] to be hanged. [the best variety of British hemp (used for the noose) was grown near Bridport, Dorset]

stabber *n.¹* [1930s+] (*Irish*) the butt end of a cigarette. [SE *stub out*]

stabber *n.²* [1940s] (*US*) a knife.

stab in the main vein *v.* [mid-17C] of a man, to have sexual intercourse.

stab in the thigh *v.* [late 19C] to have sexual intercourse.

stable *n.* (*US*) **1** [20C+] any group of people working under a single manager. **2** [1920s+] a group of prostitutes working for a pimp.

stable *v.* [1960s] (*US*) for a pimp to enroll a prostitute in his 'team'. [STABLE n. (2)]

stable-boss *n.* [1930s–40s] (*US Und.*) a pimp who runs a string of prostitutes (cf. BROTHER-IN-LAW n.). [STABLE n. (2) + BOSS n.² (1)]

stable mind *n.* [late 19C] (*UK society*) one that has no other interests than horseflesh and its performance on a racecourse. [play on SE *stable* (for horses)/*stable,* balanced + SE *mind*]

stable sister *n.* [1970s] (*US Black*) one of a group of prostitutes working for a single pimp (cf. BROTHER-IN-LAW n.). [STABLE n. (2) + SE *sister*]

stable up *v.* [1960s] (*US Black*) of a prostitute, to join those girls working for a given pimp. [STABLE n. (2)]

stab oneself and pass the dagger *v.* [mid-19C] to take a glassful then circulate the bottle.

stach *see under* STASH.

stache *n. see* STASH n.³.

stache *v. see* STASH v.¹.

stack *n.¹* [late 19C+] (*orig. US*) **1** a large amount of money; something valuable, e.g. a piece of jewellery. **2** a large amount.

stack *n.²* [1950s–70s] (*drugs*) a pack of marijuana cigarettes.

stack *n.³* [1960s+] (*US*) a 'stacked', i.e. prepared, deck of cards; also in fig. use.

stack *v.¹* **1** [late 19C] (*also* **stack it**) to cease from an action. **2** [1930s–60s] to hide away. **3** [1980s] to put to one side. **4** [1990s+] (*US Black gang/campus*) (*also* **stack chips**) to save money. [SE *stack,* to pile up one's chips in a casino]

stack *v.²* *see* STACK (ON) v.

stack asses *v.* [1970s] (*US*) to defeat heavily, to thrash. [SE *stack* + ASS n. (2)]

stack chips *v. see* STACK v.¹ (4).

stacked *adj.¹* (*also* **stacked up**) **1** [1920s+] wealthy; sometimes ext. as *well-stacked.* **2** [1930s+] of a woman, attractively well-built, esp. with large breasts. **3** [1950s] of a man, muscular. **4** [1970s] (*Irish*) drunk. **5** [1970s+] (*US gay*) having a large penis.

stacked *adj.²* [1970s+] (*US prison*) of sentences, served consecutively.

stacked like a brick backhouse *phr. see* BUILT LIKE A BRICK SHITHOUSE phr.

stacked up *adj. see* STACKED adj.¹.

stacking *n.* [1990s+] (*US Black teen*) making money. [STACK v.¹ (4)]

stack it *v.¹* [1970s–80s] (*N.Z. prison*) to boast, to exaggerate. [one *stacks* up fantasies]

stack it *v.²* *see* STACK v.¹ (1).

stack it up *v.* [late 19C] (*US*) to charge exorbitant prices.

stack of bones *n. see* BAG OF BONES n.¹.

stackola *n.* [1990s+] (*US Black*) a large amount of money, a pile of money. [STACK n.¹ (1) + -OLA sfx]

stack (on) *v.* [1940s+] (*Aus.*) to contrive, to produce. [SE *stack,* to pile up]

stack on a blue *v. see* BUNG ON A BLUE v.

stack on an act *v.* [1940s+] (*Aus.*) to lose one's temper and deliver a stream of obscenities/oaths.

stack on a turn *v.* [1940s+] (*Aus.*) to make a fuss. [var. on STACK ON AN ACT v.]

stack one's drapery *v.* (*also* **stack one's apparel**) [1910s+] (*Aus.*) to put one's jacket (and at one time hat) on the ground before starting a fight.

stacks *n.¹* [late 19C+] (*orig. US*) a great many, a good deal, a large amount; often of money.

stacks *n.²* [1970s] (*US*) stack- or high-heeled shoes.

stack the deck *v.* (*also* **stack the cards**) [20C+] (*US*) to arrange things in one's favour, usu. dishonestly. [poker imagery]

stack up *v.¹* **1** [late 19C] to challenge. **2** [late 19C–1900s] to meet. **3** [late 19C+] to emerge, to develop, to maintain, to appear as it should; also in negative phr. *that doesn't/don't stack up,* that isn't logical, that fails to reach a standard. **4** [20C+] to compare with; usu. as *stack up against.*

stack up v.[2] [1940s–60s] of a woman, to look attractive. [STACKED adj.[1] (2)]

stack up v.[3] [1950s–60s] (US teen) to crash a car.

stack up (to) v. [1920s] (US tramp) to give, to provide.

stack z's v. [1950s+] (US) to have a sleep, to nap. [SE stack + z n.[1]]

stadsjapie n. [1970s+] (S.Afr.) a city-dweller, esp. when ignorant of country ways. [Afk. stad, city + JAAP n.]

staff n. see STAFF (OF LIFE) n.

staff breaker n. (also **staff climber**) [19C] the vagina; thus a woman (cf. BITE n.[2]). [STAFF (OF LIFE) n. + SE breaker/climber]

staff-naked n. [mid-19C] gin. [? a misprint of the synon. STARK-NAKED n.]

staff (of life) n. [mid-17C–1900s] the penis (cf. BAT n.[7]). [punning on SE staff of life, bread or any other staple]

staff of love n. [mid-17C–mid-18C] the penis (cf. BAT n.[7]).

stafford law n. [late 16C–mid-17C] a beating, often in the context of a punishment. [pun on SE staff, a stick]

staffrider n. [1960s+] (S.Afr.) one who clings to the outside (or stands on the roof) of a moving train, having boarded it while it is in motion. [RIDE STAFF v.]

stag n.[1] **1** [early 18C–1950s] an informer; thus TURN STAG v. **2** [early–mid-19C] a man who attends courts in order to hire himself out as a defence witness, usu. to provide an alibi for an otherwise guilty defendant. **3** [1930s–50s] (US) a detective (cf. BEAGLE n.[3]). [orig. dial.; deer supposedly turn on any one of their number that is being hunted]

stag n.[2] [mid–late 19C] a shilling. [? play on HOG n.[1] (1)]

stag n.[3] [20C+] (orig. US) **1** an unaccompanied man at a dance or similar gathering; thus go stag, to attend a social event without a female partner. **2** any form of party or similar entertainment attended only by men. [STAG adj.]

stag n.[4] **1** [1910s+] (Irish) a cruel, selfish woman. **2** [1920s] a large, energetic woman. [(2) orig. Yorks. dial.]

stag adj. (also **staggish**) (orig. US) **1** [mid-19C+] of a man, by oneself in a social situation, e.g. a dance, where other men have partners. **2** [mid-19C+] pertaining to men, usu. in a sexual context. **3** [late 19C+] for men only.

stag v.[1] **1** [mid-18C–19C] to find, to observe. **2** [early 19C+] to inform against. [STAG n.[1] (1)]

stag v.[2] [early–mid-19C] **1** to refuse a request for a loan. **2** to demand money, to cadge, to trick.

stag v.[3] [20C+] (US) for a man, to attend a social function without a female companion. **2** [1920s] to be a bachelor. **3** [1960s] (US campus) to reject a request for a date. [STAG n.[3] (1)]

stag-dance n. [mid-19C–1910s] (US) a men-only dance, usu. performed in bar-rooms or taverns. [STAG adj. (1) + SE dance]

stage-door johnnie n. (also **johnnie**, **stage-door johnny**) [late 19C+] a man, poss. rich, who hangs around theatre stage doors hoping to meet his female idols. [SE stage-door + JOHNNIE n.[2] (3)]

stage fright n. [1970s] light (ale). [rhy. sl.]

stag film/flick n. see STAG MOVIE n.

stagger n.[1] [mid-19C] a watcher, a lookout. [STAG v.[1] (1)]

stagger n.[2] [mid-19C–1930s] (US) an effort, a try.

stagger-back n. [1950s] (W.I.) a form of toffee that is so tough that one 'staggers back' as one attempts to chew it.

staggering bob n. [19C+] meat declared unfit to eat. [meat trade jargon bob, bobby, inedible meat, esp. that taken from animals that have died rather than been slaughtered; note dial. staggering bob (with his yellow pumps), a newborn calf (with yellow hooves) that is killed for veal]

stagger juice n. [1910s+] (orig. Aus./N.Z.) alcohol; thus stagger juicery, a public house. [SE stagger + JUICE n.[3]; note Charles Dickens, Martin Chuzzlewit (1843–44): 'A pint of the the celebrated staggering ale, or Real Old Brighton Tipper']

staggers n. (also **blind staggers**) [mid-19C+] extreme drunkenness. [SE stagger; puns on staggers, a disease of horses and sl.

use/staggering through excess drinking; note also the SE hungry staggers, suffered by those weakened by starvation]

stagger-soup n. [1930s–40s] (US) strong, if not very high-quality, whisky.

staggish adj. see STAG adj.

stag line n. **1** [1920s+] (US) a number of unescorted men at a dance, who usu. stand in line eyeing the women. **2** [1960s] (US gay) a gathering of gay male prostitutes in a park or similarly well-known area. [STAG n.[3] (1) + SE line]

stag-month n. [late 19C] the first month that follows childbirth. [dial. stag, a gander; at such a time a man's infidelities were considered acceptable]

stag movie n. (also **stag**, **stag film**, **...flick**, **...show**) [1950s+] a pornographic film. [STAG adj. (2) + SE movie]

stag night n. [1960s+] **1** any social event from which women are excluded (cf. BUCK NIGHT n.). **2** the trad. uproarious eve-of-wedding party held by the groom and his male cronies. [STAG adj. + SE night]

stag or shag? phr. [1940s+] (orig. US) will you be coming, usu. to a party, alone or with a female companion? [STAG n.[3] (1) + SHAG n.[1] (1)]

stag party n. [mid-19C+] (orig. US) an all-male party, esp. on the night preceding the wedding of one of the men. [STAG adj. (2) + SE party]

stag show n. see STAG MOVIE n.

stained adj. [early 17C] drunk.

stainless steel ride n. see BIG JAB n.

stair-dancer n. [1950s+] a thief who steals from buildings that have not been properly secured. [SE stair + DANCER n.]

stair-steps n. (also **stair-steppers**) [1920s–50s] a family with children ranged at equal intervals. [their respective heights resemble a flight of stairs]

stairs without a landing n. [mid-19C] a prison treadmill.

stairway to heaven n. **1** [1960s] (US Black) the female thighs. **2** [1980s] (Aus.) a ladder in a stocking. **3** [2000s] the vagina.

stair-work n. [late 16C–early 17C] casual or clandestine sexual intercourse.

Stait, the n. see START, THE n. (1).

stake n.[1] **1** [mid-18C; late 19C+] a large sum of money. **2** [early 19C] the booty gained in a robbery. **3** [early 19C] gambling winnings. **4** [late 19C+] money saved up for future use.

stake n.[2] see STAKE(-OUT) n.

stake v.[1] (also **stake to**) [mid-19C+] to lend money, to put up funds for someone's enterprise. [STAKE n.[1] (1)]

stake v.[2] see STAKE (OUT) v.

stake long and deep v. [1970s] (US Black) to invest large sums of cash. [STAKE n.[1] (1) + SE long and deep]

stake-man n. [late 19C–1930s] (US) a hobo, a tramp. [the need for a STAKE n.[1] on which to survive]

stake one's bottom dollar v. see BET ONE'S BOTTOM DOLLAR v.

stake(-out) n. **1** [1930s+] (orig. US) the surveillance of a suspect by police stationed in clandestine hiding places. **2** [1960s] (orig. US) one who conducts such a surveillance. **3** [1960s–70s] (US Und.) the preparatory surveillance of the target of a robbery, e.g. a bank or diamond merchant. [STAKE (OUT) v.]

stake (out) v. (orig. US) **1** [1900s] to subject to preliminary analysis. **2** [1930s+] to conduct a surveillance. **3** [1990s+] to wait in a place in the hope of making an encounter, e.g. of the media. [the placing of stakes to mark out a piece of land, e.g. a mining claim]

stakes n. [late 19C+] used fig. to indicate some form of profession or occupation in which there is an implication of challenges that must be overcome, e.g. the matrimonial stakes, the novel-writing stakes. [racing jargon stakes, a race for money, usu. defined by a specific name, e.g. St Leger Stakes]

stake to v. see STAKE v.[1].

stakey *adj.* [1950s] (*US*) in possession of money. [STAKE n.¹ (4)]

staky *n.* [1940s] (*US Und.*) one who has made enough money to retire. [STAKE n.¹ (4)]

stale *n.*¹ **1** [late 16C–early 17C] a thief's or card-sharp's accomplice; a stool-pigeon. **2** [mid-17C] (*UK Und.*) a pickpocket or cut-purse. [10C SE *stale* and OHG *stala*, theft, stealing]

stale *n.*² [1980s+] (*US drugs*) the cannabis equivalent of a hangover.

stale drunk *adj.* [late 19C] hungover. [SE *stale*]

stale mutton *n.* [17C] a prostitute (cf. BANGTAIL n.¹; BIT OF MUTTON n.). [SE *stale* + MUTTON n.¹ (1)]

stalewhimper *n. see* STALL-WHIMPER n.

stalk *n.*¹ [17C–mid-18C; 1920s+] the erect penis.

stalk *n.*² **1** [mid-19C] the gallows; thus *climb the stalk*, to be hanged. **2** [late 19C] (*UK Und.*) a policeman.

stalk *n.*³ [1930s] a tie-pin. [resemblance]

stalk *n.*⁴ [1970s] cheek.

stalk a judy *v.* [late 19C+] to follow a woman in the hope of sex. [SE *stalk* + JUDY n.¹ (1)]

stalk-fever *n.* [1970s] priapism. [STALK n.¹ + SE *fever*]

stalks *n.* [1970s] (*US Black*) the human legs.

stall *n.*¹ **1** [late 16C+] (*also* **staller**) a pickpocket's helper who distracts the attention of the victim whose pocket is being emptied or purse cut. **2** [17C+] any form of decoy who works with a criminal gang. **3** [late 18C] (*UK Und.*) a pickpockets' manoeuvre whereby a target is pinioned and rendered open to theft. **4** [late 18C+] a pretext, which offers an opportunity to steal. **5** [mid-19C] (*UK Und.*) the act of rendering a victim vulnerable to a pickpocket. **6** [mid-19C+] an act of time-wasting or prevarication, an excuse. **7** [1910s] (*Aus.*) a hoax; a disappointment. **8** [1920s] (*US Und.*) a fraudulent alibi. **9** [1920s] a misdirection. [SE *stall*, a decoy bird]

stall *n.*² [20C+] (*Irish*) an act of sexual intercourse. [? Irish *stail*, a stallion]

stall *n.*³ [1900s] (*US*) a walk.

stall *v.*¹ (*UK Und.*) **1** [mid-16C–early 19C] to apprentice or to work with, i.e. 'to stall a beggar to a rogue'. **2** [mid-19C] to attach oneself (to a criminal gang). [SE *stall*, to set in a place, itself the root of *install*]

stall *v.*² **1** [late 16C+] (*UK Und.*) to shield a pickpocket, confidence trickster or thief. **2** [17C–early 18C] (*UK Und.*) to steal, to pick a pocket. **3** [mid-18C+] (*US*) to loiter or linger around. **4** [mid-19C] (*UK Und.*) to use something to shield one's face. **5** [late 19C+] to play for time, to make excuses, to delay; thus (*US*) *quit stalling*, stop wasting time, stop making excuses. **6** [1900s] (*UK Und.*) to jostle and distract one whose pocket is about to be picked. **7** [1940s+] to make someone wait. **8** [1970s] (*Aus. Und.*) to abandon an attempt, to give up. [STALL n.¹]

stall *v.*³ **1** [mid–late 19C] to spend the night in a room provided by a public house. **2** [mid-19C–1950s] to travel about. **3** [mid-19C+] to walk off. [SE *stall*, to live with]

staller *n. see* STALL n.¹ (1).

stall-fed *adj.* [early 17C; 20C+] (*Irish*) pampered. [synon. dial.; the image is of an indulged horse]

stalling (for a dip) *n.* [19C] (*UK Und.*) the shielding of a pickpocket by an accomplice. [STALL v.² (1) + DIP n.⁴ (1)]

stalling-ken *n.* (*also* **stuling-ken**) [mid-16C–mid-19C] (*UK Und.*) a depository for stolen goods, esp. as used by the RUFFLER n. to hide his booty. [SE (*in*)*stall*, to put in place + KEN n.¹ (1)]

stallion *n.* **1** [mid-16C+] a sexual athlete; a womanizer. **2** [late 16C–17C] a courtesan, a kept woman. **3** [17C–early 19C] a heterosexual male prostitute or kept man. **4** [late 17C–18C] (*UK Und.*) a pimp (cf. ABBOT ON THE CROSS n.). **5** [mid-18C+] the penis (cf. ANTEATER n.). **6** [1950s+] (*US Black*) a tall, good-looking woman, poss. highly sexed. **7** [1970s] (*US Black/Und.*) a female prostitute. **8** [1970s+] (*US gay*) a 'masculine' lesbian with a large clitoris. [(2) ? Fr. *estalon*, a decoy, an enticement, or *stale*, the lowest class of prostitute]

stall-off *n.* **1** [early–mid-19C] one who gets away with a successful ruse for a friend. **2** [early 19C+] any form of evasive story or trick. [STALL OFF v. (2)]

stall off *v.* **1** [mid-18C+] to impede, to get in the way of, to hinder; thus one who gets away with a successful ruse for a friend has *stalled him off in prime twig*. **2** [early 19C] (*UK Und.*) to save an accomplice from arrest or disgrace. **3** [early 19C] (*UK Und.*) to avoid a person or place. **4** [early 19C; 1950s] to use artifice to avoid punishment or problems. **5** [early–mid-19C] (*UK Und.*) of a villain's accomplice, to screen or disguise a robbery. **6** [1920s–50s] to defer, to postpone. [ext. of STALL v.²]

stall one's mug *v.* [mid-19C] to run off, to leave quickly; esp. in imper., go away! [? STALL OFF v. (1) + MUG n.¹ (2)]

stallsman *n.* (*also* **stalsman**) [mid–late 19C] a pickpocket's or other thief's assistant. [STALL n.¹ (1) + SE *man*]

stall to the rogue *v.* (*also* **stall to the order of rogues**) [mid-16C–early 19C] to enlist a beggar as a full member of the underworld; thus *stalling*, the enlistment or 'ordaining' process. [ext. of STALL v.¹ (1)]

stall up *v.* [early 19C] (*UK Und.*) to surround a person, forcing them to hold their hands in the air while they are stripped of their possessions; thus *staller-up*, one who robs in this way. [STALL v.² (1)]

stall-whimper *n.* (*also* **stalewhimper**) [late 17C–mid-19C] (*UK Und.*) an illegitimate child.

stalsman *n. see* STALLSMAN n.

stam flash *v.* (*also* **stam flesh**, **stamp flash**) [late 17C–early 19C] (*UK Und.*) to talk in thieves' cant. [? Ger. *stimmen*, to make one's voice heard, to sing + FLASH n.¹ (2)]

stamina daddy *n.* (*also* **stamina mummy**) [1980s+] (*W.I./UK Black teen*) a man or woman known for their powers of sexual endurance.

stammel *n.* (*also* **strammel**) [late 17C–early 19C] 'a brawny, lusty, strapping Wench' (B.E.). [SE *stammel*, a coarse woollen petticoat]

stammer *n.* [early 19C] (*Scot Und.*) an indictment.

stammer and stutter *n.* [20C+] butter. [rhy. sl.]

stamp *n.*¹ [1980s] (*UK Und.*) the post office.

stamp *n.*² [1990s+] (*Aus. Und.*) of the police, an attempt to extort a bribe.

stamp *v.* [1990s+] (*Aus. Und.*) of a policeman, to extort a bribe. [STAMP n.²]

stamp a bitch *v.* [2000s] (*US Black*) for a man to hit a woman hard enough to leave the imprint of his rings in her flesh. [SE *stamp*, to imprint + BITCH n.¹ (1)]

stamp-crab *n.* [late 19C–1900s] one who walks heavily. [SE *stamp* + CRABS n.²]

stamp-drawers *n.* [17C–early 19C] stockings. [STAMPS n.¹ (1) + DRAWERS n.]

stamped paper *n.* [early–mid-19C] a promissory note.

stampers *n.*¹ **1** [mid-16C–mid-19C] boots or shoes. **2** [mid-18C] (*UK Und.*) feet or legs.

stampers *n.*² *see* DEUSEAVILE-STAMPERS n.

stamp flash *v. see* STAM FLASH v.

stamping ground *n.*¹ (*also* **stomping ground**) [mid-19C+] one's home territory, one's area of operation. [18C SE, a place frequented by animals]

stamping ground *n.*² [1900s] anywhere known as a 'lover's lane'. [the stamping of a stallion in rut]

stamp-in-the-ashes *n.* [early 16C] a form of mixed drink, no ingredients stated.

stamp-picker *n.* [late 19C] a typographer, a compositor. [printers' jargon *stamp*, a piece of type + SE *picker*]

stamps *n.*¹ (*UK Und.*) **1** [mid-16C–mid-19C] legs, feet. **2** [mid-18C–19C] boots or shoes. [SE *stamp*]

stamps *n.*² [mid-19C–1920s] (*US*) money. [the stamping of money-orders and similar documents]

stan *n.* [1970s] (*Aus. teen*) a fool, an insignificant person, a socially inept individual.

Stan and Ollie *n.* [1990s+] an umbrella. [rhy. sl. = BROLLY n.; for ety. *see* LAUREL AND HARDY n.]

stanch (out) *v.* [1930s–40s] (*US Black*) to begin. [? SE *start out*]

stand *n.*[1] [late 16C–mid-17C] (*UK Und.*) a lookout, spec. for a team of lock-pickers.

stand *n.*[2] **1** [17C–1900s] (*also* standing) an erection. **2** [late 19C] a prostitute who specializes in fellatio. [abbr. COCKSTAND n.]

stand *n.*[3] [early 19C; 1920s] (*UK/US Und.*) a hold-up.

stand *v.*[1] [mid-16C+] of a man, to have an erection.

stand *v.*[2] [17C+] (*US Und.*) to suffer, to be subjected to, to experience.

stand *v.*[3] **1** [early 18C+] to cost, to be charged. **2** [mid-18C+] to bear the company's expenses, to pay for everyone with whom one is eating or drinking. **3** [mid–late 19C] to make an investment; to wager. **4** [mid-19C+] to give as a present. [abbr. SE *stand treat*]

stand ace (with) *v.* (*also* stand ace-high with) [late 19C–1900s] (*US*) to be held in the highest esteem by someone. [SE *stand* + ACE n.[2] (2)]

stand a good fag *v.* [late 18C–mid-19C] to resist tiredness, to persevere. [SE *stand*, to bear + FAG n.[2] (1)]

stand and shiver *n. see* SHAKE AND SHIVER n.

stand a queer lock *v. see* LOCK n.[2].

stand a rap (for) *v.* [1940s] (*US Und.*) to resemble someone closely.

standard *n.* [2000s] (*UK Black/teen*) something unexciting.

stand around with one's finger/thumb up one's ass *v. see* SIT THERE WITH ONE'S FINGER UP ONE'S ASS v.

stand at ease *n.* **1** [20C+] fleas. **2** [1910s+] (*orig. milit.*) cheese. [rhy. sl.]

stand ben *v.* [early 19C] to treat one's companions at an inn or tavern. [STAND v.[3] (2) + BEN n.[2] (1)]

stand bitch *v.* **1** [late 18C–early 19C] to make tea. **2** [late 18C–mid-19C] (*also* bitch the pot) to preside as hostess at a tea party. [SE *stand* + pre-sl. use of *bitch*, woman as a species; thus to perform in a (typically) female role; note BITCH n.[1] (8)]

stand bluff *v.* [late 18C] to swear, to be adamant. [SE *stand* + *bluff*, rough, abrupt, blunt]

stand buff *v.* **1** [late 17C–mid-19C] to suffer without complaining, to bear the brunt. **2** [late 17C+] to swear, to be adamant. [SE *stand* + fig. use of BUFF adj.[1]]

stand-by guy *n. see* STAND-UP GUY n.

stand dixie *v.* [1990s+] to keep guard, to keep a lookout.

stand down *v.* [1970s] (*US*) to humiliate.

stander *n.* **1** [early 17C] a lookout for a criminal gang. **2** [1920s] (*US*) the victim of a confidence trickster. [(1) he *stands* and watches; (2) he 'stands for' the trick]

stander-up *n.* [19C] a street thief who robs drunks under the pretence of helping them up from the gutter into which they have fallen (or been pushed).

stand for *v.* **1** [mid-19C] (*UK Und.*) to pay for. **2** [mid-19C] to hold back. **3** [mid-19C+] (*orig. US*) to tolerate, to put up with. [(1) STAND v.[3] (2); (2) SE *stand back* (from); (3) STAND v.[2]]

stand frisk *v.* [19C] to be searched. [SE *stand* + FRISK n.[2]]

stand from under *n.* [20C+] thunder. [rhy. sl.]

stand-in *n.* [late 19C–1920s] (*US*) a friendly or profitable arrangement; a corrupt arrangement, a 'put-up job'.

stand in *v.*[1] **1** [mid-19C–1910s] to go shares with, to join, to be a partner with. **2** [late 19C+] to have a friendly or profitable understanding with, to be in league with, to be on good terms with.

stand in *v.*[2] **1** [mid-19C+] (*orig. UK society*) to cost, e.g. *it stands me in £10*. **2** [1910s] (*Aus.*) to hand over (money). [SE mid-15C–mid-19C]

standing *n. see* STAND n.[2] (1).

standing ague *n.* [mid-17C] the state of erection. [STAND v.[1] + SE *ague*, the 'shaking sickness', i.e. the erect penis is lit. shaking with lust]

standing budge *n.* [late 17C] a thief's accomplice or a lookout. [SE *stand* + BUDGE n.[1] (1)]

standing on one's head *phr. see* DO (STANDING) ON ONE'S HEAD v.

standing on the top step *phr.* [1940s–50s] (*UK Und.*) a phr. used of a man on trial who is facing the likely prospect of a maximum sentence.

standing patterer *n.* [mid-19C] a man who takes 'a stand on the curb of a public thoroughfare, and deliver[s] prepared speeches to effect a sale of any articles [he has] to vend' (Hotten, 1859). [SE *stand* + PATTERER n. (1)]

standing room for one *n.* [19C] the vagina; thus *give standing room for one*, of a woman, to have sexual intercourse. [pun on SE/STAND v.[1]]

standings *n.* [1930s–40s] (*Irish*) a second-hand clothes stall. [? the stallholder *stands* behind it]

standing ware *n.* [early 18C–19C] the erect penis. [STAND v.[1] + SE *ware*, goods]

stand jiggers *v.* (*also* hold jiggers) [1950s–70s] (*US prison*) to keep a lookout. [SE *stand* + JIGGER! excl.[2]]

stand Moses *v.* **1** [17C–early 19C] to have another man's illegitimate child fathered upon one's wife; one is obliged by the parish to maintain it. **2** [mid-19C] (*US*) to act as a surrogate father and, for money, to impregnate another man's wife. **3** [mid-19C–1930s] to adopt a child. [biblical myth]

stand-off *n.* **1** [mid-19C+] a deadlock, a stalemate. **2** [late 19C–1900s] (*US*) an extension of credit, a postponement of payment. **3** [late 19C–1910s] aloofness. [STAND OFF v.]

stand-off *adj.* [late 19C–1920s] (*Aus./Irish*) haughty, unfriendly. [abbr. SE *standoffish*]

stand off *v.* **1** [late 19C–1900s] to put off, to evade (a creditor, a questioner). **2** [late 19C+] (*US*) to keep at a distance, to repel, to hold at bay. **3** [1910s–20s] to gain or extend credit.

stand-on *n.* **1** [1900s] (*US*) a leg. **2** [1940s+] an erection. [(1) SE; (2) STAND n.[2] (1) on model of HARD-ON n. (1)]

stand on *v.* **1** [late 19C] to wager on. **2** [late 19C+] to trust, to rely on.

stand one down *v.* [1920s+] (*Aus.*) to cost. [ext. STAND v.[3] (1)]

stand one's corner *v.* [late 19C+] to take or pay for one's share of anything, to do one's share. [ext. STAND v.[3] (2)]

stand one's hand *v.* [late 19C–1950s] (*Aus.*) to treat the assembled company. [ext. STAND v.[3] (2)]

stand on me! *excl.* [1950s+] believe me!

stand on one's hind leg *v. see* GET ON ONE'S HIND LEGS v.

stand on one's joint *v.* [1940s] (*US*) to have an erect penis. [SE *stand*/STAND v.[1] + JOINT n.[1]]

stand on one's (own) bottom *v.* (*also* stand on one's (own) pantofles) [16C–18C] to act in an independent manner. [later use SE; SE *stand* + BOTTOM n.[1] (2)/SE *pantofles*, high-corked shoes]

stand on velvet *v.* [mid-19C–1920s] to be in a financially advantageous position, esp. following successful gambling.

stand-out *n.*[1] [1920s+] (*US/Can.*) one who distinguishes themselves from a crowd.

stand-out *n.*[2] *see* STICK-OUT n. (1).

stand-out *adj.* [1930s+] (*orig. US*) conspicuous, better than average. [STAND-OUT n.[1]]

stand out like... *v.* [20C+] used in various combs. meaning to be very obvious, very large, e.g. *stand out like chapel hatpegs* (usu. of erect nipples), *...cod's ballocks*, *...dog's ballocks*, *...a sore thumb*, (*Can.*) *...a shit-house in the fog*.

stand-over *n.*[1] [1900s] (*Aus.*) a shoe. [one 'stands over' the sole]

stand-over *n.*[2] [1930s+] (*Aus.*) **1** a threat, an act of intimidation.

2 one who engages in intimidatory actions or words. [STAND OVER v.]

stand over v. (1930s+) (Aus./N.Z.) to intimidate, spec. to demand money with menaces. [the menacing position the demander adopts]

stand-over man n. (also **stand-over merchant**) [1930s+] (Aus.) a bully, esp. one who demands money with menaces. [STAND OVER v. + SE man/MERCHANT n.]

stand pad v. (also **sit pad**) [mid-19C–1900s] to beg at the roadside, usu. with a small piece of paper attached to one's jacket, declaring 'I am hungry'; also displaying deformities or handicaps. [SE stand + PAD n.[1] (1)]

stand pat v. (also **sit pat, stand peter**) [late 19C+] to stay as one is, to refuse to move, to refuse to speak or betray someone. [poker jargon]

stand patter v. see STAND (THE) PATTER v.

stand point v. [1960s+] (Can. prison) to be on the alert. [milit. point, the lead man of a patrol]

stand Sam v. [early 19C] to be likened to. [? the commonness of the name Sam]

stand sam v. (also **stand sammy**) **1** [19C] to buy a drink or round of drinks. **2** [mid-19C–1900s] (orig. US) to pay for, to pick up a bill. [? generic use of proper name Sam(uel); US icon Uncle Sam, and the letters 'US' stencilled on US Army knapsacks; he 'pays for all']

stand shot v. see STAND (THE) SHOT (TO) v.

stand slang v. [mid-18C] (UK Und.) of a pickpocket team, for a member to stand at a distance from the actual theft, ready to receive what has been stolen and run off with it. [SE stand + SLANG n.[1] (2)]

stand someone on their ear v. (also **stand someone on their head**) [20C+] (US) to knock down, to defeat.

stand squire v. [late 18C–early 19C] to treat the company. [STAND v.[3] (2) + SE squire]

stand still for v. (also **hold still for**) [1950s+] to tolerate, to permit, to accept.

stand the acid v. [late 19C–1910s] (US) to stand up under pressure, to maintain one's composure. [STAND v.[2] + SE acid]

stand the bears v. [early 18C] to suffer. [STAND v.[2] + ? SE bear, the animal or ? SE bear, to endure]

stand the gaff v. [late 19C+] (US) **1** to receive severe treatment, criticism etc. **2** to suffer interrogation, beatings or any adverse conditions. **3** to sustain a situation, good or bad. [STAND v.[2] + GAFF n.[2]]

stand the gag v. [late 18C] to cry out. [? earlier use of GAG n. (3)]

stand the grin v. [early 19C] to suffer ridicule. [STAND v.[2] + SE grin]

stand the huff v. [late 18C–early 19C] to take responsibility for the bill in the public house. [STAND v.[3] (2) + SE huff/HUFF v.[1] (1); the image is of the boastfulness that can underpin the gesture]

stand the nonsense v. see STAND THE RACKET v. (1).

stand (the) patter v. [late 18C–early 19C] (UK Und.) to be tried in a court. [STAND v.[2] + PATTER n. (1)]

stand the push v. (also **do the push**) [late 19C] of a woman, to have sexual intercourse (cf. CATCH AN OYSTER v.). [STAND v.[2]/ SE do + PUSH n.[1]]

stand the racket v. **1** [late 18C–1930s] (also **stand the non-sense**) to pay the bill, to treat one's companions. **2** [early 19C–1910s] to take the blame for the crimes of one's confederates. **3** [mid-19C–1940s] to put up with a situation; to overcome a challenge. [(1) STAND v.[3] (2); (2) and (3) STAND v.[2] + RACKET n.[1]; (3) in a non-criminal use]

stand the rap v. [1920s–30s] (US Und.) to take the blame, sometimes on behalf of another; to face criminal charges. [var. TAKE THE RAP v. (1)]

stand there like a tit in a trance v. [20C+] to be lost in thought, to be completely abstracted. [SE stand + TIT n.[4] + SE trance]

stand there with one's bare face hanging out v. [20C+] (US) to speak openly, candidly, brazenly.

stand (the) shot (to) v. [19C] to pay the bill for everyone else. [STAND v.[3] (2) + SHOT n.[1]]

stand to (attention) n. [20C+] a pension. [rhy. sl.]

stand to attention v. [1990s+] to have an erection. [STAND v.[1] + pun on SE]

stand to one's lick-log(, salt or no salt) v. see STAND (UP) ONE'S LICK LOG(, SALT OR NO SALT) v.

stand to pan-pudding v. [late 17C–early 18C] to stand one's ground, in lit. or fig. use. [SE stand + pan-pudding, a heavy pudding made of flour, with small pieces of bacon in it, baked in a pan]

stand-up n.[1] **1** [mid-19C] a dance. **2** [mid-19C] a seatless carriage used on the early railways. **3** [late 19C] a snack taken standing up, the snack bar where this takes place. **4** [late 19C+] sexual intercourse when both partners are standing up.

stand-up n.[2] [1900s–40s] (US) a police identification parade.

stand-up n.[3] [1930s+] (orig. US) the act of 'standing someone up', i.e. breaking an appointment; thus give the stand-up, to miss a scheduled meeting, esp. to break a date. [STAND UP v.[2] (1)]

stand-up n.[4] [1990s+] (US prison) a loyal, dependable friend. [STAND-UP adj.]

stand-up adj. [1940s+] (US Und.) honest, trustworthy, dependable. [STAND UP AND BE COUNTED v.]

stand up v.[1] [20C+] to have sexual intercourse when both partners are standing.

stand up v.[2] **1** [20C+] (orig. US) to fail to keep an appointment with someone. **2** [1930s–40s] (US Black) to treat someone as second-rate, unimportant. **3** [1940s] to keep someone waiting. [i.e. one 'leaves them standing']

stand up v.[3] **1** [20C+] of a situation, a statement, to withstand criticism, to 'hold water'. **2** [1920s+] (orig. US) to withstand pressure, esp. police questioning or criminal intimidation. **3** [1910s] (US) to hold out for, to exert pressure on. [SE stand up to]

stand up v.[4] [1970s] (orig. US) to confess. [SE stand up for]

stand up and be counted v. [20C+] (orig. US) to make one's presence felt, to join in a group action or decision, esp. at a certain risk to oneself.

stand up drinks v. [20C+] (Aus.) to set out drinks.

stand-up guy n. (also **stand-by guy, stand-up dude**) [1920s+] (US) an honest, dependable person, one who 'stands up to be counted'. [STAND-UP adj. + GUY n.[2] (1)/DUDE n. (1)]

stand upon one's pantables v. (also **stand upon one's pantacles, …pantap, …pantaphels, …pantofles**) [late 16C–mid-18C] to stand upon ceremony, to act in a dignified manner. [SE stand upon + pantofle (ult. Fr. pantoufle), a slipper, esp. one with a high heel and a built-up sole to make the wearer appear taller and more imposing]

stand-up supper n. [late 19C] (UK society) anything mean or parsimonious. [SE stand-up supper, a late supper at which those invited ate while on their feet; such a supper was, de facto, less grand (and less expensive to cater for) than a full-scale sit-down meal]

stand (up) to one's lick-log(, salt or no salt) v. [mid-19C+] (US) to stand by one's decision come what may; thus come to the lick-log, to face up to a tough decision. [SE stand up + SAmE lick-log, a notched log (occas. a wooden trough) used to hold salt for livestock]

stand up to the rack v. see COME UP TO THE RACK (OR JUMP THE FENCE) v.

stand up with v. **1** [early 19C] to dance with. **2** [mid-19C–1900s] to act as a bridesmaid or male attendant to the groom.

'Stang n. [1990s+] (US) a Ford Mustang automobile.

stangey n.[1] (also **stangy**) [late 18C–mid-19C] a tailor. [SE stang, a sting or prick, i.e. the needle]

stangey *n.*[2] (*also* **stangy**) [mid-19C] a man who is dominated by his wife. [phr. *ride the stang*, 'to be mounted astride of a pole borne on the shoulders of two men, and carried through the streets for the derision of the spectators' (*OED*). This custom, however, once popular in Scot. and the north, focused on unpopular, rather than spec. wife-dominated people, but the implication is that he has to ride a pole, since he cannot 'ride' his wife]

stank *n.* [1960s+] **1** (*US Black*) the anus. **2** (*US Black*) (*also* **stank-stank**) the vagina. **3** (*US campus*) an ugly woman. **4** (*US Black*) the smell of sex. **5** (*US campus*) any form of unpleasant smell. [SE *stink*]

stank *adj. see* STANKY *adj.*

stank ho *n.* (*also* **stank bitch**) [1970s+] (*US Black/campus*) an ugly woman, with suggestions of promiscuity. [STANKY *adj.* (1) + HO *n.*[1] (1)]

stank-stank *n. see* STANK *n.* (2).

stanky *adj.* (*also* **stank, stanking**) (*orig. US, mainly Black*) **1** [1960s+] smelly, dirty, unattractive, foul-smelling. **2** [1990s+] in fig. use, a general negative; useless, disgusting etc. [STANK *n.*]

Stanley facial *n.* [2000s] slashing the face with a Stanley knife.

Stanley knife *n.* [1990s+] one's wife. [rhy. sl.]

staph *n.* [1930s+] *staph*ylococcus, a genus of disease-inducing bacteria. [abbr.]

stapled down *adj.* [2000s] (*US Black*) of a man, dominated by one's female partner.

stap me! *excl.* [20C+] an oath orig. popular among upper-class dandies. [despite earlier STAP MY VITALS! *excl.*, based on a mispron., more likely SE *stab*]

stap my vitals! *excl.* (*also* **stap my breath! stop my vitals!**) [late 17C+] an oath popular among upper-class dandies. [SE *stop* + *vitals*; the first printed use appears in the play *The Relapse, or, Virtue in Danger* (1696) by John Vanbrugh; it is spoken by Lord Foppington, among whose affectations is the consistent pron. of 'o' as 'a']

Star, the *n.* [mid-19C] the Star and Garter public house, in Richmond, south of London.

star *n.*[1] [mid-18C] (*UK Und.*) a ring. [like a SE *star* it gives off light]

star *n.*[2] **1** [19C] a conspicuous member of society, who shines out among their peers. **2** [mid-19C] one who is exceptional within their own world. **3** [mid-19C] (*US*) a police officer, esp. in New York. **4** [1950s+] (*US Black*) a man's favourite woman, a very attractive woman. **5** [1960s+] the most favoured or successful prostitute in a pimp's string of girls. **6** [1970s] (*US Black*) a top-level pimp (cf. BOSS PLAYER *n.*). **7** [1980s+] (*W.I./UK Black*) (*also* **star-boy, star-bwai**) an attractive, sophisticated, articulate, brave, well-dressed man; esp. as ext. to a leading gangster. **8** [1980s+] (*UK Black*) a term of address between Black people, esp. friends. **9** [1990s+] a very unpleasant person, e.g. *what a fucking star!* [the theatrical/film/sports/rock music use of *star*, while obviously linked, has been SE since its early 19C coinage]

star *n.*[3] (*also* **star man**) [late 19C+] (*UK prison*) a first offender. [abbr. prison jargon *star prisoner*; a star is affixed to their name in the prison records]

star *n.*[4] [1980s+] (*W.I./UK Black teen*) **1** a term of respect, synon. with SE *sir.* **2** a general term of address, synon. with MAN *n.*[1] (1), e.g. *Wha' apen star?* What's up man?

star, the *n.* [early 19C] (*UK Und.*) the practice of cutting a hole in a shop's window, then extracting such items as can be reached. [STAR THE GLAZE *v.* (1)]

star *adv.* [1990s+] (*UK Black*) proudly, e.g. *walk star.* [SE *star*]

star boarder *n.* [1930s] (*US Und.*) the best-performing prostitute in a brothel.

starbolic (naked) *adj. see* STARK BALLOCK NAKED *adj.*

star-boy/-bwai *n. see* STAR *n.*[2] (7).

starch *n.* **1** [mid-19C+] courage, well being. **2** [late 19C+] semen (cf. BABY GRAVY *n.*). **3** [1900s] (*US*) face powder.

starch *v.* [mid-19C–1910s] (*UK Und.*) to smarten oneself up.

starcher *n.* [late 19C–1900s] a starched cravat; a stiff white tie.

starchy *adj.* **1** [mid-19C] of clothes, showy, fashionable. **2** [mid-19C+] drunk. **3** [mid-19C+] stiff, unbending, reserved, lacking in social warmth.

stardust *n.* (*drugs*) **1** [1950s+] cocaine (cf. BIRDIE POWDER *n.*). **2** [1980s] phencyclidine (cf. ACE *n.*[4]). [ext. of DUST *n.*[5] (2)/DUST *n.*[5] (5), underpinned in (1) by the popularity of cocaine among rock and film stars]

stare-cat *n.* [mid-19C+] (*orig. US*) an inquisitive neighbour, usu. a woman. [SE *stare* + CAT *n.*[1] (2)]

stare like a dead pig *v.* (*also* **stare like a stuck pig**) [late 17C–early 18C] to gape, to stare at fixedly.

starfish *n. see* BROWN STAR *n.*

star-fucker *n.* [1960s+] a sycophant, a hanger-on, esp. of celebrities. [SE *star* + FUCKER *n.* (1)]

star-fucking *n.* [1960s+] **1** acting as a toady, a parasite. **2** living as a GROUPIE *n.*[2] (1). [STAR-FUCKER *n.*]

star-gazer *n.* **1** [17C–18C] the erect penis. **2** [mid-17C–early 19C] a horse that persistently throws its head up. **3** [late 18C–mid-19C] a country prostitute who plies her trade in the open air or under hedges.

star-gazing *n.* [1900s] unconscious.

star-glazer *n.* [mid-19C] (*UK Und.*) one who cuts the panes out of shop-windows.

star-glazing *n.* [mid-late 19C] smashing and removing a pane of glass in order to steal items from a shop display or to break into a house. [the star-shaped hole in the glass + play on SE *star-gazing*]

star hotel *n.* (*also* **starlight boarding house/hotel**) [1930s–50s] the open air; esp. in phr. *sleep/doss in the star hotel*, to sleep in the open air.

stariben *n. see* STURRABIN *n.*

staring quarter *n.* [late 18C–early 19C] an ox-cheek. [note dial. *staring-quarter*, a laughing-stock]

stark *adj. see* STARK STARING BONKERS *adj.*

stark ballock naked *adj.* (*also* **starbolic, starbolic naked, stark bollock naked, stark bollux naked, starko-bollocko, stark rollock naked**) [late 19C+] absolutely naked. [SE *stark* + BALLOCK NAKED *adj.*]

starkers *adj.*[1] (*also* **starko**) [1910s+] nude. [SE *stark naked* + -ER sfx/-O sfx (3)]

starkers *adj.*[2] *see* STARK STARING BONKERS *adj.*

stark-naked *n.* [early–mid-19C] neat, undiluted gin. [the neat alcohol comes without 'clothing' + the poverty that results from excessive consumption]

stark-naked *adj.* [mid-late 19C] unadulterated, esp. of drinks. [STARK-NAKED *n.*]

starko *adj. see* STARKERS *adj.*[1].

starko-bollocko/stark rollock naked *adj. see* STARK BALLOCK NAKED *adj.*

stark staring bonkers *adj.* (*also* **stark, starkers, stark raving bats, stark raving bonkers, stark staring (crackers/dippy)**) [1910s+] absolutely crazy. [ext. of BONKERS *adj.*]

star lay *n.* [early 19C] robbery by breaking shop or house windows. [STAR, THE *n.* + LAY *n.*[4] (1)]

starlight boarding house/hotel *n. see* STAR HOTEL *n.*

star man *n. see* STAR *n.*[3].

starn *n.* [late 19C+] the buttocks. [SE *stern*]

star of the line *n.* [1960s+] (*US Black*) a pimp's favourite prostitute. [STAR *n.*[2] (5) + LINE *n.*[2] (3)]

star-pitch *n.* [late 19C] (*UK/US tramp*) sleeping in the open air.

starps *n.* [mid-19C] sprats. [backsl.]

starrer *n. see* ANGLER *n.* (1).

stars and stripes *n.*[1] [late 19C] Bostonians, esp. the more puritanically religious of them. [their trad. Sunday meal of STARS AND STRIPES *n.*[2]]

stars and stripes *n.*[2] [late 19C–1950s] (*US*) a dish of pork (belly) and baked beans; frankfurters and baked beans. [the baked beans resemble stars and the pork belly resembles stripes]

stars for studs *n.* [1970s+] (*US campus*) a course in basic astronomy. [SE *star* + STUD *n.*[1] (1)]

Starsky and Hutch *n.* [1980s+] the crotch. [rhy. sl.; ult. popular US 1970s TV detective series *Starsky and Hutch*]

Star's Nap *n.* [1990s+] a loan; the act of borrowing. [rhy. sl. = TAP *n.*[2] (2)]

Start, the *n.* **1** [mid-18C–19C] (*UK Und.*) (*also* **Stait, the**) London; also attrib., pertaining to or from London. **2** [mid-18C–early 19C] a prison, esp. Newgate (cf. ABBOTT'S PRIORY *n.*). **3** [mid-19C] the Old Bailey. [? SE *start*, a shock, a surprise; thus the effect of entering prison + a new *start* to one's life, whether good or bad; (1) because London is the starting point for a tramp's journeying round Britain; (2) ? Newgate as the start of one's journey along Holborn towards Tyburn]

start *n.*[1] [mid-19C–1900s] an odd circumstance, a surprise; often as *rum* or *rummy start*. [SE *start*, a shock]

start *n.*[2] **1** [late 19C+] (*Aus.*) a job. **2** [1970s+] (*S.Afr.*) money. [? a lit. or fig. SE *start* on a project or activity]

start *v.* [20C+] to commence complaining, nagging, being a nuisance etc; usu. in phr. *now, don't you start*. [SE *start*, to begin; *nagging* etc are assumed]

start a fowl-roost *v.* [20C+] (*Aus.*) to take on a 'double-barrelled' surname. [ety. unknown]

start a jolly *v.* [late 19C] to start the applause, for a performer or turn, at a music hall or theatre. [SE *start* + JOLLY *n.*[4] (2)]

starter *n.*[1] [late 17C–18C] (*UK Und.*) a question. [SE *start*, to jump in surprise; a question, esp. as to one's clandestine activities, may cause one to do this]

starter *n.*[2] [late 17C–early 19C] **1** a restless person, one who leaves a convivial company. **2** one who cannot stay in the same job for any length of time. [SE *start*, to jump in surprise]

starter *n.*[3] [late 19C–1920s] a laxative. [it starts one's stomach working]

starter *n.*[4] **1** [1940s–50s] (*Aus.*) one who makes a brave attempt. **2** [1960s+] (*N.Z.*) one who is keen to initiate a new activity. [SE *start*, to begin]

starter *n.*[5] [1980s+] (*Aus. prison*) any form of lubricant used to facilitate anal intercourse.

starters *n.* [1960s+] initial actions, plans etc.

star the glaze *v.* **1** [late 18C–mid-19C] (*UK Und.*) to break shop windows for the purpose of theft. **2** [mid-19C] (*UK Und.*) to break any window. **3** [mid-19C] (*US*) to vandalize plate glass by scratching it with a glazier's diamond. [SE *star*, to make a star-shaped crack or hole + GLAZE *n.* (1)]

start on *v.* (*also* **start in on, ...up on**) (*orig. US*) **1** [late 19C+] to nag, to assail verbally; to criticize. **2** [20C+] to attack physically. **3** [1960s–70s] to seduce, to have sexual intercourse with.

start one's stumps *v. see* STIR ONE'S STUMPS *v.*

start shit *v.* [1950s+] (*US Black*) to initiate trouble, to start an argument. [SE *start* + SHIT *n.*[3]]

start up on *v. see* START ON *v.*

starvation *adv.* [late 19C+] a negative intensifier, excessively, extremely; lit. 'productive of starvation', e.g. *starvation cruel*, very cruel.

starver *n.* [1900s–50s] (*Aus.*) **1** a roll. **2** a saveloy. [a large sausage, it fills the stomach of a starving person]

starve the...! *excl.* [1910s+] (*Aus.*) in combs., a general excl.; combs. include *starve the bardies! ...crows! ...lizards! ...mopokes! ...ninnies! ...rats! ...roan bullocks!* [SE *starve* (+ *bardy*, an edible Aus. wood-boring grub (*Bardistus cibarius*) or its larva)]

stash *n.*[1] [20C+] (*W.I., Guyn.*) a woman who dresses flashily; thus as *v.*, to dress showily. [? SE *ostentatious*]

stash *n.*[2] **1** [1910s+] any form of cache. **2** [1920s] (*US*) money. **3** [1920s+] (*orig. US*) (*also* **stach**) a hiding place. **4** [1930s+] (*drugs*) (*also* **sach, stasch**) a hiding place for drugs. **5** [1930s+] (*drugs*) a cache of any drug, esp. cannabis. **6** [1940s+] a place (to stay). [STASH *v.*[1] (2)]

stash *n.*[3] (*also* **stache**) [1940s+] (*US*) a mou*stache*. [abbr.]

stash *v.*[1] (*also* **stach, stache**) **1** [late 18C–1910s] (*UK Und.*) to stop, to refrain, to give up; esp. in excl. *stash it!* stop that! *stash the glim*, douse the light. **2** [late 18C+] to hide, esp., since 1930s, drugs. **3** [1930s–40s] (*US Black*) to go to sleep. **4** [1930s+] to place, whether clandestinely or in view. [18C Und. *stash*, put a stop to + influences f. SE *stop, stow, squash* + Fr. *cacher*, to hide; orig. cant, the term was dormant during the 19C but has been revived, mainly among drug users, since mid-20C]

stash *v.*[2] **1** [late 19C] to leave. **2** [1940s–80s] (*US Black*) to stand around, to stay. **3** [1970s] (*US*) to walk in, to enter; to visit, to arrive at.

stash catcher *n.* (*also* **catcher**) [1980s+] (*drugs*) one who stands outside a window to catch drugs that are thrown out during a police raid. [STASH *n.*[2] (5) + SE *catcher*]

stashed *adj.* **1** [1920s+] hidden. **2** [1930s–40s] (*US Black*) to stand; to remain. [(1) STASH *v.*[1] (2); (2) STASH *v.*[2] (2)]

stash-house *n.* [1990s+] (*US drugs*) a place where a drug dealer can store a cache of drugs. [STASH *n.*[2] (4) + SE *house*]

stashie *adj.* (*also* **stashied up, stashy**) [20C+] (*W.I./Irish*) smartly or showily dressed. [STASH *n.*[1]]

stash it *v.* **1** [early 19C–1920s] to give up one's bad habits. **2** [mid–late 19C] (*US*) to stop doing something; also as imper. [fig. use of STASH *v.*[1] (1)]

stash pad *n.* [1980s+] (*drugs*) a room, apartment or house where drugs are stored. [STASH *n.*[2] (4) + PAD *n.*[2] (2)]

stash up *v.* [1900s] to stop doing something instantly, abruptly. [fig. use of STASH IT *v.* (2)]

stashy *adj. see* STASHIE *adj.*

stat *n.* **1** [1940s+] usu. in pl., a *stat*istic, *stat*istics. **2** [1960s+] a photo*stat*, a Xerox copy. [abbr.]

statch *n.* [1950s+] statutory rape. [abbr./mispron. of SE]

state *n.* **1** [mid-19C+] a condition of emotional distress or mental agitation. **2** [late 19C+] an unkempt, dirty condition of dress or cleanliness. **3** [1980s] a state of drunkenness.

state college *n.* [1940s] (*US prison/Und.*) a state prison; thus *state grad*, a former prisoner (cf. BIG SCHOOL *n.*). [SE *state* + COLLEGE *n.* (3)]

state con *n.* (*also* **state man**) [mid-19C; 1990s+] (*US Und.*) a prisoner who is seen as overly friendly with the authorities. [SE *state* + CON *n.*[1] (8)/SE *man*, i.e. on the side of the state authorities]

state house *n.* [1900s] (*US Und.*) a public lavatory (cf. BACKHOUSE *n.*).

state-o *n.* [1950s+] (*US prison*) **1** a prisoner's official prison clothing. **2** anything to do with prison.

state of you *phr.* [1980s+] a phr. used to express disgust or disbelief at the way somebody is behaving, or at something they have said. [STATE *n.* (2)]

state-raised *adj.* [1970s+] (*US*) used of one who has been brought up in institutions.

Stateside *n.* [1940s+] (*US*) the USA, as opposed to foreign countries; also attrib., of or pertaining to the USA.

state tea *n.* [late 19C] (*UK society*) a grand tea party at which the full range of one's best tea service, cutlery and the like can be put on display. [SE *state occasion*, when the nation's finest – be it soldiers or plate – is put on display]

static *n.* [1920s+] (*orig. US*) difficulties, aggravation, impudent or argumentative talk. [SE *static*, atmospherics, radio noise]

static! *excl.* [1980s+] a cry of warning, e.g. from a street dealer's lookout at the approach of the police. [STATIC *n.*]

Statie *n.* [1940s+] (*US Und.*) a *State* policeman.

station-jack *n.* [mid-19C] (*Aus.*) a boiled meat pudding, usu. cooked in the bush or at a sheep station. [ety. unknown]

statue act *n.* [1950s] (*US Black*) standing still.

stavin chain *n.* [1900s–20s] (*US Black*) a ladies' man, a wanderer. [the mythical hero of the ballad 'Wining Boy Blues' by Jellyroll Morton (1890–1941), Stavin Chain's prowess was sexual]

staving *adj.* [mid-19C–1910s] big, excessive; hence *staver*, someone or something exceptional. [SE *stave*, to go with a rush or dash]

staving *adv.* [mid-19C–1900s] (*US*) very, excessively. [SE *stave*, to go with a rush or dash]

stay *n.* [early 19C] a cuckold. [? SE *stays*, which the errant wife might also discard for the pleasures of sex]

stay and be hanged! *excl.* [late 19C] a general excl. of resigned exasperation, oh all right! see if I care! do what you want!

stay cool *v. see* KEEP COOL *v.*

stay down *v.* [1990s+] (*US prison*) to maintain one's role as a professional criminal or gangster.

stay down low *v.* [1970s+] (*US Black*) to remain inconspicuous, to behave normally.

stay-home sauce *n.* (*also* **stay-home soup/tea**) [20C+] (*W.I.*) food that supposedly contains 'magic' ingredients that will influence a man to choose a particular woman.

stay loose *v.* (*orig. US*) **1** [1950s+] to relax, to remain calm (cf. HANG LOOSE *v.*). **2** [1980s] to keep an open mind. [SE *stay* + LOOSE *adj.*[1] (2)]

stay loose *phr.* [1970s+] goodbye, esp. in communities influenced by California's post-HIPPIE *n.*[2] (3) era 'new therapies'. [STAY LOOSE *v.*]

stay on someone's case *v.* [1960s+] to attack, to harass continually and consistently. [SE *stay* + ON SOMEONE'S CASE *phr.*]

stay put *v.* [mid-19C+] (*orig. US*) to remain, to stay where one is, to keep steady.

staytape *n.* [late 18C–early 19C] a tailor. [SE *staytape*, material used for binding the edges of fabric]

stay up *phr.* [1990s+] (*US teen*) goodbye, see you later.

stay with *v.*[1] **1** [late 19C] (*US*) to court. **2** [1930s+] to have sexual intercourse (cf. ARRIVE AT THE END OF THE SENTIMENTAL JOURNEY *v.*). [euph.]

stay with *v.*[2] **1** [late 19C] (*US*) of food, to assuage or satisfy one's hunger. **2** [late 19C+] to keep up with, to persist in an endeavour. [SE *stay*, to last]

steady (company) *n.* [late 19C+] (*orig. US*) a regular girl- or boyfriend.

steady lapper *n.* [1910s] (*Aus.*) an inveterate drunkard.

steady on the case *phr.* [1950s–60s] (*US Black*) persistent, unremitting.

steak *n.* [1970s–80s] (*UK Black*) a young woman, usu. attractive. [var. on BEEF *n.*[1] (6)]

steaka-da-oyst *n. see* STEAKDAHOYST *n.*

steak and ale *n. see* GINGER ALE *n.* (2).

steak and bull's eyes *n.* [1930s] steak-and-kidney pudding.

steak and kidney *n.* **1** [20C+] the proper name Sidney. **2** [1940s+] (*Aus.*) Sydney. [rhy. sl.]

steakdahoyst *n.* (*also* **steaka-da-oyst**) [1910s–20s] (*Aus.*) an Italian restaurant specializing in *steak* and *oysters*. [the 'Italian' pron.]

steak drapes *n.* [1990s+] the labia majora (cf. BACON STRIPS *n.*; BEEF CURTAINS *n.*).

steal *n.* **1** [late 19C–1950s] an act of theft. **2** [1930s+] (*orig. US*) a bargain; esp. in phr. *it's a steal*, often with a sum of money, e.g. *it's a steal at £5*.

steal *v.* [1980s+] (*US prison*) to attack without warning. [SE *steal up on*]

steal a shive off a cut loaf *v.* [late 16C–early 17C] of a man, to have adulterous intercourse with a married woman. [SE *steal* + *shive*, a slice of bread]

steal blind *v.* [1920s+] (*US*) to rob or cheat to an extreme extent. [SE *steal* + BLIND *adv.*[1]]

stealers *n.* (*also* **ten stealers**) [mid-17C; 1940s] the fingers. [1940s use is US Black]

stealth *n.* [1990s+] (*US Black*) self-possession; character.

stealth *adj.* [1990s+] (*US campus*) underhand, deceitful.

steam *n.*[1] **1** [late 19C–1970s] (*US Black*) beer, wine; a glass of beer. **2** [1930s+] (*Aus./N.Z.*) cheap wine, esp. if laced with methylated spirits, methylated spirits drunk by itself. **3** [1970s] (*drugs*) phencyclidine (cf. ACE *n.*[4]). [it 'gets one's steam up'; but note late 19C US proprietary *steam beer* (*pump*)]

steam *n.*[2] [1970s] (*US*) **1** problems, difficulties, trouble. **2** blame, sarcasm, intense criticism.

steam *adj.* [1970s+] old-fashioned. [the obs. railway *steam* engines, long displaced by diesel]

steam *v.*[1] **1** [mid-19C; 1910s+] (*orig. US*) to be annoyed, to be angry, to talk aggressively. **2** [mid-19C; 1990s+] (*also* **get someone's steam up**) to annoy, to infuriate. **3** [1960s] to make someone amorous.

steam *v.*[2] (*also* **steam ahead/away**) **1** [mid-19C+] to work vigorously, to make great progress. **2** [1940s+] to go fast in a vehicle.

steam *v.*[3] *see* STEAM IN *v.* (2).

steam-and-cream *n.* [1970s] (*US*) a brothel, masquerading/doubling as a sauna. [SE *steam*, i.e. of the sauna + CREAM *v.*[1] (1)]

steamboat *v.* [1960s] (*drugs*) 'to inhale the butt of a marijuana cigarette stuck in a hole in a toilet roll, the hand enclosing one end, the mouth on the other end' (Lingeman, *Drugs from A to Z*, 1969).

steamboated *adj.* (*also* **steamboats**) [1990s+] very drunk. [? STEAMED (UP) *adj.* (2)]

steam daddy *n.* (*also* **steam queen**) [1970s] (*US gay*) 'a middle-aged homosexual spending most of his time in the cloudy steam-room of a bath' (Rodgers, *The Queen's Vernacular*, 1972). [SE *steam* + DADDY *n.* (8)/QUEEN *n.*[2] (1)]

steamed (up) *adj.* **1** [1920s+] tense, annoyed. **2** [1920s+] fighting drunk. **3** [1920s+] excited. **4** [1930s+] sexually excited. **5** [1950s] (*US drugs*) under the effects of narcotics.

steam-engine *n.* [1930s] (*US prison*) a potato pie, a cooked potato. [? the steam that emanates from the hot dish]

steamer *n.*[1] **1** [early 19C] a tobacco pipe. **2** [1950s+] (*W.I.*) a form of hookah or water-pipe used for smoking marijuana. **3** [1990s+] a cigarette. **4** [2000s] a piece of excrement. [the smoke or SE *steam* produced]

steamer *n.*[2] [1930s] (*US*) an attractive woman.

steamer *n.*[3] **1** [1930s+] a fool, a gullible person (cf. BEECHAM'S PILL *n.*). **2** [1970s+] (*US gay*) the client of a male prostitute. [rhy. sl.; SE *steam tug* = MUG *n.*[2] (1)]

steamer *n.*[4] [1960s+] a male homosexual who prefers passive partners. [? STEAM IN *v.*]

steam in *v.* **1** [1940s+] (*also* **steam up**) to arrive in an energetic manner. **2** [1960s+] (*also* **steam, steam into**) to attack; to commit oneself completely, esp. in a fight.

steaming *n.*[1] [late 19C] any form of steamed pudding.

steaming *n.*[2] [1980s+] the act of mugging, esp. when performed *en masse* against a 'captive audience' by a gang on a bus or, more likely, an underground train. [? STEAM IN *v.* (2)]

steaming *adj.*[1] [1950s+] a general intensifier with euph. overtones, since usu. in negative use, e.g. *steaming prawn*, a complete fool.

steaming *adj.*[2] [1960s+] drunk. [STEAM *n.*[1]]

steam into *v.*[1] [2000s] to approach, e.g. sexually.

steam into *v.*[2] *see* STEAM IN *v.* (2).

steam-packet *n.* [mid-late 19C] a jacket. [rhy. sl.]

steam queen *n. see* STEAM DADDY *n.*

steamroll *v.* [1920s] (*US Black*) to commit adultery, to deceive a lover.

steamroller *n.* [20C+] a bowler hat. [rhy. sl.]

steam tug *n.* **1** [1930s+] a fool, a gullible person (cf. BEECHAM'S PILL *n.*). **2** [1930s+] a bug. **3** [2000s] (*Aus.*) a prize-fighter. [rhy. sl.; (1) = MUG *n.*[2] (1); (3) = PUG *n.*[5] (1)]

steam up v.[1] [1910s+] to stimulate emotionally, to arouse.

steam up v.[2] *see* STEAM IN v. (1).

steamy adj. **1** [1910s] angry. **2** [1960s] sweaty. **3** [1960s+] (orig. US) sexually arousing, erotic, salacious. **4** [1970s+] (US gay) sexually excited. [euph.]

steeazick n. [1940s] (US drugs) a cannabis cigarette. [STICK n.[9] (3) + -IZ- ifx]

steed n. [1970s] a sexual expert. [SE steed, a horse, although he does the 'riding']

Steel, the n. **1** [19C] Coldbath Fields prison (cf. ABBOTT'S PRIORY n.). **2** [early 19C–1950s] a prison. **3** [mid-19C] a treadmill. [abbr. BASTILLE n.]

steel n.[1] **1** [late 19C+] (US Und.) a knife. **2** [20C+] (US Black) a gun. [metonymy]

steel n.[2] [1940s–50s] (US Black) Whiteness.

steel v. [20C+] (US) to stab. [STEEL n.[1] (1)]

steel and concrete cure n. *see* IRON CURE n.

steel balls n. *see* BRASS BALLS n.

steel bar n. [late 18C–early 19C] a needle.

steel bar flinger n. (also **steel bar driver**) [late 18C–early 19C] a tailor. [STEEL BAR n. + SE flinger/driver]

steel bottom n. (W.I.) **1** [1950s] an alcoholic cocktail that mixes gin and wine. **2** [1970s] a drink of white rum with a beer chaser. [? the need for a SE steel bottom in one's stomach to drink such a thing]

steele rudds n. [20C+] (Aus.) spuds, potatoes. [rhy. sl.; ult. author *Steele Rudd*, pseudonym of Arthur Hoey Davis (1868–1935)]

steel jockey n. [1940s] (Aus.) one who rides a train without paying. [SE steel, i.e. the railway + JOCKEY n.[3] (2)]

steel-nose n. [mid-17C] a form of strong drink. [? it gives one a red nose that 'glows' like molten steel]

steel-pen n. [late 19C] (US) a 'swallow-tail' or tail-coat, worn for formal evening wear. [the resemblance of the tail to a steel pen nib]

steen n. [1900s] (US) an indefinite or large amount of. [? on model of UMPTEEN n.]

steep adj. [mid-19C+] (orig. US) **1** over-priced, exorbitant, excessive, exaggerated. **2** extreme, beyond the limit.

steeples n. [1910s] (Aus.) steeplechasing.

steer n. **1** [late 19C+] (US) facts, a useful piece of information. **2** [1900s–40s] (US/UK Und.) someone who gives directions. **3** [1910s] (US) an inaccurate piece of information. [SE steer, to direct]

steer v. [late 19C+] (orig. US Und.) to decoy someone into a place, activity or situation. [backform. f. STEERER n. (1)]

steerer n. **1** [mid-19C+] (US Und.) that member of a confidence trick team who engages the prospective victim and lures him into the con. **2** [late 19C+] (US Und.) anyone, e.g. a cab driver, hotel doorman or similar figure, who points a searcher towards the variety of self-indulgence they seek, e.g. sex, drugs, gambling. **3** [1920s–40s] a crooked lawyer; an agent who supplies such a lawyer with clients. **4** [1950s] (US gay) a man who runs a string of homosexual male prostitutes. [SE steer]

steer joint n. [1930s+] (orig. US) a nightclub to which patrons are directed by a cab-driver, doorman etc, who is paid by the establishment. [SE steer + JOINT n.[4] (3)]

steer the ship v. [1980s] (Aus.) to buy a drink.

steeven n. [early–mid-19C] money. [STIVER n. (1); although here the coins are presumably far from worthless]

steever n.[1] [2000s] (Irish) a kick in the buttocks.

steever n.[2] *see* STIVER n.

steez n. [1990s+] (US Black) one's personal style.

Steffi Graf n. [1990s+] **1** a laugh. **2** a bath. [rhy. sl.; ult. Ger. tennis player *Steffi Graf* (b.1969)]

Steffi Graf v. [2000s] to laugh. [rhy. sl.; ult. *see* prev.]

steiver n. *see* STIVER n.

stella dallas n. [1930s–50s] (camp gay) a loser, an unfortunate. [film title *Stella Dallas* (1937), a celebrated tear-jerker starring Barbara Stanwyck]

stellar adj. [1980s+] excellent, wonderful, 'out of this world'.

stem n.[1] (also **the stem**) **1** [late 19C+] (US, orig. tramp) a street; usu. as MAIN STEM, THE n. **2** [1920s] the area where tramps beg. **3** [1920s–30s] (US tramp) an act of begging. **4** [1930s–50s] (US Black) the world of the street, as a generic.

stem n.[2] (drugs) **1** [1900s–50s] an opium pipe; thus *up against the stem*, smoking opium. **2** [1970s] in pl., marijuana stems, as unsmokeable debris. **3** [1980s+] a crack cocaine pipe (laboratory pipette); thus *on the stem*, smoking crack cocaine.

stem n.[3] [1910s–40s] (US Und.) a drill, used in safebreaking.

stem, the n. *see* STEM n.[1].

stem v.[1] (US) **1** [1920s] to grab, to get hold of. **2** [1920s–60s] to beg. [STEM n.[1] (3)]

stem v.[2] [1920s–40s] (US Und.) to drill a safe as part of breaking it open. [STEM n.[3]]

stemmer n. [1920s–60s] (US tramp) a tramp who begs on a main street. [STEM v.[1] (2)]

stemming n. [1920s–30s] (US) begging. [STEM v.[1] (2)]

stems n. [mid-19C+] the legs, esp. of an attractive woman.

stem-wheeler n. [20C+] (US) a homosexual man. [play on SE stem-wheeler, a truck powered from *behind*]

stem-winder n.[1] [late 19C+] (US) anything considered excellent, first-rate; thus *stem-winding*, persuasive, powerful. [the then newly invented *stem-winding* watch, which, with its rejection of any need for the usual key, was seen as the finest example of state-of-the-art technology. The term currently exists only in US political speech, meaning a rousing speech]

stem-winder n.[2] *see* KEY WINDER n.

stem-winder n.[3] *see* WORK THE STEM v.

stench-trench n. [1990s+] **1** the anus. **2** the vagina (cf. AGREEABLE RUTS OF LIFE n.).

stencil n. [1970s–80s] (drugs) an extra-long marijuana cigarette. [? play on SE pencil]

stenner n. [1990s+] (UK juv.) a person who has a larger than average forehead. [abbr. Frankenstein, whose monster had such a forehead]

steno n. [20C+] (US) a stenographer, a typist. [abbr.]

stenog n. [1900s–60s] (US) a (shorthand) typist, a stenographer. [abbr.]

stenog v. [1900s–40s] (US) to work as a (shorthand) typist or stenographer. [STENOG n.]

step n. [late 19C–1940s] a slice of bread. [abbr. DOORSTEP n.]

step v.[1] (also **step it**) **1** [mid-19C+] to leave. **2** [1900s] to exist. **3** [1920s+] (US Black) to dance. **4** [1960s+] to start a fight. **5** [1970s+] to carry on with one's life.

step v.[2] [late 19C] to clean doorsteps; thus STEPPER n.[3].

step v.[3] [1970s–80s] (US Black) to work as a prostitute. [? stepney, a White-slaver's temporary best woman; more simply her 'street-walking']

step fast v. [1960s+] (US Black) to do what is necessary to survive in a harsh world.

stephen n. (also **steven**) [late 18C–mid-19C] money; thus *Steven's at home*, one has money. [? STIVER n.; STEEVEN n.]

Stephenson's Rocket n. [1990s+] a pocket. [rhy. sl.; ult. the early railway engine, 'The *Rocket*', invented by engineer George Stephenson (1781–1848)]

stepinfetchit n. **1** [1900s] (US) an old man with a lively step. **2** [1930s+] (US Black) a subservient Black person, fitting willingly into the stereotyped and inferior image refined by generations of White supremacy. [lit. 'step and fetch it'; (2) nickname of Lincoln Perry (1892–1985), who specialized in playing stereotypical 'dumb nigger' roles for Hollywood; he chose the nickname after a winning racehorse]

step it v. *see* STEP v.[1].

stepmother's breath n. [20C+] (Ulster) a sudden draught of cold air. [the trad. negative image of the 'wicked stepmother']

step-off n. [1940s] (US Black) a street curb.

step off v. **1** [1900s–20s] (US) to get married. **2** [1920s–40s] (US) to be executed. **3** [1920s+] (US) to die. **4** [1990s+] (US Black) to leave. **5** [1990s+] (US teen) to leave alone, to stop interfering.

step off! excl. [1990s+] (US Black/campus/teen) go away! leave me alone! [STEP OFF v. (5)]

step off the carpet v. [mid-19C] (US) to get married. [the carpet that runs down the church aisle]

step-on n. [1970s+] (drugs) the adulteration of a narcotic drug. [STEP ON v.]

step on v. (also **jump on**) [1970s+] (drugs) to adulterate narcotics for more profitable sales. [the image of lit. squashing something and thus making it appear larger than it is]

step on it v. (also **step on her**) [1920s+] (orig. US) to move or drive faster, esp. as an imper.; also sometimes in fig. use. ['it' being the accelerator]

step on one's cock v. (also **trip on one's dick**) [1970s+] (orig. US) to get oneself into serious trouble, to make a major blunder. [SE step on/trip + COCK n.² (1)/DICK n.⁴ (1)]

step on one's dick v. (also **step on one's foreskin/prick**) [1950s+] to make a fool of oneself; to blunder badly. [SE step + DICK n.⁴ (1)/SE foreskin/PRICK n. (2)]

step on one's motor v. [1950s] (US Black) to boast, to make (empty) threats.

step on one's tongue v. [1970s] to say something one will regret.

step on someone's buzz v. see RAPE SOMEONE'S BUZZ v.

step on someone's toes v. (also **tread on someone's toes**) [mid-19C+] to annoy, to give offence to.

step on the gas v. [1920s+] (orig. US) **1** to accelerate a motorcar. **2** to go faster, esp. in imper. **3** to liven up, to take action.

step out v.¹ [mid-19C–1900s] (US) to die or disappear.

step out v.² **1** [20C+] (orig. US Black) to go to a party, dance or some form of entertainment. **2** [1920s+] (US) to escort or go out with someone socially; usu. as step out with.

step out v.³ [1970s–80s] (N.Z.) to challenge to a fight. [the challenging phr. 'do you want to step outside?']

step out on v. [1950s+] (orig. US Black) to cuckold, to commit adultery. [ext. of SE step out, to go, to leave]

stepper n.¹ [mid-late 19C] the treadmill.

stepper n.² [mid-19C–1900s] a trotting-horse.

stepper n.³ [late 19C] a door-step cleaner, a 'step-girl'. [STEP v.²]

stepper n.⁴ **1** [1920s+] (US) a promiscuous woman. **2** [1980s] (US Black) a prostitute. [(1) a judgmental use of STEP OUT v.² (1); (2) STEP v.³]

stepper n.⁵ [1920s+] an ambitious man. [he takes steps for self-advancement]

stepper n.⁶ [1920s+] (US) a good dancer. [STEP OUT v.² (1)]

stepper n.⁷ see HIGH-STEPPER n.¹.

steppers n. [mid-19C] the feet.

stepping n.¹ [1950s+] (US Black) working as a prostitute. [STEP v.³]

stepping! n.² [2000s] (US Black) pursuing the opposite (or same in gay context) sex. [STEP OUT v.² (2)]

stepping ken n. [mid-19C] (US) a cheap dancehall. [SE step, to dance + KEN n.¹ (1)]

step someone out on the green v. [1970s] (US Black) to challenge someone to a fight. [the image of 'going outside' to some supposed turf]

step to v. (also **step up**) [1980s+] (US Black) **1** to challenge. **2** to make sexual advances towards. [SE step towards or step up to]

step up v. [1980s+] (drugs) to move from selling drugs retail to distributing larger quantities wholesale.

-ster sfx [mid-16C+] a sfx implying agency. [ult. ME, where it represents nouns of action; in SE such terms include jokester,

trickster, punster etc. Recent sl. uses have adopted the sfx, adding it to a surname or nickname and prefixing that with the, e.g. the US wrestler 'Hulk' Hogan is The Hulkster etc]

sterics n. [mid-late 18C] hysteria. [abbr. SE hysterics]

sterks n. (also **sturks**) [1930s+] (Aus.) a fit of anger or exasperation; thus **give someone the sterks**, to aggravate, to irritate. [abbr. SE hysterics]

sterky adj. [1930s+] (Aus.) frightened, terrified; thus suffering a bout of diarrhoea, engendered by fear. [STERKS n., but note SE stercoraceous, consisting of, containing or pertaining to faeces]

sterling n. [19C] (Aus.) one born in Britain who has emigrated to Australia. [play on SE (pound) sterling/sterling, of high quality]

stern n. [late 16C+] the buttocks. [SE stern, the back of a ship]

Sterno Hilton n. [1990s+] (US) a campsite. [the use of Sterno ('canned heat') to power a camping stove]

stern over appetite phr. [1930s+] (Aus.) head over heels. [euph. ARSE OVER APPETITE phr.]

sternpost n. **1** [early 19C] the buttocks. **2** [mid-late 19C] the penis. [naut. imagery]

sternwheeler n. [1940s–70s] (US gay) a passive male homosexual. [play on SE sternwheeler, a boat propelled by a wheel at its rear]

sterrika n. [1980s] a hard case. [? Yid.]

stetson adj. [1920s] (US tramp) of a person or thing, first-rate, best. [the perceived excellence of the Stetson hat]

steve n. [1910s] (Aus.) a generic term of address to a man.

steve hart v. **1** [20C+] (US Und.) to start. **2** [1980s] (Aus.) to fart. [rhy. sl.]

Steve McQueens n. [2000s] jeans. [rhy. sl.; ult. US film star Steve McQueen (1930–80)]

steven n. see STEPHEN n.

steve's mission n. [1950s] (US drugs) a place where a narcotics addict may buy and/or use drugs. [OLD STEVE n.]

Stevie Wonder n. [1990s+] thunder. [rhy. sl.; ult. US singer Stevie Wonder (b.1950)]

stew n.¹ [19C] a mess, a troublesome situation. [20C+ use is SE]

stew n.² [mid-late 19C] one who studies hard but still learns nothing. [they stew in a hot room]

stew n.³ **1** [mid-19C+] (US) a drunkard. **2** [1900s–60s] a drunken carouse. [STEWED adj.¹ (1)]

stew n.⁴ [1940s] (US Und.) nitroglycerine. [var. on SOUP n.² (1)]

stew n.⁵ (also **stewie**) [1960s+] a stewardess, an air hostess. [abbr.]

stew n.⁶ [1980s+] (Aus. prison) a prearranged fight.

stew v.¹ [mid-19C–1950s] to study hard. [STEW n.²]

stew v.² [20C+] (W.I.) to abort a pregnancy. [? obs. SE stew, to check, to restrain]

stew v.³ [1940s] (US Und.) to be executed in the electric chair.

stew and blue v. [1980s] (Aus.) to look round at the wrong time.

Stewart Granger n. [1980s+] **1** danger. **2** a chance, an opportunity. [rhy. sl.; ult. film actor Stewart Granger (1913–93); (2) is fig. use of danger (cf. NO DANGER phr.)]

stew bum n. **1** [late 19C+] a down-and-out alcoholic, the most deprived of vagrants. **2** [1920s] (US tramp) one who eats only cheap foods. **3** [1920s+] a term of abuse. [(1) and (3) STEW n.³ (1); (2) SE stew + BUM n.³ (1)]

stewed adj.¹ (also **stewed up**) **1** [mid-17C+] drunk (cf. DAMP adj.). **2** [1920s+] crazy or easily fooled. **3** [2000s] (drugs) intoxicated by a drug.

stewed adj.² [1980s+] (US campus) in trouble. [STEW n.¹]

stewed as an owl phr. see DRUNK AS A BOILED OWL phr.

stewed as a prune phr. [1910s+] extremely drunk (cf. DAMP adj.). [STEWED adj.¹ (1) + SE prune]

stewed prune n. **1** [1920s+] in pl., nonsense, rubbish. **2** [1950s] a tune. [(1) on the lines of APPLE SAUCE n.¹; (2) rhy. sl.]

stewed Quaker n. [late 18C–early 19C] (US) burnt rum with a piece of butter, 'an American remedy for a cold' (Grose, 1785). [? its brown colour, the Quaker colour; or the use of such a remedy among Quakers]

stewed to the gills *phr.* [1920s+] extremely drunk (cf. ARSE-HOLED adj.; DAMP adj.). [STEWED adj.¹ (1) + TO THE GILLS adv.]

stewed up *adj. see* STEWED adj.¹.

stewer *n.* [1940s] (*US Black*) a malicious, gossiping old woman. [her *stewing* up of gossip, rumours, slander etc or play on OLD HEN n./SE *old hen*, which would be stewed]

stew-for-beans *adj.* [1950s] (*US Und.*) equal, 'fifty-fifty'.

stewie *n.*¹ [1940s] (*US Black*) a drunkard. [STEWED adj.¹ (1)]

stewie *n.*² *see* STEW n.⁵.

stew-pit *n.* [1990s+] (*Irish*) an idiot.

stewpot *n.* [early–mid-17C] the vagina, spec. of a prostitute (cf. BAG n.¹). [SE *stew*, a brothel + *pot*]

S the spot *v.* [1990s+] (*W.I.*) to leave.

stibber-gibber *n.* [mid-16C] a habitual liar. [Paul Beale in *DSUE* (8th edn, 1984) suggests a corruption of 2 typical contemporary names, *Stephen* and *Gilbert*, generic for lying clerks]

Stick, the *n.* [1990s+] (*US Black teen*) Candle*stick* Park, in San Francisco. [abbr.]

stick *n.*¹ **1** [18C+] the penis; thus (*US gay*) *bent stick*, *dead stick*, an impotent penis (cf. BAT n.⁷). **2** [1980s+] (*US Black*) a knife. [note RMC Duntroon (Aus.) *stick*, the act of reading pornography for the purposes of masturbation; thus *stick book/stick mag/ stick vid*, a pornographic book, magazine or video (cf. STICK BOOK n.)]

stick *n.*² [19C+] an awkward or dull person; since the 1950s also used affectionately, e.g. *not a bad old stick*. [the image is of being 'wooden' or 'cross-grained']

stick *n.*³ [mid–late 18C] a sermon. [? the 'wooden' delivery of some sermons, or the wooden pulpit]

stick *n.*⁴ [late 18C+] (*UK Und.*) a pistol, usu. in pl.; thus *stow your sticks!* hide your pistols!; *flash one's sticks*, to draw but not (yet) fire one's pistols. [abbr. SE *shooting stick*]

stick *n.*⁵ **1** [19C–1950s] a shot of spirits, usu. rum or brandy, added to coffee or tea; usu. in phr. *with a stick in it*. **2** [1920s] a small glass of beer. **3** [1930s] (*US*) one who deals in illicit liquor. **4** [1940s] (*US Black*) a drunkard. [? one *sticks* it in the cup or glass]

stick *n.*⁶ **1** [19C+] a piece of furniture; usu. in pl. **2** [1940s+] (*US*) (*also* **plank**) a bar; thus *behind the stick*, working as a bartender. [i.e. wooden furniture]

stick *n.*⁷ **1** [mid-19C+] (*US*) a baseball bat. **2** [late 19C–1960s] (*UK Und.*) a crowbar, a jemmy. **3** [late 19C+] a policeman's truncheon. **4** [1920s–40s] (*US Und./prison*) a blackjack. **5** [1930s–40s] a clarinet. **6** [1940s+] (*US*) a billiard or pool cue; thus *stick hall*, a poolroom. **7** [2000s] (*US*) a manual gear lever; thus a car with manual gears.

stick *n.*⁸ [late 19C+] a cigarette.

stick *n.*⁹ **1** [1910s] (*drugs*) a quantity of opium. **2** [1930s–40s] (*drugs*) an opium pipe. **3** [1930s+] (*drugs*) a marijuana cigarette; ext. as *stick of tea*, *stick of weed*; thus *stick man*, a marijuana smoker; *break a stick*, to smoke a marijuana cigarette (cf. BAT n.⁸). **4** [1940s] (*US drugs*) a very thinly rolled marijuana cigarette. **5** [1990s+] (*US drugs*) an injection of heroin.

stick *n.*¹⁰ **1** [1920s+] a reprimand, a criticism; verbal aggression in general; usu. as *get stick*, to be on the receiving end of these attacks; thus GIVE SOMEONE (SOME) STICK v. **2** [1970s] violence.

stick *n.*¹¹ **1** [1920s+] (*US Und.*) a criminal's accomplice who poses as an ordinary person to distract or influence the victims of an intended crime or swindle. **2** [1920s+] (*US Und./gambling*) an accomplice who loses deliberately so as to encourage the victim to continue playing. **3** [2000s] (*US prison*) a close friend. [ext. of STICK n.²]

stick *n.*¹² [1930s+] (*US gambling*) a croupier. [the croupier's rake or *stick*]

stick *n.*¹³ [1960s–70s] (*UK/US Black*) a prostitute. [her role as a *stick*, i.e. tool, who solves a pimp's financial problems]

stick *n.*¹⁴ (*also* **long stick**, **sharp stick**) [1990s+] (*US prison*) influence, 'clout'.

stick *n.*¹⁵ *see* SCHTICK n.

stick, the *n.* [late 19C+] venereal disease. [? the *sticky* discharge of gonorrhoea]

stick *adj.* [mid-19C+] a synon. of SE *stark*, as in the phr. *stick, staring wild*.

stick *v.*¹ **1** [late 17C+] to cheat or swindle, esp. to overcharge. **2** [mid-19C+] to take in, to impose upon. **3** [1910s+] (*also* **stick for**) to demand money from. **4** [1950s] to give to, to pass over. **5** [1950s] to link one to.

stick *v.*² **1** [late 17C+] (*also* **stick up**) of a man, to have heterosexual intercourse; thus *double stick*, 2 bouts of intercourse in succession. **2** [1960s] to sodomize another man. [STICK n.¹ (1)]

stick *v.*³ **1** [mid-18C–mid-19C; 1950s+] (*US*) to hit; thus *stuck*. **2** [20C+] (*US/UK prison*) to charge with a crime. **3** [1920s+] (*US Black*) to attack, verbally or physically. **4** [1920s+] (*US*) to defeat. **5** [1950s] to punish.

stick *v.*⁴ **1** [mid-18C+] to stab with a knife. **2** [late 19C] to bayonet. **3** [1940s+] (*US*) to inject with a hypodermic syringe.

stick *v.*⁵ [mid–late 19C] to stymie, to bring to a stop, to render unable to move.

stick *v.*⁶ [late 19C+] to tolerate, to put up with.

stick *v.*⁷ [1940s–60s] (*drugs*) to supply or use marijuana; esp. in the phr. *are you sticking?* [STICK n.⁹ (3)]

stick *v.*⁸ [1940s+] *fig.* to dump something in the rubbish, to throw it away, usu. used in a hostile conversation. [abbr. STICK IT UP YOUR ARSE! excl.]

stick *v.*⁹ *see* STICK AROUND v.

stickability *n.* [late 19C+] the ability to endure or persevere. [STICK v.⁶]

stick a bust *v.* [late 19C] (*UK Und.*) to commit a burglary. [ext. use of STICK v.³ + BUST n.² (1)]

stick a fork in them, they're done *phr.* [1940s+] (*US*) a phr. of condemnatory dismissal, e.g. *stick a fork in him, he's done*.

stick and bangers *n.* [late 19C] **1** a billiard cue and the balls with which one plays. **2** the penis and testes. [SE *stick*/STICK n.¹ (1) + SE *banger*, that which bangs together]

stick and lift *v.* [late 19C–1920s] to eke out an impoverished life. [the actions of digging]

stick a pin there! *excl.* **1** [early–mid-18C] wait! hold it! **2** [mid-19C–1940s] note carefully! bear in mind!

stick a point *v.* [mid-17C; late 19C–1920s] to settle an argument.

stick around *v.* (*also* **stick**, **stick on**) [late 19C+] (*orig. Can./US*) to stay close by; often as imper.

stick as close as shit to a blanket *v.* [1930s+] to stay very close. [SE *stick as close* + SHIT n.¹ (1)]

stick a tail on *v.* [1960s+] to admire sexually; usu. in phr. *I could stick a tail on that.*

stick-at-it *n.* [1900s] a persistent, dedicated person. [STICK v.⁶]

stick away *v.* [20C+] to hide something or someone away.

stick book *n.* [1980s] (*Aus.*) a pornographic book or magazine. [STICK n.¹ (1) + SE *book*]

stick dick to *v. see* STICK (THE) DICK TO v.

sticker *n.*¹ **1** [mid-19C] (*UK Und.*) a lengthy period, a stay. **2** [mid-19C–1900s] a guest who overstays their welcome. **3** [late 19C–1950s] one who 'sticks' to his beliefs, job etc. **4** [1970s] (*UK police/Und.*) a prisoner who stays on remand without bail until their trial.

sticker *n.*² **1** [mid–late 19C] a butcher. **2** [mid-19C+] a pointed, stabbing weapon, e.g. a knife, rather than one that is used to slash. **3** [1920s–60s] (*US tramp*) a scarf pin. **4** [1960s] the penis. [SE *stick*, to pierce]

sticker *n.*³ [mid-19C–1910s] a commodity that does not find a ready sale. [it SE *sticks* in the shop]

sticker *n.*⁴ [mid-19C–1950s] a difficult, surprising, embarrassing or pointed question. [one is *stuck* for a response]

sticker *n.*⁵ [late 19C–1940s] (*US*) a thorn, a burr. [it SE *sticks* to one's clothes]

sticker *n.*⁶ [1900s–40s] (*US*) a postage stamp.

sticker-licker *n.* [1980s] (*S.Aus.*) a parking policeman (cf. BEAT-POUNDER n.). [the SE *stickers* they affix to cars]

stickers *n.* [1910s] (*US tramp*) beggars who pretend to be selling sticking plaster to gain an approach to a possible donor.

sticker shock *n.* [1970s+] (*US*) a shock from learning the price of something. [the price sticker]

sticker-up *n.* [late 19C] (*Aus.*) one who stages hold-ups and robberies. [STICK UP v.³ (1)]

Stickeys, the *n. see* STICKIES, THE n.

stick fat *v.* [1980s+] **1** (*Aus. Und.*) to maintain silence rather than betraying one's peers. **2** (*Aus.*) to maintain one's loyalty.

stick-flams *n.* [late 17C–mid-19C] gloves. [SE *stick* + FAM n.¹ (1), for which *flams* is prob. a misprint; thus lit. 'stick to hands']

stick for *v.*¹ *see* STICK v.¹ (3).

stick for *v.*² *see* STICK UP FOR v.

stick for drinks *v.* [late 19C] to play and win a toss of the dice (occas. turn of cards) to determine who pays for the next round of drinks.

Stickies, the *n.* (*also* **Stickeys, the**) [1960s+] the Official Irish Republican Army. [? the Officials *stick to* trad. IRA policies or they *stick on* their Easter lilies while the Provisionals use pins. Share suggests 'adhesive employed on identity badge']

stickies *n.* [1980s+] (*N.Z. drugs*) the potent flowering tops of marijuana plants. [play on SE *sticky-buds*]

stick in *v. see* STICK IT v.

stick in for *v. see* STICK SOMEONE FOR v. (1).

sticking *adj.* (*US Black*) **1** [1960s–70s] of a person, attractive. **2** [2000s] of clothes, looking good on the wearer.

sticking plaster *n.*¹ **1** [1910s–20s] a very boring visit, made by an acquaintance. **2** [1940s] (*UK Und.*) a (lengthy) prison sentence. [(1) the visitor *sticks around*; (2) the criminal *sticks in* prison]

sticking plaster *n.*² *see* PLASTER n.³ (4).

stickings *n.* [mid–late 19C] a butcher's off-cuts laid out on the chopping board, to which they stick.

stick in one's gizzard *v.* [late 17C+] to be unpalatable, to infuriate, to be unacceptable.

stick-in-the-middle *n.* [1950s] (*W.I.*) a form of dumpling. [although the dumpling is shaped like a doughnut and might have had a stick pushed through its centre to make the requisite hole, the term more likely refers to the way the heavy dumpling *sticks* to one's stomach]

stick-in-the-mud *n.* (*also* **stick-in-the-ditcher**) [early 19C+] an old-fashioned, conservative person.

stick-in-the-ribs *n.* [19C] a thick soup.

stick it *v.* (*also* **stick in**) **1** [mid-19C+] to persist, to continue in something, esp. a job. **2** [2000s] (*US teen*) to succeed in an achievement or trick.

stick it! *excl.* [1920s+] (*orig. US*) a derog. reply to a question, i.e. 'What shall I do with this?', or in response to an opinion with which one disagrees. [*up your arse/ass* is assumed]

stick it in *v.* (*also* **stick it on**) **1** [early 19C+] to charge extortionately. **2** [20C+] (*Aus.*) to work hard.

stick it into *v.* **1** [mid-19C] to victimize. **2** [20C+] (*Aus.*) to beg for a loan. **3** [20C+] (*Irish*) to have sexual intercourse (cf. BANG v.¹).

stick it in your ear! *excl.* [1920s+] a general dismissive excl.

stick it on *v.*¹ [1950s] to accuse unfairly, to 'frame up'.

stick it on *v.*² **1** [1950s+] to hit, to beat. **2** [1980s] (*N.Z.*) to have sexual intercourse (cf. BANG v.¹).

stick it on *v.*³ *see* STICK IT IN v.

stick it on *v.*⁴ *see* STICK IT UP v.¹.

stick it out *v.* [mid-19C+] to persist, to tolerate a situation (esp. an unpleasant one). [ext. of STICK v.⁶]

stick it to *v.* **1** [1940s+] (*US*) to treat harshly, to assault violently. **2** [1970s+] to defraud. **3** [1970s+] (*US*) to copulate. **4** [1990s+] to tease, to malign, to attack.

stick it up *v.*¹ (*also* **stick it on**) [mid-19C+] to place on account. [i.e. to *stick it* on the running bill]

stick it up *v.*² [mid-19C+] **1** to take advantage of, esp. financially. **2** to act uncompromisingly in pursuit of victory. [the image is of *sticking* something sharp *up* the victim]

stick it up someone's ass *v.* [1980s+] **1** (*US*) to betray, to let down. **2** to humiliate.

stick it up to *v.* [early 19C+] to charge to someone, to give responsibility to.

stick it up your arse! *excl. see* SHOVE IT UP YOUR ARSE! excl.

stick it up your arse sideways *phr.* [1990s+] a general phr. of dismissal, abuse.

stick it up your cunt! *excl.* [1930s+] (*Aus.*) a general expression of disdain, dismissal, rejecting the previous speaker's idea, opinion, insult etc. [SE *stick it up* + CUNT n.¹ (1)]

stick it up your jacksy! *excl.* [1940s+] a general excl. of dismissal or derision. [SE *stick it up* + JACKSY n.]

stick it up your jumper! *excl.* (*also* **stuff it up your jumper!**) [1930s+] (*mainly UK teen*) an excl. rejecting the previous speaker's idea, opinion, insult etc.

stick-jaw *n.* **1** [early 19C–1950s] any sweet food, e.g. a pudding, a sweet such as toffee, that is hard to chew. **2** [1910s–20s] anything seen as extremely tedious.

stickman *n.*¹ [mid-19C] the member of a pickpocket gang who is handed the stolen goods by the actual pickpocket and who must also try to hinder any attempts to capture their confederate by police or public.

stickman *n.*² [1910s+] (*US*) a croupier. [the rake or *stick* with which they collect and distribute chips]

stickman *n.*³ [1950s+] a good lover, a potent, experienced man. [STICK n.¹ (1) + SE *man*]

stickman *n.*⁴ [1960s–70s] (*US Black*) a policeman. [STICK n.⁷ (3) + SE *man*]

stickman *n.*⁵ [1990s+] (*US Black*) a close ally, a backup, a lookout. [he *sticks with* his friends]

stick of chalk *n.* [20C+] (*Aus.*) a walk. [rhy. sl.]

stick of gage *n.* (*also* **stick of dynamite, …pot, …tea**) [1940s–60s] a marijuana cigarette (cf. BAT n.⁸). [STICK n.⁹ (3) + GAGE n.²/POT n.¹⁰/TEA n.² (1)]

stick of rock *n.* [1990s+] the penis (cf. ALMOND n.). [rhy. sl. = COCK n.² (1)]

stick of wood *n.* [early 18C] a fool. [note STICK n.²]

stick on *v. see* STICK AROUND v.

stick one on *v.* (*also* **stick one into**) [1910s+] to hit. ['one' is a blow or punch]

stick one's bib in *v.* (*also* **poke one's bib in**) [1940s+] (*Aus.*) to interfere, to intrude; thus the reverse *keep one's bib out*.

stick one's duck in the mud *v.* (*also* **get some mud for the duck**) **1** [1970s] (*US*) of a man, to have sexual intercourse (cf. BURY IT v.). **2** [1980s+] (*US gay*) to have anal intercourse (cf. ASK FOR THE RING v.).

stick oneself up (to be) *v.* [late 19C] to claim, to make oneself out to be.

stick one's neck out *v.* (*also* **stick out one's neck**) [1920s+] (*orig. US campus*) to exceed one's brief, to interfere in affairs in which one is not directly concerned and often, having stuck out one's neck, fig. to have one's head cut off.

stick one's oar in *v. see* SHOVE ONE'S OAR IN v.

stick one's spoon in the wall *v.* [mid–late 19C] to die.

stick on someone like white on rice *v.* [20C+] (*W.I.*) to nag continually, to harass. [SE *stick on* + LIKE WHITE ON RICE adv.]

stick on (the price) *v.* [mid-19C+] to overcharge.

stick-out *n.* [1930s+] (*US*) **1** (*also* **stand-out**) a horse that seems a certain winner. **2** an outstanding sportsman. [STICK OUT v.]

stick out *v.* [20C+] to be conspicuous. [prior use was SE]

stick out (for) *v.* [mid-19C+] to persist in one's demand.

stick out like a sore thumb *v.* (*also* **stick out a foot/mile,**

...like a fly on a wedding cake, stick up like a sore thumb) [late 19C+] to be very conspicuous or obvious. [STICK OUT v.]

stick out one's neck v. see STICK ONE'S NECK OUT v.

stick out one's shingle v. see HANG OUT ONE'S SHINGLE v.

stick partner n. [1990s+] (US Black) a close friend, a fellow member of a street gang. [var. on STICKMAN n.⁵]

stick pussy n. [1970s+] (US gay/prison) **1** the penis, in a homosexual context. **2** a young inmate, forced into homosexuality. [STICK n.¹ (1) + PUSSY n. (2)]

sticks n.¹ **1** [early–mid-19C] the legs. **2** [1910s–40s] a person missing one or both legs. **3** [1930s+] (US Black) matches.

sticks n.² (S.Afr.) **1** [late 19C] an obstinate horse. **2** [20C+] an obstinate person. [they both SE *stick in their heels*]

sticks n.³ [20C+] (orig. US) the world beyond the big cities, esp. small towns and hamlets. [SE *stick*, as a generic for the world of trees and nature + theatrical jargon *stick*, a town outside the regular touring circuits and far beyond New York City]

sticks and stones n.¹ [mid–late 19C] furniture. [ext. STICK n.⁶ (1)]

sticks and stones n.² [20C+] bones. [rhy. sl.]

sticksing n. [1970s+] (UK Black) the practice of picking pockets. [STICKSMAN n.¹]

stick slinger n. [mid-19C] **1** (Aus.) a pimp (cf. ABBOT ON THE CROSS n.). **2** a violent thief. [(1) STICK n.¹ (1); (2) SE *stick* + SE *sling*]

sticksman n.¹ [1970s+] (UK Black) a pickpocket. [? he *sticks* his hand in another's pocket]

sticksman n.² [1980s] a womanizer. [STICK n.¹ (1) + SE *man*]

stick solid v. [1990s+] (Aus. Und.) to remain silent under interrogation. [STICK v.⁶ + SOLID adv.¹ (1)]

stick someone for v. **1** [late 19C+] (also **stick in for**) to take from someone, usu. but not invariably money. **2** [1910s+] (also **stick someone with**) to make someone pay a bill; to borrow money without repaying it. **3** [1920s+] (also **stick someone with**) in fig. use, to burden someone with something, e.g. a jail sentence.

sticksville n. see STICKVILLE n.

stick the boot in v. see PUT THE BOOT IN v.

stick (the) dick to v. [1960s] to treat badly, to exploit. [SE *stick* +DICK n.⁸; synon. for FUCK OVER v.]

stick the frighteners on v. see PUT THE FRIGHTENERS ON v.

stick the nut on v. see NUT v.².

stick to v. [17C+] **1** to remain loyal. **2** to maintain a position or opinion.

stick-to-it-iveness n. [mid-19C+] persistence, determination. [STICK TO v. (2)]

stick to one's knitting v. (also **mind one's knitting, tend one's own knitting**) [mid-18C; late 19C+] (US) to mind one's own business; to get down to the task in hand.

stickum n. (US) **1** [20C+] glue, cement. **2** [1960s+] any viscous substance.

stick-up n. **1** [20C+] a hold-up, an armed robbery. **2** [20C+] an armed robber. **3** [1980s] (Aus./N.Z.) a hold-up, a delay, a problem; also as v. [STICK UP v.³]

stick up v.¹ [mid-19C] to hold one's ground in an argument.

stick up v.² [mid-19C+] to place on account. [the sum is *stuck on* a running account]

stick up v.³ **1** [mid-19C+] (orig. Aus.) to rob, to hold up. **2** [late 19C+] to blackmail, to extort from; to beg. **3** [1900s] (Aus.) to summon, e.g. a bus to stop. **4** [1910s] to take money legally, e.g. through gambling. **5** [1930s+] in fig. use, to cost money. **6** [1940s] (US/N.Z. Und.) of the police, to hold for questioning. [the shout of 'stick up your hands!']

stick up v.⁴ [late 19C–1950s] (Aus./N.Z.) to hinder, to impede, to puzzle, to confuse.

stick up v.⁵ [late 19C+] (US) to break an appointment.

stick up v.⁶ [1920s+] (UK Und.) to put forward, usu. to offer a name to the police.

stick up v.⁷ see STICK v.² (1).

stick-up artist/boy n. see STICK-UP MAN n.

stick up for v. (also **stick for**) [mid-19C+] to defend, to champion. [STICK UP v.¹]

stick up like a sore thumb v. see STICK OUT LIKE A SORE THUMB v.

stick-up man n. (also **stick-up artist, ...boy, ...guy, ...kid**) [1910s+] an armed robber. [STICK UP v.³ (1) + SE *man*/ARTIST sfx/SE *boy*/GUY n.² (1)/KID n.¹ (4)]

stick-ups n. [mid-19C] stiff shirt collars.

stick up to v.¹ [mid-19C; 1900s] to court, to pursue sexually.

stick up to v.² [mid-19C+] to challenge, to oppose, esp. when one is ostensibly at a disadvantage. [ext. STICK UP v.¹]

stickville n. (also **sticksville**) [20C+] the predominantly rural or suburban world beyond the big cities. [STICKS n.³ + -VILLE sfx¹]

sticky n.¹ **1** [mid-19C] sealing wax. **2** [late 19C+] sticking plaster. **3** [1920s–60s] sticky buns. **4** [1930s+] sticky tape. **5** [1970s+] (US gay) semen (cf. BOLLOCK SNOT n.).

sticky n.² [1980s+] a cannabis cigarette (cf. AFRICAN WOODBINE n.). [one *sticks* 2 or more cigarette papers together]

sticky adj.¹ **1** [mid-19C+] (US) mawkish, sentimental. **2** [late 19C+] of weather, muggy. **3** [late 19C+] of a person, awkward, uncooperative, punctilious, prone to cause trouble. **4** [1910s+] of circumstances, awkward, presenting great difficulty, disagreeable because of hardship or danger. **5** [1930s+] of a social function, slow to start, stiff, uncomfortable. **6** [1930s+] unpleasant. **7** [2000s] pertaining to (commercial) sex.

sticky adj.² [1940s+] (Aus./N.Z.) inquisitive, curious. [STICKYBEAK n.]

stickybeak n. [1920s+] (Aus./N.Z.) **1** an inquisitive person. **2** an inquisitive look; thus *have a sticky*, have a look around. [one who *sticks* in their BEAK n.² (1)]

stickybeak v. [1930s+] (Aus./N.Z.) to pry, to snoop; thus *stickybeaking*, prying, 'poking one's nose in'. [STICKYBEAK n.]

sticky bun n. [20C+] a son. [rhy. sl.]

sticky spud gun n. [1990s+] the penis (cf. AX n.²). [the ejaculated semen]

sticky toffee n. [1970s] coffee. [rhy. sl.]

sticky wicket n. [1950s+] difficulties, problems. [cricket imagery]

stiff n.¹ (also **stiff one**) [late 18C+] an erection; thus [1970s+] (US Black) *sport a stiff*, to have an erection.

stiff n.² **1** [late 18C+] a corpse, also in fig. use. **2** [mid-19C+] a drunkard. **3** [mid-19C+] (also **stiff 'un**) in horseracing, a useless, losing horse and thus an erroneous, losing wager; thus *stiff*, second-rate, uncompetitive. **4** [late 19C+] (US) a penniless man, a wastrel, a tramp, a migratory or unskilled worker. **5** [late 19C+] (orig. N.Z./US) a disagreeable, or contemptible person; also joc./affectionate use. **6** [late 19C+] (US) a mean, grasping person. **7** [late 19C+] an average person, often with a description, e.g. WORKING STIFF n. **8** [1900s–40s] (US tramp) a tramp who has a job or occupation. **9** [20C+] (US) any failure, a flop; in sport, a second-rater. [(1) rigor mortis; subseq. defs. all fig. use of (1)]

stiff n.³ **1** [early 19C–1930s] (also **cross-stiff**) paper, a document, esp. a promissory note or bill of exchange, a clandestine letter. **2** [mid-19C–1900s] (US Und.) a newspaper. **3** [mid-19C–1930s] a currency note or cheque, whether genuine or forged. **4** [mid-19C+] (Aus./N.Z./US/UK Und.) a note, usu. between prisoners or passed illicitly into a prison by a relation etc. **5** [late 19C] a poster. **6** [late 19C–1910s] a hawker's licence, or similar licence. **7** [late 19C–1930s] paper money (cf. BANK-RAG n.). **8** [late 19C–1940s] (US Und.) a piece of counterfeit money. **9** [late 19C–1960s] a letter. **10** [20C+] (Aus./N.Z.) a summons from the police. **11** [1910s] the identification of a person targeted to be murdered. **12** [1910s] (US Und.) a prescription.

stiff n.⁴ [1900s] (US) a lie.

stiff *adj.*[1] **1** [mid-18C+] (*orig. US*) drunk, esp. very drunk and passed out cold. **2** [mid-18C+] dead. **3** [late 19C] unconscious. **4** [1960s] (*US*) (*also* **stiffened**) intoxicated by a drug. [SE *stiff*, rigid]

stiff *adj.*[2] **1** [early 19C+] strong, usu. of liquor, e.g. *a stiff drink*, *a stiff one*, *a* STIFF '*UN* n.[1] (2). **2** [early 19C+] demanding, difficult. **3** [mid-19C+] (*US*) expensive; thus *stiffish*, expensively. **4** [1920s+] of a blow, hard, painful. [fig. uses of SE]

stiff *adj.*[3] [mid-19C] pertaining to a bill as opposed to cash.

stiff *adj.*[4] [late 19C–1930s] **1** of a competitor, certain to win. **2** of a competition, a certainty.

stiff *adj.*[5] [late 19C+] (*orig. Aus./N.Z.*) **1** impoverished; thus *stiff and swagless*, with neither money nor possessions. **2** unlucky, unfortunate. **3** unacceptable.

stiff *v.*[1] [late 19C–1960s] to curse, to swear. [? the response, 'I say, that's a bit stiff,' to such an outburst]

stiff *v.*[2] (*orig. US*) **1** [20C+] to lie, to mislead. **2** [1950s+] to cheat, to swindle, to rob. **3** [1950s+] to fail to tip a waiter, doorman etc. **4** [1960s] to transmit misleading or lying information. **5** [2000s] to fail, e.g. of a film release. [i.e. to treat as a form of STIFF n.[2]; (3) to become a STIFF n.[2] (6)]

stiff *v.*[3] **1** [1910s+] to cause death, to kill, to murder. **2** [1990s+] to destroy. [STIFF n.[2] (1)]

stiff *v.*[4] [1930s+] of a man, to have sexual intercourse (cf. BAGAGA v.). [STIFF n.[1]]

stiff *v.*[5] [1970s+] (*US*) to mistreat, to snub, to push aside. [ext. of STIFF v.[2] (2)]

stiff *adv.* [mid-19C+] to a great (and unpleasant) extent.

stiff and jive *v.* [1930s–50s] (*US Black*) to show off, to boast. [jazz use *stiff and jive*, to play flashily but with little genuine skill]

stiff and stout *n.* [mid-17C–19C] the erect penis.

stiff-arm *v.* [1940s+] (*US*) to mistreat, to snub, to push aside.

stiff as a crutch *phr.* [late 19C+] (*Aus./N.Z.*) **1** physically stiff. **2** completely penniless. [(1) SE *stiff*; (2) ext. of STIFF adj.[5] (1)]

stiff as a poker *phr.* (*also* **stiff as a pike-staff/ramrod**) [mid-18C+] very stiff.

stiff-ass *adj.* [1960s–70s] a general term of derision. [STIFF n.[2] (5) + -ASS sfx]

stiff-assed *adj.* [1930s+] (*US*) supercilious, arrogant, standoffish. [SE *stiff* + -ASSED sfx]

stiff bickkies *n.* (*also* **stiff biccies, …bickies, tough biccies, …bickies, …bickksh**) [1970s+] (*Aus./N.Z.*) bad luck; also as (unsympathetic) phr. meaning that's your bad luck. [STIFF adj.[2] (2)/TOUGH adj. (3) + BIKKIE n. (1)]

stiff cheddar/cheese *n. see* HARD CHEESE n.

stiff-dealer *n.* [early 19C] a dealer in promissory notes. [STIFF n.[3] (1) + SE *dealer*]

stiff deity *n.* [late 17C–19C] the erect penis.

stiff-dodger *n.* [late 19C] one who borrows against fraudulent promissory notes. [STIFF n.[3] (1) + SE *dodger*]

stiffen *v.*[1] **1** [late 19C] (*also* **stiffen out**) (*Aus.*) to die. **2** [late 19C] (*Aus.*) in fig use, to punish. **3** [late 19C–1900s] to kill, to murder; lit. or fig. **4** [late 19C+] (*Aus.*) to knock someone unconscious. **5** [1900s] (*Aus.*) in fig. use, to ruin, to undermine, to 'put paid to'. [ext. STIFF v.[3] (1)]

stiffen *v.*[2] **1** [late 19C–1930s] to bribe, to corrupt; of a horse, to 'pull'. **2** [late 19C+] to swindle, usu. in passive. [STIFF v.[2] (2)]

stiffened *adj. see* STIFF adj.[1] (4).

stiffener *n.*[1] (*also* **stiffner**) [early–mid-19C] (*UK Und.*) a letter.

stiffener *n.*[2] **1** [mid-19C+] (*orig. US*) a fortifying alcoholic drink. **2** [1900s] (*Aus.*) a knockout punch.

stiffener *n.*[3] *see* DOG-STIFFENER n.

stiffen it, God! *excl.* [late 19C–1940s] a general excl. [lit. 'let it grow dead and stiff']

stiffen out *v. see* STIFFEN v.[1] (1).

stiffen the…! *excl.* (*also* **stiffen me!**) [1910s+] (*Aus.*) in combs.,

an excl. of surprise, shock etc; combs. include *stiffen the crows! …snakes! …wombats!*

stiffer *n.* [1990s+] an erection. [STIFF n.[1]]

stiff-fencer *n.* [mid-19C] a street-seller of writing paper. [STIFF n.[3] (1) + -FENCER sfx]

stiffie *n.*[1] (*also* **stiffy**) [1960s+] an erection. [STIFF n.[1]]

stiffie *n.*[2] [1980s+] an invitation. [the thick card on which it is printed]

stiffie *n.*[3] *see* STIFFY n.[1].

stiffin' and jivin' *phr.* [1930s–50s] (*US Black*) making unreal, empty conversation. [STIFF v.[2] + JIVE v.[1] (2)]

stiffing *n.* [1990s+] robbery, swindling. [STIFF v.[2] (2)]

stiffner *n. see* STIFFENER n.[1].

stiff on *adj.* [1910s] (*Aus.*) keen on.

stiff one *n.*[1] *see* STIFF n.[1].

stiff one *n.*[2] *see* STIFF '*UN* n.[1] (2).

stiff (on) the stroll *v.* [1940s] (*US Black*) to stand on the corner. [one stands *stiff*, i.e. upright + STROLL n. (1)]

stiff out *n.* [1990s+] to die. [STIFF n.[2] (1)]

stiff-rump *n.* [early 18C–early 19C] a pompous, arrogant person; thus *stiff-rumped*, arrogant, pompous.

stiff shit *phr.* [1980s+] (*Aus.*) that's your hard luck; the inference is that the speaker has very little actual sympathy. [STIFF adj.[2] (2) + fig. use of SHIT n.[1] (1)]

stiff-stander *n.* [mid-17C–19C] an erection; the erect penis; thus as adj., *stiff-standing*.

stiff the stroll *v. see* STIFF (ON) THE STROLL v.

stiff trot *n. see* ROUGH TROT n.

stiff 'un *n.*[1] **1** [mid-19C+] a corpse. **2** [mid-19C+] (*also* **stiff one**) a strong drink. **3** [late 19C] a difficult racecourse. **4** [late 19C] (*Aus.*) a general term of abuse. [(1) ext. STIFF n.[2] (1); (2) STIFF adj.[2] (1); (3) STIFF adj.[2] (2); (4) SE *stiff*, formal + ext. STIFF n.[2] (1)]

stiff 'un *n.*[2] *see* STIFF n.[2] (3).

stiffy *n.*[1] (*also* **stiffie**) [late 19C+] a corpse. [STIFF n.[2] (1)]

stiffy *n.*[2] [1910s–20s] (*US tramp*) a tramp who poses as being paralyzed. [SE *stiff*]

stiffy *n.*[3] [1950s–60s] a fool, an irritating person. [STIFF n.[2]]

stiffy *n.*[4] *see* STIFFIE n.[1].

stifle *v.* [early 17C] to slip money surreptitiously into another person's hand. [SE *stifle*, to conceal]

stifler *n.* **1** [early 19C] the gallows. **2** [early 19C] a dram of spirits. **3** [late 19C] a severe blow. [all 'take one's breath away']

stifle the squeaker *v.* (*also* **stifle a squeaker**) **1** [late 17C–1900s] to murder a child 'and throw it into a House of Office [privy]' (*B.E.*). **2** [19C–1900s] to procure an abortion. [SE *stifle* + SQUEAKER n.[1] (1)]

stig *n.* [1990s+] (*UK juv.*) an impoverished person, resembling a vagrant. [the book/TV series *Stig of the Dump*]

still *n.*[1] [mid–late 19C] a *still*-born child. [abbr.]

still *n.*[2] [late 19C–1920s] (*US*) a quiet drunkard. [pun on SE *still*, quiet/*still*, a distillery]

still *v.* [late 18C] to silence, by murdering or knocking out.

still hill *n. see* HILL n.

stillie *n.* [2000s] a *stil*etto heeled shoe. [abbr.]

still sow *n.* **1** [late 16C–early 17C] 'a close, slie lurking knave' (Florio, *World of Wordes*, 1598). **2** [early 18C] a prostitute (cf. ALLEY CAT n.). [pvb 'the still sow eats up half the draff', i.e. the quiet pig eats more than its share of fodder]

stilly *n.* [1940s] (*W.I.*) a faithful lover. [? they are *still there*]

stilting *n.* [mid-19C] (*UK Und.*) the highest level of pickpocketing.

Stilton, the *n.* [mid–late 19C] of people, objects, experiences, the best of a type or style, the superlative. [play on CHEESE, THE n. (1)/CHESHIRE, THE n.]

stilts *n.* **1** [late 18C+] (*US Black*) the human legs. **2** [1920s–60s] crutches.

stimulate *v.* [mid-19C–1910s] (*US*) to drink alcohol.

stimulated *adj.* [mid-19C] (*US*) a euph. for drunk. [STIMULATE v.]

sting n.[1] [17C–early 18C] the penis, esp. in the context of impotence.

sting n.[2] **1** [20C+] any form of robbery, esp. as a complex fraud planned well in advance; thus *put the sting on*, to cheat, to swindle, to defraud. **2** [1930s–40s] (*US Black*) a wallet. **3** [1930s+] (*US Und.*) a reasonably large sum of money ($500 average) obtained by some form of deception or trickery. **4** [1970s+] a police undercover operation designed to entrap alleged criminals.

sting n.[3] (*Aus.*) **1** [1910s+] strong (cheap) drink; occas. methylated spirits. **2** [1940s–50s] a drug, esp. as given to a racehorse.

sting n.[4] [1990s+] (*W.I.*) the currently favoured object, person, experience.

sting v. **1** [early 19C+] (*orig. UK Und.*) to steal, to cheat, both in fact and as merely overcharging. **2** [20C+] (*US*) to levy a charge upon, usu. financial but also fig., e.g. a prison sentence. **3** [1900s–30s] (*US*) to unmask, to reveal. **4** [1910s+] to demand or beg for something. **5** [1920s+] (*US Und.*) to make a successful coup as a confidence trickster. **6** [1930s] (*US prison*) to report a convict for a disciplinary offence. **7** [1940s] (*US Und.*) to arrest.

stingaree n.[1] **1** [1900s–20s] (*US Und.*) a swindle based on short-changing a cashier. **2** [1920s] (*US*) a mean person. [STING v. (1)]

stingaree n.[2] [1920s+] (*US Black*) the penis. [? link to STING n.[1] but prob. SE *stinger*]

sting-bum n. [late 17C–early 19C] a miser, a mean person. [SE *sting* + BUM n.[1] (1); poss. earlier use of STING v. (1)]

stinger n.[1] **1** [17C+] 'something that stings or smarts, e.g. a sharp blow, or the hand that delivers it; something that causes sharp distress, a pungent speech or crushing argument; a sharp frost' (*OED*). **2** [mid-19C] a swig of alcohol. **3** [mid-19C; 1940s] something noteworthy. **4** [mid-19C+] (*Aus./US*) any period of extreme weather, hot or cold.

stinger n.[2] [1930s–40s] (*US prison*) a disciplinary report.

stinger n.[3] [1950s] (*US drugs*) a hypodermic syringe.

stinger n.[4] (*also* **stringer**) [1970s+] (*US Black/prison*) a hotplate that is run from 2 wires attached to a light socket. [STING v. (1) or SE *string*, i.e. the wires; note Maledicta V:1–2 267: 'The stinger consists of wires with both ends exposed. One end is inserted into an electrical socket and the other is placed in the water to heat it, to prepare coffee']

sting for v. [20C+] (*orig. US*) to extort money from someone by begging or borrowing it in a demanding manner. [ext. of STING v. (1)]

stingo n.[1] [mid-17C+] very strong ale. [it *stings* the drinker]

stingo n.[2] [1900s] (*Aus. Und.*) an arrest. [STING n.[2] (1)]

stingo adj. [late 19C] energetic, spirited, lively. [SE *sting*/fig. use of STINGO n.[1]]

stingtail n. [17C] a prostitute (cf. BANGTAIL n.[1]). [the *sting* in a scorpion's *tail*/a whore's TAIL n.[2] (3), in this context venereal disease; note Ned Ward, *Hudibras Redivivus* (1705–07): 'For am'rous Joys, we alays find, / Leave a repenting Sting behind']

stingy-brim n. (*also* **short-brim, stingy-rim**) [1930s–80s] (*orig. US Black*) a hat with a narrow brim. [lit. a 'mean brim']

stink n. **1** [early 19C+] a fuss, a furore, a scandal; esp. in *kick up a stink, raise a stink*, to make a fuss. **2** [1910s+] a contemptible person. **3** [1940s+] a fight. **4** [1980s] (*US Black*) the vagina.

stink adj. [1940s+] (*US*) good, fine.

stink v. **1** [mid-19C+] to behave offensively, to appear offensive to someone. **2** [1920s+] (*orig. US*) to be morally inadequate or physically incompetent; generally to be rubbish. **3** [1930s] to fail, in a monetary sense. **4** [1930s+] in ironic use, to be full of, redolent of. **5** [1930s+] to be highly improbable, to lack verisimilitude.

stinka n. see STINKER n.[2].

stinkaroo n. [late 19C–1930s] a cigar or pipe.

stinkarooed adj. [1940s] (*US*) drunk. [var. STINKING adj.[2] (1)]

stink bomb n. [1930s–50s] (*US*) something disgusting or deplorable. [STINK n. (1) + SE *bomb*]

stink-car n. **1** [1900s] a motorcar. **2** [1910s] a motorcycle. [SE *stink* + *car*; (1) also pun on STINKER n.[1] (3)]

stinker n.[1] **1** [17C+] a loathsome, unpleasant person or object; occas. used teasingly/affectionately. **2** [early 19C–1950s] a black eye. **3** [mid-19C+] anything that emits an offensive smell, orig. aimed at cigars and cigarettes. **4** [20C+] (*Aus.*) a very hot or humid day. **5** [1900s] (*Aus.*) a Chinese person (cf. AH CABBAGE n.). **6** [1900s] a brandy-ball sweet. **7** [1910s+] a strongly worded letter; a disagreeable review or other communication. **8** [1910s+] anything considered unpleasant because of the difficulty in accomplishing it, e.g. a school essay; thus [1920s+] *come a stinker*, to fall into difficulties. **9** [1910s+] an exceptional example of. **10** [1930s] an unfunny 'joke'. **11** [1940s+] a failure. **12** [1990s+] a promiscuous woman. **13** [1990s+] a bad mood. [SE *stink*; (2) 20C use is Aus.]

stinker n.[2] (*also* **stinka**) [1970s+] (*S.Afr. Black*) a passbook. [the wholly negative image it enjoyed in the Black community; such passes were scrapped in 1985]

stinkeroo n. [1930s+] (*Aus./US*) something disgusting or deplorable. [STINKER n.[1] (1) + -EROO sfx]

stink-eye n. [1990s+] (*US*) an aggressive, hostile look; usu. in phr. *give* (*someone*) *the stink-eye*.

stink-finger n. (*also* **stinky-finger, stinky-pinky**) [late 19C+] **1** the middle finger. **2** manual stimulation of the female genitals; thus *play* (*at*) *stink-finger*, to manually stimulate a woman's genitals. [(1) its use in sexual foreplay]

stink-finger v. [late 19C+] to manipulate a woman's genitals.

stink-hole bay n. [early 19C] the anus (cf. A-HOLE n.).

stinkibus n. [early 18C] bad beer or liquor, esp. when adulterated. [SE *stink*; note smugglers' use, a case of liquor that has been left under the water so long as to be undrinkable]

stinkies n. [2000s] (*Irish*) excrement.

stinking adj.[1] **1** [late 17C+] (*also* **stinking-ass**) a general negative intensifier, disgusting, repellent, odious. **2** [20C+] a general intensifier, a euph. for DAMNED adj., FUCKING adj. etc. [prior use from 13C is SE]

stinking adj.[2] **1** [late 19C+] very drunk. **2** [1940s] under the influence of drugs. **3** [1940s+] very well-off. [(3) abbr. of *stinking rich*]

stinkingly adv. (*also* **stinking**) [20C+] excessively, extraordinarily.

stinking with adj. [1910s+] in possession of a large amount of something, usu. money (cf. FILTHY WITH adj.).

stinkious n. [18C] gin. [? a misprint for STINKIBUS n.]

stinko n. **1** [1920s+] (*Aus.*) wine. **2** [1930s–40s] (*US*) an alcoholic tramp. [STINKO adj. (2); (2) + ref. to *Sterno* or 'canned heat', i.e. solidified alcohol drunk by down-and-outs]

stinko adj. [1920s+] **1** very poor, less than mediocre. **2** (*also* **stinky**) very drunk.

stink of v. (*also* **stink with**) [20C+] (*orig. US*) to be full of, characterized by, e.g. *stink of success, stink with money*.

Stinkomalee n. [mid-19C] London University. [coined by the Tory wit and writer Theodore Hook (1788–1841) with ref. to contemporary concerns over Trincomalee, to the fact that the university, founded in 1836, allowed in Nonconformists (Oxford and Cambridge did not), and to the farms and their animals that formerly occupied the site]

stink on ice v. [1930s+] (*US*) to be disgusting or deplorable. [ext. of STINK v.]

stinkpot n. **1** [18C] a chamberpot. **2** [20C+] a general term of abuse, aimed usu. at people rather than things. **3** [20C+] (*Aus.*) a small firework. **4** [20C+] an engine that emits foul fumes; thus a vehicle with such an engine. **5** [1910s] a large cap, called a mushroom. **6** [1910s] a stink-bomb. **7** [1950s–70s] (*US Black*) the vagina (cf. BAG n.[1]). [(2) esp. refers in N.Z. to a child who wets itself]

stinks n. [mid-19C+] (*mainly UK public school*) chemistry, as a subject.

stinks like Hogan's goat *phr.* [1950s+] (*US*) used of something bad, objectionable, a failure etc. [SE *stinks* + HOGAN'S GOAT phr.]

stink to high heaven *v.* [1970s+] (*orig. US*) to be very disgusting and unpleasant. [STINK v. + TO HIGH HEAVEN adv.]

stink up *v.* [1930s+] (*US*) **1** to soil, to sully. **2** to 'smell' suspicious.

stink weed *n.* **1** [1940s–70s] (*drugs*) marijuana (cf. AFRICAN BUSH n.). **2** [1950s] a smoker of marijuana.

stink with *v. see* STINK OF v.

stinky *adj.*[1] [1910s+] (*orig. US*) disgusting, nasty, inferior; dangerous. [STINK v.]

stinky *adj.*[2] *see* STINKO adj. (2).

stinky-butt *adj.* [1960s] (*US Black*) a general term of abuse, lit. 'stinking anus'.

stinky-finger *n. see* STINK-FINGER n.

stinky-pie rich *phr.* [1990s+] (*US Black*) extremely rich. [var. on STINKING adj.[2] (3) + SE *rich*]

stinky-pinky *n. see* STINK-FINGER n.

stipe *n.* **1** [mid-19C+] a *stipe*ndiary magistrate. **2** [1940s+] (*Aus.*) a *stipe*ndiary racing steward. [abbr.]

stir *n.*[1] (*also* **stur**) [mid-19C+] prison; thus STIR LAWYER n. [abbr. Rom. *sturiben*, a prison, *staripen*, to imprison; ult. *štar*, to imprison]

stir *n.*[2] [late 19C] a crowd. [SE *stir*, movement]

stir *n.*[3] **1** [1940s+] (*Ulster*) a plan, a scheme. **2** [1940s+] (*orig. Ulster*) fun, enjoyment, a party. **3** [1970s+] (*N.Z.*) a bout of trouble-making. [SE *stir*, movement]

stir *adj.* [1930s+] pertaining to prison. [STIR n.[1]]

stir *v.* [1960s+] **1** to gossip maliciously, to cause trouble deliberately by so doing. **2** (*orig. Aus.*) to tease, to provoke; thus *for a stir*, for trouble's sake. **3** (*Aus.*) to cause trouble (other than through gossip etc). [abbr. SE *stir up trouble*]

stir-about *n.* **1** [late 18C+] porridge. **2** [late 19C] any pudding that requires stirring. **3** [1910s] prison.

stir a peg *v. see* STIR ONE'S STUMPS v.

stir belly *n.* [1940s+] (*US prison*) indigestion caused by tension or fear. [STIR n.[1] + SE *belly*]

stir-bug *n.* (*also* **stir-nut**) [1920s+] (*US prison*) one who has gone mad due to the pressures of incarceration. [STIR n.[1] + BUG n.[5] (4)/NUT n.[4] (1)]

stir cramps *n.* [1970s] (*US prison*) psychological/physical problems that come with a jail sentence. [STIR n.[1] + SE *cramps*]

stir-crazy *adj.* (*also* **stirry, stir-simple**) [1920s+] (*orig. US prison*) used of a prisoner who has succumbed to insanity, usu. from too long a confinement; thus *stir-craziness*, psychosis induced by imprisonment. [STIR n.[1] + SE *crazy/simple*]

stir croaker *n.* [1950s] (*US prison*) a second-rate, barely qualified doctor, assigned to prison work. [STIR n.[1] + CROAKER n.[5] (1)]

stir fudge *v. see* FUDGE n.[2].

stir hustler *n.* [1940s+] (*US prison*) one who has mastered the 'art' of incarceration. [STIR n.[1] + HUSTLER n. (4)]

stir it up *v.* [1950s+] of a woman, to masturbate (cf. APPLY LIP GLOSS v.).

stir lawyer *n.* [1950s] (*US prison*) a fellow prisoner who offers advice based on his own purported legal expertise. [STIR n.[1] + SE *lawyer*]

Stirling Moss *n.* [20C+] a DAMN n., a curse; usu. in phr. *I don't give a stirling.* [rhy. sl. = TOSS n.[1] (1); ult. UK racing driver *Stirling Moss* (b.1929)]

stir-nut *n. see* STIR-BUG n.

stir one's stew *v.* (*also* **stir the batter/sauce**) [1950s+] to masturbate, usu. of a woman (cf. APPLY LIP GLOSS v.).

stir one's stumps *v.* (*also* **start one's stumps, stir a peg, stir one's pins**) [late 16C+] to get a move on; to dance; to do one's duty keenly. [SE *stir* + *stump*, a leg, STUMPS n.]

stirred *adj.* [1940s+] provoked, incited to violence or action, gone crazy. [STIR v.]

stirrer *n.*[1] [1940s] (*US*) a penis.

stirrer *n.*[2] [1960s+] (*Aus.*) one who stirs up trouble or discontent, an agitator, a trouble-maker; an unpleasant, malicious gossip. [STIR v.]

stirrup *v.* [early–mid-18C] to thrash someone with a shoemaker's *stirrup*.

stirry *adj. see* STIR-CRAZY adj.

stir-shit *n.* [late 19C–1900s] a sodomite, a male homosexual. [SE *stir* + SHIT n.[1] (1)]

stir shit *v. see* STIR (THE) SHIT v.

stir shit out of *v.* [1940s+] (*N.Z.*) to criticize harshly, to reprimand severely. [SE *stir* + SHIT n.[1] (1)]

stir-simple *adj. see* STIR-CRAZY adj.

stir the batter *v. see* STIR ONE'S STEW v.

stir the porridge *v.* [1980s+] (*orig. Aus.*) to have sexual intercourse with a woman immediately after she has had intercourse with another man, esp. used of the final man in a gang-rape.

stir the possum *v.* (*also* **rouse the possum**) [20C+] (*Aus.*) to create a disturbance, to start things moving, to jolt the general apathy. [the animal's habit of keeping quite still for long periods]

stir the sauce *v. see* STIR ONE'S STEW v.

stir (the) shit *v.* [1950s+] to go out of one's way to make trouble, esp. by gossiping or telling tales. [SE *stir* + SHIT n.[1] (1)]

stir the stew *v.* [1900s–10s] of a man, to have sexual intercourse.

stir up *v.* [late 19C] to visit without any previous announcement.

stir-up Sunday *n.* [mid-19C] the Sunday before Advent. [the collect for that day begins with the words 'Stir up…']

stirwise *adj.* [1930s–50s] (*US Und.*) well-adjusted to prison life, capable of sustaining one's existence in prison. [STIR n.[1] + -WISE sfx (1)]

stitch *n.*[1] [mid-17C–early 19C] a tailor. [metonymy]

stitch *n.*[2] [1960s+] (*US campus/teen*) anything or anyone seen as amusing; intensified as *stitch and a half.* [the physical SE *stitch* that can accompany laughter]

stitch *v.* **1** [18C–mid-19C] (*also* **go on the stitch**) to have sexual intercourse (cf. BANG v.[1]). **2** [1930s+] to beat in a fight or contest. **3** [1960s] (*US*) to shoot dead, to kill. [the in and out SE *stitching* movement of the penis or of the fists]

stitch-back *n.* [late 17C–early 19C] very strong ale. [? its back-strengthening properties. Note early 17C SE *steelback*, Alicante wine, which was supposed to help back problems]

stitched *adj.* **1** [mid-18C+] drunk. **2** [1920s+] (*Aus.*) defeated. [(1) STITCH-BACK n.; (2) STITCH v. (2)]

stitched up *adj.* [2000s] (*US prison*) of a problem, dealt with, usu. after a fight.

stitch-louse *n.* [mid-19C] a tailor.

stitch-up *n.* [1970s+] a false arrest, based on concocted or fraudulent evidence; also in non-police contexts. [STITCH UP v. (1)]

stitch up *v.* **1** [1970s+] (*UK Und./police*) for the police to ensure a conviction by planting evidence, faking confessions etc; also in non-police use. **2** [1970s+] to complete a task to one's complete satisfaction. **3** [1980s+] to cheat someone. **4** [2000s] to place in one's power. [sewing up a garment neatly and conclusively]

stiver *n.* (*also* **steever, steiver, stuiver, stuyver**) [mid-17C+] **1** something of little value; thus in cash terms, a penny. **2** in pl., money. [Du. *stiver*, a low-valued coin, the smallest monetary unit in use at the Cape under the Dutch East India Company, one-twentieth of a florin or gulden, worth a little more than 1 (old) penny; Nares suggests 'an inhabitant of the stews' i.e. a prostitute]

stiver-cramped *adj.* [late 18C–early 19C] impoverished. [STIVER n. + SE *cramped* (for)]

stoat *n. see* STOAT-THE-BAW n.

stoater *n.* (*also* **stoter**) **1** [17C–18C] a violent blow; thus *tip someone a stoater*, give someone a blow. **2** [20C+] a bruise. [Du. *stooter, stooten,* to knock, to push]

stoater v. (also **stoter**) [17C–early 18C] to hit. [STOATER n.]

stoat-the-baw n. (also **stoat**) [1990s+] (Scot.) a statutory rapist; a man who has intercourse with a girl below the legal age of consent. [? Scot. stoat/stot, a bullock or SE stoat; but stoat = hit, so poss. just a fool, cognate with head-the-ball]

stoat-the-baw adj. [1990s+] pertaining to statutory rape and those who commit it. [STOAT-THE-BAW n.]

stoat-the-baw v. [1990s+] to commit statutory rape. [STOAT-THE-BAW n.]

stob v. see STAB v.

stocious adj.¹ (also **stotious**) [1930s+] (Irish/Scot.) drunken. [? Scot. stot, staggering]

stocious adj.² (also **stoosh, stoshious, stoshus, stotious**) [1950s+] (W.I.) 1 well-dressed, stylish, high-class. 2 good-looking. 3 snobbish. [? SE ostentatious]

stock n.¹ [late 18C–early 19C] cheek; often as good stock. [abbr. SE stock of impudence]

stock n.² see STOOK n.

stock v. [mid–late 19C] in card-games, to stack the cards in a certain way to facilitate cheating; also in fig. use.

stockbanger n. [1930s] (Aus.) a stockman; thus stockbanging, working on a cattle farm.

stockdolager n. see SOCKDOLAGER n.

stock-drawers n. (also **stock-draers**) [mid-17C–early 19C] (UK Und.) stockings. [? the stockings are drawn on]

stocker n. [1970s+] (US) a stock-car racer.

stockholder n. [1930s–40s] (US prison) a convict who curries favour with the authorities. [ironic use of SE]

stocking n. (also **stocking stuffer**) [mid-19C+] (UK Und.) money.

stockings n. [1970s] (US Black) the female legs.

stock-in-trade n. [late 19C–1900s] the genitals. [SE stock-in-trade, a workman's tools]

stocks and shares n. [20C+] stairs. [rhy. sl.]

stodge n. 1 [mid-19C+] heavy, filling, nutritionless food; thus stodgepot, a container of such food. 2 [mid-19C+] heavy, demanding but relatively unrewarding work. 3 [mid-19C+] heavy, tedious writing or speech. 4 [late 19C–1940s] food in general. 5 [1900s] a snack. 6 [1980s] (Aus.) a cake. [SE stodge, thick, liquid, viscous mud]

stodge v. 1 [mid-19C+] to gorge, to eat to excess; thus stodging, eating heavily, gorging. 2 [1900s–50s] to work steadily at something tedious. [STODGE n.]

stodger n. 1 [late 19C] an old-fashioned person. 2 [late 19C–1920s] a glutton. 3 [1900s–20s] (also **stodge, stodgy**) a dull, spiritless person; thus stodgery, the manner in which such a person behaves. 4 [1910s] (US) a slovenly cook. [STODGE v.]

stoepkakker n. [1980s+] (S.Afr.) 'a small, fat and old dog of the spoiled rotten variety which has found its sunny spot on the stoep [verandah] and refuses, with miniature fangs at full snarl, to budge for anyone or anything, not even to take care of its bodily functions' (Cyberbraai, Internet, 1997). [Afk. stoep, porch, verandah + kakker, SHITTER n.¹]

stoep-sitter n. [1930s+] (S.Afr.) a farmer who is not primarily dependent on agriculture for their income. [Afk. stoep, verandah + SE sitter]

stog n. [1990s+] (US Black) a cigarette. [STOGIE n.]

stoggs n. [1990s+] the male genitals. [dial. stog, a sharp-pointed instrument]

stogie n. (also **stogey, stogy**) 1 [late 19C+] (US) a cigar. 2 [1980s] (US drugs) an over-sized marijuana cigarette. [abbr. Conestoga; supposedly smoked by the 'stoga drivers', i.e. the drivers of the Conestoga wagons plying between Wheeling and Pittsburgh, Pennsylvania]

stoinker n. [1990s+] a malodorous (whether lit. or fig.) and promiscuous woman. [STINKER n.¹]

stoke v.¹ [20C+] (W.I.) to humiliate, to treat badly. [? obs. SE stoke, to make a thrust at]

stoke v.² [1970s+] (Aus./US) of a person, to have a good time; of an object, to prove first-rate.

stoked adj. (also **stoked on/up**) 1 [1910s] (Aus.) full (of food). 2 [1960s+] (orig. Aus.) drunk (cf. ABOUT RIGHT phr.¹). 3 [1960s+] (US campus/teen, esp. California) elated, delighted, thrilled. 4 [1960s+] (also **stoked in**) sexually excited, lustful. 5 [1970s+] intoxicated by a drug. 6 [1980s] (also **stoked out**) tired out. 7 [1980s] (US campus) fully prepared. 8 [1990s+] (US campus) surprised, amazed. [SE stoke, to build up and stir a furnace]

stoke me (up)! excl. [1980s+] (US campus) a general excl. of approval, that's wonderful! I'm so happy! great! [STOKED adj. (3)]

stoke on trent n. [1970s+] a male homosexual. [rhy. sl. = BENT n.]

stoke on trent adj. [1980s+] 1 illegal. 2 homosexual. [rhy. sl.; (1) = BENT adj. (4); (2) = BENT adj. (5)]

stoke up v. 1 [late 19C+] to eat. 2 [1980s+] (US campus) to please, to encourage. [(1) SE; (2) STOKED adj. (3)]

stokkies n. [20C+] (S.Afr. Und.) a prison. [? Afk. stok, the stocks]

stolen a manchet out of the brewer's basket phr. (also **stolen a roll out of the brewer's basket**) [late 17C–early 19C] tipsy. [SE stolen + manchet, a small loaf or roll made from the finest wheat flour]

stole (on) v. [1990s+] (US Black) to hit with a surprise punch. [? SE steal a march]

Stoli n. (also **Stoly**) [1970s+] Stolichnaya vodka. [abbr.]

stoll v.¹ [mid-19C] (Ulster) to understand. [SE stall, to put in place]

stoll v.² [late 19C] to drink; thus stolled, tipsy. [? Norfolk dial. stole, to drink, to swallow]

Stoly n. see STOLI n.

stomach ache n. [1990s+] a steak. [rhy. sl.]

stomach habit n. [1950s–70s] (drugs) heroin addiction (through inhalation rather than injection). [SE stomach + HABIT n. (1)]

stomach Steinway n. (also **stomach pump**) [1930s] (US) a piano accordion. [SE stomach, against which it is held + Steinway, a piano]

stomp n.¹ (US Black) 1 [1940s] a foot. 2 [1940s+] a shoe. [SAmE stomp, to stamp]

stomp n.² see STOMPING n.

stomp-ass adj. [1940s+] (US) violent, aggressive. [STOMP (ON) v. (1) + -ASS sfx]

stomp-down adj. [1950s+] a general intensifier, very, complete, utter.

stomp-down woman n. (also **stomp-down whore**) [1950s–70s] (US Black) the hardest working woman in a pimp's STABLE n. (2) of prostitutes. [STOMP-DOWN adj. + SE woman/whore]

stompers n. (also **stomps, stumpers**) 1 [late 19C+] (US) large, heavy boots, esp. cowboy boots. 2 [1940s+] (US Black) shoes. [SAmE stomp, to stamp]

stompie n. [1940s+] (S.Afr.) a cigarette butt, a partially smoked cigarette, esp. one stubbed out and kept for relighting later; thus a worthless remnant. [Afk. stomp, stump]

stomping n. (also **stomp**) [1940s+] (orig. US) a beating, esp. one in which the victim is kicked or trampled on. [STOMP (ON) v. (1)]

stomping ground n. see STAMPING GROUND n.¹

stomp it phr. [1930s] hurry, go fast, esp. in a vehicle. [one 'stomps' on the accelerator]

stomp (on) v. (also **stomp out**) 1 [1940s+] (US) to beat up, to defeat. 2 [1950s+] (Aus. teen) to dance. 3 [1980s] (US Black) to use language that is likely to cause a fight. [SE stamp/SAmE stomp]

stomps n. see STOMPERS n.

stomp someone's buzz v. see KILL SOMEONE'S BUZZ v.

stoms n. see STUMBLERS n.

stone n.¹ 1 [mid-18C+] a testicle; often in pl. (cf. AGATES n.). 2 [1900s–50s] (US Und.) a diamond or jewel. 3 [1960s+] in fig. use of (1), courage, bravery; usu. in pl. 4 [1990s+] (drugs) crack cocaine (cf. BASE n.). [(1) SE mid-12C–early 18C]

stone n.² [1950s–60s] (US Black) a dollar.

stone *n.*[3] [1950s+] a state of drunken or drugged intoxication. [STONED (OUT) adj.]

stone *adj.* [1910s+] complete, absolute, e.g. *stone addict*, one who is deeply addicted to a drug. [STONE adv.]

stone *v.*[1] [1940s] (*US*) to criticize, to upbraid. [SE *stone*, to hurl stones at]

stone *v.*[2] [1940s+] **1** (*drugs*) (*also* **stone up**) to render intoxicated with a drug, usu. marijuana or hashish. **2** in fig. use, to create the same effect without drugs. [the image of being knocked over with a rock]

stone *adv.* (*also* **stone-cold, stony**) [17C+] absolutely, purely, completely, to the highest degree, e.g. *stone blind*, extremely drunk; *stone bonkers*, absolutely crazy. [i.e. the solidity of a stone]

stone-blind *adj.* [1950s] extremely intoxicated with a drug. [STONED (OUT) adj. (2) + BLIND adj.[1]]

stone broke *adj.* (*also* **stone motherless broke, stony broke**) [late 19C+] penniless, absolutely impoverished; thus *stone-broke, stone-broker, stony-broker*, one who is impoverished. [STONE adv. + BROKE adj.[1]]

stone butch *n.* [1960s+] (*US gay*) a very masculine lesbian. [STONE adj. + BUTCH n.[4] (3) + fig. uses of SE *stone*: 'The term comes from African American slang, in which "stone" means "very." It has come to have other meanings as well. A butch can be sexually stone, as in, not being able to permit herself to be touched on the genitals for sex; emotionally stone, meaning that she has locked away her emotions and has trouble acknowledging or expressing them; or physically stone, having trouble being touched at all. A stone butch is usually some combination of all of these' (Scott, *Rebecca's Dict. of Queer Slang and Culture*, 1998)]

stone-cold *n.* [1930s+] (*Aus. Und.*) a villain who would never betray his or her fellows whatever the circumstances.

stone-cold *adv. see* STONE adv.

stone-cold fox *n. see* STONE FOX n.

stone crock *n.* [1920s–30s] (*US tramp*) a state prison; orig. Sing Sing, New York. [SE *stone + crock*, a jug, thus play on STONE JUG n.[1] (1)]

stone doublet *n.* [late 17C–18C] a prison, esp. Newgate prison. [SE *stone + doublet*, tight-fitting body armour]

stoned (out) *adj.* [1950s+] **1** drunk. **2** intoxicated with some form of drug; thus *stoned out of one's brain/gourd/head/mind/skull*, very intoxicated on drink or, more usu., drugs.

stone dump *n.* [20C+] (*US Und.*) a prison. [SE *stone* + DUMP n.[3] (2)]

stone end *n.* (*also* **stone finish**) [1950s+] (*Aus.*) the absolute end, an intolerable situation. [STONE adv. + SE *end/finish*]

stoneface *n.* [1940s+] a totally unemotional person. [the first (SE) use of the phr. is in Nathaniel Hawthorne's story 'The Great Stone Face' (*National Era*, 16 January 1850), in which it referred to a natural rock formation. The unsmiling silent era comedian Buster Keaton (1898–1966) was known as the 'Great Stone Face']

stone femme *n.* [1990s+] (*US gay*) **1** a lesbian who invariably accepts a passive role. **2** a lesbian who does not wish to be touched. [STONE adj./SE *stone* + FEMME n. (3); *see also* ety. at STONE BUTCH n.]

stone fence *n.* (*also* **stone-wall**) (*US*) **1** [19C–1940s] whisky or another spirit mixed with cider. **2** [mid-19C–1900s] ginger beer and brandy. [ety. unknown]

stone finish *n. see* STONE END n.

stone fox *n.* (*also* **stone-cold fox**) [1970s+] (*US Black/campus*) a beautiful woman. [STONE adv. + FOX n.[5] (1)]

stone fruit *n.* [late 19C–1900s] children. [STONE n.[1] (1) + SE *fruit*; lit. the 'fruit of one's loins']

stone-getter *n. see* PROP-GETTER n.

stone ginger *n.* [1910s+] an absolute certainty. [the N.Z. racehorse *Stone Ginger*, known as phenomenally successful; ult. STONE adj. + racing *ginger*, a showy, fast horse]

stone hotel *n.* [1970s+] (*US*) a prison (cf. BOARDING HOUSE n.).

stone house *n.* [1930s–60s] a prison (cf. BANDHOUSE n.).

stone jacket *n.* [late 18C] (*US*) a prison.

stone jug *n.*[1] (*also* **stone pitcher**) **1** [early 17C–1940s] (*also* **stone john**) a generic term for any prison. **2** [late 18C–mid-19C] Newgate prison, the main criminal prison in London. [SE *stone* + JUG n.[2] (1); note synon. USN 1900s *stone frigate*]

stone jug *n.*[2] [1920s+] a fool, a dupe (cf. BEECHAM'S PILL n.). [rhy. sl. = MUG n.[2] (1)]

stone killer *n.* [1970s] (*US*) an outstanding example of a person or thing. [STONE adj. + KILLER n.[1] (4)]

stone mansion *n.* [1920s] (*US Und.*) a prison.

stone mason *n. see* CHARLEY MASON n.

stone me! *excl.* [1930s+] an excl. of surprise. [SE *stone*, to throw stones at]

stone motherless broke *adj. see* STONE BROKE adj.

stone out *v.* [1940s–50s] (*drugs*) to become over-intoxicated by a drug, usu. marijuana or hashish. [STONED (OUT) adj. (2)]

stone pitcher *n. see* STONE JUG n.[1]

stoner *n.* **1** [1970s+] a drug user, spec. of marijuana. **2** [1990s+] (*US teen*) a delinquent. [STONED (OUT) adj. (2)]

stones, the *n.* [mid-19C] the streets (of London). [abbr. SE *cobblestones*]

stones and bones *n.* [1970s+] (*US campus*) a course in prehistory.

stone tavern *n.* [late 18C–early 19C] a prison.

stone the crows! *excl.* [1920s+] (*orig. Aus./N.Z.*) an excl. of surprise, wonder, alarm.

stone to the bone *phr.* [1950s+] (*US Black*) said of one who is considered wholly admirable in every respect. [STONE adj. + TO THE BONE phr.]

stone up *v. see* STONE v.[2] (1).

stonewall *v.* [late 19C+] (*orig. Aus.*) to put up barriers, to obfuscate, to prevaricate; thus *stonewall*, a person or thing that obstructs. [the earliest cited use is late 19C cricket jargon, thence to political use and thence to general, but note US General Thomas 'Stonewall' Jackson, nicknamed for the implacable stand he conducted during the US Civil War Battle of Bull Run, 21 July 1861]

stone-wall *n. see* STONE FENCE n.

stonewall horrors *n.* [1900s–20s] (*Anglo-Irish*) delirium tremens. [SE *stonewall* + HORRORS, THE n. (2)]

stoney *adj. see* STONY adj.

stonicky *n.* [1970s] (*UK Und.*) a cosh. [naut. *stonicky*, a rope's end, used for punishment]

stonk *v.* [1980s] to hurl abuse. [milit. term for bombarding a target]

stonker *n.* [1980s+] **1** anything large, or impressive of its type. **2** (*also* **stonk, stonk-on**) an erection. [STONKER v.]

stonker *v.* [1910s+] (*Aus.*) **1** to render useless, to put out of action, to thwart. **2** to kill, to destroy. **3** to defeat, to outwit. [echoic; orig. milit. use; ? link to dial. *stonk*, the game of marbles, echoic of the click of one marble on another]

stonkered *adj.* [1910s+] (*orig. Aus.*) **1** drunk; thus *stonkering*, drinking (cf. ANNIHILATED adj.). **2** satiated. **3** beaten, defeated, in serious trouble. **4** exhausted. **5** dead. [STONKER v.]

stonking *adv.* [1980s+] a general intensifying term of approval; also as adj., enormous, excellent etc; esp. as *stonking great*. [STONKER n. (1)]

stonk-on *n. see* STONKER n. (2).

stony *adj.* (*also* **stoney**) [late 19C+] absolutely penniless. [abbr. STONE BROKE adj.]

stony *adv. see* STONE adv.

stony blind *adj.* [1920s–30s] (*Aus.*) absolutely drunk (cf. AFFLICTED adj.). [STONE adv. + BLIND adj.[1] (1)]

stony broke *adj. see* STONE BROKE adj.

stoob *n.* [mid-19C] boots. [backsl.]

stood *adj.* [1920s] (*US*) drunk.

stooge n. 1 [1910s+] (orig. US) any despised underling. 2 [1940s–60s] (US Und.) an informer. 3 [1960s+] (US campus) a general term of abuse. [? SE student; orig. show business, a comedian's assistant or 'straight man']

stooge adj. [1990s+] (Aus.) hoaxing, deceitful. [STOOGE v. (4)]

stooge v. 1 [1930s+] (orig. US) to work as an assistant or underling. 2 [1940s] to idle, to wait around. 3 [1940s–60s] to inform against someone. 4 [1990s+] (Aus.) to fool, to deceive. [STOOGE n.]

stook n. (also stock, stuke) [mid-19C–1910s] a pocket handkerchief; thus stook buzzer/hauler, a pickpocket who specialized in stealing handkerchiefs. [? Ger. Stück, a piece of cloth]

stook v. [20C+] (S.Afr.) to stir up trouble. [S.Afr.E. stook, to distil spirits]

stooked adj. [mid-19C+] of stolen goods or money, hidden.

stool n. 1 [1910s+] an informer. 2 [1920s] a plain-clothes detective. [abbr. STOOL-PIGEON n.[1]]

stool v. 1 [20C+] (US) to act as an informer. 2 [1920s] (US Und.) to search premises for drugs. [abbr. STOOL-PIGEON n.[1]]

stoolie n. (also stooley, stoolo, stooly) [1920s+] (orig. US) an informer. [abbr. STOOL-PIGEON n.[1]]

stooling n. [1920s+] (US) acting as an informer. [abbr. STOOL-PIGEON v. (2)]

stool-pigeon n.[1] 1 [mid-19C+] (orig. US) an informer, one who makes a confession implicating others; also in fig. use. 2 [1920s] (orig. US) a time-and-motion overseer. 3 [1920s] (US Und.) an 'inside man' who takes a job to gain information about the proposed site of a robbery. [SE stool-pigeon, a bird that is tied to a stool in order to lure other birds towards the waiting hunter; in this case the 'stool' is that in a police station. Apparently coined for the game of faro – see Asbury, Sucker's Progress (1938), 16: 'Stool- pigeon – Originally this word meant a pigeon used to decoy others into a trap. A few years before the turn of the nineteenth century it came into general use among American gamblers to designate a capper or a hustler for a Faro bank, and was still used as late as 1915']

stool-pigeon n.[2] [1900s] (Aus.) a drinker in a public house. [he is sitting on a bar-stool; play on STOOL-PIGEON n.[1]]

stool-pigeon n.[3] [1980s+] (US gay) one who loiters in men's lavatories in order to offer fellatio. [SE stool, excrement or seat + pun on STOOL-PIGEON n.[1]]

stool-pigeon v. (US) 1 [mid-19C] to make a false arrest; the victim is then released on payment of a bribe and all records are expunged. 2 [mid-19C+] for one villain to inform on another.

stooly n. see STOOLIE n.

stoom out v. [1900s] (Aus.) to render someone silent; thus to kill. [SHTUM adj.]

stoop n.[1] [mid-18C–early 19C] the pillory; thus stooped, placed in the pillory. [the position one adopts while thus confined]

stoop n.[2] [1940s+] (Aus.) a petty thief. [he stoops to pick up things]

stoop n.[3] see STUPE n.

stoop v.[1] 1 [late 16C] to be ensnared by a confidence trickster or thief. 2 [1980s] (US Black) to have sexual intercourse.

stoop v.[2] [early 19C] to put someone in the pillory. [STOOP n.[1]]

stooper n. 1 [1920s–30s] (US tramp) (also stoop tobacco) a cigarette stub, picked up in the street. 2 [1960s] (US) a person who forages for betting tickets on the ground at racetracks. [SE stoop, to bend down]

stooping-match n. [early 19C] the placing of a number of people in the pillory at the same time. [STOOP n.[1] + SE match]

stoop-napper n. [late 18C–early 19C] (UK Und.) a man standing in a pillory. [STOOP n.[1] + NAPPER n.[1] (1)]

stoop tobacco n. see STOOPER n. (1).

stoosh adj. see STOCIOUS adj.[2].

stop n.[1] [mid-19C] a detective (cf. BEAT-POUNDER n.). [he stops malefactors]

stop n.[2] [1930s–40s] (US Und.) a receiver of stolen goods. [play on FENCE n.[1] (1)]

stop n.[3] [1940s+] (S.Afr. drugs) 1 marijuana. 2 a single pipeful of marijuana or enough to roll a single cigarette. 3 the smallest measure of marijuana sold. [Afk. stop, a plug or fill of tobacco]

stop v. [1920s+] (Aus.) in a fight, to knock down or knock out one's opponent; also in fig. use.

stop a bullet v. see STOP A SLUG v.

stop and go n. [20C+] a toe. [rhy. sl.]

stop and start n. [20C+] the heart. [rhy. sl.]

stop a packet v. see COP A PACKET v.

stop a pot v. (also stop a pint) [1910s–40s] (Aus.) to have a drink. [SE stop + pot (of ale)/pint]

stop a slug v. (also stop a bullet, stop lead) [1930s–50s] (US) to be shot (dead). [SE stop + SLUG n.[2] (1)/SE bullet/LEAD n.[1] (1)]

stop-gap n. [1910s–20s] the last child born to a family. [GAP n.[1] (1)]

stop-hole abbey n. [late 17C–early 19C] (UK Und.) the headquarters of the contemporary London underworld. [SE stophole, a plug + abbey; presumably some large if otherwise abandoned and decaying building, poss. in the criminal zone of ALSATIA n. (1), to which easy entrance, i.e. by the authorities, was barred]

stop it v. see STOP ONE v.[1] (2).

stople v. [1990s+] (Irish) to have sexual intercourse. [SE stopple, to close with a bung]

stop lead v. see STOP A SLUG v.

stop my vitals! excl. see STAP MY VITALS! excl.

stop off v. [late 19C–1900s] (N.Z.) to stop doing something, often as imper.

stop on a dime v. [1950s+] (US) to stop quickly and precisely. [the tiny size of the 10-cent coin]

stop one v.[1] 1 [late 19C–1910s] to be hit by. 2 [20C+] (also stop it) to be wounded. [as in a bullet (cf. STOP A SLUG v.)]

stop one v.[2] [1900s–30s] (Aus.) to have a drink.

stop one's jaw v. see HOLD ONE'S JAW v.

stop-out n. [20C+] one who stays out enjoying themselves longer than the speaker considers respectable.

stopper n. 1 [early 19C] (boxing) a heavy blow. 2 [early 19C+] anything that causes events to come to a halt; esp. in phr. put a stopper on, to bring to a halt. 3 [mid-19C] (UK Und.) a policeman (cf. BEAT-POUNDER n.).

stoppers n. [1970s] (drugs) depressants, barbiturates (cf. BARBIT n.). [they SE stop one moving]

stopping oyster n. see CHOKING OYSTER n.

stoppo n. 1 [1930s] a break from work. 2 [1930s+] an escape, a getaway; thus stoppo driver, a getaway driver; stoppo car, the car in which criminals escape. [SE stop + -O sfx (1)]

stoppo v. [1950s] (UK Und.) to make an escape.

stoppo! excl. [1950s] stop what you are doing!

stop someone's blubber v. [early 18C] (UK Und.) to silence, poss. by murder. [SE stop + BLUBBER n.[1]]

stop someone's clock v. 1 [20C+] to defeat heavily. 2 [1950s+] to kill.

stop-the-clock n. [20C+] (Ulster) a pessimist. [the custom of stopping the clocks following a death in the house]

stop thief n. [mid-19C+] 1 beef. 2 stolen meat. [rhy. sl.; note HOT BEEF! excl. = stop thief!]

stop two gaps with one bush v. [16C] to accomplish 2 tasks simultaneously. [later use is SE]

stop work n. [1940s+] (bingo) the number 65 (cf. ALDERSHOT LADIES n.). [the male retirement age]

stop your andrew makins! excl. [20C+] (Anglo-Irish) stop fooling! [? var. on ANDRAMARTINS n.; E.P. notes dial. andrew, a clown + SE merry-Andrew + SE making, i.e. doing]

stop your gab! excl. [early 19C–1900s] be quiet! [SE stop + GAB n. (1)]

stop your gap! excl. [late 19C+] shut up! be quiet! [SE stop + GAP n.[1] (2)]

store *n.* [1900s–40s] (*US Und.*) anywhere that provides the site for a confidence trick. [note US carnival use *store*, any form of carnival concession]

store-bought hair *n.* [1900s–30s] (*US Black*) a wig, a hairpiece.

stored away *phr.* [1940s–50s] (*US Und.*) in prison.

storefront preacher *n.* [1950s+] (*US Black*) a local gossip, who 'preaches' only to those who idle away their days outside the general store of some small town.

storekeeper *n.* [late 19C] (*US*) an article that has remained unsold for so long that it may never leave the shop.

stork *v.* [1970s] (*US campus*) to make pregnant. [the myth of storks bringing babies]

storm and strife *n.* [late 19C–mid-20C] (*mainly US*) one's wife. [rhy. sl.]

storm-buzzard *n.* [1930s–40s] (*US Black*) a homeless or unemployed person, a beggar.

stormer *n.* **1** [mid-19C] (*US gambling*) a heavy winner. **2** [1920s+] a success.

storm-stick *n.* [1930s+] (*Aus.*) an umbrella.

stormy dick *n.* [20C+] (*US*) the penis (cf. ALMOND *n.*). [rhy. sl. = PRICK *n.* (2)]

stormy end *n.* [1920s] (*US tramp*) the windowless or 'blind' baggage car of a passenger train.

storrac *n.* [mid-19C] carrots. [backsl.]

story *n.* **1** [late 17C+] a euph. for a lie; thus [mid-18C+] *story-teller*, a liar; *story-telling*, lying; also *story along*, to deceive, to tell a false tale. **2** [1900s–20s] a liar. **3** [1950s] (*US*) a fuss. **4** [1970s] (*US campus*) an afternoon television soap opera. ['a Puritanism that came into fashion with the trade against romances, all novels and stories being considered as dangerous and false' (Hotten, 1864)]

story of a cock and a bull *n. see* BANBURY STORY *n.*

stoshious/stoshus *adj. see* STOCIOUS *adj.*[2].

stoshy *n.* [1940s–50s] (*W.I.*) a boyfriend. [? STOCIOUS *adj.*[2]; but note UK dial. *stoushie*, a stout and healthy child]

stoter *see under* STOATER.

stotious *see under* STOCIOUS.

stotor *n.* [mid-19C] (*UK Und.*) a heavy blow, a 'settler'. [for ety. *see* STOATER *n.*]

stott-on *n.* [1990s+] (*UK juv.*) the erect penis.

stoush *n.* (*also* **stouch, stoush-up**) **1** [20C+] (*Aus./N.Z.*) a fight, fighting; thus *stoush-artist/-merchant*, a habitual and competent fighter, a bully; *deal out stoush, put in the stoush*, to attack violently, to fight enthusiastically; *take stoush*, to take a beating; *the Big Stoush*, WW1; *reinstoushments*, reinforcements. **2** [1910s] a beating. [STOUSH *v.*]

stoush *adj.* [1990s+] (*UK Black teen*) aggressive, ready to fight. [? STOUSH *n.* (1); poss. independent origin]

stoush *v.* (*also* **stouch, stoush up**) **1** [late 19C+] (*Aus./N.Z.*) to have a fight; to beat, to hit. **2** [1900s] to stop, to cease. **3** [1900s–30s] in fig. uses, e.g. to steal; *stoushed*, beaten (in a race). **4** [1910s] wounded. [? UK dial. *stashie*, a quarrel, an uproar]

stousher *n.* [20C+] (*Aus./N.Z.*) a fighter; thus *stoushie*, a soldier; *stoushing*, fighting, beating up. [STOUSH *v.* (1)]

stoush-up *n. see* STOUSH *n.*

stoush up *v. see* STOUSH *v.*

stout *n.* [late 17C–mid-18C] (*UK Und.*) strong beer. [the modern use, as a synon. for SE *porter* emerged *c.*1750]

stove *n.* [20C+] (*Ulster*) a strong or unpleasant smell, esp. of drink; thus *stoving*, drunk. [SE *stove*, to fumigate with sulphur]

stoved-up *adj. see* STOVE-UP *adj.*

stove lid *n.* [1930s+] a derog. term for a Black person (cf. BLACK-BELLY *n.*). [the blackening of the utensil]

stove-pipe *n.* (*also* **stove-pipe hat**) **1** [mid-19C–1950s] (*US*) a tall hat, a top hat. **2** [mid-19C; 1960s+] tight, narrow trousers.

stove-up *adj.* (*also* **stoved up**) [1930s–60s] (*US*) usu. of people, run-down, exhausted, worn-out. [SE *stave*, to smash]

stow *v.* **1** [mid-16C–mid-19C] to stop talking; esp. in phrs. *stow it! shut up! stow that! that's not true! stow your noise! stow your yap!* be quiet! **2** [18C+] to stop, to desist (other than speech). [SE *stow*, to put away, to put on one side]

stowed *adj.* [1990s+] packed closely, very full. [dial. *stow*, to fill up]

stow faking! *excl.* [early–mid-19C] stop that! [STOW *v.* (2) + FAKE *v.*[1] (2)]

stow one's jaw *v.* [1920s] (*US*) to stop talking, usu. as imper.

stow one's whids *v.* (*also* **stow one's whidds**) [17C–mid-19C] (*UK Und.*) to be quiet, to stop talking, to be careful. [STOW *v.* (1) + WHID *n.* (1)]

stow you! *excl.* [mid-16C–17C] (*UK Und.*) hold your peace! shut up! [STOW *v.* (1)]

stow your gaff! *excl. see* GAFF *n.*[2] (1).

s.t.p. *n.* (*drugs*) **1** [1960s+] a form of hallucinogen. **2** [1980s+] phencyclidine (cf. ACE *n.*[4]). [(1) either abbr. of serenity, tranquillity and peace, or play on scientifically treated petroleum, a gasoline additive; (2) is a mistaken use of (1)]

stract *adj.* [1990s+] (*US prison*) neat and clean in appearance and dress. [orig. synon. US milit. *strac*; note Dave Wilton on *American Dialect Society-List* (Internet, 10 August 2002): '"STRAC." Originally an 1950s acronym for Strategic Army Corps, a group of four, elite divisions maintained at a high readiness for overseas deployment. It began to be used as an adjective, to be "STRAC" was to be prepared […] After the demise of the Corps, the adjectival use hung on. A new, unofficial backronym was formed for it, "Skilled, Tough, Ready, Around the Clock." It was very common in the US Army of the 1980s']

straddle *v.* [early–mid-18C] to draw lots or throw dice to determine who shall pay a bill.

straddle a chamber-pot *v. see* PEE BETWEEN TWO HEELS *v.*

straight *n.*[1] **1** [mid-19C–1950s] (*US*) unadulterated or very strong whisky. **2** [1950s+] (*S.Afr. Black*) a 750ml (26fl oz) bottle of spirits or beer. **3** [1950s+] (*drugs*) a tobacco cigarette. **4** [1960s+] an unfiltered cigarette.

straight *n.*[2] **1** [late 19C] (*UK Und.*) someone trustworthy in criminal terms, and thus usu. not at all 'straight'. **2** [1910s+] a conventional, respectable person; by ext. one who does not use drugs. **3** [1930s+] (*orig. gay*) a heterosexual person. **4** [1930s+] conventional heterosexual intercourse in the face to-face 'missionary position'; thus pornography featuring this. **5** [1990s+] (*US campus*) one who stands outside the current social norms.

straight *n.*[3] *see* STRAIGHT SHOOTER *n.*[2] (2).

straight, the *n.* [mid-19C–1940s] (*US*) the facts, the truth, trustworthy information.

straight *adj.*[1] **1** [early 17C+] of accounts, satisfactorily settled, balanced; also in fig. use. **2** [mid-19C+] esp. of language, unadorned, undiluted, expressed in a straightforward manner. **3** [mid-19C+] of a woman, chaste; of a man, honest. **4** [mid-19C+] of a situation, honest, satisfactory, as one desires. **5** [mid-19C+] respectable, law-abiding, honest. **6** [late 19C] of a wager, definite. **7** [late 19C+] of information etc, trustworthy, undisputable. **8** [late 19C+] in criminal terms, trustworthy. **9** [20C+] a synon. for SE *right*. **10** [1920s+] aware, understanding, comprehending. **11** [1930s+] in the sex industry, used of normal heterosexual intercourse, with no 'perversions', e.g. flagellation or bestiality. **12** [1940s+] heterosexual. **13** [1960s+] conventional, as opposed to the values of the 'counterculture'. **14** [2000s] successful.

straight *adj.*[2] **1** [mid-19C+] (*drugs*) of liquor, unadulterated; subseq. of a powdered narcotic. **2** [mid-19C+] sober. **3** [1950s+] (*drugs*) not currently using drugs; orig. of narcotics but ext. to any drug. **4** [1950s+] (*drugs*) cured of one's withdrawal pains by an injection of heroin. **5** [1950s+] (*drugs*) of an addict, having had the first dose of the day. **6** [1950s+] (*drugs*) in possession of drugs. **7** [1950s+] (*US*) under the influence of drugs; thus free from withdrawal symptoms.

straight *adj.*[3] [1970s+] (*orig. US Black*) a general intensifier, e.g. *straight chilling* (lit. unadulterated).

straight *adj.*[4] (*also* **strizzy**) [1990s+] (*US teen*) cheerful, satisfied.

straight *adv.*[1] **1** [late 16C–17C; late 19C+] without any reservations. **2** [mid-19C] (*US*) properly, efficiently. **3** [mid-19C+] honestly, really. **4** [1950s] sensibly. **5** [2000s] (*US Black*) very well.

straight *adv.*[2] [late 19C+] (*orig. US*) consecutively, in a row.

straight! *excl.* **1** [late 19C+] an excl. of affirmation, honestly! really! **2** [1990s+] (*US Black*) a general term of agreement.

straight-ahead *adj.* [late 19C+] (*Aus./US*) committed, reliable, e.g. *a straight-ahead guy*.

straight ahead! *excl.* [1960s+] (*US Black*) an excl. of encouragement, support, affirmation.

straight and narrow, the *n.* [1910s+] conventionally moral and law-abiding behaviour; thus *keep on the straight and narrow*, to maintain a regular, law-abiding life. [Matt. 7:14: 'Because strait is the gate, and narrow is the way which leadeth unto life, and few there be that find it.' Note the mid-19C hymn: 'Loving Shepherd, ever near, / Teach Thy lamb Thy voice to hear; / Suffer not my steps to stray / From the straight and narrow way']

straight arrow *n.* **1** [1960s+] (*US*) an honest, clean-living, clean-cut, upright, if naïve and unsophisticated, person. **2** [1970s] (*US gay*) a heterosexual male.

straight-arrow *adj.* [1960s+] honest, upright, respectable, clean-living. [STRAIGHT ARROW n. (1)]

straight-arrow *adv.* [1960s] (*US*) honestly. [STRAIGHT-ARROW adj.]

straight as a dog's hind leg *phr.* (*also* **straight as a butcher's hook/a loon's leg**) [mid-19C–1940s] crooked. [canine physiology]

straight bit of goods *n.* [late 19C] a respectable young woman. [STRAIGHT adj.[1] (3) + BIT OF GOODS n.]

straight crip *n.* [1920s–40s] (*US tramp*) one whose handicap is not faked. [STRAIGHT adj.[1] (3) + CRIP n.[1] (1)]

straight down the pike *phr.* [1990s+] (*US*) a general intensifier, indicating a supreme example of the preceding n.

straight drinking *n.* [late 19C] drinking while upright, i.e. standing at a bar rather than sitting at a table.

straighten *v.*[1] [late 19C–1900s] (*Aus.*) to defeat, to overcome; to beat up.

straighten *v.*[2] (*also* **straighten out/up**) [20C+] (*UK Und.*) to bribe, usu. to bribe a policeman. [i.e. to make STRAIGHT adj.[1] (8)]

straighten *v.*[3] **1** [20C+] to sort someone out, to make them aware, to initiate. **2** [1940s+] to look after.

straighten *v.*[4] (*also* **straighten out/up**) **1** [1910s+] to settle an account or debt. **2** [1950s–60s] to calm down, to defuse a situation. [STRAIGHT adj.[1]]

straighten *v.*[5] [1910s+] to settle an argument or a grudge by fighting. [SE *straighten things out*]

straighten *v.*[6] (*also* **straighten out**) **1** [1920s+] (*drugs*) to give an injection of narcotics to relieve someone's withdrawal symptoms. **2** [1930s+] (*also* **straighten up**) to stop (someone) taking addictive drugs. **3** [1960s] in a general sense, to give or sell drugs. [STRAIGHT adj.[2]]

straighten *v.*[7] *see* STRAIGHTEN OUT v. (1).

straightener *n.*[1] [1900s] (*Aus.*) a reviving drink; a drink that renders an alcoholic 'normal'.

straightener *n.*[2] [1950s+] **1** an argument that may escalate into a physical fight. **2** an act of punishment, retribution.

straightener *n.*[3] [1950s+] a bribe. [STRAIGHTEN v.[2]]

straighten out *v.* **1** [late 19C+] (*also* **straighten**) to teach someone manners, to make them socially acceptable within a context. **2** [1920s+] to 'teach someone a lesson', to punish. **3** [1920s+] (*US*) to give an explanation; to sort a situation out. **4** [1920s+] to act in an acceptable manner, to remedy one's mistakes. **5** [1940s+] to soothe one's emotions; to cheer someone up. **6** [1950s] (*US Und.*) to introduce.

straighten out *see also under* STRAIGHTEN.

straighten up *v.* [20C+] to take up an honest, respectable life. [i.e. to make oneself STRAIGHT adj.[1] (5)]

straighten up *see also under* STRAIGHTEN.

straighten up and fly right *v.* [late 19C+] (*orig. US Black*) to behave oneself, to mend one's ways and live a sensible, respectable life. [orig. used in a folktale, recorded by Joel Chandler Harris in *Short Stories Told After Dark* (1889)]

straight-faced *adj.* [1940s+] (*US*) stern, unflinching.

straight flounging *n.* [1990s+] (*US teen*) acting in whatever manner is dictated by one's current circumstances. [STRAIGHT adj.[3] + SE *lounge*]

straight from the bog *phr.* [late 19C+] a derog. term used of an Irish immigrant to the UK. [racial stereotyping]

straight from the feed box *phr.* (*also* **straight from the nosebag**) [1900s–30s] of news, information, absolutely reliable, from 'inside' sources. [SE *straight* + FEED BOX n. (1); earlier var. on STRAIGHT FROM THE HORSE'S MOUTH phr.]

straight from the fridge *phr.* [1960s] (*US Black/teen*) excellent, first-rate. [i.e. COOL adj.[1] (6)]

straight from the horse's mouth *phr.* [1920s+] (*orig. racing*) of news or information, absolutely reliable, gleaned from 'inside' sources.

straight from the nosebag *phr. see* STRAIGHT FROM THE FEED BOX phr.

straight goer *n.* [20C+] (*orig. Aus.*) an honest, dependable person. [STRAIGHT adj.[1] (3) + GOER n. (3)]

straight going *n.* [late 18C] (*Aus.*) honest behaviour. [STRAIGHT adj.[1] + SE *going*]

straight goods *n.* [late 19C+] (*US*) **1** the absolute truth. **2** a person who tells the truth; also attrib. [STRAIGHT adj.[1] (2) + GOODS, THE n.[1] (2)]

straight-hair *n.* (*Aus.*) **1** [mid-19C] a convict. **2** [late 19C+] a Western Australian. [the convict crop; thus a derog. ref. to Western Australia]

straight line shooter *n.* [1930s] (*US drugs*) a drug addict who injects into the vein. [SE *straight* + LINE n.[4] (1) + SHOOTER n.[2] (1)]

straight-neck *n.* [1960s] (*US*) a conventional, disapproving person.

straightnik *n.* [1970s] (*US gay*) a heterosexual male. [STRAIGHT n.[2] (3) + -NIK sfx; but note STRAIGHT-NECK n.]

straight off *adv.* [1930s+] immediately.

straight off the banana boat *phr.* [1970s] (*US campus*) strange, eccentric, weird.

straight off the turnips *phr.* [1930s+] (*Aus./N.Z.*) used of a country bumpkin.

straight oil *n.* [1930s+] (*Aus.*) the honest truth, the facts. [STRAIGHT adj.[1] (2) + OIL n.[2] (3)]

straight-out *adj.* [20C+] (*US*) uncompromising, absolute.

straight out of the trees *phr.* [1950s+] a derog. phr. used of Black immigrants to the UK, irrespective of background (cf. AFRICAN APE n.).

straight-peg *n.* [1980s+] a law-abiding person.

straight pitching *n.* [mid-19C] (*UK Und.*) working without accomplices.

straight poop *n. see* POOP n.[4] (2).

Straights, the *n.* [17C] a network of alleyways and small courts in an area bounded by St Martin's Lane, Half Moon Street and Chandos Street, all in Covent Garden, London, the haunt of pimps, thugs and similar unsavoury characters.

straight shit *n.* [1960s+] **1** the truth. **2** utter lies. [STRAIGHT adj.[1] (2) + SHIT n.[3] (4)]

straight shooter *n.*[1] [1920s+] (*US*) an honest, dependable, trustworthy person. [fig. use of SE]

straight shooter *n.*[2] (*US drugs*) **1** [1970s] one who injects narcotics. **2** [1990s+] (*also* **straight**) a hypodermic, a syringe.

straight shot *n.* [1970s+] (*US Black*) sexual intercourse without contraception.

straight skinny n. [1960s–70s] (US) the truth. [STRAIGHT adj.[1] (2) + SKINNY n.[3] (2)]

straight tip n. [mid–late 19C] honest advice. [STRAIGHT adj.[1] (2) + TIP n.[5] (1)]

straight trick n. [1970s+] a prostitute's client who requires no 'extras' beyond normal intercourse. [STRAIGHT adj.[1] (11) + TRICK n.[1] (3)]

straight up adj.[1] **1** [late 19C] (US) of eggs, 'sunny-side up'. **2** [1960s] (US prison) of a sentence, served without parole. **3** [1960s+] simple. **4** [1970s+] (US) of drinks, served without ice cubes. [ext. of SE straight, undiluted]

straight up adj.[2] **1** [late 19C+] a general term of emphasis, implying honesty and genuineness; thus excl. straight up! honestly! really! **2** [20C+] respectable. **3** [1930s+] honest, trustworthy. **4** [1970s+] undeniable. **5** [1990s+] (US Black) rigid, strict.

straight up adv. [late 19C+] (US) honestly. [STRAIGHT UP adj.[2] (1)]

straight up six o'clock girl n. [1940s] (US Black) a very thin woman. [the position of the clock's hands]

straight walk-in n. [1920s–30s] a woman who is seen as easy to seduce. [i.e. one needs only walk in and introduce oneself]

straight wire n. [late 19C+] (Aus./N.Z.) the honest truth; also used without an article to emphasize the truth of an assertion. [STRAIGHT adj.[1] (2) + WIRE n.[2] (1)]

strained out adj. [1960s] (US drugs) to be experiencing a drug's maximum effect.

strain hard v. [late 17C–18C] to tell a substantial lie. [ext. use of SE]

strain off v. [20C+] to urinate (cf. BLEED ONE'S TURKEY v.).

strain one's greens v. **1** [1900s–30s] of a man, to have sexual intercourse. **2** [1980s+] to urinate (cf. BLEED ONE'S TURKEY v.). [SE strain + pun on greens/GREENS n.[2]]

strain the main vein v. [1950s+] to masturbate.

strain the potatoes v. (also strain the spuds/taters) [1960s+] (Aus.) to urinate (cf. BLEED ONE'S TURKEY v.).

stram, the n. (also stramm, the) [late 19C] the profession of street-walking. [? SE strumpet, or US stram, to walk some distance or dial. stram, to bang, to strike and the widespread equation of sexual intercourse with 'banging']

stramel/strammel n. see STROMMEL n.

strammel n. see STAMMEL n.

strammer n. [mid–late 19C] anything exceptional, whether in size or effect. [fig. use of dial. stram, to bang]

strange n. [1960s+] an unknown woman, usu. in a sexual context; thus piece of strange. [STRANGE adj.[1]]

strange adj.[1] [20C+] of women, unknown, hitherto unencountered. [note Leaves from the Diary of a Celebrated Burglar and Pickpocket (1865): 'Jimmy Glindon […] had left her because of her great relish for strange "blokes" during Jimmy's absence on the "dip".']

strange adj.[2] [1990s+] (US campus) on bad = good model, excellent, first-rate.

strange fruit n. [1940s–60s] (US Black) an odd, unpredictable person.

strangely weird n. [20C+] a beard. [rhy. sl.]

strange-o n. [1950s–60s] an eccentric, a madman. [SE strange + -o sfx (1)]

stranger n.[1] **1** [late 18C–19C] (mainly UK tramp) a guinea. **2** [mid-19C] (US) a barrel of whisky. **3** [1900s–30s] a sovereign. [(1) and (3) to encounter so large a sum is a rare event; (2) in a 'dry' county the whisky has to be imported from a distance]

stranger n.[2] **1** [19C+] (orig. US) a term of address to one whose name is unknown. **2** [1930s+] anyone one knows but has not seen for some time; thus hello stranger, a greeting to a long-absent friend.

strangle a darkie v. see CHOKE A DARKIE v.

strangle and smother n. [20C+] (Aus.) a mother. [rhy. sl.]

strangle a parrot v. see SMOTHER A PARROT v.

strangle-goose n. [late 18C–19C] a poulterer.

strangler n. [1920s–30s] a necktie. [? SE + pun on SE choker, a necktie/choke]

strangle the goose v. **1** [1940s] (N.Z.) (also strangle the gander) to urinate (cf. FLOG THE LIZARD v.). **2** [1970s+] (also strangle the snake/stogie) to masturbate (cf. BEAT ONE'S HOG v.). [SE goose, i.e. its long neck/SNAKE n.[3] (1)/fig. use of STOGIE n. (1)]

strap n.[1] (also streepach, streepo) [mid–late 17C; mid-19C+] (Irish) a prostitute; thus fig. an unpleasant woman. [Irish straip, a prostitute]

strap n.[2] [mid-19C] a barber. [the SE strop used to sharpen razors. Note Hugh Strap, a barber, in Tobias Smollett's Roderick Random (1748)]

strap n.[3] [mid-19C+] credit; thus on strap, on credit. [? it 'holds one together']

strap n.[4] [1900s–40s] (US Und.) 'a short-con game played with a coiled strap, one coil of which the mark tries to catch with a pencil' (Maurer, The Big Con, 1940).

strap n.[5] **1** [1940s] (US Und.) a cosh, a blackjack. **2** [1970s] (Can.) a thug.

strap n.[6] [1980s+] (US Black) a gun; thus strap me, give me a gun. [one 'straps' it to one's waist or into a holster]

strap v.[1] **1** [early 19C] (also strap at/to) to work hard, to get on with, to buckle down to. **2** [1980s] to interrogate. [? (1) one applies the fig. strap to one's own back; (2) to another's back]

strap v.[2] [mid–late 19C] to give credit. [STRAP n.[3]]

strap-oil n. (also oil of strap'em/strappem) [mid-19C–1930s] a flogging with a strap. [thus popular April Fool's joke of sending a boy for 'a pennyworth of strap-oil']

strap-on n. [1950s+] a dildo, with straps that anchor it to the user's body.

strap on v. [1960s+] to have sexual intercourse. [coarse use of SE]

strapped adj. (also strapped down, strapping) [1980s+] carrying a gun. [STRAP n.[6]]

strapped (for cash) adj. [mid-19C+] (orig. US) **1** impoverished, poor. **2** in non-monetary contexts. [? the consequent 'tightening of one's belt', usu. a leather strap; or dial. strap, to drain dry, esp. of a cow's udder; ? STRAP n.[3]]

strapper n. [late 17C–mid-19C] a big, strong person, a notably hard worker; thus 19C strapping-shop, any workplace where an especially large volume of work is required of the employees. [one who is fig. 'bound together with straps']

strapping n. [late 17C–early 19C] sexual intercourse. [SE strapping, a beating, i.e. image of intercourse as violence]

strapping adj. see STRAPPED adj.

strapponia n. [mid-19C] (US) a physical beating. [SE strap]

straps n.[1] [late 19C] sprats. [joc. mispron.]

straps n.[2] [1940s] (US Black) braces, called suspenders in US.

strap to v. see STRAP v.[1] (1).

strap up v.[1] [20C+] (Aus.) to obtain on credit; to offer credit. [ext. of STRAP v.[2]]

strap up v.[2] [1990s+] (US) to carry a gun. [STRAPPED adj.]

strat n. [1960s+] a Stratocaster guitar. [abbr.]

stratocruiser n. [1980s] (W.I. drugs) a large marijuana and tobacco cigarette (cf. BOMB n.[4]).

straw n.[1] [20C+] a person with light blond hair. [abbr. SE straw blond(e)]

straw n.[2] [1900s–60s] (US Black) a hat, although not necessarily a straw hat. [note 19C SE use, a straw hat]

straw n.[3] (drugs) **1** [1940s–50s] an opium pipe. **2** [1960s] a marijuana cigarette or marijuana generally. **3** [1960s] rolling papers.

straw n.[4] see STRAWING n.

strawb n. see STRAWBERRY (RIPPLE) n.

strawberries n. [1970s] (drugs) **1** tablets of mescaline. **2** amphetamines (cf. A n.[2]). [the colour of the tablets]

strawberries and cream *n.* [1950s] (*UK prison*) the punishment diet of bread and water.

strawberry *n.*[1] **1** [late 19C] a broken-veined, bloated nose that exhibits signs of its possessor's heavy drinking. **2** [20C+] a red nose. [the colour]

strawberry *n.*[2] **1** [1920s+] a bruise, esp. a graze or sore that results from friction with the ground. **2** [1980s+] (*US teen*) a promiscuous woman, esp. one who barters sex for drugs. **3** [1990s+] (*US campus*) a good-looking woman. [(1) resemblance; (2) ? the premise is that the woman spends so much time on her knees (for fellatio) or on her back (for intercourse) that it results in (1)]

strawberry *n.*[3] *see* STRAWBERRY (RIPPLE) n.

strawberry box *n.* [1930s+] (*Aus./N.Z.*) a receptacle used for vomit on ships and aeroplanes.

strawberry dip *n.* [1980s+] (*Aus. prison*) LSD (cf. A n.[3]). [rhy. sl. = TRIP n.[4] (2)]

strawberry fields *n.* [1970s] (*drugs*) LSD (cf. A n.[3]). [The Beatles' song 'Strawberry Fields Forever' (1967)]

strawberry kiss *n.* [2000s] cunnilingus with a menstruating woman.

strawberry (ripple) *n.* (*also* **strawb, vanilla ripple**) [1980s+] a disabled person. [var. on RASPBERRY (RIPPLE) n. (2)]

strawberry tart *n. see* RASPBERRY TART n.

straw boss *n.* **1** [late 19C+] (*US*) a person who is second-in-command, the assistant to the boss. **2** [1920s+] (*US tramp*) the foreman of a work crew. [orig. a threshing crew hierarchy in which the chief deals with the grain, the subordinate with the straw]

strawbug *n.* [1950s] (*UK juv.*) a strawberry. [joc. mispron.]

straw-chipper *n.*[1] [early–mid-19C] a barber.

straw-chipper *n.*[2] [mid-19C] a straw bonnet maker.

strawer *n. see* STRAWING n.

strawfoot *n. see* HAYFOOT n.

straw hall *n. see* STRAW YARD n. (1).

straw hat *n.* **1** [early 18C] a Billingsgate fish-wife. **2** [1900s–30s] (*Aus.*) a dandy, a fashionable person; thus **straw hat push**, the social élite. [metonymy]

strawhead *n.* [1950s–60s] (*US*) a derog. term for an immigrant, lit. one, i.e. a peasant, with straw in their hair.

strawing *n.* (*also* **straw**) [mid-19C] a form of illicit street-selling by which the buyer purchases a straw, usu. for 1 penny, and is given, as a 'free gift', a pamphlet (either pornographic or political) or a gold ring, neither of which items, the seller claims, are they allowed to sell; thus **strawer**, the seller. [Ebsworth (introduction to *Bagford Ballads*, 1880) notes: '"Jack Straw" selling [...] single straws, "a penny a piece, choice from the corn-stack;" while to each winking purchaser he gave, with a rich leer, "gratooitously," a copy of the ditty he was singing']

straw yard *n.* **1** [early 19C] (*Anglo-Irish*) (*also* **straw hall**) a debtor's prison. **2** [mid-19C] a night-shelter or casual ward, occupied by impoverished street-dwellers. [the straw laid down for bedding]

stray *n.* (*also* **stray bit/piece**) [1920s+] a pick-up, a casual sexual partner; thus casual sexual intercourse. [SE *stray* + BIT n.[2] (1)/PIECE n.[1] (1)]

strayway *adj.* [20C+] (*W.I., Gren.*) **1** given to wandering the streets. **2** undisciplined, unsettled. [SE *stray away*]

streak *n.*[1] **1** [mid-19C+] (*orig. US*) a rapid journey or rapid move; usu. in phr. *make a streak for*. **2** [1910s] (*US*) a fast runner. **3** [1970s] (*US campus*) an exciting time, esp. at a party.

streak *n.*[2] [1940s+] (*orig. Aus.*) a tall, lean person. [abbr. *long thin streak*]

streak *n.*[3] [1970s+] an act of discarding one's clothes in public, usu. at a sporting occasion, and disporting oneself in front of the crowd. [STREAKER n.]

streak *v.* **1** [mid-19C–1950s] (*also* **make streaks, streak it**) to run away. **2** [1900s] (*also* **streak it**) to go, to walk. **3** [1970s+] to strip in public and run naked in front of the crowd; thus *streaking*, performing this exhibition. [(1) and (2) SE *streak*, to go quickly; (3) STREAKER n.]

streaked *adj.* [early–mid-19C] (*US*) irritable, irascible, ill-tempered, embarrassed.

streaker *n.* [1970s+] (*orig. US*) one who runs naked through a public place. [originated on US campuses, where it amounted to the trad. *mooning* (cf. MOON n.[1] (2)), writ much larger, then transferred into a variety of larger arenas, notably the venues of major sporting events around the world]

streak it *v. see* STREAK v.

streak of lavender *n.* [1930s] an effeminate man. [SE *streak* + LAVENDER adj.]

streak of lightning *n.* [mid-19C] gin. [SE *streak* + LIGHTNING n.[1] (1)]

streak of weasel shit *n.* [1960s] (*N.Z.*) a very fast runner.

streaky *adj.* **1** [mid-19C] irritable, irascible. **2** [late 19C–1900s] (*also* **stripy**) variable in character, unstable, changeable. [(2) one is neither one emotional 'colour' nor another]

streamer issue *n.* [1930s–40s] (*US Black*) a necktie.

streamline *v.* [1980s+] (*Aus. prison*) to endure one's sentence with a minimum of problems.

streeler *n.* (*also* **streel, strool**) [mid-19C+] (*Irish*) of women, a slattern; of men, a slovenly, lazy person; also as adj., *streely*; n. *streelishness*. [Irish *straoill*, a slattern]

streepach/streepo *n. see* STRAP n.[1].

Street, The *n.* **1** [19C+] (*US*) Wall Street. **2** [19C+] (*US*) Madison Avenue. **3** [20C+] Fleet Street, London EC4, home to the main newspaper offices. **4** [1900s–10s] (*US*) Broadway. **5** [1930s–40s] (*US*) 52nd Street, between Fifth and Sixth Avenues, then the centre of New York jazz clubs. [all but (3) refer to New York City]

street, the *n.* (*also* **street, the streets**) **1** [20C+] (*orig. US*) the mythical world of 'real life', which exists on the streets, rather than in the protected environments of home, office, family etc. **2** [1940s+] (*orig. US Und.*) the world of freedom, as opposed to that of prison; thus *on the street*, at liberty; *street time*, time on parole or between prison sentences. **3** [1960s] the world of commercial homosexual encounters.

street *adj.* [1970s+] (*orig. US Black*) used of people believed to be of the 'real life', of the world which exists on the streets; sophisticated and aware, trendy. [STREET, THE n.]

street *v.* **1** [1920s] (*US Und.*) to throw someone out, e.g. of a bar. **2** [1940s] (*US Und.*) to guide a victim away from the site of a confidence trick. **3** [1950s+] (*drugs*) of a prisoner, to send out money so that a confederate can buy and smuggle back in some drugs. **4** [1960s] (*US Und.*) to release a prisoner.

street *adv.* [1980s+] (*orig. US Black*) in a manner typical of the world that exists on 'the street', in a STREET adj. manner. [STREET adj.]

street *sfx* [1960s+] (*orig. US*) a general sfx meaning place or situation, whether concrete or abstract, e.g. *money street*.

street Arab *n.* [1940s–50s] (*US Black*) a member of the Black Muslims. [the Muslims' identification with (mainly Arabic) Islam + play on SE *street Arab*, a homeless urchin]

street beef *n.* [1990s+] (*US Und.*) crimes committed inside prison by a serving prisoner who is tried in a normal court rather than facing internal prison discipline; such crimes include murder, escape, sex- or drug-related offences; also as v. [STREET, THE n. (2) + BEEF n.[2] (2)]

streetcleaner *n.* [1930s–50s] (*US Black*) a promiscuous woman; a prostitute. [the term underpins the presumed 'dirtiness' of such women]

street cred *n.* [1980s+] acceptability on a mass cultural level. [STREET, THE n. (1) + abbr. SE *credibility/credible*. Coined in the rock business and subseq. popular in any industry that targets the young consumer, it is based in the belief that the 'artist' must relate genuinely to the 'people', i.e. the working-class youth of the streets and housing estates, and thus, sincerely or otherwise, offer an air of rebellion and informality]

streeter n. [1960s] one who lives in the streets or regularly frequents a given street.

street-grizzling n. [1930s] (*UK tramp*) the practice of singing pitiful songs to beg money; thus *grizzler*, a singing tramp. [SE *street* + GRIZZLE (ONE'S GUTS) v.]

streetified adj. [1970s+] (*US Black*) well-versed with the ways of the urban lifestyle as seen on inner-city streets. [STREET, THE n. (1)]

streetman n. [20C+] a petty criminal who 'works' on the street, usu. as a drug dealer or pickpocket.

street money n. [1960s+] (*US*) money earned on the street, usu. through drug-dealing, pickpocketing or prostitution.

street nigger n. 1 [late 19C] a burnt cork artiste, who plays and sings for a living blacked up. 2 [1970s] a sophisticated 'streetwise' Black man. [(1) SE *street*/(2) STREET, THE n. (1) + NIGGER n.¹ (1)]

street people n. [1960s–70s] a form of HIPPIE n.² (3), who wear the clothes but espouse more of a trad. begging ethic than that of the 'love and peace' generation.

street-pitcher n. [mid-19C] anyone who makes a living from selling articles, singing ballads etc in the street. [SE *street* + PITCHER n.³ (3), i.e. declaiming ballads or songs (with or without accompanying sheet music), selling 'true confessions', posing as a 'nigger minstrel' etc]

street pizza n. (*also* **road pizza**) [1990s+] (*US Black*) the remains of any creature killed by a vehicle on the roads. [visual pun on ROADKILL n.¹ (1)]

street rat n. [20C+] (*US*) a street child, usu. the homeless offspring of Irish immigrants.

streets, the n. *see* STREET, THE n.

streetside n. [2000s] (*UK Black*) the street; the world of the street. [STREET, THE n. (1) + SIDE n.² (3)]

street smart adj. [1970s+] (*orig. US*) able to survive in the inner city or the ghetto streets, despite a lack of material, bourgeois advantages. [STREET, THE n. (1) + SE *smart*; var. on STREETWISE adj.]

street smarts n. [1970s+] instinctive knowledge as opposed to learned knowledge. [STREET, THE n. (1) + SMARTS n.]

street talk n. [1940s+] gossip, rumour. [such information, the product of the *street* culture of petty crime, is considered valueless]

streetwise adj. [1960s+] (*orig. US*) able to survive in the inner city or the ghetto streets despite a lack of material, bourgeois advantages. [STREET, THE n. (1) + -WISE sfx (1)]

street-yelp n. [late 19C] any street-orientated catchphrase, e.g. DOES YOUR MOTHER KNOW YOU'RE OUT? phr.

strel n. (*also* **strell**) [late 19C+] (*Polari*) a banjo; thus *strel/strell-homey*, a banjo-player. [Ital. *strillare*, to shriek]

strength, the n. [20C+] (*orig. Aus./N.Z.*) the facts, the details of a situation; usu. as the *strength of*; thus *get the strength of*, to understand. [note 'Get with the Strength', the advertising slogan of the Commonwealth Bank of Australia, whose emblem is an elephant]

strep n. 1 [1920s+] *strep*tococcus, a form of bacterium, esp. in *strep throat*. 2 [1950s+] *strep*tomycin, an antibiotic orig. used to combat tuberculosis, but now usu. used in combination with other drugs because of its toxicity. [abbr.]

stress n. [2000s] (*US Black*) weak, second-rate marijuana.

stress v. [1980s+] 1 to worry, to panic, to lose control. 2 (*US campus*) to work hard.

stress case n. [1980s+] (*US campus*) a very nervous, tense person.

stress-monger n. (*also* **stress–monster**) [1980s+] (*US campus*) a stressed, nervous person. [SE *stress* + -MONGER sfx/MONSTER sfx]

stress out v. [1980s+] 1 to cause someone to become stressed. 2 to become stressed. [ext. of STRESS v. (1)]

stretch n.¹ 1 [19C] (*UK/US Und./prison*) a year. 2 [early 19C+] (*UK/US Und./prison*) (*also* **stretcher**) a 12-month sentence; thus *two stretch*, 2 years; *three stretch*, 3 years etc. 3 [mid-19C+] (*UK/US Und./prison*) a prison sentence of undetermined length. 4 [1950s] (*UK/US Und./prison*) a long time. 5 [1980s] (*US*) a period of enlistment in the armed forces. [abbr. SE *stretch of time*]

stretch n.² 1 [early 19C] a yard (3ft/91cm). 2 [mid-19C] a march, a long journey.

stretch n.³ [1940s] (*US*) a general term of address, usu. to a tall thin person.

stretch n.⁴ [1980s+] a *stretch* limousine.

stretch v.¹ [17C–1960s] to hang, to be hanged; thus *stretcher*, a hangman; *stretched*, hanged. [abbr. SE *stretch one's neck*]

stretch v.² 1 [late 19C+] (*also* **stretch out**) to knock down, to kill. 2 [1940s+] of a man, to have sexual intercourse. [abbr. SE *stretch out on the ground*; (2) ? link to STRETCH LEATHER v.]

stretch v.³ *see* STRETCH (IT) v.

stretch a pipe v. [early 19C] to cry. [SE *stretch* + PIPE v.¹ (2)]

stretch a line v. *see* STRETCH (THE) HEMP v.

stretched adj.¹ [late 19C] whipped. [the fabric of one's trousers is SE *stretched* over the bent-over buttocks]

stretched adj.² *see* STRETCH v.¹.

stretcher n.¹ [late 17C–19C] a lie. [it SE *stretches* the truth]

stretcher n.² 1 [mid-18C–19C] a large penis. 2 [1940s] (*US Und.*) a sodomite. [it SE *stretches* the vagina/he *stretches* the anus]

stretcher n.³ [late 19C] (*Anglo-Irish*) a layer-out of the dead.

stretcher n.⁴ [1920s] a long stretch of road, the journey taken upon it. [SE *stretch*, a (long) distance]

stretcher n.⁵ [1930s–40s] (*US Black*) 1 a necktie. 2 a belt.

stretcher n.⁶ *see* STRETCH n.¹ (2).

stretcher case n. [1940s+] a liar. [STRETCHER n.¹ + play on SE]

stretcher-fencer n. [mid-19C] a street-seller of braces. [STRETCHERS n. (1) + -FENCER sfx]

stretchers n. 1 [mid-19C+] braces. 2 [1900s–60s] shoelaces.

stretch hemp v. *see* STRETCH (THE) HEMP v.

stretching n. [late 19C–1900s] helping oneself at table without waiting for a servant to offer the relevant dish.

stretching match n. 1 [mid-19C] a judicial hanging. 2 [1930s] (*US*) a double hanging. 3 [1940s] (*US*) a lynching. [STRETCH v.¹ + SE *match*]

stretch (it) v. [late 17C+] to exaggerate, to lie. [SE *stretch the truth*]

stretch leather v. [17C–19C] to have sexual intercourse; thus *go leather-stretching*; *get one's leather stretched*. [SE *stretch* + LEATHER n.¹ (1)]

stretch one n. [1930s] (*US*) a large glass of Coca-Cola.

stretch out v.¹ [1950s–60s] (*US Black*) to live one's life without restraint, to act uninhibitedly. [jazz use *stretch out*, to play to one's limits, with no restraints other than one's stamina and skill]

stretch out v.² *see* STRETCH v.² (1).

stretch some jeans v. [1980s+] (*US prison/gay*) to have (anal) sexual intercourse. [the removal of one's jeans or trousers]

stretch someone's breeches v. [late 19C] to administer a thrashing; thus *have one's breeches stretched*, to suffer a beating. [the bent-over buttocks tighten the cloth that covers them]

stretch someone's neck v. [mid-19C–1950s] to hang.

stretch the fox v. [mid-18C–19C] to exaggerate, to 'tell the tale'. [the image of huntsmen exaggerating the day's chase]

stretch (the) hemp v. (*also* **pull hemp, stretch a line**) [mid-19C–1950s] to be hanged or hang oneself. [the hempen noose]

'strewth! excl. (*also* **'struth!**) [mid-19C+] a mild, euph. oath, lit. 'God's truth'. [20C+ use is mainly Aus.]

strib n. [20C+] (*US Und.*) a prison warden. [? fig. use of dial. *strib*, to drain]

strictly adv. [1930s+] (*orig. US*) totally, entirely.

strictly! excl. [1970s+] (*US campus*) really! honestly! absolutely!

strictly from adv. [1930s+] in the style of, derivative of, exactly like.

strictly from hunger phr. [1930s+] 1 driven by dire necessity, usu. financial. **2** emptily, foolishly, to a distressing degree. **3** most unsatisfactorily. [STRICTLY adv. + SE *hunger*]

strictly union *phr.* [1930s–40s] (*US Black*) of music, banal, unadventurous. [as prescribed by union regulations]

stride *v.* [1970s] (*US Black*) to perform with great skill.

striders *n.* [1940s] (*US Black*) trousers. [var. on STRIDES n.]

strides *n.* **1** [mid-19C+] (*now mainly Aus.*) trousers. **2** [1910s+] (*Aus.*) knickers, panties. **3** [1960s] (*US*) shoes.

stride-wide *n.* [late 16C] a strong beer. [? its effects]

strife *n.* **1** [1910s+] (*Aus.*) trouble, disgrace, difficulties; esp. as in *strife*. **2** [1950s–60s] (*UK Und.*) a life sentence. [weak use of SE]

strike *n.*[1] [early 18C–mid-19C] (*UK Und.*) a sovereign, a guinea. [SE *strike*, to mint a coin]

strike *n.*[2] [late 19C–1900s] a watch. [SE *strike*, to ring the time]

strike *n.*[3] [1900s–50s] (*US*) a failure to seduce. [baseball imagery]

strike *n.*[4] [1910s+] **1** (*US Und.*) an arrest and the prison sentence that follows; thus *two strikes*, 2 terms in prison; *three strikes*, 3 arrests and the mandatory life sentence that follows in many states. **2** (*US prison*) a disciplinary charge. **3** (*US*) any position of weakness. [baseball imagery, *three strikes and you're out*]

strike *v.* **1** [mid-16C–mid-18C] to steal goods, to rob a person. **2** [17C] to borrow money. **3** [mid-18C–19C] to make a sudden and pressing demand upon someone for money. **4** [late 19C–1900s] to get money suddenly. **5** [late 19C–1920s] to ask for, e.g. food. **6** [1910s] to persuade someone to spend money.

strike! *excl.* [1910s+] (*Aus.*) an excl. of amazement, irritation etc; usu. ext. to STRIKE ME BLIND! excl.; STRIKE ME PINK! excl.

strike a blow for liberty *v.* [1920s–30s] (*US*) in the Prohibition era, to take a clandestine drink.

strike a bright *v.* [late 19C–1900s] to have a sudden, pleasant thought, to have a piece of good luck. [SE *strike* + *bright thought*]

strike a jigger *v.* [mid-19C] (*UK Und.*) to pick a lock, to break down a door. [STRIKE v. (1) + JIGGER n.[1] (1)]

strike a light *v. see* LIGHT n.[1] (1).

strike a light! *excl.* [20C+] (*orig. Aus.*) a general excl. of surprise, shock, amazement etc.

strike all of a heap *v.* (*also* **knock all of a heap**) [mid-18C+] to shock. [SE *strike* + ALL OF A HEAP adv.]

strike breaker *n.* [1920s] (*US*) a woman who takes advantage of a temporary estrangement to date the male of a couple.

strike-fire *n.* [early 18C] gin. [? play on LIGHTNING n.[1] (1)]

strike for tall timber *v. see* TAKE TO THE (TALL) TIMBER v.

strike ile *v. see* STRIKE OIL v.

strike (it) lucky *v.* [1930s+] to become lucky.

strike it rich *v.* [mid-19C+] to gain sudden wealth. [orig. used in oil-/goldfields]

strike-me *n.* [20C+] bread. [rhy. sl. on *strike me dead*]

strike me! *excl.* (*also* **strike me a dead 'un!**) [mid-19C+] a mild excl. [abbr. STRIKE ME BLIND! excl.; STRIKE ME PINK! excl.]

strike me balmy! *excl. see* STRIKE ME SILLY! excl.

strike-me-blind *n.* [late 19C] boiled rice and black-strap molasses. [the belief that rice would make one blind; thus naut. jargon *strike-me-blind*, rice]

strike me blind! *excl.* (*also* **strike me paralytic!**) [18C+] a general excl. of surprise, amazement; implies calling on God/the gods to make some concomitant gesture.

strike me blue! *excl.* [late 19C+] (*Aus./N.Z.*) a mild oath.

strike-me-dead *n.*[1] [mid-19C] small beer.

strike-me-dead *n.*[2] [late 19C+] bread. [rhy. sl.]

strike me dead! *excl.* [late 18C+] a mild oath.

strike me doleful! *excl.* [early 19C] (*US*) a mild excl.

strike me fat! *excl.* [late 19C+] (*Aus./N.Z.*) a mild excl.

strike me funny! *excl.* [early 19C] a mild excl.

strike me handsome! *excl.* [1910s+] (*Aus./N.Z.*) a mild excl.

strike me lucky! *excl.* [early 19C+] a general oath, esp. on the sealing of a bargain by slapping hands together. [UK in 19C, it

re-emerged in mid-20C+ Aus. use; Nares notes earlier 17C *strike me luck*, 'a familiar phrase, which seems to have arisen from striking a bargain, and giving earnest upon it', i.e. by shaking or striking each other's palm]

strike me paralytic! *v. see* STRIKE ME BLIND! excl.

strike me perpendicular! *excl.* (*also* **strike me perpendicular!**) [late 19C–1900s] a general excl. of surprise, alarm, shock etc. [var. ON STRIKE ME DEAD! excl.]

strike me pink! *excl.* (*also* **strike me purple!**) [20C+] a mild excl. of surprise, irritation etc.

strike me roan! *excl.* [1910s+] (*Aus./N.Z.*) a mild excl.

strike me silly! *excl.* (*also* **strike me balmy!** ...**stupid!**) [early 18C; 1910s–20s] a mild excl. of surprise, irritation etc.

strike me sober! *excl.* [1900s] (*Aus.*) a mild excl.

strike me sunburnt! *excl.* [late 19C] a mild excl. of surprise, irritation etc. [STRIKE ME PINK! excl.]

strike oil *v.* (*also* **strike ile**) [mid-19C+] (*orig. US*) to do well, to prosper.

strike out *v.* [20C+] (*US*) **1** to die. **2** to fail, esp. in an attempt to seduce a woman or trick a potential victim for a confidence trick. [baseball jargon *strike out*, for the batter to fail to make legal contact with the ball in 4 attempts]

strike paydirt *v. see* HIT PAYDIRT v.

striker *n.*[1] **1** [late 16C–mid-17C] a womanizer, a pimp (cf. ABBOT ON THE CROSS n.). **2** [late 16C–mid-17C] a prostitute. **3** [19C] the penis. [the equation of sex and violence]

striker *n.*[2] [mid-19C] (*US Und.*) a street tout who entices players into a gambling club; he doubles as a thug in the case of complaints.

striker *n.*[3] **1** [1900s] (*US milit.*) an officer's servant. **2** [1980s] (*US Und.*) a recruit for a motorcycle gang.

striker *n.*[4] **1** [1950s+] a match. **2** [2000s] (*US prison*) a home-made device used to light cigarettes.

strike the gag *v.* [mid-19C] to stop playing around, to stop joking. [SE *strike*, to desist from + GAG n. (1)]

strike the mace *v.* [early 19C] to persuade a shopkeeper to sell one goods on credit, although one has no intention of ever making that credit good. [SE *strike* + MACE n. (2)]

striking *adj.* [1950s] (*W.I.*) a general intensifier. [linked to such excl. as STRIKE ME DEAD! excl.; STRIKE ME PINK! excl. etc]

strill *n.* [late 19C+] (*Ling. Fr./Polari*) a musical instrument, esp. a portable harmonium or a piano; thus *strill-homey*, a male pianist; *strill-polone*, a female pianist. [Ital. *strillare*, to shriek, to cry out]

strilla *adj.* [2000s] (*US Black*) good, satisfactory.

string *n.*[1] **1** [early 19C–1910s] a hoax, a fraud. **2** [early 19C+] a condition, a restriction; usu. in phr. NO STRINGS phr. **3** [late 19C–1920s] (*US Und.*) a form of confidence trick. [STRING (ALONG) v.[1] (1)]

string *n.*[2] [1950s+] (*US*) the penis; thus *string and nuggets*, the penis and testicles.

string *n.*[3] *see* STRING (OF PONIES) n.

string a line *v.* [1950s] (*Aus.*) to deceive, to tell a 'tall story'. [STRING (ALONG) v.[1] + LINE n.[1] (3)]

string (along) *v.*[1] (*also* **string on**) **1** [early 19C+] to fool, to deceive someone, esp. over a drawn-out period of time; to tease. **2** [late 19C+] (*Aus./N.Z./US*) to encourage, to egg on. [the image of dragging someone along on the end of a string]

string (along) *v.*[2] **1** [mid-19C] (*US*) to progress, to walk along. **2** [20C+] to accompany. [the image of dragging a toy along on the end of a string]

string along with *v.* (*also* **string with**) [1910s+] (*orig. US*) **1** to accompany; to associate with. **2** to agree with. **3** to support.

string and top *n.* (*also* **silk and top**) [1920s–50s] a policeman (cf. BOTTLE (AND STOPPER) n.). [rhy. sl. = COP n.[1] (1)]

string and twine *n. see* SILK AND TWINE n.

string bean *n.* **1** [1920s+] a tall, skinny person; thus as a nickname; also attrib. **2** [1970s] (*US Black*) a very thin, long penis (cf.

BANANA n.[2]). [(1) D'Urfey, *Pills to Purge Melancholy* (1719–20), (of a woman): 'The one thin and lean, As a Garden French Bean']

string beans *n.* [1970s+] jeans. [rhy. sl.]

string city *n.* [2000s] suburban ribbon development. [it is 'strung out' along the road]

stringer *n.*[1] [17C; 1910s+] (*US*) a pimp. [? *string* of prostitutes/ STRING n.[2]]

stringer *n.*[2] **1** [early–mid-19C] (*UK Und.*) a confidence trickster, a swindler. **2** [mid-19C] a hoax, a trick. [STRING n.[1]]

stringer *n.*[3] [late 19C–1910s] (*N.Z.*) a woman who works in a bar encouraging the patrons to drink. [STRING (ALONG) v.[1] (2)]

stringer *n.*[4] *see* STINGER n.[4].

stringers *n.* [late 19C–1900s] handcuffs.

stringing *n.* [1900s] (*US*) teasing, deceiving. [STRING (ALONG) v.[1] (1)]

string (of ponies) *n.* [1920s+] a group of prostitutes working for a single pimp (cf. BROTHER-IN-LAW n.). [SE *string*, a set or stud of horses]

string on *v. see* STRING (ALONG) v.[1].

string oneself out *v.* [20C+] (*US*) to be disturbed, upset or worried.

string out *v.* [1960s+] **1** (*drugs*) to use and be addicted to narcotic drugs. **2** (*US campus*) to be suffering from some minor ailment. [STRUNG OUT adj.]

string someout out *v.* [1960s+] **1** to keep someone in suspense. **2** to deceive someone over a period of time. [var. on STRING (ALONG) v.[1] (1)]

string the fives on *v.* [1950s] to beat up. [BUNCH OF FIVES n.]

string up *v.* [late 19C–1910s] to garrotte. [note *string up*, to hang, is SE]

string vest *n.* [1990s+] a pest, an annoying person. [rhy. sl.]

string with *v. see* STRING ALONG WITH v.

stringybark *n.*[1] **1** [late 19C] beer. **2** [late 19C–1950s] (*Aus.*) a supposed 'whisky', actually made of turpentine and fuel oil; thus bad liquor in general. [for ety. *see* STRINGYBARK adj.]

stringybark *n.*[2] *see* STRINGYBARKER n.

stringybark *adj.* **1** [mid–late 19C] (*Aus.*) unsophisticated, rural, remote. **2** [1950s] tough, brave, hardy. [SE *stringybark*, one of many trees, typically the eucalyptus, that has a thick, rough and fibrous bark and is found in the bush of SE Aus.]

stringybark cockatoo *n.* [20C+] (*Aus.*) a small farmer, often a failed prospector forced to turn to farming in order to survive. [STRINGYBARK adj. (1) + COCKATOO n.[3]]

stringybarker *n.* (*also* **stringybark**) [late 19C–1950s] (*Aus.*) one who lives in the outback. [STRINGYBARK adj. (1)]

Strip, the *n.* [1930s+] (*US*) any main street or central area of a city devoted to entertainment, esp. Las Vegas.

strip *v.* **1** [late 17C–18C] (*UK Und.*) to rob a house, esp. to empty it of all moveable contents. **2** [late 17C+] to rob a person. **3** [1980s] (*US campus*) to upset or harm a person.

strip (act) *n.* [1930s+] (*orig. US*) a striptease show; similarly *strip club*, *strip joint*, *strip show*.

strip a peg in Plunket Street *v.* [late 18C] (*Irish*) to dress in second-hand clothes. [*Plunket Street*, the old-clothes market in Dublin]

strip-bush *n.* [mid-19C] one who steals washing from drying lines. [laundry was orig. laid out on hedges to dry]

strip-down *n.* [1950s] (*US*) an automobile that has been modified to improve its performance.

stripe *n.* **1** [1950s+] a scar, usu. the result of being slashed with an open razor. **2** [1990s+] a police patrol car, carrying some form of fluorescent stripe on its sides.

stripe *v.* **1** [1950s+] to slash with a cut-throat razor or other edged weapon. **2** [1970s] in fig. use, to harm (in a non-physical manner). **3** [1970s] to defraud. [STRIPE n. (1)]

striped *adj.* [mid-19C] (*US*) drunk.

strip-eel *n.* [early 18C] a fishmonger. [one of his jobs]

stripes *n.*[1] (*US*) **1** [mid-19C–1940s] a prison uniform; thus *wear the stripes*, to serve a prison sentence. **2** [1990s+] a referee.

stripes *n.*[2] *see* OLD STRIPES n.

stripey fat *v.* [1980s+] (*Aus. prison*) to masturbate (cf. COTTON WOOL v.). [rhy. sl. = GO OFF THE BAT v.]

striping *n.* [2000s] a reprimand. [STRIPE v. (2)]

strip joint *n.* [1950s+] (*US*) a bar or club that offers striptease shows. [SE *strip* + JOINT n.[4] (3)]

strip me! *excl.* [mid-18C] a general excl. of imprecation.

strip-me-naked *n.*[1] [mid-18C–mid-19C] a fiery drink, esp. raw gin.

strip-me-naked *n.*[2] [1950s] (*W.I.*) any form of food made from flour, e.g. biscuits, cake. [? the quantity of the food fills one up and one gets relief by taking off one's clothes; or ? the expense involved in purchasing the food leaves one 'naked' of cash]

stripped *adj.* [mid-19C–1900s] of spirits, neat.

stripped to the buff *phr.* [mid-19C+] naked, without one's clothes. [SE *stripped* + BUFF n.[1]]

stripper *n.*[1] **1** [mid–late 19C] a thief, usu. a woman, who specializes in luring young children into secluded places, where they are stripped of their clothes (which are later sold) and left naked in the street. **2** [1920s] (*US Und.*) a thief who removes all valuable parts from a car.

stripper *n.*[2] [1930s+] (*orig. US*) a striptease performer. [abbr. SE *striptease*]

strippers *n.* (*also* **low belly strippers**) [mid-19C+] (*US gambling*) playing cards of which the sides and/or ends have been slightly trimmed to help cheating.

stripping law *n.* [late 16C–early 17C] (*UK Und.*) the practice of stripping prisoners of their valuable possessions as carried out by prison staff. [SE *stripping* + LAW n.[1]]

strip teeth and bite *v.* [1900s] (*Aus.*) to become fiercely argumentative.

stripy *adj. see* STREAKY adj. (2).

Strivers' Row *n.* [1910s+] (*US Black*) a generic name for well-off Blacks who hope to move up in society by buying large properties, taking out large mortgages etc. [the orig. *Striver's Row* was a development designed by architect Stanford White (1853–1906) on West 138th and 139th Streets, New York. The 130 terraced houses, named King's Model Houses, were completed in 1891 and remained a Whites–only block until 1919. When they did come on the market, Harlem's wealthiest Blacks competed to move in; *c.*2001 Villard Books of New York City established the imprint *Strivers Row*, for Black authors]

strizzy *adj. see* STRAIGHT adj.[4].

strobe-light honey *n.* [1990s+] (*US Black teen*) a woman who is attractive at a distance or in poor light, e.g. in a club, but less so in close-up. [SE *strobe light* + HONEY n.[1] (4)]

stroke *n.*[1] [17C+] sexual intercourse; thus *take a stroke*, to have sexual intercourse; *strokability*, sexual potential. [20C+ use is mainly US Black]

stroke *n.*[2] [mid-19C+] (*UK Und./police*) an action considered audacious or daring; sometimes criminal activity. [PULL A STROKE v.]

stroke *n.*[3] [1920s] (*US*) a monopoly; rights to do something.

stroke *n.*[4] [1960s+] a gesture or action designed to comfort and reassure. [coined by Eric Berne in *Games People Play* (1964): '"stroking" may be employed colloquially to denote any act implying recognition of another's presence']

stroke *v.*[1] **1** [mid-17C+] to have sexual intercourse. **2** [1950s+] (*also* **stroke it off**) to masturbate; also used in a number of combs., e.g. *stroke one's beef*, *...one's ego*, *...one's poker*, *...one's steven*, *...the bloke*, *...the dog*, *...the goat*, *...the trumpet* (cf. BALL OFF v.[2]; BOFF v.; BUFF THE BANANA v.; STROKE ONE'S OAR v.). [(1) 20C+ use is mainly US Black]

stroke *v.*[2] **1** [1960s+] (*US prison*) to curry favour with a more powerful inmate or with the authorities. **2** [1980s] (*US campus*) to trick, to deceive.

stroke *v.*[3] [1990s+] (*UK juv.*) to steal. [the thief's hands run gently over the desired object]

stroke book *n.* (*also* **stroke mag, ...magazine, ...rag**) [1960s+] a pornographic book or magazine. [STROKE *v.*[1] (2) + SE *book/magazine*/RAG *n.*[4] (2)]

Stroke City *n.* [1960s+] (*Ulster*) Derry/Londonderry, Ireland. [SE *stroke*, a solidus + CITY sfx; the dual names of the city, claimed respectively by Catholics/Protestants and the futile attempt to rename it 'Londonderry/Derry']

stroked out *adj.* [1960s] exhausted. [fig. use of STROKE *v.*[1] (2)]

stroke house *n.* [1970s] a cinema showing pornographic films. [STROKE *v.*[1] (2) + SE *house*]

stroke it off *v. see* STROKE *v.*[1] (2).

stroke mag(azine) *n. see* STROKE BOOK *n.*

stroke one's oar *v.* [1970s] (*US*) to masturbate (cf. BUFF THE BANANA *v.*).

stroke out *v.* [1970s+] to die.

stroker *n.* [1960s+] a masturbator. [STROKE *v.*[1] (2)]

stroke rag *n. see* STROKE BOOK *n.*

stroke the beaver *v.* (*also* **stroke the dog**) [late 17C; 1990s+] (*US*) to have sexual intercourse. [SE *stroke* + BEAVER *n.*[5] (1)]

stroll *n.* **1** [mid-19C; 1920s+] (*mainly US Black*) the main street, esp. when used as a social centre. **2** [1930s+] (*US*) anything requiring only minimal effort, an easy task. **3** [1950s+] (*US pimp*) those streets or blocks on which prostitutes ply their trade; thus *stroll*, to work as a street prostitute; *stroll*, a prostitute. **4** [2000s] (*US Black*) a place where drugs are sold. [SE *stroll*, to wander along; the original *stroll* was situated between 26th and 63rd Streets on New York's West Side, the mid–late 19C centre of the Black population. During the 1890s the stroll moved to Seventh Avenue between 23rd and 34th Streets and when the focus of Black life moved again, to Harlem (*c.*1920), the stroll moved uptown on Seventh Avenue between 131st and 132nd Streets]

stroll *v.* [1940s+] to get away with something, to go free, to do well. [to walk away with something]

stroller *n.* [1980s+] (*S.Afr.*) a homeless young street beggar. [Scot. *stroller*, a vagabond; ult. SE *stroll*]

strollers *n.* [1940s] (*US Black*) trousers.

strolling mort *n.* (*also* **strowling mort**) [mid-17C–early 19C] (*UK Und.*) an unmarried female beggar, often accompanied by a child, who claims to be widowed and begs for her and her offspring's keep. [SE *stroll* + MORT *n.*]

stroll on! *excl.* [1950s+] a general excl. of dismissal or disbelief, 'you must be joking!'

strommel *n.* (*also* **stramel, strammel, stromell, strumil**) **1** [mid-16C–1900s] (*UK Und.*) straw. **2** [mid-17C–mid-18C] hair; thus *strummolo*, false pubic hair. [alternatives are dated 17C–18C *stromell*, 18C *stramel*, 18C *strumil*, 18C–19C *strammel*]

strommel-faker *n.* [late 18C–early 19C] a barber. [STROMMEL *n.* (2) + FAKER *n.* (1)]

strommel-patch *n.* [late 16C–early 17C] a pej. name for a person. [STROMMEL *n.* (1) + SE *patch*]

strong, the *n.* [20C+] (*Aus.*) the truth, the facts, the essential information; thus *what's the strong of it?* what is the truth? what are the precise facts? [var. on STRENGTH, THE *n.*]

strong *adj.* **1** [mid-17C; mid-19C+] extreme, excessive. **2** [mid-19C+] of people, uncompromising, zealous. **3** [late 19C–1900s] competent, able, well-versed. **4** [late 19C–1950s] in funds, rich; thus phr. of enquiry, *how strong are you?* how much money do you have? **5** [1910s+] (*US*) popular. **6** [1960s+] pornographic, usu. found in advertisements in such magazines.

strong *adv.* **1** [early 19C+] keenly, enthusiastically. **2** [1910s] intimately.

strong and thin *n.* **1** [1930s–40s] gin. **2** [1940s] (*US*) a hand. [rhy. sl.; (2) = FIN *n.*[1]]

strongarm *n.* **1** [mid-19C+] violence. **2** [late 19C] (*US tramp*) the act of throttling a victim so as to immobilize him or her for theft. **3** [20C+] a thug. **4** [1960s] strength.

strong-arm *adj.* [late 19C+] violent; used of a person who gets things done through threats of, as well as actual, physical violence. [STRONGARM *n.*]

strong-arm *v.* [20C+] (*orig. US*) to rob or otherwise influence someone through threats and potential, rather than actual, violence. [STRONGARM *n.*]

strongarming *n.* [1930s–40s] **1** violence, esp. when allied to robbery or extortion. **2** (*US Und.*) a form of robbery whereby a woman, posing as a prostitute, lures a man into a dark alleyway or similar space; she then puts a stranglehold around his neck and her male partner(s) rob the victim who is thus held captive. [STRONG-ARM *v.*]

strong-arm man *n.* (*also* **arm man, strong-arm boy, strong-armer, strong-arm guy**) [20C+] a thug, a hoodlum, a gangster. [STRONG-ARM *adj.* + SE *man*]

strong-arm woman *n.* [late 19C] (*US Und.*) a thuggish, violent woman, very often a street thief or the madame of a brothel. [STRONG-ARM *adj.* + SE *woman*]

strong box *n.* [1930s+] (*UK prison*) a prison, a punishment cell.

strong-eye *n.* [1900s] (*W.I.*) covetousness.

strong-eye *adj.* [1900s–10s] (*W.I.*) **1** covetous, greedy. **2** selfish, domineering. **3** determined. [STRONG-EYE *n.*]

strong for *phr.* [1900s–50s] keen on.

strong game *n. see* HEAVY GAME *n.*

strong it *v.* [1960s+] to act in an aggressive or extreme manner. [i.e. to pose as a SE *strong man*]

strong joint *n.* [1910s+] **1** (*US*) a crooked or cheating gambling game. **2** (*US*) a crooked casino or gambling house. **3** (*Aus. Und.*) a swindler. [SE *strong* + JOINT *n.*[4] (3)]

strong man *n.* [1930s+] (*Aus.*) a confidence trickster. [he 'pushes through' one's resistance]

strong-mouth *n.* [mid–late 19C] (*W.I.*) bullying, brow-beating.

strong-physic *n.* [mid–late 19C] (*W.I.*) a self-willed person. [lit. 'strong medicine']

strong-physic *adj.* [mid–late 19C] (*W.I.*) hot-tempered, irascible. [STRONG-PHYSIC *n.*]

strong suit *n.* [mid-19C+] (*orig. US*) an advantage or special talent. [card-playing imagery]

strool *n. see* STREELER *n.*

strop *n.* [1980s+] **1** (*S.Afr.*) trouble, 'backchat', obstreperous behaviour. **2** a bad temper. [STROP *v.*[1]]

strop *v.*[1] [1970s+] to display one's bad temper; thus *strop around*, to wander about in a bad mood. [? backform. f. STROPPY *adj.*]

strop *v.*[2] [1990s+] (*Aus.*) to masturbate (cf. BOFF *v.*).

strop one's beak *v.* [19C] of a man, to have sexual intercourse (cf. BURY IT *v.*). [SE *strop*, to sharpen + BEAK *n.*[2] (3)]

stropper *n.*[1] [1910s] (*US*) a large, husky man.

stropper *n.*[2] [1960s] (*Aus.*) one who is testy, irritable, dissatisfied. [STROPPY *adj.*]

stroppy *adj.* [1950s+] bad-tempered, irritable. [mispron. OBSTROPOLOUS *adj.*, i.e. SE *obstreperous*; note naut. jargon *jack strop*, a know-it-all, a braggart]

strowling mort *n. see* STROLLING MORT *n.*

struck *adj.* [20C+] (*W.I.*) greedy, gluttonous. [abbr. STRUCK ON *adj.*]

struck (on) *adj.* (*also* **struck upon/with**) [mid-19C+] obsessed with, esp. in a sexual sense.

structure *n.* [1950s+] (*W.I. Rasta*) the body, health.

struesbob! *excl.* [1970s+] (*S.Afr.*) a general excl. of assertion. [lit. *it's true as Bob*, i.e. God (cf. BOB *n.*[2])]

struggle *n.* [1920s–30s] (*US*) a party or dance. [STRUGGLE *v.*]

struggle *v.* [1920s–60s] (*US*) to dance.

struggle and strain *n.* [1910s+] a railway train. [rhy. sl.]

struggle and strainers *n.* [1980s+] trainers. [rhy. sl.]

struggle and strife *n.* [20C+] **1** one's wife. **2** life. [rhy. sl.]

struggle-buggy *n.* [1920s–60s] (*US*) a run-down old car, esp. an early model Ford. [it 'struggles along']

struggle-town *n.* [1990s+] (*Aus.*) a state of penury and/or unemployment.

struggle valley *n.* [1930s+] (*Aus.*) a tramps' encampment. [the SE *struggle* to survive]

strum *n.*[1] [late 17C–early 19C] a wig. [STROMMEL *n.*]

strum *n.*[2] (*also* **strump**) [late 17C+] a sexually available (young) woman; a prostitute. [abbr. SE *strumpet*]

strum *v.* (*also* **strump**) **1** [late 18C+] to have sexual intercourse. **2** [1960s+] (*US*) (*also* **strum heads**) to hit; to fight. **3** [1990s+] to masturbate (cf. BOFF *v.*). [SE *strum*, to play on a stringed instrument]

strum and stroll *n.* [20C+] (*Aus.*) unemployment benefit, the dole (cf. BLESS MY SOUL *n.*). [rhy. sl.]

strumil *n. see* STROMMEL *n.*

strummel *n.* **1** [mid-16C–early 19C] straw. **2** [mid-17C–mid-19C] human hair, pubic hair. [? OF *estramer*, to spread with straw or rushes]

strummolo *n. see* STROMMEL *n.* (2).

strummond *n.* [mid-19C] a pot of liquor, a 'bumper'. [? STRAM-MER *n.*]

strump *see under* STRUM.

strung out *adj.* **1** [late 19C+] obsessively in love, infatuated with someone. **2** [1930s+] (*also* **strung up**) nervous, unhappy, depressed. **3** [1940s+] obsessed with a topic or activity. **4** [1950s+] (*drugs*) (*also* **strung**) addicted to narcotics, esp. when suffering the pain of withdrawal. **5** [1980s+] (*drugs*) under the influence of any drug (with no suggestion of actual addiction).

strunt *n.* [early 17C] the penis. [SE *strunt*, the fleshy part of an animal's tail]

strut *n.* [1930s+] (*orig. US Black*) a party where the guests buy their refreshments to help pay the rent (cf. FISH-FRY *n.*). [SE *strut*]

'struth! *excl. see* 'STREWTH! *excl.*

strut-noddy *n.* [19C] an arrogant fool with no idea of his or her own stupidity. [SE *strut* + NODDY *n.*[1]]

strut one's stuff *v.* (*also* **strut some**) **1** [1920s] (*US*) to act on stage. **2** [1920s+] (*orig. US Black*) to act proudly, uninhibitedly. [SE *strut* + STUFF *n.*[7] (1)]

strychnine *n. see* QUININE *n.*

stu *n.* [1990s+] a *stu*pid person. [abbr.]

stub *n.* **1** [19C] a short person. **2** [1940s] a child.

stubbie *n.* (*also* **stubby**) (*Aus.*) **1** [1950s+] a short, squat beer bottle holding 375ml (13fl oz). **2** [1970s+] shorts. [(2) under-pinned by brandname *Stubbies*]

stubble *n.* [late 18C–1900s] female pubic hair. [SE *stubble*]

stubble it! *excl.* [late 17C–19C] (*UK Und.*) hold your tongue! be quiet! [SE *stubble*, to clear the land of stubble, to cut it short]

stubble-jumper *n.* [1920s+] (*Can./US*) a poor farmer.

stubble one's whids *v.* (*also* **stubble one's whidds**) [late 17C–mid-19C] (*UK Und.*) to be quiet, to stop talking. [STUBBLE IT! *excl.* + WHID *n.* (1)]

stubbs *n.* [19C] nothing. [SE *stub*, the end of a cigar or cigarette]

stubby *n. see* STUBBIE *n.*

stub-faced *adj.* [late 18C–19C] having one's face pitted with the scars of smallpox (cf. CRIBBAGE-FACED *adj.*). [SE *horse stubs*, horse nails; thus 'the devil run over his face with horse stubs in his shoes' (Grose, 1796)]

stub one's toe *v.* [20C+] to menstruate. [euph.]

stuccoed *adj.* [1920s–30s] (*US*) drunk.

stuck *adj.*[1] [mid-19C+] **1** left in an impossible position, deceived, completely mistaken. **2** out of money, impoverished. [fig. uses of SE, but note IN SHTUCK *phr.*]

stuck *adj.*[2] *see* STUCK (ON) *phr.*

stuckadee *n.* (*also* **stuckedee**) [1940s] (*W.I.*) a faithful lover. [ext. of STUCKY *n.*]

stuck for *phr.* [late 19C+] at a loss, unable to think of, unable to obtain.

stuck (on) *phr.* (*also* **stuck after**) **1** [mid-19C+] (*orig. US*) obsessed with, devoted to. **2** [late 19C+] (*orig. US*) in love with, pleased with. **3** [1910s] (*US*) hostile towards.

stuck out *phr.* [1970s+] (*US prison*) lazy, forgetful; deprived.

stuck-up *n.* [late 19C–1940s] an arrogant, snobbish or reserved person. [STUCK-UP *adj.*[1]]

stuck-up *adj.*[1] (*also* **stuckuppy**) [mid-19C+] (*mainly UK juv.*) arrogant, snobbish, reserved. [one SE *sticks one's nose in the air*]

stuck-up *adj.*[2] [late 19C] penniless. [STUCK *adj.*[1] (2)]

stuck with *phr.* [mid-19C+] (*orig. US*) saddled with, unable to get rid of either a person or an object.

stucky *n.* [1930s–50s] (*W.I.*) a faithful lover. [? STUCK (ON) *phr.* (2)]

stud *n.*[1] **1** [late 19C+] (*US White*) a man, not invariably but usu. sexually successful. **2** [20C+] a general form of address, usu. congratulatory. **3** [1920s+] a man, irrespective of race or colour. **4** [1930s+] (*US Black*) a sophisticated man, but with no sexual connotation. **5** [1940s+] a masculine lesbian. **6** [1960s+] a male prostitute catering to either sex. **7** [1960s+] a man as a sexual performer. **8** [1960s+] a 'masculine' male homosexual. **9** [1960s+] (*US prison*) a 'masculine' jail homosexual (who usu. reverts to heterosexuality on release). **10** [1970s+] (*US gay*) the penis. **11** [1980s+] (*US campus*) a physically strong or athletically powerful man or woman. [SE *stud*, a stallion or mare kept for breeding]

stud *n.*[2] *see* STUD (GIN) *n.*

stud *adj.*[1] [1940s+] (*US*) fine, excellent, outstanding. [STUD *n.*[1]]

stud *adj.*[2] **1** [1960s] aggressive. **2** [1970s] of homosexuals, overtly masculine. [STUD *n.*[1] (8)]

stud *v.*[1] [1940s+] (*US*) **1** to pursue sexually. **2** to work as a pimp. [STUD *n.*[1]]

stud *v.*[2] [2000s] (*US Black*) to listen to; to learn. [SE *study*]

stud broad *n.* [1960s+] (*US*) a masculine lesbian. [STUD *n.*[1] (5) + BROAD *n.*[2] (3)]

stud dog *n.* [1960s] (*US*) a male sexual predator. [STUD *n.*[1] (1) + SE *dog*]

studdy *n.* [1940s] (*US Black*) a general term of address, friend, 'old boy'. [STUD *n.*[1] (4)]

Stude *n.* [1960s–70s] (*US*) a *Stude*baker automobile. [abbr.]

stude *n.* [1910s–30s] (*US*) a *stude*nt. [abbr.]

student *n.* **1** [1930s–50s] (*drugs*) an inexperienced or novice drug-taker. **2** [1940s] (*US Und.*) a political heeler, living off the city payroll.

studette *n.* [1980s+] (*US teen*) a sexually and socially successful, physically attractive woman. [STUD *n.*[1] (1) + SE fem. sfx *-ette*]

Studey *n. see* STUDIE *n.*

stud (gin) *n.* [1910s+] (*Aus.*) an Aboriginal woman seen as an object of sexual pleasure for a White man. [STUD *n.*[1] (1) + GIN *n.*[1] (1)]

stud horse *n.* (*also* **studhoss**) [1940s+] a man with sexual and/ or athletic prowess, usu. as a term of address whether self-referentially or to a friend. [STUD *n.*[1] (1) + SE *horse*]

stud horse! *excl.* (*also* **stud hoss!**) [20C+] (*US*) a general form of greeting between men. [STUD HORSE *n.*]

studhunk *n.* [1980s] a 'masculine' man, a 'ladykiller'. [STUD *n.*[1] (1) + HUNK *n.*[1] (6)]

stud-hustler *n.* [1960s–70s] (*US gay*) a male prostitute (cf. ASS PEDDLER *n.*). [STUD *n.*[1] (6) + HUSTLER *n.* (7)]

Studie *n.* (*also* **Studey**) [1930s+] (*US*) a *Stude*baker automobile. [abbr. + sfx *-ie/-y*]

studio gangsta *n.* [1990s+] (*US Black teen*) one who poses as a GANGSTA *n.* (2) purely for the purpose of making records; their experience of street life, however, is marginal.

studly *adj.* [1960s+] (*US campus*) displaying the characteristics of a sexually successful man. [STUD *n.*[1] (1)]

stud-muffin *n.* [1980s+] (*orig. US campus*) an exceptionally successful and attractive person; occas. of an animal. [STUD n.¹ (1) + MUFFIN n.¹ (3)]

studola n. [1980s+] (US campus) a concentration of sexually successful men. [STUD n.¹ (1) + -OLA sfx]

stud out n. (US campus) **1** [1960s] to play a good-natured practical joke. **2** [1980s+] to achieve something, to do well; usu. in past tense, referring to a proven success. [fig. use of STUD n.¹ (1)]

stud up n. [1970s] (US prison) a homosexual male who tries to revert to being a heterosexual. [STUD n.¹]

stud with many fingers n. [1940s] (US Black) the Federal Bureau of Investigation (FBI) and its director, J. Edgar Hoover (1895–1972). [STUD n.¹ (4) + SE fingers; the 'fingers' were in a variety of criminal 'pies']

study n. [late 19C+] an expression of incredulity, shock; usu. in phr. you should have seen your face – it was a study! [SE study, a portrait]

study v. **1** [late 19C+] (W.I./UK Black) (also **study on**) to think about. **2** [1950s+] (gay) to appraise a potential sexual conquest or partner. **3** [1960s] (US campus) to indulge in sexual caresses short of intercourse.

study astronomy on one's back v. see GO STAR-GAZING (ON ONE'S BACK) v. (1).

study mongrel n. (also **study hog**) [1990s+] (US campus) someone who studies hard.

study on v. see STUDY v. (1).

stuff n.¹ **1** [late 16C+] things or activities in general, varying as to context. **2** [mid-17C+] anything that has no proper name, things that one cannot be bothered to describe properly. **3** [late 17C+] nonsense; lies. **4** [late 19C+] arguments. **5** [late 19C+] a person. **6** [1900s] (US Und.) an unappealing person. **7** [1900s–30s] stolen goods. **8** [1980s] a term of address.

stuff n.² [17C+] semen (cf. CRUD n.¹).

stuff n.³ **1** [18C+] (also **liquid stuff**) alcohol, esp. bootleg liquor. **2** [20C+] (drugs) drugs, esp. heroin, morphine (cf. AUNTIE EMMA n.; CACA n.). [euph.; 'William Lee', Junkie (1953): 'General terms for opium and all derivatives of opium: morphine, heroin, Delaudid, pantopon, codeine, dionine']

stuff n.⁴ [late 18C+] money.

stuff n.⁵ [mid-19C] (US Und.) a copper watch which has been galvanized and is sold as 'gold'.

stuff n.⁶ **1** [mid-19C+] the vagina, the buttocks; fig. used as female sexuality (cf. ARTICLE n.). **2** [late 19C+] a woman, usu. attractive and often out, enjoying herself. **3** [1960s+] (US prison) a male homosexual. [20C+ use is usu. US Black]

stuff n.⁷ **1** [late 19C+] (US) personality, character; ability. **2** [20C+] (US) something important, meaningful. **3** [20C+] (US prison) someone, or something, of value.

stuff n.⁸ [1960s+] (US prison) a knife.

stuff, the n. **1** [mid-18C+] what one wants, the ideal; usu. in phr. that's the stuff. **2** [1990s+] an important (or self-important) person.

stuff v.¹ **1** [18C+] to have sexual intercourse (cf. BANG v.¹; FRIG v.). **2** [1940s+] as a general euph. for FUCK v.¹. [SE stuff, to fill up but increasingly seen as a euph. for FUCK v.¹; note double entendre in D'Urfey, Pills to Purge Melancholy (1719–20): 'Three things must be stuffed, I'll tell you if I can; / A pudding, a cushion, and a Woman']

stuff v.² [mid-19C] (US Und.) to sell brass or galvanized copper watches as 'gold' ones; often as watch-stuffing or watch-stuffer; thus stuffer, a person who does this; stuff cover, his assistant. [STUFF n.⁵]

stuff v.³ **1** [mid-19C+] (also **stuff up**) to tease, to tell lies, to fool, to hoax. **2** [1940s+] to defeat, to outwit. **3** [1980s] (US Black) to attack, verbally or physically. **4** [1990s+] to cause trouble for. [SE stuff, to fill up]

stuff v.⁴ [late 19C] to sit indoors when one could/should be out enjoying the fresh air. [SE stuffy]

stuff! excl. [late 17C–1930s] nonsense! rubbish!

stuff a sock in it v. see PUT A SOCK IN IT v.

stuff cuff n. [1940s] (US Black) the padded cuff of a draped suit.

stuffed adj.¹ **1** [mid-late 19C] put-down, mocked, denigrated. **2** [1940s+] defeated, ruined, exhausted; drunk (cf. ANNIHILATED adj.). [(2) STUFF v.³ (2)]

stuffed adj.² [1930s+] bothered, concerned; usu. in phr. can't/won't be stuffed. [euph. synon. for FUCKED adj.¹ (1)]

stuffed adj.³ see STUFFED SHIRT adj.

stuffed eel-skin n. [mid-19C] an old, prob. impotent, man.

stuffed monkey n. [late 19C] (East London Jewish) 'a very pleasant close almond biscuit' (Ware).

stuffed rat n. [1930s+] (Aus.) a loaded die.

stuffed shirt n. (also **stuffed polony/suit**) [late 16C; 20C+] (orig. US) a pompous, aristocratic but ineffectual person, a bore. [i.e. the shirt is there, but there is no one inside it]

stuffed shirt adj. (also **stuffed**) [1920s+] pompous, self-satisfied. [STUFFED SHIRT n.]

stuffer n.¹ [1940s] (US Und.) a male homosexual. [the active/passive 'stuffing' of the anus]

stuffer n.² [1970s+] (drugs) a smuggler who hides drugs in the anus or vagina. [SE stuff]

stuffer n.³ [1990s+] (UK juv.) one who is very pleased with himor herself. [he or she is stuffed full of ego]

stuffing n.¹ (also **stuffings**) [late 19C+] (orig. US) the insides, the essence, as in beat/knock the stuffing out of; also used fig. (cf. DAYLIGHTS n.).

stuffing n.² [1970s] (US Black) the practice of tricking or conning a victim. [STUFF v.³ (1)]

stuff it! excl. [1940s+] a euph. excl. for FUCK IT! excl. [STUFF v.¹ (2)]

stuff it up your arse! excl. see SHOVE IT UP YOUR ARSE! excl.

stuff it up your jumper! excl. see STICK IT UP YOUR JUMPER! excl.

stuff me (sideways)! excl. [1950s+] an excl. of surprise, astonishment. [euph. for FUCK ME! excl.; STUFF v.¹ (2)]

stuff one's craw v. [20C+] (W.I.) to overeat. [ext. use of SE]

stuff up v.¹ [1900s] (Aus.) to hand over money, to pay a bill. [var. on STUMP UP v.; note STUFF n.⁴]

stuff up v.² see STUFF v.³ (1).

stuffy n. [mid-19C–1900s] a woman. [STUFF n.⁶ (2)]

stuffy adj.¹ **1** [19C–1920s] angry, sulky. **2** [late 19C+] stuffy-nosed, pompous, snobbish.

stuffy adj.² [1930s+] (orig. US) wealthy, rich. [STUFF n.¹ (1)/STUFF n.⁴]

stug n. [late 19C–1930s] courage, bravery, staying power. [backsl. = GUTS n.² (1)]

stuiver n. see STIVER n.

stuk n. [1940s] (S.Afr.) a (promiscuous) woman. [Afk. stuk, a piece, a part]

stuke n. see STOOK n.

stuling-ken n. see STALLING-KEN n.

stum v. [1970s+] (drugs) to be intoxicated by a drug. [abbr. SE stumble]

stumble (and fall) v. [1940s] **1** (US Black) to suffer serious misfortunes. **2** (US Und.) to be arrested. **3** to be killed. [SE stumble + FALL v.² (1)]

stumblebum n. [1930s+] (US) **1** a shambling, useless, foolish person. **2** a third-rate boxer. **3** a drunk, a homeless drifter; also attrib. [SE stumble + BUM n.³ (1)]

stumble bumble n. [1970s+] (drugs) a barbiturate. [play on STUMBLEBUM n.]

stumblers n. (also **stoms, stums**) [1960s+] (drugs) barbiturates (cf. BARBIT n.). [their effects]

stumer n.¹ **1** [late 19C+] a dud cheque or other fraudulent monetary draft, a counterfeit banknote. **2** [late 19C+] (Aus./N.Z.) a person without money, a defaulter, a bankrupt; thus stumered, bankrupt. **3** [late 19C+] something or someone worthless, useless, a 'flop'; thus *in a stumer*, in a (financial) mess. **4** [1910s–20s] (*UK Und.*) a certainty. **5** [1920s+] a fool. **6** [1930s] a state of agitation. **7** [1960s+] a blunder, a mistake. [ety. unknown; ? fig. use of SHTUM adj.; UK northeast dial. *stumor*, n. a 'difficult person to handle', adj. stupid; note WW1 milit. *stumer*, a dud shell that fails to explode]

stumer *n.*[2] [1910s+] a deaf mute. [SHTUM adj.]

stumm *see under* SHTUM and its combs.

stumm and crum *phr.* [1970s+] extremely quiet, 'silent as the grave'. [ext. of SHTUM adj.]

stump *n.*[1] [17C; late 19C+] the penis; thus *stump*, to enter, to have intercourse (cf. BAT n.[7]).

stump *n.*[2] [early–mid-19C] money. [it is 'stumped up']

stump *n.*[3] [late 19C] a fool. [i.e. one who is short and THICK adj.[1]]

stump *n.*[4] [mid–late 19C] (*US*) a dare, a challenge to do something difficult or dangerous.

stump *v.*[1] [late 18C–1940s] (*Can.*) to challenge (usu. to a fight), to dare.

stump *v.*[2] [19C+] to go on foot, to be off, to leave; esp. as *stump it*. [SE *stump*, to walk clumsily]

stump *v.*[3] [early 19C] to pay. [STUMP n.[2]]

stump *v.*[4] [mid-19C–1900s] to ruin economically; usu. as STUMPED (UP) adj. (1). [? SE *stump*, to confuse or to reduce to a fig. *stump* of wood]

stump *v.*[5] [1970s] (*US Black*) to rob or mug a person. [? SE *stomp*]

stump-break *v.* [1970s+] (*US*) to commit bestiality with an animal.

stumped (up) *adj.* [mid-19C+] **1** ruined, impoverished. **2** lost for ideas. [STUMP v.[4]]

stumpers *n. see* STOMPERS n.

stumpf *adj. see* SHTUM adj.

stump for *v.* [20C+] (*US*) actively to support someone or something. [SAmE *stump*, to conduct a political campaign; the image is of standing on a *tree stump* to make a speech]

stump-glim *n.* [mid-19C] (*US Und.*) a lamp-post.

stump-jumper *n.* [1930s+] (*US*) **1** a rural person, a yokel, a farmer (cf. ACORN-CRACKER n.). **2** an unsophisticated person. [stereotyping]

stump-knocker *n.* (*also* **stump orator**) [mid-19C+] (*US*) an unprofessional, part-time lay preacher; also *stump-speech*, a preacher's sermonizing. [he jumps up on a *tree stump* to preach]

stumps *n.* **1** [17C+] the legs; esp. in phr. STIR ONE'S STUMPS v. **2** [early 18C] the teeth. **3** [mid-18C] (*UK Und.*) shoes. [SE *stump*, something broken off; only the pl. is sl.]

stump the pew *v.* [early–mid-19C] to pay up. [STUMP v.[3] + ? abbr. PEWTER n. (1)]

stump up *v.* [early 19C+] to hand over, esp. of money. [ext. STUMP v.[3]]

stumpy *n.*[1] [early–mid-19C] money. [STUMP n.[2]]

stumpy *n.*[2] (*US*) **1** [mid-19C] a short person. **2** [late 19C+] a crippled beggar, esp. one with a leg missing; also as adj. [SE *stump* of a tree/leg]

stums *n. see* STUMBLERS n.

stun *n.* [mid–late 19C] nuts. [backsl.]

stun *v.* [mid-19C] (*UK Und.*) to cheat, to swindle; esp. in phr. *stun out of*, to defraud.

stun! *excl.* (*also* **stunner!**) [1980s+] (*UK juv.*) an excl. used to underline the amusement one derives from another's misfortune.

stung *adj.*[1] **1** [late 19C+] (*also* **stung for**) tricked out of money (or some other commodity). **2** [1900s] enamoured of. **3** [1910s+] (*orig. Aus.*) persuaded to lend money. **4** [1930s+] subjected to some form of problem. [(1), (2) and (4) STING v. (1); (2) fig. use of SE]

stung *adj.*[2] [1910s+] (*Aus.*) drunk. [STING n.[3] (1)]

stung by a serpent *phr.* [late 19C] of a woman, pregnant.

stung for *adj. see* STUNG adj.[1] (1).

stunlaws *n.* [mid-19C] walnuts. [backsl.]

stunna(h) *n. see* STUNNER n. (3).

stunned *adj.* **1** [1910s–30s] (*Aus./N.Z.*) drunk (cf. ADDLED adj.). **2** [1970s] (*US gay*) intoxicated by a drug.

stunned on skilly *phr.* [mid-19C] (*UK Und.*) sent to prison and thus forced to endure a diet of gruel. [SE *stun* + SKILLY n. (1)]

stunner *n.* **1** [mid–late 19C] an expert in his or her own job or profession. **2** [mid-19C+] a first-rate person or object. **3** [mid-19C+] (*also* **stunna**, **stunnah**) a notably attractive young woman, revived in the late 1980s+ to describe a woman posing as a pin-up for the tabloid press or for softcore pornographic magazines. **4** [mid-19C+] a stunning blow. **5** [late 19C] (*US*) an unusually good story or anecdote. **6** [late 19C+] a surprise, something that 'stuns'.

stunner! *excl. see* STUN! excl.

stunning *adj.* (*also* **stunny**) **1** [mid-19C] clever, knowing. **2** [mid-19C+] very attractive. **3** [mid-19C+] excellent, first-rate.

stunning *adv.* [mid-19C] excellently, wonderfully. [STUNNING adj. (3)]

stunning joe banks *adj.* [mid–late 19C] excellent to the highest degree. [STUNNING adj. (3) + proper name *Joe Banks*, a contemporary publican-cum-receiver, based in Dyott Street, Seven Dials, London, and later in the Cranbourne Street ROOKERY n. (2), who always gave a fair price to the thieves with whom he dealt. Like many receivers, he added to his income by returning, for a price, the stolen goods to their original owners. His neckties, adds Hotten (1860), were as *stunning* as his character and the aristocracy, as well as the underworld, patronized his after-hours drinking club]

stunny *adj. see* STUNNING adj.

stunt *n.* [late 19C+] **1** anything done with the intention of improving or advertising one's image or gaining an advantage over rivals, a gimmick or device for attracting attention. **2** a scheme, a plan. [orig. US campus sports use, 'an act which is striking for the skill, strength, or the like, required to do it; a feat' (*Webster* Supplement, 1900)]

stunt *v.* [2000s] **1** (*US prison*) to lie, or to pretend to have knowledge of something. **2** (*US Black*) to show off.

stunt cock *n.* [1990s+] in pornographic film-making, one who can achieve an erection on demand. [SE *stunt* + COCK n.[2] (1)]

stunty *adj.* [1920s] (*US*) ostentatious. [STUNT n. (1)]

stupe *n.* (*also* **stoop**) [mid-18C+] a fool, an idiot. [abbr. SE *stupid*]

stupe-head *n.* [1950s+] (*US*) a fool. [STUPE n./SE *stupid* + -HEAD sfx (1)]

stupid *n.* [early 18C+] a fool.

stupid *adj.* **1** [early 19C+] drunk (cf. ADDLED adj.). **2** [20C+] (*W.I.*) insignificant, small, contemptible. **3** [1980s+] (*US campus*) crazy, insane, absurd. **4** [1980s+] (*US campus*) pleasant, popular, excellent.

stupid *adv.* **1** [1960s+] (*US*) extremely, very. **2** [1990s+] (*US teen*) used of a large quantity of something.

stupid as arseholes *phr.* [1920s+] extremely stupid (cf. DUMB AS A BOX OF ROCKS phr.). [SE *stupid* + ARSEHOLE n.]

stupid-head *n.* [mid-19C] a fool. [SE *stupid* + -HEAD sfx (1)]

stupidie *n.* [20C+] (*W.I.*) a fool, an idiot. [SE *stupid* + sfx -*ie*]

stupidie *adj.* [20C+] (*W.I.*) stupid, idiotic. [STUPIDIE n.]

stupo *n.* [1920s] (*Anglo-Irish*) a fool (cf. BOBO n.[1]). [SE *stup(id)* + -o sfx (2)]

stupp *v. see* SCHTUP v.

stur *n. see* STIR n.[1].

sturks *n. see* STERKS n.

sturrabin *n.* (*also* **stariben**, **sturaban**, **sturbin**) [mid-19C–1900s] a prison. [Rom. *sturiben*, a prison, *staripen*, to imprison]

stutter and stammer *n.* [20C+] a hammer. [rhy. sl.]

stuyver *n. see* STIVER n.

style *n.* [1910s+] (*US Black*) anything one needs (fancy clothes, a clever line of patter, a personal style, a mental attitude) for the successful promotion of one's schemes; thus *styler*, a person preoccupied with appearance.

-style *sfx* (*also* **-stylee**) [1960s+] used in comb. with a n. to create an adv. meaning 'in that manner'.

style (off) *v.* [1960s+] (*orig. US Black*) to show off, to strut around. [STYLE n.]

styles *n.* [1980s] (*US Black*) clothing.

stylie *n.* [1980s+] a White person wearing trad. Black dreadlocks.

styling *n.* **1** [1960s+] showing off, acting ostentatiously. **2** [1980s+] (*US campus*) doing well, succeeding, academically as well as socially. [STYLE (OFF) v.]

styling *adj.* [1990s+] (*US Black*) ostentatious, fashionable. [STYLE n.]

styling and profiling *n.* [1980s+] (*US Black/campus*) posing as a cool, sophisticated individual, and backing that image with smart, fashionable clothes. [STYLE (OFF) v. + PROFILE v.]

stymie *n.* [1910s–40s] a frustrating situation. [STYMIED adj.; ? a P.G. Wodehouse nonce-use]

stymie *v.* **1** [1920s+] to frustrate, to destroy. **2** [1980s] (*US campus*) to deprive others by taking the last of anything. [STYMIED adj.]

stymied *adj.* [20C+] (*orig. US*) confused, frustrated, in difficulties. [golfing imagery; SE *stymie*, 'an opponent's ball which lies on the putting green in a line between the ball of the player and the hole he is playing for, if the distance between the balls is not less than six inches' (*OED*)]

suave *n.* (*also* **swave**) [1980s–90s] (*US campus/teen*) smooth style, charm; as v., to be charming. [SE *suave*, soothingly agreeable; ult. Lat. *suavis*, sweet]

suavo *n.* [1970s] a sophisticate. [SE *suave* + -o sfx (2)]

sub *n.*[1] **1** [mid-18C–1910s] a sub*altern*. **2** [mid-19C] a sub*ject* of the monarch. **3** [mid-19C] a sub*scriber*. **4** [mid-19C+] (*also* **subbie**) a loan, esp. an advance on wages; thus *do a sub*, to borrow money. **5** [mid-19C+] a sub*stitute*. **6** [late 19C] (*US*) a sub*ject*, e.g. of conversation. **7** [late 19C+] a sub*scription*. **8** [1910s+] a sub*marine*. [abbr.; (4) SE *subsistence*]

sub *n.*[2] [mid-19C–1940s] everything, all, the lot. [Hind. *sab*, all]

sub *n.*[3] [late 19C; 1990s+] a general term of abuse, denoting a despised, poverty-stricken or otherwise inadequate person. [abbr. SE *sub-human*]

sub *n.*[4] *see* SUBMARINE n.[1].

sub *v.*[1] **1** [mid-19C+] (*also* **sub up**) to give or get an advance on wages, a loan. **2** [1900s] to hand over money (as a bet). **3** [1960s] to hand over money as a bribe. [SE *subsistence money*]

sub *v.*[2] [mid-19C+] to fill in for (on a job), to deputize for; in sport to substitute for or to be substituted. [abbr. SE *substitute*]

subaltern's butter *n.* [late 19C–1920s] the flesh of an avocado pear. [the officer's preference]

subaltern's luncheon *n.* [late 19C–1900s] a glass of water and the tightening of one's belt.

sub-beau *n.* [late 17C–mid-18C] an aspirant dandy. [SE *sub*, secondary + *beau*, a dandy]

subbie *n.* *see* SUB n.[1] (4).

subby *n.*[1] (*also* **subbie**) [1950s+] a sub-contractor. [abbr.]

subby *n.*[2] *see* SUB n.[3].

sub-chaser *n.* [1920s] (*US teen*) a man who attempts to pick up girls in the street. [? SUB-DEB n.]

sub-cheese *n.* [mid-19C+] (*mainly Anglo-Ind.*) everything, the lot, all there is. [SE *sub*, inferior + CHEESE, THE n.]

sub-deb *n.* [1910s–40s] (*US*) a girl who is on the verge of 'coming out' as a debutante.

sub-human *n.* [1980s+] (*US campus*) a socially unacceptable person; thus *sub-human*, distasteful, gross, stupid.

sublime rascal *n.* [mid-19C] a lawyer.

submarine *n.*[1] **1** [1930s–40s] (*US Und.*) a doughnut. **2** [1940s+] (*US*) (*also* **sub**) a type of large, over-filled sandwich; thus *super-sub*. **3** [1980s+] (*US campus*) a tampon. [resemblance]

submarine *n.*[2] [1990s+] (*Aus.*) a male homosexual. [rhy. sl. = QUEEN n.[2] + ? ref. to GO DOWN v.[6] (1)]

submarine races *n.* [1960s–70s] (*US teen*) petting.

submarine turkey *n.* *see* DEEP-SEA TURKEY n. (3).

submerged *adj.* [1910s] drunk.

sub up *v.* *see* SUB v.[1] (1).

suburb *n.* [late 16C–early 19C] used in a variety of phrs., all denigrating suburban life and poss. virtually SE, e.g. *suburb-garden*, a house in which one installs a mistress; *suburb-humour*, unpleasant humour, usu. at another's expense; *suburb justice*, corrupt justice, one easily amenable to bribes; *suburb-trade*, prostitution; *suburb tricks*, sexual amusements; *suburb sinner*, a prostitute; *aunt of the suburbs*, a prostitute; *suburban roarer*, a pimp or male 'heavy' in a brothel; *house in the suburbs*, a brothel; *minion of the suburbs*, a male prostitute. [the 17C suburbs – Holborn, Wapping, Mile End, Bermondsey, Clerkenwell – are now parts of central London; then, however, they were beyond the City proper, and were home to various 'stink' industries, e.g. tanning, leper hospitals, playhouses and brothels]

suburban (wench) *n.* (*also* **suburban roarer, suburb lady/ whore**) [17C–early 18C] a prostitute who works in the suburbs rather than the West End of London. [SUBURB n.]

suburbian *n.* [17C–early 18C] a prostitute; also as adj. [SUBURB n.]

suburb trade *n.* [late 17C] the world of suburban prostitution; thus *suburbian-trader*, a prostitute's client. [SUBURB n.]

subway alumni *n.* [1940s+] (*US*) supporters of college sports teams who are not actually *alumni*, i.e. members or former members of the college. [they turn up at the college by *subway*]

subway dealer *n.* [20C+] (*US Und.*) a card-sharp who deals from the bottom of the pack. [SE *subway* as 'underground']

subway silver *n.* [1980s] (*US drugs*) a (mythical) form of marijuana growing in the NY subways, the result of the drug being flushed away to avoid police raids.

such *adj.* [mid-16C+] 'used as an absolute intensive, the implied clause of comparison being indeterminate and quite lost sight of' (*OED*), e.g. 'such an argument', 'such an awful place'.

such-a-much *adj.* **1** [1900s] (*US*) of a thing, important. **2** [1960s] (*US Black*) of a person, (self-)important.

such a reason pissed my goose *phr.* (*also* **such a reason my goose pissed**) [late 18C–early 19C] used in response to anything the speaker considers foolish or absurd. [PISS v.[1] (1)]

suck *n.*[1] (*also* **sucky**) [late 17C–mid-19C] (*UK Und.*) wine or strong drink. [SE *suck*, a small measure or glass of liquid]

suck *n.*[2] [early–mid-19C] (*UK Und.*) the breast pocket.

suck *n.*[3] [mid-19C–1950s] some form of suckable sweetmeat.

suck *n.*[4] (*also* **suckie**) **1** [mid-19C–1950s] a parasite, a toady, a sycophant. **2** [1910s+] (*Irish*) a first-year schoolboy. **3** [1970s+] (*Can.*) a worthless, contemptible person. [SUCK UP v. (1)]

suck *n.*[5] **1** [mid-19C+] (*orig. US*) a disappointment. **2** [20C+] (*US Black*) empty words, nagging, pointless arguments.

suck *n.*[6] [1940s+] the act of fellatio (cf. COCKSUCK n.). [SUCK v.[1] (1)]

suck *n.*[7] *see* SUCKER n.[3] (1).

suck *adj.* [1970s] worthless, second-rate. [SUCK v.[1] (3)]

suck *v.*[1] **1** [mid-17C+] to perform fellatio or cunnilingus (cf. COCKSUCK n.; CUNT-LICK v.). **2** [1940s+] in the dismissive or challenging phr. *suck this*. **3** [1960s+] (*also* **suck a big dog's dick, suck out loud**) to be worthless, contemptible, pointless, objectionable.

suck *v.*[2] **1** [19C] to pump someone for information. **2** [1950s] (*W.I.*) to nag.

suck *v.*[3] [mid-19C] (*US campus*) to cheat in an examination.

suck *v.*[4] [1970s+] (*US campus*) to be on one's last legs, to be struggling. [one *sucks for air*]

suck *v.*[5] [1970s+] (*US campus*) to make someone into a victim of one's plans, tricks etc. [? backform. f. SUCKER n.[3] (2)]

suck *v.*[6] *see* SUCK UP v. (1).

suck! *excl.* [1980s+] (*US campus*) a general excl., a euph. synon. for FUCK! excl.

sucka *n.* [1990s+] (*orig. US Black teen*) **1** a foolish, gullible person. **2** a general term of abuse. [deliberate mis-sp. of SUCKER n.³ (2)]

suck a fatty! *excl.* [1990s+] (*US*) a general excl. of dismissal, aggression. [lit. *go and suck a fat penis!*]

Sucka Free *n.* [1990s+] (*US Black teen*) San Francisco. [SUCKA n. (2) + SE *free*]

suck air *v.* **1** [1950s+] (*US*) to be fearful, to encounter problems. **2** [1980s] (*US campus*) to laugh. [var. on SUCK WIND v.]

suck a kumara *v.* [1980s] (*N.Z.*) of a machine, to break down, to crash.

suck and swallow *n.* [19C] the vagina (cf. BITE n.²). [the role of the vagina as a predator]

suck-around *n.* [1950s] (*US*) a toady. [SUCK (A)ROUND v.]

suck (a)round *v.* [1910s+] (*US*) to act in a toadying manner. [var. on SUCK UP v. (1)]

suck arse *v. see* SUCK (SOMEONE'S) ASS v.

suck-ass *n.* (*also* suck-arse) [1950s+] (*US*) a toady, a sycophant. [SUCK (SOMEONE'S) ASS v.]

suck-ass *adj.* (*also* suck-arse) [1970s+] useless, pointless, unpleasant – all deriving from the need to be obsequious. [SUCK (SOMEONE'S) ASS v.]

suck-ass *v. see* SUCK (SOMEONE'S) ASS v.

suck-back *n.* [1990s+] (*Aus.*) an extremely obnoxious person. [one who should have been *sucked back* into the womb at birth]

suck-bottle *n.* [mid-17C–mid-18C] a drinker.

suckbutt *n.* [1980s+] a sycophant. [SE *suck*/SUCK UP v. (1) + BUTT n.¹ (2)]

suck-can *n.* [19C] a drinker. [SE]

suck-casa *n.* [mid-19C] a public house, a tavern. [SUCK n.¹ + CASA n.¹]

suck-crib *n.* [late 19C] a public house, a tavern. [SUCK n.¹ + CRIB n.¹ (2)]

suck dick *v.* [1960s+] (*US*) to be reprehensible, of the lowest standard. [SUCK v.¹ (1) + DICK n.⁴ (1)]

suck diesel *v.* [2000s] (*Irish*) to enjoy oneself.

sucked *adj.* [early–mid-19C] (*UK Und.*) (very) drunk.

suck-egg *n.* [mid-19C] a foolish person. [17C SE *suck-egg*, a young man]

suck-egg *adj.* [mid-19C+] (*US*) despicable, foolish. [SUCK-EGG n.]

suck eggs *v.* [20C+] **1** (*US, esp. Southern*) to be mean and irritable, to be overbearing and unpleasant. **2** (*US*) of a person or thing or situation, to behave in a disgusting manner, to be reprehensible, e.g. *that sucks eggs.*

sucker *n.¹* [early 17C; mid-19C; 1980s] a parasite. [SE *sucker*, one who sucks, in this case money and favours]

sucker *n.²* **1** [mid-18C] the vagina (cf. BITE n.²). **2** [late 19C] the penis. **3** [1940s] (*N.Z.*) in pl., the buttocks. **4** [1970s] (*Irish*) a woman's breast.

sucker *n.³* (*orig. US*) **1** [mid-18C+] (*also* suck) an innocent, a dupe. **2** [mid-19C+] the victim of any kind of crooked plan. **3** [mid-19C+] a person (occas. animal) or object, irrespective of status. **4** [mid-19C+] an unpleasant, mean person. **5** [1910s+] a general term of address, either derog. or teasing. **6** [1940s+] an enthusiast, a 'pushover'. **7** [1950s] a fan. [14C *sucker*, an animal before it is weaned, a child at the breast; thus the innocence of both; the term was popularized by NY nightclub hostess Texas Guinan whose celebrated greeting was 'Hello sucker!']

sucker *n.⁴* [mid-19C] (*US*) a drunkard.

sucker *n.⁵* [mid-19C+] (*US*) an inhabitant of Illinois. [? the state fish (*Catostomus commersoni*), the sucker; the sucking of much-needed water from the natural artesian wells; the gullibility of the early settlers in the hands of unscrupulous land speculators; for detailed discussion see R.H. Thornton, *An American Glossary*, I pp.32–3 (1912)]

sucker *n.⁶* [late 19C+] **1** a fellatrix. **2** a lesbian (cf. CARPET-BITER n.). **3** (*US Und.*) a male homosexual (cf. BONE-EATER n.). [SUCK v.¹ (1)]

sucker *n.⁷* **1** [1930s+] a generally pej. description. **2** [1980s+] an

object, irrespective of quality. [? euph. for FUCKER n.; abbr. of COCK-SUCKER n.]

sucker *n.⁸* [1950s] (*W.I.*) a nagging old woman. [note dial. *old suck*, a blood-sucking demon in the shape of an old woman]

sucker *adj.* **1** [mid-19C] mean, untrustworthy. **2** [1910s+] (*orig. US*) foolish, naïve. [SUCKER n.³ (1)]

sucker *v.* [1930s+] (*orig. US*) (*also* suckerize) **1** to cheat, to trick; thus *sucker in*, to ensnare, to entrap. **2** to be deceived, to 'fall for'. [SUCKER n.³ (1)]

sucker-ass *adj.* [1990s+] (*US Black*) a general term of abuse. [SUCKER n.³ (2) + -ASS sfx]

sucker-bait *n.* [1940s+] (*US Und.*) **1** young women hired by casinos to appear available and thus lure and distract gamblers. **2** any form of fraudulent enticement. [SUCKER n.³ (2) + SE *bait*]

sucker-bashing *n.* [1940s+] (*Aus.*) cutting down saplings that persist in growing on newly cleared land. [SE *sucker*, a shoot thrown out from the base of a plant]

suckerize *v. see* SUCKER v.

sucker list *n.* [1930s+] (*US*) a client list, a mailing list. [SUCKER n.³ (2)]

sucker out *v.* [1960s] (*US*) to act like a fool, to make a mistake. [SUCKER n.³ (2)]

sucker play *n.* **1** [late 19C–1950s] (*US*) any form of scheme intended to trap a gullible victim. **2** [1910s] a foolish action. [SUCKER n.³ (2) + PLAY n.¹ (2)]

sucker-punch *n.* [1940s+] a surprise punch. [SUCKER n.³ (1) + SE *punch*]

sucker-punch *v.* [1960s+] (*US*) **1** to hit when the victim is not looking or is otherwise unprepared. **2** in fig. use, to shock. **3** to fool, to trick. [SUCKER-PUNCH n.]

sucker stroking *n.* [2000s] (*US prison*) to become tearful at the thought of one's absent girlfriend. [SUCKER n.³ (5)]

sucker town *n.* [1940s] (*US Und.*) a town or city in which any criminal activity is unwise – the authorities have proved impervious to corruption. [SUCKER n.³ (2); the inference is that the populace are too innocent to accept bribes]

sucker weed *n.* [1950s+] (*US Black/drugs*) poor-quality marijuana, esp. as sold to gullible consumers (cf. AFRICAN BUSH n.). [SUCKER n.³ (2) + WEED n.¹ (4)]

suck face *v.* (*also* suck heads) [1970s+] (*orig. US campus*) to kiss. [note synon. 18C *suck one's jowl*]

suck gas! *excl.* [1950s] (*US*) a dismissive excl.

suck hind tit *v.* (*also* suck hind titty) [1920s+] (*US*) **1** to be inferior, to take a secondary role. **2** to curry favour.

suck-hole *n.* **1** [late 19C+] (*orig. Aus./Can.*) (*also* suck-holer) a toady, a flatterer. **2** [1970s+] (*US gay*) a hole drilled or carved between the partitions of 2 toilet stalls in a men's room and used for sex. [(1) SUCK UP v. + HOLE n.¹ (1); (2) SUCK v.¹ (1) + SE *hole*]

suck hole *v.* [1960s+] (*Aus./Can.*) to toady, to curry favour. [SUCK-HOLE n. (1)]

suckie *n. see* SUCK n.⁴.

suck-in *n.* **1** [mid-19C–1920s] a disappointment. **2** [1910s] (*Aus.*) sharp practice; a cunning scheme, deceit. **3** [1940s] (*US Und.*) a swindler. [SUCK IN v.]

suck in *v.* **1** [mid-19C] to accept, to believe. **2** [mid-19C+] to deceive, to cheat.

sucking *n.* [1920s+] (*orig. US*) fellatio (cf. COCKSUCK n.). [SUCK v.¹ (1)/abbr. COCKSUCKING n.]

sucking *adj.¹* [mid-19C] ripe for duping; thus naut. jargon *sucking Nelson*, a midshipman. [SE *suck*, at the maternal breast, i.e. still young and inexperienced]

sucking *adj.²* [mid-19C+] (*US*) worthless, useless, contemptible. [despite synonymy, chronology appears to eliminate a link to SUCK v.¹ (3)]

sucking duppy *n.* [1940s] (*W.I.*) tuberculosis. [SE *sucking* + dial. *duppy*, a ghost, a malevolent spirit (allegedly of the dead)]

suck it and see *phr.* [late 19C+] a phr. aimed derisively at someone who has asked what is considered a stupid or impudent question. [lollipop image]

suck it easy *v.* [1980s+] (*US campus*) to relax, to lie around. [the image of lying peacefully sucking on a cool drink]

suck it up *v.* [1970s+] (*US campus*) to tolerate, to endure, to deal with.

suck job *n.* [2000s] fellatio (cf. COCKSUCK n.). [SUCK n.⁶ + JOB n.⁴]

suck lemons *v.* [20C+] (*US*) to act sourly, to complain, to sulk. [play on the SE *sour* flavour of a lemon]

suck my arse! *excl.* (*also* **suck my ass!**) [1920s+] a general statement of contempt or dismissal. [SUCK (SOMEONE'S) ASS v.]

suck my dick! *excl.* [1970s+] (*orig. US*) a general excl. of contempt, dismissal. [SUCK SOMEONE'S DICK v.]

suck-o! *excl.* [1980s+] (*Aus. prison*) an excl. of satisfaction in someone else's misfortune. [SUCK v.¹ (3) + -o sfx (7)]

suck-off *n.* **1** [1920s+] (*US*) a despicable person, esp. a toady; thus as adj., repellent, contemptible. **2** [1930s] an act of oral sex (cf. COCKSUCK n.). [SUCK SOMEONE OFF v.]

suck one's face *v.* (*also* **suck one's muns**) [17C–mid-18C] to drink.

suck out loud *v. see* SUCK v.¹ (3).

suck-pint *n.* [early 17C] a drinker.

suck-pot *n.* [18C; 19C] a drinker.

suck rope *v.* [1960s+] (*US*) to be worthless, contemptible. [ext. of SUCK v.¹ (3)]

suck round *v. see* SUCK (A)ROUND v.

suck salt *v.* [20C+] (*W.I.*) to suffer hardship.

suck-silly *adj.* [1940s] (*US*) deranged.

suck someone off *v.* **1** [20C+] to fellate (cf. COCKSUCK n.). **2** [1920s+] (*US*) to toady to. **3** [1930s+] to peform cunnilingus. **4** [1980s] to make a fool of. [(1) SUCK UP v.; (2) SUCK v.¹ (1); the *off* (cf. COME OFF v.¹) implies orgasm]

suck (someone's) ass *v.* (*also* **suck (someone's) arse**) [1930s+] (*orig. US Black*) to toady to, to be subservient, to curry favour. [SUCK v.¹ (1) + ASS n. (2); the perceived humiliation of anilingus]

suck someone's dick *v.* (*also* **kiss someone's dick**, **suck someone's can**) (*orig. US*) to flatter, to toady to, to congratulate effusively. [SUCK v.¹ (1) + DICK n.⁴ (1); the perceived self-abasement of (homosexual) fellatio]

suck someone's titty *v.* [1970s] (*US*) to depend on, to act as a parasite towards. [SE *suck* + TITTY n.¹ (1); the image of dependency implicit in breastfeeding]

suck-spigot *n.* [late 16C–early 17C] a drinker.

suck spit *v. see* SWAP SPIT v. (2).

suckster *n.* (*also* **suckstress**) [late 19C+] a fellator, a fellatrix. [SUCKER n.⁶]

sucks to be you *phr.* [1990s+] (*US campus*) an expression of commiseration. [SUCK v.¹ (3)]

sucks (to you)! *excl.* [1910s+] (*mainly UK teen*) a disdainful, dismissive excl. [? euph. for FUCK! excl.]

suckstress *n. see* SUCKSTER n.

suck suds *v.* [1940s+] (*US*) to drink beer. [SE *suck* + SUDS n.¹ (1)]

suck the bag *v.* [early 19C] to spend money.

suck the monkey *v.* **1** [late 18C–19C] to suck liquor through a straw from the ship's barrel which has been bored with a gimlet. **2** [mid-19C] to replace the milk of a coconut with rum, and consume through a straw. **3** [mid-19C] to drink from the bottle. [note Hotten (1873): 'Originally, as Captain Marryatt states, to SUCK THE MONKEY, was to suck rum from the cocoa-nuts, which spirit had been inserted in place of the milk, for the private use of the sailors']

suck the mop *v.* [mid–late 19C] for one omnibus to lose its passengers to those of a rival firm, which has boxed it in; thus *left sucking the mop*, rendered impotent and beyond hope, to be put at an utter disadvantage. [play on NURSE v. (2); SE *mop*, a baby's dummy]

suck the sugar-stick *v.* [19C] **1** of a woman, to have sexual intercourse (cf. CATCH AN OYSTER v.). **2** usu. of a woman, to fellate (cf. COCKSUCK n.). [SE *suck* + SUGAR-STICK n.]

suck tonsils *v.* [1990s+] (*US campus*) to kiss passionately.

suck-up *n.* [1960s+] one who curries favour with others, a toady, a parasite. [SUCK UP v. (1)]

suck up *v.* **1** [mid-19C+] (*also* **suck**, **suck up to**) to curry favour, to be obsequious, to grovel shamelessly in return for favours, esteem etc. **2** [1950s+] to drink.

suck wind *v.* [1960s+] (*US*) to be on one's last legs, to be struggling. [one fig. gasps for air]

sucky *adj.*¹ [late 17C–18C] tipsy, slightly drunk. [SUCK n.¹]

sucky *adj.*² (*US campus*) **1** [1910s+] awful, terrible, unpleasant. **2** [1960s+] toadying, sycophantic. [(1) ? link to SUCK v.¹ (3) but chronology appears to negate this; *OED*, quoting Paul Beale in *DSUE* (1984), suggests that which makes one *suck* in one's cheeks with pain; (2) SUCK UP v.]

sucky-sucky *n.* (*also* **sucky-fucky**) [1970s+] fellatio. [SUCK v.¹ (1)]

suction *n.*¹ [early 19C–1910s] the heavy drinking of alcohol; thus [mid-19C] *power of suction*, one's drinking capacity; [1900s] *live on suction*, to drink heavily.

suction *n.*² [1950s–70s] (*US Black*) empty words, nagging, pointless arguments. [? fig. use of SE or play on SUCK WIND v.]

sud-buster *n.* [1940s] (*US Black*) a cleaner.

sudden *adj.* [1900s–20s] **1** (*Aus.*) fast, efficient, keen. **2** (*orig. Aus.*) brutal, ruthless, drastic; of clothes, garish.

sudden death *n.*¹ **1** [mid-19C] (*Anglo-Ind.*) a spatch-cocked fowl. **2** [mid-19C–1910s] (*US*) a strong alcoholic drink, esp. cheap whisky. **3** [mid-19C+] (*sporting*) in a variety of games (orig. coin-tossing), a way of deciding the victor in a tied contest by giving the judgement to the next individual or team to score; thus [20C+] *sudden-death play-off*. **4** [late 19C] a plain boiled pudding. **5** [late 19C–1900s] coffee. **6** [late 19C+] a crumpet or bun. **7** [1950s] (*Aus.*) one who is overwhelmed or infatuated, impulsively. [(1) the bird was caught and killed as the putative eater dismounted from his horse and by the time he had washed and dressed was ready for the table]

sudden death *n.*² [1970s+] (*Aus.*) breath. [rhy. sl.]

sudden death on *phr.* [1920s+] (*Aus.*) **1** expert, skilled at. **2** unnecessarily cruel or harsh towards. [ext. SUDDEN adj. (1)]

suds *n.*¹ **1** [late 19C+] (*US*) beer; thus *suds slinger/jerker*, a bartender. **2** [1900s] drink in general. **3** [1920s+] coffee. [(1) the product's intense soap-suds-like fizziness and (to UK palates) taste. The link to 18C LITTLE IN THE SUDS, a phr. is presumably coincidental]

suds *n.*² [1910s] (*US campus*) money.

sudser *n.* [1950s+] (*US*) a soap opera. [SE *soap suds*]

sud-up *adj.* [1990s+] (*W.I.*) referring to the mix of vaginal secretions and semen that follows intercourse.

sue *n.* [1980s+] (*US campus*) a usu. derog. term for a stereotypical sorority member; thus *sue out*, to dress, look and act like a sorority member. [generic use of the proper name; note also SUZI (SORORITY) n.]

sue city *n.* [1960s+] (*US*) involvement in a court case or similar legal situation. [SE *sue* + CITY sfx + pun on *Sioux City*]

suede *n.* [1940s–70s] (*US Black*) a dark-skinned Black person.

suede *adj.* [1960s–70s] (*US Black*) dark-skinned. [SUEDE n.]

suedehead *n.* (*also* **suede**) [1970s+] a form of SKINHEAD n. (3) whose hair was grown slightly longer than the usual absolute bald look and thus presents a slight fuzz, somewhat reminiscent of suede.

suet-headed *adj.* [late 19C] foolish, stupid (cf. AIRHEADED adj.). [along the lines of PUDDING-HEADED adj.]

suety Isaac *n.* (*also* **soapy Isaac**) [1900s–20s] a suet pudding. [? its sallow 'complexion', supposedly reminiscent of a Jew, i.e. the 'Jewish' proper name *Isaac*]

suey bowl *n.* [1940s–50s] (*US Und.*) an opium den.

suey pow *n.* (*also* **sui gow**) [1900s–50s] (*drugs*) a cloth or sponge used to cool or clean an opium pipe or bowl.

suff *n.* (*also* **suffish**) [late 19C–1910s] (*N.Z./UK*) sufficient. [abbr.]

suffer *n.* [1940s] (*US Black*) a lengthy story, tediously recounted. [the listeners 'suffer' through it]

suffer a recovery *v.* [1910s–40s] to have a hangover. [joc. euph.]

sufferer *n.*[1] [mid-19C] a tailor. [? his professional problems, usu. poverty]

sufferer *n.*[2] [mid–late 19C] a sovereign. ['Cockney' mispron.]

suffering —! *excl.* [mid-19C+] used with suitable n. to create a mild oath.

suffering catfish! *excl. see* CATFISH! excl.

suffer with the shorts *v.* [1940s] (*US Black*) to be out of cash, to be impoverished. [i.e. *short* of cash]

suffier *n.* [late 16C] (*UK Und.*) that member of a team of confidence tricksters passing off fake gold who poses as a drunk. [? Netherlands High Ger. *suff*, drink]

suffish *n. see* SUFF n.

sug *n.*[1] [20C+] (*S.Afr.*) a moan, a whinge; thus as v., to whinge. [Du. *zuchten*, to sigh, to groan]

sug *n.*[2] *see* SHUG n.

sug *n.*[3] *see* SUGAR n.[5] (2).

sugan *n.* (*also* **soogan, suggan**) [1900s–40s] (*US tramp*) a quilt.

sugar *n.*[1] **1** [mid-19C+] money (cf. BEES (AND HONEY) n.). **2** [late 19C] a premium, an unexpected bonus. **3** [late 19C+] monetary gifts or bribes. [rhy. sl. on *sugar and honey*; Cohen (ed.), *Studies in Slang* II (1989), suggests that on the basis of *honey* = gold, *sugar* = silver as well as the plain generic]

sugar *n.*[2] [late 19C] a grocer. [their stock-in-trade]

sugar *n.*[3] **1** [late 19C+] a euph. for SHIT n.[1]. **2** [1910s] a contemptible person, a euph. for SHIT n.[2] (1).

sugar *n.*[4] [1920s+] (*US Black*) semen (cf. BABY GRAVY n.). [*double entendre*, e.g. Bessie Smith, 'Want Some Sugar in My Bowl']

sugar *n.*[5] (*also* **sugarpie**) **1** [1920s+] a general term of endearment, can be used of and to either sex. **2** [1930s+] (*orig. US*) (*also* **sug**) an attractive female. **3** [1930s+] (*US Black*) (*also* **sugar lump**) an attractive male.

sugar *n.*[6] (*drugs*) **1** [1930s+] morphine or heroin; thus [1970s] *sugar people*, rich young heroin addicts (cf. AUNTIE EMMA n.). **2** [1930s+] (*also* **booger sugar**) cocaine (cf. BIRDIE POWDER n.). **3** [1960s+] LSD (cf. A n.[3]). [note that *sugar people* is also influenced by SUGAR DADDY n.; (2) BOOGER n.[1]]

sugar *n.*[7] [1960s+] (*US Black*) a kiss; usu. as *give (me) some sugar*. [the 'sweetness' thereof]

sugar *n.*[8] *see* SUGAR DADDY n.

sugar *adj.* [mid-19C] easy, comfortable.

sugar *v.*[1] **1** [late 16C; 1930s] to flatter, to pander to. **2** [late 19C–1900s] to bribe. **3** [late 19C–1950s] to present a fake appearance, to 'cook the books', to pose as something one is not. [fig. uses of SE *sweeten* or phr. *sugar the pill*]

sugar *v.*[2] [late 19C+] a euph. for SHIT v.[1] or BUGGER v.[1] in various uses.

sugar! *excl.* **1** [mid-19C] a cry of exultation after a victory, supposedly given as one stands on one leg and waves the other about. **2** [mid-19C+] (*also* **ginger!**) a euph. for SHIT! excl. or BUGGER! excl. **3** [late 19C] a euph. for 'the hell with'.

sugar and honey *n.* [mid-19C–1970s] money (cf. BEES (AND HONEY) n.). [rhy. sl.]

sugar and salt *n.* [1930s] (*US drugs*) any powdered narcotic.

sugar and spice *n.* [20C+] ice. [rhy. sl.]

sugar and spice *adj.* [20C+] nice. [rhy. sl.]

sugar-baby *n.* [1920s+] (*US*) anyone or anything attractive, pleasing; also as a direct term of address. [SUGAR n.[5] (1) + BABY n.[3] (2)]

sugar-bag *n.* [late 19C+] (*Aus.*) one who accepts bribes. [they are willing to take a SE *sweetener*]

sugar-bag *adj.* [1970s] (*Aus./N.Z.*) second-rate, cheap, impover-

ished. [the Depression-era use of *sugar bags* (made of fine sacking) for a variety of makeshift and do-it-yourself tasks]

sugar-bag *v.* [1980s] (*Aus.*) to bribe. [SUGAR-BAG n.]

sugar basin *n.* [19C] the vagina (cf. APPLE n.[6]). [it contains the SUGAR-STICK n.]

sugar-candy *n.* [mid-19C+] brandy. [rhy. sl.]

sugar-candy *adj.* [20C+] handy. [rhy. sl.]

sugar cubes *n.*[1] [1940s] dice.

sugar cubes *n.*[2] (*also* **sugar lumps**) [1960s+] (*drugs*) LSD (cf. A n.[3]). [early doses of LSD came on *sugar cubes/lumps*]

sugar daddy *n.* (*also* **sugar, sugar papa, sugar pops, sweet sugar**) [1920s+] (*orig. US*) an older man who is willing to provide the various material wants of a younger mistress or, if gay, a younger male lover.

sugared *adj.* [late 19C+] a euph. for BUGGERED adj.[1] etc, usu. in phr. *I'll be sugared! I'm sugared!*

Sugar Hill *n.* (*US Black*) **1** [1920s–40s] that area of Harlem otherwise known as Coogan's Bluff, between Amsterdam and Edgecombe Avenues, between 138th and 155th Streets. As well as the rich, many Black intellectuals and artists chose to live in the area, known for its grand apartment houses, once the original White population had moved out during the 1920s. **2** [1930s–50s] the brothel and red-light area of the Black part of any southern town. [(1) SUGAR n.[1] (1); (2) SUGAR n.[5] (1) + SE *hill*; note Lincoln University (Oxford, Penn.) use *c.*1934: 'Sugar Hill. The newest dormitory, where rentals and appointments are relatively high']

sugar lump *n. see* SUGAR n.[5] (3).

sugar lumps *n. see* SUGAR CUBES n.[2].

sugar mama *n.* **1** [1970s–80s] (*US gay*) an effeminate older gay man providing material support for his younger lover. **2** [1970s+] (*US*) an older woman who keeps a (usu.) younger lover. [feminization of SUGAR DADDY n.]

sugar-man *n. see* SWEETBACK (MAN) n.

sugar mummy *n.* [1980s+] (*S.Afr. township*) **1** a wealthy White woman who pays for the companionship of attractive, younger Black men. **2** an older woman who provides for the material wants of a younger male lover. [on model of SUGAR DADDY n.]

sugar on *adj.* [late 19C] in love with, infatuated with. [var. on SWEET ON adj. (1)]

sugar papa *n. see* SUGAR DADDY n.

sugarpie *n. see* SUGAR n.[5].

sugar pimp *n.* (*also* **sweet pimp**) [1970s] a pimp who prefers charm and persuasion to threats and violence when dealing with his women. [SE *sugar* + *pimp*]

sugar pimp *v.* [1950s–70s] to be a pimp who treat one's prostitutes with charm and persuasion rather than threats and violence. [SE *sugar* + *pimp*]

sugar pops *n. see* SUGAR DADDY n.

Sugar Ray *v.* [1980s] (*Aus.*) to pay. [rhy. sl.; ult. US boxer *Sugar Ray Robinson* (1921–89)]

sugar report *n.* [1940s+] (*US campus*) a letter from one's sweetheart. [SUGAR n.[5] (1) + SE *report*; orig. milit. WW2]

sugar-scoop *n.* [1950s] the vagina (cf. APPLE n.[6]).

sugar shack *n.* [1960s] (*US Black*) spare space used for putting up a temporary guest.

sugar-shop *n.* [late 19C] a place where, during an election, voters can expect to receive bribes in return for the promise of their votes. [SUGAR n.[1] (3) + SE *shop*]

sugar-stick *n.* [mid-17C+] the penis (cf. BAT n.[7]). [Puxley, *Cockney Rabbit: A Dick 'n' Arry of Rhyming Slang* (1992), suggests rhy. sl. on PRICK n. (2), but rhy. sl. tends to be coined later]

sugar tit *n.* [1910s+] (*US*) something comforting, something desirable. [SE *sugar* + TIT n.[3] (1); the use of a cloth dipped in sugar water as a way of soothing a baby]

sugar up *v.* [1910s–20s] to flatter, to toady to. [ext. SUGAR v.[1] (1)]

sugar weed *n.* [1960s–80s] (*drugs*) second-rate, adulterated marijuana (cf. AFRICAN BUSH n.). [SE *sugar* + WEED n.[1] (4); the marijuana is compressed into a block mixed with sugar or honey]

suggan *n. see* SUGAN n.

suicide *n.* **1** [mid-19C] 4 horses driven in a line. **2** [1940s+] (*Aus.*) a punning ref., used by motorists, to the 'side' of a vehicle on which one should not attempt to pass. **3** [1970s+] (*Aus.*) used in Northern Territory to refer to the rainy season or 'wet', considered unendurable by many people.

suicide blonde *n.* [1930s+] (*orig. US*) a woman with dyed blonde or peroxide blonde hair. [? she drives men to *suicide*]

sui gow *n. see* SUEY POW n.

suit *n.*[1] [early 18C–mid-19C] a gold watch and seals. [SE *suit*, a full set of clothes]

suit *n.*[2] [mid-18C+] nudity. [abbr. BIRTHDAY SUIT n.]

suit *n.*[3] [early–mid-19C] a trick, a scheme. [SE *suit*, a pursuit]

suit *n.*[4] **1** [1940s] (*US*) a plain-clothes detective (cf. BABY-BLUES n.[2]). **2** [1950s+] (*also* **grey suit, three-piece suit**) a member of management, a businessman, anyone who has to wear a suit for their daily work, as opposed to more casually dressed creative or freelance workers, or those in jobs that in any case have no need for suits; thus an uncreative, authoritarian person.

suit and cloak *n.* [late 17C–19C] a drink, esp. brandy. [? the liquor warms one up]

suitcase *n.*[1] **1** [1930s–40s] (*US Black*) a drum kit. **2** [1990s+] (*US*) the anus.

suitcase *n.*[2] *see* BRIXTON SUITCASE n.

suitcase *v.* (*US prison*) to conceal drugs in the rectum. [SUITCASE n.[1] (2)]

suit one as a saddle fits a sow *v.* [18C] to be utterly unsuitable, to be highly incongruous.

suits *n. see* MEN IN SUITS n.

suit up *v.* [1990s+] to dress oneself in a suit.

sukey *n.* **1** [early 18C] a male homosexual. **2** [mid-18C] a lower servant girl. **3** [19C–1950s] a kettle. **4** [mid–late 19C] a fool. [*Sukey*, a dimin. of proper name *Susan*, but ? Welsh Gypsy *sukar*, to hum, to whisper (cf. BLACK SAL n.); the immediate root was presumably mid-18C+ nursery rhyme 'Polly put the kettle on']

sukey-tawdry *n.* [mid-19C] a slatternly woman, dressed in a flashy, vulgar style. [SUKEY n. (2) + SE *tawdry*]

sulph *n.* [1980s+] (*drugs*) amphetamine *sulph*ate (cf. A n.[2]). [abbr.]

sulphate *n.* [1970s+] amphetamine *sulphate* (cf. A n.[2]). [abbr.]

sultry *adj.* [late 19C–1900s] of language, writing or pictures, coarse, obscene, vulgar, 'smutty'.

sumbitch *n. see* SONOFABITCH n.

summer bird *n.* [mid-16C–early 17C] a cuckold. [play on SE *cuckoo*, which appears in summer]

summer cabbage *n.* [19C] an umbrella. [the spread of its leaves]

summer teeth *n.* [2000s] (*US Black*) crooked or missing teeth. [i.e. *some are…some are…*]

summertime *n.* [late 19C] (*US*) **1** oatmeal. **2** bread and milk.

summertime ho *n.* [1970s+] an occasional prostitute who works, not necessarily in summer, but only when she needs the money or the mood takes her; often includes high-school girls, who turn to whoring in the summer holidays. [HO n.[1] (1)]

sunbake *n.* [1950s] (*Aus.*) a sunbathe. [SUNBAKE v.]

sunbake *v.* (*also* **sun off**) [1910s+] (*Aus.*) to sunbathe.

sunbeam *n.*[1] [1950s+] (*Aus.*) an item of crockery or cutlery laid out on the table but still unused. [*as bright as a sunbeam*]

sunbeam *n.*[2] *see* SUNSHINE n.[2].

sunburned *adj.*[1] (*also* **sunburnt**) **1** [late 16C–19C] infected with a venereal disease. **2** [early 17C] drunk. [(1) pun on SE *burned/ BURNED* adj.[1]]

sunburned *adj.*[2] (*also* **sunburnt**) [late 17C–early 19C] having too many male children. [pun on SE *son*]

sunburned Irishman *n.* (*also* **smoked Irishman**) [1950s+] a derog. term for a Black person (cf. BLACKBELLY n.). [Blacks and the Irish occupy the same low social position]

Sun City *n.* [1980s+] (*S.Afr.*) an ironic nickname for Diepkloof prison, Gauteng Province (cf. ABBOTT'S PRIORY n.). [*Sun City*, the luxury hotel and entertainment complex near Rustenberg, North-West Province]

Sunday *n. see* SUNDAY PUNCH n. (1).

Sunday *v.* [late 19C] (*UK society*) to spend Sunday with a person or persons.

Sunday below Monday *phr. see* MONDAY COMES BEFORE SUNDAY phr.

Sunday best *n.* [1920s] a vest (undershirt). [rhy. sl.]

Sunday face *n.* **1** [19C] the backside. **2** [20C+] (*US Black*) a very attractive face. [play on SE *Sunday face*, a sanctimonious expression]

Sunday flash togs *n.* [late 19C–1900s] one's best clothes. [SE *Sunday* + FLASH adj.[1] (1) + TOGS n.]

Sunday go-to-meeting *adj.* [mid-19C+] (*US*) of clothes and other things, one's best.

Sunday jinal *n.* [1950s] (*W.I.*) any variety of clergyman or preacher. [SE *Sunday* + dial. *jinal*, a clever person; thus a con-man, a crook; ult. pron. of SE *general*]

Sunday man *n.*[1] [late 18C–early 19C] a criminal who only dares go out on Sunday, when the police are inactive.

Sunday man *n.*[2] [late 19C] a pimp (cf. ABBOT ON THE CROSS n.). [Sunday is the only day he can go out with his woman; the remainder of the time she will be working]

Sunday morn *n.* (*also* **early morn**) [20C+] an erection. [rhy. sl. = HORN n.[2] (3)]

Sunday promenader *n.* [early 19C] a debtor, one who risks going out on Sundays only.

Sunday punch *n.* [1920s+] (*orig. US*) **1** (*also* **Sunday**) a very hard or knockout blow; thus COP A SUNDAY v. **2** one's best effort. [on the pattern of *Sunday*, therefore best, suit]

Sunday saint *n.* [late 19C+] one whose degenerate weekday behaviour is replaced every Sunday by an air of sanctimonious and ultimately hypocritical piety.

Sunday-school story *n.* [1920s] (*US*) a fantasy, a lie.

Sunday-school words *n.* [1900s] (*US*) curses, swearing.

sundodger *n.* [1910s–40s] (*Aus./US*) one who loiters around in the hope of hand-outs, which will save them from having to earn a living. [since his likely job would be on a farm, such indolence keeps him out of the sun]

sundown *n. see* SUNSHINE n.[2].

sundown *adj.* [late 19C–1940s] (*US*) used of one who works outside their normal hours of practice, e.g. lawyers, doctors.

sundown *v.* [late 19C–1920s] (*Aus.*) to beg someone for food and drink. [SUNDOWNER n. (1)]

sundowner *n.* **1** [mid-19C+] (*Aus./N.Z.*) a tramp or vagrant who arrives at a station about sundown under the pretence of seeking work, but really, since work stops at dusk, to obtain food and a night's lodging. **2** [late 19C–1900s] (*US*) a professional who takes on extra work outside their normal hours of practice. **3** [1940s] (*Aus.*) a lazy sheepdog or cattle-dog.

sunk *adj.* **1** [1920s+] hopeless, finished, no chance. **2** [1980s+] (*Aus. prison*) found guilty in court. [naut. imagery]

sunnies *n.* [1990s+] (*Aus./N.Z.*) *sun*glasses. [abbr.]

sunny bank *n.* [late 18C–early 19C] a good fire in winter. [pun on SE *banking*, a fire]

sunny Jim *n.* [1910s+] a general term of address, esp. affectionate. [the slogan for Force breakfast food: 'High o'er the fence leaps Sunny Jim "Force" is the food that raises him', coined 1903]

sunny side, the *n.* [20C+] the good, easy, materially satisfying life. [the *sunny side of the street*]

sunny south *n.* [late 19C] the mouth. [rhy. sl.]

sun off *v. see* SUNBAKE v.

sunrise *v.* [1940s] (*US Und.*) to jail a tramp overnight, prior to expelling him from town in the morning.

sunsey *n. see* SONSY adj.

sunshades *n. see* SHADES n.[2].

sunshine *n.*[1] **1** [late 18C] prosperity. **2** [1930s] (*US Und.*) gold.

sunshine *n.*[2] (*also* **sunbeam, sundown**) [1950s+] a general form of address, e.g. *oi! sunshine!*

sunshine *n.*[3] [1960s–70s] (*drugs*) a variety of LSD (cf. A n.[3]). [abbr. *orange sunshine*, i.e. the orange-coloured pills of the drug]

sunspecs *n.* [1970s+] *sunglasses.* [abbr. + SPECS n.]

sup *n.*[1] (*also* **supp**) **1** [1920s+] a *supplement.* **2** [1960s+] a newspaper colour *supplement* and spelled with double *p*, often as *colour supp.* [abbr.; note mid-19C theatrical jargon *sup*, a supernumerary or extra]

sup *n.*[2] *see* SUPER n.[1] (5).

's up? *phr.* (*also* **zup?**) [1980s+] (*US Black/campus/teen*) a greeting. [contraction of WHAT'S UP? phr.]

supe *n.*[1] **1** [mid-19C] (*US campus*) a toady, a sycophant. **2** [mid-19C–1910s] a minor stage character, a 'walk-on'. [abbr. SE *super-numerary*]

supe *n.*[2] *see* SUPER n.[1].

supe *adj. see* SUPER adj.

supe *v.* [mid–late 19C] (*US campus*) to act as a toady. [SUPE n. (1)]

super *n.*[1] **1** [mid-19C–1920s] (*US*) a theatrical understudy. **2** [mid-19C+] the superintendent of a sheep station. **3** [late 19C+] (*also* **supe**) a police or prison superintendent. **4** [1900s–30s] (*US*) a film extra. **5** [1910s+] (*US*) (*also* **sup, supe**) a superintendent, e.g. of a work crew. **6** [1930s+] (*orig. US*) a building superintendent, a janitor. [abbr.; (1) and (4) SE *supernumerary*]

super *n.*[2] (*also* **soup, souper**) [mid-19C+] (*UK Und.*) **1** a watch; thus *super/souper and slang*, a watch and chain; *super twister*, a watch thief. **2** the ring that secures a watch-chain to one's garment. [? SE *soup-plate*, i.e. the size and shape of a watch]

super *n.*[3] [1970s+] (*Aus.*) a *super*annuation pension. [abbr.]

super *n.*[4] [1980s+] (*UK Black*) **1** a star, an important figure. **2** thus a form of respectful address.

super *n.*[5] *see* SOUPBONE n.

super *adj.* (*also* **supe**) **1** [mid-19C+] very good or pleasant, first-rate, excellent. **2** as an intensifier. [Lat. *super*, above]

super *v.* [1970s+] (*Aus.*) to dismiss, to *super*annuate. [abbr.]

super *adv.* [1970s+] (*US*) an intensifier, extremely.

superbad *adj. see* SUPERFLY adj.

super buick *n.* [1990s+] (*US drugs*) a cocktail of heroin and/or cocaine plus various prescription drugs, including scopolamine. [SE pfx *super-* + BUICK v.; the effects are unpleasant and poss. nauseating]

super c *n.* [1980s+] (*drugs*) ketamine.

supercharge *n.* [1980s+] (*drugs*) crack cocaine (cf. BASE n.). [its effects]

supercloud *n.* [1980s+] (*drugs*) crack cocaine (cf. BASE n.). [the clouds of smoke that accompany its use]

supercolossal *adj.* [1930s+] extremely large, outsized, remarkable, stupendous.

supercool *adj.* [1960s+] extremely relaxed, sophisticated. [SE pfx *super-* + COOL adj.[1] (2)]

super-duper *adj.* (*also* **sooper-dooper**) [1950s+] (*UK juv.*) excellent, first-rate, wonderful. [SE pfx *super-* + redup.]

super ecstasy *n.* [1990s+] (*drugs*) a far stronger form of MDMA known as DOB n. [ECSTASY n.]

superfatted *adj.* [1920s–40s] very fat.

superfly *n.* [1970s+] cocaine, usu. of high quality. [SUPERFLY adj. + play on FLY v.[4] (1)]

superfly *adj.* (*also* **superbad**) [1970s+] (*US Black*) of people, situations, drugs etc, excellent, first-rate. [SE pfx *super-* + FLY adj. (7)/BAD adj. (2)]

superfly *adv.* [1960s+] excellently. [SUPERFLY adj.]

supergrass *n.*[1] (*also* **superpot, superweed**) **1** [1960s+] (*drugs*) particularly strong marijuana (cf. AFRICAN BUSH n.). **2** [1970s+] phencyclidine (cf. ACE n.[4]). [SE pfx *super-* + GRASS n.[5]]

supergrass *n.*[2] [1970s+] (*UK Und.*) an informer who betrays a large number of important fellow criminals, thus helping solve many hitherto unresolved crimes. [SE pfx *super-* + GRASS n.[4]]

super-honkie *n.* [1960s–80s] (*US Black*) an exceptionally authoritarian or otherwise powerful White person. [SE pfx *super-* + HONKIE n. (1)]

superintendent of the pavement *n.* (*also* **superintendent of the sidewalk, supervisor of the pavement**) [1950s+] **1** (*Aus.*) anyone, other than those employed at the site, who enjoys standing staring at buildings under construction. **2** (*US*) any unofficial critic or observer.

super joint *n.* [1970s+] (*drugs*) phencyclidine (cf. ACE n.[4]). [SE pfx *super-* + JOINT n.[5] (3)]

supermarket conversation *n.* [1990s+] (*US Black*) empty, meaningless chatter. [with no more intrinsic quality than the Muzak played in supermarkets]

supermax *n.* [1990s+] (*US prison*) extreme lockdown.

supernaculum *n.* (*also* **supernagulum**) **1** [late 16C–mid-19C] exceptionally good liquor; thus *supernaculum*, to the last drop, to the bottom. **2** [early 19C] any first-rate commodity. [Lat. *supernaculum*, over the nail. The tradition of upending one's emptied glass onto the left thumbnail, thus proving that one had drunk every drop]

superpot *n. see* SUPERGRASS n.[1].

super saucy *adj.* [2000s] (*US Black*) excellent, first-rate.

superscrew *n.* [1980s+] (*Aus. prison*) an over-officious warder. [SE pfx *super-* + SCREW n.[2] (3)]

super-screwing *n.* [mid-19C] (*UK Und.*) watch-stealing. [SUPER n.[2] (1) + SCREW v.[4] (1)]

superskunk *n.* [1990s+] (*drugs*) an extremely potent form of marijuana. [SE pfx *super-* + SKUNK n.[2] (1)]

supersnagative *adj.* [late 19C] (*Aus./N.Z.*) excellent, wonderful, superb.

supersonic *adj.* [1940s+] (*UK juv.*) absolutely wonderful.

supersoul *n.* [1970s] (*US campus*) of Black students, an exceptionally sophisticated individual. [SE pfx *super-* + SOUL n.[2]]

superstitious pie *n.* [late 17C–early 18C] a mince pie or Christmas pie, as made by Puritans or Precisians sometime before Christmas.

superstud *n.* [1970s+] a man who is obsessed with and notably successful at sex. [SE pfx *super-* + STUD n.[1] (1)]

super toke *v.* [1980s+] (*US drugs*) to inhale a cannabis cigarette from both ends. [SE pfx *super-* + TOKE v.]

super twister *n. see* THIMBLE-TWISTER n.

supervisor of the pavement *n. see* SUPERINTENDENT OF THE PAVEMENT n.

superweed *n. see* SUPERGRASS n.[1].

supouch *n.* [late 17C–18C] a hostess or landlady. [? SE *sup*, to drink]

supp *n. see* SUP n.[1].

suppelar *n.* [mid-19C+] (*Ling. Fr./Polari*) a hat. [Ital. *suppelettile*, household fittings]

supper sneak *n.* (*also* **supper man**) [1900s–50s] (*US Und.*) a robbery that takes place while the oocupants of a house are gathered together eating.

suppose *n.* [mid-19C+] a nose. [rhy. sl.]

sup with Sir Thomas Gresham *v. see* DINE WITH SIR THOMAS GRESHAM v.

surat *n.* [mid-19C] any article of inferior quality, made from a mix of first- and second-rate materials. [textile jargon *surat*, second-rate cotton made from a mix of US (good) cotton and *surat* (bad) cotton]

sure *adv.* [mid-19C+] a general intensifier, definitely, absolutely.

sure! *excl.* [early 18C+] definitely! absolutely! [coined in the UK, the term moved to the US by the mid-19C, although it returned to the UK in the early 20C+]

sure as eggs ain't chicken *phr. see* SURE AS HOGS ARE MADE OF BACON phr.

sure as fuck *phr.* [1990s+] definitely, without the slightest doubt. [AS FUCK adv.]

sure as God made little (green) apples *phr.* (*also* **sure as God made daisies**) [late 19C+] (*US*) definitely, for sure.

sure as hell *phr.* (*also* **sure as heck, sure as hell's hot, sure hell, sure in hell, sure to hell**) [20C+] without a doubt, certainly.

sure as hogs are made of bacon *phr.* (*also* **sure as eggs ain't chicken, sure as mutton's mutton**) [19C] certainly.

sure as shit *phr.* (*also* **sure as shit and taxes, ...shite on your shoe, ...shit rolls downhill from a privy**) **1** [1950s+] certainly, definitely. **2** [1970s+] (*US*) a general affirmation. [SHIT n.¹ (1)]

sure as shooting *phr.* (*also* **sure as pop**) [mid-19C+] (*US*) definitely, for sure.

sure as twopence *phr.* [mid-18C] undoubtedly.

sure as you're a foot high *phr.* (*also* **sure as I'm a foot high, ...a man fit to wear britches, sure as you're alive/born, sure as you live**) [mid-19C–1950s] (*US*) absolutely, without a doubt.

sure card *n.* [late 16C–mid-18C] a safe plan, a trustworthy person. [SE *sure* + *card*; note mid-16C SE *sure card*, an expedient to gain a desired object, a person whose name will help one]

sure cop *n.* [1940s+] (*Aus.*) an absolute certainty, a 'sure thing', a 'dead cert'. [SE *sure* + COP n.² (1)]

sure-enough *adj.* [early 19C+] (*US*) definite, absolute, certain.

sure find *n.* [mid-19C] something that will definitely be found where one expects it. [fox-hunting use *sure find*, a place where a 'find' is sure to be made]

sure-fire *adj.* [20C+] (*orig. US*) certain, definite, unassailable. [the image of an efficient firearm]

sure five *n.* [1910s] (*Irish*) a certainty.

sure-God *adv.* [1920s] (*US*) definitely.

sure (in) hell *phr. see* SURE AS HELL phr.

sure model *n. see* SURE THING n.

sure 'nuff *see under* SHO' 'NUFF.

sure pop *n.* [mid-19C+] (*US*) a certainty, an absolute fact. [SE *sure* + POP n.³ (3)]

sure-shot *adj.* [1910s+] (*US*) successful, influential.

sure thing *n.* (*also* **sure model/shot**) [mid-19C+] (*US*) an absolute certainty, a guarantee; also attrib.

sure-thing *adj.* [late 19C+] **1** definite, certain, regular. **2** (*US Und.*) of a situation or deal, major and extremely lucrative. [SURE THING n.]

sure thing! *excl.* [mid-19C+] an affirmative excl., absolutely! certainly! I agree! [SURE THING n.]

sure to hell *phr. see* SURE AS HELL phr.

surf and turf *n.* [1960s+] (*orig. US*) **1** a restaurant specializing in seafood and steak. **2** a meal of seafood and steak.

surf bunny *n.* [1950s+] (*US*) a woman who associates with surfers. [SE *surf* + BUNNY n.¹ (2)]

surfer *n.* [1970s+] (*drugs*) phencyclidine (cf. ACE n.⁴). [? one *surfs* inner space]

surfie *n.* [1960s+] (*Aus.*) a surfer; thus *surfie chick*, a woman who associates with surfers.

surfoholic *n.* [1990s+] (*US teen*) one who is addicted to browsing the Internet. [SE *surf*, to browse the Internet]

surf or die! *excl.* [1980s+] (*US campus*) ironic use of a popular slogan to belittle those who are obsessed with surfing to the exclusion of any other activity.

surf the crimson wave *v.* [1990s+] (*US teen*) to menstruate.

surgical truss *n.* [1990s+] a bus. [rhy. sl.]

surly-boots *n.* (*also* **surly-chops**) [early 18C–mid-19C] a surly, morose person. [SE *surly* + sfx *-boots/-chops*]

surprise package *n.* [1970s] (*US gay*) a penis that is substantially larger than expected when erect. [SE *surprise* + PACKAGE n.¹ (6)]

surprise pie *n.* [2000s] a pie served in prison, with dubious or unknown contents.

surprise, surprise! *excl.* [1960s+] an ironic or sarcastic rejoinder to a piece of supposedly revelatory information.

surreverence *n. see* SIR-REVERENCE n.

Surrey docks *n.* [1970s] venereal disease. [rhy. sl. = POX n.¹ (2)]

Surro *n.* [1940s] (*Aus.*) Surry Hills, a run-down district of Sydney (latterly gentrified). [*Surrey* + -o sfx (4)]

surround *v.* [late 19C–1910s] (*Aus.*) to drink or eat. [? 'get your mouth around that']

surveyor of the highways *n.* [late 18C–early 19C] a drunkard. [the drunkard's frequent falling over]

surveyor of the pavement *n. see* INSPECTOR OF THE PAVEMENT n. (1).

sus *n.* (*also* **suss**) [1930s+] **1** a suspected person. **2** a suspicion. **3** an understanding. [abbr.; (3) SE *suspect/suspicion*]

sus *adj.* (*also* **suss**) [1950s+] suspicious; thus the *sus laws*, controversial powers that permitted the police to stop and search persons allegedly suspected of a crime and that were considered racist by the Black and Asian communities. [abbr.; note RMC Duntroon (Aus.) 1. *sus*, angry, annoyed, upset, rebellious; 2. *sus*, suspect, used of a cadet who may not 'make the grade']

sus *v.* (*also* **suss**) [1950s+] to suspect. [abbr.]

sus *adv.* (*also* **suss**) [1950s] suspiciously.

susancide *n.* [late 19C] suicide. [joc. blend of SE *Susan* + *suicide*]

susan saliva *n.* [1950s–70s] (*camp gay*) a fellator, esp. one who works as a male prostitute (cf. BABY JANE n.). ['he lives by his spits']

s.u.s.f.u. *phr.* [1940s+] (*orig. milit.*) situation unchanged, still *fucked up* (cf. S.N.A.F.U. n.). [abbr.]

sushi nigger *n.* [2000s] (*US Black*) a derog. term for an Oriental person (cf. BROWNIE n.²). [*sushi*, the popular Japanese dish + NIGGER n.¹]

sushi socialist *n. see* CHAMPAGNE SOCIALIST n.

sushi taco *n.* [1990s+] the labia majora (cf. BACON STRIPS n.). [mix of popular Japanese (*sushi*, i.e. raw fish) and Mexican (*taco*) dishes]

susie *n. see* SUSY n.

Susie-Q wagon *n.* [1940s] (*US prison*) a small cart carrying cleaning equipment.

susie (sorority) *n. see* SUZI (SORORITY) n.

sus out *v. see* SUSS OUT v.

suspended *n.* [1970s+] a *suspended* sentence. [abbr.]

sus. per coll. *adj.* [late 18C–early 19C] hanged. [Lat. *suspensus per collum*, hanged by the neck; this notation was entered in the prison ledger]

suspish *n.* [1900s–10s] a *suspicion*. [abbr.]

suspish *adj.* [1940s+] from the authority's point of view, *suspicious*; as adv. *suspishly*.

suss *see also under* SUS.

suss *n.* [1970s+] natural intelligence, instinctive knowledge, esp. as used in petty crime or other marginal occupations. [backform. f. SUSS OUT v.]

sussed (out) *adj.* [1970s+] **1** worked out. **2** clever, sophisticated, aware. **3** (*UK Und.*) arrested.

sussies *n.* [1990s+] *suspenders*. [abbr.]

susso *n.* [1930s] (*Aus.*) **1** state government relief paid to the unemployed, esp. during the 1930s Depression. **2** one who is receiving the relief; thus *on the susso*, receiving state benefits. [abbr. SE *sustenance* + -o sfx (4)]

suss out *v.* (*also* **suss, sus out**) [1960s+] **1** to understand, to work out. **2** to discover. [SE *suspicious/suspect*]

sussy *adj.* [1970s+] of a situation or person, suspicious, dubious. [SUSS OUT v.]

su-su *n.* [1950s+] (*W.I. Rasta*) gossip, the sound of whispering. [SUSU v.]

susu *v.* [1950s+] (*W.I.*) to gossip, to malign. [? echoic; or ? Twi *susuw ka*, to utter a suspicion + SE *sussurate*, to whisper]

susy *n.* (*also* **susie**) [1930s+] a sixpence. [rhy. sl.; *Susy Anna* = TANNER n.]

sutler *n.* [late 17C–early 19C] 'He that Pockets up, Gloves, Knives, Handkerchiefs, Snuff and Tobacco-boxes, and all the lesser Moveables' (B.E.). [SE *sutler*, one who sells provisions to soldiers, whether in the garrison or in camp]

suzie wang *n.* (*also* **suzie wong**) [1960s] (*camp gay*) an Oriental homosexual. [the musical/film *The World of Suzie Wong* (1960) + pun on WANG n.² (1)]

Suzie Wong *n.* [1980s+] **1** a smell. **2** a song. **3** (*Aus. prison*) a cannabis pipe. [rhy. sl.; (1) = PONG n.¹; (3) = BONG n.¹; ult. novel and film *The World of Suzie Wong* (1960) by Richard Mason (1919–97)]

suzi (sorority) *n.* (*also* **susie (sorority), suzy…**) [1970s+] (*US campus*) a stereotypical sorority member. [play on proper name]

Suzy Slut *n.* [1970s] (*US teen*) a promiscuous girl.

swab *n.¹* (*also* **swob**) **1** [late 17C+] an unpleasant person. **2** [1920s] (*Aus.*) a derog. term for an Aboriginal woman. [SE *swab*, a washcloth or mop]

swab *n.²* **1** [late 18C–mid-19C] a naval officer. **2** [mid-19C] the epaulette worn by a naval officer. **3** [20C+] (*US*) a merchant seaman, a sailor in the US Navy. [SE *swab*, a washcloth or mop, used to clean the decks]

swab *v.* [1910s+] to grab, to steal.

swabber *n.* **1** [late 16C–early 19C] a general term of abuse. **2** [mid-17C] a promiscuous woman. [SE *swabber*, one of a ship's crew whose business it was to swab the decks etc; thus one who behaves like a sailor of low rank]

swabbers *n.* [late 17C–early 19C] in cards, the ace of hearts, the knave of clubs, the ace and deuce of trumps. [? SE *swab*, to mop up; in the variety of whist known as *whisk and swabbers* a player that held these cards was automatically entitled to a share of the pot]

swabble *v.* (*also* **swobble**) [1920s–40s] (*US Black/Harlem*) to eat fast and greedily. [? SE *swill* + *gobble*]

swabby *n.* (*also* **swabbie**) [20C+] (*US*) a sailor. [SWAB n.² (3)]

swab jockey *n.* [1940s+] (*US*) a merchant seaman, a sailor in the US Navy. [SWAB n.² (3) + JOCKEY n.³ (2)]

swab (one's) tonsils *v.* [1920s+] to kiss.

swack *n.* [1970s+] (*US Black*) the penis. [? dial. *swack*, a blow]

swacked *adj.* [1930s+] very drunk. [dial. *swack*, a blow, but note Scot. *swack*, to drink deeply]

swacko *adj.* [1930s+] very drunk. [SWACKED adj.]

swack-up *n.* [mid-19C] a lie.

swad *n.* [18C–mid-19C] (*UK Und.*) a soldier. [SE *swad*, a country bumpkin]

swadder *n.* (*also* **swaddler**) [mid-16C–early 19C] (*UK Und.*) a criminal peddler (cf. CANTING CREW n.). [SWADDLE v.; Harman claims they are 'not at all evil, but of an indifferent behaviour' but by 1725 the *New Canting Dict.* condemns them as 'not content to rob and plunder, but beat and barbarously abuse, and often murder the Passengers']

swaddie *n. see* SWADDY n.

swaddle *v.* [mid-16C–mid-19C] to beat up, to assault. [SE *swaddle*, to wrap up, to restrict movement]

swaddler *n.¹* **1** [mid-18C–19C] (*also* **swadler**) a Methodist; thus *swaddling*, Methodism. **2** [mid–late 19C] any type of Protestant. [Charles Wesley, *Journal*, 10 September 1747: 'We dined with a gentleman, who explained our name to us. It seems we are beholden to Mr Cennick for it, who abounds in such like expressions as, "I curse and blaspheme all the gods in heaven, but the babe that lay in the manger, the babe that lay in Mary's lap, the babe that lay in swaddling clouts", &c. Hence they nicknamed him, "Swaddler, or Swaddling John"; and the word sticks to us all, not excepting the Clergy.' Hotten (1860) adds that during the sermon, 'an ignorant Romanist, to whom the words of the

English Bible were a novelty […] shouted out in derision "A swaddler! a swaddler!", as if the whole story were the preacher's invention']

swaddler *n.²* **see** SWADDER n.

swaddy *n.* (*also* **swaddie, swoddy**) [early 19C+] a soldier. [SWAD n.]

swad-gill *n.* (*also* **swod-gill**) [early 18C–early 19C] a soldier. [dial. *swad* + GILL n.¹ (2)]

swadkin *n.* [early 18C–mid-19C] (*UK Und.*) a newly enlisted soldier. [dial. *swad* + dimin. sfx *-kin*]

swadler *n. see* SWADDLER n.¹ (1).

swag *n.¹* **1** [mid-17C–early 19C] (*UK Und.*) a shop (and its contents) viewed as booty. **2** [mid-18C+] (*orig. UK Und.*) a thief's booty (esp. linen or clothes as opposed to jewels or plate) or a peddler's wares. **3** [mid-18C+] any form of goods. **4** [early 19C–1920s] (*orig. Aus.*) money. **5** [mid-19C] (*UK Und.*) a share in booty. **6** [mid-19C] a trader in small articles, the keeper of a SWAG-SHOP n. **7** [mid-19C] the trade in small articles. **8** [mid-19C+] a lot or plenty of anything. **9** [mid-19C+] (*UK/Aus./N.Z.*) the pack carried by an itinerant or vagrant. **10** [mid-19C+] paper money, currency. [14C SE *swag*, a bulgy bag]

swag *n.²* [1970s+] (*US Black*) hard liquor. [? SE *swig* or Scot. *swag*, a deep draught of liquid]

swag *n.³* [1980s] (*US campus*) a wild guess, used to answer homework or examination questions.

swag *n.⁴* [1990s+] (*drugs*) cannabis.

swag *v.* **1** [mid-19C+] to steal, to take forcibly. **2** [mid-19C+] to drag away, to arrest. **3** [mid-19C+] (*UK Und.*) to sell stolen property. **4** [mid-19C+] to place, to put, to carry. **5** [1930s+] to hustle along, to hurry. **6** [1950s+] to smuggle. [SWAG n.¹ (2)]

swag away *v.* [1950s+] to abduct, to kidnap. [ext. of SWAG v. (2)]

swag-barrow man *n.* [mid-19C] a street-seller of miscellaneous goods; thus *swag-barrow*, his cart. [SWAG n.¹ (7)]

swag-chovey *n.* [mid–late 19C] (*UK Und.*) a criminal receiver's shop or store; thus *swag-chovey bloke*, a marine store dealer. [SWAG n.¹ (2) + CHOVEY n.]

swagger *see also under* SWAGMAN.

swagger *n. see* SWAGSMAN n. (2).

swagger *adj.* [late 19C–1930s] (*UK society*) smart, fashionable. [SE *swagger*, to flaunt oneself]

swaggery *adj.* [late 19C] smart, fashionable. [working-class version of SWAGGER adj.]

swaggie *n.* (*also* **swaggy**) [late 19C+] (*Aus./N.Z.*) a vagrant, a tramp. [abbr. SWAGMAN n.²]

swagging *n.* **1** [mid-19C+] (*N.Z.*) walking in the mountains with a pack. **2** [late 19C+] (*Aus./N.Z.*) living as a tramp, esp. in the outback. [SWAG n.¹ (9)]

swag in *v.* [1910s–20s] to cause one to enter surreptitiously. [SE *swag*, to make someone sway or sag]

swag it *v.* [mid-19C–1910s] (*Aus.*) to live as a tramp. [SWAG n.¹ (9)]

swagman *n.¹* (*also* **swagger, swag-woman**) [mid-19C–1930s] a man (or woman) in the SWAG-SHOP n. trade, a street-seller of miscellaneous goods. [SWAG n.¹ (7)]

swagman *n.²* (*also* **swagger, swag seller, swagsman**) [late 19C+] (*Aus./N.Z.*) an itinerant worker, who travels with his pack on his back while looking for employment. [SWAG n.¹ + sfx *-man*]

swag-shop *n.* [early 19C–1920s] a shop that sells cheap articles wholesale, usu. to street-sellers. [SWAG n.¹ (6) + SE *shop*]

swagsman *n.* (*UK Und.*) **1** [mid-19C] (*also* **swagman**) one who takes the booty away after a successful burglary. **2** [late 19C–1940s] (*also* **swagger**) a receiver of stolen goods. [SWAG n.¹ (2)]

swag-woman *n. see* SWAGMAN n.¹.

swailer *n.* [1970s] (*UK Und.*) a cosh. [? dial. *swail*, to swing the arms while walking; thus to swing the cosh]

swain *v.* [1990s+] (*US*) spontaneously to revoke or take back, as in words or actions.

swak *adj.* [20C+] (*S.Afr.*) weak, feeble. [Du. *zwak*, feeble]

S.W.A.L.K. *phr.* [1910s+] sealed with *a loving* kiss; usu. found on the back of envelopes; other vars. include *S.W.A.K.*, sealed with *a* kiss; *S.W.A.N.K.*, sealed with *a nice* kiss, and *S.W.A.L.C.A.K.W.S.*, sealed with *a lick 'cos a* kiss won't stick (cf. B.O.L.T.O.P. phr.). [abbr.]

swallow *n.* **1** [late 18C–1910s] the throat. **2** [late 19C] a mouthful. **3** [20C+] a puff of a cigarette.

swallow *v.* (*also* **swallow it, swallow it whole**) **1** [17C+] to accept, esp. a false story that one is told. **2** [mid-19C] to be accepted. **3** [20C+] to abandon life as a professional criminal, to 'go straight'. **4** [20C+] to accept defeat, i.e. in a game.

swallow a hare *v.* (*also* **swallow a hair**) [mid-17C–early 19C] to become very drunk. [? the drunkard may leap around like the animal; or SE *hair*, which must be washed down the throat]

swallow a sailor *v.* [late 19C] (*UK port/harbour*) to get drunk on rum. [the naval predilection for rum]

swallow a tavern token *v.* [late 16C–mid-18C] to become drunk. [SE *swallow* + *tavern token*, a token given as part of one's change; it can be used in payment for subseq. drinks]

swallow bobby *v.* [mid-19C] (*Aus.*) to make a false witness. [? link to BOBBY *n.* (1); or ? dial. *bobby*, neat, smart]

swallower *n.*[1] [1980s] (*drugs*) a drug smuggler who swallows carefully wrapped drugs to take them through customs.

swallower *n.*[2] [1980s] (*Aus.*) a derog. term for a woman. [she swallows the semen after performing fellatio]

swallow it (whole) *v. see* SWALLOW *v.* (1).

swallow one's spit *v.* (*also* **swallow one's neck**) [1920s+] (*W.I.*) to keep quiet, to hold one's tongue.

swallow-pipe *n.* [20C+] (*W.I., Bdos*) the throat.

swallow someone's bird *v. see* BIRD *n.*[8] (1).

swallow tail *n.* [mid-19C–1930s] a swallow-tailed coat; thus *swallow-tailed*, dresssed in such a coat.

swallow the anchor *v.* **1** [late 19C+] (*UK Und.*) to change course, to stop doing something. **2** [1980s] to give oneself up to the police. [orig. naut. jargon]

swally *n.* (*Scot./Irish*) **1** [1950s+] alcohol, a drink. **2** [1990s+] a drinking binge. [SE *swallow*]

swally *v.* [late 19C+] (*Irish*) to drink, to eat. [SE *swallow*]

Swamp, the *n.* [late 19C] (*US*) a rough area of New Orleans comprising several blocks from the river.

swamp *v.*[1] **1** [mid-19C–1910s] to spend one's entire earnings on alcohol; ext. as *swamp a cheque*. **2** [20C+] (*Aus.*) to exchange, to barter. [? SE *swap*]

swamp *v.*[2] [mid-19C–1920s] (*Aus.*) to drink. [SE *swamp*, to engulf in water]

swamp *v.*[3] **1** [late 19C+] to work as a bullock driver's assistant; or to help in another occupation. **2** [1950s+] (*Aus.*) to travel, to travel with. [SWAMPER *n.*]

swamp *v.*[4] [1930s+] (*US prison*) to arrest. [Scot. *swamped*, arrested]

swamp-angel *n. see* SWAMP-RAT *n.*

swamp ass *n.* [1990s+] (*US teen*) sweat gathering between the cleft of the buttocks.

swamp breath *n.* [1980s] a contemptible person.

swamp donkey *n.* [1990s+] a very unattractive woman, or occas. man.

swamper *n.* **1** [mid-19C+] (*orig. US*) an assistant to a driver of horses, mules or bullocks. **2** [1900s–40s] (*US tramp*) a bar room cleaner. **3** [1920s+] a truck- or van-driver's assistant. **4** [1920s+] (*Aus.*) one who travels on foot but has his pack carried on a wagon. **5** [1920s+] (*Aus.*) one who obtains a lift. **6** [1950s] (*US prison*) a prisoner working as a cleaner. [? logging jargon *swamper*, one who clears a way for the loggers to move through the woods]

swamp guinea *n.* [1960s–70s] a derog. name for an Italian; the inference is of utter stupidity (cf. DAGO *n.*). [SE *swamp* + GUINEA *n.* (1)]

swamp-hog *n.* [1980s+] (*Aus.*) a general term of abuse, usu. aimed at girls or women.

swamp jig *n. see* JIG *n.*[5].

swamp-rat *n.* [20C+] (*US*) (*also* **swamp-angel/-rabbit**) a rural Southerner from the southern coastal states, a Cajun.

Swamps, the *n.* [1990s+] (*US*) a derog. term for the Sunnydale projects in the southern part of San Francisco.

swan *n.* [1980s] (*US*) a swan-dive.

swan *v.* [late 19C+] to wander, to drift, to amble. [the image of a swan gliding over water]

swan about *v.* (*also* **swan around**) [1940s+] (*orig. milit.*) to wander blithely and carelessly without a care in the world. [SWAN *v.*]

swanger *n.* [mid-19C] (*US*) a dandy.

swank *n.* **1** [mid-19C+] arrogant, showing-off behaviour. **2** [late 19C–1910s] insincere flattery. **3** [1900s–50s] a show-off, a braggart. **4** [1920s+] an aristocrat, a member of the upper classes. **5** [1990s+] (*US Black*) stolen goods. [SWANK *v.*]

swank *adj.* **1** [1910s+] showy, vulgar, arrogant. **2** [1920s+] classy, sophisticated. [SWANK *v.* (1)]

swank *v.* **1** [early 18C; 1910s+] to swagger. **2** [late 19C–1910s] to work hard at school or university. **3** [late 19C+] to pretend, to make as if. **4** [1910s+] to show someone or something off. **5** [1910s+] to boast. [? OHG *swanc*, swing the body; orig. use Midlands dial., then general sl. *c*.1900]

swankee *adj. see* SWANKY *adj.*

swanker *n.* [mid-19C–1950s] a braggart, a show-off. [SWANK *v.* (1)]

swankey *see under* SWANKY and its combs.

swanking *n.* [20C+] showing off, acting in an arrogant or vulgar manner. [SWANK *v.* (1)]

swankpot *n.* [20C+] a boaster, a braggart. [SWANK *v.* (1) + -POT sfx]

swank-pot *adj.* [1950s] showy, ostentatious. [SWANKPOT *n.*]

swanky *n.*[1] (*also* **swankey**) [mid–late 19C] an arrogant, showy, vulgar person. [SWANK *v.* (1)]

swanky *n.*[2] (*also* **swankey**) [mid-19C–1900s] table beer, weak beer (cf. SWANKY (SWIPES) *n.*). [? Essex dial. *swank*, the last portion of liquor or beer in a glass, enough for a single draught]

swanky *adj.* (*also* **swankee**) **1** [late 19C+] smart, sophisticated, chic. **2** [1900s–50s] of a person, conceited, arrogant, vulgar. **3** [2000s] of an object, vulgar, showy. [SWANK *v.* (1)]

swanky (swipes) *n.* (*also* **swankey (swipes)**) [mid-19C] weak beer. [SWANKY *n.*[2] + SWIPES *n.* (1)]

swan lake *n.* [20C+] a cake. [rhy. sl.]

Swannee River *n.* [20C+] the liver, whether human or animal. [rhy. sl.]

Swannee Rivers, the *n.* (*also* **the Swannees**) [20C+] (*Aus.*) the shivers. [rhy. sl.]

swannie *n.* [1980s+] (*N.Z.*) a large woollen bush-shirt-cum-coat. [proprietary name *Swanndri*]

swans *n.* [1990s+] (*drugs*) MDMA (cf. ECSTASY *n.*). [the picture of a *swan* stamped on some MDMA pills]

Swan Stream *n.* [mid-19C] Perth, Australia. [the city is on the Swan River]

swap *n.* (*also* **swop**) [late 18C+] an act of exchange. [SWAP *v.* (1); Grose (1796) suggests 'Irish cant']

swap *v.* (*also* **swop**) **1** [late 16C+] to exchange. **2** [mid-19C–1900s] to dismiss from a job. **3** [late 19C] (*US*) to cheat, to take in. **4** [1900s] to change one's clothes. [echoic *swap*, the sound of a slap; thus the slaps exchanged on sealing a bargain. Orig. Irish tinker's/horse-dealer's term, to *swap a bargain*, to strike a deal. Despite these origins, *swap* is now effectively SE]

swap cans *v.* [1940s+] (*US prison*) to take alternate active and passive roles in anal intercourse. [SWAP *v.* (1) + CAN *n.*[1] (2)]

swap gravy *v.* [2000s] (*US Black*) to have sexual intercourse. [SWAP v. (1) + GRAVY n.¹]

swap-out *n.* [1990s+] (*Aus. Und.*) an act of barter whereby one criminal offers the police an alternative victim in order to evade his own prosecution for a crime. [SWAP v. (1)]

swap out *v.¹* [1970s] (*US prison*) to take alternate active and passive roles in anal intercourse.

swap out *v.²* [1990s+] (*Aus. Und.*) to betray a fellow criminal in order to escape one's own prosecution for a crime. [SWAP-OUT n.]

swapper *n.¹* (*also* **swopper**) [late 17C–19C] one who effects swaps or exchanges. [SWAP v. (1)]

swapper *n.²* (*also* **swopper**) [early 18C–early 19C] something large of its type, e.g. a barefaced lie. [SWAPPING adj.]

swapping *n.* (*also* **swopping**) [late 17C+] exchanging one thing for another, bartering. [SWAP v. (1)]

swapping *adj.* (*also* **swopping**) [mid-15C–19C] very big, enormous, huge. [SE *swap/swop*, to hit]

swap spit *v.* (*also* **swap spits**) **1** [1930s+] to perform oral intercourse. **2** [1940s+] (*also* **suck spit, swap tongues**) to kiss, usu. a French kiss. **3** [1970s+] in joc./fig. use, to become intimate, to bond. [SWAP v. (1) + SE *spit*]

swarry *n.* [mid-19C+] an evening party, gathering, or social meeting. [joc. mispron. of SE *soiree*]

swart varkie *n.* [1970s–80s] (*S.Afr.*) a 20-litre (35-pint) black plastic container, used for buying wine in bulk. [Afk. *swart*, black + *varkie*, a piglet; such bulk purchases were banned in July 1982]

swartzer *n. see* SCHWARTZE n.

swash-bucket *n.* [late 19C] a slatternly woman. [SE *swash-bucket*, a receptacle for household rubbish; orig. dial.]

swassle-box *n. see* SWATCHEL-BOX n.

swat *see also under* SWOT and its combs.

swat *n.* [20C+] (*US*) a heavy blow; also in fig. use. [SWAT v.; the term had faded in UK before re-appearing in the US, most noticeably in the nickname of the big-hitting 1920s baseball star 'Babe' Ruth (1895–1948), the 'Sultan of Swat']

swat *v.* [mid-19C+] to hit. [northern dial.]

swatched *adj.* [1950s] tipsy. [? Warwickshire dial. *swatched*, of a woman, untidily dressed]

swatchel-box *n.* (*also* **schwassle-box, swassle-box**) [mid-19C] a Punch and Judy show, esp. the booth in which it is performed. [showman's jargon *Swatchel*, Mr Punch; ult. *swatchel*, the distorting instrument a puppeteer holds in his mouth in order to produce Punch's characteristic squeaky tones or Ger. *schwätzeln*, usual form of *schwatzen*, to chatter, to tattle]

swatchel-cove *n.* [mid–late 19C] a Punch and Judy man. [for ety. *see* SWATCHEL-BOX n. + COVE n. (1)]

swat flies *v.* [1920s+] (*US tramp*) to beg from a person who is standing on the curb or in front of a shop window.

swattled *adj.* [late 19C] drunk (cf. ANNIHILATED adj.). [SE *swat*]

swave *n. see* SUAVE n.

swave and blaze *adj.* [1960s+] deliberate mispron. of *suave* and *blasé*.

sway away on all top ropes *v.* (*also* **carry on top ropes**) [early 19C] to live in a hedonistic, self-indulgent manner.

swazzled *adj. see* SWIZZLED adj.

swear *n.* [mid-17C–19C] an oath. [SE *swear*]

swear and curse *n.* (*also* **swear and cuss**) [20C+] a bus. [rhy. sl.]

swear (at) *v.* [late 19C] of colours, to clash.

swear blind *v.* [1930s+] to affirm emphatically and without qualification. [SE *swear* + BLIND adv.¹]

swear by *v.* [mid-18C+] to accept as the truth, to have complete faith in.

swearing apartment *n.* [late 19C] the street. [the disapproval of swearing – however unlikely this may seem – found inside taverns and public houses]

swear off *v.* [late 19C+] to give up, to abandon, to renounce. [? one's oath of self-denial]

swear on a stack of Bibles (a mile high) *v.* (*also* **swear on a truckload of Bibles**) [mid-19C+] (*orig. US*) to make an elaborate or exaggerated oath, usu. in the face of another's disbelief.

swear to beef? *phr.* [2000s] (*US Black*) a general interrogatory phr., is that the truth?

sweat *n.¹* [late 18C] a form of amusement practised by such street gangs as the Mohocks, who surrounded a victim, pricking him with their swords and thus keeping him 'dancing' until through his exertions he had sweated sufficiently; thus *sweater*, one who practised this urban terrorism.

sweat *n.²* [late 18C+] a problem, a worry, a struggle, anything that works up real or fig. sweat. [SWEAT v.² (1)]

sweat *n.³* [1960s–70s] an occupation, a job.

sweat *n.⁴ see* OLD SWEAT n.

sweat *v.¹* **1** [late 16C] to spend money. **2** [late 18C–early 19C] to intimidate. **3** [late 18C–19C] (*UK Und.*) to lighten gold coins by immersing them in acid; thus *sweater*, one who practises such deception. **4** [early 19C] to pawn. **5** [early 19C] to remove some of the contents of. **6** [early 19C–1930s] to deprive someone of something. **7** [mid-19C] (*UK Und.*) of pickpockets etc, to subject a person or place to criminal activities. **8** [mid–late 19C] to extract money, usu. through menaces or violence. **9** [mid–late 19C] to squander money, whether one's own or someone else's. **10** [late 19C] (*UK Und.*) to melt down the solder that holds together an otherwise impenetrable strong-box. **11** [1950s] (*Aus.*) to borrow (usu. a horse) without its owner's permission. **12** [1950s] (*US Und.*) to break up stolen high denomination notes into smaller, legal bills. [fig. uses of SE]

sweat *v.²* **1** [early 17C; mid-19C+] to suffer, esp. in the context of an interrogation. **2** [mid-18C+] to put someone, esp. a prisoner, under pressure. **3** [late 19C+] to work very hard. **4** [late 19C+] to make someone work hard. **5** [1910s] to travel with difficulty. **6** [1920s] to wait for. **7** [1920s] to need, to be deprived of. **8** [1920s+] (*orig. US*) (*also* **sweat it**) to worry about, to take trouble over. **9** [1970s+] (*US Black*) to proposition. **10** [1990s+] (*US Black*) to get involved in someone's business. **11** [1990s+] (*US Black*) to be obsessed with someone to the extent of sweating in their presence; to like something very much. **12** [1990s+] (*US prison*) to cause trouble for, to annoy. **13** [1990s+] to enthuse over (to an excessive extent), to flirt eagerly.

sweat a cheque *v.* [late 19C] (*Aus./N.Z.*) to spend all one's pay on drink.

sweat back *n.* [1940s] (*US Und.*) a womanizer, a dandy. [? he sweats during intercourse]

sweat bird turds *v.* [1960s] (*US*) to work hard.

sweat board *n.* (*also* **sweat cloth**) [mid–late 19C] (*UK/US Und.*) the board or cloth upon which a game of 3-card trick is played.

sweat-box *n.* **1** [mid-19C+] (*orig. US*) an oppressively small cell, a punishment cell. **2** [late 19C+] a cell for prisoners waiting to appear in a magistrate's court. **3** [late 19C] (*US*) the upper gallery of a theatre. **4** [late 19C–1950s] any small, hot room. **5** [20C+] a room, usu. in a police station, in which prisoners undergo interrogation. **6** [1970s] (*US Black*) a crowded party. **7** [1970s+] a prison van, used to transport prisoners from court to prison etc. ['the original "sweat box" used during the period following the (US) Civil War [...] was a cell in close proximity to a stove, in which a scorching fire was built and fed with old bones, pieces of rubber shoes etc, all to make great heat and offensive smells, until the sickened and perspiring inmate of the cell confessed in order to get released' (deposition to the Republican National Committee of Law Observance & Enforcement, 1931)]

sweat bricks *v.¹* [1970s+] to work very hard.

sweat bricks *v.² see* SHIT A BRICK v. (2).

sweat bullets v. [1950s+] (US) **1** to worry excessively, to be terrified. **2** to work very hard.

sweat cloth n. see SWEAT BOARD n.

sweat cobs v. [1950s+] to perspire very heavily. [SE *sweat* + *cob*, a rounded lump, but cf. HAVE A COB ON v.]

sweat cure n. **1** [1940s] (US Und.) a synon. for the THIRD DEGREE, THE n. **2** [1940s–50s] (US drugs) withdrawal from narcotics by simple abstinence.

sweat drink n. [1960s+] (Irish) a trad. 'after-work' drink. [one is still sweating from one's labours]

sweat duds v. [19C] to pawn one's clothes. [SWEAT v.¹ (4) + DUDS n.¹ (1)]

sweater n.¹ **1** [mid-19C] a hard, demanding job. **2** [mid-19C–1900s] a harsh, demanding employer. **3** [1960s] (US campus) a worrier. [SWEAT v.²]

sweater n.² **1** [1940s] (US Und.) a strait jacket. **2** [1990s+] a condom. [SE *sweater*]

sweat hog n. [1970s+] (US campus) **1** an exceptionally difficult student, singled out at school or college for special attention. **2** an exceptionally unattractive woman. **3** a sexually promiscuous woman. [SE *sweat* + (1) SE *hog*; (2) and (3) HOG n.⁷ (1)]

sweating n. [early 19C+] (US) an interrogation. [SWEAT v.² (2)]

sweating groins! excl. [1920s] (US) an excl. of shock.

sweat it v. see SWEAT v.² (8).

sweat it out v. see SWEAT OUT v. (1).

sweat like a nigger (at election) v. [1900s–50s] (US) **1** to sweat profusely. **2** to work very hard. [SE *sweat* + NIGGER n.¹ (1)]

sweat like a paedophile in a playground v. [2000s] to sweat profusely.

sweat on v. [1910s+] (US) to be near to attaining, to wait for.

sweat one's arse off v. (also **sweat one's ass off, …balls off, …bollocks off, …butt off, …can off**) [1920s+] to work extremely hard. [SE *sweat* + ARSE n.¹ (1)/ASS n. (2)/BALLS n.¹ (1)/BALLOCKS n.¹/BUTT n.¹ (2)/CAN n.¹ (2)]

sweat one's guts out v. (also **slog one's guts out**) [late 19C+] to work to one's utmost.

sweat one's tail off v. see WORK ONE'S TAIL OFF v.

sweat on the top line v. [1910s+] (Aus.) to be within a touch of obtaining what one desires. [SWEAT v.² (6) + the 'lines' that must be filled in the game of lotto or bingo]

sweat out v. (also **sweat it out**) **1** [1920s+] (orig. US) to endure hardships and difficulties in the hope of achieving solutions or successes in the end. **2** [1940s–50s] (drugs) to withdraw from narcotics addiction, usu. by sudden and complete abstention. **3** [1940s+] to worry. **4** [1950s] to work out, to elucidate. [(2) SWEATS n. (1)]

sweat pads n. [1930s–40s] (Can./US) pancakes.

sweat-rag n. [mid-19C+] (US) a rag used for wiping the sweat from one's eyes; thus, a handkerchief.

sweat room n. **1** [1940s–50s] (US drugs) a room (in jail or hospital) in which a narcotic addict is confined during withdrawal. **2** [1960s+] (US Und.) a room in a police station where suspects are interrogated and/or beaten up. [(1) SE *sweat*; (2) SWEAT v.² (2) + SE *room*]

sweats n. [1930s+] (drugs) **1** the sweating that is part of a heroin addict's withdrawal symptoms; thus *sweat cure*, the sudden and unsupported withdrawal from drugs; SWEAT IT OUT. **2** the sweating that accompanies excessive use of cocaine.

sweat something out of v. [late 19C+] (US) to extract information from someone, usu. by intimidation. [ext. SWEAT v.² (2)]

sweat the fence v. [1990s+] (US prison) to fantasize about escape. [SWEAT v.² (11) + SE *fence*]

sweat thing n. [1960s] a stressful situation. [SWEAT n.²]

sweat up v. [1910s] to learn, to commit to memory. [SWEAT v.² (3)]

sweaty adj. **1** [1910s+] harsh, demanding. **2** [1990s+] (UK juv.) of a person, very unpleasant or unattractive.

sweaty sock n. [20C+] a Scot. [rhy. sl. = JOCK n. (2)]

sweave v. [1980s+] (US campus) to *swerve* and *weave* when drunk or drugged.

Swede n. [20C+] (US) a blunderer. [the stereotype of Swedish immigrants as strong but stupid]

swede n.¹ **1** [1910s+] the head; thus *crash* (*down*) *the swede*, *set the swede down*, to go to sleep. **2** [1990s+] a haircut.

swede n.² [1940s+] an ignorant country person; thus *swedeland*, the countryside; *swede language/talk*, rural talk; also as adj., *swede-eating/-gnawing* (cf. BUCKWHEAT n.). [SE *swede* (US rutabaga); the urban conception of the country's main product, foodstuff etc; thus *Swedey*, Metropolitan Police nickname (punning on SWEENEY (TODD), THE n.) for Operation Countryman, an investigation into corruption carried out by officers of rural and provincial forces]

swede adj. [1950s+] rural, unsophisticated. [SWEDE n.²]

swede-basher n. [1930s+] a country bumpkin, an unsophisticated peasant (cf. ACORN-CRACKER n.). [ext. of SWEDE n.²]

swede-bashing adj. [1930s+] unsophisticated, rustic and peasantlike. [SWEDE-BASHER n.]

swedge n. [20C+] (Scot.) a fight. [? SE *swedge*, a type of chisel with a bevelled edge, orig. used for making a groove around a horseshoe and latterly for various jobs requiring the bend of cold metal]

swedge v. [20C+] (Scot.) to fight. [SWEDGE n.]

Swedish n. [1960s+] **1** masturbation or mutual masturbation. **2** the use of rubber garments in sex. [the companionship and the sweating one experiences in a Swedish sauna bath]

Swedish adj. [1990s+] (US) homosexual. [? misreading of the sex-change operations carried out in Denmark]

Swedish culture n. [1960s+] the use of rubber, PVC etc in sex. [SWEDISH n. (2)]

Swedish fiddle n. [late 19C+] (US) an accordion. [its popularity among Swedish immigrants]

Swedish headache n. [1930s+] (US) intense sexual frustration. [? a problem of Swedish immigrants]

sweedle v. [1910s–30s] to trick with flattery, to 'sweet-talk'. [SE *swindle* + *wheedle*]

sweeney n. [1920s+] a barber. [the fictional *Sweeney Todd*, the 'demon barber' of Fleet Street, who sold 'golopshious' pies made from the flesh of those he had murdered]

Sweeney (Todd), the n. [1930s+] the Flying Squad; thus *sweenies*, members of the Flying Squad. [rhy. sl.; ult. see prev.]

sweenies n. [1980s+] (UK juv.) large sideboards or sideburns. [TV police series *The Sweeney*, in which such sideboards were displayed by stars John Thaw and Dennis Waterman]

sweep n. [mid-19C–1960s] an unpleasant person. [SE *chimney sweep* whose job, if not person, is regarded as unpleasant]

sweep v. [1930s] (US prison) to disappear quickly. [play on BROOM (IT) v.]

sweep one's own doorstep v. [20C+] (US) to mind one's own business.

sweep's frill n. [late 19C] a beard and whiskers that run round the line of the chin, leaving the rest of the face clean-shaven. [such facial hair was typical of a chimney sweep]

sweep's trot n. [mid-19C] a high-stepping form of amble, the best way to carry the chimney sweep's load of brushes etc.

sweep up the kitchen n. see CLEAN UP THE KITCHEN n.

sweet n. **1** [mid-19C–1940s] (also **confectionery**) a pretty young girl. **2** [1920s] (US Black) money. **3** [1960s–80s] (US Black) (also **sweet boy**) a male homosexual. **4** [1980s] an attractive heterosexual male. [(1), (3) and (4) SE; (2) play on SUGAR n.¹ (1)]

sweet adj.¹ **1** [early 17C+] (orig. Aus.) excellent, perfect, simple, correct, in order, also used negatively, e.g. a *sweet mess*. **2** [19C+] a general term of approval, applicable to people, objects, actions and events. **3** [late 19C] (UK Und.) not suspicious. **4** [1910s–50s] substantial. **5** [1940s+] (Aus.) ready, prepared. **6** [1940s+] safe, devoid of problems. **7** [1980s+] (US campus) easy.

sweet *adj.*[2] **1** [late 17C–early 19C] gullible. **2** [mid-19C+] amenable; usu. in phr. *keep/have someone sweet*, to keep someone well-disposed towards oneself, esp. by complaisance or bribery. **3** [1930s+] (*Aus.*) affectionate, amorous toward. **4** [2000s] intimate with (in a non-sexual context).

sweet *adj.*[3] [early 18C+] dextrous, expert.

sweet *adj.*[4] (*W.I.*) **1** [1940s] tipsy, slightly drunk (cf. ABOUT RIGHT phr.[1]). **2** [1950s] of a man, fashionably dressed, smart.

sweet *adj.*[5] [1950s–70s] effeminate.

sweet *v.* [late 19C] (*US Und.*) to lose.

sweet *adv.*[1] [mid-19C] amorously.

sweet *adv.*[2] [mid-19C+] without any problems, easily.

sweet *adv.*[3] [1920s] of a man, living from the wages of a woman, e.g. as a pimp.

sweet! *excl.* [1920s+] excellent! wonderful!

sweet air *n.* [1980s+] nitrous oxide.

sweet-arse *adj.* [1990s+] excellent, wonderful.

sweet as a nut *phr.* (*also* **sweet as nut, ...a clock**) [mid-17C+] (*orig. UK Und.*) easy, simple, no problems, delightful, esp. of a robbery or other 'job'.

sweet as pie *phr. see* NICE AS PIE phr. (1).

sweet b.a. *n.* [1940s+] nothing at all. [abbr. *sweet b*ugger *a*ll]

sweetback *n.* [1930s] **1** (*US tramp*) a 'part-time' tramp, who can and will opt out of the lifestyle when he wishes. **2** in fig. use, of someone who poses as having 'dropped out' of conventional society or as being unsuccessful.

sweetback (man) *n.* (*also* **sugar-man**) **1** [1920s–30s] (*US Und./ Black*) a pimp (cf. CANDYMAN n.). **2** [1920s–60s] (*US Black*) a womanizer, a ladies' man. [his physique, which women like to touch]

sweet bleeding Jesus! *excl.* [20C+] a general excl.

sweetbread *n.* [mid–late 17C] a bribe. [SE *sweetbread*, the pancreas or thymus gland of an animal, a delicacy]

sweet briar *n.* [17C] female pubic hair.

sweet bugger-all *n. see* BUGGER-ALL n.

sweet but-all *n. see* SWEET FUCK-ALL n.

sweet bwai *n.* [1970s–80s] (*UK Black*) a ghetto dandy; a womanizer. [SE *sweet* + BWOY n.]

sweetcakes *n.* **1** [1960s+] (*also* **sweet chips**) a term of affection. **2** [1980s+] (*US gay*) the buttocks (cf. BAKERY GOODS n.).

sweetcheeks *n.* [1980s+] (*US gay*) the buttocks (cf. BAKERY GOODS n.).

sweet chocolate *n. see* HOT CHOCOLATE n.

sweet con *n.* [1950s] (*US*) a form of begging in which the beggar uses persuasion and promises rather than threats. [SE *sweet* + CON n.[1] (7)]

sweet cop *n.* [20C+] **1** (*Aus.*) a pleasant, enviable situation. **2** (*Aus Und.*) a successful scheme or criminal enterprise. [SWEET adj.[1] (2) + COP n.[2]]

sweetcorn shiner *n.* [1990s+] a male homosexual (cf. BONE-EATER n.). [coarse ref. to sodomy]

sweet daddy *n.* [1970s+] (*US Black*) a lover or any man who provides for a woman. [SE *sweet* + DADDY n. (7)]

sweet damn-all *n.* [1920s+] nothing whatsoever. [DAMN-ALL n.]

sweeten *v.* **1** [late 17C+] (*UK Und.*) to lure, to decoy, to swindle, to flatter. **2** [early 19C+] to bribe, to corrupt. **3** [mid-19C–1930s] to calm down, to assuage someone's worries; in criminal contexts, to calm a suspicious victim. **4** [1930s] to add alcohol to a non-alcoholic drink.

sweetener *n.*[1] (*also* **sweetner**) (*UK Und.*) **1** [late 17C–mid-19C] a rogue who specializes in dropping something supposedly valuable where it will be found by a potential victim, who is either lured into a game or persuaded to buy the 'valuable', while the con-man claims that although they should, by rights, share the profits, he will sell his share and let the victim have the whole benefit. **2** [late 19C] one who poses as an innocent player in order to ensnare a genuine innocent into playing a game in which he will invariably find himself the defrauded loser.

sweetener *n.*[2] **1** [mid-19C] (*US*) a drink. **2** [mid-19C] a hard blow. **3** [mid-19C+] something pleasant, something encouraging, a bribe. **4** [1900s] the penis.

sweeteners *n.* [late 19C] (*UK Und.*) the lips.

sweetening (lay) *n.* [late 17C–mid-18C] a confidence trick based on deliberately dropping a guinea and swindling the dupe who picks it up. [ext. of SWEETENER n.[1] (1) + LAY n.[4] (1)]

sweeten the pot *v.* [1920s+] to make a proposition more alluring, to improve a situation. [poker jargon, to add money to a pot, to raise the betting]

sweet-eye *n.* [20C+] (*W.I.*) a lustful glance or wink; thus *make sweet-eye*, to glance in this way; *get sweet-eye*, for a woman to receive such a glance.

sweet Fanny Adams *n.* (*also* **sweet F.A.**) [1910s+] **1** absolutely nothing at all. **2** as excl., rubbish! piffle! [euph. for SWEET FUCK-ALL n.; the identity of Fanny Adams remains a mystery and is presumably based only on the initial letters]

sweet fuck-all *n.* (*also* **sweet but-all**) [1910s+] absolutely nothing. [FUCK-ALL n.]

sweet fucking Jesus! *excl.* [20C+] (*US*) an expletive with no particular meaning, conveying annoyance and surprise.

sweet go *n.* [1990s+] (*Aus. Und.*) an easy crime. [SWEET adj.[1] (2) + GO n.[3] (1)]

sweetheart *n.* **1** [20C+] a term of address; no affection is implied. **2** [1920s+] a person, usu. used in a derog. sense. **3** [1930s–40s] anything considered good. **4** [1940s] (*US Und.*) a stolen automobile in good condition. [ext. of SE, often ironic]

sweetheart *adj.* [1970s] (*US*) easy, simple.

sweetheart *v.* **1** [mid–late 19C] to make advances to, to 'chat up.' **2** [1960s] (*US Black*) to have a (sexual) relationship with.

sweetheart contract *n.* (*also* **sweetheart deal**) [1950s+] (*orig. US*) a union-employer contract that favours the company over its employees; a union-employer contract that favours all those negotiating, but not the workers the union supposedly represents.

sweetheart life *n.* [1950s] (*W.I.*) the state of living together but not being married.

sweetie *n.* (*also* **sweety**) **1** [late 19C+] an attractive girl. **2** [20C+] a beloved child. **3** [1910s+] (*orig. US*) a boy- or girlfriend. **4** [1920s+] a term of address, not necessarily implying intimacy. **5** [1920s+] used ironically to mean an unpleasant person, e.g. *he's a real sweetie*. **6** [1930s+] a pleasant person. **7** [1960s–70s] an effeminate homosexual.

sweetie-pie *n.* (*also* **sweetie-pops**) [1920s+] a general term of affection; a girlfriend. [ext. SWEETIE n. (3), praising the beloved as 'good enough to eat']

sweeties *n. see* SWEETS n.[2].

sweet Jesus *n.* [1960s+] (*drugs*) morphine, heroin (cf. AUNTIE EMMA n.; YELLOW JESUS n.). [the addict's 'saviour']

sweet Jesus! *excl.* [late 18C+] a mild, if blasphemous, oath.

sweet kid *n.* (*also* **sweetmeat**) [1970s+] (*Can./US prison*) a younger prisoner who joins up with an older man. [SWEET adj.[5] + KID n.[1] (10)/MEAT n. (1)]

sweet lady *n.* [1950s] (*US gay*) a woman who runs a string of homosexual male prostitutes.

sweet-lick *v.* [1980s] (*UK Black*) to apply deodorant. [SE *sweet* + weak use of LICK v.[1] (1)]

sweet-lips *n.* [late 19C–1900s] a glutton.

sweet Lucy *n.* (*drugs*) **1** [1950s+] hashish dissolved into wine. **2** [1960s] marijuana (cf. AUNT MARY n.[2]). **3** [1960s] barbiturates dissolved into muscatel wine. **4** [1960s+] a variety of cheap, sweet wine.

sweet mack *n.* [1960s–70s] a pimp who treats his women well. [SE *sweet* + MACK n.[1] (1)]

sweet mama *n.* [1920s+] (*US Black*) (*also* **sweet momma**) a Black man's female lover. [SE *sweet* + MAMA n. (2)]

sweet mama! *excl.* [1920s] an excl. of praise.

sweetman *n.* **1** [1920s–60s] (*US Black*) a male lover; occas. a pimp (cf. CANDYMAN n.). **2** [1920s+] (*UK Und.*) a pimp who runs only 1 prostitute and lives off her earnings alone (cf. CHILE CHUMP n.). **3** [1970s+] (*W.I.*) a married woman's lover, to whom she gives money and presents.

sweetmeat *n.*[1] **1** [mid–late 19C] an underage or child prostitute (cf. BIT OF MUTTON n.). **2** [mid–late 19C] a mistress. **3** [1940s+] (*US Und.*) a young woman. **4** [1960s+] a general term of affectionate address. [SE *sweet* + MEAT n. (1)/SE *sweetmeat*, which is 'good enough to eat']

sweetmeat *n.*[2] [late 19C; 1970s+] the penis. [SE *sweet* + MEAT n. (2) + pun; 1970s+ use is US gay]

sweetmeat *n.*[3] *see* SWEET KID n.

sweet momma *n. see* SWEET MAMA n.

sweet morpheus *n.* [1970s+] (*drugs*) morphine (cf. AUNTIE EMMA n.). [*Morpheus*, the Greek god of dreams; the root of *morphine*]

sweetmouth *n.* [mid–19C+] (*W.I.*) **1** (*also* **sweet-mouth man**) a flatterer, a persuasive person. **2** flattery, persuasiveness.

sweetmouth *adj.* (*W.I.*) **1** [1930s] flattering. **2** [1950s] greedy, gluttonous. [SWEETMOUTH n.]

sweetmouth *v.* [1940s+] (*orig. W.I.*) to flatter. [SWEETMOUTH n.]

sweet-mouth man *n. see* SWEETMOUTH n.

sweetner *n. see* SWEETENER n.[1].

sweetness and light *n.* [1950s] (*Aus.*) whisky.

sweet nothings *n.* (*also* **soft nothings**) [late 19C+] sentimental trivia, esp. the clichés of seduction.

sweet on *adj.* **1** [late 17C+] (*also* **sweet upon**) in love with, infatuated by; very fond of, in non-amatory sense. **2** [mid-19C] in a non-sexual context, satisfied with, happy about.

sweet papa *n.* (*also* **sweet poppa**) [1920s+] (*US Black*) a man who provides for the material wants of his lover.

sweet papa! *excl.* [1920s] (*US*) a general excl.

sweet patootie *n.* [1910s+] a woman, a girlfriend. [SE *sweet* + PATOOTIE n. (1)]

sweet patootie! *excl.* [1900s–20s] (*US*) a general excl.

sweet pea *n.*[1] **1** [early 19C] whisky. **2** [late 19C] urine. **3** [1960s+] tea. **4** [1970s] LSD (cf. A n.[3]). [rhy. sl.; (2) = PEE n.[1]; note (1) E.P. suggests 'the colour of the resulting urine']

sweet pea *n.*[2] [1930s–40s] (*US Und.*) **1** anything easy. **2** a gullible, vulnerable individual.

sweet pea *n.*[3] [1930s+] **1** a girl- or boyfriend. **2** a term of affection; also in ironic use.

sweet pimp *n. see* SUGAR PIMP n.

sweet poppa *n. see* SWEET PAPA n.

sweet potato pie *n.* **1** [1920s+] (*US Black*) an attractive young man or woman. **2** [1920s+] (*also* **sweet potato**) male or female genitals. **3** [1980s] sexual intercourse. **4** [1980s] a general term of endearment. [the common equation of sex and food]

sweets *n.*[1] [1920s+] (*US/W.I.*) a general term of address, both friendly and otherwise.

sweets *n.*[2] (*also* **sweeties**) [1960s+] (*drugs*) amphetamines (cf. A n.[2]). [resemblance]

sweet stuff *n.* [1930s–50s] (*drugs*) **1** heroin or morphine (cf. AUNTIE EMMA n.). **2** cocaine. [SE *sweet* + STUFF n.[3] (2)]

sweet sugar *n.*[1] [1980s] (*US Black*) an attractive male.

sweet sugar *n.*[2] *see* SUGAR DADDY n.

sweet talk *n.* (*also* **sweet talking**) [late 19C+] persuasive, seductive talk.

sweet talk *v.* [1930s+] (*orig. US Black*) **1** to persuade, to charm, to lull into false confidence. **2** to seduce.

sweet tits *n.* [1990s+] a male-to-female term of affection. [TIT n.[3] (1)]

sweet-tooth *n.* [1960s] (*US drugs*) a craving for, or addiction to, narcotics.

sweet upon *adj. see* SWEET ON adj. (1).

Sweet Willie *n.* [1970s] (*US Black*) a kindly, attentive man, esp. as a pose practised by a pimp when 'catching' a new prostitute (cf. CANDYMAN n.).

sweety *n. see* SWEETIE n.

swell *n.* **1** [late 18C+] an aristocrat, a sophisticated, stylish, rich person; thus *swellism*, the world of a 'swell'; *swellness*, being a 'swell'; *cut/do a swell*, to swagger. **2** [early 19C] a good time, a spree. **3** [early 19C–1910s] the outstanding member of any profession or occupation. **4** [mid-19C–1900s] used ironically as one who unsuccessfully emulates the style and manners of (1). [for the connoisseur of such gradations, the *swell* differed from the older aristocracy in the need and capacity for display; the aristocracy had position but no fashion, the swell had fashion and used it to win position, but his social position might be fractionally less grand. In time he, or at least his children, might attain the absolute social peaks]

swell *adj.* [early 19C+] (*orig. US Und.*) **1** excellent, wonderful, delightful; thus *swell article*, anything of high quality; *swell crib*, a genteel house; also in ironic use. **2** pertaining to the upper classes. **3** showy, ostentatious, fashionable, usu. as regards dress; thus *swell mollisher*, a very well-dressed woman. [SWELL n.; 20C+ use mainly US]

swell *v.* [early 19C–1920s] to act in an aristocratic, ostentatious manner. [SWELL n.]

swell *adv.* [mid-19C+] (*US*) very well, excellently, kindly.

swell! *excl.* [1930s+] (*US*) excellent! wonderful!

swell-cove *n.* (*also* **swell kidder**) a gentleman, a dandy. [SWELL adj. (2) + COVE n. (1)]

swell dona *n.* [late 19C] a working-class woman affecting airs of grandeur. [SWELL adj. (2) + DONA n. (1)]

swelled *adj. see* SWELLED (UP) adj.

swelled bean *n. see* SWELLHEAD n.[1] (2).

swelled-head *see under* SWELLHEAD.

swelled (up) *adj.* [1910s–20s] (*US*) snobbish, pleased with oneself. [SWELL n. (1)]

sweller *n.* [1900s] (*US*) a braggart, one who 'swells' the truth.

swell-fencer *n.* [mid-19C] a street-seller of needles. [SWELL n. (1) + -FENCER sfx; needles are required for the tailoring that garbs a swell]

swellhead *n.*[1] [early 19C+] **1** (*also* **swelled-head**) a braggart, a boaster, a show-off. **2** (*also* **swelled bean**) conceit, arrogance; also in phr. *have the swell-head*. [backform. f. SWELL-HEADED adj.]

swellhead *n.*[2] **1** [mid-19C] (*also* **swell-skull**) strong whisky, esp. when illegally distilled (cf. BUSTSKULL n.). **2** [mid-19C] a drunkard. **3** [1960s+] (*US Black*) one who has passed out through drug use. [SE *swell* + *head*]

swell-headed *adj.* (*also* **swelled-headed**) [early 19C+] arrogant, conceited. [SE *swell* + *head*]

swell hung in chains *n.* [mid-19C] a rich or ostentatious man given to wearing quantities of jewellery. [SWELL n. (1)]

swelling *n.* [1900s] an erection.

swellish *adj.* **1** [mid-19C] gentlemanly. **2** [mid-19C–1910s] fashionably dressed. [SWELL n. (1)]

swell it *v.* [late 19C] to behave or pose as an aristocrat or a rich man.

swell kidder *n. see* SWELL-COVE n.

swell mob *n.* (*UK Und.*) **1** [mid-19C–1920s] leading pickpockets whose dress reflects their success (as well as facilitating their entry into the wealthy world on which they prey). **2** [mid-19C–1940s; 2000s] a major criminal gang, irrespective of their specialities; also attrib. [SWELL adj. (1) + MOB n.[2] (3)]

swell mobsman *n.* [mid-19C–1920s] a leading pickpocket. [SWELL MOB n. (1)]

swell-nose *n.* [early 16C–18C] strong beer. [its effects]

swell-skull *n. see* SWELLHEAD n.[2] (1).

swell's lush *n.* [mid–late 19C] (*Aus.*) champagne. [SWELL n. (1) + LUSH n.[1] (1)]

Swell Street *n.* [mid-19C] the West End of London. [SWELL n. (1) + SE *street*]

swell woman *n.* [late 19C] an élite prostitute, a woman kept by a rich lover (cf. FANCY WOMAN n.). [SWELL adj. (1) + SE *woman*]

swelp me...! *excl. see* S'ELP ME (BOB)! excl.

swelter *n.* [late 19C] hot, hard work.

swep' *adj.* (*also* **swept**) [1980s+] (*US Black/campus*) sexually or emotionally obsessed with, or overwhelmed by. [abbr. SE phr. *swept off one's feet*]

swept *adj.* [1910s+] (*N.Z.*) totally without money. [it has been *swept away*]

swerve *v.* [1950s+] (*Aus.*) **1** to practise coitus interruptus. **2** to avoid; thus as n., an act of avoidance. [(1) motoring imagery; one 'avoids a child']

swi *n. see* SWY n.

swift *n.* [1920s] (*US Und.*) a fast horse, used for getaways in the pre-motorcar era.

swift *adj.* **1** [late 19C–1900s] exciting. **2** [late 19C+] sexually forward. **3** [late 19C+] smart, clever, cunning. **4** [1960s–70s] (*US campus*) dull, stupid, ignorant. **5** [1970s+] of a policeman, carrying out any illegal activities, esp. during an arrest. **6** [1980s] (*US campus*) good, excellent. **7** [1990s+] healthy.

swifter *n. see* SWIFT ONE n.

swiftie *n.*[1] (*also* **swifty**) [1940s+] (*Aus./N.Z.*) a hoax, a fraud, a deception; esp. in *pull a swiftie*, to deceive.

swiftie *n.*[2] (*also* **swifty**) [1940s+] (*US*) one who moves fast, either physically or mentally; also in ironic use.

swiftly flow *v.* [late 19C–1900s] (*Aus.*) to go. [rhy. sl.]

swift one *n.* (*also* **swifter**) [mid-19C+] a quick drink.

swift 'un *n.* [1970s+] (*UK Und.*) corrupt police procedure when arresting a suspect. [SWIFT adj. (5)]

swifty *see under* SWIFTIE.

swigman *n.* [mid-16C–mid-19C] (*UK Und.*) a criminal beggar, posing as a legitimate peddler. [? unrecorded early use of SWAG n.[1] (2)]

swill *n.* **1** [mid-19C+] unpleasant food or drink. **2** [late 19C–1950s] alcohol. **3** [1930s+] in fig. use, anything disgusting, second-rate, distasteful. **4** [1940s–60s] a cup of tea. [? SE *swill*, kitchen refuse]

swill *v.* (*also* **swill one's guts**) [mid-16C+] to drink heavily. [SE *swill*, to drink heavily; from 1916 to 1955 New South Wales pubs took 'last orders' at 6 p.m. and the resultant rush of the all-male drinkers was termed the SIX O'CLOCK SWILL n.; other states maintained the law for longer]

swillery *n.* (*also* **swill pot**) [1940s+] (*Aus.*) a hotel with a bar, a pub. [SWILL v.]

swill tub *n.* (*also* **swill bowl/pail**) [mid-16C–early 19C; 1970s] a drunkard. [SE *swill* + SE *swill tub*, a refuse container]

swim *n.* [mid-19C–1900s] a scheme, a plan; thus *in a good swim*, having a spell of good luck. [SE *swim*, a section of river well stocked with fish]

swim *v.* [1980s] (*US prison*) to conform to prison society.

swim in golden grease *v.* (*also* **swim in golden lard/oil**) [17C] to be offered and to take an abundance of bribes.

swimmer *n.*[1] [late 17C–18C] (*UK Und.*) a counterfeit coin. [? the metal used was light enough to float]

swimmer *n.*[2] **1** [early 19C] a tender or guard-ship. **2** [early 19C] a thief who escapes a prison sentence by enlisting in the Royal Navy. **3** [1980s] one who retrieves drug packages which have been purposely dropped into the sea during importation.

swimmer *n.*[3] (*also* **swimmers, swimmies**) [1920s+] a bathing costume.

swindging *adj. see* SWINGEING adj.

swindle *n.* **1** [19C] tossing to decide who pays for the next round of drinks. **2** [mid-19C] (*US*) the cost, the bill; esp. in phr. *what's the swindle?* **3** [mid-19C–1910s] a disappointment, something that proves to be a fraud and not what it was advertised as being. **4** [late 19C] a lottery. **5** [2000s] (*UK Und.*) any form of criminal

activity, e.g. drug dealing; there is no necessary implication of confidence trickery.

swindle *v.* [1990s+] (*US prison*) to fight with one's fists.

swindlecat *n. see* SHINDYKIT n.

swindler *n.* [mid-18C–mid-19C] (*UK Und.*) a trickster, a fraud. Yid. *schwindeln*, to be giddy, to act thoughtlessly or extravagantly, to swindle. Orig. Und. and supposedly imported to the UK by German Jewish immigrants *c.*1762, it entered SE during the 19C]

swindle sheet *n.* [1910s+] (*orig. US*) an expense account, any form of charges. [orig. boxing use, the accounts made up by a manager and shown to his fighter; bitter fighters felt that these were rarely relevant to the actual money involved]

swine *n.* **1** [late 19C+] anything considered as difficult or exhausting to achieve. **2** [1940s] (*UK prison*) prison guards. **3** [1980s+] (*Aus. prison*) the police. [(3) var. on PIG n.[3] (1)]

swine, the *n.* [1970s+] (*US Black*) the police. [PIG n.[3] (1)]

swine-eater *n.* (*also* **swine**) [1980s+] (*US Black Muslim*) **1** a White person. **2** a policeman (cf. ANIMAL n.[1]). [the Muslim prohibition on pig products; (2) PIG n.[3] (1)]

swing *n.*[1] [1910s+] (*US*) a rest period between 2 shifts.

swing *n.*[2] [1970s+] (*US Black*) stimulation, excitement, something that makes things 'go with a swing'.

swing, the *n.* [late 18C–mid-19C] the gallows. [SWING v.[1] (1)]

swing *v.*[1] **1** [mid-16C+] to hang. **2** [early 19C] to have someone hanged.

swing *v.*[2] **1** [mid-19C+] (*also* **swing it**) to arrange, to achieve. **2** [1900s] (*US Und.*) of a crime, to be remunerative. **3** [1930s+] to cope, to deal with a situation, to make sure that things work out as one desires, often through trickery or manipulation. **4** [1950s] (*US Und.*) of a pimp, to run a prostitute. **5** [1950s–60s] (*US drugs*) to cheat. **6** [1950s+] (*US*) to be a member of a teenage street gang, to fight as a member of a teenage street gang. **7** [1960s] to involve oneself in corruption or illegality. **8** [1960s–70s] (*US Black*) to be dealing narcotics. **9** [2000s] (*US*) to give, to hand over, to pay.

swing *v.*[3] **1** [1920s+] to make a sneering remark. **2** [1930s+] (*US*) to act, to live in a given manner.

swing *v.*[4] **1** [1930s+] to enjoy an active and varied sex life, to have sexual intercourse. **2** [1930s+] to enjoy oneself, to have a good time. **3** [1950s+] (*orig. gay*) to achieve the supreme level of well-being and satisfaction. **4** [1960s] to carry on an affair with someone. **5** [1960s] for anything to work out well, as planned. **6** [1960s] of a place, to be devoted to sex. **7** [1960s+] of a party, a club, a place of entertainment, to go well, to be enjoyable. **8** [1970s+] to arrange and participate in husband-and-wife swapping parties.

swing *v.*[5] [1940s+] (*gay*) to fellate.

swing *v.*[6] [1950s] (*US teen*) to leave, to go.

swing *v.*[7] *see* SWING BOTH WAYS v.

swing *v.*[8] *see* TAKE A SWING (AT) v.

swing a bag *v.* [1940s+] (*Aus.*) to work as a street-walker. [the prostitute's inevitable handbag]

swing around *v. see* SWING BY v.

swing ass *v. see* BLOW ASS v.

swing at *v. see* TAKE A SWING (AT) v.

swing both ways *v.* (*also* **swing, swing either way, swing three-sixty**) [1960s+] to practise bisexuality. [SWING v.[4] (1)]

swing by *v.* (*also* **swing around**) [1980s+] (*orig. US*) to visit. [SE *swing*, a trip]

swing daddy *n.* [1970s+] (*US Black*) **1** an attractive, well-dressed man. **2** a male lover. **3** a pimp (cf. BIG DADDY n.; CANDYMAN n.). [SWING v.[4] + DADDY n. (7)]

swingdog *n.* [1990s+] (*US teen*) a fashionable dresser. [SWING v.[4] (2) + DOG n.[2] (2)]

swinge *v.* **1** [early 16C–mid-17C] to drink up, to drink off. **2** [17C] to have sexual intercourse (cf. BANG v.[1]). [SE *swinge*, to beat, to castigate]

swingeing *adj.* (*also* **swindging**) [late 16C+] a general intensifier, very large, very forceful, very powerful; 17C use often describing venereal disease. [SE *swinge*, to beat; SE in 20C+, typically as *swingeing cuts* in the health budget]

swing either way *v. see* SWING BOTH WAYS *v.*

swinge off *v.* (*also* **swinge up**) **1** [early 16C–mid-17C] to toss down a drink. **2** [17C–18C] to infect with a bad case of venereal disease. [ext. of SWINGE *v.*]

swinger *n.*[1] **1** [late 16C–19C] anything notably large or forceful of its type. **2** [late 17C–early 18C] an outrageous lie. **3** [1920s+] (*Aus.*) an admirable person. **4** [1960s–70s] an exciting or lively place (usu. a club or bar).

swinger *n.*[2] **1** [mid–late 17C; 1960s+] one who leads an active and varied sex life. **2** [1950s+] one who leads an active and sophisticated social life. **3** [1960s+] one who participates in husband-and-wife swapping parties. [SWING *v.*[4]; (1) 1960s + use orig. US]

swingers *n.* **1** [17C; 1920s+] (*Aus.*) the female breasts, esp. when unsupported but still firm (cf. BOBBER *n.*[2]). **2** [19C+] the testicles (cf. BANGERS *n.*).

swinge someone's jacket *v. see* TRIM SOMEONE'S JACKET *v.*

swinge up *v. see* SWINGE OFF *v.*

swing for *v.* [mid-19C+] a general threat. [SWING *v.*[1] (1); the implication is that the speaker is willing to commit murder to get what they want and thus face the gallows]

swing in a halter *v.* [mid–late 16C] to be hanged. [ext. of SWING *v.*[1] (1)]

swinging *n.*[1] [mid-17C–19C] hanging; a hanging. [SWING *v.*[1] (1)]

swinging *n.*[2] [1960s+] indulging in husband-and-wife swapping parties. [SWING *v.*[4] (8)]

swinging *adj.*[1] [late 17C+] a general intensifier, e.g. *swinging fellow*, a very large man; *swinging lie*, an outrageous lie. [var. on SWINGEING *adj.*]

swinging *adj.*[2] [1950s+] (*orig. US*) **1** uninhibited, lively, fashionable; esp. in phrs. *swinging London*, *swinging '60s*. **2** a general term of approval. [SE *swing* + SWING *v.*[4]]

swinging *adj.*[3] [1960s+] **1** referring to those who participate in husband-and-wife swapping parties or those who enjoy a promiscuous sex life. **2** sexually active, used for sexual contacts. [SWING *v.*[4]]

swinging *adj.*[4] [1970s] (*Aus. Und.*) of a court case, adjourned. [i.e. in motion]

swinging! *excl.* [1950s–80s] (*orig. US Black*) a general term of approval. [SWING *v.*[4]; the term migrated to UK as the catchphrase of entertainer Norman Vaughan, compere of television's *Saturday Night at the London Palladium*, who alternated the positive *swinging* with the negative DODGY *adj.*; it was further associated with the image of 'swinging London' and the 'swinging Sixties']

swinging dick *n.* [1970s+] **1** (*US*) a person; usu. in phr. *every swinging dick*. **2** an aggressive person. [SE *swinging* + DICK *n.*[4] (1). Popularized in Tom Wolfe's novel *Bonfire of the Vanities* (1987) where *big swinging dicks* was used to characterize the most successful of Wall Street's financial wheeler-dealers]

swinging door *n.* [1930s] a prostitute (cf. BOAT AND OAR *n.*). [rhy. sl. = SE *whore*]

swingingly *adv.* [late 17C–18C] very much, extensively. [SWINGING *adj.*[1]]

swinging single *n.* (*also* **swingle**) [1960s+] (*US*) a sexually promiscuous unmarried person. [SWING *v.*[4]]

swinging the stick *n.* [mid-19C] robbery with violence. [the physical action of the bludgeoner]

swing into *v.* [1960s] (*US*) to arrive. [SE *swing*, a tour]

swing it *v. see* SWING *v.*[2] (1).

swing it on *v.* (*also* **swing it across**) [20C+] (*mainly Aus./N.Z.*) to deceive, to impose on, to do a bad turn to. [ext. SWING *v.*[2] (3)]

swingle *n. see* SWINGING SINGLE *n.*

swing like sixty *v.* [1960s+] (*US teen*) to perform at one's peak, to achieve ultimate success or pleasure. [SWING *v.*[4] (2) + LIKE SIXTY *adv.*]

swing low *v.* [1990s+] (*US Black teen*) to have oral sex. [SWING *v.*[4] (1) + SE *low*]

swing man *n.* [1950s–60s] a drug dealer. [? he makes things go *with a swing*]

swing of the door *n.* [1930s] the seventh drink of a session, supposedly the very last before leaving the pub.

swing on *v.* **1** [1910s+] (*US*) to hit or punch. **2** [1960s] in fig. use, to talk forcefully. **3** [1960s] (*Aus.*) to keep, to take.

swing on someone's balls *v.* [2000s] (*US Black*) of a woman, to be sexually obsessed with a man.

swing-out *n.* [1950s–70s] (*US Black/P.R.*) a violent street fight between rival urban gangs. [SWING OUT *v.* (1)]

swing out *v.* **1** [1950s–70s] to fight. **2** [1960s] (*US campus*) to lose emotional control. **3** [1960s] to associate with.

swing party *n.* [1970s+] (*orig. US*) an orgy, esp. when the participants are husband-and-wife swapping couples. [SWING *v.*[4] (8)]

swing-tail *n.* [late 18C–early 19C] a hog.

swing the bag *v.* [1960s+] (*Aus.*) of a bookmaker, to take bets at a racetrack. [the bookmaker's money *bag*]

swing the billy *v. see* SLING THE BILLY *v.*

swing the cuff *v. see* ON THE CUFF *phr.*[1].

swing the dice *v.* [1990s+] (*US Black*) to accept that much of life is a matter of luck and to live it accordingly.

swing the gate *v.* [1930s+] (*Aus.*) to work hard, to do well, to win in a contest. [sheep-shearing jargon, used of a fast and expert shearer]

swing three-sixty *v. see* SWING BOTH WAYS *v.*

swing to the left *v.* [1970s] (*US*) to be a homosexual. [SWING *v.*[4] + negative image of homosexuality/the 'sinister' left]

swing with *v.*[1] [1950s–70s] (*US*) to steal.

swing with *v.*[2] **1** [1950s+] to associate with. **2** [1960s+] to ally oneself to a group or individual, to agree with a concept. **3** [1960s] to have a relationship with, to have sex with. **4** [1960s+] to enjoy, to appreciate. [SWING *v.*[4]]

swingy *adj.* [1970s] (*US gay*) **1** bisexual. **2** enjoyable. [SWING *v.*[4]; SWING BOTH WAYS *v.*]

swinjer *n.* [1940s–50s] (*Aus.*) something excellent; also as *adj.* [? SWINGEING *adj.*]

swinny *adj.* [19C] drunk. [dial. *swinny*, giddy]

swipe *n.*[1] [mid-19C+] cheap, inferior, home-brewed alcohol.

swipe *n.*[2] **1** [1900s–50s] (*US*) an unpleasant, objectionable person. **2** [1920s] objectionable people considered collectively. [? obs. SE *swip*, to hit, to slip away]

swipe *n.*[3] [1910s–50s] (*US*) a stable-boy.

swipe *n.*[4] [1950s–80s] (*US Black*) (*also* **swipestake**) the penis. [? SE *swipe*, to hit; or ? abbr. KIDNEY-WIPER *n.*]

swipe *v.*[1] [late 19C–1900s] to drink hastily and copiously. [orig. northern dial.]

swipe *v.*[2] **1** [late 19C–1900s] (*US campus*) to defeat. **2** [late 19C+] (*orig. US*) to steal. **3** [1900s–40s] (*US Und.*) to assault. [SE *swipe*, to strike]

swiped *adj. see* SWIPEY *adj.*

swipe me! *excl.* [1970s+] an excl. of surprise. [? S'ELP ME (BOB)! *excl.*; or ? SE *swipe*]

swiper *n.* [early–mid-19C] a heavy drinker. [SWIPE *v.*[1]]

swipes *n.* **1** [late 18C–19C] weak beer, sour beer (cf. SWANKY (SWIPES) *n.*). **2** [late 18C–1920s] any beer. **3** [early–mid-19C] a public house potman. [naut. jargon *swipes*, weak or 'small' beer furnished by the purser; a sailor was allowed 4 quarts (5 litres) a day, but the quality was atrocious; ult. SWIPE *v.*[1]]

swipestake *n. see* SWIPE *n.*[4].

swipey *n.* [mid-19C] a brewery drayman. [SWIPES *n.*]

swipey *adj.* (*also* **swiped**) [19C] drunk, tipsy. [SWIPES *n.*]

swipington *n.* (*also* **swippington**) [1930s+] (*Aus.*) a drunkard. [SWIPES *n.* + LUSHINGTON *n.*]

swips *v.* [1950s] (*W.I.*) to drink off at a single draught, to 'knock back'. [SWIPE *v.*[1]]

swirly *n.* (*also* **swirlie**) [1980s+] (*US campus*) a ducking of someone's head in a toilet bowl.

swish *n.*[1] **1** [1930s] soda water, e.g. *scotch and swish*. **2** [1950s] (*N.Z.*) (*also* **swisher**) any dispenser worked by a pump.

swish *n.*[2] (*also* **swishy**) [1930s+] (*orig. US*) **1** (*also* **swisher**) a homosexual man. **2** his effeminate style. [SWISH *v.*[2]]

swish *n.*[3] **1** [1960s+] (*Aus.*) (*also* **swisho**) physical violence. **2** [1980s+] (*N.Z. prison*) abuse, harassment, heckling. [SE *swish*, echoic of a cane used in corporal punishment]

swish *adj.*[1] [20C+] fancy, elegant, 'posh'. [? the SE *swishing* of a fashionable woman's dress]

swish *adj.*[2] *see* SWISHY *adj.*

swish *v.*[1] **1** [mid-19C–1950s] (*UK juv.*) to cane; thus *swishing*, a caning. **2** [1970s–80s] (*N.Z. prison*) to hit, to punch. [the sound of the cane]

swish *v.*[2] [1940s+] of a man, to act in an effeminate manner. [SE *swish*, to move with a swish]

swish *v.*[3] [1980s+] (*N.Z. drugs*) to distribute or sell drugs; esp. in *swish on luckies*, to distribute or sell LSD or DMA (a designer hallucinogen).

swish! *excl.* [1920s] a disdainful, ironic excl., is that it? is that all?

Swish Alps *n.* [1950s–60s] (*US gay*) a gay area in the Hollywood Hills. [play on SWISH *n.*[2] (1)/*Swiss*]

swished *adj.* (*also* **switched**) [mid-19C] married. [? one is *switched* from the single to the marital state]

swisher *see under* SWISH.

swishiness *n.* [1940s+] effeminacy. [SWISH *n.*[2] (1)]

swishing *adj.* [1970s] of a (usu. gay) man, openly and extremely effeminate. [SWISH *v.*[2]]

swisho *n. see* SWISH *n.*[3] (1).

swish-tail *n.* **1** [late 18C–mid-19C] a pheasant. **2** [mid-19C] a schoolmaster. **3** [late 19C] a horse with an undocked tail. [(1) and (3) SE; (2) SWISH *v.*[1] (1) + TAIL *n.*[2] (1)]

swishy *n. see* SWISH *n.*[2].

swishy *adj.* (*also* **swish**) [1930s+] effeminate, exhibiting the supposed characteristics of a male homosexual. [SWISH *n.*[2] (1)]

Swiss *adj.* **1** [1970s+] (*US teen*) neutral, of no specific opinion. **2** [1990s+] unimpressive, second-rate. [negative stereotyping]

Swiss Army (knife) *n.* [1990s+] one's wife. [rhy. sl.]

Swiss banker *n. see* MERCHANT BANKER *n.*

Swiss itch *n.* [1920s–60s] a popular method of drinking tequila; one places a pinch of salt on the back of the hand, licks it off, drinks down a shot of tequila and immediately bites into a segment or a slice of lime. [ety. unknown; ? anecdotal]

swiss-roll *n.* [2000s] (*Irish*) the anus (cf. BAKERY GOODS *n.*; BOTTLE AND GLASS *n.*). [rhy. sl. = HOLE *n.*[1] (1)]

swissy *adj.* [1990s+] (*US teen*) bizarre, fashionable, daring.

switch *n.*[1] **1** [20C+] an exchange, esp. when it involves criminal deception. **2** [1930s–40s] (*US Und.*) subsisituting one thing, e.g. a deck of cards or a pair of dice, for another to facilitate cheating. **3** [1940s] (*US Und.*) in a confidence trick, the transfer of the victim's trust from the man who first befriended him to the principal trickster, to whom he has been introduced. **4** [2000s] (*US*) a change. [SE *switch*, to swap]

switch *n.*[2] [1930s–50s] (*US Black*) the movement of a woman's hips as she walks; also of a man; thus as *v.*, to walk with a sway of the hips. [SE *switch*, to flourish]

switch *n.*[3] **1** [1940s–60s] (*US*) a *switch*-blade knife. **2** [1940s–90s] (*Aus.*) a telephone *switch*board. [abbr.]

switch *n.*[4] **1** [1960s] (*US Und.*) one who enjoys non-standard sexual activity, e.g. flagellation. **2** [1990s+] (*US gay*) one who varies their sexual preferences, i.e. masculine to feminine, sadist

to masochist. **3** [1990s+] (*W.I.*) a heterosexual who has become homosexual.

switch *v.* [late 18C; late 19C–1930s] to have sexual intercourse (cf. BANG *v.*[1]). [SE *switch*, to whip]

switch and bone *n.* [1930s–40s] a telephone. [rhy. sl.]

switched *adj. see* SWISHED *adj.*

switched off *adj.* [1960s+] (*orig. US*) unfashionable.

switched on *adj.* [1960s+] (*orig. US*) **1** intoxicated by drugs. **2** sexually stimulated. **3** aware, sophisticated, up to the minute. [SWITCH ON *v.*; note RMC Duntroon (*Aus.*) *switched on*, used of a cadet who is alert, well-organized and generally performing as required]

switched out *adj.* [1970s] alienated. [on pattern of SWITCHED ON *adj.* (3)]

switcher *n.* [early 19C] (*UK Und.*) a hangman. [he *switches* his victim from life to death]

switcheroo *n.* [1930s+] (*US*) the opposite, the reverse, an exchange. [SE *switch* + -EROO sfx]

switch-hitter *n.* [1960s+] (*orig. US*) a bisexual. [baseball jargon *switch-hitter*, an ambidextrous batter]

switching *n.* [mid-late 19C] a marriage. [SWISHED *adj.*]

switch off! *excl.* [1900s–20s] shut up! be quiet! [electrical imagery]

switch on *v.* [1960s+] **1** (*US drugs*) to become intoxicated by drugs. **2** (*US*) to excite, to arouse sexually. **3** (*US*) to participate in the latest cultural trends. [electrical imagery]

switch up *v.* [1910s+] to fail, to malfunction.

swive *v.* **1** [18C+] to have sexual intercourse. **2** [mid-18C] to have anal intercourse (cf. ASK FOR THE RING *v.*). [OE *swīfan*, to move in a course + ON *svífa*, to rove, to ramble, to drift. Coined *c.*1440, *swive* was SE until *c.*1700. Like a number of 'obscenities' it is not genuine sl., but was for many years excluded from SE dictionaries as a taboo vulgarism]

swivel *n.* [1930s] a glance, a look at. [the head *swivels*]

swivel-eye *n.* **1** [mid-19C] a squint. **2** [late 19C] a swindler, a term of abuse.

swivel-eyed *adj.* **1** [late 18C+] squint-eyed. **2** [late 19C] a general term of abuse.

swivelly *adj.* [late 19C] drunk.

swivel-neck *n.* [1970s–80s] (*N.Z. prison*) a passive male homosexual. [the head swivels up and down when giving oral sex]

swivet *n.* [late 19C+] (*US*) an irritable mood. [dial. *swivet*, haste, hurry, passion]

swiz *n.*[1] (*also* **swizz**) [19C] intoxicating liquor. [abbr. SWIZZLE *n.*[1] (1)]

swiz *n.*[2] (*also* **swizz, swizzle**) [1910s+] (*mainly UK teen*) a fraud, a hoax, a disappointment. [SE *swindle*]

swiz *n.*[3] (*also* **swizz**) [1930s–50s] (*Aus.*) an excellent, first-rate thing. [SWINJER *n.*]

swiz *v.* (*also* **swizz**) [1950s] (*mainly UK teen*) to cheat, to swindle. [SWIZ *n.*[2]]

swizzle *n.*[1] [mid-18C–mid-19C] **1** any form of intoxicating liquor. **2** (*US*) a mix of spruce ('Prussian') beer, rum and sugar.

swizzle *n.*[2] *see* SWIZ *n.*[2].

swizzle *v.*[1] [mid-late 19C] to drink. [SWIZZLE *n.*[1] (1)]

swizzle *v.*[2] [1930s] to hoax, to trick. [SWIZ *v.*]

swizzled *adj.* (*also* **swazzled, swozzled**) [mid-19C+] drunk. [SWIZZLE *v.*[1]]

swizzler *n.* [1930s+] a cheater, a swindler. [SWIZZLE *v.*[2]]

swizzy *n.* [late 18C] any form of intoxicating drink. [var. on SWIZZLE *n.*[1] (1)]

swizzy *v.* [mid-late 19C] to drink. [SWIZZY *n.*]

swob *see also under* SWAB.

swob! *excl.* [1910s–20s] a general excl. of intensification and affirmation. [var. on S'ELP ME (BOB)! excl.]

swobble *v. see* SWABBLE *v.*

swock *v.* [1960s] (*US*) to hit, to attack. [dial. *swack*, a blow]

swoddy *n. see* SWADDY *n.*

swod-gill *n. see* SWAD-GILL *n.*

swole *adj.* [1990s+] (*US campus*) muscled. [SE *swollen*]

swoll *adj.* (*also* **swole**) [2000s] (*US prison*) angry.

swonie *n. see* SWOON UNIT *n.*

swoon! *excl.* [1980s+] (*US campus*) an excl. of approval used by a woman on seeing an attractive man.

swooner *n.* [1950s] (*US Black*) a very attractive person. [he causes girls to *swoon*]

swoon time *n.* [1950s] (*US Black*) a time of day when young people meet to chat and enjoy themselves.

swoon unit *n.* (*also* **swonie**) [1990s+] (*US teen*) a particularly attractive woman. [SE *swoon*, to faint]

swoony *adj.* [1930s+] distractingly attractive, delightful. [lit. inducing a *swoon*]

swoop *v.* **1** [1920s+] (*US Black*) to move fast, to approach or leave quickly. **2** [1950s+] (*US Black*) to steal someone else's lover, esp. when the manoeuvre is conducted quickly. **3** [1960s–80s] (*N.Z. prison*) to steal, to take; to arrest. **4** [1960s+] (*US campus*) to overtake in a car. **5** [1970s+] (*US Black*) to assault in a group. **6** [1970s+] (*US Black/campus*) to make a pass at, to make sexual advances towards.

swooper *n.* [1990s+] (*UK prison*) a prisoner who is constantly swooping down to pick up discarded cigarette ends.

swop *see also under* SWAP and its combs.

swop me...! *excl. see* S'ELP ME (BOB)! *excl.*

swop slob *v.* [1940s] (*US Black/campus*) to kiss. [abbr. SE *swap slobber*]

sword *n.* [late 16C–mid-19C; 1970s+] the penis (cf. AX *n.*²). [note D'Urfey, *Pills to Purge Melancholy* (1719–20): 'Brave Carpet Knights in *Cupid*'s Fights, their milk-white Rapiers drew']

sword fight *n.* [1990s+] a primarily male party. [SWORD *n.*]

sword-fighter *n.* [1970s+] (*UK juv.*) a male homosexual; thus swordfighting, mutual masturbation (cf. BONE-EATER *n.*). [SWORD *n.*]

swordfish *n.* [mid-19C] (*US*) a form of liquor.

sword-racket *n.* [early 19C] a means of making money by enlisting in a regiment, taking the bounty, deserting and moving on to a new regiment. [SE *sword* + RACKET *n.*¹ (1)]

swordsman *n.* [1950s+] a male sexual athlete. [SWORD *n.*; Williams notes a similar 17C use of *fencer*]

sword-swallower *n.* **1** [1940s] (*Aus.*) one who eats from his knife. **2** [1960s+] (*orig. Aus.*) a fellator or fellatrix; thus *swallow a sword*, to fellate. [SWORD *n.* + SE *swallow*]

sword-swallowing *n.* [1910s] (*US*) eating.

sworn at Highgate *phr.* [late 18C–early 19C] clever, smart. ['a ridiculous custom formerly prevailed at the public houses in Highgate [then a village north of London], to administer a ludicrous oath to all travellers of the middling rank who stopped there. The party was sworn on a pair of horns, fastened on a stick, the substance of the oath was never to kiss the maid when he could kiss the mistress, never to drink small beer when he could get strong, with many other injunctions of the like kind to all of which was added the saving clause of "unless you like it best"' (Grose, 1785)]

swosh *n.* [late 19C–1920s] rubbish, nonsense. [HOGWASH *n.*]

swot *n.* (*also* **swat**) [mid-19C+] a hard worker. [SWOT (UP) *v.*]

swotter *n.* [1900s–10s] a very hard worker. [SWOT (UP) *v.*]

swot (up) *v.* (*also* **swat (up)**) [mid-19C+] to work extremely hard, esp. on the eve of examinations or tests. [supposedly via Dr William Wallace, an instructor at the Royal Military College, Sandhurst, whose Scot. pron. turned the word 'sweat' (as in work that is so hard as to make one sweat) into *swot*. The 20C+ implication is slightly derog. – to work harder than seen as necessary by your peers]

'swounds! *excl.* (*also* **'swouns!**) [late 16C–early 17C] a mild oath, lit. 'God's wounds'.

swozzled *adj. see* SWIZZLED *adj.*

swret-sio *n. see* SRET-SIO *n.*

swuft *adj.* [1970s] (*US campus*) smart, clever, cunning. [var. on SWIFT *adj.* (3)]

swy *n.* (*also* **swi**) [1920s+] **1** the number 2, esp. a 2-shilling (10p) coin or a 2-year prison sentence. **2** (*also* **swy game, swy-up**) (*Aus.*) the game of two-up; thus *swy school*, a group of persons who have gathered to play two-up. [Ger. *zwei*, 2]

sycher *n.* (*also* **zoucher**) [late 19C] an objectionable, unpleasant person. [dial. *sycher*, a bad man]

Sydney blanket *n.* [late 19C+] (*Aus.*) a rough blanket, used by vagrants and tramps and made of a sack or bag.

Sydney duck *n.* (*also* **Sydney cove**) [mid-19C] (*US*) an Australian who joined the Californian Gold Rush of 1849; thus a former Aus. convict who pursued his villainies in San Francisco.

Sydney Harbour *n.* (*also* **coff's harbour, Dover harbour**) [1920s+] (*Aus./US*) a barber. [rhy. sl.]

Sydney or the bush *phr.* [20C+] (*Aus.*) all or nothing. [the comparison between making a fast fortune in the big city or eking out a much harder life in the outback]

Sydneysider *n.* (*Aus.*) **1** [mid–late 19C] a convict. **2** [mid-19C+] a native of New South Wales; thus *adj. Sydneyside*. [*Sydney*, the state capital]

syebuck *n.* [mid-18C–mid-19C] a sixpence.

sylvester *n.* [1950s] (*US Black*) a White man.

Sylvester (Stallone) *adj.* [1990s+] alone. [rhy. sl.; ult. US film actor *Sylvester Stallone* (b.1946)]

sympathy *n.* [20C+] sexual caresses. [a pun on 'a fellow feeling']

sympathy sticks *n.* [1940s] (*US Und.*) a beggar's crutches.

synagogue *n.* [late 19C] a shed – its use is not specified – standing at that time in the northeast corner of Covent Garden, London WC2. [by late 19C, Covent Garden market was very much a Jewish enterprise]

synagogue twins *n.* [1930s] (*US*) ham and eggs. [mocking the Jewish prohibition of pork]

syntax *n.* [late 18C–early 19C] a schoolmaster. [SE; popularized through *The Tour of Dr Syntax* (1813) by William Combe]

synth *n.* [1970s+] a synthesizer. [abbr.]

syph *n.* (*also* **sif(f), siph, the syphs**) [late 19C+] syphilis; thus *adj., syphy.* [abbr.]

sypho *n.* **1** [1910s+] (*Aus.*) syphilis. **2** [1970s+] (*US gay*) a syphilitic. [abbr. SE *syphilis* + -o sfx (4)]

syphon the python *v. see* SIPHON THE PYTHON *v.*

syphy *adj. see* SYPH *n.*

syrup *n.* **1** [1900s] alcohol, a drink. **2** [1930s] (*US*) nitroglycerin, as used as an explosive.

syrup (of figs) *n.* **1** [1970s+] a wig. **2** [1980s] (*Aus.*) an eavesdropper. [rhy. sl.; (1) = SE *wig*; (2) = FIZGIG *n.*²]

S.Y.T. *n.* [1970s] (*US gay*) a teenage male homosexual. [*sweet young thing*]

T

T *n*.[1] [1950s+] (*drugs*) marijuana (cf. AFRICAN BUSH n.). [abbr. TEA n.[2] (1)]

T *n*.[2] **1** [1960s+] (*US drugs*) a gram of methamphetamine. **2** [1970s] phencyclidine (cf. ACE n.[4]). **3** [1970s+] (*also* tee) Tuinal. [abbr.; (2) = PCP which is misreading of THC, i.e. tetra*hydro*cannabinol]

T *n*.[3] (*also* tee) [1970s+] (*orig. US*) a T-shirt. [abbr.]

t.a. *see under* TITS AND ASS.

ta *phr*. [late 18C+] thank you; thus (*S.Afr.*) *ta for niks*, thanks for nothing; *ta, hey!* thank you very much! *no ta, hey!* absolutely not, thank you very much! [orig. juv.; 'Ex a young child's difficulty with *th* and *nks*' (E.P.)]

tab *n*.[1] (*also* tabhole) [mid-19C+] the human ear. [dial.]

tab *n*.[2] **1** [late 19C–1910s] an elderly woman. **2** [1910s+] (*Aus.*) a young woman. [TABBY n.]

tab *n*.[3] **1** [late 19C+] (*US*) the bill, credit, an IOU, used fig. to imply that an action, good or bad, will be paid for later. **2** [20C+] (*US prison*) any form of prison documentation, esp. reports on prisoners that are submitted to the parole board. **3** [1930s–40s] (*US prison*) letters passed between inmates; a letter smuggled out of prison. [abbr. SE *table*]

tab *n*.[4] [1910s+] a cigarette. [dial. *tab*, the pointed end of anything]

tab *n*.[5] [1930s–40s] (*US*) a project, a line of activity, a programme; thus I AIN'T COMING (ON THAT TAB) phr.

tab *n*.[6] [1930s+] a *tab*loid newspaper. [abbr.]

tab *n*.[7] (*drugs*) **1** [1950s+] a *tab*let, esp. one containing a hallucinogenic drug (cf. PILL n.[4]). **2** [1980s] a dose of LSD in non-tablet form. [abbr.]

tab, the *n*. [1980s] (*Aus.*) the *Totalizator Agency Board*. [abbr.]

tab *v*.[1] (*also* tab up) (*US*) **1** [late 19C–1940s] to charge with a crime. **2** [1910s+] to identify, to categorize. **3** [1920s] to survey a place prior to robbing it. [abbr. SE *tabulate*]

tab *v*.[2] [1920s–40s] to follow a person, to place someone under surveillance. [KEEP TABS ON v.]

tab action *n*. (*also* tab issue) [1940s] (*US Black*) a line of credit at a bar or any other type of business. [TAB n.[3] (1) + ACTION n. (3)/ACTION sfx/SE *issue*]

tabankca *n*. (*also* tabanka) [20C+] (*W.I.*) love-sickness, sexual obsession. [? Fr. *t'as bon ça*, you are good]

tabankca *adj*. [20C+] (*W.I.*) passionate, obsessed. [TABANKCA n.]

tabasco *n*. [1920s] spirit. [play on *Tabasco* hot sauce]

tabasco *adj*. [1920s] excited, dramatic, 'hot'. [play on *Tabasco* hot sauce]

tabbed *adj*. [1970s+] (*US Black*) well-dressed. [? SE *tab*, a label]

tabbed to the bone *phr*. [1970s+] (*US Black*) dressed in one's very best, most fashionable clothes. [TABBED adj. + TO THE BONE phr.]

tabby *n*. **1** [late 17C+] an old lady, usu. as a pej.; thus *tabbyism*, acting as a querulous, interfering old woman. **2** [early 19C; 1910s–50s] a young woman, esp. an attractive one. **3** [1930s] (*US Und.*) a prostitute (cf. ALLEY CAT n.). [SE *tabby cat*, ult. *tabby*, striped or watered silk (orig. produced in the Baghdad suburb of Attabiy),

and thus applied to the colouring of the cat; thus theatrical jargon *tabs*, an old woman; note Aus. WW1 milit. *tabby*, a woman (irrespective of age)]

tabby *adj*. [1920s] (*US*) **1** interfering, inquisitive, judgemental. **2** like an old woman. [TABBY n. (1)]

tabby meeting *n*. [late 19C–1900s] a meeting of evangelists and their congregations at Exeter Hall, London. [? proper name *Tabitha*, a typically 'religious' name; note TABBY n. (1)]

tabby party *n*. [19C] a party consisting only of women. [TABBY n. (1) + SE *party*]

tabhole *n*. *see* TAB n.[1].

tab issue *n*. *see* TAB ACTION n.

table-end man *n*. [late 19C+] a man whose sexual desire is so intense that he makes love to his partner over the dining/kitchen table rather than waiting until they reach the bedroom.

table-hop *v*. [1950s+] (*orig. US*) to circulate among the tables at a restaurant, greeting and chatting with friends and acquaintances.

table-hopper *n*. *see* TABLE-TOPPER n.

tablet *n*. [1990s+] an MDMA tablet (cf. ECSTASY n.).

table-tapper *n*. [20C+] (*US*) an unprofessional, part-time lay preacher. [their thumping of the *table* as they preach]

table-topper *n*. (*also* table-hopper) [1980s+] a necrophile. [the mortuary *table* or slab]

t.a.b.u. *n*. *see* S.A.B.U. n.

tab up *v*. *see* TAB v.[1].

tac *n*. [1960s+] (*drugs*) phencyclidine (cf. ACE n.[4]). [PCP is a misappropriation of initials *THC*, i.e. tetra*hydro*cannabinol]

tach *n*.[1] [mid-19C] a hat. [backsl.]

tach *n*.[2] (*also* tacho, tack) [1960s+] a *tach*ometer, an instrument that measures the velocity of machines. [abbr.]

tache *n*. *see* TASH n.

tack *n*.[1] [mid-19C+] (*later use Irish*) anything mouldy or sour, esp. a taste (in food or drink) that is other than one expects. [SE *tack*, an alien, odd or unpleasant flavour; ? ult. Lat. *tactus*, infection]

tack *n*.[2] **1** [mid-19C+] (*orig. naut.*) food, ship's biscuit. **2** [late 19C+] drink. **3** [1950s] money. [? SE *tackle*]

tack *n*.[3] **1** [1930s–60s] (*US Black*) a nickel, 5 cents. **2** [1950s+] (*W.I. Rasta*) a bullet.

tack *n*.[4] (*US Black*) **1** [1950s–60s] a fool. **2** [1950s–60s] a conservative. **3** [1950s+] an unsophisticated person. **4** [1960s–70s] a clever person. [? SE *tacit*, silent; (4) phr. *smart as a tack*]

tack *n*.[5] [1980s+] (*orig. US*) bad taste; thus [1990s+] *tack attack*, a rush of bad taste or an experience of bad taste. [TACKY adj.[1]]

tack *n*.[6] [1990s+] (*US Und.*) a (prison-created) tattoo.

tack *n*.[7] *see* TACH n.[2].

tack *v*. [late 17C–19C] to join in marriage.

tacked down *adj*. [1960s–70s] (*US Black*) well-dressed. [SE *tack*, to join]

tacker *n*. [1940s+] (*Aus.*) a small boy. [dial. *tacker*, a child]

tackhead *n*. (*also* tacky, tackyhead) **1** [20C+] (*US*) a stupid person. **2** [20C+] (*US*) an overdressed or excessively stylish person.

3 [1960s+] (*US Black*) an unattractive, unkempt woman. **4** [1990s+] (*US*) a troublemaker. [TACKY adj.¹ + -HEAD sfx (1); (3) equating ill-kempt or unfashionable hair with an unappetizing person]

tackie *n. see* TAKKIE n.

tackie *v.* [1990s+] (*S.Afr.*) to drive fast, to accelerate. [S.Afr.E. *fat tackie*, a large tyre, used for racing or beach-driving]

tackle *n.*¹ **1** [mid-16C–19C; 1980s+] the genitals. **2** [early 17C–mid-19C] one's best clothes. **3** [late 17C–mid-19C] a prostitute, a mistress (cf. BANGTAIL n.¹). **4** [19C+] any clothes. **5** [mid-19C–1900s] food or drink. **6** [1980s+] (*Ulster*) a showily or bizarrely dressed woman. **7** [2000s] drugs. [SE *tackle*, equipment, appliances etc]

tackle *n.*² [late 19C–1940s] a watch chain; often as TOY AND TACKLE n.

tackle *n.*³ [1980s+] (*Ulster*) **1** a cantankerous, verbally abusive woman. **2** a difficult child. [SE *tackle*, to handle; here one who is 'hard to tackle']

tackle *v.* **1** [early 19C–1910s] to grip, to lay hold of. **2** [mid-19C–1910s] to attack. **3** [mid-19C–1920s] to take in hand, to deal with. **4** [mid-19C–1960s] to enter into a discussion with, to approach or question some subject. **5** [mid-19C+] to grapple with, to attempt to deal with. **6** [late 19C–1910s] to fall upon (food), to eat. **7** [1950s+] (*W.I.*) to get to know someone with the specific aim of initiating an affair.

tack together *v.* [mid-18C–19C] to marry. [ext. of TACK v.]

tack up *v.* [2000s] (*US prison*) to approach someone in a confrontational manner.

tacky *n. see* TACKHEAD n.

tacky *adj.*¹ **1** [mid-19C+] (*orig. US*) unattractive, second-rate. **2** [late 19C+] off-putting, in poor taste. **3** [1900s] (*US campus*) drunk. **4** [1900s] (*US campus*) untidy, unkempt. [ety. unknown; ? link to SAmE *tack*, a run-down horse, a poor Southern White]

tacky *adj.*² [1950s] (*W.I.*) **1** tricky, hard to beat, cunning. **2** good, skilled, clever. [SE *tack*, a new or altered course or line of action, endurance, stability, strength]

tackyhead *n. see* TACKHEAD n.

taco *n.* **1** [1960s+] (*US*) a derog. term for a Mexican; also used adj. to stereotype anything 'Mexican', i.e. cheap, stupid and/or lazy (cf. BEAN n.⁸). **2** [1980s] (*US Black/L.A.*) used as a derog. to a fellow Black; the premise being one is no better than a Mexican. [Sp. *taco*, a fried, unleavened cornmeal pancake or tortilla holding a variety of seasoned fillings, a popular Mexican food]

taco (bell) *n.* [1990s+] (*US teen*) the penis (cf. BURRITO n.). [play on *Taco Bell*, chain of US restaurants selling Mexican fast food/BELL END n.]

taco belle *n.* [1980s+] a Latin American woman. [TACO n. (1) + SE *belle* + pun on *Taco Bell* (see prev.)]

taco-eater *n.* (*also* **taco-bender**) [1960s+] (*US*) a derog. term for a Mexican, a Chicano (cf. BEAN n.⁸). [Sp. *taco* + SE *eater/bender*; see TACO n.]

taco-head *n.* [1960s+] (*US*) a derog. term for a Mexican or a Chicano (cf. BEAN n.⁸). [TACO n. (1) + -HEAD sfx (2)]

tacoland *n.* [1960s+] a derog. name for that part of a town in which the Mexicans live. [TACO n. (1) + SE *land*]

taco queen *n.* [1970s+] (*US gay*) a White homosexual who prefers Hispanic partners. [TACO n. (1) + QUEEN n.² (1)/QUEEN sfx (2)]

Taco Town *n.* (*also* **Tamaleville**) [1960s+] (*US*) a derog. term for San José, US. [TACO n. (1) + SE *town*, the Mexican population/ SAmE *tamale*, a Mexican dish consisting of corn husks wrapped around a variety of fillings + SE sfx -*ville*]

tacou *adj.* [20C+] (*W.I.*) foolish, stupid. [ety. unknown]

taco wagon *n.* [1960s+] (*US*) a derog. term for a car with its rear end lowered. [TACO n. (1) + SE *wagon*; such cars are popular among Mexican youths]

tad *n.*¹ **1** [mid-19C–1900s] (*US*) one who attempts to avoid paying a bill. **2** [mid-19C+] (*US*) a person, esp. a young boy. **3** [1940s+]

(*orig. US*) a small amount; usu. as *a tad*, slightly. [ety. unknown; ? SE *tadpole*]

tad *n.*² [20C+] (*US*) an Irish Catholic. [*Thaddeus*, a popular Irish name]

tad blame it! *excl.* [1950s] (*US*) a euph. for GOD-DAMN IT! excl.

taddler *n.* [1900s–20s] **1** a large sausage. **2** the penis. [? link to TADGER n.]

tadger *n.* (*also* **todger**, **togger**) [late 19C+] the penis. [northern UK dial.]

tad-larruping *adj. see* LARRUPING adj.

tadpole *n.* [mid-19C–1940s] (*US*) a native of Mississippi.

tadpole carrier *n.* [1990s+] the scrotum (cf. BALL-BAG n.). [sperm's resemblance to tadpoles]

taepo *n. see* TAIPO n.

taf *adj.* (*also* **taff**, **taffy**) [mid–late 19C] fat. [backsl.]

Tafee *n. see* TAFFY n.

Taff *n.* [mid-17C; mid-19C+] a Welshman, also as a direct term of address. [abbr. TAFFY n.]

taffeta girl *n. see* TIFFITY-TAFFETY n.

Taffy *n.* (*also* **Tafee**, **Taffie**) [early 17C+] a Welshman or a nickname for a Welshman; thus *Taffy's day*, St David's Day; *Taffyland*, Wales. [Welsh *Dafydd*, David]

taffy *n.*¹ [late 19C–1920s] (*US*) insincere and obvious flattery. [SE *taffy*, toffee]

taffy *n.*² (*also* **taffy goat/ram**) [1900s–50s] (*W.I.*) an old person. [? the white ram that is the regimental symbol of the Royal Welch Fusiliers regiment, which has been stationed in Jamaica. This use, lit. an 'old goat', is used respectfully]

taffy *adj.*¹ [1970s+] Welsh. [TAFFY n.]

taffy *adj.*² *see* TAF adj.

taffy *v.* [late 19C] (*US*) to tease. [TAFFY n.¹]

taffy goat *n. see* TAFFY n.².

taffy-head *n.* [1970s] a braggart, a boaster, a 'big-head'. [TAFFY n.¹ + -HEAD sfx (1)]

taffy ram *n. see* TAFFY n.².

taffy-tugger *n.* [1990s+] a masturbator. [TUG ONE'S TAFFY v.]

tag *n.*¹ **1** [mid-19C] a servant, esp. an under-servant who assists another. **2** [1960s+] one who 'tags along' behind another person, esp. for detective or spying purposes. [SE *tag along*]

tag *n.*² [mid–late 19C] an actor. [the SE *tag* or 'moral' added to the end of a play]

tag *n.*³ **1** [1920s+] (*UK/US Black*) a name. **2** [1930s] (*US prison*) a letter smuggled out of prison. **3** [1930s+] a vehicle number-plate. **4** [1930s+] (*US Und.*) an arrest warrant. **5** [1940s] a car licence. **6** [1960s+] a label commonly given to a person or thing. **7** [1980s+] the 'signature' used by a graffiti artist, spraying their name on walls, subway trains etc. **8** [2000s] (*US prison*) a piece of information. [SE *tag*, a label]

tag *v.*¹ **1** [1910s+] to punch. **2** [1930s+] to arrest. **3** [1950s+] to imprison. **4** [1950s+] to blame, to accuse. **5** [1960s+] to identify. **6** [1970s] in fig. use, to suffer, to be punished. **7** [1980s] to give a parking ticket. **8** [2000s] (*US Black*) of a man, to have sexual intercourse. [SE *tag*, to label]

tag *v.*² (*also* **tag up**) [1980s+] (*orig. US*) of graffiti artists, to affix one's name to a picture, a wall etc. [TAG n.³ (7)]

tag-a-long *n.* [1950s–60s] (*Aus.*) a girl- or boyfriend.

tagger *n.* [1980s+] one who writes their TAG n.³ (7) or personal label on walls and other visible sites, a graffiti artist. [TAG v.²]

tagnuts *n.* [1990s+] small pieces of excrement adhering to the anal hairs (cf. CLAGNUT n.).

tag up *v. see* TAG v.².

Taig *n.* (*also* **Tague**, **Teague**, **Teg**, **Teig**) [mid-17C+] **1** a Roman Catholic, spec. as used by Protestants in Northern Ireland. **2** a generic term for an Irishman (cf. DONOVAN n.¹). [Irish name *Tadhg*, usu. rendered as Thaddeus in English]

tail *n.*¹ **1** [late 13C–19C] the train attached to a woman's dress, usu. for formal use only. **2** [16C–19C] (*UK Und.*) the tail of a man's coat, usu. in the context of pickpocketing; thus *tail kick*, the pocket in a tailcoat. [SE *tail* of an animal; both SE until 18C]

tail *n.*² **1** [14C+] the posterior, the buttocks; thus in fig. use synon. with ARSE n.¹ (4)/ASS n. (5), oneself. **2** [mid-14C–1940s] the penis; thus synons. *tail-pike*, *tail-pin*, *tail-tackle*, *tail-trimmers*. **3** [mid-15C+] (*also* **tale**) the vagina; thus synons. *tail-gap*, *tail-gate*, *tail-hole*; also *tail-feathers*, pubic hair; *tail-fruit*, children; *tail-juice*, urine; *tale-bearer*, a prostitute; *tail-trading*, prostitution; *tail-wagging*, *tail-work*, sexual intercourse. **4** [late 18C+] a prostitute (cf. BANGTAIL n.¹). **5** [1910s+] women viewed collectively and as sex objects; thus PIECE OF TAIL n. **6** [1930s+] sexual intercourse. **7** [1940s] young boys viewed collectively as suitable for homosexual relationships. **8** [1950s+] a woman. [(1) SE until 1750; (2) and (3) SE until 18C]

tail *n.*³ [late 17C–mid-19C] (*UK Und.*) a sword; thus TAIL-DRAWER n. [the way it projects beyond the wearer's body]

tail *n.*⁴ **1** [20C+] (*orig. US*) one who carries out a surveillance, esp. when following the target in the street. **2** [1910s+] (*also* **tail job**) an act of surveillance. **3** [1970s] (*US prison*) an informer. [they become a SE *tail*]

tail *n.*⁵ [1990s+] (*drugs*) the long-term effect of a drug, as opposed to the initial RUSH n.³ (1).

tail *n.*⁶ [1990s+] (*US prison*) parole.

tail *v.*¹ [late 18C+] to have sexual intercourse with, to work as a prostitute. [TAIL n.² (4)]

tail *v.*² [20C+] to follow, to keep under (police) surveillance. [TAIL n.⁴]

tail ass *v. see* HAUL ASS v.

tailbone *n.* [20C+] (*US*) the buttocks. [ext. of TAIL n.² (1)]

tail-buzzer *n.* (*also* **tail-dip/-diver**) [mid–late 19C] (*UK Und.*) a thief who specializes in the picking of coat pockets. [TAIL n.¹ (2) + BUZZER n.¹/DIP n.⁴ (1)/DIVE v.¹]

tail-buzzing *n.* [mid–late 19C] (*UK Und.*) stealing a wallet from a tailcoat pocket. [TAIL-BUZZER n.]

tail-chaser *n.* [1940s+] (*US*) a womanizer. [TAIL n.² (5) + SE *chaser*]

tail-dip/-diver *n. see* TAIL-BUZZER n.

taildraft *n.* [20C+] (*Ulster*) an idler, one who holds back. [SE *tail* + *draught/draft*, the act of pulling]

tail-drawer *n.* [late 17C–early 19C] (*UK Und.*) a thief who steals gentlemen's swords from their sides. [TAIL n.³ + SE *drawer*]

tail-end charlie *n.* [1940s+] the person or vehicle that comes last in a queue. [RAF jargon *tail-end charlie*, a tail-gunner, the last aircraft in a flying formation]

tail fodder *n. see* BUM-FODDER n. (1).

tailgate *v.* **1** [1950s+] to drive a car closely (too closely) behind the one in front. **2** [1970s+] in fig. use, to follow, esp. of things that are endlessly repetitive. **3** [1990s+] (*US campus*) to watch women passing by. [SAmE *tailgate*, the tailboard of a truck or wagon]

tailgater *n.* [1960s+] (*US*) **1** a hijacker. **2** one who drives too close to the car in front. [(1) the hijacker stops the truck, lowers the *tailgate* and removes the load; (2) TAILGATE v. (1)]

tailgunner *n.* [1940s+] (*US*) a male homosexual. [TAIL n.² (1) + SE *gunner*]

tailie *n.* [1910s+] (*Aus.*) in the game of two-up, one who favours betting on 'tails' (cf. HEADIE n.). [SE *tail*, of a coin]

tailing *n.* [late 19C+] sexual intercourse. [TAIL v.¹]

tail it *v.* [1920s+] to die. [SE *tail*, the end]

tail job *n. see* TAIL n.⁴ (2).

tail light alley *n.* [1940s+] (*Aus.*) a Lovers' Lane, used by 'parking' couples. [the SE *tail lights* of the parked car but note pun on TAIL n.² (3)]

tailman *n.* [1960s] (*US campus*) a womanizer, a sexual athlete. [TAIL n.² (5) + SE *man*]

tail-off *n.* [1970s+] a lowering of demand, a withering away. [SE *tail off*]

tailor *n.* [1920s+] (*US prison/Aus.*) a factory-made cigarette,

whether prison-issue or commercially produced. [abbr. TAILOR-MADE n. (2)]

tailor *v.* [late 19C–1900s] to shoot badly at birds so as to wound rather than actually kill them. [? snobbish dismissal of 'trade' shooters; or one 'cuts them up']

tailor-made *n.* **1** [late 19C–1900s] (*US*) a personally tailored garment. **2** [1920s+] (*mainly US prison*) a factory-produced cigarette.

tailor's helper *n.* [1930s] (*US tramp*) a vicious dog.

tailor's ragout *n.* [late 18C–early 19C] bread soaked in the dressing in which cucumbers have stood. [? its popularity with tailors; they could not afford a proper meat ragout]

tail out *v.* [late 19C] (*US*) to run away, to make one's escape. [SE *tail*/TAIL n.² (1), i.e. one 'moves one's arse']

tailpiece *n.* [mid-19C] (*UK Und.*) 3 months' imprisonment.

tailpipe *n.* [1990s+] (*US*) the anus. [SE *tailpipe* + pun on TAIL n.² (1)]

tail pit *n.* [1900s–30s] (*US Und.*) a side pocket.

tails *n.* [late 19C+] a formal tailcoat; thus *white tie and tails*. [abbr.; note TAIL n.¹ (2)]

tail tea *n.* [late 19C] (*UK society*) an afternoon tea attended by aristocratic ladies who had already been at the day's 'royal drawing room' (Queen Victoria's formal receptions) where trains were a part of formal dress. [TAIL n.¹ (1) + SE *tea*. Once Victoria had died, her son Edward VII (r.1901–10) moved the 'drawing rooms' to the evening, a time more congenial to his own lifestyle]

tail timber *n.* [late 19C] lavatory paper. [TAIL n.² (1) + SE *timber*]

tail-trader *n.* [19C] a prostitute (cf. ASS PEDDLER n.; BANGTAIL n.¹). [TAIL n.² (3) + SE *trader*]

tail-tree *n.* [mid-18C–19C] the penis. [TAIL n.² (2) + SE *tree*]

tail-wagger *n.* [1940s+] **1** a dog. **2** a general insult. [(2) is synon. with the pej. use of SE *cur*]

tail water *n.* [18C] urine. [TAIL n.² (2)/TAIL n.² (3) + SE *water*]

tail-worker *n.* [19C] a prostitute (cf. BANGTAIL n.¹). [TAIL n.² (3) + SE *worker*/WORKER n.¹ (1)]

t'aint *n.* (*also* **taint, taintmeat, tent**) [1970s+] (*orig. US*) the perineum, the space between the vagina and the anus. [i.e. *t'aint pussy and t'aint asshole*]

taipo *n.* (*also* **taepo**) [mid-19C+] (*N.Z.*) a vicious horse, often used as the name for a dog. [? Maori *taepo*, the Devil, but ? pidgin f. Maori pron. of SE *devil*]

taj *adj.* [late 19C–1910s] (*UK teen*) excellent, wonderful, luscious. [abbr. proper name *Taj Mahal*, synon. with fabulous luxury]

take *n.*¹ **1** [late 19C+] (*orig. US*) money acquired by theft or fraud, bribery; thus ON THE TAKE phr. **2** [1930s+] (*US*) a share of money that is deducted for tax or some other form of levy. **3** [1930s+] (*US*) a portion, an extract, a bit. **4** [1930s+] (*US*) profits, e.g. the entrance money taken at a musical, sporting or gambling event. **5** [1930s+] (*Aus.*) a thief, a villain, esp. a cheat at cards. **6** [1930s+] (*Aus.*) a swindle. **7** [1930s+] (*Aus./US*) a theft, a robbery. **8** [1990s+] wages.

take *n.*² [1950s+] (*US*) an opinion, a view, e.g. *what's your take on it?* [abbr. SE *take a stance*]

take *n.*³ [1990s+] a parody. [SE *take*, a continuous section of film photographed at one time]

take *v.*¹ [late 17C+] to succeed, to become popular. [SE *take*, of a plant, to start flourishing]

take *v.*² [19C+] to become, to fall into a state of, e.g. *take ill*, *take sick*. [note late 17C nonce use *take with child*, to become pregnant]

take *v.*³ **1** [mid-19C+] to swindle, to cheat, to extort money from; often ext. as TAKE SOMEONE FOR v. **2** [late 19C+] to overcome, to defeat, to kill. **3** [1920s+] to accept bribery. **4** [1920s+] to break in, to rob. **5** [1920s+] to confront, to attack.

take *v.*⁴ [20C+] to accept, to put up with (something or someone), used esp. in negative, e.g. *I'm not taking that*.

take *v.*⁵ [1940s+] (*US Und.*) to take the passive role in homosexual anal intercourse.

take a back seat *v.* [late 19C+] to accept without complaint a subordinate, second-rate position.

take a bag *v.* [1960s] (*US campus*) to experience an undesirable situation.

take a bath *v.* (*also* **take a beating**) [1930s+] to lose or suffer badly, esp. in business, sport or gambling.

take a bit of doing *v.* (*also* **take a lot of doing, take some doing**) [1910s+] to require all one's efforts, to be difficult to do.

take a blinder *v.* [mid-19C–1900s] to die. [lit. 'take a blind leap' into the next world]

take a blue *v.* [1910s] to drink a glass of absinthe.

take a box *v.* [1990s+] (*Irish*) to defecate.

take a brace *v.* [late 19C+] (*US*) to pull oneself together, to smarten up. [SE *brace*, used of straps, belts etc that tighten]

take a Brodie *v.* (*also* **do a Brodie**) [late 19C+] **1** to commit suicide. **2** to fail, to slip back into bad habits. [Steve *Brodie*, a 23-year-old New York saloon-keeper who on 23 July 1886 allegedly leaped some 45m (135ft) from the city's Brooklyn Bridge in order to win a $200 wager. He survived the fall and was scooped out of the East River by a friend in a small boat. He was subseq. charged by the police with attempted suicide. Whether he actually made the jump remains unproven (the witnesses, all of them his friends, claimed that he did, but the general consensus was that a dummy was tossed over the bridge and Brodie, hiding on shore, quickly swam underwater to the point where it had hit the river, in time to be 'rescued'). This scepticism is reflected in theatrical jargon; a *brodie*, a (much touted) flop]

take a burn *v. see* BURN *v.*[2] (6).

take a bust (at) *v.* [1920s+] (*US*) to hit (with the fist). [BUST n.[4]]

take a butcher's (at) *v. see* HAVE A BUTCHER'S (AT) *v.*

take a bye *v.* [20C+] (*US*) to refuse or decline to act or participate in something. [sporting imagery]

take a carrot! *excl.* [mid-19C] an insulting excl., usu. used to women. [the potential of a *carrot* as a dildo. Note naut. jargon *carrots!* go away!; note correspondence from John Geipel (7 June 2000): 'Partridge records the Victorian expression: "Take a carrot" (piss off), which may stem from the Romani root *kar*. The word *corey* (penis) is certainly known to English Romanies, (even the decorous George Borrow listed it in the two senses, "thorn" and "membrum virile") and John Sampson recorded such derivatives as *koriakeri* ("prick-hungry"), applied to a lustful woman by one tribe of Welsh Gypsies']

take a chill (pill) *v.* [1980s+] (*US Black/campus*) to relax, to calm down. [SE *take* + CHILL PILL n.]

take a count *v.* [1970s] (*US*) to be shocked. [boxing imagery; the number, from 1 to 10, indicates the intensity]

take a course with *v.* [early 17C–early 19C] **1** to cause problems for, to interfere with. **2** to follow closely.

take a crack at *v.*[1] *see* CRACK n.[5]

take a crack at *v.*[2] *see* HAVE A CRACK AT *v.*

take a crap *v.* [1920s+] to defecate. [CRAP n.[3]]

take a dim view *v.* [1940s+] (*orig. US milit.*) to disapprove.

take a dip *v.* [1980s+] (*US campus*) to chew tobacco. [SE *dip*, a pinch of snuff, thus ext. for chewing tobacco]

take a dirt nap *v.* [1990s+] (*US Black*) **1** to be buried. **2** to die. **3** to be knocked out.

take a dive *v.* (*orig. US*) **1** [1910s+] in boxing, or any competition, for a fighter deliberately to lose a fight (cf. GO IN THE TANK *v.*[1]). **2** [1980s+] to compromise oneself. **3** [1980s+] to fail. [one lit. + fig. *dives* to the canvas]

take a douche *v.* [1960s+] (*US teen*) to leave hurriedly; esp. as imper. *take a douche!* go away!

take a drop *v.*[1] [late 19C+] to run off. [one *drops* out of sight]

take a drop *v.*[2] *see* TAKE A FALL *v.*

take a drop on *v.* [late 19C] (*US*) to take control, to 'get a grip'.

take a drop to *v.* [late 19C+] to realize, to understand. [play on TUMBLE TO *v.*]

take a dump *v.* [1940s+] (*orig. US*) to defecate, usu. in sense of incontinence. [DUMP n.[4] (1)]

take a fall *v.* (*also* **get a fall, take a drop**) **1** [1920s+] (*US Und.*) to be arrested, to be imprisoned. **2** [1920s+] (*US*) to fall in love. **3** [1950s+] (*US*) to tumble, to slip over. **4** [1970s+] (*US*) to find oneself in difficulties, to come to grief.

take a fall out of *v.* (*also* **get a fall out of**) [late 19C–1910s] (*US/Aus.*) **1** to get the better of someone. **2** to involve oneself with something. **3** to reprimand someone.

take a fashion risk *v.* [1980s+] (*US campus*) to dress in an unfashionable or outlandish manner.

take a feather out of *v.* [20C+] (*Irish*) to confuse, to surprise, to astonish. [the pulling out of a *feather* will make a bird jump]

take a flier *v.* (*also* **take a flyer**) **1** [late 18C–19C] to have quick and spontaneous sexual intercourse with both parties fully or partially dressed. **2** [mid-19C+] to go out on a spree. **3** [late 19C+] (*US*) to take a chance, to gamble, esp. financially. **4** [20C+] (*US prison*) to escape from prison. **5** [1920s+] to fall heavily. **6** [1950s] to escape, to run away from. [SE *take a flying leap*]

take a flourish *v.* [late 18C–early 19C] to have swift and spontaneous sexual intercourse, usu. when both parties are wholly or partially dressed.

take a flying fuck *v.* (*also* **take a flying frig, …jump, …leap**) **1** [20C+] (*orig. US*) used in derisory, dismissive phrs.; also ext. by *…at a galloping goose; …rolling doughnut; …rubber duck; …the moon; …yourself.* **2** [1960s] (*US Black*) to leave, to travel. [FUCK n.[1] (1)/FRIG n. (3)/JUMP n.[3] (1)/SE *jump/leap*]

take a fright *n.* [mid–late 19C] the night. [rhy. sl.]

take a gander (at) *v.* [1930s+] (*orig. US*) to look at, to glance at. [GANDER n.[3]]

take a grinder *v.* [mid-19C] to make a coarse gesture similar to thumbing one's nose and using the other hand to work an imaginary coffee-grinder. [GRINDER n.[3]]

take a hand of *v. see* MAKE A HAND OF *v.*

take a harp *v.* [late 19C] (*US campus*) to die.

take a hike *v.* [20C+] (*orig. US*) to leave; esp. as imper. *take a hike!* [SE *hike*, to walk]

take a hinge at *v.* [1930s–50s] (*US*) to look at. [the turning of one's head]

take a holiday *v.* **1** [late 19C–1900s] to be dismissed. **2** [1950s+] to jump bail.

take a hosing *v.* [1940s+] (*US*) to be cheated or badly treated. [HOSE *v.*[1] (3)]

take a jerry (to) *v.* [1910s+] (*Aus./N.Z.*) to investigate and understand something, to work something out. [JERRY *v.*[1] (2)]

take a knock down *v.* [1950s] (*US Black*) to take note.

take a lark *v. see* GO ON A LARK *v.*

take a leaf out of someone's book *v.* (*also* **take a page out of someone's book, …from someone's book**) [mid-19C+] (*US*) to imitate or emulate someone.

take a leak *v.* (*also* **spring a leak**) [1910s+] to urinate (cf. BLEED ONE'S TURKEY *v.*). [LEAK n.[2] (1)]

take a leap in the dark *v.* [17C–early 18C] to be hanged. [note Thomas Brown, *Amusements Serious and Comical* (1702): 'A brother player, who pretends he received all his memoirs from your own mouth, a little before you made a leap into the dark', where the phr. simply means 'to die']

take a load of *v. see* GET A LOAD OF *v.*

take a load off one's feet *v.* [20C+] to sit down and rest, esp. used as an invitation.

take a lot of doing *v. see* TAKE A BIT OF DOING *v.*

take a Midol! *excl.* [1980s+] (*US campus*) relax! calm down! [brandname *Midol*, menstrual relief tablets]

take a mope *v. see* COP A MOPE *v.*

take an application *v.* (*also* **take a test drive**) [1960s–80s] (*US*) to interview a woman as a prospective prostitute.

take an attitude v. see COP AN ATTITUDE v.

take and give v. [late 19C–1900s] to live, esp. as man and wife. [rhy. sl.]

take a nose-dive v. [1920s+] to collapse, to fail utterly. [flying imagery]

take an outing with tom thumb and his four brothers v. [20C+] to masturbate (cf. CONVERSE WITH HARRY PALM v.).

take a passer v. [1970s] (US) to pass out, to faint.

take a pew phr. see PARK YOURSELF IN A PEW phr.

take a picture! excl. [1980s+] (US campus) stop staring!

take a piece out of v. [1940s+] (Aus.) **1** to scold, to reprimand severely. **2** to tease.

take a pill! excl. [1990s+] (US campus/teen) calm down! [abbr. TAKE A CHILL (PILL) v.]

take a pipe v. [late 19C] to cry. [PIPE v.[1] (2)]

take a poke at v. **1** [1910s+] (orig. US) to assault, to aim a blow at. **2** [1930s+] to have a try, to attempt. **3** [1950s] to attack verbally, to cause problems for.

take a pop (at) v. (also **have a pop (at)**) **1** [mid-19C] to fire a gun, to shoot at. **2** [1920s+] to make an attempt (at). **3** [1930s+] to hit (someone). **4** [1990s+] to attack verbally. [POP n.[3]; (1) note POP n.[1] (1)]

take a potshot at v. [1920s+] (orig. US) to criticize someone severely.

take a powder v. (also **do a powder**) **1** [1910s+] to escape, to run away; also as imper. *take a powder!* go away! **2** [1940s+] to leave without paying one's rent. **3** [1940s+] of a boxer, to lose deliberately. [abbr. TAKE A RUN-OUT POWDER v.]

take a pull v. [late 19C+] (orig. Aus.) to stop, to desist; thus *take a pull on yourself*, stop it.

take a punt v. [1940s+] (orig. Aus.) to have a try at something, to make a bet on. [PUNT n.[1] (2)]

take a rain check v. [1930s+] (mainly US) to defer something until a later, unspecified, time, e.g. parole. [sporting use, a check (ticket) issued for future use if a baseball game is cancelled due to rain]

take a rap v. see TAKE THE RAP v.

take a red-hot potato! excl. (also **hold your hot-potato!**) [mid-19C–1920s] be quiet! shut up! [the effect of a *red-hot potato* in the mouth]

take-artist n. [1950s] (US) one who regularly gains income from the taking of bribes, illicit 'commissions' etc. [TAKE n.[1] (1) + ARTIST sfx]

take a run phr. [late 19C+] a general expression of contempt, dismissal.

take a run at someone v. [20C+] (US) to attempt to capture, assault or seduce someone.

take a run at yourself! excl. [1920s+] (Aus.) a general excl. of dismissal, dislike, i.e. GO TO HELL! excl. [ext. of TAKE A RUN phr.]

take a running jump (at the moon)! excl. [1930s+] a general excl. of dismissal. [ext. of TAKE A RUN phr.]

take a run-out powder v. (also **take a run-out**) [20C+] to escape, to run away. [a fig. SE *powder* that inspires speed; note POWDER v.[1]]

take a set on v. see HAVE A SET ON v.

take a shine to v. (also **have the shiners for, take a shindy to**) [mid-19C+] (orig. US) to find attractive or appealing, to have a fancy or affection for. [UK dial. *shiner*, a sweetheart]

take a shit v. **1** [early 17C; 1920s+] to defecate. **2** [1960s–70s] in fig. use, to cause trouble for, to attack. [(1) SHIT n.[1] (3); (2) SHIT n.[3] (2)]

take a shot (at) v. [1970s+] to try, to make an attempt. [SHOT n.[5] (1)]

take a shot at v. [late 19C+] to attack, whether physically or verbally. [SHOT n.[3] (1)/SHOT n.[9] (2)]

take a sight v. (also **take double sights**) [mid–late 19C] to place the thumb against the nose and close all the fingers except the little one, which is agitated as a token of derision.

take a slice off a cut cake v. [1960s] (Aus.) to commit adultery.

take a slice (off the joint) v. see CUT A SLICE (OFF THE JOINT) v.

take a snout on someone v. see HAVE A SNOUT ON SOMEONE v.

take a spin v. see GO FOR A SPIN v.

take a squat v. [1970s+] to defecate. [SQUAT n.[1] (2)]

take a stink for a nosegay v. [late 18C–mid-19C] to make a foolish blunder, to be very gullible. [a *nosegay* smells sweet, a *stink* does not]

take a stone up in the ear v. [late 17C–early 18C] of a woman, to fall into an immoral lifestyle. [ety. unknown; ? link to SE *stone*, a testicle; or to the *stoning* of adulteresses in some cultures]

take a stretch v. [late 19C+] (Aus.) to exercise, usu. to exercise a horse.

take a sweep (with both barrels) v. [1930s–50s] (US drugs) to inhale cocaine (through both nostrils).

take a swing (at) v. (also **take swing (at)**) [1910s+] **1** to aim a blow (at), to punch. **2** in fig. use, to criticize. [in boxing, a *swing*, a swinging blow]

take a test drive v. see TAKE AN APPLICATION v.

take a toss v. [1930s] to be attracted to a person, to fall in love with. [i.e. 'to fall for']

take a trick v. [late 19C] (Aus.) to show promise; to be successful. [card imagery]

take a trip to the West Indies v. [early 19C] (UK Und.) of a suspect criminal, to leave a town or place to avoid arrest.

take a tumble v.[1] [late 19C+] (orig. Aus.) to come to a realization, to work something out. [TUMBLE n.[3]]

take a tumble v.[2] [1900s] (US Und.) to 'fall for' a confidence trick.

take a tumble v.[3] see TUMBLE n.[1] (2).

take a turn among her frills v. (also **take a turn up her petticoats**) [19C] to have sexual intercourse (cf. DO HER JOB FOR HER v.).

take a turn among the cabbages v. (also **take a turn among the parsley**) [late 19C] to have sexual intercourse. [CABBAGE n.[7] (1)/PARSLEY n.[1]]

take a turn in Bushey Park v. [late 19C] to have sexual intercourse. [pun on proper name *Bushey Park*, Middlesex, UK and BUSH n.[2] (1)]

take a turn in Cock Alley v. (also **take a turn in Cock Lane**) [late 19C] to have sexual intercourse. [pun on a fictitious street COCK n.[2] (1) + SE *alley/lane*]

take a turn in Cupid's alley v. (also **take a turn in Cupid's corner and hair court**) [late 19C] to have sexual intercourse. [proper name *Cupid* + SE *alley/corner*/HAIR COURT n.]

take a turn in Love Lane on Mount Pleasant v. [late 19C] to have sexual intercourse. [facetious use of London street names]

take a turn in the stubble v. (also **take a turn through the stubble**) [18C–19C] to have sexual intercourse. [STUBBLE n.]

take a turn on hair court v. [late 19C] to have sexual intercourse. [HAIR COURT n.]

take a turn on one's back v. [late 19C] to have sexual intercourse. [facetious use of SE *back*]

take a turn on Shooter's Hill v. [late 19C; 1970s+] (US Black) to have sexual intercourse. [SHOOT v.[1] (1)]

take a turn through the stubble v. see TAKE A TURN IN THE STUBBLE v.

take a turn up her petticoats v. see TAKE A TURN AMONG HER FRILLS v.

take a vegetable breakfast v. [18C–19C] to be hanged. [pun on SE *artichoke*, a vegetable + SE *choke*]

take a walk v. (orig. US) **1** [late 19C+] to leave, to be dismissed;

esp. as imper. *take a walk!* go away! **2** [1910s+] to escape criminal proceedings. **3** [1930s+] to run off. **4** [1930s+] of a group of workers, to resign.

take a walk up back *v.* [1920s–30s] (*US prison*) to be moved from one's cell to the execution chamber.

take a whack at *v. see* HAVE A WHACK AT *v.*

take a whirl *v. see* GIVE SOMETHING A WHIRL *v.*

take beef *v.*¹ [mid-late 19C] (*UK Und.*) to run away. [CRY (HOT) BEEF *v.*]

take beef *v.*² [1990s+] (*US Black*) to get into arguments, to face criticism. [SE *take* + BEEF *n.*² (2)]

take bread and salt *v.* [late 16C–17C] to swear. [the taking of one's master's *bread and salt* provided a symbolic underpinning of an oath of fealty]

take care mines *v. see* GO FOR MINES *v.*

take care of *v.* **1** [late 19C–1910s] to arrest. **2** [20C+] to beat up; to kill. **3** [1920s+] to bribe; to exert (political) pressure on. **4** [1940s+] to have sexual intercourse with. **5** [1950s+] to cause trouble for. **6** [1970s] to pay, to give a tip. [euphs.]

take-care-of-business *adj.* [1970s] efficient. [TAKE CARE OF BUSINESS *v.*]

take care of business *v.* (*also* T.C.B.) [1950s+] (*orig. US Black*) to deal efficiently with matters in hand.

take care of number one *v.* (*also* take care of numero uno) [mid-19C+] to put oneself first, no matter what the situation. [NUMBER ONE *n.*¹/NUMERO UNO *n.*²]

take double sights *v. see* TAKE A SIGHT *v.*

take-down *n.* [late 19C–1930s] **1** a swindle, a deception. **2** (*Aus.*) a deceiver, a swindler, a cheat. **3** (*US*) a win, e.g. in gambling. [TAKE DOWN *v.*¹ (3)]

take down *v.*¹ **1** [17C] to abuse. **2** [mid-18C+] to challenge, to overcome, to surpass; to kill. **3** [mid-19C+] (*orig. Aus.*) to cheat, to swindle, to rob. **4** [late 19C+] to destroy, to dispose of. **5** [1960s] (*US prison*) to have homosexual sexual intercourse.

take down *v.*² [1940s+] (*US Und./police*) to arrest. [DOWNTOWN *n.*²]

take down someone's particulars *v.* [1920s+] of a man, to remove a woman's underwear. [pun on stereotyped police activity at the outset of an interrogation]

take five *v.* (*also* take ten) **1** [1910s+] (*US*) to take a short break, i.e. a 5-minute (or 10-minute) break; also in fig. use. **2** [1960s] (*US campus*) to leave. [FIVE *n.*¹ (2)]

take foot *v. see* MAKE FOOT *v.*

take for a ride *v.*¹ (*US Und.*) **1** [1920s+] (*also* take for an airing, …a trip) to assassinate, usu. by taking the victim out in a car and killing them at some stage, then dumping the body far from one's base; thus *go for a ride*, to suffer this form of death. **2** [1930s–40s] (*also* ride, take for a walk) to arrest.

take for a ride *v.*² (*also* give a ride, take for a trot) [1920s+] (*orig. US*) to deceive, to fool, to trick, usu. for financial gain.

take French lessons *v.* [20C+] to contract venereal disease. [FRENCH *adj.* (1); stereotyping]

take game *n.* [1940s] (*US Und.*) a confidence trick. [TAKE *v.*³ (1) + GAME *n.*² (3)]

take gas *v.* **1** [1950s+] (*US*) to be scolded and abused. **2** [1960s] (*US campus*) to do badly. **3** [1960s+] to kill oneself, by any method.

take gruel *v.* [late 19C–1900s] to die. [the giving of gruel to those on or near their deathbed]

take gruel together *v.* [late 19C–1900s] to live together as man and wife. [a clergyman who, as reported in *The Referee* of 14 December 1884, offered this euph. to explain his relations with his elderly 'housekeeper']

take heat *v.* [1920s+] (*US*) **1** to suffer or endure punishment or criticism. **2** to lose money. [HEAT *n.*³ (2)]

take-in *n.* **1** [late 18C–1920s] a hoax, a swindle. **2** [early 19C] a swindler. [TAKE IN *v.*¹]

take-in *adj.* [early 19C] deceptive, swindling. [TAKE-IN *n.* (1)]

take in *v.*¹ [mid-18C+] to hoax, to cheat, to deceive.

take in *v.*² [late 19C+] (*US*) to arrest.

take in and do for *v.* [19C] of a woman, to have sexual intercourse (cf. CATCH AN OYSTER *v.*). [pun on the same phr. used in lodging house advertisements, 'Single men taken in and done for'; note DO *v.*¹ (1)]

take in beef *v.* [19C] of a woman, to have sexual intercourse (cf. CATCH AN OYSTER *v.*). [BEEF *n.*¹ (1)]

take in cream *v. see* CREAM *n.*¹ (1).

take in snuff *v. see* TAKE SNUFF *v.*

take into the woodshed *v.* [20C+] (*US*) to scold, to punish. [the practice of taking an errant child into the woodshed for a thrashing]

take in wood *v.* (*also* wood up) [mid-19C+] (*US*) to drink; usu. in question *do you take in wood?* will you have a drink? [? the *wooden* barrels that hold liquor]

take it *v.* **1** [20C+] to suffer adversity and unhappiness without complaint. **2** [1900s–10s] to surpass others, to beat all rivals. **3** [1920s] (*US Und.*) to accept a bribe. **4** [1920s+] to have sexual intercourse.

take it! *excl.* [1930s–60s] (*gay*) an excl. used by one demanding fellatio.

take it any way *v.* [1930s–40s] (*gay*) to enjoy fellatio.

take it big *v.* (*also* take it hard) **1** [1930s+] (*US*) to react emotionally, usu. when distressed or angry. **2** [1960s] to fall in love.

take it cool *v.* [mid-19C+] to relax, to remain undisturbed by events. [COOL *adj.*¹ (2)]

take it down a thousand! *excl.* [1980s+] (*US campus*) relax! calm down! [image of some form of gauge or dial]

take it easy *v.* **1** [mid-19C+] to relax, to not worry about anything, to take time off. **2** [mid-19C+] to act calmly. **3** [1930s+] to drive more slowly. **4** [1950s+] to treat leniently. [naut. jargon *take it easy*, to neglect one's duties]

take it easy *phr.* **1** [mid-19C+] relax, don't worry, calm down, be careful. **2** [1950s+] (*US*) a phr. meaning goodbye, see you later. [TAKE IT EASY *v.*]

take it fighting *v.* [late 19C] (*US*) to approach in a courageous manner, to act aggressively. [antithesis of TAKE IT LYING DOWN *v.* (1)]

take it from the head *v.* [1990s+] (*US gang*) to be murdered. [the gunshot to the head]

take it from the top *v.* [1930s+] (*US*) to start at the beginning. [jazz use, i.e. *the top* of the score]

take it hard *v. see* TAKE IT BIG *v.*

take it in the blind *v.* [20C+] (*US prison*) to fight in private in order to settle a score. [i.e. no one else is aware of the activity]

take it in the ear *v.* [1960s+] (*US campus*) to be severely criticized.

take it light *v.* [1960s+] (*US Black*) to act in a restrained manner, to resist excess, to go slowly. [var. on TAKE IT EASY *v.* (2)]

take it lying down *v.* **1** [late 19C+] to give in without a fight, to act weakly. **2** [1950s+] of a woman, to submit, willingly or otherwise, to sexual intercourse.

take it on! *excl.* [1980s+] (*US campus*) a general excl. of encouragement.

take it on one's toes *v. see* HAVE IT AWAY *v.*

take it on the Arthur Duffy *v.* (*also* take it on the Dan O'Leary, take it on the Jesse Owens) [1900s–50s] (*US*) to run, to run off, to escape. [proper names *Arthur F Duffy*, US world record-holder of the 100-yard (100m) dash (1902–5); *Dan O'Leary*, the champion long-distance walker of the world, *fl.*1900s; *Jesse Owens* (b.1913), winner of 4 Olympic Gold medals in 1936, including 100m dash]

take it on the chin *v.* [1920s+] (*orig. US*) **1** to suffer hardship and adversity without complaint. **2** to be defeated, to be trounced. [boxing imagery]

take it on the hoof v. [1900s] (US) to run off, to leave quickly. [HOOF n. (1)]

take it on the hop v. [1960s] (US Black) to leave, to go away.

take it on the Jesse Owens v. see TAKE IT ON THE ARTHUR DUFFY v.

take it on the lam v. [20C+] (US Und.) to run away, to escape (esp. from prison). [LAM n.[1]]

take it on the nut v. [1940s] (US Und.) to lose.

take it on the run v. [1900s–30s] (US) to run away.

take it on the trot v. [1930s] to run off, to leave at speed.

take it out v. [late 19C+] (Aus.) to serve a prison term rather than pay a fine.

take it out in trade v. [1940s+] (Can./US) to have sexual intercourse as the 'price' of taking a woman out.

take it out of one v. (also knock it out of one) [mid-19C+] to tire, to exhaust. ['it' being one's breath]

take it out of someone v. 1 [early 19C+] to take revenge on, to get one's satisfaction from. 2 [1900s] to surpass.

take it out on v. [20C+] (US) to treat badly, to punish, often an innocent victim.

take it slow phr. [1930s+] (orig. US Black) 1 goodbye, see you later. 2 calm down, quieten down, relax. 3 be careful.

take it to the hoop v. [1980s+] (US Black) to take something to its limit, to do something with maximum commitment. [basketball imagery]

take it to the square v. [2000s] (US prison) to call out for a fight.

take it to the street v. [20C+] (US) to take a private conflict or issue into the public arena.

take it up the ass v. (also take it up the arse/bum) (orig. US) 1 [1940s+] to submit to anal intercourse; also used as an expression of contempt (cf. ASK FOR THE RING v.). 2 [1980s+] to be victimized, treated unfairly or harshly. [ASS n. (2)/ARSE n.[1]/BUM n.[1] (3)]

take it up the dirt road v. [1950s+] to be sodomized. [DIRT ROAD n.[2]]

take lag v. [1950s] (W.I./UK Black) to criticize, to attack verbally. [LAG v.[3] (1)]

take (large) stock v. [mid-19C+] (orig. US) to care about, to see as important, to take account of. [SE stock, a company share]

take low v. [late 19C+] (W.I./US Black) to adopt a humble attitude in order to forward one's aims.

take man n. [1970s] (Aus. Und.) in a shoplifting team, the member who actually steals the targeted object. [SE take]

take matters into one's own hands v. [20C+] to masturbate (cf. AUDITION THE FINGER PUPPETS v.). [pun]

take Mr Foot's horse v. (also travel by Mr Foot's horse) [early 19C] to go on foot.

taken bad, be v. (also took bad, be) 1 [mid-19C+] to have fallen ill. 2 [1900s] in fig. use, discomfited.

take Nebuchadnezzar out to grass v. [19C] of a woman, to have sexual intercourse.

take no prisoners v. [1980s+] to make no compromises, to act resolutely; thus as adj., uncompromising.

take no shorts v. [1980s+] (US Black) to refuse to be fooled, cheated or put at a disadvantage. [SE short change]

taken short adj. [mid-19C+] feeling desperate to make an emergency visit to the lavatory (cf. CAUGHT SHORT adj.). [the short time one has to reach the lavatory, or the short steps one takes on one's way]

take-off n.[1] [mid-19C+] an imitation, a parody, usu. mocking. [TAKE OFF v.[1]]

take-off n.[2] [1940s] (US Black) the hips.

take-off n.[3] [1940s–50s] (US prison) an escape. [TAKE OFF v.[3] (1)]

take-off n.[4] [1940s+] (US Und.) an armed street robbery or mugging. [TAKE OFF v.[2] (4)]

take off v.[1] [mid-18C+] to imitate, to mimic, to parody. [ext. of SE take off, to draw a likeness of someone]

take off v.[2] (US Black/Und.) 1 [mid–late 19C] to execute. 2 [late 19C–1900s] to deprive of money. 3 [late 19C+] to hurt, to kill. 4 [20C+] to rob. 5 [1960s+] to obtain, e.g. money. 6 [1970s] to make a raid on. [SE take off, to remove]

take off v.[3] 1 [20C+] to leave; also as imper. take off! go away! 2 [20C+] to die. 3 [1940s] (US Black) to start talking. 4 [1950s–60s] to go to, to visit. [the sl. use derives immediately from aircraft imagery, but take off, to go off, to start off, to run away, has been SE since early 19C]

take off v.[4] [1930s+] (US) to be suddenly successful or very active.

take off v.[5] [1940s+] (drugs) 1 to take narcotics. 2 to feel the effects of a drug. [i.e. to get HIGH adj.[1] (2)]

take-off artist n. 1 [1940s+] (US Und.) a successful robber, rapist or killer. 2 one who does the job then 'takes off'. [TAKE OFF v.[2]/TAKE OFF v.[3] (1) + ARTIST sfx]

take off corner-pieces v. [late 19C–1900s] to beat, usu. one's wife.

take off like a big-assed bird v. (also take off like a bat out of hell) [1940s+] (US) to leave very quickly. [TAKE OFF v.[3] (1) + SE + -ARSED sfx[1]]

take off one's coat v. [late 19C–1900s] to challenge someone to a fight. [the preparatory action]

take-on n.[1] [1920s+] (Aus.) a fight, usu. with the fists. [TAKE ON v.[1] (2)]

take-on n.[2] [1960s] an illusion.

take on v.[1] 1 [early 19C; 1910s+] (US) to become angry. 2 [late 19C+] to engage in a fight, to challenge. 3 [1910s+] (US police) to stop and search. 4 [1930s+] (US) to have sexual intercourse with.

take on v.[2] [late 19C] to become popular; to enjoy (and therefore render something popular). [var. on SE catch on]

take one off the wrist v. [1960s+] to masturbate. [ONE OFF THE WRIST n.]

take one's best hold v. [1970s+] (US) to prepare oneself emotionally for dealing with a problem. [wrestling imagery]

take one's best shot v. (also shoot one's best shot) [1960s+] (orig. US) to do the best one can, to try one's hardest. [SHOT n.[5] (1); ult. boxing imagery]

take one's daniel v. see SLING ONE'S DANIEL v.

take one's degrees v. [early–mid-19C] to be imprisoned, to serve a sentence. [play on ACADEMY n. (4)]

take one's drops v. [18C–19C] to drink heavily. [SE drop (of liquor)]

take oneself in hand v. [1950s+] (orig. naut.) to masturbate (cf. AUDITION THE FINGER PUPPETS v.). [pun]

take oneself out v. [1960s+] (US) to commit suicide. [TAKE OUT v. (2)]

take one's end v. [20C+] (Irish) to be convulsed with laughter. [SE end, death, i.e. 'to laugh oneself to death']

take one's eye(s) pass somebody v. see MAKE ONE'S EYE(S) PASS SOMEBODY v.

take one's finger out v. see PULL ONE'S FINGER OUT v.

take one's hair down v. see LET ONE'S HAIR DOWN v. (1).

take one's hank v. [1960s–70s] (US prison) to masturbate. [HANK n.[4] (3)]

take one's hat off to v. [mid-19C+] to compliment, to praise; thus excl. hats off!

take one's hook v. see HOOK v.[4] (1).

take one's lumps v. (also get one's lumps) [1930s+] (orig. US) to accept and deal with one's problems and setbacks, to 'get one's deserts'. [LUMPS n.[1]]

take one's meat out of the basket v. [1940s+] (gay) to reveal one's genitals to another man. [MEAT n. (2) + SE basket/BASKET n.[1] (2)]

take one's medicine v. 1 [mid–late 19C] to have sexual

intercourse. **2** [mid-19C–1930s] to drink. **3** [late 19C+] to accept a (deserved) punishment or reprimand.

take one's shirt off *v.* [late 19C] to lose one's temper.

take one's snake for a gallop *v.* [1940s+] **1** to masturbate (cf. BEAT ONE'S HOG *v.*). **2** to urinate (cf. FLOG THE LIZARD *v.*). [SNAKE *n.*[3]]

take one's toe *v.* [20C+] (*Ulster*) to affect, to 'get into'.

take one's whack *v. see* HAVE ONE'S WHACK *v.*

take on some backs *v.* [1970s+] (*US Black*) to have anal intercourse (cf. ASK FOR THE RING *v.*).

take on with *v.* [1910s–20s] to form an association with (a man or woman).

take out *v.* **1** [late 19C+] to knock out. **2** [1930s+] (*orig. US*) to kill, to destroy (a specific target). [abbr. SE *take out of the picture*]

take outdoors on someone *v.* [1930s] to leave alone, to avoid someone.

take over the hurdles *v.* [1940s–50s] (*US prison*) to attack in a group. [horseracing imagery]

taker *n.* **1** [mid-19C+] (*US*) a person who accepts an offer or challenge. **2** [1940s+] (*UK Und.*) a receiver of stolen goods. **3** [1950s+] (*US gay/prison*) a passive prison homosexual.

taker-up *n.* (*also* **taker**) [mid-16C–18C] the member of a criminal gang who keeps watch or entices a victim into a crooked gambling game, spec. part of a BARNARD'S LAW *n.* team.

take shit *v.* [1950s+] (*orig. US*) to suffer (and accept) humiliation, annoyance or (in weak form) teasing; often in negative. [SHIT *n.*[3] (8)]

take snuff *v.* (*also* **take in snuff**) [late 16C–mid-19C] to be offended; thus *in snuff*, offended. [SE *snuff*, the unpleasant smell of a snuffed candle, thus one fig. 'turns up one's nose']

take some doing *v. see* TAKE A BIT OF DOING *v.*

take someone apart *v.* **1** [20C+] to beat severely. **2** [1950s] to reprimand someone.

take someone down (a buttonhole) *v.* (*also* **take someone a buttonhole lower, let someone down a buttonhole**) [late 16C–1920s] to humiliate someone, to deflate someone. [the image of humiliating someone by undressing them in public]

take someone for *v.* [1930s+] to trick, to deceive, to obtain from one who is unwilling otherwise to give, esp. in the extraction of money, e.g. *I took him for a tenner.* [TAKE *v.*[3] (1)]

take someone for bad *v.* [1980s+] (*US Black*) to treat someone as a weakling and exploit them accordingly.

take someone napping *v. see* CATCH SOMEONE NAPPING *v.*

take someone off the calendar *v.* [1980s] (*US*) to kill, to murder.

take someone off the count *v.* [1980s] to murder, to kill. [milit./prison imagery, to remove from the roster of personnel or inmates]

take someone out of winding *v.* [1920s+] (*Aus.*) to silence someone, to leave someone 'at a loss for words'. [SE *wind*, breath]

take someone's back *v. see* WATCH SOMEONE'S BACK *v.*

take someone's measure *v. see* GET SOMEONE'S MEASURE *v.*

take someone's mind *v.* [1940s–60s] (*US Black*) to manipulate someone's mind, usu. for negative purposes.

take someone's number *v. see* HAVE SOMEONE'S NUMBER *v.*

take someone's pulse *v.* [1970s] (*gay*) to fondle someone's genitals.

take someone through the hoop(s) *v. see* PUT SOMEONE THROUGH THE HOOP(S) *v.*

take someone to the bridge *v.* (*also* **take someone to the hoop**) [1980s+] (*US Black*) to attack, physically or verbally.

take someone to the cleaners *v.* (*also* **send someone to the cleaners**) **1** [1900s] (*US*) to reduce someone to penury. **2** [1920s+] to defraud, outwit and otherwise remove all of a victim's assets in a wager, by extortion or by similar legal or illegal means. **3** [1920s+] to defeat thoroughly, to trounce.

take someone up on something *v.* [1910s+] to accept a proposal, an invitation.

take stock *v. see* TAKE (LARGE) STOCK *v.*

take stripes *v.* [late 19C–1940s] (*US*) to be sent to prison. [the old striped uniforms]

take ten *v. see* TAKE FIVE *v.*

take the acid off *v.* [1910s] (*Aus.*) to speak honestly, without sarcasm.

take the air *v.* (*also* **take the breeze**) [1910s–40s] to leave, to escape; often as imper.

take the baker's shop/bakery *v. see* TAKE THE CAKE *v.*

take the bayonet course *v.* [1910s–40s] to be subjected to a cure of bismuth subcarbonate and neoarsphenamine for venereal disease; injections of the drugs continued weekly over a period of years.

take the belt *v.* [late 19C] (*US teen*) to be exceptional, to 'take the biscuit'. [boxing imagery, the belt awarded to a champion]

take the big slide *v.* [1960s] (*US*) to die.

take the biscuit *v. see* TAKE THE CAKE *v.*

take the breeze *v. see* TAKE THE AIR *v.*

take the burnt chops *v.* [late 19C–1940s] (*N.Z.*) to take up work as a musterer or drover. [the campfire meals musterers eat]

take the cake *v.* (*also* **take the baker's shop, ...bakery, ...biscuit, ...bun, ...cookie, ...flour, ...pastry, capture the crumb, cop the cake/curranty**) **1** [mid-19C+] to surpass, to outdo, esp. in excessive or extreme behaviour or of a near-intolerable situation or happening. **2** [1960s+] to be highly improbable. [the perceived 'tastiness' of the *cake*]

take the cane out *v.* [1980s] to lay down the law.

take the cheese *v.* [late 19C+] of a negative circumstance or objectionable person, to surpass, to outdo. [CHEESE, THE *n.* (1); var. on TAKE THE CAKE *v.*]

take the cookie *v. see* TAKE THE CAKE *v.*

take the count *v.* [late 19C–1920s] **1** to die, lit. and fig. **2** to give up, to leave. [boxing imagery]

take the cure *v.* [20C+] (*US*) to give up something, to refrain from doing something. [SE *take the cure*, to withdraw from alcohol/drug addiction]

take the dairy off *v.* [1910s+] to divert suspicion. [corruption of SE *direction*, i.e. redirect attention]

take the day off to carry bricks *v.* [1970s+] (*N.Z.*) to take a day off to do some of one's own work, e.g. do-it-yourself.

take the Dublin packet *v.* [mid-19C–1900s] to run round the corner. [? SE *double*, to evade escape or the image of a lit. escape from the UK to Ireland by the SE *packet-boat*, e.g. by a debtor or criminal]

take the dust *v.* (*also* **chew dust**) [late 19C–1950s] (*US*) to be overtaken in a car. [the *dust* emanating from the passing vehicle]

take the Dutch route *v.* [20C+] (*US prison*) to commit suicide. [ext. of DUTCH ACT *n.*]

take the easy way out *v.* [20C+] to commit suicide. [ironic use of SE]

take the egg *v.* [late 19C–1900s] (*US*) to win. [the perceived excellence of a SE *egg*]

take the electric cure *v.* [1920s] (*US prison/Und.*) to be executed in the electric chair.

take the fall *v.* [1920s+] (*US*) **1** to volunteer oneself as a victim, usu. as the alleged perpetrator of a crime, in the place of the real villain. **2** to be accused (and condemned) unfairly of a crime. [FALL *n.* (3)]

take the fifth *v. see* PLEAD THE FIFTH *v.*

take the flour *v. see* TAKE THE CAKE *v.*

take the foot out of one's ass *v.* [1960s] (*US Black*) to rid oneself of ill treatment, of victimization, exploitation.

take the gap *v.* **1** [1950s+] to leave a party while it is still at its height. **2** [1960s+] (*S.Afr.*) to leave the country. [rugby jargon *take the gap*, to break past one's opponents]

take the gas v. [20C+] to endure punishment, esp. in a boxing ring. [the *gas* that knocks one out at the dentist's]

take the gas pipe v. [1940s+] (*US*) to commit suicide by inhaling gas.

take the gilt off the gingerbread v. [mid-19C+] to disillusion, to remove one's fantasies, to downgrade. [according to Ware, 'the past-away annual fairs were made ghastly gay with flat gingerbread cakes, covered with Dutch metal (a zinc-copper mix that counterfeited gold leaf), which tried to look like gilt']

take the heat v. [1950s+] (*orig. US*) to accept responsibility. [HEAT n.[3]]

take the heat off v. [1950s+] to relieve pressure on (a person). [HEAT n.[3]]

take the Hershey highway v. [1980s+] (*US*) to perform (homosexual) anal intercourse (cf. ASK FOR THE RING v.). [HERSHEY HIGHWAY n.]

take the horse laugh v. *see* GIVE SOMEONE THE HORSE LAUGH v.

take the hot squat v. [1920s+] (*US*) to be executed in the electric chair. [HOT SQUAT n.]

take the huff v. *see* HUFF n.[2] (1).

take the inside out v. [mid-19C] to finish, to empty, esp. a glass of beer etc.

take the kettle v. [late 19C–1900s] (*Can.*) to win, to take the prize. [Ware suggests that a kettle had been the trad. prize at spelling bees]

take the kids to the pool v. (*also* **drop the kids off**) [1990s+] to defecate. [coarse euph.]

take the knock v. (*also* **get the knock**) 1 [late 19C+] (*orig. US*) to accept the blame. 2 [late 19C+] to suffer an unpleasant surprise. 3 [late 19C+] to suffer financial losses, often in gambling. 4 [1900s–10s] of a bookmaker, to be defrauded. 5 [1930s+] of a bookmaker, to defraud a bettor. 6 [2000s] to be overcome by drink or drugs. [KNOCK n.[2]]

take the last count v. (*also* **take the long count/rest**) [1930s+] (*US*) to die. [boxing imagery]

take the michael v. *see* EXTRACT THE MICHAEL v.

take the mickey (out of) v. (*also* **take the mick/mike (out of)**) [1920s+] to tease; thus *mickey-take* (cf. EXTRACT THE MICHAEL v.). [rhy. sl.; *take the mickey bliss* = TAKE THE PISS (OUT OF) v.]

take the monkey off one's back v. [1960s+] to withdraw from narcotics addiction; also in fig. use. [MONKEY ON ONE'S BACK n.[2]]

take the monkey off your back! excl. [late 19C] calm down! [MONKEY ON ONE'S BACK n.[1]]

take the needle v. [late 19C+] (*Irish*) to get angry. [var. on GET THE NEEDLE v.]

take the oath v. [late 19C–1900s] to have a drink.

take the pants off v. (*also* **thrash the pants off**) [1930s+] to beat convincingly, to overwhelm. [SE *take/thrash* + PANTS, THE n.]

take the pastry v. *see* TAKE THE CAKE v.

take the pipe v. [1960s+] (*US*) to fail to act or achieve under pressure, esp. in sports; thus to be punished. [ety. unknown]

take the piss (out of) v. 1 [1920s+] to tease, esp. aggressively. 2 [1930s+] to attack verbally, to sneer or jeer at. 3 [1980s+] of a situation or statement, to appear ludicrous, to be a joke. 4 [1990s+] of a person, to act absurdly, to play the fool. 5 [1990s+] of a man, to have sexual intercourse. [PISS, THE n.]

take the rap v. (*also* **take a rap**) [1920s+] (*US Und.*) to take a punishment, often a prison sentence, that is actually due to someone else. 2 (*US*) to take the blame when one is not the guilty party. [RAP n.[3] (1)]

take the rip out of v. [1990s+] to mock, to criticize, to attack verbally. [? SE *rip*, a tear]

take the road to Buenos Aires v. *see* GO TO BUENOS AIRES v.

take the roof off v. *see* RAISE THE ROOF v.

take the rust out of v. [mid-19C] (*US*) to discomfit, to deflate.

take the Sabine slide v. [mid-19C] (*US*) to run off, leaving one's debts unpaid. [? play on G.T.T. phr.; the *Sabine* river is in Texas]

take the scenic route v. [1960s+] (*orig. US teen*) 1 to concentrate on pleasure at the expense of efficiency or speed. 2 to do things 'the hard way'.

take the seconds v. [1930s] (*UK Und.*) to give up, to abandon on second thoughts.

take the shine out of v. (*also* **take the shine off**) 1 [early 19C–1940s] to beat, to surpass. 2 [mid–late 19C] (*Aus.*) to take the pleasure away.

take the shit with the sugar v. [1990s+] (*Aus.*) to accept that one must have both bad and good experiences.

take the soles off someone's shoes v. [late 19C] to surprise someone.

take the soup v. [mid-19C+] to convert from Catholicism to Protestantism. [for ety. *see* SOUPER n.[1]]

take the starch out of v. 1 [mid-19C–1920s] of a woman, to have sexual intercourse with (cf. CATCH AN OYSTER v.). 2 [mid-19C+] to break the spirit of someone or something, to make weary or less arrogant. [the wilted post-orgasmic penis]

take the tiles off v. [late 19C] (*UK society*) to live in an extremely extravagant manner. [? one's fig. disposal of all one's assets, up to the house tiles]

take the tip v. [early–mid-19C] to accept a bribe. [TIP n.[2] (1)]

take the track v. [1910s+] (*N.Z.*) to be dismissed from a job.

take the veil v. [1940s–70s] (*US gay*) to abandon the homosexual lifestyle.

take the weight v. [1950s+] (*US*) to take responsibility.

take the whiskers off v. [1920s] (*US tramp*) to work for a farmer gathering the harvest.

take the wind v. [1930s+] to leave. [sailing imagery]

take the wizz v. [2000s] to tease. [WHIZ n.[6]; thus var. on TAKE THE PISS (OUT OF) v.]

take the wrinkles out of one's belly v. [late 18C–early 19C] to assuage one's hunger.

take the zero v. [1980s+] (*US campus*) to pass something by, to turn down an offer, to reject. [ZERO n. (2)]

take to v. [20C+] (*Aus./N.Z.*) to attack, usu. with the fists. [abbr. SE *take one's fists to*]

take to one's scrapers v. (*also* **set to one's pumps**) [late 18C–1960s] (*Irish*) to run off. [one's shoes 'scrape' the ground]

take to school v. *see* SCHOOL v.[2].

take to the fair v. [1940s+] (*Irish*) to amaze, to astonish; thus *take things to the fair*, to exaggerate. [the excitements of a *fair*]

take to the (tall) timber v. (*also* **break for tall timber, pull for..., put for..., strike for...**) [mid-19C+] to run off. [TALL TIMBER n.]

take to the toe v. (*also* **hit the toe**) [1950s+] (*Aus./N.Z.*) to leave quickly, to run off.

take tracks v. *see* MAKE TRACKS v.

take up v. (*also* **tuck up**) [early 18C+] to arrest; usu. as *taken/took up*, arrested.

take up one's foot and run v. *see* MAKE FOOT v.

take up slack v. *see* CUT SOME SLACK v.

take water v. [20C+] (*Aus.*) to leave a bar or public house after spending all one's cash on drink.

take your pick adj. [1990s+] stupid, foolish. [rhy. sl. = THICK adj.[1]]

Taki-Taki n. [20C+] (*W.I.*) Sranan, the Surinamese Creole language. [i.e. 'talky-talky']

takkie n. (*also* **tackie**) [1910s+] (*S.Afr.*) a rubber-soled, laced canvas shoe. [SE *tacky*, sticky]

talcum queen n. [1980s+] (*US Black*) a Black homosexual who prefers White partners. [SE *talcum powder*, usu. white + QUEEN n.[2] (1)/QUEEN sfx (2)]

tale n.[1] 1 [20C+] any form of words designed to ensnare the listener for commercial purposes, e.g. the story told by a confidence trickster to ensnare the victim. **2** [20C+] a womanizer's 'line'. **3** [1940s] (*UK Und.*) a specific con where someone is persuaded to pay the con-man, who is posing as a bookmaker, for a lost bet that he did not ask to be made.

tale *n.*[2] *see* TAIL n.[2] (3).

talent *n.* **1** [mid-19C+] attractive young women, esp. those standing around at a party, in a club or dancehall etc. **2** [late 19C–1940s] (*Aus.*) a rascal, a LARRIKIN n. **3** [late 19C–1960s] (*orig. Aus.*) a generic term for the criminal underworld. **4** [1950s+] attractive young men. **5** [1960s+] in police terms, a suspect.

tale of a cock and a bull *n. see* BANBURY STORY n.

tale of two cities *n.* [1950s–70s] the female breasts (cf. BRACE AND BITS n.). [rhy. sl. = *titties* (TITTY n.[1] (1))]

tale-pitcher *n.* [late 19C–1900s] one who tells a good story, a romantic. [thus the popular nickname of the racing journalist, raconteur and bon viveur Arthur Binstead (1861–1914), whose fund of stories, retailed to cronies as well as the readers of *The Sporting Times* (cf. PINK 'UN, THE n.), gave him the nickname *Tale-Pitcher*, usu. abbr. to *Pitcher*]

tale-teller *n.* [1940s] (*UK Und.*) a confidence trickster. [TALE n.[1]]

talk *n.* [late 19C+] a seducer's 'line' of conversation; nonsense.

talk *v.* [1920s+] (*UK Und.*) to confess or turn informer to the police or similar authority.

talk a big game *v. see* TALK A GOOD GAME v.

talk a blue streak *v.* (*also* **talk blind streaks, curse a blue streak, cuss…**) [late 19C+] (*orig. US*) to talk both fast and at great length. [SE *blue streak*, that which resembles a flash of lightning]

talk about it *phr. see* TELL ME ABOUT IT phr.

talk about Uganda *v. see* UGANDAN DISCUSSION n.

talk a good game *v.* (*also* **talk a big game**) [1950s+] (*orig. US*) to talk persuasively, but with the implication that nothing is ever actually done (cf. TALK GAME v.). [sporting imagery]

talk back (to) *v.* [mid-19C+] to make a rude response to, to be impudent.

talk big *v.* (*also* **speak big, talk bigger than a bullock**) [early 17C+] to boast, to exaggerate.

talk blind streaks *v. see* TALK A BLUE STREAK v.

talk bullock *v.* [mid-late 19C] (*N.Z.*) to use a good deal of bad language. [the typical vocabulary of a *bullock*-driver + play on BALLOCKS n.[1]]

talk business *v.* **1** [1950s] (*US Und.*) to offer a bribe to the police or other officials in the hope of securing immunity or leniency. **2** [1960s+] (*US Black*) to seduce, to charm.

talk by a bow *v.* [mid-late 19C] to argue, to quarrel. [ety. unknown; ? link to DRAW A LONG BOW v.]

talk church *v.* [mid-19C] to talk solely of one's occupation, to TALK SHOP v. (1). [? orig. in clerical circles]

talk cock *v.* [1940s+] to talk nonsense. [COCK n.[5] (2); although the assumed link is to COCK n.[2] (1)]

talk cold turkey *v.* [1930s+] (*orig. US*) to speak frankly and without reserve, to talk hard facts, to get down to business. [COLD TURKEY adv. (1); ext. of TALK TURKEY v. (3)]

talk crap *v.* [1920s+] (*orig. US*) to talk nonsense. [CRAP n.[3] (3)]

talk crisp *v.* [1910s–20s] to say unpleasant things. [note SE *talk sharply*]

talk doctor *n.* [1990s+] (*US*) a psychoanalyst, a psychotherapist.

talk-down *n.* [1960s+] the comforting of someone who is having a bad experience, usu. through injudicious use of drugs, esp. a hallucinogen. [TALK SOMEONE DOWN v.]

talkee-talkee *n.* **1** [early 19C–1900s] chatter, conversation. **2** [late 19C] a talkative person. [fake pidgin, to underpin the image of empty chatter]

talkfest *n. see* BLABFEST n.

talk French *v.* [1940s] (*US*) to fellate. [FRENCH n.[2] (3)]

talk from the teeth out *v.* [20C+] (*Ulster*) to speak hypocritically. [i.e. such talk does not come 'from the heart']

talk fuck *v.* **1** [late 19C] to talk about sex. **2** [1960s+] to murmur or shout obscenities during sexual intercourse for the gratification of one or both partners. [FUCK n.[1] (1)]

talk funny *v.* [1920s+] to speak in a manner other than that customary to the speaker.

talk game *v.* (*also* **spit game**) [1970s+] (*US Black*) to talk, to chatter, but spec. of a pimp, to chatter about pimping, whoring and those involved. [GAME n.[2] (9)]

talk greasy *v.* [2000s] (*US Black*) to rap smoothly and stylishly.

talk head *v.* [1980s+] (*US campus*) to talk in a negative manner. [TALKING HEAD n. (1)]

talk horse *v.* [late 19C–1900s] to boast, to 'talk big'.

talking *n.*[1] **1** [1950s+] (*US Black/campus*) being involved in a relationship, dating. **2** [1970s+] (*lesbian*) having a relationship with another woman while in prison. [euph.]

talking *n.*[2] [1960s+] a use of SE *talking* with the word 'about' unstated, implying not so much person-to-person communication, but as a way of emphasizing the importance and immediacy of the topic in hand, e.g. *we're talking telephone numbers*, this will be a very large sum of money. [originated in Hollywood where hyperbole is dominant, the implication is often one of slight reproof, i.e. don't forget, we are not discussing any old topic, sum of money etc but something quite exceptional or startling]

talking head *n.* [1960s+] **1** (*also* **talking hairdo**) a television presenter or interviewee (usu. in the role of 'expert') who is shot in head-and-shoulders close-up, the director eschewing any background or other movement. **2** (*US Black*) one who is in a bad temper and on the verge of fighting.

talking iron *n. see* SHOOTING IRON n. (1).

talking shit *phr.* (*also* **talking trash**) [1940s+] (*US Black*) any verbal by-play, banter between men, flirtation between a man and a woman etc. [TALK SHIT v.[1]/TALK TRASH v.]

talking-to *n.* [mid-19C+] a scolding, a reprimand. [TALK TO v.]

talk like a book *v.* [early 19C+] to appear well-educated and literate.

talk like a halfpenny book *v.* (*also* **talk like a ha'penny book**) [20C+] (*Irish*) to talk nonsense. [SE *ha'penny book*, a comic, a cheap paperback]

talk like pound notes *v.* [1950s] to talk in an affected, supposedly 'classy' manner.

talk like the back of a cigarette card *v.* [1930s] to pretend to greater knowledge than one has. [the cards that were once supplied in every pack of cigarettes and which carried a picture on one side and text (a description, a potted biography) on the other]

talk one's head off *v.* (*also* **talk one's ass off**) [1910s+] (*orig. US*) to talk incessantly.

talkorexia *n.* [1980s+] (*US campus*) a state of talking incessantly (and thus irritating others). [SE *talk* + -OREXIA sfx]

talk out of one's arse *v.* (*also* **talk out of one's arsehole, …ass, …asshole, …bum, talk through one's…**) [1970s+] to talk nonsense; thus coarse phr. *be quiet/shut your mouth and give your ass a rest.* [ARSE n.[1] (1)/ASS n. (2)/ARSEHOLE n. (1)/ASSHOLE n.[1] (1)/BUM n.[1] (1)]

talk out of one's head *v.* (*also* **talk out of one's hat**) [20C+] (*US Black*) to talk nonsense. [note TALK THROUGH ONE'S HAT v.]

talk out of school *v.* [20C+] to tell tales, to talk unguardedly.

talk out of the other side of one's mouth *v.* [mid-19C+] to change one's mind, to contradict an earlier statement.

talk out of the side of one's neck *v.* **1** [1950s+] (*US Black*) to talk nonsense. **2** [1970s+] (*US Black*) to ensure that one's conversation remains unheard by eavesdroppers. **3** [1990s+] (*US prison*) (*also* **come out of the side of one's neck**) to talk disrespectfully.

talk out of the wrong end *v.* [1990s+] to talk nonsense. [euph. for TALK OUT OF ONE'S ARSE v.]

talk packthread *v.* [late 18C–early 19C] to talk in *double entendres*. ['to use indecent language, well wrapt up' (Grose,

1796). SE *packthread*, heavyweight cord or twine used for tying bundles]

talk poor mouth *v.* [20C+] (*US*) to deny one's assets or advantages. [POOR MOUTH *v.*]

talk pretty *v. see* SPEAK PRETTY *v.*

talk proper *v.* [20C+] to talk Standard English.

talk shit *v.*[1] [1940s+] (*US Black*) to seduce, to 'chat someone up'. [SHIT n.[4]]

talk shit *v.*[2] [1960s+] **1** (*orig. US*) to talk nonsense. **2** (*US campus*) to criticize someone behind their back. **3** (*US campus*) to boast, to brag. **4** (*US Black*) to talk sl. **5** (*US Black*) to talk aggressively, to challenge verbally. [SHIT n.[3] (4)/SHIT n.[3] (8)]

talk shop *v.* **1** [mid-19C+] of people in the same trade or profession, to discuss one's job. **2** [late 19C+] to talk business, to discuss a deal. [SHOP n.[2]]

talk sideways *v.* [1910s+] (*US prison*) to talk disrespectfully, to talk 'clever'.

talk smack *v.* [1980s+] (*US Black/teen*) to gossip maliciously. [SMACK n.[6] (1), heroin, punning on words like SHIT n.[5] (1), heroin/SHIT n.[3] (8), nonsense, and JUNK n.[5] (1), heroin/JUNK n.[3] (4), nonsense (cf. POP JUNK *v.*)]

talk someone blind *v.* [1910s+] (*Aus.*) to overwhelm with talk.

talk someone down *v.* [1960s+] (*drugs*) to comfort a person who is having a bad experience, usu. after taking drugs, esp. LSD. [the comforter brings them down from the 'high' and back to normality]

talk someone's arm off *v.* (*also* **talk someone's leg off**) [mid-19C+] (*US*) to talk incessantly at someone, to harangue.

talk someone's ear off *v.* [1930s+] (*orig. US*) to talk incessantly at someone.

talk someone's head off *v.* (*also* **jaw someone's head off**) [1920s+] (*orig. US*) to talk incessantly at someone. [SE *talk*/JAW *v.*[1] (1); ext. of TALK SOMEONE'S EAR OFF *v.* but note TALK ONE'S HEAD OFF *v.*]

talk someone's leg off *v. see* TALK SOMEONE'S ARM OFF *v.*

talk that talk *v.* [1930s+] (*US Black*) **1** to chatter inconsequentially; to make empty promises. **2** to indulge in ritual name-calling, esp. based on insulting one's opponent's mother.

talk that talk and walk that walk *phr.* [1960s+] (*US Black*) a phr. of encouragement for one's verbal skills.

talk the leg off an iron pot *v.* (*also* **talk the leg off a chair**) [late 19C+] (*N.Z.*) to be overly talkative.

talk thirty bob to the pound *v.* [1950s] to talk very fast and unintelligibly. [var. on SE phr. *talk forty to the dozen*]

talk through one's arse/arsehole/ass/asshole/bum *v. see* TALK OUT OF ONE'S ARSE *v.*

talk through one's braces *v.* [1920s+] (*Aus.*) to talk nonsense, to talk rubbish. [var. on TALK THROUGH ONE'S HAT *v.* (1)]

talk through one's fly-buttons *v.* [1960s] **1** to talk nonsense, to talk rubbish. **2** to talk in a sexually provocative or sex-obsessed manner. [(1) var. on TALK THROUGH ONE'S HAT *v.* (1)]

talk through one's hat *v.* (*also* **talk through one's hair**) [late 19C+] (*orig. US*) **1** to talk nonsense. **2** to boast and exaggerate. [late 19C+]

talk through one's socks *v.* [1900s] (*Aus.*) to talk nonsense. [var. on TALK THROUGH ONE'S HAT *v.* (1)]

talk through (the back of) one's neck *v.* [late 19C+] to talk nonsense, to talk rubbish.

talk through the top of one's neck *v.* [1900s] (*Aus.*) to talk in an aristocratic manner. [as opposed to TALK THROUGH (THE BACK OF) ONE'S NECK *v.*]

talk to *v.*[1] [mid-19C+] (*orig. US*) to scold, to 'tell off'; usu. as TALKING-TO n.

talk to *v.*[2] [1990s+] (*US campus*) to date. [note TALKING n.[1] (1)]

talk to one's plate *v.* [20C+] (*US*) to say grace before a meal.

talk to the big white (tele)phone *v.* (*also* **talk into a porcelain telephone, talk to God/Ralph on the big white (tele)phone**) [1970s+] (*orig. US campus*) to vomit (cf.

DRIVE THE (PORCELAIN) BUS *v.*). [the *big white phone* being the lavatory]

talk to the canoe-driver *v.* [1960s+] (*US*) to perform cunnilingus. [play on SE *canoe/cunnilingus* + LITTLE MAN (IN THE BOAT) n. (2)]

talk to the engineer, not the oily rag *v.* [1940s+] to deal with the boss, not an assistant.

talk to the hand *phr.* [1990s+] (*US teen*) a dismissive phr., don't waste my time; often ext. with *because the face don't understand* or other vars.

talk to the mike *v.* [1980s+] (*US teen*) to perform fellatio (cf. BLOW *v.*[2]). [fig. use of MIC n.[1]]

talk to the organ-grinder, not the monkey *v.* [1940s+] to deal with the boss, not an assistant.

talk-trap *n.* [20C+] (*US*) the mouth. [SE *talk* + TRAP n.[3]]

talk trash *v.* [1950s+] (*US Black*) to talk insincerely, to boast, to lie, esp. when pursuing sex; thus *let's talk trash*, a phr. of greeting. [note Joyce, *Ulysses* (1922): 'he was going about with some of them Sinner Fein lately or whatever they call themselves talking his usual trash and nonsense']

talk turkey *v.* [early 19C+] (*orig. US*) **1** to talk agreeably or affably, to say pleasant things. **2** to talk foolishly. **3** (*also* **turkey**) to speak frankly and without reserve, to talk hard facts, to get down to business. **4** to use high-flown language. [the bird's central role in a trad. Christmas dinner]

talk up a breeze *v.* [1940s+] to talk in a fluent, persuasive manner. [var. on TALK UP A STORM *v.*]

talk up a storm *v.* (*also* **beg up a storm**) [1940s+] (*US*) to talk loudly, at length and impressively. [SE *storm*]

talk wet *v.* [1910s+] to talk in a sentimental, 'soft' manner; to talk stupidly. [WET adj.[3] (1)]

talky *adj.* [late 19C–1900s] (*US*) chatty, verbose; self-opinionated.

talky-talk *n.* (*also* **talky-talky**) [late 19C+] idle, futile, empty talk; thus adj. *talky-talky*.

talky-talky boots *n.* [late 19C] (*W.I.*) squeaky shoes or boots.

tall *adj.*[1] **1** [mid-17C–19C] of speech, boastful, high-flown. **2** [mid-19C] of speech, intense, melodramatic. **3** [mid-19C+] of speech, extravagant, untrue; esp. in phr. TALL STORY n.

tall *adj.*[2] **1** [mid-19C] (*UK Und.*) well-supplied. **2** [mid-19C] (*UK Und.*) many, a large number of. **3** [mid-19C+] (*orig. US*) large, esp. in quantity, e.g. of money; also in phr. TALL ORDER n. **4** [mid-19C+] serious, substantial; usu. with v., such as *tall drinking*; thus TALL WEEPING n.

tall *adj.*[3] [mid-19C+] (*orig. US*) excellent in quality; thus *tallest*, best. [? TALL adj.[1] (3), i.e. the boastfulness of *tall stories*, in which everything appears to be marvellous, superlative etc; or TALL adj.[2] (3)]

tall *adj.*[4] **1** [mid-19C+] (*orig. UK Und.*) drunk (cf. ELEVATED adj.). **2** [1930s–60s] (*US drugs*) intoxicated by marijuana. [play on HIGH adj.[1]; (1) 20C+ use is US Black]

tallawah *adj.* [1950s+] (*W.I.*) **1** honest, honourable, decent. **2** sturdy, fearless, physically capable. [synon. Ewe *talala*]

tall boy *n.* **1** [late 17C–early 19C] (*also* **tallen**) a large wine glass. **2** [late 17C–early 19C] a 2-quart (2.5-litre) pot filled with wine. **3** [1970s+] (*US*) a tall glass or can of beer.

tall cotton *n. see* HIGH COTTON n.

tallie *n.* [1930s+] (*Aus.*) a 'tall' story. [TALL adj.[1] (3)]

tall money *n.* [1940s+] (*US Black*) a large amount of money, substantial wealth. [TALL adj.[2] (3)]

tall order *n.* (*also* **big/large order**) [late 19C+] an excessive or extreme demand. [TALL adj.[2] (3)]

tallow *n.* [19C] semen (cf. BOLLOCK SNOT n.). [resemblance]

tallow-breeched *adj.* [18C–19C] having fat buttocks. [SE *tallow*, fatness + *breech*, the posterior]

tallow-gutted *adj.* [18C–19C] pot-bellied. [SE *tallow*, fatness + SE *guts*]

tallow pot n. [1910s–40s] (*US tramp/railroad*) a locomotive fire man.

tallow up one's pole v. [19C–1950s] to have sexual intercourse, esp. after a period of abstinence (cf. BURY IT v.). [the image is of a saddle that becomes dried out with inactivity and needs rubbing with tallow soap, in this case TALLOW n.]

tall paper n. see BIG PAPER n.

tall poppy n. [1930s+] (*Aus.*) a conspicuously high earner or other VIP. [SE *tall*; the idea being that they can be knocked down]

tall story n. (*also* **tall tale**) [mid-19C+] an extravagant, boastful story, a lie. [TALL adj.¹ (3)]

tall talk n. [mid-19C+] (*orig. US*) boasting, bragging, the telling of far-fetched stories and anecdotes. [TALL adj.¹ (3) + SE *talk*]

tall-talker n. [mid-late 19C] a braggart, a boaster. [TALL TALK n.]

tall timber n. (*US*) **1** [mid-19C+] the rural areas, the backwoods, lit. and fig. **2** [1920s] the gallows.

tall 'un n. [late 19C–1900s] a pint of coffee. [SE *tall one*]

tall weeping n. [late 19C] (*US*) intense grief. [TALL adj.¹ (4) + SE *weeping*]

tally-boy n. see TARRY-BOY n.

tally ho n.¹ [20C+] (*Irish*) confusion, fuss. [SE excl. *tally ho!*, esp. in foxhunting]

tally ho n.² [2000s] (*US prison*) rubber cement found in prison shoes, used as an inhalant.

tally-ho v. see LIVE TALLY v.

tally-husband n. (*also* **tally-man**) [18C–19C] the man with whom a woman cohabits. [LIVE TALLY v. although this seems to predate it; cf. TALLY-WIFE n.]

tallywag n. (*also* **tallywock, tooleywag**) [late 18C–19C] the penis. [TALLYWAGS n.]

tallywagger n.¹ [20C+] (*Anglo-Irish*) a thread dangling from the hem of a garment or from the edge of a rug, carpet etc. [TALLYWHACKER n.]

tallywagger n.² see TALLYWHACKER n.

tallywags n. (*also* **tarrywags**) [18C–early 19C] the testicles; the male genitals. [? SE *tally*, a notched stick or TAIL n.² (2)]

tally water n. [2000s] (*US prison*) an intoxicant that is inhaled.

tallywhacker n. (*also* **dillywhacker, tallywagger, tilly-whacker**) [20C+] the penis. [later ext. of TALLYWAG n.]

tally-wife n. (*also* **tally-woman**) [19C] the woman with whom a man cohabits. [LIVE TALLY v.; cf. TALLY-HUSBAND n.]

tallywock n. see TALLYWAG n.

t.a.l.o.i.a. phr. [1950s+] there's *a lot of it about*. [abbr.]

tam n. **1** [1930s+] (*US, later use gay*) any form of hat. **2** [1950s+] (*W.I. Rasta*) the large woollen hat used by Rastafarians to cover their dreadlocks. [abbr. SE *tam o'shanter*]

tamale n.¹ [1960s+] (*US gay*) gaudy ceramic crockery typical of that sold to tourists in Mexico. [Sp. *tamale*, a Mexican dish consisting of corn husks wrapped around a variety of fillings]

tamale n.² see HOT TAMALE n.

Tamaleville n. see TACO TOWN n.

Tambaroora n. [late 19C–1940s] (*Aus.*) a bar game in which the winner buys drinks for the players; thus *Tambaroora muster*, a group of drinkers pooling their money and buying one 'wholesale' round, since in this way more alcohol can be purchased. [*Tambaroora*, a town in New South Wales, home of the game]

tambourine man n. [1960s+] (*US drugs*) a drug dealer. [? the Bob Dylan song *Mr Tambourine Man* (1964)]

tamp v. [1940s+] (*US Black*) **1** to walk, to go. **2** to pump, to fill.

tampax n. [1990s+] (*UK juv.*) a general term of abuse. [*Tampax*, a proprietary brand of tampons]

tamp braces n. see TAMPON BRACES n.

tampi n. [1970s+] marijuana. [ety. unknown]

tamping n. [1960s] (*US prison*) a beating. [TAMP SOMEONE UP v.]

tampon n. [2000s] a snobbish person. [they are both 'stuck up']

tampon braces n. (*also* **tamp braces**) [1930s–40s] (*US Black*) a derog. term for unattractive legs on a woman.

tamp someone up v. [1920s–60s] (*US*) to beat someone up. [SE *tamp*, to ram down hard]

tamtart n. see JAM TART n. (2).

ta muchly phr. [late 19C+] thank you very much. [TA phr. + MUCHLY adv.]

t.a.n. adj. [1980s+] (*US campus*) aggressively masculine. [abbr. tough *as nails*]

Tan n. [2000s] (*Irish*) an English person. [*Black and Tans*, pro-Ulster Protestants]

tan v. **1** [17C+] to hit, to attack; usu. in phr. TAN SOMEONE'S HIDE v. **2** [1970s+] (*also* **tan it**) in fig. use, to do something aggressively or to extreme, e.g. *tan the bevvy*, to drink heavily. [SE *tan*, to process skins into leather]

tancy lee n. see NANCY LEE n. (2).

T & A see under TITS AND ASS.

tang n.¹ [1960s] (*US*) the vagina. [SE *tangy*]

tang n.² [1970s+] (*US campus*) someone who puts a damper on things. [SE *tang*, a flavour; such a person gives the situation an 'unpleasant flavour']

tangi n. [20C+] (*N.Z.*) a party involving (heavy) drinking. [Maori *tangi*, a tribal gathering at a funeral]

Tangier n. [18C–19C] a room in Newgate jail, dedicated to the imprisonment of debtors, who were known as *tangerines*. [the sufferings imposed on the victims of the contemporary Tangiers pirates]

tangle n. [late 19C–1900s] (*Aus.*) alcoholic liquor. [its effects]

tangle v. [mid-late 19C] to add alcohol to a drink. [TANGLE n.]

tangle (assholes) v. (*also* **tangle ass, tangle holes**) [1920s+] (*US*) to fight. [SE *tangle* + ASSHOLE n.¹ (1)/ASS n. (2)/HOLE n.¹ (1)]

tangled adj. [late 19C–1910s] (*Aus.*) drunk (cf. ALED UP adj.). [TANGLE n.]

tangle-foot n. (*also* **tanglehoof**) **1** [mid-19C–1930s] whisky. **2** [1910s–50s] (*Aus.*) second-rate liquor; occas. beer. [its effects]

tangle-footed adj. [mid-19C–1940s] drunk. [TANGLE-FOOT n.]

tangle holes v. see TANGLE (ASSHOLES) v.

tanglehoof n. see TANGLE-FOOT n.

tangle-leg n. [mid-19C–1900s] whisky. [its effects]

tangle-legged adj. [mid-19C] drunk (cf. ARSEHOLED adj.). [TANGLE-LEG n.]

tangle-monger n. [late 19C] (*UK society*) a woman scandal-monger. [SE *tangle*, a knotted mess + -MONGER sfx]

tangler n. [1940s] a small-time crook who deals in smuggled or stolen property. [SE *tangle*, a mess]

tangle with v. **1** [1910s+] to fight with; lit. or fig. **2** [1940s+] (*also* **tangle up with**) to become involved with. **3** [1970s] to meet.

tango pirate n. [20C+] (*US*) a gigolo. [such men took advantage of the tango craze of the early 20C to meet, seduce and even live off the affluent women at tea-dances]

tang out v. [1970s+] (*US campus*) to abandon, to put an end to. [TANG n.²]

tan it v. see TAN v. (2).

tank n.¹ **1** [late 19C–1940s] (*also* **beer-tank**) a drinker, a drunkard. **2** [1930s–50s] (*Aus./US*) a pint of beer. [TANK (UP) v.; (2) ? influenced by SE *tankard*]

tank n.² **1** [late 19C+] (*Aus./US prison*) a cell. **2** [1910s+] (*Can./US prison*) a holding cell. **3** [1930s+] (*N.Z. Und.*) a safe; thus *tank artist, tankblower, tankman*, a safe-cracker. **4** [1950s+] (*Can./US prison*) a prison, a prison wing. **5** [1970s+] a bank. [SE *tank*, a storage receptacle]

tank n.³ **1** [1910s+] a worn-out old prostitute. **2** [1960s–70s] (*US campus*) an unattractive woman. [the then newly invented SE *tank*, a bulky and mis-shapen form of weapon]

tank n.⁴ [1930s–40s] (*US Und.*) a bulletproof car.

tank n.⁵ [2000s] money. [TANK n.² (5)]

tank *n.*[6] *see* TANK TOWN n.

tank *v.*[1] [1920s+] **1** (*also* **go in the tank**) to abandon deliberately, to give up, poss. for illicit monetary gain, esp. in boxing; thus *tank fight*, *tank job*, a contest in which one fighter has been bribed to lose; *tanking*, the deliberate losing of matches. **2** to fail. [SE *tank*, a swimming pool, thus the boxer 'takes a dive']

tank *v.*[2] **1** [1940s+] (*US*) to beat up. **2** [1990s+] (*Ulster*) to administer a paramilitary 'punishment beating'. [(1) also linked to TANK v.[1]]

tank *v.*[3] *see* TANK (INTO) v.

tank *v.*[4] *see* TANK (UP) v.

tanka *n.* [1980s+] (*US campus*) a large container of soft drink. [SE *tanker*, i.e. a large receptacle]

tank act *n. see* TANK JOB n.

tanked (up) *adj.* **1** [late 19C+] drunk; thus intensified in phr. *tanked to the wide*. **2** [1960s] intoxicated by a drug. **3** [1960s] in fig. use, satiated, filled up with. [TANK (UP) v.]

tanker *n.*[1] [1910s–30s] a heavy drinker. [TANK (UP) v.]

tanker *n.*[2] [1920s+] **1** a prize-fighter who has agreed to accept cash in return for losing a fight. **2** in fig. use, a second-rate person. [TANK v.[1]]

tankie *n.* [1990s+] (*UK juv.*) a very fat person. [they are 'built like a tank']

tanking *n.* [1980s] (*UK tramp*) the act of concealing money on one's person; thus *deep tanking*, concealing money deep within one's clothing.

tank (into) *v.* [1990s+] to rush towards, to attack.

tank job *n.* (*also* **tank act**) [1930s] a corrupt sporting contest with a pre-arranged result. [TANK v.[1] (1)]

tank time *n.* [1980s+] (*US campus*) time to start drinking. [TANK (UP) v.]

tank town *n.* (*also* **tank**) [20C+] (*US*) a small, insignificant town. [the positioning of water tanks at such railway stops, the only reason why a train might stop there; note late 19C US theatrical *water tank show*, a small touring company]

tank town *adj.* [1930s+] (*US*) insignificant, petty. [TANK TOWN n.]

tank-up *n.* [1950s] a heavy drinking session. [TANK (UP) v.]

tank (up) *v.* **1** [late 19C+] to drink heavily. **2** [1970s+] in fig. use, to satisfy one's appetite, to fill up with food. [SE *tank*, a cistern]

tanky *adj.* [1930s+] (*US*) drunk. [TANK (UP) v.]

tanna *n. see* TOMMY TANA n.

tanner *n.* [early 19C–1970s] a sixpence (2½p); thus [late 19C–1910s] *tannergram*, a sixpenny telegram; [1900s–10s] *tannercab*, a sixpenny cab. [Rom. *tawno*, small, or f. a ponderous biblical joke about St Peter's supposed banking transaction when he 'lodged with one Simon a tanner']

tanner case *n.* [early 19C] a pocket. [TANNER n.]

tannery *n.* **1** [late 19C] (*US*) a pair of outsize boots or shoes. **2** [1910s] (*Aus.*) a school. [(1) SE *tannery*, a leather-maker's; (2) errant pupils will receive a TANNING n.]

tannie *n.* [1950s+] (*S.Afr.*) a narrow-minded, puritan, small-town woman. [Afk. *tante*, aunt; used affectionately or respectfully the word simply means 'auntie']

tanning *n.* [mid-19C+] a beating, a thrashing.

tan-pan-mi *n.* [1950s] (*W.I.*) ragged old work-clothes, esp. when very filthy. [lit. 'stand upon me', the clothing has become stiffened through the accretion of dirt]

tan pon it long *phr.* [1980s+] (*W.I./UK Black teen*) sexual stamina. [lit. 'stand up on it for a long time']

tan so back *phr.* [1990s+] (*W.I.*) calm down, stop being aggressive. [lit. 'stand back']

tan someone's hide *v.* [17C+] to beat someone severely, to spank someone severely. [TAN v. (1) + HIDE n.[1] (1)]

tan-study *phr.* [1990s+] (*W.I.*) calm down, relax. [lit. 'stand steady']

tantadlin *n. see* TANTOBLIN n.

tantany *n. see* ANTHONY n.

tantaria *n.* [20C+] (*W.I.*) an abusive, loud, shrewish woman. [? SE *tantara*, imitation word for the sound of a trumpet or drum]

tante *n. see* AUNTIE n.[2] (1).

tantivy *n.* **1** [mid-17C–18C] (*also* **tantwivy**) imitative of the sound of a hunting horn. **2** [late 17C–mid-18C] (*also* **tantivy boy**) a nickname given to the post-Restoration High Churchmen and Tories, esp. in the reigns of Charles II (1660–85) and James II (1685–88). [SE *tantivy*, a gallop at full tilt. The nickname use arose *c.*1680, when a caricature was publ. in which a number of High Church clergymen were represented as mounted upon the Church of England and 'riding tantivy' to Rome, behind the Duke of York]

tantoblin *n.* (*also* **tantoblin tart, tantadlin**) [mid-17C–early 19C] a piece of excrement (cf. TOLY n.). [SE *tantoblin*, a large, round sweet tart/dial. *tantablin tart*, cow dung]

tantony *n. see* ANTHONY n.

tan track *n.* [late 19C] the anus (cf. ALLEY WAY n.). [Rodgers, *The Queen's Vernacular* (1972), suggests an origin in hobo use]

tan-tracker *n.* (*also* **tan-track rider**) [1930s+] (*orig. Aus.*) a homosexual man (cf. BROWN ARTIST n.). [TAN TRACK n.]

tantrems *n.* [mid–late 19C] pranks, games, jollification. [var. on TANTRUM n.[2] + dial. *tantrum*, a freak, a whimsy]

tan trouser snake *n. see* ONE-EYED TROUSER-SNAKE n.

tantrum *n.*[1] [late 17C–18C] the penis. [northern dial. *tantril*, a wanderer]

tantrum *n.*[2] [early 18C–19C] a burst of petulant ill-temper, seen as childish or actually produced by a child. [SE 20C+; ? Ital. *tarantella*, a whirling dance which may reduce the dancers to near- or apparent hysteria]

tantwivy *n. see* TANTIVY n. (1).

tanyok *n.* [18C+] a halfpenny. [Shelta]

taoc *n.* [mid–late 19C] a coat. [backsl.]

tap *n.*[1] [late 19C+] (*US*) a very small amount.

tap *n.*[2] **1** [1930s] (*US tramp*) a house known to be a good place to beg. **2** [1990s+] a loan, an act of requesting a loan. [TAP v.[3] (2)]

tap *n.*[3] [1930s–60s] (*US*) a robbery; a confidence trick. [TAP v.[4]]

tap *n.*[4] *see* TAP (ON THE SHOULDER) n.

tap *v.*[1] [early 18C; 1930s] to spend freely and generously. [the image is of 'turning on a *tap*' of gifts etc]

tap *v.*[2] **1** [mid-18C–19C] to hit and thus draw blood from a victim's nose; thus TAP SOMEONE'S CLARET v. **2** [1920s+] (*US Und.*) to hit on the head. **3** [1940s+] to have sexual intercourse. **4** [2000s] to shoot (dead). [SE *tap*, to hit + *tap*, a valve]

tap *v.*[3] **1** [mid-19C–1940s] to arrest. **2** [late 19C+] (*also* **tap for, tap up**) to beg for, to accost someone for something, to ask for a loan, whether of money or fig. **3** [20C+] to obtain money (other than as a loan). **4** [1910s] (*US*) to exhaust one's finances. **5** [1920s+] (*also* **tap up**) to defraud, to cheat. [the lit. or fig. *tap* on the shoulder]

tap *v.*[4] [mid-19C+] (*US Und.*) to rob, to steal from.

tap *v.*[5] **1** [1920s+] (*US*) to select for a college fraternity or society. **2** [1940s+] to select, to 'line up'. [a *tap* on the shoulder]

tap a damper *v. see* TAP A TILL v.

tap a girl *v.* [late 17C–early 19C] to deflower a woman. [SE *tap*, to open; but note TAP v.[2] (3)]

tap a house *v.* [late 19C] to burgle a house. [SE *tap*, to open]

tap a judy *v.*[1] [mid–late 19C] to deflower a girl. [SE *tap*, to hit + JUDY n.[1] (1); there is a sub-ref. to TAP SOMEONE'S CLARET v., given the release of blood; but note TAP v.[2] (3)]

tap a judy *v.*[2] [mid–late 19C] to cause one's nose to bleed with a blow. [ext. of TAP A JUDY v.[1]]

tap a kidney *v.* (*also* **tilt a kidney**) [1970s+] (*US*) to urinate (cf. BLEED ONE'S TURKEY v.).

tap a till *v.* (*also* **tap a damper, till-tap**) [mid-19C+] to rob, to steal, usu. from a cash register; thus *till-tapping*, TILL-TAPPER n. [TAP v.[4] + SE *till*]

tap city *n.* **1** [1920s+] the state of being unable to raise a stake for further betting. **2** [1920s+] a metaphorical place devoted to borrowing or begging money. **3** [1930s+] (*also* **tapsville**) a state of poverty. [SE *tap*, f. the tradition of tapping the table to signify passing in poker/TAP v.³ (2)/TAP OUT v. (1) + CITY sfx/-VILLE sfx¹]

tapdance v. **1** [1920s+] (*orig. US*) to wriggle out of trouble, to evade something cleverly. **2** [1940s] (*US gay*) to masturbate; thus *tapdancer*, a masturbator (of others) (cf. DANCE WITH JOHNNIE ONE-EYE v.).

tap dancer n. [1980s] (*Aus.*) cancer. [rhy. sl.]

tape n. [early 18C–19C] a fiery drink, spirits, usu. gin. [ety. unknown; ? link to SE *taphouse*]

taped adv. [1910s+] (*US*) sized up, fully understood; usu. as *have someone taped*. [the use of a fig. *tape measure*]

taped-up adj. [1970s–80s] (*US Black*) of a woman, already with a boyfriend, thus secured from other admirers.

tape off v. [1920s+] (*Aus.*) **1** to prepare, to get ready, to put into place. **2** to reprimand. **3** to measure out correctly. [SE *tape measure*]

taper adj. [mid-19C] of money or supplies, diminishing, running out. [SE *taper off*]

taper (off) v. **1** [late 19C] to gradually diminish the quantity or potency of one's drink. **2** [1910s–40s] (*drugs*) to withdraw from narcotics by gradual reduction of dosage. **3** [1940s] (*drugs*) to force someone to withdraw from narcotics by reducing their dose.

tape the gerbil v. [1990s+] (*US teen*) to study hard. [ety. unknown]

tap for v. *see* TAP v.³ (2).

tapioca adj. [1930s–70s] (*US*) absolutely penniless. [TAP OUT v. (1)]

tap-lash n. **1** [early 17C–early 19C] inferior liquor, esp. its dregs. **2** [mid-17C–early 18C] a publican. [SE *tap* + *lash*, lit. 'beat the tap', i.e. thump it in order to extract the very last drips from the cask or barrel]

tap off v. [1990s+] to pick up or seduce. [ext. of TAP v.² (3), on model of COP OFF v.⁴]

tap (on the shoulder) n. [late 18C–early 19C] an arrest.

tap out v. **1** [1930s+] (*orig. US*) to come to the end of one's finances. **2** [1960s] to fail, to 'draw a blank'. **3** [1960s–70s] to relieve someone of their last money. **4** [1970s] (*Aus.*) in a fight, to give in, to surrender by indicating with a tap on the ground. **5** [1980s+] (*US campus*) to be exhausted. **6** [2000s] to reach a conclusion. [SE *tap* running out, also gambling use of tapping on the table to signify passing; (5) is fig. use of (1)]

tapped adj. [1910s+] insane, crazy. [DOOLALLY TAP n.]

tapped-out adj. (*also* **tapped**) **1** [1930s+] drunk. **2** [1950s+] out of money, having nothing to use for further betting. **3** [1970s+] emotionally or mentally destroyed. **4** [1980s+] (*US*) exhausted. **5** [1990s+] intoxicated by a drug, usu. crack cocaine. [TAP OUT v.]

tapper n.¹ **1** [late 18C–early 19C] a bailiff. **2** [20C+] a cadger, a beggar. [(1) SE *tap* on the shoulder; (2) TAP v.³]

tapper n.² [1910s–30s] one who cuts into casks of wine or spirits and uses a straw to drink the contents. [SE *tap*, to broach a cask]

tapper and sucker racket n. [1940s–50s] (*UK Und.*) a scheme to arrange for typewriters and vacuum cleaners to be left on approval at a residence, the goods would then be sold and the premises quickly vacated by the con-man and his partner.

taps n. [mid-18C–19C] the ears. [because they tap conversations]

tap someone's claret v. [early 19C–1920s] to cause someone's nose to bleed with a blow.

tapsville n. *see* TAP CITY n. (3).

tap the admiral v. [mid–late 19C] to suck liquor through a straw from the ship's barrel which has been bored with a gimlet. [according to Hotten (1864), the practice originated when sailors sucked out the liquor from the barrel in which Admiral Horatio Nelson's body had been preserved on the journey home after his death at the battle of Trafalgar, 'to such an extent as to leave the gallant Admiral high and dry']

tap-tub n. [early–mid-19C] the *Morning Advertiser* newspaper, also known as the *Gin and Gospel Gazette*. [SE *tap*, to broach a cask + *tub* (of liquor); the paper was the virtual house journal of the great and powerful brewing families]

tap up v.¹ [2000s] (*drugs*) to tap a vein in order to make it stand out from the surrounding flesh preparatory to an injection of narcotics.

tap up v.² *see* TAP v.³.

tar n.¹ [late 17C+] a sailor. [the use of tar on board ship]

tar n.² [1900s] (*US*) money. [appearance]

tar n.³ [1930s+] (*drugs*) opium, heroin (cf. APOSTLE n.; BLACK n.³). [colour and consistency of Mexican heroin]

ta-ra n. [1970s+] a goodbye; usu. as *say ta-ra*. [TA-RA phr.]

ta-ra phr. [1950s+] (*mainly northern*) goodbye.

taradiddle n. (*also* **tarradiddle**) [late 18C–1970s] a petty lie; thus *taradiddler*, a petty liar. [DIDDLE v.² (2)]

taradiddle! excl. [mid-19C] rubbish! nonsense! [TARADIDDLE n.]

Taranaki bullshit n. [1940s+] (*N.Z.*) excessive boasting. [BULLSHIT n. (1) + *Taranaki*, an area of the South Island, which has many dairy herds]

Taranaki cow n. [1940s+] (*N.Z.*) a nondescript, inferior cow. [for ety. *see* TARANAKI BULLSHIT n.]

Taranaki gate n. [20C+] (*N.Z.*) a gate made of strands of barbed wire interwoven with palings for strength. [for ety. *see* TARANAKI BULLSHIT n.]

Taranaki sunshine n. [1990s+] (*N.Z.*) rain or drizzle. [*Taranaki*, an area of the South Island]

Taranaki top dressing n. [1940s+] (*N.Z.*) cattle dung. [for ety. *see* TARANAKI BULLSHIT n.]

tar and feather n. [20C+] **1** leather, usu. a leather jacket. **2** weather. [rhy. sl.]

tarantula-juice n. [mid-19C–1930s] inferior whisky. [its alcoholic 'bite']

tar baby n. **1** [20C+] (*US*) a 'sticky' problem. **2** [1940s+] (*US*) (*also* **tarpot**) a derog. term for a Black person (cf. BLACKBELLY n.). **3** [1950s] (*N.Z.*) a derog. term for a Maori. [the *Tar Baby*, created by Joel Chandler Harris in 1881, when in one of his 'Uncle Remus' tales the scheming Br'er Fox, determined to catch Harris's lapine hero Br'er Rabbit, 'got im some tar, en mix it wid some turkentime, en fix up a contrapshun what he call a Tar-Baby']

tar-boiler/-burner n. *see* TARHEEL n.

tar bucket n. [1920s] (*US*) coffee.

tard n. [1970s+] (*US*) a fool. [abbr. RETARD n.]

tare an' ages! excl. (*also* **blur-an-age/-ouns! tare an' ouns!**) [mid-19C–1950s] (*Irish*) a euph. oath. [lit. 'tears and aches'; also blood/wounds (of Christ)]

t.a.r.f.u. phr. [1940s+] (*orig. US milit.*) things are really fucked-up (cf. S.N.A.F.U. n.). [abbr.]

target n.¹ [late 17C–19C] the vagina (cf. BEST IN CHRISTENDOM n.). [coined by John Wilmot, Earl of Rochester (1642–80)]

target n.² [1920s–40s] (*US Und.*) a lookout man.

target n.³ [1970s–80s] (*S.Afr. township*) anything, esp. a motor vehicle owned by a White-run company, seen as symbolic of apartheid and as such liable to criminal and violent acts.

tarheel n. (*also* **tar-boiler/burner**) [late 18C+] a native of North Carolina. [SE *tar* as a principal product of the state]

tarheel adj. [1920s] (*US*) pertaining to North Carolina or the state's culture. [TARHEEL n.]

tariff n. [2000s] a prison sentence.

tarleather n. [16C–17C] a general term of abuse directed at women. [SE *tarleather*, a strip of leather used in a flail. The women thus described are presumably seen as 'scolds' and, given that *leather* means vagina, the word is a distant precursor of PUSSY-WHIPPED adj. (1)]

tarman n. [1990s+] (*UK juv.*) a tampon.

tarnal adj. (*also* **eternal**) [late 18C+] (*US*) used as a usu. negative intensifier, cussed, DAMNED adj. [SE *eternal*]

tarnation *n.* [late 18C+] (*US*) a euph. for *hell*. [lit. DAMNATION *n.*; note 18C abbr. SE *nation*, damnation]

tarnation *adj.* [late 18C+] (*US*) hellish, damnable. [TARNATION n.]

tarnation *adv.* [late 18C+] (*US*) damnably. [TARNATION n.]

tarnation! *excl.* [late 18C+] (*US*) a euph. substitute for DAMNATION! excl. [TARNATION n.]

tar out *v.* [mid-19C–1900s] to punish, to beat. [i.e. BEAT THE TAR OUT OF v.]

tarp *n.* [20C+] *tarp*aulin. [abbr.]

tarpaulin *n.* [mid-17C–1920s] a sailor, esp. (in the days when appointments were made as much on connections as on ability) a sailor with practical experience of seamanship. [use of SE *tarpaulin* on ships]

tarpaulin *adj.* [late 17C] pertaining to sailors or sea-travel. [TARPAULIN n.]

tarpaulin muster *n.* (*also* **blanket muster, calico…, canvas…**) [late 19C+] (*Aus./N.Z.*) a collection of money, either for a round of drinks or for donation to a third party or a cause. [naut. jargon *tarpaulin muster*, a collection or pooling of money among seamen]

tar pit *n.* [1970s] (*US*) the anus. [the resemblance of *tar* to excrement]

tarpot *n.*[1] [1930s+] (*Aus./N.Z.*) a derog. term for a Maori or Aborigine; thus *hit the tarpot*, to pursue a Maori woman. [SE *tar* is black]

tarpot *n.*[2] *see* TAR BABY n. (2).

tarradiddle *n. see* TARADIDDLE n.

tarra-warra *n.* [1950s+] (*W.I. Rasta*) a polite way of expressing omitted bad words, a verbal asterisk. [? echoic of the hesitation over or mumbling of 'bad' words]

tarry-boy *n.* (*also* **tally-boy**) [1970s] (*Irish*) a dishonest, dubious or randy person. [Scot. *tarry-fingers*, dishonest person]

tarry-breeks *n.* (*also* **tarry brecks, …jacket, …john**) [late 18C–mid-19C] a sailor. [lit. 'tarry breeches'; TAR n.[1]]

tarry rope *n.* [1940s–60s] (*Aus.*) a woman, poss. a prostitute, who associates with sailors. [SE *tarry*, covered in tar + *rope*]

tarrywags *n. see* TALLYWAGS n.

tart *n.*[1] **1** [mid-19C+] a woman, a girlfriend; thus dimin. *tartlet*. **2** [late 19C+] a promiscuous woman, a prostitute; also of heterosexual men since 1960s. **3** [1930s+] (*gay*) an older man's young male lover. **4** [1930s+] (*gay*) a gay prostitute. **5** [1990s+] a promiscuous homosexual. **6** [2000s] a fool, irrespective of gender (cf. APPLEHEAD n.). [although (1) can still be found, usu. in dial., (2) has come to dominate since early 20C+, apart from Aus./N.Z., where the term remains positive or neutral]

tart *n.*[2] *see* TARTAR n. (2).

tart *adj.* [late 19C] (*US*) mediocre, second-rate.

tart *v.* [1940s] (*Aus./N.Z.*) to pursue women. [TART n.[1] (1)]

tart (about) *v. see* TART AROUND v.

tartan *n.* [2000s] (*UK Und.*) cocaine. [? rhy. sl.]

tartar *n.* **1** [late 16C–18C] a strolling vagabond, a beggar, a criminal mendicant. **2** [late 16C–1940s] (*also* **tart**) a general derog. description. **3** [late 17C–19C] a champion, an expert; thus CATCH A TARTAR v. [proper name *Tartar*, an inhabitant of the region of Central Asia extending east from the Caspian Sea, and formerly known as Independent and Chinese Tartary; ult. Persian *Tatar*, but linked in Western ears and superstitions with Lat. *tartarus*, hell]

tartarian *n.* [early–mid-17C] a thief. [ext. of TARTAR n. (1)]

tart around *v.* (*also* **tart (about)**) [1930s+] of a woman, to act in a promiscuous manner. [TART n.[1] (2)]

tarted up *adj.* **1** [1930s+] usu. of women, flashily overdressed. **2** [1950s+] applied to anything overdecorated, e.g. a 'theme pub'. [TART UP v.]

tart fuel *n.* [2000s] alcopops. [TART n.[1] (2)]

tart up *v.* **1** [1930s+] of a person, to dress up. **2** [1950s+] of an object, to decorate, to ornament. [TART n.[1] (2)]

tart with *v.* [1940s] to flirt with. [TART n.[1] (2)]

tarty *adj.* [1910s+] cheap, gaudy, vulgar, thus fig. reminiscent of a prostitute. [TART n.[1] (2)]

Tas *adj.* (*also* **Tassie**) [late 19C+] (*Aus.*) Tasmanian. [abbr.]

tash *n.* (*also* **tache, tasche, tush**) [mid-19C+] mous*tache*. [abbr.]

taste *n.* **1** [late 19C+] (*UK Und.*) a share of e.g. a bribe, the proceeds of a robbery. **2** [late 19C+] a very small amount, an almost imperceptible degree, a little. **3** [1920s+] a sample, a piece. **4** [1930s+] a drink, alcohol. **5** [1950s–60s] a sum of money. **6** [1960s+] a sample of drugs; a small measure of drugs. **7** [1970s+] sexual intercourse. **8** [1980s+] (*Aus./US*) an injection of heroin.

taste *adj.* [1980s] (*US campus*) enviable, appealing, attractive. [backform. f. TASTY adj. (2)]

taste *v.* [17C–19C] to have sexual intercourse.

taste bud *n.* [1960s+] the clitoris (cf. BABY IN THE BOAT n.). [esp. in the context of cunnilingus]

taste the sun *v.* [late 19C] of a Londoner, to spend a day in the country.

-tastic *sfx* [1990s+] an intensifying sfx, added to a n. to make it an adj. expressing an extreme, usu. positive (cf. PIMPTASTIC adj.; SHAGTASTIC adj.; SMACKTASTIC adj.). [SE fan*tastic*]

tasty *adj.* **1** [late 18C+] pleasant, admirable, well-dressed. **2** [late 19C+] sexually alluring, attractive. **3** [1970s+] of a person, smart, sharp, prob. criminal; thus *tasty villain*, a known criminal. **4** [1980s+] of a thing (usu. some form of criminal plan), valuable, worthwhile.

tasty (bit of) pastry *n.* [1940s+] a sexy woman. [TASTY adj. (1) + PASTRY n.]

Taswegian *n.* [1930s+] (*Aus.*) a person from Tasmania. [play on SE *Glaswegian*]

tat *n.*[1] [mid-19C–1900s] (*Anglo-Ind.*) a pony. [Hind. *tatti*, a native-bred pony; Ind. army officers imported their own horses]

tat *n.*[2] **1** [mid-19C–1900s] (*also* **tatter**) an old rag; thus *milky tats*, linen or otherwise white cloth rags. **2** [1920s+] anything seen as mediocre, vulgar, rubbishy. [Hind. *tat*, a strip of coarse canvas, used to make mats or screens; thus as SE, coarse canvas made esp. of jute and used for sacking]

tat *n.*[3] [20C+] (*US*) any confidence trick, usu. performed with dice; thus *ring a tat into*, to fool, to play a confidence trick on. [TATS n. (1)]

tat *n.*[4] (*also* **tatt**) [1960s+] (*orig. US prison*) a *tat*too. [abbr.]

tat *adj.* [1950s+] second-rate. [TAT n.[2] (2)]

tat *v.*[1] [early–mid-19C] to flog, to thrash. [Hampshire dial. *tat*, to pat]

tat *v.*[2] **1** [mid-19C] to gather rags for a living. **2** [1970s+] (*US gay*) to piece together, to create something out of left-over bits and pieces. [TAT n.[2]]

ta-ta *n.* **1** [late 19C+] a goodbye, an act of farewell. **2** [1930s] a hat. [TA-TA phr.]

ta-ta *v.* [1910s–30s] to say goodbye, to leave. [TA-TA n. (1)]

ta-ta *phr.* [mid-19C+] goodbye. [earlier use in nursery context]

tata *n.*[1] [early 19C+] (*W.I.*) father, an affectionate and respectful title for an old man. [infant mispron. but note its use in many African languages, e.g. Ewe, Ge, N'gombe]

tata *n.*[2] [1920s+] a foolish person. [such a person tends to use baby talk, e.g. *go for a tata*, go for a walk]

tataram *n.* [1930s+] (*W.I.*) a foolish old man, esp. one with sex on his mind. [TATA n.[1] + RAM n.[1] (2)]

ta-tas *n.*[1] [1960s] (*Aus.*) delirium tremens.

ta-tas *n.*[2] [1980s+] (*US*) the female breasts. [TITTY n.[1] (1)]

tat-box *n.* [mid–late 19C] a dice-box. [TATS n. (1) + SE *box*]

tate *n.* [1950s] the buttocks (cf. ALA n.). [rhy. sl. = DATE n.[3] (2)]

Tate and Lyle *n.* [20C+] style, i.e. cheek, audacity. [rhy. sl.; ult. a well-known brand of sugar]

tater *n.* (*also* **tatur**) **1** [mid-18C+] a po*tato*; often in pl. **2** [late 19C+] a hole in one's sock. [(1) abbr.; (2) fig. use of (1) i.e. the exposed, dirty flesh resembles the vegetable]

tater and point *n.* [mid–late 19C] a meal made up almost entirely of potatoes. [dial. *taties and point*, potatoes plus a small piece of fish or meat, so tiny as only to be pointed at, rather than providing any nutrition]

tater-eater *n. see* POTATO-EATER *n.*

tater-pillin' *n.* [20C+] a shilling (5p). [rhy. sl.; TATER *n.* (1) + pron. of SE *peeling*]

taters (in the mould) *adj.* [20C+] cold. [rhy. sl.; ult. TATER *n.* (1)]

tater-trap *n.* (*also* **tatoe-trap, tatur-trap**) [early 19C–1910s] the mouth. [TATER *n.* (1) + SE *trap*/TRAP *n.*³; var. on POTATO-TRAP *n.*]

tatie *n.* (*also* **tato, tattie**) [19C+] a po*tato*. [abbr.]

tatler *n.* (*also* **tattler**) [late 17C–mid-19C] a watch, esp. a striking watch or a repeater. [SE *tattler*, one who tattles or gossips, use revived by US Blacks]

tatlers *n.* [early 19C] (*US*) money. [ety. unknown; ? the noise of coins rattling in the pocket]

tat-monger *n.* [late 17C–early 19C] a professional dice-cheat. [TATS *n.* (1) + -MONGER sfx]

tato *n. see* TATIE *n.*

tatoe-trap *n. see* TATER-TRAP *n.*

Tat's *n. see* TATT's *n.* (1).

tats *n.* (*also* **tatts**) **1** [late 17C+] dice, esp. crooked dice. **2** [1910s+] (*Aus./N.Z.*) teeth. **3** [1960s+] (*Aus./N.Z.*) a set of false teeth. [ety. unknown; ? the rattle of the dice as they hit the table; (2) and (3) refers to the ivory in dice and teeth]

tats and all! *excl.* [early 19C] nonsense! rubbish! humbug! [fig. use of TATS *n.* (1)]

Tatt *n. see* TATT's *n.* (2).

tatt *n. see* TAT *n.*⁴.

tatter *n.*¹ [17C] a beggar. [SE *tatter*]

tatter *n.*² *see* TAT *n.*² (1).

tatter a kip *v.* [mid-18C] to wreck a brothel. [SE *tatter*, to tear to pieces + KIP *n.*¹ (1)]

tatterdemallion *n.* [17C–1920s] **1** (*UK Und.*) a wandering beggar who deliberately adopts ragged, filthy clothes in the hope of extracting more money from the kind-hearted. **2** a rascal. [SE *tatterdemallion*, a person in ragged clothing]

tattie *n. see* TATIE *n.*

tatting *n.* **1** [mid-19C–1930s] gathering old rags. **2** [1990s+] collecting scrap iron. [TAT *n.*²]

tattle-basket *n.* (*also* **tattle, tattle-box**) [18C] a gossip.

tattler *n.*¹ [18C] (*UK Und.*) the moon. [its light 'tells tales' on criminal activity]

tattler *n.*² *see* TATLER *n.*

tattle-tale *n.* **1** [late 19C+] a gossip. **2** [1920s+] an informer.

tatt man *n.* [mid-19C] (*UK Und.*) a professional dice gambler. [TATS *n.* (1)]

tattogey *n.* [mid-18C] **1** a dice-cloth, onto which one tosses the dice. **2** one who cheats by using loaded dice. [elision of TATTY TOG *n.*]

tattoo *n.*¹ [1960s] (*US drugs*) the mark of a narcotics injection.

tattoo *n.*² *see* DEVIL'S TATTOO *n.*

Tatt's *n.* **1** [mid–19C–1900s] (*also* **Tat's**) *Tattersall's* horse market in London. **2** [late 19C–1960s] (*Aus.*) (*also* **Tatt**) *Tatt's* sweep, a lottery established in 1881 on that year's Sydney Gold Cup by George Adams (1839–1904), licensee of Tattersall's Hotel, Sydney; thus *fair/square as Tatt's*, absolutely honest. [abbr.]

tatts *n. see* TATS *n.*

tatty *adj.* [1930s+] **1** inferior, cheap, badly made, shabby. **2** unkempt, untidy, dishevelled. [TAT *n.*²]

tatty muncher *n.* [1980s+] a derog. term for a Roman Catholic. [TATIE *n.*; stereotyping of the Irish, seen as Catholics, and a diet of potatoes]

tatty tog *n.* [early–mid-19C] a gaming cloth. [TATS *n.* (1) + TOG *n.*]

tatur *see under* TATER and its combs.

Taunton turkey *n.* [mid-19C–1950s] a salt herring. [the trade in such herrings in the town]

tavern treat *n.* [early 18C] sexual intercourse. [the physical and metaphorical proximity of taverns to brothels]

taw *n.* [1920s+] (*US Und.*) cash in hand, funds. [? SE *taw*, the large marble with which a player shoots]

tax *n.* **1** [1970s+] (*UK Black*) any form of entry charge, e.g. to a dance. **2** [1990s+] (*drugs*) (*also* **taxing**) a charge paid to enter a building where crack cocaine is sold. The charge is based either on the race of the customer (Whites pay more) or on the frequency of their custom. **3** [2000s] a stolen item, an act of theft.

tax *v.* **1** [mid-19C–1900s] (*US, esp. New England*) to set a price on, to charge. **2** [1980s+] to extort, to demand money with menaces. **3** [1980s+] to rob, to steal.

tax bite *n.* [1950s+] (*US*) the amount of tax one has to pay on a sum of money or salary cheque.

tax break *n.* [1960s+] (*orig. US*) a way of legally minimizing one's taxes.

tax-collector *n.* [mid–late 19C] a highwayman.

tax-fencer *n.* [late 19C] a disreputable shopkeeper, whose prices are set extortionately high. [SE *tax* + -FENCER sfx]

tax fiddle *n.* [1950s+] a way in which one can cheat or bypass the proper payment of one's taxes; thus *tax-fiddler*, one who cheats in this way. [FIDDLE *n.*³ (2)]

taxi *n.*¹ [1910s+] a small passenger aeroplane; thus *taxi-driver*, the pilot of such an aeroplane.

taxi *n.*² [1930s+] (*US*) a sentence of 5 to 15 years. [New York cabs which displayed these figures, indicating their rates per mile, on the side]

taxicabs *n.* [20C+] body lice. [rhy. sl. = CRAB *n.*²]

taxi eleven *n.* [1950s+] (*W.I.*) one's legs; thus *catch taxi eleven*, to walk. [the supposed similarity in shape of legs to the number 11]

taxing *n.*¹ [1980s+] (*drugs*) the robbery by small-time dealers of their more successful peers. [TAX *v.* (2)]

taxing *n.*² *see* TAX *n.* (2).

taxi rank *n.* [1990s+] a bank. [rhy. sl.]

taxi-rank *v.* [1970s+] to masturbate (cf. COTTON WOOL *v.*). [rhy. sl. = WANK *v.*]

taz *n.* [1920s+] **1** a beard. **2** a moustache. **3** light adolescent facial hair. [var. on TASH *n.*]

t.b. *n.*¹ (*US*) **1** [1920s–40s] a sufferer from tuberculosis. **2** [1930s–40s] a confidence trickster. [abbr. *TB*, tuberculosis; (2) tuberculosis = consumption, abbr. = *con* = CON *n.*¹ (6)]

t.b. *n.*² [1920s+] (*Aus.*) a pair of large and shapely breasts. [abbr. *two beauts*]

t.b. *n.*³ [1990s+] (*UK juv.*) a good-looking girl. [TIDY *adj.* (1) + BOILER *n.*³ (2)]

t-bagging *n. see* TEABAGGING *n.*

t.b.h. *n.* [1970s+] (*gay*) a potential sexual conquest. [abbr. *to be had*]

T-bird *n.* **1** [1950s+] a Ford *Thunderbird*. **2** [1980s+] *Thunderbird* wine, a cheap wine drunk primarily by alcoholics. [abbr.]

T-bone *n.* [1950s+] (*US Black*) a common Black nickname. [? SE *T-bone steak*, thus implying virility; however, Major, *Juba to Jive: A Dict. of Afro-American Slang* (1994), associates the def. with blues musician Aaron 'T-bone' Walker (1910–75), who took the name from his own middle name, Thibeaux, thus implying that the man, not the meat, was the paradigm]

T-bone *v.* [1990s+] (*US*) to crash into a car at a right angle, usu. by going over a red light at a junction.

T-buzz *n.* [1970s+] (*drugs*) phencyclidine (cf. ACE *n.*⁴). [T *n.*² + BUZZ *n.*³ (3)]

TCB *phr.* [2000s] (*US Black*) behaviour seen as stereotypically White. [abbr. typical *c*racker *b*ehaviour; CRACKER *n.*³ (2)]

t.c.b. *v. see* TAKE CARE OF BUSINESS *v.*

tchi *v.* (*also* **chy**) [late 19C–1950s] (*US drugs*) to roll an opium pellet preparatory to smoking. [? SE *Chinese*]

tchotchke *n.* (*also* chotchkie, tchatchka, tchotzke, tsatske) [1960s+] (*US*) **1** any small decorative thing. **2** an adorable person, esp. a small child. **3** a woman considered as a plaything. [Yid. *tsatske*, Slav *shaleh*, a plaything]

t'd off *adj. see* TEED OFF *adj.*

tea *n.*[1] **1** [late 17C–18C] strong liquor; often as COLD TEA *n.*[1], brandy. **2** [early 18C–early 19C; 1970s+] urine. **3** [late 19C+] (*US*) whisky. [reflecting the colour of tea without milk; (2) 1970s+ use is gay]

tea *n.*[2] (*drugs*) **1** [1930s+] marijuana (cf. AFRICAN BUSH *n.*). **2** [1930s+] a marijuana cigarette. **3** [1970s+] phencyclidine (cf. ACE *n.*[4]). [note the *OED* cit. from the *Boston Sunday Herald* (26 March 1967), 'Marijuana [...] when brewed with hot water', is surely no more than a teasing HIPPIE *n.*[2] (3) gulling a foolish journalist]

tea and cocoa *n.* [20C+] say-so. [rhy. sl.]

tea and sugar burglar *n.* (*also* **tea and sugar bandit**) **1** [late 19C–1900s] (*Aus.*) a vagrant. **2** [1960s+] a petty thief. [(1) the fig. 'theft' of the commodities, which are more likely offered free; (2) the smallness of the objects that are stolen]

tea and sugar man *n.* [1930s] (*UK tramp*) a casual labourer, who works for as long as it takes him to supply himself with his basic needs, before moving on.

tea-and-tattle *n.* [1920s+] (*Aus.*) a formal afternoon tea for a number of guests, a minor social get-together.

tea-and-toast *n.* [20C+] the post, the mail. [rhy. sl.]

tea and toast *v.* [1980s] (*Aus.*) to scold, to reprimand. [rhy. sl. = ROAST *v.* (3)]

tea-and-toast struggle *n.* [late 19C–1900s] a Wesleyan tea meeting, where the supply of tea rarely meets the demand.

teabag *n.* [2000s] a general term of abuse, a worthless, irrelevant person. [rhy. sl. = SLAG *n.*[1] (1)]

teabag *adj.* [1990s+] tear-jerking.

teabagging *n.* (*also* **t-bagging**) [1990s+] the sucking of a man's testicles by his partner. [the dipping action]

tea-bottle *n.* [late 19C–1900s] (*UK middle class*) an unmarried woman, a spinster. [her supposedly preferred beverage]

tea caddy *n.* [2000s] an Irish person (cf. BOG ARAB *n.*). [rhy. sl. = PADDY *n.* (1)]

teach *n.* [1940s+] **1** (*US*) (*also* **teech**) a teacher. **2** (*US Black*) anyone considered intelligent or intellectual. [abbr. SE *teacher*]

teach school *v.* [1970s+] (*US gay*) to initiate someone into the world of homosexuality.

teach someone a thing or two *v. see* KNOW A THING OR TWO *v.*

tea'd/tead up/teaed up *adj. see* TEED UP *adj.*

tea fight *n.* **1** [mid-19C] an evening party. **2** [mid-19C–1920s] a tea party.

tea fighter *n.* [late 19C] (*Aus.*) one who attends a tea party (and by implication dislikes alcohol). [TEA FIGHT *n.* (2)]

tea-for-two and a bloater *n.* [1900s–50s] a car. [rhy. sl. = MOTOR *n.*[2] (1)]

tea grout *n.* [20C+] a Boy Scout. [rhy. sl.]

Teague *n. see* TAIG *n.*

Teagueland *n.* [late 17C–mid-19C] Ireland. [TEAGUE *n.* + SE *land*]

Teaguelander *n.* [late 17C–mid-19C] an Irishman (cf. DONOVAN *n.*[1]). [TEAGUELAND *n.*]

tea-head *n.* [1940s+] (*drugs*) a marijuana smoker. [TEA *n.*[2] (1) + -HEAD sfx (3)]

tea-hound *n.*[1] [1920s] (*US*) **1** a man who frequents tea parties. **2** a womanizer. [SE *tea* + HOUND sfx]

tea-hound *n.*[2] [1930s+] (*orig. US Black*) a marijuana smoker. [TEA *n.*[2] (1) + HOUND sfx]

teahouse *n.*[1] [1930s+] (*drugs*) a house or apartment where people gather to buy and enjoy marijuana. [TEA *n.*[2] (1)]

teahouse *n.*[2] *see* TEAROOM *n.*

teaich gens *n. see* THEG GENS *n.*

teaich-gir *adj.* (*also* **teatchgir**) [mid-19C–1900s] right (quality, not direction); thus *tadging*, first-rate, excellent. [backsl., pron. 'tadger']

teaich guy *n.* [mid-19C] 8 shillings (40p). [backsl.]

teaich-yenneps *n.* [mid-19C] 8 pence. [backsl.]

tea joint *n.* [1940s] (*US*) a place, e.g. a bar or club, where marijuana can be smoked. [TEA *n.*[2] (1) + JOINT *n.*[4] (3)]

teakettle purger *n.* [mid-19C–1900s] a total abstainer. [? one who *purges*, i.e. cleans *teakettles* or uses tea to purge out alcohol; note def. in Ducange Anglicus, *The Vulgar Tongue* (1857): 'men who exchange their old clothes']

tea-leaf *n.* [late 19C+] a thief. [rhy. sl.]

tea-leaf *v.* **1** [late 19C+] (*orig. UK Und.*) to work as a thief; thus *tea-leafing*, thieving. **2** [1990s+] to rob. [TEA-LEAF *n.*]

team *n.* **1** [1930s+] a gang of criminals. **2** [1950s+] a squad of police. **3** [1980s+] (*Aus. prison*) a group of inmates.

team *adj.* [1980s+] (*US campus*) wearing clothes or accessories that brand one as part of an identifiable subculture.

tea-man *n.* [1930s–50s] (*US*) a smoker of marijuana. [TEA *n.*[2] (1) + SE sfx *-man*]

team cream *n.* [1960s+] (*orig. gay*) an orgy. [SE *team* + CREAM *v.*[1] (1)]

teameo *n.* (*also* **teamio**) [1920s–30s] (*US*) a member of the Teamsters' Union.

team-handed *adv.* [1950s+] (*UK Und.*) working in a group. [TEAM *n.* (1) + -HANDED sfx]

team Xerox *n.* [1980s+] (*US campus*) cheating. [TEAM XEROX *v.*]

team Xerox *v.* [1980s+] (*US campus*) to cheat. [*Xerox*, generic for to photocopy]

tea-oh! *excl.* [1940s+] (*N.Z.*) a call to indicate that it is time for a tea-break.

tea pad *n.* [1930s–60s] (*drugs*) a place for smoking marijuana. [TEA *n.*[2] (1) + PAD *n.*[2] (2)]

tea party *n.* [1930s–60s] (*drugs*) a gathering of people for the purpose of communal smoking of marijuana. [TEA *n.*[2] (1) + SE *party*]

teapot *n.*[1] [mid-19C] a Black person. [the colour of the typical brown/black *teapot*]

teapot *n.*[2] **1** [late 19C–1900s] a total abstainer. **2** [late 19C+] one who drinks an excessive amount of tea; often as *old teapot*, *regular teapot*.

teapot *n.*[3] [1990s+] (*UK juv.*) a male homosexual. [the children's song 'I'm a little teapot, short and stout...' and the gestures that accompany it; while designed to represent the teapot's handle and spout, they can also be interpreted as those of the stereotypical camp gay man with a 'broken', drooping wrist]

teapot (lid) *n.* [1920s+] **1** a Jew (cf. BILLY THE KID *n.*). **2** a child (cf. BILLY LID *n.*). **3** £1 sterling (cf. CHERRY-PICKER *n.*[5]). [rhy. sl.; (1) = YID *n.*[1]; (2) = KID *n.*[1] (1); (3) = QUID *n.* (2)]

teapot sucker *n.* [20C+] a teetotaller or other spoilsport.

tear *n.* **1** [mid-19C–1900s] (*US campus*) a perfect recitation. **2** [mid-19C+] (*orig. US*) a spree, a jollification; thus GO (OUT) ON A TEAR *v.*; [1900s] (*Aus.*) *hit up a tear*, to get drunk. **3** [1990s+] a state of excitement. [SE *tear*, to go at full tilt]

tear *v.* (*also* **tear up**) [late 16C+] to rush around excitedly, energetically; often as TEAR OFF *v.*[1].

tear and ages/wounds! *excl. see* TARE AN' AGES! *excl.*

tear-arse *n.*[1] (*also* **tear-ass**) **1** [20C+] cheese. **2** [1920s+] (*Aus.*) treacle, golden syrup. [their effect on the stomach; ARSE *n.*[1] (1)/ASS *n.* (2)]

tear-arse *n.*[2] (*also* **tear-ass**) [1920s+] a very busy, energetic person. [TEAR ARSE *v.*]

tear arse *v.* (*also* **tear ass**) [1920s+] to leave very quickly, to rush off; to rush around; often with prep., e.g. ...*about*, ...*away*. [TEAR *v.* + ARSE *n.*[1] (1)/ASS *n.* (2)]

tear-ass *adj.* [1970s+] agitated and angry. [TEAR ARSE *v.*]

tear a strip off *v. see* TEAR OFF A STRIP *v.*

tearaway *n.* [1930s+] a minor gangster, a small-time villain. [SE *tearaway*, an unruly person]

tearcat *n.* (*also* **tearer**) [17C–early 18C] a thug, a bully. [SE *tear*, to rip apart; note Nares: 'To TEAR A CAT. To rant, and behave with violence; probably from a cruel act of that kind having been performed by some daring ruffian, to excite surprise and alarm']

tear down *v.* **1** [late 19C+] (*US*) to reprimand severely, to attack verbally. **2** [1940s+] (*also* **tear the place down**) to demonstrate great emotion, to act intensely and wildly. **3** [1950s–60s] to depress. **4** [1970s] to destroy. [the victim's confidence is *torn down*]

tearing *adj.* **1** [mid-17C–1900s] impressive, splendid, first-rate. **2** [mid-17C–1920s] violent, rowdy or reckless in behaviour. **3** [1920s] of work, exhausting. [TEAR *v.*]

tear into *v.* [20C+] **1** (*also* **tear in**) to throw oneself enthusiastically into a task. **2** to attack physically or verbally.

tear it *v.* [20C+] to spoil one's chances, to put an end to one's plans etc; esp. in phr. *that's torn it!*

tear-it-down *n.* [1990s+] (*W.I.*) a fantastic performance.

tear it up *v. see* TEAR UP *v.*[1] (1).

tearjerker *n.* [1910s+] (*orig. US*) **1** a heavily romantic film with either a sad or happy conclusion, either of which should guarantee a weeping audience. Similarly used to describe mawkish ballads and love-songs, or a sad situation. **2** one who creates such material.

tearjerking *n.* [1940s+] an act of inducing sentimental feelings in someone. [backform. f. TEARJERKER *n.*]

tearjerking *adj.* (*also* **tearjerker, tear-yanking**) [1930s+] maudlin, sentimental. [backform. f. TEARJERKER *n.*]

tear loose *v.* [1970s+] (*US Black*) to escape from a person or situation.

tear off *v.*[1] [mid-19C+] to rush away, to leave at speed. [TEAR *v.*]

tear off *v.*[2] **1** [late 19C+] (*US*) to perform an action or activity. **2** [20C+] (*US Und.*) to steal. **3** [1940s] (*US Und.*) to cheat one's partner of their share of criminal profits. [SE *tear off*, to rip off a piece]

tear off *v.*[3] [1910s] (*US*) to speak in an aggressive manner.

tear off a lump *v.* [1910s] (*Aus.*) to succeed, to accomplish something.

tear off a piece *v.* (*also* **tear off a bit/chunk**) [1930s+] (*orig. Aus.*) of a man, to have sexual intercourse (cf. BREAK A BIT OFF *v.*). [SE *tear off* + PIECE *n.*[1] (3)/BIT *n.*[3]/SE CHUNK *n.*[1]]

tear off a strip *v.* (*also* **tear a strip off**) [1940s+] (*orig. RAF/milit.*) to criticize severely, to reprimand. [the fig. removal of a *strip(e)* of rank]

tear one's arse off *v.* (*also* **tear one's asshole out, tear one's guts out**) **1** [20C+] to work furiously. **2** [1960s+] to do something fast, to run away. [SE *tear* + ARSE *n.*[1] (1)/ASS *n.* (2)/ASSHOLE *n.*[1] (1)/GUTS *n.*[1] (2)]

tear one's ass *v.* (*also* **tear one's pants**) [1930s+] (*US*) to injure oneself, thus fig. to get into trouble. [SE *tear* + ARSE *n.*[1] (1)/ASS *n.* (2)/SE *pants*]

tearoom *n.* (*also* **teahouse, T-room**) [1920s+] (*US gay*) a public lavatory popular for casual sex and assignations. [SE *toilet* + *room* + play on SE *tearoom*]

tearoom queen *n.* (*also* **tearoom cruiser, T-room queen**) [1960s+] (*US gay*) a homosexual who hangs around public lavatories for sex. [TEAROOM *n.* + QUEEN *n.*[2] (1)/QUEEN *sfx* (2)/CRUISER *n.*[1] (5)]

tearoom trade *n.* (*also* **tea trade**) [1950s+] (*US gay*) **1** the world of sexual assignations, pick-ups and consummation practised in public lavatories. **2** men who enjoy being fellated in public lavatories. [TEAROOM *n.* + TRADE *n.* (3)]

tear open *v.* [1900s–50s] (*US Und.*) to rob extensively.

tear out *v.* [20C+] (*US Black*) to rush away, to leave fast. [TEAR *v.*]

tears *n.* [1930s–40s] (*US*) pearls. [resemblance]

tears and cheers *n.* [1920s–40s] (*US*) ears. [rhy. sl.]

tears of the tankard *n.* [late 17C–mid-19C] drops of liquor that fall onto the careless drinker's clothing.

tear someone a new ass(hole) *v.* (*also* **cut/rip someone a new ass(hole), tear someone a new one**) [1960s+] (*US*) to attack someone savagely, either physically or verbally. [ASS *n.* (2)/ASSHOLE *n.*[1] (1)]

tear someone's ass(hole) *v.* (*also* **cut someone's ass(hole), rip...**) **1** [1930s+] (*US*) to criticize someone severely. **2** [1930s+] (*W.I., Guyn.*) to thrash severely, to flog; usu. with *out* or *up*. **3** [1960s+] (*US*) in fig. use, e.g. to lose when gambling. [SE *tear* + ASS *n.* (2)/ASSHOLE *n.*[1] (1)]

tear someone's meat-house down *v.* [20C+] (*US*) to defeat, to thrash. [SE *meat-house*, a larder, here meaning one's body]

tear someone's playhouse down *v.* [1950s] (*US Black*) to render someone's life unhappy or unpleasant.

tear someone up for arse-paper *v.* (*also* **tear someone up for dunny paper**) [1910s+] (*mainly N.Z.*) to scold, to reprimand, to attack and totally overcome in an argument; thus ext. in excl. *well, I'll be torn up for arse-paper!*, an excl. of surprise or disbelief. [SE *tear up* + ARSE-PAPER *n.*/DUNNY *n.* + SE *paper*]

tear the arse out of *v.* (*also* **tear the bollocks off**) [1940s+] to destroy completely, to render useless.

tear the end off *v.* [1920s] to finish with a person or thing.

tear the place down *v. see* TEAR DOWN *v.* (2).

tear the roof off *v. see* RAISE THE ROOF *v.*

tear-up *n.*[1] [mid-19C+] a commotion, esp. as [1950s+] (*US jazz*) a spell of wild, destructive behaviour, a mêlée.

tear-up *n.*[2] [late 19C] (*UK tramp*) a rag, ragged clothing.

tear up *v.*[1] **1** [1920s+] (*US Black*) (*also* **tear it up, tear up shit**) to enjoy oneself, to do something with relish or well. **2** [1930s–60s] (*US Black*) to have sexual intercourse. **3** [1940s+] to criticize, to attack verbally. **4** [1940s+] to make a great impression (on). **5** [1950s+] (*US*) to distress, to upset; often in ironic use. **6** [1950s+] to destroy, lit. and fig., occas. to beat up.

tear up *v.*[2] *see* TEAR *v.*

tear up jack *v. see* CUT UP JACK *v.*

tear up shit *v. see* TEAR UP *v.*[1] (1).

tear up the pea patch *v.* [1910s+] (*US*) to go on a rampage.

tear-yanking *adj. see* TEARJERKING *adj.*

tea-scramble *n. see* BUN-STRUGGLE *n.*

tease *n.* **1** [mid-19C] one who can be teased easily. **2** [mid-19C+] (*also* **teaze**) one who likes to tease. **3** [1920s+] a woman or homosexual man who provokes a man sexually but then resists intercourse; occas. used of heterosexual men. **4** [1920s+] the act of teasing somebody else sexually.

tease *v.*[1] (*also* **teaze**) [19C] to flog, to whip. [SE *tease*, to 'thrash' out the fibres of wool, flax etc, before spinning]

tease *v.*[2] [1920s+] of a woman, to provoke a man sexually but to refuse him actual intercourse. [SE *tease*/abbr. COCKTEASE *v.*]

teaser *n.*[1] (*also* **teazer**) [mid-18C–1930s] something that causes annoyance or is difficult or hard to deal with. [boxing jargon *teaser*, a tricky opponent, hard to beat]

teaser *n.*[2] (*also* **teazer**) [mid-19C] a sixpence (2½p). [? TIZZY *n.*[1]]

teaser *n.*[3] [late 19C+] a woman who allows, even encourages, some physical intimacies but, however daring, will always stop short of intercourse. [abbr. COCKTEASER *n.*]

teaser *n.*[4] [20C+] (*orig. US*) a sample of something to arouse or whet one's appetite, a taste.

tease someone's cock *v. see* COCKTEASE *v.*

teaspoon *n.* [1950s+] (*drugs*) a measure of narcotic drugs. [it is half a SPOON *n.*[3]]

tea squall *n.* [early–mid-19C] a tea party.

teaster *n. see* TESTER *n.*[1].

tea-stick *n.* [1930s–50s] (*US drugs*) a marijuana cigarette (cf. BAT *n.*[8]). [TEA *n.*[2] (1) + STICK *n.*[9] (3)]

tea strainers *n.* [1980s+] trainers. [rhy. sl.]

teatchgir *adj. see* TEAICH-GIR *adj.*

tea-timers n. [1970s+] (US gay) dark glasses. [TEA n.² (1); the need to wear sunglasses to hide one's marijuana-affected pupils]

tea-towel head n. see TOWEL-HEAD n.

tea-towel holder n. [1990s+] the anus. [the small round plastic holder that a teatowel is pushed into resembles the anus]

tea trade n. see TEAROOM TRADE n.

tea up v. 1 [mid-19C] to make tea. 2 [1910s–20s] to get drunk. [SE tea/TEA n.¹ (3)]

tea voider n. [late 18C–early 19C] a chamberpot. [TEA n.¹ (2) + SE void]

teaze/teazer see under TEASE/TEASER and its combs.

teazle n. [19C] the vagina (cf. BEAUTY SPOT n.).

tec n. 1 [mid-19C+] (also **teck, tect**) a detective. 2 a detective story. [abbr.]

tecata n. [1960s+] (US drugs) heroin. [synon. Sp.]

tecato n. [1960s+] (US drugs) 1 a heavy user of marijuana. 2 a morphine or heroin addict. [TECATA n.]

tech n. [1940s+] (orig. US) a technician. [abbr.]

tech- pfx see TECHNO- pfx

techie n.¹ [1960s+] a technician. [abbr. + sfx -ie]

techie n.² [1980s+] (orig. US) 1 a computer enthusiast or expert. 2 technology. [abbr. SE technology + sfx -ie]

techie n.³ [2000s] (US Black) someone who first steals one's possessions and then displays them openly.

technicolour yawn n. (also **living color yawn, technicolour cough/spit**) [1960s+] (orig. Aus.) the act of vomiting. [the multicoloured effluvia so produced]

techno- pfx (also **tech-**) [1980s+] (US) a combining form used to indicate technological expertise or involvement, esp. as regards computing, e.g. technofreak.

teck/tect n. see TEC n. (1).

Ted n.¹ [1940s–50s] (N.Z. milit.) a German soldier. [Ital. tedesco, German]

Ted n.² 1 [1950s+] a teddy boy. 2 [1990s+] a person. [abbr.; the youth cult orig. known as 'Edwardians' and named for their sartorial style, borrowed from the contemporary upper-class dandies who in turn had recreated the fashions of their own grandfathers; (2) f. (1)]

ted adj. [1980s+] (US campus) drunk. [abbr. WASTED adj. (4)]

teddy bear n.¹ 1 [20C+] a pear. 2 [1930s+] (Aus.) a show-off, esp. a cricketer who jokes around on the field and plays to the crowd. [rhy. sl.; (2) = LAIR n.]

teddy bear n.² [20C+] (Irish) a large, brown shawl. [similarity to the covering of the child's toy]

teddy bear n.³ [1940s–50s] (Aus.) a koala.

teddy bear n.⁴ [1950s+] (US Black) a plump, sexy woman.

teddy bear n.⁵ [1990s+] a sanitary towel. [euph.]

ted frazer n. [1960s+] a razor, always a cut-throat, 'open' model. [rhy. sl.]

Ted Heath n. [1970s+] 1 a thief. 2 teeth. [rhy. sl.; pron. 'heef'; ult. Edward Heath (1916–2005), British prime minister 1970–74]

tee see under T.

teech n. see TEACH n. (1).

teed off adj. (also **t'd off**) [1950s+] (US) annoyed, irritated, upset. [TEE OFF (ON) v.]

teed up adj. (also **tea'd, tead up, teaed up, tee'd, teed out, t-oed**) 1 [late 19C+] (US) drunk; ext. as teed up to the tits (cf. ALED UP adj.). 2 [1930s+] (US drugs) intoxicated by marijuana. 3 [1940s] in a state of tense excitement due to circumstances. [(1) TEA n.¹ (3); (2) TEA n.² (1); (3) fig. use of (2)]

teef see under T'IEF.

teen- pfx [1950s+] (orig. US) a combining form for anything applicable to or enjoyed by teenagers, e.g. teenflick, teenzine, a magazine for teenagers.

teenchy-weenchy/teencie-weencie adj. see TEENSIE-WEENSIE adj.

teener n.¹ (also **teenie, teeny**) [1950s+] (US) a teenager. [abbr.]

teener n.² [1990s+] (US drugs) 1/16th of an ounce of a given (powdered) drug. [abbr.]

teenie weenie n. [1970s+] (US gay) a teenager available for being fellated. [teenie (see TEENER n.¹) + WEENIE n.¹ (4)]

teensie-weensie adj. (also **eensie-teensie, eensy-beensy, eensy-weensy, eentsy-weentsy, teenchy-weenchy, teencie-weencie, teensy, teensy-weensy, teeny-weeny, tintsy-wintsy, weeny-teeny**) [late 19C+] (orig. US juv.) very small, minuscule. [infant pron. of SE tiny]

teenth n. [1990s+] (drugs) a very small amount of cannabis. [abbr. one-sixteenth of an ounce (2g)]

teeny n. see TEENER n.¹.

teeny adj. [1960s+] pertaining to a teenager, usu. a girl. [SE teen]

teenybopper n. (also **teenybobber, teenybop, teenyrocker**) 1 [1960s+] a young girl, usu. in very early teens, with a predilection for rock music and the boys who play it; occas. used of a trend-obsessed boy. 2 [1960s+] anybody teenage or considered too young for the situation. 3 [1960s+] (US Black) a young, inexperienced (and as such unpopular) person. 4 [1970s+] (US gay) an underage boy. [TEENY n. + BOP v. (5)]

teenybopper adj. 1 [1960s+] pertaining to a teenager, usu. a young girl. 2 [1990s+] in fig. use, insignificant, 'lightweight'. [TEENYBOPPER n.]

teeny-weeny adj. see TEENSIE-WEENSIE adj.

tee off (on) v. [1950s+] (US) 1 to criticize, to reprimand, to attack verbally, to irritate or anger someone. 2 to feel anger or irritation. 3 to hit very hard. [? fig. use of golfing jargon tee off + euph. for PEE OFF v.²/PISS OFF v.; or ? var. on TICK OFF v.¹]

tee (something) up v. [1930s+] to get (something) ready, to prepare (something). [golfing jargon]

teeth n. 1 [1950s] (W.I. Rasta) bullets. 2 [1980s+] (drugs) cocaine, crack cocaine (cf. BASE n.; BLANCA n.). [similarity in (1) in shape and (2) colour/size]

teether n. [1960s] an immature person, a 'baby'.

teetotal hotel n. [late 19C] 1 a workhouse. 2 a prison (cf. BOARDING HOUSE n.). [where there would be absolutely no liquor]

teetotally adv. [early 19C–1930s] completely.

tee up v. see TEE (SOMETHING) UP v.

teevee n. see T.V. n.

Tefal n. [1990s+] (UK juv.) one who has a notably large forehead. [a series of advertisements for Tefal non-stick pans in which such individuals featured]

Teflon kid n. [1980s+] (Aus. prison) a tough young person. [nothing 'sticks' to him, ult. the advert for the Teflon brand of non-stick frying pan that 'really doesn't stick']

teg a wen eno v. see WEN adj.

tegebreg n. (also **teggereg**) [1950s+] (W.I.) a loud-mouthed domineering person.

Teg/Teig n. see TAIG n.

tekeesha n. [1990s+] (W.I.) a woman who bases her relationships on the partner's wealth. [W.I. pron. of SE take, + ?]

tek life n. [1980s+] (W.I./UK Black teen) a fashionable, popular person, a fashionable thing or place. [W.I. pron. of SE take, i.e. one who 'takes hold of' life]

tekram n. [mid-19C+] market, esp. Covent Garden; thus ogging ot tekram, going to market. [backsl.]

Tel n. [1970s+] the almost invariable nickname for working-class Londoners called Terry.

tele n. see TELLY n.

telegram carrier n. [1990s+] (W.I.) a man who prematurely ejaculates. [he 'comes fast']

telegraph n. 1 [early 19C–1900s] a scout or spy. 2 [mid-19C–1900s] (Aus.) a member of a bushranging gang whose task is to keep the others informed of the whereabouts of potential victims or efforts to capture them. 3 [mid-19C+] a network of gossip and rumour that brings news (often inaccurate) before the official sources. 4 [1960s+] (UK prison) a means of inter-cell communication in prison, by tapping mutually understood codes on the walls.

telegraph *v.* [1920s+] (*US*) to communicate one's intentions, usu. inadvertently.

telegraph one's punches *v.* [1930s+] (*orig. US*) to reveal one's intentions to an opponent inadvertently. [boxing imagery]

telephone *n.*¹ [1950s+] (*Can.*) a bilingual or multilingual Canadian who moves between the 2 national groups – Anglo*phone* and Franco*phone* – and is generally despised by both.

telephone *n.*² [1970s+] (*US campus*) a euph. for toilet, e.g. *I have to use the men's telephone* (cf. BIG WHITE TELEPHONE n.; FAIRY'S PHONEBOOTH n.).

telephone *n.*³ [1980s+] (*Aus. prison*) a means of inter-cell communication in prison by tapping the plumbing pipes.

telephone *n.*⁴ [2000s] (*UK Und.*) a type of scar inflicted on an informer's face.

telephone number *n.* [1940s+] extremely large sums of money; recent use is pl.; also in phr. *we're talking telephone numbers.* [the digits used in big city exchanges]

telephone number bit *n.* [1930s] (*US prison*) a sentence of 20 years plus, but not a life sentence.

telescope *n.*¹ [1930s] (*US tramp*) a nested set of tin cans used for cooking.

telescope *n.*² *see* SCOPE n.¹.

telescope *v.* [late 19C–1950s] (*Aus.*) to silence, to suppress.

teletubby *n.* [1990s+] one's husband. [rhy. sl. = HUBBY n.; ult. *Teletubbies*, the children's TV program]

tell a French joke *v.* [1960s+] (*gay*) to stimulate the anus orally. [FRENCH adj. (2)]

tell a lie *phr.* [1920s+] a phr. used to reverse one's previous statement or emphasize that in speaking one has just made a mistake, e.g. *they were all blondes, tell a lie, there was one brunette.*

teller *n.* [mid-18C–mid-19C] (*boxing*) a heavy, telling blow.

tell it like it is *phr.* (*also* **say it like it is, t.i.l.i.s**) [1940s+] (*orig. US Black*) to be absolutely honest, to reject dissembling; often as an exhortatory imper.

tell it to Jesus! *excl.* [1930s] (*US tramp*) a request to be quiet.

tell it to Sweeney! *excl.* (*also* **save it for Sweeney!**) [20C+] (*US*) a dismissive excl. of disbelief at a far-fetched statement. [? anecdotal or *Sweeney* as generic]

tell me about it *phr.* (*also* **talk about it**) [1920s+] (*US campus*) an expression of agreement, usu. when the first speaker is recounting some tale of problems.

tell someone what time it is *v. see* SHOW SOMEONE WHAT TIME IT IS v.

tell someone what to do with something *v.* [20C+] (*orig. US*) to reject something vehemently. ['what they should do' is SHOVE IT UP YOUR ARSE! excl.]

tell someone where they get off *v.* (*also* **show someone where they get off, tell someone (where) to get off, ...where to go**) [20C+] (*orig. US*) to scold someone for interfering. ['where they get off' or 'go to' is hell]

tell someone where to head in *v.* [1910s–50s] (*US*) to scold, to reprimand.

tell someone where to shove it *v.* (*also* **tell someone where to put it, ...stick it**) [20C+] (*orig. US*) to reject something vehemently. [i.e. SHOVE IT UP YOUR ARSE! excl.]

tell-tale *n.*¹ [mid-19C] the mouth.

tell-tale *n.*² [1950s+] (*Aus.*) a motor vehicle's indicator light. [it shows where one/the car is]

tell the tale *v.* [20C+] **1** to deceive, to hoax, to cheat through verbal dexterity. **2** to engage in amorous talk. **3** to tell a story designed to elicit a loan or a monetary gift. **4** to tell any kind of unbelievable or pathetic story. [ext. use of SE]

tell the works *v. see* GIVE SOMEONE THE WORKS v. (1).

telly *n.* (*also* **tele**) [1930s+] *tele*vision. [abbr.]

temazzy *n.* [1990s+] (*UK drugs*) *temaze*pam. [abbr.]

temmies *n.* (*also* **temazies, tems**) [1980s+] (*drugs*) *tema*zepam (a tranquillizer and short-acting hypnotic). [abbr.]

temp *n.*¹ [late 19C+] *temp*erature. [abbr.]

temp *n.*² [1930s+] a *temp*orary worker, usu. a secretary. [abbr.]

temp *v.* [1970s+] to take on a job as a temporary worker, usu. a secretary. [TEMP n.²]

temple *n.* **1** [late 18C] a brothel (cf. ABBESS n.). **2** [mid-19C+] the lavatory (cf. ALTAR n.).

temple balls *n.* [1960s+] (*drugs*) strong Nepalese hashish, sold in small balls and allegedly manufactured in Buddhist temples (cf. AFGHAN n.).

temple of Venus *n. see* VENUS'S HIGHWAY n.

temple-pickling *n.* [late 17C–early 19C] (*UK Und.*) the ducking of court officials beneath a pump. [proper name *the Temple*, 2 of the Inns of Court (the Inner and Middle Temple) + SE *pickle*, i.e. to 'bathe' in liquid. During 17C any bailiff caught within the limits of the temple was automatically thus punished]

tems *n. see* TEMMIES n.

Ten, the *n.* [1930s+] (*US Und.*) America's 10 Most Wanted Criminals list. [established as a publicity stunt in 1930s by J. Edgar Hoover (1895–1972), head of the FBI, but still in existence today]

ten *n.*¹ [1940s] (*US Black*) the human toes.

ten *n.*² [1980s+] the ideal woman or man. [the 'perfect' score of 10 out of 10, reinforced by the film *10* (1979)]

ten *n.*³ [1990s+] (*US Black*) a Mac-*10* automatic. [abbr.]

tenant at will *n.*¹ [mid-17C–early 19C] one whose wife arrives at the alehouse to make him come home. [legal jargon, *tenant at will*, one whose tenancy only exists according to the will of the landlord]

tenant at will *n.*² [early 19C] a male lover. [APARTMENT TO LET n. (1)]

tenant for life *n.* [19C] a married man. [pun on legal jargon]

tenant in tail *n.* **1** [mid-17C] one whose drunkenness promotes indiscriminate displays of affection; 'he that will be stil kissing all commers in' (*English Liberal Science*). **2** [early 18C–19C] the penis. **3** [late 18C–early 19C] one whose wife arrives at the alehouse to make him come home. [legal jargon *tenant in tail*, a tenancy held under certain specific limitations + note TAIL n.² (2)]

ten-bob squats *n.* [late 19C] the stalls in a theatre. [the price (10 shillings/50p) of the seats]

ten bob taxi *n.* [1960s–80s] (*Aus.*) a police car.

ten-cent *adj. see* TWO-CENT adj.

ten-cent bag *n.* (*also* **ten cents**) [1950s+] (*drugs*) a $10 bag of marijuana or any other drug, e.g. crack cocaine.

tench *n.*¹ **1** [mid-19C] (*Aus.*) the convict prison in Hobart, Tasmania; thus *tenchman*, an inmate of that prison. **2** [mid-late 19C] the Clerkenwell House of Detention. [abbr. SE peni*tent*iary]

tench *n.*² [mid-late 19C] the vagina (cf. BEARDED CLAM n.). [? image of the vagina as a prison (TENCH n.¹), or SE *tench*, and thus another term that equates the vagina with fish]

ten commandments *n.* [mid-16C–1910s] a woman's fingernails, esp. in the context of scratching someone's face. [stereotyping of a domineering wife or an aggressive woman]

tender *n.* [1960s+] (*US Black*) a young desirable man or woman.

tender box *n.* [1970s+] (*gay*) a young boy with alluring buttocks. [SE *tender* + BOX n.¹ (4)]

tender dick *n.* [1960s+] (*US Black*) the sexual equivalent of a soft heart, i.e. one's actions are dictated by sexual rather than emotional or intellectual feelings. [SE *tender* + DICK n.⁴ (1)]

tenderfoot *n.* [mid-19C+] (*orig. US*) a novice, an inexperienced person. [orig. used of the new arrivals in the mining or ranching areas of the Western US]

tenderloin *n.* [late 19C+] (*US*) **1** the area of a city devoted to pleasure and entertainment, typically containing restaurants, theatres, gambling houses and brothels. **2** an area where the homeless gather. [SE *tenderloin*, a tender cut of beef, pork etc. Coined for an area of New York City, the term was ext. to cover similar areas of other major US cities, notably San Francisco, where it is still in use. The concept was linked to police corruption and so great were the bribes and pay-offs available to officers of the 29th Precinct, who administered the area, that they termed it 'the juicy part of the service'. First used in 1876 by a notably corrupt policeman, Alexander S. 'Clubber' Williams (nicknamed for his propensity for violence rather than any love of nightspots), who had just moved to the 29th Precinct. 'I have been living on rump steak in the Fourth District,' he remarked, 'I will have some tenderloin now']

tenderoni *n.* [1980s+] (*US Black teen*) a sweet young girl. [SE *tender* + cod Ital.]

tender parnel *n.* [late 17C–early 19C] **1** a squeamish, oversensitive person. **2** a prostitute who works in a brothel. [ironic uses of SE *tender parnel*, a tenderly educated and gently brought-up woman, but note 'Tender Parnell, who broke her finger in a posset drink' (Grose, 1785)]

ten-dollar word *n.* [1940s+] (*US*) any form of writing or speech seen as exceeding the style or vocabulary limits of a 'normal' person; the number of dollars is variable.

tend one's own knitting *v. see* STICK TO ONE'S KNITTING *v.*

ten, eight, two-and-a-quarter *n. see* TEN, TEN, TWO-AND-A-QUARTER *n.*

tenement house in Greenwich Village *n.* [late 19C] (*US short order*) an order of soup with greens in it.

tenements to let *n. see* APARTMENT TO LET *n.*

ten-four *adv.* (*also* **10-4**) **1** [1960s+] message received and understood. **2** [1990s+] in fig. use, ready, prepared. [US police '10 codes', e.g. 10–15 civil disturbance, 10–31 crime in progress]

ten furlongs *n.* [20C+] (*Aus.*) a daughter. [rhy. sl.; *10 furlongs* = a mile and a quarter]

ten-hut *n.* [1970s] (*US*) an erection. [milit. order *ten-hut*, stand to attention]

ten in the hundred *n.* [early 17C–early 19C] a usurer. [interest of 10% was considered extortionate]

tenip *n.* [mid–late 19C] a pint. [backsl.]

ten miles of bad road *n.* (*also* **five miles of bad road**) [1960s+] (*US Black*) bad luck, esp. if it persists.

Tennant Creek *n.* [1980s+] (*Aus.*) a Greek. [rhy. sl.]

tenner *n.* **1** [mid-19C+] £10, a £10 note. **2** [late 19C+] (*US*) a $10 bill. **3** [late 19C+] (*UK/US prison*) a 10-year prison sentence.

Tennessee *n.* [mid-19C] (*US*) hot corned bread.

tennies *n.* (*also* **tenny pumps/runners, tenners**) [1960s+] (*US*) tennis shoes or trainers. [abbr.]

tennis fan *n.* [1990s+] a lesbian. [a variety of modern lesbian tennis stars]

tennis racket *n.* [20C+] a jacket. [rhy. sl.]

tenny pumps/runners *n. see* TENNIES *n.*

ten o'clock girl *n.* [1930s–50s] a London prostitute (cf. AWAYDAY GIRL *n.*). [they had to surrender to their bail at the Magistrates' Court at that time in the morning]

tenpence to the shilling *phr.* [mid-19C+] not very intelligent, slightly eccentric, odd; one of a number of phrs. meaning stupid or eccentric. [a shilling had 12 pence; var. on NOT ALL THERE phr.]

tenpenny *n.* [1940s] (*W.I.*) a bloated, fat stomach. [? size of a tenpenny piece, an obs. coin since 18C; or ? SE *tenpenny nail*, a large (5cm/3in) nail]

10% *n.* [1990s+] (*US Black*) that percentage of (Black) people who are rich, are only interested in personal gain and material wealth and who exploit the poor. [for ety. *see* 5% NATION *n.*]

ten-percent *adj.* [1940s+] inadequate, useless. [TEN-PERCENTER *n.*[2]]

ten-percenter *n.*[1] (*also* **ten-percent man**) [1920s+] (*orig. US*) an agent; thus *ten-percenterie*, an agency. [their cut]

ten-percenter *n.*[2] [1940s+] an inadequate, a failure. [their success rate/popularity]

ten-percent house *n.* [mid-19C] (*US*) a cheap, poss. crooked casino.

tenpin *v.* (*also* **do the bowling hold, hold a bowling ball**) [1970s+] to insert the thumb into a woman's anus and the middle finger into her vagina simultaneously, doing a rhythmic swinging motion of the arm to provide sexual stimulation. [simulating the effect of holding a bowling ball]

ten pounds of shit in a five pound bag *phr.* [20C+] (*US*) anything considered ugly, esp. someone obese or overweight.

tens *n.* [1960s+] (*US drugs*) amphetamines (cf. A *n.*[2]). [the 10mg tablets]

tens and twos *n.* [20C+] (*Aus.*) shoes. [rhy. sl.]

tense *adj.* [1990s+] a general term of approval. [on bad = good model]

tenski *n.* (*also* **tensky**) [1950s+] (*US*) **1** 10 per cent. **2** a $10 bill. [SE *ten* + -SKI sfx]

ten-spot *n.* **1** [mid-19C+] (*US*) a $10 bill or £10 note. **2** [1900s] (*US campus*) (*also* **ten-strike**) a perfect recitation. **3** [1900s–60s] (*US prison*) a 10-year prison sentence. [SE *ten* + -SPOT sfx; (2) f. (1) but also the idea of 10 out of 10]

ten stealers *n. see* STEALERS *n.*

tent *n.*[1] **1** [1900s] (*Anglo-Irish*) an umbrella. **2** [1910s] (*US Und.*) a prison cell. **3** [1920s–40s] (*US prison*) prison uniform, or a civilian suit. **4** [1970s] a fat woman dressed in a kaftan or similarly voluminous garment.

tent *n.*[2] *see* T'AINT *n.*

ten, ten, two-and-a-quarter *n.* (*also* **ten, eight, two-and-a-quarter; ten, twelve…**) [mid-19C–1910s] (*Aus.*) the regular weekly ration of food, as issued to hands on a rural property. [10lb (4.5kg) of flour, 10lb/8lb/12lb (4.5kg/3.6kg/5.4kg) of meat, 2lb (0.9kg) of sugar and ¼lb (113g) of tea]

tenth part of a man *n. see* NINTH PART OF A MAN *n.*

Tenth Street *n.* [1940s] (*US Black*) $10.

ten times ten *n.* [mid-19C] (*US*) $100.

ten to two *n.* [1930s+] a Jew (cf. BILLY THE KID *n.*). [rhy. sl.]

tent peg *n.*[1] [19C] the penis. [the shape, but note the biblical story of Jael and Sisera, i.e. the penis as a weapon (cf. AX *n.*[2])]

tent peg *n.*[2] [late 19C+] an egg. [rhy. sl.]

ten, twelve, two-and-a-quarter *n. see* TEN, TEN, TWO-AND-A-QUARTER *n.*

ten, twenty, thirty joint *n.* [1900s–40s] (*US*) a cheap theatre. [the seat prices: 10¢, 20¢, 30¢ + JOINT *n.*[4] (3)]

ten-two *n.* [1960s] (*US*) the trad. payment for sex, $10 for the woman, $2 for the room.

tenuc *n.* [late 19C] the vagina. [backsl. = CUNT *n.*[1] (1)]

ten wedding *n.* (*also* **10 wedding**) [late 19C] a wedding in which the wife, 1, is superior to the husband, 0.

ten yards *n.* [1940s] (*US Und.*) $1000. [SE *ten* + YARD *n.*[3] (1)]

ter *n. see* TERR *n.*

tercel-gentle *n.* [late 16C–early 19C] (*UK Und.*) a well-off knight or any rich gentleman. [SE *tercel-gentle*, a male falcon]

termage *n.* [late 16C–early 17C] (*UK Und.*) winnings at crooked gambling, esp. through cheating at bowls and later cards. [SE *term*, a limit, a full extent]

terminal *n.* [1990s+] death, murder.

terminal *adj.* [1970s+] extreme, total. [SE *terminal*, used of disease that will kill the sufferer]

term of endearment among sailors, a *n.* [20C+] a euph. for BUGGER *n.*[1] (1).

terr *n.* (*also* **ter, terro**) **1** [1930s+] (*Irish*) an ignorant but provocative individual. **2** [1970s+] (*S.Afr.*) a terrorist. **3** [1980s+] a tourist, esp. from Transvaal. [abbr./pron.]

terrace *n.* [1940s+] (*Aus.*) trousers. [rhy. sl.; *terrace of houses* = SE *trousers*]

terra firma *n.* [late 17C–early 19C] a landed estate. [Lat. *terra firma*, land, as opposed to sea]

terrible *adj.* [1950s–80s] (*US Black/teen*) wonderful, admirable, first-rate. [on bad = good model]

terrible Turk *n.* (*also* **slave and Turk**) [20C+] work; also as v. [rhy. sl.]

terrier crop *n.* [mid–late 19C] a bristly haircut, denoting a person's recent stay in prison, where hair is cropped short. [resemblance to a short-haired breed of dog]

Terries *n.* [1930s–50s] (*N.Z.*) the Territorial Army. [abbr.]

terrif *adj.* [1970s+] wonderful, marvellous. [abbr. TERRIFIC adj. (2)]

terrific *adj.* **1** [19C] very severe, excessive. **2** [1930s+] a general term of approval, wonderful, very good indeed, great. [SE *terrific*, terrifying]

terro *n. see* TERR *n.*

terrorist *n.* [1980s+] (*S.Afr., West and Southwest Cape*) a tourist, usu. from Transvaal. [joc. mispron.]

terror to cats *n.* [late 19C] an ill-behaved small boy.

terry toon *n.* **1** [1970s+] (*Aus.*) a pimp, one who lives off a prostitute. **2** [1980s+] (*Aus. prison*) a derog. term for a Black person (cf. ALPHONSE n.²). [rhy. sl.; (1) = HOON n. (1); (2) = COON n. (5)]

Terry Waite *adj.* [1990s+] late. [rhy. sl.; ult. *Terry Waite* (b. 1939), British humanitarian, also a famous hostage in Lebanon]

test *n.* (*also* **tess**) [20C+] (*UK Black/W.I.*) a person, a fellow. [? obs. SE *test*, a witness]

tester *n.*¹ (*also* **teaster, teston(e)**) **1** [late 16C–1920s] a sixpence. **2** [mid-19C–1940s] (*Aus.*) 25 strokes of the lash (cf. BOB n.⁵). [Fr. *teston*, a silver coin struck at Milan by Duke Galeazzo Sforza (1468–76). It had his own head on it, as did similar testons coined by Louis XII (r.1498–1515) and his successor François I (r.1515–47) of France and by Henry VIII (r.1509–47) of England; (2) reflects the association of numbers of lashes with denominations of coins]

tester *n.*² [1990s+] (*US drugs*) a free sample of a given drug, given out so as to encourage word-of-mouth reports that the dealer's stock is worth buying.

testicles to you! *excl.* [20C+] a general excl. of dismissal or disdain. [var. on BALLS! excl.]

testicular elevation *n.* [20C+] somewhat ponderous synon. for the coarser BALLS-UP n.

testiculating *n.* [1970s+] talking nonsense in an extremely animated manner. [SE *testicles* + *gesticulating*, the ref. is to talking BALLS n.²]

testoed *adj.* [2000s] macho, invigorated. [SE *testosterone*]

teston(e) *n. see* TESTER n.¹.

Tetbury portion *n.* [late 18C–early 19C] sexual intercourse that is followed by a dose of venereal disease; 'a **** [CUNT n.¹] and a clap' (Grose, 1796). [the poor image of the town of *Tetbury* in Gloucestershire]

tetched *adj.* [1930s+] (*US*) eccentric. [SE *touched*]

tete *n.* [20C+] (*W.I.*) a bacterial skin disease, usu. attacking the feet. [? SE *tetter*, any pustule that erupts on the skin]

tetes *n.* [1960s] (*W.I.*) a large-breasted woman. [TITTY n.¹ (1)]

tether one's nags on *v.* (*also* **tip the nags**) [19C] (*Scot.*) to have sexual intercourse. [SE *tether*, tie up + NAG n.²]

tetra *n.* [2000s] (*US Black/drugs*) cannabis, usu. marijuana. [SE *tetrahydrocannabinol*, the active ingredient of cannabis]

teuf-teuf *phr.* [1900s–20s] goodbye.

teviss *n.* [mid–late 19C] **1** a shilling. **2** a sixpence. [backsl. form of Du. *stiver*, a small coin]

tew *v.* [late 17C] of a man, to have sexual intercourse (cf. BANG v.¹). [SE *tew*, to beat, flog, belabour]

texan rude *n.* [mid-19C+] next door; thus *texan rude nam*, lit. 'next-door man', thus neighbour. [backsl.]

Texas-league *adj.* [1940s] (*US*) nouveau riche, vulgar. [the stereotyping of the ostentatious taste of Texan millionaires; note earlier baseball jargon *Texas league*, second-rate]

Texas mickey *n.* [1930s+] (*Can.*) a 84l cc (130fl oz) bottle of rye whisky. [proper name *Texas* + MICKEY n.⁵]

Texas steel *n.* [1970s+] (*US prison*) a prison.

Texas tea *n.* (*also* **Texas pot**) [1930s+] (*drugs*) marijuana (cf.

ACAPULCO (GOLD) n.; AFRICAN BUSH n.). [proper name *Texas* + TEA n.² (1); the easy availability of wild marijuana in the state]

Texas turkey *n.* [20C+] (*US*) an armadillo, as eaten *faute de mieux* during the Great Depression. [the armadillo is common in the state]

Tex Ritter *n.* [1990s+] **1** bitter (beer). **2** the lavatory (cf. ANGUS ARMANASCO n.). [rhy. sl.; (2) = SHITTER n.¹ (4); ult. Country and Western star *Tex Ritter* (1905–74); note THELMA (RITTER) n.]

textile *n.* [1990s+] a person who frequents a beach with clothes on. [the opposite of a SE *naturist*]

t.f.a. *adj.* [1980s+] (*US campus*) wonderful, exceptional, very good. [abbr. *too fucking awesome*]

t.g. *n.* [1990s+] (*US Black gang*) a junior member of a gang, under the age of 10. [abbr. *tiny gangsta*]

t.g.i.f. *phr.* [1930s+] (*orig. US*) thank God it's Friday. [abbr.]

Thai (stick) *n.* (*also* **ti-stick**) [1960s+] (*drugs*) a form of marijuana grown in Thailand, soaked in hashish oil and sold tied around a thin stick resembling a satay skewer (cf. ACAPULCO (GOLD) n.).

Thai white *n.* [1990s+] (*drugs*) a variety of heroin, refined in Thailand (cf. CHINA WHITE n.).

Thames butter *n.* [late 19C–1900s] totally rancid butter. [the 'South London Press' [...] published a paragraph to the effect that a Frenchman was making butter out of Thames mud at Battersea. In truth this chemist was extracting yellow grease from Thames mud-worms' (Ware)]

— than a nigger in a — *phr.* (*also* **— than a nigger's —**) [mid-19C+] (*US*) used in various phrs., usu. racist similes.

thang *n.* [1960s+] (*US Black teen*) thing, esp. in phr. *do your own thang* etc. [pron.]

thank Christ *phr.* (*also* **thank fuck**) [1930s+] a var. on *thank God*.

thanks a bunch *phr.* (*also* **thanks a bundle, …a heap, …a million**) [1950s+] thank you very much, often ironic.

thanks a pile *phr.* [1990s+] (*Irish*) thank you very much, often in ironic use. [PILE n.¹ (2)]

thanks, but no thanks *phr.* [1970s+] a phr. implying that a specific offer is very generous and/or alluring, but is ultimately not wanted.

thanks for nothing *phr.* [late 19C+] a phr. of annoyance and contempt.

thank you and good night *phr.* [1970s+] a dismissive, sarcastic phr., what a load of nonsense, is that the best you can offer?

that *n.* **1** [mid-17C; 1940s] sexual intercourse. **2** [19C] the penis. **3** [19C] the vagina. [euph.]

that *adj.* [mid-19C+] a mildly derog. use of 'that' to imply one's disapproval, e.g. *are you seeing that Terry tonight?*

thataboy! *excl. see* ATTABOY! excl.

that accounts for the milk in the coconut *phr. see* MILK IN THE COCONUT n.

that ain't hay *phr.* (*also* **that isn't chopped liver, …hay, …peanuts, there ain't no persimmons**) [1930s+] (*US*) a phr. used to mean that something is a large and/or significant amount. [the perceived insignificance of the various items]

that all depends *phr. see* IT ALL DEPENDS phr.

that and a dime will get you a cup of coffee *phr.* (*also* **that and a nickel will get you a cup of coffee, that and a quarter…**) [1950s+] (*US*) used of something considered unimportant or worthless.

that and this *n.* [20C+] urination (cf. ANGEL'S KISS n.). [rhy. sl. = PISS n. (2)]

that beats cockfighting *phr.* (*also* **this beats cockfighting, …thunder**) [early 19C–1920s] that is really amazing, that's beyond the bounds of possibility.

that bites (the big one) *phr.* [1980s+] (*US campus*) an expression of commiseration. [i.e. that must hurt very much]

that cat won't fight *phr. see* THAT COCK WON'T FIGHT *phr.*

thatch *n.* **1** [17C+] (*also* **top thatch**) the human hair. **2** [mid-19C+] female pubic hair.

-thatched *adj.* [late 19C+] describing a person's hair; thus *well-thatched*, having a good growth of hair. [THATCH n. (1)]

thatched head *n.* [early 17C] an Irishman (cf. BOG ARAB n.). [his stereotyped unkempt appearance]

thatched house (under the hill) *n.* (*also* **reed-roof'd cot**) [late 18C–19C] the vagina. [THATCH n. (2), but note *Thatched House* Lodge, Surrey, built for the keepers of Richmond Park in 1673 and subseq. owned by prime minister Sir Robert Walpole (1676–1745)]

thatch-gallows *n.* [late 18C–mid-19C] a worthless person. [all they are good for]

that cock won't fight *phr.* (*also* **that cat won't fight**) [early 19C–1900s] a phr. used to denigrate the previous statement, that won't do, you must be joking, I'm not having that.

that figures *phr.* [1940s+] (*orig. Aus.*) that's right, that adds up as it should. [FIGURE v.[1] (4)]

that hot shit *n. see* HOT SHIT n.

that isn't chopped liver/hay/peanuts *phr. see* THAT AIN'T HAY *phr.*

that'll be frosty Friday *phr.* [1940s+] (*Can./N.Z.*) never, that is very unlikely, that'll be the day.

that'll do for Sweeney *phr.* [1910s] (*US*) a phr. used in response to a piece of information that is considered unreliable, nonsensical. [var. on TELL IT TO SWEENEY! excl.]

that's all she wrote *phr.* (*also* **that's what she wrote**) [1940s+] (*orig. US milit.*) a general term of finality, that's all there is. [? the unhappy man's remark on reaching the terminal statements of a DEAR JOHN n. letter]

that's an idea *phr. see* IT'S AN IDEA *phr.*

that's another pair of sleeves *phr.* [1920s+] (*Aus.*) that's another matter.

that's another something *phr.* [1970s] (*US Black*) that's a different matter.

that's close *phr.* [1960s+] (*US campus*) an ironic comment implying that something is far from the truth or excessive.

that's cool *phr.* [1950s+] (*orig. US*) that's satisfactory, that's all right, don't worry. [COOL adj.[1] (5)]

that's fair *phr.* [1970s+] (*US campus*) an ironic comment that something is not fair.

that's gear! *excl. see* THAT'S (THE) GEAR! excl.

that's my eye (and Betty Martin) *phr. see* ALL MY EYE AND BETTY MARTIN *phr.*

that's news *phr.* [1970s+] (*US*) a phr. used to acknowledge one's interest in whatever one has just been told.

that's not cunt, that's peehole *phr.* [1970s] (*US*) a phr. used to suggest that a girl is not yet ready for intercourse. [CUNT n.[1] (3) + PEE n.[1] (1) + SE *hole*; note THINK IT'S JUST TO PEE THROUGH v.]

that's quacked! *excl.* [1980s+] (*US campus*) that's unfair! [play on SE *cracked*]

that's telling — *phr.* [1920s+] a phr. used to express approval or admiration for a statement, usu. an admonition of someone else, e.g. *that's telling her.*

that's the barber! *excl.* [mid-18C–early 19C] a general excl. of approbation. [ety. unknown; Grose (1785) describes it as 'a ridiculous and unmeaning phrase']

that's the chicken! *excl.* [1910s] (*Aus.*) a general excl. of approbation.

that's (the) gear! *excl.* [1920s+] (*orig. milit.*) a general excl. of approval (cf. THAT'S THE STUFF! excl.). [SE *gear*]

that's the hammer! *phr. see* JUST THE HAMMER *phr.*

that's the man as married Hannah! *excl.* [mid–late 19C] excellent! that's the way! good for you! [generic/assonant use of proper name, i.e. pron. 'man a'/Hannah]

that's the play! *excl.* [1930s] (*US*) a general excl. of agreement or approval. [SE *play*]

that's the shot! *excl.* [1940s+] (*Aus.*) a general excl. of agreement or approval. [SHOT n.[5] (3)]

that's the story! *excl.* [1940s+] (*N.Z.*) a general excl. of encouragement.

that's the stuff! *excl.* [20C+] a general excl. of approval (cf. THAT'S (THE) GEAR! excl.).

that's the tatur! *excl.* [mid-19C] (*US*) an excl. of affirmation. [TATER n. (1)]

that's the ticket! *excl.* [mid-19C+] just what is wanted, the ideal thing; occas. as *that's the ticket for soup!* [TICKET n.[3] (2); the *soup* ref. stems from the cards given out to beggars entitling them to a free meal at a soup kitchen]

that's the way it goes *phr.* [late 19C+] that is the way things work out and one must accept the facts, like it or not.

that's together! *excl.* [1970s] (*US Black/campus*) an expression of approval.

that's what she wrote *phr. see* THAT'S ALL SHE WROTE *phr.*

that's your sort! *excl.* [late 18C–mid-19C] a general excl. of approval, agreement.

thattaboy! *excl. see* ATTABOY! excl.

that takes it! *excl.* [late 19C+] that is the absolute limit! that is simply too much to bear!

that there *n.* [20C+] the vagina; thus *a bit of that there*, sexual intercourse (cf. ARTICLE n.). [euph.]

that thing *n.* (*orig. US Black*) **1** [1900s–40s] sexual intercourse. **2** [1900s–40s] the vagina (cf. ARTICLE n.). **3** [1960s+] the penis. [euph.]

that way *adj.* **1** [late 19C+] (*US*) pregnant. **2** [1920s] drunk. **3** [1920s+] homosexual. **4** [1930s+] in love. **5** [1930s+] of a given character, e.g. voyeuristic. [euphs.]

that won't hogya *phr. see* HO-GYA adj.

that won't pay the old woman her ninepence *phr.* [late 19C–1900s] used to describe an evasive act or statement. [coined at the Bow Street Police Court in London]

THC *n.* [1970s+] (*drugs*) phencyclidine (cf. ACE n.[4]). [misreading of *tetra*hydro*c*annabinnol, the active ingredient of cannabis]

the *adj.* [mid-18C+] used before the names of certain well-known figures, esp. singers and actresses. [in imitation of a similar practice with the definite article in Fr. and Ital.]

theatre *n.* [mid-19C–1900s] a police court. [the accused, whether guilty or not, will 'act' their role; also the ironic acceptance that justice often depends more on image than facts]

theg gens *n.* (*also* **teaich gens**) [mid–late 19C] 8 shillings (40p). [backsl.; GEN n.[1]]

theg yeneps *n.* [mid-19C] 8 pence. [backsl.; YENNEP n.]

Thelma (Ritter) *n.* [1990s+] **1** the anus (cf. BOTTLE AND GLASS n.). **2** a lavatory (cf. ANGUS ARMANACO n.). [rhy. sl. = SHITTER n.[1] (1)/SHITTER n.[1] (4); ult. US actress *Thelma Ritter* (1905–69); note TEX RITTER n.]

Thelonius Monk *n.* [1940s+] semen. [rhy. sl. = SPUNK n. (4); ult. jazz pianist *Thelonius Monk* (1917–82)]

them things *n.* [20C+] (*drugs*) marijuana cigarettes. [euph.]

the rabbit died *phr.* [1940s+] a phr. meaning a woman is pregnant. [the test formerly used to determine pregnancy]

therapy *n.* [1980s+] (*Aus. prison*) a beating by prison guards.

there *adj.* **1** [late 19C] (*Aus.*) of a person, attractive. **2** [20C+] (*US*) of a person, well informed, empathetic. **3** [1930s] (*US*) drunk. **4** [1930s–40s] (*US Und.*) reliable, trustworthy. **5** [1960s+] (*drugs*) intoxicated by drugs.

there, be *v.* (*US*) **1** [late 19C] to be in one's element. **2** [late 19C+] to make a definite plan, usu. in the form of a statement, *I'm there*, I'm definitely doing that.

there ain't no persimmons *phr. see* THAT AIN'T HAY *phr.*

there he goes with his eye out! *excl.* (*also* **there she goes**

with her eye out!) [mid-19C] an all-pupose excl. aimed at passers-by.

there's a kangaroo loose in the top paddock *phr.* [1990s+] (*Aus.*) a phr. describing a fool. [SE *top paddock*, used fig. for the head]

there's a letter in the post office *phr.* (*US*) **1** [mid-19C+] a warning to a man that his fly is undone or his shirt is out; also used to a woman when her slip is showing (cf. CHARLIE'S DEAD phr.). **2** [late 19C–1910s] said of a woman who is menstruating.

there's corn growing for some *phr. see* ACRE (OF CORN) n.

there's hair! *excl.* [late 19C–1920s] a general excl., lit. 'there's a woman with a lot of *hair*'. [ref. is to a hairstyle featuring the side hair being pulled up and then shaped]

there she goes with her eye out! *excl. see* THERE HE GOES WITH HIS EYE OUT! excl.

there's no intelligent life here *phr.* [1970s+] (*US campus*) a phr. denoting one's generally negative reaction to a given situation. [coined in the *Star Trek* TV series, usu. accompanying the phr. 'Beam me up, Scotty']

there's no work in Bourke *phr.* (*also* **there's no lucre at Echuca**) [1960s+] (*Aus.*) phrs. used to denote an unsatisfactory situation. [assonant phr. based on Aus. place-names]

there's one born every minute *phr.* [mid-19C+] a phr. referring to an absurd event or a person who has exhibited great foolishness. [the dictum of master showman P.T. Barnum (1810–91) to whom 'one' was a gullible victim]

there you are *n.* **1** [late 19C+] a bar. **2** [20C+] tea. [rhy. sl.; (2) = CHA n.[1]]

there you go *phr.* [1950s+] (*orig. US*) **1** a general phr. of agreement and approval. **2** a usu. negative phr. implying that the person is acting in their own particular way (yet) again.

these and those *n.* [20C+] **1** a suit of clothes. **2** toes. [rhy. sl.] **— the socks off** *phr. see* — ONE'S SOCKS OFF phr.

thesp *n.* [1960s+] an actor. [abbr. SE *thespian*]

thespian *n.* (*also* **West End thespian**) [1970s+] a lesbian. [pun on SE + ? alleged prevalence of homosexual men in theatre]

thesping *adj.* [1990s+] acting, e.g. *thesping business*. [THESP n.]

they *n.* **1** [late 19C+] those in authority or power, the Establishment. **2** [1940s] (*US Black*) a wife or mistress.

Theydon Bois *n.* [20C+] noise. [rhy. sl., pron. 'boyze'; ult. *Theydon Bois*, a town in Essex]

they're off, Mr Cutts! *excl.* [1940s+] (*N.Z.*) things have started! now we're getting down to business! [the racehorse trainer *Mr* E. Cutts, starter of the Auckland races]

they sing in our choir *phr.* [1990s+] (*US gay*) used of a fellow male/female homosexual.

thick *n.*[1] **1** [mid-19C–1940s] any drink having a dense consistency, e.g. porter, cocoa, coffee. **2** [late 19C] mud. **3** [late 19C–1910s] a thick slice of buttered bread. **4** [1930s–60s] a thick fog. **5** [1990s+] (*US Black*) one who has a muscular, well-developed physique. [SE *thick*]

thick *n.*[2] [mid-19C+] (*mainly juv./Irish*) a fool, an ignoramus. [THICK adj.[1]]

thick *adj.*[1] [late 16C+] stupid, dull, foolish; often as THICK AS... phr.[1]. [abbr. SE *thick-headed*]

thick *adj.*[2] **1** [mid-18C+] close, intimate; also as THICK AS... phr.[2]. **2** [1930s+] (*US campus*) emotionally involved, romantically attached.

thick *adj.*[3] [late 19C–1920s] drunken.

thick *adj.*[4] [late 19C+] unacceptable due to its excess, too much to handle; usu. in phr. *a bit thick*.

thick *adj.*[5] [late 19C+] intense.

thick *adj.*[6] [1990s+] (*US Black*) **1** of money, plentiful. **2** in ext. use of objects or people, displaying wealth. [i.e. a thick roll of cash]

thick *adj.*[7] [1990s+] **1** (*UK/US Black*) of a woman, physically

attractive. **2** of a man, having a large penis. **3** (*US campus*) overweight.

thick *adv.*[1] **1** [late 18C–mid-19C] heavily. **2** [mid-19C+] intensely, severely. **3** [late 19C+] densely.

thick *adv.*[2] [late 19C+] intimately. [THICK adj.[2] (1)]

thick and dense *n.* [1920s–40s] (*US*) expenses. [? rhy. sl.]

thick and thin *n.* [20C+] **1** the chin. **2** gin. **3** (*Aus.*) the skin. **4** (*US*) a grin. [rhy. sl.]

thick as... *phr.*[1] [late 16C+] stupid; used in a variety of combs., for the best known of which *see* below (cf. DUMB AS A BOX OF ROCKS phr.). [THICK adj.[1]]

thick as... *phr.*[2] [mid-18C+] very close, extremely intimate; used in a variety of combs., for the best known of which *see* below. [THICK adj.[2] (1)]

thick as two bricks *phr. see* THICK AS TWO SHORT PLANKS phr.

thick as two inkle-weavers *phr.* [mid-18C–early 19C] very close. [THICK AS... phr.[2] + SE *inkle*, linen tape]

thick as two Jews on payday *phr.* [late 19C] very close. [THICK AS... phr.[2] + racial stereotyping]

thick as two short planks *phr.* (*also* **thick as two bricks**) [1970s+] very stupid (cf. DUMB AS A BOX OF ROCKS phr.). [THICK AS... phr.[1]]

thick dick *n.* [1980s] a fool. [THICK adj.[1] + DICK n.[4] (6)]

thick ear *n.* (*also* **thick earhole**) **1** [late 19C+] an ear that has swollen up after a blow; usu. in phr. *give someone a thick ear*. **2** [1970s] in fig. use, a thug.

thick end *n.* [mid-19C+] the larger portion.

thicker *n.* [mid–late 19C] £1. [? THICK 'UN n. (1)]

thicket *n.* [late 19C+] pubic hair, usu. female.

thick head *n.* [20C+] a hangover.

thickhead *n.* [early 19C+] a fool, a simpleton; also as a term of address. [THICK-HEADED adj.]

thick-headed *adj.* [mid-18C+] stupid, foolish (cf. AIRHEADED adj.).

thickie *n.* [1960s+] a fool. [THICK adj.[1]]

thick in the clear *phr.* [mid–late 19C] confused, at a loss for coherence.

thick-legs *n.* [late 19C–1900s] navvies. [their physique]

thick lip *n.* [1930s+] a minor beating, lit. a lip that has swollen up after receiving a blow. [var. on THICK EAR n.]

thicklugged *adj.* [1920s] very stupid (cf. LONG-EARED adj.).

thickneck *n.* [1900s–50s] a large, thuggish person.

thick 'n' thins *n.* [1950s–70s] (*US Black*) stylish nylon socks, usu. black or brown. [? the pattern which may include stripes of varying widths]

thicko *n.* [1970s+] a fool (cf. BOBO n.[1]). [THICK adj.[1]]

thick one *n. see* THICK 'UN n.

thick on the ground *phr.* [late 19C+] usu. of people, plentiful, in large (crowded) numbers.

thick-skulled *adj.* (*also* **thick-sculled**) [late 17C–18C; 1940s] stupid, foolish (cf. CLOD-SKULLED adj.).

thick starch double blue *n.* [late 19C–1900s] a holiday dress worn in the summer (such dresses were heavily laundered).

thick 'un *n.* (*also* **thick one**) **1** [mid-19C–1950s] a sovereign (£1). **2** [1900s] 5 shillings, a crown (25p). **3** [1900s–40s] a slice of bread and butter. **4** [1930s] a silver dollar. [the dimensions of the coin/foodstuff]

thief *v.* [1950s+] to steal.

thief and robber *n.* [20C+] (*Aus.*) a friend. [rhy. sl. = COBBER n.[2]]

thieftaker *n.* [mid-18C] a man who hires himself out to swear on oath.

thieves' kitchen *n.* **1** [late 19C] the Law Courts in the Strand, London WC2. **2** [1910s–20s] the Athenaeum Club, London. **3** [1920s+] the Stock Exchange. [ironic ref. to the supposed respectability and actual venality of such places]

thieving hooks *n.* [early 19C] the fingers. [HOOK n.[1] (1)]

thieving irons n. **1** [early 19C] scissors. **2** [early 19C–1910s] (*Aus.*) hands. [(1) ? their use in cutting purses]

thigh-slapper n. [1960s+] (often used ironically) a supposedly very amusing joke. [the exaggerated slapping of one's thighs to intimate the intensity of one's hilarity]

thimble n. (*also* **thim**) [late 18C–1940s] (*UK Und.*) a watch. [naut. *thimble*, a thick ring of metal, through which a rope can be pushed; thus the similarity in shape]

thimble and thumb n. [1940s+] rum. [rhy. sl.]

thimble-crib n. [early–mid-19C] (*UK Und.*) a watchmaker's or jeweler's shop. [THIMBLE n. + CRIB n.[1] (1)]

thimbled adj.[1] [early 19C] wearing a watch. [THIMBLE n.]

thimbled adj.[2] [early 19C] arrested. [pun on THIMBLED adj.[1] = wearing a watch, i.e. the police watching someone]

thimble-rig n. [mid-19C–1930s] a version of the 3-card trick, in which victims are asked to bet on which of 3 rapidly manipulated thimbles contains a pea; it is very rare that anyone other than the sharper's accomplice manages to bet correctly. [SE *thimble* + RIG n.[2] (2). Sante, *Low Life* (1991), suggests that this is one of 'the only major gambling games actually invented in the United States'. However, neither E.P. nor the *OED*'s first cit. (*Hone's Every-day Book*, 1825) mentions this and Sante himself places its US appearance around 1860]

thimble-rigger n. (*also* **thimble-rig**) [mid-19C+] one who operates a game of THIMBLE-RIG n.

thimble-twister n. (*also* **thimble-screwer, super twister**) [mid-19C–1930s] (*UK Und.*) a thief who specializes in stealing watches from their wearers. [THIMBLE n. + TWISTER n.[4] (1)/SCREW v.[4] (1)]

thin n.[1] [mid-19C–1910s] a *thin* slice of bread and butter.

thin n.[2] [1920s–40s] (*US*) 10 cents. [THIN DIME n.]

thin adj. **1** [1920s+] (*US tramp*) without money, broke. **2** [1970s+] (*US Black*) of money, insubstantial. [backform. f. THIN DIME n.]

thin and thick n. [1980s] (*Aus.*) the penis (cf. ALMOND n.). [rhy. sl. = DICK n.[4] (1)]

thin city n. [1960s+] (*US campus*) a problematic or unpleasant situation. [antonym of FAT CITY n.[1]]

thin dime n. [1920s–60s] (*US*) a tiny amount of money (cf. CENT n.). [the dime (10 cents) is the thinnest coin, as well as the smallest]

Thing n. [20C+] used when one cannot remember a person's actual surname, e.g. *Mr Thing, Lady Thing*. [THING n.[1]]

thing n.[1] [late 13C+] a person, esp. someone whose name one does not know or who is unimportant.

thing n.[2] **1** [early 16C+] seduction, sexual intercourse. **2** [late 16C+] the vagina (cf. ARTICLE n.). **3** [17C+] the penis (cf. BAUBLE n.). **4** [1920s+] the buttocks; usu. in phr. *shake that thing*. **5** [1940s] in pl., the testicles (cf. GINGAMBOBS n.). **6** [1950s] (*US*) menstruation. [euph.]

thing n.[3] [20C+] (*US*) a non-specific descriptor, used when one either cannot or does not wish to use the correct term, e.g. *shall we do the coffee shop thing? I have to do the work thing.*

thing n.[4] **1** [1920s–30s] (*US campus*) a male homosexual. **2** [1980s+] (*Aus. prison*) a term of abuse for an informer.

thing n.[5] **1** [1920s+] anything to which one cannot or does not wish to give a name. **2** [1930s+] an obsession, a preoccupation with (whether negative or positive), e.g. *I have a thing about…* **3** [1930s+] one's lifestyle, one's opinion etc; usu. as *one's own thing* and in DO ONE'S (OWN) THING v. **4** [1940s+] a relationship, usu. sexual. **5** [1970s+] any activity one enjoys. **6** [1980s+] (*US Black*) a thing of importance; usu. as *it ain't no thing*, it is not important. **7** [1990s+] (*W.I.*) a girlfriend.

thing n.[6] [1930s+] an argument, a fuss.

thing n.[7] [1960s+] (*drugs*) **1** heroin, cocaine, marijuana, whatever is one's current drug of choice. **2** an addiction to heroin or another narcotic. **3** a portion – a capsule, a bag – of a narcotic (cf. PILL n.[4]). **4** marijuana. [euph.; or ? ext. of THING n.[5] (3)]

thing, the n. **1** [18C+] whatever is correct or fashionable within the context; thus *un-thing*, unfashionable. **2** [1940s] in good health.

thingahoochie n. [1970s] anything otherwise unnamed, whether through choice or one's inability to recall the correct title.

thing-a-ling n. see DINGALING n.[3].

thingamadoodle n. see THINGUM n.

thingamadoodles n. see THINGUMABOB n.

thingamajig/thingamajigger n. see THINGUMAJIG n.

thingamerry n. (*also* **thingamerrybob, thingumsmeribob**) [20C+] (*W.I.*) anything otherwise unnamed, whether through choice or one's inability to recall the correct title.

thingamy/thingammy n. see THINGUMMY n.

thingembob n. see THINGUMABOB n.

thingie n. see THINGY n.

thingio n. see THINGY n. (1).

thingmadodger n. see THINGUMABOB n.

thingmejig n. see THINGUMAJIG n.

thingmy n. see THINGY n. (1).

thingmybob n. see THINGUMABOB n.

thingo n. [20C+] (*Aus.*) a nameless object. [abbr. THINGUMABOB n.]

thing-o-me n. see THINGUMMY n.

things n. **1** [late 16C+] clothes in general, esp. those that women put on to go out, in addition to their indoor dress. **2** [17C+] one's possessions carried at a particular time, e.g. on a journey. **3** [late 17C–19C] implements or equipment for some special use, utensils.

things, the n. [mid-19C] (*UK Und.*) counterfeit money.

things and stuff phr. [1930s] (*US Black*) well-dressed, sophisticated.

things are crook in Musclebrook phr. (*also* **things are crook at Musselbrook, …in Tallarook, …weak at Julia Creek, things is weak in Werris Creek**) [1960s+] (*Aus.*) various assonant/rhyming phrs. used to denote an unsatisfactory situation.

things curry phr. [1990s+] (*W.I.*) everything is great, satisfactory. [? rhy. sl.; *curry and rice* = SE *nice*]

thingstable n. see MR THINGSTABLE n.

thingum n. (*also* **thingamadoodle**) [late 17C–1900s] an unnamed object or person; often used as a euph.

thingumabob n. (*also* **thingamadoodles, thingembob, thingmadodger, thingmybob, thingumbob, thingumjybob, thingummibob, thingumydoochy**) [late 17C+] anything, often small, to which one cannot put a name, also an unnamed person or place; often used as a euph.

thingumabobs n. (*also* **thingumbobs**) **1** [mid-18C+] the testicles (cf. GINGAMBOBS n.). **2** [late 19C–1900s] trousers (cf. DON'T-KNOW-WHAT-TO-CALL-'EMS n.). [euph. use of THINGUMABOB n.]

thingumajig n. (*also* **thingamajig, thingamajigger, thingmegig, thingummijig, thingummyjig**) [mid-19C+] a nameless object, or person.

thingumbob/thingumjybob/thingummibob n. see THINGUMABOB n.

thingummies n. **1** [early 19C+] the testicles (cf. GINGAMBOBS n.). **2** [late 19C–1900s] trousers (cf. DON'T-KNOW-WHAT-TO-CALL-'EMS n.). [euph.]

thingummy n. (*also* **thingamy, thingammy, thing-o-me**) **1** [late 18C+] any nameless object, person or situation. **2** [late 19C+] the penis (cf. BAUBLE n.). [(2) is euph. use of (1)]

thingummyjig n. see THINGUMAJIG n.

thingumsmeribob n. see THINGAMERRY n.

thingumydoochy n. see THINGUMABOB n.

thin-gut n. [17C] a very thin, starving person.

thingy n. (*also* **thingie**) **1** [1930s+] (*also* **thingio, thingmy**) an unnamed object or person. **2** [1930s+] the penis (cf. BAUBLE n.). **3** [1950s] a woman's breasts; in pl. **4** [2000s] the vagina (cf. ARTICLE n.).

thin-hips n. [1930s–40s] (US drugs) a veteran opium smoker who has lain on his hips for so long that they are mis-shapen.

think and thank phr. [late 19C–1900s] thanks, thank you. [Eng. translation of the Heb. morning prayer as used by Jewish Londoners]

thinkbox n. (also thinkpad, thoughtbox) **1** [late 19C–1940s] (Aus.) the head. **2** [1910s+] (US) the brain.

thinker n. (also thinky) [mid-19C+] the mind, the brain.

think factory n. [1950s+] (US) a research institution.

thinking box n. **1** [mid-19C+] (Aus./US) (also thinking stall) the brain. **2** [20C+] a study. **3** [1900s] the head.

think it's just to pee through v. (also think it's just to piss through) [20C+] used to denigrate an unsophisticated, inexperienced youth who supposedly has yet to appreciate the alternative function of his penis; also used of a similarly unsophisticated female. [PEE v.¹ (1)/PISS v.¹ (1)]

think one has sugar on one's dick v. [1960s] (US) to have a high (but unjustifiable) view of one's own physical attractiveness.

think one hung the moon v. see HANG THE MOON v.

think one is king shit v. [1940s+] (US) to be extremely conceited. [KING SHIT n.]

think one's asshole squirts perfume v. [1940s+] (US) to have a high (but unjustifiable) view of one's own abilities.

think one's penny silver v. [late 16C–early 18C] to have a good opinion of oneself.

think one's shit doesn't stink v. see ACT LIKE ONE'S SHIT DON'T STINK v.

think one's shit smells like ice-cream v. [1940s+] (US) to behave affectedly and in an arrogant manner. [var. on ACT LIKE ONE'S SHIT DON'T STINK v.]

thinkpad n. see THINKBOX n.

thinkpiece n. [1970s] (US Black) the brain, the mind.

think pumpkins of oneself v. [late 19C–1900s] to admire oneself. [i.e. a fig. ref. to the size of the vegetable]

think small beer of v. (also think small coals of) [19C] to have a low opinion of. [SMALL BEER n./SE small coals, slack, useless for a blazing fire]

think-tank n. [20C+] the brain.

think that the sun shines out of someone's ass v. (also think that the sun sets in someone's ass, ...arse) [1930s+] (orig. US) to worship someone, to act extremely sycophantically. [ARSE n.¹ (1)/ASS n. (2)]

thinky n. see THINKER n.

thin one n. (also thin 'un) [1920s–60s] (US Black/tramp) a dime, 10 cents. [the coin's dimensions]

thin time n. [1920s+] a period of suffering or discomfiture.

thin 'un n.¹ [mid-19C–1920s] a half-sovereign (50p). [the coin's dimensions]

thin 'un n.² see THIN ONE n.

third base n. [1940s+] (US) the vagina or penis, in the context of sexual exploration (cf. FIRST BASE n.). [baseball imagery (a 'home run' would be intercourse)]

third degree, the n. (orig. US Und.) **1** [late 19C+] the beating up and similar physical abuse of suspects by policemen in order to extract confessions; although allegedly outlawed in the last couple of decades, reality proves otherwise. **2** [1910s+] in fig. use, referring to intense questioning but devoid of physical abuse. [the first and second degrees of interrogation are never specified]

third degree v. [1910s+] to interrogate forcefully and/or violently. [THIRD DEGREE, THE n.]

third eye n. [20C+] (US) the anus. [SE third + EYE sfx]

third fiddle n. see SECOND FIDDLE n.

third leg n. [1970s+] the penis (cf. ARM n.¹). [note RMC Duntroon (Aus.) tripod, a man with a large penis]

third rail n.¹ [1910s–60s] (US) extremely strong liquor. [like the subway's electrified third rail, such liquor 'gives you a jolt']

third rail n.² [1930s–40s] (US Und.) one who cannot be bribed. [play on 'untouchable'/TOUCH v.¹]

third-rail adj. [1900s] (US) dangerous. [for ety. see THIRD RAIL n.¹]

third sexer n. [20C+] (US) a homosexual (cf. BOY-GIRL n.¹). [SE third sex, homosexuality, coined by sexologist Magnus Hirschfeld]

third-world briefcase n. [1980s+] a large portable stereophonic tape deck/radio, particularly popular among Black youths in the US and UK (cf. BRIXTON SUITCASE n.). [SE third-world, i.e. non-White]

thirst n. [1980s+] (drugs) the need for crack cocaine; thus thirst monster, one who smokes crack cocaine to excess.

thirst bazaar n. (also thirst emporium) [1900s] (US) a bar; a tavern.

thirsty adj. [1980s+] (US drugs) in desperate need of drugs.

thirteen n.¹ (also 13) [1960s+] (drugs) marijuana. [the initial letter M, 13th in the alphabet]

thirteen n.² see THIRTEENER n.

13 n. [1990s+] (US prison) a symbol showing affiliation to a Mexican gang. [the initial letter of Mexican is 13th in the alphabet]

13½ n. [2000s] (US prison) 'the sum total of 12 jurors, one judge, and one half-chance, often featured in tattoos' (The Other Side of the Wall, A Prisoner's Dictionary, 2000).

thirteen and a washout n. [1930s–40s] (US prison) the execution chamber. [the supposed unluckiness of thirteen; the WASH-OUT n. (1) is death; some prisons, using hanging, have thirteen steps onto the gallows]

thirteen and the odd n. [1910s–30s] a tail-coat, as worn with 'white tie and tails'. [ety. unknown]

thirteence n. [1920s–40s] a shilling (5p). [there were 12 pence in a shilling; presumably a child could count 'elevenpence, twelvepence, one shilling', the 13 number]

thirteen clean shirts n. [late 19C–1950s] (UK prison) a 3-month sentence. [prisoners were allotted 1 clean shirt every week]

thirteener n. (also thirteen) [late 18C–19C] a shilling.

thirteen inches n. see TWELVE INCHES n.

thirty n.¹ [late 19C+] (US) the end. [the notation –30– used orig. by printers and telegraphers to indicate the end of a story or despatch]

thirty n.² [1940s] (US Black) 1 month, i.e. 30 days.

thirty cents (shy of a quarter) phr. (also twenty-four cents shy of a quarter) [20C+] (US Black) very poor. [a quarter is 25¢, thus lit. '–5¢']

thirty-eight n. (orig. US) **1** [1920s+] a .38 calibre pistol. **2** [1930s+] a bullet from a .38 pistol. [abbr.; note TWENTY-TWO n.]

thirty-eight and/plus two adj. see FORTY adj.².

thirty-first of May n. [1920s+] (Aus.) a fool, a simpleton (cf. BEECHAM'S PILL n.). [rhy. sl. = GAY n.¹]

thirty-one n. [1930s] (US) lemonade. [a short order code]

30 on the hype n. see 20 ON THE HYPE n.

thirty-three-oh-five n. [1950s–60s] (US drugs/New York) an arrest for possession of drugs. [the statute number of the New York penal code]

thirty-two n. [1920s+] (US) a .32 calibre pistol.

— this! excl. [1980s+] (US campus) used in comb. with a n. to negate the previous speaker's suggestion, e.g. 'Let's play pool.' 'Pool this! I've got work to do.' [euph. for fuck this]

this and that n. [20C+] **1** a hat. **2** a cricket bat. **3** a cat. [rhy. sl.]

this beats cockfighting/thunder phr. see THAT BEATS COCK-FIGHTING phr.

this chicken pron. [late 19C] I, myself, me.

this child pron. [mid-19C+] (orig. US Black) I, myself, e.g. this child don't need no more trouble.

thises and thats n. [1900s–10s] spats. [rhy. sl.]

this is all right *phr.* [late 19C] a phr. of disappointment or complaint that implies quite the opposite.

this is an A and B conversation, C yourself out *phr.* [1990s+] (*US Black*) a phr. used to dismiss a third party who butts into a private conversation. [pun on SE phr. *see yourself out*]

this is protected by the red, the black and the green (with a key) *phr.* [1990s+] (*US Black teen*) **1** keep out, this is none of your business. **2** this is for Blacks only, you couldn't understand, optionally ext. by *sisseeeee*, i.e. SISSY n. (1). [the colours of Black nationalism; play on the minatory signs that indicate a building's security system]

this lime has no juice *phr. see* LIME n.[1].

this piece *n.* [2000s] (*US teen*) a place.

this, that and the other *n.* [late 19C+] a euph. for any form of obscenity.

thistledown *n.* [late 19C–1900s] (*Anglo-Irish*) children, esp. those of 'a wandering nature' (Ware). [like blowing *thistledown*, they wander. Note Devon dial. *thistleseed*, gypsies]

thistledown *adj.* [late 19C–1910s] young, unsophisticated, childish. [THISTLEDOWN n.]

this trip *phr.* [mid-18C+] on this occasion.

this won't buy baby a new frock *phr.* (*also* **this won't buy baby a new dress**) [20C+] this is useless, this is pointless.

thomas *n.*[1] **1** [mid-18C–mid-19C] the penis. **2** [mid-19C] a liveried servant. [abbr. JOHN THOMAS n.]

thomas *n.*[2] [1950s] (*W.I.*) a stubborn, conceited man. [biblical figure Doubting *Thomas*]

thomas *n.*[3] *see* TOMMY ATKINS n.

Thomas Atkins *n. see* TOMMY ATKINS n.

Thomas Cook *n.* [1990s+] a look, a glance. [rhy. sl.; ult. UK travel agent *Thomas Cook*]

Thomas Tilling *n.* [late 19C–1930s] a shilling (5p). [rhy. sl.; ult. 19C haulier *Thomas Tilling*]

thonic *n. see* TONIC n.[1].

thornback *n.* [late 17C–early 19C] an old maid. [SE *thornback*, a ray or stickleback. The usage puns on the female child of a stickleback, a *maid* or (Scot.) *maiden-skate*]

thorough *adj.* **1** [1980s+] (*US campus*) of a person, admirable. **2** [1980s+] (*US campus*) used of one who is acting arrogantly or cheekily. **3** [1990s+] (*US teen*) in absolute and complete control of a situation.

thoroughbred *n.* **1** [20C+] an admirable person, a dependable person. **2** [1950s+] (*drugs*) a dealer who sells pure or high-quality narcotics. **3** [1960s] (*US Black*) a male sexual athlete. **4** [1960s+] (*US Black*) a sophisticated hustler. **5** [1960s+] (*UK Und.*) a successful, trustworthy villain. **6** [1960s+] a prostitute with style, sophistication and knowledge, generally considered among the élite of her profession (cf. ALLEY CAT n.; BANBURY n.). [horseracing imagery; (6) note Cleland, *Memoirs of a Woman of Pleasure* (1748–9): '*Phoebe* herself, that hackney'd, thorough-bred *Phoebe*, to whom all modes and devices of pleasure were known']

thoroughbred *adj.* **1** [late 19C] sophisticated, upper-class. **2** [20C+] admirable, dependable, trustworthy.

thoroughbred Black *n.* [1950s+] (*US Black*) the ideal Black woman.

thorough churchman *n.* [late 18C–early 19C] one who goes in at one door of a church and out of the other without stopping for prayer. [pun on SE *through*]

thorough cough *n.* [late 17C–mid-19C] a cough accompanied by a simultaneous breaking of wind. [the wind goes 'through' the body]

thoroughfare *n.* [1930s] (*US Black*) a promiscuous woman (cf. BANBURY n.). [orig. W.I. use, many men have 'ridden' down her]

thorough-go-nimble *n.* [late 17C–early 19C] **1** diarrhoea (cf. APPLE-BLOSSOM TWO-STEP n.). **2** sour or second-rate beer. [(1) + pun on SE *trot*/TROTS, THE n.[2]; (2) f. (1)]

thorough good-natured wench *n.* [late 18C–early 19C] a promiscuous woman. ['one who being asked to sit down, will lie down' (Grose, 1785)]

thorough-handed man *n.* [late 19C–1900s] (*US*) a generous person.

thorough passage *phr.* [late 17C–early 19C] going 'in one ear and out the other'.

thou *n.* [mid-19C+] (*orig. US*) 1000, esp. dollars. [abbr. SE *thousand*]

thoughtbox *n. see* THINKBOX n.

thought foundry *n.* [1900s] (*US*) the brain.

thousand eyes *n.* [1980s] (*US Black*) brogues.

thousand-miler *n.* (*also* **one thousand miles, thousand-mile shirt**) [1920s+] a dark shirt, made of black or navy twill, that does not show dirt. [orig. naut., its being washed after every 1000 miles of a voyage]

thousand-on-a-plate *n.* [late 19C–1950s] (*US*) a dish of peas or beans.

thousand pities *n.* [late 19C–1900s] a woman's breasts (cf. BRACE AND BITS n.). [rhy. sl. = TITTY n.[1] (1)]

thrap *v.* (*also* **throp**) [1990s+] to masturbate (cf. BANG THE BISHOP v.; BOFF v.). [dial. *threap*, to beat, to flog]

thrash *n.* **1** [1930s+] a rumbustious, uninhibited party. **2** [1950s+] a drinking spree. **3** [1980s+] a form of fast, loud and harsh-sounding rock music.

thrash *v.* **1** [1960s+] (*Aus./N.Z.*) to overwork a piece of machinery, e.g. an automobile. **2** [1960s+] (*orig. Aus./N.Z.*) to drive at great speed. **3** [1980s+] (*US campus*) to wreck, to make a mess of.

thrashed *adj.* [1980s+] (*US campus*) **1** worn-out, broken, exhausted. **2** drunk, intoxicated by a drug.

thrasher *n.* [1990s+] (*US campus*) **1** a show-off. **2** a destructive person. **3** a skateboarder. **4** a wild party at which there are breakages. [THRASH v. (3)]

thrash on *v.* [1980s+] (*US campus*) to criticize negatively.

thrash or die! *excl.* [1980s+] (*US campus*) an ironic reversal of a clichéd slogan i.e. *march or die!*, to belittle those who are obsessed with skateboarding. [THRASHER n. (3)]

thrash someone's jacket *v.* [late 17C–early 19C] to beat, to thrash.

thrash the pants off *v. see* TAKE THE PANTS OFF v.

thrattle-pipe *n. see* THROTTLE n.

thray *n.* [1900s–70s] (*N.Z.*) a threepenny piece. [TRAY-BIT n.]

thread *v.* **1** [1940s–50s] of a man, to have sexual intercourse. **2** [1960s+] (*US gay*) to have anal intercourse (cf. ASK FOR THE RING v.). [*play at thread the needle* (*see* PLAY (AT)...)]

threaded (down) *adj.* [1950s] (*US Black*) dressed up. [THREADS n.]

threads *n.* [1920s+] (*orig. US*) clothes; occas. in sing. [metonymy]

threateners *n.* [1990s+] breasts, usu. large.

three *n.*[1] [1950s–70s] (*drugs*) a $3 bag of heroin.

three *n.*[2] *see* FINGER n.[2].

three-a-dayer *n.* [1930s] (*US drugs*) one who smokes opium 3 times a day; thus multiples, i.e. *four-a-dayer*.

three and sixpenny thoughtful *n.* [late 19C] (*UK society*) 'a feminine theory novel' (Ware), e.g. those of Mrs Craik (1826–87) or Mrs Humphry Ward (1851–1920), who wrote on social and religious themes, often dealing with women (but never suffragism). [pun on PENNY DREADFUL n.; SHILLING SHOCKER n.]

three bags *v.* [1980s] (*Aus.*) to masturbate (cf. COTTON WOOL v.). [rhy. sl.; *three bags full* = PULL v.[7]]

three bags full *n.* **1** [20C+] (*Aus.*) a pack of lies. **2** [1980s+] (*Aus. prison*) an act of masturbation. [rhy. sl.; (1) = a load of BULL n.[11] (1); (2) = PULL v.[7]]

three balls *n.* **1** [mid-19C+] (*also* **Mr Three Balls, three ball joint, three-ball man**) a pawnbroker or pawnbroker's shop (cf. FAST-TALKING CHARLIE n.). **2** [1930s+] (*US Black*) a Jew. [the trad. 3 brass balls that hang outside a pawnshop. The stereotypical pawnbroker was Jewish. The 3 balls themselves supposedly come from the arms of the Medicis (although these were 6 red balls, rather than the 3 gold ones of pawnbroking) and were imported to London by the Lombard bankers and thence to the US]

three blind mice *n.* [20C+] (a sack of) rice. [rhy. sl.; ult. the nursery rhyme]

three blue beans in a blue bladder *n.* (*also* **three blue beans in one blue bladder**) [late 16C–early 18C] futile, pointless (if noisy) talk. [the image of a jester and his trad. bladder on a stick, made noisier by the dried beans it contains]

three Bs *phr.* **1** [late 19C–1900s] as used by churchmen, *b*right, *b*rief and *b*rotherly, 3 precepts for a good service, which the younger clergy felt that the very conservative contemporary church was distinctly lacking. **2** [1920s+] (*Aus.*) *b*urn, *b*ash and *b*ury, what should be done with rubbish that accumulates in the outback. **3** [1960s+] (*US gay*) *b*low job, *b*ed and *b*reakfast. [(3) BLOW JOB n. (1)]

three-bulb plant *n.* [late 19C–1900s] (*US*) a pawnbroker. [for ety. *see* THREE BALLS n.]

three-bullet Joey *n.* [1960s–80s] (*US Black*) the police. [their being armed + generic use of proper name *Joey*]

three-card monte *n.* (*also* **three-card molly**) [late 19C+] (*orig. US*) the 3-card trick; thus *3-card man*, one who runs such a game. [Sp. *monte*, a 19C game of chance, played with 45 cards. The modern game is played only by confidence tricksters. There is no gambling unless the trickster desires otherwise – to entice a new victim – the house invariably wins; however, note Asbury *Sucker's Progress* (1938): 'ThreeCard Monte was a Mexican invention, and a misnomer if ever there was one, for it had no more actual relationship to *Monte* than to Old Maid']

three-card trick *n.* [2000s] the penis (cf. ALMOND n.). [rhy. sl. = PRICK n. (2)]

three-cents *adj.* [20C+] (*W.I.*) insignificant, unimportant, worthless. [the tiny sum]

three cheers and a tiger *phr. see* TIGER n.[2].

three-chinned dame *n.* [17C] a procuress, a bawd. [the 3 chins that come with age and loss of looks]

three cold Irish *n. see* FENIAN n.[1].

three-cornered *adj.* [mid-19C+] (*Aus.*) of a quadruped, usu. a horse, awkwardly shaped, scraggy, weak.

three-cornered scraper *n. see* SCRAPER n.[2].

three-cornered tree *n.* [mid-17C–18C] the gallows, esp. the great 'triple tree' at Tyburn.

three Cs *n.* **1** [late 19C] the Central Criminal Court, London, i.e. the Old Bailey, technically the main court for the County of Middlesex, but acknowledged as the most important court in the UK. **2** [1910s] (*UK public school*) *C*hristianity, *C*old bath and *C*ricket.

three-d masher *n.* [late 19C–1900s] a young man who poses as a gentleman but lacks the savoir-faire, not to mention the funds. [SE *three d*, i.e. 3d. or 3 old pence + MASHER n.[1] (2)]

three-dollar bill *n.* [1960s+] (*US campus*) anyone or anything eccentric or odd. [no such currency exists]

three draws and a spit *n.* (*also* **two draws and a spit**) [late 19C–1910s] a cigarette. [SE *draw*, a puff]

three-ed up *adj.* [1960s+] (*UK prison*) living 3 to a cell.

311 *phr.* (*also* **three-eleven**) [1990s+] (*US campus*) happy, keen, enthusiastic. [? police code]

three-er *n.* [1940s] a 3-year prison sentence.

three eyes *n.* [1980s] (*US Black*) the police. [? they have an eye in the back of their heads]

three-fingered hand jig *n. see* HAND JIG n.

three halfporth of gawdelpus *n.* [late 19C+] a street urchin. [GAWDELPUS n.[2] (1)]

three hots and a cot *phr.* [1960s+] (*US*) 3 meals a day plus a bed for the night, often used as a rate of payment. [HOT n.[2]]

365 *n.* [19C–1950s] any frequently served dish, e.g. ham and eggs, bacon and eggs, mutton. [the inevitable appearance of the dish on a café menu every day of the year]

three-inch fool *n.* [late 16C] one who has a short penis.

three jerks of a lamb's tail *phr. see* TWO SHAKES OF A LAMB'S TAIL phr.

three-legged beaver *n.* [1970s+] a male homosexual. [THIRD LEG n. + BEAVER n.[5] (1)]

three-legged instrument *n.* [17C] the gallows.

three-legged mare *n.* [late 17C–early 19C] the gallows, esp. the 'triple tree' at Tyburn.

three-legged stool *n.* [late 17C–18C] the Tyburn gallows. [for ety. *see* TYBURN n.]

three-letter man *n.* [1930s+] **1** (*orig. RN*) an unpleasant person. **2** (*orig. US campus*) a euph. for a homosexual. [(1) the letters are *c-a-d*; (2) they were orig. *f-a-g*, now *g-a-y*; note O. Henry 'An Unfinished Story' (1906): 'The words-of-three-letters lesson in the old blue spelling book begins with Piggy's biography. He was fat; he had the soul of a rat, the habits of a bat, and the magnanimity of a cat']

three links of the Atlantic cable *n.* [late 19C] (*US*) sausage.

3M *n.* [2000s] (*Irish*) a young man who only cares for his *ma*, his MOTH n. (2) and his *moustache. [abbr.]

three Ms *n.* [1900s] (*Aus.*) rough liquor, drunk in the Aus. outback. [Mulga Madness Mixture]

three of the best *n.* [1920s+] (*Aus.*) a packet of condoms, usu. containing 3.

three on *n.* [late 19C] (*US short order*) 3 butter cakes.

Three Ones (Hotel) *n.* [1910s] (*Aus.*) Nelson's Column, Trafalgar Square, London SW1. [a popular meeting place for Australians in London at the time; Downing, *Digger Dialects* (1919), suggests 'one arm, one eye and one pedestal', but the un-bowdlerized appendage is 'one arsehole']

three-out *n.* [early 19C–1900s] a glass that holds one third of a quart (of beer).

three pennorth of God help us *n.* (*also* **six pennyworth of God help us**) [20C+] (*Aus.*) a weakling, an insignificant person.

threepenny bits *n.* [20C+] **1** diarrhoea (cf. BANANA (SPLITS) n.). **2** a woman's breasts (cf. BRACE AND BITS n.). [rhy. sl.; (1) = SHITS, THE n. (1); (2) = TIT n.[3] (1)]

threepenny dodger *n.* (*also* **threepenny Johnnie**) [1900s–10s] a silver threepenny bit. [SE *dodge*, i.e. one is hard to get hold of/generic use of proper name]

threepenny shot *n.* [late 19C–1900s] a round steak and kidney pudding, sold at threepence a portion.

threepenny upright *n.* (*also* **threepenny ordinary, threepenny upright, twopenny upright, twopenny uprighter**) [mid-17C–early 19C; 2000s] a cheap prostitute who has no room of her own and must stand against a wall for intercourse; thus the intercourse itself (cf. DOLLAR-WOMAN n.). [her fee of 3d/2d + SE *upright*]

threepen'orth *n.* [1930s] (*UK Und.*) a 3-year prison sentence.

three-piece suit *n. see* SUIT n.[4] (2).

three-piece suite *n.* (*also* **three-piece set, three-piece suit**) [1920s+] **1** the male genitals. **2** in fig. use, a term of abuse. [furnishing/ tailoring imagery]

three planks *n.* [late 19C–1900s] a coffin.

three-point drinker *n.* [1920s–40s] one who drinks sixpenny-worth of gin with bitters, a shot of lime juice and soda. [the 3 additives]

three-pointer *n.* [1940s–60s] (*US Black*) an urban street corner; thus *three-pointer of the ace trill in the twirling top*, any corner of Seventh Avenue in Harlem.

three-quarter clift *n. see* CLIFT n.

three quarters of a peck *n.* (*also* **¾ of a neck**) [mid-19C–1940s] the neck. [rhy. sl.]

three-ring circus *n.* [1970s+] (*US gay*) a heterosexual woman. [the *three rings* = the anus, mouth and vagina]

three-rounder *n.* [1950s–60s] a petty criminal. [junior or amateur boxing matches are restricted to 3 rounds, professional bouts run to 12 or (formerly) 15]

three screws *n.* [1920s+] (*Can.*) an aluminium container holding 3 condoms. [brandname, *Three Screws* + pun on SCREW n.[1] (2)]

three shakes of a lamb's tail *phr. see* TWO SHAKES OF A LAMB'S TAIL phr.

three-sheet *v.* [20C+] (*US*) to advertise, thus to boast, to brag. [carnival/theatre use, a 3-sheet poster is larger than usual; note Philipp 'Vaudeville' (Federal Writers' Project ms. 1939): 'When an egotistic performer loitered about the lobby, or the sidewalk in front of the theatre, – perhaps to "date up a town gal" or merely to let the natives know he was an actor, – this was called "three-sheeting." (A three-sheet is a poster measuring 44 by 84 inches.) Managers generally frowned upon this practise, for to permit the public to view the performers in their private characters was supposed to detract from the mystery and glamour of the stage. And so the managers regarded with disfavor certain actors who were addicted to the debunking proclivities known as "three-sheeting in front of the theatre"']

three sheets (in the wind) *phr.* (*also* **three sheets to the wind**) [early 19C+] drunk; also as *one/two/four/six/seven sheets to the wind*; occas. intoxicated by a drug. [naval imagery, a ship carrying 'three sheets (sails) to the wind' is 'top-heavy']

threesome *n.* [1970s+] group sex involving 3 people of the same or mixed sexes.

three square *n.* [mid-19C] a penis.

three squares *n.* [20C+] *three square* meals, regular eating. [abbr.]

threeswins *n.* (*also* **treewins, treswins**) [late 17C–early 19C] (*UK Und.*) 3 pence. [SE *three* + WIN n.]

three tears and a bucket *phr.* [1970s–80s] (*US Black*) a phr. of dismissal, disinterest. [the insignificant effect of *three tears* in *a bucket*]

three threads *n.* [late 18C–early 19C] 'half common ale, mixed with stale and double beer' (Grose, 1796).

three-time loser *n.* **1** [20C+] (*orig. US Und.*) a prisoner who has been convicted of 2 crimes worthy of a prison sentence and faces a life sentence or execution if convicted a third time; also occas. *four-time, five-time* etc. **2** [1980s+] a failure, a social inadequate. [LOSER n. (2); (2) fig. use of (1) + ext. of LOSER n. (1)]

three times as queer as a three dollar bill *phr.* [1960s+] homosexual; in the eyes of the speaker, exceptionally or ostentatiously so. [QUEER adj.[1] (3) + THREE-DOLLAR BILL n.; note NINE-DOLLAR BILL n.]

three-times-seven *adj.* [late 19C–1950s] (*US Black*) 21, i.e. legally adult in the US.

three-time winner *n.* [1900s] (*US*) a lucky person or thing. [gambling imagery]

three trees *n.* [late 16C–mid-17C] the gallows. [the early gallows was made of 3 vertical posts joined by a long horizontal bar]

three-way *n.* [1970s+] sexual activity involving 3 people.

three-way *adj.* [1930s+] (*US*) of a prostitute, willing to offer her vagina, anus and mouth to clients; usu. as THREE-WAY GIRL n.

three-way deal *n.* [1960s+] sex involving 3 partners at once; thus *four-way deal* etc.

three-way girl *n.* (*also* **three-way bitch, three-way broad, three-way wench**) [1930s+] a prostitute (or woman) who will offer her vagina, anus and mouth to clients (cf. AWAYDAY GIRL n.).

three ways (and Sunday) *adv. see* NINE WAYS FROM BREAKFAST adv.

three weeks *n.* [1900s–10s] an intense but brief sexual relationship. [the title of the then racy novel by Elinor Glyn, *Three Weeks* (1907)]

three-wheeled trike *n.* [1990s+] a lesbian. [rhy. sl. = DYKE n.]

three-wheeler *n.* [1980s+] (*Aus. prison*) a woman. [rhy. sl. = SHEILA n. (1)]

three-wheel motion *n.* [1990s+] (*US Black teen*) riding one's car on 3 wheels.

three-wheel (skid) *n. see* FRONT-WHEEL SKID n.

three-year-old *n.* [early–mid-19C] (*Anglo-Irish*) a stone weighing approx. 1.36kg (3lb), used as a weapon. [the 3-pound weight]

threp *n.* (*also* **threps, thrip, thrips, thrups**) [late 17C–1910s] threepence; the smallest coin. [colloq. pron.]

thresh *n.* (*also* **thresh-up**) [1930s+] (*Aus.*) a fight. [? SE *thrash/ thresh*]

thrifty *n.* [1930s–50s] a threepenny bit. [the 12-sided coin, minted only 1937–52, carried a picture of the plant *thrift* on its reverse + play on SE]

thrill *n.* **1** [late 19C] a sensational story, a 'thriller'. **2** [1920s+] an orgasm. **3** [1950s+] (*Irish*) a promiscuous woman. [ext. uses of SE]

thrill and chill *n.* [1970s+] (*US Black*) a sexual experience so wonderful it 'sends chills up one's spine'. [THRILL n. (2) + SE *chill*]

thrilled skinny *phr.* [20C+] (*Irish*) very excited, very enthusiastic.

thriller *n.* **1** [late 19C+] a sensational play, film or story. **2** [1900s] a company of actors, specializing in melodrama. **3** [1950s+] a sensational person.

thriller-diller *adj. see* KILLER-DILLER adj.

thrip/thrips *n. see* THREP n.

throat *n.*[1] [20C+] the frenum, the small ligament that links the head of the penis to the shaft. [SE *throat*, linking the head to the body]

throat *n.*[2] [1960s+] (*US campus*) someone who works harder than average, and enjoys it. [SE *cut-throat*]

throat *v.* [1960s] (*US campus*) to work very hard. [THROAT n.[2]]

throat burner *n.* [1900s] (*US*) a drink of spirits.

throat latch *n.* [late 19C–1920s] (*US*) the Adam's apple.

throat oil *n.* [1990s+] (*Aus.*) beer or alcohol generally.

throatwash *n.* [1900s] (*US*) bourbon whisky.

throb *n. see* HEART-THROB n.

throbbing gristle *n.* [1990s+] the penis. [GRISTLE n.]

throg *v.* [1980s+] (*US campus*) to drink. [? THROW DOWN v.[4] (1) + GROG n.[1] (1)]

throne *n.* (*also* **king's throne, throne room**) [1920s+] a lavatory; thus *throne up*, to use the lavatory; *on the throne*, in the process of defecating (cf. ALTAR n.).

throp *v. see* THRAP v.

throttle *n.* (*also* **thrattle-pipe**) [mid-16C+] the throat. [northern UK dial.]

throttle-box *n.* [1940s] (*Aus.*) the throat.

throttle-jockey *n.* [1940s–60s] (*US*) **1** a pilot. **2** a HOT-RODDER n. [SE *throttle* + JOCKEY n.[3] (2)]

throttle one *v.* [1960s] (*Aus.*) to defecate (cf. BACK ONE OUT v.). [play on CHOKE A DARKIE v.]

throttling pit *n.* [1960s+] the lavatory. [play on CHOKE A DARKIE v.]

through *adj.* [1990s+] **1** (*US Black/teen*) drunk or intoxicated by drugs to the point of virtual collapse. **2** (*US campus*) annoyed, disgusted. [SE *through*, exhausted]

through and through *n.* [1970s+] (*US Black*) a wholly admirable (Black) person. [ext. of SE use]

through oneself *phr.* [20C+] (*Ulster*) confused.

throw *n.*[1] [late 19C+] a go, each, usu. in comb. with a sum of money, e.g. *10 pence a throw*.

throw *n.*[2] [20C+] an act of vomiting. [THROW v.[1]]

throw *v.*[1] [19C+] to vomit (cf. BLOW v.[3]).

throw *v.*[2] **1** [mid-19C+] (*orig. US*) to disconcert, to surprise, to worry. **2** [20C+] (*US*) to get rid of, to overcome. **3** [1900s] (*US Und.*) to send to prison.

throw *v.*[3] [mid-19C+] to lose deliberately, esp. in sports. [SE *throw away*]

throw *v.*[4] [20C+] (*US*) to do, to perform, to put across. **2** [1930s]

(*US Black*) to cast a spell. **3** [1940s–50s] (*US Und.*) to rob at gunpoint. **4** [1940s+] (*US*) to shoot a bullet. **5** [1980s+] (*US*) to sell, e.g. *throw joints*, to sell marijuana cigarettes.

throw v.[5] **1** [1920s+] (*US*) to host a party or social event. **2** [1930s] to go out on a spree. **3** [1970s+] to have sexual intercourse.

throw a benny v. [1990s+] (*UK juv.*) to lose one's temper, to throw a tantrum.

throw a boff/bop (into) v. *see* THROW A FUCK (INTO) v.

throw a brick v. **1** [1950s–60s] (*US Black*) to act violently, to kill someone, to commit a crime. **2** [1960s–70s] (*US*) to commit a minor crime. [the *throwing of a brick* through a shop window]

throw a brodie v. *see* DO A BRODIE v.

throw a buttonhole on v. [1960s+] (*US Black*) to have anal intercourse (cf. ASK FOR THE RING v.). [pun on BUTT n.[1] (2) + HOLE n.[1] (1)]

throw a crab v. *see* CRAB v.[1] (1).

throw a curve v. [1930s+] (*orig. US*) to act unpredictably or illegally, to surprise, to trick, to take advantage of someone. [CURVE n. (2)]

throw a fit v. (*also* **throw forty fits**) [late 19C+] to lose all emotional control.

throw a fuck (into) v. (*also* **throw a boff (into)**, **...a bop (into)**, **...a screw (into)**) [1940s+] (*US*) to have sexual intercourse with. [FUCK n.[1] (1)/BOFF n.[1] (2)/BOP v. (6)/SCREW n.[1] (2)]

throw a leg over v. (*also* **throw one's leg over**) [18C; 1960s+] of a man, to seduce, to have sexual intercourse (cf. GET ONE'S LEG OVER v.; LIFT A LEG OVER v.).

throw a levant v. [mid-19C–1900s] to leave, to run off. [SE *levant*, to 'steal away', esp. of a gambler, ult. Sp. *levantar la casa*, to break up housekeeping, *levantar el campo*, to break up the camp]

throw a lick v.[1] [1940s] (*W.I.*) to strike, to beat. [SE *lick*, a blow]

throw a lick v.[2] [1950s] (*W.I.*) to give someone a drink of *liquor*, esp. a 'shot' from a bottle. [abbr.]

throw a maddie v. [1960s+] to go mad, to go crazy. [SE *mad*]

throw a map v. [1940s+] (*Aus.*) to vomit. [the supposed similarity of a pool of vomit to a map of Australia]

throw a mickey v. *see* CHUCK A MICKEY v.

throw a monkey wrench into the machinery v. (*also* **hurl a monkey wrench into the machinery**) [20C+] (*orig. US*) to obstruct something deliberately, to go out of one's way to wreck a plan or project; thus *monkey-wrenching*, this form of industrial sabotage, esp. performed by ecologists; *monkey-wrencher*, one who does this.

throw a moody v. [1930s+] to become sulky, truculent, ill-tempered. [SE *moody*]

throw a natural v. *see* NATURAL n.[2] (2).

throw a pass v. *see* MAKE A PASS v.

throw a punch v. [1950s+] to defend oneself, verbally as well as physically. [boxing imagery]

throw a scare into v. [20C+] to terrorise, to intimidate.

throw a screw (into) v. *see* THROW A FUCK (INTO) v.

throw a seven v. (*orig. US*) **1** [late 19C+] (*also* **do the seven**) to die. **2** [late 19C+] to suffer misfortune. **3** [late 19C+] (*also* **chuck a sixer, chuck the seven, throw a six, throw a sixer**) to lose emotional control, to become hysterical. **4** [20C+] to faint. **5** [20C+] (*also* **chuck sevens, throw sixers**) to vomit. **6** [1920s] to succeed. [? craps dice, where 7, other than in one's initial pass, is a losing throw; Downing, *Digger Dialects* (1919), suggests that this is because it is 'impossible to throw a seven', presumably he means with a single dice; craps uses a pair; note also Aus. rules *sixer*, a scoring kick]

throw a sickie v. (*also* **chuck a sickie, pull...**) [1970s+] to take the day off sick, esp. when one is perfectly healthy. [SICKIE n.[1]]

throw a six/sixer v. *see* THROW A SEVEN v. (3).

throw a spanner in(to) the works v. [1920s+] to destroy or disable something that had hitherto been working perfectly, to

ruin someone else's plans or system. [var. on THROW A MONKEY WRENCH INTO THE MACHINERY v.]

throw ass v. *see* THROW (SOME) ASS v.

throw a thing in someone's dish v. [late 18C–19C] to tease, to reproach. [? the image of tossing something other than money into a beggar's dish]

throw attitude v. (*also* **give attitude/'tude, throw 'tude**) [1980s+] (*US campus*) to act in an arrogant, surly, obnoxious manner. [ATTITUDE n.]

throwaway n. [1980s+] (*US Und.*) a garment, e.g. a shirt, which is worn for a street crime, then immediately discarded so as to alter one's identity.

throwaway adj. [1950s+] (*US*) useless, hopeless, e.g. a *throwaway man*.

throw away belly v. (*also* **dash away belly, throw away a baby, ...a child**) [20C+] (*W.I.*) to procure an abortion, to terminate a pregnancy.

throw a willy v. *see* CHUCK A WILLIE v.

throw a wing-ding v. [1930s–60s] (*drugs*) to pretend to be suffering severe withdrawal pains in order to persuade a doctor to give one some heroin; also (*US prison*) to take illness to gain leniency or to avoid a work detail. [SE *throw* + WING-DING n.]

throw a wobbly v. (*also* **throw a wobbler, chuck a..., do a...**) [1970s+] of people, to panic, to suffer a fit of nerves; also used fig. of things. [SE *throw* + WOBBLY n.[2]]

throw back v.[1] [late 19C–1910s] to revert to ancestral type. [SE *throwback*, a reversion (to type)]

throw back v.[2] [1940s+] (*US*) to eat or drink, esp. in quantity.

throw blows v. [1980s] (*US Black*) to fight.

throw bouquets at v. [20C+] (*US*) to praise.

throw bricks at the jailhouse v. [1960s] to take foolish chances, to tempt fate.

throw craps v. [20C+] (*US*) **1** to fail. **2** to experience bad luck. [craps jargon; *craps*, a losing throw]

throw donuts v. *see* BLOW DOUGHNUTS v.

throw-down n.[1] [late 19C–100s] **1** a defeat. **2** a rejection. [wrestling jargon *throw-down*, a fall]

throw-down n.[2] [1990s+] (*US Black*) a (gang) fight. [THROW DOWN v.[3] (4)]

throw down v.[1] [late 19C] to overcome, to prove too much for. [wrestling imagery]

throw down v.[2] [late 19C+] (*US*) to discard, to abandon.

throw down v.[3] **1** [1900s–20s] (*US*) to get someone into trouble, to betray. **2** [1910s+] (*US*) to challenge. **3** [1980s+] (*US Black/campus*) to enjoy oneself vigorously, to dance. **4** [1980s+] (*US Black*) to get into a fight with. **5** [1980s+] (*US teen*) to challenge a rival break-dancer. **6** [1980s+] (*US campus*) to have sexual intercourse. **7** [1980s+] (*US Black/campus*) to work hard on a major project. [SE *throw down the gauntlet*]

throw down v.[4] **1** [1930s+] (*US campus*) to eat or drink voraciously. **2** [1980s+] (*US drugs*) to give someone some drugs, usu. pills.

throw (down) on v. **1** [late 19C+] (*US Und.*) to hold a gun on. **2** [1960s+] to blame. [ext. THROW DOWN v.[3]]

throw dust v. *see* SCRATCH GRAVEL v. (2).

throwed adj. [1990s+] (*US campus*) defeated, humiliated. [SE *thrown*]

throw for a loop v. (*also* **put someone's head in a loop**) [1960s+] to disturb, to worry considerably, to put someone off their stride. [KNOCK FOR A LOOP v.]

throw forty fits v. *see* THROW A FIT v.

throw gravel v. *see* SCRATCH GRAVEL v. (2).

throw hands v. [1970s+] (*orig. US Black*) to punch, to hit; to fight.

throw-in n. [late 19C–1900s] (*Aus.*) an unexpected piece of good luck. [SE *throw in*, to add (something) on for free, esp. in a transaction]

throw in and in *v. see* PLAY (AT) IN AND IN *v.*

throw in one's alley *v.* [1900s–20s] (*Aus.*) **1** (*also* **chuck in one's alley, pass..., roll..., sky..., sling...**) to die. **2** to give up, to cease from an action. [SE *throw in*, to toss + *alley*, a marble]

throw in one's gears *v.* [1930s] (*US Black*) to leave quickly.

throw in one's hand *v.* [1920s+] to give in, to surrender. [cards]

throw in one's marble(s) *v. see* PASS IN ONE'S MARBLE(S) *v.*

throw in one's toe *v.* [1900s] (*Aus.*) to die.

throw in the towel *v.* (*also* **chuck up the sponge, throw up...**) **1** [mid-19C+] to give in, to capitulate. **2** [1900s] to resign. **3** [1910s–30s] to die. [boxing use, whereby a towel or sponge thrown into the ring indicates the retirement of a fighter who is losing badly]

throw iron *v. see* PUMP IRON *v.*

throw it *v.* (*also* **throw the bull**) [20C+] (*US*) to brag, to boast, to claim what one cannot achieve.

throw it in *v.* [1910s+] (*Aus.*) to stop doing something. [abbr. THROW IN THE TOWEL *v.*]

throw it into *v.* **1** [late 19C] to tease. **2** [late 19C–1950s] (*US*) (*also* **chuck it into, shoot it into**) to impose upon. **3** [1930s] as *throw — into*, to force something upon someone. **4** [1950s] to assault, to kill. **5** [1970s] (*US gay*) to sodomize.

throw it up against *v.* (*also* **throw it into someone's teeth, throw it up at, throw it up in someone's face, throw it up to**) [late 19C+] (*US*) to criticize someone, to hold someone up as an object of reproach.

throw lead *v.* (*also* **spill lead**) [late 19C+] (*US*) to shoot a gun.

throw leather *v.* [1930s+] to box.

throw me in the dirt *n.* [mid-19C+] a shirt. [rhy. sl.]

throw money around like a man with no hands *v.* [1950s] (*Aus.*) to be very mean.

throw money at *v.* [1970s+] (*US*) to spend an extravagant amount of money on something, esp. in the hope of remedying a problem.

throw-off *n.* [1900s–30s] **1** a hostile or critical remark or allusion. **2** an illusion, a disguise. **3** (*US Und.*) a supposedly legitimate business which in fact masks a criminal one. [THROW OFF *v.*]

throw off *v.* **1** [late 18C+] (*orig. Und.*) to deride, to ridicule. **2** [early–mid-19C] (*UK Und.*) to boast of one's successful crimes. **3** [mid-late 19C] (*US*) to abandon, to neglect. **4** [1980s+] (*Aus. prison*) to avoid an issue.

throw off (upon) *v.* [1940s+] (*W.I.*) to give away things one no longer needs to a poorer person.

throw on *v. see* THROW (DOWN) ON *v.*

throw on a face *v.* (*also* **catch a face**) [1970s+] (*US*) to get drunk or intoxicated by drugs. [the face one 'throws on' is one's bleariness]

throw one *v.* [1990s+] to lose one's temper, to have an emotional outburst. ['one' is a fit]

throw one's cap at *v. see* SET ONE'S CAP AT *v.*

throw one's cookies *v.* (*also* **throw one's guts**) [1930s+] (*US*) to vomit (cf. BLOW CHOW *v.*). [COOKIES *n.*[1]/SE *guts*]

throw one's feet *v.* [late 19C–1930s] (*US*) to beg, to 'hustle', usu. for money. [SE *throw the feet*, of a horse, to move its feet well, esp. when crossing rough ground]

throw one's guts *v.* [1920s–60s] (*US tramp*) to inform (cf. COME ONE'S GUTS *v.*). [SE *throw* + GUTS *n.*[1] (2)]

throw one's leg over *v. see* THROW A LEG OVER *v.*

throw one's mug away *v. see* MUG *n.*[1] (2).

throw one's voice *v.* [1960s+] (*Aus.*) to vomit.

throw sets on *v. see* RUN SETS ON *v.*

throw shade *v.* (*also* **shade**) [1990s+] (*US campus*) to humiliate (someone) exceedingly. [? to 'put in the shade']

throw shapes *v. see* SHAPE *v.*[1].

throw sixers *v. see* THROW A SEVEN *v.* (5).

throw sixes *v.* [20C+] to die. [craps dice, a throw of 12 (double 6) is a losing throw]

throw (some) ass *v.* [1950s+] (*US Black*) **1** of a woman, to walk in an exaggeratedly sexy manner. **2** of a woman, to have sexual intercourse (cf. CATCH AN OYSTER *v.*). [ASS *n.* (2)]

throw some dirt on *v.* [1970s+] (*US Black*) to malign, to slander.

throw someone a hump *v. see* HUMP *n.*[4] (1).

throw someone for *v.* [1940s–50s] (*Aus.*) to cheat, to swindle, to persuade someone to give up something.

throw someone in the air *v.* (*also* **toss someone in the air**) [late 19C] (*US*) to jilt, to break off a relationship with.

throw someone out on their ass *v.* (*also* **throw someone out on their ear**) [20C+] (*Aus./US*) to eject someone forcibly.

throw something at *v.* [1970s+] (*US*) to attempt to solve a problem with an excess of some resource.

throw the baby out with the bathwater *v.* [1940s+] to be so keen on eliminating the large-scale errors that one simultaneously tosses out the less visible but highly valuable entities hidden among them.

throw the book at *v.* [1910s+] (*orig. US*) to discipline heavily, to reprimand severely (cf. HIT SOMEONE WITH THE BOOK *v.*). [the 'book of rules' that one has contravened, orig. in legal context, to *throw the book at*, to give someone a maximum sentence]

throw the boots to *v. see* PUT THE BOOTS TO *v.*

throw the bull *v. see* THROW IT *v.*

throw the cat *v. see* SLING A CAT *v.*

throw the dagger *v.* [1980s+] (*US campus*) to have sexual intercourse (cf. BURY IT *v.*). [SE *throw* + DAGGER *n.*[1]]

throw the feet *v.* [late 19C–1930s] (*orig. US*) **1** to beg. **2** to hurry off. [(1) THROW ONE'S FEET *v.*]

throw the hammer *v.* **1** [late 19C–1900s] to obtain money under false pretences. **2** [1900s] (*US*) to criticize negatively, to disparage. [HAMMER *n.*[3] (1)/HAMMER *n.*[3] (2)]

throw the harpoon in(to) *v.* (*US*) **1** [late 19C–1900s] to persuade, to trick, to attack. **2** [1960s+] to have sexual intercourse (with) (cf. BURY IT *v.*). **3** [1960s+] to flirt with. [HARPOON *n.*]

throw the hatchet *v.* [mid-19C] to tell lies, to exaggerate.

throw the hooks (into) *v.* (*US*) **1** [late 19C–1940s] to criticize viciously. **2** [late 19C+] to cheat or swindle, to lure a victim. [fishing imagery]

throw the mitts *v. see* MITT *n.* (3).

throw the skids under *v. see* PUT THE SKIDS TO *v.* (3).

throw 'tude *v. see* THROW ATTITUDE *v.*

throw-up *n.* [2000s] (*orig. US*) a simple piece of graffiti art, using only 2 colours, such as the artist's own name. [THROW UP *v.*[4]]

throw up *v.*[1] [mid-18C+] to vomit (cf. BLOW UP *v.*[3]). [abbr. THROW UP ONE'S ACCOUNTS *v.*]

throw up *v.*[2] [1920s+] to give up all hope. [abbr. SE *throw up*, to give up, thus abbr. of *throw up one's hopes*]

throw up *v.*[3] [1930s+] to produce, to provide.

throw up *v.*[4] [1990s+] to place one's name on a piece of graffiti.

throw up Jonah *v. see* HEAVE UP JONAH *v.*

throw up one's accounts *v.* [mid-late 18C] to vomit. [var. on CAST UP ONE'S ACCOUNTS *v.*]

throw up one's boots *v.* [mid-19C+] (*US*) to vomit intensely. [a melodramatic ext. of THROW UP *v.*[1]]

throw up one's heels *v.* (*also* **throw up one's heel taps, ...one's toes**) [20C+] (*US*) to vomit copiously. [ext. of THROW UP *v.*[1]; note VOMIT UP ONE'S TOENAILS *v.*]

throw up one's ring *v. see* SPEW ONE'S RING *v.* (1).

throw up the sponge *v. see* THROW IN THE TOWEL *v.*

throw words *v. see* DROP WORDS *v.*

thruff *n.* [early 19C] (*US Und.*) a pickpocket. [ety. unknown]

thrum *n.*[1] [early 18C] a prostitute. [THRUM *v.* (1)]

thrum *n.*[2] *see* THRUMS *n.* (1).

thrum *v.* **1** [mid-16C–19C] (*also* **thrum one's jacket**) to have sexual intercourse. **2** [17C–early 19C] to thrash. [SE *thrum*, to play on a stringed instrument]

thrum-cap *n.* [17C–19C] any form of roughly made or

improvised headgear. [SE *thrum*, a short piece of waste thread or yarn]

thrums *n.* **1** [late 17C–1950s] (*UK Und.*) (*also* **thrum, thrumbuskins, thrummer, thrum-mop, thrumms, thrum-mup, thrum wins**) 3 pence. **2** [late 18C] ? the shell game, the 3-card trick.

thrups *n.*[1] (*also* **thrupennies**) [late 19C+] the breasts (cf. BRACE AND BITS n.). [play on THRUPS n.[2]; ult. rhy. sl. = THREEPENNY BITS n. (2) = TIT n.[3] (1)]

thrups *n.*[2] *see* THREP n.

thrush *n.* (*US*) **1** [1920s–50s] a woman singer. **2** [1940s+] female pubic hair.

thrush *v.* [1920s–50s] (*US*) to sing. [THRUSH n. (1)]

thrust *n.* [late 18C] (*UK Und.*) an apparently luxurious and expensive waistcoat used by a confidence trickster to obtain money from a landlord.

thrusters *n.* [1960s+] (*drugs*) amphetamines (cf. A n.[2]). [the effects; it makes the user 'go faster']

thud *n.* [1910s] (*Aus.*) a bad fall (usu. in fig. contexts). [THUD v.]

thud *v.* [1910s+] (*Aus.*) to hit someone. [SE *thud*, onomat. for an object hitting something hard]

thug *n.* [1990s+] (*US Black*) a ghetto Black male. [the image of the successful SE *thug* as a cool role model; note *The Source*, October 1998: 'See a thug doesn't mean anything bad. All a thug means is you're doing something that one particular group doesn't agree with']

thugette *n.* [1990s+] (*US Black*) a female THUG n. [THUG n. + SE fem. sfx -*ette*]

thugged out *adj.* [1990s+] (*US Black*) filled with gun-carrying Black males. [THUG n.]

thugging *n.* [1990s+] (*US Black*) relaxing, acting in a cool manner. [THUG n.]

thumb *n.* [1960s+] (*drugs*) marijuana, a marijuana cigarette (cf. BONE n.[11]). [one sucks it]

thumb *v.* **1** [late 18C–19C] of a man, to have sexual intercourse; thus *well-thumbed girl*, a worn-out prostitute. **2** [20C+] (*Irish*) of a woman, to masturbate (cf. APPLY LIP GLOSS v.). [SE *thumb*, to riffle through, to press or soil with the thumb]

thumber *n.*[1] [1950s] a shilling.

thumber *n.*[2] [1980s+] (*US campus*) a beggar, a borrower, someone constantly scrounging from their friends. [SE *thumb*, to put up one's thumb in the hope of getting a free ride]

thumb in *v.* [1950s] (*US*) to be included, to be given a job. [the individual is given the 'thumbs-up']

thumb in bum and mind in neutral *phr.* [1960s+] (*orig. Aus.*) a phr. used of one who seems to have fallen into a vacant reverie. [BUM n.[1] (1)]

thumb in one's eye *n.* [20C+] (*US*) an irritation, an annoyance.

thumb of love *n.* [late 19C+] the penis.

thump *n.* [1970s+] **1** (*US Black*) a street-fight, esp. with fists or knives. **2** (*US teen*) sexual intercourse.

thump *v.* **1** [late 16C–early 18C] to have sexual intercourse (cf. BANG v.[1]). **2** [late 16C; late 18C+] to defeat heavily, esp. in battle or, more recently, in sport. **3** [1960s+] (*US Black*) to fight, usu. of a gang. **4** [1980s+] (*US teen*) of a man, to have sexual intercourse.

thump! *excl.* [20C+] used to accentuate one's rejection of a statement or idea, e.g. *do I thump! is she thump!* etc. [THUMP v. (1); euph. for FUCK! excl.]

thumper *n.*[1] [early-mid 16C] a rank of villain. [the details are unknown, presumably the 16C equivalent of a mugger: 'Tynckers [...] tryfullers, turners, and trumpers, Tempters, traytoures, trauaylers, and thumpers' (Anon., *A New Interlude called Thersites*, c.1537)]

thumper *n.*[2] **1** [mid-17C–19C] anything, occas. anyone, notably large in size. **2** [late 17C–1900s] a major lie. **3** [late 19C–1900s] (*US*) a dedicated liar.

thumper *n.*[3] [1990s+] (*US Black*) a street gangster, a thug.

thumping *adj.* [late 16C+] enormous, very large.

thumping *adv.* [mid-19C+] very, extremely, often as *thumping great*. [THUMPING adj.]

thumpingly *adv.* [late 17C+] very, exceedingly; to a very great extent. [THUMPING adj.]

thump seven kinds of shit out of *v.* (*also* **kick seven kinds of shit out of**) [1950s+] (*orig. milit.*) to beat up severely. [SHIT n.[1] (1)/SHIT, THE n.[2]]

thump the mutton *v. see* FLOG ONE'S MUTTON v.

thunder *n.* [18C+] (*US*) a euph. for *hell* or the 'daylights'.

thunder *v.* [1980s+] (*US campus*) to succeed, to do well. [i.e. to 'make a noise']

thunder! *excl.* [18C+] a euph. for HELL! excl. or DAMN! excl. in a variety of phrs., e.g. *for thunder's sake, by thunder, like thunder, what in thunder, why in thunder, who the thunder, go to thunder.*

thunder and lightning *n.* **1** [19C] gin and bitters. **2** [early 19C+] (*Irish*) a mixture of shrub and whisky. **3** [late 19C–1900s] treacle and clotted cream. **4** [1900s] brandy sauce when ignited. [LIGHTNING n.[1]]

thunder and lightning *adj.* [mid-18C–19C] 'applied to articles of apparel of a "loud" or "flashy" style, or combining two strongly contrasted colours' (*OED*); also as n.

thunder and ouns! *excl.* [mid-19C+] (*Irish*) a mild excl. [var. on Ger. *donner und blitzen!* thunder and lightning! + *ouns*, (Christ's) wounds]

thunder and rain *n.* [20C+] (*Aus.*) a train. [rhy. sl.]

thunder and tommy *n. see* HELL AND TOMMY n.

thunder and turf! *excl.* [19C] a general excl. of fury, surprise, indignation etc.

thunderation! *excl.* [mid-19C+] (*orig. US*) a mild expletive. [SE *thunder* + sfx -*ation*; var. on DAMNATION! excl.]

thunderbags *n.* [20C+] (*Aus.*) men's underpants. [SE *thunder* + SE *bags*/BAGS n.[1], i.e. the noise of breaking wind]

thunderbox *n.* **1** [20C+] (*US*) the buttocks. **2** [1930s+] a lavatory. **3** [1930s+] a portable commode. [SE *thunder* + *box*, i.e. the noise of defecation]

thunder chicken *n.* (*also* **thunder chick**) [1970s+] (*US Black*) an unkempt, unattractive woman, esp. with messy hair.

thundergob *n.* [1990s+] (*Irish*) a loud talkative person.

thunderhead *n. see* DUNDERHEAD n.

thundering *adj.* [17C+] a general intensifier, excessive, immense; also in phrs. e.g. *thundering cats!*

thundering *adv.* [mid-18C+] a general intensifier, excessively, immensely, greatly.

thundermug *n.* (*also* **thunder jug**) [mid-19C+] a chamber-pot. [SE *thunder* + MUG n.[4]/SE *jug*, i.e. the noise of defecation/urination]

thunder-thighs *n.* [1980s+] an overweight person, esp. a woman with fat thighs.

thunk *v.* [late 19C+] (*US*) to have thought. [joc. past tense of SE *think*]

thusly *adv.* [mid-19C–1900s] (*US*) thus, to sum things up.

thuzzy-muzzy *n.* [late 19C–1910s] enthusiasm. [mispron. of SE]

tib *n.*[1] [mid-16C–17C] a prostitute. [SE *tib*, 'a typical name for a woman of the lower classes' (*OED*)]

tib *n.*[2] [mid–late 19C] a bit, a piece. [backsl.]

tib *n.*[3] [2000s] (*US prison*) a cell.

tib *n.*[4] *see* TIB (OF THE BUTTERY) n.

tibby *n.*[1] [late 18C–mid-19C] a cat. [SE *tib*, a female cat]

tibby *n.*[2] [19C–1900s] the head. [Fr. *tête*, the head]

tibby *n.*[3] [1930s+] (*Aus.*) a tabloid newspaper. [? SE *tabloid*]

tibby drop *n.* [mid-19C+] hop. [rhy. sl.]

tib (of the buttery) *n.* [mid-16C–mid-19C] a goose. [SE *tib*, a young woman or a cat, presumably the femininity is the point rather than the specific animal]

Tib's eve *n. see* ST TIBB'S EVE n.

tic n. [1970s+] (*drugs*) phencyclidine (cf. ACE n.[4]). [misreading of THC, i.e. tetrahydrocannabinol; like TAC n.]

tical n. [1990s+] (*orig. US Black*) marijuana. [? abbr. SE *practical*]

tick n.[1] [17C–early 18C] a signature.

tick n.[2] **1** [17C+] an unpleasant, insignificant person, usu. male. **2** [1970s+] (*US campus*) an overweight person. **3** [1970s+] (*US campus*) a greedy or selfish person. [SE *tick*, a parasitical mite]

tick n.[3] **1** [17C+] credit; thus [1990s+] *tick list*, a large number of debts; [1990s+] *ticking*, obtaining goods on credit; also *River Tick*, debtor's prison. **2** [early 19C] a creditor. **3** [mid-19C–1910s] a dunning letter, a bill. [abbr. SE *ticket*, the writing down of one's debt]

tick n.[4] **1** [late 18C–early 19C] a watch. **2** [late 19C+] a second; thus [20C+] *on the tick, to the tick*, precisely on time; TWO TICKS n. **3** [1930s–40s] (*US Black*) used to indicate time, usu. with the number doubled as a means of confusing outsiders, e.g. *tick twenty*, 10 o'clock. **4** [20C+] (*US*) a small degree or amount, usu. an increase. [the sound and thus its minimal duration]

tick n.[5] [mid-19C] (*US campus*) a recitation by a student who is ignorant of what the text actually means.

tick v.[1] **1** [late 17C+] to obtain or place on credit. **2** [19C+] to grant someone credit, to place a debt on credit. [TICK n.[3] (1)]

tick v.[2] [1980s+] (*US campus*) **1** to talk in class without having prepared the assignment. **2** to talk nonsense. [image of a clock which *ticks* mindlessly on]

tickadyboo adj. see TICKETTY-BOO adj.

ticked (off) adj. [1950s+] (*orig. US*) irritated, annoyed. [TICK OFF v.[1]]

ticker n.[1] **1** [early 19C+] a watch. **2** [mid-19C] (*US campus*) one who recites by rote, but with no knowledge of the text. **3** [1930s+] the human heart. **4** [1930s+] (*Aus./US*) courage. [(1) and (3) the regular *ticking* or beating; (2) TICK n.[5]; (4) from (3)]

ticker n.[2] [1970s+] an accountant. [SE *tick off*, they tick off sums of money]

ticket n.[1] [early 19C] a blow, a punch. [? play on SE *punch tickets*]

ticket n.[2] **1** [mid–late 19C] (*UK Und.*) a ticket of leave, parole. **2** [late 19C–1930s] (*US*) a playing card, as used in a game of 3-card trick. **3** [1900s] a prescription. **4** [1910s] (*UK Und.*) probation. **5** [1920s–40s] (*US*) a betting slip. **6** [1920s–40s] (*US Und.*) a prison sentence. **7** [1930s] track record, history. **8** [1930s+] (*US prison*) a disciplinary record. **9** [1940s] (*US prison*) a certificate of release. **10** [1940s] a certificate of demobilization from the armed forces. **11** [1940s–70s] (*UK Und.*) an arrest warrant. **12** [1950s+] (*US*) a licence. **13** [1960s–70s] a pass or passport, whether valid or counterfeit. **14** [2000s] (*US Black*) a lottery ticket, usu. in pl. [(9) note WW1 Aus. milit. *ticket*, a discharge from the Army]

ticket n.[3] **1** [mid-19C–1900s] the facts, the truth. **2** [mid-19C+] the right, proper, best or fashionable thing to do. **3** [mid-19C+] the task in hand, the relevant procedure. **4** [1990s+] (*US*) the ideal person. [? SE *winning ticket*; or ? Fr. *étiquette* (Hotten, 1867); or ? SE *ticket*, a bill or invoice]

ticket n.[4] [1960s+] (*Aus. drugs*) a single dose of LSD, dripped onto a small piece of absorbent paper. [resemblance to a SE *ticket*, or TICKET n.[3] (2), i.e. its positive effects; note The Beatles song title 'Ticket To Ride']

ticket n.[5] [1960s+] a person (as used esp. by a MOD n.[2] (1) in the early 1960s). [TICKET n.[3] (2)]

ticket v. [late 19C–1940s] to sentence to prison. [SE *ticket*, a written pass]

ticket o' leave n. [late 19C] a holiday. [SE *ticket of leave*, a parole licence]

tickets n. [1960s+] (*S.Afr.*) the end, the finish. [? the tearing up of betting slips or tickets after one's choice has failed to win]

ticket-skinner n. [late 19C] (*US*) a ticket tout. [play on SE *mule-skinner*, a mule-driver]

ticketty-boo adj. (*also* **tickadyboo, tickety-boo, tiggerty-boo**) [1910s+] (*orig. services*) fine, wonderful, all in order. [? TICKET n.[3] (2); or ? Hind. *tikai babu*, it's all right, sir]

tickey n. (*also* **tickie, ticky**) [mid-19C+] (*S.Afr.*) **1** a threepenny piece (2½ cents post-decimalization). **2** anything or anyone very small; thus phrs. *half a brick/two bricks and a tickey high*, very small. [? dial. *ticky*, small, or Du. *stukje*, a little bit, or Hind. *taka*, a stamped silver coin]

tickey-box n. [1970s+] (*S.Afr.*) a public telephone. [TICKEY n. (1), the then charge for a call]

tickey-line n. [1960s+] (*S.Afr.*) a cheap prostitute; thus fig. *tickey-line*, cheap, second-rate. [TICKEY n. (1)]

tickey-snatching adj. [mid-19C+] (*S.Afr.*) **1** making quick profits. **2** close-fisted, mean. [TICKEY n. (1) + SE *snatch*]

tickey wire n. see LONG TICKEY n.

tickie n. see TICKEY n.

tickieman n. (*also* **tickman, tick-merchant**) [1960s+] (*Ulster*) a doorstep salesman. [one gets the goods 'on tick']

tickle n. **1** [1930s+] (*UK Und.*) a robbery or other crime, esp. a successful and lucrative one. **2** [1930s+] a piece of information. **3** [1970s+] a success in gambling. [? it *tickles one's fancy* or the image of SE *tickling* trout]

tickle v.[1] [late 16C+] to amuse, to make laugh; thus *tickle it*, to enjoy oneself.

tickle v.[2] **1** [late 19C–1910s] to puzzle, to confuse. **2** [1920s+] to rob, to steal from. **3** [1920s+] (*Aus.*) to ask someone for a loan.

tickled adj. [late 16C+] amused, pleased. [TICKLE v.[1]]

tickle-faggot n. [19C] the penis. [SE *tickle* + *faggot*, a woman]

tickle-gizzard n. [mid-17C–19C] the penis. [it tickles the woman's GIZZARD n. (1)]

tickle one's fancy v. [mid-19C+] to masturbate. [play on SE]

tickle one's innards v. [late 19C+] (*US*) to take a drink.

tickle one's pickle v. [1970s+] to masturbate (cf. BEAT ONE'S MEAT v.). [PICKLE n.[2]]

tickle-pitcher n. **1** [late 17C–early 19C] a drunkard. **2** [mid-18C] a promiscuous person of either sex. [SE *pitcher*/PITCHER n.[1]]

tickler n.[1] **1** [17C] a sword. **2** [19C] (*US*) a small knife or pistol. [it 'tickles the ribs']

tickler n.[2] [late 18C–1900s] a puzzle, something or someone that is hard to deal with or understand. [it *tickles* one's brain]

tickler n.[3] [19C–1920s] (*US*) a small measure of spirits (approx. 300ml/½ pint), a hip-flask. [it *tickles* the palate]

tickler n.[4] **1** [mid-19C] (*US*) a blow. **2** [mid–late 19C] a whip or cane. **3** [late 19C] a short poker used to preserve the smarter, 'best' one. **4** [late 19C+] the penis (cf. ARSE-OPENER n.). **5** [late 19C+] the vagina. **6** [1930s] (*Aus.*) an electric battery. **7** [1970s+] a junior official or assistant who is used by their superior(s) to pass on policies etc to still lower ranks, so that the superiors don't have to make face-to-face contact themselves.

tickler n.[5] [1920s–40s] (*US*) a moustache.

tickler n.[6] [1950s+] (*US*) a piano-player. [abbr. IVORY-TICKLER n.; note Ward, 'The Dancing School' (1700): 'the Ticklers of Cat-Guts' i.e. violinists]

tickler n.[7] see FRENCH TICKLER n.

ticklers n. [20C+] the fingers.

tickle someone's back v. [late 19C] (*Aus. Und.*) to inflict a judicial lashing.

tickle someone's ears v. [1900s–20s] to flatter.

tickle someone's hole v. [1920s–50s] to masturbate a woman, usu. performed by someone else.

tickle someone's liver v. [late 19C] (*Aus.*) to stab.

tickle someone's ribs v. see RIB TICKLE v.

tickle someone's toby v. [late 17C–19C] **1** to thrash, to beat. **2** to have sexual intercourse. [TOBY n.[1]]

tickle-tail n. **1** [mid-15C–19C] a prostitute, a promiscuous woman (cf. BANGTAIL n.[1]). **2** [late 17C–early 19C] a schoolmaster. **3** [late 18C–19C] a cane. **4** [early 19C] the penis. [SE *tickle* + (1) TAIL n.[2] (2); (2) and (3) TAIL n.[2] (1); (4) TAIL n.[2] (3)]

tickle-tail function *n.* [late 17C–early 18C] a prostitute (cf. BANGTAIL n.[1]). [ext. of TICKLE-TAIL n. (1)]

tickle-text *n.* [early 18C–1900s] a parson.

tickle the ivories *v.* [1920s+] to play the piano (cf. IVORY-TICKLER n.). [IVORY n. (6)]

tickle the minikin *v.* [17C] to play the lute or fiddle. [usu. used with sexual innuendo, thus John Marston (?), *The Comedie of Pasquil & Katherine/Jacke Drums Entertainment* (1601): 'When I was a yong man and could tickle the Minikin, I had the best stroke, the sweetest touch, but now I am falne from the Fidle, and betooke me to thee (the Pipe)']

tickle the peter *v.* [1940s+] (*mainly Aus./N.Z.*) to rob a safe, till or cashbox. [SE *tickle* + PETER n.[2] (2)]

tickle the piss out of *v.* (*also* tickle the shit out of) [1950s+] (*US*) to please or amuse someone. [PISS, THE n./SHIT, THE n.[1]]

tickle-thomas *n.* [19C] the vagina. [SE *tickle* + THOMAS n.[1] (1)]

tickle-toby *n.* **1** [late 17C–19C] a sword. **2** [late 17C–19C] the penis. **3** [late 17C–19C] the vagina. **4** [late 17C–19C] a promiscuous woman. **5** [mid-19C] a rod or birch. [SE *tickle* + TOBY n.[1]]

tickle your fancy *n.* [20C+] a homosexual. [rhy. sl. = NANCY n.[2] (2)]

tickman/tick-merchant *n. see* TICKIEMAN n.

tick off *v.[1]* **1** [late 19C+] (*orig. milit.*) to scold, to reprimand; thus *tick-off, ticking-off*, a scolding. **2** [1910s+] to identify, to mark.

tick off *v.[2]* [1950s+] (*US*) to irritate, to annoy. [? euph. PISS OFF v. (2) or TICK OFF v.[1] (1)]

tickrum *n.* (*also* tick-rome) [mid-17C–early 19C] (*UK Und.*) a licence. [SE *ticket*]

tick-tack *n.[1]* (*also* trick-track) [mid-16C+] sexual intercourse. [SE *ticktack*, 'an old variety of backgammon, played on a board with holes along the edge, in which pegs were placed for scoring' (*OED*) + the rhythmical movements]

tick-tack *n.[2]* (*also* tic-tac) [late 19C+] a system of telegraphy used on racecourses to keep the bookmakers abreast of the changing odds; thus *tick-tack man* or *ticktacker*, one who performs such telegraphy (by using a 'vocabulary' of hand and arm movements and signals). [TIC-TAC n.[1]]

tick-tock *n.* **1** [1940s] (*US Black*) the heart, the heartbeat. **2** [1950s] (*Aus. Und.*) a clock or watch. [its regular beating]

ticky *n. see* TICKEY n.

ticky-tacky *n.* [1960s+] cheap or inferior-quality material, which is used to build houses. [coined by American folksong writer Malvina Reynolds, 1900–78; redup. TACKY adj.[1]]

ticky-tacky *adj.* [1960s+] vulgar and banal, unsophisticated, corny. [TICKY-TACKY n.]

ticky-ticky *adj.* [1990s+] (*W.I.*) insignificant, worthless.

Tico-tico Land *n.* [1970s] (*US*) Brazil.

tic-tac *n.[1]* [20C+] a fact. [rhy. sl.]

tic-tac *n.[2] see* TICK-TACK n.[2].

tid *n.* [1920s+] (*Aus.*) a drunkard. [abbr. TIDDLY adj.]

tid-bit *n. see* TIT-BIT n. (3).

tiddivate *v. see* TITIVATE v.

tiddle *v.[1]* **1** [mid-16C–19C] to fondle or indulge to excess, to tend carefully, to cherish. **2** [mid-18C–1940s] to fidget, to 'mess around', to play with trifles. **3** [mid-19C+] to move forward in slow stages. [? SE *tid*, to move forward in slow stages, Norfolk dial. *tid*, of a boat, to drift with the tide]

tiddle *v.[2]* [20C+] to urinate. [var. on PIDDLE v. (1)]

tiddle a girl *v.* [mid-19C+] to seduce a woman very slowly. [TIDDLE v.[1]]

tiddle-a-wink *n.* [mid-19C] an unlicensed beerhouse. [var. on TIDDLEYWINK n.[1] (1)]

tiddled *adj.* [1920s+] slightly drunk, tipsy (cf. ALED UP adj.). [TIDDLY adj.]

tiddler *n.* **1** [late 19C+] anything small, esp. a small fish. **2** [20C+] a penis, usu. that of a small boy. **3** [1920s–60s] (*Aus.*) £1 sterling.

tiddler's bait *adj.* [20C+] late. [rhy. sl.]

tiddley *see also under* TIDDLY and its combs.

tiddley *n.* [1920s–60s] (*Aus.*) a threepenny bit. [the smallness of the coin]

tiddleywink *n.[1]* (*also* tiddlywink) **1** [mid-late 19C] an unlicensed establishment (e.g. a beerhouse, pawnbroker's or brothel). **2** [late 19C] a snack, a bite of food. [? TITLEY n. + (*on the*) *wink*, surreptitiously]

tiddleywink *n.[2]* (*also* tiddley, tiddlywink) **1** [late 19C+] a drink, usu. a spirit rather than beer or wine. **2** [1970s+] a Chinese person (cf. AH CABBAGE n.). [rhy. sl.; (2) = CHINK n. (1)]

tiddleywink *v.* (*also* tiddlywink) [late 19C–1900s] to potter about, to fiddle; thus *tiddlywinking*, insignificant, unimportant. [? the relative triviality of the game of *tiddlywinks*]

tiddly *n.* (*also* tiddley) [20C+] a drink. [abbr. TIDDLEYWINK n.[2] (1)]

tiddly *adj.* (*also* tiddy, tiddley) [20C+] slightly drunk, tipsy (cf. ALED UP adj.). [TIDDLY n. (+ ? SE *tiddly*, small)]

tiddly-push *n.* [1930s] (*Irish*) the male genitals.

tiddlywink *adj.* [mid-19C–1920s] slim, thin, puny. [? the dimensions of a SE *tiddlywink*]

tiddy *n. see* TITTY n.[1].

tiddy *adj. see* TIDDLY adj.

tiddy umpty *adv. see* UMPTY adv.

tiddyvate *v. see* TITIVATE v.

tidemark *n. see* HIGH-WATER MARK n.

tidgen *n.* [1930s] night-time; thus *on tidgen*, on night-work. [backsl.]

tidy *adj.* **1** [mid-17C; mid-19C+] usu. of a woman, attractive. **2** [early 19C+] good, satisfactory. **3** [early 19C+] substantial; usu. of money, e.g. *a tidy sum.* **4** [late 19C] in good health. **5** [20C+] competent, e.g. in a fight. **6** [1990s+] smart, clever.

tidy *adv.* [early 19C+] a general intensifier, usu. satisfactorily or very. [TIDY adj. (2)]

tidy! *excl.* [20C+] a general excl. of agreement or admiration. [TIDY adj. (2)]

tidy and neat *v.* [20C+] to eat. [rhy. sl.]

tie *n.* (*also* tie-off) [1960s+] (*drugs*) any form of tourniquet, e.g. a belt or bandanna, used to isolate the vein into which a drug is to be injected.

tie a bag on *v.* (*also* tie a load on) [1940s+] (*US*) to get drunk. [TIE ONE ON v. (1) + BAG n.[5]/LOAD n.[2]]

tie a can on *v. see* GET A CAN ON v.

tie a can to *v.* **1** [late 19C+] (*US*) to play an unpleasant trick on. **2** [1900s–40s] to reject or dismiss (a person). **3** [1920s+] to stop (an activity). [a child's tying of a can to an animal's tail]

tie a knot with the tongue that cannot be undone with the teeth *v.* [late 16C–19C] to get married.

tie a load on *v. see* TIE A BAG ON v.

tie a loop in one's chin! *excl.* [1910s] (*US*) stop talking!

tie a noose *v. see* TIE THE NOOSE v.

tied up *adj.[1]* **1** [early 17C; mid-19C+] (*also* tied) married. **2** [early 19C+] (*orig. boxing jargon*) finished, completed. **3** [late 19C] constipated. **4** [20C+] busy, involved with.

tied up *adj.[2]* [1920s–30s] **1** hanged. **2** dressed.

t'ief *n.* (*also* teef, tief) [late 19C+] (*orig. UK Black*) a thief. [W.I. pron. of SE *thief*]

t'ief *v.* (*also* teef, tief) [mid-19C+] (*UK Black*) to steal. [W.I. pron. of SE *thieve*]

tiefiness *n.* (*also* tiefness) [1950s+] (*W.I.*) theft, thieving. [T'IEF v.]

tiefin tief *n.* [1950s] (*W.I.*) an absolute, uncompromising thief. [W.I. pron.; lit. 'a thieving thief']

tief-tief *v.* [1950s] (*W.I.*) to steal continually. [T'IEF v. + redup.]

tie-head *n.* [20C+] (*W.I.*) a member of the Spiritual Baptist Church. [they *tie* their *heads* in white scarves]

tie into *v.* [20C+] (*US*) **1** to assault, to attack. **2** to get to work on someone or something. **3** to start eating voraciously.

tie it v. [late 19C] (US) to walk (from town to town). [the railroad ties and tracks that one follows]

tie it! excl. [1930s] shut up! ['it' is the mouth; note TIE A LOOP IN ONE'S CHIN! excl.]

tie-off n. see TIE n.

tie off v. [1960s+] (drugs) to tie up a vein and isolate it before injecting narcotic drugs.

tie on v. [1950s+] **1** (orig. US Black) to fight. **2** (US) to be drunk. [abbr. TIE ONE ON v.]

tie one on v. [1950s+] **1** (UK/US) to get drunk. **2** (Aus.) to provoke a fight. **3** (Ulster) to get dressed.

tiersman n. [1940s] (Aus.) one who lives in the mountains of Tasmania. [abbr. SE frontiersman]

tie-teeth n. [1910s+] (W.I.) a form of very tough toffee. [chewing it 'ties up' one's teeth]

tie that bull outside phr. (also **tie that bull to another ashcan**) [1920s] (US) stop talking nonsense. [BULL n.[11] (1)]

tie the knot v. **1** [17C+] (also **knit the knot**) to get married; thus knot-tying, a wedding. **2** [late 19C] of a clergyman, to marry a couple.

tie the noose v. [mid-18C+] to marry. [NOOSE v.[1]]

tie to v. see TIE (UP) TO v.

tie-tongue adj. [20C+] (W.I.) suffering from any form of speech impediment.

tie-up n.[1] [1920s+] (US Und.) connection, association. [TIE UP v.[1] (4)]

tie-up n.[2] [1950s+] (drugs) the rubber tube, handkerchief, string or other object used for tying off a vein before injecting narcotics. [TIE UP v.[4]]

tie-up n.[3] [1990s+] (UK Und.) an act of burglary during the day that requires tying up the occupants.

tie up v.[1] **1** [19C–1900s] to get a woman pregnant. **2** [late 19C–1900s] to perform a marriage ceremony, to join in marriage. **3** [late 19C–1950s] to get married; to cohabit. **4** [late 19C+] to associate with, to join in partnership. **5** [20C+] (W.I.) to secure a (usu. male) partner's affections, to make infatuated. **6** [1920s–40s] to link 2 people, ideas etc together. **7** [1920s–50s] to have a relationship with.

tie up v.[2] [early 19C–1900s] (UK Und.) to abandon, to give up, e.g. tie up prigging, to give up one's criminal life, to become honest. [the image of tying up one's villainy and putting it away]

tie up v.[3] **1** [early 19C–1900s] to defeat or disable in a contest, to finish. **2** [1920s] to fight.

tie up v.[4] [1950s+] (US drugs) to inject a narcotic after tying a rubber tube around the arm to find a vein.

tie up a dog v. [20C+] (Aus.) to get credit at a public house or hotel. [DOG n.[10] (2)]

tie (up) to v. [mid-19C–1940s] (US) to trust to something or someone, to look to someone for support.

tie with St Mary's knot v. [17C–18C] to hamstring. [Scot.; ult. ety. unknown]

tiff n.[1] **1** [mid-17C–mid-19C] a drink, esp. a thin or diluted one. **2** [early 18C–early 19C] a small bowl (of liquor). [? SE tipple]

tiff n.[2] **1** [early 18C–19C] a fit of temper. **2** [mid-18C+] (also **tift**) a petty quarrel, esp. an argument between lovers. [? echoic of an exhalation of gas or breath, as in shouting]

tiff v.[1] [late 17C–early 19C] (UK Und.) to have sexual intercourse. [? TIFFITY-TAFFETY n. or 15C SE tiff, to be busy with trifles]

tiff v.[2] [early 18C–early 19C] to drink, esp. in small sips. [TIFF n.[1]]

tiff v.[3] [mid-18C+] to have a petty argument. [TIFF n.[2] (2)]

tiffany trader n. see TIFFITY-TAFFETY n.

tiffin n. [mid-19C+] (orig. Anglo-Ind.) breakfast, a mid-morning snack, a light midday meal, luncheon. [TIFFING n.]

tiffing n. [early 18C–early 19C] snacking, eating other than at mealtimes. [TIFF v.[2]]

tiffity-taffety n. (also **taffeta girl**, **tiffany trader**) [late 16C–17C] a prostitute. [SE tiffany + taffeta, silks used for dresses]

tiffle up v. [early 18C] to dress oneself up. [SE tiff, to adorn oneself, to dress up]

tiffy adj. [mid–late 19C] **1** quick to take offence. **2** overly particular, petty. **3** angry, irritated, 'tetchy'. [TIFF n.[2]]

tift n. see TIFF n.[2] (2).

tig v. [1910s] (Aus.) to obtain a loan.

tiger n.[1] **1** [19C] (Aus.) a groom (often Black). **2** [19C] (Aus.) a menial outdoor worker. **3** [early–late 19C] an overdressed, showy man. **4** [early 19C–1930s] a smartly dressed manservant, esp. a boy who accompanies his master in his coach. **5** [mid-19C] an omnibus conductor. **6** [mid-19C] a parasite, a sponger, a rake. **7** [mid-19C] a ferocious woman. **8** [mid–late 19C] any male servant. **9** [late 19C] (US) a 'bouncer' in a casino. **10** [late 19C+] (Aus.) a (hard) worker in a shearing shed.

tiger n.[2] [mid-19C–1940s] (US) a form of college cheer; esp. in phr. three cheers and a tiger, the 3 usual 'hip-hip-hoorays' plus a long-drawn-out shriek, often of the word 'tiger'.

tiger n.[3] **1** [mid-19C+] (US) the game of faro; a faro table; thus BUCK (THE TIGER) v.; FIGHT THE TIGER v. **2** [1940s] (US Black) the worst hand in poker. [the card-game faro itself originated in mid-17C France, moving thence via Fr. immigrants to New Orleans and thus across the US. It takes its name f. the Egyptian Pharaoh, for unknown reasons, although it has been claimed that the early faro decks had a card with a picture of the Egyptian monarch]

tiger n.[4] [late 19C–1900s] (US) **1** a prostitute (cf. ALLEY CAT n.). **2** a wife. [? she claws her partner + play on CAT n.[1] (1)]

tiger n.[5] [late 19C–1900s] streaky bacon. [its stripes]

tiger n.[6] [late 19C–1900s] (UK juv.) bread with a tough crust. [its strength]

tiger n.[7] [late 19C+] (UK Und.) a convict who tears another convict's yellow prison suit to pieces.

tiger n.[8] [20C+] (Aus.) **1** alcoholic liquor; thus ON THE TIGER phr. **2** a heavy drinker. [its 'bite']

tiger n.[9] [1920s+] **1** an outstanding sportsman. **2** any outstanding person. [the reverse of RABBIT n.[6] (3)]

tiger n.[10] [1970s] (US/P.R.) a newly arrived Puerto Rican immigrant (cf. BATO n.). [the ship Marine Tiger, which brought many Puerto Ricans to the US]

tiger n.[11] [1980s+] (drugs) heroin. [its 'bite']

tiger n.[12] [1980s+] (S.Afr. Black) a 10-rand note; thus five tiger, 50 rand; half tiger, 5 rand. [its design]

tiger n.[13] see BLIND TIGER n.

tiger n.[14] see TIGER (TIM) n.

tiger v. [1950s+] (Aus.) to work hard, to labour. [TIGER n.[1] (10)]

tiger bit them hard, the phr. [mid–late 19C] (US) said of one who loses heavily in a casino, esp. when playing faro. [TIGER n.[3] (1)]

tiger cage n. [1990s+] (US Und.) an underground high-security or punishment cell. [the tiny, cramped underground cells or pits used illegally by South Vietnamese and US forces c.1970. Such 'cages' were deemed to be instruments of torture]

tiger for n. [late 19C+] (Aus.) an enthusiast for a task. [one's 'tigerish' appetite for work]

tiger-hunter n. [late 19C–1930s] a gambler. [TIGER n.[3] (1)]

tigerish adj. [19C] flashily dressed. [TIGER n.[1] (3)]

tiger piss n. [1970s] (US) beer.

tiger's milk n. [mid-19C–1910s] (US/S.Afr.) **1** gin. **2** (also **tiger snake**) any form of strong liquor. [SE tiger milk/Afk. tiermelk, liquor]

tiger sweat n. [1930s] (US Black) cheap, homemade gin or whisky.

tiger (tim) n. [20C+] (Aus.) a swim. [rhy. sl.]

tiggerty-boo adj. see TICKETTY-BOO adj.

tiggy n. [late 19C–1910s] a detective. [? TEC n. (1) or game of tig, a juv. catching game]

tight n.[1] [mid-19C] (US) alcohol.

tight *n.*[2] [1960s+] (*US Black gang*) one's intimate friend. [TIGHT adj.[6]]

tight *adj.*[1] **1** [late 16C+] a general positive epithet, meaning competent, skilful, admirable etc. **2** [late 17C+] (*later use US Black*) spruce, neat, well-dressed, fashionable, dressed up. **3** [1920s+] (*US Black*) of circumstances, secure, properly worked out, organized. **4** [1970s+] (*US campus*) good-looking, well-built. **5** [1990s+] (*US teen*) used of something that one likes very much, fantastic.

tight *adj.*[2] **1** [mid-18C+] of a situation or thing, hard to deal with, difficult, tough; often in phrs. *in a tight place/spot/squeeze*, in a difficult situation. **2** [early 19C+] of a contest, one in which the contestants are evenly matched. **3** [mid-19C] of a sale, offering very little profit.

tight *adj.*[3] **1** [19C+] impoverished, in financial difficulties. **2** [mid-19C+] hard to obtain, usu. of money; thus TIGHT MONEY n.

tight *adj.*[4] **1** [19C+] of an individual, mean, avaricious, ungenerous. **2** [1910s+] (*US*) of an individual, tough, unyielding, aggressive. **3** [1970s] (*Aus. teen*) sexually unresponsive, frigid. **4** [1990s+] (*US*) very unfair.

tight *adj.*[5] [early 19C+] (mildly) drunk.

tight *adj.*[6] [1910s+] very close, friendly, intimate.

tight *adj.*[7] *see* UPTIGHT adj.[2].

tight-arse *n.* (*also* **tight-ass/-butt**) **1** [1960s+] (*orig. US*) a mean person, a skinflint. **2** [1970s+] a puritan, a moral conservative. **3** [2000s] (*Aus.*) an irritating parent. [SE *tight* + ARSE n.[1] (1)/-ASS sfx/BUTT n.[1] (2); (2) and (3) f. (1)]

tight-arse *adj.* (*also* **tight-arsed, tight-ass, tight-assed**) **1** [late 19C+] of a woman, chaste. **2** [1960s+] mean. **3** [1970s+] repressed, self-denying, puritanical. [TIGHT-ARSE n.; (1) lit. use of SE *tight* + ARSE n.[1] (2)]

tight as... *see also under* DRUNK AS...

tight as a crab's arse *phr.* **1** [1940s+] (*also* **tight as a bull's arse, ...a crow's arse, ...a duck's arse, ...a fish's arse(hole), tighter than a bull's ass in fly time, ...a clam's ass**) very tight. **2** [1960s] very mean. [SE *tight*/TIGHT adj.[4] (1) + ARSE n.[1] (1)]

tight as a gnat's twat *phr.* [2000s] very mean. [TIGHT adj.[4] (1) + TWAT n. (1)]

tight as a lord *phr.* [1910s–20s] very drunk. [TIGHT adj.[5]]

tight as a mouse's earhole *phr.* [1950s+] of a vagina, very tight.

tight as a tick *phr.* (*also* **tight as a mink**) [20C+] drunk. [TIGHT adj.[5]]

tight as Dick's hatband *phr.* (*also* **tight as Jimmy's hatband, tighter than Dick's hatband**) [early 19C+] (*US*) **1** extremely tight. **2** of one's finances, impoverished. [SE *tight*/TIGHT adj.[3] (1) + DICK'S HATBAND n.]

tight as Kelsey's nuts *phr. see* KELSEY'S NUTS n.

tight as peep *phr.* (*also* **drunk as (a) peep**) [mid–late 19C] very drunk. [TIGHT adj.[5]]

tight-ass *n. see* TIGHT-ARSE n.

tight-ass/tight-assed *adj. see* TIGHT-ARSE adj.

tight-butt *n. see* TIGHT-ARSE n.

tight cheeks *n. see* TIGHT JAWS n.

tight cravat *n.* (*also* **cravat**) [late 18C–19C] a hangman's noose.

tighten *v.*[1] **1** [mid-19C+] (*Irish*) to drink heavily. **2** [late 19C] to wear a tight corset or stays.

tighten *v.*[2] (*also* **tighten up**) **1** [1940s+] to persuade, to make someone do what one desires, esp. in the context of a confidence game. **2** [1980s+] (*drugs*) to give or sell narcotics (to a desperate addict). **3** [1980s+] (*US drugs*) to take another dose of a drug, to maintain a state of intoxication. **4** [1990s+] (*US Black*) to criticize, to urge someone to a better life.

tightener *n.* (*also* **tightner**) [mid-19C–1950s] a large, heavy meal; thus *do the tightener*, to dine. [its effects on one's stomach]

tighten one's action *v.* [1970s+] (*US*) to begin behaving in a more effective or positive manner. [SE *tighten* + ACTION n. (4)]

tighten one's game *v. see* TIGHTEN (UP) ONE'S GAME v.

tighten one's wig *v.* [1940s+] **1** to smoke marijuana. **2** to give someone else marijuana. **3** to delight. [SE *tighten* + WIG n.[3] (1); the sensation of tightening of the skull that sometimes accompanies smoking]

tighten someone's jaws *v.* (*also* **grind someone's jaw**) [1960s–70s] (*US Black*) to annoy, to irritate.

tighten someone up *v.* [1980s+] (*US*) to repay a debt.

tighten up *v. see* TIGHTEN v.[2].

tighten (up) one's game *v.* [1950s+] (*US Black*) **1** to take control of one's life or of a situation in which one is interested. **2** (*also* **keep one's game tight**) to behave in a sensible, positive manner, to maintain one's image, to act in a self-beneficial manner. [GAME n.[2] (9)]

tighter than a bull's ass in flytime/tighter than a clam's ass *phr. see* TIGHT AS A CRAB'S ARSE phr.

tighter than a turtle's snatch *phr.* [1990s+] very tight.

tighter than a witch's cunt *phr.* (*also* **tighter than a nun's cunt**) [20C+] extremely tight-fitting. [CUNT n.[1] (1)]

tighter than Dick's hatband *phr. see* TIGHT AS DICK'S HATBAND phr.

tight eyes *n.* [1980s+] (*US Black*) a pej. term for an Asian, usu. a Japanese (cf. BROWNIE n.[2]).

tight hand *n.* [1950s] (*W.I.*) a miser.

tight head *n.* [1930s–40s] (*US Black*) a head of kinky black hair.

tightie whities *n. see* TIGHTY WHITIES n.

tight jaws *n.* (*also* **tight cheeks**) [1960s–70s] (*US Black*) intense anger; usu. as *have tight jaws/cheeks*, to get angry, to be angry; thus TIGHTEN SOMEONE'S JAWS v. [a grimace of fury]

tight jeff *n. see* JEFF v. (3).

tight-laced *adj.* [mid-18C+] puritanical, censorious; thus *tight-lacing*, restraining, repressive.

tight money *n.* [mid-19C+] (*US*) money in times of scarcity or high inflation. [TIGHT adj.[3] (2)]

tightner *n. see* TIGHTENER n.

tightwad *n.* [late 19C+] an ungenerous, mean person. [SE *tight* + WAD n.[1] (1)]

tightwad *adj.* [20C+] miserly. [TIGHTWAD n.]

tight-wadded *adj.* [1980s+] (*US campus*) drunk.

tight with *adj.* [1950s+] very friendly with. [TIGHT adj.[6]]

tighty whities *n.* (*also* **tightie whities**) **1** [1980s+] (*US campus*) men's briefs. **2** [2000s] (*US*) a tight, white T-shirt.

tigress *n.* [mid–late 19C] a flashily overdressed woman. [TIGER n.[1] (3)]

Tijuana bible *n.* [1940s+] a small, illustrated pornographic book. [named for the era when US citizens saw Tijuana, Mexico, as the vice capital of Central America]

Tijuana queen *n.* [1970s+] (*US gay*) a Hispanic homosexual. [*Tijuana*, Mexico + QUEEN n.[2] (1)]

Tijuana racetrack *n.* [1950s+] (*US*) stains on the underwear that result from an attack of diarrhoea. [derog. ref. to Tijuana, Mexico, and thus Mexicans]

Tijuanero *n.* (*also* **Tijuanera**) [1960s+] (*US*) a newly arrived immigrant from Mexico. [Sp., a citizen of Tijuana, the border town through which legal immigrants often pass]

tik *n.* [1990s+] (*UK Black*) a prospective victim. [? SE *tick*, one ticks them off as a potential victim]

tike-lurking *n. see* BUFFER-LURKING n.

Tilbury *n.* [late 18C–mid-19C] a sixpence (2½p). [the fare charged by the trans-Thames ferry from Gravesend to *Tilbury* Fort]

Tilbury docker *n.* [1970s] (*UK prison*) a prisoner who does not pay his debts. [rhy. sl. = KNOCKER n.[9]; ult. *Tilbury docks* (in East London)]

Tilbury docks *n.* [late 19C+] **1** (*orig. navy*) socks. **2** venereal disease. [rhy. sl.; (2) = POX n.[1] (2); ult. *Tilbury docks* (in East London)]

'tilda *n.* (*also* **tilder**) [late 19C–1950s] (*Aus.*) a vagrant's pack. [abbr. MATILDA n.]

tile *n.* [early 19C–1910s] a hat. [it sits on top of one's ROOF n. (2)]

tiled *adj.* [early–mid-19C] **1** snug, comfortable. **2** arrested, locked up, confined. [having a (*tiled*) roof over one's head]

t.i.l.i.s. *phr. see* TELL IT LIKE IT IS phr.

till *n.* [19C] the vagina (cf. BANK n.¹). [its commercial potential/one puts 'money', i.e. the penis, into it]

till *v.* [late 16C–mid-18C; 1970s+] to have sexual intercourse. [1970s+ use is US Black]

till all is blue *phr.* **1** [early 17C–19C] to the extreme, esp. used of excessive drinking. **2** [19C–1900s] (*US*) to the very end, the 'bitter' end. [the effect of the alcohol on one's eyesight. According to Smyth, *Sailor's Wordbook* (1867): 'a phrase borrowed from the idea of a vessel making out of port, and getting into blue water']

till-boy *n.* [mid-19C] a shop assistant who steals from the till.

till-diving *n. see* TILL-LIFTING n.

tilley-vally *n. see* TILLY-VALLY n.

till-frisker *n.* [mid-19C] (*UK Und.*) a person who steals from a shop cash register. [FRISK v.² (2)]

tillie-vallie *n. see* TILLY-VALLY n.

till-lifting *n.* (*also* **till-diving**) [late 19C] (*UK Und.*) the robbery of a shop cash register. [SE *till* + LIFT v.¹ (1)]

till-tap *v. see* TAP A TILL v.

till-tapper *n.* [mid-19C+] (*US Und.*) one who steals from a cash register, esp. when employed as the cashier. [TAP A TILL v.]

till the last dog is hung *phr.* [mid-19C+] to the very end, until everything is resolved.

till-tilting *n.* [mid-19C] (*US Und.*) the robbery of shop cash registers. [the tilting of the till until it opens]

tilly *n.*¹ [1950s+] (*Aus.*) a utility vehicle. [abbr. SE *utility*]

tilly *n.*² [1960s+] (*gay*) the police. [the use of a woman's name to 'feminize' the force]

tilly *n.*³ *see* MATILDA n.

tilly-vally *n.* (*also* **tilley-vally, tillie-vallie, tully-vally**) [late 15C–19C] piffle, rubbish, nonsense. [ety. unknown]

tillywhacker *n. see* TALLYWHACKER n.

tillywhiz *n.* [1970s] (*US*) the penis. [var. on TALLYWHACKER n.]

tilt *n.* [early–mid-18C] (*UK Und.*) a picklock key.

tilt *v.* [1910s] (*US*) in cards, to raise the bet.

tilt a kidney *v. see* TAP A KIDNEY v.

tilt-boat *n.* [17C] a promiscuous woman; a prostitute. [SE *tilt-boat*, 'a large rowing boat having a tilt or awning, formerly used on the Thames, esp. as a passenger boat between London and Gravesend' (OED), i.e. pun on RIDE v.¹ (1)]

tilter *n.* [late 17C–early 18C] a rapier, a sword. [SE *tilter*, one who takes part in a joust or tournament]

Tim *n.* [1960s+] (*Scot.*) a derog. term for a Roman Catholic. [the proper name Tim Malloy, stereotyped as Catholic]

timber *n.* **1** [early 19C] (*Anglo-Irish*) a wooden leg. **2** [early 19C–1960s] (*also* **small timber**) a match. **3** [mid-19C] the stocks. **4** [late 19C] a clubbing at the hands of the toughs of a town unfriendly to tramps. **5** [1930s–40s] (*US Black*) a toothpick. **6** [1930s–40s] (*US Und.*) a police nightstick. **7** [1970s] (*drugs*) stems and stalks found in a batch of marijuana.

timber-doodle *n.* [mid-late 19C] (*US*) any form of spirituous liquor. [ety. unknown]

timber-head *n.* [mid-late 17C; mid-19C] a fool. [SE *timber* + -HEAD sfx (1)]

timber merchant *n.* [early 19C–1930s] a match-seller. [TIMBER n. (2) + MERCHANT n.]

timbers *n.*¹ **1** [late 16C+] the legs. **2** [1930s] (*US tramp*) one who has a wooden leg. [SE *timber*, a wooden foundation]

timbers *n.*² [1910s–40s] (*US tramp*) a beggar who poses as a pencil-seller.

timber-stairs *n.* [mid-18C] the treadmill. [its wooden construction]

timber-toe *n.* [late 18C–1900s] **1** a wooden leg. **2** a person who has a wooden leg.

timber-toed *adj.* **1** [late 18C+] having a wooden leg. **2** [late 19C] (*US Und.*) cowardly, easily scared. [TIMBER-TOE n.; (2) ? fig. use of (1)]

timber-topper *n.* [late 19C] (*Aus.*) a horse specializing in steeplechases rather than flat-racing.

Timbucktoo *n.* [1980s+] a euph. for SE *hell*; usu. in phr. *go to Timbucktoo*. [the perceived distance]

time *n.*¹ [mid-19C+] a prison sentence; thus DO TIME v.

time *n.*² [late 19C; 1970s] (*US*) a good time, a drinking spree. [backform. f. SE phr. *a good time was had by all*]

time *n.*³ [20C+] (*US*) credit.

time *prep.* [1910s+] at the time, by the time, once, e.g. *time the day be done*, once the day is over.

time bandit *n.* [1990s+] a thief who specializes in snatching expensive watches. [SE *time* + BANDIT sfx (1); ult. Terry Gilliam's 1981 film *Time Bandits*]

time-drunk *adj.* [1970s] (*US prison/Und.*) intellectually depleted after a long jail sentence. [TIME n.¹]

time of day *n.* (*also* **time o' day**) **1** [late 17C; early 19C+] the current situation, what is going on; thus *put someone up to the time of day*, explain the situation to someone. **2** [mid-19C] the correct or pertinent thing or situation. **3** [mid-19C] a trick, a ruse.

timer *n.* [late 19C+] (*UK Und.*) a criminal who has served time in jail; often in combs., e.g. FIRST-TIMER n., SHORT-TIMER n. (1). [TIME n.¹]

times *n.* [mid-19C] multiples of a shilling (5p), e.g. *9 times*, 9 shillings (45p).

timothy *n.* [1940s+] (*Aus.*) a brothel. [? rhy. sl.; *timothy grass* = ARSE n.¹ (2) or *timothy titmouse* = HOUSE n.¹ (1)]

timothy-tool *n.* [late 19C] the penis (cf. ABRAHAM n.¹). [TOOL n.¹ (1)]

Tims *n.* [1990s+] *Timberland* boots. [abbr.]

tim-tim *n.* [20C+] (*W.I.*) an unreliable story, a fantasy. [Carib.E. excl. *tim-tim!* used by a story-teller to indicate that he/she is about to tell a folk-tale; ? ult. Fr. *tiens*, hello! look! or SE (*it's*) *time*]

tin *n.*¹ **1** [mid-19C–1960s] money, esp. silver. **2** [1920s–30s] (*US*) a trifling amount of money.

tin *n.*² **1** [1900s] (*US*) a drink. **2** [1930s] a 1-gallon can of alcohol. **3** [1980s+] (*US campus*) beer. [the can that contains it]

tin *n.*³ **1** [1910s–60s] (*US*) a small container of opium. **2** [1950s+] (*drugs*) 1oz (28g) of marijuana. **3** [1960s–70s] (*US*) a few grains of cocaine. [the selling of marijuana in measures based on the size of a popular brand tobacco tin; the use for cocaine may be a misinterpretation]

tin *n.*⁴ [1920s+] (*US*) a policeman's or sheriff's badge; thus police jargon *tin wife*, an officer's wife; *on the tin*, free, gratis, i.e. a meal. [its main component; thus those gifts and favours – free meals, drinks – obtained by showing one's official badge]

tin, the *n.* [20C+] (*Aus.*) tin-mining country.

tin *adj.* [1900s–10s] (*US campus*) best, admirable.

tin and tap *n.* (*also* **tip and tap**) [1930s–50s] (*US Und.*) a cap. [rhy. sl.]

tin-arse *n.* (*also* **tin-back, tin-bum**) [late 19C+] (*Aus./N.Z.*) an extremely lucky person. [TIN n.¹ (1) + ARSE n.¹ (1)/SE *back*/BUM n.¹ (1)]

tin-arsed *adj.* (*also* **tin-arse**) [1930s+] (*Aus./N.Z.*) thick-skinned, impervious to pain, lucky. [TIN-ARSE n.]

tin bath *n.* [20C+] scarf. [rhy. sl., pron. 'barf']

tin-bum *n. see* TIN-ARSE n.

tin can *n.* **1** [1910s+] a dilapidated old car. **2** [1920s–50s] (*US milit.*) a destroyer. **3** [1920s–60s] (*US Und.*) a safe; thus *tin-opener*, an implement for opening a safe.

tin-can *v.* **1** [1900s–20s] (*US*) to retreat, to run away. **2** [1920s] (*US Und.*) to cheat, to deceive. [the image of a dog with a tin can tied to its tail]

tin can cop *n.* [1970s+] (*US*) a rural sheriff. [TIN CAN n. (1) + COP n.¹ (1)]

tin chapel *n. see* TIN TABERNACLE n.

tin cow *n.* [1920s–40s] (*US tramp*) tinned milk. [SE *tin* + COW n.[5] (1); note synon. WW2 US Army *armored cow*]

tincture *n.* [1910s+] a drink. [hugely popularized by the 'Dear Bill' column in the magazine *Private Eye*, lampooning Denis Thatcher, husband of Margaret Thatcher (b.1925), UK Conservative prime minister (1979–90)]

tinder-box *n. see* FIRELOCK n.

tin dog *n.* (*also* **tinned dog**) [20C+] (*Aus./N.Z.*) canned meat. [note WW1 milit. *corned dog*, canned beef]

tin ear *n.* (*Aus./US*) **1** [1910s+] an eavesdropper. **2** [1930s+] a fool, a simpleton.

tin-ear *v.* [1910s+] (*Aus./US*) to eavesdrop. [TIN EAR n. (1)]

tin-eared *adj.* [1930s+] foolish (cf. LONG-EARED adj.). [TIN EAR n. (2)]

tin flute *n.* [20C+] a suit. [rhy. sl.]

ting-a-ling *n.* [1940s–80s] (*Aus.*) a ring. [rhy. sl.]

tingle *n.* [1940s+] (*Aus.*) a call on the telephone.

tin grin *n.* [1970s+] (*US campus/UK teen*) a person wearing orthodontic braces.

tin hare *n.* **1** [1920s+] (*mainly Aus.*) the electric hare used for greyhound racing. **2** [1930s+] a train, esp. a rail-motor, i.e. a small passenger train consisting of the engine and 1 coach.

tin hat *n.*[1] **1** [20C+] a helmet. **2** [1910s] a senior officer. [(2) rare var. ON BRASS HAT n.]

tin hat *n.*[2] [1960s+] a fool (cf. BEECHAM'S PILL n.). [rhy. sl. = PRAT n.[1] (6)]

tin hat *v.* [1910s–40s] (*Aus.*) to indicate one's contempt; to patronize, to talk down to. [TIN HAT n.[1] (2)]

tinhorn *n.* [late 19C+] a contemptible person, esp. if superficially flashy, a fool, usu. referring to a smalltime gambler.

tinhorn *adj.* [late 19C+] second-rate, inferior, superficially flashy. [abbr. gambling use *tinhorn gambler*, a second-rate class of gambler: 'Chuck-a-luck operators shake their dice in a "small churn-like affair of metal" – hence the expression, "tinhorn gambler", for the game is rather looked down upon as one for "chubbers" and chuck-a-luck gamblers are never admitted within the aristocratic circle of faro-dealers' (G.F. Willison, *Here They Dug Gold*, 1931)]

tink *n.* [mid-19C+] **1** a *tinker*. **2** a foul-mouthed, obstreperous person. [(1) abbr.; ? (2) the stereotype of (1)]

tinkard *n.* [16C] (*UK Und.*) a tinker who alternates legitimate work with begging. [SE *tinker*; 'He leaveth his bag a sweating at the ale house [...] and in the mean season goeth abroad begging' (Awdeley, *Fraternitie of Vagabondes*, c.1561)]

tinker *n.*[1] [mid-19C] (*UK Und.*) a sixpence.

tinker *n.*[2] **1** [20C+] an affectionate term usu. used to a child by an exasperated parent, a rascal. **2** [1920s] (*US Und.*) a novice burglar. [SE *tinker*, a peddler/'a clumsy or inefficient mender' (*OED*)]

Tinker Bell *n.* [1950s–70s] (*camp gay*) a pleasingly plump person. [the character *Tinker Bell*, the fairy in J.M. Barrie's Peter Pan (1904)]

tinker's age, a *n. see* DONKEY'S AGE, A n.

tinker's budget *n.* (*also* **tinker's news**) [mid–late 19C] stale news. [SE *tinker* + *budget*, a long letter full of news/*news*; a tinker, being on the move, would catch up with news late]

tinker's time *n.* [20C+] (*Irish*) unpunctuality (cf. AFRICAN (PEOPLE'S) TIME n.). [the slow progress and unreliability of the SE *tinker*]

tinkerty-tonk *phr.* [1920s–30s] goodbye. [nonsense]

tinkle *n.* **1** [1930s+] a ring on the telephone; usu. in phr. *give someone a tinkle*. **2** [1940s] (*US Black*) a doorbell. **3** [1960s] money (cf. CHING n.[2]). **4** [1960s+] an act of urination. [the sounds involved]

tinkle *v.* [1960s+] (*mainly US juv.*) to urinate. [TINKLE n. (4)]

tinkle-box *n.*[1] (*also* **tinkler**) [1900s–40s] (*US*) a piano.

tinkle-box *n.*[2] [1960s] (*US campus*) a lavatory. [TINKLE v. + SE *box*]

tinkler *n.*[1] [18C–19C] a mendicant tramp. [? his bell or SE *tinker*]

tinkler *n.*[2] [mid-19C–1940s] a (front-door) bell. [20C use is US Black]

tinkler *n.*[3] *see* TINKLE-BOX n.[1].

tinkle-tinkle *n.* [1910s] (*Aus.*) an effeminate man.

tin lid *n.* **1** [20C+] (*Aus.*) a child (cf. BILLY LID n.). **2** [1940s+] a Jew (cf. BILLY THE KID n.). [rhy. sl.; (1) = KID n.[1] (1); (2) = YID n.[1]]

tin lizzie *n.* (*also* **tin lizard, Liz**) **1** [1910s+] (*orig. US*) a Model T Ford. **2** [1920s+] (*oig. Aus.*) any kind of ageing, broken-down vehicle. [affectionate nickname]

tinman *n.* [mid–late 19C] (*UK sporting*) a very rich man, a millionaire. [TIN n.[1] (1) + SE *man*]

tin mittens *n.* [1930s–40s] (*US Und.*) a person who arranges something at a high price. [TIN n.[1] (1) + MITTEN n. (1)]

tinned *adj.* [1940s+] drunk. [tin beer cans]

tinned dog *n. see* TIN DOG n.

tinner *n.* [1910s] (*US Und.*) a policeman, by metonymy from his tin badge (cf. BADGE n.[2]).

tinnie *n.*[1] (*also* **tinny**) [1960s+] **1** (*orig. Aus. surfing*) a can of beer. **2** (*Aus.*) a small aluminium boat.

tinnie *n.*[2] [1980s+] (*N.Z. drugs.*) **1** silver foil, as used in smoking heroin. **2** silver foil, used for wrapping measures of cannabis; thus the measure of cannabis as sold as a single unit.

tinny *n.*[1] [mid-18C–early 19C] a fire. [? Gaelic/Erse *teine*, fire, Shelta *tini*, fire or SE *tinder*, use in lighting fires]

tinny *n.*[2] [1930s] (*US Und.*) a thief. [? TIN n.[1] (1)]

tinny *n.*[3] *see* TINNIE n.[1].

tinny *adj.*[1] **1** [mid–late 19C] wealthy, rich. **2** [1910s+] (*Aus./N.Z.*) lucky; thus *on the tinny luck*, by a fortunate chance. **3** [1930s+] (*Aus./N.Z.*) mean, grasping. [TIN n.[1] (1)]

tinny *adj.*[2] [1920s+] cheap, second-rate. [SE *tin*]

tinny house *n. see* BULLET HOUSE n.

tinny-hunter *n.* [late 18C–early 19C] a thief who robs people whose homes are burning down, while pretending to give assistance. [TINNY n.[1] + SE *hunter*: 'No beast of prey is so noxious to Society, or so destitute of feeling, as these wretches' (George Parker, *A View of Society*, 1781)]

tin of beans *n.* [1960s+] jeans. [rhy. sl.]

tin-opener *n. see* TIN CAN n. (3).

tin-pan *adj. see* TIN-POT adj.

Tin Pan Alley *n.* [late 19C+] (*orig. US*) the centre of the music business, esp. that area where music writers, lyricists and song pluggers have their offices, in its inter-war heyday the Times Square area of New York City and Denmark Street, London W1. [musician's jargon *tin-pan*, a piano + derog. description of the music as sounding like *tin pans* being clashed together. The term prob. evolved through popular use within the business, although journalist/songwriter Monroe Rosenfeld claimed its coinage *c.*1892; alternately credited to US songwriter Harry von Tilzer (1873–1946) and thus stated in his obituary (*New York Herald Tribune*, 11 January 1946)]

tin plate *n.* [20C+] a friend. [rhy. sl. = SE *mate*]

tin-pot *adj.* (*also* **tin-pan**) [mid-19C+] of a place, small, insignificant; of a person, mediocre, second-rate; of an event, irrelevant. [note naut. jargon *tin-potter*, an idler, one who shirks their duties by claiming to be ill. The use of *tin-pot* as cheap, inferior is SE]

tin ribs *n.* [late 19C] (*UK Und.*) a policeman (cf. BADGE n.[2]). [? TIN n.[4] although this predates it, or ? bullet-proof vest]

tin-roofer *n.* [1900s] (*US*) a confidence trickster. [? TIN n.[1] (1)]

tinsel teeth *n.* [1970s+] (*US campus*) a person wearing orthodontic braces.

Tinseltown *n.* **1** [1930s+] Hollywood, California. **2** [1980s+] (*Aus.*) Sydney. [the towns' glittering images]

tin shield *n.* [1990s+] (*US*) a policeman (cf. BADGE n.[2]). [metonymy]

tin shin off *v.* [late 19C–1900s] (*US*) to abscond with money. [TIN n.[1] (1) + SHIN OFF v.]

tin shirt *n.* [1920s] (*US Und.*) a bullet-proof vest.

tin soldier *n.* [1970s+] a prostitute's client, usu. middle- or upper-class, who doesn't want sex but only to act as a servant or 'slave' to the prostitute.

tin star *n.* [20C+] (*US*) a private detective; a country policeman (cf. BADGE n.²). [his identification; note TIN n.⁴]

tint *n.* [20C+] (*Irish*) a measure of liquor. [abbr. SE *tincture*]

tin tabernacle *n.* (*also* **tin chapel**) [late 19C+] any church with an iron or tin roof, esp. a Noncomformist church. [the material used for the roof]

tin-tack *n.* **1** [1930s–50s] dismissal from a job. **2** [1940s+] a bed. [rhy. sl.; (1) = SACK, THE n. (1); (2) = SACK n.³ (1)]

tin tacks *n.* [20C+] the facts; usu. in phr. GET DOWN TO TIN TACKS v.; also the basics, the smallest components. [rhy. sl.]

tin tank *n.* [20C+] a bank. [rhy. sl.]

tin throne *n.* [1930s–40s] (*US prison*) a cell latrine. [SE *tin* + *throne*/THRONE n.]

tints *n.* [1970s+] (*US Black*) **1** tinted or dark glasses. **2** tinted windows in an automobile. [SE *tinted*]

tintsy-wintsy *adj. see* TEENSIE-WEENSIE adj.

tiny tim *n.* [20C+] a £5 note (cf. BEEHIVE n.²). [rhy. sl. = FLIM n.¹ (1)]

Tío Taco *n.* (*also* **Tío Tomás**) [1970s+] (*US*) a derog. term for a Mexican who is considered insufficiently nationalistic by others. [Mex. *tío*, uncle + *taco*, the foodstuff; ult. a play on UNCLE TOM n. (1)]

tip *n.¹* [early 17C–mid-19C] **1** a draught of liquor. **2** drink in general. [SE *tip a glass* or abbr. TIPPLE n. (1)]

tip *n.²* **1** [early–mid-19C] a bribe. **2** [early–late 19C] money as used in any form of contract. [SE *tip*, a gratuity]

tip *n.³* **1** [mid-19C; 1930s+] (*orig. US Und.*) a crowd of people; thus [mid-19C] *working the tip*, working as a pickpocket. **2** [1990s+] (*US Und.*) a prison gang. [ety. unknown]

tip *n.⁴* [mid-late 19C] (*Aus.*) an Irishman, esp. a gold-miner. [proper name *Tipperary*]

tip *n.⁵* **1** [mid-19C+] a piece of 'inside' information, esp. as regards a sporting contest, usu. racing or boxing. **2** [late 19C] the subject of the tip, usu. a horse. **3** [late 19C] one's point, one's intention. **4** [late 19C+] a special hint or trick. **5** [20C+] a tip-off, but used as any reason for an arrest, not simply information given to the police. **6** [1900s] (*US Und.*) a warning. **7** [1910s–40s] (*US Und.*) a confidence trick in cards where the victim is lured with the offer of being given information about another player's hand.

tip *n.⁶* [late 19C+] the end, the ultimate. [SE *tip*, the point]

tip *n.⁷* [1940s+] (*US Black*) the aspect, the point of view, the angle, e.g. *on the art tip*, from the artistic point of view; *on the sales tip*, from the aspect of sales; ult. synon. with SE *thing*; thus *hipped to the tip*, to be very knowledgeable. [SE *tip*, advice, guidance]

tip *n.⁸* [1970s+] a very untidy, messy place, e.g. a child's bedroom. [abbr. SE *rubbish tip*]

tip *v.¹* **1** [early 17C+] to give, to hand over, to lend. **2** [18C+] to give a monetary gratuity. **3** [late 18C–1910s] to pay. [? SE *tip*, to touch lightly, orig. Und., but sl. by mid-18C]

tip *v.²* **1** [mid-17C–mid-19C] to drink, to toast. **2** [1970s] (*US campus*) to drink heavily. [abbr. SE *tipple*, to drink]

tip *v.³* [late 17C+] to do, to make, to perform; usu. in phrs., e.g. TIP A DADDLE v.; TIP (SOMEONE) THE WINK v.

tip *v.⁴* **1** [mid-18C–mid-19C] to indicate surreptitiously by a wink or similar gesture. **2** [late 19C+] to give information, esp. secret, privileged, 'inside' information, to warn. **3** [1900s] (*US Und.*) to introduce. **4** [1910s] (*Aus.*) to plan. **5** [1910s–40s] (*Aus.*) to guess, to recognize. **6** [1950s+] (*US Black*) to gain knowledge of, to understand.

tip *v.⁵* [early–mid-19C] to bribe. [TIP n.² (1)]

tip *v.⁶* [19C] to die. [abbr. TIP OFF v.¹]

tip *v.⁷* [1920s+] (*US Black*) to cheat on one's lover or mate.

2 [1980s+] to perform an illicit act. **3** [1980s+] to be in a place where one should not be. [? SE *tip*, to knock over]

tip *v.⁸* (*also* **tip out**) **1** [1930s+] (*US Black*) to leave. **2** [1980s+] (*Aus. prison*) to forcibly transfer. [SE *tip*, to move lightly or tiptoe]

tip a daddle *v.* [late 18C–19C] to shake hands. [TIP v.³ + DADDLE n.]

tip a hint *v.* [late 18C] to warn, to inform. [TIP v.³ + SE *hint*]

tip and tap *n. see* TIN AND TAP n.

tip a nod *v.* **1** [late 18C+] to warn, to signal. **2** [mid–late 19C] to recognize someone. [TIP v.³ + SE *nod*]

tip-an-pawn *n.* [1950s] (*W.I.*) one who limps. [dial. *tip*, to strike lightly + *pawn*, to grasp, to pick up. The image is of the jerky movement of the legs]

tip a pike *v.* [early 18C–mid-19C] to run off, to make an escape. [TIP v.³ + PIKE v.¹ (1)]

tip a rise *v.* [late 19C] to fool, to deceive. [TIP v.³ + RISE n.¹ (2)]

tip a settler *v.* [early 19C] to hit hard, to knock out. [TIP v.³ + SETTLER n. (2)]

tip a slang *v.* [late 18C] (*UK Und.*) to raise the forefinger of the right hand to one's nose as a sign of understanding. [TIP v.³ + SLANG n.¹]

tip a snitch *v.* [mid-18C] (*UK Und.*) to give someone a blow, to punch. [TIP v.³ + SNITCH n.¹ (1)]

tip a sock *v.* [late 17C–19C] to hit hard, to knock out. [TIP v.³ + SOCK n.³ (1)]

tip a yarn *v.* [19C] to tell a story. [TIP v.³ + YARN n. (1)]

tip grand *v.* [1930s] (*US Und.*) to leave quickly, to run away. [? fig. use of TIP v.¹ (2) + GRAND adv. (2)]

tip in *v.* [1960s+] to inform against. [TIP v.⁴ (2)]

tip into *v.* [1960s–70s] (*US*) to visit briefly; to arrive at.

tip leg bail (and land security) *v. see* LEG BAIL n.

tip-merry *adj.* [17C] tipsy. [TIP n.¹ + SE sfx *-merry*]

tip-off *n.* **1** [20C+] a piece of information, esp. concerning criminal activity. **2** [1940s+] (*also* **tip-off man**) an informer, an 'inside man'. [TIP OFF v.²]

tip off *v.¹* (*also* **tip off the perch**) [late 17C–early 19C] to die.

tip off *v.²* **1** [late 19C+] to warn. **2** [late 19C+] to provide someone with information. **3** [1910s–20s] to expose someone. [ext. of TIP v.⁴ (2)]

tip-off man *n. see* TIP-OFF n. (2).

tip off the blarney *v.* [late 18C–early 19C] to deceive, to trick by verbal facility. [TIP OFF v.² + BLARNEY n.]

tip off the perch *v. see* TIP OFF v.¹.

tip one's ditto *v.* [late 19C] to agree.

tip one's duke *v. see* TIP ONE'S MITT v.

tip one's fin *v.* (*also* **tip one's flipper**) [19C–1940s] to shake hands; usu. in phr. *tip us your fin/flipper*. [TIP v.³ + FIN n.¹/FLIPPER n.¹]

tip one's lid *v. see* DIP ONE'S LID v.

tip one's mitt *v.* (*also* **tip one's duke/hand**) **1** [early 19C+] (*also* **tip one's fist,** ...**mauley,** ...**mauns,** ...**mawley**) to shake hands. **2** [late 19C+] (*US*) to disclose one's plans inadvertently; to inform. [TIP v.³ + MITT n. (3)/MITT n. (2)/DUKE n.³ (1)/DUKE n.³ (3)/MAULEY n. (1)]

tip one's rags a gallop *v.* [19C] to leave, to depart. [TIP v.³ + SE *rags* as fig. for clothes; RAGS n. (1) is a later development]

tip out *v.¹* [1920s+] (*US Black*) to have sex with someone other than one's spouse or regular lover. [ext. of TIP v.⁷ (1)]

tip out *v.² see* TIP v.⁸.

tip over *v.¹* [1910s–30s] (*US*) to drink. [SE *tip over*]

tip over *v.²* **1** [1920s+] (*US Und.*) to raid; also as n., a police raid. **2** [1940s+] (*US*) to rob. [? ext. of TIP v.⁷ (2)]

tip-over-charley *phr.* [1910s] (*Aus.*) head-over-heels.

tip over the perch *v.* [late 16C–17C] to die. [var. on TIP OFF v.¹]

tipped *adj.* [early 17C–early 18C] drunk. [TIP v.² (1)]

tipped up *adj.* [2000s] (*US prison*) having a membership in a prison gang or clique. [TIP n.³ (2)]

tipper *n.* [mid–late 19C] a beer brewed in Brighton, with a nationwide reputation. [proper name of the brewer *Thomas Tipper*. It was brewed from notably brackish water from one specific well]

Tipperary *adj.* [late 18C] drunk, tipsy. [one 'tips' over]

Tipperary fortune *n.* [late 18C–early 19C] **1** an Irish woman with no fortune other than her body. **2** the breasts, vagina and anus. ['Two *town lands* (the breasts), *stream's town* (the pudenda) and *ballinocack* (the anus)' (Grose, 1785)]

Tipperary lawyer *n.* [mid–late 19C] a cudgel. [racial stereotyping]

Tipper Gore *n.* [1990s+] (*US teen*) one who is narrow-minded, puritanical, repressive. [*Tipper Gore*, wife of politician Al Gore (b.1948), apostrophized by her critics as a byword for narrow-minded stupidity]

tippery *n.* [early 19C–1900s] payment, i.e. the 'world of tips'. [SE *tip*/TIP v.¹ (3)]

tippet *n.*¹ [16C; 19C] a generous person, someone who treats their companions. [pun on TIP v.¹]

tippet *n.*² *see* ST JOHNSTONE'S TIPPET n.

tippet-de-witchet *n.* [early 18C] the vagina. [? SE *tippet*, 'a long narrow slip of cloth or hanging part of dress, formerly worn, either attached to and forming part of the hood, head-dress, or sleeve, or loose, as a scarf or the like' (*OED*)]

tippin' *adj.* [1970s+] (*US Black*) in full control, on top of one's game. [TIP-TOP adj. (1)]

tipple *n.* **1** [late 16C+] any alcoholic drink. **2** [late 17C+] any drink, esp. that which one prefers, i.e. *one's tipple*. [SE *tipple*, to drink]

tipple *v.* [1990s+] to appreciate, to understand, to work out. [i.e. they 'get a tip']

tippling ken *n.* (*also* **tippling house**, **...office**, **...school**, **...shop**, **...tenement**) [late 16C–mid-19C] a public house, a tavern. [SE *tipple* + KEN n.¹ (1)/SE *house*/OFFICE n.¹/SE *school*/*shop*/*tenement*]

tipply *adj.* **1** [1900s] unsteady. **2** [1910s–30s] drunk (cf. AFFLICTED adj.; ALED UP adj.). [SE *tipple over*/TIPPLE n.]

tippy *n.* [late 18C–mid-19C] **1** as *the tippy*, the height of fashion. **2** a dandy or a smart young woman. [TIP-TOP n. + ? TIP n.² (2)]

tippy *adj.* [19C] **1** in the height of fashion, smart, fine. **2** clever, ingenious. [TIPPY n. (1)]

tippybob *n.* **1** [late 18C–19C] a dandy. **2** [late 19C] (*US*) in ext. use, a derog. name for a member of the social élite. [ext. of TIPPY n.]

tippy toe *n.* [1980s] (*Aus.*) dismissal from a job.

tips *n.* [1950s] filter-*tipped* cigarettes.

tip sheet *n.* [1930s] (*US Und.*) a fake financial guide used in swindles. [TIP n.⁵ (4)]

tip-slang *adj.* [mid-19C] abusive, foul-mouthed. [? TIP A SLANG v.]

tipslinger *n.* [1920s+] (*Aus.*) a racecourse tipster. [TIP n.⁵ (1) + SE *slinger*, lit. 'thrower']

tip someone a queer chant *v. see* CHANT n. (4).

tip someone the fives *v.* [late 18C] to shake hands. [TIP v.³ + FIVES n.¹ (2)]

tip someone the office *v.* [19C] to warn someone. [TIP v.³ + OFFICE n.³ (1)]

tip someone the token *v.* [late 18C–early 19C] to give a partner a venereal disease. [TIP v.³ + TOKEN n. (2)]

tip someone the turnips *v.* [late 18C] to jilt, to 'chuck'.

tip (someone) the wink *v.* **1** [mid-17C+] to warn, to signal, usu. with an actual wink, but also fig. **2** [mid–late 19C] to acknowledge, to pay one's respects. [TIP v.³ + SE *wink*]

tipster *n.* **1** [mid–late 19C] one who gives out or sells advice on horseracing, dog-racing etc. **2** [late 19C] one who gives monetary tips to servants, employees etc. **3** [20C+] one who gives out any

form of 'inside' information; spec. (*US Und.*) a 'civilian' who alerts criminals to potential vctims, places to rob etc. [TIP n.⁵; (3) SE *tip*; (1) SE 20C+]

tip street *n.* [early 19C] a state of wealth. [fig. use of TIP n.² (2)]

tipsy as David's sow *phr. see* DRUNK AS DAVID'S SOW phr.

tip the brads *v.* [19C] **1** to be generous. **2** to be a gentleman. [TIP v.¹ (1) + BRAD n.¹ (2)]

tip the bucket on *v. see* DROP THE BUCKET ON v.

tip the chaff *v.* [early 19C] to tease, to banter with.

tip the claws (for breakfast) *v.* [18C] to be whipped, as a judicial punishment. [TIP v.³ + SE *claws*, those of the cat-o'-nine-tails]

tip the cole *v.* [mid-17C–mid-19C] to pay (a bill). [TIP v.¹ (1) + COLE n.]

tip the double *v.* [late 18C–mid-19C] **1** to run off, from a creditor or from the authorities; thus *tip the double to sherry*, to elude the sheriff. **2** to jilt. [TIP v.³ + SE phr. *at the double*]

tip the Dublin packet *v.* [early 19C] (*UK Und.*) to run off, to escape. [TIP v.³ + pun on *Dublin*/SE *double*, to run; the Dublin packet also being a boat on which one could escape to Ireland]

tip the finger *v. see* TIP THE (LITTLE) FINGER v.

tip the gam *v.* [early 19C] to talk (in a given manner). [TIP v.³ + GAM v.¹ (1)]

tip the go-by *v.* [late 18C–early 19C] **1** to avoid, to disregard deliberately. **2** to allow, to turn a blind eye to. **3** to dismiss, to get rid of. **4** to go fast. [TIP v.³ + var. on GIVE SOMEONE THE GO-BY v.]

tip the gripes in a dangle *v.* (*also* **tip the gripes in a tangle**) [late 18C] to shake hands. [TIP v.³ + SE *gripe*, to grasp]

tip the lag *v.* [mid-18C] (*UK Und.*) to have someone transported. [TIP v.³ + LAG n.² (1)]

tip the lion *v.* [late 18C–mid-19C] to squeeze someone's nose flat against their face and either poke their eyes with one's extended fingers or place them in the person's mouth. [the expression this hostile gesture produces is supposedly similar to that of a lion]

tip the (little) finger *v.* [late 19C+] (*Aus.*) to have a drink.

tip the long 'un *v.* [late 19C–1900s] of a man, to have sexual intercourse (cf. BURY IT v.). [TIP v.³ + SE *long one*]

tip the lowyer *v. see* TIP THE QUIDS v. (1).

tip the mag *v. see* MAG n.⁴ (1).

tip the nags *v. see* TETHER ONE'S NAGS ON v.

tip the queer on *v.* [early 19C–1900s] to pass a sentence of imprisonment on. [TIP v.³ + QUEER adj.¹ (1)]

tip the quids *v.* [late 17C–early 19C] **1** (*also* **tip the lowyer**) to spend money. **2** to lend money. [TIP v.³ + QUID n.]

tip the scroby (for breakfast) *v.* [late 18C–mid-19C] to be whipped, as a judicial punishment. [TIP v.³ + ? SE *scrub*]

tip the velvet *v.* **1** [late 17C–1900s] to kiss with the tongue. **2** [early–mid-19C] to tell off, to scold. **3** [early–mid-19C] to use flowery language in the hopes of a seduction. [TIP v.³ + VELVET n.¹; (1) has subseq. been interpreted as cunnilingus, notably in Sarah Waters' novel *Tipping the Velvet* (1999) but other than in a single 1684 ref. to 'kissing and tonguing' the vagina, tonguing did not mean cunnilingus until *c.*1890]

tip the whistle *v.* [late 19C] to warn. [TIP v.³ + SE *whistle*]

tip the wink *v. see* TIP (SOMEONE) THE WINK v.

tip-toe *adj.* [1950s] (*US Black*) excellent, first-rate.

tip-top *n.* **1** [18C–19C] the very best, the ultimate, the epitome. **2** [mid-18C–mid-19C] a collective n. for the cream of society, the 'bon-ton'; also in pl. meaning 'swells'. [SE *tip* + *top*, i.e. the top of the top]

tip-top *adj.* **1** [early 18C+] excellent, supreme, ultimate; thus the superlative *tip-toppest*, *tippest-toppest*. **2** [late 19C] snobbish. [TIP-TOP n.]

tip-top *adv.* [late 19C–1920s] excellently, superbly, in an excellent manner. [TIP-TOP adj. (1)]

tip-topmost *adj.* [1930s+] very good, excellent, best. [TIP-TOP adj. (1)]

tip-topper *n.* **1** [mid-19C–1910s] anything excellent, first-rate, the best. **2** [mid-19C–1940s] a dandy, a fashionable man; a first-rate person. [TIP-TOP n.]

tip up *v.* [mid-19C+] to hand over (money); usu. as imper. [ext. of TIP v.[1] (1)]

tip us the monish *phr.* [mid-19C] give us the money. [TIP v.[3] + ? mockery of the immigrant Jewish pron. of SE *money*]

tip us your fin/flipper *phr. see* TIP ONE'S FIN v.

tired *adj.*[1] [mid-19C+] drunk; thus *that tired feeling*, euph. for a state of drunkenness (cf. ADDLED adj.). [euph.]

tired *adj.*[2] [late 19C–1940s] extremely lazy; thus BORN (A BIT) TIRED adj.

tired *adj.*[3] [late 19C+] of people, things or events, tedious, dull, hackneyed; usu. in phr *to make someone tired*, to bore someone.

tired and emotional *adj.* (*also* **tired and overwrought**) [1960s+] extremely drunk (cf. ADDLED adj.). [coined as 'tired and overwrought' in the magazine *Private Eye* f. the popular euph. to mask the activities of the famous. The orig. cit. read: 'Mr George Brown [MP] had been tired and overwrought on many occasions' (*Private Eye*, 29 September 1967)]

tired-ass *adj.* [1960s+] (*US*) tedious, clichéd. [TIRED adj.[3] + -ASS sfx]

tired blood *n.* [1950s+] (*US*) a condition of listlessness. [an advertising slogan for a tonic, which promised to combat the condition]

tired people *n.* [1930s+] (*orig. US Black*) weak or displeasing people. [TIRED adj.[3]]

tired woman *n.* [1970s+] (*US Black*) a woman who lacks sophistication. [TIRED adj.[3]]

tirly-whirly *n.* [late 18C–19C] the vagina. [coined by Robert Burns (1759–96); SE *tirly-whirly*, a whirligig or, Scot. *tirly-whirly*, winding, intricate]

tirret *n.* (*also* **tirrit**) [late 16C] a fit of temper. [? SE *tirl*, St Vitus's Dance]

tish *n.* (*also* **titch**) [1970s+] (*drugs*) phencyclidine (cf. ACE n.[4]). [var. on TIC n.]

tish *adj. see* ISH adj.

tish *v.*[1] [1950s] (*US*) to pad or enhance something. [abbr. SE *tissue paper*, used as a protective wadding]

tish *v.*[2] *see* TISSUE v.

tishy *n. see* TISSUE n.

tishy *adj.* [1910s–30s] drunk. ['drunken' mispron. of *tipsy*]

tisket *n.* [1940s] a bastard. [song lyric 'A tisket, a tasket, a little yellow basket', thus BASKET n.[2]]

tissick *n.* (*also* **tissic**) [20C+] (*Irish*) a cough; thus *tizicky*, fastidious about one's food, self-conscious. [SE *phthisis*]

tissied up *adj.* [1960s+] (*Aus.*) dressed up. [TIZ UP v.]

tissue *n.* (*also* **tishy**) [1950s+] (*Aus./N.Z.*) a cigarette paper.

tissue *v.* (*also* **tish**) [1920s–40s] (*US Und.*) of a con-man, to perform a practical joke where he pretends to place a large denomination bill in a woman's stocking, promising her that if she removes it before morning it will turn into tissue paper. Inevitably she cannot wait – and invariably it is indeed tissue paper. [SE *tissue*/abbr.]

ti-stick *n. see* THAI (STICK) n.

tit *n.*[1] **1** [mid-16C–1910s] a small or half-grown horse. **2** [early–late 19C] a coach horse. [for ety. *see* TIT n.[2]; (2) f. (1)]

tit *n.*[2] **1** [late 16C+] a girl or woman, esp. in derog. or generic use, e.g. *a tasty bit of tit*, but also as a term of affection, often as *little tit*. **2** [18C+] a generic for a person of either sex. **3** [early 18C–1900s] the vagina. [despite SE *teat*/TIT n.[3] (1), ety. is onomat. term meaning anything small + Scand. dial. terms *titta*, a little girl, *tita*, a small fish etc; (1) SE until *c*.1800]

tit *n.*[3] **1** [late 19C+] a breast, usu. a woman's; usu. in pl. (cf. BORDENS n.). **2** [1910s+] (*orig. milit.*) anything considered to resemble a breast or, more often, the nipple, e.g. a button or a small switch etc. **3** [1950s+] (*also* **nipple**) in fig. use, something on which one 'feeds', e.g. a hand-out, a government grant. **4** [1960s+] something extremely simple and usu. rewarding, esp. a criminal scheme. **5** [1970s+] the nipple. **6** [2000s] (*also* **bluetit**) a UK policeman's helmet. [SE *tit* is an archaic var. sp. of *teat*; (3) suggests the simplicity of a child's finding its mother's breast; (6) is resemblance]

tit *n.*[4] [1940s+] a fool; thus *look an absolute tit*, *look a right tit*, to appear a total fool, thus the tired school 'witticism', *I feel a right tit*. [? TIT n.[3] (1) or TIT n.[2] (1)]

tit *n.*[5] [2000s] (*US prison*) heroin.

tit *adj.*[1] [1950s+] pertaining to the female breast, usu. in the context of pornography, e.g. TIT ART n.; TIT-BOOK n. [TIT n.[3] (1)]

tit *adj.*[2] **1** [1960s+] (*S.Afr.*) a general term of approval meaning excellent, wonderful, good-looking. **2** [1990s+] (*US campus*) easy. [ext. of TIT n.[3] (4)]

tit about *v.* (*also* **tit around**) [1940s+] to play around, to waste time, to act in a trivial, pointless manner. [TIT n.[4]]

tit art *n.* [1950s+] (*US*) pictures of attractive young women. [TIT adj.[1]]

tit-bit *n.* [mid-17C–18C] **1** the vagina. **2** the penis. **3** (*also* **tid-bit**) a young girl. [TIT n.[2]]

tit-book *n.* [1970s] a soft-core pornographic magazine. [TIT adj.[1] + SE *book*]

titch *n. see* TISH n.

titchy *adj.* [1950s+] (*mainly UK juv.*) small, tiny, undersized; thus *Tich* or *Titch*, popular nickname for a short person (and, with heavy humour, for an exceptionally tall one). [according to *OED* the nickname preceded the wider use: 'The stage name Little Tich of the dwarfish music-hall comedian Harry Relph (1868–1928), who was given the nickname as a child because of a resemblance to the Tichborne claimant.' The claimant was Arthur Orton (1834–98), who claimed in 1866 to be Roger Charles Tichborne (1829–54), the heir to an English baronetcy, who was lost at sea. Orton was finally discredited and imprisoned in 1874]

titfer *n.* (*also* **titfa, tit-for**) [1910s+] a hat. [abbr. TIT FOR TAT n. (1)]

tit for tat *n.* **1** [1910s+] a hat. **2** [2000s] (*Aus.*) a rat, i.e. a non-trade unionist. [rhy. sl.]

tit for tats *n.* [1940s+] (*Aus.*) the female breasts.

tit fuck *n.* (*also* **titty fuck**) [1970s+] (*orig. US*) intercourse in which the man rubs his penis between the woman's breasts. [TIT n.[3] (1)/TITTY n.[1] (1) + FUCK n.[1] (1)]

tit fuck *v.* (*also* **titty fuck**) [1990s+] to have intercourse or to masturbate between female breasts. [TIT FUCK n.]

tithead *n.* [1980s+] **1** a general term of abuse. **2** a weakling. **3** a policeman. [TIT n.[3] (1)/TIT n.[3] (6)]

ti-ti *adj.* [2000s] (*US Black*) small, little.

titire-tu *n. see* TITTERY-TU n.

titivate *v.* (*also* **tiddivate, tiddyvate, tittivate**) **1** [19C–1910s] to smarten oneself up, to put the finishing touches to. **2** [1920s] to treat kindly or gently. [? SE *tidy*]

tit-kisser *n.* [1970s] (*US*) a womanizer. [TIT n.[3] (1)]

title page *n.* [mid-19C] the face.

titless wonder *n.* [1930s+] (*orig. RAF*) a flat-chested woman. [TIT n.[3] (1); pun on CHINLESS WONDER n.]

titley *n.* [mid-19C–1930s] a drink; thus *titley and binder*, a glass of beer and a piece of bread and cheese. [? dial. *titley* tickle, i.e. one's palate, or SE *tiddly*, small, i.e. a small portion; var. on TIDDLY n.]

titley *adj.* [mid-19C+] slightly drunk, tipsy (cf. ALED UP adj.). [TITLEY n.]

tit mag *n.* (*also* **tit magazine**) [1960s+] a magazine which features scantily clad women. The pictures are interspersed with varying amounts of prose, reviews etc but despite all other pretensions, they are in the end an aid to masturbation. [TIT adj.[1] + colloq. SE *mag*, a magazine]

tit man *n.* (*also* **tits man**) [1950s+] a man who finds a woman's breasts her most appealing feature (cf. ASS-MAN n.). [TIT n.³ (1) + SE *man*]

titmouse *n.* [mid-17C–19C] the vagina.

tit-off *n.* [1970s] (*Aus.*) the caressing of a woman's breasts. [TIT OFF v.]

tit off *v.* [1970s] (*Aus.*) to caress a woman's breasts. [TIT n.³ (1); on the model of JERK OFF v.¹ (1)]

tit-proud *adj.* [1950s] (*N.Z.*) used of a woman who is proud of her breasts. [TIT n.³ (1) + SE *proud*]

tits *n.* [1980s] (*US campus*) two incomes, two stinkers: a working couple with 2 children. [abbr.]

tits, the *n.* [1950s+] perfection, excellence, an ideal situation. [fig. use of TIT n.³ (1)]

tits *adj.* **1** [1960s+] (*US*) wonderful, excellent. **2** [1990s+] (*US campus*) easy, simple. [TIT n.³ (4)]

tits! *excl.* [mid-19C+] nonsense! rubbish! [TIT n.³ (1); on model of BALLS! excl.]

tits and ass *n.* (*also* **t.a.**, **T & A**, **tits and arse**, **tits and bums**) [1950s+] (*orig. US*) **1** a burlesque show, cheap sex-orientated entertainment which features strippers etc. **2** any soft-core pornography. **3** sex appeal; women viewed as nothing more than sex objects. [TIT n.³ (1) + ASS n. (2)/ARSE n.¹ (1)/BUM n.¹ (2)]

tits and ass *adj.* (*also* **t.a.**, **T & A**, **tits and arse**, **tits and bum**, **titties and cans**) [1950s+] (*orig. US*) relating to sex-orientated entertainment or soft-core pornography. [TITS AND ASS n.]

tits and zits *adj.* [1970s+] (*US*) pertaining to teenage love and sex. [TIT n.³ (1) + ZIT n. (1)]

tits-deep *adj. see* ASS-DEEP *adj.*

tit show *n.* [1960s+] a burlesque or striptease show. [TIT adj.¹ + SE *show*]

tits man *n. see* TIT MAN n.

tits off! *excl.* [1950s–70s] go away! [euph. for PISS OFF! excl.]

tits on a bull *phr.* (*also* **tits on a boar/canary**) [1940s+] something utterly useless; usu. in phr. *no more use than tits on a bull* etc.

tits on toast *n.* [1900s–50s] (*N.Z.*) belly-pickled pork on toast. [the belly-pork often has nipples still attached]

tit spanners *n.* [1970s+] (*S.Afr.*) the hands, not necessarily in a sexual context. [TIT n.³ (1) + SE *spanner*; the image of a man playing with a woman's tits in an ungainly fashion]

tit-sucker *n.* [1940s] (*US*) a weak, babyish person. [TIT n.³ (1) + SE *suck*]

titsun *n. see* DITSOON n.

tits-up *adj.* [1970s+] (*orig. Can. prison*) dead, i.e. laid out on one's back; thus in fig. use, ruined, destroyed; esp. in phr. *go tits-up*. [TIT n.³ (1)]

titsy *adj.* [1970s+] (*US*) featuring bare-breasted women; having attractive breasts. [TIT n.³ (1)]

titted *adj.* [1990s+] drunk (cf. ARSEHOLED adj.). [var. on CUNTED adj.² + fig. use of TIT n.⁴]

titter *n.* [19C] a young woman. [SE *titter*, to giggle, or TITTY n.¹ (1)]

tittery *n.* [early–mid-18C] gin. [dial. *tittery*, unstable, on the verge of falling, i.e. its effects]

tittery-tu *n.* (*also* **titire-tu**, **tityre-tu**, **tytere-tu**) [early 17C–19C] a street gang, esp. of well-to-do roughs who infested the London streets, committing their crimes for amusement rather than gain. [the first words of Virgil's first eclogue, 'Tityre, tu patulae recubans sub tegmine fagi'. The Lat. tag implied that these privileged rogues were men of leisure and fortune, who 'lay at ease under their patrimonial beech trees']

tittie bar *n. see* TITTY BAR n.

tittivate *v. see* TITIVATE v.

tittle *v.* [20C+] (*Ulster*) to walk in a mincing manner. [? SE *teeter* or dial. *tittle*, very lightly]

tittle-tat *n.* [1950s+] **1** (*Aus.*) a gossip. **2** (*UK juv.*) a piece of gossip. [abbr. SE *tittle-tattle*]

tittup *n. see* TITUP n.

titty *n.¹* (*also* **tiddy**) **1** [late 19C+] a woman's breast; usu. in pl. (cf. BORDENS n.). **2** [1930s+] in fig. use, a source of nourishment. [dimin. of TIT n.³ (1); note earlier use as dimin. of SE *tit*, var. sp. of SE *teat*, meaning the nipple only]

titty *n.²* [20C+] milk. [TIT n.³ (1), in this case a cow's udder]

titty bar *n.* (*also* **tittie bar**) [1980s+] (*US*) a striptease or lap-dancing bar. [TITTY n.¹ (1) + SE *bar*]

titty fuck *see under* TIT FUCK.

titty girl *n.* [2000s] (*UK Black*) a consciously sexy young woman. [TITTY n.¹ (1) + SE *girl*]

titty magazine *n.* [1990s+] (*US*) a (softcore) pornographic magazine. [TITTY n.¹ (1) + SE *magazine*]

titty oggy *n.* [1960s] (*US*) intercourse in which the man rubs his penis between the woman's breasts. [TITTY n.¹ (1) + ?]

titup *n.* (*also* **tittup**) [late 19C–1930s] the correct or fashionable thing. [SE *tittup*, a horse's canter]

tit up *v.* [1960s] to fondle a woman's breasts.

titwank *n.* [1990s+] **1** an act of intercourse in which the man rubs his penis between the woman's breasts. **2** a general term of abuse. [TIT n.³ (1) + WANK n.¹]

tit willow *n.* [1930s+] a pillow. [rhy. sl.; ult. f. *The Mikado* (1885) opera]

tityre-tu *n. see* TITTERY-TU n.

tius *n.* [late 19C–1900s] a suit of clothes. [backsl.]

Tiv, the *n.* **1** [late 19C–1910s] the *Tivoli* Music Hall, London. **2** [1910s–50s] the *Tivoli* Music Hall, Sydney. [abbr.]

tives *n.* [1970s+] (*US campus*) one's relatives. [abbr.]

tivvy *n.* [19C] the vagina. [SE *activity*]

'Tizer, the *n.* [mid-19C] the *Morning Advertiser* newspaper. [abbr.]

tizicky *adj. see* TISSICK n.

tiz up *v.* [1930s+] (*Aus.*) to dress up. [? TITIVATE v.]

tizzy *n.¹* [late 18C–1910s] a sixpence. [? TILBURY n. or TESTER n.¹ (1); note WW1 RN *tizzy snatcher*, an Assistant Paymaster]

tizzy *n.²* (*also* **tiz-wizz**, **tizz**) [1930s+] (*orig. US*) a panic, a 'state', a flap. [ety. unknown; ? echoic of one's rushing around, whether lit. or fig.]

tizzy *adj.¹* [1930s+] (*Aus.*) **1** showily or flashily overdressed. **2** of a person, ostentatious, showy, vulgar. **3** of an object, flashy but cheaply manufactured. [TIZ UP v.]

tizzy *adj.²* [2000s] (*US Black*) a general term of approval. [? ext. of TIGHT adj.¹ (5)]

tizzy *v.* (*also* **tizzy up**) [1960s+] (*Aus.*) to titivate, to dress up in one's finery. [TIZ UP v.]

T.J. *n.* [1960s+] (*US*) *Ti*juana, Mexico. [abbr.]

tjeers *phr.* [1950s+] (*S.Afr.*) goodbye.

tjommie *n. see* CHOMMIE n.

T-Jones *n.* [1970s+] (*US prison*) the mother of a prisoner.

tjorie/tjorrie *n. see* CHORRIE n.

t.k.o. *v.* [1950s+] (*orig. US*) to defeat in theory, if not in practice. [boxing jargon *t.k.o.*, a technical *k*nock-*o*ut]

T.L. *n.* [1920s+] (*US*) a compliment, esp. one given in return for a previous compliment paid to oneself; also a compliment passed onto its subject by an intermediary, when the original speaker is too shy to speak themself. [SAmE trade *last*, 'a compliment offered in exchange for one that is directed towards the speaker; also, in weakened sense, a compliment, whether reciprocal or not' (OED)]

TL *n.* [1990s+] (*US*) the Tenderloin district of San Francisco. [abbr. TENDERLOIN n.]

t.l. *n.* [1950s+] (*US*) a toady, a sycophant. [abbr. Yid. *toches lecher*, ARSE-LICKER n. (1)]

t.l.c. *n.* [1960s+] (*orig. US*) kindness, consideration etc. [abbr. *tender loving care*]

t.m. *n.* [1930s+] (*Aus./Can.*) a factory-made cigarette. [abbr. TAILOR-MADE n. (2)]

T-man *n.*[1] [1920s+] (*US*) a law enforcement officer of the US Treasury Department. [lit. *Treasury-man*]

T-man *n.*[2] [1960s] (*US*) a man who likes (large) breasts. [TIT n.[3] (1) + SE *man*]

t.n.t. *n.*[1] [1950s+] the female breasts. [abbr. *two nifty tits*; TIT n.[3] (1)]

t.n.t. *n.*[2] [1960s+] (*US Black*) anyone or anything that is metaphorically 'dynamite', wonderful, exceptional etc. [SE *TNT*, trinitrotoluene]

t.n.t. *n.*[3] [1980s+] (*drugs*) **1** heroin. **2** fentanyl. [? SE *TNT*, trinitrotoluene, i.e. the 'explosive' effects]

T.O. *n.* [1950s+] (*US*) Toronto, Ontario. [abbr.]

toac *n.* [mid-19C] a coat. [backsl.]

toac-tisaw *n.* [mid-19C] a waistcoat. [backsl.]

toad *n.*[1] **1** [1920s+] (*US campus*) an unpleasant or unattractive person. **2** [1970s+] (*US*) a Black person. **3** [1980s] (*US gay*) an unattractive middle-aged gay man.

toad *n.*[2] [1980s+] (*US*) the penis (cf. ANTEATER n.).

toad in the hole *n.* **1** [mid–late 19C] a 'sandwich man' who carries 4, rather than the usual 2, boards; he is thus completely surrounded by advertising displays. **2** [1930s–40s] a bankroll. [SE *toad-in-the-hole*, meat surrounded with batter and baked; (2) rhy. sl.]

toadskin *n.* **1** [mid-19C] (*US*) a 5-cent stamp; thus *his purse is made of toadskin*, he is a mean, grasping person. **2** [1900s–40s] (*US/Aus.*) (*also* **toad**) a banknote (cf. BAT HIDE n.). [play on FROG n.[3] (1)]

toad-stabber *n.* [late 19C–1960s] (*US*) a large pocketknife or jackknife. [note synon. army jargon *cat-stabber*]

toad-sticker *n.* (*US*) **1** [mid–late 19C] a sword. **2** [20C+] a large knife.

to a fare-thee-well *adv.* (*also* **to a fare-ye-well, …fare-you-well**) [20C+] (*US*) thoroughly, completely.

to and fro *n.* **1** [20C+] snow. **2** [1960s–80s] (*Aus.*) a moustache. [rhy. sl.; (2) = MO n.[1]]

to and fro *v.* [1960s–80s] (*Aus.*) to leave, to go. [rhy. sl.]

to-and-from *n.*[1] [1910s+] a concertina. [the movements of the player's arms]

to-and-from *n.*[2] [1940s+] (*Aus.*) a British immigrant to Australia. [rhy. sl. = POM n.[2]]

toast *n.*[1] [late 17C–19C] **1** the Devil. **2** a lively old man. **3** a drunkard. [abbr. OLD TOAST n.[1]]

toast *n.*[2] [1950s+] (*US Und.*) a long and epic poem, often trad. in prisons. [SE *toast*, a dedicatory remark prefacing the taking of a drink]

toast *n.*[3] **1** [1950s+] (*US Black*) the best, the finest, anything outstanding. **2** [1970s] in phr. *on toast*, an intensifier. [i.e. that which deserves a SE *toast*; (2) SE *toast*, hot bread]

toast *n.*[4] (*also* **toaster**) [2000s+] (*US Black*) a gun. [it turns people into SE *toast*]

toast *adj.*[1] [1950s+] (*US Black/teen*) excellent, wonderful. [TOAST n.[3]]

toast *adj.*[2] [1980s+] **1** useless, finished. **2** (*US campus*) (*also* **toasty**) tipsy or hungover. [SE *toast*]

toast *adj.*[3] [1980s+] (*US campus*) in big trouble, the victim of misfortune; esp. in phr. *you're toast*. [SE *toast*]

toast *v.* **1** [1950s+] (*US Black*) to recount a lengthy epic poem, usu. based in the pimping or underworld experience. **2** [1960s+] (*W.I.*) of a disc jockey, to perform one's own lyrics to the background of a reggae song, usu. in a dub (no lyrics, only bass and rhythm lines) version. [SE *toast*, to make a speech when drinking someone's health]

toasted *adj.* **1** [1940s] (*US Und.*) executed in the electric chair. **2** [1980s+] (*US*) physically or mentally exhausted. **3** [1980s+] tipsy, either slightly or extremely drunk (cf. ANNIHILATED adj.). **4** [1980s+] (*drugs*) intensely intoxicated by a drug. [SE *toast*]

toasted bread *adj.* [1990s+] dead. [rhy. sl.]

toaster *n.*[1] [1960s] (*US*) a flamethrower. [it turns things into SE *toast*]

toaster *n.*[2] [1960s+] (*US Black*) a singer of reggae rap music. [TOAST v. (2)]

toaster *n.*[3] *see* TOAST n.[4].

toasting fork *n.* (*also* **toasting iron, toaster**) [late 16C–1900s] a sword. [note WW1 milit. *toasting fork*, a bayonet]

toast rack *n.* **1** [20C+] a horse-drawn tram as found at Douglas, Isle of Man. **2** [1920s–50s] (*Aus.*) a footboard tram in Sydney. [supposed resemblance]

toasty *adj.* *see* TOAST adj.[2] (2).

toast your blooming eyebrows! *excl.* [late 19C–1910s] a general excl. of disdain or dismissal; 'a delicate way of telling a man to go to blazes' (Ware).

toat *v.* *see* TOTE v.[1].

tobacco baron *n.* *see* BARON n.

Tobacco Road *n.* [1930s+] (*US*) any primitive rural area; thus used pej. of those who live there. [Erskine Caldwell's novel *Tobacco Road* (1932)]

to beat four of a kind *phr.* [late 19C] (*US campus*) to a very great extent. [poker imagery]

to beat hell *phr.* [late 19C+] to the utmost, very much, decisively. [BEAT HELL v.]

to beat the band *phr.* [late 19C+] (*US*) to the utmost, very much. [one drowns out the band]

tober omee *n.* [late 19C+] (*Ling. Fr./Polari*) a toll collector, e.g. a fairground or market stall superintendent. [Rom. *tober*, road + OMEE n.]

toboggan *n.* [late 19C+] (*US*) a rapid decline, usu. towards ultimate disaster; esp. in phr. *on the toboggan*. [play on ON THE SKIDS phr.]

to buggery *adv.* **1** [20C+] a synon. for TO HELL adv. **2** [1950s+] to the limit, to extremes.

to burn *adv.* [late 19C+] (*US*) in very large quantities; often ext. as *to burn a wet dog/mule with*; usu. MONEY TO BURN n. [the size/dampness of the animal requires a large fire]

toby *n.*[1] **1** [late 17C–mid-19C] the posterior, the buttocks. **2** [late 17C–1920s] a woman's genitals. [*Toby*, dimin. of proper name Tobias; thus euph.]

toby *n.*[2] **1** [19C–1940s] (*US Und.*) highway robbery; as *low toby*, on foot, and *high toby*, mounted robbery. **2** [19C–1950s] the road, the highway, esp. as a place where robbers and highwaymen can find their victims. **3** [1930s] (*also* **tobyman**) a tramp, the life of tramping. [Shelta *tobar* or Rom. *tober*, the road, ? ult. Irish *bothar*, road. Note police jargon *toby*, an area, a police division]

toby *n.*[3] [late 19C] (*UK society*) a frilled collar worn by women. [the style of collar trad. worn in Punch and Judy shows by the dog *Toby*]

toby *n.*[4] [late 19C–1940s] (*US*) a second-rate brand of cigar. [abbr. brandname *Conestoga*; STOGIE n.]

toby *n.*[5] [1920s+] (*Aus.*) **1** a simple, foolish man, but one who is kind and amenable and thus popular; thus *have a toby on*, to feel kindly or friendly towards. **2** an expert. [proper name *Tobias* + ref. to *Toby*, Mr Punch's dog]

toby *n.*[6] [1990s+] (*UK juv.*) a male homosexual. [the presumed 'poshness' and thus effeminacy of the name]

toby *v.* **1** [19C] (*also* **ply the toby**) to rob someone on the highway. **2** [1930s–50s] (*UK tramp*) to walk the roads as a tramp; thus *on the toby*, tramping. [TOBY n.[2]]

toby concern *n.* *see* TOBY LAY n.

toby-gill *n.* [early–mid-19C] a highwayman. [TOBY n.[2] (2) + GILL n.[1] (2)]

toby-gloak *n.* (*also* **tobyman**) [19C–1900s] a highwayman. [TOBY n.[2] (2) + GLOAK n./SE *man*]

toby jug *n.* [20C+] **1** a fool (cf. BEECHAM'S PILL n.). **2** an ear. [rhy. sl.; (1) = MUG n.[2] (1); (2) = LUG n.[1]]

toby lay *n.* (*also* **toby concern**) [19C] highway robbery. [TOBY n.² (2) + LAY n.⁴ (1)/SE *concern*]

tobyman *n.*¹ *see* TOBY n.² (3).

tobyman *n.*² *see* TOBY-GLOAK n.

toch eno! *excl.* [mid-19C+] look out! take care! etc. [backsl. = *hot one!*]

toches *n.* (*also* **dokus, tochus, tocus, tokis, tokus, tookus, tooky, tuchas, tuches, tuchis, tuckus**) **1** [late 19C+] the posterior, the buttocks. **2** [1900s] the vagina. [synon. Yid. *toches*]

toches-licker *n.* (*also* **tokus-licker**) [1950s+] (*orig. US*) a toady, a sycophant. [TOCHES n. (1) + SE *licker*, i.e. ARSE-LICKER n. (1)]

to Christ *phr.* (*also* **to Christmas**) [1910s+] a general intensifier.

tochus *n. see* TOCHES n.

tockley *n.* [1990s+] (*Aus.*) the penis. [ety. unknown; ? link to SE *tag*]

toco *n.* (*also* **toko**) [early 19C–1940s] punishment; thus *give someone toco*, to beat, to thrash. [? Gk *tokoz*, interest (*OED*), Hind. *tokna*, to censure (Y&B), Maori *toko*, a rod (E.P.)]

tocus *n. see* TOCHES n.

tod *n.* [late 18C–1910s] (*US*) a drink. [abbr. SE *toddy*]

today *adj.* [1960s+] (*orig. US*) fashionable, up-to-the-minute.

toddle *v.* (*also* **toddle along, toddle off**) [early 18C+] to move, to walk, to go or leave. [Vaux cites *toddle* as 'Und.' in 1812, but *OED* says SE. E.P. suggests that only upper-class 20C+ use is colloq.]

toddler *n.* **1** [late 18C–1920s] a walker. **2** [early 19C] a foot. [TODDLE v.; note *toddler*, 'one who toddles', e.g. a child or an infirm old person, is UK Und. in Vaux but is SE in the *OED*]

toddlers *n.* [mid-19C] the legs. [TODDLE v.]

toddles *n.* [mid-19C] a pretty young woman. [SE *toddles*, an infant]

toddy blossom *n.* [19C] a red face caused by the bursting of blood vessels through excessive long-term drinking. [SE *toddy* + *blossom*(-*faced*), having a red, bloated face]

toddy-stick *n.* [mid–late 19C] a muddler, one who 'messes (things) around'. [SE *toddy-stick*, a spatula, usu. of glass or metal, for stirring toddy]

todge *v.* [late 18C–early 19C] to beat, to thrash. [dial. *todge*, a very thick soup, spoon-meat, i.e. meat boiled almost to paste]

todger *n. see* TADGER n.

to die (for) *phr.* [late 19C; 1950s+] (*US*) excellent, wonderful, perfect, e.g. *that boy is to die pretty*. [note *OED* cites a single late 19C use, but then nothing until 1980s]

to-do *n.* [1990s+] (*US*) an important person. [one who makes a SE *to-do*]

todoment *n.* [20C+] (*W.I., Bdos*) **1** noise, confusion. **2** open-air fun and excitement. [SE *to-do* + sfx *-ment*]

Tod Sloan *adj.* [20C+] alone. [rhy. sl.; ult. the US jockey Tod Sloan (1874–1933)]

Tod Sloan *v. see* SLOAN v.

toe *n.* [late 19C+] (*Aus./N.Z.*) strength, speed. [the use of the *toe*, i.e. the foot, in running]

toe *adj.*¹ [1970s+] (*S.Afr.*) very stupid. [Afk. *toe*, closed]

toe *adj.*² (*also* **toe up**) [1970s+] (*US Black/campus*) **1** drunk; hungover. **2** emotionally shattered. **3** unfashionable, badly dressed. [US Black pron. of TORE UP adj.]

toe-cheese *n. see* TOE-JAM n.

toecutter *n.* [1980s+] **1** (*Aus. Und.*) a criminal who specializes on preying on other, successful and thus wealthy criminals. **2** (*US*) an aggressively selfish and single-minded individual.

t-oed *adj. see* TEED UP adj.

toeface *n.* [1910s–20s] an unpleasant or dirty person.

toe it (away) *v.* [1970s+] (*UK Und.*) to escape.

toe-jam *n.* (*also* **toe-cheese**) [1930s+] (*US*) dead skin and dirt found between unwashed toes; thus also a term of abuse.

toe-jam queen *n.* [1960s–70s] (*US gay*) a male homosexual foot-fetishist. [TOE-JAM n. + QUEEN n.² (1)/QUEEN sfx (2)]

toeology *n.* [1950s] (*US Black*) dancing, esp. of a high standard.

toe party *n.* [1920s–30s] (*US Black*) a party game whereby all the women present line up behind a sheet with nothing visible but their toes. The men then take turns to choose their preferred toes and pair off accordingly.

toe queen *n.* [1950s+] (*gay*) a foot fetishist. [SE *toe* + QUEEN n.² (1)/QUEEN sfx (2)]

toerag *n.*¹ [late 19C] (*Aus.*) a £1 note. [SE *toerag*, the foot-bindings used by tramps]

toerag *n.*² [late 19C] a second-rate, inferior newspaper. [TOERAG n.³ + RAG n.⁴ (1)]

toerag *n.*³ **1** [late 19C–1950s] a tramp. **2** [late 19C+] a general term of abuse. [SE *toerag*, the foot-bindings used by tramps; (2) Puxley, *Cockney Rabbit: A Dick 'n' Arry of Rhyming Slang* (1992), suggests rhy. sl. = SLAG n.¹ (1)]

toerag *n.*⁴ [1930s] a cigarette. [rhy. sl. = FAG n.⁴ (3)]

toe-ragger *n.* (*also* **toe-rigger**) (*Aus./N.Z.*) **1** [late 19C+] a down-and-out vagrant, a tramp. **2** [late 19C+] a general term of contemptuous abuse. **3** [1910s+] one who is given a short prison sentence. [TOERAG n.³]

toerag Tommy *n.* [late 19C] (*Aus.*) a small bookmaker.

toe-soldier *n.* [1900s] (*Aus.*) an infantryman. [play on SE *foot soldier*]

toes up *adj.* **1** [mid-19C–1950s] lying dead. **2** [late 19C] ill, indisposed. [abbr. SE *turn one's toes up*]

toe the carpet *v. see* ON THE CARPET phr.².

toe the chalk/crack/mark *v. see* WALK THE CHALK v. (2).

toe to toe *n.* [1980s+] a fight, a brawl. [SE *toe to toe*, in close combat]

toe-to-toe *v.* [1990s+] (*US*) to fight. [TOE TO TOE n.]

toe up *adj. see* TOE adj.².

toey *n.*¹ (*Aus./N.Z.*) **1** [late 19C–1900s] a fashionable, smart person, a 'swell'. **2** [1900s] (*Aus.*) an infantryman. **3** [1970s+] an alert person; one who is 'on their toes'. [? fig. use of TOE n.]

toey *n.*² *see* TOY n.³ (1).

toey *adj.* [1930s+] **1** (*Aus./N.Z.*) nervous, touchy. **2** (*Aus. prison*) liable to attempt an escape. **3** (*Aus.*) of a horse, fast. [TOE n.]

toff *n.* **1** [mid-19C] a male house-owner. **2** [mid-19C+] (*also* **toft**) an aristocrat, an upper-class person in general. **3** [late 19C+] anyone considered either to be or to be posing as a superior person. **4** [late 19C+] one who acts bravely or 'nobly'. **5** [late 19C+] one who behaves kindly, generously; thus in phr. *you're a toff*, you're very kind, thank you very much. [? SE *tuft* as in TUFT-HUNTER n. (any link to TOFFEE-NOSED adj. is invalidated by chronology)]

toffed up *adj.* [late 19C+] dressed up, esp. showily. [TOFF n. (2)]

toffee *n.*¹ [20C+] nonsense, flattery. [? the 'sweetness' of its content]

toffee *n.*² **1** [1930s] tobacco. **2** [1940s+] gelignite. [the colour or shape]

toffee-nose *n.* [1940s+] (*orig. milit.*) a snobbish or supercilious person. [TOFFEE-NOSED adj.]

toffee-nosed *adj.* (*also* **toffee**) [1910s+] snobbish, arrogant. [TOFF n. (2) + a nose fig. stuck in the air to avoid the noxious smells of everyday life]

toffee whizz *n.* [1990s+] (*drugs*) amphetamine (cf. A n.²). [SE *toffee* + WHIZ n.⁷; ? ult. a brandname]

toffee wrapper *n.* [1990s+] the head. [rhy. sl. = NAPPER n.² (2)]

toffer *n.* [mid–late 19C] a well-dressed prostitute. [TOFF n. (2)]

tofficky *adj.* [mid–late 19C] showily or ostentatiously dressed. [TOFF n. (2)]

toffish *adj.* (*also* **toffy**) [mid-19C+] aristocratic, stylish, 'swell'. [TOFF n. (2)]

toffishness *n.* [mid–late 19C] affectation, 'putting on airs'. [TOFFISH adj.]

toff ken *n.* (*also* **tuff ken**) [mid–late 19C] the house of prosperous owners. [TOFF n. (2) + KEN n.¹ (1)]

toff omee n. [late 19C–1900s] a very fine gentleman. [TOFF n. (2) + OMEE n. (3)]

toff-shoving n. [late 19C] (*UK Und.*) pushing about well-dressed gentlemen in a crowd, presumably to facilitate picking their pockets. [TOFF n. (2) + SE *shove*]

toffy adj. see TOFFISH adj.

toft n. see TOFF n. (2).

to fuck adv. [1910s+] a general intesifier, utterly, completely. [FUCK n.[5]]

tog n. (*also* **togg, togge, tugg**) **1** [18C–1960s] an outer garment, a coat; thus *long tog, upper tog, tog and kicks*, coat and trousers; *under tog*, an under petticoat. **2** [1910s] (*US Und.*) among pick-pockets, an overcoat used as a shield. [abbr. TOGE n./TOGE-MANS n.]

tog v. **1** [early–late 19C] to supply someone with clothing. **2** [early 19C–1960s] to dress up, to get dressed. [TOG n. (1)]

togamans n. see TOGEMANS n.

tog-bound adj. [late 19C–1900s] lacking decent or fashionable clothes. [TOG n. (1) + sfx -*bound*, limited]

toge n. [late 17C–early 19C] a coat. [OE *toge*, a toga; ult. Lat. *toga*, a toga or cloak. As toga, it dates back to *c.*1400, as found in the line 'Alle with taghte mene and towne in togers fulle ryche' (Sir Thomas Malory, *Morte d'Arthur*)]

togemans n. (*also* **togamans, togeman, togman**) [mid-16C–mid-19C] a coat or cloak. [Fr. *toge* or Lat. *toga*, toga + -MANS sfx]

together adj. [1960s+] **1** aware, in control, self-assured, au fait, sophisticated. **2** of a place or situation, excellent, first-rate. **3** united. **4** happy. **5** prepared, organized.

together adv. [1960s+] competently, in an emotionally worked-out manner.

tog-fencer n. **1** [late 19C–1910s] a tailor. **2** [1930s] (*UK tramp*) a market seller of second-hand clothes. [TOG n. (1) + -FENCER sfx]

togg/togge n. see TOG n.

togged adj. [19C+] dressed; thus *rum togged*, well-dressed. [TOG v. (2)]

togged down adj. [1930s–60s] (*US Black*) very well-dressed. [TOG v. (2)]

togged out (to the nines) phr. **1** [early 19C+] dressed up, usu. in one's finest clothes. **2** [1910s] equipped with a wardrobe. [TOG v. (2) + UP TO THE NINES adv.]

togged to the bricks phr. [1930s–60s] (*US Black*) dressed in style. [TOG v. (2) + BRICKS n. (1)]

togged to the knocker phr. [1910s] (*Aus.*) well-dressed. [TOG v. (2) + ? KNOCKER n.[2]]

togged to the teeth phr. [1970s] (*US Black*) very well-dressed. [TOG v. (2) + SE phr. *to the teeth*]

togged up adj. [mid-19C+] dressed up. [TOG UP v.]

togger n. see TADGER n.

toggery n. **1** [early 19C–1940s] clothing, harness, 'domestic paraphernalia of any kind' (Hotten, 1859). **2** [late 19C–1940s] any variety of official or vocational dress. [ext. of TOG n. (1)]

togging/toggs n. see TOGS n. (1).

toggy n. [mid-18C–1900s] a cloak, a coat. [TOG n. (1)]

tog it v. see TOG UP v.

togman n. see TOGEMANS n.

tog out v. see TOG UP v.

togs n. **1** [mid-18C+] (*also* **togging, toggs, tuggs**) clothes, often in combs., e.g. *long togs, sporting togs, Sunday togs.* **2** [1940s+] (*Aus./N.Z.*) a swimming costume. [TOG n. (1)]

tog-up n. [late 19C] a suit of clothes. [TOG UP v.]

tog up v. (*also* **tog it, tog out**) **1** [early 19C–1960s] to get dressed up, esp. in preparation for a night out, a party or similar event. **2** [mid-19C–1900s] to dress someone up (in their best clothes). [TOG v. (2)]

to heaven adv. [17C; late 19C+] (*US*) strongly, very much.

to hell adv. [late 19C+] a general intensifier.

to hell and go phr. [1930s+] (*W.I., Guyn.*) a general intensifier. [abbr. TO HELL AND GONE phr. (2)]

to hell and gone phr. (*US*) **1** [1910s+] very far away, a very long time. **2** [1920s+] (*also* **to hell and back**) irretrievably, thoroughly.

to hell with —! excl. [early 19C+] a dismissive excl., go away! be done with!

to hell with it! excl. [mid-19C+] a mild dismissive excl., I'm done with it!

to high heaven adv. [1940s+] (*US*) strongly, very much; usu. as STINK TO HIGH HEAVEN v. [ext. of TO HEAVEN adv.]

toilet n. **1** [1930s+] an incompetent, undesirable person. **2** [1950s] (*US*) of a woman, a good figure. **3** [1950s+] (*orig. US*) anywhere considered disgusting, esp. in show business use, a third-rate venue. **4** [1960s+] a position of complete failure. **5** [1970s+] (*US gay*) the anus.

toilet-mouthed adj. [2000s] using obscene language.

toilet roll n. [20C+] unemployment benefit, the dole (cf. BLESS MY SOUL n.). [rhy. sl.]

toilet talk n. [1950s+] obscenities, coarse language.

to it v. [1950s] (*UK prison*) to run off, to abscond, to escape.

toity n. [1980s+] (*N.Z.*) a lavatory.

Tojo n. [1940s–60s] (*Aus./US*) the Japanese nation, esp. its armed forces; thus *Tojoland*, Japan. [proper name *Hideki Tojo* (1884–1948), Japanese general and milit. dictator during WW2]

toke n.[1] **1** [mid-19C] a lump, a chunk, a portion. **2** [mid-19C–1950s] dry bread; esp. in comb. *skilly and toke*, gruel and dry bread, as served in prisons and workhouses. **3** [late 19C–1910s] bread. **4** [late 19C–1910s] food in general. [ety. unknown; ? link to Scot. *token*, a small quantity]

toke n.[2] [1950s+] (*orig. US Black*) **1** a puff or drag of any kind of cigarette (usu. cannabis), or a pipe. **2** a marijuana cigarette; a pipeful of marijuana. [TOKE v.]

toke n.[3] [1970s+] **1** (*US gambling*) a gambling chip, esp. one given to a dealer as a gratuity. **2** (*US*) a tip given to a cab-driver for bringing clients to a gambling establishment, brothel etc. [abbr. SE *token*]

toke v. (*also* **toke up**) **1** [1950s+] (*drugs*) to take a puff on a (usu. cannabis) cigarette or a pipe of crack cocaine. **2** [2000s] (*US*) to drink alcohol. [? ext. of TOKE n.[1] (1), i.e. a portion of the drug]

toke-and-streamy n. [late 19C–1900s] a period of time in prison. [TOKE n.[1] (2) + ?]

token n. **1** [early 16C] the vagina. **2** [17C–early 19C] (signs of) venereal disease. [SE *token*, a sign, in this case of disease]

tokens n. [mid-17C–early 18C] the plague. [SE *token*, a sign, in this case the gangrenous spots on the body that indicated the disease]

toke up v. see TOKE v.

tokis n. see TOCHES n.

toko n.[1] [1920s+] (*Aus.*) praise, esp. if 'laid on with a trowel'. [fig. use of TOCO n.]

toko n.[2] see TOCO n.

tokus see under TOCHES and its combs.

Tokyo rose n. [1940s–50s] the nose. [rhy. sl.; ult. WW2 pro-Japanese propagandist *Tokyo Rose* (Iva Toguri D'Aquino)]

tol n.[1] [late 17C–early 19C] (*UK Und.*) a sword. [abbr. proper name *Toledo*, from where the best swords came; thus note Ned Ward, *Writings* (1704): 'I have a long Sword; you may tak't on my Word, / For the blade is a Toledo Trusty']

tol n.[2] [mid–late 19C] a lot, a share. [backsl.]

tolbobbishly adv. [late 19C] fairly cheerily, fairly healthily, often used as a farewell in letters. [elision of SE *tolerably* + BOBBISHLY adv.]

told out adj. [mid-19C] exhausted, run-down, 'finished'. [SE *tell*, to count, to enumerate; lit. 'counted out']

tole-dish n. see TOLL-DISH n.

tolerable adv. [early 18C–1920s] acceptably, not too badly, moderately; as an intensifier. [SE adv. *tolerably*]

toley *n. see* TOLY n.

tolibon *n.* [mid-19C] (*UK Und.*) the tongue.

toll-dish *n.* (*also* **tole-dish**) [18C–19C] the vagina. [SE *toll dish*, a vessel used to measure the grain ground at a mill; thus added inferences of *grinding* etc]

toller *n.* (*also* **rifler**) [late 16C–early 17C] (*UK Und.*) a horse-stealer. [SE *toller*, tax gatherer]

tol-lol *adj.* (*also* **tollollish**) **1** [mid-19C–1900s] tolerable, bearable. **2** [late 19C+] (*Aus.*) overbearing. **3** [late 19C+] (*Aus.*) foppish. [SE *tolerable*]

tol-lollish *adv.* [mid-19C] tolerably. [TOL-LOL adj. (1)]

toll the bell on *v.* [1900s] to put an end to, to forbid. [the church bell that tolls the death-knell]

tollywhacker *n.* [1920s+] a roll of paper used as a club in a children's play. [juv. *tolly*, a candle (the similarity in shape) + WHACK v.[1] (1)]

toly *n.* (*also* **toley**) [1960s+] a piece of excrement (cf. TANTOBLIN n.). [? Scot. *toalie*, a small round cake]

Tom *see also under* UNCLE TOM.

Tom *n. see* TOM (THUMB) n.

Tom *adv.* [1960s] (*US Black*) in a subservient, White-pleasing manner. [UNCLE TOM n.]

tom *n.*[1] **1** [mid-16C–mid-19C] a generic term for a man, esp. a foolish one. **2** [early 18C] a generic for a waiter, a servant. [abbr. SE *tom fool*]

tom *n.*[2] (*also* **tommy, tom-tom**) [mid–late 19C; 1960s+] the penis (cf. ABRAHAM n.[1]).

tom *n.*[3] [late 19C; 1970s+] (*UK society/US gay*) a lesbian (cf. AMY-JOHN n.). [the male name; euphemized by Ware as 'one who does not care for the society of others than of her own sex']

tom *n.*[4] [20C+] (*Aus.*) a woman; also a generic term for women in general. [abbr. TOM-TART n.]

tom *n.*[5] [20C+] a British soldier. [abbr. TOMMY ATKINS n.]

tom *n.*[6] [1920s+] a *tomato*. [abbr.]

tom *n.*[7] [1940s+] a prostitute, esp. one working in Mayfair (cf. BABY JANE n.). [abbr. TOMMY n.[6]]

tom *n.*[8] [1950s+] jewellery. [abbr. TOMFOOLERY n.]

tom *n.*[9] [1990s+] (*US campus*) a computer. [abbr. *totally obedient moron*]

tom *n.*[10] *see* TOM (AND FUNNY) n.

tom *n.*[11] *see* TOM MIX n.

tom *n.*[12] *see* TOM TIT n.

tom *v.*[1] [19C] of a man, to have sexual intercourse. [SE *tom-cat*]

tom *v.*[2] (*mainly US Black*) [1960s+] **1** (*also* **tom it (up)**) of a Black person, to act in an inferior and obsequious manner to Whites, to act as a Black stereotype; thus *tomming*. **2** to toady. **3** (*also* **tom out**) to betray, to inform. [abbr. UNCLE TOM v.]

tom-a-doodle *n. see* TOM-DOODLE n.

tomahawk *n.* [late 19C] a policeman's truncheon.

tomahawk *v.* (*also* **tommyhawk**) [mid-19C+] (*Aus.*) to shear incompetently.

tomahawker *n.* [20C+] (*Aus.*) a rough, incompetent shearer. [TOMAHAWK v.]

tom-a-lee *n.* [1940s–80s] (*US Black*) a subservient Black person. [a Black subservient enough to have worked for the Confederate general Robert E. Lee (1807–70)]

tom and dick *n.* [2000s] a sick person. [TOM AND DICK adj.]

tom and dick *adj.* [1970s+] sick, ill. [rhy. sl.]

tom (and funny) *n.* [late 19C+] money (cf. BEES (AND HONEY) n.). [rhy. sl.; 20C+ use as *tom* is S.Afr. only, the rhy. sl. origin has presumably been forgotten]

tom and jerry *n.*[1] **1** [19C–1900s] a hard round hat. **2** [early 19C] (*US*) a rowdy celebrant. **3** [mid-19C–1940s] a highly spiced punch. [for ety. *see* TOM AND JERRY (SHOP) n.]

tom and jerry *n.*[2] *see* TOM AND JERRY (SHOP) n.

tom and jerry *adj.* [early–late 19C] merry. [rhy. sl.; note also TOM AND JERRY (SHOP) n.]

tom and jerry *v.* [early–mid-19C] to indulge in drinking, to go on a spree. [for ety. *see* TOM AND JERRY (SHOP) n.]

tom and jerry days *n.* [19C] the Regency, the reign of George IV. [for ety. *see* TOM AND JERRY (SHOP) n.]

tom and jerry gang *n.* [early–mid-19C] a gang of rowdy men, devoted to womanizing, drinking, gaming and other pleasures. [for ety. *see* TOM AND JERRY (SHOP) n.]

tom-and-jerryism *n.* [early–mid-19C] rowdiness. [for ety. *see* TOM AND JERRY (SHOP) n.]

tom and jerry (shop) *n.* [mid–late 19C] a cheap tavern. [*Tom and Jerry*, 2 fictional men-about-town created by Pierce Egan in *Life in London, or Days and Nights of Jerry Hawthorne and his elegant friend Corinthian Tom* (1821), who lent their name to this low inn (note synon. JERRY SHOP n., with no bearing on the book and found a year earlier), and to a drink (which is still being drunk in Damon Runyon's short stories more than a century later); and eventually to the Warner Bros. cartoon cat and mouse and the male leads of the 1970s BBC TV series *The Good Life*]

tom and sam *n.* [20C+] (*Aus.*) jam. [rhy. sl.]

tom-and-try *v.* [1960s–70s] (*US Black*) to advance oneself professionally by conforming to White stereotypes of Black behaviour. [TOM v.[2] (1) + SE *try*]

tomasso di rotto *n.* [late 19C–1900s] (*UK middle class teen*) nonsense, rubbish. [cod Ital. 'translation' of TOMMYROT n.]

tomato *n.* (*US*) **1** [1920s–30s] the buttocks, the posterior. **2** [1920s–30s] a fool (cf. APPLEHEAD n.). **3** [1920s+] an attractive woman; thus *ripe tomato*, a woman who is ready for seduction or even marriage. **4** [1930s] an attractive (effeminate) young man. **5** [1930s] a pimp. **6** [1930s] a prostitute. **7** [1930s+] a woman. **8** [1990s+] the vagina (cf. APPLE n.[6]). [the luscious ripeness of the fruit]

tomato can *n.* **1** [1920s–40s] (*US*) the badge worn by a local or small-town policeman. **2** [1970s] a second-rate boxer. [(1) the cheapness of its manufacture; (2) he is easily crushed]

tomato-can vag *n.* (*also* **can moocher, tomato-can stiff/tramp**) [late 19C–1940s] (*US tramp*) the lowest rank of vagrant.

tomato-picker *n.* [1960s–70s] (*US*) a derog. term for a Puerto Rican or Mexican (cf. BATO n.). [their employment as farm labourers]

tomato purée *n.* [1990s+] a jury. [rhy. sl.]

tomato sauce *n.* [20C+] a horse; thus *tomato sauces*, the horses, i.e. horseraces. [rhy. sl.]

tomb *n.* [20C+] (*US*) the anus. [i.e. it is 'deep and dark']

tombhead *n.* [1960s] (*W.I.*) **1** a large head. **2** a person who has such a head. [the rounded top of the head supposedly resembles a tombstone]

Tom Bray's bilk *n.* [early–mid-19C] (*gambling*) laying out the ace and deuce when playing cribbage. [? anecdotal]

Tom Brown *n.* [early–mid-19C] (*gambling*) the game of 'twelve in hand', generally known as cribbage. [? anecdotal]

Tombs, the *n.* [mid-19C+] (*US*) New York City prison (cf. ABBOTT'S PRIORY n.). [one is 'buried' there]

tombstone *n.*[1] [mid-19C–1900s] a pawn ticket. [the inscription 'in memory of' and the implication that once pawned, items are rarely possessed again]

tombstone *n.*[2] [mid-19C–1930s] a snaggle- or crooked tooth. [resemblance]

tombstone *n.*[3] [1980s+] (*drugs*) a capsule or pill of amphetamine (cf. A n.[2]).

tom-carding *v.* [1990s+] to distribute cards advertising prostitute's services; thus *tom-carder*. [TOM n.[7]]

tomcat *n.*[1] [20C+] a doormat. [rhy. sl.]

tomcat *n.*[2] **1** [1920s+] (*orig. US*) a womanizer, a philanderer. **2** [1940s] (*US*) a promiscuous woman. [reverse anthropomorphism]

tomcat *n.*[3] **1** [1930s] (*US Und.*) a machine gun. **2** [1930s–50s] (*US drugs/prison*) an improvised hypodermic needle made from a sewing-machine needle.

tom cat v. [1920s+] (orig. US) to strut around looking for sexual conquests. [TOMCAT n.² (1)]

Tom Collins n. [1940s] (Aus.) a rumour. [the mythical figure Tom Collins, fl.1890 in southeastern states, to whom rumours and dubious information was attributed; the name was subseq. adopted as a pseudonym by the writer Joseph Furphy (1843–1912), brother to John, the creator of FURPHY n.]

Tom coney n. (also **Tom cony/conney**) [late 17C–early 19C] a fool, the victim of a confidence trick (cf. BEN n.¹). [TOM n.¹ (1) + CONY n.²]

Tom Cruise n. [1990s+] drink, a drink. [rhy. sl. = BOOZE n. (1); ult. US film star Tom Cruise (b.1962)]

Tom, Dick and Harry n. [mid-17C+] any men, young or old, irrespective of given names. [orig. sl. but SE by mid-19C; also in a number of vars. esp. in 18C, e.g. Dick and Harry; Dick, Tom and Harry; Dick, Tom and Joe; Jack, Dick and Harry; Jack, Tom and Harry; Tom and Dick]

tom-doodle n. (also **tom-a-doodle**) [18C] a fool (cf. BEN n.¹). [TOM n.¹ (1) + DOODLE n.¹]

tom doolies n. [1950s+] the testicles (cf. CHEESE AND CRACKERS n.). [rhy. sl. = GOOLIES n. (1); ult. the popular song 'Hang Down Your Head, Tom Dooley' by the Kingston Trio, 1958]

tom double n. [18C–mid-19C] an equivocator, a cheat, a 'double-dealer'. [TOM n.¹ (1) + DOUBLE n.¹]

Tom Drum's entertainment n. see JACK DRUM'S ENTERTAINMENT n.

tom essence n. [late 17C–early 18C] a fop, a dandy. [TOM n.¹ (1) + SE essence, a perfume]

tom-farthing n. [late 17C–19C] a fool (cf. BEN n.¹). [TOM n.¹ (1) + FARTHING n.]

Tom Finney adj. [1990s+] skinny. [rhy. sl.; ult. UK footballer Tom Finney (b.1922)]

tomfoolery n. [20C+] jewellery, often imitation. [rhy. sl.]

tom-fuck v. [1970s+] (US gay) to have anal intercourse (cf. ASK FOR THE RING v.).

tom, harry and dick adj. [20C+] sick. [rhy. sl.]

tom it (up) v. see TOM v.².

tom long n. [early 17C–early 19C] a bore, a teller of long and tedious stories with neither end nor point. [the pvb figure, John Long (16C) or Tom Long (17C), 'the carrier who will never do his errand']

tommie n. see TOMMY ATKINS n.

tom (mix) n. 1 [1930s+] the number 6. 2 [1940s+] a problem, a predicament. 3 [1970s+] an injection of heroin (cf. HAMMER (AND TACK) n.). [rhy. sl.; (2) = FIX n.¹; (3) = FIX n.⁴ (1); ult. US film cowboy Tom Mix (1880–1940)]

tom molly n. see MOLLY n.¹ (1).

Tommy n. [late 19C–1910s] used as a term of address to a young boy whose real name is unknown.

tommy n.¹ 1 [late 18C–1930s] (a loaf of) bread; thus BROWN TOMMY n. 2 [mid-19C–1940s] solid food in general. 3 [late 19C+] (Aus.) bread baked with sugar and currants. [orig. milit. jargon tommy, the bread supplied as part of rations. This in turn had evolved from orig. 18C brown george to brown tommy to tommy brown and thence to its abbr. Note that St Thomas' Day, on which bread was distributed by charities, preceded the milit. coinage]

tommy n.² [mid-19C] a worn-out shirt. [Gk tomé, a section, orig. Trinity College, Dublin]

tommy n.³ [late 19C] 1 a tomato. 2 (US) tomato soup. [abbr.]

tommy n.⁴ [late 19C–1930s] (Aus./N.Z.) an axe. [SE tomahawk]

tommy n.⁵ [late 19C+] menstruation. [euph.]

tommy n.⁶ [late 19C+] (US) a prostitute, or promiscuous young woman (cf. BABY JANE n.). [? TOM-TART n.]

tommy n.⁷ [1910s–20s] a pimp. [? generic use of proper name]

tommy n.⁸ [1920s+] (Aus./N.Z.) 1 a bookmaker. 2 a bookmaker's ledger. [ety. unknown; unless a derog. ref. to TOMMY n.⁷; DNZE suggests rhy. sl. tommy rook = SE book]

tommy n.⁹ [1990s+] a male homosexual.

tommy n.¹⁰ see TOM n.².

tommy n.¹¹ see TOMMY ATKINS n.

tommy n.¹² see TOMMY GUN n.

tommy n.¹³ see TOMMYROT n.

tommy v.¹ [20C+] (Aus.) to leave. [ety. unknown]

tommy v.² see TOMMY TRIPE v.

tommy and exes n. [late 19C–1900s] bread, beer and tobacco. [TOMMY n.¹ (1) + abbr. SE extras]

Tommy Atkins n. (also **thomas, Thomas Atkins, tom, tommie, tommy**) 1 [late 19C+] a generic for a typical private soldier in the British army. 2 [1980s] an Englishman. ['arising out of the casual use of this name in the specimen forms given in the official regulations from 1815 onward [...] In some of the specimen forms other names are used; but "Thomas Atkins" being that used in all the forms for privates in the Cavalry or Infantry, is by far the most frequent, and thus became the most familiar; thus 1815 (Aug. 31) War Office, Collection of Orders, Regulations etc 75 (Form of a Soldier's Book in the Cavalry when filled up). Description, Service, &c. of Thomas Atkins, Private, No. 6 Troop, 6th Regt. of Dragoons. Where Born [...] Parish of Odiham, Hants [...] Bounty, £ Received, Thomas Atkins, his x mark' (OED); thus WW1 milit. Thomasina Atkins, a WAAC]

tommy buster n. [1940s] (US Und.) a rapist; one who physically abuses women. [TOMMY n.⁶ + BUST v.¹ (7)]

tommy dodd n.¹ [mid-late 19C] 1 in coin-tossing, the 'odd man' who goes out. 2 the game of coin-tossing itself. 3 the winner or loser in coin-tossing, the choice for the name allotted by previous agreement. [rhy. sl. = SE odd]

tommy dodd n.² 1 [late 19C] a sodomite. 2 [late 19C–1950s] God. 3 [1920s+] (US) a gun. [rhy. sl.; (1) = SOD n.¹ (2); (3) = ROD n.¹ (2)]

tommy dodd n.³ 1 [late 19C–1910s] (Aus.) a style of hat. 2 [late 19C+] (Aus./N.Z.) a small glass of beer. 3 [1910s] a walking stick. [? anecdotal]

Tommy Farr n. [20C+] a bar. [rhy. sl.; ult. UK boxer Tommy Farr (1913–86)]

tommy gee n. [1930s] (US Und./prison) a machine-gunner.

tommy geebung n. see GEEBUNG n. (1).

Tommy get out and let your father in n. see LET YOUR FATHER IN n.

tommy gun n. (also **tommy**) [1920s+] (orig. US Und.) a sub-machine gun. [one of the earliest brands, the .45 calibre Thomson]

tommy-gun v. [1960s] to blast with a sub-machine gun. [TOMMY GUN n.]

tommy-gunner n. [1940s+] (orig. US Und.) someone bearing a sub-machine gun. [TOMMY GUN n.]

tommy guns n. [1990s+] diarrhoea (cf. BANANA (SPLITS) n.). [rhy. sl. = RUNS, THE n.; ult. TOMMY GUN n.]

tommyhawk v. see TOMAHAWK v.

tommy man n. [1920s–30s] (US Und.) an armed gangster. [TOMMY GUN n. + SE man]

tommy nonsense n. see TOMMYROT n.

tommy o'rann n. [mid-19C+] food. [rhy. sl. = SCRAN n. (2)]

tommy rabbit n. [late 19C–1900s] a pomegranate. [rhy. sl., if weak]

tommy rocks n. see JOE ROCKS n.

tommy roller n. (also **charley roller**) [late 19C+] a collar. [rhy. sl.]

tommy rollocks n. (also **jimmy rollocks, rollocks**) [20C+] the testicles (cf. CHEESE AND CRACKERS n.). [rhy. sl. = BALLOCKS n.¹ (1)]

tommyrot n. (also **tommy, tommy nonsense, tommy tripe**) [late 19C+] absolute nonsense. [? the red coat of a TOMMY ATKINS n. (1), thus euph. for BLOODY adj.¹ (1)]

tommyrot v. [late 19C+] 1 to fool around, to mess about. 2 to hoax, to deceive, to humbug; thus tommy rotter, a confidence trickster. [TOMMYROT n.]

Tommy Steeles *n.* [20C+] eels. [rhy. sl.; ult. UK pop star *Tommy Steele* (b.1936)]

tommy talker *n.* [1930s+] **1** a kazoo. **2** a ventriloquist's dummy with a pull string. [generic/assonant use of proper name *tommy* + its sound]

tommy tana *n.* (*also* **tanna, tommy tanna, tommy tanner**) [1900s–10s] (*Aus.*) a nickname for a Pacific Islander imported as a labourer. [generic use of proper name *Tommy* + *Tanna*, an island near Vanuatu (the Near Hebrides)]

tommy tit *n.* [18C–early 19C] a smart young fellow. [generic/assonant use of proper name *tommy* + SE *tit*, a person]

Tommy Trinder *n.* [1990s+] a window. [rhy. sl.; Cockney pron. 'winder'; ult. UK comedian *Tommy Trinder* (1909–89)]

tommy tripe *n.*[1] [20C+] a (tobacco) pipe. [rhy. sl.]

tommy tripe *n.*[2] *see* TOMMYROT n.

tommy tripe *v.* (*also* **tommy**) [mid-19C–1900s] to examine, to survey, to keep a watch. [rhy. sl. = PIPE v.[3] (2)]

tommy tucker *n.* **1** [1930s+] (*also* **tom tucker**) supper. **2** [1990s+] a person. **3** [1990s+] (*UK Und.*) a gullible individual. [rhy. sl. + ref. to the nursery rhyme; (2) = FUCKER n. (6); (3) = SUCKER n.[3] (1)]

tommy tupper *n.* [20C+] supper. [rhy. sl.]

tom noddy *n.* [20C+] (*US*) a body, i.e. a corpse. [rhy. sl.]

Tom of Bedlam *n.* [17C–19C] a genuine (rather than criminal and thus fake) beggar. [proper name *Bedlam*, by the 16C a generic term for lunatic asylums, but orig. applied spec. to the Hospital of St Mary of Bethlehem in London. A general hospital by 1330, in 1402 it became a hospital for the insane]

tomorrow *v.* [20C+] to borrow; usu. in abbr. phr. *on the tommy*, looking for a loan. [rhy. sl.]

tom out *v. see* TOM v.[2] (3).

tom pat *n.*[1] [late 17C–18C] a parson. [abbr. PATRICO n. (1)]

tom pat *n.*[2] [19C] a shoe. [Rom. *tom pat*, a foot]

tom patrol *n.* (*also* **toms patrol, tom squad**) [1940s+] (*UK Und./police*) the vice squad, esp. as regards prostitution. [TOM n.[7] + SE *patrol/squad*]

tom pepper *n.* [early 19C+] a liar. [orig. naut., a mythical sailor ejected from Hell for lying; note WW1 RN *tom pepper*, a pvb story-teller]

tom rig *n.* [late 17C–early 19C] a promiscuous young woman; also a tomboy. [TOM n.[1] (1) + SE *rig*, a wanton woman]

tom right *n.* [mid-19C] the night. [rhy. sl.]

toms *n. see* TOM TITS n.

Tom Sawyer *n.* [late 19C+] a lawyer. [rhy. sl.; ult. *Tom Sawyer*, novel (1876) by US writer Mark Twain (Samuel Langhorne Clemens, 1835–1910)]

tom slick *n.* [1960s+] (*US Black*) a Black police informer. [TOM n.[2] + SLICK n.[1] (1), i.e. they charm their friends and inform on them to the police]

toms patrol/tom squad *n. see* TOM PATROL n.

tom-tart *n.* [late 19C–1950s] (*Aus.*) a woman. [? rhy. sl. = SE *sweetheart*]

tom tell-troth *n.* [mid-17C–19C] an honest man. [ext. of 14C SE *tom true-tongue*]

Tom (Thumb) *n.* **1** [late 19C+] (*orig. Aus.*) rum. **2** [20C+] the buttocks (cf. ALA n.). **3** [1940s+] (*Aus.*) inside information. [rhy. sl.; (2) = BUM n.[1] (1); (3) = DRUM n.[7]; ult. the famous dwarf 'General' Tom Thumb, real name Charles Sherwood Stratton (1838–83), who grew to a height of 25 inches and was exhibited around the US and Europe as a curiosity]

tom tiddler's ground *n.* **1** [mid-19C–1940s] anywhere that money or other items can be obtained easily. **2** [late 19C] a no-man's-land, a debatable territory. [the children's game *Tom Tiddler's ground*, in which one player is 'Tom', who stands behind a 'land' which marks the 'ground'. The other players dash forward over the ground, singing 'We're on Tom Tiddler's ground, picking up gold and silver', and the first or sometimes last child caught

becomes Tom; Brewer, *Dict. of Phrase and Fable* (1894) suggests that *Tiddler* is an elision of *t'idler*]

tom tiler *n.* (*also* **tom tyler**) [late 16C–19C] **1** an ordinary man, 'Mr Average'. **2** a henpecked husband. [TOM n.[1] (1) + SE *tiler*, used as generic for any ordinary job or just assonance]

tom tit *n.* (*also* **tom**) [20C+] **1** an act of defecation (cf. ANDY CAPP n.). **2** a piece of excrement (cf. ALI OOP n.). **3** a contemptible person. [rhy. sl. = SHIT n.[1]/SHIT n.[2] (1)]

tomtit *v.* [late 19C+] to defecate (cf. BOB AND HIT v.). [rhy. sl. = SHIT v.[1] (1)]

tom tits *n.* (*also* **toms**) [1940s+] (*Aus.*) diarrhoea (cf. BANANA (SPLITS) n.). [rhy. sl. = SHITS, THE n. (1)]

tom-tom *n. see* TOM n.[2].

tom topper *n.* (*also* **tom tug**) [late 18C–19C] a ferryman, a waterman. [popular song]

tom tripe *n.* [mid-19C] a pipe. [rhy. sl.]

tom tucker *n. see* TOMMY TUCKER n.

tom tug *n.*[1] **1** [late 19C] a bedbug. **2** [late 19C–1940s] a fool, a victim (cf. BEECHAM'S PILL n.). [rhy. sl.; (2) = MUG n.[2] (1)]

tom tug *n.*[2] *see* TOM TOPPER n.

tom turdman *n.* [late 17C–early 19C] a nightsoil cleaner; thus *tom turdman's fields, tom turdman's hole*, the dump where the nightsoil is deposited. [TOM n.[1] (1) + TURD n. (1)]

tom tyler *n. see* TOM TILER n.

ton *n.*[1] **1** [late 18C+] a very large (unspecified) amount; thus TONS n. **2** [1940s+] £100; thus HALF-A-TON n. **3** [1950s+] 100mph. **4** [1960s+] any unit of 100, e.g. 100 years, 100 runs (in cricket). [SE *ton*, 100 cubic feet]

ton *n.*[2] [1960s] *tonic* water. [abbr.]

tondalayo *n.* [1950s–70s] (*camp gay*) an ostentatious, flagrant homosexual. [proper name of any 'African queen'/QUEEN n.[2] (1)]

toney *adj. see* TONY adj.

tongue *n.* [1930s+] (*US Und.*) a public defender, a lawyer. [metonymy]

tongue *v.*[1] **1** [mid-19C] to talk down. **2** [20C+] (*Ulster*) to scold.

tongue *v.*[2] **1** [late 19C] to fellate (cf. COCKSUCK n.). **2** [late 19C+] (*also* **tongue-fuck**) to perform cunnilingus (cf. CUNT-LICK v.). **3** [late 19C+] to kiss with tongues in each other's mouth.

tongue bath *n.* [1930s+] licking and sucking the partner's body, including the genitals and sometimes the anus. [TONGUE v.[2]]

tongued *adj.* [mid-19C] talkative. [TONGUE v.[1]]

tongue-diving *n.* [1970s] (*US*) kissing.

tongue-fuck *v. see* TONGUE v.[2] (2).

tongue job *n.* [1960s+] (*orig. US*) oral sex, whether fellatio or cunnilingus (cf. COCKSUCK n.; CUNT-LICK v.). [SE *tongue* + JOB n.[4]]

tongue lash *v.* [1930s+] (*US gay*) to perform fellatio or anilingus (cf. AUSTRALIAN n.; COCKSUCK n.).

tongue pad *n.* **1** [late 17C–early 19C] a talkative person, esp. someone who persuades one to act foolishly or against one's will. **2** [early 18C] a confidence trickster. [SE *tongue* + PAD n.[1], on model of FOOTPAD n.]

tongue pad *v.* [late 17C–early 19C] **1** to scold, to tell off, to reprimand. **2** to persuade, to talk someone into something. [TONGUE PAD n.]

tongue party *n.* [1940s] (*US*) mutual oral-genital intercourse.

tongue pie *n.* **1** [mid-19C–1920s] a scolding, a telling off. **2** [1980s+] cunnilingus (cf. CUNT-LICK v.).

tongue-plating *n. see* PLATING n.

tongue sandwich *n.* **1** [1970s+] (*US gay*) anilingus (cf. AUSTRALIAN n.). **2** [1980s+] a deep kiss.

tongue sushi *n.* [1980s+] (*US campus*) deep kissing with tongues. [SE *tongue* + *sushi*, a form of Japanese snack, usu. based on rice and raw fish]

tongue tally *n.* [1950s] (*W.I.*) a gossip. [SE *tongue* + *tally*, to count up, to reckon; ? the image of someone tallying up the performances of their friends and acquaintances]

tongue-wang v. [1900s] (Aus.) to harangue, to berate. [? SE wag or WANGLE v.]

tongue-wrestle v. [1980s+] to kiss deeply, using tongues.

tonguing for phr. [1990s+] (Aus.) desperate for, usu. alcohol.

tonic n.[1] (also **thonic**) [early–late 19C] a halfpenny. [ety. unknown; ? link to TANNER n.]

tonic n.[2] [late 19C+] alcohol; thus (Aus.) tonicked, drunk.

tonk n.[1] [1930s+] (US/N.Z.) a seedy, 'lowlife' bar. [abbr. HONKYTONK n.[1] (1)]

tonk n.[2] [1940s+] (Aus.) 1 a male homosexual, or an effeminate heterosexual man. 2 a fool. 3 someone whose speech appears to set them above their peers. [ety. unknown; ? link to TONKY adj.]

tonk adj. [2000s] (UK teen) very large.

tonk v. [1910s+] 1 to hit. 2 to have sexual intercourse (cf. BANG v.[1]). 3 to punish. 4 to masturbate (cf. BOFF v.). 5 to run. [echoic]

tonkie n. [1980s] a condom. [ety. unknown]

tonky adj. [1930s+] (N.Z.) smart, fashionable. [? TONY adj. + SWANKY adj. (1) or Fr. (bon) ton]

ton o' my rocks n. [20C+] (Aus.) socks. [rhy. sl.]

tons n. [late 19C+] a very large amount, a great deal. [TON n.[1] (1)]

tons adv. [20C+] (US campus) very, extremely, really, e.g. I feel tons better now. [TONS n.]

tonsil hockey n. [1980s+] kissing.

tonsil polish n. (also **tonsil lubricator**, **...paint**, **...varnish**) [20C+] alcohol; occas. tea.

tonsil swab v. see SWAB (ONE'S) TONSILS v.

tonsil-tickler n. [1930s] (US) a penis, esp. a large one (cf. ARSE-OPENER n.).

tonsil varnish n. see TONSIL POLISH n.

tons of fun n. [1980s+] (US) a cynical term of address. [TONS n. + SE fun]

Tonto n. [1950s+] a Native American who is considered insufficiently nationalistic and overly subservient to the White man by other Native Americans; occas. of Blacks. [the character Tonto, the 'Red Indian' sidekick, played by Jay Silverheels (1919–80), who rode with TV's Lone Ranger (1952–6)]

tonto adj. [1980s+] crazy. [Sp. tonto, stupid]

Tonto no go to town phr. [1990s+] (US Black teen) it wouldn't be prudent at this juncture. [for ety. see TONTO n., the line was a catchphrase of the TV show]

ton-up boy n. [1960s+] a member of a motorcycle gang. [TON n.[1] (3)]

tony n. [early 17C–mid-19C; 1960s] a fool. [abbr. of proper name; coined in Middleton's play The Changeling (1623)]

tony adj. (also **toney**) [late 18C+] (orig. US) classy, sophisticated, chic. [SE tone, style]

Tony Benn n. [1990s+] £10 (cf. AYRTON (SENNA) n.). [rhy. sl.; ult. UK politician Tony Benn (b.1925)]

Tony Blair n. [1990s+] 1 hair. 2 a nightmare. [rhy. sl.; ult. Tony Blair (b.1953), UK prime minister (1997+)]

tonygle v. see NIGGLE v. ety.

Tony Hatch n. [1990s+] 1 the vagina (cf. ALL QUIET n.). 2 a (young) girl. 3 a match. [rhy. sl.; (1) = SNATCH n.[1] (2); (2) = SNATCH n.[1] (3); ult. UK pop composer Tony Hatch (b.1939)]

Tony's den n. see WILSON'S DEN n.

too-a-roo phr. see TOOROO phr.

too bloody Irish (stew)! excl. [20C+] too true! [rhy. sl.]

toodle n. [early 19C] a walk. [TOODLE v.]

toodle v. [early 19C+] to move, to go, to wander. [TODDLE v.]

toodle-oo phr. (also **tootle-oo**) [20C+] goodbye, occas. hello. [? SE toot, the tooting of a horn, in this case as a coach moves off; or ? Fr. à tout à l'heure, goodbye]

toodle-pip phr. (also **tootle-pip**) [1970s+] a nonsense word used to say goodbye. [var. on TOODLE-OO phr.]

toodley-oodley adj. [mid-late 19C] satisfactory, useful, a general term of approval. [nonsense word]

too drunk to see through a ladder phr. see CAN'T SEE THROUGH A LADDER phr. (1).

toofah/toofer n. see TWOFER n. (2).

tooies n. (also **tooeys, tooles, toolies, tuies**) [1960s+] (drugs) barbiturates, esp. Tuinal (cf. BARBIT n.). [abbr.]

took bad, be v. see TAKEN BAD, BE v.

tookus/tooky n. see TOCHES n.

tool n.[1] 1 [mid-16C+] the penis. 2 [late 17C] the vagina. 3 [late 17C+] a stupid, useless, socially inept person. [(1) (meaning any bodily organ, but primarily the penis) was SE mid-16C–mid-19C; (3) f. (1) on model of PRICK n.]

tool n.[2] 1 [late 17C–mid-19C] an unskilful workman; usu. as dull tool, poor tool. 2 [19C] a whip. 3 [mid-19C] (UK Und.) a small boy who is put through a window that is too small for the adult members of the gang to enter and who then opens the door to admit them. 4 [mid-19C–1960s] (UK/US Und.) that member of the pickpocket team who does the actual stealing; the WIRE n.[3]. 5 [mid-19C+] a weapon, usu. a gun, knife or razor. 6 [late 19C+] a burglar's implement, spec. a jemmy. 7 [1960s+] (US campus) (also **power tool**) a very hard worker. 8 [1990s+] (US drugs) a hypodermic syringe. [SE tool, an instrument of manual operation; ult. ON tol, to prepare or make]

tool n.[3] [late 19C] a drive (in a horse-drawn vehicle). [TOOL v.[1] (1)]

tool n.[4] [1990s+] (US) a sexually promiscuous woman. [abbr. GARDEN TOOL n.]

tool v.[1] 1 [early 19C–1930s] to drive a mail coach or any other horse-drawn vehicle. 2 [mid-19C+] to be driven in a horse-drawn vehicle; thus to drive or travel in a car or any other vehicle; usu. as TOOL ALONG v. 3 [mid-19C+] to proceed in a leisurely, aimless way; usu. as TOOL ALONG v. 4 [late 19C+] to leave at speed; usu. as TOOL ALONG v. [SE tool, i.e. the harness etc]

tool v.[2] [mid-19C] to pick pockets. [TOOL n.[2] (4)]

tool v.[3] 1 [mid–late 19C] to murder, usu. with a knife. 2 [1940s+] to stab; to slash with a razor. [coined by Thomas De Quincey (1785–1859), punning on SE tool, a dagger + the decoration or 'tooling' of a blade; (2) underpinned by TOOL n.[2] (5)]

tool v.[4] (also **power tool**) [1960s+] (US campus) to study. [TOOL n.[2] (7) (+ SE power)]

tool along v. (also **tool around**) [mid-19C+] 1 to drive around, esp. to drive fast. 2 to walk or travel leisurely. 3 to walk off fast. [ext. of TOOL v.[1]]

tool (around) v.[1] [1920s+] to behave in an aimless, irresponsible manner, to waste time. [TOOL n.[1] (3)]

tool (around) v.[2] [1960s+] (US campus) to mistreat someone. [TOOL n.[1] (3)]

toolbox n.[1] [19C+] the vagina (cf. BAG n.[1]). [TOOL n.[1] (1) + SE box]

toolbox n.[2] (also **toolshed**) [1990s+] a group of idiots, or just a very extreme idiot. [TOOL n.[1] (3)]

tool chest n. [19C] the vagina (cf. BAG n.[1]). [TOOL n.[1] (1) + SE chest]

tooled (up) adj. 1 [1940s+] carrying a weapon. 2 [1970s+] carrying house-breaking implements. 3 [1990s+] in fig. use, kitted out with something. [TOOL UP v.[2]]

tooler n. [mid-19C] a pickpocket. [TOOL v.[2]]

Tooleries n. [late 19C–1900s] Toole's Theatre, sited in William IV Street, London WC2.

tooles n. see TOOIES n.

Tooley Street tailor n. [late 19C–1900s] a braggart, a boaster. [the 3 tailors of Tooley St (SE1) who supposedly put together a petition to Parliament. It carried none but their own signatures but was headed grandiosely, 'We the people of England...']

tooleywag n. see TALLYWAG n.

toolhead n. [1970s+] (US campus) a fool, an idiot. [TOOL n.[1] (3) + -HEAD sfx (1)]

tool house n. [1960s] (Irish) a urinal. [TOOL n.¹ (1) + SE house]

toolie n. [1970s+] (US campus) an engineering student. [SE tool]

toolies n. see TOOIES n.

tool in v. [1960s+] (US campus) to arrive, usu. at speed. [TOOL v.¹ (4)]

tooling n. [mid-19C–1910s] skilful pickpocketing. [TOOL v.²]

toolman n. **1** [1940s+] a lock-picker, one who deals with alarms etc. **2** [1940s+] (US) a safe-breaker. **3** [2000s] a gun-carrying robber. [TOOL n.² (6)/TOOL n.² (5) + SE man]

tool off v. (also **tool out**) [late 19C–1960s] to leave, to go away. [TOOL v.¹ (4)]

tools n.¹ **1** [early 19C+] (UK Und.) any implements used in the commission of crime, e.g. house-breaking implements, guns, pistols or other weapons. **2** [mid-19C–1900s] the human hands. **3** [late 19C+] (US) eating utensils.

tools n.² [1960s+] (drugs) equipment used for injecting drugs.

toolshed n. see TOOLBOX n.².

tool up v.¹ [1920s+] of a man, to prepare oneself for sexual intercourse. [pun on SE tool up/TOOL n.¹ (1) + SE up, i.e. an erection]

tool up v.² **1** [1940s+] to arm oneself. **2** [1970s+] to carry house-breaking implements. [TOOL n.² (5)/TOOL n.² (6)]

too many adj. [mid-19C–1920s] (US) overwhelming.

too mean to part with one's shit phr. [late 19C+] very mean indeed.

too much adj. [1930s+] (orig. US) **1** wonderful, excellent, very best; sometimes ext. as too fucking much. **2** unpleasant, disgusting or overwhelming. **3** extreme, with an inference of absurd, ludicrous. [abbr. SE too much to take]

too much! excl. [1930s+] **1** an excl. of surprise or shock. **2** an excl. of pleasure, satisfaction, excitement. [TOO MUCH adj.]

too much of the monkey phr. [late 19C] (Aus.) extreme, 'asking too much'.

toon n. [1980s+] an animated cartoon, and the animations that 'populate' it. [abbr. SE cartoon, coined for the film Who Killed Roger Rabbit? (1987), which mixed animation and live action]

to one's own cheek phr. [early 19C–1900s] to oneself, for one's own private use. [metonymic use of SE cheek, the side of the face]

too numerous to mention phr. [late 19C] extremely and angrily drunk. [euph.]

tooraladi phr. see TOOROO phr.

tooraloorals n. [late 19C–1900s] (orig. theatre) a woman's breasts, esp. as exposed by a notably decolleté dress. [SE tooraalooralay, a popular, often ribald, song chorus]

too right! excl. [1910s+] (orig. Aus.) a general excl. of agreement.

tooroo phr. (also **too-a-roo**, **tooraladi**) [1910s+] (Aus.) goodbye. [var. on TOODLE-OO phr.]

toosh n. [1990s+] a girl, a woman. [TOCHES n. (1)]

tooshie n. [1930s+] (US) the buttocks. [TOCHES n.]

toot n.¹ **1** [late 18C] (also **tout**) a drinking match. **2** [late 18C+] (also **tout**) a drunken binge or spree; usu. in phr. on a/the toot; also in fig. use. **3** [late 18C+] a tea party. **4** [late 18C+] (also **tout**) a swallow of a drink, a drink. **5** [1970s+] cocaine (cf. BLOW n.⁶). **6** [1970s+] a device for inhaling cocaine. **7** [1970s+] a measure of a narcotic, usu. cocaine, enough for a single inhalation; thus an inhalation. [Scot. tout, to drink copiously, to take a large draught, thus ext. to drug use]

toot n.² [late 19C–1960s] money (cf. BEES (AND HONEY) n.). [? rhy. sl. with LOOT n.¹]

toot n.³ [1960s+] **1** excrement. **2** (Aus.) a lavatory. [? dial. tut, a small seat or TOOT v.²]

toot n.⁴ [1970s+] (S.Afr.) the whole thing, the lot. [Ital. tutti, Fr. tout, everything, all]

toot adj. [1910s] insignificant, no good.

toot v.¹ [1910s–50s] (Aus./US) to hurry along. [Fr. tout de suite, immediately]

toot v.² [1940s+] to break wind. [the noise]

toot v.³ see TOOT (UP) v.

tooted adj. [1960s] (US campus) drunk (cf. ALED UP adj.). [TOOT n.¹ (4)]

tooter n. [1910s] (US) the nose. [the noise it makes when blown]

toothache n. [19C] an erection. [euph.]

tooth booth n. [1940s] (US Black) a dentist's surgery.

tooth box n. [1900s] (Aus.) the mouth.

tooth carpenter n. [mid-19C–1940s] (US) a dentist.

toothful n. [early 19C–1930s] a measure of alcohol, a dram; thus do a toothful, to have a drink; occas. in fig. use. [Scot. toothful, to tipple]

tooth-harp n. [1960s] (Aus.) a mouth organ. [var. on MOUTH HARP n.]

toothless gibbon n. [1990s+] the vagina.

toothman n. [1950s–60s] (Aus.) a hearty eater.

tooth music n. [late 18C–early 19C] chewing.

toothpick n.¹ **1** [19C] a heavy club, a shillelagh, a watchman's stick. **2** [mid-19C+] (orig. US) a pocketknife. **3** [late 19C–1900s] a narrow, pointed boat. **4** [late 19C–1910s] (US) a long, narrow shoe. **5** [1900s] (UK Und.) a house-breaker's short crowbar. **6** [1930s–60s] a derog. term for something small and insignificant. **7** [1960s+] (US Black) a thin marijuana cigarette (cf. BONE n.¹¹). [note WW1 milit. toothpick, a bayonet; an entrenching tool]

toothpick n.² [late 19C–1940s] (US) a native of Arkansas. [generic use of ARKANSAS TOOTHPICK n.]

toothpicker n. [late 19C] a fashionable man about town and/or 'stage-door johnnie', with a uniform of crutch-handled walking-stick and a toothpick. [CRUTCH AND TOOTHPICK BRIGADE n.]

toothy adj. [2000s] (US) smiling.

toothy-pegs n. (also **tooty**) [early 19C+] (UK/Aus. juv.) the teeth. [SE tooth]

tootie n.¹ see PATOOTIE n. (3).

tootie n.² see TOOTSIE n.

tooti-frooti n. (also **tootie fruitie**) [1960s+] (US Black) a homosexual man. [play on FRUIT n.² (2) + lit. Ital. tutti-frutti, 'all the fruits', a type of ice-cream filled with chopped preserved fruits, nuts etc]

tooting adj. [1910s+] (orig. US/US Black) **1** a general intensifier; usu. in combs., e.g. darn/durn tooting, plumb tooting, too damn tooting. **2** correct. [SE toot, to make a noise (of e.g. a siren or horn). The image is the intensity of one's statement having a 'noisy' impact]

Tooting (Bec) n. [20C+] **1** a light kiss. **2** food. [rhy. sl; (1) = SE peck; (2) = PECK n.¹ (1); ult. Tooting Bec, south London]

tooting-ken n. (also **touting-ken**) [late 17C–early 19C] (UK Und.) a tavern, an alehouse. [Scot. tout, the act of drinking a large draught, a large draught of liquor + KEN n.¹ (1)]

tooting stomps n. [1940s] (US Black) a fashionable style of shoe. [SE toot + STOMP n.¹ (2)]

too tired to pull a greased stick out of a dog's arse phr. [1980s+] (Aus.) exhausted.

tootle n. [1990s+] the penis; thus in fig. use, a male homosexual. [SE tootle, to blow a wind instrument (thus punning on BLOW v.² (3))]

tootle v. [1990s+] to fellate, usu. in a homosexual context. [TOOTLE n.]

tootle v. (also **tootle along**, **...around**, **...off**) [late 19C+] to walk, to wander casually or aimlessly. [TODDLE v.]

tootledum-pattick n. [19C] a fool. [Cornish dial.]

tootle merchant n. [1990s+] a male homosexual (cf. BONE-EATER n.). [TOOTLE n. + MERCHANT n.]

tootle-oo phr. see TOODLE-OO phr.

tootling stick n. [1990s+] the penis (cf. BAT n.⁷). [SE tootle + STICK n.¹ (1)/play on FLUTE n.² (1)]

tootmobile n. [1970s] (US Black) a car. [the 'toot-toot' of its horn + -MOBILE sfx]

toot one's horn *v. see* BLOW ONE'S HORN *v.*[2] (2).

too-too *adj.* (*also* **tutu**) [late 19C+] a general term of approval, usu. regarded as somewhat affected. [redup. of SE *too*, which emphasizes the adj.]

toots *n.* **1** [1910s+] a general form of address, usu. to a woman. **2** [1930s–40s] a girl or girlfriend. [abbr. TOOTSIE n. (2)]

tootsie *n.* (*also* **tootie, tootsey-wootsey, tootsie-wootsie, tootsy-wootsy**) **1** [mid-19C+] (*orig. US*) a playful or affectionate name for a foot, usu. a child's foot; thus also toes; mostly in pl. **2** [late 19C+] (*orig. US*) an affectionate name, usu. for a woman or girl, occas. a male lover. **3** [1910s] (*orig. US*) a baby. **4** [1960s+] (*Aus.*) a lesbian. [development of baby-talk that created (1)]

Tootsie Roll *n.*[1] **1** [1920s] (*US*) the penis. **2** [1970s+] (*US Black*) an attractive woman. [brandname *Tootsie Roll*, a small chocolate cake + ref. to JELLY ROLL n.[1]]

Tootsie Roll *n.*[2] (*drugs*) **1** [1960s+] a marijuana cigarette (cf. BONE n.[11]). **2** [1970s+] Mexican heroin (cf. BLACK n.[3]). **3** [1970s+] methadone. [brandname *Tootsie Roll*, a small chocolate cake. (1) plays on SE *roll*; (2) on the consistency and colour of Mexican heroin and CHOCOLATE (STUFF) n.; (3) the image is of 'fake' heroin of no more worth to an addict than a *Tootsie Roll*]

Tootsie Roll *n.*[3] [1990s+] (*US Black teen*) a dance in which the knees are moved inwards and outwards, supposedly showing off one's buttocks. [? TOCHES n. + SE *roll*; ult. *Tootsie Roll*, the small chocolate cake]

tootsie-wootsie/tootsy-wootsy *n. see* TOOTSIE n.

toot the ringer *v.* (*also* **toot the ding-dong**) [late 19C–1940s] (*US tramp*) to ring a doorbell.

toot (up) *v.* **1** [1950s–60s] to smoke marijuana. **2** [1970s+] (*orig. US drugs*) to inhale cocaine. [TOOT n.[1] (7)]

tooty *n. see* TOOTHY-PEGS n.

tooty fruity *adj.* [1970s] (*US Black*) effeminate, poss. homosexual. [TOOTI-FROOTI n.]

too utterly too *adj.* [late 19C] a general term of approval, usu. regarded as somewhat affected. [TOO-TOO adj.]

top *n.*[1] [1920s+] (*US Black*) the head; thus phr. *not much on top*, lacking intelligence.

top *n.*[2] [1950s+] (*US Und.*) a maximum prison sentence.

top *n.*[3] [1970s+] in a sado-masochistic relationship, the dominant partner. [as opposed to a BOTTOM n.[4]; note earlier TOP MAN n. (3)]

top *n.*[4] *see* TOP END n. (2).

top *adj.* **1** [1920s+] excellent, first-rate. **2** [1960s] extreme.

top *v.*[1] **1** [17C; 1960s] to have sexual intercourse with. **2** [mid-17C] to oppose. **3** [late 17C–mid-18C] to impose upon, to intrude. **4** [late 17C–early 19C] to insult. [i.e. one places oneself 'on top' of the other person]

top *v.*[2] [mid-17C–early 19C] (*UK Und.*) to cheat, esp. at cards; thus [late 19C] *top the deck*, to use a mechanical device hidden beneath one's cuff to hold a card until it is required, when it is slipped surreptitiously onto the deck. [SE *top*, the required card is made to appear at the top of the deck]

top *v.*[3] **1** [mid-17C+] to execute by hanging; thus as excl. *top me!* i.e. HANG ME! excl. **2** [late 19C+] to kill, to murder.

top a clout *v.* [early 19C] (*UK Und.*) to position a handkerchief in a victim's pocket in readiness for removing it at an apposite moment. [SE *top* + CLOUT n.[1] (1)]

top ballocks *n.* (*also* **top bollocks/buttocks**) **1** [late 19C+] a woman's breasts. **2** the best or most popular of a kind. [SE *top* + BALLOCKS n.[1] (1)/SE *buttocks*; (2) TOP adj. (1) + var. on DOG'S BALLOCKS n. (2)]

top banana *n.* [1950s+] (*orig. US*) the chief, the boss, the president. [show business *top banana*, the leading comic in a burlesque show]

top brass *n.* **1** [1940s+] (*orig. US*) in the services or the police, the most senior officers. **2** [1950s+] (*orig. US*) in business or industry, the highest executive manager. **3** [1960s+] a leader, a chief, someone or something of importance. [BRASS n.[3] (1)]

top buttocks *n. see* TOP BALLOCKS n.

top cat *n.* [1950s+] (*orig. US Black*) the leader of a group, esp. of a clique of down-and-outs. [SE *top* + CAT n.[11] (4)]

top deck *n.* [1920s+] (*Aus.*) the head.

top-diver *n.* **1** [late 17C–early 19C] a lecher, a womanizer. **2** [1970s+] (*US gay*) a lesbian (cf. CARPET-BITER n.). [SE *dive on top (of)* + cunnilingus imagery]

top dog *n.* [20C+] a dominant figure, usu. in an institution, the boss, a senior member of an organization, a leader.

top dollar *n.* [1950s+] (*US*) a high price.

top drawer *adj.* **1** [1920s+] socially élite, aristocratic, upper-class. **2** [1950s+] first-rate.

top drawing room *n.* [late 19C–1900s] a garret.

top dressing *n.* [19C] the hair.

top end *n.* **1** [late 19C] the head. **2** [1910s+] (*Aus.*) (*also* **top, top half**) northern Australia; thus *top-ender, topsider*, one who lives there.

toper *n.* [mid–late 19C] the road. [Rom. *tober*, the road]

top-fencer *n.* (*also* **top-seller**) [mid-19C] a seller of dying speeches and 'famous last words'. [TOP *v.*[3] (1) + -FENCER sfx/SE *seller*]

top flat *n.* [late 19C; 1940s] the head.

top gun *n.* [1990s+] £100. [rhy. sl. = TON n.[1] (2)]

top half *n. see* TOP END n. (2).

top hamper *n.* [1900s] (*US*) the head, the brain.

top hat *n.*[1] [20C+] **1** a fool (cf. BEECHAM'S PILL n.). **2** a rat (the rodent). **3** a chat. [rhy. sl.; (1) = PRAT n.[1] (6)]

top hat *n.*[2] [1930s] (*UK Und.*) a detective. [? their attire]

top-heavy *adj.* [mid-17C–1910s] drunk (cf. AFFLICTED adj.).

topher *adj.* [2000s] (*US Black*) unable to achieve an erection, impotent. [ety. unknown]

top-hole *adj.* [20C+] excellent, first-rate, best; thus *top-holer*, an excellent person or object. [synon. with TOPNOTCH adj., i.e. the *top hole* in any measure]

top-hole! *excl.* [20C+] excellent! wonderful! perfect! [TOP-HOLE adj.]

topi *n.* (*also* **tops**) [1960s+] (*drugs*) **1** peyote. **2** mescaline. [? the top of the peyote cactus]

topital *adj.* [1990s+] (*US teen*) excellent, first-rate.

top joint *n.* [mid-19C] a pint (590ml) of beer. [rhy. sl.; note pron. 'jint']

top kick *n.* (*also* **top kicker**) [1910s–40s] (*orig. US*) the boss, the head of a group, whether legal or criminal. [US army jargon *top kick*, a first sergeant]

top knocker *n. see* KNOCKER n.[2] (2).

topknot *n.* [early 19C–1950s] the head. [SE *topknot*, a tuft of hair or ribbon on top of the head]

toplights *n.* [18C–19C] the eyes; thus *douse my toplights!* a mild oath, a synon. for DAMN MY EYES! excl.

top-lofty *adj.* (*also* **top-loftical**) [mid-19C–1930s] haughty, arrogant. [SE *top* + *lofty*]

top man *n.* **1** [late 18C+] a leading villain. **2** [late 19C+] a police superintendent. **3** [1930s+] the dominant partner in a homosexual (sado-masochistic) couple.

topman *n.* [early 17C+] a hangman. [TOP *v.*[3] (1) + SE *man*]

topnobber *n.* [1900s–20s] (*Anglo-Irish*) an important person. [SE *top* + NOB n.[2] (1)]

topnotch *adj.* (*also* **top-note**) [mid-19C+] excellent, first-class.

top-notcher *n.* [late 19C+] an expert, a leader in a given occupation, one of the best of any kind. [TOPNOTCH adj.]

top-off *n.* (*also* **top-off man, ...merchant**) [1930s+] (*Aus.*) an informer. [TOP OFF *v.*[2]]

top off *v.*[1] **1** [mid-19C+] to finish off, to put the finishing touches to. **2** [1910s] (*Aus.*) to kill. **3** [1910s] (*Aus.*) (*also* **top on**) to beat up. **4** [1930s] (*US Und.*) to cheat at a dice game. **5** [1930s+] to fill up, to complete a cargo. **6** [1940s+] to fill up a tank with petrol.

top off v.[2] [1930s+] (*Aus./N.Z.*) to inform against. [? TIP OFF v.[2] (2) or fig. use of TOP OFF v.[1]]

top-off man/merchant n. *see* TOP-OFF n.

top of Rome n. (*also* **top o' Rome**) [mid-19C–1920s] home. [rhy. sl.]

top of the bill phr. (*also* **top of the pot**) [20C+] the best, the ultimate. [theatrical/culinary imagery]

top of the house n. (*also* **top of the shop**) [20C+] (*bingo*) the number 99 or 100 (cf. ALDERSHOT LADIES n.). [the highest numbers on a card]

top of the tree phr. [late 18C+] upper-class, superior, aristocratic.

top on v. *see* TOP OFF v.[1] (3).

top oneself v. [1930s+] to commit suicide. [TOP v.[3] (2) + SE *oneself*]

top o' reeb n. [mid-late 19C] a pot of beer. [backsl.]

top o' Rome n. *see* TOP OF ROME n.

top out v. [1950s+] to reach a limit. [building trade jargon *top out*, to finish off a high building, to construct the very top floor]

topped adj. **1** [early 18C+] hanged. **2** [late 19C+] killed, murdered. [TOP v.[3]]

topped up adj. [1960s+] drunk.

topper n.[1] **1** [late 17C+] an outstanding person or thing of its kind. **2** [18C] the boss, the master. **3** [mid-19C+] the final word in an argument. **4** [late 19C] as *the toppers*, the upper classes. **5** [late 19C] as *my topper*, a term of affectionate address. **6** [1910s] (*US milit.*) the top sergeant. **7** [1930s+] a supposedly (but prob. not very) funny story or joke, it 'tops' or surpasses all others; a punchline. **8** [1950s+] the last in a series, the 'last straw'.

topper n.[2] [late 18C–19C] a blow to the head, either with a fist or a weapon.

topper n.[3] **1** [early–late 19C] (*UK Und.*) a hat (but not a top hat). **2** [early 19C+] a top hat. **3** [late 19C–1900s] a tall, thin person. **4** [late 19C–1950s] (*mainly US*) a loosely cut jacket or coat, generally worn by women and children.

topper n.[4] [mid-19C–1900s] **1** the stub of a cigar or cigarette. **2** the remains of burnt tobacco left in a pipe; thus *topper-hunter*, one who scavenges for cigar or cigarette stubs.

topper n.[5] [1920s] (*UK tramp*) a sovereign. [it is the *top*, i.e. the best coin]

topper n.[6] **1** [1920s–30s] a hangman. **2** [1940s+] (*UK/US prison*) someone who has attempted suicide. [TOP v.[3]]

topper n.[7] [1940s–50s] (*UK Und.*) a man who acts as a lookout man or a diversion for a DROPPER n.[1].

topper n.[8] [1940s+] (*Aus./N.Z.*) an informer. [TOP OFF v.[2]]

topper v. [19C] to kill with a blow on the head. [TOPPER n.[2]]

topper-off n. [1950s] (*Aus. prison*) an informer. [TOP OFF v.[2]]

toppie n. [1960s+] (*S.Afr.*) an old person of either sex. [? Zulu *thopi*, growing sparsely (e.g. of hair) or Hind. *topi*, a hat]

top piece n. **1** [mid-19C–1920s] a hat. **2** [mid-19C+] (*also* **top storey**) the head, the brain.

topping n.[1] [late 17C–early 18C] (*UK gambling*) a form of cheating with dice.

topping n.[2] **1** [late 18C+] execution by hanging. **2** [1990s+] suicide. [TOP v.[3]]

topping adj. (*also* **toppingly**) [late 17C+] excellent, enjoyable, first-rate. [SE *top*, 20C+ use is either ironic or consciously archaic]

topping cheat n. [late 17C–mid-19C] (*UK Und.*) the gallows. [TOP v.[3] (1) + CHEAT n. (1); lit. 'hanging thing']

topping cove n. [mid-17C–mid-19C] (*UK Und.*) a hangman. [TOP v.[3] (1) + COVE n. (1)]

topping fellow n. [mid-17C–mid-19C] a hangman. [TOP v.[3] (1) + pun on SE *topping fellow*, an admirable man]

toppingly adj. *see* TOPPING adj.

topping man n. [late 18C–early 19C] a superior, rich man. [TOPPING adj. + SE *man*]

toppings n. [1920s+] (*US tramp*) something sweet, esp. old cakes.

topping school n. [mid-17C–early 18C] a brothel (cf. ACADEMY n.). [TOP v.[1] (1)]

topping shed n. [mid-19C–1950s] that part of a prison in which the gallows is kept. [TOP v.[3] (1) + SE *shed*]

topple up one's heels v. *see* KICK UP ONE'S HEELS v.[1].

toppy adj. **1** [20C+] excessive. **2** [1900s] (*US*) upper-class.

top ramen n. [2000s] (*US Black*) an unpopular, ill-regarded person. [ety. unknown; ? Japanese noodles]

top-ropes adv. [1990s+] (*Aus.*) stylishly.

top-row adj. [late 19C] aristocratic, socially superior.

top-row adv. [late 19C] in a superior position, successfully.

top-rung adj. *see* TOP-SHELF adj.[1] (2).

tops n.[1] [mid-late 19C] pamphlets and broadsheets that purport to detail last words from the gallows, deathbed confessions etc. [TOP v.[3]]

tops n.[2] [1920s+] (*gambling*) doctored dice used for cheating purposes. [the predicted side rolls to the *top*]

tops n.[3] **1** [1930s] (*US Black*) as an admiring form of address. **2** [1930s+] (*orig. US*) the best, the ultimate, the winner.

tops n.[4] *see* TOPI n.

tops adj. [1940s+] excellent. [TOPS n.[3] (2)]

tops adv. [1930s+] at the most, at the top estimate, e.g. *5 years tops, 10 quid tops*. [SE *at a top estimate*]

tops and bottoms n. [1930s+] **1** a roll of notes in which only those on the very top and bottom are genuine, the rest being paper trimmed to fit and to bulk out the roll; also of precious stones. **2** (*US gambling*) crooked dice.

top sawyer n. [early 19C–1910s] **1** the leader in any profession, job, occupation. **2** the best of its kind. [timber trade: 'it is a piece of Norfolk slang and took its rise from Norfolk being a great timber country, where the top sawyers get double the wages of those beneath them' (Egan's Grose)]

top-seller n. *see* TOP-FENCER n.

top sergeant n. [1940s–70s] (*gay*) a masculine lesbian. ['she takes command of the girls' privates']

top set n. [1970s+] a woman's breasts. [SET n.[2] (1)]

top-shackled adj. [early 17C] drunk, fuddled, confused in the head.

top shelf n. [1950s+] (*Aus./N.Z.*) spirits. [as stored in a bar]

top-shelf adj.[1] **1** [late 19C] upper-class. **2** [20C+] (*also* **top-rung**) excellent, first-class, best.

top-shelf adj.[2] [20C+] usu. of magazines, pornographic. [euph.; the positioning of such material in a newsagent's]

top-shelfer n. [late 19C] an upper-class person. [TOP-SHELF adj.[1]]

top shot n. *see* BIG SHOT n.

topside adj. [mid-late 19C] in charge, in control. [? pidgin use]

topsider n. [1910s+] (*Aus.*) a lazy dog. [? TOPSIDE adj.; the image is that such a dog controls the master rather than vice versa]

topsman n. [18C–mid-19C] a hangman. [TOP v.[3] (1) + SE *man*]

top storey n. *see* TOP PIECE n. (2).

top storey worker n. [1930s–40s] (*UK Und.*) a cat burglar. [SE *top storey* + SE *worker*/WORKER n.[1] (1)]

topsy boozy adj. [late 19C] tipsy, half-drunk. [TOPSY FRIZY adj. + BOOZY adj. (1)]

topsy frizy adj. [late 18C–19C] tipsy, drunk. [one's *top* is SE *frizy*, curled]

topsy-versy adv. [mid-18C–1910s] upside down. [SE *topsy-turvy* + ARSEY-VARSEY phr. (1)]

top thatch n. *see* THATCH n. (1).

top the house v. [1930s] (*US Und.*) of a brothel prostitute, to make the most money during a given evening or night. [SE *top* + HOUSE n.[1] (1)]

top 'uns n. [1940s–50s] a woman's breasts.

top up v. [mid-19C+] to end up, to conclude. [to place a fig. *top* on]

to put it mildly phr. [1910s+] a phr. meaning that one is downplaying one's language, usu. ironic, i.e. the underlying sentiment is much stronger.

top whack n. [1970s+] the highest price or rate possible. [TOP WHACK adv.]

top whack *adv.* (*also* **top wack**) [1950s+] at the most. [WHACK n.² (1)]

top-yob *n.* [mid-19C] a pot-boy. [backsl.]

to raas *phr.* [1980s] (*W.I.*) a general intensifier, absolutely, to the utmost extent, 'to a T'.

torah *n. see* BIBLE n.² (1).

torch *n.* **1** [1900s] (*US*) a large cigar. **2** [1920s+] (*orig. US*) an arsonist. **3** [1920s+] (*orig. US*) an act of arson. **4** [1930s–60s] (*US tramp*) a revolver, a pistol. **5** [1960s–70s] (*US Black*) an oversized cigarette lighter. **6** [1960s+] (*US prison*) the murder of a fellow inmate by tossing a Molotov cocktail or petrol bomb into the cell. **7** [1970s+] (*drugs*) a marijuana cigarette (cf. BONE n.¹¹). **8** [1980s+] (*drugs*) a butane lighter used to ignite a crack cocaine pipe; thus *torch cooking*, using such a lighter and pipe.

torch *v.*¹ **1** [1930s+] (*orig. US*) to commit arson, to set on fire. **2** [1980s+] to light a cigarette. **3** [1990s+] (*US prison*) to throw a Molotov cocktail into an inmate's cell.

torch *v.*² *see* TORCH (FOR) v.

torch-carrier *n. see* CARRY A TORCH v.

torch-cul *n.* (*also* **torchecul**) [mid-17C–early 19C] lavatory paper. [synon. Fr. sl. *torchecul*, lit. 'give one's arse a quick smack']

torched *adj.* [1960s+] (*US*) submitted to an arsonous attack, burned out. [TORCH v.¹ (1)]

torcher *n.* [1940s+] (*US*) a 'torch' singer, a singer of maudlin, romantic songs.

torch (for) *v.* **1** [1930s+] (*orig. US*) to mourn a dead love-affair; to feel unrequited love. **2** [1960s+] to lust after. [CARRY A TORCH v.]

torch job *n.* [1930s+] (*US*) an act of arson. [TORCH v.¹ (1) + JOB n.³ (1)]

torch man *n.* [1940s] (*US Und.*) an expert in the use of an oxy-acetylene torch.

torch of love *n. see* CUPID'S TORCH n.

torch song *n.* [1920s+] a song that focuses on unrequited or lost love; thus *torch singer*, a singer of such songs. [CARRY A TORCH v.]

torch up *v.* **1** [1910s–20s] (*US*) to get drunk. **2** [1950s+] (*drugs*) to light a cannabis cigarette or pipe; thus to smoke marijuana. **3** [1990s+] to light a cigarette.

torchy *n.* [1930s] (*US Und.*) a profesional, criminal arsonist. [TORCH v.¹ (1)]

torchy *adj.* [1930s+] (*US*) suffering unrequited love; thus painful emotionally. [TORCH (FOR) v. (1)]

torcida, la *n.* [1980s+] (*US teen gang*) prison. [Sp.]

tore down *adj.* (*also* **tore, torn down**) **1** [1940s+] (*US Black*) depressed, miserable. **2** [1940s+] (*US Black*) unattractive, ugly. **3** [1950s+] (*drugs*) drunk or intoxicated by a drug. [(1) DOWN adj.² (1)]

tore out of the frame *phr.* (*US campus*) **1** [1970s+] drunk. **2** [1980s] shocked.

tore up *adj.* (*also* **all tore up, all torn up, torn up**) **1** [late 19C; 1950s+] (*US Black/campus*) miserable, depressed. **2** [1950s+] (*US Black/campus*) drunk or intoxicated by a drug (cf. ANNIHILATED adj.). **3** [1950s+] physically beaten. **4** [1970s] physically exhausted, very tired. **5** [1990s+] broken, wrecked, in a mess. **6** [2000s] ugly. [TEAR UP v.¹ (6)]

to rights *adj.* [early 19C–1900s] first-rate, excellent; also as excl. of approval. [legal jargon *to be to rights*, to have a legal case against]

to rights *adv.* [mid-19C+] **1** completely. **2** as required or desired. [note Bartlett, *Dict. Americanisms* (1848): 'to rights, directly; soon']

tormented *adj.* [early 19C–1930s] (*US*) a mild synon. for DAMNED adj.

tormentor *n.* **1** [early 19C–1900s] a water-squirter. **2** [late 19C–1910s] a back-scratcher.

tormentor of catgut *n.* [late 18C–early 19C] a fiddle-player, a violinist.

tormentor of sheepskin *n.* [early 19C] a drummer.

tormentors *n.* [mid–late 19C] riding spurs.

torn down *adj. see* TORE DOWN adj.

torn up *adj. see* TORE UP adj.

torp *n. see* TORPEDO JUICE n.

torpedo *n.*¹ [1920s+] (*US*) a thug, a hoodlum, the 'weapon' used by a gang boss and sent out to destroy enemies.

torpedo *n.*² **1** [1930s–60s] a drink containing chloral hydrate. **2** [1940s] a fat marijuana cigarette (cf. BOMB n.⁴). **3** [1970s+] (*drugs*) a tablet or capsule of a narcotic drug (cf. PILL n.⁴). **4** [1980s+] (*drugs*) a cigarette made of crack cocaine and marijuana. [the explosive imagery implicit in SE *torpedo*, i.e. it gets one HIGH adj.¹ (2); (2) + imagery]

torpedo *n.*³ [1990s+] (*US teen*) a penis that is wide at the base but grows narrower as it reaches the head. [resemblance]

torpedo *v.*¹ [1930s–60s] to drug with chloral hydrate. [TORPEDO n.² (1)]

torpedo *v.*² [1960s] (*Aus.*) of a man, to have sexual intercourse (cf. BANG v.¹).

torpedo juice *n.* (*also* **torp**) [1940s+] (*orig. milit.*) extremely strong, home-distilled liquor. ['a combination of bush beer and toddy and acquires its name from its lethal effect. The original torpedo juice was the neat alcohol extracted from torpedoes during the war by American servicemen and sometimes mixed with local bush beers' (*The Guardian*, 26 September 1961)]

torque *v.* [1980s] (*US campus*) to try to seduce someone.

torqued *adj.* **1** [1960s+] (*US*) angry. **2** [1980s+] (*US campus*) drunk, intoxicated by a drug.

torrac *n.* [mid–late 19C] **1** a carrot. **2** the penis; thus *phr.* of dismissal *ekat a torrac*, take a carrot (presumably + *and shove it…*). [backsl.]

torrid *adj.* [late 18C–1900s] drunk.

torril *n.* [19C] a general insult referring to a woman or a horse. [dial.]

torso-tosser *n.* [1920s–50s] an erotic dancer.

Tortoise Town *n.* [1900s] (*Aus.*) Adelaide. [? its slow pace in comparison to Sydney]

Tory *n.* **1** [mid-17C–19C] any of the dispossessed Irish who became outlaws, subsisting by plundering and killing the English settlers and soldiers. **2** [mid-17C–mid-19C] any outlaw, including Rajput marauders and Highland rebels. **3** [late 17C–early 18C] the nickname given to one who opposed the exclusion of James, duke of York (a Roman Catholic) from the succession to the British crown. [Irish *tóraidhe*, pursuer, although some sources define a *tory* as the one pursued, and therefore an outlaw. The Bill of Exclusion 'led to a common Use of slighting and opprobrious Words; such as Yorkist. That did not scandalize or reflect enough. Then they came to Tantivy, which implied Riding Post to Rome […] Then, observing that the Duke favoured Irish Men, all his Friends, or those accounted such by appearing against the Exclusion, were straight become Irish, and so wild Irish, thence BOGTROTTER n. (1), and in the Copia of the factious Language, the Word Tory was entertained, which signified the most despicable Savages among the Wild Irish' (Roger North, *Examen*, 1740)]

tory rory *n.* [mid-18C–mid-19C] one who wears their hat cocked distinctly to one side. [TORY n. (3) + proper name *Rory*]

tory-rory *adv.* [late 18C] lop-sided, all over the place. [TORY RORY n.]

tosh *n.*¹ [19C] (*UK Und.*) a pocket. [Fr. *poche*, a pocket]

tosh *n.*² [late 19C–1900s] a hat. [backsl.]

tosh *n.*³ [late 19C+] (*orig. Oxford University*) nonsense, rubbish. [? BOSH n.¹ or dial. *toshy*, muddy; Puxley, *Fresh Rabbit: A Dick 'n' Arry of Rhyming Slang* (1998), suggests a link to the items scavenged by a TOSHER n. (1)]

tosh *n.*⁴ [1900s] (*Aus.*) a raincoat. [abbr. SE *mackintosh*]

tosh *n.*⁵ [1940s+] a form of familiar address to someone whose name one does not know. [? Scot. *tosh*, smart, neat or dial. *toshy*, of masculine appearance, hairy-faced]

tosh *n.*[6] *see* TOSHEROON *n.*

tosh! *excl.* [1910s] rubbish! nonsense! [TOSH *n.*[3]]

tosher *n.* **1** [mid-19C] one who scavenges copper from ships' bottoms, items from the Thames mud, the sewers etc. **2** [1970s+] a painter and decorator. [dial. *toshy*, muddy]

tosheroon *n.* (*also* **tosh, tosher, tush, tusheroon, tusseroon**) [mid-19C–1980s] (*orig. Ling. Fr./Polari*) half-a-crown, 2s 6d (12½p). [? mispron. of Polari MADZA CAROON *n.*]

to shit *adv.* [1910s+] a general intensifier.

toshy *adj.* [1900s] trashy, rubbishy. [TOSH *n.*[3]]

toss *n.*[1] **1** [late 19C+] in fig. use, something of infinitesimal or zero importance; usu. in NOT GIVE A TOSS *v.* **2** [1940s+] nonsense. [TOSS (OFF) *v.*[1]]

toss *n.*[2] [1950s+] (*orig. US prison*) a search, esp. one carried out by police. [TOSS *v.*[3]]

toss *n.*[3] *see* TOSSER *n.*[1] (3).

toss *n.*[4] *see* TOSS-OFF *n.* (1).

toss *n.*[5] *see* TOSS-UP *n.*[1].

toss *v. see also under* TOSS (OFF).

toss *v.*[1] **1** [1940s] to overcome. **2** [1950s] (*Aus.*) to criticize harshly, to assault verbally. **3** [1970s+] to throw out. **4** [1980s] (*US*) to bribe. **5** [1980s] to take money from. **6** [1990s+] (*US*) to expose someone as a homosexual against their will. **7** [2000s] (*US Black*) to beat up. [SE *toss*, to throw]

toss *v.*[2] [1950s+] (*US campus*) to vomit (cf. BLOW *v.*[3]). [abbr. TOSS ONE'S COOKIES *v.* (1)]

toss *v.*[3] [1950s+] (*orig. US prison*) to search an apartment, car or person, esp. for weapons etc.

toss a party *v.* [1950s+] (*Aus.*) to 'throw' a party.

toss a reverse lunch *v.* [1970s+] (*N.Z.*) to vomit (cf. BLOW CHOW *v.*). [the regurgitation of food]

toss arse *n.* [1990s+] (*UK juv.*) a habitual masturbator. [TOSS (OFF) *v.*[1] + ARSE *n.*[1] (5)]

toss a slug *v. see* CHUCK A SLUG *v.*

toss-bag *n.* (*also* **toss-bags**) [1990s+] an unpleasant, worthless person. [TOSS (OFF) *v.*[1] + -BAG *sfx*]

toss-bottle *n. see* TOSSPOT *n.*

tossed salad *n.* [1990s+] **1** (*US Black teen*) anilingus embellished by an application of jam or syrup (cf. AUSTRALIAN *n.*). **2** (*gay*) anilingus and anal intercourse. [TOSS SALAD *v.*]

tossel *n.* (*also* **tossle**) [1980s+] (*Aus.*) a penis, usu. a child's penis. [? SE *tassel*]

tosser *n.*[1] **1** [late 19C+] (*Aus.*) an affectionate term of address. **2** [1970s+] a masturbator. **3** [1970s+] (*also* **toss**) a despicable, worthless person. [TOSS (OFF) *v.*[1]; note the chronology of (1) suggests a much earlier if uncited use of (2) and (3)]

tosser *n.*[2] **1** [1900s–50s] (*also* **tosseroon**) any coin, esp. a sovereign. **2** [1930s+] (*Irish*) a low-value coin. [SE *toss*, to throw]

tosser *adj.* [2000s] of a person, despicable, second-rate, unimportant. [TOSSER *n.*[1] (3)]

tosser sign *n.* [1990s+] a coarse gesture whereby the hand is moved up and down, imitating the action of masturbation. [TOSSER *n.*[1] (2)]

tossicate *v.* [20C+] (*Ulster*) to disturb, to worry. [SE *intoxication* + *toss*]

toss in *v. see* TOSS (IT) IN *v.*

tossing *n.* [1930s+] useless, worthless, a euph. for FUCKING *adj.* [TOSS (OFF) *v.*[1]]

toss in one's agate *v.* [1900s] (*Aus.*) to die; lit. or fig. [SE *agate*, a type of marble]

toss (it) in *v.* [1940s–60s] (*Aus./N.Z./US*) to give up, to finish.

toss it to *v.* [1960s+] (*US*) of a man, to have sexual intercourse (cf. BURY IT *v.*). [SE *toss*, to throw]

toss it up airy *v.* [1920s] to put on airs.

tossle *n. see* TOSSEL *n.*

toss-off *n.* **1** [mid-18C+] (*also* **toss**) an act of masturbation. **2** [20C+] a worthless, unpleasant person. [TOSS (OFF) *v.*[1]]

toss (off) *v.*[1] [mid-17C; mid-18C+] to masturbate; often as *toss oneself off* (cf. BALL OFF *v.*[2]).

toss (off) *v.*[2] **1** [mid-19C+] to get rid of, to discard. **2** [1910s+] to give up, to abandon (a task), to lose. [SE *toss away*]

toss off! *excl.* [1980s+] a euph. for FUCK OFF! excl. [TOSS (OFF) *v.*[1]]

toss one's cookies *v.* (*also* **toss one's groceries/tacos**) **1** [1950s+] (*orig. US campus*) to vomit (cf. BLOW CHOW *v.*). **2** [1970s] as *toss my cookies*, a derisory retort. **3** [1990s+] to make someone sick. [COOKIES *n.*[1]]

toss oneself off *v. see* TOSS (OFF) *v.*[1].

toss one's lollies *v.* (*also* **chuck one's lollies, lose…**) [1980s+] (*N.Z.*) to vomit (cf. BLOW CHOW *v.*). [SE *lollipop*]

toss one's lump *v. see* LUMP *n.*[3].

toss one's tacos *v. see* TOSS ONE'S COOKIES *v.*

tossout *n.*[1] [1930s] (*US Und.*) a beggar who specializes in throwing their limbs out of joint in order to excite pity.

tossout *n.*[2] [1940s] (*US drugs*) an addict who feigns fits. [TOSS OUT *v.*]

toss out *v.* [1930s–70s] (*US drugs*) of a drug addict, to fake a fit.

toss parlour *n.* [1990s+] a brothel. [TOSS (OFF) *v.*[1]]

tosspot *n.* (*also* **toss-bottle**) [1940s+] a fool. [TOSS (OFF) *v.*[1] + -POT *sfx* but note earlier SE *tosspot*, a drunkard]

tossprick *n.* [20C+] a general term of abuse. [TOSS (OFF) *v.*[1] + PRICK *n.* (2)]

toss-rag *n.* [1950s] a piece of tissue that has been or will be used to wipe the penis after masturbation. [TOSS (OFF) *v.*[1] + SE *rag*]

toss salad *v.* [1970s+] (*US prison*) to engage in anilingus, seen by otherwise heterosexual participants as a 'clean' non-homosexual form of quick and easy gratification; thus insulting excl. *toss my salad!* (cf. AUSTRALIAN *n.*). [? the general mixing of flesh and embellishments]

toss someone around *v.* (*also* **toss someone across**) [1910s–30s] **1** (*US Und.*) to cheat, to swindle. **2** (*US*) to mistreat, to deceive, to cheat, e.g. a lover.

toss someone in the air *v. see* THROW SOMEONE IN THE AIR *v.*

toss the boards *v.* [1950s] (*US Und.*) **1** to conduct a game of the 3-card trick. **2** to deal cards, esp. in a crooked or illegal manner. [SE *toss* + BOARDS *n.*]

toss the bull (around) *v.* [1920s+] (*US*) to chatter, to gossip. [SE *toss* + BULL *n.*[11] (1)]

toss the hooks *v. see* HOOK *n.*[1] (1).

toss the squares *v.* [1970s–80s] (*US Black*) to pass a pack of cigarettes. [SE *toss* + SQUARE *n.*[5]]

toss the tiger *v.* [1960s+] (*N.Z.*) to vomit. [SE *tiger*, echoic of vomiting]

toss-up *n.*[1] (*also* **toss**) [late 18C+] a wager (esp. fig.) in which chances are even and either eventuality is equally likely. [SE *toss up coins*]

toss-up *n.*[2] **1** [1980s+] (*drugs*) a woman who trades sex for crack cocaine or for money to buy crack cocaine. **2** [1990s+] (*Aus.*) a promiscuous woman. [SE *toss*, to throw; she 'throws herself up to' the man]

tossy *adj.*[1] [1910s–20s] arrogant, supercilious, conceited. [SE *tossy*, contemptuous]

tossy *adj.*[2] [1940s] second-rate, useless, inferior. [TOSS *n.*[1] (1)]

tostado *n.* [1960s–80s] (*US Black*) a derog. term for a Latino or Chicano (cf. BEAN *n.*[8]). [Mex. *tostado*, a popular toasted snack composed of a deep-fried cornmeal pancake topped with a seasoned mixture of beans, mincemeat and vegetables]

to stink *adv. see* LIKE STINK *adv.*

tot *n.*[1] **1** [early 18C+] a very small or tiny child, an infant. **2** [early–late 19C] a very small drinking vessel. **3** [early 19C+] a small glass of alcohol, e.g. a *tot of rum*. **4** [early 19C+] a very small quantity of anything. [ety. unknown]

tot *n.*[2] (*also* **totte**) [mid-18C–1910s] the total, the sum. [abbr.]

tot *n.*[3] (*also* **tote**) [mid-19C–1910s] a very heavy drinker. [TOT n.[1] (3)]

tot *n.*[4] (*also* **tote**) [late 19C] a *to*tal abstainer from alcohol. [abbr. + ? joc. ref. to TOT n.[1] (3)]

tot *n.*[5] [late 19C+] a rag or bone; thus *tot-picker, tot-raker,* a scavenger, a 'rag-and-bone man'. [Ger. *tod,* dead]

tot *n.*[6] (*also* **tott**) [1990s+] a young woman. [dimin. of TOTTIE n.[2] (2)]

tot *v.*[1] [mid-19C–1930s] to drink a dram. [TOT n.[1] (3)]

tot *v.*[2] [mid-19C+] to go rag-picking or scavenging. [TOT n.[5]]

tot *v.*[3] *see* TOT (UP) v.

totacho *n.* [1960s+] (*US/Hisp.*) the sl. used in the barrío.

total *adj.* [1960s+] (*orig. US teen*) a general intensifier, absolute, complete.

total *v.* [1950s+] (*orig. US*) **1** to crash a vehicle so badly as to render it beyond repair. **2** to destroy, kill or maim anything or anyone. [i.e. to destroy *totally*]

total *adv.* [1960s+] (*US teen/campus*) utterly, completely, totally.

total blowchoice *n.* [1980s+] (*US teen*) something appealing but essentially irrelevant. [TOTAL adj. + BLOW v.[5] (1) + SE *choice,* i.e. it would be a wasted choice]

total lame-out *n.* [1990s+] (*US teen*) something really stupid or boring. [TOTAL adj. + LAME adj. (2)]

totalled (out) *adj.* (*also* **totaled (out)**) [1960s+] (*orig. US*) **1** unattractive. **2** wrecked (usu. of a car). **3** drunk or drugged (cf. ANNIHILATED adj.). **4** physically or emotionally exhausted. [TOTAL v.]

totally! *excl.* [1980s+] (*orig. US campus*) a general excl. of approval or enthusiasm, absolutely! exactly! really! [SE *totally*]

totally clueless *adj.* [1950s+] (*orig. US teen*) ignorant, unaware. [note earlier but poss. distinct 1930s RAF use]

total wreck *n. see* NERVOUS WRECK n.[2].

Tote, the *n.* [late 19C+] (*orig. Aus.*) **1** the *Tot*alizator, a machine that calculates the number of tickets sold to betters on each horse/greyhound in a race. **2** the system of betting based on these calculations. [abbr.]

tote *n.*[1] *see* TOT n.[3].

tote *n.*[2] *see* TOT n.[4].

tote *v.*[1] (*also* **toat**) **1** [late 17C+] (*US*) to carry, to haul a load; thus *tote fair,* to carry one's fair share; *tote load,* to carry as much as one can; also fig. to carry around, not lit. a load. **2** [mid-18C+] to take someone, to lead or conduct someone; thus reflexively, to take oneself, to go. [the *OED* dismisses either Black or Ind. origins, but Farmer, *Americanisms Old New* (1889), suggests OE *totian,* to lift up, to elevate and legal jargon *tolt,* a writ by which a cause was removed from a court baron to the county court, itself f. Lat. *tolle,* to lift or remove]

tote *v.*[2] [1930s+] (*US*) to add up. [SE *total*]

tote guts to a bear *v. see* CARRY GUTS TO A BEAR v.

tote the mail *v. see* HAUL THE MAIL v.

to the bad *phr.* **1** [early 19C+] in debt, 'in the red'. **2** [late 19C–1920s] out of order, lit. and fig.

to the bone *phr.* [1910s+] (*orig. US Black*) to the extreme, to the ultimate extent, usu. in combs.

to the bricks *phr.* [1920s+] (*US Black*) to the limit, to the furthest extent. [the *bricks* are those of the walls]

to the curb *phr.* [1980s+] (*US Black/campus*) **1** ugly, distasteful, unpleasant. **2** impoverished. [synon. of SE phr. *in the gutter*]

to the curb, be *v.* [1980s+] (*US campus*) to vomit. [the polite person steps off the pavement and carefully vomits into the gutter]

to the dogs with —! *excl.* [1900s+] a dismissive excl. [GO TO THE DOGS v. (1)]

to the gills *adv.* [1920s+] absolutely, completely. [GILLS n.]

to the max *phr.* [1970s+] completely, to the extreme. [SE *maximum,* orig. in the California youth cultures]

to the nines *adv. see* UP TO THE NINES adv.

t'other side *n.* [mid-19C+] (*Aus.*) **1** used in West Australia to refer to the eastern states. **2** used in Tasmania to refer to the Australian mainland. [SE *the other side*]

t'other sider *n.* (*also* **othersider**) (*Aus.*) **1** [19C] a transported felon. **2** [late 19C+] a Western Australian. **3** [1900s] an Australian from the eastern part of the country. [he has come from 'the other side of the world'; (2) and (3) note T'OTHER SIDE n.]

to the ruffian *adv.* [19C] to the utmost perfection. [RUFFIN (, THE) n.]

to the shithouse *adv.* [1970s] (*Aus.*) a euph. for TO HELL adv. [SHITHOUSE n. (3) as a euph. for SE *hell*]

to the tick *adv. see* TICK n.[4] (2).

to the tits *adv.* [1970s+] completely; esp. in RIPPED TO THE TITS phr. [TIT n.[3] (1)]

to the wide *adv.* [1900s–30s] used as an intensifier, completely, totally; thus BROKE TO THE WIDE phr.; DONE TO THE WIDE phr.

tot-hunter *n.* [late 19C–1900s] lit. a collector of bones, which were recycled in a variety of manufacturing processes; used as a term of abuse. [TOT n.[5] + SE *hunter*]

tot-hunting *n.* [late 19C–1900s] wandering the streets in search of pretty women. [TOTTIE n.[2] (2) + SE *hunting* + play on TOT-HUNTER n.]

totsi *n. see* TSOTSI n.

totsie *n.* [1930s–40s] a young woman, usu. one who is sexually available. [var. on TOTTIE n.[2] (2)]

tott *n. see* TOT n.[6].

totte *n. see* TOT n.[2].

tot-teaser *n.* [1970s] (*US gay*) a pederast. [TOTTIE n.[2] (2)]

totter *n.* [late 19C+] a 'rag-and-bone man', a scavenger. [TOT v.[2]]

tottie *n.*[1] (*also* **totty**) [early 19C–1930s] (*S.Afr.*) **1** a Khoikhoi. **2** any Black or esp. Coloured person. [abbr. (*Hotten*)*tot,* the orig. and derog. name for the Khoikhoi]

tottie *n.*[2] (*also* **totty**) **1** [late 19C–1920s] a high-class prostitute. **2** [late 19C+] a young woman, or boy, usu. one who is sexually available; also collectively. **3** [1900s] (*Aus.*) a chorus-girl (the inference is of on-stage vulgarity and off-stage promiscuity). [TOT n.[1] (1)]

tottie *adj.* [early 19C–1930s] (*S.Afr.*) unpopular, vulgar, unfashionable. [TOTTIE n.[1]]

tottie fie *n.* (*also* **tottie fay/hardbake**) [late 19C+] a woman, usu. a prostitute or at least an 'enthusiastic amateur', who dominates her surroundings. [TOTTIE n.[2] (2) + SE *fie!*/SE *hardbake,* almond toffee, which is 'hard' albeit sweet]

totty *see also under* TOTTIE.

totty all colours *n.* [late 19C–1900s] a woman whose dress resembles a 'coat of many colours'. [TOTTIE n.[2] (2)]

totty-headed *adj.* [late 17C–early 19C] **1** foolish, giddy (cf. AIRHEADED adj.). **2** drunk (cf. ARSEHOLED adj.). [SE *totty,* unsteady, dizzy, befuddled]

totty one-lung *n.* [late 19C–1900s] an asthmatic or a sufferer from tuberculosis who still manages to muster some degree of style. [TOTTIE n.[2] (2)]

tot (up) *v.* [mid-18C+] to add up. [TOT n.[2]]

touch *n.*[1] **1** [16C] a trick, a dodge. **2** [early 18C–1920s] any item that will persuade purchasers to buy, albeit within certain price limits; thus *a sixpence touch, a guinea touch.* **3** [early 19C+] (*also* **touch-off**) an act of stealing or theft, esp. of pocket-picking; thus *touch merchant,* a petty thief. **4** [mid-19C] (*UK Und.*) an arrest. **5** [late 19C+] the act of cadging a loan, usu. small; thus the loan; thus *on the touch,* begging. **6** [1900s] (*US Und.*) the climax of a confidence trick, when the victim hands over their money. **7** [20C+] (*US Und.*) the money gained illegally, e.g. that which is 'stolen' by a confidence trickster's scheme; also in fig. use. **8** [1930s] one from whom one obtains a loan or a monetary gift. **9** [1930s] the victim of a confidence trick. **10** [1980s+] (*N.Z.*) one's turn to buy a round of drinks.

touch *n.*[2] [1910s] (*Aus.*) style, fashion, manner. [SE *touch*, ability, esp. of a performer]

touch *n.*[3] [1910s+] (*Aus.*) a simpleton. [SE *touched*, eccentric, mad]

touch *n.*[4] [1930s+] a piece of good fortune, e.g. an acquittal.

touch *n.*[5] [1950s+] a woman who can be easily picked up. [? SOFT TOUCH *n.*]

touch *v.*[1] **1** [early 17C+] to take money into one's own hands, to steal; often as TOUCH (SOMEONE) FOR *v.* **2** [mid-18C] to offer a loan. **3** [mid-18C+] to borrow something from, usu. money, to cadge; often as TOUCH (SOMEONE) FOR *v.* **4** [mid-19C–1930s] to pick someone's pocket. **5** [late 19C] (*US*) to defeat a bookmaker; to win a bet. **6** [late 19C+] (*Aus.*) to swindle, to cheat; usu. as TOUCH (SOMEONE) FOR *v.* **7** [1910s–40s] to ask for a favour.

touch *v.*[2] [early 18C+] to equal, to rival, to compare with.

touch *v.*[3] (*also* **get a touch on**) [late 18C+] (*UK Und./Aus.*) to arrest.

touchable *adj.* [1940s] (*US Und.*) susceptible to corruption. [? TOUCH *v.*[1] (1)]

touch all bases *v.* [20C+] (*US*) to be very thorough, or adaptable and versatile. [baseball imagery]

touch and tap *n.* [20C+] a cap. [rhy. sl.]

touch artist *n.* [1940s–60s] (*US*) a beggar, one who is always asking for a loan. [TOUCH *v.*[1] (3) + ARTIST sfx]

touch base *v.* (*also* **touch ground**) [1970s+] to communicate with, to make contact. [baseball imagery]

touch bone and whistle! *excl.* [late 18C–early 19C] an excl. used when someone breaks wind. ['Anyone having broken wind backwards, according to the vulgar law, may be pinched by any of the company till he has touched bone (i.e. his teeth) and whistled' (Grose, 1788)]

touch crib *n.* [19C] a brothel (cf. BADGER-CRIB *n.*). [SE *touch* + CRIB *n.*[1] (2)]

touched *adj.* [early–late 19C] tipsy. [SE *touched*, mentally unstable]

touch 'em up *n.* [19C] the vagina.

toucher *n.*[1] **1** [early 19C] a very tight fit, an instance of very close contact. **2** [early 19C+] a near thing. **3** [1980s+] (*US Black/drugs*) one who becomes physically affectionate after smoking crack cocaine. [SE *touch*; (3) note NON-TOUCHER *n.*]

toucher *n.*[2] **1** [mid-19C] (*US Und.*) a pickpocket. **2** [mid-19C–1900s] one who practises the TOUCH GAME *n.* **3** [mid-19C–1950s] (*US*) a thief. **4** [mid-19C+] a cadger, one who solicits small loans. [TOUCH *v.*[1]]

touch for *v. see* TOUCH (SOMEONE) FOR *v.*

touch game *n.* [mid-19C] (*US Und.*) a synon. for the MURPHY GAME *n.*[1].

touch ground *v. see* TOUCH BASE *v.*

touch guy *n.* [1970s] (*US*) one who is constantly scrounging. [TOUCH *v.*[1] (3) + GUY *n.*[2] (1)]

touch-hole *n.* **1** [17C–early 18C] the anus (cf. A-HOLE *n.*). **2** [17C–19C] the vagina (cf. BLACK HOLE *n.*[1]). [SE *touch-hole*, the vent of a firearm, through which the charge is ignited]

touch house *n.* [mid-19C] (*US Und.*) any tavern or similar establishment where victims are robbed, beaten and even killed; they may also be subjected to the MURPHY GAME *n.*[1]. [TOUCH *n.*[1] (3) + SE *house*]

touchie-feelie *adj.* (*also* **touchy-feely**) [1970s+] (*US*) pertaining to therapies and sensitivity training which encourage people to touch, hug and support one another physically.

touching *n.* [mid-18C–19C] **1** obtaining money through theft or pickpocketing. **2** bribery. [TOUCH *v.*[1] (3)]

touching the dog's arse *n.* [1980s] (*UK Und.*) the act of stealing a car. [the initials *t*aking and *d*riving *a*way]

touching-up *n. see* TOUCH-UP *n.*[1].

touch lucky *v.* [late 19C–1950s] to experience good fortune.

touch-me *n.* [late 19C–1930s] a shilling (5p). [rhy. sl.; *touch-me-on-the-nob* = BOB *n.*[4] (1)]

touch merchant *n. see* TOUCH *n.*[1] (3).

touch-my-nob *n.* [late 19C] a shilling (5p). [var. on TOUCH-ME *n.*]

touch of 'em *n.* **1** [late 19C–1900s] (*Aus.*) delirium tremens. **2** [1920s–60s] diarrhoea. [euph.]

touch-off *n. see* TOUCH *n.*[1] (3).

touch-off man *n.* [1920s–40s] (*US Und.*) a professional, criminal arsonist. [he *touches off* the fire]

touch of Laurence *n. see* LAZY LAURENCE *n.*

touch of the — *phr.* (*also* **case of the —**) [1970s+] used with pl. (often proper) nouns to imply a condition that is seen as typical of the *n.*, e.g. *touch of the New Labours, case of the Princess Di's.* [adapted from SE phr. *touch of the —*, but always used with a pl. *n.*]

touch of the hairy heel *phr.* [late 19C] (*UK society*) betraying one's working-class origins. [the image is of a carthorse as compared to a racehorse]

touch of the holy bone *phr.* [19C+] (*orig. Irish, then US*) sexual intercourse. [ironic ref. to the supposed power of holy 'relics', but note BONE *n.*[1] (1)]

touch of the Jim Brits *phr.* [1950s] (*Aus.*) nerves, edginess. [JIMMY BRITTS *n.*]

touch of the seconds *phr.* [1970s+] last minute hesitation. [abbr. SE *second thoughts*]

touch of the tarbrush *phr.* (*also* **lick of the tarbrush**) [late 18C+] a derog. term used to described someone who supposedly has a degree of Black ancestry; thus *adj.* *tar-brush*, Black; as *n.*, a Black person (cf. BLACKBELLY *n.*). [SE f. 1900; note Haliburton (1843): (to a black slave) 'You one werry good nigger [...] I make a man of you, you dam old tarbrush']

touch oneself up *v.* [1960s+] to masturbate. [TOUCH UP *v.*[1] (2)]

touch one's kick *v.* (*also* **touch one's pants, ...strides, ...tweeds**) [1950s+] (*N.Z.*) **1** to pay for a round of drinks. **2** to make a small loan. [SE *touch* + KICK *n.*[4]/SE *pants*/STRIDES *n.* (1)/SE *tweeds*]

touch one's sky *v. see* SKY (ROCKET) *n.*

touch (someone) for *v.* **1** [mid-18C+] to cadge. **2** [19C+] to remove, to take, to steal. **3** [late 19C+] (*Aus.*) to swindle, to cheat. [ext. of TOUCH *v.*[1]]

touch the bun for luck *v.* [late 18C–early 19C] to touch one's wife's or girlfriend's genital area for luck before leaving on a journey. [BUN *n.*[2] (1), orig. a RN tradition]

touch the can *v. see* CAN *n.*[4].

touch the mopusses *v. see* MOPUS *n.* (3).

touch the spot *v.* [late 19C+] to suit the circumstances, to be absolutely satisfactory in the context.

touch-trap *n.* [17C–19C] the penis. [SE *touch-trap*, a contrivance that operates when *touched*]

touch-tripe *n.* [late 17C] the penis.

touch-up *n.*[1] (*also* **touching-up**) [1950s+] an act of sexual fondling. [TOUCH UP *v.*[1] (2)]

touch-up *n.*[2] [1990s+] (*Aus. Und.*) a beating. [SE *touch up*, to strike with a whip]

touch up *v.*[1] **1** [late 18C–19C] of a man, to have sexual intercourse. **2** [late 18C+] to fondle or molest sexually.

touch up *v.*[2] **1** [late 18C–mid-19C] to urge someone into action, to exert influence on. **2** [19C] to jog someone's memory. **3** [late 19C] to stimulate or interest someone. [SE *touch up*, to tap (a horse) with a whip]

touch up *v.*[3] **1** [early 19C–1900s] to rob someone. **2** [mid-19C] to blackmail someone. [ext. of TOUCH *v.*[1] (1)]

touch up *v.*[4] [late 19C–1900s] (*US*) to approach for a loan or a favour.

touchy-feely *adj. see* TOUCHIE-FEELIE *adj.*

tough *n.* (*US Black*) **1** [1960s] an attractive or admirable person. **2** [1970s] money gained from theft or confidence tricks that is used for buying drugs. [various defs. of TOUGH *adj.*]

tough *adj.* **1** [20C+] (*orig. US*) resolute, vigorously uncompromising, severe. **2** [20C+] (*orig US*) aggressive, menacing. **3** [20C+]

unfair, 'mean', difficult. **4** [1920s+] unfortunate, pertaining to hard luck; usu. as *that's tough*. **5** [1930s] bad, depressed. **6** [1930s+] (*US Black/campus*) admirable, excellent. **7** [1950s+] of clothes or people, fashionable. **8** [1960s+] of objects or people, attractive. [SE *tough*, capable of great physical or moral endurance; (6), (7) and (8) on bad = 'good' model; (4) backform. f. TOUGH LUCK n.]

tough *adv.* **1** [1920s+] intensely, enthusiastically, committedly. **2** [1930s+] in an aggressive manner. **3** [1950s–60s] attractively. **4** [1990s+] resolutely. [TOUGH adj.]

tough act to follow *n. see* HARD ACT TO FOLLOW n.

tough apples! *excl.* [1970s+] (*US*) a response indicating a lack of sympathy with the speaker. [? euph./abbr. ROAD APPLE n.]

tough as (shoe) leather *phr.* (*also* **tough as a biled owl,** ...fencing wire, ...old boots) [mid-19C+] used of one who is considered 'hard' or 'tough'.

tough baby *n.* **1** [1910s+] a thug, a violent, lawless person. **2** [1920s–40s] (*US gang*) a girl who associates with gang members. **3** [1960s] a challenging proposition, a problem. [SE *tough* + BABY n.[3]]

tough beans *phr.* [1960s+] (*US*) an unsympathetic phr. meaning that's your bad luck.

tough biccies/bickies/bickkies *n. see* STIFF BICKKIES n.

tough boy *n.* [1920s+] a thug, a violent, lawless person.

tough cat *n.* [1950s+] (*US Black*) a man who is a successful womanizer. [TOUGH adj. (6) + CAT n.[11] (4)]

tough cheddar *n. see* HARD CHEESE n.

tough cheese *adj. see* TOUGH SHIT adj.

tough cookie *n.* [1950s+] (*US*) a survivor, an emotionally or physically strong person. [TOUGH adj. (1) + COOKIE n.[2]]

tough cud *n. see* TOUGH NUT n.

tough dancing *n.* [20C+] physically close dancing, emphasizing (and offering an opportunity for) sexual intimacy. [the term and style originated in the brothels of San Francisco's BARBARY COAST n. and spread into the mainstream dancehalls, or their less salubrious counterparts]

tough darts *phr.* [1960s+] (*US*) a phr. of dismissal, uninterest, that's your bad luck. [euph. for TOUGH TITTY n.]

toughed up *adj.* [1950s] (*US*) aggressive. [TOUGH adj. (2)]

tough egg *n.* (*also* **hard egg**) **1** [1910s+] a thug, a violent person. **2** [1920s] an uncompromising individual. [TOUGH adj. (2)/TOUGH adj. (1) + play on HARD-BOILED adj.]

tough fit *n.* [1950s–70s] (*US Black*) a well-cut suit or other garment. [TOUGH adj. (7) + SE *fit*]

tough guy *n.* **1** [1920s+] (*orig. US*) (*also* **tough monkey**) a thug. **2** [1930s+] someone who cannot easily be checked or thwarted. [TOUGH adj. (2)/TOUGH adj. (1) + GUY n.[2] (1)/MONKEY n.[1] (3)]

tough-guy *adj.* [1950s+] aggressive, uncompromising. [TOUGH GUY n.]

toughie *n.* **1** [1920s] (*US*) an attractive girl. **2** [1920s–60s] one who enjoys playing very 'rough' sports. **3** [1930s+] a 'hard', ruthless, callous person. **4** [1960s+] something that one finds 'tough' to do, understand, accept etc. **5** [1940s+] a thug. [TOUGH adj. + sfx *-ie*]

tough it out *v.* (*also* **tough it, tough out**) [mid-19C+] to withstand abuse or a bad situation.

tough lines *n. see* HARD LINES n.

tough luck *n.* [late 19C+] bad luck; esp. as an unsympathetic phr. meaning that's your bad luck.

tough monkey *n. see* TOUGH GUY n. (1).

tough noogies *phr.* [1970s+] (*US*) an unsympathetic phr. meaning that's your bad luck. [SE *tough* + fig. use of NOOGIE n.]

tough nut *n.* (*also* **tough cud, rough nut**) [mid-19C+] (*orig. US*) a person difficult, obstinate or dangerous to deal with; also of a place. [TOUGH adj. (1) + NUT n.[1] (2)]

tough-nut *adj.* [1990s+] aggressive, obstinate. [TOUGH NUT n.]

tough on *adj.* [late 19C+] (*orig. US*) hostile towards, making life hard for someone. [TOUGH adj.]

tough out *v. see* TOUGH IT OUT v.

tough shit *n.* [1940s+] (*orig. US*) unfortunate or unpleasant circumstances. [var. on TOUGH LUCK n.]

tough shit *adj.* (*also* **tough cheese**) **1** [1940s+] unfortunate. **2** [1970s] essential, basic. [TOUGH SHIT n.]

tough shit *phr.* [1950s+] an unsympathetic phr. meaning that's your bad luck, see if I care. [TOUGH SHIT n.]

tough sledding *n.* (*also* **hard sledding**) [1920s+] a problematic, demanding situation, hard times.

tough stuff *n.* [1970s–80s] (*US Black*) anything appealing or pleasing in the realms of sex or drugs. [TOUGH adj. (6)]

tough takkie *n.* [1910s+] (*S.Afr.*) hard luck. [SE *tough* + fig. use of TAKKIE n.]

tough titty *n.* (*also* **tough tiddy,** ...tit, ...tits, ...titties, **hard titty**) [1920s+] bad luck; esp. as an unsympathetic phr. meaning that's your bad luck. [var. on TOUGH LUCK n. + TITTY n.[1] (1)/TIT n.[3] (1)]

tough toenails *n.* [1950s] bad luck. [euph. for TOUGH TITTY n.]

tough turkey *n.* [1900s] (*US*) bad luck. [? euph. for TOUGH TITTY n.]

tough 'un *n.* **1** [late 19C] a very great lie. **2** [20C+] an aggressive person. [TOUGH adj. (1)/TOUGH adj. (2)]

toup *n.* [1950s+] a toupee. [abbr.]

toupee *n.* [mid-18C–19C] **1** female pubic hair. **2** a pubic wig or merkin. [SE *toupee*, a wig]

tour *v.* (*also* **toure, towre**) [mid-16C–1900s] (*UK Und.*) to see, to survey, to spy on. [? SE *tower*, to stand high above (so as to look down on); Ribton-Turner, *A History of Vagrants* (1887), suggests Erse *tòirigh*, Gaelic *tòirich*, to search after, to pursue]

tour guide *n.* [1960s+] (*US drugs*) a person who aids and supports someone having a psychedelic drug experience. [play on TRIP n.[4] (1)]

tourist *n.* **1** [1920s–40s] (*US tramp*) a tramp who travels south to avoid the cold northern winters. **2** [1940s+] (*gay*) one who occasionally enjoys homosexual sex, but is not a member of the subculture.

touristas *n.* (*also* **turistas**) [1950s+] diarrhoea or any form of stomach upset contracted on a foreign holiday (cf. AZTEC HOP n.). [Sp., lit. 'tourists']

tousle *n.* (*also* **touzle**) [mid–late 19C] bushy whiskers.

tout *n.[1]* **1** [early 18C–early 19C] a thief's lookout; thus *strong tout*, a very observant eye. **2** [late 18C–early 19C] a 'look-out house' (Grose, 1785). **3** [early–mid-19C] the act of spying or surveying; thus KEEP TOUT v. **4** [mid-19C+] (*US*) a person who sells betting advice. **5** [late 19C] a lookout for a criminal gang. **6** [1900s] (*Aus.*) one who spies for the purpose of blackmail. **7** [1940s] a spy working for a casino owner, checking the honesty of the dealers. **8** [1950s+] (*Irish/Scot.*) an informer. [TOUT v.[1]; note *tout*, a person who solicits custom, is SE]

tout *n.[2]* [1980s+] (*drugs*) an assistant to a street drug dealer, directing buyers to the seller. [TOUT n.[1]]

tout *n.[3] see* TOOT n.[1].

tout *v.[1]* [late 17C–19C] **1** to watch, to spy on. **2** (*UK Und.*) to keep a careful lookout, to be on one's guard. [SE *tout*, to peep, to peer; note *tout*, to solicit for custom, is SE]

tout *v.[2]* [1990s+] (*US drugs*) to work as an assistant to a drug dealer. [TOUT n.[2]]

touter *n.* **1** [early–mid-19C] in horseracing, one who keeps an eye on horses when training, the health of jockeys, the orders given by owners etc. **2** [mid-19C] (*UK Und.*) a thief's lookout. [TOUT v.[1]]

touting-ken *n. see* TOOTING-KEN n.

touze *v. see* TOUZLE v.

touzery gang *n.* (*also* **towzery gang**) [mid–late 19C] mock-auction swindlers. [? SE *touse*, to pull about, to abuse]

touzle *n. see* TOUSLE n.

touzle *v.* (*also* **touze**) [late 18C–19C] of a man, to have sexual intercourse (cf. BANG v.[1]). [Scot. *touzle*, to handle (esp. a woman) rudely or indelicately]

tow *n*. [mid–late 19C] money. [SE *tow*, strands of flax used for a light (money, like tow, 'burns' fast)]

towel *n*. [mid-18C–mid-19C] a cudgel. [abbr. OAKEN TOWEL n.]

towel *v*. [18C+] to beat, to cudgel, to thrash. [OAKEN TOWEL n.]

towel-head *n*. (*also* **tea-towel head, towlie**) [1980s+] a derog. term for an Arab from the Middle East (cf. ABDUL n.). [SE *towel* + -HEAD sfx (2)/SE *head*; the term became particularly popular during and after the Gulf War of 1991]

towelling *n*. [mid-19C–1900s] a thrashing, a beating. [TOWEL v.]

towel up *v*. [1910s+] (*Aus.*) to beat, to thrash. [TOWEL v.]

tower *n*.[1] [late 17C–early 18C] false hair. [SE *tower*, a very high head-dress worn by women at the time]

tower *n*.[2] [late 18C–early 19C] (*UK Und.*) clipped money. [*Tower Hill*, London, a centre of contemporary criminality]

tower *v*. [late 18C–early 19C] to spy upon. [SE *tower*, to rise to a great height (and thus be able to spy on the surrounding area)]

Tower Bridge *n*. [20C+] a fridge. [rhy. sl.]

Tower Bridge *phr*. [1930s] a phr. used in reply to 'How are you?', meaning 'up and down', 'so-so'. [*Tower Bridge* in London goes 'up and down' to let boats pass through]

tower dock *n*. [2000s] the penis (cf. ALMOND n.). [rhy. sl. = COCK n.[2] (1)]

Tower Hill *v*. [1990s+] to kill. [rhy. sl.; ult. the area *Tower Hill* in London]

Tower Hill play *n*. [late 17C–early 19C] 'a slap on the face and a kick on the breech' (Grose, 1785). [the criminal environs of *Tower Hill* where such rough-housing would have been common]

Tower Hill vinegar *n*. [16C–17C] the swordsman's block. [the sword preceded the noose as a means of execution; criminals, esp. political ones, were executed at the Tower of London]

towhead *n*. [mid–late 19C] (*US, Western*) one who is considered effeminate, a 'city slicker'. [SE *tow-head*, a light-haired boy, from SE *tow*, flax]

towie *n*. [1970s+] (*Aus.*) the driver of a *tow*-truck. [abbr.]

towlie *n. see* TOWEL-HEAD n.

towline *v. see* TOW OUT v.

town *n*. [late 19C–1900s] a halfpenny. [rhy. sl. = BROWN n.[2] (1)]

town bike *n*. (*also* **town bicycle**) [1940s+] (*orig. Aus.*) a very promiscuous woman, one who is constantly 'ridden'; thus *ride like a/the town bike*, to copulate with great vigour (cf. BANBURY n.). [BIKE n. (1)]

town bull *n*. **1** [late 17C–18C] a promiscuous man; thus *lawless as a town bull*, of a man, extremely promiscuous. **2** [late 18C–early 19C; 1910s–20s] a pimp or procurer (cf. ABBOT ON THE CROSS n.). [SE *town bull*, a bull housed in turn by the cow-keepers of a village]

town clown *n*. (*also* **clown**) [1920s–60s] (*US*) a policeman working in a village or small town.

townie *n*. **1** [early 19C–1950s] a fellow *town*sman. **2** [early 19C+] a *town*-dweller, esp. a Londoner. **3** [mid-19C+] (*mainly US campus/private school*) an inhabitant of the *town* rather than of the campus/school. **4** [2000s] a working-class 'lad', dressed in sportswear. [abbr.]

townie *adj*. (*also* **towney**) [early 19C] cunning, duplicitous; usu. in phr. *come towney over*. [as seen by a peasant, the supposed characteristics of a TOWNIE n. (2)]

town lands *n*. [late 18C–early 19C] the female breasts. [for ety. *see* TIPPERARY FORTUNE n.]

town miss *n. see* MISS n.[1].

Town of the Wind *n. see* WINDY CITY n. (1).

town pump *n*. (*also* **town punch**) [1970s+] a very promiscuous woman. [SE *town* + PUMP n.[1] (3)/PUNCH n.[1]]

towns *n*. [2000s] the testicles (cf. CHEESE AND CRACKERS n.). [rhy. sl.; *town halls* = BALLS n.[1] (1)]

towns and cities *n*. [1900s–40s] a woman's breasts (cf. BRACE AND BITS n.). [rhy. sl. = TITTY n.[1] (1)]

town shift *n*. **1** [mid-17C–mid-18C] a scoundrel, esp. a card-sharp. **2** [early 18C] a male homosexual. [(1) and poss. (2) his constantly changing his address to keep ahead of the authorities and outraged victims]

town stallion *n*. [late 17C–18C] a womanizer, a lecher. [STALLION n. (1)]

town tabby *n*. [mid-19C] a smart dowager. [colloq. *Town*, London + TABBY n. (1)]

town toddler *n*. [late 18C–mid-19C] (*UK Und.*) a gullible person, prey to confidence tricksters. [TODDLER n. (1), i.e. one who wanders around open to exploitation]

town trap *n*. [late 17C–early 18C] a pimp (cf. ABBOT ON THE CROSS n.). [SE *town* + *trap*]

towny *n. see* TOWNIE n.

tow out *v*. (*also* **towline**) [early–mid-19C] (*UK Und.*) to decoy a potential victim away from the victim's premises so that one's accomplice can enter and rob them. [naut. imagery]

towre *v. see* TOUR v.

tow row *adj*. [late 18C–19C] drunk (and disorderly). [SE *tow row*, a hubbub, a din. Note milit. jargon *tow row*, a grenadier]

Tow Street *n*. [19C] a fig. 'street' in which one is decoyed; thus *be in Tow Street*, to be decoyed, to be persuaded (against one's will). [SE *tow*, to drag]

tow-wow *n*. [mid-18C] the vagina. [? TOWZE v.]

towze *v*. [early 17C–mid-18C] of a man, to have sexual intercourse (cf. BANG v.[1]). [Scot. *touse*, to pull (a woman) about rudely or indelicately]

towzery gang *n. see* TOUZERY GANG n.

tox *v*. [mid-17C] to intoxicate; thus *toxed*, *toxt*, intoxicated, drunk. [abbr.]

toxic waste dump *n*. [1980s+] (*US campus*) a person who uses drugs or drink to excess.

toxy *n*. [1960s+] (*drugs*) a small container of opium. [? misreading of TOY n.[3] (1)]

toy *n*.[1] **1** [17C–19C] the penis. **2** [mid-17C–19C] the vagina. **3** [early 19C] a prostitute (cf. BANGTAIL n.[1]).

toy *n*.[2] [early 19C+] a watch; thus TOY AND TACKLE n.

toy *n*.[3] (*drugs*) **1** [1910s–60s] (*also* **pin-yen toy, toey**) a small container, approx. 2.5cm (1in) in diameter, used to hold prepared opium. **2** [1930s–60s] a measure of opium, a small ball, approx. the size of a pea. **3** [1960s–80s] a hypodermic syringe. [(1) + PEN YEN n.]

toy *n*.[4] [1910s+] (*US Black teen*) a gullible person, a fool.

toy *v*. [1990s+] (*US Black/teen*) to destroy another graffiti artist's work by drawing over it; thus *toy someone out*; as n., one who is inferior in the hierachy of graffiti artists. [? SE *toy*, to play with, to tease + implication of acting childishly]

toy and tackle *n*. [late 19C–1910s] a watch and chain. [TOY n.[2] + TACKLE n.[2]]

toy boy *n*. (*also* **boy toy**) [1950s+] a young attractive man popular among older, richer women; thus *boy toy*, which can mean the same or a young attractive woman popular among older men. [i.e. his/her role as a plaything]

toy-getter *n*. [late 19C] a thief specializing in stealing watches. [TOY n.[2] + SE *getter*]

toys *n*.[1] [early 18C] in fig. use of SE, sexual 'wares'.

toys *n*.[2] **1** [1960s+] (*drugs*) equipment for injecting narcotics. **2** [1970s+] any appliances designed to increase sexual pleasure or fantasies.

toy soldier *n*. [1940s] (*US Black*) an officer cadet. [derisive use of SE]

t.p.t. *n*. [1990s+] (*US teen*) trailer park trash. [abbr.]

trac *n*. [1960s+] (*Aus.*) a prisoner who refuses to accept the rules. [abbr. SE *intractable*]

trace (off) *v*. [1950s+] (*W.I. Rasta*) to curse or speak abusively to someone. [? link to UK dial. *trace*, to tell stories of old times or SE *trace*, to track, to pursue]

Tracey *n. see* SHARON *n.*

Track, the *n.* (*also* **the Bitumen**) [1930s+] (*Aus.*) the Stuart Highway running from Darwin to the south.

track *n.*¹ (*also* **trag**) [mid-19C] 1 quart (2 pints/1.14 litres). [backsl.]

track *n.*² 1 [mid-19C+] the highway or street as the home of tramps, prostitutes, pickpockets etc. 2 [late 19C–1950s] (*Aus.*) any outback road. 3 [1940s–70s] (*US Black*) a dancehall, a ballroom, esp. the Savoy Ballroom in Harlem. 4 [1940s–70s] (*US Black*) the world of pimping, hustling, confidence tricks etc; thus FAST TRACK *n.*; SLOW TRACK *n.* 5 [1960s+] (*US Black*) that area of a street where a prostitute works.

track *n.*³ [1960s+] (*Aus. prison*) a warder who is bribed to smuggle items for the inmates. [TRACK *v.*²]

track *n.*⁴ *see* TRACKS *n.*².

track, the *n. see* TURF, THE *n.*

track *v.*¹ 1 [late 17C–19C] (*UK Und.*) to go. 2 [late 19C–1920s] (*US*) to wander aimlessly. 3 [1910s–50s] to leave, to run off.

track *v.*² [1960s+] (*N.Z. prison*) to smuggle goods into/out of prison.

track *v.*³ 1 [1970s+] to maintain emotional or verbal stability, to 'keep on the right track'. 2 [1990s+] (*US Black*) to talk.

tracked up *adj.* [1960s+] (*drugs*) of a narcotics addict, having one's arms (and other parts of the body) covered in scars from injections. [TRACKS *n.*²]

trackie *n.* (*also* **trackies**) [1990s+] a *track*suit. [abbr.]

track marks *n. see* TRACKS *n.*².

track record *n.* [1960s+] (*US*) the reputation of a person or thing, based on past performance.

tracks *n.*¹ [1940s] (*US Und.*) fingerprints.

tracks *n.*² (*also* **track, track marks**) [1960s+] (*drugs*) punctures and scar tissue that accumulate along the veins of a regular drug addict.

track square *v.* (*also* **track straight**) [1910s] (*Aus.*) to pursue a love affair with honourable intentions (i.e. eventual marriage rather than short-term sex). [TRACK WITH *v.* + SQUARE *adv.* (2)/ STRAIGHT *adv.*¹ (3)]

track star *n.* [1980s] (*US police*) a fugitive on the run, a suspect being chased by the police.

track thirteen *n.* (*also* **track 13**) [1910s–40s] (*US Und.*) a life sentence. [the trad. unlucky number]

track up the dancers *v.* [late 17C–mid-19C] to rush quickly up the stairs. [SE *track*, to make one's way + DANCERS *n.* (1)]

track with *v.* [1910s+] (*Aus.*) to associate with someone of the opposite sex.

trade *n.* 1 [late 16C+] (*also* **trading**) prostitution, sexual intercourse. 2 [1920s+] a prostitute's client. 3 [1920s+] (*gay*) a man with whom one has (commercial) sex, a male prostitute, a male prostitute's customer (cf. ASS PEDDLER *n.*). 4 [1940s] one who works as a prostitute.

trade, the *n.* [mid–late 19C] (*UK Und.*) burglary.

trade *adj.* [1930s+] (*gay*) used of someone involved in commercial sex. [TRADE *n.* (3)]

trade *v.* 1 [early 17C–early 18C; 1950s] to work as a prostitute; to run a brothel. 2 [late 18C] to go looking for sexual partners. 3 [1990s+] of a heterosexual man, to have sex with a homosexual partner. [TRADE *n.*]

trademark *n.* [late 19C] a scratch on the face.

trader *n.* 1 [17C–early 19C] a prostitute, a promiscuous woman (cf. ASS PEDDLER *n.*). 2 [mid-17C–early 18C] an adulterer; a womanizer. 3 [1970s+] (*US gay*) a male homosexual prostitute. [TRADE *n.* (3)]

tradesman *n.* [mid-18C–early 19C] a thief. [joc. euph.]

tradesman's entrance *n.* (*also* **tradesman's**) [1990s+] the anus; thus *go in by/up the tradesman's*, to have anal intercourse;

thus phr. *he doesn't mind if he uses the front door or the tradesman's entrance*, he is bisexual (cf. ARSE-END *n.*). [a pun on *back passage*]

tradey *adj.* [1950s] (*gay*) pertaining to commercial sex. [TRADE *n.* (3)]

trading *n. see* TRADE *n.* (1).

trading dame *n.* (*also* **trading lady/woman**) [early 17C–early 19C] a prostitute (cf. ASS PEDDLER *n.*). [TRADE *n.* + SE *dame*]

trading justices *n.* [late 18C–early 19C] 'broken mechanics, discharged footmen, and other low fellows, smuggled into the commission of the peace, who subsist by fomenting disputes, granting warrants, and otherwise retailing justice' (Grose, 1796).

Trafalgar Square *n.* [1990s+] a chair. [rhy. sl.; ult. *Trafalgar Square*, London WC2]

traffic *n.* (*also* **trafficker, traffique**) [late 16C–18C] (*UK Und.*) a prostitute, esp. one working as a confidence trickster (cf. ASS PEDDLER *n.*). [SE *traffic*, the buying and selling of goods or the goods themselves]

traffic cop *n.* [20C+] (*orig. US*) a traffic policeman. [SE *traffic* + COP *n.*¹ (1)]

traffic ticket *n.* [2000s] (*US prison*) a minor disciplinary offence.

traffique *n. see* TRAFFIC *n.*

trag *n. see* TRACK *n.*¹.

tragic *adj.* [1970s+] an all-purpose negative meaning disastrous, appalling, very bad.

tragic magic *n.* (*US drugs*) 1 [1970s+] heroin. 2 [1980s+] crack cocaine dipped in phencyclidine. [the potentially unpleasant, if exciting, effects]

trago *n.* [1960s+] (*US*) a drink. [Sp.]

trail *n.* [mid-19C–1900s] a hoax. [TRAIL *v.*]

trail *v.* [mid-19C–1900s] to hoax, to fool. [18C SE *trail*, to persuade, to seduce (non-sexually)]

trailer *n.*¹ (*also* **traylor**) 1 [late 16C] a highway robber, usu. on foot. 2 [late 16C–early 17C] a horse thief. [they *trail* their victims]

trailer *n.*² 1 [1900s–20s] a helper. 2 [1920s–40s] (*US tramp*) a tramp who follows the circus.

trailer *n.*³ [1990s+] (*US prison*) a conjugal visit.

trailer-load *n.* [1990s+] (*W.I.*) a large quantity.

trailer trash *n.* [1990s+] (*US*) poor Whites living in trailers (large, static caravans), exhibiting a lack of sophistication and enjoying what is seen as a distasteful lifestyle. [SE *trailer* + WHITE TRASH *n.*]

trails *n.* [1980s+] (*drugs*) colourful incandescent paths in the air, 'seen' in the wake of moving objects by those who have taken hallucinogens such as LSD. [the SE *vapour trails* produced by jet aircraft]

trail the wing *v.* [20C+] (*Ulster*) to seek sympathy. [ornithological imagery]

train *n.*¹ (*also* **choo-choo**) [1960s+] (*orig. US*) group sex, usu. involving a single woman and a number of men; it can be voluntary or not.

train *n.*² [1960s+] (*US Und.*) transportation from one prison to another, the mode of transport is irrelevant.

train *v.*¹ [late 19C] (*US, mainly New England*) to romp, to play around, to 'carry on'. [pun on CARRY ON *v.*/SE *carry on*, to keep going]

train *v.*² 1 [1970s+] (*Aus./US*) of a woman, to have sex with several men in a single session. 2 [1990s+] of a man or men, to indulge in group sex with a single woman. [PULL A TRAIN *v.* (3) + undertone of SE *train*, to teach (someone) disciplined behaviour. This is not gang-rape as such, since the woman is ostensibly willing, but she may in reality have little option but to accede. Originated during a well-publicized incident at Ingham, N. Queensland in 1977; but note TRAIN *n.*¹ which predates it]

train *v.*³ *see* TRAIN (WITH) *v.*

trained nurse *n.* [1930s–50s] (*US drugs/prison*) narcotics smuggled into jail.

trainies *n.* [1990s+] a trainer, a training shoe. [abbr.]

train jockey n. [1930s] (*Aus.*) an unemployed vagrant. [JOCKEY n.[3] (2)/SE *jockey*]

trainspotter n. [1980s+] an obsessive, one who specializes in the collection of trivia, the knowledge of minutiae etc. [generic use of SE]

train with v. [late 19C–1940s] (*US*) to associate with, to cooperate with.

train wreck n. [1920s] (*US*) the neck. [rhy. sl.]

traipse *see under* TRAPES.

trake n. [1990s+] (*US Black teen*) a general term of abuse, lit. somebody down whose throat you want to thrust your fingers. [SE *tracheostomy*, the operation of making an opening in the trachea (the windpipe) near its upper end, so that the patient can breathe through it]

tra-la-la phr. [late 19C–1900s] goodbye.

tra-la-las n. [late 19C] 'one of the wealthiest and most dissipated class of dissipated men' (B&L). [? his ability to say 'tra-la-la!' to cares and problems that might cause trouble for less wealthy or dissipated people]

trallywagger n. [20C+] (*Irish*) a loose thread hanging from the hemline of one's clothing. [SE *trail*, to drag behind + *wag*]

tram fare n. [late 19C] 2 pence, esp. as a euph. used by the lowest ranks of prostitutes.

tram it v. see BUS (IT) v.

tramline n. 1 [1940s+] a scar. 2 [1990s+] a thin shaved line in an eyebrow, or a thin line of short hair on a shaved head; usu. in pl.

trammie n. (*also* **trammy**) [1940s+] (*Aus./N.Z.*) the driver or conductor of a *tram*. [abbr.]

tramp n. (*also* **trampie**) 1 [1910s+] (*orig. US*) a promiscuous woman; occas. used of a man. 2 [1910s+] (*orig. US*) a general term of abuse, esp. of someone incompetent or second rate. 3 [1960s] (*US gay*) a male prostitute. 4 [1980s] (*US campus*) an affectionate term of address. [(1) her 'wandering' from man to man]

tramp adj. [1910s+] (*US Black*) second-rate, inferior. [TRAMP n. (2)]

tramp v.[1] [1940s+] (*Aus.*) to dismiss (from a job). [SE *tramp*, to stamp on, to crush]

tramp v.[2] *see* TRAMP (IT) v.

tramp-ass adj. (*also* **trampish-ass**) [1970s] (*US Black*) of a woman, promiscuous. [TRAMP n. (1) + -ASS sfx]

tramped adj. [1920s+] (*Aus.*) dismissed from one's job. [TRAMP v.[1]]

trampers n. [late 18C–19C] the feet or shoes. [SE *tramp*]

trampie n. see TRAMP n.

trampish-ass adj. see TRAMP-ASS adj.

tramp (it) v. 1 [mid–late 19C] to cure oneself of feeling ill or 'out of sorts' by 'walking it off'. 2 [mid-19C+] to travel or wander, esp. as a beggar. [SE *tramp*, to stride]

trample v. [1990s+] (*W.I.*) to have sexual intercourse (cf. BANG v.[1]).

trampler n. [early–mid-17C] a go-between, an intermediary, a lawyer. [they *trample* the path]

trampo n. [1940s] (*US*) a good-for-nothing. [TRAMP n. (2) + -O sfx (1)]

tramp on it! excl. [1940s] (*US*) hurry up! [abbr. TRAMP ON THE GAS v.]

tramp on the gas v. [1940s] to accelerate.

trampooze v. (*also* **trampoose**) 1 [late 18C–1930s] (*US*) to wander around. 2 [1920s+] (*W.I.*) to go out on the town.

tramp's lagging n. [1940s+] (*UK Und.*) a sentence of 90 days in imprisonment, commonly that meted out for vagrancy. [SE *tramp* + LAGGING n. (2)]

trampy adj. [1980s] (*orig. US*) promiscuous, usu. but not invariably of women. [TRAMP n. (1)]

tram troub/trube n. see TROUB n.

trank n. (*drugs*) 1 [1960s+] (*also* **tranc, tranq, tranx**) any type of tranquillizer; thus **tranked (out)**, drugged by tranquillizers. 2 [1980s+] phencyclidine (cf. ACE n.[4]). [abbr.; (2) is used non-recreationally as an animal tranquillizer]

tranklement n. [19C] the stomach, the intestines. [ety. unknown, logically SE *tracklement*, a jelly to accompany meat, but this was unknown until its coinage in 1954]

tranny n. (*also* **trannie**) 1 [1960s+] a *transistor* radio. 2 [1960s+] an automobile *transmission*. 3 [1960s+] a Ford *Transit* van. 4 [1980s+] a *transvestite*. 5 [1980s+] a *transsexual*. [abbr.]

tranq n. see TRANK n. (1).

tranquillo adj. [1990s+] (*US Black/W.I.*) calm, relaxed, COOL adj.[1] (2). [SE *tranquil*]

Trans, the n. [1920s+] (*Aus.*) the train that runs from Adelaide to Perth across. [SE *trans*, across the Nullarbor Plain]

trans n. [1990s+] (*gay*) a transgender, transsexual or transvestite person. [abbr.]

transfag n. [1990s+] (*US gay*) a female to male transsexual who becomes a homosexual man.

transfer v. [late 19C–1900s] (*UK society*) to steal. [euph.]

transformer n. [1990s+] (*US Black gang*) a spy. [the toy *Transformers*, popular in the 1980s, which appear to be one thing, e.g. a car, but can be changed into another, e.g. a robot]

translated adj. [late 19C–1900s] (*UK society*) very drunk, poss. to the extent of passing out. [satirical play on SE *translate*, to be taken to heaven]

translate the truth v. [late 19C] (*UK society*) to lie. [euph.]

translators n. 1 [late 17C–mid-19C] shoemakers specializing in restoring and reselling second-hand shoes. 2 [mid-19C] shoes that have been restored and resold. [SE *translate*, i.e. from old to new]

transmogrify v. (*also* **transmigrafy, transmogriphy, transmugrify**) 1 [mid-17C–19C] to metamorphose, to alter. 2 [late 19C] to astonish, to confound. [(1) subseq. SE; OED suggests orig. version was *transmigrafy* and links it to illiterate corruption of SE *transmigure* or *transmigrate*, to move from one place to another]

transnear v. [late 17C–early 19C] (*UK Und.*) to come up with or draw level with (a person). [? 17C SE *transnear*, to cross a street so as to meet]

transporter n. [mid-19C] (*UK Und.*) the mouth. [the sentence of *transportation* that comes from a judge's *mouth*]

tranx n. see TRANK n. (1).

trap n.[1] 1 [late 17C–19C] trickery, fraud; thus **understand trap**, to be aware, to know what is in one's interest; **up to trap**, aware; **trap is down**, the trick has failed. 2 [early 18C–early 19C] one who blackmails a prostitute's client.

trap n.[2] [18C+] usu. in pl., a policeman or similar agent of the law; thus (*Aus.*) **trap-stronghold**, a police station. [metonymy, by late 19C Aus. only]

trap n.[3] [late 18C+] the mouth; esp. in phrs. KEEP ONE'S TRAP SHUT v.; SHUT ONE'S TRAP v. [it is a trap for food, often used in combs., e.g. BREAD TRAP n., MEAT TRAP n.]

trap n.[4] [19C] a small, sprung, 2-wheeled carriage, a gig. [abbr. SE *rattletrap*, anything shaky or rickety]

trap n.[5] 1 [1920s+] a place, a house or apartment, a nightclub. 2 [1930s] (*US tramp*) a hiding-place for liquor or other illegal goods. 3 [1960s] (*drugs*) a hiding place for drugs. 4 [1970s] a cubicle or stall in a public lavatory.

trap n.[6] [1940s] (*US Black*) the military draft during WW2.

trap n.[7] [1950s+] (*US*) a trapezoid muscle. [abbr.]

trap n.[8] [1970s+] (*US Black*) the number of customers a prostitute is assigned as a daily tally by her pimp to reach a financial target; thus **trap money**, her daily earnings. [i.e. those whom she SE *traps*]

trap n.[9] [1980s+] (*US campus*) a woman who appears to be taking an interest in a man and then turns indifferent. [? SE *trap*, i.e. 'a snare and a delusion']

trap n.[10] *see* WOLF-TRAP n.

trapan *n.* (*also* **trepan**) [mid-17C–18C] (*UK Und.*) **1** a person who benefits by ensnaring other people into actions that will harm them. **2** a trick or snare. [SE *trap*]

trapan *v.* (*also* **trappan, trepan**) [mid-17C–mid-19C] (*UK Und.*) to ensnare, to deceive. [TRAPAN *n.*]

trapanner *n.* (*also* **trappanner, trepanner**) [mid-17C–mid-18C] a cheat, a deceiver. [TRAPAN *v.*]

trapes *n.* (*also* **traipse, trapse**) **1** [late 17C–19C] a slatternly woman. **2** [mid-19C] a tedious, laborious task. [TRAPES *v.*]

trapes *v.* (*also* **traipse**) [late 16C+] to trudge about, to walk in a slovenly, aimless manner (with the image or actuality of one's clothes dragging on the ground). [? synon. SE *trape*, although chronology is dubious; ? OFr. *trapasser, trepasser*, to pass over or beyond]

trapeze artist *n.* **1** [1930s–40s] (*US tramp*) a tramp who rides the trains. **2** [1930s+] a sexual contortionist. **3** [1940s] a woman who enjoys cunnilingus, esp. as part of sex exhibitions. **4** [1940s] (*US gay*) a fellator. [ARTIST sfx]

trap house *n.* [mid-19C] (*US Und.*) a brothel where clients are robbed while *in flagrante* by an accomplice who reaches in through a concealed panel (cf. ACCOMMODATION HOUSE *n.*). [SE *trap* + HOUSE *n.*[1] (1)]

trap (number) two *n.* [1990s+] the anus; thus *take it up trap two*, to submit to anal intercourse. [joc. use of greyhound terminology]

trappan *v. see* TRAPAN *v.*

trappanner *n. see* TRAPANNER *n.*

trapper *n.* [late 19C] a horse that draws a small 2-wheeled carriage. [ext. of TRAP *n.*[4]]

traps *n.*[1] **1** [early 19C+] one's personal effects. **2** [mid-19C] (*UK Und.*) clothes. **3** [mid–late 19C] (*Aus.*) a pack. **4** [late 19C] tools, equipment. **5** [1970s] (*gay*) men's underwear. [SE *trappings*]

traps *n.*[2] [20C+] drums or other percussion devices. [ety. unknown; ? fig. use of SE]

trapse *n. see* TRAPES *n.*

trapstick *n.* **1** [mid-17C–18C] the penis; thus *well-trapped*, well-endowed (cf. BAT *n.*[7]). **2** [early 18C–mid-19C; 1950s] usu. in pl., legs, esp. thin legs. [SE *trapstick*, a stick used in the game of trap or trap-ball]

trap two *n. see* TRAP (NUMBER) TWO *n.*

trash *n.*[1] [late 16C–19C] money (cf. CHAFF *n.*[2]). [the identification of money and dirt]

trash *n.*[2] [1950s+] (*US Black*) loose talk, banter, teasing.

trash *n.*[3] *see* WHITE TRASH *n.*

trash *v.* **1** [1960s+] (*orig. US*) to break windows, destroy appliances etc as part of a political demonstration, a prison search, a robbery etc; thus *trasher*, a (political) vandal; *trashing*, the action of political vandalism. **2** [1970s+] (*orig. US*) to beat up, to injure badly. **3** [1970s+] (*orig. US*) to criticize (a work of art or similar creative effort) so as to undermine its validity, to malign. **4** [1970s+] (*US*) to scavenge discarded goods, other people's rubbish. **5** [1970s+] (*US*) to go out to find casual sex. **6** [1970s+] (*orig. US*) to vandalize, to destroy, to render a mess (with no political overtones). [SAmE *trash*, rubbish, garbage. (1) coined by the radical Weatherman movement. Note the 1960s 'underground' revolutionary cartoon hero 'Trashman', created by Spain Rodriguez]

trash (an' ready) *adj.* [1990s+] (*W.I./UK Black teen*) attractive, fashionable, trendy. [ety. unknown]

trashed(-out) *adj.* **1** [1960s+] very drunk (cf. ANNIHILATED *adj.*). **2** [1980s+] very intoxicated by a drug. **3** [1980s+] extremely ill or emotionally disturbed. **4** [1980s+] exhausted, tired, overworked. **5** [1980s+] of an object, wrecked, ruined, destroyed. [fig. use of TRASH *v.* (2)]

trashmouth *n.* [1970s+] (*US campus*) one who regularly uses profanity or obscenity. [SAmE *trash* + SE *mouth*]

trash one's act *v.* [1970s] (*US campus*) to cease what one is doing; usu. as imper. [fig. use of TRASH *v.* (2)]

trash talk *n.* [1990s+] (*US Black*) nonsense. [TRASH TALK *v.*]

trash talk *v.* [1960s+] (*orig. US Black*) **1** to talk nonsense, to lie. **2** to talk insultingly, disparagingly. [SAmE *trash*, rubbish]

trashy *adj.* **1** [mid-19C+] of people, worthless, disreputable. **2** [1930s+] (*US*) characteristic of poor WHITE TRASH *n.* **3** [1970s+] sluttish, tarty. [SE *trashy*, of objects, worthless]

trasseno *n. see* TROSSENO *n.*

trat *n.* [late 19C–1900s] a young and attractive prostitute. [backsl. = TART *n.*[1] (2)]

tratt *n.* (*also* **trat**) [1960s+] a trattoria or small, Italianate restaurant, esp. fashionable in the 1960s. [abbr.]

travel *v.* [mid-19C+] to move quickly, to leave, to depart.

travel agent *n.* **1** [1960s] (*drugs*) LSD (cf. A *n.*[3]). **2** [1960s] an LSD guide. **3** [1960s+] an LSD supplier. [play on TRIP *n.*[4] (1)]

travel by Harry Pannell *v.* [1920s+] (*N.Z.*) to go by foot, to walk. [*H(arry) Pannell* & Co, makers of stout walking boots]

travel by Mr Foot's horse *v. see* TAKE MR FOOT'S HORSE *v.*

travel by rail *v.* [1930s+] (*Aus.*) to be so drunk that one can only proceed by hanging onto things.

traveller *n.*[1] **1** [18C–mid-19C] a highwayman. **2** [mid-18C–1900s] (*mainly Aus.*) a tramp. **3** [19C] an itinerant peddler. **4** [19C] (*UK Und.*) a thief who moves from town to town. **5** [mid-19C+] a gypsy. **6** [late 19C–1900s] a sermon which can be delivered by the same preacher on different occasions and in different places. **7** [1980s+] a young itinerant who travels the UK by car or caravan but has no Romany connections and is often from a HIPPIE *n.*[2] (3), punk or similar youth subculture and is usu. interested in a variety of 'green' or allied issues.

traveller *n.*[2] [mid-18C] a shilling. [? it travels about from person to person or it enables one to travel]

traveller at Her Majesty's Expense *n.* [mid-19C–1900s] a convict condemned to be transported. [see GALLOPING DANDRUFF *n.*]

travelling dandruff *n. see* GALLOPING DANDRUFF *n.*

travel on one's thumb *v.* [1920s+] to hitchhike. [the raising of one's thumb in the hope of a lift]

trawler *n.* [1920s+] (*Aus.*) a police car or van; a 'Black Maria'. [it *trawls* the streets looking for suspects]

tray *n.* (*also* **tre, trey**) **1** [late 15C+] the number 3, whether as a digit or a set of 3. **2** [late 19C+] (*also* **treemoon, treyer**) a 3-month or 3-year prison sentence. **3** [1950s] £3. **4** [1950s+] (*also* **treyer**) $3. **5** [1960s+] (*US Black/drugs*) a $3 packet of heroin. [Ital. *tre*, three]

tray-bit *n.* (*also* **tray, tray-piece, trey, trey-bit**) [late 19C+] (*orig. Aus./N.Z.*) **1** a threepenny piece. **2** a term of contempt for an insignificant person.

traylor *n. see* TRAILER *n.*[1].

tray-trapper *n.* [1900s–50s] (*Aus.*) one who takes round a collection or 'passes round the hat'. [TRAY-BIT *n.* + SE *trapper*]

tre *n. see* TRAY *n.*

treach *adj.* (*also* **treacherous**) [1980s+] (*US Black/teen*) very good, excellent. [abbr./ext. of SE *treacherous*, on bad = good model]

treacle *n.* **1** [late 18C+] inferior port. **2** [early 19C+] glutinously sentimental love-making. **3** [late 19C–1930s] insincere, empty talk, typically that of a politician.

treacle! *excl. see* TREACLE-TROUSERS! *excl.*

treacle-arse *n.* [1940s–50s] (*Aus.*) a passive homosexual. [SE *treacle* + ARSE *n.*[1] (1)]

treacle-billy *n.* [20C+] (*Irish*) a lodging house. [TREACLE-MAN *n.* (2)]

treacle-man *n.* [late 19C–1900s] **1** a good-looking man who works as a decoy for burglars by charming the housemaid while the gang slip in unnoticed. **2** a smooth-talking, good-looking travelling salesman, who 'sweet-talks' the 'lady of the house' into buying his wares. **3** a shop assistant, esp. in a draper's, who has the same effect on customers. [the stickiness and sweetness of SE *treacle*]

treacle-miner *n.* [1910s] (*Aus.*) a man who boasts of his wealth or position.

treacle plaster *n.* [1920s–30s] (*UK Und.*) a sticky piece of brown paper used by a thief to remove glass carefully.

treacle sleep *n.* [mid-19C] deep, uninterrupted sleep. [the slow pouring of thick SE *treacle*]

treacle tart *n.* [1990s+] an act of breaking wind. [rhy. sl. = FART n. (1)]

Treacle Town *n.* [late 19C] **1** Bristol. **2** Macclesfield. [(1) its treacle refineries; (2) F&H posit an unlikely story of a treacle hogshead bursting and inundating the town's gutters]

treacle-trousers! *excl.* (*also* **treacle!**) [1920s–40s] (*Aus.*) a jibe aimed at one whose trousers are too short. [? they stick to the wearer's legs]

tread *v.* [mid-16C–17C; late 19C–1950s] of a man, to have sexual intercourse (cf. BANG v.¹). [SE *tread*, of the male bird, to copulate with]

treaders *n.* [late 19C; 1940s] shoes. [1940s use is US Black]

tread on someone's toes *v. see* STEP ON SOMEONE'S TOES v.

treads *n.* [1960s] (*US campus*) trainers.

treasure *n.*¹ **1** [mid-16C+] an admirable person. **2** [1920s+] (*also* **treas**) an affectionate term of address.

treasure *n.*² **1** [17C–19C; 1980s+] the vagina. **2** [18C–19C] the penis. [a relatively rare positive image; also note TREASURE OF LOVE n.]

treasure hunt *n.* [1990s+] the vagina (cf. ALL QUIET n.). [rhy. sl. = CUNT n.¹ (1)]

treasure of love *n.* [mid–late 18C] the vagina (cf. ADAM'S OWN (ALTAR) n.).

Treasure State *n.* [1930s–50s] (*US*) Montana. [its reserves of precious metals]

treasure trail *n. see* HAPPY TRAIL n.

treasury of love *n. see* NATURE'S TREASURY n.

treat *n.* **1** [19C+] anything (or occas. anyone) admirable, enjoyable or pleasurable; also used ironically. **2** [1980s] (*US campus*) a good-looking woman.

treat *v.* [2000s] (*US teen*) to teach someone, to correct someone's behaviour, to punish.

treat, a *adv.* (*also* **a treato**) [late 19C+] wonderfully, extremely, excessively, e.g. *that'll go down a treat*.

treat like shit *v.* [1970s+] to treat in a vile and unpleasant manner, deservedly or not. [SE *treat* + LIKE SHIT adv. (2)]

treble chance *n.* [20C+] a dance. [rhy. sl.]

tree *n.*¹ [1960s] (*US Black, Los Angeles*) a policeman who is susceptible to bribery. [play on SE *green* of a tree and GREEN n.² (1)]

tree *n.*² [1960s+] (*US campus*) a very tall woman of 6ft or more; thus CHERRY TREE n.

tree *n.*³ [2000s] (*US*) a gearstick.

tree *n.*⁴ *see* TRIPLE TREE n.

tree *n.*⁵ *see* WOOD n.⁴.

tree and sap *n.* [20C+] (*Aus.*) a tap (faucet). [rhy. sl.]

tree chopper *n. see* TREE-JUMPER n.

treed *adj.*¹ [1980s+] **1** (*US drugs*) extremely intoxicated by a drug. **2** (*US campus*) thrilled.

treed *adj.*² *see* UP A TREE phr.¹ (2).

tree-dweller *n.* [1990s+] a fool, a peasant.

tree-hugger *n.* (*also* **tree nymph**) [1960s+] (*US campus*) an environmentalist; thus *adj.* **tree-hugging**.

tree-jumper *n.* (*also* **tree-chopper**) [1970s+] (*US prison*) a rapist or sexual molester. [their jumping out of trees to attack their victims]

treemoon *n. see* TRAY n. (2).

tree nymph *n. see* TREE-HUGGER n.

tree of knowledge *n.* [1940s+] (*S.Afr. drugs*) marijuana (cf. AFRICAN BUSH n.).

tree of the triple crook *n.* (*also* **crooked tree**) [17C–19C] the gallows.

trees *n.* [1990s+] (*US Black/drugs*) marijuana (cf. AFRICAN BUSH n.). [pun on GREEN n.³ (1)]

tree suit *n.* [1940s–70s] (*US Black*) a coffin. [SE *tree*, i.e. wood]

tree that bears fruit all year round *n.* (*also* **tree that bears twelve times a year**) [mid-17C–mid-19C] the gallows.

treewins *n. see* THREESWINS n.

tremblers *n.*¹ **1** [19C] (*Anglo-Irish*) the stairs. **2** [1960s+] a woman's breasts, esp. when large, thus able to tremble (cf. BOBBER n.²).

tremblers *n.*² [1970s] (*drugs*) the shakes that accompany heroin withdrawal.

trembles *n.* [19C] delirium tremens.

tremendous *adj.* (*also* **tremenjous**) [early 19C+] extraordinary, esp. admirable, remarkable.

trench *n.*¹ [late 15C+] the vagina (cf. AGREEABLE RUTS OF LIFE n.).

trench *n.*² [1970s+] (*orig. US Black*) a *trench*coat. [abbr.]

trenches *n.* [1990s+] (*US Black teen*) any impoverished area.

trendoid *n.* [1980s+] one who is slavishly devoted to following the latest trends (but never quite achieves the correct effect). [SE *trend* + -OID sfx]

trendy *n.* (*also* **trend**) [1960s+] a devoted, if not always wholly successful, trend-follower. [SE *trend*]

trendy *adj.* [1980s] (*US campus*) excellent. [SE *trendy*, fashionable]

trepan *see under* TRAPAN.

trepanner *n. see* TRAPANNER n.

très *adj.* [1920s+] very. [synon. Fr.]

treswins *n. see* THREESWINS n.

Trev *n.* [1990s+] (*UK juv.*) a generic for any stupid, working-class teenager. [abbr. of the stereotyped 'proletarian' name *Trevor*]

T. Rex *n.* [1970s+] sex. [rhy. sl.; ult. *T. Rex*, a pop group of the early 1970s]

trey *see also under* TRAY and its combs.

trey-bits *n.* [1950s+] (*Aus./N.Z.*) **1** the female breasts (cf. BRACE AND BITS n.). **2** diarrhoea (cf. BANANA (SPLITS) n.). [rhy. sl.; (1) = TIT n.³ (1); (2) = SHITS, THE n. (1); ult. TRAY-BIT n. (1)]

trey eight *n.* [1980s+] (*US Black*) a .38 calibre gun. [TRAY n. (1) + SE *eight*]

treyning *see under* TRINING and its combs.

trey of knockers *n.* [1940s] (*US Black*) a pawnbroker's shop. [TRAY n. (1); the 3 balls hanging above such shops]

trey of sous *n.* [1940s] (*US Black*) 3 dimes, 30 cents; thus *trey of sous and a double ruff*, 4 nickels, 40 cents. [TRAY n. (1) + SOU n. (+ RUFF n.)]

trezzie *n. see* TRIZZIE n.

triangle *n.* [1930s+] a 3-way relationship, in any combination of sexes and sexualities.

triangles *n.* [mid-19C] delirium tremens. [due to the hallucinations, nothing is 'on the square']

trib *n.* [late 17C–1910s] (*UK Und.*) a prison. [SE *tribulation*]

tribe *n.* [late 19C+] (*US Und.*) a gang, a given group of criminal specialists.

trichi *n.* [mid–late 19C] (*Anglo-Ind.*) a *Trichi*nopoly cigar. [abbr.]

trick *n.*¹ **1** [late 16C+] sexual intercourse, occas. other forms of sexual encounter, esp. a prostitute's intercourse (or other activity) with a client. **2** [20C+] a girl, a young woman. **3** [1920s+] a prostitute's client, whether hetero- or homosexual, the implication being of deceiving any such client into parting with money. **4** [1920s+] any casual sex partner. **5** [1950s+] a general term of abuse, equating the subject with a prostitute's client. **6** [1970s+] (*US Black*) one who can be easily manipulated, e.g. a long-term admirer who is never allowed sex, but merely kept in tow for the material pleasures they offer. **7** [1970s+] a boyfriend; hetero- or homosexual. **8** [1990s+] (*US prison*) a prisoner who can be easily exploited for money or presents. [note Dillard, *Lexicon of Black English* (1977): 'The term *trick* for the sexual performance of a prostitute probably comes, ultimately, from the voodoo term for achieving control (often sexual control), possibly reinforced by the nautical term meaning "a task"]

trick n.² [early 18C+] (*UK/US Und.*) a crime, esp. a robbery or theft; thus *pull a trick*, TURN A TRICK v.¹.

trick n.³ [mid-18C–early 19C] (*US Und.*) a watch.

trick n.⁴ **1** [mid-19C+] a period of work, usu. one that is physically demanding or unpleasant. **2** [late 19C–1900s] any period spent within an institution, e.g. a hospital. **3** [late 19C+] (*US*) a prison sentence. **4** [1900s–50s] (*US*) a term of service, e.g. in the army, on a ship. **5** [1910s] a situation one dislikes. [naut. use *trick*, a turn at the wheel]

trick n.⁵ **1** [late 19C+] (*US/Aus.*) (*also* **tricksie**) a small or amusing adult, animal or child. **2** [20C+] a clever person; also used sarcastically.

trick adj.¹ [1950s+] **1** relating to commercial or casual sex. **2** used lit. or fig. to imply the foolish gullibility of anyone who is, or might as well be, a prostitute's client. [TRICK n.¹]

trick adj.² [1980s+] (*US campus*) **1** interesting, pleasing. **2** technologically sophisticated. [SE *tricky, tricksy*]

trick v.¹ **1** [1930s+] (*US*) to work as a prostitute, to have sex with a client; thus TRICKING n. **2** [1960s+] (*US*) to have casual sex. **3** [1960s+] (*gay*) to pick up a partner for casual, unpaid sex. **4** [1960s+] (*US Black*) of a man, to spend money on a woman other than one's regular partner. **5** [1960s+] (*US*) of a man, to pay for sex with a prostitute. **6** [1990s+] (*US*) of a man, to spend money on a woman in the hope of being repaid with sex. [TRICK n.¹ (3); (1) note Miler & Milner (1972): 'By implication, one is literally tricking a man by taking money for doing what women should do for free']

trick v.² *see* TRICK (ON) v.

trick-acting n. [20C+] (*Irish*) showing off.

trick-ass adj. [1960s+] (*US Black*) a general derog. term. [TRICK n.¹ (1) + -ASS sfx]

trick baby n. [1960s+] (*orig. US Black*) an illegitimate child born to a prostitute. [TRICK n.¹ (3) + SE *baby*. Given no positive evidence to the contrary, she assumes the father to have been one of the paying customers; note TRICK DADDY n.]

trick bag n.¹ [1960s+] (*US Black*) an unpleasant and disadvantaged position, a no-win situation. [TRICK n.¹ (3) + SE *bag*, a receptacle, on model of SCUMBAG n.; the pimp assumption that only victims pay for sex and that such a victim deserves whatever happens to him]

trick bag n.² [1970s] (*US*) a fig. repository of secrets and surprises.

trick broad n. [1970s] (*US Black*) a prostitute. [TRICK n.¹ (3) + BROAD n.² (2)]

trick bunk n. [1990s+] (*US prison*) that bunk in a convict dormitory which is used for clandestine sex. [TRICK n.¹ (1) + SE *bunk*]

trick cyclist n. [1950s+] (*orig. milit.*) a psychiatrist. [joc. derog. mispron.]

trick daddy n. [2000s] (*US Black*) the father of a prostitute's child. [TRICK n.¹ (3) + SE *daddy*; note TRICK BABY n.]

tricker n. [late 16C–early 17C] (*UK Und.*) a burglar's tool, spec. a gadget used to force open a window. [SE *trick*, some form of pincers or expandable wedge; 'engines of Iron so cunningly wrought, that he wil cut a barre of Iron in two with them' (Robert Greene in *The Blacke Bookes Messenger*, 1592)]

trickeration n. **1** [1930s–40s] (*US Black*) showing off, boasting, flaunting oneself or one's possessions. **2** [1940s–60s] (*US Black/prison*) the act of fooling, deceiving and otherwise manipulating someone. [SE *trick* + sfx *-eration*]

trickett n. [late 19C–1900s] (*Aus., New South Wales*) a long drink of beer. [the New South Wales champion sculler *Trickett*, who stated, for advertising purposes, that 'beer's best for an A1 nation']

trick flick n. [1950s+] (*gay*) a pornographic film. [TRICK n.¹ (1) + FLICK n.³ (1)]

trick house n. [1940s+] (*US Black*) a brothel (cf. ACCOMMODATION HOUSE n.). [TRICK n.¹ (1) + HOUSE n.¹ (1)]

trickie n. [20C+] (*Irish*) an amusing, 'sharp' person. [TRICK n.⁵ (1)]

tricking n. [1930s+] (*orig. US Black*) having sex for money. [TRICK v.¹ (1)]

trickle n. [2000s] (*US juv.*) the vagina.

trickle v. [1910s–20s] to go, to make one's way, usu. in combs., e.g. *trickle down, trickle down to, trickle over, trickle over to*. [? a P.G. Wodehouse nonce-use]

trick money n. [1940s+] (*US Black*) the money a prostitute earns and hands over to her pimp. [TRICK n.¹ (3) + SE *money*]

trickology n. [1970s] subterfuge, deception. [SE *trick* + -OLOGY n.]

trick (on) v. [1970s] (*US Black*) to inform on; to betray.

trick-pad n. [1990s+] (*US Und.*) an apartment, room or hotel room used by prostitutes to entertain their clients; also attrib. [TRICK n.¹ (3) + PAD n.² (2)]

trick rider n. [1980s] (*US*) a homosexual man. [TRICK n.¹ (7) + RIDE v.¹ (1)]

trick room n. [1920s+] a room, in a hotel or motel, where a prostitute can take clients. [TRICK n.¹ (3) + SE *room*]

tricks n. [1930s+] circumstances, one's life. [backform. f. HOW'S TRICKS? phr.]

tricksie n. *see* TRICK n.⁵ (1).

trick suit n. [1950s+] a prostitute's dress that can be removed easily and is thus suitable for business. [TRICK n.¹ (3) + SE *suit*]

trick the books v. [1910s] (*Aus.*) to deceive a bookmaker. [SE *trick* + BOOK n.² (2)]

trick towel n. [1950s+] (*gay*) a towel for wiping oneself after intercourse. [TRICK n.¹ (3) + SE *towel*]

trick-track n. *see* TICK-TACK n.¹.

trickum legis n. [late 18C–early 19C] a legal trick. [cod Lat., 'trick of the law']

trick up v. [1920s+] (*Aus.*) to take advantage of, to confuse, to outwit.

trick willy n. [1950s+] (*US Black*) a gullible Black man. [TRICK n.¹ (3) + generic *Willy*]

tried at Stafford Court, be v. [early 17C] to be beaten, to be thrashed. [pun on SE *staff*]

trif adj. (*also* **trife**) [1990s+] worthless, disgusting. [SE *trifling/TRIFLIN'* n.]

trifecta n. [1960s+] (*US*) any chance situation involving 3 components. [gambling *trifecta*, a bet on the first 3 places in a horserace]

triff n. [1900s] a *trifle*. [abbr.]

trifle n. [late 19C] the penis (cf. BAUBLE n.). [euph.]

triflin' n. [1950s+] (*US Black*) acting irresponsibly, esp. as a parasite, e.g. *don't trust a word he says, that boy is just triflin'*. [SE *trifling*]

trig n.¹ [mid-19C+] *trigon*ometry. [abbr.]

trig n.² [late 19C] a trot, a hurried walk, a trip. [17C SE *trig*, to go in a hurry]

trigger n.¹ (*also* **triggerboy, triggerman**) **1** [1930s] the index finger. **2** [1930s+] (*US*) a gunman, esp. one working for organized crime. **3** [1940s–50s] an armed bodyguard. **4** [1950s+] that member of a criminal gang who uses a gun. **5** [1990s+] (*US prison*) an armed prison guard.

trigger n.² [1940s] the penis (cf. AX n.²). [on model of GUN n.¹ (2)]

trigger happy adj. [1940s+] (*orig. US*) overemotional, keen to put action before thought. [SE *trigger happy*, over-eager to use a gun]

triggerman n. *see* TRIGGER n.¹.

trig it v. [late 18C–19C] to play truant. [SE *trig*, to walk off quickly]

trig one's wig v. [1940s] (*US Black*) to think fast. [SE *trig(ger)*, to set off, to launch + WIG n.³ (1)]

trigry-mate n. **1** [late 17C–1900s] an idle female companion.

2 [late 19C] an intimate friend. [SE *trig*, to walk briskly + SE *mate*; they are both people with whom one walks around]

trike *n.* [late 19C+] a *tricycle*. [abbr.]

trilby *n.* [late 19C–1930s] (*US*) a foot. [the heroine of the novel *Trilby* (1894) by George du Maurier, whose feet were particularly attractive. Note SE *trilby*, a type of shoe fashionable in US *c*.1900]

trilby hat *n.* [1960s+] a fool (cf. BEECHAM'S PILL n.). [rhy. sl. = PRAT n.¹ (6)]

trill *n.*¹ [late 17C–19C] the anus. [? punning Lat. *ars musica*, the musical art]

trill *n.*² [1930s–40s] (*US Black*) **1** departure. **2** an affected way of walking; thus *knock one's trill*, to walk in an affected manner. [TRILBY n.]

trill *v.* (*also* **trilly, trilly-walk**) **1** [1930s–40s] (*US Black/P.R.*) to leave, to walk off. **2** [1970s] to arrive, to enter. [? SE *trill*, to trundle, to move on wheels or TRILBY n.]

trill like a canary *v. see* SING LIKE A CANARY v.

trim *n.* (*orig. US Black*) **1** [1930s+] a woman's genitalia; female pubic hair. **2** [1930s+] (*also* **trimming**) a woman, always in a sexual context; thus GET SOME TRIM v. **3** [1950s+] cunnilingus. [? SE *trim*, neat, attractive, pretty]

trim *v.* **1** [early 16C+] (*also* **trim up**) to beat, to trounce, to defeat. **2** [early 16C+] to reprimand, to scold. **3** [17C–18C; 1960s+] to have sexual intercourse (cf. BANG v.¹). **4** [late 17C+] to cheat of money or possessions. [SE *trim*, to cut the hair, thus to 'fleece']

trimble *adj.* [20C+] (*W.I., Gren.*) selfish, greedy, fearful of sharing what one has. [? SE *tremble*]

trimmer *n.*¹ **1** [mid-18C–19C] a thing that defeats another, e.g. a blow, a stiff reply etc. **2** [19C–1930s] a person who beats, scolds, reprimands etc. **3** [late 19C–1900s] a thieving prostitute. **4** [late 19C+] (*US Und.*) a swindler, a confidence trickster; also a crooked lawyer. [TRIM v.]

trimmer *n.*² [1940s+] (*Aus./N.Z.*) something or someone that is excellent, wonderful, approved of. [SE *trimming*, excellent, first-rate]

trimming *n.*¹ **1** [early 16C; late 17C+] a beating, a defeat. **2** [17C] (*UK Und.*) sleight-of-hand used by a confidence trickster. **3** [late 17C+] a reprimand, a dressing down, a verbal beating. **4** [1910s–40s] (*UK Und.*) the final stage of a confidence game, in which the victim loses his money. [SE *trim*, to cut the hair, thus to 'fleece']

trimming *n.*² *see* TRIM n. (2).

trimmings *n.* [late 19C–1940s] secretly drunk alcohol, usu. consumed by a woman. [a period when shops (as opposed to 'sinful' public houses) were allowed to sell alcohol. Shopkeepers, typically drapers and silk-merchants, thus itemized as 'trimmings' the drinks their female customers consumed, on the bills that were sent to their husbands]

trim someone's jacket *v.* (*also* **swinge someone's jacket**) [mid-18C–early 19C] to beat, to thrash someone. [TRIM v. (1); cf. SE *dress, array*, to beat/*swinge*, to trash]

trim someone's lamps *v.* [1940s–50s] to beat someone up. [TRIM v. (1) + ? SE *lampblack*, thus to black one's eyes]

trim someone's rim *v.* [1970s] (*US*) to have anal intercourse (cf. ASK FOR THE RING v.). [assonance]

trim the buff *v.* [late 18C] to deflower a woman. [SE *trim*, to clip + BUFF n.¹]

trim up *v. see* TRIM v. (1).

trindle-tail *n. see* TRUNDLE-TAIL n.

trine *n.* [mid-17C–mid-19C] the gallows, thus Tyburn. [TRINE v.¹]

trine *v.*¹ [17C–19C] (*UK Und.*) to hang. [? abbr. TRINE TO THE CHEATS v. or TRINING n.]

trine *v.*² [early 17C–mid-18C] to go, to step. [synon. 14C–16C SE *trine*, ult. OSwed. *trina*, to go]

trine to the cheats *v.* [17C–18C] to go to the gallows, to be hanged. [SE *trine*, to march + CHEAT n. (3)]

tringham-trangham/tringum-trangum *n. see* TRINKUM-TRANKUM n.

trining *n.* (*also* **treyning, tryning**) [mid-16C–early 19C] (*UK Und.*) a hanging. [prob. SE *trine*, threefold; the ref. is to the 3-part Tyburn gallows; or ? SE *trine*, to march]

trining cheat *n.* (*also* **treyning cheat**) [early 17C] the gallows. [TRINING n. + CHEAT n. (3)]

trinity kiss *n.* [late 19C] (*UK society*) a triple kiss given to children at bedtime by their parents.

trinket *n.* **1** [17C–early 18C] the vagina (cf. ARTICLE n.). **2** [mid-19C–1910s] a baby's or small boy's penis (cf. BAUBLE n.). [SE *trinket*; note TRINKETS n.]

trinkets *n.* [mid-17C; 19C] the male genitals. [note TRINKET n. (2)]

trinkum-trankum *n.* (*also* **tringham-trangham, tringum-trangum**) **1** [late 17C–1900s] a whim or fancy. **2** [18C–1900s] a trifle. [SE *trinket*]

trip *n.*¹ **1** [mid-19C–1930s] a prostitute or a thief's female companion, esp. one who decoys and then robs drunks. **2** [1900s–50s] (*US Und.*) a prison sentence. **3** [1920s+] (*US Und.*) an arrest. **4** [1950s–60s] (*UK Und.*) a prostitute's client.

trip *n.*² [1910s–20s] an affectionate term of address. [neutral form of TRIP n.¹ (1)]

trip *n.*³ [1930s] (*US prison*) a transfer from one prison to another.

trip *n.*⁴ (*drugs*) **1** [1950s+] the experience that follows the ingestion of LSD or another hallucinogenic. **2** [1960s+] a dose of a hallucinogenic drug, usu. LSD. **3** [1970s+] any form of drug experience.

trip *n.*⁵ **1** [1960s+] any form of experience, event, lifestyle or attitude. **2** [1960s+] a challenging, surprising or otherwise out of the ordinary experience; often as *it's a trip*. **3** [1970s] anything considered simple. **4** [1970s+] (*US campus*) an odd, eccentric person; a funny person. **5** [1980s+] (*US campus*) a cheering, pleasing event. [fig. use of TRIP n.⁴]

trip *v.*¹ [1960s+] (*US drugs*) **1** to take LSD. **2** to take any hallucinogenic drug. [TRIP n.⁴ (1)]

trip *v.*² **1** [1960s+] to play around, to 'mess about'. **2** [1970s+] to be delighted, to be ecstatic; often as *trip for, trip over*; thus TRIP OFF (OF) v. **3** [1980s+] (*US Black*) to lose control, to go mad, to act under a misapprehension, to overreact. **4** [1980s+] to be passionately interested or involved in; thus TRIP OFF v. **5** [1990s+] to worry. **6** [1990s+] to be surprised. **7** [1990s+] to suffer. [fig. non-drug uses of TRIP v.¹]

trip *v.*³ **1** [1980s+] (*US Black gang/campus*) to make an error, to blunder. **2** [1990s+] (*US*) to lie.

trip down *v.* [1960s–80s] (*US*) to go to, to leave. [SE *trip*, to walk lightly]

tripe *n.*¹ (*also* **tripes**) [mid-18C+] the guts, the intestines; thus DOUBLE TRIPE n.¹; *don't bust your tripe*, don't get over-excited, don't overdo things; *have someone by the tripes*, to have someone at a disadvantage. [SE mid-15C–mid-18C]

tripe *n.*² [late 19C+] nonsense, utter rubbish; thus *tripe merchant*, a purveyor of such material. [virtually SE by 20C]

tripe and trillibub *n.* (*also* **tripes and trullibubs**) [17C–early 19C] a nickname for a fat person. [SE *tripes and trillibubs*, animal intestines]

tripe-hound *n.* **1** [20C+] an unpleasant or contemptible person. **2** [20C+] (*Aus./N.Z.*) a dog, esp. a sheepdog. **3** [1920s] a newspaper reporter or an informant. [SE *tripe*/TRIPE n.² + HOUND sfx]

tripes *n. see* TRIPE n.¹.

tripes and trillibubs *n. see* TRIPE AND TRILLIBUB n.

tripey *adj.* [1940s+] rubbishy. [TRIPE n.²]

triphead *n.* [1990s+] (*drugs*) a regular consumer of LSD. [TRIP n.⁴ (2) + -HEAD sfx (3)]

trip in *v.* [1960s–80s] (*US*) to arrive, to enter. [SE *trip*, to walk lightly]

triple *n.* [1980s+] a sexual act involving 3 particpants.

triple burger with cheese *n. see* BURGER (WITH CHEESE) n.

triple-clutcher *n.* [1950s+] a euph. for MOTHERFUCKER n. (1).

triple-decker sandwich *n. see* SANDWICH n.[2].

triple-hip *adj.* [1940s+] (*US Black*) extra smart, very wise. [SE *triple* + HIP adj. (1)]

triple master blaster *n.* [1980s+] (*drugs*) a situation in which one smokes crack cocaine while simultaneously being fellated and sodomized. [SE *triple* + MASTER BLASTER n.]

triple nine *v.* [2000s] to call the police. [the UK emergency phone number: 999]

triple-take *n. see* DOUBLE-TAKE n.

triple-threat queen *n.* [1960s+] (*US gay*) a gay man who is happy to put his penis into a mouth, an anus or an armpit. [SE + QUEEN n.[2] (1)]

triple tree *n.* (*also* **tree, triple trestle**) [late 16C–1930s] the gallows, orig. that sited at Tyburn, London; thus ext. to other gallows. [this giant 3-cornered gallows, capable of dispatching 21 villains at a time, stands menacingly in the background of Hogarth's 1747 engraving of a public hanging]

triple W *n.* [1970s] (*US Black*) a very sexy and accommodating woman. [i.e. a warm, wet, womb]

triple whammy *n.* [1950s+] (*US*) a 3-part attack, threat or difficulty. [ext. of DOUBLE WHAMMY n.]

trip off *v.* [1980s+] (*US*) to turn against, to become emotionally distanced. [opposite of TRIP v.[2] (4)]

trip off (of) *v.* [1960s+] (*orig. US*) to enjoy. [TRIP v.[2] (2); the image is of an experience so intense that it replicates the effects of LSD]

trip on one's dick *v. see* STEP ON ONE'S COCK v.

trip out *v.*[1] [1960s+] to experience a hallucinogenic drug or a simulacrum thereof. [ext. of TRIP v.[1]]

trip out *v.*[2] (*US Black/campus*) **1** [1960s+] to leave. **2** [1980s] to fool, to trick, to 'con'.

trip out *v.*[3] **1** [1960s+] to lose control, to leave normality. **2** [1960s+] to strike one as funny, crazy, extraordinary or amazing. **3** [1970s+] to obsess or fantasize about. **4** [1980s+] to be amazed, delighted. **5** [1990s+] to feel confused. **6** [1990s+] to confuse, to render emotionally unstable, to worry. [fig. use of TRIP OUT v.[1], i.e. ext. of TRIP v.[2]]

tripped-out *adj.*[1] [1960s+] (*drugs*) under the influence of LSD or another hallucinogen. [TRIP OUT v.[1]]

tripped-out *adj.*[2] [1970s+] disorientated, confused, upset. [TRIP OUT v.[3] (6)]

tripped-up *adj.* [1980s] (*US campus*) experiencing the effects of excessive drinking. [var. on TRIPPED-OUT adj.[1] with the added image of falling over]

tripper *n.* [1960s+] (*drugs*) one who takes LSD or similar hallucinogens. [TRIP v.[1]]

tripper(-up) *n.* [19C] a thief who robs innocent pedestrians who have been deliberately tripped up by a confederate. Often women, they preyed on drunken seamen. [SE *trip*]

tripping *n.*[1] **1** [1960s+] taking a drug, usu. LSD. **2** [1990s+] (*US Black*) responding to the effects of a narcotic. [TRIP v.[1]]

tripping *n.*[2] **1** [1960s+] fantasizing, acting in an irrational manner. **2** [1960s+] (*US Black*) doing something beyond the norm, in a positive way. **3** [1960s+] daydreaming. **4** [1990s+] (*US Black*) becoming angry, overreacting. [TRIP v.[2], i.e. fig. use of TRIPPING n.[1]]

tripping *adj.* [1980s+] (*US campus*) excellent, admirable. [TRIP v.[2] (2)]

-tripping *sfx* [1960s+] a general sfx denoting a style of action or opinion, e.g. *power-tripping*, asserting oneself over others; *head-tripping*, thinking. [TRIPPING n.[2]]

trippy *adj.* **1** [1960s+] (*orig. US*) bizarre, strange, disturbing (fig. approximating the sensation of taking a hallucinogen). **2** [1960s+] (*drugs*) characteristic of an LSD-taking HIPPIE n.[2] (3). **3** [1990s+] (*US teen*) excellent, first-rate. **4** [1990s+] (*drugs*) pertaining to MDMA. [TRIP n.[4]]

trippy-hippie *adj. see* HIPPY-TRIPPY adj.

trip to the moon *n.* [1940s+] (*orig. gay*) anal intercourse. [SE *trip* + MOON n.[1] (1)]

trip up on *v.* [1980s] (*US Black*) to betray a lover, to commit adultery.

triss *n.*[1] (*also* **trizz**) [1920s+] (*Aus.*) a threepenny bit. [abbr. TRIZZIE n.]

triss *n.*[2] (*also* **trizz**) [1950s+] (*Aus.*) an effeminate male homosexual. [TRISS ABOUT v.]

triss about *v.* [1940s+] (*Aus.*) to act in an effeminate manner. [synon. with SWISH v.[2]]

trissy *adj.* (*also* **trizzy**) [1950s+] (*Aus.*) homosexual, effeminate. [TRISS ABOUT v.]

triznann *n.* [2000s] (*US Black*) sexual intercourse; also as v. [? TRIM n. + -IZ- ifx]

trizz *see under* TRISS.

trizzer *n.* [1920s+] (*Aus.*) a public lavatory. [a time when the charge for a 'wash-and-brush-up' was 3 pence, i.e. a TRIZZIE n.]

trizzie *n.* (*also* **trezzie**) [1920s–60s] (*orig. Aus.*) a threepenny piece. [TRAY n. (1) or SE *three*]

trizzoe *n.* [2000s] (*US Black*) a derog. term for a woman. [TRICK n.[1] (2) + -IZ- ifx + HO n.[1]]

trizzy *adj. see* TRISSY adj.

Troc, the *n.* **1** [late 19C+] the *Troc*adero Music Hall, Piccadilly Circus, London W1. **2** [1940s] the *Troc*adero Music Hall, Sydney, Australia. [abbr.; (1) now recreated as a vast amusement arcade]

trod *n.* [1970s–80s] (*UK Black*) a journey on foot. [TROD v.]

trod *v.* [1970s–80s] (*UK Black*) to walk; thus *trodder*, a pedestrian. [SE *trod*, past tense of *tread*]

trodder boots *n.* [1980s] (*UK Black*) heavy boots. [TROD v. + SE *boots*]

trods *n.* [1940s] (*US Black*) the feet. [SE *tread*]

troepie *n. see* TROOPIE n.

trog *n.* [1950s+] (*orig. naut.*) a general term of disdain. [SE *troglodyte*, a prehistoric cave dweller, loosely defined in sl. contexts as 'the lowest form of human life'; note RMC Duntroon (Aus.) *trog*, an ugly woman]

Trojan *n.* (*also* **trusty Trojan**) **1** [17C–19C] an intimate companion, esp. as a fellow drinker and roisterer. **2** [17C–1910s] a generally good fellow. **3** [early–mid-19C] a professional gambler. [proper name *Trojan*, a brave or plucky person, a person of great energy or endurance, ult. the Homeric legends]

Trojan horse *n.* [1960s+] (*US gay*) a gay man who poses as a 'straight' masculine person. [the Homeric myth of deception]

troll *n.*[1] [mid-19C+] (*also* **trol**) a sluttish, idling woman. [abbr. SE *trollop*; 20C+ use is N.Z.]

troll *n.*[2] **1** [1940s+] (*US campus*) an ugly man or woman. **2** [1960s] (*US campus*) a notably hard worker. **3** [1980s] (*US campus*) a small girl or woman (in contrast to a tall one). **4** [1980s] (*US campus*) a lecherous older man. **5** [1980s+] (*US gay*) an unattractive middle-aged gay man. [SE *troll*, a monster]

troll *v.* (*also* **troll about/around**) **1** [late 14C+] to wander around, to saunter; also in fig. use. **2** [1950s+] of a prostitute, to look for clients. **3** [1950s+] (*gay*) to walk the streets in search of a sexual partner. **4** [1960s+] to search, to root around for. **5** [1980s] (*US campus*) to go drinking in a succession of bars. [ult. OF *troller*, to search for game (without purpose) or Fr. *trôler*, to ramble]

troll and troll by *n.* [mid-16C] (*UK Und.*) one who is esteemed by no-one and esteems no-one. [? TROLL v. (1)]

trolley *see also under* TROLLEY (AND TRUCK).

trolley *n.* [1900s–50s] (*US drugs/prison*) any means of moving illegal drugs or other commodities around a jail.

trolley *v.* (*US*) **1** [20C+] of a person, to move (fast). **2** [1910s] to travel by tram or trolley-bus.

trolley and tram *n.* [20C+] ham (cf. BEEF AND HAM n.). [rhy. sl.]

trolley (and truck) *n.* [1910s+] an act of sexual intercourse. [rhy. sl. = FUCK n.[1] (1)]

trolley (and truck) *v.* [1910s+] to have sexual intercourse. [TROLLEY (AND TRUCK) n.]

trolley dolly *n.* [1980s+] (*orig. gay*) an air steward.

trolleyed *adj.* [1990s+] drunk or under the influence of drugs. [OFF ONE'S TROLLEY phr.]

trolleys *n. see* TROLLIES n.

troll for faggots *v.* [1970s] (*gay*) to search the streets for a sexual partner. [TROLL v. (3) + FAGGOT n.² (3)]

troll hazard of trace *n.* [mid-16C] (*UK Und.*) someone who follows their master as far as the master can be seen. [TROLL v. (1) + *trace*, a track or line of footprints]

troll hazard of tritrace *n.* [mid-16C] (*UK Und.*) one who 'goeth gaping after his master' (Awdeley, *Fraternitie of Vagabondes*, c.1561). [TROLL v. (1) + *tritrace*, an unknown word which ? linked to *treytrace*, itself another mystery; but note prev.]

trollies *n.* (*also* **trolleys, trollys**) **1** [1950s+] underpants. **2** [1990s+] trousers. [Lancashire dial. *trollys*, a woman's drawers, itself linked to Scot. *trolly*, any object with its length disproportionate to its width; ? ult. SE *trail*]

trolling *n.* **1** [mid-19C+] idling, sauntering. **2** [1930s+] working as a prostitute. **3** [1960s+] (*gay*) strolling the streets looking for possible partners. [TROLL v.]

trollocks *n.* [mid-19C] a sluttish, idling woman.

trollop *n.* [20C+] (*US Black*) an unattractive, ugly woman. [SE *trollop*, but without the sexual implications]

trollopee *n.* [mid-18C] a loose dress. [? pun on SE *trollop*, i.e. 'loose']

trollopping *adj.* [mid-18C–early 19C] **1** behaving like a SE *trollop*. **2** ungainly, gauche. [SE *trollop*]

troll with *n.* [mid-16C] (*UK Und.*) a servant who walks alongside his master; 'no man shall know the seruaunt from ye Maister' (Awdeley, *Fraternitie of Vagabondes*, c.1561). [TROLL v. (1)]

trolly lolly *n.* [late 17C–early 19C] a type of lace, coarsely made but once very fashionable. [Flem. *tralje/traalj*, trellis, lattice, mesh]

trollys *n. see* TROLLIES n.

trolly-wags *n.* [19C] trousers. [? rhy. sl. = BAGS n.¹ (1)]

trom *n.* [1990s+] (*drugs*) marijuana. [ironic abbr. of SE *traumatize*, to damage psychologically]

trombone *n.* [1930s+] a telephone. [partial rhy. sl., i.e. only 1 element rather than the usual 2- or 3-word phr.]

trombone *v.* [1990s+] to rack the slide of a shotgun, loading a cartridge into the breech.

tromboning *n.* **1** [late 19C] sexual intercourse. **2** [1990s+] a sex act in which a woman or gay man licks their partner's anus while simultaneously masturbating him.

tromp *adj.* (*also* **trong, trueing, trung**) [2000s] (*UK Black*) attractive.

trompie *n.* [1970s+] (*S.Afr. drugs*) a long, conically shaped marijuana cigarette (cf. BONE n.¹¹). [Afk. *trompie*, a trumpet, a jew's harp]

tron *n.* [2000s] (*US*) a waitress or waiter; thus as v., to work as a waiter or waitress. [abbr. SE *waitron*, preferred non-sexist term]

trong *adj. see* TROMP adj.

tronk *n.* [late 18C–1900s] (*S.Afr.*) prison. [Fr. *tronc*, box, Du. *tronk* or Buganese *tarunka*, a prison. The word could have been imported by Buganese and Balinese slaves; also used in mid-20C Pennsylvania as n., a prison, and v., to imprison]

T-room *see under* TEAROOM and its combs.

troop *n.¹* [2000s] (*US teen*) a long walk.

troop *n.² see* TROUPE n.

troop *v. see* TROOP OFF v.

trooper *n.¹* **1** [mid-17C; mid-19C] a prostitute. **2** [mid-17C] a prostitute's customer. **3** [1930s+] a brave or stalwart person. [milit. *trooper*, but note theatrical/SE *trouper*, a veteran, stalwart actor; (3) backform. f. LIKE A TROOPER adv.]

trooper *n.²* [late 17C–18C] (*UK Und.*) half-a-crown, 2s 6d (12½p). [? its making up part of a SE *trooper's* pay]

troopie *n.* (*also* **troepie**) [1970s+] (*S.Afr.*) a soldier, esp. the lowest rank of national serviceman. [SE *trooper*]

troop off *v.* (*also* **troop, troop out**) [early 18C+] to leave, to go off. [SE *troop*, to walk; late 20C+ use is mainly US campus]

troops *n.* [1930s+] (*US*) a gang, a mob.

trophy *n.* [1970s] (*US campus*) half a gallon (1.9 litres) of alcohol.

tropical *adj.* **1** [late 19C+] of language, obscene. **2** [1940s+] (*Aus.*) of stolen goods, illegal, dishonest. **3** [1990s+] (*Aus.*) intense. **4** [1990s+] (*Aus. Und.*) highly suspicious, very dangerous for criminal activity. [fig. uses of HOT adj.¹/HOT adj.²]

tropical fish *n.* [2000s] an act of urination (cf. ANGEL'S KISS n.). [half rhy. sl. = PISS n. (2)]

troppo *adj.* [1940s+] (*Aus./N.Z.*) mad, insane; thus *go troppo*, to go mad. [SE *tropical*, i.e. the effects of the heat + -O sfx (5)]

tross *n.* (*also* **tros**) [mid-late 19C] a sort. [backsl.]

trosseno *n.* (*also* **trasseno, troseno**) [mid-late 19C] anything that is bad. [backsl., lit. 'one sort']

trossy *adj.* [late 19C–1910s] dirty, unkempt. [? dial. *make a trossle of oneself*, to be slatternly]

trot *n.¹* **1** [late 16C–mid-18C] a prostitute. **2** [18C–19C] the vagina. **3** [1910s–30s] a fellow; esp. as *old trot*. **4** [1920s+] (*N.Z.*) a woman. [SE *trot*, a hag, an old woman]

trot *n.²* **1** [mid-19C–1920s] a child just learning to walk or run. **2** [late 19C] a baby animal. **3** [late 19C+] a walk, a journey; thus [1940s] (*US Black*) *cop a trot*, to walk, to move. **4** [1910s+] (*Aus.*) a sequence of consecutive events, a run of good or bad luck; thus BAD TROT n.; LEAN TROT n.; ROUGH TROT n.; *long trot*, a winning streak. **5** [1950s] an escape (from prison). [SE *trot*, the horse's gait]

trot *n.³* [late 19C+] (*US campus*) a translation of a text, classical or otherwise, for the illegitimate use of students; a study aid (cf. ANIMAL n.³). [play on HORSE n.⁶/PONY n.³]

trot *n.⁴* [1960s+] a *Trots*kyite, used indiscriminately for any hard-left group in the UK; thus media use *trot-slot*, a programme that concerns itself with, or apparently propagandizes for, such groups. [abbr.]

trot, the *n. see* TROTS, THE n.².

trot *v.¹* **1** [early 19C+] (*also* **trot along/off**) to leave, to move off. **2** [late 19C] to steal openly, in broad daylight. **3** [late 19C–1960s] to take out (a woman), to 'walk out with'. [SE *trot*, to go or move quickly; ult. from the horse's gait]

trot *v.²* [1950s] to escape (from prison). [TROT v.¹ (1)]

trot in *v.* [late 19C] to arrest and take to trial.

trot off *v. see* TROT v.¹.

trot out *v.* **1** [mid–late 19C] to spend one's money; usu. as *trot out the pieces*. **2** [mid-19C+] to produce, esp. of an excuse or a lie. **3** [mid-19C+] (*also* **trot up**) to exhibit (someone or something), to put on display. [horseracing jargon *trot out*, to exhibit, to display a horse; (1) and (2) f. (3)]

trot round *v.* [mid-19C+] to go round (to), to pay a call (on). [SE *trot*, to go or move quickly]

trots *n.* **1** [mid-19C–1900s] policemen. **2** [late 19C–1900s] feet. [presumably (1) is fig. use of (2) but cits. predate]

trots, the *n.¹* [late 19C+] (*Aus.*) trotting races.

trots, the *n.²* (*also* **the trot**) [early 19C+] diarrhoea. [note synon. US Appalachian use *johnny trots*]

trot someone round *v.* [late 19C+] to show someone around a place. [var. on TROT OUT v. (3)]

trotter *n.¹* **1** [late 17C+] a foot; usu. in pl. **2** [late 18C+] a racehorse; usu. in pl. meaning horseracing in general. **3** [1920s] a dancing person. [SE *trot*]

trotter *n.²* [1960s+] (*UK Und.*) a deserter from the armed forces. [TROT v.¹ (1)]

trotter-box *n.* (*also* **trotter-case**) [early–mid-19C] a shoe. [TROTTER n.¹ (1) + SE *box/case*]

trotter-shaking *n.* [mid-19C] dancing. [TROTTER n.¹ (1) + SE *shaking*]

trottery *n.* [1920s–60s] (*US*) a dancehall. [SE *trot*]

trot the udyju Pope o' Rome *phr.* [late 19C] an enigmatic phr. asking usu. another man to take one's wife home. [cod Lat. *udyju*, JUDY n.[1] (1) + POPE (OF ROME) n.]

trotting-cases *n.* [mid-19C] shoes. [SE *trot*]

trotty *adj.* (*also* **trottie**) [late 19C] of a person's figure, small, dainty; of clothes neat, fashionable. [TROT n.[2] (1)]

trot up *v. see* TROT OUT v. (3).

troub *n.* (*also* **tram troub/trube**) [1910s+] (*Aus.*) a tram conductor. [SE *troubador*, a wandering singer, i.e. the conductor 'sings out' the stops]

trouble *n.* [late 19C] **1** (*US*) a day of public festivity. **2** (*US*) any interruption of ordinary work. **3** (*Aus.*) a criminal conviction.

trouble *v.* [late 19C+] to bother, to worry (about).

trouble and fuss *n.* [1960s+] a bus. [rhy. sl.]

trouble and strife *n.* **1** [20C+] one's wife. **2** [1900s] life. [rhy. sl.]

trouble-gusset *n.* [mid-17C] the penis. [SE *trouble* + GUSSET n. (2)]

trouble monkey *n.* [2000s] the penis (cf. ANTEATER n.). [SE *trouble* as euph. for sexual intercourse + MONKEY n.[10] (2)]

troubles and cares *n.* [20C+] stairs. [rhy. sl.]

trough *n.* **1** [mid-19C+] eating. **2** [20C+] the place at which one eats.

trough (out) *v.* [1980s+] (*US campus*) to eat voraciously.

trounce *v.* [mid-19C–1900s] to have sexual intercourse (cf. BANG v.[1]).

trouncer *n.* **1** [19C] a strong drink. **2** [20C+] a highly capable or expert individual. **3** [20C+] something amazing or astounding. **4** [20C+] (*Ulster*) an attractive woman.

troupe *n.* (*also* **troop**) [1930s–50s] (*US Und.*) a gang of thieves.

trouper *n. see* TROOPER n.[1].

troused *adj. see* TROUSERED adj.

trouser *n.* (*also* **trowser**) [late 19C] a jack of all trades, an odd-job man. [? he will turn his hand to anything so long as he *trousers* his payment]

trouser *v.* [late 19C+] to pocket.

trouser bandit *n.* [1990s+] a male homosexual (cf. BONE-EATER n.). [SE *trouser* + BANDIT sfx (2)]

trouser cakes *n.* [1990s+] the buttocks (cf. BAKERY GOODS n.). [SE *trouser* + CAKES n.[1] (2)]

trouser chuff *n.* (*also* **trouser cough**) [1980s+] a fart. [SE *trousers* + CHUFF n.[3]; note synon. 17C *cough in the breech*, i.e. buttocks]

trousered *adj.* (*also* **troused**) [1990s+] drunk.

trouser mauser *n.* [1990s+] the penis. [SE *trouser* + *Mauser*, a type of pistol]

trouser off *v.* [1920s+] (*Irish*) to ejaculate.

trouser snake *n. see* ONE-EYED TROUSER-SNAKE n.

trouser trout *n.* [1980s+] (*US*) the penis (cf. ANTEATER n.).

trouser trumpet *n.* [1990s+] the penis (cf. ACCORDION n.).

trout *n.*[1] **1** [mid–late 17C; mid-19C+] a woman; often as OLD TROUT n. **2** [1950s–60s] (*US Black*) the vagina (cf. BEARDED CLAM n.). [the identification of women and fish; note FISH n.[1]]

trout *n.*[2] [mid-17C–early 19C] a boon companion, a true friend, a trusted servant; often as TRUSTY TROUT n. [? on pattern of FISH n.[3]; note SE *trow*, faith, trust, belief]

trout-fishing *n.* [1960s+] (*US gay*) of a gay man, seeking out rich old women who offer money in return for companionship. [TROUT n.[1] (1) + SE *fishing*]

trout's ankle *n. see* EEL'S ANKLE n.

trowser *n. see* TROUSER n.

troy (school) *n.* [1940s–60s] (*Aus.*) a gambling game. [ety. unknown]

trubs *n.* [20C+] (*Aus.*) troubles, problems. [abbr.]

trucha *v.* [1960s+] (*US*) to be alert, to watch out. [Sp.]

truck *n.*[1] [mid–late 19C] a hat. [naut. jargon *truck*, the 'cap' on the very top of a mast]

truck *n.*[2] [1980s+] (*US campus*) someone who moves very slowly. [TRUCK v. (5)]

truck *v.* **1** [mid-17C; 1930s] (*US Black*) to have sexual intercourse.

2 [1930s–70s] to dance the truck, a contemporary popular dance. **3** [1930s+] to move, to travel; often in comb. with *along, around* etc. **4** [1930s+] (*US Black*) to leave, to depart. **5** [1980s+] (*US campus*) to move slowly. [? 17C *truck*, to trudge, ult. synon. Ital. *truccare*; (2) 'that jerky yet rhythmic dance which combines a bend of the body, a tightening of the hand muscles and a slight strut with the legs' (Baltimore *Sun*, 15 November 1935)]

truck-driver *n.* [1950s+] (*US Black*) an ostentatiously 'masculine' homosexual, poss. dressed as a trucker or in similar macho clothes.

truck-drivers *n.* [1970s+] (*drugs*) amphetamines (cf. A n.[2]). [their use by *truck-drivers* and others in staying awake]

truckie *n.* [1950s+] (*Aus./N.Z.*) a long-distance truck-driver, or his lorry. [var. on SAmE *trucker*]

trucking *n.* **1** [1930s+] (*US Black*) strutting, strolling. **2** [1930s+] dancing the truck. **3** [1960s+] moving, struggling along, getting on with it; esp. as in HIPPIE n.[2] (3) slogan *keep on trucking*, an exhortation to continue with one's life. [TRUCK v.]

truck jewellery *n.* [1990s+] (*US Black teen*) items of large, gold jewellery. [? one needs a SE *truck* to carry it or SE *truck*, miscellaneous articles suitable for barter]

truckload *n.* [1980s+] a large amount.

trucks *n.* [mid-19C–1900s] trousers. [? TROLLY-WAGS n. or SE *trucks*, odds and ends]

trudging house *n. see* TRUGGING HOUSE n.

true *adj.* [1990s+] (*US Black teen*) loyal, faithful, dependable. [revival of 11C–19C SE]

true blue *adj.* [mid–late 17C] used of a regular, dedicated drinker. [play on SE *true blue*, orig. the colour of 17C Scot. Covenanters (the reversal of the monarchy's red), subseq. of 19C+ Tories]

true dat *phr.* [1990s+] (*US Black*) an affirmative phr. [pron. of SE *true that*]

true dinkum *n.* (*also* **true dink**) [1900s–40s] (*Aus.*) the absolute truth. [SE *true* + DINKUM adj.]

true grit *n. see* REAL GRIT n. (2).

trueing *adj. see* TROMP adj.

truepenny *n.* [late 16C–17C; early 19C–1900s] a trusty, honest person. [the image of a sound coin]

true trout *n. see* TRUSTY TROUT n.

truff *n.* [18C] a purse. [SE *truffle*]

truff *v.* [mid-19C+] (*northern*) to steal, to pilfer; thus (*Irish*) *truff*, stolen goods. [Scot. *truff*, to pilfer, to obtain by deceit]

trug *n.* (*UK Und.*) **1** [late 16C–18C] (*also* **trugmallion**) a prostitute, a mistress (cf. JAMETTE n.). **2** [17C] a catamite or young homosexual boy. [Ital. *trucca*, 'a fustian or rogish word for a trull, a whore, or a wench' (Florio, *World of Wordes*, 1598); ? cognate with SE *truck*, to barter or exchange commodities]

trugging house *n.* (*also* **trugging ken/place, trudging house**) [late 16C–early 17C] a brothel (cf. ACCOMMODATION HOUSE n.). [TRUG n. (1) + HOUSE n.[1] (1)/KEN n.[1] (1)/SE *place*]

trugmoldy *n.* [mid-17C–early 19C] a prostitute. [? var. on *trugmallion* (see TRUG n.)]

trull *n.* (*UK Und.*) **1** [early 16C–1950s] a prostitute (cf. JAMETTE n.). **2** [mid-17C–early 19C] a tinker's or soldier's companion. [Ger. *Trulle*, a prostitute]

trump *n.*[1] [18C–1900s] an act of breaking wind audibly; occas. also a similar sound emitted from the vagina during intercourse. [TRUMP v.]

trump *n.*[2] **1** [early 19C+] an admirable person, an excellent fellow. **2** [mid-19C] an excellent thing. **3** [1910s–60s] (*also* **trump of the dump**) (*Aus./N.Z.*) a person in charge. [card-playing imagery]

trump *adj.* [1990s+] (*US Black*) rich and successful, with overtones of flashiness. [millionaire property developer, Donald Trump (b.1946)]

trump *v.* [mid-17C+] to break wind loudly; occas. also of the vagina, to make a similar noise during sexual intercourse. [SE *trump*, to trumpet]

trumper *n*. [early–mid-19C] one who breaks wind loudly. [TRUMP v.]

trumpery *n*. [mid-18C–early 19C] a worn-out old prostitute. [SE *trumpery*, valueless goods]

trumpet *n*. **1** [19C] the nose. **2** [late 19C; 1990s+] an act of breaking wind. **3** [1970s+] the telephone. **4** [1990s+] (*US teen*) one who has an extremely large ego.

trumpet *v*. [1920s+] to break wind.

trumpeter *n*. **1** [mid-17C–early 18C] one who belches or breaks wind. **2** [late 18C–early 19C] one who has bad breath. **3** [late 19C] a general term of affectionate address. [(2) to play the trumpet one needs 'strong', here 'bad' breath]

trumpeters *n*. [late 19C] (*Aus. Und.*) 'irons which connect [...] ordinary leg-chains with a bazil [bezel] riveted around each leg immediately below the knees' (Price Warung, *Tales of the Early Days*, 1894). [? the noise of the chains]

trumpeter's lips *n*. [1990s+] the involuntary clenching of the anus at moments of great fear.

trumpie *n*. [1970s] a braggart, a boaster.

trump the hump *v*. [1930s–40s] (*US Black*) to climb a hill. [SE *tramp*]

trump tight *adj*. [2000s] (*US Black*) first-class, fully worked out.

trumpy *adj*. [early 19C] of a person, admirable, first-rate. [TRUMP n.² (1)]

truncheon *n*. [18C–19C; 1990s+] the penis.

trundlers *n*. [late 17C–early 19C] (*UK Und.*) peas. [SE *trundle*, to roll along (around one's plate)]

trundle-tail *n*. (*also* **trindle-tail**) [17C] a derog. description of a person. [SE *trundle-tail*, a cur, a mongrel, lit. a dog with a curly tail]

trundle the bones *v. see* ROLL THE BONES v.

trundling-cheat *n*. [17C] any form of wheeled vehicle. [SE *trundle* + CHEAT n. (1)]

trung *adj. see* TROMP adj.

trunk *n*.¹ [17C–mid-19C] the vagina. [the idea of it being a chest filled with treasure]

trunk *n*.² [late 17C–1900s] the human nose; thus mocking phr. addressed to one who has a prominent nose, *how fares your old trunk?* [an elephant's *trunk*]

trunk *n*.³ [19C] a fool. [SE *trunk*, the body, bereft of the head]

trunk *v*. [1960s] of a man, to have sexual intercourse.

trunk and tree *n*. [1990s+] the human knee. [rhy. sl.]

trunkmaker-like *adj*. [late 18C–early 19C] used of someone who makes more noise than they do real work. [SE *trunkmaker*, one who makes trunks or boxes; thus the noise so created]

trunk-work *n*. [late 16C–early 17C] casual or clandestine sexual intercourse.

trus mi *phr. see* TRUS WI phr.

trustafarian *n*. [1980s+] someone fortunate enough to have a trust fund to insulate them from work or 'real life'. [SE *trust* (*fund*) + joc. abbr. (*Rasta*)*farian*]

trust-buster *n*. [20C+] (*US*) a campaigner against the power of monopolistic industrial or business trusts. [SE *trust* + BUST v.¹ (1)]

trusty *n*.¹ [19C] (*Anglo-Irish*) an overcoat. [it can be trusted to keep one warm/dry]

trusty *n*.² (*also* **trustee, trustie**) [early 19C+] (*Aus./UK/US prison*) a convict who, on the grounds of good behaviour and trust-worthiness, is allotted a priviliged position in the jail.

trusty Trojan *n. see* TROJAN n.

trusty trout *n*. (*also* **true trout**) [mid-17C–early 19C] a boon companion, a true friend. [TROUT n.²]

trus wi *phr*. (*also* **trus mi**) [1980s+] (*W.I./UK Black teen*) believe (in) us/me, trust (in) us/me. [pron. SE *trust we/me*]

trut *n*. [1930s–60s] (*Aus.*) a threepenny bit. [SE *thruppence/ threepence*]

try for White *v*. [1940s+] (*S.Afr.*) to attempt to pass oneself off as White; less common are *try for Black, try for Coloured*.

try-hard *n*. [1990s+] (*Aus. teen*) a general term of abuse. [i.e. the person is trying too hard to be liked or accepted]

try it on *v*. **1** [19C] (*also* **try on**) to live by thieving. **2** [early 19C+] to attempt to get away with something, usu. that which one is not entitled to have. **3** [early 19C+] to make a sexual pass (at someone).

try it on the dog *v*. [late 19C+] usu. of a play or film, to experiment with, to try out. [the testing of poss. poisoned meat by giving it to an unfortunate dog; or theatre jargon *try it on the matinée dog*, the implication being that a matinée is less well-acted than an evening performance]

try it on with *v*. [early 19C+] to attempt to persuade someone who is otherwise unwilling. [ext. of TRY IT ON v. (2), 'it' being one's persuasive 'line']

tryke *n*. [1990s+] (*US gay*) a female transsexual lesbian. [SE *transsexual* + DYKE n.]

tryning *n. see* TRINING n.

try-on *n*. [early 19C+] **1** an attempt at imposition or deceit. **2** the subject of the attempt. **3** any form of attempt at something.

try on *v. see* TRY IT ON v. (1).

try-out *n*. [20C+] a trial run, a trial period, an experimental attempt.

try (something) on for size *v*. [1940s+] (*orig. US*) to try out, to see if something (often fig.) will work.

try to front *v*. (*also* **want to front**) [1980s+] (*US campus*) to denigrate, to make negative comments. [FRONT v.¹ (4)]

t.s. *n*. [1940s+] (*orig. US milit.*) tough shit, often used ironically or mockingly as well as sympathetically. [abbr. TOUGH SHIT n.]

t/s *n*. (*also* **t.s.**) [1970s+] a transsexual. [abbr.]

Ts and Blues *n*. [1980s] (*US drugs*) a combination of Talwin and PBZ (an anti-histamine), used as a cheap subsitute for heroin. [abbr. Talwin + BLUE n.⁹ (2)]

tsang *n*. [1960s–70s] (*S.Afr. township*) money. [ety. unknown; ? echoic of chinking coins]

tsatske *n. see* TCHOTCHKE n.

t.s.h. *phr*. [1980s+] (*US campus*) an expression of commiseration or resignation. [abbr. *that shit happens*]

tsotsi *n*. (*also* **totsi**) [1940s+] (*S.Afr.*) **1** a flashily dressed township thug or gangster; thus *tsotsi taal*, the sl. of the tsotsi world. **2** the tight trousers worn by such gangsters. [Sotho pron. of ZOOT SUIT n.]

tsuris *n*. (*also* **tsooris, tsoris, tsouris, tzuris**) [20C+] troubles, worries, suffering. [Yid. *tsuris*, ult. Heb. *tsarah*, trouble]

t.t. *n*. [1910s+] a *teetotaller*. [abbr.]

t/t *phr*. [1970s+] used in sex contact advertisements, *tit torture*. [abbr.]

t.t.f.n. *phr*. [1940s+] goodbye. [*ta-ta* for *now*, orig. created and popularized on comedian Tommy Handley's BBC Radio show *ITMA* (*It's That Man Again*, 1939–49). Dorothy Summers, as 'Mrs Mopp' (the comic charlady) actually used the phr., which was revived by BBC Radio 2 disc jockey Jimmy Young (b.1923)]

tub *n*.¹ **1** [17C+] a boat; thus [1920s–40s] transatlantic liners, esp. as venues for crime, thus WORK THE TUBS v. (1). **2** [mid-17C–1910s] a pulpit. **3** [late 17C–mid-19C] a coach, esp. a form of covered carriage known as a 'chariot'. **4** [mid–late 19C] a seatless carriage used on the early railways. **5** [mid-19C–1900s] (*US*) a fire engine. **6** [1900s] a glass containing approx. 1 pint. **7** [1910s–50s] a car. **8** [1920s–70s] (*UK Und.*) an omnibus; thus WORK THE TUBS v. (2). **9** [1930s] a truck. **10** [1960s] (*Aus. prison*) a sanitary bucket.

tub *n*.² [late 19C+] a fat person. [abbr. SE *tubby*]

tub *n*.³ [1980s] £100.

tub *v*. [early 17C; mid-19C+] to wash oneself (in a bath or *tub*). [SE *tub*, a bath]

tubbichon *n*. [mid–late 19C] a single curled lock of back hair, worn pulled forwards over the left shoulder. [Fr. *tire-bouchon*, corkscrew, a term used to describe this hairstyle, popularized *c*.1860 by the Empress Eugénie]

tubbing n.[1] [19C] (*UK prison*) a prison sentence. [one is placed inside a *tub*, i.e. a cell]

tubbing n.[2] [late 19C] an act of washing (in a bath). [TUB v.]

tubby n. [late 19C+] (*US*) a fat person, often used as a (usu.) affectionate nickname. [SE *tubby* adj.]

tub-drubber n. see TUB-THUMPER n.

tube n.[1] **1** [mid-18C+] the penis. **2** [20C+] the London Underground, orig. the TWOPENNY TUBE n. **3** [1920s–50s] (*US*) the New York Subway. **4** [1940s–70s] a cigarette. **5** [1950s+] (*Aus.*) a tall, thin beer glass. **6** [1960s] (*US prison*) a Benzedrine inhaler, esp. used recreationally. **7** [1960s] (*US campus*) a very promiscuous girl. **8** [1960s+] (*orig. Aus.*) a bottle or can of beer. **9** [1980s+] (*US drugs*) a large water pipe. [SE *tube*]

tube n.[2] **1** [late 19C–1950s] a telephone. **2** [1940s+] (*UK prison*) a prison officer who makes a habit of listening for information from prison informers. **3** [1950s+] (*Ulster*) a general term of contempt. [the telephone's short-range predecessor, the SE *speaking tube*; (3) f. (2)]

tube n.[3] [1950s+] (*orig. US*) **1** television, as a medium, the industry. **2** a television set. [abbr. cathode ray *tube*, a basic component of the TV]

tube n.[4] [1960s] (*US campus*) an easy course.

tube n.[5] [1980s+] (*Scot.*) a person, usu. with derog. overtones. [ety. unknown]

tube v. [1960s+] (*US campus*) to do badly at work. [GO DOWN THE TUBE(S) v.]

tubed (out) adj. **1** [1960s+] very drunk. **2** [1990s+] (*Irish*) worn-out, useless. [GO DOWN THE TUBE(S) v.; (1) + TUBE n.[1] (8)]

tube (it) v. [1910s+] to travel on the London Underground. [TUBE n.[1] (2)]

tube it v. [1950s+] to watch television. [TUBE n.[3] (2)]

tubesteak n. **1** [1960s+] (*US*) a hot dog, a frankfurter, bologna. **2** [1970s+] (*orig. US*) the penis (cf. BACON n.[1]). [(2) f. (1)]

tubesteak of love n. [1980s+] (*US campus*) the penis (cf. BACON n.[1]). [ext. of TUBESTEAK n. (2)]

tubesteak tarzan n. [1990s+] a homosexual (cf. BONE-EATER n.). [TUBESTEAK n. (2) + *Tarzan*]

tub house n. [1900s] (*US*) a mission. [TUB n.[1] (2) + SE *house*]

tub-man n. (*also* **tub-preacher**) [mid-17C–early 18C] a preacher, a parson. [TUB n.[1] (2) + SE *man/preacher*]

tub of blood n. see BLOODY BUCKET n.

tub of lard n. (*also* **tub of blubber, ...'gator guts, ...guts, ...hog fat, ...soapgrease, bundle of lard, gourd..., butter tub**) [mid-19C+] a fat person.

tub of turds n. [mid-17C] (*UK Und.*) an ugly fat person. [TURD n. (1)]

tub-pounder n. see TUB-THUMPER n.

tub-preacher n. see TUB-MAN n.

tubs n.[1] [mid–late 19C] a butter seller. [the butter *tubs*]

tubs n.[2] [1940s–60s] (*orig. US*) drums. [the shape]

tubs n.[3] [1960s+] (*US gay*) a gay bathhouse. [SE *tub*, a bath]

tubster n. [early 18C] a parson. [TUB n.[1] (2) + -STER sfx]

tub-thumper n. (*also* **tub-drubber/-pounder**) [18C+] a vehement preacher or orator, either clerical or secular. [TUB n.[1] (2) + SE *thumper/drubber*]

tub-thumping n. [mid-19C+] preaching or speechifying, whether or not on religious topics. [TUB-THUMPER n.]

tubular adj. [1980s+] (*US teen*) the ultimate in perfection. [? surfer jargon *tube*, the inside curve of a good wave]

tub worker n. see WORK THE TUBS v. (1).

tuchas/tuches/tuchis n. see TOCHES n.

tuck n. **1** [early–mid-19C] a hearty meal; more usu. TUCK-IN n. or TUCK-OUT n.[1]. **2** [mid-19C] a hearty appetite. **3** [mid-19C+] (*mainly UK juv.*) food, esp. sweet cakes and pastries. **4** [1970s] (*UK Und.*) a successful robbery. [TUCK v.[2]; + ? ref. to the strain placed on the tucks in one's garments]

tuck v.[1] [late 17C–early 19C] to hang; usu. as TUCK UP v.[1] (1). [SE *tuck*, to tug or snatch]

tuck v.[2] [late 18C+] to eat, esp. heartily or greedily; usu. with a prep.; thus TUCK IN v.

tuck v.[3] [1960s+] to tape the penis to the groin (usu. in the context of transvestism). [one 'tucks it away']

Tuckahoe n. [mid-19C–1950s] (*US*) an inhabitant of Virginia.

tucked away adj. (*also* **tucked under**) [20C+] (*Aus./US*) dead and buried.

tucked up adj.[1] [late 17C–mid-19C] hanged. [TUCK UP v.[1] (1)]

tucked up adj.[2] **1** [mid-19C] dazed, unconscious. **2** [late 19C–1910s] worn down, deprived, exhausted. **3** [20C+] (*UK Und.*) captured without any chance of escape. **4** [1990s+] under control. [? TUCKED UP adj.[1]]

tucked up adj.[3] [1920s] well fed. [TUCKER v.]

tuck 'em fair n. [18C] a judicial hanging; thus *dance at tuck 'em fair*, to be hanged. [TUCK v.[1] + SE *fair*]

tucker n. [mid-19C+] (*Aus./N.Z.*) food, rations; thus *hard tucker*, meagre rations; *tucker job*, a poorly paid job (which just covers the cost of one's rations); *tucker money*, a pittance; *tucker chute*, the anus (occas. the mouth); TUCKER-FUCKER n. [ext. of TUCK n. (3), orig. rations of 19C gold diggers]

tucker v. **1** [late 19C+] to provide someone with food. **2** [20C+] to eat a meal. [TUCKER n.]

tuckerbox n. [1970s+] an informer. [Jack Moses poem (*c.*1920s) 'the dog sat on the tuckerbox / nine miles from Gundagai', usu. recited as '*shat* on...' thus the derog.]

tuckered (out) adj. [mid-19C+] (*Aus./US*) exhausted, worn-out. [TUCKER OUT v.]

tucker-fucker n. [1980s+] (*Aus.*) **1** a cook, esp. institutional. **2** a microwave. **3** tomato sauce. [TUCKER n. + FUCKER n. (10)]

tucker out v. [mid-19C+] (*orig. US*) to become exhausted, to collapse. [9C–13C SE *tuck*, to punish, to ill-treat]

tuck-hunter n. [mid-19C] one who is keen to seek out sources of feasting. [TUCK n. (3) + SE *hunter*]

Tuckie n. (*also* **Tuk, Tukkie**) [1910s–30s] (*S.Afr.*) a student of the Transvaal University College, since 1930 renamed University of Pretoria. [initials *T.U.C.* + dimin. *-kie*]

tuck-in n. [mid-19C+] a good meal. [TUCK IN v. or ext. of TUCK n. (1)]

tuck in v. [early 19C+] to eat or drink, heartily or greedily. [SE *tuck in*, in the sense of 'put away']

tuck on a price v. [late 19C] to put a price up to unacceptable heights.

tuck-out n.[1] [early 19C+] a feast, a hearty meal. [ext. of TUCK n. (1)]

tuck-out n.[2] [mid-19C] (*Aus.*) a fight, a beating. [9C–13C SE *tuck*, to punish, to ill-treat]

tucks of time n. [20C+] (*Irish*) plenty of time.

tuck up v.[1] **1** [early 18C–19C] to hang. **2** [1940s–80s] to defraud, to steal from. [TUCK v.[1]]

tuck up v.[2] see TAKE UP v.

tuck up fair n. [mid-19C] the gallows. [TUCK v.[1] + SE *fair*; note TUCK 'EM FAIR n.]

tuckus n. see TOCHES n.

Tucson blanket n. see CALIFORNIA BLANKET n.

'tude n. see ATTITUDE n.

Tuesday is longer than Monday phr. see MONDAY COMES BEFORE SUNDAY phr.

tuff adj. [1960s+] (*US teen*) good or cool. [mis-sp. SE *tough*]

tuff ken n. see TOFF KEN n.

Tufnell Park n. [1990s+] a game, an amusing episode. [rhy. sl. = LARK n.[1]; ult. *Tufnell Park*, an area of north London]

tuft n.[1] [mid-17C–mid-18C; 1970s+] female pubic hair.

tuft n.[2] [mid-18C–19C] an aristocratic, titled undergraduate. [the *tuft* was that adorning the mortarboards of titled students – of gold threads rather than the usual black]

tuft-hunter n. 1 [mid–late 18C] an undergraduate who pursues the acquaintance of rich or titled students. 2 [mid-19C+] a snob, a toady, a social climber. [TUFT n.²]

tuft-hunting n. [late 18C–19C] social climbing, pursuing aristocratic connections. [TUFT-HUNTER n.]

tuft-hunting adj. [mid-19C+] socially aspirant. [TUFT-HUNTER n. (2)]

tug n.¹ [late 19C–1930s] (Aus.) 1 a card-sharp. 2 a confidence trickster. [? they tug cards from the bottom of the pack]

tug n.² [late 19C–1940s] (mainly Aus.) a dirty, uncouth, repellent person. [? generalized use of Etonian public school jargon tug, a scholar, a clever person, a (too) hard worker; itself abbr. SE tug-mutton, a ref. to their meals but ? also to masturbation. Such figures are disdained by their aristocratic peers]

tug n.³ 1 [1940s–60s] (Irish) the act of breaking someone out of prison. 2 [1960s+] an arrest. 3 [1970s] the act of picking up, meeting, introducing oneself. 4 [1970s+] a warning.

tug v. 1 [17C; 2000s] of a man, to have sexual intercourse. 2 [1950s+] (orig. Aus.) to masturbate (cf. BOFF v.). [SE tug; (1) 2000s use is US Black]

tug (a head) v. [1970s] (Aus. Und.) to distract someone's attention while a crime is being committed.

tug-button Tuesday n. [mid-19C] the Tuesday before Advent.

tugg n. see TOG n.

tugger n.¹ [20C+] (Irish) a woman who deals in old clothes. [the wicker boxcar in which she collects her stock and which she tugs around the streets]

tugger n.² [2000s] a male masturbator. [TUG v. (2)]

tuggs n. see TOGS n. (1).

tug-mutton n. 1 [17C] a pimp (cf. ABBOT ON THE CROSS n.). 2 [late 19C] the penis. [SE tug + MUTTON n.¹ (1)/MUTTON n.³]

tug one's slug v. [1990s+] to masturbate (cf. BEAT ONE'S HOG v.). [TUG v. (2) + SLUG n.⁵ (2)]

tug one's taffy v. (also **pull one's taffy**) [1990s+] (US) to masturbate. [TUG v. (2) + SAmE taffy, toffee]

tug o' war n. [20C+] a prostitute (cf. BOAT AND OAR n.). [rhy. sl. SE = whore]

tug someone's coat v. see PULL SOMEONE'S COAT v. (1).

tuies n. see TOOIES n.

t.u.i.f.u. n. [1940s+] (US) a terrible blunder (cf. S.N.A.F.U. n.). [abbr. the ultimate in fuck ups]

Tuk/Tukkie n. see TUCKIE n.

tulip n.¹ 1 [early 19C] a dandy. 2 [mid-19C] a bishop's mitre. 3 [mid-19C] the penis. 4 [mid-19C–1910s] the female genitals. [resemblance]

tulip n.² 1 [mid-19C] a person, used affectionately. 2 [1950s+] (Irish) a fool, usu. a funny one. [the flower as attractive/ insignificant]

tulips n. [2000s] multiple sclerosis. [rhy. sl.; tulips and roses = multiple sclerosis]

tulip-sauce n. [late 19C–1900s] a kiss, the act of kissing. [pun on 'two lips']

tulips of the goes n. [early–mid-19C] the cream of the fashionable world. [SE tulip + GO n.² (1)]

tully-vally n. see TILLY-VALLY n.

tum n. (also **tum-tum**) [mid-19C+] (mainly UK juv.) the stomach. [abbr. + redup.]

tumbe n. [1970s] (US/P.R. Und.) a swindle, a confidence trick. [Sp. tumbar, to knock down]

tumble n.¹ 1 [mid-19C–1930s] (UK Und.) an act of discovery. 2 [20C+] (US Und.) an arrest; thus take a tumble, to be arrested and jailed. [TUMBLE v.³]

tumble n.² [late 19C+] an act of sexual intercourse; thus GIVE SOMEONE A TUMBLE v.¹. [TUMBLE v.¹ (1)]

tumble n.³ [late 19C+] (US) a sign of recognition, a response; usu. in phrs. GIVE SOMEONE A TUMBLE v.²; TAKE A TUMBLE v.¹. [TUMBLE v.² (1)]

tumble n.⁴ [1920s] (US Und.) a chance, an opportunity.

tumble n.⁵ see TUMBLE (DOWN THE SINK) n.

tumble v.¹ 1 [early 16C+] to seduce, to have sexual intercourse. 2 [1960s] to murder. 3 [1960s+] (Aus.) to confuse, to throw off balance. [SE tumble, to cause to fall]

tumble v.² [mid-19C+] 1 to realize, to notice, to recognize; thus TUMBLE TO v. 2 to agree (to), to take a liking (to). 3 (UK Und.) to understand. [fig. uses of SE tumble on, to chance on]

tumble v.³ 1 [mid-19C+] (UK Und.) to alert, to make someone suspicious. 2 [20C+] (US Und.) to be arrested. [ext. of TUMBLE v.²]

tumble v.⁴ [1930s+] to have a drink. [TUMBLE (DOWN THE SINK) n.]

tumble-a-bed n. [late 18C–19C] a chambermaid. [her stereotypical availability]

tumble and trip n. [20C+] a collection of money. [rhy. sl. = WHIPROUND n.]

tumble and trips n. [1920s] (US) lips. [rhy. sl.]

tumbledown n. [early–mid-19C] grog. [it makes one tumble down but note next]

tumble (down the sink) n. [1910s+] a drink. [rhy. sl.]

tumble down to grass v. [late 19C–1900s] to go to rack and ruin. [the image of once cultivated fields returning to grass]

tumble-in n. [mid–late 19C] an act of sexual intercourse. [TUMBLE IN v.]

tumble in v. [mid-19C+] 1 to have sexual intercourse. 2 to go to bed. [ext. of TUMBLE v.¹ (1)]

tumbler n.¹ [17C–mid-19C] the member of a confidence tricking team who searches out and ensnares a suitable victim. [SE tumbler, a dog like a small greyhound, formerly used to catch rabbits (i.e. pun on CONY n.²)]

tumbler n.² [late 17C–mid-19C] a cart. [SE tumbler, a tumbril]

tumblers n. [early–mid-17C] the testicles (cf. BANGERS n.).

tumble to v. 1 [mid–late 19C] to involve oneself energetically or enthusiastically. 2 [mid-19C+] (US) to discover, to become aware of. [TUMBLE v.² (1)]

tumble to pieces v. [mid–late 19C] to go successfully through childbirth. [the pieces are the mother and the newborn child]

tumble-turd n. [1940s–50s] (W.I.) a short, stocky person. [18C US regional dial. tumble-turd, a large black beetle that rolls and buries pieces of dung]

tumble up v. [early–late 19C] (orig. naut.) 1 to rush, to hurry. 2 to rise from bed. [SE tumble]

tummler n. (also **tumler**) [1960s+] (US) 1 the 'life and soul of the party', a person who talks a great deal but accomplishes little. 2 in show business, the MC of a (Jewish) hotel in Catskill Mountains, New York. [Yid./Ger. Tummel, disorder]

tummy n. [mid-19C+] (mainly UK juv.) the stomach. [abbr.]

tummy banana n. [1960s+] the penis (cf. BANANA n.²).

tummy-timber n. see BELLY-TIMBER n.

tump v. [19C] to have sexual intercourse (cf. BANG v.¹). [SE tump, to strike]

tumpa adj. [1940s+] (W.I. Rasta) a stump; thus tumpa-foot man, a 1-footed man.

tump over v. [1970s+] (US campus) to knock over. [SE tump, to strike]

tum-tum n. see TUM n.

tun n. [mid-19C–1900s] a drunkard. [abbr. LUSHINGTON n. + pun on SE tun, a large barrel]

tuna n. [1970s] 1 (US) one who believes themselves to be far more sophisticated than is the reality. 2 (US gay) a homosexual sailor who only takes the passive role in fellatio. 3 (US campus/gay) an attractive man; thus hot tuna! an excl. said on seeing a sexy man.

tunaface n. [1990s+] a lesbian. [TUNA (FISH) n. (2) + SE sfx -face]

tuna (fish) n. [1960s+] 1 (US campus/Black) a girlfriend, a woman. 2 (orig. US Black) the vagina (cf. BEARDED CLAM n.). [the identification of women with fish/FISH n.¹ (1)]

tuna naan n. (also **tuna taco**) [1990s+] a woman's genitals, esp.

in the context of cunnilingus. [TUNA (FISH) n. (2) + *naan*, a variety of Ind. bread/*taco*, a Mexican cornmeal pancake]

tuna wagon n. [1970s+] (*US*) an old, decrepit car. [its only use would be to convey fish]

tune v. 1 [late 18C+] to beat, to thrash. 2 [1960s+] (*US teen*) to talk to, esp. flirtatiously. 3 [1980s] (*S.Afr.*) to enjoy life. 4 [1980s+] (*S.Afr.*) to tease, to hoax, to deceive. [? to get a fig. *tune* – positive or otherwise – from one's target]

tuned adj. (*also* **tuned in/up**) [1920s+] (*US*) stimulated by alcohol but not drunk. [fig. use of TUNE v. (1) but note TUNE UP v. (1)]

tuned in adj. [1950s+] aware of what is going on, at one with the nuances of a situation or conversation. [TUNE IN v.]

tuned out adj. [1950s+] 1 out of touch, unaware. 2 daydreaming, inattentive. [radio imagery]

tuned up *see* TUNED adj.

tune in v. [1920s+] 1 (*orig. US*) to be aware, to be culturally sophisticated; thus 1960s HIPPIE n.[2] (3) slogan 'turn on, *tune in*, drop out'. 2 to make someone aware, to explain. [radio imagery]

tune in one's mike v. [1940s] (*US Black*) to listen. [fig. use of MIC n.[1]]

tune one's pipes v. [18C] to cry. [pun on SE *pipe one's eye*]

tune out v. [1920s+] 1 to lose concentration, deliberately or otherwise. 2 to dismiss a topic or person from one's mind. [radio imagery]

tunes n. [1980s+] (*US campus*) music.

tune someone grief v. (*also* **tune someone skeef**) [1970s+] (*S.Afr.*) to abuse someone verbally, to give someone trouble. [TUNE v. + SE *grief*/S.Afr. *skeef*, disapprovingly, ult. Afk. *skeef*, askew, crooked]

tune the old cow died of n. (*also* **tune the old cow died on**) 1 [early 19C–1910s] (*also* **tune the old cat died of**) a discordant or unpleasant piece of music. 2 [late 19C+] a lecture or homily delivered to a beggar instead of money.

tune up v. 1 [1920s+] to get drunk. 2 [1960s] (*US campus*) to become intoxicated by drugs. 3 [1970s+] to beat, to thrash. [ext. of TUNE v. (1); fig. use of SE *tune up*, of musical instruments]

tunker n. [late 18C–1900s] a street preacher. [Penn Du. *dunken*, a Baptist, lit. 'dipped']

tunnel n. 1 [1970s+] (*US gay*) the anus (cf. ALLEY WAY n.). 2 [1980s+] (*Aus. prison*) a woman.

tunnel-grunters n. [19C] potatoes. [dial.]

tunnel (of love) n. [19C] the vagina (cf. AGREEABLE RUTS OF LIFE n.). [note synon. RMC Duntroon (Aus.) in 1980s+ (also used as a generic for a woman)]

tunnel rat n. 1 [20C+] (*US prison*) one who escapes by digging their way out of prison. 2 [1990s+] (*New York City*) a transit policeman (cf. ANIMAL n.[1]). [note Vietnam era milit. *tunnel rat*, a soldier who entered – and fought in – the extensive enemy tunnel system]

Tunnels n. [late 19C] the Opera Comique in the Strand. [the theatre, which was demolished in 1899 during the building of the Aldwych, was built largely underground and featured a number of subterranean passages, leading patrons from the street to the auditorium]

tunnel stiff n. [20C+] (*US*) an underground tunnel worker. [SE *tunnel* + STIFF n.[2] (7)]

tunti n. [1950s+] (*W.I. Rasta*) the vagina. [for ety. *see* TUN-TUN n.]

tun-tun n. [1950s+] (*W.I., USVI*) 1 the vagina. 2 a term of affection. [suggested links to DUNDUS n. or Carib.E. *tun-tun*, turned cornmeal, are unlikely; ? SE *turn* + redup., the movements of intercourse]

tup n.[1] 1 [17C–early 19C] a cuckold. 2 [early 17C] a lecher. [TUP v.]

tup n.[2] [late 19C–1950s] (*W.I.*) 1 1½ (old) pence. 2 a very small amount. [abbr. SE *tuppence*]

tup adj. [late 19C] arrested. [pron. SE (*locke*)*d up*]

tup v. 1 [late 16C+] to have sexual intercourse (cf. BANG n.[1]). 2 [early 17C] to render a cuckold. [SE *tup*, a ram; thus

Shakespeare's *Othello* (1604), when Iago informs Brabantio that: 'An old Blacke Ram Is tupping your White Ewe'; (2) the ram's HORNS n.]

tup-an-gill n. [mid-19C+] (*W.I.*) 2½ (old) pence. [TUP n.[2] + GILL n.[2] (1)]

tuppence n. [1940s+] (*Aus.*) a fool, a halfwit. [phr. '(only) *tuppence* in the quid']

tuppence coloured adj. [late 19C] exciting. [from toy theatres, advertised as 'penny plain, tuppence coloured']

tuppenny damn n. *see* DAMN n.

tuppenny-ha'penny adj. (*also* **tuppence-ha'penny**, **twopenny**, **twopenny-halfpenny/-ha'penny**, **twopence-halfpenny**) [early 19C+] virtually worthless, insignificant, paltry, cheap, second-rate. [the low value; Williams notes a *twopenny whore* as the cheapest 17C prostitute]

tupper n. [late 19C–1900s] (*UK society*) a bore. ['takes its rise from Mr Martin *Tupper* who wrote a phenomenally successful book called *Proverbial Philosophy* – composed entirely of self-evident propositions' (Ware)]

tuppy adj. [late 19C–1950s] (*Aus.*) of an animal, worn-out, thus worthless. [? SE *tupped*, used for breeding; also Aboriginal use *tuppy*, vagina]

tu quoque n. [early 17C–19C] the vagina. [lit. Lat. 'you also'; ? play on QUIM n. and similar terms for the vagina beginning with *q*; Williams suggests it began as a Lat. rejoinder to the insult 'you're a cunt']

turbo n. 1 [1980s+] (*drugs*) crack cocaine and marijuana smoked together. 2 [1990s+] (*US campus*) a very energetic, 'speedy' person; as adj., slightly crazy. [SE *turbo*-charged]

turbobitch n. [1980s+] (*US campus*) an unpleasant, irritable, negative woman. [SE *turbo* + BITCH n.[1] (1)/SE *slut*]

turbo-charged adj. [1990s+] (*W.I.*) of a woman, extremely attractive.

turboslut n. [1980s] (*US campus*) a notably promiscuous woman.

turd n. 1 [11C+] a piece of excrement. 2 [mid-15C+] (*also* **bugturd**, **turdball**) an unappealing person or object. [OE *tord*, ult. presumed Indo-Eur. root **der*, tear or split. Orig. use, *c.*1000, was simply excrement, the additional pej. meaning was added mid-15C. Thus Harman's *Caveat* (1567) translates the Und. phr. 'Gerry gan the Ruffian cly thee' as 'A torde in thy mouth, the deuill take thee' (*Gerry*, JERE n.[1]). As with many similar terms that are vulgar rather than actual sl., *turd* was excluded from polite speech (and dictionaries) by late 18C. It has remained off-limits, although like many of the 'milder' obscenities, it has crept gradually into spoken, if not written English, esp. where, like its cognate SHIT n.[2] (1), it refers not to excrement, but to a human object of derision or dislike]

turdburger n. [2000s] (*Aus.*) a term of abuse. [TURD n. (1) + SE *burger*]

turd-burglar n. [1960s+] (*orig. Aus.*) a homosexual man; also attrib. (cf. BROWN ARTIST n.). [TURD n. (1) + SE *burglar*, his predilection for anal intercourse; note synon. RMC Duntroon (Aus.) *bowel burglar*]

turd for —!, a excl. [mid-17C–19C] a general excl. of dismissal. [TURD n. (1)]

turdhead n. [1940s+] a term of abuse. [TURD n. (1)/TURD n. (2) + -HEAD sfx (1)]

turd in the punchbowl phr. [1990s+] (*US*) a general term of abuse. [TURD n. (1)]

turd in your teeth! excl. [mid-16C–mid-17C] go to hell! (and stay there). [TURD n. (1)]

turdish adj. [1930s+] unpleasant, obnoxious. [TURD n. (2)]

turd-packer n. (*also* **shit-packer**, **turd-tapper**) [1930s+] (*orig. US*) a homosexual (cf. BROWN ARTIST n.). [TURD n. (1)/SHIT n.[1] (1) + SE *packer/tapper*]

turd poodle n. [1980s+] (*US campus*) an unappealing or stupid person. [TURD n. (2) + play on DOG n.[3] (2)]

turd-puncher n. [1970s+] a homosexual (cf. BROWN ARTIST n.). [TURD n. (1) + SE *puncher*]

turf n. 1 [mid-19C+] the highway or street as the home of the criminal underworld; thus spec. TURF, THE n. 2 [1940s+] the area with which one is familiar and where one is recognized as a regular figure. 3 [1950s+] (*US Und.*) the area controlled by a street or prison gang. 4 [1960s] (*US Und.*) the ground. 5 [1960s+] that area of life, work or other activity in which a person's authority or influence is recognized. [note SE *turf*, as a general n. for the world of horseracing]

turf, the n. (*also* **the track**) [mid-19C+] the occupation of prostitution; thus ON THE TURF phr. (1). [TURF n. (1)]

turf v.[1] [1940s–50s] (*Aus.*) to have sexual intercourse in the open air. [SE *turf*, the grass]

turf v.[2] *see* TURF OUT v. (2).

turfer n. [late 19C] a prostitute. [TURF, THE n.]

turf it v. 1 [mid-19C] to work as a prostitute. 2 [late 19C–1930s] to sleep outdoors, usu. under a tent. 3 [late 19C–1940s] to live as a tramp. [TURF, THE n./TURF n. (1)]

turf it! excl. [1930s+] (*Aus.*) be quiet! shut up! [TURF OUT v.]

turfite n. 1 [mid-19C–1900s] a gambler. 2 [1990s+] (*W.I.*) a veteran. [SE *turf*, as a general n. for the world of horseracing]

turf out v. (*also* **turf off**) 1 [late 19C+] to eject, to throw out, supposedly onto some grass; to dismiss from a job. 2 [1950s] (*N.Z.*) (*also* **turf**) to reject a lover.

turf patrol n. [1980s+] (*Irish*) a session of smoking marijuana. [play on GRASS n.[5]]

turf up v. [1920s+] (*Aus.*) to abandon, to leave a job. [TURF OUT v.]

turistas n. *see* TOURISTAS n.

turk n.[1] 1 [late 16C–17C] (*also* **mahomet**) a low-class prostitute. 2 [late 17C+] a boorish, unpleasant person. 3 [early 18C; 1930s+] (*gay*) one who enjoys anal intercourse. 4 [late 19C+] (*US*) an Irish immigrant. 5 [1950s+] (*US prison*) a 'masculine', predatory prison homosexual. 6 [1970s+] a sexually active man. [racist stereotyping; (2) prob. underpinned by Irish *torc*, a boar or hog]

turk n.[2] 1 [late 19C+] (*Aus.*) a turkey. 2 [1910s–60s] a Turkish cigarette. [abbr.]

turk v. [20C+] of a man, to have sexual intercourse, esp. with a degree of brutality. [racial stereotyping]

turkey n.[1] [mid-19C] a state of drunkenness; thus *catch a turkey*, *carry/have a turkey on one's back*, to be drunk. [DRIVE TURKEYS TO MARKET v.]

turkey n.[2] [20C+] (*US*) an Irish immigrant. [TURK n.[1] (4)]

turkey n.[3] 1 [20C+] an appalling, unquestionable disaster, esp. in show business. 2 [1920s+] a failure, an incompetent, a dull person. 3 [1930s+] (*drugs*) inferior-quality or even fake drugs. 4 [1940s] (*US gang*) a gang member who won't or can't fight, but runs messages etc. 5 [1940s+] an unappealing or worthless thing, a disappointment. 6 [1950s+] a general derog. term of address. 7 [1950s+] an unattractive man or woman. 8 [1980s+] (*US Und./teen*) the victim of a mugging. [according to Cohen (ed.), *Studies in Slang* IV (1995), pp.100–19, originating in the theatrical *turkey show*, a touring show, usu. burlesque, mounted at a moment's notice and staffed by a third-rate cast, even stage-struck amateurs]

turkey n.[4] 1 [1900s–40s] (*Aus./US*) a vagrant's pack, a lumberman's kit pack. 2 [1910s–40s] (*US Und.*) a suitcase, a large traveling bag. [resemblance to the bulky bird which has been 'stuffed']

turkey n.[5] 1 [1970s+] amphetamine (cf. A n.[2]). 2 [1980s+] (*drugs*) cocaine. [ety. unknown]

turkey n.[6] *see* PLAIN-TURKEY n.

turkey adj. 1 [1910s] (*US*) easily accomplished and enjoyed or desired. 2 [1950s] (*US gang*) cowardly; thus *turn turkey*, to back down due to fear. [? TURKEY n.[3] (2)]

turkey v.[1] [1960s] (*US campus/drugs*) to breathe marijuana smoke through the nose. [resemblance to a puffed-up SE *turkey*]

turkey v.[2] *see* TALK TURKEY v. (3).

turkey-buyer n. [late 19C–1900s] a rich person. [orig. use is Leadenhall Market; turkeys were beyond the pockets of the poor]

Turkey Day n. [1910s–40s] (*US Black*) Thanksgiving. [the trad. dish]

turkey gobble n. [1980s+] (*Aus. prison*) fellatio; thus *turkey gobbler*, a felaltor/fellatrix (cf. BASKET LUNCH n.). [TURKEY NECK n.]

turkey merchant n. 1 [late 17C–mid-19C] one who buys and sells turkeys, a poulterer. 2 [mid-19C] (*UK Und.*) a dealer in smuggled silk. [puns on SE *Turkey merchant*, one who trades with Turkey; (2) the play was on *merchant*, i.e. a legitimate dealer; (1) allegedly credited to Horne Tooke, when questioned by fellow Etonians as to his father's occupation]

turkey neck n. [1950s+] the penis. [supposed resemblance]

turkey off v. [20C+] (*Aus./N.Z.*) to leave in a hurry, to run off. [imitative of the farmyard bird]

turkey on a string n. [1970s+] (*US Black*) one who is infatuated and thus easily led and controlled. [ext. of TURKEY n.[3] (2)]

Turkey puddle n. [early 18C] coffee.

turkey's elbow n. *see* BEE'S KNEES n.

turkey shoot n. [1940s+] 1 (*US*) a combat in which one's own side wins without any difficulty, killing and destroying on a large scale; also in fig. use. 2 anything exceptionally easy. [the large SE *turkey* presents an easy target; SAmE *turkey shoot*, a shooting match at which turkeys are the targets and the prizes]

Turkey trot n. [1960s+] diarrhoea suffered by tourists (cf. AZTEC HOP n.). [TROTS, THE n.[2]]

turking n. [20C+] sexual intercourse, copulating. [TURK v.]

Turkish adj. *see* TURKISH (DELIGHT) adj.

Turkish (bath) n. [1990s+] a laugh. [rhy. sl.; Cockney pron. 'barf']

Turkish culture n. [1960s+] (*gay*) the practice of anal intercourse. [note Cleland, *Memoirs of a Woman of Pleasure* (1748–9): 'The round bulge of those Turkish beauties of her's tallying with the hollow made by the bent of his belly and thighs, as they curv'd inwards']

Turkish delight n. 1 [1960s+] (*gay*) pederasty. 2 [1970s+] (*US gay*) an anal vigin. [racial stereotyping + pun]

Turkish (delight) adj. 1 [1990s+] mean, grasping. 2 [2000s] rubbishy. [rhy. sl.; (1) = TIGHT adj.[4] (1); (2) = SHITE adj.]

Turkish rope n. [1990s+] (*US Black gang*) a gold neck-chain, with large links, as worn by successful street thugs. [? the gold or chain comes from *Turkey*]

Turkish shore n. [late 17C–early 19C] Lambeth, Southwark, Rotherhithe, all areas south of the River Thames where the innocent visitor to London was liable to meet trouble. [the negative image of *Turkey*]

turkish towel n. [1930s] tripe.

Turk McGurk n. [1970s] (*US*) a deceitful, untrustworthy person.

turn n.[1] [17C–18C] a judicial hanging. [SE *turn off*, to kill]

turn n.[2] [17C–19C; 2000s] an act of sexual intercourse. [SE *turn-up*, a prostitute + *turn*, an act, a performance]

turn n.[3] [mid-19C+] a shock, usu. unpleasant, e.g. *a nasty turn*.

turn n.[4] [1910s] a robbery.

turn n.[5] [1950s+] (*Aus., mainly teen*) a party. [TURN IT ON v.]

turn v.[1] [17C–19C] to deceive or rob.

turn v.[2] [1910s+] (*US Und.*) 1 to betray to the authorities. 2 to give state's evidence. 3 of a policeman, to become corrupt. 4 to persuade a villain to give evidence against or spy on fellow criminals.

turn v.[3] 1 [1930s] (*US drugs*) to sell drugs; of a doctor or dentist, to write prescriptions for narcotics. 2 [1960s] (*US Und.*) to sell, usu. stolen goods.

turn v.[4] [1970s] to distract someone's attention. [they lit. 'turn' away]

turn v.[5] *see* TURN A TRICK v.[2] (3).

turnabout n.[1] 1 [20C+] (*Aus.*) sodomy. 2 [1960s+] (*US Black*) sexual intercourse. [the turning to present one's buttocks]

turnabout *n.*[2] [1980s+] (*drugs*) amphetamine (cf. A *n.*[2]). [the drug's effects]

turn a trick *v.*[1] (*also* **turn the trick**) [late 19C+] (*US*) to carry out a successful robbery, theft or confidence trick. [TRICK *n.*[2]]

turn a trick *v.*[2] (*orig. and chiefly US*) **1** [late 19C+] to make something happen as required/desired. **2** [1920s+] to have sexual intercourse. **3** [1930s+] (*also* **do a trick, turn, turn a date, turn tricks**) to be paid for sexual intercourse, either as a professional prostitute or on a one-off or occasional basis in between working as a student, actress or model. [TRICK *n.*[1] (1)]

turn belly to belly *v. see* PLAY AT BELLY-TO-BELLY *v.*

turn blue! *excl.* [1950s–60s] a euph. version of GO TO HELL! excl.

Turnbull Street bee *n.* [early 17C] a venereally diseased prostitute. [Turnbull Street was a well-known centre of whoring]

Turnbull Street flea *n.* [early–mid-17C] a crab-louse. [for ety. *see* prev.]

Turnbull Street rogue *n.* [early 17C] a dissipated villain, a pimp (cf. ABBOT ON THE CROSS *n.*). [for ety. *see* TURNBULL STREET BEE *n.*]

turn charlie *v.* [1930s+] to act in a cowardly manner, esp. when one thus lets down one's companions. [SE *turn* + CHARLEY HOWARD *n.*]

turn cock-tail *v.* [late 19C] (*UK Und.*) to act in a cowardly manner. [SE *turn* + COCK-TAIL *n.*[3]]

turn copper *v.* [late 19C–1950s] (*US*) to become an informer (cf. CALL COPPER *v.*). [SE *turn* + COPPER *n.*[3] (2)]

turn dog *v.* (*Aus.*) **1** [mid-19C–1940s] to become an informer, to inform on. **2** [1900s] to become unkind (and treat someone cruelly). **3** [1910s] to let someone down, to 'bite the hand that feeds you'. **4** [1910s] to betray; to take a bribe. [SE *turn* + DOG *n.*[3] (7)]

turn down *v.*[1] [mid-18C–1930s] to drink down, to 'toss back' a drink. [the tilting of the glass or bottle]

turn down *v.*[2] [19C] (*orig. US*) to reject, to snub, to rebuke. [20C+ use is SE]

-turned *sfx* [1930s+] (*US*) of a certain type, disposed, natured; always in combs., e.g. *nice-turned, mild-turned.*

turned around *adj.* [1960s+] (*US*) confused, disorientated.

turned off *adj.*[1] [mid-19C–1910s] (*UK society*) married.

turned off *adj.*[2] **1** [1950s+] unexcited (in a sexual context). **2** [1960s+] out of touch, unaware, daydreaming. **3** [1960s+] (*US campus*) unenthusiastic. [TURN (SOMEONE) OFF *v.*]

turned on *adj.* **1** [1950s+] (*US*) intoxicated, esp. by drugs. **2** [1960s+] sexually stimulated. **3** [1960s+] aware, sophisticated, up-to-the-minute. [TURN ON *v.*/TURN (SOMEONE) ON *v.*]

turned over *adj.* [mid-19C] **1** remanded in custody pending one's trial. **2** stopped and searched by the police. [? *turned over* to the authorities]

turned up *adj.*[1] [early 19C] ruined.

turned up *adj.*[2] [early–mid-19C] **1** stopped and searched by the police. **2** acquitted of a crime in court, esp. through lack of evidence.

turned up *adj.*[3] [1980s] disgusted. [? turn up one's nose]

turner out *n.* [mid-19C] (*UK Und.*) a counterfeiter. [SE *turn out*, to manufacture]

turn flip-flops *v. see* FLIP-FLOP *v.* (1).

turnie *n.* [1990s+] a turnstile. [abbr.]

turn-in *n.*[1] [late 19C] a bed. [TURN IN *v.* (1)]

turn-in *n.*[2] *see* TURN-UP *n.*[1] (3).

turn in *v.* **1** [late 17C+] to go to bed. **2** [1910s+] to stop doing something, to abandon. **3** [1920s] to die.

turn Indian *v.* [mid-19C] (*US*) to revert to nature, to abandon one's 'civilized' habits. [racist stereotyping]

turning over *n.* [late 19C–1900s] (*US*) a reprimand, a telling-off.

turning-tree *n.* [mid-16C–mid-17C] the gallows. [SE *turn off*,

to hang + TRIPLE TREE *n.*; also an image of the turning, hanging corpse]

turn in one's dinner pail *v. see* HAND IN ONE'S DINNER PAIL *v.*

turn into fish food *v.* [20C+] to drown.

turnip *n.*[1] [early 19C+] an old-fashioned watch; thus *cut turnip-tops*, to steal a watch, chain and seals. [its rotundity and thickness]

turnip *n.*[2] **1** [mid-19C+] a simpleton, a fool. **2** [mid-19C+] the head. **3** [1910s–20s] a term of affectionate address; usu. as *old turnip.*

turnip greens *n. see* GREENS *n.*[4].

turnip-pate *n.* [late 17C–early 19C] a very fair head of hair; thus *turnip-pated*, having white hair or very light blond hair.

turnips *n.* [late 18C] (*US Und.*) acquitted. [? joc. pron. of *turn up*]

turnip-snagger *n.* (*also* **turnip-sucker**) [20C+] (*Irish*) a peasant, a country person (cf. ACORN-CRACKER *n.*). [SE *turnip* + *snag*, to snatch]

turn it down *v.* [1960s+] (*gay*) to moderate one's more flagrantly homosexual behaviour. [radio/TV imagery]

turn it on *v.* **1** [1920s+] to make things happen, to intensify things, to 'hot up' the atmosphere. **2** [1940s+] (*Aus.*) to start a fight. **3** [1940s+] (*Aus.*) to provide food and drink, to host a party. **4** [1940s+] (*Aus.*) to allow or offer sex, often with more than 1 partner.

turn it up *v.*[1] **1** [early 19C+] to stop doing something. **2** [1900s–10s] (*Aus.*) in ext. use, to die. [TURN (SOMEONE) UP *v.*]

turn it up *v.*[2] [1980s+] (*N.Z.*) of a woman, to offer oneself for sex.

turn it up! *excl.* [late 19C+] stop doing that! don't exaggerate! [TURN IT UP *v.*[1] (1)]

turnkey *n.* [2000s] (*US prison*) a guard who does the bare minimum required for his/her shift. [i.e. no more than open and shut the doors]

turn-off *n.* [1960s+] anything or anyone repellent, whether physically (esp. sexually) or emotionally. [TURN (SOMEONE) OFF *v.* (3)]

turn off *v.*[1] [mid-17C–1930s] to execute by hanging.

turn off *v.*[2] [mid-19C–1920s] (*US Und.*) to break open, often using some form of picklock.

turn off *v.*[3] [late 19C–1900s] (*Aus.*) to marry or be married.

turn off *v.*[4] [1960s+] to lose interest in, esp. sexually; often in passive, to be repelled by. [TURN (SOMEONE) OFF *v.*]

turn off (the gas) *v.* [late 19C–1960s] to stop bragging or boasting. [SE *turn off* + GAS *n.*[1] (1)]

turn Old-Mas *v. see* OLE-MAS *n.*

turn-on *n.* **1** [1950s–60s] (*Can.*) something done by an 'in-group' to provoke outsiders. **2** [1960s+] of objects or people, a thrill, sexual or otherwise. **3** [1960s+] (*drugs*) enough of a drug to produce its desired effects. [TURN ON *v.*/TURN (SOMEONE) ON *v.*]

turn on *v.* **1** [1950s+] (*orig. US*) to take drugs, esp. heroin, morphine or cannabis. **2** [1950s+] (*orig. US*) to become stimulated. **3** [1970s] (*US*) to drink liquor. [TURN (SOMEONE) ON *v.* (4); (1) note exhortation by Timothy Leary (1920–96) to '*turn on*, tune in and drop out']

turn on a cabbage-leaf *v.* [1940s] (*Aus./N.Z.*) of a horse, to react immediately to the rider's control. [the small dimensions of the leaf]

turn on a dime *v.* (*also* **turn on a dollar**) [1940s+] (*US*) usu. of a vehicle or horse, to turn in a very small space. [SE *dime/ dollar*]

turn one's crank *v.* [1940s+] to be enjoyable.

turn one's damper down *v.*[1] [1900s–30s] (*US Black*) to calm down, to relax; esp. as imper. *turn your damper down!* [SE *damper*, a device to slow down machinery]

turn one's damper down *v.*[2] [1920s–50s] (*US Black*) to satisfy sexually; also in fig. use.

turn one's face to the wall *v.* [1940s+] to die.

turn on one's lights v. [1990s+] to start thinking, to act sensibly.

turn on the fan v. [20C+] (US) to hurry, to move quickly. [FAN v.[2] (1)]

turn on the heat v. [1930s+] **1** (orig. US) to pressurize, to put pressure on. **2** (US) to cover or shoot with a gun. [HEAT n.[3]]

turn on the leaks v.[1] [1930s] to start crying. [LEAK v.[1] (2)]

turn on the leaks v.[2] see LEAK n.[2] (2).

turn on the tap v. (also **turn the tap(s) on**) [late 19C+] to start crying; thus *turn off the tap*, to stop crying. [the implication is of a lack of sincerity]

turn on the toe v. [late 16C–early 17C] to push the victim off the ladder at the climax of a judicial hanging. [a ladder was employed before the early 19C development of the drop]

turn on the waterworks v. [mid-19C+] to start crying. [WATERWORKS n.]

turn-out n.[1] [early 19C+] a fist-fight. [the participants *turn out* to fight]

turn-out n.[2] **1** [late 19C+] any kind of activity. **2** [1900s–50s] a resolution, a solution.

turn-out n.[3] [1950s] (US Und.) a discharge from prison. [TURN OUT v.[2] (2)]

turn-out n.[4] [1960s–70s] **1** (US) a novice, a recent initiate, e.g. a new prostitute. **2** (US prison) (also **penitentiary turn-out**) a young prisoner who is forced into life as a homosexual. [TURN (SOMEONE) OUT v.]

turn out v.[1] [19C+] to get out of bed. [SE *turn-out*, a getting up from one's bed]

turn out v.[2] **1** [late 19C–1900s] (Aus.) to leave home and become a bushranger. **2** [1910s] (US Und.) to free a criminal from arrest. **3** [1960s] (US Und.) to become a professional thief. [SE *turn out*, to leave home and start work]

turn out v.[3] **1** [20C+] to beat up. **2** [1930s+] (US Black) to turn a place over, to cause trouble, e.g. at a party, in school. **3** [1950s+] (US Black) to dominate, to take over. [? TURN-OUT n.[1]]

turn out v.[4] **1** [1920s–40s] (US Und.) to commence a career as a confidence trickster. **2** [1960s] to start using a drug (cf. TURN (SOMEONE) OUT v.). **3** [1980s] (US Black) to start living/working on the streets.

turn out the set v. (also **turn the set/shit out**) [1970s+] (US Black) to disrupt a situation or occasion, esp. permanently. [TURN OUT v.[3] (2) + SET n.[1] (3)/SHIT n.[4]]

turn-over n.[1] **1** [mid-late 19C] (UK Und.) a body search. **2** [1940s] (US prison) the last night of a sentence. **3** [1950s+] (UK prison) a search of a prisoner's cell.

turn-over n.[2] [1980s+] (US) one who is seen as betraying their race, usu. Black or Puerto Rican, by assimilating into or at least succeeding in White society. [TURN OVER (ON) v.]

turn over v.[1] **1** [mid-19C+] (UK Und.) to search a house or apartment or prison cell, usu. with the maximum of damage and mess. **2** [mid-19C+] to search a person. **3** [late 19C–1910s] to rob. **4** [1950s+] (also **turn up**) to beat up, to attack. **5** [1980s+] to destroy a place.

turn over v.[2] (also **turn up**) [mid-19C+] to distress, to make nauseous. [it turns one's stomach over or up]

turn over v.[3] [1930s+] (gay) to allow anal intercourse. [the physical act that may precede the intercourse]

turn over (on) v. [late 19C+] (UK/US Und.) **1** to inform on (a fellow inmate). **2** to cheat, to defraud.

turn over the perch v. [late 16C–early 17C] **1** to upset, to humiliate. **2** to overcome, to conquer. **3** to kill.

turn paper collars v. [late 19C–1900s] (US) to live in poverty. [SE *paper collar*, a symbolically 'poor' garment]

turnpike n. [mid-17C–19C] the vagina (cf. ALLEY n.[1]).

turnpike man n. [late 18C–mid-19C] a parson. [from the fees or tolls the clergy collect for christenings and funerals: 'our entrance into and exit from the world' (Grose, 1785)]

turnpike sailor n. [mid-late 19C] a wandering beggar who poses as the victim of a shipwreck.

turn rabbit v. see RABBIT v.[3].

turn-round pudding n. [late 19C–1900s] porridge or any form of pudding that requires stirring.

turn snitch v. [late 18C–mid-19C] to become an informer. [SNITCH n.[1] (3)]

turn someone around v. [1960s+] (US) **1** to change someone's attitude or behaviour, esp. to persuade a criminal to turn informer. **2** to disorientate.

turn someone every which way but loose v. see CUT SOMEONE EVERY WHICH WAY BUT LOOSE v.

turn someone in v. [1920s+] to betray; to give up someone to the authorities.

turn (someone) off v. **1** [1950s+] to alienate, to repel someone (cf. TURN OFF v.[4]). **2** [1960s] (drugs) to deprive someone of a supply of drugs. **3** [1960s+] to repel someone sexually.

turn (someone) on v. **1** [late 19C–1920s] to persuade someone to do something. **2** [1940s–60s] (US Black) to render angry. **3** [1940s+] (Aus./N.Z.) to provide liquor, e.g. for a party. **4** [1950s+] (orig. US) to offer or introduce drugs to another person (cf. TURN ON v.). **5** [1950s+] (orig. US) to introduce someone or something (non-drugs) to another person. **6** [1950s+] (orig. US) to stimulate someone, usu. sexually, to appeal to someone (cf. TURN ON v.).

turn (someone) out v. **1** [1940s+] (orig. US Black) to initiate a newcomer in a variety of situations, e.g. (pimp) to put a prostitute on the streets; (Hell's Angels) to use a woman for multiple sex; (US Und.) to make a new inmate into a prison homosexual (cf. TURN OUT v.[4]). **2** [1970s+] (US Black) to use unconventional means to introduce someone to any important first experience. **3** [1990s+] to take someone's virginity.

turn someone's mouth behind their back v. [20C+] (W.I.) to beat up severely, to 'knock someone's face through the back of their neck'.

turn (someone) up v. **1** [19C–1930s] to ignore a former friend or end a sexual relationship, to abandon or betray someone (cf. TURN UP v.[2]). **2** [early 19C–1930s] to set someone free, to release (a prisoner), to acquit; usu. in passive as *turned up*, acquitted. **3** [mid-19C] to dismiss from a job. **4** [mid-19C+] (UK Und.) to inform against someone, to turn someone over to the police. **5** [late 19C] (US) to rob; usu. in passive as *turned up*, robbed. [SE *turn up*, to turn a horse loose]

turn square v. [mid-19C–1940s] of a criminal, to reform, to join the world of the law-abiding. [SQUARE adj. (2)]

turn stag v. [late 18C–mid-19C] to betray someone, to inform against someone. [STAG n.[1]]

turn state v. (also **turn state's**) [20C+] (US Und.) to give state's evidence. [abbr.]

turn the corner v. [1970s+] of a man, to become homosexual or acknowledge one's homosexuality.

turn the corner of Bolt Street v. [19C] to escape, to run off. [play on BOLT v. (1)]

turn the key on v. [1930s] (UK Und.) to give a life sentence.

turn the set/shit out v. see TURN OUT THE SET v.

turn the tables v. [1930s+] (gay) of a male homosexual prostitute, to blackmail a client. [SE *turn the tables*, to reverse the relations between 2 parties]

turn the tap(s) on v. see TURN ON THE TAP v.

turn the trick v. see TURN A TRICK v.[1].

turn ticks on v. [1950s] (W.I.) to beg from. [? TICK n.[3] (1)]

turn to bag and wallet v. [late 16C] to become a professional beggar. [SE *bag* + *wallet*, a pedlar's bag]

turn-tongue adj. [20C+] (W.I.) duplicitous, hypocritical, lying.

turn tricks v. see TURN A TRICK v.[2] (3).

turn Turk v. [late 16C–17C; 20C+] to become a renegade, a rebel. [racial stereotyping, note TURK n.[1]]

turn turtle v. [late 19C+] (orig. US) **1** to turn upside down. **2** to back down, to act in a cowardly manner.

turn-up n.[1] **1** [early 19C–1900s] a boxing or wrestling match or contest. **2** [early 19C–1900s] a street fight. **3** [early 19C+] (also **turn-in**) any form of argument or altercation. **4** [mid-19C–1900s] a sudden exit, a speedy departure. **5** [late 19C–1910s] (UK society) a minor quarrel, a tiff. [SE turn up, to throw into disorder]

turn-up n.[2] [mid-19C+] a surprise, usu. pleasant, a piece of good luck; thus phr. a turn-up for the books. [racing jargon turn-up, an unexpected piece of luck, ult. SE turn up, to arrive, to appear]

turn up v.[1] **1** [early 17C–early 18C] to prostitute oneself or another. **2** [19C] of a woman, to have sexual intercourse (cf. CATCH AN OYSTER v.). [OED cites sense (1) only as 'apparently'. Note TURN UP ONE'S TAIL v.]

turn up v.[2] **1** [early–late 19C] to run away. **2** [early 19C+] to abandon a habit or occupation, to desist from (cf. TURN (SOMEONE) UP v.). **3** [mid–late 19C] to alter or change something. **4** [1920s] (US) to give up, to weaken. **5** [1960s] (Aus. Und.) to take the blame for someone else's crime. [SE turn up, to turn a horse loose]

turn up v.[3] [mid–late 19C] (UK Und.) to hand (something) over.

turn up v.[4] [mid-19C–1920s] (UK/US) to search. [? SE turn upside down]

turn up v.[5] see TURN OVER v.[1] (4).

turn up v.[6] see TURN OVER v.[2].

turn up a trump v. see TURN UP TRUMPS v.

turn up jack v. see CUT UP JACK v.

turn up one's heels v. see KICK UP ONE'S HEELS v.[1].

turn up one's tail v. [mid-17C–early 18C] of a woman, to have sexual intercourse (cf. CATCH AN OYSTER v.). [SE turn up + TAIL n.[2] (3)/TAIL n.[2] (1)]

turn-ups n. [late 19C–1900s] the rejection of a suitor. [TURN (SOMEONE) UP v. (1)]

turn up sweet v. [early 19C] (UK Und.) to abandon somebody but leave them unaware or happy. [TURN (SOMEONE) UP v.]

turn up trumps v. (also **turn up a trump**) [late 18C+] to turn out right in the end, esp. when this result comes as a surprise. [card-playing imagery]

Turpentine/Turps n. see SERPS n.

turps n. **1** [mid-19C+] any form of alcohol; thus on the turps, drinking (heavily). **2** [late 19C+] (Aus.) beer. [abbr. SE turpentine]

turps nudger n. [1990s+] a heavy drinker. [TURPS n. (1)]

turret n. **1** [mid-19C] in boxing, the face. **2** [1910s] (Aus.) the head.

turtle n.[1] [1900s] (US) a racehorse (presumably slow).

turtle n.[2] [1940s+] (orig. Aus.) a promiscuous woman. [i.e. 'once she's on her back, she's fucked']

turtle v. [1940s] (US Black) to turn.

turtle (dove) n.[1] [15C+] a lover, a term of affection. [E.P. claims this is rhy. sl. but it certainly originated long before]

turtle (dove) n.[2] [mid-19C+] usu. in pl., a glove, esp. those worn by house-breakers to hide fingerprints. [rhy. sl.]

turtle (dove) v. [mid-19C+] to love, to be in a romantic state. [TURTLE (DOVE) n.[1]]

turtle-frolic n. [mid-18C–19C] (orig. US) a feast, the centrepiece of which is a turtle.

turtlehead n. (also **turtle's head**) [1990s+] a piece of excrement poking out of the anus, due to the urgent need to defecate.

turtleneck (sweater) n. (also **winter wear**) [1970s+] (US campus/gay) an uncircumcised penis (cf. BALD-HEADED HERMIT n.). [resemblance]

turtle shit n. (US) **1** [1950s+] (also **cat shit**) nonsense, rubbish. **2** [1990s+] the 'stuffing', the 'daylights', the insides. [SE turtle + SHIT n.[3] (4)/SHIT, THE n.[2]; (1) var. on BULLSHIT n.]

turtle soup n. [late 19C–1900s] sheep's head broth.

tush n.[1] [1940s] (W.I.) human excrement. [Djerma tosi, excrement; but note TUSH n.[2] (1)]

tush n.[2] (also **tooshy, tushie, tushy**) **1** [1950s+] the buttocks. **2** [1970s+] (US gay) the vagina. [TOCHES n.]

tush n.[3] see TASH n.

tush n.[4] see TOSHEROON n.

tush v. [1910s] (W.I.) to excrete. [TUSH n.[1]]

tusheroon n.[1] [mid–late 19C] a crown piece, 5 shillings. [OED suggests that (2) is 'erroneous']

tusheroon n.[2] see TOSHEROON n.

tush hog n. **1** [1930s+] (US) a bully, an aggressive person. **2** [1940s] (US Black) an aggressive sexual athlete. **3** [1950s+] (US) an aggressive homosexual. [ety. unknown]

tushie n. see TUSH n.[2].

tushroon n. [1900s–50s] (US Black) money. [var. on TOSHEROON n.]

tush-teeth n. [20C+] (W.I.) buckteeth, protruding teeth. [SE tusk]

tushy n. see TUSH n.[2].

tusk n. [1910s] (US Und.) a tooth. [SE elephant's tusk]

tuskee n. (also **tuskie**) [1970s–80s] (US Black) a large marijuana cigarette (cf. BONE n.[11]). [? resemblance to an elephant's tusk]

tuskin n. [late 18C–early 19C] a country carter or ploughman. [? dial. tush, the broad part of a ploughshare, ult. tusk, tooth]

tusseroon n. see TOSHEROON n.

tussle n. [1960s+] (US) sexual intercourse. [TUSSLE v. (3)]

tussle v. **1** [mid–late 19C] to argue. **2** [1950s+] (US Black) to fight. **3** [1960s+] (US) to engage in sexual activity. [Scot. tousle, to push around roughly, to struggle or contend with; (1) SE post-1890]

tussocker n. [late 19C+] (Aus.) a tramp or vagrant pretending to seek work but actually keener on board and lodging. [Aus./N.Z. tussock land, uncultivated grassland used for sheep-grazing, across which he has travelled]

tussock-jumper n. [1960s+] (N.Z.) a musterer. [for ety. see prev.]

tussy n. [19C] a drunkard. [abbr. SE intoxicated]

tussy-mussy n. see TUZZY-MUZZY n.

tute n. [mid-19C+] **1** a tutor. **2** a tutorial. [abbr.]

Tuttle Nask n. [late 17C–18C] the Tothill house of correction in Tothill Fields, London. [Tuttle, i.e. Tothill + NASK n.]

tut-tut-tut n. [1900s] (Aus.) a hut. [rhy. sl.]

tutu adj. see TOO-TOO adj.

tutus n. [1940s] (W.I.) the male genitals. [Carib.E. tutu, a conch shell]

tux n. **1** [1910s+] (US) (also **tuck**) a dinner jacket. **2** [1940s] (US Und.) a strait jacket. [abbr. SE tuxedo, a dinner jacket, named for Tuxedo Park, New York, where the jacket was first introduced at the country club in 1886]

tuxed up adj. [1990s+] (orig. US) wearing a dinner jacket. [TUX UP v.]

tux up v. [1930s+] to put on a dinner jacket. [TUX n. (1)]

tuzzy-muzzy n. (also **tussy-mussy, tuz, tuzimuzzy, tuzzy**) [late 17C–19C] the vagina. [dial. tuzzy-muzzy, dishevelled, ragged, rough; alternative def. as a nosegay or bouquet garni and for 'old man's beard' (i.e. clematis]

t.v. n. (also **teevee**) [1970s+] a transvestite.

t.v. adj. [1980s+] pertaining to transvestism. [T.V. n.]

TV style n. [1950s–70s] (gay) anal intercourse with one partner on his knees. [TV, television, which can optionally be watched when adopting this position for sex]

twachel n. see TWATCHEL n.

twack n. [1980s+] (US campus) a 12-pack of beer. [abbr. SE twelve + pack]

twaddle n. [late 18C–early 19C] a bore. ['a fashionable term that for a while succeeded that of bore' (Grose, 1785). SE twaddle, idle talk, nonsense, itself f. synon. twattle, ? ult. tattle]

twaddle v. [late 18C–19C] to trifle, to 'mess around'. [SE twaddle]

twag v. [1990s+] (UK juv.) to play truant; thus twag lady/man, an official who searches out truants. [? abbr. HOP THE WAG v.]

twak n.[1] [mid-19C+] (S.Afr.) tobacco. [Afk. tabak]

twak n.[2] [1950s+] (S.Afr.) nonsense, rubbish. [Afk. twak, nonsense]

twam *n.* (*also* **twammy, twim**) [20C+] the vagina. [? TWAT *n.* (1) + QUIM *n.* (1)]

twang *n.*[1] **1** [late 17C–18C] a prostitute. **2** [18C] a pimp or a prostitute's male accomplice, who appears to beat up victims whom she has robbed, under the guise of offering them intercourse. [TWANG *v.*[1]]

twang *n.*[2] [late 19C–1930s] (*Aus.*) opium (cf. APOSTLE *n.*). [Chinese or cod Chinese; ? f. *twankay*, green tea]

twang *v.*[1] (*also* **twangle**) [mid-16C–18C; 1980s+] to engage in spontaneous sexual intercourse. [? SE *twang*, to fire an arrow; note D'Urfey, *Pills to Purge Melancholy* (1719–20): 'Twangdillo, A New Ballad', which deals with the many female pursuers of one 'Roger Twangdillo']

twang *v.*[2] [1940s+] (*UK Black*) to persuade, to sweet-talk.

twang adam cove *n.* [mid-18C] (*UK Und.*) the act – through plausible, beguiling speech – of luring victims into the hands of confidence tricksters. [? SE *twang* + ? ADAM *n.*[1] + COVE *n.* (1)]

twange *n.* [1990s+] the vagina. [TWAT *n.* (1) + MINGE *n.* (1)]

twanger *n.* **1** [late 16C–mid-17C; late 19C] the penis. **2** [late 19C] something very large or fine of its kind. [fig. uses of SE *twang*, to reverberate]

twanging *adj.* [early 17C] excellent, first-rate; thus *go off twanging*, to turn out very well. [SE *twang*, to give off a ringing note]

twangle *v. see* TWANG *v.*[1].

twangman *n.* [20C+] (*Irish*) a pimp. [TWANG *n.*[1] (2) + sfx *-man*]

twang one's wire *v.* (*also* **twang the wire**) [1950s+] to masturbate.

twangy *adj.* [1980s+] (*US*) pertaining to male prostitution. [TWANG *v.*[1]]

twangy boy *n.* [1980s+] (*US*) a young male prostitute. [TWANGY *adj.*]

twank *n.* [1960s+] **1** (*gay*) an older man. **2** in prostitute usage, an older man who enjoys watching young women at work but has no personal interest in sex. [? the pantomime 'dame' *Widow Twankey* or WANK *n.*[1] (1)]

twankay *n.* (*also* **twankey**) [1900s] gin. [tea trade jargon *twankey*, green tea, thus ? the root of the pantomime dame Widow Twankey]

twanky *n.* [2000s] (*US Black*) the number 20. [pron.]

twat *n.* **1** [mid-17C+] (*also* **twat-hole, twattle, twit-twat, twoit, twot**) the vagina; in pl. the labia. **2** [20C+] a derog. term for a woman. **3** [1910s+] (*also* **twatt, twot**) a term of abuse, irrespective of gender (cf. BAMBA *n.*[1]). **4** [1950s+] (*US*) the buttocks. **5** [1970s+] (*US gay*) the anus. **6** [1980s+] something unpleasant, second-rate. **7** [2000s] (*US Black*) used as a deliberately coarse substitute for SE *what?* **8** [2000s] a neutral term for a person. [? dial. *twitchel*, a narrow passage; (1) *twit-twat* is lit. abbr. SE *twittle-twattle*, idle talk]

twat *v.* **1** [1980s+] to hit someone. **2** [1990s+] to behave in an unsophisticated manner. **3** [1990s+] to waste time. [TWAT *n.* (3)]

twat burglar *n.* [1990s+] an adulterer. [TWAT *n.* (1) + SE *burglar*]

twatchel *n.* (*also* **twachel, twatchil, twatchylle**) [mid-17C–early 19C] the vagina. [dimin. of TWAT *n.* (1) + dial. *twitchel*, a passage]

twat-faker *n.* [1900s–20s] a pimp. [TWAT *n.* (1) + FAKER *n.*]

twathead *n.* [2000s] a general term of abuse. [TWAT *n.* (1) + -HEAD sfx (1)]

twat-hole *n. see* TWAT *n.* (1).

twat-hooks *n. see* CUNT-HOOKS *n.*

twatling-strings *n. see* TWATTLING-STRINGS *n.*

twat-mag *n.* [1990s+] a pornographic magazine. [TWAT *n.* (1) + colloq. SE *mag*, a magazine]

twatman *n.* [1990s+] (*UK juv.*) a general term of abuse. [play on the superhero Batman + TWAT *n.* (3)]

twat-masher *n.* [1900s–20s] a pimp, a procurer. [TWAT *n.* (1) + MASH *v.*[1] (1)]

twatmaster *n.* [1990s+] a term of abuse or hostility. [TWAT *n.* (3) + sfx *-master*]

twat on *v.* [1990s+] to talk inconsequentially, to chatter. [TWAT *n.* (3)]

twat-rug *n.* [late 19C–1900s] female pubic hair. [TWAT *n.* (1) + SE *rug*]

twat-scourer *n.* **1** [late 17C] a general term of abuse. **2** [early 18C] a surgeon, a doctor. [TWAT *n.* (1) + SE *scourer*, a cleaner, a polisher]

twat-scouring *adj.* [late 17C] a general term of abuse. [TWAT-SCOURER *n.* (1)]

twat-seller *n.* [20C+] a prostitute (cf. ASS PEDDLER *n.*; BANGTAIL *n.*[1]). [TWAT *n.* (1) + SE *seller*]

twatt *n. see* TWAT *n.* (3).

twatted *adj.* [1990s+] intoxicated by drink or drugs. [fig. use of TWAT *v.* (1)]

twatting *n.* **1** [19C] sexual intercourse. **2** [1980s+] a beating. [TWAT *v.* (1)]

twatting *adj.* [2000s] a general negative intensifier. [TWATTING *n.* (1), i.e. a euph. for FUCKING *adj.*]

twattle *n. see* TWAT *n.* (1).

twattling-strings *n.* (*also* **twatling-strings**) [late 16C–early 19C] the anal sphincter, esp. in the context of breaking wind. [joc. use of dial. *twattle*, to chatter, to talk idly]

twatty *adj.* [1970s+] stupid. [TWAT *n.* (3)]

tweague *n.* (*also* **tweak**) [late 17C–mid-19C] a state of excitement or agitation. [SE *tweak*, a wrench, a sharp tug]

tweaguey *adj.* [late 18C–early 19C] angry, irritated. [TWEAGUE *n.*]

tweak *n.*[1] (*also* **tweake**) **1** [early 17C–early 18C] a prostitute. **2** [early 18C–early 19C] a whoremonger. [? SE *tweak*, the act of tugging, thus fig. sexual intercourse]

tweak *n.*[2] *see* TWEAGUE *n.*

tweak *n.*[3] *see* TWEAKS *n.*

tweak *v.*[1] [late 19C] to hit a target with a missile from a catapult. [TWEAKER *n.*[1]]

tweak *v.*[2] **1** [1970s] (*drugs*) to inject narcotics. **2** [1980s+] (*drugs*) to be intoxicated with heroin or crack cocaine. **3** [1980s+] (*drugs*) to suffer heroin or crack cocaine withdrawal. **4** [1980s+] (*US Black/campus*) to act as if one were intoxicated by drugs, to act energetically or strangely. [SE *tweak*, to wrench, to pull sharply]

tweake *n. see* TWEAK *n.*[1].

tweaked *adj.* [1980s+] (*US, mainly campus/Black*) **1** drunk or under the influence of a drug (cf. AFFLICTED *adj.*). **2** experiencing the effects of crack cocaine. **3** mad. **4** broken, out of order, messy. **5** exhausted. **6** on edge, tense, nervous, upset. [TWEAK *v.*[2]]

tweaker *n.*[1] [late 19C] a catapult. [SE *tweak*, to pinch]

tweaker *n.*[2] [1980s+] (*drugs*) **1** a drug user. **2** a crack cocaine user. [TWEAK *v.*[2] (2)]

tweakified *adj.* [1990s+] (*US drugs*) suffering the paranoia-inducing effects of smoking crack cocaine. [TWEAK *v.*[2] (2)]

tweaking *n.* [1990s+] (*US Black*) talking inappropriately or tactlessly. [SE *tweak*, i.e. to 'pinch' someone's sensibilities]

tweaking *adj.* [1990s+] **1** (*US Black/drugs*) intoxicated by drugs. **2** (*US campus*) tense, emotional, hyperactive. [TWEAK *v.*[2]]

tweak out *v.* (*also* **twig out**) [1980s+] (*US campus*) **1** to hurt, to damage. **2** to lose control, to act eccentrically. [ext. of TWEAK *v.*[2] (4); *twig* is mispron.]

tweaks *n.* (*also* **tweak**) [2000s] (*US drugs*) crack cocaine (cf. BASE *n.*). [TWEAK *v.*[2] (2)]

tweaky *adj.* [2000s] (*US drugs*) exhibiting the signs of addiction to crack cocaine. [TWEAKS *n.*]

tweed *n.* [1950s+] (*US Black/drugs*) marijuana. [*the* WEED *n.*[1] (4)]

tweed-capper *n.* [1910s] (*Aus.*) an immigrant from the UK. [the headgear worn]

tweedle, the *n.* **1** [late 19C+] (*UK Und.*) the substitution of fake jewellery for the real thing, usu. by sleight of hand in a jewellery store, esp. in the form of a *tweedle*, a fake ring studded with paste diamonds. **2** [1910s+] the sale of any dubious goods. [SE *twiddle*, to twist]

tweedledum sir *n*. [late 19C–1900s] (*UK society*) usu. in pl., a baronet or knight who is given his honours for 'services to music', e.g. Sir Arthur Sullivan (1842–1900).

tweedler *n*. (*UK Und.*) **1** [1920s+] a small-time confidence trickster. **2** [1970s] a stolen vehicle which is passed off as perfectly legitimate. [TWEEDLE, THE n.]

tweedling *n*. [1920s+] (*UK Und.*) selling stolen property or even non-existent property to innocent purchasers who assume the goods are legitimate. [TWEEDLE, THE n.]

tweeds *n*. **1** [1950s+] (*Aus.*) trousers. **2** [1960s] (*US campus*) a suit.

tweegat jakkals *n*. [1990s+] (*S.Afr.*) a term of extreme vilification. [Afk. *twee gat jakkals*, a jackal with 2 anuses]

tweek *n*. (*also* **tweeker**) [1980s+] (*drugs*) methcathinone. [SE *tweak*, i.e. its effects]

tweeked *adj*. *see* TWEAKED adj.

tween *n*. (*also* **tweenie**) [1990s+] a sophisticated pre-teenager. [on model of SE *teen*; ? ult. SE *between*; note children's TV programme, *The Tweenies*]

tweenie *n*. [2000s] (*Aus.*) a male homosexual. [? pun on TWEEN n.]

tweer *n*. *see* TWIRE n.

twelve *n*. *see* TWELVER n. (1).

twelve godfathers *n*. (*also* **the twelve**) [early 18C–mid-19C] the jury; thus *you will be christened by twelve godfathers someday before long*. [they 'give a name' to one's crime]

1200 *n*. [1990s+] in rap music, the Technics SL *1200* turntable, regarded as the best turntable for DJ-ing.

twelve inches *n*. [mid-18C; 1960s+] (*also* **one foot, thirteen inches**) a (large) penis.

twelve-inch rule *n*. [20C+] a fool (cf. BEECHAM'S PILL n.). [rhy. sl.]

twelve o'clock! *excl*. [late 19C–1900s] time to be moving! time for action! [used by workmen with ref. to 12 o'clock midday, dinner time, when things are likely to speed up]

12:01 *n*. [2000s] (*US prison*) a discharge. [? the time]

twelver *n*. **1** [late 17C–19C] (*orig. UK Und.*) (*also* **twelve**) a shilling (5p). **2** [late 19C] (*Aus. Und.*) a 12-month sentence. [(1) the 12 pennies it represented, use after 1730s mainly Aus.]

12/12 *v*. [2000s] (*US prison*) to serve the whole of one's sentence without parole.

twenty *n*. (*also* **twennie**) [1980s+] (*US drugs*) $20 worth of crack cocaine.

twenty and a ten *n*. *see* FIVE AND TWO n.

twenty and forty *n*. [2000s] (*US Black*) $20 worth of marijuana and a 40oz (1-litre) bottle of malt liquor.

twenty cents *n*. [1930s–70s] (*US Black*) **1** $2; $20. **2** a $20 bag of marijuana.

twenty-five *n*.[1] [1960s+] (*drugs*) LSD (cf. A n.[3]). [its chemical name, *d-lysergic acid diethylamide-25*]

twenty-five *n*.[2] [1980s+] (*US drugs*) a $25 bag of cocaine.

twenty-five, the *n*. [2000s] the M25 motorway, encircling Greater London and the adjacent home counties.

25 boffos *n*. [20C+] (*US Und.*) a 25-year sentence. [fig. use of BOFF n.[1] (1)]

25 with an izl *n*. [1990s+] (*US*) a prison sentence of 25 years to life. [SE *izl*, i.e. the * notation next to the years of one's sentence, denoting 'life']

twenty-four carat *adj*. (*also* **twenty-carat, twenty-two..., forty-eight...**) **1** [20C+] complete, authentic. **2** [1900s–50s] very wealthy. **3** [1960s] totally reliable, wholly trustworthy. [fig. use of the SE descriptions of the purity of gold]

twenty-four cents shy of a quarter *phr*. *see* THIRTY CENTS (SHY OF A QUARTER) phr.

24/24 *adv*. [1980s+] (*orig. US prison*) all day, continually. [24 hours out of the daily 24]

twenty in the pounder *n*. [late 19C–1900s] one who pays their debts in full rather than opting to pay in instalments. [i.e. 20 shillings to a (pre-decimal) pound]

twenty-minute man *n*. [1900s] (*US Und.*) a con-man who is unable to keep the victim from complaining after he has lost his money. [his con-man persona only lasts 20 minutes]

twenty-nine and a wake-up *n*. [1960s+] (*US prison*) the period between receiving a notice of parole and one's actual release, i.e. 1 month. [29 whole days and the WAKE-UP n.[2]; i.e. the last, on which one only wakes up in prison]

20 on the hype *n*. (*also* **30 on the hype**) [1950s+] (*drugs*) a very heavy intake of heroin. [the number of millilitres on the HYPE n.[2] (1)]

twenty-percent man *n*. [1950s] a money lender. [note TEN-PERCENTER n.[1]]

twenty-sack *n*. [1990s+] (*US*) $20 worth of drugs, usu. marijuana or crack cocaine.

twenty-six girl *n*. (*also* **26 girl**) [1940s] a young woman who runs a dice game played in a bar.

twenty-spot *n*. [mid-19C+] a £20 note or $20 bill. [SE *twenty* + -SPOT sfx (2)]

twenty-three skidoo! *excl*. (*also* **23 (skidoo)!**) [late 19C+] (*US*) go away! get out! [ety. unknown; theories include: downdraughts created by the Flatiron Building at the corner of Broadway and 23rd St, New York City, which would blow up women's skirts to the delight of male observers – the phr. developed f. the police who saw these men at *23* (the corner) and shooed them away with a shout of *skiddoo*; railway telegraph jargon *23*, a message of the greatest urgency (however, as listed in the generally used *Phillips Code* [1925 edn] 23 does not mean this – rather 'all copy'); or a number signifying finality or completion; *skid* from SKID ROW n., *23* from NYC's 23rd St which once had the ferries and depots for 80% of those – including the skid row tramps – who wished to leave the city; note SKIDOO v.]

twenty-twenty vision *n*. [20C+] perfect vision, in a fig. sense; thus *twenty-twenty hindsight*, a fig. perfect understanding or appreciation of what has already been seen. [ophthalmic jargon *20/20*, perfect vision]

twenty-two *n*. [1920s+] (*US*) a .22 calibre pistol. [abbr.; note THIRTY-EIGHT n. (1)]

twenty-two carat *n*. [1940s] (*UK drugs*) high-quality, pure cocaine. [TWENTY-TWO CARAT adj.]

twenty-two carat *adj*. *see* TWENTY-FOUR CARAT adj.

twerp *n*. (*also* **twirp**) [1910s+] an idiot, a nincompoop. [ety. unknown; J.R.R. Tolkien (letter, 6 October 1944) suggests an early 20C+ Oxford contemporary *T.W. Earp*]

twerpy *adj*. [1960s+] foolish, idiotic. [TWERP n.]

twibill *n*. [17C; late 19C] a thug, a bully. [SE *twibill*, a 2-edged axe]

twice *v*. [late 19C–1940s] to cheat, to deceive. [TWO-TIME v.]

twice laid *n*. **1** [mid–late 19C] a dish of fried fish and potatoes. **2** [20C+] (*US*) a dish of minced meat on toast. [i.e. the remains of a previous meal]

twicer *n*.[1] **1** [late 17C; late 19C–1900s] one who attends church twice on a Sunday. **2** [mid-19C] (*Aus. Und.*) one who has twice been convicted of a criminal offence. **3** [mid–late 19C] something or someone very important, i.e. doubly valuable, relevant, forceful etc. **4** [late 19C+] (*Aus.*) a sycophant. **5** [20C+] a widow or widower who marries for the second time. **6** [1910s+] (*orig. Aus.*) a confidence trickster, one who engages in any form of 'double-dealing'. **7** [1910s+] (*Aus.*) a very demanding person, lit. one who asks for 2 helpings of food. **8** [1910s+] 2 of something, e.g. a whipping, a 2-year prison sentence. **9** [1940s] (*UK Und.*) 2 shilling pieces. [SE *twice*; (4) SE *two-faced*]

twicer *n*.[2] *see* ONCER n.[1] (1).

twicers *n*. [late 19C–1900s] twins.

twice twenty *adj*. *see* FORTY adj.[2].

twiddle *n.* [1950s] (*UK prison*) letting a warder suspect one of holding contraband, only to reval that one is holding something completely innocuous; once suspicions have been allayed, one can then reveal or pass on the actual contraband, e.g. tobacco.

twiddle-diddles *n.* [late 18C–early 19C] the testicles. [SE *twiddle*, to play with + redup.]

twiddlepoop *n.* [late 18C–early 19C] an effeminate-looking man. [SE *twiddle*, to twirl around + POOP n.¹ (3)]

twig *n.*¹ **1** [late 18C–mid-19C] style, fashion; usu. as *in twig*, smartly or fashionably dressed. **2** [early–mid-19C] (*orig. boxing*) condition, fettle, spirits; often as IN FINE TWIG phr. **3** [early–mid-19C] a stylish (young) man. [ety. unknown; ? TWIG v.²]

twig *n.*² [mid–late 19C] (*UK Und.*) a look. [TWIG v.² (1)]

twig *n.*³ **1** [1940s] (*US Black*) a tree. **2** [1960s–70s] a marijuana cigarette (cf. BONE n.¹¹). **3** [1980s+] (*US campus*) a notably thin person. **4** [2000s] (*US drugs*) a very small piece of crack cocaine (cf. BASE n.).

twig *v.*¹ [early 18C–19C] to disengage, to break off; thus (*UK Und.*) *twig the darbies*, knock off the handcuffs or irons. [? SE *tweak* or *twitch*]

twig *v.*² **1** [mid-18C–1910s] to observe, to watch. **2** [late 18C+] to understand, to work out. **3** [late 18C+] to recognize. **4** [19C–1930s] to catch sight of, to become aware of. [? fig. uses of dial. *twick*, to jerk]

twig and berries *n.* [20C+] a young boy's penis and testes.

twigged *adj.* [1980s+] (*US drugs*) intoxicated by drugs. [TWIG n.³ (2)]

twigger *n.* [late 16C–17C] **1** a promiscuous woman, a prostitute. **2** a womanizer. [SE *twigger*, a ewe that is a prolific breeder]

twiggez-vous (the chose)? *phr.* (*also* **twiggy-vous (the chose)?**) [late 19C–1950s] do you understand (what this is?/what's happening?). [a 'macaronic' or mixed-language phr. based on a Frenchified form of TWIG v.² (2) + Fr. *vous*, you + *chose*, thing]

twig out *v. see* TWEAK OUT v.

twigs *n.* [1930s–40s] (*US Black*) the human legs.

twillip *n.* [1940s] a general term of abuse. [TWERP n. + ?]

twim *n. see* TWAM n.

twin-coat *n.* [1970s] (*W.I.*) a hypocrite. [i.e. one who has 2 fig. *coats*]

twine *n.* [1960s] (*Aus. Und.*) a confidence trick. [TWINE v.]

twine *v.* [mid-19C; 1980s+] (*Aus. prison*) to trick, to deceive; as in passing a counterfeit coin for a good one. [? SE *twine*]

twink *n.*¹ (*also* **twinkle, twinky**) [17C–19C] a moment, a very brief period of time; usu. as *in a twink*. [SE *twinkling* (of a star)]

twink *n.*² (*also* **twinkle toes**) **1** [1960s] (*US campus*) a male homosexual, or a person who is suspected of being one. **2** [1960s+] (*US gay*) an available attractive young boy, whether working for money or not. [? the SE *twinkle* in his eye]

twink *n.*³ [1960s+] (*US campus*) someone unusual, crazy or stupid.

Twinkie *n.* [1990s+] (*US campus*) an Asian who identifies with Caucasians. [a *Twinkie* biscuit, which is 'brown on the outside and White inside']

twinkie *n.* (*also* **twinky, twink**) **1** [1970s+] (*US gay*) a young, inexperienced homosexual man. **2** [1980s+] a young (underage) sex object, whether male or female and seen as suitable for exploitation. **3** [1980s+] anyone considered odd or eccentric. **4** [1990s+] the penis. [? fig. use of *Twinkie*, a variety of sweet biscuit; or ? ext. of TWINK n.²/TWINK n.³]

twinkies *n.* [2000s] (*US Black*) chrome car wheels.

twinklers *n.* **1** [mid-17C–mid-19C; 1940s] the eyes. **2** [18C+] the stars. **3** [1900s–20s] diamonds. [SE *twinkle*, to sparkle; (1) 1940s use is US Black]

twinkle toes *n. see* TWINK n.².

twinkle/twinky *n. see* TWINK n.¹.

twinky *n. see* TWINKIE n.

twin-mouth *n.* [1970s] (*W.I.*) a hypocrite. [i.e. one who speaks with 2 fig. mouths]

twire *n.* (*also* **tweer**) [late 17C–early 18C] a glance, esp. a leer. [dial. *twire*, to look covertly, to peer, to peep]

twirl *n.* [late 19C+] **1** (*UK/US Und.*) a key, esp. a skeleton or duplicate key. **2** (*UK prison*) a prison officer.

twirl, the *n.* [1950s–60s] **1** (*UK Und.*) working as a fraudulent bookmaker, typically taking large bets but putting them down on a less popular horse – if the horse originally betted on wins, the bookmaker simply claims the bettor was mistaken. **2** a confidence trick that involves the substitution of a fake jewel for a real one.

twirl *v.* [1980s+] (*US campus*) to party, to dance.

twirler *n.*¹ [late 18C–mid-19C] (*UK Und.*) a seller of (old) clothes.

twirler *n.*² [1920s+] a key, esp. a skeleton or duplicate key. [TWIRL n. (1)]

twirl the pearls *v.* [1960s+] (*US camp gay*) to dance.

twirp *n. see* TWERP n.

twiss *n.* [late 18C–early 19C] (*Irish*) a chamberpot. [an attack on the English writer Richard *Twiss* (1747–1821), who had publ. the highly critical 'Tour in Ireland'. To take their revenge the Irish produced a chamberpot with a picture of Richard Twiss inside it, beneath which was inscribed the rhyme 'Let everyone piss / On lying Dick Twiss']

twist *n.*¹ **1** [late 17C–early 19C] a drink of tea and coffee mixed together. **2** [late 18C–mid-19C] any mixed alcoholic drink, typically brandy and eggs or brandy, beer and eggs, brandy and gin or a *gin twist*, gin and hot water.

twist *n.*² [late 18C–1950s] an appetite, a capacity for eating. [TWIST (DOWN) (APACE) v.]

twist *n.*³ **1** [early 19C] the hangman's noose. **2** [mid-19C+] the arm lock forced on a person who is being arrested. **3** [late 19C] (*UK Und.*) a hold on something or someone.

twist *n.*⁴ **1** [20C+] (*Irish*) a quarrel, an argument; thus phrs. *in good twist*, on good terms; *in bad twist*, on bad terms; *in twist*, in agreement. **2** [20C+] cheating, dishonesty, treachery; thus *at the twist*, double-crossing; *on the twist*, thieving. **3** [1970s+] (*Irish*) a turn.

twist *n.*⁵ [1910s+] (*Aus.*) a professional criminal. [abbr. TWISTER n.⁴; or ? not being STRAIGHT adj.¹ (5)]

twist *n.*⁶ **1** [1920s+] (*US Und.*) a girl, a woman. **2** [1950s+] the passive member of a lesbian relationship. **3** [1970s] (*US prison*) a prostitute. [abbr. TWIST AND TWIRL n.]

twist *n.*⁷ (*drugs*) **1** [1930s+] a marijuana cigarette (cf. AFRICAN WOODBINE n.). **2** [2000s] a small bag of heroin secured with a twist tie. [it is *twisted* into shape; note TWIST v.⁴]

twist *n.*⁸ [1980s] (*Aus.*) a key.

twist *v.*¹ **1** [early 18C–mid-19C] to be hanged; thus as excl. *twist me!* a synon. for HANG ME! excl. **2** [20C+] (*Aus.*) to be convicted of a crime. [lit./fig. twisting on the rope]

twist *v.*² **1** [mid–late 19C] to steal. **2** [20C+] to cheat, to defraud. **3** [1920s] to lie. [i.e. 'twisting' the rules]

twist *v.*³ [mid-19C–1900s] (*UK Und.*) to steal a watch by first snapping its ring.

twist *v.*⁴ **1** [1910s+] (*US*) (*also* **twist a burn**) to roll a cigarette. **2** [1940s+] (*drugs*) to roll a marijuana cigarette.

twist *v.*⁵ [1950s] to leave.

twist *v.*⁶ *see* TWIST (DOWN) (APACE) v.

twist and twine *v.* [20C+] (*Irish*) to whine. [rhy. sl.]

twist and twirl *n.* [20C+] a girl. [rhy. sl.]

twist (down) (apace) *v.* [late 17C–early 19C] to eat, esp. heartily. [? the twisting of the wrist in eating or tearing pieces of bread from a loaf; note Worcestershire dial. *twist something down one*, to eat heartily]

twisted *adj.*¹ [late 18C–early 19C] hanged. [TWIST v.¹ (1)]

twisted *adj.*² **1** [20C+] annoyed, out of emotional control. **2** [20C+] odd, bizarre, extraordinary. **3** [20C+] confused. **4** [1930s+] (*orig. US*) very drunk (cf. AFFLICTED adj.). **5** [1960s+]

(*orig. US*) extremely intoxicated by a drug, esp. a hallucinogen or cannabis. **6** [1960s+] cynical, disenchanted. **7** [1990s+] (*US campus*) of a woman, bisexual.

twisted *adj.*[3] [1950s–70s] (*US*) **1** arrested. **2** serving time in jail.

twister *n.*[1] **1** [late 17C] a voracious eater. **2** [mid-19C] (*US*) a spree. [TWIST (DOWN) (APACE) v.]

twister *n.*[2] [mid–late 19C] (*US*) a story, a 'tall tale'.

twister *n.*[3] **1** [mid-19C–1950s] (*US*) something that causes a person to go into fig. contortions; thus *knock a twister*, to disconcert very much. **2** [1950s] (*US Und.*) a beggar or drug addict who can fake convincing fits in order to obtain money or drugs.

twister *n.*[4] **1** [mid-19C+] (*US Und.*) a pickpocket, a thief. **2** [late 19C] as a term of address, with no negative inference. **3** [1910s+] an untrustworthy person, a crook, a liar. **4** [1920s–30s] one who, through their own corruption, is impervious to the cheating and trickery of others.

twister *n.*[5] **1** [late 19C+] (*Aus./US*) a cyclone, a tornado; also in fig. use. **2** [1930s–50s] (*UK Und.*) a fit.

twister *n.*[6] **1** [20C+] (*US prison*) a prison guard. **2** [1930s–70s] (*US Black*) a frontdoor key; thus *twister to the slammer*, the door key. [the 'twisting' or turning of the key]

twister *n.*[7] [1930s–50s] (*drugs*) **1** a user of marijuana. **2** an injection of mixed narcotic drugs. **3** violent retching or vomiting of blood or mucus during withdrawal sickness. **4** fake withdrawal symptoms; one who is exhibiting them; thus *frame a twister*, to throw a fake withdrawal fit in the hope of obtaining narcotics from a doctor. **5** a ration of narcotics. [one is SE *twisted* up by the drugs or their effects]

twist hay *v.* [2000s] (*Irish*) to start trouble, usu. playfully.

twistical *adj.* [19C] crooked, morally ambiguous. [SE *twisted*]

twisting *n.* **1** [mid-19C–1900s] a scolding, a telling-off. **2** [1910s–20s] a cause of anxiety or unhappiness. [one's emotions are *twisted*]

twist it, choke it, and make it squeal *v.* [1930s] (*US short order*) an order for an egg malted milk.

twisto *n.* [1990s+] (*US*) a sexual pervert. [TWISTED adj.[2] (2)]

twist one's wig *v.* [1960s] (*orig. US Black*) to make the utmost effort, to stretch one's mind. [SE *twist* + WIG n.[3] (1)]

twist someone's arm *v.* [1950s+] to force someone to do something against their will, often ironic.

twist someone's cap *v.* [2000s] (*US prison*) to shoot, to kill.

twist the tiger's tail *v. see* FIGHT THE TIGER v.

twit *n.* **1** [1920s+] a fool, an idiot. **2** [1960s–70s] (*gay*) an effeminate male homosexual. [TWERP n. + TWAT n. (3)]

twit *v.* [late 16C+] to tease, to make fun of.

twitch *n.* [1930s] (*US Und.*) an instrument of torture. [SE *twitch*, 'a noose or loop; spec. a noose which may be tightened by twisting the stick to the end of which it is attached, used to compress the lip or muzzle of a horse to restrain him during a painful operation' (*OED*)]

twitch, the *n.* [1980s+] (*drugs*) a nervous mannerism that afflicts regular users of crack cocaine.

twitched *adj.* [late 19C+] nervous, irritable. [SE *twitch*]

twitcher *n.* **1** [1950s] (*US drugs*) a drug addict. **2** [1980s+] a crack cocaine addict who is afflicted by nervous twitching. [SE *twitch*/TWITCH, THE n.]

twitchety *adj.* (*also* **twitchetty**) [mid–late 19C] nervous, fidgety. [SE *twitch*]

twitching *n.* [early 19C] (*Scot. Und.*) stealing shawls from women wearing them in the street.

twitter *n.* [1900s] either an effeminate man or a masculine woman.

twitting *adj.* [1920s+] foolish, stupid. [TWIT n. (1)]

twittoc *n.* [late 18C–mid-19C] (*UK Und.*) the number 2. [corruption of SE *two*]

twit-twat *n. see* TWAT n. (1).

twitty *adj.* [1980s+] (*US campus*) silly, foolish, ineffectual. [TWIT n. (1)]

twize *n.* [1970s+] (*US campus*) Budweiser beer. [abbr./pron.]

t.w.k. *adj.* [mid–late 19C] (*Anglo-Ind.*) ? of a woman, *too well known*. [abbr.]

two *n.* **1** [late 19C–1930s] 2 pennyworth (of spirits). **2** [20C+] (*UK Und.*) a 2-year sentence.

two and eight *n.* [1910s+] a state, a panic. [rhy. sl.]

two bad boys from Illinois *n.* [20C+] (*US*) in craps dice, a throw of 2 (cf. ADA FROM DECATUR n.).

two-bagger *n. see* DOUBLE-BAGGER n.

two bit *n.* [mid-19C+] (*W.I.*) 9 (old) pence.

two-bit *adj.* (*also* **two-bits**) [20C+] (*US*) second-rate, inferior. [SE *two* + BIT n.[1] (4), lit. worth 25 cents]

two-bit Annie *n.* [1940s] (*US*) a cheap prostitute (cf. DOLLAR-WOMAN n.). [TWO-BIT adj. + proper name]

two-bit hustler *n.* [1940s–50s] (*US Und.*) **1** a promiscuous woman; a low-priced prostitute (cf. DOLLAR-WOMAN n.). **2** a second-rate confidence trickster. **3** a passive homosexual or low-priced male homosexual prostitute. [TWO-BIT adj. + HUSTLER n.]

two bits *n.* **1** [mid-19C+] (*US*) 25 cents. **2** [1940s–60s] (*orig. US Black*) $2. **3** [1940s–60s] (*US Und.*) $25. [BIT n.[1] (4)]

two-bits *adj. see* TWO-BIT adj.

two-bitty *adj.* [1940s] (*W.I.*) feeling poorly, not up to much. [TWO-BIT adj.]

two-blink *adj.* [20C+] (*US*) extremely small, insignificant. [the equivalent of blinking twice]

two-bob *adj.* [1940s+] (*orig. Aus.*) inferior, useless, second-rate. [BOB n.[4] (1), lit. worth 2 shillings (10p)]

two-bob bit *n.* (*also* **two-bob bits**) [1930s+] **1** an act of defecation (cf. ANDY CAPP n.). **2** diarrhoea (cf. BANANA (SPLITS) n.). **3** a female breast (cf. BRACE AND BITS n.). **4** a contemptible person. [rhy. sl.; (1) = SHIT n.[1] (3); (2) = SHITS, THE n. (1); (3) = TIT n.[3] (1); (4) = SHIT n.[2] (1)]

two-bob each way *phr.* [1960s+] (*Aus.*) uncommitted. [the cheapness of such a bet]

two-bob hop *n.* [1920s+] (*Aus.*) a cheap dance. [SE *two* + BOB n.[4] (1) + HOP n.[1] (1)]

two bowers and an ace *n.* [late 19C] (*US*) something excellent; an advantage. [euchre terminology *bowers*, the name of the 2 highest cards – the knave of trumps, and the knave of the same colour, called right and left bower respectively]

two bulb *n.* [2000s] (*Irish*) a police car. [the 2 flashing lights on the roof]

two by four *n.* (*also* **five to four, six to four, sixty-four**) [1930s+] a prostitute (cf. BOAT AND OAR n.). [rhy. sl. = SE *whore*]

two-by-four *adj.* [late 19C+] (*US*) small, insignificant. [the minimal dimensions]

twoc *n. see* TWOCKER n.

twoc *v. see* TWOCK v.

two camels *n.* [1940s] (*US Black*) 10 minutes. [? the time needed to smoke 2 *Camel* cigarettes]

2CB *n. see* NEXUS n.

two-cent *adj.* (*also* **ten-cent**) [late 19C+] inferior, second-rate. [var. on TWO-BIT adj.; worth only 2 cents]

two-cent dosser *n.* [late 19C] a man who lives in stale-beer shops, which specialized in stale or old and strong beer. [SE *two cents* + DOSSER n. (1); note UK, despite US denomination]

two cents *n.* [1930s–40s] (*US Black*) $2.

two cents' worth *n.* (*also* **two cents**) **1** [1900s–50s] (*US*) a little, a trivial amount. **2** [1910s+] one's personal opinion, a remark about a topic.

twock *v.* (*also* **twoc**) [1990s+] to steal cars, usu. for joy-riding. [abbr. take without owner's consent]

twocker *n.* (*also* **twoc, twocer, twok**) [1990s+] a youth who steals cars to use in a crime or for amusement; developed into a non-specific term of abuse. [TWOCK v.]

two dicks *n.* [1990s+] (*UK juv.*) a general term of abuse. [the image of one who is such a WANKER n. (2) that he requires 2 penises]

two dog night n. [1970s+] (Aus./US) a very cold night. [orig. Aboriginal term, the need to sleep between a pair of dogs to batten onto their warmth]

two-dollar adj. [1990s+] (US) second-rate. [var. on TWO-CENT adj.]

two-dollar words n. (also **five-dollar expression/words**) [20C+] (US) language that the speaker considers to be unnecessarily 'difficult' or 'intellectual'.

two dots and a dash n. 1 [1910s–20s] fried eggs and bacon. 2 [1960s+] (US gay) the male genitals. [visual likeness]

two dozen n. [late 19C] (Aus. Und.) a punishment of 25 lashes.

two drinks and a sandwich n. see COFFEE AND CAKES n.

two ducks n. see TWO (LITTLE) DUCKS n.

twoed-up adv. (also **two'd up**) [1960s+] (UK prison) having 2 prisoners sharing a cell; thus **threed-up** etc.

two ends of a clift n. see CLIFT n.

twoer n. 1 [late 19C] a 2-wheeled cab. 2 [late 19C] a 2-shilling (10p) piece. 3 [1930s] a 2-year prison sentence. 4 [1940s+] £20; £200 (cf. ONER n.[3]).

two-eyed steak n. (also **two-eyed beefsteak**) [late 19C–1930s] a kipper, a salted herring. [its flatness]

two eyes of blue! excl. [1920s+] too true! [rhy. sl.]

twoface v. [1930s+] (Can.) to treat in a duplicitous manner. [SE two-faced]

two faces under one hood n. [late 16C–early 19C] double-dealing, cheating, duplicity; a deceitful person. [SE two-faced]

two fat cheeks (and ne'er a nose) n. [18C–19C] the posterior, the buttocks.

two fat ladies n. (also **two old ladies**) [1940s+] (bingo) the number 88 (cf. ALDERSHOT LADIES n.). [the supposedly similar shapes (cf. ONE FAT LADY n.)]

twofer n. 1 [late 19C] a harlot (cf. DOLLAR-WOMAN n.). 2 [late 19C–1930s] (US) (also **toofah, toofer**) a cheap cigar. 3 [20C+] a prostitute who is amenable to vaginal and/or anal intercourse. 4 [1940s–50s] (US) a theatre ticket sold at half price, or similar offer. [? 'two for the price of one']

two-fifth n. [2000s] (US) a .25 calibre pistol.

two-finger v. [1940s] (US police) to pickpocket.

two-fingered salute n. [1960s+] an obscene gesture of dismissal; a 'V-sign'.

two-fisted adj. 1 [late 18C+] good at fist-fighting, thus tough, manly. 2 [early–mid-19C] clumsy. 3 [20C+] ext. use of (1) with ref. to inanimate objects, e.g. two-fisted yarn, a tough, male-orientated story.

two-foot rule n. [mid–late 19C] a fool (cf. BEECHAM'S PILL n.). [rhy. sl.]

two-for-a-nickel adj. [1920s–60s] (US) cheap, second-rate.

two Fs n. [late 19C] (UK middle class) fringe and followers. [abbr.; the supposed characteristics of a woman servant, whose hair was worn in a fringe and whose potential charms attracted a variety of suitors]

two-handed adj. 1 [late 17C–1920s] usu. of people, large, strapping; thus two-handed fellow, two-handed wench. 2 [mid-19C–1920s] clumsy, maladroit. 3 [1910s–30s] (US) dedicated, committed, generous.

two-handed put n. [late 18C–19C] sexual intercourse. [SE two-handed, wholehearted + put, an act of thrusting or pushing]

two-handful n. see HANDFUL n.[3] (2).

two hearts in a pond n. [late 19C–1900s] 2 baked hearts, cooked in a 'pond dish', i.e. a round dish divided in 2 halves by a 'wall'.

two hoots n. see HOOT n.[3] (1).

200 on a plate n. [1940s] (US) pork and beans.

two in a bowl n. [late 19C] (US short order) a plate of oyster stew. [2 oysters]

two-inched adj. [1990s+] (US Black) of a woman, given insufficient sexual gratification. [the lit./fig. dimensions of the man's penis]

two inches beyond upright n. [late 19C–1900s] a hypocritical liar. [such a person cannot be considered 'upright']

two in one n. [1960s] (US drugs) cocaine and heroin injected together.

two in the air n. [late 19C] (US short order) 2 fried eggs.

twoit n. see TWAT n. (1).

two jerks of a lamb's tail phr. see TWO SHAKES OF A LAMB'S TAIL phr.

two Jews n. [1940s] the number 2.

twok n. see TWOCKER n.

two-leaved book n. [late 16C–17C] the vagina.

two-legged mare n. [mid-16C–17C; late 19C] the gallows.

two-legged tree n. [19C] the gallows.

two-legged tympany n. (also **tympany with two heels**) [mid-16C–early 18C] a baby, esp. in the embryonic stage; thus have a two-legged tympany, to be pregnant. [SE tympany, a morbid swelling or tumour]

two little crutches n. [1940s+] (bingo) the number 77 (cf. ALDERSHOT LADIES n.). [the supposedly similar shapes]

two (little) ducks n. [late 19C+] (bingo) the number 22 (cf. ALDERSHOT LADIES n.). [the supposedly similar shapes]

two looking at you n. (also **two looking up**) [20C+] (US) 2 fried eggs 'sunny-side up'. [orig. short order cooking jargon]

two-mac n. [1950s+] (W.I.) 2 shillings. [SE two + MAC n.[1]]

two-minute brother n. [1990s+] (US Black) a man who suffers from premature ejaculation. [SE two minutes, the length of the copulation + BROTHER n. (2)]

two-mouth n. [1950s] (W.I.) a hypocrite. [dial. two-mouth, a double-edged machete]

twonk n. [1980s] a fool. [TWAT n. (3) + PLONKER n. (3)]

two old ladies n. see TWO FAT LADIES n.

211 n. [1990s+] (US Black) an armed robbery; also as v. [California police code number]

213 n. [1990s+] (US Black) Los Angeles. [the telephone area code]

twoonie n. [1990s+] (Can.) a 2-dollar coin. [SE two + LOONIE n.[1]]

twoosie(-woosie) n. [1940s] an attractive young girl. [? play on FLOOZIE n.]

two-out n. [mid-19C] a small measure or glass of gin, prob. worth 2 pence.

two out adv. [1980s+] (Aus. prison) having 2 prisoners sharing a cell. [TWOED-UP adv.]

two-peg n. [1900s–60s] (Aus.) a florin, a 2-shilling piece (10p). [SE two + PEG n.[3]]

two pence short of a bob phr. [20C+] not very intelligent, slightly eccentric, odd. [a BOB n.[4] (1) was composed of 12 pence; var. on NOT ALL THERE phr.]

two pence wet and two pence dry n. [18C] a brief act of intercourse with a prostitute, either vaginal, i.e. wet, or anal, i.e. dry, or masturbation (cf. DOLLAR-WOMAN n.). [? a 'low' gambling game, see C. Johnson, History of Highwaymen, p.59: 'Come, said he, what shall we do with all this Drink? We will play Two pence wet, and Fourpence dry [...] at this low Gaming Rumbold had, in short, won of his Confederate ten shillings']

twopenny n.[1] [mid-19C–1930s] the head. [rhy. sl. twopenny loaf = loaf of bread = head; note the later LOAF (OF BREAD) n.]

twopenny n.[2] [late-19C–1910s] a pawnbroker's professional go-between, who charges 2 pence to take one's goods to the pawnshop and negotiate a deal.

twopenny n.[3] [1910s–20s] a general term of affection.

twopenny adj. see TUPPENNY-HA'PENNY adj.

twopenny burster n. [early 19C] a loaf of bread. [its price and its effect on the stomach]

twopenny damn n. see DAMN n.

twopenny-halfpenny adj. see TUPPENNY-HA'PENNY adj.

twopenny hop *n.* [mid–late 19C] a cheap dancehall or dance held at one. [the 2d price of admission + HOP n.[1]; 'the clog hornpipe, the pipe dance, flash jigs, and horn pipes in fetters, à la Jack Sheppard, are the favourite movements' (Hotten, 1867)]

twopenny rope *n.* [mid-19C–1930s] (*UK tramp*) a hostel, a casual ward. [orig. 2 ropes strung across a room, with rough bedding (usu. sacking) strung between them, on which bedless tramps could fitfully sleep for a 2d payment; note Dickens, *Pickwick Papers* (1836–7): ''Ven the lady and gen'lm'n as keeps the Hot-el, first begun business, they used to make the beds on the floor; but this wouldn't do at no price, 'cos instead o' taking a moderate twopenn'orth o' sleep, the lodgers used to lie there half the day. So now they has two ropes, 'bout six foot apart, and three from the floor, which goes right down the room; and the beds are made of slips of coarse sacking, stretched across em']

twopenny tube *n.* [1900s–30s] the London Underground. [the original fare of 2d + TUBE n.[1] (2)]

twopenny upright/uprighter *n. see* THREEPENNY UPRIGHT n.

two-pipe *n.* [1940s] (*US Und.*) a double-barrelled shotgun.

two-pot screamer *n. see* ONE-POT SCREAMER n.

two Ps *n. see* MAY YOUR PRICK AND PURSE NEVER FAIL YOU! excl.

two puppies fighting in a bag *n.* [1970s+] very large, poorly contained and mobile breasts; also of buttocks. [coined to describe the actress Elizabeth Taylor (b.1932)]

two-quidder *n.* [late 19C] one who earns £2 per week, thus a member of the lower middle classes.

twos *n.* [1970s+] (*UK prison*) the second landing of cells in a prison block; similarly *threes, fours* etc.

two's and fews *phr.* [1940s–50s] having no or very little money. [orig. of prostitutes who charge 2 dollars, but often have to take less, i.e. whatever they can get]

twos and threes *n.* [1960s–80s] **1** keys. **2** knees. [rhy. sl.]

two sandwiches short of a picnic *phr. see* ONE SANDWICH SHORT OF THE PICNIC phr.

two shakes *n.* (*also* **a brace of shakes, a couple of shakes**) [mid-19C+] a very short time; usu. in phr. *in two shakes*, quickly, immediately. [abbr. of TWO SHAKES OF A LAMB'S TAIL phr.; SE *brace*, *pair*; but note also SHAKE n.[2] (2)]

two shakes of a lamb's tail *phr.* (*also* **two shakes of a (dead) sheep's tail, ...a donkey's tail, ...a duck's tail, ...a frog's whisker, ...the mainbrace, three shakes of..., a whisk of..., two jerks of..., three jerks of..., two twists of a lamb's tail, a fling of a cow's tail**) [mid-19C+] a very short time, usu. in phr. *in two shakes...*, extremely quickly, at once.

two-shoes *n.* [mid-19C+] a little girl. [the popular children's tale *The History of Little Goody Two-Shoes* (1765), supposedly written by Oliver Goldsmith (?1730–74) for the children's publisher John Newbury]

two-slice *n.* [1990s+] an office. [rhy. sl.]

two snaps up *phr.* [1990s+] (*US campus*) an expression of approval. [referring to the snapping of one's fingers, and a play on the phr. 'two thumbs up' used by US TV film critics Roger Ebert and Gene Siskel]

two spaces *n.* [20C+] (*US Und.*) a 2-year prison sentence. [i.e. 2 year-long spaces in one's life]

two-spot *n.* **1** [mid-19C+] (*US*) a $2 bill. **2** [late 19C–1930s] a low-value playing card. **3** [late 19C–1930s] in fig. use, an insignificant person. **4** [1900s–40s] (*US prison/Und.*) (*also* **two-spotter**) a 2-year sentence. **5** [1970s–80s] (*Aus. Und.*) A$200. **6** [1990s+] (*Aus. drugs*) A$200 worth of heroin. [SE *two* + -SPOT sfx]

two-stemmer *n.* [late 19C–1950s] (*US*) a small town. [STEM n.[1] (1), i.e. the 2 major streets that such a town could boast]

two-step *n.* [1920s–40s] (*US tramp*) a chicken.

two stone underweight *phr.* (*also* **two stone wanting**) [late 18C–1900s] castrated, thus as n., a eunuch. [pun on STONE n.[1] (1)]

two-storey lorry *n.* [1940s] (*US Black*) a double-decker bus.

twos up *n.* **1** [1960s+] sexual intercourse involving 2 men and 1 woman. **2** spec. when a woman has 2 men simultaneously penetrating her anus and her vagina.

two's up! *excl.* [1970s] an excl. used to denote one's desire to share a cigarette.

twot *n. see* TWAT n.

two tacos short of a combination plate *phr.* [1980s] (*US*) not very intelligent, slightly eccentric, odd. [var. on NOT ALL THERE phr.]

two thieves beating a rogue *phr.* [late 18C–early 19C] a phr. said of a person beating their hands against their sides to get warm on a cold day.

two-thirty *adj.* [late 19C+] dirty. [rhy. sl.]

two ticks *n.* (*also* **a couple of ticks, two-twos**) [20C+] a very short time; usu. in phr. *in two ticks*, very quickly, virtually immediately. [SE *tick*, the movement of a clock, i.e. seconds; TICK n.[4] (2)]

two-time *adj. see* TWO-TIMING adj.

two-time *v.* **1** [1910s+] (*also* **five-time**) to deceive sexually. **2** [1920s+] (*orig. US*) to cheat, esp. to double-cross.

two-time loser *n.* **1** [1910s+] (*US Und.*) a person who already has 2 convictions and so risks a higher sentence the third time. **2** [1950s+] (*US*) a person who has been divorced twice.

two-timer *n.* [1920s+] (*orig. US*) a cheat, a double-crosser. [TWO-TIME v.]

two-timey *adj.* [1940s] (*US*) indecisive.

two-timing *adj.* (*also* **two-time**) [1920s+] (*orig. US*) duplicitous, esp. in a sexual context. [TWO-TIME v. (1)]

two-to-one *n.* [19C] (*US*) a pawnbroker. [either the arrangement of the trad. 3 balls hanging outside the pawnbroker's (1 above, 2 below) or the popular belief that it was 2–1 odds that one's pledge would never be redeemed]

two to one against you *phr.* [late 19C–1900s] you have no hope, the odds are stacked against you. [for ety. *see* TWO-TO-ONE n.]

two-to-one shop *n.* [late 18C–early 19C] a pawnbroker's shop. [for ety. *see* TWO-TO-ONE n.]

two twists of a lamb's tail *phr. see* TWO SHAKES OF A LAMB'S TAIL phr.

two-twos *n. see* TWO TICKS n.

two UEs *n.* (*also* **2 UEs**) [20C+] (*Aus.*) fleas. [rhy. sl.]

two-upper *n.* [1910s+] (*Aus.*) a player of the gambling game of two-up; thus *two-up school*, on the model of SE *card-school*, the place where the game is played.

two-way baby *n.* [1960s+] (*US*) a bisexual.

two-way girl *n.* (*also* **two-way bitch**) [1930s+] a woman who is amenable to vaginal and anal intercourse.

two-way guy *n. see* ONE-WAY adj. (1).

two-way man *n.* [1930s+] a male prostitute who is willing to act as the passive or active partner in sodomy or fellatio.

two ways from the jack *phr. see* FORTY WAYS (FROM THE JACK) phr.

two-wheeler *n.* [20C+] (*Aus.*) a woman. [rhy. sl. = SHEILA n.]

two white, two red, and after you with the blacking brush *phr.* [mid-19C] 2 dabs of white powder, 2 of red and a blacking brush for the eyebrows; often abbr. as *two white, two red and the brush.* [a ref. to the excessive use of coloured cosmetics imported from Fr. *c.*1860–7]

two whoops and a holler *n. see* WHOOP AND A HOLLER n.

two with their eyes closed *n.* [20C+] (*US*) 2 fried eggs turned over in the pan.

two with their eyes open *n.* [1940s] (*US*) 2 eggs fried on one side only.

two with you *phr.* [late 19C] let's have a (twopenny) drink.

two years *n.* [1940s] (*US Und.*) a 2-dollar bill.

twunt *n.* [1990s+] a despicable, unpleasant person. [TWAT n. (3) + CUNT n.[2] (1)]

ty *n.* [1920s] (*Aus.*) typhoid fever. [abbr.]

Tyburn *n.* [16C–19C] sited near what is now Marble Arch, the village of Paddington, the principal site of public executions in London between 1388–1783, when it was replaced by Newgate; not sl. as such but occurring in many combs., e.g. FETCH A TYBURN STRETCH *v.*; MAKE A TYBURN SHOW *v.*; PREACH AT TYBURN CROSS *v.* [later use is historical]

Tyburn bird *n.* [late 17C] a criminal, destined to be hanged at Tyburn. [TYBURN *n.* + BIRD *n.*² (1)]

Tyburn blossom *n.* [late 18C–early 19C] a young thief or pickpocket. ['who in time will ripen unto fruit born by the DEADLY NEVERGREEN *n.*' (Grose, 1796)]

Tyburn check *n.* [16C–early 19C] a hangman's noose.

Tyburn collar *n.* [mid-19C] a fringe of beard worn under the chin.

Tyburn collop *n.* [16C] a miserable face.

Tyburn face *n.* [late 17C–18C] a miserable, down-in-the-mouth look.

Tyburn foretop *n.* (*also* **Tyburn top**) [late 18C–early 19C] **1** a wig with its foretop combed forward over the eyes; such wigs were esp. popular among the underworld. **2** a hairstyle associated with criminals.

Tyburnian tree *n. see* TYBURN TREE *n.*

Tyburn jig *n.* [late 17C–early 19C] a hanging.

Tyburn piccadill *n.* (*also* **piccadill**) [mid-17C–early 19C] a hangman's noose; thus *put on a Tyburn piccadill*, to be hanged. [*Tyburn*, generic for the execution ground + SE *piccadill*, an ornamented collar fashionable in the early 17C. The term comes from the Sp. *picadillo*, the dimin. of *picado*, meaning pricked, pierced, punctured, slashed or minced (thus *picada*, a puncture and *picadillo*, minced meat). The piccadill was brought to the UK either by Robert Baker (*The London Encyclopedia*, 1983) or by 'one Higgins' (*The Atheneum*, 1901), but, whichever individual, he made a fortune from his import, sufficient to buy land around what is now Piccadilly Circus and to erect, *c.*1622, a large mansion which was promptly and irreverently christened Piccadilly Hall. The surrounding area soon became known as Piccadilly. However, the *OED* cites a source writing in 1656 who claimed that the house was thus named because, being at the furthest edge of the parish of St Martin in the Fields, in which it lay, it was therefore serving as a 'collar', or outer edge of the area]

Tyburn stretch *n.* [mid-16C–early 19C] a hanging. [SE *stretch* one's neck]

Tyburn string *n.* [mid-17C–18C] a hangman's noose.

Tyburn tiffany *n.* [17C–18C] a hangman's noose. [SE *tiffany*, a transparent gauze muslin, often used as a headcover]

Tyburn tippet *n.* [mid-16C–early 19C] a hangman's noose. [TYBURN *n.* + SE *tippet*, a scarf, a band of silk or fur worn around the neck]

Tyburn top *n. see* TYBURN FORETOP *n.*

Tyburn tree *n.* (*also* **Tyburnian tree**) [mid-17C+] the gallows sited at Tyburn. [the best-known *Tyburn tree*, a great triple gallows on which 21 malefactors could be 'turned off' simultaneously, was erected in June 1751. Its first victim was 'Romish Canonical Doctor' John Story; although this gallows was the first permanent such structure on the site, hangings had taken place at Tyburn since 1388. Tyburn was in the then village of Paddington, thus note synon. *Paddington-tree*, e.g. in broadside 'Cromwell's Coronation' *c.*1656; later use is historical]

tyee *n.* (*also* **tyhee**) [late 18C+] (*US*) an important person. [Chinook jargon *tyee*, a chief]

tying-up *n.* [1900s] (*Aus.*) a marriage ceremony, a wedding. [TIE UP *v.*¹ (2)]

tyke *n.* [20C+] (*Aus./N.Z.*) a Roman Catholic; thus *Tykeland*, Ireland. [TEAGUE *n.*]

tyke-boy *n.* [19C] a dog fancier; one who supports dog fights. [SE *tyke*, dog]

tympany with two heels *n. see* TWO-LEGGED TYMPANY *n.*

typer *n.* [1930s–50s] **1** (*orig. US*) a typewriter. **2** (*US Und.*) a machinegun. [abbr. SE TYPEWRITER *n.*¹]

typewriter *n.*¹ [1910s+] a machinegun or sub-machinegun. [the tapping noise]

typewriter *n.*² [1930s+] a fighter (lit. or fig.). [rhy. sl.]

tyrekicker *n.* [1980s+] (*N.Z.*) of a politician or other decision-maker, one who discusses and debates, but fails to act. [car sales use *tyrekicker*, one who examines a car at length, then does not buy it]

Tyrone Power *n.* [1940s+] (*Aus.*) a shower. [rhy. sl.; ult. US actor *Tyrone Power* (1914–58)]

tyrooger *n.* [1960s] (*US*) the penis (cf. BAUBLE *n.*). [nonsense word]

tytere-tu *n. see* TITTERY-TU *n.*

tzing-tzing *adj.* [late 19C] excellent, first-rate. [? CHIN-CHIN! excl.]

tzuris *n. see* TSURIS *n.*

U

Ubangi *n.* [1980s] (*US*) a Black person. [central Afr. *Ubangi* tribe]

u.b.d.'d! *excl.* [1910s–20s] *you be d*amned! [abbr./pron.]

ubrown *n.* [1980s+] (*S.Afr. township*) brandy. [the colour]

u.b.s *n.* [1970s] (*US campus*) underwear, usu. female. [abbr. *underbodies*]

u.c. *n.* [1980s] (*US*) an *u*ndercover agent.

u/c *adj.* [1970s+] used in contact advertisements, uncircumcised. [abbr. *uncut*]

ucky *adj. see* YUCKY *adj.*

u-clever *n. see* CLEVER *n.*

ud *n.* (*also* **cud**) [17C–mid-18C] a euph. for *God*, used in a variety of oaths, such as *ud's wount-likins!* (cf. BOB n.[2]).

udders *n.* [early 18C; 1930s+] the female breasts (cf. BORDENS n.).

udso! *excl. see* ODSO! excl.

ud's wount-likins! *excl. see* UD n.

U-ey *n. see* U-IE n.

uff *n. see* OOF n.

Ugandan discussion *n.* [1970s+] sexual intercourse; also vars., such as *talk about Uganda, Ugandan affairs.*

uggies *n.* (*also* **ugg boots**) [1990s+] sheepskin boots or slippers. [SE *ugly*]

uglee *n. see* UGLY n.[2] (2).

uglies, the *n.* **1** [mid-19C+] a fit of depression or bad temper. **2** [late 19C] delirium tremens. **3** [1950s+] the state of being unattractive. **4** [1970s] nitrogen narcosis, 'rapture of the deep'.

ugly *n.*[1] [mid–late 19C] (*UK society*) a shade for a bonnet. [what was generally seen as its lack of style or taste]

ugly *n.*[2] **1** [mid–late 19C] a derog. term of address; thus *Mr Ugly.* **2** [1950s+] (*also* **uglee**) an unattractive person, usu. female.

ugly *adj.* [1990s+] (*US campus*) difficult.

ugly as a bagful of busted boils *phr.* (*also* **ugly as a bagful of busted arseholes**) [1980s+] (*Aus./N.Z.*) very ugly.

ugly as a hatful of arseholes *phr.* [1960s+] (*Aus./US*) very ugly. [SE *ugly* + *hatful* + ARSEHOLE n. (1)]

ugly as a hatful of bronzas *phr. see* BRONZE n.[2] (1).

ugly as a shithouse rat *phr.* [1990s+] (*Aus.*) extremely unattractive.

ugly as a tarantula *phr.* [late 19C] very angry, unpleasant.

ugly as bull-beef *phr.* [mid-19C] a general term of contempt; thus *go to the billy-fencer and sell yourself for bull-beef.*

ugly customer *n.* [early 19C+] an unpleasant, menacing individual. [SE *ugly* + CUSTOMER n. (1); the format dates to 16C *lewd customer*]

uglyman *n.* [mid–late 19C] that member of the garrotting team who actually does the choking.

ugly plug *n.* [19C] (*US*) an ugly face. [SE *ugly* + PLUG n.[5] (4)/play on PLUG-UGLY n. (1)]

ugly sister *n.* [20C+] a blister. [rhy. sl.; note SKIN-AND-BLISTER n. = SE *sister*]

U-haul *n.* [1990s+] (*US gay*) a lesbian who falls in love at first sight and moves in right away with a new lover. [the US truck rental company *U-Haul*]

U-ie *n.* (*also* **U-ey, yewie, yoo-ee, youee**) [1960s+] (*orig. Aus.*) a U-turn; thus *do/chuck/bang a U-ie*, to make a U-turn.

uke *n.* [1920s+] (*orig. US*) a *uke*lele. [abbr.]

ullage *n.* [late 19C] the dregs in the bottom of wine glasses or casks. [SE *ullage*, the amount of wine or other liquor by which a cask or bottle falls short of being quite full; note WW1 RN *ullage*, an incompetent]

ultimate *n.* [1980s+] (*drugs*) **1** cocaine. **2** crack cocaine (cf. BASE n.). [the potency and effects]

ultimatum *n.* [early 19C] the buttocks, the posterior. [SE *ultimatum*, the final point, the extreme limit]

ultra! *excl.* [1980s+] excellent! first-rate! wonderful! [SE *ultra*, on pattern of MEGA adj., but note Polari *ultra*, very]

ultracool *adj.* [1960s+] (*orig. US*) extremely sophisticated. [SE *ultra* + COOL adj.[1] (3)]

ultramarine *adj.* [late 19C–1910s] obscene, 'smutty'. [play on BLUE adj.[3]]

ultraswoopy *adj.* [2000s] (*US*) very stylish, streamlined.

umac *n.* [1960s+] (*S.Afr. Black*) a young man about town. [pfx *u-* + ? MACK n.[1] (2)]

umberstick *n.* [20C+] (*Ulster*) an umbrella. [SE *umbrella* + *stick*]

umble-cum-stumble *v.* [late 19C] to understand comprehensively.

umbrella *n.*[1] [1930s] **1** a cowardly boxer, one who cannot take the punches. **2** cowardice. [he 'folds up', thus FOLD v.]

umbrella *n.*[2] [1960s–70s] (*US*) police protection, obtained through bribery. [it keeps one from being 'rained on' – *see* RAIN ON v. (1)]

umbrella *n.*[3] [1990s+] a fellow, usu. a husband, boyfriend or lover. [rhy. sl.; Cockney pron. 'fella']

umbrella branch *n.* (*also* **umbrella brigade**) [1970s+] the Special Branch. [they may dress in the bowler hat and rolled umbrella uniform of their bureaucratic masters in Whitehall]

ump *n.* [20C+] (*US*) an *ump*ire. [abbr.]

umpchay *n.* [1920s–30s] a fool. [cod Lat. = CHUMP n.[1] (2)]

umph *n. see* OOMPH n.

umpteen *n.* [1910s+] an unspecified large number or amount; thus adj. *umpteenth.* [orig. WW1 milit. use, deliberately replacing a specific number with a noncommittal *um* for communications secrecy]

umpty *adj.* (*also* **umpty-umph**) [1910s+] (*orig. milit.*) **1** of an indefinite number, usu. a large one; in combs., e.g. *umpty-nine, umpty-eleven*; thus *umptieth.* **2** unpleasant, difficult. [(1) UMPTEEN n.; (2) ? GET THE HUMP v. (1)]

umpty *adv.* (*also* **tiddy umpty**) [1930s] (*US Black*) completely, entirely. [UMPTY adj. (1)]

umpty-doo *adj.* (*also* **humpty-doo**) [1910s+] (*Aus.*) **1** drunk. **2** in general fig. uses. [the nursery rhyme *Humpty-Dumpty*, who 'fell off a wall']

umpty-umph *adj. see* UMPTY *adj.*

u.m.s. *n.* [1980s+] (*US campus*) a sudden, unpredictable change of mood. [abbr. *ugly mood swing*]

un *n.* [1990s+] (*US campus*) an outsider, someone who does not fit in. [negative SE pfx *un-*]

una *n.* [mid-19C+] (*Ling. Fr./Polari*) the number 1. [Ital. *uno*, one]

un-ass *v.* [1960s+] (*US Black*) to hand over, to give up. [SE pfx *un-* + ASS *n.* (2)]

unavoidable circumstances *n.* [late 19C] (*US*) formal dress breeches worn for Court appearances.

unavoidable wreck *n.* [1930s] the neck. [rhy. sl.]

unbelt *v.* [late 19C–1920s] (*US*) to hand over money. [SE *unbelt*, to remove a sword]

unbenefit *v.* [1990s+] (*US teen*) to disassociate oneself from someone after a disagreement or an unpleasant occurrence. [lit. 'to withdraw one's benefits from']

unbetty *v.* **1** [early–mid-19C] to unlock. **2** [1930s] (*US Und.*) of a prostitute, to unbutton the customer's trousers. [SE pfx *un-* + BETTY *v.*]

unbleached American *n.* [mid-19C–1940s] an African-American. [one of the earliest efforts to find a euph. for such derog. terms as NIGGER *n.*[1] (1)]

unbleached Australian *n.* [late 19C+] a Native Australian, an Aboriginal. [for ety. *see* UNBLEACHED AMERICAN *n.*]

unboiled lobster *n.* [mid-19C] a policeman (cf. ANIMAL *n.*[1]; BABY-BLUES *n.*[2]). [the uncooked lobster is blue, like a police uniform; the cooked lobster turns red/pink, like a soldier's jacket]

unbooted *adj.* [1940s–50s] (*US Black*) naïve, ignorant. [a country person, who does not wear shoes]

unc *n.* [20C+] (*US*) uncle (cf. UNK *n.*). [abbr.]

unchubb *v. see* CHUBB (UP) *v.*

unchummy *adj.* [1920s] unfriendly. [SE pfx *un-* + CHUMMY *adj.*]

Uncle *n.* (*also* **my uncle, our uncle**) [mid-19C+] the USA, esp. the US armed forces or other federal/national authorities; thus *duck Uncle*, to avoid the draft. [abbr. UNCLE SAM *n.*[1]]

uncle *n.*[1] (*also* **mine uncle('s), my uncle('s)**) **1** [mid-18C+] a pawnbroker; usu. as *my uncle*. **2** [late 18C–early 19C] a privy (cf. AUNTIE *n.*[1]). **3** [late 19C–1910s] as *your uncle*, oneself. **4** [1920s–40s] (*US*) a receiver of stolen goods. [SE *uncle*; thus the avuncular help he gives 'relatives' in temporary financial distress]

uncle *n.*[2] (*also* **unkey, unky**) **1** [mid-19C–1960s] (*US*) a form of address to a Black male whose name one does not know or ignores. **2** [20C+] a general term of address to a man; there need be neither prior acquaintance or any form of relationship.

uncle *n.*[3] [1940s–70s] (*US gay/prison*) an older homosexual male with a taste for young men or boys.

uncle *n.*[4] *see* DUTCH UNCLE *n.*

uncle *adj. see* UNCLE TOM *adj.*

uncle *v. see* UNCLE TOM *v.*

uncle! *excl.* [1910s+] (*US*) an excl. used to signify one's surrender, usu. in a physical confrontation. [CRY UNCLE *v.*]

Uncle Arthur *n.* (*also* **Arthurs**) [20C+] (*Irish*) a generic for Guinness and the family who own it; thus *Arthur Guinness talk*, drunken language. [founder *Arthur* Guinness (1725–1803)]

Uncle Ben *n.*[1] [1940s+] (*bingo*) the number 10 (cf. ALDERSHOT LADIES *n.*). [rhy. sl.]

Uncle Ben *n.*[2] [1970s+] (*US gay*) a homosexual Black man who prefers White men; thus a term of abuse. [play on UNCLE TOM *n.* (1) + whiteness of *Uncle Ben's* brand of rice]

Uncle Benny *n.* (*also* **Uncle Ben**) [1920s–40s] (*US Und.*) a pawnbroker. [typical Jewish name *Benjamin*; pawnbroking is seen as a 'Jewish' occuption]

Uncle Bert *n.* [20C+] a shirt. [rhy. sl.]

Uncle Bill *n.* [1930s–50s] a policeman, the police (cf. BILLY *n.*[6]). [OLD BILL *n.* (1)]

Uncle Bob *n.*[1] [20C+] the penis (cf. ALMOND *n.*). [rhy. sl. = KNOB *n.*[1] (3)]

Uncle Bob *n.*[2] [1940s] a policeman (cf. BILLY *n.*[6]). [SE *uncle* + BOBBY *n.* (1)]

Uncle Bob *n.*[3] [1990s+] a job. [rhy. sl.]

Uncle Dick *n.* [1950s+] the penis (cf. ALMOND *n.*). [rhy. sl. = PRICK *n.* (2)]

Uncle Dick *adj.* [1940s+] ill, sick. [rhy. sl.]

Uncle Dick *v.* [1970s+] to be ill. [rhy. sl. = SE *sick*]

Uncle Fred *n.* [1930s+] bread. [rhy. sl.]

uncle from Fiji *n. see* FIJI UNCLE *n.*

Uncle George *n. see* UNCLE TOM *n.* (1).

uncle in Fiji *n. see* FIJI UNCLE *n.*

Uncle Joe *n.* [1940s] (*W.I.*) a large, dense cake. [? anecdotal]

Uncle John *n.* [2000s] a penis (cf. ABRAHAM *n.*[1]).

Uncle Lester *n.* [1990s+] a child molester. [rhy. sl.]

Uncle Mac *n.* [1980s+] (*drugs*) heroin (cf. HAMMER (AND TACK) *n.*). [rhy. sl. = SMACK *n.*[6] (1)]

Uncle Melvin/Merv *n. see* MELVIN *n.* (1).

Uncle Merv *v.* [1990s+] (*Aus.*) of a man, to ogle, to leer. [rhy. sl. = PERV *v.*]

Uncle Nabs *n.* [1970s+] (*US Black*) the police. [SE *Uncle* + NAB *n.*[2] (1)]

Uncle Ned *n.*[1] **1** [20C+] (*Aus.*) bread. **2** [1910s+] a bed. **3** [1930s+] (*also* **old ned**) the head. [rhy. sl.]

Uncle Ned *n.*[2] [1900s] (*Aus.*) a Black South African.

Uncle Payther *n.* [20C+] (*Irish*) a whingeing complainer. [the characteristics of Uncle *Payther* (Peter Flynn), a character in *The Moon and the Stars* (1926) by Sean O'Casey]

Uncle Sam *n.*[1] (*also* **Aunt Sam, Sam, Uncle Sammy, …Samuel, …Samwell**) [19C+] a generic term for the USA and American culture, esp. the armed forces or federal agencies of the USA. [created during the War of 1812 as the equivalent symbol to the UK's John Bull. 'He' is always pictured as a bewhiskered, high-hatted old gentleman, garbed in red, white and blue. The figure is supposed to have been based on a Samuel Wilson, an inspector of provisions based in Troy, New York. The symbol gained further currency during WW1 when he was painted by James Montgomery Flagg as a stern figure pointing a finger at passers-by in a celebrated recruiting poster; note Bartlett, *Dict. Americanisms* (1848): 'Immediately after the last declaration of war with England, Elbert Anderson of New York, then a contractor, visited Troy, on the Hudson; where was concentrated, and where he purchased, a large quantity of provisions, beef, pork, &c. The inspectors of these articles at that place were Messrs. Ebenezer and Samuel Wilson. The latter gentleman (invariably known as '*Uncle Sam*') generally superintended in person a large number of workmen, who, on this occasion, were employed in overhauling the provisions purchased by the contractor for the army. The casks were marked "E. A. – U. S." This work fell to the lot of a facetious fellow in the employ of the Messrs. Wilson, who, on being asked by some of his fellow-workmen the meaning of the mark (for the letters U. S. for United States, were then almost entirely new to them), said, "he did not know, unless it meant *Elbert Anderson* and *Uncle Sam*" – alluding exclusively, then, to the said "*Uncle Sam*" Wilson. The joke took among the workmen, and passed currently; and "*Uncle Sam*" himself being present, was occasionally rallied by them on the increasing extent of his possessions']

Uncle Sam *n.*[2] [20C+] a cut of lamb. [rhy. sl.]

Uncle Samantha *n.* [1950s–60s] (*camp gay*) the US government. [a camp feminization of UNCLE SAM *n.*[1]]

Uncle Sammy *n. see* UNCLE SAM *n.*[1]

Uncle Sam's action *n.* [1940s] (*US Black*) induction into one of the services (after being drafted). [UNCLE SAM *n.*[1] + ACTION *n.* (4)]

Uncle Sam's I.O.U. *n.* [1940s] money, a note (cf. ABE *n.*[2]). [UNCLE SAM *n.*[1]]

Uncle Sam's pets *n.* [1940s] (*US Black campus*) soldiers. [UNCLE SAM n.[1] + SE *pets*]

Uncle Samuel/Samwell *n.* see UNCLE SAM n.[1].

uncles and aunts *n.* [1920s–40s] pants. [rhy. sl.]

Uncle Sham *n.* [1960s–70s] (*US Black*) a derog. version of UNCLE SAM n.[1]. [SE *Uncle* + *sham*, fake; coined by the US protest movement to ridicule the hollowness at the heart of the so-called 'American dream']

Uncle Thomas *n.* [1920s] (*US*) the penis (cf. ABRAHAM n.[1]; MR TOM n.[1]). [JOHN THOMAS n. (1)]

uncle three balls *n.* [late 19C] a pawnbroker. [UNCLE n.[1] (1) + the 3 golden balls that trad. indicate a pawnshop]

Uncle Tom *n.* (*orig. US Black*) **1** [20C+] (*also* **Dr Thomas, Mr Thomas, Mr Tom, Tom, Uncle George, Uncle Thomas**) a subservient Black person, fitting willingly into the stereotyped and inferior image refined by generations of White supremacy; a middle-class Black who wishes to distance himself from the ghetto; an affected or pretentious Black person. **2** [1940s+] a tattle-tale, a person who befriends another, usu. in the workplace, only to deceive them. [*Uncle Tom*, the hero of Harriet Beecher Stowe's anti-slavery novel *Uncle Tom's Cabin* (1852)]

Uncle Tom *adj.* (*also* **Tom, uncle, Uncle Tomish**) [20C+] (*orig. US Black*) outwardly subservient, in the context of Black/White relations. [UNCLE TOM n. (1)]

Uncle Tom *v.* (*also* **uncle**) [1940s+] (*US Black*) to act in a subservient, obsequious manner to Whites. [UNCLE TOM n. (1)]

Uncle Tomahawk *n.* [1970s+] (*US*) a Native American who is condemned as insufficiently nationalistic. [play on UNCLE TOM n. (1) + SE *tomahawk*, the trad. 'Red Indian' weapon]

Uncle Tomish *adj.* see UNCLE TOM adj.

Uncle Whiskers *n.* [1920s+] (*US Und.*) a federal agent or agency. [the facial hair trad. adorning images of UNCLE SAM n.[1]]

Uncle Wilf *n.* [20C+] the police. [rhy. sl. = FILTH n.[2], pron. 'filf']

Uncle Willie *adj.* **1** [1920s+] chilly. **2** [1930s+] silly. [rhy. sl.]

unco *n.* [1990s+] (*Aus. teen*) an uncoordinated person or object. [abbr. SE *uncoordinated*]

unconked *adj.* see CONKED adj.[1].

unconscious *n.* [1920s–30s] **1** a day-dreamer. **2** (*US campus*) a fool.

unconscious *adj.* [1990s+] (*US campus*) performing instinctively (and successfully).

uncool *adj.* [1950s+] (*orig. US*) unpleasant, emotional, rude, tactless, unsophisticated, unfair; various negative meanings as to a particular context. [pfx *un-* + COOL adj.[1]]

uncunt *v.* (*also* **decunt**) [late 19C] **1** for a man to withdraw the penis from the vagina. **2** for a woman to remove the penis from the vagina.

uncunty *adj.* [1970s] unattractive, lacking sex appeal. [SE *un-* + CUNTY adj.[2] (1)]

uncut *adj.* **1** [1930s+] (*mainly drugs*) pure, unadulterated. **2** [1970s+] (*US gay*) uncircumcised.

undeniable *n.* [19C] the vagina.

under *n.* [1930s–50s] sexual intercourse. [i.e. the place of the genitals *under* the body]

under *adj.* [1930s+] drunk; thus *put under*, to render drunk. [abbr. *under the influence*]

under and over *n.* [late 19C] sexual intercourse.

under-arm *adj.* [1950s–70s] pornographic. [? UNDER THE ARM phr.]

under-belongings *n.* [19C] the vagina.

underbeneaths *n.* [1920s] (*US*) teeth. [rhy. sl.]

under board *phr.* see ABOVE BOARD phr. (2).

under breeze *adv.* [20C+] (*W.I.*) very fast. [sailing imagery]

undercarriage *n.* [1990s+] the penis.

underchunders *n.* [1990s+] (*Aus.*) underpants.

undercomestumble *v.* (*also* **undercumstumble, understumble**) [mid-19C] to understand. [play on SE *stumble upon*]

undercover *n.*[1] [1930s+] a plain-clothes detective or *undercover* agent. [abbr.]

undercover *n.*[2] [1950s+] (*US Black*) sexual intercourse.

undercover man *n.* [1940s–60s] a male homosexual. [play on UNDERCOVER n.[1]]

undercrackers *n.* [1990s+] male underwear.

undercumestumble *v.* see UNDERCOMESTUMBLE v.

underdaks *n.* [1940s+] (*Aus.*) male underpants. [SE *under* + DAKS n.]

underdig *v.* [2000s] (*US Black*) to understand fully. [SE *understand* + DIG v.[5]]

under-dimple *n.* [19C] the vagina.

underdone *adj.* [late 19C–1900s] said of one who has a pale complexion. [cooking imagery]

underdubber *n.* [early 19C] (*UK prison*) a turnkey. [SE *under* + DUB v.[1] (2)]

underdungers *n.* [1980s+] (*N.Z.*) underpants. [SE *under* + *dungarees* + play on *dung*]

under-entrance *n.* [19C] the vagina (cf. BELLY ENTRANCE n.).

underfugs *n.* [1910s] underpants. [SE *under* + FUG n.[1] (1)]

under full sail *phr.* [1930s] (*US*) drunk. [like a ship, one is reeling from side to side]

under glass *phr.* [1920s+] (*orig. US*) imprisoned, arrested. [the image of a show case]

underground mutton *n.* (*also* **underground chicken**) [1930s+] (*Aus.*) rabbit. [the animal's habitat and edibility]

underhung *adj.* see HUNG adj.[1] (1).

under manners *phr.* [1990s+] (*W.I./UK Black*) behaving as required, submitting to another person's orders.

under one's hat *phr.* [late 19C+] (*US*) secret (cf. KEEP IT UNDER ONE'S HAT v.).

underpinners *n.* [mid-19C] (*US*) the legs.

underpinnings *n.* [mid-19C+] the legs.

underput *n.* [early 17C] a mistress. [SE *put under*, i.e. the position of sexual intercourse]

under rations *n.* see GROUND RATIONS n.

under-rigging *n.*[1] see RIGGING n.[1].

under-rigging *n.*[2] see UNDER-WORKS n.

undershell *n.* [19C] a waistcoat.

understandings *n.*[1] **1** [late 18C–19C] boots or shoes. **2** [early 19C–1920s] the legs. [puns]

understandings *n.*[2] [late 19C] of a woman, sexual conquests. [pun + play on SE *understanding*, a relationship + STAND n.[2] (1), an erection]

understand what's what *v.* see KNOW WHAT'S WHAT v.

understumble *v.* see UNDERCOMESTUMBLE v.

undertaker *n.* [19C] the vagina. [17C use of SE *undertake* as euph./pun for *copulate with*]

undertaker's job *n.* **1** [1930s+] (*orig. US*) a hopeless, i.e. 'dead', proposition. **2** [1970s+] (*gambling*) a horse or greyhound which is deliberately – for the sake of the odds – not meant to win, whatever legitimate gamblers may presume. [SE *undertaker* + JOB n.[4]]

under the arm *phr.* [1930s–60s] second-rate, inferior, bad. [? the smell or the image of secrecy and hiding]

under the bed *phr.* see UNDER THE TABLE phr. (1).

under the cosh *phr.* **1** [1950s+] (*also* **under the hammer**) in trouble, at a disadvantage; thus *have under the cosh*, to have at a disadvantage. **2** [2000s] under pressure, usu. at work. [SE *under* + fig. use of COSH n. (1)]

under the gun *phr.* [1940s+] (*orig. US*) under great pressure, stress. [chaingangs who work supervised by gun-carrying guards]

under the hatches *phr.* [mid-16C–1910s] in trouble, dead, in jail.

under the lap *phr.* (*Aus.*) **1** [1930s+] confidentially. **2** [1940s+] clandestinely.

under the screw *phr.* [mid-19C] in prison. [SE *under* + SCREW n.² (3)]

under the screws *phr.* [early 19C] under pressure. [SE *under* + *thumbscrews*]

under the table *phr.* 1 [mid-19C+] (*also* **under the bed**) clandestine, secret, corrupt. 2 [late 19C+] drunk, i.e. one has fallen there; thus *drink under the table*, to outdrink a fellow-drinker. [(2) allegedly coined by George Washington 'Chuck' Connors, a New York character known as 'the Bowery philosopher']

under the whip *phr.* [1900s] (*Aus.*) at a disadvantage.

under the wire *phr.* [1930s+] at the very last minute. [horse-racing imagery]

underwear *n.* [1960s+] (*US gay*) an unshaven chin; thus *phr. your underwear is showing*, you need a shave.

under-works *n.* (*also* **under-rigging**) [early 19C] the male genitalia.

underworld *n.* [late 19C] the vagina (cf. BLACK HOLE n.¹).

under wraps *adv.* [20C+] restrainedly.

undies *n.* [20C+] underwear, usu. women's. [abbr. SE *underwear*, *under-garments*]

undigested Ananias *n.* [late 19C] a triumphant liar. [SE *undigested* + the biblical figure *Ananias*, one who, 'with Sapphira his wife, sold a possession and kept back part of the price' (Acts, 5:1,2); used allusively for a liar]

undub *v.* [mid-18C–early 19C] (*UK Und.*) to unlock. [SE pfx *un-* + DUB v.¹ (2)]

undue perversity *n.* [1980s+] (*US campus*) Purdue University, West Lafayette, Indiana. [joc. reversal]

unfair shake *n.* (*also* **rough shake**) [1950s+] bad luck. [reverse of FAIR SHAKE n.]

unfledged *adj.* [1910s–20s] naked. [lit. 'featherless']

unfortunate *n.* [late 18C–1900s] a prostitute, a 'fallen woman'. [euph. SE *unfortunate woman*]

unfuckingbelievable *adj.* (*also* **unfucking real**) [1960s+] an intensified form of SE *unbelievable/*UNREAL adj. (1). [FUCKING adj. (4)]

unglued *adj.* [1950s+] unstable, emotional, lacking control.

ungodly *adj.* (*also* **ungoddamly**) 1 [late 19C+] appalling, awful; esp. as *ungodly hour*, very late. 2 [1970s] (*US campus*) extremely good.

ungodly *adv.* [1960s+] (*US*) extremely. [UNGODLY adj. (1)]

ungood *adj.* (*also* **double plus ungood**) [1980s] (*US*) bad. [part of the basic lexicon of Newspeak, the language of George Orwell's *1984*]

ungrateful man *n.* [late 18C–early 19C] a parson, 'who at least once a week abuses his best benefactor, i.e. the devil' (Grose, 1785).

ungroovy *adj.* [1940s] (*US Black*) unsophisticated, unaware. [SE pfx *un-* + GROOVY adj.²]

unguentum aureum *n.* 1 [late 16C–early 19C] a bribe. 2 [early 19C] an advance payment. [Lat.; lit.'golden ointment']

unhip *adj.* (*also* **unhep, unhipped**) [1930s+] (*orig. US*) unaware, unsophisticated, ignorant. [SE pfx *un-* + HIP adj. (1)]

unhook *v.* 1 [1950s] to release from being arrested or from prison. 2 [1950s–60s] (*drugs*) to stop taking narcotics. [SE pfx *un-* + (1) fig. use of SE; (2) HOOKED adj.³]

uni *n.* 1 [late 19C+] (*orig. Aus.*) *university*. 2 [1960s] (*US campus*) a *uniform*. [abbr.]

unicorn *n.* 1 [17C] a cuckold. 2 [late 18C–mid-19C] a coach drawn by 3 horses, 2 abreast and 1 in the lead. 3 [late 19C] a woman and 2 men or 2 women and 1 man in league for criminal purposes. [the image of the *unicorn's* protruding horn, thus (1) play on HORN n.¹ (1)]

uniform *n.* 1 [1920s+] a uniformed policeman; often in pl. (cf. BABY-BLUES n.²). 2 [1940s+] (*gay*) a member of the armed or uniformed services; often in pl. 3 [1970s] (*gay*) a gay man who dresses in some form of uniform, e.g. military or police. 4 [1970s] a prison officer. [metonymy]

Union, the *n.* [late 19C+] the workhouse. [*Union House*]

union card *n.* [1970s] (*US campus*) a university degree certificate. [its use in gaining work]

union jack *n.¹* [1900s] Argentine frozen beef. ['cut it where you will when it's cooked it's red, white and blue' (Binstead, *Pitcher in Paradise*, 1903)]

union jack *n.²* [1990s+] the human back. [rhy. sl.]

union wage *n.* [1970s+] (*US Black*) the police. [? the primary motivation for their activities]

unit *n.* 1 [1960s+] (*US campus*) a person; a thing. 2 [1970s] the vagina (cf. ARTICLE n.). 3 [1970s+] the penis. 4 [1980s+] (*US campus*) (*also* **female unit**) a young woman.

units *n. see* RENTAL UNITS n.

universal staircase *n.* [19C] a prison treadmill.

university of hard knocks *n. see* SCHOOL OF HARD KNOCKS n.

university of life *n.* [20C+] the fig. 'college' attended by those who claim personal experience as infinitely superior to academic knowledge.

unjazzed *adj. see* JAZZED (UP) adj. (2).

unk *n.* (*also* **unkie**) [20C+] *uncle* (cf. UNC n.) [abbr.]

unkey *n. see* UNCLE n.²

unkie *n.¹* [1950s–70s] (*drugs*) morphine (cf. AUNTIE EMMA n.). [abbr. JUNKIE n.]

unkie *n.² see* UNK n.

unkjay *n.* [1940s–50s] a heroin addict. [cod Lat. for JUNKIE n.]

unky *n. see* UNCLE n.²

unlaid *adj.* [1960s+] of a woman or man, virgin. [SE pfx *un-* + LAY v.¹ (1)]

unlax *v.* [1920s–30s] (*US*) to relax, to unwind. [popularized by the 1930s–40s US radio series *Amos and Andy*]

unload *v.* 1 [mid-18C; late 19C–1930s] to take someone's money or possessions. 2 [mid-19C; 1930s+] to ejaculate. 3 [mid-19C+] to drop, to dispose of, to get rid of. 4 [20C+] (*US*) to get off or out of a vehicle. 5 [20C+] to throw a punch, to beat up. 6 [1900s] to offer one's opinion. 7 [1910s+] (*US*) to fire one's gun. 8 [1940s] to defecate.

unloading *n.* [1990s+] masturbation. [UNLOAD v. (2)]

unload pewter *v.* [mid-19C] to drink from a quart pot.

unlucky for some *n.* [1940s+] 1 (*bingo*) the number 13 (cf. ALDERSHOT LADIES n.). 2 £13. [the number most prone to superstitious interpretation]

unmarked *n.* [1950s+] (*US police*) an unmarked police car.

unmentionable *n.* [1950s] a euph. for a variety of negative personal descriptions.

unmentionables *n.* (*also* **unspeakables, untalkaboutables, unutterables, unwhisperables**) [mid-19C–1920s] trousers (cf. DON'T-KNOW-WHAT-TO-CALL-'EMS n.).

unmonkeyable *adj.* [1910s–20s] of a person, impervious to trickery. [SE pfx *un-* + MONKEY v.]

unoofy *adj.* [late 19C] impoverished, poor. [SE pfx *un-* + OOFY adj.]

unpalled *adj.* [early 19C] (*UK Und.*) used to describe a thief whose gang has been arrested and is thus forced to work solo. [SE pfx *un-* + PAL n. (1)]

unparliamentary *adj.* [mid-19C] obscene. [SE *unparliamentary language*, as laid down in *Erskine May*, which covers all Parliamentary procedure]

unpaved *adj.* 1 [early 17C] castrated. 2 [late 19C] aggressively drunk. [(1) one has 'lost one's stones', i.e. STONE n.¹ (1)]

unpick one's teeth *v. see* NOT PICK ONE'S TEETH v.

unpin one's back hair *v.* 1 [mid-19C+] (*orig. US*) to relax one's inhibitions. 2 [1930s+] to admit to being homosexual.

unreal *adj.* (*also* **not real**) 1 [1960s+] (*Aus./US*) unbelievable, unacceptable, unpleasant, an all-purpose negative that depends for precise meaning on context. **2** [1980s] (*Aus./N.Z./US campus*) a term of all-encompassing approbation, esp. as used by teenage girls.

unrig *v.* **1** [late 17C–mid-19C] to get undressed. **2** [late 18C–early 19C] to strip someone of their clothes; thus *unrigged*, stripped. [SE pfx *un-* + RIG *v.*[1] (1)]

unruly member *n.* [19C] the penis (cf. DEAREST MEMBER *n.*). [SE *unruly* + MEMBER *n.*[1] + play on usu. def. = the tongue, from General Epistle of James, 3:5–8: 'Even so the tongue is a little member [...] But the tongue can no man tame; it is an unruly evil, full of deadly poison']

unsheik *v.* [1920s] (*US Black*) to divorce. [SE pfx *un-* + brandname *Sheik*, a popular US condom]

unshingle *v.* [early–mid-19C] (*Aus.*) to knock off someone's hat. [SE pfx *un-* + *shingle*, a roof tile]

unshop *v.* [1910s–20s] to dismiss a workman. [SE pfx *un-* + *shop*, a workshop, a place of work]

unsliced *adj.* [1970s+] (*US gay*) uncircumcised. [var. on UNCUT *adj.* (2)]

unslough *v.* [mid-19C–1940s] (*UK Und.*) to unlock, to open. [SE pfx *un-* + SLOUGH *v.* (1)]

unslour *v.* [early 19C] (*UK Und.*) to unlock. [SE pfx *un-* + SLOUR (UP) *v.* (2)]

unspeakables *n.* *see* UNMENTIONABLES *n.*

unspit *v.* [late 19C] to vomit (cf. BLOW *v.*[3]).

unswallow *v.* [1930s] to vomit (cf. BLOW *v.*[3]).

unsweetened *n.* [late 19C–1910s] gin.

untalkaboutables *n.* *see* UNMENTIONABLES *n.*

unthimble *v.* [early 19C] (*UK Und.*) to rob a man of his watch. [SE pfx *un-* + THIMBLE *n.*]

untie *v.* [1960s+] (*drugs*) to remove the tourniquet – a belt, a shoelace – used to isolate a vein for injecting narcotics.

untogether *adj.* [1960s+] **1** a general negative, of a person, not in full possession of their faculties, of a situation, less than satisfactorily under control. **2** (*US*) unstylish, lacking social awareness. [antonym of TOGETHER *adj.*]

untwisted *adj.* [late 17C–18C] ruined, 'undone'.

unutterables/unwhisperables *n.* *see* UNMENTIONABLES *n.*

unwind *v.* [1910s] (*Aus.*) to cheat, to deceive.

u.p. *adv.* [early 19C–1930s] up; usu. in phr. *it's all u.p. for him.* [spelling out of SE *up*]

up *n.*[1] [mid-18C+] an excited mood, a feeling of stimulation, intoxication.

up *n.*[2] [1940s+] a prospective purchaser in a store. [? they pick things *up*]

up *n.*[3] *see* UPPER *n.*[2].

up *adj.* **1** [1940s+] (*orig. US*) mentally stimulated, excited, hopeful. **2** [1940s+] (*also up on*) intoxicated by a drug. **3** [1950s+] (*US Black*) of a person, ready, prepared. **4** [1960s+] (*US campus*) sexually aroused. **5** [1970s] intoxicating. **6** [1970s] (*US*) upset. **7** [1970s+] stimulating, uplifting. **8** [1990s+] (*US Black*) tense, nervous.

up *v.*[1] [17C+] to begin, to push oneself forward, to say or do something; usu. in phr. *ups and...*, e.g. *he ups and starts saying...*

up *v.*[2] **1** [mid-18C–19C] of mood or spirits, to raise, to pick up, to lift. **2** [1930s+] (*orig. US*) to raise, to increase prices, charges etc. **3** [1950s+] (*orig. US*) to improve, to boost; to promote.

up *v.*[3] **1** [late 19C+] to have sexual intercourse with. **2** [1950s] (*Aus./N.Z.*) a euph. for FUCK *v.*[3], i.e. a term of contempt or dismissal. **3** [2000s] (*UK Und.*) to beat up. [the man puts his penis *up* the vagina]

up *v.*[4] [1950s] (*US Black*) to play music.

up *v.*[5] [1960s–70s] (*US*) to hand over, to produce. [SE *come up with*]

up *v.*[6] [2000s] to mock.

up *adv.*[1] [mid-19C+] going on, happening; usu. in a negative context, e.g. *I think something is up.*

up *adv.*[2] [late 19C+] having sexual relations with.

up *adv.*[3] [late 19C+] (*orig. UK Und.*) arrested, in prison; thus *have (someone) up*, to bring someone before the courts. [SEND UP *v.*[1]]

up *adv.*[4] **1** [1900s] of an object, offered, put in place. **2** [1910s+] of food, ready, e.g. *tea's up, grub's up.*

up *prep.*[1] [mid-19C] in possession of, usu. used with a *v.*, e.g. *sugared up*, in possession of money.

up *prep.*[2] [1930s+] at, e.g. *up the market.*

up above *phr.* [1910s] (*Aus.*) in prison.

up a flume! *excl.* [mid-19C] (*US*) a dismissive, insulting excl.

up against *phr.* **1** [late 19C+] (*orig. US*) facing problems, in difficulties; esp. in phr. *up against it.* **2** [1900s] to the responsibility of. **3** [1930s+] (*US prison*) addicted to drugs.

up against one's duckhouse *phr.* (*also up against one's fowlhouse*) [1930s+] (*Aus.*) a setback, a problem; usu. in phr. *that's one up against your duckhouse.*

up against the wall *phr.* (*also up against the bit, ...gun, ...ropes, ...wire*) **1** [1910s+] (*orig. milit.*) facing serious problems. **2** [1960s+] (*US campus*) foolish, stupid. [the putting of prisoners against a wall to face a firing squad, reinforced in (2) by 1960s radical slogan, *Up against the wall, motherfucker!*]

up a gum tree *phr.* **1** [20C+] (*orig. Aus.*) (*also up a wattle*) in trouble or difficulties, facing a problem. **2** [1950s+] in error, wrong. **3** [1950s+] (*N.Z.*) easily. [the chasing of an animal into such a tree where it is very hard to dislodge]

up an alley *phr.* [1900s] (*US*) a general phr. of dismissal.

up-and-down *n.*[1] [early 17C; 1970s] sexual intercourse.

up-and-down *n.*[2] [20C+] brown (ale). [rhy. sl.]

up-and-down *n.*[3] [1900s] a housemaid. [her running up- and downstairs]

up-and-down *n.*[4] [1930s] a town. [rhy. sl.]

up-and-down, the *n.* **1** [1910s] an official investigation. **2** [1910s+] a look, scrutiny; usu. in phr. *give — an/the up-and-down*; also attrib. [the movement of one's eyes]

up-and-down *adj.* **1** [mid–late 19C] (*also up-and-down-stairs*) absolute, complete. **2** [mid-19C+] honest, law-abiding, straightforward.

up-and-down *adv.* **1** [mid-19C] (*US*) in a straightforward, open and honest manner. **2** [late 19C+] unrestrainedly; often as *swear up and down.*

up-and-downer *n.* [1910s+] a fight, a tussle. [the fluctuating fortunes of the fighters]

up-and-down-stairs *adj.* *see* UP-AND-DOWN *adj.* (1).

up and dust *v.* [20C+] (*US Black*) to leave in a hurry, to run away. [UP *v.*[1] + DUST *v.*[2] (1)]

up and under *n.* [1990s+] thunder. [rhy. sl.]

up and under *v.* [1950s+] (*Aus.*) to vomit (cf. HALLEY'S COMET *n.*). [rhy. sl. = CHUNDER *v.*]

up and up *adj.* **1** [1900s] (*Aus.*) evenly matched. **2** [1920s+] (*orig. US*) fair, honest, straightforward. [ON THE UP AND UP *phr.* (1)]

up and up gee *n.* [20C+] (*US Und.*) an inmate who has not properly learned prison survival. [UP AND UP *adj.* (2) + GEE *n.*[3] (1)]

up arsehole street *phr.* (*also in arsehole street*) [1950s+] in difficulties, facing problems. [SE *up* + ARSEHOLE *n.* + SE *street*]

up a tree *n.* [1980s+] (*bingo*) the number 3 (cf. ALDERSHOT LADIES *n.*). [rhy. sl.]

up a tree *phr.*[1] **1** [mid-19C] impoverished. **2** [mid-19C+] (*also treed*) in (temporary) difficulties. [the image of a cat perched, spitting down at an adversary, high in a tree]

up a tree *phr.*[2] **1** [1910s+] annoyed, emotionally unstable. **2** [1930s+] drunk.

up a wattle *phr.* *see* UP A GUM TREE *phr.* (1).

upbeat *adj.* [1940s+] (*orig. US*) optimistic, positive. [orig. jazz use]

up cack street *phr.* *see* IN SHIT STREET *phr.*

upchuck *v.* [1920s+] (*orig. US*) to vomit; thus *upchucking*, the act of vomiting (cf. BLOW *v.*[3]). [SE *up* + CHUCK *v.*[1] (3)]

up each other *phr.* [1940s+] (*Aus.*) indulging in mutual flattery. [UP v.³ (1) + SE *each other*; the image is of buggery]

up-foot *v.* [late 19C] to get to one's feet.

up for *phr.* [mid-19C+] keen on, willing to do; thus UP FOR IT *phr.*

up for it *phr.* [1980s+] enthusiastic, ready for anything. [UP FOR *adv.*]

up front *adj.* (*also* **in front, out front**) **1** [1950s+] (*orig. US*) open, honest. **2** [1970s] foremost.

up front *adv.* (*also* **in front, out front**) **1** [1950s+] in advance, esp. of money paid for illegal activities, e.g. drug purchases. **2** [1970s] in the foreground. **3** [1970s+] openly, without deception. **4** [1970s+] (*orig. US Black*) first, at the start.

upful *adj.* (*also* **uphill**) [1950s+] (*W.I. Rasta*) positive, encouraging. [SE *hopeful*]

up goes the donkey *phr.* **1** [mid–late 19C] a phr. used to extract as much money as possible before agreeing to perform any task. **2** [1910s] used to denote the imminence of (dramatic) events. [the old showman's exhibition, as a finale to his act a donkey is hoisted into the air, but before he will do it, the crowd is exhorted to hand over some extra pennies to make it worth his while. The usu. phr. is *three more and up goes the donkey!* (the *OED* cites 'a penny more...']

up her like a rat up a drain(pipe), be *v.* (*also* **be up her like a rat up a rhododendron**) [1960s+] (*orig. Aus.*) **1** the assumption that a woman will be freely, easily and speedily sexually available to the speaker. **2** in non-sexual contexts, suggesting speed. [i.e. 'I could be UP v.³ (1) her...']

up her way *phr.* [late 19C+] of a man, having sexual intercourse.

uphill *adj. see* UPFUL *adj.*

uphill gardener *n.* [1980s] a male homosexual; thus *uphill gardening*, homosexual intercourse. [the ref. is to anal intercourse]

uphills *n.* [late 17C–early 19C] (*UK Und.*) fixed dice that will always show high numbers.

up in *phr.* [mid-19C+] well versed in, expert at.

up in G *phr.* (*also* **up to G**) **1** [late 19C–1920s] (*US*) very best, superlative. **2** [1900s] with a loud voice. [? play on the musical note G]

up in one's hat *phr.* **1** [late 19C] drunk. **2** [1920s] (*Irish*) elated.

up in someone's grits *phr.* [2000s] (*US Black*) of a man, having sexual intercourse.

up in someone's guts *phr.* [2000s] (*US Black*) of a man, having sexual intercourse.

up in someone's shit *phr.* [2000s] (*US Black*) interfering, 'poking one's nose in'. [SE *up in* + SHIT n.⁶]

up in the air *phr.* **1** [late 19C–1910s] (*US*) crazy. **2** [20C+] annoyed, irritated. **3** [20C+] happy, in a good mood. **4** [20C+] doubting, speculative, hypothetical. **5** [1910s] (*US*) incompetent. **6** [1910s+] (*US*) cocky, self-opinionated. **7** [1930s] (*US drugs*) intoxicated.

up in the boughs *phr.* [late 17C+] angry, irritated.

up in the bucks *phr.* [1920s–30s] (*US*) wealthy, prospering. [SE *up* + BUCK n.³ (1)]

up in the paints *phr.* (*also* **up in the paint cards**) [1930s+] (*US*) depending on context, old, high, superior; all meanings imply something more extreme. [gambling jargon *paints* = high (royal) cards]

up in the stirrups *phr.* [early–mid-19C] prospering, doing well. [riding imagery]

upjump *n.* [1910s] (*Aus.*) an upstart, a nouveau riche, a general term of abuse. [SE *jumped up*]

up King Street *phr.* [1950s] (*Aus.*) in financial difficulties; thus *go up King Street*, to become bankrupt. [*King Street*, Sydney, the site of the Supreme Court, which hears bankruptcy cases; note SE phr. *in carey street*]

up large *phr.* [1980s+] (*N.Z.*) heavy drinking.

up on *phr.*¹ [late 19C+] aware of what is happening, alert. [var. on UP IN phr.]

up on *phr.*² *see* UP adj. (2).

up on blocks *phr.* [1990s+] menstruating. [automobile imagery, of a car that is unavailable for use, i.e. a ref. to sex]

up one's arse *phr.* (*also* **up one's ass, ...butt, ...hole**) [1970s+] (*US*) immediately behind and thus irritating, bothering. [SE *up* + ARSE n.¹ (1)/ASS n. (2)/BUTT n.¹ (2)/HOLE n.¹ (1)]

up oneself *phr.* [1940s+] (*Aus.*) arrogant, self-satisfied, full of oneself. [image of auto-sodomy]

up one's own arse *phr.* [2000s] self-important. [UP adv.² + ARSE n.¹ (1), i.e. auto-sodomizing]

up on it *phr.* [1980s+] (*US Black*) aware, knowledgeable. [ext. of UP ON phr.¹]

upon my sam! *excl.* [late 19C+] a general excl. of emphasis; thus ext. as *upon my sacred Sam! upon my sainted Sam!* [SE *upon* + ? SOLOMON n.¹]

upon my sivvy! *excl.* (*also* **upon my civvy/sivey!**) [mid-19C–1910s] a mild oath, on my soul! on my oath! [SE *upon* + ? *asservation*, keeping one's word. E.P. rejects this, opting for SE *affidavit* or *soul*]

upon the square *phr. see* ON THE SQUARE phr.

up on the stickers *phr.* [1940s] (*US Black*) aware, appreciative of what is important.

upped *adj.* [1930s] raped. [UP adv.²]

upper *n.*¹ [1940s+] a member of the *upper* classes. [abbr.]

upper *n.*² (*also* **up, uppie, ups**) **1** [1960s+] (*drugs*) amphetamine or a similar form of drug, e.g. Methedrine; often in pl. (cf. A n.²). **2** [1960s+] (*US*) a state of optimistic excitement (poss. the result of ingesting (1)).

upper and downer *n.* **1** [late 19C] a form of wrestling match in which the opponents attempt to throw each other, but do not use blows; thus any form of physical fight. **2** [1990s+] an argument.

upper apartment *n.* [19C] the head.

upper benjamin *n.* (*also* **upper ben**) **1** [late 18C–19C] (*orig. UK Und.*) an overcoat, a greatcoat. **2** [mid-19C] in pl., a pair of trousers. [according to Hotten (1874) an acknowledgement of the large number of (? Jewish) tailors called *Benjamin*]

upper crust *n.* **1** [early–mid-19C] the head, esp. in boxing use. **2** [mid-19C] a hat. **3** [mid-19C+] the social élite, the aristocracy; thus *upper-crusted*, aristocratic.

upper crust *adj.* [mid-19C+] conceited, snobbish; upper-class. [UPPER CRUST n. (3)]

upper deck *n.* **1** [1930s–40s] the neck. **2** [1940s+] (*Aus.*) female breasts. [(1) rhy. sl.]

upper extremity/garret *n. see* UPPER STOREY n.

upper Holloway *n.* [19C] the vagina (cf. ANTIPODES n.). [SE *upper* + HOLLOWAY n. (1)]

upper loft *n. see* UPPER STOREY n.

upper miserys *n.* [2000s] (*US Black*) the state of feeling physically sick.

upper roger *n.* [19C] (*Anglo-Ind.*) the heir apparent to a rajah's or other throne. [Hind. *yuva-raja*, a young king]

uppers and beneath *n.* [1920s–40s] (*US Und.*) the teeth.

uppers and downers *n.* (*also* **uppers and unders**) [1910s–60s] the teeth.

upper shell *n.* [mid-18C–19C] an overcoat.

upper stock *n.* [late 18C–early 19C] breeches. [SE *upper stock*, the upper part of the stockings]

upper storey *n.* (*also* **upper extremity, ...garret, ...loft, ...works**) **1** [mid-18C+] the head, the brain, the mental capacity that resides within it; thus *his upper storey/garret is unfurnished*, he is a foolish or 'empty' person, he is 'not all there'. **2** [late 19C+] (*US*) the female breasts. [(1) note GARRET n.]

upper ten *n.* **1** [mid-19C–1940s] (*orig. US*) the social élite; thus *uppertendom*, the world of the social élite. **2** [late 19C] in fig. use, any superior group. [abbr. SE *upper ten thousand*, coined by the journalist Nathaniel Parker Willis (1806–67) in a piece entitled 'Necessity for a Promenade Drive' (1848) in which he stated 'At present there is no distinction among the upper ten thousand of the city']

upper ten *adj.* [mid–late 19C] socially élite, of or pertaining to the social élite. [UPPER TEN n.]

upper ten push *n.* [late 19C] (*Aus. prison*) a grouping of upper-class prisoners. [UPPER TEN adj. + PUSH n.² (4)]

upper ten set *n.* [late 19C] those servants who work for the 'upper ten thousand'. [UPPER TEN adj. + SE *set*]

upper-tog *n.* (*also* **upper togger**) [early–mid-19C] a greatcoat, an overcoat. [SE *upper* + TOGS n. (1)]

upper works *n. see* UPPER STOREY n.

uppie *n.*¹ [1970s+] (*S.Afr.*) a student of the University of Port Elizabeth. [University of Port Elizabeth]

uppie *n.*² *see* UPPER n.².

uppish *adj.* **1** [late 17C–mid-19C] well-off, provided with sufficient money. **2** [late 17C+] proud, arrogant. **3** [early 18C] tipsy. **4** [late 18C–early 19C] irritable, easily offended. [Johnson, *Dictionary* (1755), terms (2) a 'low word', thus its inclusion here, but *OED* lists it as SE]

uppities *n.* [late 19C–1950s] (*US*) social climbers. [UPPITY adj. (1)]

uppity *n.* [1940s+] arrogance, nerve, gall.

uppity *adj.* (*also* **uppity-ass**) **1** [late 19C+] (*orig. US*) cheeky, arrogant, one who refuses to 'know their place'; esp. in phr. *uppity nigger*, a Black person who refuses to accept his or her second-class status. **2** [1910s+] (*also* **uppity-up**, **upty-up**) snobbish, élitist. [SE *up*]

upright *n.*¹ [late 18C–mid-19C] a pint or quart measure of liquor, thus a pot of that size.

upright *n.*² (*also* **uprighter**) [late 18C+] sexual intercourse performed while standing up.

upright *n.*³ [early 19C] a cheap bed, rented out for 3d or 4d.

upright grand *n.* [1920s+] (*Aus.*) sexual intercourse while standing up. [UPRIGHT n.² + pun on SE *upright grand* piano]

upright grin *n.* (*also* **upright wink**) [late 19C] the vagina; thus *flash the upright grin*, to expose one's vagina. [physiognomy (+ FLASH v.² (3))]

upright man *n.* [mid-16C–early 19C] (*UK Und.*) a senior criminal beggar, outranked, if at all, only by the RUFFLER n. Such a villain held absolute power, demanding and receiving both cash and kind, including their women, from his inferiors and beating them without fear of revenge (cf. CANTING CREW n.). [his stance: he adopted no form of counterfeit physical deformity, as did many of his peers, in his pose as a solid citizen. As such he both gulled the public and commanded loyalty and financial dues from lesser thieves]

uprights *n.* [late 19C–1940s] (*US Black*) the legs.

upright sneak *n.* [late 18C–early 19C] (*UK Und.*) one who steals pewter pots from the boys employed by taverns to collect them. [SE *upright* + SNEAK n.¹ (2)]

upright wink *n. see* UPRIGHT GRIN n.

uproar *n.* [mid-18C–mid-19C] an opera. [a heavy pun]

ups *n. see* UPPER n.².

upsadaisy! *excl.* (*also* **oops-a-daisy!**) [mid-19C+] a soothing excl. offered to a fallen child as one picks them up; thus as phr. head-over-heels, upside down. [? the image of plucking a daisy from a lawn; ? SE *upside down*]

up salt creek *phr. see* UP SHIT('S) CREEK (WITHOUT A PADDLE) phr.

upsee *adj.* (*also* **upsey, upsie**) [late 16C–17C] in the manner or style of, esp. as applied to drinking habits; thus *upsee-Dutch*, in the Dutch manner; *upsee-English*, in the English manner; *upsee-Freeze* (1) in the Friesian manner, or (2) strong drink; to drink *upsee-freeze cross*, to drink with arms intertwined. [Du. *op zijn*, on

his. A second ety. suggests Du. *op zee*, overseas or imported, and thus refers to the drink itself, whether English, Dutch or whatever, rather than the manner of drinking; Nares sees this as 'near to another English phrase for drunkenness, being *half-seas over*'; note Ebsworth, *Roxburghe Ballads* (1876): 'Like "Wassael" and "Trinkael" the phrase upsie-friese, or vrijster, seems to have been used as a toast, perhaps for "To your sweetheart"']

upset Mrs Jones *v. see* MRS JONES n.

upset the lobster-cart *v.* [early 19C] (*mainly US*) to knock a person down.

upsey *adj. see* UPSEE adj.

up shit('s) creek (without a paddle) *phr.* (*also* **up salt creek**) [20C+] (*orig. US*) in serious trouble; thus (*Aus.*) pregnant out of wedlock (cf. UP THE CREEK (WITHOUT A PADDLE) phr.). [SE *up* + SHIT CREEK n.]

up shit street *phr. see* IN SHIT STREET phr.

upshot *n.* [early 19C] a riotous frolic. [dial. *upshot*, a feast, a celebration]

upside *prep.* [1960s+] (*US Black*) next to, up against; thus *upside one's head*, of a blow, against the head.

upsie *adj. see* UPSEE adj.

up someone's daily *phr. see* DAILY (MAIL) n. (1).

up South *n.* [1950s–60s] (*US Black*) the Northern states. [the implication is that racism and prejudice is just as widespread as it is 'down South']

up stacks *v. see* UP STICKS v.

upstage *adj.* (*also* **upstageish**) [1900s–30s] (*US*) conceited, snobbish. [theatre jargon]

upstage *v.* [late 19C+] (*US*) to outwit, to win or be superior to another person. [theatrical jargon]

upstairs *n.*¹ [late 19C] the best brands of spirits. [kept on a special high shelf in the public house]

upstairs *n.*² **1** [1910s+] (*US*) heaven. **2** [1920s+] (*US*) the mind, esp. as regards its intelligence. **3** [1930s] (*US prison*) the gallows. **4** [1930s–40s] (*US Und.*) an inside breast pocket. **5** [1950s+] a higher authority, a senior position. **6** [1970s] a lavatory (cf. ALTAR n.). **7** [2000s] (*UK Und.*) the Crown Court.

upstairs *adj.* [1950s] (*US Black*) superior.

upstairs *adv.* [1990s+] into a senior position.

up stakes *v.* (*also* **upstakes**) [mid-19C+] (*US*) to leave, esp. abruptly. [SE *pick up one's stakes*, the boundary posts of a property]

upstate *n.* [1930s+] (*New York Und.*) prison. [the main New York state prisons are upstate]

upstate *adj.* [1950s] (*US Black*) socially or economically superior. [SE *upscale*]

up sticks *v.* (*also* **up stacks, up stick**) [mid-19C+] to move, to pack up and leave. [naut. jargon *up stick*, to ship the mast or *stick* before moving]

upta *adj.* (*also* **upter**) [1910s+] (*Aus.*) useless, no use whatsoever. [UP TO PUTTY phr.]

up the ante *v.* (*also* **raise the ante**) [late 19C+] (*US*) lit. and fig., to increase the amount, to demand a higher price. [poker imagery]

up the ass *adv.* (*also* **up the arse**) [1950s+] (*US*) **1** to excess, in large amounts. **2** thoroughly, very well. [SE *up* + ASS n. (2)/ARSE n.¹ (1)]

up the booai *phr. see* BOOAI n.

up the butt *adv.* [1980s+] (*orig. US*) to an excess, to the extreme. [SE *up* + BUTT n.¹ (2)]

up the chute *phr.* [1930s+] (*Aus./N.Z.*) useless, worthless, failed. [SE *up* + ? CHUTE n.²]

up the creek (without a paddle) *phr.* **1** [1920s+] in trouble, facing problems; thus (*Aus.*) pregnant out of wedlock. **2** [1960s+] mad, crazy. [euph. for UP SHIT('S) CREEK (WITHOUT A PADDLE)'S phr.]

up the duff *phr.* [1940s+] (*orig. Aus.*) pregnant. [SE *up* + *duff*, a pudding, same imagery as HAVE A BUN IN THE OVEN v.; PUDDING CLUB n.]

up the fairground *phr.* [1980s] likely to be lucky. [? the fairground's gambling sideshows]

up the flue *adv. see* IN THE FLUE phr.

up the gargoyle *phr. see* UP THE SPOUT phr. (6).

up the gazoo *adv.* (*also* **up the wazoo**) [1950s+] (*orig. US*) full up, as much as one can handle, to excess.

up the kite *phr.* [1990s+] pregnant.

up the loop *phr.* [1950s] insane, eccentric (cf. CLEAN AROUND THE BEND phr.; UP THE POLE phr.[1]; UP THE STICK phr.[2]; UP THE WALL phr.).

up the pole *phr.*[1] **1** [late 19C–1900s] (*US*) teetotal. **2** [late 19C–1920s] drunk; thus *half up the pole,* tipsy. **3** [late 19C+] wrong, in error, in trouble, facing difficulties. **4** [late 19C+] insane, eccentric (cf. UP THE LOOP phr.). [note late 19C US milit. *up the pole,* sober, 'military' and within regulation; the *pole* was the flagpole bearing the nation's emblem]

up the pole *phr.*[2] [20C+] pregnant.

up there Cazaly! *excl.* [1940s+] (*Aus.*) a cry of encouragement. [Australian rules football player Roy *Cazaly* (1893–1963), star of the South Melbourne team and noted for his leaps into the air for a 'mark']

up the river *phr.* [late 19C+] (*orig. US*) in prison; sometimes ext. as *sanitarium/summer hotel…*; thus SEND UP THE RIVER v. [orig. the penitentiary at Ossining ('Sing-Sing'), which is sited *up the river* from New York City]

up the shit *adv.* [1980s] (*US campus*) in large quantities. [SE *up* + SHITLOAD n.]

up the spank *phr.* [late 19C] at the pawnbroker's. [? var. UP THE SPOUT phr. (2)]

up the spout *phr.* **1** [early 19C–1920s] hospitalized, imprisoned. **2** [early 19C+] in the pawnshop. **3** [early 19C+] having problems, 'in a bad way'. **4** [mid-19C+] (*orig. US*) gone to waste, ruined. **5** [late 19C+] dead. **6** [1900s–10s] (*also* **up the gargoyle**) bankrupt. **7** [1940s+] pregnant. [SE *up* + *spout,* a lift formerly in use in pawnbrokers' shops, up which the articles pawned were taken for storage, thus the pawnshop itself]

up-the-spout and Charley-Wag *phr.* [late 19C] a general phr. used of something that has gone to waste, been squandered or lost. [UP THE SPOUT phr. (5) + PLAY THE CHARLEY WAG v.]

up the stairs *phr.* (*also* **down the steps, up the steps**) **1** [1930s+] on trial; thus *go up the stairs/steps,* to be tried at the Old Bailey, to be sent to the Old Bailey from a lower court. **2** [1950s] to be sent to prison. [the steps that lead from the cells beneath the Old Bailey up into the dock]

up the stick *phr.*[1] [1930s+] crazy, eccentric (cf. UP THE LOOP phr.). [var. on UP THE POLE phr.[1] (4)]

up the stick *phr.*[2] [1930s+] (*orig. Aus.*) pregnant. [var. on UP THE POLE phr.[2]]

up the wall *phr.* (*also* **up the walls**) [1940s+] (*US*) crazy, eccentric, or over-excited, anxious (cf. UP THE LOOP phr.). [CLIMB UP THE WALLS v.]

up the way *phr.* [1930s+] (*Aus.*) pregnant. [IN THE FAMILY WAY phr.]

up the wazoo *adv. see* UP THE GAZOO adv.

up the wop *phr.* [1980s+] (*N.Z.*) **1** pregnant. **2** broken, out of order.

up the ying-yang *adv.* [1960s+] to an excess, to the extreme. [fig. use of YING-YANG n.]

uptight *adj.*[1] **1** [1930s+] in difficulties. **2** [1940s+] (*US Black*) trapped, in a position from which there is no escape. **3** [1970s] addicted.

uptight *adj.*[2] (*also* **tight**) **1** [1930s+] tense, nervous, annoyed. **2** [1960s+] formal, unbending, strait-laced. **3** [1960s+] under emotional control. [SE *tight,* tense]

uptight *adj.*[3] **1** [1950s+] close, friendly. **2** [1960s] (*US campus*) very attractive. **3** [1960s+] satisfactory, good. **4** [1960s+] having sexual intercourse. [SE *tight,* faithful]

uptight *adj.*[4] [1960s–70s] out of money, impoverished. [TIGHT adj.[3]]

up to *prep.* [late 19C+] incumbent upon, obligatory.

up to *phr.* [late 18C+] aware of, knowledgeable about. [20C+ use is SE]

up to all lurks *phr. see* LURK n. (3).

up to dick *phr.* (*also* **up to door**) [late 19C–1910s] up to standard, as required; thus, in negative, unwell, sick, wretched. [SE *up* + DICK n.[3], i.e. one 'could swear by it'; *door* appears to be a corruption]

up to dolly's wax *phr.* (*also* **up to pussy's bow**) [1940s+] (*Aus.*) absolutely full of food. [nursery use, dolls used to have solid bodies surmounted with carefully modelled wax heads]

up to G *phr. see* UP IN G phr.

up to here *phr.* **1** [late 19C+] bored, disgusted, utterly intolerant of an event, someone's statements, actions etc. **2** [1900s] full of food and/or drink. [HAVE HAD IT UP TO HERE v.]

up to mud *phr.* [1930s+] (*Aus.*) unsatisfactory. [the innate worthlessness of mud]

up to no good *phr.* [1980s+] having sexual intercourse with someone.

up to one's ass *phr.* (*also* **up to one's arse/asshole**) [1960s+] (*orig. US*) totally involved in, overwhelmed by.

up to one's ass in alligators *phr.* (*also* **up to one's ass in rattlesnakes, …ears in alligators, …ears in rattlesnakes**) [1980s+] (*US*) in very serious troubles, facing overwhelming problems. [the saying *when you're up to one's ass/ears in alligators, you don't worry about draining the swamp,* often used to imply that one has no time for (long-term liberal) social action, when faced by the immediate threat of criminality]

up top *n.* [1950s+] (*Aus.*) northern Australia; thus *uptoppers,* those who live there.

up to pussy's bow *phr. see* UP TO DOLLY'S WAX phr.

up to putty *phr.* (*also* **up to shit**) [1910s+] (*Aus.*) worthless, ineffectual. [the innate worthlessness of putty]

up to slum *phr.* [early–mid-19C] knowing, aware, on the look out for tricks. [UP TO phr. + SLUM n.[2] (3)]

up to snuff *phr.* [early 19C+] efficient, capable, aware; ext. as *up to snuff and twopenny, up to snuff and a pinch above it.*

up to the arms in wood *phr.* [early 19C] standing in the pillory.

up to the arse in *phr.* (*also* **up to the ass in, …your arse in, …your ass in**) [20C+] (*orig. US*) completely overwhelmed by. [SE *up* + ARSE n.[1] (1)/ASS n. (2)]

up to the cackle *phr.* (*also* **up to the gossip, …the try-on**) [late 18C–mid-19C] aware of what is going on, shrewd, very experienced or knowledgeable. [UP TO phr. + CACKLE n.[1]/SE *gossip*/TRY-ON n.]

up to the dodge *phr.* [mid-19C–1910s] (*US*) aware, shrewd, knowledgeable. [UP TO phr. + DODGE n. (1)]

up to the knocker *phr.* **1** [mid-19C–1910s] capable, up to a task. **2** [mid-19C] fashionably dressed or over-dressed. **3** [late 19C] in prime condition; enjoying oneself. [SE *up* + KNOCKER n.[2] (1) or fig. use of SE (*door*) *knocker*]

up to the nines *adv.* (*also* **to the nines**) [late 18C+] to the highest degree, to perfection; usu. as DRESSED TO THE NINES phr. or TOGGED OUT (TO THE NINES) phr. [ety. unknown; ? the numerologistic attribution of 9 as a mystic number or (according to Ware) a corruption of an older phr. *up to the eyen,* up to the eyes, i.e. the satisfaction of the eyes]

up to the stump *phr.* [mid-19C] (*US*) out of money, impoverished.

up to the try-on *phr. see* UP TO THE CACKLE phr.

up to trap *phr. see* TRAP n.[1] (1).

up to tripe *phr.* [1900s–10s] worthless, unpleasant, distasteful. [SE *up* + TRIPE n.[2]]

uptown *n.* **1** [1950s+] (*W.I. Rasta*) the upper classes. **2** [1970s]

(*US drugs*) cocaine, always considered the drug of the more affluent. [UPTOWN adj.]

uptown *adj.* [1920s+] (*US*) sophisticated, worldly, rich; thus *go uptown (on)*, to act in a snobbish manner (towards). [SE *uptown*, the residential area of a US city]

uptucker *n.* **1** [mid-19C] the hangman. **2** [1930s] (*US prison*) the noose. [SE *up* + TUCK v.[1]]

upty-up *adj. see* UPPITY adj. (2).

upways *n.* [1970s+] (*US Black*) a snobbish, stand-offish person. [SE *upways*, in an upward direction]

up West *n.* [late 19C+] the West End of London, as seen either from the East End or from the further western or suburban areas.

upya! *excl.* [1940s+] (*Aus.*) a dismissive, contemptuous excl., lit. *up you!* [UP YOU! excl.]

up you! *excl.* [late 19C+] a dismissive, contemptuous excl. [euph. for FUCK YOU! excl., esp. when accompanied by the (orig. US) raised middle-finger gesture]

up you for the rent! *excl.* [1940s+] (*Aus.*) a dismissive, contemptuous excl. [ext. of UP YOU! excl.]

up your arse! *excl.* (*also* **up your ass! ...back! ...brown! ...bum! ...butt! ...flue! ...gig! ...giggy! ...gunga! ...hole! ...jacksie!**) [1910s+] a dismissive, insulting excl. [a preceding 'stick it...' is taken as read; ARSE n.[1] (1)/ASS n. (2)/SE *back*/BROWN n.[3] (1)/BUM n.[1] (1)/BUTT n.[1] (2)/FLUE n.[1] (3)/GIG n.[9]/GUNGA n.[1] (1)/HOLE n.[1] (1)/JACKSIE n.[1]]

up your jumper! *excl.* [1920s+] (*Aus.*) a euph. synon. of UP YOUR ARSE! excl.

up your pipe! *excl.* [1930s+] a euph. synon. of UP YOUR ARSE! excl. [coarse use of SE]

up yours! *excl.* [1930s+] (*orig. US*) an excl. of contempt. [euph. abbr. of UP YOUR ARSE! excl.]

urban surfing *n.* [1970s+] riding on the outside of moving vehicles.

urger *n.* **1** [1910s+] (*Aus.*) a man who obtains money illegally or dishonourably, esp. as a tipster at a racecourse. **2** [1920s–60s] a sponger or idler.

uriah heep *n.* [20C+] an unpleasant person. [rhy. sl. = CREEP n. (3); ult. *Uriah Heep*, a villain in Dickens' *David Copperfield* (1849–50)]

urinal of the planets *n.* [late 17C–early 19C] Ireland. [a literary usage that reflects the country's high rainfall]

u.s. *adj.* (*also* **u/s**) [1940s+] (*orig. RAF*) useless.

u.s.a. *n.* [1990s+] (*UK juv.*) a girl's upper thighs and genital area. [*under skirt area*]

use *v.*[1] (*also* **use up**) [mid-19C; 1970s+] (*US*) to criticize or abuse. [clipping of SE *abuse*; 1970s+ use is US campus]

use *v.*[2] [1910s+] to need, to desire, to 'do with', e.g. *I could use a decent meal*.

use *v.*[3] **1** [1920s+] (*drugs*) to take narcotic drugs, esp. heroin. **2** [1940s] to consume a drink.

use at *v.* [late 19C] to frequent, to visit.

used-beer department *n.* [1920s+] (*Aus./Can.*) the lavatory in a bar.

used food tube *n.* [1980s] (*Aus.*) the anus (cf. ALLEY WAY n.).

used fruit chute *n.* [1990s+] (*Aus.*) the anus, esp. in a homosexual context (cf. ALLEY WAY n.).

used-to-be *n.* [1920s–60s] (*US Black*) an ex-lover.

used up *adj.* **1** [mid-18C–mid-19C] dead, killed in battle. **2** [mid-19C] beaten up. **3** [mid-19C] bankrupt. **4** [mid-19C] brokenhearted. **5** [mid-19C+] exhausted, whether of a person, a vehicle, a place. [a message sent by General John Guise during his attack

on Cartagena during the war with Spain *c.*1740 when he requested that he be sent more grenadiers because of the 1200 he already had, 50 per cent were 'used up', in other words killed or wounded]

useful *n.* [mid-19C+] (*Aus.*) a general helper, esp. in a public house. [SE *general/generally useful*]

useful *adj.* [2000s] sexually attractive.

useful as pockets on a singlet *phr.* (*also* **useful as a hip pocket on a singlet**) [2000s] (*Aus.*) absolutely useless.

useless as a one-legged man at an ass-kicking contest *phr.* [1960s+] (*US*) absolutely worthless.

useless as a spare prick at a (lesbian) wedding *phr.* [1960s+] totally useless.

useless as tits on a nun *phr.* (*also* **useless as a tit on a hand, ...tits on a boar (hog), ...tits on a bull, ...tits on a gumdigger's dog**) [1930s+] (*US/Aus.*) utterly useless.

use one's block *v.* [1980s] (*N.Z.*) to act sensibly. [SE *use* + BLOCK n.[1] (2)]

use one's loaf *v.* (*also* **use one's bean, ...one's skull, ...one's turnip, ...the old bean**) [1930s+] to think, to act intelligently, to work things out; also as imper. *use your loaf!* be sensible! [SE *use* + LOAF (OF BREAD) n./BEAN n.[5]/SE *skull*/TURNIP n.[2] (2)]

use one's nut *v. see* NUT n.[1] (3).

user *n.* [1920s+] a drug addict. [USE v.[3] (1)]

use the chump *v.* [20C+] to act intelligently. [SE *use* + CHUMP n.[1] (1)]

use the English *v.* [1940s+] (*US gay*) to wriggle one's buttocks while being penetrated anally. [snooker jargon *English*, a swerving shot]

use the five-fingered chequebook *v.* [1980s+] (*N.Z.*) to shoplift.

use the glass *v.* [1900s–30s] to use a broken glass or bottle as a weapon in a fight, typically in a public house.

use the noggin *v.* [early 19C+] (*orig. US*) to act intelligently, to be aware. [SE *use* + NOGGIN n.[1] (1)]

use the old bean *v. see* USE ONE'S LOAF v.

use up *v. see* USE v.[1].

u.s.g. *n.* [1990s+] (*US Black*) the American Black community, i.e. the status of Blacks, governmental statements of equal rights notwithstanding, as regards the larger US world. [abbr. *United States ghettos*]

usher! *excl.* [late 19C–1920s] yes! [? Yid. *user*, it is so]

usher of the back door *n. see* GENTLEMAN OF THE BACK DOOR n.

usher of the hall *n.* [late 19C] (*UK society*) the odd-job man in a great house.

usual, the *n.* **1** [mid-19C+] one's habitual choice of drink or beverage. **2** [1990s+] sexual intercourse.

U.T.B.N.B. *phr.* [1990s+] anal intercourse as a means of contraception. [*Up The Bum, No Babies*]

ute *n.* [1940s+] (*Aus.*) a utility vehicle, a small truck. [abbr.]

utopiate *n.* [1970s] (*US drugs*) a hallucinogen. [pun on SE *opiates* + *Utopia*]

utzpay *n.* [1930s] a fool, an idiot. [cod Lat. for PUTZ n. (2)]

UVs *n.* [1960s+] (*US teen*) sunshine; thus *soak up UVs*, to get a tan. [abbr. *ultra-violet rays*]

uxter *n.* [late 19C] money. [dial. *uxter/oxter*, an armpit or armhole of a jacket, thus the wallet that is carried in an inside pocket; note dial. *come with a crooked oxter*, to bring a present, to come with a good dowry]

u.y.b. *n.* [1980s] (*US campus*) a derog. term for a woman. [abbr. *uppity yankee bitch*, i.e. UPPITY adj. (1)]

V

V *n.*[1] **1** [mid-19C–1960s] (*US*) (*also* **V-spot**) a 5-dollar bill (cf. C *n.*[1]). **2** [1930s–60s] (*US prison*) a 5-year prison sentence. [Lat. numeral V, 5]

V *n.*[2] [1930s–40s] (*US Und.*) a bank vault.

V *n.*[3] [1950s–80s] (*UK Black*) the crotch; the genitals.

V *n.*[4] [1970s] (*US*) volume, e.g. on a stereo. [abbr.]

V *n.*[5] [1970s] (*US Black/campus*) television. [abbr. SE *TV*]

V *n.*[6] [1970s] (*US Und.*) a suit. [abbr. VINE *n.*[1]]

V *n.*[7] [1980s+] (*drugs*) the mild tranquilizer Valium. [abbr.]

v *adv.* [late 19C+] very. [abbr.]

Vaalie *n.* (*also* **Vaaljapie**) [1970s+] (*S.Afr.*) a native of the Transvaal, generally looked down upon by the citizens of Cape Town, esp. when they appear there on holiday. [*Transvaal* + JAAP *n.*]

vacant lot *n.* [1980s] (*US campus*) a person who is not in touch with reality.

vacation *n.* **1** [late 19C] the period a criminal spends out of prison. **2** [1920s+] (*US*) time spent in prison.

vacuum *n.* **1** [19C] the vagina (cf. BITE *n.*[2]). **2** [1980s+] (*US campus*) a hearty eater. [both 'suck']

vacuum cleaner *n.* [1940s–50s] a sports car. [it helps one 'pick up bits of fluff']

vacuum cleaners *n.* [1940s] (*US Black*) the human lungs.

vada *v. see* VARDA *v.*

vade-mecum *n.* [19C] the vagina (cf. ARTICLE *n.*). [Lat. *vade mecum*, lit. 'come with me', fig. 'a useful thing']

vag *n.*[1] [mid-19C+] (*Aus./N.Z./US*) **1** a vagrant. **2** a charge of vagrancy; thus *on the vag, under the vag*, on a charge of vagrancy. [abbr.]

vag *n.*[2] (*also* **vadge**) [1980s+] **1** the vagina. **2** in fig. use, a general term of abuse (cf. BAMBA *n.*[1]).

vag *v.* [mid-19C+] (*Aus./US*) to charge and/or arrest someone for vagrancy. [VAG *n.*[1]]

vagabond *n.* (*also* **vargybin'**, **vargybun'**, **wagabone**) **1** [mid-19C–1920s] a lazy but inoffensive young man. **2** [20C+] (*W.I.*) a lecherous old man.

vaggerie *v.* [mid-19C+] (*Ling. Fr./Polari*) to go, to leave. [Ital. *viaggiare*, to travel]

vagina little-finger *n.* [1960s–70s] (*camp gay*) a snob. [*vagina* puns on Virginia, seen as a typical upper-class name. *Little-finger* refers to the affected crooking of the little finger when drinking]

vagitarian *n.* [1990s+] (*US gay*) a lesbian. [play on *vagina/ vegetarian* although she too will EAT *v.*[3] (1) someone's MEAT *n.* (3)]

vague *v.* [1990s+] to be more precise. [coined in late 1990s US TV show *Buffy the Vampire Slayer*]

vakeel *n.* [mid-19C] (*Anglo-Ind.*) a barrister. [Urdu *vakil*, an attorney, an authorized representative]

Val *n.* [1980s+] (*US*) **1** a Valley Girl. **2** San Fernando Valley, California. [abbr.]

val *n.* [2000s] *val*ue. [abbr.]

valentine *n.* [1920s–40s] **1** (*US prison*) a short sentence, maximum 1 year. **2** (*US police*) a reprimand, a punishment. [ironic uses of SE]

Valentine Dyalls *n.* [1990s+] piles. [rhy. sl.; ult. UK film actor *Valentine Dyall* (1908–85)]

valentino *v.* [1960s] to make love.

Vallie *n.* (*also* **vally, vals**) [1990s+] *Vali*um, a mild tranquillizer. [abbr.]

vamoose *v.* (*also* **vamoose the ranch, vamos, vamose**) [mid-19C+] (*orig. US*) to go away, to leave; esp. as imper. *vamoose!* go away! be off!; thus *vamoosed*, missing, lost. [Sp. *vamos!* let's go!]

vamoosing *n.* [mid-19C] flight. [VAMOOSE *v.*]

vamp *n.*[1] [mid-19C] an old stocking that has had the foot repaired. [SE *vamp*, that part of the stocking that covers the ankle and foot]

vamp *n.*[2] **1** [mid–late 19C] a robbery. **2** [1900s] a robber. [VAMP *v.*[1] (1)]

vamp *v.*[1] **1** [mid-17C–19C; 1990s+] to pawn, to steal. **2** [1990s+] to beg (from). [SE *vamp*, to repair, to patch up; 20C+ use is US Black]

vamp *v.*[2] **1** [20C+] (*US*) to vanish, to disappear; to travel. **2** [1920s+] to play the seductress. **3** [1950s] to walk.

vamper *n.* [mid-19C–1920s] a thief, esp. one who deliberately starts fights between others in order to rob them in the confusion. [SE *vamp*, to improvise + VAMP *v.*[1] (1)]

vampers *n.* [late 17C–18C] (*UK Und.*) stockings. [SE *vamp*]

vampire's teabag *n.* (*also* **vampire-bag**) [1990s+] (*US Black*) a sanitary napkin. [coarse use of SE]

vamp on *v.* [1970s+] (*US Black*) **1** to make an unjust attack, to arrest. **2** when aimed at the oppressor, to correct, to force him to mend his ways. [? SE *vampire*; (2) was esp. popular with 1960s–70s radicals]

Van *n. see* VAN DER MERWE *n.*

vancouver *n.* [1990s+] a vacuum cleaner, a hoover. [rhy. sl.]

vandemonianism *n.* [mid–late 19C] (*Aus.*) rowdyism, riotousness. [the one-time prison colony of Van Dieman's Land or Tasmania + ref. to SE *pandemonium*]

Vanderbilt *n.* [late 19C] (*US*) a very rich man. [New York's multi-millionaire *Vanderbilt* family]

Van der Merwe *n.* (*also* **Van**) [1960s+] (*S.Afr.*) the generic, stereotypical Afrikaner, the subject of a wide range of 'Van der Merwe' jokes characterizing him as loutish, bigoted and stupid; thus *the real Van der Merwe*, synon. with REAL McCOY, THE *n.* (1); *meet one's Van der Merwe*, meet one's Waterloo. [the common Afrikaner surname]

van dragger *n.* [20C+] a thief who specializes in stealing goods from the back of vans and carts; thus *van-dragging*.

V and V *n.* [1970s] (*US*) a combination of Valium and Vermouth. [abbr.]

V and X (store) *n.* [1940s] (*US Black*) a corner store. [Lat. *V*, 5 + *X*, 10, i.e. a '5 and 10 cent' store]

van dyke n.[1] [1930s+] (*Aus.*) a lavatory. [pun on DIKE n.[1]/Sir Anthony *Van Dyke*, portraitist (1599–1641)]

van dyke n.[2] [1960s+] (*US gay*) **1** a lesbian with a trace of a moustache on her upper lip. **2** a lesbian truck driver. [puns on DYKE n. + portraitist Anthony *Van Dyke* (1599–1641) who was thus bearded; (2) also puns on SE *van*, a truck]

vanilla n. **1** [1930s+] (*US Black*) a White person, esp. a woman. **2** [1980s+] (*US*) a heterosexual who practises normal sexual behaviour. **3** [1980s+] (*US gay*) non-penetrative sex, i.e. cuddling and mutual masturbation. [for ety. *see* VANILLA adj.]

vanilla adj. (*also* **plain vanilla**) [1970s+] plain, simple, no frills, esp. of sexual activity. [the plainest ice-cream flavour; the term was popularized in the 1980s+ but ? coined by the saxophonist Lester Young *c*.1935]

vanilla dinge n. [1960s] (*US*) a Black man who prefers White women. [VANILLA n. (1) + DINGE n. (2)]

vanilla fudge n. [1980s] (*Aus.*) a judge. [rhy. sl.]

vanilla queen n. **1** [1980s+] (*US Black*) a gay Black male who prefers White partners. **2** [2000s] a gay man who practises 'tame', non-experimental sex. [VANILLA n. (1) + QUEEN n.[2] (1)/QUEEN sfx (2)]

vanilla ripple n. *see* STRAWBERRY (RIPPLE) n.

vanilla sex n. [1990s+] (*gay*) a term for relatively conventional forms of sexual activity, usu. in contrast to sado-masochistic sex. [VANILLA adj. + SE *sex*]

vanilla suburb n. [1970s+] (*US*) the White suburbs, as opposed to the Black inner city. [VANILLA n. (1) + SE *suburb*]

vanity n. [late 19C] one's favourite liquor. [SE *vanity*, a thing of which one is vain]

vanity fair n. [20C+] a chair. [rhy. sl.]

van John n. [mid-19C] in cards, the game of pontoon or 21. [Fr. *vingt-et-un*, (the game of) 21]

vank v. [1990s+] (*W.I.*) to dismiss someone; to die. [? SE *vanquish*]

vanny n. [2000s] a van-driver.

vantage loaf n. [19C] the thirteenth loaf in a 'baker's dozen'. [SE *vantage*, an advantage, in this case to the buyer + *loaf*; note synon. 17C SE *vantage of bread*]

vap n. [20C+] (*W.I./UK Black*) **1** a bad mood. **2** an impulse. [? Fr. *vapeur*, dizziness, light-headedness + obs. SE *the vapours*]

vapors n.[1] [1980s+] (*US drugs*) the smoke issuing from a crack pipe.

vapors n.[2] [1990s+] (*US Black*) **1** a newly realized desire for an individual who, once shunned, has now gained status/material possessions and is thus suddenly alluring. **2** jealousy. [? obs. SE *vapours*, a fantasy, a foolish boast]

varda v. (*also* **vada, varder, vardi, vardo, vardy, verda**) [mid-19C+] (*Ling. Fr./Polari*) to look at, esp. in imper., e.g. *varda the riah!* look at that hair!; thus *varda d'amour*, a loving look; *bona vardering*, good-looking. [Venetian *vardia*, a look; however, note Polari etymologist W.S. Wilcox in a letter, 25 November 1999: 'Partridge and others derive the word *varder* from Italian *vedere*, but *guardare* (look, regard) fits the form better. *Guarda, guardare* tend to sound *warda, wardare* (and indeed are pronounced so in some Italian dialects) and given the well-attested wavering between *v-* and *w-* in 19C English the progression to *varder* is predictable (no doubt reinforced by *vedere*)']

vardo n. [early 19C+] a gypsy wagon; thus *vardo-gill*, a waggoner. [Rom. *vardo, wardo*, a cart]

vardy n. [late 18C–mid-19C] an opinion, a viewpoint. [SE *verdit*, obs. form of *verdict*]

vardy v. *see* VARDA v.

vargybin'/vargybun' n. *see* VAGABOND n.

varicose-vein flat n. [1990s+] a flat in poor maintenance. [the cracked plaster is reminiscent of varicose veins]

vark n. [1950s+] (*S.Afr.*) a general term of abuse, esp. of a police-man. [Afk. *vark*, pig; note PIG n.[3] (1)]

varment n. (*also* **varmint**) [late 18C–early 19C] an amateur

sportsman who has the skill of a professional. [? E.P. suggests dial. *varment/vermin*, any animal destructive of game but *OED* disputes this, rejecting any such link]

varmint adj. (*also* **varment**) **1** [early-mid-19C] fashionable, 'swell', dashing. **2** [19C] shrewd, knowing, 'au fait'. [VARMENT n.]

varnish n. **1** [late 19C] (*UK society*) second-rate champagne. **2** [1900s] (*UK society*) a second-rate person, an inadequate. **3** [1900s] sauce offered with food sold from a coffee-stall. **4** [1920s] (*US Und.*) bootleg liquor, esp. 'rye' whisky.

varnisher n. [mid-19C] a counterfeiter of fake sovereigns.

varnish one's pole v. (*also* **varnish the flagpole**) [1980s+] to masturbate (cf. BUFF THE BANANA v.). [SE *varnish* + POLE n./SE *flagpole*]

varnish remover n. [1950s+] (*US*) cheap, inferior whisky.

varnish the cane v. (*also* **varnish the stick**) [1900s–60s] (*US*) of a man, to have sexual intercourse. [SE *varnish* + CANDY CANE n.[1]/STICK n.[1] (1)]

varnish the flagpole v. *see* VARNISH ONE'S POLE v.

varoom v. *see* VROOM v.

vasbyt v. [1960s+] (*S.Afr., orig. milit.*) to keep going, to 'tough it out', to 'bite the bullet'. [Afk. *vasbyt*, to bite hard, to seize with the jaws]

Vaseline n. [1910s; 1970s] (*Aus./US*) butter or margarine.

Vaseline brown n. *see* HIGH BROWN n.

Vaseline valley n. [1980s+] (*Aus.*) a stretch of Oxford Street, Sydney acknowledged as the city's gay centre. [the use of Vaseline to ease anal intercourse + ? pun on California's Silicon Valley]

Vaseline villa n. [1960s+] (*US gay*) a YMCA frequented by gay men. [for ety. *see* VASELINE VALLEY n.]

v.a.t. n. [1980s+] *vodka and tonic* (cf. G. AND T. n.). [abbr.; coined in the TV series *Minder* (1979–81)]

vat en sit n. [1950s+] (*S.Afr. township*) a 'live-in lover', a common-law partner, an unsolemnized marriage; also as adj. [Afk. *vat en sit*, stay put, lit. 'take and sit']

vat hom Fluffie! excl. [1970s+] (*S.Afr.*) an exhortation, esp. in the context of sports events or business meetings when the subject(s) of the cry has to pull something special out of the hat. [Afk. lit. 'go get him Fluffie'; no record exists of the original Fluffie (a dog, presumably)]

vatican roulette n. [1960s+] the notoriously undependable rhythm method of contraception. [the only form permitted by the Catholic Church]

vato n. [1970s+] (*US Hisp.*) **1** a member of a Mexican teen gang; thus VATO LOCO n. **2** in Chicano use, a man, irrespective of race.

vato loco n. *see* BATO LOCO n.

vatterig adj. [1970s+] (*S.Afr.*) used of one who has 'wandering' hands. [Du. *vatten*, to take, to catch]

vault v. [late 16C–17C] to have sexual intercourse. [SE *vault*, to jump, to leap]

vaulter n. (*also* **vawter**) [late 16C–17C] a prostitute. [VAULT v.]

vaulting house n. (*also* **vaulting school**) [late 16C–early 19C] a brothel (cf. ACCOMMODATION HOUSE n.). [VAULT v. + HOUSE n.[1] (1)]

vaykay n. [1970s] (*US*) a holiday, a *vaca*tion. [abbr./pron.]

vay-ki-vay adj. [20C+] (*W.I.*) unplanned, haphazard. [Fr. *vaille que vaille*, come what may, any old how]

vay-ki-vay adv. [20C+] (*W.I.*) carelessly, shabbily. [VAY-KI-VAY adj.]

v.b.c. phr. [1980s+] (*US campus*) having the outline of one's buttocks showing through tight trousers; or revealing the top of one's buttocks due to wearing one's trousers lower than the waist. [abbr. *visible butt crack*]

v.b.d. n. [1960s] (*US Black*) an unsatisfactory evening with a member of the opposite sex. [abbr. *very bad date*]

v.c. adj. [late 19C] plucky, courageous. [abbr. *Victoria Cross*]

veal n.[1] [1920s] (*US*) a young woman who flirts maliciously.

veal n.[2] *see* CALF n.[1] (1).

veal will be cheap – calves fall! *excl.* [late 17C–19C] a mocking cry aimed at one who has very thin legs.

vee-dub *n.*[1] [1970s+] (*Aus.*) a Volkswagen car. [abbr. of *vee-double-you*, pron. of *VW*]

vee-dub *n.*[2] [1990s+] (*US teen*) the shaved female genitals. [the shaved genital area supposedly resembles the bonnet of a Volkswagen *VW*]

vee-in *n.* [1980s+] (*US Black gang*) an initiation ritual whereby the new member is beaten by other gang members for an allotted time, e.g. 1 minute. [? VAMP ON v./SE *violence*]

veejay *n. see* V.J. n.

veeno *n. see* VINO n.

veep *n.* [1940s+] (*US*) a vice-president. [pron. of initial letters]

vee-wee *n.* [1960s+] a Volkswagen car. [pron. of *VW*]

veg *n.*[1] (*also* **veggies**) [late 19C+] vegetables. [abbr.]

veg *n.*[2] [1980s+] a moron, a madman. [abbr. SE *vegetable*]

veg *v.* (*also* **veg out**) [1960s+] to do nothing, to lapse into a totally apathetic and passive state. [abbr. SE *vegetate*]

vega *n.* [1990s+] (*US Black teen*) a marijuana cigarette rolled inside the outer leaves of a cigar (cf. BLUNT n.[3]). [the cigar brand Garcia y *Vega*, the West Coast version of Phillies Blunts]

vege *n. see* VEGGIE n.

Vegemite Valley *n.* [1990s+] (*Aus.*) the anus or rectum, in the context of (homosexual) anal intercourse (cf. BOURNEVILLE BOULEVARD n.). [the Aus. brown yeast spread *Vegemite*, the vegetarian equivalent of UK *Marmite*]

vegetable *n.* [1970s+] (*US gay*) a lesbian. [play on FRUIT n.[2] (2)]

vegetable *adj.* [1970s] **1** (*US campus*) very drunk or intoxicated with drugs. **2** brainless, very stupid.

vegetable John *n.* [1920s] (*Aus.*) a Chinese greengrocer (cf. AH CABBAGE n.). [SE *vegetable* + JOHN CHINAMAN n.]

vegetarian *n.* [1960s+] (*US*) a female prostitute or male homosexual who will not perform fellatio, i.e. will not EAT SOMEONE'S MEAT v.

vegged (out) *adj.* [1980s+] (*US campus*) **1** heavily intoxicated by drugs. **2** exhausted. [VEG v.]

veggie *n.* (*also* **vege, veggy, vegie, vegy**) **1** [1950s+] a vegetable. **2** [1970s+] a vegetarian. **3** [1980s+] a person reduced to a vegetative state. **4** [1980s+] (*Irish*) a derog. term for a physically or mentally disabled child. [abbr.]

veggie *adj.* [1980s+] vegetarian.

veggie-meat *n.* [1990s+] (*W.I.*) an available young woman; a virgin.

veggies *n. see* VEG n.[1].

veggy/vegie *n. see* VEGGIE n.

veg out *v. see* VEG v.

vegy *n. see* VEGGIE n.

V-8 *n.* [1940s] (*US Black*) a solitary woman who prefers her own company to that of others, esp. of men. [? abbr. SE *deviate*, i.e. she 'must' be a lesbian]

veil up *v.* [1930s–40s] (*US*) to get married.

vein shooter *n.* [1930s–50s] (*US drugs*) one who injects into the vein; thus a veteran addict. [VEIN SHOT n.]

vein shot *n.* [1930s–50s] (*US drugs*) an injection of narcotics directly into a vein. [SE *vein* + SHOT n.[6] (2)]

veiny bang-stick *n.* (*also* **veiny love-stalk**) [1990s+] a penis (cf. BAT n.[7]). [SE *veiny* + BANG n.[2] (2) + STICK n.[1] (1)]

velcro grin *n.* [1990s+] (*US*) a false rigid smile.

velcro head *n.* [1970s+] (*US*) a derog. term for a Black person (cf. BRILLOHEAD n.). [*Velcro* + -HEAD sfx (1); the supposed resemblance of the material to tightly curled hair]

velveeta *adj.* [1980s+] (*US campus*) unappealing or unpleasant. [*Velveeta*, a processed cheese spread, thus play on CHEESY adj.[2] (1)]

velvet *n.*[1] [late 17C–19C] the tongue.

velvet *n.*[2] [late 19C+] gain, profit, winnings; thus *to the velvet*, to the good.

velvet *n.*[3] [1950s] (*Aus./N.Z.*) any dark-skinned woman; thus *a bit of velvet*. [abbr. BLACK VELVET n. (1)]

velvet *n.*[4] [1980s] female pubic hair.

velvet-lined meat grinder *n.* (*also* **velvet cone**) [1940s–70s] (*US*) the vagina (cf. BAG n.[1]; BITE n.[2]).

velvet orbs *n. see* ORBS n.

velvet room *n.* [mid-19C] (*US*) the back room of a saloon where patrons might enjoy a slightly quieter and more salubrious atmosphere than in the rowdier front.

velvet tunnel *n.* [1990s+] the vagina (cf. AGREEABLE RUTS OF LIFE n.).

venerable monosyllable *n. see* MONOSYLLABLE n.

venison out of Tup Park *n.* [late 17C–mid-18C] mutton. [SE *venison + tup*, a ram]

ventilate *v.* **1** [late 19C] to stab. **2** [late 19C+] (*orig. US*) to shoot, to kill with a bullet. [i.e. to 'let air into']

vent man *n.* [2000s] (*US*) a tramp, a street person. [their sleeping over warm subway air vents]

venture girl *n.* [mid-19C] a single woman sent out to India in the hope of winning herself a husband.

Venus's anvil/cave/court/cup *n. see* VENUS'S HIGHWAY n.

Venus's curse *n.* [early 19C] venereal disease.

Venus's field *n. see* VENUS'S HIGHWAY n.

Venus's game *n. see* GAME n.[1].

Venus's glove *n.* [late 16C–early 17C] the vagina (cf. ADAM'S OWN (ALTAR) n.; BAG n.[1]).

Venus's highway *n.* (*also* grove of Venus, gulf of Venus, hill of Venus, shrine of Venus, temple of Venus, Venus's anvil, ...cave, ...court, ...cup, ...field, ...garden, ...hall, ...honeypot, ...mark, ...secret cell) [late 16C–1900s] the vagina (cf. ADAM'S OWN (ALTAR) n.; ALLEY n.[1]). [literary euph.]

vep *n.* [20C+] (*W.I.*) a lift, a free ride. [Fr. *vêpres*, vespers, a service at which there is no collection and is thus 'free']

Vera Lynn *n.* (*also* **vera**) [1940s+] **1** thus a gin-drinker. **2** skin. **3** (*UK/Aus.*) the chin. **4** (*Irish*) in pl., cigarette papers. [rhy. sl.; (4) = SKIN n.[18]; ult. UK singer *Vera Lynn* (b.1917)]

verandah *n.* **1** [late 19C] the gallery of the Old Vic Theatre, London. **2** [20C+] (*Aus./US*) a pot belly.

vera vice *n.* (*also* **victoria vice**) [1950s+] (*gay*) the police vice squad. [joc. 'feminization' of the squad]

verbal *n.* (*also* **verbals**) [1960s+] **1** a statement (usu. untrue), by a policeman, designed to ensure the conviction of a suspect. **2** (*UK Und.*) a statement, often self-incriminatory, to the police either voluntarily or during and after interrogation. **3** insults, abuse, 'backchat'; thus *give someone the verbals*, to abuse; *give it the verbal*, to talk aggressively. **4** a conversation.

verbal *v.* [1960s+] (*UK/Aus. Und.*) **1** of the police, to fake a confession by claiming that one's statement under interrogation admitted the crimes for which in court one is pleading not guilty. **2** to talk. **3** to confess under interrogation. **4** to talk aggressively, to abuse. [VERBAL n.]

verbal diarrhoea *n.* [1940s+] excessive talk, esp. when meaningless, pointless and irritating to the hearer. [note late 17C–19C fig. use of SE *diarrhoea*, an excessive flow of words etc]

verbals *n. see* VERBAL n.

verb-grinder *n.* [early 19C] a nit-picking schoolmaster.

verda *v. see* VARDA v.

verdomde *adj.* [mid-19C+] (*S.Afr.*) DAMNED adj., infernal. [Du. *verdoemd*, damned]

verification shot *n.* [1930s–50s] (*US drugs*) the drawing of blood back into the syringe to make sure that one has hit a vein. [SE *verification* + SHOT n.[6] (2)]

vermilion *adj.* [late 19C] (*Aus.*) a euph. for BLOODY adj.[1] (1).

vermilion *v.* [early 19C] (*Aus.*) to cover or smear someone with blood.

Vermont charity *n.* [1910s–40s] (*US tramp*) sympathy. [? the meanness of that state's authorities]

verneuk v. [late 19C+] (*S.Afr.*) to cheat, to swindle. [Du. sl. *verneuken*]

Veronica Lake n. [1950s+] a steak. [rhy. sl.; ult. the film star *Veronica Lake* (1919–73)]

versatile adj. [1950s–60s] **1** bisexual. **2** (*US gay*) able to enjoy both active and passive sexual roles. [euph.]

verse v. [16C] (*UK Und.*) to practise a fraud or deceit by verbal means. [SE *verse*, to pour out the voice]

verser n. (*also* **retriever**) [mid-16C–early 17C] (*UK Und.*) that member of a confidence trickster team (practising the BARNARD'S LAW n.) who actually plays the game of chance through which a victim is defrauded and who would often claim to be a friend of one of the victim's friends. [VERSE v.; the imagery reflects the world of hunting (cf. BEATER n.¹)]

versing law n. [16C] (*UK Und.*) those confidence tricks that focus on the use of counterfeit gold to entrap the victim. [VERSE v. + LAW n.¹]

vertical bacon sandwich n. [1990s+] (*US*) the labia majora (cf. BACON STRIPS n.).

vertical care-grinder n. [mid–late 19C] the prison treadmill.

vertical drinking n. [1950s+] (*N.Z.*) drinking while standing at the bar, esp. in a crowd.

vertical smile n. [20C+] the vagina.

very famillionaire adj. [mid-19C] (*UK society*) typical of a nouveau riche. [play on SE *very familiar*]

very froncey adj. [late 19C] (*UK society*) vulgar. [Fr. *très français*, very French]

very idea!, the excl. see IDEA!, THE (VERY) excl.

very well adj. [mid-19C+] acceptable; thus *that's all very well*. [lit. an intensifier of *well*]

vessel n. [early 19C] the nose. [when 'tapped' it 'overflows' with blood]

vest n. **1** [1930s+] (*US*) a bullet-proof vest. **2** [1950s] (*US Und.*) watches and/or jewellery worn on the waistcoat.

vestal n. [early 19C] a sexually unrestrained person. [SE *vestal virgin*, a Roman priestess supposedly dedicated to absolute chastity]

vestry n. [19C] the vagina.

vestryman n. [19C] the penis. [VESTRY n. + SE *man*]

vet n. **1** [mid-19C+] an ex-serviceman. **2** [1910s+] an old-timer, an ageing or experienced person. **3** [1960s+] an ageing, experienced or worn-out prostitute. [abbr. SE *veteran*]

vet, the n. [1930s+] (*orig. milit.*) a doctor; thus (*S.Afr.*) a prison doctor. [SE *vet*, a veterinary surgeon]

vet adj. [1930s–50s] (*US*) veteran, experienced. [VET n.]

veterano n. [1980s] (*US*) a veteran of gang life. [Sp.]

Vette n. [1950s+] a Cor*vette* automobile. [abbr.]

vex adj. (*also* **vexed**, **vexed up**) [1930s+] (*orig. W.I.*) annoyed, angry; thus *vexness*, bad temper. [SE *vexed*]

vex-money n. [20C+] (*W.I., Trin.*) money a woman carries with her on a date. If, for whatever reason (usu. the denial of sex), she is forced to make her own way home, she has some funds. [Carib.E. *vex*, irritating, annoying + SE *money*]

v.g. adj. [1940s+] very good. [abbr.]

V-girl n. [1940s] (*US*) a woman willing to have sex with (or at least go out with) servicemen for patriotic reasons. [abbr. *Victory-girl* + play on B-GIRL n.]

vibe n. (*also* **vibes**) [1960s+] **1** atmosphere; thus *good vibes, bad vibes*. **2** feelings, intuitions. **3** of a person, personality, style. [abbr. SE *vibrations*]

vibe v. **1** [1960s+] (*US*) to experience, to enjoy. **2** [1960s+] to give off an atmosphere. **3** [1980s+] (*US Black*) to carry on a relationship, usu. sexual. **4** [1990s+] to create a pleasant, exciting atmosphere. [VIBE n.]

vibe out v. [1990s+] (*W.I.*) to relax, to take a break. [VIBE n.]

vibes n.¹ [1930s+] a *vib*raphone or *vib*raharp. [abbr.]

vibes n.² see VIBE n.

vibe someone out v. [1960s+] to produce emotional effects, usu. negative and confusing, in someone. [VIBE n.]

Vic n. **1** [mid–late 19C] the Victoria Theatre, London. **2** [mid-19C+] (*also* **Viccy**) Queen *Vic*toria; also as a name for a public house. **3** [late 19C] *Vic*toria railway station, London. **4** [late 19C] (*Aus.*) the *Vic*toria Theatre, Sydney. **5** [1910s–40s] (*US*) a *Vic*trola brand phonograph. **6** [1930s+] (*Aus.*) the state of *Vic*toria. [abbr.]

vic n. (*US Und.*) **1** [1920s–40s] a convict, i.e. a self-styled *vic*tim of justice. **2** [1930s+] (*also* **vick**) a *vic*tim of crime. [abbr.]

vic v. [1990s+] to *vic*timize, to make the subject of a crime. [abbr.]

vicar of Bray n. [20C+] in cards, a 3. [rhy. sl. = TRAY n. (1)]

Viccy n. see VIC n. (2).

vice n. [1950s+] the *vice* squad. [abbr.]

vice v. [1950s+] (*US Black*) to do harm, to cheat, to steal, to cause physical pain. [SE *vice*, to force, to strain, but note 15C *vice*, to treat arrogantly or oppressively]

vice-admiral (of the narrow seas) n. [mid-17C–early 19C] 'a drunken man that pisses under the table into his companions' shoes' (Grose, 1796).

vice versa n. [1960s] (*US gay*) mutual cunnilingus or fellatio.

vice-whipper n. [late 17C] a clergyman; a pious person.

vicey-versey adv. (*also* **vicky-verky**, **wisey warcy**) [mid-19C+] vice versa. [deliberate joc. mispron.]

vicious adj. (*US Black/teen*) **1** [1980s] serious. **2** [1980s+] wonderful, excellent, admirable. [on bad = good model]

vick n. see VIC n. (2).

vicky n. **1** [1960s] a dismissive 'V' hand sign. **2** [1990s+] a virgin. [the initial 'V']

vicky-verky adv. see VICEY-VERSEY adv.

vict n. [1930s–60s] (*US Black*) a crime *vic*tim. [abbr.]

victoria monk n. [late 19C–1900s] semen. [rhy. sl. = SPUNK n. (4); ult. music hall star *Victoria Monks* (1884–1972), best known for her version of 'Won't you come home, Bill Bailey?']

victoria vice n. see VERA VICE n.

Victor Trumper n. [20C+] (*Aus.*) a cigarette butt. [rhy. sl. = BUMPER n.³; ult. Aus. cricketer *Victor Trumper* (1877–1915)]

victory n. [1940s–50s] (*W.I.*) a style of haircut that gave a man's hair a V-shape at the back. [the 'V for Victory' campaign of WW2]

victory V n. [1990s+] an act of urination (cf. ANGEL'S KISS n.). [rhy. sl. = PEE n.¹ (2)/WEE n.]

victualler n. [late 16C–early 17C] a pimp; thus *victualling-house*, a brothel (cf. ABBOT ON THE CROSS n.). [innkeepers who doubled as pimps]

victualling department n. (*also* **victualling office**) [late 17C–1900s] the stomach. [SE *victuals*, food + *department/office*]

vid n. **1** [1980s+] *vid*eotape. **2** [1990s+] a hallucination, presumably drug-induced. **3** [1990s+] a striking image or memory. [abbr.; (2) and (3) f. (1)]

vidaholic n. [1980s+] (*US*) a TV/video addict. [SE *video* + -AHOLIC sfx]

viddle-de-vop n. [1940s] (*US Black*) a low whistle. [? echoic]

vide-ho n. [1990s+] an attractive (young) woman, who dances on TV shows. [play on SE *video* + HO n.¹ (4)]

vietas n. see FIETAS n.

Vietnik n. [1960s–70s] (*US*) an active protester against the US involvement in the Vietnam War (1964–75). [*Viet*(*nam*) + -NIK sfx]

viewy adj. [early–mid-19C] flashy, showy, attractive. [it/one becomes a SE *view*]

vigorish n. (*also* **vig**, **vigerage**, **viggerish**, **viggresh**) **1** [1910s+] (*US*) interest on a loan or debt. **2** [2000s] profit. [? Yid./Rus. *vyigrysh*, profit, winnings]

vig ounce n. [1970s+] (*US drugs*) 1oz (28g) of narcotics. [VIGORISH n. (1)]

Viking n. [2000s] (*US prison*) an inmate who has a very dirty or untidy cell.

Viking v. [2000s] (*US prison*) to live a good life, with plenty of material comforts, despite being incarcerated.

Viking cheat n. [1990s+] (*W.I.*) a member of the Establishment, an authority, thus an oppressor.

Viking queen n. [1960s+] (*gay*) **1** a (dyed) blond male. **2** one who prefers Nordic partners. [*Viking* + SE *queen*/QUEEN n.² (1)/QUEEN sfx (2)]

vile n. (*also* **ville, voil, vyle**) [late 17C+] a town or village. [Fr. *ville*, town; note -VILE sfx]

-vile sfx (*also* **-ville**) [mid-16C–mid-19C] used in combs. to mean town or village; thus DEUSEAVILE n.; RUMVILE n. [Fr. *ville*, town]

Village, the n. **1** [19C] London, mainly in hunting/horseracing use. **2** [late 19C–1900s] (*US*) the Lower East Side, New York City. **3** [1910s+] (*US*) Greenwich Village, New York City. [abbr.]

village bike n. *see* RALEIGH BIKE n.

village butler n. [late 18C] 'old thieves, that would rather steal a dishclout than discontinue the practice of thieving' (Potter, *New Dict. of Cant, c.1790*).

village ram n. [1930s+] (*W.I.*) a local philanderer and ladies' man. [SE *village* + RAM n.¹ (2)]

villain n. [1960s+] a professional criminal. [specific use of SE]

Ville, the n. **1** [1920+] Penton*ville* prison, London N1. **2** [2000s] (*US*) Greenwich *Village*, New York City. [abbr.]

ville n. *see* VILE n.

-ville sfx¹ [mid-19C+] (*mainly US*) used to emphasize a particular characteristic, e.g. *dragsville*, a very boring place or situation, STICKVILLE n. [first use is UK, but popularized by 1950s US beatniks]

-ville sfx² *see* -VILE sfx.

vin blong n. (*also* **vin blank, vin blinc, ving blong, von blink, vonblong**) [1910s] (*orig. milit.*) cheap white wine; thus *vongrooge*, cheap red wine. [mispron. of Fr. *vin blanc*/*vin rouge*, white wine/red wine]

vincent n. [late 16C–early 17C] (*UK Und.*) the victim of a crooked gambling game. [VINCENT'S LAW n.]

Vincent Price n. [1990s+] ice. [rhy. sl.; ult. film star *Vincent Price* (1911–93)]

vincent's law n. [late 16C–early 19C] (*UK Und.*) cheating for profit at bowls and later cards. [Lat. *vincens*, victorious; the use is ironic + LAW n.¹]

vine n.¹ (*also* **vines**) [1930s+] (*orig. US Black*) a suit, usu. for a male; often in pl. [SE *vine*, i.e. a well-cut suit clings to the figure as does the plant to a tree]

vine n.² [1960s] (*orig. UK Und.*) any unofficial underground network of information. [GRAPEVINE n.¹]

vine, the n. [1970s+] (*US Black*) wine.

vined adj. [1960s] dressed. [VINE n.¹]

vinegar n.¹ [late 17C–early 19C] (*UK Und.*) a cloak, an overcoat. [? its being worn in 'sharp' weather]

vinegar n.² [2000s] semen (cf. BABY GRAVY n.).

vinegar pisser n. [early 17C] a miser, a mean person. [SE *vinegar* + PISS v.¹ (1)]

vinegar stick n. **1** [1930s] (*US Und.*) a thin, stiletto-like knife. **2** [2000s] the penis (cf. BAT n.⁷). [(2) STICK n.¹ (1); they are both 'sharp']

vinegar strokes n. (*also* **gravy strokes**) [1970s+] the final thrusts of sexual intercourse. [? one 'puts a bit of vinegar' into them; note Barry Humphries, *The Traveller's Tool* (1985), in 'Les's Large Appendix': 'The penultimate phase in sexual connection when the active partner experiences a facial rictus similar to that produced by drinking vinegar (information supplied by a doctor)']

vines n. *see* VINE n.¹.

vineyard n. [1970s+] (*US Black*) an ironic ref. to anywhere that alcoholics congregate.

ving blong n. *see* VIN BLONG n.

vinnies n. (*also* **Vinny's**) [1980s+] (*Aus./N.Z.*) the Society of St Vincent de Paul; thus their second-hand clothes shops. [abbr.]

vino n. (*also* **veeno**) **1** [late 19C+] wine, usu. cheap. **2** [1990s+] (*Aus.*) a glass of wine. [Ital. *vino*, wine]

vintage n. [late 19C] (*orig. US*) the year of one's birth. [SE *vintage*, the year of a wine's creation]

vintner n. [early 18C] a heavy drinker. [play on SE]

vinyl n. [1970s+] records (as opposed to tapes or CDs); thus *vinyl junkie*, one who is obsessed by records, rejecting all other forms of recorded music.

violate v. [1960s+] (*US*) to forfeit one's parole through a violation of the rules and to be returned to prison.

violet n. (*also* **garden violet**) **1** [late 19C–1940s] an onion; in pl., spring onions or sage and onion stuffing. **2** [1920s–30s] cabbage. [although the terms are found in several dictionaries, none, including *OED*, provides an actual cit.]

violet crumble v. [1990s+] (*Aus.*) to understand. [rhy. sl. = TUMBLE v.² (3); ult. an Aus. sweet]

violin n. [1980s+] (*Aus. drugs/prison*) a hypodermic syringe; thus *play the violin*, to inject oneself.

violin-case n. [1910s–40s] (*US*) an oversized shoe.

vip n. [1930s–50s] (*Aus.*) a miser. [? SE *viper*]

vipe v. [1930s–60s] (*drugs*) to smoke marijuana. [VIPER n. (1)]

viper n. (*drugs*) **1** [1930s+] a regular user of marijuana. **2** [1970s] a regular user of heroin. **3** [1980s] an injection of morphine and heroin. [ety. unknown; obviously f. SE *viper*, but unclear which characteristics]

viperish adj. [1950s] (*drugs*) regularly using marijuana. [VIPER n. (1)]

viperland n. [1940s] the world of marijuana smokers. [VIPER n. (1) + SE *land*]

viper's drag n. [1930s] a marijuana cigarette. [VIPER n. (1) + DRAG n.⁹]

viper's weed n. [1930s–50s] marijuana (cf. AFRICAN BUSH n.). [VIPER n. (1) + WEED n.¹ (4)]

virgie n. [1930s–60s] a virgin; also as adj., virginal. [abbr.]

virgin n.¹ [1910s–20s] **1** a cigarette made of *Virgin*ia tobacco. **2** (*US*) a martini, i.e. a mix of *ver*mouth and *gin*. [abbr.]

virgin n.² [1970s] (*US Und.*) a criminal with no convictions. [note 1940s US Army *virgin*, a soldier who has yet to contract venereal disease]

virgin bride n. [20C+] (*Aus.*) a ride. [rhy. sl.]

virginia n. [1990s+] (*US*) the vagina. [joc. mispron.]

Virgin Mary n. [1960s] (*US*) 'an obviously pregnant single girl who insists she is merely gaining weight, then leaves town to go on a diet' (Trimble, *5,000 Adult Sex Words & Phrases*, 1966). [Christ's supposedly parthenogenic mother]

virgin pullet n. [early 19C] 'a young woman who though often trod has never laid' (Bee), i.e. no longer a virgin but not yet a mother. [SE *virgin* + PULLET n.]

virgins' bus n. [late 19C] the last bus to run westward from Piccadilly Circus. ['so named satirically in reference of the chief patronesses at that late hour' (Ware), i.e. girls who have resisted male advances]

virgin vault n. [1990s+] (*US campus*) a female residence hall.

virtue rewarded n. [late 19C] prison. [the initials *V.R.*, i.e. *Victoria Regina*, on the side of the prison van]

virtuoso of the skin flute n. [20C+] a masturbator. [SE *virtuoso* + SKIN FLUTE n.]

virus, the n. [1980s+] (*orig. US*) HIV, the virus that causes AIDS. [euph.]

vi's n. [1960s] (*US campus*) Levi-Strauss jeans. [abbr. Le*vi's*]

visa-body n. [1990s+] (*W.I.*) a human object of desire.

vision n. [1970s] television. [abbr.]

visit from the stork n. [late 19C+] (*UK society*) the arrival of a new baby. [the child's version of childbirth]

visiting café la mamma n. [1990s+] (*US*) breastfeeding. [play on SE *mama*, a mother/the New York City theatre group *Café la Mama* (founded 1961)]

visiting fireman *n.* [1920s+] (*orig. US*) **1** a person or group who are particularly well looked after when visiting an organization of kindred spirits. **2** tourists who are expected to spend freely. **3** parasites, hangers-on. [orig. 1855 when the Baltimore *Sun* reported that 'A company of firemen from Rochester, N.Y. [...] continue to receive the attentions of their brother firemen of Baltimore. [...] This evening the visiting firemen will be the guests of the Washington Hose Company' (25 October 1855)]

visit Miss Murphy *v.* [20C+] to visit the lavatory (cf. AUNTIE n.[1]). [euph.]

visit Miss White *v.* [1920s] to visit the lavatory (cf. AUNTIE n.[1]). [? the white lavatory bowl]

visit Mrs Jones *v. see* MRS JONES n.

visit one's Indian cousin *v.* [1940s+] (*W.I.*) to have one's hair straightened (cf. CONK n.[2]). [Indian hair is straight; note the big immigration to the W.I. from east India]

visitor *n.* [1940s+] a menstrual period. [euph.]

visitor to Vegemite valley *n.* [1990s+] a male homosexual (cf. BROWN ARTIST n.). [SE *visitor* + VEGEMITE VALLEY n.]

visit Sir Harry *v.* [mid-19C] to visit the lavatory (cf. AUNTIE n.[1]). [euph.]

visit the sandbox *v.* [1960s] (*US campus*) to visit the lavatory. [SE *visit* + *sandbox*, a pet's litter tray]

vitamin A *n.* [1980s+] **1** LSD (cf. A n.[3]). **2** MDMA (cf. ECSTASY n.). [SE *vitamin* + abbr. (1) ACID n.[3]; (2) ACID n.[4]]

vitamin C *n.* [1980s+] cocaine (cf. AUNT NORA n.). [SE *vitamin* + C n.[2] (1)]

vitamin E *n.* [1980s+] MDMA (cf. ECSTASY n.). [SE *vitamin* + E n.]

vitamin H *n.* [1980s+] (*Aus. drugs/prison*) heroin (cf. BIG H n.). [SE *vitamin* + H n.[2] (1)]

vitamin K *n. see* SPECIAL K n.

vitamin M *n.* [1970s] (*US drugs*) Methedrine (cf. M n.).

vitamins *n.* **1** [1950s] money. **2** [1980s+] (*drugs*) any drugs available in pill or capsule form (cf. PILL n.[4]). [play on the supposedly health-giving properties of SE *vitamins*]

vitamin T *n.* [1980s+] (*drugs*) marijuana (cf. AFRICAN BUSH n.). [SE *vitamin* + TEA n.[2] (1)]

Vitamin V *n.* [2000s] vodka. [ironic use of SE *vitamin* + initial letter of *vodka*]

vitamin X *n.* [1990s+] MDMA (cf. ECSTASY n.). [SE *vitamin* + X n.[3] (3) or pron. of ECSTASY n.]

vitamin XXX *n.* [1980s+] alcohol. [SE *vitamin* + XXX, a mark of a beer's strength]

viz *n.* [1990s+] a face. [abbr. SE *visage*]

v.j. *n.* (*also* **veejay**) [1980s+] (*US*) video jockey, a television presenter of music videos. [abbr.; on pattern of DJ n.]

vlam *n.* [1970s+] (*S.Afr.*) methylated spirits (as drunk by alcoholics); thus *vlam-drinker*. [Afk. *vlam*, flame]

voce *n.* (*also* **voche, votch**) [mid-19C+] (*Ling. Fr./Polari*) the voice. [Ital. *voce*, a voice]

vodders *n.* (*also* **vod**) [1990s+] *vod*ka.

voddy *n.* [1980s+] *vod*ka. [abbr.]

vodeodo *n.* [1930s] plunder, booty, cash. [play on musical *vo-do-deo-do*, a meaningless refrain used to produce rhythm + DOUGH n.[1] (1)]

voetjie-voetjie *n.* [1910s+] (*S.Afr.*) the surreptitious nudging of someone's foot out of sight of anyone else, typically beneath a table; the contact is usu. a prelude to greater intimacy. [Afk. *voet*, foot; PLAY FOOTSIE v. (1)]

voetsak *n.* [1970s+] (*S.Afr.*) an infinite, non-specific number, e.g. *straight from the year voetsak*, the equivalent of 'God knows when' or 'the year dot'. [Afk. *voertsek*, forward, more usu. found as a dismissive command (*see* next)]

voetsak! *excl.* [mid-19C+] (*S.Afr.*) (*also* **voetsek!**) a general excl. of dismissal, go away! be off! get out! [Du. *voort seg ik*, lit. 'be off, I say!']

vogel grafter *n.* [1900s] (*US Und.*) one who robs young children. [Ger. *vogel*, a bird or FOGLE n. + GRAFTER n.[1] (1)]

vogue *n.* [1960s–70s] (*gay*) a cigarette. [? its fashionability]

voil *n. see* VILE n.

voker *v.* [mid-19C+] **1** to speak. **2** to understand. [Lat. *vocare*, to speak]

volkie *n.* [1940s+] (*S.Afr.*) a derog. term for a Coloured farm labourer. [Du. *volk*, people]

Volks *n.* [1950s+] a *Volks*wagen car. [abbr.]

Volksie *n.* [1960s+] (*S.Afr.*) a *Volks*wagen 'Beetle'. [abbr.]

voluntary knee drill *n.* [late 19C] abject adulation. [subjects throw themselves to their knees]

vom *n.* [1990s+] **1** vomit. **2** bad, disgusting food. [VOM v.[1]]

vom *v.* [1990s+] to be sick. [abbr. SE *vomit*]

vomatose *adj.* [1980s+] (*US campus*) disgusting. [SE *vomit* + *comatose*]

vomit up one's toenails *v.* [2000s] (*US*) to vomit copiously.

vomity *adj.* (*also* **vomitrocious**) [1970s–80s] (*orig. US*) very disgusting; thus as n., a disgusting person. [SE *vomit*]

von blink *n. see* VIN BLONG n.

von-blinked *adj.* [1910s] (*Aus.*) drunk (cf. ADRIAN (QUIST) adj.). [VIN BLONG n.]

vonblong *n. see* VIN BLONG n.

vonce *n.* **1** [1950s] (*US Black/jazz*) marijuana. **2** [1960s] (*US*) a term of abuse. [(1) Yid. *vonce*, a bedbug, thus = ROACH n.[2]; (2) ? abbr. of SCHWANTZ n. (2)]

vongrooge *n. see* VIN BLONG n.

Von Trappe *n.* [2000s] trouble, difficulties, problems. [rhy. sl. = CRAP n.[5] (2); ult. the *Von Trapp* family in the film *Sound of Music* (1965)]

voom *v. see* VROOM v.

voompse *v.* (*also* **vumpse**) [20C+] (*W.I.*) to pay attention to; usu. in negative, thus *not even voompse at/upon*, to ignore, to cut dead. [ety. unknown]

votch *n. see* VOCE n.

vote for the alderman *v.* [early–mid-19C] to take a drink. [joc. ref. to ALDERMAN LUSHINGTON n.]

voucher *n.* [late 17C–mid-18C] (*UK Und.*) an accomplice who passes the counterfeit money produced by the coiner. [he *vouches* for its authenticity]

vowel *v.* [early 18C–mid-19C] of a losing gamester, to pay off one's debts with an IOU. [the *vowels* IOU]

voyager *n.* [1960s] one who is under the influence of LSD. [they are on a TRIP n.[4] (1)]

v.p.l. *n.* [1980s+] of a woman, the line of one's underwear visible through a tight outer garment. [abbr. *visible pantie line*]

v.r. *n.* [mid–late 19C] a prison van. [the monarch's initials (for Victoria Regina), painted on its sides; also joc. abbr. *vagabonds removed*]

vreet *v.* [1970s+] (*S.Afr.*) to devour, to gobble up. [Du. *vreten*, to eat; usu. of an animal and thus sl. when used of a person]

vrek *v.* [1910s+] (*S.Afr.*) to die; thus *gaan vrek*, to drop dead. [Afk. *vrek*, to die, usu. of animals]

vrij *v. see* VRY v.

vroe *n. see* FROE n.[1].

vroom *v.* (*also* **varoom, voom**) [1950s+] (*US*) to go fast, esp. to drive a vehicle at speed. [echoic of the sound of an engine]

vrot *adj.* (*S.Afr.*) **1** [1910s+] rotten, lousy, esp. as a catch-all negative or intensifier, i.e. very much. **2** [1990s+] drunk. [fig. use of Du. *verotten*, to rot]

vrow *n. see* FROE n.[1].

vrow-case *n.* [late 17C–mid-19C] a brothel. [Du. *vrouw*, a woman/VROW n. + CASA n.[1]/CASE n.[3] (3)]

vry *v.* (*also* **fraai, fray, frey, vrij**) [late 19C+] (*S.Afr.*) to caress amorously, to pet; to court, to woo. [synon. Afk. *vry*]

v.s. *n.* [1930s–50s] (*US drugs*) a vein shot, i.e. an intravenous injection of narcotics; a VEIN SHOT n.

V-spot *n. see* V n.[1] (1).

V-town *n.* [1990s+] (*US Black teen*) Vallejo, California. [abbr.]

vuilgat *n.* (*also* **vuilgoed**) [1910s+] (*S.Afr.*) a general term of abuse, esp. to an extremely dirty person. [Afk. *vuil*, foul + GAT n.[2]]

vu ja de *phr.* [1980s+] (*US campus*) a phr. meaning I have never done anything of this sort before, this situation or experience is a complete novelty. [inverse of Fr. *déjà vu*, already seen, used as a phr. to describe the sense that one has been somewhere before, seen or done something previously]

vumpse *v. see* VOOMPSE v.

vut *n.* [1990s+] (*UK juv.*) a failure, an inadequate. [? GO PHUT v.]

v. w/e *adj.* (*also* **v.w.e.**) [1960s+] used in sex contact advertisements, having notably large genitals. [abbr. *very* WELL-ENDOWED adj.]

vyle *n. see* VILE n.

W

W *n.*[1] [1950s+] a lavatory. [abbr. *W.C.*]

W *n.*[2] [1950s+] (*UK Und.*) a warrant for arrest, search etc. [abbr.]

w *v.* [1900s] to cheat, to swindle. [WELCH v.]

waai *v.* [1960s+] (*S.Afr.*) to leave. [Afk. *waai*, to blow]

wabbler *n.*[1] (*also* **wobbler**) [19C] a boiled leg of mutton. [SE *wobble*]

wabbler *n.*[2] *see* FOOT-WABBLER n.

wabbly *adj. see* WOBBLY adj.[2].

wack *see also under* WHACK and its combs.

wack *n. see* WHACKO n.

wack *adj.* (*also* **wacked, whack**) **1** [1980s+] (*US Black*) (*also* **wack-ass, whacked**) second-rate, phoney, unsatisfactory; a general term of opprobrium. **2** [1990s+] positive, extremely good. [orig. popularized in 1986 through the anti-CRACK n.[13] mural by Keith Haring (1958–90), which bore the slogan: 'Crack is wack'. Note W.I. *wacka-tac*, a disagreeable person]

wack around *v.* [1980s] (*US campus*) to act lazily. [WACK adj. (1) + SE *around*]

wacker *n.* [1990s+] a penis (cf. AX n.[2]). [WHACK v.[1] (1)]

wacker *adj.* (*also* **whacker**) [1940s+] (*Aus.*) excellent, wonderful. [WHACK v.[1] (1)]

wack job *n.* [1980s+] (*US*) an eccentric or insane person. [WHACKO n. + JOB n.[6] (1)]

wackness *n.* [2000s] (*US Black*) mediocrity. [WACK adj. (1)]

wacky *see also under* WHACKY and its combs.

wacky dust *n.* [1930s] (*US drugs*) cocaine (cf. BIRDIE POWDER n.). [WHACKY adj. + SE *dust*]

wacky house *n.* [1930s] (*US Und.*) a psychiatric institution. [WHACKY adj. + SE *house*]

wad *n.*[1] **1** [early 19C+] a roll of money or money in general. **2** [late 19C+] (*Aus./US*) a large quantity of a commodity. [repopulared *c.*1985 by UK comedian Harry Enfield's character 'Loadsamoney', with his Thatcherite credo, 'Wad is God'; note RMC Duntroon (*Aus.*) *wad*, one who spends heavily on clothes]

wad *n.*[2] [mid–late 19C] straw used for bedding. [abbr. SE *wadding*]

wad *n.*[3] **1** [20C+] (*orig. US campus*) (*also* **wad-waste**) a fool, an idiot, an unpleasant person. **2** [1970s] (*US campus*) a sexually aggressive male. [WAD n.[6], although this predates it so perhaps just SE *wad*, esp. when used to describe a bundle of post-masturbatory/defecatory tissue (cf. BUNGWAD n./JERKWAD n.); note also the earlier TIGHTWAD n.]

wad *n.*[4] [1900s] (*US campus*) the mouth.

wad *n.*[5] **1** [1910s–30s] a drink of alcohol. **2** [1910s+] (*orig. milit.*) food, esp. a bun, cake or sandwich; in all cases its filling qualities are more important than taste etc; thus *char and wads*, tea and buns. **3** [2000s] (*drugs*) a bag of tobacco or marijuana. [SE *wad*, a bundle]

wad *n.*[6] [1920s+] semen, esp. an ejaculation of semen. [SE *wad*, a bundle; note RMC Duntroon (*Aus.*) *wad*, a womanizer]

-wad *sfx* [1970s+] (*US campus*) an all-purpose usu. negative sfx that can be added freely to any word to mean a fool (cf. BUNGWAD n.; CHEAPWAD n.; DICKWAD n.; DIPWAD n.; DUMBWAD n.; FUCKWAD n.; JERKWAD n.; NIMWAD n.; PUFFWAD n.). [WAD n.[3] (1)]

waddie *n.* (*also* **waddy**) (*US, Western*) **1** [late 19C–1900s] a cowrustler, a person who steals or rebrands cattle. **2** [1900s–50s] a cowboy, esp. a temporary cowhand. [SE *wadding*, something that 'fills in']

waddy *n.* (*also* **waddie**) [early 19C+] (*Aus.*) a club or cudgel. [Dharuk *wadi*, a tree, a stick]

waddy *v.* (*Aus.*) **1** [mid-19C+] to hit someone, usu. with a club or cudgel. **2** [late 19C] to beg, to implore. [WADDY n.]

wade *n.* [19C] a ford. [SE *wade*, to step through water]

wade in *v.* (*also* **wade into**) [mid-19C+] **1** to commit oneself wholeheartedly, esp. to a fight. **2** to commence an action.

waders *n.* [1940s] (*US Black*) boots (there is no suggestion of water as in SE *waders*).

wadge *n.* (*also* **wodge**) **1** [mid-19C+] a thick, chunky, dense lump. **2** [1990s+] (*Irish*) a thick slice of bread. [orig. synon. dial.]

wad-shifter *n.* [1910s–30s] a teetotaller. [WAD n.[5] (2) + SE *shifter*]

wad that would choke a wombat, a *n.* (*also* **a wad that would choke a coal chute, …a donkey**) [20C+] (*Aus./US*) an exceptionally impressive roll of cash (cf. ROLL JACK RICE COULDN'T JUMP OVER, A n.). [WAD n.[1] (1) + SE *choke*]

wad-waste *n. see* WAD n.[3] (1).

wafer-woman *n.* [early 17C–mid-18C] a madame. [? her posing as a legitimate maker of *wafers*, i.e. filigree]

waffle *n.*[1] **1** [1930s+] (*US Und.*) a male homosexual. **2** [1940s] a woman. [SE *waffle*, a form of batter-cake; ? play on SE *waffle iron* and IRON n.[1]]

waffle *n.*[2] [1930s+] nonsense, rubbish. [orig. late 19C printers' jargon; 'twaddle, gossip, or "jaw"' (*OED*)]

waffle *v.*[1] (*also* **whaffle, woffle**) [late 19C+] to dither, to talk nonsense. [orig. Scot./northern dial.; ult. *waff*, to yelp]

waffle *v.*[2] [1970s+] (*US*) to tread or trample. [play on WAFFLE STOMPERS n.]

waffle iron *n.* [1910s] (*US*) a sidewalk or pavement grating. [resemblance]

waffles *n.* [mid-19C] an idler, a loafer. [WAFFLE v.[1]]

waffle stompers *n.* [1970s+] (*US campus*) heavy boots with thick cleated soles that resemble a waffle iron.

wag *n.*[1] [late 19C–1950s] (*Aus./US*) a vagrant. [abbr./pron.]

wag *n.*[2] [late 19C+] **1** a general term of contempt. **2** anyone without firm opinions, a 'yes-man'. [their wagging head, whether through stupidity or the desire to affirm whatever has been said]

wag *n.*[3] *see* WAG-AT-THE-WALL n.

wag *v.*[1] **1** [late 17C+] (*also* **wag off**) to leave, to walk slowly. **2** [19C+] (*US Black*) to procrastinate, to find it hard to make any decisions. **3** [mid-19C+] (*Aus.*) (*also* **wag it, wag off**) to play truant. [SE *vagrant*]

wag *v.*[2] *see* WAG (ONE'S TAIL) v.

wagabone *n. see* VAGABOND n.

wag-at-the-wall *n.* (*also* **wag**) [20C+] (*Irish*) a clock.

wage *n. see* WEDGE n.[1] (1).

wager one's beaver *v. see* BET ONE'S BUTTONS v.

wages *n.* [1920s+] any form of illicit earnings.

wagga *n.* (*also* **wagga blanket/rug**) [20C+] (*Aus.*) an improvised covering, made by stitching together a pair of chaff bags, sacks etc. [*Wagga Wagga*, a town in New South Wales; ult. Aboriginal phr. *many crows*]

wagga-wagga *adj.* [1990s+] (*W.I.*) plentiful, abundant. [Yoruba *waga-waga*, bundled together]

wagger *n.* [late 19C] a truant. [HOP THE WAG v.]

waggle *v.* [late 19C–1900s] (*US*) to overcome, to surpass.

waggon *n.* [1900s–40s] (*S.Afr.*) a cigarette. [? brandname]

waggon lay *n.* [18C] (*UK Und.*) waiting in the street to waylay and rob waggons. [SE *waggon* + LAY n.[4] (1)]

wag hemp in the wind *v.* [mid-16C–early 17C] to be hanged. [the hempen rope]

wag it *v. see* WAG v.[1] (3).

wag off *v. see* WAG v.[1].

wagon *n.*[1] (*also* **bill-wagon**) **1** [late 19C+] (*US*) a police patrol *wagon*. **2** [20C+] an ambulance. **3** [20C+] an automobile.

wagon *n.*[2] [1920s+] (*Irish/US*) **1** a derog. name for a woman. **2** a prostitute (cf. BANBURY n.). [she gives you a 'ride']

wagon *n.*[3] [1930s] (*US Und.*) a revolver. [? the revolving chamber resembles a wagon wheel]

wagon-chasing *adj.* [1950s] of a lawyer, one who fig. pursues the police wagon in the hope of picking up otherwise unrepresented cases.

wag one's bottom *v.* [late 19C+] to work as a prostitute. [var. on WAG (ONE'S TAIL) v.]

wag one's chin *v.* (*also* **wag one's chops, …jaw, …tongue**) [early 18C; late 19C+] to talk, to gossip, to complain. [SE *wag* + SE *chin*/CHOPS n.[1] (1)/JAW n. (1)/SE *jaw/tongue*]

wag one's heels *v. see* KICK UP ONE'S HEELS v.[1].

wag (one's tail) *v.* [late 17C–19C] of a woman, to act in a promiscuous manner; to be a prostitute. [SE *wag* + TAIL n.[2] (3)]

wag one's tongue *v. see* WAG ONE'S CHIN v.

wagon-hunter *n.* [mid-18C] a brothel-keeper's agent who solicited for customers at coaching inns.

wagoning *n.* [mid-late 19C] coach-driving.

wagon-wheel *n. see* WHEEL n.[1] (1).

wagtail *n.* (*also* **water-wagtail**) [late 16C–early 19C] a promiscuous woman, a prostitute; occas. a dissolute man (cf. BANGTAIL n.[1]); also attrib. [SE *wag* + TAIL n.[2] (3)]

wagtailed *adj.* [mid-17C] promiscuous. [WAGTAIL n.]

wail *n.* [1930s] (*US Und.*) a legal trial. [SE *wail*, i.e. the unhappiness occasioned]

wail *v.*[1] **1** [1950s+] (*orig. US Black*) to abandon one's inhibitions, to lose oneself in an activity, esp. of musicians during an improvised solo, or of sexual pleasure. **2** [1960s–70s] (*W.I.*) to behave badly, aggressively; thus *wail down the place*, to dance and sing with utter abandon. **3** [1970s+] (*orig. US Black*) to sing.

wail *v.*[2] *see* WHALE v.[1] (1).

wailing *adj.* (*also* **whaling**) [1950s+] (*US Black/campus*) excellent, wonderful. [WAIL v.[1] (1)]

wail on *v. see* WHALE v.[1] (1).

waistcoateer *n.* (*also* **wastcotier**) [17C–1920s] a prostitute. [the *waistcoat* that served her as a 'badge of office'; 20C use historical]

waistcoat piece *n.* [late 19C] the breast and neck of mutton. [its supposed resemblance to that part of a suit]

waist tog *n.* [mid-19C–1900s] a waistcoat. [SE *waist* + TOG n. (1)]

wait and linger *n.* [20C+] a finger. [rhy. sl.]

waiter *n.* [late 19C] (*Aus.*) a losing horse. [it 'waits' for the rest of the field to finish]

wait for dead men's shoes *v.* [mid-17C–1900s] to expect an inheritance, to hope to succeed to someone else's job.

wajan *n.* (*also* **wajang, wajank**) [20C+] (*W.I., Trin.*) **1** a prostitute, a promiscuous woman, esp. from the slums. **2** an expert. [ety. unknown; ? pron. of SE *wait, John*]

waka blonde *n.* [1980s+] (*N.Z.*) a derog. term for a Maori woman.

wake *n. see* WIDE-AWAKE n.

wake *v. see* WISE UP v.

wake-amine *n.* [1990s+] (*drugs*) amphetamine (cf. A n.[2]). [it 'wakes one up']

wake it! *excl.* [1980s+] (*US campus*) an exhortation to action, get with it!

wake it up! *excl.* [1950s+] (*Aus./N.Z.*) hurry up! get on with it!

wake-me-up *n. see* WAKE-UP n.[3] (1).

wake 'n' bake *v.* [1990s+] (*US drugs*) to smoke marijuana upon waking.

wake snakes *v.* [mid–late 19C] (*US*) to drive to utmost fury, to start moving; also as adj., fast, intense.

wake the dead *v.* [1990s+] to masturbate. [the 'resurrection' of one's flaccid penis]

wake-up *n.*[1] [1930s+] (*Aus.*) an alert and resourceful person, always aware of the possibilities of a situation; thus *to be a (full) wake-up(s)*.

wake-up *n.*[2] [1940s+] (*US prison*) the last day of one's sentence or term of milit. service. [the days left are calculated as 'X and a wake-up'; thus one 'wakes up' in an institution, but goes to bed in freedom; similarly used in US milit. for the final morning of one's service]

wake-up *n.*[3] (*also* **wake-up boost, …hit, …shot**) **1** [1940s+] (*also* **wake-me-up**) the first drink of the day. **2** [1950s+] a narcotics user's first injection of the day; a crack cocaine user's first pipe. **3** [1960s+] any form of stimulant and amphetamine; also as *wake-up pill* (cf. A n.[2]).

wake up *v. see* WISE UP v.

wake up and smell the coffee *v.* [1980s+] to come to one's senses.

wake-up boost/hit/shot *n. see* WAKE-UP n.[3].

wakey, wakey! *excl.* [1940s+] **1** up you get! **2** get a move on! stop day-dreaming! [orig. milit. use; the *locus classicus* was as used on the 1950s radio show the *Billy Cotton Bandshow*, where the eponymous bandleader adopted it as a catchphrase]

wal *n.* [1940s–60s] (*Aus.*) a policeman (cf. BEAT-POUNDER n.). [abbr. WALLOPER n.[1] (4)]

wale *v. see* WHALE v.[1] (1).

Waler *n.* (*also* **whaler**) (*Aus.*) **1** [mid–late 19C] a horse reared in the colony and exported to India. **2** [late 19C+] a native of New South Wales. [abbr.]

waler *see under* WHALER.

walk *n.*[1] **1** [mid-19C; 1970s] the area walked by a street prostitute. **2** [1990s+] (*US prison*) the regular patrol route of a prison warder.

walk *n.*[2] **1** [1950s+] a release from a charge. **2** [1980s] (*US campus*) a release from a class.

walk *v.*[1] [mid-19C] to die.

walk *v.*[2] [late 19C–1900s] (*US campus*) to take an examination without using any form of cheating aid.

walk *v.*[3] [late 19C+] of objects, to go missing (presumed stolen).

walk *v.*[4] **1** [1940s] (*US tramp*) to banish, to eject from a place. **2** [1960s+] to leave, to walk off; to resign. [SE *walk away, walk off*]

walk *v.*[5] [1950s] (*US*) to beat up. [i.e. to 'walk all over']

walk *v.*[6] [1950s+] **1** (*UK Und.*) to be found not guilty. **2** (*US prison/Und.*) to be released from prison or arrest. **3** (*US prison*) to release someone from prison.

walk-about *n.* (*also* **walk-a-leg, walk-a-picky, walker-leg, walker-picky**) [20C+] (*W.I.*) of a woman, a busybody, a gossip. [her tale-telling perambulations]

walk-about money *n.* [1930s+] daily expenses, petty cash rather than a large amount that needs investing or depositing.

walk a chalk line/a crack *v. see* WALK THE CHALK v.

walk-a-leg *n. see* WALK-ABOUT *n.*

walk all over *v. (also* **walk over**) [mid-19C+] **1** to defeat someone comprehensively. **2** to treat someone with contempt.

walkalone *n.* [2000s] (*US prison*) a prisoner who has to exercise alone.

walk and nyam *n.* [early 19C+] (*W.I.*) a poor White; thus a sponger of any race. [SE *walk* + NYAM *v.* (1)]

walk-a-picky *n. see* WALK-ABOUT *n.*

walk around *v. (also* **walk round**) **1** [mid-19C] (*US*) to cheat. **2** [1900s] to defeat easily.

walk-back *n.* [1940s] (*US Black*) an apartment at the rear of the block.

walk backwards up Holborn Hill *v. (also* **push the cart up Holborn Hill, ride backwards up…, ride in a cart up…**) [mid-17C–18C] to go to the gallows. [the road to Tyburn led from Newgate jail along Holborn. Criminals trad. stood in the cart facing backwards, poss. to increase their ignominy, but more likely to avoid seeing the approaching gallows until the last possible moment]

walkboy *n.* [1980s+] (*US Black*) a close male friend. [they *walk* together]

walk-by *n.* [1990s+] (*US Black gang*) a shooting in which the attacker walks past the victim or the victim's home and fires. [on model of DRIVE-BY *n.* (1)]

walk cool *v.* [1960s] (*US Black*) to act in an unconcerned, relaxed manner, esp. in the face of problems or menaces. [SE *walk* + COOL *adv.* (1)]

walk dandy-dude *v.* [1940s] (*W.I.*) to kick out one's legs when walking, the result of a deformity. [SE *walk* + *dandy* + DUDE *n.* (1)]

walk-down *n.* [1940s] (*US Black*) a basement apartment.

walk down one's throat *v.* [late 19C+] to tell off, to scold, to reprimand.

walked off *adj.* [1910s–20s] taken off to prison. [the condemned person is escorted from court]

walker *n.* **1** [mid-19C] a postman, a courier. **2** [mid-19C] (*UK Und.*) a street-walker, a prostitute (cf. NIGHT WALKER *n.*). **3** [1980s+] a man, often rich, invariably personable and socially acceptable, who accompanies the wives of prominent men to parties, on shopping expeditions, to the theatre etc.

walker *v.* [late 19C] to pawn.

walker! *excl.* [19C] an all-purpose teasing, dismissive excl., nonsense! humbug! rubbish! [abbr. HOOKEY WALKER! excl.]

Walker & Co. *n.* [20C+] (*W.I.*) a notional place used fig. to mean a state of unemployment. [one *walks* around searching for work]

walker-leg/-picky *n. see* WALK-ABOUT *n.*

walkers *n.* [early 17C–mid-19C] the feet.

walk-foot *n.* [1900s] (*W.I.*) **1** a poor White. **2** a beggar. [any White who walks rather than rides is assumed to be poor]

walk heavy *v.* [1960s] (*US Black*) to impose oneself on the world, to walk about in a deliberately self-assured manner.

walkie-talkie *n.* [1990s+] (*Aus./US prison*) a prisoner who is overly friendly towards the authorities. [he *walks* and *talks* to the guards]

walk-in *n.* (*US*) **1** [1920s] one who gatecrashes parties. **2** [1960s] a sexually available woman; thus by ext., a prostitute.

walk in *v. see* WALK IT *v.*

walking buckra *n.* [early 19C] (*W.I.*) **1** a poor White. **2** a beggar. [SE *walking* + BUCKRA *n.*; a White man who had no horse and was thus forced to walk was considered of the lowest rank]

walking dandruff *n. see* GALLOPING DANDRUFF *n.*

walking dick with eyes *n.* [1980s] (*US campus*) an insignificant male, a loser. [SE *walking* + DICK *n.*[4] (1); sexually frustrated, he ogles women but dares not make an advance]

walking distiller *n.* [early 19C] one who is easily annoyed, unable to take a joke. [CARRY THE KEG *v.*]

walking gentleman *n.* [late 19C] one who poses as something but lacks the expertise to back the image. [orig. theatrical *walking*

gentleman, 'walking gentleman: an actor playing a part requiring gentlemanlike appearance, but with little or nothing to say' (*OED*)]

walking mort *n.* [mid-16C–17C] (*UK Und.*) an unmarried female beggar, often accompanied by a child, who claimed to be widowed and begged for her and her offspring's keep (cf. CANTING CREW *n.*). [SE *walking* + MORT *n.*]

walking Moses! *excl.* [1910s–20s] a general excl. of surprise, excitement, alarm etc.

walking orders *n.* [early–mid-19C] a notice of dismissal. [var. on WALKING PAPERS *n.* (1)]

walking papers *n.* **1** [early 19C+] (*US*) a notice of dismissal. **2** [early 19C+] an announcement that a relationship is over; divorce papers. **3** [1960s+] (*US prison*) an official notice to inform a prisoner that they have finished their sentence.

walking poulterer *n.* [late 18C–early 19C] a rural thief who steals fowls, then hawks them from door to door.

walking stationer *n.* [late 18C–mid-19C] a hawker of pamphlets, gallows confessions, popular songs and similar materials. [ext. of SE *walking* + *stationer*, a bookseller; cf. early 17C SE *standing stationer*, one who has a stall in a market]

walking the line *phr.* [1980s+] (*Aus. prison*) serving a jail sentence. [rhy. sl. = DO TIME *v.* (1)]

walking ticket *n.* **1** [mid-19C–1900s] (*US*) a notice of dismissal. **2** [1950s+] (*Aus./US prison*) an official notice to inform a prisoner that they have finished their sentence.

walking train *n.* [1920s+] (*W.I.*) a local train. [its lack of velocity]

walking wounded *n.* [1960s+] (*US*) anyone who, despite substantial problems in their life, is still able to function. [orig. WW1 milit.]

walk into *v.* **1** [mid-19C] in fig. use, to approach aggressively, to concentrate on. **2** [mid-19C] to be indebted to, e.g. a tradesman. **3** [mid-19C] to defeat in a game of chance; to win money from. **4** [mid-19C] to spend money freely. **5** [mid-19C] (*US Und.*) to cheat, to defraud. **6** [mid-19C–1900s] to scold, to reprimand. **7** [mid-19C+] to attack, to overcome, to demolish. **8** [mid-19C+] to eat or drink to excess. [all come from the image of making a space or hole, whether in a meal, a purse or a person and *walking into it*]

walk into someone's affections *v.* [mid-19C] **1** to beat, to scold. **2** to run up debts. [ironic uses of SE, to gain someone's love effortlessly]

walk it *v.* (*also* **walk in**) [1930s+] to win easily, usu. in a sporting context. [the relative lack of effort put out]

walk like she can't mash ants *phr.* [20C+] (*W.I.*) used of a woman, implying that she appears far more innocent than her behaviour suggests she is. [note SE phr. *butter wouldn't melt in their mouth*]

walk Matilda *v. see* WALTZ MATILDA *v.*

walk of shame *n.* [1990s+] (*orig. US campus*) a woman's public appearance after spending the night with a new lover.

walk on! *excl.* [1970s+] (*US campus*) a term of dismissal, disbelief, contempt.

walk one's chalks *v.* [mid-19C] to leave, to go away; also as imper. [SE *walk* + CHALKS *n.*]

walk one's dog *v.* [1960s+] (*US*) to urinate or to defecate (cf. DESPATCH ONE'S CARGO *v.*; FLOG THE LIZARD *v.*). [the euph. excuse one makes when leaving the room]

walk one's ferret *v.* [1940s] (*N.Z.*) to masturbate (cf. BEAT ONE'S HOG *v.*).

walk on one's tongue *v.* [1900s] (*Aus.*) to have one's tongue hanging out with thirst.

walk on rocky socks *v.* [20C+] (*US*) to walk unsteadily owing to an excess of drink.

walk out together *v.* (*also* **walk out with**) [1930s+] (*UK society*) to have a clandestine affair. [ironical use of SE *walk out*, to go out with one's fiancé or boy- or girlfriend, usu. in the context of the middle or working classes]

walk over v. see WALK ALL OVER v.

walk round v.[1] [late 19C–1900s] to prepare oneself to face an attack. [the image of a dog circling warily on the lookout for enemies]

walk round v.[2] see WALK AROUND v.

walk soft v. [1970s+] (US Black) to behave modestly.

walk someone's log v. [late 19C] (US campus) to hurt someone.

walktalk n. [1910s+] (Aus.) a stroll on which the walkers chatter together.

walk tall v. [mid-19C+] (orig. US) to behave proudly, courageously and honestly.

walk the barber v. [mid-19C] to seduce a woman. [? ref. to the pubic hair or the trad. link between barbers and blood – hence the red-and-white-striped pole – and the blood of a lost virginity]

walk the black dog on v. [late 18C–early 19C] (UK prison) to inflict a punishment on a new fellow-prisoner who refuses to pay the automatic fine that is levied on him as a new inmate.

walk the boodle v. [early 19C] (US Und.) to distribute counterfeit notes. [SE walk + BOODLE n.[1] (2)]

walk the carpet v. [early 19C] to receive a reprimand, esp. of household servants. [such errant servants were summoned into the carpeted parlour to be told off by the master or mistress]

walk the chalk v. (also **walk a chalk line, …a crack**) **1** [early 19C+] to walk along a chalked line in order to prove one's sobriety. **2** [mid-19C+] (also **toe the chalk, …the crack, …the mark**) to behave in a sober, respectable manner. [(2) is fig. use of (1)]

walk the check v. [1970s+] (US campus) to walk deliberately out of a restaurant without paying the bill. [abbr. SE walk away from the check (SAmE for cheque)]

walk the dog v. [1910s+] (US) to show off by driving or walking at speed.

walk the piazzas v. [early 19C] to (start) work as a prostitute. [the piazzas of Covent Garden were popular among prostitutes]

walk the plank v. [late 19C+] (US) to be dismissed from a job. [the trad. punishment of Caribbean pirates]

walk the pony v. [1980s] to visit the lavatory. [SE walk + PONY (AND TRAP) n.]

walk the way of a trollop v. [1990s+] (US campus) a woman, to signal sexual availability. [a play on the more usu. walk the way of the warrior, much loved by martial arts films etc]

walk turkey v. [late 19C] to walk around in a strutting manner. [such a promenade supposedly resembles a turkey's walk]

walk-up n. **1** [1910s+] (US) an apartment on an upper floor that has to be reached by the stairs because no lift exists. That which lacks not only lifts but also proper plumbing is a coldwater walk-up. Less common terms are the WALK-DOWN n., a basement apartment, and the walk-back, an apartment at the back of the block. **2** [1990s+] a shooting that is carried out on foot. [(1) abbr. SE walk-up apartment; (2) var. on WALK-BY n.]

walk up (against) the wall v. [late 18C–early 19C] to run up credit at a public house. [the landlord chalks one's running debts on the wall]

walk-up fuck n. [20C+] (Aus.) a woman who is readily available for sex. [SE walk up + FUCK n.[1] (1); one needs only to walk up and ask]

walk up Ladder Lane and down Hemp Street v. [19C] to be hanged. [orig. naut. jargon]

walk up the wall v. see WALK UP (AGAINST) THE WALL v.

wallaby n. [mid-19C+] (Aus.) a vagrant; a swagman; also attrib. [his nomadic life]

wallaby v. [1900s] (Aus.) to wander around. [WALLABY n.]

wallaby track n. [mid-19C+] (Aus.) the route followed by an itinerant moving from station to station in search of work; thus

hit the wallaby, to set off down the road, as a tramp. [WALLABY n. + SE track]

Wallace and Gromit v. [2000s] to vomit (cf. HALLEY'S COMET n.). [rhy. sl.; ult. Oscar-winning animated plasticine characters Wallace and Gromit created by Nick Park]

Wallace Beery n. [1990s+] a query, a question. [rhy. sl.; ult. US film star Wallace Beery (1885–1949)]

wallah n. **1** [mid-18C+] a man, esp. in the sense of a man who is pertaining to or connected with something, usu. a job. **2** [1960s+] a bureaucrat, an administrator. [Hind. sfx wala, pertaining to or connected with, in turn from the Arabic wal, proximity. It is the equivalent, therefore, of the Lat. -arius. Although found today as a single term, its 19C uses tended to be in combs., such as Agra wallah, a native of Agra; banghy-wallah, a porter who carries loads with a banghy, or shoulder-yoke; howdah-wallah, an elephant accustomed to carry a howdah; and the Anglo-Indian competition wallah, those who entered the Civil Service competitive exams, established in 1856 to replace the old system of personal patronage]

wall-banger n. [1960s+] (US teen/drugs) **1** a Quaalude or methaqualone capsule. **2** anyone who is so intoxicated by drugs that they cannot walk straight. [the effect of methaqualone is to slow and 'soften' one's movements]

wallbanging n. [1980s+] (US gang) painting graffiti, esp. gang slogans or gang nicknames, on walls. [SE wall + bang, i.e. one 'hits' a wall]

Wall City n. [1930s] (US Und.) San Quentin prison, California (cf. ABBOTT'S PRIORY n.). [the prison walls + CITY sfx]

waller n. [2000s] (US Black) a general derog. term.

wall-eyed adj. **1** [mid–late 19C] of any work, badly done. **2** [20C+] of any odd or irregular action. **3** [1910s+] (US) drunk (cf. ARSE-HOLED adj.). **4** [2000s] under the influence of marijuana. [SE wall-eyed, squinting]

wall-falling adj. [1970s+] (Irish) exhausted, tired out.

wallflower n. **1** [early 19C+] a woman (occas. a man) who does not join in dancing at a ball or dance, either through her inability to find a partner or through her desire to remain solo; thus a retiring, shy person. **2** [1980s] (UK prison) a prisoner obsessed with the possibility of escape. [(1) fig. use of SE; (2) fig. use of (1)]

wallflowers n. [early–mid-19C] old or second-hand clothes hanging up for sale. [joc. use of WALLFLOWER n. (1)]

wallflower week n. [20C+] those days during which a woman is menstruating and is, trad., sexually inactive. [WALLFLOWER n. (1) + SE week]

wall fruit n. [mid-19C] kissing up against a wall.

wall-hugger n. [1980s+] an eccentric, a mad person; thus wall-hugging, crazed.

wallio n. see WALYO n.

wall it v. [late 18C–mid-19C] to chalk up a debt on the wall of a public house.

wall job n. [1950s] (US gay) anal intercourse performed in a standing position. [SE wall + JOB n.[4]]

wallop n.[1] **1** [early 19C+] (orig. boxing) (also **whollop, wollop**) a resounding blow; lit. or fig.; thus come a wallop, to take a fall. **2** [1910s] a time, a share. **3** [1910s+] a try. **4** [1930s] a success. [WALLOP v. (2)]

wallop n.[2] [late 19C+] (orig. Aus.) beer, alcohol in general. [ext. of WALLOP n.[1] (1), i.e. its strength; in WW2 beer only]

wallop v. **1** [early 18C–1910s] to make violent, noisy movements, to move clumsily or convulsively, to flounder. **2** [early 19C+] (also **whollop, wollop**) to beat, to thrash, to hit hard. **3** [late 19C+] to overcome, to surpass, to defeat. **4** [1990s+] to have sexual intercourse (cf. BANG v.[1]). [? Walloon waloper, to beat linen in water or Fr. galoper/Ital. gallopare, to gallop]

wallop! excl. [20C+] indicative of a sudden action.

walloper n.[1] **1** [early 19C] a blow. **2** [early 19C+] anyone who beats up their victims with a cudgel or stick. **3** [1910s+] one who beats, e.g. hits a child. **4** [1930s+] (*Aus.*) a policeman (cf. BEAT-POUNDER n.). **5** [1940s] a clumsy fellow. **6** [1980s+] (*Aus.*) the penis (cf. AX n.²). [WALLOP v. (2)]

walloper *n.²* [late 19C+] (*US*) anything or anyone exceptional in quality, size, character etc. [WALLOPING adj. (2)]

walloper *n.³* [1930s] a hotel, a bar. [WALLOP n.²]

wallopies *n.* [1970s+] (*US campus*) female breasts, esp. large ones (cf. BOBBER n.²). [Scot. *wallop*, to dangle, to flop about]

walloping *n.* [1990s+] an act of sexual intercourse. [WALLOP v. (4)]

walloping *adj.* **1** [early 19C] clumsy, awkward. **2** [mid-19C+] (*also* **wholloping**) a general intensifier, usu. as to size and often ext. as *walloping great*. **3** [late 19C+] in fig. use, powerful. [WALLOP v.]

wallop it in *v.* [late 19C+] to penetrate sexually, therefore to have sexual intercourse (cf. BANG v.¹; BURY IT v.). [WALLOP v. (1)]

wallop someone's block off *v. see* KNOCK SOMEONE'S BLOCK OFF v.

wallpaper *n.* **1** [1940s+] (*US*) worthless paper money such as counterfeit notes. **2** [1980s+] (*drugs*) money (cf. BANK-RAG n.). [(1) it has no monetary use; (2) one has enough to use it as wallpaper]

wall-prop, be a *v. see* MAKE WALLPAPER v.

wall queen *n.* [1970s] (*US gay*) **1** a man who leans against a wall while he has sex. **2** a gay man who enjoys reading the inscriptions on public lavatory walls. [SE *wall* + QUEEN n.² (1)/QUEEN sfx (2)]

wall-to-wall *adj.* [1960s+] everywhere, all over. [abbr. SE *wall-to-wall carpet*]

wally *n.¹* [late 19C+] a pickled cucumber.

wally *n.²* (*also* **wolly**) **1** [1920s+] an unfashionable, unintelligent, 'suburban' person, lacking in taste and sophistication. **2** [1930s] (*US tramp*) a tramp who stays within a given radius of his home town. **3** [1970s] a person with learning difficulties. **4** [1970s+] (*Aus.*) a bungler. **5** [1990s+] (*US campus*) an otherwise socially unacceptable person who is accepted into a social group because needed for intelligence, athletic ability or good looks. [ety. unknown; ? abbr. Scot. *wally-drag*, a feeble, ill-grown or worthless person. The proper name *Walter* is sometimes categorized as a 'silly' name. In police jargon, a *wally* is a trainee and thus incompetent policeman; ext. of WALLY n.¹; but note CORNICHON n. ety.]

wally *n.³* [1980s+] (*US campus*) used as a nickname for someone seen as acting like a big brother or sister. [the older brother character *Wally* in US TV show *Leave It to Beaver*]

Wally Grout *n.* [1990s+] (*Aus.*) one's turn to buy a round of drinks. [rhy. sl. = SHOUT n.¹ (2); ult. Aus. wicket keeper *Wally Grout* (1927–68)]

Wally-O *n. see* WALYO n.

wally the monk *adj.* [1980s] (*Aus.*) drunk (cf. ADRIAN (QUIST) adj.). [rhy. sl.]

walnut-shell *n.* [early 19C] a very light carriage. [resemblance]

walnut whip *n.* [1990s+] **1** a sleep. **2** a nipple. **3** a vasectomy. [rhy. sl.; (1) = KIP n.¹ (4); (2) = NIP n.⁵; (3) = SE *snip*]

walrus *n.* **1** [1910s–60s] a large, bushy moustache, supposedly reminiscent of the animal. **2** [1920s+] (*US*) a short, fat person. **3** [2000s] (*Irish*) £50 (cf. FOAL n.).

walter joyce *n.* [late 19C] the voice. [rhy. sl.]

Walter Mitty *n.* [1980s+] (*Aus.*) the female breast (cf. BRACE AND BITS n.). [rhy. sl. = TITTY n.¹ (1); ult. the novel *The Secret Life of Walter Mitty* (1941) by James Thurber]

Walter Scott *n.* [1950s+] a pot (of beer). [rhy. sl.; ult. novelist Sir *Walter Scott* (1771–1832)]

waltz *n.* [1920s+] **1** anything that can be accomplished with minimum effort. **2** an easy success, esp. in sporting use, e.g. a boxing match in which neither fighter makes much effort. [WALTZ v.²]

waltz *v.¹* (*also* **waltz along, ...around, ...in, ...into, ...off, ...up**) **1** [late 19C+] to move lightly, blithely, unconcernedly. **2** [late 19C+] to move or to take someone. **3** [1970s] (*US*) to evade or deceive someone.

waltz *v.²* [1960s+] to achieve something easily, esp. in sporting use.

waltz into *v.* [1910s+] to attack.

waltz Matilda *v.* (*also* **walk Matilda**) [late 19C+] (*Aus.*) to go on the tramp, carrying one's pack; thus *Matilda-waltzer*, a tramp. [SE *waltz* + MATILDA n.]

waltz me around *n.* [1980s] (*Aus.*) a pound. [rhy. sl.]

waltz off *v. see* WALTZ v.¹.

waltz off on the ear *v.* [late 19C] (*US*) to act precipitately, on the basis of hearing a statement but not considering its implications. [ext. WALTZ OFF v. + ON THE EARIE phr. (2)]

waltz up *v. see* WALTZ v.¹.

walyo *n.* (*also* **wallio, Wally-O**) [20C+] (*US*) **1** a young man, often used affectionately by an older man. **2** an Italian man (cf. DAGO n.). [? Ital. dial. *uaglio*, a young one]

wamba *n. see* WONGA n.

wamble *n.* [mid–late 17C] a feeling of nausea, queasiness; often as *the wambles*; thus *wamble-cropped, wamble-stomached*, feeling nauseous, sick. [SE *wamble*, to feel queasy, to walk unsteadily; ? ult. Dan. *vamle*, to feel nausea + Norw. *vamla*, to stagger]

wamblety-cropped *adj.* (*also* **wamble-cropped, womble-script, womblety-cropped**) [late 17C–mid-19C] suffering from an upset stomach due to excessive drinking. [SE *wamble-cropped*, sick in the stomach]

wame *n.* [late 18C–early 19C] the vagina. [Scot. *wame*, the womb, the stomach]

wampo *n.* [1940s+] beer slops or overflow, recycled and served as fresh beer. [? RAF sl. *wampo*, intoxicating liquor; ? note *Wampole*, a preparation of alcohol, quinine and strychnine sold by an eponymous US drug firm *c.*1910]

wampum *n.* [mid-19C+] (*orig. US*) money. [Algonquin *wampumpeag*, beads made from quahog shells and used as money; often abbr. to *wampum* itself]

wampum and warpaint *n.* [late 19C] evening dress. [*wampum*, beads, worn as ornamental garments or jewellery + WARPAINT n. (3)]

wampus *n.* [1950s] (*W.I.*) a large man. [? abbr. CATAWAMPUS n. (2)]

wampy *adj.* [1950s–70s] (*N.Z.*) mad, insane. [? WAMPO n.]

wana *n.* [1970s+] (*drugs*) marijuana. [abbr./pron.]

wan and wan *n. see* ONE-AND-ONE n.¹.

wand *n.* [17C+] the penis.

Wanda Wandwaver *n.* [1960s–70s] (*camp gay*) an exhibitionist. [WAND n. + SE *waver*]

wander! *excl.* [late 19C] go away!

wandering star *n.* [mid-19C] a woman who coyly seduces men in the street in order to rob them.

Wandering Willie *n.* [1910s–30s] (*US*) a vagrant, a tramp.

wang *n.¹* [1920s–40s] a notable person.

wang *n.²* (*also* **wanger, wang-wang, wing-wang**) **1** [1930s+] (*orig. US*) the penis. **2** [1990s+] (*S.Afr.*) a cigarette. [WHANG n.⁵; (2) resembles the shape of (1)]

wanga *n. see* WONGA n.

wanga-gut *n.* (*also* **wonga-gut**) [1980s+] (*W.I./UK Black teen*) greediness or jealousy. [? WONGA n. + SE *gut*, i.e. one is 'hungry' for cash]

wangdoodle *see under* WHANGDOODLE.

wanger *n. see* WANG n.².

wangle *n.* [late 19C–1910s] (*Irish*) a thin, tall, weak young man. [dial. *wangling*, sickly, weak, delicate]

wangle *v.* [late 19C+] to obtain what one wants, often through a degree of manipulation or cunning.

wangled *adj.* [1940s] stolen. [WANGLE v.]

wangler *n.* [1910s–20s] one who uses a variety of irregular means to accomplish a purpose. [WANGLE v.]

wanglo-saxon *n.* [1970s] (*US*) a White *Anglo-Saxon*.

wang-tang *n.* [1970s] (*US Black*) anything, esp. on a sexual level, that is particularly desirable. [? fig. use of WANG n.² (1) + SE *tang*, a flavour]

wang-wang *n. see* WANG n.².

wangy *n.* [1910s] (*US tramp*) a beggar who sells bootlaces as a front for his basic trade of begging.

wank *n.*¹ **1** [1940s+] an act of masturbation. **2** [1970s+] in fig. use, self-indulgence. **3** [1980s] (*US campus*) a person who is logged on to a computer (usu. the Internet or involved in hacking) for a long time. **4** [1990s+] nonsense. **5** [2000s] something worthless. [WANK v.]

wank *n.*² *see* WANKER n. (2).

wank *adj.* [1980s+] a general pej. epithet, unpleasant, distasteful, useless etc.

wank *v.* (*also* **whank**) [1940s+] **1** to masturbate (cf. BOFF v.); also ext. as WANK OFF v. **2** to waste time. **3** to abuse someone else. **4** to be logged onto a computer for a long time. [ety. unknown, but note the many 'beating' synons., the orig. sp. *whank* and late 18C Scot./dial. *whank*, to beat, to thrash]

wank! *excl.* [1970s+] (*US campus*) a general negative retort. [WANK v.]

wank-bag *n.* [1990s+] a general term of abuse. [WANK n.¹ (1) + -BAG sfx]

wanked *adj. see* WANKERED adj.

wanked out *adj.* [1970s+] exhausted. [fig. use of WANK v. + SE *out*]

wanker *n.* [1940s+] **1** a masturbator. **2** (*also* **wank**) a general derog. description of a lazy, incompetent, unpleasant person. **3** (*US campus*) an undesirable situation or thing. **4** the penis. [WANK v. (1); note late 19C Yorks./Norfolk dial. *wanker*, a simpleton; E.P. suggests origin in 'late C.19' but offers no evidence]

wankered *adj.* (*also* **wanked**) [1990s+] **1** exhausted, worn-out. **2** having consumed a large quantity of alcohol or drugs. [fig. use of WANK v. (1)]

wanker's doom *n.* [1940s+] (*orig. RAF*) a fig. unpleasant fate. [WANK v. (1), i.e. the insanity that awaits those who believe that masturbation is indeed a debilitating sin]

wankily *adv.* [1990s+] in a second-rate manner. [WANKY adj. (3)]

wanking *n.* [1940s+] masturbation. [WANK v. (1)]

wanking spanners *n.* [1940s+] the hands. [WANKING n. + SE *spanners*]

wank mag *n.* [1960s+] a pornographic magazine. [WANK v. (1) + colloq. SE *mag*, a magazine]

wank off *v.* [1940s+] **1** to masturbate (cf. BALL OFF v.²). **2** to masturbate another person, usu. male. [ext. of WANK v. (1)]

wank on *v.* [1980s+] to bore, to talk nonsense for a long time. [fig. use of WANK v. (1)]

wankshaft *n.* [1990s+] (*UK juv.*) the penis. [WANK v. (1) + SE *shaft*/SHAFT n.¹]

wanksta *n.* [2000s] **1** a White person espousing Black gangster culture. **2** a would-be gangster. [WACK adj. (1)/WANNABE adj./WANKER n. (2) + GANGSTA n. (2)]

wankstain *n.* [1990s+] an ineffectual person. [WANK n.¹ + SE *stain*]

wankstain *adj.* [2000s] ineffectual, worthless. [WANKSTAIN n.]

wank-tank *n.* [2000s] a large, ostentatious car, purchased for the enhancement of its owner's ego and the display of his material success. [WANK n.¹ (2) + SE *tank*]

wank the crank *v.* [1960s+] to masturbate. [WANK v. (1) + CRANK n.⁵ (1)]

wanky *adj.* **1** [1920s+] pretentious. **2** [1940s+] covered in post-masturbatory semen. **3** [1970s+] inferior, second-rate. **4** [1970s+] sexually titillating, conducive to masturbation. **5** [1980s] (*US juv.*) crazy. [fig./lit. uses of WANK v. (1); however, note the 1923 use by 'Bartimeus' in *Seaways*: 'Wanky Willy,' the First Lieutenant who

sometimes drank rather more port than was good for him – anyhow, when there was an 'occasion']

wannabe *n.* **1** [1970s+] an aspirant, one who yearns to be a certain individual, usu. more talented and famous than they are. **2** [1990s+] (*US prison*) a young prisoner who poses as a prison-wise veteran. [SE *I want to be…*, orig. US Black, where the term simply meant a fantasist and latterly a White person wishing to be Black + from surfing jargon for a learner. Popularized with the rise of the pop star Madonna (Madonna Louise Veronica Ciccone, b.1958), whose fans declared, either verbally or in the way they dressed, *I wanna be like Madonna*]

wannabe *adj.* [1980s+] aspirant. [WANNABE n. (1)]

wannabe raped look *n.* [1980s+] of a woman, a sluttish, provocative style of dressing. [ext. of SE *want to be raped*]

wanna bet? *phr. see* WANT TO BET (ON IT)? phr.

wanna do a thing? *phr.* [1960s+] (*US Black*) asking a passing woman if she fancies intercourse. [SE *want* + DO A THING v. (1)]

Wanno *n.* [1990s+] (*UK Und.*) HMP *Wandsworth*, in south London. [abbr. + -O sfx (6)]

wansteads *n.* [1920s–30s] spats. [rhy. sl.; *Wanstead Flats* = spats; ult. East London area *Wanstead Flats*]

want *n.* **1** [20C+] (*Irish*) any form of mental deficiency. **2** [1970s] (*US police*) a charge. [(1) such a person is *in want* of some brains]

want an apron *v.* [late 19C] to be out of work. [an era when workmen wore some form of apron – before the modern overall – while at work]

want in *v.* [20C+] to desire to make oneself part of.

wanting *adj.* [mid-19C] mentally unbalanced, insane. [SE *wanting* intelligence, brains etc]

wanton ace *n.* [19C] the vagina. [SE *wanton* + ACE OF SPADES n.²]

want one's hip buttons *v.* [20C+] (*Ulster*) to be less than wholly intelligent.

want out *v.* [late 19C+] to wish to be disassociated from.

want portholes in one's coffin *v.* [1910s] (*Aus.*) to be hard to please.

want salt *v.* [late 19C] (*US*) to be a weakling; to need 'grit' of character. [SE *want* + *salt*, that which enhances flavour]

want some *v.* [1970s+] (*US campus*) to search for sex. [SE *want* + SOME n. (2)]

want some? *phr.* [1970s+] a form of verbal challenge that may lead onto a fight. [SE *want* + SOME n. (1)]

want something yesterday *v.* (*also* **need something yesterday**) [1970s+] to want something as quickly as possible.

want to bet (on it)? *phr.* (*also* **wanna bet?**) [1940s+] a challenging refutation of the previous speaker's assertion.

want to front *v. see* TRY TO FRONT v.

want to make something of it? *phr.* (*also* **want to do something about it?**) [1920s+] (*orig. US*) a ritual request that may well herald a fight, but still gives the other person the chance to back down.

want to piss like a dressmaker *v.* [late 19C] to be desperate to urinate. [? a dressmaker working in a sweatshop and not permitted to take a break]

wantz *n.* [1970s] (*US*) the penis. [abbr. SCHWANTZ n. (1)]

wap *n.* [early 18C] the act of copulation. [WAP v.]

wap *v.* [mid-16C–early 19C] to have sex, usu. used of a woman. [SE *wap*, to throw violently, to pull down; Henke, *Gutter Life and Language* (1988), suggests link to *wap*, a mongrel and thence to BITCH n.¹ (1)]

wapi *n.* [1950s] (*W.I.*) sexual intercourse. [? WAP n.]

wap-john *n.* [mid-19C] a gentleman's coachman. [SE *wap*, to hit + JOHN n.¹ (1)]

wappen-bappen *n.* [1930s+] (*W.I.*) a tumbledown slum shed or shanty made of old tins, bits of wood, discarded packaging and similar found objects. [echoic of hammering such a shack together]

wapper-eyed adj. [early 17C–early 19C] sore-eyed, squinting. [dial. wapper, to have sore eyes, to blink]

wapper-jawed adj. see WHOPPER-JAWED adj.

wapping n. [mid-16C–18C] sexual intercourse. [WAP v.]

wapping adj. see WHOPPING adj.

wapping-dell n. (also **wapping-mort**) [17C–mid-18C] a prostitute. [WAP v. + DELL n. (2)/MORT n.]

wapping ken n. [mid-18C] (UK Und.) a brothel (cf. BADGER-CRIB n.). [WAPPING n. + KEN n.¹ (1)]

wappy adj. [1950s–60s] sentimental, idealistic. [? SE wet + soppy]

waps n. (also **wap-waps**) [1990s+] the female breasts. [SE wap, to move, to shake]

warahoon n. [1960s+] (W.I.) a noisy ill-bred person. [? name of a tribe of (unidentified) South American coastal Amerindians, poss. the Warrau of the Orinoco Delta and northwest Guyana]

war and strife n. [1900s–70s] one's wife. [rhy. sl.]

warap n. [20C+] (W.I.) **1** a cheap, tasteless meal, esp. a soup. **2** a cheap meal made of fish or meat and 'ground-provisions', i.e. locally available starchy roots, all boiled up together. [Carib.E. warap, a drink made from fermented sugar-cane, drunk by poor peasants]

wara-wara n. [20C+] (W.I., Jam.) bits and pieces. [WARA-WARA adj.]

wara-wara adj. [20C+] (W.I., Guyn.) cheap, of inferior quality, esp. of clothing. [Yoruba wara-wara, half done, in a hurry]

warb n. [1930s+] **1** (Aus.) a fool, a simpleton. **2** (Aus.) a dirty, unkempt person; a loafer. **3** (UK Und.) a drunkard, a down-and-out. **4** (Aus.) a low-paid manual worker. [? SE warble, the maggot of a warble-fly]

war baby n. **1** [1910s–20s] (UK/Aus.) a young or newly conscripted soldier. **2** [1920s; 1940s] an illegitimate child, conceived and born while the mother's husband is away on active service. **3** [1920s–40s] (US) a bond that is sold during wartime with the presumption that it will 'grow' in value. **4** [1940s] (US Und.) money gained through the successful hoaxing of a man who had made his money in the still-recent WW1.

warble v. [late 19C+] to talk in a pleasant manner.

warbler n. **1** [mid-18C; late 19C–1920s] a male singer. **2** [early 19C] a singer who 'go[es]' about to "free and easy" meetings, to chaunt for pay, for grog, or for the purpose of putting off benefit-tickets' (Bee). **3** [early 19C; 1920s+] a female singer. **4** [1940s–50s] (US Und.) a public defender. **5** [1970s+] a telephone whose bell warbles rather than rings.

warby adj. [1940s+] (Aus.) **1** unprepossessing in appearance or disposition, unkempt, disreputable, decrepit. **2** insecure, unwell. [WARB n.]

war club n. [20C+] (US) a baseball bat.

war cry n. [late 19C] a mixture of stout and mild ale. [a satire on the Salvation Army newspaper The War Cry and the belief that while the Army spoke 'stoutly' it used only 'mild' terms]

war daddy n. [2000s] (US prison) an inmate who protects another from problems while incarcerated; the protected inmate will be expected to offer homosexual services.

warden n. [1950s–60s] (US teen) a parent or any other authority figure.

ware n. **1** [17C–early 19C] the vagina; the maidenhead; thus generic for a woman (cf. BANK n.¹). **2** [late 18C] the penis. [SE ware, goods on sale, thus the commercial potential of sex]

ware hawk! excl. see WARE (THE) HAWK! excl.

warehouse n. **1** [1900s–20s] (UK society) a large, fashionable pawn shop. **2** [1930s] (US) a bank. **3** [1960s+] a large and impersonal institution offering shelter to the mentally ill, the old or the poor. **4** [2000s] (US prison) an overcrowded prison.

warehouse v. **1** [late 19C] to imprison. **2** [1900s–20s] (UK society) to place in pawn. **3** [1970s+] (US) to place an individual, usu. a mental patient, in a large and impersonal institution, i.e. to 'put them away'. [WAREHOUSE n.]

ware (the) hawk! excl. (also **ware the bull!**) [17C–1900s] a warning cry, orig. indicating that a bailiff or constable is approaching; thus war-hawk, a bailiff. [hunting jargon ware hawk! a warning cry either to or of animals. The hawk personifies any 'grasping' person, whether working for or against the law]

warhorse n. **1** [late 19C+] (US) a veteran, an old-timer. **2** [1930s] (US campus) an uncompromising, determined woman.

warlord n. [1950s+] **1** (US Black/teen) a street-gang leader. **2** (US prison) a gang leader, who takes control of gang fights and killings, although not the absolute head of a gang.

warm adj.¹ **1** [17C–1900s] rich, well-off. **2** [mid-18C] enthusiastic, zealous. **3** [mid-18C] slightly drunk (cf. ABOUT RIGHT phr.¹). **4** [mid-18C+] sharp-tempered. **5** [early 19C–1920s] of speech, suggestive. **6** [mid-19C–1920s] unpleasant, uncomfortable. **7** [mid-19C–1950s] (UK Und.) under suspicion; of a place, dangerous for criminal activity. **8** [mid-19C+] of a situation or place, exciting, active. **9** [late 19C] of a bill, large, poss. exorbitant. **10** [late 19C] of a picture, smutty. **11** [late 19C–1910s] (US) able, competent. **12** [late 19C+] of a woman, sexy, provocative. **13** [1910s–30s] (Aus.) intimate. **14** [1990s+] (US Black) human, affectionate, the opposite of COOL adj.¹ (1).

warm adj.² see HOT adj.¹ (14).

warm v. [late 18C+] to thrash, to beat, esp. in descriptive combs., such as WARM SOMEONE'S JACKET v., warm someone's arse, to thrash.

warm adv. [20C+] (W.I.) a great deal, much.

warm as they make them phr. [late 19C] of a woman, very sexy. [ext. of WARM adj.¹ (12)]

warm baby n. see HOT BABY n.

warm beer n. [1970s+] urine. [its colour]

warm bit n. [late 19C] a promiscuous, sexy woman. [WARM adj.¹ (12) + BIT n.² (1)]

warm body n. [20C+] (US) an insignificant person, someone who is present but does not participate.

warm corner n. [mid-19C–1900s] anywhere frequented by prostitutes. [WARM adj.¹ (12) + SE corner]

warmed over adj. [late 19C+] (US) derivative, unimaginative. [SE warm over, of food, to reheat, to warm up]

warm flannel n. see HOT FLANNEL n.

warm fuzzy n. [2000s] (US) a compliment, praise. [its effects on the listener]

warming pan n.¹ **1** [17C] the vagina. **2** [mid-17C–mid-18C] a female bed companion. **3** [mid-19C–1900s] a place-holder, a deputy, used orig. of clergy.

warming pan n.² [late 17C–19C] a large, gold pocket watch. [the shape]

warm in the tail phr. see HOT IN THE TAIL phr.

warm member n. [late 19C–1920s] (US) a promiscuous man, a philanderer. [WARM adj.¹ (12) + SE member, a participant/MEMBER n.¹]

warm-mouth n. [1950s] (W.I.) the very first meal of the day, eaten between 4 a.m. and 6 a.m. and preceding a proper breakfast.

warm shop n. (also **warm show**) [1910s–20s] a brothel (cf. BANGING-SHOP n.). [WARM adj.¹ (12) + SE shop/SHOP n.¹ (1)]

warm someone's ear v. **1** [20C+] (Ulster) to hit someone across the ear; usu. in unexecuted threat, I'll warm your ear (for you!). **2** [1920s–30s] (US) to chatter and gossip incessantly.

warm someone's jacket v. [late 18C–1930s] to thrash someone, esp. in the context of school beatings.

warm the cockles (of the heart) v. [late 17C; late 18C+] to cheer up, to delight. [? the resemblance of the heart to a cockleshell or the zoological name of the cockle, cardium, which in Gk means heart]

warm the husband's supper v. (also **warm the husband's dinner, ...the old man's supper**) [19C] to stand in front of the fire with lifted skirts.

warm the oven v. [mid-19C] to drink, to get drunk.

warm the wax of someone's ear v. [mid-19C–1910s] to box someone's ears. [WARM v. + SE *wax + ear*]

warm the whole of one's body v. [20C+] to stand with one's back to the fire. [pun on *whole/hole*, i.e. the anus]

warm 'un n. [late 19C] a prostitute. [WARM adj.¹ (12) + SE *one*]

warm up n. [1970s+] **1** sexual foreplay. **2** a wash before intercourse. [(1) WARM UP v.; (2) sporting imagery, i.e. exercising to prepare oneself for the match]

warm up v. [1900s–70s] to indulge in sexual foreplay. [WARM adj.¹ (12)]

warm with n. [mid-late 19C] a drink of *warm* spirits and water *with* sugar (cf. HOT WITH n.).

warp n. (*also* **warpe**) [late 16C–mid-17C] (*UK Und.*) the lookout man for a team of thieves who steal by hooking objects from stalls or shop windows. [? SE *ward*, to watch]

warpaint n. **1** [mid-19C] military uniform. **2** [mid-19C–1920s] court dress, formal dress. **3** [mid-19C+] cosmetics, make-up.

warped adj. [2000s] (*Irish*) drunk.

warp out v. (*also* **warp away**) [1990s+] (*US*) to leave hastily. [the use of *warp speed* in the *Star Trek* TV series (from 1966) and films (from 1980)]

warp-seven adj. [1990s+] (*US Black*) very fast. [WARP OUT v.]

warrab n. [mid-19C] a barrow. [backsl.]

warra-warra n. [1950s+] (*W.I. Rasta*) a euph. for politely omitted obscenities. [the mumbling that replaces the actual words]

warren n.¹ **1** [late 16C–early 19C] a brothel (cf. BIRDCAGE n.¹). **2** [late 17C–early 19C] a boarding school. [abbr. CUNNY WARREN n.]

warren n.² [17C–early 19C] a creditor, part of a confidence team that encourages rich young men to run up large bills and then DUN v. them. [? SE *warrant*]

warrior bold adj. (*also* **warrior's hold**) [20C+] cold; also as n., a cold in the head. [rhy. sl.]

warrocks! excl. [late 19C] (*US*) beware! look out! [SE *war hawks!* i.e. tomahawks, and presumably referring to a native American attack]

war stories n. [1960s+] (*US*) stories of one's adventurous exploits, e.g. in a street gang; real war plays no part.

wart n. [late 19C+] (*orig. US*) an unpleasant, obnoxious person. [note milit. use *wart*, (RN) a junior midshipman, (British Army) a young subaltern]

warts and all phr. [1910s+] not excluding any deficiencies or negative characteristics. [the story of Oliver Cromwell (1599–1658) ordering the painter Sir Peter Lely (1618–80) to 'use all your skill to paint my picture truly like me, and not flatter me at all; but remark all these roughnesses, pimples, warts and everything as you see me, otherwise I will never pay a farthing for it']

Warwick Farm n. [1940s+] (*Aus.*) an arm. [rhy. sl.; ult. *Warwick Farm*, a Sydney racecourse]

waser n. (*also* **wasser**) [1900s–10s] a young woman. [Fr. *oiseau*, a bird]

wash n.¹ **1** [early 18C; mid-19C] tea. **2** [mid-19C+] beer, also as an accompaniment to a spirit. **3** [late 19C] (*Aus.*) a tea-party. **4** [1940s] (*US*) soda water. **5** [1940s+] (*US*) a second drink, one to wash down the first.

wash n.² [1910s] verbal nonsense. [abbr. EYEWASH n. (1)]

wash n.³ **1** [1960s+] (*W.I.*) the mash of cheap grain and sugar that is distilled to produce the homemade spirit sold in illicit drinking clubs. **2** [1970s] (*US drugs*) a mix of heroin, water and blood that is injected by the user. [SE *wash*, malt etc steeped in water to undergo fermentation]

wash n.⁴ [1980s+] crack cocaine (cf. BASE n.). [the process of chemical purification, known as WASHING n., that is used when making the drug]

wash n.⁵ see WHITEWASH n.².

wash v.¹ [mid-19C+] to stand a test, to face questioning; usu. in negative phr. *it/that won't wash*, the topic will not bear analysis or investigation.

wash v.² [1930s–70s] (*US Und.*) to kill, to murder, to assassinate; thus *wash day* in prison, execution day. [fig. use of SE *wash out*]

wash v.³ [1970s+] to 'de-criminalize' corruptly or illegally gained money by 'washing' it through a casino till or bank. [var. on LAUNDER v.]

wash v.⁴ [1980s+] (*drugs*) to alter the properties of cocaine base by a chemical process.

wash and go n. [1990s+] (*gay*) one who leaves immediately after sex. [play on the brandname shampoo]

wash a Negro white v. (*also* **wash the Ethiopian white**) [late 16C–19C] to attempt the impossible. [racist fantasies]

wash away v. [1940s+] (*US*) **1** to kill, to murder. **2** in fig. use, to overwhelm.

wash-belly n. [1950s] (*W.I.*) a woman's last child. [the image of finally 'cleaning out' the womb]

washed rock n. [1980s+] (*drugs*) crack cocaine (cf. BASE n.). [WASH v.⁴ + ROCK n.³ (4)]

washed up adj.¹ (*also* **all washed up**) **1** [20C+] (*orig. US*) (*also* **washed out, wash up**) useless, exhausted, failed. **2** [1920s+] of a relationship, ended. **3** [1930s] finished doing something. **4** [1930s–40s] upset, depressed. [theatrical use *washed up*, finished for the night]

washed up adj.² [1930s+] (*drugs*) no longer using drugs. [i.e. one is CLEAN adj.¹ (10)]

washer n.¹ [1900s–10s; 1970s] (*US*) a dollar. [SE *washer*, a small metal disk]

washer n.² [1940s] (*US Black*) a tavern, a bar, a fast-food restaurant. [? BELLY WASH n.¹ (2)]

washer n.³ [1970s+] (*US gay*) a condom. [SE *washer*, anything placed between 2 surfaces to relieve friction]

washer-dona n. (*also* **water-dona**) [late 19C] a washerwoman. [SE *washer/water* + DONA n. (1)]

washer-dryer n. [1980s] (*US Black*) a douche-bag and towel.

washer-upper n. [1960s+] one who washes dishes, usu. in a restaurant, hotel etc.

washicong(s) n. (*also* **watchekong(s)**) [1950s] (*W.I., Gren./Trin.*) sandals, plimsolls; spec. sandals with open-work in the pattern of a flower. [Chinese *hua xie kong hong*, lit. 'flower shoes (which are) full of holes'; 'this cheap footwear was most popular among the chinese indentured labourers in Trin. in the late 19C' (Allsopp)]

washing n. [1980s+] (*drugs*) preparing crack cocaine. [WASH v.⁴]

washing powder n. [1970s+] (*US Black*) a douching solution.

wash it down one's neck v. see WASH ONE'S NECK v.

washman n. [mid-16C] (*UK Und.*) a criminal mendicant sporting fake sores and wounds. Their superior in the criminal hierarchy, the PALLIARD n. (1), saw them as inferior rivals and would treat them accordingly.

wash one's brain v. (*also* **wash one's head**) [early 19C] to drink wine.

wash one's dirty linen v. (*also* **air one's dirty linen, wash one's dirty laundry**) [mid-19C+] to discuss private family matters in public; usu. as *wash one's dirty linen in public*; occas. also antonym *wash one's dirty linen at home*, to keep such matters private.

wash one's foot in the tank v. [1940s] (*US Black*) to drive a car very fast.

wash one's head v. see WASH ONE'S BRAIN v.

wash one's ivories v. see SLUICE THE IVORIES v.

wash one's liver of milk v. [late 17C–mid-18C] to stop behaving in a cowardly manner. [the idea that *milk* rather than blood is running through one's veins]

wash one's mouth v. [late 19C–1910s] to have a drink.

wash one's mouth upon v. (*also* **wash one's tongue on**) [1940s+] (*W.I.*) to gossip about, to denigrate.

wash one's neck v. (also **put it down one's neck, wash it down…**) [late 19C–1920s] to drink.

wash one's skin v. [20C+] (*W.I.*) to beat, to thrash, to defeat comprehensively.

wash one's tongue on v. see WASH ONE'S MOUTH UPON v.

wash-out n. **1** [20C+] a disappointment, a failure. **2** [1910s] (*US prison*) a life sentence. **3** [1910s+] a useless or unsuccessful person.

wash out v. **1** [1910s+] (*orig. milit.*) to remove, to cancel, to dismiss (e.g. from a course). **2** [1910s+] to fail, e.g. a course. **3** [1930s] (*US*) to lose all one's money, esp. from gambling.

wash-rock n. [1990s+] (*drugs*) crack cocaine (cf. BASE n.). [WASH n.⁴ + ROCK n.³ (4)]

wash the Ethiopian white v. see WASH A NEGRO WHITE v.

wash the ivories v. see SLUICE THE IVORIES v.

wash-up n. [1900s–50s] (*mainly Aus.*) the final assessment, the outcome, the 'bottom line'. [WASH UP v. (1)]

wash up adj. see WASHED UP adj.¹ (1).

wash up v. **1** [1900s–50s] (*US*) to bring to a conclusion, to end. **2** [1930s] to finish a relationship. **3** [1950s] (*US drugs*) to withdraw from narcotics addiction. [supposedly coined thus: '"That guy might be all right if he washed up [washed, cleaned himself]," commented Buck […] Just then the stage manager called out, "What will I do with this act, Mr. Ziegfeld?" "Wash up him and the bird," said Flo [Ziegfeld] and that was the last of the Italian and his trained canary […] Hype Igoe, the World's sporting writer, heard of the incident […] and in commenting […] upon Frank Moran, heavy weight pugilist, advised that matchmakers "wash him up". The phrase […] has become a colloquial fixture […] as a meaty synonym for finals and farewell' (N.Y. *World*, 25 October 1925); however, note date]

wash-your-foot-and-come n. [20C+] (*W.I.*) an impromptu dance, with no special dressing-up required.

was my face red! excl. [1930s+] an excl. of embarrassed regret, usu. when recounting some shameful solecism.

WASP n. [1950s+] White Anglo-Saxon Protestant, the predominant racial group in the USA; thus *wasp, waspish, waspy,* characteristic of this social grouping. [abbr; orig. Chicago sl./Ohio Valley social workers' jargon *WASP, White Appalachian Southern Protestants*]

wasp n.¹ [late 18C–early 19C] a diseased prostitute (cf. ALLEY CAT n.). ['she carries a sting in her tail']

wasp n.² [1960s+] (*Irish*) a traffic warden. [the black and yellow colours of the uniform]

wasp v. [1940s] (*US*) to tease maliciously; thus adj., *waspish.*

wasp and bee n. [20C+] (*Aus.*) tea. [rhy. sl.]

wasser n. see WASER n.

was she worth it? n. (also **seven and six**) [1940s+] (*bingo*) the number 76 (cf. ALDERSHOT LADIES n.). [the then price of a UK marriage licence, 7s 6d (35 pence)]

wassock n. see WAZZOCK n.

wassup? phr. see WHAT'S UP? phr.

wassy adj. see WAXY adj.².

wastcotier n. see WAISTCOATEER n.

waste v. **1** [1940s+] (*orig. US milit.*) to kill, to beat up. **2** [1960s+] (*US teen/gang*) to defeat, to trounce. **3** [1960s+] to get drunk or intoxicated by a drug. **4** [1960s+] to smash, to destroy.

waste-butt n. **1** [early 19C] a landlord, a publican. **2** [early–mid-19C] a drunkard. **3** [late 19C] an eating-house.

waste case n. (also **waste machine**) [1980s+] (*US campus*) a drunkard. [WASTED adj. (8) + SE *case*]

wasted adj. **1** [1950s+] (*orig. US*) killed. **2** [1950s+] (*US*) ruined, destroyed. **3** [1950s+] (*US*) penniless. **4** [1950s+] utterly overcome by a drug. **5** [1950s+] feeling very ill. **6** [1950s+] exhausted. **7** [1960s–70s] badly beaten up. **8** [1960s+] very drunk (cf. ANNIHILATED adj.). **9** [1970s] in serious trouble. **10** [1980s] (*US Black*) of a woman, unattractive. [WASTE v.]

wastepipe n. [19C] the vagina.

waste product n. **1** [1960s+] a general term of abuse. **2** [1980s+] (*US campus*) a drunkard. [SE *waste/*WASTE v. (3) + SE *product*]

waster n. [1980s] (*UK Black*) a gun. [WASTE v. (1)]

wat n. [early 16C–17C] a hare. [dial.]

watch n. [mid-16C–early 18C] self; usu. as *my watch, his watch* etc. [perhaps the image is of the idea of a person being synon. with one who is watching, i.e. is alive]

watch and chain n. [20C+] the brain. [rhy. sl.]

watch (chain) and seals n. **1** [early–mid-19C] a sheep's head and pluck, i.e. heart, liver and lungs. **2** [late 19C] the male genitals.

watchekong(s) n. see WASHICONG(S) n.

watchie n. (also **watchy**) [early–mid-19C; 2000s] a *watch*man. [abbr.]

watch it v. [late 19C+] to look out, to be careful; esp. in imper. *watch it!* used as a warning or a threat.

watch-maker n. [mid-19C] a pickpocket, esp. one who specializes in stealing watches.

watch my dust! excl. [1910s+] (*US*) see me go! [the SE *dust* of departure; note DUST v.² (1)]

watch one's ass v. (also **watch one's arse**) [1960s+] (*orig. US*) to take care, to take note, to be warned. [SE *watch* + ARSE n.¹ (1)/ASS n. (2)]

watch one's back v. [1950s+] to take care of oneself.

watch oneself v. [1950s+] to take care; esp. as an imper. when the implication is of a threat from the speaker.

watch one's lip v. (also **watch one's mouth/tongue**) [1950s+] to mind one's manners, to talk politely; also as imper. [SE *watch* + LIP n.¹ (1)/MOUTH n.¹ (3)/SE *tongue*]

watch one's step v. (also **mind one's step**) [1910s+] to be careful, lit. or fig.

watchpot n. [late 19C–1910s] (*Irish*) one who hangs around at mealtimes in the hope of being offered a meal. [they *watch* the cooking *pot*]

watch queen n. [1970s+] a male homosexual voyeur. [SE *watch* + QUEEN n.² (1)/QUEEN sfx (2)]

watch someone's back v. (also **get someone's back, take…**) [1950s+] **1** to look after or protect someone else. **2** to take care of someone else.

watch someone's waters v. [early 18C–early 19C] to keep a close watch on someone's actions. [SE *hold one's water*, to delay urination]

watch submarines v. see WATCH (THE) SUBMARINE RACES v.

watch the ant races v. [1970s+] to be excessively drunk. [the image of having collapsed on the floor]

watch the store v. see MIND THE STORE v.

watch (the) submarine races v. (also **watch submarines**) [1960s+] (*US*) to indulge in sexual activity in a parked car.

watchy n. see WATCHIE n.

watch your arse! excl. (also **watch your ass!**) [1960s+] behave yourself! mind your manners! [ARSE n.¹ (1)/ASS n. (2)]

watch your hip! excl. [1950s+] (*W.I.*) watch your manners! [SE *watch* + euph. *hip*, the buttocks, the backside]

water n.¹ [late 18C] tears. [early var. on WATERWORKS n. (1)]

water n.² (*drugs*) **1** [1960s+] injectable amphetamine (cf. A n.²). **2** [1970s+] phencyclidine (cf. ACE n.⁴). **3** [1990s+] furanon di-hydro, a substance used medically to encourage sleep and assist muscle recovery and growth. **4** [2000s] gamma hydroxy-butyrate. [ety. unknown]

water, the n. **1** [17C+] the River Thames in London; thus *over the water*, south of the Thames, or vice versa. **2** [19C] the English Channel. **3** [mid-19C–1930s] (*also* **big water**) the Atlantic Ocean, thus *over the water*, in America/Britain/Europe (cf. BIG DITCH n.). **4** [1950s] (*UK Black*) Bayswater, London W2. **5** [1980s+] the River Mersey in Liverpool.

water v.¹ [mid-18C] to stand treat, to entertain. [SE *water*, to provide water for, usu., a horse]

water v.[2] [late 18C] (US) to 'pack' a jury with members who are likely to deliver a biased verdict. [SE water, to dilute]

water v.[3] [1970s] (US) to drink (alcohol).

waterbag n. [1930s+] (Aus.) a fanatical teetotaller.

water-barrel n. see WATER-BUTT n.

water bewitched n. [late 17C–1900s] weak tea, punch or any other liquor.

water-bobby n. [late 19C] a river policeman (cf. BILLY n.[6]). [SE water + BOBBY n. (1)]

water-bonse n. [late 19C–1910s] a 'cry-baby'. [SE water + BONCE n. (1), lit. 'water-head']

water-bottle n.[1] [mid-17C] the penis. [its urinary function]

water-bottle n.[2] [late 19C] a total abstainer, a teetotaller.

waterbox n. (also **watercourse**, **watergap**) [mid-17C–early 18C] the vagina (cf. DAMP n.). [note D'Urfey, Pills to Purge Melancholy (1719–20): 'She knew him for a Workman that had the ready skill / To open well her Water-gate, and best supply her Mill']

waterboy n. (also **waterman**) [1930s+] (US) a useless boxer who accepts money to lose fights. [play on TAKE A DIVE v. (1)]

water buffalo v. [1980s+] (US campus) to vomit. [? echoic]

water burner n. [1950s+] (Aus.) a cook.

waterbury watch n. [1930s] Scotch (whisky). [rhy. sl.; the popular watches made in Waterbury, Connecticut]

water-butt n. (also **water-barrel**) [mid-19C] the stomach.

water-cart v. [mid-19C–1920s] to weep, to cry.

watercourse n. see WATERBOX n.

watercress n. [1970s+] a dress. [rhy. sl.]

water-dog n. [mid-19C–1900s] a Norfolk dumpling, a plain dumpling made from bread dough. [the ref. is to the Norfolk Broads; note a Norfolk dumpling also means a native of Norfolk]

water-dona n. see WASHER-DONA n.

water-engine n. [late 19C] the urinary organs, irrespective of gender.

waterfall n. **1** [19C] a handkerchief worn in the top pocket. **2** [mid-19C] pubic hair. **3** [mid-19C] a neckcloth, scarf or tie with long pendant ends. **4** [mid-19C–1920s] false hair. [resemblance]

water-funk n. [late 19C] one who is afraid to go into water. [SE water + FUNK n.[2] (4)]

watergap n. see WATERBOX n.

water-gate n. [mid-16C] the vagina when wet with sexual excitement (cf. BELLY ENTRANCE n.).

waterhead n. [1960s+] a foolish person. [lit. one who has 'water on the brain']

water hen n. [1960s+] the number 10. [rhy. sl.]

watering hole n. (also **water hole**) **1** [1950s+] a restaurant, a bar, anywhere where alcoholic refreshment is available. **2** [1970s] (gay) an area where one can wander in search of sexual partners, usu. a park or a bar. [SE water-hole, a pool or reservoir, esp. as used by animals for drinking]

watering place n.[1] [early 18C] the vagina.

watering place n.[2] **1** [late 18C–1900s] (also **watering-house**) any place where alcohol is available. **2** [late 19C–1930s] (US) a restaurant or similar place of entertainment for public drinking favoured by the rich.

waterlogged adj. [1910s–20s] very drunk (cf. DAMP adj.).

waterloo n.[1] [late 19C] a halfpenny. [the halfpenny toll to cross Waterloo Bridge]

waterloo n.[2] [20C+] a stew. [rhy. sl.]

waterman n.[1] [1950s] (W.I.) a heavy drinker, an alcoholic. [SE water, a euph. for white rum]

waterman n.[2] see WATERBOY n.

waterman n.[3] see WATER'S MAN n.

watermelon man n. [1970s] (US Black) a drug seller. [euph.; stereotyped association of watermelons and US Blacks]

watermelons n. [1960s+] (orig. US campus) large female breasts (cf. APPLES n.[1]). [ext. of MELONS n.]

watermill n. [mid-17C–early 19C] the vagina (cf. DAMP n.).

water of life n. **1** [19C] whisky. **2** [early–mid-19C] gin. **3** [1930s] (US drugs) any drug. **4** [1950s+] (US Black) semen (cf. BABY FLUID n.).

water one's cheeks v. [1990s+] (US Black) to cry.

water one's horse/mule v. see WATER THE MULE v.

water one's nag v. [mid-19C] to urinate (cf. PAY ONE'S WATER BILL v.). [SE water + play on SE nag, a horse/NAG n.[2]]

water one's plants v. [late 16C] to weep.

water one's pony v. see WATER THE MULE v.

water pad n. [late 17C–mid-19C] a thief who specializes in robbing ships on the River Thames. [SE water + PAD n.[1] (3)]

water pistol n. [1970s] the penis (cf. AX n.[2]).

water plant n. [early–mid-19C] an umbrella. [joc. resemblance]

water rat n. **1** [late 19C] a sergeant in the Thames River Police. **2** [1950s+] (Ulster) a customs officer. [they both check travellers/goods using 'the water']

waters n. [1940s] (US Black) wellington boots, galoshes. [their use on wet days]

water scriger n. [late 18C–early 19C] a doctor who diagnoses on the basis of a patient's urine. [SE water, urine + ? corruption of scriver, a scribe]

water's man n. (also **waterman**) [mid–late 19C] a costermonger's handkerchief, coloured light or dark blue. [the light and dark blue colours sported by Cambridge and Oxford university oarsmen]

water sneak n. (also **water sneaksman**) [late 18C–early 19C] a thief who works on a river. [SE water + SNEAK n.[1] (2)]

water sports n. [1970s+] urolognia, urinating on a partner for sexual stimulation.

water-sprinkler n. [1900s] (Aus.) a priest, a clergyman. [the act of christening with holy water]

water the dragon v. [mid–late 19C] to urinate (cf. PAY ONE'S WATER BILL v.). [euph.; ? significantly predates DRAGON n.[4]]

water the flowers v. [1980s] to urinate (cf. BURN THE GRASS v.; PAY ONE'S WATER BILL v.). [euph.]

water the mule v. (also **water one's horse, ...one's mule, ...one's pony, ...the horses**) [1970s+] (US) to urinate (cf. PAY ONE'S WATER BILL v.). [euph. but note MULE n.[5] (1)]

water-wagon n. (also **ice wagon**) [late 19C+] a fig. state of sobriety; usu. in ON THE WAGON phr.

water-wagtail n. see WAGTAIL n.

waterworks n. **1** [mid-19C+] tears; thus TURN ON THE WATERWORKS v. **2** [late 19C+] the urinary organs. **3** [1910s] the vagina. **4** [1930s] rain.

watery-headed adj. [late 18C–19C] tearful, prone to crying.

wattle n. [1940s–50s] (Aus.) a dirty, grubby person. [rhy. sl.; wattle and daub = WARB n. (2)]

wattles n. [late 17C–mid-19C] (orig. UK Und.) ears. [SE wattles, the 'ears' of a turkey or cock]

waunds!/wauns! excl. see WOUNDS! excl.

wave a flag of defiance v. [late 19C–1910s] to be drunk. [one's temporary boldness]

wave maker n. see MAKE WAVES v. (1).

wave one's willy v. [1960s+] of a man, to act in an exaggeratedly macho manner; thus WILLIE-WAVING n. [SE wave + WILLIE n.[5]]

wave the (magic) wand v. [1970s+] to masturbate.

Wavy Navy n. [1910s+] the Royal Naval Volunteer Reserve. [the wavy braid worn by its officers on their uniform sleeves until 1956]

wax n.[1] **1** [mid-19C–1910s] a temper, a state of anger; thus WAXY adj.[1]; on the wax, angry; waxiness, fury. **2** [1990s+] (US Black) sexual intercourse. [archaic SE wax wrath, to become angry; (2) WAX v.[2]]

wax n.[2] (US Black) **1** [20C+] chewing gum. **2** [2000s] a deposit of dried, shiny vaginal secretions on the buttocks and/or thighs.

wax *n.*[3] [1920s+] (*orig. US*) a gramophone record; thus *put on wax*, to record. [the *wax* master discs in which the recording stylus cuts its groove]

wax *n.*[4] *see* BODY WAX *n.*

wax *v.*[1] [late 19C–1900s] **1** to mark down. **2** (*UK Und.*) to remember clearly.

wax *v.*[2] [late 19C+] to defeat in competition. **2** [late 19C+] to beat up, to thrash. **3** [1960s+] to kill. **4** [1990s+] to have sexual intercourse (cf. BANG *v.*[1]). **5** [2000s] (*US Black*) to leak vaginal secretions onto the buttocks and/or thighs. [SE *wax*, to grown in intensity + WHACK *v.*[1] (1)]

wax *v.*[3] [1930s+] (*orig. US*) to make a record. [WAX *n.*[3]]

wax *v.*[4] [1980s+] (*Aus. prison*) to share; thus *waxer*, one who is entitled to a share. [? WHACK *n.*[2] (1)]

wax ass *v.* [1970s+] (*US Black*) to have sexual intercourse (cf. BANG *v.*[1]). [WAX *v.*[2] (4) + ASS *n.* (3)]

wax-borer *n.* [1950s+] (*Aus.*) a talkative bore; thus *wax-bore*, to talk tediously at someone. [i.e. they 'bore' through one's ear *wax*]

waxed *adj.* [1900s–70s] having a personality and characteristics that are known well. [? SE *wax*, to polish, i.e. they 'shine' in a crowd]

waxed, buffed and simonized *phr.* [1980s+] (*US Black*) **1** comprehensively defeated, beaten up. **2** describing something that is superlative, impressive. [WAX *v.*[2] (2) + car valeting imagery]

waxhead *n.* [1980s+] (*Aus.*) a surfer. [SE *wax*, as used on surfboards + -HEAD sfx (4)]

waxie *n.* (*also* **waxey**) [late 19C] (*UK Und.*) a 'nigger minstrel', a burnt cork artiste, who works on the street.

wax one's carrot *v.* [1980s+] to masturbate (cf. BEAT ONE'S MEAT *v.*; BUFF THE BANANA *v.*).

wax pilot *n.* [2000s] (*US Black*) a highly talented disc jockey. [WAX *n.*[3] + SE *pilot*]

wax-pot *n.* [1910s–20s] an ill-tempered person. [WAX *n.*[1] (1) + -POT sfx; on pattern of SE *fusspot*]

wax someone's ass *v.* (*also* **wax someone's head/tail**) [1960s+] (*US*) to beat up, to thrash. [WAX *v.*[2] (2) + ASS *n.* (2)/SE *head*/TAIL *n.*[2] (1)]

wax (something) up *v.* [late 19C] to ruin, to make a mess of; to cause trouble. [WAX *v.*[2] (2)]

wax the buick *v.* (*also* **wax the candle-stick, ...the car, ...the carrot, ...the dolphin, ...the surfboard, ...the womb**) [1980s+] to masturbate (cf. BUFF THE BANANA *v.*).

wax up *v.*[1] [1970s+] (*US Black*) **1** to propitiate someone whom one has insulted or annoyed. **2** to hide evidence. [SE *wax*, to polish; (2) suggests making things look better]

wax up *v.*[2] *see* WAX (SOMETHING) UP *v.*

waxworks *n.* **1** [1960s] (*US*) a record company. **2** [1980s+] (*US gay*) anywhere, e.g. a bar, mainly frequented by older, less attractive gay men. [(1) WAX *n.*[3] + SE *works*; (2) derog. use of SE]

waxy *n.* [mid-19C–1900s] a cobbler. [the *waxed* thread he uses]

waxy *adj.*[1] [mid-19C–1950s] angry. [WAX *n.*[1] (1)]

waxy *adj.*[2] (*also* **wassy**) [1940s+] (*W.I.*) **1** lively, exciting, enjoyable. **2** of a person, attractive. [SE *waxy*, i.e. an image of 'shininess']

way *adv.* [late 19C+] (*US*) very, extremely, a general intensifier. [SE *a long way*, reinforced by WAY-OUT *adj.*[1] (2), WAY TO GO! excl.; but note W.I. *waay! waay-ou!*, an excl. of great amusement, excitement, exultation]

way! *excl.* [1990s+] the affirmative response to the negative NO WAY! excl. (2).

wayback *n.* **1** [late 19C–1910s] (*US*) an old-fashioned person. **2** [late 19C–1930s] (*Aus./N.Z./US*) the Aus. outback or the US West or any rural nowhere. **3** [1900s–30s] (*Aus./US*) (*also* **waybacker**) a person or animal from the outback or any rural nowhere.

way back *adj.* [1940s–60s] (*US Black*) well-established, traditional, tried and tested. [SE *from way back*, from a long time ago]

way down south in Dixie *n.* [1980s] fellatio.

way-in *n.* [late 19C] the vagina (cf. BELLY ENTRANCE *n.*). [SE *way in*, an entry]

way in *adj.* [1970s] fashionable, chic.

way of all flesh *phr.* [19C] dead; thus *go the way of all flesh*, to die. [var. on orig. Bible phr. *go the way of all the earth*; popularized in trans. of the Douay Bible (1609)]

way of life *n.* [early 19C] the profession of prostitution. [euph.]

way-oh! *excl.* [late 19C] a dismissive excl., not likely!

way-out *n.* [1960s–70s] (*US*) an unconventional or eccentric person; thus *way-outness*, unconventionality. [WAY-OUT *adj.*[1]]

way-out *adj.*[1] [1950s+] (*orig. US*) **1** bizarre. **2** fantastic, exceptional. [orig. jazz use]

way-out *adj.*[2] [1950s+] (*US*) wholly wrong, greatly mistaken. [abbr. *way out of line*]

way past *adv.* [1980s+] (*orig. US Black*) a general intensifier, e.g. *way past bad, way past cool*. [lit. 'beyond']

way poo cow! *excl.* [20C+] (*W.I., Gren.*) watch out for yourself! look out for the consequences! [Fr. *voir pour corps-vous*, lit. 'see for your body', hence *look out for yourself*]

wayside ditch *n.* (*also* **wayside fountain**) [late 19C] the vagina (cf. AGREEABLE RUTS OF LIFE *n.*).

way to go! *excl.* [1940s+] an excl. of approval, i.e. *that's the right way to go...* [allegedly coined for the 1940 film *Knute Rockne*]

way to heaven *n. see* ROAD TO A CHRISTENING *n.*

way-up *adj.* **1** [late 19C–1900s] (*US*) top-rank, first-class, socially and otherwise superior. **2** [1940s] (*US drugs*) in a very positive mood, poss. drug-induced. [(2) play on HIGH *adj.*[1]]

way up! *excl.* [late 19C] (*US*) definitely! very much so!

waz *n.* (*also* **wazz**) [1990s+] **1** urination. **2** masturbation. [WAZ *v.*]

waz *v.* (*also* **wazz**) [1990s+] **1** of a man, to urinate. **2** of a woman, to masturbate (cf. APPLY LIP GLOSS *v.*; BOFF *v.*). **3** to waste. [dial. *wass*, to urinate]

wazoo *n.* **1** [1960s+] the vagina. **2** [1970s+] (*US*) the buttocks, the anus. [? var. GAZOO *n.*/KAZOO *n.*]

wazzed *adj.* [1990s+] **1** drunk (cf. ADDLED *adj.*). **2** vomiting. **3** exhausted. [(1) play on PISSED *adj.*[1]]

wazzock *n.* (*also* **wassock**) [1990s+] a fool. [? WAZOO *n.*]

wazzocked *adj.* [1980s+] drunk or intoxicated by a drug. [var. on WAZZOOED *adj.*]

wazzooed *adj.* [1970s+] (*drugs*) extremely intoxicated by a drug. [echoic or play on WAZZED *adj.* (1)]

wazzup? *phr. see* WHAT'S UP? phr.

w/e *adj.* [1960s+] used in sex contact advertisements, having notably large genitals. [abbr. WELL-ENDOWED *adj.* (1)]

weak *n.* [late 19C] tea. [as opposed to coffee]

weak *adj.* **1** [1950s] lacking in funds, poor. **2** [1950s+] poor, disappointing, ineffectual. **3** [1970s+] stupid.

weak as gin's piss *phr.* (*also* **weak as cat breath, ...nun's piss, ...puppy's piss**) [1940s+] (*orig. Aus.*) extremely weak. [SE *weak* + GIN *n.*[1] (1) + PISS *n.* (1)]

weak-ass *adj.* [1980s+] a derog. term for second-rate, unimpressive, powerless. [WEAK *adj.* (2) + -ASS sfx]

weak down *v.* [1900s–40s] (*US Black*) to become demoralized, to show a lack of courage or determination. [WEAK *adj.* (2) + SE *down*]

weakheart *n.* [1970s] (*UK/W.I.*) a derog. term for a policeman.

weakie *n.* [1940s+] (*Aus.*) an unreliable, untrustworthy person. [WEAK *adj.* (2) + sfx -*ie*]

weak in the arm *n.* [late 19C–1900s] a short measure of beer. [the publican has supposedly not pulled the beer tap to its fullest extent]

weak-jointed *adj.* [mid-19C] (*US*) a euph. for drunk.

weaksauce *n.* [2000s] (*US teen*) an unfunny joke.

weak shit *n.* [1960s+] **1** second-rate, weak, inadequate words or actions. **2** (*drugs*) second-rate, relatively ineffective drugs. [WEAK *adj.* (2) + (1) SHIT *n.*[3] (6); (2) SHIT *n.*[5] (3)]

weak sister *n.* [mid-19C+] (*orig. US*) the weakest member of a group, the sex is irrelevant. [a play on the earlier, biblical *weaker brethren*, a translation of the Gk term *asthenes* 'applied by St Paul (esp. in Rom. 14 and 1 Cor. 8) to believers whose scruples, though unsound, should be treated with tenderness, lest they should be led by the example of the more enlightened into acts condemned by their conscience' (*OED*)]

weak tap *n.* [1950s] one who has a low income. [SE *weak* + TAP v.³ (2)]

weak-wristed *adj. see* LIMP-WRISTED *adj.*

weapon *n.*¹ [late 16C+] the penis (cf. AX n.²). [first cited in an 11C glossary and in Langland's *Piers Plowman* (1377): 'While thou art young and thy weapon keen...'. It was used more widely from the mid-18C]

weapon *n.*² [2000s] (*Irish*) a good and positive thing; as in phr. *it's a weapon.*

weaponhead *n.* [1980s+] (*Aus. prison*) a foolish person. [? WEAPON n.¹ + -HEAD sfx (1); thus play on DICKHEAD n.]

wear *n.* [1950s+] (*Irish*) an open-mouthed kiss. [the 2 mouths are so entwined that it appears that one is 'wearing' the other]

wear *v.* [1910s+] to tolerate, to stand, to believe.

wear a cut-glass veil *v.* (*also* **wear a crystal veil**) [1940s–70s] (*US gay*) to attempt unsuccessfully to hide one's homosexual preferences. [such a transparent 'veil' hides nothing]

wear a forker *v.* [early 17C] to be cuckolded. [SE *wear* + *fork*, i.e. the 'horns' that a cuckold wears]

wear a green bonnet *v.* [19C] to be bankrupt. [the defunct tradition of a bankrupt wearing a green cap to denote his status]

wear a green sweater/tie *v. see* WEAR A RED SWEATER *v.*

wear a hat *v.* [1960s] (*US teen*) **1** to have a steady girlfriend; to be married; to bring one's partner to a party. **2** to lead a respectable life. [the once universal hat was seen as a badge of dull respectability in the 1960s]

wear a head *v.* [early 19C] to be intelligent.

wear a mourning veil *v.* [1940s–70s] (*US gay*) to attempt to hide one's homosexual proclivities. [such a 'veil' is black and thus impenetrable]

wear a red sweater *v.* (*also* **wear a green sweater, ...a green tie, ...a red tie**) [1960s+] (*US gay*) to act in an obviously homosexual manner. [? the brightness of the colours, i.e. one cannot hide one's sexuality; ? or the belief that such clothes denote a homosexual wearer (red was a stereotypical 'queer' colour)]

wear-arse *n.* [late 18C–early 19C] a 1-horse chaise or light, open carriage. [SE *wear out* + ARSE n.¹ (1); from the jolting]

wear a smile *v.* [1900s–70s] (*US Black*) to be naked.

wear a straw in one's ear *v.* [1910s–20s] of a woman, to seek a new husband. [? custom of standing with a straw in one's mouth, which indicates one's desire to find a new job; + ? dial. *draw a straw across*, to beguile]

wear bifocals *v.* [1970s+] (*US gay*) to be bisexual.

Wearie *n.* (*also* **Weary**) [20C+] (*Ulster*) the Devil. [SE *weary* but note OE *wearg*, the accursed one]

wearies, the *n.* [1950s] (*US*) tiredness, boredom, apathy.

wear iron boots *v.* [1950s] (*US Black*) to be very well-off.

wear it *v.* **1** [early–mid-19C] (*UK Und.*) to be accused of becoming an informer. **2** [20C+] (*US Und.*) to take the blame for a crime even when not actually guilty. [WEAR v.]

wear it upon *v.* [early 19C] (*UK Und.*) to inform against. ['it' is the nose, i.e. NOSE n.¹ (1)]

wear one's badge *v.* [1940s–60s] (*US gay*) to wear an outward sign of being a homosexual. [formerly this was a red tie, although this practice is now obs.]

wear one's business *v.* [1990s+] (*US Und.*) to act in an obvious manner, to betray one's secrets. [SE *wear* + BUSINESS n.¹ (5); var. on SE *to wear one's heart on one's sleeve*]

wear one's head large *v.* [late 19C] to be suffering from a hangover. [SE *wear* + HEAD n.⁵ (1) + *large*]

wear one's sitting breeches *v. see* HAVE ONE'S SITTING BREECHES ON *v.*

wear out one's soul-case *v. see* BURST ONE'S SOUL-CASE *v.*

wear someone's balls for a necktie *v.* [1920s+] used as a threat of violence, e.g. *try that again and I'll wear...*

wear someone's guts for earmuffs *v. see* HAVE SOMEONE'S GUTS FOR GARTERS *v.*

wear the bands *v.* [early 19C] (*mainly UK Und.*) to be hungry. [SE *wear* + BANDED adj.]

wear the beard *v.* (*also* **don the beard**) [1990s+] usu. of a man, to perform cunnilingus (cf. BEARD RIDE n.). [SE *wear* + BEARD n.¹ (1)]

wear the blanket *v.* [mid-19C] (*US*) to have native American blood. [the stereotyped association of *blankets* and Native Americans]

wear the blue *v. see* BLUE n.⁸ (3).

wear the blue and buttons *v.* [late 19C] (*US*) to be a member of the police. [the uniform]

wear the blues *v.* (*also* **wear the stripes**) [1900s] (*US*) to be in prison. [the colour/pattern of prison uniforms]

wear the broad arrow *v.* [late 19C] to be imprisoned; thus *broad arrow suit, arrows,* prison uniform. [the *arrows* that were printed onto prison clothing]

wear the bull's feather *v.* [mid-16C–early 19C] to be a cuckold. [pun on the bull's 'feather', i.e. its SE *horn*/HORN n.¹]

wear the dog *v.* [1970s] (*US Black*) to go around looking deeply depressed. [SE *wear* + *hangdog* look]

wear the horns *v.* [17C+] to be cuckolded. [SE *wear* + HORNS n.]

wear the leek *v.* [late 19C] to be Welsh. [SE *wear* + *leek,* the national emblem]

wear the pants *v.* [late 19C+] (*orig. US*) to be the dominant member of a heterosexual partnership. [coined in an era when only men were thought to wear pants (trousers)]

wear the ring *v.* [1970s+] (*US Black*) to be in a regular relationship, whether actually married or not, and thus to reject any alternative entanglements. [the wedding *ring* + the image of a *ring* through a bull's nose]

wear the stripes *v. see* WEAR THE BLUES *v.*

wear the trousers *v.* [1930s+] to dominate, usu. implying that the woman in a relationship is the one who dictates the rules.

wear the vine leaf *v.* [1900s] (*Aus.*) to be drunk.

wear the willow *v.* [late 16C–1900s] to have been abandoned by one's mistress or lover. [abbr. SE *wear the willow garland*; the symbolic role of the weeping *willow*]

wear two pairs of shoes *v.* [1970s+] (*US gay*) to be bisexual.

Weary *n. see* WEARIE n.

weary *adj.* [late 17C–1900s] drunk (cf. ADDLED adj.). [euph.]

wear yellow hose *v.* (*also* **wear yellow stockings**) [17C] to be jealous. [play on YELLOW adj.¹; thus the yellow stockings of Malvolio in Shakespeare's *Twelfth Night* (1599)]

weary willie *n.* [20C+] (*US*) a tramp, a migrant worker. [SE *weary* + assonant/generic *Willie*]

weary willie and tired tim *n.* (*also* **weary willie and tired thomas**) [1900s–30s] a pair of idling, loafing individuals. [the cartoon tramps created in *Illustrated Chips* in April 1898 by Tom Browne (1870–1910)]

weasel *n.*¹ **1** [mid-17C; 20C+] (*also* **weasle**) a general derog. term. **2** [1920s+] (*US*) an informer. **3** [1930s] (*US Und.*) a private detective (cf. BEAGLE n.³). **4** [1940s+] (*N.Z.*) a sly or devious person. [reverse anthropomorphism; Williams has 17C use of *weasel,* a lecher]

weasel *n.*² [mid-19C+] (*US*) a native of South Carolina. [the state has a large population of the animal]

weasel *n.*³ [1920s+] (*orig. US*) the penis (cf. ANTEATER n.). [it 'burrows']

weasel (and stoat) *n.* [1950s+] an overcoat. [rhy. sl.]

weasel (out) *v.* (*also* **weasel-word**) (*orig. US*) **1** [20C+] to evade, to equivocate. **2** [1940s+] to wriggle out of a promise or duty. [reverse anthropomorphism]

weasle *n. see* WEASEL n.[1] (1).

weathercock *n.* [late 19C] the head.

weather gig *n.* [late 17C–early 18C] the vagina. [SE *wether*, a castrated ram + GIG n.[1] (2)]

weatherhead *n.* [late 17C–mid-19C] a fool, a simpleton; thus adj. *weatherheaded*. [SE *weather* + -HEAD sfx (1); the image is of the fool's head turning like that of a *weathercock*; Hotten (1864) prefers SE *wether*, a ram, thus the person has a 'sheepish' look]

weather-sharp *n.* [1900s] (*US*) a weather-forecaster. [SE *weather* + SHARP n.[1] (2)]

weave *n.*[1] [1970s] (*US Black*) a trick; thus *put the weave on*, to deceive, to trick.

weave *n.*[2] (*US Black*) **1** [1970s] clothing. **2** [1980s+] false hair; hair extensions.

weave hustling *n. see* WORM HUSTLING n.

weaver *n.* [1950s+] (*US*) a poor driver who *weaves* from lane to lane along the road.

weave the four F's *v.* [1940s] (*orig. US Black*) of a man, to seduce. [SE *weave* + FOUR-Fs n.]

weaving *n.* [19C] in cards, cheating by secreting a number of cards on one's knee, or wedged between a knee and the underside of the table. These cards can be brought into the hand, swapping them for those one has been dealt, as and when required.

webbed up *phr.* [1980s+] **1** involved or caught up in. **2** having a relationship (with). [SE (spider's) *web*]

web-foot *n.* **1** [mid-19C–1910s] (*US*) an infantryman. **2** [mid-19C+] (*US*) a native of Oregon. **3** [late 19C] a native of Lincolnshire. **4** [1970s+] (*US*) an environmentalist. [they all encounter wet paths etc]

Webster Avenue walking stick *n.* [1960s] (*US gang*) a baseball bat studded with razorblades.

wedded to the Duke of Exeter's daughter *phr.* [late 16C] suffering the torture of the rack. [the rack had been introduced into England by John Holland, 4th *Duke of Exeter*, in 1447]

wedding *n.*[1] [late 18C] the emptying of a privy. [? SE *weeding*]

wedding *n.*[2] *see* IRISH WEDDING n.

wedding bells *n.* [1970s] (*drugs*) LSD (cf. A n.[3]). [ety. unknown; ? it 'rings' in one's skull]

wedding kit *n.* (*also* **wedding tackle**) [1910s+] the male genitals. [SE *wedding* + *kit*/TACKLE n.[1] (1)]

wedge *n.*[1] **1** [18C+] (*also* **wage**) silver, money in general. **2** [early 18C–1910s] silver plate. **3** [late 19C] (*UK Und.*) a receiver. **4** [1970s+] a thick, chunky roll of banknotes, usu. folded in half; thus a large amount of money or wealth in general. [(3) the silver plate was melted down into *wedges* by receivers]

wedge *n.*[2] **1** [early 18C+] the penis (cf. ARSE-OPENER n.). **2** [1960s] (*US campus*) in fig. use, a derog. term for a hard worker. [(1) it SE *wedges* open the vagina]

wedge *n.*[3] (*also* **wej**) [mid-19C] a Jew. [backsl.]

wedge *n.*[4] (*also* **wedges, wedgies**) [1960s+] (*drugs*) LSD (cf. A n.[3]). [? the shape of the pill]

wedge *adj.* [mid-19C] silver, silver-plated. [WEDGE n.[1] (2)]

wedgeass *n.* [1940s–50s] (*US*) a general term of abuse; thus adj. *wedge-assed*. [SE *wedge* + -ASS sfx]

wedged (up) *adj.* [1990s+] well-off, rich. [WEDGE n.[1] (4)]

wedge feeder *n.* [late 18C–mid-19C] a silver spoon. [WEDGE adj. + FEEDER n.[1]]

wedgehead *n.* [1990s+] one who has a 'wedge' haircut.

wedge-hunter *n.* [mid-19C–1900s] (*UK Und.*) a thief specializing in silver plate and silver watches. [WEDGE adj. + SE *hunter*]

wedge-hunting *n.* [late 19C] (*UK Und.*) stealing silver-plate or silver watches. [WEDGE-HUNTER n.]

wedge-lobb *n.* [early 19C] a silver snuff-box. [WEDGE adj. + LOB n.[1] (1)]

wedges *n. see* WEDGE n.[4].

wedge-super *n.* [mid-19C] (*UK Und.*) a silver watch. [WEDGE adj. + SUPER n.[2] (1)]

wedge up *v.* [2000s] to amass money. [WEDGE n.[1] (4) + SE *up*]

wedgie *n.* (*also* **snuggy, wedgy**) [1970s+] a trick whereby one pulls an unsuspecting victim's underpants up between their buttocks. [SE *wedge*, to stick or thrust between]

wedgies *n.*[1] [1940s+] women's *wedge*-heeled shoes. [abbr.]

wedgies *n.*[2] *see* WEDGE n.[4].

wedgy *n. see* WEDGIE n.

wee *n.* (*also* **wee-wee**) [late 19C+] (*mainly UK juv.*) urine, urination. [? juv. mispron. of 'u-ween' (urine) or var. on PEE n.[1] (1)]

wee *v.* (*also* **make wee-wee, wee-wee**) [late 19C+] (*mainly UK juv.*) to urinate. [WEE n.]

wee buns! *excl.* (*also* **onions!**) [20C+] (*Ulster*) no problem!

weed *n.*[1] **1** [17C+] tobacco. **2** [mid-19C–1940s] a cigar. **3** [late 19C+] a cigarette. **4** [1920s+] (*drugs*) (*also* **weeds**) marijuana (cf. AFRICAN BUSH n.). **5** [1930s–40s] a marijuana cigarette. [ext. uses of SE]

weed *n.*[2] [mid-19C] a hatband. [SE *weed*, a mourning garment, often a black hatband]

weed *n.*[3] **1** [mid-late 19C] an ill-conditioned, weak horse. **2** [20C+] a weakling, a feeble and thus contemptible person. **3** [1930s–60s] (*US Und./Black/teen*) (*also* **weed in the garden**) a stranger, an ousider.

weed *v.*[1] [late 18C] (*US Und.*) to speak.

weed *v.*[2] **1** [early 19C] (*UK Und.*) to steal small amounts, so as not to alert the victim. **2** [early 19C–1930s] (*orig. UK Und.*) to steal part rather than all of a potential booty. **3** [mid-19C+] to take, to steal; thus *weed a leather*, to steal a wallet and strip out its contents.

weed *v.*[3] [1930s–40s] (*US Black/Und.*) **1** to lend, esp. money; thus *weed a holler note until mother comes in*, to lend someone $100 until their gambling luck changes. **2** to give, to hand.

weed *v.*[4] [1990s+] (*US drugs*) to smoke marijuana. [WEED n.[1] (4)]

weeder *n.* **1** [early–mid 19C] (*UK Und.*) a villain who steals a proportion of the gang's joint booty. **2** [1940s+] (*US Und.*) one who steals in small amounts to avoid detection. [WEED v.[2]]

Weedgie *n. see* WEEDJIE n.

weedhead *n.* [1930s+] (*drugs*) a marijuana smoker. [WEED n.[1] (4) + -HEAD sfx (3)]

weedheaded *adj.* [1940s] (*US Black/drugs*) intoxicated by marijuana. [WEEDHEAD n.]

weed hound *n.* [1940s–50s] (*US*) a marijuana user. [WEED n.[1] (4) + HOUND sfx]

weeding dues *n.* [early 19C] (*UK Und.*) 'speaking of any person, place, or property, that has been weeded [i.e. robbed], it is said "weeding dues have been concerned"' (Vaux). [WEED v.[2] (2) + SE *dues*]

weed in the garden *n. see* WEED n.[3] (3).

Weedjie *n.* (*also* **Weedgie**) [1990s+] (*Scot.*) a native of Glasgow. [a Glaswegian]

weed out *v.* [1950s+] (*drugs*) to smoke marijuana to excess. [WEED n.[1] (4) + SE *out*]

weeds *n.*[1] [late 16C+] clothes.

weeds *n.*[2] *see* WEED n.[1] (4).

weeds, the *n.* **1** [1920s–30s] (*US tramp*) a hobo camp. **2** [1950s] (*US Und.*) the outskirts, the suburbs. [its position on the edge of town]

weed tea *n.* [1960s–70s] (*drugs*) marijuana tea. [WEED n.[1] (4) + SE *tea*]

weed the swag *v.* [early 19C] (*UK Und.*) to embezzle part of the booty before dividing what remains with one's gang. [WEED v.[2] (2) + SWAG n.[1] (2)]

weedy *adj.* **1** [19C] of a horse, weak-legged, lacking strength. **2** [mid-19C+] of humans, weak, cowardly, spineless. **3** [1920s+] of things, boring, troublesome, small, insignificant. [WEED n.[3]]

weedy-weedy *v.* [2000s] (*US prison*) to inform.

wee georgie wood *adj.* [1930s+] (*Aus.*) good. [rhy. sl.; ult. the eponymous musical hall star, popular 1920s–30s]

weejee *n.* (*also* **wejee**) [mid–19C] **1** a chimneypot hat. **2** a chimneypot hat. **3** anything outstanding of its type, esp. an invention.

weejuns *n.* [1950s+] (*US teen*) moccasins, loafers. [brandname, *Weejuns*]

weekend *n.* [1940s–50s] (*UK prison*) a very short period of imprisonment.

weekend *adj.* [1930s+] part-time, infrequent, irregular; usu. in combs., *see* below.

weekender *n.* **1** [19C] a prostitute who only works at the weekend. **2** [1940s+] a weekend cottage. **3** [1950s+] (*drugs*) someone who is not a serious drug taker, thus not addicted. **4** [1960s+] a suitcase suitable for packing those items needed for a weekend's trip or holiday.

weekend habit *n.* [1930s+] (*drugs*) the occasional use of drugs. [SE *weekend*/WEEKEND adj. + HABIT n. (1)]

weekend ho *n.* [1970s+] (*US Black*) **1** a part-time prostitute, often without a pimp but poss. helping out her boyfriend with cash. **2** (*also* **weekend warrior**) an underage prostitute. [SE *weekend*/WEEKEND adj. + HO n.¹ (1)/SE *warrior*]

weekend man *n.* [1970s+] (*US Black*) a family man who can only manage the street life at weekends.

weekend pussy *n.* [1990s+] (*US Black*) an adulterous female lover, lit. one whom one only visits at the weekend. [SE *weekend* + PUSSY n. (1)]

weekend warrior *n.*¹ **1** [1960s+] (*US*) a member of the National Guard. **2** [1970s+] anyone deemed to be insufficiently dedicated to a given activity or occupation. **3** [1980s] (*Aus.*) a member of the Australian Army's Reservist units. **4** [1980s] (*US drugs*) one who takes potentially addictive narcotic drugs at weekends (or on similarly special occasions) only.

weekend warrior *n.*² *see* WEEKEND HO n. (2).

wee man *n.* [1990s+] (*Irish*) the penis.

ween *n.* (*also* **weenie**, **weeny**, **wiener**) [1950s+] (*US campus*) **1** (*also* **ween bucket**) a boring, socially unappealing or unacceptable person. **2** a hard-working student. [WEENIE n.¹ (5)]

weenchy *adj.* [20C+] (*US*) tiny, very little. [WEENY adj.]

weenie *n.*¹ (*also* **weener**, **weeney**, **weeny**, **weinie**, **wiener**, **wienie**, **winnie**) **1** [late 19C+] (*US*) a frankfurter sausage, a HOT DOG n.¹ (1). **2** [1900s] (*US Und.*) bread. **3** [1920s+] (*US*) a young woman, an effeminate man. **4** [1930s+] (*US, mainly juv.*) the penis (cf. BACON n.¹). **5** [1950s+] (*US*) a general derog.; thus *wienie* (*out*), to act cowardly, wimpishly. [SAmE *wiener*, a Vienna sausage; ult. Ger. *Wienenwurst*]

weenie *n.*² [1940s–60s] (*US*) a good idea, a scheme.

weenie *n.*³ *see* WEEN n.

weenie *adj.*¹ [1960s–80s] (*US campus*) second-rate, insignificant. [WEENIE n.¹ (5)]

weenie *adj.*² *see* WEENY adj.

weenie bin *n.* [1970s+] (*US campus*) a separate study room in a library. [WEENIE n.¹ (4)/WEENIE n.¹ (5) + SE *bin*, i.e. either the sexual encounters that take place there or a general disparaging term]

weenie waver *n.* (*also* **weenie/weinie/wienie wagger**, **weinie wiggler**) [1970s+] an exhibitionist. [WEENIE n.¹ (4) + SE *waver*]

weenie woman *n.* [1990s+] (*US*) an effeminate homosexual. [WEENIE n.¹ (4) + SE *woman*]

weeny *n.*¹ *see* WEEN n.

weeny *n.*² *see* WEENIE n.¹.

weeny *adj.* (*also* **weenie**) [late 18C+] tiny. [infant pron.]

weeny-bopper *n.* [1970s+] a very young pop fan. [WEENY adj. + BOP v. (5), on pattern of TEENYBOPPER n. (1)]

weeny-teeny *adj. see* TEENSIE-WEENSIE adj.

weep and wail *n.* [late 19C–1950s] a tale, esp. a beggar's tale of woe. [rhy. sl.]

weep city *n.* [1940s] (*US Black*) crying, tearfulness. [SE *weep* + CITY sfx]

weeper *n.*¹ [mid-17C] (*UK Und.*) a Jew (cf. BIGNOSE n.). [? long sideburns or *payes* as worn by orthodox Jews; ? long noses for weeping]

weeper *n.*² **1** [mid–late 19C] a piece of black crepe worn around the hat of a mourner or undertaker. **2** [late 19C–1910s] usu. in pl., a long, sweeping moustache, long sidewhiskers. [? the trailing ends of crepe once worn at funerals – where mourners wept]

weepers *n.* [mid-19C–1940s] (*US*) one's best clothes; thus those one wears to funerals.

weepie *n.* (*also* **weeper**) [1920s+] a film or story whose main effect is to reduce its audience to tears, usu. consciously romantic; thus *three-handkerchief weepie*, a very emotional film.

weeping willow *n.*¹ [late 19C+] a pillow. [rhy. sl.]

weeping willow *n.*² [1920s] (*US*) a pessimist, a killjoy.

weep Irish *v.* [mid-17C–early 18C] to talk nonsense, to shed crocodile tears. [racial stereotyping]

weeps *n.* [late 19C+] (*US*) tears.

weeps, the *n.* [late 19C+] **1** tearfulness, crying. **2** (*US tramp*) a hard-luck story.

wee small hours *n.* [mid-19C+] the very early morning.

wee-wee *n.*¹ (*also* **oui-oui**) **1** [mid-19C] (*orig. Aus./N.Z.*) a French person. **2** the French language. [the excl. *oui oui!* yes, yes! + derog. pun on WEE n.]

wee-wee *n.*² [1970s+] the penis.

wee-wee *n.*³ *see* WEE n.

wee-wee *v. see* WEE v.

wee-wee off *v.* [1960s] (*N.Z.*) to annoy, to infuriate. [euph. for PISS OFF v. (2)]

Wee Willie Winky *n.* [1990s+] a derog. term for a Chinese person (cf. AH CABBAGE n.). [rhy. sl. = CHINKY n.]

weezo *n.* [2000s] (*US prison*) an informer. [? play on SE *wheeze*]

wegro *n.* [2000s] (*US Black*) a White person who takes on Black culture and style. [SE *white* + *negro*]

we had one but the wheel came off *phr.* [1910s+] a phr. used to indicate that the speaker has not understood the subject of a conversation.

we here *phr.* [1990s+] (*US campus*) an expression of support. [US Black var. on SE *we are here*]

weigh forty *v.* [early 19C] (*UK Und.*) of a thief, to move into more serious crime, and thus be worthy of arrest. [the £40 cash bonus awarded to any policeman who secured a 'Tyburn ticket', i.e. captured a murderer]

weigh in *v.* **1** [late 19C+] (*US*) to assert oneself. **2** [late 19C+] to pay or give one's share. **3** [20C+] to join in, esp. in an argument. **4** [1910s+] to play one's part. **5** [1920s+] to arrive. [horseracing use, i.e. the pre-race *weigh-in*]

weigh in the sacks on *v.* [1930s–40s] (*US*) to criticize.

weigh into *v.* [1930s+] (*orig. Aus.*) to attack verbally or physically, to criticize.

weigh-meat *n.* [late 19C+] (*W.I.*) bones that are weighed up by the butcher and charged for along with the meat that accompanies them.

weigh off *v.* **1** [1910s+] (*UK Und.*) to sentence a convicted prisoner; thus *weighed off*, sent off to prison. **2** [1930s+] to get one's own back, to take revenge on. **3** [2000s] in fig. use, to estimate, to consider as. **4** [2000s] in fig. use, to injure, to hurt. **5** [2000s] in fig. use, to deal with. [orig. milit.]

weigh on *v.* [2000s] to repay a favour. [i.e. to add some fig. 'weight' to a relationship]

weigh one's thumb *v.* [late 19C] to give short measure. [the age-old practice of a shopkeeper keeping his thumb pressing on the scales when weighing goods]

weigh one's weight *v.* [19C] to commit a capital offence. [under an act of William and Mary the reward for the capture of a highwayman or coiner had been set at £40]

weigh out *v.* **1** [late 19C] to apportion shares. **2** [late 19C+] to hand over money.

weight *n.*[1] (*orig. US*) **1** [late 18C+] influence, importance; thus *hold no weight*, to be unimpressive, to lack credibility or influence. **2** [1930s+] blame, responsibility, obligation, duty; thus CARRY WEIGHT *v.* (2); *that's your weight*, that's your responsibility. **3** [1940s+] emotional or psychological pressure. [one is bowed beneath the *weight* of one's influence/responsibility]

weight *n.*[2] **1** [1940s] (*US Und.*) a policeman's truncheon. **2** [1960s+] (*US Black*) a gun, a pistol. [its lit. + fig. SE *weight*]

weight *n.*[3] **1** [1960s+] (*drugs*) a large quantity of drugs (esp. pounds of hashish/marijuana, kilos of cocaine/heroin). **2** [1960s+] 1lb of marijuana, cannabis. **3** [1990s+] 1oz of heroin. **4** [1990s+] a measure of a given drug, differing as to the drug in question. [(2) may be qualified by number, e.g. *five weight of hash*, 5lb of hashish]

weight pile *n. see* IRON PILE n. (2).

weighty *adj.* [2000s] (*UK teen*) good.

weigh up *v.* [late 19C+] to appraise, to assess.

weinie *n. see* WEENIE n.[1].

weinie wagger/wiggler *n. see* WEENIE WAVER n.

weird *adj.* [20C+] (*orig. UK society*) wonderful, excellent.

weird-ass *adj.* [1960s+] (*US*) strange, eccentric, mad. [SE *weird* + -ASS sfx]

weird beard *n.* (*also* **weirdie-beardie**) [1960s+] (*UK juv.*) a derog. term for one who looks like a beatnik, an eco-activist, an anti-nuclear protestor etc.

weirdie *n.* (*also* **weirdy**) **1** [late 19C+] an eccentric person; esp. as *bearded weirdie*, a man with long hair and/or a beard and as such negatively stereotyped as an 'intellectual'. **2** [1940s+] anything, typically a book or film, that is considered fantastic, bizarre or grotesque. **3** [1960s] a male homosexual. **4** [1960s] (*US campus*) an unattractive woman. [SE *weird* + sfx *-ie*]

weirdie *adj.* (*also* **weirdy**) [1950s+] odd, eccentric, peculiar.

weirdie-beardie *n. see* WEIRD BEARD n.

weirdo *n.* **1** [1950s+] an eccentric, a peculiar person. **2** [1960s+] one who enjoys non-standard sexual practice. [SE *weird* + -O sfx (7)]

weirdo *adj.* [1960s+] eccentric, odd, bizarre, out of the ordinary. [WEIRDO n. (1)]

weird out *v.* [1970s+] **1** to horrify, to play mental games. **2** (*drugs*) to experience hallucinations from intoxication by narcotics. **3** to feel confused or at a loss.

weirdsville *n.* [1950s+] (*US*) anywhere considered off or out of the ordinary. [SE *weird* + -VILLE sfx[1]]

weirdy *see under* WEIRDIE.

weisenheimer *n. see* WISENHEIMER n.

wej *n. see* WEDGE n.[3].

wejee *n. see* WEEJEE n.

welch *n.* [late 19C–1900s] (*US*) the act of defrauding a bettor. [WELCH v. (1)]

welch *v.* (*also* **welsh**) **1** [mid-19C+] to refuse to pay a gambling debt or other bill; to refuse to hand over any sum of money. **2** [late 19C+] in fig. use, to let down, to disappoint. **3** [1920s+] (*US campus*) to reject, to stand aside from, to turn down (all relate to a social engagement). **4** [1920s+] to renege on one's words or on a promised action. [racist stereotyping, but note Ger. *Welsch*, foreigner]

Welch comb *n.* (*also* **Welsh comb**) [mid-17C–early 19C] the thumb and 4 fingers, used to smooth one's hair. [racial stereotyping]

welcher *n.* (*also* **welsher**) **1** [mid-19C+] anyone who refuses to pay their debts, gambling or otherwise. **2** [1920s–60s] an informer. [WELCH v.]

welch out *v.* [1980s] (*US campus*) to opt out of an activity. [WELCH v.]

welcome green *n. see* GREEN n.[2] (1).

welcome, I'm sure! *excl.* [late 19C+] you're welcome to it! [an equivalent to the various European forms of acknowledgement that greet 'please', e.g. Ital. *prego*. In the UK, however, the form is strictly lower-/lower-middle-class]

welcome wagon *n.* [1970s+] (*US gay/prison*) the man who is first in line in a gang-rape.

welfare mother *n.* [1970s+] (*US Black*) any woman, irrespective of status vis-à-vis welfare, who is poorly dressed and unkempt. [ironic use of SE]

welfare pimp *n.* [2000s] (*US Black*) a pimp who collects the welfare checks due to his prostitutes (cf. CANDYMAN n.).

welk! *excl.* [1980s+] (*US campus*) you're *welc*ome! [abbr.]

well *v.* **1** [early 19C] (*UK Und.*) to defraud one's criminal confederates, to divide booty unfairly. **2** [mid-19C+] to pocket; thus *well it*, to be well-off, to make a good income. **3** [late 19C+] to conceal a proportion of one's income or estate from one's creditors.

well *adv.*[1] [mid-19C+] a general intensifier, very, definitely, extremely etc; thus *well tasty, well sus* etc. [Ware labels late 19C use 'society' but earlier use general]

well *adv.*[2] [late 19C] used as an intensifier in such combs. as *bloody well, damn well, jolly well* etc.

well away *phr.* **1** [1920s+] (*also* **well on**) drunk or on one's way towards being so (cf. ABOUT RIGHT phr.[1]). **2** [1940s] asleep. **3** [1960s+] making headway in a seduction.

well-breeched *adj. see* WELL-HEELED adj.[1].

well-bushed *adj.* [20C+] of a man, having notably large genitals, of a woman, having plentiful pubic hair. [SE *well* + BUSH n.[2] (1)]

well-cemented *adj.* [1950s] (*Aus.*) rich.

well-covered *adj. see* WELL-UPHOLSTERED adj.

well-endowed *adj.* **1** [1950s+] (*also* **well-end**) of a man, having notably large genitals. **2** [1960s+] of a woman, having notably large breasts. [euph.]

well-fixed *adj.* (*also* **well-got**) [early 19C+] (*US*) reasonably affluent, comfortable. [SE *well* + *fixed*, sorted out]

well fucked and far from home *phr.* [20C+] of a man, conducting an adulterous relationship.

well-furnished *adj.* [mid-18C] of a man, having notably large genitals. [euph.]

well-got *adj. see* WELL-FIXED adj.

well-heeled *adj.*[1] (*also* **all-heeled, well-breeched**) [mid-19C+] rich. [the quality of a rich person's footwear]

well-heeled *adj.*[2] *see* HEELED adj.[1].

well hove! *excl.* [1910s–20s] well done! well played! [SE *well* + *hove*, past tense of *heave*]

well-hung *adj.*[1] [late 17C+] of a man, having notably large genitals.

well-hung *adj.*[2] [20C+] young. [rhy. sl.]

wellie *n.* (*also* **welly**) [1950s+] a *welling*ton boot; usu. in pl. [abbr.]

wellied *n.* [1990s+] drunk (cf. ANNIHILATED adj.). [WELLY v. (2)]

wellies *n.* (*also* **green wellies**) [1980s+] public-school educated, upper-middle and upper-class students, who are seen as playing rather than working their way through university. [SE *wealthy* + the green wellington boots that such students wear for various rural pleasures]

well, I'll be dipped in shit! *excl.* [1960s+] (*US*) a general excl. of surprise or amazement. [SE *dipped* + SHIT n.[1] (1)]

well-in *adj.* **1** [mid-19C+] (*Aus.*) well-off, affluent. **2** [late 19C+] popular, secure, entrenched. **3** [20C+] successfully ingratiated, on the way to a successful seduction.

wellington *n.* [1960s+] (*Aus.*) sexual intercourse. [rhy. sl.; *wellington boot* = ROOT n.[1] (5)]

well-inlaid/-inlayed *adj. see* INLAID adj.

well-lined *adj.* [late 19C] rich, prosperous. [one *lines one's pockets*]

well-loaded *adj.*[1] [1920s+] of a man, having notably large genitals.

well-loaded *adj.*[2] [1930s+] (*orig. US*) drunk.

well-mended *adj.* [20C+] (*Irish*) of an ill person, improved in health.

well-oiled *adj.* [late 19C+] very drunk (cf. DAMP adj.). [SE *well* + OILED (UP) adj.]

well on *phr. see* WELL AWAY phr. (1).

well put-on *adj.* [1920s+] (*Scot./Ulster*) well-dressed.

well-shod *adj.* [late 19C] (*US*) rich. [fig., but also, no doubt, lit. 'wearing good shoes']

well-sinking *n.* [late 18C–19C] (*Anglo-Ind.*) making money. [digging for buried treasure]

well-sprung *adj.* [1910s–30s] drunk. [one is 'bouncing up and down']

well-stacked *adj.*[1] [1950s+] (*orig. US*) of a woman, attractive, esp. having a good figure, spec. large breasts and buttocks. [ext. of STACKED adj.[1] (2)]

well-stacked *adj.*[2] *see* STACKED adj.[1] (1).

well to live *phr.* [late 17C–mid-19C] tipsy. [one is enjoying life]

well under *phr.* [1910s+] (*Aus.*) drunk. [note SE *under the influence*]

well under way *phr.* [mid-19C] (*US*) drunk (cf. ABOUT RIGHT phr.[1]).

well up *phr.* [1990s+] (*Irish*) very tall.

well-upholstered *adj.* (*also* **well-covered**) [1930s+] plump, fleshy, fat.

welly *n.*[1] [2000s] a beating. [WELLY v. (2)]

welly *n.*[2] *see* WELLIE n.

welly *v.* [1980s+] **1** to kick, to trip up. **2** to beat up, to assault. [the use of a WELLIE n. to kick]

welsh *see also under* WELCH and its combs.

Welsh bait *n. see* SCOTCH BAIT n.

Welsh cricket *n.* [late 16C–early 17C] a louse. [negative stereotyping]

Welsh ejectment *n.* [early 19C] removing the roof of a tenant's house, with the purpose of making the house uninhabitable. [the stereotyped meanness of the Welsh]

Welsh fiddle *n. see* SCOTCH FIDDLE n.

Welshie *n.* (*also* **Welshy**) **1** [1920s] (*Aus.*) a native of New South Wales. **2** [1950s+] a Welshman.

Welsh parsley *n.* [early–mid-17C] hemp, as used in the hangman's rope.

welt *n.* [2000s] (*Scot.*) the penis. [dial. *welter*, something large or heavy of its type]

wem *n.* [mid-17C–early 18C] the vagina. [SE *wem*, a blemish, a defilement or by confusion with *wen*, a protruberance]

wembleys *n.* [1960s] (*US campus*) the female breasts.

wen *adj.* [mid-19C+] new; thus *teg a wen eno*, get a new one. [backsl.]

wench *n.* **1** [late 14C+] a woman. **2** [16C+] a promiscuous woman, a prostitute. **3** [1940s+] (*US campus*) an unpleasant or unattractive woman. [SE use, coined *c.*1290, is archaic]

wendy *n.* [1980s+] (*UK juv.*) a schoolchild (of either sex) who has been rejected by his or her peers. [? *Wendy*, the 'goody-goody' daughter in J.M. Barrie's *Peter Pan* (1904)]

went mad and they shot him, he *phr.* [1940s+] (*Aus.*) a general phr. used in the reply to the question 'Where is X?'

wentworth falls *n.* (*also* **wentworth's balls**) [1920s+] (*Aus.*) the testicles (cf. CHEESE AND CRACKERS n.). [rhy. sl. = BALLS n.[1] (1); ult. the *Wentworth Falls*, near Katoomba in the Blue Mountains of New South Wales]

werris *n.* [1960s+] (*Aus.*) a Greek. [rhy. sl.; abbr. of *Werris Creek*]

Wessi *n.* [1990s+] an occupant of the former West Germany; as opposed to OSSI n. [Ger. sl.; ult. from *Westdeutsche*, West German]

Westbound, the *n.* [1930s] (*US tramp*) death.

West Broadway *n.* [mid-19C] (*US*) hash, stew. [ety. unknown]

west central *n.* [mid-19C] a water closet. [a pun on SE *WC*/the W.C. (west central) London postal district]

west coast turnarounds *n.* [1980s+] (*drugs*) amphetamines;

MDMA (cf. A n.[2]; ECSTASY n.). [their use in keeping long-distance drivers awake]

West End thespian *n. see* THESPIAN n.

western guy *n.* [1930s–40s] (*US Und.*) an out-of-town thief.

West Ham(s) (Reserves) *n.* [1970s+] nerves. [rhy. sl.; ult. *West Ham United*, London football team]

West Hell *n.* (*also* **East Hell**) [1930s+] (*US*) anywhere considered far away, unpleasant and culturally alien.

westie *n.* (*Aus.*) **1** [1980s+] one who lives in the *western* suburbs of Sydney. **2** [2000s] one who totally lacks fashion sense.

Westminster Abbey *n.* [20C+] a cabbie. [rhy. sl.]

Westminster brougham *n. see* WHITECHAPEL BROUGHAM n.

Westminster wedding *n.* [mid-17C–early 19C] 'a Whore and a Rogue Married together' (B.E.); a visit to a prostitute. [the contemporary negative reputation of Westminster; thus the pvb 'who goes to Westminster for a wife, to Paul's for a man, and to Smithfield for a horse may meet with a whore, a knave, and a jade']

Westphalia *n.* [late 19C–1920s] the posterior, the buttocks. [pun on *Westphalia* ham/SE *ham*, the back of the thigh and buttock]

Westralia *n.* [late 19C+] (*Aus.*) Western Australia; thus *Westralian*, *Westralienne*, a Western Australian. [abbr.]

wet *n.*[1] **1** [late 17C+] (*also* **whet**) a drink; thus *wet stuff*, alcohol; *do a wet*, to have a drink. **2** [1960s] (*US campus*) a drinking party.

wet *n.*[2] [late 19C–1930s] (*US*) an anti-Prohibitionist, who wants alcohol to remain legal.

wet *n.*[3] [1920s+] the act of urination. [SE *wet*, to urinate]

wet *n.*[4] (*also* **wet end**, **wetso**) [1930s+] (*orig. UK juv.*) an ineffectual, weak, foolish person.

wet *n.*[5] *see* WETBACK n.

wet, the *n.* [late 19C+] (*Aus.*) the rainy season.

wet *adj.*[1] **1** [late 17C; late 19C+] of a woman, sexually excited, 'secreting lech-water'. **2** [early 18C+] drunk; sometimes *all wet* (cf. DAMP adj.). **3** [mid-19C–1920s] drunken; often as *wet night*. **4** [mid-19C+] (*US*) permitting the sale of alcohol; thus a *wet state*.

wet *adj.*[2] [1910s–50s] (*Aus.*) angry.

wet *adj.*[3] [1910s+] **1** (*mainly UK upper-middle/upper class*) weak, spineless; thus *wetness*, weakness, ineffectuality, spinelessness. **2** incorrect, mistaken, no good; usu. as ALL WET phr.

wet *adj.*[4] [1920s–40s] of a horse, stolen and smuggled from Mexico. [WET n.[5]]

wet *adj.*[5] [1970s] (*US Black*) suspicious. [play on FISHY adj.[3] (1)]

wet *adj.*[6] *see* WET QUAKER n.

wet *v.*[1] (*also* **wet it**, **wet one's nose**, **wet up**, **whet**) **1** [late 17C+] to drink; thus *wet the other eye*, to have another drink. **2** [mid-19C] (*US campus*) to 'christen' new clothes by treating one's friends to a drink on the first occasion of wearing them. **3** [mid–late 19C] to treat to a drink for any form of celebration.

wet *v.*[2] (*also* **wet up**) [1970s–80s] (*UK Black*) to slash or stab with a knife. [blood is *wet*]

wet *v.*[3] [1990s+] (*US Black*) to excite a woman. [vaginal secretions, i.e. to make her WET adj.[1] (1)]

wet *adv.* [1910s+] foolishly, weakly.

wet affairs *n. see* WET WORK n.

wet and damp *n.* [1980s+] (*Aus. prison*) a homosexual. [rhy. sl. = CAMP n.[2] (1)]

wet arts *n. see* WET WORK n.

wetback *n.* (*also* **wet**) [1920s+] a derog. term for an illegal Mexican immigrant to the USA; thus used of Mexicans and Hispanics in general (cf. BATO n.). [the condition of the immigrants who trad. swim the Rio Grande as the best means of beating border checks. Despite its reputation as a racist slur, Hispanics accept it; thus US Mex. self-description *los mojados*, the wet ones]

wetback *adj.* [1940s+] (*US*) pertaining to illegal Mexican immigrants. [WETBACK n.]

wet bargain *n.* [early 19C] a deal concluded over drinks.

wet behind the ears *phr.* (*also* **before one was dry behind the ears, wet-eared, wet from the borning time**) [20C+] naïve, inexperienced, gauche.

wet blanket *n.* **1** [mid-19C+] a dreary person, a spoilsport, a 'killjoy'. **2** [20C+] a depressing event or situation. [the use of a wet blanket to quench fires]

wet both eyes *v. see* WET THE OTHER EYE *v.*

wetbox *n.* [2000s] (*US*) the vagina. [WET adj.¹ (1) + BOX n.¹ (1)]

wetbrain *n.* [1950s+] a state of stupidity induced by alcoholism; thus an alcoholic; non-specifically a fool (cf. BAKEBRAIN n.). [SE *water on the brain*, i.e. encephalitis]

wet check *n.* [1990s+] (*Aus.*) a contraceptive sheath, a condom.

wet day *n. see* WET WEEK n.

wet deck *n.* [late 19C+] (*Can./US*) a woman or prostitute who performs serial sex acts. [the accumulation of sexual fluids]

wet dream *n.* **1** [1910s–40s] something pathetic. **2** [1920s+] a fantasy, esp. a particularly optimistic one. [ext. uses of SE]

wet-eared *adj. see* WET BEHIND THE EARS phr.

wet end *n. see* WET n.⁴.

wet foot *n.* [1970s] a naïve, inexperienced, innocent person; also as adj.

wet from the borning time *phr. see* WET BEHIND THE EARS phr.

wet goods *n.* [late 18C; mid-19C–1940s] alcohol. [opposite of SE *dry goods*, groceries etc]

wet goose *n.* [late 19C] a foolish, naïve person. [WET adj.³ (1) + GOOSE n.¹ (1)]

wet hand *n.* (*also* **wet 'un**) [late 19C] a drunkard, a heavy drinker. [WET adj.¹ (2) + HAND n.¹]

wethead *n.* [1970s+] (*US Black*) a simpleton, an innocent, a novice. [SE *wet* + -HEAD sfx (1)]

wet hen *n.* [late 19C] (*US*) a prostitute (cf. ALLEY CAT n.). [? WET adj.¹ (1) + HEN n.¹ (1)]

wet in *v.* [1970s] to celebrate a promotion by drinking (to excess).

wet it *v. see* WET v.¹.

wet leg *n.* [1920s–30s] a self-pitying person. [? they are fig. urinating down their own leg]

wet-nosed *adj.* [1960s+] (*US*) innocent, naïve.

wet one *n.*¹ [early 19C] a drinker. [WET adj.¹ (2) + SE *one*]

wet one *n.*² [late 19C+] a loose breaking of wind.

wet oneself *v.* [1930s+] to become over-excited. [i.e. WET ONE'S PANTS v. (1)]

wet one's goozle *v.* [1920s] (*US*) to have a drink. [SE *wet* + GOOZLE n.]

wet one's jacket *v.* [early 19C] (*US*) to get drunk. [SE *wet* + JACKET n.¹]

wet one's knickers *v. see* WET ONE'S PANTS v.

wet one's luck *v.* [1900s] (*Aus.*) to drink in celebration of one's good fortune.

wet one's neck *v.* **1** [early 19C; 1910s] to have a drink. **2** [early–mid-19C] to get drunk.

wet one's nose *v. see* WET v.¹.

wet one's pants *v.* (*also* **spot one's pants, wet one's knickers**) **1** [1930s+] to panic, to lose control, to get over-excited. **2** [1960s+] to find extremely exciting or attractive. [the involuntary urination that may follow great fear]

wet one's tonsils *v.* [1940s–60s] (*US*) to drink.

wet one's whistle *v.* **1** [late 14C+] to take a drink; thus *whistle-wetter*, a drink. **2** [early 17C–early 18C; 1960s] to give someone a drink. [SE *wet* + WHISTLE n.¹ (1)]

wet parson *n.* [late 18C–early 19C] a parson with a taste for liquor. [WET adj.¹ (2) + SE *parson*]

wet Quaker *n.* [late 17C–mid-19C] one who pretends to be religious and abjure alcohol, but in fact drinks regularly in secret; also in fig. use. [WET adj.¹ (2) + *Quaker*]

wet rag *n.* [1940s+] **1** an emotional, sentimental person. **2** (*US campus*) an unpleasant, unpopular person.

wet smack *n.* [1920s+] (*US*) a weakling, an ineffectual person. [WET adj.³ (1) + fig. use of SE *smack*]

wetso *n. see* WET n.⁴.

wet someone's ass *v.* [2000s] (*US Black*) to shoot someone. [the wetness of blood]

wet soul *n.* [early 19C] a regular and reasonably heavy drinker. [WET adj.¹ (2) + SE *soul*, a person]

wet suit *n.* [1990s+] (*Aus.*) a contraceptive sheath, a condom.

wet the baby's head *v.* [late 19C+] to drink in celebration of a baby's birth.

wet the clay *v. see* MOISTEN THE CLAY v.

wet the deal *v.* (*also* **wet the bargain/coat**) [mid-19C+] to seal a deal with a drink.

wet-thee-through *n.* [early 19C] gin.

wet the other eye *v.* (*also* **wet both eyes, …t'other eye**) [mid-18C–19C] to follow one drink immediately by another.

wettie *n.* [1990s+] (*Aus./N.Z.*) a wet suit. [abbr.]

wet 'un *n.*¹ [mid-19C] a diseased cow, technically unfit for human consumption, but often sold for conversion into sausages. [*wet 'un* presumably means 'wet brain' and the disease must have been the same as, or at least similar to, the late 20C+ BSE, 'mad cow disease']

wet 'un *n.*² *see* WET HAND n.

wet 'uns *n.* [late 19C] tears.

wet up *v.*¹ *see* WET v.¹.

wet up *v.*² *see* WET v.².

wet week *n.* (*also* **wet day**) [20C+] (*Irish*) a short time. [? being *wet* it 'shrinks']

wet work *n.* (*also* **wet affairs/arts**) [1960s+] murder, assassination, esp. as carried out by secret services; thus *get wet*, to be assassinated. [translation of KGB sl. *Mokryye Dela*, the department of wet affairs]

wetworks *n.* [1900s] (*US*) a bar. [WET n.¹ (1) + SE *works*]

we wuz robbed! *excl.* [1930s+] we were cheated! [coined by US boxing manager Joe Jacobs (1896–1940), manager in 1932 of the German world heavyweight champion Max Schmeling. Defending his title in America, Schmeling systematically destroyed his opponent but was still declared the loser, outpointed by the challenger, local boy Jack Sharkey. Jacobs' phr. made his feelings plain]

WGB *n.* [2000s] (*US Black*) a White girl's buttocks.

w.g.f. *phr.* [1960s+] used by transsexuals to mean *whole girl fantasy* or *fetish*. [abbr.]

wha'appen? *phr. see* WHAT HAPPEN? phr.

whack *see also under* WACK and its combs.

whack *n.*¹ (*also* **wack**) **1** [late 18C+] a blow, usu. with some form of stick. **2** [1940s] (*US Und.*) a sentence. **3** [1960s+] (*Scot./Aus.*) a punishment, one's deserts; thus *cop one's whack*, to get one's deserts. **4** [1980s+] (*drugs*) the act of diluting bulk drugs, e.g. heroin, for retail sale. [WHACK v.¹]

whack *n.*² (*also* **wack**) **1** [late 18C+] a share, a portion. **2** [early 19C+] a swig of a drink, a gulp of food. **3** [late 19C+] (*US*) a try, an attempt; often in phr. HAVE A WHACK AT v. **4** [late 19C+] a 'go', a time. **5** [1980s+] (*W.I.*) a large sum of money. **6** [1990s+] (*drugs*) a portion of a drug, e.g. a 'line' of a narcotic, a puff of cannabis. [ext. uses of WHACK v.¹ (1)]

whack *n.*³ [early 19C] (*Anglo-Irish*) a pickpocket.

whack *n.*⁴ (*also* **wack**) [mid-19C–1910s] (*Anglo-Irish*) food, sustenance. [Scot. *whack*, a slice, appetite]

whack *n.*⁵ (*also* **wack**) **1** [1940s+] (*US*) a mad or eccentric person; occas. of a place. **2** [1980s+] (*US campus*) (*also* **whacker**) a fool. [abbr. WHACKO n.]

whack *n.*⁶ *see* WHACKER n.¹.

whack *v.*¹ (*also* **wack**) **1** [late 18C+] to hit. **2** [20C+] to hit in a fig. sense, e.g. to sentence to prison. **3** [20C+] (*also* **whack out**) to defeat in a competition, to outdo. **4** [1900s] (*US*) to lie. **5** [1930s+] (*also* **wack out, whack out**) to murder, to kill; also in fig. use. **6** [1930s+] (*US*) to cut or chop. **7** [1950s+] (*also* **wack off, whack off**) to masturbate; thus *whack-silly*, addicted to masturbation and as such, mad (cf. BANG THE BISHOP v.; BOFF v.). **8** [1970s+] (*US drugs*) (*also* **whack up**) to dilute or 'cut' a narcotic.

whack v.[2] (*also* **wack**) **1** [early 19C] (*also* **whack out**) to share or divide equally; thus *whack the blunt*, to share out the money. **2** [1960s+] to charge money; usu. *whack someone for*. [WHACK n.[2]]

whack-a-doo *adj.* [20C+] lunatic, eccentric. [ext. of WHACKO n.]

whackatabacky *n. see* WHACKY BACCY n.

whack attack n.[1] (*also* **wack attack**) [1980s+] (*US Black*) the onset of apparent insanity, usu. through the use of drugs. [WHACK n.[5] (1) + SE *attack*]

whack attack n.[2] (*also* **wack attack**) [1980s+] an act of masturbation; often as *have a whack attack*. [WHACK IT v. + SE *attack* + play on McDonalds' hamburger's coinage, *Mac attack*, a sudden craving for a hamburger]

whack down v.[1] (*also* **wack down**) [20C+] to lay down money, to write down notes. [WHACK v.[1] (1) + SE *down*]

whack down v.[2] (*also* **whack off**) **1** [1960s+] to consume, to eat or drink. **2** [2000s] to inhale. [fig. uses of WHACK v.[1] (1)]

whacked *adj.* (*also* **wacked**, **wacked to the wide**, **whacked to the wide**) **1** [20C+] completely shocked, overcome. **2** [20C+] beaten, defeated. **3** [1910s+] absolutely exhausted. **4** [1940s+] (*US campus*) eccentric (cf. WHACKED OUT adj.[2]; WHACKO adj.[1]; WHACKY adj.). **5** [1990s+] overcome by an excess of drink or drugs. **6** [1990s+] (*US campus*) stupid. **7** [2000s] ruined, in disrepair. [WHACK v.[1]]

whacked out *adj.*[1] (*also* **wacked**, **wacked out**, **whacked**) [1960s+] **1** [*orig. US*] murdered. **2** exhausted. **3** having lost all one's money gambling. **4** under the influence of a drug or of alcohol. **5** emotionally drained. [WHACK v.[1]]

whacked out *adj.*[2] (*also* **wacked out**) [1960s+] crazy, insane, eccentric (cf. WHACKED adj.). [WHACKO n.]

whacked to the wide *adj. see* WHACKED adj.

whacked up *adj.* [1940s+] (*US*) **1** absurd, ludicrous, crazy. **2** (*also* **wacked up**) badly injured. [(1) WHACKED adj. (4); (2) WHACK v.[1] (1)]

whacker n.[1] (*also* **whack**) [late 18C+] anything particularly large or notable, e.g. a lie. [WHACK v.[1] (1)]

whacker n.[2] [1910s] (*UK Und.*) a police truncheon. [WHACK v.[1] (1)]

whacker n.[3] [1930s] (*Irish*) a small glass of brandy. [WHACK n.[2] (2)]

whacker n.[4] (*also* **wacker**) [1940s+] (*US*) a masturbator, lit. and fig. [WHACK v.[1] (7)]

whacker n.[5] (*also* **wacker**) [1960s+] (*Aus.*) **1** a fool. **2** a person who is seriously mentally unstable. [WHACKY adj. but note WHACK v.[1] (7), i.e. the mythical links of masturbation and insanity]

whacker n.[6] *see* WHACK n.[5] (2).

whacking *n.* **1** [mid-19C+] a blow, a beating. **2** [2000s] a murder. [WHACK v.[1]]

whacking *adv.* [early 19C+] a general intensifier; usu. in *whacking great*, *whacking horrible* etc; also as adj. [WHACKER n.[1]]

whack it *v.* (*also* **wack it**) [1960s+] to masturbate (cf. BANG THE BISHOP v.). [fig. use of WHACK v.[1] (7)]

whack it in *v.* (*also* **wack it in**, **wack it up**, **whack it up**) [late 19C+] of a man, to have sexual intercourse (cf. BANG v.[1]; BURY IT v.). [fig. use of WHACK v.[1]]

whack it out *v.* (*also* **wack it out**) [1910s–20s] to defend or support successfully. [WHACK v.[1]]

whack it up v.[1] [1910s] (*Aus.*) to do something energetically. [fig. use of WHACK v.[1]]

whack it up v.[2] *see* WHACK IT IN v.

whack job *n.* [1970s+] (*US*) an insane person, a madman. [WHACKO n. + JOB n.[6]]

whackle out *v.* [1910s] (*Aus.*) to consider deeply.

whacko *n.* (*also* **wack**, **wacko**) [1970s+] **1** an unstable or mentally ill person. **2** a crazy, eccentric or extreme person. [WHACKO adj.[1]]

whacko adj.[1] (*also* **wacko**) [1940s+] crazy, insane, eccentric (cf. WHACKED adj.). [WHACKY adj.]

whacko adj.[2] [1950s–60s] (*Aus.*) exciting, pleasurable. [WHACKO! excl.]

whacko! *excl.* (*also* **wacko!**) [1910s+] (*Aus.*) a general excl. of pleasure.

whack off v.[1] *see* WHACK v.[1] (7).

whack off v.[2] *see* WHACK DOWN v.[2].

whacko-the-chook *adj.* (*also* **whacko-the-goose**) [1970s+] (*Aus.*) excellent, first-rate, absolutely wonderful. [WHACKO! excl. + CHOOK n. (1)/SE *goose*]

whacko-the-diddle-oh *adj.* [1940s+] (*Aus.*) excellent, splendid, first-rate. [WHACKO THE DIDDLE-OH! excl.]

whacko the diddle-oh! *excl.* [1940s+] (*Aus.*) a general excl. of pleasure, esp. on seeing an attractive woman. [ext. WHACKO! excl.]

whacko-the-goose *adj. see* WHACKO-THE-CHOOK adj.

whack-out *n.* [1960s] (*US*) an absolute failure. [WHACK OUT v.[2], i.e. one is 'dead']

whack out v.[1] (*also* **wack out**) **1** [20C+] to create, to make. **2** [1910s+] to play (music), to 'knock out' (a tune). [fig. uses of WHACK v.[1] (1)]

whack out v.[2] (*also* **wack out**) **1** [1960s] of objects, to destroy; as *whack something out*. **2** [1990s+] to render unconscious; often as *whack someone out*. [WHACK v.[1] (5)]

whack out v.[3] *see* WHACK v.[1].

whack out v.[4] *see* WHACK v.[2] (1).

whack the crap out of *v.* [1960s] (*orig. US*) to beat hard. [WHACK v.[1] (1) + CRAP n.[3] (6)]

whack the one-eyed worm *v.* (*also* **whack the weasel**) [1960s+] to masturbate (cf. BANG THE BISHOP v.; BEAT ONE'S HOG v.). [WHACK v.[1] (7) + ONE-EYED (WONDER) WORM n./WEASEL n.[3]]

whack-up *n.* [late 19C+] a division of the spoils. [WHACK UP v.[2]]

whack up v.[1] **1** [late 19C+] (*US*) to make a contribution, a donation. **2** [late 19C+] to come up with, to create. **3** [1980s+] (*US*) to acquire money, esp. by bribery. [WHACK n.[2]]

whack up v.[2] [late 19C+] (*orig. US*) to divide loot. [ext. WHACK v.[2] (1)]

whack up v.[3] [20C+] of an engine, a vehicle, to accelerate. [ext. use of WHACK v.[1] (1)]

whack up v.[4] [1980s+] (*Aus. prison*) to inject narcotics. [ext. use of WHACK v.[1], i.e. HIT v.[3] (4)]

whack up v.[5] *see* WHACK v.[1] (8).

whacky *adj.* (*also* **wacky**) [1930s+] (*orig. US*) eccentric; thus *w(h)ackiness*, eccentricity (cf. WHACKED adj.). [Yorks. dial. *whacky*, a fool, a simpleton, a blockhead; also Warwickshire dial. *whacky*, left-handed]

-whacky *sfx* (*also* **-wacky**) [1930s+] (*US*) a comb. adj. to describe an enthusiasm or habit, e.g. *car-wacky*, car crazy. [WHACKY adj.]

whacky baccy *n.* (*also* **wackey dust**, **wacky baccy**, **wacky weed**, **whackatabacky**, **whacky weed**) [1930s; 1980s+] (*drugs*) marijuana. [WHACKY adj. + *baccy* (see BACCA n.)/DUST n.[5] (4)/WEED n.[1] (4)]

whacky for *phr.* [1960s+] (*US*) keen on, fascinated by. [WHACKY adj.]

whaddaya whaddaya? *phr.* [1950s+] a general interrog. phr.; lit. what do you?

whaddup? *phr.* [1990s+] (*US Black*) a phr. of greeting. [var. on WHAT'S UP? phr. (1)]

whaddya know? *phr. see* WHAT DO YOU KNOW? phr.

whaffle *v. see* WAFFLE v.[1].

wha' gwaan *phr. see* WHAT A GWAAN? phr.

whail *v.* (*also* **whale**) [1940s–60s] (*US Black*) to do something particularly well or efficiently.

whale *n.* **1** [mid-19C–1920s] (*US, orig. campus*) an exceptionally brilliant scholar; thus in general a very competent person. **2** [late 19C–1910s] (*Aus.*) an exceptional performer in a given discipline; thus phr. *be a whale on*. **3** [late 19C+] (*US*) an exceptionally large or fat person. **4** [late 19C+] (*also* **gale**) a large quantity; a general intensifier; esp. in phr. *whale of a*. **5** [1900s–10s] a fanatic, an obsessive. [joc. uses of SE, the size of the creature]

whale *v.*[1] (*also* **whale on**) **1** [mid-19C+] (*US*) (*also* **wail, wail on, wale**) to hit, to thrash or trounce; also in fig. use. **2** [1950s+] (*US Black/campus*) to act or do well. [? SE *wale*, to mark the flesh with wales (weals), or a *whale*bone whip]

whale *v.*[2] *see* WHAIL *v.*

whale and whitewash *n.* [1930s] (*UK tramp*) fish in white sauce.

whale away *v.* (*also* **whale into/it**) [mid-19C+] (*US*) to attack or work at something vigorously, esp. when vocalizing a point; usu. with *at*. [ext. of WHALE *v.*[1] (1)]

whale belly *n.* [1930s] (*US tramp*) a steel coal-car.

whalebone lay *n.* [early 18C] (*UK Und.*) using a piece of whalebone daubed with an adhesive to rob a shop till. [SE *whalebone* + LAY *n.*[4] (1)]

whale down *v.* [1950s+] to eat furiously. [ext. WHALE *v.*[1] (1)]

whale in the bay *n.* (*Aus.*) **1** [1930s] someone who has money to spend and uses it on the assembled company. **2** [1980s+] a person at work behind the scenes, usu. in a negative way.

whale into/it *v. see* WHALE AWAY *v.*

whale of a *phr.*[1] [1910s+] someone or something exceptional, outstanding, enjoyable.

whale of a *phr.*[2] *see* WHALE *n.* (4).

whale on *v. see* WHALE *v.*[1].

whaler *n.*[1] (*also* **waler**) [mid-19C–1960s] (*US*) anything considered large of its kind. [SE *whale*]

whaler *n.*[2] (*also* **waler**) [late 19C–1940s] (*Aus.*) a tramp, a vagrant.

whaler *n.*[3] *see* WALER *n.*

whaler's delight *n.* [1900s–20s] (*Aus.*) brown sugar mixed with cold tea to make a thick paste. [WHALER *n.*[2] + SE *delight*]

whales on *phr.* [late 19C] (*US*) obsessed with, devoted to. [WHALE *n.* (5) + SE *on*]

whale the piss out of *v.* (*also* **whale the shit out of**) [1970s+] to beat viciously. [WHALE *v.*[1] (1) + PISS, THE *n.*/SHIT, THE *n.*[2]]

whale the tar out of *v. see* BEAT THE TAR OUT OF *v.*

whale up the Lachlan *v.* [1950s] (*Aus.*) to live as a tramp. [WHALER *n.*[2] + *Lachlan*, a river in southeast Australia]

whaling *n.* [mid-19C+] a beating. [WHALE *v.*[1] (1)]

whaling *adj.*[1] [1900s–10s] (*US*) a general intensifier, enormous. [SE *whale*]

whaling *adj.*[2] *see* WAILING *adj.*

wham *n.* **1** [1910s+] a blow, usu. from a fist; also in fig. use. **2** [1980s] (*US Black*) a large, aggressive man. **3** [1980s] an unpleasant woman. [WHAM *v.* (1)]

wham *v.* **1** [1910s+] (*orig. US*) to hit or strike; also in fig. use. **2** [1920s] to throw hard. [echoic]

wham! *excl.* (*also* **whammo!**) [1920s+] (*US*) used to express surprise or convey the impact of a sudden violent attack or blow; also attrib.; thus *whammo*, energy, spirit. [echoic]

wham bam! *excl.* [1940s+] (*orig. US*) used to express sudden or speedy movement.

wham bam, thank you ma'am *phr.* (*also* **gangbang, thank you ma'am; ram, bam, thank you ma'am; slam, bam, thank you ma'am**) [1940s+] **1** epitomizing brief sexual intercourse intended on the whole for male satisfaction only. **2** anything, in a non-sexual sense, that has to be done quickly and perfunctorily; also attrib. **3** thank you, usu. cynical. [echoic]

whambang *adj.* [1950s+] (*US*) loud, large and impressive.

whamdanglers *n.* [1990s+] an extremely large pair of breasts (cf. BOBBER *n.*[2]). [WHAM *v.* (1) + SE *dangle*]

whammer *n.* [1990s+] the penis (cf. AX *n.*[2]). [WHAM *v.* (1)]

whammo! *excl. see* WHAM! *excl.*

whammy *n.* **1** [1930s+] a 'hex', an evil influence, the evil eye. **2** [1950s+] a punchline, anything devastating and beyond a similarly powerful response. **3** [1960s] spiritual force. **4** [1960s] (*US drugs*) (*also* **whammie**) a portion of a given drug that will induce the desired level of intoxication. **5** [1980s+] (*US campus*) an extremely unattractive woman. [WHAM *v.*; note *Whammy*, a character who can paralyse with a stare in comic strip *Li'l Abner*]

whang *n.*[1] [late 18C+] a reverberating blow. [WHANG *v.* (1)]

whang *n.*[2] [20C+] (*Irish*) a thin, lanky person. [Scot. *whang*, a bootlace]

whang *n.*[3] **1** [1910s+] (*Aus.*) a large piece, a share, a portion. **2** [1930s–40s] (*US*) (*also* **whangdanger**) an excellent thing.

whang *n.*[4] [1920s–30s] (*US Und.*) a stupid person.

whang *n.*[5] [1930s+] (*orig. US*) the penis, usu. large. [fig. use of WHANG *v.* (1), i.e. the aggressive image of the penis as that which 'hits' the vagina]

whang *v.* **1** [late 18C+] to hit. **2** [19C+] to throw, to drive, to pull, to shoot etc with force or with violent impact. [SE *thong*, to flog or lash with a thong; ult. f. ON *ßvengja*, to secure or fasten with a thong]

whangdanger *n. see* WHANG *n.*[3] (2).

whangdoodle *n.*[1] (*also* **wangdoodle, wingdoodle**) (*US*) **1** [mid-19C] a mythical beast of uncertain character. **2** [late 19C+] an unspecified object, something one does not know the name of. **3** [1920s] nonsense. **4** [1920s] jazz music. [nonsense word; (2) is fig. use of (1)]

whangdoodle *n.*[2] (*also* **wangdoodle, wingdoodle**) [1970s+] (*US*) the penis (cf. BAUBLE *n.*). [WHANGDOODLE *n.*[1] (2) + ext. of WHANG *n.*[5]; note DOODLE *n.*[2] (1) although the link is unlikely]

whangee *n.* [1900s–60s] a cane. [Chinese *huang*, bamboo sprouts that were too old for eating; thus the *whangee* was a cane made from the stem of one or other species of *Phyllostachys*, Chinese and Japanese plants allied to and resembling bamboos]

whanger *n.* **1** [late 19C] anything large or unusual of its kind. **2** [1910s+] the penis, usu. larger than average. [fig. use of WHANG *v.* (1); note WHANG *n.*[5]]

whank *v. see* WANK *v.*

whap *see also under* WHOP.

whap *n.* [1920s–60s] a hit, a blow. [echoic/WHOP *n.* (1)]

wha'ppen *phr. see* WHAT'S HAPPENING? *phr.*

whap that thing! *excl.* [1960s–70s] (*US Black*) a congratulatory remark to a passing woman, implying her supreme sexiness. [WHOP *v.* (2) + SE *thing*]

wharfie *n.* [1910s+] (*Aus./N.Z.*) a docker. [SE *wharf*, the usu. Aus./N.Z. term for SE *dock*]

wharf-rat *n.* [mid-19C–1940s] (*orig. US*) anyone who hangs around wharfs, looking out for an opportunity to steal from a cargo. [SE *wharf* + RAT *n.*[2] (5)]

what! *excl.* **1** [early 19C+] an excl. meaning what did you say? or what is it? **2** [mid-18C+] (*also* **eh, what!**) an expletive tacked onto the end of a sentence to give it greater emphasis or act as an affirmative, meaning isn't it? isn't he? etc, e.g. *that's a nasty fellow, what!*

what about it? *phr.* [1910s] (*Aus.*) an invitation to drink.

what a gwaan? *phr.* (*also* **wha' gwaan**) [1970s+] (*W.I./UK Black teen*) what is going on? what's happening? how are things?

what-all *n.* [1940s+] anything for which one has no proper name; often as *I don't know what-all*.

what are you pushing? *phr.* [1970s] (*US Black*) what sort of car do you drive? [PUSH *v.*[5]]

what a trip! *excl.* [1960s+] how bizarre! how strange! what an odd experience! [TRIP *n.*[5] (2)]

what can I do you for? *phr.* [1920s+] a facetious reversal of SE *what can I do for you?* [DO *v.*[2] (1)]

whatchamacallit *n.* (*also* **whatchacallit, watchumajigger, what-sha-call-him, what-you-call-it**) [late 16C; mid-19C+]

anything to which one cannot give a name when required; also used euph.

what cooks? *phr. see* WHAT'S COOKING? phr.

what does it look like? *phr.* [1970s] (*US campus*) hello.

what-do-you-call-it *n.* (*also* **what d'ye callum**) [17C–18C] the genitals. [euph.]

what do you know? *phr.* (*also* **whaddya know? what do you think?**) **1** [20C+] an expression of surprise, usu. ironic. **2** [1910s+] a greeting, hello, how are you, what have you been doing?

what do you say? *phr.* [1920s+] (*US*) how are you?

what do you want, jam on it? *phr. see* DO YOU WANT JAM ON IT? phr.

whatd'youcallhim *n.* (*also* **whatd'youcallher, what-d'ye-call'em**) [late 16C+] anyone for whom one cannot provide the name.

what-d'you-call-it *n.* (*also* **whatdayacallit, whatdyecall, whatd'yecall'em, whatd'yecallum, whatyermecallems, whatyermycalit**) [late 16C+] anything for which one has no precise name.

what else is new? *phr.* [1950s+] (*orig. US*) a deprecating comment on anything the previous speaker has said, esp. if that speaker had intended to make a big impression.

what-er? *n.* (*also* **what-y?**) [late 19C] a form of 'what' used when questioning the previous speaker's self-description, e.g. *'I'm a butcher.' 'A what-er?'*.

whatever *adv.* **1** [20C+] whatever happens, at all events. **2** [1970s+] (*orig. US Black/teen*) a general expression of dismissal, disinterest.

whatever bakes one's biscuit *phr.* [2000s] (*US*) whatever makes one happy or satisfied.

whatever floats your boat *phr.* (*also* **whatever blows your skirt up**) [1980s+] (*US*) a general phr. of acquiescence; whatever you like, whatever makes you happy.

whatever turns you on *phr.* [1970s+] whatever you like, whatever makes you happy, esp. as a slightly sarcastic response to a revelation of a particularly bizarre or distasteful pleasure (usu. sexual). [SE *whatever* + TURN (SOMEONE) ON v. (6)]

what-for *n.* (*also* **what-sort**) [late 19C+] a punishment, trouble, a fuss; usu. in phr. GIVE SOMEONE WHAT-FOR v. [? abbr. of the question 'what are you doing this to me for?' or 'what is this happening for?']

what gives? *phr.* (*also* **what's giving?**) [1940s+] a general greeting; thus *what gives with —?*, how is —?, what is happening with —? [Yid. *vi geht's?* how goes it?]

what happen? *phr.* (*also* **wha'appen? what happening?**) [1950s+] (*W.I./UK Black*) a general form of greeting, hello, how are you?

what Harry gave Doll *n.* (*also* **what Robin gave Nell**) [late 17C–19C] sexual intercourse; thus *get what Harry gave Doll*, of a woman, to have sexual intercourse. [generic use of proper names]

what-ho *adj.* [1930s] (*US*) enjoyable, fun. [WHAT HO! excl.]

what ho! *excl.* [late 17C; early 19C+] a general excl., usu. of greeting.

what ho, she bumps! *excl.* [late 19C+] an excl. used on seeing a special display of energy, esp. by a woman. [orig. used of a boat moving through choppy seas]

what in Cain? *phr.* [mid-19C] a general intensifier of a question. [euph. for WHAT IN HELL? phr.]

what in hell? *phr.* (*also* **how in (holy) hell? where in hell? who in hell? why in hell?**) [mid-19C+] a general intensifier of a query.

what in time? *phr.* (*also* **why in time?**) [mid-19C–1920s] (*US*) a question, often deriving from one's incomprehension or surprise, i.e. what on earth? what in the world? etc.

whatisit *n. see* WHATSIT n.

what is (it)? *phr.* [1970s+] (*US Black/campus*) a greeting. [the usual response is 'What it was']

what is this, Christmas? *excl.* [1980s+] a general excl. of pleasurable surprise.

what it is? *phr.* [1970s+] (*US Black*) a friendly greeting, hello, how are you?

what it takes *n.* [1920s–30s] (*orig. US*) money (cf. ACTUAL, THE n.). [the centrality of money to daily life]

what-nosed *adj.* [19C] drunk. [play on 'what do they know?', being so drunk + the swollen/red *nose* of drunkenness]

what-not *n.* **1** [late 16C+] used when the correct description or name eludes the speaker; also of an unnamed action. **2** [1930s] the penis (cf. BAUBLE n.).

what odds? *phr.* (*also* **what's the odds?**) [mid-19C+] what's the difference?

what-oh *n.* [1910s–20s] a 'fast' young woman. [the appreciative *what, oh!* remark of a watching male]

what Paddy gave the drum *n.* [mid-19C+] (*orig. milit.*) a thrashing, a beating.

what price (the)... *phr.* [late 19C+] what do you think of (something/someone) now? [racing use *price*, the odds]

what Robin gave Nell *n. see* WHAT HARRY GAVE DOLL n.

whatsamajig *n.* [1990s+] (*Aus.*) something the name of which one does not know or has forgotten.

what say? *phr.* [early 19C+] (*orig. US*) what did you say? what was that? what do you think?

what's biting you? *phr.* (*also* **what's itching you?**) [1910s+] what's the matter? what's the problem?

what's buzzin' cousin? *phr.* [1940s–50s] (*US*) what's happening? how have you been? [BUZZ v.[6] (1) + assonance]

what's cooking? *phr.* (*also* **what cooks?**) [1930s+] **1** (*orig. US*) a phr. of greeting, WHAT'S GOING ON? phr. **2** lit. what's going on?, i.e. what is happening? [orig. swing band use]

what's cracking? *phr.* [1990s+] (*orig. US Black*) a general phr. of greeting.

what's crackulatin'? *phr. see* WHAT'S KRACKALACKIN? phr.

what's crawling you? *phr.* [1910s+] what's the matter? [ref. is to lice]

what's doing? *phr.* [20C+] (*Aus./US*) a greeting; an inquiry as to what is happening.

whatsername *n. see* WHATSHISNAME n.

what's giving? *phr. see* WHAT GIVES? phr.

what's going down *n. see* WHAT'S HAPPENING n.

what's going down? *phr.* [1970s+] (*US Black/campus*) a greeting. [GO DOWN v.[7] (1)]

what's going on? *phr.* (*also* **what's going?**) [1950s+] a common greeting.

what-sha-call-him *n. see* WHATCHAMACALLIT n.

what shakes? *phr.* [mid-19C] (*UK Und.*) what chance is there of stealing something? [SE *shake*]

what-shall-call-um *n.* **1** [early 17C] a need to urinate. **2** [early–mid-19C] a prostitute, a promiscuous woman. [euph.]

what's hanging? *phr. see* HOW'S IT HANGING? phr.

what's happening *n.* (*also* **what's going down**) [1960s+] (*orig. US Black*) the fashionable, chic, smart event, place, show etc; thus *not what's happening*, the opposite, somewhere unfashionable. [HAPPENING adj.]

what's happening? *phr.* (*also* **wha'ppen? what's the haps?**) [1950s+] a greeting, hello and how are you? what are you doing? what have you been doing?

whatsisface *n.* (*also* **whatsherass, whatsherface, what-shisass, whatzerface**) [1960s+] used for a name one has temporarily forgotten.

whatshisname *n.* (*also* **whatshername, whatsiname, whatsisname, whatsname, whatsoname, what's-their-names, what's your name, whatzername, whatzisname,**

wotsaname) [mid-17C+] any person or thing to which one cannot give a proper name.

whatsie *n.* [1950s+] (*Aus.*) any person or thing to which one cannot give a proper name. [abbr. WHATSISNAME n.]

whatsit *n.* (*also* whatisit, whatsis, what's it, whatzis, wotsit) **1** [late 19C+] (*US*) an unspecified or unspecifiable person or object. **2** [1980s] a homosexual or lesbian.

what's itching you? *phr. see* WHAT'S BITING YOU? phr.

what's it going to be? *phr. see* WHAT WILL YOU HAVE? phr.

whatsits *n.* **1** [1950s+] (*also* wotsit) the male genitals. **2** [1960s] the menstrual period.

what's its name *n.* (*also* whatsitsname) **1** [mid-19C+] (*also* whatsyname) an unspecified object. **2** [late 19C] the penis (cf. BAUBLE n.). **3** [late 19C] the vagina (cf. ARTICLE n.). [euph.]

what's it to you? *phr.* [early 18C; mid-19C+] an aggressive reply to a questioner implying that whatever the answer may be, it is none of their business.

what's jumping? *phr.* [1980s+] (*US campus*) a general greeting. [JUMP v.⁶ (1)]

what's krackalackin? *phr.* (*also* what's crackulatin'?) [2000s] (*US Black*) a greeting.

whatsname *n. see* WHATSISNAME n.

what's new? *phr.* (*also* what's the new?) [1910s+] a general greeting.

whatsoname *n. see* WHATSHISNAME n.

what's on the rail for the lizard? *phr.* [1940s] (*US Black*) what have you got to offer? esp. in the context of money, sexual favours and other exciting, if unrespectable, pleasures. [note later LIZARD n.³]

what-sort *n. see* WHAT-FOR n.

what's popping? *phr.* [2000s] (*US teen*) a phr. of greeting, enquiry. [POP v.³ (1)]

what's shaking? *phr.* (*US*) **1** [1950s+] (*also* how's it shaking?) a greeting, hello and how are you? **2** [1960s] what's the matter? [SE *shake*/SHAKE v.⁶ (2)]

what's that when it's at home? *phr.* (*also* who's he/she when he's/she's at home?) [late 19C+] a deliberate misunderstanding of a word or statement, which the speaker is implying to be too 'clever' for them to understand.

what's the (big) idea? *phr.* [1910s+] (*orig. US*) more a threat than a question, usu. asked when someone is doing or saying something of which the speaker disapproves.

what's the deal? *phr.* **1** [1940s+] (*US*) what's happening? what's going on? **2** [1990s+] what's the problem?

what's the dilly? *phr.* (*also* what's the dills? what's the dilly-o?) [1990s+] (*US Black*) a phr. of greeting. [? DILLY n.³; or pron. of *deal*/*dealie* in WHAT'S THE DEAL? phr.]

what's the good word? *phr.* **1** [1910s+] what are the facts? **2** [1940s+] (*US*) a cordial greeting, how are you?

what's the haps? *excl. see* WHAT'S HAPPENING? phr.

what's the idea? *phr. see* WHAT'S THE (BIG) IDEA? phr.

what's-their-names *n. see* WHATSHISNAME n.

what's the new? *phr. see* WHAT'S NEW? phr.

what's the odds? *phr. see* WHAT ODDS? phr.

what's the scam? *phr.* [1970s+] (*US*) what's happening? what's going on? [SCAM n.¹ (1)]

what's the scoop? *phr.* [1950s] (*US*) a general greeting, what's going on? [SE *scoop*, a revelatory newspaper story]

what's the shit? *phr.* [1960s] (*US*) what's going on? what's happening? [SHIT n.³ (6)]

what's the story (morning glory)? *phr.* (*also* what's your story (morning glory)?) **1** [1930s+] (*US Black*) explain yourself, what are you up to? **2** [1940s+] (*orig. US Black*) a general greeting, how are you? [(2) grew in popularity in the UK after the 1995 release of the album (*What's the Story*) *Morning Glory?* by Oasis]

what's the verdict? *phr.* [1990s+] (*US Black*) what's happening? what's going on?

what's the word? *phr.* [1950s–70s] (*US Black*) a greeting; always with the response *Thunderbird*. [assonance + ref. to *Thunderbird*, a sweet, fortified wine]

what's-this *n.* [1930s] (*US*) a euph. for *hell*.

what's to it? *phr.* [1940s–50s] (*US Black/teen*) a phr. of greeting.

what's up? *phr.* (*also* wassup? wazzup? what up?) **1** [mid-19C+] a general enquiry or greeting. **2** [mid-19C+] what's the matter? esp. in *what's up with you/her etc.* **3** [1910s+] what is happening? what is going on?

what's up, G? *phr.* [1990s+] (*orig. US Black*) (*also* what up toe?) a greeting. [WHAT'S UP? phr. (1) + G n.³ (2)]

what's with —? *phr.* [1930s+] (*US*) what's the meaning of —? what's the matter with —?

whatsyname *n. see* WHAT'S ITS NAME n. (1).

what's your game? *phr. see* GAME n.² (7).

what's your jive/lick? *phr. see* WHAT'S YOUR TALE? phr.

what's your name *n. see* WHATSHISNAME n.

what's your poison? *phr.* (*also* what's your medicine? what's your nourishment?) [mid-19C+] a general invitation to have a drink. [POISON n.¹/MEDICINE n. (1)/SE *nourishment*]

what's yours? *phr.* [late 19C+] an invitation to take a drink.

what's your song, King Kong? *phr.* [1940s] (*US Black*) how are you? how do you feel? [assonance]

what's your story (morning glory)? *phr. see* WHAT'S THE STORY (MORNING GLORY)? phr.

what's your tale? *phr.* (*also* what's your jive? what's your lick?) [1940s] (*US Black campus*) a greeting, how are you? [SE *tale*/JIVE n.¹ (4)/LICK n.² (6)]

what the blazes! *excl.* (*also* what the blazing! what the blue blazes! who the blazes! why the blazes!) [early 19C+] a general excl. of extreme surprise, absolute confusion etc. [BLAZES n. (1)/BLUE BLAZES n.]

what the Connaught man shot at *n.* [late 19C] (*Anglo-Irish*) nothing. [negative stereotyping]

what the devil! *excl.* (*also* how the devil! where the devil! who the devil!) [mid-14C+] a general interrog. intensifier, a euph. for *what the hell!/why the hell!* etc.

what the dickens! *excl.* (*also* what the diggings!) [late 16C+] a euph. for WHAT THE DEVIL! excl.; also used as an intensifier. [DICKENS n. (1)]

what the dogs! *excl.* [late 18C–mid-19C] a mild oath, a euph. of WHAT THE HELL! excl.

what the fuck...? *phr.* (*also* what the fug...? ...piss...? ...shit...?) [20C+] (*orig. US*) a phr. used to indicate one's incomprehension; also abbr. to just *the fuck...* [FUCK, THE n. (1)/PISS n. (1)/SHIT n.¹ (1)]

what the fuck! *excl.* (*also* what the shit! W.T.F.!) [1960s+] **1** an excl. of shock, surprise. **2** an excl. of resignation, acceptance, disinterest. [WHAT THE FUCK...? phr.]

what the hell *phr.* [1920s+] whatever.

what the hell! *excl.* (*also* what the heck! what the sweet hell!) [mid-19C+] **1** a statement of resignation, acceptance. **2** a general excl. indicative of annoyance or surprise. [HELL, THE phr.²]

what the hey! *excl. see* HEY n.

what the Jesus! *excl.* [1920s–40s] (*US tramp*) an excl. of irritation.

what the piss...? *phr. see* WHAT THE FUCK...? phr.

what the Sam Hill! *excl.* [early 19C+] (*US*) an excl. of surprise, shock, alarm or resignation etc. [SAM HILL! excl.; euph., via the initial 'h', for WHAT THE HELL! excl.; note A.K. Sokol in *American Speech* XV:1 (1940) who suggests the name *Samael*, 'the prince of the demons', which appeared, as *Samiel*, in the opera *Der Freischütz*, premiered in the US in 1825]

what the shit...? *phr. see* WHAT THE FUCK...? phr.

what the shit! *excl. see* WHAT THE FUCK! excl.

what the sweet hell! *excl. see* WHAT THE HELL! excl.

what up? *phr. see* WHAT'S UP? phr.

what up dog? *phr.* [1990s+] (*US Black teen*) a general greeting. [WHAT'S UP? phr. (1) + DOG n.² (3)]

what up toe? *phr. see* WHAT'S UP, G? phr.

what will you have? *phr.* (*also* **what's it going to be?**) [mid-19C+] a general invitation to have a drink.

what will you liq? *phr.* [late 19C] (*UK middle class*) what would you like to drink? [LIQ n. (2)]

what-y? *n. see* WHAT-ER? n.

whatyermecallems/whatyermycalit *n. see* WHAT-D'YOU-CALL-IT n.

what-you-call-it *n. see* WHATCHAMACALLIT n.

what you know *n. see* YOU KNOW WHAT n. (4).

what you know? *phr.* (*also* **what you know, Joe? what you say? what you saying?**) [1940s+] (*US campus*) a greeting, hello.

whatzerface *n. see* WHATSHISFACE n.

whatzername *n. see* WHATSHISNAME n.

whatzis *n. see* WHATSIT n.

whatzisname *n. see* WHATSHISNAME n.

whazood *adj.* [1970s+] (*US campus*) drunk. [var. on WAZZOOED adj.]

w.h.b. *phr.* [late 19C–1900s] men who take unwanted liberties with women, 'gropers'. [abbr. wandering hand brigade]

wheadle *n.* (*also* **wheedle, wheedler**) [late 17C–mid-19C] (*UK Und.*) a sharper, a confidence trickster; thus *cut a wheadle*, to ensnare a victim. [WHEADLE v.]

wheadle *v.* (*also* **wheedle**) [mid-17C–19C] (*UK Und.*) to cheat. [SE *wheedle*, to flatter]

Wheadler *n.* [early 18C] (*UK Und.*) the Moon. [*see* oliver widdles at OLIVER n.¹]

wheat *n.*¹ [1900s] (*US*) a rustic, a peasant (cf. BUCKWHEAT n.).

wheat *n.*² [1960s+] (*drugs*) marijuana (cf. AFRICAN BUSH n.).

wheat belt *n.* [1920s+] (*Aus.*) a prostitute. [? pun on OATS n.¹]

Wheatlander *n.* [1900s] (*Aus.*) a South Australian.

wheedle *see also under* WHEADLE.

wheedle *v. see* WHIDDLE v.

wheek *v.* [20C+] (*Ulster*) to steal. [Antrim dial. *wheek*, to snatch away]

wheeker *n.* [20C+] (*Ulster*) anything exceptionally good. [WHEEK v., i.e. something worth stealing]

wheel *n.*¹ **1** [late 18C–1930s] (*US*) (*also* **wagon-wheel**) a $1 coin. **2** [19C] a 5-shilling coin. [abbr. CARTWHEEL n.¹]

wheel *n.*² [late 19C–1940s] (*orig. Aus./US*) a bicycle.

wheel *n.*³ (*also* **wheels, wheels of steel**) [1980s+] the record turntable or turntables as used by HIP-HOP n. and RAP n.⁵ DJs. [the circular shape of the turntable, usu. used in pl. The DJ manipulates 2 turntables (some use 3) simultaneously, selecting bits of records and mixing them together]

wheel *n.*⁴ *see* BIG WHEEL n.

wheel *v.* **1** [mid-19C+] (*US*) to drive fast, to ride fast. **2** [late 19C–1900s] to ride a bicycle or similar pedal-powered vehicle; thus WHEELER n. **3** [1930s+] (*US Black*) to drive an automobile. **4** [1940s+] to drive someone, as in a taxi. **5** [1980s] (*US campus*) (*also* **wheel on over**) to make a visit, to travel.

wheel! *excl.* [1980s+] (*W.I./UK Black teen*) a demand that a DJ replay a favourite song; thus phr. *wheel and come again*. [? WHEEL n.³]

wheel and deal *v.* (*also* **wheeler-deal**) **1** [1940s–50s] (*US Black*) to have a good time, to dance. **2** [1950s+] (*US*) to engage in many business arrangements expressly to make a profit, or achieve a satisfactory outcome. [(2) abbr. BIG WHEEL n. + SE *deal*; (1) is poss. a discrete use]

wheel a spiel *v.* [1950s] (*US Black*) to talk, esp. in a persuasive, fluent manner. [WHEEL IN v./WHEEL AND DEAL v. (2) + SPIEL n. (4)]

wheel-band in the nick *phr.* [late 17C–early 19C] drinking in the normal fashion, tilting the glass over the left thumb. [SE *wheelband in the nick*, a tyre that runs along a regular groove]

wheelchair *n.* [1940s] (*US Black*) a motor vehicle.

wheelchair set *n.* [1970s] (*US gay*) old homosexuals, considered as a group.

wheeled *adj.* [late 19C] **1** conveyed in a cab. **2** successful, rich, important. [WHEEL v. (4), i.e. one who goes about in a *wheeled* cab]

wheeler *n.* **1** [late 19C–1910s] a cyclist. **2** [1940s] (*US Und.*) a motorcycle policeman. **3** [1950s+] a driver. [WHEEL v. (2)]

wheeler-deal *v. see* WHEEL AND DEAL v.

wheeler-dealer *n.* (*also* **wheeler and dealer**) **1** [1960s] (*Aus.*) a petty confidence trickster. **2** [1960s+] an entrepreneur, an 'operator'. [WHEEL AND DEAL v. (2)]

wheelie *n.*¹ [1960s+] the stunt of riding on the back wheel only of a motorcycle or bicycle.

wheelie *n.*² [1990s+] a *wheel*chair. [abbr.]

wheelie *v.* **1** [1960s+] to perform the stunt of riding on the back wheel only of a motorcycle or bicycle. **2** [1970s] (*US campus*) to drive a car fast and recklessly causing the tyres to screech. [WHEELIE n.¹]

wheel in *v.* (*also* **wheel out/up**) [1910s+] (*orig. US*) of a person or an object, to bring into or remove from a meeting, an interview etc; esp. in imper. *wheel one in!* bring one in!

wheelman *n.*¹ [late 19C] (*US*) a cyclist. [WHEEL n.² + SE *man*]

wheelman *n.*² [1930s+] (*orig. UK Und.*) an expert car driver, either for the police or for criminals. [i.e. one who drives the WHEELS n.¹ (3)]

wheel of life *n.* [19C] a prison treadmill. [SE *wheel* + pun on SE *life*, existence/*life sentence*]

wheel on over *v. see* WHEEL v. (5).

wheel out/up *v. see* WHEEL IN v.

wheels *n.*¹ **1** [late 19C] a bicycle. **2** [1910s+] (*US*) the legs. **3** [1930s+] a car; thus *on wheels*, driving a car. **4** [1960s–70s] a truck. **5** [1990s+] a motorcycle.

wheels *n.*² **1** [1940s] influence. **2** [1970s] (*US*) brains. [the image is of machinery working in the head/government etc]

wheels *n.*³ [2000s] (*US*) the female breasts (cf. BAGS n.¹). [they too are round]

wheels *n.*⁴ *see* WHEEL n.³.

wheels come off *phr.* [1960s+] of a situation or events, to detoriate, to go wrong; usu. as excl. *the wheels came off!* [automobile imagery]

wheels of steel *n. see* WHEEL n.³.

wheen *n.* [1910s+] (*Irish*) a small or large number. [Anglo-Saxon *hwaene*, few]

wheesht! *excl. see* WHISHT! excl.

whee up *v.* [1940s] (*US*) to excite, to stimulate. [echoic excl. *whee*. inferring speediness + GEE UP n. (2)]

wheeze *n.* **1** [late 19C] (*orig. theatre*) a joke, a catchphrase. **2** [late 19C–1930s] a piece of special information, a 'tip'. **3** [late 19C+] a trick or dodge frequently used. **4** [1960s] a theory, a concept. [orig. theatre use, a joke or comic gag introduced into the performance by a clown or comedian, esp. a constantly repeated catchphrase]

wheeze *v.* [late 19C–1900s] to pass on information, to inform on.

wheezer *n.* **1** [1970s] the penis. **2** [2000s] a cigar.

wheezy anna *n.* [20C+] a spanner. [rhy. sl.]

Whelan the Wrecker *n.* [1930s+] (*Aus.*) a vandal. [the name of a demolition firm, *Whelan the Wrecker*, Sydney Road, Coburg, Melbourne]

whelk *n.* [mid–late 19C] the vagina; thus the fake-threatening phr. *I'll have your whelk* (cf. BEARDED CLAM n.). [equation of the vagina with fish (FISH n.¹ (1))]

whelp *n.* [mid-19C+] a native of Tennessee.

whelp *v.* [late 19C–1940s] to give birth. [SE *whelp*, of a dog, to give birth]

when Adam was an oakum boy *phr.* [mid-19C–1910s] a

very long time ago; often ext. by *…in Brooklyn Navy Yard, …in Chatham.*

when Christ was a corporal *phr.* [1970s] (*US*) a very long time ago.

when cock get teeth *phr.* (*also* **when cock make teeth, when fowl cut…, when fowl get…**) [20C+] (*W.I.*) absolutely never.

when push comes to shove *phr.* [1940s+] (*orig. US*) in the final assessment, when all other alternatives have been exhausted. [SE *push* is seen as less aggressive than *shove*]

when-shee *n. see* YEN-SHEE *n.* (1).

when the balloon goes up *phr.* [1910s+] (*orig. milit.*) the start of proceedings, esp. when there is a potential for controversy or argument. [? raising of an observation *balloon* immediately before an attack]

when the band begins to play *phr.* [late 19C–1940s] when matters become serious.

when the chips are down *phr.* [1940s+] in the final event, at the denouement, when one has no option. [CHIPS *n.*[2]/SE *chips*, counters used in gambling]

when the crow shits *phr.* [1970s+] (*Aus.*) payday. [Aus. var. on US WHEN THE EAGLE SHITS *phr.*; a bird is engraved on the reverse of an Aus. dollar coin]

when the eagle shits *phr.* (*also* **when the eagle flies, …screams, …walks**) [1940s+] (*orig. US milit./Aus.*) payday. [the *eagle* engraved on the US silver dollar coin]

when the jack takes the ace *phr.* [mid-19C] sexual intercourse. [JACK *n.*[3] (1) + ACE *n.*[1] (1)]

when the mark buss *phr.* (*also* **when the mark burst/bust**) [20C+] (*W.I.*) when the truth comes out, when the facts are revealed. [Carib.E. *mark*, one of the 36 symbols – a centipede, a hog, an old lady – used in the gambling game of *Whe-Whe*. Each is identified by a number and players bet on which number will be found to reveal the winning symbol in a round]

when the numbers are up *phr.* (*also* **when the numbers go up**) [late 19C+] (*Aus.*) when the result is known. [the raising of a board carrying the numbers of the winning horses after a horserace]

when the plate-fleet comes in *phr.* [late 17C–early 19C] when one finally makes a fortune, 'when one's ship comes in'. [SE *Plate fleet*, the fleet that brought home the annual yield of silver from the Indies to Spain]

when the red is over the pink, go for the brown *phr.* [1990s+] a phr. meaning when a woman is menstruating, opt for anal intercourse. [snooker imagery]

when the road runs red, hit the dirt track *phr.* [1990s+] a phr. meaning when a woman is menstruating, opt for anal intercourse. [SE *road*/ROAD *n.*[1] (2) + DIRT TRACK *n.*]

when the whips are cracking *phr.* [20C+] (*Aus.*) when the action begins.

when-we *n.* [1980s+] (*S.Afr.*) an immigrant from a country once part of the British Empire who maintains his or her old beliefs, including feelings of racial superiority. Such figures, who were often middle-ranking administrators, also despise the South Africans among whom they have been forced to live. The type, drawn to South Africa by apartheid, have presumably all but died out since majority rule. [the common use of *when we were in…* to start a bitterly nostalgic sentence]

when you were… *phr.* [1920s+] a phr. based on one's childhood, or even earlier life, meaning a very long time ago, e.g. (*Aus.*) *when you were just a dirty look, …just a gleam/twinkle in your father's eye, …still in/wearing short pants, …running up and down your father's backbone,* (*Aus.*) *…when your mother was cutting bread on you.*

whereabouts *n.* [1930s+] (*Aus.*) male underpants. [pun on SE *wear-abouts*]

where are you at? *phr. see* WHERE IT'S AT *phr.* (2).

where did you get that hat? *phr.* [late 19C–1910s] (*orig. US*) a general jeer or shout of derision.

where did you get your licence? *phr.* [1970s+] (*Aus.*) a general phr. of annoyance aimed at a poor or allegedly poor driver, often with a suggestion such as 'Woolworths?' 'off a Weetabix packet?' etc.

where do we go from here? (*also* **where do we go from there?**) [1920s+] what happens now/next?

where in hell? *phr. see* WHAT IN HELL? *phr.*

where it's at *phr.* (*also* **where it is, where it's happening**) **1** [mid-19C+] the truth, the right place, the ideal situation, opinion, experience; an expression of approval/affirmation. **2** [1970s+] (*also* **where are you at?**) as a greeting.

where one is at *phr.* (*also* **where one is coming from, …one is coming out, …one's head is at**) [1940s+] (*orig. US Black*) one's lifestyle, attitudes, philosophy, mood or overall emotional state.

where one lives *phr.* [mid-19C+] (*orig. US*) at a vital or central point of one's emotions, e.g. *that gets me right where I live.*

wheresis *n.* [1930s] (*US*) an otherwise unidentified place.

where's the beef? *phr.* [1980s+] (*US*) what's the real point, importance, inner meaning, content etc. [slogan for Wendy's hamburgers in 1984 + play on BEEF *n.*[2] (2)/SE *beef*]

where's the fire? *phr.* [1920s+] (*orig. US*) where are you running to? what's the hurry?

where the chicken has the axe *phr.* [1910s] in the neck.

where the crows fly backwards to keep the dust out of their eyes *phr.* [late 19C+] (*Aus.*) of anywhere that is considered beyond the bounds of civilization.

where the devil! *excl. see* WHAT THE DEVIL! *excl.*

where the five'n'arf? *phr.* [1920s–30s] where in God's name? [rhy. sl.; 5½ yards = one rod (unit of measurement) = God]

where the monkey shoves his nuts *n.* [late 19C+] a euph. for the anus; usu. as *you can shove/put it/them where the monkey…*

where the sun doesn't shine *n.* [20C+] (*US*) a euph. for the anus (cf. PART THAT GOES OVER THE FENCE LAST *n.*).

where uncle's doodle goes *n.* [mid–late 19C] the vagina; thus *be where uncle's doodle goes*, of a man, to have sexual intercourse. [SE *uncle* + DOODLE *n.*[2] (1)]

wherewith *n.* (*also* **wherewithal**) [19C] money (cf. ACTUAL, THE *n.*). [the role of money in sustaining life]

where you at? *phr.* [2000s] (*US Black*) a phr. of greeting. [WHERE ONE IS AT *phr.*]

wherry-go-nimble *n.* [20C+] **1** the lavatory. **2** diarrhoea (cf. APPLE-BLOSSOM TWO-STEP *n.*). [? SE *where he go nimbly* + pun on SE *trot*/TROTS, THE *n.*[2]]

whet *n. see* WET *n.*[1] (1).

whet *v. see* WET *v.*[1] (1).

whetshire cully *n.* [mid-18C] (*UK Und.*) a goldsmith.

Whetstone Park deer *n.* (*also* **Whetstone, Whetstone Park lady, Whetstone park mutton**) [17C–18C] prostitutes. [proper name *Whetstone Park*, a lane between Holborn and Lincoln's Inn Fields, well known for its 'nest of wenches' (B.E.) + SE *deer*/MUTTON *n.*[1] (1); thus Wycherley, *Love in a Wood* (1672), attacking a loose woman: 'If I had met you in *Wheatstones*-Park with a drunken Foot-Soldier, I should not have been jealous of you'; and Ned Ward, *The London Spy* (1699), on the prostitutes available in the women's section of Bedlam Hospital: ''Tis a new *Whetstone's Park* […] where a *Sports–man*, at any Hour in the Day, may meet with *Game* for his purpose']

whetting corn *n.* (*also* **whetting stone**) [early 17C–mid-19C] the vagina. [lit. a 'grindstone']

whib-bob *n.* (*also* **whibb-bob**) [mid-17C] the female genitals. [Henke, *Gutter Life and Language* (1988), suggests that the term exists only in the five *Wandering Whore* pamphlets]

whiblin *n.* [early–mid-17C] **1** anything for which one has no proper name. **2** the testicles (cf. GINGAMBOBS *n.*). [ety. unknown]

whichever way you slice it *phr. see* NO MATTER HOW YOU SLICE IT phr.

whid *n.* (*also* **whidd**) **1** [mid-16C–mid-19C] (*UK Und.*) a word; usu. in pl.; thus *hold one's whid*, to be quiet. **2** [mid-19C] a salesman's patter. **3** [mid-19C] a lie. [SE *word* and OE *cwide*, a statement]

whid *v.* (*also* **whiddy**) [17C–early 19C] to talk criminal jargon, to lie. [WHID n. (1)]

whidding cheat *n.* [mid-18C] (*UK Und.*) the tongue. [WHID v. + CHEAT n. (1)]

whiddle *n.* [early 19C] a trial, an interrogation. [WHIDDLE v.]

whiddle *v.* (*also* **wheedle**) [late 17C–mid-19C] (*UK Und.*) **1** to tell, to recount. **2** to inform against, to raise a hue and cry. [? WHID v.]

whiddle beef *v.* [late 17C–early 19C] to raise the alarm. [WHIDDLE v. (2) + HOT BEEF! excl.]

whiddler *n.* [late 17C–mid-19C] an informer. [WHIDDLE v. (2)]

whiddy *v. see* WHID v.

whiff *n.* (*also* **wif, wiff**) **1** [mid-19C–1910s] a cigar, or tobacco. **2** [1900s–60s] an inhalation of cocaine. **3** [1970s+] (*US drugs*) cocaine (cf. BLOW n.⁶). **4** [1980s] a puff of cannabis. [SE *whiff*, to inhale, to sniff; note 17C SE *take the whiff*, to smoke]

whiff *adj. see* WHIFFY adj.

whiff *v.*¹ [late 19C+] to smell unpleasantly; thus *whiff out*, to 'stink out' a room. [ME *weffe*, an offensive odour or taste]

whiff *v.*² [late 19C+] (*US drugs*) to inhale a drug, orig. opium, usu. cocaine. [SE *whiff*, to inhale, to sniff]

whiff *v.*³ [1910s+] (*US*) **1** to miss a ball; thus as n., a miss. **2** to make someone miss. [SE *whiff*, to move as a puff of air, and so one hits air rather than the ball]

whiff *v.*⁴ [1930s] (*US*) to kill, to murder. [play on SE *whiff*, to blow away]

whiffed *adj.* [1910s] (*US drugs*) incapacitated from an excess of cocaine. [WHIFF v.²]

whiffet *n.* [mid-19C–1920s] (*US*) an insignificant person, a whippersnapper. [SE *whiffet*, a small dog]

whiffle *n.* [early 19C] a blow. [SE *whiffle*, to blow on, as with a puff of air]

whiffle *v.* [20C+] (*Ulster*) to make an evasive answer. [SE *whiffle*, to talk idly]

whiffled *adj.* [1920s–30s] drunk. [? SE *whiffle*, to move lightly as if blown by a puff of air]

whifflegig *adj.* [mid-19C] trivial, trifling. [SE *whiffle*, to talk idly + GIG n.⁴ (1)]

whiffles *n.* [late 18C–early 19C] 'a relaxation of the scrotum' (Grose, 1785). [SE *whiffle*, to move lightly]

whiffmagig *n.* [mid-19C] a trifler, an insignificant or contemptible fellow. [SE *whiff*, a puff of wind + GIG n.⁴ (1)]

whiffy *adj.* (*also* **whiff, wiffy**) [late 19C+] smelly; also in fig. use. [SE *whiff*, an unpleasant smell]

whig *n.* [late 19C] an irresolute person, someone who constantly changes their mind. [the refusal of the parliamentary *Whig* party to stay firmly on one side or the other]

whigger *n. see* WIGGA n.

whiggish *adj.* [late 17C] 'Factious, Seditious, Restless, Uneasy' (B.E.). [for ety. *see* WHIG n.]

Whigland *n.* [late 17C–mid-19C] Scotland; thus *Whiglander*, a Scot. [its being a centre of *Whig* politics]

whilk *n.* (*also* **giddy whilk**) [1910s–20s] a silly young woman. [var. on WHELK n.]

whim *n. see* WHIM-WHAM n. (2).

whimble-wambles *n.* [mid-19C] stomach cramps. [redup. of WAMBLE n.]

whimp *n. see* WIMP n.².

whimsy *n.* [early 17C] a promiscuous woman. [like WHIM-WHAM n. (1), a play on a SE term for 'trifle']

whim-wham *n.* **1** [17C; mid-19C] the penis (cf. BAUBLE n.).

2 [17C–18C] (*also* **whim**) the vagina (cf. ARTICLE n.). **3** [early–mid-19C] nonsense, rubbish. [SE *whim-wham*, a trifle, a trinket; (1) + link to QUIM n. (1)]

whim-whams *n.* [late 19C+] (*US*) anxiety, nervousness. [SE *whim-wham*, a trifle, a fantasy]

whin-bush *n.* [late 19C] pubic hair. [SE *whin-bush*, a furze-bush + BUSH n.² (1)]

whiners *n.* [late 17C–mid-19C] prayers; thus phr. *chop (up) the whiners*, to mumble one's prayers speedily and with no interest in their meaning. [note B.E. (*c.*1698): 'To Whine, to cry squeekingly, as at Conventicles']

whing-ding *n. see* WING-DING n.

whings *n. see* WINGS n.

whing-whang *n.* [late 19C] something, typically a small gadget, for which one has no specific name.

whip *n.*¹ [late 19C+] (*Aus./N.Z.*) an abundance. [play on SE *lashings*]

whip *n.*² [1940s] (*US Und.*) a bail bond. [abbr. WHIPROUND n.]

whip *n.*³ [1960s+] (*Aus.*) rum; esp. in phr. *crack of the whip*. [its effects, i.e. one is 'whipped' into action]

whip *n.*⁴ [1990s+] (*US Black*) an automobile.

whip *n.*⁵ *see* WHIPROUND n.

whip *v.*¹ (*orig. US*) **1** [mid-17C+] to steal, to make off with. **2** [mid-19C+] to swindle. [SE *whip*, to take briskly, suddenly]

whip *v.*² [late 17C; mid-19C+] (*US Und.*) to walk, to travel, to go.

whip *v.*³ **1** [early 19C+] (*US*) to defeat. **2** [1930s+] to beat up. [ext. of SE *whip*]

whip *v.*⁴ **1** [mid-19C] to drag someone, to force someone to do something; usu. in comb. with a prep., e.g. *in, along, up.* **2** [mid-19C+] to place, to move.

whip *v.*⁵ [1980s+] (*US*) to give.

whip *v.*⁶ [1990s+] (*US campus*) to fall asleep while sitting up. [? SE *whiplash*, the way in which one's head slumps suddenly onto one's shoulder]

whip a game on *v.* [1940s+] (*US Black*) to hoax, to trick, to deceive, esp. when selling drugs. [WHIP v.⁵ + GAME n.² (3)]

whip and lash *n.* [20C+] a moustache. [rhy. sl.]

whip and top *v.* [20C+] to masturbate (cf. COTTON WOOL v.). [rhy. sl. = STROP v.²]

whip-around *n. see* WHIPROUND n.

whip-arse *n.* [early 17C] a schoolmaster. [SE *whip* + ARSE n.¹ (1)]

whip-belly (vengeance) *n.* (*also* **pinch-gut vengeance**) [18C–early 19C] very thin beer. [its unpleasant effects]

whip boss *n.* [1940s–50s] (*US prison*) the chief officer on a prison farm. [BOSS n.²; he carries a *whip*]

whip-cat *n.* [mid-19C] a tailor. [WHIP THE CAT v.⁴]

whip-cat *adj.* [late 16C–early 17C] drunken. [WHIP THE CAT v.² (1)]

whip-handle *n.* [mid-17C] (*Scot.*) an unimportant, small man.

whip-her-ginny/whip-her-jenny *n. see* WHIPPERGINNIE n.

whip it *v.* **1** [18C; 1970s+] (*also* **whip it in**) to have sexual intercourse; esp. in modern phr. *whip it in, whip it out and wipe it* (cf. BANG v.¹). **2** [20C+] to masturbate.

whip it on *v.* [1950s+] (*US street gang*) to attack, to start a fight.

whip it on someone *v.*¹ **1** [1940s+] (*US drugs*) to inject someone other than oneself with narcotics. **2** [1970s] (*US*) of a man, to have sexual intercourse (cf. BURY IT v.).

whip it on someone *v.*² [1960s+] (*US*) **1** to explain and inform someone of facts and events. **2** to give, to hand over.

whip-jack *n.* **1** [16C–19C] (*UK Und.*) a mendicant villain who posed as a discharged mariner, backed by a counterfeit licence, suitably adorned with fake seals; he also specialized in robbing stalls, fairground booths and similar open displays of goods (cf. CANTING CREW n.). **2** [early 19C] as a general derog. [SE *whip*, to beat + *Jack*, a general nickname; an alternative ety., WHIP v.¹ + JACK n.², requires a substantially later coinage]

whip off *v.*¹ **1** [early 17C–early 19C] to drink greedily. **2** [late

17C–18C] (*UK Und.*) to steal. **3** [late 18C+] to run off. [SE *whip*, to move suddenly, to take briskly]

whip off *v.*[2] [20C+] (*US campus*) to masturbate (cf. BALL OFF v.[2]).

whip on *v.*[1] **1** [mid-19C] (*UK Und.*) to lay (the blame) on. **2** [1960s] (*US*) to beat up. **3** [1970s+] (*US*) to subject to.

whip on *v.*[2] *see* WHIP (SOMETHING) ON v.

whip one's dripper *v.* [1990s+] to masturbate.

whip one's weight in wildcats *v.* (*also* **whip one's weight in bear, …catamounts, …polecats**) [early 19C+] (*US*) to be fit and strong, to fight hard.

whip-out *n.* [1970s+] (*US*) money, esp. a first payment or investment. [WHIP OUT v.]

whip out *v.* [early 18C; late 19C+] to produce, usu. quickly.

whip-out man *n.* [1960s] (*US*) an exhibitionist. [WHIP OUT v. + SE *man*]

whipped *adj.*[1] **1** [mid-19C+] defeated. **2** [mid-19C+] (*US*) drunk, intoxicated (cf. ANNIHILATED adj.). **3** [1940s] (*US Black*) hungover. **4** [1950s+] (*US*) exhausted. [WHIP v.[3]]

whipped *adj.*[2] **1** [1920s+] dominated, subservient, meek; thus *get whipped*, to get married. **2** [1960s+] willing to do anything one's partner demands. **3** [1980s+] (*US campus/teen*) in love, infatuated. [fig. use of SE; (2) underlined by abbr. PUSSY-WHIPPED adj. (1)]

whipped cream *n.* [1970s+] (*US Black*) semen (cf. BABY GRAVY n.). [resemblance]

whipped up *adj.* [1930s–50s] (*US Black*) exhausted, worn-out, physically wrecked. [WHIPPED adj.[1] (4)]

whipped with an ugly stick, be *v.* [1960s–80s] to be unattractive. [often cited as a supposed reason for the lack of good looks]

whipper *n.* [1980s] (*US campus*) a very tedious class. [WHIP v.[6]]

whipperginnie *n.* (*also* **whip-her-ginny, whip-her-jenny**) [late 16C–early 17C] a term of abuse for a woman. [lit. 'whip her, Jenny']

whippets *n.* (*also* **whippet**) [1970s] (*drugs*) nitrous oxide. [as dispensed from a can of *whipped* cream]

whipping *n.* **1** [mid-19C+] (*US*) a sound, comprehensive beating or defeat. **2** [1900s] punishment, physical discipline. [WHIP v.[3] (1)]

whippit quick *n.* [1990s+] the penis (cf. ALMOND n.). [rhy. sl. = PRICK n. (2)]

whippy *n.* [1960s+] (*Aus.*) **1** a pocket. **2** a hiding place, esp. for money. **3** a wallet. [WHIP v.[1]]

whippy *adj.* [1960s–70s] **1** (*US*) smart, well-dressed. **2** cheeky, mocking. **3** (*US campus*) intelligent, clever. [smart as a *whip*]

whipround *n.* (*also* **whip, whip-around**) [mid-19C+] a collection, an appeal for money. [SE *whip up*, to enthuse a group of people towards a united action, also note naval jargon *whip*, 'after the usual allowance of wine is drunk at mess, those who wish for more put a shilling each into a glass handed round to procure a further supply' (Hotten, 1867)]

whip round *v.* [mid-19C+] to make a financial collection, e.g. for a leaving present. [WHIPROUND n.]

whips *n.* [1970s+] (*US Black*) **1** the White establishment. **2** the police. [the repressive imagery of their institutions]

whipsaw *v.* **1** [late 19C+] (*US*) to have at a complete disadvantage, to overcome completely; to benefit or to win by manipulating a situation so that one's rivals attack one another. **2** [1900s] to attack, to assault. [SE *whip-saw*, something that is disadvantageous in 2 ways]

whipsey *adj.* [1920s] (*US*) tipsy. [? WHIPPED adj.[1] (2)]

whip-shack *n.* [1970s+] (*US Black*) anywhere one can have sexual intercourse. [WHIP IT ON SOMEONE v.[1] (2)]

Whipshire *n.* [late 17C–early 19C] Yorkshire. [? the hunting gentry who live there]

whips of *n.* [20C+] (*Aus.*) a great deal, an abundance. [dial.]

whip someone's ass *v.* (*also* **whip someone's arse, whoop someone's ass, whup someone's ass**) [1950s+] (*orig. US*) **1** to beat completely and comprehensively, whether or not with violence. **2** in fig. use, to defeat intellectually. [SE *whip* + ARSE n.[1] (1)/ASS n. (2)]

whip someone's head to the red *v.* [1930s–40s] (*US Black*) to threaten injury or retaliation (whether genuinely or as a bluff).

whip some skull on *v.* [1970s+] to fellate (cf. BRAIN n.[2]). [WHIP v.[5] + SKULL n.[7] (1)]

whip (something) on *v.* [1970s] (*US*) to give, to hand over.

whipster *n.* **1** [17C–early 19C] a clever, cunning person. **2** [20C+] (*Irish*) a forward, impudent woman; also occas. a man. [they are 'sharp as a whip'; (2) WHIP v.[1] (1), as they are inclined to steal]

whip-stitch! *excl.* [late 17C–early 18C] an excl. used to indicate a sudden movement or action. [note SAmE phr. *every whip-stitch*, at short or frequent intervals]

whip the baloney pony *v.* (*also* **whip the dummy, …lizard, …pony, …weasel, …wire**) [1990s+] to masturbate (cf. BEAT ONE'S HOG v.; BEAT ONE'S MEAT v.). [SE *whip* + BALONEY n.[2]/DUMMY n.[3]/LIZARD n.[3]/SE *pony*/WEASEL n.[3]/WIRE n.[5]]

whip the cat *v.*[1] [early 17C+] to play a practical joke. ['a trick often practised on ignorant country fellows, by laying a wager with them that they may be pulled through a pond by a cat; the bet being made, a rope is fastened round the waist of the person to be catted and the end thrown across the pond, to which the cat is also fastened by a pack-thread, and three or four sturdy fellows are appointed to lead and whip the cat; these on a signal given, seize the end of the cord, and pretending to whip the cat, haul the astonished booby through the water' (Grose, 1785)]

whip the cat *v.*[2] **1** [mid-17C–mid-18C] to get drunk. **2** [mid-17C–19C] to vomit through excessive drinking.

whip the cat *v.*[3] **1** [late 18C] to lay the blame for one's offences on someone else. **2** [late 19C+] (*Aus./N.Z.*) to suffer guilt and remorse for past errors, to worry about something about which one can do nothing. **3** [20C+] (*Aus.*) to complain *ad nauseam*, to whinge at length. [i.e. *whip the cat* that has spilt the milk over which one is crying]

whip the cat *v.*[4] **1** [19C] to be extremely mean as regards money. **2** [19C] to work as an itinerant tailor, carpenter, locksmith, knife-grinder etc. **3** [19C+] to shirk work on Mondays. **4** [early 19C] to idle on the job. [19C dial. *whip the cat*, to go from house to house as an itinerant tailor; such a job was unlikely to reap very rich rewards]

whip the dog *v.* [1910s+] (*US*) **1** to waste time and loaf on the job. **2** to bungle, to blunder. [euph. var. on FUCK THE DOG (AND SELL THE PUPS) v.]

whip the dummy/lizard/pony/weasel/wire *v. see* WHIP THE BALONEY PONY v.

whip-up *n.* [1920s] a monetary collection. [WHIP UP v. (1)]

whip (up) *v.* [early 17C–early 19C] to drink greedily, quickly.

whip up *v.* **1** [early 18C+] to collect, to organize. **2** [1930s+] to create, e.g. a suit of clothes.

whirl *n.* **1** [20C+] (*US*) a chance, an opportunity, a 'go'. **2** [1910s] an outing.

whirligig *n.* **1** [late 18C–mid-19C] (*UK Und.*) the pillory. **2** [1910s+] an unspecified gadget.

whirligigs *n.* [late 17C–early 19C] the testicles (cf. BANGERS n.). [SE *whirligig*, a variety of toy that is whirled or spun around]

whirling spray *n.* [1940s+] (*Aus.*) a talkative bore. [the words 'spray out']

whirlpit *n.* [mid-17C] the vagina (cf. BLACK HOLE n.[1]).

whirlybird *n.* [1950s+] (*US*) a helicopter.

whisht! *excl.* (*also* **wheesht! whist!**) [late 16C+] be quiet!, also as a n., silence; thus phr. *hold one's whist*, to be quiet.

whisk *n.* [mid-17C–early 19C] an insignificant person, a whippersnapper. [they make no more impression on the world than does a quick *whisk* on dirt]

whiskbroom 'with' *n.* [late 19C] (*US*) drunkenness. [an anecdote of late 19C Prohibition (then restricted to certain states rather than the nationwide version of 1920–33): a temperance campaigner, on entering a haberdasher's to buy a whiskbroom was offered one 'with' and one 'without'. On asking what this meant she was shown that a broom 'with' had a small bottle of whisky hidden amid its bristles]

whisker *n.*[1] [late 17C–early 19C] anything excessive, esp. a great lie. [SE *whisk*, to move briskly]

whisker *n.*[2] [1910s] (*US*) a country dweller.

whisker *n.*[3] [1910s+] (*orig. US*) a very small, infinitesimal amount or distance.

whisker *n.*[4] **1** [1920s–60s] a young woman. **2** [1930s+] (*Aus.*) pubic hair. **3** [1990s+] the penis.

whiskerando *n.* [mid-19C] a man who is heavily whiskered. [the character Don Ferolo *Whiskerandos* in R.B. Sheridan's play *The Critic* (1779)]

whisker-bed *n.* [mid-19C] the jaw; the face.

Whiskeries *n.* (*also* **Whiskyries**) [late 19C] the Irish Exhibition held in London in 1888. [Irish *whisky*]

whiskers *n.*[1] **1** [mid-19C+] (*US*) an old man; thus *his whiskers*, the head of the household; also as a term of address. **2** [1930s+] (*US Und.*) the US government, Army, or any other institution. [(2) the bewhiskered UNCLE SAM *n.*[1]]

whiskers *n.*[2] **1** [late 19C] (*US short order*) mutton chops. **2** [1940s] (*US*) pubic hair.

whiskers *n.*[3] [1940s–50s] (*US Und.*) a lesbian; a male homosexual.

whiskers *n.*[4] [1980s] (*US*) courage.

whisker-splitter *n.* [late 18C–early 19C] a womanizer. [NETHER WHISKERS *n.* + SE *splitter*]

whiskey-jerker *n. see* JERKER *n.*[1] (3).

whiskey-mill *n. see* GIN-MILL *n.* (1).

whiskin *n.* [mid-17C] a pimp (cf. ABBOT ON THE CROSS *n.*). [abbr. *pimp-whiskin* (*see* PIMP WHISK *n.* (1))]

whisking *adj.* **1** [early 17C–mid-19C] brisk, lively, smart. **2** [late 17C–early 18C] great, excessive. [SE *whisk*, to move briskly]

whisk of a lamb's tail, a *phr. see* TWO SHAKES OF A LAMB'S TAIL *phr.*

whisky-bottle *n.* [late 19C] a Scottish drunkard. [stereotyping]

whisky-frisky *adj.* [late 18C; 1910s] flighty. [SE *whisk* + *frisk*]

whiskyhead *n.* [1930s+] (*US*) **1** one who drinks a great deal of whisky. **2** delirium tremens. [SE *whisky* + (1) -HEAD sfx (3); (2) HEAD *n.*[5] (1)]

Whiskyries *n. see* WHISKERIES *n.*

whisky-skin *n.* [mid–late 19C] (*US*) a mixed drink containing a large proportion of whisky.

whisky's talking *phr. see* IT'S THE BEER TALKING *phr.*

whisky-straight *n.* [mid-19C] (*US*) whisky without additional water.

whisper *n.*[1] [mid-19C+] (*UK Und.*) a request for money; thus SLING (SOMEONE) THE WHISPER *v.* (1). [the surreptitious tones of the request]

whisper *n.*[2] **1** [late 19C; 1970s] a criminal's lookout man or tipster. **2** [late 19C+] a rumour, usu. of impending crimes, a tip; thus SLING (SOMEONE) THE WHISPER *v.* (2).

whisper *n.*[3] [late 19C+] a walk. [rhy. sl.; *whisper and talk* = walk]

whisper *n.*[4] [1900s] (*US Und.*) a sentence of 15–30 days.

whisper *v.*[1] [mid–late 19C] **1** to borrow money from. **2** to persuade someone to give money. [WHISPER *n.*[1]]

whisper *v.*[2] *see* SLING (SOMEONE) THE WHISPER *v.* (2).

whispering dudder *n. see* DUDDER *n.*[1].

whispering gallery *n.* [late 19C] the bar of the Gaiety Theatre. [a play on the more respectable *Whispering Gallery* encircling the dome of St Paul's Cathedral, and from the less well-off patrons whispering 'Can you lend me…?']

whist! *excl. see* WHISHT! *excl.*

whister-clister *n.* [late 18C–mid-19C] a blow on the ear. [dial. *whister*, whisper + SE *clyster*, an enema]

whister-snefet *n.* (*also* **whister-snivit**) [mid-16C] a blow on the ear. [dial. *whister*, whisper + SE/dial. *snite*, to wipe/SE *snivel*, nasal mucus]

whisticaster *n.* [early 19C] a blow on the ear. [dial. *whister*, whisper + SE *cast*, to throw]

whistle *n.*[1] **1** [late 14C–mid-19C] the mouth, the throat; subseq. used only in WET ONE'S WHISTLE *v.* **2** [late 19C] a flute. **3** [1910s] the lungs. [? the sounds]

whistle *n.*[2] **1** [mid-18C] a eunuch. **2** [late 19C] the penis (cf. ACCORDION *n.*). [(2) resemblance; Williams notes the 'lascivious' 17C stories/ballads of the 'Carman's whistle'; note earlier WHISTLE AND BELLS *n.*]

whistle *n.*[3] *see* WHISTLE (AND FLUTE) *n.*

whistle *v.* [1930s+] to smell unpleasantly. [the smell makes a 'noise']

whistle and bells *n.* [late 18C] the penis and testes.

whistle (and flute) *n.* **1** [1910s+] a suit of clothes. **2** [1960s] (*Aus.*) in pl., boots. **3** [2000s] cocaine (cf. BARLEY *n.*[2]). [rhy. sl.; (3) = TOOT *n.*[1] (5)]

whistle and toot *n.* [1910s+] money (cf. BEES (AND HONEY) *n.*). [rhy. sl. = LOOT *n.*[1] (2)]

whistle bait *n.* [1940s–50s] (*US*) an attractive woman. [one at whom men *whistle*]

whistle-belly-thumps *n.* [1990s+] stomach aches associated with diarrhoea. [rumbling and the pain in the stomach]

whistle-belly-vengeance *n.* [mid-19C] bad or thin beer. [var. on WHIP-BELLY (VENGEANCE) *n.*; the rumbling it produces in the drinker's stomach]

whistle-blower *n.* **1** [1970s+] a scandalmonger, an investigator who reveals facts that disturb a hitherto satisfactory, though corrupt, status quo. **2** [1990s+] (*US Und.*) a police informer.

whistlecock *n.* (*also* **whistleprick**) [late 19C+] (*Aus.*) a derog. name for a Native Australian, an Aborigine. [an initiation ritual-cum-prophylactic whereby the underside of the penis is slit to make a permanent incision in the urethra; the effect is to prevent the normal ejaculation of semen into one's partner]

whistled *adj.* [1930s–40s] (*orig. milit.*) drunk.

whistle Dixie *v.* [20C+] (*US*) **1** to engage in wishful fantasies. **2** to pursue without hope of success. **3** to boast, to brag without substance; usu. as *not just whistling Dixie*. [for ety. *see* DIXIE *n.*]

whistle drunk *adj.* [mid-18C] very drunk. [despite appearances, the chronology suggests there is no connection between this and WHISTLED *adj.*]

whistle for *v.* [early 16C+] to hope vainly for something; often used in the dismissive phr. *you can go whistle for it*, following someone's plea.

whistle for wind *n.* [late 19C] a fool.

whistle in the cage *v.* [early 19C] for a villain, on being arrested, to betray his accomplices. [fig. use of SE *whistle* + CAGE *n.* (1)]

whistle in the dark *v.*[1] [1930s+] **1** to hazard a guess, to speculate wildly. **2** to put on a brave front, to appear more confident than one really is.

whistle in the dark *v.*[2] [1960s–70s] (*US*) to perform cunnilingus.

whistle off *v.* [late 17C–18C] to run away, to leave at speed.

whistleprick *n. see* WHISTLECOCK *n.*

whistler *n.*[1] **1** [19C] a broken-down horse, whose breath whistles in his lungs. **2** [mid-19C] a bullet. **3** [1910s–20s] a revolver. **4** [1910s–20s] anything particularly large. **5** [1930s] (*US Und.*) a police car. **6** [1940s] a female railway porter. **7** [1940s+] (*US Und.*) an informer. [(2) abbr. BLUE WHISTLER *n.*]

whistler *n.*[2] [early 19C] (*UK Und.*) a counterfeit halfpenny or farthing. [the false ring when tapped]

whistler *n.*[3] [early–mid-19C] the proprietor of an unlicensed spirit-shop in a prison. [his drinks are kept hidden so that when the police raid they can *whistle for them*]

whistler *n.*[4] **1** [early–mid-19C] the mouth. **2** [1970s] an audible breaking of wind. **3** [1970s+] (*US gay*) a fellator. **4** [1980s+] (*drugs*) a nasal hole resulting from excessive cocaine use.

whistler *n.*[5] [late 19C] a casual labourer at the docks. [he attempts to *whistle up* work]

whistlers *n. see* WHISTLING-BREECHES *n.*

whistle stop *n.* [1930s+] (*US*) a small town; also attrib. [orig. railroad jargon *whistlestop town*; trains do not halt at such a town unless a passenger informs the conductor who then signals the fact by pulling on the signal cord and the engineer acknowledges the request by 2 whistles. The derog. sl. use led to the abandoning of the term by the railroads, who substituted *flag stop* or *flag station* to spare local feelings]

whistle up a breeze *v. see* RAISE THE WIND *v.* (1).

whistle-wetter *n. see* WET ONE'S WHISTLE *v.* (1).

whistling berries *n.* [1930s] (*US*) beans. [their effect on breaking wind]

whistling-breeches *n.* (*also* **whistlers**) [late 19C–1930s] corduroy trousers. [the swishing noise the material makes as the legs brush together]

whistling shop *n.* **1** [late 18C–mid-19C] a room in the King's Bench (or any other) prison where one could buy drink illicitly. **2** [mid-19C] any illicit drinking house. [WHISTLE *n.*[1] (1)/WHISTLER *n.*[3] + SHOP *n.*[1] (3)]

Whit, the *n.* (*also* **Whitt, the**) [late 17C–early 19C] (*UK Und.*) Newgate prison, Tothill prison (cf. ABBOTT'S PRIORY *n.*). [abbr. WHITTINGTON('S) COLLEGE *n.*]

white *n.*[1] **1** [early 19C–1920s] gin. **2** [1930s] (*US*) any form of alcohol.

white *n.*[2] [late 19C+] (*Aus.*) a shilling. [WHITE *adj.*[1]]

white *n.*[3] **1** [20C+] (*drugs*) morphine, heroin (cf. AUNTIE EMMA *n.*; BLACK *n.*[3]). **2** [1930s+] (*orig. UK Und.*) cocaine (cf. BLANCA *n.*). **3** [1960s+] (*drugs*) amphetamine (cf. A *n.*[2]). **4** [1980s+] crack cocaine (cf. BASE *n.*). [the colour of the respective drugs]

white *adj.*[1] [late 16C–1940s] silver.

white *adj.*[2] **1** [mid-19C+] honest, upright, fair-dealing. **2** [1960s] (*US Black*) patronizing, exploitative (but not necessarily White-skinned). [(1) coined without any consciously negative overtones and representing a rare (if unsurprisingly) positive racial stereotype, the term has been used in an increasingly ironic manner, esp. since the 1960s]

white *adj.*[3] [1970s+] (*S.Afr.*) cheeky, insubordinate. [used of a Black person 'getting above themselves' and thus trespassing on perceived White prerogatives]

white *adv.* [late 19C+] honestly, fairly. [WHITE *adj.*[2] (1)]

white about the gills *phr.*[1] (*also* **pale in the gills**) [mid-19C+] frightened. [SE *white* + GILLS *n.* (1)]

white about the gills *phr.*[2] *see* GREEN ABOUT THE GILLS *phr.*

white alley *n.* [late 19C–1930s] (*US*) an opportunity, one's 'best shot'. [marbles imagery]

white-ant *v.* **1** [1930s+] (*Aus.*) to sabotage, during a labour dispute; thus *white-anter*, a saboteur; *white-anting*, sabotage. **2** [1980s] to slander. [reverse anthropomorphism; note RMC Duntroon (Aus.) *white ant*, for a cadet to steal another's girlfriend]

white ants *n.* [1900s–50s] (*Aus.*) eccentricity, insanity; thus *have white ants*, to be crazy. [the supposed eating away of one's brain by white ants]

white apron *n.* [late 16C–mid-17C] a prostitute. [the SE *white apron* that was recognized as a prostitute's 'uniform'; note D'Urfey, *Pills to Purge Melancholy* (1719–20): 'And first for those ladies that walk in the Night, / Their Aprons and handkerchiefs they should be White'; the aim was 'the better to be seen']

white around the gills *phr. see* GREEN ABOUT THE GILLS *phr.*

white-arsed *adj.* (*also* **white-ass**) [1920s+] a general term of abuse. [SE *white* + -ARSED *sfx*]

white ash *n.* [mid-19C] (*US*) an oar; thus *white-ash breeze*, the oar's impetus through the water. [the *white ash* (*Fraxinus americana*), from which oars are made]

white as midnight's arsehole *phr.* [mid-16C–mid-17C] absolutely dark, totally black.

white-ass *adj. see* WHITE-ARSED *adj.*

white bag *n.* [1970s] (*US Black/drugs*) high-quality heroin (cf. BLACK *n.*[3]). [the colour of the drug; cheaper Mexican heroin is brown]

white-bag-man *adj.* [early 19C] a pickpocket.

white-belly rat *n.* [1920s–50s] (*W.I.*) a hypocrite. [this variety of rat supposedly blows on the thing it bites to minimize the pain]

white boy *n.* (*also* **white son**) [mid-16C–mid-18C] an especial favourite, a 'mother's darling'. [the image of SE *white* as denoting purity and innocence]

white bread *n.* **1** [1980s] (*US Black*) a derog. term for a Black person with a light complexion. **2** [1990s+] a pasty, unhealthy complexion.

white bread *adj.* **1** [1970s+] (*US*) used of anything pertaining to White, middle-class, mainstream styles; bland, unexciting, suburban. **2** [1980s] (*US campus*) used of anything good, pleasing, admirable.

white brick *n.* [1980s+] (*drugs*) cocaine (in bulk) (cf. BLANCA *n.*). [its colour + BRICK *n.*[6] (4)]

white broth ken *n.* [mid-19C] (*UK/US Und.*) a place where stolen silver is melted down. [WHITE *adj.*[1] + SE *broth* (as a precursor of SOUP *n.*[1]) + KEN *n.*[1] (1)]

white buzman *n.* [mid-19C] (*UK Und.*) a pickpocket, esp. one who steals silver or white handerchiefs. [WHITE *adj.*[1] + BUZMAN *n.*]

white callies *n.* (*also* **yellow callies**) [1990s+] (*drugs*) MDMA (cf. ECSTASY *n.*). [SE *white* + ? *California*]

Whitechapel *n.*[1] [mid-19C] in coin-tossing, a score of 2 out of 3 wins. [presumably popular in this area of London's East End]

Whitechapel *n.*[2] [mid-19C] an upper-cut. [? a blow favoured by East Enders]

Whitechapel *n.*[3] [late 19C] a sex murder. [the 'Jack the Ripper killings', which took place in Whitechapel in 1888]

Whitechapel *n.*[4] [20C+] an apple. [rhy. sl.]

Whitechapel *adj.* [late 17C–19C] used in various combs. to denote poverty, roughness and criminality; *see* below. [*Whitechapel*, the home of Cockney London and the heart of London's impoverished and thus often criminal East End]

Whitechapel beau *n.* [late 18C] one 'who dresses with a needle and thread, and undresses with a knife' (Grose, 1785). [WHITECHAPEL *adj.* + ironic use of SE *beau*]

Whitechapel breed *n.* [late 18C] a woman who is 'fat, ragged and saucy' (Grose, 1785). [WHITECHAPEL *adj.*]

Whitechapel brougham *n.* (*also* **Westminster brougham**) [mid-19C] a costermonger's donkey-barrow. [the closed carriage known as a *brougham* was beyond the income of the average Whitechapel costermonger]

Whitechapel fortune *n. see* WHITECHAPEL PORTION *n.*

Whitechapel oner *n.* [late 19C] a fashionable young man-about-Whitechapel, an East End dandy. [SE *Whitechapel* + ONER *n.*[1] (1), i.e. he is *number one* in local estimation]

Whitechapel play *n.* **1** [mid-18C–early 19C] in whist, the leading of all one's best cards, with no attempt to finesse the opponent. **2** [mid-19C] in billiards, to pot an opponent's ball. [WHITECHAPEL *adj.*; both uses stress the snobbish assumption that East Enders are unable to play ostensibly patrician games with the correct skill and subtlety]

Whitechapel portion *n.* (*also* **Whitechapel fortune**) **1** [late 17C–18C] the vagina, 'two torn smocks and what Nature gives' (B.E.). **2** [19C] 'a clean gown and a pair of pattens' (Hotten, 1864). [WHITECHAPEL *adj.*]

Whitechapel shave *n.* [mid-19C] whitening applied to the face to lighten the 'five o'clock shadow'. [WHITECHAPEL adj.; the poor cannot afford a barber to shave them]

Whitechapel warriors *n.* [late 19C] the Aldgate militia. [Aldgate, in *Whitechapel* + SE *warriors*]

white-choker *n.* [late 19C–1910s] a clergyman. [the white bands that are part of his dress]

white-chokery *n.* [late 19C] the upper classes. [i.e. those who wear a *white choker* or large white neckerchief as part of their evening dress]

White Cliffs (of Dover) *adv.* [20C+] over; usu. in phr. *all White Cliffs*. [rhy. sl.]

white cloud *n.* [1980s+] (*drugs*) crack cocaine smoke.

white corner *n.* (*also* **white mouth**) [20C+] (*W.I.*) an unpleasant, white discharge from the corner of one's mouth, usu. caused by vitamin deficiency.

white cow *n.* (*US*) **1** [1920s+] a vanilla milkshake. **2** [1940s+] a vanilla ice-cream soda. [SE *white* + COW n.⁵ (1)]

white cross *n.* (*drugs*) **1** [1900s–20s] cocaine (cf. BLANCA n.). **2** [1940s–50s] morphine; heroin (cf. AUNTIE EMMA n.; BLACK n.³). **3** [1970s] amphetamine pills with a white cross cut into one surface (cf. A n.²).

white dove *n.* [1990s+] a variety of MDMA (cf. ECSTASY n.). [SE *white*, i.e. the colour of the pill + DOVE n. (1)]

white dust *n.* [1970s] (*drugs*) **1** phencyclidine (cf. ACE n.⁴). **2** LSD (cf. A n.³). [the form in which the drug is sometimes sold]

white dynamite *n.* [1990s+] (*drugs*) heroin (cf. BLACK n.³). [its colour and effects]

white ewe *n.* [late 17C–18C] a beautiful and important woman in a band of villains.

white eye *n.* [early 19C–1910s] cheap, rough whisky. [its alleged effect; one's eyes apparently roll up in their sockets, exposing the whites]

white-eyes *n.* **1** [20C+] (*Native American*) White people. **2** [1970s+] (*US Black*) a White person. [the term *paleface* is generally fictional and invariably used by Whites rather than the 'Red Indians' to whom they attribute it]

white fever *n. see* PADDY FEVER n.

white fish *n.* [mid-19C] a silver dollar. [WHITE adj.¹ + FISH n.² (2)]

white-flighter *n.* [2000s] (*US*) a White person who has left the inner city through fear of its non-White population. [SAmE *white flight*, the migration of White people from inner-city areas]

white girl *n.* [1970s+] (*drugs*) cocaine, heroin (cf. BLACK n.³; BLANCA n.). [SE *white* + GIRL n.²]

white goods *n.* [1920s] (*US Und.*) narcotics. [their white powder form]

white guy *n. see* WHITE MAN n.¹.

white-haired boy *n.* (*also* **white-headed boy**) [19C+] (*orig. US*) an especial favourite, one who can, in the right eyes, do no wrong. [15C–17C SE *white*, precious, 'pet', 'darling'; Share suggests the 'Celtic preference for fair hair'; note synon. 16C SE *white*, son]

Whitehall warrior *n.* [1960s+] **1** a civil servant. **2** an officer in the services who has been seconded to administrative rather than active duties. [*Whitehall*, the home of the UK government + SE *warrior*]

white hat *n.* [1970s+] a hero, a 'good' character (as opposed to a 'bad' one) in any fictional medium. [*white hats* were worn by the heroes and black hats by the villains in the old, silent Western films]

Whitehaven docks *n.* [1970s] venereal disease. [rhy. sl. = POX n.¹ (2)]

white-headed *adj.* [1900s] (*Aus.*) angry, indignant.

white-headed boy *n. see* WHITE-HAIRED BOY n.

white horse *n.*¹ [late 19C] (*Irish*) cowardice. [tradition has it that King James II fled the battle of the Boyne riding a *white horse*]

white horse *n.*² [1900s–30s] (*US*) pure alcohol, diluted for drinking. [its translucency and its effects]

white horse *n.*³ [1950s+] (*drugs*) cocaine; occas. heroin; thus RIDE THE WHITE HORSE v.¹ (cf. BLACK n.³; BLANCA n.). [SE *white* + HORSE n.⁸; heroin is usu. brown, cocaine is white]

white house *n.* [1950s–70s] (*US Black*) the world of White society. [underpinned by a ref. to the *White House*, home of the US presidency]

white it out *v.* [late 19C–1950s] (*Aus.*) to serve a jail sentence. [? one SE *whites out*, i.e. erases, that period of one's life]

white jenny *n.* [18C–19C] a watch made of foreign silver. [WHITE adj.¹ + ? abbr. SE *engine*]

white kaffir *n.* (*S.Afr.*) **1** [mid-19C] a derog. term for a White perceived as behaving badly by their peers. **2** [mid-19C] a White who has become overly close to or assimilated into the Black community. **3** [1930s+] an albino. [SE *white* + KAFFIR n.¹]

white Kanaka *n.* [1910s] (*Aus.*) a White person seen as having 'gone native' and as such disdained. [SE *white* + KANAKA n.¹]

white-knuckle *adj.* [1970s+] (*orig. US*) terrifying, very frightening; often of a fairground ride or horror film. [the *whitening* of one's *knuckles* as one grips onto something to control one's emotions]

white-knuckle *v.* [1990s+] to suffer bravely, irrespective of the pain.

white-knuckler *n.* [1970s+] (*US*) **1** an aeroplane flight. **2** a tense, anxious person. [WHITE-KNUCKLE adj.]

white lady *n.*¹ [1930s+] (*Aus.*) methylated spirits. [SE *white lady*, a cocktail made of 2 parts of dry gin, 1 of orange liqueur and 1 of lemon juice]

white lady *n.*² [1960s+] (*drugs*) **1** cocaine (cf. BLANCA n.). **2** heroin; thus *white queen*, good-quality heroin (cf. BLACK n.³). [its colour, although the bulk of late 20C+ heroin is light brown; note cocaine is a 'feminine' drug, *see* GIRL n.²]

white lightning *n.* **1** [1920s+] (*US*) illicit home-brewed whisky or poteen. **2** [1970s+] (*drugs*) (*also* **white light**) LSD (cf. A n.³). [the effects]

white lilies *n.* [1940s] (*US Black*) bed linen.

white line *n.* **1** [late 19C–1920s] (*US tramp*) alcohol that has been diluted. **2** [1910s] a drinker. **3** [1910s–30s] (*also* **white lime**) alcohol; thus *white-liner*, a dealer in or drinker of alcohol. [ety. unknown]

white-line fever *n.*¹ [1970s+] the obsessive use of cocaine. [the *white lines* of the powdered drug that are inhaled by users]

white-line fever *n.*² [1970s+] (*US*) an obsessive driver. [the *white lines* that divide traffic lanes]

white liver *n.* **1** [1930s–60s] a homosexual who has no interest whatsoever in women. **2** [1960s] a lesbian with no interest whatsoever in men. **3** [1990s+] (*US/W.I.*) nymphomania. [SE *white*, pure + *liver*]

white-livered *adj.* (*also* **liver-faced**) [mid-16C+] cowardly. [the assumption that a coward has insufficient bile or 'choler' in his liver, so rendering it white and him weak]

white lot *n.* [19C] a silver watch. [WHITE adj.¹ + SE *lot*, an article]

white magic *n.* [late 19C] (*UK society*) extremely beautiful women.

white man *n.*¹ (*also* **white guy**) [mid-19C+] (*UK/US*) an honourable person. [SE *white*/WHITE adj.² (1) + SE *man*/GUY n.²; modern use usu. ironic]

white man *n.*² [1950s] (*W.I.*) an albino.

white man's burden *n.* [1940s–50s] work; the matter in hand. [Kipling's poem 'The White Man's Burden', in which the task was the ruling of the 'new-caught sullen peoples / Half-devil and half-child']

white man's chance *n.* [mid–late 19C] (*US*) a fair chance. [as opposed to the treatment of non-Whites]

white man's disease *n.* [1980s+] (*US Black*) the relative inability of Caucasians to jump; a term of derision almost exclusively used in a basketball context.

white meat *n.* (*also* **light meat**) **1** [1930s] (*US*) an easy target;

something desirable. **2** [1930s+] (*US Black/W.I.*) a White person; usu. a woman and in a sexual context. **3** [1970s] (*gay*) young (underage) boys. **4** [1970s+] a White penis (cf. BACON n.¹). [(1) SE *white* + MEAT n. (1), pun on the genteel euph. for the 'breast' of a chicken; (2) and (3) the tenderness of young SE *chicken*/CHICKEN n.⁴ (4); note printers' jargon *white meat*, an actress; (4) MEAT n. (2)]

white mice *n.* **1** [1930s] (*Aus.*) lice. **2** [1940s–50s] dice. [rhy. sl.]

white money *n.* **1** [mid-16C–early 17C; mid-19C+] silver coins. **2** [20C+] (*US*) an illegal political contribution. **3** [1940s] large banknotes (cf. BANK-RAG n.). [(1) WHITE adj.¹; (2) it is seen as 'invisible', unlike green dollars; (3) the old large 'white' £5 note]

white mosquitoes *n.* [1940s–50s] (*drugs*) cocaine or any powdered drug (cf. BLANCA n.). [the mosquito-bite-like mark left after an injection]

white mouth *n. see* WHITE CORNER n.

white mouth *v.* **1** [1930s] (*US Black*) to pretend servility in one's conversations with Whites. **2** [2000s] to fellate (cf. COCKSUCK n.). [(1) one 'talks their language'; (2) the white semen]

white mule *n.* [1900s–60s] (*US*) homemade whisky made from grain alcohol (cf. MULE n.³). [SE *white* + MULE n.³ (1)]

white nigga *n. see* WIGGA n.

white nigger *n.* **1** [mid-19C; 1960s+] a Black person who is regarded as deferring to White people or accepting a role prescribed by them. **2** [mid–late 19C] a derog. term for a White person who does menial labour. **3** [late 19C] (*Sierra Leone*) a European. **4** [1930s] (*US*) a Jew (cf. ARAB n.²). **5** [1940s+] a Mediterranean and thus relatively dark-skinned immigrant to the US, e.g. a Greek or Italian (cf. DAGO n.). **6** [1950s–70s] beatniks, hippies and other counter-cultural groups who see their alienation from mainstream culture as analogous with the everyday role of any Black person. **7** [1960s+] (*Can.*) a self-description by embittered French Canadians who see themselves as second-class citizens in a primarily British country. [SE *White* + NIGGER n.¹ (1); (6) note Norman Mailer, *The White Negro* (1957): 'The hipster had absorbed the existentialist synapses of the Negro, and for practical purposes could be considered a White Negro'; (2) note Ned Ward, *The London Spy* (1700): '[The Irishman is] a Valuable Slave in our *Western-Plantations*, where they are distinguish'd by the Ignominious Epithet of *White-Negroes*']

white night *n.* [late 19C+] a sleepless night.

white nurse *n.* [1930s+] (*drugs*) any form of powdered white drugs. [the 'health-giving' effects; note Rolling Stones' song 'Sister Morphine' (1969)]

white one *n.* **1** [1920s] (*US Und.*) a diamond. **2** [1920s–40s] (*US Und.*) a silver watch. **3** [1940s] (*US Black*) a white shirt. [(1) and (3) SE *white*; (2) WHITE adj.¹]

white-on-white *n.* **1** [1940s+] (*US Black*) a white Cadillac with white interior finish and white upholstery; thus *white-on-white-in-white*, a Black person who seeks the supposed status of association with White people, esp. through a White girlfriend and a white Cadillac. **2** [1950s+] a white shirt.

whiteout *n.* **1** [1980s+] (*drugs*) isobutyl nitrite (cf. AIMIES n.). **2** [2000s] (*US*) a temporary loss of consciousness. [(1) its effect on the brain; (2) as opposed to a full-scale SE *blackout*]

white owl *n.* **1** [1900s] (*US*) a chamberpot. **2** [1970s] a White penis (cf. ANTEATER n.).

white Owsley's *n. see* OWSLEY ACID n.

white pipe *n.* [1990s+] (*S.Afr.*) a mixture of marijuana, tobacco and a crushed tablet of Mandrax (the brandname of methaqualone). [SE *white* + PIPE n.⁴]

white pointer *n.* [1990s+] (*Aus.*) a highway patrolman. [SAusE *white pointer* shark, the 'Great White Shark']

white port *n.* [mid-18C–mid-19C] (*UK Und.*) gin.

white powder *n.* [1940s+] any form of narcotic or other drug that comes in the form of white powder.

white prop *n.* [mid-19C] a diamond scarf or tie stickpin. [SE *white* + PROP n.⁴ (1)]

white pudding *n. see* PUDDING n.¹ (1).

white quarter *n. see* RED CENT n.

white queen *n. see* WHITE LADY n.² (2).

white rat *n.* [1980s+] (*Aus. prison*) an albino prisoner.

white ribbon *n.* (*also* **white ribbin**) [early 19C] gin. [SE *white* + RIBBON n.¹]

white Russian *n.* [1960s+] (*gay*) the oral exchange of semen. [the similarity of white semen to the colour of a *white Russian* cocktail]

whites *n.*¹ [late 17C–mid-18C; late 19C+] venereal disease, spec. a vaginal discharge, gonorrhoea. [the colour of the discharge; late 20C+ use is Aus.]

whites *n.*² [early 19C–1900s] silver coins; thus in counterfeiters' jargon *large whites*, half-crowns; *small whites*, shillings. [WHITE adj.¹]

whites *n.*³ [1960s] (*W.I.*) a drink of white rum.

whites *n.*⁴ [1960s+] (*drugs*) amphetamines (cf. A n.²).

white satin *n.*¹ [mid-19C–1900s] gin. [the term is still in use as a proprietary name for a brand of gin, *Sir Robert Burnett's White Satin Gin*]

white satin *n.*² [1950s] (*Aus.*) a White woman, esp. as considered sexually. [play on BLACK VELVET n. (1)]

white serjeant *n.* [late 18C–19C] a wife who dominates her husband.

white serpent *n.* [1990s+] heroin (cf. BLACK n.³).

white sheep *n. see* BLACK CAP n.

white shirt *n.* [1950s+] (*UK/US prison*) a senior prison officer, who (in the UK) wears a white shirt rather than the blue of the junior ranks.

white shit *n.* [1990s+] (*drugs*) **1** heroin (cf. BLACK n.³; CACA n.). **2** cocaine (cf. BLANCA n.). [SE *white* + SHIT n.⁵]

white-shoe *adj.* **1** [1950s+] (*US*) immature, effeminate. **2** [1960s+] pertaining to the US establishment, e.g. a *white-shoe law firm*. **3** [1990s+] (*Aus.*) describing businessmen who prefer casual clothes to the trad. 'uniform' of black shoes and dark suits.

white sidewall *n. see* WHITEWALL n.

white silk *n.* [1930s–50s] (*US drugs*) morphine crystals (cf. AUNTIE EMMA n.).

white slang *n.* [1910s] (*US Und.*) a silver watch chain. [WHITE adj.¹ + SLANG n.² (2)]

white slufe *n. see* WHITE STUFF n. (5).

white sneaker set *n.* [1960s] (*US gay*) homosexual society.

white son *n. see* WHITE BOY n.

white soup *n.* [late 18C–19C] (*UK Und.*) silver that has been melted down from the original, stolen plate. [WHITE adj.¹ + SOUP n.¹]

white space *n.* [1980s+] free time. [the space in question is in the speaker's diary]

white-staff *n.* [mid-18C] the penis (cf. BAT n.⁷). [SE *white staff*, 'a white rod or wand carried as a symbol of office by certain officials, e.g. the steward of the king's household and the lord high treasurer' (*OED*)]

white stone *n.* **1** [1910s] (*US Und.*) a diamond. **2** [1940s–50s] (*US Black*) a fake diamond, esp. as used in a confidence trick. [SE *white* + STONE n.¹ (2)]

white stuff *n.* **1** [mid–late 19C] anything made of silver. **2** [20C+] (*drugs*) morphine or heroin (cf. AUNTIE EMMA n.; BLACK n.³). **3** [1920s] (*US*) grain alcohol used for making illicit liquor. **4** [1920s+] (*drugs*) cocaine (cf. BLANCA n.). **5** [1930s] (*also* **white slufe**) opium (cf. APOSTLE n.). **6** [1940s] diamonds. **7** [1950s] large denomination notes. **8** [1980s] Demerol. [(1) WHITE adj.¹; (2), (4) and (5) SE *white* + STUFF n.³ (2); (7) large 'white' £5 notes]

white swallow *n.* [1990s+] (*US, mainly West Coast*) semen; usu. in the context of fellatio.

white tail deer hunting *n.* [2000s] (*US Black*) having anal intercourse with a White woman. [SE *white* + play on SE *tail*/TAIL n.² (1)]

white tape *n.* (*also* **white wool**) [early 18C–mid-19C] gin or genever. [SE *white* + TAPE n./SE *wool*]

white toy *n.* [mid–late 19C] a silver watch. [WHITE adj.[1] + TOY n.[2]]

white trash *n.* (*also* **ofay trash, trash**) [mid-19C+] (*orig. US Black*) a derog. term for the poor White population of the Southern states; thus ext. to non-US contexts; occas. in sing. [lit. 'White rubbish']

white trash *adj.* [1940s+] (*orig. US*) pertaining to the culture and mores of the White underclass population of the Southern states; latterly describing any poor White. [WHITE TRASH n.]

white 'un *n.* [mid–late 19C] a silver watch. [WHITE adj.[1] + SE *one*]

whitewall *n.* (*also* **white sidewall**) [1970s+] (*orig. US milit.*) a very severe 'short back and sides' haircut, orig. in the US Marines.

whitewash *n.*[1] [mid-19C–1900s] a glass of sherry taken as the finale after a meal spent drinking port and claret. [its relatively 'white' colour and its 'washing' away of the red wines]

whitewash *n.*[2] (*also* **wash**) [mid-19C+] in sport, the complete defeat of one team by another; thus any crushing defeat.

whitewash *v.*[1] [mid-18C–1900s] to free oneself of debts by becoming a bankrupt.

whitewash *v.*[2] [mid-19C+] (*US*) to win decisively. [WHITEWASH n.[2]]

whitewash *v.*[3] [1960s+] **1** to have sexual intercourse. **2** to ejaculate. **3** (*US gay*) to perform anilingus (cf. AUSTRALIAN n.). [the whiteness of the semen]

whitewashed *adj.* [mid-18C–1900s] freed of one's debts by becoming a bankrupt. [WHITEWASH v.[1]]

whitewasher *n.* [late 19C] a glass of white wine taken at the end of dinner. [var. on WHITEWASH n.[1]; one 'cleans up' the palate with the lighter drink]

whitewashing *n.*[1] [mid-18C] (*W.I.*) insincerely accepting religious conversion when the alternative is to be killed. [the Black man or woman is 'washed white' through baptism]

whitewashing *n.*[2] [early 19C] declaring oneself bankrupt (and serving the concomitant prison sentence) to nullify one's debts. [WHITEWASH v.[1]]

whitewash someone's kidneys *v.* [1950s+] (*Aus.*) to have anal intercourse (cf. ASK FOR THE RING v.). [WHITEWASH v.[3] (2) + SE *kidneys*]

whitewash someone's tonsils *v.* (*also* **massage someone's tonsils**) [1960s+] (*US*) to ejaculate in someone's mouth, following fellation. [WHITEWASH v.[3] (2)/SE *massage* + *tonsils*]

whitewater wristing *v.* [1990s+] masturbation. [play on SE *whitewater rafting* + *whiteness* of semen]

white widow *n.* [1990s+] (*drugs*) a form of marijuana (i.e. super-compacted SUPERSKUNK n.) that is so dense as to exude white crystals (cf. BLACK DOMINA n.).

white wine *n.* [early–mid-19C] gin. [euph.; gin was seen as a degenerate drink]

white wing *n.* [late 19C–1950s] (*US*) any wearer of a white uniform. [the *locus classicus* was the nickname of the New York City street sweepers, who wore white uniforms after the reforms of the city's street cleaning by Colonel George F. Waring in 1895]

white wings *n.* [late 19C–1900s] (*US*) eggs. [those of the hens that lay them]

white wog *n.* [1970s] (*US*) a derog. term for an Irish person (cf. BOG ARAB n.; BOG-WOG n.[1] (3))

white wool *n.*[1] **1** [early 17C] (*UK Und.*) the silver pieces that are left with the victim of a substitution fraud. **2** [late 17C–mid-19C] silver in general. [WHITE adj.[1] + SE *wool*]

white wool *n.*[2] *see* WHITE TAPE n.

whitey *n.*[1] (*US/UK Black*) **1** [early 19C; 1930s+] any White individual; occas. ext. to Latinos and Chicanos. **2** [mid-19C+] the White race in general.

whitey *n.*[2] [1990s+] (*Aus.*) Carlton draft beer.

whitey *n.*[3] [1990s+] (*UK juv.*) a short-term attack of panic and increased heart-rate caused by an excess of cannabis. [the white pallor of the victim's skin]

whitey mcfly *n.* (*US Black*) a White person attempting to adopt Black culture and style. [WHITEY n.[1] (1) + MCFLY n.]

whitey-whitey *n.* [1950s] (*W.I.*) an albino.

whither-go-ye *n.* (*also* **whither-do-go**) [late 17C–early 19C] a wife. [the question asked by a stereotypically nagging, over-inquisitive wife]

Whit's Palace *n.* [late 19C] Newgate prison (cf. ABBOTT'S PRIORY n.).

Whitt, the *n. see* WHIT, THE n.

Whittington priory *n.* [late 19C] Holloway prison (cf. ABBOTT'S PRIORY n.). [its association with Dick *Whittington* (c.1358–1423), who 'turned again' at nearby Highgate]

Whittington('s) college *n.* [17C–early 19C] (*UK Und.*) Newgate prison (cf. ABBOTT'S PRIORY n.; BIG SCHOOL n.). [the name of a Warden or the rebuilding of Newgate in 1423 by the executors of Richard ('Dick') Whittington, the former Lord Mayor + COLLEGE n. (2)]

whittle *v.* [early 18C] to inform, to betray one's confederates. [WHIDDLE v. (2)]

whittled as a penguin *phr.* [1960s] (*Aus.*) extremely drunk. [16C–17C SE *whittled*, drunk + *penguin*]

whittler *n.* [1920s–40s] (*US tramp*) a small-town sheriff or constable. [lacking big-city crimes, he sits *whittling* a piece of wood]

whittle the stick *v.* (*also* **whittle one's tool**) [1960s] to masturbate. [SE *whittle* + play on SE *stick*/*tool* + STICK n.[1] (1)/TOOL n.[1] (1)]

whit-whit *n.* [2000s] (*US Black*) an untrustworthy woman; a woman whose vagina smells and is prob. infected. [? WHITES n.]

whiz *n.*[1] **1** [late 18C–early 19C] noise, commotion, a 'buzz'; thus *hold your whiz!* be quiet! shut up! **2** [1900s] (*US*) a spree. **3** [1910s+] (*Aus.*) energy, spirit. [echoic]

whiz *n.*[2] [mid-19C] (*US*) a deal, a bargain. [ety. unknown; ? the speed, i.e. SE *whiz*, of its conclusion]

whiz *n.*[3] (*also* **whizz, wiz**) **1** [late 19C+] a general term of approbation, esp. of a highly satisfying thing or event. **2** [1910s+] a general term of approbation, esp. of a very skilful or talented person. [SE *wizard*]

whiz *n.*[4] (*also* **whizz, wizz**) [1920s+] a pickpocket; also in combs., e.g. *whiz artist, whiz-boy, whizman*. [SE *whiz*, to move fast]

whiz *n.*[5] [1950s–60s] (*US*) whiskey. [abbr.]

whiz *n.*[6] (*also* **whizz, wizz**) [1960s+] an act of urination. [WHIZ v.[2]]

whiz *n.*[7] (*also* **whizz**) [1990s+] amphetamine, amphetamine sulphate (cf. A n.[2]). [SE *whiz*, to move fast]

whiz *adj.* [1910s+] a general term of admiration. [WHIZ n.[3]]

whiz *v.*[1] (*also* **whizz, wizz**) **1** [1920s+] (*US Und.*) to pickpocket. **2** [1960s+] to steal. [WHIZ n.[4]]

whiz *v.*[2] (*also* **whizz**) [1920s+] to urinate. [echoic of urine hitting the lavatory bowl]

whiz! *excl.* [mid-18C–mid-19C] a general excl.

whiz bang *n.*[1] [1910s+] (*US*) any person or thing that is impressive or successful. [WHIZ n.[3] + SE *bang*]

whiz bang *n.*[2] [1930s–50s] (*drugs*) an injection of cocaine plus heroin or morphine. [the *whiz* of the cocaine + the *bang* of the opiate]

whiz bang *adj.* [1910s+] (*US*) describing a person or thing that is impressive or successful. [WHIZ BANG n.[1]]

whiz gang *n. see* WHIZ MOB n.

whiz jizzum *v.* [20C+] to masturbate. [WHIZ v.[2] + JISM n.]

whiz-kid *n.* (*also* **whizz-kid**) [1960s+] an exceptional person, a genius, somebody who is very good at a particular trade or skill. [WHIZ n.[3] (2)]

whiz mob *n.* (*also* **whiz gang, whizz mob**) [1920s+] the world of pickpockets; a gang of pickpockets. [WHIZ n.[4] + MOB n.[2] (3)]

whiz off *v. see* RACE OFF v.

whiz pop *n.* [1970s] (*US campus*) a stupid person. [such a person emulates a dud firework, which *whizzes* then sputters out with an anti-climactic *pop*]

whizz *see also under* WHIZ and its combs.

whizz-bomb *n.* [2000s+] (*drugs*) MDMA (cf. ECSTASY n.).

whizzer *n.*[1] [late 19C+] something or someone extraordinary or wonderful. [WHIZ n.[3]]

whizzer *n.*[2] (*also* **wizzer**) [20C+] a pickpocket. [WHIZ n.[4]]

whizzer *n.*[3] [1960s] a spree, a drinking bout. [SE *whiz*; ? WHIZ n.[1] (2)]

whizzing *n.* [1920s–40s] working as a pickpocket. [WHIZ v.[1] (1)]

whizzing *adj.* [1900s–50s] (*mainly UK juv.*) wonderful, first-rate; also as a positive intensifier. [WHIZ n.[3] (1)]

whizzo *adj.* (*also* **wizz, wizzo**) [1940s+] (*mainly UK juv., except when ironic*) wonderful, brilliant, amazing; also as excl. [WHIZ n.[3] (1)]

whizz off *v. see* RACE OFF v.

whizzy-whizzy *v. see* WIZZY-WIZZY v.

who *n. see* HO n.[1] (2).

whoaball *n.* (*also* **whoball, whow-ball, woball**) [late 17C–mid-19C] a milkmaid. [SE *whoa*, stop + *Ball*, a common name for a cow]

whoa, bust me! *excl.* [19C] a general excl. of anger, amazement. [SE *whoa* + BUST v.[1] (5)]

whoady *n.* [2000s] (*US Black*) a friend, a partner.

whoa, Emma (mind the paint)! *excl.* [late 19C] an excl. used to a woman who either looks odd or is behaving strangely or excessively in public. [an inquest on one *Emma* who had died suddenly and whose husband had attempted to revive her with this excl.]

whoa, Jameson! *excl.* [late 19C] an excl. used, with a certain degree of admiration, to restrain one who the speaker feels is 'going too far'. [the audacious but politically disastrous *Jameson* Raid, 1896]

who are you? *phr.* **1** [mid–late 19C] an aggressive phr. used in London streets; usu. greeted with the equally aggressive rejoinder 'Who are *you*?' **2** [1980s+] (*US campus*) what's the matter? what's your problem? **3** [1980s+] (*US campus*) as excl., be quiet!

whoball *n. see* WHOABALL n.

who cares? *phr.* [mid-19C+] a dismissive phr. indicating one's lack of concern.

whocker-jawed *adj. see* WHOPPER-JAWED adj.

who cut the cheese? *phr.* [1950s+] (*orig. US, mainly juv.*) who broke wind? [the smell associated with some soft cheeses]

whodunnit *n.* [1940s–50s] (*UK prison*) meat pie. [SE *whodunnit*, a murder mystery; the 'murder victim' is the prison cat, the supposed origin of the meat in the pie]

whodyamaflick *n.* [2000s] used for a name one has temporarily forgotten.

whoe *n. see* HO n.[1].

who has any lands in Appleby? *phr.* [late 17C–early 19C] a phr. addressed to 'the man at whose door the glass stands long, or who does not circulate it in due time' (Grose, 1785).

who in hell? *phr. see* WHAT IN HELL? phr.

who is he/she when he's/she's at home? *phr. see* WHAT'S THAT WHEN IT'S AT HOME? phr.

who kicked your kennel? *phr.* (*also* **who kicked your pigsty?**) [1910s+] mind your own business.

whole bag of tricks, the *n.* (*also* **the whole box of tricks**) [mid-19C+] everything necessary to deal with a situation.

whole ball of wax, the *n.* [mid-19C+] (*US*) absolutely everything.

whole bang shoot, the *n.* (*also* **the bang shoot, the whole bang lot, the whole shoot(ing)**) [late 19C+] everything or everybody, relevant and involved (cf. WHOLE SHOT, THE n.).

whole bit, the *n.* [1960s+] everything. [SE *whole* + BIT n.[8] (1)]

whole boiling lot, the *n.* (*also* **the whole biling, ...boiling, ...boiling bunch**) [19C+] absolutely everything, absolutely everyone.

whole boodle, the *n. see* BOODLE n.[1] (1).

whole box and dice, the *n.* [late 19C+] (*Aus.*) everything.

whole box of tricks, the *n. see* WHOLE BAG OF TRICKS, THE n.

whole caboodle, the *n. see* WHOLE KIT AND CABOODLE, THE n.

whole caboose, the *n.* (*also* **the whole caboosh**) [late 19C+] (*Aus./Irish*) everything, the lot.

whole can of worms, the *n.* [1970s] everything, everyone. [ext. of CAN OF WORMS n.]

whole cheese, the *n.* (*US*) **1** [1900s] everything. **2** [1900s–30s] an important person.

whole circus, the *n.* [1910s] (*Aus.*) everything that one might require.

whole cooloo, the *n.* [1930s] everything, 'the lot'. [Arabic *cooloo*, all, or CABOODLE n.]

whole enchilada, the *n.* (*also* **the full enchilada**) [1950s+] (*US*) everything, the lot.

whole famn damily, the *n.* (*also* **the whole famdamily**) [2000s] (*US*) a euph. for the *whole damn family.*

whole-footed *adj.* [mid-18C–mid-19C] unreserved, frank, free and easy. [SE *whole-footed*, treading with one's whole foot, not just the toes]

whole gimbang, the *n. see* WHOLE SHEBANG, THE n.

whole hog, the *n.* [mid-19C+] absolutely everything, the very best of something; usu. in phr. GO THE WHOLE HOG v.

whole-hog *adj.* [mid-19C+] complete, absolute, unswerving, devoted; usu. with regard to politics. [WHOLE HOG, THE n.]

whole issue, the *phr. see* ISSUE n.

whole jingbang, the *n.* [late 19C+] the whole thing, the whole affair, the whole lot. [Scot., ? echoic of people moving]

whole kit, the *n.* (*also* **the whole kip**) [late 18C–mid-19C] the entire lot, the full collection.

whole kit and biling, the *n.* (*also* **the kit and boiling, the whole shool and boiling**) [mid-19C–1940s] (*US*) absolutely everything and everyone, the lot. [WHOLE KIT, THE n. + SE *boiling*/dial. *biling*]

whole kit and caboodle, the *n.* (*also* **the kit and caboodle, the whole caboodle, the whole kit and boodle, the whole kit and kaboodle**) [mid-19C+] (*orig. US*) the lot, everything there is. [WHOLE KIT, THE n. + CABOODLE n.]

whole kit and cargo, the *n.* (*also* **the whole kit and crew, ...kit and killybang, ...kit and parcel, ...kit and posse, ...kit and tolic, ...kit and tuck**) [mid-19C+] (*US*) the lot. [WHOLE KIT, THE n. + SE *cargo*]

whole new ball game *n.* [1960s+] (*US*) a totally revised or new situation. [baseball imagery]

whole nine yards, the *n.* (*also* **the whole nine**) [1960s+] everything, the complete package. [ety. unknown, but most of the many suggestions involve supposed standards of measurement, from the dimensions of a nun's habit to the capacity of a cement truck and the length of an ammunition clip to that of a hangman's rope. However, few, when checked, actually run to 9 yards. It is most likely to be the use of 9 as a form of 'mystic' number]

whole 'nother thing *n.* [1960s+] (*US*) a totally different situation; something else entirely.

whole outfit, the *n.* [1910s+] the lot, everything.

whole route, the *n.* [1900s] (*US*) everything.

whole schmear, the *n.* (*also* **the whole schmeer, ...shmear, ...shmeer, ...smear**) [1910s+] (*US*) everything, the whole lot; everyone. [despite ety. of SCHMEER v., authorities claim that *whole schmeer* is not Yid.; Nathan Süsskind (in Cohen (ed.), *Studies in Slang* II, 1989) suggests Ger. *Schmiere*, a small, insignificant and third-rate piece of art or performance; transferred to the artist or theatre company that produces it, and thence to the company, its props, and everything it possesses; thus *whole schmeer* = WHOLE

KIT AND CABOODLE, THE n. = everything; note Rosten, *The Joys of Yiddish* (1968), who includes v. but does not mention n.]

whole shebang, the n. (*also* **the whole gimbang**) [mid-19C+] absolutely everything. [SE *whole* + US milit. jargon *shebang*, a soldier's tent, where his possessions were kept, ult. SE *shebang*, a hut, a dwelling]

whole shool and boiling, the n. *see* WHOLE KIT AND BILING, THE n.

whole shoot(ing), the n. *see* WHOLE BANG SHOOT, THE n.

whole shooting match, the n. (*also* **the whole shooting gallery, ...lot**) [late 19C+] (*orig. US*) absolutely everything.

whole shot, the n. [1960s+] (*US*) everything; a complete version (cf. WHOLE BANG SHOOT, THE n.).

whole smear, the n. *see* WHOLE SCHMEAR, THE n.

whole team (and the dog under the wagon) n. (*also* **full team**) [mid-19C–1910s] (*US*) a phr. used to indicate one's own or another's importance, energy etc; usu. as *ain't I/he/she/they a whole team...*

who let you out? phr. [late 19C–1940s] a deliberately deflating response to someone who is behaving far too self-confidently. [one has been released from an asylum]

wholewheat bread n. [1970s+] (*US Black*) a light-skinned person.

whole works, the n. *see* WORKS, THE n.

whollop *see under* WALLOP.

whomp n. (*also* **whump, wump**) (*US*) 1 [1920s+] a heavy, low sound. 2 [1950s] a spree. 3 [1970s+] a heavy blow. [echoic]

whomp v. (*also* **whomp on, whump, womp, womp on**) 1 [1930s+] to hit; also in fig. use. 2 [1950s+] (*US*) to defeat, to trounce. 3 [1980s+] to have sexual intercourse (cf. BANG v.[1]). [WHOMP n.]

whomp! excl. (*also* **whump!**) [1950s+] echoic of the sound of a sudden blow, used to indicate suddenness, immediacy. [WHOMP n. (3)]

whomp up v. (*also* **whump up**) [1950s+] (*US*) 1 to create, to devise, to make up. 2 to stimulate, to stir up. [ext. of WHOMP v.]

whoobang v. [2000s] (*US teen*) to gossip maliciously; to talk nonsense.

whoof it in v. (*also* **whoomf**) [1950s+] to push something in(to). [echoic]

whoogie n. [1990s+] (*US Black*) a derog. term for a White person. [SE *white* + BOOGIE n.[2] (1)]

whoop v. *see* WHOP v.

whoop and a holler n. [early 19C+] (*US*) a short distance; also *two whoops and a holler*. [SE *whoop* + *holler*, both meaning shout, and so the distance such cries would carry]

whoop-de-do n. (*also* **whoop-de-doodle**) (*US*) 1 [1920s+] an uproar, a noisy celebration, a significant event. 2 [1940s] praise.

whoop-de-do adj. (*also* **whoop-de-doodle**) [1940s+] (*US*) uproarious, noisy. [WHOOP-DE-DO n. (1)]

whoop-de-do! excl. (*also* **whoop-dee-doo! whoopty-woo!**) [late 19C+] an excl. of joy, excitement; often ironic. [ext. of WHOOPEE!]

whooped adj. (*also* **whupped**) [1980s] (*US campus*) drunk; also in fig. use, infatuated, in love (cf. ANNIHILATED adj.). [WHOP v. (2)]

whoopee n. [1920s+] (*US*) a wild party; self-indulgence of any sort; also attrib. [WHOOPEE! excl.]

whoopee! excl. [mid-19C+] (*orig. US*) a cry of intense delight. [SE *whoop*, a cry + sfx -*ee*]

whoopee mama n. [1920s–30s] a flighty young woman, usu. middle-class, in her late teens or very early 20s, pursuing a lifestyle as far as possible removed from that desired by her parents. [WHOOPEE n. + MAMA n. (1)]

whoopee water n. [1940s] (*US*) alcohol. [WHOOPEE n. + SE *water*]

who opened their lunch? phr. [1960s–70s] (*Aus.*) a phr. meaning who broke wind?

whooper-dooper n. [1930s+] (*US*) a wild celebration, a carouse. [SE *whoop* + redup.]

whooperup n. [late 19C] a second-rate singer who produces noise rather than music. [SE *whoop*]

whooper-up n. *see* WHOOP IT UP v. (1).

whooping adj. [mid-19C+] very large of its type.

whoop it up v. (*also* **hoop up, whoop things up, whoop up**) 1 [late 19C+] (*orig. US*) to have a noisy, ostentatious good time; thus *whooper-up*, one who acts in this way. 2 [late 19C+] (*also* **whoop on**) to stir things up, to create excitement, to praise something and thus arouse support for it. 3 [1910s] (*US*) to vomit. 4 [1940s] (*US*) to raise, to increase. [SE *whoop*, a cry]

whoops v. [1920s+] (*US*) to vomit (cf. BARF v.). [SE *whoops!* an excl. of apology + echoic]

whoopsie n. (*also* **whoopsie-boy, whoops-m'dear**) [1940s+] a homosexual.

whoopsie adj. [1940s–50s] (*US*) homosexual, effeminate. [WHOOPSIE n.]

whoopsie-doodle adj. [1950s] eccentric.

whoops-m'dear n. *see* WHOOPSIE n.

whoop someone's ass v. *see* WHIP SOMEONE'S ASS v.

whoop things up v. *see* WHOOP IT UP v.

whoopty-woo! excl. *see* WHOOP-DE-DO! excl.

whoop-up n. 1 [1900s] (*Aus.*) praise, support. 2 [1950s] a plan, a scheme. [WHOOP IT UP v. (2)]

whoop up v. *see* WHOOP IT UP v.

whooray n. *see* HOORAY n.

whoosh v. [1910s] (*Aus.*) to hit.

whoozis n. (*also* **whoosis**) 1 [20C+] (*US*) (*also* **whoozit, whosis, whosit, whosthis, whozis**) an unknown or unspecifiable thing or person. 2 [2000s] a penis (cf. BAUBLE n.). [SE *who's this/it*]

whoozy adj. *see* WOOZY adj.

whop n. 1 [mid-19C–1960s] (*UK juv.*) a beating, a caning. 2 [1900s] (*US Und.*) a sentence of 15–30 days. 3 [1920s] a fine example. 4 [1940s] (*US Black campus*) (*also* **whupp**) a hangover. 5 [1950s+] (*US*) an attempt, a try. 6 [1990s+] (*US drugs*) a go, a time. [WHOP v. (2)]

whop v. (*also* **whap, whoop, wop**) 1 [mid-17C] to have sexual intercourse (cf. BANG v.[1]). 2 [19C+] to hit, to beat, to flog. 3 [mid-19C+] to overcome, to surpass, to defeat; thus *whopping*, a severe beating or defeat. 4 [1910s] (*US*) to shoot. [? SE *quap*, to beat, to throb, ult. Ger. *quappen*, to flop, *quappeln*, to quiver]

whop! excl. (*also* **whap!**) [mid-19C+] echoic of the sound of a sudden blow.

whopcacker n. (*also* **wopcacker**) [1920s+] (*Aus.*) anything notable, amazing etc. [? WOOPKNACKER n.]

whop it up v. (*also* **whop it in**) [1960s+] of a man, to have sexual intercourse; esp. in *I could whop it up her/that*, I would like to have sex with that woman (cf. BANG v.[1]; BURY IT v.). [fig. use of WHOP v. (2)]

whopper n. (*also* **whapper, wopper**) 1 [early 18C+] a notably large object or creature. 2 [late 18C+] a notably large person. 3 [mid-19C+] a notably large blow. 4 [mid-19C+] a particularly gross lie. 5 [1960s+] a large or erect penis. 6 [1990s+] a very stupid person. [fig. use of WHOP v. (2)]

whopper-jawed adj. (*also* **wapper-jawed, whocker-jawed, womper-jawed**) 1 [1910s+] (*US*) crooked, out of place, damaged, broken. 2 [1920s] crazy. [WHOP v. (2) + SE *jaw*]

whoppie n. [1970s] (*US*) sexual intercourse. [WHOP IT UP v.]

whopping n. [mid-19C–1960s] a beating, a thrashing. [WHOP v. (2)]

whopping adj. (*also* **wapping, whapping, wopping**) [early 17C+] enormous, very large; esp. ext. as *whopping great*. [fig. use of WHOP v. (2)]

whop-straw n. (*also* **Johnny whop-straw, ...wopstraw**) [mid–late 19C] a countryman, a peasant (cf. ACORN-CRACKER n.). [his SE *whopping* or threshing straw]

who pulled your chain? *phr.* [1910s+] a derisive phr. to one who has 'butted in' to a private conversation, who asked you to make a comment?

who put the quarter in your slot? *phr.* [1980s+] (*US campus*) a sarcastic admonition to mind one's own business.

whore *n.* **1** [20C+] a general derog. term of address, irrespective of sex. **2** [1950s] in cards, the queen. **3** [1950s] (*US prison*) a passive male homosexual, a catamite. **4** [1950s+] a promiscuous woman, but not necessarily, and not even usu., an actual prostitute; also of homosexual men. **5** [1960s] (*US Black*) a girlfriend. [rooted in SE *whore*, but carrying no commercial overtones]

whore *sfx* [1980s+] (*US campus*) used in comb. with a n. to denote a fanatic, someone who is obsessed by the object in question, e.g. *bookwhore*, *partywhore*.

whorebag *n.* [2000s] an unattractive woman, poss. a prostitute (cf. BAG n.⁴). [SE *whore* + -BAG sfx]

whore car *n.* [1960s] (*US*) an unmarked car used by police to patrol street prostitutes.

whore-chaser *n.* [1960s] (*US Black*) a womanizer, whether pursuing actual prostitutes or merely available women. [fig. use of SE]

whoredog *n.* [1980s+] (*US campus*) **1** an unrespectable or criminal person. **2** a promiscuous woman. [WHORE n. + (1) DOG n.³ (1); (2) DOG n.³ (8)]

whore-eater *n.* [early 18C] a pimp (cf. ABBOT ON THE CROSS n.).

whore-hopper *n.* (*also* whore-fucker) [1940s+] (*US*) a sexually voracious man who frequently visits prostitutes. [SE *whore* + HOP v.¹ (8)]

whorehound *n.* [1940s+] a man who enjoys sex with prostitutes. [SE *whore* + HOUND sfx]

whorehouse *adj.* [1940s+] (*US*) cheap, tawdry, in bad taste. [SE *whorehouse*]

whorehouse broad *n.* (*also* whorehouse chick, …girl, …woman) [1970s+] (*US Black*) a prostitute who works in a brothel rather than on the streets. [SE *whorehouse* + BROAD n.² (2)/CHICK n.⁴ (2)/SE *girl*/SE *woman*]

whore-pipe *n.* [late 18C–early 19C] the penis. [SE *whore* + PIPE n.² (1)]

whore's bath *n. see* WHORE SPLASH n.

whore's bird *n.* [mid-16C–early 19C] a term of abuse; a debauchee. [SE *whore* + BIRD n.² (1)]

whore scars *n. see* SCARS n.

whore's curse *n.* [late 18C–early 19C] 5s 3d (26p), thus presumably the telling-off one received for offering only 5s 3d. [the going rate for a prostitute's favours was half a guinea (10s 6d), the gold coin worth 5s 3d was substituted by mean customers who liked to be seen giving the woman gold, but saw no reason to be over-generous]

whore's get *n. see* GET n.¹ (1).

whore's ghost *n.* (*Irish*) **1** [1970s+] anything seen as intractable or obnoxious. **2** [1990s+] a child of a prostitute.

whore splash *n.* (*also* whore's bath) [1950s+] a brief, cursory wash, often a quick shower, as taken by a prostitute between clients; also in non-prostitution use.

whoride *n.* [1990s+] (*US Black*) any form of extreme activity, a shooting, a riot etc. [WHORIDE v.]

whoride *v.* [1990s+] (*US Black*) to mock; to be noisy.

whosermybob *n.* (*also* whosamajig, whosemawhat, whosemyjig, whosemyjig) [1930s+] (*Aus.*) anything or anyone that one has forgotten the name of. [vars. on THINGUMABOB n./THINGUMAJIG n.]

whosis/whosit *n. see* WHOOZIS n. (1).

who's milking this cow? *phr.* [late 19C+] mind your own business.

who's robbing this coach? *phr.* [1930s+] (*Aus.*) mind your own business. [a joke based on the bush-ranging era, cited at length in E.P., *DSUE* (1984) p.1336/2]

whosthis *n. see* WHOOZIS n. (1).

who stole the donkey? *phr.* [mid–late 19C] a phr. shouted after anyone wearing a white hat, and the reply is 'the man in the white hat'. [certainly anecdotal, but Hotten (1864) is 'unable to explain the phrase']

who struck Buckley? *phr.* [mid-19C] 'a common phrase used to irritate Irishmen' (Hotten, 1864). [ety. unknown; presumably anecdotal, although poss. merely assonant]

who's your daddy? *phr.* [2000s] (*US Black*) a deliberately insulting form of address. [? DADDY n. (11)/DADDY n. (14), i.e. a mocking statement of the speaker's domination/humiliation of their target]

who the blazes! *excl. see* WHAT THE BLAZES! excl.

who the devil! *excl. see* WHAT THE DEVIL! excl.

whow-ball *n. see* WHOABALL n.

who you screwin'? *phr.* [1960s+] an aggressive question aimed at someone who is staring, or perhaps is not, but whom the speaker wishes to challenge, usu. as a prelude to a fight. [SCREW v.⁶ (2)]

whozis *n. see* WHOOZIS n. (1).

whump *see under* WHOMP and its combs.

whup *v.* [20C+] (*US*) **1** to defeat, e.g. in a competition. **2** to make someone suffer, i.e. fig. to beat. **3** to attack, to beat up. **4** to punch. [SE *whip*]

whup-a-child *n.* [1970s+] (*US Black*) the police, a policeman.

whupp *n. see* WHOP n. (4).

whupped *adj.¹* [1980s] (*US campus*) henpecked. [WHUP v. (3)]

whupped *adj.² see* WHOOPED adj.

whup someone's ass *v. see* WHIP SOMEONE'S ASS v.

whup the game *v.* [1970s+] (*US Black*) to succeed in life. [WHUP v. (1) + GAME n.² (3)]

why buy a cow when milk is so cheap? *phr.* [late 17C+] why get married when sexually permissive women are so available?

why in hell? *phr. see* WHAT IN HELL? phr.

why in time? *phr. see* WHAT IN TIME? phr.

whyms *n.* [late 19C] members of the Y.M.C.A. [a supposed 'telescoping' of the initials]

why the arse! *excl.* [1950s] (*UK Black*) an intensified form of *why the hell!*

why the blazes! *excl. see* WHAT THE BLAZES! excl.

why the devil! *excl.* (*also* why the fuck! why the hell! why the shit!) [early 18C+] an exclamatory query of amazement, annoyance etc. [all intensified forms of SE *why?* + SE *devil*/FUCK, THE n. (1)/HELL, THE phr.²/SHIT n.¹ (1)]

wibble *n.* [early 18C–early 19C] any form of weak or bad drink. [it makes one's stomach *wibble*, i.e. wobble]

wibble-wobble *adv.* (*also* wibblety-wobblety, wibbly-wobbly) [mid-19C+] unsteadily. [SE *wobbly*]

wibbly-wobbly *adj.* [1910s+] uneven. [WIBBLE-WOBBLE adv.]

wibling's witch *n.* (*also* w.w.) [late 18C–19C] the 4 of clubs. [the gambler James *Wibling* (*fl.* early 17C), who made a fortune from gambling and whose lucky card was supposedly the 4 of clubs]

wicher *adj. see* WITCHER adj.

wicher-cully *n.* [mid-17C–18C] (*UK Und.*) a silversmith. [WITCHER adj. + CULLY n. (3)]

wick *n.¹* [mid-19C] the penis. [resemblance]

wick *n.² see* HACKNEY WICK n.

wick-dipping *n.* [1970s] sexual intercourse. [DIP ONE'S WICK v.]

wicked *adj.* **1** [mid-17C; late 19C+] unpleasant, terrible, awful. **2** [mid-19C+] (*orig. US*) excellent, wonderful. [although the modern bad = good model properly dates f. 1970s US Black vocabulary, the *OED*'s first cited use is in F. Scott Fitzgerald's *This Side of Paradise* (1920), while we also have 1 mid-19C cit.]

wicked *adv.* [early 19C+] very, really.

wicked! *excl.* [1990s+] a general excl. of affirmation, approval, excellent! wonderful! [WICKED adj. (2)]

wicked awesome *adj.* [1990s+] (*US teen*) used of anything especially excellent. [WICKED adj. (2) + AWESOME adj. (1)]

wicked lady *n.* [1940s–50s] (*UK prison*) the cat-o'-nine-tails.

wicked loser *n.* [1980s+] (*US campus*) a failure, esp. one who could equally well have succeeded had they so decided. [SE *wicked* + LOSER n. (1)]

wicked pisser *n.* [1990s+] (*US, mainly northeast*) something very good or very bad. When used without an article, e.g. *This food is wicked pisser*, it is taken to mean very good; when used with an article, e.g. *This job is a wicked pisser*, it is taken to mean something very bad. [WICKED adj. (2) + PISSER n.[2] (1)]

wicked rumours *n.* [20C+] bloomers. [rhy. sl.]

wicked thing *n.* [1970s+] (*US Black*) an extraordinary event or situation. [WICKED adj. (2) + SE *thing*]

wicked-wassy and wild *adj.* [1990s+] (*W.I.*) extraordinary.

wicked witch *n.* [1990s+] an unpleasant, malicious woman. [rhy. sl. = BITCH n.[1] (1)]

wicket *n.* **1** [19C] throat. **2** [late 19C] the vagina. [SE *wicket*, a gate]

wick-wack *adj.* [1990s+] (*US Black*) inferior, second-rate. [redup. of WACK adj. (1)]

widdle *n.* [1950s+] (*mainly UK juv.*) an act of urination. [WIDDLE v.]

widdle *v.* [1950s+] to urinate. [? WEE v. + PIDDLE v. (1)]

widdy *n.* [late 18C+] a widow. [abbr.]

wide *adj.* **1** [mid-19C+] (*also* **wide-o, wide-oh**) 'sharp', aware, knowledgeable. **2** [late 19C] lax, loose, immoral. **3** [1930s+] aware of. [SE *wide (of the mark)*, going astray, deviating from the proper course (of life/action); prior use f. 16C is SE]

wide-awake *n.* (*also* **wake**) [mid-19C–1930s] a soft felt hat with broad brim and low crown. [a pun on the material, which lacked a 'nap']

wide-awake *adj.* **1** [19C] vigilant, aware, knowing. **2** [mid-19C] (*UK Und.*) pertaining to the underworld. **3** [1900s] of a garment, flashy, ostentatious, i.e. as worn by a 'wide boy'.

wide boy *n.* [1930s+] a minor villain, often dabbling in 'get-rich-quick' schemes. [WIDE adj. (1) + SE *boy*]

wide load *n.* [1990s+] (*US campus*) someone with large hips and buttocks.

wide man *n.* **1** [1930s–40s] (*also* **wide chump/con**) a swindler, a con-man. **2** [1950s] (*UK Und.*) a professional thief. [WIDE adj. (1) + SE *man*]

widen *v.* [1940s] (*US Black*) to leave. [Mezzrow & Wolfe, *Really the Blues* (1946): 'To widen means to widen the gap between you and the other person – in other words, to leave']

wideness *n.* **1** [late 19C+] perspicacity, intelligence. **2** [2000s] audacity. [WIDE adj. (1)]

wide-o *n.* [1920s+] a minor villain, a 'spiv'. [WIDE adj. (1)]

wide-o *adj.* [1930s] vulnerable. [SE *wide-open*]

wide-o/-oh *adj. see* WIDE adj. (1).

wide-oh! *excl.* [late 19C] look out! take care! be on your guard! [WIDE adj. (1)]

wide-on *n.* [1960s+] female sexual excitement. [on the pattern of the male HARD-ON n., the image is of a gaping vagina (cf. WIDE-OPEN adj.[3] (1))]

wide-open *adj.*[1] **1** [mid-19C+] morally and legally unconstrained. **2** [late 19C+] vulnerable, undefended. [boxing imagery]

wide-open *adj.*[2] [1950s+] (*US*) of driving, very fast. [the throttle is 'wide open']

wide-open *adj.*[3] **1** [1950s+] (*US Black*) sexually excited. **2** [1980s] (*US campus*) drunk. **3** [1980s] (*US campus*) wild. [(1) HAVE ONE'S NOSE OPEN v.; (2) (3) fig. uses of WIDE-OPEN adj.[1] (2)]

wide open *adv.* **1** [late 19C+] of an illegal business, without constraint from the authorities. **2** [20C+] (*US*) of driving, at full speed. [WIDE-OPEN adj.[1] (1)]

wide-open beaver *n.* [1970s+] a photograph or film of the inner labia. [SE *wide-open* + BEAVER n.[5] (1)]

wide place in the road *n.* [20C+] (*US*) a derog. phr. for a small town or hamlet. [its unimportance in the eyes of those who drive through]

widgeon *n.* [early 17C–mid-18C] a fool. [note Freddie *Widgeon*, one of the foolish members of the Drones Club in the comic novels of P.G. Wodehouse (1881–1975)]

widgie *n.* [1950s+] (*Aus.*) the female counterpart of a BODGIE n. (1). [post-1960s use historical only; ? RIDGIE-DIDGIE adj.]

wido *n.* [mid-19C] an alert, aware person, one who is 'no fool'. [WIDE adj. (1) + ? earliest use of -O sfx (2)]

Widow, the *n.*[1] [late 18C+] a nickname for Veuve Cliquot champagne, therefore champagne in general. [Fr. *veuve*, a widow]

Widow, the *n.*[2] [late 19C] Queen Victoria. [widowed in 1861 on the death of her husband, Prince Albert, and ext. by the fiercely royalist Rudyard Kipling (1865–1936) as 'the widow at Windsor']

widow *n.*[1] [early 18C] an expiring fire. **2** [mid–late 19C] an extra hand dealt to the table in certain card-games.

widow *n.*[2] [1970s] (*drugs*) any black capsule that contains amphetamine (cf. A n.[2]). [abbr. BLACK WIDOW n.]

widow *sfx* [20C+] of a woman who is left behind while her husband devotes himself to an obsession, usu. sport or a hobby, e.g. *golf widow, cricket widow* etc (cf. WIDOWER sfx).

widow bewitched *n.* [early 18C–mid-19C] a woman whose husband is temporarily absent (cf. WIDOWER BEWITCHED n.).

widower *sfx* [1960s+] the male version of the more common WIDOW sfx.

widower bewitched *n.* [early 18C] a husband separated from or deserted by his wife. [male var. on WIDOW BEWITCHED n.]

widow five-finger *n. see* FIVE-FINGERED WIDOW n.

Widow Jones *n.* (*also* **Widow Jones's house**) [1900s] the lavatory (cf. AUNTIE n.[1]). [var. on MRS JONES n.]

widow-maker *n.* [1940s+] (*Can./US*) a dead branch caught high in a tree which may fall and kill or injure someone below.

widow's mite *n.* [1910s–70s] a light, usu. for a cigarette. [rhy. sl.]

widow's wink *n.* [1970s] a Chinese person (cf. AH CABBAGE n.). [rhy. sl. = CHINK n. (1)]

widow twankey *n.* [20C+] **1** a handkerchief, i.e. a *hankie*. **2** an American. [rhy. sl.; (2) = SE *Yankee*]

wiener *n.*[1] *see* WEEN n.

wiener *n.*[2] *see* WEENIE n.[1].

wienie *see under* WEENIE and its combs.

wif *n.*[1] (*also* **wiff**) [1920s] (*US*) a wife.

wif *n.*[2] *see* WHIFF n.

wife *n.*[1] **1** [19C] (*UK prison*) a key. **2** [early 19C–1930s] a fetter fixed to one's leg. [she 'locks up' her husband]

wife *n.*[2] **1** [1920s–30s] (*US campus*) one's roommate. **2** [1920s+] the supposedly subservient, 'female' partner in a gay couple. **3** [1930s+] (*US Black/UK Und.*) a pimp's favoured prostitute, or one of a group working for a pimp (cf. BROTHER-IN-LAW n.). **4** [1940s+] (*US gang*) the steady girlfriend of a gang member. **5** [1980s+] (*US campus*) a regular girlfriend.

wife-beater *n.* [1990s+] (*US*) a sleeveless singlet. [the association of such singlets with men who are prone to domestic violence]

wife-in-law *n.* [1960s+] (*US Black*) any woman in a pimp's group of prostitutes, other than his favourite and thus most privileged woman. [play on WIFE n.[2] (3)]

wife in watercolours *n.* [late 18C–early 19C] a mistress. [the image of colours fading as do the passions of the newly married or the idea that the loving (if essentially hired) mistress was less strident than an intolerant harridan of a wife. Watercolours, suggests Grose (1785), are, like mistresses, 'easily effaced, or dissolved']

wife out of Westminster *n.* [18C–19C] a wife unconstrained by monogamy. [SE *wife* + WESTMINSTER WEDDING n.]

wife's best friend *n.* [1960s+] (*orig. Aus.*) the penis.

wife's dream *n.* [1900s] (*Aus.*) a racing tip, the inference is of its unlikeliness.

wife-starver *n.* [1960s+] (*Aus.*) a man who defaults on his maintenance payments.

wifey *n.* (*also* **wifie**) [mid-19C+] a wife or regular girlfriend; also attrib.; the implication is of respectable behaviour.

wiff *n.*[1] *see* WHIFF *n.*

wiff *n.*[2] *see* WIF *n.*[1]

wiffle-woffle *n.* [1910s–20s] an arrogant person. [? WIFFLE-WOFFLES *n.* (1), i.e. a fig. stomach-ache renders them ill-humoured]

wiffle-woffles *n.* [mid-19C] **1** stomach-ache. **2** a state of depression.

wiffy *adj. see* WHIFFY *adj.*

wifie *n. see* WIFEY *n.*

wig *n.*[1] **1** [late 18C] a dignitary; lit. one who wears a wig for professional reasons. **2** [mid-19C+] a barrister or judge.

wig *n.*[2] [late 18C–1900s] a severe scolding, a telling-off. [WIG v.[2]]

wig *n.*[3] **1** [mid-19C; 1940s+] the head, the brain or its functions. **2** [mid-19C+] the pubic hair of either sex. **3** [20C+] the hair. **4** [1930s+] (*US Black*) hair that has been artificially straightened. **5** [1950s] (*W.I.*) a male haircutting style that supposedly resembles a judge's wig. The hair is cut into a peak at the front and there is no sharp razor line at the back. Those requesting such a cut would tell the barber, 'Try me'. **6** [1950s–70s] (*US Black*) an eccentric person (cf. WIGGER *n.*[2]). [(1) 1940s+ use is US Black]

wig *n.*[4] [1970s] (*US*) something of importance.

wig *v.*[1] **1** [late 18C; 1950s] (*US Black*) to inform, to explain. **2** [1930s+] (*US*) to talk, to chatter. **3** [1930s+] to annoy, to irritate. **4** [1950s] (*US Black*) to delight, to impress. **5** [1950s] to understand, to approve. **6** [1950s+] (*US*) to play cerebral, intellectual jazz music. **7** [1950s+] (*US*) to be in good spirits, to enjoy. **8** [1950s+] (*US*) to become or render nervous, hysterical, overly stressed, mentally unbalanced. **9** [1960s+] (*US*) to reach a different state through drugs. [fig. uses of WIG *n.*[3] (1)]

wig *v.*[2] [early 19C+] to scold, to reprimand. [a judge's *wig*, i.e. the scolder uses quasi-judicial authority]

wiganowns *n.* [late 18C–early 19C] a man wearing a notably large wig. [? ext. of SE *wig*]

wig-block *n.* (*also* **wig box/stand**) [late 18C–1970s] the head. [ext. WIG *n.*[3] (1)]

wig bust *n.* [1940s+] (*US Black*) the altering of a natural crinkly Black head of hair into a straight PROCESS *n.* style. [WIG *n.*[3] (3) + fig. use of BUST *v.*[1] (4)]

wig city *adj.* [1960s+] (*US teen*) eccentric, unbalanced. [WIG *n.*[3] (6) + CITY sfx]

wigeon *n.* [1940s+] (*Aus.*) an affectionate term for a young woman. [SE *widgeon/wigeon*, a wild duck, thus DUCK *n.*[1] (1)]

wig-faker *n.* [18C–19C] a wig-maker, a hairdresser. [SE *wig* + FAKER *n.* (1)]

wigga *n.* (*also* **whigger, white nigga, wigger**) [1990s+] (*orig. US*) a White person who aspires to be Black and so adopts a Black, spec. HIP-HOP *n.*/RAP *n.*[5], lifestyle (cf. CHIGGER *n.*[1]). [SE *White* + NIGGA *n.*, invariably derog. term used by Blacks to sneer at those who ape their culture and by Whites in a generally racist sense]

wigga-wagga *n.* **1** [late 19C–1910s] a walking stick. **2** [1900s–70s] (*also* **wigger-wagger**) the penis. [SE *wiggle/waggle*]

wigged (out) *adj.* **1** [1950s–60s] (*drugs*) intoxicated by a drug. **2** [1950s+] (*orig. US*) eccentric, insane, deluded, out of touch (cf. WIGGY *adj.*). **3** [1960s] (*orig. US*) inspired or intoxicated by an idea. [WIG OUT *v.*]

wiggen *n.* [mid-19C] (*UK Und.*) the neck.

wigger *n.*[1] [20C+] (*Irish*) a derog. term for a woman.

wigger *n.*[2] [1950s+] (*US Black/campus*) an unstable, eccentric person. [WIG *n.*[3] (6)]

wigger *n.*[3] *see* WIGGA *n.*

wigger-wagger *n. see* WIGGA-WAGGA *n.* (2).

wigging *n.* [mid-19C+] a reprimand, a telling-off. [WIG v.[2]; note Hotten (1860): 'If the head of a firm calls a clerk into the parlour, and rebukes him, it is an EAR-WIGGING; if done before the other clerks it is a WIGGING']

wiggin's *n. see* EARWIG *n.* (5).

wigglers *n.* [1940s] (*US Black*) the fingers; the toes. [SE *wiggle*]

wigglestick *n.* [1970s] the penis (cf. BAT *n.*[7]).

wiggy *adj.* [1960s+] **1** eccentric, bizarre, unpleasant, disturbing. **2** confused. **3** pleasing, enjoyable, exciting and up-to-date. **4** (*US drugs*) intoxicated with narcotics. [WIG *n.*[3] (6)]

wig hat *n.* [1950s+] (*orig. US Black*) a wig; a hairpiece. [WIG *n.*[3] (1) + SE *hat*]

wig out *v.* **1** [1950s+] (*US*) to lose control, to have a breakdown; thus WIGGED (OUT) *adj.* (2). **2** [1950s+] (*orig. jazz*) to enjoy oneself, to lose one's inhibitions. **3** [1960s+] (*US campus*) to shock or be shocked; to excite, to thrill. [ext. of WIG v.[1]]

wig-picker *n.* [1960s+] (*US*) a psychiatrist. [WIG *n.*[3] (1) + SE *picker*]

wigsby *n. see* MR WIGSBY *n.*

wigs on the green *phr.* (*also* **jigs on the green, mill...**) [early 19C+] (*orig. Irish*) an argument, a fight. [if one has not already removed it, one's wig is likely to fall or be knocked off in such a fight]

wig stand *n. see* WIG-BLOCK *n.*

wigster *n. see* MR WIGSBY *n.*

wig tightener *n.* [1950s] (*US Black*) a wonderful, admirable individual. [WIG *n.*[3] (1) + SE *tightener*]

wig-trig *n.* [1940s] (*US*) an idea. [WIG *n.*[3] (1)]

wig-wag *v.* [20C+] to wave or move with a writhing movement; thus *wig-wagger*, one who *wig-wags*; *wig-waggy*, tortuous, winding. [SE *wiggle + wag*]

wilbur *n.* [20C+] a flight. [rhy. sl.; air pioneer *Wilbur* Wright (1867–1912)]

wild *n.* **1** [mid-19C] (*UK tramp*) a village. **2** [1950s] in pl., the suburbs. [SE *wild*, a wild or waste place]

wild *adj.* **1** [1920s+] (*US*) exciting, wonderful. **2** [1940s+] eccentric, bizarre, weird, odd. **3** [1960s+] (*US Und.*) consecutive, referring to prison sentences. **4** [1990s+] (*W.I.*) philandering.

wild *v.* (*US Black*) **1** [1980s+] to go out looking for victims to mug and attack; usu. as *n. wilding* (sometimes pronounced *wilin'*). **2** [2000s] to have sexual intercourse. [popularized through media reports of the savage rape and beating of New York's 'Central Park jogger' in 1989. According to the accused, 'wild', like its *n.* form 'wilding', is a nonce-word, used by them alone and meaning simply going wild. It was elevated to a sl. term after a report in the *New York Times* on 22 April 1989. However, the term is used, in the criminal sense and earlier, by the rapper Ice T on his album *Rhyme Pays* (1987); note also BUCK-WILD *adj.*]

wild! *excl.* [1950s–60s] wonderful! fabulous! the best! [WILD *adj.* (1)]

wild and woolly *adj.* [late 19C+] (*US*) uncouth, raucous.

wild as a cut fox *phr. see* MAD AS A CUT SNAKE *phr.*

wild-ass *adj.* (*also* **wild-assed**) [1960s+] (*US*) crazy, insane, unbalanced. [WILD *adj.* (2) + -ASS sfx]

wild-buck *adj.* [1950s] uncontrolled, unrestrained. [SE *wild*, unrestrained]

wild card *n.* [1920s+] (*US*) something or someone unknown or unpredictable; also as *adj.* [poker imagery]

wildcat *n.*[1] **1** [mid-19C–1900s] the notes issued by a wildcat bank; thus any worthless money. **2** [mid-19C–1920s] (*US*) an unsound, dubious business, esp. a 'wildcat bank'. [wildcat banks existed in the western US before the National Bank Act of 1863 and were virtually unregulated. The notes they issued were essentially worthless]

wildcat *n.*[2] **1** [late 19C–1940s] (*US*) illicitly distilled whisky. **2** [1920s] (*US Und.*) an illicit brewery. **3** [1980s+] (*drugs*) methcathinone. **4** [1980s+] (*drugs*) cocaine. [the effects]

wildcat n.[3] [1970s+] (*US Black*) someone who participates intensely and also to his own advantage in street life. [SE *wildcat/wild/*WILD adj. (2) + CAT n.[11] (4)]

wildcat adj. **1** [mid-late 19C] describing the notes issued by a wildcat bank; thus of any money or finances, worthless, fraudulent. **2** [mid-19C–1930s] fraudulent, highly speculative. **3** [mid-19C–1940s] (*orig. US*) of a business practice, unsound, dubious; esp. in phr. *wildcat bank*. [WILDCAT n.[1]]

wildcatter n. [late 19C+] a freelance bootlegger. [SAmE *wildcatter*, a prospector who sinks wildcat wells]

wild duck n. [1980s+] (*Aus. prison*) a prisoner who does not pay his debts. [? rhy. sl. = FUCK n.[6]]

wildfire n. [mid-18C] a fiery drink. [its taste and effects]

wilding n. *see* WILD v. (1).

wild oats n. [mid-16C–early 17C] a dissolute young man, a rake. [SE *sow one's wild oats*]

wild out v. [2000s+] to party, to act crazily. [WILD adj. (1), reinforced by WILD v. (1)]

wild rogue n. [16C–early 19C] (*UK Und.*) a dedicated professional villain (cf. CANTING CREW n.). [ext. of ROGUE n.[1]]

wilds, the n. [late 19C–1900s] (*Aus.*) a fit of depression, a temper tantrum; thus *give someone the wilds*, to depress, to 'bring down', to annoy. [WILD adj. (2)]

wild squirt n. [late 17C–early 19C] diarrhoea. [ext. SQUIRT n.[1] (1)]

wild thing, the n. [1980s+] (*orig. US Black/campus*) **1** sexual intercourse. **2** rape.

wild west n. [20C+] a vest or undershirt. [rhy. sl.]

wild Willy n. [late 19C] (*US campus*) a dedicated hedonist. [SE *wild*, unrestrained + *Willy*]

Wilkie Bards n. [1910s+] playing cards. [rhy. sl.; ult. music-hall comedy star *Wilkie Bard* (1874–1944)]

Wilkinson sword adj. [1990s+] bald. [rhy. sl.]

will a fish swim? phr. *see* CAN A DUCK SWIM? phr.

willamakanka n. *see* BULLAMAKANKA n.

will do phr. [1950s+] a general affirmative, OK, I'll do it.

william n.[1] [mid-19C–1920s] **1** a bill; esp. in phr. *meet sweet William*, to pay off a bill as soon as it is presented. **2** (*US*) a dollar bill. [abbr. of *William* = bill]

william n.[2] [mid-19C+] the penis (cf. ABRAHAM n.[1]). [proper name, on pattern of JOHN THOMAS n.]

william n.[3] [1950s+] **1** excrement (cf. ALI OOP n.). **2** an act of defecation (cf. ANDY CAPP n.). [rhy. sl.; *william pitt* = SHIT n.[1]; ult. UK politician *William Pitt the Younger* (1759–1806)]

William Pitts n. [1990s+] diarrhoea (cf. BANANA (SPLITS) n.). [rhy. sl. = SHITS, THE n. (1); ult. *see* WILLIAM n.[3]]

William Powell n. [1930s+] a towel. [rhy. sl.; ult. film star *William Powell* (1892–1984)]

William Tell n. [20C+] a smell. [rhy. sl.; the 15C Swiss hero *William Tell*]

William the Third n. [1960s–70s] (*Aus.*) a piece of excrement, a stool (cf. ALI OOP n.). [rhy. sl. = TURD n. (1)]

willie n.[1] [late 19C–1900s] (*US tramp*) a tramp.

willie n.[2] (*also* **willie-boy, willie watcher, willy**) **1** [late 19C–1940s] a weak, cowardly or frightened man. **2** [late 19C+] a male homosexual. [? proper name or northern *willie*, the penis]

willie n.[3] [1940s+] (*orig. Aus.*) a tantrum. [? WILLIES n.; or ? abbr. SAusE *willy*, a whirlwind; or ? link to SE *willy-nilly*]

willie n.[4] (*also* **willy**) (*Aus.*) **1** [1940s+] money, esp. money set aside for use in betting. **2** [1960s+] a wallet. [ety. unknown; ? given the context of betting, SE *will he...won't he* (and should I bet on it)]

willie n.[5] (*also* **willy**) [1960s+] the penis. [orig. in northern but non-dial. use]

willie n.[6] *see* WILLY n.[1].

willie-boy n. *see* WILLIE n.[2].

willie lunchmeat n. (*also* **willie lump-lump**) [1980s+] (*US Und.*) a fool (cf. APPLEHEAD n.). [WILLY n.[1] + generic use of proper name + the stolidity and density of SE *lunchmeat/lump*; note the US comedian Red Skelton's 'character', the drunken *Willie Lump-Lump*]

Willies, the n. [1920s–30s] (*US tramp*) the Good Will Industries of the Methodist Church. [play on name; ? influenced by HOLY WILLIE n.]

willies n. [late 19C+] nerves, worries, tension; esp. in phr. *give (someone) the willies*, to unnerve. [ety. unknown; ? link to fig. use of dial. *willy-wambles*, stomach-rumbling]

willie watcher n. *see* WILLIE n.[2].

willie-waving n. (*also* **willy-waving**) [1970s+] acting, speaking or posing in an exaggeratedly macho fashion. [WILLIE n.[5] + SE *waving*]

willie, willie – wicked, wicked! excl. [late 19C] an excl. used when sighting an older woman chatting to a younger man. [from a case in which a middle-aged landlady sued her non-paying young lodger, whose defence was that not only would she come into his room, but she then proceeded to sit on his bed]

will I fuck! excl. *see* DO I FUCK! excl.

willing adj. [20C+] (*Aus./N.Z.*) pugnacious, aggressive, violent.

willing tit n. [early 18C–early 19C] a complaisant woman. [SE *willing* + TIT n.[2] (1); note B.E. (1698): 'Willing-Tit, a little horse that Travels chearfully']

willing winchell n. *see* WINCHELL n.

will I shit! excl. *see* DO I FUCK! excl.

will o'the wisps n. [20C+] crisps. [rhy. sl.]

willow adj. [late 17C–18C] (*UK Und.*) poor, of no reputation. [SE *willowy*, slim]

will's whiff n. [20C+] syphilis. [rhy. sl. = SYPH n.; ult. brandname of *Will's Whiff*, a small cigar]

willy *see also under* WILLIE and its combs.

willy n.[1] (*also* **willie**) [1910s] (*US*) lunchmeat.

willy n.[2] [1930s] (*US*) physical effort. [? earlier ref. to WILLIE n.[5]]

willy lees n. [1940s+] (*Aus.*) a flea, fleas. [rhy. sl.]

will you shoot? phr. [1900s–50s] (*Aus.*) will you pay for a drink? [SHOOT v.[5] (2)]

will you short? phr. [late 19C] (*Aus.*) will you have a drink of spirits? [SHORT n.[1] (2)]

willy wacht n. [late 19C] a drink, esp. of whisky. [Scot.; *Willy* Arnot (a distiller? a landlord?), good whisky + *wacht/waught*, to drink deeply]

willy wag n. [20C+] (*Aus.*) a pack. [rhy. sl. = SWAG n.[1] (9)]

willy-welly n. [1990s+] a condom. [WILLIE n.[5] + WELLIE n.]

Willy Wonka n. [1980s+] **1** the penis (cf. ALMOND n.). **2** a fool (cf. BEECHAM'S PILL n.; CHOAD n.). [rhy. sl. = PLONKER n. (2)/PLONKER n. (3); ult. fictional character *Willy Wonka* in *Charlie and the Chocolate Factory* (1964) by Roald Dahl]

willy woofter n. *see* WOOFTER n.

wilma n. [1980s+] (*US campus*) an ugly, stupid woman. [the character *Wilma* in the cartoon (1960s) and film (1994) *The Flintstones*]

Wilson Pickett n. [1970s] a ticket. [rhy. sl.; ult. soul star *Wilson Pickett* (b.1941)]

Wilson's den n. (*also* **Tony's den**) [1960s+] (*bingo*) the number 10 (cf. ALDERSHOT LADIES n.). [10 Downing Street, then home to Prime Minister Harold *Wilson* (1916–95), now *Tony* Blair (b.1953); presumably the name can be altered to fit the current incumbent]

wilt v. [late 19C] to fade, i.e. to run off, to bolt.

wimble n. [mid-17C–18C] the penis. [SE *wimble*, a gimlet, an instrument for boring into soft ground]

wimble v. [mid-late 17C] of a man, to have sexual intercourse. [WIMBLE n.; lit. to pierce with a gimlet]

wimp n.[1] [1920s–40s] a woman. [note 1910s Oxford University sl. *go wimping*, for a male undergraduate to go out on the town looking for women]

wimp *n.*[2] (*also* **whimp**) [1920s+] a weakling, an indecisive person, often male. [? ext. WIMP *n.*[1] + note Wellington *Wimpy*, a character in the cartoon film *Popeye*]

wimp *adj.* [1980s] unimportant, insignificant, irrelevant. [WIMP *n.*[2]]

wimp dog *n.* [1980s+] (*US campus*) a male with little personality or assertiveness. [WIMP *n.*[2] + DOG *n.*[2] (2)]

wimpette *n.* [1980s] an insignificant, cowardly female. [WIMP *n.*[2] + SE fem. sfx *-ette*]

wimp-guts *n.* [1980s+] a coward, a weakling. [WIMP *n.*[2] + -GUTS sfx; note RMC Duntroon (Aus.) *cunt guts*, a non-specific term of abuse]

wimpish *adj.* [1920s+] (*orig. US*) ineffectual and/or effeminate. [WIMP *n.*[1]/WIMP *n.*[2]]

wimpo *n.* (*also* **wimpoid**) [1980s+] a weakling, an ineffective person. [WIMP *n.*[2] + -O sfx (1)/-oid]

wimp out *v.* [1960s+] (*orig. US*) to act in a cowardly manner, to let someone down, to fail to live up to a commitment. [WIMP *n.*[2]]

wimpy *adj.* [1960s+] (*orig. US*) weak, ineffective, cowardly. [WIMP *n.*[2]]

win *n.* (*also* **winn, wyn**) [mid-16C–mid-19C] a penny. [origin unknown, but Vaux suggests, without further explanation, an abbr. of *Winchester*; Ribton-Turner, *A History of Vagrants* (1887), suggests synon. Erse *pinghin*, Manx *ping*]

win *v.* [late 17C–1940s] to steal. [euph.]

win a pair of gloves *v.* [late 18C–early 19C] to kiss a sleeping man. [the woman who does so was trad. rewarded with a pair of gloves]

Winchcombe Carson *n.* [20C+] (*Aus.*) a parson. [rhy. sl.; ? Aus. financial planners *Winchcombe Carson*]

winchell *n.* (*also* **willing winchell, winning...**) [1930s–40s] **1** (*US Und.*) a confidence trickster's victim, a sucker. **2** a generic term for a gossip columnist. [gossip columnist Walter Winchell (1897–1972); (1) ? the image of the gossipy writer as 'swallowing' any story]

winchester *n.* [early 19C] a penny. [WIN *n.*]

Winchester goose *n.* (*also* **goose, Winchester pigeon**) [mid-16C–17C] venereal disease. [the popular brothels of Southwark came under the jurisdiction of the Bishop of *Winchester*; thus 17C pvb referring to a well-known prostitute: 'No Goose bit so sore as Bess Broughton's']

wind *n.*[1] [early–mid-18C] strong liquor, esp. gin. [it catches one's breath]

wind *n.*[2] [early 19C] life; thus (*UK Und.*) *lagged for one's wind*, transported for one's natural life. [SE *wind*, the breath of life]

wind *v.* [late 18C+] (*W.I.*) of a woman, to move in a provocative manner, with much swishing of the hips. [SE *wind*, to writhe, to wriggle]

wind and kite *n.* [2000s] a website. [rhy. sl.]

wind and rain *n.* (*Aus.*) **1** [1960s+] a train. **2** [1980s] an airplane. [rhy. sl.]

windbag *n.* **1** [mid-19C+] a braggart, a boaster, a 'loudmouth'. **2** [1930s] (*UK Und.*) a confidence trick, based on selling envelopes that are apparently filled with valuables; in the event they contain only rubbish.

windbags *n.* (*also* **wind-pumps**) [mid-18C; 1900s–40s] (*US Black*) the lungs. [their role in one's body]

wind-cutter *n.* [19C] a cocked hat. [its shape]

wind do twirl *n.* [mid-19C] a woman. [rhy. sl. = SE *girl*]

winded-settled *adj. see* SETTLED adj. (1).

winder *n.*[1] [early–mid-19C] a sentence of transportation for life; thus *winded-settled* (*see* SETTLED adj. (1)). [WIND *n.*[2]]

winder *n.*[2] [mid-19C] something so astounding that it 'takes one's breath away'. [SE *wind*, to deprive of breath, usu. through a blow]

windgat *n.* [1980s+] (*S.Afr.*) a braggart, a boaster, a 'blowhard'. [SE *wind* + Afk. *gat*; lit. 'windy-arse']

windgat *adj.* [1980s+] (*S.Afr.*) cocky, self-opinionated. [WINDGAT *n.*]

windie *n.* [1980s+] (*N.Z.*) a *wind*-surfer. [abbr.]

Windies *n.* [1960s+] (*orig. Aus.*) the *West Indies* cricket team; thus *Windie*, a member of the team. [elision]

winding boy *n.* (*also* **winding ball**) [1930s–40s] (*US Black*) a sexual athlete. [he can 'wind up' his sexual 'machinery']

wind instrument *n.* [early 17C] the anus. [SE *break wind*]

windjammer *n.*[1] [late 19C–1950s] (*orig. US*) a talkative, loquacious person, thus a liar; thus *windjamming*, loquacity. [SE *wind*, i.e. 'hot air' + *jam*, to force; note late 19C US army *windjammer*, a trumpeter]

windjammer *n.*[2] [20C+] (*Aus.*) a hammer. [rhy. sl.]

windjammer *n.*[3] [1980s+] (*Aus.*) a male homosexual. [play on SE *jam*, to force + (the source of) *wind*, i.e. the anus]

windmill *n.* [early 19C] the anus; thus *she has no fortune but her mills*, i.e. the WINDMILL n. and WATERMILL n. [SE *wind* + *mill*, i.e. the unpleasant odours]

windmill cocktail *n.* [20C+] (*US*) **1** rainwater. **2** glass of water. [the stream that runs by a mill]

wind one's ball of yarn *v.* (*also* **ravel up one's ball of yarn**) [1930s–50s] (*US*) of a man, to have sexual intercourse.

wind one's clock *v.* [1970s] (*US*) of a woman, to be excited sexually, to have sexual intercourse (cf. CATCH AN OYSTER v.).

window *n.* (*also* **pane of glass, windowpane**) [late 19C–1920s] a monocle.

window climber *n. see* PORCH CLIMBER n.

window glass *n. see* WINDOWPANE n.[1].

window licker *n.* [1990s+] (*UK juv.*) a mentally handicapped person. ['Comes from the "special" people who ride on "special" buses, sitting on the bus, face leant against the glass, tongue hanging out' (*Online Dict. Playground Slang*, 2001)]

window man *n.* [1950s+] (*S.Afr.*) a Coloured person who is trying to pass as White and thus cuts their darker friends or relatives when they see them in public. [Afk. *vensterkies*, a little window or *vensterjies kyk*, to look at little windows, i.e. one who pretends to be gazing into shop windows when embarrassing friends appear]

windowpane *n.*[1] (*also* **pane, window glass**) [1970s+] (*drugs*) a variety of LSD (cf. A n.[3]). [a small square of gelatine impregnated with LSD]

windowpane *n.*[2] *see* WINDOW n.

window-peeper *n.* [late 18C–early 19C] a collector of the window tax. [he 'peeps' at the number of windows a house has]

windows *n.*[1] **1** [mid-19C+] the eyes. **2** [1900s–10s] (*US*) spectacles.

windows *n.*[2] *see* SQUARE PAIR n.

window shop *v.* [1970s+] (*US campus*) to go out looking for desirable members of the opposite sex. [play on SE]

window warrior *n.* [2000s] (*UK prison*) a prisoner who shouts from his cell window.

wind-pies *n.* (*also* **nutten-chops, wind-pies and air sausages, wind-sandwich and breeze-pie**) [20C+] (*W.I., Bdos/Trin.*) no food, nothing to eat.

wind pudding *n. see* AIR PUDDING n.

wind-pumps *n. see* WINDBAGS n.

wind-sandwich and breeze-pie *n. see* WIND-PIES n.

windshield *n.* [1910s] (*US*) a table napkin.

wind someone's cotton *v.* [mid-19C–1900s] to cause someone trouble, to create difficulties for someone.

Windsor Castle *n.* [20C+] the anus (cf. BOTTLE AND GLASS n.). [rhy. sl. = ARSEHOLE n. (1)]

Windsor Group hotel *n.* [1990s+] a prison (cf. BOARDING HOUSE n.). [play on Windsor, the surname of the Royal Family, and the legal phr. 'detained at Her Majesty's Pleasure']

wind-stopper *n.* [mid–late 19C] a garrotter. [SE *wind*, breath + *stop*]

wind-sucker *n.* **1** [mid-19C] a worn-out horse, fit only for slaughter. **2** [1920s] (*US*) a braggart. [(1) its heavy breathing; (2) the expulsion of *wind*, i.e. breath]

wind the horn *v.* [17C] to break wind.

wind tormentors *n.* (*also* **wind-teasers**) [1900s–20s] extremely long sideburns, e.g. the *paies* as worn by an orthodox Jew; occas. also other facial hair.

Windtown *n. see* WINDY CITY n. (1).

wind-trap *n.* [20C+] a flap, esp. of hair. [rhy. sl.]

wind-up *n.*[1] **1** [early 19C+] a conclusion, the end; death. **2** [1940s] (*US*) a fight.

wind-up *n.*[2] [1930s] (*US*) promotion, praise.

wind-up *n.*[3] [1980s+] **1** a practical joke. **2** a deliberate attempt to worry, to render unhappy. **3** a deliberate attempt to mislead. [WIND UP v.[2] (2)]

wind up *v.*[1] **1** [early 18C+] to bring to a conclusion. **2** [mid-19C+] to end up, to find oneself somewhere. **3** [mid-19C+] to result; to come to a conclusion. [SE *wind up*, i.e. the winding up of something that has been extended while in use]

wind up *v.*[2] **1** [20C+] to cause someone to become annoyed. **2** [1960s+] to tease, to misinform, usu. maliciously. [SE *wind up*, i.e. winding up a clock to 'make it go']

wind-up artist *n.* (*also* **wind-up merchant**) [1980s+] someone who specializes in teasing, poss. to the point of at least verbal retaliation. [WIND-UP n.[3] + ARTIST sfx/MERCHANT n.]

wind up the clock *v.* [late 18C] to have sexual intercourse. [based on a mildly coarse scene in Laurence Sterne's novel *Tristram Shandy* (1759–67)]

wind vertical *n. see* DRAFT UP n.

Windville *n. see* WINDY CITY n. (1).

windward passage *n.* [late 18C] the anus.

Windy, the *n. see* WINDY CITY n.

windy *adj.*[1] **1** [late 17C–19C] foolish. **2** [mid-19C+] conceited, boastful. [SE *wind*, i.e. 'hot air'; (2) prior use is SE]

windy *adj.*[2] [late 19C+] (*mainly UK juv.*) cowardly, scared. [GET THE WIND UP v.]

Windy City *n.* **1** [late 19C+] (*US*) (*also* **Town of the Wind, Windtown, Windville, the Windy**) Chicago, Illinois. **2** [1980s+] (*S.Afr.*) Port Elizabeth. [the climate; note B. Popik on *American Dialect Society-List* (Internet, 22 August 2001): 'Troy was first known as the "windy city." Later, Siena, Italy, was called the "city of winds" (*Citta dei Venti*). In the early 1880s, the Chicago Tribune wanted to promote Chicago as a summer resort. An attraction was the cool breeze off the lake. By 1885, Chicago was the "city of winds" and "windy city"']

windy wallets *n.* [late 19C–1900s] a loquacious, talkative self-aggrandizing person. [i.e. a WINDBAG n.]

wine *n.*[1] [mid–late 19C] (*orig. UK campus*) a party at which those assembled drink wine; thus *wine and dine*, to entertain others.

wine *n.*[2] [1930s–60s] (*US Black*) money. [? the turning of one into the other]

wine *n.*[3] (*also* **wining**) [1990s+] (*W.I.*) a form of highly erotic dancing, esp. as seen at carnivals; thus *wine*, to dance in this manner. [W.I. pron. of SE *wind*, i.e. the partners would *wind* round each other]

wine *v.* [mid-19C] to give or attend a party where wine is drunk. [WINE n.[1]]

winebag *n.* [late 19C] a drunkard who prefers wine to beer or spirits.

wine bum *n.* [1920s] (*US Und.*) a wine-drinking alcoholic. [SE *wine* + BUM n.[3] (1)]

wined *adj.* [late 19C] (*Aus.*) drunk (cf. ALED UP adj.).

wine-dot *n.* [1950s+] (*Aus.*) a drinker of cheap wine. [a pun on SE *Wyandotte*, a breed of medium-sized domestic fowls, orig. found in the US]

wine dump *n.* [1920s] (*US Und.*) a cheap bar, frequented by wine-drinking alcoholics. [SE *wine* + DUMP n.[3] (2)]

winehead *n.* [1950s+] (*US*) an alcoholic who opts for wine as his or her preferred intoxicant. [SE *wine* + -HEAD sfx (3)]

winey *adj.* [mid-19C–1910s] tipsy, slightly drunk (cf. ALED UP adj.).

wing *n.*[1] **1** [late 18C] an oar. **2** [early 19C+] an arm. **3** [1970s] (*US*) a car door.

wing *n.*[2] [late 19C] (*UK prison*) a single leaf of rolling tobacco.

wing *n.*[3] [late 19C–1940s] (*Aus./Irish*) a pre-decimalization penny. [WIN n.]

wing *n.*[4] *see* WING-DING n. (1).

wing *v.*[1] **1** [early 19C+] (*US*) to shoot but not kill; to wound. **2** [mid–19C+] to hit with a ball or missile. [lit. 'to hit in the SE *wing*']

wing *v.*[2] *see* WING (IT) v.

wing'd *adj. see* WINGED adj.[1].

wing-ding *n.* (*also* **whing-ding**) **1** [1920s+] (*also* **wing**) a fit, esp. as suffered by a withdrawing narcotics user (cf. THROW A WING-DING v.). **2** [1930s–60s] an outburst of emotion or temper. **3** [1930s+] a fake fit, 'thrown' by a prisoner in the hope of convincing authorities that he should be placed in the more comfortable surroundings of a mental ward. **4** [1940s+] (*orig. US*) a boisterous, noisy party. **5** [1950s+] a dramatic, noisy event. **6** [1960s] an unstable, crazy person. **7** [1960s+] a sexual encounter. [redup. of WING n.[1] (2), i.e. the image of waving one's arms in a frenzy]

wing-dinger *n.* **1** [1930s] a withdrawing narcotics user who throws a fake fit, in order to convince a doctor of the need for a supply of drugs. **2** [1940s] a fake fit. **3** [1970s] an outburst of emotion. [WING-DING n.]

wingdinging *adj.* [1960s] (*US Black*) splendid.

wingdoodle *see under* WHANGDOODLE.

winged *adj.*[1] (*also* **wing'd**) **1** [mid-19C] tipsy, slightly drunk. **2** [1950s–70s] (*US drugs*) addicted to cocaine. [(1) HIT UNDER THE WING phr.; (2) ? play on FLY v.[4] (1)]

winged *adj.*[2] [mid-19C+] wounded. [WING v.[1] (1)]

winger *n.* [mid-19C] long, bushy sideburns growing beyond the edge of the chin. [SE *wing*]

wingers *n.* [mid-19C] long whiskers.

wingey *n. see* WINGY n.

winging *adj.* [1900s] **1** (*US drugs*) suffering from withdrawal of a narcotic drug. **2** anxious.

wing (it) *v.* **1** [late 19C+] to improvise, to ad lib, to play a situation by ear without practice or rehearsal. **2** [1900s] to move fast, to 'fly'. [one fig. 'takes wing']

wingnut *n.*[1] [1980s+] an eccentric, a fool (cf. NUTBALL n.). [ext. of NUT n.[4] (1)]

wingnut *n.*[2] [1990s+] (*UK juv.*) a person with large, protruding ears. [SE *wingnut*, i.e. the shape]

wing out *v.* [1990s+] (*UK Black*) to leave, to go away. [SE *wing*, to fly]

wings *n.* (*also* **whings**) [1930s+] (*US drugs*) any powdered narcotic; thus *get one's wings*, to start using heroin; *give someone wings*, to inject someone or teach someone to inject heroin. [one becomes 'high' but also play on USAF/RAF jargon *get one's wings*, to be commissioned as a pilot]

wings over Sing Sing *n.* [1940s] (*US Black*) a girl who is under the age of consent, and with whom intercourse may lead to imprisonment for statutory rape. [? the result of statutory rape is that one will 'fly' into prison]

wing-wang *n.*[1] [1970s+] (*US gay*) the anus.

wing-wang *n.*[2] *see* WANG n.[2].

wingy *n.* (*also* **wingey**) [late 19C+] (*Aus./US*) the 'inevitable' nickname of any 1-armed man. [WING n.[1] (2)]

win in a walk *v.* [late 19C+] (*orig. US*) to win easily.

wining *n. see* WINE n.[3].

winji *adj.* [1940s+] (*W.I.*) sickly, frail, weak, puny. [UK dial. *winge*, to shrivel, as in fruit that is drying out]

wink *n.*[1] [1920s–60s] (*Aus.*) a sixpence. [? WIN n.; or resemblance to a *tiddlywink*]

wink *n.*[2] [1980s+] (*US gay*) an uncircumcised penis. [the glans 'winks' from within the foreskin]

wink at *v.* [1940s] to overlook deliberately.

wink at the blind eye *v. see* BLIND EYE n. (2).

winker *n.* [1970s] the vagina. [its supposed resemblance to a vertical 'eye']

winkers *n.* **1** [late 18C+] usu. of a horse, blinkers. **2** [early 19C; 20C+] (*Aus.*) spectacles. **3** [early 19C+] (*also* **winklers**) the eyes or eyelashes. **4** [1950s+] vehicle indicators.

winker-stinker *n.* [1960s+] (*US prison*) the anus. [the shape and the odour]

winkie *n. see* WINKY n.

winkle *n.*[1] [late 19C+] (*mainly UK juv.*) the penis.

winkle *n.*[2] *see* WRINKLE n.[1] (1).

winklebag *n.* (*also* **winkle**) [1970s+] a cigarette. [rhy. sl. = FAG n.[4] (3)]

winkle-fishing *n.* [1910s–20s] picking one's nose.

winklepickers *n.* [1960s+] highly pointed-toed boots or shoes. [orig. favoured by Teddy Boys in the 1950s, but latterly absorbed into the wide variety of teen fashions]

winkler *n.* [1970s] one who assists in the eviction of tenants, usu. by means of threats and pressure. [SE *winkle out*]

winklers *n. see* WINKERS n. (3).

wink out *v.* [late 19C–1920s] (*US*) to die.

winks *n.*[1] [mid-19C] peri*winkles.* [abbr.]

winks *n.*[2] *see* FORTY WINKS n.

wink the other eye *v.* [late 19C–1900s] to disregard and dismiss what has just been said.

winky *n.* (*also* **winkie**) [late 19C+] a very small or a child's penis; thus excl. *my winky!* [dimin. of WINKLE n.[1]]

winn *n. see* WIN n.

winner *n.* **1** [20C+] a person or project that is a potential success. **2** [1960s] (*US campus*) used ironically, a social outcast, i.e. a LOSER n.

winner *adj.* [1960s+] first-rate, excellent. [WINNER n. (1)]

winners *n. see* WINNINGS n.

winnet *n. see* WINNIT n.

winnick *adj.* [1910s] crazy, eccentric. [the asylum at *Winnick*, Lancashire]

winnie *n.*[1] [1990s+] a lesbian (cf. AMY-JOHN n.). [the bear *Winnie*-the-Pooh who 'licks the honeypot', i.e. HONEYPOT n.[1] (1)]

winnie *n.*[2] *see* WEENIE n.[1]

winnings *n.* (*also* **winners**) [late 17C–early 19C] (*UK Und.*) booty, plunder. [WIN v.]

winning winchell *n. see* WINCHELL n.

winnit *n.* (*also* **winnet**) [1990s+] a piece of excrement adhering to the anal hairs (cf. CLAGNUT n.).

winny-popper *n.* [1950s+] (*Can. juv.*) the penis. [WINKLE n.[1] + POP v.[1] (9)]

wino *n.* **1** [late 19C+] (*orig. US*) an alcoholic, usu. living in poverty; also attrib. **2** [2000s] (*US campus*) a wine connisseur. [SE *wine* + -O sfx (1)]

win on *v.* [1940s+] (*Aus.*) to seduce a woman.

Winona Ryder *n.* [2000s] cider. [rhy. sl.; ult. US film actress *Winona Ryder* (b.1971)]

win or lose *n.* [20C+] alcohol, liquor. [rhy. sl. = BOOZE n. (1)]

wino time *n.* [1940s+] (*US Und.*) a short sentence. [WINO n. (1) + TIME n.[1]; habitual drunkards generally receive short sentences, i.e. days rather than years in prison]

win-out *n.* [late 19C–1900s] (*US*) a success, esp. against the odds; also attrib.

winry *n.* [1990s+] (*W.I.*) sexual prowess.

winter bush *n.* [2000s] (*US Black*) a pronounced growth of a woman's pubic hair; shaved in the summer, it is allowed to grow in the winter. [SE *winter* + BUSH n.[2] (1)]

winter-campaign *n.* [late 19C] rioting, brawling drunkenly. [the contemporary Fenian bombing campaign]

winter cricket *n.* [late 18C–early 19C] a tailor. [the 'sewing' motions of the insect's legs]

winter Friday *n.* [20C+] (*Irish*) a chilly-looking, impoverished individual.

winter-hedge *n.* [late 19C–1920s] a clothes-horse. [the way a full clothes-horse 'hedges off' a portion of the room; summer washing is dried out of doors]

winter palace *n.* [late 19C] a prison. [impoverished criminals or tramps deliberately have themselves jailed during the cold winter months]

winter rat *n.* [1970s+] (*US*) an old car, driven in bad weather.

winter tread *n.* [1990s+] (*Aus.*) a condom, a contraceptive sheath. [i.e. a winter tread tyre, thus play on RUBBER n.[5]]

winter wear *n. see* TURTLENECK (SWEATER) n.

win the shine-rag *v.* (*also* **win the shiny rag**) [mid–late 19C] to lose one's money by gambling. [? one is thus reduced to cleaning shoes for a living]

wipe *n.*[1] [late 16C–early 17C] the act of drinking. [? one 'wipes' the glass with one's lips]

wipe *n.*[2] [late 16C+] (*UK Und.*) a blow; also in fig. use.

wipe *n.*[3] **1** [18C+] a handkerchief; thus *the wipe lay*, stealing handkerchiefs. **2** [1900s–40s] (*US Und.*) a form of confidence trick based on persuading the victim that money can be raised to a higher denomination; it is first secreted in a handkerchief.

wipe *v.* **1** [19C+] to attack, whether physically or verbally. **2** [1900s] (*Aus.*) to give in, to give up. **3** [1920s+] to destroy, to defeat. **4** [1930s] (*Aus./N.Z.*) to refuse to grant a loan or any other form of gift, e.g. food for a beggar; to render bankrupt. **5** [1940s–60s] (*Aus./N.Z.*) to repudiate, to forget, to dismiss from one's mind. **6** [1940s+] (*also* **wipe out**) to murder. **7** [1980s] (*US*) to throw. [SE *wipe out*]

wiped out *adj.* **1** [20C+] (*US*) financially ruined. **2** [1950s+] exhausted. **3** [1950s+] (*also* **wiped**) drunk, intoxicated by drugs (cf. ADDLED adj.). [SE *wipe out*, to erase]

wipe down *v.* [mid-19C] to flatter, to pacify.

wipe-drawer/-hauler *n. see* WIPER-DRAWER n.

wipe lay, the *n. see* WIPE n.[3] (1).

wipe-off *n.* [1930s+] (*Aus.*) a rejection, a dismissal. [WIPE v. (5)]

wipe off *v.* **1** [mid-19C+] to get rid of, to remove. **2** [1920s+] (*Aus.*) to bid a last farewell, esp. to a place. [(1) SE *wipe off*, to erase; (2) WIPE v. (5)]

wipe oneself out *v.* [20C+] to commit suicide.

wipe one's eye *v.* [mid-19C] to take a drink, esp. to offer or to accept another drink. [? WIPE n.[1]]

wipe-out *n.* **1** [1960s+] (*US*) a major failure; a crushing defeat, annihilation, **2** [1970s] (*US*) an overwhelming experience, esp. as the result of an excess of drugs and/or drink. **3** [1980s] (*US*) a killing. **4** [1990s+] (*Aus.*) a general term of abuse. [orig. ski/surf jargon *wipe-out*, a spectacular fall]

wipe-out *adj.* [1970s] (*US*) exhausting, physically draining.

wipe out *v.*[1] **1** [mid-19C+] to beat up. **2** [mid-19C+] to kill. **3** [mid-19C+] to ruin financially. **4** [20C+] (*US*) to defeat, to destroy. **5** [1960s] (*US campus*) to destroy something, e.g. an automobile; to harm oneself. **6** [1960s+] to astonish. **7** [1960s+] (*US campus*) to fail. **8** [1970s] to incapacitate. [(1) and (2) used by milit. mid-19C+]

wipe out *v.*[2] *see* WIPE v. (6).

wiper *n.*[1] [early 17C–19C] a handkerchief.

wiper *n.*[2] **1** [late 19C] a severe physical blow, a harsh verbal attack, anything that will overwhelm an opponent. **2** [late 19C] an impudent boy. **3** [late 19C] a thug, a person who delivers physical blows. **4** [1930s+] (*US Und.*) a hired killer. [WIPE v.]

wiper-drawer *n.* (*also* **wipe-drawer, wipe-hauler, wiper**) [late 17C–18C] (*UK Und.*) a stealer of handkerchiefs; thus *wipe-drawing, wipe-hauling.* [WIPE n.[3] (1)/WIPER n.[1] + SE *draw/haul*]

wipe round v. [late 19C] to hit; usu. in phr. *wipe someone round the face/mouth/head*. [ext. WIPE v. (1)]

wipe someone's ass v. [1970s] (*US*) to defeat comprehensively.

wipe someone's eye v. 1 [mid-19C+] to get the better of, to defeat. 2 [1920s+] to discomfit, to 'give someone a black eye'. [sporting use *wipe someone's eye*, to shoot someone else's bird]

wipe someone up v. [1930s] (*UK Und.*) to be picked up or arrested by the police.

wipe the floor (with) v. (*also* **wipe the street (with)**) [late 19C+] to beat decisively, to thrash. [note synon. RN *wipe the deck with*]

wipe your chin phr. (*also* **wipe your eye**) [20C+] (*Aus.*) a phr. used to upbraid one who is presumed to be lying. [? thus removing the 'shit' they are talking]

wire n.¹ [mid-19C] (*US campus*) a trick, a hoax, a stratagem.

wire n.² 1 [mid-19C–1960s] a telegram. 2 [20C+] a private warning; thus *get/give the wire*, get/give a warning or message. 3 [1920s–50s] (*US Und.*) 'a racing swindle in which the con men convinced the victim that with the connivance of a corrupt Western Union official they could delay the race results long enough for him to place a bet after the race had been run, but before the bookmakers received the results' (Maurer, *The Big Con*, 1940). 4 [1920s+] (*US*) a telephone. 5 [1930s] (*US prison*) a guard who does favours for the inmates. 6 [1940s] (*Aus.*) a scolding, a reprimand. 7 [1940s+] (*US Black*) the gossip circuit, the 'grapevine'. 8 [1960s] (*US Black*) a 'line' of talk. 9 [1960s+] any form of electronic eavesdropping device. 10 [1990s+] (*US*) the Internet, connected by a modem. 11 [2000s] (*US prison*) a message, a phone-call. [(1) 'telegram' is SE in 20C+; (9) abbr. SE *wire-tapping*]

wire n.³ [mid-19C–1960s] the pickpocket who actively steals from his victim, rather than the various accomplices on his team; thus as v., to pickpocket; *on the wire*, working as a pickpocket. [the SE *wire* used as an adjunct to the fingers]

wire n.⁴ [1910s] (*US tramp*) articles constructed of stolen telegraph wire and sold in the street.

wire n.⁵ [1940s+] 1 the penis; thus PULL ONE'S WIRE v. 2 (*drugs*) a vein used for the injection of drugs.

wire v.¹ 1 [mid-19C+] to send a telegram. 2 [1900s] (*Aus.*) to suggest, to instruct. 3 [1950s+] (*US*) to place an eavesdropping device in a room, 'to bug', or to conceal such a device on a person. [WIRE n.² (9)]

wire v.² [1980s] (*US*) to stimulate, to excite. [WIRED adj.¹]

wire v.³ *see* HOT-WIRE v. (1).

wire chair n. *see* CHAIR, THE n.

wired adj.¹ (*also* **wired up**) 1 [late 19C] (*US*) irritated, provoked. 2 [1960s+] (*orig. US drugs*) addicted to heroin. 3 [1960s+] using cocaine or some form of amphetamine or caffeine. 4 [1960s+] tense, nervous, irritable, full of 'electricity'. 5 [1960s+] in fig. use, addicted to a person or an activity. 6 [1970s] (*US prison*) having a homosexual lifestyle prior to entering prison. 7 [1970s] (*US gay*) sexually excited. 8 [1970s+] drunk. 9 [1970s+] highly stimulated, excited, eager. 10 [1980s+] crazy. 11 [1980s+] affected by cannabis. [SE *wired*, carrying electricity]

wired adj.² [1940s+] (*gambling*) of cards, back to back. [SE *wired together*]

wired adj.³ [1950s+] satisfactory, ideal, as one desires. [? SE *wired together*]

wired for sound phr. [1990s+] (*drugs*) experiencing the most extreme effects of cocaine or amphetamine. [ext. of WIRED adj.¹ (3)]

wired (in) adj. [1930s+] (*US*) 1 well connected in political or business circles. 2 in control, secure and assured. [SE *wire*, a connection]

wired into adj. [1960s+] (*US*) intimately involved in or with. [SE *wired together*]

wire-draw n. [late 16C–18C] (*UK Und.*) a trick that ensnares a victim; thus *wire-drawn*, tricked in this way; *wiredrawer*, a trickster. [SE *wire-draw*, to draw out, to persuade by subtle arguing]

wired up adj. *see* WIRED adj.¹.

wired up to the moon phr. [1990s+] (*Irish*) crazy.

wire in v. (*also* **wire into**) [mid–late 19C] to set about one's work enthusiastically, to set about a meal and start eating heartily. [fig. use of SE *wire*, to join together with wires]

wire in and get one's name up v. [mid–late 19C] 1 to seduce. 2 to attempt success. [ext. WIRE IN v.; orig. used as an invitation to enter a boxing ring and prepare for a contest]

wire into v. *see* WIRE IN v.

wireless n. [1920s–30s] a baseless rumour. [WIRE n.² (2) + pun on SE]

wire parlour n. [1910s] (*US Und.*) an execution chamber, using the electric chair.

wire-puller n. (*also* **wire-worker**) [mid-19C+] a person who exerts influence or manipulates, esp. in politics. [PULL (THE) WIRES v.]

wirer n. [mid-19C] an expert pickpocket who uses a wire to remove objects from his victims. [WIRE n.³]

wires n. [1920s] the electric chair.

wire-tapper n. [late 19C–1930s] (*US*) a confidence trickster who claims that he can intercept the wire bringing racecourse results and thus cheat the bookmakers; thus *wire-tapping*, the swindle itelf.

wire up v. [1970s+] (*US Black*) to explain the current situation, to tell what has been or is happening. [electronic imagery]

wire-worker n. *see* WIRE-PULLER n.

wiring n. [mid–late 19C] (*UK Und.*) working as a professional pickpocket. [WIRE n.³]

Wisacres Hall n. [mid-18C–mid-19C] Gresham College, London, esp. as home of the Royal Society. [SE *wiseacre*, one who thinks himself, or wishes to be thought, wise; thus a sneer at the Society's intellectual membership]

wisdom-weed n. [1950s+] (*W.I.*) any herb that is seen as having the effect of making one wiser, esp. marijuana (cf. AFRICAN BUSH n.). [SE *wisdom* + *weed*/WEED n.¹ (4)]

wise adj. 1 [late 19C+] (*orig. US*) shrewd, cunning, knowing, aware; usu. as GET WISE (TO) v. 2 [late 19C+] stupid, foolish, in ironic use, i.e. one who believes him- or herself shrewd. 3 [1940s–60s] homosexually experienced.

wise v.¹ [1970s] (*US Black*) to agree with; to understand.

wise v.² *see* WISE UP v.

wise adv. [1940s+] (*US*) in a sophisticated manner. [WISE adj. (1)]

-wise sfx (*orig. US*) 1 [1930s+] aware of, in the know. 2 [1940s+] with reference to, as regards, e.g. *job-wise*, *success-wise*.

wise alec(k) n. *see* SMART ALEC(K) n.

wise apple n. [1940s+] (*US*) one who is too clever for their own good. [WISE adj. (2) + APPLE n.² (1)]

wise-ass n. (*also* **wise-arse, wisepuss**) [1950s+] (*US*) one who sees himself or herself as cleverer than they really are. [WISE adj. (2) + -ASS sfx]

wise-ass adj. (*also* **wise-assed**) [1950s+] self-opinionated, self-aggrandizing. [WISE-ASS n.]

wise-ass v. [1950s+] (*US*) to act in a 'smart' manner. [WISE-ASS n.]

wise boy n. *see* WISE GUY n.

wise bull n. *see* BULL n.¹⁰ (1).

wisecrack n. [1910s+] (*orig. US*) a witty retort, a smart comment, a joke at someone else's expense. [WISE adj. (1) + CRACK n.¹¹ (1)]

wisecrack v. [1910s+] (*orig. US*) to make a witty retort or a smart comment, to make a joke at someone else's expense. [WISE-CRACK n.]

wisecracker n. [1920s+] a person who makes a witty retort or smart comment, or a joke at someone else's expense. [WISE-CRACK v.]

wisecracking adj. [1910s+] describing a person who makes smart retorts. [WISECRACK v.]

wised(-up) adj. [20C+] (US) aware, knowledgeable. [WISE adj. (1)/WISE UP v.]

wise guy n. (also **smart guy, wise boy, wise punk**) **1** [late 19C+] (gambling) gamblers who are first to favour a particular line of betting, which influences the changing odds. **2** [late 19C+] (US) a shrewd person. **3** [20C+] (US) anyone who thinks they are particularly knowing or clever; a general derog. description, the implication being that the person is too clever for their own good. **4** [1910s] (US) a criminal. **5** [1940s+] (US) as a form of personal address. **6** [1970s+] (orig. US) a member of an organized crime syndicate, usu. the US Mafia. [WISE adj. (1) + GUY n.² (1)]

wise-guy adj. (also **smart-guy**) (US) **1** [1920s+] clever in a showy kind of way. **2** [1950s+] related to the US Mafia or its culture and lifestyle. [WISE GUY n.]

wise-head n. **1** [mid-19C] an ironic ref. to one who sees himself or herself as clever. **2** [1910s–30s] (Aus./US) a clever, cunning person. [WISE adj.]

wise hombre n. [20C+] (US) a shrewd, clever person. [WISE adj. (1) + HOMBRE n. (1)]

wise Injun n. [1910s] (US) an expert. [WISE adj. (1) + INJUN n.]

wise money n. see SMART MONEY n. (1).

wise monkey n. [20C+] a condom. [rhy. sl. = FLUNKY n.²]

wisenheimer n. (also **weisenheimer, wisenstein**) [20C+] a know-it-all, a self-appointed smart fellow. [WISE adj. (1) + Ger./Jewish sfx -heimer, usu. part of a surname]

wise off v. [1950s+] (US) **1** to make jokes at someone's expense. **2** to boast, to brag. [WISECRACK v.]

wise punk n. see WISE GUY n.

wisepuss n. see WISE-ASS n.

wise to phr. [late 19C+] aware of what is going on, 'in the know'. [WISE adj. (1)]

wise up v. (also **wake, wake up, wise**) [late 19C+] (orig. US) **1** to inform, to explain to someone. **2** to (begin to) understand, to appreciate; also to start acting sensibly, to cease being stupid; often as imper. wise up! [WISE adj. (1)]

wisey n. [1940s] (US) a clever, showy person, a WISE GUY n. (3).

wisey warcy adv. see VICEY-VERSEY adv.

wishbone n. [1970s] the penis. [SE wish (for sex) + SE bone/BONE n.¹ (1)]

wish book n. [1920s+] (Can./US) a mail-order catalogue.

wish to hell v. (also **hope to hell, wish to Christ, wish to hell and little centipedes, wish to Pete**) [late 19C+] (orig. US) to desire intensely.

wisty-castor n. [early 19C] a punch, a blow. [var. on WHISTER-CLISTER n.]

witblits n. [1930s+] (S.Afr.) home-distilled spirits, often sold as 'brandy'. [Du. wit, white + blits, lightning]

witch n. **1** [1940s–50s] a girlfriend. **2** [1950s] an ugly woman. **3** [1950s–70s] (US Black) a prostitute.

witch, the n. [1940s–60s] (drugs) heroin, cocaine, morphine (cf. AUNTIE EMMA n.). [? it 'bewitches' the user; note cocaine is a 'feminine' drug, see GIRL n.² (1)]

witcher adj. (also **wicher**) [late 17C–early 19C] (UK Und.) silver. [? WHITE adj.¹ + SE silver]

witcher(-bubber) n. [late 17C–early 19C] (UK Und.) a silver bowl. [WITCHER adj. + BUBBER n.¹ (2)]

witcher-cully n. (UK Und.) **1** [late 17C–early 19C] a silversmith. **2** [mid-18C] silverware. [WITCHER adj. + CULLY n. (3)]

witcher-tilter n. [late 17C–early 19C] (UK Und.) a silver-hilted sword. [WITCHER adj. + TILTER n.]

witchetty grub n. [20C+] (Aus.) a cub scout. [rhy. sl.]

witch hazel n. see HAZEL n.

witch-tit adj. [1960s+] of weather, very cold. [COLD AS A WITCH'S TIT phr.]

with prep.¹ [mid-19C] of a mix of warmed or chilled alcohol, with sugar; thus without, without sugar.

with prep.² [20C+] understanding a person's line of thought, following their reasoning, e.g. I'm definitely with you on that.

with a continuando phr. [late 17C–early 18C] for a very long time, usu. referring to a drinking bout and thus prefaced by 'drunk...'. [Sp.]

with a few jars on phr. see JAR n.¹ (2).

with a hey nonny-nonny and a hotcha-cha phr. see HOTCHA! excl.

with a hook! excl. see HOOKEY WALKER! excl.

with bells on phr. (also **with tits on**) **1** [late 19C+] in a joyous mood, enthusiastic. **2** [20C+] (US) (also **with bells**) definitely, without doubt. **3** [1960s+] (also **with spangles**) with melodramatic, lurid and otherwise exciting embellishments. [? the bells that adorned a jester's outfit or the practice in the Old West of outfitting the lead animals of a freight-hauling team with bells, to announce their presence and thus minimize accidents]

with ears adv. (also **with earflaps/earlaps**) [1970s+] (US) to an extreme and insufferable degree. [the creation of fig. 'noise']

with hot feet adv. see HOT FOOT adv.

within (a) cooee of phr. [late 19C+] (Aus./N.Z.) within hailing distance, within easy reach, near; thus out of cooee, at a distance. [Aboriginal cooee, a bush call later adopted by the colonists and thence by UK English-speakers]

within a kick phr. [1910s] (Aus.) very nearly.

within the kick of a brown cow phr. [1900s] (Aus.) very close to.

with it adj. [1940s+] au fait, aware, knowledgeable, fashionable, up-to-date. [esp. popular during the Beatnik era of the 1950s + 'Swinging London' period of the 1960s]

with it! excl. [1960s] (US gay) yes!

with knobs on phr. (also **with nobs on**) [1920s+] embellished, with 'add-ons', decorations. [i.e. with 'extras' but ? ref. to KNOB n.¹ (3)]

with knobs on! excl. (also **with nobs on!**) [1930s+] (mainly UK juv.) an excl. retort meaning the same to you and more so! [WITH KNOBS ON phr.]

with no error phr. see AND NO MISTAKE (ABOUT IT) phr.

with one's tail on fire phr. [mid-18C] infected with venereal disease. [TAIL n.² (2)/TAIL n.² (3) + FIRE n.¹]

without prep. see WITH prep.¹

without a mintie phr. [1930s] (Aus.) penniless. [SE without + MINTIE n.¹]

without a pot to pee/piss in v. see NOT HAVE A POT TO PISS IN (OR A WINDOW TO THROW IT OUT OF) v.

with spangles phr. see WITH BELLS ON phr. (3).

with the bark on phr. [mid-19C–1940s] (US) of a statement, absolutely unvarnished, totally honest.

with the birdies phr. [1990s+] (Aus.) eccentric, insane.

with the program phr. [1970s+] in tune with the prevailing situation in a positive manner; thus (US Black teen) imper. get with the program, pay attention. [PROGRAM n.; from the recovery techniques of Alcoholics Anonymous/Narcotics Anonymous and other groups that offer their variously habituated members a 12-point program of self-help]

with tits on phr. see WITH BELLS ON phr.

wit ou n. [1970s+] (S.Afr. Indian) a White person. [Afk. wit, white + OU n.]

witpyp v. [1960s+] (S.Afr.) to smoke a mixture of marijuana and powdered methaqualone (Mandrax). [Afk. 'white pipe'; the capsules of Mandrax are white]

witter v. [1950s+] to chatter on pointlessly. [? Scot. whitter, to twitter]

wittol n. (also **wittal**) [late 16C–early 18C] a complaisant husband who makes no effort to discourage his wife's adventuring. [SE *woodwale*, a bird that is often the target of a cuckoo, who lays its egg in the woodwale's nest]

wix *adj.* [2000s] (*UK teen*) good, excellent. [WICKED adj. (2)]

wiz *n.*[1] [1940s] (*US drugs*) cocaine (cf. WHIZ n.[7]). [SE *whiz*, to move fast]

wiz *n.*[2] *see* WHIZ n.[3].

wizard *adj.* [1920s+] (*orig. US*) a general term of approval, excellent, wonderful. [despite US origin, the main use has been UK society, esp. by those who attended prep schools]

wizz *see also under* WHIZ.

wizzer *n. see* WHIZZER n.[2].

wizzo *adj. see* WHIZZO adj.

wizzy-wizzy *v.* (*also* **whizzy-whizzy**) [20C+] (*W.I., Bdos*) to whisper together. [SE *whisper*]

wob *n.* [1910s–30s] (*US*) the trade union Industrial Workers of the World or IWW, their collective members; also attrib. [abbr. WOBBLY n.[1]]

woball *n. see* WHOABALL n.

wobbegong *n.* [1920s+] (*Aus.*) **1** any form of unnamed insect. **2** anything excellent or outstanding. [? Aboriginal *wobbegong*, a carpet-shark + play on SE *wobegone*]

wobble *n.*[1] [20C+] (*Irish*) shaving lather. [the stirring of the lather before its use]

wobble *n.*[2] (*also* **wobble-weed**) [1980s+] (*US drugs*) phencyclidine (cf. ACE n.[4]). [its effects]

wobbler *n.*[1] *see* WABBLER n.[1].

wobbler *n.*[2] *see* WOBBLY n.[2].

wobbler *n.*[3] *see* WOBBLY n.[3].

wobblers *n.* **1** [late 19C] eggs. **2** [1980s] pills, usu. amphetamine. **3** [1990s+] the female breasts (cf. BOBBER n.[2]).

wobble-shop *n.* [mid-19C] an unlicensed liquor store. [the effects of the liquor one buys there]

wobble-weed *n. see* WOBBLE n.[2].

wobbly *n.*[1] [1910s+] (*US*) a member of the trade union Industrial Workers of the World or IWW.

wobbly *n.*[2] (*also* **wobbler**) [1930s+] a fit of nerves, of panic, of bad temper; thus one who has such attacks.

wobbly *n.*[3] (*also* **wobbler**) [1960s+] a dubious or untrustworthy story.

wobbly *adj.*[1] [1910s+] (*US*) pertaining to the trade union Industrial Workers of the World. [WOBBLY n.[1]]

wobbly *adj.*[2] (*also* **wabbly**) [1920s+] unlikely, 'shaky', e.g. of plans or prospects.

wobbly eggs *n.* [1990s+] Temazepam. [the oval shape + the effect on the user]

wobbly pop *n.* [1990s+] (*US*) beer. [SE *wobbly* + POP n.[2] (1); its fizziness + its impairing effects]

wodge *n. see* WADGE n.

woejus *adj. see* WOJUS adj.

woema *n.* [1970s+] (*S.Afr.*) energy, power. [? Zulu *vuma*, to thrive]

woes *adj.* [1970s+] (*S.Afr., mainly juv.*) furious, ill-tempered. [Du. *woest*, fierce]

woffle *v.*[1] [early 19C] to eat. [? dial. *woffle*, to chew]

woffle *v.*[2] *see* WAFFLE v.[1].

woffle dust *n.* [20C+] (*Aus.*) a fig. term for luck, esp. if gambling when one *puts a bit of woffle dust* on the cards/dice. [? nonce-word]

wog *n.*[1] [1910s+] (*also* **woggo, woggy**) a derog. term for any non-White, esp. an Indian or Pakistani and latterly, in the UK, Bangladeshi (cf. BROWNIE n.[2]). **2** [1920s+] (*Aus. juv.*) a very young child. **3** [1940s+] any foreigner; esp. in the phr. *the wogs begin at Calais*. **4** [1960s+] a derog. term for a Black person (cf. ALLIGATOR BAIT n.[2]). **5** [1970s+] an Indian meal, an Indian restaurant. **6** [1980s+] (*Aus.*) a Mediterranean immigrant, e.g. a Greek or Yugoslav (cf. DAGO n.). [ety. unknown; it appears to have been used in the East End of London from *c*.1910;

suggestions include that of F.C. Bowen in *Sea Slang* (1929), who includes 'Wogs, lower class Babu shipping clerks on the Indian coast', but provides no further detail. Popular belief has always chosen the acronym westernized oriental *gentleman* or wily oriental *gentleman*, while E.P. opts for abbr. of SE *golliwog*, and certainly this once-popular doll, with its caricatured 'Black' features, has long since been marginalized as politically incorrect]

wog *n.*[2] [1930s+] (*Aus.*) **1** a germ or parasite, an insect. **2** an illness or disease, a 'bug'. **3** a tiny fragment. [ety. unknown; ? link to dial. *wog*, to twitch, to move; (2) is fig. use of (1)]

wog *adj.* [1940s+] (*also* **woggy**) pertaining to an Indian, Arab etc; ext. to anyone with a dark complexion. [WOG n.[1] (1)]

wog box *n.* [1980s+] a large, portable stereo tape-recorder-cum-radio, particularly beloved of ghetto youths. [WOG n.[1] (1) + BOX n.[5] (7)]

woggie *adj.* [1940s+] foreign, esp. Asian. [WOG n.[1] (1)]

woggo *n. see* WOG n.[1] (1).

wog gut *n.* [1940s] diarrhoea or any stomach upset that assails a tourist in any exotic part of the world (cf. AZTEC HOP n.). [WOG n.[1] (1) + SE *gut*]

woggy *n. see* WOG n.[1] (1).

woggy *adj. see* WOG adj.

wojus *adj.* (*also* **woejus, wojious**) [1980s+] (*Irish*) bad, terrible. [SE *woeful* + *atrocious*]

wok *v.* [1990s+] (*UK Black/teen*)) to have sexual intercourse. [? WHACK IT IN v.]

wolf *n.*[1] **1** [mid-19C+] a male overtly pursuing women for sex. **2** [1910s] (*US*) an obsessive, one who is very keen. **3** [1910s] (*US Und.*) a tramp who rides on passenger trains by virtue of strength rather than cunning. **4** [1910s+] (*US gay*) a predatory male or female homosexual, esp. in the context of prison; thus *wolf's handshake*, the tweaking of a new inmate's cheek by a veteran homosexual. **5** [1920s+] (*US*) an older, usu. homosexual, tramp who travels with a young boy. **6** [1990s+] a professional poker-player.

wolf *n.*[2] [1930s] (*US Und.*) a criminal who works alone. [SE *lone wolf*]

wolf *n.*[3] [1950s+] (*W.I. Rasta*) one who is not a Rastafarian but has a dreadlock hairstyle.

wolf *n.*[4] [1970s] (*drugs*) phencyclidine (cf. ACE n.[4]). [its non-recreational use as an animal tranquillizer]

wolf *n.*[5] [1970s] (*US prison*) a 15-year sentence.

wolf *v.*[1] **1** [1910s] (*US*) to complain. **2** [1960s+] (*US prison*) to banter. [? SE *woof*/WOOF v.[1]]

wolf *v.*[2] [1920s–40s] (*US*) to pursue women. [WOLF n.[1] (1)]

wolf *v.*[3] [2000s] to whistle at a passing woman in an admiring, lustful way. [abbr. WOLF-WHISTLE v.]

wolf-call *v.* [1940s+] to whistle at a passing woman in an admiring, lustful way; also as n. [WOLF n.[1] (1) + SE *call*]

wolfess *n.* [1940s+] a sexually aggressive woman, both hetero- and homosexual. [WOLF n.[1] (1) + fem. sfx -*ess*]

wolfies *n. see* ROOFIE n.[2].

wolfing *n.* (*also* **wolfing it**) [1920s+] (*US Black*) talking grandiloquently, but not always backing up one's words with action. [WOOF v.[1]]

wolf in the breast *n.* [mid-18C–19C] (*UK Und.*) a trick practised by strolling beggar women, who ask for alms to obtain medicine to deal with a gnawing pain in their breast.

wolfish *adj.* [19C+] (*US*) extremely hungry. [SE *wolf*, to eat ravenously]

wolf pack *n.* [1950s+] (*US*) a juv. or prison gang; also as v., to sit around or attack in a gang (cf. RAT PACK n.).

wolf-pussy *n.* [1970s] (*US Black*) unpleasant vaginal odours. [? *whiff* + PUSSY n. (2)]

wolf ticket *n.* [1970s+] (*US Black*) a threat; an empty boast. [WOOF v.[1] + SE *ticket*]

wolf-trap *n.* (*also* **trap**) [mid–late 19C] (*US*) a cheap, poss. crooked, casino.

wolf-whistle *n.* [1950s+] a 2-note whistle aimed at a passing woman by an admiring, lustful man; or vice versa. [WOLF n.[1] (1) + SE *whistle*]

wolf-whistle *v.* [1950s+] to whistle at a passing woman in an admiring, lustful way. [WOLF-WHISTLE n.]

wollapalooza *n. see* LALLAPALOOSA n.

wollie *n.* (*also* **woola, woolah, woolas, woolie, woolies, wooly**) [1980s+] (*drugs*) a cigarette of crack or base cocaine, mixed with marijuana and wrapped in a cigar leaf.

wollied *adj.* [1980s] drunk (cf. ADDLED adj.). [WALLY n.[2] (1), i.e. one is rendered stupid]

wollies *n.* [late 19C] olives. [? joc. excl. *oh olive!*]

wollop *see under* WALLOP.

wolly *n. see* WALLY n.[2].

Wolverine *n.* [mid-19C+] (*US*) an inhabitant of Michigan.

wolverine *n.* [1930s–50s] (*US Black*) a sexually aggressive woman. [fem. var. on WOLF n.[1] (1)]

woman *n.*[1] [late 18C–1900s] in coin-tossing, the reverse of a coin. [the engraving of Britannia; the face of the coin had the then male monarch's head]

woman *n.*[2] **1** [1920s] a tramp's young boy companion. **2** [1960s+] (*US prison*) a prisoner's male lover; the homosexuality may only exist for the length of the sentence. **3** [1980s+] (*US juv.*) an effeminate boy, an unpopular boy.

woman about town *n.* (*also* **girl about town, girl/lady/ woman of the town**) [late 17C–1900s] a prostitute, esp. a street-walker (cf. FANCY WOMAN n.). [as opposed to a *man about town* or *man of the town*, a generally congratulatory phr., these female counterparts were invariably condemnatory, however much of a euph. the term might be; note GIRL n.[1] (1)]

woman and her husband *n.* [late 18C–early 19C] a married couple where the wife is larger than the husband. [reverse of the usual order, SE *man and wife*]

woman-be-damned *n.* [1940s–50s] (*W.I.*) any form of cooking that is done by men only, e.g. a labouring gang.

woman in comfortable shoes *n.* [1990s+] a lesbian.

woman-jessie *n. see* JESSIE n.[1] (2).

woman-killer *n. see* LADY-KILLER n.

woman-lover *n. see* LADY-LOVER n.

woman-man *n.* [20C+] (*W.I., Gren.*) an effeminate male homosexual (cf. BOY-GIRL n.[1]).

woman of all work *n.* [late 18C–early 19C] a maidservant 'who refuses none of her master's commands' (Grose, 1796), i.e. who not only waits upon but sleeps with her master. [pun on SE *maid of all work*]

woman of pleasure *n. see* LADY OF PLEASURE n.

woman of the town *n. see* WOMAN ABOUT TOWN n.

woman trouble *n.* [1950s+] **1** from a female point of view, gynaecological problems. **2** from a male point of view, problems in a relationship.

womba *n. see* WONGA n.

wombat *n.*[1] **1** [20C+] (*Aus./US*) a fool, an eccentric (cf. AIREDALE n.; DINGBAT n.[9]). **2** [1980s] (*US campus*) an ugly person. **3** [2000s] a pointless occupation, i.e. *waste of money, brains and time*. [SE *wombat*, a burrowing marsupial resembling a small bear; (3) is an acronym]

wombat *n.*[2] [1980s+] an unappreciative male. [pun on he 'eats roots and leaves'/*eats*, ROOT v.[3] (1) and leaves]

wombat *adj.* [20C+] (*Aus.*) dead. [rhy. sl. = *hors de combat*]

womb-beater *n.* (*also* **womb-sweeper**) [1960s–70s] (*US Black*) a man with a large penis (cf. ARSE-OPENER n.).

womble *n.* [1970s+] a fool, a socially unacceptable individual. [the *Wombles*, stars of a 1970s UK children's TV series]

womblescropt/womblety-cropped *adj. see* WAMBLETY-CROPPED adj.

womb-sweeper *n. see* WOMB-BEATER n.

women-drawers *n.* [early 17C] prostitutes. [SE *woman drawer*, a barmaid; what the prostitute 'draws' is semen]

womp *adj.* [1990s+] (*US*) of a situation, bad, problematic. [WHOMP v. (1)]

womp *v. see* WHOMP v.

womper-jawed *adj. see* WHOPPER-JAWED adj.

womp on *v. see* WHOMP v.

won *adj.* [late 17C–19C] stolen. [WIN v.]

wong *n.*[1] (*also* **Mr Wong**) [1940s+] (*US*) the penis. [var. on WANG n.[2] (1)]

wong *n.*[2] [1990s+] (*UK Black*) money. [abbr. WONGA n.]

wonga *n.* (*also* **wamba, wanga, womba**) [late 19C+] money. [Rom. *wanger*, coal, fig. money; thus Rom. *wongar-camming mush*, a miser, lit. 'one who loves coal' + ? pun on COLE n. (1)]

wonga-gut *n. see* WANGA-GUT n.

wonk *n.*[1] **1** [1910s–40s] a weak-looking, ungainly person. **2** [1930s–60s] (*Aus.*) a White person, usu. as an insult. **3** [1940s+] (*Aus.*) an effeminate or homosexual male. **4** [1960s+] (*US campus*) anyone who works harder than the rest of the students see fit. [? WONKY adj.; note political jargon *policy wonk*, an expert in the minutiae of policy; Martin Amis (2000) suggests backsl. f. SE *know*; (1) note Hong Kong *wonk*, a scruffy mongrel, lit. a 'yellow dog' (from Ning Po pron. of letters *y.d.*)]

wonk *n.*[2] [1940s] echoic of an explosion, a blow, a loud noise.

wonk one's conker *v.* [1990s+] to masturbate. [assonance, but note WANK v. (1)]

wonky *adj.* [1910s+] **1** of a person or object, unsteady, unstable, out of kilter; thus phr. *on a wonk*. **2** (*Aus.*) mad; thus *wonkite*, a mad person. **3** nervous. [ety. unknown; note synon. Ger. *wankel*]

won't quit *phr.* (*also* **won't stop**) [1960s+] (*orig. US*) outstanding, wonderful, beyond compare, e.g. *she's got legs that just won't quit.*

woo *n.* [1930s+] (*N.Z.*) a petting session. [SE *woo*, to court]

wood *n.*[1] [early 19C; 1940s+] money. [the barrels in which liquor is stored]

wood *n.*[2] [mid–late 19C] the pulpit. [its manufacture]

wood *n.*[3] (*US Und.*) **1** [1920s] a beer keg, holding bootleg alcohol. **2** [1940s] a policeman's truncheon.

wood *n.*[4] (*also* **tree**) **1** [1950s+] the penis (cf. BAT n.[7]). **2** [1980s+] an erection; thus *get good wood*, to have a strong erection; *give/slip someone wood*, of a man, to have sexual intercourse. [the solidity of the erection]

wood *n.*[5] [1960s+] **1** (*US Black*) a derog. term for a White person. **2** (*US prison*) a term of address between White males. [abbr. PECKERWOOD n.]

wood *n.*[6] *see* WOODIE n.[1].

wood *v.* [1960s] (*Aus.*) to hit.

wood-and-water joey *n.* [late 19C+] (*Aus.*) **1** a general labourer. **2** a sycophant, a hanger-on. [SE *wood-and-water* + JOEY n.[2] (1), they run for firewood, drinking water etc]

woodbine *n.* **1** [1910s] any cheap cigarette, irrespective of brand. **2** [1910s; 1940s] (*Aus.*) an Englishman, esp. a soldier. [Wills' *Woodbine* cigarettes, a cheap UK brand and as such popular among WW1 troops]

wood-butcher *n.* [19C+] a second-rate carpenter.

woodcock *n.*[1] [early 16C–mid-18C] a fool, a gullible person (cf. AIREDALE n.; HORSECOCK n.[1]). [the ease with which the SE *woodcock* can be caught in a snare]

woodcock *n.*[2] [late 18C–early 19C] a tailor who has presented a long bill. [pun on the bird's long *bill*]

woodcock *n.*[3] [mid-19C] (*US*) pork and beans. [? misreading of *Scotch Woodcock*: hard boiled eggs chopped up with anchovy sauce and then laid on slices of buttered toast]

woodcock's head *n.* [late 16C] a pipe. [the shape]

wood duck *n.* [1980s+] **1** (*Aus.*) a fool (cf. AIREDALE n.). **2** (*Aus. prison*) an inexperienced prisoner. [Aus. *wood duck*, technically classified as a *maned goose*, thus pun on GOOSE n.[1] (1)]

wooden *n. see* WOODEN (SPOON) n.

wooden *v. see* WOODEN (OUT) v.

wooden aspro *n.* [1970s+] (*N.Z. prison*) a blow on the head with a truncheon; the truncheon itself. [SE *wooden* + *Aspro*, a painkiller]

wooden casement *n.* (*also* **wooden cravat**) [late 17C] the pillory.

wooden coat *n. see* WOODEN OVERCOAT n.

wooden doublet *n.* [mid-18C] a coffin.

woodener *n.*[1] [late 19C–1920s] (*Aus./N.Z.*) **1** a staggering blow; a knockout punch. **2** in fig. use, something, e.g. an excess of drink, that 'knocks one out'. [it renders the recipient 'dead wood']

woodener *n.*[2] [1920s–60s] (*Irish*) a cheap wooden seat at the cinema.

woodener *n.*[3] [1940s–50s] (*UK prison*) a 1-month sentence. [the *wooden* spoon once issued + rhy. sl. = MOON n.[2] (1)]

wooden fit *n.* [late 19C–1900s] a fainting. [one drops rigidly to the ground]

wooden habeas *n.* [late 18C–early 19C] a coffin; thus *go out with a wooden habeas*, to die in prison. [SE *wooden* + pun on *habeas corpus*, lit. 'thou shalt have the body', a writ whereby an accused and jailed person must be brought before the court and the reason for their imprisonment justified]

wooden horse *n.* [mid-16C–17C] the gallows.

wooden kimono *n.* (*also* **wooden kimino/kimona**) [1910s+] a coffin.

wooden leg *n.* [1990s+] an egg. [rhy. sl.]

wooden-legged mare *n.* [early 18C–mid-19C] the gallows.

wooden nickel *n.* (*also* **copper nickel, wooden money**) [1920s+] (*orig. US*) something worthless; thus in phr. *don't take any wooden nickels*, meaning 'be watchful'. [a non-existent and undoubtedly worthless coin]

wooden nutmeg *n.* [mid–late 19C] (*US*) **1** a native of Connecticut. **2** a confidence trickster. [the use of such 'nutmegs' in confidence trickery; thus the negative image of such individuals]

wooden (out) *v.* [20C+] (*Aus./N.Z.*) to knock down, to knock out. [WOODENER n.[1] (1)]

wooden overcoat *n.* (*also* **wooden coat, ...suit, ...uniform**) [mid-19C+] a coffin, often used in fictional versions of organized crime; thus *wooden overcoat man*, an undertaker.

wooden parenthesis *n.* [early 19C] the pillory. [the sides of the pillory supposedly resemble the curves of a *parenthesis*, i.e. ( )]

wooden pegs *n.* [20C+] the legs. [rhy. sl.]

wooden plank *n.* [1980s+] an American. [rhy. sl. = YANK n. (1)]

wooden ruff *n.* (*also* **wooden shoes**) [late 17C–mid-19C] (*UK Und.*) a pillory or the stocks; thus *wear the wooden ruff*, to stand in the pillory. [like the SE *ruff* it encircles the neck]

wooden shoes *n.* **1** [late 17C–mid-18C] the supporters of the Old Pretender, James Stuart (1688–1766). **2** [mid-18C] the French, France; thus foreigners in general. **3** [1940s] (*US Und.*) a Dutchman. [the wearing of wooden *sabots* by the French]

wooden (spoon) *n.* [1930s–50s] (*UK prison*) a 1-month sentence. [rhy. sl. = MOON n.[2] (1)]

wooden spoon *n.*[1] **1** [mid-19C] (*US campus*) at Yale, a prize conferred at the end of the junior year for the 'most popular man in class'. **2** [late 19C] a fool. **3** [20C+] (*orig. sporting*) a metaphorical prize for the competitor or team who comes last in a sporting contest. [the actual *wooden spoon* trad. awarded to that Cambridge undergraduate unfortunate enough to come bottom in the year's mathematical tripos. Note the synon. *wooden wedge*, named after the philologist Hensleigh Wedgwood, who took last place in the Cambridge classical tripos of 1824]

wooden spoon *n.*[2] [1920s] an erect penis (cf. BAT n.[7]). [like *wood*, it is hard; note this predates WOOD n.[4] (1)]

wooden suit *n. see* WOODEN OVERCOAT n.

wooden surtout *n.* [late 18C–mid-19C] a coffin. [SE *wooden* + *surtout*, an overcoat]

wooden swear *n.* [20C+] slamming a door and leaving the room as the final punctuation of an argument. [the *wooden* door 'swears' as it slams shut]

woodentop *n.* [1970s+] **1** a uniformed policeman. **2** a simpleton. [the UK children's TV series]

wooden ulster *n.* [late 19C] a coffin. [SE *ulster*, a long, loose overcoat]

wooden uniform *n. see* WOODEN OVERCOAT n.

woodheap *v.* [1910s+] (*Aus.*) **1** to ostracize a fellow worker. **2** to force an itinerant to chop firewood in return for food and accommodation. [SE *woodheap*, a stack of firewood]

wood hick *n.* [19C] (*US*) a derog. term for a rustic, a peasant (cf. BOONIE n.[1]). [SE *wood(land)* + HICK n.[1] (1)]

woodie *n.*[1] (*also* **wood, woody**) [20C+] **1** a Wills *Woodbine* cigarette. **2** any cheap cigarette. [abbr.; (2) is fig. use of (1)]

woodie *n.*[2] (*also* **woody**) [1940s+] (*orig. US*) an erection; the erect penis (cf. BAT n.[7]). [ext. of WOOD n.[4] (2)]

woodie *n.*[3] (*also* **woody**) [1960s+] (*orig. US surfing*) a wood-panelled station wagon. [abbr.]

wood merchant *n.* [late 19C–1910s] a street seller of matches.

woodpecker *n.*[1] **1** [17C–early 19C] (*UK Und.*) in a crooked gambling game, the accomplice who urges on the victim, helping him by providing a succession of small stakes. **2** [1940s] (*US/Aus.*) a machinegun. **3** [1940s–50s] (*US Und.*) a typist. [SE *woodpecker*, which takes repeated small pecks at a tree, gradually creating a substantial hole; (2) adds the tapping noise]

woodpecker *n.*[2] [1950s] (*W.I.*) a district policeman (cf. ANIMAL n.[1]; BABY-BLUES n.[2]). [the red stripes on his uniform, reminiscent of the bird's colouring]

woodpecker *n.*[3] *see* PECKERWOOD n.

woodpile *n.* [1930s] (*US*) a xylophone. [its manufacture]

woodpile cousin *n.* [20C+] (*US*) a distant relation, e.g. a third or fourth cousin, a family friend. [the sharing of a common woodpile]

wood-pusher *n.* [1940s+] (*US*) a bad chess-player. [they have no strategy and merely move the pieces]

wood-pussy *n.* (*also* **woods–pussy**) [late 19C+] (*Can./US*) a skunk, a polecat. [lit. 'wood-cat']

wood rash *n.* [1970s–80s] (*N.Z. prison*) an injury inflicted by a truncheon.

woodrow *n.* [1990s+] an erection; usu. *slip her the woodrow*, to have sexual intercourse. [ext. of WOOD n.[4]]

Woods *n.* [1950s] a Wills *Woodbine* cigarette. [abbr.]

woods *n.* **1** [1900s] (*US Und.*) whiskers. **2** [1960s] (*US campus*) the female pubic area.

woods colt *n.* [late 19C+] (*US*) an illegitimate child. [SAmE, *woods colt*, a horse of unknown paternity; such a *colt* is conceived and/or reared in the *woods*, rather than in a stable]

woodser *n. see* JIMMY WOODSER n.

woodsman *n.* [1960s+] a sexual athlete. [WOOD n.[4] + sfx *-man*]

woods-pussy *n. see* WOOD-PUSSY n.

Woodstock wannabe *n.* [1990s+] (*US campus*) one whose lifestyle and attitudes are reminiscent of the HIPPIE n.[2] (3) 1960s. [the *Woodstock* Festival of 1969 (seen as the high-watermark of hippiedom) + WANNABE n. (1)]

wood up *v. see* TAKE IN WOOD v.

woody *see under* WOODIE.

woof *v.*[1] [1910s+] (*mainly US*) to speak in a variety of ways; the meaning differs as to context, e.g. flirtatious, aggressive, meaningless, threatening, bullying, bluffing, joking. [US Black pron. of SE *wolf* + SE *woof*, the sound of barking]

woof *v.*[2] [1940s] (*Aus.*) to poke.

woof *v.*[3] [1970s+] (*US campus*) to vomit (cf. BARF v.). [echoic]

woof! *excl.* [1920s+] used by a man on seeing a passing attractive young woman; or vice versa. [? an imitation of the howl of a lovesick dog]

woof (down) v. [1920s+] to consume voraciously. [SE *wolf* + *down*]

woofer n. [1930s+] (*US Black*) a loud, loquacious talker who says a good deal, but with little actual meaning. [WOOF v.[1]]

woofers n. [1980s] (*Aus.*) greyhounds.

woofing n. [1920s+] (*US Black*) speaking in a variety of ways; the meaning differs as to context, e.g. flirtatiously, aggressively, meaninglessly, threateningly, in a bullying or bluffing manner. [WOOF v.[1]]

woofing session n. (*also* **lugging session**) [1980s] (*US Black*) a session of amicable chatter, of joking. [WOOF v.[1] + SE *session*]

woof it v. [1980s+] (*US gay*) to perform fellatio energetically and voraciously (cf. BASKET LUNCH n.). [SE *wolf*, to eat ravenously/play on EAT v.[3] (1)]

woofits n. [1910s–20s] nerves, tension, esp. with a hangover; thus *get the woofits*, to become tense, nervous. [ety. unknown; ? link to SE *fit*, a seizure]

woofled adj. [1930s] (*US*) drunk.

woof on someone v. [1980s] **1** (*US Black*) to brag, to boast; to trick, to lie; to play the DOZENS n. **2** (*US campus*) to be irritatingly curious. [ext. of WOOF v.[1]]

woofter n. (*also* **willy woofter**) [1980s+] a male homosexual. [var. on POOFTER n. (1)]

woofterish adj. [1980s+] (*Aus./N.Z.*) of an argument, indecisive, unconvincing. [WOOFTER n.]

woof-woof n. [1990s+] a dog.

woof! woof! excl. [1920s] (*US*) an excl. of ridicule or indignation.

woogie n. [1960s] (*US Black*) a Black person. [var. on BOOGIE n.[2] (1) + SE *boogie-woogie* music]

woo-hah! excl. [1990s+] (*US Black teen*) an excl. implying one's domination of a situation.

wook n. [1980s+] an individual who is completely committed to an alternative lifestyle, living far outside mainstream society. [the *wookie*, the hair-covered quasi-ape who co-pilots the space ship *Millenium Falcon* in the *Star Wars* films]

wool n.[1] [mid-19C–1910s] courage, fortitude, character. [orig. boxing jargon]

wool n.[2] **1** [mid-19C+] hair. **2** [1960s+] (female) pubic hair and by extension, a woman as a sex object. [(2) is metonymic use of (1)]

wool n.[3] [1990s+] an unsophisticated person, a peasant. [abbr. WOOLLY-BACK n.]

wool v. **1** [mid-19C] to confuse, to discomfit. **2** [1930s–50s] (*US*) to pull someone's hair in play or anger. [(1) SE *pull the wool over someone's eyes*; (2) WOOL n.[2] (1)]

woola/woolah/woolas n. see WOLLIE n.

wool-barber n. (*also* **wool-chopper**) [late 19C+] (*Aus.*) a sheep-shearer.

wool-bird n. (*also* **woolly bird**) [late 18C–mid-19C] (*UK Und.*) a sheep, a lamb; thus [mid-19C] *wing of a woolbird*, a shoulder of lamb.

wool-bug n. [late 19C–1930s] (*N.Z.*) a sheep-shearer. [SE *wool* + BUG n.[1] (1)/BUG n.[5] (2)]

wool-chopper n. see WOOL-BARBER n.

wool-grower n.[1] [mid-18C] in boxing, the head. [WOOL n.[2] (1) + SE *grower*]

wool-grower n.[2] [1960s] (*Aus.*) a sheep farmer.

wool hat n. (*also* **wool-hat boy**) [mid-19C–1950s] (*US*) a rural person. [their stereotypical headgear; urbanites wear silk hats]

wool-hawk n. [20C+] (*Aus.*) a skilful shearer.

wool-hole n. [mid-19C–1900s] the workhouse. [orig. printers' jargon, an old or unemployed printer described himself as being *in the wool-hole*, a fig. use of *wool-hole*, defined in Savage's *Dict. of Printing* (1841) as: 'a place boxed off sometimes under a stair case, or in any situation where the dust will not affect the press room, in which the wool is carded wherewith to make the balls']

woolie n. see WOLLIE n.

Woolies n. [1930s+] a nickname for the *Wool*worths stores founded by F.W. Woolworth (1852–1919). [abbr.]

woolies n.[1] [late 19C+] long woollen underwear.

woolies n.[2] see WOLLIE n.

woolloomooloo adj. [late 19C+] (*Aus.*) rough, unsophisticated, thuggish; thus *Woolloomooloo bushman*, one who rides a horse badly; *Woolloomooloo upper-cut*, a kick to the groin. [*Woolloomooloo*, a waterside suburb in Sydney]

woolloomooloo Yank n. (*also* **woolloomooloo Frenchman**) [1940s] (*Aus.*) a relatively unsophisticated person who attempts to ape the supposedly more sophisticated style of an American or Frenchman. [WOOLLOOMOOLOO adj. + YANK n. (1)/SE *Frenchman*]

woolly n. **1** [late 19C–1900s] (*Aus./US*) a blanket. **2** [20C+] (*Aus./US*) a sheep. **3** [1900s] (*US*) a cigarette or cigar end. **4** [1960s+] (*Aus./US*) a farmer.

woolly adj.[1] **1** [mid-19C] ill-tempered. **2** [1930s] tipsy, a little drunk (cf. ADDLED adj.). [(1) given WOOL n.[2] (1), ? link to KEEP YOUR HAIR ON! excl.]

woolly adj.[2] [late 19C+] pertaining to a country person or peasant. [SE *woolly*, i.e. like a sheep; later use f. WOOL n.[3]]

woolly-back n. [1960s+] an unsophisticated country person. [the resemblance to their sheep; esp. used by Liverpudlians]

woolly bird n. see WOOL-BIRD n.

woolly crown n. [late 17C–mid-19C] a fool, i.e. a 'soft-headed fellow' (Grose, 1785).

woolly dog n. [1910s] (*Aus.*) a term of abuse.

woolly hoof n. [1980s] (*Aus.*) a male homosexual. [rhy. sl. = POOF n. (1)]

woolly vest n. [1990s+] a pest, an irritating person. [rhy. sl.]

woolly woofter n. (*also* **woolly woof**) [1980s+] a male homosexual. [WOOFTER n. + assonance]

Woolwich and Greenwich n. [20C+] spinach. [rhy. sl.; popular with Cockney greengrocers]

Woolwich ferry n. [20C+] sherry. [rhy. sl.]

Woolwich pier n. [20C+] an ear. [rhy. sl.]

woolworm n. [1940s] (*US Und.*) a shoplifter specializing in woollen garments.

Woolworth marriage n. (*also* **Woolworth wedding**) [1920s–60s] a 'marriage' that exists only in the cheap Woolworths' ring purchased for the occasion. [an era when hoteliers looked askance if a couple had no visible proof of their wedded status]

wooly n. see WOLLIE n.

wooly scarf n. [2000s] a laugh. [rhy. sl.]

wooly west n. [1920s] (*US*) the breast, the chest (cf. BRACE AND BITS n.). [rhy. sl.]

woo number n. [1950s] (*US Black*) a girlfriend or boyfriend. [SE *woo* + NUMBER n.[1] (1)]

woop n. [1920s+] (*Aus./N.Z.*) **1** a tough but isolated and backward country-dweller, a 'hayseed'. [WOOP-WOOP n.]

woopknacker n. [1920s+] (*N.Z.*) a very tough, recalcitrant person, a 'hard case'. [? WOOP n. (1) + SE *knacker*, a horse-slaughterer]

Woop-Woop n. [1910s+] (*Aus.*) **1** an imaginary place that is a byword for backwardness and remoteness. **2** an unsophisticated rural person. [? redup. based on the style of Aborigine language]

woop-woop pigeon n. [1930s+] (*Aus.*) **1** a kookaburra. **2** a swamp pheasant. [WOOP-WOOP n. (1) + SE *pigeon*]

woosey adj. see WOOZY adj.

woozed (up) adj. see WOOZLED adj.

woozie adj. see WOOZY adj.

woozily adv. [late 19C+] (*orig. US*) vaguely or unsteadily. [WOOZY adj. (1)]

woozled adj. (*also* **woozed, woozed up**) [late 19C–1920s] tipsy, drunk. [WOOZY adj. (5)]

woozy adj. (*also* **hoozy, whoozy, woosey, woozie**) [late 19C+] **1** (*orig. US*) vague, befuddled, dizzy or unwell. **2** (*orig. US*) sentimental, affectionate; thus *wooziness*, sentimentality. **3** (*US campus*) pleasant, enjoyable. **4** (*US*) keen on, interested in (other than romantically). **5** (*orig. US*) under the influence of drugs or drink, poss. of a blow on the head; thus backforms. *wooze*, *woozishness*, drunkenness. **6** (*orig. US*) mad, eccentric. [? echoic of one's blurred mumblings]

wop *see also under* WHOP *and its combs.*

wop *n.*[1] **1** [20C+] (*also* **woppe**) a derog. term for an Italian; thus *wopalina*, an Italian girl or woman (cf. DAGO n.). **2** [1900s] (*US*) a peasant, a country-dweller. **3** [1910s] (*US*) a manual labourer. **4** [1910s–40s] any non-specific foreigner. **5** [1910s+] the Italian language. [Sp. *guapo*, a dandy, which was taken up in Sicily during an occupation by Spain and thus imported to the US by 19C immigrants; note Edwin Torres, *After Hours* (1979): 'Plenty of the *guapi* (pretty ones), Neapolitan and Sicilian, around in those days. But they wasn't all pretty, at least to the Irish, who tagged them "wops"'; note Tosches, *Where Dead Voices Gather* (2001): 'The probable root of "wop" is the Latin *uappu*, which was used literally to describe wine gone bad, but which was also used figuratively as early as the first century B.C., by Horace, to describe a good-for-nothing, a worthless character. From *uappu* came the Sicilian *vappu* and *guappu*, which connoted arrogance, bluster, and maleficence entwined. It was these Sicilian words that were commonly used to describe the work-bosses who lured their greenhorn *paesani* into servitude in New York City in the early years of the twentieth century. In New York and other American seaports, the lowly labor of the Italian immigrants' servitude – the dockside toil and offal-hauling that others shunned came to be called, after the work-bosses, *guappu* work; and eventually the laborer himself, and not the boss, was known as *guappu*. The peasant immigrants' tendency to clip the final vowels from standard Italian and Sicilian [...] rendered *guappu* as *guapp'*, which was pronounced, more or less, as *wop'*]

wop *n.*[2] [1910s–40s] (*US prison*) the very last few weeks or days of one's sentence. [ety. unknown]

wop *n.*[3] [1950s] a 'go', a time. [? var. on POP n.[3] (1)]

wop *adj.* **1** [1910s+] referring to an Italian person or to Italian culture; as a nickname for an Italian. **2** [2000s] referring to a Spaniard or South American or to their culture. [WOP n.[1]]

wop flat *n. see* WOP TOWN n.

woppe *n. see* WOP n.[1] (1).

woppidown *n.* [1910s+] (*Aus.*) a damper. [? WHOP v. (2) *it down* on the plate]

wop stick *n.* [1930s–40s] (*US*) a clarinet. [WOP adj. (1) + STICK n.[7] (5)]

wop town *n.* (*also* **wop flat**) [1930s+] (*US*) that part of a town in which the Italian community lives. [WOP adj. (1) + SE *town*]

wop-wop *n.* **1** [1900s–50s] (*Aus.*) a roustabout, a handyman, a casual labourer. **2** [1950s+] (*N.Z.*) a sheep farm; thus the country as opposed to the town. [? WHOP v. (2), i.e. the noise of the man running up and down the shearing shed carrying fleeces to the wool tables]

word, the *n.* [late 19C+] (advance) information; thus *put the word out (on)*, to mark for assassination or arrest.

word *adj.* [1980s+] (*US campus*) fashionable; a term of general approval. [phr. *the last word in...*, ult. Fr. *le dernier cri*]

word *v.* **1** [late 19C+] to tip off, to warn, to inform. **2** [20C+] (*Aus.*) to speak to, to accost, to tell, to pass word to, to rebuke or to tell off. **3** [1910s] to make sexual advances, to 'chat up'. **4** [2000s] (*US Black*) to swear (an oath).

word! *excl.* [1980s+] (*orig. US Black*) **1** an excl. of approval, admiration, agreement etc. **2** an expression of greeting or farewell. **3** used to signify that one is having the final say in an argument. [abbr. WORD UP! excl. + ? SE *the last word in, that's my last word*]

-word *sfx* [1980s+] a euph. sfx used, with a single initial letter, to denote a variety of 'unsayable' terms, e.g. the *C-word*,

CUNT n.[1]; the *F-word*, FUCK n.[1]; also, often in a newspaper context, to denote a topic of importance, a device that has become so over-used as to become tediously clichéd, e.g. the *M-word*, Maastricht.

word-grubber *n.* [late 18C–early 19C] a critic; one who deliberately uses hard words in their conversation. [SE *word* + *grub up*]

wordhole *n.* [1990s+] (*US*) the mouth.

word in your ear, a *n.* [mid-19C+] a quick, confidential chat.

word is bond *phr.* (*also* **word is born**) [1990s+] (*orig. US Black*) a general term of affirmation, I mean it, I promise. [SE phr. *my word is my bond*]

word-pecker *n.* [late 17C–mid-19C] a punster. [pun on SE *woodpecker*]

word-slinger *n.* [1930s] (*US*) a newspaper reporter.

word to the mother (bird)! *excl.* [1990s+] (*US Black*) an excl. of approval, admiration etc. [ext. of WORD! excl.]

word up *v.* [1990s+] (*US Black*) to speak plainly, openly. [WORD UP! excl.]

word up! *excl.* [1980s+] (*orig. US Black*) an excl. of approval, admiration, agreement etc.

work *n.*[1] **1** [late 18C+] (*also* **piece of work**) the criminal life or a criminal act; thus *work clothes*, clothes used for committing a crime. **2** [20C+] (*US Und.*) the written records held by illegal bookmakers. [ext. uses of SE]

work *n.*[2] [1920s+] (*US Und.*) **1** the marking of cards by a card-sharp. **2** some form of weight used to make 'loaded' dice.

work *n.*[3] [1990s+] (*W.I.*) a sexual relationship.

work *v.* **1** [17C+] to have sexual intercourse. **2** [late 18C+] to do, to perform, to carry through a plan of action; usu. in combs., e.g. WORK THE BULLS v.; WORK THE ORACLE v. etc. **3** [late 18C+] to exploit. **4** [late 18C+] to practise one's occupation as a criminal, e.g. a thief or confidence trickster. **5** [late 19C+] (*US*) to charm or enthral, esp. an audience. **6** [late 19C+] to get or to get rid of, esp. by artifice. **7** [late 19C+] of an object, to be in active use, e.g. *here's a dollar that's not working*. **8** [1930s+] to work as a street prostitute. **9** [1960s–70s] (*orig. US Black*) to exchange sexual favours for money; thus to work as a call-girl, 'escort' or prostitute. **10** [1960s+] (*US*) to place under pressure; to interrogate; to cause strong feelings. **11** [1960s+] to deal with in some way. **12** [1980s+] (*US campus*) to beat up. **13** [1990s+] to stimulate sexually. **14** [1990s+] to work as a street seller.

work a clout *v.* [late 18C] to steal a handkerchief. [WORK v. (4)]

work a crowd *v.* (*also* **work a room**) **1** [late 19C] of a pick-pocket, to make one's way through a crowd, robbing opportunistically. **2** [1930s+] to ply one's trade to an audience, begging, preaching, entertaining etc. [WORK v. (4)/WORK v. (2)/WORK v. (5)]

work a door *v.* [1920s+] to work as a prostitute, standing or sitting in one's own doorway; thus DOOR n.[1]. [SE *work*]

work a game *v.* [1950s] to pursue a (usu. criminal) scheme or plan. [WORK v. (4) + GAME n.[2] (3)]

work a ginger *v. see* GINGER n.[3] (3).

workaholic *n.* (*also* **workoholic**) [1960s+] anyone who is obsessed by working and thus very rarely stops. [SE *work* + -AHOLIC sfx]

work a point *v.* (*also* **work points**) [late 19C+] (*Aus.*) to live by one's wits, to take advantage by trickery and deception. [WORK v. (2) + SE *point* (that one scores)]

work a ready *v.* [1910s+] (*Aus.*) to concoct a swindle or fraud. [WORK v. (2) + READY n.[2]]

work a room *v. see* WORK A CROWD v.

work a spot *v.* [1990s+] (*US Black*) to sell drugs or sex from a specific location. [WORK v. (2) + SE *spot*]

workbench *n.* [early 19C; 1960s] a bedstead. [WORK v. (1) + SE *bench*]

work both sides of the street *v.* **1** [20C+] (*also* **play both sides of the game/street**) to ally oneself to both sides in a dispute or division, to behave in an opportunistic manner. **2** [1960s+] (*also* **play both sides of the fence**) to be bisexual. **3** [1990s+] (*US*) to work exceptionally hard.

worker *n.*[1] **1** [mid-19C+] a criminal; usu. in combs., e.g. BADGER WORKER n.; DUNNIGAN WORKER n.; LUSH WORKER n.; SKIN WORKER n.; TAIL-WORKER n. **2** [1910s] in a pickpocket team, the member who actual picks the victim's pocket. [WORK v.]

worker *n.*[2] [1970s+] (*Aus.*) a prostitute. [WORK v. (8)]

work for Street and Walker *v.* [1930s–50s] (*Aus.*) to be unemployed and walking the streets in search of a job. [puns]

work from a book *v.* (*US Black*) **1** [1940s+] for a pimp to run his professional life by the recognized 'rules and regulations' of the pimping life, supposedly enshrined in an authoritative *Book*. **2** [1960s+] to conduct business through an address book, so eliminating many of the problems (esp. police interference) that are met in street prostitution. [SE *work* + (1) BOOK, THE n.; (2) BOOK n.[1] (2)]

work high *v.* [1930s] (*US Und.*) **1** to rob in broad daylight. **2** to work out of one's criminal class.

work hot *v.* [1980s+] (*Aus. prison*) to do something illegal. [SE *work* + HOT adj.[2] (1)]

workie *n.*[1] [1930s–40s] (*US*) the *workhouse*. [abbr.]

workie *n.*[2] *see* WORKY n.

working *n.* **1** [1900s] (*US Und.*) stealing. **2** [1980s+] (*drugs*) selling crack cocaine. [WORK v.]

working classes *n.* [20C+] glasses (spectacles). [rhy. sl.]

working girl *n.* **1** [1930s+] (*US*) (*also* **working broad, …chick, …woman**) a prostitute (cf. AWAYDAY GIRL n.). **2** [1970s+] an effeminate male prostitute. [WORK v. (8) + SE *girl*/BROAD n.[2] (2)/CHICK n.[4] (2)/SE *woman*]

working john *n. see* WORKING STIFF n.

working-man's smile *n.* [1980s+] (*US*) the top of the crevice between a man's buttocks, visible when he bends over and the waist of his low-cut trousers is forced downwards.

working-over *n.* [1920s+] **1** a beating. **2** a search. **3** in fig. use, non-physical harsh treatment. [WORK OVER v.]

working stiff *n.* (*also* **working john, working plug, work stiff**) [20C+] an average, unexceptional working man. [SE *work* + STIFF n.[2] (7)/JOHN n.[1] (1)/PLUG n.[5] (4)]

working the cuts *phr.* [20C+] used of a prostitute who works on the street rather than in a brothel. [WORK v. (8) + SE *cut*, a passage, a route]

working woman *n. see* WORKING GIRL n. (1).

work it *v.*[1] [late 19C+] to arrange, often by underhand or duplicitous methods. [WORK v. (2)]

work it *v.*[2] *see* WORK (ONESELF) OFF v.

work like a kaffir *v.* [1970s+] (*S.Afr.*) to work very hard. [SE *work* + KAFFIR n.[1] (2)]

work like a nigger *v.* (*also* **work like a black, …like a nig**) [mid-19C+] (*orig. US*) to work very hard. [SE *work* + NIGGER n.[1]]

work like a wop *v.* [1920s] (*US Black*) to work very hard. [SE *work* + WOP n.[1] (1); var. on WORK LIKE A NIGGER v.]

work low *v.* [1930s] (*US Und.*) to take on a less prestigious criminal job than usual. [antonym of WORK HIGH v.]

workman *n.* **1** [16C] a dice cheat. **2** [mid-19C–1900s] a cardsharp. **3** [1910s] (*US Und.*) a pickpocket. [WORK v. (4) + SE *man*]

workman's entrance *n.* [1990s+] the anus (cf. ARSE-END n.). [i.e. the BACK DOOR n. (1)]

work off *v.*[1] **1** [mid–late 19C] to hang; to execute. **2** [late 19C] (*UK Und.*) to make a forged banknote.

work off *v.*[2] *see* WORK (ONESELF) OFF v.

workoholic *n. see* WORKAHOLIC n.

work on *v.* [1930s–60s] (*US prison*) to beat up. [SE/var. on WORK OVER v. (2)]

work one's arse off *v.* (*also* **work one's ass off, …one's balls off, …one's bollocks off, …one's can off, …one's fanny off, …one's nuts off, …one's pants off, …one's tits off**) [1920s+] to work extremely hard; thus *work someone's arse off*, to make another person work hard. [SE *work* + ARSE n.[1]/ASS n. (2)/BALLS n.[1] (1)/BALLOCKS n.[1] (1)/CAN n.[1] (2)/FANNY n.[1] (2)/NUTS n.[2] (1)/PANTS n.[1] (2)/TIT n.[3] (1)]

work one's bot *v.* [20C+] to have sexual intercourse. [SE *work* + abbr. SE *bottom*]

work one's butt off *v.* (*also* **act one's butt off, battle one's butt off, work one's buns off**) [1960s+] (*orig. US*) to work very hard. [SE *work* + BUTT n.[1] (2)/BUNS n. (2); var. on WORK ONE'S ARSE OFF v.]

work one's can off *v. see* WORK ONE'S ARSE OFF v.

work (oneself) off *v.* (*also* **work it**) [16C+] to masturbate (cf. BALL OFF v.[2]).

work one's fanny off *v. see* WORK ONE'S ARSE OFF v.

work one's mealie off *v.* [1990s+] (*S.Afr.*) to work very hard. [euph. var. on WORK ONE'S ARSE OFF v.]

work one's nut *v.* [1910s+] to scheme, to plot, to use one's brains to avoid work; thus synon. phrs. [20C+] (*Aus.*) *work one's head*; [1950s] (*Aus.*) *work one's skull*; [1970s] *work one's loaf*. [WORK v. (2) + NUT n.[1] (2)/SE *head*/SE *skull*/LOAF (OF BREAD) n.]

work one's nuts off/pants off *v. see* WORK ONE'S ARSE OFF v.

work one's points *v.* [1940s] (*US*) to get on with something, to do or perform.

work one's tail off *v.* (*also* **sweat one's tail off**) [1920s+] (*orig. US*) to work very hard. [SE *work* + fig. use of TAIL n.[2] (1)]

work one's ticket *v.* [1910s+] to malinger, to escape onerous duties by shamming illness or similar unsuitability. [orig. British Army use, obtaining a discharge through faking illness]

work one's tits off *v. see* WORK ONE'S ARSE OFF v.

work on shorts *v.* [1920s] (*US Und.*) to work as a pickpocket by oneself. [the pickpocketing team is *short*, i.e. composed of just 1 person]

work-out *n.* **1** [1900s–30s] the simultaneous sacking or dismissal of a large number of a firm's workers. **2** [1930s+] (*US*) a beating. [SE *work out*, to loosen, to get rid of]

work out *v.* **1** [1940s–50s] (*US Und.*) to beat up; to give the 'third degree'. **2** [1960s+] (*US Black*) to have sexual intercourse. [SE *work out*, to exercise]

work out! *excl.* [1970s] (*US Black*) an excl. of exhortation.

work out of one's hat *v.* [1990s+] (*US*) to freelance; to work independently of a specific organization. [the wearing of a *hat* as one travels around]

work out one's soul-case *v. see* BURST ONE'S SOUL-CASE v.

work over *v.* **1** [1910s+] to search and steal from somebody's clothes. **2** [1920s+] (*orig. US*) to beat up, to hurt to any extent short of murder; thus *work-over*, a thrashing, a beating (cf. WORKING-OVER n.); also in fig. use.

work points *v. see* WORK A POINT v.

Works, the *n.* [late 19C] (*UK prison*) any of the convict prisons at Chatham, Portsmouth, Portland or Dartmoor (cf. ABBOTT'S PRIORY n.).

works *n.*[1] (*Aus./US*) **1** [1900s] the intestines of an animal. **2** [1910s] the brain. **3** [1910s+] the human stomach or its contents. [SE *works*, the internal parts of a machine]

works *n.*[2] **1** [1930s+] (*drugs*) the equipment used by a narcotics user for injecting him- or herself. **2** [1990s+] the equipment used for smoking crack cocaine, heroin etc. [SE *works*, machinery]

works, the *n.* (*also* **the whole works**) **1** [late 19C+] everything, the lot. **2** [1900s–20s] the leader, the 'boss'. **3** [1920s] the situation. **4** [1920s+] the finest example. **5** [1920s+] a beating; the 'third degree'; murder; thus GIVE SOMEONE THE WORKS v. (2). **6** [1930s–40s] (*US Und.*) an informer; a confession. **7** [1930s–50s] (*US gay*) a passive homosexual. **8** [1930s+] sexual intercourse. **9** [1950s] (*US teen*) a machine. **10** [1980s+] in prostitution, the full range of a prostitute's services.

work someone's arse off *v. see* WORK ONE'S ARSE OFF v.

work someone's nerves v. (also **work someone's last nerve**) [1990s+] (US Black/campus) **1** to annoy, to irritate. **2** to exert emotional pressure upon someone.

work the biz v. [1990s+] (Can.) to work as a prostitute. [WORK v. (8) + BIZ n.[1] (1)]

work the boards v. [1970s] (UK Und.) to run the 3-card trick. [WORK v. (4) + BOARDS n.]

work the broads v. see FAKE THE BROADS v.

work the bulls v. [mid-19C] (Aus./UK Und.) to pass counterfeit crown coins. [WORK v. (4) + BULL n.[4] (2)]

work the growler v.[1] [late 19C–1910s] to hire a cab to accompany one on a 'pub-crawl'. [SE work + GROWLER n.[2]]

work the growler v.[2] see RUSH THE GROWLER v.

work the hole v. (also **make the hole**) [1940s–50s] (US Und.) to rob drunks who have passed out in the subway. [WORK v. (4) + HOLE n.[2] (5)]

work the kid v. see KID LAY n.

work the knocker v. [1950s–60s] (UK Und.) touring houses, ostensibly to buy or sell goods, but spec. to trick or bully people into selling heirlooms, antiques etc for minimal prices. [WORK v. (4) + SE knocker]

work the noble v. [late 19C] (UK tramp) to beg, posing as an impoverished clergyman or upper-class person. [WORK v. (4) + SE noble]

work the oracle v. **1** [19C] to raise money. **2** [mid-19C+] to plan, to manoeuvre, to succeed through cunning. **3** [1910s] (Aus.) to reach a satisfactory conclusion. [WORK v. + SE oracle, a prophet]

work the rattlers v. [1920s] (US Und.) to rob the passengers on subway trains. [WORK v. (4) + RATTLER n.[1] (10)]

work the room v. [1950s+] to chatter to people at a party or meeting. [show business use, for an entertainer to move through the audience, chatting to people and involving them in the act]

work the stem v. [1910s+] (US tramp) to beg on the streets; thus stem-winder, a tramp who goes begging. [WORK v. (4) + STEM n.[1] (1)]

work the tear-pump v. [late 19C–1900s] to burst, prob. insincerely, into tears.

work the tubs v. [1920s–40s] (UK Und.) **1** to commit crimes, usu. card-sharping, on board transatlantic liners; thus tub worker, a confidence trickster who focuses on the passengers of such boats. **2** to pickpocket on the buses or at bus-stops. [WORK v. (4) + TUB n.[1] (1)/TUB n.[1] (8)]

work (the) wires v. [late 19C] (US) to engage in political chicanery. [WORK v. (2) + SE wires, i.e. the connections]

work things v. [late 19C+] to make things work out in the way one wishes, sometimes but not necessarily illicitly. [WORK v. (2) + SE things]

work under the armpits v. [early 19C] (UK Und.) to confine one's criminality to such activities that would be classed as petty larceny, bringing a maximum sentence of 7 years' transportation, rather than hanging; thus work above the armpits, to commit crimes that could lead to one's execution. [SE work/WORK v. (4) + SE armpits; ? or the armpits as a fig. line above which is the neck from which one can be hung, below which one is 'safe']

work up v.[1] [mid-19C] (US) of a detective, to follow a suspect. [ext. WORK v. (1)]

work up v.[2] [late 19C+] of a man, to have sexual intercourse. [ext. WORK v. (1)]

workus n. [mid–late 19C] **1** a workhouse. **2** a derog. term for a Methodist chapel. [(1) Cockney pron.; (2) from its deliberate plainness]

work wires v. see WORK (THE) WIRES v.

work with the bogies v. [late 19C–1930s] to act as an informant. [SE work + BOGEY n.[1] (3)]

worky n. (also **workie**) [mid-19C+] an employed person. [SE work]

world n. [late 18C] (UK society) a knowledge of the fashionable world, the beau monde.

world, the n. **1** [1960s] (US gay) the world of homosexuality. **2** [1960s+] (US) the world as lived outside an institution, e.g. the army, a prison. **3** [1990s+] (US) everything.

worlds n. see FREE WORLD n. (2).

worm n.[1] [17C–early 18C; 1940s+] the penis; thus BURP THE WORM v.

worm n.[2] [mid-19C] a policeman (cf. ANIMAL n.[1]). [? SE worm, an unpleasant, despicable person]

worm n.[3] [1910s–40s] (US Und.) silk; thus worm-worker, a thief who specializes in stealing silk. [play on SE silkworm]

worm n.[4] [1960s] (US campus) a notably hard worker.

worm n.[5] [1980s+] (drugs) phencyclidine (cf. ACE n.[4]). [ety. unknown]

worm v. [mid-19C] to remove the beard from an oyster or mussel. [SE worm, to remove intestinal worms from an animal]

wormbait n. (also **worm food**) [1940s+] a corpse.

wormdick n. see WORMROD n.

worm farm n. [1960s+] (orig. US) an eccentric, one whose mind is 'full of worms'; thus living on a worm farm, crazy, eccentric.

worm food n. see WORMBAIT n.

worm hustling n. (also **weave hustling, worm work**) [1930s–40s] (US Und.) selling fake silk. [WORM n.[3] + HUSTLE v. (2)]

wormrod n. (also **wormdick**) [1990s+] a very unpleasant person; thus a general term of abuse. [SE worm + ROD n.[1] (1)/DICK n.[4] (6)]

worms n. [1920s–40s] (US) spaghetti; thus worms in blood, spaghetti in tomato sauce.

worms and snails n. [20C+] fingernails. [rhy. sl.]

worm work n. see WORM HUSTLING n.

worrab n. [mid-19C+] (costermonger) a barrow. [backsl.]

worrit n. [mid-19C–1910s] anxiety, worry; thus a person suffering from such problems. [WORRIT v. (2)]

worrit v. [early–mid-19C] **1** to worry someone, to nag. **2** to be worried, anxious. [orig. dial.]

worry and strife n. [1930s+] one's wife. [rhy. sl.; var. on TROUBLE AND STRIFE n. (1)]

worryguts n. [1930s+] a pathological worrier, esp. as a term of address. [SE worry + -GUTS sfx]

worry wart n. [1930s+] (US) a pathological worrier. [SE worry + WART n.]

worse for wear phr. [mid-19C+] drunk, intoxicated by drugs.

worse half n. see INFERIOR HALF n.

worse luck! excl. [mid-19C+] that's a shame! more's the pity!

worse than a (two-bob) fart in a bottle phr. see NOT WORTH A FART phr.

worship at the altar v. [1970s+] (US gay) to fellate.

worship the porcelain god(dess)/the throne v. see KISS THE PORCELAIN GOD(DESS) v.

worst adj. [mid-19C] (US campus) a general superlative, used sarcastically.

worst kind, the phr. [mid-19C+] (US) to the greatest extent, extremely, very badly.

worst part n. [16C] the vagina.

worth a bob or two phr. [20C+] **1** of things, valuable. **2** of people, wealthy. [understatement + betting imagery]

worth a cent phr. (also **worth a busted nickel, ...a copper, ...twopence**) [late 19C+] (Aus./US) to the least amount, e.g. you ain't helping your Mom worth a cent.

worth a plum phr. [mid-19C] wealthy. [SE worth + PLUM n.[1] (1)]

worth a whoop phr. [1900s] (US) valuable. [SE worth + whoop, a shout]

worth one's weight in burnt copper phr. [late 19C] worthless, worth very little. [pun on SE phr. worth one's weight in gold; copper has little value compared with gold]

worth twopence phr. see WORTH A CENT phr.

wossname n. [20C+] a popular mis-sp. of WHATSHISNAME n.

wotcher! excl. (also **wotcha!**) [mid-19C+] a stereotypical

Cockney greeting. [elision of 16C+ SE *what cheer*; the trad. response to the extended *wotcher, cock!* is 'How's yer mother off for dripping?']

wotchero! *excl.* [late 19C] hello! [ext. of WOTCHER! excl.]

wotsaname *n. see* WHATSHISNAME *n.*

wotsit *n.*[1] *see* WHATSIT *n.*

wotsit *n.*[2] *see* WHATSITS *n.* (1).

would fuck up a wet dream *phr. see* COULD FUCK UP A WET DREAM *phr.*

would I had Kemp's shoes to throw after you *phr.* [late 16C–early 19C] a phr. used to wish someone good luck. [William *Kemp* (*fl.*1600), who had played the original Dogberry in the first performance of *Much Ado About Nothing*. In 1600 he was thrown out of Shakespeare's troupe at the Globe, and to restore his image and win some needed publicity, he danced his way from London to Norwich in 9 days. The account he then printed and circulated was entitled *Kemp's Nine Days Wonder*]

would I shit you? you're my favourite turd *phr.* (*also* **I wouldn't shit you...**) [1960s+] (*US*) an assertion of one's sincerity, in answer to the previous speaker's 'Don't bullshit me...'. [SHIT v.[1] (1)/SHIT v.[3] (1) + TURD n.]

wouldn't believe daylight out of *phr.* [20C+] (*Ulster*) a phr. meaning that one does not believe a single word somebody speaks.

wouldn't be seen dead with someone in a forty-acre paddock *phr.* [late 19C+] (*orig. Aus.*) an expression of extreme dislike.

wouldn't it! *excl.* [1940s+] (*Aus./N.Z.*) a general excl. of dismay, exasperation or disgust. [abbr. *wouldn't it make you sick, wouldn't it root you, wouldn't it make you spit chips* and similar phrs. (*see also* next)]

wouldn't it rotate you? *phr.* (*also* **wouldn't it rip yer? ...rock yer? ...rot yer sock?**) [1940s+] (*Aus./N.Z.*) a general excl. of dismay, exasperation or disgust.

wouldn't touch it with a dog's prick *phr.* [1960s] a general phr. of aversion, esp. in a sexual context.

wouldn't touch it with a fishing pole/forty-foot (barge) pole *phr. see* WOULDN'T TOUCH IT WITH A TEN-FOOT (BARGE) POLE *phr.*

wouldn't touch it with a red-hot poker *phr.* [1930s+] (*Aus.*) a phr. indicating one's absolute aversion.

wouldn't touch it with a rotten stick *phr.* [mid-19C] a phr. indicating one's absolute aversion.

wouldn't touch it with a ten-foot (barge) pole *phr.* (*also* **wouldn't touch it with a fishing pole, ...forty-foot (barge) pole**) **1** [mid-19C+] an expression of a lack of interest in something or a refusal to do something. **2** [20C+] used by one man to another to express his lack of interest in a woman they are observing. **3** [1970s] (*US*) describing a person or thing that is inferior to something else.

wouldn't touch it with yours *phr.* [late 19C+] a popular phr. between 2 men observing a woman whom the speaker finds unattractive. [i.e. *your* penis]

wouldn't touch — with a pitchfork *phr.* [late 19C] used by one man to another to express his lack of interest in a woman they are observing.

wounded *adj.* [2000s] (*US campus*) exhausted; hungover.

wounded soldier *n.* [1990s+] (*US campus*) a partially empty beer container. [play on DEAD SOLDIER n., which is completely empty]

woundily *adv. see* WOUNDY *adv.*

wounds! *excl.* [mid-16C–mid-19C] (*also* **waunds! wauns!**) a euph. excl., lit. 'God's wounds!'

wound-up *adj.* **1** [mid-19C] drunk. **2** [1910s+] (*also* **wound up like an eight-day clock, woundy**) annoyed, tense and irritated.

woundy *adv.* (*also* **woundily**) [18C–19C] a general intensifier, very, extremely; also as adj., very great.

wow *n.* [1910s+] (*US*) an exciting, admirable or astonishing thing or person. [SE excl. *wow!*]

wow, the *n.* [1940s+] (*N.Z.*) a psychiatric institution. [*Whaw*, a local nickname for an area of Avondale, Auckland, associated with such institutions since the mid-19C]

wow *v.* [1920s+] to delight, to enthral, to please very much. [SE excl. *wow!*]

wowse *v.* [1900s–10s] (*Aus.*) to behave as a puritan and/or censor. [backform. f. WOWSER n.[1] (1)]

wowser *n.*[1] **1** [late 19C+] (*Aus./N.Z.*) a puritan, a self-appointed censor, a 'Mrs Grundy'; thus *wowserdom*, the world of puritanism; *wowserish*, puritanical; *wowseristic*, prudish; *wowserly*, puritanically. **2** [1900s–10s] a general term of abuse. **3** [1950s] a bluestocking. **4** [1950s] a teetaller. [UK dial. *wow*, to howl like a dog, to grumble, to complain. Claimed by John Norton (1858–1916), editor of the Sydney *Truth*, as his coinage. However, a correspondent (5 June 1910) cited him as the popularizer but not the coiner of a term that 'in the ordinary parlance of the proletariat [...] signifies a "bald-headed, bad-breathed, bible-banging bummer, who ought to be banged with a bowser"' (Norton, as noted by Seal, *The Lingo*, 1999); Seal declares it a FURPHY n., i.e. a fantasy, and claimed the term was an acronym for 'We Only Want Social Evils Righted/Rectified/Removed']

wowser *n.*[2] (*also* **wowzer**) [1910s+] (*US*) something, or somebody, impressive, sensational, successful. [SE *wow!*]

wowzers! *excl.* [1990s+] (*US teen*) a general excl. of approval. [ext. SE *wow!*]

w.p. *n.* [mid-19C–1900s] a place-holder, a deputy; used orig. of a clergyman who holds a living *pro tempore*. [abbr. WARMING PAN n.[1] (3)]

w.p.b. *n.* [late 19C+] waste paper basket. [abbr.]

wrap *n.*[1] [1950s+] (*Aus.*) a boost, a commendation. [RAP n.[4] (8)]

wrap *n.*[2] [1970s+] a conclusion, something over and done with, finished. [movie jargon *wrap*, the end of a day's filming; WRAP (IT) UP v. (1)]

wrap *n.*[3] [1980s+] (*US campus*) a girlfriend. [? SE *rapture*; ? SE *wrap around each other*]

wrap *n.*[4] [1990s+] (*drugs*) a small quantity of powder-based drugs, e.g. heroin, cocaine, folded into a small square of paper.

wrap *v. see* RAP v.[3] (5).

wrap around *v.* (*also* **wrap round**) [1950s+] (*orig. US*) to crash one's car; usu. as *wrap around a tree*.

wrap (it) up *v.* (*also* **wrap**) **1** [1930s+] to bring to an end, to conclude, to stop doing something, esp. as imper. *wrap it up!* stop! **2** [1940s–50s] (*N.Z./US Und.*) to win.

wrap oneself around *v.* [late 19C+] (*orig. US*) to eat and drink; often as imper. *wrap yourself around that.*

wrapped *adj.*[1] [1960s+] (*orig. Aus./US campus*) **1** besotted with, infatuated by, in love with. **2** fascinated by, enthused with. [abbr. SE *wrapped up in*]

wrapped *adj.*[2] *see* WRAPPED UP *adj.* (3).

wrapped *adj.*[3] *see* WRAP UP v.[2].

wrapped tight *adj.* [1960s+] (*US campus/teen*) **1** sane, balanced, esp. in negative uses, e.g. *he's not wrapped too tight.* **2** feeling fine, happy. [the image of a neatly *wrapped* package]

wrapped up *adj.* **1** [1900s–40s] (*US*) aware, 'in tune', sophisticated. **2** [1910s+] affected, in love with. **3** [1930s+] (*also* **wrapped**) sorted out.

wrapper *n.* **1** [early–mid-19C] an overcoat. **2** [1930s+] (*Aus./US prison*) a cigarette paper. [note US *wrapper*, a woman's loose robe or gown]

wrapping *n.* [1920s–70s] (*US teen*) clothes, esp. female.

wrap-rascal *n.* **1** [early 18C–19C] a loose overcoat or greatcoat, worn mainly in the 18C. **2** [late 18C–early 19C] a red greatcoat. [despite SE origin, not necessarily worn by criminals]

wrap round *v. see* WRAP AROUND v.

wraps n. [2000s] (*UK Black*) dark glasses. [they 'wrap around' the face]

wrapt up in the tail of his mother's smock phr. [late 18C–early 19C] a phr. said of one who has notable success with women.

wrapt up in warm flannel phr. [late 18C–early 19C] drunk on spirits, esp. gin. [ref. to such terms as WHITE RIBBON n.; WHITE SATIN n.[1] that, like FLANNEL n.[1], are 'textiles' that describe gin]

wrap-up n.[1] **1** [1930s] (*US Und.*) a gullible person who has been successfully tricked. **2** [1960s+] the end, the conclusion. [(1) one who can be 'wrapped up' in deceit; (2) movie jargon *wrap*, the end of a day's shooting]

wrap-up n.[2] [1940s+] (*Aus.*) a flattering account. [RAP v.[3] (5) + image of SE *wrapping* the subject in fine words]

wrap-up n.[3] [1940s+] a sexually available young woman. [fig. use of WRAP (IT) UP v. (1); the easy conclusion of a seduction]

wrap-up n.[4] [1960s] (*Irish*) a parcel of scraps from the butcher.

wrap up v.[1] [1940s+] to stop talking, esp. as a command, *wrap up!*

wrap up v.[2] [1950s+] (*Aus.*) to praise, to flatter; thus *wrapped*, overjoyed. [WRAP-UP n.[2]]

wrap up v.[3] *see* RAP v.[3] (5).

wrap up v.[4] *see* WRAP (IT) UP v.

wreath of roses n. [1900s–30s] a venereal ulcer. [the ring of ulcers that surround the diseased genitals]

wreck v. [1960s–70s] (*gay*) **1** to degrade a fellow homosexual when he is not expecting it. **2** to exaggerate one's effeminacy deliberately as a shock tactic.

wrecked adj. **1** [1960s+] very drunk (cf. ANNIHILATED adj.). **2** [1970s+] (*drugs*) heavily affected by a drug. **3** [1980s] (*US campus*) very upset. **4** [2000s] exhausted.

wreck somone's beads v. [1970s] (*US gay*) to beat someone up; to shock or startle. [SE *wreck* + BEADS n.[2]]

wreck the head n. [2000s] (*Irish*) one who is highly infuriating.

wren n. **1** [mid-19C] a prostitute who specialized in army camps (cf. ALLEY CAT n.). **2** [1910s–60s] (*US*) an attractive woman.

wrester n. [late 16C–early 17C] (*UK Und.*) a picklock. [SE *wrest*, to twist]

wrestle the hash v. (*also* **wrestle the chuck**) [mid–late 19C] (*US*) to dine. [SE *wrestle* + *hash*/CHUCK n.[3] (2)]

wretch n. [1980s+] (*US campus*) an involuntary celibate, someone unable to find a sexual partner despite their best efforts. [SE *wretch*, a miserable, wretched person]

wretch-claat n. (*also* **wretch-claht**) [1980s] (*UK Black*) a term of abuse. [SE *wretch* + Jam. *claat* or *cloth*]

wriggle-diggle n. [1960s+] petting, mutual fondling; thus sexual intercourse. [the woman SE *wriggles*, the man SE *digs*]

wriggle like a cut snake v. [1940s+] (*Aus.*) **1** to act the toady. **2** to be evasive.

wriggle navels v. [18C] to have sexual intercourse (cf. BELLY BUMP v.). [note Williams 17C ref.: '*wriggle*, allusive of copulatory motion']

wriggle off v. [late 19C] to leave.

wriggling pole n. (*also* **wriggling stick**) [early 18C] the penis (cf. BAT n.[7]). [SE *wriggling* + POLE n.]

wrinch v. [1990s+] (*W.I.*) to scowl.

wring v. [late 19C] (*US*) to pick someone's pocket. [SE *wring*, to press or squeeze, to clasp]

wringer n. *see* RINGER n.[1].

wring in v. [mid-19C] (*US Und.*) to include, to pay for. [? prior use of RING IN v.[2]]

wringing and twisting n. [1940s] (*US Black*) suffering racial discrimination and dealing with it either by rebellion or acquiescence. [i.e. the SE *wringing* and *twisting* is of other people's heads or one's own hands]

wring-jaw n. [late 18C–mid-19C] (*US*) rough cider. [its effects]

wring neck n. *see* RING NECK n.

wring oneself v. [late 19C] (*UK Und.*) to change clothes.

wring out one's sock v. [1980s+] of a man, to urinate.

wring the dew off the branch v. [2000s] to urinate.

wring the rattlesnake v. [1960s–70s] to urinate (cf. FLOG THE LIZARD v.).

wrinkle n.[1] **1** [late 16C+] (*also* **winkle**) an idea, device or trick, esp. a new one. **2** [early 19C] a lie. **3** [mid-19C] (*US*) a bit, a small amount. **4** [mid-19C+] a useful piece of information. [? 14C–16C SE *wrinkle*, a tortuous, sinuous movement]

wrinkle n.[2] [1990s+] (*US campus*) an unpleasant, unsophisticated male. [abbr. PENIS WRINKLE n.]

wrinkle n.[3] *see* WRINKLY n.

wrinkle v. [early 19C] to lie; thus *wrinkler*, a habitual liar. [WRINKLE n.[1] (2)]

wrinkle-bellied adj. [late 18C–early 19C] having had a number of children; usu. used of a prostitute, i.e. *wrinkle-bellied whore*. [her stretch-marks]

wrinkle room n. [1970s+] (*gay*) a bar, a club or that area of a club where older gay men gather.

wrinkles n. [1970s] (*US Black*) chitterlings. [? resemblance]

wrinkly n. (*also* **wrinkle, wrinklies**) **1** [1920s+] (*mainly UK upper/upper-middle class juv.*) an old person, the old. **2** [1980s+] (*Aus. prison*) an old prisoner.

wrist n. (*also* **wristjob**) [1990s+] an unpleasant person. [the movement of the wrist in masturbation, usu. accompanied by using the forefinger of 1 hand to point to the wrist of the other]

wrist aerobics n. (*also* **wrist marathon**) [1990s+] masturbation. [the movement of the wrist]

wristy adj. *see* LIMP-WRISTED adj.

writ bug n. (*also* **writ writer**) [1940s+] (*US prison*) a prison inmate who becomes a self-taught lawyer, either to pursue their own case, to combat prison corruption or to help fellow inmates, a JAILHOUSE LAWYER n. [SE *writ* + BUG n.[5] (2)]

write v. **1** [1930s–60s] (*drugs*) of a doctor, to write prescriptions for narcotics. **2** [1960s] to pass dud cheques.

write a letter to a man about a dog v. *see* SEE A MAN ABOUT A DOG v. (3).

write-off n. (*orig. milit.*) **1** [1910s+] anything or anyone that is completely destroyed, beyond all hope of repair. **2** [1970s] a farewell, a termination. [in orig. service use, it is *written off* the inventory]

write off v. [1910s+] (*orig. RAF*) to completely destroy something, so that it is beyond all hope of repair.

write one's name across another's v. [late 19C] (*orig. sporting*) to hit in the face.

write one's name on v. [mid-19C+] to reserve for oneself, to have the first go at.

write one's (own) ticket v. [late 19C+] to be able to stipulate one's own conditions, to be in an advantageous position.

write out v. [1930s] (*US Und.*) to order to be killed. [fig. a role *written out* of a script]

writer n.[1] [1930s+] (*drugs*) a doctor who will write prescriptions for narcotics and ask no questions about the user. [WRITE v. (1)]

writer n.[2] [1980s+] (*US*) a graffiti artist.

write scrip v. (*also* **write script**) [1930s+] (*drugs*) to give out prescriptions for narcotics. [WRITE v. (1) + SCRIP n.[2]/SCRIPT n.]

write-up n. [1920s+] (*US prison*) a disciplinary report.

write up v. [1920s+] **1** (*US prison*) to report a convict for misconduct. **2** (*US*) to report a worker for inadequate work or a misdemeanor. [WRITE-UP n.]

writing n. **1** [1930s–50s] (*US drugs/prison*) a means of smuggling drugs into prison; a letter is soaked in some form of narcotized solution and the text of the letter makes it clear, with simple codes, that this has been done. **2** [1930s–50s] (*US drugs*) a narcotics prescription. **3** [1990s+] graffiti. [(1) and (2) WRITE v. (1); (3) WRITER n.[2]]

writing doctor n. (*also* **writing croaker**) [1930s+] (*drugs*) a doctor who will write prescriptions for narcotics and ask no questions about the user. [WRITE v. (1) + SE *doctor*/CROAKER n.⁵ (1)]

writ writer *n. see* WRIT BUG n.

wrokin *n.* [17C–19C] a Dutch woman. [? Du. *vrouw*, a woman + dimin. sfx *-kin*]

wrong *adj.* **1** [mid-19C] (*UK Und.*) unsafe (for criminal activity). **2** [mid-19C] (*UK Und.*) of money, counterfeit. **3** [20C+] (*US Und.*) untrustworthy (in criminal terms), too close to the authorities, thus honest; thus *go wrong*, to turn informer. **4** [1900s–50s] in respectable terms, corrupt. **5** [1940s–50s] (*Aus.*) eccentric, insane (cf. WRONG IN ONE'S GARRET phr.). **6** [1960s] (*US Black/campus*) irritating, contrary. **7** [1980s] (*US campus*) grumpy, unfriendly. **8** [1990s+] right, good.

wrong *adv.* [mid-19C] in a criminal, illegal manner.

wrong for *adj.* [1970s] (*US Und.*) biased against. [WRONG adj. (3)]

wronggo *n. see* WRONGO n.

wrong guy *n.* (*also* **wrong gee/Injun**) [1920s+] (*US Und.*) **1** an incompetent, an untrustworthy person. **2** an informer. [WRONG adj. (3) + GUY n.² (1)/GEE n.³ (1)/INJUN n.; (2) is spec. use of (1)]

wrong in one's garret *phr.* [mid-19C] insane, eccentric (cf. WRONG IN ONE'S NUT phr.; WRONG IN ONE'S UPPER STOREY phr.). [SE *wrong* + GARRET n. (1)]

wrong in one's nut *phr.* [late 19C] mad, eccentric (cf. WRONG IN ONE'S GARRET phr.). [SE *wrong* + NUT n.¹ (2)]

wrong in one's upper storey *phr.* [mid-19C+] insane (cf. WRONG IN ONE'S GARRET phr.). [SE *wrong* + UPPER STOREY n. (1)]

wrong number *n.* [1920s+] (*US*) **1** a mistaken idea. **2** a dangerous person. **3** a dishonest, untrustworthy person.

wrongo *n.* (*also* **wrong-o, wronggo**) [1930s+] (*orig. US*) **1** a criminal; in weak use, an undesirable person. **2** a mistake, error or lie. [SE *wrong* + -O sfx (2)]

wrongo *adj.* [1950s+] (*US*) **1** mistaken, inept, prone to error. **2** unpleasant, undesirable. [WRONGO n. (2)]

wrong riff *n.* [1930s–40s] (*US Black*) a mistake, a blunder. [orig. jazz use]

wrong steer *n.* [20C+] (*US*) misdirection, both lit. and fig.

wrong 'un *n.* [late 19C+] **1** an untrustworthy, incompetent person, animal, action, circumstance, event. **2** a piece of counterfeit money. **3** a prostitute. **4** a law-breaker, a criminal. [racing jargon *wrong 'un*, a horse that had been deliberately pulled up during a race; ult. SE *wrong one*]

wrought *see under* RORT.

wrought iron! *excl.* [1970s] (*US campus*) an excl. of approval. [joc. var. on the excl. RIGHT ON! excl.]

wrung out (like a dishcloth) *phr.* [1950s+] (*orig. US*) exhausted.

wrung-up *adj.* [1980s] (*US campus*) over-excited, out of control. [play on UPTIGHT adj.² (1)]

wry mouth and a pissen pair of breeches *n.* [late 18C–early 19C] a hanging. [SE *wry*, contorted, twisted + *pissen*, pissed upon, i.e. the effect on the victim's bodily functions]

wry neck day *n.* [late 18C–early 19C] the hanging day. [for ety. *see* WRY MOUTH AND A PISSEN PAIR OF BREECHES n.]

w/s *n.* [1970s+] used in sex contact advertisements, urolagnia. [abbr. WATER SPORTS n.]

w.t. *n.* [2000s] (*UK juv.*) a derog. ref. to poor, working-class or underclass pupils. [abbr. WHITE TRASH n.]

W.T.F.! *excl. see* WHAT THE FUCK! excl.

W2 *n.* [late 19C] the German Kaiser Wilhelm II (reigned 1888–1918); thus ext. to any military-looking man. [the signature affixed to his telegram sent to Paul Kruger (1825–1904), president of the South African Republic and leader of the Boers, on New Year's Day 1896]

wuckless *adj.* [1990s+] (*UK juv.*) homosexual. [ety. unknown]

wuk *v.* [1990s+] (*UK Black*) to have sexual intercourse. [pron. of/var. on WORK v. (1)/WHACK IT IN v./WAX v.² (4)]

wukka *n.* [1980s+] (*US campus*) a very good-looking man or woman. [? WICKED adj. (2) + PUKKA adj.]

wump *n. see* WHOMP n.

wuppie *n.* [1990s+] a young urban professional who has made money via the Internet. [initial letter of SE *website* + YUPPIE n.]

wurp *n.* [1920s] (*US*) a social inadequate. [? abbr. TWERP n.]

wuss *n.* (*also* **wuss bag, wussette, wussy**) [1970s+] (*orig. US teen*) a weakling, someone who cannot be depended on. [WIMP n.² + PUSSY n. (10)]

wusser *n.* [late 19C] a canal boat. [? play on Ger. *wasser*, water]

wuss out *v.* [1970s+] to lose courage, to back down. [WUSS n.]

wussy *n. see* WUSS n.

wussy *adj.* [1970s+] cowardly, weak, effeminate. [WUSS n.]

w.w. *n. see* WIBLING'S WITCH n.

Wyatt Earp *n.*¹ [1970s] the penis (cf. ABRAHAM n.¹). [rhy. sl. = CURP n.; ult. US lawman *Wyatt Earp* (1848–1929)]

Wyatt Earp *n.*² [2000s] a burp. [rhy. sl.; ult. US lawman *Wyatt Earp* (1848–1929)]

wylin' *adj.* [2000s] (*US teen*) excellent. [ext. WILD adj. (1)]

wylo *v.* [late 19C] (*UK Und.*) to run away. [orig. Anglo-Chinese]

wyn *n. see* WIN n.

Wyoming ketchup *n.* **1** [1920s] opium (cf. APOSTLE n.). **2** [1930s] (*US*) alcohol.

XYZ

X *n.*[1] [mid-19C+] (*US*) a $10 bill, $10 cash (cf. C n.[1]). [Roman numeral *X*, 10]

X *n.*[2] [1950s] (*US drugs*) a narcotic injection.

x *n.*[1] [mid-19C] a method of arrest whereby a policeman grasps the villain's collar and holds their arm in such a way that the more they struggle, the more likely it is for the arm to be broken. [the crossed position of the arm]

x *n.*[2] [1920s–60s] (*US prison*) an ex-convict.

x *n.*[3] **1** [1950s] (*drugs*) an injection. **2** [1990s+] (*drugs*) marijuana. **3** [1990s+] (*US drugs*) MDMA (cf. ECSTASY n.). [the use of *x* as a code, i.e. because drugs are prohibited; (3) pron. of ECSTASY n.]

x *n.*[4] [1950s+] (*W.I.*) the *ac*celerator on a car. [pron.]

x *adj.* (*also* **ex**) [1950s+] angry. [*x* = lit. 'cross']

x *v.* (*also* **ex**) [1950s+] (*Aus./US campus*) to stop, to eliminate. [*x*, a cross, thus *cross out*]

X amount *n.* [1980s+] (*US*) a very large amount. [? X n.[1] + SE *amount*]

X-cat *n.* [2000s] (*US prison*) an inmate who is in need of mental health care.

x'ed out *adj.* [1970s] (*US Black*) used of something that, while once important, is no longer relevant. [X OUT v.[1]]

Xerox *v.* **1** [1960s–70s] (*US campus*) to cheat on a test. **2** [1990s+] (*US Black*) to copy, to imitate. [brandname of Rank *Xerox* Corp., leading copier manufacturers]

Xerox copy *n.* [1950s+] (*Aus.*) a Remembrance Day poppy. [rhy. sl.; ult. *see* XEROX v.]

Xerox queen *n.* [1960s+] (*US gay*) a man who prefers all his sexual partners to resemble each other. [*Xerox* (*see* XEROX v. + QUEEN n.[2] (1)/QUEEN sfx (2)]

X Files *n.* [1990s+] piles. [rhy. sl.]

x-ing *n.* [1980s+] (*US drugs*) experiencing MDMA (cf. X OUT v.[2]). [x n.[3] (3)]

xippie *n.* [1990s+] a modern young person who wishes to adopt the lifestyle of the hippies of the 1960s. [the *X* of Douglas Coupland's *Generation X* + HIPPIE n.[2] (3)]

xis *n. see* EXIS n.

X kegger *n. see* KEGGER n. (2).

X-man *n.* [1990s+] (*UK juv.*) a male homosexual. [such men are not 'real' men but '(e)x-men']

x out *v.*[1] [1970s+] (*US Black*) to dismiss something as no longer important or relevant. [the use of an 'X' to cross out text]

x out *v.*[2] [1980s+] (*US drugs*) to experience MDMA (cf. X-ING n.). [x n.[3]]

x-ray *v.* [1950s] (*US Black*) to watch closely, to stare at.

X-ray dress *n.* [1920s] (*US*) a translucent dress.

x-row *n.* [20C+] (*US prison*) the condemned cells. [fig. use of *x* as 'nameless', or the inmates are the *ex*-living, i.e. looking forward only to execution]

x's *n.* (*also* **x.s.**) [mid-19C+] *ex*penses. [abbr.]

X's hall *n.* [late 19C] the London session house. [*X*, one Hicks, a notoriously punitive judge]

XTC *n.* [1980s+] (*drugs*) MDMA (cf. ECSTASY n.). [pron. of ECSTASY n.]

XX *n. see* DOUBLE-X n.[2].

xyz *n.* [1950s] (*US drugs*) an infected lesion that results from injecting with an improvised syringe. [x n.[3] (1)]

Y *n.* [1910s+] (*orig. US*) the *Y*oung Men's Christian Association (YMCA); often as *the Y*. [abbr.]

yaba *n.* (*also* **ya ba**) [1990s+] a form of hallucinogen, derived from synthetic amphetamine and orig. created by Nazi chemists during WW2.

yabber *n.* [mid-19C+] (*Aus.*) talk, chatter. [? pidgin; ult. Wuy-wurung *yaba*, to speak, but note SE *jabber*]

yabber *v.* [mid-19C+] (*Aus.*) to talk, to chatter; thus *yabberer*, a talkative, loquacious person. [YABBER n.]

yabbos *n.* (*also* **yarbos**) [1980s] (*US campus*) breasts.

yabby *n.* [1980s+] (*Aus.*) in cricket, a wicket-keeper. [SAusE *yabby*, a crayfish; the crouching, padded and gauntleted keeper supposedly resembles one]

yachtie *n.* [1940s+] (*Aus./N.Z.*) a yachting enthusiast.

yack *n.*[1] [late 18C–19C] a watch. [? Welsh gypsy *yakengeri*, a clock, lit. 'a thing of the eyes']

yack *n.*[2] (*also* **yak**) [1950s+] **1** (*US*) empty, tedious, trivial talk. **2** (*US*) a laugh. **3** (*US*) an accent, a tone of voice. **4** (*US, Western*) a fool. [echoic]

yack *adj.* [2000s] disgusting. [YUCK adj.]

yack *v.* (*also* **yak**) **1** [1940s+] (*also* **yak it up**) to chatter tediously. **2** [1950s+] to laugh. **3** [1980s] to make a sharp noise. **4** [1980s+] (*US campus*) to vomit (cf. BARF v.). [YACK n.[2] (1)]

yacker *n.*[1] (*also* **yakker**) [late 19C+] (*Aus.*) food. [YAKKA n.; i.e. the result of work is money to buy food]

yacker *n.*[2] (*also* **yakkapukee, yakker**) [1950+] (*Aus.*) **1** talk, chatter. **2** a gossip, one who talks too much. [ext. YACK n.[2] (1)]

yacker *n.*[3] *see* YAKKA n.

yacker *v.* (*also* **yakker**) [1950s+] (*Aus.*) to talk, to chatter, to gossip. [YACK v. (1)]

yackety-yak *n.* (*also* **yackety-yack, yacky-yak, yakety-yack/-yak, yakkety-yack/-yak, yak-yak**) [early 18C; 1940s+] aimless chatter. [early 18C use presumably echoic; later use YACK n.[2] (1) + redup.]

yackety-yak *v.* (*also* **yackety-yack, yakety-yack, yakety-yak, yakkety-yack, yakkety-yak**) [1940s+] to chatter aimlessly. [YACKETY-YAK n.]

yacking *n.* (*also* **yakking**) [1950s+] inconsequential chatter. [YACK v. (1)]

yacky-yak *n. see* YACKETY-YAK n.

yacoo *n.* (*also* **yakoo**) [1960s+] (*US Black*) a White racist bigot. [*Yacub*, the white devil-figure of Black Muslim theology]

yad *n.* [mid-19C] a day. [backsl.]

yadda yadda yadda *phr.* (*also* **yada yada yada**) [1990s+] predictable, repetitive, essentially meaningless chatter. [YATTER n. + redup.]

yadnab *n.* (*also* **yadnarb**) [mid-19C] brandy. [backsl.]

yaffle *v.*[1] [late 18C–1930s] (*orig. UK Und.*) to eat or drink, esp. noisily or greedily. [? Yorks. dial. *yaffle*, to mumble or yelp (like a dog)]

yaffle *v.*[2] [1910s–50s] (*US Und.*) to arrest, to snatch, to take. [? SNAFFLE v. (1)]

yaffner *n.* [late 19C–1930s] (*US Black*) an untrustworthy person, a tell-tale. [ety. unknown]

yaga yaga *n.* [1980s+] (*W.I., Rasta*) a friend, an intimate. [YAGA-YAGA! excl.]

yaga-yaga! *excl.* [1980s+] (*W.I./UK Black teen*) a greeting, a means of attracting attention to oneself. [fig. use of RAGA-RAGA adj.; the y/r substitution comes from the folk-tales of Anansi, the spider, whose 'Bungo' talk uses 'y' for 'r']

yagga-yagga *n.* [20C+] (*W.I.*) unmannerly behaviour.

yahoo *n.*[1] **1** [18C+] a person lacking cultivation or sensibility, a philistine, a hooligan. **2** [1970s] a person. [Jonathan Swift's *Gulliver's Travels* (1727), in which the *yahoos* were an imaginary race of brutes having the form of men; note Aus. *yahoo*, a prob. mythical creature resembling a large hairy man, said to haunt eastern Australia]

yahoo *n.*[2] *see* YEYO n.

yak *see also under* YACK and its combs.

yak *n.* [1980s+] (*US*) a general term of abuse. [YACK v. (1), i.e. one who talks rubbish all the time; ? and/or someone who looks like a SE *yak*]

yakka *n.* (*also* **yacker, yakker**) [late 19C+] (*Aus.*) exhausting work. [Jagara *yaga*, work; but note Ulster *yokkin*, a spell of work, lit. the 'yoking' of horses]

yakka *v.* (*also* **yakker**) [late 19C+] (*Aus.*) to work hard, to labour. [YAKKA n.; note J.D. Lang, *Cooksland* (1847), p.447: 'The word *yacca* in the Moreton Bay dialect of the Aboriginal language, is one of those unfortunate words that has more than double duty to perform. It signifies everything in the shape of service or performance from the first incipient attempts at motion, to the most violent exertion, and it usually takes its signification from the noun to which it is appended, as in the instance I have given above, mooyoom yacca, to read, to write, or to cast accounts']

yakkapukee *n. see* YACKER n.[2].

yakoo *n. see* YACOO n.

yaks *n. see* YOKS n.

yale *n.* **1** [1960s–70s] (*US drugs*) a hypodermic syringe. **2** [1980s+] (*drugs*) crack cocaine (cf. BASE n.). [brandname of the syringe; (2) is a misreading of (1)]

yalla *n. see* HIGH YELLOW n.

yaller boy *n. see* YELLOW BOY n.[1].

yaller gal *n. see* YELLOW GIRL n.

yam *n.*[1] [early 18C+] food; 'this word is used by the lowest class all over the world; by the Wapping sailor, West India negro, or Chinese coolie' (Hotten, 1867). [West African words such as Hausa *nama*, flesh, meat, Swahili *nyama*, meat, Fulah *nyama*, to eat; all these in turn based on SE *yam*, a variety of edible tuber]

yam *n.*[2] [mid-19C–1920s] (*US Black*) a West Indian. [SE *yam*, an edible tuber; stereotyped as central to the W.I. diet]

yam *v.* [early 18C+] to eat. [YAM n.[1]]

yanepatine *n. see* YENNEPATINE n.

yang *n.* [1960s+] the penis. [var. on WANG n.[2] (1)]

yanga *n. see* NYANGA n.

yang yang *n.* [1980s+] (*US campus*) nonsense, rubbish. [nonsense word + ? play on YANG n. on pattern of COCK n.[5] (2)]

Yank *n.* **1** [late 18C+] a usu. derog. term for an American. **2** [mid-19C–1920s] (*also* **Yanky**) a Northerner, a New Englander; a Union soldier. [abbr. SE *Yankee*; ult. Du. *Janke*, a dimin. of Jan (John) and coined as a derisive nickname by either the Dutch or the English in the New England states. Substantial documentary evidence bears this out, with many late 18C–early 19C records of sailors, pirates and one Black slave nicknamed *yankey, yanky*

or *yankee*. The term is most likely an elision of *Jan Kees* (Kees being a dimin. of Cornelius), the Dutch equivalent of 'Joe Doakes' or 'John Doe' and based in its turn on *Jan Kaas*, lit. 'John Cheese'. It seems to have been coined as a nickname for the Dutch settlers, then, with the appearance of the English in Connecticut, turned on the newcomers by the Dutch and then extended to the whole of New England]

Yank *adj.* (*also* **yankee, yanky**) [mid-19C+] American.

Yank *v.* [1940s] of British women, to pick up American servicemen during WW2. [YANK n. (1)]

yank *n.*[1] **1** [early 19C+] a tug, a pull, a wrench. **2** [2000s] an act of masturbation. [YANK v.[1] (1)]

yank *n.*[2] *see* YANKEE n.[2] (1).

yank *v.*[1] **1** [mid-19C+] (*orig. US*) to drag, to pull. **2** [late 19C–1900s] (*orig. US*) a var. on PULL DOWN v. (3), to earn, to win money; thus *yank-down*, a profit, a commission. **3** [late 19C+] (*orig. US*) to arrest. **4** [1900s] (*US*) to victimize, to harass or to dupe. **5** [1940s+] (*orig. US*) to remove. **6** [1990s+] (*US campus*) to steal. [ety. unknown]

yank *v.*[2] [1980s] (*US campus*) to vomit (cf. BARF v.). [echoic]

yankee *n.*[1] [mid-19C] (*US*) a glass of whisky sweetened with molasses. [a popular drink]

yankee *n.*[2] **1** [mid-19C–1900s] (*also* **yank**) a cheater, a swindler. **2** [1900s] (*also* **yankee-trick**) an act of cheating. [YANKEE v.]

yankee *n.*[3] [1970s–80s] (*gay*) masturbation; a masturbator. [YANK OFF v.]

yankee *adj. see* YANK adj.

yankee *v.* (*also* **come yankee over, play yankee with**) [19C+] to cheat, to drive a hard bargain. [SE *Yankee*, i.e. the poor reputation of New England businessmen and lawyers + COME OVER v.[1]/SE *play*]

Yankee Doodles *n.* [1990s+] noodles. [rhy. sl.]

Yankee heaven *n.* (*also* **Yankee paradise**) [late 19C] Paris. [the dictum 'When good Americans die, they go to Paris', coined *c.*1860 by Thomas G. Appleton (1812–84)]

Yankeeland *n.* (*also* **Yankland, Yankieland**) [early 19C+] America. [SE *Yankee*/YANK n. (1)]

yankeeries *n.* [late 19C] Buffalo Bill's Wild West Show, which arrived in London in 1887 (and was seen at Earl's Court by Queen Victoria). [SE *Yankee*]

Yankee shout *n.* (*also* **Scotchman's shout, Scotch shout**) [1940s–60s] (*Aus./N.Z.*) a round of drinks for which each individual buys their own drink; anything where people pay for themselves. [stereotyping of SE *Yankees* or *Scots* as mean + SHOUT n.[1] (2); such individual payments run contrary to the Aus. tradition of buying rounds for one's whole company]

yankee's yawn *n.* [1950s–60s] (*US gay*) the open mouth of a climaxing male. [SE *Yankee* + SE *yawn*]

yankee-trick *n. see* YANKEE n.[2] (2).

Yankieland/Yankland *n. see* YANKEELAND n.

Yank mags *n. see* YANKS n.

yank off *v.* [1990s+] to masturbate (cf. BALL OFF v.[2]). [YANK v.[1] (1)]

yank one's crank *v.* [20C+] (*US*) to masturbate. [YANK v.[1] (1) + CRANK n.[5] (1)]

yank one's meat *v.* [1970s+] to masturbate (cf. BEAT ONE'S MEAT v.). [YANK v.[1] (1) + MEAT n. (2)]

yank one's wank *v.* [20C+] to masturbate. [YANK v.[1] (1) + WANK n.[1] (1)]

Yanks *n.* (*also* **Yank mags**) [1930s] American pulp magazines, as distributed in the UK. [play on YANK n. (1)/YANK v.[1] (1) + colloq. SE *mag*, a magazine]

yank someone's chain *v.* [1960s+] to irritate someone, to annoy someone, to remind or distract someone forcibly. [YANK v.[1] (1) + SE *chain*]

yank someone's coat *v.* [2000s] (*US prison*) to confront a fellow inmate with a secret they do not wish revealed. [YANK v.[1] (1); ext. of PULL SOMEONE'S COAT v. (1)]

Yank tank n. [1980s+] (N.Z.) a large US car.

yank the plank v. [1990s+] to masturbate (cf. COTTON WOOL v.). [rhy. sl. = WANK v. (1); or YANK v.¹ (1) + PLANK n.³]

yank up v. [1930s+] to bring up or educate a child roughly, without controls, manners or discipline. [YANK v.¹ (1); ext. of DRAG UP v.¹]

Yanky n. see YANK n. (2).

yanky adj. see YANK adj.

yannep/yannup n. see YENNEP n.

yanta n. [1990s+] (US) a derog. term for a Black person (cf. ALLIGATOR BAIT n.²). [ety. unknown; ? link to YENTA n.]

yaoh n. see YEYO n.

y.a.p. n. [1980s] (US) a young aspiring professional. [abbr.]

yap n.¹ **1** [mid-19C+] (orig. US) (also **yop**) idle, trivial chatter. **2** [late 19C+] (US) (also **yapper, yop**) the mouth; usu. in derog. sense, shut your yap! etc. **3** [20C+] (Irish) (also **yawp, yerp**) a whining, complaining person. **4** [20C+] (US) (also **yap yap**) a chatterer. **5** [1910s–20s] (US) a tell-tale, an informer. **6** [1950s] a sound. **7** [1950s+] (orig. US) a chat, a conversation. **8** [1980s] a petty swindler. [SE yap, a yelping dog or its bark]

yap n.² **1** [late 19C–1940s] (US) a contemptible person, irrespective of class or background. **2** [late 19C+] (US) a derog. term for a peasant, a rustic simpleton. **3** [20C+] (US Und.) a criminal's victim. **4** [1920s] (US tramp) a novice within the tramp community. [fig. uses of YAP n.¹]

yap n.³ [1950s] (W.I.) a Chinese person (cf. AH CABBAGE n.). [? Chinese surname]

yap v.¹ (also **yawp, yerp**) **1** [early 19C+] (also **yap it up**) to talk, to make a noise, esp. to shout at, like a dog; thus yapper, a chatterer. **2** [20C+] (US) to complain, to nag. [dial. yap, to talk loudly, foolishly; note synon. RMC Duntroon (Aus.); also as n., one who talks excessively]

yap v.² [mid-19C] to pay back; thus YAP-POO v. [backsl.]

yap it up v. see YAP v.¹ (1).

yapper n.¹ see YAP n.¹ (2).

yapper n.² see YAP v.¹ (1).

yappies, the n. [1940s+] (Aus.) 'the dogs', i.e. greyhound racing. [SE yap, to bark]

yappiness n. see YAPPY adj.³.

yappy adj.¹ **1** [mid-19C+] foolish, soft. **2** [1990s+] (US campus) over-generous. [YAP n.²]

yappy adj.² [20C+] (Ulster) thin, hungry-looking. [YAP n.¹ (2); one's mouth is fig. open with hunger]

yappy adj.³ [1930s+] (orig. US) noisy, talkative; thus yappiness, verbosity. [YAP v.¹ (1); the image is of an irrepressible puppy]

yapster n. [late 18C–19C+] a dog. [SE yap, to bark + sfx -ster]

yap wagon n. [1920s] (US) a vehicle taking tourists on sightseeing tours. [YAP n.² (1) + SE wagon]

yap yap n. see YAP n.¹ (4).

yap-yap v. [1950s] (W.I.) to open one's mouth wide through hunger. [YAP n.¹ (2) + redup.]

yar adj. [1960s] (US) in love. [ety. unknown]

yaram n. see YARRUM n.

yarbles n. [1970s+] **1** testicles. **2** courage, guts. [? link to dial. yarb, 'an opprobrious epithet' (EDD) + BALLS n.¹; popularized by the film A Clockwork Orange (1971)]

yarbos n. see YABBOS n.

Yard, the n.¹ [20C+] Scotland Yard; later New Scotland Yard, the headquarters of London's Metropolitan Police. [abbr.]

Yard, the n.² see YARD n.² (5).

yard n.¹ (also **yeard**) [19C] the penis. [prior use SE f. late 14C; Old Teut. gazdjo, a thin pole + ? link to Lat. hasta, a spear + Ital. cazzo, penis; note double entendre in D'Urfey, Pills to Purge Melancholy (1719–20): 'A fine dapper Taylor, with a Yard in his hand, / Did profer his Service to be at Command']

yard n.² **1** [20C+] (W.I./UK Black) one's home. **2** [1920s+] a house or other dwelling place. **3** [1930s+] (US prison) the recreation area of a prison; thus back on the yard, out of solitary confinement. **4** [1980s+] (US campus) the campus. **5** [1980s+] (also **the Yard**) Jamaica. **6** [1990s+] (Irish) a toilet (cf. ALTAR n.).

yard n.³ **1** [1920s+] (US) 100 or 1000; usu. of dollars (cf. HALF-A-YARD n.). **2** [1930s+] (US prison) a year; thus a sentence of 1 year. **3** [1960s] (drugs) $100 worth of heroin. **4** [1990s+] (US Und.) a sentence of 100 years.

yard adj. [1990s+] (W.I./UK Black) Jamaican. [YARD n.² (5)]

yard v.¹ [1900s] (Aus.) to marry.

yard v.² (US Black) **1** [1950s+] (also **yard on**) to be sexually unfaithful. **2** [1960s] to chat, to make small talk. [(1) abbr. fig. SE play in someone's back-yard; (2) ? chatting over the fence between 2 backyards]

yardbird n.¹ [1940s+] (US) **1** a civilian dock worker in a naval dockyard. **2** anyone confined by authority to a restricted area, usu. prison. [SE yard + BIRD n.² (1)/BIRD n.³ (2)]

yardbird n.² (also **pigeon**) [1990s+] (US prison) fried chicken.

yardbird lawyer n. [1940s+] (US Und.) a prison inmate who has become a self-taught lawyer, either to pursue his own case, to combat prison corruption or to help fellow inmates. [YARDBIRD n.¹ (2) + SE lawyer]

yard boy n. [1990s+] (US gay) one who prefers sex outdoors.

yard bull n. **1** [1910s+] (US) (also **railroad dick, yard dick**) a railroad police officer, guard or detective (cf. BEAGLE n.³). **2** [1930s+] a prison guard. [(1) SE marshalling yard; (2) YARD n.² (3) + BULL n.¹⁰ (5)]

yard dog n. [1930s–40s] (US Black) **1** a fool, a gullible person (cf. AIREDALE n.). **2** an ill-dressed, badly behaved individual.

yard hack n. [20C+] (US) a prison guard. [YARD n.² (3) + HACK n.⁵ (4)]

yardie n. [1980s+] (orig. W.I.) **1** a Jamaican. **2** one of a gang of organized Jamaican criminals who specialize in purveying drugs and violence on an international level. [YARD n.² (5); Francis-Jackson, Official Dancehall Dict. (1995), defines (1) as 'a Jamaican residing overseas']

yardman n. [1980s+] (W.I./UK Black teen) a Jamaican. [YARD n.² (5) + SE man]

yardnarb n. [late 19C] brandy. [backsl.]

yard nigger n. [20C+] a subservient, acquiescent Black. [SE yard + NIGGER n.¹ (1); the differentiation under slavery between the 'domesticated' Blacks who worked as house servants and those who, seen as more rebellious, merely toiled in the plantation fields]

yard of clay n. [19C] a clay pipe with a notably long stem.

yard of pump water n. [late 19C] a tall, thin person.

yard of satin n. [early 19C–1920s] a glass of gin. [SE yard, a glass + SATIN n.¹ (1)]

yard of tin n. [mid-19C] a horn, esp. in hunting or coaching.

yard of tripe n. [mid-19C] a pipe. [rhy. sl.]

yard on v. see YARD v.² (1).

yard patrol n. [20C+] (US prison) **1** a group of convicts. **2** a prison guard. [YARD n.² (3) + SE patrol]

yard queen n. [2000s] (US prison) a prison homosexual. [YARD n.² (3) + QUEEN n.² (1)]

yard rat n. [1990s+] (US prison) a prisoner who frequents the prison yard, socializing with friends. [YARD n.² (3) + RAT n.² (6)]

yarm n. see YARRUM n.

Yarmouth bloater n.¹ [mid-19C] an inhabitant of Yarmouth. [the town's main occupation of fishing]

Yarmouth bloater n.² [1910s+] an automobile. [rhy. sl. = MOTOR n.² (1)]

Yarmouth capon n. (also **Norfolk capon**) **1** [mid-17C–1900s] a red herring. **2** [early 19C] a soldier, i.e. his red coat. **3** [mid-19C] a bloater. [the local fishing industry]

yarn n. (orig. naut.) **1** [early 19C+] a story, esp. a long and poss.

implausibly wonderful one. **2** [1910s+] a chat, a conversation. [the stories told by sailors during the lengthy processes of making ropes; note Hall Caine, *The Deemster* (1897): 'Without motive a story is not a novel, but only a yarn'; in other words, a *yarn* implies the dichotomy between 'literary' and 'popular' writing]

yarn *v.* **1** [early 19C+] to tell tales, prob. implausible or far-fetched ones. **2** [mid-19C+] to talk to, to chatter with. [YARN *n.*]

yarn-chopper *n.* (*also* **yarn-slinger/-spinner**) [late 19C–1920s] a story-teller, a chatterer. [YARN *n.* + SE *chop/sling/spin*]

yarpie *n.* [1980s+] (*Aus.*) a South African; thus *Yarpieland*, South Africa. [JAAP *n.* (1)]

yarra *adj.* [late 19C+] (*Aus.*) insane; also as *n.*, a stupid person. [the mental hospital at Yarra Bend, Victoria]

Yarra banker *n.* [late 19C–1940s] (*Aus.*) **1** (*also* **Yarra-sider**) a soap-box orator. **2** (*also* **Yarra bender**) an idler, a loafer found on the banks of Melbourne's Yarra River. [the *banks* of the *Yarra* are the equivalent of London's Hyde Park Corner]

yarrum *n.* (*also* **yaram, yarm, yarum**) [mid-16C–mid-19C] (*UK Und.*) milk; thus *poplars of yarrum*, milk porridge. [? a corruption of SE *yellow* or *yallow*; Ribton-Turner, *A History of Vagrants* (1887), suggests Gaelic *uaram*, fresh water]

yasha *n.* [1970s] (*camp gay*) an idiot, a fool. [Rus. *yasha*, a peasant]

yasser *n.* [1990s+] (*US*) an erection. [abbr. *Yasser* CRACK A FAT *v.*, a pun on PLO leader *Yasser* Arafat (1929–2004)]

yat *n. see* YATTY *n.* (1).

yatata *n.* [1940s–50s] (*US*) talk, chatter; also as *v.*, to talk monotonously, tediously. [YATTER *v.*]

yatter *n.* [early 19C+] talk, chatter, gabble. [orig. Scot.]

yatter *v.* [early 19C+] to talk, to chatter, to gabble. [YATTER *n.*]

yatty *n.* [2000s] (*UK Black*) **1** (*also* **yat**) a girl, a girlfriend, esp. derog., i.e. a promiscuous girl, a prostitute. **2** a cowardly man.

yaup *v. see* YAWP *v.*

yaupy *adj.* (*also* **yaupish**) [19C] drunk. [YAWP *v.* (1); note SE *yawpish*, hungry]

yawn *n.* [late 19C+] anything or anyone considered tedious, boring and thus producing SE *yawns*.

yawner *n.* [1940s+] (*US*) anything boring, yawn-producing. [YAWN *n.* + sfx *-er*]

yawney *n.* (*also* **yawny**) [19C; 1950s] a fool, a simpleton; also as *adj.*, simple. [dial.; their mouth *yawns* open in stupidity]

yawp *see also under* YAP.

yawp *v.* (*also* **yaup**) **1** [late 19C+] (*orig. US*) to talk loudly or foolishly, to nag; also as *n.* **2** [1940s] to vomit (cf. BARF *v.*). [dial./YAP *n.*[1] (3)]

yay *adj. see* YEA *adj.*

yay-nay *n.* [mid-19C] a simpleton, an unsophisticated person. [bereft of communicative powers, they can only answer 'yea' or 'nay' to any question]

yayo *n.* [2000s] (*US Black/drugs*) **1** money. **2** marijuana. [? YEYO *n.*]

yayo/yayoo *n. see* YEYO *n.*

y-bone steak *n.* [1970s] the female genitals. [the fork of the thighs + play on SE *T-bone steak*]

yea *adj.* (*also* **yay**) [1950s+] (*orig. US Black*) this, e.g. *yea big*, this big; *yea high*, this high.

yea and nay man *n.* (*also* **yea and nay**) [late 17C–early 19C] **1** a Quaker; also attrib., pertaining to a Quaker. **2** a simpleton, capable of answering only 'yes' or 'no'; thus a poor conversationalist, a monosyllabic person. [the Quakers' supposed predilection for simple, black and white answers]

yeah *adv.* (*also* **yeah, bubba; yeh**) [late 19C+] (*orig. US*) yes. [pron.]

yeah man *n.* [1980s+] (*US campus*) a boring person. [they chatter on; one intersperses their monologue by saying 'Yeah, man' occasionally]

yeaho *n. see* YEYO *n.*

yeah, right *phr. see* RIGHT *phr.*

year *n.* [1940s–50s] (*US Und.*) a dollar; thus *five years*, $5 etc.

yeard *n. see* YARD *n.*[1].

year dot *n.* (*also* **year one**) [late 19C+] a very long time ago; usu. *from year dot*, for ever.

yearn *n.* [1970s] (*drugs*) an obsession with and desire for narcotic drugs that precedes a full-blown physical addiction.

yeasting *n.* [1940s–60s] (*US Black*) exaggerating, boasting. [the way in which yeast makes otherwise flat dough rise]

yecch/yech *see under* YUCK.

yegg *n.* (*also* **johnny yeg, yeggman**) (*US Und.*) **1** [20C+] a thief, spec. a safe-cracker; thus *yegg mob*, a gang of safe-breakers. **2** [20C+] any variety of criminal. **3** [1910s–20s] (*also* **yegger**) a hold-up man, a robber with violence. **4** [1910s–30s] a beggar. [? John *Yegg*, a contemporary villain and the first safe-breaker to use nitroglycerine; however, Cohen (ed.), *Studies in Slang* VI (1999), notes an article in the *San Francisco Chronicle*, 6 March 1904, citing criminal John Yeager who led a gang of tramps who robbed the Reading railroad; his name was the basis of the generic 'John Yegg', the notional leader of all similar gangs; note also Jack Black (1926): 'Yegg [...] is a corruption of "yekk," a word from one of the many dialects spoken in Chinatown, and it means beggar. When a hypo or beggar approached a Chinaman to ask for something to eat, he was greeted with the exclamation, "yekk man, yekk man." The underworld is quick to seize upon strange words, and the bums and hypos in Chinatown were calling themselves yeggmen years before the term was taken out on the road and given currency by eastbound beggars. In no time it had a verb hung on it, and to yegg meant to beg. The late William A. Pinkerton was responsible for its changed meaning [...] A burglar with some humor fell into Pinkerton's hands and when asked who was breaking open the country "jugs" he whispered to the detective that it was the yeggs. Investigation convinced Pinkerton that there were a lot of men drifting about the country who called themselves yeggs. The word went into a series of magazine articles Pinkerton was writing at the time and was fastened upon the "box" men. Its meaning has since widened until now the term "yegg" includes all criminals whose work is "heavy"'; Irwin, *American Tramp and Und. Slang* (1931), suggests: 'Originally a man too wise, too cautious, too old or too cowardly to risk crime in a city, where police and private detectives were alert, and who took to "the road" for easier "graft" and "pickings"']

yegg *v.* [1900s–30s] (*US Und.*) **1** to hold up and rob. **2** to break open a safe. [YEGG *n.*]

ye gods (and little fishes)! *excl.* [early 18C–1950s] a mild oath.

yeh *adv. see* YEAH *adv.*

Yehudi *n.* [20C+] (*US*) a Jew (cf. ARAB *n.*[2]). [Heb. *yehudi*, a Jew]

yeknod *n.* (*also* **jerk-nod, jirk-nod, keynod, yerknod**) [mid-19C] a donkey. [backsl.]

yell *n.*[1] [mid–late 19C] beer. [its *yellow* colour]

yell *n.*[2] **1** [1920s+] something or someone hilarious. **2** [1950s] (*US Und.*) the betrayal of one's confederates. **3** [1950s] (*US Black*) someone considered excellent, attractive. **4** [1960s+] an act of vomiting.

yell *v.* [1940s–50s] (*US Und.*) to confess; to betray and/or testify against an accomplice.

yell (bloody) murder *v. see* HOLLER (BLOODY) MURDER *v.*

yell calf-rope *v. see* HOLLER CALF-ROPE *v.*

yell copper *v. see* HOLLER COPPER *v.*

yeller *n.* [1950s] (*US Und.*) a lawyer. [SE *yell*, i.e. his verbosity]

yeller feller *n. see* YELLOW FELLOW *n.*

yellow *n.*[1] [late 19C+] cowardice; often as *streak of yellow*. [YELLOW *adj.*[3] (1)]

yellow *n.*[2] **1** [1910s+] a sovereign, £1 sterling (cf. CANARY *n.*[5]). **2** [1920s] (*US tramp*) a gold watch. [the golden, i.e. *yellow*, colour]

yellow *n.*[3] [1920s+] a light-skinned Black person.

yellow *n.*[4] **1** [1940s] (*US Und.*) a (fake) telegram used in confidence tricks. **2** [1970s] (*US*) a taxi.

yellow *n.*[5] *see* MELLOW YELLOW n.[2].

yellow *adj.*[1] [17C+] jealous; thus *yellows*, jealousy. [corruption of SE]

yellow *adj.*[2] **1** [late 18C+] (*US*) of a Black person, light-skinned. **2** [1920s] a person of mixed race, half-White, half-Black.

yellow *adj.*[3] **1** [mid-19C+] (*also* **yellow around the gills**) cowardly. **2** [late 19C–1970s] (*orig. US*) unsatisfactory, second-rate, of dubious quality. [the negative image of the colour; ? reinforced, even subconsciously, by the widespread use of some form of identification, usu. yellow, forced on European Jews by the Catholic Church; the stereotypical Jew is not a hero]

yellow *adj.*[4] [late 19C] pertaining to money. [the golden/*yellow* colour]

yellow *adj.*[5] [20C+] pertaining to the Orient, e.g. Japan or China.

yellow *v.* [1930s–50s] (*US Und.*) to turn cowardly. [YELLOW adj.[3] (1)]

yellow *adv.* [1920s] in a cowardly manner. [YELLOW adj.[3] (1)]

yellow agony *n.* [late 19C–1910s] (*Aus.*) **1** (*also* **agony**) a generic for Chinese immigrants to Australia (cf. AH CABBAGE n.). **2** a single immigrant. [generic use of SE *yellow* for Chinese; the *agony* was that of Aus. workers, esp. sailors, who saw their jobs threatened by such immigrants]

yellow and black *n.* [late 19C] (*Aus.*) an Aboriginal.

yellow and white *n.* [late 19C] (*US Und.*) a watch. [SE *yellow*, i.e. gold + WHITE adj.[1]]

yellow around the gills *phr. see* YELLOW adj.[3] (1).

yellow ass *n.* [1930s–60s] (*US*) a light-skinned Black girl. [YELLOW adj.[2] (1) + ASS n. (2)]

yellow-ass/-assed *adj. see* YELLOW-BELLIED adj.

yellow-back *n.*[1] (*US*) **1** [1900s–10s] a $500 note. **2** [1900s–40s] a $20 note (cf. BLUE-BACKS n.; CANARY n.[5]). **3** [1920s] a $1000 note. [the former printing of certain denominations of US dollar-bills in yellow rather than the usual green]

yellow-back *n.*[2] [1920s] a coward; thus *yellow-backed*, cowardly. [ext. of YELLOW adj.[3] (1)]

yellow-back *n.*[3] [1940s+] (*Aus.*) a gob of phlegm. [its colour]

yellow-bellied *adj.* (*also* **yellow-ass, -assed, -belly**) [1910s+] cowardly. [ext. of YELLOW adj.[3] (1)]

yellow belly *n.*[1] [late 18C+] a native of Lincolnshire, esp. of the southern or fenland part of the county. [the yellow-stomached frog or the eels that abound there]

yellow belly *n.*[2] (*US*) **1** [mid-19C–1910s] a Mexican, esp. a soldier (cf. BATO n.). **2** [late 19C] a Dutchman. [(1) the colour of their uniforms and stereotyping of Mexicans as YELLOW adj.[3] (1); (2) the link of the Dutch to butter]

yellow belly *n.*[3] **1** [mid-19C–1910s] a Chinese person (cf. AH CABBAGE n.). **2** [late 19C–1930s] (*UK/US*) a half-caste; a Eurasian. **3** [1940s] (*Aus.*) a Japanese person (cf. BUDDHAHEAD n.). [the 'yellow' Oriental complexion]

yellow belly *n.*[4] (*also* **yellow guts/heel**) [1920s+] a coward. [YELLOW-BELLIED adj./YELLOW adj.[3] (1) + SE *guts/heel*]

yellow-belly *adj. see* YELLOW-BELLIED adj.

yellow bird *n.* [mid-19C] (*US*) a dollar (cf. CANARY n.[5]). [the eagle engraved upon it]

yellow-black *n.* [1940s] (*US Und.*) a mulatto. [YELLOW adj.[2] (1) + SE *black*]

yellow-born *adj.* [1940s] cowardly. [YELLOW adj.[3] (1) + SE *born*]

yellow boy *n.*[1] (*also* **yaller boy**) **1** [mid-17C–19C] a sovereign; a guinea (£1.05) or a golden guinea (cf. CANARY n.[5]). **2** [1910s–30s] (*US*) money. [(1) the colour of the golden coin; (2) *see* YELLOW-BACK n.[1]]

yellow boy *n.*[2] [mid-19C–1900s] (*US*) a mulatto. [YELLOW adj.[2] (1) + SE *boy*]

yellow brick road *n.* [2000s] (*US prison*) yellow lines on the ground that indicate areas beyond which prisoners are forbidden to step. [ref. to the Yellow Brick Road of the book/movie *The Wizard of Oz* (publ. 1900, filmed 1939)]

yellow callies *n. see* WHITE CALLIES n.

yellow dimples *n.* [1970s] (*drugs*) LSD, esp. combined with another drug (cf. A n.[3]). [ety. unknown]

yellow dog *n.* (*also* **yellow pup**) [late 19C+] (*US*) a general term of contempt for a person or thing.

yellow dog contract *n.* [1920s+] (*US*) an employee's work contract forbidding union membership. [YELLOW DOG n. + SE *contract*]

yellow eye *n.* [1940s] (*US Black*) an egg.

yellow face *n.* [late 19C–1900s] a Chinese person, usu. derog. (cf. AH CABBAGE n.).

yellow fancy *n.* [mid–late 19C] a costermonger's handkerchief, yellow with white spots.

yellow fellow *n.* (*also* **yeller feller**) [20C+] (*Aus.*) a mulatto, a half-White, half-Aborigine male. [YELLOW adj.[2] (1) + SE *fellow*]

yellow fever *n.* [1950s–60s] (*orig. US gay*) an obsession, either hetero- or homosexual, with Oriental lovers. [SE *yellow*, i.e. the skin tone, + *fever*]

yellow fish *n.* [20C+] (*US*) an illegal Chinese immigrant (cf. AH CABBAGE n.). [SE *yellow*, the Oriental complexion + FISH n.[3]]

yellow george *n.* [18C–19C] a guinea. [SE *yellow*, its golden colour + GEORGE n.[1] (3)]

yellow girl *n.* (*also* **yaller gal**) [mid-19C+] (*US*) a mulatto. [YELLOW adj.[2] (1) + SE *girl*]

yellow gloak *n.* [early–mid-19C] a jealous man, esp. a jealous husband. [YELLOW adj.[1] + GLOAK n.]

yellow goods *n.* [1940s] (*US Und.*) smuggled Chinese immigrants. [SE *yellow*, i.e. the skin tone, + *goods*]

yellow guts *n. see* YELLOW BELLY n.[4].

yellow-gutted *adj.* [1940s+] cowardly. [YELLOW adj.[3] (1) + SE *gut*]

yellowhammer *n.*[1] [early–mid-17C] a golden guinea. [the colour of the golden coin]

yellowhammer *n.*[2] [mid-19C–1930s] (*US*) an unsophisticated rustic. [SAmE *yellowhammer*, the golden-winged woodpecker, thus a synon. for PECKERWOOD n.]

yellowhammer *n.*[3] [1900s] (*US*) a Chinese person (cf. AH CABBAGE n.). [SE *yellow*, i.e. the skin tone]

yellowhammer *n.*[4] [1910s] (*US*) a coward. [YELLOW adj.[3] (1)]

yellow heel *n. see* YELLOW BELLY n.[4].

yellow jack *n.*[1] (*also* **yellow johnnies**) [mid-19C+] yellow fever. [SE *yellow* + generic use of *jack*]

yellow jack *n.*[2] *see* YELLOW JACKETS n.

yellow jacket *n.*[1] [late 18C+] (*US*) a wasp or hornet.

yellow jacket *n.*[2] [mid-19C] (*Aus.*) a convict. [his yellow uniform]

yellow jacket *n.*[3] [mid-19C] (*US*) a gold piece (cf. CANARY n.[5]).

yellow jackets *n.* (*also* **yellow jack**) [1950s+] (*orig. US Black*) Nembutal, a proprietary brand of pentobarbital sodium. [the yellow capsule]

yellow Jesus *n.* [1990s+] (*Aus. drugs*) home-manufactured heroin (cf. BLACK n.[3]; SLEEPING JESUS n.). [its light-brown colour]

yellow johnnies *n. see* YELLOW JACK n.[1].

yellow kelter *n.* [20C+] (*Irish*) a gold coin (cf. CANARY n.[5]). [SE *yellow* + KELTER n.]

yellow leg *n.*[1] **1** [mid-19C] (*US*) an East Tennessean. **2** [late 19C] (*US*) a US cavalryman. **3** [1940s+] (*Can.*) a member of the Royal Canadian Mounted Police. [(2) and (3) the yellow stripe running down their uniform trousers]

yellow leg *n.*[2] [1900s–10s] (*US*) a strikebreaker. [YELLOW adj.[3] (1) + pattern of SE *blackleg*]

yellow man *n.* [early–mid-19C] a costermonger's handkerchief, coloured plain yellow.

yellow mellow *n. see* MELLOW YELLOW n.[3].

yellowness *n.* [1940s] cowardice. [YELLOW adj.[3] (1)]

yellow nigger *n.* (*also* yellow nig) **1** [mid-19C–1940s] (*US*) a derog. term for a mulatto. **2** [1960s+] an Asian (cf. BROWNIE n.²). [(1) YELLOW adj.² (1); (2) SE *yellow* skin tone of Orientals + NIGGER n.¹]

yellow one *n.* [late 19C–1920s] a gold watch. [its *yellow*, i.e. golden, colour]

yellow pack *n.* [1990s+] (*Irish*) low-paid employment of young people and the concomitant dismissal of more expensive senior employees. [the yellow packaging of the 'own-brand' goods sold by the Quinnsworth chain of supermarkets]

yellow packet *adj.* [1980s+] (*UK juv.*) cheap, indicative of poverty. [in the 1980s Fine Fare supermarkets offered a range of 'Yellow Packet' goods, generally seen as second-rate and good only for the very poor]

yellow peril *n.* **1** [20C+] a derog. term for any Oriental person; the concept that the teeming yellow races are poised to overtake White 'civilization' (cf. BROWNIE n.²). **2** [1910s+] a Gold Flake cigarette. **3** [1960s+] the Communist Chinese. **4** [1980s] (*UK prison*) vegetable soup. [(2) joc. use of (1)]

yellow pup *n. see* YELLOW DOG n.

yellow route *n.* [1980s] (*S.Afr.*) the departure of White South Africans in the face of the imminent take-over by a multiracial government. [YELLOW adj.³ (1) + SE *route*]

yellows *n.*¹ [1960s+] (*drugs*) Nembutal, a depressant. [the colour of the pills]

yellows *n.*² *see* YELLOW adj.¹.

yellows, the *n.* [mid-17C] a venereal infection, esp. gonorrhoea. [the pus-filled discharge]

yellow sheet *n.* [1960s+] (*US Und.*) a criminal's record of arrests. [its colour; SHEET n. (4)]

yellow silk *n.* [late 19C–1900s] milk. [rhy. sl.]

yellow snake *n.* [late 18C] (*W.I.*) a mulatto. [YELLOW adj.² (2) + SE *snake*]

yellow stuff *n.* [early 19C–1910s] gold; thus money, wealth (cf. CANARY n.⁵).

yellow sunshine *n.* [1970s+] (*drugs*) a form of LSD (cf. A n.³). [var. on *orange sunshine*, cf. ORANGE n.²]

yellowtail *n.* [1920s] (*US*) a Japanese person (cf. BUDDHAHEAD n.). [SE *yellow* skin tone + TAIL n.² (1)]

yellow up *v.* [1930s] (*US*) to turn cowardly. [YELLOW adj.³ (1)]

yellow velvet *n.* [1970s–80s] an Asiatic woman, esp. in the context of sex. [SE *yellow*, skin tone/YELLOW adj.⁵; var. on BLACK VELVET n. (1)]

yelper *n.* **1** [early 18C–early 19C] (*also* yelp) a town crier. **2** [early 19C] a wild beast. **3** [early–mid-19C] a whiner, a complainer. **4** [1930s–40s] (*US Und.*) an informer. **5** [1950s+] (*US*) a police car or emergency vehicle siren.

yen *n.*¹ [late 19C+] (*drugs*) a desperate desire for a narcotic, usu. heroin; thus *get one's yen off*, to satisfy one's need for narcotics when suffering withdrawal symptoms. **2** [20C+] in non-drug contexts, a craving, an intense desire. **3** [1920s–40s] opium (cf. APOSTLE n.). [Beijing dial. Chinese *yen*, smoke, poss. reinforced by SE *yearn* (cf. YEARN n.)]

yen *n.*² [1900s–20s] (*US Und.*) money; a dollar.

yen *v.* **1** [1920s–60s] (*drugs*) to desire narcotics. **2** [1930s–50s] to desire someone or something. [YEN n.¹]

yenams *n.* (*also* yenems, yenhams) [1920s–70s] someone else's property, cigarettes etc. [synon. Yid. *yenams*, lit. 'his']

yen-chee *n. see* YEN-SHEE n. (1).

yen chiang *n. see* YEN TSIANG n.

yen dong *n.* [late 19C–1930s] (*US drugs*) the lamp used to heat 'pills' of opium. [Chinese or mock-Chinese]

yenep *n. see* YENNEP n.

yenhams *n. see* YENAMS n.

yen hock *n.* (*also* yen hanck, yen hawk, yen hok, yen hoke) [late 19C–1960s] (*US drugs*) the needle used to prepare a pipe of opium; thus attrib., pertaining to opium and/or its smoking; and in fig. use, pertaining to a thin object or person. [Chinese or mock-Chinese; poss. *yen*, as generic for opium + SE *hook*]

yen hop *n.* [late 19C–1930s] (*US drugs*) the box that contains opium paraphernalia. [Chinese or mock-Chinese]

yennep *n.* (*also* yannep, yannup, yenep, yennap, yennop) [mid-19C+] a penny. [backsl.]

yennepatine *n.* (*also* yanepatine) [mid-19C] a penny a time. [backsl.; YENNEP n.]

yennep flatch *n.* [mid-19C] 3 halfpence. [backsl.; YENNEP n. + FLATCH n.]

yennop *n. see* YENNEP n.

yennork *n. see* YENORK n.

yenom *n.* [mid-19C] money. [backsl.]

yen on *n.* [1940s] (*US drugs*) withdrawal from opium addiction.

yenork *n.* (*also* yennork) [mid-19C] a crown, 5 shillings (25p); thus FLATCHENORC n. [backsl.]

yen pok *n.* [late 19C–1930s] (*US drugs*) a pill of opium (cf. APOSTLE n.). [Chinese or mock-Chinese]

yen pop *n.* [1930s–50s] (*US drugs*) marijuana. [Chinese or mock-Chinese]

yen pox *n.* [1940s–60s] (*drugs*) pills of opium; William Burroughs in *Junkie* (1953) prefers opium ashes/residue (which can still be recycled when desperate) (cf. APOSTLE n.). [YEN POK n.]

yen-shee *n.* (*drugs*) **1** [late 19C+] (*also* when-shee, yen-chee, yen-she) opium (cf. APOSTLE n.). **2** [late 19C+] opium residue; thus *yen-shee hop*, the box used to hold opium ashes, sold to impoverished users; YEN-SHEE GOW n. **3** [1910s–40s] tincture of opium, sometimes mixed with whisky. **4** [1950s] heroin. [Chinese or mock-Chinese; note Irwin, *American Tramp and Und. Slang* (1931): 'Despite the declaration of several educated Chinese that they know of no word in their own language anything like the preceding as representing opium, it is easy to see that the underworld has taken the term from some Chinese root word or sentence']

yen-shee baby *n.* [1930s+] (*drugs*) hard impacted faeces produced, often painfully, by a heroin addict during a period of withdrawal. [YEN-SHEE n. (1) + SE *baby*; one effect of addiction is long-term constipation]

yen-shee boy *n.* [1930s–50s] (*US drugs*) an opium addict. [YEN-SHEE n. (1) + SE *boy*]

yen-shee gow *n.* [late 19C–1950s] (*US drugs*) the tool used to remove opium residue from a pipe. [YEN-SHEE n. (1)/Chinese or mock-Chinese]

yen-shee quay *n.* (*also* yen-shee-kwoi) [late 19C–1950s] (*US drugs*) an opium addict. [YEN-SHEE n. (1)/Chinese or mock-Chinese]

yen-shee suey *n.* [1930s–50s] (*drugs*) opium residue dissolved into wine. [YEN-SHEE n. + SE (*chop*) *suey*]

yen sleep *n.* [1970s+] (*drugs*) a restless, drowsy sleep that accompanies opiate withdrawal. [YEN n.¹ (1) + SE *sleep*]

yenta *n.* [1920s+] (*orig. US*) a nagging, whining person, usu. female. [Ital. *gentile*, a lady; thence adopted by Yid. speakers and popularized through the fictional *Yenta Telebende*, created in the Jewish New York press by the humorist 'B. Kovner' (Jacob Adler)]

yen tsiang *n.* (*also* yen chiang) [mid-19C–1930s] (*US drugs*) an opium pipe. [Chinese *yen tsiang*, 'opium pistol']

yentz *v.* **1** [1930s] to cheat, to swindle, to deceive. **2** [1930s–70s] to have sexual intercourse. [for ety. *see* YENTZER n.]

yentzer *n.* [1930s+] (*US*) a cheat, a deceiver, a liar. [Yid. *yenzter*, lit. FUCKER n. (3)]

yen yen *n.* (*also* yenyen) [late 19C–1950s] (*US drugs*) a craving for opium. [the term uses both the orig. Chinese and the derived SE term; however, note Cantonese *yinyan*, craving for opium]

yeo *n. see* YEYO n.

yeoman of the vinegar bottle *n.* [late 16C] a sufferer from venereal disease. [the use of vinegar as a 'cure' for the disease; as well as internal or external use some doctors suggested that the mercury used in the treatment of syphilis should first be boiled in vinegar]

yep *adv.* (*also* **yump, yup**) [late 19C+] (*orig. US*) yes. [pron.]

yer actual *adj. see* YOUR ACTUAL adj.

yerba *n.* [1960s+] (*drugs*) marijuana; thus *yerba buena*, good marijuana; *yerba mala*, bad marijuana (cf. AFRICAN BUSH n.). [Sp. *yerba*, herb]

yerknod *n. see* YEKNOD n.

yernt *n.* [1980s] (*US campus*) a socially inept person. [? YENTA n.]

yerp *see under* YAP.

yerquick *n.* [2000s] (*Aus.*) an absolute fool. [sarcastic use of SE *quick*, intelligent]

yerriso *n.* [20C+] (*W.I.*) gossip, rumour. [pron. of SE *I hear so*]

yes *v.* [20C+] to act in an obsequious manner.

yes-baas *n.* [1960s+] (*S.Afr.*) a servile, subservient Black. [lit. 'yes, boss']

yesca *n.* (*also* **llesca, yesco**) [1940s+] (*US drugs*) marijuana. [Sp. *llesca*, tinder, fuel; pron. 'yesca']

yes-girl *n.* [1960s] a sexually complaisant young woman. [play on YES-MAN n.]

yes-man *n.* (*also* **yes-wife**) [1910s+] (*orig. US*) an obsequious, subservient person, esp. in business, one who always says 'yes' to their superiors, in the belief that this is what they like to hear. [? borrowed from synon. 19C Ger. *jaherr*]

yes sir! *excl.* (*also* **yes siree!**) [late 18C+] (*orig. US*) an emphatic assertion.

yes siree bob! *excl.* [mid-19C+] a general excl. of affirmation; definitely, certainly, absolutely.

yest *n.* [early 18C–early 19C] yesterday. [abbr.]

ye stars! *excl. see* MY STARS! excl.

yesty *n.* [1950s] (*Aus.*) yesterday. [abbr.]

yes-wife *n. see* YES-MAN n.

yet *adv.* [1930s+] (*orig. US*) an ironic intensive placed at the end of a sentence. [Yid. *noch*, another]

yettie *n.* [2000s] a young internet technocrat. [acronym]

yet to be *phr.* [1950s+] free (referring both to behaviour and cost). [rhy. sl.]

yewie *n. see* U-IE n.

yeyo *n.* (*also* **jejo, llello, yahoo, yaoh, yayo, yayoo, yeaho, yeo**) [1990s+] (*drugs*) **1** cocaine. **2** crack cocaine (cf. BASE n.). [synon. Sp. *llello*, pron. 'yeayo']

yicky *adj. see* ICKY adj. (3).

Yid *n.*[1] (*also* **Yiddel, Yiddo, Yit, Yitt**) [mid-19C+] a Jew; both derog. and general use, depending on context; thus pl. *Yidden* (cf. ARAB n.[2]). [Ger. *Jude*, Jew, ult. Yehuda or Judah, one of the biblical Jacob's sons. The term, as Rosten, *The Joys of Yiddish* (1968), points out, is neutral if pronounced 'yeed' as it would be by Jews speaking the Judaeo-German language Yiddish, but unashamedly offensive if pronounced 'yid']

Yid *n.*[2] (*also* **Yit, Yitt**) [1950s–70s] (*Aus.*) a sovereign; thus *half a Yid*, a half sovereign, 10 shillings (50p) (cf. BEES (AND HONEY) n.). [rhy. sl. = QUID n. (2), but note stereotyped link of Jews and money]

Yiddisher *n.* [late 19C–1910s] a Jew (cf. ARAB n.[2]).

Yiddisher *adj.* (*also* **Yid, Yiddish**) [late 19C+] Jewish. [Yid. *yiddishe*, Jewish]

Yiddisher fiddle *n.* [1920s–50s] minor cheating or other illegality. [pun on YIDDISHER adj. + SE *fiddle*/FIDDLE n.[3] (2)]

Yiddisher piano *n.* [1910s+] a cash register. [YIDDISHER adj. + SE *piano*; negative stereotyping]

Yiddish highway *n.* [20C+] (*US*) highway US-301, the route from New York City to Miami. [YIDDISHER adj. + SE *highway*; New York Jews trad. move to Miami for their retirement; the relatives use the highway for visits]

Yiddish Renaissance *n.* [1950s+] over-elaborate furniture in doubtful taste (cf. EARLY HALLOWEEN n.). [YIDDISHER adj. + SE *Renaissance*; racial stereotyping]

Yiddish screwdriver *n. see* JEWISH SCREWDRIVER n.

Yiddle *n.* [20C+] a derog. term for a Jew (cf. ARAB n.[2]). [dimin. of YID n.[1]]

Yiddo *n. see* YID n.[1].

yike *n.* **1** [1930s–60s] (*Aus.*) an argument, a dispute, a fight, a brawl. **2** [1940s] a boxing match. [ety. unknown; ? echoic or dial. *yike*, the call of the woodpecker]

yikes *n.* [1970s+] worries, nervousness. [? backform. f. YIKES! excl.]

yikes! *excl.* [1940s+] an excl. of surprise or shock. [? link to SE *yoicks!* or CRIKEY! excl.]

ying-yang *n.* (*also* **yin-yang**) **1** [1950s] (*US*) sexual intercourse. **2** [1950s+] the penis. **3** [1960s+] the anus; esp. in UP THE YING-YANG phr. **4** [1970s] in fig. use, nonsense. [? var. on WANG n.[2] (1); the link to 'Hindu' *yin* and *yang* in Wentworth & Flexner, *Dict. American Slang* (1960, 1975) seems spurious; note RMC Duntroon (*Aus.*) *ying-yang*, an Asian]

yip *n.* **1** [1910s] (*US*) talk. **2** [1930s+] (*US Und.*) a complaint. [SE *yip*, a short, sharp bark]

yip *v.*[1] [1910s+] (*US*) to talk in a petulant or irritating manner. [SE *yip*, to bark]

yip *v.*[2] [1930s+] to feel nervous, twitchy. [YIPS n.]

yippee beans *n.* [1960s] (*Aus.*) amphetamines (cf. A n.[2]). [rhy. sl.]

yips *n.* [1930s+] nerves. [popularly linked to golf use]

yip-yap drug *n.* [1990s+] (*Aus. drugs*) any drug that makes one talk fast and usu. meaninglessly, e.g. amphetamine, cocaine (cf. A n.[2]). [YIP v.[1] + SE *yap*]

yit *n.* [1970s–80s] (*UK juv.*) a general term of abuse.

Yit/Yitt *see under* YID.

yi-yen *n. see* GEE YEN n.

Y.M. *n.* [1910s+] (*orig. US*) the *Young Men's Christian Association* (cf. Y.W.). [abbr.]

Y.M.C.A. *adj.*[1] [late 19C–1930s] priggish, puritan, 'goody-goody'. [the religiously based organization]

Y.M.C.A. *adj.*[2] [1950s] of food, disgusting, unappetizing. [*yesterday's muck cooked again*]

yo *n.* [1990s+] (*US*) a young Black man, esp. one who deals drugs on the street. [YO! excl. (2)]

yo *v.* [1980s+] (*UK Black*) to greet with a shout of 'Yo!' [YO! excl. (2)]

yo! *excl.* **1** [1910s+] yes! **2** [1960s+] (*US*) a general term of address. **3** [1990s+] used to add emphasis to a statement. [orig. used in 15C as excl. of warning; ? abbr. US Black/Southern *y'all*]

yob *n.* **1** [mid-19C–1900s] a boy. **2** [mid-19C+] an uncouth, vulgar youth. **3** [1910s] a man. **4** [1910s–50s] (*Aus.*) a spec. abusive term for a man. [backsl.; note WW1 milit. use, *yob*, a young, gullible officer]

yobbo *n.* [1920s+] a lout, a hooligan; a general derog. used of working-class youths. [ext. of YOB n. (2)]

yobby *adj.* [1960s+] loutish. [YOB n. (2)]

yo-boy *n.* [1980s+] (*US Black*) a White youth who apes his Black contemporaries. [his use of the common Black greeting YO! excl.]

yock *n.* (*also* **yockele, yok**) **1** [20C+] a gentile. **2** [1930s+] a fool. [backsl. = GOY n.]

yock *v.* **1** [1950s+] to laugh or shout loudly; thus *yocks*, laughter. **2** [1990s+] to spit. [(1) YOKS n.; (2) ? SE *hawk*]

yocker *n.* **1** [1990s+] (*UK juv.*) a lump of spit. **2** [2000s] (*Irish*) a testicle. [(1) YOCK v. (2)]

yocks *n. see* YOKS n.

yodel *v.* (*also* **yodel over the mahogany**) [1960s+] (*Aus./N.Z.*) to vomit (cf. BARF v.).

yodel in the canyon (of love) *v.* (*also* **grin in the canyon, yodel from the highest tower, yodel in the valley, yodel up the valley**) [1930s+] to perform cunnilingus.

yoghurt truck *n. see* SALTY YOGURT SLINGER n.

Yogi Bear *n.* [1960s+] (*Aus.*) a prison dandy. [rhy. sl. = LAIR n.; ult. US cartoon character *Yogi Bear*]

yok *n. see* YOCK n.

yoke *n.*[1] (*Irish*) **1** [mid-19C–1940s] a horse-drawn carriage. **2** [late 19C–1900s] a riding horse, as opposed to a racehorse. **3** [20C+] any form of unspecified gadget or object. **4** [1910s+] a car, a vehicle, e.g. a police wagon; a boat. **5** [1930s+] (*also* **yokibus**) a person. **6** [1960s+] a (young) woman.

yoke *n.*[2] **1** [1940s–50s] (*US Black/teen*) a job. **2** [1980s+] the act of grabbing someone around the neck as part of a mugging. [SE *yoke*, a form of collar]

yoke *v.* **1** [mid-19C+] (*US*) to murder by strangulation or by cutting someone's throat from behind. **2** [1940s+] to rob while choking or strangling the victim, either with a rope or stick; one person does the *yoking*, the other rifles the victim's pockets. [SE *yoke*, a collar placed across the neck]

yoked *adj.* [1980s+] (*US campus*) muscular, well-built. [? one's shoulders resemble a SE *yoke*]

yokibus *n. see* YOKE n.[1] (5).

yoks *n.* (*also* **yaks, yocks, yuks**) [1940s+] (*US*) laughs; thus *get one's yuks*, to derive pleasure. [echoic]

yokuff *n.* [mid-19C] a large box, a chest. [SE *coffer*]

yola *n.* [1900s–40s] (*US Black*) a light-skinned young woman. [? Sp.]

yold *n.* (*also* **yuld**) [1940s–50s] (*US*) a gullible victim. [Heb. *yeled*, a boy]

yom *n.* (*also* **yomo**) [1970s+] (*US*) **1** a Black street boy. **2** a Black girl. [their frequent use of YO' MAMA! excl.]

yom *adj.* [1970s] pertaining to Black and Puerto Rican culture, lifestyle. [YOM n.]

yo' mama! *excl.* (*also* **yo' Momma!**) [1940s] (*US Black*) a general excl. which, like MOTHERFUCKER n., varies as to context, from the jovially teasing to the deliberately insulting; usu. used as a retort. [US Black pron. of YOUR MOTHER! excl.]

yomo *n. see* YOM n.

yomp *v.* [1980s+] to march, to walk (in difficult conditions). [orig. Royal Marine term for the marching with weapons and a 120lb pack across appalling terrain in extremely hostile conditions on the premise that once this ultimate in route marches is concluded, the troops will be prepared to fight a battle at the other end; poss. Norw. word used by skiers to describe the crossing of obstacles. The term gained widespread currency during the Falklands War of 1982]

yonker *n. see* YOUNKER n.

yonks *n.* [1960s+] a long time; esp. in phr. *for yonks*. [ety. unknown; ? DONKEY'S (YEARS) n.]

yonnie *n.* [1940s+] (*Aus.*) a small stone, a pebble. [ety. unknown; ? Aboriginal language]

yoo-ee *n. see* U-IE n.

yoof *adj.* [1980s+] used of anything, esp. TV programmes, that is high on pop gossip and fashion, low (in critical eyes) on intelligence and is aimed at the young. [deliberate mispron. of SE *youth* + mimicry of the 'street-cred' London accents of presenters of such programmes and of their doyenne, the then TV executive Janet Street-Porter]

yoo-hoo *v.* [1940s+] to shout 'hello', to attract someone's attention. [YOO-HOO! excl.]

yoo-hoo! *excl.* [1940s+] a cry of hello!

yoo-hoo boy *n.* [1940s–70s] (*US*) an effeminate homosexual. [his camp shrieks of YOO-HOO! excl.]

yook *n.* [mid-19C] (*UK Und.*) venereal disease.

yoot *n. see* YOUT n.

yop *n.*[1] [late 19C] (*US*) a lout. [YOB n. (2)]

yop *n.*[2] *see* YAP n.[1].

York *n.* [mid-19C–1960s] (*US tramp*) New York City. [abbr.]

York *adj.* [early 18C; mid–late 19C] (*US*) of or pertaining to New York City. [YORK n.]

york *n.* [early 19C] a stare, a glance. [YORK v.]

york *v.* [early 19C] to stare at. [? Cheshire dial. *york*, to pierce or the stereotyped Yorkshireman's shrewd appraisal]

Yorker *n.* [mid-18C–1940s] a New Yorker. [YORK n.]

Yorkie *n.* (*also* **Yorky**) **1** [mid-19C+] a *York*shireman; also in direct address. **2** [1950s+] a *York*shire terrier. [abbr.]

York Minster to a brass farthing *phr.* [early–mid-19C] the longest possible odds (cf. ALL THE WORLD TO A CHINA ORANGE phr.).

Yorkshire *n.* [mid-19C–1900s] sharp practice. [Ware defines as 'fair and square payments', but this may be ironic; ult. UK county *Yorkshire*]

Yorkshire *adj.* [early 17C; late 18C–mid-19C] mean, grasping; also used in combs. below. [stereotyping of *Yorkshire* people as mean]

Yorkshire *v.* [late 19C] to defraud, to deceive. [negative stereotyping]

Yorkshire bite *n.* **1** [late 18C–mid-19C] over-reaching, greediness. **2** [mid-19C] a grasping person.

Yorkshire compliment *n.* [mid-19C–1900s] a gift that means nothing to the donor and is useless to the recipient. [negative stereotyping]

Yorkshire estate *n.* [mid-19C–1900s] money that is in prospect but not yet handed over; thus *when I come into my Yorkshire estates*, when I finally have some money. [negative stereotyping of Yorks. business or legal methods]

Yorkshire hog *n.* [late 18C] a fat wether or castrated ram. [SE *Yorkshire hog*, a very large pig, but note 'The Old Yorkshire Pig is by some considered as the very worst of the large varieties, very long legged, weak loined, not of strong constitution, nor good stye pigs, but yet quicker feeders' (*Encycl. Metrop.*, 1845)]

Yorkshire penny bank *n.* [20C+] masturbation; usu. in phr. *not worth a Yorkshire penny bank*. [rhy. sl. = WANK n.[1] (1)]

Yorkshire reckoning *n.* [mid-19C] a situation where every member of the company pays for themselves. [COME YORKSHIRE OVER v.]

Yorkshire rippers *n.* [1980s+] slippers. [rhy. sl.]

Yorkshire tyke *n.* [1940s+] a microphone. [rhy. sl. = MIC n.[1]]

York Street concerned *phr.* (*also* **there York Street is concerned**) [19C] someone is staring (cf. MR KNAP IS CONCERNED phr.[1]). [YORK v.]

Yorky *n. see* YORKIE n.

yo thang *n. see* YOUR THING n.

you ain't just whistling 'Dixie' *phr.* [20C+] (*US*) you really mean what you're saying, you're not just being flippant. [for ety. see DIXIE n.]

you ain't know! *excl.* [2000s] (*US Black*) an excl. of affirmation, esp. when confirming what the speaker seems only to be questioning. [lit. 'you didn't know that already?'; a synon. with SE *you don't say!*]

you ain't saying nothing *phr.* [1970s] (*US Black*) a dismissive phr. meaning nothing you say is of the slightest importance.

you and me *n.* **1** [20C+] tea. **2** [20C+] urination, urine (cf. ANGEL'S KISS n.). **3** [1910s–30s] a flea. **4** [1940s+] (*bingo*) the number 3 (cf. ALDERSHOT LADIES n.). **5** [1960s+] (*Aus.*) a pea. [rhy. sl.; (2) = PEE n.[1]]

you and whose army? *phr.* (*also* **you and who else?**) [1930s+] (*mainly US teen*) a phr. addressed to anyone who is threatening violence.

you are a thief and a murderer and you have killed a baboon and stole his face *phr.* [late 18C–early 19C] a general phr. of hostility and contempt.

you are Josephus rex *phr.* [late 18C–early 19C] you are joking. [pun on SE abbr. *jo* + Lat. *rex*, king]

you be hanged! *excl.* [17C–1900s] a general excl. of dismissal, contempt.

you bet! *excl.* (*also* **you betcha/betcher!**) [mid-19C+] (*orig. US*) a general excl. of affirmation, agreement, certainly! I'll say so! indeed!

you can fuck me but you can't make me like the baby

phr. [1980s+] (*Aus. prison*) a prisoner may endure his punishment but need not necessarily enjoy it.

you can have it! *excl.* (*also* **you can keep it!**) [1930s+] no thanks! it's all yours! I don't want it!

you can take that to the bank *phr. see* BANK ON v.

you can't fart against thunder *phr.* [late 19C+] don't try to do the impossible.

you can't fight city hall *phr.* (*also* **go fight city hall**) [1940s+] (*US*) you can't win against the establishment.

you can't fly on one wing *phr.* [1940s+] (*Can.*) have another drink before you go.

you can't walk on one leg *phr.* [1980s] (*Aus.*) a phr. used to encourage someone to have another drink. [var. on YOU CAN'T FLY ON ONE WING phr.]

you can't win 'em all *phr.* [1920s+] a consolatory phr. used to say that one cannot be successful every time.

you couldn't box kippers *phr.* [1920s+] a phr. used to decry a person as a physical weakling.

you couldn't see —'s arse for dust *phr.* (*also* **you couldn't see —'s ass for dust**) [late 19C+] said of someone who has run off very quickly. [SE *see* + ARSE n.[1](1)/ASS n. (2) + SE *dust*]

you couldn't throw your hat over the workhouse wall *phr.* [1900s–30s] a phr. used to tease someone who has, or allegedly has, a number of illegitimate children. [such children were usu. sent to the workhouse]

you don't get many of those to the pound *phr.* [20C+] a phr. used by leering men observing a woman with large breasts.

you don't know whether you want a shit or haircut *phr.* (*also* **you don't know whether your arsehole's bored or punched**) [20C+] a phr. used to indicate that a person is very stupid. [SE *know* + SHIT n.[1](3)/ARSEHOLE n. (1)]

you don't look at the mantelpiece when you're poking the fire *phr.* [20C+] a phr. meaning that a woman's looks are irrelevant if she's sexually available.

you don't want to go there *phr.* [1990s+] a phr. meaning this is not an area of conversation that you should pursue (cf. DON'T (EVEN) GO THERE phr.).

you down with o.p.p.? *phr.* [1990s+] (*US Black teen*) do you respect other people's property? [DOWN adj.[1] (1) + O.P.P. n. (1)]

youee *n. see* U-IE n.

you got it *phr.* [1960s–70s] a phr. implying that nothing new has happened, there is no information to pass on; usu. as a response to the query WHAT'S HAPPENING? phr.

you got it! *excl.* [1970s+] (*orig. US, esp. Black*) a general affirmative reply, usu. to a yes/no question.

you-know *n.*[1] [1920s–30s] (*US*) the posterior, the buttocks (cf. PART THAT GOES OVER THE FENCE LAST n.). [euph.]

you-know *n.*[2] [1930s+] (*drugs*) cocaine (cf. BARLEY n.[2]). [rhy. sl. = SNOW n.[2] (1)]

you know *phr.* [late 19C+] a verbal punctuation, with no real meaning. [abbr. earlier *don't you know*]

you-know-his-name *n. see* YOU KNOW WHO n.

you know it (is) *phr.* [late 19C; 1960s+] (*orig. US*) any form of emphatic agreement, yes indeed, you're right etc.

you know what *n.* **1** [17C] the vagina (cf. ARTICLE n.). **2** [mid-17C–mid-18C] the penis (cf. BAUBLE n.). **3** [late 17C–early 18C; 1950s+] sexual intercourse. **4** [late 17C+] (*also* **what you know**) anything the speaker does not wish to name; often as a euph. **5** [2000s] the buttocks.

you know what you can do *phr.* [1920s+] a dismissive phr. used to counter a suggestion, an unacceptable offer etc; often describing something as *you know what you can do with…* [i.e. SHOVE IT UP YOUR ARSE! excl.]

you know where *n.* **1** [mid-18C+] a euph. depending on context; if sexual, a ref. to the vagina or penis; if hostile, the anus or the testicles (cf. ARTICLE n.; GINGAMBOBS n.; PART THAT GOES OVER THE FENCE LAST n.). **2** [mid-19C+] hell. **3** [1920s] the lavatory.

you know who *n.* (*also* **you-know-his-name**) [late 17C+] used of a person whose name one knows, but prefers not to mention.

you'll have to do the other thing *phr.* [mid-19C+] a phr. meaning if you don't like it this way, then… [i.e. *go to hell*]

you'll know me again, won't you? *phr. see* DO YOU THINK YOU'LL KNOW ME AGAIN? phr.

you make a better door than a window *phr.* [20C+] a phr. used to someone who is blocking one's view.

you make me tired *phr.* (*also* **you make my butt tired**) [late 19C+] (*orig. US*) you bore me. [supposedly imported to the UK by the contemporary Duchess of Marlborough, a fashion leader]

You Must Come Across *n.* [1930s] (*US tramp*) the YMCA. [COME ACROSS v. (1)]

young *adj.* **1** [mid-19C+] diminutive, miniature, a small version of. **2** [1930s+] (*US Black*) immature, un-versed in street life. **3** [1940s] (*Irish*) tipsy.

young and frisky *n.* [20C+] (*Aus.*) whisky. [rhy. sl.]

young-ass *adj.* [1950s+] (*US Black*) immature. [SE *young* + -ASS sfx]

young bantam *n.* [1940s] (*US Black*) a very young girl. [SE *young* + BANTAM n. (2)]

young bleed *n.* [2000s] (*US Black*) a female virgin. [? she will *bleed* when deflowered]

young blood *n.* [early 19C+] a young man, making his way in the world; thus (*orig. US Black*) the up-and-coming youth who is learning the mores of street life; also as a term of address.

young devil *n.* [17C+] a term of mildly reproving affection.

young, dumb and full of cum *phr.* [1970s+] (*US*) used of a teenager or young person whose enthusiasm for life (and esp. sex) outweighs their intelligence. [SE *young* + *dumb* + CUM n.[1] (1)]

young hemp *n.* [late 18C–early 19C] an ill-behaved young man or boy. [? link to adj. *hempen*, e.g. HEMPEN CRAVAT n., thus a candidate for the gallows]

young horse *n.* [1930s] (*US prison*) roast beef. [? play on OLD HORSE n.[2]]

youngie *n.* **1** [1960s+] (*Aus.*) a young woman. **2** [1990s+] a young person. [SE *young* + dimin./affectionate sfx *-ie*; on pattern of OLDIE n. (1)]

young in the head *phr.* [1970s+] (*US Black*) childish, immature.

young kipper *n.* [20C+] an inadequate meal. [a pun on the Jewish festival of *Yom Kippur*, the Day of Atonement, at which time it is customary to spend the day fasting]

young set-me-up *n. see* SET-ME-UP n.

young suit *n.* [1930s–40s] (*US Black*) a badly fitting or too small suit.

young 'un *n.* [mid-19C+] a young person, often as a direct term of address.

younker *n.* (*also* **yonker, yunker**) [mid-16C–1960s] a lad, a boy; sometimes a female child. [Du. *jonker, jonkheer*, young master]

your actual *adj.* (*also* **yer actual**) [1960s+] an emphatic intensifier of a person or object, e.g. *your actual Rolls Royce*. [coined by Barry Took and Marty Feldman for the 1950s–60s BBC radio show *Round the Horne*]

your arse! *excl.* (*also* **your ass!**) [1920s+] a dismissive excl. meaning I don't believe you!

your asshole's sucking wind *phr.* [1940s+] (*orig. US*) you are talking nonsense. [ARSEHOLE n. (1) + SUCK WIND v.]

your ass is mine *phr.* [1950s+] a general threat, usu. following a conditional, e.g. *if you don't — your ass is mine*. [ASS n. (5) + SE *mine*]

your dime *phr.* [1970s] (*US*) a phr. used on answering the phone to tell the caller 'tell me why you rang'. [i.e. you are paying for the call, it's up to you to speak]

you're all about – like shit in a field *phr.* [20C+] you are a useful, alert, efficient person – like hell you are! [SHIT n.[1] (1) + SE *field*]

you're another *phr.* [mid-18C+] a meaningless or vaguely contemptuous and ultimately childish retort, responding to a speaker who has made the offensive comment, 'You're a —'.

you're darn tootin' *phr.* (*also* **you're damn tootin', you're durn tootin'**) [1930s+] (*orig. US*) you're absolutely right. [DARN adj. + TOOTING adj. (1); abbr. *you're darn tootin' right*]

you're having a laugh! *excl.* [1990s+] an excl. of astonishment or disbelief.

you're it *phr.* [1970s] (*US campus*) used as a response to the greeting 'What's happening (man)?'

you're so sharp you'll cut yourself *phr.* [20C+] a mocking phr. directed at someone who seems to think him- or herself exceptionally clever, well-informed etc. [SHARP adj. (2) + SE *cut*]

you're so tan I hate you *phr.* [1990s+] (*US campus*) goodbye.

you're telling me! *excl.* [1930s+] that's absolutely right! I don't disagree at all! I know only too well! [? Gus Kahn song-title 'You're Telling Me' (1932)]

your face and my arse/ass/butt! *excl. see* KISS MY ARSE! excl.

your father's a glazier? *phr. see* IS YOUR FATHER A GLAZIER? phr.

your granny! *excl.* (*also* **your grandmother!**) [early 19C+] (*US*) a general response of incredulity, disbelief, you must be joking!

your man *n.* (*also* **your woman**) [1930s+] (*Irish*) **1** an unnamed, although quite poss. specified, individual. **2** a specific thing, a good thing. **3** the Devil.

Your Man Upstairs *n.* [1990s+] (*Irish*) God. [YOUR MAN n. (1) + UPSTAIRS n.² (1)]

your mother *n.* [1940s+] (*camp gay*) oneself; thus *your mother needs a drink* etc. [the 'feminization' underpinning much camp gay sl.]

your mother! *excl.* (*also* **your mom!**) [1940s+] (*orig. US, mainly teen*) a rejoinder to an insult, implying that whatever that insult is, it applies most to the speaker's own mother (cf. YO' MAMA! excl.). [euph. for GO FUCK YOUR MOTHER! excl.]

your mother's cunt! *excl.* (*also* **your mother's box! ...twat!**) [1950s+] a derisive, dismissive excl. [SE *mother* + CUNT n.¹ (1)/BOX n.¹ (1)/TWAT n. (1)]

your nibs *n.* [mid-19C] yourself. [NIBS n. (1)]

your other eye! *excl.* [20C+] (*Irish*) an excl. of disbelief, rubbish! nonsense!

your roof is leaking *phr.* [1940s] a phr. used of an eccentric, an unstable person. [ROOF n. (2) + SE *leaking*]

yours and ours *n.* [20C+] flowers. [rhy. sl., used by Covent Garden Market porters and street vendors]

— yourself *phr.* [late 19C+] used as a retort, mocking or rebutting what has just been said, e.g. 'Hello.' 'Hello yourself!'

yours truly *n.* (*also* **yours faithfully, yours sincerely**) [mid-19C+] a joc. ref. by a speaker to him- or herself.

your thing *n.* (*also* **yo thang**) [1960s+] (*orig. US Black*) one's preference, one's own style, one's role within the group. [THING n.⁵ (3)]

your uncle *n. see* UNCLE n.¹ (3).

your woman *n. see* YOUR MAN n.

you said it! *excl.* [20C+] (*orig. US*) a general excl. of emphasis and agreement.

you scratch my back and I'll scratch yours *phr.* [mid-19C+] (*orig. US*) an invitation to reciprocate mutually, let's do a favour for each other.

you should be so lucky *phr.* [1950s+] usu. in ironic use, you should be so lucky – but there's almost no hope that you will be. [? a Yid. phr.; certainly orig. identified with Jewish use]

yout *n.* (*also* **yoot**) (*W.I./UK Black*) [1970s+] **1** a child, a young man, an immature man. **2** in general, politically active young people. [SE *youth*; the deliberate mispron. accentuates the oppositional stance of such young men]

you the man *phr. see* MAN, THE n. (2).

yout'man *n.* [1980s+] (*W.I./UK Black teen*) a young person, man or woman. [YOUT n. + sfx -*man*]

you've got a nerve *phr.* [late 19C+] how dare you. [NERVE n. (2)]

you what? *excl.* [1920s+] an excl. spoken as a challenge, say that again! [SE *what?*, the speaker pretends not to have heard what has been said]

you wouldn't give it to a Jap on ANZAC day *phr.* [1970s+] (*Aus.*) said of anything that is absolutely unacceptable. [ANZAC *day*, the Aus./N.Z. memorial to their joint forces landing at Gallipoli in 1915; then ext. to WW2]

you wouldn't read about it *phr.* (*also* **you wouldn't know about it**) [1940s+] (*orig. Aus.*) a phr. describing anything amazing or unbelievable and proving that nature is infinitely more bizarre than mere art.

yowza(h)! *excl.* [1930s+] (*US teen*) a general excl., either of approval or of vaguely non-committal agreement. [YES SIR! excl.]

yoxter *n.* [mid-19C] a convict who has returned from transportation before the full expiry of their sentence. [ety. unknown; ? link to Scot./dial. *yox*, to vomit, to cough up, i.e. the convict has 'come up again']

yoyo *n.¹* **1** [1920s+] the penis, esp. when small. **2** [1940s+] (*US*) an unpredictable or inconsistent person whose moods and actions go up and down; thus a fool; also as adj. (cf. CHOAD n.). **3** [1980s] (*US campus*) a bisexual person. [(2) is fig. use of (1) which also goes 'up and down']

yoyo *n.²* (*also* **yoyo boy**) [1980s+] (*US Black*) a street youth. [YO! excl.]

Y.T. *n.* [1940s+] oneself, i.e. YOURS TRULY n.

yuck *n.* (*also* **yecch, yech, yuk**) [1940s+] (*US*) anything or anyone seen as disgusting or repulsive. [YUCK! excl.]

yuck *adj.* [1970s+] disgusting, repulsive. [YUCK n.]

yuck *v.* [1960s+] (*US campus/teen*) to vomit (cf. BARF v.). [echoic]

yuck! *excl.* (*also* **yecch! yuk!**) [1960s+] (*mainly juv.*) an all-purpose excl. of distaste. [echoic]

yuck mouth *n.* (*US Black*) an extremely proficient fellatrix.

yuck up *v.* [1960s+] **1** (*W.I.*) to annoy, to irritate. **2** to vomit (cf. BARF v.). **3** (*US*) to laugh. [ext. of YUCK v.]

yucky *n.* [1980s] an act of defecation.

yucky *adj.* (*also* **ucky, yecchy, yucko, yukky**) [1960s+] (*mainly juv.*) unpleasant, disgusting, with overtones of stickiness or smelliness. [YUCK! excl.]

Yug *n.* (*also* **Yugo**) [1950s+] **1** a Yugoslav. **2** (*Aus.*) an immigrant from former Yugoslavia. [abbr.]

yuk *see also under* YUCK.

yuk *n.¹* [1930s] (*US prison*) a friend.

yuk *n.²* [1970s+] (*US*) a laugh, the sound of laughter. [YUK v. (1)]

yuk *v.* **1** [1960s+] (*US*) to laugh. **2** [1970s+] (*US gay*) to be excited.

yuke *v.* [1990s+] (*US campus*) to vomit (cf. BARF v.). [echoic]

yukker *n.* [1990s+] (*UK juv.*) a baby, a toddler. [YUCK n.]

yuks *n. see* YOKS n.

yuld *n. see* YOLD n.

Yuletide log *n.* [1970s] a dog. [rhy. sl.]

yum! *excl.* (*also* **yum-yum!**) [late 19C+] an expression of praise for anything delightful, usu. delicious food. [echoic]

yummies *n.* [1970s+] (*US gay*) the male genitalia; thus *get some yummies*, to have anal intercourse. [YUMMY adj. (2), i.e. 'good enough to eat'/EAT v.³ (1)]

yummy *n.* [1960s+] **1** an attractive teenage girl. **2** an attractive young man. [YUMMY adj. (2), i.e. 'good enough to eat']

yummy *adj.* [late 19C+] **1** tasty, delicious, flavoursome. **2** used similarly, of people, objects, experiences etc. [YUM! excl.]

yummy *v.* [1950s] to have sexual intercourse. [YUMMY adj. (2)]

yump *adv. see* YEP adv.

yumpie *n.* [1980s] (*US*) a young, *upwardly-mobile professional*. [abbr.; var. on YUPPIE n.]

yum-yum n. 1 [late 19C] a pretty young woman. 2 [late 19C] the vagina. 3 [late 19C–1920s] anything deliciously pleasurable, esp. love-making; thus *yum-yum girl*, a prostitute. [YUM! excl.; note naut. jargon *yum-yum*, love letter]

yum-yum adj. 1 [late 19C] of a young woman, very attractive. 2 [late 19C–1920s] deliciously pleasurable.

yum-yum! excl. see YUM! excl.

yum-yums n. [1970s+] (*drugs*) any drugs in pill or capsule form (cf. PILL n.4). [YUM-YUM n. (3)]

yunk n. [1910s+] (*Aus.*) a lump, a chunk; thus *yunk of dodger*, a slice of bread. [? SE *hunk*]

yunker n. see YOUNKER n.

yuntry adj. [1990s+] (*W.I.*) a rural area.

yup adv. see YEP adv.

yuppie n. (*also* **yup**) [1980s+] (*orig. US*) a young, upwardly-mobile professional; hence v. *yuppify*, n. *yuppification*. [abbr.; the term created a variety of often one-off derivations, e.g. *pumpie*, previously *upwardly mobile prat*, i.e. a failed or former yuppie]

yuppie v. [1980s] (*US campus*) to defecate.

yuppie flu n. (*also* **yuppie disease**) [1980s+] ME, myalgic encephalomyelitis. [the condition, which appeared to become more prevalent during the 1980s and which resembled the most deleterious form of 'flu. It was often dismissed by doctors as no more than hypochondria, although its sufferers were able to demonstrate a variety of definite symptoms]

yuppie puppie n. [1990s+] a child of the generation for whom children were seen as something of a fashion accessory in the early 1990s. [YUPPIE n. + SE *puppy*]

yupster n. [1990s+] a synon. with YUPPIE n. [YUPPIE n. + -STER sfx]

yush! excl. [1980s+] (*W.I./UK Black teen*) a general expression of greeting.

yutz n. [1980s+] 1 a penis. 2 a fool, an idiot (cf. ALTER KACKER n.; CHOAD n.). [US Yid. *yutz*, a penis]

Y.W. [1910s+] (*orig. US*) the Young Women's Christian Association (cf. Y.M. n.). [abbr.]

Z n.1 [1980s] (*US*) a Mercedes model 300Z. [abbr.]

Z n.2 see ZIP (GUN) n.

z n.1 (*also* **zee**, **Zs**, **z's**, **zzzs**) [1960s+] (*orig. US*) a nap, a sleep; usu. in pl., sleep in general; thus BAG Z's v.; BLOW Z's v.; BUST SOME Z's v.; CATCH (SOME) Z's v.; COP (SOME) Z's v.; STACK Z's v. and other vars., to go to sleep. [echoic of the sound of one's breathing; note RMC Duntroon (*Aus.*) *land of zzz*, sleep; *punch a few zeds, suck in (some/the) zeds*, to sleep]

z n.2 (*also* **zee**) [1970s+] (*US drugs*) 1 1oz (28g) of cannabis. 2 1oz (28g) of heroin. [abbr. *oz*]

z v. (*also* **ze**, **z-out**, **z's**) [1960s+] (*US Black/teen*) to sleep. [z n.1]

'z abbr. see 's abbr.1.

za n. [1960s+] (*US teen/campus*) pizza; thus *do a za*, to buy or eat a pizza. [abbr.]

zac n. (*also* **sac**, **zack**) (*Aus./N.Z.*) 1 [late 19C+] a sixpence, a very small sum of money, 5 cents. 2 [1930s+] a 6-month prison sentence. [? SE *six* or Scot. *saxpence*]

Zacatecas purple n. [1960s+] (*drugs*) a variety of marijuana from Mexico (cf. ACAPULCO (GOLD) n.). [the town of *Zacatecas*, Mexico, near which the marijuana is assumed to have been grown; the buds are coloured *purple*]

zachary scotts n. [1940s–50s] diarrhoea (cf. BANANA (SPLITS) n.). [rhy. sl. = TROTS, THE n.2; ult. film star *Zachary Scott* (1914–65)]

zack n. see ZAC n.

'zack n. see BOZACK n.

zad n. [early 18C–early 19C] a crooked person or thing. [the crooked shape of the letter Z]

zaftig adj. (*also* **zoftick**, **zoftig**) [1920s+] usu. of a woman, plump, buxom. [Ger. *zaftig*, juicy]

zak n. [1960s–70s] (*S.Afr. township*) money. [? ZAC n. (1)]

Zambuck n. (*also* **Zambuk**) [1920s+] (*Aus.*) a St John's Ambulance man. [name of *Zambuk*, a proprietary antiseptic

ointment; Zambuk website: 'The word Zam-Buk originated in New Zealand, and was used to describe someone who administered first aid to wounded sportsmen. A "Zambuck" was a member of the Order of St. John, which was established at the time of the Crusades to care for the injured. Today, South Africa's most popular ointment is still used for every-day battle-scars – at school, work and home!']

zamie (girl) n. [1950s+] (*W.I.*) a lesbian; thus *make zamie*, to have a relationship with another woman. [? Fr. *les amies*, female friends]

zamietess n. [1950s+] (*W.I.*) a tough, brawling, noisy woman. [ZAMIE (GIRL) n. + sfx *-ess*]

zane n.1 [mid-19C–1960s] (*US gay*) a male homosexual (cf. ABIGAIL n.).

zane n.2 [1910s] (*US*) 10 cents, a dime. [Ger. *zehn*, ten]

Zane Grey n. [1930s+] (*Aus.*) pay, wages. [rhy. sl.; ult. Western writer *Zane Grey* (1875–1939)]

zanzy adj. [1960s] (*US Black*) attractive, first-rate. [*Zanzibar*, a part of Africa and thus good and authentic]

zap n. [1960s+] (*orig. US*) energy, enthusiasm. [ZAP! excl.]

zap v. 1 [1940s+] (*orig. US milit.*) to kill. 2 [1950s+] (*US Black*) to move quickly. 3 [1960s+] to put an end to, to do away with. 4 [1960s+] to attack, to criticize. 5 [1960s+] (*US campus*) to fail someone in a test or examination. 6 [1960s+] to overwhelm emotionally; to shock, to alarm. 7 [1960s+] to send, to put or to hit forcefully. 8 [1960s+] to engage in sexual relations. 9 [1960s+] to encounter problems; of a criminal, to get arrested, imprisoned. 10 [1960s+] to shoot. 11 [1980s+] (*US campus*) to cook in a microwave. 12 [1990s+] to steal. [ZAP! excl.]

zap! excl. [1920s+] (*orig. US*) used to describe the force of a sudden impact. [? echoic of the noise of a speeding bullet]

zapped adj. 1 [1950s+] killed, destroyed; exhausted; overwhelmed. 2 [1970s+] intoxicated by drink and/or drugs. [ZAP v.]

zappy adj. [1960s+] energetic, spirited, amusing. [ZAP v.]

zar n. [1900s–50s] (*US Black*) anywhere considered far away, unpleasant and culturally alien. [? SE *it's there*]

zarndrer n. [mid-19C] a long, single curl brought from the back hair over the left shoulder and allowed to fall on the breast. [abbr. of the name of its originator, Princess, later Queen *Alexandra*, wife of King Edward VII]

zarp n. [late 19C–1900s] (*S.Afr.*) a policeman. [abbr. *Zuid Afrikaansche Republik Politie*, Republic of South Africa Police]

Zasu Pitts n. [1930s–50s] diarrhoea (cf. BANANA (SPLITS) n.). [rhy. sl. = SHITS, THE n. (1); ult. film star *Zasu Pitts* (1898–1963)]

zat n. see ZIT n. (1).

zatch v. [1990s+] to have sexual intercourse.

zazzle n. [1950s] (*US Black*) sexual desire or sensuality. [? abbr. of PIZZAZZ n.]

zazzy adj. [1930s–60s] (*US Black*) sexy, sensuous, erotic. [ZAZZLE n.]

Z'd out adj. [1960s+] (*US teen*) unable to wake up properly, still sleepy. [z v.]

ze v. see z v.

zeb adj. [mid–late 19C] best; thus *zeb taoc*, best coat. [backsl.]

zebbled adj. [1990s+] (*UK juv.*) circumcised.

zebra n. 1 [late 19C–1920s] (*US*) a striped prison uniform. 2 [late 19C–1920s] (*US*) a convict. 3 [1970s+] (*US*) a stripe-shirted sports umpire. 4 [1970s–80s] (*UK Black*) a half-caste. 5 [1990s+] (*US Black teen*) a White person who poses as Black. [in all cases, the image is of a mixture of black and white]

zeb taoc n. see ZEB adj.

zed n. [1980s+] (*orig. US Black*) a sleep, a nap. [var. on z n.1]

zed about v. [late 19C] (*UK society*) to wander about in a zigzag manner. [the shape of the letter Z]

Zedland n. [late 18C–19C] the southwestern counties of England; Somerset, Devon, Cornwall, Dorset. [the local dials. in which 's' tends to be pronounced as 'z']

zee see also under z.

zeek out v. (also **zoom out**) [1980s+] (US teen) to act outrageously, to lose control, esp. through drugs or drink; thus **zeeked out**, exhausted, stupid, a general negative. [nonsense word *zeek* (the image is of going to extremes, in this case the last letter of the alphabet)/fig. use of SE *zoom*]

zees n. [2000s] (US Black/drugs) cigarette papers. [*Zig-Zag* rolling papers]

zef n. [1970s+] (S.Afr. teen) a member of the working class.

zelda n.[1] [1950s+] (US teen) a dull, uninteresting girl. [? the 'old-fashioned' name]

zelda n.[2] [1970s] (S.Afr. gay) a pure blooded Zulu. [initial letter]

zelda gooch n. [1970s] (camp gay) anyone considered unfashionable. [? anecdotal; note late 1970s erotic gay male oriented 'Zelda Gooch' Coloring Book, created by Wilton David]

zen n. [1960s+] (drugs) LSD (cf. A n.[3]). [SE *Zen* Buddhism, i.e. its spiritual effects]

zep n. [1910s+] a *Zeppelin* airship. [abbr.]

zerked (out) adj. [1980s] (drugs) completely intoxicated on a drug. [? abbr. SE *berserk*]

zero n. [1920s+] **1** (also **double zero**) a nobody, a totally useless and insignificant person. **2** nothing. **3** an insignificant or otherwise lacking place.

zero adj. [1970s] useless, worthless. [ZERO n.]

zero v. [1990s+] (US/W.I.) to kill, to murder. [i.e. to reduce to *zero*, or nothing]

zero cool adj. [1950s–60s] (US campus) extremely aware, sophisticated. [SE *zero* + COOL adj.[1] (3)/SE *cool*, i.e. 'no heat whatsoever']

zeroed adj. [1960s] (US campus) drunk to unconsciousness. [i.e. reduced to a ZERO n. (1)]

zero-hero n. [1990s+] (UK teen) the designated non-drinking driver escorting drinking friends for a night out. [their alcohol consumption is *zero*]

zero minus adj. [1970s+] (US campus) utterly, completely impossible, unacceptable. [i.e. 'less than nothing']

zetz n. [1970s+] (US) a blow or punch, often fig. [synon. Yid.; ult. Ger. *Zurücksetzung*, a setting back]

z-head n. [1980s] (US campus) a stupid person. [Z n.[1] + -HEAD sfx (1)]

zhlob/zhlub n. see SCHLUB n.

zhlubby adj. [1960s+] (US) coarse, boorish. [SCHLUB n.]

zhoosh v. [mid-19C+] (Polari) to fix, to tidy. [echoic of one's rushing about]

zib n. [1920s–40s] (US) an eccentric person. [ety. unknown; ? ZIP n.[1] (1), i.e. a human *zero*]

ziff n.[1] [mid-19C] a young thief. [? SE *thief*]

ziff n.[2] [1910s+] (Aus./N.Z.) a beard. [ety. unknown]

zig n. [1920s–60s] (US) a derog. name for a Black person (cf. ALLIGATOR BAIT n.[2]). [var. on JIG n.[5]]

zigabo/zigaboo/ziggerboo n. see JIGABOO n.

ziggy n. see ZOOK n. (2).

zigzagged adj. (also **zig-a-zag**, **zigzag**) **1** [1910s–20s] drunk (cf. AFFLICTED adj.). **2** [1950s] (drugs) intoxicated by a drug. [(1) one's unsteady gait; reinforced in (2) by *Zig-Zag* rolling papers]

zig-zig n. [1910s+] sexual intercourse; often found in pidgin slangs. [var. on JIG-A-JIG n.]

zilch n.[1] (orig. US campus/teen) **1** [1940s+] zero, nothing, something unimportant; also as adj. **2** [1960s] an ordinary or insignificant person. [? US campus *Joe Zilsch*, an insignificant person, popularized in 1930s magazine *Ballyhoo* as Joe Zilch]

zilch n.[2] [1960s+] (US teen) a spot or skin blemish. [? var. on ZIT n. (1)]

zilch v. [1960s+] **1** (US campus) to fail or do badly in an examination. **2** to make into nothing. [ZILCH n.[1]]

zillion n. (also **b'zillion**, **gajillion**) [1930s+] (orig. US) an unspecified, very large number.

zillion, a adv. [1970s] to a very great extent, very successfully.

zillionaire n. [1940s+] an uncountably rich person. [ZILLION n.]

zim-zim n. [1980s] (S.Afr.) a member of a politically orientated Black youth gang. [SE *-ism*, i.e. shorthand for politico-ideological beliefs]

zinc n. [1990s+] (UK juv.) something extremely unfashionable.

-zine sfx [1960s+] (US) used to describe a type of magazine, e.g. fanzine, teenzine. [abbr. SE *fanzine*]

zing n. (orig. US) **1** [20C+] a high-pitched noise. **2** [1910s+] energy, enthusiasm. **3** [1920s] in pl., a state of drunkenness. [echoic]

zing v. (orig. US) **1** [1920s+] to rush around energetically or at high speed. **2** [1940s+] to make a high-pitched noise. **3** [1960s+] to insult, to tease. **4** [1960s+] to make a snappy delivery of a witticism. **5** [1960s+] to shock with an unforeseen revelation. **6** [1960s+] to bet heavily, usu. at dice. [ZING n.]

zinger n. **1** [1940s+] (also **zingie**) something exceptional, whether good or bad. **2** [1940s+] a witty line, a one-line joke or repartee; a slanderous or disparaging comment. **3** [1970s+] a surprise question, an unexpected turn of events. [ZING v. (4)]

zingo! excl. see BINGO! excl. (1).

zing up v. [1970s] (orig. US) to enliven something, e.g. food. [i.e. to impart ZING n. (2)]

zingy adj. [1930s+] (orig. US) enthusiastic, energetic. [ZING n. (2)]

zip n.[1] (also **zippo**) **1** [late 19C+] (orig. US campus) a grade or mark of zero (cf. ACE n.[6]). **2** [1950s+] (US) nothing. **3** [1960s+] (US prison) zero, used in specifying the maximum length of a sentence, e.g. *zip-five*, from 0–5 years; *zip-ten*, 0–10 years etc. **4** [1970s+] an insignificant person, an unpleasant person with no good qualities. [SE *zero*]

zip n.[2] (also **zipp**, **zippo**) **1** [20C+] energy, a stimulus. **2** [1960s] a highly energetic person.

zip n.[3] [1950s] a sip of a drink; a single measure of alcohol. [SE *sip*]

zip n.[4] [1960s+] (US) a derog. term for a Vietnamese (or other Indo-Chinese) person. [ZIP n.[1] (1), i.e. their alleged lack of intelligence; or abbr. ZIPPERHEAD n.]

zip n.[5] [2000s] (US drugs) 1oz (28g) of a given drug. [ext. of Z n.[2]]

zip n.[6] see ZIP (GUN) n.

zip adj. [1980s] (US campus) unpleasant, bad, generally negative. [ZIP n.[1] (1)]

zip v.[1] (orig. US) **1** [mid-19C+] of a vehicle or a driver or any object, to move fast. **2** [late 19C+] of a person, to run around energetically, to be highly energetic, to do something energetically. **3** [1920s+] of a situation, e.g. a stage performance, to move fast. [echoic, esp. of a speeding bullet]

zip v.[2] (also **zip up**) [1930s+] to be quiet, to shut up. [var. on ZIP ONE'S LIP v.]

zip v.[3] [1960s+] (US) to shoot (dead). [echoic of the *zip* sound of a bullet but note ZIP n.[1], i.e. one renders the target 'nothing']

zipalid n. (also **zipperhead**, **zipperlid**) [1970s+] a complete fool. [i.e. one whose head has been 'unzipped' and their brain removed]

zip coon n. [mid-19C–1920s; 1980s] (US Black) a subservient Black person. [song 'Ole Zip Coon'; ult. COON n. (5); thus defined in Major, *Juba to Jive: A Dict. of Afro-American Slang* (1994), but note Tosches, *Where Dead Voices Gather* (2001): 'The figure of the black dandy, the Northern zip coon, was introduced...']

zip (gun) n. (also **Z**) [1940s+] (US) a homemade firearm capable of firing single bullets. [SE *zip*, the noise of a fired bullet. One takes a short length of pipe, 4–10 ins long with its inside diameter that of a bullet; a bullet is placed at one end and detonated by a sharp tap from a pointed steel rod which in turn is hit by the heel of one's hand or by a small object]

zip it (up)! excl. [1930s+] be quiet! shut up! [ZIP ONE'S LIP v.]

zip one's lip v. (also **zip one's mouth**, **zipper one's trap**) [1930s+] (orig. US) to stop talking, esp. in imper. [SE *zip* + *lip/mouth*/TRAP n.[3]]

zipp n. see ZIP n.[2].

zipper *n.* [1920s–30s] a promiscuous woman. [? she is full of ZIP n.² (1)]

zipper club *n.* [1970s+] (*US gay*) anywhere that plays host to repeated oral sex, e.g. a lavatory or bath-house. [the lowering of the *zipper* of one's fly; one goes there to EAT v.³ (1)]

zipper dinner *n. see* ZIPPER SEX n.

zippered *adj.* [1940s+] drunk. [? ZAP v. or ZIP n.² (1)]

zipperfish *n.* [1990s+] **1** the penis (cf. ANTEATER n.). **2** the female genitals. [SE zip(*per*)]

zipperhead *n.* [1960s+] (*US*) a Vietnamese, any Asian person (cf. BROWNIE n.²).

zipperhead/zipperlid *n. see* ZIPALID n.

zipper one's trap *v. see* ZIP ONE'S LIP v.

zipper pockets *n.* [1970s] (*US*) a mean, grasping person.

zipper sex *n.* (*also* **zipper dinner**) [1970s+] (*US gay*) quick, spontaneous fellatio without even dropping one's trousers, just unzippping and pulling out the penis.

zippo *see under* ZIP.

zippy *adj.* **1** [1920s] (*US*) fashionable. **2** [1920s+] energetic, full of 'pep'. **3** [1920s+] fast, speedy. **4** [1990s+] (*drugs*) containing amphetamine or a similar stimulant. [ZIP n.² (1)]

zip squat *n.* [1990s+] (*US campus*) a very small amount, nothing. [ZIP n.¹ (2) + SQUAT n.²]

zip up *v. see* ZIP v.².

zircon *n.* [1960s] (*US*) a fool. [SE *zircon*, a fake diamond]

zit *n.* **1** [1950s+] (*orig. US teen*) (*also* **zat, zitz, zort**) a spot, pimple or blackhead; thus *adj. zitty*, spotty; n., *zitty*, a person with acne. **2** [1960s] (*US campus*) any form of mark. **3** [1960s] (*US campus*) a general insult. **4** [1960s] (*US gay*) an underage boy. **5** [1970s+] a skin blemish left by a lovebite. [ety. unknown]

zit doctor *n.* [1980s] (*US teen*) a dermatologist. [ZIT n. (1) + SE *doctor*]

zit-features *n.* [1990s+] a general term of abuse, delivered to one who has acne. [ZIT n. (1) + SE *features*]

zithead *n.* [1990s+] (*US*) a teenager; the image is of acned mediocrity. [ZIT n. (1) + -HEAD sfx (1)]

zitz *n. see* ZIT n. (1).

zizz *n.¹* [1940s+] (*US*) gaiety, liveliness. [abbr. PIZZAZZ n.]

zizz *n.²* (*also* **ziz**) [1940s+] (*orig. milit.*) a nap, a snooze, a brief sleep. [ZIZZ v.]

zizz *v.* [1930s+] **1** to have a nap or snooze; thus *zizzing*, dozing, napping. **2** (*US*) to move fast. [echoic]

znees *n.* (*also* **znus, znuz**) [18C–mid-19C] frost; thus *zneesy*, frosty (weather). [? SE *sneeze*, the product of such weather]

zo *n.* [1960s] (*US campus*) zoology. [abbr.]

zob *n.* [1900s–40s] (*US*) a good-for-nothing, a weak person. [note Jan Ivarsson on *American Dialect Society-List* (Internet, 23 March 2003): '"Zob" with the variants "zobi", "zeb" or "zébi" is well established in French slang since at least 1870 [...] It comes from maghrebin Arabic "zebbi" or classical Arabic "zubb". The sense of the word is "penis", and it is very often used pejoratively about a person']

zod *n.* [1980s+] (*US campus/teen*) an eccentric, a strange person. [SE *he's odd*]

zoftick/zoftig *adj. see* ZAFTIG adj.

zogs *n.* [1960s] (*US campus*) the female breasts.

zoid *n.* [1980s+] **1** a schoolchild who has been rejected by his or her peers. **2** (*US campus*) a fan of punk rock and its attendant styles. [-ZOID sfx]

-zoid *sfx* [1970s+] (*orig. US*) used to invest a variety of terms, usu. negative and derog. descriptions of people, with a 'space-age', SF aura.

zol *n.* [1940s+] (*S.Afr. drugs*) **1** a hand-rolled cigarette. **2** a marijuana cigarette; thus *zol-rooker*, a marijuana smoker. **3** a measure of marijuana, enough to make a single cigarette. **4** cannabis. [ety. unknown; *zol* is recorded as 1950s US/Mex. border drug use, but no provable link exists; Branford, *Dict. of South African English*

(4th edn, 1993), notes the obs. trade name of miniature cheroots but gives no date; if it precedes drug use it would be an obvious root]

Zola Budd *n.* [1980s+] (*S.Afr.*) **1** a black taxi. **2** a slow armoured police vehicle. [the S.Afr. runner *Zola Budd* Pieterse (b.1966) was permitted to represent England after a lengthy press campaign; she ran against the US champion Mary Decker Slaney and stepped on her foot; Decker was considered the superior athlete; thus Budd is equated with the slow vehicles]

zombie *n.¹* **1** [1930s+] (*US Black/campus*) a bizarre-looking person. **2** [1940s+] a dullard, a slow-witted person; thus *zombied out*, slow-witted; *zombie up*, to 'freeze'; *zombie off*, to lose consciousness. **3** [1980s+] (*UK prison*) a prison officer who looks permanently miserable and humourless. **4** [1980s+] a policewoman (cf. COPESS n.). **5** [1980s+] (*US Black*) a very African-looking person, short of stature, with a dark complexion and broad features. **6** [1980s+] a crack addict. [SE *zombie*, 'a soulless corpse said to have been revived by witchcraft; formerly, the name of a snake-deity in voodoo cults of or deriving from West Africa and Haiti' (*OED*); ult. Kongo *nzambi*, god, *zumbi*, fetish]

zombie *n.²* (*also* **zom box**) [1940s+] (*US/UK Black*) a radio or television. [radio/television renders its listener/watcher a *zombie*; BOX n.⁵ (2)/BOX n.⁵ (6)]

zombie (weed) *n.* (*also* **zombie buzz**) [1970s+] (*drugs*) phencyclidine (cf. ACE n.⁴). [its effects render one zombie-like]

zonched *adj. see* ZORCHED adj.

zone *n.* (*also* **zoner**) [1980s+] (*US drugs*) a habitual drug user. [ZONE v. (3)]

zone *v.* (*also* **zone out**) **1** [1970s+] to lose consciousness or concentration; thus *in a zone*, daydreaming. **2** [1990s+] to relax. **3** [1990s+] to be intoxicated by a hallucinogenic drug. [one is in one's own private SE *zone*]

zoned *adj.* (*also* **zoned out**) [1970s+] **1** (*US*) drunk or intoxicated by a given drug (cf. ADDLED adj.). **2** exhausted, burned out. **3** disorientated. [ZONE v.]

zoner *n. see* ZONE n.

zonk *n.* [1940s+] (*S.Afr.*) a sandwich. [ety. unknown]

zonk *v. see* ZONK (OUT) v.

zonked (out) *adj.* (*also* **zonkers**) **1** [1950s+] intoxicated by a given drug or by drink. **2** [1960s+] (*also* **zonky**) confused, mentally impaired. **3** [1960s+] completely exhausted. **4** [1970s+] (*US*) enthusiastic or excited. [ZONK (OUT) v.]

zonker *n.* **1** [1960s+] (*US campus*) an unpleasant or unpopular person. **2** [1970s+] anyone who takes drugs to excess. [ZONK (OUT) v.]

zonko *n.* [1970s+] (*US campus*) a boring, dull, thus socially unacceptable, person. [ZONK (OUT) v. + -o sfx]

zonk (out) *v.* **1** [1950s+] to hit or strike. **2** [1960s+] to fail. **3** [1960s+] to fall asleep. **4** [1970s+] (*US*) to die, to lose consciousness, esp. from alcohol or drugs. **5** [1970s+] to overcome, to knock out, lit. or fig. [SE *zonk*, echoic of a blow or solid impact]

zonky *adj. see* ZONKED (OUT) adj. (2).

zoo *n.¹* **1** [1920s–60s] a prison. **2** [1930s] a brothel whose workers come from 'all nations' (cf. BIRDCAGE n.¹). **3** [1960s+] (*US campus*) a wild party; thus as v., to be noisy and rowdy.

zoo *n.²* [1970s+] (*US campus*) the lowest grade possible; thus as v., to fail an exam. [in a scale where A is best, Z is worst]

zoo *n.³* **1** [1980s] (*US campus*) an amusing person. **2** [1990s+] (*W.I.*) a very unattractive person. [SE *zoo*, the meanings suggest contradictory images]

zoodikers! *excl. see* ZOOKS! excl.

zooed *adj.* **1** [1960s+] (*US campus*) drunk. **2** [1980s+] (*US drugs*) highly intoxicated by a drug. [i.e. reduced to animal-like inarticulacy]

zooie *n.* [1960s–70s] (*drugs*) an implement that holds the butt of a marijuana cigarette. [ety. unknown]

zook *n.* **1** [1930s–70s] (*UK Black*) a veteran prostitute. **2** [1990s+]

(*also* **ziggy**) a marijuana cigarette, esp. when laced with crack cocaine. [(1) ety. unknown; (2) ? var. on ZOOM n.³ (2) + SE *cigarette*]

zooks! *excl.* (*also* **zoodikers! zookers!**) [mid-17C+] a general excl. [abbr. GADZOOKS! excl.; 20C+ use is historical/joc.]

zoolooed *adj.* [1970s+] (*US campus*) drunk. [? *Zulu*; the image is of a charging warrior as portrayed in the 1964 film]

zooly *adj.* [1960s] (*US teen*) fine, good, exciting.

zoom *n.*¹ [1930s] (*US Und.*) a police raid. [ZOOM v.¹ (1)]

zoom *n.*² [1960s+] zest, vivacity, enthusiasm. [ZOOM v.¹ (1)]

zoom *n.*³ (*drugs*) **1** [1970s] amphetamine (cf. A n.²). **2** [1980s+] phencyclidine; marijuana laced with phencyclidine (cf. ACE n.⁴). [its effects]

zoom *v.*¹ (*also* **zoom around/off**) **1** [1920s+] to rush, to move fast. **2** [1930s] to drag someone off quickly. **3** [1950s+] (*drugs*) to start to feel a drug working; to exhibit (drug-fuelled) energy. [SE *zoom*, echoic of moving at speed]

zoom *v.*² [1930s–40s] (*US Black*) to get something without paying for it, e.g. a ticket to a show; thus *on a zoom*, for free. [i.e. one 'zooms off' with it/'zooms' it away]

zoom buggy *n.* [1940s–60s] (*US teen*) a fast car. [ZOOM v.¹ (1) + BUGGY n.¹ (1)]

zoomer *n.* [2000s] a female breast (cf. BAZONGAS n.). [abbr. of BAZOOM n.]

zoom-in *n.* [1990s+] (*US*) a sudden, unexpected and sometimes unwanted kiss. [ZOOM v.¹ (1)]

zoom off *v. see* ZOOM v.¹.

zoom out *v. see* ZEEK OUT v.

zooms *n.* [1960s] (*US campus*) the female breasts (cf. BAZONGAS n.). [abbr. of BAZOOM n.]

zoom someone off *v.* [1970s] (*US Black*) to deceive, to betray someone emotionally. [fig. use of ZOOM v.¹ (1)]

zoom someone out *v.* [1970s–80s] (*US Black*) **1** to amaze, to fascinate, to surprise. **2** to overwhelm someone by the force of one's speech, to take over someone's mind. [fig. use of ZOOM v.¹ (1)]

zoomy *adj.* [1940s+] (*US*) fast, stylish, high-flying. [ZOOM v.¹ (1)]

zoons! *excl. see* ZOUNDS! excl.

zoot *n.*¹ (*also* **zootie, zut**) [1970s+] (*UK Black*) a cannabis cigarette. [ety. unknown]

zoot *n.*² *see* ZOOT SUIT n.

zoot *adj.* [1930s+] (*US Black*) overexaggerated as applied to clothes.

zoot *v.* [1930s–40s] (*US Black*) to dress flashily or vulgarly. [ZOOT SUIT n. (2)]

zooted (up) *adj.* [1980s+] (*US Black/campus*) (*also* **zootied**) under the influence of drink or drugs. [ZOOT n.¹]

zooted up *adj.* [1940s] (*US*) wearing a ZOOT SUIT n.

zooter *n. see* ZOOT-SUITER n.

zootie *n.*¹ (*US drugs*) [1980s+] phencyclidine (cf. ACE n.⁴).

zootie *n.*² *see* ZOOT n.¹.

zootied *adj. see* ZOOTED (UP) adj.

zoot suit *n.* (*also* **zoot**) **1** [1930s–40s] (*US Black*) overexaggerated clothes. **2** [1940s+] (*orig. US Black*) a style of suit worn in the 1940s and 1950s, characterized by a long, draped jacket with padded shoulders and high-waisted tapering trousers; thus *zoot-shirt*, a brightly coloured shirt designed to be worn with a zoot suit; *zoot pants*, trousers designed like those of a zoot suit; *zoot suit action*, a fashion competition in which a wearer of a zoot suit attempts to outdo rivals. **3** [1970s+] (*UK prison*) prison clothing worn in the punishment cell. [? New Orleans patois *zoot*, cute]

zoot-suiter *n.* (*also* **zooter**) [1930s–60s] (*US*) **1** a wearer of a zoot-suit; thus a fashionable, COOL adj.¹ person. **2** in derog. use, a foolish, arrogant, vulgar young man, esp. when his image is boosted by flashy clothes. [ZOOT SUIT n.]

zooty *adj.* [1940s–60s] (*US*) flashily dressed, smart. [ZOOT SUIT n. (2)]

zoo-zoos and wham-whams *n. see* ZUUZUUS AND WHAM-WHAMS n.

zorba *n.* [1980s] (*Aus.*) a Greek. [*Zorba the Greek* (1952), the novel and later film by Nikos Kazantakis]

zorba *v.* [1950s+] to urinate (cf. APPLE AND PIP v.). [rhy. sl.; *Zorba the Greek* = LEAK v.¹ (1)]

zorba'd *adj.* [1990s+] annoyed, angry. [rhy. sl.; *Zorba the Greeked* = leaked = pissed, i.e. PISSED OFF adj.]

zorched *adj.* (*also* **zonched**) [1960s] experiencing the effects of an excess of drink or drugs; thus *zorch out*, to drink heavily, to take drugs. [? ZONKED (OUT) adj. (1) + SE *torched*, set on fire]

zort *n.*¹ [1970s] (*US*) a dollar. [ety. unknown]

zort *n.*² *see* ZIT n. (1).

zortch *n.* [1970s] (*US*) sex. [? ZOT v. (1)]

zot *n.*¹ (*also* **zotz**) [1960s+] (*US campus*) zero, e.g. as in an examination. [SE *zero* + ? SQUAT n.²]

zot *n.*² [1970s] (*Aus.*) an act of sexual intercourse. [ZOT v. (1)]

zot *v.* **1** [1960s] (*Aus./US*) to hit. **2** [1960s+] (*orig. US*) to move quickly; thus *zot along, zot down* etc. **3** [1970s] (*Aus.*) to act in a speedy manner, to do something abruptly, e.g. down a drink. [ety. unknown; ? use of initial 'z' to denote speed]

zot! *excl.* [1960s–70s] (*Aus.*) an excl. denoting suddenness. [echoic]

zotz *n. see* ZOT n.¹.

zotz *v.* [1990s+] (*US*) to kill, to murder. [ZETZ n.]

zouch *n.* [18C] a slovenly, ungenteel man, one who walks with a slouch. [? SE *slouch*, 'an awkward, slovenly, or ungainly man; a lubber, lout, clown; also, a lazy, idle fellow' (*OED*)]

zoucher *n. see* SYCHER n.

zounds! *excl.* (*also* **zoons! zouns!**) [late 16C+] a euph. excl. for *God!* sometimes intensified to *zounds and blood!* lit. 'God's wounds!'; *zounds and death!* 'God's death!'

z-out *v. see* Z v.

zowie *n.* [1910s+] keenness, enthusiasm, energy. [ZOWIE! excl.]

zowie! *excl.* [20C+] (*orig. US*) an excl. used to describe sudden impact or fig. amazement. [echoic of speed]

Zs/z's *n. see* Z n.¹.

z's *v. see* Z v.

zubrick *n.* [1960s] (*US gay*) the penis.

zuch *n.* [1940s+] (*US Und.*) an informer. [? ZOUCH n.]

zug up *v.* [20C+] (*W.I., Gren.*) to cut a man's or boy's hair in an amateurish, raggedy manner. [ety. unknown; ? the shape of the letter 'Z' implies raggedness]

zuke *v.* [1980s+] (*US campus*) to vomit (cf. BARF v.). [echoic]

Zulu *n.* [1930s+] (*US*) a derog. term for a Black person (cf. AFRICAN APE n.). [SE *Zulu*, a member of a Bantu people inhabiting Zululand or Natal]

zulu *n.* [1920s] (*US*) a thug.

Zulu princess *n.* [1960s–70s] (*US gay*) a young, handsome Black man. [ZULU n. + PRINCESS n. (3)]

zum-zum *n.* [2000s] (*W.I.*) the vagina. [? var. on PUM-PUM n.²]

zup *n.* [2000s] (*UK Black*) an escape. [ZUP v.]

zup *v.* [2000s] (*UK Black*) to make an escape. [one 'ups and' leaves]

zup? *phr. see* 'S UP? phr.

zurucker *n.* [1940s] (*Aus.*) a police trooper. [Ger. *zurück*, backwards; thus ? detectives follow a line of clues *backwards* to the perpetrator]

zut *n. see* ZOOT n.¹.

zutt *n.* [1950s] (*UK Black*) a cigarette end, a butt.

zutupeck *n.* [1990s+] (*W.I.*) an unattractive woman.

zuuzuus and whamwhams *n.* (*also* **zoo-zoos a[nd wham-]whams**) [1960s+] (*US prison*) confectionery sold t[o] [ety. unknown; but note SAmE *Zu-Zu* or *Zou-[?]* for the Zouaves in the Union Army]

zweideener *n.* [late 19C] (*Aus./N.Z.*) a [?] [Ger. *zwei*, two + DEENER n.]

zybo-fucker *n.* [2000s] (*US Black*) a [?] Black man's woman, esp. by force [?]

zzzs *n. see* Z n.¹.